American Statistics Index 1992

Covering Publications Issued
January 1–December 31, 1992

A comprehensive guide to the statistical publications of the U.S. Government

Index

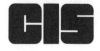

CIS Congressional Information Service, Inc.

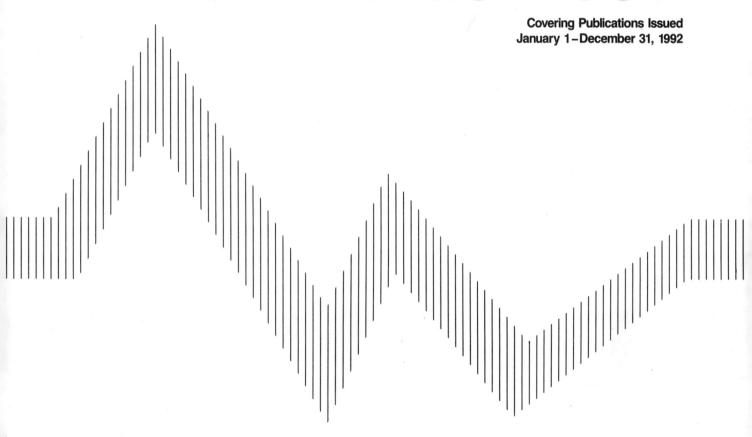

ISSN 0091 - 1658
Key Title: American Statistics Index

The Library of Congress Cataloged the First Issue of This Title as Follows:

American Statistics Index, 1973-
Washington. Congressional Information Service. annual.

"A comprehensive guide and index to the statistical publications of the U.S. Government."

1. United States-Statistics-Bibliography.
2. United States-Statistics-Abstracts. I. Congressional Information Service.

Z7554.U5A46 016.3173 73-82599
ISSN 0091 - 1658 MARC-S

International Standard Book Number
For the Set: 0-88692-267-4
For Index Volume: 0-88692-268-2
For Abstract Volume: 0-88692-269-0

Published by Congressional Information Service, Inc.
4520 East-West Highway
Bethesda, MD 20814 U.S.A.

∞™

The paper used in this publication meets the minimum requirements of American National Standard for Information Sciences-Permanence of Paper for Printed Library Materials, ANSI Z39.48-1984.

A privately organized reference service.
Printed and Bound in the United States of America.

CONTENTS

The American Statistics Index 1992 Annual is published in two volumes, the contents of which are summarized below.

Index

Detailed Table of Contents: Index Volume v

User Guide vii

Introduction to the American Statistics Index vii
Coverage of ASI Annual and Monthly Editions vii
Statistical Publications Covered by ASI viii
Organization of ASI Abstracts and Indexes ix
How ASI Abstracts Statistical Publications xi
How ASI Indexes Statistical Publications xii
Acquiring the Documents xx
Additional CIS Services xx
Sample Abstracts xxiii
Sample Search xxvi
Where To Write for Statistical Publications xxviii
Document Availability Symbols xxxii
Acronyms and Selected Abbreviations xxxiii
Issuing Agencies and ASI Accession Numbers xxxiv

Index by Subjects and Names 1

Index by Categories 837

Index by Titles 915

Index by Agency Report Numbers 983

Index of Superintendent of Documents Numbers 1001

Guide to Selected Standard Classifications 1019

Abstracts

Detailed Table of Contents: Abstracts Volume

Issuing Agencies and ASI Accession Numbers v

User Guide xvii

Abstracts of Statistical Publications 1

Detailed Table of Contents: Index Volume

Index by Subjects and Names 1
(This index contains references to subjects, to corporate authors, and to individual authors of articles and publications.)

Index by Categories 837
(This index contains references to publications tables, and groups of tables that contain breakdowns of statistical data by State, by industry, by age, or by some other standard category.)

Geographic Breakdowns

By Census Division 837
By City 838
By County 841
By Foreign Country 843
By Outlying Area 850
By Region 853
By SMSA or MSA 859
By State 860
By Urban-Rural and Metro-Nonmetro 873

Economic Breakdowns

By Commodity 875
By Federal Agency 878
By Income 880
By Individual Company or Institution 882
By Industry 888
By Occupation 892

Demographic Breakdowns

By Age 894
By Disease 899
By Educational Attainment 900
By Marital Status 902
By Race and Ethnic Group 904
By Sex 909

Index by Titles 915
(This index contains an alphabetical listing of all publication titles abstracted.)

Index by Agency Report Numbers 983
(This index contains a listing of all publications abstracted for which there are agency report numbers available, arranged by issuing agency.)

Index of Superintendent of Documents Numbers 1001
(This index contains a listing of Superintendent of Documents Classification Numbers for publications abstracted by ASI.)

Guide to Selected Standard Classifications 1019
(This guide outlines the major standard classification systems used by various Federal agencies to arrange and present social and economic statistical data.)

Census Regions and Divisions 1019
Outlying Areas of the U.S. 1019
Standard Federal Administrative Regions 1019
Farm Production Regions 1019
Federal Reserve Districts 1020
Federal Home Loan Bank Districts 1020
Bureau of Labor Statistics Regions (and Regional Offices) 1020
Metropolitan Statistical Areas 1021
Consolidated Metropolitan Statistical Areas 1022
Cities with Population over 100,000 1023
Consumer Price Index Cities 1023
Standard Industrial Classification 1024
Standard Occupational Classification 1032
Standard International Trade Classification, Revision 3 1035

USER GUIDE

INTRODUCTION TO THE AMERICAN STATISTICS INDEX

The U.S. Government is the world's most important and prolific publisher of statistics. Federal agencies produce a continual flow of facts and figures on virtually every aspect of life in America and on most matters of world-wide concern.

Until the initiation of the American Statistics Index (ASI) and related services in 1972, use of Government statistics was hampered by the absence of adequate tools to identify relevant publications and pinpoint the data within them, as well as by the difficulty of locating and acquiring the publications themselves.

Major statistical agencies, such as the Census Bureau, index their own publications and disseminate them widely; other agencies issue publications lists and partial indexes; many agencies do neither. Nowhere in the Government is this wealth of data indexed, or even listed, completely. Many of these publications are not available through the Government Printing Office nor listed in its *Monthly Catalog;* and many are unavailable at depository libraries.

ASI aims to be a master guide and index to all the statistical publications of the U.S. Government. It was created to meet the need expressed in 1971 by the President's Commission on Federal Statistics, for "a central catalog of data available in government agencies . . . a single source in which one could locate all data currently collected by the Federal Government on a particular subject."

Specifically, the purpose of ASI is to perform the following functions, promptly and comprehensively:

- **Identify** the statistical data published by all branches and agencies of the Federal Government.
- **Catalog** the publications in which these data appear, providing full bibliographic information about each publication.
- **Announce** new publications as they appear.
- **Describe** the contents of these publications fully.
- **Index** this information in full subject detail.
- **Micropublish** virtually all the publications covered by ASI, thereby providing, on a continuing basis, reliable access to the statistics themselves.

To assure comprehensiveness, ASI staff members monitor all published document listings and regularly visit or contact over 500 Federal offices. In 1992, ASI collected, abstracted, and micropublished approximately 5,000 titles, including 600 periodicals. To assure prompt coverage during the year, full abstracts and indexing for all publications, including statistical articles within individual issues of periodicals, are published in an ASI Monthly Supplement issued 5 to 6 weeks after the month in which publications are obtained. The source documents themselves are issued on ASI microfiche about two weeks later.

This ASI 1992 Annual cumulates and enhances ASI Monthly Supplement coverage of Federal statistical publications issued during 1992. It is meant to be used in coordination with other ASI publications and services that provide comprehensive coverage of Federal statistical publications issued since the 1960s.

The following User's Guide discusses how the ASI system is organized; what kinds of statistical publications and statistics are issued by the Federal Government and accessible through ASI; how these publications are cataloged for retrieval through ASI; how their contents are abstracted and indexed in ASI; and where one can obtain the publications in hardcopy or on ASI microfiche.

COVERAGE OF ASI ANNUAL AND MONTHLY EDITIONS

ASI full coverage of U.S. Government statistical publications dates from the 1960s. This coverage is achieved through a base ASI Retrospective Edition, covering publications issued from 1960-73; Annual editions, each covering publications issued during a single year of coverage, 1974–92; and Monthly Supplement editions, issued throughout each year.

Each ASI edition is issued in 2 sections: an Abstracts Section that contains full descriptions of the content and format of each publication, organized by ASI accession number; and an Index Section that contains comprehensive subject and name, category, title, and report number indexes, with references keyed to abstract accession numbers.

The separate ASI editions are more fully described below.

ASI 1992 Annual

The ASI 1992 Annual, covering publications issued Jan. 1–Dec. 31, 1992, cumulates coverage of all publications originally abstracted and indexed in the ASI 1992 Monthly Supplements. It replaces and fully supersedes those Monthly Supplements.

In addition, the 1992 Annual contains full abstracts and indexing for all periodicals actively being published in 1992. In this respect, it is also designed to serve as the base reference source for all periodicals currently publishing in 1993, and to be used in conjunction with ASI 1993 Monthly Supplements for locating data contained in current periodicals. Abstracts of periodicals and other recurring publications in the 1992 Annual reflect the format and content of the latest issue received during the year, and include notations of any significant changes occurring during the year.

ASI 1993 Monthly Supplements

ASI 1993 Monthly Supplements provide current abstracts and indexing for all new publications issued during each month of 1993. These include wholly new publications, new items in series, and updates or new editions of annuals, semiannuals, or other publications covered in previous ASI editions.

Monthly Supplements may also include abstracts for some publications that were issued prior to 1993, but that only recently came to our attention. Such publications are covered, provided they are still current enough to be of general interest.

All statistical periodicals covered by ASI, whether quarterly, monthly, weekly, or daily, are reviewed by the ASI staff on a continuing basis, and the issues received are listed in each Monthly Supplement in the "Periodicals Received and Reviewed" section. However, Monthly Supplements do not re-abstract or re-index periodicals that have remained substantially unchanged since this 1992 Annual.

Only those periodicals that show significant changes in content or format since the basic description in this 1992 Annual are re-abstracted and indexed in the detail necessary to describe the change.

Periodical articles that contain statistical data are abstracted and indexed individually each month.

Monthly Supplements are issued 5 to 6 weeks after the end of the month covered, generally by the 10th-12th of each month.

ASI Retrospective Coverage

This ASI 1992 Annual is the nineteenth annual cumulation issued since the publication of ASI's base 1974 Annual and Retrospective Edition. The Retrospective Edition covers statistical publications in print as of Jan. 1, 1974, as well as significant publications issued since the early 1960s.

In the case of repetitive or continuing publications, such as annuals or periodicals, which present continuing series of statistics over long periods of time, the Retrospective Edition does not describe each issuance published since 1960. Rather, it describes in full the format and contents of the most recent edition received at the time, and, where possible, characterizes major changes in format that occurred prior to 1974.

Subsequent annual cumulations, taken together, provide comprehensive coverage of statistical publications issued since Jan. 1, 1974. These annuals are published as hardcover abstracts and index volumes in the spring following the year of coverage.

ASI Multi-year Cumulative Indexes

ASI has published three multiple-year cumulative indexes to date. The 1974–79 Cumulative Index, published in May 1990, which revises and supersedes the separate Annual Index volumes issued for 1974 through 1979, is designed to be used in conjunction with ASI First through Sixth Annual Supplements as originally published. A cumulation covering ASI 1980 through 1984 Index volumes was published in 1985, and a cumulation covering ASI 1985 through 1988 Index volumes was published in 1989. A cumulation covering ASI 1989 through 1992 Index volumes will be published in late 1993. For more information about these multiple-year indexes, consult the most recent CIS catalog.

STATISTICAL PUBLICATIONS COVERED BY ASI

Publications included in ASI cover a wide range of subjects, reflecting the many concerns of hundreds of central and regional Federal agencies. These issuing agencies are listed in the detailed table of contents in each Abstracts volume and in the list of "Issuing Agencies and ASI Accession Numbers" in the Index volume. ASI abstracts and indexes all Federal agency publications that contain social, economic, demographic, or natural resources data, and a selection of publications with scientific and technical data.

ASI includes all Federal publications that contain primary data of research value or secondary data collected on a special subject, and also special studies and analyses or other statistics-related materials. All types of publications are covered, whether published as periodicals, as special one-time reports, as items within a large continuing report series, or as annual or biennial reports.

For purposes of inclusion in ASI, the term "publication" is defined as all printed or duplicated materials that may be distributed by an agency to members of the public, whether on a broad or a limited basis. In a few cases, ASI has obtained single copies of materials that are not generally available for distribution, and has micropublished them for distribution. Press releases and other ephemera are included only if they contain basic data not readily available in another form.

In addition to printed reports, ASI covers CD-ROM releases, microfiche, and wall maps that present statistics. Coverage of CD-ROM products issued by Federal agencies began in 1990; ASI has covered nearly 100 individual CD-ROM titles since 1990.

The sections below describe selected examples of the approximately 5,000 titles covered every year by ASI.

Basic Social and Economic Statistical Data

Since its early organization, and as required by the U.S. Constitution, the Federal Government has been responsible for gathering basic national social and economic data. Today, six large Federal statistical agencies, each in a specialized field, have as their major function the regular collection, analysis, and publication of such data. Data published by these agencies are broadly characterized below:

- **Agricultural Statistics Board, Department of Agriculture** — Monthly to annual reports on every important U.S. crop, with data on production, yield, prices, prospective plantings, and indicated production for the season.
- **Bureau of the Census** — Decennial census of population and housing; quinquennial economic and agricultural censuses; Census of Governments; Current Housing Reports, Current Industrial Reports, monthly foreign trade data, and reports from the monthly Current Population Survey; and methodological studies, indexes, and guides.
- **Bureau of Labor Statistics** — Monthly reports on the Consumer Price Index and unemployment rate; and other periodic, serial, and annual reports on prices, wages and hours, benefits, collective bargaining, work stoppages, and productivity.
- **Energy Information Administration** — Weekly to annual reports on U.S. production, consumption, stocks, trade, and prices of all major energy resources; finances and operations of oil companies, electric utilities, and other energy industries; and projections of energy supply and demand.
- **National Center for Education Statistics** — Annual and other collections of data on elementary, secondary, and higher education schools, staff, students, finances, curricula, and graduates.
- **National Center for Health Statistics** — Monthly and annual collections of vital statistics; and periodic surveys of the health condition of the population, and of health care, personnel, and facilities.

Many additional departments and agencies regularly compile primary data, both from required reports in their areas of responsibility and from special surveys; for example: Bureau of Mines' *Mineral Industry Surveys,* Justice Department's *Uniform Crime Reports* and victimization surveys, Treasury Department income tax statistics, Federal Reserve data on finances and banking, Department of Transportation data on highways and air traffic, and National Science Foundation's Surveys of Science Resources.

Program Related Statistics

Almost all executive departments and administrative or regulatory agencies publish statistics on their own funding and programs.

These data cover agency financial statements, personnel, processing efficiency, workloads, accidents, persons served, and payments made. Some of these data are of interest well beyond the functioning of the agency; for example, social security recipients and payments, food stamp recipients, aliens admitted, speed of handling court cases, nuclear power plant shutdowns and accidents, Federal civilian workforce, and military troop strengths.

ASI provides full coverage of these types of program statistics, but, where possible, selects agency-wide reports for inclusion, and excludes subagency reports that only repeat data in the reports of the larger unit.

For example, the basic financial publication for the entire Government, the *Budget of the U.S.*, is fully covered by ASI; but ASI does not also cover budget requests or justifications from individual agencies unless they present significant data not available elsewhere. ASI generally covers the annual report of each separate agency, but not those of sub-agencies unless they include unique data. Also, ASI covers data on grants, contracts, and procurements, as reported by a large agency as a whole (such as DOD *Prime Contract Awards),* but usually excludes reports by individual divisions.

Special Studies

Many agencies produce a steady stream of monographs, analyses, and studies on subjects within their areas of activity; these are covered by ASI whenever they include statistical data of probable research value. Some agencies also undertake large special studies from time to time; an example of this kind of study covered by ASI in 1992 is the Department of Health and Human Services' *Characteristics of Physicians* State report series, which presents detailed data on practicing physicians.

In some cases, special commissions are created specifically for the purpose of studying a problem of current concern. Studies of this nature have been covered by ASI beginning with those from the early 1960s. For instance, this 1992 Annual covers *Speaking of Kids: A National Survey of Children and Parents,* a report of the National Commission on Children.

Some original studies are included which, although not primarily quantitative in nature, present statistics unavailable anywhere else; a number of reports by the General Accounting Office fall into this category. Other publications in ASI which are primarily non-statistical, may contain significant statistical sections. Congressional committee hearings and prints are prime examples.

Non-Tabular Statistics-Related Materials

Publications selected for inclusion in ASI generally contain statistical data in tabular form. However, maps, charts, listings, and narrative materials have also been covered if they provide aid in locating statistical data or in understanding statistical programs. Thus, we cover narrative discussions of statistical methodology, classification guides, directories, and bibliographies that include references to a significant body of statistical materials.

In general, we have attempted to cover all such material issued by the major statistical agencies, but we have applied somewhat more rigid standards for inclusion of material from other agencies.

Exclusions and Selective Coverage

The following kinds of material are either excluded from ASI or covered only on a selective basis:

- **Scientific and technical data** — Highly technical studies, scientific and experimental observations, engineering data, clinical medical studies, and animal laboratory studies are generally excluded from ASI. These data are disseminated through such information services as NTIS, NASA, ERIC, and the National Library of Medicine; ASI makes no attempt to duplicate this coverage.

  We do provide selective coverage of technical data with broad social or economic implications or particular current interest, as well as the less technical publications of technically oriented agencies. For instance, we do cover epidemiological studies; a large number of reports on energy resources, use, and conservation; EPA publications presenting monitoring data and pollution abatement measures; NOAA weather observations and forecasting techniques; and selected NASA publications.
- **Contract studies** — ASI coverage of contract studies by private organizations is typically limited to those that have been issued by a Federal agency as its own publication, either directly through the agency, through GPO, or through NTIS. In special cases, additional contract studies are covered that we would normally exclude but that have been recommended by an agency as being of particular importance.
- **Classified and confidential data** — These data are not included.
- **Congressional publications** — Congressional publications that contain substantial statistical information are included in ASI. However, ASI does not include any appropriations hearings, which contain primarily Federal program data, and which are abstracted and indexed in detail in the comprehensive *CIS/Index to Publications of the U.S. Congress.*

  When ASI covers a congressional publication also covered by the CIS/Index, it is completely re-abstracted and indexed to highlight the statistical data.

ORGANIZATION OF ASI ABSTRACTS AND INDEXES

ASI provides access to statistical data through companion volumes of indexes and abstracts. In making a subject search, you should consult this 1992 Annual for descriptions of publications issued during 1992, and for basic descriptions of periodicals that continue publication in 1993. The 1993 Monthly Supplements will cover new publications issued during 1993, including new editions of annual reports, and will change and update information regarding 1993 issues of periodicals. To search for material issued prior to 1992, you should consult the ASI Retrospective Edition and the subsequent Annuals, and all multi-year ASI cumulative indexes.

ASI Indexes

Ordinarily, research in ASI will begin with the Index volume. The ASI indexes are designed to lead you to the information you seek from a variety of starting points. The five basic ASI indexes are designed to answer the following types of questions:

- **Subject and Name Index** — "What publications provide statistical data on cost of living and related matters?" and "What publications were issued by the Office of Management and Budget?"
- **Category Index** — "What publications provide cost of living data broken down by city, or some other geographic category?"
- **Title Index** — "What statistical data are included in a periodical entitled *Monthly Labor Review*?"
- **Agency Report Number Index** — "Where in ASI will I find reports in the BLS Bulletin 3065 series?"
- **SuDoc Number Index** — "Does ASI cover the report with the Superintendent of Document number E3.49:990?"

Each ASI index reference will lead you to an abstract. Descriptive abstracts are provided for every publication; they are designed to tell you enough about the information content of the publication to enable you to decide whether or not it is likely to contain the specific data for which you are looking.

This system depends upon a basic key — the ASI accession number — which identifies publications (or specific parts of publications) in both the index and the abstract volumes.

ASI Accession Numbers

Each ASI abstract carries a unique accession number, which identifies not only the individual publication, but also the issuing agency and the publication type (see Sample Abstracts on p. xxiii-xxv for an illustration of how accession numbers appear on abstracts). The accession number has four basic components, the form and functions of which are described below.

- **Issuing Agency** — In the accession number for any one publication's abstract, the first two to four digits (up to the digit before the hyphen) are keyed to an overall coding scheme and represent the agency that issued the publication. (Coding for large agencies may be broken down by subagency or subject matter area.)
- **Publication type** — The last digit before the hyphen is keyed to the document's publication type, as follows:

  2 = Current periodicals, daily through semiannual
  4 = annuals and biennials
  6 = publications in series
  8 = special and irregular publications
  1, 3, 5, 7, 9 = special series and special groups of publications (such as census reports or crop reports) that do not fall into one of the four basic types or which are most clearly represented if kept together under a special heading.
- **Sequential ASI serial number** — The digits after the hyphen form a unique serial number, sequentially assigned, basically in order of ASI acquisition, so that every publication has its own unique number that can be easily found in the Abstracts volumes of ASI.
- **Analytic number** — In many cases, ASI describes publications by using a main abstract in coordination with subordinate abstracts called "analytics," which are printed after the main abstract and are identified and sequenced by decimal numbers (.1, .2, or .3, etc.) following the main abstract accession number.

  Analytics are frequently used to describe and individually index distinct parts of a large publication. They are also used to abstract and separately index the individual publications comprising a series, or the statistical articles appearing in individual issues of periodicals.

To use the ASI indexes and abstracts effectively, you do not need to know the ASI agency-coding or publication-type coding schemes, which are incorporated into accession numbers, but familiarity with codes can speed interpretation of entries in the indexes.

Arrangement of Abstracts by Accession Number

All abstracts are arranged by accession number in ascending order. This system automatically catalogs all publications, first by issuing agency, then by publication type, and then by individual publication serial number. All index references are made to these accession numbers. For ease in referring from index to abstract, every page of

Sample: ASI Accession Numbers

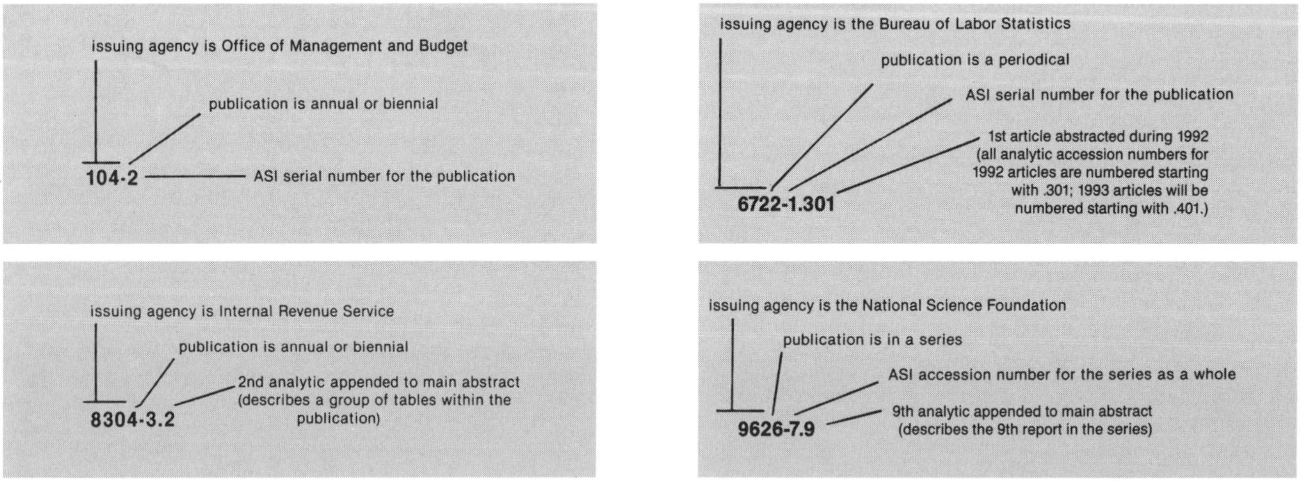

abstracts in the Abstracts volume carries a locator number in the upper right or left corner.

Continuity of Accession Numbers

Generally, once ASI has assigned an accession number to a publication, all successive issues or updates of that publication will receive the same accession number. If the number is changed, cross-references between the old and new numbers are included in the abstracts. The accession number will change if, for example, the periodicity of the publication changes from quarterly to annual, or if the issuing agency of the publication changes.

HOW ASI ABSTRACTS STATISTICAL PUBLICATIONS

All ASI abstracts are original and are based upon examination of the entire document. Abstracts differ substantially in degree of detail, depending on the type of publications and the kind of data being described. However, all abstracts are written to fulfill certain objectives.

These objectives are to describe a publication fully enough to allow you to determine if it is likely to contain the specific statistical data you seek; to provide the bibliographic data you need to identify and locate the publication if you wish to borrow or acquire it; and to tell you where in the publication you can find the data, often with specific page ranges.

Guidelines for Describing Statistical Contents

In describing the basic subject matter or statistical data of a publication, ASI does not attempt to summarize observations or conclusions. Rather, we attempt to state consistently what a publication is about; what specific data are presented, from what source, and at what level of detail; and what relationship the publication has to other statistical series. In describing a publication, ASI abstractors observe the following guidelines:

- State the subject matter and purpose of the publication as a whole.
- Identify sources of data presented, whether primary (based on original collection) or whether selected or reprinted from other published sources.
- Describe, if data are primary, the sample type and size, the survey methodology, or the information reporting requirement by which the data were gathered.
- Specify time span and geographic coverage of the data (special methods, discussed below, are used to describe time coverage and currency of data in periodicals).
- State periodicity of data collection and publication.
- Indicate breakdowns of the data and the level of detail they provide.
- Outline physical contents of the publication, such as number of charts and tables, and presence of narrative discussion, appendices, bibliographies, and index. Include page ranges to indicate the quantity and location of each type of material.
- List individual titles of all tables in publications that present continuing time series data or data from basic censuses (handling of table listings is further discussed below).
- Review continuity and length of time series data, providing references to ASI abstracts of earlier publications in the series and any breaks in publishing continuity since ASI coverage began.
- Indicate when a serial publication was first issued (if known), when ASI began covering it, and when an ASI accession number changed. [This information is a new feature within ASI abstracts, beginning with this 1992 Annual.]
- Provide references to known related publications that present similar or identical source data in different analytical or publication formats.

In all cases, the aim is to specify as precisely as possible the actual data to be found in a publication. Particular pains are taken to distinguish among publications providing different data on similar subject matter.

Listing of Table Titles

For every publication, ASI attempts to identify, mention, and index the subjects and categories for which significant amounts of statistical data are presented. Often, the best way to describe in detail the data in a statistical publication is to list the titles of the tables it contains.

In general, ASI lists individual titles of tables that carry forward a continuing time series of data in biennial, annual or periodical publications. We also list table titles for publications presenting data from basic surveys and censuses. We usually list the titles exactly as they appear in the original publication. Where necessary for clarity or additional detail, these titles are augmented by material in brackets. Pagination for each table, or group of tables, is given.

Abstracts of special or irregular publications generally do not list tables, but describe the tables in varying degrees of detail, depending upon their number and complexity. If listing table titles is the clearest and briefest way to indicate the exact data present, it is done for any type of publication.

Special Aspects of Abstracts Describing Periodicals

This 1992 Annual contains full descriptions of all statistical periodicals that published any issues during 1992. Since most statistical periodicals retain constant format, features, and tables, it would be redundant to provide full abstracts for each issue. Therefore, abstracts of periodicals indicate the features common to all issues and list tables that appear in each issue or at regular intervals. Periodicals that were discontinued during 1992 are so annotated in this 1992 Annual; All others may be presumed to be continuing publication in 1993.

Statistical articles in periodicals are individually abstracted and indexed each month, and special tables that appear only in certain issues are listed. All such articles and special tables appearing in periodical issues during 1992 are included in this 1992 Annual.

In listing tables for periodicals, we do not give the time coverage of the data as a specific month or year, but describe it in a way that will apply to all issues. The abstracts do not include page ranges, which may change from issue to issue.

All abstracts of periodicals in this annual include a notation of issues received, reviewed, and microfilmed during 1992. The cover dates of the issues are labeled (P) if they approximate the publication date: or (D) if they represent the period covered by the data presented. The body of the abstract usually indicates the time lag between the data date and the publication date.

Periodical abstracts in the 1992 Annual serve as the base abstracts for continuing periodicals, to be used in conjunction with the 1993 Monthly Supplements. Issues of those periodicals received during 1993 will be listed in the Monthly Supplements "Periodicals Received and Reviewed" section as they are received, but will not be re-abstracted of re-indexed unless their contents change significantly.

Provision of Bibliographic Data

ASI abstracts for each publication provide, at a minimum, primary bibliographic information, such as title, date, collation, agency report number (if any), and periodicity. In addition, we include, whenever possible, the Superintendent of Documents classification number, the Library of Congress card number, the Government Printing Office (GPO) *Monthly Catalog* entry number, the GPO stock number, and the depository Item Number.

However, many Government publications covered in ASI have not been assigned all, or in some cases any, identification or classification numbers. Many of the publications we cover are not cataloged either in the GPO *Monthly Catalog* or in the issuing agency's own catalog or publication list, if one exists.

Each document abstract provides as much specific information on hardcopy availability as we are able to obtain at time of publication, and includes information on ASI microfiche availability and price. (For more information about the availability of documents or microfiche, see below "Acquiring the Documents.")

Usually, all bibliographic information for a publication is given at the head of the main abstract, following the title (see Sample Abstracts on p. xxiii-xxv for detailed labeling of bibliographic information provided). When analytic abstracts are being used to describe separate documents in a series, however (see sample abstract for publications in series), only bibliographic data common to the entire series are included in the main abstract, and information individual to each document is shown in its respective analytic abstract.

Frequently, a publication that is going to be cataloged by the GPO *Monthly Catalog* will not have been cataloged by the time ASI monthly abstracts are published. If such *Monthly Catalog* entries appear prior to the ASI Annual, information from them is included in the published Annual. Occasionally, items have not yet been covered in the *Monthly Catalog,* but are documents within continuing series for which established classification data exist; in such cases, we will publish classification data, based on precedent, in the absence of *Monthly Catalog* verification. In addition, ASI publishes bibliographic data revisions and additions in a special section at the end of each quarterly Monthly Supplement index volume. These revisions and additions are then cumulated annually and issued as separate pamphlets to supplement the bibliographic data in each past ASI Annual.

References to Publication Dates

When a date is included in the title of a publication, ASI prints it as part of the title; this date usually represents the period covered by the data or, sometimes, the year the report was prepared. When a date is given anywhere within a publication to indicate date of transmittal, final preparation, or printing, ASI lists this date in the bibliographic data. The user should remember, however, that schedules are often delayed and the publication may not actually have become available until later.

Some publications contain no date at all, and, for these, ASI lists in the bibliographic data the closest approximation it can determine of the year of actual release.

Uses of Main Abstracts and Analytic Abstracts

To handle the broad variety of materials it includes, ASI developed a flexible approach to document accessioning and abstracting. As described earlier in the section on the ASI accession number, we use a structured abstract system that provides for main abstracts and subordinate abstracts (analytics).

ASI uses analytics for the following purposes:

- To single out part of a publication for more detailed abstracting, or to divide the publication into parts, generally into groups of tables, which are then listed. Analytics may also be used for sections or chapters of a publication, each of which is then further described.
- To abstract individual publications in a series. The title and bibliographic data unique to the publication are given in the analytic; data common to the series as a whole are given in the main abstract.
- To abstract articles in periodicals. Article abstracts are identified by 3-digit analytics, beginning with .301 for the first article abstracted in 1992. Thus, article abstracts always follow table listings, which begin with .1.

ASI provides for each individual publication the descriptive information outlined in the above sections. For periodicals, annuals, or one-time publications, the basic information is usually given in the main abstract (see the Sample Abstracts on p. xxiii and xxiv).

For publications in series, information common to the series as a whole is given in the main abstract, and that peculiar to each individual publication in the series is given in its respective analytic (see Sample Abstract on p. xxv). This system allows complete descriptions of individual, related publications without extensive repetition of common characteristics.

The use of analytics also allows ASI to index to specific parts or even single tables in publications. Any index terms may be assigned to an analytic to indicate data specific only to that analytic, and the ASI accession number, with a decimal, will lead the user to it.

For example, the accession number 6224-2.2, under a given index term means that the second analytic, not the publication as a whole, contains data on that topic. The main abstract, however, will contain the basic information on the subject, data type and source, and overall contents of the publication.

When index terms apply to the entire publication or to many of the analytics used, these terms are assigned to the main abstract only and are not repeated for the individual analytics to which they apply.

HOW ASI INDEXES STATISTICAL PUBLICATIONS

ASI indexes are designed to serve a wide range of needs and search approaches for locating statistical materials.

To accomplish this, the following five separate indexes have been provided:

- **Index by Subjects and Names,** which contains references to specific subject areas, places, and personal and corporate authors.
- **Index by Categories** (and accompanying Guide to Selected Standard Classifications), which contains references to tabular data breakdowns by twenty-one common geographic, demographic, and economic categories (e.g., by State, by sex, or by specific industry).
- **Index by Titles**
- **Index by Agency Report Numbers**
- **Index of Superintendent of Documents Numbers**

This section reviews basic ASI objectives and policies in building these five indexes; provides instructions and suggestions for using each of them; and gives specific hints on which indexes to use for answers to a number of different types of questions.

INDEX BY SUBJECTS AND NAMES

The Index by Subjects and Names provides access to:

- **Subjects** of publications and of specific data within publications.
- **Place names,** including names of cities, counties, States, and foreign countries to which data relate.
- **Government agency names,** including the Federal national or regional agencies, commissions, or congressional committees that issue publications or that are the subjects of data contained in publications.
- **Major Government programs or proposals** to which data relate (e.g., Work Incentive Program, Medicare).
- **Special classes of publications or data** (e.g., publications under the terms "Opinion and attitude surveys," "Statistical programs and activities," "Projections," "Directories," and "Bibliographies").
- **Individual personal names, companies, and institutions,** both as authors and as subjects of publications.
- **Major surveys** through which significant bodies of data have been collected (e.g., Current Population Survey).

Sample: INDEX BY SUBJECTS AND NAMES

subject term — **Grains and grain products**

Labor productivity, indexes of output, hours, and employment by SIC 2- to 4-digit industry, 1967-90, annual rpt, 6824-1.3 — ASI accession number for analytic abstract describing tables in publication

Production inputs, output, and productivity for farms, by commodity and region, 1947-89, annual rpt, 1544-17 — ASI accession number for main abstract for this publication

notation of content characterizing data contained in publication — Tax (income) returns of corporations, income and tax items by asset size and detailed industry, 1989, annual rpt, 8304-21

see also reference to narrower or related ASI subject terms where additional publications are listed —
see also Alcohol fuels
see also Animal feed
see also Baking and bakery products
see also Corn
see also Hops
see also Rice
see also Soybeans
see also Wheat

see also reference to relevant data breakdown in "Index by Categories" — *see also* under By Commodity in the "Index by Categories"

Grand Island, Nebr. — place name term
Wages by occupation, and benefits for office and plant workers, 1991 survey, periodic labor market rpt, 6785-3.10

Graves, Edmund J. — author term
"1989 Summary: National Hospital Discharge Survey", 4146-8.198 — notation indicating report title and ASI accession number

subject term not used by ASI — **Great Plains**
see reference to appropriate ASI term — *see* North Central States

As illustrated in the above sample, this index consists of the following four basic structural elements:

- Subject and author terms (subject terms are based upon a controlled vocabulary).
- *See* and *see also* cross references directing the user to the appropriate index term or to terms under which additional related data may be found.
- Notations of content, which summarize the relevant data content and time coverage of each publication indexed to a particular term. Under an author's name the title is used as a notation of content.
- ASI accession numbers, which refer the user to the full ASI abstract for that publication.

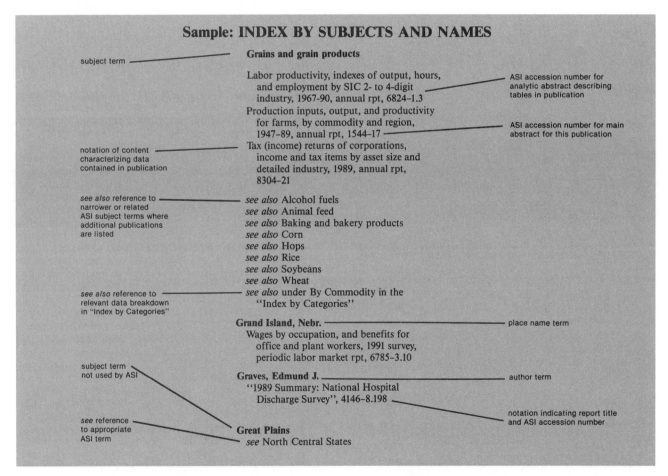

ASI Subject Terms

Subject terms and cross references in the Index by Subjects and Names are based on a controlled vocabulary developed by ASI to meet the particular needs of ASI data coverage. This vocabulary is constantly reviewed and enlarged to respond to the ever expanding range of subjects receiving attention in Government publications.

Publications abstracted in ASI cover an extremely wide variety of subjects, and the data presented range from the very general to the very specific. In selecting subject index terms for the ASI controlled vocabulary, we have strived to maintain a middle level of specificity, which allows for adequate flexibility in indexing to specific subjects, but avoids too great a fragmentation and scattering of subject references. For example, in dealing with data on commodities, the ASI controlled vocabulary generally contains terms for commodity groups, such as the terms "Grains and grain products," "Animal feed," and "Baking and bakery products," found in the preceding sample. However, in the case of selected specific commodities, which are frequently dealt with in publications covered by ASI, we have established separate index terms (e.g., "Wheat," "Corn," "Rice," and "Soybeans" in the preceding sample).

ASI policy is to index to subject terms that reflect the principal subject matters and data contents of each publication abstracted. In addition, unusual items or items of special interest that occur in the body of a report or article, or in individual tables or groups of tables, will be indexed whether or not they relate to the primary focus of the publication at hand.

When indexing a publication to which a hierarchy of vocabulary terms might apply, we select the most specific applicable term or terms in the controlled vocabulary, and do not also index to broader or narrower terms that do not reflect so well its particular focus. But when the focus of the document is equally upon the more general and the more particular subject term, we place index entries under both terms.

For example, when indexing large compendia that present major data on commodities, we index both to the terms for commodity groups and also to those terms for specific commodities that have been established in the controlled vocabulary. Publications primarily focusing on a single commodity, such as wheat, corn, or rice, will be indexed only to the specific commodity terms and not to the more general term "Grains and grain products." Publications that focus on the general subject of grains, but contain a considerable amount of data on one or more of these specific commodities, will be indexed both to the specific commodity terms and to "Grains and grain products." Finally, publications that include some data on the specific commodities, but have a main focus that is on grains will be indexed only to "Grains and grain products."

Cross References

The *see also* references provided by ASI, such as those shown in the preceding sample, are designed to guide you to additional material to be found under the related or narrower terms cited, and to remind you of the need to check the Index by Categories where additional data may be available.

ASI also provides *see* references to aid in locating the specific form of phraseology of subject terms used by ASI. ("Great Plains," for example, is not a term used by ASI, but relevant entries will be found under the term "North Central States.")

Notations of Content

Each index entry under a subject or category term contains an ASI accession number and a "notation of content," a brief description of a report's subject matter or data content. These notations assist you in selecting relevant entries under any particular term and restricting the number of abstracts to which you need refer.

Notations of content are individually written for each publication indexed by ASI. They include, at a minimum, the main subject or subjects of the publication as they relate to the specific index term, and the data date. Additional information that may be noted, as relevant, includes geographic area of coverage, major data breakdowns, and periodicity of publication. Under an author term, the publication title is used as the notation of content.

In selecting the first words for notations of content, we have attempted to choose key words that will automatically group index entries according to their prime subject content. The key words perform some of the functions of a "second-level" index term (e.g., the word "Production" used in the preceding sample to group entries relating to grain farming). Although the informal type of grouping thus achieved can be helpful to you, these groups will not always bring together all related material. A complete search should include examination of all notations of content under a given term.

In general, only one notation of content for any one publication appears under a specific index term. This entry must reflect the full scope of the publication being indexed as it relates to that subject term. As a result, in many cases, the notation of content must be quite general, subsuming coverage of a great deal of specific data. In those cases, however, when the material relating to an index term is too diverse to be covered by a single notation of content, a second notation may be used under that term.

As stated above, usually only one notation of content for any one publication will appear under a specific index term. However, the wording of the notation of content for a single publication may be different for each of the index terms under which it appears. In such cases, the differences reflect an effort to relate the wording and initial key word of the notation of content to the specific index term under which it appears.

For example, the publication in the above index sample with the notation of content, "Tax (income) returns of corporations, income and tax items by asset size and detailed industry, 1989, annual rpt," contains financial data for a number of industries. Under most of the index terms for these industries, "Tax" is effective as an initial key word, but under "Income taxes" and other tax-related terms, an alternative key word is needed. Under those terms, the notation of content reads, "Corporations income tax returns, income and tax items by asset size and detailed industry, 1989, annual rpt."

In all cases, it must be remembered that notations of content are brief and highly condensed guides, and cannot be used as substitutes for the abstracts. The full abstracts will further describe the extent and limitations of the data indicated in the index entry, and will often note the existence of related data that could not be indicated in the brief space occupied by the index entry.

Other Indexing Conventions

- **Alphabetization —** Following Library of Congress practice, ASI alphabetizes on a word-by-word basis. For example, "New Jersey" and "New York" precede "Newark," and "Fire departments" precedes

"Firearms." It is important to know if there is a word break in a term, since a compound word like "Airlines" will follow all terms beginning with the word "Air" (i.e., "Air pollution"). Hyphenated words are alphabetized as if they were two separate words.

- **Proper Names —** These have been entered in natural word order. Thus, you will find "Department of Labor" rather than "Labor Department," and "Bureau of Labor Statistics" rather than "Labor Statistics Bureau." However, names of individuals always have last name first, such as "Boyd, Gayle M."
- **References to the United States —** Because of the nature and scope of most U.S. Government statistical publications, "U.S." is an implied prefix for many of the subjects in the ASI Subject Index. Thus, you will find "Army" rather than "U.S. Army," and "Foreign relations" rather than "U.S. Government-foreign relations." In agency titles, the prefix "U.S." has been dropped whenever possible, except where necessary to conform to *U.S. Government Manual* usage (e.g., U.S. Postal Service). In notations of content, "U.S." is always implied unless "foreign," "world," or "by country" is specified.

Making a Subject Index Search

If you are seeking a specific piece of information in ASI, you will often find it quickly by referring to the obvious subject term or terms, locating the relevant group of notations of content, and selecting the one or ones most pertinent to your search. You should then consult the abstract for a full description of the publication and its availability.

If such a search does not yield the information required, or if you desire a more complete survey of possible data on the subject, additional steps should be taken. As previously noted, your first step should be to consult the more specific and related *see also* terms listed under the relevant subject terms in order to obtain additional leads.

Your next step should be to consult more general terms that encompass the subject matter sought. Despite our efforts to index to the most specific available term, some statistical publications are so wide-ranging or so detailed in their subject coverage that it is impractical to include references to all the specific topics they mention. It is wise, therefore, when checking the specific subject term in which you are interested, also to check the more general terms related to it.

Searching the subject terms, however, is only part of making a successful subject search in ASI. For instance, a publication that contains data on agriculture may break down these data by hundreds of different commodities, one of which is likely to be grains. The existence of these breakdowns by category adds a new dimension to statistical data retrieval. To help the researcher locate this kind of information quickly, ASI has provided an Index by Categories, which is discussed in detail below.

A limited amount of overlapping (or "double posting") occurs between the Index by Subjects and Names and the Index by Categories. Detailed data subject matter shown in tabular breakdowns (e.g., occupational breakdowns) are always indexed in the Index by Categories. In selected cases, where tabular breakdowns or cross-tabulations provide an extensive or particularly significant body of data on a given subject, references to these data have been included in both the Index of Subjects and Names (e.g., indexed to the subject terms "Clerical workers," "Nurses and nursing," "Blue-collar workers," etc.) and the Index by Categories (e.g., "By Occupation"). The existence of this limited overlap should not mislead the user with respect to the large amount of additional data available through the Index by Categories.

INDEX BY CATEGORIES

As mentioned above, to provide a ready access to the multiplicity of detailed statistical data in tabular breakdowns and cross-classifications, ASI has created a special type of supplementary index: the Index by Categories. This index includes references to all publications that contain comparative tabular data broken down in any or several of the following twenty-one standard categories:

- **Geographic Categories —** By census division; By city; By county; By foreign country; By outlying area (territories of the U.S.); By region; By SMSA or MSA; By State; and By urban-rural and metro-nonmetro.
- **Economic Categories —** By commodity; By Federal agency; By income; By individual company or institution; By industry; and By occupation.
- **Demographic Categories —** By age; By disease; By educational attainment; By marital status; By race and ethnic group; and By sex.

For easier use, index entries within each of the categories are grouped according to subject matter, under one of the following nineteen subheadings:

Agriculture and Food
Banking, Finance, and Insurance
Communications and Transportation
Education
Energy Resources and Demand
Geography and Climate
Government and Defense
Health and Vital Statistics
Housing and Construction
Industry and Commerce
Labor and Employment
Law Enforcement
Natural Resources, Environment, and Pollution
Population
Prices and Cost of Living
Public Welfare and Social Security
Recreation and Leisure
Science and Technology
Veterans Affairs

In those instances where a reference might logically fit under two or more of the subheadings, we have tried to select the most obvious one and to place it there. A brief listing of the kinds of material referenced under each subheading is given at the beginning of the Index by Categories.

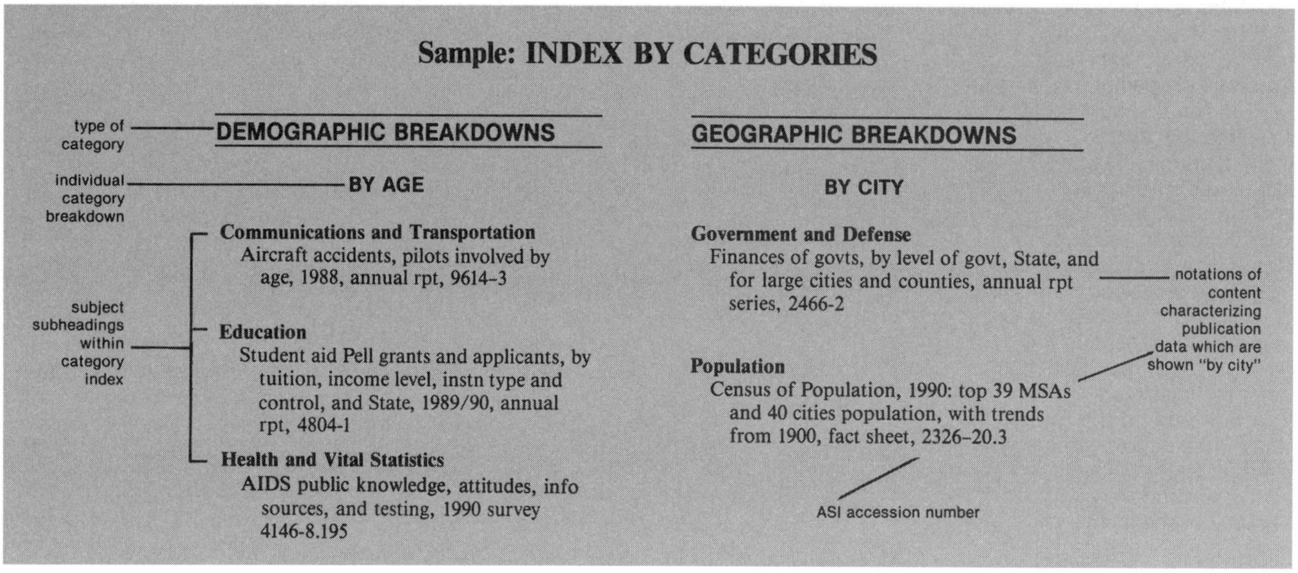

As illustrated in the above sample, this index consists of the following four basic structural elements:

- Category terms, for the twenty-one categories listed above.
- Subject subheadings, to group entries within each category by subject matter. These are listed above.
- Notations of content, which are used just as in the Index by Subjects and Names to characterize further the data indexed to the category.
- ASI accession numbers, which refer the user to the full ASI abstract for that publication.

In the Index by Categories, data in the specified categories can be identified with greater detail and specificity than in the Index by Subjects and Names. This index also provides the best and most complete source for locating comparative data on a wide variety of subjects.

Breakdowns in individual tables, to which references are made in the Index by Categories, may vary considerably in the detail provided. Breakdowns "By sex" are, by definition, complete. Breakdowns "By State" are usually, but not always, for all 50 States. However, detail in breakdowns of such categories as "By city," "By SMSA," "By Federal agency," "By industry," "By commodity," and "By occupation," varies widely. In the abstracts of publications containing such breakdowns, we have, when possible, tried to include an indication of the degree of detail provided (i.e., "by detailed industries," "by major cause of death," "for 20 large cities," etc.).

In searching the Index by Categories for very detailed data, such as those on a small city, minor industry, or other specific entity, you are likely to find several entries referring to publications that could possibly contain the information you want. You will usually find it necessary to go back to the abstract to ascertain which publication has or is most likely to have that information. In some cases, where a high degree of specificity is desired, an examination of the Index by Categories and the abstracts will help to narrow the field of possibilities, but it may still be necessary actually to examine the text of two or three publications to be certain the exact information needed is there.

Examples and further instructions for making various types of Category Index searches follow.

Making a Search by Geographic Categories

Much data on Chicago can be located under the term "Chicago, Ill." in the Index by Subjects and Names. These entries represent instances where Chicago is the principal subject of a publication or where a significant body of information relating to Chicago can be found. There are considerable additional data, however, to be found in individual tables that have a breakdown by city, including Chicago. These data are located in the Index by Categories under the term "By city."

Similarly, you can find data on individual States, counties, SMSAs, MSAs, or foreign countries in the Index by Categories. The number of places included in reports indexed to these categories may vary considerably. Breakdowns by State or county are usually complete, unless the notation of content indicates that data are limited to a specific part of the country, or to "large counties" or "selected counties." In the case of cities or foreign countries, there may be wider variation; when practical, the notation of content indicates the degree of detail provided (e.g., "40 cities" in the sample above).

Data on the regions of the U.S. can be found under the category "By region." Since, however, the different Federal agencies use a variety of regional delineations, such data may not be comparable from one report to another. To assist the user, ASI has provided lists of six major regional structures in the Guide to Selected Standard Classifications, further described below.

Making a Search by Economic Categories

The Index by Categories term "By Industry" will lead to reports and to individual tables which present a wealth of detailed data on both major and minor industries. These data can often be found only through the Index by Categories, since the Subject Index would become unwieldy if ASI attempted to index each column of every table.

In the same way as for cities, explained above, the notation of content will generally indicate the level of industry detail provided in each publication, and the abstract will specify further. In some cases, the degree of detail in the breakdowns may be based upon a standard classification system, such as the Standard Industrial Classification (SIC) which classifies all types of industries, businesses, and services for purposes of developing comparable statistical data. Whenever such a standard classification is used, this fact is noted in the abstract and frequently in the notation of content as well. Several of the most frequently used classifications, including the SIC, are listed in ASI's Guide to Standard Statistical Classifications, further described below.

The use of the SIC listing to find data on a specific industry is illustrated in the sample below. For example, if you want data on the typesetting industry, an industry for which there is no separate entry in the Subject Index, you can refer to the SIC listing to determine at what SIC level the typesetting service industry is specified. Since it is specified at the 4-digit level, you can then examine the entries under "By Industry" in the Category Index, and check the abstracts of likely references, to find reports and specific tables that present data broken down to the SIC 4-digit level.

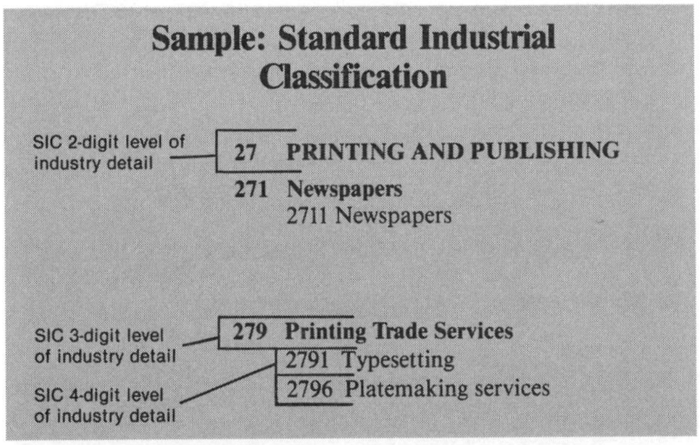

Very detailed data on commodities can be found in the same way, using the category term "By Commodity." The industry and commodity categories only partially overlap, since many firms produce a wide range of commodities but are classified only in the industry of their major activity. ASI policy is to follow the classification— industry-based or commodity-based—used by the publication. To make a complete search for such economic data, you will probably want to examine both categories.

Data shown for individual entities of all kinds, including companies or their brand name products, universities, hospitals, foundations, and government projects may be found under "By Individual Company or Institution." Category indexing is also provided for data "By Federal Agency," "By Occupation," and "By Income," including both salary levels and total family income.

Making a Search by Demographic Categories

When you want data about specific groups of the population, the Category Index is a versatile tool to augment the Subject Index. For example, the following subjects can be thoroughly searched using this two-pronged approach:

- **Women** — Data may be found under the subject terms "Women," "Women's employment," or "Maternity." Quantities of additional data may be found under the category term "By Sex."
- **Age groups** — Look under subject terms "Children," "Youth," or "Aged and aging." Look also under the category term "By Age."
- **Blacks** — Look under such subject terms as "Black Americans," "Black students," or "Racial discrimination." More data can be found under the category term "By Race."
- **The poor** — The subject term "Poverty" will lead to reports dealing specifically with the poor. Additional data can be extracted from reports with breakdowns "By Income," found in the Category Index.
- **Divorced persons** — The subject term "Marriage and divorce" will lead to reports specifically on this subject. The category term "By Marital Status" will lead to additional data.

In a similar way you can find data on demographic groups under the categories "By Occupation," "By Industry," "By Educational Attainment," or "By Disease."

Making a Search for Comparative Data

A major advantage of the Index by Categories is the ease with which it enables you to locate comparative data on a subject. This index is the logical starting point for such search questions as: "Which cities have the highest unemployment rate?" "Which States have the lowest taxes?" "Which are the largest industries in the U.S. in specified States?" "Do people with more education really earn more money?" (These last two questions each combine two category terms: "By Industry" and "By State," and "By Income" and "By Educational Attainment.") Data pertinent to these questions will also be found under the subject terms "Employment and unemployment, general," "State and local taxes," etc. However, the most efficient search for such comparative data will begin with the Index by Categories.

ASI's Guide to Selected Standard Classifications

As stated above, Federal statistical data breakdowns are frequently presented in terms of several standard classification systems, and ASI abstracts generally make note of their use. To provide an easily accessible reference for the user, we have printed a number of major classification systems or lists in the "Guide to Selected Standard Classifications." The Guide, which appears at the end of the Index volume, includes the following listings:

- Census regions and divisions; outlying areas of the U.S.; Standard Federal Administrative Regions; farm production regions; Federal Reserve Districts; Federal Home Loan Bank Districts; and Bureau of Labor Statistics Regions.
- Metropolitan Statistical Areas (MSAs); Consolidated Metropolitan Statistical Areas; cities with population over 100,000 (based on the 1990 Census of Population) and Consumer Price Index cities.
- Standard Industrial Classification (SIC), providing 1- to 4-digit codes for industry divisions through individual industries.
- Standard Occupational Classification, providing 1- to 3-digit codes for major and minor occupational groups.
- Standard International Trade Classification (SITC), a system of 3-digit codes for commodities in world trade, developed by the United Nations, used for foreign trade data, and consistent with the 7-digit codes used for U.S. import-export data.

Even when data breakdowns do not correspond with one of these standard classification systems, these listings can still serve as useful guides to what may be included in breakdowns at varying levels of detail (i.e., "by major industry group" will approximate the 2-digit SIC level, and "by detailed industries" will approximate the 4-digit level).

Government publications that describe these and

other standard classification systems, survey methods, glossaries, and directories are abstracted and microfilmed by ASI, and can usually also be obtained in hardcopy by the user. Such publications are generally indexed to "Methodology" or "Classifications" as well as to their respective subjects.

INDEX BY TITLES

This index lists titles of all publications covered by ASI in the 1992 Annual. It also lists titles of periodical articles, conference papers, and reports within larger publications when these are separately abstracted.

This index lists all main titles and also analytic titles of individual monographs within a series, except when series reports are essentially identical, e.g., a series of State reports or country reports. In these cases, the name of each State or country can be found in the Index by Subjects and Names; the reports will also be listed, usually in alphabetical order, in the Abstracts volume under the ASI accession number for the series. Series reports on individual commodities or industries are listed in the Index by Titles under the name of the commodity, followed by the name of the series, e.g., "Footwear, Current Industrial Report."

Titles are listed alphabetically in natural word order, as they appear in the abstract. ASI routinely omits initial articles (a, an, the) in titles, both in the abstracts and in this index. Titles that begin with Arabic numbers (e.g., "1991 Joint Economic Report") appear at the end of the index.

To assist users in locating a publication, we provide in certain cases alternate word orders for titles, including all of those beginning with Arabic numerals. For example, census reports are generally listed under the overall title of the census and under the title of the individual report as well.

Sample: INDEX BY TITLES

publication title	Cancer Statistics Review, 1973-88, 4474-35
title of individual report in a series	Capital Punishment, 1990, 6066-25.42
article title	Career of Conceptualizing and Quantifying in Social Science, 1502-3.203

Each title is followed by the ASI accession number, which directs the user to the abstract of the publication.

Anyone knowing the title of the publication desired can locate it most quickly in this index. Users should keep in mind that notations of content in the Index by Subjects and Names and in the Index by Categories bear no necessary relationship to a publication's title and should not be confused with it.

INDEX BY AGENCY REPORT NUMBERS

This index lists the report numbers assigned to publications by the issuing agency. It can be useful both for identifying one specific document and for locating an entire series of numbered publications.

We have grouped numbers in this index under the names of each issuing executive department, independent agency or commission, or congressional body, but generally have not attempted to group them by bureau, office, or committee within a department or independent agency. (Frequently, the alphabetical prefixes of the numbers themselves serve to identify agencies.)

Exceptions to this general rule are Census Bureau publication numbers, which are preceded with the word "Census" so that they group together and are not intermixed with other Commerce Department reports. Also, the "DHHS" prefix in the Department of Health and Human Services report numbers has been omitted so that numbers will group more meaningfully.

Sample: INDEX BY AGENCY REPORT NUMBERS

Federal department or agency — **DEPARTMENT OF EDUCATION**

Agency Report Number —

LP 91-740	4874-1
LP 91-743	4874-6
NCES 91-074	4834-20

INDEX OF SUPERINTENDENT OF DOCUMENTS NUMBERS

This index presents, in shelf list order, the Superintendent of Documents (SuDocs) Classification Numbers of publications abstracted by ASI during 1992, and provides references from the SuDocs numbers to ASI accession numbers.

The index enables a user who has obtained a SuDocs number from the Monthly Catalog or some other source to quickly locate the ASI abstract and then obtain the document.

Sample: INDEX OF SUPERINTENDENT OF DOCUMENTS NUMBERS

SuDocs number	ASI accession number
A67.18:FS(nos.)	1925-14
A67.18:FS1-91	1925-14.2
A67.18:FS1-91/supp	1925-14.1
A67.18:FS2-91	1925-14.3
A67.18:FT(nos.)	1925-16
A67.18:FTEA(nos.)	1925-15
A67.18:FTEA1-91	1925-15.1
A67.18:FTEA2-91	1925-15.2
A67.18:FTEA3-91	1925-15.3

Suggestions for Making Information Searches

The "best" information search technique to use with ASI abstracts and indexes depends upon the type of information needed and upon the amount and type of information with which the search begins. Listed below are some examples of the types of information you can obtain through ASI, together with suggested routes for searching.

IN ORDER TO . . .	YOU SHOULD . . .
Pinpoint specific statistical data on any subject treated in Federal Government publications.	Use the subject index.
Locate broad analyses of comprehensive studies.	Use the subject index; concentrate on the more general subject terms.
Determine whether data are available for specific parts of the U.S., such as States, cities, or counties; for specific industries or commodities; or for specific groups of people, such as races, men and women, or age, income, or occupational groups.	Use both the subject and category indexes.
Find comparative data for States, cities, foreign countries, Government agencies, commodities, industries, or groups of people.	Use the category index.
Find out what Federal Reserve district Florida is in.	Look in the Guide to Selected Standard Classifications.
Determine whether a large report, with a breakdown by industry, will include data on the dog food industry.	Look at the Standard Industrial Classification Codes listed in the Guide to Selected Standard Classifications to determine that the industry you are looking for has a 4-digit code. Look in the indexes for notations of content specifying detailed industry breakdowns. Look at the table listing in the abstract for tables specifying 4-digit detail.
Find data on Minneapolis.	Look in the subject index under "Minneapolis, Minn." Look also in the category index under "By city."
Be confident that you have found the latest data available.	Look at the dates in the notations of content that interest you in the ASI 1992 Annual. Check ASI 1993 Monthly Supplements under the same index terms to see if there are similar notations with later dates. ASI is current to 6-10 weeks after publication of the reports covered. If the notations of content indicate a periodical, locate the latest issue in the "Periodicals Received and Reviewed" section.
Find the latest issue of a periodical carrying forward a statistical time series.	Look in ASI 1992 Annual for description of the periodical. Look for the title in the "Periodicals Received and Reviewed" section of the latest ASI Monthly Supplements; the issues received each month will be listed.
Locate continuing monthly or quarterly reports on a particular subject.	Look in the subject index. The notations of content include the periodicity of the reports.
Determine the availability of comparable historical data.	Look in the abstract to see if the report is part of a continuing time series (e.g. Twentieth annual report) and when ASI coverage began. Also look in the abstract for changes in ASI accession numbers or breaks in continuity.
Locate the report of a specific Board or Commission.	Look in the subject index under the name of the issuing agency.
Locate an agency publication list.	Look in the subject index under "Government publications lists."
Review the entire statistical output of any particular Federal Government agency or office.	Look in the detailed table of contents for the ASI accession number and page of the agency that interests you. Look in the Abstracts Section for all publications under this accession number.
Find out how many Federal Government agencies publish data on the same subject.	Look in the subject index, at the ASI accession numbers following the notations of content. The first two to four digits (minus the digit before the hyphen) indicate the issuing agency of the publication.
Locate a specific statistical article in a periodical.	Look in the title index or in the subject index under the author's name.
Determine the content of a specific publication when you know the title or agency report number.	Use the title index or the agency report number index to locate the pertinent abstract.
Locate all the reports in a specific series.	Look in the title index of each edition of ASI under the title of the series. If it is a numbered series, use the agency report number index.
Find a report you remember hearing about in the 1970s.	Start out by checking the ASI Retrospective Edition Index and 1974-79 Cumulative Index.
Locate reports describing specific statistical methods; locate reports containing projected data.	Look in the subject index under "Methodology;" look in the subject index under "Projections."

ACQUIRING THE DOCUMENTS

Once you have identified a publication that appears to contain the data you seek, you may wish to borrow or acquire the publication itself, either in its original hardcopy form or in microform.

Acquiring Documents From a Library

Although there are no complete collections in existence, Government documents can be found in many libraries, particularly those that have been designated as U.S. Government depository libraries. There are usually at least two depositories in each congressional district, approximately 1,300 throughout the country.

The publication abstracts that contain a bullet (•) and an Item Number indicate publications that have been made available to depository libraries by the Government Printing Office. However, fewer than 50 depositories receive *all* the publications that are theoretically available to them, and even these libraries receive only about three-quarters of all the publications covered by ASI.

Libraries that subscribe to the ASI Microfiche Library will have complete collections of the materials abstracted and indexed in ASI.

Requesting or Purchasing Publications From the Government

Whether or not they are sent to depositories, many Government publications can be purchased while the supply lasts, either from the Government Printing Office, or, in certain cases, from the National Technical Information Service, or the issuing agency.

If a publication listed in ASI is available for sale, the price and source, when known, are listed in the abstract. It should be noted that the prices of Government publications are subject to frequent change. The price listed is that printed on the publication or in the GPO *Monthly Catalog,* or is based on firm information about a later price from another source.

When the publication abstract contains a single dagger (†), inquiries should be addressed directly to the issuing agency in order to determine whether copies are available for distribution. Principal agency addresses are listed in each Annual Abstracts volume in the section labeled "Where to Write for Statistical Publications."

Some publications intended for internal or official use only have been printed in small editions, and copies generally are not available for distribution. In some cases, the agency will honor a written request for a copy of one of these publications, but this will be decided by the agency on a case-by-case basis. Abstracts of publications in this category carry a double dagger (‡).

In some cases, we have been informed by the agency that there are absolutely no copies available for distribution outside the agency. Abstracts of publications in this category carry a diamond symbol (♦). In most of these cases, the agencies have cooperated with our attempt to make the data available to the public by permitting ASI to microfilm the publications for inclusion in the ASI Microfiche Library. The agency itself will not honor requests for publications that carry this symbol.

The ASI Microfiche Program

Because of the enormous difficulty of acquiring, cataloging, and maintaining a collection of all the publications covered by ASI, no complete hardcopy collection of these publications now exists in any library. For this reason, CIS has undertaken to make these publications available in American Standard microfiche on a continuing basis.

Our microfiche sheets measure 105 × 149 mm (approximately 4″ × 6″), and contain up to 98 document pages. Each has an eye-readable "title header" that conclusively identifies the accession number, series title (if any), dates of periodical issues, and document title of each publication filmed. Documents are separated from each other, and they are plainly sequenced for file integrity and quick retrieval according to ASI accession number.

Researchers may view microfiche with the aid of a simple reader, such as those found in most libraries and offices. Individual pages from a microfiche can be reproduced in full size with the aid of a reader-printer; these machines are becoming increasingly available in libraries and offices.

With a few specific exclusions, all printed publications abstracted and indexed in ASI are available on ASI microfiche. The microfiche availability and unit count for a given publication are indicated by the notation "ASI/MF" in the publication's abstract. We have systematically excluded only publications that reprint other items in the ASI Microfiche Library, large or colored maps that are unsuitable for reproduction in standard microfiche, and large appendix volumes that are nonstatistical (such as public hearing testimony) or highly technical. Also excluded are Federal CD-ROM releases, although any printed manuals or guides for individual CD-ROMs are included in the microfiche collection.

Automatically updated collections of current publications, on silver-halide, archival-quality microfiche, are available on a subscription basis. Retrospective collections, shipped in their entirety and ready for use, may also be purchased. Collections may be ordered to contain the entire range of ASI publications, may be limited to "non-depository" publications (i.e., those not included in Government documents classes sent to depository libraries), or may be limited to publications of a single Government agency. For details, please write: CIS Library Services Manager.

ASI Documents on Demand

Since June 1, 1975, individual publications covered in ASI have been available on diazo microfiche or paper copy for purchase through our ASI DOCUMENTS ON DEMAND service. The price of any document is based on the "unit count" data indicated for the document, e.g. ASI/MF/3. (Note that a unit count of 3 is the minimum order for any document, regardless of size; each additional 100 pages or less equals 1 additional unit.) Please ask your librarian for additional ordering information; or write CIS Documents on Demand, P.O. Box 30056, Bethesda, MD 20814.

ADDITIONAL CIS SERVICES

Index to International Statistics and Statistical Reference Index

Beginning in January 1983, Congressional Information Service initiated publication of the Index to International

Statistics (IIS), a comprehensive monthly index and abstracting service, covering the statistical publications of international intergovernmental organizations, including UN, OECD, EC, OAS, and approximately 90 other important organizations.

Since 1980, Congressional Information Service has published the Statistical Reference Index (SRI), a monthly abstract and index publication with annual cumulations, covering statistical reports from a broad range of U.S. sources other than the Federal Government. These sources include trade, professional, and other nonprofit associations; business organizations; commercial publishers; independent research centers; State government agencies; and university research centers. SRI has selected from these sources a cross-section of documents presenting basic national and State data on business, industry, finance, economic and social conditions, the environment, and the population.

SRI and IIS complement ASI's coverage of statistical materials by providing access to data not collected by the Federal Government and to alternative sources and analyses of data. Because the abstracting and indexing styles of the two publications are quite similar, researchers can use ASI, SRI, and IIS without significantly changing their search methods.

Most of the documents covered in SRI and IIS are included in their respective Microfiche Libraries, available on a subscription basis. For more information about SRI, IIS, and their microfiche programs, contact the CIS Marketing Department.

Statistical Masterfile

In 1989, CIS introduced a new CD-ROM product, the Statistical Masterfile, which allows users to search simultaneously the abstracts and indexing from ASI, SRI, and IIS. The three component data bases may be purchased separately or in any combination. Both current year service and retrospective coverage are available for each data base. Current service subscribers receive quarterly CD-ROM disk updates.

For additional information, contact the CIS Marketing Department.

CIS On-Line Services

Through cooperative arrangements with on-line computer services, the CIS data base is made available to the public. This service makes possible direct on-line computer searching of the abstracts and indexing contained in all American Statistics Indexes and all CIS/Indexes, from our first publication to the present.

CIS/Indexes to Publications of the U.S. Congress

Since 1970, Congressional Information Service has published the CIS/Index, a monthly abstract and index publication with annual cumulations, which covers all publications of the U.S. Congress. Selected congressional publications containing statistical data are covered in ASI as well as CIS. Those covered by ASI are re-abstracted and re-indexed to focus on their statistical contents.

However, ASI does not repeat CIS/Index coverage of the wide range of congressional publications that contain no substantial statistical data. Nor does ASI abstract or index the publications of the Senate and House Appropriations Committees. Since CIS/Indexes provide detailed access to the extensive program statistics and background information contained in publications of these committees, we believe that reabstracting them for ASI would be a duplication of effort and service.

The CIS/Microfiche Library and CIS Documents on Demand services provide full-text availability of CIS/ Index publications in a manner paralleling ASI microfiche services.

Other Services

In early 1993 Congressional Information Service will publish a new edition of the *Guide to 1990 U.S. Decennial Census Publications* covering all decennial census publications issued in 1990, 1991, and 1992, as well as some key background reports on possible undercounts and other methodological issues. A cumulative edition of the Guide is issued each spring to include coverage of reports issued within the past year. The abstracts and indexing in the Guide are substantially reprinted from ASI annual editions and combined in a single volume for the convenience of researchers. A companion microfiche collection is also available. CIS issued a similar Guide and microfiche collection for the 1980 Census.

The Census Guides and other CIS publications and microform collections are fully described in the CIS catalog, available on request.

Sample Abstract—Individual Publication

8304
INTERNAL REVENUE SERVICE
Annuals and Biennials

8304–2 INDIVIDUAL INCOME TAX RETURNS, 1987
Annual. 1990. 161 p.
IRS Pub. 1304(Rev.8-90).
•Item 964. GPO $9.00.
ASI/MF/4
S/N 048-004-02296-6.
°T22.35/8:987. LC 61-037567.

Final detailed annual tabulation of 1987 individual income tax returns, filed during 1988. Presents data on number of returns, sources of income, deductions and exemptions, tax computation and tax rates, age and blindness exemption, credit for the elderly, and high income returns; with breakdowns by marital status and selected financial items, including size of adjusted gross income.

Data are estimates based on a stratified sample of all individual tax returns filed for income year 1987.

Contains the following 7 sections:

1. Introduction and data sources, with 3 tables showing summary data, selected years 1975-87; and selected data items, by income class, for 2 alternative definitions of income, 1987. (p. 1-12)
2. Sample description and methodology, with 2 tables. (p. 13-17)
3. 15 basic tables, listed below. (p. 19-66)
4. High income returns, with 12 tables showing 1987 total and high income returns ($200,000 or more), and tax item amounts, by selected income, deduction, credit, and tax status characteristics, under 4 alternative income definitions. (p. 67-90)
5. Explanation of terms. (p. 91-108)
6. 1987 tax forms. (p. 109-152)
7. Index. (p. 153-161)

Report has been published annually since 1916. ASI coverage began with report for 1970 (see ASI Retrospective Edition under this number).

Preliminary income tax return data are reported in the *Statistics of Income Bulletin* (see 8302- 2).

TABLES:

[Data are for 1987. Data are shown by size of adjusted gross income, unless otherwise noted.]

8304–2.1: Returns Filed and Sources of Income

1.1. Selected income and tax items, by accumulated size of adjusted gross income. (p. 20)

1.2. All returns: adjusted gross income, itemized deductions, exemptions, and tax items, by marital status. (p. 23)

issuing agency
publication type
ASI accession number for publication as a whole
title
collation
periodicity and date
agency report number
depository item number
hardcopy source and price
ASI microfiche availability and unit count*
Superintendent of Documents classification number
GPO stock number
Library of Congress number
data sources
description of publication as a whole
organization of contents
ASI coverage history
reference to related publications
detailed table listing
note on coverage of all tables
ASI accession number for group of related tables within publication
titles and page locations of individual tables

*for calculating ASI Documents on Demand fees; the number of physical fiche is generally two less than the ASI/MF unit count

Sample Abstract—Periodical Publication

6722 BUREAU OF LABOR STATISTICS: GENERAL

Current Periodicals

6722–1 MONTHLY LABOR REVIEW

Monthly. Approx. 110 p.
•Item 770.
GPO: $22.00 per yr; single copy $5.00. ASI/MF/4
S/N 729-007-00000-5.
°L2.6:(v.nos.&nos.)
MC 91-1079. LC 15-026485.

Monthly journal on labor conditions; with current statistics on employment, earnings, prices, productivity, and labor-management relations.

Each issue contains feature articles, individually described below; current labor statistics, with 51 tables, listed below; and all or most of the following regular features:

a. Labor month in review.

b. Research summaries and communications; selectively described below when they contain statistics and are not readily available as separate reports.

TABLES:

[Data are current to 1-3 months prior to cover date. Tables show monthly data for the past 13 months, and annual averages for previous 2 years, unless otherwise noted.]

6722–1.1: Comparative Indicators

[Tables show data for current and previous 5-7 quarters. Tables 1-2 include totals for previous 2 years.]

1. Labor market indicators.
2. Annual and quarterly percent changes in compensation, prices, and productivity.

ARTICLES:

MARCH 1991
Vol. 114, No. 3

6722–1.217: Changes in Hospital Staffing Patterns

By Kay Anderson and Barbara Wootton (p. 3-9). Article on hospital employment, by detailed occupation, 1989 with trends from 1983. Data are from Occupational Employment Statistics surveys of hospitals conducted Apr. 1989 and earlier.

Includes 2 tables showing hospital employment, and percent of hospitals reporting, by detailed occupation, Apr. 1989 with summary comparisons to 1986 and 1983.

A related triennial report presents complete survey results. For description of report for 1986 survey, see ASI 1989 Annual, 6748-60.

- ASI accession number for periodical as a whole
- title of periodical
- approximate pagination of each issue
- hardcopy availability information
- ASI microfiche availability and unit count* per issue
- Superintendent of Documents classification number
- GPO Monthly Catalog entry number
- Library of Congress number
- description of periodical as a whole
- note on coverage of all tables
- ASI accession number for group of related tables within publication
- titles of individual tables
- individual issue date, volume, and number
- ASI accession number for abstract of article within individual issue
- title, author, and page range of article within individual issue
- description of individual article

*for calculating ASI Documents on Demand fees; the number of physical fiche is generally two less than the ASI/MF unit count

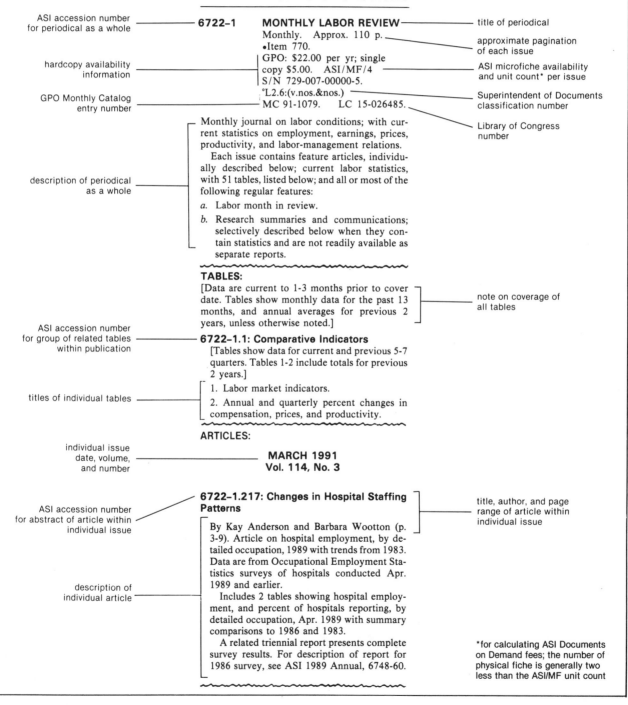

Sample Abstract—Publications in Series

2546
BUREAU OF CENSUS: POPULATION
Publications in Series

ASI accession number for series as a whole

2546-1 **CURRENT POPULATION REPORTS. Series P-20: Population Characteristics**

title of series

•Item 142-C-1.

depository item number for all publications in series

GPO: subscription with series P-23, and -60, $96.00 per yr; single copy prices vary. For individual bibliographic data, see below. P-20, (nos.) S/N 803-005-00000-1.

hardcopy availability for all publications in series

GPO Stock number

LC 52-002169.

Library of Congress number

description of series as a whole

Continuing series of reports presenting current data on selected characteristics of persons, families, and households, with some historical trends. Subjects covered include education and enrollment, fertility, mobility, voting, marital status and living arrangements, ethnic origin, and rural population.

major subjects

Data are from Current Population Surveys conducted in the month or months indicated in the title, with comparisons to previous surveys.

data sources

Series contains recurring and special reports, and, for some topics, both advance data and final reports.

Reports are described below in order of receipt.

ASI accession number for individual report in series

2546-1.448: Hispanic Population in the U.S.: March 1990

[No. 449. Mar. 1991. iii+34 p.+errata. °C3.186/14-2:990. S/N 803-005-00048-6. $2.25. ASI/MF/3]

agency report number
date
collation
Superintendent of Documents classification number
GPO stock number
price
ASI microfiche availability and unit count*

description of report subject matter

By Jesus M. Garcia and Patricia A. Montgomery. Report presenting summary data on socioeconomic characteristics of the Hispanic origin population, 1990. Data are from the Mar. 1990 Current Population Survey (CPS).

Contents: introduction, with 4 charts and 1 summary table (p. 1-5); 4 detailed tables, listed below (p. 6-15); and appendices, with definitions, notes on data source and reliability, 5 standard error tables, and facsimile questionnaire (p. 17-34).

organization of contents

Previous report, for Mar. 1989, is described in ASI 1990 Annual under 2546-1.443.

reference to previous annual report

TABLES:

titles and page locations of individual tables

1. Selected social characteristics of all persons and Hispanic persons [age, sex, marital status, and years of school completed]. (p. 6)

2. Selected economic characteristics of all persons and Hispanic persons [labor force status, occupational group, percent distribution by earnings, and median earnings, by sex;

*for calculating ASI Documents on Demand fees; the number of physical fiche is generally two less than the ASI/MF unit count

Sample ASI Search

"How much did the chemicals industry invest in pollution control equipment in New Jersey?"

Step 1

Check the ASI Index Volume

Start with a "subject" approach where extensive cross-references will lead to the proper index reference from almost any likely point of entry.

Index by Subjects and Names

Pollution
see Acid rain
see Air pollution
see Dioxins
see Environmental pollution and control
see Global climate change
see Marine pollution
see Mercury pollution
see Motor vehicle exhaust
see Noise
see Radiation
see Radon
see Soil pollution
see Water pollution

Chemicals and chemical industry
Acid rain, emissions of contributing pollutants, by source, State, and Canada Province, 1985, 9198–121

Pollution abatement capital and operating costs, by SIC 2-to 4-digit industry and State, 1988, annual Current Industrial Rpt, 2506–3.6

Environmental pollution and control
Abatement and control equipment industry financial and operating data, by MSA, county, and city, 1987 Census of Manufactures, State rpt series, 2495–1
Abatement spending by govts, business, and consumers, 1984-88, annual article, 2702–1.137
Abatement spending, capital and operating costs by SIC 2- to 4-digit industry and State, 1988, annual Current Industrial Rpt, 2506–3.6

Index by Categories

An alternate approach is through the "Index by Categories." Since you are looking for information about a particular state, you can find it under "By State."

BY STATE

Natural Resources, Environment, and Pollution
Acid rain, emissions of contributing pollutants, by source, State, and Canada Province, 1985, 9198–121

Pollution abatement capital and operating costs, by SIC 2-to 4-digit industry and State, 1988, annual Current Industrial Rpt, 2506–3.6

Step 2

Go from the index to the data description in the appropriate Abstracts volume

The ASI accession number in the index will lead to a publication entry that fully describes the document and pinpoints the tables containing the statistics you need.

2506
BUREAU OF CENSUS: MANUFACTURING
Publications in series

2506–3.6: Manufacturers' Pollution Abatement Capital Expenditures and Operating Costs, Final Report for 1988

[Annual. Sept. 1990. 55 p. MA200(88)-1. °C3.158:MA200(88)-1/990. LC 77-646295. Price not given. ASI/MF/3]

Annual report for 1988 on pollution abatement control capital expenditures and operating costs, for U.S. by SIC 4-digit industry, and for States by 2-digit industry. Data are from a sample survey of approximately 20,000 establishments with 20 or more employees, in industries with abatement capital expenditures or annual operating costs of at least $1 million.

Contents: introduction (p. 1); and 6 tables, listed below (p. 2-55).

Advance annual report for 1988 was received in Apr. 1990 and is also available on ASI microfiche under this number [Apr. 1990. 2 p. MA200(88)-1. C3.158:MA200(88)-1. Price not given. ASI/MF/3]. No advance or final reports were issued for 1987. Final report for 1986, titled *Pollution Abatement Costs and Expenditures,* is described in ASI 1989 Annual under this number.

TABLES:

[Data are for 1988. Tables show data for U.S. by SIC 2- to 4-digit industry ("a" tables) and for States by SIC 2-digit major industry groups ("b" tables). Tables 1-2 show hazardous and nonhazardous solid waste pollutants.]

1a-1b. Pollution abatement capital expenditures [for air and solid waste pollution, by pollutant type; and for air and water pollution, by abatement technique (end-of-line, production process change)]. (p. 2-21)

2a-2b. Pollution abatement operating costs by form of abatement [payments for public sewage services and solid waste collection and disposal; and for pollutants abated from air, water, and solid waste]. (p. 22-38)

3a-3b. Pollution abatement operating costs by kind of cost [depreciation; labor; materials and supplies; and services, equipment leasing, and other costs] and cost recovered by form of pollutants [air, water, solid waste]. (p. 39-55)

Step 3

Retrieve the publication

The ASI abstract contains the bibliographic information you need to locate the publication in a library's hardcopy collection or to obtain it from the issuing source, if copies are available.

Alternatively, if you have access to an ASI Microfiche Library collection, the ASI accession number will lead you directly to the correct microfiche. Or, individual publications abstracted in any ASI Monthly or Annual Supplement are available for purchase on microfiche directly from Congressional Information Service through our CIS & ASI Documents on Demand Service.

Order kits supplied to all ASI subscribers provide the necessary information about costs and how to place microfiche orders. Details are also available by writing CIS Documents on Demand.

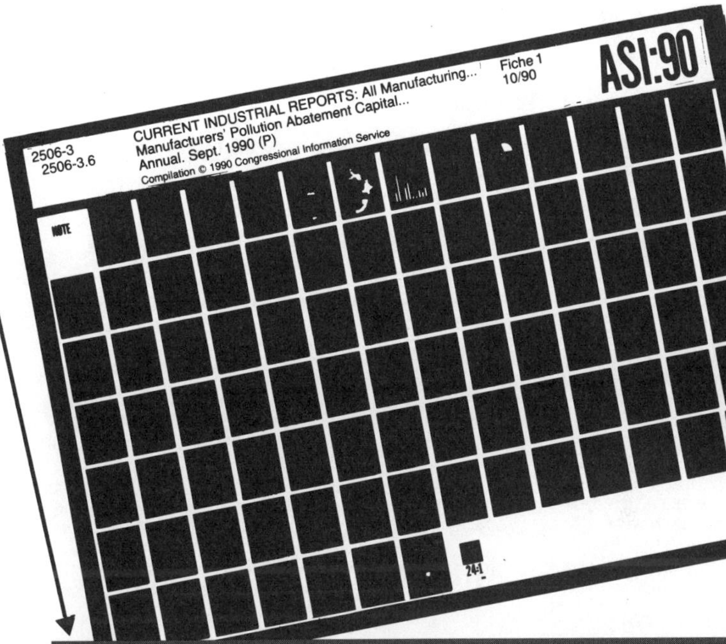

Table 1b. **Pollution Abatement Capital Expenditures for States and Major Groups: 1988**—Con.

[Million dollars. Totals may not agree with detail because of independent rounding. Statistics in this table cover manufacturing establishments with 20 employees or more. See text for a

SIC code	Industry	Total pollution abatement capital expenditures	Air: Total	Air: By type of pollutant abated: Particulates	Sulfur oxides	Nitrogen oxides and carbon monoxide	Hydrocarbon volatile organic compounds	Lead	Hazardous air pollutants	Other
	Massachusetts—Con.									
34	Fabricated metal products	(D)	(D)	(D)	-	-	(Z)	(D)	-	(D)
35	Machinery, except electrical	2.8	.6	.1	.1	-	(D)	-	(D)	-
36	Electric and electronic equipment	4.3	.9	(Z)	-	-	.4	(D)	.2	.3
38	Instruments and related products	(D)	(D)	(D)	(D)	-	(D)	-	-	(D)
	Michigan	**154.4**	**58.7**	**39.7**	**.2**	**.6**	**11.6**	**-**	**3.9**	**2.6**
20	Food and kindred products	7.0	2.9	2.4	(D)	-	.5	-	-	(D)
24	Lumber and wood products	1.1	.9	.9	-	-	-	-	-	-
26	Paper and allied products	11.8	(D)	(D)	(D)	-	-	-	(D)	(D)
27	Printing and publishing	1.3	-	-	-	-	-	-	-	-
28	Chemicals and allied products	30.7	10.2	2.4	.1	(Z)	6.0	-	.8	.9
30	Rubber and miscellaneous plastics products	1.7	1.0	.4	-	-	.6	-	-	-
31	Leather and leather products	1.2	.1	(Z)	-	-	.1	-	-	(Z)
32	Stone, clay, and glass products	1.9	1.3	1.3	(Z)	-	-	-	-	-
33	Primary metal industries	29.4	13.6	13.0	-	(D)	-	-	(Z)	(D)
34	Fabricated metal products	5.4	1.4	(D)	(Z)	-	(Z)	-	(D)	.3
35	Machinery, except electrical	3.1	2.1	.1	(D)	(D)	.1	-	1.8	(Z)
36	Electric and electronic equipment	1.8	(D)	(D)	-	-	(Z)	-	(Z)	(D)
37	Transportation equipment	57.0	23.9	18.1	(D)	(D)	4.2	-	(D)	.7
	New Jersey	**84.6**	**24.2**	**8.3**	**(D)**	**(D)**	**7.6**	**.1**	**2.3**	**1.8**
20	Food and kindred products	9.2	1.8	1.4	(Z)	.1	.1	-	-	.2
28	Chemicals and allied products	48.2	9.3	2.5	.1	.2	4.0	(Z)	1.5	.9
29	Petroleum and coal products	11.7	(D)	(D)	(D)	(D)	.9	-	(D)	(D)
32	Stone, clay, and glass products	3.4	3.0	2.1	-	.1	.8	-	(Z)	(Z)
33	Primary metal industries	1.1	.7	(D)	(Z)	.4	(Z)	.1	(Z)	(D)
34	Fabricated metal products	2.4	1.5	(Z)	(D)	(D)	1.3	-	(Z)	(Z)
36	Electric and electronic equipment	1.8	.4	.3	-	-	(D)	-	(D)	(D)
37	Transportation equipment	2.2	(D)	(D)	-	-	-	-	-	-
39	Miscellaneous manufacturing industries	1.3	.8	(D)	-	-	(D)	-	-	.1
	New Mexico	**(D)**	**(D)**	**(D)**	**(D)**	**-**	**(D)**	**-**	**(D)**	**(D)**
33	Primary metal industries	(D)	(D)	(D)	(D)	-	-	-	-	(D)
	New York	**102.1**	**45.8**	**16.4**	**1.3**	**.6**	**16.9**	**1.4**	**6.2**	**2.8**
20	Food and kindred products	2.7	1.4	.8	(D)	(D)	.1	-	[illegible]	.4
26	Paper and allied products	[illegible]	6.7	(D)	(D)	[illegible]	4.7	-	[illegible]	(D)
27	Printing and publishing	[illegible]	2.9	.5	.1	[illegible]	.1	(D)	[illegible]	-
28	Chemicals and allied products	[illegible]	13.7	2.5	[illegible]	[illegible]	6.5	(D)	[illegible]	[illegible]
30	Rubber and miscellaneous plastics products	[illegible]	(D)	.5	[illegible]	[illegible]	[illegible]	-	[illegible]	[illegible]

Where to Write for Statistical Publications

Publications abstracted in ASI are frequently available to the public from the Government Printing Office, the National Technical Information Service, or the issuing agency. In addition, a complete collection of abstracted publications is available in the ASI Microfiche Library.

Information about the source and availability of specific publications is given in each ASI abstract. (For illustrations, see the Sample Abstracts; for background information, see the section headed "Acquiring the Documents" on p. xx.)

The mailing addresses of GPO, NTIS, and principal issuing agency sources of publications are listed below.

When ordering publications from the issuing agency, requests should be directed to the specific subagency, Information Division, c/o the parent agency. Where the subagency has a separate mailing address, it is given.

There has been no attempt to list regional or field offices for every agency and subagency. Listings and addresses of these offices can be found in most agency catalogs, and in local telephone directories for the cities in which they are located.

Addresses have been provided for the sources of publications, periodicals, and/or specials and irregulars, which may be available only, or more conveniently, from offices in other locations than the central information office for an agency. Identification of other unusual sources will appear with the abstract of a publication.

GOVERNMENT PRINTING OFFICE (GPO)
Superintendent of Documents
Washington, DC 20402

NATIONAL TECHNICAL INFORMATION SERVICE (NTIS)
5285 Port Royal Rd
Springfield, VA 22161

EXECUTIVE OFFICE OF THE PRESIDENT
Publications Unit, Rm G236
New Executive Office Bldg
Washington, DC 20503

COUNCIL OF ECONOMIC ADVISERS
New Executive Office Bldg
Washington, DC 20506

COUNCIL ON ENVIRONMENTAL QUALITY
722 Jackson Pl., N.W.
Washington, DC 20006

OFFICE OF MANAGEMENT & BUDGET
Publications Unit, Rm G236
New Executive Office Bldg
Washington, DC 20503

OFFICE OF NATIONAL DRUG CONTROL POLICY
750 17th St., N.W.
Washington, DC 20500

OFFICE OF SCIENCE AND TECHNOLOGY POLICY
New Executive Office Building
Washington, DC 20506

OFFICE OF THE U.S. TRADE REPRESENTATIVE
600 17th St., N.W.
Washington, DC 20506

DEPARTMENT OF AGRICULTURE
(Subagency Name)
Information Division
Washington, DC 20250

AGRICULTURAL MARKETING SERVICE
Information Staff Room 3510-S
Washington, DC 20250

Cotton Division
4841 Summer Ave.
Memphis, TN 38122

AGRICULTURAL STATISTICS
5820 S. Building
Washington, DC 20250

ECONOMIC RESEARCH SERVICE
ERS-NASS Publications
341 Victory Dr.
Herndon, VA 22070

FOREST SERVICE—Forest Experiment Stations

Intermountain (INT)
324 25th St.
Ogden, UT 84401

North Central (NC)
1992 Folwell Ave.
St. Paul, MN 55108

Northeastern (NE)
370 Reed Rd
Broomall, PA 19008

Pacific Northwest (PNW)
P.O. Box 3890
Portland, OR 97208

Pacific Southwest (PSW)
1960 Addison St. P.O. Box 245
Berkeley, CA 94701

Rocky Mountain (RM)
11177 W 8th Ave.
Lakewood, CO 80225

Southeastern (SE)
P.O. Box 2680
Asheville NC 28802

Southern (SO)
T-10210 Postal Services Bldg
701 Loyola Ave.
New Orleans, LA 70113

SOIL CONSERVATION SERVICE
(Western U.S.)
West Technical Service Center, Rm 510
511 N.W. Broadway
Portland, OR 97209

DEPARTMENT OF COMMERCE
(Subagency Name)
Office of Public Affairs
Washington, DC 20230

BUREAU OF ECONOMIC ANALYSIS
Information Services Division
1401 K St., N.W.
Washington, DC 20235

BUREAU OF THE CENSUS
Customer Services
Data User Services Division
Washington, DC 20233

NATIONAL INSTITUTE OF STANDARDS AND TECHNOLOGY
Office of Information Activities
Rm 640, Administration Bldg
Washington, DC 20234

NATIONAL OCEANIC AND ATMOSPHERIC ADMINISTRATION
Office of Public Affairs
WSC-5
Rockville, MD 20852

Environmental Satellite, Data, and Information Service
Library and Information Services Division
Rockville, MD 20852

Environmental Research Laboratories
Public Information Office
Boulder, CO 80302

National Climatic Data Center
EDIS
Federal Building
Asheville, NC 28801

National Marine Fisheries Service
Public Affairs
Rm 6268, 1335 East-West Highway
Silver Spring, MD 20910

National Ocean Service
Public Information Office
WSC-1
Rockville, MD 20852

National Weather Service
Rm 400, Gramax Bldg
8060 13th St.
Silver Spring, MD 20910

PATENT AND TRADEMARK OFFICE
Office of Public Affairs
2021 Jefferson Davis Highway
Arlington, VA 20231

DEPARTMENT OF COMMERCE DISTRICT OFFICES— INTERNATIONAL TRADE ADMINISTRATION

319 World Trade Center Alaska
4201 Tudor Center Dr.
Anchorage, AK 99508

4360 Chamblee-Dunwoody Rd.
Atlanta, GA 30341

Rm 415, U.S. Customhouse
Baltimore, MD 21202

Berry Bldg., 2015 2nd Ave. N.,
Birmingham, AL 35203

Suite 307, World Trade Center
Commonwealth Pier Area
Boston, MA 02210

Rm 1312, 111 W. Huron St.
Buffalo, NY 14202

Suite 809, 405 Capitol St.
Charleston, WV 25301

55 E. Monroe St.
Chicago, IL 60603

550 Main St.
Cincinnati, OH 45202

Rm 600, 666 Euclid Ave.
Cleveland, OH 44114

Suite 172, 1835 Assembly St.
Columbia, SC 29201

Rm 7A5, 1100 Commerce St.
Dallas, TX 75242

Suite 600, 1625 Broadway
Denver, CO 80202

Rm 817, 210 Walnut St.
Des Moines, IA 50309

1140 McNamara Bldg, 477 Michigan Ave.
Detroit, MI 48226

Rm 203, 324 W. Market St.
Greensboro, NC 27402

Rm 610-B, 450 Main St.
Hartford, CT 06103

P.O. Box 50026, 400 Ala Moana Blvd.
Honolulu, HI 96850

Rm 2625, 515 Rusk Ave.
Houston, TX 77002

Suite 520, One N. Capitol St.
Indianapolis, IN 46204

328 Jackson Mall Office Center
Jackson, MS 39213

Rm 635, 601 E. 12th St.
Kansas City, MO 64106

Suite 635, 320 W. Capitol Ave.
Little Rock, AR 72201

Rm 9200, 11000 Wilshire Blvd.
Los Angeles, CA 90024

Rm 636B, 601 W. Broadway
Louisville, KY 40202

Suite 224, 51 SW 1st Ave.
Miami, FL 33130

517 E. Wisconsin Ave.
Milwaukee, WI 53202

Rm 108, 110 S. 4th St.
Minneapolis, MN 55401

Suite 1114, Parkway Towers
Nashville, TN 37219

2 Canal St.
New Orleans, LA 70130

Rm 3718, Federal Office Bldg
New York, NY 10278

6601 Broadway Extension
Oklahoma City, OK 73116

11133 O St.
Omaha, NE 68137

Suite 202, 475 Allendale Rd.
King of Prussia, PA 19406

Rm 3412, Federal Bldg and U.S. Courthouse
Phoenix, AZ 85025

Rm 2002, 1000 Liberty Ave.
Pittsburgh, PA 15222

Suite 242, 1 World Trade Center
121 SW Salmon St.
Portland, OR 97204

1755 E. Plumb La., No. 152
Reno, NV 89502

Rm 8010, 400 N. 8th St.
Richmond, VA 23240

Rm 105, 324 S. State St.
Salt Lake City, UT 84111

6363 Greenwich Dr.
San Diego, CA 92122

14th Fl., 250 Montgomery St.
San Francisco, CA 94104

Rm G-55, Federal Bldg, Chardon Ave.
San Juan, PR 00918

120 Barnard St., A-107
Savannah, GA 31401

Suite 290, 3131 Elliott Ave.
Seattle, WA 98121

Suite 610, 7911 Forsyth Blvd.
St. Louis, MO 63105

Suite 100, Bldg 6, 3131 Princeton Pike
Trenton, NJ 08648

DEPARTMENT OF DEFENSE

Office of the Assistant Secretary of Defense
(Public Affairs)
The Pentagon
Washington, DC 20301

Directorate for Information Operations
and Reports (DIOR)
Suite 1204, 1215 Jefferson Davis Hwy.
Arlington, VA 22202-4302

DEFENSE LOGISTICS AGENCY
Defense Fuel Supply Center
Public Affairs
Bldg 8, Cameron Station
Alexandria, VA 22314

U.S. AIR FORCE PUBLICATIONS
Office of the Secretary of the Air Force
Office of Information
Public Information Division
Headquarters, USAF
Washington, DC 20330

U.S. ARMY PUBLICATIONS
Public Information Office
Office of the Chief of Information
Headquarters, Department of the Army
Washington, DC 20310

U.S. ARMY CORPS OF ENGINEERS
Public Affairs Office
Forrestal Bldg
Washington, DC 20314

U.S. ARMY CORPS OF ENGINEERS REGIONAL OFFICES
Alaska District
P.O. Box 7002
Anchorage, AK 99510

Detroit District
P.O. Box 1027
Detroit, MI 48281

Louisville District
P.O. Box 59
Louisville, KY 40201

Lower Mississippi Valley Division
P.O. Box 60
Vicksburg, MS 39180

Missouri River Division
Downtown Station, P.O. Box 103
Omaha, NE 68101

Mobile District
P.O. Box 2288
Mobile, AL 36828

Nashville District
P.O. Box 1070
Nashville, TN 37202

New England Division
424 Trapelo Rd
Waltham, MA 02154

New Orleans District
P.O. Box 60267
New Orleans, LA 70160

North Atlantic Division
90 Church St.
New York, NY 10007

North Central Division
536 S. Clark St.
Chicago, IL 60605

Ohio River Division
P.O. Box 1159
Cincinnati, OH 45201

South Atlantic Division
510 Title Bldg
30 Pryor St., S.W.
Atlanta, GA 30303

South Pacific Division
630 Sansome St.
San Francisco, CA 94111

Southwest Division
1114 Commerce St.
Dallas, TX 75242

U.S. NAVY PUBLICATIONS
Public Information Division
Office of Information
Department of the Navy
Washington, DC 20350

DEPARTMENT OF EDUCATION

(Specified Office)
400 Maryland Ave., S.W.
Washington, DC 20202

NATIONAL CENTER FOR EDUCATION STATISTICS
OERI
555 New Jersey Ave., N.W.
Washington, DC 20208

NATIONAL ASSESSMENT OF EDUCATIONAL PROGRESS (NAEP)
CN6710
Princeton, NJ 08541-6710

DEPARTMENT OF ENERGY

(Subagency Name)
Washington, DC 20585

BONNEVILLE POWER ADMINISTRATION
Public Involvement
P.O. Box 12999
Portland, OR 97212

ENERGY INFORMATION ADMINISTRATION
National Energy Information Center
EI-20, Mail Station 1F048
1000 Independence Ave., S.W.
Washington, DC 20585

FEDERAL ENERGY REGULATORY COMMISSION
Public Information Office, Rm 1000
825 North Capitol St., N.E.
Washington, DC 20426

OAK RIDGE NATIONAL LABORATORY
Technical Information Center
P.O. Box 62
Oak Ridge, TN 37831

DEPARTMENT OF HEALTH AND HUMAN SERVICES

Office of Public Affairs
Rm 647-D, HHH Bldg
200 Independence Ave., S.W.
Washington, DC 20201

AGENCY FOR HEALTH CARE POLICY AND RESEARCH
AHCPR Clearinghouse
P.O. Box 8547
Silver Spring, MD 20907-8547

CENTERS FOR DISEASE CONTROL AND PREVENTION
1600 Clifton Rd, N.E.
Atlanta, GA 30333

FOOD AND DRUG ADMINISTRATION
HFE 88
5600 Fishers La.
Rockville, MD 20857

HEALTH CARE FINANCING ADMINISTRATION
648 East High Rise Bldg
6401 Security Blvd
Baltimore, MD 21235

HEALTH RESOURCES AND SERVICES ADMINISTRATION
(Subagency Name)
14-43 Parklawn Bldg
5600 Fishers La.
Rockville, MD 20857

National Maternal and Child Health
Clearinghouse
38th & R Sts., N.W.
Washington, DC 20057

Clearinghouse for Primary Care Information
8201 Greensboro Dr., Suite 600
McLean, VA 22102

NATIONAL CENTER FOR HEALTH STATISTICS
Rm 1-57, Federal Center Bldg #2
3700 East-West Hwy
Hyattsville, MD 20782

NATIONAL CLEARINGHOUSE FOR ALCOHOL AND DRUG INFORMATION
P.O. Box 2345
Rockville, MD 20847-2345

NATIONAL INSTITUTES OF HEALTH
Office of Information
Rm 307, Bldg 1
9000 Rockville Pike
Bethesda, MD 20205

NATIONAL INSTITUTE OF MENTAL HEALTH
Public Inquiries
Rm 11A-21, 5600 Fishers La.
Rockville, MD 20857

NATIONAL INSTITUTE FOR OCCUPATIONAL SAFETY AND HEALTH
Publications, DTS
4676 Columbia Parkway
Cincinnati, OH 45226

OFFICE OF HUMAN DEVELOPMENT SERVICES
Rm 329D, HHH Bldg
200 Independence Ave., S.W.
Washington, DC 20201

OFFICE ON SMOKING AND HEALTH
Rm 158, 5600 Fishers La.
Rockville, MD 20857

PUBLIC HEALTH SERVICE
Office of Public Affairs
Rm 740-G, HHH Bldg
200 Independence Ave., S.W.
Washington, DC 20201

OHIC/ODPHP
P.O. Box 1133
Washington, DC 20013-1133

SOCIAL SECURITY ADMINISTRATION
Printing and Records Management Branch
1121 Operations Bldg
6401 Security Blvd
Baltimore, MD 21235

DEPARTMENT OF HOUSING AND URBAN DEVELOPMENT

Publication Service Center
Rm B-258
Washington, DC 20410

OFFICE OF POLICY DEVELOPMENT AND RESEARCH
HUD USER
P.O. Box 6091
Rockville, MD 20850

DEPARTMENT OF THE INTERIOR

(Subagency Name)
Office of Information
Washington, DC 20240

BUREAU OF MINES
Publication Distribution Section
4800 Forbes Ave.
Pittsburgh, PA 15213

FISH AND WILDLIFE SERVICE
Natl Coastal Ecosystems Team
NASA Slidell Computer Complex
1010 Gause Blvd.
Slidell, LA 709458

U.S. GEOLOGICAL SURVEY
USGS Books and Open-File Rpts. Section
Box 25425, Federal Center
Denver, CO 80225

DEPARTMENT OF JUSTICE

Office of Public Information
10th and Constitution Ave., N.W.
Washington, DC 20530

BUREAU OF PRISONS
320 1st St., N.W.
Washington, DC 20534

DRUG ENFORCEMENT ADMINISTRATION
1405 I St., N.W.
Washington, DC 20537

FEDERAL BUREAU OF INVESTIGATION
9th and Pennsylvania Ave., N.W.
Washington, DC 20535

FOREIGN CLAIMS SETTLEMENT COMMISSION OF THE U.S.
Vanguard Building
1111 20th St., N.W.
Washington, DC 20579

IMMIGRATION AND NATURALIZATION SERVICE
425 I St., N.W.
Attn: Tariff Rm 235
Washington, DC 20536

NATIONAL CRIMINAL JUSTICE REFERENCE SERVICE (NCJRS)
Box 6000
Rockville, MD 20850

OFFICE OF JUSTICE PROGRAMS
633 Indiana Ave., N.W.
Washington, DC 20531

DEPARTMENT OF LABOR

Office of Information, Publications, and Reports
200 Constitution Ave., N.W.
Washington, DC 20210

BUREAU OF LABOR STATISTICS
Information Office
Postal Square Bldg.
2 Massachusetts Ave., N.W.
Washington, DC 20212

BUREAU OF LABOR STATISTICS REGIONAL OFFICES
Region I
Rm 1603, JFK Federal Bldg
Government Center
Boston, MA 02203

Region II
201 Varick St.
New York, NY 10014

Region III
3535 Market St.
P.O. Box 13309
Philadelphia, PA 19104

Region IV
1371 Peachtree St., N.E.
Atlanta, GA 30367

Region V
Federal Office Bldg
230 S. Dearborn St.
Chicago, IL 60604

Region VI
555 Griffin St., Rm 221
Dallas, TX 75202

Regions VII and VIII
911 Walnut St.
Kansas City, MO 64106

Regions IX and X
71 Stevenson St.
San Francisco, CA 94119-3766

EMPLOYMENT AND TRAINING ADMINISTRATION
Rm 10426, 601 D St., N.W.
Washington, DC 20213

MINE SAFETY AND HEALTH ADMINISTRATION
Office of Information
Ballston Tower #3, Rm 902
4015 Wilson Blvd
Arlington, VA 22203

DEPARTMENT OF STATE

(Subagency Name)
Bureau of Public Affairs
Washington, DC 20520

DEPARTMENT OF TRANSPORTATION

Office of Public & Consumer Affairs (S-81)
400 7th St., S.W.
Washington, DC 20590

Transporation Systems Center
Kendall Sq.
Cambridge, MA 02142

FEDERAL AVIATION ADMINISTRATION
Public Inquiry Center (APA-420)
800 Independence Ave., S.W.
Washington, DC 20590

FEDERAL HIGHWAY ADMINISTRATION
Office of Public Affairs (HPA-1)
400 7th St., S.W.
Washington, DC 20590

FEDERAL RAILROAD ADMINISTRATION
Office of Public Affairs (ROA-30)
400 7th St., S.W.
Washington, DC 20590

FEDERAL TRANSIT ADMINISTRATION
Office of Public Affairs (UPA-1)
400 7th St., S.W.
Washington, DC 20590

MARITIME ADMINISTRATION
Office of Public Affairs (MAR-240)
400 7th St., S.W.
Washington, DC 20590

NATIONAL HIGHWAY TRAFFIC SAFETY ADMINISTRATION
400 7th St., S.W.
Washington, DC 20590

SAINT LAWRENCE SEAWAY DEVELOPMENT CORPORATION
P.O. Box 44090
Washington, DC 20026-4090

U.S. COAST GUARD
Public Affairs Division (G-BPA)
2100 2nd St., S.W.
Washington, DC 20593

DEPARTMENT OF THE TREASURY

Public Affairs Office
15th and Pennsylvania Ave., N.W.
Washington, DC 20220

BUREAU OF ALCOHOL, TOBACCO AND FIREARMS
Office of Public Affairs
1200 Pennsylvania Ave., N.W.
Washington, DC 20226

BUREAU OF ENGRAVING AND PRINTING
Public Affairs Section, Rm 602-11A
14th and C Sts., S.W.
Washington, DC 20228

BUREAU OF THE PUBLIC DEBT
Washington, DC 20226

COMPTROLLER OF THE CURRENCY
Communications Division
490 L'Enfant Plaza East, S.W.
Washington, DC 20219

FINANCIAL MANAGEMENT SERVICE
Pennsylvania Ave. and Madison Pl., N.W.
Washington, DC 20226

INTERNAL REVENUE SERVICE
Office of Public Affairs
1111 Constitution Ave., N.W.
Washington, DC 20224

OFFICE OF REVENUE SHARING
Office of Public Affairs
2401 E St., N.W.
Washington, DC 20226

OFFICE OF THRIFT SUPERVISION
1700 G St., N.W.
Washington, DC 20552

U.S. CUSTOMS SERVICE
Office of Public Affairs
1301 Constitution Ave., N.W.
Washington, DC 20229

U.S. MINT
Assistant to the Director for Public Affairs
501 13th St., N.W.
Washington, DC 20220

U.S. SAVINGS BOND DIVISION
Washington, DC 20226

U.S. SECRET SERVICE
Office of Public Affairs
1800 G St., N.W.
Washington, DC 20223

DEPARTMENT OF VETERANS AFFAIRS

Office of Public Affairs
810 Vermont Ave., N.W.
Washington, DC 20420

INDEPENDENT AGENCIES

ACTION
Office of Public Affairs
1100 Vermont Ave., N.W.
Washington, DC 20525

AFRICAN DEVELOPMENT FOUNDATION
1400 Eye St., N.W.
Washington, DC 20005

AMERICAN BATTLE MONUMENTS COMMISSION
20 Massachusetts Ave., N.W.
Washington, DC 20314

APPALACHIAN REGIONAL COMMISSION
Archivist
1666 Connecticut Ave., N.W.
Washington, DC 20235

CENTRAL INTELLIGENCE AGENCY
Photoduplication Service
Library of Congress
Washington, DC 20540

CONSUMER PRODUCT SAFETY COMMISSION
Bureau of Information and Education
Product Safety Information Division
5401 Westbard Ave.
Bethesda, MD 20207

ENVIRONMENTAL PROTECTION AGENCY
(Subagency Name)
401 M St., S.W.
Washington, DC 20460

Documents Distribution Division
1901 Ross Ave.
Cincinnati, OH 45212

Office of Air Quality Planning and Standards
Research Triangle Park, NC 27711

ENVIRONMENTAL PROTECTION AGENCY REGIONAL OFFICES
Region I
Rm 2203, JFK Federal Bldg
Boston, MA 02203

Region II
Rm 1009, 26 Federal Plaza
New York, NY 10278

Region III
841 Chestnut St.
Philadelphia, PA 19107

Region IV
345 Courtland St., N.E.
Atlanta, GA 30365

Region V
230 South Dearborn St.
Chicago, IL 60604

Region VI
1445 Ross Ave.
Dallas, TX 75202

Region VII
726 Minnesota Ave.
Kansas City, KS 66101

Region VIII
999 18th St., Suite 500
Denver, CO 80202-2405

Region IX
215 Fremont St.
San Francisco, CA 94105

Region X
1200 6th Ave.
Seattle, WA 98101

EQUAL EMPLOYMENT OPPORTUNITY COMMISSION
1801 L St., N.W.
Washington, DC 20507

EXPORT-IMPORT BANK OF THE UNITED STATES
Public Affairs Office
811 Vermont Ave., N.W.
Washington, DC 20571

FARM CREDIT ADMINISTRATION
Information Division
1501 Farm Credit Dr.
McLean, VA 22102

FEDERAL COMMUNICATIONS COMMISSION
Public Information Office
1919 M St., N.W.
Washington, DC 20554

FEDERAL DEPOSIT INSURANCE CORPORATION
Information Office
550 17th St., N.W.
Washington, DC 20429

FEDERAL ELECTION COMMISSION
999 E St., N.W.
Washington, DC 20463

FEDERAL EMERGENCY MANAGEMENT AGENCY
Office of Public Affairs
500 C St., S.W.
Washington, DC 20472

FEDERAL HOME LOAN BANKS
Federal Home Loan Bank of Atlanta
Peachtree Center Station
P.O. Box 56527
Atlanta, GA 30343

Federal Home Loan Bank of Boston
P.O. Box 2196
Boston, MA 02106

Federal Home Loan Bank of Chicago
111 E. Wacker Dr.
Chicago, IL 60601

Federal Home Loan Bank of Cincinnati
2500 DuBois Tower
P.O. Box 598
Cincinnati, OH 45201

Federal Home Loan Bank of Dallas
500 E. John Carpenter Freeway
P.O. Box 619026
Dallas/Ft. Worth, TX 75261

Federal Home Loan Bank of Des Moines
907 Walnut St.
Des Moines, IA 50309

Federal Home Loan Bank of Indianapolis
1350 Merchants Plaza, South Tower
115 W. Washington St.
P.O. Box 60
Indianapolis, IN 46206

Federal Home Loan Bank of New York
One World Trade Center
New York, NY 10048

Federal Home Loan Bank of Pittsburgh
11 Stanwix St.
Gateway Center
Pittsburgh, PA 15222

Federal Home Loan Bank of San Francisco
600 California St.
P.O. Box 7948
San Francisco, CA 94120

Federal Home Loan Bank of Seattle
600 Stewart St.
Seattle, WA 98101

Federal Home Loan Bank of Topeka
3 Townsite Plaza
P.O. Box 176 120 East 6th St.
Topeka, KS 66601

FEDERAL HOME LOAN MORTGAGE CORPORATION
1770 G St., N.W.
Washington, DC 20552

FEDERAL HOUSING FINANCE BOARD
1777 F St., N.W.
Washington, DC 20066

FEDERAL MARITIME COMMISSION
Public Information Office
1100 L St., N.W.
Washington, DC 20573

FEDERAL MEDIATION AND CONCILIATION SERVICE
2100 K St., N.W.
Washington, DC 20427

FEDERAL NATIONAL MORTGAGE ASSOCIATION
3900 Wisconsin Ave., N.W.
Washington, DC 20016

FEDERAL RESERVE SYSTEM
Board of Governors
Publications Section
Division of Administrative Services
Washington, DC 20551

Federal Reserve Bank of Atlanta
Research Department
P.O. Box 1731
Atlanta, GA 30301

Federal Reserve Bank of Boston
Bank & Public Information Center
600 Atlantic Ave.
Boston, MA 02106

Federal Reserve Bank of Chicago
Publications Division
P.O. Box 834
Chicago, IL 60690

Federal Reserve Bank of Cleveland
Research Department
P.O. Box 6387
Cleveland, OH 44101

Federal Reserve Bank of Dallas
Research Department
Station K
Dallas, TX 75222

Federal Reserve Bank of Kansas City
Research Department
925 Grand Ave.
Kansas City, MO 64198

Federal Reserve Bank of Minneapolis
Office of Public Information
Minneapolis, MN 55480

Federal Reserve Bank of New York
Public Information Department
33 Liberty St.
New York, NY 10045

Federal Reserve Bank of Philadelphia
Public Information Department
PO Box 66
Philadelphia, PA 19105

Federal Reserve Bank of Richmond
Bank and Public Relations Department
P.O. Box 27622
Richmond, VA 23261

Federal Reserve Bank of St. Louis
Research Department
Box 442
St. Louis, MO 63166

Federal Reserve Bank of San Francisco
Research Information Center
P.O. Box 7702
San Francisco, CA 94120

FEDERAL TRADE COMMISSION
Public Reference Room
Pennsylvania Ave. at 6th St., N.W.
Rm 130
Washington, DC 20580

GENERAL SERVICES ADMINISTRATION
Director of Information
18th & F Sts., N.W.
Washington, DC 20405

INTERSTATE COMMERCE COMMISSION
Public Information Office
12th St. and Constitution Ave., N.W.
Washington, DC 20423

MERIT SYSTEMS PROTECTION BOARD
1120 Vermont Ave., N.W.
Washington, DC 20419

NATIONAL AERONAUTICS AND SPACE ADMINISTRATION
Headquarters, Information Center
Washington, DC 20546

NATIONAL ARCHIVES AND RECORDS ADMINISTRATION
Publications Services
Washington, DC 20408

NATIONAL CREDIT UNION ADMINISTRATION
Office of Public Information
1776 G St., N.W.
Washington, DC 20456

NATIONAL FOUNDATION ON THE ARTS AND HUMANITIES
1100 Pennsylvania, Ave., N.W.
Washington, DC 20506

NATIONAL LABOR RELATIONS BOARD
1717 Pennsylvania Ave., N.W.
Washington, DC 20570

NATIONAL MEDIATION BOARD
1425 K St., N.W.
Washington, DC 20572

NATIONAL SCIENCE FOUNDATION
Public Information Branch, Rm 531
1800 G St., N.W.
Washington, DC 20550

NATIONAL TRANSPORTATION SAFETY BOARD
Publications Unit
490 L'Enfant Plaza, S.W.
Washington, DC 20594

OFFICE OF PERSONNEL MANAGEMENT
Office of Public Affairs
1900 E St., N.W.
Washington, DC 20415

PANAMA CANAL COMMISSION
2000 L St., N.W.
Washington, DC 20036

PEACE CORPS
1990 K St., N.W.
Washington, DC 20526

PENSION BENEFIT GUARANTY CORPORATION
2020 K St., N.W.
Washington, DC 20006

RAILROAD RETIREMENT BOARD
Division of Information Service
844 Rush St.
Chicago, IL 60611

RESOLUTION TRUST CORPORATION
Corporate Communications Office
Washington, DC 20434

SECURITIES AND EXCHANGE COMMISSION
Office of Public Information
450 5th St., N.W.
Washington, DC 20549

SELECTIVE SERVICE SYSTEM
600 E St., N.W.
Washington, DC 20435

SMALL BUSINESS ADMINISTRATION
Office of Public Communications
409 Third St., S.W.
Washington, DC 20416

SMITHSONIAN INSTITUTION
Office of Public Affairs
Washington, DC 20560

TENNESSEE VALLEY AUTHORITY
Suite 300, 412 First St., S.E.
Washington, DC 20444

Public Affairs Office
400 W. Summit Hill Dr.
Knoxville, TN 37902-1499

Division of Energy Use and Distributor Relations
721 Power Building
Chattanooga, TN 37401

Division of Land and Forest Resources
Norris, TN 37828

National Fertilizer Development Center
Muscle Shoals, AL 35660

Technical Library
NFD 1A 100E
Muscle Shoals, AL 35660-1010

U.S. ARMS CONTROL AND DISARMAMENT AGENCY
Office of Public Affairs
320 21st St., N.W.
Washington, DC 20451

U.S. INFORMATION AGENCY
Office of Public Liaison
301 Fourth St., S.W.
Washington, DC 20547

U.S. INTERNATIONAL DEVELOPMENT COOPERATION AGENCY
Office of Public Affairs
Washington, DC 20523-0001

Agency for International Development
Director, Office of Public Affairs
Washington, DC 20523-0001

AID Development Information Services Clearinghouse
1500 Wilson Blvd., Suite 1010
Arlington, VA 22209-2404

Overseas Private Investment Corporation
1615 M St., N.W.
Washington, DC 20527

U.S. INTERNATIONAL TRADE COMMISSION
Office of the Secretary
500 E St., S.W.
Washington, DC 20436

U.S. OFFICE OF SPECIAL COUNSEL
1730 M St., N.W.
Washington, DC 20036-4505

U.S. POSTAL SERVICE
475 L'Enfant Plaza West, S.W.
Washington, DC 20260

SPECIAL BOARDS, COMMITTEES, AND COMMISSIONS

ADVISORY COMMISSION ON INTERGOVERNMENTAL RELATIONS
800 K St., N.W.
South Building, Suite 450
Washington, DC 20575

ARCHITECTURAL AND TRANSPORTATION BARRIERS COMPLIANCE BOARD
Suite 501, 1111 18th St., N.W.
Washington, DC 20036

BOARD FOR INTERNATIONAL BROADCASTING
Suite 400, 1201 Connecticut Ave., N.W.
Washington, DC 20036

COMMISSION ON CIVIL RIGHTS
624 9th St., N.W.
Washington, DC 20425

COMMODITY FUTURES TRADING COMMISSION
Office of Public Information
2033 K St., N.W.
Washington, DC 20581

Suite 4600, 233 S. Wacker Dr.
Chicago, IL 60606

Rm 400, 4901 Main St.
Kansas City, MO 64112

510 Grain Exchange Building
Minneapolis, MN 55415

Suite 4747, One World Trade Center
New York, NY 10048

FEDERAL FINANCIAL INSTITUTIONS EXAMINATION COUNCIL
Suite 850B, 1776 G St., N.W.
Washington, DC 20006

FEDERAL LABOR RELATIONS AUTHORITY
500 C St., S.W.
Washington, DC 20424

HARRY S. TRUMAN SCHOLARSHIP FOUNDATION
712 Jackson Place, N.W.
Washington, DC 20006

INTER-AMERICAN FOUNDATION
1515 Wilson Blvd, 5th Fl.
Rosslyn, VA 22209

INTERNATIONAL JOINT COMMISSION, U.S. AND CANADA
United States Section
2001 S St., N.W.
Washington, DC 20440

J. WILLIAM FULBRIGHT FOREIGN SCHOLARSHIP BOARD
U.S. Information Agency
Rm 247, 301 4th St., S.W.
Washington, DC 20547

JAPAN-U.S. FRIENDSHIP COMMISSION
Rm 3416, 1200 Pennsylvania Ave., N.W.
Washington, DC 20004

MARINE MAMMAL COMMISSION
Rm 512, 1825 Connecticut Ave., N.W.
Washington, DC 20009

MIGRATORY BIRD CONSERVATION COMMISSION
18th & C Sts., N.W., 622 ARL.SQ
Washington, DC 20240

NATIONAL ADVISORY COUNCIL ON ADULT EDUCATION
Rm 323, 425 13th St., N.W.
Washington, DC 20004

NATIONAL ADVISORY COUNCIL ON INDIAN EDUCATION
330 C St., S.W., Room 4072
Switzer Bldg, Mail Stop 2419
Washington, DC 20202-7556

NATIONAL ADVISORY COUNCIL ON INTERNATIONAL MONETARY AND FINANCIAL POLICIES
Rm 5410
Department of the Treasury
Washington, DC 20220

NATIONAL CAPITAL PLANNING COMMISSION
Suite 301, 801 Pennsylvania Ave., N.W.
Washington, DC 20576

NATIONAL COMMISSION FOR EMPLOYMENT POLICY
1522 K St., N.W., Rm 300
Washington, DC 20005

NATIONAL COMMISSION ON LIBRARIES AND INFORMATION SCIENCE
1111 18th St., N.W., Suite 310
Washington, DC 20036

OFFICE OF NAVAJO AND HOPI INDIAN RELOCATION
P.O. Box KK
Flagstaff, ZA 86002

PRESIDENT'S COMMITTEE ON EMPLOYMENT OF PEOPLE WITH DISABILITIES
1111 20th St., N.W., Suite 636
Washington, DC 20036

PROSPECTIVE PAYMENT ASSESSMENT COMMISSION
300 7th St., S.W.
Washington, DC 20024

U.S. ADVISORY COMMISSION ON PUBLIC DIPLOMACY
Rm 1008, 1750 Pennsylvania Ave., N.W.
Washington, DC 20547

JUDICIAL BRANCH

ADMINISTRATIVE OFFICE OF U.S. COURTS
Washington, DC 20544

FEDERAL JUDICIAL CENTER
1 Columbus Circle, N.E.
Washington, DC 20002

SPECIAL COURTS
U.S. Court of International Trade
1 Federal Plaza
New York, NY 10007

U.S. Court of Claims
717 Madison Pl., N.W.
Washington, DC 20005

U.S. Tax Court
400 2nd St., N.W.
Washington, DC 20217

UNITED STATES CONGRESS

(House Committee Name)
U.S. House of Representatives
Washington, DC 20515

(Senate Committee Name)
U.S. Senate
Washington, DC 20510

(Joint Committee Name)
U.S. Congress
Washington, DC 20510

CONGRESSIONAL BUDGET OFFICE
Office of Intergovernmental Relations
2nd and D Sts., S.W.
Washington, DC 20515

LIBRARY OF CONGRESS
Publications Officer
Washington, DC 20540

OFFICE OF TECHNOLOGY ASSESSMENT
Office of Public Affairs
Washington, DC 20510

U.S. GENERAL ACCOUNTING OFFICE
Document Handling and Information Services Facility
P.O. Box 6015
Gaithersburg, MD 20877

QUASI-OFFICIAL AGENCIES

AMERICAN NATIONAL RED CROSS
Office of Public Affairs and Financial Development
17th and D Sts., N.W.
Washington, DC 20006

NATIONAL RAILROAD PASSENGER CORPORATION (AMTRAK)
Public Affairs Department
60 Massachusetts Ave., N.E.
Washington, DC 20002

U.S. INSTITUTE OF PEACE
1550 M St., N.W.
Washington, DC 20005-1708

Document Availability Symbols

The following abbreviations and symbols are used to indicate the availability of documents abstracted by ASI. The symbols are provided in the bibliographic data section given at the head of each abstract.

GPO For sale by Government Printing Office, Washington, D.C., 20402.

The GPO stock number (S/N) is also given. The price is given if it has been announced at the time ASI goes to press; GPO prices change frequently, however.

NTIS For sale by National Technical Information Service, 5285 Port Royal Rd., Springfield, Va., 22161.

Order number and price are also given if available.

† or ‡ Inquire of the issuing agency.

† Copies are available at the time the document is issued, often free of charge, but supplies may be limited.

‡ Limited or restricted distribution has been specified by the agency. In some cases a request for a copy will be honored.

Addresses of major issuing agency offices are given in the Abstracts Volume, p. xxxvii; Index Volume, p. xxviii. If documents are available from another office, the name and address will be given in the bibliographic data section of the abstract.

◆ No distribution. Issuing agency has specified it should not be contacted.

ASI/MF Available on ASI microfiche. Microfiche collections are available in many libraries. The number following this notation indicates the unit count for ordering individual documents on microfiche through ASI "Documents on Demand." For information, see p. xxx.

● Item Depository item number, assigned to classes of documents issued to depository libraries.

ACRONYMS AND SELECTED ABBREVIATIONS

The following acronyms and abbreviations may be used without further identification:

ADAMHA	Alcohol, Drug Abuse and Mental Health Administration
Admin	Administration
AFDC	Aid to Families with Dependent Children
AID	Agency for International Development
AIDS	Acquired immune deficiency syndrome
Amtrak	National Railroad Passenger Corporation
Assn	Association
BEA	Bureau of Economic Analysis
Bibl	Bibliography
BLS	Bureau of Labor Statistics
Bull	Bulletin
Bur	Bureau
CAB	Civil Aeronautics Board
CBO	Congressional Budget Office
CCC	Commodity Credit Corporation
CDC	Centers for Disease Control
CES	Center for Education Statistics
CETA	Comprehensive Employment and Training Act
CIA	Central Intelligence Agency
Conf	Conference
CPI	Consumer Price Index
CRS	Congressional Research Service
CY	Calendar year
DEA	Drug Enforcement Administration
Dept	Department
Dev	Development
Div	Division
DOD	Department of Defense
DOE	Department of Energy
DOT	Department of Transportation
EC	European Community (formerly European Economic Community, EEC)
EDA	Economic Development Administration
EIA	Energy Information Administration
EPA	Environmental Protection Agency
ERS	Economic Research Service
ESEA	Elementary and Secondary Education Act
Eximbank	Export-Import Bank
FAA	Federal Aviation Administration
FAO	Food and Agriculture Organization (UN)
FAS	Foreign Agricultural Service
FBI	Federal Bureau of Investigation
FCC	Federal Communications Commission
FDA	Food and Drug Administration
FDIC	Federal Deposit Insurance Corporation
Fed	Federal
FERC	Federal Energy Regulatory Commission
FHA	Federal Housing Administration
FHLB	Federal Home Loan Bank
FHLBB	Federal Home Loan Bank Board
FmHA	Farmers Home Administration
FSLIC	Federal Savings and Loan Insurance Corporation
FTC	Federal Trade Commission
FY	Fiscal year
GAO	General Accounting Office
GATT	General Agreement on Tariffs and Trade
GDP	Gross Domestic Product
GNP	Gross National Product
Govtl	Governmental
GPO	Government Printing Office
GSA	General Services Administration
GS	General Schedule
HCFA	Health Care Financing Administration
HHS	Department of Health and Human Services
HMO	Health maintenance organization
HRSA	Health Resources and Services Administration
HUD	Department of Housing and Urban Development
Hwy	Highway
ICC	Interstate Commerce Commission
IMF	International Monetary Fund
Info	Information
Inst	Institute
Instn	Institution
Intl	International
IRA	Individual retirement arrangement
IRS	Internal Revenue Service
ITA	International Trade Administration
LC	Library of Congress
MarAd	Maritime Administration
Mgmt	Management
MSA	Metropolitan Statistical Area (formerly SMSA)
NASA	National Aeronautics and Space Administration
NASS	National Agricultural Statistics Service
Natl	National
NATO	North Atlantic Treaty Organization
NCES	National Center for Education Statistics
NCHS	National Center for Health Statistics
NIH	National Institutes of Health
NIMH	National Institute of Mental Health
NLRB	National Labor Relations Board
NOAA	National Oceanic and Atmospheric Administration
NOW	Negotiable orders of withdrawal
NRC	Nuclear Regulatory Commission
NSF	National Science Foundation
NTIS	National Technical Information Services
OAS	Organization of American States
OASDHI	Old-Age, Survivors, Disability, and Health Insurance Program
OCS	Outer continental shelf
OECD	Organization for Economic Cooperation and Development
OHDS	Office of Human Development Services
OMB	Office of Management and Budget
OPEC	Organization of Petroleum Exporting Countries
OPM	Office of Personnel Management
OSHA	Occupational Safety and Health Administration
PAD	Petroleum Administration for Defense (abolished in 1954 but acronym still in use)
PHS	Public Health Service
PPI	Producer Price Index
PRC	People's Republic of China
Pub	Publication
R&D	Research and Development
REA	Rural Electrification Administration
Res	Research
Rpt	Report
S&L	Savings and Loan Association
SALT	Strategic Arms Limitation Talks
SBA	Small Business Administration
SEC	Securities and Exchange Commission
SIC	Standard Industrial Classification
SITC	Standard International Trade Classification
SMSA	Standard Metropolitan Statistical Area (see MSA)
SRS	Statistical Reporting Service
SSA	Social Security Administration
SSI	Supplemental Security Income
TSUSA	Tariff Schedules of the U.S., Annotated
TTPI	Trust Territory of the Pacific Islands
TVA	Tennessee Valley Authority
USDA	Department of Agriculture
USGS	U.S. Geological Survey
USIA	U.S. Information Agency
USITC	U.S. International Trade Commission
USPS	U.S. Postal Service
VA	Department of Veterans Affairs

Issuing Agencies and ASI Accession Numbers

Listed below are issuing agencies for all publications abstracted in this Annual. Agencies are arranged to reflect current departmental organizations.

EXECUTIVE OFFICE OF THE PRESIDENT

040 Office of the Vice President
100 Office of Management and Budget
200 Council of Economic Advisers
230 Office of National Drug Control Policy
440 Office of the U.S. Trade Representative
480 Council on Environmental Quality

DEPARTMENT OF AGRICULTURE

1000 General
1120 Agricultural Cooperative Service
1180 Farmers Home Administration
1200 Forest Service
1240 Rural Electrification Administration
1260 Soil Conservation Service
1270 Office of Transportation
1290 Federal Grain Inspection Service
Agricultural Marketing Service
- 1300 General
- 1309–1319 Commodity Reports

1350 Human Nutrition Information Service
1360 Food and Nutrition Service
1370 Food Safety and Inspection Service
1380 Packers and Stockyards Administration
1390 Animal and Plant Health Inspection Service
Economic Research Service
- 1500 General
- 1520 International
- 1540 National Economics
- 1560 National Economics, Commodities
- 1580 Natural Resources
- 1590 Economic Development

National Agricultural Statistics Service
- 1610–1631 Agricultural Statistics Board

1700 Agricultural Research Service
1740 Cooperative State Research Service
1760 Office of Grants and Program Systems
Agricultural Stabilization and Conservation Service
- 1800 General
- 1820 Commodity Credit Corp.

1920 Foreign Agricultural Service
1950 Office of International Cooperation and Development

DEPARTMENT OF COMMERCE

2000 General
2020 Bureau of Export Administration
2040 International Trade Administration
2060 Economic Development Administration
2100 Minority Business Development Agency
National Oceanic and Atmospheric Administration
- 2140 General
- 2150 National Environmental Satellite, Data, and Information Service
- 2160 National Marine Fisheries Service
- 2170 National Ocean Service
- 2180 National Weather Service

2210 National Institute of Standards and Technology
2220 National Technical Information Service
2240 Patent and Trademark Office
Bureau of Census
- 2300 Bibliographies and Guides
- 2320 General
- 2340 Agriculture
- 2380 Construction
- 2399 1987 Census of Retail Trade
- 2410 Business
- 2420 Foreign Trade
- 2460 Governments
- 2471 1990 Census of Housing
- 2480 Housing
- 2497 1987 Census of Manufactures
- 2500 Manufacturing
- 2531 1990 Census of Population
- 2540 Population
- 2551 1990 Census of Population and Housing
- 2620 Methodology

2700 Bureau of Economic Analysis
2800 National Telecommunications and Information Administration
2900 U.S. Travel and Tourism Administration

DEPARTMENT OF ENERGY

3000 General
3020 Office of the Secretary of Energy
3080 Federal Energy Regulatory Commission
3160 Energy Information Administration
3220 Bonneville Power Administration
3230 Southeastern Power Administration
3240 Southwestern Power Administration
3250 Western Area Power Administration
3300 Conservation and Renewable Energy
3320 Environment, Safety, and Health
3330 Fossil Energy
3340 Defense Programs
3350 Nuclear Energy

- 3360 Civilian Radioactive Waste Management
- 3400 International Affairs and Energy Emergencies

DEPARTMENT OF DEFENSE

- 3500 General
- 3540 Office of the Secretary of Defense
- 3700 Department of Army
- 3750 Army Corps of Engineers
- 3800 Department of Navy
- 3900 Defense Agencies

DEPARTMENT OF HEALTH AND HUMAN SERVICES

- 4000 General

Public Health Service

- 4040 General
- 4060 Food and Drug Administration
- 4080 Indian Health Service
- 4090 Substance Abuse and Mental Health Services Administration
- Health Resources and Services Administration
  - 4100 General
  - 4110 Bureau of Health Professions
- National Center for Health Statistics
  - 4120 Bibliographies and Guides
  - 4140 General
  - 4160 Methodology
- 4180 Agency for Health Care Policy and Research
- Centers for Disease Control
  - 4200 General
  - 4240 National Institute for Occupational Safety and Health
- National Institutes of Health
  - 4430 General
  - 4470 NIH Research Institutes
  - 4480 National Institute on Alcohol Abuse and Alcoholism
  - 4490 National Institute on Drug Abuse
  - 4500 National Institute of Mental Health

Administration for Children and Families

- 4580 General
- 4590 Office of Refugee Resettlement
- 4600 Office of Human Development Services
- 4650 Health Care Financing Administration
- 4690 Family Support Administration
- Social Security Administration
  - 4700 General
  - 4740 Office of Policy

DEPARTMENT OF EDUCATION

- 4800 General
- Office of Educational Research and Improvement
  - 4810 General
  - National Center for Education Statistics
  - 4820 General
  - 4830 Elementary and Secondary Education
  - 4840 Postsecondary Education
  - 4870 Library Programs
- 4880 Office of Research
- 4890 National Assessment of Educational Progress
- 4940 Office of Special Education and Rehabilitative Services

DEPARTMENT OF HOUSING AND URBAN DEVELOPMENT

- 5000 General
- 5120 Community Planning and Development
- 5140 Housing (FHA)
- 5180 Policy Development and Research

DEPARTMENT OF INTERIOR

- 5300 General
- 5500 Fish and Wildlife Service
- 5540 National Park Service
- Bureau of Mines
  - 5600 General
  - 5610 Mineral Industry Surveys
- 5640 Office of Surface Mining Reclamation and Enforcement
- 5660 Geological Survey
- 5700 Bureau of Indian Affairs
- 5720 Bureau of Land Management
- 5730 Minerals Management Service
- 5820 Bureau of Reclamation

DEPARTMENT OF JUSTICE

- 6000 General
- 6060 Office of Justice Programs
- 6220 Federal Bureau of Investigation
- 6240 Bureau of Prisons
- 6260 Immigration and Naturalization Service
- 6280 Drug Enforcement Administration
- 6290 U.S. Marshals Service

DEPARTMENT OF LABOR

- 6300 General
- 6360 Bureau of International Labor Affairs
- 6400 Employment and Training Administration
- 6500 Employment Standards Administration
- 6560 Women's Bureau
- 6600 Occupational Safety and Health Administration
- 6660 Mine Safety and Health Administration
- 6680 Pension and Welfare Benefits Administration
- Bureau of Labor Statistics
  - 6720 General
  - 6740 Employment Analysis and Trends
  - 6760 Prices and Living Conditions
  - 6780 Wages and Industrial Relations
  - 6820 Productivity and Technology
  - 6840 Occupational Safety and Health
  - 6880 Methodology
  - 6940 Regional Office 4, Atlanta
  - 6960 Regional Office 6, Dallas

DEPARTMENT OF STATE

- 7000 General
- 7140 Bureau of Intelligence and Research
- 7180 Bureau of Consular Affairs

DEPARTMENT OF TRANSPORTATION

7300 General
7400 Coast Guard
7500 Federal Aviation Administration
7550 Federal Highway Administration
7600 Federal Railroad Administration
7700 Maritime Administration
7740 Saint Lawrence Seaway Development Corp.
7760 National Highway Traffic Safety Administration
7880 Federal Transit Administration

DEPARTMENT OF TREASURY

8000 General
8100 Financial Management Service
8140 U.S. Customs Service
8200 U.S. Mint
8240 Bureau of the Public Debt
8300 Internal Revenue Service
8400 Office of the Comptroller of Currency
8430 Office of Thrift Supervision
8440 U.S. Savings Bonds Division
8460 U.S. Secret Service
8480 Bureau of Alcohol, Tobacco and Firearms

DEPARTMENT OF VETERANS AFFAIRS

8600 General
8700 Veterans Health Administration

INDEPENDENT AGENCIES

9020 ACTION
9030 African Development Foundation
9060 American Battle Monuments Commission
9080 Appalachian Regional Commission
9110 Central Intelligence Agency
9160 Consumer Product Safety Commission
Environmental Protection Agency
- 9180 General
- 9190 Air and Radiation
- 9200 Water
- 9210 Solid Waste and Emergency Response
- 9230 Pesticides and Toxic Substances

9240 Equal Employment Opportunity Commission
9250 Export-Import Bank
9260 Farm Credit Administration
9270 Federal Election Commission
9280 Federal Communications Commission
9290 Federal Deposit Insurance Corp.
9300 Federal Home Loan Banks
9330 Federal Maritime Commission
9340 Federal Mediation and Conciliation Service
9360 Federal Reserve Board of Governors
Federal Reserve Banks
- 9371 Federal Reserve Bank of Atlanta
- 9373 Federal Reserve Bank of Boston
- 9375 Federal Reserve Bank of Chicago
- 9377 Federal Reserve Bank of Cleveland
- 9379 Federal Reserve Bank of Dallas
- 9381 Federal Reserve Bank of Kansas City
- 9383 Federal Reserve Bank of Minneapolis
- 9385 Federal Reserve Bank of New York
- 9387 Federal Reserve Bank of Philadelphia
- 9389 Federal Reserve Bank of Richmond
- 9391 Federal Reserve Bank of St. Louis
- 9393 Federal Reserve Bank of San Francisco

9400 Federal Trade Commission
9410 Federal Home Loan Mortgage Corp.
9430 Federal Emergency Management Agency
9440 Federal Housing Finance Board
9450 General Services Administration
9470 Federal National Mortgage Association
9480 Interstate Commerce Commission
9490 Merit Systems Protection Board
9500 National Aeronautics and Space Administration
9510 National Archives and Records Administration
9530 National Credit Union Administration
9560 National Foundation on the Arts and the Humanities
9580 National Labor Relations Board
9600 National Mediation Board
9610 National Transportation Safety Board
9620 National Science Foundation
9630 Nuclear Regulatory Commission
9650 Peace Corps
9660 Panama Canal Commission
9670 Pension Benefit Guaranty Corp.
9700 Railroad Retirement Board
9720 Resolution Trust Corp.
9730 Securities and Exchange Commission
9740 Selective Service System
9760 Small Business Administration
9780 Student Loan Marketing Association
9800 Tennessee Valley Authority
9820 U.S. Arms Control and Disarmament Agency
9830 Office of Government Ethics
9840 Office of Personnel Management
9850 U.S. Information Agency
9860 U.S. Postal Service
9880 U.S. International Trade Commission
9890 U.S. Office of Special Counsel
U.S. International Development Cooperation Agency
- 9900 General
- 9910 Agency for International Development

SPECIAL BOARDS, COMMITTEES, AND COMMISSIONS

10040 Advisory Commission on Intergovernmental Relations
10100 Advisory Committee on Federal Pay
10170 Advisory Council on Social Security
10310 Board for International Broadcasting
10320 J. William Fulbright Foreign Scholarship Board
10400 Barry M. Goldwater Scholarship and Excellence in Education Foundation
11040 Commission on Civil Rights
11710 Committee for Purchase from the Blind and Other Severely Handicapped
11920 Commodity Futures Trading Commission
12800 Federal Financing Bank
12900 Federal Council on the Aging

13000 Federal Financial Institutions Examination Council
13360 Federal Labor Relations Authority
14300 Interagency Forum on Aging-Related Statistics
14310 Harry S. Truman Scholarship Foundation
14350 Interagency Task Force on Acid Precipitation
14360 Interagency Council on the Homeless
14420 Inter-American Foundation
14640 International Joint Commission, U.S. and Canada
14730 Marine Mammal Commission
14780 Migratory Bird Conservation Commission
14870 National Advisory Council on Indian Education
15030 National Advisory Commission on Semiconductors
15340 National Advisory Council on International Monetary and Financial Policies
15450 National Capital Planning Commission
15490 National Commission for Employment Policy
15520 National Commission on Children
15630 National Commission on Libraries and Information Science
15910 National Education Goals Panel
16000 Office of Navajo and Hopi Indian Relocation
17200 Prospective Payment Assessment Commission
17260 Physician Payment Review Commission
17610 U.S. Architectural and Transportation Barriers Compliance Board
17660 U.S. Sentencing Commission

UNITED STATES COURTS

18200 Administrative Office of the U.S. Courts
18220 Special Courts

UNITED STATES CONGRESS

House Committees

21140 House Aging Committee, Select
21240 House Banking, Finance and Urban Affairs Committee
21260 House Budget Committee
21300 House District of Columbia Committee
21340 House Education and Labor Committee
21360 House Energy and Commerce Committee
21380 House Foreign Affairs Committee
21400 House Government Operations Committee
21420 House Administration Committee
21440 House Interior and Insular Affairs Committee
21560 House Merchant Marine and Fisheries Committee
21620 House Post Office and Civil Service Committee
21640 House Public Works and Transportation Committee
21700 House Science and Technology Committee
21720 House Small Business Committee
21760 House Veterans Affairs Committee
21780 House Ways and Means Committee
21940 House Special Publications
21960 House Temporary Committees

Joint Committees

23840 Joint Economic Committee

Senate Committees

25140 Senate Aging Committee, Special
25160 Senate Agriculture, Nutrition, and Forestry Committee
25240 Senate Banking, Housing, and Urban Affairs Committee
25260 Senate Commerce, Science and Transportation Committee
25310 Senate Energy and Natural Resources Committee
25360 Senate Finance Committee
25380 Senate Foreign Relations Committee
25400 Senate Governmental Affairs Committee
25420 Senate Intelligence, Select
25520 Senate Judiciary Committee
25540 Senate Labor and Human Resources Committee
25720 Senate Small Business Committee
25920 Senate Documents
25940 Senate Special Publications

General Accounting Office

26102–26106 General
26109 Office of the Comptroller General
26111 Accounting and Financial Management
26113 Resources, Community and Economic Development
26119 General Government
26121 Human Resources
26123 National Security and International Affairs
26125 Information Management and Technology
26131 Program Evaluation and Methodology

26200 Government Printing Office
26300 Congressional Budget Office
26350 Office of Technology Assessment
26400 Library of Congress

QUASI-OFFICIAL AGENCIES

29250 American National Red Cross
29520 National Railroad Passenger Corp. (AMTRAK)
29570 Smithsonian Institution
29590 U.S. Institute of Peace

Index by Subjects and Names

Index by Subjects and Names

This index contains references to subjects, to corporate authors, and to individual authors.

References to individual items within a tabular breakdown (e.g. data about a particular State in a table that is broken down State-by-State) have been included only on a very selective basis. For complete references to information of this kind, please use the Index by Categories.

For information on how to make best use of both indexes, please consult the User Guide.

Abel, Daft & Earley
"Study of the Food and Kindred Products Industry in Appalachia", 9088–37
Abilene, Tex.
Wages by occupation, for office and plant workers, 1992 survey, periodic MSA rpt, 6785–17.3
Abken, Peter
"Corporate Pensions and Government Insurance: Deja Vu All Over Again?", 9371–1.302
Abnormalities
see Birth defects
see Genetic defects and diseases
Abortion
Contraceptives failures and health risks to women, with pregnancy, abortion, and cancer death rates, 1980s, conf paper, 4164–2
Deaths related to pregnancy, 1989, US Vital Statistics advance annual rpt, 4146–5.124
Health condition and care indicators, 1950s-90 with health improvement and disease prevention goals for 1990, annual data compilation, 4144–11
Infant health, deaths and risk factors, and prevention issues, for US and selected countries, 1990 conf, 4148–28
Performance of abortions by method, patient characteristics, and State, and related deaths, 1970-89, annual article, 4202–7.324
Pregnancy outcome probabilities, by gestation week, 1980, article, 4042–3.324
Public opinion on abortion, by respondent characteristics, data compilation, 1992 annual rpt, 6064–6.2
Soviet Union and US economic and sociodemographic indicators, selected years 1970-90, handbook, 2328–80
Statistical Abstract of US, 1992 annual data compilation, 2324–1.2
Teenage abortion and late prenatal care initiation, risk relation to season of conception, 1979-86, article, 4042–3.372
Vietnam population size, components of change, and selected characteristics, 1979, 1989, and projected to 2050, 2326–18.65
Youth health condition, risk factors, and preventive and treatment services use and availability, 1970s-80s, 26358–234.2
Abraham, Sidney
"Fats, Cholesterol, and Sodium Intake in the Diet of Persons 1-74 Years: U.S.", 4147–16.6
"Overweight Adults in the U.S.", 4147–16.6
Abrahams, Edward D.
"Competitive Assessment of the U.S. Power Tool Industry", 2046–12.46
Abramowitz, Molly
"American Housing Survey: Housing Data Between the Censuses", 2328–89
Abrasive materials
Employment, earnings, and hours, by SIC 1- to 4-digit industry, monthly 1989-Feb 1992, annual rpt, 6744–4
Exports and imports between US and outlying areas, by detailed commodity and mode of transport, 1991, annual rpt, 2424–11
Exports and imports of US, by country and detailed commodity, monthly rpt, 2422–12
Exports and imports of US, by Harmonized System 6-digit commodity and country, 1991, annual rpt, 2424–13
Exports and imports of US, by transport mode, country, and SITC 1- to 3-digit commodity, 1991, annual rpt, 2424–12
Exports of US, detailed Schedule B commodities with countries of destination, 1991, annual rpt, 2424–10
Input-output structure of US economy, detailed interindustry transactions for 541 industries, and components of final demand, 1982 benchmark data, 2708–17
Manufacturing annual survey, 1990: finances and operations, by SIC 2- to 4-digit industry, series, 2506–14
Manufacturing census, 1987: concentration of largest firms measured by value added, and for shipments by SIC 2- and 4-digit industry, subject rpt, 2497–6
Manufacturing census, 1987: shipments of manufacturers products, by customer class and SIC 2- and 4-digit industry, subject rpt, 2497–4
Mineral Industry Surveys, commodity review of production, trade, stocks, and use, quarterly rpt, 5612–2.19
Mineral Industry Surveys, commodity reviews of production, trade, stocks, and use, monthly rpt series, 5612–1
Mineral Industry Surveys, commodity reviews of production, trade, use, and industry operations, advance annual rpt series, 5614–5
Mineral Industry Surveys, State reviews of production, 1991, preliminary annual rpt, 5614–6
Minerals Yearbook, Vol 1, 1989: commodity reviews of production, use, trade, prices, and mining operations, annual rpt, 5604–33
Minerals Yearbook, Vol 1, 1990: commodity reviews of production, reserves, supply, use, and trade, annual rpt series, 5604–20
Minerals Yearbook, Vol 1, 1991: commodity reviews of production, reserves, supply, use, and trade, annual rpt series, 5604–15
Minerals Yearbook, Vol 2, 1989: State reviews of production and sales by commodity, and business activity, annual rpt series, 5604–16
Minerals Yearbook, Vol 2, 1990: State reviews of production and sales by commodity, and business activity, annual rpt series, 5604–22
Minerals Yearbook, Vol 3, 1989: foreign country reviews of production, trade, and policy, by commodity, annual rpt, 5604–35
Occupational injuries and incidence, employment, and hours in nonmetallic minerals mines and related operations, 1990, annual rpt, 6664–1
Occupational injury and illness rates, by SIC 2- to 4-digit industry, 1989-90, annual rpt, 6844–7
Occupational injury and illness rates, by SIC 2- to 4-digit industry, 1990, annual rpt, 6844–1
Price indexes (producer), by stage of processing and detailed commodity, monthly rpt, 6762–6
Price indexes (producer), by stage of processing and detailed commodity, monthly 1991, annual rpt, 6764–2
Production, prices, trade, use, employment, tariffs, and stockpiles, by mineral, with foreign comparisons, 1987-91, annual rpt, 5604–18
Statistical Abstract of US, 1992 annual data compilation, 2324–1.25
Stockpiling of strategic material by Fed Govt, activity, and inventory by commodity, as of Sept 1991, semiannual rpt, 3542–22
Stockpiling of strategic material, inventories and needs, by commodity, 1992, annual rpt, 3544–37
Absenteeism
Aircraft pilot and flight attendant occupational injuries, illnesses, and lost workdays, for commercial carriers, mid 1970s-88, article, 6722–1.320
Auto and auto parts trade, production, and labor conditions, for US and compared to Canada and Mexico, 1950s-90, 6366–3.28
Child care arrangements of mothers employed and in school, and costs, by age of child and characteristics of mother, 1988, Current Population Rpt, 2546–20.24
Child care arrangements of younger working mothers, and costs, by selected characteristics, 1988, 6726–2.1
Child day care and early childhood education programs availability, demand, use, costs, and provider and enrollee characteristics, 1990 survey, 4808–39
Child infectious disease cases, and related disability and health care, by disease, health insurance status, and other characteristics, 1988, 4147–10.181

Crime victimization rates, by victim and offender characteristics, circumstances, and offense, 1990 survey, annual rpt, 6066–3.47
Disability, acute and chronic health conditions, absenteeism, and health services use, by selected characteristics, 1990, annual rpt, 4147–10.182; 4147–10.183
Education (public elementary and secondary) system mgmt by higher education instn, Chelsea, Mass and Boston University demonstration program operations and results, 1988-90, 4808–38
Education data compilation, 1992 annual rpt, 4824–2
Educational attainment relation to health condition and care, indicators by selected characteristics, 1989, 4147–10.180
Grocery stores occupational injury and illness rates, and lost workdays by State, 1990, article, 6722–1.339
Health condition and care indicators, 1950s-90 with health improvement and disease prevention goals for 1990, annual data compilation, 4144–11
High school dropout rates, and subsequent completion, by student and school characteristics, alternative estimates, 1991, annual rpt, 4834–23
Japan and US occupational injuries and illnesses, and lost workday and death rates, late 1950s-88, article, 6722–1.318
Kindergarten absence rate correlation to sudden infant death syndrome incidence, local area study, 1992 article, 4042–3.331
Labor force not at work, and hours lost, for illness and other reasons, by worker characteristics and industry div, monthly rpt, periodic data, 6742–2
Labor force not at work, unemployed, and working less than 35 hours, by reason, sex, race, region, and State, 1991, annual rpt, 6744–7.1; 6744–7.2
Longshore workers injuries resulting in lost time, FY76-91, annual rpt, 6504–10
Metal structural fabrication industry occupational injury and illness rates and lost workdays, by State, 1989, 6722–1.301
Mines (coal) and related operations occupational injuries and incidence, employment, and hours, 1990, annual rpt, 6664–4
Mines (metal) and related operations occupational injuries and incidence, employment, and hours, 1990, annual rpt, 6664–3
Mines (nonmetallic minerals) and related operations occupational injuries and incidence, employment, and hours, 1990, annual rpt, 6664–1
Mines (sand and gravel) and related operations occupational injuries and incidence, employment, and hours, 1990, annual rpt, 6664–2
Mines (stone) and related operations occupational injuries and incidence, employment, and hours, 1990, annual rpt, 6664–5
NASA accidents, casualties, damage, and safety activities, FY91, annual rpt, 9504–4
Occupational injuries, illnesses, and lost workdays, by SIC 2-digit industry, 1990-91, annual press release, 6844–3
Occupational injury and illness rates and lost workdays, for selected industries, 1978-89, compilation of papers, 6728–41
Occupational injury and illness rates by circumstances and establishment size, and methodology for computing rates, industry rpt series, 6886–4
Occupational injury and illness rates, by SIC 2- to 4-digit industry, 1989-90, annual rpt, 6844–7
Occupational injury and illness rates, by SIC 2- to 4-digit industry, 1990, annual rpt, 6844–1
Railroad accidents, casualties, and damage, by cause, railroad, and State, 1991, annual rpt, 7604–1
Soft drink industry occupational injury and illness rate and lost workdays, for 7 States, mid 1970s-90, article, 6722–1.319
Statistical Abstract of US, 1992 annual data compilation, 2324–1.3; 2324–1.13
Traffic accidents direct and indirect costs, by cost type, payment source, and severity, 1980s, 7558–114
Youth health condition, risk factors, and preventive and treatment services use and availability, 1970s-80s, 26358–234.2; 26358–234.3

Abt Associates, Inc.
"Certification Requirements for Nursing Homes: Final Report", 17206–2.37
"Federal Sentencing in Transition, 1986-90", 6066–19.68
"Medicaid Payment Methodologies for Inpatient Hospital Services", 17206–2.35
"Pre- and Postoperative Visits Associated with Surgical Global Services", 17266–2.6
"Prosecution of Felony Arrests, 1988", 6064–27
"Report on Quality Assurance in Non-PPS Settings", 17206–2.41
"Study of Health Care Access in Counties Where the Only Hospital Closed", 17206–2.30
"Volume Adjustments Used in State Medicaid Programs and Rate Setting Systems", 17206–2.34

Abu Dhabi
see United Arab Emirates

Accident insurance
see Automobile insurance
see Property and casualty insurance

Accidental deaths
Aircraft accidents and circumstances, for US operations of domestic and foreign airlines and general aviation, periodic rpt, 9612–1
Aircraft accidents, casualties, and damage, for commercial operations by detailed circumstances, 1988, annual rpt, 9614–2
Aircraft accidents, deaths, and circumstances, by carrier and carrier type, preliminary 1991, annual press release, 9614–9
Aircraft accidents, deaths, and rates, for airlines and general aviation by type of service, 1981-90, annual rpt, 7504–1.9
Aircraft hijackings, on-board explosions, and other crimes, US and foreign incidents, 1986-90, annual rpt, 7504–31
Alaska occupational injury deaths, by cause, occupation, and industry, early 1980s, article, 4042–3.307
Arson cases, civilian and fire fighter casualties, and property damage, 1986-89, 9438–14
Boat registrations, and accidents, casualties, and damage by cause, by vessel characteristics and State, 1991, annual rpt, 7404–1
Bombing incidents and casualties, by target, circumstances, and State, 1987-91, annual rpt, 8484–4.1
Bombing incidents, casualties, and damage, by target, circumstances, and State, 1991, annual rpt, 6224–5
Coast Guard search and rescue missions, and lives and property lost and saved, by district and assisting unit, FY91, annual rpt, 7404–2
Consumer Product Safety Commission activities, recalls by brand, and casualties and medical costs, by product type, FY90, annual rpt, 9164–2
Costa Rica and Guatemala life expectancy, and death rate by cause and age, by sex, 1984 and trends from 1900, working paper, 2326–18.64
Deaths and rates, by cause, age, sex, marital status, race, and State, 1989, US Vital Statistics advance annual rpt, 4146–5.124
Deaths and rates, by cause and age, preliminary 1990-91, US Vital Statistics annual rpt, 4144–7
Deaths and rates, by cause and selected social, demographic, and employment characteristics, 1979-85, natl longitudinal study, 4478–186
Deaths and rates, by cause, provisional data, monthly rpt, 4142–1.2
Deaths and rates, by detailed location, cause, and demographic characteristics, 1989, US Vital Statistics annual rpt, 4144–3
Disasters and natl security incidents and mgmt, with data by major event and State, 1992 annual rpt, 9434–6
Diving (underwater) accidents, illnesses, and deaths, by circumstances, diver characteristics, and location, 1970-90, annual rpt, 2144–29
Fire fighter deaths, by cause, circumstances, and location, 1990, annual rpt, 9434–8
Fire-related injuries by severity, and deaths, by ignition source, victim age, and treatment location, 1984-85 local area study, article, 4042–3.340
Fires, casualties, losses, and US Fire Admin activities, funding, and training programs, FY91, annual rpt, 9434–7
Floods in Mississippi River and Gulf of Mexico basins, precipitation and water levels by site, damage, and deaths, 1982-83, 5666–27.33
Foreign countries disasters, casualties, damage, and aid by US and others, FY91 and trends from FY64, annual rpt, 9914–12
Grain handling facility explosions and casualties, by firm, FY92, annual rpt, 1294–1
Hazardous material transport accidents, casualties, and damage, by mode of transport, with DOT control activities, 1990, annual rpt, 7304–4

Health condition and care indicators, 1950s-90 with health improvement and disease prevention goals for 1990, annual data compilation, 4144–11
Hospital trauma center cases and deaths by injury type, costs, and payment sources, with data for selected areas, 1991 hearing, 21348–123
Hurricane Andrew atmospheric pressure, wind speeds, deaths, and damage, by location, Aug 1992, article, 2152–8.304
Indian Health Service and tribal facilities and use, and Indians health and other characteristics, by IHS region, 1980s-90, annual chartbook, 4084–7
Indian Health Service facilities, funding, operations, and Indian health and other characteristics, 1950s-91, annual chartbook, 4084–1
Insurance (life) coverage and claims, for Federal civilian employees, FY90 with trends from FY86, annual rpt, 9844–37.3
Law enforcement officer assaults and deaths by circumstances, agency, victim and offender characteristics, and location, 1990, annual rpt, 6224–3
Military deaths by cause, age, race, and rank, and personnel captured and missing, by service branch, FY91, annual rpt, 3544–40
Military training accidents, and deaths by cause, by service branch, FY88-91, GAO rpt, 26123–397
Mines (coal) and related operations occupational injuries and incidence, employment, and hours, 1990, annual rpt, 6664–4
Mines (coal) disabling injuries and deaths, 1937-90, biennial rpt, 3164–79
Mines (metal) and related operations occupational injuries and incidence, employment, and hours, 1990, annual rpt, 6664–3
Mines (nonmetallic minerals) and related operations occupational injuries and incidence, employment, and hours, 1990, annual rpt, 6664–1
Mines (sand and gravel) and related operations occupational injuries and incidence, employment, and hours, 1990, annual rpt, 6664–2
Mines (stone) and related operations occupational injuries and incidence, employment, and hours, 1990, annual rpt, 6664–5
Mines and mills injuries by circumstances, employment, and hours, by type of operation and State, quarterly rpt, 6662–1
Mines occupational deaths, by circumstances and selected victim characteristics, semiannual rpt series, 6662–3
Morbidity and Mortality Weekly Report, infectious notifiable disease cases by State, and public health issues, 4202–1
NASA accidents, casualties, damage, and safety activities, FY91, annual rpt, 9504–4
Occupational deaths, by equipment type, circumstances, and OSHA standards violated, series, 6606–2
Occupational injury and illness rates by SIC 2- to 4-digit industry, and deaths by cause and industry div, 1990, annual rpt, 6844–1
PHS Commissioned Corps members deaths, by cause, 1965-89, article, 4042–3.316
Prevention of accidental injury and death, and treatment, 1991 conf papers, 4208–35
Prevention of accidental injury and death, 1991 conf summary, 4206–2.56
Prison deaths in State and Fed Govt facilities, by cause, 1990, quinquennial rpt, 6068–218
Prisoners and movements, by offense, location, and selected other characteristics, data compilation, 1992 annual rpt, 6064–6.6
Prisoners in Federal and State instns, deaths by cause, sex, and State, 1990, annual rpt, 6064–26.3; 6064–26.4
Railroad accidents, casualties, and damage, by cause, railroad, and State, 1991, annual rpt, 7604–1
Railroad accidents, casualties, and damage, Fed Railroad Admin activities, and safety inspectors by State, 1990, annual rpt, 7604–12
Railroad accidents, casualties, circumstances, and railroad involved, 1988, annual rpt, 9614–8
Railroad accidents, casualties, damage, and circumstances, by incident, 1988, annual rpt, 7604–3
Railroad accidents involving hazardous materials, casualties, and circumstances, 1984-89, 9618–18
Ships wrecked off Alaska, characteristics, deaths, cargo, and whale catch, by vessel and location, 1763-1937, 5738–34
Statistical Abstract of US, 1992 annual data compilation, 2324–1.2
Terrorism incidents in US, related activity, and casualties, by attack type, target, group, and location, 1991, annual rpt, 6224–6
Transit systems accidents and casualties by circumstances, damage, and ridership, by mode, 1990, annual rpt, 7884–13
Transit systems finances and operations, by mode, size of fleet and urban area, region, and for 518 systems, 1990, annual rpt, 7884–4
Transportation accident deaths, by mode, 1990-91, annual press release, 9614–6
Transportation Natl Safety Board investigations and recommendations, and accidents and casualties by mode, 1990, annual rpt, 9614–1
Vital statistics provisional data, monthly rpt, 4142–1
Weather phenomena and storm characteristics, casualties, and property damage, by State, monthly listing, 2152–3
see also Drowning
see also Homicide
see also Poisoning and drug reaction
see also Suicide
see also Traffic accident fatalities
see also War casualties
see also under By Disease in the "Index by Categories"

Accidents and accident prevention
Bicycle helmet use by children relation to safety knowledge and attitudes, 1989 local area survey, article, 4042–3.326
Child and maternal health condition and services use, indicators by age, race, and poverty status, 1988, 4478–197
Developing countries injury surveillance activities, and CDC recommendations, 1992 narrative article, 4202–7.308
Disability, acute and chronic health conditions, absenteeism, and health services use, by selected characteristics, 1990, annual rpt, 4147–10.182; 4147–10.183
Disabled workers labor force status, type and cause of disability, and other characteristics, 1970s-89, chartbook, 4948–11
Head injuries involving selected consumer products and household structures, 1990 annual rpt, feature, 9164–7
Health condition and care indicators, 1950s-90 with health improvement and disease prevention goals for 1990, annual data compilation, 4144–11
HHS financial aid, by program, recipient, State, and city, FY91, annual regional listings, 4004–3
Hospital discharges and length of stay, by diagnosis, patient and instn characteristics, procedure performed, and payment source, 1990, annual rpt, 4147–13.112
Hospital discharges and length of stay by region and diagnosis, and procedures performed, by age and sex, 1990, annual rpt, 4146–8.211
Hospital discharges and length of stay under old and new survey designs, by diagnosis, patient and instn characteristics, and procedure, Jan-Mar 1988, 4147–13.110
Hospital discharges by detailed diagnostic and procedure category, primary diagnosis, and length of stay, by age, sex, and region, 1990, annual rpt, 4147–13.111
Hunter safety funding by Fish and Wildlife Service, by State, FY90, annual rpt, 5504–1
Hunter safety funding by Fish and Wildlife Service, by State, FY92, semiannual press release, 5502–1
Hydroelectric power plants licensing by FERC, impacts of environmental laws, with staffing and plant safety incidents, 1980s-90s, GAO rpt, 26113–599
Indian Health Service outpatient services provided, by reason for visit and age, FY90, annual rpt, 4084–2
Indian Health Service, tribal, and contract facilities hospitalization, by diagnosis, age, sex, and service area, FY91, annual rpt, 4084–5
Morbidity and Mortality Weekly Report, infectious notifiable disease cases by State, and public health issues, 4202–1
OECD members health care costs, hospital use, resources, and economic and health indicators, by country, 1960s-90, article, 4652–1.322
Physicians visits, by patient and practice characteristics, diagnosis, and services provided, 1989, annual rpt, 4147–13.109
Prevention of accidental injury and death, and treatment, 1991 conf papers, 4208–35
Prevention of accidental injury and death, 1991 conf summary, 4206–2.56
Prevention of disease and injury, activities effectiveness, evaluation methodologies, 1992 rpt, 4206–2.53

Statistical Abstract of US, 1992 annual data compilation, 2324–1.3
see also Accidental deaths
see also Agricultural accidents and safety
see also Aviation accidents and safety
see also Disasters
see also Driving while intoxicated
see also Drowning
see also Emergency medical service
see also Fires and fire prevention
see also Marine accidents and safety
see also Mine accidents and safety
see also Motor vehicle safety devices
see also Nuclear accidents and safety
see also Occupational health and safety
see also Poisoning and drug reaction
see also Product safety
see also Property damage and loss
see also Railroad accidents and safety
see also Space program accidents and safety
see also Spinal cord injuries
see also Traffic accident fatalities
see also Traffic accidents and safety
see also Traffic engineering
see also Transportation accidents and safety
see also Workers compensation
see also under By Disease in the "Index by Categories"

Accounting and auditing
Air Force fiscal mgmt system operations and techniques, quarterly rpt, 3602–1
Banks assets valuation impact of market value accounting for debt securities, by bank asset size, 1990, GAO rpt, 26111–77
Banks in Fed Reserve System, expenses and operations itemized by service, office, and district, 1991, annual rpt, 9364–11
Banks portfolio valuation at market value, with assets and liabilities by type, ease of estimation, and bank asset size, Dec 1990, article, 9375–1.301
Budget of US, conversion of deposit insurance and Pension Benefit Guarantee Corp budget authority and outlays from cash to accrual accounting basis, FY93, 108–46.1
County Business Patterns, 1989: employment, establishments, and payroll, by SIC 2- to 4-digit industry and county, annual State rpt series, 2326–8
County Business Patterns, 1990: employment, establishments, and payroll, by SIC 2- to 4-digit industry and county, annual State rpt series, 2326–6
Employment, earnings, and hours, by SIC 1- to 4-digit industry, monthly 1989-Feb 1992, annual rpt, 6744–4
Employment, unemployment, and labor force characteristics, by region and census div, 1991, annual rpt, 6744–7.1
Fed Govt agencies administrative records and other holdings of Natl Archives, final inventories, series, 9516–2
Fed Govt agencies and program operations investigations, summaries of findings, as of 1991, annual GAO rpt, 26104–5.4
Fed Govt labor productivity, indexes of output and labor costs by function, FY67-90, annual rpt, 6824–1.6
Fed Govt loans, loan guarantees, and grants, administrative costs budget accounting, by program and agency, 1992 rpt, 26306–6.166
Fed Transit Admin grants by State, and oversight, 1988-92, GAO rpt, 26113–600
Finances and operations, by SIC 2- to 4-digit industry, forecast 1992, annual rpt, 2044–28
Financial instns loan loss computations for tax returns under alternative methods, 1991 rpt, 8008–157
GAO activities, operations, and resulting cost savings to Fed Govt, FY91, annual rpt, 26104–1
HUD programs fraud and abuse, financial and program mgmt improvement activities, FY91, annual rpt, 5004–9
Input-output structure of US economy, detailed interindustry transactions for 541 industries, and components of final demand, 1982 benchmark data, 2708–17
Labor demand, turnover, and training completions, by detailed occupation, 1990 and projected to 2005, biennial rpt, 6744–3
Military and personal property shipments by commercial cariers, and cost savings from bill audits and rate negotiations, FY99-91, GAO rpt, 26123–369
Minority Business Dev Centers mgmt and financial aid, and characteristics of businesses, by region and State, FY91, annual rpt, 2104–6
Multinatl US firms and foreign affiliates finances and operations, by industry and country, 1989 benchmark survey, annual rpt, 2704–5
OASDHI future cost estimates, actuarial study series, 4706–1
OASDHI programs actuarial studies, series, 4706–2
OASDI and Medicare trust fund finances, economic assumptions, outlook, and health care system reform issues, series, 10176–1
Occupational injury and illness rates, by SIC 2- to 4-digit industry, 1989-90, annual rpt, 6844–7
Occupational injury and illness rates, by SIC 2- to 4-digit industry, 1990, annual rpt, 6844–1
Occupational Outlook Handbook, 1992-93, biennial rpt, 6744–1
Pension plans health benefits accounting standards changes, and impacts on firm finances, with background data, 1986-89, technical paper, 9366–6.298
Railroad retirement system actuarial evaluation, 1991 and projected to 2016, annual rpt, 9704–1
Small Business Admin loan guarantee program participants finances, operations, characteristics, and views, 1991 survey, 9768–25
Tax (income) compliance issues for large firms, with income, taxes paid, and tax credits, 1988, GAO rpt, 26119–405
Tax (income) compliance of corporations, and IRS enforcement activities, 1970s-92, hearing, 25408–118
Tax (income) returns of corporations, income and tax items by asset size and detailed industry, 1989, annual rpt, 8304–4; 8304–21
Tax (income) returns of partnerships, income statement and balance sheet items, by industry group, 1990, annual article, 8302–2.314
Tax (income) returns of sole proprietorships, income statement items, by industry group, 1990, annual article, 8302–2.317; 8302–2.320
Tax collection, enforcement, and litigation activity of IRS, with data by type of tax, region, and State, FY91, annual rpt, 8304–3
Tax deductions for amortization of intangible assets from acquired businesses, IRS unresolved audits, and claims allowed, 1991 GAO rpt, 26119–365
Tax preparation services fraud and other IRS undercover criminal investigations, and costs, by region, mid 1980s-90, GAO rpt, 26119–394
Tax preparation services use for individual income tax returns, 1991, annual article, 8302–2.319
see also Federal Inspectors General reports
see also Financial disclosure
see also Government forms and paperwork

Acharya, Sankarshan
"Debt Buybacks Signal Sovereign Countries' Creditworthiness: Theory and Tests", 9366–6.294
"Efficient Resolution of Moral Hazard via Capital Market: Monitoring Banks", 9366–6.292
"Maximizing the Market Value of a Firm To Choose Dynamic Policies for Managerial Hiring, Compensation, Firing and Tenuring", 9366–6.293
"Value of Double Leverage, Bank Holding Companies and Capital Regulation", 9366–6.291

Achievement tests
see Educational tests

Acid rain
Coal-fired power plants air pollutant reduction technology funding, and impacts on energy costs and emissions, 1950s-87 and projected to 2010, annual rpt, 3334–5; 3338–4
Coal-fired power plants air pollutant reduction technology funding, and project descriptions, 1991, annual rpt, 3334–4
Distribution, pH levels, and composition of acid rain, monitoring results by site, 1989, annual rpt, 9194–20
Electric power plants coal and oil deliveries by sulfur content and location, and sulfur removal capacity use by plant, 1990-91, annual rpt, 3164–42
Emissions of acid rain constituents, and environmental, economic, and health effects, 1985-89 and alternative projections to 2030, 14358–4
Research on acid rain, activities, and funding by Federal agency, FY91-92, 14358–3
Sulfur dioxide and other air pollutants levels, and measurements exceeding natl standards, by site, 1990-91, annual rpt, 9194–5
Water supply and quality in streams and lakes, and groundwater levels in wells, by drainage basin, 1990, annual State rpt series, 5666–10
Water supply and quality in streams and lakes, and groundwater levels in wells, by drainage basin, 1990-91, annual CD-ROM, 5664–18
Water supply and quality in streams and lakes, and groundwater levels in wells, by drainage basin, 1991, annual State rpt series, 5666–12

Water supply in US and southern Canada, streamflow, surface and groundwater conditions, and reservoir levels, by location, monthly rpt, 5662–3
Acids
see Chemicals and chemical industry
Ackermann, Susan P.
"Cancer Screening Behaviors Among U.S. Women: Breast Cancer, 1987-89, and Cervical Cancer, 1988-89", 4202–7.313
Ackert, Lucy F.
"Rational Expectations and Security Analysts' Earnings Forecasts", 9371–10.84
Acquired immune deficiency syndrome
Blood banks safety violations, FDA enforcement, disease transmittal, and Houston regional center activities and finances, 1970s-91, hearings, 21368–134
Cancer deaths of AIDS patients from non-AIDS-related cancers, 1985-91 study, article, 4472–1.351
Cases of AIDS by risk group, race, sex, age, State, and SMSA, and deaths, quarterly rpt, 4202–9
Child AIDS cases hospitalization and charges, by instn and patient characteristics, and payment source, 1986-87, 4186–6.16
Criminal justice systems of States, activities, employment, funding, and data collection, by State, 1970s-91, annual rpt, 6064–40
Data on health condition and care, indicators, 1988 natl survey, CD-ROM, 4147–10.184
Deaths and rates, by cause, age, sex, marital status, race, and State, 1989, US Vital Statistics advance annual rpt, 4146–5.124
Deaths from AIDS, by age, race, and sex, preliminary 1990-91, annual rpt, 4144–7
Developing countries economic and social conditions from 1960s, and Intl Dev Cooperation Agency and AID activities and funding, FY91-93, annual rpt, 9904–4
Drug abuse and treatment, research on biological and behavioral factors and addiction potential of new drugs, 1991 annual conf, 4494–11
Drug abuse indicators for selected metro areas, research results, data collection, and policy issues, 1992 semiannual conf, 4492–5
Drug abuse treatment services costs, effectiveness, and financing issues, 1991 conf papers, 4498–80
Drug abusers and sexual partners AIDS prevention programs, client characteristics, and outcomes, for selected metro areas, 1989 annual conf, 4494–12
Drug abusers with HIV, disease progression longitudinal studies, 1987 conf papers, 4498–79
Fed Govt financial and nonfinancial domestic aid, 1992 base edition, annual listing, 104–5
Fed Govt funding of AIDS patients health care and support services under Ryan White CARE Act, and grants by metro area, 1991, article, 4042–3.352
Health condition and care indicators, 1950s-90 with health improvement and disease prevention goals for 1990, annual data compilation, 4144–11
HHS financial aid, by program, recipient, State, and city, FY91, annual regional listings, 4004–3
Idiopathic CD4+ T-lymphocytopenia epidemiology and patient characteristics, 1992 conf, 4208–36
Latin America young unmarried adults sexual activity, contraceptives use, and AIDS risk knowledge, by sex and country, 1984-91, article, 4202–7.323
Medicaid claims and payments for HIV patients, by sex, age, risk group, eligibility, and source of care, for Michigan, mid 1980s, article, 4042–3.348
Medicaid costs, and service use and needs, for AIDS patients in New Jersey waiver program, 1987-89, article, 4652–1.317
Medicaid costs and service use, for AIDS patients in California, 1984-86, article, 4652–1.301
Minority youth AIDS prevention, interactive videodisc presentation effectiveness, 1992 article, 4042–3.332
Morbidity and Mortality Weekly Report, infectious notifiable disease cases by age, race, and State, and deaths, 1940s-91, annual rpt, 4204–1
Morbidity and Mortality Weekly Report, infectious notifiable disease cases by State, and public health issues, 4202–1
Natl Cancer Inst activities, grants by recipient, and cancer deaths and cases, FY91 and trends, annual rpt, 4474–13
Natl Inst of Allergy and Infectious Diseases activities, grants by recipient and location, and disease cases, FY84-91, annual rpt, 4474–30
Natl Inst of Neurological Disorders and Stroke activities, and disorder cases, FY91, annual rpt, 4474–25
Opportunistic diseases diagnosed in AIDS patients, by age group, quarterly rpt, annual data, 4202–9
Pneumonia (*Pneumocystis carinii*) prevention in AIDS patients, vaccination schedules, dosages, and precautions, CDC recommendations, 1992 rpt, 4206–2.54
Prevention and control plans for AIDS, with cases and Federal funding, 1980s-94, 4048–22
Prevention, prevalence, and treatment issues for AIDS, series, 26356–6
Prison deaths in State and Fed Govt facilities, by cause, 1990, quinquennial rpt, 6068–218
Prison testing programs by region and State, data compilation, 1992 annual rpt, 6064–6.1
Prisoners AIDS and tuberculosis cases, test results, and control and treatment policies, by location, 1990 survey, annual rpt, 6064–22
Prisoners in Federal and State instns, deaths by cause, sex, and State, 1990, annual rpt, 6064–26.3; 6064–26.4
Prisoners in jails, deaths by cause, 1990-91, annual rpt, 6066–25.48
Public knowledge, attitudes, info sources, and testing for AIDS, 1991 survey, 4146–8.218
Sexual partner notification by men with HIV infection, relation to risk behavior and other characteristics, 1988-89 local area study, article, 4042–3.310
Statistical Abstract of US, 1992 annual data compilation, 2324–1.2; 2324–1.3
Teenage boys AIDS risk behavior, sexual activity, and drug and condom use, 1988, article, 4042–3.313
Testing for AIDS, public opinion on mandatory testing, data compilation, 1992 annual rpt, 6064–6.2
Testing for HIV-2 antibodies, CDC recommendations, 1992 rpt, 4206–2.62
Testing of HIV patients for T-lymphocytes, specimen handling, and lab worker safety, CDC guidelines, 1992 rpt, 4206–2.58
Tuberculosis (drug resistant) cases, and AIDS-related cases, 1990-92, article, 4042–3.362
Veterans health care centers AIDS cases by sex, race, risk factor, and facility, and AIDS prevention and treatment issues, quarterly rpt, 8702–1
Women in methadone maintenance programs, AIDS knowledge, attitudes, and risk behavior, effects of life skills training, 1988-89 local area study, article, 4042–3.353
Youth health condition, risk factors, and preventive and treatment services use and availability, 1970s-80s, 26358–234.2
Acquisitions, business
see Business acquisitions and mergers
ACTION
Activities and funding of ACTION, by program, FY91, annual rpt, 9024–2
Budget of US, authoritative financial statements with appropriations, outlays, and receipts, by category and agency, FY91, annual rpt, 8104–2.2
Budget of US, obligations and authority by function, agency, and program, with summaries and analyses, FY93, annual rpt, 104–2
Education funding by Federal agency, program, and recipient type, and instn spending, 1960s-91, annual rpt, 4824–8
Expenditures of Fed Govt in States, by type, program, agency, and State, FY91, annual rpt, 2464–2
Labor unions recognized in Fed Govt, agreements and membership by agency and facility, as of Jan 1991, biennial listing, 9844–14
see also Foster Grandparent Program
see also Retired Senior Volunteer Program
see also Senior Companion Program
see also Student Community Service Program
see also VISTA
Adams, Andrea
"Educational Attainment in the U.S.: March 1991 and 1990", 2546–1.460
"School Enrollment—Social and Economic Characteristics of Students: October 1990", 2546–1.459
Adams, Gwyn
"German Unification and the European Monetary System: A Quantitative Analysis", 9366–7.275
Adams, Patricia F.
"Current Estimates from the National Health Interview Survey, 1990", 4147–10.182
"Current Estimates from the National Health Interview Survey, 1991. Vital and Health Statistics Series 10", 4147–10.183

Aday, Lu Ann
"Health Insurance and Utilization of Medical Care for Chronically Ill Children with Special Needs: Health of Our Nation's Children, U.S., 1988", 4146–8.216
Adelman, Clifford
"The Way We Are: The Community College as American Thermometer", 4888–7
Aden
see Yemen, South
Adhesives
Exports and imports between US and outlying areas, by detailed commodity and mode of transport, 1991, annual rpt, 2424–11
Exports and imports of US, by Harmonized System 6-digit commodity and country, 1991, annual rpt, 2424–13
Exports of US, detailed Schedule B commodities with countries of destination, 1991, annual rpt, 2424–10
Injuries from use of consumer products, by severity, victim age, and detailed product, 1991, annual rpt, 9164–6
Input-output structure of US economy, detailed interindustry transactions for 541 industries, and components of final demand, 1982 benchmark data, 2708–17
Manufacturing annual survey, 1990: finances and operations, by SIC 2- to 4-digit industry, series, 2506–14
Manufacturing census, 1987: concentration of largest firms measured by value added, and for shipments by SIC 2- and 4-digit industry, subject rpt, 2497–6
Manufacturing census, 1987: shipments of manufacturers products, by customer class and SIC 2- and 4-digit industry, subject rpt, 2497–4
Manufacturing finances and operations, by SIC 2- to 4-digit industry, forecast 1992, annual rpt, 2044–28
Occupational injury and illness rates, by SIC 2- to 4-digit industry, 1989-90, annual rpt, 6844–7
Price indexes (producer), by stage of processing and detailed commodity, monthly rpt, 6762–6
Price indexes (producer), by stage of processing and detailed commodity, monthly 1991, annual rpt, 6764–2
Adkins, Daniel C.
"U.S. Petroleum Supply", 3164–2.1
Adlakha, Arjun
"Excess Mortality in Guatemala: A Comparison of Causes of Death in Guatemala and Costa Rica", 2326–18.64
Adler, Robert K.
"Changes in Energy Intensity in the Manufacturing Sector, 1980-88. Manufacturing Energy Consumption Survey", 3166–13.7
Administration
see Administration of justice
see Administrative law and procedure
see Business management
see Executives and managers
see Health facilities administration
see Public administration
see School administration and staff
Administration for Children and Families
AFDC beneficiaries by county, payments, application processing and disposition, hearings, and fraud cases, by State, FY90, annual rpt, 4584–3
AFDC beneficiaries demographic and financial characteristics, by State, FY90, annual rpt, 4584–7
AFDC provisions, by State, FY89-90, annual rpt, 4584–8
Assistance (financial) of HHS, by program, recipient, State, and city, FY91, annual regional listings, 4004–3
Budget of US, obligations and authority by function, agency, and program, with summaries and analyses, FY93, annual rpt, 104–2
Child support overdue payments deducted from wages, and employer compliance, by State, FY85-89, 4588–1
Energy aid for low income households, coverage and impacts on energy use and costs, selected years FY79-89, 4588–2
Energy aid for low income households, funding sources, costs, and participation, by State, FY90, annual rpt, 4584–1
Energy aid for low income households, program characteristics by State, FY91, annual rpt, 4584–2
Expenditures of Fed Govt in States, by type, program, agency, and State, FY91, annual rpt, 2464–2
see also Administration for Children, Youth, and Families
see also Family Support Administration
Administration for Children, Youth, and Families
Head Start enrollment, funding, and staff, annual rpt, issuing agency transfer, 4604–8
Head Start enrollment, funding, and staff, FY91, annual rpt, 4584–5
Head Start handicapped enrollment, by handicap, State, and for Indian and migrant programs, annual rpt, issuing agency transfer, 4604–1
Head Start handicapped enrollment, by handicap, State, and for Indian and migrant programs, 1988/89, annual rpt, 4584–4
see also National Center on Child Abuse and Neglect
Administration of justice
Budget of US, obligations and authority by function, agency, and program, with summaries and analyses, FY93, annual rpt, 104–2
Data on crime, criminal justice admin and enforcement, and public opinion, data compilation, 1992 annual rpt, 6064–6
Employment and payroll, by function and level of govt, annual rpt series, 2466–1
Energy use in commercial buildings, costs, and conservation, by building characteristics, survey rpt series, 3166–8
Expenditures (direct) and employment, by function and level of govt, selected years 1962-87, 10048–53
Expenditures, employment, and payroll, by activity, level of govt, and State, FY90, annual rpt, 6066–25.50
Fed Govt agencies and program operations investigations, summaries of findings, as of 1991, annual GAO rpt, 26104–5.4
Foreign countries human rights conditions in 170 countries, 1991, annual rpt, 21384–3
Govt finances, by level of govt, State, and for large cities and counties, annual rpt series, 2466–2
Judicial Conf proceedings and findings, spring 1992, semiannual rpt, 18202–2
Justice Dept activities, FY91, annual rpt, 6004–1
State and local govt employment of minorities and women, by occupation, function, and pay level, 1991, annual rpt, 9244–6.4
States criminal justice systems activities, employment, funding, and data collection, by State, 1970s-91, annual rpt, 6064–40
see also Administrative law and procedure
see also Arrest
see also Civil procedure
see also Correctional institutions
see also Courts
see also Crime and criminals
see also Crime victim compensation
see also Criminal procedure
see also Due process of law
see also Evidence
see also Extradition
see also Federal aid to law enforcement
see also Fines and settlements
see also Judges
see also Judicial reform
see also Juries
see also Law enforcement
see also Lawyers and legal services
see also Legal aid
see also Legal arbitration and mediation
see also Military law
see also Pardons
see also Parole and probation
see also Pretrial detention and release
see also Sentences, criminal procedure
see also Trials
see also Witnesses
see also under names of specific types of courts (listed under Courts)
Administration on Aging
Assistance (financial) of HHS, by program, recipient, State, and city, FY91, annual regional listings, 4004–3
Administrative agencies
see under Executive Office of the President
see under Federal boards, committees, and commissions
see under Federal executive departments
see under Federal independent agencies
Administrative Conference of the U.S.
Budget of US, authoritative financial statements with appropriations, outlays, and receipts, by category and agency, FY91, annual rpt, 8104–2.2
Budget of US, obligations and authority by function, agency, and program, with summaries and analyses, FY93, annual rpt, 104–2
Administrative law and procedure
Advisory committees of Fed Govt, and members, staff, meetings, and costs by agency, FY91, annual rpt, 9454–18
AFDC hearings dispositions, and fraud cases, referrals, and actions, by State, FY90, annual rpt, 4584–3.4; 4584–3.5
Airport security operations to prevent hijacking, screening results, enforcement actions, and hijacking attempts, 1990, annual rpt, 7504–49
Court criminal case processing in Federal district courts, and dispositions, by offense, district, and offender characteristics, 1989, annual data compilation, 6064–29

Criminal case processing in Federal district courts, and dispositions, by offense, 1980-91, annual rpt, 6064–31
Criminal prison and parole admissions and releases, sentence length, and time served, by offense and offender characteristics, 1988, annual rpt, 6064–33
Disability benefit applications under OASDI and SSI, dispositions, awards, and administrative law judge hearing outcomes, by race, 1988, GAO rpt, 26121–459
Fed Govt agencies administrative records and other holdings of Natl Archives, final inventories, series, 9516–2
Fed Govt agencies ethics regulation, activities, and staff, 1991, biennial rpt, 9834–1
Fed Govt labor productivity, indexes of output and labor costs by function, FY67-90, annual rpt, 6824–1.6
Jails under court order to reduce overcrowding and to improve conditions, by State, 1990, annual rpt, 6064–26.1
Jails under court order to reduce overcrowding and to improve conditions, 1990-91, annual rpt, 6066–25.48
Judges views toward establishment of separate ALJ agency, 1992, GAO report, 26119–428
OASDHI and SSI admin, case processing, staff, and client problems with contacting SSA offices, 1980s-90, hearing, 25148–45
OASDI Disability Insurance eligibility determinations by States, caseloads, Federal funding, and State directors views, 1980s-91, hearing, 21148–63
Prisons under court order, by reason, 1990, quinquennial rpt, 6068–218
Prisons under court order to reduce overcrowding and to improve conditions, by State, 1990, annual rpt, 6064–26.3
SSA activities, litigation, finances, and staff, FY91, annual rpt, 4704–6
Unemployment insurance programs of States, quality appraisal results, FY91, annual rpt, 6404–16
US attorneys case processing and collections, by case type and Federal district, FY91, annual rpt, 6004–2
Veterans Appeals Board appeals and hearings, 1967-91, annual rpt, 8604–5.2
see also Antitrust law
see also Civil procedure
see also Commercial law
see also Consumer protection
see also Environmental impact statements
see also Environmental regulation
see also Federal Inspectors General reports
see also Financial institutions regulation
see also Fines and settlements
see also Freedom of information
see also Government and business
see also Government forms and paperwork
see also Labor law
see also Licenses and permits
see also Maritime law
see also Medical regulation
see also Price regulation
see also Tax laws and courts
see also Tax protests and appeals
see also under names of individual regulatory commissions (listed under Federal independent agencies)

Administrative Office of the U.S. Courts
Budget of US, authoritative financial statements with appropriations, outlays, and receipts, by category and agency, FY91, annual rpt, 8104–2.2
Budget of US, obligations and authority by function, agency, and program, with summaries and analyses, FY93, annual rpt, 104–2
Caseloads (civil and criminal) for Federal district, appeals, and bankruptcy courts, by offense, circuit, and district, 1991, annual rpt, 18204–11
Caseloads (civil and criminal) for Federal district, appeals, and special courts, by offense, circuit, and district, 1991, annual rpt, 18204–8
Judicial Conf proceedings and findings, spring 1992, semiannual rpt, 18202–2
Juror (grand and petit) use and costs, trials, and trial days, by Federal district court, annual rpt, discontinued, 18204–4
Wiretaps authorized, costs, arrests, trials, and convictions, by offense and jurisdiction, 1991, annual rpt, 18204–7

Administrators
see Business management
see Executives and managers

Adolescents
see Youth

Adoption
Alien children adopted by US citizens, by sex, age, region, and country of birth, FY91, annual rpt, 6264–2.1
Assistance programs under Ways and Means Committee jurisdiction, finances, operations, and participant characteristics, FY70s-91, annual rpt, 21784–11
Child living arrangements, and women's marriage and divorce experience, by race, 1970s-90, Current Population Rpt, 2546–2.166
HHS financial aid, by program, recipient, State, and city, FY91, annual regional listings, 4004–3
Immigrant and nonimmigrant visas of US issued and refused, by class, issuing office, and nationality, FY90, annual rpt, 7184–1
Statistical Abstract of US, 1992 annual data compilation, 2324–1.12

Adult day care
Family members and others caring for aged, caregiver quit probability related to selected characteristics, 1982, article, 4652–1.305

Adult education
Enrollment and other data for adult and vocational education programs, by student characteristics, 1980s-91, annual rpt, 4824–2.26
Enrollment, funding, and activities of adult education and literacy programs, fact sheet series, 4806–4
Enrollment, tuition, control, location, and other characteristics of higher education instns, 1991/92, biennial listing, 4844–3
Homeless adults educational services, program activities, and participation, by State, FY88-89, annual rpt, 4804–39
Homeless persons aid programs of Fed Govt, program descriptions and funding, by agency and State, FY87-91, annual GAO rpt, 26104–21
Indian education funding of Fed Govt, with enrollment, program grants, and fellowships by State, 1980s-FY91, annual rpt, 14874–1
Job Training Partnership Act education and worker training program participants, by selected characteristics, 1986-88, 15496–1.15
Literacy and English as a second language programs for adults, Education Dept and State programs, enrollment, and funding, by State, 1988-91, 4808–41
Literacy program for preschoolers and parents, Even Start program activities and grants by recipient, FY90, annual listing, 4804–41
Natl Education Goals progress indicators, by State, 1992, annual rpt, 15914–1
Participation in adult education, by selected characteristics, 1991 survey, 4826–10.5
Prison and community-based facilities, population, employment, spending, and other characteristics, by State and for Fed Govt, 1990, quinquennial rpt, 6068–218
see also Correspondence courses

Advanced materials
Ceramics (advanced) research publication releases in 6 countries, by subfield, selected years 1965-90, hearing, 21708–130
Competitiveness (intl) of US high technology industries, with background data by industry and foreign comparisons, 1960s-91, GAO rpt, 26123–406
Manufacturing finances and operations, by SIC 2- to 4-digit industry, forecast 1992, annual rpt, 2044–28
Minerals Yearbook, Vol 1, 1990: commodity review of production, reserves, supply, use, and trade, annual rpt, 5604–20.64
Production, trade, use, and foreign investment in US industry, for minerals, 1985-90 and projected to 2000, annual rpt, 5304–5
see also Biotechnology
see also Polymers

Advertising
Airline consumer complaints to DOT about service by US and foreign carrier, and for travel and cargo service, by reason, monthly rpt, 7302–11
Alcoholic beverages ads appeal to youth, industry guidelines, and review by govts, consumer groups, and TV networks, 1991 rpt, 4006–10.5
Banks and thrifts finances and operations by deposit size, Fed Reserve functional cost analysis, 1991, annual rpt, 9364–6
Business statistics, detailed data for major industries and economic indicators, *Survey of Current Business*, monthly rpt, 2702–1.6
Business statistics, detailed data for major industries and economic indicators, 1960-91, *Survey of Current Business* biennial supplement, 2704–1
Cigarette ad and promotion costs by media, and market shares, by cigarette type, with sales and use, 1963-89, annual rpt, 9404–4
Communications services revenue and expenses, itemized by SIC 2- to 4-digit kind of business, 1990, annual rpt, 2413–15

County Business Patterns, 1989: employment, establishments, and payroll, by SIC 2- to 4-digit industry and county, annual State rpt series, 2326–8
County Business Patterns, 1990: employment, establishments, and payroll, by SIC 2- to 4-digit industry and county, annual State rpt series, 2326–6
Department store advertised sale prices and references to competitors prices, and actual consumer savings, 1990-91 local area study, 9408–57
Drug (prescription) advertising in medical journals, accuracy, info completeness, and violations of FDA regulations, 1990, 4008–119
Drug abuse prevention services evaluation, methodological issues, 1991 conf, 4498–78
Electric utilities privately owned, finances and operations, detailed data, 1990, annual rpt, 3164–23
Employment, earnings, and hours, by SIC 1- to 4-digit industry, monthly 1989-Feb 1992, annual rpt, 6744–4
Employment in advertising, by detailed occupation, 1990, article, 6722–1.341
Exports and imports of services, direct and among multinatl firms affiliates, by industry and world area, 1986-91, article, 2702–1.336
Exports, imports, tariffs, and industry operating data for advertising, 1992 rpt, 9885–12.3
Finances and operations, by SIC 2- to 4-digit industry, forecast 1992, annual rpt, 2044–28
Fishing (sport) anglers using charter and partyboat services, age, income, and sources of advertising influencing vessel choice, 1974-86, article, 2162–1.301
Food marketing cost indexes, by expense category, monthly rpt with articles, 1502–4
Food marketing sector finances, operations, and merger activity, for processors and distributors, 1991, annual rpt, 1544–22
Help-wanted ads index and ratio to unemployment, *Survey of Current Business*, cyclical indicators, monthly rpt, 2702–1.1
Input-output structure of US economy, detailed interindustry transactions for 541 industries, and components of final demand, 1982 benchmark data, 2708–17
Mammography use and promotion costs, by recruitment method, 1988-90 study, article, 4472–1.318
Manufacturing annual survey, 1990: value of shipments, by SIC 4- to 5-digit product class, 2506–14.1
Manufacturing census, 1987: concentration of largest firms measured by value added, and for shipments by SIC 2- and 4-digit industry, subject rpt, 2497–6
Military competitive and formally advertised awards, by contractor type and service branch, various periods FY82-1st half FY92, semiannual rpt, 3542–1.2
Milk order advertising and promotion finances, and producer participation, by region, 1991, annual article, 1317–4.304
Multinatl US firms and foreign affiliates finances and operations, by industry and country, 1989 benchmark survey, annual rpt, 2704–5
Natural gas interstate pipeline company detailed financial and operating data, by firm, 1990, annual rpt, 3164–38
New England States economic indicators, Fed Reserve 1st District, monthly rpt, 9373–2
Nutrition public service announcements displayed in supermarkets, effectiveness, local area study, 1992 article, 4042–3.371
Occupational injury and illness rates, by SIC 2- to 4-digit industry, 1989-90, annual rpt, 6844–7
Price indexes (producer), by stage of processing and detailed commodity, monthly rpt, 6762–6
Price indexes (producer), by stage of processing and detailed commodity, monthly 1991, annual rpt, 6764–2
Smoking cessation TV promotion campaign, hotline calls by sex, race, age, and education, aggregate 1983-87, article, 4472–1.313
Statistical Abstract of US, 1992 annual data compilation, 2324–1.18
Tax (income) returns filed, by type of filer, selected income items, quarterly rpt, 8302–2.1
Tax (income) returns of corporations, income and tax items by asset size and detailed industry, 1989, annual rpt, 8304–4; 8304–21
Tax (income) returns of sole proprietorships, income statement items, by industry group, 1990, annual article, 8302–2.317; 8302–2.320
Tax exempt organizations with unrelated business income, finances by organization type, 1987, article, 8302–2.306
Telephone and telegraph firms detailed finances and operations, 1990, annual rpt, 9284–6.2
see also Direct marketing
see also Labeling
see also Sales promotion

Advisory Commission on Intergovernmental Relations
Activities and finances of ACIR, 1991, annual rpt, 10044–3
Boundary review commission activities in 12 States, 1989, 10048–85
Budget of US, authoritative financial statements with appropriations, outlays, and receipts, by category and agency, FY91, annual rpt, 8104–2.2
Budget of US, obligations and authority by function, agency, and program, with summaries and analyses, FY93, annual rpt, 104–2
Fed Govt block and categorical grant programs for State and local govts, FY91, biennial listing, 10044–8
Govt direct spending and employment, by function and level of govt, selected years 1962-87, 10048–53
Govt finances, tax systems and revenue, and fiscal structure, by level of govt and State, 1992 with historical trends, annual rpt, 10044–1
Intergovernmental Perspective, quarterly journal, 10042–1
Local govts in metro areas, finances, structure, and service delivery, local area rpt series, 10046–9
Mail order sales from out of State, tax revenue losses by State, 1990-92, 10048–84
Medicaid coverage, funding, and costs, with reform recommendations, mid 1960s-92, 10048–83
Taxes, spending, and govt efficiency, public opinion by respondent characteristics, 1992 survey, annual rpt, 10044–2
Water supply mgmt for surface and groundwater, with groundwater depletion and use by purpose, 1980s, 10048–82

Advisory Commission on Regulatory Barriers to Affordable Housing
Housing affordability and availability, impacts of govt land use regulations and rent control, and low income housing condition, 1991 hearing, 21248–174

Advisory Committee on Federal Pay
Budget of US, authoritative financial statements with appropriations, outlays, and receipts, by category and agency, FY91, annual rpt, 8104–2.2
Pay comparability of Fed Govt with private industry, and recommended and actual pay adjustments, annual rpt, discontinued, 10104–1

Advisory Council on Historic Preservation
Budget of US, authoritative financial statements with appropriations, outlays, and receipts, by category and agency, FY91, annual rpt, 8104–2.2
Budget of US, obligations and authority by function, agency, and program, with summaries and analyses, FY93, annual rpt, 104–2

Advisory Council on Social Security
Findings and recommendations on OASDHI and health care system status and reform, series, 10176–3
Findings and recommendations on OASDHI and health care system status and reform, 1991 quadrennial rpt, 10178–1
Public opinion on OASDHI and health care system operations and reform issues, series, 10176–2
Trust funds of OASDI and Medicare, finances, economic assumptions, and outlook, with health care system reform issues, series, 10176–1

Aerial surveys
Bears (grizzly) in Yellowstone Natl Park area, monitoring results, 1991, annual rpt, 5544–4
Birds (waterfowl) population, habitat conditions, and migratory flight forecasts, for Canada and US by region, 1992 and trends from 1955, annual rpt, 5504–27
Wetlands acreage and losses, by wetland type, 1970s-80s, 5508–89
Wetlands acreage in Florida, by wetland type, 1970s-80s, 5508–119
Whales (bowhead and white) migration through Beaufort Sea, behavior impacts of oil drilling and aircraft noise, spring 1990, 5738–27
Whales population and behavior in Chukchi and Beaufort Seas, by endangered species, 1982-91, 5738–32
Whales population and behavior in Chukchi and Beaufort Seas, by endangered species, 1990, 5738–36

Aeronautical engineering
see Aviation sciences
Aeronautical navigation
Airport capacity improvement projects and funding, traffic, and delays, by major airport, 1988-90 and forecast to 2000, annual rpt, 7504–43
Equipment PPI, monthly 1991, annual rpt, 6764–2
Exports and imports between US and outlying areas, by detailed commodity and mode of transport, 1991, annual rpt, 2424–11
Exports and imports of US, by Harmonized System 6-digit commodity and country, 1991, annual rpt, 2424–13
Exports of US, detailed Schedule B commodities with countries of destination, 1991, annual rpt, 2424–10
FAA air traffic control and airway facilities and services, finances and operations, FY86-90, annual rpt, 7504–37
FAA air traffic control and airway facilities improvement under Aviation System Capital Investment Plan, 1981-91 and projected to 2006, annual rpt, 7504–12
FAA air traffic control facility traffic levels, including instrument operations, by airport and State, FY91, annual rpt, 7504–27
FAA certifications for pilots and nonpilots by type, age, sex, region, and State, 1991, annual rpt, 7504–2
Flight service station workload of FAA, pilot briefs, contacts, and flight plans by facility, projected FY92-2002 and trends from FY83, annual rpt, 7504–39
Instrument flight rule aircraft handled, by user type, FAA traffic control center, and region, FY85-91 and projected to FY2005, annual rpt, 7504–15
Instruments and related products shipments, trade, use, and firms, by detailed type, 1991, annual Current Industrial Rpt, 2506–12.26
Traffic, aircraft, pilots, airports, and fuel use, forecast FY92-2003 and trends from FY82, annual rpt, 7504–6
Traffic and passenger enplanements, by airport, region, and State, projected FY92-2005 and trends from FY83, annual rpt, 7504–7
see also Radar
Aerospace industry
Business statistics, detailed data for major industries and economic indicators, *Survey of Current Business*, monthly rpt, 2702–1.22
Business statistics, detailed data for major industries and economic indicators, 1960-91, *Survey of Current Business* biennial supplement, 2704–1
Capital expenditures for plant and equipment, by major industry group, quarterly rpt, 2502–2
Competitiveness (intl) of US high technology industries, with background data by industry and foreign comparisons, 1960s-91, GAO rpt, 26123–406
Competitiveness (intl) of US manufacturing industry, trade and economic policies with background data and foreign comparisons, 1991 rpt, 26358–252
County Business Patterns, 1989: employment, establishments, and payroll, by SIC 2- to 4-digit industry and county, annual State rpt series, 2326–8
County Business Patterns, 1990: employment, establishments, and payroll, by SIC 2- to 4-digit industry and county, annual State rpt series, 2326–6
EC govt subsidies, by industry sector and for Airbus Industrie, by country, 1980s-91, hearing, 21708–132
Employment and Earnings, detailed data, monthly rpt, 6742–2.6
Employment Cost Index and alternative measure of compensation costs, by component, occupation, industry group, union status, and location, 1975-92, annual rpt, 6744–20
Employment Cost Index and percent change by occupational group, industry div, region, and metro-nonmetro area, quarterly press release, 6782–5
Employment Cost Index in aerospace manufacturing, by occupational group and industry, monthly rpt, 6782–1.1
Employment, earnings, and hours, by SIC 1- to 4-digit industry, monthly 1989-Feb 1992, annual rpt, 6744–4
Employment of minorities and women, by occupation, SIC 1- to 3-digit industry, State, and MSA, 1991, annual rpt, 9244–1
Exports, imports, tariffs, and industry operating data for aircraft, spacecraft, and related equipment, 1991 rpt, 9885–9.1
Imports of US given duty-free treatment for value of US material sent abroad, by commodity and country, 1987-90, annual rpt, 9884–14
Input-output structure of US economy, detailed interindustry transactions for 84 industries, and components of final demand, 1987, annual article, 2702–1.316
Input-output structure of US economy, detailed interindustry transactions for 541 industries, and components of final demand, 1982 benchmark data, 2708–17
Labor hourly costs, by component, occupational group, industry div, union coverage, and region, 1992, annual rpt, 6744–21
Manufacturing annual survey, 1990: finances and operations, by SIC 2- to 4-digit industry, series, 2506–14
Manufacturing census, 1987: concentration of largest firms measured by value added, and for shipments by SIC 2- and 4-digit industry, subject rpt, 2497–6
Manufacturing census, 1987: shipments of manufacturers products, by customer class and SIC 2- and 4-digit industry, subject rpt, 2497–4
Manufacturing corporations financial statements, by selected SIC 2- to 3-digit industry, quarterly rpt, 2502–1
Manufacturing finances and operations, by SIC 2- to 4-digit industry, forecast 1992, annual rpt, 2044–28
Occupational injury and illness rates, by SIC 2- to 4-digit industry, 1989-90, annual rpt, 6844–7
Occupational injury and illness rates, by SIC 2- to 4-digit industry, 1990, annual rpt, 6844–1
Price indexes (producer), by stage of processing and detailed commodity, monthly rpt, 6762–6
Price indexes (producer), by stage of processing and detailed commodity, monthly 1991, annual rpt, 6764–2
Production, shipments, and trade of civil aircraft, by type, 1981-90, annual rpt, 7504–1.10
Sales, orders, backlog, and firms, by product for govt, military, and other customers, 1991, annual Current Industrial Rpt, 2506–12.22
Science, engineering, and technical employment in manufacturing, by field and industry, 1989, triennial rpt, 9627–23
Shipments, trade, use, and firms, by type of craft and engine, monthly Current Industrial Rpt, 2506–12.24
Statistical Abstract of US, 1992 annual data compilation, 2324–1.22
Tax (income) returns of corporations, income and tax items by asset size and detailed industry, 1989, annual rpt, 8304–4; 8304–21
see also Aircraft
see also Missiles and rockets
see also Spacecraft
Aetna Life Insurance Co.
Fed Govt civilian employee health insurance programs enrollment, profits, and administrative costs, by plan, 1984-90, GAO rpt, 26119–376
Fed Govt civilian employees retirement, health, and life insurance benefits, coverage and finances of 4 programs, FY86-90, annual rpt, 9844–37.2
AFDC
see Aid to Families with Dependent Children
Afghanistan
Agricultural trade of US, by detailed commodity and country, 1991, annual rpt, 1524–8
Agricultural trade of US, by detailed commodity and country, 1991, semiannual rpt, 1522–4
AID economic aid to developing countries, obligations and disbursements by country, quarterly rpt, 9912–4
AID loans repayment status and terms by program and country, and status of predecessor agency loans, quarterly rpt, 9912–3
Economic and military aid and loans from US and intl agencies, by program and country, FY46-91, annual rpt, 9914–5
Economic and social conditions of developing countries from 1960s, and Intl Dev Cooperation Agency and AID activities and funding, FY91-93, annual rpt, 9904–4
Economic, social, political, and geographic summary data, by country, 1992, annual factbook, 9114–2
Exports and imports of US, by transport mode, country, and SITC 1- to 3-digit commodity, 1991, annual rpt, 2424–12
Exports and imports of US with Communist and transitional economy countries, by detailed commodity and country, quarterly rpt with articles, 9882–2
Exports of US, detailed Schedule B commodities with countries of destination, 1991, annual rpt, 2424–10
Hostages kidnapped in Afghanistan, listing as of 1991, 7004–22

Human rights conditions in 170 countries, and US economic and military aid, 1991, annual rpt, 21384–3
Military aid of US, arms sales, and training programs costs and budget requests, by program, world region, and country, FY91-93, annual rpt, 7144–13
Military spending, arms trade, and force strengths, with govt spending and population, by country, 1979-89, annual rpt, 9824–1
Minerals Yearbook, Vol 3, 1989: foreign country review of production, trade, and policy, by commodity, annual rpt, 5604–35.2
Population size, growth rates, and components of change, by country, projected 1990-2020 and trends from 1950, biennial rpt, 2324–9
Refugee migration, and intl aid programs, by world area and country of origin and asylum, 1991, annual rpt, 7004–15
UN voting record and share of votes in agreement with US, by issue, country, and world area, 1991, annual rpt, 7004–18

Africa
Agricultural exports of US, for grains, oilseed products, hides, skins, and cotton, by country, weekly rpt, 1922–3
Agricultural trade by commodity and country, prices, and world market devs, monthly rpt, 1922–12
Agricultural trade of US, by commodity and country, bimonthly rpt, 1522–1
Agricultural trade of US, by detailed commodity and country, 1991, annual rpt, 1524–8
Agricultural trade of US, by detailed commodity and country, 1991, semiannual rpt, 1522–4
AID contracts and grants for technical and support services, by instn, country, and State, FY91, annual listing, 9914–7
AID economic aid to developing countries, obligations and disbursements by country, quarterly rpt, 9912–4
AID loans repayment status and terms by program and country, and status of predecessor agency loans, quarterly rpt, 9912–3
Air traffic and passengers, for intl routes over north Atlantic, by aviation type and route, alternative forecasts 1992-2010 and trends from 1982, annual rpt, 7504–44
Construction contract awards and billings, by country of contractor and world area of award, 1990, annual article, 2042–1.304
Dracunculiasis cases, and surveillance and eradication programs, for India, Pakistan, and Africa, 1980s-91, article, 4202–7.307
Economic and military aid and loans from US and intl agencies, by program and country, FY46-91, annual rpt, 9914–5
Economic and social conditions of developing countries from 1960s, and Intl Dev Cooperation Agency and AID activities and funding, FY91-93, annual rpt, 9904–4
Economic dev grants and fellowships of African Dev Foundation, FY84-91, annual rpt, 9034–1
Economic, social, and political conditions in sub-Saharan Africa, with US aid by program and country, 1991 rpt, 7008–58
Energy producers finances and operations, by energy type for US firms domestic and foreign operations, 1990, annual rpt, 3164–44.2
Energy production by type, and oil trade, and use, by country group and selected country, monthly rpt, 9112–2
Energy use and production, by fuel type, country, and country group, projected 1995-2010 and trends from 1970, annual rpt, 3164–84
Exports and imports (waterborne) of US, by type of service, customs district, port, and world area, monthly rpt, 2422–7
Exports and imports of OECD, total and for 4 major countries, and US trade by country, by commodity, 1980-90, world area rpt, 9116–1.2
Exports and imports of US, by Harmonized System 6-digit commodity and country, 1991, annual rpt, 2424–13
Exports and imports of US, by selected country, country group, and commodity group, 1991, annual rpt, 2044–37
Exports and imports of US, by transport mode, country, and SITC 1- to 3-digit commodity, 1991, annual rpt, 2424–12
Exports, imports, and balances of US for manufactured goods, by SITC 2-digit commodity and country, quarterly rpt, 2042–35
Family planning and population activities of AID, grants by project and recipient, and contraceptive shipments, by country, FY91, annual rpt series, 9914–13
Food supply, needs, and aid for developing countries, status and alternative forecasts, 1992 world area rpt, 1526–8.2
Immigrant and nonimmigrant visas of US issued and refused, by class, issuing office, and nationality, FY90, annual rpt, 7184–1
Immigrants admitted to US, by class of admission, country of birth, and MSA of destination, FY91, advance annual rpt, 6264–4
Immigrants and legalized aliens, by occupational group and country of birth, preliminary FY91, annual tables, 6264–1
Immigrants and nonimmigrants admitted to US, alien workers, visitors, deportations, and naturalizations, FY91, annual summary rpt, 6264–7
Immigration to US, alien workers, visitors, deportations, and naturalizations, by country, FY91 and trends from 1820, annual rpt, 6264–2
Income tax returns of foreign corporations and individuals, and US entities abroad, detailed data compilation, 1970s-89, quinquennial rpt, 8308–31
Investment (foreign direct) of US, by industry group and world area, 1989-91, annual article, 2702–1.332
Loans of US banks to foreigners at all US and foreign offices, by country group and country, quarterly rpt, 13002–1
Military aid of US, arms sales, and training, by country, FY50-91, annual rpt, 3904–3
Military spending, arms trade, and force strengths, with govt spending and population, by country, 1979-89, annual rpt, 9824–1
Minerals production, reserves, and industry role in domestic economy and world supply, 1991 world area rpt, 5606–1.19
Minerals Yearbook, Vol 3, 1989: foreign country review of production, trade, and policy, by commodity, annual rpt, 5604–35.1
Multinatl firms US affiliates finances and operations, by industry, country of parent firm, and State, 1987, 2708–48
Multinatl firms US affiliates, finances, and operations, by industry, world area of parent firm, and State, 1989-90, annual rpt, 2704–4
Multinatl US firms and foreign affiliates finances and operations, by industry and country, 1989 benchmark survey, annual rpt, 2704–5
Multinatl US firms foreign affiliates, income statement items by asset size, industry, and country, 1988, biennial article, 8302–2.322
Peace Corps activities, funding by program, and volunteers, by country, FY93, annual rpt, 9654–1
Population size, growth rates, and components of change, by country, projected 1990-2020 and trends from 1950, biennial rpt, 2324–9
Refugee arrivals in US by world area and country of origin, and quotas, monthly rpt, 7002–4
Refugee arrivals in US by world area of origin and State of settlement, and Federal aid, FY91-92 and proposed FY93 allocations, annual rpt, 7004–16
Refugee migration, and intl aid programs, by world area and country of origin and asylum, 1991, annual rpt, 7004–15
Sahel rainfall correlation with northwest Atlantic Ocean hurricanes, 1947-90, 2148–61
Tax (income) returns for foreign corporate activity in US, selected income and tax items, by industry div and selected country, 1988, article, 8302–2.309
Terrorism (intl) incidents, casualties, and attacks on US targets, by attack type and country, 1991, annual rpt, 7004–22
Terrorism (intl) incidents, casualties, and attacks on US targets, by attack type and world area, 1991, annual rpt, 7004–13
Tide height and time daily at coastal points, forecast 1993, annual rpt, 2174–2.4; 2174–2.5
Travel to and from US, and travel receipts and payments, by world area, with data by country, 1985-90, annual rpt, 2904–10
Travel to and from US on US and foreign flag air carriers, by country, world area, and US port, monthly rpt, 7302–2
Travel to US, by characteristics of visit and traveler, country, port city, and State of destination, quarterly rpt, 2902–1
Travel to US, spending by world area of residence, and economic impact, by spending category and State, 1989, 2908–28
UN voting record and share of votes in agreement with US, by issue, country, and world area, 1991, annual rpt, 7004–18
US military and civilian personnel and dependents, by service branch, world area, and country, quarterly rpt, 3542–20
Weather conditions and effect on agriculture, by US region, State, and city, and world area, weekly rpt, 2182–7

Weather events and anomalies, precipitation and temperature for US and foreign locations, weekly rpt, 2182–6
see also African Development Bank
see also African Development Fund
see also Algeria
see also Angola
see also Benin
see also Botswana
see also Burkina Faso
see also Burundi
see also Cameroon
see also Cape Verde
see also Central African Republic
see also Chad
see also Comoros
see also Congo
see also Djibouti
see also Egypt
see also Equatorial Guinea
see also Ethiopia
see also Gabon
see also Gambia
see also Ghana
see also Guinea
see also Guinea-Bissau
see also Ivory Coast
see also Kenya
see also Lesotho
see also Liberia
see also Libya
see also Madagascar
see also Malawi
see also Mali
see also Mauritania
see also Mauritius
see also Morocco
see also Mozambique
see also Namibia
see also Niger
see also Nigeria
see also Reunion
see also Rwanda
see also Sao Tome and Principe
see also Senegal
see also Seychelles
see also Sierra Leone
see also Somalia
see also South Africa
see also Sudan
see also Swaziland
see also Tanzania
see also Togo
see also Tunisia
see also Uganda
see also Western Sahara
see also Zaire
see also Zambia
see also Zimbabwe
see also under By Foreign Country in the "Index by Categories"

African Americans
see Black Americans

African Development Bank
AID loans repayment status and terms by program and country, and status of predecessor agency loans, quarterly rpt, 9912–3
Loan activity by purpose and country, FY90, annual rpt, 15344–1.9
Loans and grants for economic and military aid from US and intl agencies, by program and country, FY46-91, annual rpt, 9914–5

African Development Foundation
Grants and fellowships of ADF, by country, FY84-91, annual rpt, 9034–1

African Development Fund
Loan activity by purpose and country, FY90, annual rpt, 15344–1.9

Age
see Age discrimination
see Aged and aging
see Children
see Life expectancy
see Population characteristics
see Youth
see under By Age in the "Index by Categories"

Age discrimination
Auto rental age restrictions impacts on military personnel, with personnel by age, and rental receipts by company, 1991, GAO rpt, 26123–391
Labor laws enacted, by State, 1991, annual article, 6722–1.309

Aged and aging
Asian and Pacific Islands Americans social and economic characteristics, for West and total US, 1990-91, Current Population Report, 2546–1.462
Births to older women, for US and other countries, 1985, article, 4652–1.324
Black Americans social and economic characteristics, for South and total US, 1991 and trends from 1950, annual Current Population Rpt, 2546–1.463
Blind persons by age, older blind persons by State, and State rehabilitation services, 1989, 21148–64
Board and care home violations of State drug handling and dispensing regulations, for 3 metro areas, 1990-91, GAO rpt, 26121–447
Business owner and business characteristics, for minority- and women-owned firms, by industry, employment and sales size, and form of ownership, 1987 survey, 2328–59
Census of Population and Housing, 1990: population and housing characteristics, detailed geographic coverage, State CD-ROM series, 2551–10
Census of Population and Housing, 1990: summary characteristics, by county, subdiv, and place, State rpt series, 2551–7
Census of Population and Housing, 1990: summary characteristics, households, and land area, by county, subdiv, and place, State rpt series, 2551–1
Census of Population, 1990: population characteristics and living arrangements, by county, place, and urban-rural location, State rpt series, 2531–1
Census of Population, 1990: population characteristics and living arrangements, for Native American, urban, and metro areas, series, 2531–2
Consumer Income, socioeconomic characteristics of persons, families, and households, detailed cross-tabulations, Current Population Rpt series, 2546–6
Criminal justice systems activities, spending, and employment, by level of govt, data compilation, 1992 annual rpt, 6064–6.1
Data on aged population, Fed Govt sources, interagency forum activities, and contacts, 1989-90, annual rpt, 14324–1
Deaths and rates, by cause and selected social, demographic, and employment characteristics, 1979-85, natl longitudinal study, 4478–186
Deaths and rates, by detailed location, cause, and demographic characteristics, 1989, US Vital Statistics annual rpt, 4144–3
Developing countries aged population and selected characteristics, 1980s and projected to 2020, country rpt series, 2326–19
Earnings of aged, impacts of 1983 OASI earnings test repeal, 1970-85, technical paper, 4746–26.13
Employment and earnings covered under OASDHI, and social security contributions, by age, sex, race, State, and county, 1988, annual rpt, 4744–29
Family members and others caring for aged, caregiver quit probability related to selected characteristics, 1982, article, 4652–1.305
Financial status of families, income, net worth, and assets and debt by type, by income and selected characteristics, 1983 and 1989, article, 9362–1.301
Foreign and US aged population and characteristics, by country, 1991 and projected to 2020, wallchart, 2328–82
Foreign and US savings rates, and ratio of aged to working age population, for US, Japan, and West Germany, 1980s-90, article, 9387–1.302
Health care and long-term care needs of aged, financial issues with background data, 1991 rpt, 10176–1.3
Health care costs of aged, indicators of ability to pay out of pocket costs by selected characteristics, 1984, article, 4742–1.307
Health care system and OASDHI status and reform, Advisory Commission on Social Security findings and recommendations, series, 10176–3
Health condition and care indicators, 1950s-90 with health improvement and disease prevention goals for 1990, annual data compilation, 4144–11
Health promotion program for aged, costs and effectiveness of case mgmt and health education, 1980-83 local area study, article, 4042–3.342
Households and family characteristics, by location, 1991, annual Current Population Rpt, 2546–1.457
Households and housing characteristics, and unit and neighborhood quality, by MSA location for 11 MSAs, 1987 survey, supplement, 2485–8
Households and housing characteristics, MSA surveys, fact sheet series, 2485–11
Households and housing detailed characteristics, and unit and neighborhood quality, by location, 1989, biennial rpt supplement, 2485–13
Households and housing detailed characteristics, and unit and neighborhood quality, MSA surveys, series, 2485–6
Households and housing unit summary characteristics, 1989 and trends, chartbook, 2486–2.1
Households composition, income, benefits, and labor force status, Survey of Income and Program Participation methodology, working paper series, 2626–10

Housing (rental) units, total, with HUD assistance by program, and eligible for aid, by unit, household, and neighborhood characteristics, and location, 1989, biennial rpt, 5184–11
Housing census, 1990: summary unit characteristics, by householder race and age, county, place, and urban-rural location, State rpt series, 2471–1
Hypertension cases, stroke and heart disease risk, and drug dosages, with diagnosis and treatment methods, 1992 quadrennial rpt, 4478–198
Income (household) and poverty status under alternative income definitions, by recipient characteristics, 1979-91, annual Current Population Rpt, 2546–6.78
Income (household) and wealth distribution by selected characteristics, with foreign comparisons, 1992 compilation of papers, Current Population Rpt, 2546–6.79
Income (household) of aged and younger adults, by source, household composition, and age group, 1984 and 1989, article, 4742–1.304
Income (household) of aged and younger adults, by source, household composition, and age group, 1984-89, 4746–26.20
Income (personal) relative to median, by race and selected other characteristics, mid 1960s-89, Current Population Rpt, 2546–6.73
Income and sources of aged, by OASDI beneficiary and poverty status, and other characteristics, 1990, biennial rpt, 4744–25
Income and sources of aged, by whether OASDI beneficiary, poverty status, and other characteristics, 1990, biennial rpt, 4744–26
Income and wealth of older persons compared to other age groups, 1990 and trends from 1947, 4746–26.24
Income, net worth, and poverty status of aged, compared to other age groups, 1988-90, article, 4742–1.320
Influenza vaccination schedules, dosages, and precautions, CDC recommendations, 1992 rpt, 4206–2.59
Injuries from use of consumer products and related activities, by severity and victim age and sex, 1990, annual rpt, 9164–7
Injuries from use of consumer products, by severity, victim age, and detailed product, 1991, annual rpt, 9164–6
Labor force status, income sources, and reasons for not working for aged, with data by occupation, sex, and race, 1989-90 and projected to 2050, 21148–65
Living arrangements, family relationships, and marital status, by selected characteristics, 1991, annual Current Population Rpt, 2546–1.461
Living arrangements of aged, by poverty status, 1991, annual rpt, 4744–3.1
Longitudinal Study of Aging survey design and data collection and estimation procedures, 1984-90, 4147–1.28
Mammography use by older women, relation to views and participation in promotional workshop, local area study, 1992 article, 4042–3.337
Mental illness (serious) among adults, functional limitations, govt aid, drugs used, visits to professionals, and other characteristics, 1989, 4146–8.220
OECD members health care costs, hospital use, resources, and economic and health indicators, by country, 1960s-90, article, 4652–1.322
Older persons labor force status, and retirement age, by sex, 1950s-90 and projected to 2005, article, 6722–1.332
Pacific territories population and housing detailed characteristics, by location, 1990 Census of Population and Housing, series, 2551–8
Poor aged persons, by health, nutrition, assistance, and other characteristics, 1990, GAO rpt, 26131–100
Population economic well-being indicators, by selected characteristics and household income and income-to-poverty ratio, 1984, 2546–20.22
Population of aged, and health, economic, and other characteristics, with foreign comparisons, 1980s-91 with trends and projections, Current Population Rpt, 2546–2.165
Population of aged, social and economic characteristics, 1900s-1990 and projected to 2050, biennial chartbook, 12904–1
Population size and characteristics of aged, series, 2326–25
Poverty relation to low earnings, by work experience during year, household relationship, sex, race, age, and education, 1960s-90, Current Population Rpt, 2546–6.74
Poverty status of population and families, by detailed characteristics, 1991, annual Current Population Rpt, 2546–6.77
Rural areas aged health and social characteristics, 1991 annual chartbook, 1504–8
Rural areas aged health and social characteristics, 1991 annual conf, 1504–9
Single person and nonfamily households social, economic and housing characteristics, by tenure, 1989, 2486–1.15
Southeastern US layoff events and separations, by State, industry div, and reason for separation, 1990-91, press release, 6946–3.25
Statistical Abstract of US, 1992 annual data compilation, 2324–1
Tax (income) returns of individuals, by filing status, tax item, and income level, 1991, annual article, 8302–2.319
Traffic accidents and casualties, by driver age and sex, 1990, 7768–105
Unemployed displaced workers, layoffs and unemployment insurance claims by reason, industry, selected characteristics, and State, quarterly press release, 6742–23
Unemployed displaced workers, layoffs and unemployment insurance claims by reason, industry, selected characteristics, MSA, and State, 1990, annual rpt, 6744–18
Voting age population, by sex, age, race, and State, forecast 1992 general elections, with votes cast from 1930, Current Population Rpt, 2546–3.170
Wages and productivity relation to worker age, by sex and occupation, model description and results, 1991 working paper, 9377–9.128
Women (older) living alone, income by source, and expenses by type, by marital status, 1988-89, article, 1702–1.301
see also Adult day care
see also Age discrimination
see also Alzheimer's disease
see also Civil service pensions
see also Foster Grandparent Program
see also Geriatrics
see also Individual retirement arrangements
see also Medicare
see also Military benefits and pensions
see also Nursing homes
see also Old age assistance
see also Old-Age, Survivors, Disability, and Health Insurance
see also Pensions and pension funds
see also Retired Senior Volunteer Program
see also Retirement
see also Senior Companion Program
see also Social security
see also Supplemental Security Income
see also Veterans benefits and pensions
see also under By Age in the "Index by Categories"

Agency for Health Care Policy and Research
Assistance (financial) of HHS, by program, recipient, State, and city, FY91, annual regional listings, 4004–3
Budget of US, obligations and authority by function, agency, and program, with summaries and analyses, FY93, annual rpt, 104–2
Health care services use and costs, methodology and findings of natl survey, series, 4186–8
Hospital costs and use, data compilation project analyses, series, 4186–6
Medicare coverage of new health care technologies, risks and benefit evaluations, series, 4186–10

Agency for International Development
Activities and funding of Intl Dev Cooperation Agency and AID, FY91-93, and developing countries economic and social conditions from 1960s, annual rpt, 9904–4
Activities, finances, and staff of AID, by program and country, FY90, GAO rpt, 26123–382
Budget of US, authoritative financial statements with appropriations, outlays, and receipts, by category and agency, FY91, annual rpt, 8104–2.2
Budget of US, obligations and authority by function, agency, and program, with summaries and analyses, FY93, annual rpt, 104–2
Contracts and grants of AID for technical and support services, by instn, country, and State, FY91, annual listing, 9914–7
Contracts, grants, and cooperative agreements of AID to higher education instns, by project, instn, and country, FY91, annual listing, 9914–6
Currency (foreign) accounts owned by US under AID admin and by foreign govts with joint AID control, status by program and country, quarterly rpt, 9912–1
Dev projects of AID, and socioeconomic impacts, evaluation rpt series, 9916–1
Disaster preparedness and economic, population, and political data, discontinued series, 9916–2

Disasters, casualties, damage, and aid by US and others, by country, FY91 and trends from FY64, annual rpt, 9914–12
Economic aid to developing countries, obligations and disbursements by country, quarterly rpt, 9912–4
Economic, population, and agricultural data, US and other aid sources, and AID activity, country rpt series, 9916–12
Education funding by Federal agency, program, and recipient type, and instn spending, 1960s-91, annual rpt, 4824–8
Family planning and population activities of AID, grants by project and recipient, and contraceptive shipments, by country, FY91, annual rpt series, 9914–13
Housing and urban dev program of AID, FY91, annual rpt, 9914–4
Labor unions recognized in Fed Govt, agreements and membership by agency and facility, as of Jan 1991, biennial listing, 9844–14
Latin America economic and social conditions, resources, trade, and aid, 1992, annual factbook, 9914–14
Latin America economic conditions, trade, and foreign aid, working paper series, 9916–13
Liabilities (contingent) and claims paid by Fed Govt on federally insured and guaranteed contracts with foreign obligors, by country and program, periodic rpt, 8002–12
Loan activity, terms, and purpose, by country, FY90, annual rpt, 15344–1.10
Loan repayment status and terms by program and country, AID and predecessor agencies, quarterly rpt, 9912–3
Loans and grants for economic and military aid from US and intl agencies, by program and country, FY46-91, annual rpt, 9914–5
R&D and related funding of Fed Govt to higher education and nonprofit instns, by field, instn, agency, and State, FY90, annual rpt, 9627–17
Voluntary agencies foreign aid programs, funding, and outlays, by agency, 1990, annual rpt, 9914–9

Agent Orange
see Dioxins

Agocs, Mary M.
"Respiratory Disease Surveillance in Hungary", 4202–7.319

Agrarian reform
see Land reform

Agricultural accidents and safety
Grain handling facility explosions and casualties, by firm, FY92, annual rpt, 1294–1
Injuries from use of consumer products, by severity, victim age, and detailed product, 1991, annual rpt, 9164–6
Injuries, illnesses, and lost workdays, by SIC 2-digit industry, 1990-91, annual press release, 6844–3
Injury and illness rates by SIC 2- to 4-digit industry, and deaths by cause and industry div, 1990, annual rpt, 6844–1
Injury and illness rates, by SIC 2- to 4-digit industry, 1989-90, annual rpt, 6844–7
Pesticide applicators dioxin serum levels, by exposure duration, 1988 study, article, 4472–1.303
Workers compensation laws of States and Fed Govt, 1992 annual rpt, 6504–11

Agricultural chemicals
see Fertilizers
see Pesticides

Agricultural commodities
see also Agricultural exports and imports
see also Agricultural marketing
see also Agricultural prices
see also Agricultural production
see also Agricultural production costs
see also Agricultural production quotas and price supports
see also Agricultural stocks
see also Agricultural subsidies
see also Animal feed
see also Animals
see also Census of Agriculture
see also Citrus fruits
see also Cocoa and chocolate
see also Coffee
see also Corn
see also Cotton
see also Dairy industry and products
see also Flowers and nursery products
see also Food and food industry
see also Food consumption
see also Food prices
see also Food supply
see also Fruit and fruit products
see also Grains and grain products
see also Gum and wood chemicals
see also Hides and skins
see also Honey and beekeeping
see also Hops
see also Livestock and livestock industry
see also Lumber industry and products
see also Meat and meat products
see also Natural fibers
see also Nuts
see also Oils, oilseeds, and fats
see also Peanuts
see also Poultry industry and products
see also Rice
see also Seeds
see also Soybeans
see also Spices and herbs
see also Sugar industry and products
see also Tea
see also Tobacco industry and products
see also Vegetables and vegetable products
see also Wheat
see also Wool and wool trade
see also under By Commodity in the "Index by Categories"

Agricultural Cooperative Service
Budget of US, obligations and authority by function, agency, and program, with summaries and analyses, FY93, annual rpt, 104–2
Cooperatives finances, aggregate for top 100 assns by commodity group, 1990, annual rpt, 1124–3
Cooperatives, finances, and membership, by type of service, commodity, and State, 1990, annual rpt, 1124–1
Cooperatives finances, operations, activities, and current issues, monthly journal, 1122–1
Cooperatives, finances, operations, activities, and membership, commodity rpt series, 1126–1
Exports of food marketing cooperatives under intl business arrangements, 1985-88, 1128–69
Milk handlers (cooperative and proprietary) performance, views of dairy farmers in southern States, 1989 survey, 1128–67
Milk producer prices received from cooperatives and proprietary handlers, by characteristics of cooperative membership and operation, 1989 survey, 1128–68

Agricultural cooperatives
see Rural cooperatives

Agricultural credit
Agricultural Outlook, production, prices, marketing, and trade, by commodity, forecast and current situation, monthly rpt with articles, 1502–4
Agricultural Statistics, 1991, annual rpt, 1004–1
Assets and debts of private sector, balance sheets by segment, 1960-91, semiannual rpt, 9365–4.1
Banks (insured commercial and savings) finances, for foreign and domestic offices, by asset size, 1990, annual rpt, 9294–4.2
Banks (natl) charters, mergers, liquidations, enforcement cases, and financial performance, with data by instn and State, quarterly rpt, 8402–3
Banks agricultural loans share of all loans, with market shares and returns on assets, by bank size, 1970s-80s, working paper, 9381–10.122
Banks seasonal borrowing from Fed Reserve, participants financial and other characteristics, Fed Reserve 8th District, 1984-90, article, 9391–1.311
Business statistics, detailed data for major industries and economic indicators, 1960-91, *Survey of Current Business* biennial supplement, 2704–1
CCC certificate exchange activity, by commodity, biweekly press release, 1802–16
CCC loan activities by commodity, and agency operating results, monthly press release, 1802–7
CCC price support and other program outlays, with production and marketing outlook, by commodity, projected 1991-97, annual rpt, 26306–6.171
Costs of production, itemized by farm sales size and region, 1991, annual rpt, 1614–3
Cotton loan rates, and micronaire differentials of CCC, monthly rpt, annual tables, 1309–12
Cotton prices at selected spot markets, NYC futures prices, and CCC loan rates, 1991/92 and trends from 1944, annual rpt, 1309–2
Debt (real and nonreal estate) of farm sector, and assets by type, including and excluding operator households, by sales size, 1960-89, 1548–387
Debt outstanding, by sector and type of debt and holder, monthly rpt, 9362–1.1
Economic Indicators of the Farm Sector, balance sheets, and receipts by detailed commodity, by State, 1986-90, annual rpt, 1544–18
Fed Govt finances, cash and debt transactions, daily tables, 8102–4
Finances of farms, assets, liabilities, and debt by lender type, by State, 1960-89, 1548–384
Financial and marketing conditions of farms, forecast 1992, annual chartbook, 1504–8

Financial and marketing conditions of farms, forecast 1992, annual conf, 1504–9
Flow-of-funds accounts, savings, investments, and credit statements, quarterly rpt, 9365–3.3
FmHA activities, and loans and grants by program and State, FY91 and trends from FY70, annual rpt, 1184–17
FmHA guaranteed loan program, characteristics of borrowers, lenders, and loans, FY88, 1548–386
FmHA loans and borrower supervision activities in farm and housing programs, by type and State, monthly rpt, 1182–1
FmHA loans, by type, borrower characteristics, and State, quarterly rpt, discontinued, 1182–8
FmHA loans, by type, borrower race, and State, quarterly rpt, 1182–5
FmHA loans, delinquencies, and lending practices, by loan program, FY88-91, GAO rpt, 26113–569
FmHA property acquired through foreclosure, acreage, value, and sales, for farm and nonfarm property by State, monthly rpt, 1182–6
Grain support loan programs of USDA, activity and status by grain and State, monthly rpt, 1802–3
Honey production, prices, trade, stocks, marketing, and CCC honey loan and distribution activities, monthly rpt, 1311–2
Interest rates and terms on farm loans, by size of loan, 1990, annual rpt, 9364–5.3
Land transfers, by source of credit financing and region, 1982-92, article, 1561–16.302
Loans (farm) at risk of default, lender losses, and selected farm financial indicators, by type of farm and lender, 1984-89, 1548–383
Loans (farm) outstanding, and lenders financial condition, quarterly rpt with articles, 1541–1
Loans (farm), terms, delinquency, agricultural bank failures, and credit conditions by Fed Reserve District, quarterly rpt, 9365–3.10
Lumber and wood products trade and export promotion of US by country, and trade balance, by commodity, FAS periodic circular, 1925–36
Mortgage loan activity, by type of lender, loan, and mortgaged property, monthly press release, 5142–18
Mortgage loan activity, by type of lender, loan, and mortgaged property, quarterly press release, 5142–30
North Central States business and economic conditions, Fed Reserve 9th District, quarterly journal, 9383–19
North Central States farm credit conditions and economic devs, Fed Reserve 7th District, monthly rpt, 9375–10
North Central States farm credit conditions, earnings, and expenses, Fed Reserve 9th District, quarterly rpt, 9383–11
South Central States agricultural and small banks financial ratios, by State, as of 1991 and trends from 1985, article, 9391–16.306
South Central States agricultural banks financial ratios, and farm finances and production growth, by State, 1980s-92, annual article, 9391–16.308
Southeastern States, Fed Reserve 5th District insured commercial banks financial statements, by State, quarterly rpt, 9389–18
Southeastern States, Fed Reserve 8th District banking and economic conditions, quarterly rpt with articles, 9391–16
Southwestern US farm credit conditions and real estate values, Fed Reserve 11th District, quarterly rpt, 9379–11
Storage facility and equipment loans to farmers under CCC grain program, by State, monthly table, 1802–9
West Central States farm real estate values, farm loan trends, and regional farm price index, Fed Reserve 10th District, quarterly rpt, 9381–16.1
see also Agricultural production quotas and price supports
see also Farm Credit System

Agricultural education
Degrees awarded in higher education, by level, field, race, and sex, 1989/90 and trends from 1980/81, annual rpt, 4844–17
Digest of Education Statistics, 1992 annual data compilation, 4824–2
Enrollment in science and engineering grad programs, by field, source of funds, and characteristics of student and instn, 1990, annual rpt, 9627–7
Expenditures and staffing for agricultural research by USDA, State agencies, and other instns, by topic, FY91, annual rpt, 1744–2
Expenditures for research and education, USDA appropriations by program and subagency, FY83-91, annual rpt, 1004–19
Expenditures for research and education, USDA competitive awards by program and recipient, FY91, annual listing, 1764–1
High school enrollment in vocational education, and academic and other credits earned, by subject and student characteristics, classes of 1982 and 1987, 4838–50
Teachers of vocational education, by subject area and selected characteristics, for public high schools, 1987/88, 4836–3.9
Vocational education enrollment, student and teacher characteristics, and outcomes, for secondary and postsecondary instns, 1970s-90, 4828–42
see also Agricultural extension work

Agricultural energy use
Conservation of energy, State programs aid from Fed Govt, and energy savings, by State, 1990, annual rpt, 3304–1
Developing countries energy efficiency improvement issues and devs, with data by end use and country, 1980s-90, 26358–260
Economic Indicators of the Farm Sector, itemized production costs, receipts, and returns, by commodity and region, 1975-90, annual rpt, 1544–20
Energy use by mode of transport, fuel supply, and demographic and economic factors of vehicle use, 1970s-90, annual rpt, 3304–5
Financial and marketing conditions of farms, forecast 1992, annual conf, 1504–9
Fuel oil and kerosene sales and deliveries, by end-use, PAD district, and State, 1990, annual rpt, 3164–94
Gasoline and other motor fuel use, by consuming sector and State, 1991, annual rpt, 7554–1.1
Irrigated farmland, farm characteristics, and water and fuel sources, by State and leading county, 1950s-88, 1588–122
Pacific basin countries energy supply and demand, and implications for US trade, country rpt series, 3406–6
Prices received and paid by farmers, by commodity and State, monthly rpt, 1629–1
Prices received and paid by farmers, by commodity and State, 1991, annual rpt, 1629–5
Production inputs, finances, mgmt, and land value and transfers, periodic situation rpt with articles, 1561–16
Production itemized costs, by farm sales size and region, 1991, annual rpt, 1614–3
Production itemized costs, receipts, and returns, by crop and State, 1987-89, annual rpt, 1544–24
Rice production, practices, costs, and land tenure, by production area, 1988, 1568–309
Soybean tillage systems impacts on yield and inputs use and costs, 1990, article, 1561–3.304

Agricultural exports and imports
Agricultural Outlook, production, prices, marketing, and trade, by commodity, forecast and current situation, monthly rpt with articles, 1502–4
Agricultural situation and farm-related topics, monthly rpt, 1502–6
Agricultural Stabilization and Conservation Service programs, annual commodity fact sheet series, 1806–4
Agricultural Statistics, 1991, annual rpt, 1004–1
Business statistics, detailed data for major industries and economic indicators, *Survey of Current Business*, monthly rpt, 2702–1.13
Business statistics, detailed data for major industries and economic indicators, 1960-91, *Survey of Current Business* biennial supplement, 2704–1
Canada-US trade agreement issues, with data on Canada fertilizer and agricultural production and trade, 1960s-90s, hearing, 25368–179
Caribbean Basin Initiative export and investment incentives, contact listing, bibl, and US imports country, 1983-91, annual rpt, 2044–36
Chile agricultural trade, total and with US, by selected commodity, 1990, article, 1502–4.301
Chile trade and investment policies, foreign direct investment, and US agricultural trade and tariffs, 1985-91, GAO rpt, 26119–408
Communist and transitional economy countries trade with US, by detailed commodity and country, quarterly rpt with articles, 9882–2
Cooperatives (food marketing) exports under intl business arrangements, 1985-88, 1128–69

Costa Rica exports to US by commodity group, and role in stimulating economic growth, 1980s, working paper, 9916–13.2
Cuba trade, by commodity and country, mid 1980s-91, 9118–8
Developing countries economic, population, and agricultural data, US and other aid sources, and AID activity, country rpt series, 9916–12
Developing countries food supply, needs, and aid, status and alternative forecasts, world area rpt series, 1526–8
Eastern Europe agricultural trade with US, by commodity group and country, 1988-91, 1928–11
EC economic integration impacts on domestic and intl agricultural conditions, 1990 conf, 1528–325
Export credit sales agreement terms, by commodity and country, FY90, annual rpt, 15344–1.11
Export licensing, monitoring, and enforcement activities, FY91, annual rpt, 2024–1
Export promotion activities of FAS trade offices, operating costs, and funding by program, by country, 1989-90, GAO rpt, 26123–370
Exports (agricultural) info and service sources, 1991 annual listing, 1924–11
Exports and imports (agricultural), by selected commodity, 1940-91, annual rpt, 204–1.8
Exports and imports (agricultural) commodity and country, prices, and world market devs, monthly rpt, 1922–12
Exports and imports (agricultural) of US, by commodity and country, bimonthly rpt, 1522–1
Exports and imports (agricultural) of US, by detailed commodity and country, 1991, annual rpt, 1524–8
Exports and imports (agricultural) of US, by detailed commodity and country, 1991, semiannual rpt, 1522–4
Exports and imports (agricultural) of US, outlook and current situation, quarterly rpt, 1542–4
Exports and imports between US and outlying areas, by detailed commodity and mode of transport, 1991, annual rpt, 2424–11
Exports and imports of US, by country and detailed commodity, monthly rpt, 2422–12
Exports and imports of US by country, and trade shifts by commodity, 1991, annual rpt, 9884–25
Exports and imports of US, by Harmonized System 6-digit commodity and country, 1991, annual rpt, 2424–13
Exports and imports of US, by selected country, country group, and commodity group, 1991, annual rpt, 2044–37
Exports and imports of US, by transport mode, country, and SITC 1- to 3-digit commodity, 1991, annual rpt, 2424–12
Exports, imports, and balances of US, by selected country, country group, and commodity group, preliminary data, monthly rpt, 2042–34
Exports, imports, and balances of US for manufactured goods, by SITC 2-digit commodity and country, quarterly rpt, 2042–35
Exports, imports, and balances of US with major trading partners, by product category, 1987-91, annual chartbook, 9884–21
Exports, imports, and trade flows, by country and commodity, with background economic indicators, data compilation, monthly CD-ROM, 2002–6
Exports, imports, supply, consumption, prices, spending, and indexes, by food commodity, 1990, annual rpt, 1544–4
Exports, imports, tariffs, and industry operating data for agricultural, fishery, and forest products, commodity rpt series, 9885–8
Exports of agricultural products and nonelectrical machinery, *Survey of Current Business*, monthly rpt, 2702–1.1
Exports of grains, oilseed products, hides, skins, and cotton, by country, weekly rpt, dropped data, 1922–3
Exports of US, detailed commodities by country, monthly CD-ROM, 2422–13
Exports of US, detailed Schedule B commodities with countries of destination, 1991, annual rpt, 2424–10
FDA detention of imports, by reason, product, shipper, brand, and country, monthly listing, 4062–2
Financial and marketing conditions of farms, forecast 1992, annual chartbook, 1504–8
Foreign and US agricultural supply and demand indicators, by selected crop, monthly rpt, 1522–5
Foreign and US fresh and processed fruit, vegetable, and nut production and trade, FAS monthly circular with articles, 1925–34
Foreign countries agricultural production, consumption, and policies, and US export dev and promotion, monthly journal, 1922–2
Foreign countries agricultural production, prices, and trade, by country, 1980-91 and forecast 1992, annual world area rpt series, 1524–4
Imports, exports, and employment impacts, by SIC 2- to 4-digit industry and commodity, quarterly rpt, 2322–2
Imports of US, detailed commodities by country, monthly CD-ROM, 2422–14
Imports of US given duty-free treatment for value of US material sent abroad, by commodity and country, 1987-90, annual rpt, 9884–14
Indexes of trade dependency for total, merchandise, and agricultural products, by country, 1960s-88, 1528–328
Input-output structure of US economy, detailed interindustry transactions for 541 industries, and components of final demand, 1982 benchmark data, 2708–17
Intl transactions summary, 1980s-91, annual article, 9362–1.304
Latin America economic and social conditions, resources, trade, and aid, 1992, annual factbook, 9914–14
Marketing and financial conditions of farms, forecast 1992, annual conf, 1504–9
Mexico agricultural trade with US and Canada, and impacts of North American Free Trade Agreement, 1980s-90, 1528–330
Mexico agricultural trade with US, and impacts of North American Free Trade Agreement, 1980s-2000, article, 9381–1.307
Mexico and US economic and trade impacts of proposed North American Free Trade Agreement, with data on maquiladora plants, 1980s-90, hearings, 21788–210
Mexico imports from US, by industry and State, 1987-91, 2048–154
Natl income and product accounts, comprehensive accounts and components, benchmark revisions, 1929-88, 2708–5
Natl income and product accounts, comprehensive accounts and components, *Survey of Current Business*, monthly rpt, 2702–1.27
North Central States farm credit conditions and economic devs, Fed Reserve 7th District, monthly rpt, 9375–10
OECD intl trade position for US and 4 countries, and factors affecting US competition, quarterly pamphlet, 2042–25
OECD trade, total and for 4 major countries, and US trade by country, by commodity, 1980-90, world area rpt series, 9116–1
Panama Canal traffic and tolls, by commodity, flag of vessel, and trade route, FY91, annual rpt, 9664–3.1
Pesticide residue in food imports, FDA enforcement, with contaminated shipments distributed, damages assessed and paid, and repeat offenders, FY88-90, GAO rpt, 26113–598
Price indexes for exports and imports, by selected end-use category, monthly press release, 6762–15
Price indexes for exports and imports of goods and services, and dollar exchange rate indexes, quarterly press release, 6762–13
Processed food production and stocks by State, shipments, exports, ingredients, and use, periodic Current Industrial Rpt series, 2506–4
Quarantined fruits and vegetable imports, by crop, country, and port of entry, FY89, annual rpt, 1524–7
Statistical Abstract of US, 1992 annual data compilation, 2324–1.23
Tariff Schedule of US, classifications and rates of duty by detailed imported commodity, 1993 base edition, 9886–13
Uganda cash transfers from AID linked to nontraditional crop export programs, 1988-90, 9916–1.77
Waterborne commerce (domestic and foreign) of US, freight by commodity, traffic, and passengers, by port and waterway, 1989, annual rpt, 3754–3
West Central States economic indicators, Fed Reserve 10th District, quarterly rpt, 9381–16.2
see also Public Law 480
see also under names of specific commodities or commodity groups (listed under Agricultural commodities)

Agricultural extension work
Expenditures for research and education, USDA appropriations by program and subagency, FY83-91, annual rpt, 1004–19
Expenditures of Fed Govt in States, by type, program, agency, and State, FY91, annual rpt, 2464–2
Foreign countries agricultural research grants of USDA, by program, subagency, and country, FY92, annual listing, 1954–3

Agricultural finance
Agricultural Economics Research, quarterly journal, 1502–3
Agricultural Statistics, 1991, annual rpt, 1004–1
Assets and debts of private sector, balance sheets by segment, 1960-91, semiannual rpt, 9365–4.1
Assets of farm sector by type, and real and nonreal estate debt, including and excluding operator households, by sales size, 1960-89, 1548–387
Capital investment in farm sector relation to net worth, model description and results, 1991 working paper, 9375–13.77
Dairy farms financial statement, by size and region, 1987-90, annual article, 1561–2.301
Data on agriculture, collection, methodology, and use for major time series of USDA, series, 1506–1
Economic Indicators of the Farm Sector, balance sheets, and receipts by detailed commodity, by State, 1986-90, annual rpt, 1544–18
Equity of farms, by State, 1990, article, 1541–1.303
Exports, imports, tariffs, and industry operating data for agricultural, fishery, and forest products, commodity rpt series, 9885–8
Family farms financial condition, 1970s-88, annual rpt, 1504–4
Finances of farms, assets, liabilities, and debt by lender type, by State, 1960-89, 1548–384
Finances of farms, debts, assets, and receipts, and lenders financial condition, quarterly rpt with articles, 1541–1
Financial and marketing conditions of farms, forecast 1992, annual chartbook, 1504–8
Financial and marketing conditions of farms, forecast 1992, annual conf, 1504–9
Financial condition of farm sector, and prices, supply, and demand by commodity, 1980s-91 and forecast 1992, annual article, 9381–1.303
Financial condition of farms, selected years 1939-91, annual rpt, 204–1.8
Flow-of-funds accounts, savings, investments, and credit statements, quarterly rpt, 9365–3.3
Foreign direct investment in US, major transactions by type, industry, country, and US location, 1990, annual rpt, 2044–20
Gross State Product by component, industry div, and State, 1977-89, article, 2702–1.303
Income tax returns of foreign corporations and individuals, and US entities abroad, detailed data compilation, 1970s-89, quinquennial rpt, 8308–31
Japan investment in US farmland and agricultural industries, with data by State and county, late 1960s-90, 1528–332
Multinatl US firms and foreign affiliates finances and operations, by industry and country, 1989 benchmark survey, annual rpt, 2704–5
Multinatl US firms foreign affiliates, income statement items by asset size, industry, and country, 1988, biennial article, 8302–2.322
Natl income and product accounts, comprehensive accounts and components, benchmark revisions, 1929-88, 2708–5
Natl income and product accounts, comprehensive accounts and components, *Survey of Current Business*, monthly rpt, 2702–1.29
North Central States farm credit conditions and economic devs, Fed Reserve 7th District, monthly rpt, 9375–10
North Central States farm credit conditions, earnings, and expenses, Fed Reserve 9th District, quarterly rpt, 9383–11
Puerto Rico and other US possessions corporations income tax returns, income and tax items, and employment, by selected industry, 1989, article, 8302–2.326
SEC registration, firms required to file annual rpts, as of Sept 1991, annual listing, 9734–5
South Central States agricultural banks financial ratios, and farm finances and production growth, by State, 1980s-92, annual article, 9391–16.308
Statistical Abstract of US, 1992 annual data compilation, 2324–1.23
Tax (estate) returns property and tax data, by size of gross estate and State, 1989-90, article, 8302–2.305
Tax (income) returns filed, by type of filer, selected income items, quarterly rpt, 8302–2.1
Tax (income) returns for foreign corporate activity in US, selected income and tax items, by industry div and selected country, 1988, article, 8302–2.309
Tax (income) returns of corporations, income and tax items by asset size and detailed industry, 1989, annual rpt, 8304–4; 8304–21
Tax (income) returns of corporations with foreign tax credit, income and tax items by industry group, 1988, biennial article, 8302–2.316
Tax (income) returns of individuals, by filing status, tax item, and income level, 1991, annual article, 8302–2.319
Tax (income) returns of partnerships, income statement and balance sheet items, by industry group, 1990, annual article, 8302–2.314
Tax returns filed, by type of tax and IRS region and service center, projected 1991-98 and trends from 1978, annual rpt, 8304–9
Vegetable farms financial condition, 1990, article, 1561–11.304
West Central States economic indicators, Fed Reserve 10th District, quarterly rpt, 9381–16.2
see also Agricultural credit
see also Agricultural insurance
see also Agricultural prices
see also Agricultural production costs
see also Agricultural production quotas and price supports
see also Agricultural subsidies
see also Farm Credit System
see also Farm income
see also Rural cooperatives

Agricultural forecasts
Agricultural Economics Research, quarterly journal, 1502–3
Agricultural Outlook, production, prices, marketing, and trade, by commodity, forecast and current situation, monthly rpt with articles, 1502–4
Apple seasonal price forecasts based on production, price, and stocks, 1970s-91, article, 1561–6.303
Coffee production, trade, and use, by country, with US and intl prices, FAS periodic circular, 1925–5
Cotton production, trade, and use, for selected countries, FAS monthly circular, 1925–4.2
Cotton production, trade, use, and stocks, USDA forecast accuracy, 1980-90, article, 1561–1.302
Dairy production, trade, use, and prices, for US and selected countries, forecast 1992 and trends from 1987, FAS semiannual circular, 1925–10
Developing countries food supply, needs, and aid, status and alternative forecasts, world area rpt series, 1526–8
Exports and imports (agricultural) commodity and country, prices, and world market devs, monthly rpt, 1922–12
Exports and imports (agricultural) of US, outlook and current situation, quarterly rpt, 1542–4
Fed Crop Insurance Corp financial performance, and effect of alternative price forecasts on program costs, 1983-89, GAO rpt, 26131–95
Financial and marketing conditions of farms, forecast 1992, annual chartbook, 1504–8
Fish and shellfish catch and stocks in northwest Atlantic, by species and location, 1887-1991 and forecast to 1993, semiannual conf, 2162–9
Foreign and US agricultural supply and demand indicators, by selected crop, monthly rpt, 1522–5
Foreign countries agricultural production, prices, and trade, by country, 1980-91 and forecast 1992, annual world area rpt series, 1524–4
Fruit and nut season production forecasts of USDA, analysis of accuracy, mid 1970s-90, article, 1561–6.302
Grain production, supply, trade, and use, by country and world region, forecasts and trends, FAS monthly circular, 1925–2.1
Livestock grazing forage demand, and meat supply and demand, indicators, 1960s-90 and projected to 2030, 1208–404
Marketing and financial conditions of farms, forecast 1992, annual conf, 1504–9
Meat production, inventory, and price forecasts of USDA, accuracy, 1980s, GAO rpt, 26131–93
Mexico agricultural trade with US, and impacts of North American Free Trade Agreement, 1980s-2000, article, 9381–1.307
Molasses (feed) production forecasts, weekly rpt, supplement, 1311–16
Production, acreage, and yield for selected crops, forecasts by selected world region and country, FAS monthly circular, 1925–28
Production inputs, finances, mgmt, and land value and transfers, periodic situation rpt with articles, 1561–16
Rice season average price forecasts using futures settlement prices, 1990-92, article, 1561–8.301

Soybean acreage and production, USDA forecast accuracy, 1965-91, article, 1561–3.306
Soybean season average price forecasts using futures settlement prices, 1986-92, article, 1561–3.303
Timber in western US, insect and disease infestation from lumber imports from USSR, economic and environmental impacts, 1991 and projected to 2040, 1208–389
USDA price, production, and supply forecasts used for commodity program outlays, accuracy, 1975-88, GAO rpt, 26131–94
Vegetable production, acreage, and yield, current and forecast for selected fresh and processing crops by State, periodic rpt, 1621–12
Wheat season average price forecasts using futures settlement prices, 1986-92, article, 1561–12.301

Agricultural income
see Farm income

Agricultural industries
see Agricultural finance
see Agricultural labor
see Agricultural marketing
see Agricultural production
see Agricultural services
see Agricultural wages
see Agriculture
see Dairy industry and products
see Farms and farmland
see Flowers and nursery products
see Food and food industry
see Fruit and fruit products
see Grains and grain products
see Honey and beekeeping
see Livestock and livestock industry
see Meat and meat products
see Poultry industry and products
see Rural cooperatives
see Sugar industry and products
see Tobacco industry and products
see Vegetables and vegetable products
see Veterinary medicine

Agricultural insurance
Agricultural Statistics, 1991, annual rpt, 1004–1
Budget of US, obligations and authority by function, agency, and program, with summaries and analyses, FY93, annual rpt, 104–2
Costs of production, itemized by farm sales size and region, 1991, annual rpt, 1614–3
Economic Indicators of the Farm Sector, balance sheets, and receipts by detailed commodity, by State, 1986-90, annual rpt, 1544–18
Expenditures of Fed Govt for disaster aid by program, with farm crop insurance participation and finances of private insurers and Fed Crop Insurance Corp, 1980s-92, GAO rpt, 26113–556
Expenditures of Fed Govt in States, by type, program, agency, and State, FY91, annual rpt, 2464–2
Fed Crop Insurance Corp financial performance, and effect of alternative price forecasts on program costs, 1983-89, GAO rpt, 26131–95

Agricultural labor
Agricultural situation and farm-related topics, monthly rpt, 1502–6
Agricultural Statistics, 1991, annual rpt, 1004–1
Alien workers legal residence applicants share of population, and farm workers share of applicants, by MSA, 1989, working paper, 6366–6.9
Black Americans social and economic characteristics, for South and total US, 1991 and trends from 1950, annual Current Population Rpt, 2546–1.463
Business statistics, detailed data for major industries and economic indicators, 1960-91, *Survey of Current Business* biennial supplement, 2704–1
County Business Patterns, 1989: employment, establishments, and payroll, by SIC 2- to 4-digit industry and county, annual State rpt series, 2326–8
County Business Patterns, 1990: employment, establishments, and payroll, by SIC 2- to 4-digit industry and county, annual State rpt series, 2326–6
Deaths and rates, by cause and selected social, demographic, and employment characteristics, 1979-85, natl longitudinal study, 4478–186
Economic indicators and components, current data and annual trends, monthly rpt, 23842–1.2
Economic Indicators of the Farm Sector, production inputs, output, and productivity, by commodity and region, 1947-90, annual rpt, 1544–17
Educational attainment, by social and demographic characteristics and location, 1991 and trends from 1940, biennial Current Population Rpt, 2546–1.460
Employment and Earnings, detailed data, monthly rpt, 6742–2
Employment and economic conditions, alternative BLS projections to 2005 and trends 1975-90, biennial rpt, 6744–19
Employment and labor productivity, 1947-90, annual rpt, 204–1.8
Employment, earnings, and hours, monthly press release, 6742–5
Employment on farms, wages, hours, and perquisites, by State, monthly rpt, 1631–1
Employment situation, earnings, hours, and other BLS economic indicators, transcripts of BLS Commissioner's monthly testimony, periodic rpt, 23846–4
Employment, unemployment, and labor force characteristics, by region and State, 1991, annual rpt, 6744–7.1; 6744–7.2
Employment, wages, hours, and payroll costs, by major industry group and demographic characteristics, *Survey of Current Business*, monthly rpt, 2702–1.7
Exports, imports, tariffs, and industry operating data for agricultural, fishery, and forest products, commodity rpt series, 9885–8
Food stamp recipient household size, composition, income, and income and deductions allowed, summer 1989, annual rpt, 1364–8
Hired and contract labor costs, by farm type and sales size, and for top States and counties, 1987, article, 1541–1.305
Hired farm workers and earnings, by selected characteristics, 1990, 1598–278
Immigrant and nonimmigrant visas of US issued and refused, by class, issuing office, and nationality, FY90, annual rpt, 7184–1
Immigrants and legalized aliens, by occupational group and country of birth, preliminary FY91, annual tables, 6264–1
Immigration to US, alien workers, visitors, deportations, and naturalizations, by country, FY91 and trends from 1820, annual rpt, 6264–2
Indian and govt lands under Bur of Indian Affairs mgmt, acreage, leases, and use, 1989, annual rpt, 5704–12
Labor demand, turnover, and training completions, by detailed occupation, 1990 and projected to 2005, biennial rpt, 6744–3
Labor laws enacted, by State, 1991, annual article, 6722–1.309
Minimum wage rates, 1938-91, annual rpt, 4744–3.1
Minority group and women employment, by occupation, SIC 1- to 3- digit industry, State, and MSA, 1991, annual rpt, 9244–1
Occupational Outlook Handbook, 1992-93, biennial rpt, 6744–1
Pacific territories population and housing detailed characteristics, by location, 1990 Census of Population and Housing, series, 2551–8
Population on farms, by employment, social, and economic characteristics, and region, 1990, annual Current Population Rpt, 2546–1.458
Sheep and wool production, use, and prices, and operations costs and returns, for western US, 1920s-90, 1548–382
Statistical Abstract of US, 1992 annual data compilation, 2324–1.23
Tobacco (flue-cured) farms and farm operators, by region and selected characteristics, 1970s-87, 1568–307
Training for job qualification and skill improvement, workers participating by training source, occupation, age, sex, and race, 1991, 6728–32
Youth labor force status, by sex, race, and industry div, summer 1988-92, annual press release, 6744–14
see also Agricultural accidents and safety
see also Agricultural wages
see also Farm operators
see also Migrant workers
see also under By Occupation in the "Index by Categories"

Agricultural land
see Farms and farmland

Agricultural machinery and equipment
Accidents (fatal), deaths, and rates, by circumstances, characteristics of persons and vehicles involved, and location, 1990, annual rpt, 7764–10
Agricultural Outlook, production, prices, marketing, and trade, by commodity, forecast and current situation, monthly rpt with articles, 1502–4
Capital (fixed), govt and private nonresidential structures and equipment, residential capital, and consumer-owned durable goods, 1925-90, annual article, 2702–1.305; 2702–1.327

County Business Patterns, 1989: employment, establishments, and payroll, by SIC 2- to 4-digit industry and county, annual State rpt series, 2326–8
County Business Patterns, 1990: employment, establishments, and payroll, by SIC 2- to 4-digit industry and county, annual State rpt series, 2326–6
Drivers licenses issued and in force by age and sex, fees, and renewal, by license class and State, 1990, annual rpt, 7554–16
Employment, earnings, and hours, by SIC 1- to 4-digit industry, monthly 1989-Feb 1992, annual rpt, 6744–4
Employment of minorities and women, by occupation, SIC 1- to 3-digit industry, State, and MSA, 1991, annual rpt, 9244–1
Exports and imports (agricultural) of US, by commodity and country, bimonthly rpt, 1522–1
Exports and imports (agricultural) of US, by detailed commodity and country, 1991, annual rpt, 1524–8
Exports and imports (agricultural) of US, by detailed commodity and country, 1991, semiannual rpt, 1522–4
Exports and imports between US and outlying areas, by detailed commodity and mode of transport, 1991, annual rpt, 2424–11
Exports and imports of US, by country and detailed commodity, monthly rpt, 2422–12
Exports and imports of US, by Harmonized System 6-digit commodity and country, 1991, annual rpt, 2424–13
Exports and imports of US, by transport mode, country, and SITC 1- to 3-digit commodity, 1991, annual rpt, 2424–12
Exports, imports, tariffs, and industry operating data for farm machinery and lawn equipment, 1992 rpt, 9885–9.3
Exports of US, detailed Schedule B commodities with countries of destination, 1991, annual rpt, 2424–10
Farm credit, terms, delinquency, agricultural bank failures, and credit conditions by Fed Reserve District, quarterly rpt, 9365–3.10
Farm finances, assets, liabilities, and debt by lender type, by State, 1960-89, 1548–384
Farm production inputs, finances, mgmt, and land value and transfers, periodic situation rpt with articles, 1561–16
Farm production inputs, output, and productivity, by commodity and region, 1947-90, annual rpt, 1544–17
Farm production itemized costs, by farm sales size and region, 1991, annual rpt, 1614–3
Farm production itemized costs, receipts, and returns, by commodity and region, 1975-90, annual rpt, 1544–20
Farm production itemized costs, receipts, and returns, by crop and State, 1987-89, annual rpt, 1544–24
Farm sector assets by type, and real and nonreal estate debt, including and excluding operator households, by sales size, 1960-89, 1548–387
Farm sector balance sheet, and marketing receipts by detailed commodity, by State, 1986-90, annual rpt, 1544–18
Grain storage facility and equipment loans to farmers under CCC program, by State, monthly table, 1802–9
Injuries from use of consumer products, by severity, victim age, and detailed product, 1991, annual rpt, 9164–6
Input-output structure of US economy, detailed interindustry transactions for 84 industries, and components of final demand, 1987, annual article, 2702–1.316
Input-output structure of US economy, detailed interindustry transactions for 541 industries, and components of final demand, 1982 benchmark data, 2708–17
Irrigated farmland, farm characteristics, and water and fuel sources, by State and leading county, 1950s-88, 1588–122
Labor productivity, indexes of output, hours, and employment by SIC 2- to 4-digit industry, 1967-90, annual rpt, 6824–1.3
Manufacturing annual survey, 1990: finances and operations, by SIC 2- to 4-digit industry, series, 2506–14
Manufacturing census, 1987: concentration of largest firms measured by value added, and for shipments by SIC 2- and 4-digit industry, subject rpt, 2497–6
Manufacturing census, 1987: shipments of manufacturers products, by customer class and SIC 2- and 4-digit industry, subject rpt, 2497–4
Manufacturing finances and operations, by SIC 2- to 4-digit industry, forecast 1992, annual rpt, 2044–28
Military prime contract awards, by detailed procurement category, FY88-91, annual rpt, 3544–18
Multinatl US firms and foreign affiliates finances and operations, by industry and country, 1989 benchmark survey, annual rpt, 2704–5
Natl income and product accounts, comprehensive accounts and components, benchmark revisions, 1929-88, 2708–5
Natl income and product accounts, comprehensive accounts and components, *Survey of Current Business*, monthly rpt, 2702–1.28
North Central States farm credit conditions and economic devs, Fed Reserve 7th District, monthly rpt, 9375–10
Occupational injury and illness rates, by SIC 2- to 4-digit industry, 1989-90, annual rpt, 6844–7
Occupational injury and illness rates, by SIC 2- to 4-digit industry, 1990, annual rpt, 6844–1
OECD trade, total and for 4 major countries, and US trade by country, by commodity, 1980-90, world area rpt series, 9116–1
Price indexes (producer), by stage of processing and detailed commodity, monthly rpt, 6762–6
Price indexes (producer), by stage of processing and detailed commodity, monthly 1991, annual rpt, 6764–2
Prices received and paid by farmers, by commodity and State, monthly rpt, 1629–1
Prices received and paid by farmers, by commodity and State, 1991, annual rpt, 1629–5
Productivity of labor and capital, and indexes of output, hours, and employment, 1967-90, annual rpt, 6824–1.5
Rice production, practices, costs, and land tenure, by production area, 1988, 1568–309
Science, engineering, and technical employment in manufacturing, by field and industry, 1989, triennial rpt, 9627–23
Soviet Union and US economic and sociodemographic indicators, selected years 1970-90, handbook, 2328–80
Soybean tillage systems impacts on yield and inputs use and costs, 1990, article, 1561–3.304
Statistical Abstract of US, 1992 annual data compilation, 2324–1.23
Tax (income) returns of corporations, income and tax items by asset size and detailed industry, 1989, annual rpt, 8304–4; 8304–21
see also Lawn and garden equipment

Agricultural marketing
Agricultural Outlook, production, prices, marketing, and trade, by commodity, forecast and current situation, monthly rpt with articles, 1502–4
Agricultural Statistics, 1991, annual rpt, 1004–1
Business statistics, detailed data for major industries and economic indicators, 1960-91, *Survey of Current Business* biennial supplement, 2704–1
Consumer research, food marketing, legislation, and regulation devs, and consumption and price trends, quarterly journal, 1541–7
Costs of food marketing by component, farm-retail food prices, and industry finances and productivity, 1920s-91, annual rpt, 1544–9
Costs of production, itemized by farm sales size and region, 1991, annual rpt, 1614–3
County Business Patterns, 1989: employment, establishments, and payroll, by SIC 2- to 4-digit industry and county, annual State rpt series, 2326–8
County Business Patterns, 1990: employment, establishments, and payroll, by SIC 2- to 4-digit industry and county, annual State rpt series, 2326–6
Economic indicators and components, current data and annual trends, monthly rpt, 23842–1.1
Economic Indicators of the Farm Sector, balance sheets, and receipts by detailed commodity, by State, 1986-90, annual rpt, 1544–18
Economic Indicators of the Farm Sector, itemized production costs, receipts, and returns, by commodity and region, 1975-90, annual rpt, 1544–20
Employment, earnings, and hours, by SIC 1- to 4-digit industry, monthly 1989-Feb 1992, annual rpt, 6744–4
Fed Govt financial and nonfinancial domestic aid, 1992 base edition, annual listing, 104–5
Finances, operations, and merger activity, for food processors and distributors, 1991, annual rpt, 1544–22
Foreign countries agricultural research grants of USDA, by program, subagency, and country, FY92, annual listing, 1954–3

Income of farms, cash marketing receipts ranked by commodity and State, 1990, 1548–385
Input-output structure of US economy, detailed interindustry transactions for 84 industries, and components of final demand, 1987, annual article, 2702–1.316
Marketing and financial conditions of farms, forecast 1992, annual chartbook, 1504–8
Marketing and financial conditions of farms, forecast 1992, annual conf, 1504–9
Military prime contract awards, by detailed procurement category, FY88-91, annual rpt, 3544–18
Occupational injury and illness rates, by SIC 2- to 4-digit industry, 1989-90, annual rpt, 6844–7
Occupational injury and illness rates, by SIC 2- to 4-digit industry, 1990, annual rpt, 6844–1
Research (agricultural) funding and staffing for USDA, State agencies, and other instns, by topic, FY91, annual rpt, 1744–2
Research and education grants, USDA competitive awards by program and recipient, FY91, annual listing, 1764–1
Sales of farm products by stage of processing and marketing, and trade, by selected commodity, 1987, young readers pamphlet, 2346–1.5
Tax (income) returns of corporations, income and tax items by asset size and detailed industry, 1989, annual rpt, 8304–4; 8304–21
Truck and warehouse services finances and inventory, by SIC 2- to 4-digit industry, 1990 survey, annual rpt, 2413–14
Truck rates for fruit and vegetables weekly by growing area and market, and shipments monthly by State and country of origin, 1991, annual rpt, 1311–15
Wholesale trade sales and inventories, by SIC 2- to 3-digit kind of business, monthly rpt, 2413–7
Yearbook of Agriculture, special topics, 1992 annual compilation of papers, 1004–18
see also Agricultural exports and imports
see also Agricultural prices
see also Agricultural production quotas and price supports
see also Agricultural stocks
see also Agricultural surpluses
see also Food inspection
see also Food prices
see also Food stores
see also Rural cooperatives
see also under names of specific commodities or commodity groups (listed under Agricultural commodities)

Agricultural Marketing Service
Apple production, marketing, and prices, for Appalachia and compared to other States, 1989-92, annual rpt, 1311–13
Bean (dried) prices by State, market activity, and foreign and US production, use, stocks, and trade, weekly rpt, 1311–17
Bean (dried) production and prices by State, exports and foreign production by country, and USDA food aid purchases, by bean type, 1986-91, annual rpt, 1311–18
Budget of US, obligations and authority by function, agency, and program, with summaries and analyses, FY93, annual rpt, 104–2
Chile fruit exports to US, sales by port of entry, and prices in 5 terminal cities, by commodity, 1990/91, annual rpt, 1311–27
Cotton (long staple) production, prices, exports, stocks, and mill use, monthly rpt, 1309–12
Cotton acreage planted by State and county, and fiber quality, by variety, 1992, annual rpt, 1309–6
Cotton fiber and processing test results, by variety, region, State, and production area, 1991, annual rpt, 1309–16
Cotton fiber grade, staple, and mike, for upland and American pima cotton by State, monthly rpt, 1309–11
Cotton fiber grade, staple, mike, and other quality indicators, for upland cotton by classing office, weekly rpt, 1309–15
Cotton linters production, stocks, use, and prices, monthly rpt, 1309–10
Cotton prices at selected spot markets, NYC futures prices, and CCC loan rates, 1991/92 and trends from 1944, annual rpt, 1309–2
Cotton prices in 7 spot markets, futures prices at NYC exchange, farm prices, and CCC loan stocks, monthly rpt, 1309–1
Cotton quality, by State, 1991, annual rpt, 1309–7
Cotton quality, supply, and carryover, 1991-92, annual rpt, 1309–8
Cottonseed prices and quality, by State, seasonal weekly rpt, 1309–14
Cottonseed quality factors, by State, 1991 crop, annual rpt, 1309–5
Dairy prices, by product and selected area, with related marketing data, 1991, annual rpt, 1317–1
Expenditures of Fed Govt in States, by type, program, agency, and State, FY91, annual rpt, 2464–2
Flower and foliage shipments from Florida by State and mode of transport, US imports by country, and prices, by variety, mid 1980s-91, annual rpt, 1311–24
Food aid programs purchases, by commodity, firm, and shipping point or destination, weekly rpt, 1302–3
Fruit and vegetable shipments, and arrivals by city, by mode of transport and State and country of origin, 1991, annual rpt series, 1311–4
Fruit and vegetable shipments by mode of transport, arrivals, and imports, by commodity and State and country of origin, weekly rpt, 1311–3
Fruit and vegetable wholesale prices in NYC by State, and shipments and arrivals by mode of transport, by commodity, weekly rpt, 1311–20
Fruit and vegetable wholesale prices in NYC, Chicago, and selected shipping points, by crop, 1991, annual rpt, 1311–8
Fruit and vegetable wholesale prices in NYC-Newark, and arrivals by mode of transport, by commodity and State, 1990, annual rpt, 1311–21
Fruit shipments, production, and marketing, for Florida, with US trade and prices, by commodity, 1970s-91, annual rpt, 1311–23
Grain production, prices, trade, and export inspections by US port and country of destination, by grain type, weekly rpt, 1313–2
Grain stocks by region and market city, and grain inspected for export, by type, weekly rpt, 1313–4
Grape shipments from California and arrivals by city by mode of transport, prices, and production, by variety, 1970s-90, annual rpt, 1311–25
Grapes crushed and purchased, and grower prices and returns, for California, by type and variety, 1990-91, annual rpt, 1311–30
Hay (alfalfa and prairie) prices, for selected areas, weekly rpt, 1313–5
Honey production, prices, trade, stocks, marketing, and CCC honey loan and distribution activities, monthly rpt, 1311–2
Hops production, stocks, use, and US trade by country, monthly rpt, 1313–7
Livestock, meat, and wool, market news summary data by animal type and market, weekly rpt, 1315–1
Milk order market prices and detailed operations, by State and market area, 1990-91, annual rpt, 1317–3
Milk order market prices and detailed operations, monthly rpt with articles, 1317–4
Molasses (feed) wholesale prices by market area, and trade, weekly rpt, 1311–16
Molasses supply, use, wholesale prices by market, and imports by country, 1986-91, annual rpt, 1311–19
Peaches production, marketing, and prices in 3 southeastern States and Appalachia, 1991, annual rpt, 1311–12
Peanut production and US exports by country, prices, and stocks, weekly rpt, 1311–1
Peanut production, prices, stocks, exports, use, inspection, and quality, by region and State, 1982-91, annual rpt, 1311–5
Pecan production and prices by State, and US trade by country, late 1980s-91, annual rpt, 1311–28
Potato production, acreage, prices, and shipments, for 7 major producer States, and compared to other States, 1970s-92, annual rpt, 1311–29
Potato production, acreage, shipments, and arrivals, for Maine by variety, and compared to other States and Canada, 1991-92, annual rpt, 1311–26
Poultry and egg prices and marketing, by selected region, State, and city, monthly and weekly 1991, annual rpt, 1317–2
Revenue of USDA, by source and subagency, FY88-92, GAO rpt, 26113–602
Rice market activities, prices, inspections, sales, trade, supply, and use, for US and selected foreign markets, weekly rpt, 1313–8
Tobacco leaf stocks, production, sales, and import inspections by country, by product, quarterly rpt, 1319–3
Tobacco marketing activity, prices, and sales, by grade, type, market, and State, 1991, annual rpt series, 1319–5
Tobacco production, prices, stocks, taxes by State, and trade and production by country, 1991, annual rpt, 1319–1
Truck rates for fruit and vegetables paid by shippers and receivers, by commodity and city, and fleet itemized costs per mile, weekly rpt, 1311–22

Truck rates for fruit and vegetables weekly by growing area and market, and shipments monthly by State and country of origin, 1991, annual rpt, 1311–15
Wool prices, sales, trade, and stocks, and sheep inventory, weekly and biweekly rpt, 1315–2

Agricultural policy
Agricultural Economics Research, quarterly journal, 1502–3
Agricultural Outlook, production, prices, marketing, and trade, by commodity, forecast and current situation, monthly rpt with articles, 1502–4
Court criminal case processing in Federal district courts, and dispositions, by offense, 1980-91, annual rpt, 6064–31
Criminal case processing in Federal district courts, and dispositions, by offense, district, and offender characteristics, 1989, annual data compilation, 6064–29
Farm financial and marketing conditions, forecast 1992, annual conf, 1504–9
Foreign countries agricultural production, consumption, and policies, and US export dev and promotion, monthly journal, 1922–2
Investigations of Federal agency and program operations, summaries of findings, as of 1991, annual GAO rpt, 26104–5.2
see also Agricultural credit
see also Agricultural finance
see also Agricultural marketing
see also Agricultural prices
see also Agricultural production quotas and price supports
see also Agricultural subsidies
see also Food prices
see also Land reform

Agricultural prices
Agricultural Economics Research, quarterly journal, 1502–3
Agricultural Outlook, production, prices, marketing, and trade, by commodity, forecast and current situation, monthly rpt with articles, 1502–4
Agricultural situation and farm-related topics, monthly rpt, 1502–6
Agricultural Statistics, 1991, annual rpt, 1004–1
Business statistics, detailed data for major industries and economic indicators, 1960-91, *Survey of Current Business* biennial supplement, 2704–1
CCC commodities for sale, and prices, monthly press release, 1802–4
Economic indicators and components, current data and annual trends, monthly rpt, 23842–1.4
Export and import price indexes, by selected end-use category, monthly press release, 6762–15
Exports, imports, tariffs, and industry operating data for agricultural, fishery, and forest products, commodity rpt series, 9885–8
Financial and marketing conditions of farms, forecast 1992, annual conf, 1504–9
Financial condition of farm sector, and prices, supply, and demand by commodity, 1980s-91 and forecast 1992, annual article, 9381–1.303
Financial condition of farms, selected years 1939-91, annual rpt, 204–1.8
Foreign and US agricultural prices and US import prices, for selected commodities, bimonthly rpt, 1522–1.3
Foreign and US agricultural supply and demand indicators, by selected crop, monthly rpt, 1522–5
Foreign and US economic conditions, for major industrial countries, monthly rpt, 9112–1
Foreign countries agricultural production, prices, and trade, by country, 1980-91 and forecast 1992, annual world area rpt series, 1524–4
Global climate change impacts on agricultural production and GDP, with data by crop and world area, mid 1970s-86, 1528–326
North Central States farm credit conditions and economic devs, Fed Reserve 7th District, monthly rpt, 9375–10
Prices (farm-retail) for food, marketing cost components, and industry finances and productivity, 1920s-91, annual rpt, 1544–9
Prices received and paid by farmers, by commodity and State, monthly rpt, 1629–1
Prices received and paid by farmers, by commodity and State, 1991, annual rpt, 1629–5
Prices received by farmers and production value, by detailed crop and State, 1989-91, annual rpt, 1621–2
Producer Price Index, by major commodity group and subgroup, and processing stage, monthly press release, 6762–5
Producer price indexes, by stage of processing and detailed commodity, monthly rpt, 6762–6
Producer price indexes, by stage of processing and detailed commodity, monthly 1991, annual rpt, 6764–2
Production itemized costs, receipts, and returns, by crop and State, 1987-89, annual rpt, 1544–24
Southeastern States, Fed Reserve 8th District banking and economic conditions, quarterly rpt with articles, 9391–16
Statistical Abstract of US, 1992 annual data compilation, 2324–1.23
Survey of Current Business, detailed data for major industries and economic indicators, monthly rpt, 2702–1.4
West Central States economic indicators, Fed Reserve 10th District, quarterly rpt, 9381–16.2
West Central States farm real estate values, farm loan trends, and regional farm price index, Fed Reserve 10th District, quarterly rpt, 9381–16.1
see also Agricultural production quotas and price supports
see also Food prices
see also under names of specific commodities or commodity groups (listed under Agricultural commodities)

Agricultural production
Acreage planted and harvested, by crop and State, 1990-91 and planned as of June 1992, annual rpt, 1621–23
Agricultural Economics Research, quarterly journal, 1502–3
Agricultural Outlook, production, prices, marketing, and trade, by commodity, forecast and current situation, monthly rpt with articles, 1502–4
Agricultural situation and farm-related topics, monthly rpt, 1502–6
Agricultural Stabilization and Conservation Service programs, annual commodity fact sheet series, 1806–4
Agricultural Statistics, 1991, annual rpt, 1004–1
Business statistics, detailed data for major industries and economic indicators, *Survey of Current Business*, monthly rpt, 2702–1.13
Business statistics, detailed data for major industries and economic indicators, 1960-91, *Survey of Current Business* biennial supplement, 2704–1
Diversification of farm production, measures with data by commodity, 1990, article, 1541–1.314
Exports, imports, tariffs, and industry operating data for agricultural, fishery, and forest products, commodity rpt series, 9885–8
Financial and marketing conditions of farms, forecast 1992, annual chartbook, 1504–8
Indian and govt lands under Bur of Indian Affairs mgmt, acreage, leases, and use, 1989, annual rpt, 5704–12
Input-output structure of US economy, detailed interindustry transactions for 84 industries, and components of final demand, 1987, annual article, 2702–1.316
Input-output structure of US economy, detailed interindustry transactions for 541 industries, and components of final demand, 1982 benchmark data, 2708–17
Irrigation projects of Reclamation Bur in western US, crop production and acreage by commodity, State, and project, 1990, annual rpt, 5824–12
Natl income and product accounts and components, *Survey of Current Business*, monthly rpt, 2702–1.23
Natl income and product accounts, comprehensive accounts and components, benchmark revisions, 1929-88, 2708–5
Natl income and product accounts, comprehensive accounts and components, *Survey of Current Business*, monthly rpt, 2702–1.24; 2702–1.31
Occupational injury and illness rates, by SIC 2- to 4-digit industry, 1990, annual rpt, 6844–1
Palau admin, and social, economic, and govtl data, FY91, annual rpt, 7004–6
Production, farms, acreage, and related data, by selected crop and State, monthly rpt, 1621–1
Production indicators for farms, 1947-90, annual rpt, 204–1.8
Production, prices, trade, and use, for foreign and US agriculture, periodic rpt, discontinued, 1522–3
Statistical Abstract of US, 1992 annual data compilation, 2324–1.23
Weather conditions and effect on agriculture, by US region, State, and city, and world area, weekly rpt, 2182–7
Weather phenomena and storm characteristics, casualties, and property damage, by State, monthly listing, 2152–3
see also Agricultural forecasts
see also Agricultural production costs

see also Agricultural production quotas and price supports
see also Agricultural productivity
see also Agricultural stocks
see also Agricultural surpluses
see also Aquaculture
see also Fertilizers
see also Food supply
see also Foreign agriculture
see also under names of specific commodities or commodity groups (listed under Agricultural commodities)

Agricultural production costs

Acid rain environmental, economic, and health effects, and pollutant emissions, 1985-89 and alternative projections to 2030, 14358–4
Agricultural Outlook, production, prices, marketing, and trade, by commodity, forecast and current situation, monthly rpt with articles, 1502–4
Agricultural situation and farm-related topics, monthly rpt, 1502–6
Appalachia food processing firms, employment, and shipments, and farm production, by commodity and State, 1960s-90, 9088–37
Business statistics, detailed data for major industries and economic indicators, *Survey of Current Business*, monthly rpt, 2702–1.13
Costs of food marketing by component, farm-retail food prices, and industry finances and productivity, 1920s-91, annual rpt, 1544–9
Costs of production (itemized), receipts, and returns, by crop and State, 1987-89, annual rpt, 1544–24
Costs of production, itemized by farm sales size and region, 1991, annual rpt, 1614–3
Data on agriculture, collection, methodology, and use for major time series of USDA, 1990 rpt, 1506–1.1
EC economic integration impacts on domestic and intl agricultural conditions, 1990 conf, 1528–325
Economic indicators and components, current data and annual trends, monthly rpt, 23842–1.1; 23842–1.4
Economic Indicators of the Farm Sector, balance sheets, and receipts by detailed commodity, by State, 1986-90, annual rpt, 1544–18
Economic Indicators of the Farm Sector, itemized production costs, receipts, and returns, by commodity and region, 1975-90, annual rpt, 1544–20
Finances of farms, debts, assets, and receipts, and lenders financial condition, quarterly rpt with articles, 1541–1
Finances of farms, production inputs, mgmt, and land value and transfers, periodic situation rpt with articles, 1561–16
Financial and marketing conditions of farms, forecast 1992, annual chartbook, 1504–8
Financial condition of farms, selected years 1939-91, annual rpt, 204–1.8
Irrigated farmland, farm characteristics, and water and fuel sources, by State and leading county, 1950s-88, 1588–122
North Central States farm credit conditions, earnings, and expenses, Fed Reserve 9th District, quarterly rpt, 9383–11
Prices received and paid by farmers, by commodity and State, monthly rpt, 1629–1
Prices received and paid by farmers, by commodity and State, 1991, annual rpt, 1629–5
Tax (income) returns of corporations, income and tax items by asset size and detailed industry, 1989, annual rpt, 8304–4; 8304–21
Value-added calculation for farm production, methodology with background data, 1988-91, article, 1541–1.321
see also Agricultural marketing
see also under names of specific commodities or commodity groups (listed under Agricultural commodities)

Agricultural production quotas and price supports

Acreage reduction program compliance, enrollment, and yield on planted acreage, by commodity and State, annual press release series, 1004–20
Agricultural Outlook, production, prices, marketing, and trade, by commodity, forecast and current situation, monthly rpt with articles, 1502–4
Agricultural Stabilization and Conservation Service producer payments and certificate value, by program, monthly rpt, discontinued, 1802–10
Agricultural Stabilization and Conservation Service producer payments, by program and State, 1991, annual table, 1804–12
Agricultural Stabilization and Conservation Service programs, annual commodity fact sheet series, 1806–4
Agricultural Statistics, 1991, annual rpt, 1004–1
Budget of US, CBO analysis of revenue and spending alternatives and projections of economic indicators, FY93-97, annual rpt, 26304–3
CCC financial condition and major commodity program operations, FY63-88, annual chartbook, 1824–2
CCC loan activities by commodity, and agency operating results, monthly press release, 1802–7
CCC price support and other program outlays, with production and marketing outlook, by commodity, projected 1991-97, annual rpt, 26306–6.171
Certificate exchange activity of CCC, by commodity, biweekly press release, 1802–16
Crop subsidies of USDA, deficiency payments by payment size and producer form of organization, 1990, GAO rpt, 26113–574
Dairy production by State, stocks, prices, and CCC price support activities, by product type, monthly rpt, 1627–3
Dairy production, prices, trade, and use, periodic situation rpt with articles, 1561–2
Dairy products price support purchases, sales, donations, and inventories of CCC, monthly rpt, 1802–2
Dairy storage holdings and purchases of USDA by product, and milk order deliveries and prices by market area, 1991, annual rpt, 1317–1.1; 1317–1.5
Economic Indicators of the Farm Sector, balance sheets, and receipts by detailed commodity, by State, 1986-90, annual rpt, 1544–18
Expenditures (direct) and employment, by function and level of govt, selected years 1962-87, 10048–53
Expenditures of Fed Govt in States, by type, program, agency, and State, FY91, annual rpt, 2464–2
Feed and feed additives production, use, and prices, by commodity, State, and country, various periods 1949-92, 1568–308
Feed production, acreage, stocks, use, trade, prices, and price supports, periodic situation rpt with articles, 1561–4
Forecasts of prices, production, and supply used for USDA commodity program outlays, accuracy, 1975-88, GAO rpt, 26131–94
Grain and feed trade policy impacts on importing and exporting countries, FAS monthly circular, 1925–2.4
Grain production, prices, trade, and export inspections by US port and country of destination, by grain type, weekly rpt, 1313–2
Grain support loan programs of USDA, activity and status by grain and State, monthly rpt, 1802–3
Loans (farm) at risk of default, lender losses, and selected farm financial indicators, by type of farm and lender, 1984-89, 1548–383
Milk order market prices and detailed operations, by State and market area, 1990-91, annual rpt, 1317–3
Milk order market prices and detailed operations, monthly rpt with articles, 1317–4
Peanut production and US exports by country, prices, and stocks, weekly rpt, 1311–1
Production inputs, finances, mgmt, and land value and transfers, periodic situation rpt with articles, 1561–16
Rice foreign and US production, prices, trade, stocks, and use, periodic situation rpt, 1561–8
Rice production, practices, costs, and land tenure, by production area, 1988, 1568–309
Statistical Abstract of US, 1992 annual data compilation, 2324–1.23
Sugar and sweeteners production, prices, trade, supply, and use, quarterly situation rpt with articles, 1561–14
Tobacco (flue-cured) farms and farm operators, by region and selected characteristics, 1970s-87, 1568–307
Tobacco and cigarette production, use, trade, and subsidies, by EC member country, 1991, article, 1925–16.306
Tobacco marketing activity, prices, and sales, by grade, type, market, and State, 1991, annual rpt series, 1319–5
Tobacco production, marketing, use, price supports, and trade, quarterly situation rpt with articles, 1561–10
Tobacco quotas, support levels, and loan receipts, by type of tobacco, 1983-91, annual rpt, 1319–1.2
Wheat and rye price supports and loan rates, quarterly situation rpt with articles, 1561–12
Wool support and market prices, 1950-89, 1548–382

Agricultural productivity
Agricultural Statistics, 1991, annual rpt, 1004–1
Brazil agricultural productivity indicators, 1968-87, 1528–331
Economic Indicators of the Farm Sector, itemized production costs, receipts, and returns, by commodity and region, 1975-90, annual rpt, 1544–20
Economic Indicators of the Farm Sector, production inputs, output, and productivity, by commodity and region, 1947-90, annual rpt, 1544–17
Feed production, acreage, stocks, use, trade, prices, and price supports, periodic situation rpt with articles, 1561–4
Foreign and US agricultural production, acreage, and yield for selected crops, forecasts by selected world region and country, FAS monthly circular, 1925–28
Foreign and US agricultural supply and demand indicators, by selected crop, monthly rpt, 1522–5
Foreign countries agricultural production, prices, and trade, by country, 1980-91 and forecast 1992, annual world area rpt series, 1524–4
Global climate change impacts on agricultural production and GDP, with data by crop and world area, mid 1970s-86, 1528–326
Irrigation projects of Reclamation Bur in western US, crop production and acreage by commodity, State, and project, 1990, annual rpt, 5824–12
Ozone levels impacts on grain yields, by region, 1991 rpt, 14358–4
Production, farms, acreage, and related data, by selected crop and State, monthly rpt, 1621–1
Production indicators for farms, 1947-90, annual rpt, 204–1.8
Production itemized costs, receipts, and returns, by crop and State, 1987-89, annual rpt, 1544–24
Research (agricultural) funding and staffing for USDA, State agencies, and other instns, by topic, FY91, annual rpt, 1744–2
Vegetable production, prices, trade, stocks, and use, for selected fresh and processing crops, periodic situation rpt with articles, 1561–11
Wheat acreage, yield, and profitability impacts of using purchased rather than leftover seed, 1986-88, 1548–388
Wheat and rye foreign and US production, prices, trade, stocks, and use, quarterly situation rpt with articles, 1561–12
see also under names of specific commodities or commodity groups (listed under Agricultural commodities)

Agricultural Research Service
Budget of US, obligations and authority by function, agency, and program, with summaries and analyses, FY93, annual rpt, 104–2
Family Economics Review, consumer goods prices and supply, and home economics, quarterly journal, 1702–1
Sugarcane clones yields, stability, and fungi resistance, 1991/92, annual rpt, 1704–2
see also Cooperative State Research Service

Agricultural sciences and research
Agricultural Economics Research, quarterly journal, 1502–3
Bovine somatotropin (bST) dairy industry use, effectiveness of FDA testing for human and animal safety, 1991, GAO rpt, 26131–101
Budget of US, obligations and authority by function, agency, and program, with summaries and analyses, FY93, annual rpt, 104–2
Expenditures and staffing for agricultural research by USDA, State agencies, and other instns, by topic, FY91, annual rpt, 1744–2
Expenditures for R&D and related activities of higher education and nonprofit instns by Fed Govt, by field, instn, agency, and State, FY90, annual rpt, 9627–17
Expenditures for R&D by Fed Govt, by detailed function, program, and agency, FY91-93, annual rpt, 9627–9
Expenditures for R&D by higher education instns and federally funded centers, by field, instn, and State, FY90, annual rpt, 9627–13
Expenditures for research and education, USDA appropriations by program and subagency, FY83-91, annual rpt, 1004–19
Expenditures for research and education, USDA competitive awards by program and recipient, FY91, annual listing, 1764–1
Exports, imports, tariffs, and industry operating data for agricultural, fishery, and forest products, commodity rpt series, 9885–8
Facilities of higher education instns for R&D, space and equipment adequacy, needs, and funding by source, by instn type and control, 1992, biennial rpt, 9624–25
Fed Govt block and categorical grant programs for State and local govts, FY91, biennial listing, 10044–8
Foreign countries agricultural research grants of USDA, by program, subagency, and country, FY92, annual listing, 1954–3
Labor demand, turnover, and training completions, by detailed occupation, 1990 and projected to 2005, biennial rpt, 6744–3
Occupational Outlook Handbook, 1992-93, biennial rpt, 6744–1
Science and Engineering Indicators, employment, education, R&D funding, and industry impacts, with foreign comparisons, 1960s-91, biennial rpt, 9624–10
Seed varieties patent protection, and wheat farmer profitability of using purchased seed, 1986-89, 1548–388
Sugarcane clones yields, stability, and fungi resistance, 1991/92, annual rpt, 1704–2
Weather services activities and funding, by Federal agency, planned FY92-93, annual rpt, 2144–2
Yearbook of Agriculture, special topics, 1992 annual compilation of papers, 1004–18
see also Agricultural education

Agricultural services
Bee colony rentals, and pollinated crop value, by crop, 1989, hearings, 25168–78
Cooperatives, finances, and membership, by type of service, commodity, and State, 1990, annual rpt, 1124–1
Costs of production (itemized), receipts, and returns, by crop and State, 1987-89, annual rpt, 1544–24
County Business Patterns, 1989: employment, establishments, and payroll, by SIC 2- to 4-digit industry and county, annual State rpt series, 2326–8
County Business Patterns, 1990: employment, establishments, and payroll, by SIC 2- to 4-digit industry and county, annual State rpt series, 2326–6
Economic Indicators of the Farm Sector, itemized production costs, receipts, and returns, by commodity and region, 1975-90, annual rpt, 1544–20
Farm production itemized costs, by farm sales size and region, 1991, annual rpt, 1614–3
Input-output structure of US economy, detailed interindustry transactions for 84 industries, and components of final demand, 1987, annual article, 2702–1.316
Input-output structure of US economy, detailed interindustry transactions for 541 industries, and components of final demand, 1982 benchmark data, 2708–17
Multinatl firms US affiliates finances and operations, by industry, country of parent firm, and State, 1987, 2708–48
Occupational injury and illness rates, by SIC 2- to 4-digit industry, 1989-90, annual rpt, 6844–7
Occupational injury and illness rates, by SIC 2- to 4-digit industry, 1990, annual rpt, 6844–1
Rice production, practices, costs, and land tenure, by production area, 1988, 1568–309
Tax (income) returns of corporations, income and tax items by asset size and detailed industry, 1989, annual rpt, 8304–4
Tax (income) returns of sole proprietorships, income statement items, by industry group, 1990, annual article, 8302–2.317; 8302–2.320
see also Veterinary medicine

Agricultural Stabilization and Conservation Service
Activities of ASCS, annual commodity fact sheet series, 1806–4
Budget of US, obligations and authority by function, agency, and program, with summaries and analyses, FY93, annual rpt, 104–2
CCC commodities for sale, and prices, monthly press release, 1802–4
CCC loan activities by commodity, and agency operating results, monthly press release, 1802–7
Colorado River Salinity Control Program participation and payments, FY87-91, annual rpt, 1804–23
Conservation program of USDA, acreage, projects, participation, and funding, by State, 1936-90, quinquennial rpt, 1808–1
Conservation program of USDA, funding by practice, region and State, monthly rpt, 1802–15

Conservation program of USDA, participation and payments by practice and State, FY91, annual rpt, 1804–7
Cost sharing payments and eligibility requirements for USDA agricultural and water conservation programs, FY88-92, GAO rpt, 26113–572
Dairy products price support purchases, sales, donations, and inventories of CCC, monthly rpt, 1802–2
Disaster relief to farmers, Fed Govt costs by program, 1980s-92, GAO rpt, 26113–556
Emergency Conservation Program for farmland damaged by natural disaster, aid and participation by State, FY91, annual rpt, 1804–22
Emergency Conservation Program for farmland damaged by natural disaster, funding by region and State, monthly rpt, 1802–13
Grain support loan programs of USDA, activity and status by grain and State, monthly rpt, 1802–3
Pesticide production, trade, and additives, by type, with manufacturers listing, annual rpt, discontinued, 1804–5
Producer payments and certificate value, by program, monthly rpt, discontinued, 1802–10
Producer payments, by program and State, 1991, annual table, 1804–12
Rural Clean Water Program funding for control of pollution from farming, by region and State, monthly rpt, 1802–14
Storage facility and equipment loans to farmers under CCC grain program, by State, monthly table, 1802–9
Timber and orchard damage from natural disaster, USDA restoration aid and program participation by practice and State, FY91, annual rpt, 1804–24
Timber improvement program for private land, Fed Govt cost-sharing funds by region and State, monthly rpt, 1802–11
Timber improvement program for private land, participation and payments by State, FY91, annual rpt, 1804–20
Water Bank Program agreements, payments to farmers, and wetlands acreage, by State, 1972-91, annual rpt, 1804–21
Wetlands preservation under Water Bank Program, acreage, agreements, and payments, by State, monthly rpt, 1802–5
see also Commodity Credit Corp.

Agricultural Statistics Board
Acreage of farmland, and operations, by sales size, region, and State, 1990-92, annual rpt, 1614–4
Acreage planted and harvested, by crop and State, 1990-91 and planned as of June 1992, annual rpt, 1621–23
Acreage planted, by selected crop and State, 1983-91 and planned 1992, annual rpt, 1621–22
Cattle and calves for beef and milk, by State, as of July 1992, semiannual press release, 1623–1
Cattle and calves loss to predators, disease, and other causes, by region and State, 1991, 1618–22
Cattle and calves on feed, inventory and marketings by State, monthly release, 1623–2
Celery acreage planted and growing, by growing area, monthly rpt, 1621–14
Cold storage food stocks by commodity and census div, and warehouse space use, by State, monthly rpt, 1631–5
Cold storage food stocks by commodity, and warehouse space use, by census div, 1991, annual rpt, 1631–11
Cold storage warehouses and capacity, by State, as of Oct 1991, biennial rpt, 1614–2
Cotton ginnings, by State and county, seasonal biweekly rpt, 1631–19
Dairy cattle, milk production, and grain and other concentrates fed, by State, monthly rpt, 1627–1
Dairy production by commodity, and plants, by State, 1991, annual rpt, 1627–5
Dairy production by State, stocks, prices, and CCC price support activities, by product type, monthly rpt, 1627–3
Egg production and layer inventory, by State, 1990-91, annual rpt, 1625–7
Egg production by type of product, and eggs broken under Federal inspection by region, monthly rpt, 1625–2
Employment on farms, wages, hours, and perquisites, by State, monthly rpt, 1631–1
Fertilizer and pesticide use and application rates, by type, crop, and State, series, 1616–1
Fish (catfish) raised on farms, inventory, stocks, and production, by major producer State, quarterly rpt, 1631–18
Fish (catfish) raised on farms, production, inventory, sales, prices, and imports, monthly release, 1631–14
Fish (trout) raised on farms, production, sales, prices, and losses, 1991-92, annual rpt, 1631–16
Flower and foliage production, sales, prices, and growers, by crop and State, 1990-91 and planting planned 1992, annual rpt, 1631–8
Fruit and nut production, prices, and use, annual rpt series, 1621–18
Grain stocks on and off farms, by crop, quarterly rpt, 1621–4
Honey production, prices, stocks, and bee colonies, by State, 1990-91, annual rpt, 1631–6
Hops stocks held by growers, dealers, and brewers, 1990-92, semiannual press release, 1621–8
Livestock slaughter and meat production, by livestock type and State, monthly rpt, 1623–9
Livestock slaughter, meat production, and slaughter plants, by species and State, 1991, annual rpt, 1623–10
Meat animal production, prices, receipts, and disposition, by species and State, 1990-91, annual rpt, 1623–8
Milk of manufacturing grade, fat content and prices received by farmers in Minnesota and Wisconsin, monthly rpt, 1629–6
Milk of manufacturing grade, fat content and prices received by farmers in Minnesota and Wisconsin, 1989-91, annual rpt, 1629–2
Milk production, use, and receipts, and milk cow inventory, by State, 1989-91, annual rpt, 1627–4
Mink and pelt production, prices, and farms, selected years 1969-92, annual rpt, 1631–7
Mushroom production, sales, and prices, by State, 1966/67-1991/92 and planned 1992/93, annual rpt, 1631–9
Peanut stocks, millings, and use, by grade and type, monthly rpt, 1621–6
Potato production, prices, stocks, and use, by State, 1980s-91, annual rpt, 1621–11
Potato production, stocks, processing, yields, and harvest losses, by State, periodic rpt, 1621–10
Poultry (broiler) hatcheries eggs set and chicks placed, by State, weekly rpt, 1625–11
Poultry (chicken and turkey) hatchery production, 1990-91, annual rpt, 1625–8
Poultry (chicken, egg, and turkey) production and inventories, monthly rpt, 1625–1
Poultry (chicken, egg, and turkey) production and prices, by State, 1990-91, annual rpt, 1625–5
Poultry slaughtered under Fed Govt inspection, pounds certified, and condemnations by cause, by State, monthly rpt, 1625–3
Prices received and paid by farmers, by commodity and State, monthly rpt, 1629–1
Prices received and paid by farmers, by commodity and State, 1991, annual rpt, 1629–5
Prices received by farmers and production value, by detailed crop and State, 1989-91, annual rpt, 1621–2
Production, farms, acreage, and related data, by selected crop and State, monthly rpt, 1621–1
Production itemized costs, by farm sales size and region, 1991, annual rpt, 1614–3
Publications of ASB, releases planned 1992, annual listing, 1614–1
Rice stocks on and off farms and total in all positions, periodic rpt, 1621–7
Swine inventory, value, farrowings, and farms, by State, quarterly release, 1623–3
Turkey hatcheries egg inventory and poult placements, by region, monthly rpt, 1625–10
Turkeys raised by State, and losses by region, 1990-91, and hatchery plans, 1992, annual rpt, 1625–6
Vegetable production, acreage, and yield, current and forecast for selected fresh and processing crops by State, periodic rpt, 1621–12
Vegetable production, value, and acreage, for selected fresh and processing crops by State, 1989-91, annual rpts, 1621–25
Wheat and rye acreage seeded, by State, 1990-92, annual rpt, 1621–30
Wool and mohair production and prices, by State, 1989-91, annual press release, 1623–6

Agricultural stocks
Agricultural Outlook, production, prices, marketing, and trade, by commodity, forecast and current situation, monthly rpt with articles, 1502–4
Agricultural Stabilization and Conservation Service programs, annual commodity fact sheet series, 1806–4
Agricultural Statistics, 1991, annual rpt, 1004–1
Apple production, marketing, and prices, for Appalachia and compared to other States, 1989-92, annual rpt, 1311–13

Apple seasonal price forecasts based on production, price, and stocks, 1970s-91, article, 1561–6.303
Assets of farm sector by type, and real and nonreal estate debt, including and excluding operator households, by sales size, 1960-89, 1548–387
Bean (dried) prices by State, market activity, and foreign and US production, use, stocks, and trade, weekly rpt, 1311–17
Business statistics, detailed data for major industries and economic indicators, *Survey of Current Business*, monthly rpt, 2702–1.13
Business statistics, detailed data for major industries and economic indicators, 1960-91, *Survey of Current Business* biennial supplement, 2704–1
Cattle and calves for beef and milk, by State, as of July 1992, semiannual press release, 1623–1
Cattle and calves on feed, inventory and marketings by State, monthly release, 1623–2
Cocoa and cocoa products foreign and US production, prices, and trade, 1980s-93, FAS semiannual circular, 1925–9
Coffee production, trade, and use, by country, with US and intl prices, FAS periodic circular, 1925–5
Cold storage food stocks by commodity and census div, and warehouse space use, by State, monthly rpt, 1631–5
Cold storage food stocks by commodity, and warehouse space use, by census div, 1991, annual rpt, 1631–11
Cotton (long staple) production, prices, exports, stocks, and mill use, monthly rpt, 1309–12
Cotton linters production, stocks, use, and prices, monthly rpt, 1309–10
Cotton production and trade for US and selected countries, FAS periodic circular series, 1925–4
Cotton quality, supply, and carryover, 1991-92, annual rpt, 1309–8
Dairy production by State, stocks, prices, and CCC price support activities, by product type, monthly rpt, 1627–3
Dairy production, prices, trade, and use, periodic situation rpt with articles, 1561–2
Dairy production, trade, use, and prices, for US and selected countries, forecast 1992 and trends from 1987, FAS semiannual circular, 1925–10
Dairy products, commercial and Fed Govt storage holdings of butter, cheese, and nonfat dry milk, monthly rpt, 1317–4.2
Dairy storage holdings, total and for USDA by product, 1991, annual rpt, 1317–1.1
Developing countries food supply, needs, and aid, status and alternative forecasts, world area rpt series, 1526–8
Economic Indicators of the Farm Sector, balance sheets, and receipts by detailed commodity, by State, 1986-90, annual rpt, 1544–18
Feed production, acreage, stocks, use, trade, prices, and price supports, periodic situation rpt with articles, 1561–4
Fish (catfish) raised on farms, inventory, stocks, and production, by major producer State, quarterly rpt, 1631–18
Fish (catfish) raised on farms, production, inventory, sales, prices, and imports, monthly release, 1631–14
Fish hatcheries and farms, production, costs, prices, and sales, for catfish and trout, 1970s-92, semiannual situation rpt, 1561–15
Foreign and US agricultural supply and demand indicators, by selected crop, monthly rpt, 1522–5
Foreign countries agricultural production, prices, and trade, by country, 1980-91 and forecast 1992, annual world area rpt series, 1524–4
Fruit and nut production, prices, trade, stocks, and use, by selected crop, periodic situation rpt with articles, 1561–6
Grain production, prices, trade, and export inspections by US port and country of destination, by grain type, weekly rpt, 1313–2
Honey production, prices, stocks, and bee colonies, by State, 1990-91, annual rpt, 1631–6
Honey production, prices, trade, stocks, marketing, and CCC honey loan and distribution activities, monthly rpt, 1311–2
Hops production, stocks, use, and US trade by country, monthly rpt, 1313–7
Livestock, meat, poultry, and egg production, prices, trade, and stocks, monthly rpt, 1561–17
Livestock, meat, poultry, and egg production, prices, trade, stocks, and use, periodic situation rpt with articles, 1561–7
Natl income and product accounts, comprehensive accounts and components, benchmark revisions, 1929-88, 2708–5
Natl income and product accounts, comprehensive accounts and components, *Survey of Current Business*, monthly rpt, 2702–1.28
Oils, oilseeds, and fats foreign and US production and trade, FAS periodic circular series, 1925–1
Onions in summer storage, shrinkage and loss, 1989-91, annual rpts, 1621–25
Peanut production and US exports by country, prices, and stocks, weekly rpt, 1311–1
Peanut production, prices, stocks, exports, use, inspection, and quality, by region and State, 1982-91, annual rpt, 1311–5
Peanut stocks, millings, and use, by grade and type, monthly rpt, 1621–6
Pecan production and prices by State, and US trade by country, late 1980s-91, annual rpt, 1311–28
Potato production, acreage, prices, and shipments, for 7 major producer States, and compared to other States, 1970s-92, annual rpt, 1311–29
Potato production, acreage, shipments, and arrivals, for Maine by variety, and compared to other States and Canada, 1991-92, annual rpt, 1311–26
Potato production, prices, stocks, and use, by State, 1980s-91, annual rpt, 1621–11
Potato production, stocks, processing, yields, and harvest losses, by State, periodic rpt, 1621–10
Rice foreign and US production, prices, trade, stocks, and use, periodic situation rpt, 1561–8
Rice market activities, prices, inspections, sales, trade, supply, and use, for US and selected foreign markets, weekly rpt, 1313–8
Sugar and sweeteners production, prices, trade, supply, and use, quarterly situation rpt with articles, 1561–14
Tax (income) returns of corporations, income and tax items by asset size and detailed industry, 1989, annual rpt, 8304–4
Tobacco leaf stocks, production, sales, and import inspections by country, by product, quarterly rpt, 1319–3
Tobacco production, prices, stocks, taxes by State, and trade and production by country, 1991, annual rpt, 1319–1
Tomato production, acreage, and yield by State, trade and production by country, stocks, shipments, and prices, 1960s-91, 1568–310
Vegetable production, prices, trade, stocks, and use, for selected fresh and processing crops, periodic situation rpt with articles, 1561–11
Wheat and rye foreign and US production, prices, trade, stocks, and use, quarterly situation rpt with articles, 1561–12
Wool prices, sales, trade, and stocks, and sheep inventory, weekly and biweekly rpt, 1315–2
see also Agricultural surpluses
see also Grain storage and facilities

Agricultural subsidies
Agricultural Stabilization and Conservation Service producer payments and certificate value, by program, monthly rpt, discontinued, 1802–10
Agricultural Stabilization and Conservation Service producer payments, by program and State, 1991, annual table, 1804–12
American Samoa govt finances, with data on health and farm spending and employment, mid 1980s-91, GAO rpt, 26123–385
Assistance (block and categorical grants) programs for State and local govts, FY91, biennial listing, 10044–8
Assistance (financial and nonfinancial) of Fed Govt, 1992 base edition, annual listing, 104–5
Budget of US, balances of budget authority obligated and unobligated, by function and agency, FY90-93, annual rpt, 104–8
Budget of US, Bush Admin proposals, with detail for defense budgets, and historical data from FY34, FY93, 108–46
Budget of US, CBO analysis and review of FY93 budget by function, annual rpt, 26304–2
Budget of US, CBO analysis of revenue and spending alternatives and projections of economic indicators, FY93-97, annual rpt, 26304–3
Budget of US, House concurrent resolution, with spending and revenue targets, FY93 and projected to FY97, annual rpt, 21264–2
Budget of US, midsession review of FY93 budget, by function, annual rpt, 104–7
Budget of US, obligations and authority by function, agency, and program, with summaries and analyses, FY93, annual rpt, 104–2

Budget of US, receipts by source, outlays by agency and program, and balances, monthly rpt, 8102–3
Cameroon fertilizer producer subsidy elimination, effectiveness of AID support of govt reforms, 1987-92, 9916–1.76
Canada livestock price support payments, by species, 1986-91, semiannual rpt, 1925–33.2
Colorado River Salinity Control Program participation and payments, FY87-91, annual rpt, 1804–23
Conservation program of USDA, funding by practice, region and State, monthly rpt, 1802–15
Conservation program of USDA, participation and payments by practice and State, FY91, annual rpt, 1804–7
Conservation programs of USDA, cost sharing payments and eligibility requirements, FY88-92, GAO rpt, 26113–572
EC economic integration impacts on domestic and intl agricultural conditions, 1990 conf, 1528–325
EC export subsidies by commodity, FAS monthly circular, 1925–32
EC tomato (paste and canned) minimum grower price and processor subsidy, by country, 1985/86-1992/93, article, 1925–34.336
Economic Indicators of the Farm Sector, balance sheets, and receipts by detailed commodity, by State, 1986-90, annual rpt, 1544–18
Emergency Conservation Program for farmland damaged by natural disaster, aid and participation by State, FY91, annual rpt, 1804–22
Emergency Conservation Program for farmland damaged by natural disaster, funding by region and State, monthly rpt, 1802–13
Expenditures of Fed Govt in States, by type, program, agency, and State, FY91, annual rpt, 2464–2
Exports (agricultural) under federally financed programs, by commodity and country, bimonthly rpt, periodic data, 1522–1
Exports, imports, tariffs, and industry operating data for agricultural, fishery, and forest products, commodity rpt series, 9885–8
Foreign countries agricultural production, prices, and trade, by country, 1980-91 and forecast 1992, annual world area rpt series, 1524–4
Forest Service activities and finances, by region and State, FY91, annual rpt, 1204–1.2
Fraud and abuse in USDA programs, audits and investigations, FY92, semiannual rpt, 1002–4
Grain and feed trade policy impacts on importing and exporting countries, FAS monthly circular, 1925–2.4
Loans and loan guarantees of Fed Govt, outstanding amounts by agency and program, *Treasury Bulletin*, quarterly rpt, 8002–4.11
Mexico agricultural trade with US and Canada, and impacts of North American Free Trade Agreement, 1980s-90, 1528–330
Morocco agricultural subsidies to producers and consumers, by selected commodity, 1970s-90, 1528–329
Natl income and product accounts, comprehensive accounts and components, benchmark revisions, 1929-88, 2708–5
Natl income and product accounts, comprehensive accounts and components, *Survey of Current Business*, monthly rpt, 2702–1.26
Rice market activities, prices, inspections, sales, trade, supply, and use, for US and selected foreign markets, weekly rpt, 1313–8
Timber and orchard damage from natural disaster, USDA restoration aid and program participation by practice and State, FY91, annual rpt, 1804–24
Water Bank Program agreements, payments to farmers, and wetlands acreage, by State, 1972-91, annual rpt, 1804–21
see also Agricultural credit
see also Agricultural production quotas and price supports

Agricultural surpluses
Agricultural Stabilization and Conservation Service programs, annual commodity fact sheet series, 1806–4
CCC commodities for sale, and prices, monthly press release, 1802–4
CCC financial condition and major commodity program operations, FY63-88, annual chartbook, 1824–2
CCC loan activities by commodity, and agency operating results, monthly press release, 1802–7
Cotton prices in 7 spot markets, futures prices at NYC exchange, farm prices, and CCC loan stocks, monthly rpt, 1309–1
Dairy products price support purchases, sales, donations, and inventories of CCC, monthly rpt, 1802–2
Grain stocks on and off farms, by crop, quarterly rpt, 1621–4
Grain support loan programs of USDA, activity and status by grain and State, monthly rpt, 1802–3
see also Agricultural production quotas and price supports
see also Agricultural stocks
see also Food assistance
see also Public Law 480

Agricultural Trade Development and Assistance Act
see Public Law 480

Agricultural transportation
see Agricultural marketing

Agricultural wages
Agricultural Outlook, production, prices, marketing, and trade, by commodity, forecast and current situation, monthly rpt with articles, 1502–4
Economic Indicators of the Farm Sector, balance sheets, and receipts by detailed commodity, by State, 1986-90, annual rpt, 1544–18
Economic Indicators of the Farm Sector, itemized production costs, receipts, and returns, by commodity and region, 1975-90, annual rpt, 1544–20
Hired farm workers and earnings, by selected characteristics, 1990, 1598–278
Income (household, family, and personal), by source, detailed characteristics, and region, 1991, annual Current Population Rpt, 2546–6.76
Income (personal) per capita and by source, and employment, by industry div, State, MSA, and county, 1969-90, annual CD-ROM, 2704–7
Irrigated farmland, farm characteristics, and water and fuel sources, by State and leading county, 1950s-88, 1588–122
Natl income and product accounts, comprehensive accounts and components, benchmark revisions, 1929-88, 2708–5
Natl income and product accounts, comprehensive accounts and components, *Survey of Current Business*, monthly rpt, 2702–1.29
Occupational Outlook Handbook, 1992-93, biennial rpt, 6744–1
Production itemized costs, by farm sales size and region, 1991, annual rpt, 1614–3
Production itemized costs, receipts, and returns, by crop and State, 1987-89, annual rpt, 1544–24
Rice production, practices, costs, and land tenure, by production area, 1988, 1568–309
Statistical Abstract of US, 1992 annual data compilation, 2324–1.23
Tobacco (flue-cured) farms and farm operators, by region and selected characteristics, 1970s-87, 1568–307
Wages, employment, hours, and perquisites, for farm labor by State, monthly rpt, 1631–1

Agriculture
Agricultural Statistics, 1991, annual rpt, 1004–1
Data coverage and availability of Census Bur rpts and data files, 1992 annual listing, 2304–2
Data on agriculture, collection, methodology, and use for major time series of USDA, series, 1506–1
Data on agriculture, historic maps, Natl Archives special collection, 1976 rpt, 9516–1.7
Data on agriculture, young readers pamphlet series, 2346–1
Statistical Abstract of US, 1992 annual data compilation, 2324–1.23
TVA agriculture and fertilizer rpts, 1970-90, annual listing, 9804–28
see also Agricultural accidents and safety
see also Agricultural credit
see also Agricultural education
see also Agricultural energy use
see also Agricultural exports and imports
see also Agricultural extension work
see also Agricultural finance
see also Agricultural forecasts
see also Agricultural insurance
see also Agricultural labor
see also Agricultural machinery and equipment
see also Agricultural marketing
see also Agricultural policy
see also Agricultural prices
see also Agricultural production
see also Agricultural production costs
see also Agricultural production quotas and price supports
see also Agricultural productivity
see also Agricultural sciences and research
see also Agricultural services
see also Agricultural stocks
see also Agricultural subsidies

see also Agricultural surpluses
see also Agricultural wages
see also Botany
see also Census of Agriculture
see also Drought
see also Farm income
see also Farm operators
see also Farms and farmland
see also Fertilizers
see also Food and food industry
see also Foreign agriculture
see also Forests and forestry
see also Horticulture
see also Irrigation
see also Pesticides
see also Pests and pest control
see also Rural areas
see also Soils and soil conservation
see also Wildlife and wildlife conservation
see also under By Industry in the "Index by Categories"

Agriculture Department
see Department of Agriculture

Ahearn, Mary C.
"Life Cycle and Expectations of Farmers", 1541–1.309

Ahern, Cathaleen A.
"Good Quality Care Increases Hospital Profits Under Prospective Payment", 4652–1.316

Ahmed, Shaghil
"Importance of the Tax System in Determining the Marginal Cost of Funds", 9387–8.278
"Marginal Cost of Funds with Nonseparable Public Spending", 9387–8.265

Ahmed, Ziaul Z.
"Productivity in the Nuts and Bolts Industry, 1958-90", 6722–1.343

Ahrenholz, Dean W.
"Overview of Mark-recovery Studies on Adult and Juvenile Atlantic Menhaden, *Brevoortia tyrannus*, and Gulf Menhaden, *B. patronus*", 2162–1.303
"Population Biology and Life History of the North American Menhadens, *Brevoortia* spp.", 2162–1.303

AID
see Agency for International Development

Aid to blind
Library of Congress activities, acquisitions, services, and financial statements, FY91, annual rpt, 26404–1
Medicaid and SSI recipients, by eligibility type, from 1970s, and by State, 1990, annual rpt, 4744–3.6; 4744–3.8
Medicaid coverage, funding, and costs, with reform recommendations, mid 1960s-92, 10048–83
Older blind persons by State, and State rehabilitation services, 1989, 21148–64
Outlying areas income maintenance beneficiaries and payments, by program and area, quarterly FY90, annual rpt, 4584–3.1; 4584–3.2
Outlying areas programs and provisions, FY89-90, annual rpt, 4584–8
VA health care services, needs, availability, structure, and funding, 1991 compilation of papers, 8608–9
Vending facilities run by blind on Federal and non-Federal property, finances and operations by agency and State, FY91, annual rpt, 4944–2
Vocational rehabilitation cases of State agencies, by disposition and State, FY91 and trends from FY21, annual rpt, 4944–5
Vocational rehabilitation programs of Fed Govt and States, activities and funding, FY91, annual rpt, 4944–1
see also Supplemental Security Income

Aid to disabled and handicapped persons
Benefits, beneficiaries, and spells of participation, by aid program and recipient characteristics, 1987-88, Current Population Rpt, 2546–20.25
Education funding by Federal agency, program, and recipient type, and instn spending, 1960s-91, annual rpt, 4824–8
Election polling places accessibility and services availability for aged and disabled, by State, 1990 natl elections, hearing, 21428–11
Energy aid for low income households, funding sources, costs, and participation, by State, FY90, annual rpt, 4584–1
Energy aid for low income households, program characteristics by State, FY91, annual rpt, 4584–2
Fed Govt financial and nonfinancial domestic aid, 1992 base edition, annual listing, 104–5
Fed Govt programs under Ways and Means Committee jurisdiction, finances, operations, and participant characteristics, FY70s-91, annual rpt, 21784–11
Food stamp recipient household size, composition, income, and income and deductions allowed, summer 1989, annual rpt, 1364–8
HHS financial aid, by program, recipient, State, and city, FY91, annual regional listings, 4004–3
Housing (low income) for disabled, HUD capital advances and rental aid by recipient, FY92, press release, 5006–3.98
Housing (public) for aged, placement of younger mentally disabled tenants, behavioral problems, and services, 1990 survey, GAO rpt, 26113–590
Library of Congress activities, acquisitions, services, and financial statements, FY91, annual rpt, 26404–1
Mail (free) for blind and handicapped, volume and costs, FY91, annual rpt, 9864–2
Mail (free) for blind and handicapped, volume and weight, quarterly rpt, 9862–1
Mail (free) revenue and subsidy for revenue forgone, FY91, and volume from FY87, annual rpt, 9864–1
Mail volume, revenues, and subsidies for revenue forgone, by class of mail, FY91, annual rpt, 9864–5
Medicaid and SSI recipients, by eligibility type, from 1970s, and by State, 1990, annual rpt, 4744–3.8
Medicaid coverage, funding, and costs, with reform recommendations, mid 1960s-92, 10048–83
Outlying areas income maintenance beneficiaries and payments, by program and area, quarterly FY90, annual rpt, 4584–3.1; 4584–3.2
Outlying areas programs and provisions, FY89-90, annual rpt, 4584–8
Railroad employee benefits program finances and beneficiaries, FY91, annual rpt, 9704–1
see also Aid to blind
see also Disability benefits and insurance
see also Old-Age, Survivors, Disability, and Health Insurance
see also Sheltered workshops
see also Special education
see also Supplemental Security Income
see also Vocational rehabilitation
see also Workers compensation

Aid to Families with Dependent Children
Beneficiaries of AFDC by county, payments, application processing and disposition, hearings, and fraud cases, by State, FY90, annual rpt, 4584–3
Beneficiaries of AFDC, demographic and financial characteristics by State, FY90, annual rpt, 4584–7
Benefits and beneficiaries, from 1936, and by State, 1989, annual rpt, 4744–3.9
Benefits, beneficiaries, and spells of participation, by aid program and recipient characteristics, 1987-88, Current Population Rpt, 2546–20.25
Budget of US, obligations and authority by function, agency, and program, with summaries and analyses, FY93, annual rpt, 104–2
Child care arrangements of younger working mothers, and costs, by selected characteristics, 1988, 6726–2.1
Expenditures, coverage, and benefits for social welfare programs, late 1930s-90, annual rpt, 4744–3.1
Expenditures of Fed Govt in States, by type, program, agency, and State, FY91, annual rpt, 2464–2
Finances and operations of programs under Ways and Means Committee jurisdiction, FY70s-91, annual rpt, 21784–11
Food stamp eligibility and payment errors, by type, recipient characteristics, and State, FY90, annual rpt, 1364–15
Food stamp recipient household size, composition, income, and income and deductions allowed, summer 1989, annual rpt, 1364–8
Income from transfer payments, natl income and product account benchmark revisions, 1929-88, 2708–5
Income from transfer payments, natl income and product accounts, *Survey of Current Business*, monthly rpt, 2702–1.25
Job Training Partnership Act education and worker training program participants, by selected characteristics, 1986-88, 15496–1.15
Medicaid coverage, eligibility, and payment provisions of States, as of March 1992, annual rpt, 4654–19
Medicaid coverage, funding, and costs, with reform recommendations, mid 1960s-92, 10048–83
Ohio poverty, hunger, and public welfare program operations and indicators of need, by county, 1991 hearing, 21968–58
Population economic well-being indicators, by selected characteristics and household income and income-to-poverty ratio, 1984, 2546–20.22
Single mothers family income, and impacts of child care, govt and child support payments, taxes, and marriage, with data by State, 1970s-91, 21788–212
State AFDC provisions, FY89-90, annual rpt, 4584–8

Statistical Abstract of US, 1992 annual data compilation, 2324–1.12
Unemployed Parent program of AFDC, caseloads and payments by State, and State admin of Job Opportunities and Basic Skills Training program, 1991 GAO rpt, 26131–96
Unemployment of AFDC applicants in recent months, characteristics of prior job and unemployment insurance eligibility, for Maryland, 1988-90, hearing, 21788–207
see also Work incentive programs

AIDS
see Acquired immune deficiency syndrome

Ainsworth, Robert G.
"JTPA Education-Coordination Set-Aside: States' Implementation of the Program", 15496–1.15

Air bases
see Military bases, posts, and reservations

Air cargo
Accidents and circumstances, for US operations of domestic and foreign airlines and general aviation, periodic rpt, 9612–1
Aircraft registered with FAA, by type and characteristics of aircraft, make, carrier, State, and county, 1991, annual rpt, 7504–3
Business statistics, detailed data for major industries and economic indicators, *Survey of Current Business*, monthly rpt, 2702–1.10
Collective bargaining agreements expiring during year, and workers covered, by firm, union, industry group, and State, 1992, annual rpt, 6784–9
Consumer complaints against air carriers, agents, and cargo handlers, monthly rpt, 7302–11
Energy use by fuel type, and miles traveled, by transport mode, projected 1990-2010 and trends from 1960s, 3008–124
Exports and imports between US and outlying areas, by detailed commodity and mode of transport, 1991, annual rpt, 2424–11
Exports and imports of US, by transport mode, country, and SITC 1- to 3-digit commodity, 1991, annual rpt, 2424–12
Exports of US, detailed commodities by country, monthly CD-ROM, 2422–13
Finances of airlines, by carrier, carrier group, and for total certificated system, quarterly rpt, 7302–7
Flower and foliage shipments from Florida by State and mode of transport, US imports by country, and prices, by variety, mid 1980s-91, annual rpt, 1311–24
Fruit and vegetable shipments, and arrivals by city, by mode of transport and State and country of origin, 1991, annual rpt series, 1311–4
Fruit and vegetable shipments by mode of transport, arrivals, and imports, by commodity and State and country of origin, weekly rpt, 1311–3
Fruit and vegetable wholesale prices in NYC by State, and shipments and arrivals by mode of transport, by commodity, weekly rpt, 1311–20
Fruit and vegetable wholesale prices in NYC-Newark, and arrivals by mode of transport, by commodity and State, 1990, annual rpt, 1311–21
Fruit shipments, production, and marketing, for Florida, with US trade and prices, by commodity, 1970s-91, annual rpt, 1311–23
Grape shipments from California and arrivals by city by mode of transport, prices, and production, by variety, 1970s-90, annual rpt, 1311–25
Hazardous cargo inspections at airports, compliance and enforcement actions, 1990, annual rpt, 7504–49
Hazardous material transport accidents, casualties, and damage, by mode of transport, with DOT control activities, 1990, annual rpt, 7304–4
Imports of US, detailed commodities by country, monthly CD-ROM, 2422–14
Mail (air) carried by US certificated carriers, by airport and carrier, 1991, annual rpt, 7504–35
Mail operating costs of USPS, itemized by class of mail, FY91, annual rpt, 9864–4
Mail revenue, costs, and volume, by class of mail, FY91, annual rpt, 9864–2
Military and personal property shipments, passenger traffic, and costs, by service branch and mode of transport, FY91, annual rpt, 3704–15
Price indexes (producer), by stage of processing and detailed commodity, monthly rpt, 6762–6
Price indexes (producer), by stage of processing and detailed commodity, monthly 1991, annual rpt, 6764–2
Price indexes for exports and imports of manufactured goods and services, quarterly press release, 6762–13
Shipments and exports by air freight, by industry, 1980s, working paper, 9375–13.78
Tax (excise) collections of IRS, by source, quarterly rpt, 8302–1
Traffic (passenger and cargo), and departures by aircraft type, by carrier and airport, 1991, annual rpt, 7504–35
Traffic (passenger and cargo), carrier enplanement shares, and FAA airport improvement program grants, by airport and State, 1990, annual rpt, 7504–48
Traffic, aircraft, carriers, airports, and FAA activities, detailed data, 1981-90, annual rpt, 7504–1
Traffic, aircraft, pilots, airports, and fuel use, forecast FY92-2003 and trends from FY82, annual rpt, 7504–6
Traffic and passenger and freight enplanements, by airport, 1960s-91 and projected to 2010, hub area rpt series, 7506–7
Traffic, capacity, and performance, by carrier and type of operation, monthly rpt, 7302–6
Traffic, capacity, and performance for medium regional airlines, by carrier, quarterly rpt, 7302–8
see also Military airlift

Air conditioning
Apartment completions by region and metro-nonmetro location, and absorption rate, by size and rent class, preliminary 1991, annual Current Housing Rpt, 2484–3
Apartment market absorption rates and characteristics for nonsubsidized furnished and unfurnished units, 1990, annual Current Housing Rpt, 2484–2
Commercial buildings energy use, costs, and conservation, by building characteristics, survey rpt series, 3166–8
Energy conservation technologies for housing and commercial buildings, use, costs, efficiency, and residential tax credits, 1970s-90 and projected to 2010, 26358–259
Energy supply, demand, and prices, by fuel type and end-use sector, projections and underlying assumptions, 1995-2010, annual rpt, 3164–90
Energy use, costs, and conservation, and household and housing characteristics, survey rpt series, 3166–7
Equipment shipments, trade, use, and firms, by product, 1991, annual Current Industrial Rpt, 2506–12.7
Exports and imports between US and outlying areas, by detailed commodity and mode of transport, 1991, annual rpt, 2424–11
Exports and imports of US, by country and detailed commodity, monthly rpt, 2422–12
Exports and imports of US, by Harmonized System 6-digit commodity and country, 1991, annual rpt, 2424–13
Exports and imports of US, by transport mode, country, and SITC 1- to 3-digit commodity, 1991, annual rpt, 2424–12
Exports of US, detailed Schedule B commodities with countries of destination, 1991, annual rpt, 2424–10
Home mortgages FHA-insured, financial, property, and borrower characteristics, by metro area, 1991, annual rpt, 5144–24
Home mortgages FHA-insured, financial, property, and borrower characteristics, by State, 1991, annual rpt, 5144–1; 5144–25
Home mortgages FHA-insured, financial, property, and borrower characteristics, 1991, annual rpt, 5144–17; 5144–23
Housing (low income) energy aid, coverage and impacts on energy use and costs, selected years FY79-89, 4588–2
Housing (low income) energy aid, funding sources, costs, and participation, by State, FY90, annual rpt, 4584–1
Housing (rental) units, total, with HUD assistance by program, and eligible for aid, by unit, household, and neighborhood characteristics, and location, 1989, biennial rpt, 5184–11
Housing alteration and repair spending, by property and job characteristics, and region, quarterly rpt, annual tables, 2382–7.2
Housing and households characteristics, MSA surveys, fact sheet series, 2485–11
Housing and households detailed characteristics, and unit and neighborhood quality, MSA surveys, series, 2485–6
Housing energy use, and availability of appliances by type, selected years 1978-90, annual rpt, 3164–74.1
Housing unit and household characteristics of recent movers, and reason for move, by tenure, 1989, 2486–1.12
Housing units completed, single and multifamily units by structural and financial characteristics, and location, 1987-91, annual rpt, 2384–1

Housing units completed, single and multifamily units by structural characteristics, monthly rpt, quarterly tables, 2382–2.2
Injuries from use of consumer products and related activities, by severity and victim age and sex, 1990, annual rpt, 9164–7
Injuries from use of consumer products, by severity, victim age, and detailed product, 1991, annual rpt, 9164–6
Manufacturing finances and operations, by SIC 2- to 4-digit industry, forecast 1992, annual rpt, 2044–28
Pacific territories population and housing detailed characteristics, by location, 1990 Census of Population and Housing, series, 2551–8
Population economic well-being indicators, by selected characteristics and household income and income-to-poverty ratio, 1984, 2546–20.22
Price indexes (producer), by stage of processing and detailed commodity, monthly rpt, 6762–6
Price indexes (producer), by stage of processing and detailed commodity, monthly 1991, annual rpt, 6764–2
R&D facilities of higher education instns, space and equipment adequacy, needs, and funding by source, by instn type and control, 1992, biennial rpt, 9624–25
Shipments and PPI for building materials, by type, quarterly rpt, 2042–1.5; 2042–1.6
Single parent families in own and others homes, by financial, housing, and other characteristics, 1989, 2486–1.14
Solar collector and photovoltaic cell shipments by end-use sector and State, and trade, 1990, annual rpt, 3164–62
TVA electric power purchases of municipal and cooperative distributors, and prices and use by distributor and consumer sector, monthly rpt, 9802–1

Air Force
Accidents during training activities, and deaths by cause, by service branch, FY88-91, GAO rpt, 26123–397
Black military and civilian DOD personnel, by sex, grade, and period of service, and lists of award recipients, officers, and service academy grads, 1770s-90, 3548–22
Budget of DOD, organization, personnel, weapons, and property, by service branch, State, and country, 1992 annual summary rpt, 3504–13
Criminal case processing in military courts, and prisoners by facility, by service branch, data compilation, 1992 annual rpt, 6064–6.5
Deaths by cause, age, race, and rank, and personnel captured and missing, by service branch, FY91, annual rpt, 3544–40
Health care facilities of DOD in US and abroad, beds, admissions, outpatient visits, and births, by service branch, quarterly rpt, 3542–15
Homosexual military personnel discharges by pay grade, tenure, race, sex, and occupation, and investigations, by service branch, 1980s-90, GAO rpt, 26123–392
Officers newly commissioned, share from service academies, and academy attrition, 1970s-91 and projected to FY97, GAO rpt, 26123–389
Officials (Federal) and Congress members use of military aircraft, and aircraft inventory characteristics, 1989-91, GAO rpt, 26123–384
Officials (Federal) use of military aircraft, trips of 11 officials by reason, with costs and reimbursements, 1989-91, GAO rpt, 26111–78
Persian Gulf War costs to US by category and service branch, and offsetting contributions by allied country, monthly rpt, 102–3
Persian Gulf War Operation Desert Storm deployment, by sex, race, rank, and service branch, 1990-91, GAO rpt, 26123–394
Personnel (civilian and military) of DOD, by service branch, major installation, and State, as of Sept 1991, annual rpt, 3544–7
Personnel active duty enlisted accessions by race, and goals, by sex and service branch, quarterly press release, 3542–7
Personnel, contracts, and payroll, by service branch and location, with top 5 contractors and maps, by State and country, FY91, annual rpt, 3544–29
Personnel needs, costs, and force readiness, by service branch, FY93, annual rpt, 3504–1
Personnel occupational distribution, by race, sex, and service branch, FY90, GAO rpt, 26123–381
Personnel reductions planned by service branch, and women and minorities affected by Army and Air Force plans, FY90-91, GAO rpt, 26123–373
Personnel reserve and active duty force mix and costs under alternative reduction cases, by service branch, 1990 and projected to 1997, 26306–6.172
Personnel strengths, for active duty, civilians, and dependents, by service branch and US and foreign location, quarterly rpt, 3542–20
Personnel strengths, for active duty, civilians, and reserves, by service branch, FY91 and trends, annual rpt, 3544–1
Personnel strengths, for active duty, civilians, and reserves, by service branch, quarterly rpt, 3542–14
Personnel strengths in US and abroad, by service branch, world area, and country, quarterly press release, 3542–9
Personnel strengths, summary by service branch, monthly press release, 3542–2
Reserve forces personnel and equipment strengths, and readiness, by reserve component, FY91, annual rpt, 3544–31
Reserve forces personnel strengths and characteristics, by component, quarterly rpt, 3542–4
Training and education programs of DOD, funding, staff, students, and facilities, by service branch, FY93, annual rpt, 3504–5
see also Department of Air Force

Air freight
see Air cargo

Air National Guard
see National Guard

Air navigation
see Aeronautical navigation

Air piracy
Airport security operations to prevent hijacking, screening results, enforcement actions, and hijacking attempts, 1990, annual rpt, 7504–49
Foreign and US hijackings, on-board explosions, and other crimes, 1986-90, annual rpt, 7504–31
Hijacking attempts on US and foreign aircraft, summary data 1978-88, annual rpt, 7304–1
Hijackings, other crimes against aviation, and airport screening results, data compilation, 1992 annual rpt, 6064–6.3
Pan Am Flight 103 bombing in 1988 and other terrorist incidents, role of Libya, 1991, annual rpt, 7004–13
Sentences for Federal offenses, guidelines by offense and circumstances, series, 17668–1
Terrorism (intl) incidents, casualties, and attacks on US targets, by attack type and country, 1991, annual rpt, 7004–22

Air pollution
Abatement activity of EPA, compliance, and monitoring stations operating status, annual rpt, discontinued, 9194–4
Abatement equipment shipments by industry, and new and backlog orders, by product, 1991, annual Current Industrial Rpt, 2506–12.5
Abatement spending by govts, business, and consumers, 1972-90, annual article, 2702–1.321
Abatement spending, capital and operating costs by SIC 2- to 4-digit industry and State, 1990, annual Current Industrial Rpt, 2506–3.6
Aircraft air pollution emissions compared to other sources, by pollutant, 1989, GAO rpt, 26113–562
Assistance (financial and nonfinancial) of Fed Govt, 1992 base edition, annual listing, 104–5
Cancer (lung) risk relation to environmental smoke exposure, for nonsmoking women, local area study, 1992 article, 4472–1.342
Carbon dioxide in atmosphere, DOE R&D programs and funding at natl labs, universities, and other instns, FY92, annual summary rpt, 3004–18.10
Carbon monoxide nonattainment area supply and demand of oxygenated gasoline, forecast winter 1992/93, article, 3162–24.301
Clean Air Act 1990 amendments economic impacts with background data for Midwest and US, 1992 article, 9375–1.304
Coal coke use and costs in steel industry, effects of Clean Air Act, 1985-91 and projected to 2003, 5606–5.10
Coal-fired power plants air pollutant reduction technology funding, and impacts on energy costs and emissions, 1950s-87 and projected to 2010, annual rpt, 3334–5; 3338–4
Coal-fired power plants air pollutant reduction technology funding, and project descriptions, 1991, annual rpt, 3334–4
Detroit metro area air pollutant levels, by pollutant and site, 1970s-90, 14648–28
Developing countries energy efficiency improvement issues and devs, with data by end use and country, 1980s-90, 26358–260

DOE contractor research lab and nuclear weapons facilities radiation and other pollutant releases, monitoring results, annual site rpt series, 3324–2
Electric power industrial producers capacity, generation, and sales by industry div and State, and emissions, by census div, 1989-90, article, 3162–35.301
Electric power plants (steam), renewal and replacement of aging facilities, costs and benefits for selected units, projected 1991-2000, article, 3162–35.303
Electric power plants air pollutant emissions, by type and region, alternative projections 1990-2010, annual rpt, 3164–96
Electric utilities privately owned, air pollution emissions and abatement equipment by fuel type and State, 1986-90, annual rpt, 3164–11.5
Electric utilities privately owned, pollution abatement outlays by type of pollutant and equipment, and firm, 1990, annual rpt, 3164–23
Emissions levels for 3 pollutants, and capacity of electric plants with abatement equipment, by type, 1985-90, annual rpt, 3164–74.5
Emissions levels for 6 pollutants, and measurements exceeding natl standards, by site, 1990-91, annual rpt, 9194–5
Emissions levels for 6 pollutants, by source and selected MSA, 1982-91, annual rpt, 9194–1
Energy natl strategy plans for conservation, R&D, security, and pollution reduction, technical rpt series, 3006–13
Energy supply, demand, and prices, by fuel type and end-use sector, projections and underlying assumptions, 1995-2010, annual rpt, 3164–90
Environmental Quality, status of problems, protection programs, research, and intl issues, 1991 annual rpt, 484–1
EPA pollution control grant program activities, monthly rpt, 9182–8
EPA R&D programs and funding, planned FY92, annual listing, 9184–17
Health condition and care indicators, 1950s-90 with health improvement and disease prevention goals for 1990, annual data compilation, 4144–11
Health effects of selected pollutants, concentrations in food and environment, sources, human intake, and regulation, series, 9186–8
Health effects of selected pollutants on animals by species and on humans, and environmental levels, series, 5506–14
Hungary child respiratory disease cases, by type, age, and air pollution levels, for Sopron, 1990, article, 4202–7.319
Industrial hazardous substances releases and reduction methods under EPA regulation, by chemical, source, industry, and location, 1989, annual rpt, 9234–6
Industrial hazardous substances releases and reduction methods under EPA regulation, with chemical stocks and use, facility directory, 1987-89, annual CD-ROM, 9234–7
Justice Dept enforcement of environmental laws, activities, FY83-92, annual press release, 6004–22
Kuwait oil fires set by Iraq, pollution levels, disease cases, and US remediation and monitoring spending, 1991 rpt, 9188–117
Kuwait oil fires set by Iraqi forces, air pollution levels by substance and site, as of Mar 1991, 9188–116
Kuwait oil fires set by Iraqi forces, air pollution levels, health effects, intl monitoring activities, and wells affected, 1991, GAO rpt, 26113–566
Minerals offshore lease sales environmental and economic impacts in coastal areas, final statement series, 5736–7
Mines (underground) diesel engine exhaust emissions measurement and control, 1992 conf, 5608–177
Ozone levels impacts on grain yields, by region, 1991 rpt, 14358–4
Recycling in manufacturing industries, fuel savings, and CO2 emissions reductions, 1988 and projected to 1995, hearing, 21368–140
Statistical Abstract of US, 1992 annual data compilation, 2324–1.6
see also Acid rain
see also Global climate change
see also Motor vehicle exhaust
see also Radiation
see also Radon

Air safety
see Aviation accidents and safety

Air traffic control
Airport capacity improvement projects and funding, traffic, and delays, by major airport, 1988-90 and forecast to 2000, annual rpt, 7504–43
Certificates for pilots and nonpilots held, by type of certificate, age, sex, region, and State, 1991, annual rpt, 7504–2
Drug testing and results for airline and aviation safety employees, by drug type and occupational group, 1991, semiannual rpt, 7502–17
Employment in ATC facilities, by selected characteristics of staff, FY90, annual rpt, 7504–41
Employment of DOT, by subagency, occupation, and selected personnel characteristics, FY91, annual rpt, 7304–18
FAA tower, instrument, flight center, and flight services operations, quarterly rpt, 7502–16
Flight service station workload of FAA, pilot briefs, contacts, and flight plans by facility, projected FY92-2002 and trends from FY83, annual rpt, 7504–39
Instrument flight rule aircraft handled, by user type, FAA traffic control center, and region, FY85-91 and projected to FY2005, annual rpt, 7504–15
Labor demand, turnover, and training completions, by detailed occupation, 1990 and projected to 2005, biennial rpt, 6744–3
Medical research and test results for aviation, technical rpt series, 7506–10
Occupational Outlook Handbook, 1992-93, biennial rpt, 6744–1
Operational errors, and other incidents, monthly rpt, 7502–15
Operations and finances of FAA, and staff by region, FY90-91, annual rpt, 7504–10
Operations and finances of FAA ATC and airway facilities and services, FY86-90, annual rpt, 7504–37
Operations of FAA ATC facilities, by service and aviation type, and facility, 1981-90, annual rpt, 7504–1.2
Operations of FAA ATC facilities, improvement under Aviation System Capital Investment Plan, 1981-91 and projected to 2006, annual rpt, 7504–12
Traffic, aircraft, pilots, airports, and fuel use, forecast FY92-2003 and trends from FY82, annual rpt, 7504–6
Traffic and other aviation activity forecasts of FAA, 1992 annual conf, 7504–28
Traffic and passenger and freight enplanements, by airport, 1960s-91 and projected to 2010, hub area rpt series, 7506–7
Traffic and passenger enplanements, by airport, region, and State, projected FY92-2005 and trends from FY83, annual rpt, 7504–7
Traffic levels at FAA ATC facilities, by airport and State, FY91, annual rpt, 7504–27
User fees financing of transportation infrastructure, with data on hwys, airports, and waterways, 1985-91, 26306–6.170
see also Aviation accidents and safety

Air transportation
see Air cargo
see Air travel
see Airlines
see Airports and airways
see Military aviation

Air travel
Amtrak finances, executive office travel expenses and staff years, and membership dues by assn, FY88-92, GAO rpt, 26113–573
Atlantic Ocean intl air traffic and passengers, by aviation type and route, alternative forecasts 1992-2010 and trends from 1982, annual rpt, 7504–44
Consumer complaints against air carriers, agents, and cargo handlers, monthly rpt, 7302–11
Consumer spending, natl income and product account benchmark revisions, 1929-88, 2708–5
Consumer spending, natl income and product accounts, comprehensive accounts and components, *Survey of Current Business*, monthly rpt, 2702–1.25
Diving (underwater) accidents, illnesses, and deaths, by circumstances, diver characteristics, and location, 1970-90, annual rpt, 2144–29
Energy use by mode of transport, fuel supply, and demographic and economic factors of vehicle use, 1970s-90, annual rpt, 3304–5
Fed Govt financial and nonfinancial domestic aid, 1992 base edition, annual listing, 104–5
Fed Govt officials and Congress members use of military aircraft, and aircraft inventory characteristics, 1989-91, GAO rpt, 26123–384
Fed Govt officials use of military aircraft, trips of 11 officials by reason, with costs and reimbursements, 1989-91, GAO rpt, 26111–78
Foreign travel to and from US on US and foreign flag air carriers, by country, world area, and US port, monthly rpt, 7302–2
Foreign travel to US and Canada, market analyses with detailed trip and traveler characteristics, country rpt series, 2906–2

Foreign travel to US, by characteristics of visit and traveler, country, port city, and State of destination, monthly rpt, 2902–1
Foreign travel to US, by characteristics of visit and traveler, world area of origin, and US destination, 1991 survey, annual rpt, 2904–12
Hawaii humpback whale habitat impacts of human activities, with data on shipping, whale watching, coastal construction, and aircraft, 1980s-90, 14738–14
Marshals Service activities, FY91, annual rpt, 6294–1
Multinatl firms US affiliates finances and operations, by industry, country of parent firm, and State, 1987, 2708–48
Pacific Ocean intl air traffic and passengers, by route, alternative forecasts 1992-2010 and trends from 1980, annual rpt, 7504–51
Passenger cost and travel time, for buses, air travel, and Amtrak, by selected route, 1980s-1992, GAO rpt, 26113–583
Passenger enplanements and traffic, by airport, region, and State, projected FY92-2005 and trends from FY83, annual rpt, 7504–7
Passenger traffic, aircraft, pilots, airports, and fuel use, forecast FY92-2003 and trends from FY82, annual rpt, 7504–6
Passenger traffic, capacity, and performance, by carrier and type of operation, monthly rpt, 7302–6
Passenger traffic, capacity, and performance for medium regional airlines, by carrier, quarterly rpt, 7302–8
Price indexes for exports and imports of manufactured goods and services, quarterly press release, 6762–13
Soviet Union and US economic and sociodemographic indicators, selected years 1970-90, handbook, 2328–80
Tax (excise) collections of IRS, by source, quarterly rpt, 8302–1; 8302–2.1
Traffic (passenger and cargo), and departures by aircraft type, by carrier and airport, 1991, annual rpt, 7504–35
Traffic (passenger, cargo, and mail), and airline operations, by type of service, air carrier, State, and country, 1981-90, annual rpt, 7504–1.4; 7504–1.6
Traffic and passenger and freight enplanements, by airport, 1960s-91 and projected to 2010, hub area rpt series, 7506–7
see also Aeronautical navigation
see also Aircraft
see also Airlines
see also Airports and airways
see also Aviation accidents and safety
see also Civil aviation
see also General aviation
see also Military aviation
see also Pilots

Airbus Industrie
EC govt subsidies, by industry sector and for Airbus Industrie, by country, 1980s-91, hearing, 21708–132

Aircraft
Business statistics, detailed data for major industries and economic indicators, *Survey of Current Business*, monthly rpt, 2702–1.22
Business statistics, detailed data for major industries and economic indicators, 1960-91, *Survey of Current Business* biennial supplement, 2704–1
Exports and imports between US and outlying areas, by detailed commodity and mode of transport, 1991, annual rpt, 2424–11
Exports and imports of US, by country and detailed commodity, monthly rpt, 2422–12
Exports and imports of US, by Harmonized System 6-digit commodity and country, 1991, annual rpt, 2424–13
Exports and imports of US, by transport mode, country, and SITC 1- to 3-digit commodity, 1991, annual rpt, 2424–12
Exports, imports, tariffs, and industry operating data for aircraft, spacecraft, and related equipment, 1991 rpt, 9885–9.1
Exports of US, detailed Schedule B commodities with countries of destination, 1991, annual rpt, 2424–10
Flight and engine hours, and shutdown rates, by aircraft and engine model, and air carrier, monthly rpt, 7502–13
Foreign countries economic, social, political, and geographic summary data, by country, 1992, annual factbook, 9114–2
Freight (waterborne domestic and foreign) by commodity, traffic, and passengers, by port and waterway, 1989, annual rpt, 3754–3
Input-output structure of US economy, detailed interindustry transactions for 541 industries, and components of final demand, 1982 benchmark data, 2708–17
Manufacturing annual survey, 1990: value of shipments, by SIC 4- to 5-digit product class, 2506–14.1
Manufacturing census, 1987: shipments of manufacturers products, by customer class and SIC 2- and 4-digit industry, subject rpt, 2497–4
OECD trade, total and for 4 major countries, and US trade by country, by commodity, 1980-90, world area rpt series, 9116–1
Police employment, spending, and operations, for State, city, county, and special district agencies, 1990, annual rpt, 6064–39
Pollution (air) emissions of aircraft compared to other sources, by pollutant, 1989, GAO rpt, 26113–562
Price indexes (producer), by stage of processing and detailed commodity, monthly rpt, 6762–6
Price indexes (producer), by stage of processing and detailed commodity, monthly 1991, annual rpt, 6764–2
Registration of aircraft with FAA, by type and characteristics of aircraft, make, carrier, State, and county, 1991, annual rpt, 7504–3
Rice production, practices, costs, and land tenure, by production area, 1988, 1568–309
Shipments of general aviation aircraft, and commercial carriers orders and deliveries, by aircraft type, quarterly rpt, 7502–16
Shipments, trade, use, and firms, by type of craft and engine, monthly Current Industrial Rpt, 2506–12.24
Statistical Abstract of US, 1992 annual data compilation, 2324–1.22
Tax (luxury) revenue, and related IRS administrative costs, FY91 and projected to FY95, GAO rpt, 26119–385
Traffic (passenger and cargo), and departures by aircraft type, by carrier and airport, 1991, annual rpt, 7504–35
Traffic, aircraft, carriers, airports, and FAA activities, detailed data, 1981-90, annual rpt, 7504–1
Traffic, aircraft, pilots, airports, and fuel use, forecast FY92-2003 and trends from FY82, annual rpt, 7504–6
Traffic and other aviation activity forecasts of FAA, 1992 annual conf, 7504–28
see also Aerial surveys
see also Aeronautical navigation
see also Aerospace industry
see also Aircraft noise
see also Aviation accidents and safety
see also Aviation fuels
see also Helicopters
see also Military aircraft

Aircraft accidents
see Aviation accidents and safety

Aircraft noise
Whales (bowhead and white) migration through Beaufort Sea, behavior impacts of oil drilling and aircraft noise, spring 1990, 5738–27

Airlines
Aircraft registered with FAA, by type and characteristics of aircraft, make, carrier, State, and county, 1991, annual rpt, 7504–3
Business statistics, detailed data for major industries and economic indicators, *Survey of Current Business*, monthly rpt, 2702–1.10
Business statistics, detailed data for major industries and economic indicators, 1960-91, *Survey of Current Business* biennial supplement, 2704–1
Capital expenditures for plant and equipment, by major industry group, quarterly rpt, 2502–2
Collective bargaining agreements expiring during year, and workers covered, by firm, union, industry group, and State, 1992, annual rpt, 6784–9
Consumer complaints by reason, passengers denied boarding, and late flights, by reporting carrier and airport, monthly rpt, 7302–11
County Business Patterns, 1989: employment, establishments, and payroll, by SIC 2- to 4-digit industry and county, annual State rpt series, 2326–8
County Business Patterns, 1990: employment, establishments, and payroll, by SIC 2- to 4-digit industry and county, annual State rpt series, 2326–6
CPI by component for US city average, and by selected metro area, region, and population size, monthly rpt, 6762–2
Employment, earnings, and hours, by SIC 1- to 4-digit industry, monthly 1989-Feb 1992, annual rpt, 6744–4
Employment of minorities and women, by occupation, SIC 1- to 3-digit industry, State, and MSA, 1991, annual rpt, 9244–1
Finances and operations, by SIC 2- to 4-digit industry, forecast 1992, annual rpt, 2044–28
Finances and operations of airlines, summary data, quarterly rpt, 7502–16
Finances of airlines, by carrier, carrier group, and for total certificated system, quarterly rpt, 7302–7

Flight and engine hours, and shutdown rates, by aircraft and engine model, and air carrier, monthly rpt, 7502–13
Hijackings, on-board explosions, and other crime, US and foreign incidents, 1986-90, annual rpt, 7504–31
Input-output structure of US economy, detailed interindustry transactions for 541 industries, and components of final demand, 1982 benchmark data, 2708–17
Labor disputes of airlines, Natl Mediation Board activities and caseloads, with data by carrier and union, FY87-88, annual rpt, 9604–1
Labor productivity, indexes of output, hours, and employment by SIC 2- to 4-digit industry, 1967-90, annual rpt, 6824–1.4
Military and personal property shipments, passenger traffic, and costs, by service branch and mode of transport, FY91, annual rpt, 3704–15
Occupational Outlook Handbook, 1992-93, biennial rpt, 6744–1
Passenger miles and fuel use, projected 1990-2010, 3008–124
Price indexes (producer), by stage of processing and detailed commodity, monthly rpt, 6762–6
Price indexes (producer), by stage of processing and detailed commodity, monthly 1991, annual rpt, 6764–2
Statistical Abstract of US, 1992 annual data compilation, 2324–1.22
Tax (income) returns of corporations, income and tax items by asset size and detailed industry, 1989, annual rpt, 8304–4; 8304–21
Tax (income) returns of sole proprietorships, income statement items, by industry group, 1990, annual article, 8302–2.317; 8302–2.320
Traffic (passenger and cargo), and departures by aircraft type, by carrier and airport, 1991, annual rpt, 7504–35
Traffic (passenger and cargo), carrier enplanement shares, and FAA airport improvement program grants, by airport and State, 1990, annual rpt, 7504–48
Traffic, aircraft, carriers, airports, and FAA activities, detailed data, 1981-90, annual rpt, 7504–1
Traffic, aircraft, pilots, airports, and fuel use, forecast FY92-2003 and trends from FY82, annual rpt, 7504–6
Traffic and other aviation activity forecasts of FAA, 1992 annual conf, 7504–28
Traffic and passenger and freight enplanements, by airport, 1960s-91 and projected to 2010, hub area rpt series, 7506–7
Traffic and passenger enplanements, by airport, region, and State, projected FY92-2005 and trends from FY83, annual rpt, 7504–7
Traffic, capacity, and performance, by carrier and type of operation, monthly rpt, 7302–6
Traffic, capacity, and performance for medium regional airlines, by carrier, quarterly rpt, 7302–8
Traffic levels at FAA air traffic control facilities, by airport and State, FY91, annual rpt, 7504–27
see also Aviation accidents and safety

Airports and airways
Alaska airport dev plans, annual rpt, discontinued, 7504–36
Atlantic Ocean intl air traffic and passengers, by aviation type and route, alternative forecasts 1992-2010 and trends from 1982, annual rpt, 7504–44
Budget of US, obligations and authority by function, agency, and program, with summaries and analyses, FY93, annual rpt, 104–2
Capacity improvement projects and funding, traffic, and delays, by major airport, 1988-90 and forecast to 2000, annual rpt, 7504–43
Crimes against civil aviation, and circumstances, US and worldwide, 1986-90, annual rpt, 7504–31
DOT planning and safety grants, by program, State, and for 40 SMSAs, FY89, annual rpt, 7304–7
Employment in airports, air cargo shipments by industry, and convention attendance, for Chicago and other locations, mid 1970s-90, working paper, 9375–13.78
FAA activities and finances, and staff by region, FY90-91, annual rpt, 7504–10
FAA airport improvement program activities and grants, by State and airport, FY91, annual rpt, 7504–38
FAA airport planning and dev project grants, by airport and location, quarterly press release, 7502–14
Fed Govt Airport and Airway Trust Fund financial condition, monthly rpt, 8102–9.5
Fed Govt spending in States, by type, program, agency, and State, FY91, annual rpt, 2464–2
Foreign countries economic, social, political, and geographic summary data, by country, 1992, annual factbook, 9114–2
Govt direct spending and employment, by function and level of govt, selected years 1962-87, 10048–53
Govt employment and payroll, by function, level of govt, and jurisdiction, annual rpt series, 2466–1
Govt finances, by level of govt, State, and for large cities and counties, annual rpt series, 2466–2
Hub airports air carrier operations, by airport, quarterly rpt, 7502–16
Pacific Ocean intl air traffic and passengers, by route, alternative forecasts 1992-2010 and trends from 1980, annual rpt, 7504–51
Passenger complaints, boarding denials, and late flights, by reporting carrier and airport, monthly rpt, 7302–11
Passenger travel to and from US on US and foreign flag air carriers, by country, world area, and US port, monthly rpt, 7302–2
Security operations of airports to prevent hijacking, screening results, enforcement actions, and hijacking attempts, 1990, annual rpt, 7504–49
Statistical Abstract of US, 1992 annual data compilation, 2324–1.22
Traffic (passenger and cargo), and departures by aircraft type, by carrier and airport, 1991, annual rpt, 7504–35
Traffic (passenger and cargo), carrier enplanement shares, and FAA airport improvement program grants, by airport and State, 1990, annual rpt, 7504–48
Traffic, aircraft, carriers, airports, and FAA activities, detailed data, 1981-90, annual rpt, 7504–1
Traffic, aircraft, pilots, airports, and fuel use, forecast FY92-2003 and trends from FY82, annual rpt, 7504–6
Traffic and other aviation activity forecasts of FAA, 1992 annual conf, 7504–28
Traffic and passenger and freight enplanements, by airport, 1960s-91 and projected to 2010, hub area rpt series, 7506–7
Traffic and passenger enplanements, by airport, region, and State, projected FY92-2005 and trends from FY83, annual rpt, 7504–7
Traffic levels at FAA air traffic control facilities, by airport and State, FY91, annual rpt, 7504–27
User fees financing of transportation infrastructure, with data on hwys, airports, and waterways, 1985-91, 26306–6.170
see also Air traffic control
see also Aircraft noise
see also Aviation accidents and safety

Aizcorbe, Ana M.
"Procyclical Labor Productivity, Increasing Returns to Labor, and Labor Hoarding in U.S. Auto Assembly Plant Employment", 6886–6.89

Ajman
see United Arab Emirates

Akhtar, M. A.
"Supply-Side Consequences of U.S. Fiscal Policy in the 1980s", 9385–1.304; 9385–8.125

Akron, Ohio
CPI by component for US city average, and by region, population size, and for 15 metro areas, monthly rpt, 6762–1
CPI by component for US city average, and by selected metro area, region, and population size, monthly rpt, 6762–2
see also under By City and By SMSA or MSA in the "Index by Categories"

Alabama
Appalachian Regional Commission funding, by project and State, planned FY92, annual rpt, 9084–3
Banks (insured commercial and savings) deposits by instn, State, MSA, and county, as of June 1991, annual regional rpt, 9295–3.4
Coal production and mines by county, prices, productivity, miners, and reserves, by mining method and State, 1990-91, annual rpt, 3164–25
County Business Patterns, 1990: employment, establishments, and payroll, by SIC 2- to 4-digit industry and county, annual State rpt, 2326–6.2
Deaths and rates, by detailed location, cause, and demographic characteristics, 1989, US Vital Statistics annual rpt, 4144–3.1
Economic indicators by State and MSA, Fed Reserve 6th District, quarterly rpt, 9371–14
Employment and housing indicators by State, FHLB 4th District, quarterly rpt, 9302–36
Employment by industry div, earnings, and hours, for 8 southeastern States, quarterly press release, 6942–7

Employment, earnings, and hours, by selected SIC 1- to 4-digit industry, State, and for 275 MSAs, 1987-92, 6748–81
Estuary environmental and fishery conditions, research results and methodology, 1992 rpt, 2176–7.28
Fed Govt spending in States and local areas, by type, State, county, and city, FY91, annual rpt, 2464–3
Fed Govt spending in States, by type, program, agency, and State, FY91, annual rpt, 2464–2
Fish (catfish) raised on farms, inventory, stocks, and production, by major producer State, quarterly rpt, 1631–18
HHS financial aid, by program, recipient, State, and city, FY91, annual regional listing, 4004–3.4
Hospital deaths of Medicare patients, actual and expected rates by diagnosis, and hospital characteristics, by instn, FY90, annual State rpt, 4654–14.1
Hospitals in rural areas, Medicare admission rates and charges, by instn, patient, and care characteristics, mid 1980s, 17206–2.33
Housing census, 1990: summary unit characteristics, by householder race and age, county, place, and urban-rural location, State rpt, 2471–1.2
Medicare payment of physicians, reforms impacts on services, and monitoring methods, 1992 annual rpt, 4004–34
Military prime contract awards, by contractor, service branch, State, and city, FY91, annual rpt, 3544–22
Mineral Industry Surveys, State reviews of production, 1991, preliminary annual rpt, 5614–6
Minerals Yearbook, Vol 2, 1990: State review of production and sales by commodity, and business activity, annual rpt, 5604–22.2
Multinatl firms US affiliates finances and operations, by industry, country of parent firm, and State, 1987, 2708–48
Physicians, by specialty, age, sex, and location of training and practice, 1990, State rpt, 4116–6.1
Population and housing census, 1990: detailed geographic coverage, State CD-ROM, 2551–9.6
Population and housing census, 1990: summary characteristics, by county, subdiv, and place, State rpt, 2551–7.2
Population census, 1990: population characteristics and living arrangements, by county, place, and urban-rural location, State rpt, 2531–1.2
Statistical Abstract of US, 1992 annual data compilation, 2324–1
Textile mill employment, earnings, and hours, for 8 Southeastern States, quarterly press release, 6942–1
Timber in Alabama, acreage and volume by species, forest type, ownership, and county, 1990, series, 1206–30
Timber in Alabama, pine acreage converted from nonforest use, reforested, and harvested, 1950s-90, 1208–409
Water supply and quality in streams and lakes, and groundwater levels in wells, by drainage basin, 1991, annual State rpt, 5666–12.1
see also Birmingham, Ala.
see also Dothan, Ala.
see also Huntsville, Ala.
see also Mobile, Ala.
see also Montgomery, Ala.
see also under By State in the "Index by Categories"

Alameda County, Calif.
Housing and households characteristics, unit and neighborhood quality, and journey to work by MSA location, for 11 MSAs, 1985 survey, supplement, 2485–8
Housing and households detailed characteristics, and unit and neighborhood quality, by location, 1989 survey, MSA rpt, 2485–6.8

Alami, Tarik
"Would Monetary Policy Be Effective if the OASDI Trust Funds Held Most Treasury Debt?", 4746–26.19

Alaska
Agricultural Statistics, 1991, annual rpt, 1004–1
Airport dev plans for Alaska, annual rpt, discontinued, 7504–36
Arctic Natl Wildlife Refuge oil reserves and production, alternative forecasts 1985-2015, 3166–6.64
Banks (insured commercial and savings) deposits by instn, State, MSA, and county, as of June 1991, annual regional rpt, 9295–3.6
Coal production and mines by county, prices, productivity, miners, and reserves, by mining method and State, 1990-91, annual rpt, 3164–25
Deaths and rates, by detailed location, cause, and demographic characteristics, 1989, US Vital Statistics annual rpt, 4144–3.1
Employment, earnings, and hours, by selected SIC 1- to 4-digit industry, State, and for 275 MSAs, 1987-92, 6748–81
Environmental conditions and oil dev impacts for Alaska OCS, compilation of papers, series, 2176–1
Fed Govt spending in States and local areas, by type, State, county, and city, FY91, annual rpt, 2464–3
Fed Govt spending in States, by type, program, agency, and State, FY91, annual rpt, 2464–2
Fish and shellfish resources and catch, marine mammal and sea turtle population, and mgmt, by species and region, 1988-90, annual rpt, 2164–22
Freight (waterborne domestic and foreign) by commodity, traffic, and passengers, by port and waterway, 1989, annual rpt, 3754–3.4
HHS financial aid, by program, recipient, State, and city, FY91, annual regional listing, 4004–3.10
Hospital deaths of Medicare patients, actual and expected rates by diagnosis, and hospital characteristics, by instn, FY90 annual State rpt, 4654–14.2
Housing census, 1990: inventory, occupancy, and costs, State fact sheet, 2326–21.3
Housing census, 1990: summary unit characteristics, by householder race and age, county, place, and urban-rural location, State rpt, 2471–1.3
Ice conditions of Bering Sea and Alaska north coast, monthly rpt, 2182–5
Marine mammals protection activities and funding, populations, and harvests, by species, 1990, annual rpt, 5504–12
Marine mammals tissue pollutant concentrations, by species and pollutant type, for Alaska, 1987-91, 2218–87
Military and DOD civilian personnel and dependents, by service branch and US and foreign location, quarterly rpt, 3542–20
Military prime contract awards, by contractor, service branch, State, and city, FY91, annual rpt, 3544–22
Mineral Industry Surveys, State reviews of production, 1991, preliminary annual rpt, 5614–6
Minerals resources of Alaska, and geologic characteristics, compilation of papers, 1990, annual rpt, 5664–15
Minerals resources of Alaska, production, oil and gas leases, reserves, and exploratory wells, with maps and bibl, 1990, annual rpt, 5664–11
Minerals Yearbook, Vol 2, 1990: State review of production and sales by commodity, and business activity, annual rpt, 5604–22.3
Multinatl firms US affiliates finances and operations, by industry, country of parent firm, and State, 1987, 2708–48
Occupational injury deaths in Alaska, by cause, occupation, and industry, early 1980s, article, 4042–3.307
Oil and gas OCS reserves of Fed Govt, leasing and exploration activity, production, revenue, and costs, by ocean area, FY91, annual rpt, 5734–4
Oil and lease condensate production on Alaska North Slope and other US areas, 1949-91, annual rpt, 3164–74.2
Oil crude, gas liquids, and refined products supply, demand, and movement, by PAD district and State, 1991, annual rpt, 3164–2
Oil, gas, and coal reserve acreage in Alaska, by ownership, 1991 rpt, 5608–174
Physicians, by specialty, age, sex, and location of training and practice, 1990, State rpt, 4116–6.2
Pollution (air) contributing to global warming, emissions by monitoring site and country, and temperature change by world area and US region, 1860s-1990, annual rpt, 3004–33
Population and housing census, 1990: detailed geographic coverage, State CD-ROM, 2551–9.9
Population and housing census, 1990: population and housing characteristics, detailed geographic coverage, State CD-ROM, 2551–10.2
Population and housing census, 1990: summary characteristics, by county, subdiv, and place, State rpt, 2551–7.3
Population census, 1990: population characteristics and living arrangements, by county, place, and urban-rural location, State rpt, 2531–1.3
Radionuclide concentrations in air, water, humans, animals, and milk near Nevada and other nuclear test sites, 1990, annual rpt, 9194–17
Rural areas in Alaska, population characteristics and energy resources dev effects, series, 5736–5

Shipborne commerce (domestic) of US, freight by major commodity group, vessel type, and port, 1987-89, annual rpt, 7704–7
Ships wrecked off Alaska, characteristics, deaths, cargo, and whale catch, by vessel and location, 1763-1937, 5738–34
Statistical Abstract of US, 1992 annual data compilation, 2324–1
Telecommunications domestic and intl rates, by type of service and area served, 1990, annual rpt, 9284–6.6
Tide height and time daily at coastal points, forecast 1993, annual rpt, 2174–2.1
Timber in Alaska, acreage and resources by species, ownership class, and inventory unit, series, 1206–9
Timber in northwestern US and British Columbia, production, prices, trade, and employment, quarterly rpt, 1202–3
Water supply and quality in streams and lakes, and groundwater levels in wells, by drainage basin, 1990, annual State rpt, 5666–10.2
Water supply, and snow survey results, monthly State rpt, 1266–2.1
Water supply, and snow survey results, 1991, annual State rpt, 1264–14.5
Wetlands environmental conditions, for Alaska Copper River Delta, 1987, 1208–401
Whales population and behavior in Chukchi and Beaufort Seas, by endangered species, 1982-91, 5738–32
Whales population and behavior in Chukchi and Beaufort Seas, by endangered species, 1990, 5738–36
see also Alaska Natives
see also Aleutian Islands
see also Anchorage, Alaska
see also Cook Inlet, Alaska
see also Gulf of Alaska
see also Nikishka, Alaska
see also Prince William Sound, Alaska
see also Seldovia, Alaska
see also Trans-Alaska Pipeline System
see also Valdez, Alaska
see also under By State in the "Index by Categories"

Alaska Natives
AFDC Job Opportunities and Basic Skills Training programs operated by Indian and Alaska Native organizations, funding and persons eligible, FY91, GAO rpt, 26121–460
Census of Population and Housing, 1990: population and housing characteristics, detailed geographic coverage, State CD-ROM series, 2551–10
Census of Population and Housing, 1990: summary characteristics, by county, subdiv, and place, State rpt series, 2551–7
Census of Population, 1990: population characteristics and living arrangements, by county, place, and urban-rural location, State rpt series, 2531–1
Census of Population, 1990: population characteristics and living arrangements, for Native American, urban, and metro areas, series, 2531–2
Education data compilation, 1992 annual rpt, 4824–2
Education funding of Fed Govt, with enrollment, program grants, and fellowships by State, for Indians, 1980s-FY91, annual rpt, 14874–1
Employment of minorities and women, by occupation, SIC 1- to 3-digit industry, State, and MSA, 1991, annual rpt, 9244–1
Health condition and other characteristics of Indians, and Indian Health Service facilities and use, by IHS region, 1980s-90, annual chartbook, 4084–7
Health condition and other characteristics of Indians, and Indian Health Service facilities, funding, and operations, 1950s-91, annual chartbook, 4084–1
Hospitalization in Indian Health Service, tribal, and contract facilities, by diagnosis, age, sex, and IHS service area, FY91, annual rpt, 4084–5
Housing census, 1990: summary unit characteristics, by householder race and age, county, place, and urban-rural location, State rpt series, 2471–1
Libraries (public) services for Indians and Hawaii Natives, project listing and funding by tribe and State, FY90, annual rpt, 4874–5
Oil, gas, and coal reserve acreage in Alaska, by ownership, 1991 rpt, 5608–174
Polar bear harvest by Alaska Natives, by village, 1989/90, annual rpt, 5504–12
Rural areas in Alaska, population characteristics and energy resources dev effects, series, 5736–5
Wastewater treatment and collection facility construction funding needs and Fed Govt grants, by State, 1990 and projected to 2010, biennial rpt, 9204–7
Whales (bowhead) catch and quota for Eskimos, and other marine mammals harvest, 1970s-91, annual rpt, 14734–1

Alaska Power Administration
Finances and operations of Federal power admins and electric utilities, 1990, annual rpt, 3164–24.2

Alban, David H.
"Aspen Ecosystem Properties in the Upper Great Lakes", 1208–418

Albania
Agricultural trade of US, by detailed commodity and country, 1991, annual rpt, 1524–8
Agricultural trade of US, by detailed commodity and country, 1991, semiannual rpt, 1522–4
Agricultural trade of US with Eastern Europe, by commodity group and country, 1988-91, 1928–11
Economic and military aid and loans from US and intl agencies, by program and country, FY46-91, annual rpt, 9914–5
Economic and social conditions of developing countries from 1960s, and Intl Dev Cooperation Agency and AID activities and funding, FY91-93, annual rpt, 9904–4
Economic, social, political, and geographic summary data, by country, 1992, annual factbook, 9114–2
Export licensing, monitoring, and enforcement activities, FY91, annual rpt, 2024–1
Exports and imports of US, by commodity and country, 1980-90, world area rpt, 9116–1.1
Exports and imports of US, by transport mode, country, and SITC 1- to 3-digit commodity, 1991, annual rpt, 2424–12
Exports and imports of US with Communist and transitional economy countries, by detailed commodity and country, quarterly rpt with articles, 9882–2
Exports and imports of US with Eastern Europe, by commodity and country, 1987-91 and outlook for 1992, 2048–158
Exports of US, detailed Schedule B commodities with countries of destination, 1991, annual rpt, 2424–10
Human rights conditions in 170 countries, and US economic and military aid, 1991, annual rpt, 21384–3
Military aid of US, arms sales, and training programs costs and budget requests, by program, world region, and country, FY91-93, annual rpt, 7144–13
Military spending, arms trade, and force strengths, with govt spending and population, by country, 1979-89, annual rpt, 9824–1
Population size, growth rates, and components of change, by country, projected 1990-2020 and trends from 1950, biennial rpt, 2324–9
Refugee migration, and intl aid programs, by world area and country of origin and asylum, 1991, annual rpt, 7004–15
UN voting record and share of votes in agreement with US, by issue, country, and world area, 1991, annual rpt, 7004–18

Albany, N.Y.
Wages by occupation, for office and plant workers, 1991 survey, periodic MSA rpt, 6785–3.1
see also under By City and By SMSA or MSA in the "Index by Categories"

Albright, John L.
"U.S. Petroleum Trade, 1991", 3162–6.303

Albuquerque, N.Mex.
Wages by occupation, and benefits for office and plant workers, 1992 survey, periodic MSA rpt, 6785–3.4
see also under By City and By SMSA or MSA in the "Index by Categories"

Alcohol abuse and treatment
Abuse of alcohol, and related injury and illness, series, 4486–1
Abuse of drugs and alcohol, by selected characteristics, 1991 survey, annual rpt series, 4494–5
Assistance (financial and nonfinancial) of Fed Govt, 1992 base edition, annual listing, 104–5
Costs (direct and indirect) of alcohol abuse, 1985, article, 4482–1.311
Crime, criminal justice admin and enforcement, and public opinion, data compilation, 1992 annual rpt, 6064–6
Data on health condition and care, indicators, 1988 natl survey, CD-ROM, 4147–10.184
DC metro area drug, alcohol, and tobacco use, user characteristics, and consequences, series, 4496–12
Deaths and rates, by cause, age, sex, marital status, race, and State, 1989, US Vital Statistics advance annual rpt, 4146–5.124
Deaths related to alcohol, by cause, State, and county, annual averages 1979-80 and 1983-85, 4488–10.4
Drug abuse in combination with alcohol, indicators for selected metro areas, research results, data collection, and policy issues, 1992 semiannual conf, 4492–5

Education data compilation, 1992 annual rpt, 4824–2
Health condition and care indicators, 1950s-90 with health improvement and disease prevention goals for 1990, annual data compilation, 4144–11
Health effects of alcohol abuse, 1979-85, series, 4488–10
Health risk behavior, prevalence of 7 habits, by age, State, and other characteristics, 1986-90, article, 4202–7.305
HHS financial aid, by program, recipient, State, and city, FY91, annual regional listings, 4004–3
Homeless persons aid programs of Fed Govt, program descriptions and funding, by agency and State, FY87-91, annual GAO rpt, 26104–21
Homeless persons transitional housing and support services, HUD grants by community, 1991, press release, 5006–3.80
Hospital discharges and length of stay for alcohol-related diagnoses, by age, sex, race, and region, 1979-85, 4488–10.5
Indian and Alaska Native youth health condition and behavioral patterns, by sex and grade, 1988-90, 4088–3
Indian Health Service and tribal facilities and use, and Indians health and other characteristics, by IHS region, 1980s-90, annual chartbook, 4084–7
Indian Health Service facilities, funding, operations, and Indian health and other characteristics, 1950s-91, annual chartbook, 4084–1
Insurance (health) coverage and provisions of employee benefit plans, by plan type, for State and local govt employees, 1990, biennial rpt, 6784–21
Palau admin, and social, economic, and govtl data, FY91, annual rpt, 7004–6
Parole and probation clients in program for drug- and alcohol-dependent Federal offenders, as of various dates 1987-91, annual rpt, 18204–8.8
Prevalence of mental illness among adults by diagnosis, and health services use, 1980-83, article, 4042–3.368
Prevention of drug abuse, evaluation of services, methodological issues, 1991 conf, 4498–78
Prison and community-based facilities, population, employment, spending, and other characteristics, by State and for Fed Govt, 1990, annual rpt, 6064–26.3
Prison treatment units, and clients by age, sex, and race, by State, data compilation, 1992 annual rpt, 6064–6.6
Probation population, by offender characteristics, sentence conditions, whether rearrested, and offense, 1986-89, 6066–19.65
Public opinion on drinking and alcoholism, by respondent characteristics, data compilation, 1992 annual rpt, 6064–6.3
Research on alcoholism, treatment programs, and patient characteristics, quarterly journal, 4482–1
Research on drug abuse and treatment, biological and behavioral factors, and addiction potential of new drugs, 1991 annual conf, 4494–11
States criminal justice systems activities, employment, funding, and data collection, by State, 1970s-91, annual rpt, 6064–40
Statistical Abstract of US, 1992 annual data compilation, 2324–1.3
Veterans post-traumatic stress cases by period of service, and VA treatment and rehabilitation program operations and staff, by site, FY91, annual rpt, 8704–6
Women in jail, by criminal background and sociodemographic characteristics, with comparisons to men, 1989, 6066–19.66
Youth alcohol use and abuse, by sex, race, Hispanic origin, and grade, 1987, article, 4482–1.302
Youth alcohol use, knowledge, attitudes, and info sources, series, 4006–10
Youth drug, alcohol, and cigarette use and attitudes, by substance type and selected characteristics, 1975-91 surveys, press release, 4008–116; 4494–4
Youth health condition, risk factors, and preventive and treatment services use and availability, 1970s-80s, 26358–234.2
see also Driving while intoxicated
see also Drug and alcohol testing

Alcohol, Drug Abuse and Mental Health Administration
Assistance (financial) of HHS, by program, recipient, State, and city, FY91, annual regional listings, 4004–3
Budget of US, obligations and authority by function, agency, and program, with summaries and analyses, FY93, annual rpt, 104–2
Expenditures of Fed Govt in States, by type, program, agency, and State, FY91, annual rpt, 2464–2
see also Center for Mental Health Services
see also National Institute of Mental Health
see also National Institute on Alcohol Abuse and Alcoholism
see also National Institute on Drug Abuse

Alcohol fuels
Auto alternative fuels use in Federal fleet, energy economy performance at 4 sites, FY91, annual rpt, 3304–28
Consumption of wood, waste, and alcohol fuels, by region, 1981-90, annual rpt, 3164–74.7
Corn and barley feed and industrial use, revised estimates 1980s-91, article, 1561–4.301
Electric power plants and capacity, by fuel used, owner, location, and operating status, 1991 and for units planned 1992-2001, annual listing, 3164–36
Farm financial and marketing conditions, forecast 1992, annual conf, 1504–9
Oxygenate supply and blending in gasoline, by PAD district, monthly data, weekly rpt, 3162–32.3
Oxygenate supply, blending in gasoline, and plant capacity and use, by PAD district, monthly rpt, 3162–6.4
Production, feedstock availability, inputs, and auto emissions, for alcohol fuels, 1991 hearing, 25318–82
Production of denatured alcohol for fuel use, monthly rpt, 8486–1.3
Research and education grants, USDA competitive awards by program and recipient, FY91, annual listing, 1764–1
Supply, demand, and movement of crude oil, gas liquids, and refined products, by PAD district and State, 1991, annual rpt, 3164–2
Supply, demand, and prices, by fuel type and end-use sector, alternative projections by region, 1990-2010, annual rpt, 3164–96
Supply, demand, and prices, by fuel type and end-use sector, alternative projections 1990-2010, annual rpt, 3164–75
Supply, demand, and prices, by fuel type and end-use sector, with foreign comparisons, 1981-90, annual fact book, 3164–76
Tax (income) returns filed, by type of filer, selected income items, quarterly rpt, 8302–2.1
Tax (income) returns of corporations, income and tax items by asset size and detailed industry, 1989, annual rpt, 8304–21
Tax (income) returns of individuals, by filing status, tax item, and income level, 1991, annual article, 8302–2.319
TVA biomass energy program, operations, finances, and technological characteristics, series, 9806–9
see also Biomass energy
see also Gasohol

Alcohol use
Births and rates, by characteristics of birth, infant, and mother, and presence of maternal risk factors and birth defects, 1989, 4146–5.125
Cancer (breast) risk relation to estrogen replacement therapy use, body mass index, and other risk factors, 1987-89 NYC study, article, 4472–1.350
Cancer (nasopharyngeal) death risk by level of smoking and alcohol use, 1986, article, 4472–1.312
Cancer (stomach) risk relation to smoking and alcohol use, 1989-90 local area study, article, 4472–1.334
Consumption of alcohol, by beverage type, region, and State, 1977-88, annual rpt, 4486–1.11
Consumption of alcohol, by beverage type, region, and State, 1977-89, annual rpt, 4486–1.15
Consumption of alcohol, by selected characteristics, 1991 survey, annual rpt series, 4494–5
Consumption, supply, trade, prices, spending, and indexes, by food commodity, 1990, annual rpt, 1544–4
DC metro area drug, alcohol, and tobacco use, user characteristics, and consequences, series, 4496–12
Deaths during 1986, decedents health condition, services use, habits, and social, employment, and other characteristics, 4147–20.19
Diving (underwater) accidents, illnesses, and deaths, by circumstances, diver characteristics, and location, 1970-90, annual rpt, 2144–29
Health condition and care indicators, 1950s-90 with health improvement and disease prevention goals for 1990, annual data compilation, 4144–11
Heart disease hospitalization and death risk related to alcohol use level, 1990 article, 4482–1.301
Indian health risk behavior, by region and for Montana, mid 1980s, article, 4042–3.346

Maternal and child health indicators and services use, by age, race, and poverty status, 1988, 4478–197
Mexican American women's alcohol use, by whether immigrant and occupational group, 1992 article, 4482–1.309
see also Alcohol abuse and treatment
see also Driving while intoxicated

Alcoholic beverages
see Alcohol use
see Alcoholic beverages control laws
see Beer and breweries
see Liquor and liquor industry
see Wine and winemaking

Alcoholic beverages control laws
Arrests, by offense, offender characteristics, and location, 1991, annual rpt, 6224–2.2
Court civil and criminal caseloads for Federal district, appeals, and bankruptcy courts, by type of suit and offense, circuit, and district, 1991, annual rpt, 18204–11
Court civil and criminal caseloads for Federal district, appeals, and special courts, 1991, annual rpt, 18204–8
Court criminal case processing in Federal district courts, and dispositions, by offense, district, and offender characteristics, 1989, annual data compilation, 6064–29
Court criminal case processing in Federal district courts, and dispositions, by offense, 1980-91, annual rpt, 6064–31
Juvenile arrests, by sex, race, disposition, and offense, 1990, 6066–27.8
Juvenile courts drug and alcohol offenses cases, by disposition and offender age, sex, and race, 1985-88, 6066–27.7
Sale permits for alcohol revoked and suspended, fines, and inspections, for Bur of Alcohol, Tobacco, and Firearms, FY78-90, hearing, 21788–217
Sentences for Federal offenses, guidelines by offense and circumstances, series, 17668–1
US attorneys civil and criminal cases by type and disposition, and collections, by Federal district, FY91, annual rpt, 6004–2.1
Youth alcohol purchase, consumption, and sale laws, penalties, and enforcement problems, 1991 survey, 4006–10.4

Alcoholism
see Alcohol abuse and treatment

Aleutian Islands
Environmental conditions and oil dev impacts for Alaska OCS, compilation of papers, series, 2176–1

Alexander, Greg R.
"Seasonal Variation in Adolescent Conceptions, Induced Abortions, and Late Initiation of Prenatal Care", 4042–3.372

Alexander, Henrietta B.
"Investigation of Passing Accidents on Two-Lane, Two-Way Roads", 7552–3.301

Alexandria, Va.
Fed Govt land acquisition and dev projects in DC metro area, characteristics and funding by agency and project, FY92-96, annual rpt, 15454–1

Alfalfa
see Animal feed

Algal blooms
see Eutrophication

Algeria
Agricultural trade by commodity and country, prices, and world market devs, monthly rpt, 1922–12
Agricultural trade of US, by detailed commodity and country, 1991, annual rpt, 1524–8
Agricultural trade of US, by detailed commodity and country, 1991, semiannual rpt, 1522–4
Cuba trade, by commodity and country, mid 1980s-91, 9118–8
Economic and military aid and loans from US and intl agencies, by program and country, FY46-91, annual rpt, 9914–5
Economic and social conditions of developing countries from 1960s, and Intl Dev Cooperation Agency and AID activities and funding, FY91-93, annual rpt, 9904–4
Economic conditions, policy, and trade practices, by country, 1989-91, annual rpt, 21384–5
Economic, social, political, and geographic summary data, by country, 1992, annual factbook, 9114–2
Exports and imports of US, by commodity and country, 1980-90, world area rpt, 9116–1.6
Exports and imports of US, by Harmonized System 6-digit commodity and country, 1991, annual rpt, 2424–13
Exports and imports of US, by selected country, country group, and commodity group, 1991, annual rpt, 2044–37
Exports and imports of US, by transport mode, country, and SITC 1- to 3-digit commodity, 1991, annual rpt, 2424–12
Exports, imports, and balances of US for manufactured goods, by SITC 2-digit commodity and country, quarterly rpt, 2042–35
Exports of US, detailed Schedule B commodities with countries of destination, 1991, annual rpt, 2424–10
Food supply, needs, and aid for developing countries, status and alternative forecasts, 1992 world area rpt, 1526–8.2
Human rights conditions in 170 countries, and US economic and military aid, 1991, annual rpt, 21384–3
Military aid of US, arms sales, and training programs costs and budget requests, by program, world region, and country, FY91-93, annual rpt, 7144–13
Military spending, arms trade, and force strengths, with govt spending and population, by country, 1979-89, annual rpt, 9824–1
Minerals Yearbook, Vol 3, 1989: foreign country review of production, trade, and policy, by commodity, annual rpt, 5604–35.1
Natural gas and liquefied gas trade of US with 5 countries, by US firm, 1955-91, annual article, 3162–4.301
Oil production, and exports and prices for US, by major exporting country, detailed data, monthly rpt with articles, 3162–24
Oil production, and exports and prices for US, by major exporting country, detailed data, monthly 1973-88, 3168–123
Oil production, stocks, use, and trade, by selected country and country group, monthly rpt, 3162–42
Population size, growth rates, and components of change, by country, projected 1990-2020 and trends from 1950, biennial rpt, 2324–9
Refugee migration, and intl aid programs, by world area and country of origin and asylum, 1991, annual rpt, 7004–15
Steel trade, by product, country, and customs district, with US industry operating data, 1989-June 1992, semiannual rpt, 9882–15
UN voting record and share of votes in agreement with US, by issue, country, and world area, 1991, annual rpt, 7004–18
see also under By Foreign Country in the "Index by Categories"

Ali, Mir B.
"State-Level Costs of Production: Major Field Crops, 1987-89", 1544–24

Alien workers
Admissions to US of immigrants, alien workers, and visitors, deportations, and naturalizations, by country, FY91 and trends from 1820, annual rpt, 6264–2
Admissions to US of immigrants and legalized aliens, by occupational group and country of birth, preliminary FY91, annual table, 6264–1
Admissions to US of immigrants and nonimmigrants, alien workers, deportations, and naturalizations, FY91, annual summary rpt, 6264–7
Clothing and other industries employment of aliens, and impacts on local economies, with background data, 1990 working paper, 6366–6.6
Discrimination and other employment-related problems of alien workers in NYC, hotline calls, 1988, 6366–6.7
Employer sanctions under Immigration Reform and Control Act, impacts on labor markets, with data for selected industries and metro areas, 1980s, working paper, 6366–6.10
Fed Govt civilian employees work-years, pay rates, and benefits use and costs, by agency, FY90, annual rpt, 9844–31
Los Angeles wages and working conditions impacts of Immigration Reform and Control Act, 1980s-91, working paper, 6366–6.9
Military health care personnel, and accessions by training source, by occupation, specialty, and service branch, FY90, annual rpt, 3544–24
Palau admin, and social, economic, and govtl data, FY91, annual rpt, 7004–6
Science and engineering labor force, Federal and university research funding, and educational data, series, 9626–6
Visas of US issued and refused to immigrants and nonimmigrants, by class, issuing office, and nationality, FY90, annual rpt, 7184–1
Wages impacts of immigration reform provisions for alien legalization and employer sanctions, model results, 1987-89, working paper, 6366–6.8

Aliens
Admissions to US of aliens, by class of admission and selected port and country, FY90-91, fact sheet, 6266–2.9
Admissions to US of immigrants, alien workers, and visitors, deportations, and naturalizations, by country, FY91 and trends from 1820, annual rpt, 6264–2
Admissions to US of immigrants and nonimmigrants, alien workers, deportations, and naturalizations, FY91, annual summary rpt, 6264–7
AFDC application denials, by reason and State, FY90, annual rpt, 4584–3.3
AFDC beneficiaries demographic and financial characteristics, by State, FY90, annual rpt, 4584–7
AIDS cases in US among persons from countries with predominantly heterosexual transmission patterns, and among their sexual contacts, quarterly rpt, 4202–9
Assistance (financial and nonfinancial) of Fed Govt, 1992 base edition, annual listing, 104–5
Business statistics, detailed data for major industries and economic indicators, 1960-91, *Survey of Current Business* biennial supplement, 2704–1
Education (bilingual) enrollment, and eligible students not enrolled, by State, 1990-91, annual rpt, 4804–14
Food stamp eligibility and payment errors, by type, recipient characteristics, and State, FY90, annual rpt, 1364–15
Food stamp recipient household size, composition, income, and income and deductions allowed, summer 1989, annual rpt, 1364–8
HHS financial aid, by program, recipient, State, and city, FY91, annual regional listings, 4004–3
Illegal aliens applications for legal residence under Immigration Reform and Control Act, periodic rpt, discontinued, 6262–3
Illegal aliens applying for legal residence, share of population, and farm workers share of applicants, by MSA, 1989, working paper, 6366–6.9
Illegal aliens enforcement activity of Coast Guard, by nationality, 1st half FY92, semiannual rpt, 7402–4
Illegal aliens held in Immigration and Naturalization Service detention facilities pending hearings, and legal aid requests, 1980s-91, GAO rpt, 26119–409
Illegal entry and smuggling of aliens, Federal sentencing guidelines by offense and circumstances, series, 17668–1
Income from US sources and tax withheld for alien nonresidents, by country and tax treaty status, detailed data compilation for income tax returns, 1984-88, quinquennial rpt, 8308–31
Income from US sources and tax withheld for foreign natls not residing in US, by country and tax treaty status, 1989, annual article, 8302–2.308
Malaria cases in US, for military personnel and US and foreign natls, and by country of infection, 1966-90, annual rpt, 4205–4
Pacific territories population and housing detailed characteristics, by location, 1990 Census of Population and Housing, series, 2551–8
Prison and community-based facilities, population, employment, spending, and other characteristics, by State and for Fed Govt, 1990, quinquennial rpt, 6068–218
Residency (temporary) applications of aliens, by occupation, age, sex, marital status, and country, 1988-91, 4808–41
Supplemental Security Income alien recipients, by legal status, for applications made 1974-90, annual rpt, 4744–3.8
Tax (estate) returns for nonresident aliens, property and tax data, by estate size and decedent country of residence, 1986, article, 8302–2.310
Tuberculosis cases and rates, by patient characteristics, 1985 and 1990, article, 4202–7.302
see also Alien workers
see also Citizenship
see also Deportation
see also Foreign medical graduates
see also Foreign students
see also Immigration and emigration
see also Mexicans in the U.S.
see also Refugees

Alig, Joanne T.
"Wastepaper Recycling and the Future Timber Market", 1504–9.1

Alimony
see Child support and alimony

Allegheny County, Pa.
Govt finances, structure, and service delivery, 1992 local area rpt, 10046–9.2
Housing and households characteristics, and unit and neighborhood quality, by MSA location for 11 MSAs, 1986 survey, supplement, 2485–8

Allen, Nancy L.
"NAEP 1990 Technical Report", 4896–8.5

Allentown, Pa.
see also under By City and By SMSA or MSA in the "Index by Categories"

Allergies
Cases of acute and chronic conditions, disability, absenteeism, and health services use, by selected characteristics, 1990, annual rpt, 4147–10.182; 4147–10.183
Disability and work limitations of persons with chronic health conditions, by condition, age, and sex, 1983-86, 4946–1.2
Natl Inst of Allergy and Infectious Diseases activities, grants by recipient and location, and disease cases, FY84-91, annual rpt, 4474–30

Allied health personnel
Health condition and care indicators, 1950s-90 with health improvement and disease prevention goals for 1990, annual data compilation, 4144–11
HHS financial aid, by program, recipient, State, and city, FY91, annual regional listings, 4004–3
Hospital employees and wages by occupation, and benefits, by region and selected MSA, 1991 survey, 6787–6.254
Hospital employment and job vacancy rate, by occupation, and instn size and control, 1981-88, annual rpt, 4114–12
Labor demand, turnover, and training completions, by detailed occupation, 1990 and projected to 2005, biennial rpt, 6744–3
Labor supply and education of health professionals, by professional and other characteristics, and location, 1960s-92 and projected to 2020, biennial rpt, 4114–8
Medicare reimbursement of hospitals under prospective payment system, and effect on services, finances, and beneficiary payments, 1980-91, annual rpt, 17204–2
Military health care personnel, and accessions by training source, by occupation, specialty, and service branch, FY90, annual rpt, 3544–24
Occupational Outlook Handbook, 1992-93, biennial rpt, 6744–1
Pacific territories population and housing detailed characteristics, by location, 1990 Census of Population and Housing, series, 2551–8
VA health care facilities trainees, by detailed program and city, FY91, annual rpt, 8704–4
see also Clinical laboratory technicians
see also Dietitians and nutritionists
see also Midwives

Allshouse, Jane E.
"Food Consumption, Prices, and Expenditures, 1970-90", 1544–4

Almonds
see Nuts

Alpers, Charles N.
"Compilation and Interpretation of Water-Quality and Discharge Data for Acidic Mine Waters at Iron Mountain, Shasta County, California, 1940-91", 5666–27.35

Altig, David
"Ebbing Tide Lowers All Boats: Monetary Policy, Inflation, and Social Justice", 9377–1.306
"Efficiency and Welfare Effects of Tax Reform: Are Fewer Tax Brackets Better Than More?", 9377–9.143

Aluminum and aluminum industry
Building materials PPI, by type, quarterly rpt, 2042–1.5
Business statistics, detailed data for major industries and economic indicators, *Survey of Current Business*, monthly rpt, 2702–1.16
Business statistics, detailed data for major industries and economic indicators, 1960-91, *Survey of Current Business* biennial supplement, 2704–1
Castings (nonferrous) shipments, by metal type, 1991, annual Current Industrial Rpt, 2506–10.5
China minerals production and trade, by commodity, 1989-90, annual rpt, 5604–38
County Business Patterns, 1989: employment, establishments, and payroll, by SIC 2- to 4-digit industry and county, annual State rpt series, 2326–8
County Business Patterns, 1990: employment, establishments, and payroll, by SIC 2- to 4-digit industry and county, annual State rpt series, 2326–6
Employment, earnings, and hours, by SIC 1- to 4-digit industry, monthly 1989-Feb 1992, annual rpt, 6744–4
Energy use and prices for manufacturing industries, 1988 survey, series, 3166–13
Exports and imports between US and outlying areas, by detailed commodity and mode of transport, 1991, annual rpt, 2424–11
Exports and imports of US, by country and detailed commodity, monthly rpt, 2422–12

Exports and imports of US, by Harmonized System 6-digit commodity and country, 1991, annual rpt, 2424–13
Exports and imports of US, by transport mode, country, and SITC 1- to 3-digit commodity, 1991, annual rpt, 2424–12
Exports of US, detailed Schedule B commodities with countries of destination, 1991, annual rpt, 2424–10
Financial and economic performance indicators and indexes for metals industries, by commodity, monthly rpt, 5602–5
Foreign and US aluminum plant ownership, capacity, energy and aluminum sources, and startup and closing dates, by plant and location, 1990, annual listing, 5604–49
Foreign countries mineral production, reserves, and industry role in domestic economy and world supply, world area and country rpt series, 5606–1
Freight (waterborne domestic and foreign) by commodity, traffic, and passengers, by port and waterway, 1989, annual rpt, 3754–3
Futures and options trading volume, by commodity and exchange, FY91, annual rpt, 11924–2
Imports of US given duty-free treatment for value of US material sent abroad, by commodity and country, 1987-90, annual rpt, 9884–14
Injuries from use of consumer products, by severity, victim age, and detailed product, 1991, annual rpt, 9164–6
Input-output structure of US economy, detailed interindustry transactions for 541 industries, and components of final demand, 1982 benchmark data, 2708–17
Labor productivity, indexes of output, hours, and employment by SIC 2- to 4-digit industry, 1967-90, annual rpt, 6824–1.3
Manufacturing annual survey, 1990: finances and operations, by SIC 2- to 4-digit industry, series, 2506–14
Manufacturing census, 1987: concentration of largest firms measured by value added, and for shipments by SIC 2- and 4-digit industry, subject rpt, 2497–6
Manufacturing census, 1987: shipments of manufacturers products, by customer class and SIC 2- and 4-digit industry, subject rpt, 2497–4
Manufacturing finances and operations, by SIC 2- to 4-digit industry, forecast 1992, annual rpt, 2044–28
Mineral Industry Surveys, commodity review of production, trade, stocks, and use, monthly rpt, 5612–1.1
Mineral Industry Surveys, commodity review of production, trade, stocks, and use, quarterly rpt, 5612–2.2
Minerals Yearbook, Vol 1, 1989: commodity reviews of production, use, trade, prices, and mining operations, annual rpt, 5604–33
Minerals Yearbook, Vol 1, 1990: commodity review of production, reserves, supply, use, and trade, annual rpt, 5604–20.4
Minerals Yearbook, Vol 2, 1989: State reviews of production and sales by commodity, and business activity, annual rpt series, 5604–16
Minerals Yearbook, Vol 2, 1990: State reviews of production and sales by commodity, and business activity, annual rpt series, 5604–22
Minerals Yearbook, Vol 3, 1989: foreign country reviews of production, trade, and policy, by commodity, annual rpt, 5604–35
Mines (metal) and related operations occupational injuries and incidence, employment, and hours, 1990, annual rpt, 6664–3
Occupational injury and illness rates, by SIC 2- to 4-digit industry, 1989-90, annual rpt, 6844–7
Occupational injury and illness rates, by SIC 2- to 4-digit industry, 1990, annual rpt, 6844–1
OECD trade, total and for 4 major countries, and US trade by country, by commodity, 1980-90, world area rpt series, 9116–1
Pacific Northwest aluminum industry electricity purchased from Bonneville Power Admin, by customer, FY91, annual rpt, 3224–1
Pacific Northwest aluminum industry electricity purchased from Bonneville Power Admin, by customer, 1991, semiannual rpt, 3222–1
Price indexes (producer), by stage of processing and detailed commodity, monthly rpt, 6762–6
Price indexes (producer), by stage of processing and detailed commodity, monthly 1991, annual rpt, 6764–2
Production, prices, trade, and foreign and US industry devs, by commodity, bimonthly rpt, 5602–4
Production, prices, trade, use, employment, tariffs, and stockpiles, by mineral, with foreign comparisons, 1987-91, annual rpt, 5604–18
Production, trade, use, and foreign investment in US industry, for minerals, 1985-90 and projected to 2000, annual rpt, 5304–5
Recycling of municipal and industrial waste, costs, revenues, and secondary products trade and related energy use and pollution reductions, 1991 hearings, 21368–139
Shipments (defense and total), trade, use, and inventories of aluminum ingots and mill products, monthly Current Industrial Rpt, 2506–10.9
Statistical Abstract of US, 1992 annual data compilation, 2324–1.25
Stockpiling of strategic material by Fed Govt, activity, and inventory by commodity, as of Sept 1991, semiannual rpt, 3542–22
Stockpiling of strategic material, inventories and needs, by commodity, 1992, annual rpt, 3544–37
Wire and cable (insulated) shipments, trade, use, and firms, by product, 1991, annual Current Industrial Rpt, 2506–10.8

Aluminum Co. of America
Tennessee Valley river control activities, and hydroelectric power generation and capacity, 1990, annual rpt, 9804–7

Alvarez, Fernando
"Banking in Computable General Equilibrium Economies: Technical Appendices I and II", 9383–20.25

Alzheimer's disease
Caregivers hours and other characteristics, services costs and payment source, and patient functioning, by location, 1990, conf paper, 4164–2
Deaths during 1986, decedents health condition, services use, habits, and social, employment, and other characteristics, 4147–20.19
Natl Inst of Neurological Disorders and Stroke activities, and disorder cases, FY91, annual rpt, 4474–25

Ambrose, Michael P.
"Federal Civilian Work Years and Personnel Costs in the Executive Branch for FY91", 9842–1.303

Ambulatory aids
see Prosthetics and orthotics

Amerasians
see Refugees

American Bar Association
"Income Withholder's Role in Child Support", 4588–1

American Battle Monuments Commission
Activities, expenses, and visitors by site, FY87, annual rpt, 9064–1
Budget of US, authoritative financial statements with appropriations, outlays, and receipts, by category and agency, FY91, annual rpt, 8104–2.2
Budget of US, obligations and authority by function, agency, and program, with summaries and analyses, FY93, annual rpt, 104–2

American Forces Information Service
"Defense '92: Almanac", 3504–13

American Historical Association
Financial statements of AHA, and membership by State, 1990, annual rpt, 29574–2

American Housing Survey
Current Housing Reports, unit and household characteristics, subject rpt series, 2486–1; 2486–2
Data coverage and availability of Census Bur rpts and data files, 1992 annual listing, 2304–2
Data coverage and products of AHS, and metro areas surveyed 1974-94, 2328–89
Energy-related data coverage and availability from Census Bur, 1991 pamphlet, 2326–7.84
Housing and households characteristics, and unit and neighborhood quality, by MSA location for 11 MSAs, 1987 survey, supplement, 2485–8
Housing and households characteristics, MSA surveys, fact sheet series, 2485–11
Housing and households detailed characteristics, and unit and neighborhood quality, by location, 1989, biennial rpt supplement, 2485–13
Housing and households detailed characteristics, and unit and neighborhood quality, MSA surveys, series, 2485–6
Housing and households detailed characteristics, and unit and neighborhood quality, 1989, wallchart, 2485–12
Rental housing units, total, with HUD assistance by program, and eligible for aid, by unit, household, and neighborhood characteristics, and location, 1989, biennial rpt, 5184–11

American Indians
see Indians
American Institutes for Research
"National Dropout Statistics Field Test Evaluation", 4838–49
American Lung Association
Smoking cessation clinics success rates, and participants smoking history, views on program, and other characteristics, 1987-88 local area study, article, 4042–3.314
American Medical Association
"Characteristics of Physicians, Jan. 1, 1990", 4116–6
American National Red Cross
Activities and finances of Red Cross, FY91, annual rpt, 29254–1
American Samoa
Banks (insured commercial and savings) deposits by instn, State, MSA, and county, as of June 1991, annual regional rpt, 9295–3.6
Economic, social, political, and geographic summary data, by country, 1992, annual factbook, 9114–2
Exports and imports between US and outlying areas, by detailed commodity and mode of transport, 1991, annual rpt, 2424–11
Fed Govt spending in States and local areas, by type, State, county, and city, FY91, annual rpt, 2464–3
Fed Govt spending in States, by type, program, agency, and State, FY91, annual rpt, 2464–2
Govt finances, with data on health and farm spending and employment, for American Samoa, mid 1980s-91, GAO rpt, 26123–385
HHS financial aid, by program, recipient, State, and city, FY91, annual regional listing, 4004–3.9
Hospital deaths of Medicare patients, actual and expected rates by diagnosis, and hospital characteristics, by instn, FY90 annual State rpt, 4654–14.12
Oil company overcharge settlements funds received, and conservation and energy aid spending, by outlying area, 1990, GAO rpt, 26113–564
Physicians, by specialty, age, sex, and location of training and practice, 1990, State rpt, 4116–6.53
Pollution (air) contributing to global warming, emissions by monitoring site and country, and temperature change by world area and US region, 1860s-1990, annual rpt, 3004–33
Population and housing census, 1990: detailed characteristics, by location, outlying area rpt, 2551–8.1
Population size, growth rates, and components of change, by country, projected 1990-2020 and trends from 1950, biennial rpt, 2324–9
see also under By Outlying Area in the "Index by Categories"
American Schools and Hospitals Abroad
AID economic aid to developing countries, obligations and disbursements by country, quarterly rpt, 9912–4
Developing countries economic and social conditions from 1960s, and Intl Dev Cooperation Agency and AID activities and funding, FY91-93, annual rpt, 9904–4
American Stock Exchange
Trading volume on American Stock Exchange, monthly rpt, 9362–1.1
Trading volume, securities listed by type, and finances, by exchange, selected years 1938-90, annual rpt, 9734–2.1; 9734–2.2
American Telephone and Telegraph Co.
Fiber optics and copper wire mileage and access lines, and fiber systems investment, by telecommunications firm, 1985-91, annual rpt, 9284–18
Finances and operations, detail for telephone firms, 1990, annual rpt, 9284–6
Finances and operations of local and long distance firms, subscribership, and charges, late 1970s-92, semiannual rpt, 9282–7
Intl telecommunications operations of US carriers, finances, rates, and traffic by service type, firm, and country, 1975-90, annual rpt, 9284–17
Ames Laboratory
see also Department of Energy National Laboratories
Amirault, Thomas A.
"How Workers Get Their Training", 6728–32
Ammon, Craig
"Sole Proprietorship Return Preliminary Statistics, 1990: Data Release", 8302–2.317
"Sole Proprietorships, 1990", 8302–2.320
Ammunition
County Business Patterns, 1989: employment, establishments, and payroll, by SIC 2- to 4-digit industry and county, annual State rpt series, 2326–8
County Business Patterns, 1990: employment, establishments, and payroll, by SIC 2- to 4-digit industry and county, annual State rpt series, 2326–6
Criminal cases by type and disposition, and collections, for US attorneys, by Federal district, FY91, annual rpt, 6004–2.1
Employment, earnings, and hours, by SIC 1- to 4-digit industry, monthly 1989-Feb 1992, annual rpt, 6744–4
Exports and imports between US and outlying areas, by detailed commodity and mode of transport, 1991, annual rpt, 2424–11
Exports and imports of US, by country and detailed commodity, monthly rpt, 2422–12
Exports and imports of US, by Harmonized System 6-digit commodity and country, 1991, annual rpt, 2424–13
Exports of US, detailed Schedule B commodities with countries of destination, 1991, annual rpt, 2424–10
Freight (waterborne domestic and foreign) by commodity, traffic, and passengers, by port and waterway, 1989, annual rpt, 3754–3
Imports of US given duty-free treatment for value of US material sent abroad, by commodity and country, 1987-90, annual rpt, 9884–14
Input-output structure of US economy, detailed interindustry transactions for 541 industries, and components of final demand, 1982 benchmark data, 2708–17
Manufacturing annual survey, 1990: finances and operations, by SIC 2- to 4-digit industry, series, 2506–14
Manufacturing census, 1987: concentration of largest firms measured by value added, and for shipments by SIC 2- and 4-digit industry, subject rpt, 2497–6
Manufacturing census, 1987: shipments of manufacturers products, by customer class and SIC 2- and 4-digit industry, subject rpt, 2497–4
Military and personal property shipments, passenger traffic, and costs, by service branch and mode of transport, FY91, annual rpt, 3704–15
Military budget, procurement appropriations by item, service branch, and defense agency, FY91-93, annual rpt, 3544–32
Military outlays and obligations, by function and service branch, quarterly rpt, 3542–3
Military prime contract awards, by category, contract and contractor type, and service branch, FY82-1st half FY92, semiannual rpt, 3542–1
Military prime contract awards, by category, contractor type, and State, FY89-91, annual rpt, 3544–11
Military prime contract awards, by detailed procurement category, FY88-91, annual rpt, 3544–18
Natl income and product accounts, comprehensive accounts and components, benchmark revisions, 1929-88, 2708–5
Natl income and product accounts, comprehensive accounts and components, *Survey of Current Business*, monthly rpt, 2702–1.26
Occupational injury and illness rates, by SIC 2- to 4-digit industry, 1989-90, annual rpt, 6844–7
Occupational injury and illness rates, by SIC 2- to 4-digit industry, 1990, annual rpt, 6844–1
OECD trade, total and for 4 major countries, and US trade by country, by commodity, 1980-90, world area rpt series, 9116–1
Price indexes (producer), by stage of processing and detailed commodity, monthly rpt, 6762–6
Price indexes (producer), by stage of processing and detailed commodity, monthly 1991, annual rpt, 6764–2
Science, engineering, and technical employment in manufacturing, by field and industry, 1989, triennial rpt, 9627–23
Tax (excise) collections of IRS, by source, quarterly rpt, 8302–1
Tax (income) returns of corporations, income and tax items by asset size and detailed industry, 1989, annual rpt, 8304–4; 8304–21
Amnesties
see Pardons
Amtrak
see National Railroad Passenger Corp.
Anaheim, Calif.
CPI by component for US city average, and by region, population size, and for 15 metro areas, monthly rpt, 6762–1
CPI by component for US city average, and by selected metro area, region, and population size, monthly rpt, 6762–2
Housing and households characteristics, and unit and neighborhood quality, by MSA location for 11 MSAs, 1986 survey, supplement, 2485–8

Housing starts and completions authorized by building permits in 40 MSAs, quarterly rpt, 2382–9
Wages by occupation, for office and plant workers, 1991 survey, periodic MSA rpt, 6785–16.3

Ancestry
Census of Population and Housing, 1990: population and housing characteristics, detailed geographic coverage, State CD-ROM series, 2551–10
Census of Population, 1990: ancestry of US population, by group and State, press release, 2328–87
see also Minority groups
see also under By Race and Ethnic Group in the "Index by Categories"

Anchorage, Alaska
CPI by component for US city average, and by selected metro area, region, and population size, monthly rpt, 6762–2
Tide height and time daily at coastal points, forecast 1993, annual rpt, 2174–2.1

Andean Group
Exports, imports, membership, and trade impacts of regional preferential trading arrangements, by group, late 1940s-91, article, 9373–1.308

Andean Trade Preference Act
Exports (duty free) under Andean Trade Preference Act from 4 countries to US, and business opportunities, 1989-91, 2048–161

Andersen, Peder A.
"Aircraft, Spacecraft, and Related Equipment, Industry and Trade Summary", 9885–9.1

Anderson, D. Michael
"Cancer Prevention Counseling on Telephone Helplines", 4042–3.325

Anderson, David E.
"Breast Cancer Risks in Relatives of Male Breast Cancer Patients", 4472–1.330

Anderson, Donnald K.
"Statistics of the Congressional Election of Nov. 6, 1990", 21944–3

Anderson, Kay E.
"Occupation Trends in Advertising, 1984-90", 6722–1.341

Anderson, Keith B.
"Review of Structure-Performance Studies in Grocery Retailing", 9408–56

Anderson, Marc R.
"Statistical Comparison of Selected Chemical Constituents in Water from Chemigation and Conventional Irrigation Wells in Kansas, 1987", 5666–28.21

Andersson, Michael
"Cancer Incidence Among Danish Thorotrast-Exposed Patients", 4472–1.338

Andorra
Economic, social, political, and geographic summary data, by country, 1992, annual factbook, 9114–2
Exports and imports of US, by transport mode, country, and SITC 1- to 3-digit commodity, 1991, annual rpt, 2424–12
Population size, growth rates, and components of change, by country, projected 1990-2020 and trends from 1950, biennial rpt, 2324–9

Andrews, Roxanne
"Longitudinal Patterns of California Medicaid Recipients with Acquired Immunodeficiency Syndrome", 4652–1.301

Andrus, Jon K.
"Surveillance Challenge: Final Stages of Eradication of Poliomyelitis in the Americas", 4202–7.309

Anesthesiology
Blue Cross-Blue Shield plans changes in physician costs per enrollee and for selected procedures, mid 1980s, article, 4652–1.320
HHS financial aid, by program, recipient, State, and city, FY91, annual regional listings, 4004–3
Labor supply and education of health professionals, by professional and other characteristics, and location, 1960s-92 and projected to 2020, biennial rpt, 4114–8
Labor supply of physicians, by specialty, age, sex, and location of training and practice, 1990, State rpt series, 4116–6
Medicare payment of physicians under fee schedule, methodology with data by procedure and specialty, 1992, annual rpt, 17264–1
Military health care personnel, and accessions by training source, by occupation, specialty, and service branch, FY90, annual rpt, 3544–24
VA health care facilities physicians, dentists, and nurses, by selected employment characteristics and VA district, quarterly rpt, 8602–6
VA health care staff and turnover, by occupation, physician specialty, and location, 1991, annual rpt, 8604–8

Angola
Agricultural trade of US, by detailed commodity and country, 1991, annual rpt, 1524–8
Agricultural trade of US, by detailed commodity and country, 1991, semiannual rpt, 1522–4
Economic and military aid and loans from US and intl agencies, by program and country, FY46-91, annual rpt, 9914–5
Economic and social conditions of developing countries from 1960s, and Intl Dev Cooperation Agency and AID activities and funding, FY91-93, annual rpt, 9904–4
Economic conditions, policy, and trade practices, by country, 1989-91, annual rpt, 21384–5
Economic, social, political, and geographic summary data, by country, 1992, annual factbook, 9114–2
Exports and imports of US, by commodity and country, 1980-90, world area rpt, 9116–1.2
Exports and imports of US, by Harmonized System 6-digit commodity and country, 1991, annual rpt, 2424–13
Exports and imports of US, by selected country, country group, and commodity group, 1991, annual rpt, 2044–37
Exports and imports of US, by transport mode, country, and SITC 1- to 3-digit commodity, 1991, annual rpt, 2424–12
Exports, imports, and balances of US for manufactured goods, by SITC 2-digit commodity and country, quarterly rpt, 2042–35
Exports of US, detailed Schedule B commodities with countries of destination, 1991, annual rpt, 2424–10
Food supply, needs, and aid for developing countries, status and alternative forecasts, 1992 world area rpt, 1526–8.2
Human rights conditions in 170 countries, and US economic and military aid, 1991, annual rpt, 21384–3
Military aid of US, arms sales, and training programs costs and budget requests, by program, world region, and country, FY91-93, annual rpt, 7144–13
Military spending, arms trade, and force strengths, with govt spending and population, by country, 1979-89, annual rpt, 9824–1
Minerals Yearbook, Vol 3, 1989: foreign country review of production, trade, and policy, by commodity, annual rpt, 5604–35.1
Oil exports to US by OPEC and non-OPEC countries, monthly rpt, 3162–24.3
Oil exports to US by OPEC and non-OPEC countries, monthly 1973-88, 3168–123.3
Population size, growth rates, and components of change, by country, projected 1990-2020 and trends from 1950, biennial rpt, 2324–9
Refugee migration, and intl aid programs, by world area and country of origin and asylum, 1991, annual rpt, 7004–15
Steel trade, by product, country, and customs district, with US industry operating data, 1989-June 1992, semiannual rpt, 9882–15
UN voting record and share of votes in agreement with US, by issue, country, and world area, 1991, annual rpt, 7004–18
see also under By Foreign Country in the "Index by Categories"

Anguilla
Agricultural trade of US, by detailed commodity and country, 1991, semiannual rpt, 1522–4
Economic and social conditions, resources, and trade, and aid, 1992, annual factbook, 9914–14
Economic, social, political, and geographic summary data, by country, 1992, annual factbook, 9114–2
Exports and imports of US, by transport mode, country, and SITC 1- to 3-digit commodity, 1991, annual rpt, 2424–12
Exports of US, detailed Schedule B commodities with countries of destination, 1991, annual rpt, 2424–10
Population size, growth rates, and components of change, by country, projected 1990-2020 and trends from 1950, biennial rpt, 2324–9

Animal and Plant Health Inspection Service
Animal protection, licensing, and inspection activities of USDA, and animals used in research, by State, FY90, annual rpt, 1394–10
Budget of US, obligations and authority by function, agency, and program, with summaries and analyses, FY93, annual rpt, 104–2
Cattle tuberculosis cases and cooperative Federal-State eradication activities, by State, FY90-91, annual rpt, 1394–13
Foreign and US animal disease outbreaks, quarterly rpt, 1392–3

Natl Veterinary Services Labs activities, biologic drug products evaluation and disease testing, FY91, annual rpt, 1394–17
Poultry Natl Improvement Plan participating hatcheries and birds, by species and disease program, 1992, annual listing, 1394–15
Revenue of USDA, by source and subagency, FY88-92, GAO rpt, 26113–602

Animal diseases and zoonoses
Cattle and calves loss to predators, disease, and other causes, by region and State, 1991, 1618–22
Cattle tuberculosis cases and cooperative Federal-State eradication activities, by State, FY90-91, annual rpt, 1394–13
Fish and shellfish aquaculture in US and Japan, mgmt, methods, and biological data for selected species, 1990 conf, annual rpt, 2164–15
Foreign and US animal disease outbreaks, quarterly rpt, 1392–3
Inspections of meat and poultry for domestic use and export, and rejections by cause, by type of animal and product, FY90, annual rpt, 1374–3
Morbidity and Mortality Weekly Report, infectious notifiable disease cases by age, race, and State, and deaths, 1940s-91, annual rpt, 4204–1
Morbidity and Mortality Weekly Report, infectious notifiable disease cases by State, and public health issues, 4202–1
Natl Veterinary Services Labs activities, biologic drug products evaluation and disease testing, FY91, annual rpt, 1394–17
Poultry Natl Improvement Plan participating hatcheries and birds, by species and disease program, 1992, annual listing, 1394–15
Poultry slaughtered under Fed Govt inspection, pounds certified, and condemnations by cause, by State, monthly rpt, 1625–3
Research (agricultural) funding and staffing for USDA, State agencies, and other instns, by topic, FY91, annual rpt, 1744–2
Sheep and lamb losses, by type of predator and disease, for western US, 1986, 1548–382
see also Rabies
see also Veterinary medicine

Animal experimentation
HHS financial aid, by program, recipient, State, and city, FY91, annual regional listings, 4004–3
Higher education instn R&D facilities space and equipment adequacy, needs, and funding by source, by instn type and control, 1992, biennial rpt, 9624–25
Licensing and inspection of facilities, and other animal protection activities of USDA, with animals used in research, by State, FY90, annual rpt, 1394–10
Public knowledge, interest, and expectations for science and technology, 1990 survey, biennial rpt, 9624–10.7
Reproduction and population research, Fed Govt funding by project, FY90, annual listing, 4474–9

Animal feed
Acreage planted and harvested, by crop and State, 1990-91 and planned as of June 1992, annual rpt, 1621–23
Acreage planted, by selected crop and State, 1983-91 and planned 1992, annual rpt, 1621–22
Acreage reduction program compliance, enrollment, and yield on planted acreage, by commodity and State, annual press release series, 1004–20
Agricultural Stabilization and Conservation Service producer payments, by program and State, 1991, annual table, 1804–12
Agricultural Statistics, 1991, annual rpt, 1004–1
Alfalfa feed products, industry competitiveness of US and Canada, investigation with background financial and operating data and foreign comparisons, 1991 rpt, 9886–4.180
Cattle and calves on feed, inventory and marketings by State, monthly release, 1623–2
Chemicals (inorganic) production by State, shipments, trade, and use, by product, 1991, annual Current Industrial Rpt, 2506–8.14
Cooperatives, finances, operations, activities, and membership, 1950s-89, commodity rpt, 1126–1.7
Corn and barley feed and industrial use, revised estimates 1980s-91, article, 1561–4.301
Costs of feeding livestock in selected locations, periodic situation rpt with articles, 1561–7
County Business Patterns, 1989: employment, establishments, and payroll, by SIC 2- to 4-digit industry and county, annual State rpt series, 2326–8
County Business Patterns, 1990: employment, establishments, and payroll, by SIC 2- to 4-digit industry and county, annual State rpt series, 2326–6
Dairy cattle, milk production, and grain and other concentrates fed, by State, monthly rpt, 1627–1
Dairy herd feed prices, by selected State, 1991, annual rpt, 1317–1.4
Dairy production by State, stocks, prices, and CCC price support activities, by product type, monthly rpt, 1627–3
Employment, earnings, and hours, by SIC 1- to 4-digit industry, monthly 1989-Feb 1992, annual rpt, 6744–4
Exports and imports (agricultural) commodity and country, prices, and world market devs, monthly rpt, 1922–12
Exports and imports (agricultural) of US, by commodity and country, bimonthly rpt, 1522–1
Exports and imports (agricultural) of US, by detailed commodity and country, 1991, annual rpt, 1524–8
Exports and imports (agricultural) of US, by detailed commodity and country, 1991, semiannual rpt, 1522–4
Exports and imports between US and outlying areas, by detailed commodity and mode of transport, 1991, annual rpt, 2424–11
Exports and imports of US, by country and detailed commodity, monthly rpt, 2422–12
Exports and imports of US, by Harmonized System 6-digit commodity and country, 1991, annual rpt, 2424–13
Exports and imports of US, by selected country, country group, and commodity group, 1991, annual rpt, 2044–37
Exports and imports of US, by transport mode, country, and SITC 1- to 3-digit commodity, 1991, annual rpt, 2424–12
Exports of grains, oilseed products, hides, skins, and cotton, by country, weekly rpt, dropped data, 1922–3
Exports of US, detailed Schedule B commodities with countries of destination, 1991, annual rpt, 2424–10
Farm financial and marketing conditions, forecast 1992, annual chartbook, 1504–8
Farm financial and marketing conditions, forecast 1992, annual conf, 1504–9
Farm income, cash marketing receipts ranked by commodity and State, 1990, 1548–385
Farm production inputs, output, and productivity, by commodity and region, 1947-90, annual rpt, 1544–17
Farm production itemized costs, by farm sales size and region, 1991, annual rpt, 1614–3
Farm production itemized costs, receipts, and returns, by commodity and region, 1975-90, annual rpt, 1544–20
Farm sector balance sheet, and receipts by detailed commodity, by State, 1986-90, annual rpt, 1544–18
FDA investigations and regulatory activities, quarterly rpt, 4062–3
Fish (processed) production by location, and trade, by species and product, 1988-91, annual rpts, 2166–6
Fish (trout) raised on farms, production, sales, prices, and losses, 1991-92, annual rpt, 1631–16
Fish and shellfish cold storage holdings, by product and species, preliminary data, monthly press release, 2162–2
Fish catch, trade, use, and fishery operations, with selected foreign data, by species, 1980s-91, annual rpt, 2164–1
Foreign and US agricultural supply and demand indicators, by selected crop, monthly rpt, 1522–5
Foreign and US grain production, prices, trade, stocks, and use, FAS periodic circular series, 1925–2
Foreign countries agricultural production, prices, and trade, by country, 1980-91 and forecast 1992, annual world area rpt series, 1524–4
Freight (waterborne domestic and foreign) by commodity, traffic, and passengers, by port and waterway, 1989, annual rpt, 3754–3
Hay (alfalfa and prairie) prices, for selected areas, weekly rpt, 1313–5
Imports and quotas of dairy products, by commodity and country of origin, FAS monthly rpt, 1925–31
Input-output structure of US economy, detailed interindustry transactions for 541 industries, and components of final demand, 1982 benchmark data, 2708–17
Irrigation projects of Reclamation Bur in western US, crop production and acreage by commodity, State, and project, 1990, annual rpt, 5824–12

Labor productivity, indexes of output, hours, and employment by SIC 2- to 4-digit industry, 1967-90, annual rpt, 6824–1.3
Livestock, meat, poultry, and egg production, prices, trade, and stocks, monthly rpt, 1561–17
Manufacturing annual survey, 1990: finances and operations, by SIC 2- to 4-digit industry, series, 2506–14
Milk (nonfat) and whey feed prices in central States, 1991, annual rpt, 1317–1.4
Molasses (feed) wholesale prices by market area, and trade, weekly rpt, 1311–16
Molasses supply, use, wholesale prices by market, and imports by country, 1986-91, annual rpt, 1311–19
Occupational injury and illness rates, by SIC 2- to 4-digit industry, 1989-90, annual rpt, 6844–7
Occupational injury and illness rates, by SIC 2- to 4-digit industry, 1990, annual rpt, 6844–1
OECD trade, total and for 4 major countries, and US trade by country, by commodity, 1980-90, world area rpt series, 9116–1
Oil and fat production, consumption by end use, and stocks, by type, monthly Current Industrial Rpt, 2506–4.4
Packers purchases and feeding, and livestock markets, dealers, and sales, by State, 1990, annual rpt, 1384–1
Potato production, prices, stocks, and use, by State, 1980s-91, annual rpt, 1621–11
Poultry and egg production, prices, receipts, trade, and disposition, by species, 1960-90, annual rpt, 1564–13
Price indexes (producer), by stage of processing and detailed commodity, monthly rpt, 6762–6
Price indexes (producer), by stage of processing and detailed commodity, monthly 1991, annual rpt, 6764–2
Price support and other CCC program outlays, with production and marketing outlook, by commodity, projected 1991-97, annual rpt, 26306–6.171
Prices (producer and retail) of meat and fish, 1987-92, semiannual situation rpt, 1561–15.3
Prices received and paid by farmers, by commodity and State, monthly rpt, 1629–1
Prices received and paid by farmers, by commodity and State, 1991, annual rpt, 1629–5
Prices received by farmers and production value, by detailed crop and State, 1989-91, annual rpt, 1621–2
Production, acreage, stocks, use, trade, prices, and price supports, periodic situation rpt with articles, 1561–4
Production, farms, acreage, and related data, by selected crop and State, monthly rpt, 1621–1
Production, prices, trade, and marketing, by commodity, current situation and forecast, monthly rpt with articles, 1502–4
Production, prices, trade, and stocks, for feedstuffs and feed grains by type, weekly rpt, 1313–2
Production, use, and prices for feed and feed additives, by commodity, State, and country, various periods 1949-92, 1568–308
Rice market activities, prices, inspections, sales, trade, supply, and use, for US and selected foreign markets, weekly rpt, 1313–8
Seed exports, by type, world region, and country, FAS quarterly rpt, 1925–13
Sheep and wool production, use, and prices, and operations costs and returns, for western US, 1920s-90, 1548–382
Wheat and rye foreign and US production, prices, trade, stocks, and use, quarterly situation rpt with articles, 1561–12
see also Pasture and rangeland
see also Pet food and supplies
see also under By Commodity in the "Index by Categories"

Animal oils
see Oils, oilseeds, and fats

Animals
Exports and imports of US, by country and detailed commodity, monthly rpt, 2422–12
Exports and imports of US, by Harmonized System 6-digit commodity and country, 1991, annual rpt, 2424–13
Exports and imports of US, by transport mode, country, and SITC 1- to 3-digit commodity, 1991, annual rpt, 2424–12
Exports of US, detailed Schedule B commodities with countries of destination, 1991, annual rpt, 2424–10
Licensing and inspection of facilities, and other animal protection activities of USDA, with animals used in research, by State, FY90, annual rpt, 1394–10
see also Animal diseases and zoonoses
see also Animal experimentation
see also Animal feed
see also Birds and bird conservation
see also Endangered species
see also Fish and fishing industry
see also Fishing, sport
see also Hunting and trapping
see also Livestock and livestock industry
see also Marine mammals
see also Pasture and rangeland
see also Pet food and supplies
see also Pets
see also Poultry industry and products
see also Rabies
see also Veterinary medicine
see also Wildlife and wildlife conservation
see also Wildlife refuges
see also Zoological parks

Ann Arbor, Mich.
Commuters, by county of residence and work, for top 10 metro areas, 1990 Census of Population, press release, 2328–84
CPI by component for US city average, and by region, population size, and for 15 metro areas, monthly rpt, 6762–1
CPI by component for US city average, and by selected metro area, region, and population size, monthly rpt, 6762–2
see also under By City and By SMSA or MSA in the "Index by Categories"

Anne Arundel County, Md.
Housing and households characteristics, and unit and neighborhood quality, by MSA location for 11 MSAs, 1987 survey, supplement, 2485–8

Annual Housing Survey
see American Housing Survey

Annual Survey of Manufactures
Data coverage and availability of Census Bur rpts and data files, 1992 annual listing, 2304–2
Finances and operations, by SIC 2- to 4-digit industry, 1990 survey, series, 2506–14
Operations and performance of manufacturing industries, analytical rpt series, 2506–16

Antarctica
Environmental summary data, and intl claims and disputes, 1992 annual factbook, 9114–2
Marine Mammal Protection Act admin, and populations, strandings, and catch permits by species and location, 1988-89, annual rpt, 2164–11
NSF activities, finances, and funding by program, FY91, annual rpt, 9624–6
Pollution (air) contributing to global warming, emissions by monitoring site and country, and temperature change by world area and US region, 1860s-1990, annual rpt, 3004–33
US military and civilian personnel and dependents, by service branch, world area, and country, quarterly rpt, 3542–20
Weather (marine) forecast areas, and broadcast schedules and stations worldwide, as of Sept 1992, annual rpt, 2184–3
Weather (marine) forecast broadcast schedules worldwide, periodic rpt, 2182–9

Anthropology
Fed Govt aid to higher education and nonprofit instns for R&D and related activities, by field, instn, agency, and State, FY90, annual rpt, 9627–17
Higher education grad programs enrollment in science and engineering, by field, source of funds, and characteristics of student and instn, 1990, annual rpt, 9627–7

Anthropometry
see Body measurements

Antigua and Barbuda
Agricultural trade of US, by detailed commodity and country, 1991, semiannual rpt, 1522–4
AID loans repayment status and terms by program and country, and status of predecessor agency loans, quarterly rpt, 9912–3
Economic and social conditions, resources, and trade, and aid, 1992, annual factbook, 9914–14
Economic, social, political, and geographic summary data, by country, 1992, annual factbook, 9114–2
Exports and imports of US, by transport mode, country, and SITC 1- to 3-digit commodity, 1991, annual rpt, 2424–12
Human rights conditions in 170 countries, and US economic and military aid, 1991, annual rpt, 21384–3
Military aid of US, arms sales, and training programs costs and budget requests, by program, world region, and country, FY91-93, annual rpt, 7144–13
Population size, growth rates, and components of change, by country, projected 1990-2020 and trends from 1950, biennial rpt, 2324–9

UN voting record and share of votes in agreement with US, by issue, country, and world area, 1991, annual rpt, 7004–18
Antimony trioxide
see Chemicals and chemical industry
Antiques
Exports and imports between US and outlying areas, by detailed commodity and mode of transport, 1991, annual rpt, 2424–11
Exports and imports of US, by country and detailed commodity, monthly rpt, 2422–12
Exports and imports of US, by Harmonized System 6-digit commodity and country, 1991, annual rpt, 2424–13
Exports of US, detailed Schedule B commodities with countries of destination, 1991, annual rpt, 2424–10
Antitrust law
Banks (natl) charters, mergers, liquidations, enforcement cases, and financial performance, with data by instn and State, quarterly rpt, 8402–3
Cases filed under antitrust law, by Fed Govt and private parties, data compilation, 1992 annual rpt, 6064–6.5
Court civil and criminal caseloads for Federal district, appeals, and bankruptcy courts, by type of suit and offense, circuit, and district, 1991, annual rpt, 18204–11
Court civil and criminal caseloads for Federal district, appeals, and special courts, 1991, annual rpt, 18204–8
Court criminal case processing in Federal district courts, and dispositions, by offense, district, and offender characteristics, 1989, annual data compilation, 6064–29
Court criminal case processing in Federal district courts, and dispositions, by offense, 1980-91, annual rpt, 6064–31
Debt delinquent on Federal accounts, cases and collections of Justice Dept and private law firms, pilot project results, FY91, annual rpt, 6004–20
Justice Dept antitrust criminal enforcement activities by industry div and offense, sentencing, and labor costs, FY90, GAO rpt, 26119–375
Merger announcements and antitrust challenges impact on stock returns of rival firms, 1980s, 9408–55
Sentences for Federal offenses, guidelines by offense and circumstances, series, 17668–1
US attorneys civil and criminal cases by type and disposition, and collections, by Federal district, FY91, annual rpt, 6004–2.1; 6004–2.7
Apartment houses
Alteration and repair of owner-occupied homes, costs and structural, household, financial, and project characteristics, 1987, 2486–1.13
Alteration and repair spending, by property and job characteristics, and region, quarterly rpt, annual tables, 2382–7.2
American Housing Survey: unit and household characteristics of recent movers, and reason for move, by tenure, 1989, 2486–1.12
American Housing Survey: unit and households characteristics, and unit and neighborhood quality, by MSA location for 11 MSAs, 1987 survey, supplement, 2485–8
American Housing Survey: unit and households detailed characteristics, and unit and neighborhood quality, MSA rpt series, 2485–6
American Housing Survey: unit and households detailed characteristics, and unit and neighborhood quality, 1989, biennial rpt supplement, 2485–13
American Housing Survey: unit and households detailed characteristics, and unit and neighborhood quality, 1989, wallchart, 2485–12
Arson incidents by whether structure occupied, property value, and arrest rate, by property type, 1991, annual rpt, 6224–2.1
Assets and debts of private sector, balance sheets by segment, 1960-91, semiannual rpt, 9365–4.1
Census of Housing, 1990: inventory, occupancy, and costs, State fact sheet series, 2326–21
Census of Housing, 1990: summary unit characteristics, by householder race and age, county, place, and urban-rural location, State rpt series, 2471–1
Construction put in place, permits, housing sales, costs, material prices, and employment, quarterly rpt with articles, 2042–1
Construction put in place, value of new public and private structures, by type, monthly rpt, 2382–4
Discrimination in housing rental and sales, for blacks and Hispanics in selected metro areas, 1989 study, series, 5186–16
Energy use, costs, and conservation, and household and housing characteristics, survey rpt series, 3166–7
Fed Govt financial and nonfinancial domestic aid, 1991 base edition with supplements, annual listing, 104–5
Fed Natl Mortgage Assn activities and finances, 1991, annual rpt, 9474–1
Households and family characteristics, by location, 1991, annual Current Population Rpt, 2546–1.457
Housing and households summary characteristics, 1989 and trends, chartbook, 2486–2.1
Input-output structure of US economy, detailed interindustry transactions for 541 industries, and components of final demand, 1982 benchmark data, 2708–17
Low income rental housing in rural areas, FmHA loans and impacts of programs to maintain supply and to deter mortgage prepayment, 1988-91, GAO rpt, 26113–586
Market absorption rates and characteristics for nonsubsidized furnished and unfurnished units, 1990, annual Current Housing Rpt, 2484–2
Market absorption rates for apartments and condominiums, and completions by rent class and sales price, quarterly rpt, 2482–2
Mortgage loan activity, by type of lender, loan, and mortgaged property, monthly press release, 5142–18
Mortgage loan activity, by type of lender, loan, and mortgaged property, quarterly press release, 5142–30
Natl income and product accounts, comprehensive accounts and components, benchmark revisions, 1929-88, 2708–5
Natl income and product accounts, comprehensive accounts and components, *Survey of Current Business*, monthly rpt, 2702–1.28
New apartment units completed by region and metro-nonmetro location, and absorption rates, by size and price class, preliminary 1991, annual Current Housing Rpt, 2484–3
New housing starts, by units per structure and metro-nonmetro location, and mobile home placements and prices, by region, monthly rpt, 2382–1
New housing units authorized, by region, State, selected MSA, and permit-issuing place, monthly rpt, 2382–5
New housing units authorized, by State, MSA, and permit-issuing place, 1991, annual rpt, 2384–2
New housing units completed and under construction, by units per structure, region, and inside-outside MSAs, monthly rpt, 2382–2
New single and multifamily units, by structural and financial characteristics, inside-outside MSAs, and region, 1987-91, annual rpt, 2384–1
North Central States, FHLB 7th District housing vacancy rates for single and multifamily units and mobile homes, by ZIP code, annual MSA rpt series, 9304–18
NYC housing supply, occupancy, condition, and household characteristics, by tenure and borough, 1991 triennial survey, 2488–3
Pacific territories population and housing detailed characteristics, by location, 1990 Census of Population and Housing, series, 2551–8
Rental housing units, total, with HUD assistance by program, and eligible for aid, by unit, household, and neighborhood characteristics, and location, 1989, biennial rpt, 5184–11
Savings instns failures, inventory of real estate assets available from Resolution Trust Corp, 1991, semiannual listing, 9722–2.4
Savings instns failures, inventory of real estate assets available from Resolution Trust Corp, 1992, semiannual listing, 9722–2.11
Single person and nonfamily households social, economic and housing characteristics, by tenure, 1989, 2486–1.15
Southeastern States, Fed Reserve 6th District, economic indicators by State and MSA, quarterly rpt, 9371–14
Statistical Abstract of US, 1992 annual data compilation, 2324–1.26
Supply and demand for housing and commercial real estate, market activity indicators by region, quarterly rpt, 9292–6
Vacant housing characteristics and costs, and occupancy and vacancy rates, by region and metro-nonmetro location, quarterly rpt, 2482–1
Vacant housing characteristics, and occupancy and vacancy rates, by tenure and location, 1960s-91, annual rpt, 2484–1

West Central States, FHLB 10th District housing vacancy rates for single and multifamily units and mobile homes, by ZIP code, annual MSA rpt series, 9304–22
Western States, FHLB 12th District housing vacancy rates for single and multifamily units and mobile homes, by ZIP code, annual MSA rpt series, 9304–21
Wiretaps authorized, costs, arrests, trials, and convictions, by offense and jurisdiction, 1991, annual rpt, 18204–7
see also Condominiums and cooperatives
see also Rooming and boarding houses

Appalachia
Apple production, marketing, and prices, for Appalachia and compared to other States, 1989-92, annual rpt, 1311–13
Cancer (cervical) and dysplasia rates in Appalachian States, compared to total US, 1986-87, article, 4472–1.327
Coal production and mines by county, prices, productivity, miners, and reserves, by mining method and State, 1990-91, annual rpt, 3164–25
Dev project funding by Appalachian Regional Commission, by project and State, planned FY92, annual rpt, 9084–3
Dev projects in Appalachia, and funding by source, by program and State, FY91, annual rpt, 9084–1
Fed Govt spending in States, by type, program, agency, and State, FY91, annual rpt, 2464–2
Food processing firms, employment, and shipments, and farm production, by commodity and State, for Appalachia, 1960s-90, 9088–37
Health care services projects of Appalachian Regional Commission by State, and project listing, 1960s-80s, 9088–38
HHS financial aid, by program, recipient, State, and city, FY91, annual regional listings, 4004–3
Housing vacancy rates for single and multifamily units and mobile homes in FHLB 5th District, discontinued annual MSA rpt series, 9304–27
Hwy system and access roads funding and completion status, by State, quarterly tables, 9082–1
Ohio poverty, hunger, and public welfare program operations and indicators of need, by county, 1991 hearing, 21968–58
Peaches production, marketing, and prices in 3 southeastern States and Appalachia, 1991, annual rpt, 1311–12
Population of Appalachia, by State and county, 1980 and 1990, annual rpt, 9084–1
Temperature annual and seasonal averages by US region, and departures from normal by world area, 1860s-1990, annual rpt, 3004–33
see also under By Region in the "Index by Categories"
see also under names of individual States

Appalachian Regional Commission
Activities of ARC, local dev projects, and funding by source, by program and State, FY91, annual rpt, 9084–1
Budget of US, authoritative financial statements with appropriations, outlays, and receipts, by category and agency, FY91, annual rpt, 8104–2.2
Budget of US, obligations and authority by function, agency, and program, with summaries and analyses, FY93, annual rpt, 104–2
Education funding by Federal agency, program, and recipient type, and instn spending, 1960s-91, annual rpt, 4824–8
Expenditures of ARC, by project and State, planned FY92, annual rpt, 9084–3
Food processing firms, employment, and shipments, and farm production, by commodity and State, for Appalachia, 1960s-90, 9088–37
Health care services projects of ARC by State, and project listing, 1960s-80s, 9088–38
Hwy system and access roads funding and completion status, by State, quarterly tables, 9082–1

Apparel
see Clothing and clothing industry

Appeals
see Court of Military Appeals
see Federal courts of appeals
see Supreme Court
see Tax protests and appeals
see U.S. Court of Appeals for the Federal Circuit

Apples
see Fruit and fruit products

Appliances
see Household appliances and equipment

Apportionment
see Congressional apportionment

Apprenticeship
Employment and Training Admin activities, funding, and participant characteristics, by program, FY86-88, annual rpt, 6404–17
Minority group and women apprentices, and earnings, by occupation, and programs regulation, 1990, GAO rpt, 26121–446
Occupational Outlook Handbook, 1992-93, biennial rpt, 6744–1

Appropriations
see Budget of the U.S.
see Defense budgets and appropriations

Aptitude tests
see Educational tests

Aquaculture
Bass (striped) stocks status on Atlantic coast, and sport and commercial catch by State, 1979-90, annual rpt, 5504–29
Catfish and trout hatcheries and farms, production, costs, prices, and sales, 1970s-92, semiannual situation rpt, 1561–15
Catfish farms, sales, and acreage, by State, 1990-91, article, 9391–16.301
Catfish raised on farms, inventory, stocks, and production, by producer State, quarterly rpt, 1631–18
Catfish raised on farms, production, inventory, sales, prices, and imports, monthly release, 1631–14
Farm financial and marketing conditions, forecast 1992, annual chartbook, 1504–8
Farm financial and marketing conditions, forecast 1992, annual conf, 1504–9
Hatcheries and research stations under Fish and Wildlife Service mgmt, acreage by site and State, as of Sept 1992, annual rpt, 5504–8
Japan and US aquaculture mgmt, methods, and biological data for selected species, 1990 conf, annual rpt, 2164–15
Natl Fish Hatchery System activities and deliveries, by species, hatchery, and jurisdiction of waters stocked, FY91, annual rpt, 5504–10
Research and education grants, USDA competitive awards by program and recipient, FY91, annual listing, 1764–1
Salmon aquaculture activities of Little White Salmon National Fish Hatchery, late 1890s-1980s, 5508–114
Salmon aquaculture production and exports, by country, 1980s-90, article, 2162–1.301
Salmon conservation spending by organization, and population, for Columbia River basin, 1970-91, GAO rpt, 26113–577
Statistical Abstract of US, 1992 annual data compilation, 2324–1.24
Trout raised on farms, production, sales, and prices, 1991-92, annual rpt, 1631–16

Arab Republic of Egypt
see Egypt

Arabian Peninsula
see Oman
see Qatar
see Saudi Arabia
see United Arab Emirates
see Yemen
see Yemen, North
see Yemen, South

Arapahoe County, Colo.
Housing and households characteristics, and unit and neighborhood quality, by MSA location for 11 MSAs, 1986 survey, supplement, 2485–8

Arbitration
see Civil procedure
see Labor-management relations, general
see Labor-management relations in government
see Legal arbitration and mediation

Architect of the Capitol
Activities of Capitol Architect, funding, costs, and contracts, FY89, annual rpt, 25944–1
Budget of US, obligations and authority by function, agency, and program, with summaries and analyses, FY93, annual rpt, 104–2
Expenditures for salaries, supplies, and services, itemized by payee and function, 2nd half FY91, semiannual rpt, 25922–2

Architectural and Transportation Barriers Compliance Board
see U.S. Architectural and Transportation Barriers Compliance Board

Architectural barriers to the handicapped
Building access for disabled to Federal and federally funded facilities, complaints by disposition and State, FY91, annual rpt, 17614–1
Election polling places accessibility and services availability for aged and disabled, by State, 1990 natl elections, hearing, 21428–11
Equipment (assistive technology) and home accessibility features, use, payment sources, and unmet needs, by age, 1990, 4146–8.219

Architecture
County Business Patterns, 1989: employment, establishments, and payroll, by SIC 2- to 4-digit industry and county, annual State rpt series, 2326–8

County Business Patterns, 1990: employment, establishments, and payroll, by SIC 2- to 4-digit industry and county, annual State rpt series, 2326–6
Degrees awarded in higher education, by level, field, race, and sex, 1989/90 and trends from 1980/81, annual rpt, 4844–17
Employment and economic conditions, alternative BLS projections to 2005 and trends 1975-90, biennial rpt, 6744–19
Historic and natural natl landmarks damaged and threatened, with owner, location, damage type, and recommended remedial action, 1990, annual listing, 5544–16
Input-output structure of US economy, detailed interindustry transactions for 541 industries, and components of final demand, 1982 benchmark data, 2708–17
Labor demand, turnover, and training completions, by detailed occupation, 1990 and projected to 2005, biennial rpt, 6744–3
Occupational Outlook Handbook, 1992-93, biennial rpt, 6744–1
see also Architectural barriers to the handicapped

Arctic
NSF R&D grant awards, by div and program, FY90, biennial rpt, 9626–7.5
see also Arctic Ocean

Arctic Ocean
Environmental conditions and oil dev impacts for Alaska OCS, compilation of papers, series, 2176–1
Environmental summary data, and intl claims and disputes, 1992 annual factbook, 9114–2
Marine Mammal Protection Act admin, and populations, strandings, and catch permits by species and location, 1988-89, annual rpt, 2164–11
Tide height and time daily at coastal points, forecast 1993, annual rpt, 2174–2.5
see also Beaufort Sea
see also Chukchi Sea

Area studies
African Dev Foundation dev grants and fellowships, by country, FY84-91, annual rpt, 9034–1
Arts Natl Endowment activities and grants, FY91, annual rpt, 9564–3
Degrees awarded in higher education, by level, field, race, and sex, 1989/90 and trends from 1980/81, annual rpt, 4844–17
Latin America dev grants of Inter-American Foundation by program area, and fellowships by field and instn, by country, FY72-91, annual rpt, 14424–2
Latin America dev grants of Inter-American Foundation by recipient, and fellowships, by country, FY91, annual rpt, 14424–1

Area wage surveys
BLS data collection, analysis, and presentation methods, by program, 1992 rpt, 6888–1
State and local govt employees wages by occupation, and benefits, periodic MSA survey rpt series, 6785–15
Wages by occupation, and benefits for office and plant workers, periodic MSA survey rpt series, 6785–3; 6785–12; 6785–16; 6785–17
Wages by occupation, for office and plant workers in selected MSAs, 1991 surveys, annual rpt, 6785–5
Wages by occupation, for office and plant workers in selected MSAs, 1991 surveys, annual summary rpts, 6785–6
see also Industry wage surveys

Argentina
Agricultural trade of US, by detailed commodity and country, 1991, annual rpt, 1524–8
Agricultural trade of US, by detailed commodity and country, 1991, semiannual rpt, 1522–4
AID loans repayment status and terms by program and country, and status of predecessor agency loans, quarterly rpt, 9912–3
Debt burden indicators for 8 developing countries, alternative projections 1991-2000 and trends from 1974, technical paper, 9366–7.271
Economic and military aid and loans from US and intl agencies, by program and country, FY46-91, annual rpt, 9914–5
Economic and social conditions of developing countries from 1960s, and Intl Dev Cooperation Agency and AID activities and funding, FY91-93, annual rpt, 9904–4
Economic and social conditions, resources, and trade, and aid, 1992, annual factbook, 9914–14
Economic conditions, policy, and trade practices, by country, 1989-91, annual rpt, 21384–5
Economic, population, and agricultural data, US and other aid sources, and AID activity, 1992 country rpt, 9916–12.64
Economic, social, political, and geographic summary data, by country, 1992, annual factbook, 9114–2
Exports and imports of US, by commodity and country, 1980-90, world area rpt, 9116–1.7
Exports and imports of US, by Harmonized System 6-digit commodity and country, 1991, annual rpt, 2424–13
Exports and imports of US, by selected country, country group, and commodity group, 1991, annual rpt, 2044–37
Exports and imports of US, by transport mode, country, and SITC 1- to 3-digit commodity, 1991, annual rpt, 2424–12
Exports, imports, and balances of US for manufactured goods, by SITC 2-digit commodity and country, quarterly rpt, 2042–35
Exports, imports, and balances of US with major trading partners, by product category, 1987-91, annual chartbook, 9884–21
Exports, investment, debt, and tariffs of 7 Latin America countries, and trade and investment policy liberalization issues, mid 1960s-91, 9886–4.184
Exports of US, detailed Schedule B commodities with countries of destination, 1991, annual rpt, 2424–10
Ferrosilicon from 6 countries, injury to US industry from foreign subsidized and less than fair value imports, investigation with background financial and operating data, 1992 rpt, 9886–19.84
Human rights conditions in 170 countries, and US economic and military aid, 1991, annual rpt, 21384–3
Imports of goods, services, and investment from US, trade barriers, impacts, and US actions, by country, 1991, annual rpt, 444–2
Inflation relation to money supply, for 5 South America countries, 1970s-90, technical paper, 9379–12.91
Military aid of US, arms sales, and training programs costs and budget requests, by program, world region, and country, FY91-93, annual rpt, 7144–13
Military spending, arms trade, and force strengths, with govt spending and population, by country, 1979-89, annual rpt, 9824–1
Multinatl US firms and foreign affiliates finances and operations, by industry and country, 1989 benchmark survey, annual rpt, 2704–5
Multinatl US firms foreign affiliates, income statement items by asset size, industry, and country, 1988, biennial article, 8302–2.322
Nuclear power generation in US and 20 countries, monthly rpt, 3162–24.10
Nuclear power generation in US and 20 countries, monthly 1973-88, 3168–123.10
Oil production, investment needs, and exports, for 8 South America countries, 1980s-90 and projected to 2010, GAO rpt, 26123–396
Population size, growth rates, and components of change, by country, projected 1990-2020 and trends from 1950, biennial rpt, 2324–9
Refugee migration, and intl aid programs, by world area and country of origin and asylum, 1991, annual rpt, 7004–15
Spacecraft and satellite launches since 1957, quarterly listing, 9502–2
Steel (carbon flat-rolled) products from 21 countries, injury to US industry from foreign subsidized and less than fair value imports, investigation with background financial and operating data, 1992 rpt, 9886–19.85
Steel trade, by product, country, and customs district, with US industry operating data, 1989-June 1992, semiannual rpt, 9882–15
Tax (income) final withholding systems use in 4 countries, and feasibility of US adoption, with background data, 1986-92, GAO rpt, 26119–400
UN voting record and share of votes in agreement with US, by issue, country, and world area, 1991, annual rpt, 7004–18
see also under By Foreign Country in the "Index by Categories"

Argonne National Laboratory
"Forecast of Transportation Energy Demand Through the Year 2010", 3008–124
see also Department of Energy National Laboratories

Arid zones
Birds in western US Great Basin sagebrush habitat, population density by species, 1978-83 studies, 1208–402
Livestock grazing on public desert areas, acreage, use, fees, and endangered species, 1988-90, GAO rpt, 26113–552

Arizona
Banks (insured commercial and savings) deposits by instn, State, MSA, and county, as of June 1991, annual regional rpt, 9295–3.6
Camping in wilderness areas, impacts on plants and soils, 1979-90 studies, 1208–395
Coal production and mines by county, prices, productivity, miners, and reserves, by mining method and State, 1990-91, annual rpt, 3164–25
County Business Patterns, 1990: employment, establishments, and payroll, by SIC 2- to 4-digit industry and county, annual State rpt, 2326–6.4
Deaths and rates, by detailed location, cause, and demographic characteristics, 1989, US Vital Statistics annual rpt, 4144–3.1
Employment, earnings, and hours, by selected SIC 1- to 4-digit industry, State, and for 275 MSAs, 1987-92, 6748–81
Fed Govt spending in States and local areas, by type, State, county, and city, FY91, annual rpt, 2464–3
Fed Govt spending in States, by type, program, agency, and State, FY91, annual rpt, 2464–2
HHS financial aid, by program, recipient, State, and city, FY91, annual regional listing, 4004–3.9
Hospital deaths of Medicare patients, actual and expected rates by diagnosis, and hospital characteristics, by instn, FY90 annual State rpt, 4654–14.3
Housing census, 1990: inventory, occupancy, and costs, State fact sheet, 2326–21.4
Housing census, 1990: summary unit characteristics, by householder race and age, county, place, and urban-rural location, State rpt, 2471–1.4
Medicare payment of physicians, reforms impacts on services, and monitoring methods, 1992 annual rpt, 4004–34
Military prime contract awards, by contractor, service branch, State, and city, FY91, annual rpt, 3544–22
Mineral Industry Surveys, State reviews of production, 1991, preliminary annual rpt, 5614–6
Minerals Yearbook, Vol 2, 1990: State review of production and sales by commodity, and business activity, annual rpt, 5604–22.4
Multinatl firms US affiliates finances and operations, by industry, country of parent firm, and State, 1987, 2708–48
Physicians, by specialty, age, sex, and location of training and practice, 1990, State rpt, 4116–6.3
Population and housing census, 1990: detailed geographic coverage, State CD-ROM, 2551–9.8
Population and housing census, 1990: summary characteristics, by county, subdiv, and place, State rpt, 2551–7.4
Population census, 1990: population characteristics and living arrangements, by county, place, and urban-rural location, State rpt, 2531–1.4
Statistical Abstract of US, 1992 annual data compilation, 2324–1
Water quality and fish population in southwestern US streams, impacts of land mgmt and forest fires, 1980s-91, 1208–390
Water supply and quality in streams and lakes, and groundwater levels in wells, by drainage basin, 1990, annual State rpt, 5666–10.3
Water supply, and snow survey results, monthly State rpt, 1266–2.2
Water supply, and snow survey results, 1991, annual State rpt, 1264–14.6
see also Douglas, Ariz.
see also Maricopa County, Ariz.
see also Mesa, Ariz.
see also Phoenix, Ariz.
see also Tucson, Ariz.
see also under By State in the "Index by Categories"

Arkansas
Banks (insured commercial and savings) deposits by instn, State, MSA, and county, as of June 1991, annual regional rpt, 9295–3.4
Coal production and mines by county, prices, productivity, miners, and reserves, by mining method and State, 1990-91, annual rpt, 3164–25
Deaths and rates, by detailed location, cause, and demographic characteristics, 1989, US Vital Statistics annual rpt, 4144–3.1
Economic and banking conditions, for Fed Reserve 8th District, quarterly rpt with articles, 9391–16
Employment by industry div, earnings, and hours, by southwestern State, monthly rpt, 6962–2
Employment, earnings, and hours, by selected SIC 1- to 4-digit industry, State, and for 275 MSAs, 1987-92, 6748–81
Fed Govt spending in States and local areas, by type, State, county, and city, FY91, annual rpt, 2464–3
Fed Govt spending in States, by type, program, agency, and State, FY91, annual rpt, 2464–2
Fish (catfish) raised on farms, inventory, stocks, and production, by major producer State, quarterly rpt, 1631–18
Floods in Mississippi River and Gulf of Mexico basins, precipitation and water levels by site, damage, and deaths, 1982-83, 5666–27.33
HHS financial aid, by program, recipient, State, and city, FY91, annual regional listing, 4004–3.6
Hospital deaths of Medicare patients, actual and expected rates by diagnosis, and hospital characteristics, by instn, FY90 annual State rpt, 4654–14.4
Housing census, 1990: inventory, occupancy, and costs, State fact sheet, 2326–21.5
Housing census, 1990: summary unit characteristics, by householder race and age, county, place, and urban-rural location, State rpt, 2471–1.5
Measles cases in Arkansas, with risk factors and vaccination rates, 1986, article, 4042–3.301
Military prime contract awards, by contractor, service branch, State, and city, FY91, annual rpt, 3544–22
Mineral Industry Surveys, State reviews of production, 1991, preliminary annual rpt, 5614–6
Minerals Yearbook, Vol 2, 1990: State review of production and sales by commodity, and business activity, annual rpt, 5604–22.5
Multinatl firms US affiliates finances and operations, by industry, country of parent firm, and State, 1987, 2708–48
Physicians, by specialty, age, sex, and location of training and practice, 1990, State rpt, 4116–6.4
Population and housing census, 1990: detailed geographic coverage, State CD-ROM, 2551–9.7
Population and housing census, 1990: summary characteristics, by county, subdiv, and place, State rpt, 2551–7.5
Population census, 1990: population characteristics and living arrangements, by county, place, and urban-rural location, State rpt, 2531–1.5
Research grants of Arkansas science agency and industry sponsors matching funds, and Federal R&D aid to higher education instns, mid 1980s-90, hearing, 21708–131
Rice market activities, prices, inspections, sales, trade, supply, and use, for US and selected foreign markets, weekly rpt, 1313–8
Rice production, practices, costs, and land tenure, by production area, 1988, 1568–309
Rice stocks on and off farms and total in all positions, periodic rpt, 1621–7
Statistical Abstract of US, 1992 annual data compilation, 2324–1
Timber in Arkansas, resources and removals by species and ownership, 1992 rpt, 1206–8.13
Water use by end use, well withdrawals, and public supply deliveries, by county, 1988, State rpt, 5666–24.11
Water use by end use, well withdrawals, and public supply deliveries, by county, 1989, State rpt, 5666–24.12; 5666–24.18
see also Little Rock, Ark.
see also Pine Bluff, Ark.
see also under By State in the "Index by Categories"

Arkansas River
Freight (waterborne domestic and foreign) by commodity, traffic, and passengers, by port and waterway, 1989, annual rpt, 3754–3.2
Water supply and quality in streams and lakes, and groundwater levels in wells, by drainage basin, 1990, annual State rpt series, 5666–10
Water supply and quality in streams and lakes, and groundwater levels in wells, by drainage basin, 1991, annual State rpt series, 5666–12

Arlington, Tex.
Housing and households characteristics, unit and neighborhood quality, and journey to work by MSA location, for 11 MSAs, 1985 survey, supplement, 2485–8
Housing and households characteristics, 1989 survey, MSA fact sheet, 2485–11.10
Housing and households detailed characteristics, and unit and neighborhood quality, by location, 1989 survey, MSA rpt, 2485–6.6

Arlington, Va.
Fed Govt land acquisition and dev projects in DC metro area, characteristics and funding by agency and project, FY92-96, annual rpt, 15454–1

Armed services
Budget of US, CBO analysis and review of FY93 budget by function, annual rpt, 26304–2
see also Air Force
see also Armed services reserves
see also Army
see also Coast Guard
see also Department of Defense
see also International military forces
see also Marine Corps
see also Military personnel
see also Navy
see also Selective service
see also Voluntary military service

Armed services reserves
Army strategic capability, force strengths, budget, and mgmt, FY79-93, annual rpt, 3704–13
Base construction, renovation, and closure, DOD budget requests by project, service branch, State, and country, FY93, annual rpt, 3544–15
Base support costs by function, and personnel and acreage by installation, by service branch, FY93, annual rpt, 3504–11
Budget of DOD, base construction and family housing appropriations by facility, service branch, and location, FY91-93, annual rpt, 3544–39
Budget of DOD, organization, personnel, weapons, and property, by service branch, State, and country, 1992 annual summary rpt, 3504–13
Budget of DOD, procurement appropriations by item, service branch, and defense agency, FY91-93, annual rpt, 3544–32
Budget of DOD, R&D appropriations by item, service branch, and defense agency, FY91-93, annual rpt, 3544–33
Budget of US, Bush Admin proposals, with detail for defense budgets, and historical data from FY34, FY93, 108–46.2
Health care personnel and turnover, by specialty for reserves, FY90, annual rpt, 3544–24.8
Labor laws enacted, by State, 1991, annual article, 6722–1.309
Navy personnel strengths, accessions, and attrition, detailed statistics, quarterly rpt, 3802–4
Pacific territories population and housing detailed characteristics, by location, 1990 Census of Population and Housing, series, 2551–8
Persian Gulf War costs to US by category and service branch, and offsetting contributions by allied country, monthly rpt, 102–3
Persian Gulf War US reserve forces mobilization, by component, 1990-91, annual rpt, 3544–31.2
Personnel and equipment strengths, and readiness, by reserve component, FY91, annual rpt, 3544–31
Personnel and payroll for reserve units, by service branch, by State and country, FY91, annual rpt, 3544–29
Personnel needs, costs, and force readiness, by service branch, FY93, annual rpt, 3504–1
Personnel reserve and active duty force mix and costs under alternative reduction cases, by service branch, 1990 and projected to 1997, 26306–6.172
Personnel strengths and characteristics, by reserve component, quarterly rpt, 3542–4
Personnel strengths for active duty, civilians, and reserves, by service branch, FY91, annual rpt, 3544–2
Personnel strengths, for active duty, civilians, and reserves, by service branch, quarterly rpt, 3542–14
Personnel strengths for reserve components, by selected characteristics, FY91, annual rpt, 3544–1.5
Statistical Abstract of US, 1992 annual data compilation, 2324–1.11
Training and education programs of DOD, funding, staff, students, and facilities, by service branch, FY93, annual rpt, 3504–5
see also Coast Guard Reserve
see also Marine Reserve
see also National Guard

Armenia
Agricultural production, prices, and trade, for former USSR republics, 1960s-91 and forecast 1992, annual rpt, 1524–4.1
Economic, social, political, and geographic summary data, by country, 1992, annual factbook, 9114–2
Embassies of US in former Soviet republics and Baltic States, positions planned by function, and filled, 1992, GAO rpt, 26123–403
Energy supply and use, and social, economic, and political indicators for former Soviet Republics and Baltic States, 1989-90, 3168–126
Energy use and production of former USSR Republics, by fuel type, 1990, annual rpt, 3164–84.2
Exports and imports of US with Communist and transitional economy countries, by detailed commodity and country, quarterly rpt with articles, 9882–2
Livestock and meat inventories, use, and imports, by former USSR republic, 1986-93, semiannual rpt, 1925–33.2
Population size and characteristics of former Soviet Republics and Baltic States, 1989-92, 9118–19

Arms and munitions
see Ammunition
see Arms control and disarmament
see Arms trade
see Bombs
see Chemical and biological warfare agents
see Defense contracts and procurement
see Defense expenditures
see Explosives
see Firearms
see Military assistance
see Military weapons
see Missiles and rockets
see Nuclear weapons

Arms control and disarmament
NATO and Warsaw Pact military forces reductions and ceilings under CFE treaty, as of Nov 1990, 9828–1
NATO and Warsaw Pact military forces reductions and ceilings under CFE treaty, inspections, and US compliance costs and savings, 1991 hearings, 25388–59
Treaties and agreements on arms control, status and Arms Control and Disarmament Agency activities, 1991, annual rpt, 9824–2
Treaties and other bilateral and multilateral agreements of US in force, by country, as of Jan 1992, annual listing, 7004–1
UN voting record and share of votes in agreement with US, by issue, country, and world area, 1991, annual rpt, 7004–18
see also Intermediate-Range Nuclear Forces Treaty
see also Strategic Arms Reduction Talks

Arms Control and Disarmament Agency
see U.S. Arms Control and Disarmament Agency

Arms trade
Criminal cases by type and disposition, and collections, for US attorneys, by Federal district, FY91, annual rpt, 6004–2.1
Criminal sentences for Federal offenses, guidelines by offense and circumstances, series, 17668–1
Debt to US of foreign govts and private obligors, by country and program, periodic rpt, 8002–6
Exports and imports between US and outlying areas, by detailed commodity and mode of transport, 1991, annual rpt, 2424–11
Exports and imports of US, by Harmonized System 6-digit commodity and country, 1991, annual rpt, 2424–13
Exports of US, detailed Schedule B commodities with countries of destination, 1991, annual rpt, 2424–10
Finances of Fed Govt, cash and debt transactions, daily tables, 8102–4
Foreign countries arms trade, for 32 countries, 1984-88, hearing, 25408–115
Foreign countries human rights conditions in 170 countries, and US economic and military aid, 1991, annual rpt, 21384–3
Foreign countries military aid of US, arms sales, and training, by country, FY50-91, annual rpt, 3904–3
Foreign countries military spending, arms trade, and force strengths, with govt spending and population, by country, 1979-89, annual rpt, 9824–1
Liabilities (contingent) and claims paid by Fed Govt on federally insured and guaranteed contracts with foreign obligors, by country and program, periodic rpt, 8002–12
Middle East arms trade and force strengths, and impacts of voluntary arms trade reductions, by country, mid 1960s-91 and projected to 2002, 26306–6.173
Sales of arms, military aid, and training programs of US, costs and budget requests, by program, world region, and country, FY91-93, annual rpt, 7144–13
Statistical Abstract of US, 1992 annual data compilation, 2324–1.11
Treaties and agreements on arms control, status and Arms Control and Disarmament Agency activities, 1991, annual rpt, 9824–2
see also Military assistance

Army
Accidents during training activities, and deaths by cause, by service branch, FY88-91, GAO rpt, 26123–397
Black military and civilian DOD personnel, by sex, grade, and period of service, and lists of award recipients, officers, and service academy grads, 1770s-90, 3548–22
Budget of DOD, organization, personnel, weapons, and property, by service branch, State, and country, 1992 annual summary rpt, 3504–13

Criminal case processing in military courts, and prisoners by facility, by service branch, data compilation, 1992 annual rpt, 6064–6.5
Deaths by cause, age, race, and rank, and personnel captured and missing, by service branch, FY91, annual rpt, 3544–40
Discrimination issues in Army, personnel, promotion, and training by race and sex, annual rpt, discontinued, 3704–10
Health care facilities of DOD in US and abroad, beds, admissions, outpatient visits, and births, by service branch, quarterly rpt, 3542–15
Helicopter (Apache) use and performance during Persian Gulf War, 1991, GAO rpt, 26123–378
Homosexual military personnel discharges by pay grade, tenure, race, sex, and occupation, and investigations, by service branch, 1980s-90, GAO rpt, 26123–392
Officers (line) accessions, involuntary separations, and strengths under alternative Army force reduction plans, FY90-95, 26306–3.121
Officers newly commissioned, share from service academies, and academy attrition, 1970s-91 and projected to FY97, GAO rpt, 26123–389
Persian Gulf War costs to US by category and service branch, and offsetting contributions by allied country, monthly rpt, 102–3
Persian Gulf War Operation Desert Storm deployment, by sex, race, rank, and service branch, 1990-91, GAO rpt, 26123–394
Personnel (civilian and military) of DOD, by service branch, major installation, and State, as of Sept 1991, annual rpt, 3544–7
Personnel active duty enlisted accessions by race, and goals, by sex and service branch, quarterly press release, 3542–7
Personnel, contracts, and payroll, by service branch and location, with top 5 contractors and maps, by State and country, FY91, annual rpt, 3544–29
Personnel needs, costs, and force readiness, by service branch, FY93, annual rpt, 3504–1
Personnel occupational distribution, by race, sex, and service branch, FY90, GAO rpt, 26123–381
Personnel reductions planned by service branch, and women and minorities affected by Army and Air Force plans, FY90-91, GAO rpt, 26123–373
Personnel reserve and active duty force mix and costs under alternative reduction cases, by service branch, 1990 and projected to 1997, 26306–6.172
Personnel strengths, for active duty, civilians, and dependents, by service branch and US and foreign location, quarterly rpt, 3542–20
Personnel strengths, for active duty, civilians, and reserves, by service branch, FY91 and trends, annual rpt, 3544–1
Personnel strengths, for active duty, civilians, and reserves, by service branch, quarterly rpt, 3542–14
Personnel strengths in US and abroad, by service branch, world area, and country, quarterly press release, 3542–9
Personnel strengths, summary by service branch, monthly press release, 3542–2
Reserve forces personnel and equipment strengths, and readiness, by reserve component, FY91, annual rpt, 3544–31
Reserve forces personnel strengths and characteristics, by component, quarterly rpt, 3542–4
Strategic capability of Army, force strengths, budget, and mgmt, FY79-93, annual rpt, 3704–13
Training and education programs of DOD, funding, staff, students, and facilities, by service branch, FY93, annual rpt, 3504–5
see also Army Corps of Engineers
see also Department of Army
see also National Guard

Army Corps of Engineers
Activities of Corps, FY90, annual rpt, 3754–1
Budget of US, obligations and authority by function, agency, and program, with summaries and analyses, FY93, annual rpt, 104–2
Columbia River Power System projects, plant investment allocation schedule, FY91, annual rpt, 3224–1
Dredging contracts of Corps to small businesses, costs and bidding activity, FY90-92, GAO rpt, 26113–589
Expenditures of Fed Govt in States, by type, program, agency, and State, FY91, annual rpt, 2464–2
Finances and operations of Federal power admins and electric utilities, 1990, annual rpt, 3164–24.2
Freight (waterborne domestic and foreign) by commodity, traffic, and passengers, by port and waterway, 1989, annual rpt, 3754–3
Freight (waterborne domestic and foreign), by port, 1990, annual rpt, 3754–7
Great Lakes and connecting channels water levels, and forecasts, semimonthly rpt, 3752–2
Great Lakes water levels and forecasts, and Corps flood prevention activities, monthly rpt and supplements, 3752–1
Hydroelectric power plants capacity and other characteristics, for western US, FY91, annual rpt, 3254–1
Ohio River basin waterway facilities, freight by commodity and port, and recreation, by waterway, 1988-89, annual rpt, 3754–6
Procurement, DOD prime contract awards by contractor, service branch, State, and city, FY91, annual rpt, 3544–22
Procurement, DOD prime contract awards in labor surplus areas, by service branch, State, and area, 1st half FY92, semiannual rpt, 3542–19
Recreation (outdoor) facilities of Corps, mgmt, acreage, visits, and non-Federal public and private dev alternatives, 1980s-90, 3758–8
Southeastern Fed Power Program financial statements, FY91, annual rpt, 3234–1
Water resources dev projects of Corps, characteristics, and costs, 1950s-89, biennial State rpt series, 3756–1
Water resources dev projects of Corps, characteristics, and costs, 1950s-91, biennial State rpt series, 3756–2
Water resources dev projects of Corps, local sponsors views on cooperation and cost sharing, 1991 survey, GAO rpt, 26113–548

Arnade, Carlos A.
"Productivity of Brazilian Agriculture: Measurement and Uses", 1528–331

Arnett, Margaret W.
"Savannah River Site Environmental Report for 1991", 3324–2.15

Arnold, Carolyn L.
"School Effects on Educational Achievement in Mathematics and Science", 4896–6.7

Arnsberger, Paul
"Charities and Other Tax-Exempt Organizations, 1988", 8302–2.315

Arrest
Airport security operations to prevent hijacking, screening results, enforcement actions, and hijacking attempts, 1990, annual rpt, 7504–49
Aliens (illegal) apprehended, deported, and required to depart from US, 1892-1991, annual rpt, 6264–2.5
Aliens (illegal) apprehended, deported, and required to depart from US, 1921-1990, annual summary rpt, 6264–7
Aliens (illegal) apprehensions and Border Patrol agent shifts, mid 1980s-91, working paper, 6366–6.9
Arrests and criminal case processing, by offense, offender characteristics, and location, data compilation, 1992 annual rpt, 6064–6.4; 6064–6.5
Arrests and rates, by offense, offender characteristics, population size, and jurisdiction, 1991, annual rpt, 6224–2.1; 6224–2.2
Coast Guard enforcement activities, 1st half FY92, semiannual rpt, 7402–4
Counterfeiting and other Secret Service investigations and arrests by type, and dispositions, FY91 and trends from FY82, annual rpt, 8464–1
Drug (illegal) production, eradication, and seizures, by substance, with US aid, by country, 1988-92, annual rpt, 7004–17
Drug abuse and trafficking reduction programs activities, funding, staff, and Bush Admin budget request, by Federal agency, FY91-93, annual rpt, 234–2
Drug abuse indicators for selected metro areas, research results, data collection, and policy issues, 1992 semiannual conf, 4492–5
Drug control street-level task forces enforcement activities, impacts on crime, and residents views, local area studies, 1992 rpt, 6068–251
Drug test results at arrest, by drug type, offense, and sex, for selected urban areas, quarterly rpt, 6062–3
Drunk driving arrests, sentencing, and prisoner drinking patterns and other characteristics, 1989, 6066–19.69
Felony case processing from arrest to sentencing, cases and duration by disposition and offense, for selected cities, 1988, annual rpt, 6064–27

Foreign countries human rights conditions in 170 countries, 1991, annual rpt, 21384–3
Fraud and forgery arrests, case dispositions, and sentencing, by age, sex, race, and offense type, 1983-88, 6066–19.64
Juvenile arrests, by sex, race, disposition, and offense, 1990, 6066–27.8
Juvenile facilities population, by resident characteristics and facility type, late 1970s-89, 6068–250
Juvenile facilities population, by resident characteristics and facility type, 1977-89, annual rpt, 6064–35
Law enforcement officer assaults and deaths by circumstances, agency, victim and offender characteristics, and location, 1990, annual rpt, 6224–3
LSD trafficking, abuse, and enforcement, and DEA field div activities, 1980s-91, 6288–9
Marijuana crop eradication activities of DEA and local agencies by State, and drug potency and prices, 1982-91, annual rpt, 6284–4
Marshals Service activities, FY91, annual rpt, 6294–1
Postal Service inspection activities, 2nd half FY92, semiannual rpt, 9862–2
Probation population, by offender characteristics, sentence conditions, whether rearrested, and offense, 1986-89, 6066–19.65
States criminal justice systems activities, employment, funding, and data collection, by State, 1970s-91, annual rpt, 6064–40
Statistical Abstract of US, 1992 annual data compilation, 2324–1.5
Warrants issued for search and arrest, caseloads of Federal district courts, by circuit and district, 1991, annual rpt, 18204–8.26
Wiretaps authorized, costs, arrests, trials, and convictions, by offense and jurisdiction, 1991, annual rpt, 18204–7
Women arrestees drug abuse history and selected other characteristics, for 4 cities, 1988-89, 6068–246
see also Pretrial detention and release

Arriaga, Eduardo
"Excess Mortality in Guatemala: A Comparison of Causes of Death in Guatemala and Costa Rica", 2326–18.64

Arson
Bombing incidents and casualties, by target, circumstances, and State, 1987-91, annual rpt, 8484–4.1
Bombing incidents, casualties, and damage, by target, circumstances, and State, 1991, annual rpt, 6224–5
Court criminal case processing in Federal district courts, and dispositions, by offense, district, and offender characteristics, 1989, annual data compilation, 6064–29
Court criminal case processing in Federal district courts, and dispositions, by offense, 1980-91, annual rpt, 6064–31
Crime, criminal justice admin and enforcement, and public opinion, data compilation, 1992 annual rpt, 6064–6
Crime Index by population size and region, and offenses by large city, 1st half 1992, semiannual rpt, 6222–1
Crimes, arrests, and rates, by offense, offender characteristics, population size, and jurisdiction, 1991, annual rpt, 6224–2.1; 6224–2.2
Homicides, by circumstance, victim and offender relationship, and type of weapon, 1991, annual rpt, 6224–2.1
Incidents of arson, civilian and fire fighter casualties, and property damage, 1986-89, 9438–14
Juvenile arrests, by sex, race, disposition, and offense, 1990, 6066–27.8
Prison and parole admissions and releases, sentence length, and time served, by offense and offender characteristics, 1988, annual rpt, 6064–33
Prisoners in Federal and contract instns, by selected characteristics, region, and Federal instn, FY89, annual rpt, 6244–1.1
Sentences for Federal offenses, guidelines by offense and circumstances, series, 17668–1
Statistical Abstract of US, 1992 annual data compilation, 2324–1.5
Terrorism (intl) incidents, casualties, and attacks on US targets, by attack type and country, 1991, annual rpt, 7004–22
Terrorism (intl) incidents, casualties, and attacks on US targets, by attack type and world area, 1991, annual rpt, 7004–13
Terrorism incidents in US, related activity, and casualties, by attack type, target, group, and location, 1991, annual rpt, 6224–6
Wildfires and acreage burned, by type of land, ownership, cause, region, and State, 1984-90, annual rpt, 1204–4
Wiretaps authorized, costs, arrests, trials, and convictions, by offense and jurisdiction, 1991, annual rpt, 18204–7
Women in jail, by criminal background and sociodemographic characteristics, with comparisons to men, 1989, 6066–19.66

Art
Copyrights Register activities, registrations by material type, and fees, FY91 and trends from 1790, annual rpt, 26404–2
Exports and imports between US and outlying areas, by detailed commodity and mode of transport, 1991, annual rpt, 2424–11
Exports and imports of US, by country and detailed commodity, monthly rpt, 2422–12
Exports and imports of US, by Harmonized System 6-digit commodity and country, 1991, annual rpt, 2424–13
Exports, imports, tariffs, and industry operating data for paints and inks, 1992 rpt, 9885–11.3
Exports of US, detailed Schedule B commodities with countries of destination, 1991, annual rpt, 2424–10
Injuries from use of consumer products, by severity, victim age, and detailed product, 1991, annual rpt, 9164–6
Labor demand, turnover, and training completions, by detailed occupation, 1990 and projected to 2005, biennial rpt, 6744–3
Library of Congress activities, acquisitions, services, and financial statements, FY91, annual rpt, 26404–1
Natl Endowment for Arts activities and grants, FY91, annual rpt, 9564–3
Occupational Outlook Handbook, 1992-93, biennial rpt, 6744–1
OECD trade, total and for 4 major countries, and US trade by country, by commodity, 1980-90, world area rpt series, 9116–1
Statistical Abstract of US, 1992 annual data compilation, 2324–1.7
Tariff Schedule of US, classifications and rates of duty by detailed imported commodity, 1993 base edition, 9886–13
see also Antiques

Artificial fibers
see Synthetic fibers and fabrics

Artificial foods
see Synthetic food products

Artificial satellites
see Communications satellites
see Meteorological satellites
see Satellites

Artificial sweeteners
see Syrups and sweeteners

Arts and the humanities
Degree (PhD) recipients in higher education, by field and selected characteristics, 1979, 1984, and 1989, 4848–44
Degrees awarded in higher education, by level, field, race, and sex, 1989/90 and trends from 1980/81, annual rpt, 4844–17
Education data compilation, 1992 annual rpt, 4824–2
Education natl goals progress indicators, by State, 1992, annual rpt, 15914–1
Govt funding for arts, by level of govt, State, and selected city, FY86-92, GAO rpt, 26119–371
Vocational education enrollment, and academic and other credits earned, by subject and student characteristics, high school classes of 1982 and 1987, 4838–50
see also Architecture
see also Art
see also Cultural activities
see also Dance
see also Federal aid to arts and humanities
see also Foreign languages
see also Language arts
see also Motion pictures
see also Museums
see also Music
see also Performing arts
see also Photography and photographic equipment
see also Social sciences
see also Theater

Aruba
Agricultural trade of US, by detailed commodity and country, 1991, semiannual rpt, 1522–4
Economic and social conditions, resources, and trade, and aid, 1992, annual factbook, 9914–14
Economic, social, political, and geographic summary data, by country, 1992, annual factbook, 9114–2
Exports and imports of US, by transport mode, country, and SITC 1- to 3-digit commodity, 1991, annual rpt, 2424–12
Exports of US, detailed Schedule B commodities with countries of destination, 1991, annual rpt, 2424–10
Population size, growth rates, and components of change, by country, projected 1990-2020 and trends from 1950, biennial rpt, 2324–9

Asbestos contamination
Carcinogens chemistry, sources, environment and health risks, and regulation, by substance and brand, 1991 annual rpt, 4044–15
Deaths from selected occupational diseases, for men by age group, 1970s-89, annual data compilation, 4144–11
Fed Govt asbestos trust fund financial condition, monthly rpt, 8102–9.13
Industrial hazardous substances releases and reduction methods under EPA regulation, by chemical, source, industry, and location, 1989, annual rpt, 9234–6
Industrial hazardous substances releases and reduction methods under EPA regulation, with chemical stocks and use, facility directory, 1987-89, annual CD-ROM, 9234–7
Schools asbestos contamination, abatement funding and costs by selected State, 1988-91, GAO rpt, 26113–560
Schools asbestos contamination, inspection and abatement effectiveness, staff and parental notification, and inspector and janitorial training, as of 1990, 9238–71
Torts for product liability, asbestos-related personal injury caseload in Federal district courts, 1991, annual rpt, 18204–8.14; 18204–8.18; 18204–11
Vermiculite with asbestos contamination, sources, human intake, and regulation, 1992 rpt, 9186–8.37

ASEAN
see Association of Southeast Asian Nations

Ash, Mark S.
"Animal Feeds Compendium", 1568–308
"U.S. Production Trends for High-Protein Soybean Meal", 1561–3.301

Ashby, Jack
"Trend and Distribution of Hospital Uncompensated Care Costs, 1980-89", 17206–2.32

Asia
Agricultural exports of US, for grains, oilseed products, hides, skins, and cotton, by country, weekly rpt, 1922–3
Agricultural trade by commodity and country, prices, and world market devs, monthly rpt, 1922–12
Agricultural trade of US, by commodity and country, bimonthly rpt, 1522–1
Agricultural trade of US, by detailed commodity and country, 1991, annual rpt, 1524–8
Agricultural trade of US, by detailed commodity and country, 1991, semiannual rpt, 1522–4
AID contracts and grants for technical and support services, by instn, country, and State, FY91, annual listing, 9914–7
AID economic aid to developing countries, obligations and disbursements by country, quarterly rpt, 9912–4
AID loans repayment status and terms by program and country, and status of predecessor agency loans, quarterly rpt, 9912–3
Air traffic and passengers, for intl routes over Pacific, by route, alternative forecasts 1992-2010 and trends from 1980, annual rpt, 7504–51
Cancer death rates, by body site, sex, and world area, 1969 and annual percent change 1969-86, article, 4472–1.306
Construction contract awards and billings, by country of contractor and world area of award, 1990, annual article, 2042–1.304
Dollar exchange rate trade-weighted index of Fed Reserve Bank of Atlanta, by world area, quarterly rpt, 9371–15
Dollar exchange rate trade-weighted index of Fed Reserve Bank of Dallas, by world area, monthly rpt, 9379–13
Drug abuse indicators, by world region and selected country, 1992 semiannual conf, 4492–5.2
Economic and military aid and loans from US and intl agencies, by program and country, FY46-91, annual rpt, 9914–5
Economic and social conditions of developing countries from 1960s, and Intl Dev Cooperation Agency and AID activities and funding, FY91-93, annual rpt, 9904–4
Energy supply and demand for Pacific basin, and implications for US trade, country rpt series, 3406–6
Export and import balances of US, and dollar exchange rates, with 5 Asian countries, 1992 semiannual rpt, 8002–14
Exports and imports (waterborne) of US, by type of service, customs district, port, and world area, monthly rpt, 2422–7
Exports and imports of China and other Asia countries with US, composition and trends, 1980s-91, article, 9385–1.303
Exports and imports of OECD, total and for 4 major countries, and US trade by country, by commodity, 1980-90, world area rpt, 9116–1.3
Exports and imports of US, by Harmonized System 6-digit commodity and country, 1991, annual rpt, 2424–13
Exports and imports of US, by selected country, country group, and commodity group, 1991, annual rpt, 2044–37
Exports and imports of US, by transport mode, country, and SITC 1- to 3-digit commodity, 1991, annual rpt, 2424–12
Exports, imports, and balances of US, by selected country, country group, and commodity group, preliminary data, monthly rpt, 2042–34
Exports, imports, and balances of US with major trading partners, by product category, 1987-91, annual chartbook, 9884–21
Family planning and population activities of AID, grants by project and recipient, and contraceptive shipments, by country, FY91, annual rpt series, 9914–13
Food supply, needs, and aid for developing countries, status and alternative forecasts, 1992 world area rpt, 1526–8.2
Heroin prices and purity in 19 metro areas and Puerto Rico, by world area of origin, quarterly rpt, 6282–2
Immigrant and nonimmigrant visas of US issued and refused, by class, issuing office, and nationality, FY90, annual rpt, 7184–1
Immigrants admitted to US, by class of admission, country of birth, and MSA of destination, FY91, advance annual rpt, 6264–4
Immigrants and legalized aliens, by occupational group and country of birth, preliminary FY91, annual tables, 6264–1
Immigrants and nonimmigrants admitted to US, alien workers, visitors, deportations, and naturalizations, FY91, annual summary rpt, 6264–7
Immigration to US, alien workers, visitors, deportations, and naturalizations, by country, FY91 and trends from 1820, annual rpt, 6264–2
Income tax returns of foreign corporations and individuals, and US entities abroad, detailed data compilation, 1970s-89, quinquennial rpt, 8308–31
Investment (foreign direct) of US, by industry group and world area, 1989-91, annual article, 2702–1.332
Labor costs (manufacturing) and productivity, by selected country, 1950s-91, press release, 6726–1.55
Labor costs and indexes, by selected country, 1991, semiannual rpt, 6822–3
Loans of US banks to foreigners at all US and foreign offices, by country group and country, quarterly rpt, 13002–1
Lumber (hardwood) exports of US to Europe and Asia, by species and country, 1981-90, 1208–373
Military aid of US, arms sales, and training, by country, FY50-91, annual rpt, 3904–3
Military aid of US, arms sales, and training programs costs and budget requests, by program, world region, and country, FY91-93, annual rpt, 7144–13
Military spending, arms trade, and force strengths, with govt spending and population, by country, 1979-89, annual rpt, 9824–1
Minerals Yearbook, Vol 3, 1989: foreign country review of production, trade, and policy, by commodity, annual rpt, 5604–35.2
Multinatl firms US affiliates finances and operations, by industry, country of parent firm, and State, 1987, 2708–48
Multinatl firms US affiliates, finances, and operations, by industry, world area of parent firm, and State, 1989-90, annual rpt, 2704–4
Multinatl US firms and foreign affiliates finances and operations, by industry and country, 1989 benchmark survey, annual rpt, 2704–5
Multinatl US firms foreign affiliates, income statement items by asset size, industry, and country, 1988, biennial article, 8302–2.322
Peace Corps activities, funding by program, and volunteers, by country, FY93, annual rpt, 9654–1
Population size, growth rates, and components of change, by country, projected 1990-2020 and trends from 1950, biennial rpt, 2324–9
Refugee arrivals in US by world area and country of origin, and quotas, monthly rpt, 7002–4
Refugee arrivals in US by world area of origin and State of settlement, and Federal aid, FY91-92 and proposed FY93 allocations, annual rpt, 7004–16
Refugee migration, and intl aid programs, by world area and country of origin and asylum, 1991, annual rpt, 7004–15
Steel trade, by product, country, and customs district, with US industry operating data, 1989-June 1992, semiannual rpt, 9882–15

Tax (income) returns for foreign corporate activity in US, selected income and tax items, by industry div and selected country, 1988, article, 8302–2.309
Terrorism (intl) incidents, casualties, and attacks on US targets, by attack type and country, 1991, annual rpt, 7004–22
Terrorism (intl) incidents, casualties, and attacks on US targets, by attack type and world area, 1991, annual rpt, 7004–13
Tidal currents, daily time and velocity by station for North America and Asia coasts, forecast 1993, annual rpt, 2174–1.2
Tide height and time daily at coastal points, forecast 1993, annual rpt, 2174–2.5
Travel to and from US, and travel receipts and payments, by world area, with data by country, 1985-90, annual rpt, 2904–10
Travel to and from US on US and foreign flag air carriers, by country, world area, and US port, monthly rpt, 7302–2
Travel to US, by characteristics of visit and traveler, country, port city, and State of destination, quarterly rpt, 2902–1
Travel to US, spending by world area of residence, and economic impact, by spending category and State, 1989, 2908–28
UN voting record and share of votes in agreement with US, by issue, country, and world area, 1991, annual rpt, 7004–18
US military and civilian personnel and dependents, by service branch, world area, and country, quarterly rpt, 3542–20
Weather conditions and effect on agriculture, by US region, State, and city, and world area, weekly rpt, 2182–7
Weather events and anomalies, precipitation and temperature for US and foreign locations, weekly rpt, 2182–6
Weather forecasts for US and Northern Hemisphere, precipitation and temperature by location, semimonthly rpt, 2182–1
see also Afghanistan
see also Asian Development Bank
see also Bahrain
see also Bangladesh
see also Bhutan
see also Brunei
see also Burma
see also Cambodia
see also China, Peoples Republic
see also Hong Kong
see also India
see also Indonesia
see also Iran
see also Iraq
see also Israel
see also Japan
see also Jordan
see also Kazakhstan
see also Korea, North
see also Korea, South
see also Kuwait
see also Kyrgyzstan
see also Laos
see also Lebanon
see also Macao
see also Malaysia
see also Maldives
see also Middle East
see also Mongolia
see also Myanmar
see also Nepal
see also Oman
see also Pakistan
see also Philippines
see also Qatar
see also Saudi Arabia
see also Singapore
see also Southeast Asia
see also Sri Lanka
see also Syria
see also Taiwan
see also Tajikistan
see also Thailand
see also Turkey
see also Turkmenistan
see also United Arab Emirates
see also Uzbekistan
see also Vietnam
see also Yemen
see also Yemen, North
see also Yemen, South
see also under By Foreign Country in the "Index by Categories"

Asian Americans
AIDS cases by risk group, race, sex, age, State, and MSA, and deaths, quarterly rpt, 4202–9
Arrests and prisoners, by offense, offender characteristics, and location, data compilation, 1992 annual rpt, 6064–6.4; 6064–6.6
Arrests, by offense, offender characteristics, and location, 1991, annual rpt, 6224–2.2
Business mgmt and financial aid from Minority Business Dev Centers, and characteristics of businesses, by region and State, FY91, annual rpt, 2104–6
Census of Population and Housing, 1990: data summary, use, and availability, fact sheet, 2326–23.2
Census of Population and Housing, 1990: detailed geographic coverage, State CD-ROM series, 2551–9
Census of Population and Housing, 1990: population and housing characteristics, detailed geographic coverage, State CD-ROM series, 2551–10
Census of Population and Housing, 1990: summary characteristics, households, and land area, by county, subdiv, and place, State rpt series, 2551–1
Census of Population, 1990: ancestry of US population, by group and State, press release, 2328–87
Census of Population, 1990: population characteristics and living arrangements, by county, place, and urban-rural location, State rpt series, 2531–1
Census of Population, 1990: population characteristics and living arrangements, for Native American, urban, and metro areas, series, 2531–2
Education data compilation, 1992 annual rpt, 4824–2
Education data, detail for elementary, secondary, and higher education, 1920s-91 and projected to 2002, annual rpt, 4824–1
Educational performance and conditions, characteristics, attitudes, activities, and plans, 1988 8th grade class, natl longitudinal survey, series, 4826–9
Educational performance of elementary and secondary students, and factors affecting proficiency, by selected characteristics, 1990 natl assessments, subject rpt series, 4896–8
Eighth grade class of 1988: Asian and Hispanic students proficiency in English and language at home, by selected characteristics, natl longitudinal survey, 1992 rpt, 4826–9.12
Employment of minorities and women, by occupation, SIC 1- to 3-digit industry, State, and MSA, 1991, annual rpt, 9244–1
Fed Equal Opportunity Recruitment Program activity, and employment by sex, race, pay grade, and occupational group, FY91, annual rpt, 9844–33
Fed Govt employment of minorities, disabled, and veterans, and years of service, by occupation, age, sex, and agency, as of Sept 1990, biennial rpt, 9844–27
FmHA loans, by type, borrower race, and State, quarterly rpt, 1182–5
Food aid program of USDA for women, infants, and children, participants by race, State, and Indian agency, 1991, annual rpt, 1364–16
Health care professionals supply and education, by professional and other characteristics, and location, 1960s-92 and projected to 2020, biennial rpt, 4114–8
Health condition and care indicators, 1950s-90 with health improvement and disease prevention goals for 1990, annual data compilation, 4144–11
Higher education degrees awarded, by level, field, race, and sex, 1989/90 and trends from 1980/81, annual rpt, 4844–17
Higher education enrollment, by level, race, and sex, fall 1980-90, biennial rpt, 4844–15
Higher education enrollment, by sex and race, 1976-2000, annual rpt, 4824–4
Housing census, 1990: summary unit characteristics, by householder race and age, county, place, and urban-rural location, State rpt series, 2471–1
Nuclear engineering enrollment and degrees granted by instn and State, and grad placement, by student characteristics, 1991, annual rpt, 3004–5
NYC housing supply, occupancy, condition, and household characteristics, by tenure and borough, 1991 triennial survey, 2488–3
Pacific territories population and housing detailed characteristics, by location, 1990 Census of Population and Housing, series, 2551–8
Population size, by race and Hispanic origin, 1992 and projected 2000-2050, press release, 2328–85
Population social and economic characteristics, for Asian and Pacific Islands Americans, for West and total US, 1990-91, Current Population Rpt, 2546–1.462
Prison and community-based facilities, population, employment, spending, and other characteristics, by State and for Fed Govt, 1990, quinquennial rpt, 6068–218
Prisoners, characteristics, and movements, by State, 1990, annual rpt, 6064–26
Radiation protection and health physics enrollment and degrees granted by instn and State, and grad placement, by student characteristics, 1991, annual rpt, 3004–7

Science and engineering employment and education of minorities, women, and disabled, by field, mid 1970s-91, biennial rpt, 9624–20
Science and engineering grad enrollment, by field, source of funds, and characteristics of student and instn, 1990, annual rpt, 9627–7
Science and Engineering Indicators, employment, education, R&D funding, and industry impacts, with foreign comparisons, 1960s-91, biennial rpt, 9624–10
State and local govt employment of minorities and women, by occupation, function, pay level, and State, 1991, annual rpt, 9244–6
Statistical Abstract of US, 1992 annual data compilation, 2324–1
see also Pacific Islands Americans
see also under By Race and Ethnic Group in the "Index by Categories"

Asian Development Bank
Loan activity by purpose and country, and funds by source, FY90, annual rpt, 15344–1.8
Loans and grants for economic and military aid from US and intl agencies, by program and country, FY46-91, annual rpt, 9914–5

Asphalt and tar
Business statistics, detailed data for major industries and economic indicators, 1960-91, *Survey of Current Business* biennial supplement, 2704–1
Carcinogens chemistry, sources, environment and health risks, and regulation, by substance and brand, 1991 annual rpt, 4044–15
Consumption of energy, by detailed fuel type, end-use sector, and State, 1960-90, State Energy Data System annual rpt, 3164–39
County Business Patterns, 1989: employment, establishments, and payroll, by SIC 2- to 4-digit industry and county, annual State rpt series, 2326–8
County Business Patterns, 1990: employment, establishments, and payroll, by SIC 2- to 4-digit industry and county, annual State rpt series, 2326–6
Exports and imports between US and outlying areas, by detailed commodity and mode of transport, 1991, annual rpt, 2424–11
Exports and imports of US, by Harmonized System 6-digit commodity and country, 1991, annual rpt, 2424–13
Exports of US, detailed Schedule B commodities with countries of destination, 1991, annual rpt, 2424–10
Freight (waterborne domestic and foreign) by commodity, traffic, and passengers, by port and waterway, 1989, annual rpt, 3754–3
Hwy construction material use by type, and spending, by State, 1940s-91, annual rpt, 7554–29
Lumber preservatives performance test results, by type, late 1930s-80s, 1208–391
Manufacturing annual survey, 1990: finances and operations, by SIC 2- to 4-digit industry, series, 2506–14
Manufacturing census, 1987: concentration of largest firms measured by value added, and for shipments by SIC 2- and 4-digit industry, subject rpt, 2497–6
Manufacturing census, 1987: shipments of manufacturers products, by customer class and SIC 2- and 4-digit industry, subject rpt, 2497–4
Occupational injury and illness rates, by SIC 2- to 4-digit industry, 1989-90, annual rpt, 6844–7
Occupational injury and illness rates, by SIC 2- to 4-digit industry, 1990, annual rpt, 6844–1
Pacific basin countries energy supply and demand, and implications for US trade, country rpt series, 3406–6
Price indexes (producer), by stage of processing and detailed commodity, monthly rpt, 6762–6
Price indexes (producer), by stage of processing and detailed commodity, monthly 1991, annual rpt, 6764–2
Price indexes (producer) for building materials, by type, quarterly rpt, 2042–1.5
Prices and spending for fuel, by type, end-use sector, and State, 1990, annual rpt, 3164–64
Production and sales of synthetic organic chemicals, and manufacturer listing, by product, 1990, annual rpt, 9884–3
Science, engineering, and technical employment in manufacturing, by field and industry, 1989, triennial rpt, 9627–23
Supply, demand, and movement of crude oil, gas liquids, and refined products, by PAD district and State, 1991, annual rpt, 3164–2
Supply, demand, trade, stocks, and refining of oil and gas liquids, by detailed product, State, and PAD district, monthly rpt with articles, 3162–6

Assassination
Terrorism (intl) incidents, casualties, and attacks on US targets, by attack type and country, 1991, annual rpt, 7004–22
Terrorism (intl) incidents, casualties, and attacks on US targets, by attack type and world area, 1991, annual rpt, 7004–13

Assault
Arrests and criminal case processing through sentencing, cases and duration by disposition and offense, for selected cities, 1988, annual rpt, 6064–27
Court civil and criminal caseloads for Federal district, appeals, and bankruptcy courts, by type of suit and offense, circuit, and district, 1991, annual rpt, 18204–11
Court civil and criminal caseloads for Federal district, appeals, and special courts, 1991, annual rpt, 18204–8
Court criminal case processing in Federal district courts, and dispositions, by offense, district, and offender characteristics, 1989, annual data compilation, 6064–29
Court criminal case processing in Federal district courts, and dispositions, by offense, 1980-91, annual rpt, 6064–31
Crime, criminal justice admin and enforcement, and public opinion, data compilation, 1992 annual rpt, 6064–6
Crime Index by population size and region, and offenses by large city, 1st half 1992, semiannual rpt, 6222–1
Crimes, arrests by offender characteristics, and rates, by offense, and law enforcement employees, by population size and jurisdiction, 1991, annual rpt, 6224–2
Drug test results at arrest, by drug type, offense, and sex, for selected urban areas, quarterly rpt, 6062–3
Juvenile arrests, by sex, race, disposition, and offense, 1990, 6066–27.8
Occupational deaths, by cause and industry div, 1990, annual rpt, 6844–1
Prison and parole admissions and releases, sentence length, and time served, by offense and offender characteristics, 1988, annual rpt, 6064–33
Prisoners in Federal and contract instns, by selected characteristics, region, and Federal instn, FY89, annual rpt, 6244–1.1
Prisoners in State and Federal instns, violations by type, 1990, quinquennial rpt, 6068–218
Probation population, by offender characteristics, sentence conditions, whether rearrested, and offense, 1986-89, 6066–19.65
Railroad accidents, casualties, and damage, by cause, railroad, and State, 1991, annual rpt, 7604–1
Sentences for Federal crimes, guidelines use and results by offense and district, and Sentencing Commission activities, 1991, annual rpt, 17664–1
Sentences for Federal offenses, guidelines by offense and circumstances, series, 17668–1
States criminal justice systems activities, employment, funding, and data collection, by State, 1970s-91, annual rpt, 6064–40
Terrorism (intl) incidents, casualties, and attacks on US targets, by attack type and country, 1991, annual rpt, 7004–22
Terrorism (intl) incidents, casualties, and attacks on US targets, by attack type and world area, 1991, annual rpt, 7004–13
Victimization rates, by victim and offender characteristics, circumstances, and offense, survey rpt series, 6066–3
Victimizations, by offense and whether reported to police, 1990-91, press release, 6068–249
Victimizations of households, by offense, household characteristics, and location, 1975-91, annual rpt, 6066–25.49
Victims of crime, compensation and support service programs funding, by offense and State, FY88-90, biennial rpt, 6064–37
Women in jail, by criminal background and sociodemographic characteristics, with comparisons to men, 1989, 6066–19.66
see also Assaults on police
see also Domestic violence

Assaults on police
Assaults and deaths of law enforcement officers, by circumstances, agency, victim and offender characteristics, and location, 1991, annual rpt, 6224–3
Assaults and deaths of law enforcement officers, by circumstances, and offender characteristics, data compilation, 1992 annual rpt, 6064–6.3

Statistical Abstract of US, 1992 annual data compilation, 2324–1.5

Assets and liabilities

see Business assets and liabilities, general
see Business assets and liabilities, specific industry
see Business inventories
see Foreign debts
see Government assets and liabilities
see International reserves
see Personal debt
see Wealth

Association of Southeast Asian Nations

Background Notes, ASEAN history, structure, and programs, 1992 rpt, 7006–2.18
Exports and imports of US by country, and trade shifts by commodity, 1991, annual rpt, 9884–25
Exports, imports, membership, and trade impacts of regional preferential trading arrangements, by group, late 1940s-91, article, 9373–1.308
UN voting record and share of votes in agreement with US, by issue, country, and world area, 1991, annual rpt, 7004–18

Associations

County Business Patterns, 1989: employment, establishments, and payroll, by SIC 2- to 4-digit industry and county, annual State rpt series, 2326–8
County Business Patterns, 1990: employment, establishments, and payroll, by SIC 2- to 4-digit industry and county, annual State rpt series, 2326–6
Election campaign-related internal communications of firms and assns, spending by organization, location, and candidate, 1991-92, biennial rpt, 9274–3
Electric utilities conservation programs, collaboration between utilities and interest groups, and effects on costs, 1992 rpt, 3308–104
Employment, earnings, and hours, by SIC 1- to 4-digit industry, monthly 1989-Feb 1992, annual rpt, 6744–4
Health care facilities excluded from Medicare prospective payment system, quality standards and review, certification, accreditation, and licensing, 1991 survey, 17206–2.41
Homeowner assns fees paid, MSA surveys, series, 2485–6
Housing (public and Indian) tenant assns, HUD project mgmt and operation training grants by recipient, FY91, press release, 5006–3.77
Housing (public and Indian) tenant assns, HUD project mgmt and operation training grants by recipient, FY92, press release, 5006–3.100
Input-output structure of US economy, detailed interindustry transactions for 541 industries, and components of final demand, 1982 benchmark data, 2708–17
Lumber and wood products export market dev, assn listing, FAS periodic circular, supplement, 1925–36
Tax (income) returns of corporations, income and tax items by asset size and detailed industry, 1989, annual rpt, 8304–4; 8304–21
see also Cooperatives
see also Credit unions
see also Labor unions
see also Membership organizations
see also Nonprofit organizations and foundations
see also Political action committees
see also Rural cooperatives
see also Tax exempt organizations
see also under By Individual Company or Institution in the "Index by Categories"

Astronautics

see Astronauts
see Communications satellites
see Meteorological satellites
see Satellites
see Space program accidents and safety
see Space programs
see Space sciences

Astronauts

NASA project launch schedules and technical descriptions, press release series, 9506–2
Spacecraft launches and other activities of NASA and USSR, with flight data, 1957-91, annual rpt, 9504–6.1

Astronomy

Fed Govt aid to higher education and nonprofit instns for R&D and related activities, by field, instn, agency, and State, FY90, annual rpt, 9627–17
Higher education grad programs enrollment in science and engineering, by field, source of funds, and characteristics of student and instn, 1990, annual rpt, 9627–7
NASA project launch schedules and technical descriptions, press release series, 9506–2
NASA R&D funding to higher education instns, by field, instn, and State, FY91, annual listing, 9504–7
Occupational Outlook Handbook, 1992-93, biennial rpt, 6744–1
Planetary space probe findings, and NASA activities and finances, 1957-91, annual rpt, 9504–6.1
R&D funding by higher education instns and federally funded centers, by field, instn, and State, FY90, annual rpt, 9627–13
Science and Engineering Indicators, employment, education, R&D funding, and industry impacts, with foreign comparisons, 1960s-91, biennial rpt, 9624–10
Star position tables, planet coordinates, time conversion factors, and listing of observatories worldwide, 1993, annual rpt, 3804–7

AT&T

see American Telephone and Telegraph Co.

Atherton, Joan

"AID Economic Policy Reform Program in Uganda", 9916–1.77

Athletics

see Physical education and training
see Sporting goods
see Sports and athletics

Atlanta, Ga.

CPI by component for US city average, and by selected metro area, region, and population size, monthly rpt, 6762–2
Drug abuse indicators for selected metro areas, research results, data collection, and policy issues, 1992 semiannual conf, 4492–5
Drug test results at arrest, by drug type, offense, and sex, for selected urban areas, quarterly rpt, 6062–3
Fruit and vegetable shipments, and arrivals by city, by mode of transport and State and country of origin, 1991, annual rpt, 1311–4.1
Heroin prices and purity in 19 metro areas and Puerto Rico, by world area of origin, quarterly rpt, 6282–2
Housing and households characteristics, and unit and neighborhood quality, by MSA location for 11 MSAs, 1987 survey, supplement, 2485–8
Housing rental and sales, discrimination against blacks and Hispanics in selected metro areas, 1989 study, 5186–16.2
Housing starts and completions authorized by building permits in 40 MSAs, quarterly rpt, 2382–9
State and local govt employees wages by occupation, and benefits, 1991 survey, periodic MSA rpt, 6785–15.1
see also under By City and By SMSA or MSA in the "Index by Categories"

Atlantic City, N.J.

Wages by occupation, and benefits for office and plant workers, 1992 survey, periodic MSA rpt, 6785–3.6
see also under By City and By SMSA or MSA in the "Index by Categories"

Atlantic Ocean

Air traffic and passengers, for intl routes over north Atlantic, by aviation type and route, alternative forecasts 1992-2010 and trends from 1982, annual rpt, 7504–44
Coastal areas environmental conditions and mgmt, for individual areas, conf series, 2146–8
Environmental summary data, and intl claims and disputes, 1992 annual factbook, 9114–2
Fish (billfish) tagged and recovered by location, and Japan catch in US waters, 1950-90, annual rpt, 2164–7
Fish (game) tagging and research activities, by species, 1990, annual rpt, 2164–24
Fish (striped bass) stocks status on Atlantic coast, and sport and commercial catch by State, 1979-90, annual rpt, 5504–29
Fish and shellfish catch and stocks in northwest Atlantic, by species and location, 1887-1991 and forecast to 1993, semiannual conf, 2162–9
Fish and shellfish distribution in Atlantic Ocean, bottom trawl survey results by species and location, periodic rpt series, 2164–18
Fish and shellfish resources and catch, marine mammal and sea turtle population, and mgmt, by species and region, 1988-90, annual rpt, 2164–22
Fish catch, trade, use, and fishery operations, with selected foreign data, by species, 1980s-91, annual rpt, 2164–1
Fishing (ocean sport) activities, and catch by species, by angler characteristics and State, 1990-91, annual coastal area rpt, 2166–17.1
Freight (waterborne domestic and foreign) by commodity, traffic, and passengers, by port and waterway, 1989, annual rpt, 3754–3.1
Hurricanes and tropical storms in north Atlantic Ocean, characteristics, 1991, annual article, 2152–8.302

Hurricanes in northwest Atlantic Ocean, correlation with Sahel Africa rainfall, 1947-90, 2148–61
Marine Fisheries Review, US and foreign fisheries resources, dev, mgmt, and research, quarterly journal, 2162–1
Marine Mammal Protection Act admin, and populations, strandings, and catch permits by species and location, 1988-89, annual rpt, 2164–11
Mariners Weather Log, quarterly journal, 2152–8
Oil and gas OCS reserves of Fed Govt, leasing and exploration activity, production, revenue, and costs, by ocean area, FY91, annual rpt, 5734–4
Port improvement capital expenditures and financing methods, by region and selected port, 1946-89, 7708–6
Research activities of Atlantic Oceanographic and Meteorological Lab, and bibl, FY91, annual rpt, 2144–19
Sharks and other fish tagged and recovered, by species, 1991, annual rpt, 2164–21
Shellfish harvest in estuaries, approved and restricted areas, and pollution sources, by estuary, State, and coastal region, 1990, quinquennial rpt, 2178–33
Temperature of sea surface by ocean and for US coastal areas, and Bering Sea ice conditions, monthly rpt, 2182–5
Tidal currents, daily time and velocity by station for North America coasts, forecast 1993, annual rpt, 2174–1.1
Tide height and time daily at coastal points, forecast 1993, annual rpt, 2174–2.3; 2174–2.4
Weather (marine) forecast areas, and broadcast schedules and stations worldwide, as of Sept 1992, annual rpt, 2184–3
Weather (marine) forecast broadcast schedules worldwide, periodic rpt, 2182–9
see also Caribbean area
see also New York Bight

Atlantic Oceanographic and Meteorological Laboratory
see National Oceanic and Atmospheric Administration

Atmospheric sciences
Atlantic Oceanographic and Meteorological Lab research activities and bibl, FY91, annual rpt, 2144–19
Carbon dioxide in atmosphere, DOE R&D programs and funding at natl labs, universities, and other instns, FY92, annual summary rpt, 3004–18.10
DOE R&D projects and funding at natl labs, universities, and other instns, FY91, annual summary rpt, 3004–18.4
Fed Govt aid to higher education and nonprofit instns for R&D and related activities, by field, instn, agency, and State, FY90, annual rpt, 9627–17
Global climate change contributing pollutants, emissions by monitoring site and country, and temperature change by world area and US region, 1860s-1990, annual rpt, 3004–33
Great Lakes Environmental Research Lab activities, FY91 annual rpt, 2144–26
Higher education grad programs enrollment in science and engineering, by field, source of funds, and characteristics of student and instn, 1990, annual rpt, 9627–7
NASA R&D funding to higher education instns, by field, instn, and State, FY91, annual listing, 9504–7
Pacific Marine Environmental Lab research activities and bibl, FY91, annual rpt, 2144–21
R&D funding by higher education instns and federally funded centers, by field, instn, and State, FY90, annual rpt, 9627–13
see also Meteorology

ATMs
see Automated tellers

Atomic bombs
see Nuclear explosives and explosions
see Nuclear weapons

Atomic energy
see Nuclear power

Attitudes
see Opinion and attitude surveys

Attorneys-at-law
see Lawyers and legal services

Audiology
see Ear diseases and infections
see Hearing and hearing disorders
see Speech pathology and audiology

Audiovisual education
see Educational broadcasting

Auditing
see Accounting and auditing

Auerbach, Alan J.
"Social Security and Medicare Policy from the Perspective of Generational Accounting", 9377–9.137

Augusta, Ga.
see also under By City and By SMSA or MSA in the "Index by Categories"

Aul, Jay C.
"Evaluation of an Alternative Method for Hiring Air Traffic Control Specialists with Prior Military Experience", 7506–10.101

Aurora, Ill.
see also under By City and By SMSA or MSA in the "Index by Categories"

Austin, Tex.
Wages by occupation, and benefits for office and plant workers, 1992 survey, periodic MSA rpt, 6785–3.4
see also under By City and By SMSA or MSA in the "Index by Categories"

Australia
Agricultural production, prices, and trade, by country, 1980s and forecast 1992, annual world region rpt, 1524–4.3
Agricultural trade of US, by detailed commodity and country, 1991, annual rpt, 1524–8
Agricultural trade of US, by detailed commodity and country, 1991, semiannual rpt, 1522–4
Cancer (invasive melanoma) cases in Queensland, Australia, by sex, 1979/80 and 1987, article, 4472–1.344
Cuba trade, by commodity and country, mid 1980s-91, 9118–8
Economic and military aid and loans from US and intl agencies, by program and country, FY46-91, annual rpt, 9914–5
Economic and monetary trends, compounded annual rates of change and annual indicators for US and 15 trading partners, quarterly rpt, annual supplement, 9391–7
Economic and social conditions of developing countries from 1960s, and Intl Dev Cooperation Agency and AID activities and funding, FY91-93, annual rpt, 9904–4
Economic conditions, policy, and trade practices, by country, 1989-91, annual rpt, 21384–5
Economic, social, political, and geographic summary data, by country, 1992, annual factbook, 9114–2
Exports and imports (waterborne) of US, by type of service, customs district, port, and world area, monthly rpt, 2422–7
Exports and imports of US, by Harmonized System 6-digit commodity and country, 1991, annual rpt, 2424–13
Exports and imports of US, by selected country, country group, and commodity group, 1991, annual rpt, 2044–37
Exports and imports of US, by transport mode, country, and SITC 1- to 3-digit commodity, 1991, annual rpt, 2424–12
Exports, imports, and balances of US for manufactured goods, by SITC 2-digit commodity and country, quarterly rpt, 2042–35
Exports of US, detailed Schedule B commodities with countries of destination, 1991, annual rpt, 2424–10
Health care costs and components, services use, resources, and economic indicators, by OECD country, 1960s-90, article, 4652–1.322
Human rights conditions in 170 countries, and US economic and military aid, 1991, annual rpt, 21384–3
Import restrictions and trade protectionism measures of US, Australia, Canada, and EC, cases initiated, 1980-85, article, 9379–1.301
Imports of goods, services, and investment from US, trade barriers, impacts, and US actions, by country, 1991, annual rpt, 444–2
Income (household) and wealth distribution by selected characteristics, with foreign comparisons, 1992 compilation of papers, Current Population Rpt, 2546–6.79
Labor conditions, union coverage, and work accidents, 1992 annual country rpt, 6366–4.18
Military spending, arms trade, and force strengths, with govt spending and population, by country, 1979-89, annual rpt, 9824–1
Minerals Yearbook, Vol 3, 1989: foreign country review of production, trade, and policy, by commodity, annual rpt, 5604–35.2
Multinatl firms US affiliates finances and operations, by industry, country of parent firm, and State, 1987, 2708–48
Multinatl firms US affiliates, finances, and operations, by industry, world area of parent firm, and State, 1989-90, annual rpt, 2704–4
Multinatl US firms and foreign affiliates finances and operations, by industry and country, 1989 benchmark survey, annual rpt, 2704–5
Multinatl US firms foreign affiliates, income statement items by asset size, industry, and country, 1988, biennial article, 8302–2.322
Oil exports to US by OPEC and non-OPEC countries, monthly rpt, 3162–24.3

Oil exports to US by OPEC and non-OPEC countries, monthly 1973-88, 3168–123.3
Oil production, stocks, use, and trade, by selected country and country group, monthly rpt, 3162–42
Oil supply, demand, and stock forecasts, by world area, quarterly rpt, 3162–34
Pollution (air) contributing to global warming, emissions by monitoring site and country, and temperature change by world area and US region, 1860s-1990, annual rpt, 3004–33
Population size, growth rates, and components of change, by country, projected 1990-2020 and trends from 1950, biennial rpt, 2324–9
Refugee migration, and intl aid programs, by world area and country of origin and asylum, 1991, annual rpt, 7004–15
Spacecraft and satellite launches since 1957, quarterly listing, 9502–2
Steel (carbon flat-rolled) products from 21 countries, injury to US industry from foreign subsidized and less than fair value imports, investigation with background financial and operating data, 1992 rpt, 9886–19.85
Steel imports of US under voluntary restraint agreement, by product, customs district, and country, with US industry operating data, quarterly rpt, 9882–13
Steel trade, by product, country, and customs district, with US industry operating data, 1989-June 1992, semiannual rpt, 9882–15
Tax (estate) returns for nonresident aliens, property and tax data, by estate size and decedent country of residence, 1986, article, 8302–2.310
Tax revenue, by level of govt and type of tax, for OECD countries, mid 1960s-90, annual rpt, 10044–1.2
UN voting record and share of votes in agreement with US, by issue, country, and world area, 1991, annual rpt, 7004–18
Weather conditions and effect on agriculture, by US region, State, and city, and world area, weekly rpt, 2182–7
Wine production, trade, use, and stocks for EC, and Australia and US exports by country, 1985-92, article, 1925–34.325
see also under By Foreign Country in the "Index by Categories"

Austria
Agricultural trade of US, by detailed commodity and country, 1991, annual rpt, 1524–8
Agricultural trade of US, by detailed commodity and country, 1991, semiannual rpt, 1522–4
AID loans repayment status and terms by program and country, and status of predecessor agency loans, quarterly rpt, 9912–3
Cuba trade, by commodity and country, mid 1980s-91, 9118–8
Economic and military aid and loans from US and intl agencies, by program and country, FY46-91, annual rpt, 9914–5
Economic and social conditions of developing countries from 1960s, and Intl Dev Cooperation Agency and AID activities and funding, FY91-93, annual rpt, 9904–4
Economic conditions, income, production, prices, employment, and trade, 1992 periodic country rpt, 2046–4.25
Economic conditions, policy, and trade practices, by country, 1989-91, annual rpt, 21384–5
Economic, social, political, and geographic summary data, by country, 1992, annual factbook, 9114–2
Exports and imports of US, by Harmonized System 6-digit commodity and country, 1991, annual rpt, 2424–13
Exports and imports of US, by selected country, country group, and commodity group, 1991, annual rpt, 2044–37
Exports and imports of US, by transport mode, country, and SITC 1- to 3-digit commodity, 1991, annual rpt, 2424–12
Exports, imports, and balances of US for manufactured goods, by SITC 2-digit commodity and country, quarterly rpt, 2042–35
Exports of US, detailed Schedule B commodities with countries of destination, 1991, annual rpt, 2424–10
Health care costs and components, services use, resources, and economic indicators, by OECD country, 1960s-90, article, 4652–1.322
Human rights conditions in 170 countries, and US economic and military aid, 1991, annual rpt, 21384–3
Labor conditions, union coverage, and work accidents, 1991 annual country rpt, 6366–4.3
Military spending, arms trade, and force strengths, with govt spending and population, by country, 1979-89, annual rpt, 9824–1
Multinatl US firms and foreign affiliates finances and operations, by industry and country, 1989 benchmark survey, annual rpt, 2704–5
Multinatl US firms foreign affiliates, income statement items by asset size, industry, and country, 1988, biennial article, 8302–2.322
Oil production, stocks, use, and trade, by selected country and country group, monthly rpt, 3162–42
Population size, growth rates, and components of change, by country, projected 1990-2020 and trends from 1950, biennial rpt, 2324–9
Refugee migration, and intl aid programs, by world area and country of origin and asylum, 1991, annual rpt, 7004–15
Steel (carbon flat-rolled) products from 21 countries, injury to US industry from foreign subsidized and less than fair value imports, investigation with background financial and operating data, 1992 rpt, 9886–19.85
Steel imports of US under voluntary restraint agreement, by product, customs district, and country, with US industry operating data, quarterly rpt, 9882–13
Steel trade, by product, country, and customs district, with US industry operating data, 1989-June 1992, semiannual rpt, 9882–15
Tax revenue, by level of govt and type of tax, for OECD countries, mid 1960s-90, annual rpt, 10044–1.2
UN voting record and share of votes in agreement with US, by issue, country, and world area, 1991, annual rpt, 7004–18
see also under By Foreign Country in the "Index by Categories"

Authors
see Writers and writing

Automated data processing
see Computer industry and products
see Computer use
see Information storage and retrieval systems

Automated tellers
Banks and thrifts finances and operations by deposit size, Fed Reserve functional cost analysis, 1991, annual rpt, 9364–6
Fees for ATM networks, by type and selected network, 1990, working paper, 9387–8.270
Service fees, minimum balances, and services offered by banks and thrifts, by service type, 1991, annual rpt, 9364–12

Automation
Air traffic control and airway facilities improvement activities under Aviation System Capital Investment Plan, 1981-91 and projected to 2006, annual rpt, 7504–12
Banks in Fed Reserve System, expenses and operations itemized by service, office, and district, 1991, annual rpt, 9364–11
Judicial Conf proceedings and findings, spring 1992, semiannual rpt, 18202–2
Labor force, composition, and productivity effects of technological devs, 1970s-90 and projected to 2005, industry rpt series, 6826–2
NSF R&D grant awards, by div and program, FY90, periodic rpt, 9626–7.3
Postal Service automation impacts on labor hours, by task, 1990-91 with projected use of selected equipment to 1995, GAO rpt, 26119–395
Technology transfer by Federal R&D labs to small manufacturers, promotional programs activities and grants to States, late 1980s-91, GAO rpt, 26113–551
Unemployed displaced workers, layoffs and recalls by layoff reason, industry, firm size, and State, 2nd half 1988, 6406–6.36
Unemployed displaced workers, layoffs and unemployment insurance claims by reason, industry, selected characteristics, and State, quarterly press release, 6742–23
Unemployed displaced workers, layoffs and unemployment insurance claims by reason, industry, selected characteristics, MSA, and State, 1990, annual rpt, 6744–18
see also Automated tellers
see also Computer industry and products
see also Computer networks
see also Computer use
see also Electronic funds transfer
see also Industrial robots
see also Information storage and retrieval systems

Automobile insurance
Consumer spending, natl income and product account benchmark revisions, 1929-88, 2708–5
Consumer spending, natl income and product accounts, comprehensive accounts and components, *Survey of Current Business*, monthly rpt, 2702–1.25

Costs of owning and operating autos, vans, and light trucks, by vehicle size and year of operation, 1991 model year, biennial rpt, 7554–21
Costs of owning and operating autos, 1980, 1985, and 1991, article, 1702–1.306
CPI by component for US city average, and by selected metro area, region, and population size, monthly rpt, 6762–2

Automobile parking
see Parking facilities

Automobile repair and maintenance
Collective bargaining agreements expiring during year, and workers covered, by firm, union, industry group, and State, 1992, annual rpt, 6784–9
Costs of owning and operating autos, vans, and light trucks, by vehicle size and year of operation, 1991 model year, biennial rpt, 7554–21
Costs of owning and operating autos, 1980, 1985, and 1991, article, 1702–1.306
County Business Patterns, 1989: employment, establishments, and payroll, by SIC 2- to 4-digit industry and county, annual State rpt series, 2326–8
County Business Patterns, 1990: employment, establishments, and payroll, by SIC 2- to 4-digit industry and county, annual State rpt series, 2326–6
CPI by component for US city average, and by selected metro area, region, and population size, monthly rpt, 6762–2
Employment, earnings, and hours, by SIC 1- to 4-digit industry, monthly 1989-Feb 1992, annual rpt, 6744–4
Input-output structure of US economy, detailed interindustry transactions for 84 industries, and components of final demand, 1987, annual article, 2702–1.316
Input-output structure of US economy, detailed interindustry transactions for 541 industries, and components of final demand, 1982 benchmark data, 2708–17
Labor productivity, indexes of output, hours, and employment by SIC 2- to 4-digit industry, 1967-90, annual rpt, 6824–1.4
Occupational injury and illness rates, by SIC 2- to 4-digit industry, 1989-90, annual rpt, 6844–7
Occupational injury and illness rates, by SIC 2- to 4-digit industry, 1990, annual rpt, 6844–1
Occupational Outlook Handbook, 1992-93, biennial rpt, 6744–1
Postal Service operating costs, itemized by class of mail, FY91, annual rpt, 9864–4
Tax (income) returns of corporations, income and tax items by asset size and detailed industry, 1989, annual rpt, 8304–4; 8304–21
Tax (income) returns of partnerships, income statement and balance sheet items, by industry group, 1990, annual article, 8302–2.314
Tax (income) returns of sole proprietorships, income statement items, by industry group, 1990, annual article, 8302–2.317; 8302–2.320

Automobiles
AFDC beneficiaries demographic and financial characteristics, by State, FY90, annual rpt, 4584–7
Arson cases, civilian and fire fighter casualties, and property damage, 1986-89, 9438–14
Arson incidents by whether structure occupied, property value, and arrest rate, by property type, 1991, annual rpt, 6224–2.1
Banks in Fed Reserve System, expenses and operations itemized by service, office, and district, 1991, annual rpt, 9364–11
Bombing incidents and casualties, by target, circumstances, and State, 1987-91, annual rpt, 8484–4.1
Bombing incidents, casualties, and damage, by target, circumstances, and State, 1991, annual rpt, 6224–5
Business statistics, detailed data for major industries and economic indicators, *Survey of Current Business*, monthly rpt, 2702–1.22
Business statistics, detailed data for major industries and economic indicators, 1960-91, *Survey of Current Business* biennial supplement, 2704–1
Census of Population and Housing, 1990: summary characteristics, by county, subdiv, and place, State rpt series, 2551–7
Commuting to work, by mode, trip duration, and work location, 1980 and 1990, 7558–120
Consumer Expenditure Survey, spending by category, and income, by selected household characteristics, 1991, annual press release, 6726–1.53
Consumer holdings of durable goods, by type, in current and constant dollars, 1925-90, annual article, 2702–1.305
Consumer holdings of durable goods, by type, in current and constant dollars, 1988-91, annual article, 2702–1.327
Costs of owning and operating autos, vans, and light trucks, by vehicle size and year of operation, 1991 model year, biennial rpt, 7554–21
Costs of owning and operating autos, 1980, 1985, and 1991, article, 1702–1.306
CPI by component for US city average, and by selected metro area, region, and population size, monthly rpt, 6762–2
Electric-powered autos, R&D activity and DOE funding shares, FY91, annual rpt, 3304–2
Energy economy and miles traveled per car, monthly rpt, annual data, 3162–24.1
Energy economy performance of autos and light trucks by make, standards, and enforcement, 1978-94 model years, annual rpt, 7764–9
Energy economy test results for US and foreign makes, 1993 model year, annual rpt, 3304–11
Energy use and vehicle registrations, by vehicle type, 1960-91, annual rpt, 3164–74.1
Energy use by fuel type, and miles traveled, by transport mode, projected 1990-2010 and trends from 1960s, 3008–124
Energy use by mode of transport, fuel supply, and demographic and economic factors of vehicle use, 1970s-90, annual rpt, 3304–5
Families financial status, income, net worth, and assets and debt by type, by income and selected characteristics, 1983 and 1989, article, 9362–1.301
Farm prices received and paid, by commodity and State, monthly rpt, 1629–1
Farm production itemized costs, by farm sales size and region, 1991, annual rpt, 1614–3
Freight (waterborne domestic and foreign) by commodity, traffic, and passengers, by port and waterway, 1989, annual rpt, 3754–3
Households and housing characteristics, MSA surveys, fact sheet series, 2485–11
Households net worth distribution under alternative sample weighting systems to account for inconsistency in survey design and response rates, 1992 rpt, 9368–91
Households with autos and trucks available, for rental units and units receiving and eligible for HUD assistance, by location, 1989, biennial rpt, 5184–11
Households with autos and trucks available, MSA surveys, series, 2485–6
Households with autos available, by selected State, 1980 and 1990, 7558–120
Housing and population census, 1990: population and housing characteristics, detailed geographic coverage, State CD-ROM series, 2551–10
Hwy Statistics, detailed data by State, 1991, annual rpt, 7554–1
Hwy Statistics, summary data by State, 1990-91, annual rpt, 7554–24
Hwy Statistics, summary data with trends and projections, 1992 chartbook, 7554–41
Hwy traffic volume on rural roads and city streets, monthly rpt, 7552–8
Input-output structure of US economy, detailed interindustry transactions for 541 industries, and components of final demand, 1982 benchmark data, 2708–17
Loan activity of savings instns insured by Savings Assn Insurance Fund by FHLB district and State, and for FDIC-insured savings banks, 1989, annual rpt, 8434–1
Loans (consumer) of banks, relation to bank-auto finance company interest rate spread, tax reform, and other factors, 1970s-91, working paper, 9379–12.88
Loans for autos, monthly rpt, 23842–1.5
Loans for autos outstanding, *Survey of Current Business*, monthly rpt, 2702–1.8
Loans for new and used autos, banks and thrifts offering loans, and fees, 1991, annual rpt, 9364–12
Loans of banks and finance companies, rates, terms, and related data, monthly rpt series, 9365–2
Natl income and product accounts and components, *Survey of Current Business*, monthly rpt, 2702–1.23
Natl income and product accounts, comprehensive accounts and components, benchmark revisions, 1929-88, 2708–5
Natl income and product accounts, comprehensive accounts and components, *Survey of Current Business*, monthly rpt, 2702–1.24; 2702–1.31
Older autos retirement programs proposals costs, savings, and emissions and energy use reductions, 1992 rpt, 26358–263
Pacific territories population and housing detailed characteristics, by location, 1990 Census of Population and Housing, series, 2551–8

Population economic well-being indicators, by selected characteristics and household income and income-to-poverty ratio, 1984, 2546–20.22
Price indexes (producer), by stage of processing and detailed commodity, monthly rpt, 6762–6
Price indexes (producer), by stage of processing and detailed commodity, monthly 1991, annual rpt, 6764–2
Prices received and paid by farmers, by commodity and State, 1991, annual rpt, 1629–5
Quality changes in autos since last model year, factory and retail value, 1993 model year, annual press release, 6764–3
Recalls of motor vehicles and equipment with safety-related defects, by make, monthly listing, 7762–12
Recalls of motor vehicles and equipment with safety-related defects, by make, quarterly listing, 7762–2
Retail trade sales and inventories, by kind of business, region, and selected State, MSA, and city, monthly rpt, 2413–3
Retail trade sales, by kind of business, advance monthly rpt, 2413–2
Retail trade sales, inventories, purchases, gross margin, and accounts receivable, by SIC 2- to 4-digit kind of business and form of ownership, 1990, annual rpt, 2413–5
Sales and prices for domestic and import autos and trucks, and auto production and inventories, 1992 model year, annual article, 2702–1.339
Sales and production of US auto industry and Japanese assembly plants in US, and imports, 1979-90, article, 6722–1.313
Sales of domestic and imported cars, monthly rpt, quarterly data, 23842–1.1
Soviet Union and US economic and sociodemographic indicators, selected years 1970-90, handbook, 2328–80
Statistical Abstract of US, 1992 annual data compilation, 2324–1.21
Tax (excise) collections of IRS, by source, quarterly rpt, 8302–1; 8302–2.1
Tax (luxury) revenue, and related IRS administrative costs, FY91 and projected to FY95, GAO rpt, 26119–385
Travel patterns, personal and household characteristics, and auto and public transport use, 1990 survey, series, 7556–6
Travel to US, spending by world area of residence, and economic impact, by spending category and State, 1989, 2908–28
Wholesale trade sales and inventories, by SIC 2- to 3-digit kind of business, monthly rpt, 2413–7
see also Automobile insurance
see also Automobile repair and maintenance
see also Drivers licenses
see also Gasoline
see also Gasoline service stations
see also Motor vehicle exhaust
see also Motor vehicle exports and imports
see also Motor vehicle fleets
see also Motor vehicle industry
see also Motor vehicle parts and supplies
see also Motor vehicle registrations
see also Motor vehicle rental
see also Motor vehicle safety devices
see also Motor vehicle theft
see also Traffic accident fatalities
see also Traffic accidents and safety
see also under By Commodity in the "Index by Categories"

Autopsies
Aviation medicine research and test results, technical rpt series, 7506–10
Diving (underwater) accidents, illnesses, and deaths, by circumstances, diver characteristics, and location, 1970-90, annual rpt, 2144–29
Drug abuse indicators for selected metro areas, research results, data collection, and policy issues, 1992 semiannual conf, 4492–5
Ethanol in blood of accident victims, analysis of levels from drinking and postmortem microbial fermentation, 1992 technical rpt, 7506–10.111
Performance of autopsies, for 15 leading causes, 1989, US Vital Statistics advance annual rpt, 4146–5.124

Avalanches
Incidents and mgmt of disasters and natl security threats, with data by major event and State, 1992 annual rpt, 9434–6

Aviation
see Aeronautical navigation
see Aerospace industry
see Air traffic control
see Air travel
see Aircraft
see Airlines
see Airports and airways
see Astronauts
see Aviation accidents and safety
see Aviation fuels
see Aviation medicine
see Aviation sciences
see Civil aviation
see General aviation
see Military aviation
see Space program accidents and safety
see Space programs
see Space sciences
see Spacecraft

Aviation accidents and safety
Accidents and casualties of aircraft by carrier, 1980-90, annual rpt, 9614–1
Accidents and circumstances, for US operations of domestic and foreign airlines and general aviation, periodic rpt, 9612–1
Accidents, casualties, and damage for air carriers, by detailed circumstances, 1988, annual rpt, 9614–2
Accidents, deaths, and circumstances, by carrier and carrier type, preliminary 1991, annual press release, 9614–9
Accidents, deaths, and rates, by type of air service, 1981-90, annual rpt, 7504–1.9
Alaska occupational injury deaths, by cause, occupation, and industry, early 1980s, article, 4042–3.307
Bombing incidents and casualties, by target, circumstances, and State, 1987-91, annual rpt, 8484–4.1
Collisions (mid-air) and near collisions, and relation to air traffic density, 1981-86, 7508–76
DOT activities by subagency, budget, and summary accident data, FY89, annual rpt, 7304–1
Drug testing and results for airline and aviation safety employees, by drug type and occupational group, 1991, semiannual rpt, 7502–17
Drug testing of air traffic control staff and job applicants, program operations and medical staff views, 1990 survey, technical rpt, 7506–10.115
Engine rotor failures on aircraft, by carrier and incident characteristics, 1988, annual rpt, 7504–50
Evacuations of aircraft and related casualties by incident, 1975-89, with proposed flight attendant work hour limitations, hearing, 21648–68
FAA activities and finances, and staff by region, FY90-91, annual rpt, 7504–10
Hazardous material transport accidents, casualties, and damage, by mode of transport, with DOT control activities, 1990, annual rpt, 7304–4
Injury and illness rates by SIC 2- to 4-digit industry, and deaths by cause and industry div, 1990, annual rpt, 6844–1
Medical research and test results for aviation, technical rpt series, 7506–10
NASA accidents, casualties, damage, and safety activities, FY91, annual rpt, 9504–4
Occupational injuries, illnesses, and lost workdays, for commercial airline pilots and flight attendants, mid 1970s-88, article, 6722–1.320
Occupational injury and illness rates, by SIC 2- to 4-digit industry, 1989-90, annual rpt, 6844–7
Pilot and air traffic control errors, runway incursions, and near collisions, monthly rpt, 7502–15
Statistical Abstract of US, 1992 annual data compilation, 2324–1.22
Weather services activities and funding, by Federal agency, planned FY92-93, annual rpt, 2144–2
see also Air piracy
see also Air traffic control
see also Space program accidents and safety

Aviation fuels
Business statistics, detailed data for major industries and economic indicators, *Survey of Current Business*, monthly rpt, 2702–1.17
Business statistics, detailed data for major industries and economic indicators, 1960-91, *Survey of Current Business* biennial supplement, 2704–1
Consumption of aviation fuels, forecast FY92-2003 and trends from FY82, annual rpt, 7504–6
Consumption of energy, by detailed fuel type, end-use sector, and State, 1960-90, State Energy Data System annual rpt, 3164–39
Consumption of energy by fuel type, and miles traveled, by transport mode, projected 1990-2010 and trends from 1960s, 3008–124
Consumption of energy by mode of transport, fuel supply, and demographic and economic factors of vehicle use, 1970s-90, annual rpt, 3304–5
Exports and imports between US and outlying areas, by detailed commodity and mode of transport, 1991, annual rpt, 2424–11

Exports and imports of US, by Harmonized System 6-digit commodity and country, 1991, annual rpt, 2424–13
Exports of US, detailed Schedule B commodities with countries of destination, 1991, annual rpt, 2424–10
Foreign and US oil production, trade, and stocks, by product and country, 1987-90, annual rpt, 3164–50.2
Freight (waterborne domestic and foreign) by commodity, traffic, and passengers, by port and waterway, 1989, annual rpt, 3754–3
Manufacturing annual survey, 1990: finances and operations, by SIC 2- to 4-digit industry, series, 2506–14
Pacific basin countries energy supply and demand, and implications for US trade, country rpt series, 3406–6
Price indexes (producer), by stage of processing and detailed commodity, monthly rpt, 6762–6
Price indexes (producer), by stage of processing and detailed commodity, monthly 1991, annual rpt, 6764–2
Prices and spending for fuel, by type, end-use sector, and State, 1990, annual rpt, 3164–64
Prices and volume of oil products sold and purchased by refiners, processors, and distributors, by product, end-use sector, PAD district, and State, monthly rpt, 3162–11; 3164–85
Prices of jet fuel for domestic and intl operations, quarterly rpt, 7502–16
Supply and demand of oil and refined products, refinery capacity and use, and prices, weekly rpt, 3162–32
Supply, demand, and movement of crude oil, gas liquids, and refined products, by PAD district and State, 1991, annual rpt, 3164–2
Supply, demand, and prices, by fuel type and end-use sector, alternative projections by region, 1990-2010, annual rpt, 3164–96
Supply, demand, and prices, by fuel type and end-use sector, alternative projections 1990-2010, annual rpt, 3164–75
Supply, demand, and prices, by fuel type and end-use sector, with foreign comparisons, 1991 and trends from 1949, annual rpt, 3164–74.1; 3164–74.2
Supply, demand, and prices, by fuel type, end-use sector, and country, detailed data, monthly rpt with articles, 3162–24
Supply, demand, and prices, by fuel type, end-use sector, and country, detailed data, monthly 1973-88, 3168–123
Supply, demand, and prices of energy, forecasts by resource type, quarterly rpt, 3162–34
Supply, demand, trade, stocks, and refining of oil and gas liquids, by detailed product, State, and PAD district, monthly rpt with articles, 3162–6
Tax (excise) collections of IRS, by source, quarterly rpt, 8302–1

Aviation industry
see Aerospace industry
see Aircraft
see Airlines
see Aviation accidents and safety

Aviation medicine
Military health care personnel, and accessions by training source, by occupation, specialty, and service branch, FY90, annual rpt, 3544–24
Research and test results for aviation medicine, technical rpt series, 7506–10

Aviation sciences
Employment of scientists, engineers, and technicians in manufacturing, by field and industry, 1989, triennial rpt, 9627–23
Fed Govt aeronautics and space activities and budgets, by agency, and foreign programs, 1957-FY91, annual rpt, 9504–9
NASA R&D funding to higher education instns, by field, instn, and State, FY91, annual listing, 9504–7
R&D funding by higher education instns and federally funded centers, by field, instn, and State, FY90, annual rpt, 9627–13
Science and Engineering Indicators, employment, education, R&D funding, and industry impacts, with foreign comparisons, 1960s-91, biennial rpt, 9624–10
see also Space sciences

Avidor, Abraham
"Agricultural Trade Policy and Trade for Central and East Europe", 1928–11

Avila, Lixion A.
"North Atlantic Hurricanes—1991", 2152–8.302

Avina, Jeffrey M.
"Evaluating the Impact of Grassroots Development Funding: An Experimental Methodology Applied to Eight IAF Projects", 14428–1

Avrigian, Anna M.
"Big Game Fishing in Northern Gulf of Mexico During 1990", 2164–23

Awards, medals, and prizes
Coin and medal production by denomination, capacity, and facility improvement funding, by mint, with monetary metals purchases, projected FY92-96, hearing, 21248–164
Drug abuse prevention programs in schools, Education Dept recognition program, 1989/90-1990/91, annual listing, 4814–2
HHS public health innovation contest winners, project descriptions and costs, 1991, article, 4042–3.322
Mint (US) activities, finances, coin and medals production and holdings, and gold and silver transactions, by facility, FY91, annual rpt, 8204–1
Nobel laureates supported by NIH, 1991 annual rpt, 4434–1
Technological innovations of industrial and Federal labs, market potential and results of annual ***R&D 100*** awards competition, 1960s-90, 2218–86
see also Employee bonuses and work incentives
see also Military awards, decorations, and medals

Azerbaijan
Agricultural production, prices, and trade, for former USSR republics, 1960s-91 and forecast 1992, annual rpt, 1524–4.1
Economic, social, political, and geographic summary data, by country, 1992, annual factbook, 9114–2
Embassies of US in former Soviet republics and Baltic States, positions planned by function, and filled, 1992, GAO rpt, 26123–403
Energy supply and use, and social, economic, and political indicators for former Soviet Republics and Baltic States, 1989-90, 3168–126
Energy use and production of former USSR Republics, by fuel type, 1990, annual rpt, 3164–84.2
Exports and imports of US with Communist and transitional economy countries, by detailed commodity and country, quarterly rpt with articles, 9882–2
Livestock and meat inventories, use, and imports, by former USSR republic, 1986-93, semiannual rpt, 1925–33.2
Population size and characteristics of former Soviet Republics and Baltic States, 1989-92, 9118–19

Babbel, David F.
"Generalized Put-Call Parity", 9371–10.67
"Quantity-Adjusting Options and Forward Contracts", 9371–10.73

Babor, Thomas F.
"Just Say Y.E.S.: Matching Adolescents to Appropriate Interventions for Alcohol and Other Drug-Related Problems", 4482–1.305

Babula, Ronald A.
"Canada's Broiler Supply Management Program: A Shield from U.S. Price Volatility?", 1502–3.302
"Regional Responsiveness of Agricultural Interest Rates to U.S. Treasury Bill Rates", 1541–1.306

Bach, Robert L.
"Impact of IRCA on the U.S. Labor Market and Economy", 6366–6.10

Bachman, Ronet
"Crime Victimization in City, Suburban, and Rural Areas: A National Crime Victimization Survey Report", 6066–3.48

Bachu, Amara
"Who's Minding the Kids? Child Care Arrangements: Fall 1988", 2546–20.24

Backus, David K.
"Dynamics of the Trade Balance and the Terms of Trade: The S-Curve", 9377–9.142
"In Search of Scale Effects in Trade and Growth", 9383–20.22
"International Real Business Cycles", 9383–20.16
"Relative Price Movements in Dynamic General Equilibrium Models of International Trade", 9377–9.144

Badzioch, Michael D.
"Breast Cancer Risks in Relatives of Male Breast Cancer Patients", 4472–1.330

Baer, Herbert
"Capital Adequacy and the Growth of U.S. Banks", 9375–13.88

Bahamas
Agricultural trade of US, by detailed commodity and country, 1991, annual rpt, 1524–8
Agricultural trade of US, by detailed commodity and country, 1991, semiannual rpt, 1522–4
Drug abuse indicators, by world region and selected country, 1991 semiannual conf, 4492–5.1

Economic and military aid and loans from US and intl agencies, by program and country, FY46-91, annual rpt, 9914–5
Economic and social conditions, resources, and trade, and aid, 1992, annual factbook, 9914–14
Economic conditions, policy, and trade practices, by country, 1989-91, annual rpt, 21384–5
Economic, social, political, and geographic summary data, by country, 1992, annual factbook, 9114–2
Exports and imports of US, by commodity and country, 1980-90, world area rpt, 9116–1.4
Exports and imports of US, by transport mode, country, and SITC 1- to 3-digit commodity, 1991, annual rpt, 2424–12
Exports, imports, and balances of US for manufactured goods, by SITC 2-digit commodity and country, quarterly rpt, 2042–35
Exports of US, detailed Schedule B commodities with countries of destination, 1991, annual rpt, 2424–10
Human rights conditions in 170 countries, and US economic and military aid, 1991, annual rpt, 21384–3
Military aid of US, arms sales, and training programs costs and budget requests, by program, world region, and country, FY91-93, annual rpt, 7144–13
Multinatl US firms and foreign affiliates finances and operations, by industry and country, 1989 benchmark survey, annual rpt, 2704–5
Multinatl US firms foreign affiliates, income statement items by asset size, industry, and country, 1988, biennial article, 8302–2.322
Oil exports to US by OPEC and non-OPEC countries, monthly rpt, 3162–24.3
Oil exports to US by OPEC and non-OPEC countries, monthly 1973-88, 3168–123.3
Population size, growth rates, and components of change, by country, projected 1990-2020 and trends from 1950, biennial rpt, 2324–9
Ships in world merchant fleet, tonnage, and new ship construction and deliveries, by vessel type and country, as of Jan 1992, annual rpt, 7704–3
Steel trade, by product, country, and customs district, with US industry operating data, 1989-June 1992, semiannual rpt, 9882–15
UN voting record and share of votes in agreement with US, by issue, country, and world area, 1991, annual rpt, 7004–18

Bahrain

Agricultural trade of US, by detailed commodity and country, 1991, annual rpt, 1524–8
Agricultural trade of US, by detailed commodity and country, 1991, semiannual rpt, 1522–4
AID economic aid to developing countries, obligations and disbursements by country, quarterly rpt, 9912–4
Apple imports of 5 Persian Gulf countries, by country of origin, 1981-90, article, 1925–34.322
Background Notes, summary social, political, and economic data, 1991 rpt, 7006–2.7
Boycotts (intl) by OPEC and other countries, US firms and individuals cooperation and tax benefits denied, 1990, article, 8302–2.323
Economic and military aid and loans from US and intl agencies, by program and country, FY46-91, annual rpt, 9914–5
Economic and social conditions of developing countries from 1960s, and Intl Dev Cooperation Agency and AID activities and funding, FY91-93, annual rpt, 9904–4
Economic conditions, policy, and trade practices, by country, 1989-91, annual rpt, 21384–5
Economic, social, political, and geographic summary data, by country, 1992, annual factbook, 9114–2
Exports and imports of US, by commodity and country, 1980-90, world area rpt, 9116–1.6
Exports and imports of US, by transport mode, country, and SITC 1- to 3-digit commodity, 1991, annual rpt, 2424–12
Exports, imports, and balances of US for manufactured goods, by SITC 2-digit commodity and country, quarterly rpt, 2042–35
Exports of US, detailed Schedule B commodities with countries of destination, 1991, annual rpt, 2424–10
Human rights conditions in 170 countries, and US economic and military aid, 1991, annual rpt, 21384–3
Military aid of US, arms sales, and training programs costs and budget requests, by program, world region, and country, FY91-93, annual rpt, 7144–13
Military spending, arms trade, and force strengths, with govt spending and population, by country, 1979-89, annual rpt, 9824–1
Minerals Yearbook, Vol 3, 1989: foreign country review of production, trade, and policy, by commodity, annual rpt, 5604–35.3
Multinatl US firms foreign affiliates, income statement items by asset size, industry, and country, 1988, biennial article, 8302–2.322
Oil production, stocks, use, and trade, by selected country and country group, monthly rpt, 3162–42
Population size, growth rates, and components of change, by country, projected 1990-2020 and trends from 1950, biennial rpt, 2324–9
UN voting record and share of votes in agreement with US, by issue, country, and world area, 1991, annual rpt, 7004–18

Bail

see Pretrial detention and release

Baillie, Richard T.

"Post-Louvre Intervention: Did Target Zones Stabilize the Dollar?", 9377–9.134

Bajwa, Rajinder S.

"Agricultural Irrigation and Water Use", 1588–122

Baker, Allen

"Revisions in Estimates of Food and Industrial Use for Feed Grains", 1561–4.301

Baker, D. A.

"Population Dose Commitments Due to Radioactive Releases from Nuclear Power Plant Sites in 1988", 9634–7

Baker, Nancy T.

"Inventory of Public Water Supplies in Arkansas", 5666–24.18
"Summary and Analysis of Water-Use Data Collection in Eastern Arkansas", 5666–24.11
"Summary of Reported Water Use for Arkansas Counties", 5666–24.12

Baker, Susan P.

"Occupational Injury Prevention", 4208–35

Baker, Timothy D.

"Uncounted Dead—American Civilians Dying Overseas", 4042–3.315

Bakersfield, Calif.

see also under By City and By SMSA or MSA in the "Index by Categories"

Baking and bakery products

Appalachia food processing firms, employment, and shipments, and farm production, by commodity and State, 1960s-90, 9088–37
Confectionery shipments, trade, use, and ingredients used, by product, 1991, annual Current Industrial Rpt, 2506–4.5
Consumption, supply, trade, prices, spending, and indexes, by food commodity, 1990, annual rpt, 1544–4
County Business Patterns, 1989: employment, establishments, and payroll, by SIC 2- to 4-digit industry and county, annual State rpt series, 2326–8
County Business Patterns, 1990: employment, establishments, and payroll, by SIC 2- to 4-digit industry and county, annual State rpt series, 2326–6
CPI by component for US city average, and by selected metro area, region, and population size, monthly rpt, 6762–2
Employment, earnings, and hours, by SIC 1- to 4-digit industry, monthly 1989-Feb 1992, annual rpt, 6744–4
Employment of minorities and women, by occupation, SIC 1- to 3-digit industry, State, and MSA, 1991, annual rpt, 9244–1
Exports and imports (agricultural) of US, by detailed commodity and country, 1991, annual rpt, 1524–8
Exports and imports (agricultural) of US, by detailed commodity and country, 1991, semiannual rpt, 1522–4
Exports and imports between US and outlying areas, by detailed commodity and mode of transport, 1991, annual rpt, 2424–11
Exports and imports of US, by country and detailed commodity, monthly rpt, 2422–12
Exports and imports of US, by Harmonized System 6-digit commodity and country, 1991, annual rpt, 2424–13
Exports and imports of US, by transport mode, country, and SITC 1- to 3-digit commodity, 1991, annual rpt, 2424–12
Exports of US, detailed Schedule B commodities with countries of destination, 1991, annual rpt, 2424–10
Input-output structure of US economy, detailed interindustry transactions for 541 industries, and components of final demand, 1982 benchmark data, 2708–17

Labor productivity, indexes of output, hours, and employment by SIC 2- to 4-digit industry, 1967-90, annual rpt, 6824–1.3
Manufacturing annual survey, 1990: finances and operations, by SIC 2- to 4-digit industry, series, 2506–14
Manufacturing census, 1987: concentration of largest firms measured by value added, and for shipments by SIC 2- and 4-digit industry, subject rpt, 2497–6
Manufacturing census, 1987: shipments of manufacturers products, by customer class and SIC 2- and 4-digit industry, subject rpt, 2497–4
Manufacturing finances and operations, by SIC 2- to 4-digit industry, forecast 1992, annual rpt, 2044–28
Multinatl US firms and foreign affiliates finances and operations, by industry and country, 1989 benchmark survey, annual rpt, 2704–5
Nutrient, caloric, and waste composition, detailed data for raw, processed, and prepared baked food products, 1992 rpt, 1356–3.18
Occupational injury and illness rates, by SIC 2- to 4-digit industry, 1989-90, annual rpt, 6844–7
Occupational injury and illness rates, by SIC 2- to 4-digit industry, 1990, annual rpt, 6844–1
Price indexes (producer), by stage of processing and detailed commodity, monthly rpt, 6762–6
Price indexes (producer), by stage of processing and detailed commodity, monthly 1991, annual rpt, 6764–2
Prices (farm-retail) for food, marketing cost components, and industry finances and productivity, 1920s-91, annual rpt, 1544–9
Retail trade sales and inventories, by kind of business, region, and selected State, MSA, and city, monthly rpt, 2413–3
Retail trade sales, inventories, purchases, gross margin, and accounts receivable, by SIC 2- to 4-digit kind of business and form of ownership, 1990, annual rpt, 2413–5
Science, engineering, and technical employment in manufacturing, by field and industry, 1989, triennial rpt, 9627–23
Tax (income) returns of corporations, income and tax items by asset size and detailed industry, 1989, annual rpt, 8304–4; 8304–21
Wheat flour bakery cost, quarterly situation rpt with articles, 1561–12

Balance of payments

Agricultural, fishery, and forest products trade, tariffs, and industry operating data, commodity rpt series, 9885–8
Agricultural Outlook, production, prices, marketing, and trade, by commodity, forecast and current situation, monthly rpt with articles, 1502–4
Agricultural trade, outlook and current situation, quarterly rpt, 1542–4
Banks (US) and nonbanking firms liabilities to and claims on foreigners, by country, 1989-90, annual rpt, 9364–5.10
Business statistics, detailed data for major industries and economic indicators, 1960-91, *Survey of Current Business* biennial supplement, 2704–1
Canada and US current accounts balance reconciliation adjustment methodology, with background data, 1990-91, article, 2702–1.341
Capital movements between US and foreign countries, *Treasury Bulletin*, quarterly rpt, 8002–4.13
Central America economic indicators, by country, 1969-89, working paper, 9916–13.4
Chemical and energy products trade, tariffs, and industry operating data, commodity rpt series, 9885–11
Developing countries economic and social conditions from 1960s, and Intl Dev Cooperation Agency and AID activities and funding, FY91-93, annual rpt, 9904–4
Developing countries economic, population, and agricultural data, US and other aid sources, and AID activity, country rpt series, 9916–12
Economic indicators and components, current data and annual trends, monthly rpt, 23842–1.7
Electronics and services trade, tariffs, and industry operating data, commodity rpt series, 9885–12
Energy producers finances and operations, by energy type for US firms domestic and foreign operations, 1990, annual rpt, 3164–44
Exports and imports of US by country, and trade shifts by commodity, 1991, annual rpt, 9884–25
Exports and imports of US, by selected country, country group, and commodity group, 1991, annual rpt, 2044–37
Exports and imports relation to balance of trade, model description and results, 1950s-90, working paper, 9377–9.142
Exports and imports relation to terms of trade and GNP, alternative models description and results, 1992 working paper, 9377–9.144
Exports, imports, and balances of US, by selected country, country group, and commodity group, preliminary data, monthly rpt, 2042–34
Exports, imports, and balances of US for manufactured goods, by SITC 2-digit commodity and country, quarterly rpt, 2042–35
Exports, imports, and balances of US with major trading partners, by product category, 1987-91, annual chartbook, 9884–21
Exports, imports, and trade flows, by country and commodity, with background economic indicators, data compilation, monthly CD-ROM, 2002–6
Fed Govt financial operations, detailed data, *Treasury Bulletin*, quarterly rpt, 8002–4
Fed Reserve Bd and Reserve banks finances, staff, and review of monetary policy and economic devs, 1991, annual rpt, 9364–1
Financial instns (intl) funds by source and disbursements by purpose, by country, with US policy review, FY90, annual rpt, 15344–1
Flow-of-funds accounts, savings, investments, and credit statements, quarterly rpt, 9365–3.3
Flows of trade and investment, and economic indicators, for selected countries and country groups, selected years 1946-91, annual rpt, 204–1.9
Foreign and US economic conditions, and trade devs and balances, with data by selected country and country group, monthly rpt, 9882–14
Foreign and US economic conditions, for major industrial countries, monthly rpt, 9112–1
Foreign and US economic indicators, trade balances, and exchange rates, for selected OECD and Asian countries, 1992 semiannual rpt, 8002–14
Foreign countries economic conditions and implications for US, periodic country rpt series, 2046–4
Haiti economic conditions, 1985-91, working paper, 9916–13.3
Intl transactions of US, and economic and monetary trends for US and 7 major industrialized countries, quarterly rpt, 9391–7
Intl transactions summary, monthly rpt, 9362–1.3
Intl transactions summary, 1980s-91, annual article, 9362–1.304
Intl transactions, *Survey of Current Business*, monthly rpt, quarterly tables, 2702–1.33
Investment (intl) position of US, by component, industry, world region, and country, 1990-91, annual article, 2702–1.323
Israel economic conditions, US investment and export opportunities, and trade practices, 1992 rpt, 2008–32
Latin America economic and social conditions, resources, trade, and aid, 1992, annual factbook, 9914–14
Latin America economic conditions, trade, and foreign aid, working paper series, 9916–13
Lumber and wood products trade and export promotion of US by country, and trade balance, by commodity, FAS periodic circular, 1925–36
Machinery and equipment trade, tariffs, and industry operating data, commodity rpt series, 9885–9
Manufacturing trade, tariffs, and industry operating data, commodity rpt series, 9885–10
Minerals and metals trade, tariffs, and industry operating data, commodity rpt series, 9885–13
Multinatl firms US affiliates, finances, and operations, by industry, world area of parent firm, and State, 1989-90, annual rpt, 2704–4
Natl income and product accounts and components, *Survey of Current Business*, monthly rpt, 2702–1.23
Natl income and product accounts, comprehensive accounts and components, benchmark revisions, 1929-88, 2708–5
Natl income and product accounts, comprehensive accounts and components, *Survey of Current Business*, monthly rpt, 2702–1.27
Natl income and product accounts revisions to GDP, personal income, and selected foreign transactions, various periods 1959-90, tables, 2702–1.313
OECD countries current account balance and net assets, relation to inflation, unemployment rate, and govt lending, 1970s-89, technical paper, 9366–7.274

OECD intl trade position for US and 4 countries, and factors affecting US competition, quarterly pamphlet, 2042–25
OPEC and other countries intl boycotts, US firms and individuals cooperation and tax benefits denied, with trade by country, 1990, article, 8302–2.323
Overseas Business Reports: economic conditions, investment and export opportunities, and trade practices, country market research rpt series, 2046–6
Productivity and capital investment relation to trade balances, for selected countries, 1960s-90, working paper, 9393–10.22
Statistical Abstract of US, 1992 annual data compilation, 2324–1.29; 2324–1.31
Telecommunications finances, rates, and traffic for US carriers intl operations, by service type, firm, and country, 1975-90, annual rpt, 9284–17
Travel to and from US, and travel receipts and payments, by world area, with data by country, 1985-90, annual rpt, 2904–10
see also Foreign debts
see also Foreign exchange
see also Foreign investments
see also Foreign trade

Balance of trade
see Balance of payments

Balance sheets
see Business assets and liabilities, general
see Business assets and liabilities, specific industry
see Business income and expenses, general
see Business income and expenses, specific industry
see Government assets and liabilities

Balanced Budget and Emergency Deficit Control Act
Budget of US, House concurrent resolution, with spending and revenue targets, FY93 and projected to FY97, annual rpt, 21264–2
Cancellation of budget authority under Act, FY93, annual rpt, 26304–6
Cancellation of budget authority under Act, OMB sequestration estimates, by category, FY92, annual rpt, 104–27

Balke, Nathan S.
"Are Deep Recessions Followed by Strong Recoveries?", 9379–12.82
"Threshold Cointegration", 9379–12.90

Ball, Jeff
"Income Withholder's Role in Child Support", 4588–1

Ball, Judy K.
"Pediatric AIDS-Related Discharges in a Sample of U.S. Hospitals: Demographics, Diagnoses, and Resource Use", 4186–6.16

Ballard, Jane E.
"Descriptive Epidemiology of Unintentional Residential Fire Injuries in King County, WA, 1984 and 1985", 4042–3.340

Ballard, John A.
"Attitudes of Patients Toward Smoking by Health Professionals", 4042–3.334

Baltic States
see Estonia
see Latvia
see Lithuania

Baltimore, Md.
Air traffic, and passenger and freight enplanements, by airport, 1960s-90 and projected to 2010, hub area rpt, 7506–7.42
Commuters, by county of residence and work, for top 10 metro areas, 1990 Census of Population, press release, 2328–84
CPI by component for US city average, and by region, population size, and for 15 metro areas, monthly rpt, 6762–1
CPI by component for US city average, and by selected metro area, region, and population size, monthly rpt, 6762–2
Freight (waterborne domestic and foreign) by commodity, traffic, and passengers, by port and waterway, 1989, annual rpt, 3754–3.1
Fruit and vegetable shipments, and arrivals by city, by mode of transport and State and country of origin, 1991, annual rpt, 1311–4.1
Housing and households characteristics, and unit and neighborhood quality, by MSA location for 11 MSAs, 1987 survey, supplement, 2485–8
Housing starts and completions authorized by building permits in 40 MSAs, quarterly rpt, 2382–9
Wages by occupation, and benefits for office and plant workers, 1991 survey, periodic MSA rpt, 6785–12.2
see also under By City and By SMSA or MSA in the "Index by Categories"

Banca Nazionale del Lavoro
Iraq loans from Banca Nazionale del Lavoro Atlanta office, with purpose and exporting country and company involved, 1991 hearing, 21248–165

Bangladesh
Agricultural trade of US, by detailed commodity and country, 1991, annual rpt, 1524–8
Agricultural trade of US, by detailed commodity and country, 1991, semiannual rpt, 1522–4
AID economic aid to developing countries, obligations and disbursements by country, quarterly rpt, 9912–4
AID loans repayment status and terms by program and country, and status of predecessor agency loans, quarterly rpt, 9912–3
Boycotts (intl) by OPEC and other countries, US firms and individuals cooperation and tax benefits denied, 1990, article, 8302–2.323
Economic and military aid and loans from US and intl agencies, by program and country, FY46-91, annual rpt, 9914–5
Economic and social conditions of developing countries from 1960s, and Intl Dev Cooperation Agency and AID activities and funding, FY91-93, annual rpt, 9904–4
Economic conditions, income, production, prices, employment, and trade, 1992 periodic country rpt, 2046–4.62
Economic conditions, policy, and trade practices, by country, 1989-91, annual rpt, 21384–5
Economic, social, political, and geographic summary data, by country, 1992, annual factbook, 9114–2
Exports and imports of US, by transport mode, country, and SITC 1- to 3-digit commodity, 1991, annual rpt, 2424–12
Exports, imports, and balances of US for manufactured goods, by SITC 2-digit commodity and country, quarterly rpt, 2042–35
Exports of US, detailed Schedule B commodities with countries of destination, 1991, annual rpt, 2424–10
Food supply, needs, and aid for developing countries, status and alternative forecasts, 1992 world area rpt, 1526–8.2
Human rights conditions in 170 countries, and US economic and military aid, 1991, annual rpt, 21384–3
Labor conditions, union coverage, and work accidents, 1991 annual country rpt, 6366–4.1
Labor conditions, union coverage, and work accidents, 1992 annual country rpt, 6366–4.47
Military aid of US, arms sales, and training programs costs and budget requests, by program, world region, and country, FY91-93, annual rpt, 7144–13
Military spending, arms trade, and force strengths, with govt spending and population, by country, 1979-89, annual rpt, 9824–1
Minerals Yearbook, Vol 3, 1989: foreign country review of production, trade, and policy, by commodity, annual rpt, 5604–35.2
Population size, growth rates, and components of change, by country, projected 1990-2020 and trends from 1950, biennial rpt, 2324–9
Refugee migration, and intl aid programs, by world area and country of origin and asylum, 1991, annual rpt, 7004–15
Towels (shop) from Bangladesh at less than fair value, injury to US industry, investigation with background financial and operating data, 1992 rpt, 9886–14.340
UN voting record and share of votes in agreement with US, by issue, country, and world area, 1991, annual rpt, 7004–18

Banister, Judith
"Rural Labor Force Trends in China", 1524–4.2
"Vietnam Population Dynamics and Prospects", 2326–18.65

Bank deposits
Assets and debts of private sector, balance sheets by segment, 1960-91, semiannual rpt, 9365–4.1
Availability of deposits, banks policies, 1980s-90, last issue of annual rpt, 9364–13
Banking and financial conditions, 1990, annual rpt, 9364–5
Banks and thrifts finances and operations by deposit size, Fed Reserve functional cost analysis, 1991, annual rpt, 9364–6
Banks balance sheets, by Fed Reserve District, for major banks in NYC, and for US branches and agencies of foreign banks, weekly rpt, 9365–1.3
Business statistics, detailed data for major industries and economic indicators, *Survey of Current Business*, monthly rpt, 2702–1.8

Business statistics, detailed data for major industries and economic indicators, 1960-91, *Survey of Current Business* biennial supplement, 2704–1
Commercial and savings banks (insured) finances, by State, 1990, annual rpt, 9294–4
Commercial and savings banks insured by FDIC, financial condition and performance, by asset size and region, quarterly rpt, 9292–1
Commercial banks (insured) domestic and foreign office consolidated financial statements, monthly rpt, quarterly data, 9362–1.4
Commercial banks profitability, balance sheet and income statement items, and financial ratios, by asset size, 1985-91, annual article, 9362–1.305
Credit unions federally insured, finances by instn characteristics and State, as of June 1992, semiannual rpt, 9532–6
Credit unions federally insured, finances, 1990-91, annual rpt, 9534–1
Credit unions with low income membership, financial, operating, and membership data, 1982-91, 9536–1.8
Debits and turnover of demand and savings deposits, monthly rpt, 9362–1.1
Debits, deposits, and deposit turnover, for commercial banks by type of account, monthly rpt, 9365–2.5
Deposits in insured commercial and savings banks, by instn, State, MSA, and county, as of June 1991, annual regional rpt series, 9295–3
Economic indicators and components, current data and annual trends, monthly rpt, 23842–1.5
Families financial status, income, net worth, and assets and debt by type, by income and selected characteristics, 1983 and 1989, article, 9362–1.301
Fed Reserve banks expenses and operations, itemized by service, office, and district, 1991, annual rpt, 9364–11
Fed Reserve banks finances and staff, 1991, annual rpt, 9364–1.1
Financial and monetary conditions, selected US summary data, weekly rpt, 9391–4
Financial, banking, and mortgage market activity, weekly rpt series, 9365–1
Financial instns reform issues, with finances, impacts of deposit insurance changes, and views of depositors and bankers, 1991 hearings, 25248–129
Flow-of-funds accounts, savings, investments, and credit statements, quarterly rpt, 9365–3.3
Households financial services use, by account type and instn type and location, 1989 survey, article, 9362–1.303
Households net worth distribution under alternative sample weighting systems to account for inconsistency in survey design and response rates, 1992 rpt, 9368–91
Interest rates on bank deposits, deregulation impacts on bank asset risk, alternative model descriptions and results, 1970s-80s, working paper, 9379–14.15
Interest rates on bank deposits, relation to market concentration, regulation, migration, and other factors, 1980s, technical paper, 9366–6.297
Interest rates on bank deposits, relation to measures of bank financial strength and other indicators, 1984-91, technical report, 9366–6.300
Intl financial markets performance of foreign and US bank and securities firms, finances and competitiveness issues, 1980s, compilation of papers, 9385–10
Intl transactions, *Survey of Current Business*, monthly rpt, quarterly tables, 2702–1.33
Mail volume to and from households, use, and views, by class, source, content, and household characteristics, FY87-90, annual rpt, 9864–10
Merger applications approved, and assets and offices involved, by bank, 1990, annual rpt, 9294–5
Monetary aggregates relation to GDP, for M2 including and excluding small time deposits and other components, 1960s-91, article, 9385–1.305
Monetary trends, Fed Reserve Bank of St Louis monthly rpt, 9391–2
New England States banks and thrifts, assets and liabilities by type, and deposits relation to capital/asset ratios, by instn type and size, 1980s-91, article, 9373–1.309
New England States banks and thrifts, deposits by type and loans relation to capital/asset ratios, by instn size, 1990-91, working paper, 9373–27.4
Nonprofit charitable organizations finances, with data by State and for top 10 instns, 1988, article, 8302–2.302
North Central States business and economic conditions, Fed Reserve 9th District, quarterly journal, 9383–19
North Central States, FHLB 6th District insured S&Ls financial condition and operations by State, quarterly rpt, 9302–23
North Central States, FHLB 8th District S&Ls, locations, assets, and savings, 1992, annual listing, 9304–9
Reserve and overdraft requirements of Fed Reserve and 3 foreign central banks, with balance sheets and deposit balances, 1989-90, article, 9377–1.307
Savings instns brokered deposits relation to size and selected financial ratios, late 1980s-91, article, 9379–15.301
Savings instns brokered deposits relation to size and selected financial ratios, 1st qtr 1991, working paper, 9379–14.17
Savings instns failure resolution activity and finances of Resolution Trust Corp, with data by asset type, State, region, and instn, monthly rpt, 9722–3
Savings instns failure resolution activity of Resolution Trust Corp, assets, deposits, and assets availability and sales, periodic press release, 9722–1
Savings instns failure resolution activity of Resolution Trust Corp, brokered deposits, fees, and interest rates by instn and region, as of July 1991, hearing, 21248–171
Savings instns failure resolution activity of Resolution Trust Corp impact on M2 growth, with deposits in resolved thrifts, 1990-91, article, 9379–1.303
Savings instns failure resolution activity of Resolution Trust Corp, with data by State and instn, and RTC finances, 1990, annual rpt, 9724–1
Savings instns financial statements, for instns insured by Savings Assn Insurance Fund by FHLB district and State, and for FDIC-insured savings banks, 1989, annual rpt, 8434–1
Savings instns holdings of low-grade (junk) bonds and relation to stock volatility and deposit interest rates, late 1980s, working paper, 9375–13.69
Savings instns insured by Savings Assn Insurance Fund, assets, liabilities, and deposit and loan activity, by conservatorship status, monthly rpt, 8432–1
Savings instns insured by Savings Assn Insurance Fund, finances by profitability group, district, and State, quarterly rpt, 8432–4
Savings instns insured by Savings Assn Insurance Fund, offices, and deposits, by region, State, MSA, and county, 1991, annual rpt, 8434–5
Service fees, minimum balances, and services offered by banks and thrifts, by service type, 1991, annual rpt, 9364–12
Southeastern States, Fed Reserve 5th District, economic indicators by State, quarterly rpt, 9389–16
Southeastern States, Fed Reserve 5th District insured commercial banks financial statements, by State, quarterly rpt, 9389–18
Southeastern States, Fed Reserve 8th District banking and economic conditions, quarterly rpt with articles, 9391–16
Statistical Abstract of US, 1992 annual data compilation, 2324–1.16
Tax exempt organizations finances, with data by type, size, State, and for largest organizations, late 1940s-80s, compilation of papers, 8308–35
Treasury tax and loan account deposits, Fed Reserve Banks mgmt of securities held as collateral, 1991, GAO rpt, 26111–80
Trust assets of banks, trust companies, and S&Ls, by type of asset and fund, selected firm, and State, 1991, annual rpt, 13004–1
Uninsured bank deposits by type and bank size, and relation to bank size and selected operating ratios, 1980s-91, technical paper, 9385–8.126
West Central States economic indicators, Fed Reserve 10th District, quarterly rpt, 9381–16.2
West Central States, Fed Reserve 10th District banking industry structure, performance, and financial devs, 1991, annual rpt, 9381–14
West Central States, FHLB 10th District thrifts, locations, assets, and deposits, 1992, annual listing, 9304–17
Western States, FHLB 11th District shareholder instns, offices, and financial condition, 1992 annual listing, 9304–23
see also Certificates of deposit
see also Checking accounts
see also Deposit insurance
see also International reserves
see also Negotiable orders of withdrawal accounts
see also Savings

Bank holding companies
Assets, offices, and deposits of BHCs, by State, 1990, annual rpt, 9364–5.11
Banks seasonal borrowing from Fed Reserve, participants financial and other characteristics, Fed Reserve 8th District, 1984-90, article, 9391–1.311
Capital requirements impacts on BHCs asset growth, 1989-91, working paper, 9375–13.88
Commercial paper ratings of BHCs relation to total commercial paper outstanding, 1980s-90, technical paper, 9366–6.299
Fed Reserve Bd and Reserve banks finances, staff, and review of monetary policy and economic devs, 1991, annual rpt, 9364–1
Financial and economic analysis, technical paper series, 9393–10
Financial ratios, banks held, and equity financing relation to regulatory capital standards, for publicly-traded and large BHCs, 1970s-90, technical paper, 9366–6.291
Leverage-related and other financial ratios relation to return on equity for BHCs, 1980s, technical paper, 9385–8.134
Merger applications approved, and assets and offices involved, by bank, 1990, annual rpt, 9294–5
Reform of banking system, impacts on consumers, with background data, 1991 hearing, 21248–167
Reform of banking system, issues, with top instn finances, fiscal impacts, and views of depositors, bankers, and regulators on deposit insurance, 1991 hearings, 21248–168
Reform of financial system, issues, with finances, impacts of deposit insurance changes, and views of depositors and bankers, 1991 hearings, 25248–129
Securities of banks, common stock dividends relation to earnings, capital, and other factors, 1989-90, article, 9292–4.302
Stock prices of BHCs relation to capital and assets, 1990-92, article, 9385–1.311
Stock returns of large BHCs, relation to returns on industrial stock and long-term bonds, model description and results, 1970s-90, article, 9393–8.301
Tax (income) returns of corporations, income and tax items by asset size and detailed industry, 1989, annual rpt, 8304–4; 8304–21
West Central States, Fed Reserve 10th District banking industry structure, performance, and financial devs, 1991, annual rpt, 9381–14

Bank Insurance Fund
Budget deficit forecasting accuracy, contributing factors, and analysis of major programs, FY91, annual GAO rpt, 26104–23
Commercial and savings banks insured by BIF, financial condition and performance, by asset size and region, quarterly rpt, 9292–1
Deposits in insured commercial and savings banks, by instn, State, MSA, and county, as of June 1991, annual regional rpt series, 9295–3
Finances and operations of FDIC, insured deposits, and finances of banks needing FDIC aid, 1991 and trends from 1934, annual rpt, 9294–1
Finances of BIF projected under alternative assumptions about bank failures and assets involved, 1991-93, hearing, 21248–166
Financial performance of banks, risk assessment, and regulation, 1991 annual conf papers, 9375–7
Losses of BIF, relation to duration of failed bank undercapitalization, 1985-90, article, 9391–1.312

Bank of Credit and Commerce International
Financial statements, audits, and selected loan data, for BCCI, 1984-90, hearing, 25388–60
Financial statements of BCCI DC office, 1984-90, GAO rpt, 26119–427

Bank Secrecy Act
Money laundering investigations by Treasury Dept, civil penalty cases workload, processing, and disposition, 1985-91, GAO rpt, 26119–390

Bankruptcy
Airline finances and operations, summary data, quarterly rpt, 7502–16
Business bankruptcy filings with SEC participation, by firm, FY91, annual rpt, 9734–2.4
Farm finances, debts, assets, and receipts, and lenders financial condition, quarterly rpt with articles, 1541–1
Federal bankruptcy cases admin, costs and efficiency of 2 programs, 1990-91, GAO rpt, 26119–421
FmHA loans and borrower supervision activities in farm and housing programs, by type and State, monthly rpt, 1182–1
Prisoners in Federal and contract instns, by selected characteristics, region, and Federal instn, FY89, annual rpt, 6244–1.1
Small business finances, operations, owner characteristics, and Federal contracts, 1980s-90, annual rpt, 9764–6
Statistical Abstract of US, 1992 annual data compilation, 2324–1.17
Unemployed displaced workers, layoffs and recalls by layoff reason, industry, firm size, and State, 2nd half 1988, 6406–6.36
Unemployed displaced workers, layoffs and unemployment insurance claims by reason, industry, selected characteristics, and State, quarterly press release, 6742–23
Unemployed displaced workers, layoffs and unemployment insurance claims by reason, industry, selected characteristics, MSA, and State, 1990, annual rpt, 6744–18
US attorneys civil and criminal cases by type and disposition, and collections, by Federal district, FY91, annual rpt, 6004–2.1
see also Business failures and closings
see also Federal bankruptcy courts

Banks and banking
Acquisitions by banks of failed and other banks, financial performance relation to asset mix, market concentration, and other factors, 1984-90, article, 9292–4.304
Acquisitions of banks, purchase price relation to target and acquiring banks financial ratios variability and asset size, 1980s, working paper, 9371–10.80
Assets and liabilities of Fed Reserve member and nonmember banks, 1990-91, annual rpt, 9364–1.2
Assets, liabilities, loans, investments, and deposits for commercial banks, total and in and outside NYC, monthly rpt, 9362–1.1
Assets of banks, composition and securitization relation to risk and liquidity indicators, model description and results, 1980s-91, technical paper, 9366–6.295
Assets valuation by banks, impact of market value accounting for debt securities, by bank asset size, Dec 1990, GAO rpt, 26111–77
Bombing incidents and casualties, by target, circumstances, and State, 1987-91, annual rpt, 8484–4.1
Boycotts (intl) invitations received by US firms, by country, FY91, annual rpt, 2024–1
Business statistics, detailed data for major industries and economic indicators, *Survey of Current Business*, monthly rpt, 2702–1.8
Business statistics, detailed data for major industries and economic indicators, 1960-91, *Survey of Current Business* biennial supplement, 2704–1
Computer data processing vendors contracts with banks and thrifts, involvement of illegal business transactions, and instn and vendor views, 1985-90, GAO rpt, 26119–374
Consumer spending, natl income and product account benchmark revisions, 1929-88, 2708–5
Consumer spending, natl income and product accounts, comprehensive accounts and components, *Survey of Current Business*, monthly rpt, 2702–1.25
County Business Patterns, 1989: employment, establishments, and payroll, by SIC 2- to 4-digit industry and county, annual State rpt series, 2326–8
County Business Patterns, 1990: employment, establishments, and payroll, by SIC 2- to 4-digit industry and county, annual State rpt series, 2326–6
Criminal cases by type and disposition, and collections, for US attorneys, by Federal district, FY91, annual rpt, 6004–2.1
Debits, deposits and turnover, consumer credit, interest rates, and status changes, monthly rpt series, 9365–2
Economies of scale and scope, impacts of bank asset quality indicators and other factors by asset size, model results, 1990, working paper, 9387–8.260
Economies of scale for large banks, alternative model results, 1984-86, working paper, 9387–8.274
Economies of scale in banking, impacts of potential mergers among large banks, model description and results, 1980s, working paper, 9387–8.256
Employment, earnings, and hours, by SIC 1- to 4-digit industry, monthly 1989-Feb 1992, annual rpt, 6744–4
Employment of minorities and women, by occupation, SIC 1- to 3-digit industry, State, and MSA, 1991, annual rpt, 9244–1
Failures of banks and assets involved, and Bank Insurance Fund finances, alternative projections, 1991-93, hearing, 21248–166
Failures of banks, FDIC resolution costs relation to bank financial and other characteristics, 1985-90, article, 9292–4.303

Failures of banks, forecasting performance of asset risk indicators and other factors, 1980s-91, article, 9379–15.302
Failures of banks relation to portfolio risk, and analysis of alternative failure warning models, 1992 working paper, 9379–14.18
Failures of banks, undercapitalization duration relation to Bank Insurance Fund losses, 1985-90, article, 9391–1.312
Finances and operations, by SIC 2- to 4-digit industry, forecast 1992, annual rpt, 2044–28
Finances and operations of banks and thrifts by deposit size, Fed Reserve functional cost analysis, 1991, annual rpt, 9364–6
Finances, examination ratings, and failure resolution costs and methods, for banks, 1980s-91, article, 9292–4.301
Finances of banks and thrifts, by instn type, 1991, annual rpt, 13004–2
Finances of banks needing FDIC aid, 1991, annual rpt, 9294–1
Finances of insured commercial and savings banks, by State, 1990, annual rpt, 9294–4
Financial and economic devs, Fed Reserve Bank of Boston bimonthly journal, 9373–1
Financial and economic devs, Fed Reserve Bank of Chicago bimonthly journal, 9375–1
Financial and economic devs, Fed Reserve Bank of New York quarterly journal, 9385–1
Financial and economic devs, Fed Reserve Bank of Philadelphia bimonthly journal, 9387–1
Financial and operating conditions of banks, 1990, annual rpt, 9364–5
Financial, banking, and mortgage market activity, weekly rpt series, 9365–1
Financial condition and performance of insured commercial and savings banks, by asset size and region, quarterly rpt, 9292–1
Financial performance indicators, by bank, 1991-92, hearings, 25248–127
Financial performance of banks and thrifts relation to market concentration, 1992 working paper, 9371–10.88
Financial performance of banks in Fed Reserve 10th District, by State, quarterly rpt, 9381–16
Financial performance of banks, relation to growth in State personal income, 1980s-90, working paper, 9377–9.135
Financial performance of banks, relative efficiency, model description and results, mid 1980s-90, article, 9391–1.305
Financial performance of banks, risk assessment, and regulation, 1991 annual conf papers, 9375–7
Financial ratios of insured commercial banks and FDIC-insured savings banks, by asset size and State, quarterly rpt, 13002–3
Financial services output and prices, model description and results, 1985-88, working paper, 6886–6.91
Foreign branches of US banks, assets and liabilities by world region and country, quarterly rpt, 9365–3.7
Foreign branches of US banks, balance sheets, monthly rpt, 9362–1.3
Foreign direct investment in US, by industry group and world area, 1989-91, annual article, 2702–1.331
Foreign direct investment of US, by industry group and world area, 1989-91, annual article, 2702–1.332
Fraud and abuse in financial instns, Justice Dept enforcement activity, staff, and case dispositions by instn type, 1988-92, 6008–35
Fraud in banks and thrifts, Justice Dept investigation and prosecution activities, 1989-92, GAO rpt, 26119–426
Households financial services use, by account type and instn type and location, 1989 survey, article, 9362–1.303
Industrial production, relation to bank deposits, reserves, and loans, 1920s-70s, article, 9377–1.302
Input-output structure of US economy, detailed interindustry transactions for 541 industries, and components of final demand, 1982 benchmark data, 2708–17
Intl financial markets performance of foreign and US bank and securities firms, finances and competitiveness issues, 1980s, compilation of papers, 9385–10
Intl transactions, *Survey of Current Business*, monthly rpt, quarterly tables, 2702–1.33
Investments and loans of commercial banks, monthly rpt, 23842–1.5
Investments and loans of commercial banks, 1972-91, annual rpt, 204–1.5
Iraq loans from Banca Nazionale del Lavoro Atlanta office, with purpose and exporting country and company involved, 1991 hearing, 21248–165
Japan *keiretsu* corporations equity and debt financing by shareholding banks, with model results, 1960s-70, article, 9393–8.302
Labor productivity, indexes of output, hours, and employment by SIC 2- to 4-digit industry, 1967-90, annual rpt, 6824–1.4
Mail volume to and from households, use, and views, by class, source, content, and household characteristics, FY87-90, annual rpt, 9864–10
Merger applications approved, and assets and offices involved, by bank, 1990, annual rpt, 9294–5
Mergers of banks, antitrust issues, with background financial data by State and selected instn, 1991 hearing, 21248–176
Mergers of banks, impact on operating costs, 1982-86, working paper, 9371–10.78
Mergers of banks, impacts on noninterest expense ratios, with background data for total and southeastern US, 1980s-90, article, 9371–1.303
Mgmt efficiency indicator for banks, with results for surviving and failed banks, mid 1980s, article, 9379–1.302
Mortgage applications, dispositions, and secondary loan market sales, by purpose, lender type, and applicant and neighborhood characteristics, 1991, article, 9362–1.307
Mortgage interest rate differential among cities, and relation to bank market conditions, 1987-88, technical paper, 9366–1.162
Multinatl firms US affiliates finances and operations, by industry, country of parent firm, and State, 1987, 2708–48
Multinatl firms US affiliates, finances, and operations, by industry, world area of parent firm, and State, 1989-90, annual rpt, 2704–4
Multinatl US firms foreign affiliates, income statement items by asset size, industry, and country, 1988, biennial article, 8302–2.322
Natl banks charters, mergers, liquidations, enforcement cases, and financial performance, with data by instn and State, quarterly rpt, 8402–3
New England States banks and thrifts, assets and liabilities by type, and deposits relation to capital/asset ratios, by instn type and size, 1980s-91, article, 9373–1.309
New England States banks and thrifts, deposits by type and loans relation to capital/asset ratios, by instn size, 1990-91, working paper, 9373–27.4
New England States banks and thrifts real estate lending impacts of capital losses, with financial ratios, 1980s-91, article, 9373–27.12
North Central States business and economic conditions, Fed Reserve 9th District, quarterly journal, 9383–19
Occupational injury and illness rates, by SIC 2- to 4-digit industry, 1989-90, annual rpt, 6844–7
Occupational injury and illness rates, by SIC 2- to 4-digit industry, 1990, annual rpt, 6844–1
Productivity, inefficiencies, and economies of scale for banks, alternative model descriptions and results, 1991 working paper, 9377–9.126
Profitability of banks, balance sheet and income statement items, and financial ratios, by asset size, 1985-91, annual article, 9362–1.305
Profitability of banks, relation to market concentration, efficiency indicators, and regulation, model description and results, 1980s, technical paper, 9366–6.290
Reform of banking system, impacts on consumers, with background data, 1991 hearing, 21248–167
Reform of banking system, issues, with top instn finances, fiscal impacts, and views of depositors, bankers, and regulators on deposit insurance, 1991 hearings, 21248–168
Reform of financial system, issues, with finances, impacts of deposit insurance changes, and views of depositors and bankers, 1991 hearings, 25248–129
Robberies, by type of premises, population size, and region, 1991, annual rpt, 6224–2.1
Robbery of banks and related crimes by State, casualties, and hostages, data compilation, 1992 annual rpt, 6064–6.3
Robbery of banks, US attorneys cases by disposition, FY91, annual rpt, 6004–2.1; 6004–2.7
Securities of banks, common stock dividends relation to earnings, capital, and other factors, 1989-90, article, 9292–4.302
Securities of banks, new issues by type of instrument, relation to primary capital ratio and other factors, 1983-86, working paper, 9371–10.79
Service fees, minimum balances, and services offered by banks and thrifts, by service type, 1991, annual rpt, 9364–12
Small Business Investment Companies capital holdings, SBA obligation, and ownership, as of July 1992, semiannual listing, 9762–4

South Central States agricultural and small banks financial ratios, by State, as of 1991 and trends from 1985, article, 9391–16.306
South Central States agricultural banks financial ratios, and farm finances and production growth, by State, 1980s-92, annual article, 9391–16.308
South Central States bank performance indicators by asset size, Fed Reserve 8th District, 1988-91, annual article, 9391–16.307
Southeastern States, Fed Reserve 6th District banks financial ratios, by asset size and State, 1987-91, annual article, 9371–1.305
Southeastern States, Fed Reserve 8th District banking and economic conditions, quarterly rpt with articles, 9391–16
Statistical Abstract of US, 1992 annual data compilation, 2324–1.16
Tax (income) returns for foreign corporate activity in US, selected income and tax items, by industry div and selected country, 1988, article, 8302–2.309
Tax (income) returns of corporations, income and tax items by asset size and detailed industry, 1989, annual rpt, 8304–4; 8304–21
Tax rates and revenue of State and local govts, by source and State, 1992 and historical trends, annual rpt, 10044–1
Texas banks loan losses relation to loan volume growth and other factors, mid 1970s-90, article, 9379–1.305
Texas banks loans and financial ratios relation to economic indicators, 1970s-90, working paper, 9379–14.16
Trust assets of banks, trust companies, and S&Ls, by type of asset and fund, selected firm, and State, 1991, annual rpt, 13004–1
West Central States economic indicators, Fed Reserve 10th District, quarterly rpt, 9381–16.2
West Central States, Fed Reserve 10th District banking industry structure, performance, and financial devs, 1991, annual rpt, 9381–14
see also Agricultural credit
see also Automated tellers
see also Bank deposits
see also Bank holding companies
see also Checking accounts
see also Commercial credit
see also Consumer credit
see also Credit
see also Credit cards
see also Credit unions
see also Deposit insurance
see also Discrimination in credit
see also Electronic funds transfer
see also Eurocurrency
see also Export-Import Bank
see also Farm Credit System
see also Federal Financing Bank
see also Federal Home Loan Banks
see also Federal Reserve System
see also Financial institutions regulation
see also Flow-of-funds accounts
see also Foreign exchange
see also Interest rates
see also International reserves
see also Loans
see also Money supply
see also Mortgages
see also Negotiable orders of withdrawal accounts
see also Savings
see also Savings institutions

Banks for Cooperatives
see Farm Credit System

Barbados
Agricultural trade of US, by detailed commodity and country, 1991, annual rpt, 1524–8
Agricultural trade of US, by detailed commodity and country, 1991, semiannual rpt, 1522–4
AID economic aid to developing countries, obligations and disbursements by country, quarterly rpt, 9912–4
Economic and military aid and loans from US and intl agencies, by program and country, FY46-91, annual rpt, 9914–5
Economic and social conditions of developing countries from 1960s, and Intl Dev Cooperation Agency and AID activities and funding, FY91-93, annual rpt, 9904–4
Economic and social conditions, resources, and trade, and aid, 1992, annual factbook, 9914–14
Economic conditions, policy, and trade practices, by country, 1989-91, annual rpt, 21384–5
Economic, social, political, and geographic summary data, by country, 1992, annual factbook, 9114–2
Exports and imports of US, by transport mode, country, and SITC 1- to 3-digit commodity, 1991, annual rpt, 2424–12
Exports of US, detailed Schedule B commodities with countries of destination, 1991, annual rpt, 2424–10
Human rights conditions in 170 countries, and US economic and military aid, 1991, annual rpt, 21384–3
Military aid of US, arms sales, and training programs costs and budget requests, by program, world region, and country, FY91-93, annual rpt, 7144–13
Military spending, arms trade, and force strengths, with govt spending and population, by country, 1979-89, annual rpt, 9824–1
Multinatl US firms and foreign affiliates finances and operations, by industry and country, 1989 benchmark survey, annual rpt, 2704–5
Population size, growth rates, and components of change, by country, projected 1990-2020 and trends from 1950, biennial rpt, 2324–9
Tax (income) returns of Foreign Sales Corps, assets, and income and tax items, by industry, country of incorporation, and transaction pricing method, 1987, article, 8302–2.311
UN voting record and share of votes in agreement with US, by issue, country, and world area, 1991, annual rpt, 7004–18

Barber and beauty shops
County Business Patterns, 1989: employment, establishments, and payroll, by SIC 2- to 4-digit industry and county, annual State rpt series, 2326–8
County Business Patterns, 1990: employment, establishments, and payroll, by SIC 2- to 4-digit industry and county, annual State rpt series, 2326–6
CPI by component for US city average, and by selected metro area, region, and population size, monthly rpt, 6762–2
Employment, earnings, and hours, by SIC 1- to 4-digit industry, monthly 1989-Feb 1992, annual rpt, 6744–4
House of Representatives salaries, expenses, and contingent fund disbursement, detailed listings, quarterly rpt, 21942–1
Input-output structure of US economy, detailed interindustry transactions for 541 industries, and components of final demand, 1982 benchmark data, 2708–17
Labor demand, turnover, and training completions, by detailed occupation, 1990 and projected to 2005, biennial rpt, 6744–3
Labor productivity, indexes of output, hours, and employment by SIC 2- to 4-digit industry, 1967-90, annual rpt, 6824–1.4
Occupational injury and illness rates, by SIC 2- to 4-digit industry, 1990, annual rpt, 6844–1
Occupational Outlook Handbook, 1992-93, biennial rpt, 6744–1
Senate receipts, itemized expenses by payee, and balances, 1st half FY92, semiannual listing, 25922–1
Tax (income) returns of partnerships, income statement and balance sheet items, by industry group, 1990, annual article, 8302–2.314
Tax (income) returns of sole proprietorships, income statement items, by industry group, 1990, annual article, 8302–2.317; 8302–2.320

Barbett, Samuel F.
"State Higher Education Profiles, Fourth Edition: A Comparison of State Higher Education Data for FY88", 4844–13

Bargas, Sylvia E.
"U.S. International Sales and Purchases of Private Services: U.S. Cross-Border Transactions, 1986-91; and Sales by Affiliates, 1989-90", 2702–1.336

Barges
Construction and operating subsidies of MarAd by firm, and ship deliveries and fleet by country, by vessel type, FY91, annual rpt, 7704–14.1
Containers (intermodal) and equipment owned by shipping and leasing companies, inventory by type and size, 1991, annual rpt, 7704–10
Foreign and US merchant ships, tonnage, and new ship construction and deliveries, by vessel type and country, as of Jan 1992, annual rpt, 7704–3
Freight (shipborne domestic), by major commodity group, vessel type, and port, 1987-89, annual rpt, 7704–7
Freight (waterborne domestic and foreign) by commodity, traffic, and passengers, by port and waterway, 1989, annual rpt, 3754–3
Grain shipments and rates for barge and rail loadings, periodic situation rpt with articles, 1561–4
Ohio River basin waterway facilities, freight by commodity and port, and recreation, by waterway, 1988-89, annual rpt, 3754–6
Oil and refined products stocks, and interdistrict shipments by mode of transport, monthly rpt, 3162–6.3

Oil crude, gas liquids, and refined products supply, demand, and movement, by PAD district and State, 1991, annual rpt, 3164–2
St Lawrence Seaway ship, cargo, and passenger traffic, and toll revenue, 1991 and trends from 1959, annual rpt, 7744–2

Barkema, Alan D.
"Farm Economy Turns Down", 9381–1.303
"North American Free Trade Agreement: What Is at Stake for U.S. Agriculture?", 9381–1.307
"Realignment in Farm Lending: Strategic Issues for the 1990s", 9381–10.122

Barker, Peggy R.
"Serious Mental Illness and Disability in the Adult Household Population: U.S., 1989", 4146–8.220

Barley
see Grains and grain products

Barnes, George P.
"Ethnicity, Location, Age, and Fluoridation Factors in Baby Bottle Tooth Decay and Caries Prevalence of Head Start Children", 4042–3.317

Barron, John M.
"Gender Differences in Training, Capital, and Wages", 6886–6.93

Barry, Robert D.
"Agriculture Outlook 1992: Panel Discussion on U.S. Sugar Program", 1504–9.1

Basketball
Injuries from use of consumer products and related activities, by severity and victim age and sex, 1990, annual rpt, 9164–7
Injuries from use of consumer products, by severity, victim age, and detailed product, 1991, annual rpt, 9164–6
NCAA Div I athletic depts staff by race, and income, by sex and position, 1990/91, GAO rpt, 26121–476

Bastian, Lisa D.
"Crime and the Nation's Households, 1991", 6066–25.49
"School Crime: A National Crime Victimization Survey Report", 6066–3.46

Batista, Juan C.
"Vital Link to Trade in Tree Fruit Between Mexico and California Is Transportation", 1504–9.1

Baton Rouge, La.
Wages by occupation, and benefits for office and plant workers, 1992 survey, periodic MSA rpt, 6785–3.6
see also under By City and By SMSA or MSA in the "Index by Categories"

Battelle Memorial Institute
"California OCS Phase II Monitoring Program: Final Report", 5734–11
"Monitoring of Olympic National Park Beaches To Determine Fate and Effects of Spilled Bunker C Fuel Oil", 5738–38.1
see also Department of Energy National Laboratories

Batteries
Auto (electric-powered) R&D activity and DOE funding shares, FY91, annual rpt, 3304–2
Auto parts trade with Japan and other countries, 1985-90 and forecast to 1994, annual rpt, 2004–10
Business statistics, detailed data for major industries and economic indicators, *Survey of Current Business*, monthly rpt, 2702–1.16
Business statistics, detailed data for major industries and economic indicators, 1960-91, *Survey of Current Business* biennial supplement, 2704–1
County Business Patterns, 1989: employment, establishments, and payroll, by SIC 2- to 4-digit industry and county, annual State rpt series, 2326–8
County Business Patterns, 1990: employment, establishments, and payroll, by SIC 2- to 4-digit industry and county, annual State rpt series, 2326–6
Employment, earnings, and hours, by SIC 1- to 4-digit industry, monthly 1989-Feb 1992, annual rpt, 6744–4
Exports and imports between US and outlying areas, by detailed commodity and mode of transport, 1991, annual rpt, 2424–11
Exports and imports of US, by country and detailed commodity, monthly rpt, 2422–12
Exports and imports of US, by Harmonized System 6-digit commodity and country, 1991, annual rpt, 2424–13
Exports of US, detailed Schedule B commodities with countries of destination, 1991, annual rpt, 2424–10
Injuries from use of consumer products and related activities, by severity and victim age and sex, 1990, annual rpt, 9164–7
Injuries from use of consumer products, by severity, victim age, and detailed product, 1991, annual rpt, 9164–6
Input-output structure of US economy, detailed interindustry transactions for 541 industries, and components of final demand, 1982 benchmark data, 2708–17
Manufacturing annual survey, 1990: finances and operations, by SIC 2- to 4-digit industry, series, 2506–14
Manufacturing census, 1987: concentration of largest firms measured by value added, and for shipments by SIC 2- and 4-digit industry, subject rpt, 2497–6
Manufacturing census, 1987: shipments of manufacturers products, by customer class and SIC 2- and 4-digit industry, subject rpt, 2497–4
Occupational injury and illness rates, by SIC 2- to 4-digit industry, 1989-90, annual rpt, 6844–7
Occupational injury and illness rates, by SIC 2- to 4-digit industry, 1990, annual rpt, 6844–1
OECD trade, total and for 4 major countries, and US trade by country, by commodity, 1980-90, world area rpt series, 9116–1
Price indexes (producer), by stage of processing and detailed commodity, monthly rpt, 6762–6
Price indexes (producer), by stage of processing and detailed commodity, monthly 1991, annual rpt, 6764–2

Bauer, Paul W.
"Inefficiency and Productivity Growth in Banking: A Comparison of Stochastic Econometric and Thick Frontier Methods", 9377–9.126

Baugher, Eleanor F.
"Poverty in the U.S.: 1991", 2546–6.77

Bauxite
see Aluminum and aluminum industry

Bayoumi, Tamim
"Taxation and Inflation: A New Explanation for Current Account Imbalances", 9366–7.274

BEA
see Bureau of Economic Analysis

Beaches
see Lakes and lakeshores
see Seashores

Bean, Judy A.
"Covariances for Estimated Totals When Comparing Between Years. Vital and Health Statistics Series 2", 4147–2.114

Beans
see Vegetables and vegetable products

Bears
see Wildlife and wildlife conservation

Beaufort Sea
Environmental conditions and oil dev impacts for Alaska OCS, compilation of papers, series, 2176–1
Fish (anadromous species) population, migration, and habitat conditions, for coastal Beaufort Sea, summer 1990, 5738–37
Pollution concentrations in Beaufort Sea sediment and marine life, by contaminant and site, 1985-89, 5738–33
Whales (bowhead and white) migration through Beaufort Sea, behavior impacts of oil drilling and aircraft noise, spring 1990, 5738–27
Whales population and behavior in Chukchi and Beaufort Seas, by endangered species, 1982-91, 5738–32
Whales population and behavior in Chukchi and Beaufort Seas, by endangered species, 1990, 5738–36

Beaumont, Tex.
Ships in Natl Defense Reserve Fleet at Beaumont harbor, as of July 1991, semiannual listing, 7702–2
see also under By City and By SMSA or MSA in the "Index by Categories"

Beauregard, Karen M.
"Persons Denied Private Health Insurance Due to Poor Health", 4186–8.23

Beauty aids
see Cosmetics and toiletries

Beauty parlors
see Barber and beauty shops

Bechter, Dan M.
"Evidence of Improved Inventory Control", 9389–1.302

Becker, Paul R.
"Alaska Marine Mammal Tissue Archival Project: Sample Inventory and Results of Analyses of Selected Samples for Organic Compounds and Trace Elements", 2218–87

Beckman, Barry A.
"Composite Index of Coincident Indicators and Alternative Coincident Indexes", 2702–1.322

Beckman, David P.
"Idaho Forest Pest Conditions and Program Summary, 1990", 1206–49.1
"Idaho Forest Pest Conditions and Program Summary, 1991", 1206–49.4

Bedore, James M.
"Do U.S. Health Care Costs Affect U.S. International Competitiveness?", 9882–16.302
"Insurance, Industry and Trade Summary", 9885–12.2

Beecher, Gary R.
"Nutrient Content of Foods Important to Health", 1504–9.1

Beemiller, Richard M.
"Regional Multipliers: A User Handbook for the Regional Input-Output Modeling System (RIMS II)", 2708–47

Beer and breweries
Appalachia food processing firms, employment, and shipments, and farm production, by commodity and State, 1960s-90, 9088–37
Business statistics, detailed data for major industries and economic indicators, *Survey of Current Business*, monthly rpt, 2702–1.13
Business statistics, detailed data for major industries and economic indicators, 1960-91, *Survey of Current Business* biennial supplement, 2704–1
Consumption of alcohol, by beverage type, region, and State, 1977-88, annual rpt, 4486–1.11
Consumption of alcohol, by beverage type, region, and State, 1977-89, annual rpt, 4486–1.15
Consumption, supply, trade, prices, spending, and indexes, by food commodity, 1990, annual rpt, 1544–4
County Business Patterns, 1989: employment, establishments, and payroll, by SIC 2- to 4-digit industry and county, annual State rpt series, 2326–8
County Business Patterns, 1990: employment, establishments, and payroll, by SIC 2- to 4-digit industry and county, annual State rpt series, 2326–6
CPI by component for US city average, and by selected metro area, region, and population size, monthly rpt, 6762–2
Employment, earnings, and hours, by SIC 1- to 4-digit industry, monthly 1989-Feb 1992, annual rpt, 6744–4
Exports and imports (agricultural) of US, by commodity and country, bimonthly rpt, 1522–1
Exports and imports (agricultural) of US, by detailed commodity and country, 1991, annual rpt, 1524–8
Exports and imports (agricultural) of US, by detailed commodity and country, 1991, semiannual rpt, 1522–4
Exports and imports between US and outlying areas, by detailed commodity and mode of transport, 1991, annual rpt, 2424–11
Exports and imports of US, by country and detailed commodity, monthly rpt, 2422–12
Exports and imports of US, by Harmonized System 6-digit commodity and country, 1991, annual rpt, 2424–13
Exports of US, detailed Schedule B commodities with countries of destination, 1991, annual rpt, 2424–10
Grain (feed) consumption, by end use, periodic situation rpt with articles, 1561–4
Grain prices for brewers, rice and corn grits, periodic situation rpt, 1561–8
Grain production, prices, trade, and export inspections by US port and country of destination, by grain type, weekly rpt, 1313–2
Hops production, stocks, use, and US trade by country, monthly rpt, 1313–7
Hops stocks held by growers, dealers, and brewers, 1990-92, semiannual press release, 1621–8
Input-output structure of US economy, detailed interindustry transactions for 541 industries, and components of final demand, 1982 benchmark data, 2708–17
Labor productivity, indexes of output, hours, and employment by SIC 2- to 4-digit industry, 1967-90, annual rpt, 6824–1.3
Manufacturing annual survey, 1990: finances and operations, by SIC 2- to 4-digit industry, series, 2506–14
Manufacturing census, 1987: concentration of largest firms measured by value added, and for shipments by SIC 2- and 4-digit industry, subject rpt, 2497–6
Manufacturing census, 1987: shipments of manufacturers products, by customer class and SIC 2- and 4-digit industry, subject rpt, 2497–4
Occupational injury and illness rates, by SIC 2- to 4-digit industry, 1989-90, annual rpt, 6844–7
Occupational injury and illness rates, by SIC 2- to 4-digit industry, 1990, annual rpt, 6844–1
Price indexes (producer), by stage of processing and detailed commodity, monthly rpt, 6762–6
Price indexes (producer), by stage of processing and detailed commodity, monthly 1991, annual rpt, 6764–2
Production of beer, monthly rpt, 1313–7
Production, stocks, materials used, and tax-free and taxable removals by State, for beer, monthly rpt, 8486–1.1
Rice shipments, by end use, package size, and State of origin and destination, 1960s-89, biennial rpt, 1564–11
Tax (income) returns of corporations, income and tax items by asset size and detailed industry, 1989, annual rpt, 8304–4; 8304–21
Tax rates and revenue of State and local govts, by source and State, 1992 and historical trends, annual rpt, 10044–1
Youth alcohol use, knowledge, attitudes, and info sources, series, 4006–10

Bees and beeswax
see Honey and beekeeping

Beeson, Patricia E.
"Components of City-Size Wage Differentials, 1973-88", 9377–1.301

Behavior
see Health risk behavior
see Intelligence levels
see Mental health and illness
see Sexual behavior
see Social sciences
see Stress

Behavioral sciences
see Anthropology
see Psychology
see Social sciences
see Sociology

Behrmann, Susan L.
"Collective Bargaining, 1991: Recession Colors Talks", 6722–1.307

Belarus
see Byelarus

Belgium
Agricultural trade of US, by detailed commodity and country, 1991, annual rpt, 1524–8
Agricultural trade of US, by detailed commodity and country, 1991, semiannual rpt, 1522–4
AID loans repayment status and terms by program and country, and status of predecessor agency loans, quarterly rpt, 9912–3
Cuba trade, by commodity and country, mid 1980s-91, 9118–8
Dollar exchange rates of selected currencies, weekly chartbook, 9365–1.5
Economic and military aid and loans from US and intl agencies, by program and country, FY46-91, annual rpt, 9914–5
Economic conditions, income, production, prices, employment, and trade, 1992 periodic country rpt, 2046–4.30
Economic conditions, policy, and trade practices, by country, 1989-91, annual rpt, 21384–5
Economic, social, political, and geographic summary data, by country, 1992, annual factbook, 9114–2
Education in science and math, intl assessment results and other indicators of proficiency, by selected country, 1960s-80s, 4838–51
Exports and imports of US, by Harmonized System 6-digit commodity and country, 1991, annual rpt, 2424–13
Exports and imports of US, by selected country, country group, and commodity group, 1991, annual rpt, 2044–37
Exports and imports of US, by transport mode, country, and SITC 1- to 3-digit commodity, 1991, annual rpt, 2424–12
Exports, imports, and balances of US for manufactured goods, by SITC 2-digit commodity and country, quarterly rpt, 2042–35
Exports of US, detailed Schedule B commodities with countries of destination, 1991, annual rpt, 2424–10
Health care costs and components, services use, resources, and economic indicators, by OECD country, 1960s-90, article, 4652–1.322
Human rights conditions in 170 countries, and US economic and military aid, 1991, annual rpt, 21384–3
Intl transactions of US with 9 countries, 1989-91, *Survey of Current Business*, monthly rpt, annual table, 2702–1.33
Labor conditions, union coverage, and work accidents, 1992 annual country rpt, 6366–4.19; 6366–4.30
Military spending, arms trade, and force strengths, with govt spending and population, by country, 1979-89, annual rpt, 9824–1
Multinatl US firms and foreign affiliates finances and operations, by industry and country, 1989 benchmark survey, annual rpt, 2704–5
Multinatl US firms foreign affiliates, income statement items by asset size, industry, and country, 1988, biennial article, 8302–2.322

Nuclear power generation in US and 20 countries, monthly rpt, 3162–24.10
Nuclear power generation in US and 20 countries, monthly 1973-88, 3168–123.10
Oil production, stocks, use, and trade, by selected country and country group, monthly rpt, 3162–42
Population size, growth rates, and components of change, by country, projected 1990-2020 and trends from 1950, biennial rpt, 2324–9
Refugee migration, and intl aid programs, by world area and country of origin and asylum, 1991, annual rpt, 7004–15
Steel (carbon flat-rolled) products from 21 countries, injury to US industry from foreign subsidized and less than fair value imports, investigation with background financial and operating data, 1992 rpt, 9886–19.85
Steel trade, by product, country, and customs district, with US industry operating data, 1989-June 1992, semiannual rpt, 9882–15
Tax (estate) returns for nonresident aliens, property and tax data, by estate size and decedent country of residence, 1986, article, 8302–2.310
Tax revenue, by level of govt and type of tax, for OECD countries, mid 1960s-90, annual rpt, 10044–1.2
UN voting record and share of votes in agreement with US, by issue, country, and world area, 1991, annual rpt, 7004–18
see also under By Foreign Country in the "Index by Categories"

Belitz, Kenneth
"Estimation of a Water Budget for the Central Part of the Western San Joaquin Valley, California. Regional Aquifer-System Analysis ", 5666–25.14

Belize
Agricultural trade of US, by detailed commodity and country, 1991, annual rpt, 1524–8
Agricultural trade of US, by detailed commodity and country, 1991, semiannual rpt, 1522–4
AID economic aid to developing countries, obligations and disbursements by country, quarterly rpt, 9912–4
AID loans repayment status and terms by program and country, and status of predecessor agency loans, quarterly rpt, 9912–3
Economic and military aid and loans from US and intl agencies, by program and country, FY46-91, annual rpt, 9914–5
Economic and social conditions of developing countries from 1960s, and Intl Dev Cooperation Agency and AID activities and funding, FY91-93, annual rpt, 9904–4
Economic and social conditions, resources, and trade, and aid, 1992, annual factbook, 9914–14
Economic, social, political, and geographic summary data, by country, 1992, annual factbook, 9114–2
Exports and imports of US, by transport mode, country, and SITC 1- to 3-digit commodity, 1991, annual rpt, 2424–12
Exports of US, detailed Schedule B commodities with countries of destination, 1991, annual rpt, 2424–10
Human rights conditions in 170 countries, and US economic and military aid, 1991, annual rpt, 21384–3
Military aid of US, arms sales, and training programs costs and budget requests, by program, world region, and country, FY91-93, annual rpt, 7144–13
Population size, growth rates, and components of change, by country, projected 1990-2020 and trends from 1950, biennial rpt, 2324–9
Refugee migration, and intl aid programs, by world area and country of origin and asylum, 1991, annual rpt, 7004–15
UN voting record and share of votes in agreement with US, by issue, country, and world area, 1991, annual rpt, 7004–18

Bell, Felicitie C.
"Life Tables for the U.S. Social Security Area: 1900-2080", 4706–1.107

Bell Operating Companies
Fiber optics and copper wire mileage and access lines, and fiber systems investment, by telecommunications firm, 1985-91, annual rpt, 9284–18
Finances and operations, detail for telephone firms, 1990, annual rpt, 9284–6
Finances and operations of local and long distance firms, subscribership, and charges, late 1970s-92, semiannual rpt, 9282–7
Local telephone rates and low-income subsidies, by region, company, and city, 1980s-91, semiannual rpt, 9282–8
Transmission and network systems dev, and indicators of use, by BOC, 1991 rpt, 2808–30

Bellamy, Donald
"Educational Attainment of Farm Operators", 1541–1.316

Belongia, Michael T.
"Foreign Exchange Intervention by the U.S.: A Review and Assessment of 1985-89", 9391–1.310

Beltz, Roy C.
"Forest Resources of Arkansas", 1206–8.13

Bender, Thomas R.
"Surveillance of Traumatic Occupational Fatalities in Alaska—Implications for Prevention", 4042–3.307

Benin
Agricultural trade of US, by detailed commodity and country, 1991, annual rpt, 1524–8
Agricultural trade of US, by detailed commodity and country, 1991, semiannual rpt, 1522–4
AID economic aid to developing countries, obligations and disbursements by country, quarterly rpt, 9912–4
AID loans repayment status and terms by program and country, and status of predecessor agency loans, quarterly rpt, 9912–3
Economic and military aid and loans from US and intl agencies, by program and country, FY46-91, annual rpt, 9914–5
Economic and social conditions of developing countries from 1960s, and Intl Dev Cooperation Agency and AID activities and funding, FY91-93, annual rpt, 9904–4
Economic conditions, income, production, prices, employment, and trade, 1992 periodic country rpt, 2046–4.15
Economic, social, political, and geographic summary data, by country, 1992, annual factbook, 9114–2
Exports and imports of US, by commodity and country, 1980-90, world area rpt, 9116–1.2
Exports and imports of US, by transport mode, country, and SITC 1- to 3-digit commodity, 1991, annual rpt, 2424–12
Exports of US, detailed Schedule B commodities with countries of destination, 1991, annual rpt, 2424–10
Human rights conditions in 170 countries, and US economic and military aid, 1991, annual rpt, 21384–3
Military aid of US, arms sales, and training programs costs and budget requests, by program, world region, and country, FY91-93, annual rpt, 7144–13
Military spending, arms trade, and force strengths, with govt spending and population, by country, 1979-89, annual rpt, 9824–1
Minerals Yearbook, Vol 3, 1989: foreign country review of production, trade, and policy, by commodity, annual rpt, 5604–35.1
Population size, growth rates, and components of change, by country, projected 1990-2020 and trends from 1950, biennial rpt, 2324–9
Refugee migration, and intl aid programs, by world area and country of origin and asylum, 1991, annual rpt, 7004–15
UN voting record and share of votes in agreement with US, by issue, country, and world area, 1991, annual rpt, 7004–18

Bennefield, Robert L.
"Who's Helping Out? Support Networks Among American Families: 1988", 2546–20.21

Bennett, Claudette E.
"Asian and Pacific Islander Population in the U.S.: March 1990-91", 2546–1.462
"Black Population in the U.S.: March 1991", 2546–1.463

Benson, Paul R.
"Clients/Patients with a Principal Diagnosis of Affective Disorder Served in the Inpatient, Outpatient, and Partial Care Programs of Specialty Mental Health Organizations, U.S., 1986", 4506–3.49

Benson, Veronica
"Current Estimates from the National Health Interview Survey, 1990", 4147–10.182
"Current Estimates from the National Health Interview Survey, 1991. Vital and Health Statistics Series 10", 4147–10.183

Benston, George J.
"Motivations for Bank Mergers and Acquisitions: Enhancing the Deposit Insurance Put Option versus Increasing Operating Net Cash Flow", 9371–10.80

Berenbrock, Charles
"Ground-Water Flow System in Indian Wells Valley, Kern, Inyo, and San Bernardino Counties, California", 5666–28.15

Bergen County, N.J.
Housing and households characteristics, and unit and neighborhood quality, by MSA location for 11 MSAs, 1987 survey, supplement, 2485–8

Wages by occupation, and benefits, for office and plant workers, 1992 survey, periodic MSA rpt, 6785–17.3

Berger, Allen N.

"Profit-Concentration Relationship in Banking", 9366–6.290

"Securitization, Risk, and the Liquidity Problem in Banking", 9366–6.295

Bering Sea

Environmental conditions and oil dev impacts for Alaska OCS, compilation of papers, series, 2176–1

Ice conditions of Bering Sea and Alaska north coast, monthly rpt, 2182–5

Marine mammals incidental catch by fishing trawl vessels, by species, vessel flag and type, and North Pacific location, 1965-88, 2168–129

Research activities of Pacific Marine Environmental Lab, and bibl, FY91, annual rpt, 2144–21

Tide height and time daily at coastal points, forecast 1993, annual rpt, 2174–2.5

Berlin, Mitchell

"Debt Covenants and Renegotiation", 9387–8.272

Bermuda

Agricultural trade of US, by detailed commodity and country, 1991, annual rpt, 1524–8

Agricultural trade of US, by detailed commodity and country, 1991, semiannual rpt, 1522–4

Economic and military aid and loans from US and intl agencies, by program and country, FY46-91, annual rpt, 9914–5

Economic and social conditions, resources, and trade, and aid, 1992, annual factbook, 9914–14

Economic, social, political, and geographic summary data, by country, 1992, annual factbook, 9114–2

Exports and imports of US, by transport mode, country, and SITC 1- to 3-digit commodity, 1991, annual rpt, 2424–12

Exports of US, detailed Schedule B commodities with countries of destination, 1991, annual rpt, 2424–10

Multinatl US firms and foreign affiliates finances and operations, by industry and country, 1989 benchmark survey, annual rpt, 2704–5

Multinatl US firms foreign affiliates, income statement items by asset size, industry, and country, 1988, biennial article, 8302–2.322

Population size, growth rates, and components of change, by country, projected 1990-2020 and trends from 1950, biennial rpt, 2324–9

Tax (income) returns, income, and tax withheld for foreign partners of US partnerships, by country, 1990, article, 8302–2.324

Berreth, Charles A.

"Workers' Compensation: State Enactments in 1991", 6722–1.310

Betting

see Gambling

see Pari-mutuel wagering

Beverages

Consumption, supply, trade, prices, spending, and indexes, by food commodity, 1990, annual rpt, 1544–4

County Business Patterns, 1989: employment, establishments, and payroll, by SIC 2- to 4-digit industry and county, annual State rpt series, 2326–8

County Business Patterns, 1990: employment, establishments, and payroll, by SIC 2- to 4-digit industry and county, annual State rpt series, 2326–6

CPI by component for US city average, and by selected metro area, region, and population size, monthly rpt, 6762–2

Employment, earnings, and hours, by SIC 1- to 4-digit industry, monthly 1989-Feb 1992, annual rpt, 6744–4

Employment of minorities and women, by occupation, SIC 1- to 3-digit industry, State, and MSA, 1991, annual rpt, 9244–1

Exports and imports (agricultural) of US, by commodity and country, bimonthly rpt, 1522–1

Exports and imports (agricultural) of US, by detailed commodity and country, 1991, annual rpt, 1524–8

Exports and imports (agricultural) of US, by detailed commodity and country, 1991, semiannual rpt, 1522–4

Exports and imports between US and outlying areas, by detailed commodity and mode of transport, 1991, annual rpt, 2424–11

Exports and imports of US, by country and detailed commodity, monthly rpt, 2422–12

Exports and imports of US, by Harmonized System 6-digit commodity and country, 1991, annual rpt, 2424–13

Exports and imports of US, by selected country, country group, and commodity group, 1991, annual rpt, 2044–37

Exports and imports of US, by transport mode, country, and SITC 1- to 3-digit commodity, 1991, annual rpt, 2424–12

Exports of US, detailed Schedule B commodities with countries of destination, 1991, annual rpt, 2424–10

Foreign and US fresh and processed fruit, vegetable, and nut production and trade, FAS monthly circular with articles, 1925–34

Manufacturing census, 1987: concentration of largest firms measured by value added, and for shipments by SIC 2- and 4-digit industry, subject rpt, 2497–6

Manufacturing census, 1987: shipments of manufacturers products, by customer class and SIC 2- and 4-digit industry, subject rpt, 2497–4

Multinatl US firms and foreign affiliates finances and operations, by industry and country, 1989 benchmark survey, annual rpt, 2704–5

Nutrient, caloric, and waste composition, detailed data for raw, processed, and prepared foods, 1992 rpt, 1356–3.17

Occupational injury and illness rates, by SIC 2- to 4-digit industry, 1989-90, annual rpt, 6844–7

Occupational injury and illness rates, by SIC 2- to 4-digit industry, 1990, annual rpt, 6844–1

OECD trade, total and for 4 major countries, and US trade by country, by commodity, 1980-90, world area rpt series, 9116–1

Orange juice (frozen) cold storage stocks, by census div, 1991, annual rpt, 1631–11

Orange juice production, imports, exports, and use, by country, various periods 1985-92, article, 1925–34.308

Orange juice production, use, exports, and stocks, and Brazil exports, by country, 1985-92, article, 1925–34.328

Pineapple (canned fruit and juice) production and exports, by country, and Mexico export prices, selected years 1987-92, annual article, 1925–34.327

Pineapple (canned fruit and juice) production and exports, for 2 countries, forecast 1992, semiannual article, 1925–34.346

Price indexes (producer), by stage of processing and detailed commodity, monthly rpt, 6762–6

Price indexes (producer), by stage of processing and detailed commodity, monthly 1991, annual rpt, 6764–2

Science, engineering, and technical employment in manufacturing, by field and industry, 1989, triennial rpt, 9627–23

Statistical Abstract of US, 1992 annual data compilation, 2324–1.3

Tax (income) returns of corporations, income and tax items by asset size and detailed industry, 1989, annual rpt, 8304–4

Vending machine shipments by product, trade, and use, 1991, Current Industrial Rpt, 2506–12.10

Weight and volume conversion factors for agricultural commodities and products, 1992 rpt, 1508–3

see also Beer and breweries

see also Coffee

see also Liquor and liquor industry

see also Soft drink industry and products

see also Tea

see also Wine and winemaking

see also under By Commodity in the "Index by Categories"

Bexar County, Tex.

Housing and households characteristics, and unit and neighborhood quality, by MSA location for 11 MSAs, 1986 survey, supplement, 2485–8

Bezirganian, Steve D.

"U.S. Affiliates of Foreign Companies: Operations in 1990", 2702–1.319

Bhutan

Economic and military aid and loans from US and intl agencies, by program and country, FY46-91, annual rpt, 9914–5

Economic, social, political, and geographic summary data, by country, 1992, annual factbook, 9114–2

Exports and imports of US, by transport mode, country, and SITC 1- to 3-digit commodity, 1991, annual rpt, 2424–12

Human rights conditions in 170 countries, and US economic and military aid, 1991, annual rpt, 21384–3

Minerals Yearbook, Vol 3, 1989: foreign country review of production, trade, and policy, by commodity, annual rpt, 5604–35.2

Population size, growth rates, and components of change, by country, projected 1990-2020 and trends from 1950, biennial rpt, 2324–9

Refugee migration, and intl aid programs, by world area and country of origin and asylum, 1991, annual rpt, 7004–15
UN voting record and share of votes in agreement with US, by issue, country, and world area, 1991, annual rpt, 7004–18
Bibliographies
Accident deaths and injuries prevention, and treatment, 1991 conf papers, 4208–35
Agent Orange exposure health effects, literature review, 1990, annual rpt series, 8706–1
Alaska OCS environmental conditions and oil dev impacts, compilation of papers, series, 2176–1
Alcohol abuse research, treatment programs, and patient characteristics and health effects, quarterly journal, 4482–1
Atlantic Oceanographic and Meteorological Lab research activities and bibl, FY91, annual rpt, 2144–19
Auto (electric-powered) R&D activity and DOE funding shares, FY91, annual rpt, 3304–2
Biomass energy program of TVA, operations, finances, and technological characteristics, series, 9806–9
Birds (northern spotted owl) conservation methods in Pacific Northwest, findings and recommendations, 1990 rpt, 1208–385
Birds (northern spotted owl) conservation methods in Pacific Northwest, timber industry impacts, and Federal and State spending, 1980s-95, 1208–388
Caribbean Basin Initiative export and investment incentives, contact listing, bibl, and US imports country, 1983-91, annual rpt, 2044–36
Coastal and estuarine pollutant concentrations in fish, shellfish, and environment, series, 2176–3
Coastal and riparian areas environmental conditions, fish, wildlife, use, and mgmt, for individual ecosystems, series, 5506–9
Coastal areas environmental conditions and mgmt, for individual areas, conf series, 2146–8
Crime, criminal justice admin and enforcement, and public opinion, data compilation, 1992 annual rpt, 6064–6
Criminal justice issues, series, 6066–25
Developing countries economic, population, and agricultural data, US and other aid sources, and AID activity, country rpt series, 9916–12
Disasters and natl security incidents and mgmt, with data by major event and State, 1992 annual rpt, 9434–6
Drug abuse and treatment, research on biological and behavioral factors and addiction potential of new drugs, 1991 annual conf, 4494–11
Employment and retirement research, bibl, 1990 listing, 4746–26.14
Employment and unemployment current statistics and articles, Monthly Labor Review, 6722–1
Energy supply and demand summary data, DOE activities and finances, and bibl, 1990, annual rpt, 3024–2
Foreign countries *Background Notes*, summary social, political, and economic data, series, 7006–2
Foreign countries economic and social conditions, working paper series, 2326–18
Foreign countries statistical abstracts and rpts, 1992 annual listing, 2324–1
Geothermal resources, power plant capacity and operating status, leases, and wells, by location, 1960s-95, 3308–87
Glaciology intl research summaries, methodology, and bibls, series, 2156–18
Global climate change and contributing pollutants emissions, literature review, 1980s and projected to 2075, 3338–3
Global climate change contributing pollutants, atmospheric concentrations by location, and monitoring activities, 1990, annual rpt, 2144–28
Global climate change contributing pollutants, emissions by monitoring site and country, and temperature change by world area and US region, 1860s-1990, annual rpt, 3004–33
Great Lakes Environmental Research Lab activities, FY91 annual rpt, 2144–26
Grocery store profits and prices relation to market concentration, literature review, 1990 rpt, 9408–56
Health condition and quality of life measurement, rpts and other info sources, quarterly listing, 4122–1
Homeless persons aid by program and Federal agency, and indicators of need, 1990, annual rpt, 14364–1
Households composition, income, benefits, and labor force status, Survey of Income and Program Participation methodology, working paper series, 2626–10
Latin America economic conditions, trade, and foreign aid, working paper series, 9916–13
Marine Fisheries Review, US and foreign fisheries resources, dev, mgmt, and research, quarterly journal, 2162–1
Marine Mammal Protection Act admin, and populations, strandings, and catch permits by species and location, 1988-89, annual rpt, 2164–11
Marine mammals protection, Federal and intl regulatory and research activities, 1991, annual rpt, 14734–1
Minerals (strategic) supply and characteristics of individual deposits, by country, commodity rpt series, 5666–21
Minerals resources of Alaska, and geologic characteristics, compilation of papers, 1990, annual rpt, 5664–15
Minerals resources of Alaska, production, oil and gas leases, reserves, and exploratory wells, with maps and bibl, 1990, annual rpt, 5664–11
Morbidity and Mortality Weekly Report, infectious notifiable disease cases by age, race, and State, and deaths, 1940s-91, annual rpt, 4204–1
NOAA Environmental Research Labs rpts, FY91, annual listing, 2144–25
Nuclear power plant decommissioning and radioactive waste site remedial actions, bibl, 1991 annual listing, 3354–12
Ocean pollution, estuary, and coastal waters monitoring and assessment, NOAA activities and funding, FY90, annual rpt, 2174–9
Oceanographic and other research activities of NOAA, FY87-88, biennial rpt, 2144–6
Oil enhanced recovery research contracts of DOE, project summaries, funding, and bibl, quarterly rpt, 3002–14
Pacific Marine Environmental Lab research activities and bibl, FY91, annual rpt, 2144–21
Pollutants health effects, concentrations in food and environment, sources, human intake, and regulation, series, 9186–8
Radiation exposure of population near Hanford, Wash, nuclear plant, with methodology, 1944-91, series, 3356–5
Radiation from electronic devices, incidents by type of device, and FDA control activities, 1991, annual rpt, 4064–13
Semiconductor industry (US) intl competitiveness, status, outlook, and Federal policy, 1980s, annual rpt, 15034–1
Smoking and health effects, with trends in smoking, related disease and death, and public attitudes, literature review, 1992 annual rpt, 4204–18
Smoking, tobacco, and health impacts research rpts, 1991 annual report, 4204–19
Solar photovoltaic R&D sponsored by DOE, projects, funding, and rpts, FY91, annual listing, 3304–20
Soviet Union trade and investment opportunities for US firms, contact listing, bibl, and background economic data, 1991 rpt, 2048–157
States statistical abstracts and rpts, 1992 annual listing, 2324–1
Survey of Income and Program Participation methodology, evaluation of errors, and bibl, 1990 rpt, 2628–34
Telecommunications and Info Natl Admin rpts, FY91, annual listing, 2804–3
Timber in northeastern US, hardwood forests ecology and mgmt, 1992, 1208–405
Timber in Pacific Northwest, old-growth forests plant and wildlife population and species diversity, 1991 compilation of papers, 1208–386
Timber research activities and bibl, annual rpt, suspended, 1204–14
Traffic safety research, literature review, with data on accidents and impact of safety measures, 1961-90, 7558–98
Transit systems research rpts, 1991, annual listing, 7884–11
Vaccination research rpts, 1991 annual listing, 4204–16
Waste (industrial) generation, disposal, and regulation, by industry and State, mid 1980s-90, 26358–256
Youth unemployment research based on natl longitudinal surveys, review of studies conducted 1977-88, 6728–42
see also CD-ROM catalogs and guides
see also Computer data file guides
see also Government publications lists
Bicycles
Accident deaths involving alcohol, by driver and victim blood alcohol levels, and other characteristics, 1977-88, annual rpt, 4486–1.12
Accident deaths involving alcohol, by driver and victim blood alcohol levels, and other characteristics, 1977-89, annual rpt, 4486–1.14

Accidents (fatal), circumstances, and characteristics of persons and vehicles involved, 1991, semiannual rpt, 7762–11
Accidents (fatal), deaths, and rates, by circumstances, characteristics of persons and vehicles involved, and location, 1990, annual rpt, 7764–10
Accidents, casualties, circumstances, and characteristics of persons and vehicles involved, 1990, annual rpt, 7764–18
Accidents involving consumer products and related activities, injuries by severity and victim age and sex, 1990, annual rpt, 9164–7
Accidents involving consumer products, injuries by severity, victim age, and detailed product, 1991, annual rpt, 9164–6
Child bicycle helmet use relation to safety knowledge and attitudes, 1989 local area survey, article, 4042–3.326
Commuting to work, by mode, trip duration, and work location, 1980 and 1990, 7558–120
Exports and imports between US and outlying areas, by detailed commodity and mode of transport, 1991, annual rpt, 2424–11
Exports and imports of US, by country and detailed commodity, monthly rpt, 2422–12
Exports and imports of US, by Harmonized System 6-digit commodity and country, 1991, annual rpt, 2424–13
Exports of US, detailed Schedule B commodities with countries of destination, 1991, annual rpt, 2424–10
Housing and households characteristics, unit and neighborhood quality, and journey to work by MSA location, for 11 MSAs, 1985 survey, supplement, 2485–8
Housing and households detailed characteristics, and unit and neighborhood quality, by location, 1989, biennial rpt supplement, 2485–13
Imports of bicycles and costume jewelry from PRC and other countries, 1986-91, article, 9882–2.301
Input-output structure of US economy, detailed interindustry transactions for 541 industries, and components of final demand, 1982 benchmark data, 2708–17
Manufacturing annual survey, 1990: finances and operations, by SIC 2- to 4-digit industry, series, 2506–14
Manufacturing finances and operations, by SIC 2- to 4-digit industry, forecast 1992, annual rpt, 2044–28
Pacific territories population and housing detailed characteristics, by location, 1990 Census of Population and Housing, series, 2551–8
Police employment, spending, and operations, for State, city, county, and special district agencies, 1990, annual rpt, 6064–39
Price indexes (producer), by stage of processing and detailed commodity, monthly rpt, 6762–6
Price indexes (producer), by stage of processing and detailed commodity, monthly 1991, annual rpt, 6764–2
Thefts, and value of property stolen and recovered, by property type, 1991, annual rpt, 6224–2.1
Travel patterns, personal and household characteristics, and auto and public transport use, 1990 survey, series, 7556–6

Biddle, Elyce A.
"Job Hazards Underscored in Woodworking Study", 6728–41

Bilingual education
Adult education and literacy programs funding, enrollment, and activities, fact sheet series, 4806–4
Adult literacy and English as a second language programs, Education Dept and State programs, enrollment, and funding, by State, 1988-91, 4808–41
Digest of Education Statistics, 1992 annual data compilation, 4824–2
Eighth grade class of 1988: Asian and Hispanic students proficiency in English and language at home, by selected characteristics, natl longitudinal survey, 1992 rpt, 4826–9.12
Enrollment in bilingual education, and eligible students not enrolled, by State, 1990-91, annual rpt, 4804–14
Expenditures for education by Federal agency, program, and recipient type, and instn spending, 1960s-91, annual rpt, 4824–8
Expenditures of Fed Govt in States, by type, program, agency, and State, FY91, annual rpt, 2464–2

Billings, Mont.
Wages by occupation, for office and plant workers, 1991 survey, periodic MSA rpt, 6785–16.3

Biloxi, Miss.
see also under By City and By SMSA or MSA in the "Index by Categories"

Bingham, R. H.
"Floods of December 1982 to May 1983 in the Central and Southern Mississippi River and the Gulf of Mexico Basins", 5666–27.33

Binghamton, N.Y.
see also under By City and By SMSA or MSA in the "Index by Categories"

Biologic drug products
County Business Patterns, 1989: employment, establishments, and payroll, by SIC 2- to 4-digit industry and county, annual State rpt series, 2326–8
County Business Patterns, 1990: employment, establishments, and payroll, by SIC 2- to 4-digit industry and county, annual State rpt series, 2326–6
Epoetin alfa treatment for anemia in kidney dialysis patients, use and costs, 1989 and 1991, 17206–1.17
Exports and imports (agricultural) of US, by detailed commodity and country, 1991, annual rpt, 1524–8
Exports and imports (agricultural) of US, by detailed commodity and country, 1991, semiannual rpt, 1522–4
Exports and imports between US and outlying areas, by detailed commodity and mode of transport, 1991, annual rpt, 2424–11
Exports and imports of US, by Harmonized System 6-digit commodity and country, 1991, annual rpt, 2424–13
Exports of US, detailed Schedule B commodities with countries of destination, 1991, annual rpt, 2424–10
FDA investigations and regulatory activities, quarterly rpt, 4062–3
Manufacturing annual survey, 1990: finances and operations, by SIC 2- to 4-digit industry, series, 2506–14
Manufacturing census, 1987: concentration of largest firms measured by value added, and for shipments by SIC 2- and 4-digit industry, subject rpt, 2497–6
Manufacturing census, 1987: shipments of manufacturers products, by customer class and SIC 2- and 4-digit industry, subject rpt, 2497–4
Manufacturing finances and operations, by SIC 2- to 4-digit industry, forecast 1992, annual rpt, 2044–28
Occupational injury and illness rates, by SIC 2- to 4-digit industry, 1989-90, annual rpt, 6844–7
Occupational injury and illness rates, by SIC 2- to 4-digit industry, 1990, annual rpt, 6844–1
Price indexes (producer), by stage of processing and detailed commodity, monthly rpt, 6762–6
Price indexes (producer), by stage of processing and detailed commodity, monthly 1991, annual rpt, 6764–2
Veterinary Services Natl Labs activities, biologic drug products evaluation and disease testing, FY91, annual rpt, 1394–17
see also Vaccination and vaccines

Biological sciences
Alaska OCS environmental conditions and oil dev impacts, compilation of papers, series, 2176–1
Degree (PhD) recipients in higher education, by field and selected characteristics, 1979, 1984, and 1989, 4848–44
Degrees awarded in higher education, by level, field, race, and sex, 1989/90 and trends from 1980/81, annual rpt, 4844–17
DOE R&D projects and funding at natl labs, universities, and other instns, FY92, annual summary rpt, 3004–18.7
Employment of scientists and engineers, and related topics, advance rpt series, 9626–8
Employment of scientists, engineers, and technicians in manufacturing, by field and industry, 1989, triennial rpt, 9627–23
Fed Govt aid to higher education and nonprofit instns for R&D and related activities, by field, instn, agency, and State, FY90, annual rpt, 9627–17
General Medical Sciences Natl Inst activities, budget, and research and training funding by program, FY91, annual rpt, 4474–38
Higher education grad programs enrollment in science and engineering, by field, source of funds, and characteristics of student and instn, 1990, annual rpt, 9627–7
Labor demand, turnover, and training completions, by detailed occupation, 1990 and projected to 2005, biennial rpt, 6744–3
Minority group, women, and disabled persons employment and education in science and engineering, by field, mid 1970s-91, biennial rpt, 9624–20

NASA R&D funding to higher education instns, by field, instn, and State, FY91, annual listing, 9504–7
NSF R&D grant awards, by div and program, FY90, periodic rpt, 9626–7.6
Occupational Outlook Handbook, 1992-93, biennial rpt, 6744–1
Oceanographic research and distribution activities of World Data Center A by country, and cruises by ship, 1990, annual rpt, 2144–15
R&D facilities of higher education instns, space and equipment adequacy, needs, and funding by source, by instn type and control, 1992, biennial rpt, 9624–25
R&D funding by higher education instns and federally funded centers, by field, instn, and State, FY90, annual rpt, 9627–13
Research on population and reproduction, Federal funding by project, FY90, annual listing, 4474–9
Research on population and reproduction, Natl Inst of Child Health and Human Dev funding and activities, 1991, annual rpt, 4474–33
Science and Engineering Indicators, employment, education, R&D funding, and industry impacts, with foreign comparisons, 1960s-91, biennial rpt, 9624–10
Small business R&D grants of Fed Govt, by program area, agency, MSA, and State, FY90, annual rpt, 9764–7
see also Biotechnology
see also Botany
see also Genetics
see also Physiology
see also Zoology

Biological warfare agents
see Chemical and biological warfare agents

Biomass energy
China biomass-fired electric power plant feasibility assessment, 1991 rpt, 3308–103
Consumption of wood, waste, and alcohol fuels, by end-use sector and region, 1990, annual rpt, 3164–97
Consumption of wood, waste, and alcohol fuels, by region, 1981-90, annual rpt, 3164–74.7
Developing countries energy efficiency improvement issues and devs, with data by end use and country, 1980s-90, 26358–260
DOE R&D projects and funding at natl labs, universities, and other instns, FY92, annual summary rpt, 3004–18.7
Electric power plants certification applications filed with FERC, for small production and cogeneration facilities, FY80-91, annual listing, 3084–13
Iowa timber resources and removals, by species, forest and tree characteristics, ownership, and county, 1988-90 and trends from 1973-74, 1208–75
Missouri timber resources and removals, by species, forest and tree characteristics, ownership, and county, 1987-89 and trends from 1959, 1208–76
Pacific basin countries energy supply and demand, and implications for US trade, country rpt series, 3406–6
Pacific Northwest nonutility electric power generation and capacity, by energy source, purchasing utility, and facility, forecasts 1991-2012, annual rpt, 3224–3.4
Supply, demand, and prices, by fuel type and end-use sector, alternative projections 1990-2010, annual rpt, 3164–75
Supply, demand, and prices, by fuel type and end-use sector, projections and underlying assumptions, 1995-2010, annual rpt, 3164–90
Supply, demand, and prices, by fuel type and end-use sector, with foreign comparisons, 1981-90, annual fact book, 3164–76
TVA biomass energy program, operations, finances, and technological characteristics, series, 9806–9
Yearbook of Agriculture, special topics, 1992 annual compilation of papers, 1004–18
see also Alcohol fuels
see also Gasohol
see also Wood fuel

Biotechnology
Agricultural research and education grants, USDA competitive awards by program and recipient, FY91, annual listing, 1764–1
Bovine somatotropin (bST) dairy industry use, effectiveness of FDA testing for human and animal safety, 1991, GAO rpt, 26131–101
Budget of US, obligations and authority by function, agency, and program, with summaries and analyses, FY93, annual rpt, 104–2
DOE R&D projects and funding at natl labs, universities, and other instns, FY92, annual summary rpt, 3004–18.7
Farm financial and marketing conditions, forecast 1992, annual conf, 1504–9
Fed Govt financial and nonfinancial domestic aid, 1992 base edition, annual listing, 104–5
HHS financial aid, by program, recipient, State, and city, FY91, annual regional listings, 4004–3
Manufacturing finances and operations, by SIC 2- to 4-digit industry, forecast 1992, annual rpt, 2044–28
Public knowledge, interest, and expectations for science and technology, 1990 survey, biennial rpt, 9624–10.7
Reproduction and population research, Fed Govt funding by project, FY90, annual listing, 4474–9
Sugarcane clones yields, stability, and fungi resistance, 1991/92, annual rpt, 1704–2

Birds and bird conservation
Alaska OCS environmental conditions and oil dev impacts, compilation of papers, series, 2176–1
Alaska rural areas population characteristics, and energy resources dev effects, series, 5736–5
Coastal and riparian areas environmental conditions, fish, wildlife, use, and mgmt, for individual ecosystems, series, 5506–9
Crane (sandhill) hunting activity and permits, by State and county, 1990/91-1991/92, annual rpt, 5504–31
Criminal case processing in Federal district courts, and dispositions, by offense, district, and offender characteristics, 1989, annual data compilation, 6064–29
Criminal case processing in Federal district courts, and dispositions, by offense, 1980-91, annual rpt, 6064–31
Duck breeding population, by species, State, and Canada Province, 1991-92 with trends from 1955, annual rpt, 5504–30
Duck hunting stamps philatelic and sales info, 1992/93, annual supplement, 5504–25
Ducks (dabbling) nesting activity in north central Iowa, by habitat characteristics and species, 1984-85, technical rpt, 5506–12.5
Ducks population and nesting success in south-central North Dakota, by species, with habitat conditions, 1960s-81, 5508–120
Environmental Quality, status of problems, protection programs, research, and intl issues, 1991 annual rpt, 484–1
Fishing (net) operations off California, marine mammals and birds incidental catch, 1984-85, 14738–13
Great Lakes Science Advisory Board research activities and water quality goals, FY91, biennial rpt, 14644–6
Idaho Snake River area birds of prey, rodent, and vegetation distribution and characteristics, research results, 1991, annual rpt, 5724–14
Migratory Bird Conservation Commission wetlands habitat acquisition, funding by State, 1992, press release, 5306–4.13; 5306–4.16
Migratory waterfowl refuge and breeding area acreage acquired by Fed Govt, and costs, by site and State, FY92, annual rpt, 14784–1
Migratory waterfowl refuge and breeding area acreage under Fish and Wildlife Service mgmt, by site and State, as of Sept 1992, annual rpt, 5504–8
Minerals offshore lease sales environmental and economic impacts in coastal areas, final statement series, 5736–7
Mourning dove population, by hunting and nonhunting State, 1966-92, annual rpt, 5504–15
Owl (northern spotted) conservation methods in Pacific Northwest, findings and recommendations, 1990 rpt, 1208–385
Owl (northern spotted) conservation methods in Pacific Northwest, timber industry impacts, and Federal and State spending, 1980s-95, 1208–388
Pacific Northwest old-growth forests plant and wildlife population and species diversity, 1991 compilation of papers, 1208–386
Pigeon population and survival rates in central New York, by harvest level, 1981-83, technical rpt, 5506–12.4
Pollutants health effects for animals by species and for humans, and environmental levels, for selected substances, series, 5506–14
Public lands acreage, grants, use, revenues, and allocations, by State, FY91, annual rpt, 5724–1.2
Research on fish and wildlife population, habitat, and mgmt, technical rpt series, 5506–12
Sagebrush habitats of western US Great Basin, bird population density, by species, 1978-83 studies, 1208–402
Terns (least) and piping plover and habitat levels of selenium and other pollutants, for Missouri River in South Dakota, 1988-90, 5508–118

Waterfowl (migratory) hunter harvest, age and sex ratios by species, State, and flyway, 1987-91, annual rpt, 5504–32
Waterfowl (migratory) hunter harvest and unretrieved kills, and duck stamps sold, by species, State, Canada Province, and flyway, 1990-91, annual rpt, 5504–28
Waterfowl (migratory) population, habitat conditions, and flight forecasts, for Canada and US by region, 1992 and trends from 1955, annual rpt, 5504–27
Waterfowl (migratory) refuge and breeding area acreage, and agreements and payments to farmers under Water Bank Program, by State, 1972-91, annual rpt, 1804–21
Waterfowl (migratory) wetlands acreage, and agreements and payments to farmers under Water Bank Program, monthly rpt, 1802–5
Woodcock population from 1968, and hunter harvest, by State, 1992, annual rpt, 5504–11
see also Poultry industry and products

Birmingham, Ala.
Drug control street-level task forces enforcement activities, impacts on crime, and residents views, local area studies, 1992 rpt, 6068–251
Drug test results at arrest, by drug type, offense, and sex, for selected urban areas, quarterly rpt, 6062–3
see also under By City and By SMSA or MSA in the "Index by Categories"

Birth control
see Abortion
see Contraceptives
see Family planning
see Sexual sterilization

Birth defects
Births and rates, by characteristics of birth, infant, and mother, and presence of maternal risk factors and birth defects, 1989, 4146–5.125
Cytomegalovirus (congenital) disease cases, by infant, mother, and birth characteristics, type of impairment, State, and Canada Province, 1990-91, 4202–7.314
Deaths and rates, by cause, age, sex, marital status, race, and State, 1989, US Vital Statistics advance annual rpt, 4146–5.124
Deaths and rates, by cause and age, preliminary 1990-91, US Vital Statistics annual rpt, 4144–7
Deaths and rates, by cause, provisional data, monthly rpt, 4142–1.2
Deaths and rates, by detailed location, cause, and demographic characteristics, 1989, US Vital Statistics annual rpt, 4144–3
Fetal alcohol syndrome rates among Indians in Canada and Southwestern US, 1970s-80s, article, 4482–1.310
Fetal alcohol syndrome treatment and rehabilitation costs, 1985, article, 4482–1.311
Head Start handicapped enrollment, by handicap, State, and for Indian and migrant programs, 1988/89, annual rpt, 4584–4
Hospital discharges and length of stay, by diagnosis, patient and instn characteristics, procedure performed, and payment source, 1990, annual rpt, 4147–13.112
Hospital discharges and length of stay by region and diagnosis, and procedures performed, by age and sex, 1990, annual rpt, 4146–8.211
Hospital discharges and length of stay under old and new survey designs, by diagnosis, patient and instn characteristics, and procedure, Jan-Mar 1988, 4147–13.110
Hospital discharges by detailed diagnostic and procedure category, primary diagnosis, and length of stay, by age, sex, and region, 1990, annual rpt, 4147–13.111
Indian Health Service and tribal facilities and use, and Indians health and other characteristics, by IHS region, 1980s-90, annual chartbook, 4084–7
Indian Health Service, tribal, and contract facilities hospitalization, by diagnosis, age, sex, and service area, FY91, annual rpt, 4084–5
Mentally retarded school-age cases, forecasts using birth defect records, accuracy, 1992 article, 4042–3.327
OECD members health care costs, hospital use, resources, and economic and health indicators, by country, 1960s-90, article, 4652–1.322
Pollutants health effects, concentrations in food and environment, sources, human intake, and regulation, series, 9186–8
Pollutants health effects for animals by species and for humans, and environmental levels, for selected substances, series, 5506–14
Pregnancy health survey, reasons for participation for mothers with and without children with birth defects, 1990, article, 4042–3.377
Spina bifida and other neural tube birth defects prevention through prenatal use of folic acid supplements, findings and CDC recommendations, 1992 rpt, 4206–2.64
Transplants of organs, failure and death risk by selected transplant and patient characteristics, 1987-89, annual rpt, 4104–17.1
see also under By Disease in the "Index by Categories"

Birthplace
Census of Population and Housing, 1990: immigrants, by period of entry, citizenship, State, birthplace, and for top cities and counties, press release, 2328–88
Census of Population and Housing, 1990: population and housing characteristics, detailed geographic coverage, State CD-ROM series, 2551–10
Census of Population and Housing, 1990: summary characteristics, by county, subdiv, and place, State rpt series, 2551–7
Immigrant and nonimmigrant visas of US issued and refused, by class, issuing office, and nationality, FY90, annual rpt, 7184–1
Immigrants admitted to US, by class of admission, country of birth, and MSA of destination, FY91, advance annual rpt, 6264–4
Immigrants and legalized aliens, by occupational group and country of birth, preliminary FY91, annual tables, 6264–1
Immigrants and nonimmigrants admitted to US, alien workers, visitors, deportations, and naturalizations, FY91, annual summary rpt, 6264–7
Immigration to US, alien workers, visitors, deportations, and naturalizations, by country, FY91 and trends from 1820, annual rpt, 6264–2
Pacific territories population and housing detailed characteristics, by location, 1990 Census of Population and Housing, series, 2551–8
Refugee arrivals and resettlement in US, by age, sex, sponsoring agency, State, and country, monthly rpt, 4592–1
Refugee arrivals in US by world area of origin and State of settlement, and Federal aid, FY91-92 and proposed FY93 allocations, annual rpt, 7004–16
Refugee migration, and intl aid programs, by world area and country of origin and asylum, 1991, annual rpt, 7004–15
Statistical Abstract of US, 1992 annual data compilation, 2324–1.1

Births
Alaska rural areas population characteristics, and energy resources dev effects, series, 5736–5
Births and rates, by characteristics of birth, infant, and mother, and presence of maternal risk factors and birth defects, 1989, 4146–5.125
Births and rates, by State, preliminary 1990-91, US Vital Statistics annual rpt, 4144–7
Cancer (liver) risk for women relation to parity and oral contraceptives use, 1985-86, article, 4472–1.331
Foreign countries population size, growth rates, and components of change, by country, projected 1990-2020 and trends from 1950, biennial rpt, 2324–9
Health condition and care indicators, 1950s-90 with health improvement and disease prevention goals for 1990, annual data compilation, 4144–11
Health service areas, indicators of service use, and residents seeking care outside area, under alternative area definitions, 1988-89, 4147–2.113
Hospital discharges and length of stay, by diagnosis, patient and instn characteristics, procedure performed, and payment source, 1990, annual rpt, 4147–13.112
Hospital discharges and length of stay by region and diagnosis, and procedures performed, by age and sex, 1990, annual rpt, 4146–8.211
Hospital discharges and length of stay under old and new survey designs, by diagnosis, patient and instn characteristics, and procedure, Jan-Mar 1988, 4147–13.110
Indian Health Service and tribal facilities and use, and Indians health and other characteristics, by IHS region, 1980s-90, annual chartbook, 4084–7
Indian Health Service and tribal hospital admissions, length of stay, beds, and births, by facility and service area, FY90-91, annual rpt, 4084–4
Indian Health Service and tribal hospital capacity, use, and births, by area and facility, quarterly rpt, 4082–1
Indian Health Service facilities, funding, operations, and Indian health and other characteristics, 1950s-91, annual chartbook, 4084–1

Military health care facilities of DOD in US and abroad, admissions, beds, outpatient visits, and births, by service branch, quarterly rpt, 3542–15
Population size and components of change, alternative projections 1990-2080 and trends from 1900, annual actuarial rpt, 4706–1.106
Population size, July 1981-89 and compared to 1980 and 1990, annual press release, 2324–10
Pregnancy outcome probabilities, by gestation week, 1980, article, 4042–3.324
Soviet Union and US economic and sociodemographic indicators, selected years 1970-90, handbook, 2328–80
Statistical Abstract of US, 1992 annual data compilation, 2324–1.2
Twin births, by birth order and weight, gestation period, mothers age, and race, 1950s-88, 4147–21.50
Vietnam population size, components of change, and selected characteristics, 1979, 1989, and projected to 2050, 2326–18.65
Vital statistics provisional data, monthly rpt, 4142–1
see also Abortion
see also Birth defects
see also Birthplace
see also Births out of wedlock
see also Birthweight
see also Fertility
see also Fetal deaths
see also Infant mortality
see also Maternal deaths
see also Maternity
see also Maternity benefits
see also Maternity homes
see also Obstetrics and gynecology
see also Prenatal care
see also Teenage pregnancy

Births out of wedlock
Abortions by method, patient characteristics, and State, and related deaths, 1970-89, annual article, 4202–7.324
Cytomegalovirus (congenital) disease cases, by infant, mother, and birth characteristics, type of impairment, State, and Canada Province, 1990-91, 4202–7.314
Health condition and care indicators, 1950s-90 with health improvement and disease prevention goals for 1990, annual data compilation, 4144–11
Latin America young unmarried adults sexual activity, contraceptives use, and AIDS risk knowledge, by sex and country, 1984-91, article, 4202–7.323
Marriage, divorce, and remarriage of women by age, and child living arrangements, by race, 1970s-90, Current Population Rpt, 2546–2.166
Poverty status of families, by detailed characteristics, 1980 and 1988, GAO rpt, 26131–102
Statistical Abstract of US, 1992 annual data compilation, 2324–1.2
see also Maternity homes

Birthweight
Births and rates, by characteristics of birth, infant, and mother, and presence of maternal risk factors and birth defects, 1989, 4146–5.125
Cytomegalovirus (congenital) disease cases, by infant, mother, and birth characteristics, type of impairment, State, and Canada Province, 1990-91, 4202–7.314
Deaths and rates, by cause and age, preliminary 1990-91, US Vital Statistics annual rpt, 4144–7
Deaths and rates, by cause, provisional data, monthly rpt, 4142–1.2
Deaths of infants, risk factors, and health and prevention issues, for US and selected countries, 1990 conf, 4148–28
Education natl goals progress indicators, by State, 1992, annual rpt, 15914–1
Food aid program of USDA for women, infants, and children, prenatal participation effects on birthweight and health and social welfare costs, 1960s-90, GAO rpt, 26121–458
Foreign and US infant mortality rate, and births of low birthweight and to teen and older mothers, 1980s, article, 4652–1.324
Health condition and care indicators, 1950s-90 with health improvement and disease prevention goals for 1990, annual data compilation, 4144–11
Hospital intensive care for newborns, assessment of alternative case mix groupings intended to improve cost homogeneity, 1985, article, 4652–1.303
Indian Health Service and tribal facilities and use, and Indians health and other characteristics, by IHS region, 1980s-90, annual chartbook, 4084–7
Indian Health Service facilities, funding, operations, and Indian health and other characteristics, 1950s-91, annual chartbook, 4084–1
Indian low birthweight births, compared to whites and blacks, for New York, 1980s, article, 4042–3.359
Low birthweight risk relation to mothers smoking, weight, and age, 1988, article, 4042–3.367
Maternal and child health indicators and services use, by age, race, and poverty status, 1988, 4478–197
Medicaid patients low birthweight births, by prenatal care source and adequacy, and other risk factors, for 2 States, late 1980s, article, 4042–3.304
Ohio poverty, hunger, and public welfare program operations and indicators of need, by county, 1991 hearing, 21968–58
Prenatal care program of Medicaid, costs and benefits, for Missouri, 1988, article, 4042–3.365
Statistical Abstract of US, 1992 annual data compilation, 2324–1.2
Twin births, by birth order and weight, gestation period, mothers age, and race, 1950s-88, 4147–21.50

Bishop, Kathryn
"Photographic Supplies, Industry and Trade Summary", 9885–10.4

Bismuth
see Metals and metal industries

Biswas, N. N.
"Synthesis of Seismicity Studies for Western Alaska", 2176–1.40

Bixby, Ann K.
"Benefits and Beneficiaries Under Public Employee Retirement Systems, FY89", 4742–1.318
"Overview of Public Social Welfare Expenditures, FY89", 4742–1.302
"Public Social Welfare Expenditures, FY89", 4742–1.319

Bjerke, Keith
"Making of the 1990 Farm Bill", 1504–9.1

Black Americans
AIDS cases by risk group, race, sex, age, State, and MSA, and deaths, quarterly rpt, 4202–9
Births and rates, by characteristics of birth, infant, and mother, and presence of maternal risk factors and birth defects, 1989, 4146–5.125
Business owner and business characteristics, for minority- and women-owned firms, by industry, employment and sales size, and form of ownership, 1987 survey, 2328–59
Cancer (breast) symptoms duration prior to seeking care, for black and white women, by selected characteristics, 1985-86 local area study, article, 4472–1.323
Cancer (cervical and breast) screening among poor black women, effects of in-home promotion program, 1989-92, article, 4042–3.338
Census of Population and Housing, 1990: data summary, use, and availability, fact sheet, 2326–23.2
Census of Population and Housing, 1990: detailed geographic coverage, State CD-ROM series, 2551–9
Census of Population and Housing, 1990: population and housing characteristics, detailed geographic coverage, State CD-ROM series, 2551–10
Census of Population and Housing, 1990: summary characteristics, households, and land area, by county, subdiv, and place, State rpt series, 2551–1
Census of Population, 1990: ancestry of US population, by group and State, press release, 2328–87
Census of Population, 1990: black population undercount, estimates by age and sex, 21628–97
Census of Population, 1990: population characteristics and living arrangements, by county, place, and urban-rural location, State rpt series, 2531–1
Census of Population, 1990: population characteristics and living arrangements, for Native American, urban, and metro areas, series, 2531–2
Consumer Income, socioeconomic characteristics of persons, families, and households, detailed cross-tabulations, Current Population Rpt series, 2546–6
Crime, criminal justice admin and enforcement, and public opinion, data compilation, 1992 annual rpt, 6064–6
Crimes, arrests, and rates, by offense, offender characteristics, population size, and jurisdiction, 1991, annual rpt, 6224–2.1; 6224–2.2
Deaths and rates, by cause and selected social, demographic, and employment characteristics, 1979-85, natl longitudinal study, 4478–186
Deaths and rates, by detailed location, cause, and demographic characteristics, 1989, US Vital Statistics annual rpt, 4144–3
Disability benefit applications under OASDI and SSI, dispositions, awards, and administrative law judge hearing outcomes, by race, 1988, GAO rpt, 26121–459

Drug, alcohol, and cigarette use, by selected characteristics, 1991 survey, annual rpt series, 4494–5
Education data compilation, 1992 annual rpt, 4824–2
Educational attainment, by social and demographic characteristics and location, 1991 and trends from 1940, biennial Current Population Rpt, 2546–1.460
Employment of minorities and women, by occupation, SIC 1- to 3-digit industry, State, and MSA, 1991, annual rpt, 9244–1
Employment, unemployment, and labor force characteristics, by region, State, and selected metro area, 1991, annual rpt, 6744–7
Farm population, by employment, social, and economic characteristics, and region, 1990, annual Current Population Rpt, 2546–1.458
Fed Equal Opportunity Recruitment Program activity, and employment by sex, race, pay grade, and occupational group, FY91, annual rpt, 9844–33
Fed Govt employment of minorities, disabled, and veterans, and years of service, by occupation, age, sex, and agency, as of Sept 1990, biennial rpt, 9844–27
FmHA loans, by type, borrower race, and State, quarterly rpt, 1182–5
Food aid program of USDA for women, infants, and children, participants by race, State, and Indian agency, 1991, annual rpt, 1364–16
Health care professionals supply and education, by professional and other characteristics, and location, 1960s-92 and projected to 2020, biennial rpt, 4114–8
Health condition and care indicators, 1950s-90 with health improvement and disease prevention goals for 1990, annual data compilation, 4144–11
Homicide and suicide among young black men, by day of week, with comparisons to whites and women, 1979-85, article, 4042–3.323
Hospital closings relation to hospital and community characteristics, by metro-nonmetro location, 1980-87, article, 4042–3.341
Households and family characteristics, by location, 1991, annual Current Population Rpt, 2546–1.457
Households and housing characteristics, and unit and neighborhood quality, by MSA location for 11 MSAs, 1987 survey, supplement, 2485–8
Households and housing detailed characteristics, and unit and neighborhood quality, by location, 1989, biennial rpt supplement, 2485–13
Households and housing detailed characteristics, and unit and neighborhood quality, MSA surveys, series, 2485–6
Households composition, income, benefits, and labor force status, Survey of Income and Program Participation methodology, working paper series, 2626–10
Housing (rental) units, total, with HUD assistance by program, and eligible for aid, by unit, household, and neighborhood characteristics, and location, 1989, biennial rpt, 5184–11
Housing census, 1990: summary unit characteristics, by householder race and age, county, place, and urban-rural location, State rpt series, 2471–1
Income (household) and poverty status under alternative income definitions, by recipient characteristics, 1979-91, annual Current Population Rpt, 2546–6.78
Income (household) and wealth distribution by selected characteristics, with foreign comparisons, 1992 compilation of papers, Current Population Rpt, 2546–6.79
Income (personal) relative to median, by race and selected other characteristics, mid 1960s-89, Current Population Rpt, 2546–6.73
Labor demand, turnover, and training completions, by detailed occupation, 1990 and projected to 2005, biennial rpt, 6744–3
Labor force status, by race, detailed Hispanic origin, and sex, quarterly rpt, 6742–18
Labor force, wages, hours, and payroll costs, by major industry group and demographic characteristics, *Survey of Current Business*, monthly rpt, 2702–1.7
Living arrangements, family relationships, and marital status, by selected characteristics, 1991, annual Current Population Rpt, 2546–1.461
Migration, immigration, and mover characteristics compared to nonmovers, 1987-90, annual Current Population Rpt, 2546–1.456
Migration since 1990, mover characteristics by same or different area, and compared to nonmovers, 1991, annual Current Population Rpt, 2546–1.464
Military and civilian DOD employment of blacks, by sex, grade, and period of service, and lists of award recipients, officers, and service academy grads, 1770s-90, 3548–22
Military personnel deployment in Operation Desert Storm, by sex, race, rank, and service branch, 1990-91, GAO rpt, 26123–394
NYC black and Hispanic health condition and care indicators, 1980s, conf paper, 4164–2
NYC housing supply, occupancy, condition, and household characteristics, by tenure and borough, 1991 triennial survey, 2488–3
Pacific territories population and housing detailed characteristics, by location, 1990 Census of Population and Housing, series, 2551–8
Population economic well-being indicators, by selected characteristics and household income and income-to-poverty ratio, 1984, 2546–20.22
Population size, by race and Hispanic origin, 1992 and projected 2000-2050, press release, 2328–85
Population social and economic characteristics, for Black Americans, for South and total US, 1991 and trends from 1950, annual Current Population Rpt, 2546–1.463
Poverty relation to low earnings, by work experience during year, household relationship, sex, race, age, and education, 1960s-90, Current Population Rpt, 2546–6.74
Prison and community-based facilities, population, employment, spending, and other characteristics, by State and for Fed Govt, 1990, quinquennial rpt, 6068–218
Prisoners, characteristics, and movements, by State, 1990, annual rpt, 6064–26
Prisoners in Federal and contract instns, by selected characteristics, region, and Federal instn, FY89, annual rpt, 6244–1.1
Science and engineering employment and education of minorities, women, and disabled, by field, mid 1970s-91, biennial rpt, 9624–20
Science and Engineering Indicators, employment, education, R&D funding, and industry impacts, with foreign comparisons, 1960s-91, biennial rpt, 9624–10
State and local govt employment of minorities and women, by occupation, function, pay level, and State, 1991, annual rpt, 9244–6
Statistical Abstract of US, 1992 annual data compilation, 2324–1
Unemployed displaced workers, layoffs and unemployment insurance claims by reason, industry, selected characteristics, and State, quarterly press release, 6742–23
Unemployed displaced workers, layoffs and unemployment insurance claims by reason, industry, selected characteristics, MSA, and State, 1990, annual rpt, 6744–18
Women's labor force status, earnings, and other economic status indicators, for blacks and compared to whites, various periods 1939-88, 11048–191
Women's occupational differences for blacks and whites, and compared to men, selected years 1940-88, article, 6722–1.321
see also Black colleges
see also Black students
see also Racial discrimination
see also under By Race and Ethnic Group in the "Index by Categories"

Black colleges
Agricultural research funding and staffing for USDA, State agencies, and other instns, by topic, FY91, annual rpt, 1744–2
AID contracts, grants, and cooperative agreements with higher education instns, by project, instn, and country, FY91, annual listing, 9914–6
Athletic depts at NCAA Div I schools, staff by race, and income, by sex and position, 1990/91, GAO rpt, 26121–476
Community Dev Block Grants technical aid programs of black colleges, HUD grants by recipient, 1991, press release, 5006–3.78
Enrollment, degrees awarded, and finances of predominantly black instns, 1985-90, annual rpt, 4824–2.17
Enrollment, finances, staff, and degrees, for traditional black instns, by instn and selected student characteristics, 1970s-90, 4848–46
HHS financial aid, by program, recipient, State, and city, FY91, annual regional listings, 4004–3

HUD grants to black colleges for economic and community dev programs, by recipient, 1991, press release, 5006–3.85
R&D and related funding of Fed Govt to higher education and nonprofit instns, by field, instn, agency, and State, FY90, annual rpt, 9627–17
R&D facilities of higher education instns, space and equipment adequacy, needs, and funding by source, by instn type and control, 1992, biennial rpt, 9624–25
R&D funding by higher education instns and federally funded centers, by field, instn, and State, FY90, annual rpt, 9627–13
Science and engineering grad enrollment, by field, source of funds, and characteristics of student and instn, 1990, annual rpt, 9627–7

Black, Dan A.
"Bidding for Workers", 6886–6.95

Black lung disease
Assistance of Fed Govt, by type, program, agency, and State, FY91, annual rpt, 2464–2
Benefits and beneficiaries by recipient type, from 1970, and by State, 1990, annual rpt, 4744–3.7
Benefits by county, FY91, annual regional listings, 4004–3
Benefits payment in natl income and product accounts, benchmark revisions, 1929-88, 2708–5
Benefits payment in natl income and product accounts, *Survey of Current Business*, monthly rpt, 2702–1.26
Benefits to miners, widows, and dependents, by State, quarterly rpt, 4742–1.3
Benefits under workers compensation, by type of program and insurer, and State, 1988-89, annual article, 4742–1.311
Compensation benefits and claims by State, trust fund receipts by source, and disbursements, 1991, annual rpt, 6504–3
Deaths from selected occupational diseases, for men by age group, 1970s-89, annual data compilation, 4144–11
Statistical Abstract of US, 1992 annual data compilation, 2324–1.12
Tax (excise) collections of IRS, by source, quarterly rpt, 8302–2.1
Tax (excise) collections of IRS for black lung benefits, quarterly rpt, 8302–1
Trust funds financial condition, for black lung, monthly rpt, 8102–9.10

Black market
see Money laundering
see Underground economy

Black students
Condition of Education, detail for elementary, secondary, and higher education, 1920s-91 and projected to 2002, annual rpt, 4824–1
Digest of Education Statistics, 1992 annual data compilation, 4824–2
Eighth grade class of 1988: educational performance and conditions, characteristics, attitudes, activities, and plans, natl longitudinal survey, series, 4826–9
Elementary and secondary students educational performance, and factors affecting proficiency, by selected characteristics, 1990 natl assessments, subject rpt series, 4896–8
Enrollment, by grade, instn type and control, and student characteristics, 1989 and trends from 1947, annual Current Population Rpt, 2546–1.459
Enrollment, finances, staff, and degrees, for traditional black instns, by instn and selected student characteristics, 1970s-90, 4848–46
Health care professionals supply and education, by professional and other characteristics, and location, 1960s-92 and projected to 2020, biennial rpt, 4114–8
Higher education degrees awarded, by level, field, race, and sex, 1989/90 and trends from 1980/81, annual rpt, 4844–17
Higher education enrollment, by level, race, and sex, fall 1980-90, biennial rpt, 4844–15
Higher education enrollment, by sex and race, 1976-2000, annual rpt, 4824–4
Nuclear engineering enrollment and degrees granted by instn and State, and grad placement, by student characteristics, 1991, annual rpt, 3004–5
Radiation protection and health physics enrollment and degrees granted by instn and State, and grad placement, by student characteristics, 1991, annual rpt, 3004–7
Science and engineering grad enrollment, by field, source of funds, and characteristics of student and instn, 1990, annual rpt, 9627–7
see also under By Race and Ethnic Group in the "Index by Categories"

Blaine, Thomas W.
"Demand for Land Information System Services: A Theoretical Framework", 1502–3.303

Blane, Diane
"AID Economic Policy Reform Program in Cameroon", 9916–1.76

Bleed, Daniel M.
"Cancer Incidence and Survival Among American Indians Registered for Indian Health Service Care in Montana, 1982-87", 4472–1.347

Blind
Disability and work limitations of persons with chronic health conditions, by condition, age, and sex, 1983-86, 4946–1.2
Education (special) enrollment by age, staff, funding, and needs, by type of handicap and State, 1990/91, annual rpt, 4944–4
Head Start handicapped enrollment, by handicap, State, and for Indian and migrant programs, 1988/89, annual rpt, 4584–4
Libraries for blind and handicapped, readership, circulation, staff, funding, and holdings, FY91, annual listing, 26404–3
Population of blind by age, older blind persons by State, and State rehabilitation services, 1989, 21148–64
Vending facilities run by blind on Federal and non-Federal property, finances and operations by agency and State, FY91, annual rpt, 4944–2
Veterans health care, patients, visits, costs, and operating beds, by VA and contract facility, and region, quarterly rpt, 8602–4
see also Aid to blind
see also Eye diseases and defects
see also Supplemental Security Income

Blocks, city
Census Bur data coverage and availability for statistics on counties, cities, and small areas, 1991 rpt, 2326–7.82
Census Bur geographic levels of data coverage, maps, and reference products, 1992 rpt, 2308–67
Census of Population and Housing, 1990: detailed geographic coverage, State CD-ROM series, 2551–9
Census of Population and Housing, 1990: population and housing characteristics, detailed geographic coverage, State CD-ROM series, 2551–10

Blodgett, James C.
"Streamflow Gains and Losses and Selected Flow Characteristics of Cottonwood Creek, North-Central California, 1982-85", 5666–27.31

Blomquist, William
"Coordinating Water Resources in the Federal System: The Groundwater-Surface Water Connection", 10048–82

Blood
AIDS cases at VA health care centers by sex, race, risk factor, and facility, and AIDS prevention and treatment issues, quarterly rpt, 8702–1
Banks (blood) safety violations, FDA enforcement, disease transmittal, and Houston regional center activities and finances, 1970s-91, hearings, 21368–134
Exports and imports between US and outlying areas, by detailed commodity and mode of transport, 1991, annual rpt, 2424–11
Exports and imports of US, by Harmonized System 6-digit commodity and country, 1991, annual rpt, 2424–13
Shipments of blood and blood products, 1990 Annual Survey of Manufactures, 2506–14.1
Transfusion recipients AIDS cases, by age group, sex, race, and presence of other risk factors, quarterly rpt, 4202–9
Transfusion recipients hepatitis cases, by strain, 1989 and trends from 1966, 4205–2
see also Blood diseases and disorders
see also Blood pressure
see also Septicemia

Blood diseases and disorders
Anemia treatment of kidney dialysis patients with Epoetin alfa, costs and use, 1989 and 1991, 17206–1.17
Bone marrow donors, minority recruitment, Federal aid, transplants, costs, payment sources, 1987-92, GAO rpt, 26121–487
Cancer (leukemia) patients ras oncogene activation risk from occupational dust and chemical exposure, 1992 article, 4472–1.352
Cancer (secondary) risk for chronic lymphocytic leukemia, by treatment method, 1992 article, 4472–1.343
Cases of acute and chronic conditions, disability, absenteeism, and health services use, by selected characteristics, 1990, annual rpt, 4147–10.182; 4147–10.183
Deaths and rates, by cause, age, sex, marital status, race, and State, 1989, US Vital Statistics advance annual rpt, 4146–5.124
Deaths and rates, by cause, provisional data, monthly rpt, 4142–1.2

Deaths and rates, by detailed location, cause, and demographic characteristics, 1989, US Vital Statistics annual rpt, 4144–3
Hemophiliac and coagulation disorder AIDS cases, by age group, sex, race, and presence of other risk factors, quarterly rpt, 4202–9
Hemophiliac hospital discharges, costs, charges, and Medicare payment, 1987-88, 17206–1.13
HHS financial aid, by program, recipient, State, and city, FY91, annual regional listings, 4004–3
Hospital discharges and length of stay, by diagnosis, patient and instn characteristics, procedure performed, and payment source, 1990, annual rpt, 4147–13.112
Hospital discharges and length of stay by region and diagnosis, and procedures performed, by age and sex, 1990, annual rpt, 4146–8.211
Hospital discharges and length of stay under old and new survey designs, by diagnosis, patient and instn characteristics, and procedure, Jan-Mar 1988, 4147–13.110
Hospital discharges by detailed diagnostic and procedure category, primary diagnosis, and length of stay, by age, sex, and region, 1990, annual rpt, 4147–13.111
Leukemia virus infection among residents of Japan island villages, by diet, occupation, and residence characteristics, 1984-86 study, article, 4472–1.319
Lymphoma deaths and rates, for Hodgkin's disease and other types, provisional data, monthly rpt, 4142–1.2
Natl Heart, Lung, and Blood Inst activities, and Advisory Council recommendations, 1991 narrative rpt, 4474–22
Natl Heart, Lung, and Blood Inst activities, and grants by recipient and location, FY91 and disease trends from 1940, annual rpt, 4474–15
Non-Hodgkin's lymphoma incidence in Italy, by sex and geographic area, aggregate 1983-87, article, 4472–1.336
OECD members health care costs, hospital use, resources, and economic and health indicators, by country, 1960s-90, article, 4652–1.322
Pollutants health effects, concentrations in food and environment, sources, human intake, and regulation, series, 9186–8
see also Septicemia
see also under By Disease in the "Index by Categories"

Blood poisoning
see Septicemia

Blood pressure
Diabetes patients physician office visits, by characteristics of patient, physician, and visit, 1989, 4146–8.212
Pulse rate relation to blood pressure and other physical, demographic, and behavioral characteristics, 1971-74, article, 4042–3.321
see also Hypertension

Bloom, Justin L.
"Survey of Direct U.S. Private Capital Investment in Research and Development Facilities in Japan", 9628–88

Bloomington, Ind.
Wages by occupation, and benefits for office and plant workers, 1992 survey, periodic MSA rpt, 6785–3.4

Blostin, Allan P.
"Employee Payments for Health Care Services", 6722–1.348

Blue collar workers
Black Americans social and economic characteristics, for South and total US, 1991 and trends from 1950, annual Current Population Rpt, 2546–1.463
Business statistics, detailed data for major industries and economic indicators, 1960-91, *Survey of Current Business* biennial supplement, 2704–1
Deaths and rates, by cause and selected social, demographic, and employment characteristics, 1979-85, natl longitudinal study, 4478–186
Earnings, annual average percent changes for selected occupational groups, selected MSAs, monthly rpt, 6782–1.1
Educational attainment, by social and demographic characteristics and location, 1991 and trends from 1940, biennial Current Population Rpt, 2546–1.460
Employment and economic conditions, alternative BLS projections to 2005 and trends 1975-90, biennial rpt, 6744–19
Employment and unemployment during recessions, 1948-91, annual article, 6722–1.312
Employment Cost Index and alternative measure of compensation costs, by component, occupation, industry group, union status, and location, 1975-92, annual rpt, 6744–20
Employment, earnings, and hours, by SIC 1- to 4-digit industry, monthly 1989-Feb 1992, annual rpt, 6744–4
Employment, earnings, and hours, monthly press release, 6742–5
Employment situation, earnings, hours, and other BLS economic indicators, transcripts of BLS Commissioner's monthly testimony, periodic rpt, 23846–4
Employment, unemployment, and labor force characteristics, by region, State, and selected metro area, 1991, annual rpt, 6744–7
Fed Govt civilian employees work-years, pay rates, and benefits use and costs, by agency, FY90, annual rpt, 9844–31
Fed Govt employment of minorities, women, and disabled, by agency and occupation, FY90, annual rpt, 9244–10
Higher education faculty and staff, by occupation, full- and part-time status, sex, and instn type and control, fall 1989, biennial rpt, 4844–18
Immigrants and legalized aliens, by occupational group and country of birth, preliminary FY91, annual tables, 6264–1
Immigration to US, alien workers, visitors, deportations, and naturalizations, by country, FY91 and trends from 1820, annual rpt, 6264–2
Income (household, family, and personal), by source, detailed characteristics, and region, 1991, annual Current Population Rpt, 2546–6.76
Labor demand, turnover, and training completions, by detailed occupation, 1990 and projected to 2005, biennial rpt, 6744–3
Labor hourly costs, by component, industry and occupational group, worker class, and firm size, monthly rpt, annual tables, 6782–1.2
Labor hourly costs, by component, occupational group, industry div, union coverage, and region, 1992, annual rpt, 6744–21
Minority group and women employment, by occupation, SIC 1- to 3- digit industry, State, and MSA, 1991, annual rpt, 9244–1
Occupational Outlook Handbook, 1992-93, biennial rpt, 6744–1
Pacific territories population and housing detailed characteristics, by location, 1990 Census of Population and Housing, series, 2551–8
State and local govt employment of minorities and women, by occupation, function, pay level, and State, 1991, annual rpt, 9244–6
Training for job qualification and skill improvement, workers participating by training source, occupation, age, sex, and race, 1991, 6728–32
Wages by occupation, and benefits, for office and plant workers, periodic MSA survey rpt series, 6785–16; 6785–17
Wages, hourly and weekly averages by industry div, monthly press release, 6742–3
see also Area wage surveys
see also Industry wage surveys
see also Production workers
see also Service workers
see also under By Occupation in the "Index by Categories"
see also under names of specific industries or industry groups

Blue Cross-Blue Shield
Benefits costs per enrollee compared to Medicare, by selected State, late 1970s-80s, annual rpt, 17266–1.3; 17266–1.7
Diabetes patients physician office visits, by characteristics of patient, physician, and visit, 1989, 4146–8.212
Fed Govt civilian employee health insurance programs enrollment, profits, and administrative costs, by plan, 1984-90, GAO rpt, 26119–376
Fed Govt civilian employees retirement, health, and life insurance benefits, coverage and finances of 4 programs, FY86-90, annual rpt, 9844–37.2; 9844–37.4
Hospital reimbursement by private insurers, standard rates proposal with data on coverage, payments, and hospital uncompensated care, 1992 rpt, 17206–1.16
Internist office visits, by characteristics of patient, physician, and visit, 1989, 4146–8.214
Physicians costs per enrollee and for selected procedures, changes under Blue Cross-Blue Shield plans, mid 1980s, article, 4652–1.320
Physicians visits, by patient and practice characteristics, diagnosis, and services provided, 1989, annual rpt, 4147–13.109
Traffic accident injury hospitalization, costs, and discharges, by payment source and State, mid 1980s-90, 7768–122

Board for International Broadcasting
Budget of US, authoritative financial statements with appropriations, outlays, and receipts, by category and agency, FY91, annual rpt, 8104–2.2
Budget of US, obligations and authority by function, agency, and program, with summaries and analyses, FY93, annual rpt, 104–2
Radio Free Europe and Radio Liberty broadcast and financial data, FY91, annual rpt, 10314–1
Board of Foreign Scholarships
see also Fulbright, J. William, Foreign Scholarship Board
Board of Governors of the Federal Reserve System
see Federal Reserve Board of Governors
Boarding houses
see Rooming and boarding houses
Boards of education
see School boards
Boats and boating
Coast Guard enforcement activities, 1st half FY92, semiannual rpt, 7402–4
County Business Patterns, 1989: employment, establishments, and payroll, by SIC 2- to 4-digit industry and county, annual State rpt series, 2326–8
County Business Patterns, 1990: employment, establishments, and payroll, by SIC 2- to 4-digit industry and county, annual State rpt series, 2326–6
Employment, earnings, and hours, by SIC 1- to 4-digit industry, monthly 1989-Feb 1992, annual rpt, 6744–4
Energy use by mode of transport, fuel supply, and demographic and economic factors of vehicle use, 1970s-90, annual rpt, 3304–5
Exports and imports between US and outlying areas, by detailed commodity and mode of transport, 1991, annual rpt, 2424–11
Exports and imports of US, by country and detailed commodity, monthly rpt, 2422–12
Exports and imports of US, by Harmonized System 6-digit commodity and country, 1991, annual rpt, 2424–13
Exports of US, detailed Schedule B commodities with countries of destination, 1991, annual rpt, 2424–10
Fish and Wildlife Service restoration programs funding, land purchases, and project listing, by State, FY90, annual rpt, 5504–1
Fishery employment, vessels, plants, and cooperatives, by State, 1990, annual rpt, 2164–1.10
Fishing (ocean sport) activities, and catch by species, by angler characteristics and State, annual coastal area rpt series, 2166–17
Fishing (ocean sport) catch, by species, mode of fishing, and coastal region, 1991, annual rpt, 2164–1.2
Hawaii humpback whale habitat impacts of human activities, with data on shipping, whale watching, coastal construction, and aircraft, 1980s-90, 14738–14
Input-output structure of US economy, detailed interindustry transactions for 541 industries, and components of final demand, 1982 benchmark data, 2708–17
Manatees killed in Florida and other US waters, by cause, 1978-91, annual rpt, 14734–1
Manufacturing annual survey, 1990: finances and operations, by SIC 2- to 4-digit industry, series, 2506–14
Manufacturing census, 1987: concentration of largest firms measured by value added, and for shipments by SIC 2- and 4-digit industry, subject rpt, 2497–6
Manufacturing census, 1987: shipments of manufacturers products, by customer class and SIC 2- and 4-digit industry, subject rpt, 2497–4
Manufacturing finances and operations, by SIC 2- to 4-digit industry, forecast 1992, annual rpt, 2044–28
Occupational injury and illness rates, by SIC 2- to 4-digit industry, 1989-90, annual rpt, 6844–7
Occupational injury and illness rates, by SIC 2- to 4-digit industry, 1990, annual rpt, 6844–1
Ohio River basin waterway facilities, freight by commodity and port, and recreation, by waterway, 1988-89, annual rpt, 3754–6
Pacific territories population and housing detailed characteristics, by location, 1990 Census of Population and Housing, series, 2551–8
Police employment, spending, and operations, for State, city, county, and special district agencies, 1990, annual rpt, 6064–39
Price indexes (producer), by stage of processing and detailed commodity, monthly rpt, 6762–6
Price indexes (producer), by stage of processing and detailed commodity, monthly 1991, annual rpt, 6764–2
Public lands acreage, grants, use, revenues, and allocations, by State, FY91, annual rpt, 5724–1.2
Recalls of recreational boats and engines with safety-related defects, by make, periodic listing, 7402–5
Registrations of boats, and accidents, casualties, and damage by cause, by vessel characteristics and State, 1991, annual rpt, 7404–1
Tax (luxury) revenue, and related IRS administrative costs, FY91 and projected to FY95, GAO rpt, 26119–385
Vermont White River basin stream recreation use by activity, time, and location, 1987, 1208–400
Washington and Oregon coastal areas tourism and recreation facilities and economic impacts, by county, 1983-88, 5738–40.3
see also Barges
see also Ferries
see also Inland water transportation
see also Marine accidents and safety
see also Ships and shipping
Boaz, Rachel F.
"Why Do Some Caregivers of Disabled and Frail Elderly Quit?", 4652–1.305
Bobbitt, Sharon A.
"Early Estimates. Public and Private Elementary and Secondary Education Statistics, School Year 1992-93", 4834–19
Boca Raton, Fla.
Housing starts and completions authorized by building permits in 40 MSAs, quarterly rpt, 2382–9
Wages by occupation, and benefits for office and plant workers, 1991 survey, periodic MSA rpt, 6785–3.1
Bodle, Jack
"Ninety Years of Salmon Culture at Little White Salmon National Fish Hatchery", 5508–114
Body measurements
Cancer (breast) risk relation to estrogen replacement therapy use, body mass index, and other risk factors, 1987-89 NYC study, article, 4472–1.350
Cancer (colon) risk relation to diet, aspirin use, exercise, and other factors, 1982-88, article, 4472–1.346
Homeless mothers and children nutrient intake, body measurements, and blood chemistry, 1989-90 local area study, article, 4042–3.330
Maternal and child health indicators and services use, by age, race, and poverty status, 1988, 4478–197
Pulse rate relation to blood pressure and other physical, demographic, and behavioral characteristics, 1971-74, article, 4042–3.321
Youth health condition, risk factors, and preventive and treatment services use and availability, 1970s-80s, 26358–234.2
see also Birthweight
see also Obesity
Boehm, Paul
"Final Report on Monitoring Hydrocarbons and Trace Metals in Beaufort Sea Sediments and Organisms", 5738–33
Boeing Petroleum Services, Inc.
DOE contractor computer system security and controls at Strategic Petroleum Reserve offices, 1991, 3006–5.27
Bogs
see Wetlands
Boise, Idaho
see also under By City and By SMSA or MSA in the "Index by Categories"
Boland, Barbara
"Prosecution of Felony Arrests, 1988", 6064–27
Boldin, Michael D.
"Using Switching Models To Study Business Cycle Asymmetries: 1. Overview of Methodology and Application", 9385–8.139
Bolivia
Agricultural trade of US, by detailed commodity and country, 1991, annual rpt, 1524–8
Agricultural trade of US, by detailed commodity and country, 1991, semiannual rpt, 1522–4
AID economic aid to developing countries, obligations and disbursements by country, quarterly rpt, 9912–4
AID loans repayment status and terms by program and country, and status of predecessor agency loans, quarterly rpt, 9912–3
Economic and military aid and loans from US and intl agencies, by program and country, FY46-91, annual rpt, 9914–5
Economic and social conditions of developing countries from 1960s, and Intl

Dev Cooperation Agency and AID activities and funding, FY91-93, annual rpt, 9904–4
Economic and social conditions, resources, and trade, and aid, 1992, annual factbook, 9914–14
Economic conditions, policy, and trade practices, by country, 1989-91, annual rpt, 21384–5
Economic, population, and agricultural data, US and other aid sources, and AID activity, 1992 country rpt, 9916–12.62
Economic, social, political, and geographic summary data, by country, 1992, annual factbook, 9114–2
Exports (duty free) under Andean Trade Preference Act from 4 countries to US, and business opportunities, 1989-91, 2048–161
Exports and imports of US, by commodity and country, 1980-90, world area rpt, 9116–1.7
Exports and imports of US, by transport mode, country, and SITC 1- to 3-digit commodity, 1991, annual rpt, 2424–12
Exports, investment, debt, and tariffs of 7 Latin America countries, and trade and investment policy liberalization issues, mid 1960s-91, 9886–4.184
Exports of US, detailed Schedule B commodities with countries of destination, 1991, annual rpt, 2424–10
Fruit, vegetable, nut, and cut flower imports of US from Andean countries, 1989 and 1991, article, 1925–34.317
Human rights conditions in 170 countries, and US economic and military aid, 1991, annual rpt, 21384–3
Inflation relation to money supply, for 5 South America countries, 1970s-90, technical paper, 9379–12.91
Military aid of US, arms sales, and training programs costs and budget requests, by program, world region, and country, FY91-93, annual rpt, 7144–13
Military spending, arms trade, and force strengths, with govt spending and population, by country, 1979-89, annual rpt, 9824–1
Natural gas composition and helium levels, analyses of individual wells and pipelines, 1985-91, annual rpt, 5604–2
Oil production, investment needs, and exports, for 8 South America countries, 1980s-90 and projected to 2010, GAO rpt, 26123–396
Population size, growth rates, and components of change, by country, projected 1990-2020 and trends from 1950, biennial rpt, 2324–9
Refugee migration, and intl aid programs, by world area and country of origin and asylum, 1991, annual rpt, 7004–15
UN voting record and share of votes in agreement with US, by issue, country, and world area, 1991, annual rpt, 7004–18

Bolling, H. Christine
"Japanese Presence in U.S. Agribusiness", 1528–332

Bombs
Aircraft hijackings, on-board explosions, and other crimes, US and foreign incidents, 1986-90, annual rpt, 7504–31
Airport security operations to prevent hijacking, screening results, enforcement actions, and hijacking attempts, 1990, annual rpt, 7504–49
Homicides, by circumstance, victim and offender relationship, and type of weapon, 1991, annual rpt, 6224–2.1
Incidents of bombing, and casualties, by target and circumstances, with explosives theft and recovery, by State, 1987-91, annual rpt, 8484–4
Incidents of bombing, casualties, and damage, by target, data compilation, 1992 annual rpt, 6064–6.3
Incidents of bombing, damage, and casualties, by target, circumstances, and State, 1991, annual rpt, 6224–5
Law enforcement officer assaults and deaths by circumstances, agency, victim and offender characteristics, and location, 1990, annual rpt, 6224–3
Prisoners in Federal and contract instns, by selected characteristics, region, and Federal instn, FY89, annual rpt, 6244–1.1
Terrorism (intl) incidents, casualties, and attacks on US targets, by attack type and country, 1991, annual rpt, 7004–22
Terrorism (intl) incidents, casualties, and attacks on US targets, by attack type and world area, 1991, annual rpt, 7004–13
Terrorism incidents in US, related activity, and casualties, by attack type, target, group, and location, 1991, annual rpt, 6224–6
see also Military weapons
see also Nuclear explosives and explosions

Bond, Ronald S.
"Analysis of Department Store Reference Pricing in Metropolitan Washington", 9408–57

Bonds
see Government securities
see Municipal bonds
see Securities
see Surety bonds
see Tax exempt securities

Bonneville Power Administration
Bonneville Power Admin mgmt of Fed Columbia River Power System, finances, operations, and sales by customer, FY91, annual rpt, 3224–1
Electric power capacity and use in Pacific Northwest, by end-use sector, projected under alternative fuel price cases, annual rpt, suspended, 3224–4
Electric power capacity and use in Pacific Northwest, by energy source, forecast under alternative load and demand cases, 1991-2012, annual rpt, 3224–3
Finances and operations of Federal power admins and electric utilities, 1990, annual rpt, 3164–24.2
Finances and sales for Fed Columbia River Power System, summary data, quarterly rpt, 3222–2
Hazardous waste mgmt and environmental protection standards compliance activities of BPA, 1991, annual rpt, 3224–6
Population, households, employment, income, and fuel prices, for Pacific Northwest, alternative projections, annual rpt, suspended, 3224–5
Sales, revenue, and rates of BPA, by customer and customer type, 1991, semiannual rpt, 3222–1

Bonuses
see Employee bonuses and work incentives

Books and bookselling
Consumer holdings of durable goods, by type, in current and constant dollars, 1925-90, annual article, 2702–1.305
Consumer holdings of durable goods, by type, in current and constant dollars, 1988-91, annual article, 2702–1.327
Copyrights Register activities, registrations by material type, and fees, FY91 and trends from 1790, annual rpt, 26404–2
County Business Patterns, 1989: employment, establishments, and payroll, by SIC 2- to 4-digit industry and county, annual State rpt series, 2326–8
County Business Patterns, 1990: employment, establishments, and payroll, by SIC 2- to 4-digit industry and county, annual State rpt series, 2326–6
Employment, earnings, and hours, by SIC 1- to 4-digit industry, monthly 1989-Feb 1992, annual rpt, 6744–4
Exports and imports between US and outlying areas, by detailed commodity and mode of transport, 1991, annual rpt, 2424–11
Exports and imports of US, by country and detailed commodity, monthly rpt, 2422–12
Exports and imports of US, by Harmonized System 6-digit commodity and country, 1991, annual rpt, 2424–13
Exports of US, detailed Schedule B commodities with countries of destination, 1991, annual rpt, 2424–10
GPO bookstores, 1992 annual listing, 2304–2
Input-output structure of US economy, detailed interindustry transactions for 541 industries, and components of final demand, 1982 benchmark data, 2708–17
Manufacturing annual survey, 1990: finances and operations, by SIC 2- to 4-digit industry, series, 2506–14
Manufacturing census, 1987: concentration of largest firms measured by value added, and for shipments by SIC 2- and 4-digit industry, subject rpt, 2497–6
Manufacturing census, 1987: shipments of manufacturers products, by customer class and SIC 2- and 4-digit industry, subject rpt, 2497–4
Manufacturing finances and operations, by SIC 2- to 4-digit industry, forecast 1992, annual rpt, 2044–28
Occupational injury and illness rates, by SIC 2- to 4-digit industry, 1989-90, annual rpt, 6844–7
Occupational injury and illness rates, by SIC 2- to 4-digit industry, 1990, annual rpt, 6844–1
OECD trade, total and for 4 major countries, and US trade by country, by commodity, 1980-90, world area rpt series, 9116–1
Price indexes (producer), by stage of processing and detailed commodity, monthly rpt, 6762–6
Price indexes (producer), by stage of processing and detailed commodity, monthly 1991, annual rpt, 6764–2
Retail trade sales and inventories, by kind of business, region, and selected State, MSA, and city, monthly rpt, 2413–3

Retail trade sales, inventories, purchases, gross margin, and accounts receivable, by SIC 2- to 4-digit kind of business and form of ownership, 1990, annual rpt, 2413–5
Science, engineering, and technical employment in manufacturing, by field and industry, 1989, triennial rpt, 9627–23
Soviet Union and US economic and sociodemographic indicators, selected years 1970-90, handbook, 2328–80
Statistical Abstract of US, 1992 annual data compilation, 2324–1.7
Tax (income) returns of corporations, income and tax items by asset size and detailed industry, 1989, annual rpt, 8304–4; 8304–21
Tax (income) returns of sole proprietorships, income statement items, by industry group, 1990, annual article, 8302–2.317; 8302–2.320
see also Libraries

Booth, Rick
"USCGC *Tamaroa*—Modern Day Lifesavers", 2152–8.303

Bordo, Michael D.
"Gold Standard as a Rule", 9377–9.136

Boschen, John F.
"Effects of Countercyclical Monetary Policy on Money and Interest Rates: An Evaluation of Evidence from FOMC Documents", 9387–8.259

Bosnia and Herzegovina
Economic, social, political, and geographic summary data, by country, 1992, annual factbook, 9114–2

Boston, Mass.
Commuters, by county of residence and work, for top 10 metro areas, 1990 Census of Population, press release, 2328–84
CPI by component for US city average, and by region, population size, and for 15 metro areas, monthly rpt, 6762–1
CPI by component for US city average, and by selected metro area, region, and population size, monthly rpt, 6762–2
Drug abuse indicators for selected metro areas, research results, data collection, and policy issues, 1992 semiannual conf, 4492–5
Fruit and vegetable shipments, and arrivals by city, by mode of transport and State and country of origin, 1991, annual rpt, 1311–4.1
Heroin prices and purity in 19 metro areas and Puerto Rico, by world area of origin, quarterly rpt, 6282–2
Housing and households characteristics, unit and neighborhood quality, and journey to work by MSA location, for 11 MSAs, 1985 survey, supplement, 2485–8
Housing and households characteristics, 1989 survey, MSA fact sheet, 2485–11.7
Housing and households detailed characteristics, and unit and neighborhood quality, by location, 1989 survey, MSA rpt, 2485–6.10
Mortgage applications of minorities, for Boston by disposition and financial characteristics, with problems in analyzing lender disclosure statements, 1990, working paper, 9373–27.15
Pollutant concentrations in coastal and estuarine fish, shellfish, and environment, late 1970s-89, local area rpt, 2176–3.14
Wages by occupation, and benefits, for office and plant workers, 1991 survey, periodic MSA rpt, 6785–16.1
Wages by occupation, and benefits, for office and plant workers, 1992 survey, periodic MSA rpt, 6785–17.3
see also under By City and By SMSA or MSA in the "Index by Categories"

Botany
Carbon dioxide in atmosphere, DOE R&D programs and funding at natl labs, universities, and other instns, FY92, annual summary rpt, 3004–18.10
DOE R&D projects and funding at natl labs, universities, and other instns, FY92, annual summary rpt, 3004–18.7
Higher education grad programs enrollment in science and engineering, by field, source of funds, and characteristics of student and instn, 1990, annual rpt, 9627–7
Research (agricultural) funding and staffing for USDA, State agencies, and other instns, by topic, FY91, annual rpt, 1744–2
Research and education grants, USDA competitive awards by program and recipient, FY91, annual listing, 1764–1
see also Flowers and nursery products
see also Forests and forestry
see also Fruit and fruit products
see also Horticulture
see also Plants and vegetation
see also Vegetables and vegetable products

BOTEC Analysis Corp.
"Hospital Readmissions", 4008–117

Botswana
Agricultural trade of US, by detailed commodity and country, 1991, annual rpt, 1524–8
Agricultural trade of US, by detailed commodity and country, 1991, semiannual rpt, 1522–4
AID economic aid to developing countries, obligations and disbursements by country, quarterly rpt, 9912–4
AID loans repayment status and terms by program and country, and status of predecessor agency loans, quarterly rpt, 9912–3
Economic and military aid and loans from US and intl agencies, by program and country, FY46-91, annual rpt, 9914–5
Economic and social conditions of developing countries from 1960s, and Intl Dev Cooperation Agency and AID activities and funding, FY91-93, annual rpt, 9904–4
Economic, social, political, and geographic summary data, by country, 1992, annual factbook, 9114–2
Exports and imports of US, by transport mode, country, and SITC 1- to 3-digit commodity, 1991, annual rpt, 2424–12
Exports of US, detailed Schedule B commodities with countries of destination, 1991, annual rpt, 2424–10
Human rights conditions in 170 countries, and US economic and military aid, 1991, annual rpt, 21384–3
Military aid of US, arms sales, and training programs costs and budget requests, by program, world region, and country, FY91-93, annual rpt, 7144–13
Military spending, arms trade, and force strengths, with govt spending and population, by country, 1979-89, annual rpt, 9824–1
Minerals Yearbook, Vol 3, 1989: foreign country review of production, trade, and policy, by commodity, annual rpt, 5604–35.1
Population size, growth rates, and components of change, by country, projected 1990-2020 and trends from 1950, biennial rpt, 2324–9
Refugee migration, and intl aid programs, by world area and country of origin and asylum, 1991, annual rpt, 7004–15
UN voting record and share of votes in agreement with US, by issue, country, and world area, 1991, annual rpt, 7004–18

Boucher, Janice L.
"Misspecification Bias in Tests of the Forward Foreign Exchange Rate Unbiasedness Hypothesis", 9371–10.68

Boulder, Colo.
CPI by component for US city average, and by selected metro area, region, and population size, monthly rpt, 6762–2
Housing starts and completions authorized by building permits in 40 MSAs, quarterly rpt, 2382–9
Housing vacancy rates for single and multifamily units and mobile homes, by city and ZIP code, 1992, annual MSA rpt, 9304–22.1

Bourdon, Karen H.
"Estimating the Prevalence of Mental Disorders in U.S. Adults from the Epidemiologic Catchment Area Survey", 4042–3.368

Bourque, Mary L.
"Levels of Mathematics Achievement: Initial Performance Standards for the 1990 NAEP Mathematics Assessment. Volume III, Technical Report", 4896–8.6

Bovine somatotropin
see Hormones

Bowen, G. Stephen
"First Year of AIDS Services Delivery Under Title I of the Ryan White CARE Act", 4042–3.352

Boy Scouts of America
Statistical Abstract of US, 1992 annual data compilation, 2324–1.7

Boycotts
Exporters (US) antiboycott law violations and fines by firm, and invitations to boycott by country, FY91, annual rpt, 2024–1
Intl boycotts by OPEC and other countries, US firms and individuals cooperation and tax benefits denied, 1990, article, 8302–2.323
Intl boycotts by OPEC and other countries, US firms and shareholders cooperation and tax benefits denied, detailed data compilation for income tax returns, 1986, quinquennial rpt, 8308–31
Tax (income) returns of corporations with foreign tax credit, income and tax items by industry group, 1988, biennial article, 8302–2.316

Boyd, N. F.
"Relationship Between Mammographic and Histological Risk Factors for Breast Cancer", 4472–1.332

Bradbury, Katharine L.
"What Past Recoveries Say About the Outlook for New England", 9373–1.315

Bradby, Denise
"Characteristics of At-Risk Students in NELS:88. National Education Longitudinal Study of 1988", 4826–9.16
"Language Characteristics and Academic Achievement: A Look at Asian and Hispanic Eighth Graders in National Education Longitudinal Study of 1988", 4826–9.12

Braddock, Douglas J.
"Scientific and Technical Employment, 1990-2005", 6722–1.314

Bradford, John J.
"U.S. Possessions Corporation Returns, 1989: Data Release", 8302–2.326

Bradley, Anne F.
"Fire Ecology of Forests and Woodlands in Utah", 1208–420

Bradner, L. A.
"Water Quality in the Upper Floridan Aquifer in the Vicinity of Drainage Wells, Orlando, Fla.", 5666–28.19

Brain diseases
see Cerebrovascular diseases
see Neurological disorders

Brand, Gary J.
"Forest Statistics for Iowa, 1990", 1208–75

Brand names
see Trademarks
see under By Individual Company or Institution in the "Index by Categories"

Bratton, Lisa
"Public Water-Supply in Massachusetts, 1986", 5666–24.16

Braun, R. Anton
"Seasonal Solow Residuals and Christmas: A Case for Labor Hoarding and Increasing Returns", 9375–13.71
"Seasonality and Equilibrium Business Cycle Theories", 9375–13.74

Bray, Mayfield S.
"Audiovisual Records in the National Archives of the U.S. Relating to World War II", 9516–1.3
"Audiovisual Records Relating to Naval History", 9516–1.6

Brazil
Agricultural productivity indicators for Brazil, 1968-87, 1528–331
Agricultural trade by commodity and country, prices, and world market devs, monthly rpt, 1922–12
Agricultural trade of US, by detailed commodity and country, 1991, annual rpt, 1524–8
Agricultural trade of US, by detailed commodity and country, 1991, semiannual rpt, 1522–4
AID economic aid to developing countries, obligations and disbursements by country, quarterly rpt, 9912–4
AID loans repayment status and terms by program and country, and status of predecessor agency loans, quarterly rpt, 9912–3
Coffee production by State, exportable production, and exports to US, for Brazil, late 1980s-1992/93, FAS periodic circular, 1925–5
Cuba trade, by commodity and country, mid 1980s-91, 9118–8
Debt burden indicators for 8 developing countries, alternative projections 1991-2000 and trends from 1974, technical paper, 9366–7.271
Economic and military aid and loans from US and intl agencies, by program and country, FY46-91, annual rpt, 9914–5
Economic and social conditions of developing countries from 1960s, and Intl Dev Cooperation Agency and AID activities and funding, FY91-93, annual rpt, 9904–4
Economic and social conditions, resources, and trade, and aid, 1992, annual factbook, 9914–14
Economic conditions, income, production, prices, employment, and trade, 1992 periodic country rpt, 2046–4.28
Economic conditions, policy, and trade practices, by country, 1989-91, annual rpt, 21384–5
Economic, population, and agricultural data, US and other aid sources, and AID activity, 1992 country rpt, 9916–12.67
Economic, social, political, and geographic summary data, by country, 1992, annual factbook, 9114–2
Exports and imports of US, by commodity and country, 1980-90, world area rpt, 9116–1.7
Exports and imports of US, by Harmonized System 6-digit commodity and country, 1991, annual rpt, 2424–13
Exports and imports of US, by selected country, country group, and commodity group, 1991, annual rpt, 2044–37
Exports and imports of US, by transport mode, country, and SITC 1- to 3-digit commodity, 1991, annual rpt, 2424–12
Exports and imports, trade agreements and relations, and USITC investigations, 1991, annual rpt, 9884–5
Exports, imports, and balances of US for manufactured goods, by SITC 2-digit commodity and country, quarterly rpt, 2042–35
Exports, imports, and balances of US with major trading partners, by product category, 1987-91, annual chartbook, 9884–21
Exports, investment, debt, and tariffs of 7 Latin America countries, and trade and investment policy liberalization issues, mid 1960s-91, 9886–4.184
Exports of US, detailed Schedule B commodities with countries of destination, 1991, annual rpt, 2424–10
Grape (table and wine) production by variety, and wine exports and imports by country, for Brazil, 1991-92, article, 1925–34.341
Human rights conditions in 170 countries, and US economic and military aid, 1991, annual rpt, 21384–3
Imports of goods, services, and investment from US, trade barriers, impacts, and US actions, by country, 1991, annual rpt, 444–2
Inflation relation to money supply, for 5 South America countries, 1970s-90, technical paper, 9379–12.91
Labor conditions, union coverage, and work accidents, 1992 annual country rpt, 6366–4.16
Military aid of US, arms sales, and training programs costs and budget requests, by program, world region, and country, FY91-93, annual rpt, 7144–13
Military spending, arms trade, and force strengths, with govt spending and population, by country, 1979-89, annual rpt, 9824–1
Multinatl US firms and foreign affiliates finances and operations, by industry and country, 1989 benchmark survey, annual rpt, 2704–5
Multinatl US firms foreign affiliates, income statement items by asset size, industry, and country, 1988, biennial article, 8302–2.322
Nuclear power generation in US and 20 countries, monthly rpt, 3162–24.10
Nuclear power generation in US and 20 countries, monthly 1973-88, 3168–123.10
Oil exports to US by OPEC and non-OPEC countries, monthly rpt, 3162–24.3
Oil exports to US by OPEC and non-OPEC countries, monthly 1973-88, 3168–123.3
Oil production, investment needs, and exports, for 8 South America countries, 1980s-90 and projected to 2010, GAO rpt, 26123–396
Orange juice production, use, exports, and stocks, and Brazil exports, by country, 1985-92, article, 1925–34.328
Pipes and tubes (welded nonalloy steel) from 6 countries at less than fair value, injury to US industry, investigation with background financial and operating data, 1992 rpt, 9886–14.361
Pollution (air) contributing to global warming, emissions by monitoring site and country, and temperature change by world area and US region, 1860s-1990, annual rpt, 3004–33
Population size, growth rates, and components of change, by country, projected 1990-2020 and trends from 1950, biennial rpt, 2324–9
Refugee migration, and intl aid programs, by world area and country of origin and asylum, 1991, annual rpt, 7004–15
Spacecraft and satellite launches since 1957, quarterly listing, 9502–2
Steel (carbon and alloy) products from Brazil at less than fair value, injury to US industry, investigation with background financial and operating data, 1992 rpt, 9886–14.356
Steel (carbon flat-rolled) products from 21 countries, injury to US industry from foreign subsidized and less than fair value imports, investigation with background financial and operating data, 1992 rpt, 9886–19.85
Steel (hot-rolled) products containing lead or bismuth from 4 countries, injury to US industry from foreign subsidized and less than fair value imports, investigation with background financial and operating data, 1992 rpt, 9886–19.82
Steel imports of US under voluntary restraint agreement, by product, customs district, and country, with US industry operating data, quarterly rpt, 9882–13
Steel trade, by product, country, and customs district, with US industry operating data, 1989-June 1992, semiannual rpt, 9882–15

Textile and apparel foreign market conditions for US exports, with domestic industry operations, 1992 country rpt, 2046–15.1
UN voting record and share of votes in agreement with US, by issue, country, and world area, 1991, annual rpt, 7004–18
see also under By Foreign Country in the "Index by Categories"

Brazoria, Tex.
CPI by component for US city average, and by region, population size, and for 15 metro areas, monthly rpt, 6762–1
CPI by component for US city average, and by selected metro area, region, and population size, monthly rpt, 6762–2
Housing and households characteristics, and unit and neighborhood quality, by MSA location for 11 MSAs, 1987 survey, supplement, 2485–8
Housing starts and completions authorized by building permits in 40 MSAs, quarterly rpt, 2382–9

Bread
see Baking and bakery products

Breast disorders
see Mammography
see Urogenital diseases

Breast-feeding
Latin America economic and social conditions, resources, trade, and aid, 1992, annual factbook, 9914–14
Maternal and child health indicators and services use, by age, race, and poverty status, 1988, 4478–197

Bredahl, Maury E.
"Product Effects of Trade Restrictions in the Japanese Pork Import Market", 1524–4.3

Brelsford, Taylor
"Social Indicators Study of Alaskan Coastal Villages I. Key Informant Summaries, Volume 1: Schedule A Regions", 5736–5.17

Brewer, Elijah, III
"Empirical Test of the Incentive Effects of Deposit Insurance: The Case of Junk Bonds at Savings and Loan Associations", 9375–13.69
"Ex Ante Risk and Ex Post Collapse of S&Ls in the 1980s", 9375–1.306

Brewster, Marge A.
"Predicting Needs for Special Education Resources for Mental Retardation from Birth Defects Records", 4042–3.327

Bribery
see Corruption and bribery

Brickey, Michael R.
"Pacific Outer Continental Shelf Region: Production Record by Platform, 1990", 5734–9

Bridegeport, Conn.
see also under By City and By SMSA or MSA in the "Index by Categories"

Bridges and tunnels
Army Corps of Engineers activities and projects, FY88 and trends from 1800s, annual rpt, 3754–1.1
Army Corps of Engineers activities and projects, FY89 and trends from 1800s, annual rpt, 3754–1.2
Army Corps of Engineers activities and projects, FY90 and trends from 1800s, annual rpt, 3754–1.3
Conditions and funding of rural hwys and bridges, discontinued series, 1276–1
Conditions of hwy bridges, and replacement and repair program funding by bridge, by State, 1990, biennial rpt, 7554–27
Forest Service activities and finances, by region and State, FY91, annual rpt, 1204–1.1
Hwy Statistics, detailed data by State, 1991, annual rpt, 7554–1
Hwy Statistics, summary data with trends and projections, 1992 chartbook, 7554–41
Mexico-US trade agreement impacts on truck traffic at border crossings, Customs Service staff needs, and hwy improvement costs, projected to 2000 with trends from 1986, GAO rpt, 26123–368
Ownership, type, use, dimensions, and location of bridges over navigable waters, 1991 regional listing series, 7406–5
Public lands acreage and use, and Land Mgmt Bur activities and finances, annual State rpt series, 5724–11
Water storage and carriage facilities of Reclamation Bur, capacity, and operating status, as of Sept 1990, biennial listing, 5824–7

Bright, Daniel J.
"Ground-Water Hydrology and Quality in the Lompoc Area, Santa Barbara County, California, 1987-88", 5666–28.17

Brill, Howard
"Impact of IRCA on the U.S. Labor Market and Economy", 6366–6.10

Brilliant, Franca
"Office of U.S. Foreign Disaster Assistance, Annual Report, FY91", 9914–12

Briscoe, William W.
"Within DRG Case Complexity Change in FY90", 17206–2.39

Bristol, Conn.
Housing and households characteristics, and unit and neighborhood quality, by MSA location for 11 MSAs, 1987 survey, supplement, 2485–8

British Columbia Province, Canada
Tidal currents, daily time and velocity by station for North America and Asia coasts, forecast 1993, annual rpt, 2174–1.2
Timber in northwestern US and British Columbia, production, prices, trade, and employment, quarterly rpt, 1202–3

British Virgin Islands
Agricultural trade of US, by detailed commodity and country, 1991, semiannual rpt, 1522–4
Economic and social conditions, resources, and trade, and aid, 1992, annual factbook, 9914–14
Economic, social, political, and geographic summary data, by country, 1992, annual factbook, 9114–2
Exports and imports of US, by transport mode, country, and SITC 1- to 3-digit commodity, 1991, annual rpt, 2424–12
Exports of US, detailed Schedule B commodities with countries of destination, 1991, annual rpt, 2424–10
Population size, growth rates, and components of change, by country, projected 1990-2020 and trends from 1950, biennial rpt, 2324–9
Tax (income) returns, income, and tax withheld for foreign partners of US partnerships, by country, 1990, article, 8302–2.324

Broach, Dana
"Air Traffic Control Specialists in the Airway Science Curriculum Demonstration Project 1984-90: Third Summative Evaluation", 7506–10.96
"Identifying Ability Requirements for Operators of Future Automated Air Traffic Control Systems", 7506–10.122

Broadcasting
see Educational broadcasting
see Public broadcasting
see Radio
see Television

Brockton, Mass.
Housing and households characteristics, unit and neighborhood quality, and journey to work by MSA location, for 11 MSAs, 1985 survey, supplement, 2485–8
Housing and households detailed characteristics, and unit and neighborhood quality, by location, 1989 survey, MSA rpt, 2485–6.10

Brokers
see Futures trading
see Real estate business
see Stockbrokers

Bronfman, Benson
"Handbook of Evaluation of Utility DSM Programs", 3308–102

Brookhaven National Laboratory
see also Department of Energy National Laboratories

Brooks, Rhonda L.
"Biodegradable Polymers", 1504–9.1

Brothers, Stephen L., Jr.
"Energy Management Annual Report, FY91", 9804–26

Broussard, Kathryn A.
"Assessment of the 50/92 Provision and the U.S. Rice Program", 1561–8.303

Brown, Bryan W.
"Stochastic Specification in Random Production Models of Cost Minimizing Firms", 9371–10.82

Brown, Patricia Q.
"Salaries of Full-Time Instructional Faculty on 9- and 10-Month and 11- and 12-Month Contracts in Institutions of Higher Education, 1980-81 Through 1990-91", 4844–8

Brown, Richard A.
"Resolution Costs of Bank Failures: An Update of the FDIC Historical Loss Model", 9292–4.303

Brown, Susan S.
"Forest Statistics for Land Outside National Forests in Southwestern Montana, 1989", 1206–25.12

Browne, Lynn E.
"Why New England Went the Way of Texas Rather than California", 9373–1.302

Brownson, Ross C.
"Role of Data-Driven Planning and Coalition Development in Preventing Cardiovascular Disease", 4042–3.302

Brownsville, Tex.
see also under By City and By SMSA or MSA in the "Index by Categories"

Broyles, Susan G.
"Integrated Postsecondary Education Data System Glossary", 4848–47
"Key Statistics on the Noncollegiate Sector of Postsecondary Education: 1990", 4844–19
Brunei
Agricultural trade of US, by detailed commodity and country, 1991, annual rpt, 1524–8
Agricultural trade of US, by detailed commodity and country, 1991, semiannual rpt, 1522–4
Economic and military aid and loans from US and intl agencies, by program and country, FY46-91, annual rpt, 9914–5
Economic, social, political, and geographic summary data, by country, 1992, annual factbook, 9114–2
Exports and imports of US, by transport mode, country, and SITC 1- to 3-digit commodity, 1991, annual rpt, 2424–12
Exports of US, detailed Schedule B commodities with countries of destination, 1991, annual rpt, 2424–10
Human rights conditions in 170 countries, and US economic and military aid, 1991, annual rpt, 21384–3
Minerals Yearbook, Vol 3, 1989: foreign country review of production, trade, and policy, by commodity, annual rpt, 5604–35.2
Population size, growth rates, and components of change, by country, projected 1990-2020 and trends from 1950, biennial rpt, 2324–9
UN voting record and share of votes in agreement with US, by issue, country, and world area, 1991, annual rpt, 7004–18
Brunner, Allan D.
"Recent Developments Affecting the Profitability and Practices of Commercial Banks", 9362–1.305
Bryan, Michael F.
"Different Kind of Money Illusion: The Case of Long and Variable Lags", 9377–9.131
Bryden, Edward J.
"Commodity Prices and P-Star", 9377–1.303
bST
see Hormones
Bucci, Michael
"Police and Firefighter Pension Plans", 6722–1.350
Buck, Germaine M.
"Comparison of Native American Births in Upstate New York with Other Race Births, 1980-86", 4042–3.359
Budget Enforcement Act
Budget of US, Bush Admin proposals, with detail for defense budgets, and historical data from FY34, FY93, 108–46
Budget of US, CBO analysis of revenue and spending alternatives and projections of economic indicators, FY93-97, annual rpt, 26304–3
Budget of US, House concurrent resolution, with spending and revenue targets, FY93 and projected to FY97, annual rpt, 21264–2
Budget of US, obligations and authority by function, agency, and program, with summaries and analyses, FY93, annual rpt, 104–2
Gramm-Rudman Act budget deficit reduction, CBO sequestration estimates, FY93, annual rpt, 26304–6
Gramm-Rudman Act budget deficit reduction, OMB sequestration estimates, by category, FY92, annual rpt, 104–27
Budget of the U.S.
Budget of US, authoritative financial statements with appropriations, outlays, and receipts, by agency, FY91, annual rpt, 8104–2
Budget of US, balances of budget authority obligated and unobligated, by function and agency, FY90-93, annual rpt, 104–8
Budget of US, Bush Admin proposals, with detail for defense budgets, and historical data from FY34, FY93, 108–46
Budget of US, CBO analysis and review of FY93 budget by function, annual rpt, 26304–2
Budget of US, CBO analysis of revenue and spending alternatives and projections of economic indicators, FY93-97, annual rpt, 26304–3
Budget of US, House Budget Committee analysis of Bush Admin proposals and economic assumptions, FY93, 21268–42
Budget of US, House concurrent resolution, with spending and revenue targets, FY93 and projected to FY97, annual rpt, 21264–2
Budget of US, midsession review of FY93 budget, by function, annual rpt, 104–7
Budget of US, obligations and authority by function, agency, and program, with summaries and analyses, FY93, annual rpt, 104–2
Budget of US, receipts and outlays on natl income and product basis, FY93, annual article, 2702–1.310
Business statistics, detailed data for major industries and economic indicators, 1960-91, *Survey of Current Business* biennial supplement, 2704–1
Deficit and other economic impacts of Reagan Admin supply-side fiscal policy, 1980s and trends from 1960s, technical paper, 9385–1.304; 9385–8.125
Deficit forecasting accuracy, factors contributing to discrepancies, and analysis of major programs, FY91, annual GAO rpt, 26104–23
Deficits impacts on GNP and public and foreign debt, projected under alternative reduction policies, 1990-2020 with intl comparisons from 1981, GAO rpt, 26109–5
Economic Report of the President for 1991, economic effects of budget proposals, and trends and projections, 1940s-95, annual hearings, 23844–4
Economic Report of the President for 1992, Joint Economic Committee critique and policy recommendations, annual rpt, 23844–2
Economic Report of the President for 1992, with economic trends from 1929, annual rpt, 204–1.6
Fed Govt agencies budget requests and program costs and characteristics, series, 26306–3
Gramm-Rudman Act budget deficit reduction, CBO sequestration estimates, FY93, annual rpt, 26304–6
Gramm-Rudman Act budget deficit reduction, OMB sequestration estimates, by category, FY92, annual rpt, 104–27
Receipts and outlays, 1990, annual rpt, 9364–5.5
Receipts by source and outlays by agency, *Treasury Bulletin*, quarterly rpt, 8002–4.1
Receipts by source and outlays by function, monthly rpt, quarterly and annual data, 23842–1.6
Receipts by source, outlays by agency and program, and balances, monthly rpt, 8102–3
Receipts, outlays, and debt, Fed Reserve Bank of St Louis monthly rpt, 9391–3
Savings instns failures, costs and budget deficit and economic impacts, 1980s and projected to 2010, 26306–6.165
Statistical Abstract of US, 1992 annual data compilation, 2324–1.10
see also Defense budgets and appropriations
see also Executive impoundment of appropriated funds
see also Fiscal policy
see also Nonappropriated funds
see also Public debt
Budgets
see Budget of the U.S.
see Defense budgets and appropriations
see Family budgets
see Foreign budgets
Buescher, Paul A.
"Comparison of Low Birth Weight Among Medicaid Patients of Public Health Departments and Other Providers of Prenatal Care in North Carolina and Kentucky", 4042–3.304
Buffalo, N.Y.
CPI by component for US city average, and by selected metro area, region, and population size, monthly rpt, 6762–2
Freight (waterborne domestic and foreign) by commodity, traffic, and passengers, by port and waterway, 1989, annual rpt, 3754–3.3
Fruit and vegetable shipments, and arrivals by city, by mode of transport and State and country of origin, 1991, annual rpt, 1311–4.1
see also under By City and By SMSA or MSA in the "Index by Categories"
Buhler, Susan E.
"Outlook for Poultry and Eggs", 1504–9.1
Building codes
Housing affordability and availability, impacts of govt land use regulations and rent control, and low income housing condition, 1991 hearing, 21248–174
Building laws
see Building codes
see Building permits
see Zoning and zoning laws
Building maintenance services
see Janitorial and maintenance services
Building materials
Acid rain environmental, economic, and health effects, and pollutant emissions, 1985-89 and alternative projections to 2030, 14358–4
Business statistics, detailed data for major industries and economic indicators, *Survey of Current Business*, monthly rpt, 2702–1.18; 2702–1.20

Business statistics, detailed data for major industries and economic indicators, 1960-91, *Survey of Current Business* biennial supplement, 2704–1
Clay (construction) production and shipments by region and State, trade, and use, by product, quarterly Current Industrial Rpt, 2506–9.2
County Business Patterns, 1989: employment, establishments, and payroll, by SIC 2- to 4-digit industry and county, annual State rpt series, 2326–8
County Business Patterns, 1990: employment, establishments, and payroll, by SIC 2- to 4-digit industry and county, annual State rpt series, 2326–6
Employment, earnings, and hours, by SIC 1- to 4-digit industry, monthly 1989-Feb 1992, annual rpt, 6744–4
Employment of minorities and women, by occupation, SIC 1- to 3-digit industry, State, and MSA, 1991, annual rpt, 9244–1
Energy use in commercial buildings, costs, and conservation, by building characteristics, survey rpt series, 3166–8
Exports and imports between US and outlying areas, by detailed commodity and mode of transport, 1991, annual rpt, 2424–11
Exports and imports of US, by country and detailed commodity, monthly rpt, 2422–12
Exports and imports of US, by Harmonized System 6-digit commodity and country, 1991, annual rpt, 2424–13
Exports and imports of US, by selected country, country group, and commodity group, 1991, annual rpt, 2044–37
Exports and imports of US, by transport mode, country, and SITC 1- to 3-digit commodity, 1991, annual rpt, 2424–12
Exports, imports, and balances of US for manufactured goods, by SITC 2-digit commodity and country, quarterly rpt, 2042–35
Exports of US, detailed Schedule B commodities with countries of destination, 1991, annual rpt, 2424–10
Farm prices received and paid, by commodity and State, monthly rpt, 1629–1
Farm prices received and paid, by commodity and State, 1991, annual rpt, 1629–5
Farm production itemized costs, by farm sales size and region, 1991, annual rpt, 1614–3
Finances and operations by SIC 4-digit construction materials industry, selected years 1977-89, article, 2042–1.302
Glass (flat) production, shipments, inventories, and trade, quarterly Current Industrial Rpt, 2506–9.6
Home mortgages FHA-insured, financial, property, and borrower characteristics, by metro area, 1991, annual rpt, 5144–24
Home mortgages FHA-insured, financial, property, and borrower characteristics, by State, 1991, annual rpt, 5144–1; 5144–25
Home mortgages FHA-insured, financial, property, and borrower characteristics, 1991, annual rpt, 5144–17; 5144–23
Housing (rental) units, total, with HUD assistance by program, and eligible for aid, by unit, household, and neighborhood characteristics, and location, 1989, biennial rpt, 5184–11
Housing alteration and repair spending for homeowner and contracted jobs, quarterly rpt, 2382–7.1
Housing units completed, single and multifamily units by structural and financial characteristics, and location, 1987-91, annual rpt, 2384–1
Hwy construction material prices and indexes for Federal-aid system, by type of material and urban-rural location, quarterly rpt, 7552–7
Hwy construction material prices and indexes for Federal-aid system, by type of material, quarterly press release, 7552–16
Hwy construction material use by type, and spending, by State, 1940s-91, annual rpt, 7554–29
Hwy receipts by source, and spending by function, by level of govt and State, 1991, annual rpt, 7554–1.3
Injuries from use of consumer products and related activities, by severity and victim age and sex, 1990, annual rpt, 9164–7
Injuries from use of consumer products, by severity, victim age, and detailed product, 1991, annual rpt, 9164–6
Injuries from use of consumer products, related deaths and costs, and recalls by brand, by product type, FY90, annual rpt, 9164–2
Input-output structure of US economy, detailed interindustry transactions for 541 industries, and components of final demand, 1982 benchmark data, 2708–17
Labor productivity, indexes of output, hours, and employment by SIC 2- to 4-digit industry, 1967-90, annual rpt, 6824–1.3
Manufacturing census, 1987: concentration of largest firms measured by value added, and for shipments by SIC 2- and 4-digit industry, subject rpt, 2497–6
Manufacturing census, 1987: shipments of manufacturers products, by customer class and SIC 2- and 4-digit industry, subject rpt, 2497–4
Manufacturing finances and operations, by SIC 2- to 4-digit industry, forecast 1992, annual rpt, 2044–28
Military prime contract awards, by category, contract and contractor type, and service branch, FY82-1st half FY92, semiannual rpt, 3542–1
Military prime contract awards, by category, contractor type, and State, FY89-91, annual rpt, 3544–11
Military prime contract awards, by detailed procurement category, FY88-91, annual rpt, 3544–18
Occupational injury and illness rates, by SIC 2- to 4-digit industry, 1989-90, annual rpt, 6844–7
Occupational injury and illness rates, by SIC 2- to 4-digit industry, 1990, annual rpt, 6844–1
Pacific territories population and housing detailed characteristics, by location, 1990 Census of Population and Housing, series, 2551–8
Price indexes (producer), by stage of processing and detailed commodity, monthly rpt, 6762–6
Price indexes (producer), by stage of processing and detailed commodity, monthly 1991, annual rpt, 6764–2
Price indexes (producer) for material inputs, by construction industry, monthly rpt, 6762–6
Production, shipments, PPI, and stocks of building materials, by type, quarterly rpt, 2042–1.5; 2042–1.6
Retail trade sales and inventories, by kind of business, region, and selected State, MSA, and city, monthly rpt, 2413–3
Retail trade sales, by kind of business, advance monthly rpt, 2413–2
Retail trade sales, inventories, purchases, gross margin, and accounts receivable, by SIC 2- to 4-digit kind of business and form of ownership, 1990, annual rpt, 2413–5
Soviet Union and US economic and sociodemographic indicators, selected years 1970-90, handbook, 2328–80
Soviet Union construction activity and building materials production, 1985-92, article, 2042–1.301
Statistical Abstract of US, 1992 annual data compilation, 2324–1.26
Tax (income) returns of corporations, income and tax items by asset size and detailed industry, 1989, annual rpt, 8304–4; 8304–21
see also Asbestos contamination
see also Cement and concrete
see also Clay industry and products
see also Floor coverings
see also Insulation
see also Lumber industry and products
see also Paints and varnishes
see also Stone products and quarries
see also Wall coverings
see also under By Commodity in the "Index by Categories"

Building permits
Business statistics, detailed data for major industries and economic indicators, *Survey of Current Business*, monthly rpt, 2702–1.5
Coastal areas construction authorized by permit, by building type, 1970-89, 2176–8.3
Construction authorized by building permits, by type of construction, region, State, and MSA, quarterly rpt, 2042–1.3
Housing starts and completions authorized by building permits in 40 MSAs, quarterly rpt, 2382–9
New England States economic indicators, Fed Reserve 1st District, monthly rpt, 9373–2
New housing units authorized, by region, State, selected MSA, and permit-issuing place, monthly rpt, 2382–5
New housing units authorized, by State, MSA, and permit-issuing place, 1991, annual rpt, 2384–2
Nuclear power plant operating licenses, and construction permits granted and pending, monthly rpt, 3162–24.8
Nuclear power plant operating licenses, and construction permits granted and pending, monthly 1973-88, 3168–123.8
Southeastern States, Fed Reserve 5th District, economic indicators by State, quarterly rpt, 9389–16

Southeastern States, Fed Reserve 6th District, economic indicators by State and MSA, quarterly rpt, 9371–14
Southeastern States, FHLB 4th District, employment and housing indicators by State, quarterly rpt, 9302–36
Statistical Abstract of US, 1992 annual data compilation, 2324–1.26
West Central States economic indicators, Fed Reserve 10th District, quarterly rpt, 9381–16.2
see also Zoning and zoning laws

Buildings
see Apartment houses
see Architectural barriers to the handicapped
see Architecture
see Building codes
see Building materials
see Building permits
see Commercial buildings
see Condominiums and cooperatives
see Construction industry
see Elevators
see Housing condition and occupancy
see Housing construction
see Housing maintenance and repair
see Housing sales
see Housing supply and requirements
see Industrial plants and equipment
see Mobile homes
see Prefabricated buildings
see Public buildings

Bulgaria
Agricultural trade of US, by detailed commodity and country, 1991, annual rpt, 1524–8
Agricultural trade of US, by detailed commodity and country, 1991, semiannual rpt, 1522–4
Agricultural trade of US with Eastern Europe, by commodity group and country, 1988-91, 1928–11
Economic and social conditions of developing countries from 1960s, and Intl Dev Cooperation Agency and AID activities and funding, FY91-93, annual rpt, 9904–4
Economic conditions, policy, and trade practices, by country, 1989-91, annual rpt, 21384–5
Economic, social, political, and geographic summary data, by country, 1992, annual factbook, 9114–2
Export industries dev potential, with trade and industry finances and operations, for 5 Eastern Europe countries, 1985-90, 9886–4.179
Export licensing, monitoring, and enforcement activities, FY91, annual rpt, 2024–1
Exports and imports of US, by commodity and country, 1980-90, world area rpt, 9116–1.1
Exports and imports of US, by transport mode, country, and SITC 1- to 3-digit commodity, 1991, annual rpt, 2424–12
Exports and imports of US with Communist and transitional economy countries, by detailed commodity and country, quarterly rpt with articles, 9882–2
Exports and imports of US with Eastern Europe, by commodity and country, 1987-91 and outlook for 1992, 2048–158
Exports of US, detailed Schedule B commodities with countries of destination, 1991, annual rpt, 2424–10
Human rights conditions in 170 countries, and US economic and military aid, 1991, annual rpt, 21384–3
Market economy transition of Eastern Europe countries, trade, and foreign investment, by country, 1990-91, 9118–13
Military aid of US, arms sales, and training programs costs and budget requests, by program, world region, and country, FY91-93, annual rpt, 7144–13
Military spending, arms trade, and force strengths, with govt spending and population, by country, 1979-89, annual rpt, 9824–1
Population size, growth rates, and components of change, by country, projected 1990-2020 and trends from 1950, biennial rpt, 2324–9
Refugee migration, and intl aid programs, by world area and country of origin and asylum, 1991, annual rpt, 7004–15
Tobacco and cigarette production, use, and trade, for Bulgaria, 1980-91, article, 1925–16.303
UN voting record and share of votes in agreement with US, by issue, country, and world area, 1991, annual rpt, 7004–18

Bunce, Vicki
"Demographic Profiles of the Airway Facilities Work Force, Annual Report, FY90 Year-End Data", 7504–41

Burbey, Thomas J.
"Water-Level and Pumpage Data for Las Vegas Valley, Clark County, Nevada, 1986-90", 5666–28.23

Bureau for Refugee Programs, State Department
Arrivals in US by world area of origin and State of settlement, and Federal aid, FY91-92 and proposed FY93 allocations, annual rpt, 7004–16
Arrivals in US, by world area of origin, processing, and nationality, monthly rpt, 7002–4
Migration of refugees, and intl aid programs, by world area and country of origin and asylum, 1991, annual rpt, 7004–15

Bureau of Alcohol, Tobacco and Firearms
Alcoholic beverages and tobacco production, removals, stocks, and material used, by State, monthly rpt series, 8486–1
Bombing incidents and casualties by target and circumstances, and explosives theft and recovery, by State, 1987-91, annual rpt, 8484–4
Budget of US, obligations and authority by function, agency, and program, with summaries and analyses, FY93, annual rpt, 104–2
Firearms dealers licensed by Bur of Alcohol, Tobacco and Firearms, views on regulatory inspections, 1992 survey, GAO rpt, 26119–429
Tax enforcement activities and collections of BATF and IRS, 1991 hearing, 21788–217

Bureau of Census
Activities, rpts, and user services of Census Bur, monthly rpt, 2302–3
Advisory committees findings and recommendations for Census Bur data collection and statistical program plans, 1992 conf, 2628–35
Agricultural summary data, young readers pamphlet series, 2346–1
American Housing Survey, data coverage, products, and metro areas surveyed 1974-94, 2328–89
American Housing Survey: unit and households characteristics, and unit and neighborhood quality, by MSA location for 11 MSAs, 1987 survey, supplement, 2485–8
American Housing Survey: unit and households characteristics, MSA fact sheet series, 2485–11
American Housing Survey: unit and households detailed characteristics, and unit and neighborhood quality, MSA rpt series, 2485–6
American Housing Survey: unit and households detailed characteristics, and unit and neighborhood quality, 1989, biennial rpt supplement, 2485–13
American Housing Survey: unit and households detailed characteristics, and unit and neighborhood quality, 1989, wallchart, 2485–12
Annual Survey of Manufactures, 1990: finances and operations, by SIC 2- to 4-digit industry, series, 2506–14
Apartment and condominium completions and absorption rates, by size and price class, preliminary 1991, annual Current Housing Rpt, 2484–3
Apartment and condominium completions by rent class and sales price, and market absorption rates, quarterly rpt, 2482–2
Apartment market absorption rates and characteristics for nonsubsidized furnished and unfurnished units, 1990, annual Current Housing Rpt, 2484–2
Budget of US, obligations and authority by function, agency, and program, with summaries and analyses, FY93, annual rpt, 104–2
Budget proposals for 2000 decennial census planning and economic statistics programs improvement, FY92, hearing, 21628–98
Buildings (commercial and public) alteration and repair spending, by type, size, age, and region, 1989, 2388–4
Capital expenditures for plant and equipment, by major industry group, quarterly rpt, 2502–2
Census Bur geographic levels of data coverage, maps, and reference products, 1992 rpt, 2308–67
Census of Housing, 1990: inventory, occupancy, and costs, State fact sheet series, 2326–21
Census of Housing, 1990: median value and rent, by State and region, and compared to 1970 and 1980, fact sheet, 2328–83
Census of Housing, 1990: summary unit characteristics, by householder race and age, county, place, and urban-rural location, State rpt series, 2471–1
Census of Manufactures, 1987: concentration of largest firms measured by value added, and for shipments by SIC 2- and 4-digit industry, subject rpt, 2497–6
Census of Manufactures, 1987: shipments of manufacturers products by customer class and SIC 2- and 4-digit industry, subject rpt, 2497–4
Census of Population and Housing, 1990: data coverage, collection procedures, products and services availability, and uses, guide, 2555–1

Census of Population and Housing, 1990: data summary, use, and availability, for selected long form questions, fact sheet series, 2326–23
Census of Population and Housing, 1990: detailed geographic coverage, CD-ROM user guide, 2308–65
Census of Population and Housing, 1990: detailed geographic coverage, State CD-ROM series, 2551–9
Census of Population and Housing, 1990: immigrants, by period of entry, citizenship, State, birthplace, and for top cities and counties, press release, 2328–88
Census of Population and Housing, 1990: Indian tribes population size, with data by State, press release, 2328–86
Census of Population and Housing, 1990: industry and occupation classification codes, alphabetical index, 2628–1
Census of Population and Housing, 1990: industry and occupation classification codes, classified index, 2628–2
Census of Population and Housing, 1990: maps and cartographic products availability, listing, 2308–66
Census of Population and Housing, 1990: Pacific territories detailed characteristics, by location, series, 2551–8
Census of Population and Housing, 1990: population and housing characteristics, detailed geographic coverage, State CD-ROM series, 2551–10
Census of Population and Housing, 1990: summary characteristics, by county, subdiv, and place, State rpt series, 2551–7
Census of Population and Housing, 1990: summary characteristics, households, and land area, by county, subdiv, and place, State rpt series, 2551–1
Census of Population and Housing, 1990: Summary Tape File 3 CD-ROM user guide, 2308–68
Census of Population, local govts participation in 1990 census and plans for 2000 census, hearing, 21628–100
Census of Population, 1990: ancestry of US population, by group and State, press release, 2328–87
Census of Population, 1990: commuters, by county of residence and work, for top 10 metro areas, press release, 2328–84
Census of Population, 1990: data accuracy and enumeration methodology issues, hearing, 21628–97
Census of Population, 1990: data accuracy, evaluation, and adjustment issues, hearing, 21628–99
Census of Population, 1990: data adjustment for undercounts, Commerce Dept decision against adjustment, hearing, 21628–101
Census of Population, 1990: data adjustment for undercounts, evaluation of advisability, with error rates by race and selected city, hearing, 21628–102
Census of Population, 1990: data adjustment for undercounts, issues, 1991, 25408–119
Census of Population, 1990: data adjustment in intercensal data for census undercounts, final decision with data by region and State, 2328–90
Census of Population, 1990: data adjustment in intercensal data for census undercounts, recommendations with alternative undercount estimates, 2628–36
Census of Population, 1990: minority group participation in census, effectiveness and quality of outreach and promotional programs, hearing, 21628–103
Census of Population, 1990: population characteristics and living arrangements, by county, place, and urban-rural location, State rpt series, 2531–1
Census of Population, 1990: population characteristics and living arrangements, for Native American, urban, and metro areas, series, 2531–2
Census of Population, 1990: post-enumeration review of planning and conduct of census, and recommendations for improvement, GAO rpt, 26119–403
Census of Population, 2000: planning activities, and review of 1990 census operations, hearing, 21628–104
Census of Retail Trade, 1987: sales and establishments, by merchandise line, State rpt series, discontinued, 2399–3
Characteristics of Business Owners Survey, 1987: minority- and women-owned firms and owner characteristics, by industry, employment and sales size, and form of ownership, 1987 survey, 2328–59
Chemical and oil products shipments, firms, trade, and use, by product, periodic Current Industrial Rpt series, 2506–8
Clay and glass production, shipments, trade, and stocks, by product, periodic Current Industrial Rpt series, 2506–9
Clothing and shoe production, shipments, trade, and use, by product, periodic Current Industrial Rpt series, 2506–6
Communications services revenue and expenses, itemized by SIC 2- to 4-digit kind of business, 1990, annual rpt, 2413–15
Construction put in place, value of new public and private structures, by type, monthly rpt, 2382–4
Corporations financial statements for manufacturing, mining, and trade, by selected SIC 2- to 3-digit industry, quarterly rpt, 2502–1
County Business Patterns, 1989: employment, establishments, and payroll, by SIC 2- to 4-digit industry and county, annual State rpt series, 2326–8
County Business Patterns, 1990: employment, establishments, and payroll, by SIC 2- to 4-digit industry and county, annual State rpt series, 2326–6
Current Housing Reports, unit and household characteristics, subject rpt series, 2486–1; 2486–2
Current Population Reports, demographic, social, and economic characteristics, series, 2546–1
Current Population Reports, demographic subjects, special study series, 2546–2
Current Population Reports, income and socioeconomic characteristics of persons, families, and households, detailed cross-tabulations, series, 2546–6
Current Population Reports, population estimates and projections, by region and State, series, 2546–3
Current Population Reports, population estimates for civilian, resident, and total population, monthly rpt, 2542–1
Data availability on CD-ROM, and use, 1992 user guide, 2308–64
Data collection methodology, programs, and measurement techniques of Census Bur, technical paper series, 2626–2
Data coverage and availability of Census Bur rpts and data files, 1992 annual listing, 2304–2
Data coverage, availability, and use, for Census Bur rpts and products, series, 2326–7
Data files and rpts of Census Bur, monthly listing, 2302–6
Developing countries aged population and selected characteristics, 1980s and projected to 2020, country rpt series, 2326–19
Developing countries population size, life expectancy, and fertility, trends and forecasts, country rpt series, 2326–24
Economic censuses and related statistics, data coverage and availability, 1992 preliminary guide, 2308–5
Economic censuses of 1987 and related programs, CD-ROM series, 2326–22
Economic censuses of 1987 and related programs, CD-ROM series, user guides, 2306–8
Economic censuses, 1987: data collection, coverage, availability, and procedural history, 2628–16
Electronic info storage and transmission costs and revenues for 4 Federal agencies, FY85-91, GAO rpt, 26125–47
Export statistics classification codes of Census Bur for countries, commodities, and customs districts, 1990 base edition and supplements, 2428–5
Exports and imports (waterborne) of US, by type of service, customs district, port, and world area, monthly rpt, 2422–7
Exports and imports between US and outlying areas, by detailed commodity and mode of transport, 1991, annual rpt, 2424–11
Exports and imports of US, by country and detailed commodity, monthly rpt, 2422–12
Exports and imports of US, by Harmonized System 6-digit commodity and country, 1991, annual rpt, 2424–13
Exports and imports of US, by transport mode, country, and SITC 1- to 3-digit commodity, 1991, annual rpt, 2424–12
Exports, imports, and trade flows, by country and commodity, with background economic indicators, data compilation, monthly CD-ROM, 2002–6
Exports of US, detailed commodities by country, monthly CD-ROM, 2422–13
Exports of US, detailed Schedule B commodities with countries of destination, 1991, annual rpt, 2424–10
Fed Govt spending in States and local areas, by type, State, county, and city, FY91, annual rpt, 2464–3
Fed Govt spending in States, by type, program, agency, and State, FY91, annual rpt, 2464–2
Food (processed) production and stocks by State, shipments, exports, ingredients, and use, periodic Current Industrial Rpt series, 2506–4
Foreign countries economic and social conditions, working paper series, 2326–18

Foreign countries population size, growth rates, and components of change, by country, projected 1990-2020 and trends from 1950, biennial rpt, 2324–9
Govt employment and payroll, by function, level of govt, and jurisdiction, annual rpt series, 2466–1
Govt finances, by level of govt, State, and for large cities and counties, annual rpt series, 2466–2
Govt retirement systems of States and local area, cash and security holdings and finances, quarterly rpt, 2462–2
Housing alteration and repair spending, by type, tenure, region, and other characteristics, quarterly rpt, 2382–7
Housing starts and completions authorized by building permits in 40 MSAs, quarterly rpt, 2382–9
Housing starts, by units per structure and metro-nonmetro location, and mobile home placements and prices, by region, monthly rpt, 2382–1
Housing units (1-family) sold and for sale by price, stage of construction, months on market, and region, monthly rpt, 2382–3
Housing units authorized, by region, State, selected MSA, and permit-issuing place, monthly rpt, 2382–5
Housing units authorized, by State, MSA, and permit-issuing place, 1991, annual rpt, 2384–2
Housing units completed and under construction, by region and units per structure, monthly rpt, 2382–2
Housing units completed, single and multifamily units by structural and financial characteristics, and location, 1987-91, annual rpt, 2384–1
Housing vacancy and occupancy rates, and vacant unit characteristics, by tenure and location, 1960s-91, annual rpt, 2484–1
Housing vacant unit characteristics and costs, and occupancy and vacancy rates, by region and metro-nonmetro location, quarterly rpt, 2482–1
Imports, exports, and employment impacts, by SIC 2- to 4-digit industry and commodity, quarterly rpt, 2322–2
Imports of US, detailed commodities by country, monthly CD-ROM, 2422–14
Lumber, paper, and related products shipments, trade, stocks, and use, periodic Current Industrial Rpt series, 2506–7
Machinery and equipment production, shipments, trade, stocks, orders, use, and firms, by product, periodic Current Industrial Rpt series, 2506–12
Manufacturing industries operations and performance, analytical rpt series, 2506–16
Manufacturing production, shipments, inventories, orders, and pollution control costs, periodic Current Industrial Rpt series, 2506–3
Map and geographic computer-readable database of Census Bur, TIGER files availability and use, 1991 rpt, 2628–32
Metals (intermediate product) shipments, trade, and inventories, by product, periodic Current Industrial Rpt series, 2506–11
Metals (primary) production, shipments, trade, stocks, and material used, by product, periodic Current Industrial Rpt series, 2506–10
Multinatl firms US affiliates finances and operations, by industry, country of parent firm, and State, 1987, 2708–48
NYC housing supply, occupancy, condition, and household characteristics, by tenure and borough, 1991 triennial survey, 2488–3
Older persons population size and characteristics, series, 2326–25
Older population and characteristics, by country, 1991 and projected to 2020, wallchart, 2328–82
Population and housing data, and policy issues, fact sheet series, 2326–17
Population size, by race and Hispanic origin, 1992 and projected 2000-2050, press release, 2328–85
Population size, July 1991-92, by region, census div, and State, annual press release, 2324–10
Retail trade sales and inventories, by kind of business, region, and selected State, MSA, and city, monthly rpt, 2413–3
Retail trade sales, by kind of business, advance monthly rpt, 2413–2
Retail trade sales, inventories, purchases, gross margin, and accounts receivable, by SIC 2- to 4-digit kind of business and form of ownership, 1990, annual rpt, 2413–5
Small business use of Census Bur economic data in planning decisions, case studies, 1991 rpt, 2628–33
Soviet Union and US economic and sociodemographic indicators, selected years 1970-90, handbook, 2328–80
Statistical Abstract of US, 1992 annual data compilation, 2324–1
Survey of Income and Program Participation, data collection, methodology, and availability, 1991 users guide, 2628–24
Survey of Income and Program Participation, data collection, methodology, and comparisons to other data bases, working paper series, 2626–10
Survey of Income and Program Participation, household income and socioeconomic characteristics, special study series, 2546–20
Survey of Income and Program Participation methodology, evaluation of errors, and bibl, 1990 rpt, 2628–34
Tax revenue, by level of govt, type of tax, State, and selected large county, quarterly rpt, 2462–3
Textile mill production, trade, sales, stocks, and material used, by product, region, and State, periodic Current Industrial Rpt series, 2506–5
Truck and warehouse services finances and inventory, by SIC 2- to 4-digit industry, 1990 survey, annual rpt, 2413–14
Wholesale trade sales and inventories, by SIC 2- to 3-digit kind of business, monthly rpt, 2413–7

Bureau of Consular Affairs, State Department
Visa (immigrant) applicants on waiting lists at consular office, by preference class, world region, and for top countries, as of Jan 1992, 7188–1
Visas of US issued and refused to immigrants and nonimmigrants, by class, issuing office, and nationality, FY90, annual rpt, 7184–1

Bureau of Diplomatic Security, State Department
Terrorism (intl) incidents, casualties, and attacks on US targets, by attack type and country, 1991, annual rpt, 7004–22

Bureau of Economic Analysis
Business cycle forecasting performance of BEA economic indicators, 1948-91, technical paper, 9379–12.95
Data coverage and availability of BEA rpts, 1992 annual rpt, 2704–6
Income (personal) per capita and by source, and employment, by industry div, State, MSA, and county, 1969-90, annual CD-ROM, 2704–7
Input-output model of BEA, regional multipliers by industry and State, and methodology, 1992 guide, 2708–47
Input-output structure of US economy, detailed interindustry transactions for 541 industries, and components of final demand, 1982 benchmark data, 2708–17
Multinatl firms US affiliates finances and operations, by industry, country of parent firm, and State, 1987, 2708–48
Multinatl firms US affiliates, finances, and operations, by industry, world area of parent firm, and State, 1989-90, annual rpt, 2704–4
Multinatl US firms and foreign affiliates finances and operations, by industry and country, 1989 benchmark survey, annual rpt, 2704–5
Natl income and product accounts, comprehensive accounts and components, benchmark revisions, 1929-88, 2708–5
Survey of Current Business, detailed data for major industries and economic indicators, monthly rpt, 2702–1
Survey of Current Business, detailed data for major industries and economic indicators, 1960-91, biennial supplement, 2704–1

Bureau of Engraving and Printing
Budget of US, obligations and authority by function, agency, and program, with summaries and analyses, FY93, annual rpt, 104–2

Bureau of Export Administration
Budget of US, obligations and authority by function, agency, and program, with summaries and analyses, FY93, annual rpt, 104–2
Licensing of exports, monitoring, and enforcement activities, FY91, annual rpt, 2024–1
Militarily strategic manufacturing industries finances, operations, and intl competitiveness, series, 2026–1

Bureau of Health Professions
Hospital employment and job vacancy rate, by occupation, and instn size and control, 1981-88, annual rpt, 4114–12
Labor supply and education of health professionals, by professional and other characteristics, and location, 1960s-92 and projected to 2020, biennial rpt, 4114–8
Physicians, by specialty, age, sex, and location of training and practice, 1990, State rpt series, 4116–6

Bureau of Indian Affairs
Budget of US, obligations and authority by function, agency, and program, with summaries and analyses, FY93, annual rpt, 104–2
Dams on Indian reservations, Bur of Indian Affairs and tribal mgmt of unsafe dams and Interior Dept funding, 1980s-91, GAO rpt, 26113–558
Education (special) enrollment by age, staff, funding, and needs, by type of handicap and State, 1990/91, annual rpt, 4944–4
Education funding of Fed Govt, with enrollment, program grants, and fellowships by State, for Indians, 1980s-FY91, annual rpt, 14874–1
Expenditures of Fed Govt in States, by type, program, agency, and State, FY91, annual rpt, 2464–2
Finances and operations of Federal power admins and electric utilities, 1990, annual rpt, 3164–24.2
Land ownership, multiple ownership, and Bur of Indian Affairs records maintenance, for 12 reservations, 1991, GAO rpt, 26113–559
Lands (Indian and govt) under BIA mgmt, acreage, leases, and use, 1989, annual rpt, 5704–12
Trust funds of Indians, BIA overpayments and shortages, by account, 1970s-91, hearing, 21408–131
Bureau of Intelligence and Research, State Department
Communist and OECD countries economic conditions, annual rpt, discontinued, 7144–11
EC trade with US by country, and total agricultural trade, annual rpt, discontinued, 7144–7
Foreign countries *Geographic Notes*, boundaries, claims, nomenclature, and other devs, quarterly rpt, 7142–3
Military aid of US, arms sales, and training programs costs and budget requests, by program, world region, and country, FY91-93, annual rpt, 7144–13
NATO members trade with Council for Mutual Economic Assistance Europe members, by country, annual rpt, discontinued, 7144–5
NATO members trade with PRC, by country, annual rpt, discontinued, 7144–14
OECD members GNP and GNP growth, by country, annual rpt, discontinued, 7144–8
OECD trade, by country, annual rpt, discontinued, 7144–10
Bureau of International Labor Affairs
Caribbean area duty-free exports to US, and imports from US, by country, and impact on US employment, by commodity, 1991, annual rpt, 6364–2
Exports and imports impacts on US industries and employment, series, 6366–3
Foreign countries labor conditions, union coverage, and work accidents, annual country rpt series, 6366–4
Immigration impacts on US labor force and employment, working paper series, 6366–6
Research contracts of Bur, FY83-91, annual listing, 6364–1
Bureau of Justice Assistance
Drug enforcement grants of Fed Govt, and allocations to local govts, by State, FY91, annual rpt, 6064–38
Women arrestees drug abuse history and selected other characteristics, for 4 cities, 1988-89, 6068–246
Bureau of Justice Statistics
Court criminal case processing in Federal district courts, and dispositions, by offense, district, and offender characteristics, 1989, annual data compilation, 6064–29
Court criminal case processing in Federal district courts, and dispositions, by offense, 1980-91, annual rpt, 6064–31
Crime and criminal justice data collection, methodology, and use, technical rpt series, 6066–23
Crime, criminal justice admin and enforcement, and public opinion, data compilation, 1992 annual rpt, 6064–6
Crime victimization, by offense and whether reported to police, 1990-91, press release, 6068–249
Crime victimization rates, by victim and offender characteristics, circumstances, and offense, survey rpt series, 6066–3
Criminal justice issues, series, 6066–19; 6066–25
Drug abuse and trafficking relationship to other crime, and enforcement data, series, 6066–29
Drug enforcement, offenses, and public opinion, summaries of BJS rpts, 1975-90, annual pamphlet, 6064–30
Felony case processing from arrest to sentencing, cases and duration by disposition and offense, for selected cities, 1988, annual rpt, 6064–27
Police employment, spending, and operations, for State, city, county, and special district agencies, 1990, annual rpt, 6064–39
Prison and community-based facilities, population, employment, spending, and other characteristics, by State and for Fed Govt, 1990, quinquennial rpt, 6068–218
Prison and parole admissions and releases, sentence length, and time served, by offense and offender characteristics, 1988, annual rpt, 6064–33
Prisoners, characteristics, and movements, by State, 1990, annual rpt, 6064–26
Prisoners in Federal and State instns by selected characteristics, releases, staff, and instn size, with data by region and State, late 1970s-91, 6068–248
States criminal justice systems activities, employment, funding, and data collection, by State, 1970s-91, annual rpt, 6064–40
Bureau of Labor Statistics
Auto quality changes since last model year, factory and retail value, 1993 model year, annual press release, 6764–3
Budget of US, obligations and authority by function, agency, and program, with summaries and analyses, FY93, annual rpt, 104–2
Collective bargaining agreements expiring during year, and workers covered, by firm, union, industry group, and State, 1992, annual rpt, 6784–9
Collective bargaining wage and benefit changes, quarterly press release, 6782–2
Consumer Expenditure Survey, spending by category, selected household characteristics, and region, quarterly rpt, 6762–14
CPI by component for US city average, and by region, population size, and for 15 metro areas, monthly rpt, 6762–1
CPI by component for US city average, and by selected metro area, region, and population size, monthly rpt, 6762–2
Dallas-Fort Worth metro area employment, earnings, hours, and CPI changes, late 1970s-91, annual rpt, 6964–2
Data collection, analysis, and presentation methods, by program, 1992 rpt, 6888–1
Data on labor turnover, job openings, and new hires and wages, pilot survey results, costs, and methodology, 1990-91, 6728–40
Department store inventory price indexes, by class of item, monthly table, 6762–7
Economic conditions and employment, alternative BLS projections to 2005 and trends 1975-90, biennial rpt, 6744–19
Economic indicators, prices, labor costs, and productivity, BLS econometric analyses and methodology, working paper series, 6886–6
Employer Cost Index by region, quarterly press release, 6942–8
Employment and Earnings, detailed data, monthly rpt, 6742–2
Employment Cost Index and alternative measure of compensation costs, by component, occupation, industry group, union status, and location, 1975-92, annual rpt, 6744–20
Employment Cost Index and percent change by occupational group, industry div, region, and metro-nonmetro area, quarterly press release, 6782–5
Employment, earnings, and hours, by selected SIC 1- to 4-digit industry, State, and for 275 MSAs, 1987-92, 6748–81
Employment, earnings, and hours, by SIC 1- to 4-digit industry, monthly 1989-Feb 1992, annual rpt, 6744–4
Employment, earnings, and hours, monthly press release, 6742–5
Employment, unemployment, and labor force characteristics, by region, State, and selected metro area, 1991, annual rpt, 6744–7
Export and import price indexes, by selected end-use category, monthly press release, 6762–15
Export and import price indexes for goods and services, and dollar exchange rate indexes, quarterly press release, 6762–13
Family members labor force status and earnings, by family composition and race, quarterly press release, 6742–21
Fed Govt labor productivity, indexes of output and labor costs by function, FY67-90, annual rpt, 6824–4
Foreign and US manufacturing hourly compensation costs, by industry and country, series, 6826–3
Foreign and US manufacturing labor costs and indexes, by selected country, 1991, semiannual rpt, 6822–3
Houston metro area employment, earnings, hours, and CPI changes, 1970s-91, annual rpt, 6964–1

Injury and illness rates by SIC 2- to 4-digit industry, and deaths by cause and industry div, 1990, annual rpt, 6844–1
Injury and illness rates, by SIC 2- to 4-digit industry, 1989-90, annual rpt, 6844–7
Labor force characteristics, press release series, 6726–1
Labor force status effects on families, series, 6726–2
Labor hourly costs, by component, occupational group, industry div, union coverage, and region, 1992, annual rpt, 6744–21
Minority group labor force status, by race, detailed Hispanic origin, and sex, quarterly rpt, 6742–18
Monthly Labor Review, current statistics and articles, 6722–1
Occupation training completions, and labor demand and turnover, by detailed occupation, 1990 and projected to 2005, biennial rpt, 6744–3
Occupational injuries, illnesses, and lost workdays, by SIC 2-digit industry, 1990-91, annual press release, 6844–3
Occupational injury and illness rates and lost workdays, for selected industries, 1978-89, compilation of papers, 6728–41
Occupational injury and illness rates by circumstances and establishment size, and methodology for computing rates, industry rpt series, 6886–4
Occupational Outlook Handbook, 1992-93, biennial rpt, 6744–1
Occupational Outlook Quarterly, journal, 6742–1
Occupational separations, replacement rates, and related job openings, estimation procedures with data by occupation, age, and sex, late 1980s and projected to 2005, 6748–84
Producer Price Index, by major commodity group and subgroup, and processing stage, monthly press release, 6762–5
Producer Price Index use in sales contract escalation clauses, methodology, 1991 rpt, 6888–23
Producer price indexes, by stage of processing and detailed commodity, monthly rpt, 6762–6
Producer price indexes, by stage of processing and detailed commodity, monthly 1991, annual rpt, 6764–2
Productivity and costs of labor for private, nonfarm business, and manufacturing sectors, revised data, quarterly rpt, 6822–2
Productivity and costs of labor, indexes, preliminary data, quarterly rpt, 6822–1
Productivity of labor, indexes of output, hours, and employment by SIC 2- to 4-digit industry, 1967-90, annual rpt, 6824–1
Southeastern US employment by industry div, earnings, and hours, for 8 States, quarterly press release, 6942–7
Southeastern US employment conditions, with comparisons to other regions, press release series, 6946–3
Southeastern US textile mill employment, earnings, and hours, for 8 States, quarterly press release, 6942–1
Southern US textile mill employment, 1951-91, annual rpt, 6944–1
Southwestern US employment by industry div, earnings, and hours, by State, with CPI by major component for 2 Texas MSAs, monthly rpt, 6962–2
State and local govt collective bargaining, wage and benefit changes and coverage, 1st half 1992, semiannual press release, 6782–6
State and local govt employees benefit plan coverage and provisions, by plan type, 1990, biennial rpt, 6784–21
State and local govt employees wages by occupation, and benefits, periodic MSA survey rpt series, 6785–15
State and local govt employment and payroll, monthly rpt, 6742–4
Statistical programs of Fed Govt, funding by agency, and BLS programs improvement spending, 1991 hearing, 23848–227
Technological devs effect on labor force, composition, and productivity, 1970s-90 and projected to 2005, industry rpt series, 6826–2
Training for job qualification and skill improvement, workers participating by training source, occupation, age, sex, and race, 1991, 6728–32
Unemployed displaced workers, layoffs and unemployment insurance claims by reason, industry, selected characteristics, and State, quarterly press release, 6742–23
Unemployed displaced workers, layoffs and unemployment insurance claims by reason, industry, selected characteristics, MSA, and State, 1990, annual rpt, 6744–18
Unemployment, by State and metro area, monthly press release, 6742–12
Unemployment, employment, and labor force, by State, MSA, and city, monthly rpt, 6742–22
Wage and benefit changes from collective bargaining and mgmt decisions, by industry div, monthly rpt, 6782–1
Wages by occupation, and benefits for office and plant workers, periodic MSA survey rpt series, 6785–3; 6785–12; 6785–16; 6785–17
Wages by occupation, for office and plant workers in selected MSAs, 1991 surveys, annual rpt, 6785–5
Wages by occupation, for office and plant workers in selected MSAs, 1991 surveys, annual summary rpts, 6785–6
Wages, hourly and weekly averages by industry div, monthly press release, 6742–3
Wages, hours, and employment by occupation, and benefits, for selected locations, industry survey rpt series, 6787–6
Wages of full- and part-time workers, by selected characteristics, quarterly press release, 6742–20
Wages of workers covered by unemployment insurance, by industry div, State, and MSA, 1990-91, annual press releases, 6784–17
Women's labor force status and characteristics, 1960s-90, chartbook, 6748–85
Women's labor force status, by age, race, and family status, quarterly rpt, 6742–17
Work stoppages, workers involved, and days idle, 1991 and trends from 1947, annual press release, 6784–12
Youth labor force status by age, Apr and July 1992 and change from 1991, annual press release, 6744–13
Youth labor force status, by sex, race, and industry div, summer 1988-92, annual press release, 6744–14
Youth unemployment research based on natl longitudinal surveys, review of studies conducted 1977-88, 6728–42

Bureau of Land Management

Acreage, grants, use, revenues, and allocations, for public lands by State, FY91 and trends, annual rpt, 5724–1
Activities and finances of BLM, and public land acreage and use, annual State rpt series, 5724–11
Activities and finances of BLM, by State, FY90, annual rpt, 5724–13
Activities of BLM in Southwestern US, FY91, annual rpt, 5724–15
Budget of US, obligations and authority by function, agency, and program, with summaries and analyses, FY93, annual rpt, 104–2
Expenditures of Fed Govt in States, by type, program, agency, and State, FY91, annual rpt, 2464–2
Grazing of livestock on public desert areas, acreage, use, fees, and endangered species, 1988-90, GAO rpt, 26113–552
Grazing of livestock on public rangeland, allotments, permits, acreage, and stocking rates, by BLM State office, as of Sept 1991, GAO rpt, 26113–582
Idaho Snake River area birds of prey, rodent, and vegetation distribution and characteristics, research results, 1991, annual rpt, 5724–14
Livestock grazing on natl rangeland, BLM mgmt, officials views, 1980s-90, GAO rpt, 26113–567
New Mexico Caballo Resource Area public land mgmt, and grazing, environmental, and leasing activities, FY90-91, annual rpt, 5724–17
Oregon lumber production, and industry operations, by county, 1988, 1208–280
Owl (northern spotted) conservation methods in Pacific Northwest, findings and recommendations, 1990 rpt, 1208–385
Private landowners restriction of access to public lands, reasons and impacts on recreation and land mgmt activities, 1991-92 surveys, GAO rpt, 26113–571
Public lands, Fed Govt payments to local govts in lieu of property taxes, by State, FY92, annual press release, 5306–4.15

Bureau of Mines

Alaska oil, gas, and coal reserve acreage, by ownership, 1991 rpt, 5608–174
Aluminum plant ownership, capacity, energy and aluminum sources, and startup and closing dates, by US and foreign plant and location, 1990, annual listing, 5604–49
Bismuth reserves, production, and US trade, by country, and US consumption by end use, 1980s-90, 5608–175
Budget of US, obligations and authority by function, agency, and program, with summaries and analyses, FY93, annual rpt, 104–2

Byproducts of primary metals mining, production and prices by commodity, 1965-90, 5608–170
China minerals production and trade, by commodity, 1989-90, annual rpt, 5604–38
Coal miners working under unsupported mine roof, reasons, supervisor reactions, and preventive measures, 1989-90 survey, 5608–173
Diesel engines exhaust in underground mines, emissions measurement and control, 1992 conf, 5608–177
Explosives and blasting agents use, by type, industry, and State, 1991, Mineral Industry Surveys, annual rpt, 5614–22
Foreign and US minerals industries operations, trends, and projections for selected countries, series, 5606–5
Foreign and US minerals supply under alternative market conditions, reserves, and background industry data, series, 5606–4
Foreign countries mineral production, reserves, and industry role in domestic economy and world supply, world area and country rpt series, 5606–1
Lime producing firms and plants, with operating data, 1991, Mineral Industry Surveys, annual listing, 5614–31
Metals (nonferrous) production in 5 western States, and prices, for 5 metals, 1848-1990, 5608–178
Metals industries economic performance indicators and indexes, by commodity, monthly rpt, 5602–5
Mineral Industry Surveys, commodity reviews of production, trade, stocks, and use, monthly rpt series, 5612–1
Mineral Industry Surveys, commodity reviews of production, trade, stocks, and use, quarterly rpt series, 5612–2
Mineral Industry Surveys, commodity reviews of production, trade, use, and industry operations, advance annual rpt series, 5614–5
Mineral Industry Surveys, State reviews of production, 1991, preliminary annual rpt, 5614–6
Minerals production, prices, trade, and foreign and US industry devs, by commodity, bimonthly rpt, 5602–4
Minerals production, prices, trade, use, employment, tariffs, and stockpiles, by mineral, with foreign comparisons, 1987-91, annual rpt, 5604–18
Minerals Yearbook, data collection and availability, annual rpt, discontinued, 5604–48
Minerals Yearbook, Vol 1, 1989: commodity reviews of production, use, trade, prices, and mining operations, annual rpt, 5604–33
Minerals Yearbook, Vol 1, 1990: commodity reviews of production, reserves, supply, use, and trade, annual rpt series, 5604–20
Minerals Yearbook, Vol 1, 1991: commodity reviews of production, reserves, supply, use, and trade, annual rpt series, 5604–15
Minerals Yearbook, Vol 2, 1989: State reviews of production and sales by commodity, and business activity, annual rpt series, 5604–16
Minerals Yearbook, Vol 2, 1990: State reviews of production and sales by commodity, and business activity, annual rpt series, 5604–22
Minerals Yearbook, Vol 3: foreign country reviews of production, trade, and policy, by commodity, annual rpt series, suspended, 5604–17
Minerals Yearbook, Vol 3, 1989: foreign country reviews of production, trade, and policy, by commodity, annual rpt, 5604–35
Natural gas composition and helium levels, analyses of individual wells and pipelines, by selected State and county, 1986-90, 5608–132
Natural gas composition and helium levels, analyses of individual wells and pipelines, 1985-91, annual rpt, 5604–2
Peat producing firms, with operating data, 1991, Mineral Industry Surveys, annual listing, 5614–32
Phosphate rock production, prices, sales, trade, and use, 1992, Mineral Industry Surveys, annual rpt, 5614–20
Potash production, prices, trade, use, and sales, 1991-92 crop years, Mineral Industry Surveys, annual rpt, 5614–19
Public lands minerals resources and availability, State rpt series, 5606–7
Publications and patents of Mines Bur, monthly listing, 5602–2
Rope (wire) used for mine hoists, characteristics by type, 1991 rpt, 5608–172
Salt production capacity, by firm and facility, 1991, annual listing, 5614–30
Soviet Union minerals production and exports, by commodity and Republic, 1975-90, annual rpt, 5604–39
Wetlands acid neutralizing capability for mining runoff, with pollutant levels and site characteristics, for Pennsylvania, 1987-90, 5608–171
Zinc production and processing losses by State, trade, use, and prices, 1850s-1990, 5608–176

Bureau of Prisons
Activities of Bur, and inmate and staff characteristics, 1991, annual rpt, 6244–2
Budget of US, obligations and authority by function, agency, and program, with summaries and analyses, FY93, annual rpt, 104–2
Costs of construction and operation, capacity, and inmates, for Federal and State prisons, 1985-89, GAO rpt, 26119–407
Crime, criminal justice admin and enforcement, and public opinion, data compilation, 1992 annual rpt, 6064–6
Debt delinquent on Federal accounts, cases and collections of Justice Dept and private law firms, pilot project results, FY91, annual rpt, 6004–20
Employment requirements for new and expanded Federal prisons, by occupation, FY87-95, GAO rpt, 26119–397
Facilities characteristics for Bur admin offices and correctional instns, 1992, annual listing, 6244–4
Fed Prison Industries finances and operations, FY91, annual rpt, 6244–3
Fed Prison Industries sales, by commodity and Federal agency, FY91, annual rpt, 6244–5
Prisoners and staff in Federal instns, by selected characteristics, region, and instn, FY89, annual rpt, 6244–1
Prisoners in Federal instns, admissions, releases, and recidivism, by region, monthly rpt series, 6242–1

Bureau of Reclamation
Budget of US, obligations and authority by function, agency, and program, with summaries and analyses, FY93, annual rpt, 104–2
Colorado River Basin Federal reservoir and power operations and revenues, 1991-92, annual rpt, 5824–6
Colorado River Storage Project finances and activities in western States, FY91, annual rpt, 5824–3
Columbia River Power System projects, plant investment allocation schedule, FY91, annual rpt, 3224–1
Drought aid of Reclamation Bur, by western State, 1992 press release, 5306–4.17
Hydroelectric power plants capacity and other characteristics, for western US, FY91, annual rpt, 3254–1
Hydroelectric power plants, generation, and capacity, for Reclamation Bur projects, 1978-90 and projected to 1995, 5828–14
Irrigation projects of Reclamation Bur in western US, crop production and acreage by commodity, State, and project, 1990, annual rpt, 5824–12
Water storage and carriage facilities of Bur, capacity, and operating status, as of Sept 1990, biennial listing, 5824–7

Bureau of Security and Consular Affairs
see Bureau of Consular Affairs, State Department

Bureau of the Mint
see U.S. Mint

Bureau of the Public Debt
Budget of US, obligations and authority by function, agency, and program, with summaries and analyses, FY93, annual rpt, 104–2
Public debt issued, redeemed, and outstanding, by series and source, and gifts to reduce debt, monthly rpt, 8242–2
Savings bonds issued, redeemed, and outstanding, by series, monthly table, 8242–1

Bureaucracy
see Civil service system
see Government efficiency
see Government employees
see International employees
see Political science
see Public administration

Burgdorf, Kenneth
"Assessment of the National Science Foundation's 1985-87 College Science Instrumentation Program", 9628–87
"Scientific and Engineering Research Facilities at Universities and Colleges: 1992", 9624–25

Burglary
see Motor vehicle theft
see Robbery and theft
see Security devices

Burial and burial laws
see Cemeteries and funerals
see Military cemeteries and funerals

Burke, Thomas P.
"Alternatives to Hospital Care Under Employee Benefit Plans", 6722–1.302
Burkina Faso
Agricultural trade of US, by detailed commodity and country, 1991, annual rpt, 1524–8
Agricultural trade of US, by detailed commodity and country, 1991, semiannual rpt, 1522–4
AID economic aid to developing countries, obligations and disbursements by country, quarterly rpt, 9912–4
Economic and military aid and loans from US and intl agencies, by program and country, FY46-91, annual rpt, 9914–5
Economic and social conditions of developing countries from 1960s, and Intl Dev Cooperation Agency and AID activities and funding, FY91-93, annual rpt, 9904–4
Economic conditions, income, production, prices, employment, and trade, 1991 periodic country rpt, 2046–4.2
Economic conditions, income, production, prices, employment, and trade, 1992 periodic country rpt, 2046–4.56
Economic, social, political, and geographic summary data, by country, 1992, annual factbook, 9114–2
Exports and imports of US, by transport mode, country, and SITC 1- to 3-digit commodity, 1991, annual rpt, 2424–12
Exports of US, detailed Schedule B commodities with countries of destination, 1991, annual rpt, 2424–10
Human rights conditions in 170 countries, and US economic and military aid, 1991, annual rpt, 21384–3
Military spending, arms trade, and force strengths, with govt spending and population, by country, 1979-89, annual rpt, 9824–1
Minerals Yearbook, Vol 3, 1989: foreign country review of production, trade, and policy, by commodity, annual rpt, 5604–35.1
Population size, growth rates, and components of change, by country, projected 1990-2020 and trends from 1950, biennial rpt, 2324–9
Refugee migration, and intl aid programs, by world area and country of origin and asylum, 1991, annual rpt, 7004–15
UN voting record and share of votes in agreement with US, by issue, country, and world area, 1991, annual rpt, 7004–18
Burma
Agricultural trade of US, by detailed commodity and country, 1991, annual rpt, 1524–8
Agricultural trade of US, by detailed commodity and country, 1991, semiannual rpt, 1522–4
AID economic aid to developing countries, obligations and disbursements by country, quarterly rpt, 9912–4
AID loans repayment status and terms by program and country, and status of predecessor agency loans, quarterly rpt, 9912–3
Economic and military aid and loans from US and intl agencies, by program and country, FY46-91, annual rpt, 9914–5
Economic conditions, income, production, prices, employment, and trade, 1992 periodic country rpt, 2046–4.12
Economic, social, political, and geographic summary data, by country, 1992, annual factbook, 9114–2
Exports and imports of US, by transport mode, country, and SITC 1- to 3-digit commodity, 1991, annual rpt, 2424–12
Exports of US, detailed Schedule B commodities with countries of destination, 1991, annual rpt, 2424–10
Human rights conditions in 170 countries, and US economic and military aid, 1991, annual rpt, 21384–3
Military spending, arms trade, and force strengths, with govt spending and population, by country, 1979-89, annual rpt, 9824–1
Minerals Yearbook, Vol 3, 1989: foreign country review of production, trade, and policy, by commodity, annual rpt, 5604–35.2
Population size, growth rates, and components of change, by country, projected 1990-2020 and trends from 1950, biennial rpt, 2324–9
Refugee migration, and intl aid programs, by world area and country of origin and asylum, 1991, annual rpt, 7004–15
see also Myanmar
Burn injuries
see Fires and fire prevention
Burros, wild
see Wildlife and wildlife conservation
Burrows, C. W.
"Occupational Radiation Exposure from U.S. Naval Nuclear Propulsion Plants and Their Support Facilities, 1991", 3804–10
Burundi
Agricultural trade of US, by detailed commodity and country, 1991, annual rpt, 1524–8
Agricultural trade of US, by detailed commodity and country, 1991, semiannual rpt, 1522–4
AID economic aid to developing countries, obligations and disbursements by country, quarterly rpt, 9912–4
Economic and military aid and loans from US and intl agencies, by program and country, FY46-91, annual rpt, 9914–5
Economic and social conditions of developing countries from 1960s, and Intl Dev Cooperation Agency and AID activities and funding, FY91-93, annual rpt, 9904–4
Economic, social, political, and geographic summary data, by country, 1992, annual factbook, 9114–2
Exports and imports of US, by transport mode, country, and SITC 1- to 3-digit commodity, 1991, annual rpt, 2424–12
Human rights conditions in 170 countries, and US economic and military aid, 1991, annual rpt, 21384–3
Military aid of US, arms sales, and training programs costs and budget requests, by program, world region, and country, FY91-93, annual rpt, 7144–13
Military spending, arms trade, and force strengths, with govt spending and population, by country, 1979-89, annual rpt, 9824–1
Minerals Yearbook, Vol 3, 1989: foreign country review of production, trade, and policy, by commodity, annual rpt, 5604–35.1
Population size, growth rates, and components of change, by country, projected 1990-2020 and trends from 1950, biennial rpt, 2324–9
Refugee migration, and intl aid programs, by world area and country of origin and asylum, 1991, annual rpt, 7004–15
UN voting record and share of votes in agreement with US, by issue, country, and world area, 1991, annual rpt, 7004–18
Burwell, Michael
"Shipwrecks of the Alaskan Shelf and Shore", 5738–34
Bus Regulatory Reform Act
Deregulation of intercity bus service in 1982, impacts on service, ridership, and State and Federal funding, with background data, 1980s-92, GAO rpt, 26113–583
Buses
Accidents (fatal), circumstances, and characteristics of persons and vehicles involved, 1991, semiannual rpt, 7762–11
Accidents (fatal), deaths, and rates, by circumstances, characteristics of persons and vehicles involved, and location, 1990, annual rpt, 7764–10
Accidents and casualties on transit systems by circumstances, damage, and ridership, by mode, 1990, annual rpt, 7884–13
Accidents at hwy-railroad grade-crossings, detailed data by State and railroad, 1991, annual rpt, 7604–2
Accidents, casualties, circumstances, and characteristics of persons and vehicles involved, 1990, annual rpt, 7764–18
Commuting to work, by mode, trip duration, and work location, 1980 and 1990, 7558–120
Consumer spending, natl income and product account benchmark revisions, 1929-88, 2708–5
Consumer spending, natl income and product accounts, comprehensive accounts and components, *Survey of Current Business*, monthly rpt, 2702–1.25
County Business Patterns, 1989: employment, establishments, and payroll, by SIC 2- to 4-digit industry and county, annual State rpt series, 2326–8
County Business Patterns, 1990: employment, establishments, and payroll, by SIC 2- to 4-digit industry and county, annual State rpt series, 2326–6
Deregulation of intercity bus service in 1982, impacts on service, ridership, and State and Federal funding, with background data, 1980s-92, GAO rpt, 26113–583
DOT activities by subagency, budget, and summary accident data, FY89, annual rpt, 7304–1
Drivers licenses issued and in force by age and sex, fees, and renewal, by license class and State, 1990, annual rpt, 7554–16
Employment, earnings, and hours, by SIC 1- to 4-digit industry, monthly 1989-Feb 1992, annual rpt, 6744–4
Energy use and vehicle registrations, by vehicle type, 1960-91, annual rpt, 3164–74.1

Energy use by fuel type, and miles traveled, by transport mode, projected 1990-2010 and trends from 1960s, 3008–124
Energy use by mode of transport, fuel supply, and demographic and economic factors of vehicle use, 1970s-90, annual rpt, 3304–5
Exhaust emissions reductions programs, funding, and alternative fuel bus dev, periodic rpt, 7882–3
Exports and imports of US, by country and detailed commodity, monthly rpt, 2422–12
Exports and imports of US, by Harmonized System 6-digit commodity and country, 1991, annual rpt, 2424–13
Finances and employment of ICC-regulated carriers, as of FY91, annual rpt, 9484–1
Finances and operations of interstate carriers, by carrier, 1990, annual rpt, 9486–5.3
Finances and operations of transit systems, by mode, size of fleet and urban area, region, and for 518 systems, 1990, annual rpt, 7884–4
Finances, equipment, and ridership characteristics of transit systems, 1985-90, biennial rpt, 7884–8
Hwy Statistics, detailed data by State, 1991, annual rpt, 7554–1
Hwy Statistics, summary data by State, 1990-91, annual rpt, 7554–24
Labor productivity, indexes of output, hours, and employment by SIC 2- to 4-digit industry, 1967-90, annual rpt, 6824–1.4
Manufacturing annual survey, 1990: finances and operations, by SIC 2- to 4-digit industry, series, 2506–14
Military and personal property shipments, passenger traffic, and costs, by service branch and mode of transport, FY91, annual rpt, 3704–15
Natl park system visits and overnight stays, by park and State, monthly rpt, 5542–4
Occupational injury and illness rates, by SIC 2- to 4-digit industry, 1990, annual rpt, 6844–1
Occupational Outlook Handbook, 1992-93, biennial rpt, 6744–1
Pacific territories population and housing detailed characteristics, by location, 1990 Census of Population and Housing, series, 2551–8
Police employment, spending, and operations, for State, city, county, and special district agencies, 1990, annual rpt, 6064–39
Price indexes (producer), by stage of processing and detailed commodity, monthly rpt, 6762–6
Price indexes (producer), by stage of processing and detailed commodity, monthly 1991, annual rpt, 6764–2
Recalls of motor vehicles and equipment with safety-related defects, by make, monthly listing, 7762–12
Ridership and selected revenue data, for individual large Class I bus carriers, quarterly rpt, 9482–13
Statistical Abstract of US, 1992 annual data compilation, 2324–1.21
Travel patterns, personal and household characteristics, and auto and public transport use, 1990 survey, series, 7556–6
Travel to US, by characteristics of visit and traveler, world area of origin, and US destination, 1991 survey, annual rpt, 2904–12
Urban areas transit systems grants of Federal Transit Admin, by city and State, FY91, annual rpt, 7884–10
see also School busing

Business acquisitions and mergers

Airline finances and operations, summary data, quarterly rpt, 7502–16
Banking system reform impacts on consumers, with background data, 1991 hearing, 21248–167
Banks (insured commercial and savings) finances, and changes in status, by State, 1990, annual rpt, 9294–4.1
Banks (natl) charters, mergers, liquidations, enforcement cases, and financial performance, with data by instn and State, quarterly rpt, 8402–3
Banks acquisitions of failed and other banks, financial performance relation to asset mix, market concentration, and other factors, 1984-90, article, 9292–4.304
Banks acquisitions purchase price relation to target and acquiring banks financial ratios variability and asset size, 1980s, working paper, 9371–10.80
Banks economies of scale, impacts of potential mergers among large banks, model description and results, 1980s, working paper, 9387–8.256
Banks finances, examination ratings, and failure resolution costs and methods, 1980s-91, article, 9292–4.301
Banks in Texas, loan losses relation to loan volume growth and other factors, mid 1970s-90, article, 9379–1.305
Banks mergers antitrust issues, with background financial data by State and selected instn, 1991 hearing, 21248–176
Banks mergers approved, and assets and offices involved, by instn, 1990, annual rpt, 9294–5
Banks mergers impacts on noninterest expense ratios, with background data for total and southeastern US, 1980s-90, article, 9371–1.303
Banks mergers impacts on operating costs, 1982-86, working paper, 9371–10.78
Credit unions federally insured, finances, mergers, closings, and insurance fund losses and financial statements, FY91, annual rpt, 9534–7
Credit unions with low income membership, financial, operating, and membership data, 1982-91, 9536–1.8
EC economic integration impacts on domestic economic conditions and US trade, with background data, 1986-91, 9886–4.181
Energy producers finances and operations, by energy type for US firms domestic and foreign operations, 1990, annual rpt, 3164–44
Energy resources of US, foreign direct investment by energy type and firm, US affiliates operations, and acquisitions, as of 1990, annual rpt, 3164–80
Fed Reserve Bd and Reserve banks finances, staff, and review of monetary policy and economic devs, 1991, annual rpt, 9364–1
Finance companies assets, operating ratios, and growth indicators, for top 20 firms, 1980s-90, article, 9385–1.309
Food marketing sector finances, operations, and merger activity, for processors and distributors, 1991, annual rpt, 1544–22
Foreign direct investment by method and industry div, and affiliated firms R&D spending, pay, employment, and trade compared to US-owned firms, 1980-90, article, 9391–1.309
Foreign direct investment in US by country, and finances, employment, and acreage owned, by industry group of business acquired or established, 1985-91, annual article, 2702–1.320
Foreign direct investment in US by top 10 countries, factors affecting rate of return, and compared to returns for US firms, 1980s-91, article, 2702–1.330
Foreign direct investment in US, major transactions by type, industry, country, and US location, 1990, annual rpt, 2044–20
Foreign direct investment in US, relation to exchange rate and relative labor costs and wealth indicators, for 7 countries, 1980s, working paper, 9373–27.10
Minority business Federal procurement set-aside contracts, status of participants as of 1990, annual rpt, 9764–8
Oil refinery capacity, openings, closings, and acquisitions by plant, and fuel used by PAD district, 1991, annual rpt, 3164–2.1
Rail line abandonment, construction, and acquisition certificate applications, by disposition, FY89-91, annual rpt, 9484–1.1
Savings instns failure resolution activity and finances of Resolution Trust Corp, with data by asset type, State, region, and instn, monthly rpt, 9722–3
Savings instns failure resolution activity of Resolution Trust Corp, assets, deposits, and assets availability and sales, periodic press release, 9722–1
Savings instns failure resolution activity of Resolution Trust Corp, with data by State and instn, and RTC finances, 1990, annual rpt, 9724–1
Savings instns, FHLB 11th District shareholder instns, offices, and financial condition, 1992 annual listing, 9304–23
Statistical Abstract of US, 1992 annual data compilation, 2324–1.17
Stock returns of rival firms, impact of merger announcements and antitrust challenges, 1980s, 9408–55
Tax deductions for amortization of intangible assets from acquired businesses, IRS unresolved audits, and claims allowed, 1991 GAO rpt, 26119–365
Unemployed displaced workers, layoffs and recalls by layoff reason, industry, firm size, and State, 2nd half 1988, 6406–6.36
Unemployed displaced workers, layoffs and unemployment insurance claims by reason, industry, selected characteristics, and State, quarterly press release, 6742–23
Unemployed displaced workers, layoffs and unemployment insurance claims by reason, industry, selected characteristics, MSA, and State, 1990, annual rpt, 6744–18

Business and industry
Business America, foreign and domestic commerce, and US investment and trade opportunities, biweekly journal, 2042–24
Census of Population and Housing, 1990: industry and occupation classification codes, alphabetical index, 2628–1
Census of Population and Housing, 1990: industry and occupation classification codes, classified index, 2628–2
Foreign countries economic and social conditions, working paper series, 2326–18
R&D funding by higher education instns and federally funded centers, by field, instn, and State, FY90, annual rpt, 9627–13
Rural areas economic conditions and dev, quarterly journal, 1502–8
Science and Engineering Indicators, employment, education, R&D funding, and industry impacts, with foreign comparisons, 1960s-91, biennial rpt, 9624–10
Survey of Current Business, detailed data for major industries and economic indicators, monthly rpt, 2702–1
Survey of Current Business, detailed data for major industries and economic indicators, 1960-91, biennial supplement, 2704–1
see also Agriculture
see also Area wage surveys
see also Automation
see also Banks and banking
see also Business acquisitions and mergers
see also Business assets and liabilities, general
see also Business assets and liabilities, specific industry
see also Business cycles
see also Business education
see also Business ethics
see also Business failures and closings
see also Business firms and establishments, number
see also Business formations
see also Business income and expenses, general
see also Business income and expenses, specific industry
see also Business inventories
see also Business management
see also Business orders
see also Business outlook and attitude surveys
see also Capital investments, general
see also Capital investments, specific industry
see also Commercial buildings
see also Commercial credit
see also Commercial law
see also Communications industries
see also Competition
see also Construction industry
see also Consultants
see also Corporations
see also Credit
see also Defense industries
see also Depreciation
see also Divestiture
see also Earnings, general
see also Earnings, local and regional
see also Earnings, specific industry
see also Economic concentration and diversification
see also Electric power plants and equipment
see also Employee benefits
see also Employee ownership
see also Employee performance and appraisal
see also Employment and unemployment, general
see also Employment and unemployment, local and regional
see also Employment and unemployment, specific industry
see also Executives and managers
see also Export processing zones
see also Financial institutions
see also Fish and fishing industry
see also Foreign corporations
see also Forests and forestry
see also Franchises
see also Government and business
see also Home-based offices and workers
see also Hours of labor
see also Industrial and commercial energy use
see also Industrial arts
see also Industrial capacity and utilization
see also Industrial plants and equipment
see also Industrial production
see also Industrial production indexes
see also Industrial purchasing
see also Industrial robots
see also Industrial siting
see also Industrial standards
see also Industry wage surveys
see also Input-output analysis
see also Insurance and insurance industry
see also Labor law
see also Labor-management relations, general
see also Labor mobility
see also Labor productivity
see also Labor supply and demand
see also Labor turnover
see also Labor unions
see also Manufacturing
see also Marketing
see also Mines and mineral resources
see also Minority businesses
see also Multinational corporations
see also Occupational health and safety
see also Occupations
see also Ownership of enterprise
see also Partnerships
see also Payroll
see also Personnel management
see also Printing and publishing industry
see also Production costs
see also Productivity
see also Proprietorships
see also Public administration
see also Public utilities
see also Real estate business
see also Repair industries
see also Retail trade
see also Service industries
see also Small business
see also Standard Industrial Classification
see also Trade adjustment assistance
see also Trademarks
see also Transportation and transportation equipment
see also Value added tax
see also Wholesale trade
see also Women-owned businesses
see also under By Individual Company or Institution in the "Index by Categories"
see also under By Industry in the "Index by Categories"
see also under names of specific industries or industry groups

Business assets and liabilities, general
Acquired businesses intangible assets, tax deductions for amortization, IRS unresolved audits, and claims allowed, 1991 GAO rpt, 26119–365
Assets and debts of private sector, balance sheets by segment, 1960-91, semiannual rpt, 9365–4.1
Boycotts (intl) by OPEC and other countries, US firms and individuals cooperation and tax benefits denied, 1990, article, 8302–2.323
Corporations financial statements for manufacturing, mining, and trade, by selected SIC 2- to 3-digit industry, quarterly rpt, 2502–1
Corporations income tax returns, income and tax items by asset size and detailed industry, 1989, annual rpt, 8304–4; 8304–21
Corporations income tax returns, summary data by asset size and industry div, 1989, annual article, 8302–2.321
Debt outstanding, by sector and type of debt and holder, monthly rpt, 9362–1.1
Debt outstanding by type of holder, and total and per capita Federal debt, 1929-89, hearing, 25368–177
Domestic Intl Sales Corps (Interest Charge) income tax returns, assets, and income and tax items, by detailed industry, 1987, article, 8302–2.312
Economic indicators and components, current data and annual trends, monthly rpt, 23842–1.5
Families financial status, income, net worth, and assets and debt by type, by income and selected characteristics, 1983 and 1989, article, 9362–1.301
Flow-of-funds accounts, assets and liabilities by type and economic sector, annual rpt, suspended, 9364–3
Flow-of-funds accounts, savings, investments, and credit statements, quarterly rpt, 9365–3.3
Foreign-controlled US firms transactions with related foreign persons, by type, industry div, and country, 1988, article, 8302–2.318
Foreign corporations and individuals, and US entities abroad, detailed data compilation for income tax returns, 1970s-89, quinquennial rpt, 8308–31
Foreign countries tax credits on corporate income tax returns, with income and tax items by industry group, 1988, biennial article, 8302–2.316
Foreign Sales Corps income tax returns, assets, and income and tax items, by industry, country of incorporation, and transaction pricing method, 1987, article, 8302–2.311
Households net worth distribution under alternative sample weighting systems to account for inconsistency in survey design and response rates, 1992 rpt, 9368–91
Imports and tariff provisions effect on US industries and products, investigations with background financial and operating data, series, 9886–4

Manufacturing annual survey, 1990: finances and operations, by SIC 2- and 3-digit industry and State, 2506–14.3
Militarily strategic manufacturing industries finances, operations, and intl competitiveness, series, 2026–1
Minority- and woman-owned businesses and owner characteristics, by industry, employment and sales size, and form of ownership, 1987 survey, 2328–59
Multinatl firms US affiliates finances and operations, by industry div, country of parent firm, and State, 1989-90, annual article, 2702–1.319; 2702–1.337
Multinatl firms US affiliates, finances, and operations, by industry, world area of parent firm, and State, 1989-90, annual rpt, 2704–4
Multinatl firms US affiliates income tax compliance issues, with income and tax data by industry group, 1987-89, press release, 8008–155
Multinatl US firms and foreign affiliates finances and operations, by industry and country, 1989 benchmark survey, annual rpt, 2704–5
Multinatl US firms and foreign affiliates finances and operations, by industry and world area, 1988, annual article, 2702–1.329
Multinatl US firms foreign affiliates, income statement items by asset size, industry, and country, 1988, biennial article, 8302–2.322
Partnership income tax returns, income statement and balance sheet items by industry group, 1990, annual article, 8302–2.314
Puerto Rico and other US possessions corporations income tax returns, income and tax items, and employment, by selected industry, 1989, article, 8302–2.326
Small business capital formation sources and issues, 1991 annual conf, 9734–4
Small business finances, operations, owner characteristics, and Federal contracts, 1980s-90, annual rpt, 9764–6
Small business loan collateral adequacy for failed firms, with loan liquidation recoveries and losses, FY89, GAO rpt, 26113–553
Statistical Abstract of US, 1992 annual data compilation, 2324–1.16; 2324–1.17
Survey of Current Business, detailed data for major industries and economic indicators, 1960-91, biennial supplement, 2704–1
Tax (estate) returns property and tax data, by size of gross estate and State, 1989-90, article, 8302–2.305
Tax (income) returns filed, by type of filer, selected income items, quarterly rpt, 8302–2.1
Tax exempt organizations finances, with data by type, size, State, and for largest organizations, late 1940s-80s, compilation of papers, 8308–35
see also Agricultural finance
see also Bankruptcy
see also Business assets and liabilities, specific industry
see also Business income and expenses, general
see also Business inventories
see also Capital investments, general
see also Depreciation
see also Divestiture
see also Foreign investments
see also Government assets and liabilities
see also Industrial plants and equipment
see also Investments
see also Mortgages
see also Operating ratios

Business assets and liabilities, specific industry
Agricultural cooperatives finances, aggregate for top 100 assns by commodity group, 1990, annual rpt, 1124–3
Agricultural cooperatives, finances, and membership, by type of service, commodity, and State, 1990, annual rpt, 1124–1
Agricultural cooperatives finances, operations, activities, and current issues, monthly journal, 1122–1
Agricultural cooperatives, finances, operations, activities, and membership, commodity rpt series, 1126–1
Airline finances, by carrier, carrier group, and for total certificated system, quarterly rpt, 7302–7
American Historical Assn financial statements, and membership by State, 1990, annual rpt, 29574–2
Bank deposits interest rates deregulation impacts on bank asset risk, alternative model descriptions and results, 1970s-80s, working paper, 9379–14.15
Bank holding companies capital requirements impacts on asset growth, 1989-91, working paper, 9375–13.88
Bank holding companies stock prices relation to capital and assets, 1990-92, article, 9385–1.311
Bank of Credit and Commerce Intl financial statements, audits, and selected loan data, 1984-90, hearing, 25388–60
Banking and economic conditions, for Fed Reserve 8th District, quarterly rpt with articles, 9391–16
Banking and financial conditions, 1990, annual rpt, 9364–5
Banking system reform impacts on consumers, with background data, 1991 hearing, 21248–167
Banking system reform issues, with top instn finances, fiscal impacts, and views of depositors, bankers, and regulators on deposit insurance, 1991 hearings, 21248–168
Banks (insured commercial) and offices, and summary assets and liabilities, 1990-91, annual rpt, 9364–1.2
Banks (insured commercial) domestic and foreign office consolidated financial statements, monthly rpt, quarterly data, 9362–1.4
Banks (insured commercial), Fed Reserve 5th District members financial statements, by State, quarterly rpt, 9389–18
Banks (insured commercial and FDIC-insured savings) assets, income, and financial ratios, by asset size and State, quarterly rpt, 13002–3
Banks (insured commercial and savings) finances, by State, 1990, annual rpt, 9294–4
Banks (insured commercial and savings) financial condition and performance, by asset size and region, quarterly rpt, 9292–1
Banks (natl) charters, mergers, liquidations, enforcement cases, and financial performance, with data by instn and State, quarterly rpt, 8402–3
Banks (US) foreign branches assets and liabilities, by world region and country, quarterly rpt, 9365–3.7
Banks (US) foreign branches, balance sheets, monthly rpt, 9362–1.3
Banks acquisitions of failed and other banks, financial performance relation to asset mix, market concentration, and other factors, 1984-90, article, 9292–4.304
Banks and thrifts finances and operations by deposit size, Fed Reserve functional cost analysis, 1991, annual rpt, 9364–6
Banks and thrifts finances by instn type, and Fed Financial Instns Exam Council financial statements, 1991, annual rpt, 13004–2
Banks and thrifts in Fed Reserve 1st District, selected assets, monthly rpt, 9373–2
Banks and thrifts in New England, assets and liabilities by type, and deposits relation to capital/asset ratios, by instn type and size, 1980s-91, article, 9373–1.309
Banks and thrifts in New England, real estate lending impacts of capital losses, with financial ratios, 1980s-91, article, 9373–27.12
Banks assets composition and securitization, relation to risk and liquidity indicators, model description and results, 1980s-91, technical paper, 9366–6.295
Banks assets valuation impact of market value accounting for debt securities, by bank asset size, 1990, GAO rpt, 26111–77
Banks balance sheets, by Fed Reserve District, for major banks in NYC, and for US branches and agencies of foreign banks, weekly rpt, 9365–1.3
Banks capital availability impacts on lending, 1992 working paper, 9379–14.19
Banks checking account and commercial loan activity by bank size, and loan sales and assets for top banks, 1970s-90, working paper, 9387–8.264
Banks economies of scale and scope, impacts of asset quality indicators and other factors by asset size, model results, 1990, working paper, 9387–8.260
Banks failures and assets involved, and Bank Insurance Fund finances, alternative projections, 1991-93, hearing, 21248–166
Banks failures forecasting performance of asset risk indicators and other factors, 1980s-91, article, 9379–15.302
Banks failures resolution costs to FDIC, relation to bank financial and other characteristics, 1986-90, article, 9292–4.303
Banks failures, undercapitalization duration relation to Bank Insurance Fund losses, 1985-90, article, 9391–1.312
Banks finances, examination ratings, and failure resolution costs and methods, 1980s-91, article, 9292–4.301
Banks in Fed Reserve 3rd District, assets, income, and rates of return, by major instn, quarterly rpt, annual table, 9387–10

Banks in Fed Reserve 8th District, financial performance indicators by asset size, 1988-91, annual article, 9391–16.307
Banks in Fed Reserve 9th District, finances and performance ratios, by State, quarterly journal, 9383–19
Banks mergers antitrust issues, with background financial data by State and selected instn, 1991 hearing, 21248–176
Banks mergers approved, and assets and offices involved, by instn, 1990, annual rpt, 9294–5
Banks mergers impacts on noninterest expense ratios, with background data for total and southeastern US, 1980s-90, article, 9371–1.303
Banks needing FDIC aid, finances and operations, 1991, annual rpt, 9294–1
Banks portfolio valuation at market value, with assets and liabilities by type, ease of estimation, and bank asset size, Dec 1990, article, 9375–1.301
Banks profitability, balance sheet and income statement items, and financial ratios, by asset size, 1985-91, annual article, 9362–1.305
Banks securities new issues by type of instrument, relation to primary capital ratio and other factors, 1983-86, working paper, 9371–10.79
Banks uninsured deposits by type and bank size, and relation to bank size and selected operating ratios, 1980s-91, technical paper, 9385–8.126
Coal industry retirees pension and health trust funds financial condition, employer contributions, and beneficiaries, late 1970s-92, GAO rpt, 26121–469; 26121–471
Credit card issuers disclosure of terms and conditions to consumers, with finances and operations, 1991 hearing, 21248–175
Credit unions (federally-insured) financial performance, by charter type and region, 1st half 1992, semiannual rpt, 9532–7
Credit unions assets, members, and location, 1992 annual listing, 9534–6
Credit unions failures, assets and losses to Natl Credit Union Share Insurance Fund by asset size and charter, and for largest failures by instn, FY86-91, 9536–1.7
Credit unions federally insured, finances by instn characteristics and State, as of June 1992, semiannual rpt, 9532–6
Credit unions federally insured, finances, mergers, closings, and insurance fund losses and financial statements, FY91, annual rpt, 9534–7
Credit unions federally insured, finances, 1990-91, annual rpt, 9534–1
Credit unions finances, operations, and regulation, series, 9536–1
Credit unions financial performance and regulation, with background data, 1960s-90, GAO rpt, 26119–364
Credit unions with low income membership, financial, operating, and membership data, 1982-91, 9536–1.8
Drug industry operating in Puerto Rico under tax-favored status, tax and income items, 1985-86, hearing, 21448–46
Electric power distribution loans from REA, and borrower operating and financial data, by firm and State, 1991, annual rpt, 1244–1
Electric power sales by customer, plants, and capacity of Southeastern Power Admin, FY91, annual rpt, 3234–1
Electric utilities finances and operations, detailed data for publicly and privately owned firms, 1990, annual rpt, 3164–11.4
Electric utilities finances and operations, detailed data for publicly owned firms, 1990, annual rpt, 3164–24
Electric utilities privately owned, finances and operations, detailed data, 1990, annual rpt, 3164–23
Energy producers finances and operations, by energy type for US firms domestic and foreign operations, 1990, annual rpt, 3164–44
Energy resources of US, foreign direct investment by energy type and firm, and US affiliates operations, as of 1990, annual rpt, 3164–80
Finance companies assets, operating ratios, and growth indicators, for top 20 firms, 1980s-90, article, 9385–1.309
Finance companies credit outstanding and leasing activities, by credit type, monthly rpt, 9365–2.7
Financial instns assets by instn type, and for top 10 finance companies by firm, 1970 and 1990, article, 9391–16.305
Financial instns holdings, for banks in and outside NYC, and for thrift instns, monthly rpt, 9362–1.1
Financial instns in Texas and Federal Reserve 11th District, financial condition and devs, periodic journal, 9379–15
Financial instns reform issues, with finances, impacts of deposit insurance changes, and views of depositors and bankers, 1991 hearings, 25248–129
Financial markets (intl) performance of foreign and US bank and securities firms, finances and competitiveness issues, 1980s, compilation of papers, 9385–10
Hospital financial performance under Medicare, 1977-89, article, 4652–1.315
Insurance (life) industry assets by type, and South Central States guaranty fund limits, 1992 article, 9391–16.310
Insurance company asset risk assessment, with financial ratios by firm type and financial status, 1990 and trends from 1900s, article, 9373–1.314; 9373–27.3
Insurance company finances, by insurance type and firm, with some intl comparisons, 1991 conf, 9373–3.35
Insurance industry finances, failures, and regulation, with data by firm and State, 1990 hearing, 25528–119
Insurance industry financial condition, operations, assets, junk bond holdings, and State regulation, with intl comparisons, 1991 hearings, 25268–79
Natural gas interstate pipeline company detailed financial and operating data, by firm, 1990, annual rpt, 3164–38
Nonprofit charitable and other tax exempt organizations finances, by category and size of assets and contributions, 1988, annual article, 8302–2.315
Nonprofit charitable organizations finances, summary data by asset size, 1989, article, 8302–2.325
Nonprofit charitable organizations finances, with data by State and for top 10 instns, 1988, article, 8302–2.302
Oil company production and imports by type, and financial data, 1975-90, annual rpt, 3164–74.1
Pension Benefit Guaranty Corp guaranteed plans, assets and liabilities of top 50 underfunded plans, 1991, annual press release, 9674–2
Pension plans terminated, liabilities, assets, and Pension Benefit Guarantee Corp recoveries and losses, with top 50 underfunded plans, mid 1970s-91, article, 9371–1.302
Railroad (Class I) finances and operations, detailed data by firm, class of service, and district, 1990, annual rpt, 9486–5.1
Railroad (Class I) finances and operations, detailed data by firm, class of service, and district, 1991, annual rpt, 9486–6.1
Railroad employment and finances, for ICC-regulated carriers, as of FY91, annual rpt, 9484–1
Savings and loan assns, FHLB 6th District insured members financial condition and operations by State, quarterly rpt, 9302–23
Savings and loan assns, FHLB 8th District members, locations, assets, and savings, 1992, annual listing, 9304–9
Savings instns assets and liabilities, by instn type, 1990, annual rpt, 9364–5.4
Savings instns conversion from mutual to stock ownership, financial performance for Fed Reserve 1st District instns, 1980s-90, article, 9373–1.307
Savings instns failure resolution activity and finances of Resolution Trust Corp, with data by asset type, State, region, and instn, monthly rpt, 9722–3
Savings instns failure resolution activity of Resolution Trust Corp, assets, deposits, and assets availability and sales, periodic press release, 9722–1
Savings instns failure resolution activity of Resolution Trust Corp, with data by State and instn, and RTC finances, 1990, annual rpt, 9724–1
Savings instns failure resolution costs, impacts of capital standards relaxation, 1979-92, working paper, 9377–9.140
Savings instns, FHLB 1st District members, financial condition, and locations, 1992, annual listing, 9304–26
Savings instns, FHLB 10th District members, locations, assets, and deposits, 1992, annual listing, 9304–17
Savings instns, FHLB 11th District shareholder instns, offices, and financial condition, 1992 annual listing, 9304–23
Savings instns financial condition and devs, working paper series, 9379–14
Savings instns financial statements, for instns insured by Savings Assn Insurance Fund by FHLB district and State, and for FDIC-insured savings banks, 1989, annual rpt, 8434–1
Savings instns insured by Savings Assn Insurance Fund, assets, liabilities, and deposit and loan activity, by conservatorship status, monthly rpt, 8432–1
Savings instns insured by Savings Assn Insurance Fund, finances by profitability group, district, and State, quarterly rpt, 8432–4

Savings instns regulatory issues, 1989 annual conf, 9304–24
Securities industry finances, for broker-dealers and individual stock exchanges and clearing agencies, 1986-90, annual rpt, 9734–2.1
Shipping firms combined financial statements, FY89-90, annual rpt, 7704–14.5
Small Business Investment Companies capital holdings, SBA obligation, and ownership, as of July 1992, semiannual listing, 9762–4
Small Business Investment Company finances, losses, and program operations, 1980s-91, 25728–44
Small Business Investment Company program financial performance, findings and recommendations, 1992 rpt, 9768–24
Stockbrokers assets and liabilities, 1990, annual rpt, 9364–5.13
Stockbrokers issuing securities credit, balance sheet, as of June 1991, annual rpt, 9365–5.1
Telephone and telegraph firms detailed finances and operations, 1990, annual rpt, 9284–6
Telephone firms borrowing under Rural Telephone Program, and financial and operating data, by State, 1991, annual rpt, 1244–2
Transit systems finances and operations, by mode, size of fleet and urban area, region, and for 518 systems, 1990, annual rpt, 7884–4
Truck, bus, and rail carriers regulated by ICC, employment and finances, as of FY91, annual rpt, 9484–1
Truck interstate carriers finances and operations, by district, 1990, annual rpt, 9486–5.2
Trust assets of banks, trust companies, and S&Ls, by type of asset and fund, selected firm, and State, 1991, annual rpt, 13004–1
Uranium mining and milling industries finances and operations, with selected foreign comparisons, 1970s-90 and projected to 2005, annual rpt, 3164–82
see also Agricultural finance
see also Business income and expenses, specific industry
see also Business inventories
see also Capital investments, specific industry
see also Depreciation
see also Educational finance
see also Government assets and liabilities
see also under By Industry in the "Index by Categories"

Business assistance
see Government and business
see Subsidies

Business cycles
Business statistics, detailed data for major industries and economic indicators, 1960-91, *Survey of Current Business* biennial supplement, 2704–1
Capital costs over business cycles relation to firm size and financial distress indicators, 1960s-91, article, 9385–1.312
Earnings relation to business cycle, 1960s-80s, article, 9377–1.304
Economic indicators and cyclical devs and outlook, by Fed Reserve Bank District, periodic rpt, 9362–8
Economic Report of the President for 1991, economic effects of budget proposals, and trends and projections, 1940s-95, annual hearings, 23844–4
Employment and unemployment during recessions, 1948-91, annual article, 6722–1.312
Employment over business cycles, relation to regional and industrial economic factors, model description and results, 1992 working paper, 9381–10.134
Employment situation, earnings, hours, and other BLS economic indicators, transcripts of BLS Commissioner's monthly testimony, periodic rpt, 23846–4
Forecasts of business cycles, performance of BEA economic indicators, 1948-91, technical paper, 9379–12.95
GDP forecasting performance of selected economic indicators over selected forecast periods and business cycles, 1960s-91, article, 9375–1.307
GNP growth over business cycles, alternative model descriptions and results, 1950s-80s, technical paper, 9385–8.139
GNP seasonal growth relation to monetary, fiscal, and demand indicators, 1991 working paper, 9375–13.74
GNP seasonal variations relation to labor hoarding and returns to scale, 1991 working paper, 9375–13.71
Great Depression monetary policy conduct of Fed Reserve, with discount rate and other policy indicators, selected qtrs 1923-31, article, 9391–1.306
Health care services employment, compared to other industries, 1960s-91, article, 6722–1.347
Industrial production during business cycle recovery, relation to depth of decline, alternative indexes, model results, 1880s-1991, technical paper, 9379–12.82
Intl business cycle impacts on economic indicators, for industrialized countries, 1950s-80s, working paper, 9383–20.16
Labor productivity over business cycle relation to hours worked, model descriptions and results, 1940s-91, article, 9383–6.302
Loans to businesses, and inventories, impacts of recessions, late 1940s-91, article, 9391–1.315
Manufacturing debt/asset ratios impact on employment changes over the business cycle, 1960s-84, technical paper, 9366–6.286
Manufacturing production over business cycles, relation to market structure and other factor inputs, for durable and nondurable goods, 1991 working paper, 9375–13.70
Metals industries economic performance indicators and indexes, by commodity, monthly rpt, 5602–5
Monetary policy impacts on money supply and interest rates, and regression results for alternative indexes, 1950s-88, working paper, 9387–8.259
New England construction, real estate, and other economic performance indicators, compared to Texas and other areas, 1970s-91, article, 9373–1.302
Productivity shocks impacts on business cycles, and relation to monetary, fiscal, and demand indicators, 1991 working paper, 9375–13.73
Recession and business cycle expansion duration indicators, 1850s-1990, working paper, 9375–13.83
Recession forecasting performance of economic indicators and experimental indexes, 1992 working paper, 9375–13.84
Recession of 1990-91, duration and depth indicators compared to previous recessions from late 1940s, article, 9373–1.301
State and local govt finances over business cycle contractions and expansions, late 1940s-91, article, 9375–1.303
Statistical Abstract of US, 1992 annual data compilation, 2324–1.17
Survey of Current Business, detailed financial and business data, and economic indicators, monthly rpt, 2702–1.1; 2702–1.2
see also Economic indicators

Business districts
see Central business districts

Business diversification
see Economic concentration and diversification

Business education
Construction (hwy) minority contractor training, funding by region, FY92, annual release, 7554–40
Degree (PhD) recipients in higher education, by field and selected characteristics, 1979, 1984, and 1989, 4848–44
Degrees awarded in higher education, by level, field, race, and sex, 1989/90 and trends from 1980/81, annual rpt, 4844–17
Digest of Education Statistics, 1992 annual data compilation, 4824–2
FmHA activities, and loans and grants by program and State, FY91 and trends from FY70, annual rpt, 1184–17
High school enrollment in vocational education, and academic and other credits earned, by subject and student characteristics, classes of 1982 and 1987, 4838–50
Housing (public and Indian) tenant assns, HUD project mgmt and operation training grants by recipient, FY91, press release, 5006–3.77
Housing (public and Indian) tenant assns, HUD project mgmt and operation training grants by recipient, FY92, press release, 5006–3.100
Minority- and woman-owned businesses and owner characteristics, by industry, employment and sales size, and form of ownership, 1987 survey, 2328–59
Teachers of vocational education, by subject area and selected characteristics, for public high schools, 1987/88, 4836–3.9
Vocational education enrollment, student and teacher characteristics, and outcomes, for secondary and postsecondary instns, 1970s-90, 4828–42

Business efficiency
see Business management
see Consultants
see Labor productivity
see Operating ratios
see Productivity

Business energy use
see Agricultural energy use
see Industrial and commercial energy use

see Transportation energy use
Business ethics
Banks and thrifts contracts with computer data processing vendors, involvement of illegal business transactions, and instn and vendor views, 1985-90, GAO rpt, 26119–374
Real estate agent fees for mortgage banker referrals, and other issues, consumer views, 1989 survey, hearings, 21248–161
Business failures and closings
Aluminum plant ownership, capacity, energy and aluminum sources, and startup and closing dates, by US and foreign plant and location, 1990, annual listing, 5604–49
Bank deposits interest rates deregulation impacts on bank asset risk, alternative model descriptions and results, 1970s-80s, working paper, 9379–14.15
Banking system reform impacts on consumers, with background data, 1991 hearing, 21248–167
Banks (agricultural) failures, quarterly rpt, 9365–3.10
Banks (insured commercial and savings) finances, and changes in status, by State, 1990, annual rpt, 9294–4.1
Banks (insured commercial and savings) financial condition and performance, by asset size and region, quarterly rpt, 9292–1
Banks (natl) charters, mergers, liquidations, enforcement cases, and financial performance, with data by instn and State, quarterly rpt, 8402–3
Banks capital aid by Reconstruction Finance Corp, impact on solvency status and financial ratios, 1920s-40, article, 9381–1.304
Banks failures and assets involved, and Bank Insurance Fund finances, alternative projections, 1991-93, hearing, 21248–166
Banks failures forecasting performance of asset risk indicators and other factors, 1980s-91, article, 9379–15.302
Banks failures relation to portfolio risk, and analysis of alternative failure warning models, 1992 working paper, 9379–14.18
Banks failures resolution costs to FDIC, relation to bank financial and other characteristics, 1986-90, article, 9292–4.303
Banks failures, undercapitalization duration relation to Bank Insurance Fund losses, 1985-90, article, 9391–1.312
Banks finances, examination ratings, and failure resolution costs and methods, 1980s-91, article, 9292–4.301
Banks mergers approved, and assets and offices involved, by instn, 1990, annual rpt, 9294–5
Banks mgmt efficiency indicator, with results for surviving and failed banks, mid 1980s, article, 9379–1.302
Banks needing FDIC aid, finances and operations, 1991, annual rpt, 9294–1
Business cycle recession and expansion duration indicators, 1850s-1990, working paper, 9375–13.83
Credit unions failures, assets and losses to Natl Credit Union Share Insurance Fund by asset size and charter, and for largest failures by instn, FY86-91, 9536–1.7
Credit unions federally insured, finances, mergers, closings, and insurance fund losses and financial statements, FY91, annual rpt, 9534–7
Credit unions federally insured, finances, 1990-91, annual rpt, 9534–1
Credit unions financial performance and regulation, with background data, 1960s-90, GAO rpt, 26119–364
Displaced workers losing job 1987-92, labor force status by employment and other characteristics, as of Jan 1992, biennial press release, 6726–1.48
Electric power plants and capacity, by fuel used, owner, location, and operating status, 1991 and for units planned 1992-2001, annual listing, 3164–36
Electric power plants summer capacity and fuel source, for new and retired units, 1990, annual rpt, 3164–11.1
Failures and formation of business, 1950-91, annual rpt, 204–1.7
Farm credit conditions, earnings, and expenses, Fed Reserve 9th District, quarterly rpt, 9383–11
Farm finances, debts, assets, and receipts, and lenders financial condition, quarterly rpt with articles, 1541–1
Farm loan guarantees of FmHA, characteristics of borrowers, lenders, and loans, FY88, 1548–386
Financial instns failures, by instn type, US and Fed Reserve 10th District, selected years 1987-91, annual rpt, 9381–14
Financial instns reform issues, with finances, impacts of deposit insurance changes, and views of depositors and bankers, 1991 hearings, 25248–129
FmHA loan guarantees to business and industry in rural areas, by State and industry, and closures and defaults, FY74-91, GAO rpt, 26113–591
FmHA loans and borrower supervision activities in farm and housing programs, by type and State, monthly rpt, 1182–1
Fruit and vegetable processing industry in California, workers affected by plant closings, 1977-86, working paper, 6366–6.5
Hospital closings, financial and operating characteristics compared to instns remaining open, 1985-88, 17206–2.27
Hospital closings, financial and operating characteristics related to instn and area characteristics, 1985-88, 17206–2.28
Hospital closings relation to hospital and community characteristics, by metro-nonmetro location, 1980-87, article, 4042–3.341
Hospital closures in 1990, operating characteristics, current use, and location, annual rpt, 4004–35
Hospital reimbursement by Medicare under prospective payment system, rural area instns financial performance and impacts of PPS policy changes, 1991 rpt, 26306–6.164
Hydroelectric power plants retired, characteristics and location, as of 1992, annual listing, 3084–12
Insurance (life and health) company failures, and State guaranty fund assessments, by State, 1975-90, GAO rpt, 26119–392
Insurance industry finances, failures, and regulation, with data by firm and State, 1990 hearing, 25528–119
Insurance industry financial condition, operations, assets, junk bond holdings, and State regulation, with intl comparisons, 1991 hearings, 25268–79
Labor laws enacted, by State, 1991, annual article, 6722–1.309
Lumber mills closed and employees affected, by mill type, for 3 western States, 1990, hearing, 21728–78
Minority business Federal procurement set-aside contracts, status of participants as of 1990, annual rpt, 9764–8
North Central States business and economic conditions, Fed Reserve 9th District, quarterly journal, 9383–19
Nuclear reactors for domestic use and export by function and operating status, with owner, operating characteristics, and location, 1991 annual listing, 3354–15
Occupational safety enforcement activities of Federal and State agencies, inspections, closure orders, and violations contested and upheld, FY91, GAO rpt, 26121–461
Oil refinery capacity, openings, closings, and acquisitions by plant, and fuel used by PAD district, 1991, annual rpt, 3164–2.1
Pension plans terminated, liabilities, assets, and Pension Benefit Guarantee Corp recoveries and losses, with top 50 underfunded plans, mid 1970s-91, article, 9371–1.302
Rural areas health care access for counties without hospitals and in which the only hospital closed, 1987-89, 17206–2.30
Savings instns failure resolution activity and finances of Resolution Trust Corp, with data by asset type, State, region, and instn, monthly rpt, 9722–3
Savings instns failure resolution activity of Resolution Trust Corp, assets, deposits, and assets availability and sales, periodic press release, 9722–1
Savings instns failure resolution activity of Resolution Trust Corp, brokered deposits, fees, and interest rates by instn and region, as of July 1991, hearing, 21248–171
Savings instns failure resolution activity of Resolution Trust Corp impact on M2 growth, 1990-91, article, 9379–1.303
Savings instns failure resolution activity of Resolution Trust Corp impact on M2 growth, 1990-91, technical paper, 9379–12.83
Savings instns failure resolution activity of Resolution Trust Corp, with data by State and instn, and RTC finances, 1990, annual rpt, 9724–1
Savings instns failure resolution costs, impacts of capital standards relaxation, 1979-92, working paper, 9377–9.140
Savings instns failures, costs and budget deficit and economic impacts, 1980s and projected to 2010, 26306–6.165
Savings instns failures, financial performance of instns under Resolution Trust Corp conservatorship, quarterly rpt, 9722–5
Savings instns failures, inventory of real estate assets available from Resolution Trust Corp, semiannual listing series, 9722–2
Savings instns failures, low-grade junk bonds holdings of Resolution Trust Corp, quarterly press release, 9722–4
Savings instns failures, Resolution Trust Corp sales of real estate and other assets, 1990-91, GAO rpt, 26119–372
Savings instns financial ratios, for high and low risk S&Ls, 1987, article, 9375–1.306

Savings instns insured by Savings Assn Insurance Fund, assets, liabilities, and deposit and loan activity, by conservatorship status, monthly rpt, 8432–1
Schools of higher education closing, by instn type and control, 1960/61-1991/92, annual rpt, 4824–2.19
Securities Investor Protection Corp regulatory activity and finances, 1970s-91, GAO rpt, 26119–419
Small Business Admin loan guarantee program participants finances, operations, characteristics, and views, 1991 survey, 9768–25
Small business finances, operations, owner characteristics, and Federal contracts, 1980s-90, annual rpt, 9764–6
Small Business Investment Company finances, losses, and program operations, 1980s-91, 25728–44
Small Business Investment Company program financial performance, findings and recommendations, 1992 rpt, 9768–24
Small business loan collateral adequacy for failed firms, with loan liquidation recoveries and losses, FY89, GAO rpt, 26113–553
Statistical Abstract of US, 1992 annual data compilation, 2324–1.17
Survey of Current Business, detailed data for major industries and economic indicators, monthly rpt, 2702–1.3
Survey of Current Business, detailed data for major industries and economic indicators, 1960-91, biennial supplement, 2704–1
Survey of Current Business, detailed financial and business data, and economic indicators, monthly rpt, 2702–1.1
Unemployed displaced workers, layoffs and recalls by layoff reason, industry, firm size, and State, 2nd half 1988, 6406–6.36
Unemployed displaced workers, layoffs and unemployment insurance claims by reason, industry, selected characteristics, MSA, and State, 1990, annual rpt, 6744–18
Uranium mill capacity by plant, and production, by operating status, 1987-91, annual rpt, 3164–65.1
West Central States economic indicators, Fed Reserve 10th District, quarterly rpt, 9381–16.2
see also Bankruptcy

Business firms
see Bank holding companies
see Business acquisitions and mergers
see Business failures and closings
see Business firms and establishments, number
see Business formations
see Corporations
see Foreign corporations
see Franchises
see Government corporations and enterprises
see Holding companies
see Home-based offices and workers
see Industrial plants and equipment
see Industrial siting
see Minority businesses
see Multinational corporations
see Partnerships
see Proprietorships
see Public utilities
see Small business
see Small Business Investment Companies
see Women-owned businesses
see under By Individual Company or Institution in the "Index by Categories"

Business firms and establishments, number
Agricultural cooperatives, finances, and membership, by type of service, commodity, and State, 1990, annual rpt, 1124–1
Agricultural cooperatives, finances, operations, activities, and membership, commodity rpt series, 1126–1
Agricultural, fishery, and forest products trade, tariffs, and industry operating data, commodity rpt series, 9885–8
Bank holding companies, financial ratios, banks held, and equity financing relation to regulatory capital standards, 1970s-90, technical paper, 9366–6.291
Banking and financial conditions, 1990, annual rpt, 9364–5
Banks (insured commercial) and offices, and summary assets and liabilities, 1990-91, annual rpt, 9364–1.2
Banks (insured commercial and FDIC-insured savings) assets, income, and financial ratios, by asset size and State, quarterly rpt, 13002–3
Banks (insured commercial and savings) deposits by instn, State, MSA, and county, as of June 1991, annual regional rpt series, 9295–3
Banks (insured commercial and savings) finances, and changes in status, by State, 1990, annual rpt, 9294–4.1
Banks (insured commercial and savings) financial condition and performance, by asset size and region, quarterly rpt, 9292–1
Banks (natl) charters, mergers, liquidations, enforcement cases, and financial performance, with data by instn and State, quarterly rpt, 8402–3
Banks agricultural loans share of all loans, with market shares and returns on assets, by bank size, 1970s-80s, working paper, 9381–10.122
Banks and thrifts finances and operations by deposit size, Fed Reserve functional cost analysis, 1991, annual rpt, 9364–6
Banks finances, examination ratings, and failure resolution costs and methods, 1980s-91, article, 9292–4.301
Building (commercial) energy use, costs, and conservation, by building characteristics, survey rpt series, 3166–8
Building materials industry finances and operations, by SIC 4-digit industry, selected years 1977-89, article, 2042–1.302
Chemical and energy products trade, tariffs, and industry operating data, commodity rpt series, 9885–11
Chemical and oil products shipments, firms, trade, and use, by product, periodic Current Industrial Rpt series, 2506–8
Chemicals (synthetic organic) production, sales, and manufacturer listing, by product, 1990, annual rpt, 9884–3
Corporations income tax returns, income and tax items by asset size and detailed industry, 1989, annual rpt, 8304–4; 8304–21
County Business Patterns, 1989: employment, establishments, and payroll, by SIC 2- to 4-digit industry and county, annual State rpt series, 2326–8
County Business Patterns, 1990: employment, establishments, and payroll, by SIC 2- to 4-digit industry and county, annual State rpt series, 2326–6
Credit unions federally insured, finances by instn characteristics and State, as of June 1992, semiannual rpt, 9532–6
Credit unions federally insured, finances, mergers, closings, and insurance fund losses and financial statements, FY91, annual rpt, 9534–7
Credit unions federally insured, finances, 1990-91, annual rpt, 9534–1
Credit unions financial performance and regulation, with background data, 1960s-90, GAO rpt, 26119–364
Dairy production by commodity, and plants, by State, 1991, annual rpt, 1627–5
Electric power distribution loans from REA, and borrower operating and financial data, by firm and State, 1991, annual rpt, 1244–1
Electronics and services trade, tariffs, and industry operating data, commodity rpt series, 9885–12
Enterprise zone programs in rural areas, jobs created and saved, and firms participating, by industry, 1986, article, 1502–7.303
Exports, imports, balances, US consumption, and operations of industries affected, by industry, 1989-91, annual rpt, 9884–25
Fertilizer (inorganic) shipments, trade, use, and firms, by product and State, with stocks, 1991, annual Current Industrial Rpt, 2506–8.13
Fish (processed) production by location, and trade, by species and product, 1988-91, annual rpts, 2166–6
Fishery employment, vessels, plants, and cooperatives, by State, 1990, annual rpt, 2164–1.10
Food marketing sector finances, operations, and merger activity, for processors and distributors, 1991, annual rpt, 1544–22
Food processing firms, employment, and shipments, and farm production, by commodity and State, for Appalachia, 1960s-90, 9088–37
Foreign-controlled US firms transactions with related foreign persons, by type, industry div, and country, 1988, article, 8302–2.318
Foreign-owned corporate activity in US, income tax returns and selected income and tax items, by industry div and selected country, 1988, article, 8302–2.309
Gasoline service stations price competition and divorcement from oil companies, issues with data by firm, city, and State, 1991 hearing, 25528–120
Glassware shipments, trade, use, and firms, by product, 1991, annual Current Industrial Rpt, 2506–9.3
Hazardous substances industrial releases and reduction methods under EPA regulation, by chemical, source, industry, and location, 1989, annual rpt, 9234–6
Hazardous waste generation and disposal taxes, rates, and firms filing returns, by substance type, 1989, annual article, 8302–2.303

Imports under Generalized System of Preferences, status, and US tariffs, with trade by country and US economic impacts, for selected commodities, 1987-91, annual rpt, 9884–23
Industry (US) intl competitiveness, with selected foreign and US operating data by major firm and product, series, 2046–12
Livestock packers purchases and feeding, and livestock markets, dealers, and sales, by State, 1990, annual rpt, 1384–1
Lumber mills, operations, log use by species and origin, and residue use, for California by product and county, 1988, 1208–108
Machinery and equipment production, shipments, trade, stocks, orders, use, and firms, by product, periodic Current Industrial Rpt series, 2506–12
Machinery and equipment trade, tariffs, and industry operating data, commodity rpt series, 9885–9
Manufacturing annual survey, 1990: establishments, employment, finances, inventories, and energy use, by SIC 2- to 4-digit industry, 2506–14.2
Manufacturing annual survey, 1990: finances and operations, by SIC 2- and 3-digit industry and State, 2506–14.3
Manufacturing census, 1987: concentration of largest firms measured by value added, and for shipments by SIC 2- and 4-digit industry, subject rpt, 2497–6
Manufacturing census, 1987: exporting establishments, shipments, and employment, by SIC 2-digit industry and State, 2506–16.2
Manufacturing trade, tariffs, and industry operating data, commodity rpt series, 9885–10
Metals (intermediate product) shipments, trade, and inventories, by product, periodic Current Industrial Rpt series, 2506–11
Minerals and metals trade, tariffs, and industry operating data, commodity rpt series, 9885–13
Minerals Yearbook, Vol 1, 1989: commodity reviews of production, use, trade, prices, and mining operations, annual rpt, 5604–33
Minority- and woman-owned businesses and owner characteristics, by industry, employment and sales size, and form of ownership, 1987 survey, 2328–59
Minority Business Dev Centers mgmt and financial aid, and characteristics of businesses, by region and State, FY91, annual rpt, 2104–6
Multinatl firms US affiliates finances and operations, by industry, country of parent firm, and State, 1987, 2702–1.340; 2708–48
Multinatl US firms and foreign affiliates finances and operations, by industry and country, 1989 benchmark survey, annual rpt, 2704–5
Multinatl US firms foreign affiliates, income statement items by asset size, industry, and country, 1988, biennial article, 8302–2.322
Partnership income and losses impact of 1986 Tax Reform Act, by profit status and selected industry, 1980s, article, 8302–2.313
Partnership income tax returns, income statement and balance sheet items by industry group, 1990, annual article, 8302–2.314
Potato chip plants and quantity used for chips, by region, 1990-91, annual rpt, 1621–11
Puerto Rico and other US possessions corporations income tax returns, income and tax items, and employment, by selected industry, 1989, article, 8302–2.326
Railroad employment and finances, for ICC-regulated carriers, as of FY91, annual rpt, 9484–1
Savings instns, FHLB 1st District members by type and State, 1991, annual rpt, 9304–2
Savings instns financial statements, for instns insured by Savings Assn Insurance Fund by FHLB district and State, and for FDIC-insured savings banks, 1989, annual rpt, 8434–1
Savings instns insured by Savings Assn Insurance Fund, assets, liabilities, and deposit and loan activity, by conservatorship status, monthly rpt, 8432–1
Savings instns insured by Savings Assn Insurance Fund, finances by profitability group, district, and State, quarterly rpt, 8432–4
Savings instns insured by Savings Assn Insurance Fund, offices, and deposits, by region, State, MSA, and county, 1991, annual rpt, 8434–5
Securities industry finances, for broker-dealers and individual stock exchanges and clearing agencies, 1986-90, annual rpt, 9734–2.1
Semiconductor materials supply and demand, and semiconductor firms by State, late 1980s and projected to 1993, hearing, 21708–130
Small business finances, operations, owner characteristics, and Federal contracts, 1980s-90, annual rpt, 9764–6
Small business loans, contracts, and financing by SBA program and firm, and SBA activities, FY91, annual rpt, 9764–1
Solar collector and photovoltaic cell shipments by end-use sector and State, and trade, 1990, annual rpt, 3164–62
Sole proprietorship income tax returns, income statement items by industry group, 1990, annual article, 8302–2.317; 8302–2.320
Statistical Abstract of US, 1992 annual data compilation, 2324–1.17
Survey of Current Business, detailed data for major industries and economic indicators, monthly rpt, 2702–1.3
Survey of Current Business, detailed data for major industries and economic indicators, 1960-91, biennial supplement, 2704–1
Telephone and telegraph firms detailed finances and operations, 1990, annual rpt, 9284–6
Telephone firms borrowing under Rural Telephone Program, and financial and operating data, by State, 1991, annual rpt, 1244–2
Telephone service subscribership, charges, and local and long distance firm finances and operations, late 1970s-92, semiannual rpt, 9282–7
Transit systems finances and operations, by mode, size of fleet and urban area, region, and for 518 systems, 1990, annual rpt, 7884–4
Truck and bus interstate carriers finances and operations, by district, 1990, annual rpt, 9486–5.3
Truck, bus, and rail carriers regulated by ICC, employment and finances, as of FY91, annual rpt, 9484–1
Truck interstate carriers finances and operations, by district, 1990, annual rpt, 9486–5.2
Trust assets of banks, trust companies, and S&Ls, by type of asset and fund, selected firm, and State, 1991, annual rpt, 13004–1
TV and radio stations on the air, by class of operation, monthly press release, 9282–4
Uranium mining and milling industries finances and operations, with selected foreign comparisons, 1970s-90 and projected to 2005, annual rpt, 3164–82
Uranium supply and industry operations, various periods 1947-91 and projected to 2001, annual rpt, 3164–65
Vending facilities run by blind on Federal and non-Federal property, finances and operations by agency and State, FY91, annual rpt, 4944–2
Warehouses (cold storage) and capacity, by State, as of Oct 1991, biennial rpt, 1614–2
Wire and cable (insulated) shipments, trade, use, and firms, by product, 1991, annual Current Industrial Rpt, 2506–10.8
see also Business acquisitions and mergers
see also Business failures and closings
see also Business formations
see also Farms and farmland
see also Industrial plants and equipment
see also under By Industry in the "Index by Categories"

Business formations

Banks (insured commercial and savings) finances, and changes in status, by State, 1990, annual rpt, 9294–4.1
Credit unions federally insured, finances, mergers, closings, and insurance fund losses and financial statements, FY91, annual rpt, 9534–7
Credit unions federally insured, finances, 1990-91, annual rpt, 9534–1
Electric power plants summer capacity and fuel source, for new and retired units, 1990, annual rpt, 3164–11.1
Foreign direct investment by method and industry div, and affiliated firms R&D spending, pay, employment, and trade compared to US-owned firms, 1980-90, article, 9391–1.309
Formation and failures of business, 1950-91, annual rpt, 204–1.7
Minority Business Dev Centers mgmt and financial aid, and characteristics of businesses, by region and State, FY91, annual rpt, 2104–6
Multinatl US firms foreign affiliates, income statement items by asset size, industry, and country, 1988, biennial article, 8302–2.322
New England States economic indicators, Fed Reserve 1st District, monthly rpt, 9373–2

North Central States business and economic conditions, Fed Reserve 9th District, quarterly journal, 9383–19
Oil refinery capacity, openings, closings, and acquisitions by plant, and fuel used by PAD district, 1991, annual rpt, 3164–2.1
Partnership income and losses impact of 1986 Tax Reform Act, by profit status and selected industry, 1980s, article, 8302–2.313
Small Business Admin guaranteed loans issued under regular, certified, and preferred lender programs, selected characteristics, FY83-90, GAO rpt, 26113–581
Small business finances, operations, owner characteristics, and Federal contracts, 1980s-90, annual rpt, 9764–6
Small business loans, contracts, and financing by SBA program and firm, and SBA activities, FY91, annual rpt, 9764–1
Small business use of Census Bur economic data in planning decisions, case studies, 1991 rpt, 2628–33
Statistical Abstract of US, 1992 annual data compilation, 2324–1.17
Survey of Current Business, detailed data for major industries and economic indicators, monthly rpt, 2702–1.3
Survey of Current Business, detailed financial and business data, and economic indicators, monthly rpt, 2702–1.1
West Central States economic indicators, Fed Reserve 10th District, quarterly rpt, 9381–16.2

Business income and expenses, general
Alien nonresidents income from US sources and tax withheld by country and US tax treaty status, 1989, annual article, 8302–2.308
Boycotts (intl) by OPEC and other countries, US firms and individuals cooperation and tax benefits denied, 1990, article, 8302–2.323
Building materials industry finances and operations, by SIC 4-digit industry, selected years 1977-89, article, 2042–1.302
Business statistics, detailed data for major industries and economic indicators, 1960-91, *Survey of Current Business* biennial supplement, 2704–1
Corporations finances, monthly rpt, 9362–1.1
Corporations financial statements for manufacturing, mining, and trade, by selected SIC 2- to 3-digit industry, quarterly rpt, 2502–1
Corporations income tax returns, income and tax items by asset size and detailed industry, 1989, annual rpt, 8304–4; 8304–21
Corporations income tax returns, summary data by asset size and industry div, 1989, annual article, 8302–2.321
Corporations under domestic and foreign control, finances and tax burdens, 1983-87, GAO rpt, 26119–411
Domestic Intl Sales Corps (Interest Charge) income tax returns, assets, and income and tax items, by detailed industry, 1987, article, 8302–2.312
Economic indicators and components, current data and annual trends, monthly rpt, 23842–1.1; 23842–1.3; 23842–1.5
Economic indicators compounded annual rates of change, monthly rpt, 9391–3
Election campaign-related internal communications of firms and assns, spending by organization, location, and candidate, 1991-92, biennial rpt, 9274–3
Electric power demand, and industrial and employment impacts of capacity shortfalls and new power plants, by selected State, 1960s-80s and projected to 2000, hearing, 21248–163
Environmental Quality, status of problems, protection programs, research, and intl issues, 1991 annual rpt, 484–1
Farm operators nonfarm self-employment income by source and farm profit and loss, and tax burden, 1987, article, 1541–1.320
Foreign-controlled US firms transactions with related foreign persons, by type, industry div, and country, 1988, article, 8302–2.318
Foreign corporations and individuals, and US entities abroad, detailed data compilation for income tax returns, 1970s-89, quinquennial rpt, 8308–31
Foreign countries tax credits on corporate income tax returns, with income and tax items by industry group, 1988, biennial article, 8302–2.316
Foreign direct investment in US by country, and finances, employment, and acreage owned, by industry group of business acquired or established, 1985-91, annual article, 2702–1.320
Foreign direct investment in US, by industry group and world area, 1989-91, annual article, 2702–1.331
Foreign direct investment in US by top 10 countries, factors affecting rate of return, and compared to returns for US firms, 1980s-91, article, 2702–1.330
Foreign direct investment of US, by industry group and world area, 1989-91, annual article, 2702–1.332
Foreign-owned corporate activity in US, income tax returns and selected income and tax items, by industry div and selected country, 1988, article, 8302–2.309
Foreign Sales Corps income tax returns, assets, and income and tax items, by industry, country of incorporation, and transaction pricing method, 1987, article, 8302–2.311
Gross State Product by component, industry div, and State, 1977-89, article, 2702–1.303
Health care spending by businesses, households, and govts, 1965-90, annual article, 4652–1.309
Housing (rental) units, total, with HUD assistance by program, and eligible for aid, by unit, household, and neighborhood characteristics, and location, 1989, biennial rpt, 5184–11
Imports and tariff provisions effect on US industries and products, investigations with background financial and operating data, series, 9886–4
Imports injury to US industries from foreign subsidized products and sales at less than fair value, investigations with background financial and operating data, series, 9886–19
Imports injury to US industries from foreign subsidized products, investigations with background financial and operating data, series, 9886–15
Imports injury to US industries from sales at less than fair value, investigations with background financial and operating data, series, 9886–14
Imports of US given duty-free treatment for value of US material sent abroad, by commodity and country, 1987-90, annual rpt, 9884–14
Income (personal) per capita and by source, and employment, by industry div, State, MSA, and county, 1969-90, annual CD-ROM, 2704–7
Industry (US) intl competitiveness, with selected foreign and US operating data by major firm and product, series, 2046–12
Industry finances and operations, by SIC 2- to 4-digit industry, forecast 1992, annual rpt, 2044–28
Input-output structure of US economy, detailed interindustry transactions for 541 industries, and components of final demand, 1982 benchmark data, 2708–17
Inventories related to sales, by industry sector, model description and results, late 1960s-91, article, 9389–1.302
Manufacturing annual survey, 1990: establishments, employment, finances, inventories, and energy use, by SIC 2- to 4-digit industry, 2506–14.2
Manufacturing census, 1987: shipments of manufacturers products, by customer class and SIC 2- and 4-digit industry, subject rpt, 2497–4
Manufacturing profits relation to real exchange rate, model description and results, 1992 technical paper, 9385–8.142
Militarily strategic manufacturing industries finances, operations, and intl competitiveness, series, 2026–1
Minority- and woman-owned businesses and owner characteristics, by industry, employment and sales size, and form of ownership, 1987 survey, 2328–59
Minority Business Dev Centers mgmt and financial aid, and characteristics of businesses, by region and State, FY91, annual rpt, 2104–6
Multinatl firms US affiliates finances and operations, by industry, country of parent firm, and State, 1987, 2702–1.340; 2708–48
Multinatl firms US affiliates finances and operations, by industry div, country of parent firm, and State, 1989-90, annual article, 2702–1.319; 2702–1.337
Multinatl firms US affiliates, finances, and operations, by industry, world area of parent firm, and State, 1989-90, annual rpt, 2704–4
Multinatl firms US affiliates gross product, by component, industry, and country of parent firm, 1987-90, article, 2702–1.342
Multinatl firms US affiliates income tax compliance issues, with income and tax data by industry group, 1987-89, press release, 8008–155
Multinatl US firms and foreign affiliates finances and operations, by industry and country, 1989 benchmark survey, annual rpt, 2704–5

Multinatl US firms and foreign affiliates finances and operations, by industry and world area, 1988, annual article, 2702–1.329
Multinatl US firms foreign affiliates, income statement items by asset size, industry, and country, 1988, biennial article, 8302–2.322
Natl income and product accounts and components, *Survey of Current Business*, monthly rpt, 2702–1.23
Natl income and product accounts, comprehensive accounts and components, benchmark revisions, 1929-88, 2708–5
Natl income and product accounts, comprehensive accounts and components, *Survey of Current Business*, monthly rpt, 2702–1.28
Pacific territories population and housing detailed characteristics, by location, 1990 Census of Population and Housing, series, 2551–8
Partnership income and losses impact of 1986 Tax Reform Act, by profit status and selected industry, 1980s, article, 8302–2.313
Partnership income tax returns, income statement and balance sheet items by industry group, 1990, annual article, 8302–2.314
Partnerships (US) foreign partners income and tax withheld, by country, 1990, article, 8302–2.324
Philadelphia metro area transit service operations, costs and benefits, and local economic and air pollution impacts, 1970s-90 and projected to 2020, 7308–205
Political campaign finances reported to Fed Election Commission, by type of filer, 1990 natl elections, biennial rpt series, 9276–2
Pollution abatement spending by govts, business, and consumers, 1972-90, annual article, 2702–1.321
Productivity and costs of labor for private, nonfarm business, and manufacturing sectors, revised data, quarterly rpt, 6822–2
Puerto Rico and other US possessions corporations income tax returns, income and tax items, and employment, by selected industry, 1989, article, 8302–2.326
R&D funding by small high technology firms relation to firm finances, 1991 working paper, 9375–13.75
Retail trade sales and inventories, by kind of business, region, and selected State, MSA, and city, monthly rpt, 2413–3
Retail trade sales, by kind of business, advance monthly rpt, 2413–2
Retail trade sales, inventories, purchases, gross margin, and accounts receivable, by SIC 2- to 4-digit kind of business and form of ownership, 1990, annual rpt, 2413–5
Sales and ratio to inventories, by industry div, 1950-91, annual rpt, 204–1.1; 204–1.3; 204–1.7
Self-employed persons farm and nonfarm business income, 1989, article, 1541–1.301
Services trade of US, direct and among multinatl firms affiliates, by industry and world area, 1986-91, article, 2702–1.336
Small Business Admin loan guarantee program participants finances, operations, characteristics, and views, 1991 survey, 9768–25
Small business finances, operations, owner characteristics, and Federal contracts, 1980s-90, annual rpt, 9764–6
Small business R&D grants of Fed Govt, project sales by type and dev funding by source, by agency and selected firm, 1984-91, GAO rpt, 26113–393
Sole proprietorship income tax returns, income statement items by industry group, 1990, annual article, 8302–2.317; 8302–2.320
Statistical Abstract of US, 1992 annual data compilation, 2324–1.17
Survey of Current Business, detailed data for major industries and economic indicators, monthly rpt, 2702–1
Survey of Current Business, detailed data for major industries and economic indicators, 1960-91, biennial supplement, 2704–1
Tax (income) and effective rates on US, foreign, and worldwide income, by company and industry, 1980s, GAO rpt, 26119–289
Tax (income) returns filed, by type of filer, selected income items, quarterly rpt, 8302–2.1
Tax (income) returns of individuals, by filing status, tax item, and income level, 1991, annual article, 8302–2.319
Tax (income) returns of individuals, detailed data, 1988, annual rpt, 8304–2
Tax (income) returns of individuals, selected income and tax items by income level, preliminary 1990, annual article, 8302–2.307
Tax (income) returns of individuals with foreign earned income, income and tax items by income level and occupation, 1987, article, 8302–2.301
Tax exempt organizations finances, with data by type, size, State, and for largest organizations, late 1940s-80s, compilation of papers, 8308–35
Wholesale trade sales and inventories, by SIC 2- to 3-digit kind of business, monthly rpt, 2413–7
see also Agricultural finance
see also Agricultural marketing
see also Agricultural production costs
see also Business assets and liabilities, general
see also Business income and expenses, specific industry
see also Capital investments, general
see also Depreciation
see also Economic indicators
see also Employee benefits
see also Energy production costs
see also Farm income
see also Industrial and commercial energy use
see also Industrial purchasing
see also Labor costs and cost indexes
see also Operating ratios
see also Payroll
see also Production costs
see also Professionals' fees
see also Royalties
see also Value added tax

Business income and expenses, specific industry
Aerospace industry sales, orders, backlog, and firms, by product for govt, military, and other customers, 1991, annual Current Industrial Rpt, 2506–12.22
Agricultural cooperatives finances, aggregate for top 100 assns by commodity group, 1990, annual rpt, 1124–3
Agricultural cooperatives, finances, and membership, by type of service, commodity, and State, 1990, annual rpt, 1124–1
Agricultural cooperatives finances, operations, activities, and current issues, monthly journal, 1122–1
Agricultural cooperatives, finances, operations, activities, and membership, commodity rpt series, 1126–1
Agricultural, fishery, and forest products trade, tariffs, and industry operating data, commodity rpt series, 9885–8
Airline finances and operations, summary data, quarterly rpt, 7502–16
Airline finances, by carrier, carrier group, and for total certificated system, quarterly rpt, 7302–7
Airline operations and passenger, cargo, and mail traffic, by type of service, air carrier, State, and country, 1981-90, annual rpt, 7504–1.6
American Historical Assn financial statements, and membership by State, 1990, annual rpt, 29574–2
Army and Air Force Exchange Service financial statements, 1990, annual rpt, 3504–21
Auto industry finances and operations, trade by country, and prices of selected US and foreign models, monthly rpt, 9882–8
Bank of Credit and Commerce Intl DC office financial statements, 1984-90, GAO rpt, 26119–427
Bank of Credit and Commerce Intl financial statements, audits, and selected loan data, 1984-90, hearing, 25388–60
Banking and financial conditions, 1990, annual rpt, 9364–5
Banks (insured commercial), Fed Reserve 5th District members financial statements, by State, quarterly rpt, 9389–18
Banks (insured commercial and FDIC-insured savings) assets, income, and financial ratios, by asset size and State, quarterly rpt, 13002–3
Banks (insured commercial and savings) finances, by State, 1990, annual rpt, 9294–4
Banks (insured commercial and savings) financial condition and performance, by asset size and region, quarterly rpt, 9292–1
Banks (natl) charters, mergers, liquidations, enforcement cases, and financial performance, with data by instn and State, quarterly rpt, 8402–3
Banks and thrifts finances and operations by deposit size, Fed Reserve functional cost analysis, 1991, annual rpt, 9364–6
Banks and thrifts finances by instn type, and Fed Financial Instns Exam Council financial statements, 1991, annual rpt, 13004–2
Banks dividends on common stock, relation to earnings, capital, and other factors, 1989-90, article, 9292–4.302

Banks economies of scale, alternative model results for large banks, 1984-86, working paper, 9387–8.274
Banks economies of scale and scope, impacts of asset quality indicators and other factors by asset size, model results, 1990, working paper, 9387–8.260
Banks economies of scale, impacts of potential mergers among large banks, model description and results, 1980s, working paper, 9387–8.256
Banks in Fed Reserve System, expenses and operations itemized by service, office, and district, 1991, annual rpt, 9364–11
Banks in Fed Reserve 3rd District, assets, income, and rates of return, by major instn, quarterly rpt, annual table, 9387–10
Banks income, expenses, and dividends, for Fed Reserve members, 1990, annual rpt, 9364–5.11
Banks mergers antitrust issues, with background financial data by State and selected instn, 1991 hearing, 21248–176
Banks mergers impacts on noninterest expense ratios, with background data for total and southeastern US, 1980s-90, article, 9371–1.303
Banks mergers impacts on operating costs, 1982-86, working paper, 9371–10.78
Banks needing FDIC aid, finances and operations, 1991, annual rpt, 9294–1
Banks profitability, balance sheet and income statement items, and financial ratios, by asset size, 1985-91, annual article, 9362–1.305
Banks relative efficiency, model description and results, mid 1980s-90, article, 9391–1.305
Bus (Class I) passengers and selected revenue data, for individual large carriers, quarterly rpt, 9482–13
CCC loan activities by commodity, and agency operating results, monthly press release, 1802–7
Chemicals (synthetic organic) production, sales, and manufacturer listing, by product, 1990, annual rpt, 9884–3
Child day care and early childhood education programs availability, demand, use, costs, and provider and enrollee characteristics, 1990 survey, 4808–39
Cigarette ad and promotion costs by media, and market shares, by cigarette type, with sales and use, 1963-89, annual rpt, 9404–4
Coal industry retirees pension and health trust funds financial condition, employer contributions, and beneficiaries, late 1970s-92, GAO rpt, 26121–469; 26121–471
Colorado River Storage Project finances and activities in western States, FY91, annual rpt, 5824–3
Communications services revenue and expenses, itemized by SIC 2- to 4-digit kind of business, 1990, annual rpt, 2413–15
Credit card issuers, and banks credit operations, costs and revenue, mid 1970s-91, article, 9362–1.306
Credit Union Natl Admin Central Liquidity Facility financial statements, FY91, annual rpt, 9534–5
Credit unions federally insured, finances by instn characteristics and State, as of June 1992, semiannual rpt, 9532–6
Credit unions federally insured, finances, mergers, closings, and insurance fund losses and financial statements, FY91, annual rpt, 9534–7
Credit unions federally insured, finances, 1990-91, annual rpt, 9534–1
Credit unions financial performance and regulation, with background data, 1960s-90, GAO rpt, 26119–364
Credit unions with low income membership, financial, operating, and membership data, 1982-91, 9536–1.8
Drug (prescription) prices in US and other countries, industry profits, and R&D and marketing spending, 1980s-91 and projected to 2000, 25148–44
Drug industry operating in Puerto Rico under tax-favored status, tax and income items, 1985-86, hearing, 21448–46
Electric power distribution loans from REA, and borrower operating and financial data, by firm and State, 1991, annual rpt, 1244–1
Electric power plants production, fuel use, stocks, and costs by fuel type, and sales, by State, monthly rpt, with articles, 3162–35
Electric power purchases of municipal and cooperative distributors, and prices and use by distributor and consumer sector, for TVA, monthly rpt, 9802–1
Electric power sales and finances, for Bonneville Power Admin mgmt of Fed Columbia River Power System, summary data, quarterly rpt, 3222–2
Electric power sales and finances of TVA, FY91, annual rpt, 9804–1
Electric power sales and revenue, by end-use sector, consumption level, and utility, 1990, annual rpt, 3164–91
Electric power sales by customer, activities by plant, and financial statements of Western Area Power Admin, FY91, annual rpt, 3254–1
Electric power sales by customer, financial statements, and operations and costs by project, for Southwestern Fed Power System, FY91, annual rpt, 3244–1
Electric power sales by customer, plants, and capacity of Southeastern Power Admin, FY91, annual rpt, 3234–1
Electric power sales, finances, and operations, for Fed Columbia River Power System, FY91, annual rpt, 3224–1
Electric power sales, revenue, and rates of Bonneville Power Admin, by customer and customer type, 1991, semiannual rpt, 3222–1
Electric utilities conservation programs energy savings and spending, with data for top 25 firms, 1990, 3308–106
Electric utilities finances and operations, detailed data for publicly and privately owned firms, 1990, annual rpt, 3164–11.4
Electric utilities finances and operations, detailed data for publicly owned firms, 1990, annual rpt, 3164–24
Electric utilities privately owned, finances and operations, detailed data, 1990, annual rpt, 3164–23
Energy producers finances and operations, by energy type for US firms domestic and foreign operations, 1990, annual rpt, 3164–44
Energy production, dev, and distribution firms revenues and income, quarterly rpt, 3162–38
Energy resources of US, foreign direct investment by energy type and firm, and US affiliates operations, as of 1990, annual rpt, 3164–80
Farm Credit System financial condition, quarterly rpt, 9262–2
Farm Credit System financial statements and loan activity by lender type, and borrower characteristics, 1991, annual rpt, 9264–2
Farm Credit System financial statements, 1991, annual rpt, 9264–5
Fed Home Loan Bank of Atlanta financial statements, quarterly rpt, 9302–37
Fed Home Loan Bank of Atlanta financial statements, 1989-91, annual rpt, 9304–1
Fed Home Loan Bank of Boston financial statements, quarterly rpt, 9302–35
Fed Home Loan Bank of Boston financial statements, 1990-91, annual rpt, 9304–2
Fed Home Loan Bank of Chicago financial statements, 1989-91, annual rpt, 9304–4
Fed Home Loan Bank of Cincinnati financial statements, 1989-91, annual rpt, 9304–6
Fed Home Loan Bank of Dallas financial statements, 1989-91, annual rpt, 9304–11
Fed Home Loan Bank of Des Moines financial statements, 1989-91, annual rpt, 9304–7
Fed Home Loan Bank of New York financial statements, 1989-91, annual rpt, 9304–12
Fed Home Loan Bank of Pittsburgh financial statements, 1989-91, annual rpt, 9304–13
Fed Home Loan Bank of San Francisco financial statements, 1989-91, annual rpt, 9304–14
Fed Home Loan Bank of Seattle financial statements, 1989-91, annual rpt, 9304–15
Fed Home Loan Bank of Topeka financial statements, 1989-91, annual rpt, 9304–16
Fed Home Loan Banks financial statements, monthly tables, 9442–1
Fed Home Loan Banks financial statements, 1989-91, annual rpt, 9444–1
Fed Home Loan Mortgage Corp activities and financial statements, 1991, annual rpt, 9414–1
Fed Home Loan Mortgage Corp financial condition and capital adequacy, 1990, annual rpt, 5184–8
Fed Natl Mortgage Assn activities and finances, 1991, annual rpt, 5184–9; 9474–1
Fed Reserve Bank of Atlanta financial statements, 1990-91, annual rpt, 9371–4
Fed Reserve Bank of Boston financial statements, 1990-91, annual rpt, 9373–26
Fed Reserve Bank of Chicago financial statements, 1990-91, annual rpt, 9375–5
Fed Reserve Bank of Cleveland financial statements, 1990-91, annual rpt, 9377–5
Fed Reserve Bank of Dallas financial statements, 1990-91, annual rpt, 9379–2
Fed Reserve Bank of Kansas City financial statements, 1990-91, annual rpt, 9381–3

Fed Reserve Bank of Minneapolis financial statements, 1990-91, annual rpt, 9383–2
Fed Reserve Bank of New York financial statements, 1990-91, annual rpt, 9385–2
Fed Reserve Bank of Philadelphia financial statements, 1990-91, annual rpt, 9387–3
Fed Reserve Bank of Richmond financial statements, 1990-91, annual rpt, 9389–2
Fed Reserve Bank of San Francisco financial statements, 1990-91, annual rpt, 9393–2
Fed Reserve Bank of St Louis financial statements, 1990-91, annual rpt, 9391–17
Fed Reserve Bd and Reserve banks finances, staff, and review of monetary policy and economic devs, 1991, annual rpt, 9364–1
Fed Reserve System, Bd of Governors, and district banks financial statements, performance, and fiscal services, 1991-92, annual rpt, 9364–10
FHA-insured mortgage activities, audits, and financial statements, FY90-91, annual rpt, 5144–26
Finance companies assets, operating ratios, and growth indicators, for top 20 firms, 1980s-90, article, 9385–1.309
Financial markets (intl) performance of foreign and US bank and securities firms, finances and competitiveness issues, 1980s, compilation of papers, 9385–10
Food marketing cost indexes, by expense category, monthly rpt with articles, 1502–4
Food marketing sector finances, operations, and merger activity, for processors and distributors, 1991, annual rpt, 1544–22
Food prices (farm-retail), marketing cost components, and industry finances and productivity, 1920s-91, annual rpt, 1544–9
Govt Natl Mortgage Assn finances, and mortgage-backed securities program, FY91, annual rpt, 5144–6
GPO activities, finances, and production, FY91, annual rpt, 26204–1
Health Care Financing Review, provider prices, price inputs and indexes, and labor, quarterly journal, 4652–1.1
Home drug infusion therapy use, equipment, industry finances, and Medicare coverage options, 1992 rpt, 26358–258
Hospital capital, operating, and total costs, model estimates of factors affecting variation, 1985-89, article, 4652–1.313
Hospital financial performance under Medicare, 1977-89, article, 4652–1.315
Hospital reimbursement by Medicaid, provisions by State, 1991, 17206–2.35
Hospital reimbursement by Medicare under prospective payment system, analyses of alternative payment plans, series, 17206–1
Hospital reimbursement by Medicare under prospective payment system, diagnosis related group code assignment and effects on care and instn finances, series, 4006–7
Hospital reimbursement by Medicare under prospective payment system, impacts on costs, industry structure and operations, and quality of care, series, 17206–2
Hospital reimbursement by Medicare under prospective payment system, impacts on operating costs and margins, 1980s, article, 4652–1.312
Hospital reimbursement by Medicare under prospective payment system, methodology, inputs, and data by diagnostic group, 1992 annual rpt, 17204–1
Hospital reimbursement by Medicare under prospective payment system, omitted services impacts on hospital revenue, FY85, article, 4652–1.316
Hospital reimbursement by Medicare under prospective payment system, rural area instns financial performance and impacts of PPS policy changes, 1991 rpt, 26306–6.164
Housing (low income) developers tax credits, subsidies, project and tenant characteristics, and investor returns, 1987-88, 5188–133
Insurance (health) private plans to supplement Medicare, loss ratio performance, by firm, 1988-89, GAO rpt, 26121–452
Insurance industry financial condition, operations, assets, junk bond holdings, and State regulation, with intl comparisons, 1991 hearings, 25268–79
Metals (primary) production, shipments, trade, stocks, and material used, by product, periodic Current Industrial Rpt series, 2506–10
Minerals offshore lease sales environmental and economic impacts in coastal areas, final statement series, 5736–7
Minerals production, prices, trade, and foreign and US industry devs, by commodity, bimonthly rpt, 5602–4
Minerals Yearbook, Vol 1, 1989: commodity reviews of production, use, trade, prices, and mining operations, annual rpt, 5604–33
Mint (US) activities, finances, coin and medals production and holdings, and gold and silver transactions, by facility, FY91, annual rpt, 8204–1
Motor vehicle industry finances, and average fleet fuel economy, by selected firm, 1991 hearings, 21368–138
Natural and supplemental gas production, prices, trade, use, reserves, and pipeline company finances, by firm and State, monthly rpt with articles, 3162–4
Natural gas interstate pipeline company detailed financial and operating data, by firm, 1990, annual rpt, 3164–38
Nonprofit charitable and other tax exempt organizations finances, by category and size of assets and contributions, 1988, annual article, 8302–2.315
Nonprofit charitable organizations finances, summary data by asset size, 1989, article, 8302–2.325
Nonprofit charitable organizations finances, with data by State and for top 10 instns, 1988, article, 8302–2.302
Nuclear power plant safety standards and research, design, licensing, construction, operation, and finances, with data by reactor, quarterly journal, 3352–4
Nursing home reimbursement rates of Medicaid, and ratio to private resident payments, by State, FY89, article, 9373–1.311
Oil company effective income tax rates, with background income and tax data for domestic and foreign operations, 1977-89, 3168–124
Oil company production and imports by type, and financial data, 1975-90, annual rpt, 3164–74.1
Oil company profits, refinery capacity, gasoline prices, and market share, by firm, 1991 hearing, 25528–120
Oil production disruption after Iraq invasion of Kuwait, impacts on futures prices, family budgets, and oil firms, 1990 hearings, 25408–116
Panama Canal Commission finances and activities, with Canal traffic and local govt operations, FY91, annual rpt, 9664–3
Pension Benefit Guaranty Corp activities and finances, FY91, annual rpt, 9674–1
Physicians payment by Medicare under fee schedule, methodology with data by procedure and specialty, 1992, annual rpt, 17264–1
Physicians payment by Medicare under fee schedule, practice expense estimates based on resource use compared to allowed charge method, 1991, 17266–2.9
Postal Service activities, finances, and mail volume and subsidies, FY91, annual rpt, 9864–5.3
Postal Service activities, financial statements, and employment, FY87-91, annual rpt, 9864–1
Postal Service operating costs, itemized by class of mail, FY91, annual rpt, 9864–4
Postal Service revenue and mail volume by class, and special service transactions, quarterly rpt, 9862–1
Postal Service revenue, costs, and volume, by service type and class of mail, FY91, annual rpt, 9864–2
Prison Industries (Federal) finances and operations, FY91, annual rpt, 6244–3
Prison Industries (Federal) sales, by commodity and Federal agency, FY91, annual rpt, 6244–5
Radio Free Europe and Radio Liberty broadcast and financial data, FY91, annual rpt, 10314–1
Radio frequency assignments for mobile communications, effects of auctioning frequencies, 1990, 26306–6.169
Railroad (Amtrak) finances and operations, FY91, annual rpt, 29524–1
Railroad (Amtrak) finances, executive office travel expenses and staff years, and membership dues by assn, FY88-92, GAO rpt, 26113–573
Railroad (Class I) finances and operations, detailed data by firm, class of service, and district, 1990, annual rpt, 9486–5.1
Railroad (Class I) finances and operations, detailed data by firm, class of service, and district, 1991, annual rpt, 9486–6.1
Railroad employment and finances, for ICC-regulated carriers, as of FY91, annual rpt, 9484–1
Railroad freight, by commodity and region of origin and destination, 1989, annual rpt, 7604–6
Railroad Retirement Accounts financial statements, FY91, annual rpt, 9704–1
Railroad revenue, income, freight, and rate of return, by Class I freight railroad and district, quarterly rpt, 9482–2
Reclamation Bur irrigation activities, finances, and project impacts in western US, 1990, annual rpt, 5824–12

Recycling of municipal and industrial waste, costs, revenues, and secondary products trade and related energy use and pollution reductions, 1991 hearings, 21368–139
Red Cross activities and finances, FY91, annual rpt, 29254–1
Resolution Trust Corp activities and finances, with data on savings instns conservatorships by State and instn, 1990, annual rpt, 9724–1
Savings and loan assns, FHLB 6th District insured members financial condition and operations by State, quarterly rpt, 9302–23
Savings instns economies of scale and scope, for mutual and stock instns by asset size, model description and results, 1989 technical paper, 8436–1.7
Savings instns failures, financial performance of instns under Resolution Trust Corp conservatorship, quarterly rpt, 9722–5
Savings instns, FHLB 6th and 11th District and natl cost of funds indexes, and mortgage and Treasury bill rates, monthly rpt, 9302–38
Savings instns, FHLB 7th District and natl cost of funds indexes, and mortgage rates, monthly rpt, 9302–30
Savings instns financial statements, for instns insured by Savings Assn Insurance Fund by FHLB district and State, and for FDIC-insured savings banks, 1989, annual rpt, 8434–1
Savings instns insured by Savings Assn Insurance Fund, finances by profitability group, district, and State, quarterly rpt, 8432–4
Securities industry finances, for broker-dealers and individual stock exchanges and clearing agencies, 1986-90, annual rpt, 9734–2.1
Semiconductor and related equipment sales, by US and Japanese firm, 1970s-88, annual rpt, 15034–1.1
Shipping firms combined financial statements, FY89-90, annual rpt, 7704–14.5
Small Business Admin loan and contract activity by program and firm, and financial condition, FY91, annual rpt, 9764–1
St Lawrence Seaway Dev Corp finances and activities, with Seaway cargo tonnage, and shipping costs compared to other US ports, 1990, annual rpt, 7744–1
Steel imports of US under voluntary restraint agreement, by product, customs district, and country, with US industry operating data, quarterly rpt, 9882–13
Steel trade, by product, country, and customs district, with US industry operating data, 1989-June 1992, semiannual rpt, 9882–15
Student Loan Marketing Assn activities and finances, 1991, annual rpt, 9784–1
Tax exempt organizations with unrelated business income, finances by organization type, 1987, article, 8302–2.306
Telecommunications finances, rates, and traffic for US carriers intl operations, by service type, firm, and country, 1975-90, annual rpt, 9284–17
Telephone and telegraph firms detailed finances and operations, 1990, annual rpt, 9284–6
Telephone firms borrowing under Rural Telephone Program, and financial and operating data, by State, 1991, annual rpt, 1244–2
Telephone local service charges and low-income subsidies, by region, company, and city, 1980s-91, semiannual rpt, 9282–8
Telephone rural cooperative bank financial statements, FY91, annual rpt, 1244–4
Telephone service subscribership, charges, and local and long distance firm finances and operations, late 1970s-92, semiannual rpt, 9282–7
Textile mill production, trade, sales, stocks, and material used, by product, region, and State, periodic Current Industrial Rpt series, 2506–5
Timber sales of Forest Service, expenses, and operations, by region, State, and natl forest, FY91, annual rpts, 1204–36
Transit systems finances and operations, by mode, size of fleet and urban area, region, and for 518 systems, 1990, annual rpt, 7884–4
Transit systems finances, equipment, and ridership characteristics, 1985-90, biennial rpt, 7884–8
Travel-related industries employment and receipts, for businesses near Blue Ridge Parkway, 1987, 7556–8.4
Truck and bus interstate carriers finances and operations, by district, 1990, annual rpt, 9486–5.3
Truck and warehouse services finances and inventory, by SIC 2- to 4-digit industry, 1990 survey, annual rpt, 2413–14
Truck, bus, and rail carriers regulated by ICC, employment and finances, as of FY91, annual rpt, 9484–1
Truck interstate carriers finances and operations, by district, 1990, annual rpt, 9486–5.2
Truck itemized costs per mile, finances, and operations, for agricultural carriers, 1991, annual rpt, 1311–15
Truck rates for fruit and vegetables paid by shippers and receivers, by commodity and city, and fleet itemized costs per mile, weekly rpt, 1311–22
Truck transport of household goods, financial and operating data by firm, quarterly rpt, 9482–14
Truck transport of property, financial and operating data by region and firm, quarterly rpt, 9482–5
TVA finances and operations by program and facility, FY91, annual rpt, 9804–32
Uranium enrichment facilities of DOE, financial statements, FY90-91, annual rpt, 3354–7
Uranium mining and milling industries finances and operations, with selected foreign comparisons, 1970s-90 and projected to 2005, annual rpt, 3164–82
Vending facilities run by blind on Federal and non-Federal property, finances and operations by agency and State, FY91, annual rpt, 4944–2
Voluntary agencies foreign aid programs, funding, and outlays, by agency, 1990, annual rpt, 9914–9
Warehouse services finances, by SIC 3- to 4-digit industry, 1990 survey, annual rpt, 2413–14
Workers compensation coverage, benefits, costs, and insurers performance, 1939-88, article, 4742–1.322
Workers compensation programs under Federal admin, finances and operations, FY91, annual rpt, 6504–10
see also Agricultural finance
see also Agricultural marketing
see also Agricultural production costs
see also Business assets and liabilities, specific industry
see also Capital investments, specific industry
see also Depreciation
see also Educational finance
see also Energy production costs
see also Farm income
see also Operating ratios
see also Payroll
see also Production costs
see also under By Industry in the "Index by Categories"

Business inventories
Alcoholic beverages and tobacco production, removals, stocks, and material used, by State, monthly rpt series, 8486–1
Assets and debts of private sector, balance sheets by segment, 1960-91, semiannual rpt, 9365–4.1
Auto industry finances and operations, trade by country, and prices of selected US and foreign models, monthly rpt, 9882–8
Auto production, inventories, and inventory/sales ratio, 1992 model year, annual article, 2702–1.339
Building materials production, shipments, and stocks, by type, quarterly rpt, 2042–1.6
Business statistics, detailed data for major industries and economic indicators, *Survey of Current Business*, monthly rpt, 2702–1
Business statistics, detailed data for major industries and economic indicators, 1960-91, *Survey of Current Business* biennial supplement, 2704–1
Chemical and oil products shipments, firms, trade, and use, by product, periodic Current Industrial Rpt series, 2506–8
Clay and glass production, shipments, trade, and stocks, by product, periodic Current Industrial Rpt series, 2506–9
Cotton (long staple) production, prices, exports, stocks, and mill use, monthly rpt, 1309–12
Cotton linters production, stocks, use, and prices, monthly rpt, 1309–10
Cotton, wool, and synthetic fiber production, prices, trade, and use, periodic situation rpt with articles, 1561–1
Department store inventory price indexes, by class of item, monthly table, 6762–7
Economic indicators and components, and Fed Reserve 4th District business and financial conditions, monthly chartbook, 9377–10
Economic indicators and components, current data and annual trends, monthly rpt, 23842–1.1; 23842–1.3
Economic indicators compounded annual rates of change, monthly rpt, 9391–3
Fertilizer (inorganic) shipments, trade, use, and firms, by product and State, with stocks, 1991, annual Current Industrial Rpt, 2506–8.13

Flow-of-funds accounts, savings, investments, and credit statements, quarterly rpt, 9365–3.3
Food (processed) production and stocks by State, shipments, exports, ingredients, and use, periodic Current Industrial Rpt series, 2506–4
Forecasts of economic indicators, 1992-93 and trends from 1948, annual article, 9383–6.301
Forecasts of economic indicators, 1993-94 and trends from 1948, annual article, 9383–6.303
Hazardous substances industrial releases and reduction methods under EPA regulation, with chemical stocks and use, facility directory, 1987-89, annual CD-ROM, 9234–7
Imports and tariff provisions effect on US industries and products, investigations with background financial and operating data, series, 9886–4
Imports injury to US industries from foreign subsidized products and sales at less than fair value, investigations with background financial and operating data, series, 9886–19
Imports injury to US industries from foreign subsidized products, investigations with background financial and operating data, series, 9886–15
Imports injury to US industries from sales at less than fair value, investigations with background financial and operating data, series, 9886–14
Input-output structure of US economy, detailed interindustry transactions for 84 industries, and components of final demand, 1987, annual article, 2702–1.316
Input-output structure of US economy, detailed interindustry transactions for 541 industries, and components of final demand, 1982 benchmark data, 2708–17
Inventories and ratio to sales, by industry div, 1950-91, annual rpt, 204–1.1; 204–1.3
Lumber, paper, and related products shipments, trade, stocks, and use, periodic Current Industrial Rpt series, 2506–7
Machinery and equipment production, shipments, trade, stocks, orders, use, and firms, by product, periodic Current Industrial Rpt series, 2506–12
Manufacturing annual survey, 1990: establishments, employment, finances, inventories, and energy use, by SIC 2- to 4-digit industry, 2506–14.2
Manufacturing annual survey, 1990: finances and operations, by SIC 2- and 3-digit industry and State, 2506–14.3
Manufacturing shipments, inventories, and orders, by SIC 2- to 3-digit industry, monthly Current Industrial Rpt, 2506–3.1
Metals (intermediate product) shipments, trade, and inventories, by product, periodic Current Industrial Rpt series, 2506–11
Metals (primary) production, shipments, trade, stocks, and material used, by product, periodic Current Industrial Rpt series, 2506–10
Middle Atlantic States manufacturing business outlook, monthly survey rpt, 9387–11
Mineral Industry Surveys, commodity reviews of production, trade, stocks, and use, monthly rpt series, 5612–1
Mineral Industry Surveys, commodity reviews of production, trade, stocks, and use, quarterly rpt series, 5612–2
Mobile home placements and prices by State, and dealer inventories, by region, monthly rpt, 2382–1
Multinatl firms US affiliates, finances, and operations, by industry, world area of parent firm, and State, 1989-90, annual rpt, 2704–4
Multinatl US firms and foreign affiliates finances and operations, by industry and country, 1989 benchmark survey, annual rpt, 2704–5
Natl income and product accounts and components, *Survey of Current Business*, monthly rpt, 2702–1.23
Natl income and product accounts, comprehensive accounts and components, benchmark revisions, 1929-88, 2708–5
Natl income and product accounts, comprehensive accounts and components, *Survey of Current Business*, monthly rpt, 2702–1.28
Nonprofit charitable and other tax exempt organizations finances, by category and size of assets and contributions, 1988, annual article, 8302–2.315
Nonprofit charitable organizations finances, with data by State and for top 10 instns, 1988, article, 8302–2.302
Recessions impacts on business loans and inventories, late 1940s-91, article, 9391–1.315
Retail trade sales and inventories, by kind of business, region, and selected State, MSA, and city, monthly rpt, 2413–3
Retail trade sales, inventories, purchases, gross margin, and accounts receivable, by SIC 2- to 4-digit kind of business and form of ownership, 1990, annual rpt, 2413–5
Rice shipments, by end use, package size, and State of origin and destination, 1960s-89, biennial rpt, 1564–11
Sales related to inventories, by industry sector, model description and results, late 1960s-91, article, 9389–1.302
Southeastern US manufacturing conditions, survey methodology and selected results, Dec 1991-July 1992, article, 9371–1.307
Statistical Abstract of US, 1992 annual data compilation, 2324–1.27; 2324–1.28
Tax (income) returns filed, by type of filer, selected income items, quarterly rpt, 8302–2.1
Tax (income) returns of corporations, income and tax items by asset size and detailed industry, 1989, annual rpt, 8304–4; 8304–21
Tax (income) returns of partnerships, income statement and balance sheet items, by industry group, 1990, annual article, 8302–2.314
Tax (income) returns of sole proprietorships, income statement items, by industry group, 1990, annual article, 8302–2.317
Tax exempt organizations finances, with data by type, size, State, and for largest organizations, late 1940s-80s, compilation of papers, 8308–35
Textile mill production, trade, sales, stocks, and material used, by product, region, and State, periodic Current Industrial Rpt series, 2506–5
Truck and warehouse services finances and inventory, by SIC 2- to 4-digit industry, 1990 survey, annual rpt, 2413–14
Vaccine and toxoid shipments, by product type, 1987-90, 4205–22
Wholesale trade sales and inventories, by SIC 2- to 3-digit kind of business, monthly rpt, 2413–7
see also Agricultural stocks
see also Business orders
see also Coal stocks
see also Energy stocks and inventories
see also Petroleum stocks

Business loans
see Commercial credit

Business machines and equipment
Banks and thrifts finances and operations by deposit size, Fed Reserve functional cost analysis, 1991, annual rpt, 9364–6
County Business Patterns, 1989: employment, establishments, and payroll, by SIC 2- to 4-digit industry and county, annual State rpt series, 2326–8
County Business Patterns, 1990: employment, establishments, and payroll, by SIC 2- to 4-digit industry and county, annual State rpt series, 2326–6
Electric utilities privately owned, finances and operations, detailed data, 1990, annual rpt, 3164–23
Employment, earnings, and hours, by SIC 1- to 4-digit industry, monthly 1989-Feb 1992, annual rpt, 6744–4
Employment of minorities and women, by occupation, SIC 1- to 3-digit industry, State, and MSA, 1991, annual rpt, 9244–1
Exports and imports between US and outlying areas, by detailed commodity and mode of transport, 1991, annual rpt, 2424–11
Exports and imports of US, by country and detailed commodity, monthly rpt, 2422–12
Exports and imports of US, by Harmonized System 6-digit commodity and country, 1991, annual rpt, 2424–13
Exports and imports of US, by selected country, country group, and commodity group, 1991, annual rpt, 2044–37
Exports and imports of US, by transport mode, country, and SITC 1- to 3-digit commodity, 1991, annual rpt, 2424–12
Exports, imports, and balances of US for manufactured goods, by SITC 2-digit commodity and country, quarterly rpt, 2042–35
Exports of US, detailed Schedule B commodities with countries of destination, 1991, annual rpt, 2424–10
Furniture (office) shipments and exports, by product, 1991, annual Current Industrial Rpt, 2506–7.8
House of Representatives salaries, expenses, and contingent fund disbursement, detailed listings, quarterly rpt, 21942–1
Imports of US given duty-free treatment for value of US material sent abroad, by commodity and country, 1987-90, annual rpt, 9884–14

Injuries from use of consumer products, by severity, victim age, and detailed product, 1991, annual rpt, 9164–6
Input-output structure of US economy, detailed interindustry transactions for 84 industries, and components of final demand, 1987, annual article, 2702–1.316
Labor productivity, indexes of output, hours, and employment by SIC 2- to 4-digit industry, 1967-90, annual rpt, 6824–1.3
Manufacturing annual survey, 1990: finances and operations, by SIC 2- to 4-digit industry, series, 2506–14
Manufacturing census, 1987: concentration of largest firms measured by value added, and for shipments by SIC 2- and 4-digit industry, subject rpt, 2497–6
Manufacturing census, 1987: shipments of manufacturers products, by customer class and SIC 2- and 4-digit industry, subject rpt, 2497–4
Military prime contract awards, by detailed procurement category, FY88-91, annual rpt, 3544–18
Multinatl US firms and foreign affiliates finances and operations, by industry and country, 1989 benchmark survey, annual rpt, 2704–5
Natl income and product accounts, comprehensive accounts and components, benchmark revisions, 1929-88, 2708–5
Natl income and product accounts, comprehensive accounts and components, *Survey of Current Business*, monthly rpt, 2702–1.28
Natural gas interstate pipeline company detailed financial and operating data, by firm, 1990, annual rpt, 3164–38
Occupational injury and illness rates, by SIC 2- to 4-digit industry, 1989-90, annual rpt, 6844–7
Occupational injury and illness rates, by SIC 2- to 4-digit industry, 1990, annual rpt, 6844–1
OECD trade, total and for 4 major countries, and US trade by country, by commodity, 1980-90, world area rpt series, 9116–1
Price indexes (producer), by stage of processing and detailed commodity, monthly rpt, 6762–6
Price indexes (producer), by stage of processing and detailed commodity, monthly 1991, annual rpt, 6764–2
Science, engineering, and technical employment in manufacturing, by field and industry, 1989, triennial rpt, 9627–23
Shipments, trade, use, and firms, for office machines by product, 1991, annual Current Industrial Rpt, 2506–12.2
Tax (income) returns of corporations, income and tax items by asset size and detailed industry, 1989, annual rpt, 8304–4; 8304–21
Technology-intensive capital investment relation to productivity growth, 1950s-89, article, 9385–1.310
Thefts, and value of property stolen and recovered, by property type, 1991, annual rpt, 6224–2.1
see also Computer industry and products
see also Office supplies
see also under By Commodity in the "Index by Categories"

Business management
Banks financial performance, risk assessment, and regulation, 1991 annual conf papers, 9375–7
Banks mgmt efficiency indicator, with results for surviving and failed banks, mid 1980s, article, 9379–1.302
Corporations securities holdings by shareholder type, and mgmt and executive pay issues, with data by company, 1991 hearing, 25248–130
County Business Patterns, 1989: employment, establishments, and payroll, by SIC 2- to 4-digit industry and county, annual State rpt series, 2326–8
County Business Patterns, 1990: employment, establishments, and payroll, by SIC 2- to 4-digit industry and county, annual State rpt series, 2326–6
Exports and imports of services, direct and among multinatl firms affiliates, by industry and world area, 1986-91, article, 2702–1.336
Input-output structure of US economy, detailed interindustry transactions for 541 industries, and components of final demand, 1982 benchmark data, 2708–17
Japan *keiretsu* and independent corporations ownership and concentration indicators, 1984, technical paper, 9366–6.288
Minority- and woman-owned businesses and owner characteristics, by industry, employment and sales size, and form of ownership, 1987 survey, 2328–59
Minority Business Dev Centers mgmt and financial aid, and characteristics of businesses, by region and State, FY91, annual rpt, 2104–6
Multinatl US firms and foreign affiliates finances and operations, by industry and country, 1989 benchmark survey, annual rpt, 2704–5
Natural gas interstate pipeline company detailed financial and operating data, by firm, 1990, annual rpt, 3164–38
Occupational injury and illness rates, by SIC 2- to 4-digit industry, 1989-90, annual rpt, 6844–7
Occupational Outlook Handbook, 1992-93, biennial rpt, 6744–1
Pacific territories population and housing detailed characteristics, by location, 1990 Census of Population and Housing, series, 2551–8
Small business use of Census Bur economic data in planning decisions, case studies, 1991 rpt, 2628–33
see also Business outlook and attitude surveys
see also Consultants
see also Employee performance and appraisal
see also Executives and managers
see also Industrial purchasing
see also Industrial siting
see also Labor-management relations, general
see also Personnel management

Business orders
Aircraft orders and deliveries of commercial carriers, by aircraft type, quarterly rpt, 7502–16
Business statistics, detailed data for major industries and economic indicators, *Survey of Current Business*, monthly rpt, 2702–1
Business statistics, detailed data for major industries and economic indicators, 1960-91, *Survey of Current Business* biennial supplement, 2704–1
Cancellation and completion of contracts, related layoffs and subsequent recalls, 2nd half 1988, 6406–6.36
Cancellation and completion of contracts, related layoffs and unemployment insurance claims, quarterly press release, 6742–23
Cancellation and completion of contracts, related layoffs and unemployment insurance claims, 1990, annual rpt, 6744–18
Economic indicators and components, current data and annual trends, monthly rpt, 23842–1.3
Machinery and equipment production, shipments, trade, stocks, orders, use, and firms, by product, periodic Current Industrial Rpt series, 2506–12
Manufacturing shipments and new and unfilled orders, 1950-91, annual rpt, 204–1.3
Manufacturing shipments, inventories, and orders, by SIC 2- to 3-digit industry, monthly Current Industrial Rpt, 2506–3.1
Metals industries economic performance indicators and indexes, by commodity, monthly rpt, 5602–5
Middle Atlantic States manufacturing business outlook, monthly survey rpt, 9387–11
Militarily strategic manufacturing industries finances, operations, and intl competitiveness, series, 2026–1
Minority Business Dev Centers mgmt and financial aid, and characteristics of businesses, by region and State, FY91, annual rpt, 2104–6
Natural gas interstate pipeline company reserves and production, by firm, 1963-91 and deliverability projected to 2011, last issue of annual rpt, 3164–33
Pollution abatement capital and operating costs, by SIC 2- to 4-digit industry and State, 1990, annual Current Industrial Rpt, 2506–3.6
Ships under foreign flag owned by US firms and foreign affiliates, by type, owner, and country of registry and construction, as of July 1991, semiannual rpt, 7702–3
Statistical Abstract of US, 1992 annual data compilation, 2324–1.27
Textile mill production, trade, sales, stocks, and material used, by product, region, and State, periodic Current Industrial Rpt series, 2506–5
Uranium marketing, contracts, prices, utility shipments, and trade, 1982-91 and projected to 2001, annual rpt, 3164–65.2
Uranium mining and milling industries finances and operations, with selected foreign comparisons, 1970s-90 and projected to 2005, annual rpt, 3164–82

Business outlook and attitude surveys
Banks and thrifts contracts with computer data processing vendors, involvement of illegal business transactions, and instn and vendor views, 1985-90, GAO rpt, 26119–374

Farm credit conditions and real estate values, Fed Reserve 11th District, quarterly rpt, 9379–11
Farm credit conditions, earnings, and expenses, Fed Reserve 9th District, quarterly rpt, 9383–11
Food processing for school lunch programs, donations processed, contracts, and processors problems with State reporting requirements, with data by State, 1989-91, GAO rpt, 26113–555
Food processing industry location factors, rankings, 1988 survey, 9088–37
Hazardous substances occupational exposure, employer compliance with info and training regulations, employer views by firm size and industry div, 1989-91, GAO rpt, 26121–456
Home-based workers by selected characteristics, and views, 1989, article, 1702–1.307
Japan R&D activities of US firms, employee characteristics, and mgmt views on benefits and drawbacks, 1991 rpt, 9628–88
Middle Atlantic States manufacturing business outlook, monthly survey rpt, 9387–11
Milk handlers (cooperative and proprietary) performance, views of dairy farmers in southern States, 1989 survey, 1128–67
Milk producer prices received from cooperatives and proprietary handlers, by characteristics of cooperative membership and operation, 1989 survey, 1128–68
North Central States business and economic conditions, Fed Reserve 9th District, quarterly journal, 9383–19
North Central States farm credit conditions and economic devs, Fed Reserve 7th District, monthly rpt, 9375–10
Office location factors, rankings of importance, and ratings for Chicago, 1992 working paper, 9375–13.78
R&D spending of major firms, by industry group, planned 1990-91, 9626–6.38
Real estate assets marketing activities of Resolution Trust Corp, real estate industry views, 1991 survey, GAO rpt, 26119–422
Real estate supply and demand, housing and commercial property market activity indicators by region, quarterly rpt, 9292–6
Sexual harassment complaints and company policies, 1988 survey, hearing, 21348–120
Small Business Admin loan guarantee program participants finances, operations, characteristics, and views, 1991 survey, 9768–25
Small business product and service R&D grants of Fed Govt, indicators of commercial success, FY88-90, chartbook, 9768–23
Small business views on economic outlook and opportunities, 1991 survey, hearings, 23848–230
Tax (income) admin and compliance issues, and taxpayer views, 1991 conf, 8304–25
West Central States farm real estate values, farm loan trends, and regional farm price index, Fed Reserve 10th District, quarterly rpt, 9381–16.1
see also Survey of Real Estate Trends
see also Survey of Southeastern Manufacturing Conditions

Business services
see Accounting and auditing
see Advertising
see Consultants
see Courier services
see Credit bureaus and agencies
see Direct marketing
see Employment services
see Public relations

Busing
see School busing

Butler, Gertrude S.
"Foreign Ownership of U.S. Agricultural Land Through Dec. 31, 1991: County-Level Data", 1584–3

Buxton, Boyd M.
"Supply Response to Price Changes for Selected Vegetables", 1561–11.302
"U.S. Fruit Industry and the North American Free Trade Agreement", 1561–6.304

Buzzanell, Peter
"Cuba's Sugar Industry—Facing a New World Order", 1561–14.302

Byce, Chuck
"Students at Less-Than-4-Year Institutions: 1987 National Postsecondary Student Aid Study", 4846–3.12

Byelarus
Agricultural production, prices, and trade, for former USSR republics, 1960s-91 and forecast 1992, annual rpt, 1524–4.1
Economic, social, political, and geographic summary data, by country, 1992, annual factbook, 9114–2
Embassies of US in former Soviet republics and Baltic States, positions planned by function, and filled, 1992, GAO rpt, 26123–403
Energy supply and use, and social, economic, and political indicators for former Soviet Republics and Baltic States, 1989-90, 3168–126
Energy use and production of former USSR Republics, by fuel type, 1990, annual rpt, 3164–84.2
Exports and imports of US with Communist and transitional economy countries, by detailed commodity and country, quarterly rpt with articles, 9882–2
Livestock and meat inventories, use, and imports, by former USSR republic, 1986-93, semiannual rpt, 1925–33.2
Population size and characteristics of former Soviet Republics and Baltic States, 1989-92, 9118–19
UN voting record and share of votes in agreement with US, by issue, country, and world area, 1991, annual rpt, 7004–18

Cable television
Copyright royalty fees from CATV, and funds available for distribution, 1990-91, annual rpt, 26404–2
County Business Patterns, 1989: employment, establishments, and payroll, by SIC 2- to 4-digit industry and county, annual State rpt series, 2326–8
County Business Patterns, 1990: employment, establishments, and payroll, by SIC 2- to 4-digit industry and county, annual State rpt series, 2326–6
CPI by component for US city average, and by selected metro area, region, and population size, monthly rpt, 6762–2
Equipment shipments, trade, use, and firms, for electronic communications systems and related products, 1991, annual Current Industrial Rpt, 2506–12.35
Finances and operations, by SIC 2- to 4-digit industry, forecast 1992, annual rpt, 2044–28
Finances of communications services, itemized revenue and expenses by SIC 2- to 4-digit kind of business, 1990, annual rpt, 2413–15
Households entertainment spending, recreation participation by activity, and video product and pet ownership, 1970s-90, article, 1702–1.303
Licensing activities of FCC, by class of operation, FY91, annual rpt, 9284–4
Mail volume to and from households, use, and views, by class, source, content, and household characteristics, FY87-90, annual rpt, 9864–10
Price indexes (producer), by stage of processing and detailed commodity, monthly rpt, 6762–6
Price indexes (producer), by stage of processing and detailed commodity, monthly 1991, annual rpt, 6764–2
Statistical Abstract of US, 1992 annual data compilation, 2324–1.18

Cacchione, David A.
"Bottom and Near-Bottom Sediment Dynamics in Norton Sound, Alaska", 2176–1.40

Caces, M. Fe
"Alcohol Use and Physically Risky Behavior Among Adolescents", 4482–1.308
"Trends in Alcohol-Related Morbidity Among Short-Stay Community Hospital Discharges, U.S., 1979-89", 4486–1.16
"U.S. Alcohol Epidemiologic Data Reference Manual. Volume 3: County Alcohol Problem Indicators, 1979-85", 4488–10.4

Cain, Glen G.
"Using SIPP To Analyze Black-White Differences in Youth Employment", 2626–10.146

Caithamer, D. F.
"Trends in Duck Breeding Populations, 1955-92", 5504–30

Calem, Paul S.
"Delaware Valley Mortgage Plan: An Analysis Using HMDA Data", 9387–8.266
"Location and Quality Effects of Mergers", 9387–8.268
"Reputation Acquisition and Persistence of Moral Hazard in Credit Markets", 9387–8.275
"Strange Behavior of the Credit Card Market", 9387–1.301

California
AIDS patients costs and service use under Medicaid, for California, 1984-86, article, 4652–1.301
Almond production, 1990-92, annual rpt, 1621–18.4
Banks (insured commercial and savings) deposits by instn, State, MSA, and county, as of June 1991, annual regional rpt, 9295–3.6

Banks (multinatl) US branches assets and liabilities, total and for 3 States, monthly rpt, quarterly data, 9362–1.4
Bean (dried) prices by State, market activity, and foreign and US production, use, stocks, and trade, weekly rpt, 1311–17
Bee colony rentals, and pollinated crop value, by crop, 1989, hearings, 25168–78
Birds (northern spotted owl) conservation methods in Pacific Northwest, findings and recommendations, 1990 rpt, 1208–385
Birds (northern spotted owl) conservation methods in Pacific Northwest, timber industry impacts, and Federal and State spending, 1980s-95, 1208–388
Celery acreage planted and growing, by growing area, monthly rpt, 1621–14
Coal production and mines by county, prices, productivity, miners, and reserves, by mining method and State, 1990-91, annual rpt, 3164–25
Dairy prices, by product and selected area, with related marketing data, 1991, annual rpt, 1317–1
Deaths and rates, by detailed location, cause, and demographic characteristics, 1989, US Vital Statistics annual rpt, 4144–3.1
Employment, earnings, and hours, by selected SIC 1- to 4-digit industry, State, and for 275 MSAs, 1987-92, 6748–81
Employment in California, impacts of changes on employment in nearby States, regression results, 1992 article, 9393–8.306
Fed Govt spending in States and local areas, by type, State, county, and city, FY91, annual rpt, 2464–3
Fed Govt spending in States, by type, program, agency, and State, FY91, annual rpt, 2464–2
Fertilizer use and application rates, by type and crop, for California, 1990, 1616–1.2
Fishing (ocean sport) activities, and catch by species, by angler characteristics and State, 1987-89, annual coastal area rpt, 2166–17.2
Fruit and vegetable processing industry in California, workers affected by plant closings, 1977-86, working paper, 6366–6.5
Grape shipments from California and arrivals by city by mode of transport, prices, and production, by variety, 1970s-90, annual rpt, 1311–25
Grapes crushed and purchased, and grower prices and returns, for California, by type and variety, 1990-91, annual rpt, 1311–30
HHS financial aid, by program, recipient, State, and city, FY91, annual regional listing, 4004–3.9
Hospital deaths of Medicare patients, actual and expected rates by diagnosis, and hospital characteristics, by instn, FY90 annual State rpt, 4654–14.5
Hospital wage index, effect of occupation mix adjustment, by California labor market area, 1988, 17206–2.31
Hospitals in rural areas, Medicare admission rates and charges, by instn, patient, and care characteristics, mid 1980s, 17206–2.33
Housing census, 1990: summary unit characteristics, by householder race and age, county, place, and urban-rural location, State rpt, 2471–1.6
Input-output model of BEA, regional multipliers by industry and State, and methodology, 1992 guide, 2708–47
Jail population and overcrowding by county, and construction funding, for California, 1980s, 6066–30.1
Lumber mills, operations, log use by species and ownership, and residue use, for California by product and county, 1988, 1208–108
Marine mammals and birds incidental catch in California net fishing operations, 1984-85, 14738–13
Metals (nonferrous) production in 5 western States, and prices, for 5 metals, 1848-1990, 5608–178
Military prime contract awards, by contractor, service branch, State, and city, FY91, annual rpt, 3544–22
Mineral Industry Surveys, State reviews of production, 1991, preliminary annual rpt, 5614–6
Minerals Yearbook, Vol 2, 1990: State review of production and sales by commodity, and business activity, annual rpt, 5604–22.6
Multinatl firms US affiliates finances and operations, by industry, country of parent firm, and State, 1987, 2708–48
Occupational repetitive motion injury rates by selected industry, with data for California, 1980s, hearing, 21408–128
Oil and gas dev impacts on California OCS water quality, marine life, and sediments, by site, 1986-90, annual rpt, 5734–11
Otters (sea) population, and relocation project results, for California, 1982-90, annual rpt, 5504–12
Otters (sea) population off California coast, 1982-91, annual rpt, 14734–1
Peppers (dried chili and paprika) acreage and production in California and New Mexico, 1971-91, FAS annual circular, 1925–15.1
Physicians, by specialty, age, sex, and location of training and practice, 1990, State rpt, 4116–6.5
Pistachio production, 1990-92, annual rpt, 1621–18.7
Pollutant concentrations in coastal and estuarine fish, shellfish, and environment, late 1970s-89, local area rpt, 2176–3.16
Population and housing census, 1990: detailed geographic coverage, State CD-ROM, 2551–9.9
Population and housing census, 1990: population and housing characteristics, detailed geographic coverage, State CD-ROM, 2551–10.5; 2551–10.6; 2551–10.7
Population and housing census, 1990: summary characteristics, by county, subdiv, and place, State rpt, 2551–7.6
Population census, 1990: population characteristics and living arrangements, by county, place, and urban-rural location, State rpt, 2531–1.6
Potato production, acreage, prices, and shipments, for 7 major producer States, and compared to other States, 1970s-92, annual rpt, 1311–29
Radiation and other pollutant releases from DOE contractor research lab and nuclear weapons facilities, monitoring results, 1991 annual site rpt, 3324–2.3; 3324–2.10; 3324–2.11; 3324–2.13
Rice market activities, prices, inspections, sales, trade, supply, and use, for US and selected foreign markets, weekly rpt, 1313–8
Rice production, practices, costs, and land tenure, by production area, 1988, 1568–309
Rice stocks on and off farms and total in all positions, periodic rpt, 1621–7
Shipborne commerce (domestic) of US, freight by major commodity group, vessel type, and port, 1987-89, annual rpt, 7704–7
Statistical Abstract of US, 1992 annual data compilation, 2324–1
Timber in northwestern US and British Columbia, production, prices, trade, and employment, quarterly rpt, 1202–3
Truck use of intermodal containers over legal weight for hwy use, California enforcement activity, and container traffic by mode, 1960s-88, hearing, 21648–65
Unemployed displaced workers job search and placement aid effectiveness, relation to previous employment and other characteristics, 1979-87 studies, 15496–1.14
Water (groundwater) supply, quality, chemistry, and use, 1987-88, local area rpt, 5666–28.17
Water (groundwater) supply, quality, chemistry, other characteristics, and use, 1992 regional rpt, 5666–25.14
Water quality, chemistry, hydrology, and other characteristics, 1991 local area study, 5666–27.32
Water quality, chemistry, hydrology, and other characteristics, 1992 local area study, 5666–27.31; 5666–27.35
Wildlife habitats assessment use of forest inventories, with data for northern coastal California, as of 1985, 1208–414
see also Alameda County, Calif.
see also Anaheim, Calif.
see also Fairfield, Calif.
see also Garden Grove, Calif.
see also Inyo County, Calif.
see also Kern County, Calif.
see also Long Beach, Calif.
see also Los Angeles, Calif.
see also Los Angeles County, Calif.
see also Monterey, Calif.
see also Napa, Calif.
see also Oakland, Calif.
see also Porterville, Calif.
see also Riverside, Calif.
see also Sacramento, Calif.
see also Salinas, Calif.
see also San Bernardino, Calif.
see also San Bernardino County, Calif.
see also San Diego, Calif.
see also San Francisco, Calif.
see also San Jose, Calif.
see also Santa Ana, Calif.
see also Santa Barbara, Calif.
see also Seaside, Calif.
see also Tulare County, Calif.
see also Vallejo, Calif.
see also Visalia, Calif.

see also under By State in the "Index by Categories"
Callis, Robert R.
"Current Housing Reports, Series H-111. Housing Vacancies and Homeownership, Annual Statistics: 1991", 2484–1
Cambodia
Agricultural trade of US, by detailed commodity and country, 1991, semiannual rpt, 1522–4
AID economic aid to developing countries, obligations and disbursements by country, quarterly rpt, 9912–4
Economic and military aid and loans from US and intl agencies, by program and country, FY46-91, annual rpt, 9914–5
Economic and social conditions of developing countries from 1960s, and Intl Dev Cooperation Agency and AID activities and funding, FY91-93, annual rpt, 9904–4
Economic, social, political, and geographic summary data, by country, 1992, annual factbook, 9114–2
Export licensing, monitoring, and enforcement activities, FY91, annual rpt, 2024–1
Exports and imports of US, by transport mode, country, and SITC 1- to 3-digit commodity, 1991, annual rpt, 2424–12
Exports and imports of US with Communist and transitional economy countries, by detailed commodity and country, quarterly rpt with articles, 9882–2
Human rights conditions in 170 countries, and US economic and military aid, 1991, annual rpt, 21384–3
Military spending, arms trade, and force strengths, with govt spending and population, by country, 1979-89, annual rpt, 9824–1
Minerals Yearbook, Vol 3, 1989: foreign country review of production, trade, and policy, by commodity, annual rpt, 5604–35.2
Population size, growth rates, and components of change, by country, projected 1990-2020 and trends from 1950, biennial rpt, 2324–9
Refugee migration, and intl aid programs, by world area and country of origin and asylum, 1991, annual rpt, 7004–15
Refugees from Indochina, arrivals, and departures, by country of origin and resettlement, camp, and ethnicity, monthly rpt, 7002–4
UN voting record and share of votes in agreement with US, by issue, country, and world area, 1991, annual rpt, 7004–18
Cambridge, Mass.
Housing and households characteristics, unit and neighborhood quality, and journey to work by MSA location, for 11 MSAs, 1985 survey, supplement, 2485–8
Housing and households detailed characteristics, and unit and neighborhood quality, by location, 1989 survey, MSA rpt, 2485–6.10
Cameroon
Agricultural trade of US, by detailed commodity and country, 1991, annual rpt, 1524–8
Agricultural trade of US, by detailed commodity and country, 1991, semiannual rpt, 1522–4
AID economic aid to developing countries, obligations and disbursements by country, quarterly rpt, 9912–4
AID loans repayment status and terms by program and country, and status of predecessor agency loans, quarterly rpt, 9912–3
Background Notes, summary social, political, and economic data, 1992 rpt, 7006–2.22
Economic and military aid and loans from US and intl agencies, by program and country, FY46-91, annual rpt, 9914–5
Economic and social conditions of developing countries from 1960s, and Intl Dev Cooperation Agency and AID activities and funding, FY91-93, annual rpt, 9904–4
Economic, social, political, and geographic summary data, by country, 1992, annual factbook, 9114–2
Exports and imports of US, by commodity and country, 1980-90, world area rpt, 9116–1.2
Exports and imports of US, by transport mode, country, and SITC 1- to 3-digit commodity, 1991, annual rpt, 2424–12
Exports of US, detailed Schedule B commodities with countries of destination, 1991, annual rpt, 2424–10
Fertilizer producer subsidy elimination, effectiveness of AID support of Cameroon govt reforms, 1987-92, 9916–1.76
Human rights conditions in 170 countries, and US economic and military aid, 1991, annual rpt, 21384–3
Military aid of US, arms sales, and training programs costs and budget requests, by program, world region, and country, FY91-93, annual rpt, 7144–13
Military spending, arms trade, and force strengths, with govt spending and population, by country, 1979-89, annual rpt, 9824–1
Minerals Yearbook, Vol 3, 1989: foreign country review of production, trade, and policy, by commodity, annual rpt, 5604–35.1
Population size, growth rates, and components of change, by country, projected 1990-2020 and trends from 1950, biennial rpt, 2324–9
Refugee migration, and intl aid programs, by world area and country of origin and asylum, 1991, annual rpt, 7004–15
UN voting record and share of votes in agreement with US, by issue, country, and world area, 1991, annual rpt, 7004–18
Camp, Linda D.
"Current Water Resources Activities in Ohio, 1991", 5666–26.23
Campaign funds
Fed Election Commission activities, and campaign finances, various periods 1975-91, annual rpt, 9274–1
Fed Election Commission activities, campaign finances, elections, and procedures, press release series, 9276–1
Finances reported to Fed Election Commission, by type of filer, 1990 natl elections, biennial rpt series, 9276–2
Independent expenditures of firms and assns for campaign-related internal communications, by organization, location, and candidate, 1991-92, biennial rpt, 9274–3
Presidential election campaign fund contribution checkoffs on tax returns, FY91 and cumulative from FY72, annual rpt, 8304–3.1
Presidential election campaign fund contributions from income tax return checkoff, receipts and outlays, mid 1970s-91 and alternative projections to 1993, hearing, 21428–10
Statistical Abstract of US, 1992 annual data compilation, 2324–1.8
see also Political action committees
Campany, Sarah O.
"Profiles in Safety and Health: Retail Grocery Stores", 6722–1.339
Campbell, Jean P.
"Water-Quality Trends in New Jersey Streams", 5666–27.27
Camping
County Business Patterns, 1989: employment, establishments, and payroll, by SIC 2- to 4-digit industry and county, annual State rpt series, 2326–8
County Business Patterns, 1990: employment, establishments, and payroll, by SIC 2- to 4-digit industry and county, annual State rpt series, 2326–6
Fires (wild) and acreage burned, by type of land, ownership, cause, region, and State, 1984-90, annual rpt, 1204–4
Forest Service activities and finances, by region and State, FY91, annual rpt, 1204–1.1
Forests (natl) recreational use, by type of activity and State, 1991, annual rpt, 1204–17
Injuries from use of consumer products, by severity, victim age, and detailed product, 1991, annual rpt, 9164–6
Natl park system visits and overnight stays, by park and State, monthly rpt, 5542–4
Natl park system visits and overnight stays, by park and State, 1991, annual rpt, 5544–12
Public lands acreage, grants, use, revenues, and allocations, by State, FY91, annual rpt, 5724–1.2
Tax (income) returns of sole proprietorships, income statement items, by industry group, 1990, annual article, 8302–2.317; 8302–2.320
Travel to US, by characteristics of visit and traveler, world area of origin, and US destination, 1991 survey, annual rpt, 2904–12
Washington and Oregon coastal areas tourism and recreation facilities and economic impacts, by county, 1983-88, 5738–40.3
Wilderness area camping impacts effects on plants and soils, 1979-90 studies, 1208–395
Campus security
Bombing incidents, casualties, and damage, by target, circumstances, and State, 1991, annual rpt, 6224–5
Condition of Education, detail for elementary, secondary, and higher education, 1920s-91 and projected to 2002, annual rpt, 4824–1
Crime victimization rates, by victim and offender characteristics, circumstances, and offense, 1990 survey, annual rpt, 6066–3.47

Eighth grade class of 1988: educational performance and conditions, characteristics, attitudes, activities, and plans, natl longitudinal survey, series, 4826–9
Juvenile facilities compensatory education programs activities, participant and staff characteristics, and outcomes, 1991 rpt, 4808–40.4
Law enforcement personnel, and crimes by offense, by higher education instn, 1991, annual rpt, 6224–2.1; 6224–2.3
Natl Education Goals progress indicators, by State, 1992, annual rpt, 15914–1
Principals views on safety, discipline, and student drug use, for elementary and secondary schools, 1991 survey, 4826–1.32
Public opinion on crime and crime-related issues, by respondent characteristics, data compilation, 1992 annual rpt, 6064–6.2
Terrorism incidents in US, related activity, and casualties, by attack type, target, group, and location, 1991, annual rpt, 6224–6

Canada

Acid rain environmental, economic, and health effects, and pollutant emissions, 1985-89 and alternative projections to 2030, 14358–4
Agricultural and beverage imports of Canada, total and from US, by commodity, 1988-91, article, 1925–34.335
Agricultural production, prices, and trade, by country, 1980s and forecast 1992, annual world region rpt, 1524–4.3
Agricultural trade by commodity and country, prices, and world market devs, monthly rpt, 1922–12
Agricultural trade of US, by detailed commodity and country, 1991, annual rpt, 1524–8
Agricultural trade of US, by detailed commodity and country, 1991, semiannual rpt, 1522–4
AIDS and tuberculosis cases in prisons, test results, and control and treatment policies, by location, 1990 survey, annual rpt, 6064–22
Alfalfa feed products, industry competitiveness of US and Canada, investigation with background financial and operating data and foreign comparisons, 1991 rpt, 9886–4.180
Auto and auto parts trade, production, and labor conditions, for US and compared to Canada and Mexico, 1950s-90, 6366–3.28
Auto industry finances and operations, trade by country, and prices of selected US and foreign models, monthly rpt, 9882–8
Auto parts trade with Japan and other countries, 1985-90 and forecast to 1994, annual rpt, 2004–10
Birds (duck) breeding population, by species, State, and Canada Province, 1991-92 and trends from 1955, annual rpt, 5504–30
Birds (waterfowl) hunter harvest and unretrieved kills, and duck stamps sold, by species, State, Canada Province, and flyway, 1990-91, annual rpt, 5504–28
Birds (waterfowl) population, habitat conditions, and migratory flight forecasts, for Canada and US by region, 1992 and trends from 1955, annual rpt, 5504–27
Birds (woodcock) population in US and Canada from 1968, and hunter harvest, by State, 1992, annual rpt, 5504–11
Boundary waters of Canada and US, Intl Joint Commission activities, biennial rpt, discontinued, 14644–3
Cancer (breast) risk relation to breast density, for Canada, 1992 article, 4472–1.332
Coal exports of US to Canada by mode of transport, and overseas, by State of origin, quarterly rpt, 3162–8; 3162–37.1
Construction contract awards and billings, by country of contractor and world area of award, 1990, annual article, 2042–1.304
Cuba trade, by commodity and country, mid 1980s-91, 9118–8
Current accounts balance of Canada and US, reconciliation adjustment methodology, with background data, 1990-91, article, 2702–1.341
Cytomegalovirus (congenital) disease cases, by infant, mother, and birth characteristics, type of impairment, State, and Canada Province, 1990-91, 4202–7.314
Dollar exchange rate trade-weighted index of Fed Reserve Bank of Atlanta, by world area, quarterly rpt, 9371–15
Dollar exchange rate trade-weighted index of Fed Reserve Bank of Dallas, by world area, monthly rpt, 9379–13
Drivers licenses requirements and admin, by State and Canada Province, as of Jan 1992, biennial rpt, 7554–18
Drug (prescription) prices in Canada and US, by brand and vendor, 1991, GAO rpt, 26121–482
Drug abuse indicators, by world region and selected country, 1991 semiannual conf, 4492–5.1
Economic and military aid and loans from US and intl agencies, by program and country, FY46-91, annual rpt, 9914–5
Economic and monetary trends, compounded annual rates of change and quarterly indicators for US and 7 major industrialized countries, quarterly rpt, 9391–7
Economic conditions, and oil supply and demand, for major industrial countries, monthly rpt, 9112–1
Economic conditions, consumer and stock prices and production indexes, for 7 OECD countries, *Survey of Current Business*, monthly rpt, 2702–1.1
Economic conditions, policy, and trade practices, by country, 1989-91, annual rpt, 21384–5
Economic indicators, and dollar exchange rates, for selected OECD countries, 1992 semiannual rpt, 8002–14
Economic, social, political, and geographic summary data, by country, 1992, annual factbook, 9114–2
Education in science and math, intl assessment results and other indicators of proficiency, by selected country, 1960s-80s, 4838–51
Electric power generation projects on Columbia River, returns to Canada, forecast 1992-2012, annual rpt, 3224–3.2
Electric underground cable from Canada at less than fair value, injury to US industry, investigation with background financial and operating data, 1992 rpt, 9886–14.341
Energy producers finances and operations, by energy type for US firms domestic and foreign operations, 1990, annual rpt, 3164–44.2
Energy production by type, and oil trade, and use, by country group and selected country, monthly rpt, 9112–2
Energy supply and demand, by fuel and end-use sector, 1950s-87 and forecast to 1995, 3166–6.58
Energy use and production, by fuel type, country, and country group, projected 1995-2010 and trends from 1970, annual rpt, 3164–84
Exchange rates relation to domestic and foreign relative prices, for US and 7 other countries, model description and results 1970s-90, working paper, 9381–10.123
Export credit activity of Eximbank and 6 OECD countries, 1990, annual rpt, 9254–3
Exports and imports (waterborne) of US, by type of service, customs district, port, and world area, monthly rpt, 2422–7
Exports and imports among US, Canada, and Japan related to domestic and foreign prices and income, 1965-87, technical paper, 9366–7.276
Exports and imports among US, Canada, and Mexico, intraindustry trade indexes by commodity, 1962-87, 1528–327
Exports and imports between Canada and US over Great Lakes, and other foreign trade, by type of vessel, 1987-89, annual rpt, 7704–7.3
Exports and imports of US by country, and trade shifts by commodity, 1991, annual rpt, 9884–25
Exports and imports of US, by Harmonized System 6-digit commodity and country, 1991, annual rpt, 2424–13
Exports and imports of US, by selected country, country group, and commodity group, 1991, annual rpt, 2044–37
Exports and imports of US, by transport mode, country, and SITC 1- to 3-digit commodity, 1991, annual rpt, 2424–12
Exports and imports of US, Canada, and Mexico, economic impacts of North American Free Trade Agreement, alternative model descriptions, 1992 conf, 9886–4.182
Exports and imports, trade agreements and relations, and USITC investigations, 1991, annual rpt, 9884–5
Exports, imports, and balances of US, by selected country, country group, and commodity group, preliminary data, monthly rpt, 2042–34
Exports, imports, and balances of US for manufactured goods, by SITC 2-digit commodity and country, quarterly rpt, 2042–35
Exports, imports, and balances of US with major trading partners, by product category, 1987-91, annual chartbook, 9884–21
Exports of US, detailed Schedule B commodities with countries of destination, 1991, annual rpt, 2424–10
Farmland in US owned by foreigners, holdings, acreage, and value by land use, owner country, State, and county, 1991, annual rpt, 1584–3

Fetal alcohol syndrome rates among Indians in Canada and Southwestern US, 1970s-80s, article, 4482–1.310
Financial markets (intl) performance of foreign and US bank and securities firms, finances and competitiveness issues, 1980s, compilation of papers, 9385–10
Freight (waterborne domestic and foreign) by commodity, traffic, and passengers, by port and waterway, 1989, annual rpt, 3754–3.3
Fruit and vegetable shipments, and arrivals by city, by mode of transport and State and country of origin, 1991, annual rpt series, 1311–4
Govt civil service merit systems operations, pay, appointments, and promotions, for Canada and US, late 1980s-91, 9498–16
Great Lakes water quality, and pollution control policy and activities, 1991 biennial rpt, 14644–1
Health care costs and components, services use, resources, and economic indicators, by OECD country, 1960s-90, article, 4652–1.322
Health care system reform issues, with data on insurance administrative and employer costs, coverage, public views, and Canada and UK systems, 1950s-91, hearings, 25368–180
Human rights conditions in 170 countries, and US economic and military aid, 1991, annual rpt, 21384–3
Immigrants admitted to US, by class of admission, country of birth, and MSA of destination, FY91, advance annual rpt, 6264–4
Immigrants and nonimmigrants admitted to US, alien workers, visitors, deportations, and naturalizations, FY91, annual summary rpt, 6264–7
Immigration to US, alien workers, visitors, deportations, and naturalizations, by country, FY91 and trends from 1820, annual rpt, 6264–2
Import restrictions and trade protectionism measures of US, Australia, Canada, and EC, cases initiated, 1980-85, article, 9379–1.301
Imports of goods, services, and investment from US, trade barriers, impacts, and US actions, by country, 1991, annual rpt, 444–2
Imports of US given duty-free treatment for value of US material sent abroad, by commodity and country, 1987-90, annual rpt, 9884–14
Income (household) and wealth distribution by selected characteristics, with foreign comparisons, 1992 compilation of papers, Current Population Rpt, 2546–6.79
Income tax returns of foreign corporations and individuals, and US entities abroad, detailed data compilation, 1970s-89, quinquennial rpt, 8308–31
Interest and exchange rates, security yields, and stock indexes, for selected foreign countries, weekly chartbook, 9365–1.5
Investment (foreign direct) in US, by industry group and world area, 1989-91, annual article, 2702–1.331
Investment (foreign direct) in US, major transactions by type, industry, country, and US location, 1990, annual rpt, 2044–20
Investment (foreign direct) of US, by industry group and world area, 1989-91, annual article, 2702–1.332
Labor conditions, union coverage, and work accidents, 1992 annual country rpt, 6366–4.32
Labor costs (manufacturing) and productivity, by selected country, 1950s-91, press release, 6726–1.55
Labor costs and indexes, by selected country, 1991, semiannual rpt, 6822–3
Livestock price support payments of Canada, by livestock type, 1986-91, semiannual rpt, 1925–33.2
Lumber (softwood) from Canada, costs and production compared to US, 1970s-91, hearing, 21728–78
Lumber (softwood) from Canada, injury to US industry from foreign subsidized imports, investigation with background financial and operating data, 1992 rpt, 9886–15.80
Lumber exports from northwestern US ports by selected country, and US imports from Canada, quarterly rpt, 1202–3
Magnesium from Canada, injury to US industry from foreign subsidized and less than fair value imports, investigation with background financial and operating data, 1992 rpt, 9886–19.86
Manufacturing industry (US) intl competitiveness, trade and economic policies with background data and foreign comparisons, 1991 rpt, 26358–252
Meat from Canada inspected and rejected, by US port of entry, 1989-91, hearing, 21368–141
Meat trade of US and Canada, inspection activity, 1989-91, GAO rpt, 26113–595
Mexico agricultural trade with US and Canada, and impacts of North American Free Trade Agreement, 1980s-90, 1528–330
Mexico trade with US and other countries, foreign investment, and maquiladoras operations, 1980s-91, GAO rpt, 26119–417
Military aid of US, arms sales, and training, by country, FY50-91, annual rpt, 3904–3
Military spending, arms trade, and force strengths, with govt spending and population, by country, 1979-89, annual rpt, 9824–1
Monetary policies and central bank regulation in US and 5 countries, 1980-91, article, 9385–1.308
Multinatl firms US affiliates finances and operations, by industry, country of parent firm, and State, 1987, 2708–48
Multinatl firms US affiliates, finances, and operations, by industry, world area of parent firm, and State, 1989-90, annual rpt, 2704–4
Multinatl US firms and foreign affiliates finances and operations, by industry and country, 1989 benchmark survey, annual rpt, 2704–5
Multinatl US firms foreign affiliates, income statement items by asset size, industry, and country, 1988, biennial article, 8302–2.322
Natural gas and liquefied gas trade of US with 5 countries, by US firm, 1955-91, annual article, 3162–4.301
Natural gas imports and contracted supply from Canada and Mexico, by US pipeline firm, 1989-90, annual rpt, 3164–33.6
Nepheline syenite from Canada at less than fair value, injury to US industry, investigation with background financial and operating data, 1992 rpt, 9886–14.344
Nuclear power generation in US and 20 countries, monthly rpt, 3162–24.10
Nuclear power generation in US and 20 countries, monthly 1973-88, 3168–123.10
Oil production, stocks, use, and trade, by selected country and country group, monthly rpt, 3162–42
Oil production, use, stocks, and exports and prices for US, by country, detailed data, monthly rpt with articles, 3162–24
Oil production, use, stocks, and exports and prices for US, by country, detailed data, monthly 1973-88, 3168–123
Oil supply, demand, and stock forecasts, by world area, quarterly rpt, 3162–34
Pension plan finances, participation, and benefits, for 9 OECD countries, with data by firm and worker characteristics, 1990 conf, 6688–2
Physicians trained in Canada and practicing in US, by activity, sex, and county, 1990, State rpt series, 4116–6
Physicians trained in Canada, supply in US, 1970s-89 and projected to 2020, biennial rpt, 4114–8
Pollution (air) contributing to global warming, emissions by monitoring site and country, and temperature change by world area and US region, 1860s-1990, annual rpt, 3004–33
Population size, growth rates, and components of change, by country, projected 1990-2020 and trends from 1950, biennial rpt, 2324–9
Potassium hydroxide from 3 countries at less than fair value, injury to US industry, investigation with background financial and operating data, 1992 rpt, 9886–14.339
Potato production, acreage, prices, and shipments, for 7 major producer States, and compared to other States, 1970s-92, annual rpt, 1311–29
Potato production, acreage, shipments, and arrivals, for Maine by variety, and compared to other States and Canada, 1991-92, annual rpt, 1311–26
Raisin imports of EC member countries and Canada, and Turkey exports, by country, 1989-93, semiannual article, 1925–34.348
Raisin imports of 3 countries, and Chile exports, by country of origin and destination, 1988-91, semiannual article, 1925–34.321
Refugee migration, and intl aid programs, by world area and country of origin and asylum, 1991, annual rpt, 7004–15
Science and Engineering Indicators, employment, education, R&D funding, and industry impacts, with foreign comparisons, 1960s-91, biennial rpt, 9624–10
Seismographs (portable) from Canada, injury to US industry from foreign subsidized imports, investigation with background financial and operating data, 1992 rpt, 9886–15.79

Spacecraft and satellite launches since 1957, quarterly listing, 9502–2

St Lawrence Seaway ship, cargo, and passenger traffic, and toll revenue, 1991 and trends from 1959, annual rpt, 7744–2

Steel (carbon flat-rolled) products from 21 countries, injury to US industry from foreign subsidized and less than fair value imports, investigation with background financial and operating data, 1992 rpt, 9886–19.85

Steel trade, by product, country, and customs district, with US industry operating data, 1989-June 1992, semiannual rpt, 9882–15

Tax (estate) returns for nonresident aliens, property and tax data, by estate size and decedent country of residence, 1986, article, 8302–2.310

Tax (income) returns for foreign corporate activity in US, selected income and tax items, by industry div and selected country, 1988, article, 8302–2.309

Tax (income) returns, income, and tax withheld for foreign partners of US partnerships, by country, 1990, article, 8302–2.324

Tax (income and capital) policies, with background data, for EC, Japan, and US, mid 1960s-91, article, 9373–1.316

Tax revenue, by level of govt and type of tax, for OECD countries, mid 1960s-90, annual rpt, 10044–1.2

Telecommunications domestic and intl rates, by type of service and area served, 1990, annual rpt, 9284–6.6

Telecommunications industry intl competitiveness, structure, and devs, with background data and foreign comparisons, 1991 rpt, 2808–30

Tide height and time daily at coastal points, forecast 1993, annual rpt, 2174–2.3

Tobacco production and use in Latin America, Canada, and US, and related economic, health, and social issues, 1950s-92, annual rpt, 4204–18

Trade agreement of Canada and US, issues with data on Canada fertilizer and agricultural production and trade, 1960s-90s, hearing, 25368–179

Transportation energy use, fuel prices, vehicle registrations, and mileage, by selected country, 1950-89, annual rpt, 3304–5.1

Travel by Canadians to US and other countries, market analysis with detailed trip and traveler characteristics, 1991, country rpt, 2906–2.24

Travel to and from US, and travel receipts and payments, by world area, with data by country, 1985-90, annual rpt, 2904–10

Travel to and from US, by world area, forecast 1992-93, annual rpt, 2904–9

Travel to and from US on US and foreign flag air carriers, by country, world area, and US port, monthly rpt, 7302–2

Travel to US and Canada, market analysis with detailed trip and traveler characteristics, country rpt series, 2906–2

Travel to US, spending by world area of residence, and economic impact, by spending category and State, 1989, 2908–28

UN voting record and share of votes in agreement with US, by issue, country, and world area, 1991, annual rpt, 7004–18

Water supply in US and southern Canada, streamflow, surface and groundwater conditions, and reservoir levels, by location, monthly rpt, 5662–3

Weather (marine) forecast areas, and broadcast schedules and stations worldwide, as of Sept 1992, annual rpt, 2184–3

Weather (marine) forecast broadcast schedules worldwide, periodic rpt, 2182–9

Weather conditions and effect on agriculture, by US region, State, and city, and world area, weekly rpt, 2182–7

Wetlands conservation projects, acreage, and costs, for Canada and Mexico, FY92, 14784–1

see also British Columbia Province, Canada

see also Ontario Province, Canada

see also Quebec Province, Canada

see also Toronto, Canada

see also under By Foreign Country in the "Index by Categories"

Canal Zone

see Panama Canal

Canals

Army Corps of Engineers activities and projects, FY88 and trends from 1800s, annual rpt, 3754–1.1

Army Corps of Engineers activities and projects, FY89 and trends from 1800s, annual rpt, 3754–1.2

Army Corps of Engineers activities and projects, FY90 and trends from 1800s, annual rpt, 3754–1.3

Bridges over navigable waters, with type of bridge and use, owner, dimensions, and location, 1991 regional listing series, 7406–5

Freight (waterborne domestic and foreign) by commodity, traffic, and passengers, by port and waterway, 1989, annual rpt, 3754–3

Ohio River basin waterway facilities, freight by commodity and port, and recreation, by waterway, 1988-89, annual rpt, 3754–6

Reclamation Bur irrigation activities, finances, and project impacts in western US, 1990, annual rpt, 5824–12

Reclamation Bur water storage and carriage facilities, capacity, and operating status, as of Sept 1990, biennial listing, 5824–7

St Lawrence Seaway ship, cargo, and passenger traffic, and toll revenue, 1991 and trends from 1959, annual rpt, 7744–2

see also Panama Canal

Cancer

see Carcinogens

see Neoplasms

Candy and confectionery products

Appalachia food processing firms, employment, and shipments, and farm production, by commodity and State, 1960s-90, 9088–37

Consumption, supply, trade, prices, spending, and indexes, by food commodity, 1990, annual rpt, 1544–4

County Business Patterns, 1989: employment, establishments, and payroll, by SIC 2- to 4-digit industry and county, annual State rpt series, 2326–8

County Business Patterns, 1990: employment, establishments, and payroll, by SIC 2- to 4-digit industry and county, annual State rpt series, 2326–6

CPI by component for US city average, and by selected metro area, region, and population size, monthly rpt, 6762–2

Employment, earnings, and hours, by SIC 1- to 4-digit industry, monthly 1989-Feb 1992, annual rpt, 6744–4

Exports and imports (agricultural) of US, by commodity and country, bimonthly rpt, 1522–1

Exports and imports (agricultural) of US, by detailed commodity and country, 1991, annual rpt, 1524–8

Exports and imports (agricultural) of US, by detailed commodity and country, 1991, semiannual rpt, 1522–4

Exports and imports between US and outlying areas, by detailed commodity and mode of transport, 1991, annual rpt, 2424–11

Exports and imports of US, by country and detailed commodity, monthly rpt, 2422–12

Exports and imports of US, by Harmonized System 6-digit commodity and country, 1991, annual rpt, 2424–13

Exports and imports of US, by transport mode, country, and SITC 1- to 3-digit commodity, 1991, annual rpt, 2424–12

Exports of US, detailed Schedule B commodities with countries of destination, 1991, annual rpt, 2424–10

Input-output structure of US economy, detailed interindustry transactions for 541 industries, and components of final demand, 1982 benchmark data, 2708–17

Manufacturing annual survey, 1990: finances and operations, by SIC 2- to 4-digit industry, series, 2506–14

Manufacturing census, 1987: concentration of largest firms measured by value added, and for shipments by SIC 2- and 4-digit industry, subject rpt, 2497–6

Manufacturing census, 1987: shipments of manufacturers products, by customer class and SIC 2- and 4-digit industry, subject rpt, 2497–4

Manufacturing finances and operations, by SIC 2- to 4-digit industry, forecast 1992, annual rpt, 2044–28

Occupational injury and illness rates, by SIC 2- to 4-digit industry, 1989-90, annual rpt, 6844–7

Occupational injury and illness rates, by SIC 2- to 4-digit industry, 1990, annual rpt, 6844–1

Price indexes (producer), by stage of processing and detailed commodity, monthly rpt, 6762–6

Price indexes (producer), by stage of processing and detailed commodity, monthly 1991, annual rpt, 6764–2

Retail trade sales and inventories, by kind of business, region, and selected State, MSA, and city, monthly rpt, 2413–3

Rice shipments, by end use, package size, and State of origin and destination, 1960s-89, biennial rpt, 1564–11

Shipments and per capita consumption of confectionery products, 1981-91, semiannual rpt, 1925–9.2

Shipments, trade, use, and ingredients, by confectionery product, 1991, annual Current Industrial Rpt, 2506–4.5
Weight and volume conversion factors for agricultural commodities and products, 1992 rpt, 1508–3
see also Cocoa and chocolate

Canfield, Dennis V.
"Enhancement of Drug Detection and Identification by Use of Various Derivatizing Reagents on GC-FTIR Analysis", 7506–10.112
"Postmortem Alcohol Production in Fatal Aircraft Accidents", 7506–10.111

Canner, Glenn B.
"Developments in the Pricing of Credit Card Services", 9362–1.306
"Expanded HMDA Data on Residential Lending: One Year Later", 9362–1.307

Canton, Ohio
see also under By City and By SMSA or MSA in the "Index by Categories"

Cantor, Richard
"Bank Capital Ratios, Asset Growth, and the Stock Market", 9385–1.311

Caouette, Terry L.
"Introduction of Seasonally Adjusted State Labor Force Data", 6742–2.305

Capacity utilization, industrial
see Industrial capacity and utilization

Cape Verde
Agricultural trade of US, by detailed commodity and country, 1991, semiannual rpt, 1522–4
AID economic aid to developing countries, obligations and disbursements by country, quarterly rpt, 9912–4
AID loans repayment status and terms by program and country, and status of predecessor agency loans, quarterly rpt, 9912–3
Economic and military aid and loans from US and intl agencies, by program and country, FY46-91, annual rpt, 9914–5
Economic and social conditions of developing countries from 1960s, and Intl Dev Cooperation Agency and AID activities and funding, FY91-93, annual rpt, 9904–4
Economic, social, political, and geographic summary data, by country, 1992, annual factbook, 9114–2
Exports and imports of US, by transport mode, country, and SITC 1- to 3-digit commodity, 1991, annual rpt, 2424–12
Human rights conditions in 170 countries, and US economic and military aid, 1991, annual rpt, 21384–3
Military aid of US, arms sales, and training programs costs and budget requests, by program, world region, and country, FY91-93, annual rpt, 7144–13
Military spending, arms trade, and force strengths, with govt spending and population, by country, 1979-89, annual rpt, 9824–1
Minerals Yearbook, Vol 3, 1989: foreign country review of production, trade, and policy, by commodity, annual rpt, 5604–35.1
Population size, growth rates, and components of change, by country, projected 1990-2020 and trends from 1950, biennial rpt, 2324–9
UN voting record and share of votes in agreement with US, by issue, country, and world area, 1991, annual rpt, 7004–18

Capehart, Tom
"Flue-Cured Tobacco Farms: Selected Characteristics", 1568–307
"Leaf and Cigarette Production and Trade in Central and East Europe", 1561–10.303

Capital gains
see Investments

Capital investments, general
Assets and debts of private sector, balance sheets by segment, 1960-91, semiannual rpt, 9365–4.1
Business natl and local outlook, North Central States business leaders views, 1992 survey, article, 9383–19.303
Capital (fixed), govt and private nonresidential structures and equipment, residential capital, and consumer-owned durable goods, 1925-90, annual article, 2702–1.305; 2702–1.306; 2702–1.327; 2702–1.338
Central America economic indicators, by country, 1969-89, working paper, 9916–13.4
Cost changes relation to changes in capital investment, by asset type and industry div, late 1950s-80s, article, 9373–1.304
Cost of capital over business cycles relation to firm size and financial distress indicators, 1960s-91, article, 9385–1.312
Economic indicators and components, current data and annual trends, monthly rpt, 23842–1.1; 23842–1.5
Economic indicators compounded annual rates of change, monthly rpt, 9391–3
Enterprise zone programs of States, business investment and jobs created, and incentive programs, by State, 1992 annual rpt, 5124–9
Expenditures for new plant and equipment, tax rates, and rates of return, alternative estimates, 1950s-80s, technical paper, 8006–6.2
Expenditures for new plants and equipment, by industry div, 1947-2nd qtr 1992, annual rpt, 204–1.3
Expenditures for new plants and equipment, monthly rpt, 9362–1.1
Expenditures for plant and equipment, by industry div, quarterly rpt, 2042–1.4
Expenditures for plant and equipment, by major industry group, quarterly rpt, 2502–2
Expenditures for plant and equipment, by major industry group, 1990, annual rpt, 9364–5.6
Export and import balances relation to productivity and capital investment, for selected countries, 1960s-90, working paper, 9393–10.22
Fiscal policy (supply side) of Reagan Admin, economic impacts, 1980s and trends from 1960s, technical paper, 9385–1.304; 9385–8.125
Flow-of-funds accounts, savings, investments, and credit statements, quarterly rpt, 9365–3.3
Foreign countries economic conditions and implications for US, periodic country rpt series, 2046–4
Gross private fixed investment, 1929-91, annual rpt, 204–1.1
Imports and tariff provisions effect on US industries and products, investigations with background financial and operating data, series, 9886–4
Imports injury to US industries from foreign subsidized products and sales at less than fair value, investigations with background financial and operating data, series, 9886–19
Imports injury to US industries from sales at less than fair value, investigations with background financial and operating data, series, 9886–14
Industry (US) intl competitiveness, with selected foreign and US operating data by major firm and product, series, 2046–12
Industry finances and operations, by SIC 2- to 4-digit industry, forecast 1992, annual rpt, 2044–28
Input-output structure of US economy, detailed interindustry transactions for 541 industries, and components of final demand, 1982 benchmark data, 2708–17
Manufacturing annual survey, 1990: establishments, employment, finances, inventories, and energy use, by SIC 2- to 4-digit industry, 2506–14.2
Manufacturing annual survey, 1990: finances and operations, by SIC 2- and 3-digit industry and State, 2506–14.3
Manufacturing capital investment relation to cash flow and other factors, 1992 working paper, 9375–13.81
Manufacturing capital investment relation to debt/collateral ratios, model description and results, 1950s-80, working paper, 9377–9.141
Manufacturing census, 1987: concentration of largest firms measured by value added, and for shipments by SIC 2- and 4-digit industry, subject rpt, 2497–6
Manufacturing investment spending relation to cash flow and other factors, model description and results, 1950s-80s, technical paper, 9385–8.129
Mexico investment spending by industry, and impacts of relative price changes and intl debt crisis, 1980s, technical paper, 9366–7.270
Middle Atlantic States manufacturing business outlook, monthly survey rpt, 9387–11
Militarily strategic manufacturing industries finances, operations, and intl competitiveness, series, 2026–1
Minority- and woman-owned businesses and owner characteristics, by industry, employment and sales size, and form of ownership, 1987 survey, 2328–59
Multinatl firms US affiliates finances and operations, by industry div, country of parent firm, and State, 1989-90, annual article, 2702–1.319
Multinatl firms US affiliates, finances, and operations, by industry, world area of parent firm, and State, 1989-90, annual rpt, 2704–4
Multinatl US firms and foreign affiliates finances and operations, by industry and country, 1989 benchmark survey, annual rpt, 2704–5
Multinatl US firms and foreign affiliates finances and operations, by industry and world area, 1988, annual article, 2702–1.329

Multinatl US firms foreign affiliates capital expenditures, by major industry group, world area, and country, 1987-92, semiannual article, 2702–1.312
Multinatl US firms foreign affiliates capital expenditures, by major industry group, world area, and country, 1988-92, semiannual article, 2702–1.335
Natl income and product accounts and components, *Survey of Current Business*, monthly rpt, 2702–1.23
Natl income and product accounts, comprehensive accounts and components, benchmark revisions, 1929-88, 2708–5
Natl income and product accounts, comprehensive accounts and components, *Survey of Current Business*, monthly rpt, 2702–1.28
Pollution abatement capital and operating costs, by SIC 2- to 4-digit industry and State, 1990, annual Current Industrial Rpt, 2506–3.6
Pollution abatement capital spending, for mining, petroleum refining, and electric utilities, 1990, annual Current Industrial Rpt, 2506–3.6
Pollution abatement spending by govts, business, and consumers, 1972-90, annual article, 2702–1.321
Productivity of labor, capital, and other inputs in manufacturing, changes by selected industry, various periods 1949-88, article, 6722–1.345
Productivity of labor for US and foreign countries, and impacts of investment spending, 1950s-91, article, 9381–1.308
Productivity relation to high technology capital investment, by industry sector, 1940s-80s, technical paper, 9385–8.130
Small business finances, operations, owner characteristics, and Federal contracts, 1980s-90, annual rpt, 9764–6
Southeastern US manufacturing conditions, survey methodology and selected results, Dec 1991-July 1992, article, 9371–1.307
Statistical Abstract of US, 1992 annual data compilation, 2324–1.17; 2324–1.27
Survey of Current Business, detailed data for major industries and economic indicators, 1960-91, biennial supplement, 2704–1
Tax (income) returns of corporations, income and tax items by asset size and detailed industry, 1989, annual rpt, 8304–4
Tax exempt organizations finances, with data by type, size, State, and for largest organizations, late 1940s-80s, compilation of papers, 8308–35
Technology-intensive capital investment relation to productivity growth, 1950s-89, article, 9385–1.310
see also Capital investments, specific industry
see also Depreciation
see also Foreign investments
see also Industrial plants and equipment
see also Venture capital

Capital investments, specific industry
Agricultural cooperatives finances, aggregate for top 100 assns by commodity group, 1990, annual rpt, 1124–3
Agricultural, fishery, and forest products trade, tariffs, and industry operating data, commodity rpt series, 9885–8
Airline finances, by carrier, carrier group, and for total certificated system, quarterly rpt, 7302–7
Airport capacity improvement projects and funding, traffic, and delays, by major airport, 1988-90 and forecast to 2000, annual rpt, 7504–43
Auto and auto parts trade, production, and labor conditions, for US and compared to Canada and Mexico, 1950s-90, 6366–3.28
Banks in Fed Reserve System, expenses and operations itemized by service, office, and district, 1991, annual rpt, 9364–11
Colorado River Storage Project finances and activities in western States, FY91, annual rpt, 5824–3
Electric power distribution loans from REA, and borrower operating and financial data, by firm and State, 1991, annual rpt, 1244–1
Electric power plants (coal-burning) air pollutant reduction technology funding, and impacts on energy costs and emissions, 1950s-87 and projected to 2010, annual rpt, 3334–5; 3338–4
Electric power plants (coal-burning) air pollutant reduction technology funding, and project descriptions, 1991, annual rpt, 3334–4
Electric power plants production and capital costs, operations, and fuel use, by fuel type, plant, utility, and location, 1990, annual rpt, 3164–9
Electric power sales by customer, activities by plant, and financial statements of Western Area Power Admin, FY91, annual rpt, 3254–1
Electric power sales by customer, financial statements, and operations and costs by project, for Southwestern Fed Power System, FY91, annual rpt, 3244–1
Electric power sales by customer, plants, and capacity of Southeastern Power Admin, FY91, annual rpt, 3234–1
Electric power sales, finances, and operations, for Fed Columbia River Power System, FY91, annual rpt, 3224–1
Electric utilities finances and operations, detailed data for publicly and privately owned firms, 1990, annual rpt, 3164–11.4
Electric utilities finances and operations, detailed data for publicly owned firms, 1990, annual rpt, 3164–24
Electric utilities privately owned, finances and operations, detailed data, 1990, annual rpt, 3164–23
Energy producers finances and operations, by energy type for US firms domestic and foreign operations, 1990, annual rpt, 3164–44
Energy production and trade for Romania, 1970s-91, with capital investment projected to 2000, GAO rpt, 26123–402
Farm Credit System financial condition, quarterly rpt, 9262–2
Farm production itemized costs, receipts, and returns, by commodity and region, 1975-90, annual rpt, 1544–20
Farm production itemized costs, receipts, and returns, by crop and State, 1987-89, annual rpt, 1544–24
Farm sector balance sheet, and marketing receipts by detailed commodity, by State, 1986-90, annual rpt, 1544–18
Fed Reserve System, Bd of Governors, and district banks financial statements, performance, and fiscal services, 1991-92, annual rpt, 9364–10
Food processing firms, employment, and shipments, and farm production, by commodity and State, for Appalachia, 1960s-90, 9088–37
Minerals production, prices, trade, use, employment, tariffs, and stockpiles, by mineral, with foreign comparisons, 1987-91, annual rpt, 5604–18
Natural gas interstate pipeline company detailed financial and operating data, by firm, 1990, annual rpt, 3164–38
Nonprofit charitable and other tax exempt organizations finances, by category and size of assets and contributions, 1988, annual article, 8302–2.315
Oil production, investment needs, and exports, for 8 South America countries, 1980s-90 and projected to 2010, GAO rpt, 26123–396
Panama Canal Commission finances and activities, with Canal traffic and local govt operations, FY91, annual rpt, 9664–3
Postal Service activities, finances, and mail volume and subsidies, FY91, annual rpt, 9864–5.3
Railroad (Amtrak) finances and operations, FY91, annual rpt, 29524–1
Railroad employment and finances, for ICC-regulated carriers, as of FY91, annual rpt, 9484–1
Reclamation Bur irrigation activities, finances, and project impacts in western US, 1990, annual rpt, 5824–12
Recycling in manufacturing industries, fuel savings, and CO2 emissions reductions, 1988 and projected to 1995, hearing, 21368–140
Red Cross activities and finances, FY91, annual rpt, 29254–1
Semiconductor industry (US) intl competitiveness, status, and outlook, working paper series, 15036–1
St Lawrence Seaway Dev Corp finances and activities, with Seaway cargo tonnage, and shipping costs compared to other US ports, 1990, annual rpt, 7744–1
Telecommunications fiber optics and copper wire mileage and access lines, and fiber systems investment, by firm, 1985-91, annual rpt, 9284–18
Telecommunications industry intl competitiveness, structure, and devs, with background data and foreign comparisons, 1991 rpt, 2808–30
Telephone and telegraph firms detailed finances and operations, 1990, annual rpt, 9284–6
Telephone firms borrowing under Rural Telephone Program, and financial and operating data, by State, 1991, annual rpt, 1244–2
Transit systems finances and operations, by mode, size of fleet and urban area, region, and for 518 systems, 1990, annual rpt, 7884–4
Truck, bus, and rail carriers regulated by ICC, employment and finances, as of FY91, annual rpt, 9484–1
Truck interstate carriers finances and operations, by district, 1990, annual rpt, 9486–5.2

TVA finances and operations by program and facility, FY91, annual rpt, 9804–32
Uranium mining and milling industries finances and operations, with selected foreign comparisons, 1970s-90 and projected to 2005, annual rpt, 3164–82
Vending facilities run by blind on Federal and non-Federal property, finances and operations by agency and State, FY91, annual rpt, 4944–2
see also Depreciation
see also Foreign investments
see also Industrial plants and equipment

Capital punishment
Federal criminal sentencing, guidelines by offense and circumstances, series, 17668–1
Habeas corpus use to appeal capital convictions, and time from crime to execution, with data by race and State, 1977-91, 6008–34
Prisoners and movements, by offense, location, and selected other characteristics, data compilation, 1992 annual rpt, 6064–6.6
Prisoners in Federal and State instns by selected characteristics, releases, staff, and instn size, with data by region and State, late 1970s-91, 6068–248
Prisoners on death row in Federal and State instns, 1990, quinquennial rpt, 6068–218
Prisoners under death sentence, and executions from 1930, by offense, prisoner characteristics, and State, 1990, annual rpt, 6064–26.6
Public opinion on crime and crime-related issues, by respondent characteristics, data compilation, 1992 annual rpt, 6064–6.2
States criminal justice systems activities, employment, funding, and data collection, by State, 1970s-91, annual rpt, 6064–40
Statistical Abstract of US, 1992 annual data compilation, 2324–1.5

Caprio, Giovanni
"Haiti Macroeconomic Assessment", 9916–13.3

Carbon dioxide
see Air pollution
see Global climate change

Carcinogens
Chemistry, sources, environment and health risks, and regulation of carcinogens, by substance and brand, 1991 annual rpt, 4044–15
Cigarette smoke tar, nicotine, and carbon monoxide content, by brand, 1990, 9408–53
Great Lakes industrial water pollution emissions, comparison of State, EPA, Intl Joint Commission, and Ontario standards, 1991 rpt, 14648–29
Natl Cancer Inst epidemiology and biometry activities, FY91, annual rpt, 4474–29
Pollutants health effects, concentrations in food and environment, sources, human intake, and regulation, series, 9186–8
Pollutants health effects for animals by species and for humans, and environmental levels, for selected substances, series, 5506–14
Research and testing activities under Natl Toxicology Program, FY90 and planned FY91, annual rpt, 4044–16
Smoking, tobacco, and health impacts research rpts, 1991 annual report, 4204–19
see also Asbestos contamination
see also Dioxins
see also Radiation
see also Radon

Cardiovascular diseases
Alcohol use related to heart disease hospitalization and death risk, 1990 article, 4482–1.301
Cases of acute and chronic conditions, disability, absenteeism, and health services use, by selected characteristics, 1990, annual rpt, 4147–10.182; 4147–10.183
Deaths and rates, by cause, age, sex, marital status, race, and State, 1989, US Vital Statistics advance annual rpt, 4146–5.124
Deaths and rates, by cause and age, preliminary 1990-91, US Vital Statistics annual rpt, 4144–7
Deaths and rates, by cause and selected social, demographic, and employment characteristics, 1979-85, natl longitudinal study, 4478–186
Deaths and rates, by cause, provisional data, monthly rpt, 4142–1.2
Deaths and rates, by detailed location, cause, and demographic characteristics, 1989, US Vital Statistics annual rpt, 4144–3
Deaths during 1986, decedents health condition, services use, habits, and social, employment, and other characteristics, 4147–20.19
Diabetes patients physician office visits, by characteristics of patient, physician, and visit, 1989, 4146–8.212
Disability and work limitations of persons with chronic health conditions, by condition, age, and sex, 1983-86, 4946–1.2
Fire fighter deaths, by cause, circumstances, and location, 1990, annual rpt, 9434–8
Health condition and care indicators, 1950s-90 with health improvement and disease prevention goals for 1990, annual data compilation, 4144–11
HHS financial aid, by program, recipient, State, and city, FY91, annual regional listings, 4004–3
Hospital deaths of Medicare patients, actual and expected rates by diagnosis, with hospital characteristics, by instn, FY90, annual State rpt series, 4654–14
Hypertension cases, stroke and heart disease risk, and drug dosages, with diagnosis and treatment methods, 1992 quadrennial rpt, 4478–198
Indian Health Service and tribal facilities and use, and Indians health and other characteristics, by IHS region, 1980s-90, annual chartbook, 4084–7
Insurance (health) denial by private carriers because of poor health, by selected characteristics, 1987, 4186–8.23
Medicare payment of physicians, reforms impacts on services, and monitoring methods, 1992 annual rpt, 4004–34
Missouri heart disease risk factors prevalence, 1989-90, article, 4042–3.302
Natl Heart, Lung, and Blood Inst activities, and Advisory Council recommendations, 1991 narrative rpt, 4474–22
Natl Heart, Lung, and Blood Inst activities, and grants by recipient and location, FY91 and disease trends from 1940, annual rpt, 4474–15
Occupational deaths, by cause and industry div, 1990, annual rpt, 6844–1
OECD members health care costs, hospital use, resources, and economic and health indicators, by country, 1960s-90, article, 4652–1.322
Older population, and health, economic, and other characteristics, with foreign comparisons, 1980s-91 with trends and projections, Current Population Rpt, 2546–2.165
Pacemaker lead implants, failures, and costs, by model, 1992 GAO rpt, 26131–103
Physicians visits, by patient and practice characteristics, diagnosis, and services provided, 1989, annual rpt, 4147–13.109
Pollutants health effects, concentrations in food and environment, sources, human intake, and regulation, series, 9186–8
Pulse rate relation to blood pressure and other physical, demographic, and behavioral characteristics, 1971-74, article, 4042–3.321
Smoking, tobacco, and health impacts research rpts, 1991 annual report, 4204–19
Statistical Abstract of US, 1992 annual data compilation, 2324–1.2
Surgical cardiac procedures and heart transplants, rehabilitation risks and benefit evaluation for Medicare coverage, 1991 rpt, 4186–10.8
Transplants of hearts and lungs, failures, deaths, and survival rates, by hospital, 1987-89, annual rpt, 4104–17.5
see also Hypertension
see also under By Disease in the "Index by Categories"

Caregivers and caregiving
Alzheimer's patients functioning, caregivers hours and other characteristics, and services costs and payment source, by location, 1990, conf paper, 4164–2
Assistance programs under Ways and Means Committee jurisdiction, finances, operations, and participant characteristics, FY70s-91, annual rpt, 21784–11
Deaths during 1986, decedents health condition, services use, habits, and social, employment, and other characteristics, 4147–20.19
Handicapped children's formal and informal care, outlays and time spent relation to diagnosis and other characteristics, 1988, article, 4042–3.329
Older persons care by family members and others, caregiver quit probability related to selected characteristics, 1982, article, 4652–1.305
see also Adult day care
see also Child day care
see also Foster home care
see also Guardianship
see also Health facilities and services
see also Health occupations
see also Hospices
see also Nursing homes
see also Parents
see also Single parents

Carey, Max L.
"Industry Output and Job Growth Continues Slow into Next Century", 6744–19

Cargo
see Air cargo
see Freight
Caribbean area
Agricultural trade of Caribbean basin with US, by whether duty levied, commodity, and country, 1983 and 1987-91, annual article, 1925–34.329
Agricultural trade of US, by commodity and country, bimonthly rpt, 1522–1
Agricultural trade of US, by detailed commodity and country, 1991, annual rpt, 1524–8
Agricultural trade of US, by detailed commodity and country, 1991, semiannual rpt, 1522–4
AID economic aid to developing countries, obligations and disbursements by country, quarterly rpt, 9912–4
AID loans repayment status and terms by program and country, and status of predecessor agency loans, quarterly rpt, 9912–3
Air traffic and passengers, for intl routes over north Atlantic, by aviation type and route, alternative forecasts 1992-2010 and trends from 1982, annual rpt, 7504–44
Clothing exports to US, and domestic and US-owned industry production costs and operations, for Caribbean area and Mexico, impacts of North American Free Trade Agreement, 1992 rpt, 9886–4.186
Economic and social conditions of developing countries from 1960s, and Intl Dev Cooperation Agency and AID activities and funding, FY91-93, annual rpt, 9904–4
Economic and social conditions, resources, and trade, and aid, 1992, annual factbook, 9914–14
Economic conditions, trade, and foreign aid, for Latin America, working paper series, 9916–13
Economic, population, and agricultural data, US and other aid sources, and AID activity, 1992 regional rpt, 9916–12.70
Export and investment incentives under Caribbean Basin Initiative, contact listing, bibl, and US imports by country, 1983-91, annual rpt, 2044–36
Exports (duty-free) of Caribbean area to US, and imports from US, by country, and impact on US employment, by commodity, 1991, annual rpt, 6364–2
Exports (duty-free) of Caribbean area to US, by commodity and country, with consumer and industry impacts, 1984-91, annual rpt, 9884–20
Exports and imports (waterborne) of US, by type of service, customs district, port, and world area, monthly rpt, 2422–7
Exports and imports of OECD, total and for 4 major countries, and US trade by country, by commodity, 1980-90, world area rpt, 9116–1.4
Exports and imports of US by country, and trade shifts by commodity, 1991, annual rpt, 9884–25
Exports and imports of US, by Harmonized System 6-digit commodity and country, 1991, annual rpt, 2424–13
Exports and imports of US, by selected country, country group, and commodity group, 1991, annual rpt, 2044–37
Exports and imports of US, by transport mode, country, and SITC 1- to 3-digit commodity, 1991, annual rpt, 2424–12
Exports of US, detailed Schedule B commodities with countries of destination, 1991, annual rpt, 2424–10
Family planning and population activities of AID, grants by project and recipient, and contraceptive shipments, by country, FY91, annual rpt series, 9914–13
Fish (billfish) tagged and recovered by location, and Japan catch in US waters, 1950-90, annual rpt, 2164–7
Fish (game) tagging and research activities, by species, 1990, annual rpt, 2164–24
Immigrants admitted to US, by class of admission, country of birth, and MSA of destination, FY91, advance annual rpt, 6264–4
Immigrants and legalized aliens, by occupational group and country of birth, preliminary FY91, annual tables, 6264–1
Immigrants and nonimmigrants admitted to US, alien workers, visitors, deportations, and naturalizations, FY91, annual summary rpt, 6264–7
Immigration to US, alien workers, visitors, deportations, and naturalizations, by country, FY91 and trends from 1820, annual rpt, 6264–2
Imports of Latin America and Caribbean countries from US, by State of origin, 1987 and 1990, 2048–160
Inter-American Foundation activities, grants by recipient, and fellowships, by country, FY91, annual rpt, 14424–1
Inter-American Foundation dev grants by program area, and fellowships by field and instn, by country, FY72-91, annual rpt, 14424–2
Investment (foreign direct) in US, by industry group and world area, 1989-91, annual article, 2702–1.331
Loans of US banks to foreigners at all US and foreign offices, by country group and country, quarterly rpt, 13002–1
Military aid of US, arms sales, and training programs costs and budget requests, by program, world region, and country, FY91-93, annual rpt, 7144–13
Multinatl US firms and foreign affiliates finances and operations, by industry and country, 1989 benchmark survey, annual rpt, 2704–5
Multinatl US firms foreign affiliates, income statement items by asset size, industry, and country, 1988, biennial article, 8302–2.322
Oil exports to US by OPEC and non-OPEC countries, monthly rpt, 3162–24.3
Oil exports to US by OPEC and non-OPEC countries, monthly 1973-88, 3168–123.3
Peace Corps activities, funding by program, and volunteers, by country, FY93, annual rpt, 9654–1
Refugee arrivals in US by world area and country of origin, and quotas, monthly rpt, 7002–4
Sharks and other fish tagged and recovered, by species, 1991, annual rpt, 2164–21
Textile imports under Multifiber Arrangement by product and country, and status of bilateral agreements, 1988-91, annual rpt, 9884–18
Tobacco production and use in Latin America, Canada, and US, and related economic, health, and social issues, 1950s-92, annual rpt, 4204–18
Travel to US, by characteristics of visit and traveler, country, port city, and State of destination, quarterly rpt, 2902–1
see also Anguilla
see also Antigua and Barbuda
see also Aruba
see also Bahamas
see also Barbados
see also Bermuda
see also British Virgin Islands
see also Caribbean Community
see also Cayman Islands
see also Cuba
see also Dominica
see also Dominican Republic
see also Grenada
see also Guadeloupe
see also Haiti
see also Jamaica
see also Martinique
see also Montserrat
see also Netherlands Antilles
see also Puerto Rico
see also St. Christopher and Nevis
see also St. Lucia
see also St. Vincent and The Grenadines
see also Trinidad and Tobago
see also Turks and Caicos Islands
see also U.S. Virgin Islands
see also under By Foreign Country in the "Index by Categories"
Caribbean Basin Economic Recovery Act
Exports (duty-free) of Caribbean area to US, and imports from US, by country, and impact on US employment, by commodity, 1991, annual rpt, 6364–2
Exports and imports of US by country, and trade shifts by commodity, 1991, annual rpt, 9884–25
Caribbean Basin Initiative
see Trade agreements
Caribbean Community
Exports, imports, membership, and trade impacts of regional preferential trading arrangements, by group, late 1940s-91, article, 9373–1.308
Carlino, Gerald
"Have Regional Per-Capita Incomes Converged?", 9387–8.257
Carlson, Kenneth E.
"Federal Sentencing in Transition, 1986-90", 6066–19.68
Carlstrom, Charles T.
"Efficiency and Welfare Effects of Tax Reform: Are Fewer Tax Brackets Better Than More?", 9377–9.143
Carney, Diane
"Shallow Subtidal Survey of the Washington Outer Coast and Olympic National Park To Determine the Distribution, Fate, and Effects of Spilled Bunker C Fuel Oil", 5738–38.3
Carpets and rugs
Business statistics, detailed data for major industries and economic indicators, *Survey of Current Business*, monthly rpt, 2702–1.21
Business statistics, detailed data for major industries and economic indicators, 1960-91, *Survey of Current Business* biennial supplement, 2704–1

County Business Patterns, 1989: employment, establishments, and payroll, by SIC 2- to 4-digit industry and county, annual State rpt series, 2326–8
County Business Patterns, 1990: employment, establishments, and payroll, by SIC 2- to 4-digit industry and county, annual State rpt series, 2326–6
Employment, earnings, and hours, by SIC 1- to 4-digit industry, monthly 1989-Feb 1992, annual rpt, 6744–4
Exports and imports between US and outlying areas, by detailed commodity and mode of transport, 1991, annual rpt, 2424–11
Exports and imports of US, by Harmonized System 6-digit commodity and country, 1991, annual rpt, 2424–13
Injuries from use of consumer products and related activities, by severity and victim age and sex, 1990, annual rpt, 9164–7
Injuries from use of consumer products, by severity, victim age, and detailed product, 1991, annual rpt, 9164–6
Manufacturing census, 1987: concentration of largest firms measured by value added, and for shipments by SIC 2- and 4-digit industry, subject rpt, 2497–6
Manufacturing census, 1987: shipments of manufacturers products, by customer class and SIC 2- and 4-digit industry, subject rpt, 2497–4
Occupational injury and illness rates, by SIC 2- to 4-digit industry, 1989-90, annual rpt, 6844–7
Price indexes (producer), by stage of processing and detailed commodity, monthly rpt, 6762–6
Price indexes (producer), by stage of processing and detailed commodity, monthly 1991, annual rpt, 6764–2
Science, engineering, and technical employment in manufacturing, by field and industry, 1989, triennial rpt, 9627–23
Shipments, trade, and use, for carpets and rugs by product, 1991, annual Current Industrial Rpt, 2506–5.9

Carroll, Irwin
"Preserving the Vital Base: America's Semiconductor Materials and Equipment Industry", 15036–1.1

Carroll, Margaret D.
"Fats, Cholesterol, and Sodium Intake in the Diet of Persons 1-74 Years: U.S.", 4147–16.6

Cartels
see Monopolies and cartels
see Organization of Petroleum Exporting Countries

Carter, Christine L.
"Segregation Analysis of Esophageal Cancer in 221 High-Risk Chinese Families", 4472–1.315

Carter, Grace M.
"Longitudinal Comparison of Charge-Based Weights and Cost-Based Weights", 4652–1.318

Carter, Michael A.
"Use of Restraint Devices To Prevent Collision Injuries and Deaths Among Welfare-Supported Children", 4042–3.312

Carter, Yvonne B.
"Directory of Library Research and Demonstration Projects 1976-1986: Abstracts of Funded Projects", 4878–5

Cartography
Census Bur geographic levels of data coverage, maps, and reference products, 1992 rpt, 2308–67
Census Bur TIGER computer-readable map and geographic data base, files availability and use, 1991 rpt, 2628–32
Census of Population and Housing, 1990: maps and cartographic products availability, listing, 2308–66
Copyrights Register activities, registrations by material type, and fees, FY91 and trends from 1790, annual rpt, 26404–2
Geological Survey activities and funding, FY91, annual rpt, 5664–8
Glaciology intl research summaries, methodology, and bibls, series, 2156–18
Library of Congress activities, acquisitions, services, and financial statements, FY91, annual rpt, 26404–1
Wetlands (coastal) mapping projects status, costs, and methods, 1990 conf, 5508–116
see also Maps

Casey, Connie H.
"Characteristics of HUD-Assisted Renters and Their Units in 1989", 5184–11

Casey, J. L.
"Coal-Fired Flow Facility, University of Tennessee Space Institute, Site Environmental Report for 1990", 3324–2.7

Casey, John G.
"Shark Tagger, 1991 Summary", 2164–21

Cashwell, C. E.
"Analysis of Transporting Highway Route-Controlled Quantities: An Overview of 1985-90", 3008–129

Caskets
see Cemeteries and funerals

Caskey, John P.
"Check-Cashing Outlets in the U.S. Financial System", 9381–1.301

Casualty insurance
see Property and casualty insurance

Catalogs
see Bibliographies
see CD-ROM catalogs and guides
see Computer data file guides
see Directories
see Government publications lists

Cataracts
see Eye diseases and defects

Catfish
see Aquaculture

Cattle
see Dairy industry and products
see Livestock and livestock industry

CATV
see Cable television

Caulkins, Peter P.
"Reregistration's Impact on Agriculture", 1504–9.1

Cayman Islands
Agricultural trade of US, by detailed commodity and country, 1991, annual rpt, 1524–8
Agricultural trade of US, by detailed commodity and country, 1991, semiannual rpt, 1522–4
Economic and social conditions, resources, and trade, and aid, 1992, annual factbook, 9914–14
Economic, social, political, and geographic summary data, by country, 1992, annual factbook, 9114–2
Exports and imports of US, by transport mode, country, and SITC 1- to 3-digit commodity, 1991, annual rpt, 2424–12
Exports of US, detailed Schedule B commodities with countries of destination, 1991, annual rpt, 2424–10
Foreign bank loans to US businesses by location of issuer, with impact of change in Fed Reserve Bd reserve requirements, 1980s-91, article, 9385–1.307
Multinatl US firms foreign affiliates, income statement items by asset size, industry, and country, 1988, biennial article, 8302–2.322
Population size, growth rates, and components of change, by country, projected 1990-2020 and trends from 1950, biennial rpt, 2324–9

Cayton, Michael
"Foreign Participation in U.S. Futures Markets Grows", 8002–4.301

CD-ROM catalogs and guides
American Housing Survey, data coverage, products, and metro areas surveyed 1974-94, 2328–89
BEA rpts data coverage and availability, 1992 annual article, 2702–1.308
BEA rpts data coverage and availability, 1992 annual rpt, 2704–6
Census Bur activities, rpts, and user services, monthly rpt, 2302–3
Census Bur data availability on CD-ROM, and use, 1992 user guide, 2308–64
Census Bur data coverage and availability for economic censuses and related statistics, 1992 preliminary guide, 2308–5
Census Bur data files and rpts, coverage and availability, 1992 annual listing, 2304–2
Census Bur geographic levels of data coverage, maps, and reference products, 1992 rpt, 2308–67
Census Bur rpts and data files, coverage, availability, and use, series, 2326–7
Census Bur rpts and data files, monthly listing, 2302–6
Census of Population and Housing, 1990: data coverage, collection procedures, products and services availability, and uses, guide, 2555–1
Census of Population and Housing, 1990: detailed geographic coverage, CD-ROM user guide, 2308–65
Census of Population and Housing, 1990: maps and cartographic products availability, listing, 2308–66
Census of Population and Housing, 1990: Summary Tape File 3 CD-ROM user guide, 2308–68
Economic censuses of 1987 and related programs, CD-ROM series, user guides, 2306–8
Hazardous substances industrial releases and reduction methods under EPA regulation, with chemical stocks and use, facility directory, 1991 CD-ROM user guide, 9238–70
Library of Congress rpts and products, 1992-93, biennial listing, 26404–6
Map and geographic computer-readable database of Census Bur, TIGER files availability and use, 1991 rpt, 2628–32

CD-ROM releases
Census of Population and Housing, 1990: detailed geographic coverage, State CD-ROM series, 2551–9
Census of Population and Housing, 1990: population and housing characteristics, detailed geographic coverage, State CD-ROM series, 2551–10
Economic censuses of 1987 and related programs, CD-ROM series, 2326–22
Exports, imports, and trade flows, by country and commodity, with background economic indicators, data compilation, monthly CD-ROM, 2002–6
Exports of US, detailed commodities by country, monthly CD-ROM, 2422–13
Hazardous substances industrial releases and reduction methods under EPA regulation, with chemical stocks and use, facility directory, 1987-89, annual CD-ROM, 9234–7
Health condition and care indicators, 1988 natl survey, CD-ROM, 4147–10.184
Imports of US, detailed commodities by country, monthly CD-ROM, 2422–14
Income (personal) per capita and by source, and employment, by industry div, State, MSA, and county, 1969-90, annual CD-ROM, 2704–7
Water supply and quality in streams and lakes, and groundwater levels in wells, by drainage basin, 1990-91, annual CD-ROM, 5664–18
see also CD-ROM catalogs and guides
see also CD-ROM technology and use

CD-ROM technology and use
Census Bur data availability on CD-ROM, and use, 1992 user guide, 2308–64
Fed Govt info storage and transmission on electronic formats, costs and revenues for 4 agencies, FY85-91, GAO rpt, 26125–47
Library of Congress activities, acquisitions, services, and financial statements, FY91, annual rpt, 26404–1
see also CD-ROM catalogs and guides
see also CD-ROM releases

CDC
see Centers for Disease Control

Cedar Rapids, Iowa
see also under By City and By SMSA or MSA in the "Index by Categories"

Celebuski, Carin A.
"Assessment of the National Science Foundation's 1985-87 College Science Instrumentation Program", 9628–87

Celery
see Vegetables and vegetable products

Cella, Margot
"Certification Requirements for Nursing Homes: Final Report", 17206–2.37
"Report on Quality Assurance in Non-PPS Settings", 17206–2.41

Cellular telephones
see Mobile radio

Cement and concrete
Business statistics, detailed data for major industries and economic indicators, *Survey of Current Business*, monthly rpt, 2702–1.20
Business statistics, detailed data for major industries and economic indicators, 1960-91, *Survey of Current Business* biennial supplement, 2704–1
County Business Patterns, 1989: employment, establishments, and payroll, by SIC 2- to 4-digit industry and county, annual State rpt series, 2326–8
County Business Patterns, 1990: employment, establishments, and payroll, by SIC 2- to 4-digit industry and county, annual State rpt series, 2326–6
Employment, earnings, and hours, by SIC 1- to 4-digit industry, monthly 1989-Feb 1992, annual rpt, 6744–4
Energy use and prices for manufacturing industries, 1988 survey, series, 3166–13
Exports and imports between US and outlying areas, by detailed commodity and mode of transport, 1991, annual rpt, 2424–11
Exports and imports of US, by country and detailed commodity, monthly rpt, 2422–12
Exports and imports of US, by Harmonized System 6-digit commodity and country, 1991, annual rpt, 2424–13
Exports and imports of US, by transport mode, country, and SITC 1- to 3-digit commodity, 1991, annual rpt, 2424–12
Exports of US, detailed Schedule B commodities with countries of destination, 1991, annual rpt, 2424–10
Foreign countries mineral production, reserves, and industry role in domestic economy and world supply, world area and country rpt series, 5606–1
Freight (waterborne domestic and foreign) by commodity, traffic, and passengers, by port and waterway, 1989, annual rpt, 3754–3
Hwy construction material prices and indexes for Federal-aid system, by type of material and urban-rural location, quarterly rpt, 7552–7
Hwy construction material prices and indexes for Federal-aid system, by type of material, quarterly press release, 7552–16
Hwy construction material use by type, and spending, by State, 1940s-91, annual rpt, 7554–29
Input-output structure of US economy, detailed interindustry transactions for 541 industries, and components of final demand, 1982 benchmark data, 2708–17
Labor productivity, indexes of output, hours, and employment by SIC 2- to 4-digit industry, 1967-90, annual rpt, 6824–1.3
Manufacturing annual survey, 1990: finances and operations, by SIC 2- to 4-digit industry, series, 2506–14
Manufacturing census, 1987: concentration of largest firms measured by value added, and for shipments by SIC 2- and 4-digit industry, subject rpt, 2497–6
Manufacturing census, 1987: shipments of manufacturers products, by customer class and SIC 2- and 4-digit industry, subject rpt, 2497–4
Manufacturing finances and operations, by SIC 2- to 4-digit industry, forecast 1992, annual rpt, 2044–28
Mineral Industry Surveys, commodity review of production, trade, stocks, and use, monthly rpt, 5612–1.2
Mineral Industry Surveys, State reviews of production, 1991, preliminary annual rpt, 5614–6
Minerals Yearbook, Vol 1, 1989: commodity reviews of production, use, trade, prices, and mining operations, annual rpt, 5604–33
Minerals Yearbook, Vol 1, 1990: commodity review of production, reserves, supply, use, and trade, annual rpt, 5604–20.13
Minerals Yearbook, Vol 2, 1989: State reviews of production and sales by commodity, and business activity, annual rpt series, 5604–16
Minerals Yearbook, Vol 2, 1990: State reviews of production and sales by commodity, and business activity, annual rpt series, 5604–22
Minerals Yearbook, Vol 3, 1989: foreign country reviews of production, trade, and policy, by commodity, annual rpt, 5604–35
Multinatl firms US affiliates finances and operations, by industry, country of parent firm, and State, 1987, 2708–48
Occupational injuries and incidence, employment, and hours in stone mines and related operations, 1990, annual rpt, 6664–5
Occupational injury and illness rates, by SIC 2- to 4-digit industry, 1989-90, annual rpt, 6844–7
Occupational injury and illness rates, by SIC 2- to 4-digit industry, 1990, annual rpt, 6844–1
OECD trade, total and for 4 major countries, and US trade by country, by commodity, 1980-90, world area rpt series, 9116–1
Pollution (air) abatement equipment shipments by industry, and new and backlog orders, by product, 1991, annual Current Industrial Rpt, 2506–12.5
Pollution (air) contributing to global warming, emissions by monitoring site and country, and temperature change by world area and US region, 1860s-1990, annual rpt, 3004–33
Price indexes (producer), by stage of processing and detailed commodity, monthly rpt, 6762–6
Price indexes (producer), by stage of processing and detailed commodity, monthly 1991, annual rpt, 6764–2
Production and PPI for building materials, and cement shipments to census divs, Puerto Rico, and foreign countries, quarterly rpt, 2042–1.5; 2042–1.6
Production, prices, trade, and foreign and US industry devs, by commodity, bimonthly rpt, 5602–4
Production, prices, trade, use, employment, tariffs, and stockpiles, by mineral, with foreign comparisons, 1987-91, annual rpt, 5604–18
Production, trade, use, and foreign investment in US industry, for minerals, 1985-90 and projected to 2000, annual rpt, 5304–5
Science, engineering, and technical employment in manufacturing, by field and industry, 1989, triennial rpt, 9627–23
Tax (income) returns of corporations, income and tax items by asset size and detailed industry, 1989, annual rpt, 8304–4; 8304–21

Cemeteries and funerals
Casket manufacturers and other industries concentration measured by shipments, 1987 Census of Manufactures, subject rpt, 2497–6
Casket manufacturers financial and operating data, 1990 Annual Survey of Manufactures, series, 2506–14
Casket manufacturers price indexes, monthly rpt, 6762–6
Casket manufacturers price indexes, monthly 1991, annual rpt, 6764–2
Casket manufacturers shipments by customer class and SIC 2- and 4-digit industry, 1987 Census of Manufactures, subject rpt, 2497–4
Consumer spending, natl income and product account benchmark revisions, 1929-88, 2708–5
Consumer spending, natl income and product accounts, comprehensive accounts and components, *Survey of Current Business*, monthly rpt, 2702–1.25
County Business Patterns, 1989: employment, establishments, and payroll, by SIC 2- to 4-digit industry and county, annual State rpt series, 2326–8
County Business Patterns, 1990: employment, establishments, and payroll, by SIC 2- to 4-digit industry and county, annual State rpt series, 2326–6
CPI by component for US city average, and by selected metro area, region, and population size, monthly rpt, 6762–2
Crime victim compensation and support service programs funding, by offense and State, FY88-90, biennial rpt, 6064–37
Employee paid leave days for funerals, for State and local govt employees, 1990, biennial rpt, 6784–21
Employment, earnings, and hours, by SIC 1- to 4-digit industry, monthly 1989-Feb 1992, annual rpt, 6744–4
Input-output structure of US economy, detailed interindustry transactions for 541 industries, and components of final demand, 1982 benchmark data, 2708–17
Tax (estate) returns property and tax data, by size of gross estate and State, 1989-90, article, 8302–2.305
Tax (income) returns of sole proprietorships, income statement items, by industry group, 1990, annual article, 8302–2.317; 8302–2.320
Tax exempt organizations and employee plans listed on IRS masterfile, determinations, applications, and rulings, FY91, annual rpt, 8304–3.2
Workers compensation laws of States and Fed Govt, 1992 annual rpt, 6504–11
see also Military cemeteries and funerals

Censorship
Foreign countries human rights conditions in 170 countries, 1991, annual rpt, 21384–3
see also Freedom of the press

Census Bureau
see Bureau of Census

Census divisions
see under By Census Division in the "Index by Categories"

Census of Agriculture
Data coverage and availability of Census Bur rpts and data files, 1992 annual listing, 2304–2
Data from economic censuses of 1987 and related programs, CD-ROM series, 2326–22
Data from economic censuses of 1987 and related programs, CD-ROM series, user guides, 2306–8
Data on agriculture, young readers pamphlet series, 2346–1
Energy-related data coverage and availability from Census Bur, 1991 pamphlet, 2326–7.84

Census of Construction Industries
Data collection, coverage, availability, and procedural history, 1987 economic censuses, 2628–16
Data coverage and availability for economic censuses and related statistics, 1992 preliminary guide, 2308–5
Data from economic censuses of 1987 and related programs, CD-ROM series, 2326–22
Data from economic censuses of 1987 and related programs, CD-ROM series, user guides, 2306–8

Census of Fatal Occupational Injuries
Occupational deaths data collection program of BLS and States, with results by selected worker characteristics, 1991, article, 6722–1.338

Census of Financial, Insurance, and Real Estate Industries
Data coverage and availability for economic censuses and related statistics, 1992 preliminary guide, 2308–5

Census of Governments
Data coverage and availability of Census Bur rpts and data files, 1992 annual listing, 2304–2
Energy-related data coverage and availability from Census Bur, 1991 pamphlet, 2326–7.84

Census of Housing
Data coverage and availability of Census Bur rpts and data files, 1992 annual listing, 2304–2
Housing inventory, occupancy, and costs, 1990 census, State fact sheet series, 2326–21
Housing median value and rent, by State and region, 1990 census compared to 1970 and 1980, fact sheet, 2328–83
Housing unit summary characteristics, by householder race and age, county, place, and urban-rural location, 1990 census, State rpt series, 2471–1
see also Census of Population and Housing

Census of Manufactures
Concentration of largest firms measured by value added, and for shipments by SIC 2- and 4-digit industry, 1987 census, subject rpt, 2497–6
Corn and barley feed and industrial use, revised estimates 1980s-91, article, 1561–4.301
Data collection, coverage, availability, and procedural history, 1987 economic censuses, 2628–16
Data coverage and availability for economic censuses and related statistics, 1992 preliminary guide, 2308–5
Data from economic censuses of 1987 and related programs, CD-ROM series, 2326–22
Data from economic censuses of 1987 and related programs, CD-ROM series, user guides, 2306–8
Operations and performance of manufacturing industries, analytical rpt series, 2506–16
Shipments of manufacturers products by customer class and SIC 2- and 4-digit industry, 1987 census, subject rpt, 2497–4

Census of Mineral Industries
Data collection, coverage, availability, and procedural history, 1987 economic censuses, 2628–16
Data coverage and availability for economic censuses and related statistics, 1992 preliminary guide, 2308–5

Census of Minority-Owned Business Enterprises
see Survey of Minority-Owned Business Enterprises

Census of Outlying Areas
Data collection, coverage, availability, and procedural history, 1987 economic censuses, 2628–16
Data coverage and availability for economic censuses and related statistics, 1992 preliminary guide, 2308–5

Census of Population
Ancestry of US population, by group and State, 1990 census, press release, 2328–87
Assistance (formula grants) of Fed Govt, use of adjusted census and intercensal data for allocation, with data by program and State, FY91, 25408–120
Budget proposals for 2000 decennial census planning and economic statistics programs improvement, FY92, hearing, 21628–98
Commuters, by county of residence and work, for top 10 metro areas, 1990 census, press release, 2328–84
Data accuracy and enumeration methodology issues, 1990 census, hearing, 21628–97
Data accuracy, evaluation, and adjustment issues, 1990 census, hearing, 21628–99
Data adjustment for undercounts, Commerce Dept decision against adjustment, 1990 census, hearing, 21628–101
Data adjustment for undercounts, evaluation of advisability, with error rates by race and selected city, 1990 census, hearing, 21628–102
Data adjustment for undercounts, issues, 1990 census, hearing, 25408–119
Data adjustment in intercensal data for 1990 census undercounts, final decision with data by region and State, 2328–90
Data adjustment in intercensal data for 1990 census undercounts, recommendations with alternative undercount estimates, 2628–36
Data coverage and availability of Census Bur rpts and data files, 1992 annual listing, 2304–2
Homeless shelter and on-street population counts, assessment of methodology and procedures, 1990 census, GAO rpt, 26119–370
Local govts participation in 1990 census and plans for 2000 census, hearing, 21628–100
Minority group participation in 1990 census, effectiveness and quality of outreach and promotional programs, hearing, 21628–103

Planning activities for 2000 census, and review of 1990 census operations, hearing, 21628–104
Population characteristics and living arrangements, by county, place, and urban-rural location, 1990 census, State rpt series, 2531–1
Population characteristics and living arrangements, for Native American, urban, and metro areas, 1990 census, series, 2531–2
Post-enumeration review of planning and conduct of 1990 census, and recommendations for improvement, GAO rpt, 26119–403
see also Census of Population and Housing

Census of Population and Housing
Data collection and statistical program plans of Census Bur, advisory committees findings and recommendations, 1992 conf, 2628–35
Data coverage and availability of Census Bur rpts and data files, 1992 annual listing, 2304–2
Data coverage by geographic level, maps, and reference products from Census Bur, 1992 rpt, 2308–67
Data coverage, collection procedures, products and services availability, and uses, 1990 census, guide, 2555–1
Data summary, use, and availability, for selected long form questions, 1990 census, fact sheet series, 2326–23
Energy-related data coverage and availability from Census Bur, 1991 pamphlet, 2326–7.84
Immigrants, by period of entry, citizenship, State, birthplace, and for top cities and counties, 1990 census, press release, 2328–88
Indian tribes population size, with data by State, 1990 census, press release, 2328–86
Industry and occupation classification codes, alphabetical index, 1990 census, 2628–1
Industry and occupation classification codes, classified index, 1990 census, 2628–2
Map and geographic computer-readable database of Census Bur, TIGER files availability and use, 1991 rpt, 2628–32
Maps and cartographic products availability, 1990 census, listing, 2308–66
Pacific territories population and housing detailed characteristics, by location, 1990 census, series, 2551–8
Population and housing characteristics, detailed geographic coverage, 1990 census, CD-ROM user guide, 2308–65
Population and housing characteristics, detailed geographic coverage, 1990 census, State CD-ROM series, 2551–9; 2551–10
Population and housing characteristics, households, and land area, by county, subdiv, and place, 1990 census, State rpt series, 2551–1
Population and housing characteristics, Summary Tape File 3 CD-ROM user guide, 1990 census, 2308–68
Population and housing summary characteristics, by county, subdiv, and place, 1990 census, State rpt series, 2551–7
see also Census of Housing
see also Census of Population

Census of Retail Trade
Data collection, coverage, availability, and procedural history, 1987 economic censuses, 2628–16
Data coverage and availability for economic censuses and related statistics, 1992 preliminary guide, 2308–5
Data from economic censuses of 1987 and related programs, CD-ROM series, 2326–22
Data from economic censuses of 1987 and related programs, CD-ROM series, user guides, 2306–8
Sales and establishments, by merchandise line, 1987 census, State rpt series, discontinued, 2399–3

Census of Service Industries
Data collection, coverage, availability, and procedural history, 1987 economic censuses, 2628–16
Data coverage and availability for economic censuses and related statistics, 1992 preliminary guide, 2308–5
Data from economic censuses of 1987 and related programs, CD-ROM series, 2326–22
Data from economic censuses of 1987 and related programs, CD-ROM series, user guides, 2306–8

Census of Transportation
Data collection, coverage, availability, and procedural history, 1987 economic censuses, 2628–16
Data from economic censuses of 1987 and related programs, CD-ROM series, 2326–22
Data from economic censuses of 1987 and related programs, CD-ROM series, user guides, 2306–8
see also Census of Transportation, Communications, and Utilities Industries

Census of Transportation, Communications, and Utilities Industries
Data coverage and availability for economic censuses and related statistics, 1992 preliminary guide, 2308–5

Census of Wholesale Trade
Data collection, coverage, availability, and procedural history, 1987 economic censuses, 2628–16
Data coverage and availability for economic censuses and related statistics, 1992 preliminary guide, 2308–5
Data from economic censuses of 1987 and related programs, CD-ROM series, 2326–22
Data from economic censuses of 1987 and related programs, CD-ROM series, user guides, 2306–8

Census of Women-Owned Businesses
see Survey of Women-Owned Businesses

Census tracts
Census Bur data coverage and availability for statistics on counties, cities, and small areas, 1991 rpt, 2326–7.82
Census Bur geographic levels of data coverage, maps, and reference products, 1992 rpt, 2308–67
Census of Population and Housing, 1990: detailed geographic coverage, State CD-ROM series, 2551–9
Census of Population and Housing, 1990: population and housing characteristics, detailed geographic coverage, State CD-ROM series, 2551–10

Center for Human Resource Research, Ohio State University
"Maternal-Child Health Data from the NLSY: 1988 Tabulations and Summary Discussion", 4478–197

Center for Mental Health Services
Facilities for mental health care, staff, patients, and finances, 1970s-91, biennial rpt, 4094–1

Centers for Disease Control
Accident deaths and injuries prevention, and treatment, 1991 conf papers, 4208–35
AIDS case definitions of CDC proposed for 1992, compared to 1982-87 definitions, 1992 rpt, 26356–6.6
AIDS cases by risk group, race, sex, age, State, and MSA, and deaths, quarterly rpt, 4202–9
Assistance (financial) of HHS, by program, recipient, State, and city, FY91, annual regional listings, 4004–3
Budget of US, obligations and authority by function, agency, and program, with summaries and analyses, FY93, annual rpt, 104–2
Computer video display terminal use relation to musculoskeletal disorders, among telephone industry workers, 1990, 4248–93
Expenditures of Fed Govt in States, by type, program, agency, and State, FY91, annual rpt, 2464–2
Hepatitis cases by infection source, age, sex, race, and State, and deaths, by strain, 1989 and trends from 1966, 4205–2
Idiopathic CD4+ T-lymphocytopenia epidemiology and patient characteristics, 1992 conf, 4208–36
Malaria cases in US, for military personnel and US and foreign natls, and by country of infection, 1966-90, annual rpt, 4205–4
Minority grads of CDC Epidemic Intelligence Service, by race and current employer, 1950s-80s, article, 4042–3.374
Morbidity and Mortality Weekly Report, infectious notifiable disease cases and deaths, and other public health issues, periodic journal, 4202–7
Morbidity and Mortality Weekly Report, infectious notifiable disease cases by age, race, and State, and deaths, 1940s-91, annual rpt, 4204–1
Morbidity and Mortality Weekly Report, infectious notifiable disease cases by State, and public health issues, 4202–1
Morbidity and Mortality Weekly Report, special supplements, series, 4206–2
Ship (passenger) sanitary inspection scores, biweekly rpt, 4202–10
Vaccination needs for intl travel by country, and disease prevention recommendations, 1992 annual rpt, 4204–11
Vaccination research rpts, 1991 annual listing, 4204–16
Vaccine and toxoid shipments, by product type, 1987-90, 4205–22
see also National Institute for Occupational Safety and Health
see also Office on Smoking and Health

CENTO
see Central Treaty Organization

Central African Republic
Agricultural trade of US, by detailed commodity and country, 1991, annual rpt, 1524–8

Agricultural trade of US, by detailed commodity and country, 1991, semiannual rpt, 1522–4
AID economic aid to developing countries, obligations and disbursements by country, quarterly rpt, 9912–4
Economic and military aid and loans from US and intl agencies, by program and country, FY46-91, annual rpt, 9914–5
Economic and social conditions of developing countries from 1960s, and Intl Dev Cooperation Agency and AID activities and funding, FY91-93, annual rpt, 9904–4
Economic conditions, income, production, prices, employment, and trade, 1992 periodic country rpt, 2046–4.11
Economic, social, political, and geographic summary data, by country, 1992, annual factbook, 9114–2
Exports and imports of US, by transport mode, country, and SITC 1- to 3-digit commodity, 1991, annual rpt, 2424–12
Human rights conditions in 170 countries, and US economic and military aid, 1991, annual rpt, 21384–3
Military aid of US, arms sales, and training programs costs and budget requests, by program, world region, and country, FY91-93, annual rpt, 7144–13
Military spending, arms trade, and force strengths, with govt spending and population, by country, 1979-89, annual rpt, 9824–1
Minerals Yearbook, Vol 3, 1989: foreign country review of production, trade, and policy, by commodity, annual rpt, 5604–35.1
Population size, growth rates, and components of change, by country, projected 1990-2020 and trends from 1950, biennial rpt, 2324–9
Refugee migration, and intl aid programs, by world area and country of origin and asylum, 1991, annual rpt, 7004–15
UN voting record and share of votes in agreement with US, by issue, country, and world area, 1991, annual rpt, 7004–18

Central America
Agricultural exports of US, for grains, oilseed products, hides, skins, and cotton, by country, weekly rpt, 1922–3
Agricultural trade of US, by detailed commodity and country, 1991, annual rpt, 1524–8
Agricultural trade of US, by detailed commodity and country, 1991, semiannual rpt, 1522–4
Economic and military aid and loans from US and intl agencies, by program and country, FY46-91, annual rpt, 9914–5
Economic and social conditions of developing countries from 1960s, and Intl Dev Cooperation Agency and AID activities and funding, FY91-93, annual rpt, 9904–4
Economic and social conditions, resources, and trade, and aid, 1992, annual factbook, 9914–14
Economic conditions, trade, and foreign aid, for Latin America, working paper series, 9916–13
Economic, population, and agricultural data, US and other aid sources, and AID activity, 1991 regional rpt, 9916–12.59
Exports (duty-free) of Caribbean area to US, and imports from US, by country, and impact on US employment, by commodity, 1991, annual rpt, 6364–2
Exports (duty-free) of Caribbean area to US, by commodity and country, with consumer and industry impacts, 1984-91, annual rpt, 9884–20
Exports and imports (waterborne) of US, by type of service, customs district, port, and world area, monthly rpt, 2422–7
Exports and imports of OECD, total and for 4 major countries, and US trade by country, by commodity, 1980-90, world area rpt, 9116–1.5
Immigrants admitted to US, by class of admission, country of birth, and MSA of destination, FY91, advance annual rpt, 6264–4
Immigrants and legalized aliens, by occupational group and country of birth, preliminary FY91, annual tables, 6264–1
Immigrants and nonimmigrants admitted to US, alien workers, visitors, deportations, and naturalizations, FY91, annual summary rpt, 6264–7
Immigrants from Central America in DC, by selected employment and other characteristics, and reasons for migration, 1985-88, working paper, 6366–6.3
Immigration to US, alien workers, visitors, deportations, and naturalizations, by country, FY91 and trends from 1820, annual rpt, 6264–2
Imports of Latin America and Caribbean countries from US, by State of origin, 1987 and 1990, 2048–160
Inter-American Foundation activities, grants by recipient, and fellowships, by country, FY91, annual rpt, 14424–1
Inter-American Foundation dev grants by program area, and fellowships by field and instn, by country, FY72-91, annual rpt, 14424–2
Investment (foreign direct) of US, by industry group and world area, 1989-91, annual article, 2702–1.332
Military aid of US, arms sales, and training programs costs and budget requests, by program, world region, and country, FY91-93, annual rpt, 7144–13
Multinatl US firms and foreign affiliates finances and operations, by industry and country, 1989 benchmark survey, annual rpt, 2704–5
Multinatl US firms foreign affiliates, income statement items by asset size, industry, and country, 1988, biennial article, 8302–2.322
Peace Corps activities, funding by program, and volunteers, by country, FY93, annual rpt, 9654–1
Refugee migration, and intl aid programs, by world area and country of origin and asylum, 1991, annual rpt, 7004–15
Terrorism (intl) incidents, casualties, and attacks on US targets, by attack type and country, 1991, annual rpt, 7004–22
Tobacco production and use in Latin America, Canada, and US, and related economic, health, and social issues, 1950s-92, annual rpt, 4204–18
Travel to US, by characteristics of visit and traveler, country, port city, and State of destination, quarterly rpt, 2902–1
Weather events and anomalies, precipitation and temperature for US and foreign locations, weekly rpt, 2182–6
see also Belize
see also Caribbean area
see also Central American Common Market
see also Costa Rica
see also El Salvador
see also Guatemala
see also Honduras
see also Inter-American Development Bank
see also Latin American Integration Association
see also Nicaragua
see also Panama
see also under By Foreign Country in the "Index by Categories"

Central American Common Market
Exports, imports, membership, and trade impacts of regional preferential trading arrangements, by group, late 1940s-91, article, 9373–1.308

Central business districts
Commuting accessibility of central business district, impact on housing prices, for Philadelphia, 1970-88, working paper, 9387–8.258

Central cities
Asian and Pacific Islands Americans social and economic characteristics, for West and total US, 1990-91, Current Population Report, 2546–1.462
Black Americans social and economic characteristics, for South and total US, 1991 and trends from 1950, annual Current Population Rpt, 2546–1.463
Census of Housing, 1990: summary unit characteristics, by householder race and age, county, place, and urban-rural location, State rpt series, 2471–1
Census of Population and Housing, 1990: summary characteristics, households, and land area, by region, State, MSA, and city, US rpt, 2551–1.1
Census of Population, 1990: population characteristics and living arrangements, by county, place, and urban-rural location, State rpt series, 2531–1
Consumer Income, socioeconomic characteristics of persons, families, and households, detailed cross-tabulations, Current Population Rpt series, 2546–6
Deaths and rates, by cause and selected social, demographic, and employment characteristics, 1979-85, natl longitudinal study, 4478–186
Definitions of MSAs and central cities, and revisions, 1992, annual listing, 104–32
Educational enrollment, by grade, instn type and control, and student characteristics, 1990 and trends from 1947, annual Current Population Rpt, 2546–1.459
Employment and unemployment in metro and nonmetro areas, monthly rpt, quarterly data, 6742–2.9
Households and family characteristics, by location, 1991, annual Current Population Rpt, 2546–1.457
Housing (rental) units, total, with HUD assistance by program, and eligible for aid, by unit, household, and neighborhood characteristics, and location, 1989, biennial rpt, 5184–11
Housing and households detailed characteristics, and unit and neighborhood quality, by location, 1989, biennial rpt supplement, 2485–13

Housing and households detailed characteristics, and unit and neighborhood quality, MSA surveys, series, 2485–6
Housing energy use, costs, and conservation, and household and housing characteristics, survey rpt series, 3166–7
Housing unit and household characteristics of recent movers, and reason for move, by tenure, 1989, 2486–1.12
Housing vacancy and occupancy rates, and vacant unit characteristics and costs, by region and metro-nonmetro location, quarterly rpt, 2482–1
Income (household) and poverty status under alternative income definitions, by recipient characteristics, 1979-91, annual Current Population Rpt, 2546–6.78
Income (personal) relative to median, by race and selected other characteristics, mid 1960s-89, Current Population Rpt, 2546–6.73
Income per capita for central cities and suburbs, by city, 1991 hearings, 21308–28
Migration, immigration, and mover characteristics compared to nonmovers, 1987-90, annual Current Population Rpt, 2546–1.456
Migration, population change, and areas losing population, by region, State, and metro-nonmetro location, 1980s and trends from 1940, Current Population Rpt, 2546–2.164
Migration since 1990, mover characteristics by same or different area, and compared to nonmovers, 1991, annual Current Population Rpt, 2546–1.464
see also Central business districts
see also Urban renewal

Central Intelligence Agency
Budget of US, authoritative financial statements with appropriations, outlays, and receipts, by category and agency, FY91, annual rpt, 8104–2.2
Budget of US, obligations and authority by function, agency, and program, with summaries and analyses, FY93, annual rpt, 104–2
Chiefs of State and Cabinet members, by country, bimonthly listing, 9112–4
China economic performance and trade, 1980-91, annual rpt, 9114–5
Cuba trade, by commodity and country, mid 1980s-91, 9118–8
Developing countries debt to foreign lenders, and IMF credit outstanding, by country, 1985-91, annual rpt, 9114–7
Eastern Europe transition to market economies, economic conditions, trade, and foreign investment, by country, 1990-91, 9118–13
Economic conditions, and oil supply and demand, for major industrial countries, monthly rpt, 9112–1
Economic, social, political, and geographic summary data, by country, 1992, annual factbook, 9114–2
Energy production by type, and oil trade, and use, by country group and selected country, monthly rpt, 9112–2
OECD trade, total and for 4 major countries, and US trade by country, by commodity, 1980-90, world area rpt series, 9116–1
Soviet Union former Republics and Baltic States population size and characteristics, 1989-92, 9118–19
Soviet Union officials public appearances in and outside USSR, annual rpt, discontinued, 9114–1

Central Treaty Organization
Economic and military aid and loans from US and intl agencies, by program and country, FY46-91, annual rpt, 9914–5

Centrally planned economies
Agricultural Outlook, production, prices, marketing, and trade, by commodity, forecast and current situation, monthly rpt with articles, 1502–4
Agricultural trade of US, by commodity and country, bimonthly rpt, 1522–1
Agricultural trade of US, by detailed commodity and country, 1991, annual rpt, 1524–8
Economic and social conditions of foreign countries, working paper series, 2326–18
Energy use and production, by fuel type, country, and country group, projected 1995-2010 and trends from 1970, annual rpt, 3164–84
Oil and gas production and trade by country, and use, for centrally planned economy countries, monthly rpt, 9112–2
see also Albania
see also Bulgaria
see also Cambodia
see also China, Peoples Republic
see also Council for Mutual Economic Assistance
see also Cuba
see also Czechoslovakia
see also East-West trade
see also Eastern Europe
see also Germany, East
see also Hungary
see also Korea, North
see also Poland
see also Romania
see also Soviet Union
see also Vietnam
see also Yugoslavia
see also under By Foreign Country in the "Index by Categories"

Ceramic products
see Advanced materials
see Clay industry and products
see Pottery and porcelain products

Cereals
see Grains and grain products

Cerebrovascular diseases
Cases of acute and chronic conditions, disability, absenteeism, and health services use, by selected characteristics, 1990, annual rpt, 4147–10.182; 4147–10.183
Deaths and rates, by cause, age, sex, marital status, race, and State, 1989, US Vital Statistics advance annual rpt, 4146–5.124
Deaths and rates, by cause and age, preliminary 1990-91, US Vital Statistics annual rpt, 4144–7
Deaths and rates, by cause and selected social, demographic, and employment characteristics, 1979-85, natl longitudinal study, 4478–186
Deaths and rates, by cause, provisional data, monthly rpt, 4142–1.2
Deaths and rates, by detailed location, cause, and demographic characteristics, 1989, US Vital Statistics annual rpt, 4144–3
Deaths during 1986, decedents health condition, services use, habits, and social, employment, and other characteristics, 4147–20.19
Health condition and care indicators, 1950s-90 with health improvement and disease prevention goals for 1990, annual data compilation, 4144–11
Hospital deaths of Medicare patients, actual and expected rates by diagnosis, with hospital characteristics, by instn, FY90, annual State rpt series, 4654–14
Hospitalization for stroke, diagnostic coding errors and impacts on Medicare costs, 1980s, 4006–7.12
Hypertension cases, stroke and heart disease risk, and drug dosages, with diagnosis and treatment methods, 1992 quadrennial rpt, 4478–198
Indian Health Service and tribal facilities and use, and Indians health and other characteristics, by IHS region, 1980s-90, annual chartbook, 4084–7
Natl Heart, Lung, and Blood Inst activities, and grants by recipient and location, FY91 and disease trends from 1940, annual rpt, 4474–15
Natl Inst of Neurological Disorders and Stroke activities, and disorder cases, FY91, annual rpt, 4474–25
see also under By Disease in the "Index by Categories"

Cerrelli, Ezio C.
"Crash Data and Rates for Age-Sex Groups of Drivers, 1990", 7768–105
"1991 Traffic Fatalities, Preliminary Report", 7762–11

Certificates of deposit
Banks (insured commercial) domestic and foreign office consolidated financial statements, monthly rpt, quarterly data, 9362–1.4
Banks (insured commercial and savings) finances, for foreign and domestic offices, by asset size, 1990, annual rpt, 9294–4.2
Banks and thrifts finances and operations by deposit size, Fed Reserve functional cost analysis, 1991, annual rpt, 9364–6
Banks and thrifts in New England, deposits by type and loans, relation to capital/asset ratios, by instn size, 1990-91, working paper, 9373–27.4
Banks uninsured deposits by type and bank size, and relation to bank size and selected operating ratios, 1980s-91, technical paper, 9385–8.126
Economic indicators and components, current data and annual trends, monthly rpt, 23842–1.5
Families financial status, income, net worth, and assets and debt by type, by income and selected characteristics, 1983 and 1989, article, 9362–1.301
Foreign and US economic conditions, and trade devs and balances, with data by selected country and country group, monthly rpt, 9882–14
Foreign and US industrial stock indexes and long-term govt bond yields, for selected countries, weekly chartbook, 9365–1.5
Households financial services use, by account type and instn type and location, 1989 survey, article, 9362–1.303
Interest rates for commercial paper, govt securities, other financial instruments, and home mortgages, monthly rpt, 9365–2.14

Interest rates in money and capital markets, weekly averages by instrument, 1990, annual rpt, 9364–5.3
New England States banks and thrifts, assets and liabilities by type, and deposits relation to capital/asset ratios, by instn type and size, 1980s-91, article, 9373–1.309
North Central States, FHLB 6th District insured S&Ls financial condition and operations by State, quarterly rpt, 9302–23
Savings instns failure resolution activity of Resolution Trust Corp, brokered deposits, fees, and interest rates by instn and region, as of July 1991, hearing, 21248–171
Savings instns financial statements, for instns insured by Savings Assn Insurance Fund by FHLB district and State, and for FDIC-insured savings banks, 1989, annual rpt, 8434–1
Savings instns insured by Savings Assn Insurance Fund, assets, liabilities, and deposit and loan activity, by conservatorship status, monthly rpt, 8432–1
Southeastern States, Fed Reserve 5th District insured commercial banks financial statements, by State, quarterly rpt, 9389–18
Southeastern States, Fed Reserve 8th District banking and economic conditions, quarterly rpt with articles, 9391–16
Yields on govt and private issues, weekly rpt, 9391–4

Certification
see Licenses and permits
see Occupational testing and certification

Ceylon
see Sri Lanka

CFE treaty
see Treaty on Conventional Armed Forces in Europe

Chad
Agricultural trade of US, by detailed commodity and country, 1991, annual rpt, 1524–8
Agricultural trade of US, by detailed commodity and country, 1991, semiannual rpt, 1522–4
AID economic aid to developing countries, obligations and disbursements by country, quarterly rpt, 9912–4
Background Notes, summary social, political, and economic data, 1992 rpt, 7006–2.20
Economic and military aid and loans from US and intl agencies, by program and country, FY46-91, annual rpt, 9914–5
Economic and social conditions of developing countries from 1960s, and Intl Dev Cooperation Agency and AID activities and funding, FY91-93, annual rpt, 9904–4
Economic conditions, income, production, prices, employment, and trade, 1991 periodic country rpt, 2046–4.3
Economic, social, political, and geographic summary data, by country, 1992, annual factbook, 9114–2
Exports and imports of US, by transport mode, country, and SITC 1- to 3-digit commodity, 1991, annual rpt, 2424–12
Exports of US, detailed Schedule B commodities with countries of destination, 1991, annual rpt, 2424–10
Human rights conditions in 170 countries, and US economic and military aid, 1991, annual rpt, 21384–3
Military aid of US, arms sales, and training programs costs and budget requests, by program, world region, and country, FY91-93, annual rpt, 7144–13
Military spending, arms trade, and force strengths, with govt spending and population, by country, 1979-89, annual rpt, 9824–1
Minerals Yearbook, Vol 3, 1989: foreign country review of production, trade, and policy, by commodity, annual rpt, 5604–35.1
Population size, growth rates, and components of change, by country, projected 1990-2020 and trends from 1950, biennial rpt, 2324–9
Refugee migration, and intl aid programs, by world area and country of origin and asylum, 1991, annual rpt, 7004–15
UN voting record and share of votes in agreement with US, by issue, country, and world area, 1991, annual rpt, 7004–18

Chadwick, Ann
"School Lunch and the Dietary Guidelines", 1504–9.1

Chaloud, D. J.
"Offsite Environmental Monitoring Report: Radiation Monitoring Around U.S. Nuclear Test Areas, 1990", 9194–17

Champaign, Ill.
Wages by occupation, for office and plant workers, 1991 survey, periodic MSA rpt, 6785–12.2
see also under By City and By SMSA or MSA in the "Index by Categories"

CHAMPUS
see Civilian Health and Medical Program of the Uniformed Services

Chance, Sean
"Farm Financial Performance by Farm Credit District, 1980, 1985, and 1990", 1541–1.317

Chancroid
see Sexually transmitted diseases

Chaney, Bradford
"Scientific and Engineering Research Facilities at Universities and Colleges: 1992", 9624–25

Chang, Clara
"Union Membership Statistics in 12 Countries", 6722–1.305

Chapman, Louisa E.
"Influenza—U.S., 1989-90 and 1990-91 Seasons", 4202–7.316

Characteristics of Business Owners Survey
Minority- and woman-owned businesses and owner characteristics, by industry, employment and sales size, and form of ownership, 1987 survey, 2328–59

Chari, V. V.
"Optimal Fiscal and Monetary Policy: Some Recent Results", 9383–20.17

Charity
see Gifts and private contributions
see Nonprofit organizations and foundations

Charleston, S.C.
Freight (waterborne domestic and foreign) by commodity, traffic, and passengers, by port and waterway, 1989, annual rpt, 3754–3.1
Wages by occupation, and benefits for office and plant workers, 1992 survey, periodic MSA rpt, 6785–3.5
see also under By City and By SMSA or MSA in the "Index by Categories"

Charleston, W.Va.
see also under By City and By SMSA or MSA in the "Index by Categories"

Charlotte, N.C.
Housing starts and completions authorized by building permits in 40 MSAs, quarterly rpt, 2382–9
see also under By City and By SMSA or MSA in the "Index by Categories"

Charrette, Susan M.
"Capital Flight from Debtor Nations When Labor Is Mobile", 9385–8.122

Chartbooks
CCC financial condition and major commodity program operations, FY63-88, annual chartbook, 1824–2
Disabled workers labor force status, type and cause of disability, and other characteristics, 1970s-89, chartbook, 4948–11
Economic indicators and components, and Fed Reserve 4th District business and financial conditions, monthly chartbook, 9377–10
Exports, imports, and balances of US with major trading partners, by product category, 1987-91, annual chartbook, 9884–21
Family life and relationships quality and other issues, views of parents and children, 1990 survey, 15528–2
Farm financial and marketing conditions, forecast 1992, annual chartbook, 1504–8
Financial data for US and selected foreign countries, including exchange rates, interest rates, gold prices, and security yields, weekly chartbook, 9365–1.5
Health care services use, spending, payment sources, and admin, with foreign comparisons, 1970s-90, chartbook, 21788–213
Housing and households summary characteristics, 1989 and trends, chartbook, 2486–2.1
Hwy Statistics, summary data with trends and projections, 1992 chartbook, 7554–41
Indian Health Service and tribal facilities and use, and Indians health and other characteristics, by IHS region, 1980s-90, annual chartbook, 4084–7
Indian Health Service facilities, funding, operations, and Indian health and other characteristics, 1950s-91, annual chartbook, 4084–1
Military health care benefits and costs under Civilian Health and Medical Program of Uniformed Services, FY85-90, annual chartbook, 3504–23
Minority group and women employment by industry sector, and govt salaries, by occupation, mid 1960s-90, chartbook, 9248–20
Older persons income and sources, by OASDI beneficiary and poverty status, and other characteristics, 1990, biennial chartbook, 4744–25
Older persons socioeconomic characteristics, 1900s-90 and projected to 2050, biennial chartbook, 12904–1
Older population and characteristics, by country, 1991 and projected to 2020, wallchart, 2328–82

Pollution (air) levels for 6 pollutants, by source and selected MSA, 1982-91, annual rpt, 9194–1
Small business product and service R&D grants of Fed Govt, indicators of commercial success, FY88-90, chartbook, 9768–23
Travel to and from US, by world area, forecast 1992-93, annual rpt, 2904–9
Weather trends and deviations, by world region, 1880s-1990, annual chartbook, 2184–9
Women's labor force status and characteristics, 1960s-90, chartbook, 6748–85
see also Maps

Chattanooga, Tenn.
see also under By City and By SMSA or MSA in the "Index by Categories"

Chatterjee, Satyajit
"Effect of Transitional Dynamics on the Distribution of Wealth in a Neoclassical Capital Accumulation Model", 9387–8.261
"Neoclassical Model of Seasonal Fluctuations", 9387–8.262

Checking accounts
Assets and debts of private sector, balance sheets by segment, 1960-91, semiannual rpt, 9365–4.1
Banks and thrifts finances and operations by deposit size, Fed Reserve functional cost analysis, 1991, annual rpt, 9364–6
Banks checking account and commercial loan activity by bank size, and loan sales and assets for top banks, 1970s-90, working paper, 9387–8.264
Budget of US, authoritative financial statements with appropriations, outlays, and receipts, by category and agency, FY91, annual rpt, 8104–2.2
Cashing of checks, outlets fees by type of check, and legal maximum in regulated States, 1991 article, 9381–1.301
Commercial banks finances, for foreign and domestic offices, by asset size, 1990, annual rpt, 9294–4.2
Commercial banks holdings of demand deposits of individuals, partnerships, and corporations, monthly rpt, 9362–1.1
Deposits, debits, and deposit turnover at financial instns, 1990, annual rpt, 9364–5.1
Deposits in banks, availability policies, with background data, 1980s-90, last issue of annual report, 9364–13
Deposits in insured commercial and savings banks, by instn, State, MSA, and county, as of June 1991, annual regional rpt series, 9295–3
Economic indicators and components, current data and annual trends, monthly rpt, 23842–1.5
Families financial status, income, net worth, and assets and debt by type, by income and selected characteristics, 1983 and 1989, article, 9362–1.301
Fed Reserve banks expenses and operations, itemized by service, office, and district, 1991, annual rpt, 9364–11
Financial and monetary conditions, selected US summary data, weekly rpt, 9391–4
Flow-of-funds accounts, savings, investments, and credit statements, quarterly rpt, 9365–3.3
Forgery of checks and bonds, Secret Service investigations and arrests, FY91 and trends from FY82, annual rpt, 8464–1
Households bill payment transactions, by method, FY87-90, annual rpt, 9864–10
Households financial services use, by account type and instn type and location, 1989 survey, article, 9362–1.303
Monetary trends, Fed Reserve Bank of St Louis monthly rpt, 9391–2
Service fees, minimum balances, and services offered by banks and thrifts, by service type, 1991, annual rpt, 9364–12
Southeastern States, Fed Reserve 5th District insured commercial banks financial statements, by State, quarterly rpt, 9389–18
West Central States economic indicators, Fed Reserve 10th District, quarterly rpt, 9381–16.2
see also Negotiable orders of withdrawal accounts

Chelsea, Mass.
Education (public elementary and secondary) system mgmt by higher education instn, Chelsea, Mass and Boston University demonstration program operations and results, 1988-90, 4808–38

Chemical and biological warfare agents
Agent Orange exposure cases at VA health centers, and exemptions from copayment requirements, 1989, GAO rpt, 26121–464
Agent Orange exposure health effects, literature review, 1990, annual rpt series, 8706–1
Disasters and natl security incidents and mgmt, with data by major event and State, 1992 annual rpt, 9434–6
Industrial hazardous substances releases and reduction methods under EPA regulation, with chemical stocks and use, facility directory, 1987-89, annual CD-ROM, 9234–7
Persian Gulf War chemical protective suits and masks contractor deliveries and field inspections, 1990-91, GAO rpt, 26123–387
Treaties and agreements on arms control, status and Arms Control and Disarmament Agency activities, 1991, annual rpt, 9824–2
Vaccination for biological warfare agents, Salk Inst dev and production, and Army contract costs by component, late 1970s-91, GAO rpt, 26123–374

Chemicals and chemical industry
Acids (inorganic) trade, tariffs, and industry operating data, 1992 rpt, 9885–11.2
Antimony trioxide from PRC at less than fair value, injury to US industry, investigation with background financial and operating data, 1992 rpt, 9886–14.342
Business statistics, detailed data for major industries and economic indicators, *Survey of Current Business*, monthly rpt, 2702–1.11
Business statistics, detailed data for major industries and economic indicators, 1960-91, *Survey of Current Business* biennial supplement, 2704–1
Capital expenditures for plant and equipment, by major industry group, quarterly rpt, 2502–2
Collective bargaining agreements expiring during year, and workers covered, by firm, union, industry group, and State, 1992, annual rpt, 6784–9
Communist and transitional economy countries trade with US, by detailed commodity and country, quarterly rpt with articles, 9882–2
County Business Patterns, 1989: employment, establishments, and payroll, by SIC 2- to 4-digit industry and county, annual State rpt series, 2326–8
County Business Patterns, 1990: employment, establishments, and payroll, by SIC 2- to 4-digit industry and county, annual State rpt series, 2326–6
Cuba trade, by commodity and country, mid 1980s-91, 9118–8
Employment, earnings, and hours, by SIC 1- to 4-digit industry, monthly 1989-Feb 1992, annual rpt, 6744–4
Employment of minorities and women, by occupation, SIC 1- to 3-digit industry, State, and MSA, 1991, annual rpt, 9244–1
Employment, unemployment, and labor force characteristics, by region and census div, 1991, annual rpt, 6744–7.1
Energy producers finances and operations, by energy type for US firms domestic and foreign operations, 1990, annual rpt, 3164–44.1
Energy use and prices, by fuel type and manufacturing industry, 1974-88, 3166–15.3
Energy use and prices for manufacturing industries, 1988 survey, series, 3166–13
Environmental Quality, status of problems, protection programs, research, and intl issues, 1991 annual rpt, 484–1
Exports and imports between US and outlying areas, by detailed commodity and mode of transport, 1991, annual rpt, 2424–11
Exports and imports of US, by country and detailed commodity, monthly rpt, 2422–12
Exports and imports of US by country, and trade shifts by commodity, 1991, annual rpt, 9884–25
Exports and imports of US, by Harmonized System 6-digit commodity and country, 1991, annual rpt, 2424–13
Exports and imports of US, by selected country, country group, and commodity group, 1991, annual rpt, 2044–37
Exports and imports of US, by transport mode, country, and SITC 1- to 3-digit commodity, 1991, annual rpt, 2424–12
Exports, imports, and balances of US for manufactured goods, by SITC 2-digit commodity and country, quarterly rpt, 2042–35
Exports, imports, tariffs, and industry operating data for energy and chemical products, commodity rpt series, 9885–11
Exports of US, detailed commodities by country, monthly CD-ROM, 2422–13
Exports of US, detailed Schedule B commodities with countries of destination, 1991, annual rpt, 2424–10
Foreign direct investment in US, by industry group and world area, 1989-91, annual article, 2702–1.331

Foreign direct investment of US, by industry group and world area, 1989-91, annual article, 2702–1.332
Freight (waterborne domestic and foreign) by commodity, traffic, and passengers, by port and waterway, 1989, annual rpt, 3754–3
Imports, exports, and employment impacts, by SIC 2- to 4-digit industry and commodity, quarterly rpt, 2322–2
Imports of US, detailed commodities by country, monthly CD-ROM, 2422–14
Imports of US given duty-free treatment for value of US material sent abroad, by commodity and country, 1987-90, annual rpt, 9884–14
Industrial hazardous substances releases and reduction methods under EPA regulation, by chemical, source, industry, and location, 1989, annual rpt, 9234–6
Industrial hazardous substances releases and reduction methods under EPA regulation, with chemical stocks and use, facility directory, 1987-89, annual CD-ROM, 9234–7
Injuries from use of consumer products, by severity, victim age, and detailed product, 1991, annual rpt, 9164–6
Input-output structure of US economy, detailed interindustry transactions for 84 industries, and components of final demand, 1987, annual article, 2702–1.316
Input-output structure of US economy, detailed interindustry transactions for 541 industries, and components of final demand, 1982 benchmark data, 2708–17
Labor productivity, indexes of output, hours, and employment by SIC 2- to 4-digit industry, 1967-90, annual rpt, 6824–1.3
Manufacturing annual survey, 1990: finances and operations, by SIC 2- to 4-digit industry, series, 2506–14
Manufacturing census, 1987: concentration of largest firms measured by value added, and for shipments by SIC 2- and 4-digit industry, subject rpt, 2497–6
Manufacturing census, 1987: shipments of manufacturers products, by customer class and SIC 2- and 4-digit industry, subject rpt, 2497–4
Manufacturing corporations financial statements, by selected SIC 2- to 3-digit industry, quarterly rpt, 2502–1
Manufacturing finances and operations, by SIC 2- to 4-digit industry, forecast 1992, annual rpt, 2044–28
Manufacturing industries operations and performance, analytical rpt series, 2506–16
Manufacturing production, shipments, inventories, orders, and pollution control costs, periodic Current Industrial Rpt series, 2506–3
Mexico imports from US, by industry and State, 1987-91, 2048–154
Military and personal property shipments, passenger traffic, and costs, by service branch and mode of transport, FY91, annual rpt, 3704–15
Military prime contract awards, by detailed procurement category, FY88-91, annual rpt, 3544–18
Minerals production, trade, use, and foreign investment in US industry, 1985-90 and projected to 2000, annual rpt, 5304–5
Multinatl firms US affiliates finances and operations, by industry, country of parent firm, and State, 1987, 2708–48
Multinatl firms US affiliates, finances, and operations, by industry, world area of parent firm, and State, 1989-90, annual rpt, 2704–4
Multinatl US firms and foreign affiliates finances and operations, by industry and country, 1989 benchmark survey, annual rpt, 2704–5
Multinatl US firms foreign affiliates, income statement items by asset size, industry, and country, 1988, biennial article, 8302–2.322
Natl income and product accounts, comprehensive accounts and components, benchmark revisions, 1929-88, 2708–5
Natl income and product accounts, comprehensive accounts and components, *Survey of Current Business*, monthly rpt, 2702–1.29
Nepheline syenite from Canada at less than fair value, injury to US industry, investigation with background financial and operating data, 1992 rpt, 9886–14.344
Occupational injury and illness rates, by SIC 2- to 4-digit industry, 1989-90, annual rpt, 6844–7
Occupational injury and illness rates, by SIC 2- to 4-digit industry, 1990, annual rpt, 6844–1
OECD trade, total and for 4 major countries, and US trade by country, by commodity, 1980-90, world area rpt series, 9116–1
Ohio River basin waterway facilities, freight by commodity and port, and recreation, by waterway, 1988-89, annual rpt, 3754–6
Pacific Northwest population, households, employment, income, fuel prices, and electricity demand, alternative forecasts 1991-2010, annual rpt, 3224–3.3
Pollution (air) abatement equipment shipments by industry, and new and backlog orders, by product, 1991, annual Current Industrial Rpt, 2506–12.5
Pollution abatement capital and operating costs, by SIC 2- to 4-digit industry and State, 1990, annual Current Industrial Rpt, 2506–3.6
Potassium hydroxide from 3 countries at less than fair value, injury to US industry, investigation with background financial and operating data, 1992 rpt, 9886–14.339
Price indexes (producer), by stage of processing and detailed commodity, monthly rpt, 6762–6
Price indexes (producer), by stage of processing and detailed commodity, monthly 1991, annual rpt, 6764–2
Production and sales of synthetic organic chemicals, and manufacturer listing, by product, 1990, annual rpt, 9884–3
Production, shipments, firms, trade, and use, by product, periodic Current Industrial Rpt series, 2506–8
Puerto Rico and other US possessions corporations income tax returns, income and tax items, and employment, by selected industry, 1989, article, 8302–2.326
Science, engineering, and technical employment in manufacturing, by field and industry, 1989, triennial rpt, 9627–23
Soviet Union and US economic and sociodemographic indicators, selected years 1970-90, handbook, 2328–80
Sulfanilic acid, economic effects of removal from US duty free status, 1992 rpt, 9886–4.188
Sulfanilic acid from Hungary and India, injury to US industry from foreign subsidized and less than fair value imports, investigation with background financial and operating data, 1992 rpt, 9886–19.83
Sulfanilic acid from PRC at less than fair value, injury to US industry, investigation with background financial and operating data, 1992 rpt, 9886–14.357
Synthetic organic chemical production, by detailed product, quarterly rpt, 9882–1
Tariff Schedule of US, classifications and rates of duty by detailed imported commodity, 1993 base edition, 9886–13
Tariff Schedule of US, classifications for pharmaceutical and intermediate chemical products, 1992 rpt, 9886–4.185
Tax (excise) collections of IRS, by source, quarterly rpt, 8302–1
Tax (excise) on hazardous waste generation and disposal, rates, and firms filing returns, by substance type, 1989, annual article, 8302–2.303
Tax (income) returns of corporations, income and tax items by asset size and detailed industry, 1989, annual rpt, 8304–4; 8304–21
Tax (income) returns of corporations with foreign tax credit, income and tax items by industry group, 1988, biennial article, 8302–2.316
Wholesale trade sales and inventories, by SIC 2- to 3-digit kind of business, monthly rpt, 2413–7
see also Adhesives
see also Chemical and biological warfare agents
see also Dioxins
see also Drugs
see Dyeing and coloring materials
see also Explosives
see also Fertilizers
see also Food ingredients and additives
see also Gases
see also Gum and wood chemicals
see also Hazardous substances
see also Hazardous waste and disposal
see also Paints and varnishes
see also Pesticides
see also Petrochemicals
see also Pharmaceutical industry
see also Plastics and plastics industry
see also Soap and detergent industry
see also Synthetic fibers and fabrics
see also under By Commodity in the "Index by Categories"
see also under By Industry in the "Index by Categories"

Chemistry
DOE R&D projects and funding at natl labs, universities, and other instns, FY91, annual summary rpt, 3004–18.3; 3004–18.4

DOE R&D projects and funding at natl labs, universities, and other instns, FY92, annual summary rpt, 3004–18.6
Employment of scientists, engineers, and technicians in manufacturing, by field and industry, 1989, triennial rpt, 9627–23
Fed Govt aid to higher education and nonprofit instns for R&D and related activities, by field, instn, agency, and State, FY90, annual rpt, 9627–17
Higher education grad programs enrollment in science and engineering, by field, source of funds, and characteristics of student and instn, 1990, annual rpt, 9627–7
Labor demand, turnover, and training completions, by detailed occupation, 1990 and projected to 2005, biennial rpt, 6744–3
NASA R&D funding to higher education instns, by field, instn, and State, FY91, annual listing, 9504–7
Occupational Outlook Handbook, 1992-93, biennial rpt, 6744–1
R&D funding by higher education instns and federally funded centers, by field, instn, and State, FY90, annual rpt, 9627–13
Science and Engineering Indicators, employment, education, R&D funding, and industry impacts, with foreign comparisons, 1960s-91, biennial rpt, 9624–10
Water quality, chemistry, hydrology, and other characteristics, local area studies, series, 5666–27
see also Chemicals and chemical industry

Chemotherapy
Cancer (secondary) risk for chronic lymphocytic leukemia, by treatment method, 1992 article, 4472–1.343
Carcinogens chemistry, sources, environment and health risks, and regulation, by substance and brand, 1991 annual rpt, 4044–15
Hyperthermia therapy used with cancer chemotherapy, risks and benefit evaluation for Medicare coverage, 1991 rpt, 4186–10.7

Chen, Ling-chun
"Heterogeneity for Allelic Loss in Human Breast Cancer", 4472–1.310

Cherries
see Fruit and fruit products

Chesapeake Bay
Army Corps of Engineers water resources dev projects, characteristics, and costs, 1950s-89, biennial State rpt series, 3756–1
Army Corps of Engineers water resources dev projects, characteristics, and costs, 1950s-91, biennial State rpt series, 3756–2
Fish (striped bass) stocks status on Atlantic coast, and sport and commercial catch by State, 1979-90, annual rpt, 5504–29
Tidal currents, daily time and velocity by station for North America coasts, forecast 1993, annual rpt, 2174–1.1
Tide height and tidal current velocity daily at Middle Atlantic coastal stations, forecast 1993, annual rpt, 2174–11
Water supply and quality in streams and lakes, and groundwater levels in wells, by drainage basin, 1990, annual State rpt series, 5666–10
Water supply and quality in streams and lakes, and groundwater levels in wells, by drainage basin, 1991, annual State rpt series, 5666–12

Cheyenne, Wyo.
Wages by occupation, for office and plant workers, 1992 survey, periodic MSA rpt, 6785–3.5

Chicago, Ill.
Airports employment, air cargo shipments by industry, and convention attendance, for Chicago and other locations, mid 1970s-90, working paper, 9375–13.78
Commuters, by county of residence and work, for top 10 metro areas, 1990 Census of Population, press release, 2328–84
CPI by component for US city average, and by region, population size, and for 15 metro areas, monthly rpt, 6762–1
CPI by component for US city average, and by selected metro area, region, and population size, monthly rpt, 6762–2
Drug abuse indicators for selected metro areas, research results, data collection, and policy issues, 1992 semiannual conf, 4492–5
Drug test results at arrest, by drug type, offense, and sex, for selected urban areas, quarterly rpt, 6062–3
Freight (waterborne domestic and foreign) by commodity, traffic, and passengers, by port and waterway, 1989, annual rpt, 3754–3.3
Fruit and vegetable shipments, and arrivals by city, by mode of transport and State and country of origin, 1990, annual rpt, 1311–4.2
Fruit and vegetable wholesale prices in NYC, Chicago, and selected shipping points, by crop, 1991, annual rpt, 1311–8
Heroin prices and purity in 19 metro areas and Puerto Rico, by world area of origin, quarterly rpt, 6282–2
Housing and households characteristics, and unit and neighborhood quality, by MSA location for 11 MSAs, 1987 survey, supplement, 2485–8
Housing rental and sales, discrimination against blacks and Hispanics in selected metro areas, 1989 study, 5186–16.2
Housing starts and completions authorized by building permits in 40 MSAs, quarterly rpt, 2382–9
Housing vacancy rates for single and multifamily units and mobile homes, by city and ZIP code, 1991, annual MSA rpt, 9304–18.1
Oil prices by product, for 4 cities, seasonal weekly rpt, 3162–45
Wages by occupation, and benefits, for office and plant workers, 1991 survey, periodic MSA rpt, 6785–16.1
see also under By City and By SMSA or MSA in the "Index by Categories"

Chicanos
see Hispanic Americans
see Mexicans in the U.S.

Chickens
see Poultry industry and products

Child abuse and neglect
Assistance for child abuse and neglect prevention and treatment, and disabled infant protection, by State, FY91, annual listing, 4584–6
Assistance for child abuse and neglect prevention and treatment, discretionary grants, FY91, annual listing, 4584–9
Cases of abuse and neglect reported, and victim characteristics, data compilation, 1992 annual rpt, 6064–6.2
Deaths and rates, by cause, age, sex, marital status, race, and State, 1989, US Vital Statistics advance annual rpt, 4146–5.124
HHS financial aid, by program, recipient, State, and city, FY91, annual regional listings, 4004–3
Indian and Alaska Native youth health condition and behavioral patterns, by sex and grade, 1988-90, 4088–3
Indian crime victim compensation and support service programs operations, 1988-90, 6066–31.1
Labor laws enacted, by State, 1991, annual article, 6722–1.309
Sentences for Federal offenses, guidelines by offense and circumstances, series, 17668–1
Statistical Abstract of US, 1992 annual data compilation, 2324–1.5
Thrownaway child rpts, and Office of Juvenile Justice and Delinquency Prevention activities for missing children and runaways, FY90, annual rpt, 6064–36
US attorneys civil and criminal cases by type and disposition, and collections, by Federal district, FY91, annual rpt, 6004–2.1
Victims of crime, compensation and support service programs funding, by offense and State, FY88-90, biennial rpt, 6064–37
Youth health condition, risk factors, and preventive and treatment services use and availability, 1970s-80s, 26358–234.2

Child day care
AFDC beneficiaries demographic and financial characteristics, by State, FY90, annual rpt, 4584–7
Arrangements for child care by mothers employed and in school, and costs, by age of child and characteristics of mother, 1988, Current Population Rpt, 2546–20.24
Arrangements for child care by younger working mothers, and costs, by selected characteristics, 1988, 6726–2.1
Arrangements for child care prior to 1st grade, by setting and parents' educational level, 1991 survey, 4826–10.2
Assistance programs under Ways and Means Committee jurisdiction, finances, operations, and participant characteristics, FY70s-91, annual rpt, 21784–11
Availability, demand, use, and costs of child day care and early childhood education programs and provider and enrollee characteristics, 1990 survey, 4808–39
County Business Patterns, 1989: employment, establishments, and payroll, by SIC 2- to 4-digit industry and county, annual State rpt series, 2326–8
County Business Patterns, 1990: employment, establishments, and payroll, by SIC 2- to 4-digit industry and county, annual State rpt series, 2326–6
CPI by component for US city average, and by selected metro area, region, and population size, monthly rpt, 6762–2

Drug abuse by mothers, treatment and other services use, referrals, needs, and barriers, for 13 NIDA-funded programs, 1990/91 survey, 4498–76
Handicapped children's formal and informal care, outlays and time spent relation to diagnosis and other characteristics, 1988, article, 4042–3.329
Hepatitis cases by infection source, age, sex, race, and State, and deaths, by strain, 1989 and trends from 1966, 4205–2
HHS financial aid, by program, recipient, State, and city, FY91, annual regional listings, 4004–3
Homeless persons transitional housing and support services, HUD grants by community, 1991, press release, 5006–3.80
Homeless persons transitional housing and support services program, outcome relation to client characteristics and services, FY87-90, GAO rpt, 26113–549
Input-output structure of US economy, detailed interindustry transactions for 541 industries, and components of final demand, 1982 benchmark data, 2708–17
Job Training Partnership Act support services and supplementary payments, and impact on single parent participation, 199091, 26106–8.15
Labor demand, turnover, and training completions, by detailed occupation, 1990 and projected to 2005, biennial rpt, 6744–3
Labor laws enacted, by State, 1991, annual article, 6722–1.309
Occupational injury and illness rates, by SIC 2- to 4-digit industry, 1989-90, annual rpt, 6844–7
Occupational injury and illness rates, by SIC 2- to 4-digit industry, 1990, annual rpt, 6844–1
Occupational Outlook Handbook, 1992-93, biennial rpt, 6744–1
Population economic well-being indicators, by selected characteristics and household income and income-to-poverty ratio, 1984, 2546–20.22
Single mothers family income, and impacts of child care, govt and child support payments, taxes, and marriage, with data by State, 1970s-91, 21788–212
Special education programs, enrollment by age, staff, funding, and needs, by type of handicap and State, 1990/91, annual rpt, 4944–4
Statistical Abstract of US, 1992 annual data compilation, 2324–1.12
Tax (income) returns filed, by type of filer, selected income items, quarterly rpt, 8302–2.1
Tax (income) returns of individuals, by filing status, tax item, and income level, 1991, annual article, 8302–2.319
Tax (income) returns of individuals, detailed data, 1988, annual rpt, 8304–2
Tax (income) returns of partnerships, income statement and balance sheet items, by industry group, 1990, annual article, 8302–2.314
Tax (income) returns of sole proprietorships, income statement items, by industry group, 1990, annual article, 8302–2.317; 8302–2.320

Child labor
Labor laws enacted, by State, 1991, annual article, 6722–1.309
States child labor certification and injury reporting procedures, relation to proposed Federal guidelines, 1991, GAO rpt, 26121–451

Child mortality
AIDS cases by risk group, race, sex, age, State, and MSA, and deaths, quarterly rpt, 4202–9
Costa Rica and Guatemala life expectancy, and death rate by cause and age, by sex, 1984 and trends from 1900, working paper, 2326–18.64
Deaths and rates, by cause, age, sex, marital status, race, and State, 1989, US Vital Statistics advance annual rpt, 4146–5.124
Deaths and rates, by cause, age, sex, race, and State, preliminary 1990-91 and trends from 1960, US Vital Statistics annual rpt, 4144–7
Deaths and rates, by detailed location, cause, and demographic characteristics, 1989, US Vital Statistics annual rpt, 4144–3
Developing countries economic and social conditions from 1960s, and Intl Dev Cooperation Agency and AID activities and funding, FY91-93, annual rpt, 9904–4
Health condition and care indicators, 1950s-90 with health improvement and disease prevention goals for 1990, annual data compilation, 4144–11
Latin America economic and social conditions, resources, trade, and aid, 1992, annual factbook, 9914–14
see also Infant mortality

Child support and alimony
AFDC application denials, by reason and State, FY90, annual rpt, 4584–3.3
Assistance programs under Ways and Means Committee jurisdiction, finances, operations, and participant characteristics, FY70s-91, annual rpt, 21784–11
Awards of child support, payment status, reasons for nonpayment, and mothers characteristics, by fathers residence in and out of State, 1990, GAO rpt, 26121–442
Child Support Enforcement Program collections for non-AFDC clients, administrative costs, and user fees, by State, with Federal shares of costs, 1990, GAO rpt, 26121–463
Family members supporting others outside household, by relationship and provider characteristics, 1988, fact sheet, 2326–17.48
Family members supporting others outside household, by relationship, recipient living arrangements, and provider characteristics, 1988, Current Population Rpt, 2546–20.21
HHS financial aid, by program, recipient, State, and city, FY91, annual regional listings, 4004–3
Housing (rental) units, total, with HUD assistance by program, and eligible for aid, by unit, household, and neighborhood characteristics, and location, 1989, biennial rpt, 5184–11
Income (household, family, and personal), by source, detailed characteristics, and region, 1991, annual Current Population Rpt, 2546–6.76
Interstate enforcement of wage deductions for overdue child support payments, effectiveness, 1991, GAO rpt, 26121–445
Mississippi poverty, hunger, and public welfare program operations and indicators of need, 1991 hearing, 21968–57
Payments of child support and alimony, and payments share of income, by selected characteristics of payer and payee, 1988-89, article, 1702–1.305
Payments of child support and visitation practices of absent fathers, and mothers with custody, by employment and other characteristics, 1988, article, 6722–1.329
Poverty rates of divorced parents, effects of child support enforcement provisions, model results, 1976-83, working paper, 6886–6.87
Poverty status of families, by detailed characteristics, 1980 and 1988, GAO rpt, 26131–102
Single mothers family income, and impacts of child care, govt and child support payments, taxes, and marriage, with data by State, 1970s-91, 21788–212
Single parent families in own and others homes, by financial, housing, and other characteristics, 1989, 2486–1.14
Statistical Abstract of US, 1992 annual data compilation, 2324–1.12
Tax (income) returns of individuals, by filing status, tax item, and income level, 1991, annual article, 8302–2.319
Tax (income) returns of individuals, detailed data, 1988, annual rpt, 8304–2
Tax (income) returns of individuals, selected income and tax items by income level, preliminary 1990, annual article, 8302–2.307
Tax returns filed subject to child support collection, FY91 and cumulative from 1981, annual rpt, 8304–3.1
Wage deductions for overdue child support payments, and employer compliance, by State, FY85-89, 4588–1

Child Support Enforcement Program
Administrative costs, collections, and user fees for non-AFDC services under Program, by State, with Federal shares of costs, 1990, GAO rpt, 26121–463

Child welfare
Appalachia local dev projects, and funding by source, by program and State, FY91, annual rpt, 9084–1
Assistance (financial and nonfinancial) of Fed Govt, 1992 base edition, annual listing, 104–5
Assistance programs under Ways and Means Committee jurisdiction, finances, operations, and participant characteristics, FY70s-91, annual rpt, 21784–11
Benefits, beneficiaries, and spells of participation, by aid program and recipient characteristics, 1987-88, Current Population Rpt, 2546–20.25
Benefits, beneficiary characteristics, and trust funds of OASDHI, Medicaid, SSI, and related programs, selected years 1937-90, annual rpt, 4744–3
Drug abuse by mothers, treatment and other services use, referrals, needs, and barriers, for 13 NIDA-funded programs, 1990/91 survey, 4498–76
Expenditures for public welfare by program, FY50s-89, annual article, 4742–1.319

Food aid program of USDA for women, infants, and children, participant referrals to social service programs, by type and reason, 1990 local area study, article, 4042–3.318
Food aid program of USDA for women, infants, and children, participants and costs by State and Indian agency, FY90, annual tables, 1364–12
Food aid program of USDA for women, infants, and children, participants by race, State, and Indian agency, 1991, annual rpt, 1364–16
Food aid program of USDA for women, infants, and children, participants, clinics, and costs, by State and Indian agency, monthly tables, 1362–16
Food aid program of USDA for women, infants, and children, State contract awards and bid prices for infant formula, late 1980s-91, hearing, 25528–118
Food stamp eligibility and payment errors, by type, recipient characteristics, and State, FY90, annual rpt, 1364–15
Food stamp recipient household size, composition, income, and income and deductions allowed, summer 1989, annual rpt, 1364–8
Health care services for mothers and children, Federal block grant beneficiary and taxpayer equity among States, issues, alternative allocation formulas, and background data, 1992 GAO rpt, 26121–454
HHS financial aid, by program, recipient, State, and city, FY91, annual regional listings, 4004–3
Homeless persons aid programs of Fed Govt, program descriptions and funding, by agency and State, FY87-91, annual GAO rpt, 26104–21
Indochina Amerasian children arriving in US and refugee camps under Orderly Departure Program, monthly rpt, 7002–4
Medicaid-eligible child health screenings, rural physicians participation effects of promotional mailing, for North Carolina, 1990, article, 4042–3.358
Mississippi poverty, hunger, and public welfare program operations and indicators of need, 1991 hearing, 21968–57
Railroad retirement, survivors, unemployment, and health insurance programs, monthly rpt, 9702–2
Statistical Abstract of US, 1992 annual data compilation, 2324–1.3
Supplemental Security Income and Medicaid eligibility and payment provisions, and beneficiaries living arrangements, by State, 1992, annual rpt, 4704–13
Supplemental Security Income child beneficiaries and benefits, by selected characteristics, family income status, and State, 1991, article, 4742–1.316
Supplemental Security Income payments and beneficiaries, by type of eligibility, State, and county, Dec 1990, annual rpt, 4744–27
Veterans compensation and pension recipients, for each US war, 1775-1991, annual rpt, 8604–2
Veterans disability and death compensation and pension cases, by type of entitlement and period of service, monthly rpt, 8602–5
Veterans disability and death compensation cases of VA, by entitlement type, period of service, and sex, as of Mar 1992, annual rpt, 8604–13
Veterans disability and death compensation cases of VA, by entitlement type, period of service, sex, age, and State, FY90, annual rpt, 8604–7
Workers compensation laws of States and Fed Govt, 1992 annual rpt, 6504–11
see also Adoption
see also Aid to Families with Dependent Children
see also Child abuse and neglect
see also Child day care
see also Child support and alimony
see also Foster home care
see also Head Start Project
see also Old-Age, Survivors, Disability, and Health Insurance
see also School lunch and breakfast programs

Childbirth
see Births
see Birthweight
see Infant mortality
see Maternal deaths
see Maternity
see Midwives
see Obstetrics and gynecology

Children
AIDS cases among children, hospital use and charges by instn and patient characteristics, and payment source, 1986-87, 4186–6.16
AIDS cases by risk group, race, sex, age, State, and MSA, and deaths, quarterly rpt, 4202–9
AIDS virus-related Medicaid claims and payments, by sex, age, risk group, eligibility, and source of care, for Michigan, mid 1980s, article, 4042–3.348
Alcohol abuse risk for preschoolers in later life, presence of selected behavior problems, 1986, article, 4482–1.303
Asian and Pacific Islands Americans social and economic characteristics, for West and total US, 1990-91, Current Population Report, 2546–1.462
Auto safety, child restraints use among Medicaid recipients by selected characteristics, local area study, 1992 article, 4042–3.312
Bicycle helmet use by children relation to safety knowledge and attitudes, 1989 local area survey, article, 4042–3.326
Black Americans social and economic characteristics, for South and total US, 1991 and trends from 1950, annual Current Population Rpt, 2546–1.463
Budget of US, House Budget Committee analysis of Bush Admin proposals and economic assumptions, FY93, 21268–42
Census of Population and Housing, 1990: population and housing characteristics, detailed geographic coverage, State CD-ROM series, 2551–10
Census of Population and Housing, 1990: summary characteristics, by county, subdiv, and place, State rpt series, 2551–7
Census of Population and Housing, 1990: summary characteristics, households, and land area, by county, subdiv, and place, State rpt series, 2551–1
Census of Population, 1990: population characteristics and living arrangements, by county, place, and urban-rural location, State rpt series, 2531–1
Census of Population, 1990: population characteristics and living arrangements, for Native American, urban, and metro areas, series, 2531–2
Consumer Income, socioeconomic characteristics of persons, families, and households, detailed cross-tabulations, Current Population Rpt series, 2546–6
Dental caries and baby bottle tooth decay prevalence among Head Start children in southwest US, by characteristics of child and area, 1992 article, 4042–3.317
Dental fluoride products use by children, by frequency of dental visits and selected characteristics, 1983-89, 4146–8.222
Disease (infectious) cases among children, and related disability and health care, by disease, health insurance status, and other characteristics, 1988, 4147–10.181
Family life and relationships quality and other issues, views of parents and children, 1990 survey, 15528–2
Farm population, by employment, social, and economic characteristics, and region, 1990, annual Current Population Rpt, 2546–1.458
Fires (wild) and acreage burned, by type of land, ownership, cause, region, and State, 1984-90, annual rpt, 1204–4
Health condition and care indicators, 1950s-90 with health improvement and disease prevention goals for 1990, annual data compilation, 4144–11
Health condition and care indicators, 1988 natl survey, CD-ROM, 4147–10.184
Health condition of children and mothers, and services use, indicators by age, race, and poverty status 1988, 4478–197
Hepatitis B eradication through universal childhood vaccination, with schedules, dosages, and precautions, CDC recommendations, 1991 rpt, 4206–2.49
Homeless mothers and children nutrient intake, body measurements, and blood chemistry, 1989-90 local area study, article, 4042–3.330
Households and family characteristics, by location, 1991, annual Current Population Rpt, 2546–1.457
Households and housing characteristics, and unit and neighborhood quality, by MSA location for 11 MSAs, 1987 survey, supplement, 2485–8
Households and housing detailed characteristics, and unit and neighborhood quality, by location, 1989, biennial rpt supplement, 2485–13
Households and housing detailed characteristics, and unit and neighborhood quality, MSA surveys, series, 2485–6
Households and housing unit characteristics of recent movers, and reason for move, by tenure, 1989, 2486–1.12
Households composition, income, benefits, and labor force status, Survey of Income and Program Participation methodology, working paper series, 2626–10
Housing (rental) units, total, with HUD assistance by program, and eligible for aid, by unit, household, and neighborhood characteristics, and location, 1989, biennial rpt, 5184–11

Hungary child respiratory disease cases, by type, age, and air pollution levels, for Sopron, 1990, article, 4202–7.319
Hypertension cases, stroke and heart disease risk, and drug dosages, with diagnosis and treatment methods, 1992 quadrennial rpt, 4478–198
Immigrant and nonimmigrant visas of US issued and refused, by class, issuing office, and nationality, FY90, annual rpt, 7184–1
Immigrants and nonimmigrants admitted to US, alien workers, visitors, deportations, and naturalizations, FY91, annual summary rpt, 6264–7
Immigration to US, alien workers, visitors, deportations, and naturalizations, by country, FY91 and trends from 1820, annual rpt, 6264–2
Income (household) and poverty status under alternative income definitions, by recipient characteristics, 1979-91, annual Current Population Rpt, 2546–6.78
Income (personal) relative to median, by race and selected other characteristics, mid 1960s-89, Current Population Rpt, 2546–6.73
Injuries from use of consumer products and related activities, by severity and victim age and sex, 1990, annual rpt, 9164–7
Injuries from use of consumer products, by severity, victim age, and detailed product, 1991, annual rpt, 9164–6
Living arrangements, family relationships, and marital status, by selected characteristics, 1991, annual Current Population Rpt, 2546–1.461
Living arrangements of children, and women's marriage and divorce experience, by race, 1970s-90, Current Population Rpt, 2546–2.166
Migration, immigration, and mover characteristics compared to nonmovers, 1987-90, annual Current Population Rpt, 2546–1.456
Migration since 1990, mover characteristics by same or different area, and compared to nonmovers, 1991, annual Current Population Rpt, 2546–1.464
Missing, abducted, runaway, and exploited children, and Office of Juvenile Justice and Delinquency Prevention activities, FY90, annual rpt, 6064–36
Pacific territories population and housing detailed characteristics, by location, 1990 Census of Population and Housing, series, 2551–8
Population economic well-being indicators, by selected characteristics and household income and income-to-poverty ratio, 1984, 2546–20.22
Poverty status of population and families, by detailed characteristics, 1991, annual Current Population Rpt, 2546–6.77
Radiation exposure of population near commercial reactors, by body site, age group, and selected plant, 1988, annual rpt, 9634–7
Radiation exposure of population near Hanford, Wash, nuclear plant, with methodology, 1944-91, series, 3356–5
Railroad accidents, casualties, and damage, by cause, railroad, and State, 1991, annual rpt, 7604–1
Reading and TV viewing activities of children at home, by grade level, 1991 survey, 4826–10.1
Statistical Abstract of US, 1992 annual data compilation, 2324–1
Tax (income) returns of individuals, by filing status, tax item, and income level, 1991, annual article, 8302–2.319
Tax (income) returns of individuals, detailed data, 1988, annual rpt, 8304–2
Vaccination for pertussis, schedules, dosages, and precautions, CDC guidelines, 1992 rpt, 4206–2.51
Vaccine (acellular) for pertussis, CDC guidelines for schedules, dosages, and precautions, 1992 rpt, 4206–2.65
see also Adoption
see also Aid to Families with Dependent Children
see also Birth defects
see also Births
see also Births out of wedlock
see also Breast-feeding
see also Child abuse and neglect
see also Child day care
see also Child labor
see also Child mortality
see also Child support and alimony
see also Child welfare
see also Compensatory education
see also Educational enrollment
see also Elementary and secondary education
see also Foster home care
see also Handicapped children
see also Head Start Project
see also Infant mortality
see also Juvenile courts and cases
see also Juvenile delinquency
see also Juvenile detention and correctional institutions
see also Old-Age, Survivors, Disability, and Health Insurance
see also Parents
see also Pediatrics
see also Preschool education
see also Remedial education
see also School lunch and breakfast programs
see also Single parents
see also Special education
see also Students
see also Youth
see also Youth employment
see also under By Age in the "Index by Categories"

Childs, Nathan W.
"U.S. Rice Distribution Patterns, 1988/89", 1564–11

Chile
Agricultural trade of Chile, total and with US, by selected commodity, 1990, article, 1502–4.301
Agricultural trade of US, by detailed commodity and country, 1991, annual rpt, 1524–8
Agricultural trade of US, by detailed commodity and country, 1991, semiannual rpt, 1522–4
AID economic aid to developing countries, obligations and disbursements by country, quarterly rpt, 9912–4
AID loans repayment status and terms by program and country, and status of predecessor agency loans, quarterly rpt, 9912–3
Background Notes, summary social, political, and economic data, 1992 rpt, 7006–2.16
Debt burden indicators for 8 developing countries, alternative projections 1991-2000 and trends from 1974, technical paper, 9366–7.271
Economic and military aid and loans from US and intl agencies, by program and country, FY46-91, annual rpt, 9914–5
Economic and social conditions of developing countries from 1960s, and Intl Dev Cooperation Agency and AID activities and funding, FY91-93, annual rpt, 9904–4
Economic and social conditions, resources, and trade, and aid, 1992, annual factbook, 9914–14
Economic conditions, policy, and trade practices, by country, 1989-91, annual rpt, 21384–5
Economic, social, political, and geographic summary data, by country, 1992, annual factbook, 9114–2
Exports and imports (agricultural) of Chile with US, US tariffs, and Chile trade and investment policies and foreign direct investment, 1985-91, GAO rpt, 26119–408
Exports and imports of US, by commodity and country, 1980-90, world area rpt, 9116–1.7
Exports and imports of US, by Harmonized System 6-digit commodity and country, 1991, annual rpt, 2424–13
Exports and imports of US, by selected country, country group, and commodity group, 1991, annual rpt, 2044–37
Exports and imports of US, by transport mode, country, and SITC 1- to 3-digit commodity, 1991, annual rpt, 2424–12
Exports, imports, and balances of US for manufactured goods, by SITC 2-digit commodity and country, quarterly rpt, 2042–35
Exports, investment, debt, and tariffs of 7 Latin America countries, and trade and investment policy liberalization issues, mid 1960s-91, 9886–4.184
Exports of US, detailed Schedule B commodities with countries of destination, 1991, annual rpt, 2424–10
Fruit exports of Chile to US, sales by port of entry, and prices in 5 terminal cities, by commodity, 1990/91, annual rpt, 1311–27
Human rights conditions in 170 countries, and US economic and military aid, 1991, annual rpt, 21384–3
Imports of goods, services, and investment from US, trade barriers, impacts, and US actions, by country, 1991, annual rpt, 444–2
Military aid of US, arms sales, and training programs costs and budget requests, by program, world region, and country, FY91-93, annual rpt, 7144–13
Military spending, arms trade, and force strengths, with govt spending and population, by country, 1979-89, annual rpt, 9824–1
Multinatl US firms and foreign affiliates finances and operations, by industry and country, 1989 benchmark survey, annual rpt, 2704–5

Multinatl US firms foreign affiliates, income statement items by asset size, industry, and country, 1988, biennial article, 8302–2.322
Oil production, investment needs, and exports, for 8 South America countries, 1980s-90 and projected to 2010, GAO rpt, 26123–396
Population size, growth rates, and components of change, by country, projected 1990-2020 and trends from 1950, biennial rpt, 2324–9
Raisin imports of 3 countries, and Chile exports, by country of origin and destination, 1988-91, semiannual article, 1925–34.321
Refugee migration, and intl aid programs, by world area and country of origin and asylum, 1991, annual rpt, 7004–15
Social security system of Chile, replacement with private pension system, economic impacts, 1970s-90, technical paper, 9385–8.123
Strawberry trade of US and Mexico, and Mexico and Chile supply and use, 1987-92, annual article, 1925–34.315
Textile and apparel foreign market conditions for US exports, with domestic industry operations, 1992 country rpt, 2046–15.2
UN voting record and share of votes in agreement with US, by issue, country, and world area, 1991, annual rpt, 7004–18
see also under By Foreign Country in the "Index by Categories"

China, Nationalist
see Taiwan

China, Peoples Republic
Agricultural exports of US, for grains, oilseed products, hides, skins, and cotton, by country, weekly rpt, 1922–3
Agricultural production, prices, and trade, for PRC, 1960s-90, annual rpt, 1524–4.2
Agricultural trade by commodity and country, prices, and world market devs, monthly rpt, 1922–12
Agricultural trade of US, by detailed commodity and country, 1991, annual rpt, 1524–8
Agricultural trade of US, by detailed commodity and country, 1991, semiannual rpt, 1522–4
Antimony trioxide from PRC at less than fair value, injury to US industry, investigation with background financial and operating data, 1992 rpt, 9886–14.342
Bicycles and costume jewelry exports of to US from PRC and other countries, 1986-91, article, 9882–2.301
Cancer (esophageal) risk for relatives of cases in Yaocun Commune, Linxian, PRC, 1989, article, 4472–1.315
Cancer (liver) patients with tumor suppression gene p53 mutations, by hepatitis B virus seropositivity, for US, Hawaii, and PRC, 1992 article, 4472–1.353
Cotton production, trade, and use, for selected countries, FAS monthly circular, 1925–4.2
Cuba trade, by commodity and country, mid 1980s-91, 9118–8
Dyes (sulfur) from 3 countries at less than fair value, injury to US industry, investigation with background financial and operating data, 1992 rpt, 9886–14.347
Economic and military aid and loans from US and intl agencies, by program and country, FY46-91, annual rpt, 9914–5
Economic conditions, income, production, prices, employment, and trade, 1992 periodic country rpt, 2046–4.64
Economic conditions, policy, and trade practices, by country, 1989-91, annual rpt, 21384–5
Economic indicators, trade balances, and dollar exchange rates, 1992 semiannual rpt, 8002–14
Economic performance and trade, for PRC, 1980-91, annual rpt, 9114–5
Economic, social, political, and geographic summary data, by country, 1992, annual factbook, 9114–2
Electric power plants (biomass-fired) feasibility assessment, for PRC Yunnan Province, 1991 rpt, 3308–103
Energy use and production, by fuel type, country, and country group, projected 1995-2010 and trends from 1970, annual rpt, 3164–84
Export licensing, monitoring, and enforcement activities, FY91, annual rpt, 2024–1
Exports and imports of China and other Asia countries with US, composition and trends, 1980s-91, article, 9385–1.303
Exports and imports of NATO members with PRC, by country, annual rpt, discontinued, 7144–14
Exports and imports of US, by commodity and country, 1980-90, world area rpt, 9116–1.3
Exports and imports of US by country, and trade shifts by commodity, 1991, annual rpt, 9884–25
Exports and imports of US, by Harmonized System 6-digit commodity and country, 1991, annual rpt, 2424–13
Exports and imports of US, by selected country, country group, and commodity group, 1991, annual rpt, 2044–37
Exports and imports of US, by transport mode, country, and SITC 1- to 3-digit commodity, 1991, annual rpt, 2424–12
Exports and imports of US with Communist and transitional economy countries, by detailed commodity and country, quarterly rpt with articles, 9882–2
Exports, imports, and balances of US for manufactured goods, by SITC 2-digit commodity and country, quarterly rpt, 2042–35
Exports, imports, and balances of US with major trading partners, by product category, 1987-91, annual chartbook, 9884–21
Exports of US, detailed Schedule B commodities with countries of destination, 1991, annual rpt, 2424–10
Ferrosilicon from 6 countries, injury to US industry from foreign subsidized and less than fair value imports, investigation with background financial and operating data, 1992 rpt, 9886–19.84
Fruit production by province, and trade, for PRC by commodity, 1980s-91, article, 1925–34.318
Human rights conditions in 170 countries, and US economic and military aid, 1991, annual rpt, 21384–3
Imports of goods, services, and investment from US, trade barriers, impacts, and US actions, by country, 1991, annual rpt, 444–2
Inflationary periods relative price changes and money demand behavior, for Germany, 1920-23, and for PRC, 1946-49, working paper, 9371–10.86
Labor conditions, union coverage, and work accidents, 1992 annual country rpt, 6366–4.50
Lockwashers (helical spring) from PRC and Taiwan at less than fair value, injury to US industry, investigation with background financial and operating data, 1992 rpt, 9886–14.362
Military spending, arms trade, and force strengths, with govt spending and population, by country, 1979-89, annual rpt, 9824–1
Minerals production and trade of PRC, by commodity, 1989-90, annual rpt, 5604–38
Minerals Yearbook, Vol 3, 1989: foreign country review of production, trade, and policy, by commodity, annual rpt, 5604–35.2
Multinatl US firms and foreign affiliates finances and operations, by industry and country, 1989 benchmark survey, annual rpt, 2704–5
Multinatl US firms foreign affiliates, income statement items by asset size, industry, and country, 1988, biennial article, 8302–2.322
Mushroom (canned) trade, supply, and demand, for selected countries, 1980s-92, article, 1925–34.333
Oil production, and exports by country, for PRC, monthly rpt, 9112–2
Oil production and exports to US, by major exporting country, detailed data, monthly rpt with articles, 3162–24
Oil production and exports to US, by major exporting country, detailed data, monthly 1973-88, 3168–123
Oil production, stocks, use, and trade, by selected country and country group, monthly rpt, 3162–42
Oil supply, demand, and stock forecasts, by world area, quarterly rpt, 3162–34
Pipe fittings (carbon steel) from 2 countries at less than fair value, injury to US industry, investigation with background financial and operating data, 1992 rpt, 9886–14.352
Pollution (air) contributing to global warming, emissions by monitoring site and country, and temperature change by world area and US region, 1860s-1990, annual rpt, 3004–33
Population size, growth rates, and components of change, by country, projected 1990-2020 and trends from 1950, biennial rpt, 2324–9
Refugee migration, and intl aid programs, by world area and country of origin and asylum, 1991, annual rpt, 7004–15
Ships in world merchant fleet, tonnage, and new ship construction and deliveries, by vessel type and country, as of Jan 1992, annual rpt, 7704–3

Spacecraft and satellite launches since 1957, quarterly listing, 9502–2
Steel imports of US under voluntary restraint agreement, by product, customs district, and country, with US industry operating data, quarterly rpt, 9882–13
Steel trade, by product, country, and customs district, with US industry operating data, 1989-June 1992, semiannual rpt, 9882–15
Sulfanilic acid from PRC at less than fair value, injury to US industry, investigation with background financial and operating data, 1992 rpt, 9886–14.357
Tidal currents, daily time and velocity by station for North America and Asia coasts, forecast 1993, annual rpt, 2174–1.2
Timber in northwestern US and British Columbia, production, prices, trade, and employment, quarterly rpt, 1202–3
UN voting record and share of votes in agreement with US, by issue, country, and world area, 1991, annual rpt, 7004–18
see also under By Foreign Country in the "Index by Categories"

Chiropractic and naturopathy
County Business Patterns, 1989: employment, establishments, and payroll, by SIC 2- to 4-digit industry and county, annual State rpt series, 2326–8
County Business Patterns, 1990: employment, establishments, and payroll, by SIC 2- to 4-digit industry and county, annual State rpt series, 2326–6
Degrees awarded in higher education, by level, field, race, and sex, 1989/90 and trends from 1980/81, annual rpt, 4844–17
Health condition and care indicators, 1950s-90 with health improvement and disease prevention goals for 1990, annual data compilation, 4144–11
Labor supply and education of health professionals, by professional and other characteristics, and location, 1960s-92 and projected to 2020, biennial rpt, 4114–8
Occupational Outlook Handbook, 1992-93, biennial rpt, 6744–1
Tax (income) returns of sole proprietorships, income statement items, by industry group, 1990, annual article, 8302–2.317; 8302–2.320

Chocolate
see Cocoa and chocolate

Chojnacky, David C.
"Forest Statistics for Land Outside National Forests in Southwestern Montana, 1989", 1206–25.12

Cholera
see Food and waterborne diseases

Cholesterol
Cancer (breast) risk of postmenopausal women relation to dietary fat and other nutrient intake, 1986-89, article, 4472–1.328
Diabetes patients physician office visits, by characteristics of patient, physician, and visit, 1989, 4146–8.212
Food composition, detailed data on nutrients, calories, and waste, for raw, processed, and prepared foods, series, 1356–3
Health condition and care indicators, 1950s-90 with health improvement and disease prevention goals for 1990, annual data compilation, 4144–11
Heart disease risk factors prevalence in Missouri, 1989-90, article, 4042–3.302
Indian (Navajo) diabetics and nondiabetics cholesterol and triglyceride levels, by age and sex, 1989-90 local area study, article, 4042–3.309
Physicians cholesterol treatment practices and views, 1986 local area study, article, 4042–3.345
Testing of serum cholesterol, public awareness and use, 1987-88 local area study, article, 4042–3.335

Choy, Susan P.
"Parental Financial Support for Undergraduate Education: 1987 National Postsecondary Student Aid Study", 4846–3.11
"Schools and Staffing in the U.S.: A Statistical Profile, 1987-88. Schools and Staffing Survey", 4836–3.10

Christiano, Lawrence J.
"Liquidity Effects and the Monetary Transmission Mechanism", 9383–20.20

Christiansen, Elaine H.
"Residential Fuelwood Consumption in the Southeastern U.S.", 9806–9.12

Christmas Island
Exports and imports of US, by transport mode, country, and SITC 1- to 3-digit commodity, 1991, annual rpt, 2424–12
Minerals Yearbook, Vol 3, 1989: foreign country review of production, trade, and policy, by commodity, annual rpt, 5604–35.2

Chronic fatigue syndrome
see Diseases and disorders

Chronic health conditions
see Diseases and disorders
see Health condition

Chronologies
Aircraft accidents, casualties, and damage, for commercial operations by detailed circumstances, 1988, annual rpt, 9614–2
Aircraft accidents, deaths, and circumstances, by carrier and carrier type, preliminary 1991, annual press release, 9614–9
Aircraft hijackings and attempts, persons involved, and location, for US and foreign carriers, 1990, annual rpt, 7504–49
Aircraft hijackings, on-board explosions, and other crimes, US and foreign incidents, 1986-90, annual rpt, 7504–31
Arms Control and Disarmament Agency activities, and treaties status, 1991, annual rpt, 9824–2
Banks mergers approved, and assets and offices involved, by instn, 1990, annual rpt, 9294–5
Capitol Architect outlays for salaries, supplies, and services, itemized by payee and function, 2nd half FY91, semiannual rpt, 25922–2
Census of Population, 1990: post-enumeration review of planning and conduct of census, and recommendations for improvement, GAO rpt, 26119–403
China economic performance and trade, 1980-91, annual rpt, 9114–5
Common markets, free trade areas, and other preferential trading arrangements membership and initiation dates, 1992 article, 9373–1.308
Consumer Product Safety Commission activities, recalls by brand, and casualties and medical costs, by product type, FY90, annual rpt, 9164–2
CPI methodology changes, 1890-1988, 6888–1
Earthquakes and other ground motion, intensity by station, 1990, annual rpt, 5664–14
Electric power disturbances, utility, location, customers affected, power losses, cause, and restoration time involved, listing, monthly rpt, 3162–35
Electric power disturbances, utility, location, customers affected, power losses, cause, and restoration time involved, listing, 1990, annual rpt, 3164–11
Energy Info Admin related legislation and impact, listing, 1974-87, annual rpt, 3164–29
Exporters (US) antiboycott law violations and fines by firm, and invitations to boycott by country, FY91, annual rpt, 2024–1
Fed Govt civilian pay legislation, 1945-90, annual rpt, 9844–6.5
Fed Govt debt subject to statutory limits, and legislative history, FY40-91 and projected to FY97, 108–46.5
Fed Govt financial and nonfinancial domestic aid programs and changes since 1965, by agency, 1992 base edition, annual listing, 104–5
Foreign countries *Geographic Notes*, boundaries, claims, nomenclature, and other devs, quarterly rpt, 7142–3
Futures and options trading volume, by commodity and exchange, FY91, annual rpt, 11924–2
Geothermal resources dev in US, listing of events, 1891-1990, 3168–122
House of Representatives salaries, expenses, and contingent fund disbursement, detailed listings, quarterly rpt, 21942–1
Income maintenance and health care financing, chronology of private and public actions, 1636-1991, quadrennial rpt, 10178–1
Labor-mgmt collective bargaining agreements expiring during year, and workers covered, by firm, union, industry group, and State, 1992, annual rpt, 6784–9
Medicaid coverage, funding, and costs, with reform recommendations, mid 1960s-92, 10048–83
Military and civilian DOD employment of blacks, by sex, grade, and period of service, and lists of award recipients, officers, and service academy grads, 1770s-90, 3548–22
Military forces reductions and ceilings for NATO and Warsaw Pact under CFE treaty, as of Nov 1990, 9828–1
Monetary policy decisions of Fed Open Market Committee, 1953-88, working paper, 9387–8.259
NIH activities, staff, funding, and facilities, historical data, 1991 annual rpt, 4434–1
OASDHI, Medicaid, SSI, and related programs benefits, beneficiary characteristics, and trust funds, selected years 1937-90, annual rpt, 4744–3
Officials (Federal) use of military aircraft, trips of 11 officials by reason, with costs and reimbursements, 1989-91, GAO rpt, 26111–78
Oil supply disruptions, shortfalls and share of world consumption disrupted, for major events, 1951-89, hearings, 21368–142

Railroad accidents, casualties, damage, and circumstances, by incident, 1988, annual rpt, 7604–3
Senate receipts, itemized expenses by payee, and balances, 1st half FY92, semiannual listing, 25922–1
Ships wrecked off Alaska, characteristics, deaths, cargo, and whale catch, by vessel and location, 1763-1937, 5738–34
Smithsonian Instn activities, rpts, and funding by donor, FY91, annual rpt, 29574–1.2
Spacecraft launches and other activities of NASA and USSR, with flight data, 1957-91, annual rpt, 9504–6.1
Spaceflights (manned) of US and USSR, 1961-91, annual rpt, 9504–9.1
Star position tables, planet coordinates, time conversion factors, and listing of observatories worldwide, 1993, annual rpt, 3804–7
Stock market decline of Nov 1991, impacts of trading related to option and futures expirations, 9738–22
Terrorism (intl) incidents, casualties, and attacks on US targets, by attack type and country, 1991, annual rpt, 7004–22
Terrorism (intl) incidents, casualties, and attacks on US targets, by attack type and world area, 1991, annual rpt, 7004–13
Terrorism incidents in US, related activity, and casualties, by attack type, target, group, and location, 1991, annual rpt, 6224–6
Transportation Natl Safety Board investigations and recommendations, and accidents and casualties by mode, 1990, annual rpt, 9614–1
UN peacekeeping operations costs by mission, and assessment rates by country, 1948-92, GAO rpt, 26123–404

Chrysler Corp.
Energy economy test results, 1993 model year, annual rpt, 3304–11
Safety of domestic and foreign autos, crash test results by model, model years 1987-91, 7768–111
Safety of domestic and foreign autos, crash test results by model, press release series, 7766–7

Chrystal, K. Alec
"How the 1992 Legislation Will Affect European Financial Services", 9391–1.308

Chu, Kenneth C.
"Implications of Birth Cohort Patterns in Interpreting Trends in Breast Cancer Rates", 4472–1.341

Chukchi Sea
Environmental conditions and oil dev impacts for Alaska OCS, compilation of papers, series, 2176–1
Whales population and behavior in Chukchi and Beaufort Seas, by endangered species, 1982-91, 5738–32
Whales population and behavior in Chukchi and Beaufort Seas, by endangered species, 1990, 5738–36

Chun, Andrew K.
"Central North Pacific Hurricanes—1991", 2152–8.302

Church and state
see also Religious liberty

Churches
see Religious organizations

Chute, Adrienne
"Public Libraries in the U.S.: 1990", 4824–6

CIA
see Central Intelligence Agency

Cigarettes and cigars
see Smoking
see Tobacco industry and products

Cimini, Michael H.
"Collective Bargaining, 1991: Recession Colors Talks", 6722–1.307

Cincinnati, Ohio
CPI by component for US city average, and by selected metro area, region, and population size, monthly rpt, 6762–2
Fruit and vegetable shipments, and arrivals by city, by mode of transport and State and country of origin, 1991, annual rpt, 1311–4.1
Housing and households characteristics, and unit and neighborhood quality, by MSA location for 11 MSAs, 1986 survey, supplement, 2485–8
Wages by occupation, and benefits, for office and plant workers, 1992 survey, periodic MSA rpt, 6785–17.3
see also under By City and By SMSA or MSA in the "Index by Categories"

Cinema
see Motion pictures

Ciocca, Daniel R.
"Correlation of HER-2/neu Amplification with Expression and with Other Prognostic Factors in 1,103 Breast Cancers", 4472–1.337

Circulatory diseases
Cases of acute and chronic conditions, disability, absenteeism, and health services use, by selected characteristics, 1990, annual rpt, 4147–10.182; 4147–10.183
Deaths and rates, by cause, age, sex, marital status, race, and State, 1989, US Vital Statistics advance annual rpt, 4146–5.124
Deaths and rates, by cause and age, preliminary 1990-91, US Vital Statistics annual rpt, 4144–7
Deaths and rates, by detailed location, cause, and demographic characteristics, 1989, US Vital Statistics annual rpt, 4144–3
Disability and work limitations of persons with chronic health conditions, by condition, age, and sex, 1983-86, 4946–1.2
Health condition and care indicators, 1950s-90 with health improvement and disease prevention goals for 1990, annual data compilation, 4144–11
Hospital discharges and length of stay, by diagnosis, patient and instn characteristics, procedure performed, and payment source, 1990, annual rpt, 4147–13.112
Hospital discharges and length of stay by region and diagnosis, and procedures performed, by age and sex, 1990, annual rpt, 4146–8.211
Hospital discharges and length of stay under old and new survey designs, by diagnosis, patient and instn characteristics, and procedure, Jan-Mar 1988, 4147–13.110
Hospital discharges by detailed diagnostic and procedure category, primary diagnosis, and length of stay, by age, sex, and region, 1990, annual rpt, 4147–13.111
Indian Health Service, tribal, and contract facilities hospitalization, by diagnosis, age, sex, and service area, FY91, annual rpt, 4084–5
OECD members health care costs, hospital use, resources, and economic and health indicators, by country, 1960s-90, article, 4652–1.322
Physicians visits, by patient and practice characteristics, diagnosis, and services provided, 1989, annual rpt, 4147–13.109
see also Blood diseases and disorders
see also Cardiovascular diseases
see also Cerebrovascular diseases
see also Hypertension
see also under By Disease in the "Index by Categories"

Cirrhosis of liver
see Digestive diseases

CIS
see Commonwealth of Independent States

Cities
Census Bur data coverage and availability for statistics on counties, cities, and small areas, 1991 rpt, 2326–7.82
Census Bur geographic levels of data coverage, maps, and reference products, 1992 rpt, 2308–67
Census of Housing, 1990: summary unit characteristics, by householder race and age, county, place, and urban-rural location, State rpt series, 2471–1
Census of Population and Housing, 1990: detailed geographic coverage, State CD-ROM series, 2551–9
Census of Population and Housing, 1990: population and housing characteristics, detailed geographic coverage, State CD-ROM series, 2551–10
Census of Population and Housing, 1990: summary characteristics, by county, subdiv, and place, State rpt series, 2551–7
Census of Population and Housing, 1990: summary characteristics, households, and land area, by county, subdiv, and place, State rpt series, 2551–1
Census of Population, 1990: population characteristics and living arrangements, by county, place, and urban-rural location, State rpt series, 2531–1
Crime victimization in cities, suburbs, and rural areas, by offense, circumstances, and victim and offender characteristics, 1987-89, 6066–3.48
Crimes, arrests by offender characteristics, and rates, by offense, and law enforcement employees, by population size and jurisdiction, 1991, annual rpt, 6224–2
Fed Govt spending in States and local areas, by type, State, county, and city, FY91, annual rpt, 2464–3.2
Foreign countries and cities population density, and distribution, life expectancy, and infant mortality by world region, 1991, fact sheet, 2326–17.50
Foreign countries *Geographic Notes*, boundaries, claims, nomenclature, and other devs, quarterly rpt, 7142–3
Govt direct spending and employment, by function and level of govt, selected years 1962-87, 10048–53
Govt employment and payroll, by function, level of govt, and State, 1991, annual rpt, 2466–1.1

Govt employment of minorities and women, by occupation, function, pay grade, and level of govt, 1991, annual rpt, 9244–6.3
Govt finances, by level of govt, State, and for large cities and counties, annual rpt series, 2466–2
Govt finances, structure, and service delivery in large metro areas, local area rpt series, 10046–9
Govt finances, tax systems and revenue, and fiscal structure, by level of govt and State, 1992 with historical trends, annual rpt, 10044–1
Labor surplus areas eligible for preferential Fed Govt contracts, monthly listing, 6402–1
Statistical Abstract of US, 1992 annual data compilation, 2324–1
Wage differentials among cities related to city size and worker characteristics, 1977-88, article, 9377–1.301
see also Blocks, city
see also Census tracts
see also Central business districts
see also Central cities
see also City and town planning
see also Harbors and ports
see also Metropolitan Statistical Areas
see also Neighborhoods
see also Suburbs
see also Urban areas
see also Wards, city
see also ZIP codes
see also under By City and By SMSA or MSA in the "Index by Categories"
see also under names of individual cities

Citizen-government relations
see Government-citizen relations

Citizen lawsuits
see Government-citizen lawsuits

Citizenship
Census of Population and Housing, 1990: immigrants, by period of entry, citizenship, State, birthplace, and for top cities and counties, press release, 2328–88
Census of Population and Housing, 1990: population and housing characteristics, detailed geographic coverage, State CD-ROM series, 2551–10
Census of Population and Housing, 1990: summary characteristics, by county, subdiv, and place, State rpt series, 2551–7
Criminal cases by type and disposition, and collections, for US attorneys, by Federal district, FY91, annual rpt, 6004–2.1
Criminal sentences for Federal offenses, guidelines by offense and circumstances, series, 17668–1
Criminal sentences under Federal mandatory minimum provisions by defendant characteristics, and views on justice system impacts, FY90, 17668–2
Education natl goals progress indicators, by State, 1992, annual rpt, 15914–1
Fed Govt civilian employment, by citizenship status and location, bimonthly rpt, 9842–1
Foreign countries human rights conditions in 170 countries, 1991, annual rpt, 21384–3
Military employment of civilians, by US citizenship, service branch, and country, quarterly rpt, 3542–20
Military health care personnel, and accessions by training source, by occupation, specialty, and service branch, FY90, annual rpt, 3544–24
Military service branches civilian employment, with summary military employment data, quarterly rpt, 3542–16
Naturalization petitions filed and granted, by Federal district court, 1991, annual rpt, 18204–8.27
Naturalizations, by Immigration and Naturalization Service district and country of origin, 1970s-90, annual summary rpt, 6264–7
Naturalizations, by selected characteristics and country, FY91 and trends from 1907, annual rpt, 6264–2.4
Pacific territories population and housing detailed characteristics, by location, 1990 Census of Population and Housing, series, 2551–8
Prisoners in Federal and contract instns, by selected characteristics, region, and Federal instn, FY89, annual rpt, 6244–1.1
Refugee arrivals and resettlement in US, by age, sex, sponsoring agency, State, and country, monthly rpt, 4592–1
Small Business Admin loan guarantee program participants finances, operations, characteristics, and views, 1991 survey, 9768–25
see also Alien workers
see also Aliens
see also Foreign medical graduates
see also Foreign students

Citrus fruits
Agricultural Statistics, 1991, annual rpt, 1004–1
Consumption, supply, trade, prices, spending, and indexes, by food commodity, 1990, annual rpt, 1544–4
CPI by component for US city average, and by selected metro area, region, and population size, monthly rpt, 6762–2
Exports and imports (agricultural) of US, by commodity and country, bimonthly rpt, 1522–1
Exports and imports (agricultural) of US, by detailed commodity and country, 1991, annual rpt, 1524–8
Exports and imports (agricultural) of US, by detailed commodity and country, 1991, semiannual rpt, 1522–4
Exports and imports between US and outlying areas, by detailed commodity and mode of transport, 1991, annual rpt, 2424–11
Exports and imports of US, by country and detailed commodity, monthly rpt, 2422–12
Exports and imports of US, by Harmonized System 6-digit commodity and country, 1991, annual rpt, 2424–13
Exports of US, detailed Schedule B commodities with countries of destination, 1991, annual rpt, 2424–10
Farm income, acreage, prices received, and production costs, for fruit, nut, and berry operations by commodity and region, 1987, article, 1561–6.301
Farm sector balance sheet, and receipts by detailed commodity, by State, 1986-90, annual rpt, 1544–18
Fertilizer and pesticide use and application rates, by type, crop, and State, 1991, 1616–1.3
Foreign and US fresh and processed fruit, vegetable, and nut production and trade, FAS monthly circular with articles, 1925–34
Foreign countries agricultural production, prices, and trade, by country, 1980-91 and forecast 1992, annual world area rpt series, 1524–4
Futures and options trading volume, by commodity and exchange, FY91, annual rpt, 11924–2
Futures trading in selected commodities and financial instruments and indexes, for NYC, Chicago, and other markets activity, biweekly rpt, 11922–5
Imports of fruits and vegetables under quarantine, by crop, country, and port of entry, FY89, annual rpt, 1524–7
Mexico fruit trade with US, 1989-91, and US tariffs under proposed North American Free Trade Agreement, 1992, by commodity, article, 1561–6.304
Orange juice (frozen) cold storage stocks, by census div, 1991, annual rpt, 1631–11
Orange juice production, imports, exports, and use, by country, various periods 1985-92, article, 1925–34.308
Orange juice production, use, exports, and stocks, and Brazil exports, by country, 1985-92, article, 1925–34.328
Price indexes (producer), by stage of processing and detailed commodity, monthly rpt, 6762–6
Price indexes (producer), by stage of processing and detailed commodity, monthly 1991, annual rpt, 6764–2
Prices (farm-retail) for food, marketing cost components, and industry finances and productivity, 1920s-91, annual rpt, 1544–9
Prices (wholesale) for fresh fruit and vegetables in NYC, Chicago, and selected shipping points, by crop, 1991, annual rpt, 1311–8
Prices (wholesale) of fruit and vegetables in NYC by State, and shipments and arrivals by mode of transport, by commodity, weekly rpt, 1311–20
Prices (wholesale) of fruit and vegetables in NYC-Newark, and arrivals by mode of transport, by commodity and State, 1990, annual rpt, 1311–21
Prices received and paid by farmers, by commodity and State, monthly rpt, 1629–1
Prices received and paid by farmers, by commodity and State, 1991, annual rpt, 1629–5
Prices received by farmers and production value, by detailed crop and State, 1989-91, annual rpt, 1621–2
Production, farms, acreage, and related data, by selected crop and State, monthly rpt, 1621–1
Production, prices, and use of fruit and nuts, annual rpt series, 1621–18
Production, prices, trade, stocks, and use, by selected crop, periodic situation rpt with articles, 1561–6
Shipments by mode of transport, arrivals, and imports, for fruit and vegetables by commodity and State and country of origin, weekly rpt, 1311–3

Shipments of fruit and vegetables, and arrivals by city, by mode of transport and State and country of origin, 1991, annual rpt series, 1311–4
Shipments, production, and marketing of fruit and vegetables, for Florida, with US trade and prices, by commodity, 1970s-91, annual rpt, 1311–23
Truck rates for fruit and vegetables paid by shippers and receivers, by commodity and city, and fleet itemized costs per mile, weekly rpt, 1311–22
Weight and volume conversion factors for agricultural commodities and products, 1992 rpt, 1508–3

City and town planning
Boundary review commission activities in 12 States, 1989, 10048–85
Community Dev Block Grant activities and funding, by program, FY75-91, annual rpt, 5124–8
Economic Dev Admin activities, and funding by program, recipient, State, and county, FY91 and cumulative from FY66, annual rpt, 2064–2
Historic and natural natl landmarks damaged and threatened, with owner, location, damage type, and recommended remedial action, 1990, annual listing, 5544–16
Labor demand, turnover, and training completions, by detailed occupation, 1990 and projected to 2005, biennial rpt, 6744–3
Occupational Outlook Handbook, 1992-93, biennial rpt, 6744–1

City taxation
see State and local taxes

Civil aviation
Pilots and nonpilots certified by FAA, by certificate type, age, sex, region, and State, 1991, annual rpt, 7504–2
Statistical Abstract of US, 1992 annual data compilation, 2324–1.22
Traffic, aircraft, carriers, airports, and FAA activities, detailed data, 1981-90, annual rpt, 7504–1
see also Aerospace industry
see also Air cargo
see also Air piracy
see also Air traffic control
see also Aircraft
see also Airlines
see also Airports and airways
see also Aviation accidents and safety
see also General aviation
see also Pilots

Civil defense
Assistance (financial and nonfinancial) of Fed Govt, 1992 base edition, annual listing, 104–5
Expenditures of Fed Govt in States, by type, program, agency, and State, FY91, annual rpt, 2464–2
Mgmt of disasters and natl security threats, with data by major event and State, 1992 annual rpt, 9434–6
Natl income and product accounts, comprehensive accounts and components, benchmark revisions, 1929-88, 2708–5
Natl income and product accounts, comprehensive accounts and components, *Survey of Current Business*, monthly rpt, 2702–1.26
see also National Guard

Civil engineering
see Bridges and tunnels
see Canals
see Dams
see Harbors and ports
see Highways, streets, and roads
see Irrigation
see Public works
see Reclamation of land
see Rivers and waterways
see Traffic engineering

Civil liberties
see Civil rights
see Due process of law
see Electronic surveillance
see Habeas corpus
see Right of privacy
see Searches and seizures

Civil-military relations
see also Defense contracts and procurement
see also Defense industries
see also Impacted areas

Civil procedure
Environmental laws enforcement activities of Justice Dept, FY83-91, press release, 6008–37
Environmental laws enforcement activities of Justice Dept, FY83-92, annual press release, 6004–22
Federal district, appeals, and bankruptcy courts, civil cases terminated by circuit and district, 1991, annual rpt, 18204–11
Federal district, appeals, and special courts civil and criminal caseloads, by offense, circuit, and district, 1991, annual rpt, 18204–8
Judicial Conf proceedings and findings, spring 1992, semiannual rpt, 18202–2
Patent and trademark litigation, by court, FY91, annual rpt, 2244–1.5
Reform recommendations for civil litigation, with background data, 1960-90, 048–3
Securities law enforcement activities of SEC, FY91, annual rpt, 9734–2.3
SSA activities, litigation, finances, and staff, FY91, annual rpt, 4704–6
US attorneys case processing and collections, by case type and Federal district, FY91, annual rpt, 6004–2
see also Administrative law and procedure
see also Adoption
see also Bankruptcy
see also Child support and alimony
see also Claims
see also Commitment
see also Contempt of court
see also Contracts
see also Divestiture
see also Domestic relations courts and cases
see also Evidence
see also Extradition
see also Fines and settlements
see also Government-citizen lawsuits
see also Guardianship
see also Habeas corpus
see also Indian claims
see also Judgments, civil procedure
see also Juries
see also Legal arbitration and mediation
see also Marriage and divorce
see also Tax protests and appeals
see also Torts
see also Trials

Civil rights
Court civil and criminal caseloads for Federal district, appeals, and bankruptcy courts, by type of suit and offense, circuit, and district, 1991, annual rpt, 18204–11
Court civil and criminal caseloads for Federal district, appeals, and special courts, 1991, annual rpt, 18204–8
Criminal sentences for Federal offenses, guidelines by offense and circumstances, series, 17668–1
Fed Govt accounts receivable, delinquent debt cases and collections of Justice Dept and private law firms, pilot project results, FY91, annual rpt, 6004–20
Foreign countries human rights conditions in 170 countries, 1991, annual rpt, 21384–3
Latin America economic and social conditions, resources, trade, and aid, 1992, annual factbook, 9914–14
UN voting record and share of votes in agreement with US, by issue, country, and world area, 1991, annual rpt, 7004–18
US attorneys case processing and collections, by case type and Federal district, FY91, annual rpt, 6004–2
see also Age discrimination
see also Discrimination against the handicapped
see also Discrimination in credit
see also Discrimination in education
see also Discrimination in employment
see also Discrimination in housing
see also Due process of law
see also Freedom of information
see also Racial discrimination
see also Religious liberty
see also Right of assembly
see also Right of privacy
see also Sex discrimination

Civil Rights Act
Employment discrimination issues in Act, EEOC cases by issue, damage awards, and sexual harassment complaints and company policies, late 1970s-91, hearing, 21348–120

Civil Rights Commission
see Commission on Civil Rights

Civil service pensions
Beneficiaries and taxes collected for social insurance programs since 1940, quarterly rpt, 4742–1.4
Benefits and beneficiaries of govt pension plans, by type of plan and eligibility, and level of govt, 1960s-80s, annual article, 4742–1.318
Budget of US, Bush Admin proposals, with detail for defense budgets, and historical data from FY34, FY93, 108–46
Budget of US, CBO analysis of revenue and spending alternatives and projections of economic indicators, FY93-97, annual rpt, 26304–3
Budget of US, obligations and authority by function, agency, and program, with summaries and analyses, FY93, annual rpt, 104–2
Budget of US, receipts by source, outlays by agency and program, and balances, monthly rpt, 8102–3
Expenditures (direct) and employment, by function and level of govt, selected years 1962-87, 10048–53
Expenditures, coverage, and benefits for social welfare programs, late 1930s-90, annual rpt, 4744–3.1; 4744–3.3

Expenditures for public welfare by program, FY50s-89, annual article, 4742–1.319
Expenditures of Fed Govt in States, by type, program, agency, and State, FY91, annual rpt, 2464–2
Fed Govt civil service retirement system actuarial valuation, FY79-91 and projected to FY2065, annual rpt, 9844–34
Fed Govt civilian employees demographic and employment characteristics, as of Sept 1991, annual article, 9842–1.301
Fed Govt civilian employees retirement, health, and life insurance benefits, coverage and finances of 4 programs, FY86-90, annual rpt, 9844–37
Fed Govt civilian employees work-years, pay rates, and benefits use and costs, by agency, FY90, annual rpt, 9844–31
Finances of govts, by level of govt, State, and for large cities and counties, annual rpt series, 2466–2
Flow-of-funds accounts, savings, investments, and credit statements, quarterly rpt, 9365–3.3
Income (household, family, and personal), by source, detailed characteristics, and region, 1991, annual Current Population Rpt, 2546–6.76
Income and sources of aged, by whether OASDI beneficiary, poverty status, and other characteristics, 1990, biennial rpt, 4744–26
Indian Health Service employment of Indians and non-Indians, training, hires, and quits, by occupation, FY90, annual rpt, 4084–6
Judicial Survivors Annuity Fund financial condition and annuitants, June 1987-91, annual rpt, 18204–8.12
Mortgage loan activity, by type of lender, loan, and mortgaged property, monthly press release, 5142–18
Mortgage loan activity, by type of lender, loan, and mortgaged property, quarterly press release, 5142–30
Mortgage, mortgage-backed security, and govt security holdings of public and private pension funds, and public funds investment in housing, 1986-90, 5188–134
Natl income and product accounts, comprehensive accounts and components, benchmark revisions, 1929-88, 2708–5
Natl income and product accounts, comprehensive accounts and components, *Survey of Current Business*, monthly rpt, 2702–1.25
New England States govt retirement systems investment policy assessment, with system assets and liabilities, by State, 1992 article, 9373–25.301
Police and firefighters pension plans, participation requirements, and earnings replacement, 1990, article, 6722–1.350
Postal Service employment and related expenses, FY91, annual rpt, 9864–5.3
Senior Executive Service members characteristics, entries, exits, and awards, FY79-91, annual rpt, 9844–36
State and local govt retirement systems, cash and security holdings and finances, quarterly rpt, 2462–2
State govt pension funds use to balance budgets, with data for 2 States, 1991 hearing, 21148–66
Statistical Abstract of US, 1992 annual data compilation, 2324–1.12
Transit systems finances and operations, by mode, size of fleet and urban area, region, and for 518 systems, 1990, annual rpt, 7884–4

Civil service system
Canada and US civil service merit systems operations, pay, appointments, and promotions, late 1980s-91, 9498–16
Equal Opportunity Recruitment Program activity, and Fed Govt employment by sex, race, pay grade, and occupational group, FY91, annual rpt, 9844–33
Fed Govt noncareer employees conversions to career appointments, by pay grade and agency, 1988-89, GAO rpt, 26119–382
Merit system oversight and enforcement activities of OPM, series, 9496–2
Merit Systems Protection Board decisions on appeals of Fed Govt personnel actions, by agency and region, FY91, annual rpt, 9494–2
Senior Executive Service members characteristics, entries, exits, and awards, FY79-91, annual rpt, 9844–36
Senior Executive Service noncareer and Schedule C appointments, by agency, 1990-91, GAO rpt, 26119–412
Violations and prohibited political activity reported by Federal employees, cases by type, FY91, annual rpt, 9894–1
see also Civil service pensions
see also Federal employees
see also Labor-management relations in government
see also State and local employees

Civil War
see War

Civil works
see Public works

Civilian Health and Medical Program of the Uniformed Services
Benefits and costs under CHAMPUS, FY85-90, annual chartbook, 3504–23
Commercial activities of DOD performed in-house, and work-years, by service branch, installation, and State, FY91, annual rpt, 3544–25

Claims
AID economic aid to developing countries, obligations and disbursements by country, quarterly rpt, 9912–4
Banks (US) and nonbanking firms claims on foreigners, by type and country, *Treasury Bulletin*, quarterly rpt, 8002–4.13
Banks (US) and nonbanking firms liabilities to and claims on foreigners, by country, 1989-90, annual rpt, 9364–5.10
Crime victim compensation and support service programs funding, by offense and State, FY88-90, biennial rpt, 6064–37
Crime victim compensation and support service programs operations, series, 6066–31
Debt delinquent on Federal accounts, cases and collections of Justice Dept and private law firms, pilot project results, FY91, annual rpt, 6004–20
Fed Govt contingent liabilities and claims paid on insured and guaranteed contracts with foreign obligors, by country and program, periodic rpt, 8002–12
Mining claims on public lands, cumulative FY76-91, annual rpt, 5724–1.2
Public lands acreage and use, and Land Mgmt Bur activities and finances, annual State rpt series, 5724–11
Radiation exposure of Navy personnel on nuclear-powered vessels and at support facilities, and injury claims, 1950s-91, annual rpt, 3804–10
Railroad safety violation claims settled, by carrier, FY91, annual rpt, 7604–10
Truck transport of household goods, performance and disposition of damage claims, for selected carriers, 1991, annual rpt, 9484–11
US attorneys civil cases, by type and disposition, FY91, annual rpt, 6004–2.5
Wolf (gray) kills of livestock, and farmer compensation claims and payments, for Minnesota, late 1970s-80s, 5508–115
see also Crime victim compensation
see also Fines and settlements
see also Indian claims
see also Insurance and insurance industry
see also under specific types of insurance (listed under Insurance and insurance industry)

Clair, Robert T.
"Loan Growth and Loan Quality: Some Preliminary Evidence from Texas Banks", 9379–1.305

Clarida, Richard H.
"Cointegration, Aggregate Consumption, and the Demand for Imports: A Structural Econometric Investigation", 9385–8.141
"Real Exchange Rate and U.S. Manufacturing Profits: A Theoretical Framework with Some Empirical Support", 9385–8.142

Clark County, Nev.
Water (groundwater) supply, quality, chemistry, and use, 1986-90, local area rpt, 5666–28.23

Clark, Joy
"Simulated Economic Impact of TED Regulations on Selected Vessels in the Texas Shrimp Fishery", 2162–1.302

Clark, Michelle A.
"Are Small Rural Banks Credit-Constrained? A Look at the Seasonal Borrowing Privilege in the Eighth Federal Reserve District", 9391–1.311
"District Bank Performance in 1991: More Ups than Downs", 9391–16.307
"District Banks Navigate Recession's Waters", 9391–16.303
"Future of Community Banking", 9391–17
"Is There Less Assurance in Life Insurance?", 9391–16.310
"When a Bank's Not a Bank—Nonbanks in the Financial Marketplace", 9391–16.305

Clark, Todd
"Business Cycle Fluctuations in U.S. Regions and Industries: The Roles of National, Region-Specific, and Industry-Specific Shocks", 9381–10.134

Clarke, Janet T.
"Aerial Surveys of Endangered Whales in the Alaskan Chukchi and Western Beaufort Seas, 1990", 5738–36
"Distribution, Abundance and Behavior of Endangered Whales in the Alaskan Chukchi and Western Beaufort Seas, 1991: with a Review, 1982-91", 5738–32

Clarksville, Tenn.
Wages by occupation, and benefits for office and plant workers, 1992 survey, periodic MSA rpt, 6785–3.5
Class actions
see Government-citizen lawsuits
Classifications
Alcohol abuse and dependence prevalence, by age, race, and sex, and diagnostic criteria, 1988, article, 4482–1.306
Census Bur geographic levels of data coverage, maps, and reference products, 1992 rpt, 2308–67
Census of Population and Housing, 1990: detailed geographic coverage, CD-ROM user guide, 2308–65
Census of Population and Housing, 1990: industry and occupation classification codes, alphabetical index, 2628–1
Census of Population and Housing, 1990: Summary Tape File 3 CD-ROM user guide, 2308–68
Computer systems purchase and use, and data recording, processing, and transfer, Fed Govt standards, series, 2216–2
Economic censuses of 1987 and related programs, CD-ROM user guide series, 2306–8
Economic censuses, 1987: data collection, coverage, availability, and procedural history, 2628–16
Export statistics classification codes of Census Bur for countries, commodities, and customs districts, 1990 base edition and supplements, 2428–5
Health service areas, indicators of service use, and residents seeking care outside area, under alternative area definitions, 1988-89, 4147–2.113
Higher education instn physical plant inventory and classification methods, 1992 guidelines, 4848–48
Library of Congress activities, acquisitions, services, and financial statements, FY91, annual rpt, 26404–1
Library of Congress rpts and products, 1992-93, biennial listing, 26404–6
Medicare reimbursement of hospitals under prospective payment system, diagnosis related group code assignment and effects on care and instn finances, series, 4006–7
MSA and central city definitions and revisions, 1992, annual listing, 104–32
Occupational Outlook Handbook, 1992-93, biennial rpt, 6744–1
Oil and gas field codes and locations, 1991, annual listing, 3164–70
Physicians time and effort in patient visits, office personnel services, and coding manual use in billing, by selected specialty, 1989 survey, 17266–2.5
Poverty income guidelines and derivation, by family size, 1992 with trends from 1965, article, 4742–1.310
Tariff Schedule of US, classifications and rates of duty by detailed imported commodity, 1993 base edition, 9886–13
Tariff Schedule of US, classifications for pharmaceutical and intermediate chemical products, 1992 rpt, 9886–4.185
Textile Agreement Category System import classification codes, correlation with TSUSA, 1993 annual rpt, 2044–31
see also Standard Industrial Classification
see also "Guide to Selected Standard Classifications" section in the back of this Index
Classified information
see Internal security
Clauson, Annette L.
"Costs of Producing and Selling Burley Tobacco: 1989, 1990 and Preliminary 1991", 1561–10.301
"Costs of Producing and Selling Flue-Cured Tobacco: 1991 and Preliminary 1992", 1561–10.305
"Flue-Cured Tobacco Farms: Selected Characteristics", 1568–307
"1990 Crop Sugarbeet and Sugarcane Production and Processing Costs", 1561–14.303
Clay industry and products
Business statistics, detailed data for major industries and economic indicators, *Survey of Current Business*, monthly rpt, 2702–1.20
Business statistics, detailed data for major industries and economic indicators, 1960-91, *Survey of Current Business* biennial supplement, 2704–1
Ceramic floor and wall tiles trade, tariffs, and industry operating data, 1992 rpt, 9885–13.2
County Business Patterns, 1989: employment, establishments, and payroll, by SIC 2- to 4-digit industry and county, annual State rpt series, 2326–8
County Business Patterns, 1990: employment, establishments, and payroll, by SIC 2- to 4-digit industry and county, annual State rpt series, 2326–6
DOE R&D projects and funding at natl labs, universities, and other instns, FY91, annual summary rpt, 3004–18.3
Employment, earnings, and hours, by SIC 1- to 4-digit industry, monthly 1989-Feb 1992, annual rpt, 6744–4
Exports and imports between US and outlying areas, by detailed commodity and mode of transport, 1991, annual rpt, 2424–11
Exports and imports of US, by country and detailed commodity, monthly rpt, 2422–12
Exports and imports of US, by Harmonized System 6-digit commodity and country, 1991, annual rpt, 2424–13
Exports and imports of US, by transport mode, country, and SITC 1- to 3-digit commodity, 1991, annual rpt, 2424–12
Exports of US, detailed commodities by country, monthly CD-ROM, 2422–13
Exports of US, detailed Schedule B commodities with countries of destination, 1991, annual rpt, 2424–10
Freight (waterborne domestic and foreign) by commodity, traffic, and passengers, by port and waterway, 1989, annual rpt, 3754–3
Hwy construction material use by type, and spending, by State, 1940s-91, annual rpt, 7554–29
Imports, exports, and employment impacts, by SIC 2- to 4-digit industry and commodity, quarterly rpt, 2322–2
Imports of US, detailed commodities by country, monthly CD-ROM, 2422–14
Input-output structure of US economy, detailed interindustry transactions for 541 industries, and components of final demand, 1982 benchmark data, 2708–17
Labor productivity, indexes of output, hours, and employment by SIC 2- to 4-digit industry, 1967-90, annual rpt, 6824–1.3
Manufacturing annual survey, 1990: finances and operations, by SIC 2- to 4-digit industry, series, 2506–14
Manufacturing census, 1987: concentration of largest firms measured by value added, and for shipments by SIC 2- and 4-digit industry, subject rpt, 2497–6
Manufacturing census, 1987: shipments of manufacturers products, by customer class and SIC 2- and 4-digit industry, subject rpt, 2497–4
Manufacturing finances and operations, by SIC 2- to 4-digit industry, forecast 1992, annual rpt, 2044–28
Mineral Industry Surveys, State reviews of production, 1991, preliminary annual rpt, 5614–6
Minerals Yearbook, Vol 1, 1989: commodity reviews of production, use, trade, prices, and mining operations, annual rpt, 5604–33
Minerals Yearbook, Vol 1, 1990: commodity review of production, reserves, supply, use, and trade, annual rpt, 5604–20.15
Minerals Yearbook, Vol 2, 1989: State reviews of production and sales by commodity, and business activity, annual rpt series, 5604–16
Minerals Yearbook, Vol 2, 1990: State reviews of production and sales by commodity, and business activity, annual rpt series, 5604–22
Minerals Yearbook, Vol 3, 1989: foreign country reviews of production, trade, and policy, by commodity, annual rpt, 5604–35
Multinatl firms US affiliates finances and operations, by industry, country of parent firm, and State, 1987, 2708–48
Occupational injuries and incidence, employment, and hours in nonmetallic minerals mines and related operations, 1990, annual rpt, 6664–1
Occupational injury and illness rates, by SIC 2- to 4-digit industry, 1989-90, annual rpt, 6844–7
Occupational injury and illness rates, by SIC 2- to 4-digit industry, 1990, annual rpt, 6844–1
Price indexes (producer), by stage of processing and detailed commodity, monthly rpt, 6762–6
Price indexes (producer), by stage of processing and detailed commodity, monthly 1991, annual rpt, 6764–2
Production, prices, trade, use, employment, tariffs, and stockpiles, by mineral, with foreign comparisons, 1987-91, annual rpt, 5604–18
Production, shipments, and PPI for building materials, by type, quarterly rpt, 2042–1.5; 2042–1.6
Production, shipments, trade, and stocks, by clay product, periodic Current Industrial Rpt series, 2506–9
Science, engineering, and technical employment in manufacturing, by field and industry, 1989, triennial rpt, 9627–23

see also Pottery and porcelain products
see also under By Industry in the "Index by Categories"

Clean Air Act
Coal coke use and costs in steel industry, effects of Clean Air Act, 1985-91 and projected to 2003, 5606–5.10
Economic impacts of 1990 amendments to Act, with background data for Midwest and US, 1992 article, 9375–1.304
Enforcement of environmental laws by EPA and State govts, activities, FY91, annual rpt, 9184–21

Clean Water Act
Enforcement of environmental laws by EPA and State govts, activities, FY91, annual rpt, 9184–21

Cleaning services
see Domestic workers and services
see Janitorial and maintenance services
see Laundry and cleaning services

Clearwater, Fla.
CPI by component for US city average, and by selected metro area, region, and population size, monthly rpt, 6762–2
Housing starts and completions authorized by building permits in 40 MSAs, quarterly rpt, 2382–9
Wages by occupation, and benefits, for office and plant workers, 1991 survey, periodic MSA rpt, 6785–16.3

Cleary, Paul D.
"Factors Affecting the Availability and Use of Hemodialysis Facilities", 4652–1.306

Clemency
Criminal case processing in Federal courts, by offense, disposition, and jurisdiction, data compilation, 1992 annual rpt, 6064–6.5
Executions, commutations of sentence, and other removals of inmates from death row, data compilation, 1992 annual rpt, 6064–6.6
Prison and parole admissions and releases, sentence length, and time served, by offense and offender characteristics, 1988, annual rpt, 6064–33
Prisoners released from sentences and death row, by reason and State, 1990, annual rpt, 6064–26.4; 6064–26.6
see also Pardons

Clement International Corp.
"Review of Literature on Herbicides, Including Phenoxy Herbicides and Associated Dioxins: Volume XVII Analysis of Recent Literature on Health Effects; and Volume XVIII Annotated Bibliography of Recent Literature on Health Effects", 8706–1.4

Clergy
Immigrants admitted to US, by class and country, FY85-91, annual rpt, 6264–2.1
Labor demand, turnover, and training completions, by detailed occupation, 1990 and projected to 2005, biennial rpt, 6744–3
Occupational Outlook Handbook, 1992-93, biennial rpt, 6744–1
VA health care facilities trainees, by detailed program and city, FY91, annual rpt, 8704–4
see also Missions and missionaries

Clerical workers
Air traffic control and airway facilities staff, by employment and other characteristics, FY90, annual rpt, 7504–41
Deaths and rates, by cause and selected social, demographic, and employment characteristics, 1979-85, natl longitudinal study, 4478–186
DOT employment, by subagency, occupation, and selected personnel characteristics, FY91, annual rpt, 7304–18
Earnings, annual average percent changes for selected occupational groups, selected MSAs, monthly rpt, 6782–1.1
Employment and economic conditions, alternative BLS projections to 2005 and trends 1975-90, biennial rpt, 6744–19
Employment Cost Index and alternative measure of compensation costs, by component, occupation, industry group, union status, and location, 1975-92, annual rpt, 6744–20
Employment, earnings, and hours, monthly press release, 6742–5
Employment situation, earnings, hours, and other BLS economic indicators, transcripts of BLS Commissioner's monthly testimony, periodic rpt, 23846–4
Employment, unemployment, and labor force characteristics, by region, State, and selected metro area, 1991, annual rpt, 6744–7
Fed Govt employment of minorities, women, and disabled, by agency and occupation, FY90, annual rpt, 9244–10
Higher education faculty and staff, by occupation, full- and part-time status, sex, and instn type and control, fall 1989, biennial rpt, 4844–18
Immigrants and legalized aliens, by occupational group and country of birth, preliminary FY91, annual tables, 6264–1
Immigration to US, alien workers, visitors, deportations, and naturalizations, by country, FY91 and trends from 1820, annual rpt, 6264–2
Income (household, family, and personal), by source, detailed characteristics, and region, 1991, annual Current Population Rpt, 2546–6.76
Labor demand, turnover, and training completions, by detailed occupation, 1990 and projected to 2005, biennial rpt, 6744–3
Minority group and women employment, by occupation, SIC 1- to 3- digit industry, State, and MSA, 1991, annual rpt, 9244–1
Occupational Outlook Handbook, 1992-93, biennial rpt, 6744–1
Pacific territories population and housing detailed characteristics, by location, 1990 Census of Population and Housing, series, 2551–8
Physicians time and effort in patient visits, office personnel services, and coding manual use in billing, by selected specialty, 1989 survey, 17266–2.5
State and local govt employment of minorities and women, by occupation, function, pay level, and State, 1991, annual rpt, 9244–6
Student Community Service Learning work-study program, earnings and operations, 1986-90, GAO rpt, 26121–449
Training for job qualification and skill improvement, workers participating by training source, occupation, age, sex, and race, 1991, 6728–32
Wages by occupation, and benefits, for office and plant workers, periodic MSA survey rpt series, 6785–16; 6785–17
see also Area wage surveys
see also Industry wage surveys
see also under By Occupation in the "Index by Categories"

Cleveland, Ohio
CPI by component for US city average, and by region, population size, and for 15 metro areas, monthly rpt, 6762–1
CPI by component for US city average, and by selected metro area, region, and population size, monthly rpt, 6762–2
Drug test results at arrest, by drug type, offense, and sex, for selected urban areas, quarterly rpt, 6062–3
see also under By City and By SMSA or MSA in the "Index by Categories"

Client/Patient Sample Survey of Inpatient, Outpatient, and Partial Care Programs
Mental health care of affective disorder patients, by patient and facility characteristics, 1986, 4506–3.49

Climate
see Global climate change
see Meteorology
see Weather

Climate Monitoring and Diagnostics Laboratory
see National Oceanic and Atmospheric Administration

Clingman, Michael D.
"Average Wages for 1985-90 for Indexing Under the Social Security Act", 4706–2.133

Clinical laboratory technicians
Hospital employment and job vacancy rate, by occupation, and instn size and control, 1981-88, annual rpt, 4114–12
Labor demand, turnover, and training completions, by detailed occupation, 1990 and projected to 2005, biennial rpt, 6744–3
Labor supply and education of health professionals, by professional and other characteristics, and location, 1960s-92 and projected to 2020, biennial rpt, 4114–8
Military health care personnel, and accessions by training source, by occupation, specialty, and service branch, FY90, annual rpt, 3544–24
Occupational Outlook Handbook, 1992-93, biennial rpt, 6744–1
VA health care facilities trainees, by detailed program and city, FY91, annual rpt, 8704–4
VA health care staff and turnover, by occupation, physician specialty, and location, 1991, annual rpt, 8604–8
Vaccination for smallpox, schedules, dosages, and precautions, CDC guidelines, 1991 rpt, 4206–2.50

Clinics
AIDS virus-related Medicaid claims and payments, by sex, age, risk group, eligibility, and source of care, for Michigan, mid 1980s, article, 4042–3.348
Appalachian Regional Commission health care services projects by State, and project listing, 1960s-80s, 9088–38

County Business Patterns, 1989: employment, establishments, and payroll, by SIC 2- to 4-digit industry and county, annual State rpt series, 2326–8
County Business Patterns, 1990: employment, establishments, and payroll, by SIC 2- to 4-digit industry and county, annual State rpt series, 2326–6
Employment, earnings, and hours, by SIC 1- to 4-digit industry, monthly 1989-Feb 1992, annual rpt, 6744–4
Food aid program of USDA for women, infants, and children, participants and costs by State and Indian agency, FY90, annual tables, 1364–12
Food aid program of USDA for women, infants, and children, participants by race, State, and Indian agency, 1991, annual rpt, 1364–16
Food aid program of USDA for women, infants, and children, participants, clinics, and costs, by State and Indian agency, monthly tables, 1362–16
HHS financial aid, by program, recipient, State, and city, FY91, annual regional listings, 4004–3
Indian Health Service and tribal facilities and use, and Indians health and other characteristics, by IHS region, 1980s-90, annual chartbook, 4084–7
Indian Health Service facilities, funding, operations, and Indian health and other characteristics, 1950s-91, annual chartbook, 4084–1
Medicaid beneficiaries and payments, by service type, FY72-90, annual rpt, 4744–3.6
Medicare admin and research, and HCFA affirmative action and accreditation programs, FY87, annual rpt, 4654–5
Medicare and Medicaid beneficiaries and program operations, 1992, annual fact book, 4654–18
Mental health care facilities, staff, and patient characteristics, *Statistical Notes* series, 4506–3
Mental health care facilities, staff, patients, and finances, 1970s-91, biennial rpt, 4094–1
Military health care facilities of DOD in US and abroad, admissions, beds, outpatient visits, and births, by service branch, quarterly rpt, 3542–15
Oregon Medicaid waiver proposal for managed care, services priorities dev procedures and issues, with background data, 1992 rpt, 26358–254
Quality standards and review for health care facilities excluded from Medicare prospective payment system, certification, accreditation, and licensing, 1991 survey, 17206–2.41
Rural areas health care access for counties without hospitals and in which the only hospital closed, 1987-89, 17206–2.30
VA Geriatric Research, Education and Clinical Centers activities and finances, FY88, annual rpt, 8704–8
Veterans health care, patients, visits, costs, and operating beds, by VA and contract facility, and region, quarterly rpt, 8602–4
Veterans in VA and non-VA health facilities, by type, FY67-91, annual rpt, 8604–5.3
Youth health condition, risk factors, and preventive and treatment services use and availability, 1970s-80s, 26358–234.3
see also Clinical laboratory technicians
see also Hospitals
see also Medical examinations and tests

Clocks
see Watches and clocks

Clothing and clothing industry
Business statistics, detailed data for major industries and economic indicators, *Survey of Current Business*, monthly rpt, 2702–1.21
Business statistics, detailed data for major industries and economic indicators, 1960-91, *Survey of Current Business* biennial supplement, 2704–1
Caribbean area and Mexico clothing exports to US, and domestic and US-owned industry production costs and operations, impacts of North American Free Trade Agreement, 1992 rpt, 9886–4.186
Collective bargaining agreements expiring during year, and workers covered, by firm, union, industry group, and State, 1992, annual rpt, 6784–9
Consumer Expenditure Survey, spending by category, and income, by selected household characteristics, 1991, annual press release, 6726–1.53
Consumer Expenditure Survey, spending by category, selected household characteristics, and region, quarterly rpt, 6762–14
Consumer spending, natl income and product account benchmark revisions, 1929-88, 2708–5
Consumer spending, natl income and product accounts, comprehensive accounts and components, *Survey of Current Business*, monthly rpt, 2702–1.25
County Business Patterns, 1989: employment, establishments, and payroll, by SIC 2- to 4-digit industry and county, annual State rpt series, 2326–8
County Business Patterns, 1990: employment, establishments, and payroll, by SIC 2- to 4-digit industry and county, annual State rpt series, 2326–6
CPI by component for US city average, and by selected metro area, region, and population size, monthly rpt, 6762–2
Cuba trade, by commodity and country, mid 1980s-91, 9118–8
Eastern Europe export industries dev potential, with trade and industry finances and operations, for 5 countries, 1985-90, 9886–4.179
Employment, earnings, and hours, by selected SIC 1- to 4-digit industry, State, and for 275 MSAs, 1987-92, 6748–81
Employment, earnings, and hours, by SIC 1- to 4-digit industry, monthly 1989-Feb 1992, annual rpt, 6744–4
Employment of aliens in US clothing and other industries, and impacts on local economies, with background data, 1990 working paper, 6366–6.6
Employment of minorities and women, by occupation, SIC 1- to 3-digit industry, State, and MSA, 1991, annual rpt, 9244–1
Employment, unemployment, and labor force characteristics, by region and census div, 1991, annual rpt, 6744–7.1
Energy use and prices, by fuel type and manufacturing industry, 1974-88, 3166–15.3
Energy use and prices for manufacturing industries, 1988 survey, series, 3166–13
Exports and imports between US and outlying areas, by detailed commodity and mode of transport, 1991, annual rpt, 2424–11
Exports and imports of US, by country and detailed commodity, monthly rpt, 2422–12
Exports and imports of US by country, and trade shifts by commodity, 1991, annual rpt, 9884–25
Exports and imports of US, by Harmonized System 6-digit commodity and country, 1991, annual rpt, 2424–13
Exports and imports of US, by selected country, country group, and commodity group, 1991, annual rpt, 2044–37
Exports and imports of US, by transport mode, country, and SITC 1- to 3-digit commodity, 1991, annual rpt, 2424–12
Exports, imports, and balances of US for manufactured goods, by SITC 2-digit commodity and country, quarterly rpt, 2042–35
Exports of US, detailed commodities by country, monthly CD-ROM, 2422–13
Exports of US, detailed Schedule B commodities with countries of destination, 1991, annual rpt, 2424–10
Exports of US textile products, and trade regulations of foreign countries, by commodity and country, 1989-91, biennial rpt, 2044–18
Exports of US textiles and apparel, by product group and country, quarterly rpt, 2042–36
Foreign countries market conditions for US textile and apparel exports, with domestic industry operations, country rpt series, 2046–15
Freight (waterborne domestic and foreign) by commodity, traffic, and passengers, by port and waterway, 1989, annual rpt, 3754–3
Hazardous substances industrial releases and reduction methods under EPA regulation, by chemical, source, industry, and location, 1989, annual rpt, 9234–6
Hazardous substances industrial releases and reduction methods under EPA regulation, with chemical stocks and use, facility directory, 1987-89, annual CD-ROM, 9234–7
Immigration Reform and Control Act employer sanctions impacts on labor markets, with data for selected industries and metro areas, 1980s, working paper, 6366–6.10
Imports, exports, and employment impacts, by SIC 2- to 4-digit industry and commodity, quarterly rpt, 2322–2
Imports of textiles, by country of origin, monthly rpt, 2042–27
Imports of textiles, by product and country of origin, monthly rpt series, 2046–8; 2046–9
Imports of textiles under Multifiber Arrangement by product and country, and status of bilateral agreements, 1988-91, annual rpt, 9884–18

Imports of US, detailed commodities by country, monthly CD-ROM, 2422–14
Imports of US given duty-free treatment for value of US material sent abroad, by commodity and country, 1987-90, annual rpt, 9884–14
Injuries from use of consumer products and related activities, by severity and victim age and sex, 1990, annual rpt, 9164–7
Injuries from use of consumer products, by severity, victim age, and detailed product, 1991, annual rpt, 9164–6
Input-output structure of US economy, detailed interindustry transactions for 84 industries, and components of final demand, 1987, annual article, 2702–1.316
Input-output structure of US economy, detailed interindustry transactions for 541 industries, and components of final demand, 1982 benchmark data, 2708–17
Labor laws enacted, by State, 1991, annual article, 6722–1.309
Labor productivity, indexes of output, hours, and employment by SIC 2- to 4-digit industry, 1967-90, annual rpt, 6824–1.3
Latin America economic and social conditions, resources, trade, and aid, 1992, annual factbook, 9914–14
Manufacturing annual survey, 1990: finances and operations, by SIC 2- to 4-digit industry, series, 2506–14
Manufacturing census, 1987: concentration of largest firms measured by value added, and for shipments by SIC 2- and 4-digit industry, subject rpt, 2497–6
Manufacturing census, 1987: shipments of manufacturers products, by customer class and SIC 2- and 4-digit industry, subject rpt, 2497–4
Manufacturing finances and operations, by SIC 2- to 4-digit industry, forecast 1992, annual rpt, 2044–28
Manufacturing production, shipments, inventories, orders, and pollution control costs, periodic Current Industrial Rpt series, 2506–3
Mexico imports from US, by industry and State, 1987-91, 2048–154
Multinatl firms US affiliates finances and operations, by industry, country of parent firm, and State, 1987, 2708–48
Natl income and product accounts and components, *Survey of Current Business*, monthly rpt, 2702–1.23
Northern Mariana Islands, Saipan garment factories occupational health and safety violations and penalties assessed by OSHA, Mar 1992, press release, 6606–3.10
Occupational injury and illness rates, by SIC 2- to 4-digit industry, 1989-90, annual rpt, 6844–7
Occupational injury and illness rates, by SIC 2- to 4-digit industry, 1990, annual rpt, 6844–1
OECD trade, total and for 4 major countries, and US trade by country, by commodity, 1980-90, world area rpt series, 9116–1
Pacific territories population and housing detailed characteristics, by location, 1990 Census of Population and Housing, series, 2551–8
Price indexes (producer), by stage of processing and detailed commodity, monthly rpt, 6762–6
Price indexes (producer), by stage of processing and detailed commodity, monthly 1991, annual rpt, 6764–2
Production, shipments, trade, and use of clothes, by product, periodic Current Industrial Rpt series, 2506–6
Puerto Rico and other US possessions corporations income tax returns, income and tax items, and employment, by selected industry, 1989, article, 8302–2.326
Retail trade sales and inventories, by kind of business, region, and selected State, MSA, and city, monthly rpt, 2413–3
Retail trade sales, by kind of business, advance monthly rpt, 2413–2
Retail trade sales, inventories, purchases, gross margin, and accounts receivable, by SIC 2- to 4-digit kind of business and form of ownership, 1990, annual rpt, 2413–5
Science, engineering, and technical employment in manufacturing, by field and industry, 1989, triennial rpt, 9627–23
Soviet Union and US economic and sociodemographic indicators, selected years 1970-90, handbook, 2328–80
Sweaters from 3 countries at less than fair value, injury to US industry, investigation supplement, 1992 rpt, 9886–14.363
Tax (income) returns of corporations, income and tax items by asset size and detailed industry, 1989, annual rpt, 8304–4; 8304–21
Tax (income) returns of sole proprietorships, income statement items, by industry group, 1990, annual article, 8302–2.317; 8302–2.320
Thefts, and value of property stolen and recovered, by property type, 1991, annual rpt, 6224–2.1
see also Shoes and shoe industry
see also under By Commodity in the "Index by Categories"
see also under By Industry in the "Index by Categories"

CMEA
see Council for Mutual Economic Assistance

Coakley, George J.
"Subequatorial Africa: International Strategic Minerals Inventory Summary Report. Mineral Perspectives", 5606–1.19

Coal and coal mining
Alaska minerals resources, production, oil and gas leases, reserves, and exploratory wells, with maps and bibl, 1990, annual rpt, 5664–11
Business statistics, detailed data for major industries and economic indicators, *Survey of Current Business*, monthly rpt, 2702–1.17
Business statistics, detailed data for major industries and economic indicators, 1960-91, *Survey of Current Business* biennial supplement, 2704–1
China minerals production and trade, by commodity, 1989-90, annual rpt, 5604–38
Coke use and costs in steel industry, effects of Clean Air Act, 1985-91 and projected to 2003, 5606–5.10
Consumption of energy, by detailed fuel type, end-use sector, and State, 1960-90, State Energy Data System annual rpt, 3164–39
County Business Patterns, 1989: employment, establishments, and payroll, by SIC 2- to 4-digit industry and county, annual State rpt series, 2326–8
County Business Patterns, 1990: employment, establishments, and payroll, by SIC 2- to 4-digit industry and county, annual State rpt series, 2326–6
Developing countries energy efficiency improvement issues and devs, with data by end use and country, 1980s-90, 26358–260
Eastern Europe export industries dev potential, with trade and industry finances and operations, for 5 countries, 1985-90, 9886–4.179
Electric power and industrial plants prohibited from oil and gas primary use, exemptions, and gas use by State, 1980-91, annual rpt, 3334–1
Electric power plants (coal-burning) air pollutant reduction technology funding, and impacts on energy costs and emissions, 1950s-87 and projected to 2010, annual rpt, 3334–5; 3338–4
Electric power plants (coal-burning) air pollutant reduction technology funding, and project descriptions, 1991, annual rpt, 3334–4
Electric power plants (coal-fired) generating capacity and replacement of energy imports, with background data, alternative forecasts 1990-2000, 3166–6.63
Electric power plants (steam) fuel receipts, costs, and quality, by fuel, plant, utility, and State, 1991, annual rpt, 3164–42
Electric power plants and capacity, by fuel used, owner, location, and operating status, 1991 and for units planned 1992-2001, annual listing, 3164–36
Electric power plants production and capital costs, operations, and fuel use, by fuel type, plant, utility, and location, 1990, annual rpt, 3164–9
Electric power plants production, capacity, sales, and fuel stocks, use, and costs, by State, 1986-90, annual rpt, 3164–11
Electric power plants production, fuel use, stocks, and costs by fuel type, and sales, by State, monthly rpt, with articles, 3162–35
Electric power supply, demand, and trade of Mexico and US, with data by fuel source, utility, and region, 1970s-89 and projected to 2000, 3408–2
Employment, earnings, and hours, by SIC 1- to 4-digit industry, monthly 1989-Feb 1992, annual rpt, 6744–4
Environmental Quality, status of problems, protection programs, research, and intl issues, 1991 annual rpt, 484–1
Explosives and blasting agents use, by type, industry, and State, 1991, Mineral Industry Surveys, annual rpt, 5614–22
Fed Govt and Indian land oil, gas, and minerals production and revenue, by State, 1991 and trends from 1920, annual rpt, 5734–2
Fed Govt power plants conversion to alternative fuels, 1992, annual rpt, 3334–2

Finances and operations, by SIC 2- to 4-digit industry, forecast 1992, annual rpt, 2044–28
Finances and operations of energy producers, by energy type for US firms domestic and foreign operations, 1990, annual rpt, 3164–44
Foreign and US energy production, trade, use, and reserves, and oil and refined products supply and prices, by country, 1981-90, annual rpt, 3164–50
Foreign and US energy supply and demand, by major fuel and end-use sector, 1950s-87 and forecast to 1995, 3166–6.58
Foreign and US energy use and production, by fuel type, country, and country group, projected 1995-2010 and trends from 1970, annual rpt, 3164–84
Foreign and US oil dependency, energy demand, and efficiency measures, for 6 OECD countries, 1970s-80s, working paper, 9375–13.79
Foreign countries mineral production, reserves, and industry role in domestic economy and world supply, world area and country rpt series, 5606–1
Foreign direct investment in US energy sources by type and firm, and US affiliates operations, as of 1990, annual rpt, 3164–80
Freight (waterborne domestic and foreign) by commodity, traffic, and passengers, by port and waterway, 1989, annual rpt, 3754–3
Housing (rental) units, total, with HUD assistance by program, and eligible for aid, by unit, household, and neighborhood characteristics, and location, 1989, biennial rpt, 5184–11
Housing and households detailed characteristics, and unit and neighborhood quality, MSA surveys, series, 2485–6
Housing energy use, costs, and conservation, and household and housing characteristics, survey rpt series, 3166–7
Input-output structure of US economy, detailed interindustry transactions for 84 industries, and components of final demand, 1987, annual article, 2702–1.316
Input-output structure of US economy, detailed interindustry transactions for 541 industries, and components of final demand, 1982 benchmark data, 2708–17
Japan energy use and imports by fuel type, and gasoline prices, 1970s-80s, hearing, 21448–45
Labor productivity, indexes of output, hours, and employment by SIC 2- to 4-digit industry, 1967-90, annual rpt, 6824–1.2
Manufacturing corporations financial statements, by selected SIC 2- to 3-digit industry, quarterly rpt, 2502–1
Manufacturing energy use and prices, by fuel type and industry, 1974-88, 3166–15.3
Manufacturing energy use and prices, 1988 survey, series, 3166–13
Methane production in coal fields, and proved reserves, by State, 1989-91, 3164–46.3
Military and personal property shipments, passenger traffic, and costs, by service branch and mode of transport, FY91, annual rpt, 3704–15
Minerals Yearbook, Vol 3, 1989: foreign country reviews of production, trade, and policy, by commodity, annual rpt, 5604–35
Multinatl firms US affiliates finances and operations, by industry, country of parent firm, and State, 1987, 2708–48
Multinatl US firms and foreign affiliates finances and operations, by industry and country, 1989 benchmark survey, annual rpt, 2704–5
Natl Energy Strategy plans for conservation, R&D, security, and pollution reduction, technical rpt series, 3006–13
Occupational deaths in mining accidents, by circumstances and selected victim characteristics, semiannual rpt series, 6662–3
Occupational injuries and incidence, employment, and hours in coal mines and related operations, 1990, annual rpt, 6664–4
Occupational injuries and incidence, employment, and hours in metal mines and related operations, 1990, annual rpt, 6664–3
Occupational injuries by circumstances, employment, and hours, for mining industries by type of operation and State, quarterly rpt, 6662–1
Occupational injury and illness rates, by SIC 2- to 4-digit industry, 1989-90, annual rpt, 6844–7
Occupational injury and illness rates, by SIC 2- to 4-digit industry, 1990, annual rpt, 6844–1
Occupational safety, coal miners working under unsupported mine roof, reasons, supervisor reactions, and preventive measures, 1989-90 survey, 5608–173
Ohio River basin waterway facilities, freight by commodity and port, and recreation, by waterway, 1988-89, annual rpt, 3754–6
Pacific basin countries energy supply and demand, and implications for US trade, country rpt series, 3406–6
Pollution (air) abatement equipment shipments by industry, and new and backlog orders, by product, 1991, annual Current Industrial Rpt, 2506–12.5
Pollution (air) contributing to global warming, emissions by monitoring site and country, and temperature change by world area and US region, 1860s-1990, annual rpt, 3004–33
Production and mines by county, prices, productivity, miners, and reserves, by mining method and State, 1990-91, annual rpt, 3164–25
Production and sales of synthetic organic chemicals, and manufacturer listing, by product, 1990, annual rpt, 9884–3
Production by State and region, weekly rpt, 3162–1
Production, dev, and distribution firms revenues and income, quarterly rpt, 3162–38
Production of coal, reserves, use, and prices by State, exports by country, and employment, 1900s-90, biennial rpt, 3164–79
Production, prices, exports, and use by sector, for coal, with data by region, projections, annual rpt, discontinued, 3164–68
Production, stocks, and shipments of coal by State, end-use sector, and mode of transport, quarterly rpt, 3162–8
Public land use restrictions on coal mining, impacts on production, costs, and demand, by region, 1985-88 and projected to 2075, 5668–125
Public lands acreage, grants, use, revenues, and allocations, by State, FY91, annual rpt, 5724–1.2
Reclamation of coal mining land, Office of Surface Mining Reclamation and Enforcement activities and funding, by State and Indian tribe, FY77-91, annual rpt, 5644–1
Retired coal industry workers pension and health trust funds financial condition, employer contributions, and beneficiaries, late 1970s-92, GAO rpt, 26121–469; 26121–471
Romania energy production and trade, 1970s-91, with capital investment projected to 2000, GAO rpt, 26123–402
Soviet Union and US economic and sociodemographic indicators, selected years 1970-90, handbook, 2328–80
Statistical Abstract of US, 1992 annual data compilation, 2324–1.25
Supply, demand, and distribution of energy, and regulatory impacts, series, 3166–6
Supply, demand, and prices, by fuel type and end-use sector, alternative projections by region, 1990-2010, annual rpt, 3164–96
Supply, demand, and prices, by fuel type and end-use sector, alternative projections 1990-2010, annual rpt, 3164–75
Supply, demand, and prices, by fuel type and end-use sector, projections and underlying assumptions, 1995-2010, annual rpt, 3164–90
Supply, demand, and prices, by fuel type and end-use sector, with foreign comparisons, 1981-90, annual fact book, 3164–76
Supply, demand, and prices, by fuel type and end-use sector, with foreign comparisons, 1991 and trends from 1949, annual rpt, 3164–74
Supply, demand, and prices, by fuel type, end-use sector, and country, detailed data, monthly rpt with articles, 3162–24
Supply, demand, and prices, by fuel type, end-use sector, and country, detailed data, monthly 1973-88, 3168–123
Supply, demand, and prices of energy, forecasts by resource type, quarterly rpt, 3162–34
Supply, demand, prices, movements, and stocks of coal, coke, and breeze, by end-use sector and State, quarterly rpt, 3162–37
Tax (excise) on coal and other black lung trust fund receipts, fund disbursements, and claims and benefits by State, 1991, annual rpt, 6504–3
Tax (income) returns of corporations, income and tax items by asset size and detailed industry, 1989, annual rpt, 8304–4; 8304–21
Tax (income) returns of sole proprietorships, income statement items, by industry group, 1990, annual article, 8302–2.317; 8302–2.320

Technological devs effect on labor force, composition, and productivity, 1970s-90 and projected to 2005, industry rpt, 6826–2.9
Water quality, chemistry, hydrology, and other characteristics, local area studies, series, 5666–27
Wetlands acid neutralizing capability for mining runoff, with pollutant levels and site characteristics, for Pennsylvania, 1987-90, 5608–171
see also Black lung disease
see also Coal exports and imports
see also Coal prices
see also Coal reserves
see also Coal stocks
see also under By Commodity in the "Index by Categories"

Coal exports and imports
Business statistics, detailed data for major industries and economic indicators, *Survey of Current Business*, monthly rpt, 2702–1.17
Business statistics, detailed data for major industries and economic indicators, 1960-91, *Survey of Current Business* biennial supplement, 2704–1
Electric utilities coal imports, by utility and country of origin, 1987-91, annual rpt, 3164–42
Exports and imports between US and outlying areas, by detailed commodity and mode of transport, 1991, annual rpt, 2424–11
Exports and imports of coal, by country of origin and destination, 1989, annual rpt, 3164–50.4
Exports and imports of US, by country and detailed commodity, monthly rpt, 2422–12
Exports and imports of US, by Harmonized System 6-digit commodity and country, 1991, annual rpt, 2424–13
Exports and imports of US, by selected country, country group, and commodity group, 1991, annual rpt, 2044–37
Exports and imports of US, by transport mode, country, and SITC 1- to 3-digit commodity, 1991, annual rpt, 2424–12
Exports of coal, by country of destination, selected years 1900-90, biennial rpt, 3164–79
Exports of coal to Canada by mode of transport, and overseas, by State of origin, quarterly rpt, 3162–8
Exports of US, detailed commodities by country, monthly CD-ROM, 2422–13
Exports of US, detailed Schedule B commodities with countries of destination, 1991, annual rpt, 2424–10
Foreign and US coal trade flows and reserves, by country, annual rpt, discontinued, 3164–77
Foreign countries mineral production, reserves, and industry role in domestic economy and world supply, world area and country rpt series, 5606–1
Imports, exports, and employment impacts, by SIC 2- to 4-digit industry and commodity, quarterly rpt, 2322–2
Imports of US, detailed commodities by country, monthly CD-ROM, 2422–14
Mexico imports from US, by industry and State, 1987-91, 2048–154
OECD trade, total and for 4 major countries, and US trade by country, by commodity, 1980-90, world area rpt series, 9116–1
Pacific basin countries energy supply and demand, and implications for US trade, country rpt series, 3406–6
Public land use restrictions on coal mining, impacts on production, costs, and demand, by region, 1985-88 and projected to 2075, 5668–125
Statistical Abstract of US, 1992 annual data compilation, 2324–1.25
Supply, demand, and prices, by fuel type and end-use sector, alternative projections by region, 1990-2010, annual rpt, 3164–96
Supply, demand, and prices, by fuel type and end-use sector, alternative projections 1990-2010, annual rpt, 3164–75
Supply, demand, and prices, by fuel type and end-use sector, with foreign comparisons, 1981-90, annual fact book, 3164–76
Supply, demand, and prices, by fuel type and end-use sector, with foreign comparisons, 1991 and trends from 1949, annual rpt, 3164–74
Supply, demand, and prices, by fuel type, end-use sector, and country, detailed data, monthly rpt with articles, 3162–24
Supply, demand, and prices, by fuel type, end-use sector, and country, detailed data, monthly 1973-88, 3168–123
Supply, demand, and prices of energy, forecasts by resource type, quarterly rpt, 3162–34
Supply, demand, prices, movements, and stocks of coal, coke, and breeze, by end-use sector and State, quarterly rpt, 3162–37
Waterborne commerce (domestic and foreign) of US, freight by commodity, traffic, and passengers, by port and waterway, 1989, annual rpt, 3754–3

Coal prices
Business statistics, detailed data for major industries and economic indicators, *Survey of Current Business*, monthly rpt, 2702–1.17
Business statistics, detailed data for major industries and economic indicators, 1960-91, *Survey of Current Business* biennial supplement, 2704–1
Electric power plants (coal-fired) generating capacity and replacement of energy imports, with background data, alternative forecasts 1990-2000, 3166–6.63
Electric power plants (steam) fuel receipts, costs, and quality, by fuel, plant, utility, and State, 1991, annual rpt, 3164–42
Electric power plants prices paid for fossil fuels, FY90-91, annual rpt, 3084–9
Electric power plants production, capacity, sales, and fuel stocks, use, and costs, by State, 1986-90, annual rpt, 3164–11
Electric power plants production, fuel use, stocks, and costs by fuel type, and sales, by State, monthly rpt, with articles, 3162–35
Housing energy prices, by fuel type and State, 1990 and forecast 1991-92, 3166–6.61
Manufacturing energy use and prices, by fuel type and industry, 1974-88, 3166–15.3
Pacific basin countries energy supply and demand, and implications for US trade, country rpt series, 3406–6
Pacific Northwest population, households, employment, income, fuel prices, and electricity demand, alternative forecasts 1991-2010, annual rpt, 3224–3.3
Prices and spending for fuel, by type, end-use sector, and State, 1990, annual rpt, 3164–64
Prices of coal, production, reserves, and use by State, exports by country, and employment, 1900s-90, biennial rpt, 3164–79
Prices of fuel, by type, end-use sector, and region, projected 1991-2030, 3166–6.60
Prices, productivity, miners, reserves, and production and mines by county, by mining method and State, 1990-91, annual rpt, 3164–25
Prices, supply, and demand, by fuel type and end-use sector, alternative projections by region, 1990-2010, annual rpt, 3164–96
Prices, supply, and demand, by fuel type and end-use sector, alternative projections 1990-2010, annual rpt, 3164–75
Prices, supply, and demand, by fuel type and end-use sector, projections and underlying assumptions, 1995-2010, annual rpt, 3164–90
Prices, supply, and demand, by fuel type and end-use sector, with foreign comparisons, 1981-90, annual fact book, 3164–76
Prices, supply, and demand, by fuel type and end-use sector, with foreign comparisons, 1991 and trends from 1949, annual rpt, 3164–74
Prices, supply, and demand of energy, forecasts by resource type, quarterly rpt, 3162–34
Prices, supply, demand, movements, and stocks of coal, coke, and breeze, by end-use sector and State, quarterly rpt, 3162–37
Producer price indexes, by stage of processing and detailed commodity, monthly rpt, 6762–6
Producer price indexes, by stage of processing and detailed commodity, monthly 1991, annual rpt, 6764–2

Coal reserves
Alaska oil, gas, and coal reserve acreage, by ownership, 1991 rpt, 5608–174
China minerals production and trade, by commodity, 1989-90, annual rpt, 5604–38
Foreign and US coal trade flows and reserves, by country, annual rpt, discontinued, 3164–77
Foreign and US energy reserves, by type of fuel and country, as of Jan 1991, annual rpt, 3164–50.6
Foreign countries mineral production, reserves, and industry role in domestic economy and world supply, world area and country rpt series, 5606–1
Pacific basin countries energy supply and demand, and implications for US trade, country rpt series, 3406–6
Producers finances and operations, by energy type for US firms domestic and foreign operations, 1990, annual rpt, 3164–44.4

Public land use restrictions on coal mining, impacts on production, costs, and demand, by region, 1985-88 and projected to 2075, 5668–125
Public lands minerals resources and availability, State rpt series, 5606–7
Reserves of coal, production, use, and prices by State, exports by country, and employment, 1900s-90, biennial rpt, 3164–79
Reserves, prices, productivity, miners, and production and mines by county, by mining method and State, 1990-91, annual rpt, 3164–25
Supply, demand, and prices, by fuel type and end-use sector, with foreign comparisons, 1991 and trends from 1949, annual rpt, 3164–74

Coal stocks
Business statistics, detailed data for major industries and economic indicators, *Survey of Current Business*, monthly rpt, 2702–1.17
Electric power plants production, capacity, sales, and fuel stocks, use, and costs, by State, 1986-90, annual rpt, 3164–11
Electric power plants production, fuel use, stocks, and costs by fuel type, and sales, by State, monthly rpt, with articles, 3162–35
Electric utilities, coke plants, and other industry stocks of coal, monthly rpt, 3162–24.6
Electric utilities, coke plants, and other industry stocks of coal, monthly 1973-88, 3168–123.6
Electric utilities, coke plants, other industrial, producer, and distributor coal stocks, and total coke and breeze stocks, quarterly rpt, 3162–37
Stocks of coal, by State, quarterly rpt, 3162–8
Supply, demand, and prices, by fuel type and end-use sector, with foreign comparisons, 1991 and trends from 1949, annual rpt, 3164–74.4
Supply, demand, and prices, by fuel type, end-use sector, and country, detailed data, monthly rpt with articles, 3162–24
Supply, demand, and prices, by fuel type, end-use sector, and country, detailed data, monthly 1973-88, 3168–123
Supply, demand, and prices of energy, forecasts by resource type, quarterly rpt, 3162–34

Coast Guard
Boat registrations, and accidents, casualties, and damage by cause, by vessel characteristics and State, 1991, annual rpt, 7404–1
Bridges over navigable waters, with type of bridge and use, owner, dimensions, and location, 1991 regional listing series, 7406–5
Budget of US, obligations and authority by function, agency, and program, with summaries and analyses, FY93, annual rpt, 104–2
Courts (military) cases and actions, FY91, annual rpt, 3504–3
Criminal case processing in military courts, and prisoners by facility, by service branch, data compilation, 1992 annual rpt, 6064–6.5
Drug (heroin) seizures by Federal agencies, with NYC street prices and purity, FY82-91, GAO rpt, 26119–404
Drug enforcement training of US for foreign govts, enrollment in US and host countries by program, FY91, annual rpt, 7004–17
Employment of DOT, by subagency, occupation, and selected personnel characteristics, FY91, annual rpt, 7304–18
Enforcement activities of USCG, 1st half FY92, semiannual rpt, 7402–4
Expenditures of Fed Govt in States, by type, program, agency, and State, FY91, annual rpt, 2464–2
Recalls of recreational boats and engines with safety-related defects, by make, periodic listing, 7402–5
Search and rescue missions, and lives and property lost and saved, by USCG district and assisting unit, FY91, annual rpt, 7404–2
Statistical Abstract of US, 1992 annual data compilation, 2324–1.11
see also Coast Guard Reserve

Coast Guard Reserve
Personnel and equipment strengths, and readiness, by reserve component, FY91, annual rpt, 3544–31
Personnel strengths and characteristics, by reserve component, quarterly rpt, 3542–4
Personnel strengths for reserve components, by selected characteristics, FY91, annual rpt, 3544–1.5

Coastal areas
Army Corps of Engineers activities and projects, FY88 and trends from 1800s, annual rpt, 3754–1.1
Army Corps of Engineers activities and projects, FY89 and trends from 1800s, annual rpt, 3754–1.2
Army Corps of Engineers activities and projects, FY90 and trends from 1800s, annual rpt, 3754–1.3
California OCS oil and gas dev impacts on water quality, marine life, and sediments, by site, 1986-90, annual rpt, 5734–11
Coast Guard search and rescue missions, and lives and property lost and saved, by district and assisting unit, FY91, annual rpt, 7404–2
Environmental conditions and mgmt, for individual coastal areas, conf series, 2146–8
Environmental conditions, fish, wildlife, use, and mgmt, for individual coastal and riparian ecosystems, series, 5506–9
Environmental impacts of coastal areas economic dev and population growth, 1960-80s and projected to 2010, series, 2176–8
Environmental mgmt of coastal areas, State activities and Federal funding, FY90-91, biennial rpt, 2174–8
Environmental Quality, status of problems, protection programs, research, and intl issues, 1991 annual rpt, 484–1
Fish catch quotas for US 200 mile zone, allocations by species and country, periodic coastal area rpt series, discontinued, 7006–5
Fish catch, trade, use, and fishery operations, with selected foreign data, by species, 1980s-91, annual rpt, 2164–1
Latin America economic and social conditions, resources, trade, and aid, 1992, annual factbook, 9914–14
Marine Fisheries Review, US and foreign fisheries resources, dev, mgmt, and research, quarterly journal, 2162–1
Marine Mammal Protection Act admin, and populations, strandings, and catch permits by species and location, 1988-89, annual rpt, 2164–11
Middle Atlantic States tide height and tidal current velocity daily at selected coastal stations, forecast 1993, annual rpt, 2174–11
NOAA activities and funding for ocean pollution, estuary, and coastal waters monitoring and assessment, FY90, annual rpt, 2174–9
Ocean surface temperature by ocean and for US coastal areas, and Bering Sea ice conditions, monthly rpt, 2182–5
Oil spill off Washington coast in 1988, pollutant levels and impacts on marine biota, by site, as of 1990, 5738–38
Pollutant concentrations in coastal and estuarine fish, shellfish, and environment, series, 2176–3
Pollution indicators for coastal zones and watersheds, by location, 1980s-90, 2178–35
Shellfish harvest in estuaries, approved and restricted areas, and pollution sources, by estuary, State, and coastal region, 1990, quinquennial rpt, 2178–33
Tidal currents, daily time and velocity by station for North America and Asia coasts, forecast 1993, annual rpts, 2174–1
Tide height and time daily at coastal points worldwide, forecast 1993, annual rpt series, 2174–2
Washington and Oregon coastal areas recreation resources, and impacts of OCS oil and gas dev, 1983-88, 5738–40
Water (saline) withdrawal and use, for coastal areas, State rpt series, 5666–24
Wetlands (coastal) conservation funding by project, 1992 press release, 5306–4.12
see also Chesapeake Bay
see also Continental shelf
see also Estuaries
see also Harbors and ports
see also New York Bight
see also Offshore mineral resources
see also Offshore oil and gas
see also Puget Sound
see also San Francisco Bay
see also Seashores
see also Territorial waters
see also Wetlands

Coates, Ralph J.
"Differences Between Black and White Women with Breast Cancer in Time from Symptom Recognition to Medical Consultation", 4472–1.323

Cobb-Clark, Deborah A.
"Immigration Reform: The Effects of Employer Sanctions and Legalization on Wages", 6366–6.8

Cobb County, Ga.
Housing and households characteristics, and unit and neighborhood quality, by MSA location for 11 MSAs, 1987 survey, supplement, 2485–8

Cobb, Kathy
"American Indian Economic Development", 9383–19.304

Cocaine
Abuse of drugs and alcohol, by selected characteristics, 1991 survey, annual rpt series, 4494–5
Abuse of drugs, indicators for selected metro areas, research results, data collection, and policy issues, 1992 semiannual conf, 4492–5
Abuse of drugs, treatment, biological and behavioral factors, and addiction potential of new drugs, research results, 1991 annual conf, 4494–11
Airline and aviation safety employees drug testing and results, by drug type and occupational group, 1991, semiannual rpt, 7502–17
Arrests for drug- and nondrug-related offenses, urine test results by drug type, offense, and sex, for selected urban areas, quarterly rpt, 6062–3
Coast Guard enforcement activities, 1st half FY92, semiannual rpt, 7402–4
Crime relationship to drug abuse and trafficking, and enforcement data, series, 6066–29
DC metro area drug, alcohol, and tobacco use, user characteristics, and consequences, series, 4496–12
Fed Govt drug abuse and trafficking reduction programs activities, funding, staff, and Bush Admin budget request, by Federal agency, FY91-93, annual rpt, 234–2
Foreign and US cocaine trafficking, with prices and purity, 1988-90, annual rpt, 6284–5
Foreign countries drug production, eradication, and seizures, by illegal substance, with US aid, by country, 1988-92, annual rpt, 7004–17
Health condition and care indicators, 1950s-90 with health improvement and disease prevention goals for 1990, annual data compilation, 4144–11
Immigration and Naturalization Service illegal alien and narcotics activities, FY84-91, annual rpt, 6264–2.5
Immigration and Naturalization Service illegal alien and narcotics activities, FY91, annual summary rpt, 6264–7
Police and sheriff depts drug enforcement activities, and employee drug testing policies, 1990, 6066–19.67
Prices of illegal drugs by type and selected metro area, and cocaine and heroin purity, quarterly rpt, 6282–1
Prices of illegal drugs by type, stage of processing, and country of origin, 1991, annual rpt, 6284–7
Public opinion on crime and crime-related issues, by respondent characteristics, data compilation, 1992 annual rpt, 6064–6.2
Research on drug abuse and treatment, summaries of findings, resource materials, and grant listings, bimonthly rpt, 4492–4
Sentences for Federal offenses, guidelines by offense and circumstances, series, 17668–1
Sentences under Federal mandatory minimum provisions, by defendant characteristics, and views on justice system impacts, FY90, 17668–2
Supply of drugs in US by country of origin, abuse, prices, and seizures, by substance, 1991, annual rpt, 6284–2
Testing for drugs, urinalysis methods accuracy by drug type, 1991, 6068–247
Women arrestees drug abuse history and selected other characteristics, for 4 cities, 1988-89, 6068–246
Youth drug, alcohol, and cigarette use and attitudes, by substance type and selected characteristics, 1975-91 surveys, press release, 4008–116; 4494–4

Cocheba, Donald J.
"Potential Effects of OCS Oil and Gas Exploration and Development on Pacific Northwest Indian Tribes: Final Technical Report", 5738–35

Cocoa and chocolate
Agricultural Statistics, 1991, annual rpt, 1004–1
Appalachia food processing firms, employment, and shipments, and farm production, by commodity and State, 1960s-90, 9088–37
Business statistics, detailed data for major industries and economic indicators, *Survey of Current Business*, monthly rpt, 2702–1.13
Business statistics, detailed data for major industries and economic indicators, 1960-91, *Survey of Current Business* biennial supplement, 2704–1
Consumption, supply, trade, prices, spending, and indexes, by food commodity, 1990, annual rpt, 1544–4
County Business Patterns, 1989: employment, establishments, and payroll, by SIC 2- to 4-digit industry and county, annual State rpt series, 2326–8
County Business Patterns, 1990: employment, establishments, and payroll, by SIC 2- to 4-digit industry and county, annual State rpt series, 2326–6
Cuba trade, by commodity and country, mid 1980s-91, 9118–8
Exports and imports (agricultural) of US, by commodity and country, bimonthly rpt, 1522–1
Exports and imports (agricultural) of US, by detailed commodity and country, 1991, annual rpt, 1524–8
Exports and imports (agricultural) of US, by detailed commodity and country, 1991, semiannual rpt, 1522–4
Exports and imports between US and outlying areas, by detailed commodity and mode of transport, 1991, annual rpt, 2424–11
Exports and imports of US, by country and detailed commodity, monthly rpt, 2422–12
Exports and imports of US, by Harmonized System 6-digit commodity and country, 1991, annual rpt, 2424–13
Exports and imports of US, by transport mode, country, and SITC 1- to 3-digit commodity, 1991, annual rpt, 2424–12
Exports of US, detailed Schedule B commodities with countries of destination, 1991, annual rpt, 2424–10
Foreign and US cocoa and cocoa products production, prices, and trade, 1980s-93, FAS semiannual circular, 1925–9
Foreign countries agricultural production, prices, and trade, by country, 1980-91 and forecast 1992, annual world area rpt series, 1524–4
Freight (waterborne domestic and foreign) by commodity, traffic, and passengers, by port and waterway, 1989, annual rpt, 3754–3
Futures and options trading volume, by commodity and exchange, FY91, annual rpt, 11924–2
Futures trading in selected commodities and financial instruments and indexes, for NYC, Chicago, and other markets activity, biweekly rpt, 11922–5
Imports and quotas of dairy products, by commodity and country of origin, FAS monthly rpt, 1925–31
Input-output structure of US economy, detailed interindustry transactions for 541 industries, and components of final demand, 1982 benchmark data, 2708–17
Manufacturing annual survey, 1990: finances and operations, by SIC 2- to 4-digit industry, series, 2506–14
Manufacturing census, 1987: concentration of largest firms measured by value added, and for shipments by SIC 2- and 4-digit industry, subject rpt, 2497–6
Manufacturing census, 1987: shipments of manufacturers products, by customer class and SIC 2- and 4-digit industry, subject rpt, 2497–4
Occupational injury and illness rates, by SIC 2- to 4-digit industry, 1989-90, annual rpt, 6844–7
Occupational injury and illness rates, by SIC 2- to 4-digit industry, 1990, annual rpt, 6844–1
OECD trade, total and for 4 major countries, and US trade by country, by commodity, 1980-90, world area rpt series, 9116–1
Price indexes (producer), by stage of processing and detailed commodity, monthly rpt, 6762–6
Price indexes (producer), by stage of processing and detailed commodity, monthly 1991, annual rpt, 6764–2
Shipments, trade, use, and ingredients, by confectionery product, 1991, annual Current Industrial Rpt, 2506–4.5
Weight and volume conversion factors for agricultural commodities and products, 1992 rpt, 1508–3

Codman Research Group, Inc.
"Utilization of Inpatient Hospital Services by Rural Medicare Beneficiaries", 17206–2.33

Coffee
Agricultural Statistics, 1991, annual rpt, 1004–1
Business statistics, detailed data for major industries and economic indicators, *Survey of Current Business*, monthly rpt, 2702–1.13
Business statistics, detailed data for major industries and economic indicators, 1960-91, *Survey of Current Business* biennial supplement, 2704–1
Cancer (pancreatic) death risk relation to occupational DDT exposure and other characteristics, 1982 article, 4472–1.314
Consumption, supply, trade, prices, spending, and indexes, by food commodity, 1990, annual rpt, 1544–4
County Business Patterns, 1989: employment, establishments, and payroll, by SIC 2- to 4-digit industry and county, annual State rpt series, 2326–8

County Business Patterns, 1990: employment, establishments, and payroll, by SIC 2- to 4-digit industry and county, annual State rpt series, 2326–6
CPI by component for US city average, and by selected metro area, region, and population size, monthly rpt, 6762–2
Cuba trade, by commodity and country, mid 1980s-91, 9118–8
Exports and imports (agricultural) of US, by commodity and country, bimonthly rpt, 1522–1
Exports and imports (agricultural) of US, by detailed commodity and country, 1991, annual rpt, 1524–8
Exports and imports (agricultural) of US, by detailed commodity and country, 1991, semiannual rpt, 1522–4
Exports and imports between US and outlying areas, by detailed commodity and mode of transport, 1991, annual rpt, 2424–11
Exports and imports of US, by country and detailed commodity, monthly rpt, 2422–12
Exports and imports of US, by Harmonized System 6-digit commodity and country, 1991, annual rpt, 2424–13
Exports and imports of US, by transport mode, country, and SITC 1- to 3-digit commodity, 1991, annual rpt, 2424–12
Exports of US, detailed Schedule B commodities with countries of destination, 1991, annual rpt, 2424–10
Foreign countries agricultural production, prices, and trade, by country, 1980-91 and forecast 1992, annual world area rpt series, 1524–4
Freight (waterborne domestic and foreign) by commodity, traffic, and passengers, by port and waterway, 1989, annual rpt, 3754–3
Futures and options trading volume, by commodity and exchange, FY91, annual rpt, 11924–2
Futures trading in selected commodities and financial instruments and indexes, for NYC, Chicago, and other markets activity, biweekly rpt, 11922–5
Input-output structure of US economy, detailed interindustry transactions for 541 industries, and components of final demand, 1982 benchmark data, 2708–17
Latin America economic and social conditions, resources, trade, and aid, 1992, annual factbook, 9914–14
Manufacturing annual survey, 1990: finances and operations, by SIC 2- to 4-digit industry, series, 2506–14
Manufacturing census, 1987: concentration of largest firms measured by value added, and for shipments by SIC 2- and 4-digit industry, subject rpt, 2497–6
Manufacturing census, 1987: shipments of manufacturers products, by customer class and SIC 2- and 4-digit industry, subject rpt, 2497–4
Occupational injury and illness rates, by SIC 2- to 4-digit industry, 1989-90, annual rpt, 6844–7
Occupational injury and illness rates, by SIC 2- to 4-digit industry, 1990, annual rpt, 6844–1
OECD trade, total and for 4 major countries, and US trade by country, by commodity, 1980-90, world area rpt series, 9116–1
Price indexes (producer), by stage of processing and detailed commodity, monthly rpt, 6762–6
Price indexes (producer), by stage of processing and detailed commodity, monthly 1991, annual rpt, 6764–2
Prices received and paid by farmers, by commodity and State, 1991, annual rpt, 1629–5
Prices received by farmers and production value, by detailed crop and State, 1989-91, annual rpt, 1621–2
Production, farms, acreage, and related data, by selected crop and State, monthly rpt, 1621–1
Production, trade, and use of coffee by country, with US and intl prices, FAS periodic circular, 1925–5
Vending machine shipments by product, trade, and use, 1991, Current Industrial Rpt, 2506–12.10
Weight and volume conversion factors for agricultural commodities and products, 1992 rpt, 1508–3

Coffman, Joseph
"Manganese Availability—Market Economy Countries: 1980's Perspective. A Minerals Availability Appraisal", 5606–4.31

Cogeneration of heat and electricity
see Electric power and heat cogeneration

Cohany, Sharon R.
"Vietnam-Era Cohort: Employment and Earnings", 6722–1.326

Cohen, Deborah A.
"Group Counseling at STD Clinics To Promote Use of Condoms", 4042–3.376

Cohen, Hugh I.
"Wild Card Option in T-Bond Futures Is Relatively Worthless", 9371–10.71

Cohen, Nathaniel
"Export Market Report, Textiles and Apparel", 2042–36

Cohen, Robyn L.
"Drunk Driving", 6066–19.69

Coins and coinage
Banks in Fed Reserve System, expenses and operations itemized by service, office, and district, 1991, annual rpt, 9364–11
Budget of US, receipts by source, outlays by agency and program, and balances, monthly rpt, 8102–3
Currency and coin outstanding and in circulation, by type and denomination, and per capita, *Treasury Bulletin*, quarterly rpt, 8002–4.10
Exports and imports between US and outlying areas, by detailed commodity and mode of transport, 1991, annual rpt, 2424–11
Exports and imports of US, by country and detailed commodity, monthly rpt, 2422–12
Exports and imports of US, by Harmonized System 6-digit commodity and country, 1991, annual rpt, 2424–13
Exports and imports of US, by selected country, country group, and commodity group, 1991, annual rpt, 2044–37
Exports and imports of US, by transport mode, country, and SITC 1- to 3-digit commodity, 1991, annual rpt, 2424–12
Exports, imports, and balances of US for manufactured goods, by SITC 2-digit commodity and country, quarterly rpt, 2042–35
Exports of US, detailed Schedule B commodities with countries of destination, 1991, annual rpt, 2424–10
Fed Reserve banks finances and staff, 1991, annual rpt, 9364–1.1
Injuries from use of consumer products and related activities, by severity and victim age and sex, 1990, annual rpt, 9164–7
Injuries from use of consumer products, by severity, victim age, and detailed product, 1991, annual rpt, 9164–6
Production of coins and medals by denomination, capacity, and facility improvement funding, by mint, with monetary metals purchases, projected FY92-96, hearing, 21248–164
Production of coins, and use and holdings of monetary metals, by metal type and US Mint facility, FY91, annual rpt, 8204–1
Production of coins by US Mint, for US by denomination and mint, monthly table, 8202–1
Seignorage in Budget of US, classified as deficit financing, FY92, annual rpt, 104–2.2
Seignorage in Budget of US, classified as deficit financing, FY93, 108–46.1
Seignorage in Fed Govt authoritative financial statements, FY91, annual rpt, 8104–2.2
Seignorage sources, use, and impacts of inflation, 1950s-90, article, 9391–1.307
Thefts, and value of property stolen and recovered, by property type, 1991, annual rpt, 6224–2.1
see also Counterfeiting and forgery
see also Money supply

Coke
see Coal and coal mining

Colby, David
"Physician Payment Under Medicaid", 17266–1.4

Colby, W. Hunter
"China's Agricultural Marketing System in the 1980's", 1524–4.2

Cold storage and refrigeration
Agricultural Statistics, 1991, annual rpt, 1004–1
Business statistics, detailed data for major industries and economic indicators, *Survey of Current Business*, monthly rpt, 2702–1.13
Capacity of refrigerated warehouses, by State, as of Oct 1991, biennial rpt, 1614–2
Containers (intermodal) and equipment owned by shipping and leasing companies, inventory by type and size, 1991, annual rpt, 7704–10
County Business Patterns, 1989: employment, establishments, and payroll, by SIC 2- to 4-digit industry and county, annual State rpt series, 2326–8
County Business Patterns, 1990: employment, establishments, and payroll, by SIC 2- to 4-digit industry and county, annual State rpt series, 2326–6
Dairy storage holdings, total and for USDA by product, 1991, annual rpt, 1317–1.1
Employment, earnings, and hours, by SIC 1- to 4-digit industry, monthly 1989-Feb 1992, annual rpt, 6744–4
Energy supply, demand, and prices, by fuel type and end-use sector, projections and underlying assumptions, 1995-2010, annual rpt, 3164–90

Energy use in commercial buildings, costs, and conservation, by building characteristics, survey rpt series, 3166–8
Energy use of households, and availability of appliances by type, selected years 1978-90, annual rpt, 3164–74.1
Equipment PPI, monthly 1991, annual rpt, 6764–2
Equipment shipments, trade, use, and firms, by product, 1991, annual Current Industrial Rpt, 2506–12.7
Exports and imports between US and outlying areas, by detailed commodity and mode of transport, 1991, annual rpt, 2424–11
Exports and imports of US, by country and detailed commodity, monthly rpt, 2422–12
Exports and imports of US, by Harmonized System 6-digit commodity and country, 1991, annual rpt, 2424–13
Exports and imports of US, by transport mode, country, and SITC 1- to 3-digit commodity, 1991, annual rpt, 2424–12
Exports of US, detailed Schedule B commodities with countries of destination, 1991, annual rpt, 2424–10
Fish (processed) production by location, and trade, by species and product, 1988-91, annual rpts, 2166–6
Fish (tuna) catch in Japan, trade, tariffs, prices, holdings, and consumption, by species, 1977-90, 2166–19.11
Fish and shellfish cold storage holdings, by product and species, preliminary data, monthly press release, 2162–2
Fish catch, trade, use, and fishery operations, with selected foreign data, by species, 1980s-91, annual rpt, 2164–1
Food stocks in cold storage by commodity and census div, and warehouse space use, by State, monthly rpt, 1631–5
Food stocks in cold storage by commodity, and warehouse space use, by census div, 1991, annual rpt, 1631–11
Fruit and nut production, prices, and use, annual rpt series, 1621–18
Grape shipments from California and arrivals by city by mode of transport, prices, and production, by variety, 1970s-90, annual rpt, 1311–25
Input-output structure of US economy, detailed interindustry transactions for 541 industries, and components of final demand, 1982 benchmark data, 2708–17
Manufacturing annual survey, 1990: finances and operations, by SIC 2- to 4-digit industry, series, 2506–14
Manufacturing finances and operations, by SIC 2- to 4-digit industry, forecast 1992, annual rpt, 2044–28
Meat, poultry, and egg production, prices, trade, and stocks, monthly rpt, 1561–17
Military and personal property shipments, passenger traffic, and costs, by service branch and mode of transport, FY91, annual rpt, 3704–15
Military prime contract awards, by detailed procurement category, FY88-91, annual rpt, 3544–18
Military Sealift Command shipping operations, finances, and personnel, FY91, annual rpt, 3804–14
Nut cold storage holdings, by type and region, weekly rpt, periodic data, 1311–1
Poultry and egg prices and marketing, by selected region, State, and city, monthly and weekly 1991, annual rpt, 1317–2
Poultry and egg production, prices, receipts, trade, and disposition, by species, 1960-90, annual rpt, 1564–13
Price indexes (producer), by stage of processing and detailed commodity, monthly rpt, 6762–6
Science, engineering, and technical employment in manufacturing, by field and industry, 1989, triennial rpt, 9627–23
Ships under foreign flag owned by US firms and foreign affiliates, by type, owner, and country of registry and construction, as of July 1991, semiannual rpt, 7702–3
Vegetable production, prices, trade, stocks, and use, for selected fresh and processing crops, periodic situation rpt with articles, 1561–11
Warehouse services finances, by SIC 3- to 4-digit industry, 1990 survey, annual rpt, 2413–14
see also Ice, manufactured

Cole, David N.
"Trends in Campsite Condition: Eagle Cap Wilderness, Bob Marshall Wilderness, and Grand Canyon National Park", 1208–395

Cole, Theodore M.
"Rehabilitation of Persons with Injuries", 4208–35

Collective bargaining
see Labor-management relations, general
see Labor unions

Colleges and universities
see Black colleges
see Federal aid to higher education
see Federal aid to medical education
see Higher education
see Junior colleges
see State funding for higher education

Collender, Robert N.
"Changes in Farm Credit System Structure", 1541–1.311
"Farm Credit System Outlook", 1504–9.1

Collier, Drew R.
"Railroad Transportation of U.S. Grain to Mexico", 1504–9.1

Collin County, Tex.
Housing and households characteristics, unit and neighborhood quality, and journey to work by MSA location, for 11 MSAs, 1985 survey, supplement, 2485–8
Housing and households detailed characteristics, and unit and neighborhood quality, by location, 1989 survey, MSA rpt, 2485–6.5

Collins, William E.
"Index of FAA Office of Aviation Medicine Reports: 1961-91", 7506–10.97

Colombia
Agricultural trade of US, by detailed commodity and country, 1991, annual rpt, 1524–8
Agricultural trade of US, by detailed commodity and country, 1991, semiannual rpt, 1522–4
AID economic aid to developing countries, obligations and disbursements by country, quarterly rpt, 9912–4
AID loans repayment status and terms by program and country, and status of predecessor agency loans, quarterly rpt, 9912–3
Cuba trade, by commodity and country, mid 1980s-91, 9118–8
Economic and military aid and loans from US and intl agencies, by program and country, FY46-91, annual rpt, 9914–5
Economic and social conditions of developing countries from 1960s, and Intl Dev Cooperation Agency and AID activities and funding, FY91-93, annual rpt, 9904–4
Economic and social conditions, resources, and trade, and aid, 1992, annual factbook, 9914–14
Economic conditions, policy, and trade practices, by country, 1989-91, annual rpt, 21384–5
Economic, social, political, and geographic summary data, by country, 1992, annual factbook, 9114–2
Exports (duty free) under Andean Trade Preference Act from 4 countries to US, and business opportunities, 1989-91, 2048–161
Exports and imports of US, by commodity and country, 1980-90, world area rpt, 9116–1.7
Exports and imports of US, by Harmonized System 6-digit commodity and country, 1991, annual rpt, 2424–13
Exports and imports of US, by selected country, country group, and commodity group, 1991, annual rpt, 2044–37
Exports and imports of US, by transport mode, country, and SITC 1- to 3-digit commodity, 1991, annual rpt, 2424–12
Exports, imports, and balances of US for manufactured goods, by SITC 2-digit commodity and country, quarterly rpt, 2042–35
Exports, imports, and balances of US with major trading partners, by product category, 1987-91, annual chartbook, 9884–21
Exports, investment, debt, and tariffs of 7 Latin America countries, and trade and investment policy liberalization issues, mid 1960s-91, 9886–4.184
Exports of US, detailed Schedule B commodities with countries of destination, 1991, annual rpt, 2424–10
Fruit, vegetable, nut, and cut flower imports of US from Andean countries, 1989 and 1991, article, 1925–34.317
Hostages kidnapped in Colombia, listing as of 1991, 7004–22
Human rights conditions in 170 countries, and US economic and military aid, 1991, annual rpt, 21384–3
Immigrants from Colombia employed in New England textile industry, by selected characteristics, 1960s-80s, working paper, 6366–6.4
Imports of goods, services, and investment from US, trade barriers, impacts, and US actions, by country, 1991, annual rpt, 444–2
Inter-American Foundation dev grants, project characteristics, area benefits, and investment returns, for 8 projects, 1970s-88, 14428–1
Military aid of US, arms sales, and training programs costs and budget requests, by program, world region, and country, FY91-93, annual rpt, 7144–13

Military spending, arms trade, and force strengths, with govt spending and population, by country, 1979-89, annual rpt, 9824–1
Multinatl US firms and foreign affiliates finances and operations, by industry and country, 1989 benchmark survey, annual rpt, 2704–5
Multinatl US firms foreign affiliates, income statement items by asset size, industry, and country, 1988, biennial article, 8302–2.322
Natural gas composition and helium levels, analyses of individual wells and pipelines, 1985-91, annual rpt, 5604–2
Oil exports to US by OPEC and non-OPEC countries, monthly rpt, 3162–24.3
Oil exports to US by OPEC and non-OPEC countries, monthly 1973-88, 3168–123.3
Oil production, investment needs, and exports, for 8 South America countries, 1980s-90 and projected to 2010, GAO rpt, 26123–396
Population size, growth rates, and components of change, by country, projected 1990-2020 and trends from 1950, biennial rpt, 2324–9
Refugee migration, and intl aid programs, by world area and country of origin and asylum, 1991, annual rpt, 7004–15
Steel trade, by product, country, and customs district, with US industry operating data, 1989-June 1992, semiannual rpt, 9882–15
UN voting record and share of votes in agreement with US, by issue, country, and world area, 1991, annual rpt, 7004–18
see also under By Foreign Country in the "Index by Categories"

Colorado

Banks (insured commercial and savings) deposits by instn, State, MSA, and county, as of June 1991, annual regional rpt, 9295–3.6
Coal production and mines by county, prices, productivity, miners, and reserves, by mining method and State, 1990-91, annual rpt, 3164–25
Deaths and rates, by detailed location, cause, and demographic characteristics, 1989, US Vital Statistics annual rpt, 4144–3.1
Drug abuse indicators for selected metro areas, research results, data collection, and policy issues, 1992 semiannual conf, 4492–5
Employment, earnings, and hours, by selected SIC 1- to 4-digit industry, State, and for 275 MSAs, 1987-92, 6748–81
Fed Govt spending in States and local areas, by type, State, county, and city, FY91, annual rpt, 2464–3
Fed Govt spending in States, by type, program, agency, and State, FY91, annual rpt, 2464–2
Financial and economic devs, Fed Reserve 10th District, quarterly rpt, 9381–16
HHS financial aid, by program, recipient, State, and city, FY91, annual regional listing, 4004–3.8
Hospital deaths of Medicare patients, actual and expected rates by diagnosis, and hospital characteristics, by instn, FY90 annual State rpt, 4654–14.6
Housing census, 1990: inventory, occupancy, and costs, State fact sheet, 2326–21.7
Housing census, 1990: summary unit characteristics, by householder race and age, county, place, and urban-rural location, State rpt, 2471–1.7
Military prime contract awards, by contractor, service branch, State, and city, FY91, annual rpt, 3544–22
Mineral Industry Surveys, State reviews of production, 1991, preliminary annual rpt, 5614–6
Minerals Yearbook, Vol 2, 1990: State review of production and sales by commodity, and business activity, annual rpt, 5604–22.7
Multinatl firms US affiliates finances and operations, by industry, country of parent firm, and State, 1987, 2708–48
Nuclear power plant (helium-cooled) at Fort St Vrain, occupational radiation exposure, 1974-89, annual rpt, 9634–3
Physicians, by specialty, age, sex, and location of training and practice, 1990, State rpt, 4116–6.6
Population and housing census, 1990: detailed geographic coverage, State CD-ROM, 2551–9.8
Population and housing census, 1990: population and housing characteristics, detailed geographic coverage, State CD-ROM, 2551–10.9
Population and housing census, 1990: summary characteristics, by county, subdiv, and place, State rpt, 2551–7.7
Population census, 1990: population characteristics and living arrangements, by county, place, and urban-rural location, State rpt, 2531–1.7
Potato production, acreage, prices, and shipments, for 7 major producer States, and compared to other States, 1970s-92, annual rpt, 1311–29
Radiation and other pollutant releases from DOE contractor research lab and nuclear weapons facilities, monitoring results, 1992 annual site rpt, 3324–2.14
Statistical Abstract of US, 1992 annual data compilation, 2324–1
Uranium tailings at inactive Gunnison mill, remedial action proposals, costs, site characteristics, and environmental, socioeconomic, and health impacts, 1992 rpt, 3356–4.12
Water quality, chemistry, hydrology, and other characteristics, 1990 local area study, 5666–27.25
Water resources data collection and analysis activities of USGS Water Resources Div District, with project descriptions, 1991 rpt, 5666–26.24
Water salinity control program for Colorado River, participation and payments, FY87-91, annual rpt, 1804–23
Water supply, and snow survey results, monthly State rpt, 1266–2.3
Water supply, and snow survey results, 1990, annual State rpt, 1264–14.1
Water supply in Colorado, streamflow, precipitation, and reservoir storage, 1992 water year, annual rpt, 1264–13
Wilderness areas acreage by State, and Colorado off-road vehicle use, owner expenses, and views on registration fee, 1986-88, hearing, 25318–85
see also Arapahoe County, Colo.
see also Boulder, Colo.
see also Colorado Springs, Colo.
see also Denver, Colo.
see also Jefferson County, Colo.
see also Longmont, Colo.
see also under By State in the "Index by Categories"

Colorado River

Reservoir and power operations and revenues of Fed Govt, for Colorado River Basin, 1991-92, annual rpt, 5824–6
Salinity control program for Colorado River, participation and payments, FY87-91, annual rpt, 1804–23
Salinity control program for Colorado River, producer payments by State, 1991, annual table, 1804–12
Water storage project for Colorado River, finances and activities in western States, FY91, annual rpt, 5824–3
Water storage project for Colorado River power sales, and Glen Canyon Dam operations, 1960s-80s, hearing, 21448–47
Water supply and quality in streams and lakes, and groundwater levels in wells, by drainage basin, 1990, annual State rpt series, 5666–10
Water supply and quality in streams and lakes, and groundwater levels in wells, by drainage basin, 1991, annual State rpt series, 5666–12

Colorado Springs, Colo.

Housing starts and completions authorized by building permits in 40 MSAs, quarterly rpt, 2382–9
see also under By City and By SMSA or MSA in the "Index by Categories"

Coloring materials

see Dyeing and coloring materials
see Paints and varnishes

Columbia River

Bonneville Power Admin mgmt of Fed Columbia River Power System, finances, operations, and sales by customer, FY91, annual rpt, 3224–1
Electric power capacity and use in Pacific Northwest, by energy source, forecast under alternative load and demand cases, 1991-2012, annual rpt, 3224–3
Fish (salmon) aquaculture activities of Little White Salmon National Fish Hatchery, late 1890s-1980s, 5508–114
Fish (salmon) conservation spending by organization, and population, for Columbia River basin, 1970-91, GAO rpt, 26113–577
Freight (waterborne domestic and foreign) by commodity, traffic, and passengers, by port and waterway, 1989, annual rpt, 3754–3.4
Indian tribes in Pacific Northwest, OCS oil and gas lease and dev environmental, economic, and cultural impacts, with background data, 1970s-92, 5738–35
Radiation exposure of population near Hanford, Wash, nuclear plant, with methodology, 1944-91, series, 3356–5
Water supply and quality in streams and lakes, and groundwater levels in wells, by drainage basin, 1990, annual State rpt series, 5666–10
Water supply and quality in streams and lakes, and groundwater levels in wells, by drainage basin, 1991, annual State rpt series, 5666–12

Water supply in US and southern Canada, streamflow, surface and groundwater conditions, and reservoir levels, by location, monthly rpt, 5662–3

Columbia, S.C.

Fruit and vegetable shipments, and arrivals by city, by mode of transport and State and country of origin, 1991, annual rpt, 1311–4.1

Wages by occupation, and benefits for office and plant workers, 1992 survey, periodic MSA rpt, 6785–3.6

see also under By City and By SMSA or MSA in the "Index by Categories"

Columbus, Ga.

Wages by occupation, for office and plant workers, 1992 survey, periodic labor market rpt, 6785–3.6

see also under By City and By SMSA or MSA in the "Index by Categories"

Columbus, Miss.

Wages by occupation, and benefits for office and plant workers, 1992 survey, periodic MSA rpt, 6785–3.6

Columbus, Ohio

Air traffic, and passenger and freight enplanements, by airport, 1960s-90 and projected to 2010, hub area rpt, 7506–7.43

Housing and households characteristics, and unit and neighborhood quality, by MSA location for 11 MSAs, 1987 survey, supplement, 2485–8

Wages by occupation, and benefits, for office and plant workers, 1991 survey, periodic MSA rpt, 6785–16.3

see also under By City and By SMSA or MSA in the "Index by Categories"

Commemorations and memorials

see Monuments and memorials

Commerce

see Foreign trade

see Interstate commerce

Commerce Department

see Department of Commerce

Commercial banking

see Banks and banking

Commercial buildings

Alteration and repair spending for commercial and public buildings, by type, size, age, and region, 1989, 2388–4

Alteration and repair spending for commercial and public buildings, by type, 1989, article, 2042–1.305

Assets and debts of private sector, balance sheets by segment, 1960-91, semiannual rpt, 9365–4.1

Bombing incidents and casualties, by target, circumstances, and State, 1987-91, annual rpt, 8484–4.1

Bombing incidents, casualties, and damage, by target, circumstances, and State, 1991, annual rpt, 6224–5

Business statistics, detailed data for major industries and economic indicators, 1960-91, *Survey of Current Business* biennial supplement, 2704–1

Capital investment changes relation to changes in costs, by asset type and industry div, late 1950s-80s, article, 9373–1.304

Child day care and early childhood education programs availability, demand, use, costs, and provider and enrollee characteristics, 1990 survey, 4808–39

Coastal areas construction authorized by permit, by building type, 1970-89, 2176–8.3

Construction put in place, permits, housing sales, costs, material prices, and employment, quarterly rpt with articles, 2042–1

Construction put in place, value of new public and private structures, by type, monthly rpt, 2382–4

Crime victimization rates, by victim and offender characteristics, circumstances, and offense, 1990 survey, annual rpt, 6066–3.47

Energy conservation programs of States, Federal aid and savings, by State, 1990, annual rpt, 3304–1

Energy conservation technologies for housing and commercial buildings, use, costs, efficiency, and residential tax credits, 1970s-90 and projected to 2010, 26358–259

Energy supply, demand, and prices, by fuel type and end-use sector, projections and underlying assumptions, 1995-2010, annual rpt, 3164–90

Energy use in commercial buildings, costs, and conservation, by building characteristics, survey rpt series, 3166–8

Flow-of-funds accounts, savings, investments, and credit statements, quarterly rpt, 9365–3.3

Historic and natural natl landmarks damaged and threatened, with owner, location, damage type, and recommended remedial action, 1990, annual listing, 5544–16

Housing units with nonresidential activities on premises, MSA surveys, series, 2485–6

Input-output structure of US economy, detailed interindustry transactions for 541 industries, and components of final demand, 1982 benchmark data, 2708–17

Lighting in commercial buildings, energy use and conservation by building characteristics, 1986, 3166–15.1

Mortgage loan activity, by type of lender, loan, and mortgaged property, monthly press release, 5142–18

Multinatl firms US affiliates finances and operations, by industry div, country of parent firm, and State, 1989-90, annual article, 2702–1.319; 2702–1.337

Multinatl firms US affiliates, finances, and operations, by industry, world area of parent firm, and State, 1989-90, annual rpt, 2704–4

Natl income and product accounts, comprehensive accounts and components, benchmark revisions, 1929-88, 2708–5

Natl income and product accounts, comprehensive accounts and components, *Survey of Current Business*, monthly rpt, 2702–1.28

Neighborhood and housing quality, indicators and attitudes, by householder type and location, for 11 MSAs, 1987 survey, supplement, 2485–8

Neighborhood and housing quality, indicators and attitudes, by householder type and location, 1989, biennial rpt supplement, 2485–13

Robberies, by type of premises, population size, and region, 1991, annual rpt, 6224–2.1

Savings instns failures, inventory of real estate assets available from Resolution Trust Corp, 1991, semiannual listing, 9722–2.1

Savings instns failures, inventory of real estate assets available from Resolution Trust Corp, 1992, semiannual listing, 9722–2.8

Statistical Abstract of US, 1992 annual data compilation, 2324–1.26

Supply and demand for housing and commercial real estate, market activity indicators by region, quarterly rpt, 9292–6

Telecommunications industry intl competitiveness, structure, and devs, with background data and foreign comparisons, 1991 rpt, 2808–30

Terrorism incidents in US, related activity, and casualties, by attack type, target, group, and location, 1991, annual rpt, 6224–6

Wiretaps authorized, costs, arrests, trials, and convictions, by offense and jurisdiction, 1991, annual rpt, 18204–7

Commercial Buildings Energy Consumption Survey

Design and questionnaire dev for 1992 survey, 3166–15.4

Lighting in commercial buildings, energy use and conservation by building characteristics, 1986, 3166–15.1

Commercial credit

Agricultural cooperatives finances, aggregate for top 100 assns by commodity group, 1990, annual rpt, 1124–3

Assets and debts of private sector, balance sheets by segment, 1960-91, semiannual rpt, 9365–4.1

Banking and financial conditions, 1990, annual rpt, 9364–5

Banks (commercial) business loans, and commercial paper of nonfinancial companies, weekly rpt, 9391–4

Banks checking account and commercial loan activity by bank size, and loan sales and assets for top banks, 1970s-90, working paper, 9387–8.264

Banks credit operations costs and revenue, by credit type, mid 1970s-91, article, 9362–1.306

Banks loan commitments impact on business investment, 1980-84, working paper, 9381–10.128

Commercial paper outstanding, by issuer and holder type, and foreign firms paper issued by US subsidiaries and foreign offices, 1980s-91, article, 9362–1.308

Economic indicators and components, current data and annual trends, monthly rpt, 23842–1.5

Finance companies business credit outstanding, 1990, annual rpt, 9364–5.7

Financial and business detailed statistics, *Fed Reserve Bulletin*, monthly rpt with articles, 9362–1

Flow-of-funds accounts, savings, investments, and credit statements, quarterly rpt, 9365–3.3

Foreign-controlled US firms transactions with related foreign persons, by type, industry div, and country, 1988, article, 8302–2.318

Intl financial markets performance of foreign and US bank and securities firms, finances and competitiveness issues, 1980s, compilation of papers, 9385–10

Minority- and woman-owned businesses and owner characteristics, by industry, employment and sales size, and form of ownership, 1987 survey, 2328–59
Minority Business Dev Centers mgmt and financial aid, and characteristics of businesses, by region and State, FY91, annual rpt, 2104–6
Monetary trends, Fed Reserve Bank of St Louis monthly rpt, 9391–2
North Central States business and economic conditions, Fed Reserve 9th District, quarterly journal, 9383–19
Overseas Business Reports: economic conditions, investment and export opportunities, and trade practices, country market research rpt series, 2046–6
Recessions impacts on business loans and inventories, late 1940s-91, article, 9391–1.315
Rural areas businesses credit assistance of Fed Govt, by program and county characteristics, 1983-89, 1548–389
Savings instns insured by Savings Assn Insurance Fund, assets, liabilities, and deposit and loan activity, by conservatorship status, monthly rpt, 8432–1
Small Business Admin guaranteed loans issued under regular, certified, and preferred lender programs, selected characteristics, FY83-90, GAO rpt, 26113–581
Small Business Admin loan guarantee program participants finances, operations, characteristics, and views, 1991 survey, 9768–25
Small Business Admin loans to tourism-related and other small businesses in rural areas, FY86-1st half FY91, hearing, 21728–79
Small business financing sources, and business financial data by size, type, and industry, 1980s-90, annual rpt, 9764–6.2
Small business loan collateral adequacy for failed firms, with loan liquidation recoveries and losses, FY89, GAO rpt, 26113–553
Southeastern States, Fed Reserve 5th District insured commercial banks financial statements, by State, quarterly rpt, 9389–18
Survey of Current Business, detailed data for major industries and economic indicators, monthly rpt, 2702–1.8
Survey of Current Business, detailed data for major industries and economic indicators, 1960-91, biennial supplement, 2704–1
Tax (income) returns of corporations, income and tax items by asset size and detailed industry, 1989, annual rpt, 8304–21
West Central States economic indicators, Fed Reserve 10th District, quarterly rpt, 9381–16.2

Commercial education
see Business education

Commercial finance companies
see Finance companies

Commercial law
Court civil and criminal caseloads for Federal district, appeals, and bankruptcy courts, by type of suit and offense, circuit, and district, 1991, annual rpt, 18204–11
Court civil and criminal caseloads for Federal district, appeals, and special courts, 1991, annual rpt, 18204–8
see also Antitrust law
see also Bankruptcy
see also Interstate commerce
see also Licenses and permits
see also Maritime law
see also Patents
see also Price regulation
see also Trademarks

Commercial treaties
see Trade agreements

Commissaries
see Military post exchanges and commissaries

Commission of Fine Arts
Budget of US, authoritative financial statements with appropriations, outlays, and receipts, by category and agency, FY91, annual rpt, 8104–2.2
Budget of US, obligations and authority by function, agency, and program, with summaries and analyses, FY93, annual rpt, 104–2

Commission on Civil Rights
Black women's labor force status, earnings, and other economic status indicators, and compared to whites, various periods 1939-88, 11048–191
Budget of US, authoritative financial statements with appropriations, outlays, and receipts, by category and agency, FY91, annual rpt, 8104–2.2
Budget of US, obligations and authority by function, agency, and program, with summaries and analyses, FY93, annual rpt, 104–2
Labor unions recognized in Fed Govt, agreements and membership by agency and facility, as of Jan 1991, biennial listing, 9844–14

Commission on the Future Structure of Veterans Health Care
VA health care services, needs, availability, structure, and funding, findings and recommendations, 1991 rpt, 8608–8
VA health care services, needs, availability, structure, and funding, 1991 compilation of papers, 8608–9

Commissions of the Federal Government
see Federal boards, committees, and commissions
see Federal independent agencies

Commitment
Mental health care of affective disorder patients, by patient and facility characteristics, 1986, 4506–3.49
Prison and community-based facilities, population, employment, spending, and other characteristics, by State and for Fed Govt, 1990, quinquennial rpt, 6068–218
Prisoners in Federal instns, admissions, releases, and recidivism, by region, monthly rpt series, 6242–1
see also Sentences, criminal procedure

Committee for Purchase from the Blind and Other Severely Handicapped
Budget of US, authoritative financial statements with appropriations, outlays, and receipts, by category and agency, FY91, annual rpt, 8104–2.2
Budget of US, obligations and authority by function, agency, and program, with summaries and analyses, FY93, annual rpt, 104–2
Workshops for blind and handicapped, finances, operations, and Federal procurement, FY82-91, annual rpt, 11714–1

Committee on Problems of Drug Dependence, Inc.
"Problems of Drug Dependence, 1991: Proceeding of the 53rd Annual Scientific Meeting, The Committee on Problems of Drug Dependence, Inc.", 4494–11

Committees of Congress
see Congressional committees
see Congressional joint committees

Commodities
see Foreign trade
see Futures trading
see Generic products
see Manufacturing
see Mines and mineral resources
see Natural resources
see Stockpiling
see Strategic materials
see under By Commodity in the "Index by Categories"
see under names of specific commodities or commodity groups

Commodity Credit Corp.
Agricultural Stabilization and Conservation Service programs, annual commodity fact sheet series, 1806–4
Agricultural Statistics, 1991, annual rpt, 1004–1
Budget of US, obligations and authority by function, agency, and program, with summaries and analyses, FY93, annual rpt, 104–2
Certificate exchange activity of CCC, by commodity, biweekly press release, 1802–16
Cotton loan rates, and micronaire differentials of CCC, monthly rpt, annual tables, 1309–12
Cotton prices at selected spot markets, NYC futures prices, and CCC loan rates, 1991/92 and trends from 1944, annual rpt, 1309–2
Cotton prices in 7 spot markets, futures prices at NYC exchange, farm prices, and CCC loan stocks, monthly rpt, 1309–1
Cotton production, trade, and use, for selected countries, FAS monthly circular, 1925–4.2
Dairy production by State, stocks, prices, and CCC price support activities, by product type, monthly rpt, 1627–3
Dairy products price support purchases, sales, donations, and inventories of CCC, monthly rpt, 1802–2
Dairy products uncommitted stocks, periodic situation rpt with articles, 1561–2
Economic Indicators of the Farm Sector, balance sheets, and receipts by detailed commodity, by State, 1986-90, annual rpt, 1544–18
Expenditures in natl income and product accounts and in unified budget, benchmark revisions, 1929-88, 2708–5
Expenditures in natl income and product accounts and in unified budget, *Survey of Current Business*, monthly rpt, 2702–1.26
Export credit sales agreement terms, by commodity and country, FY90, annual rpt, 15344–1.11

Exports (agricultural) under federally financed programs, by commodity and country, bimonthly rpt, periodic data, 1522–1
Financial condition and major commodity program operations of CCC, FY63-88, annual chartbook, 1824–2
Grain futures contracts, stocks in deliverable position by type, weekly tables, 11922–4
Grain production, prices, trade, and export inspections by US port and country of destination, by grain type, weekly rpt, 1313–2
Honey production, prices, trade, stocks, marketing, and CCC honey loan and distribution activities, monthly rpt, 1311–2
Input-output structure of US economy, detailed interindustry transactions for 541 industries, and components of final demand, 1982 benchmark data, 2708–17
Latin America economic and social conditions, resources, trade, and aid, 1992, annual factbook, 9914–14
Liabilities (contingent) and claims paid by Fed Govt on federally insured and guaranteed contracts with foreign obligors, by country and program, periodic rpt, 8002–12
Loans (farm) outstanding, and lenders financial condition, quarterly rpt with articles, 1541–1
Loans (farm) outstanding, by lender type and State, 1960-89, 1548–384
Loans of CCC, activities and operating results, monthly release, 1802–7
Lumber and wood products trade and export promotion of US by country, and trade balance, by commodity, FAS periodic circular, 1925–36
Oils, oilseeds, and fats foreign and US production and trade, FAS periodic circular series, 1925–1
Price support and other CCC program outlays, with production and marketing outlook, by commodity, projected 1991-97, annual rpt, 26306–6.171
Rice foreign and US production, prices, trade, stocks, and use, periodic situation rpt, 1561–8
Rice market activities, prices, inspections, sales, trade, supply, and use, for US and selected foreign markets, weekly rpt, 1313–8
Sale offerings of CCC commodities, and prices, monthly press release, 1802–4
Seed exports, by type, world region, and country, FAS quarterly rpt, 1925–13
Statistical Abstract of US, 1992 annual data compilation, 2324–1.23
Storage facility and equipment loans to farmers under CCC grain program, by State, monthly table, 1802–9

Commodity Exchange Authority
see Commodity Futures Trading Commission

Commodity futures
see Futures trading

Commodity Futures Trading Commission
Activities, funding, and staff of CFTC, and futures and options trading volume by commodity and exchange, FY91, annual rpt, 11924–2
Budget of US, authoritative financial statements with appropriations, outlays, and receipts, by category and agency, FY91, annual rpt, 8104–2.2
Budget of US, obligations and authority by function, agency, and program, with summaries and analyses, FY93, annual rpt, 104–2
Futures trading in selected commodities and financial instruments and indexes, for NYC, Chicago, and other markets activity, biweekly rpt, 11922–5
Grain futures contracts, stocks in deliverable position by type, weekly tables, 11922–4
Labor unions recognized in Fed Govt, agreements and membership by agency and facility, as of Jan 1991, biennial listing, 9844–14

Common carriers
see Airlines
see Buses
see Passenger ships
see Public utilities
see Railroads
see Ships and shipping
see Taxicabs
see Trucks and trucking industry

Common markets and free trade areas
Export and import agreements, negotiations, and related legislation, 1991, annual rpt, 444–1
Exports and imports, trade agreements and relations, and USITC investigations, 1991, annual rpt, 9884–5
Exports, imports, membership, and trade impacts of regional preferential trading arrangements, by group, late 1940s-91, article, 9373–1.308
Free trade and currency zones devs, and impacts on monetary policy, 1991 conf, 9381–13.1
Loans of US banks to foreigners at all US and foreign offices, by country group and country, quarterly rpt, 13002–1
see also Andean Group
see also Caribbean Community
see also Central American Common Market
see also Council for Mutual Economic Assistance
see also European Community
see also European Free Trade Association
see also Export processing zones
see also Latin American Integration Association
see also North American Free Trade Agreement

Commonwealth of Independent States
Uranium resources and production of CIS, by state, 1992 article, 3164–65
see also Armenia
see also Azerbaijan
see also Byelarus
see also Kazakhstan
see also Kyrgyzstan
see also Moldova
see also Russia
see also Soviet Union
see also Tajikistan
see also Turkmenistan
see also Ukraine
see also Uzbekistan

Communicable diseases
see Acquired immune deficiency syndrome
see Animal diseases and zoonoses
see Infective and parasitic diseases
see Pneumonia and influenza
see Rabies
see Sexually transmitted diseases
see Tuberculosis

Communications industries
Capital expenditures for plant and equipment, by major industry group, quarterly rpt, 2502–2
Collective bargaining agreements expiring during year, and workers covered, by firm, union, industry group, and State, 1992, annual rpt, 6784–9
County Business Patterns, 1989: employment, establishments, and payroll, by SIC 2- to 4-digit industry and county, annual State rpt series, 2326–8
County Business Patterns, 1990: employment, establishments, and payroll, by SIC 2- to 4-digit industry and county, annual State rpt series, 2326–6
Criminal cases by type and disposition, and collections, for US attorneys, by Federal district, FY91, annual rpt, 6004–2.1
Employment, earnings, and hours, by SIC 1- to 4-digit industry, monthly 1989-Feb 1992, annual rpt, 6744–4
Employment of minorities and women, by occupation, SIC 1- to 3-digit industry, State, and MSA, 1991, annual rpt, 9244–1
Exports and imports between US and outlying areas, by detailed commodity and mode of transport, 1991, annual rpt, 2424–11
Exports and imports of US, by Harmonized System 6-digit commodity and country, 1991, annual rpt, 2424–13
Exports of US, detailed Schedule B commodities with countries of destination, 1991, annual rpt, 2424–10
Finances of communications services, itemized revenue and expenses by SIC 2- to 4-digit kind of business, 1990, annual rpt, 2413–15
Foreign direct investment in US, major transactions by type, industry, country, and US location, 1990, annual rpt, 2044–20
House of Representatives salaries, expenses, and contingent fund disbursement, detailed listings, quarterly rpt, 21942–1
Input-output structure of US economy, detailed interindustry transactions for 84 industries, and components of final demand, 1987, annual article, 2702–1.316
Input-output structure of US economy, detailed interindustry transactions for 541 industries, and components of final demand, 1982 benchmark data, 2708–17
Licensing activities of FCC, by class of operation, FY91, annual rpt, 9284–4
Military budget, manpower needs, costs, and force readiness by service branch, FY93, annual rpt, 3504–1
Military prime contract awards, by detailed procurement category, FY88-91, annual rpt, 3544–18
Multinatl firms US affiliates finances and operations, by industry, country of parent firm, and State, 1987, 2708–48
Multinatl US firms and foreign affiliates finances and operations, by industry and country, 1989 benchmark survey, annual rpt, 2704–5
Multinatl US firms foreign affiliates, income statement items by asset size, industry, and country, 1988, biennial article, 8302–2.322

Natl income and product accounts, comprehensive accounts and components, benchmark revisions, 1929-88, 2708–5
Natl income and product accounts, comprehensive accounts and components, *Survey of Current Business*, monthly rpt, 2702–1.29
Occupational injury and illness rates, by SIC 2- to 4-digit industry, 1989-90, annual rpt, 6844–7
Occupational injury and illness rates, by SIC 2- to 4-digit industry, 1990, annual rpt, 6844–1
Pacific territories population and housing detailed characteristics, by location, 1990 Census of Population and Housing, series, 2551–8
SEC registration, firms required to file annual rpts, as of Sept 1991, annual listing, 9734–5
Senate receipts, itemized expenses by payee, and balances, 1st half FY92, semiannual listing, 25922–1
Tax (income) returns of corporations, income and tax items by asset size and detailed industry, 1989, annual rpt, 8304–4; 8304–21
Tax (income) returns of partnerships, income statement and balance sheet items, by industry group, 1990, annual article, 8302–2.314
Tax (income) returns of sole proprietorships, income statement items, by industry group, 1990, annual article, 8302–2.317; 8302–2.320
see also Books and bookselling
see also Cable television
see also Census of Transportation, Communications, and Utilities Industries
see also Communications satellites
see also Educational broadcasting
see also Home video and audio equipment
see also Information services
see also Journalism
see also Mass media
see also Motion pictures
see also Newspapers
see also Periodicals
see also Printing and publishing industry
see also Public broadcasting
see also Radio
see also Recording industry
see also Telecommunication
see also Telegraph
see also Telephones and telephone industry
see also Television
see also under By Industry in the "Index by Categories"

Communications Satellite Corp.
Finances and operations of COMSAT, 1989-90, annual rpt, 9284–6.5
Finances, rates, and traffic for US telecommunications carriers intl operations, by service type, firm, and country, 1975-90, annual rpt, 9284–17

Communications satellites
Exports of US, detailed Schedule B commodities with countries of destination, 1991, annual rpt, 2424–10
Finances and operations, by SIC 2- to 4-digit industry, forecast 1992, annual rpt, 2044–28
Foreign countries economic, social, political, and geographic summary data, by country, 1992, annual factbook, 9114–2
Launchings and other activities of NASA and Soviet Union, with flight data, 1957-91, annual rpt, 9504–6.1
Price indexes (producer), by stage of processing and detailed commodity, monthly rpt, 6762–6
Price indexes (producer), by stage of processing and detailed commodity, monthly 1991, annual rpt, 6764–2
Shipments, trade, use, and firms, for electronic communications systems and related products, 1991, annual Current Industrial Rpt, 2506–12.35
Telephone and telegraph firms detailed finances and operations, 1990, annual rpt, 9284–6
TV (satellite) copyright royalty fees, and funds available for distribution, 1990-91, annual rpt, 26404–2

Communism
see Centrally planned economies
see Communist parties

Communist countries
see Centrally planned economies
see East-West trade

Communist parties
Foreign countries economic, social, political, and geographic summary data, by country, 1992, annual factbook, 9114–2

Community-based correctional programs
Drug smuggling interdiction, inmate and staff testing, and treatment programs, by prison characteristics, 1989-90, 6066–19.70
Facilities, population, employment, spending, and other characteristics of correctional instns, by State and for Fed Govt, 1990, annual rpt, 6064–26.3; 6068–218
Federal criminal sentencing, guidelines use and results by offense and district, and Sentencing Commission activities, 1991, annual rpt, 17664–1
Juvenile facilities population, by resident characteristics and facility type, late 1970s-89, 6068–250
Juvenile facilities population, by resident characteristics and facility type, 1977-89, annual rpt, 6064–35
Probation population, by offender characteristics, sentence conditions, whether rearrested, and offense, 1986-89, 6066–19.65
Sentences for Federal offenses, guidelines by offense and circumstances, series, 17668–1
Sex offenders treatment programs for adults and juveniles, by program type and State, data compilation, 1992 annual rpt, 6064–6.1

Community colleges
see Junior colleges

Community development
Appalachia local dev projects, and funding by source, by program and State, FY91, annual rpt, 9084–1
Assistance (financial and nonfinancial) of Fed Govt, 1992 base edition, annual listing, 104–5
Black colleges grants from HUD for economic and community dev programs, by recipient, 1991, press release, 5006–3.85
Budget of US, CBO analysis and review of FY93 budget by function, annual rpt, 26304–2
Budget of US, CBO analysis of revenue and spending alternatives and projections of economic indicators, FY93-97, annual rpt, 26304–3
Budget of US, House concurrent resolution, with spending and revenue targets, FY93 and projected to FY97, annual rpt, 21264–2
Budget of US, obligations and authority by function, agency, and program, with summaries and analyses, FY93, annual rpt, 104–2
Economic Dev Admin activities, and funding by program, recipient, State, and county, FY91 and cumulative from FY66, annual rpt, 2064–2
Enterprise zone programs in rural areas, jobs created and saved, and firms participating, by industry, 1986, article, 1502–7.303
Enterprise zone programs of States, business investment and jobs created, and incentive programs, by State, 1992 annual rpt, 5124–9
Expenditures (direct) and employment, by function and level of govt, selected years 1962-87, 10048–53
Expenditures of Fed Govt in States, by type, program, agency, and State, FY91, annual rpt, 2464–2
FmHA activities, and loans and grants by program and State, FY91 and trends from FY70, annual rpt, 1184–17
Govt employment and payroll, by function, level of govt, and jurisdiction, annual rpt series, 2466–1
HHS financial aid, by program, recipient, State, and city, FY91, annual regional listings, 4004–3
HUD grants to aid housing purchase in depressed areas, by recipient, 1991, press release, 5006–3.84
HUD matching grants for neighborhood revitalization and affordable housing, by recipient, 1992, press release, 5006–3.92
Indian (Navajo and Hopi) relocation program activities and caseloads, monthly rpt, 16002–1
Natl income and product accounts, comprehensive accounts and components, benchmark revisions, 1929-88, 2708–5
Natl income and product accounts, comprehensive accounts and components, *Survey of Current Business*, monthly rpt, 2702–1.26
Neighborhood Dev Demonstration program evaluation, grantee organization characteristics, activities, finances, and private sector support, 1984-89, 5188–119
Neighborhood Reinvestment Corp contracting practices and oversight of local grantees, with grantee listing, FY88-91, GAO rpt, 26113–587
R&D funding by Fed Govt, by detailed function, program, and agency, FY91-93, annual rpt, 9627–9
State and local govt employment of minorities and women, by occupation, function, and pay level, 1991, annual rpt, 9244–6.4
see also City and town planning
see also Community Development Block Grants
see also Urban Development Action Grants

see also Urban renewal

Community Development Block Grants

Assistance (block and categorical grants) programs for State and local govts, FY91, biennial listing, 10044–8

Black colleges technical aid programs supporting CDBGs, HUD grants by recipient, 1991, press release, 5006–3.78

Expenditures and activities under CDBGs, by program, FY75-91, annual rpt, 5124–8

Expenditures of Fed Govt in States, by type, program, agency, and State, FY91, annual rpt, 2464–2

Housing (rental) rehabilitation funding and activities of HUD, by program and region, FY91, annual rpt, 5124–7

Community health services

Drug abuse treatment services costs, effectiveness, and financing issues, 1991 conf papers, 4498–80

HHS financial aid, by program, recipient, State, and city, FY91, annual regional listings, 4004–3

Indian Health Service and tribal facilities and use, and Indians health and other characteristics, by IHS region, 1980s-90, annual chartbook, 4084–7

Indian Health Service facilities, funding, operations, and Indian health and other characteristics, 1950s-91, annual chartbook, 4084–1

Mental health care facilities, staff, and patient characteristics, *Statistical Notes* series, 4506–3

Mental health care facilities, staff, patients, and finances, 1970s-91, biennial rpt, 4094–1

Physicians in community and migrant health centers, hospital admitting privileges status and issues, 1991, GAO rpt, 26121–465

Rural areas health care access for counties without hospitals and in which the only hospital closed, 1987-89, 17206–2.30

see also Group homes for the handicapped

see also Home health services

Community mental health centers

see Community health services

see Mental health facilities and services

Community Planning and Development, HUD

Budget of US, obligations and authority by function, agency, and program, with summaries and analyses, FY93, annual rpt, 104–2

Community Dev Block Grant activities and funding, by program, FY75-91, annual rpt, 5124–8

Enterprise zone programs of States, business investment and jobs created, and incentive programs, by State, 1992 annual rpt, 5124–9

Homeless persons housing and support services projects, funding, and clients, by organization, FY87 and FY90, GAO rpt, 26113–593

Housing (rental) rehabilitation funding and activities of HUD, by program and region, FY91, annual rpt, 5124–7

Community Relations Service

Activities and funding of CRS investigation and mediation of minority discrimination disputes, FY91, annual rpt, 6004–9

Community treatment centers

see Community-based correctional programs

see Community health services

see Group homes for the handicapped

Commuting

Carpool high occupancy vehicle lanes design, enforcement, and use in selected cities, 1991 conf, 7308–204

Census of Population and Housing, 1990: population and housing characteristics, detailed geographic coverage, State CD-ROM series, 2551–10

Census of Population and Housing, 1990: summary characteristics, by county, subdiv, and place, State rpt series, 2551–7

Census of Population, 1990: commuters, by county of residence and work, for top 10 metro areas, press release, 2328–84

Central business district commuting accessibility, impact on housing prices, for Philadelphia, 1970s-80s, working paper, 9387–8.258

Employees commuting to work, by mode, trip duration, and work location, 1980 and 1990, 7558–120

Employer-provided transit fare subsidies, participation, and parking costs, by selected city, 1985-92, GAO rpt, 26113–597

Energy use by mode of transport, fuel supply, and demographic and economic factors of vehicle use, 1970s-90, annual rpt, 3304–5

Housing (rental) total, HUD-assisted by program, and eligible for aid, recent movers by reason, selected characteristics, and location, 1989, biennial rpt, 5184–11

Housing and households characteristics, unit and neighborhood quality, and journey to work by MSA location, for 11 MSAs, 1985 survey, supplement, 2485–8

Housing and households detailed characteristics, and unit and neighborhood quality, by location, 1989, biennial rpt supplement, 2485–13

Hwy Statistics, summary data by State, 1990-91, annual rpt, 7554–24

Migration, population change, and areas losing population, by region, State, and metro-nonmetro location, 1980s and trends from 1940, Current Population Rpt, 2546–2.164

Pacific territories population and housing detailed characteristics, by location, 1990 Census of Population and Housing, series, 2551–8

Philadelphia metro area transit service operations, costs and benefits, and local economic and air pollution impacts, 1970s-90 and projected to 2020, 7308–205

Safety research on traffic issues, literature review, with data on accidents and impact of safety measures, 1961-90, 7558–98

Travel patterns, personal and household characteristics, and auto and public transport use, 1990 survey, series, 7556–6

see also Buses

see also High-speed ground transportation

see also Pedestrians

see also Subways

see also Urban transportation

Comoros

Agricultural trade of US, by detailed commodity and country, 1991, annual rpt, 1524–8

Agricultural trade of US, by detailed commodity and country, 1991, semiannual rpt, 1522–4

AID economic aid to developing countries, obligations and disbursements by country, quarterly rpt, 9912–4

Background Notes, summary social, political, and economic data, 1992 rpt, 7006–2.12

Economic and military aid and loans from US and intl agencies, by program and country, FY46-91, annual rpt, 9914–5

Economic and social conditions of developing countries from 1960s, and Intl Dev Cooperation Agency and AID activities and funding, FY91-93, annual rpt, 9904–4

Economic, social, political, and geographic summary data, by country, 1992, annual factbook, 9114–2

Exports and imports of US, by transport mode, country, and SITC 1- to 3-digit commodity, 1991, annual rpt, 2424–12

Human rights conditions in 170 countries, and US economic and military aid, 1991, annual rpt, 21384–3

Military aid of US, arms sales, and training programs costs and budget requests, by program, world region, and country, FY91-93, annual rpt, 7144–13

Minerals Yearbook, Vol 3, 1989: foreign country review of production, trade, and policy, by commodity, annual rpt, 5604–35.1

Population size, growth rates, and components of change, by country, projected 1990-2020 and trends from 1950, biennial rpt, 2324–9

UN voting record and share of votes in agreement with US, by issue, country, and world area, 1991, annual rpt, 7004–18

Compact disc data storage

see CD-ROM catalogs and guides

see CD-ROM releases

see CD-ROM technology and use

Companies

see Business acquisitions and mergers

see Business failures and closings

see Business firms and establishments, number

see Business formations

see Corporations

see Ownership of enterprise

see Partnerships

see Proprietorships

see under By Individual Company or Institution in the "Index by Categories"

Compensation

see Claims

see Crime victim compensation

see Earnings, general

see Earnings, local and regional

see Earnings, specific industry

see Employee benefits

see Federal pay

see Military pay

see Payroll

see State and local employees pay

see Torts

Compensatory education
Assistance for compensatory education, and allocation by function, for 8 school districts, 1990/91, GAO rpt, 26121–478
Elementary and secondary education enrollment, staff, finances, operations, programs, and policies, 1987/88 biennial survey, series, 4836–3
Expenditures of Fed Govt in States, by type, program, agency, and State, FY91, annual rpt, 2464–2
Juvenile facilities compensatory education programs activities, participant and staff characteristics, and outcomes, 1991 rpts, 4808–40
Literacy program for preschoolers and parents, Even Start program activities and grants by recipient, FY90, annual listing, 4804–41
see also Bilingual education
see also Head Start Project
see also Remedial education
see also Special education

Competition
Agricultural research and education grants, USDA competitive awards by program and recipient, FY91, annual listing, 1764–1
Banks and thrifts contracts with computer data processing vendors, involvement of illegal business transactions, and instn and vendor views, 1985-90, GAO rpt, 26119–374
Department store advertised sale prices and references to competitors prices, and actual consumer savings, 1990-91 local area study, 9408–57
Electric utilities operation under Public Utility Holding Company Act, with capacity and construction costs, late 1960s-80s, 3006–13.1
Financial instns reform issues, with finances, impacts of deposit insurance changes, and views of depositors and bankers, 1991 hearings, 25248–129
Gasoline service stations price competition and divorcement from oil companies, issues with data by firm, city, and State, 1991 hearing, 25528–120
Health sciences research and training grants and contracts of Natl Inst of General Medical Sciences, by program, FY91, annual rpt, 4474–38
Infant formula bid prices and contracts awarded by States under USDA food aid program for women, infants, and children, late 1980s-91, hearing, 25528–118
Mail volume and employment of USPS, impacts of competition and rate increases, with evaluation of alternative forecast models, 1970s-80s and forecast to 1995, GAO rpt, 26119–384
Military competitive and formally advertised awards, by contractor type and service branch, various periods FY82-1st half FY92, semiannual rpt, 3542–1.2
Military prime contract awards, by size and type of contract, service branch, competitive status, category, and labor standard, FY91, annual rpt, 3544–19
NASA procurement contract awards, by type, contractor, State, and country, FY92 with trends from 1961, semiannual rpt, 9502–6
NIH research and training grants awarded to women, by recipient characteristics, inst, and host instn, FY90, annual rpt, 4434–18
see also Antitrust law
see also Dumping
see also Economic concentration and diversification
see also Foreign competition
see also Monopolies and cartels

Compson, Michael
"Health Insurance Status of Farm Operators, Managers, and Workers, and the President's Health Care Reforms", 1541–1.318
"IRS Estimates of the Aggregate Net Farm Profit (Loss) of Farm Sole Proprietors", 1541–1.320

Comptroller General of the U.S.
see General Accounting Office

Compulsory military service
see Draft evasion and protest
see Selective service

Computer data file guides
American Housing Survey, data coverage, products, and metro areas surveyed 1974-94, 2328–89
BEA rpts data coverage and availability, 1992 annual article, 2702–1.308
BEA rpts data coverage and availability, 1992 annual rpt, 2704–6
Census Bur activities, rpts, and user services, monthly rpt, 2302–3
Census Bur data coverage and availability for economic censuses and related statistics, 1992 preliminary guide, 2308–5
Census Bur data files and rpts, coverage and availability, 1992 annual listing, 2304–2
Census Bur geographic levels of data coverage, maps, and reference products, 1992 rpt, 2308–67
Census Bur rpts and data files, coverage, availability, and use, series, 2326–7
Census Bur rpts and data files, monthly listing, 2302–6
Census of Population and Housing, 1990: data coverage, collection procedures, products and services availability, and uses, guide, 2555–1
Census of Population and Housing, 1990: detailed geographic coverage, CD-ROM user guide, 2308–65
Census of Population and Housing, 1990: maps and cartographic products availability, listing, 2308–66
Educational performance and conditions, characteristics, attitudes, activities, and plans, 1988 8th grade class, natl longitudinal survey, series, 4826–9
Energy Info Admin activities, 1991, annual rpt, 3164–29
Energy Info Admin forecasting and data analysis models, 1992, annual listing, 3164–87
Energy Info Admin rpts and data files, 1991, annual listing, 3164–98
Energy use, costs, and conservation, and household and housing characteristics, survey rpt series, 3166–7
Fed Govt standards for data recording, processing, and transfer, and for purchase and use of computer systems, series, 2216–2
Global climate change contributing pollutants, emissions by monitoring site and country, and temperature change by world area and US region, 1860s-1990, annual rpt, 3004–33
Library of Congress rpts and products, 1992-93, biennial listing, 26404–6
Map and geographic computer-readable database of Census Bur, TIGER files availability and use, 1991 rpt, 2628–32
NTIS computer software and documentation, 1992 annual listing, 2224–2
Ocean pollution research projects, rpts and data files, FY84-87, listing, 2158–51
Survey of Income and Program Participation, data collection, methodology, and availability, 1991 users guide, 2628–24
see also CD-ROM catalogs and guides

Computer industry and products
Banks in Fed Reserve System, expenses and operations itemized by service, office, and district, 1991, annual rpt, 9364–11
Capital investment changes relation to changes in costs, by asset type and industry div, late 1950s-80s, article, 9373–1.304
Competitiveness (intl) of US high technology industries, with background data by industry and foreign comparisons, 1960s-91, GAO rpt, 26123–406
Competitiveness (intl) of US manufacturing industry, trade and economic policies with background data and foreign comparisons, 1991 rpt, 26358–252
County Business Patterns, 1989: employment, establishments, and payroll, by SIC 2- to 4-digit industry and county, annual State rpt series, 2326–8
County Business Patterns, 1990: employment, establishments, and payroll, by SIC 2- to 4-digit industry and county, annual State rpt series, 2326–6
Employment, earnings, and hours, by SIC 1- to 4-digit industry, monthly 1989-Feb 1992, annual rpt, 6744–4
Exports and imports between US and outlying areas, by detailed commodity and mode of transport, 1991, annual rpt, 2424–11
Exports and imports of US, by country and detailed commodity, monthly rpt, 2422–12
Exports and imports of US, by Harmonized System 6-digit commodity and country, 1991, annual rpt, 2424–13
Exports and imports of US, by transport mode, country, and SITC 1- to 3-digit commodity, 1991, annual rpt, 2424–12
Exports of US, detailed Schedule B commodities with countries of destination, 1991, annual rpt, 2424–10
Fed Govt data processing use and dev, Natl Archives special collection, 1988 rpt, 9516–1.8
Fed Govt info storage and transmission on electronic formats, costs and revenues for 4 agencies, FY85-91, GAO rpt, 26125–47
Fed Govt standards for data recording, processing, and transfer, and for purchase and use of computer systems, series, 2216–2
GSA activities and finances, FY91, annual rpt, 9454–1

House of Representatives salaries, expenses, and contingent fund disbursement, detailed listings, quarterly rpt, 21942-1
Imports of US given duty-free treatment for value of US material sent abroad, by commodity and country, 1987-90, annual rpt, 9884-14
Input-output structure of US economy, detailed interindustry transactions for 541 industries, and components of final demand, 1982 benchmark data, 2708-17
Mail volume to and from households, use, and views, by class, source, content, and household characteristics, FY87-90, annual rpt, 9864-10
Manufacturing annual survey, 1990: finances and operations, by SIC 2- to 4-digit industry, series, 2506-14
Manufacturing census, 1987: concentration of largest firms measured by value added, and for shipments by SIC 2- and 4-digit industry, subject rpt, 2497-6
Manufacturing census, 1987: shipments of manufacturers products, by customer class and SIC 2- and 4-digit industry, subject rpt, 2497-4
Manufacturing finances and operations, by SIC 2- to 4-digit industry, forecast 1992, annual rpt, 2044-28
Memory components from South Korea at less than fair value, injury to US industry, investigation with background financial and operating data, 1992 rpt, 9886-14.348
Military prime contract awards, by detailed procurement category, FY88-91, annual rpt, 3544-18
Modem shipments, trade, use, and firms, 1991, annual Current Industrial Rpt, 2506-12.35
Natl income and product accounts, comprehensive accounts and components, benchmark revisions, 1929-88, 2708-5
Natl income and product accounts, comprehensive accounts and components, *Survey of Current Business*, monthly rpt, 2702-1.28
NTIS computer software and documentation, 1992 annual listing, 2224-2
Occupational injury and illness rates, by SIC 2- to 4-digit industry, 1989-90, annual rpt, 6844-7
Occupational injury and illness rates, by SIC 2- to 4-digit industry, 1990, annual rpt, 6844-1
OECD trade, total and for 4 major countries, and US trade by country, by commodity, 1980-90, world area rpt series, 9116-1
Price indexes (producer), by stage of processing and detailed commodity, monthly rpt, 6762-6
Price indexes (producer), by stage of processing and detailed commodity, monthly 1991, annual rpt, 6764-2
Productivity relation to high technology capital investment, by industry sector, 1940s-80s, technical paper, 9385-8.130
Shipments, trade, use, and firms, for office machines by product, 1991, annual Current Industrial Rpt, 2506-12.2
Soviet Union and US economic and sociodemographic indicators, selected years 1970-90, handbook, 2328-80
Statistical Abstract of US, 1992 annual data compilation, 2324-1.27
see also CD-ROM catalogs and guides
see also CD-ROM releases
see also CD-ROM technology and use
see also Computer data file guides
see also Computer networks
see also Computer sciences
see also Computer use
see also Industrial robots
see also Information storage and retrieval systems
see also Semiconductors

Computer networks
BEA rpts data coverage and availability, 1992 annual article, 2702-1.308
Bombings involving manufacturing instructions posted on computer bulletin boards, 1987-91, annual rpt, 8484-4.1
Fed Govt standards for data recording, processing, and transfer, and for purchase and use of computer systems, series, 2216-2
Finances and operations, by SIC 2- to 4-digit industry, forecast 1992, annual rpt, 2044-28
Telecommunications industry intl competitiveness, structure, and devs, with background data and foreign comparisons, 1991 rpt, 2808-30
see also Automated tellers
see also Electronic funds transfer

Computer programmers
see Computer use

Computer sciences
Degrees awarded in higher education, by level, field, race, and sex, 1989/90 and trends from 1980/81, annual rpt, 4844-17
DOT employment, by subagency, occupation, and selected personnel characteristics, FY91, annual rpt, 7304-18
Employment of scientists, engineers, and technicians in manufacturing, by field and industry, 1989, triennial rpt, 9627-23
Fed Govt aid to higher education and nonprofit instns for R&D and related activities, by field, instn, agency, and State, FY90, annual rpt, 9627-17
Higher education grad programs enrollment in science and engineering, by field, source of funds, and characteristics of student and instn, 1990, annual rpt, 9627-7
Labor demand, turnover, and training completions, by detailed occupation, 1990 and projected to 2005, biennial rpt, 6744-3
Minority group, women, and disabled persons employment and education in science and engineering, by field, mid 1970s-91, biennial rpt, 9624-20
NASA R&D funding to higher education instns, by field, instn, and State, FY91, annual listing, 9504-7
NSF activities, finances, and funding by program, FY91, annual rpt, 9624-6
NSF R&D grant awards, by div and program, periodic rpt series, 9626-7
Occupational Outlook Handbook, 1992-93, biennial rpt, 6744-1
R&D facilities of higher education instns, space and equipment adequacy, needs, and funding by source, by instn type and control, 1992, biennial rpt, 9624-25
R&D funding by higher education instns and federally funded centers, by field, instn, and State, FY90, annual rpt, 9627-13
Science and Engineering Indicators, employment, education, R&D funding, and industry impacts, with foreign comparisons, 1960s-91, biennial rpt, 9624-10
Small business R&D grants of Fed Govt, by program area, agency, MSA, and State, FY90, annual rpt, 9764-7

Computer software
see Computer industry and products

Computer use
Air Force fiscal mgmt system operations and techniques, quarterly rpt, 3602-1
Air traffic control and airway facilities staff, by employment and other characteristics, FY90, annual rpt, 7504-41
Banks and thrifts contracts with computer data processing vendors, involvement of illegal business transactions, and instn and vendor views, 1985-90, GAO rpt, 26119-374
Banks and thrifts finances and operations by deposit size, Fed Reserve functional cost analysis, 1991, annual rpt, 9364-6
Banks in Fed Reserve System, expenses and operations itemized by service, office, and district, 1991, annual rpt, 9364-11
County Business Patterns, 1989: employment, establishments, and payroll, by SIC 2- to 4-digit industry and county, annual State rpt series, 2326-8
County Business Patterns, 1990: employment, establishments, and payroll, by SIC 2- to 4-digit industry and county, annual State rpt series, 2326-6
Criminal justice systems activities, spending, and employment, by level of govt, data compilation, 1992 annual rpt, 6064-6.1
DOE contractor computer system security and controls at Strategic Petroleum Reserve offices, 1991, 3006-5.27
Earnings, annual average percent changes for selected occupational groups, selected MSAs, monthly rpt, 6782-1.1
Education data compilation, 1992 annual rpt, 4824-2
Education in math, elementary and secondary students computer and calculator use and availability, by grade level, 1990 natl assessment, fact sheet, 4896-9.1
Education in science and math, course participation, instruction, and performance, by selected characteristics, 1988 8th grade class, natl longitudinal survey, 1992 rpt, 4826-9.13
Educational performance of elementary and secondary students, and factors affecting proficiency, by selected characteristics, 1990 natl assessments, subject rpt series, 4896-8
Educational performance of elementary and secondary students in math, science, reading, and writing, 1969-90, 4898-32
Employment and economic conditions, alternative BLS projections to 2005 and trends 1975-90, biennial rpt, 6744-19
Employment, earnings, and hours, by SIC 1- to 4-digit industry, monthly 1989-Feb 1992, annual rpt, 6744-4

Employment, unemployment, and labor force characteristics, by region and census div, 1991, annual rpt, 6744–7.1
Exports and imports of services, direct and among multinatl firms affiliates, by industry and world area, 1986-91, article, 2702–1.336
FBI fingerprint identification system automation costs, staff, and workload, FY90 and projected to FY2000, 26358–253
Fed Govt standards for data recording, processing, and transfer, and for purchase and use of computer systems, series, 2216–2
Fed Reserve System, Bd of Governors, and district banks financial statements, performance, and fiscal services, 1991-92, annual rpt, 9364–10
Industry finances and operations, by SIC 2- to 4-digit industry, forecast 1992, annual rpt, 2044–28
Input-output structure of US economy, detailed interindustry transactions for 541 industries, and components of final demand, 1982 benchmark data, 2708–17
Labor demand, turnover, and training completions, by detailed occupation, 1990 and projected to 2005, biennial rpt, 6744–3
Military in-house commercial activities work-years, by service branch, State, and installation, FY91, annual rpt, 3544–25
Multinatl US firms and foreign affiliates finances and operations, by industry and country, 1989 benchmark survey, annual rpt, 2704–5
Occupational injury and illness rates, by SIC 2- to 4-digit industry, 1989-90, annual rpt, 6844–7
Occupational injury and illness rates, by SIC 2- to 4-digit industry, 1990, annual rpt, 6844–1
Occupational musculoskeletal disorders from computer video display terminal use, among telephone industry workers, 1990, 4248–93
Occupational Outlook Handbook, 1992-93, biennial rpt, 6744–1
Police agencies employment, spending, and operations, FY90, 6066–25.44
Police employment, spending, and operations, for State, city, county, and special district agencies, 1990, annual rpt, 6064–39
Schools (elementary and secondary) computer use, by grade level, 1992 edition, annual rpt, 4824–2.30
Sheriffs' agencies employment, spending, and operations, FY90, 6066–25.45
Statistical Abstract of US, 1992 annual data compilation, 2324–1.4; 2324–1.13; 2324–1.28
Students computer use at home and school, by selected characteristics, 1992 edition, annual rpt, 4824–2.30
Tax (income) returns filed, by type, IRS service center, and whether full-paid, refund, and electronically filed, 1990 and projected to 1998, semiannual rpt, 8302–7
Tax (income) returns filed using alternative methods, with fraud, and conventional form preparation time and processing costs, 1986-92, GAO rpt, 26119–400
Tax (income) returns of individuals, by filing status, tax item, and income level, 1991, annual article, 8302–2.319
Tax (income) returns of individuals, IRS processing and taxpayer info activity, electronic and experimental filings, and refunds, periodic press release, 8302–6
Tax (income) returns of sole proprietorships, income statement items, by industry group, 1990, annual article, 8302–2.317; 8302–2.320
Tax (income) withholding and related documents filed, by type and IRS service center, 1991 and projected 1992-99, annual rpt, 8304–22
Tax returns filed, by type of tax, whether electronically filed, and IRS region and service center, projected 1991-98 and trends from 1978, annual rpt, 8304–9
Tax returns filed electronically, by tax type, region, and State, FY86-91, annual rpt, 8304–3.1
Training for job qualification and skill improvement, workers participating by training source, occupation, age, sex, and race, 1991, 6728–32
Voter registration and verification data storage and retrieval systems use and characteristics, for selected counties, 1992 rpt, 9278–8
Workplace computer use, by selected worker characteristics, 1992 edition, annual rpt, 4824–2.30
see also Automation
see also CD-ROM technology and use
see also Computer networks
see also Computer sciences
see also Economic and econometric models
see also Mathematic models and modeling

COMSAT
see Communications Satellite Corp.

COMSIS Corp.
"Federal Transit Administration: 1990 Section 15 Annual Report. Data Tables", 7884–4.1

Comstock, George W.
"Tuberculosis in a Small Semi-Rural County", 4042–3.319

Concentration, business
see Economic concentration and diversification

Concrete
see Cement and concrete

Condemnation of property
see Property condemnation

Condominiums and cooperatives
American Housing Survey: unit and households detailed characteristics, and unit and neighborhood quality, MSA rpt series, 2485–6
Census of Population and Housing, 1990: population and housing characteristics, detailed geographic coverage, State CD-ROM series, 2551–10
Census of Population and Housing, 1990: summary characteristics, by county, subdiv, and place, State rpt series, 2551–7
HUD grants to aid purchase of multifamily housing units, by recipient, 1992, press release, 5006–3.91
Market absorption rate and characteristics, 1990, annual Current Housing Rpt, 2484–2
Market absorption rates for condominiums, and completions by sales price, quarterly rpt, 2482–2
Mortgages FHA-insured for 1-family units, by loan type and mortgage characteristics, quarterly rpt, 5142–45
New condominium units completed and absorption rates, by size and price class, preliminary 1991, annual Current Housing Rpt, 2484–3
New condominium units completed, by size, price, and location, 1991, annual rpt, 2384–1.7
New condominiums, by intended use, units per structure, tenure, and region, monthly rpt, annual tables, 2382–1
NYC housing supply, occupancy, condition, and household characteristics, by tenure and borough, 1991 triennial survey, 2488–3
Pacific territories population and housing detailed characteristics, by location, 1990 Census of Population and Housing, series, 2551–8
Rental units conversion to condos and coops, households displaced by whether receiving HUD assistance, selected other characteristics, and location, 1989, biennial rpt, 5184–11
Savings instns failures, inventory of real estate assets available from Resolution Trust Corp, 1991, semiannual listing, 9722–2.5
Savings instns failures, inventory of real estate assets available from Resolution Trust Corp, 1992, semiannual listing, 9722–2.12
Tax (income) returns filed, by type of return and IRS district, 1990 and projected 1991-98, annual rpt, 8304–24
Tax (income) returns filed, by type of tax and IRS region and service center, projected 1991-98 and trends from 1978, annual rpt, 8304–9
Tax (income) returns of corporations, income and tax items by asset size and detailed industry, 1989, annual rpt, 8304–4; 8304–21

Condoms
see Contraceptives

Confectionery products
see Candy and confectionery products

Conferences
Accident deaths and injuries prevention, and treatment, 1991 conf papers, 4208–35
AIDS-like idiopathic CD4+ T-lymphocytopenia epidemiology and patient characteristics, 1992 conf, 4208–36
AIDS prevention programs for drug abusers and their sexual partners, client characteristics, and outcomes, for selected metro areas, 1989 annual conf, 4494–12
AIDS virus infection among drug abusers, disease progression longitudinal studies, 1987 conf papers, 4498–79
Air traffic and other aviation activity forecasts of FAA, 1992 annual conf, 7504–28
Banks financial performance, risk assessment, and regulation, 1991 annual conf papers, 9375–7
Carpool high occupancy vehicle lanes design, enforcement, and use in selected cities, 1991 conf, 7308–204

Census Bur data collection and statistical program plans, advisory committees findings and recommendations, 1992 conf, 2628–35
Coastal areas environmental conditions and mgmt, for individual areas, conf series, 2146–8
Drug abuse and treatment, research on biological and behavioral factors and addiction potential of new drugs, 1991 annual conf, 4494–11
Drug abuse indicators for selected metro areas, research results, data collection, and policy issues, 1992 semiannual conf, 4492–5
Drug abuse prevention services evaluation, methodological issues, 1991 conf, 4498–78
Drug abuse treatment and education programs for prisoners and parolees, activities, costs, and outcomes, 1990 conf, 4498–77
Drug abuse treatment services costs, effectiveness, and financing issues, 1991 conf papers, 4498–80
EC economic integration impacts on domestic and intl agricultural conditions, 1990 conf, 1528–325
Farm financial and marketing conditions, forecast 1992, annual conf, 1504–9
Fed Govt agencies administrative records and other holdings of Natl Archives, final inventories, series, 9516–2
Financial and monetary studies, Fed Reserve Bank of Boston conf series, 9373–3
Financial and monetary studies, Fed Reserve Bank of Kansas City conf series, 9381–13
Fires on wildlands, ecology, mgmt, cultural impacts, and historic patterns, 1990 conf, 1208–415
Fish and shellfish aquaculture in US and Japan, mgmt, methods, and biological data for selected species, 1990 conf, annual rpt, 2164–15
Fish and shellfish catch and stocks in northwest Atlantic, by species and location, 1887-1991 and forecast to 1993, semiannual conf, 2162–9
Fish catch, driftnet fishing impacts, and fish feeding, habitat, and other characteristics, for north Pacific Ocean, 1988 conf, 2168–131
Forest Service Rocky Mountain Forest and Range Experiment Station rpts, 1980-89, listing, 1208–403
Glaciology intl research summaries, methodology, and bibls, series, 2156–18
Health and vital statistics data collection, and use for planning and evaluation, 1989 biennial conf papers, 4164–2
Health condition and quality of life measurement, rpts and other info sources, quarterly listing, 4122–1
HHS financial aid, by program, recipient, State, and city, FY91, annual regional listings, 4004–3
Hwy construction zones traffic control and safety procedures and equipment, 1991 conf, 7558–115
Infant health, deaths and risk factors, and prevention issues, for US and selected countries, 1990 conf, 4148–28
Info services, access, policy, technology, and other issues, recommendations, 1991 conf, 15638–16
Injury prevention and treatment, 1991 conf summary, 4206–2.56
Judicial Conf proceedings and findings, spring 1992, semiannual rpt, 18202–2
Library of Congress activities, acquisitions, services, and financial statements, FY91, annual rpt, 26404–1
Mines (underground) diesel engine exhaust emissions measurement and control, 1992 conf, 5608–177
Mink and otter population, breeding, trapping, pollutant levels, and research status, for Great Lakes area, 1991 conf, 14648–27
North American Free Trade Agreement proposal for Canada, US, and Mexico, economic impacts, alternative model descriptions, 1992 conf, 9886–4.182
Nuclear power plant decommissioning and radioactive waste site remedial actions, bibl, 1991 annual listing, 3354–12
Pension plan finances, participation, and benefits, for 9 OECD countries, with data by firm and worker characteristics, 1990 conf, 6688–2
Physicians payment by Medicare under fee schedule, profiling uses and impacts on practices, 1992 conf, 17266–2.10
Savings instns regulatory issues, 1989 annual conf, 9304–24
Telecommunications and Info Natl Admin rpts, FY91, annual listing, 2804–3
Timber in Pacific Northwest, old-growth forests plant and wildlife population and species diversity, 1991 compilation of papers, 1208–386
Timber in Rocky Mountains and southwest US, old growth forests ecology, mgmt, and research methods, 1992 conf, 1208–421
Timber in southeastern US, resources mgmt and research, 1990 biennial conf papers, 1204–35
VA health care services, needs, availability, structure, and funding, 1991 compilation of papers, 8608–9
Vital and Health Statistics Natl Committee activities, FY91, annual narrative rpt, 4164–1
Weather conditions and forecasts, data collection and analysis issues, 1991 annual conf, 2184–10
Weights, measures, and performance standards dev, proposals, and policies, 1992 annual conf, 2214–7
Wetlands (coastal) mapping projects status, costs, and methods, 1990 conf, 5508–116

Conflict of interests
Fed Govt agencies ethics regulation, activities, and staff, 1991, biennial rpt, 9834–1
Fed Govt employees moonlighting, selected characteristics of 2nd job and Federal position, FY88-90, GAO rpt, 26119–386
Foreign countries interests represented by former US govt officials, activities and individuals, FY86-91, GAO rpt, 26123–134
R&D licenses for university activities supported by NSF and NIH, transfer to private firms, related income, and scientists associated with licensees, FY89-90, GAO rpt, 26113–575
Sentences for Federal offenses, guidelines by offense and circumstances, series, 17668–1
US attorneys civil and criminal cases by type and disposition, and collections, by Federal district, FY91, annual rpt, 6004–2.1

Congenital malformations
see Birth defects

Conglomerates
see Business acquisitions and mergers
see Economic concentration and diversification

Congo
Agricultural trade of US, by detailed commodity and country, 1991, annual rpt, 1524–8
Agricultural trade of US, by detailed commodity and country, 1991, semiannual rpt, 1522–4
AID economic aid to developing countries, obligations and disbursements by country, quarterly rpt, 9912–4
Economic and military aid and loans from US and intl agencies, by program and country, FY46-91, annual rpt, 9914–5
Economic and social conditions of developing countries from 1960s, and Intl Dev Cooperation Agency and AID activities and funding, FY91-93, annual rpt, 9904–4
Economic conditions, income, production, prices, employment, and trade, 1992 periodic country rpt, 2046–4.43
Economic, social, political, and geographic summary data, by country, 1992, annual factbook, 9114–2
Exports and imports of US, by commodity and country, 1980-90, world area rpt, 9116–1.2
Exports and imports of US, by transport mode, country, and SITC 1- to 3-digit commodity, 1991, annual rpt, 2424–12
Exports, imports, and balances of US for manufactured goods, by SITC 2-digit commodity and country, quarterly rpt, 2042–35
Exports of US, detailed Schedule B commodities with countries of destination, 1991, annual rpt, 2424–10
Human rights conditions in 170 countries, and US economic and military aid, 1991, annual rpt, 21384–3
Military aid of US, arms sales, and training programs costs and budget requests, by program, world region, and country, FY91-93, annual rpt, 7144–13
Military spending, arms trade, and force strengths, with govt spending and population, by country, 1979-89, annual rpt, 9824–1
Minerals Yearbook, Vol 3, 1989: foreign country review of production, trade, and policy, by commodity, annual rpt, 5604–35.1
Population size, growth rates, and components of change, by country, projected 1990-2020 and trends from 1950, biennial rpt, 2324–9
Refugee migration, and intl aid programs, by world area and country of origin and asylum, 1991, annual rpt, 7004–15
UN voting record and share of votes in agreement with US, by issue, country, and world area, 1991, annual rpt, 7004–18

Congress
Air travel by Federal officials and Congress aboard military aircraft, and aircraft inventory characteristics, 1989-91, GAO rpt, 26123-384
Budget of US, authoritative financial statements with appropriations, outlays, and receipts, by agency, FY91, annual rpt, 8104-2
Budget of US, obligations and authority by function, agency, and program, with summaries and analyses, FY93, annual rpt, 104-2
Budget of US, receipts by source, outlays by agency and program, and balances, monthly rpt, 8102-3
Election voter turnout by age and sex, 1990 congressional elections, with trends from 1964, fact sheet, 2326-17.39
Financial operations of Fed Govt, detailed data, *Treasury Bulletin*, quarterly rpt, 8002-4
Mail (franked) to households, by content, FY87-90, annual rpt, 9864-10
Statistical Abstract of US, 1992 annual data compilation, 2324-1.8
see also Architect of the Capitol
see also Congressional apportionment
see also Congressional Budget Office
see also Congressional committees
see also Congressional districts
see also Congressional employees
see also Congressional-executive relations
see also Congressional investigations
see also Congressional joint committees
see also Congressional powers
see also General Accounting Office
see also Government Printing Office
see also House of Representatives
see also Library of Congress
see also Office of Technology Assessment
see also Senate

Congressional apportionment
Statistical Abstract of US, 1992 annual data compilation, 2324-1.8

Congressional Budget Office
Budget deficit reduction under Gramm-Rudman Act, CBO sequestration estimates, FY93, annual rpt, 26304-6
Budget of US, authoritative financial statements with appropriations, outlays, and receipts, by category and agency, FY91, annual rpt, 8104-2.2
Budget of US, CBO analysis and review of FY93 budget by function, annual rpt, 26304-2
Budget of US, CBO analysis of revenue and spending alternatives and projections of economic indicators, FY93-97, annual rpt, 26304-3
Budget of US, obligations and authority by function, agency, and program, with summaries and analyses, FY93, annual rpt, 104-2
Fed Govt agencies budget requests and program costs and characteristics, series, 26306-3
Fed Govt programs of congressional interest, objectives, feasibility, benefits, and costs, series, 26306-6

Congressional committees
Budget of US, House concurrent resolution, with spending and revenue targets, FY93 and projected to FY97, annual rpt, 21264-2
House of Representatives salaries, expenses, and contingent fund disbursement, detailed listings, quarterly rpt, 21942-1
Senate receipts, itemized expenses by payee, and balances, 1st half FY92, semiannual listing, 25922-1
see also Congressional joint committees
see also House Administration Committee
see also House Aging Committee, Select
see also House Banking, Finance and Urban Affairs Committee
see also House Budget Committee
see also House District of Columbia Committee
see also House Education and Labor Committee
see also House Energy and Commerce Committee
see also House Foreign Affairs Committee
see also House Government Operations Committee
see also House Hunger Committee, Select
see also House Interior and Insular Affairs Committee
see also House Merchant Marine and Fisheries Committee
see also House Post Office and Civil Service Committee
see also House Public Works and Transportation Committee
see also House Science, Space, and Technology Committee
see also House Small Business Committee
see also House Veterans Affairs Committee
see also House Ways and Means Committee
see also Joint Economic Committee
see also Joint Taxation Committee
see also Senate Aging Committee, Special
see also Senate Agriculture, Nutrition, and Forestry Committee
see also Senate Banking, Housing, and Urban Affairs Committee
see also Senate Commerce, Science and Transportation Committee
see also Senate Energy and Natural Resources Committee
see also Senate Finance Committee
see also Senate Foreign Relations Committee
see also Senate Governmental Affairs Committee
see also Senate Intelligence Committee, Select
see also Senate Judiciary Committee
see also Senate Labor and Human Resources Committee
see also Senate Small Business Committee
see also under names of individual subcommittees (starting with Subcommittee)

Congressional districts
Census Bur data coverage and availability for statistics on counties, cities, and small areas, 1991 rpt, 2326-7.82
Census Bur geographic levels of data coverage, maps, and reference products, 1992 rpt, 2308-67
Census of Population and Housing, 1990: detailed geographic coverage, State CD-ROM series, 2551-9
Census of Population and Housing, 1990: population and housing characteristics, detailed geographic coverage, State CD-ROM series, 2551-10
Election campaign finances of House and Senate candidates, by State and district, 1990 natl elections, 9276-2.2
Election campaign-related internal communications of firms and assns, spending by organization, location, and candidate, 1991-92, biennial rpt, 9274-3
Energy conservation aid of Fed Govt to public and nonprofit private instns, by building type and State, 1991, annual rpt, 3304-15
Fed Govt spending in States and local areas, by type, State, county, and city, FY91, annual rpt, 2464-3
Forests (natl) and other lands under Forest Service mgmt, acreage by forest and location, 1991 and historic trends, annual rpt, 1204-2
Forests (natl) revenue share paid to States, and acreage, by forest, county, and congressional district, FY92, annual rpt, 1204-33
HHS financial aid, by program, recipient, State, and city, FY91, annual regional listings, 4004-3
Military spending reductions, economic impacts by defense contractor, industry, State, and congressional district, 1989-90 hearings, 23848-224
NSF grants and contracts, by field, recipient, and State, FY90, annual rpt, 9624-26
Statistical Abstract of US, 1992 annual data compilation, 2324-1.8
VA programs spending, by State, county, and congressional district, FY91, annual rpt, 8604-6
see also Congressional apportionment

Congressional employees
Capitol Architect activities, funding, costs, and contracts, FY89, annual rpt, 25944-1
Capitol Architect outlays for salaries, supplies, and services, itemized by payee and function, 2nd half FY91, semiannual rpt, 25922-2
Employment and payroll (civilian) of Fed Govt, by pay system, agency, and location, 1991, annual rpt, 9844-6.1; 9844-6.2
Employment, earnings, and hours, by SIC 1- to 4-digit industry, monthly 1989-Feb 1992, annual rpt, 6744-4
Former US govt officials representing foreign interests, activities and individuals, FY86-91, GAO rpt, 26123-134
House of Representatives salaries, expenses, and contingent fund disbursement, detailed listings, quarterly rpt, 21942-1
Senate receipts, itemized expenses by payee, and balances, 1st half FY92, semiannual listing, 25922-1
Statistical Abstract of US, 1992 annual data compilation, 2324-1.8

Congressional-executive relations
Arms Control and Disarmament Agency activities, and treaties status, 1991, annual rpt, 9824-2
Block grants discretionary spending, congressional changes to set-aside and cost-ceiling requirements for 11 programs, FY82-91, GAO rpt, 26121-466
Budget of US, CBO analysis and review of FY93 budget by function, annual rpt, 26304-2
HHS cost savings from legislative actions and proposals, 1st half FY92, semiannual rpt, 4002-6

see also Executive impoundment of appropriated funds
Congressional investigations
House of Representatives salaries, expenses, and contingent fund disbursement, detailed listings, quarterly rpt, 21942–1
Senate receipts, itemized expenses by payee, and balances, 1st half FY92, semiannual listing, 25922–1
see also General Accounting Office
Congressional joint committees
Budget of US, authoritative financial statements with appropriations, outlays, and receipts, by category and agency, FY91, annual rpt, 8104–2.2
see also Joint Economic Committee
see also Joint Taxation Committee
Congressional powers
Budget of US, House concurrent resolution, with spending and revenue targets, FY93 and projected to FY97, annual rpt, 21264–2
Immigration and nationality bills introduced and laws enacted, 77th-102nd Congresses, annual rpt, 6264–2.5
see also Congressional-executive relations
Congressional Research Service
"Airbus Industrie: An Economic and Trade Perspective", 21708–132
"Demographic Change and the Economy of the Nineties", 23848–226
"Older Workers in the Labor Market", 21148–65
see also Library of Congress
Connecticut
Banks (insured commercial and savings) deposits by instn, State, MSA, and county, as of June 1991, annual regional rpt, 9295–3.1
County Business Patterns, 1990: employment, establishments, and payroll, by SIC 2- to 4-digit industry and county, annual State rpt, 2326–6.8
Deaths and rates, by detailed location, cause, and demographic characteristics, 1989, US Vital Statistics annual rpt, 4144–3.1
Economic indicators for New England States, Fed Reserve 1st District, monthly rpt, 9373–2
Employment, earnings, and hours, by selected SIC 1- to 4-digit industry, State, and for 275 MSAs, 1987-92, 6748–81
Fed Govt spending in States and local areas, by type, State, county, and city, FY91, annual rpt, 2464–3
Fed Govt spending in States, by type, program, agency, and State, FY91, annual rpt, 2464–2
HHS financial aid, by program, recipient, State, and city, FY91, annual regional listing, 4004–3.1
Hospital deaths of Medicare patients, actual and expected rates by diagnosis, and hospital characteristics, by instn, FY90 annual State rpt, 4654–14.7
Housing census, 1990: summary unit characteristics, by householder race and age, county, place, and urban-rural location, State rpt, 2471–1.8
Medicaid impacts on State budgets, and program financing, cost control measures, enrollment, and services coverage, by selected State, 1960s-80s and projected to 1997, 10176–3.6
Military prime contract awards, by contractor, service branch, State, and city, FY91, annual rpt, 3544–22
Mineral Industry Surveys, State reviews of production, 1991, preliminary annual rpt, 5614–6
Minerals Yearbook, Vol 2, 1990: State review of production and sales by commodity, and business activity, annual rpt, 5604–22.8
Multinatl firms US affiliates finances and operations, by industry, country of parent firm, and State, 1987, 2708–48
Physicians, by specialty, age, sex, and location of training and practice, 1990, State rpt, 4116–6.7
Population and housing census, 1990: detailed geographic coverage, State CD-ROM, 2551–9.1
Population and housing census, 1990: population and housing characteristics, detailed geographic coverage, State CD-ROM, 2551–10.10
Population and housing census, 1990: summary characteristics, by county, subdiv, and place, State rpt, 2551–7.8
Population census, 1990: population characteristics and living arrangements, by county, place, and urban-rural location, State rpt, 2531–1.8
Statistical Abstract of US, 1992 annual data compilation, 2324–1
Wages by occupation, for office and plant workers, 1992 survey, periodic MSA rpt, 6785–3.4
Water supply in northeastern US, precipitation and stream runoff by station, monthly rpt, 2182–3
see also Bristol, Conn.
see also Danbury, Conn.
see also Hartford, Conn.
see also New Britain, Conn.
see also under By State in the "Index by Categories"
Conrail
see Consolidated Rail Corp.
Conscription
see Draft evasion and protest
see Selective service
Conservation of natural resources
Agricultural and water conservation programs of USDA, cost sharing payments and eligibility requirements, FY88-92, GAO rpt, 26113–572
Agricultural Conservation Program acreage and projects, by State, 1936-90, quinquennial rpt, 1808–1
Agricultural Conservation Program funding, by practice, region and State, monthly rpt, 1802–15
Agricultural Stabilization and Conservation Service producer payments, by program and State, 1991, annual table, 1804–12
Agricultural Statistics, 1991, annual rpt, 1004–1
Appalachia local dev projects, and funding by source, by program and State, FY91, annual rpt, 9084–1
Assistance (block and categorical grants) programs for State and local govts, FY91, biennial listing, 10044–8
Assistance (financial and nonfinancial) of Fed Govt, 1992 base edition, annual listing, 104–5
Budget of US, balances of budget authority obligated and unobligated, by function and agency, FY90-93, annual rpt, 104–8
Budget of US, Bush Admin proposals, with detail for defense budgets, and historical data from FY34, FY93, 108–46
Budget of US, CBO analysis and review of FY93 budget by function, annual rpt, 26304–2
Budget of US, CBO analysis of revenue and spending alternatives and projections of economic indicators, FY93-97, annual rpt, 26304–3
Budget of US, House concurrent resolution, with spending and revenue targets, FY93 and projected to FY97, annual rpt, 21264–2
Budget of US, midsession review of FY93 budget, by function, annual rpt, 104–7
Budget of US, obligations and authority by function, agency, and program, with summaries and analyses, FY93, annual rpt, 104–2
Budget of US, receipts by source, outlays by agency and program, and balances, monthly rpt, 8102–3
Construction put in place, permits, housing sales, costs, material prices, and employment, quarterly rpt with articles, 2042–1
Construction put in place, value of new public and private structures, by type, monthly rpt, 2382–4
Developing countries economic, population, and agricultural data, US and other aid sources, and AID activity, country rpt series, 9916–12
Environmental Quality, status of problems, protection programs, research, and intl issues, 1991 annual rpt, 484–1
Fed Govt accounts receivable, delinquent debt cases and collections of Justice Dept and private law firms, pilot project results, FY91, annual rpt, 6004–20
Fed Govt construction spending, by type of structure, FY85-92, annual article, 2042–1.303
Fed Govt labor productivity, indexes of output and labor costs by function, FY67-90, annual rpt, 6824–1.6
Fed Govt spending in States, by type, program, agency, and State, FY91, annual rpt, 2464–2
Fish and Wildlife Service restoration programs funding, land purchases, and project listing, by State, FY90, annual rpt, 5504–1
FmHA loans, by type, borrower race, and State, quarterly rpt, 1182–5
Forest Service activities and finances, by region and State, FY91, annual rpt, 1204–1
Govt direct spending and employment, by function and level of govt, selected years 1962-87, 10048–53
Govt employment and payroll, by function, level of govt, and jurisdiction, annual rpt series, 2466–1
Govt finances, by level of govt, State, and for large cities and counties, annual rpt series, 2466–2
Interior Dept programs fraud and abuse, audits and investigations, 2nd half FY92, semiannual rpt, 5302–2

Investigations of GAO, 1991, listing, 26106–10.6
Land Mgmt Bur activities and finances, and public land acreage and use, annual State rpt series, 5724–11
Landmarks (natl historic and natural) damaged and threatened, with owner, location, damage type, and recommended remedial action, 1990, annual listing, 5544–16
Military prime contract awards, by detailed procurement category, FY88-91, annual rpt, 3544–18
Natl income and product accounts, comprehensive accounts and components, benchmark revisions, 1929-88, 2708–5
Natl income and product accounts, comprehensive accounts and components, *Survey of Current Business*, monthly rpt, 2702–1.26
R&D funding by Fed Govt, by detailed function, program, and agency, FY91-93, annual rpt, 9627–9
State and local govt employment of minorities and women, by occupation, function, and pay level, 1991, annual rpt, 9244–6.4
TVA finances and operations by program and facility, FY91, annual rpt, 9804–32
Wetlands preservation under Water Bank Program, acreage, agreements, and payments, by State, monthly rpt, 1802–5
see also Birds and bird conservation
see also Endangered species
see also Energy conservation
see also Environmental pollution and control
see also Environmental regulation
see also Flood control
see also Forests and forestry
see also International cooperation in conservation
see also Land use
see also Marine resources conservation
see also National forests
see also National parks
see also Plants and vegetation
see also Reclamation of land
see also Recycling of waste materials
see also Severance taxes
see also Soils and soil conservation
see also State forests
see also State funding for natural resources and conservation
see also Water resources development
see also Wilderness areas
see also Wildlife and wildlife conservation
see also Wildlife refuges

Consolidated Metropolitan Statistical Areas
see Metropolitan Statistical Areas
see under By SMSA or MSA in the "Index by Categories"

Consolidated Rail Corp.
Finances and operations of Class I railroads, detailed data by firm, class of service, and district, 1990, annual rpt, 9486–5.1
Finances and operations of Class I railroads, detailed data by firm, class of service, and district, 1991, annual rpt, 9486–6.1

Constitutional law
Court civil and criminal caseloads for Federal district, appeals, and bankruptcy courts, by type of suit and offense, circuit, and district, 1991, annual rpt, 18204–11
Court civil and criminal caseloads for Federal district, appeals, and special courts, 1991, annual rpt, 18204–8
US attorneys civil and criminal cases by type and disposition, and collections, by Federal district, FY91, annual rpt, 6004–2.1
see also Administrative law and procedure
see also Citizenship
see also Civil rights
see also Congressional-executive relations
see also Congressional powers
see also Due process of law
see also Federal-State relations
see also Habeas corpus
see also Interstate relations
see also Judicial powers
see also Right of assembly
see also Right of privacy

Construction industry
Appalachia hwy system and access roads funding and completion status, by State, quarterly tables, 9082–1
Business activity indicators, 1990, annual rpt, 9364–5.9
Business cycle recession and expansion duration indicators, 1850s-1990, working paper, 9375–13.83
Business statistics, detailed data for major industries and economic indicators, *Survey of Current Business*, monthly rpt, 2702–1.5
Business statistics, detailed data for major industries and economic indicators, 1960-91, *Survey of Current Business* biennial supplement, 2704–1
Census Bur data files and rpts, coverage and availability, 1992 annual listing, 2304–2
Collective bargaining agreements expiring during year, and workers covered, by firm, union, industry group, and State, 1992, annual rpt, 6784–9
Collective bargaining wage and benefit changes, quarterly press release, 6782–2
Collective bargaining wage changes and coverage, by industry and whether contract includes escalator clause and lump sum payment, 1982-91, annual article, 6722–1.325
Contracts for industrial and commercial construction, *Survey of Current Business*, cyclical indicators, monthly rpt, 2702–1.1
Correctional facilities construction issues and projects, series, 6066–30
County Business Patterns, 1989: employment, establishments, and payroll, by SIC 2- to 4-digit industry and county, annual State rpt series, 2326–8
County Business Patterns, 1990: employment, establishments, and payroll, by SIC 2- to 4-digit industry and county, annual State rpt series, 2326–6
Deaths and rates, by cause and selected social, demographic, and employment characteristics, 1979-85, natl longitudinal study, 4478–186
DOE Superconducting Super Collider particle accelerator program, conventional facility construction funding and estimated and actual costs, 1988-99, 3006–5.32
Earnings, weekly averages, monthly rpt, 23842–1.2
Electric power plants (steam), renewal and replacement of aging facilities, costs and benefits for selected units, projected 1991-2000, article, 3162–35.303
Electric utilities finances and operations, detailed data for publicly and privately owned firms, 1990, annual rpt, 3164–11.4
Electric utilities finances and operations, detailed data for publicly owned firms, 1990, annual rpt, 3164–24
Electric utilities operation under Public Utility Holding Company Act, with capacity and construction costs, late 1960s-80s, 3006–13.1
Electric utilities privately owned, finances and operations, detailed data, 1990, annual rpt, 3164–23
Employment and Earnings, detailed data, monthly rpt, 6742–2.5
Employment Cost Index and alternative measure of compensation costs, by component, occupation, industry group, union status, and location, 1975-92, annual rpt, 6744–20
Employment, earnings, and hours, by selected SIC 1- to 4-digit industry, State, and for 275 MSAs, 1987-92, 6748–81
Employment, earnings, and hours, by SIC 1- to 4-digit industry, monthly 1989-Feb 1992, annual rpt, 6744–4
Employment, earnings, and hours, monthly press release, 6742–5
Employment of minorities and women, by occupation, SIC 1- to 3-digit industry, State, and MSA, 1991, annual rpt, 9244–1
Employment situation, earnings, hours, and other BLS economic indicators, transcripts of BLS Commissioner's monthly testimony, periodic rpt, 23846–4
Employment, unemployment, and labor force characteristics, by region, State, and selected metro area, 1991, annual rpt, 6744–7
Energy use by mode of transport, fuel supply, and demographic and economic factors of vehicle use, 1970s-90, annual rpt, 3304–5
Equipment for mining and construction, trade, tariffs, and industry operating data, 1992 rpt, 9885–9.2
Explosives and blasting agents use, by type, industry, and State, 1991, Mineral Industry Surveys, annual rpt, 5614–22
Farm production itemized costs, by farm sales size and region, 1991, annual rpt, 1614–3
Fed Govt financial and nonfinancial domestic aid, 1992 base edition, annual listing, 104–5
Fed Govt land acquisition and dev projects in DC metro area, characteristics and funding by agency and project, FY92-96, annual rpt, 15454–1
Finances and operations, by SIC 2- to 4-digit industry, forecast 1992, annual rpt, 2044–28
Foreign direct investment in US, major transactions by type, industry, country, and US location, 1990, annual rpt, 2044–20
Germany construction activity in former East and West regions, 1991, article, 2042–1.306
Gross State Product by component, industry div, and State, 1977-89, article, 2702–1.303
Hawaii humpback whale habitat impacts of human activities, with data on shipping, whale watching, coastal construction, and aircraft, 1980s-90, 14738–14

Hwy construction bids and contracts for Federal-aid hwys, by State, 1st half 1992, semiannual rpt, 7552–12
Hwy construction material prices and indexes for Federal-aid system, by type of material and urban-rural location, quarterly rpt, 7552–7
Hwy construction minority contractor training, funding by region, FY92, annual release, 7554–40
Hwy construction zones traffic control and safety procedures and equipment, 1991 conf, 7558–115
Hwy interstate mileage, by completion status and State, as of June 1992, semiannual rpt, 7552–5
Hwy receipts by source, and spending by function, by level of govt and State, 1991, annual rpt, 7554–1.3
Immigration Reform and Control Act employer sanctions impacts on labor markets, with data for selected industries and metro areas, 1980s, working paper, 6366–6.10
Imports, exports, and employment impacts, by SIC 2- to 4-digit industry and commodity, quarterly rpt, 2322–2
Income tax returns of foreign corporations and individuals, and US entities abroad, detailed data compilation, 1970s-89, quinquennial rpt, 8308–31
Industry activity, construction put in place, permits, material prices, and employment, quarterly rpt with articles, 2042–1
Input-output structure of US economy, detailed interindustry transactions for 84 industries, and components of final demand, 1987, annual article, 2702–1.316
Input-output structure of US economy, detailed interindustry transactions for 541 industries, and components of final demand, 1982 benchmark data, 2708–17
Japan construction activity, by type and region, selected years 1985-91, article, 2042–1.307
Libraries (public) services for Indians and Hawaii Natives, project listing and funding by tribe and State, FY90, annual rpt, 4874–5
Loan activity for mortgages, by type of lender, loan, and mortgaged property, monthly press release, 5142–18
Loan activity for mortgages, by type of lender, loan, and mortgaged property, quarterly press release, 5142–30
Middle Atlantic States economic conditions, Fed Reserve 3rd District, quarterly rpt, 9387–10
Military aid of US, arms sales, and training, by country, FY50-91, annual rpt, 3904–3
Military base and family housing construction, DOD appropriations by facility, service branch, and location, FY91-93, annual rpt, 3544–39
Military base construction, renovation, and closure, budget requests by project, service branch, State, and country, FY93, annual rpt, 3544–15
Military contracts, payroll, and personnel, by service branch and location, with top 5 contractors and maps, by State and country, FY91, annual rpt, 3544–29
Military outlays and obligations, by function and service branch, quarterly rpt, 3542–3
Military prime contract awards, by category, contract and contractor type, and service branch, FY82-1st half FY92, semiannual rpt, 3542–1
Military prime contract awards, by category, contractor type, and State, FY89-91, annual rpt, 3544–11
Military prime contract awards, by detailed procurement category, FY88-91, annual rpt, 3544–18
Military prime contract awards, by size and type of contract, service branch, competitive status, category, and labor standard, FY91, annual rpt, 3544–19
Military weapons acquisition costs by system and service branch, DOD budget, FY91-93, annual rpt, 3504–2
Minority- and woman-owned businesses and owner characteristics, by industry, employment and sales size, and form of ownership, 1987 survey, 2328–59
Multinatl firms US affiliates finances and operations, by industry, country of parent firm, and State, 1987, 2708–48
Multinatl US firms and foreign affiliates finances and operations, by industry and country, 1989 benchmark survey, annual rpt, 2704–5
Multinatl US firms foreign affiliates, income statement items by asset size, industry, and country, 1988, biennial article, 8302–2.322
Natl Guard activities, personnel, and facilities, FY91, annual rpt, 3504–22
Natl income and product accounts, comprehensive accounts and components, benchmark revisions, 1929-88, 2708–5
Natl income and product accounts, comprehensive accounts and components, *Survey of Current Business*, monthly rpt, 2702–1.29
Natural gas interstate pipeline company detailed financial and operating data, by firm, 1990, annual rpt, 3164–38
New construction (public and private) activity, and new housing starts, 1929-91, annual rpt, 204–1.3
New construction (public and private) put in place, value by type, monthly rpt, 2382–4
New England construction, real estate, and other economic performance indicators, compared to Texas and other areas, 1970s-91, article, 9373–1.302
New England States economic indicators, Fed Reserve 1st District, monthly rpt, 9373–2
NIH grants and contracts, quarterly listing, 4432–1
Occupational injuries, illnesses, and lost workdays, by SIC 2-digit industry, 1990-91, annual press release, 6844–3
Occupational injury and illness rates by circumstances and establishment size, and methodology for computing rates, 1988, industry rpt, 6886–4.3
Occupational injury and illness rates, by SIC 2- to 4-digit industry, 1989-90, annual rpt, 6844–7
Occupational injury and illness rates, by SIC 2- to 4-digit industry, 1990, annual rpt, 6844–1
Occupational Outlook Handbook, 1992-93, biennial rpt, 6744–1
Pacific territories population and housing detailed characteristics, by location, 1990 Census of Population and Housing, series, 2551–8
Persian Gulf War allied and other countries cash and in-kind contributions, by type and country, 1990-91, GAO rpt, 26123–371
Persian Gulf War costs to US by category and service branch, and offsetting contributions by allied country, monthly rpt, 102–3
Price indexes (producer), by stage of processing and detailed commodity, monthly 1991, annual rpt, 6764–2
Price indexes (producer) for material inputs, by construction industry, monthly rpt, 6762–6
Prison construction and operating costs, capacity, and inmates, for Federal and State facilities, 1985-89, GAO rpt, 26119–407
Puerto Rico and other US possessions corporations income tax returns, income and tax items, and employment, by selected industry, 1989, article, 8302–2.326
R&D facilities of higher education instns, space and equipment adequacy, needs, and funding by source, by instn type and control, 1992, biennial rpt, 9624–25
SEC registration, firms required to file annual rpts, as of Sept 1991, annual listing, 9734–5
Small business finances, operations, owner characteristics, and Federal contracts, 1980s-90, annual rpt, 9764–6
Southeastern US employment by industry div, earnings, and hours, for 8 States, quarterly press release, 6942–7
Soviet Union construction activity and building materials production, 1985-92, article, 2042–1.301
Statistical Abstract of US, 1992 annual data compilation, 2324–1.26
Tax (income) returns filed, by type of filer, selected income items, quarterly rpt, 8302–2.1
Tax (income) returns for foreign corporate activity in US, selected income and tax items, by industry div and selected country, 1988, article, 8302–2.309
Tax (income) returns of corporations, income and tax items by asset size and detailed industry, 1989, annual rpt, 8304–4; 8304–21
Tax (income) returns of corporations with foreign tax credit, income and tax items by industry group, 1988, biennial article, 8302–2.316
Tax (income) returns of partnerships, income statement and balance sheet items, by industry group, 1990, annual article, 8302–2.314
Tax (income) returns of sole proprietorships, income statement items, by industry group, 1990, annual article, 8302–2.317; 8302–2.320
Tennessee Valley economic conditions, and compared to US, alternative projections 1992-2010 and trends from 1929, annual rpt, 9804–27
Uranium tailings at inactive mills, remedial action proposals, costs, site characteristics, and environmental, socioeconomic, and health impacts, series, 3356–4

VA health care, nursing home, and other facilities construction projects, costs and completion status by site, FY91, annual rpt, 8604–3.4
VA health care services, needs, availability, structure, and funding, 1991 compilation of papers, 8608–9
VA programs spending, by State, county, and congressional district, FY91, annual rpt, 8604–6
Wage and benefit changes from collective bargaining and mgmt decisions, by industry div, monthly rpt, 6782–1
Wages by occupation, and benefits, for office and plant workers, periodic MSA survey rpt series, 6785–16; 6785–17
West Central States economic indicators, Fed Reserve 10th District, quarterly rpt, 9381–16.2
see also Building codes
see also Building materials
see also Building permits
see also Cement and concrete
see also Census of Construction Industries
see also Housing construction
see also Housing maintenance and repair
see also Plumbing and heating
see also Shipbuilding and repairing
see also Wrecking and demolition
see also under By Industry in the "Index by Categories"

Consultants
AID and Intl Dev Cooperation Agency activities and funding, FY91-93, with developing countries economic and social conditions from 1960s, annual rpt, 9904–4
Credit unions federally insured, finances by instn characteristics and State, as of June 1992, semiannual rpt, 9532–6
Electric utilities conservation programs, collaboration between utilities and interest groups, and effects on costs, 1992 rpt, 3308–104
Employment, earnings, and hours, by SIC 1- to 4-digit industry, monthly 1989-Feb 1992, annual rpt, 6744–4
Fed Govt agencies ethics regulation, activities, and staff, 1991, biennial rpt, 9834–1
Finances and operations, by SIC 2- to 4-digit industry, forecast 1992, annual rpt, 2044–28
Foreign countries interests represented by former US govt officials, activities and individuals, FY86-91, GAO rpt, 26123–134
Higher education PhD degree recipients employment plans, by employer type, work activity, and field, 1979, 1984, and 1989, 4848–44
House of Representatives salaries, expenses, and contingent fund disbursement, detailed listings, quarterly rpt, 21942–1
Investment advisors for trust, employee benefit, and other accounts, assets advised by all and top 10 firms, 1990, annual rpt, 13004–1
Military prime contract awards, by detailed procurement category, FY88-91, annual rpt, 3544–18
Minority Business Dev Centers mgmt and financial aid, and characteristics of businesses, by region and State, FY91, annual rpt, 2104–6
Nuclear Regulatory Commission budget, staff, and activities, by program, FY91-93, annual rpt, 9634–9
Occupational Outlook Handbook, 1992-93, biennial rpt, 6744–1
Physicians consulting and attending at VA facilities, by specialty, quarterly rpt, 8602–6
Science and engineering labor force, Federal and university research funding, and educational data, series, 9626–6
Senate receipts, itemized expenses by payee, and balances, 1st half FY92, semiannual listing, 25922–1
Tax (income) returns of partnerships, income statement and balance sheet items, by industry group, 1990, annual article, 8302–2.314
Tax (income) returns of sole proprietorships, income statement items, by industry group, 1990, annual article, 8302–2.317; 8302–2.320
UNESCO fiscal mgmt, spending, staff, and funding sources, mid 1970s-92, GAO rpt, 26123–84

Consumer cooperatives
see also Rural cooperatives

Consumer credit
Airline consumer complaints to DOT about service by US and foreign carrier, and for travel and cargo service, by reason, monthly rpt, 7302–11
Assets and debts of private sector, balance sheets by segment, 1960-91, semiannual rpt, 9365–4.1
Auto, mobile home, and other consumer installment credit loans, monthly rpt, 23842–1.5
Auto, van, and light truck ownership and operating costs, by vehicle size and year of operation, 1991 model year, biennial rpt, 7554–21
Banks (insured commercial and savings) finances, for foreign and domestic offices, by asset size, 1990, annual rpt, 9294–4.2
Banks (natl) charters, mergers, liquidations, enforcement cases, and financial performance, with data by instn and State, quarterly rpt, 8402–3
Banks consumer lending relation to bank-auto finance company interest rate spread, tax reform, and other factors, 1970s-91, working paper, 9379–12.88
Banks credit operations costs and revenue, by credit type, mid 1970s-91, article, 9362–1.306
Business statistics, detailed data for major industries and economic indicators, *Survey of Current Business*, monthly rpt, 2702–1.8
Business statistics, detailed data for major industries and economic indicators, 1960-91, *Survey of Current Business* biennial supplement, 2704–1
Debt outstanding for installment and noninstallment credit, monthly rpt series, 9365–2
Families financial status, income, net worth, and assets and debt by type, by income and selected characteristics, 1983 and 1989, article, 9362–1.301
Financial and business detailed statistics, *Fed Reserve Bulletin*, monthly rpt with articles, 9362–1
Flow-of-funds accounts, savings, investments, and credit statements, quarterly rpt, 9365–3.3
Households financial services use, by account type and instn type and location, 1989 survey, article, 9362–1.303
Installment credit outstanding and terms, 1988-90, annual rpt, 9364–5.7
Installment credit outstanding, extensions, and liquidations, monthly rpt, 9362–1.1
New England States economic indicators, Fed Reserve 1st District, monthly rpt, 9373–2
North Central States business and economic conditions, Fed Reserve 9th District, quarterly journal, 9383–19
Outstanding installment credit by type, and noninstallment credit, 1950-91, annual rpt, 204–1.5
Retail trade sales, inventories, purchases, gross margin, and accounts receivable, by SIC 2- to 4-digit kind of business and form of ownership, 1990, annual rpt, 2413–5
Savings instns financial statements, for instns insured by Savings Assn Insurance Fund by FHLB district and State, and for FDIC-insured savings banks, 1989, annual rpt, 8434–1
Savings instns insured by Savings Assn Insurance Fund, assets, liabilities, and deposit and loan activity, by conservatorship status, monthly rpt, 8432–1
Southeastern States, Fed Reserve 5th District, economic indicators by State, quarterly rpt, 9389–16
Southeastern States, Fed Reserve 5th District insured commercial banks financial statements, by State, quarterly rpt, 9389–18
Southeastern States, Fed Reserve 8th District banking and economic conditions, quarterly rpt with articles, 9391–16
Statistical Abstract of US, 1992 annual data compilation, 2324–1.16
Survey of Current Business, detailed financial and business data, and economic indicators, monthly rpt, 2702–1.1
West Central States economic indicators, Fed Reserve 10th District, quarterly rpt, 9381–16.2
see also Credit bureaus and agencies
see also Credit cards
see also Credit unions
see also Discrimination in credit
see also Finance companies
see also Personal debt

Consumer Expenditure Survey
Child support and alimony payments, and payments share of income, by selected characteristics of payer and payee, 1988-89, article, 1702–1.305
Economic indicators, prices, labor costs, and productivity, BLS econometric analyses and methodology, working paper series, 6886–6
Expenditures by category, and income, by selected household characteristics, 1991 survey, annual press release, 6726–1.53
Expenditures by category, selected household characteristics, and region, quarterly rpt, 6762–14
Expenditures on selected durable goods and services, 1980-90, article, 6722–1.324

Food spending at and away from home, by selected characteristics, 1989, article, 1702–1.308
Housing costs exceeding 28% of gross income, families income by source and expenses by type, by tenure and other characteristics, 1989, article, 1702–1.304
Married couples aged 18-25, income and expenses by wife's employment status and family size, 1988-89, article, 1702–1.302
Women (older) living alone, income by source, and expenses by type, by marital status, 1988-89, article, 1702–1.301

Consumer expenditures
see Personal consumption

Consumer income
see Personal and household income

Consumer Price Index
Agricultural Outlook, production, prices, marketing, and trade, by commodity, forecast and current situation, monthly rpt with articles, 1502–4
BLS data collection, analysis, and presentation methods, by program, 1992 rpt, 6888–1
Budget of US, CBO analysis of revenue and spending alternatives and projections of economic indicators, FY93-97, annual rpt, 26304–3
Business cycle duration and strength indicators, late 1940s-91, article, 9373–1.301
Business statistics, detailed data for major industries and economic indicators, 1960-91, *Survey of Current Business* biennial supplement, 2704–1
CPI by component for US city average, and by region, population size, and for 15 metro areas, monthly rpt, 6762–1
CPI by component for US city average, and by selected metro area, region, and population size, monthly rpt, 6762–2
CPI by component, monthly for last 13 months with trends from 1940, quarterly rpt, 4742–1.5
CPI changes for selected items, 1982-91, annual article, 6722–1.322
Dairy products CPI for all urban consumers, US city average, monthly rpt, 1317–4.2
Dallas-Fort Worth metro area employment, earnings, hours, and CPI changes, late 1970s-91, annual rpt, 6964–2
Economic indicators and components, and Fed Reserve 4th District business and financial conditions, monthly chartbook, 9377–10
Economic indicators and components, current data and annual trends, monthly rpt, 23842–1.4
Economic indicators and relation to govt finances by level of govt, selected years 1929-91, annual rpt, 10044–1
Economic indicators compounded annual rates of change, monthly rpt, 9391–3
Economic indicators, monthly rpt, 9362–1.2
Economic indicators, prices, labor costs, and productivity, BLS econometric analyses and methodology, working paper series, 6886–6
Energy use by mode of transport, fuel supply, and demographic and economic factors of vehicle use, 1970s-90, annual rpt, 3304–5
Family Economics Review, consumer goods prices and supply, and home economics, quarterly journal, 1702–1
Food consumption, supply, trade, prices, spending, and indexes, by commodity, 1990, annual rpt, 1544–4
Footwear production, employment, use, prices, and US trade by country, quarterly rpt, 9882–6
Forecasts of economic indicators, 1992-93 and trends from 1948, annual article, 9383–6.301
Forecasts of economic indicators, 1993-94 and trends from 1948, annual article, 9383–6.303
Foreign and US consumer price indexes, for 7 OECD countries, *Survey of Current Business*, monthly rpt, 2702–1.1
Foreign and US economic conditions, for major industrial countries, monthly rpt, 9112–1
Foreign and US industrial production indexes and CPI, for US and 6 OECD countries, current data and annual trends, monthly rpt, 23842–1.7
Foreign countries economic and monetary trends, compounded annual rates of change and quarterly indicators for US and 7 major industrialized countries, quarterly rpt, 9391–7
Foreign countries economic conditions and implications for US, periodic country rpt series, 2046–4
Health Care Financing Review, provider prices, price inputs and indexes, and labor, quarterly journal, 4652–1.1
Health care spending, and CPI for selected services, 1980s-91, and nursing home population by sex, projected to 2040, article, 1702–1.309
Health care spending by funding source, 1990, with trends and indexes by service type from 1960, article, 4652–1.323
Health condition and care indicators, 1950s-90 with health improvement and disease prevention goals for 1990, annual data compilation, 4144–11
Higher education instn revenue by source and spending by function, by State and instn control, FY82-90, annual rpt, 4844–6
Houston metro area employment, earnings, hours, and CPI changes, 1970s-91, annual rpt, 6964–1
Latin America economic and social conditions, resources, trade, and aid, 1992, annual factbook, 9914–14
Metro area CPI and components, relation to CPI of other MSAs, for 4 major MSAs, 1967-92, article, 9373–1.312
Monthly Labor Review, CPI and PPI current statistics, 6722–1.4
New England States economic indicators, Fed Reserve 1st District, monthly rpt, 9373–2
North Central States business and economic conditions, Fed Reserve 9th District, quarterly journal, 9383–19
North Central States farm credit conditions and economic devs, Fed Reserve 7th District, monthly rpt, 9375–10
OECD members health care costs, hospital use, resources, and economic and health indicators, by country, 1960s-90, article, 4652–1.322
Price indexes (consumer and producer), by commodity group, selected years 1929-91, annual rpt, 204–1.4
Southeastern States, Fed Reserve 8th District banking and economic conditions, quarterly rpt with articles, 9391–16
Statistical Abstract of US, 1992 annual data compilation, 2324–1.15
Survey of Current Business, detailed data for major industries and economic indicators, monthly rpt, 2702–1.4
Survey of Current Business, detailed financial and business data, and economic indicators, monthly rpt, 2702–1.1
Telephone local service charges and low-income subsidies, by region, company, and city, 1980s-91, semiannual rpt, 9282–8
Telephone service subscribership, charges, and local and long distance firm finances and operations, late 1970s-92, semiannual rpt, 9282–7
Texas, Dallas-Ft Worth and Houston MSAs, CPI by major component, monthly rpt, 6962–2

Consumer Product Safety Commission
Activities of CPSC, recalls by brand, and casualties and medical costs by product type, FY90, annual rpt, 9164–2
Budget of US, authoritative financial statements with appropriations, outlays, and receipts, by category and agency, FY91, annual rpt, 8104–2.2
Budget of US, obligations and authority by function, agency, and program, with summaries and analyses, FY93, annual rpt, 104–2
Injuries from use of consumer products and related activities, by severity and victim age and sex, 1990, annual rpt, 9164–7
Injuries from use of consumer products, by severity, victim age, and detailed product, 1991, annual rpt, 9164–6
Labor unions recognized in Fed Govt, agreements and membership by agency and facility, as of Jan 1991, biennial listing, 9844–14

Consumer protection
Airline consumer complaints by reason, passengers denied boarding, and late flights, by reporting carrier and airport, monthly rpt, 7302–11
Bank deposits availability policies, with background data, 1980s-90, last issue of annual report, 9364–13
Banks customer complaints received by Fed Reserve System, by type and disposition, 1991, annual rpt, 9364–1
Banks in Fed Reserve System, expenses and operations itemized by service, office, and district, 1991, annual rpt, 9364–11
Building access for disabled to Federal and federally funded facilities, complaints by disposition and State, FY91, annual rpt, 17614–1
Carcinogens chemistry, sources, environment and health risks, and regulation, by substance and brand, 1991 annual rpt, 4044–15
Child day care and early childhood education programs availability, demand, use, costs, and provider and enrollee characteristics, 1990 survey, 4808–39
Claims Court caseload by type of suit, and judgments, FY92, annual rpt, 18224–1

Consumer Product Safety Commission activities, recalls by brand, and casualties and medical costs, by product type, FY90, annual rpt, 9164–2
Credit card issuers disclosure of terms and conditions to consumers, with finances and operations, 1991 hearing, 21248–175
Criminal sentences for Federal offenses, guidelines by offense and circumstances, series, 17668–1
FDA investigations and regulatory activities, quarterly rpt, 4062–3
Fed Govt financial and nonfinancial domestic aid, 1992 base edition, annual listing, 104–5
Gasoline service stations price competition and divorcement from oil companies, issues with data by firm, city, and State, 1991 hearing, 25528–120
Health care facilities excluded from Medicare prospective payment system, quality standards and review, certification, accreditation, and licensing, 1991 survey, 17206–2.41
Health Care Financing Admin research activities and grants, by program, FY91, annual listing, 4654–10
HHS financial aid, by program, recipient, State, and city, FY91, annual regional listings, 4004–3
Hospital deaths of Medicare patients, actual and expected rates by diagnosis, with hospital characteristics, by instn, FY90, annual State rpt series, 4654–14
Hospital reimbursement by Medicare under prospective payment system, impacts on costs, industry structure and operations, and quality of care, series, 17206–2
Hospital reimbursement by Medicare under prospective payment system, omitted services impacts on hospital revenue, FY85, article, 4652–1.316
Imports detained by FDA, by reason, product, shipper, brand, and country, monthly listing, 4062–2
Medicare supplemental private insurance loss ratio performance, by firm, 1988-89, GAO rpt, 26121–452
Physicians payment and participation in Medicaid by service type, and cost compared to Medicare, by State, FY89, 17266–1.4
Physicians payment by Medicare, impacts of reforms on services, and monitoring methods, 1992 annual rpt, 4004–34
Physicians payment by Medicare, payment reforms impact on service availability, monitoring activity, 1991, annual rpt, 17266–1.5
Physicians payment by Medicare under assigned fee, participation and additional billing, by specialty, service, and State, late 1980s-92, 17266–1.6
Physicians payment by Medicare, vulnerable beneficiaries services use prior to fee schedule implementation, 1986-90, annual rpt, 17266–1.8
Postal Service customer complaints received, by type, FY91, annual rpt, 9864–5.2
Postal Service inspection activities, 2nd half FY92, semiannual rpt, 9862–2
Securities Investor Protection Corp regulatory activity and finances, 1970s-91, GAO rpt, 26119–419
Shellfish harvest in estuaries, approved and restricted areas, and pollution sources, by estuary, State, and coastal region, 1990, quinquennial rpt, 2178–33
State govt protective inspection and regulation funding, by State, FY90, 10044–1
Truck transport of household goods, performance and disposition of damage claims, for selected carriers, 1991, annual rpt, 9484–11
US attorneys civil and criminal cases by type and disposition, and collections, by Federal district, FY91, annual rpt, 6004–2.1
VA health care facilities inpatient deaths, results of quality of care reviews, 1986 and 1989, 8708–1
see also Defective products
see also Food ingredients and additives
see also Food inspection
see also Hazardous substances
see also Labeling
see also Licenses and permits
see also Medical regulation
see also Motor vehicle safety devices
see also Product safety

Consumer surveys
Banking system reform issues, with top instn finances, fiscal impacts, and views of depositors, bankers, and regulators on deposit insurance, 1991 hearings, 21248–168
Consumer attitude indexes, *Survey of Current Business*, monthly rpt, 2702–1.1
Financial instns reform issues, with finances, impacts of deposit insurance changes, and views of depositors and bankers, 1991 hearings, 25248–129
Food consumer research, marketing, legislation, and regulation devs, and consumption and price trends, quarterly journal, 1541–7
Forecasts of durable goods spending, performance of consumer sentiment index and other economic indicators, 1950s-90, article, 9393–8.304
Health care system and OASDHI operations and reform issues, public opinion, 1991 surveys, 10176–2.2
Industrial production and unemployment forecasting performance of consumer sentiment surveys, 1991 working paper, 9371–10.69
Mail volume to and from households, use, and views, by class, source, content, and household characteristics, FY87-90, annual rpt, 9864–10
New England States economic indicators, Fed Reserve 1st District, monthly rpt, 9373–2
Oregon Medicaid waiver proposal for managed care, services priorities dev procedures and issues, with background data, 1992 rpt, 26358–254
Physicians billing and payment under Medicare, beneficiaries knowledge and experience by selected characteristics, 1988-89, 17266–2.1
Postal Service on-time delivery of 1st class mail, impacts of standards revisions, 1990-91, GAO rpt, 26119–431
Real estate agent fees for mortgage banker referrals, and other issues, consumer views, 1989 survey, hearings, 21248–161
Smoking cessation programs ratings by consumers, 1992 article, 4042–3.308
Travel to US, by characteristics of visit and traveler, world area of origin, and US destination, 1991 survey, annual rpt, 2904–12
Wilderness visitors recreation choices, impacts of fires, 1989 local area survey, 1208–422
see also American Housing Survey
see also Consumer Expenditure Survey
see also National Medical Expenditure Survey
see also Nationwide Food Consumption Survey
see also Survey of Consumer Finances

Consumers
see Boycotts
see Consumer credit
see Consumer Price Index
see Consumer protection
see Consumer surveys
see Cost of living
see Personal and household income
see Personal consumption

Consumption
see Food consumption
see Personal consumption
see under names of specific commodities or commodity groups

Containerization
Fruit and vegetable shipments, and arrivals by city, by mode of transport and State and country of origin, 1991, annual rpt series, 1311–4
Fruit and vegetable shipments by mode of transport, arrivals, and imports, by commodity and State and country of origin, weekly rpt, 1311–3
Intermodal containers and equipment owned by shipping and leasing companies, inventory by type and size, 1991, annual rpt, 7704–10
Military and personal property shipments by commercial cariers, and cost savings from bill audits and rate negotiations, FY99-91, GAO rpt, 26123–369
Military and personal property shipments, passenger traffic, and costs, by service branch and mode of transport, FY91, annual rpt, 3704–15
Military Sealift Command shipping operations, finances, and personnel, FY91, annual rpt, 3804–14
Oil refinery crude received, by mode of transport and PAD district, 1991, annual rpt, 3164–2.1
Railroad (Class I) finances and operations, detailed data by firm, class of service, and district, 1990, annual rpt, 9486–5.1
Railroad (Class I) finances and operations, detailed data by firm, class of service, and district, 1991, annual rpt, 9486–6.1
Shipborne trade of US, by type of service, customs district, port, and world area, monthly rpt, 2422–7
Shipbuilding and repair facilities, capacity, and employment, by shipyard, 1991, annual rpt, 7704–9
Ships, cargo, and passenger traffic, and toll revenue on St Lawrence Seaway, 1991 and trends from 1959, annual rpt, 7744–2
Ships in world merchant fleet, tonnage, and new ship construction and deliveries, by vessel type and country, as of Jan 1992, annual rpt, 7704–3

Ships under foreign flag owned by US firms and foreign affiliates, by type, owner, and country of registry and construction, as of July 1991, semiannual rpt, 7702–3
Truck trailer shipments, exports, and firms, by trailer type, monthly Current Industrial Rpt, 2506–12.25
Truck use of intermodal containers over legal weight for hwy use, California enforcement activity, and container traffic by mode, 1960s-88, hearing, 21648–65

Containers
see Containerization
see Packaging and containers

Contempt of court
Court civil and criminal caseloads for Federal district, appeals, and bankruptcy courts, by type of suit and offense, circuit, and district, 1991, annual rpt, 18204–11
Court civil and criminal caseloads for Federal district, appeals, and special courts, 1991, annual rpt, 18204–8
Sentences for Federal offenses, guidelines by offense and circumstances, series, 17668–1
US attorneys civil and criminal cases by type and disposition, and collections, by Federal district, FY91, annual rpt, 6004–2.1

Continental shelf
Alaska OCS environmental conditions and oil dev impacts, compilation of papers, series, 2176–1
California OCS oil and gas dev impacts on water quality, marine life, and sediments, by site, 1986-90, annual rpt, 5734–11
Environmental conditions, fish, wildlife, use, and mgmt, for individual coastal and riparian ecosystems, series, 5506–9
Oregon OCS rocky banks fish and invertebrate population and habitats, 1988-90, 5738–39
Ships wrecked off Alaska, characteristics, deaths, cargo, and whale catch, by vessel and location, 1763-1937, 5738–34
Workers compensation programs under Federal admin, finances and operations, FY91, annual rpt, 6504–10
see also Coastal areas
see also Offshore mineral resources
see also Offshore oil and gas
see also Territorial waters

Continuing education
see Adult education

Contraband
see also Drug and narcotics offenses

Contraception
see Contraceptives
see Family planning
see Sexual sterilization

Contraceptives
AIDS prevention programs for drug abusers and their sexual partners, client characteristics, and outcomes, for selected metro areas, 1989 annual conf, 4494–12
AIDS public knowledge, attitudes, info sources, and testing, 1991 survey, 4146–8.218
Alcohol use and contraceptives use at first intercourse, by whether intercourse planned, for US and Scotland, 1991 article, 4482–1.304
Cancer (breast) risk relation to estrogen replacement therapy use, body mass index, and other risk factors, 1987-89 NYC study, article, 4472–1.350
Cancer (liver) risk for women relation to parity and oral contraceptives use, 1985-86, article, 4472–1.331
Condom use promotion effectiveness in prevention of sexually transmitted disease reinfection, 1988 local area study, article, 4042–3.376
Developing countries family planning and population activities of AID, grants by project and recipient, and contraceptive shipments, by country, FY91, annual rpt series, 9914–13
Developing countries population size, life expectancy, and fertility, trends and forecasts, country rpt series, 2326–24
Exports and imports between US and outlying areas, by detailed commodity and mode of transport, 1991, annual rpt, 2424–11
Exports and imports of US, by Harmonized System 6-digit commodity and country, 1991, annual rpt, 2424–13
Exports of US, detailed Schedule B commodities with countries of destination, 1991, annual rpt, 2424–10
Failures and health risks to women of contraceptives, with pregnancy, abortion, and cancer death rates, 1980s, conf paper, 4164–2
Foreign countries contraception use by women, by age and country, 1991 biennial rpt, 2324–9
Health condition and care indicators, 1950s-90 with health improvement and disease prevention goals for 1990, annual data compilation, 4144–11
Indian and Alaska Native youth health condition and behavioral patterns, by sex and grade, 1988-90, 4088–3
Latin America economic and social conditions, resources, trade, and aid, 1992, annual factbook, 9914–14
Latin America young unmarried adults sexual activity, contraceptives use, and AIDS risk knowledge, by sex and country, 1984-91, article, 4202–7.323
Oral contraceptives use by age and race, for persons dying in 1986, 4147–20.19
Research on population and reproduction, Federal funding by project, FY90, annual listing, 4474–9
Research on population and reproduction, Natl Inst of Child Health and Human Dev funding and activities, 1991, annual rpt, 4474–33
Shipments, trade, and use of drugs, by product, 1991, annual Current Industrial Rpt, 2506–8.5
Statistical Abstract of US, 1992 annual data compilation, 2324–1.2
Teenage boys AIDS risk behavior, sexual activity, and drug and condom use, 1988, article, 4042–3.313
Vietnam population size, components of change, and selected characteristics, 1979, 1989, and projected to 2050, 2326–18.65
Youth health condition, risk factors, and preventive and treatment services use and availability, 1970s-80s, 26358–234.2

Contracts
Banks and thrifts contracts with computer data processing vendors, involvement of illegal business transactions, and instn and vendor views, 1985-90, GAO rpt, 26119–374
Construction (industrial and commercial) contracts, *Survey of Current Business*, cyclical indicators, monthly rpt, 2702–1.1
Court civil and criminal caseloads for Federal district, appeals, and bankruptcy courts, by type of suit and offense, circuit, and district, 1991, annual rpt, 18204–11
Court civil and criminal caseloads for Federal district, appeals, and special courts, 1991, annual rpt, 18204–8
Housing alteration and repair spending, by job category and for work under contract, quarterly rpt, 2382–7
Labor laws enacted, by State, 1991, annual article, 6722–1.309
Mental health care facilities, staff, patients, and finances, 1970s-91, biennial rpt, 4094–1
Natural gas interstate pipeline capacity, use, contract deliveries, and prices, by region, State, and firm, 1990, 3168–125
Petrochemicals industries contract labor accidents, injuries, safety programs operations, and employee characteristics, 1986-91, 6608–6
Shipping industry structure, rates, and effects of Shipping Act, by route, 1980s, 9408–54
Uranium marketing, contracts, prices, utility shipments, and trade, 1982-91 and projected to 2001, annual rpt, 3164–65.2
Western Area Power Admin activities by plant, financial statements, and sales by customer, FY91, annual rpt, 3254–1
see also Agricultural production quotas and price supports
see also Business orders
see also Defense contracts and procurement
see also Defense industries
see also Escalator clauses
see also Futures trading
see also Government contracts and procurement
see also Labor-management relations, general
see also Labor-management relations in government

Contributions
see Campaign funds
see Gifts and private contributions

Controlled substances
see Alcoholic beverages control laws
see Cocaine
see Drug abuse and treatment
see Drug and narcotics offenses
see Marijuana

Convalescent homes
see Nursing homes

Conventions
see Exhibitions and trade fairs
see Political conventions
see Treaties and conventions

Convictions, criminal
see Sentences, criminal procedure

Conway, Roger K.
"Impact of the Clean Air Act on Agriculture", 1504–9.1

Cook County, Ill.
Housing and households characteristics, and unit and neighborhood quality, by MSA location for 11 MSAs, 1987 survey, supplement, 2485–8

Cook Inlet, Alaska
Tide height and time daily at coastal points, forecast 1993, annual rpt, 2174–2.1
Cook Islands
Economic, social, political, and geographic summary data, by country, 1992, annual factbook, 9114–2
Exports and imports of US, by transport mode, country, and SITC 1- to 3-digit commodity, 1991, annual rpt, 2424–12
Population size, growth rates, and components of change, by country, projected 1990-2020 and trends from 1950, biennial rpt, 2324–9
Cooking equipment
see Household appliances and equipment
Cooking utensils
see Household supplies and utensils
Cooperative State Research Service
Budget of US, obligations and authority by function, agency, and program, with summaries and analyses, FY93, annual rpt, 104–2
Expenditures and staffing for agricultural research by USDA, State agencies, and other instns, by topic, FY91, annual rpt, 1744–2
Expenditures of Fed Govt in States, by type, program, agency, and State, FY91, annual rpt, 2464–2
Cooperatives
Political action committees, by type, 1974-91, semiannual press release, 9276–1.96
Political action committees, by type, 1974-92, semiannual press release, 9276–1.107
Political action committees contributions by party, and finances, by PAC type, 1991-92, press release, 9276–1.106; 9276–1.110
Political campaign finances reported to Fed Election Commission, by type of filer, 1990 natl elections, biennial rpt series, 9276–2
Tax (income) withholding and related documents filed, by type and IRS service center, 1991 and projected 1992-99, annual rpt, 8304–22
Tax exempt organizations with unrelated business income, finances by organization type, 1987, article, 8302–2.306
see also Condominiums and cooperatives
see also Credit unions
see also Rural cooperatives
Copper and copper industry
Building materials PPI, by type, quarterly rpt, 2042–1.5
Business statistics, detailed data for major industries and economic indicators, *Survey of Current Business*, monthly rpt, 2702–1.16
Business statistics, detailed data for major industries and economic indicators, 1960-91, *Survey of Current Business* biennial supplement, 2704–1
Byproducts of primary metals mining, production and prices by commodity, 1965-90, 5608–170
Castings (nonferrous) shipments, by metal type, 1991, annual Current Industrial Rpt, 2506–10.5
Coin and medal production by denomination, capacity, and facility improvement funding, by mint, with monetary metals purchases, projected FY92-96, hearing, 21248–164
Coin production and monetary metals use and holdings of US Mint, by metal type, FY91, annual rpt, 8204–1
County Business Patterns, 1989: employment, establishments, and payroll, by SIC 2- to 4-digit industry and county, annual State rpt series, 2326–8
County Business Patterns, 1990: employment, establishments, and payroll, by SIC 2- to 4-digit industry and county, annual State rpt series, 2326–6
Eastern Europe export industries dev potential, with trade and industry finances and operations, for 5 countries, 1985-90, 9886–4.179
Employment, earnings, and hours, by SIC 1- to 4-digit industry, monthly 1989-Feb 1992, annual rpt, 6744–4
Exports and imports between US and outlying areas, by detailed commodity and mode of transport, 1991, annual rpt, 2424–11
Exports and imports of US, by country and detailed commodity, monthly rpt, 2422–12
Exports and imports of US, by Harmonized System 6-digit commodity and country, 1991, annual rpt, 2424–13
Exports and imports of US, by transport mode, country, and SITC 1- to 3-digit commodity, 1991, annual rpt, 2424–12
Exports of US, detailed Schedule B commodities with countries of destination, 1991, annual rpt, 2424–10
Financial and economic performance indicators and indexes for metals industries, by commodity, monthly rpt, 5602–5
Foreign and US supply under alternative market conditions, reserves, and background industry data, 1992 rpt, 5606–4.30
Foreign countries mineral production, reserves, and industry role in domestic economy and world supply, world area and country rpt series, 5606–1
Freight (waterborne domestic and foreign) by commodity, traffic, and passengers, by port and waterway, 1989, annual rpt, 3754–3
Futures and options trading volume, by commodity and exchange, FY91, annual rpt, 11924–2
Futures trading in selected commodities and financial instruments and indexes, for NYC, Chicago, and other markets activity, biweekly rpt, 11922–5
Input-output structure of US economy, detailed interindustry transactions for 541 industries, and components of final demand, 1982 benchmark data, 2708–17
Labor productivity, indexes of output, hours, and employment by SIC 2- to 4-digit industry, 1967-90, annual rpt, 6824–1.2; 6824–1.3
Manufacturing annual survey, 1990: finances and operations, by SIC 2- to 4-digit industry, series, 2506–14
Manufacturing census, 1987: concentration of largest firms measured by value added, and for shipments by SIC 2- and 4-digit industry, subject rpt, 2497–6
Manufacturing census, 1987: shipments of manufacturers products, by customer class and SIC 2- and 4-digit industry, subject rpt, 2497–4
Manufacturing finances and operations, by SIC 2- to 4-digit industry, forecast 1992, annual rpt, 2044–28
Mineral Industry Surveys, commodity review of production, trade, stocks, and use, monthly rpt, 5612–1.6
Mineral Industry Surveys, State reviews of production, 1991, preliminary annual rpt, 5614–6
Minerals Yearbook, Vol 1, 1989: commodity reviews of production, use, trade, prices, and mining operations, annual rpt, 5604–33
Minerals Yearbook, Vol 1, 1990: commodity review of production, reserves, supply, use, and trade, annual rpt, 5604–20.18
Minerals Yearbook, Vol 2, 1989: State reviews of production and sales by commodity, and business activity, annual rpt series, 5604–16
Minerals Yearbook, Vol 2, 1990: State reviews of production and sales by commodity, and business activity, annual rpt series, 5604–22
Minerals Yearbook, Vol 3, 1989: foreign country reviews of production, trade, and policy, by commodity, annual rpt, 5604–35
Mines (metal) and related operations occupational injuries and incidence, employment, and hours, 1990, annual rpt, 6664–3
Occupational injury and illness rates, by SIC 2- to 4-digit industry, 1989-90, annual rpt, 6844–7
Occupational injury and illness rates, by SIC 2- to 4-digit industry, 1990, annual rpt, 6844–1
OECD trade, total and for 4 major countries, and US trade by country, by commodity, 1980-90, world area rpt series, 9116–1
Price indexes (producer), by stage of processing and detailed commodity, monthly rpt, 6762–6
Price indexes (producer), by stage of processing and detailed commodity, monthly 1991, annual rpt, 6764–2
Production in 5 western States, and prices, for 5 nonferrous metals, 1848-1990, 5608–178
Production, prices, trade, and foreign and US industry devs, by commodity, bimonthly rpt, 5602–4
Production, prices, trade, use, employment, tariffs, and stockpiles, by mineral, with foreign comparisons, 1987-91, annual rpt, 5604–18
Production, trade, use, and foreign investment in US industry, for minerals, 1985-90 and projected to 2000, annual rpt, 5304–5
Stockpiling of strategic material by Fed Govt, activity, and inventory by commodity, as of Sept 1991, semiannual rpt, 3542–22
Stockpiling of strategic material, inventories and needs, by commodity, 1992, annual rpt, 3544–37
Telecommunications fiber optics and copper wire mileage and access lines, and fiber systems investment, by firm, 1985-91, annual rpt, 9284–18
Wire and cable (insulated) shipments, trade, use, and firms, by product, 1991, annual Current Industrial Rpt, 2506–10.8

Copyright
Claims Court caseload by type of suit, and judgments, FY92, annual rpt, 18224–1
Court civil and criminal caseloads for Federal district, appeals, and bankruptcy courts, by type of suit and offense, circuit, and district, 1991, annual rpt, 18204–11
Court civil and criminal caseloads for Federal district, appeals, and special courts, 1991, annual rpt, 18204–8
Criminal cases by type and disposition, and collections, for US attorneys, by Federal district, FY91, annual rpt, 6004–2.1
Criminal sentences for Federal offenses, guidelines by offense and circumstances, series, 17668–1
Exports of goods, services, and investment, trade barriers, impacts, and US actions, by country, 1991, annual rpt, 444–2
Foreign countries economic conditions, policy, and trade practices, by country, 1989-91, annual rpt, 21384–5
Intl agreements of US establishing copyright relations, by country, as of Jan 1992, annual listing, 7004–1
Register of Copyrights activities, registrations by material type, and fees, FY91 and trends from 1790, annual rpt, 26404–2
Registrations and claims and fees collected by type of material, claims and fees, and fee transfers, for Library of Congress Copyright Office, FY91, annual rpt, 26404–1
Statistical Abstract of US, 1992 annual data compilation, 2324–1.18
see also Patents
see also Trademarks

Copyright Royalty Tribunal
Royalty fees from cable and satellite TV available for distribution by Tribunal, 1990-91, annual rpt, 26404–2

Coral reefs and islands
Alaska OCS environmental conditions and oil dev impacts, compilation of papers, series, 2176–1

Corey, Roger L., Jr.
"Fresh or Frozen Fish, Industry and Trade Summary", 9885–8.7

Corn
Acreage planted and harvested, by crop and State, 1990-91 and planned as of June 1992, annual rpt, 1621–23
Acreage planted, by selected crop and State, 1983-91 and planned 1992, annual rpt, 1621–22
Acreage reduction program compliance, enrollment, and yield on planted acreage, by commodity and State, annual press release series, 1004–20
Agricultural Statistics, 1991, annual rpt, 1004–1
Alcoholic beverages production, stocks, materials used, and taxable and tax-free removals, for beer and distilled spirits by State, monthly rpt, 8486–1.1; 8486–1.3
Business statistics, detailed data for major industries and economic indicators, *Survey of Current Business*, monthly rpt, 2702–1.13
Business statistics, detailed data for major industries and economic indicators, 1960-91, *Survey of Current Business* biennial supplement, 2704–1
CCC certificate exchange activity, by commodity, biweekly press release, 1802–16
CCC financial condition and major commodity program operations, FY63-88, annual chartbook, 1824–2
Consumption of corn and barley for feed and industrial use, revised estimates 1980s-91, article, 1561–4.301
Consumption, supply, trade, prices, spending, and indexes, by food commodity, 1990, annual rpt, 1544–4
County Business Patterns, 1989: employment, establishments, and payroll, by SIC 2- to 4-digit industry and county, annual State rpt series, 2326–8
County Business Patterns, 1990: employment, establishments, and payroll, by SIC 2- to 4-digit industry and county, annual State rpt series, 2326–6
Exports and imports (agricultural) commodity and country, prices, and world market devs, monthly rpt, 1922–12
Exports and imports (agricultural) of US, by commodity and country, bimonthly rpt, 1522–1
Exports and imports (agricultural) of US, by detailed commodity and country, 1991, annual rpt, 1524–8
Exports and imports (agricultural) of US, by detailed commodity and country, 1991, semiannual rpt, 1522–4
Exports and imports between US and outlying areas, by detailed commodity and mode of transport, 1991, annual rpt, 2424–11
Exports and imports of US, by country and detailed commodity, monthly rpt, 2422–12
Exports and imports of US, by Harmonized System 6-digit commodity and country, 1991, annual rpt, 2424–13
Exports and imports of US, by transport mode, country, and SITC 1- to 3-digit commodity, 1991, annual rpt, 2424–12
Exports of grains, oilseed products, hides, skins, and cotton, by country, weekly rpt, dropped data, 1922–3
Exports of US, detailed Schedule B commodities with countries of destination, 1991, annual rpt, 2424–10
Farm income, cash marketing receipts ranked by commodity and State, 1990, 1548–385
Farm sector balance sheet, and receipts by detailed commodity, by State, 1986-90, annual rpt, 1544–18
Fed Crop Insurance Corp financial performance, and effect of alternative price forecasts on program costs, 1983-89, GAO rpt, 26131–95
Feed production, acreage, stocks, use, trade, prices, and price supports, periodic situation rpt with articles, 1561–4
Fertilizer and pesticide use and application rates, by type, crop, and State, 1991, 1616–1.1
Fertilizer use and application rates, by type and crop, for California, 1990, 1616–1.2
Foreign and US agricultural production, acreage, and yield for selected crops, forecasts by selected world region and country, FAS monthly circular, 1925–28
Foreign and US agricultural supply and demand indicators, by selected crop, monthly rpt, 1522–5
Foreign and US grain production, prices, trade, stocks, and use, FAS periodic circular series, 1925–2
Foreign and US oils, oilseeds, and fats production and trade, FAS periodic circular series, 1925–1
Foreign countries agricultural production, prices, and trade, by country, 1980-91 and forecast 1992, annual world area rpt series, 1524–4
Freight (waterborne domestic and foreign) by commodity, traffic, and passengers, by port and waterway, 1989, annual rpt, 3754–3
Futures and options trading volume, by commodity and exchange, FY91, annual rpt, 11924–2
Futures contracts, stocks in deliverable position by type, weekly table, 11922–4.3
Futures trading in selected commodities and financial instruments and indexes, for NYC, Chicago, and other markets activity, biweekly rpt, 11922–5
Input-output structure of US economy, detailed interindustry transactions for 541 industries, and components of final demand, 1982 benchmark data, 2708–17
Inspections of grain for domestic use and export, and foreign buyers complaints, FY92, annual rpt, 1294–1
Irrigation projects of Reclamation Bur in western US, crop production and acreage by commodity, State, and project, 1990, annual rpt, 5824–12
Labor productivity, indexes of output, hours, and employment by SIC 2- to 4-digit industry, 1967-90, annual rpt, 6824–1.3
Loan support programs of USDA for grains, activity and status by grain and State, monthly rpt, 1802–3
Manufacturing annual survey, 1990: finances and operations, by SIC 2- to 4-digit industry, series, 2506–14
Manufacturing census, 1987: concentration of largest firms measured by value added, and for shipments by SIC 2- and 4-digit industry, subject rpt, 2497–6
Manufacturing census, 1987: shipments of manufacturers products, by customer class and SIC 2- and 4-digit industry, subject rpt, 2497–4
OECD trade, total and for 4 major countries, and US trade by country, by commodity, 1980-90, world area rpt series, 9116–1
Price indexes (producer), by stage of processing and detailed commodity, monthly rpt, 6762–6
Price indexes (producer), by stage of processing and detailed commodity, monthly 1991, annual rpt, 6764–2
Price support and other CCC program outlays, with production and marketing outlook, by commodity, projected 1991-97, annual rpt, 26306–6.171
Prices received and paid by farmers, by commodity and State, monthly rpt, 1629–1
Prices received and paid by farmers, by commodity and State, 1991, annual rpt, 1629–5
Prices received by farmers and production value, by detailed crop and State, 1989-91, annual rpt, 1621–2

Production, farms, acreage, and related data, by selected crop and State, monthly rpt, 1621–1
Production itemized costs, receipts, and returns, by commodity and region, 1975-90, annual rpt, 1544–20
Production itemized costs, receipts, and returns, by crop and State, 1987-89, annual rpt, 1544–24
Production of oil and fat, consumption by end use, and stocks, by type, monthly Current Industrial Rpt, 2506–4.4
Production of oil, crushings, and stocks, by oilseed type and State, monthly Current Industrial Rpt, 2506–4.3
Production, price, and supply forecasts used for USDA commodity program outlays, accuracy, 1975-88, GAO rpt, 26131–94
Production, prices, trade, and export inspections by US port and country of destination, by grain type, weekly rpt, 1313–2
Production, prices, trade, and marketing, by commodity, current situation and forecast, monthly rpt with articles, 1502–4
Production, prices, trade, and use of oils and fats, periodic situation rpt with articles, 1561–3
Soviet Union and US economic and sociodemographic indicators, selected years 1970-90, handbook, 2328–80
Stocks of grain by region and market city, and grain inspected for export, by type, weekly rpt, 1313–4
Stocks of grain on and off farms, by crop, quarterly rpt, 1621–4
Sweeteners (refined corn) trade, use, and wholesale prices, by commodity, quarterly situation rpt with articles, 1561–14
Weather conditions and effect on agriculture, by US region, State, and city, and world area, weekly rpt, 2182–7
Weight and volume conversion factors for agricultural commodities and products, 1992 rpt, 1508–3

Corporate profits
see Business income and expenses, general
see Business income and expenses, specific industry
see Operating ratios

Corporation for Public Broadcasting
Budget of US, authoritative financial statements with appropriations, outlays, and receipts, by category and agency, FY91, annual rpt, 8104–2.2
Budget of US, obligations and authority by function, agency, and program, with summaries and analyses, FY93, annual rpt, 104–2
Expenditures of Fed Govt in States, by type, program, agency, and State, FY91, annual rpt, 2464–2

Corporations
Aluminum plant ownership, capacity, energy and aluminum sources, and startup and closing dates, by US and foreign plant and location, 1990, annual listing, 5604–49
Assets and debts of private sector, balance sheets by segment, 1960-91, semiannual rpt, 9365–4.1
Boycotts (intl) by OPEC and other countries, US firms and individuals cooperation and tax benefits denied, 1990, article, 8302–2.323
Capital (fixed), govt and private nonresidential structures and equipment, residential capital, and consumer-owned durable goods, 1925-90, annual article, 2702–1.305; 2702–1.327
Capital costs over business cycles relation to firm size and financial distress indicators, 1960s-91, article, 9385–1.312
Election campaign-related internal communications of firms and assns, spending by organization, location, and candidate, 1991-92, biennial rpt, 9274–3
Finances and tax burdens of corporations under domestic and foreign control, 1983-87, GAO rpt, 26119–411
Financial data, security issues, profits, taxes, and dividends, monthly rpt, 9362–1.1
Financial statements for manufacturing, mining, and trade corporations, by selected SIC 2- to 3-digit industry, quarterly rpt, 2502–1
Flow-of-funds accounts, savings, investments, and credit statements, quarterly rpt, 9365–3.3
Income tax and other govt finances, by level of govt and State, 1992 and historical trends, annual rpt, 10044–1
Japan *keiretsu* and independent corporations ownership and concentration indicators, 1984, technical paper, 9366–6.288
Japan *keiretsu* corporations equity and debt financing by shareholding banks, with model results, 1960s-70, article, 9393–8.302
Minority- and woman-owned businesses and owner characteristics, by industry, employment and sales size, and form of ownership, 1987 survey, 2328–59
Natl income and product accounts, comprehensive accounts and components, benchmark revisions, 1929-88, 2708–5
Natl income and product accounts, comprehensive accounts and components, *Survey of Current Business*, monthly rpt, 2702–1.24
Patents (US) granted to US and foreign applicants, by applicant and country, 1960s-91, annual rpt, 2244–3
Political action committees, by type, 1974-91, semiannual press release, 9276–1.96
Political action committees, by type, 1974-92, semiannual press release, 9276–1.107
Political action committees contributions by party, and finances, by PAC type, 1991-92, press release, 9276–1.106; 9276–1.110
Political campaign finances reported to Fed Election Commission, by type of filer, 1990 natl elections, biennial rpt series, 9276–2
Productivity and costs of labor for private, nonfarm business, and manufacturing sectors, revised data, quarterly rpt, 6822–2
Profits by industry div, profit tax liability, and dividends, monthly rpt, quarterly data, 23842–1.1
Profits by industry div, stockholders equity, and costs per unit of output, 1947-91, annual rpt, 204–1.1; 204–1.7
Public confidence in people running selected social instns, 1972-88 surveys, biennial rpt, 9624–10.7
Puerto Rico and other US possessions corporations income tax returns, income and tax items, and employment, by selected industry, 1989, article, 8302–2.326
Puerto Rico statehood referendum proposal, with background data on Federal outlays, economic conditions, and finances of corporations with tax-favored status, 1940s-88, hearing, 21448–46
Retail trade sales, inventories, purchases, gross margin, and accounts receivable, by SIC 2- to 4-digit kind of business and form of ownership, 1990, annual rpt, 2413–5
SEC registration, firms required to file annual rpts, as of Sept 1991, annual listing, 9734–5
Securities holdings by shareholder type, and mgmt and executive pay issues, with data by company, 1991 hearing, 25248–130
Small Business Admin loan guarantee program participants finances, operations, characteristics, and views, 1991 survey, 9768–25
Small business finances, operations, owner characteristics, and Federal contracts, 1980s-90, annual rpt, 9764–6
Statistical Abstract of US, 1992 annual data compilation, 2324–1.17
Survey of Current Business, detailed data for major industries and economic indicators, monthly rpt, 2702–1
Survey of Current Business, detailed data for major industries and economic indicators, 1960-91, biennial supplement, 2704–1
Tax (income) collection, enforcement, and litigation activity of IRS, with data by type of tax, region, and State, FY91, annual rpt, 8304–3
Tax (income) compliance issues for large firms, with income, taxes paid, and tax credits, 1988, GAO rpt, 26119–405
Tax (income) compliance of corporations, and IRS enforcement activities, 1970s-92, hearing, 25408–118
Tax (income) returns and supplemental documents filed, by type, FY91 and projected to FY2000, semiannual rpt, 8302–4
Tax (income) returns filed, by type of filer, selected income items, quarterly rpt, 8302–2.1
Tax (income) returns filed, by type of return and IRS district, 1990 and projected 1991-98, annual rpt, 8304–24
Tax (income) returns filed, by type of tax and IRS region and service center, projected 1991-98 and trends from 1978, annual rpt, 8304–9
Tax (income) returns of corporations, income and tax items by asset size and detailed industry, 1989, annual rpt, 8304–4; 8304–21
Tax (income) returns of corporations, summary data by asset size and industry div, 1989, annual article, 8302–2.321
Tax (income) returns of corporations with foreign tax credit, income and tax items by industry group, 1988, biennial article, 8302–2.316
Tax collections of State govts by detailed type of tax, and tax rates, by State, FY91, annual rpt, 2466–2.7

Tax returns and supplemental documents filed, by type, 1990 and projected to 1999, annual article, 8302–2.304
Tax revenue, by level of govt, type of tax, State, and selected large county, quarterly rpt, 2462–3
Terrorism (intl) incidents, casualties, and attacks on US targets, by attack type and country, 1991, annual rpt, 7004–22
Terrorism (intl) incidents, casualties, and attacks on US targets, by attack type and world area, 1991, annual rpt, 7004–13
Truck and warehouse services finances and inventory, by SIC 2- to 4-digit industry, 1990 survey, annual rpt, 2413–14
see also Bank holding companies
see also Business acquisitions and mergers
see also Economic concentration and diversification
see also Foreign corporations
see also Government corporations and enterprises
see also Holding companies
see also Monopolies and cartels
see also Multinational corporations
see also Public utilities
see also under By Individual Company or Institution in the "Index by Categories"

Corps of Engineers
see Army Corps of Engineers

Corpus Christi, Tex.
Wages by occupation, and benefits for office and plant workers, 1992 survey, periodic MSA rpt, 6785–3.5
see also under By City and By SMSA or MSA in the "Index by Categories"

Correctional institutions
AIDS and tuberculosis cases in prisons, test results, and control and treatment policies, by location, 1990 survey, annual rpt, 6064–22
Budget of US, obligations and authority by function, agency, and program, with summaries and analyses, FY93, annual rpt, 104–2
Construction issues and projects at correctional facilities, series, 6066–30
Costs of construction and operation, capacity, and inmates, for Federal and State prisons, 1985-89, GAO rpt, 26119–407
Data on crime, criminal justice admin and enforcement, and public opinion, data compilation, 1992 annual rpt, 6064–6
Drug abuse and trafficking reduction programs activities, funding, staff, and Bush Admin budget request, by Federal agency, FY91-93, annual rpt, 234–2
Drug smuggling interdiction, inmate and staff testing, and treatment programs, by prison characteristics, 1989-90, 6066–19.70
Employment, earnings, facilities, and inmates of State and local correctional instns, by level of govt, facility characteristics, and State, data compilation, 1992 annual rpt, 6064–6.1; 6064–6.6
Employment requirements for new and expanded Federal prisons, by occupation, FY87-95, GAO rpt, 26119–397
Expenditures (direct) and employment, by function and level of govt, selected years 1962-87, 10048–53
Expenditures by function, and revenues by source, natl income and product account benchmark revisions, 1929-88, 2708–5
Expenditures by function, and revenues by source, natl income and product accounts, *Survey of Current Business*, monthly rpt, 2702–1.26
Expenditures, employment, and payroll, by activity, level of govt, and State, FY90, annual rpt, 6066–25.50
Facilities, population, employment, spending, and other characteristics of correctional instns, by State and for Fed Govt, 1990, annual rpt, 6064–26.3; 6068–218
Fed Bur of Prisons activities, and inmate and staff characteristics, 1991, annual rpt, 6244–2
Fed Bur of Prisons admin offices and correctional instns, facility characteristics, 1992, annual listing, 6244–4
Fed Govt spending in States, by type, program, agency, and State, FY91, annual rpt, 2464–2
Federal and State correctional instns population by sex, admissions, and instn capacity and overcrowding, by State, 1980s-91, annual rpt, 6066–25.47
Federal correctional instns prisoners and staff, by selected characteristics, region, and instn, FY89, annual rpt, 6244–1
Foreign countries human rights conditions in 170 countries, 1991, annual rpt, 21384–3
Govt employment and payroll, by function, level of govt, and jurisdiction, annual rpt series, 2466–1
Govt finances, tax systems and revenue, and fiscal structure, by level of govt and State, 1992 with historical trends, annual rpt, 10044–1
Jail population by sex, race, and for 25 jurisdictions, and instn conditions, 1990-91, annual rpt, 6066–25.48
Jail population, capacity, and instns under court order to reduce overcrowding and improve conditions, by State, 1990, annual rpt, 6064–26.1
Mental health care facilities, staff, patients, and finances, 1970s-91, biennial rpt, 4094–1
Occupational Outlook Handbook, 1992-93, biennial rpt, 6744–1
Palau admin, and social, economic, and govtl data, FY91, annual rpt, 7004–6
Police employment, spending, and operations, for State, city, county, and special district agencies, 1990, annual rpt, 6064–39
Sheriffs' agencies employment, spending, and operations, FY90, 6066–25.45
State prisons housing space by region, and employees by occupation, 1984 and 1990, 6068–248
States criminal justice systems activities, employment, funding, and data collection, by State, 1970s-91, annual rpt, 6064–40
Statistical Abstract of US, 1992 annual data compilation, 2324–1.5
see also Community-based correctional programs
see also Juvenile detention and correctional institutions
see also Military prisons
see also Parole and probation
see also Prison work programs
see also Prisoners
see also Rehabilitation of criminals

Correspondence courses
Occupational qualification and skill improvement training, workers participating by training source, occupation, age, sex, and race, 1991, 6728–32
Student guaranteed loan participation and default rates, for correspondence schools, FY87-89, GAO rpt, 26121–448

Corruption and bribery
Arrests for fraud and forgery, case dispositions, and sentencing, by age, sex, race, and offense type, 1983-88, 6066–19.64
Court civil and criminal caseloads for Federal district, appeals, and bankruptcy courts, by type of suit and offense, circuit, and district, 1991, annual rpt, 18204–11
Court civil and criminal caseloads for Federal district, appeals, and special courts, 1991, annual rpt, 18204–8
Court criminal case processing in Federal district courts, and dispositions, by offense, district, and offender characteristics, 1989, annual data compilation, 6064–29
Court criminal case processing in Federal district courts, and dispositions, by offense, 1980-91, annual rpt, 6064–31
Govt officials prosecuted and convicted for corruption, by judicial district and level of govt, 1970-90, annual rpt, 6004–13
IRS internal audits, and employee and nonemployee violations, FY91, annual rpt, 8304–3.1
Sentences, arrests, and convictions, by offense, data compilation, 1992 annual rpt, 6064–6.5
Sentences for Federal crimes, guidelines use and results by offense and district, and Sentencing Commission activities, 1991, annual rpt, 17664–1
Sentences for Federal offenses, guidelines by offense and circumstances, series, 17668–1
Statistical Abstract of US, 1992 annual data compilation, 2324–1.5
US attorneys civil and criminal cases by type and disposition, and collections, by Federal district, FY91, annual rpt, 6004–2.1; 6004–2.7
Wiretaps authorized, costs, arrests, trials, and convictions, by offense and jurisdiction, 1991, annual rpt, 18204–7
see also Federal Inspectors General reports

Cosmetics and toiletries
Carcinogens chemistry, sources, environment and health risks, and regulation, by substance and brand, 1991 annual rpt, 4044–15
County Business Patterns, 1989: employment, establishments, and payroll, by SIC 2- to 4-digit industry and county, annual State rpt series, 2326–8
County Business Patterns, 1990: employment, establishments, and payroll, by SIC 2- to 4-digit industry and county, annual State rpt series, 2326–6
CPI by component for US city average, and by selected metro area, region, and population size, monthly rpt, 6762–2

Employment, earnings, and hours, by SIC 1- to 4-digit industry, monthly 1989-Feb 1992, annual rpt, 6744–4
Exports and imports between US and outlying areas, by detailed commodity and mode of transport, 1991, annual rpt, 2424–11
Exports and imports of US, by country and detailed commodity, monthly rpt, 2422–12
Exports and imports of US, by Harmonized System 6-digit commodity and country, 1991, annual rpt, 2424–13
Exports and imports of US, by transport mode, country, and SITC 1- to 3-digit commodity, 1991, annual rpt, 2424–12
Exports of US, detailed Schedule B commodities with countries of destination, 1991, annual rpt, 2424–10
FDA investigations and regulatory activities, quarterly rpt, 4062–3
Imports detained by FDA, by reason, product, shipper, brand, and country, monthly listing, 4062–2
Injuries from use of consumer products and related activities, by severity and victim age and sex, 1990, annual rpt, 9164–7
Injuries from use of consumer products, by severity, victim age, and detailed product, 1991, annual rpt, 9164–6
Input-output structure of US economy, detailed interindustry transactions for 541 industries, and components of final demand, 1982 benchmark data, 2708–17
Labor productivity, indexes of output, hours, and employment by SIC 2- to 4-digit industry, 1967-90, annual rpt, 6824–1.3
Manufacturing annual survey, 1990: finances and operations, by SIC 2- to 4-digit industry, series, 2506–14
Manufacturing census, 1987: concentration of largest firms measured by value added, and for shipments by SIC 2- and 4-digit industry, subject rpt, 2497–6
Manufacturing census, 1987: shipments of manufacturers products, by customer class and SIC 2- and 4-digit industry, subject rpt, 2497–4
Manufacturing finances and operations, by SIC 2- to 4-digit industry, forecast 1992, annual rpt, 2044–28
Occupational injury and illness rates, by SIC 2- to 4-digit industry, 1989-90, annual rpt, 6844–7
Occupational injury and illness rates, by SIC 2- to 4-digit industry, 1990, annual rpt, 6844–1
OECD trade, total and for 4 major countries, and US trade by country, by commodity, 1980-90, world area rpt series, 9116–1
Price indexes (producer), by stage of processing and detailed commodity, monthly rpt, 6762–6
Price indexes (producer), by stage of processing and detailed commodity, monthly 1991, annual rpt, 6764–2
Production and sales of synthetic organic chemicals, and manufacturer listing, by product, 1990, annual rpt, 9884–3
Toxicology Natl Program research and testing activities, FY90 and planned FY91, annual rpt, 4044–16

Cost of living
Business statistics, detailed data for major industries and economic indicators, 1960-91, *Survey of Current Business* biennial supplement, 2704–1
Economic indicators, prices, labor costs, and productivity, BLS econometric analyses and methodology, working paper series, 6886–6
Energy use by mode of transport, fuel supply, and demographic and economic factors of vehicle use, 1970s-90, annual rpt, 3304–5
Farm prices received and paid, by commodity and State, monthly rpt, 1629–1
Foreign countries living costs, State Dept indexes, housing allowances, and hardship differentials by country and major city, quarterly rpt, 7002–7
Statistical Abstract of US, 1992 annual data compilation, 2324–1.15
see also Consumer Price Index
see also Energy prices
see also Family budgets
see also Food prices
see also Housing costs and financing
see also Inflation
see also Medical costs
see also Prices
see also Producer Price Index
see also Rent

Cost of living adjustments
see Escalator clauses

Cost of production
see Agricultural production costs
see Business income and expenses, general
see Business income and expenses, specific industry
see Energy production costs
see Producer Price Index
see Production costs

Costa Rica
Agricultural trade of US, by detailed commodity and country, 1991, annual rpt, 1524–8
Agricultural trade of US, by detailed commodity and country, 1991, semiannual rpt, 1522–4
AID economic aid to developing countries, obligations and disbursements by country, quarterly rpt, 9912–4
AID loans repayment status and terms by program and country, and status of predecessor agency loans, quarterly rpt, 9912–3
Background Notes, summary social, political, and economic data, 1992 rpt, 7006–2.21
Death rates by cause and age, and life expectancy, by sex, for Costa Rica and Guatemala, 1984 and trends from 1900, working paper, 2326–18.64
Economic and military aid and loans from US and intl agencies, by program and country, FY46-91, annual rpt, 9914–5
Economic and social conditions of developing countries from 1960s, and Intl Dev Cooperation Agency and AID activities and funding, FY91-93, annual rpt, 9904–4
Economic and social conditions, resources, and trade, and aid, 1992, annual factbook, 9914–14
Economic conditions, policy, and trade practices, by country, 1989-91, annual rpt, 21384–5
Economic indicators and reform issues in Costa Rica, mid 1970s-90, working paper, 9916–13.5
Economic indicators for Central America by country, 1969-89, working paper, 9916–13.4
Economic, population, and agricultural data, US and other aid sources, and AID activity, 1992 country rpt, 9916–12.61
Economic, social, political, and geographic summary data, by country, 1992, annual factbook, 9114–2
Exports and imports of US, by commodity and country, 1980-90, world area rpt, 9116–1.5
Exports and imports of US, by Harmonized System 6-digit commodity and country, 1991, annual rpt, 2424–13
Exports and imports of US, by selected country, country group, and commodity group, 1991, annual rpt, 2044–37
Exports and imports of US, by transport mode, country, and SITC 1- to 3-digit commodity, 1991, annual rpt, 2424–12
Exports, imports, and balances of US for manufactured goods, by SITC 2-digit commodity and country, quarterly rpt, 2042–35
Exports, investment, debt, and tariffs of 7 Latin America countries, and trade and investment policy liberalization issues, mid 1960s-91, 9886–4.184
Exports of Costa Rica to US by commodity group, and role in stimulating economic growth, 1980s, working paper, 9916–13.2
Exports of US, detailed Schedule B commodities with countries of destination, 1991, annual rpt, 2424–10
Human rights conditions in 170 countries, and US economic and military aid, 1991, annual rpt, 21384–3
Labor conditions, union coverage, and work accidents, 1992 annual country rpt, 6366–4.33
Military aid of US, arms sales, and training programs costs and budget requests, by program, world region, and country, FY91-93, annual rpt, 7144–13
Military spending, arms trade, and force strengths, with govt spending and population, by country, 1979-89, annual rpt, 9824–1
Multinatl US firms and foreign affiliates finances and operations, by industry and country, 1989 benchmark survey, annual rpt, 2704–5
Multinatl US firms foreign affiliates, income statement items by asset size, industry, and country, 1988, biennial article, 8302–2.322
Population size, growth rates, and components of change, by country, projected 1990-2020 and trends from 1950, biennial rpt, 2324–9
Refugee migration, and intl aid programs, by world area and country of origin and asylum, 1991, annual rpt, 7004–15
Steel trade, by product, country, and customs district, with US industry operating data, 1989-June 1992, semiannual rpt, 9882–15
UN voting record and share of votes in agreement with US, by issue, country, and world area, 1991, annual rpt, 7004–18

see also under By Foreign Country in the "Index by Categories"
Costantini, Adele S.
"Incidence of Non-Hodgkin's Lymphomas in Italy", 4472–1.336
Cote d'Ivoire
see Ivory Coast
Cotterill, Philip G.
"Prospective Payment for Medicare Hospital Capital: Implications of the Research", 4652–1.313
Cotton
Acreage planted and harvested, by crop and State, 1990-91 and planned as of June 1992, annual rpt, 1621–23
Acreage planted, by selected crop and State, 1983-91 and planned 1992, annual rpt, 1621–22
Acreage planted by State and county, and fiber quality, by cotton variety, 1992, annual rpt, 1309–6
Acreage reduction program compliance, enrollment, and yield on planted acreage, by commodity and State, annual press release series, 1004–20
Agricultural Stabilization and Conservation Service cotton programs, 1955-92, annual fact sheet, 1806–4.14
Agricultural Stabilization and Conservation Service producer payments, by program and State, 1991, annual table, 1804–12
Agricultural Statistics, 1991, annual rpt, 1004–1
Business statistics, detailed data for major industries and economic indicators, *Survey of Current Business*, monthly rpt, 2702–1.21
Business statistics, detailed data for major industries and economic indicators, 1960-91, *Survey of Current Business* biennial supplement, 2704–1
CCC certificate exchange activity, by commodity, biweekly press release, 1802–16
CCC cotton and grain loan activity, by commodity, weekly rpt, 1313–2
CCC financial condition and major commodity program operations, FY63-88, annual chartbook, 1824–2
Clothing and shoe production, shipments, trade, and use, by product, periodic Current Industrial Rpt series, 2506–6
County Business Patterns, 1989: employment, establishments, and payroll, by SIC 2- to 4-digit industry and county, annual State rpt series, 2326–8
County Business Patterns, 1990: employment, establishments, and payroll, by SIC 2- to 4-digit industry and county, annual State rpt series, 2326–6
Employment, earnings, and hours, by SIC 1- to 4-digit industry, monthly 1989-Feb 1992, annual rpt, 6744–4
Export licensing, monitoring, and enforcement activities, FY91, annual rpt, 2024–1
Exports and imports (agricultural) commodity and country, prices, and world market devs, monthly rpt, 1922–12
Exports and imports (agricultural) of US, by commodity and country, bimonthly rpt, 1522–1
Exports and imports (agricultural) of US, by detailed commodity and country, 1991, annual rpt, 1524–8
Exports and imports (agricultural) of US, by detailed commodity and country, 1991, semiannual rpt, 1522–4
Exports and imports between US and outlying areas, by detailed commodity and mode of transport, 1991, annual rpt, 2424–11
Exports and imports of textiles, raw fiber equivalents by product, country, and world region, 1989-90, article, 1561–1.301
Exports and imports of US, by country and detailed commodity, monthly rpt, 2422–12
Exports and imports of US, by Harmonized System 6-digit commodity and country, 1991, annual rpt, 2424–13
Exports and imports of US, by transport mode, country, and SITC 1- to 3-digit commodity, 1991, annual rpt, 2424–12
Exports of grains, oilseed products, hides, skins, and cotton, by country, weekly rpt, dropped data, 1922–3
Exports of US, detailed Schedule B commodities with countries of destination, 1991, annual rpt, 2424–10
Exports of US textiles and apparel, by product group and country, quarterly rpt, 2042–36
Farm financial and marketing conditions, forecast 1992, annual chartbook, 1504–8
Farm financial and marketing conditions, forecast 1992, annual conf, 1504–9
Farm income, cash marketing receipts ranked by commodity and State, 1990, 1548–385
Farm sector balance sheet, and receipts by detailed commodity, by State, 1986-90, annual rpt, 1544–18
Fertilizer and pesticide use and application rates, by type, crop, and State, 1991, 1616–1.1
Fiber and processing test results, by cotton staple, region, State, and production area, 1991, annual rpt, 1309–16
Fiber grade, staple, and mike, for upland and American pima cotton by State, monthly rpt, 1309–11
Fiber grade, staple, mike, and other quality indicators, for upland cotton by classing office, weekly rpt, 1309–15
Fiber quality, by State, 1991, annual rpt, 1309–7
Fiber quality, supply, and carryover, 1991-92, annual rpt, 1309–8
Foreign and US agricultural production, acreage, and yield for selected crops, forecasts by selected world region and country, FAS monthly circular, 1925–28
Foreign and US agricultural supply and demand indicators, by selected crop, monthly rpt, 1522–5
Foreign and US cotton production and trade, FAS periodic circular series, 1925–4
Foreign countries agricultural production, prices, and trade, by country, 1980-91 and forecast 1992, annual world area rpt series, 1524–4
Foreign countries market conditions for US textile and apparel exports, with domestic industry operations, country rpt series, 2046–15
Freight (waterborne domestic and foreign) by commodity, traffic, and passengers, by port and waterway, 1989, annual rpt, 3754–3
Futures and options trading volume, by commodity and exchange, FY91, annual rpt, 11924–2
Futures trading in selected commodities and financial instruments and indexes, for NYC, Chicago, and other markets activity, biweekly rpt, 11922–5
Ginnings of cotton, by State and county, seasonal biweekly rpt, 1631–19
Imports of textiles, by country of origin, monthly rpt, 2042–27
Imports of textiles, by product and country of origin, monthly rpt series, 2046–8; 2046–9
Imports of textiles under Multifiber Arrangement by product and country, and status of bilateral agreements, 1988-91, annual rpt, 9884–18
Input-output structure of US economy, detailed interindustry transactions for 541 industries, and components of final demand, 1982 benchmark data, 2708–17
Irrigation projects of Reclamation Bur in western US, crop production and acreage by commodity, State, and project, 1990, annual rpt, 5824–12
Linters production, stocks, use, and prices, monthly rpt, 1309–10
Manufacturing annual survey, 1990: finances and operations, by SIC 2- to 4-digit industry, series, 2506–14
Manufacturing census, 1987: concentration of largest firms measured by value added, and for shipments by SIC 2- and 4-digit industry, subject rpt, 2497–6
Manufacturing census, 1987: shipments of manufacturers products, by customer class and SIC 2- and 4-digit industry, subject rpt, 2497–4
Occupational injury and illness rates, by SIC 2- to 4-digit industry, 1989-90, annual rpt, 6844–7
Occupational injury and illness rates, by SIC 2- to 4-digit industry, 1990, annual rpt, 6844–1
OECD trade, total and for 4 major countries, and US trade by country, by commodity, 1980-90, world area rpt series, 9116–1
Price indexes (producer), by stage of processing and detailed commodity, monthly rpt, 6762–6
Price indexes (producer), by stage of processing and detailed commodity, monthly 1991, annual rpt, 6764–2
Price support and other CCC program outlays, with production and marketing outlook, by commodity, projected 1991-97, annual rpt, 26306–6.171
Prices in selected spot markets, futures prices at NYC exchange, farm prices, and CCC loan stocks, monthly rpt, 1309–1
Prices of cotton at selected spot markets, NYC futures prices, and CCC loan rates, 1991/92 and trends from 1944, annual rpt, 1309–2
Prices received and paid by farmers, by commodity and State, monthly rpt, 1629–1
Prices received and paid by farmers, by commodity and State, 1991, annual rpt, 1629–5
Prices received by farmers and production value, by detailed crop and State, 1989-91, annual rpt, 1621–2

Production, farms, acreage, and related data, by selected crop and State, monthly rpt, 1621–1
Production inputs, output, and productivity for farms, by commodity and region, 1947-90, annual rpt, 1544–17
Production itemized costs, receipts, and returns, by commodity and region, 1975-90, annual rpt, 1544–20
Production itemized costs, receipts, and returns, by crop and State, 1987-89, annual rpt, 1544–24
Production, price, and supply forecasts used for USDA commodity program outlays, accuracy, 1975-88, GAO rpt, 26131–94
Production, prices, exports, stocks, and mill use of long staple cotton, monthly rpt, 1309–12
Production, prices, trade, and marketing, by commodity, current situation and forecast, monthly rpt with articles, 1502–4
Production, prices, trade, and use of cotton, wool, and synthetic fibers, periodic situation rpt with articles, 1561–1
Production, trade, sales, stocks, and material used, by product, region, and State, periodic Current Industrial Rpt series, 2506–5
Production, trade, use, and stocks of cotton, USDA forecast accuracy, 1980-90, article, 1561–1.302
Science, engineering, and technical employment in manufacturing, by field and industry, 1989, triennial rpt, 9627–23
Soviet Union and US economic and sociodemographic indicators, selected years 1970-90, handbook, 2328–80
Weight and volume conversion factors for agricultural commodities and products, 1992 rpt, 1508–3

Cottonseed
see Oils, oilseeds, and fats

Cottrell, Benjamin H. Jr.
"Final Case Study for the National Scenic Byways Study: Study of the Highway Safety Aspects of the Blue Ridge Parkway", 7556–8.2

Cotugna, Nancy
"Development and Supermarket Field Testing of Videotaped Nutrition Messages for Cancer Risk Reduction", 4042–3.371

Coughlin, Cletus C.
"Foreign-Owned Companies in the U.S.: Malign or Benign?", 9391–1.309
"How Foreign-Owned Firms Benefit the Eighth District", 9391–16.302
"How the 1992 Legislation Will Affect European Financial Services", 9391–1.308

Coulam, Robert F.
"Medicare's Prospective Payment System: A Critical Appraisal", 4652–1.312

Council for Mutual Economic Assistance
Exports and imports of NATO members with CMEA Europe members, by country, annual rpt, discontinued, 7144–5

Council of Economic Advisers
Budget of US, authoritative financial statements with appropriations, outlays, and receipts, by category and agency, FY91, annual rpt, 8104–2.2
Budget of US, obligations and authority by function, agency, and program, with summaries and analyses, FY93, annual rpt, 104–2
Economic indicators and components, current data and annual trends, monthly rpt, 23842–1
Economic Report of the President for 1992, with economic trends from 1929, annual rpt, 204–1

Council on Environmental Quality
Budget of US, authoritative financial statements with appropriations, outlays, and receipts, by category and agency, FY91, annual rpt, 8104–2.2
Budget of US, obligations and authority by function, agency, and program, with summaries and analyses, FY93, annual rpt, 104–2
Environmental Quality, status of problems, protection programs, research, and intl issues, 1991 annual rpt, 484–1

Counselors and counseling
Alien workers discrimination and other employment-related problems in NYC, hotline calls, 1988, 6366–6.7
Education (special) enrollment by age, staff, funding, and needs, by type of handicap and State, 1990/91, annual rpt, 4944–4
Education data compilation, 1992 annual rpt, 4824–2
Educational enrollment, finances, staff, and high school grads, for elementary and secondary public school systems by State, FY89-90, annual rpt, 4834–6
HHS financial aid, by program, recipient, State, and city, FY91, annual regional listings, 4004–3
Homeless persons transitional housing and support services program, outcome relation to client characteristics and services, FY87-90, GAO rpt, 26113–549
Hospital discharges by detailed diagnostic and procedure category, primary diagnosis, and length of stay, by age, sex, and region, 1990, annual rpt, 4147–13.111
Juvenile facilities compensatory education programs activities, participant and staff characteristics, and outcomes, 1991 rpts, 4808–40
Labor demand, turnover, and training completions, by detailed occupation, 1990 and projected to 2005, biennial rpt, 6744–3
Occupational Outlook Handbook, 1992-93, biennial rpt, 6744–1
Physicians (internists) office visits, by characteristics of patient, physician, and visit, 1989, 4146–8.214
Physicians visits, by patient and practice characteristics, diagnosis, and services provided, 1989, annual rpt, 4147–13.109
Physicians visits, by patient and practice characteristics, diagnosis, and services provided, 1990, advance rpt, 4146–8.215
Prison and community-based facilities, population, employment, spending, and other characteristics, by State and for Fed Govt, 1990, annual rpt, 6064–26.3; 6068–218
VA health care facilities trainees, by detailed program and city, FY91, annual rpt, 8704–4
Veterans (Persian Gulf) post-traumatic stress disorder cases, and VA program use, by site, 1991, annual rpt, 8704–7
Veterans rehabilitative and educational counseling provided, 1967-91, annual rpt, 8604–5.2
see also Clergy
see also Psychiatry
see also Social work
see also Vocational guidance

Counterfeiting and forgery
Arrests, by offense, offender characteristics, and location, 1991, annual rpt, 6224–2.2
Arrests for fraud and forgery, case dispositions, and sentencing, by age, sex, race, and offense type, 1983-88, 6066–19.64
Court civil and criminal caseloads for Federal district, appeals, and bankruptcy courts, by type of suit and offense, circuit, and district, 1991, annual rpt, 18204–11
Court civil and criminal caseloads for Federal district, appeals, and special courts, 1991, annual rpt, 18204–8
Court criminal case processing in Federal district courts, and dispositions, by offense, district, and offender characteristics, 1989, annual data compilation, 6064–29
Court criminal case processing in Federal district courts, and dispositions, by offense, 1980-91, annual rpt, 6064–31
Crime, criminal justice admin and enforcement, and public opinion, data compilation, 1992 annual rpt, 6064–6
Currency (counterfeit) seized and in circulation, and operations suppressed by Secret Service, data compilation, 1992 annual rpt, 6064–6.4
Juvenile arrests, by sex, race, disposition, and offense, 1990, 6066–27.8
Postal Service inspection activities, 2nd half FY92, semiannual rpt, 9862–2
Prison and parole admissions and releases, sentence length, and time served, by offense and offender characteristics, 1988, annual rpt, 6064–33
Prisoners in Federal and contract instns, by selected characteristics, region, and Federal instn, FY89, annual rpt, 6244–1.1
Secret Service counterfeiting and other investigations and arrests by type, and disposition, FY91 and trends from FY82, annual rpt, 8464–1
Sentences for Federal crimes, guidelines use and results by offense and district, and Sentencing Commission activities, 1991, annual rpt, 17664–1
Sentences for Federal offenses, guidelines by offense and circumstances, series, 17668–1
US attorneys civil and criminal cases by type and disposition, and collections, by Federal district, FY91, annual rpt, 6004–2.1

Counties
Agricultural Conservation Program, counties served by State, FY91, annual rpt, 1804–7
Census Bur data coverage and availability for statistics on counties, cities, and small areas, 1991 rpt, 2326–7.82
Census Bur geographic levels of data coverage, maps, and reference products, 1992 rpt, 2308–67
Census of Housing, 1990: summary unit characteristics, by householder race and age, county, place, and urban-rural location, State rpt series, 2471–1

Census of Population and Housing, 1990: detailed geographic coverage, State CD-ROM series, 2551–9
Census of Population and Housing, 1990: population and housing characteristics, detailed geographic coverage, State CD-ROM series, 2551–10
Census of Population and Housing, 1990: summary characteristics, by county, subdiv, and place, State rpt series, 2551–7
Census of Population and Housing, 1990: summary characteristics, households, and land area, by county, subdiv, and place, State rpt series, 2551–1
Census of Population, 1990: population characteristics and living arrangements, by county, place, and urban-rural location, State rpt series, 2531–1
Census of Population, 1990: population characteristics and living arrangements, for Native American, urban, and metro areas, series, 2531–2
Crimes, arrests by offender characteristics, and rates, by offense, and law enforcement employees, by population size and jurisdiction, 1991, annual rpt, 6224–2
Farmland damaged by natural disaster, Emergency Conservation Program aid and participation by State, FY91, annual rpt, 1804–22
Govt direct spending and employment, by function and level of govt, selected years 1962-87, 10048–53
Govt employment and payroll, by function and population size, for 424 largest counties, 1991, annual rpt, 2466–1.2
Govt employment and payroll, by function, level of govt, and State, 1991, annual rpt, 2466–1.1
Govt employment of minorities and women, by occupation, function, pay grade, and level of govt, 1991, annual rpt, 9244–6.3
Govt finances, by level of govt, State, and for large cities and counties, annual rpt series, 2466–2
Govt finances, structure, and service delivery in large metro areas, local area rpt series, 10046–9
Govt finances, tax systems and revenue, and fiscal structure, by level of govt and State, 1992 with historical trends, annual rpt, 10044–1
Health service areas, indicators of service use, and residents seeking care outside area, under alternative area definitions, 1988-89, 4147–2.113
Income (personal) per capita and by source, and employment, by industry div, State, MSA, and county, 1969-90, annual CD-ROM, 2704–7
Labor surplus areas eligible for preferential Fed Govt contracts, monthly listing, 6402–1
Migration, immigration, and mover characteristics compared to nonmovers, 1987-90, annual Current Population Rpt, 2546–1.456
Migration, population change, and areas losing population, by region, State, and metro-nonmetro location, 1980s and trends from 1940, Current Population Rpt, 2546–2.164
Migration since 1990, mover characteristics by same or different area, and compared to nonmovers, 1991, annual Current Population Rpt, 2546–1.464
Rural areas economic and social conditions, dev, and problems, periodic journal, 1502–7
Soil surveys and maps for counties, 1899-1991, annual listing, 1264–11
Statistical Abstract of US, 1992 annual data compilation, 2324–1
see also County Business Patterns
see also under By County in the "Index by Categories"

County Business Patterns
Employment, establishments, and payroll, by SIC 2- to 4-digit industry and county, 1989, annual State rpt series, 2326–8
Employment, establishments, and payroll, by SIC 2- to 4-digit industry and county, 1990, annual State rpt series, 2326–6

Courier services
Tax (income) returns of sole proprietorships, income statement items, by industry group, 1990, annual article, 8302–2.317; 8302–2.320

Court of International Trade
Budget of US, authoritative financial statements with appropriations, outlays, and receipts, by category and agency, FY91, annual rpt, 8104–2.2
Budget of US, obligations and authority by function, agency, and program, with summaries and analyses, FY93, annual rpt, 104–2
Caseloads of Court, decisions, and appeals, FY91-92, annual rpt, 18224–2
Cases filed and terminated, 1990-91, annual rpt, 18204–8.21

Court of Military Appeals
Cases and actions of military courts, FY91, annual rpt, 3504–3

Courtless, Joan C.
"Trends in Transportation", 1702–1.306

Courts
Budget of US, authoritative financial statements with appropriations, outlays, and receipts, by agency, FY91, annual rpt, 8104–2
Budget of US, obligations and authority by function, agency, and program, with summaries and analyses, FY93, annual rpt, 104–2
Budget of US, receipts by source, outlays by agency and program, and balances, monthly rpt, 8102–3
Employment, earnings, and hours, by SIC 1- to 4-digit industry, monthly 1989-Feb 1992, annual rpt, 6744–4
Expenditures, employment, and payroll, by activity, level of govt, and State, FY90, annual rpt, 6066–25.50
Fed Govt labor productivity, indexes of output and labor costs by function, FY67-90, annual rpt, 6824–1.6
Judicial Conf proceedings and findings, spring 1992, semiannual rpt, 18202–2
Marshals Service activities, FY91, annual rpt, 6294–1
Sheriffs' agencies employment, spending, and operations, FY90, 6066–25.45
Statistical Abstract of US, 1992 annual data compilation, 2324–1.5
see also Administrative Office of the U.S. Courts
see also Civil procedure
see also Contempt of court
see also Court of International Trade
see also Court of Military Appeals
see also Courts-martial and courts of inquiry
see also Criminal procedure
see also D.C. courts
see also Domestic relations courts and cases
see also Federal bankruptcy courts
see also Federal courts of appeals
see also Federal district courts
see also Federal Judicial Center
see also Judges
see also Judicial Conference of the U.S.
see also Judicial powers
see also Judicial reform
see also Juries
see also Juvenile courts and cases
see also Parole and probation
see also Sentences, criminal procedure
see also State courts
see also Supreme Court
see also Tax Court of the U.S.
see also Tax laws and courts
see also Traffic laws and courts
see also Trials
see also U.S. Claims Court
see also U.S. Court of Appeals for the Federal Circuit
see also Witnesses

Courts-martial and courts of inquiry
Cases and actions of military courts, FY91, annual rpt, 3504–3
Criminal case processing in military courts, and prisoners by facility, by service branch, data compilation, 1992 annual rpt, 6064–6.5; 6064–6.6

Cousins, Jennifer H.
"Family Versus Individually Oriented Intervention for Weight Loss in Mexican American Women", 4042–3.356

Covey, Ted
"Managing Farm Lender Interest Rate Risk with Financial Futures", 1541–1.308

Cowan, Cathy A.
"Business, Households, and Governments: Health Care Costs, 1990", 4652–1.309

Cows
see Dairy industry and products
see Livestock and livestock industry

Cox, Christine S.
"Plan and Operation of the NHANES I Epidemiologic Followup Study, 1987. Vital and Health Statistics Series 1", 4147–1.29

Cox, Donald F.
"Fee Update and Medicare Volume Performance Standards for 1993", 17266–1.7

Coyle, William T.
"Future of Agriculture and Trade in the Pacific: An Overview", 1524–4.3

CPI
see Consumer Price Index

Crabbe, Leland
"Effect of a Rating Change on Commercial Paper Outstandings", 9366–6.299

Craig, R. Sean
"Fiscal Implications of the Transition from Planned to Market Economy", 9366–7.278

Cranberries
see Fruit and fruit products

Crawford, Everett
"Changing Nation—Its Changing Labor Force", 15496–1.16
Creasey, William A.
"Review of Literature on Herbicides, Including Phenoxy Herbicides and Associated Dioxins: Volume XIX Analysis of Recent Literature on Health Effects and Volume XX Annotated Bibliography of Recent Literature on Health Effects", 8706–1.5
Credit
Assets and debts of private sector, balance sheets by segment, 1960-91, semiannual rpt, 9365–4.1
Budget of US, Bush Admin proposals, with detail for defense budgets, and historical data from FY34, FY93, 108–46.2
Budget of US, House concurrent resolution, with spending and revenue targets, FY93 and projected to FY97, annual rpt, 21264–2
Budget of US, obligations and authority by function, agency, and program, with summaries and analyses, FY93, annual rpt, 104–2
Demand for credit, activity indicators, 1982-91, annual rpt, 204–1.5
Economic indicators and components, current data and annual trends, monthly rpt, 23842–1.5
Economic indicators performance, and Fed Reserve monetary policy objectives, as of July 1992, semiannual rpt, 9362–4
Financial and business detailed statistics, *Fed Reserve Bulletin*, monthly rpt with articles, 9362–1
Statistical Abstract of US, 1992 annual data compilation, 2324–1.16
see also Agricultural credit
see also Business assets and liabilities, general
see also Business assets and liabilities, specific industry
see also Commercial credit
see also Commodity Credit Corp.
see also Consumer credit
see also Credit bureaus and agencies
see also Credit cards
see also Credit unions
see also Discrimination in credit
see also Finance companies
see also Foreign debts
see also Government assets and liabilities
see also Interest payments
see also International finance
see also Loan delinquency and default
see also Loans
see also Mortgages
see also Public debt
Credit bureaus and agencies
County Business Patterns, 1989: employment, establishments, and payroll, by SIC 2- to 4-digit industry and county, annual State rpt series, 2326–8
County Business Patterns, 1990: employment, establishments, and payroll, by SIC 2- to 4-digit industry and county, annual State rpt series, 2326–6
Employment, earnings, and hours, by SIC 1- to 4-digit industry, monthly 1989-Feb 1992, annual rpt, 6744–4
Mortgage loan activity, by type of lender, loan, and mortgaged property, monthly press release, 5142–18
Mortgage loan activity, by type of lender, loan, and mortgaged property, quarterly press release, 5142–30
Multinatl US firms foreign affiliates, income statement items by asset size, industry, and country, 1988, biennial article, 8302–2.322
Tax (income) returns of corporations, income and tax items by asset size and detailed industry, 1989, annual rpt, 8304–4; 8304–21
Tax (income) returns of sole proprietorships, income statement items, by industry group, 1990, annual article, 8302–2.317; 8302–2.320
Credit cards
Banks (natl) charters, mergers, liquidations, enforcement cases, and financial performance, with data by instn and State, quarterly rpt, 8402–3
Banks and other credit card issuers costs and revenue, mid 1970s-91, article, 9362–1.306
Banks and thrifts finances and operations by deposit size, Fed Reserve functional cost analysis, 1991, annual rpt, 9364–6
Debt outstanding on credit cards, consumer payments share of disposable income, and bank and retail debt held, 1980s-90, article, 9387–1.301
Economic indicators and components, current data and annual trends, monthly rpt, 23842–1.5
Families financial status, income, net worth, and assets and debt by type, by income and selected characteristics, 1983 and 1989, article, 9362–1.301
Households financial services use, by account type and instn type and location, 1989 survey, article, 9362–1.303
Households holding credit cards by income, age, and card type, and debt outstanding, with issuer costs and revenue, 1970s-80, article, 9362–1.306
Issuers of credit cards, disclosure of terms and conditions to consumers, with finances and operations, 1991 hearing, 21248–175
Mail volume to and from households, use, and views, by class, source, content, and household characteristics, FY87-90, annual rpt, 9864–10
Minority- and woman-owned businesses and owner characteristics, by industry, employment and sales size, and form of ownership, 1987 survey, 2328–59
Statistical Abstract of US, 1992 annual data compilation, 2324–1.16
Credit Reform Act
Loans, loan guarantees, and grants of Fed Govt, administrative costs budget accounting, by program and agency, 1992 rpt, 26306–6.166
Credit unions
Assets and liabilities of financial instns, by instn type, 1990, annual rpt, 9364–5.4
Assets, members, and location of credit unions, 1992 annual listing, 9534–6
Assets of depository instns, monthly rpt, 9362–1.1
Business statistics, detailed data for major industries and economic indicators, 1960-91, *Survey of Current Business* biennial supplement, 2704–1
County Business Patterns, 1989: employment, establishments, and payroll, by SIC 2- to 4-digit industry and county, annual State rpt series, 2326–8
County Business Patterns, 1990: employment, establishments, and payroll, by SIC 2- to 4-digit industry and county, annual State rpt series, 2326–6
Failures of credit unions, assets involved and losses to Natl Credit Union Share Insurance Fund by asset size and charter, and for largest failures by instn, FY86-91, 9536–1.7
Farm loan guarantees of FmHA, characteristics of borrowers, lenders, and loans, FY88, 1548–386
Finances and operations, by SIC 2- to 4-digit industry, forecast 1992, annual rpt, 2044–28
Finances, mergers, and closings of federally insured credit unions, and insurance fund losses and financial statements, FY91, annual rpt, 9534–7
Finances of banks and thrifts, by instn type, 1991, annual rpt, 13004–2
Finances of federally insured credit unions, by instn characteristics and State, as of June 1992, semiannual rpt, 9532–6
Finances of federally insured credit unions, 1990-91, annual rpt, 9534–1
Finances, operations, and regulation of credit unions, series, 9536–1
Financial performance and regulation of credit unions, with background data, 1960s-90, GAO rpt, 26119–364
Financial performance of federally-insured credit unions, by charter type and region, 1st half 1992, semiannual rpt, 9532–7
Flow-of-funds accounts, savings, investments, and credit statements, quarterly rpt, 9365–3.3
Fraud and abuse in financial instns, Justice Dept enforcement activity, staff, and case dispositions by instn type, 1988-92, 6008–35
Households financial services use, by account type and instn type and location, 1989 survey, article, 9362–1.303
Installment credit outstanding and terms, by lender and credit type, monthly rpt, 9365–2.6
Installment credit outstanding, by type of holder, *Survey of Current Business*, monthly rpt, 2702–1.8
Low income credit unions financial, operating, and membership data, 1982-91, 9536–1.8
Reform of financial system, issues, with finances, impacts of deposit insurance changes, and views of depositors and bankers, 1991 hearings, 25248–129
Rural Credit Unions cooperatives, memberships, and loans, by State, 1990, annual rpt, 1124–1
Statistical Abstract of US, 1992 annual data compilation, 2324–1.16
Tax (income) returns of corporations, income and tax items by asset size and detailed industry, 1989, annual rpt, 8304–4; 8304–21
Tax exempt organizations and employee plans listed on IRS masterfile, determinations, applications, and rulings, FY91, annual rpt, 8304–3.2

West Central States economic indicators, Fed Reserve 10th District, quarterly rpt, 9381–16.2

Crime and criminals

Alcohol abuse direct and indirect costs, 1985, article, 4482–1.311

Aliens excluded and deported from US by cause and country, 1892-1991, annual rpt, 6264–2.5

Crimes, arrests by offender characteristics, and rates, by offense, and law enforcement employees, by population size and jurisdiction, 1991, annual rpt, 6224–2

Data on crime and criminal justice, collection, methodology, and use, technical rpt series, 6066–23

Data on crime and criminal justice, research results, series, 6066–20

Data on crime, criminal justice admin and enforcement, and public opinion, data compilation, 1992 annual rpt, 6064–6

Data on criminal justice issues, series, 6066–19; 6066–25

Drug abuse and trafficking relationship to other crime, and enforcement data, series, 6066–29

Drug abuse treatment services costs, effectiveness, and financing issues, 1991 conf papers, 4498–80

Homicides and rate, by weapon, circumstances, and victim characteristics, and years of potential life lost, 1980s, article, 4202–7.315

Immigrant and nonimmigrant visa applicants refused, and refusals overcome, by reason, FY90, annual rpt, 7184–1.3

Immigrants and nonimmigrants admitted to US, alien workers, visitors, deportations, and naturalizations, FY91, annual summary rpt, 6264–7

Index of crime by population size and region, and offenses by large city, 1st half 1992, semiannual rpt, 6222–1

Index of crime, victimizations and arrest by offense, circumstances, and location, data compilation, 1992 annual rpt, 6064–6.3; 6064–6.4

Neighborhood and housing quality, indicators and attitudes, by householder type and location, for 11 MSAs, 1987 survey, supplement, 2485–8

Neighborhood and housing quality, indicators and attitudes, by householder type and location, 1989, biennial rpt supplement, 2485–13

Neighborhood and housing quality, indicators and attitudes, MSA surveys, series, 2485–6

Neighborhood quality, indicators and attitudes of renter households, by whether receiving and eligible for HUD assistance, householder characteristics, and location, 1989, biennial rpt, 5184–11

Palau admin, and social, economic, and govtl data, FY91, annual rpt, 7004–6

States criminal justice systems activities, employment, funding, and data collection, by State, 1970s-91, annual rpt, 6064–40

Statistical Abstract of US, 1992 annual data compilation, 2324–1.5

Victimization rates, by victim and offender characteristics, circumstances, and offense, survey rpt series, 6066–3

Victimizations, by offense and whether reported to police, 1990-91, press release, 6068–249

Wiretaps authorized, costs, arrests, trials, and convictions, by offense and jurisdiction, 1991, annual rpt, 18204–7

see also Air piracy
see also Arrest
see also Arson
see also Assassination
see also Assault
see also Assaults on police
see also Bombs
see also Child abuse and neglect
see also Correctional institutions
see also Corruption and bribery
see also Counterfeiting and forgery
see also Courts
see also Crime victim compensation
see also Criminal investigations
see also Criminal procedure
see also Detective and protective services
see also Domestic violence
see also Driving while intoxicated
see also Drug and narcotics offenses
see also Fraud
see also Gambling
see also Homicide
see also Hostages
see also International crime
see also Juvenile delinquency
see also Kidnapping
see also Law enforcement
see also Money laundering
see also Motor vehicle theft
see also Organized crime
see also Parole and probation
see also Pretrial detention and release
see also Prisoners
see also Prostitution
see also Rape
see also Recidivism
see also Rehabilitation of criminals
see also Robbery and theft
see also Sentences, criminal procedure
see also Sex crimes
see also Smuggling
see also Tax delinquency and evasion
see also Terrorism
see also Trials
see also Vandalism
see also Violence
see also War crimes

Crime victim compensation

Activities of crime victim compensation and support service programs, series, 6066–31

Expenditures for crime victim compensation and support service program, by offense and State, FY88-90, biennial rpt, 6064–37

Financial instns fraud and abuse, Justice Dept enforcement activity, staff, and case dispositions by instn type, 1988-92, 6008–35

Probation population, by offender characteristics, sentence conditions, whether rearrested, and offense, 1986-89, 6066–19.65

Savings instns failure resolution activity of Resolution Trust Corp, with fraud and abuse Federal indictments and case dispositions, 1990, annual rpt, 9724–1

Savings instns fraud and abuse, Federal indictments and case dispositions, periodic press release, 6002–3; 6008–33

States criminal justice systems activities, employment, funding, and data collection, by State, 1970s-91, annual rpt, 6064–40

Criminal investigations

Antitrust criminal enforcement activities of Justice Dept by industry div and offense, sentencing, and labor costs, FY90, GAO rpt, 26119–375

Banks and thrifts fraud cases, Justice Dept investigation and prosecution activities, 1989-92, GAO rpt, 26119–426

Data on crime, criminal justice admin and enforcement, and public opinion, data compilation, 1992 annual rpt, 6064–6

Drug abuse and trafficking reduction programs activities, funding, staff, and Bush Admin budget request, by Federal agency, FY91-93, annual rpt, 234–2

Financial instns fraud and abuse, Justice Dept enforcement activity, staff, and case dispositions by instn type, 1988-92, 6008–35

IRS undercover criminal investigations and costs by criminal activity, and success rates, by region, mid 1980s-90, GAO rpt, 26119–394

Justice Dept employee misconduct investigations, by type of allegation and penalty, 1988-90, GAO rpt, 26119–380

Marijuana crop eradication activities of DEA and local agencies by State, and drug potency and prices, 1982-91, annual rpt, 6284–4

Military homosexual personnel discharges by pay grade, tenure, race, sex, and occupation, and investigations, by service branch, 1980s-90, GAO rpt, 26123–392

Military supplies theft and fraud losses, and inventory control measures adequacy, 1988-91, GAO rpt, 26123–377

Police employment, spending, and operations, for State, city, county, and special district agencies, 1990, annual rpt, 6064–39

Postal Service inspection activities, FY91, annual rpt, 9864–9

Postal Service inspection activities, 2nd half FY92, semiannual rpt, 9862–2

Savings instns failure resolution activity of Resolution Trust Corp, with fraud and abuse Federal indictments and case dispositions, 1990, annual rpt, 9724–1

Savings instns fraud and abuse, Federal indictments and case dispositions, periodic press release, 6002–3; 6008–33

Secret Service counterfeiting and other investigations and arrests by type, and disposition, FY91 and trends from FY82, annual rpt, 8464–1

Securities law enforcement activities of SEC, FY91, annual rpt, 9734–2.3

Tax (income) compliance of corporations, and IRS enforcement activities, 1970s-92, hearing, 25408–118

Tax litigation and enforcement activity of IRS, FY91, annual rpt, 8304–3.1

Terrorism incidents in US, related activity, and casualties, by attack type, target, group, and location, 1991, annual rpt, 6224–6

Wiretaps authorized, costs, arrests, trials, and convictions, by offense and jurisdiction, 1991, annual rpt, 18204–7

see also Searches and seizures

Criminal procedure
Aliens (illegal) held in Immigration and Naturalization Service detention facilities pending hearings, and legal aid requests, 1980s-91, GAO rpt, 26119–409
Antitrust criminal enforcement activities of Justice Dept by industry div and offense, sentencing, and labor costs, FY90, GAO rpt, 26119–375
Court civil and criminal caseloads for Federal district, appeals, and bankruptcy courts, by type of suit and offense, circuit, and district, 1991, annual rpt, 18204–11
Data on crime and criminal justice, collection, methodology, and use, technical rpt series, 6066–23
Data on crime and criminal justice, research results, series, 6066–20
Data on crime, criminal justice admin and enforcement, and public opinion, data compilation, 1992 annual rpt, 6064–6
Data on criminal justice issues, series, 6066–19; 6066–25
Drug abuse and trafficking reduction programs activities, funding, staff, and Bush Admin budget request, by Federal agency, FY91-93, annual rpt, 234–2
Drug abuse and trafficking relationship to other crime, and enforcement data, series, 6066–29
Drug abuse, treatment, and enforcement issues, series, 236–1; 236–3
Environmental laws enforcement activities of EPA and State govts, FY91, annual rpt, 9184–21
Environmental laws enforcement activities of Justice Dept, FY83-91, press release, 6008–37
Environmental laws enforcement activities of Justice Dept, FY83-92, annual press release, 6004–22
Federal district, appeals, and special courts civil and criminal caseloads, by offense, circuit, and district, 1991, annual rpt, 18204–8
Federal district court criminal case processing and dispositions, by offense, 1980-91, annual rpt, 6064–31
Felony case processing from arrest to sentencing, cases and duration by disposition and offense, for selected cities, 1988, annual rpt, 6064–27
Fraud and forgery arrests, case dispositions, and sentencing, by age, sex, race, and offense type, 1983-88, 6066–19.64
Immigration and nationality violations, convictions, and deportations, FY91, annual summary rpt, 6264–7
Immigration and nationality violations, prosecutions, fines, imprisonment, and convictions, and deportation and exclusion cases, FY85-91, annual rpt, 6264–2.5
Judicial Conf proceedings and findings, spring 1992, semiannual rpt, 18202–2
Juvenile arrests, by disposition and population size, 1991, annual rpt, 6224–2.2
Secret Service counterfeiting and other investigations and arrests by type, and disposition, FY91 and trends from FY82, annual rpt, 8464–1
State court chief prosecutors employment characteristics, and felony case prosecution procedures, 1990 survey, 6066–25.46
States criminal justice systems activities, employment, funding, and data collection, by State, 1970s-91, annual rpt, 6064–40
US attorneys case processing and collections, by case type and Federal district, FY91, annual rpt, 6004–2
see also Arrest
see also Capital punishment
see also Commitment
see also Crime victim compensation
see also Evidence
see also Extradition
see also Fines and settlements
see also Habeas corpus
see also Juries
see also Pardons
see also Parole and probation
see also Pretrial detention and release
see also Searches and seizures
see also Sentences, criminal procedure
see also Trials

Croatia
Economic, social, political, and geographic summary data, by country, 1992, annual factbook, 9114–2

Cromwell, Brian A.
"Does California Drive the West? An Econometric Investigation of Regional Spillovers", 9393–8.306

Crone, Theodore M.
"Estimating House Price Appreciation: A Comparison of Methods", 9387–8.284
"Slow Recovery in the Third District: Evidence from New Time-Series Models", 9387–1.303
"Vector-Autoregression Forecast Models for the Third District States", 9387–8.282

Crook, Frederick W.
"Building a New Rural Socialist Order: Implications for Production, Income, and Trade", 1524–4.2
"China's Barley: An Analysis of Production, Consumption, and Trade", 1524–4.2

Crop insurance
see Agricultural insurance

Crop yields
see Agricultural productivity

Croushore, Dean D.
"Importance of the Tax System in Determining the Marginal Cost of Funds", 9387–8.278
"Marginal Cost of Funds with Nonseparable Public Spending", 9387–8.265
"Ricardian Equivalence Under Income Uncertainty", 9387–8.269

CSR, Inc.
"U.S. Alcohol Epidemiologic Data Reference Manual", 4488–10

Cuba
Agricultural trade of US, by detailed commodity and country, 1991, semiannual rpt, 1522–4
Aliens (illegal) enforcement activity of Coast Guard, by nationality, 1st half FY92, semiannual rpt, 7402–4
Economic and military aid and loans from US and intl agencies, by program and country, FY46-91, annual rpt, 9914–5
Economic and social conditions, resources, and trade, and aid, 1992, annual factbook, 9914–14
Economic, social, political, and geographic summary data, by country, 1992, annual factbook, 9114–2
Export licensing, monitoring, and enforcement activities, FY91, annual rpt, 2024–1
Exports and imports of Cuba, by commodity and country, mid 1980s-91, 9118–8
Exports and imports of US, by transport mode, country, and SITC 1- to 3-digit commodity, 1991, annual rpt, 2424–12
Exports and imports of US with Communist and transitional economy countries, by detailed commodity and country, quarterly rpt with articles, 9882–2
Human rights conditions in 170 countries, and US economic and military aid, 1991, annual rpt, 21384–3
Immigrants and nonimmigrants admitted to US, alien workers, visitors, deportations, and naturalizations, FY91, annual summary rpt, 6264–7
Immigration to US, alien workers, visitors, deportations, and naturalizations, by country, FY91 and trends from 1820, annual rpt, 6264–2
Military spending, arms trade, and force strengths, with govt spending and population, by country, 1979-89, annual rpt, 9824–1
Population size, growth rates, and components of change, by country, projected 1990-2020 and trends from 1950, biennial rpt, 2324–9
Refugee migration, and intl aid programs, by world area and country of origin and asylum, 1991, annual rpt, 7004–15
Sugar production, acreage, use, and trade by country, for Cuba, mid 1950s-92, article, 1561–14.302
UN voting record and share of votes in agreement with US, by issue, country, and world area, 1991, annual rpt, 7004–18

Culliton, Thomas J.
"Building Along America's Coasts: 20 Years of Building Permits, 1970-89", 2176–8.3

Cultural activities
Education natl goals progress indicators, by State, 1992, annual rpt, 15914–1
see also Anthropology
see also Area studies
see also Art
see also Arts and the humanities
see also Dance
see also Educational exchanges
see also Exchange of persons programs
see also Federal aid to arts and humanities
see also International cooperation in cultural activities
see also Language arts
see also Motion pictures
see also Museums
see also Music
see also Performing arts
see also Theater

Cummins, Carol L.
"Savannah River Site Environmental Report, 1990", 3324–2.2

Cummins, J. David
"Structure, Conduct, and Regulation of the Property-Liability Insurance Industry", 9373–3.35

Cunniff, Mark A.
"Recidivism of Felons on Probation, 1986-89", 6066–19.65

Cunningham, H. Wilson
"Soy Printing Ink", 1504–9.1
Curran, Thomas C.
"National Air Quality and Emissions Trends Report, 1991", 9194–1
Currency
see Coins and coinage
see Flow-of-funds accounts
see Foreign exchange
see Money supply
see Special foreign currency programs
Current Employment Survey
Employment and Earnings, detailed data, monthly rpt, 6742–2
Current Population Reports
see Current Population Survey
see Survey of Income and Program Participation
Current Population Survey
BLS data collection, analysis, and presentation methods, by program, 1992 rpt, 6888–1
Consumer Income, socioeconomic characteristics of persons, families, and households, detailed cross-tabulations, series, 2546–6
Data collection and statistical program plans of Census Bur, advisory committees findings and recommendations, 1992 conf, 2628–35
Data collection, methodology, and comparisons to other data bases, Survey of Income and Program Participation, working paper series, 2626–10
Data coverage and availability of Census Bur rpts and data files, 1992 annual listing, 2304–2
Employment and Earnings, detailed data, monthly rpt, 6742–2
Employment, unemployment, and labor force characteristics, by region, State, and selected metro area, 1991, annual rpt, 6744–7
Farm population, by employment, social, and economic characteristics, and region, 1990, annual rpt, 2546–1.458
Housing unit and household characteristics, subject rpt series, 2486–1; 2486–2
Income, tax, and transfer payments distribution and equity, analyses and alternative estimates, series, 4746–14
Industry and occupation classification codes, alphabetical index, 1990 census, 2628–1
Industry and occupation classification codes, classified index, 1990 census, 2628–2
Labor force characteristics, press release series, 6726–1
Older persons income and sources, by whether OASDI beneficiary, poverty status, and other characteristics, 1990, biennial rpt, 4744–26
Population and housing data, and policy issues, fact sheet series, 2326–17
Population demographic, social, and economic characteristics, series, 2546–1
Population demographic subjects, special study series, 2546–2
Population estimates and projections, by region and State, series, 2546–3
Population estimates for civilian, resident, and total population, monthly rpt, 2542–1
Unemployment, by State and metro area, monthly press release, 6742–12
Curricula
Black higher education instns enrollment, finances, staff, and degrees, by instn and selected student characteristics, 1970s-90, 4848–46
Condition of Education, detail for elementary, secondary, and higher education, 1920s-91 and projected to 2002, annual rpt, 4824–1
Digest of Education Statistics, 1992 annual data compilation, 4824–2
Eighth grade class of 1988: educational performance and conditions, characteristics, attitudes, activities, and plans, natl longitudinal survey, series, 4826–9
Elementary and secondary schools, teachers, staff, and enrollment, by selected characteristics, 1987/88-88/89, 4836–3.10
High school classes of 1980 and 1982: education, employment, and family characteristics, activities, and attitudes, natl longitudinal study, series, 4826–2
Higher education enrollment, faculty, finances, and degrees, by instn level and control, and State, FY88, annual rpt, 4844–13
Natl Education Goals progress indicators, by State, 1992, annual rpt, 15914–1
Occupation training completions, and labor demand and turnover, by detailed occupation, 1990 and projected to 2005, biennial rpt, 6744–3
Private elementary and secondary schools, students, and staff characteristics, by school type and affiliation, 1987/88, 4836–3.8
States elementary and secondary curricula, competency, and attendance requirements, with background data, 1970s-90, 4838–52
Statistical Abstract of US, 1992 annual data compilation, 2324–1.4
see also Agricultural education
see also Area studies
see also Arts and the humanities
see also Astronomy
see also Biological sciences
see also Business education
see also Chemistry
see also Earth sciences
see also Economics
see also Educational reform
see also Environmental sciences
see also Foreign languages
see also Geography
see also Health education
see also History
see also Home economics
see also Industrial arts
see also Information sciences
see also Journalism
see also Language arts
see also Legal education
see also Mathematics
see also Medical education
see also Military education
see also Physical education and training
see also Physical sciences
see also Physics
see also Political science
see also Psychology
see also Scientific education
see also Sex education
see also Social sciences
see also Social work
see also Sociology
see also Teacher education
see also Vocational education and training
Curry, Jeffrey B.
"Individual Income Tax Returns, 1991: Taxpayer Usage Study", 8302–2.319
Customs administration
Court of Intl Trade caseloads, decisions, and appeals, FY91-92, annual rpt, 18224–2
Criminal cases by type and disposition, and collections, for US attorneys, by Federal district, FY91, annual rpt, 6004–2.1
Customs Service mgmt and trade law enforcement effectiveness, staff and broker survey results, 1992 GAO rpt, 26119–420
FDA detention of imports, by reason, product, shipper, brand, and country, monthly listing, 4062–2
FDA investigations and regulatory activities, quarterly rpt, 4062–3
Fruit and vegetable imports under quarantine, by crop, country, and port of entry, FY89, annual rpt, 1524–7
Grain inspected for domestic use and export, foreign buyers complaints, and handling facilities explosions, FY92, annual rpt, 1294–1
Meat and poultry inspection for domestic use and export, and rejections by cause, by type of animal and product, FY90, annual rpt, 1374–3
Meat plants inspected and certified for exporting to US, by country, 1991, annual listing, 1374–2
Meat trade of US and Canada, inspection activity, 1989-91, GAO rpt, 26113–595
Mexico-US trade agreement impacts on truck traffic at border crossings, Customs Service staff needs, and hwy improvement costs, projected to 2000 with trends from 1986, GAO rpt, 26123–368
Overtime pay for customs inspectors, issues, 1991 hearing, 21788–214
Pesticide residue in food imports, FDA enforcement, with contaminated shipments distributed, damages assessed and paid, and repeat offenders, FY88-90, GAO rpt, 26113–598
Tea imports inspected by FDA, by type and country, 1985-91, FAS annual circular, 1925–15.3
Tobacco leaf stocks, production, sales, and import inspections by country, by product, quarterly rpt, 1319–3
see also Smuggling
Customs duties
see Tariffs and foreign trade controls
Customs Service
see U.S. Customs Service
Cyprus
Agricultural trade of US, by detailed commodity and country, 1991, annual rpt, 1524–8
Agricultural trade of US, by detailed commodity and country, 1991, semiannual rpt, 1522–4
AID loans repayment status and terms by program and country, and status of predecessor agency loans, quarterly rpt, 9912–3

Background Notes, summary social, political, and economic data, 1992 rpt, 7006–2.13
Economic and military aid and loans from US and intl agencies, by program and country, FY46-91, annual rpt, 9914–5
Economic and social conditions of developing countries from 1960s, and Intl Dev Cooperation Agency and AID activities and funding, FY91-93, annual rpt, 9904–4
Economic conditions, income, production, prices, employment, and trade, 1992 periodic country rpt, 2046–4.54
Economic, social, political, and geographic summary data, by country, 1992, annual factbook, 9114–2
Exports and imports of US, by transport mode, country, and SITC 1- to 3-digit commodity, 1991, annual rpt, 2424–12
Exports of US, detailed Schedule B commodities with countries of destination, 1991, annual rpt, 2424–10
Human rights conditions in 170 countries, and US economic and military aid, 1991, annual rpt, 21384–3
Military aid of US, arms sales, and training programs costs and budget requests, by program, world region, and country, FY91-93, annual rpt, 7144–13
Military spending, arms trade, and force strengths, with govt spending and population, by country, 1979-89, annual rpt, 9824–1
Minerals Yearbook, Vol 3, 1989: foreign country review of production, trade, and policy, by commodity, annual rpt, 5604–35.3
Population size, growth rates, and components of change, by country, projected 1990-2020 and trends from 1950, biennial rpt, 2324–9
Refugee migration, and intl aid programs, by world area and country of origin and asylum, 1991, annual rpt, 7004–15
Ships in world merchant fleet, tonnage, and new ship construction and deliveries, by vessel type and country, as of Jan 1992, annual rpt, 7704–3
UN voting record and share of votes in agreement with US, by issue, country, and world area, 1991, annual rpt, 7004–18

Cytomegalovirus
see Infective and parasitic diseases

Czechoslovakia
Agricultural trade of US, by detailed commodity and country, 1991, annual rpt, 1524–8
Agricultural trade of US, by detailed commodity and country, 1991, semiannual rpt, 1522–4
Agricultural trade of US with Eastern Europe, by commodity group and country, 1988-91, 1928–11
Economic and military aid and loans from US and intl agencies, by program and country, FY46-91, annual rpt, 9914–5
Economic and social conditions of developing countries from 1960s, and Intl Dev Cooperation Agency and AID activities and funding, FY91-93, annual rpt, 9904–4
Economic conditions, policy, and trade practices, by country, 1989-91, annual rpt, 21384–5
Economic, social, political, and geographic summary data, by country, 1992, annual factbook, 9114–2
Export industries dev potential, with trade and industry finances and operations, for 5 Eastern Europe countries, 1985-90, 9886–4.179
Export licensing, monitoring, and enforcement activities, FY91, annual rpt, 2024–1
Exports and imports of US, by commodity and country, 1980-90, world area rpt, 9116–1.1
Exports and imports of US, by transport mode, country, and SITC 1- to 3-digit commodity, 1991, annual rpt, 2424–12
Exports and imports of US with Communist and transitional economy countries, by detailed commodity and country, quarterly rpt with articles, 9882–2
Exports and imports of US with Eastern Europe, by commodity and country, 1987-91 and outlook for 1992, 2048–158
Exports of US, detailed Schedule B commodities with countries of destination, 1991, annual rpt, 2424–10
Health care system, spending, and population health condition indicators, for Czechoslovakia, 1988-89, article, 4042–3.363
Human rights conditions in 170 countries, and US economic and military aid, 1991, annual rpt, 21384–3
Imports of goods, services, and investment from US, trade barriers, impacts, and US actions, by country, 1991, annual rpt, 444–2
Labor conditions and work accidents, 1992 annual country rpt, 6366–4.41
Market economy transition of Eastern Europe countries, trade, and foreign investment, by country, 1990-91, 9118–13
Military aid of US, arms sales, and training programs costs and budget requests, by program, world region, and country, FY91-93, annual rpt, 7144–13
Military spending, arms trade, and force strengths, with govt spending and population, by country, 1979-89, annual rpt, 9824–1
Military weapons production in Czech and Slovak regions, and domestic and export arms sales, 1987-90, hearing, 25408–115
Pension systems finances and provisions in Eastern Europe, 1950s-90 and alternative projections to 2025, technical paper, 8006–6.7
Pollution (air) contributing to global warming, emissions by monitoring site and country, and temperature change by world area and US region, 1860s-1990, annual rpt, 3004–33
Population size, growth rates, and components of change, by country, projected 1990-2020 and trends from 1950, biennial rpt, 2324–9
Refugee migration, and intl aid programs, by world area and country of origin and asylum, 1991, annual rpt, 7004–15
Spacecraft and satellite launches since 1957, quarterly listing, 9502–2
Steel imports of US under voluntary restraint agreement, by product, customs district, and country, with US industry operating data, quarterly rpt, 9882–13
Steel trade, by product, country, and customs district, with US industry operating data, 1989-June 1992, semiannual rpt, 9882–15
Tax reform issues in transition to market economy, with tax rates, revenue, and govt spending compared to EC, by selected country, late 1960s-91, technical paper, 9366–7.278
UN voting record and share of votes in agreement with US, by issue, country, and world area, 1991, annual rpt, 7004–18

Daberkow, Stan
"Outlook for Production Inputs", 1504–9.1

Dacquel, Laarni T.
"Residents of Farms and Rural Areas: 1990", 2546–1.458

Dade County, Fla.
Housing and households characteristics, and unit and neighborhood quality, by MSA location for 11 MSAs, 1986 survey, supplement, 2485–8

Dahl, Carol
"Energy Security: A Comparison of Protectionist Policies", 9379–12.96

Dahl, David S.
"Bankers Decry New Regulations, But Recognize Need to Protect Deposit Insurance Fund", 9383–19.305
"Leaders Give Their Schools High Marks", 9383–19.301
"Poll Respondents Voice Concerns over Region's Water Quality and Quantity", 9383–19.302
"Regional and National Economies Expected To Continue Expansion", 9383–19.303

Dahl, Thomas E.
"Wetlands: Status and Trends in the Conterminous U.S. Mid-1970's to Mid-1980's", 5508–89

Dahmann, Donald C.
"Residents of Farms and Rural Areas: 1990", 2546–1.458

Dahomey
see Benin

Dairy industry and products
Agricultural Stabilization and Conservation Service dairy programs, 1949-92, annual fact sheet, 1806–4.8
Agricultural Stabilization and Conservation Service producer payments, by program and State, 1991, annual table, 1804–12
Agricultural Statistics, 1991, annual rpt, 1004–1
Appalachia food processing firms, employment, and shipments, and farm production, by commodity and State, 1960s-90, 9088–37
Bovine somatotropin (bST) dairy industry use, effectiveness of FDA testing for human and animal safety, 1991, GAO rpt, 26131–101
Business statistics, detailed data for major industries and economic indicators, *Survey of Current Business*, monthly rpt, 2702–1.13
Business statistics, detailed data for major industries and economic indicators, 1960-91, *Survey of Current Business* biennial supplement, 2704–1
Cattle and calves for beef and milk, by State, as of July 1992, semiannual press release, 1623–1

Cattle, milk production, and grain and other concentrates fed, by State, monthly rpt, 1627–1
CCC financial condition and major commodity program operations, FY63-88, annual chartbook, 1824–2
Cold storage food stocks by commodity and census div, and warehouse space use, by State, monthly rpt, 1631–5
Cold storage food stocks by commodity, and warehouse space use, by census div, 1991, annual rpt, 1631–11
Confectionery shipments, trade, use, and ingredients used, by product, 1991, annual Current Industrial Rpt, 2506–4.5
Consumption, supply, trade, prices, spending, and indexes, by food commodity, 1990, annual rpt, 1544–4
County Business Patterns, 1989: employment, establishments, and payroll, by SIC 2- to 4-digit industry and county, annual State rpt series, 2326–8
County Business Patterns, 1990: employment, establishments, and payroll, by SIC 2- to 4-digit industry and county, annual State rpt series, 2326–6
CPI by component for US city average, and by selected metro area, region, and population size, monthly rpt, 6762–2
Employment, earnings, and hours, by SIC 1- to 4-digit industry, monthly 1989-Feb 1992, annual rpt, 6744–4
Employment of minorities and women, by occupation, SIC 1- to 3-digit industry, State, and MSA, 1991, annual rpt, 9244–1
Exports and imports (agricultural) commodity and country, prices, and world market devs, monthly rpt, 1922–12
Exports and imports (agricultural) of US, by commodity and country, bimonthly rpt, 1522–1
Exports and imports (agricultural) of US, by detailed commodity and country, 1991, annual rpt, 1524–8
Exports and imports (agricultural) of US, by detailed commodity and country, 1991, semiannual rpt, 1522–4
Exports and imports between US and outlying areas, by detailed commodity and mode of transport, 1991, annual rpt, 2424–11
Exports and imports of dairy, livestock, and poultry products, by commodity and country, FAS monthly circular, 1925–32
Exports and imports of US, by country and detailed commodity, monthly rpt, 2422–12
Exports and imports of US, by Harmonized System 6-digit commodity and country, 1991, annual rpt, 2424–13
Exports and imports of US, by selected country, country group, and commodity group, 1991, annual rpt, 2044–37
Exports and imports of US, by transport mode, country, and SITC 1- to 3-digit commodity, 1991, annual rpt, 2424–12
Exports, imports, tariffs, and industry operating data for dairy products, 1992 rpt, 9885–8.3
Exports of US, detailed Schedule B commodities with countries of destination, 1991, annual rpt, 2424–10
Farm credit, terms, delinquency, agricultural bank failures, and credit conditions by Fed Reserve District, quarterly rpt, 9365–3.10
Farm financial and marketing conditions, forecast 1992, annual chartbook, 1504–8
Farm financial and marketing conditions, forecast 1992, annual conf, 1504–9
Farm income, cash marketing receipts ranked by commodity and State, 1990, 1548–385
Farm sector balance sheet, and receipts by detailed commodity, by State, 1986-90, annual rpt, 1544–18
Farms (dairy) financial statements, by size and region, 1987-90, annual article, 1561–2.301
Foreign and US dairy production, trade, use, and prices, forecast 1992 and trends from 1987, FAS semiannual circular, 1925–10
Foreign countries agricultural production, prices, and trade, by country, 1980-91 and forecast 1992, annual world area rpt series, 1524–4
Freight (waterborne domestic and foreign) by commodity, traffic, and passengers, by port and waterway, 1989, annual rpt, 3754–3
Herd Improvement Program cooperatives and cows tested, by State, 1990, annual rpt, 1124–1
Imports and quotas of dairy products, by commodity and country of origin, FAS monthly rpt, 1925–31
Infant formula bid prices and contracts awarded by States under USDA food aid program for women, infants, and children, late 1980s-91, hearing, 25528–118
Input-output structure of US economy, detailed interindustry transactions for 541 industries, and components of final demand, 1982 benchmark data, 2708–17
Labor productivity, indexes of output, hours, and employment by SIC 2- to 4-digit industry, 1967-90, annual rpt, 6824–1.3
Manufacturing annual survey, 1990: finances and operations, by SIC 2- to 4-digit industry, series, 2506–14
Manufacturing census, 1987: concentration of largest firms measured by value added, and for shipments by SIC 2- and 4-digit industry, subject rpt, 2497–6
Manufacturing census, 1987: shipments of manufacturers products, by customer class and SIC 2- and 4-digit industry, subject rpt, 2497–4
Manufacturing finances and operations, by SIC 2- to 4-digit industry, forecast 1992, annual rpt, 2044–28
Milk handlers (cooperative and proprietary) performance, views of dairy farmers in southern States, 1989 survey, 1128–67
Milk of manufacturing grade, fat content and prices received by farmers in Minnesota and Wisconsin, monthly rpt, 1629–6
Milk of manufacturing grade, fat content and prices received by farmers in Minnesota and Wisconsin, 1989-91, annual rpt, 1629–2
Milk order market prices and detailed operations, by State and market area, 1990-91, annual rpt, 1317–3
Milk order market prices and detailed operations, monthly rpt with articles, 1317–4
Multinatl US firms and foreign affiliates finances and operations, by industry and country, 1989 benchmark survey, annual rpt, 2704–5
Nutrient, caloric, and waste composition, detailed data for raw, processed, and prepared foods, 1992 rpt, 1356–3.17
Occupational injury and illness rates, by SIC 2- to 4-digit industry, 1989-90, annual rpt, 6844–7
Occupational injury and illness rates, by SIC 2- to 4-digit industry, 1990, annual rpt, 6844–1
OECD trade, total and for 4 major countries, and US trade by country, by commodity, 1980-90, world area rpt series, 9116–1
Price indexes (producer), by stage of processing and detailed commodity, monthly rpt, 6762–6
Price indexes (producer), by stage of processing and detailed commodity, monthly 1991, annual rpt, 6764–2
Price support and other CCC program outlays, with production and marketing outlook, by commodity, projected 1991-97, annual rpt, 26306–6.171
Price support purchases, sales, donations, and inventories of CCC, for dairy products, monthly rpt, 1802–2
Prices (farm-retail) for food, marketing cost components, and industry finances and productivity, 1920s-91, annual rpt, 1544–9
Prices of dairy products, by type and selected area, with related marketing data, 1991, annual rpt, 1317–1
Prices received and paid by farmers, by commodity and State, monthly rpt, 1629–1
Prices received and paid by farmers, by commodity and State, 1991, annual rpt, 1629–5
Prices received by milk producers from cooperatives and proprietary handlers, by characteristics of cooperative membership and operation, 1989 survey, 1128–68
Production inputs, output, and productivity for farms, by commodity and region, 1947-90, annual rpt, 1544–17
Production itemized costs, receipts, and returns, by commodity and region, 1988-90, annual rpt, 1544–20
Production of dairy products by type, and plants, by State, 1991, annual rpt, 1627–5
Production of manufactured dairy products by State, stocks, prices, and CCC price support activities, by product type, monthly rpt, 1627–3
Production, price, and supply forecasts used for USDA commodity program outlays, accuracy, 1975-88, GAO rpt, 26131–94
Production, prices, trade, and marketing, by commodity, current situation and forecast, monthly rpt with articles, 1502–4
Production, prices, trade, and use for dairy products, periodic situation rpt with articles, 1561–2
Production, prices, trade, and use of oils and fats, periodic situation rpt with articles, 1561–3
Production, use, and receipts, and milk cow inventory, by State, 1989-91, annual rpt, 1627–4
Radiation and radionuclide concentrations in air, water, and milk, monitoring results by site, quarterly rpt, 9192–5

Radiation exposure of population near Hanford, Wash, nuclear plant, with methodology, 1944-91, series, 3356–5
Radionuclide concentrations in air, water, humans, animals, and milk near Nevada and other nuclear test sites, 1990, annual rpt, 9194–17
Science, engineering, and technical employment in manufacturing, by field and industry, 1989, triennial rpt, 9627–23
Soviet Union and US economic and sociodemographic indicators, selected years 1970-90, handbook, 2328–80
Statistical Abstract of US, 1992 annual data compilation, 2324–1.23
Supply and demand indicators for livestock and dairy products, and for selected foreign and US crops, monthly rpt, 1522–5
Tax (income) returns of corporations, income and tax items by asset size and detailed industry, 1989, annual rpt, 8304–4; 8304–21
Tax (income) returns of partnerships, income statement and balance sheet items, by industry group, 1990, annual article, 8302–2.314
Weight and volume conversion factors for agricultural commodities and products, 1992 rpt, 1508–3
see also under By Commodity in the "Index by Categories"

Daley, Judy R.
"Profiles in Safety and Health: Work Hazards of Mobile Homes", 6728–41

Dallas County, Tex.
Housing and households characteristics, unit and neighborhood quality, and journey to work by MSA location, for 11 MSAs, 1985 survey, supplement, 2485–8
Housing and households detailed characteristics, and unit and neighborhood quality, by location, 1989 survey, MSA rpt, 2485–6.5

Dallas, Tex.
Commuters, by county of residence and work, for top 10 metro areas, 1990 Census of Population, press release, 2328–84
CPI by component for US city average, and by region, population size, and for 15 metro areas, monthly rpt, 6762–1
CPI by component for US city average, and by selected metro area, region, and population size, monthly rpt, 6762–2
CPI by major component for 2 Texas MSAs, monthly rpt, 6962–2
Drug test results at arrest, by drug type, offense, and sex, for selected urban areas, quarterly rpt, 6062–3
Employment, earnings, hours, and CPI changes, for Dallas-Fort Worth metro area, late 1970s-91, annual rpt, 6964–2
Fruit and vegetable shipments, and arrivals by city, by mode of transport and State and country of origin, 1990, annual rpt, 1311–4.2
Heroin prices and purity in 19 metro areas and Puerto Rico, by world area of origin, quarterly rpt, 6282–2
Housing and households characteristics, unit and neighborhood quality, and journey to work by MSA location, for 11 MSAs, 1985 survey, supplement, 2485–8
Housing and households characteristics, 1989 survey, MSA fact sheet, 2485–11.6
Housing and households detailed characteristics, and unit and neighborhood quality, by location, 1989 survey, MSA rpt, 2485–6.5
Housing starts and completions authorized by building permits in 40 MSAs, quarterly rpt, 2382–9
School districts in Dallas, educational quality relation to property values, model description and results, 1985-87, technical paper, 9379–12.94
Wages by occupation, and benefits, for office and plant workers, 1991 survey, periodic MSA rpt, 6785–16.4
see also under By City and By SMSA or MSA in the "Index by Categories"

Dams
Agricultural Conservation Program acreage and projects, by State, 1936-90, quinquennial rpt, 1808–1
Army Corps of Engineers activities and projects, FY88 and trends from 1800s, annual rpt, 3754–1.1
Army Corps of Engineers activities and projects, FY89 and trends from 1800s, annual rpt, 3754–1.2
Army Corps of Engineers activities and projects, FY90 and trends from 1800s, annual rpt, 3754–1.3
Army Corps of Engineers water resources dev projects, characteristics, and costs, 1950s-89, biennial State rpt series, 3756–1
Army Corps of Engineers water resources dev projects, characteristics, and costs, 1950s-91, biennial State rpt series, 3756–2
Colorado River Storage Project finances and activities in western States, FY91, annual rpt, 5824–3
Failures of dams, deaths, and unsafe dams by State, 1874-1982, 9434–6
Indian reservations dams with safety problems, Bur of Indian Affairs and tribal mgmt, and Interior Dept funding, 1980s-91, GAO rpt, 26113–558
Input-output structure of US economy, detailed interindustry transactions for 541 industries, and components of final demand, 1982 benchmark data, 2708–17
Ohio River basin waterway facilities, freight by commodity and port, and recreation, by waterway, 1988-89, annual rpt, 3754–6
Reclamation Bur water storage and carriage facilities, capacity, and operating status, as of Sept 1990, biennial listing, 5824–7
Tennessee Valley river control activities, and hydroelectric power generation and capacity, 1990, annual rpt, 9804–7
TVA finances and operations by program and facility, FY91, annual rpt, 9804–32
see also Reservoirs

Danbury, Conn.
Wages by occupation, and benefits, for office and plant workers, 1992 survey, periodic MSA rpt, 6785–17.1

Dance
County Business Patterns, 1989: employment, establishments, and payroll, by SIC 2- to 4-digit industry and county, annual State rpt series, 2326–8
County Business Patterns, 1990: employment, establishments, and payroll, by SIC 2- to 4-digit industry and county, annual State rpt series, 2326–6
Injuries from use of consumer products and related activities, by severity and victim age and sex, 1990, annual rpt, 9164–7
Injuries from use of consumer products, by severity, victim age, and detailed product, 1991, annual rpt, 9164–6
Labor demand, turnover, and training completions, by detailed occupation, 1990 and projected to 2005, biennial rpt, 6744–3
Natl Endowment for Arts activities and grants, FY91, annual rpt, 9564–3
Occupational Outlook Handbook, 1992-93, biennial rpt, 6744–1

Darby, James T.
"Coordinating Rural Development with National Strategies", 1504–9.1

Darby, Michael R.
"Impact of Government Deficits on Personal and National Saving Rates", 8006–6.5

Daronco, Karla M.
"Corporate Foreign Tax Credit, 1988: An Industry Focus", 8302–2.316

Data processing
see Computer industry and products
see Computer networks
see Computer sciences
see Computer use
see Information storage and retrieval systems

Dates
see Chronologies

Daugherty, Andrea L.
"1990 Update: AIDS in Correctional Facilities", 6064–22

Davenport, Edgar L.
"Changes in Florida's Industrial Roundwood Products Output, 1987-89", 1208–352
"Pulpwood Prices in the Southeast, 1990", 1204–22

Davenport, Iowa
Wages by occupation, and benefits, for office and plant workers, 1992 survey, periodic MSA rpt, 6785–17.1
see also under By City and By SMSA or MSA in the "Index by Categories"

Davies, Sally M.
"Accounting for Prediction Variance in Event Studies", 9366–6.287

Davis, Letitia K.
"Use of Death Certificates for Mesothelioma Surveillance", 4042–3.351

Davis, Robert E.
"Rating Northeasters", 2152–8.301

Davis, Robert L.
"Smoking During Pregnancy Among Northwest Native Americans", 4042–3.306

Davis, Stacy C.
"Transportation Energy Data Book: Edition 12", 3304–5

Davison, Cecil W.
"Forecasting U.S. Soybean Prices with Futures Prices", 1561–3.303

DAWN
see Drug Abuse Warning Network

Dawson, John M.
"Prosecutors in State Courts, 1990", 6066–25.46

Day care programs
see Adult day care
see Child day care
Day, Kelly
"Energy Efficiency, Technological Change, and the Dieselization of U.S. Agriculture", 1561–16.301
Daylight hours
see Time of day
Dayton, Ohio
see also under By City and By SMSA or MSA in the "Index by Categories"
Daytona Beach, Fla.
see also under By City and By SMSA or MSA in the "Index by Categories"
D.C.
Air traffic, and passenger and freight enplanements, by airport, 1960s-90 and projected to 2010, hub area rpt, 7506–7.42
Auto alternative fuels use in Federal fleet, energy economy performance at 4 sites, FY91, annual rpt, 3304–28
Banks (insured commercial), Fed Reserve 5th District members financial statements, by State, quarterly rpt, 9389–18
Banks (insured commercial and savings) deposits by instn, State, MSA, and county, as of June 1991, annual regional rpt, 9295–3.2
Budget of US, authoritative financial statements with appropriations, outlays, and receipts, by category and agency, FY91, annual rpt, 8104–2.2
Budget of US, obligations and authority by function, agency, and program, with summaries and analyses, FY93, annual rpt, 104–2
Commuters, by county of residence and work, for top 10 metro areas, 1990 Census of Population, press release, 2328–84
CPI by component for US city average, and by region, population size, and for 15 metro areas, monthly rpt, 6762–1
CPI by component for US city average, and by selected metro area, region, and population size, monthly rpt, 6762–2
Deaths and rates, by detailed location, cause, and demographic characteristics, 1989, US Vital Statistics annual rpt, 4144–3.1
Drug abuse indicators for selected metro areas, research results, data collection, and policy issues, 1992 semiannual conf, 4492–5
Drug, alcohol, and tobacco use, user characteristics, and consequences, for DC metro area, series, 4496–12
Drug test results at arrest, by drug type, offense, and sex, for selected urban areas, quarterly rpt, 6062–3
Economic indicators by State, Fed Reserve 5th District, quarterly rpt, 9389–16
Education funding by Federal agency, program, and recipient type, and instn spending, 1960s-91, annual rpt, 4824–8
Employment and housing indicators by State, FHLB 4th District, quarterly rpt, 9302–36
Employment, earnings, and hours, by selected SIC 1- to 4-digit industry, State, and for 275 MSAs, 1987-92, 6748–81
Fed Govt civilian employment and payroll, by agency in DC metro area, total US, and abroad, bimonthly rpt, 9842–1
Fed Govt civilian employment and payroll, by pay system, agency, and location, 1991, annual rpt, 9844–6
Fed Govt land acquisition and dev projects in DC metro area, characteristics and funding by agency and project, FY92-96, annual rpt, 15454–1
Fed Govt spending in States and local areas, by type, State, county, and city, FY91, annual rpt, 2464–3
Fed Govt spending in States, by type, program, agency, and State, FY91, annual rpt, 2464–2
Fruit and vegetable shipments, and arrivals by city, by mode of transport and State and country of origin, 1991, annual rpt, 1311–4.1
Govt finances, revenue by source, financial statements, and employment for DC, with income in central city and suburbs compared to other cities, 1991 hearings, 21308–28
Heroin prices and purity in 19 metro areas and Puerto Rico, by world area of origin, quarterly rpt, 6282–2
HHS financial aid, by program, recipient, State, and city, FY91, annual regional listing, 4004–3.3
Hospital deaths of Medicare patients, actual and expected rates by diagnosis, and hospital characteristics, by instn, FY90 annual State rpt, 4654–14.9
Housing and households characteristics, unit and neighborhood quality, and journey to work by MSA location, for 11 MSAs, 1985 survey, supplement, 2485–8
Housing and households characteristics, 1989 survey, MSA fact sheet, 2485–11.3
Housing and households detailed characteristics, and unit and neighborhood quality, by location, 1989 survey, MSA rpt, 2485–6.1
Housing census, 1990: summary unit characteristics, by householder race and age, county, place, and urban-rural location, State rpt, 2471–1.10
Housing starts and completions authorized by building permits in 40 MSAs, quarterly rpt, 2382–9
Immigrants from Central America in DC, by selected employment and other characteristics, and reasons for migration, 1985-88, working paper, 6366–6.3
Immigration Reform and Control Act employer sanctions impacts on labor markets, with data for selected industries and metro areas, 1980s, working paper, 6366–6.10
Military and DOD civilian personnel in DC metro area, FY91, and in Pentagon from FY45, annual rpt, 3544–1.1
Military prime contract awards, by contractor, service branch, State, and city, FY91, annual rpt, 3544–22
Multinatl firms US affiliates finances and operations, by industry, country of parent firm, and State, 1987, 2708–48
Physicians, by specialty, age, sex, and location of training and practice, 1990, State rpt, 4116–6.9
Population and housing census, 1990: detailed geographic coverage, State CD-ROM, 2551–9.5
Population and housing census, 1990: population and housing characteristics, detailed geographic coverage, State CD-ROM, 2551–10.11
Population and housing census, 1990: summary characteristics, by county, subdiv, and place, State rpt, 2551–7.10
Population census, 1990: population characteristics and living arrangements, by county, place, and urban-rural location, State rpt, 2531–1.10
Prisoners in Federal and contract instns, by selected characteristics, region, and Federal instn, FY89, annual rpt, 6244–1.1
Statistical Abstract of US, 1992 annual data compilation, 2324–1
Wages by occupation, and benefits, for office and plant workers, 1992 survey, periodic MSA rpt, 6785–17.2
Water resources dev projects of Army Corps of Engineers, characteristics, and costs, 1950s-91, biennial State rpt, 3756–2.9
Workers compensation programs under Federal admin, finances and operations, FY91, annual rpt, 6504–10
see also D.C. courts
see also under By City, By SMSA or MSA, and By State in the "Index by Categories"

D.C. courts
Caseloads (civil and criminal) for Federal district, appeals, and bankruptcy courts, by offense, circuit, and district, 1991, annual rpt, 18204–11
Caseloads (civil and criminal) for Federal district, appeals, and special courts, 1991, annual rpt, 18204–8

De Long, J. Bradford
"Macroeconomic Policy and Long-Run Growth", 9381–1.308

de Vos, Klaas
"Evaluation of Subjective Poverty Definitions Comparing Results from the U.S. and the Netherlands", 6886–6.84

De Wilde, Carolyn
"Projections of Returns To Be Filed in CY92-99", 8302–2.304

De Wire, Elinor
"Savers of Lives", 2152–8.303

Deaf
Disability and work limitations of persons with chronic health conditions, by condition, age, and sex, 1983-86, 4946–1.2
Education (special) enrollment by age, staff, funding, and needs, by type of handicap and State, 1990/91, annual rpt, 4944–4
Election polling places accessibility and services availability for aged and disabled, by State, 1990 natl elections, hearing, 21428–11
Head Start handicapped enrollment, by handicap, State, and for Indian and migrant programs, 1988/89, annual rpt, 4584–4

Dean, Debra
"Local Boundary Commissions: Status and Roles in Forming, Adjusting and Dissolving Local Government Boundaries", 10048–85

DeAre, Diana
"Geographical Mobility: March 1987-March 1990", 2546–1.456
"Geographical Mobility: March 1990-March 1991", 2546–1.464

Death penalty
see Capital punishment

Deaths
AFDC beneficiaries demographic and financial characteristics, by State, FY90, annual rpt, 4584–7
AIDS deaths and rates, by age group, quarterly rpt, 4202–9
AIDS patient deaths from non-AIDS related cancers, 1985-91 study, article, 4472–1.351
AIDS patients costs and service use under Medicaid, for California, 1984-86, article, 4652–1.301
AIDS prevention and control plans, cases, and Federal funding, 1980s-94, 4048–22
Alaska rural areas population characteristics, and energy resources dev effects, series, 5736–5
Alcohol abuse direct and indirect costs, 1985, article, 4482–1.311
Alcohol-related deaths, by cause, State, and county, annual averages 1979-80 and 1983-85, 4488–10.4
Blood banks safety violations, FDA enforcement, disease transmittal, and Houston regional center activities and finances, 1970s-91, hearings, 21368–134
Cancer (breast) cases, survival, and death rates, by age, and change by birth cohort, 1970s-90s, article, 4472–1.341
Cancer (breast) research funding, cases, and deaths, 1970s-90, GAO rpt, 26131–92
Cancer (breast and cervical) deaths and rates by State, and in situ case rates by age, by race, 1970s-86, article, 4202–7.312
Cancer (colon) risk relation to diet, aspirin use, exercise, and other factors, 1982-88, article, 4472–1.346
Cancer (mesothelioma) patient deaths, by cause of death reported on death certificates, for Massachusetts, 1982-89, article, 4042–3.351
Cancer (nasopharyngeal) death risk by level of smoking and alcohol use, 1986, article, 4472–1.312
Cancer death rates and annual change, by body site, sex, and race, comparability of local registry and natl data, 1975-88, article, 4472–1.320
Cancer death rates, by body site, sex, and world area, 1969 and annual percent change 1969-86, article, 4472–1.306
Cancer deaths by age, and cases, by sex, 1988 and 1991, annual rpt, 4474–13
Cirrhosis of liver deaths, by age, sex, race, and whether alcohol involved, 1988 and trends from 1910, annual rpt, 4486–1.13
Contraceptives failures and health risks to women, with pregnancy, abortion, and cancer death rates, 1980s, conf paper, 4164–2
Costa Rica and Guatemala life expectancy, and death rate by cause and age, by sex, 1984 and trends from 1900, working paper, 2326–18.64
Death rates by cause, and life expectancy, by sex and age, 1900s-89 and projected to 2080, actuarial rpt, 4706–1.107
Deaths and rates, by cause, age, sex, marital status, race, and State, 1989, US Vital Statistics advance annual rpt, 4146–5.124
Deaths and rates, by cause, age, sex, race, and State, preliminary 1990-91 and trends from 1960, US Vital Statistics annual rpt, 4144–7
Deaths and rates, by cause and selected social, demographic, and employment characteristics, 1979-85, natl longitudinal study, 4478–186
Deaths and rates, by detailed location, cause, and demographic characteristics, 1989, US Vital Statistics annual rpt, 4144–3
Deaths recorded in 121 cities, weekly rpt, 4202–1
Developing countries aged population and selected characteristics, 1980s and projected to 2020, country rpt series, 2326–19
Disability Insurance beneficiaries deaths and survival, by selected characteristics, for persons entitled 1972 and 1985, article, 4742–1.321
Drug abuse treatment services costs, effectiveness, and financing issues, 1991 conf papers, 4498–80
Foreign countries deaths of US civilians, by selected cause, 1975 and 1984, article, 4042–3.315
Foreign countries population size, growth rates, and components of change, by country, projected 1990-2020 and trends from 1950, biennial rpt, 2324–9
Health condition and care indicators, 1950s-90 with health improvement and disease prevention goals for 1990, annual data compilation, 4144–11
Heart disease hospitalization and death risk related to alcohol use level, 1990 article, 4482–1.301
Heart, Lung, and Blood Natl Inst activities, and grants by recipient and location, FY91 and disease trends from 1940, annual rpt, 4474–15
Hepatitis cases by infection source, age, sex, race, and State, and deaths, by strain, 1989 and trends from 1966, 4205–2
Home health care for Medicare and non-Medicare patients, services use and nursing visits, for Virginia, 1983-85, article, 4652–1.302
Hospital deaths of Medicare patients, actual and expected rates by diagnosis, with hospital characteristics, by instn, FY90, annual State rpt series, 4654–14
Hospital reimbursement by Medicare under prospective payment system, omitted services impacts on hospital revenue, FY85, article, 4652–1.316
Indian cancer cases, and incidence and survival rates, with comparisons to whites, for 2 States, 1982-87, article, 4472–1.347
Indian Health Service and tribal facilities and use, and Indians health and other characteristics, by IHS region, 1980s-90, annual chartbook, 4084–7
Indian Health Service facilities, funding, operations, and Indian health and other characteristics, 1950s-91, annual chartbook, 4084–1
Japan and US occupational injuries and illnesses, and lost workday and death rates, late 1950s-88, article, 6722–1.318
Juvenile facilities population, by resident characteristics and facility type, 1977-89, annual rpt, 6064–35
Kidney end-stage disease treatment facilities, Medicare enrollment and reimbursement, survival, and patient characteristics, 1984-90, annual rpt, 4654–16
Medicare coverage of new health care technologies, risks and benefit evaluations, series, 4186–10
Medicare payment of physicians, reforms impacts on services, and monitoring methods, 1992 annual rpt, 4004–34
Medicare payment of physicians, vulnerable beneficiaries services use prior to fee schedule implementation, 1986-90, annual rpt, 17266–1.8
Mental illness (schizophrenia) cases, share by disposition 10 and 30 years after diagnosis, 1992 rpt, 26356–9.4
Military deaths by cause, age, race, and rank, and personnel captured and missing, by service branch, FY91, annual rpt, 3544–40
Morbidity and Mortality Weekly Report, infectious notifiable disease cases by age, race, and State, and deaths, 1940s-91, annual rpt, 4204–1
OECD members health care costs, hospital use, resources, and economic and health indicators, by country, 1960s-90, article, 4652–1.322
Older persons socioeconomic characteristics, 1900s-90 and projected to 2050, biennial chartbook, 12904–1
Older population, and health, economic, and other characteristics, with foreign comparisons, 1980s-91 with trends and projections, Current Population Rpt, 2546–2.165
Philippines Mount Pinatubo volcanic eruptions, evacuation camps infective disease cases and deaths, 1991, article, 4202–7.320
PHS Commissioned Corps members deaths, by cause, 1965-89, article, 4042–3.316
Population size and components of change, alternative projections 1990-2080 and trends from 1900, annual actuarial rpt, 4706–1.106
Population size, July 1981-89 and compared to 1980 and 1990, annual press release, 2324–10
Prison and parole admissions and releases, sentence length, and time served, by offense and offender characteristics, 1988, annual rpt, 6064–33
Prison deaths in State and Fed Govt facilities, by cause, 1990, quinquennial rpt, 6068–218
Prisoners and movements, by offense, location, and selected other characteristics, data compilation, 1992 annual rpt, 6064–6.6
Prisoners, characteristics, and movements, by State, 1990, annual rpt, 6064–26
Prisoners in jails, deaths by cause, 1990-91, annual rpt, 6066–25.48
Refugees, displaced persons, and population affected by famine, CDC recommendations for disease surveillance, control, and prevention, with background data, 1978-91, 4206–2.63
Research on population and reproduction, Federal funding by project, FY90, annual listing, 4474–9
Retirees health and other characteristics related to Medicare use and charges 2 years later, 1984, article, 4652–1.319
San Antonio, Tex, govt funding for public housing and health, with background data, 1989-91, hearing, 21248–172

Smoking and health effects, with trends in smoking, related disease and death, and public attitudes, literature review, 1992 annual rpt, 4204–18
Smoking control strategies effectiveness, with data on research funding, smoking prevalence, cancer deaths, and taxation, 1900s-91, 4476–7.1
Soviet Union and US economic and sociodemographic indicators, selected years 1970-90, handbook, 2328–80
Statistical Abstract of US, 1992 annual data compilation, 2324–1.2
Tobacco production and use in Latin America, Canada, and US, and related economic, health, and social issues, 1950s-92, annual rpt, 4204–18
Transplants of organs, failures, deaths, and survival rates, by hospital, 1987-89, annual rpt series, 4104–17
VA health care facilities inpatient deaths, results of quality of care reviews, 1986 and 1989, 8708–1
Veterans and servicepersons life insurance, actuarial analyses of VA programs, 1991, annual rpt, 8604–1
Veterans disability and death compensation and pension cases, by type of entitlement and period of service, monthly rpt, 8602–5
Veterans disability and death compensation cases of VA, by entitlement type, period of service, and sex, as of Mar 1992, annual rpt, 8604–13
Veterans disability and death compensation cases of VA, by entitlement type, period of service, sex, age, and State, FY90, annual rpt, 8604–7
Veterans disability by type, and deaths, by period of service, and VA activities, FY91, annual rpt, 8604–3.3
Vietnam population size, components of change, and selected characteristics, 1979, 1989, and projected to 2050, 2326–18.65
Vital and Health Statistics series: death rates for selected causes and population groups, 4147–20
Vital statistics provisional data, monthly rpt, 4142–1
see also Accidental deaths
see also Autopsies
see also Capital punishment
see also Cemeteries and funerals
see also Child mortality
see also Drowning
see also Fetal deaths
see also Homicide
see also Infant mortality
see also Maternal deaths
see also Poisoning and drug reaction
see also Suicide
see also Traffic accident fatalities
see also War casualties

DeBraal, J. Peter
"Foreign Ownership of U.S. Agricultural Land Through Dec. 31, 1991", 1584–2
"Foreign Ownership of U.S. Agricultural Land Through Dec. 31, 1991: County-Level Data", 1584–3

Debt
see Agricultural credit
see Business assets and liabilities, general
see Business assets and liabilities, specific industry
see Commercial credit
see Consumer credit
see Credit
see Credit bureaus and agencies
see Foreign debts
see Government assets and liabilities
see Government securities
see Loans
see Mortgages
see Municipal bonds
see Personal debt
see Public debt
see U.S. savings bonds

DeCaro, Teresa
"Role of Specialty Societies and Physicians in the Commission's Evaluation of Relative Work Values", 17266–2.8

Decatur, Ill.
Wages by occupation, for office and plant workers, 1991 survey, periodic MSA rpt, 6785–12.2

Decker, Ella M.
"Water Resources Activities of the USGS in South Dakota, FY89-90", 5666–26.16

Decontrol of prices
see Price regulation

Default
see Bankruptcy
see Loan delinquency and default

Defective products
Aircraft accidents, casualties, and damage, for commercial operations by detailed circumstances, 1988, annual rpt, 9614–2
Aircraft engine rotor failures, by carrier and incident characteristics, 1988, annual rpt, 7504–50
Auto and auto equipment recalls for safety-related defects, by make, monthly listing, 7762–12
Auto and auto equipment recalls for safety-related defects, by make, quarterly listing, 7762–2
Boats (recreational) and engines recalls for safety-related defects, by make, periodic listing, 7402–5
Consumer Product Safety Commission activities, recalls by brand, and casualties and medical costs, by product type, FY90, annual rpt, 9164–2
Diving (underwater) accidents, illnesses, and deaths, by circumstances, diver characteristics, and location, 1970-90, annual rpt, 2144–29
Imports detained by FDA, by reason, product, shipper, brand, and country, monthly listing, 4062–2
Pacemaker lead implants, failures, and costs, by model, 1992 GAO rpt, 26131–103
Railroad accidents, casualties, and damage, by cause, railroad, and State, 1991, annual rpt, 7604–1

Defense
see Civil defense
see Department of Defense
see Military intervention
see Military invasion and occupation
see National defense
see War

Defense Advanced Research Projects Agency
Semiconductor industry R&D consortium funding, outlays, and effectiveness in improving US competitive position, 1980s-92, GAO rpt, 26113–588

Defense agencies
Base construction, renovation, and closure, DOD budget requests by project, service branch, State, and country, FY93, annual rpt, 3544–15
Budget of DOD, base construction and family housing appropriations by facility, service branch, and location, FY91-93, annual rpt, 3544–39
Budget of DOD, personnel needs, costs, and force readiness by service branch, FY93, annual rpt, 3504–1
Budget of DOD, procurement appropriations by item, service branch, and defense agency, FY91-93, annual rpt, 3544–32
Budget of DOD, R&D appropriations by item, service branch, and defense agency, FY91-93, annual rpt, 3544–33
Commercial activities of DOD performed in-house, and work-years, by service branch, installation, and State, FY91, annual rpt, 3544–25
Expenditures and obligations of DOD, by function and service branch, quarterly rpt, 3542–3
Personnel (civilian) of DOD, by service branch and defense agency, with summary military employment data, quarterly rpt, 3542–16
Personnel (civilian and military) of DOD, by service branch and defense agency, quarterly rpt, 3542–14.1
see also Defense Advanced Research Projects Agency
see also Defense Communications Agency
see also Defense Contract Audit Agency
see also Defense Intelligence Agency
see also Defense Investigative Service
see also Defense Logistics Agency
see also Defense Mapping Agency
see also Defense Nuclear Agency
see also Defense Security Assistance Agency

Defense budgets and appropriations
Air Force fiscal mgmt system operations and techniques, quarterly rpt, 3602–1
Army strategic capability, force strengths, budget, and mgmt, FY79-93, annual rpt, 3704–13
Base construction, renovation, and closure, DOD budget requests by project, service branch, State, and country, FY93, annual rpt, 3544–15
Budget authority and outlays of DOD, FY85-93, GAO rpt, 26123–399
Budget deficit reduction under Gramm-Rudman Act, CBO sequestration estimates, FY93, annual rpt, 26304–6
Budget deficit reduction under Gramm-Rudman Act, OMB sequestration estimates, by category, FY92, annual rpt, 104–27
Budget of DOD, itemized account of legislative history, annual rpt, discontinued, 3504–7
Budget of DOD, organization, personnel, weapons, and property, by service branch, State, and country, 1992 annual summary rpt, 3504–13
Budget of DOD, programs, policies, and operations, FY91, annual rpt, 3544–2
Budget of US, authoritative financial statements with appropriations, outlays, and receipts, by category and agency, FY91, annual rpt, 8104–2.2

Budget of US, balances of budget authority obligated and unobligated, by function and agency, FY90-93, annual rpt, 104–8
Budget of US, Bush Admin proposals, with detail for defense budgets, and historical data from FY34, FY93, 108–46.2
Budget of US, CBO analysis and review of FY93 budget by function, annual rpt, 26304–2
Budget of US, CBO analysis of revenue and spending alternatives and projections of economic indicators, FY93-97, annual rpt, 26304–3
Budget of US, House Budget Committee analysis of Bush Admin proposals and economic assumptions, FY93, 21268–42
Budget of US, House concurrent resolution, with spending and revenue targets, FY93 and projected to FY97, annual rpt, 21264–2
Budget of US, midsession review of FY93 budget, by function, annual rpt, 104–7
Budget of US, obligations and authority by function, agency, and program, with summaries and analyses, FY93, annual rpt, 104–2
Budget of US, receipts by source, outlays by agency and program, and balances, monthly rpt, 8102–3
Civilian Health and Medical Program of Uniformed Services benefits and costs, FY85-90, annual chartbook, 3504–23
Construction of military bases and family housing, DOD appropriations by facility, service branch, and location, FY91-93, annual rpt, 3544–39
Economic Report of the President for 1992, Joint Economic Committee critique and policy recommendations, annual rpt, 23844–2
Foreign countries military aid of US, arms sales, and training programs costs and budget requests, by program, world region, and country, FY91-93, annual rpt, 7144–13
Investigations of Federal agency and program operations, summaries of findings, as of 1991, annual GAO rpt, 26104–5.1
Natl Guard activities, personnel, and facilities, FY91, annual rpt, 3504–22
NATO and Warsaw Pact military forces reductions and ceilings under CFE treaty, inspections, and US compliance costs and savings, 1991 hearings, 25388–59
Persian Gulf War costs to US by category and service branch, and offsetting contributions by allied country, monthly rpt, 102–3
Persian Gulf War impacts on US budget deficit, FY91, annual GAO rpt, 26104–23
Personnel needs, costs, and force readiness, by service branch, FY93, annual rpt, 3504–1
Procurement appropriations, by item, service branch, and defense agency, FY91-93, annual rpt, 3544–32
R&D funding by item, service branch, and defense agency, FY91-93, annual rpt, 3544–33
Reductions in defense spending, economic impacts by defense contractor, industry, State, and congressional district, 1989-90 hearings, 23848–224
Reductions in defense spending, economic impacts of alternative plans, with data by industry and State, various periods 1949-87, article, 9385–1.313
Reductions in defense spending, economic impacts of Bush Admin plans by industry and State, FY92-97, 26306–6.167
Reserve forces personnel and equipment strengths, and readiness, by reserve component, FY91, annual rpt, 3544–31
Statistical Abstract of US, 1992 annual data compilation, 2324–1.11
Training and education programs of DOD, funding, staff, students, and facilities, by service branch, FY93, annual rpt, 3504–5
Weapons acquisition costs by system and service branch, DOD budget, FY91-93, annual rpt, 3504–2
see also Defense expenditures

Defense Communications Agency
Commercial activities of DOD performed in-house, and work-years, by service branch, installation, and State, FY91, annual rpt, 3544–25
Labor unions recognized in Fed Govt, agreements and membership by agency and facility, as of Jan 1991, biennial listing, 9844–14
Personnel (civilian and military) of DOD, by service branch and defense agency, quarterly rpt, 3542–14.1

Defense Contract Audit Agency
Labor unions recognized in Fed Govt, agreements and membership by agency and facility, as of Jan 1991, biennial listing, 9844–14
NASA programs fraud and abuse, audits and investigations, 2nd half FY92, semiannual rpt, 9502–9
Personnel (civilian and military) of DOD, by service branch and defense agency, quarterly rpt, 3542–14.1

Defense contracts and procurement
Aerospace industry sales, orders, backlog, and firms, by product for govt, military, and other customers, 1991, annual Current Industrial Rpt, 2506–12.22
Biological warfare agent vaccine dev and production of Salk Inst, and Army contract costs by component, late 1970s-91, GAO rpt, 26123–374
Budget of DOD, itemized account of legislative history, annual rpt, discontinued, 3504–7
Budget of DOD, organization, personnel, weapons, and property, by service branch, State, and country, 1992 annual summary rpt, 3504–13
Budget of DOD, procurement appropriations by item, service branch, and defense agency, FY91-93, annual rpt, 3544–32
Budget of DOD, programs, policies, and operations, FY91, annual rpt, 3544–2
Budget of US, authoritative financial statements with appropriations, outlays, and receipts, by category and agency, FY91, annual rpt, 8104–2.2
Budget of US, Bush Admin proposals, with detail for defense budgets, and historical data from FY34, FY93, 108–46.2
Chemical protective suits and masks contractor deliveries and field inspections during Persian Gulf War, 1990-91, GAO rpt, 26123–387
Debts of contractors owed to Fed Govt and deferred, status by service branch and firm, 1980-91, GAO rpt, 26123–400
Drug enforcement activities of DOD, funding by purpose, FY89-91, GAO rpt, 26123–390
Expenditures and obligations of DOD, by function and service branch, quarterly rpt, 3542–3
Expenditures of Fed Govt in States and local areas, by type, State, county, and city, FY91, annual rpt, 2464–3
Expenditures of Fed Govt in States, by type, program, agency, and State, FY91, annual rpt, 2464–2
Fraud and abuse in DOD programs, audits and investigations, 2nd half FY92, semiannual rpt, 3542–18
Fraud by DOD contractors, dispositions, fines, and settlements for top 100 firms, 1981-92, GAO rpt, 26119–423
Fuel oil and kerosene sales and deliveries, by end-use, PAD district, and State, 1990, annual rpt, 3164–94
Input-output structure of US economy, detailed interindustry transactions for 84 industries, and components of final demand, 1987, annual article, 2702–1.316
Input-output structure of US economy, detailed interindustry transactions for 541 industries, and components of final demand, 1982 benchmark data, 2708–17
Investigations of Federal agency and program operations, summaries of findings, as of 1991, annual GAO rpt, 26104–5.1
Minority business funding, by program and Federal agency, FY91, annual rpt, 2104–5
Natl Guard activities, personnel, and facilities, FY91, annual rpt, 3504–22
Natl income and product accounts and components, *Survey of Current Business*, monthly rpt, 2702–1.23
Natl income and product accounts, comprehensive accounts and components, benchmark revisions, 1929-88, 2708–5
Natl income and product accounts, comprehensive accounts and components, *Survey of Current Business*, monthly rpt, 2702–1.26
Navy ship construction contract costs and funding, FY83-91, GAO rpt, 26123–401
Navy weapons systems parts purchases from foreign suppliers and US contractors, by State and country, 1988, 2026–1.3
Persian Gulf War costs to US by category and service branch, and offsetting contributions by allied country, monthly rpt, 102–3
Post exchange operations, listing by facility and location worldwide, 1991-92, annual rpt, 3504–10
Prime contract awards of DOD, by category, contract and contractor type, and service branch, FY82-1st half FY92, semiannual rpt, 3542–1
Prime contract awards of DOD, by category, contractor type, and State, FY89-91, annual rpt, 3544–11
Prime contract awards of DOD, by contractor, service branch, State, and city, FY91, annual rpt, 3544–22

Prime contract awards of DOD, by detailed procurement category, FY88-91, annual rpt, 3544–18
Prime contract awards of DOD, by service branch and State, 1st half FY92, semiannual rpt, 3542–5
Prime contract awards of DOD, by size and type of contract, service branch, competitive status, category, and labor standard, FY91, annual rpt, 3544–19
Prime contract awards of DOD, for top 100 contractors, FY91, annual listing, 3544–5
Prime contract awards of DOD in labor surplus areas, by service branch, State, and area, 1st half FY92, semiannual rpt, 3542–19
Prime contractors, contract actions, and contracts, FY85-93, GAO rpt, 26123–399
Prime contracts, payroll, and personnel, by service branch and location, with top 5 contractors and maps, by State and country, FY91, annual rpt, 3544–29
R&D prime contract awards of DOD, for top 500 contractors, FY91, annual listing, 3544–4
R&D prime contract awards of DOD to US and foreign nonprofit instns and govt agencies, by instn and location, FY91, annual listing, 3544–17
Reductions in defense spending, economic impacts by defense contractor, industry, State, and congressional district, 1989-90 hearings, 23848–224
Reserve forces personnel and equipment strengths, and readiness, by reserve component, FY91, annual rpt, 3544–31
Semiconductor integrated circuit sales to DOD, for top 10 firms, 1991, GAO rpt, 26113–588
Shipments of military and personal property by commercial cariers, and cost savings from bill audits and rate negotiations, FY99-91, GAO rpt, 26123–369
Small business finances, operations, owner characteristics, and Federal contracts, 1980s-90, annual rpt, 9764–6
Small business R&D grants of Fed Govt, project sales by type and dev funding by source, by agency and selected firm, 1984-91, GAO rpt, 26113–393
Statistical Abstract of US, 1992 annual data compilation, 2324–1.11
Subcontract awards by DOD contractors to small and disadvantaged business, by firm and service branch, quarterly rpt, 3542–17
Survey of Current Business, defense activity indicators, monthly rpt, 2702–1.1
Weapons acquisition costs by system and service branch, DOD budget, FY91-93, annual rpt, 3504–2
Workers compensation programs under Federal admin, finances and operations, FY91, annual rpt, 6504–10

Defense Department
see Department of Defense

Defense expenditures
Air Force fiscal mgmt system operations and techniques, quarterly rpt, 3602–1
Assistance (block and categorical grants) programs for State and local govts, FY91, biennial listing, 10044–8
Base support costs by function, and personnel and acreage by installation, by service branch, FY93, annual rpt, 3504–11
Developing countries economic and social conditions from 1960s, and Intl Dev Cooperation Agency and AID activities and funding, FY91-93, annual rpt, 9904–4
Drug enforcement activities of DOD, funding by purpose, FY89-91, GAO rpt, 26123–390
Economic indicators compounded annual rates of change, monthly rpt, 9391–3
Expenditures (direct) and employment, by function and level of govt, selected years 1962-87, 10048–53
Expenditures and budget authority of DOS, FY85-93, GAO rpt, 26123–399
Expenditures and obligations of DOD, by function and service branch, quarterly rpt, 3542–3
Expenditures for contracts and payroll, and personnel, by service branch and location, with top 5 contractors and maps, by State and country, FY91, annual rpt, 3544–29
Expenditures of Fed Govt, by function, FY90, annual rpt, 2466–2.2
Expenditures of Fed Govt by type, and other finances, selected years 1952-90, annual rpt, 10044–1
Expenditures of Fed Govt in States and local areas, by type, State, county, and city, FY91, annual rpt, 2464–3
Expenditures of Fed Govt in States, by type, program, agency, and State, FY91, annual rpt, 2464–2
Foreign countries economic, social, political, and geographic summary data, by country, 1992, annual factbook, 9114–2
Foreign countries military spending, arms trade, and force strengths, with govt spending and population, by country, 1979-89, annual rpt, 9824–1
Gross State Product by component, industry div, and State, 1977-89, article, 2702–1.303
Hazardous waste site remedial action at military installations, activities and funding by site and State, FY91, annual rpt, 3544–36
Investigations of Federal agency and program operations, summaries of findings, as of 1991, annual GAO rpt, 26104–5.1
Loans and loan guarantees of Fed Govt, outstanding amounts by agency and program, *Treasury Bulletin*, quarterly rpt, 8002–4.11
Natl Guard activities, personnel, and facilities, FY91, annual rpt, 3504–22
Natl income and product accounts and components, *Survey of Current Business*, monthly rpt, 2702–1.23
Natl income and product accounts, comprehensive accounts and components, benchmark revisions, 1929-88, 2708–5
Natl income and product accounts, comprehensive accounts and components, *Survey of Current Business*, monthly rpt, 2702–1.26
NATO, Japan, and South Korea military spending and indicators of ability to support common defense, by country, 1970s-90, annual rpt, 3544–28
NATO military base construction projects, and US funding, by project status, 1985-93, GAO rpt, 26123–388
New England States employment growth after recessions, relation to selected economic factors, various periods 1969-90, article, 9373–1.315
Persian Gulf War costs to US by category and service branch, and offsetting contributions by allied country, monthly rpt, 102–3
Presidential approval rating and political party affiliation impact on defense spending and transfer payments, model description and results, 1950s-88, working paper, 9393–10.17
Reductions in defense spending, economic impacts by defense contractor, industry, State, and congressional district, 1989-90 hearings, 23848–224
Reductions in defense spending, economic impacts of alternative plans, with data by industry and State, various periods 1949-87, article, 9385–1.313
Sealift Military Command shipping operations, finances, and personnel, FY91, annual rpt, 3804–14
Service academies prep schools costs and student performance indicators, 1988-90, GAO rpt, 26123–380
Statistical Abstract of US, 1992 annual data compilation, 2324–1.11
Survey of Current Business, defense activity indicators, monthly rpt, 2702–1.1
Training and education programs of DOD, funding, staff, students, and facilities, by service branch, FY93, annual rpt, 3504–5
see also Budget of the U.S.
see also Defense budgets and appropriations
see also Defense contracts and procurement
see also Defense research
see also Military pay

Defense industries
Aluminum ingot and mill product defense and total shipments, trade, use, and inventories, monthly Current Industrial Rpt, 2506–10.9
Business statistics, detailed data for major industries and economic indicators, 1960-91, *Survey of Current Business* biennial supplement, 2704–1
Commercial activities of DOD performed in-house, and work-years, by service branch, installation, and State, FY91, annual rpt, 3544–25
Czechoslovakia military weapons production in Czech and Slovak regions, and domestic and export arms sales, 1987-90, hearing, 25408–115
Employment of defense industries, FY85-93, GAO rpt, 26123–399
Manufacturing industries important to military, finances, operations, and intl competitiveness, series, 2026–1
Reductions in defense spending, economic impacts by defense contractor, industry, State, and congressional district, 1989-90 hearings, 23848–224
Reductions in defense spending, economic impacts of alternative plans, with data by industry and State, various periods 1949-87, article, 9385–1.313
Reductions in defense spending, economic impacts of Bush Admin plans by industry and State, FY92-97, 26306–6.167
Shipments of military and nonmilitary capital goods, and Federal defense spending, 1970s-91, fact sheet, 2326–17.43

Survey of Current Business, defense activity indicators, monthly rpt, 2702–1.1
see also Arms trade
see also Defense contracts and procurement

Defense Intelligence Agency
Persian Gulf War costs to US by category and service branch, and offsetting contributions by allied country, monthly rpt, 102–3

Defense Investigative Service
Personnel (civilian and military) of DOD, by service branch and defense agency, quarterly rpt, 3542–14.1

Defense Logistics Agency
Commercial activities of DOD performed in-house, and work-years, by service branch, installation, and State, FY91, annual rpt, 3544–25
Hazardous waste site remedial action at military installations, activities and funding by site and State, FY91, annual rpt, 3544–36
Labor unions recognized in Fed Govt, agreements and membership by agency and facility, as of Jan 1991, biennial listing, 9844–14
Persian Gulf War costs to US by category and service branch, and offsetting contributions by allied country, monthly rpt, 102–3
Personnel (civilian and military) of DOD, by service branch and defense agency, quarterly rpt, 3542–14.1
Procurement, contractor debts owed to Fed Govt and deferred, status by service branch and firm, 1980-91, GAO rpt, 26123–400
Procurement, DOD prime contract awards by category, contract and contractor type, and service branch, FY82-1st half FY92, semiannual rpt, 3542–1
Procurement, DOD prime contract awards by contractor, service branch, State, and city, FY91, annual rpt, 3544–22
Procurement, DOD prime contract awards by detailed procurement category, FY88-91, annual rpt, 3544–18
Procurement, DOD prime contract awards by service branch and State, 1st half FY92, semiannual rpt, 3542–5
Procurement, DOD prime contract awards by size and type of contract, service branch, competitive status, category, and labor standard, FY91, annual rpt, 3544–19
Procurement, DOD prime contract awards in labor surplus areas, by service branch, State, and area, 1st half FY92, semiannual rpt, 3542–19
Procurement, subcontract awards by DOD contractors to small and disadvantaged business, by firm and service branch, quarterly rpt, 3542–17
Shipments by DOD of military and personal property, passenger traffic, and costs, by service branch and mode of transport, FY91, annual rpt, 3704–15
Stockpiling of strategic material, inventories and needs, by commodity, 1992, annual rpt, 3544–37

Defense Mapping Agency
Commercial activities of DOD performed in-house, and work-years, by service branch, installation, and State, FY91, annual rpt, 3544–25
Labor unions recognized in Fed Govt, agreements and membership by agency and facility, as of Jan 1991, biennial listing, 9844–14
Persian Gulf War costs to US by category and service branch, and offsetting contributions by allied country, monthly rpt, 102–3
Personnel (civilian and military) of DOD, by service branch and defense agency, quarterly rpt, 3542–14.1

Defense Nuclear Agency
Commercial activities of DOD performed in-house, and work-years, by service branch, installation, and State, FY91, annual rpt, 3544–25
Labor unions recognized in Fed Govt, agreements and membership by agency and facility, as of Jan 1991, biennial listing, 9844–14
Personnel (civilian and military) of DOD, by service branch and defense agency, quarterly rpt, 3542–14.1

Defense research
Basic R&D program of DOD, activities and funding, FY62-88, biennial rpt, 3504–12
Biological warfare agent vaccine dev and production of Salk Inst, and Army contract costs by component, late 1970s-91, GAO rpt, 26123–374
Budget of DOD, organization, personnel, weapons, and property, by service branch, State, and country, 1992 annual summary rpt, 3504–13
Budget of DOD, personnel needs, costs, and force readiness by service branch, FY93, annual rpt, 3504–1
Budget of DOD, programs, policies, and operations, FY91, annual rpt, 3544–2
Budget of DOD, R&D appropriations by item, service branch, and defense agency, FY91-93, annual rpt, 3544–33
Budget of DOD, weapons acquisition costs by system and service branch, FY91-93, annual rpt, 3504–2
Budget of US, Bush Admin proposals, with detail for defense budgets, and historical data from FY34, FY93, 108–46.2
Commercial activities of DOD performed in-house, and work-years, by service branch, installation, and State, FY91, annual rpt, 3544–25
Drug enforcement activities of DOD, funding by purpose, FY89-91, GAO rpt, 26123–390
Expenditures and obligations of DOD, by function and service branch, quarterly rpt, 3542–3
Expenditures for DOD base support by function, and personnel and acreage by installation, by service branch, FY93, annual rpt, 3504–11
Expenditures for R&D by Fed Govt, by detailed function, program, and agency, FY91-93, annual rpt, 9627–9
Manufacturing industries important to military, finances, operations, and intl competitiveness, series, 2026–1
Nuclear reactors for domestic use and export by function and operating status, with owner, operating characteristics, and location, 1991 annual listing, 3354–15
Prime contract awards of DOD, by category, contract and contractor type, and service branch, FY82-1st half FY92, semiannual rpt, 3542–1
Prime contract awards of DOD, by category, contractor type, and State, FY89-91, annual rpt, 3544–11
Prime contract awards of DOD, by detailed procurement category, FY88-91, annual rpt, 3544–18
Prime contract awards of DOD for R&D, for top 500 contractors, FY91, annual listing, 3544–4
Prime contract awards of DOD for R&D to US and foreign nonprofit instns and govt agencies, by instn and location, FY91, annual listing, 3544–17
Prime contracts, payroll, and personnel, by service branch and location, with top 5 contractors and maps, by State and country, FY91, annual rpt, 3544–29
Radioactive waste and spent fuel generation, inventory, and disposal, 1960s-90 and projected to 2020, annual rpt, 3364–2
Science and Engineering Indicators, employment, education, R&D funding, and industry impacts, with foreign comparisons, 1960s-91, biennial rpt, 9624–10.4
Small business R&D grants of Fed Govt, by program area, agency, MSA, and State, FY90, annual rpt, 9764–7
Weather services activities and funding, by Federal agency, planned FY92-93, annual rpt, 2144–2
see also Military science

Defense Security Assistance Agency
Foreign countries military aid of US, arms sales, and training, by country, FY50-91, annual rpt, 3904–3
Foreign countries military aid of US, arms sales, and training programs costs and budget requests, by program, world region, and country, FY91-93, annual rpt, 7144–13
Liabilities (contingent) and claims paid by Fed Govt on federally insured and guaranteed contracts with foreign obligors, by country and program, periodic rpt, 8002–12

DeGennaro, Ramon P.
"Capital Forbearance and Thrifts: An Ex Post Examination of Regulatory Gambling", 9377–9.140

Degrees, educational
see Degrees, higher education
see Educational attainment
see under By Educational Attainment in the "Index by Categories"

Degrees, higher education
Black higher education instns enrollment, finances, staff, and degrees, by instn and selected student characteristics, 1970s-90, 4848–46
Census of Population and Housing, 1990: summary characteristics, by county, subdiv, and place, State rpt series, 2551–7
Condition of Education, detail for elementary, secondary, and higher education, 1920s-91 and projected to 2002, annual rpt, 4824–1
Data on education, enrollment, degrees, teachers, and spending, 1977/78-1990/91 and alternative projections to 2002/2003, annual rpt, 4824–4
Data on education, enrollment, finances, teachers, and other characteristics, by State, 1969-89, 4828–33

Data on education, selected trends and projections 1979-2002, annual pamphlet, 4824–9
Degrees awarded and enrollment in higher education, by sex, full- and part-time status, and instn level and control, fall 1991, annual rpt, 4844–16
Degrees awarded in higher education, by level, field, race, and sex, 1989/90 and trends from 1980/81, annual rpt, 4844–17
Degrees awarded in higher education, by level, 1980s-93, annual press release, 4804–19
Degrees awarded in higher education, highest level by instn, 1991/92, biennial listing, 4844–3
Degrees, faculty, finances, and enrollment in higher education, by instn level and control, and State, FY88, annual rpt, 4844–13
Digest of Education Statistics, 1992 annual data compilation, 4824–2
Environmental Quality, status of problems, protection programs, research, and intl issues, 1991 annual rpt, 484–1
Fed Govt civilian employees demographic and employment characteristics, as of Sept 1991, annual article, 9842–1.301
Health care professionals supply and education, by professional and other characteristics, and location, 1960s-92 and projected to 2020, biennial rpt, 4114–8
High school class of 1972: community college attendance, by selected characteristics, natl longitudinal study, 1970s-86, 4888–7
Income (household, family, and personal), by source, detailed characteristics, and region, 1991, annual Current Population Rpt, 2546–6.76
Indian education funding of Fed Govt, and enrollment, degrees, and program grants and fellowships by State, late 1970s-FY90, annual rpt, 14874–1
Labor force status, job degree requirements, and earnings of college grads, with data by occupation, 1960s-90, article, 6722–1.330
Labor force status, job degree requirements, and outlook for college grads, 1980s-90 and projected to 2005, article, 6722–1.331
Minority group higher education enrollment, completion, and degrees, by race, sex, and type of instn, 1970s-90, 26306–3.122
Minority group, women, and disabled persons employment and education in science and engineering, by field, mid 1970s-91, biennial rpt, 9624–20
Natl Education Goals progress indicators, by State, 1992, annual rpt, 15914–1
Nuclear engineering enrollment and degrees by instn and State, and women grads plans and employment, 1991, annual rpt, 3006–8.18
Nuclear engineering enrollment and degrees granted by instn and State, and grad placement, by student characteristics, 1991, annual rpt, 3004–5
Occupation training completions, and labor demand and turnover, by detailed occupation, 1990 and projected to 2005, biennial rpt, 6744–3
Pacific territories population and housing detailed characteristics, by location, 1990 Census of Population and Housing, series, 2551–8
PhD degree recipients, by field and selected characteristics, 1979, 1984, and 1989, 4848–44
Population economic well-being indicators, by selected characteristics and household income and income-to-poverty ratio, 1984, 2546–20.22
Productivity relation to degree awards, effects of selection bias, model description and results, 1991 working paper, 6886–6.81
Radiation protection and health physics enrollment and degrees granted by instn and State, and grad placement, by student characteristics, 1991, annual rpt, 3004–7
Radiation protection and health physics enrollment and degrees granted by instn and State, and women grads plans and employment, 1991, annual rpt, 3006–8.19
Science and engineering employment and education of minorities, women, and disabled, by field, mid 1970s-91, biennial rpt, 9624–20
Science and Engineering Indicators, employment, education, R&D funding, and industry impacts, with foreign comparisons, 1960s-91, biennial rpt, 9624–10
Science and engineering labor force, Federal and university research funding, and educational data, series, 9626–6
Science and engineering PhDs, by field, instn, employment prospects, sex, race, and other characteristics, 1960s-90, advance annual rpt, 9626–8.1
Science, engineering, and technical employment by industry and occupation, and degrees awarded, 1970s-90 and projected to 2005, article, 6722–1.314
Soviet Union and US economic and sociodemographic indicators, selected years 1970-90, handbook, 2328–80
Statistical Abstract of US, 1992 annual data compilation, 2324–1.4; 2324–1.20
Teachers and administrators in private schools, pay, work conditions, and selected characteristics, by school type and affiliation, 1987/88, 4836–3.8
Teachers and other special education staff, training, degrees, and certification, by field and State, FY89, annual rpt, 4944–4
see also under By Educational Attainment in the "Index by Categories"

DeKalb County, Ga.
Housing and households characteristics, and unit and neighborhood quality, by MSA location for 11 MSAs, 1987 survey, supplement, 2485–8

Del Bene, Linda
"Income, Assets, and Health Insurance: Economic Resources for Meeting Acute Health Care Needs of the Aged", 4742–1.307

Delaware
Banks (insured commercial and savings) deposits by instn, State, MSA, and county, as of June 1991, annual regional rpt, 9295–3.2
Deaths and rates, by detailed location, cause, and demographic characteristics, 1989, US Vital Statistics annual rpt, 4144–3.1
Employment, earnings, and hours, by selected SIC 1- to 4-digit industry, State, and for 275 MSAs, 1987-92, 6748–81
Employment growth and unemployment rates, Fed Reserve 3rd District, quarterly rpt, 9387–10
Fed Govt spending in States and local areas, by type, State, county, and city, FY91, annual rpt, 2464–3
Fed Govt spending in States, by type, program, agency, and State, FY91, annual rpt, 2464–2
HHS financial aid, by program, recipient, State, and city, FY91, annual regional listing, 4004–3.3
Hospital deaths of Medicare patients, actual and expected rates by diagnosis, and hospital characteristics, by instn, FY90 annual State rpt, 4654–14.8
Housing census, 1990: summary unit characteristics, by householder race and age, county, place, and urban-rural location, State rpt, 2471–1.9
Medicaid impacts on State budgets, and program financing, cost control measures, enrollment, and services coverage, by selected State, 1960s-80s and projected to 1997, 10176–3.6
Military prime contract awards, by contractor, service branch, State, and city, FY91, annual rpt, 3544–22
Mineral Industry Surveys, State reviews of production, 1991, preliminary annual rpt, 5614–6
Minerals Yearbook, Vol 2, 1990: State review of production and sales by commodity, and business activity, annual rpt, 5604–22.9
Multinatl firms US affiliates finances and operations, by industry, country of parent firm, and State, 1987, 2708–48
Physicians, by specialty, age, sex, and location of training and practice, 1990, State rpt, 4116–6.8
Population and housing census, 1990: detailed geographic coverage, State CD-ROM, 2551–9.5
Population and housing census, 1990: population and housing characteristics, detailed geographic coverage, State CD-ROM, 2551–10.11
Population and housing census, 1990: summary characteristics, by county, subdiv, and place, State rpt, 2551–7.9
Population census, 1990: population characteristics and living arrangements, by county, place, and urban-rural location, State rpt, 2531–1.9
Statistical Abstract of US, 1992 annual data compilation, 2324–1
see also Kent County, Del.
see also Wilmington, Del.
see also under By State in the "Index by Categories"

Delaware County, Pa.
Housing and households characteristics, unit and neighborhood quality, and journey to work by MSA location, for 11 MSAs, 1985 survey, supplement, 2485–8
Housing and households detailed characteristics, and unit and neighborhood quality, by location, 1989 survey, MSA rpt, 2485–6.4

Delaware River
Army Corps of Engineers water resources dev projects, characteristics, and costs, 1950s-89, biennial State rpt series, 3756–1
Army Corps of Engineers water resources dev projects, characteristics, and costs, 1950s-91, biennial State rpt series, 3756–2
Freight (waterborne domestic and foreign) by commodity, traffic, and passengers, by port and waterway, 1989, annual rpt, 3754–3.1
Tidal currents, daily time and velocity by station for North America coasts, forecast 1993, annual rpt, 2174–1.1
Water supply and quality in streams and lakes, and groundwater levels in wells, by drainage basin, 1990, annual State rpt series, 5666–10
Water supply and quality in streams and lakes, and groundwater levels in wells, by drainage basin, 1991, annual State rpt series, 5666–12
Water supply in northeastern US, precipitation and stream runoff by station, monthly rpt, 2182–3
Water supply in US and southern Canada, streamflow, surface and groundwater conditions, and reservoir levels, by location, monthly rpt, 5662–3

Delaware River Basin Commission
Budget of US, authoritative financial statements with appropriations, outlays, and receipts, by category and agency, FY91, annual rpt, 8104–2.2
Budget of US, obligations and authority by function, agency, and program, with summaries and analyses, FY93, annual rpt, 104–2

Delivery services
see Courier services

Della Rocco, Pamela S.
"Comparison of Performance on the Shipley Institute of Living Scale, Air Traffic Control Specialist Selection Test, and FAA Academy Screen", 7506–10.126

Dellagiarino, George
"Geological and Geophysical Data Acquisition, Outer Continental Shelf Through FY90", 5738–41

Delman, Farrell
"Tobacco Taxes, Employment, and Income", 1504–9.1

Delray Beach, Fla.
Wages by occupation, and benefits for office and plant workers, 1991 survey, periodic MSA rpt, 6785–3.1

Delucia, R. A.
"Statistics on Aircraft Gas Turbine Engine Rotor Failures That Occurred in U.S. Commercial Aviation During 1988", 7504–50

Delvo, Herman
"Peanut Production Practices and Input Use: 1991", 1561–16.304

Demand deposits
see Checking accounts
see Negotiable orders of withdrawal accounts

Demirors, Umran
"Price-Adjustment Delays in the Secondary Market for Developing Country Debt and the Estimation of Asset Pricing Models", 9385–8.132

Democratic Party
Campaign finances, elections, procedures, and Fed Election Commission activities, press release series, 9276–1
Campaign finances reported to Fed Election Commission, by type of filer, 1990 natl elections, biennial rpt series, 9276–2
Campaign-related internal communications of firms and assns, spending by organization, location, and candidate, 1991-92, biennial rpt, 9274–3
Statistical Abstract of US, 1992 annual data compilation, 2324–1.8
Votes cast by party, candidate, and State, 1990 natl elections, biennial rpt, 21944–3

Democratic Peoples Republic of Korea
see Korea, North

Demography
see Population characteristics
see Population size
see Vital statistics
see under Demographic Breakdowns in the "Index by Categories"

Demolition
see Wrecking and demolition

Demonstration and pilot projects
AIDS prevention programs for drug abusers and their sexual partners, client characteristics, and outcomes, for selected metro areas, 1989 annual conf, 4494–12
Assistance (financial and nonfinancial) of Fed Govt, 1992 base edition, annual listing, 104–5
Auto alternative fuels use in Federal fleet, energy economy performance at 4 sites, FY91, annual rpt, 3304–28
Child abuse and neglect prevention and treatment, and disabled infant protection, grants by State, FY91, annual listing, 4584–6
Child abuse and neglect prevention and treatment, discretionary grants, FY91, annual listing, 4584–9
Coal-fired power plants air pollutant reduction technology funding, and impacts on energy costs and emissions, 1950s-87 and projected to 2010, annual rpt, 3334–5
Coal-fired power plants air pollutant reduction technology funding, and project descriptions, 1991, annual rpt, 3334–4
Debt delinquent on Federal accounts, cases and collections of Justice Dept and private law firms, pilot project results, FY91, annual rpt, 6004–20
Disabled persons rehabilitation, Federal and State activities and funding, FY90, annual rpt, 4944–1
Economic Dev Admin activities, and funding by program, recipient, State, and county, FY91 and cumulative from FY66, annual rpt, 2064–2
Education (early childhood) for handicapped children, project descriptions, 1991/92, annual listing, 4944–10
Education (public elementary and secondary) system mgmt by higher education instn, Chelsea, Mass and Boston University demonstration program operations and results, 1988-90, 4808–38
Educational equity program for women, grants and contracts by project, type, and State, 1988-92, annual rpt, 4804–2
EPA pollution control grant program activities, monthly rpt, 9182–8
Health Care Financing Admin research activities and grants, by program, FY91, annual listing, 4654–10
Health Care Financing Review, quarterly journal, 4652–1
Heart, Lung, and Blood Natl Inst activities, and grants by recipient and location, FY91 and disease trends from 1940, annual rpt, 4474–15
HHS financial aid, by program, recipient, State, and city, FY91, annual regional listings, 4004–3
Homeless persons aid programs of Fed Govt, program descriptions and funding, by agency and State, FY87-91, annual GAO rpt, 26104–21
HUD housing and community development programs, press release series, 5006–3
Hwy traffic mgmt and info electronic system, demonstration program results, late 1980s, 7558–119
Indian education funding of Fed Govt, with enrollment, program grants, and fellowships by State, 1980s-FY91, annual rpt, 14874–1
Kidney end-stage disease research of CDC and HCFA, project listing, 1991, annual rpt, 4654–16
Labor turnover, job openings, and new hires and wages, pilot survey results, costs, and methodology, 1990-91, 6728–40
Lead paint abatement costs and results, demonstration project design and findings, 1991 rpt, 5188–131
Libraries (research) funding of Education Dept, by project, instn, and State, FY90, annual listing, 4874–2
Library research and demonstration projects and funding, FY67-86, listing, 4878–5
Literacy and English as a second language programs for adults, Education Dept and State programs, enrollment, and funding, by State, 1988-91, 4808–41
Literacy programs in workplaces, demonstration projects funding and participants, FY88-90, 4808–43
Mentally retarded SSI beneficiaries transitional job training demonstration project participant characteristics, 1985-87, article, 4742–1.301
Neighborhood Dev Demonstration program evaluation, grantee organization characteristics, activities, finances, and private sector support, 1984-89, 5188–119
Occupational Safety and Health Admin activities and grants, press release series, 6606–3
Oil enhanced recovery research contracts of DOE, project summaries, funding, and bibl, quarterly rpt, 3002–14
Older persons health promotion program, costs and effectiveness of case mgmt and health education, 1980-83 local area study, article, 4042–3.342
Public Health Reports, bimonthly journal, 4042–3

Dempster, Dan
"North American Trade Issues", 1504–9.1

DeNavas, Carmen
"Money Income of Households, Families, and Persons in the U.S.: 1991", 2546–6.76

Denmark
Agricultural trade of US, by detailed commodity and country, 1991, annual rpt, 1524–8
Agricultural trade of US, by detailed commodity and country, 1991, semiannual rpt, 1522–4
AID loans repayment status and terms by program and country, and status of predecessor agency loans, quarterly rpt, 9912–3
Cancer risk relation to radiologic Thorotrast exposure, Denmark study, 1992 article, 4472–1.338
Cuba trade, by commodity and country, mid 1980s-91, 9118–8
Economic and military aid and loans from US and intl agencies, by program and country, FY46-91, annual rpt, 9914–5
Economic conditions, income, production, prices, employment, and trade, 1992 periodic country rpt, 2046–4.40
Economic conditions, policy, and trade practices, by country, 1989-91, annual rpt, 21384–5
Economic, social, political, and geographic summary data, by country, 1992, annual factbook, 9114–2
Exports and imports of US, by Harmonized System 6-digit commodity and country, 1991, annual rpt, 2424–13
Exports and imports of US, by selected country, country group, and commodity group, 1991, annual rpt, 2044–37
Exports and imports of US, by transport mode, country, and SITC 1- to 3-digit commodity, 1991, annual rpt, 2424–12
Exports, imports, and balances of US for manufactured goods, by SITC 2-digit commodity and country, quarterly rpt, 2042–35
Exports of US, detailed Schedule B commodities with countries of destination, 1991, annual rpt, 2424–10
Health care costs and components, services use, resources, and economic indicators, by OECD country, 1960s-90, article, 4652–1.322
Human rights conditions in 170 countries, and US economic and military aid, 1991, annual rpt, 21384–3
Labor conditions, union coverage, and work accidents, 1992 annual country rpt, 6366–4.24; 6366–4.48
Military spending, arms trade, and force strengths, with govt spending and population, by country, 1979-89, annual rpt, 9824–1
Multinatl US firms and foreign affiliates finances and operations, by industry and country, 1989 benchmark survey, annual rpt, 2704–5
Multinatl US firms foreign affiliates, income statement items by asset size, industry, and country, 1988, biennial article, 8302–2.322
Oil production, stocks, use, and trade, by selected country and country group, monthly rpt, 3162–42
Population size, growth rates, and components of change, by country, projected 1990-2020 and trends from 1950, biennial rpt, 2324–9
Refugee migration, and intl aid programs, by world area and country of origin and asylum, 1991, annual rpt, 7004–15
Tax revenue, by level of govt and type of tax, for OECD countries, mid 1960s-90, annual rpt, 10044–1.2
UN voting record and share of votes in agreement with US, by issue, country, and world area, 1991, annual rpt, 7004–18
see also Faeroes
see also under By Foreign Country in the "Index by Categories"

Dental condition
Acute and chronic health conditions, disability, absenteeism, and health services use, by selected characteristics, 1990, annual rpt, 4147–10.182; 4147–10.183
Child dental caries and baby bottle tooth decay prevalence among Head Start children in southwest US, by characteristics of child and area, 1992 article, 4042–3.317
Health condition and care indicators, 1950s-90 with health improvement and disease prevention goals for 1990, annual data compilation, 4144–11
HHS financial aid, by program, recipient, State, and city, FY91, annual regional listings, 4004–3
Research and training grants of Natl Inst of Dental Research, by recipient instn, FY90, annual listing, 4474–19
Youth health condition, risk factors, and preventive and treatment services use and availability, 1970s-80s, 26358–234.2

Dentists and dentistry
Child and maternal health condition and services use, indicators by age, race, and poverty status, 1988, 4478–197
Child dental fluoride products use, by frequency of dental visits and selected characteristics, 1983-89, 4146–8.222
Consumer spending, natl income and product account benchmark revisions, 1929-88, 2708–5
Consumer spending, natl income and product accounts, comprehensive accounts and components, *Survey of Current Business*, monthly rpt, 2702–1.25
County Business Patterns, 1989: employment, establishments, and payroll, by SIC 2- to 4-digit industry and county, annual State rpt series, 2326–8
County Business Patterns, 1990: employment, establishments, and payroll, by SIC 2- to 4-digit industry and county, annual State rpt series, 2326–6
CPI by component for US city average, and by selected metro area, region, and population size, monthly rpt, 6762–2
Degrees awarded in higher education, by level, field, race, and sex, 1989/90 and trends from 1980/81, annual rpt, 4844–17
Education in science and engineering, grad programs enrollment by field, source of funds, and characteristics of student and instn, 1990, annual rpt, 9627–7
Employment, earnings, and hours, by SIC 1- to 4-digit industry, monthly 1989-Feb 1992, annual rpt, 6744–4
Expenditures for health care by funding source, 1990, with trends and indexes by service type from 1960, article, 4652–1.323
Fed Govt financial and nonfinancial domestic aid, 1992 base edition, annual listing, 104–5
Health Care Financing Review, provider prices, price inputs and indexes, and labor, quarterly journal, 4652–1.1
Health condition and care indicators, 1950s-90 with health improvement and disease prevention goals for 1990, annual data compilation, 4144–11
Hepatitis cases by infection source, age, sex, race, and State, and deaths, by strain, 1989 and trends from 1966, 4205–2
Hospital employment and job vacancy rate, by occupation, and instn size and control, 1981-88, annual rpt, 4114–12
Indian Health Service and tribal facilities and use, and Indians health and other characteristics, by IHS region, 1980s-90, annual chartbook, 4084–7
Indian Health Service facilities, funding, operations, and Indian health and other characteristics, 1950s-91, annual chartbook, 4084–1
Input-output structure of US economy, detailed interindustry transactions for 541 industries, and components of final demand, 1982 benchmark data, 2708–17
Insurance (health) coverage and provisions of employee benefit plans, by plan type, for State and local govt employees, 1990, biennial rpt, 6784–21
Labor demand, turnover, and training completions, by detailed occupation, 1990 and projected to 2005, biennial rpt, 6744–3
Labor supply and education of health professionals, by professional and other characteristics, and location, 1960s-92 and projected to 2020, biennial rpt, 4114–8
Medicaid beneficiaries and payments, by service type, FY72-90, annual rpt, 4744–3.6
Medicare and Medicaid beneficiaries and program operations, 1992, annual fact book, 4654–18
Medicare reimbursement of hospitals under prospective payment system, and effect on services, finances, and beneficiary payments, 1980-91, annual rpt, 17204–2
Military health care personnel, and accessions by training source, by occupation, specialty, and service branch, FY90, annual rpt, 3544–24
Navy personnel strengths, accessions, and attrition, detailed statistics, quarterly rpt, 3802–4
Occupational Outlook Handbook, 1992-93, biennial rpt, 6744–1
Research and training grants of Natl Inst of Dental Research, by recipient instn, FY90, annual listing, 4474–19
Soviet Union and US economic and sociodemographic indicators, selected years 1970-90, handbook, 2328–80
Statistical Abstract of US, 1992 annual data compilation, 2324–1.3
Tax (income) returns of corporations, income and tax items by asset size and detailed industry, 1989, annual rpt, 8304–4; 8304–21
Tax (income) returns of sole proprietorships, income statement items, by industry group, 1990, annual article, 8302–2.317; 8302–2.320
VA health care facilities employment, FY67-91, annual rpt, 8604–5.1

VA health care facilities physicians, dentists, and nurses, by selected employment characteristics and VA district, quarterly rpt, 8602-6
VA health care facilities trainees, by detailed program and city, FY91, annual rpt, 8704-4
VA health care professionals employment, by district and facility, quarterly rpt, 8602-4
VA health care services, needs, availability, structure, and funding, 1991 compilation of papers, 8608-9
VA health care staff and turnover, by occupation, physician specialty, and location, 1991, annual rpt, 8604-8
see also Dental condition

Denver, Colo.
CPI by component for US city average, and by selected metro area, region, and population size, monthly rpt, 6762-2
Drug abuse indicators for selected metro areas, research results, data collection, and policy issues, 1992 semiannual conf, 4492-5
Drug test results at arrest, by drug type, offense, and sex, for selected urban areas, quarterly rpt, 6062-3
Heroin prices and purity in 19 metro areas and Puerto Rico, by world area of origin, quarterly rpt, 6282-2
Housing and households characteristics, and unit and neighborhood quality, by MSA location for 11 MSAs, 1986 survey, supplement, 2485-8
Housing starts and completions authorized by building permits in 40 MSAs, quarterly rpt, 2382-9
Housing vacancy rates for single and multifamily units and mobile homes, by city and ZIP code, 1992, annual MSA rpt, 9304-22.2
Wages by occupation, and benefits, for office and plant workers, 1991 survey, periodic MSA rpt, 6785-16.4
see also under By City and By SMSA or MSA in the "Index by Categories"

Department of Agriculture
Acreage reduction program compliance, enrollment, and yield on planted acreage, by commodity and State, annual press release series, 1004-20
Activities and programs of USDA, by subagency, FY91, annual rpt, 1004-3
Agricultural Statistics, 1991, annual rpt, 1004-1
Budget of US, authoritative financial statements with appropriations, outlays, and receipts, by category and agency, FY91, annual rpt, 8104-2.2
Budget of US, obligations and authority by function, agency, and program, with summaries and analyses, FY93, annual rpt, 104-2
Credit sales agreement terms, by commodity and country, FY90, annual rpt, 15344-1.11
Education funding by Federal agency, program, and recipient type, and instn spending, 1960s-91, annual rpt, 4824-8
Electronic info storage and transmission costs and revenues for 4 Federal agencies, FY85-91, GAO rpt, 26125-47
Expenditures of Fed Govt in States, by type, program, agency, and State, FY91, annual rpt, 2464-2
Farm financial and marketing conditions, annual conf, issuing agency change, 1004-16
Fraud and abuse in USDA programs, audits and investigations, FY92, semiannual rpt, 1002-4
Labor unions recognized in Fed Govt, agreements and membership by agency and facility, as of Jan 1991, biennial listing, 9844-14
Meat production, inventory, and price forecasts of USDA, accuracy, 1980s, GAO rpt, 26131-93
Production, price, and supply forecasts used for USDA commodity program outlays, accuracy, 1975-88, GAO rpt, 26131-94
R&D and related funding of Fed Govt to higher education and nonprofit instns, by field, instn, agency, and State, FY90, annual rpt, 9627-17
Research and education appropriations of USDA, by program and subagency, FY83-91, annual rpt, 1004-19
Revenue of USDA, by source and subagency, FY88-92, GAO rpt, 26113-602
Rural areas dev aid by Fed Govt, Bush Admin programs and initiatives, FY91, annual rpt, 1004-17
Science and engineering grad enrollment, by field, source of funds, and characteristics of student and instn, 1990, annual rpt, 9627-7
Yearbook of Agriculture, special topics, 1992 annual compilation of papers, 1004-18
see also Agricultural Cooperative Service
see also Agricultural Marketing Service
see also Agricultural Research Service
see also Agricultural Stabilization and Conservation Service
see also Agricultural Statistics Board
see also Animal and Plant Health Inspection Service
see also Commodity Credit Corp.
see also Cooperative State Research Service
see also Economic Research Service
see also Farmers Home Administration
see also Federal Crop Insurance Corp.
see also Federal Grain Inspection Service
see also Food and Nutrition Service
see also Food Safety and Inspection Service
see also Foreign Agricultural Service
see also Forest Service
see also Human Nutrition Information Service
see also National Agricultural Statistics Service
see also Office of Grants and Program Systems, USDA
see also Office of International Cooperation and Development, USDA
see also Office of Transportation, USDA
see also Packers and Stockyards Administration
see also Rural Electrification Administration
see also Soil Conservation Service
see also under By Federal Agency in the "Index by Categories"

Department of Air Force
Base closings in Germany, US liability for local natl employee severance pay, projected FY91-95, GAO rpt, 26123-383
Base construction, renovation, and closure, DOD budget requests by project, service branch, State, and country, FY93, annual rpt, 3544-15
Base support costs by function, and personnel and acreage by installation, by service branch, FY93, annual rpt, 3504-11
Budget of DOD, base construction and family housing appropriations by facility, service branch, and location, FY91-93, annual rpt, 3544-39
Budget of DOD, procurement appropriations by item, service branch, and defense agency, FY91-93, annual rpt, 3544-32
Budget of DOD, programs, policies, and operations, FY91, annual rpt, 3544-2
Budget of DOD, R&D appropriations by item, service branch, and defense agency, FY91-93, annual rpt, 3544-33
Budget of DOD, weapons acquisition costs by system and service branch, FY91-93, annual rpt, 3504-2
Budget of US, Bush Admin proposals, with detail for defense budgets, and historical data from FY34, FY93, 108-46.2
Commercial activities of DOD performed in-house, and work-years, by service branch, installation, and State, FY91, annual rpt, 3544-25
Courts (military) cases and actions, FY91, annual rpt, 3504-3
Expenditures and obligations of DOD, by function and service branch, quarterly rpt, 3542-3
Fiscal mgmt system operations and techniques of Air Force, quarterly rpt, 3602-1
Hazardous waste site remedial action at military installations, activities and funding by site and State, FY91, annual rpt, 3544-36
Health care personnel, and accessions by training source, by occupation, specialty, and service branch, FY90, annual rpt, 3544-24
Labor unions recognized in Fed Govt, agreements and membership by agency and facility, as of Jan 1991, biennial listing, 9844-14
Personnel (civilian) of DOD, by service branch and defense agency, with summary military employment data, quarterly rpt, 3542-16
Personnel (civilian and military) of DOD, by service branch, major installation, and State, as of Sept 1991, annual rpt, 3544-7
Physicians, by specialty, age, sex, and location of training and practice, 1990, State rpt series, 4116-6
Procurement, contractor debts owed to Fed Govt and deferred, status by service branch and firm, 1980-91, GAO rpt, 26123-400
Procurement, DOD prime contract awards by category, contract and contractor type, and service branch, FY82-1st half FY92, semiannual rpt, 3542-1
Procurement, DOD prime contract awards by contractor, service branch, State, and city, FY91, annual rpt, 3544-22
Procurement, DOD prime contract awards by detailed procurement category, FY88-91, annual rpt, 3544-18
Procurement, DOD prime contract awards by service branch and State, 1st half FY92, semiannual rpt, 3542-5

Procurement, DOD prime contract awards by size and type of contract, service branch, competitive status, category, and labor standard, FY91, annual rpt, 3544–19
Procurement, DOD prime contract awards in labor surplus areas, by service branch, State, and area, 1st half FY92, semiannual rpt, 3542–19
Procurement, subcontract awards by DOD contractors to small and disadvantaged business, by firm and service branch, quarterly rpt, 3542–17
Shipments by DOD of military and personal property, passenger traffic, and costs, by service branch and mode of transport, FY91, annual rpt, 3704–15
see also Air Force
see also terms beginning with Defense and with Military

Department of Army
Base closings in Germany, US liability for local natl employee severance pay, projected FY91-95, GAO rpt, 26123–383
Base construction, renovation, and closure, DOD budget requests by project, service branch, State, and country, FY93, annual rpt, 3544–15
Base support costs by function, and personnel and acreage by installation, by service branch, FY93, annual rpt, 3504–11
Biological warfare agent vaccine dev and production of Salk Inst, and Army contract costs by component, late 1970s-91, GAO rpt, 26123–374
Budget of DOD, base construction and family housing appropriations by facility, service branch, and location, FY91-93, annual rpt, 3544–39
Budget of DOD, procurement appropriations by item, service branch, and defense agency, FY91-93, annual rpt, 3544–32
Budget of DOD, programs, policies, and operations, FY91, annual rpt, 3544–2
Budget of DOD, R&D appropriations by item, service branch, and defense agency, FY91-93, annual rpt, 3544–33
Budget of DOD, weapons acquisition costs by system and service branch, FY91-93, annual rpt, 3504–2
Budget of US, Bush Admin proposals, with detail for defense budgets, and historical data from FY34, FY93, 108–46.2
Commercial activities of DOD performed in-house, and work-years, by service branch, installation, and State, FY91, annual rpt, 3544–25
Courts (military) cases and actions, FY91, annual rpt, 3504–3
Discrimination issues in Army, personnel, promotion, and training by race and sex, annual rpt, discontinued, 3704–10
Expenditures and obligations of DOD, by function and service branch, quarterly rpt, 3542–3
Expenditures of Fed Govt in States, by type, program, agency, and State, FY91, annual rpt, 2464–2
Hazardous waste site remedial action at military installations, activities and funding by site and State, FY91, annual rpt, 3544–36
Health care personnel, and accessions by training source, by occupation, specialty, and service branch, FY90, annual rpt, 3544–24
Labor unions recognized in Fed Govt, agreements and membership by agency and facility, as of Jan 1991, biennial listing, 9844–14
Personnel (civilian) of DOD, by service branch and defense agency, with summary military employment data, quarterly rpt, 3542–16
Personnel (civilian and military) of DOD, by service branch, major installation, and State, as of Sept 1991, annual rpt, 3544–7
Physicians, by specialty, age, sex, and location of training and practice, 1990, State rpt series, 4116–6
Procurement, DOD prime contract awards by category, contract and contractor type, and service branch, FY82-1st half FY92, semiannual rpt, 3542–1
Procurement, DOD prime contract awards by contractor, service branch, State, and city, FY91, annual rpt, 3544–22
Procurement, DOD prime contract awards by detailed procurement category, FY88-91, annual rpt, 3544–18
Procurement, DOD prime contract awards by service branch and State, 1st half FY92, semiannual rpt, 3542–5
Procurement, DOD prime contract awards by size and type of contract, service branch, competitive status, category, and labor standard, FY91, annual rpt, 3544–19
Procurement, DOD prime contract awards in labor surplus areas, by service branch, State, and area, 1st half FY92, semiannual rpt, 3542–19
Procurement, subcontract awards by DOD contractors to small and disadvantaged business, by firm and service branch, quarterly rpt, 3542–17
Shipments by DOD of military and personal property, passenger traffic, and costs, by service branch and mode of transport, quarterly rpt, periodicity change, 3702–1; 3704–15
Strategic capability of Army, force strengths, budget, and mgmt, FY79-93, annual rpt, 3704–13
see also Army
see also Army Corps of Engineers
see also National Guard
see also Reserve Officers Training Corps
see also terms beginning with Defense and with Military

Department of Commerce
Activities, funding, and staff of Commerce Dept, by subagency, FY91, annual rpt, 2004–1
Auto parts trade with Japan and other countries, 1985-90 and forecast to 1994, annual rpt, 2004–10
Budget appropriations and staff for Commerce Dept, by subagency, FY91-93, annual rpt, 2004–6
Budget of US, authoritative financial statements with appropriations, outlays, and receipts, by category and agency, FY91, annual rpt, 8104–2.2
Budget of US, Bush Admin proposals, with detail for defense budgets, and historical data from FY34, FY93, 108–46.3
Budget of US, obligations and authority by function, agency, and program, with summaries and analyses, FY93, annual rpt, 104–2
Education funding by Federal agency, program, and recipient type, and instn spending, 1960s-91, annual rpt, 4824–8
Expenditures of Fed Govt in States, by type, program, agency, and State, FY91, annual rpt, 2464–2
Exports, imports, and trade flows, by country and commodity, with background economic indicators, data compilation, monthly CD-ROM, 2002–6
Fraud and abuse in Commerce Dept programs, audits and investigations, 2nd half FY92, semiannual rpt, 2002–5
Israel economic conditions, US investment and export opportunities, and trade practices, 1992 rpt, 2008–32
Labor unions recognized in Fed Govt, agreements and membership by agency and facility, as of Jan 1991, biennial listing, 9844–14
Publications of Commerce Dept, with economic indicator performance from 1961, biweekly listing, 2002–1
R&D and related funding of Fed Govt to higher education and nonprofit instns, by field, instn, agency, and State, FY90, annual rpt, 9627–17
see also Bureau of Census
see also Bureau of Economic Analysis
see also Bureau of Export Administration
see also Economic Development Administration
see also Foreign Trade Zones Board
see also International Trade Administration
see also Minority Business Development Agency
see also National Environmental Satellite, Data, and Information Service
see also National Institute of Standards and Technology
see also National Marine Fisheries Service
see also National Ocean Service
see also National Oceanic and Atmospheric Administration
see also National Technical Information Service
see also National Telecommunications and Information Administration
see also National Weather Service
see also Patent and Trademark Office
see also U.S. Travel and Tourism Administration
see also under By Federal Agency in the "Index by Categories"

Department of Defense
Base support costs by function, and personnel and acreage by installation, by service branch, FY93, annual rpt, 3504–11
Black military and civilian DOD personnel, by sex, grade, and period of service, and lists of award recipients, officers, and service academy grads, 1770s-90, 3548–22
Budget of DOD, itemized account of legislative history, annual rpt, discontinued, 3504–7
Budget of DOD, organization, personnel, weapons, and property, by service branch, State, and country, 1992 annual summary rpt, 3504–13
Budget of DOD, personnel needs, costs, and force readiness by service branch, FY93, annual rpt, 3504–1

Budget of DOD, programs, policies, and operations, FY91, annual rpt, 3544–2
Budget of DOD, weapons acquisition costs by system and service branch, FY91-93, annual rpt, 3504–2
Budget of US, authoritative financial statements with appropriations, outlays, and receipts, by category and agency, FY91, annual rpt, 8104–2.2
Budget of US, Bush Admin proposals, with detail for defense budgets, and historical data from FY34, FY93, 108–46.2
Budget of US, obligations and authority by function, agency, and program, with summaries and analyses, FY93, annual rpt, 104–2
Civilian Health and Medical Program of Uniformed Services benefits and costs, FY85-90, annual chartbook, 3504–23
Commercial activities of DOD performed in-house, and work-years, by service branch, installation, and State, FY91, annual rpt, 3544–25
Courts (military) cases and actions, FY91, annual rpt, 3504–3
Dependents Schools basic skills and college entrance test scores, 1991-92, annual rpt, 3504–16
Drug enforcement activities of DOD, funding by purpose, FY89-91, GAO rpt, 26123–390
Drug enforcement communications network for Federal agencies, funding for equipment and DOD support, FY88-91 and projected to FY87, GAO rpt, 26123–372
Education funding by Federal agency, program, and recipient type, and instn spending, 1960s-91, annual rpt, 4824–8
Employment, earnings, and hours, by SIC 1- to 4-digit industry, monthly 1989-Feb 1992, annual rpt, 6744–4
Exchange service financial statements, 1990, annual rpt, 3504–21
Expenditures of Fed Govt in States and local areas, by type, State, county, and city, FY91, annual rpt, 2464–3
Expenditures of Fed Govt in States, by type, program, agency, and State, FY91, annual rpt, 2464–2
Fraud and abuse in DOD programs, audits and investigations, 2nd half FY92, semiannual rpt, 3542–18
Homosexual military personnel discharges by pay grade, tenure, race, sex, and occupation, and investigations, by service branch, 1980s-90, GAO rpt, 26123–392
Labor unions recognized in Fed Govt, agreements and membership by agency and facility, as of Jan 1991, biennial listing, 9844–14
Natl Guard activities, personnel, and facilities, FY91, annual rpt, 3504–22
Personnel (civilian) of DOD, by service branch and defense agency, with summary military employment data, quarterly rpt, 3542–16
Personnel (civilian and military) of DOD, by service branch, major installation, and State, as of Sept 1991, annual rpt, 3544–7
Personnel strengths, for active duty, civilians, and reserves, by service branch, FY91 and trends, annual rpt, 3544–1
Personnel strengths, for active duty, civilians, and reserves, by service branch, quarterly rpt, 3542–14
Post exchange operations, listing by facility and location worldwide, 1991-92, annual rpt, 3504–10
Procurement, DOD prime contract awards by category, contract and contractor type, and service branch, FY82-1st half FY92, semiannual rpt, 3542–1
Procurement, DOD prime contract awards by contractor, service branch, State, and city, FY91, annual rpt, 3544–22
Procurement, DOD prime contract awards by service branch and State, 1st half FY92, semiannual rpt, 3542–5
Procurement, DOD prime contract awards in labor surplus areas, by service branch, State, and area, 1st half FY92, semiannual rpt, 3542–19
R&D (basic) program of DOD, activities and funding, biennial rpt, discontinued, 3504–12
R&D and related funding of Fed Govt to higher education and nonprofit instns, by field, instn, agency, and State, FY90, annual rpt, 9627–17
Science and engineering grad enrollment, by field, source of funds, and characteristics of student and instn, 1990, annual rpt, 9627–7
Shipments of military and personal property by commercial cariers, and cost savings from bill audits and rate negotiations, FY99-91, GAO rpt, 26123–369
Spacecraft launches and other activities of NASA and USSR, with flight data, 1957-91, annual rpt, 9504–6.1
Survey of Current Business, defense activity indicators, monthly rpt, 2702–1.1
Training and education programs of DOD, funding, staff, students, and facilities, by service branch, FY93, annual rpt, 3504–5
see also Armed services
see also Army Corps of Engineers
see also Court of Military Appeals
see also Defense Advanced Research Projects Agency
see also Defense agencies
see also Defense Communications Agency
see also Defense Contract Audit Agency
see also Defense Intelligence Agency
see also Defense Investigative Service
see also Defense Logistics Agency
see also Defense Mapping Agency
see also Defense Nuclear Agency
see also Defense Security Assistance Agency
see also Department of Air Force
see also Department of Army
see also Department of Navy
see also Marine Corps
see also Office of the Secretary of Defense
see also terms beginning with Defense and with Military
see also under By Federal Agency in the "Index by Categories"

Department of Education
Adult literacy and English as a second language programs, Education Dept and State programs, enrollment, and funding, by State, 1988-91, 4808–41
Bilingual education enrollment, and eligible students not enrolled, by State, 1990-91, annual rpt, 4804–14
Budget of US, authoritative financial statements with appropriations, outlays, and receipts, by category and agency, FY91, annual rpt, 8104–2.2
Budget of US, Bush Admin proposals, with detail for defense budgets, and historical data from FY34, FY93, 108–46.3
Budget of US, obligations and authority by function, agency, and program, with summaries and analyses, FY93, annual rpt, 104–2
Child day care and early childhood education programs availability, demand, use, costs, and provider and enrollee characteristics, 1990 survey, 4808–39
Elementary and secondary school system mgmt by higher education instn, Chelsea, Mass and Boston University demonstration program operations and results, 1988-90, 4808–38
Enrollment, staff, and spending, by instn level and control, and teacher salaries, 1980s-93, annual press release, 4804–19
Expenditures for education by Federal agency, program, and recipient type, and instn spending, 1960s-91, annual rpt, 4824–8
Expenditures of Fed Govt in States, by type, program, agency, and State, FY91, annual rpt, 2464–2
Financial aid programs of Education Dept, 1992 annual listing, 4804–3
Fraud and abuse in Education Dept programs, audits and investigations, 2nd half FY92, semiannual rpt, 4802–1
Fulbright-Hays academic exchanges, grants by purpose, and foreign govt share of costs, by country, FY91, annual rpt, 10324–1
Handicapped children early education project descriptions, 1991/92, annual listing, 4944–10
Homeless adults educational services, program activities, and participation, by State, FY88-89, annual rpt, 4804–39
Indians and Alaska Natives education condition, indicators and comparisons to other groups, 1980s-90, 4808–42
Juvenile facilities compensatory education programs activities, participant and staff characteristics, and outcomes, 1991 rpts, 4808–40
Labor unions recognized in Fed Govt, agreements and membership by agency and facility, as of Jan 1991, biennial listing, 9844–14
Literacy program for preschoolers and parents, Even Start program activities and grants by recipient, FY90, annual listing, 4804–41
Literacy programs in workplaces, demonstration projects funding and participants, FY88-90, 4808–43
Literacy programs in workplaces, project descriptions and Education Dept funding, FY91, annual listing, 4804–40
Pell grants and applicants, by tuition, family and student income, instn type and control, and State, 1990/91, annual rpt, 4804–1
Preschool students transition to kindergarten, programs and factors affecting activities, 1989-90 study, 4808–44

R&D and related funding of Fed Govt to higher education and nonprofit instns, by field, instn, agency, and State, FY90, annual rpt, 9627–17
States elementary and secondary curricula, competency, and attendance requirements, with background data, 1970s-90, 4838–52
Student aid funding and participation, by Federal program, instn type and control, and State, annual rpt, discontinued, 4804–28
Student guaranteed loan activity, by program, guarantee agency, and State, quarterly rpt, 4802–2
Student guaranteed loan Stafford program, Education Dept collection of lender origination fees, 1980s-91, GAO rpt, 26121–467
Student guaranteed loans, defaults, and collections, by type of loan, lender, and guarantee agency, with data by State and top lender, FY91, annual rpt, 4804–38
Student loans of Fed Govt in default, losses, and rates, by instn and State, as of June 1991, annual rpt, 4804–18
Student supplemental grants, loans, and work-study awards, Federal share by instn and State, 1992/93, annual listing, 4804–17
Vocational education enrollment, and academic and other credits earned, by subject and student characteristics, high school classes of 1982 and 1987, 4838–50
Women's educational equity program grants and contracts, by project, type, and State, 1988-92, annual rpt, 4804–2
see also National Assessment of Educational Progress
see also Office of Educational Research and Improvement
see also Office of Special Education and Rehabilitative Services
see also Office of Vocational and Adult Education
see also under By Federal Agency in the "Index by Categories"

Department of Energy
Activities and finances of DOE, summary energy supply and demand data, and bibl, 1990, annual rpt, 3024–2
Budget of US, authoritative financial statements with appropriations, outlays, and receipts, by category and agency, FY91, annual rpt, 8104–2.2
Budget of US, obligations and authority by function, agency, and program, with summaries and analyses, FY93, annual rpt, 104–2
Contracts and grants of DOE, by category, State, and for top contractors, FY91, annual rpt, 3004–21
Data collection forms of DOE and related rpts, 1991, annual listing, 3164–86
Education funding by Federal agency, program, and recipient type, and instn spending, 1960s-91, annual rpt, 4824–8
Employment in energy-related fields, manpower studies and devs, series, 3006–8
Energy use, costs, and conservation, for DOE, by end use, fuel type, and field office, FY91, annual rpt, 3004–27
Expenditures of Fed Govt in States, by type, program, agency, and State, FY91, annual rpt, 2464–2
Finances and mgmt of DOE programs, audits and investigations, series, 3006–5
Fraud and abuse in DOE programs, audit resolution activities, 2nd half FY92, semiannual rpt, 3002–15
Fraud and abuse in DOE programs, audits and investigations, 2nd half FY92, semiannual rpt, 3002–12
Global climate change contributing pollutants, emissions by monitoring site and country, and temperature change by world area and US region, 1860s-1990, annual rpt, 3004–33
Inventions recommended by Natl Inst of Standards and Technology for DOE support, awards, and evaluation status, 1991, annual listing, 2214–5
Jordan oil shale-fired electric power plants, feasibility assessment with background data, 1990 rpt, 3008–127
Labor unions recognized in Fed Govt, agreements and membership by agency and facility, as of Jan 1991, biennial listing, 9844–14
Natl Energy Strategy plans for conservation and pollution reduction, funding for R&D and basic science activities, FY91-93, 3008–128
Natl Energy Strategy plans for conservation, R&D, security, and pollution reduction, technical rpt series, 3006–13
Nuclear engineering enrollment and degrees granted by instn and State, and grad placement, by student characteristics, 1991, annual rpt, 3004–5
Oil company overcharge settlements funds received, and conservation and energy aid spending, by outlying area, 1990, GAO rpt, 26113–564
Oil enhanced recovery research contracts of DOE, project summaries, funding, and bibl, quarterly rpt, 3002–14
Property (real) of DOE owned and leased, by type, subagency, contractor, and site, FY91, annual rpt, 3004–28
R&D and related funding of Fed Govt to higher education and nonprofit instns, by field, instn, agency, and State, FY90, annual rpt, 9627–17
R&D field offices and facilities of DOE, activities, staff, and finances, FY91, biennial rpt, 3004–4
R&D projects and funding of DOE at natl labs, universities, and other instns, periodic summary rpt series, 3004–18
Radiation protection and health physics enrollment and degrees granted by instn and State, and grad placement, by student characteristics, 1991, annual rpt, 3004–7
Radioactive materials shipments on US hwys, by material type, carrier, and shipper, 1985-90, 3008–129
Small business procurement contract awards of DOE, by business type and subagency, FY90, annual rpt, 3004–35
Strategic Petroleum Reserve capacity, inventory, fill rate, and finances, quarterly rpt, 3002–13
Supply, demand, and price projections, by fuel type and end-use sector, biennial rpt, discontinued, 3004–13
Toxicology Natl Program research and testing activities, FY90 and planned FY91, annual rpt, 4044–16
Transportation energy use by fuel type, and miles traveled, by mode, projected 1990-2010 and trends from 1960s, 3008–124
see also Alaska Power Administration
see also Bonneville Power Administration
see also Department of Energy: Civilian Radioactive Waste Management
see also Department of Energy: Conservation and Renewable Energy
see also Department of Energy: Defense Programs
see also Department of Energy: Environment, Safety, and Health
see also Department of Energy: Fossil Energy
see also Department of Energy: International Affairs and Energy Emergencies
see also Department of Energy National Laboratories
see also Department of Energy: Nuclear Energy
see also Energy Information Administration
see also Federal Energy Regulatory Commission
see also Office of the Secretary of Energy
see also Southeastern Power Administration
see also Southwestern Power Administration
see also Western Area Power Administration
see also under By Federal Agency in the "Index by Categories"

Department of Energy: Civilian Radioactive Waste Management
Nuclear Waste Fund finances, and CRWM Program costs, quarterly rpt, 3362–1
Nuclear Waste Fund finances, and CRWM R&D costs, FY90-91, annual rpt, 3364–1
Nuclear Waste Fund utility payments and liabilities by State, and uranium enrichment customers costs of regulation and waste mgmt, 1991 hearings, 21368–137
Nuclear waste repository research, transport, and disposal costs under alternative systems, 1983-89 and projected to 2094, 3368–5
Radioactive waste repository sites, storage containers radionuclide releases at proposed Nevada site, 1990 rpt, 3368–4
Spent fuel and radioactive waste generation, inventory, and disposal, 1960s-90 and projected to 2020, annual rpt, 3364–2
Spent fuel deliveries to DOE for disposal, by utility and reactor, projected 1998-2007, annual rpt, 3364–5

Department of Energy: Conservation and Renewable Energy
Auto (electric-powered) R&D activity and DOE funding shares, FY91, annual rpt, 3304–2
Auto alternative fuels use in Federal fleet, energy economy performance at 4 sites, FY91, annual rpt, 3304–28
Auto engine and power train R&D projects, DOE contracts and funding by recipient, FY91, annual rpt, 3304–17
Auto fuel economy test results for US and foreign makes, 1993 model year, annual rpt, 3304–11
China biomass-fired electric power plant feasibility assessment, 1991 rpt, 3308–103

Conservation aid of Fed Govt to public and nonprofit private instns, by building type and State, 1991, annual rpt, 3304–15
Electric utilities conservation programs alternative planning strategies cost effectiveness, model results, 1991 rpt, 3308–100
Electric utilities conservation programs, collaboration between utilities and interest groups, and effects on costs, 1992 rpt, 3308–104
Electric utilities conservation programs data reporting guidelines, with background data, 1991 rpt, 3308–101
Electric utilities conservation programs energy savings and spending, with data for top 25 firms, 1990, 3308–106
Electric utilities conservation programs, energy savings measurement methodology, 1991, compilation of papers, 3308–102
Electric utilities conservation programs, impacts on prices and revenue requirements, alternative projections 1990-2010, 3308–105
Geothermal resources, power plant capacity and operating status, leases, and wells, by location, 1960s-95, 3308–87
Solar energy and passive solar design for buildings, costs, savings, and characteristics, discontinued series, 3306–5
Solar photovoltaic R&D sponsored by DOE, projects, funding, and rpts, FY91, annual listing, 3304–20
State govt energy conservation programs, Federal aid and savings, by State, 1990, annual rpt, 3304–1
Transportation energy use by mode, fuel supply, and demographic and economic factors of vehicle use, 1970s-90, annual rpt, 3304–5

Department of Energy: Defense Programs
Nuclear material inventory discrepancies at DOE and contractor facilities, 1990/91, annual rpt, 3344–2

Department of Energy: Environment, Safety, and Health
Nuclear weapons facilities of DOE, security deficiencies by type and facility, 1989-90, GAO rpt, 26113–557
Radiation and other pollutant releases from DOE contractor research lab and nuclear weapons facilities, monitoring results, annual site rpt series, 3324–2

Department of Energy: Fossil Energy
Coal-fired power plants air pollutant reduction technology funding, and impacts on energy costs and emissions, 1950s-87 and projected to 2010, annual rpt, 3334–5; 3338–4
Coal-fired power plants air pollutant reduction technology funding, and project descriptions, 1991, annual rpt, 3334–4
Electric power and industrial plants prohibited from oil and gas primary use, exemptions, and gas use by State, 1980-91, annual rpt, 3334–1
Environmental regulation impacts on oil resources recovery, under alternative oil price, technology, and regulatory assumptions, projected 1990-2015, 3338–2
Fed Govt power plants conversion to alternative fuels, 1992, annual rpt, 3334–2
Global climate change and contributing pollutants emissions, literature review, 1980s and projected to 2075, 3338–3
Naval Petroleum and Oil Shale Reserves production and revenue by fuel type, sales by purchaser, and wells, by reserve, FY91, annual rpt, 3334–3
Strategic Petroleum Reserve crude oil specifications and physical and chemical analyses results, 1991, 3338–5

Department of Energy: International Affairs and Energy Emergencies
Electric power seasonal peak demand and generating capacity, by region, annual rpt, suspended, 3404–6
Electric power supply, demand, and trade of Mexico and US, with data by fuel source, utility, and region, 1970s-89 and projected to 2000, 3408–2
Pacific basin countries energy supply and demand, and implications for US trade, country rpt series, 3406–6

Department of Energy National Laboratories
Activities, staff, and finances of DOE R&D field offices and facilities, FY91, biennial rpt, 3004–4
Argonne Natl Lab procurement from govt supply sources, FY91, 3006–5.29
Contracts and grants of DOE, by category, State, and for top contractors, FY91, annual rpt, 3004–21
Expenditures for R&D and related activities of higher education and nonprofit instns by Fed Govt, by field, instn, agency, and State, FY90, annual rpt, 9627–17.1
Expenditures for R&D by higher education instns and federally funded centers, by field, instn, and State, FY90, annual rpt, 9627–13
Nuclear material inventory discrepancies at DOE and contractor facilities, 1990/91, annual rpt, 3344–2
Nuclear reactors for domestic use and export by function and operating status, with owner, operating characteristics, and location, 1991 annual listing, 3354–15
Nuclear weapons facilities of DOE, contractor fees, environmental and safety enforcement activity, and salaries, by contractor and facility, 1987-88, hearing, 21408–127
Oak Ridge Natl Lab contractors excise tax refunds due from off-highway use of motor vehicle fuels, 1988-90, 3006–5.26
Oil enhanced recovery research contracts of DOE, project summaries, funding, and bibl, quarterly rpt, 3002–14
Property (real) of DOE owned and leased, by type, subagency, contractor, and site, FY91, annual rpt, 3004–28
R&D projects and funding of DOE at natl labs, universities, and other instns, periodic summary rpt series, 3004–18
Radiation and other pollutant releases from DOE contractor research lab and nuclear weapons facilities, monitoring results, annual site rpt series, 3324–2
Radioactive low-level waste from DOE military activities, disposal methods and costs, 1991, 3006–5.30
Radioactive materials shipments on US hwys, by material type, carrier, and shipper, 1985-90, 3008–129
Radioactive waste and spent fuel generation, inventory, and disposal, 1960s-90 and projected to 2020, annual rpt, 3364–2
Security at DOE nuclear weapons facilities, deficiencies by type and facility, 1989-90, GAO rpt, 26113–557
Solar photovoltaic R&D sponsored by DOE, projects, funding, and rpts, FY91, annual listing, 3304–20
Superconducting super collider construction costs, and funding by source, FY88-91 and projected to FY99, 3006–5.28

Department of Energy: Nuclear Energy
Hanford, Wash, nuclear plant, nearby population radiation exposure, with methodology, 1944-91, series, 3356–5
Power plants decommissioning and nuclear waste site remedial actions, bibl, 1991 annual listing, 3354–12
Radioactive low-level waste disposal activities of States and interstate compacts, annual rpt, issuing agency transfer, 3354–14
Radioactive low-level waste disposal activities of States and interstate compacts, with data by disposal facility and reactor, 1990, annual rpt, 3004–36
Reactors for domestic use and export by function and operating status, with owner, operating characteristics, and location, 1991, annual listing, 3354–15
Safety standards and research, design, licensing, construction, operation, and finances, for nuclear power plants with data by reactor, quarterly journal, 3352–4
Spent fuel from nuclear power plants and additional storage capacity needed, by reactor, projected 1991-2040, annual rpt, 3354–2
Uranium enrichment facilities of DOE, financial statements, FY90-91, annual rpt, 3354–7
Uranium imports impacts on US industry, with data on DOE enrichment program and stocks, 1980s-92, GAO rpt, 26113–584
Uranium tailings at inactive mills, remedial action activities by site, and funding, FY91, annual rpt, 3354–9
Uranium tailings at inactive mills, remedial action proposals, costs, site characteristics, and environmental, socioeconomic, and health impacts, series, 3356–4

Department of Health and Human Services
Alcohol use, knowledge, attitudes, and info sources of youth, series, 4006–10
Assistance (financial) of HHS, by program, recipient, State, and city, FY91, annual regional listings, 4004–3
Budget of US, authoritative financial statements with appropriations, outlays, and receipts, by category and agency, FY91, annual rpt, 8104–2.2
Budget of US, Bush Admin proposals, with detail for defense budgets, and historical data from FY34, FY93, 108–46.3
Budget of US, obligations and authority by function, agency, and program, with summaries and analyses, FY93, annual rpt, 104–2
Drug (prescription) advertising in medical journals, accuracy, info completeness, and violations of FDA regulations, 1990, 4008–119
Drug, alcohol, and cigarette use and attitudes of youth, by substance type, 1975-91 surveys, press release, 4008–116

Education funding by Federal agency, program, and recipient type, and instn spending, 1960s-91, annual rpt, 4824–8
Expenditures of Fed Govt in States and local areas, by type, State, county, and city, FY91, annual rpt, 2464–3.2
Expenditures of Fed Govt in States, by type, program, agency, and State, FY91, annual rpt, 2464–2
Fraud and abuse in HHS programs, audits and investigations, 1st half FY92, semiannual rpt, 4002–6
Freedom of Info Act requests, disposition, costs, and fees, for HHS, 1991, annual rpt, 4004–21
Health care professionals licensing and disciplinary actions of State medical boards, 1950s-88, series, 4006–8
Hospital closures in 1990, operating characteristics, current use, and location, annual rpt, 4004–35
Labor unions recognized in Fed Govt, agreements and membership by agency and facility, as of Jan 1991, biennial listing, 9844–14
Medicaid eligibility expansion for prenatal care, coverage, use, and costs, by State, 1990-91, 4008–120
Medicare beneficiaries multiple hospital admissions, by reason and characteristics of instn and patient, 1985, 4008–117
Medicare financial and admin issues, Inspector General rpts, series, 4006–11
Medicare payment of physicians, reforms impacts on services, and monitoring methods, 1992 annual rpt, 4004–34
Medicare payment of physicians under fee schedule, adjustment factor recommendations, 1993, annual rpt, 4004–33
Medicare payment of physicians, volume performance standard recommendations, FY93, annual rpt, 4004–32
Medicare reimbursement of hospitals under prospective payment system, diagnosis related group code assignment and effects on care and instn finances, series, 4006–7
Oil company overcharge settlements funds received, and conservation and energy aid spending, by outlying area, 1990, GAO rpt, 26113–564
Poor families self-sufficiency aid and Head Start programs, HUD and HHS joint funding by recipient, 1991, press release, 5006–3.83
R&D and related funding of Fed Govt to higher education and nonprofit instns, by field, instn, agency, and State, FY90, annual rpt, 9627–17
Science and engineering grad enrollment, by field, source of funds, and characteristics of student and instn, 1990, annual rpt, 9627–7
see also Administration for Children and Families
see also Administration on Aging
see also Agency for Health Care Policy and Research
see also Alcohol, Drug Abuse and Mental Health Administration
see also Bureau of Health Professions
see also Centers for Disease Control
see also Division of Research Grants, NIH
see also Family Support Administration
see also Food and Drug Administration
see also Health Care Financing Administration
see also Health Resources and Services Administration
see also Indian Health Service
see also National Cancer Institute
see also National Center for Health Statistics
see also National Center on Child Abuse and Neglect
see also National Heart, Lung, and Blood Institute
see also National Institute for Occupational Safety and Health
see also National Institute of Allergy and Infectious Diseases
see also National Institute of Child Health and Human Development
see also National Institute of Environmental Health Sciences
see also National Institute of General Medical Sciences
see also National Institute of Mental Health
see also National Institute on Alcohol Abuse and Alcoholism
see also National Institute on Drug Abuse
see also National Institutes of Health
see also National Library of Medicine
see also Office of Policy, SSA
see also Office on Smoking and Health
see also Public Health Service
see also Social Security Administration
see also under By Federal Agency in the "Index by Categories"

Department of Housing and Urban Development
Activities of HUD, and housing programs operations and funding, 1990, annual rpt, 5004–10
Apartment and condominium completions by rent class and sales price, and market absorption rates, quarterly rpt, 2482–2
Assistance for housing and community dev programs of HUD, press release series, 5006–3
Budget of US, authoritative financial statements with appropriations, outlays, and receipts, by category and agency, FY91, annual rpt, 8104–2.2
Budget of US, Bush Admin proposals, with detail for defense budgets, and historical data from FY34, FY93, 108–46.3
Budget of US, obligations and authority by function, agency, and program, with summaries and analyses, FY93, annual rpt, 104–2
Education funding by Federal agency, program, and recipient type, and instn spending, 1960s-91, annual rpt, 4824–8
Expenditures of Fed Govt in States, by type, program, agency, and State, FY91, annual rpt, 2464–2
Fraud and abuse in HUD programs, audits and investigations, FY92, semiannual rpt, 5002–8; 5002–11
Fraud and abuse in HUD programs, financial and program mgmt improvement activities, FY91, annual rpt, 5004–9
Labor unions recognized in Fed Govt, agreements and membership by agency and facility, as of Jan 1991, biennial listing, 9844–14
Low income housing eligibility, tenants reported income agreement with tax records, 1989-90, GAO rpt, 26121–468
R&D and related funding of Fed Govt to higher education and nonprofit instns, by field, instn, agency, and State, FY90, annual rpt, 9627–17
see also Community Planning and Development, HUD
see also Government National Mortgage Association
see also Housing (FHA), HUD
see also Policy Development and Research, HUD
see also under By Federal Agency in the "Index by Categories"

Department of Interior
Activities and finances of DOI, historic administrative records and other materials, Natl Archives final inventory, 1987 rpt, 9516–2.1
Activities of Interior Dept, press release series, 5306–4
Budget of US, authoritative financial statements with appropriations, outlays, and receipts, by category and agency, FY91, annual rpt, 8104–2.2
Budget of US, Bush Admin proposals, with detail for defense budgets, and historical data from FY34, FY93, 108–46.3
Budget of US, obligations and authority by function, agency, and program, with summaries and analyses, FY93, annual rpt, 104–2
Education funding by Federal agency, program, and recipient type, and instn spending, 1960s-91, annual rpt, 4824–8
Expenditures of Fed Govt in States, by type, program, agency, and State, FY91, annual rpt, 2464–2
Fraud and abuse in DOI programs, audits and investigations, 2nd half FY92, semiannual rpt, 5302–2
Labor unions recognized in Fed Govt, agreements and membership by agency and facility, as of Jan 1991, biennial listing, 9844–14
Minerals production, trade, use, and foreign investment in US industry, 1985-90 and projected to 2000, annual rpt, 5304–5
R&D and related funding of Fed Govt to higher education and nonprofit instns, by field, instn, agency, and State, FY90, annual rpt, 9627–17
see also Bureau of Indian Affairs
see also Bureau of Land Management
see also Bureau of Mines
see also Bureau of Reclamation
see also Fish and Wildlife Service
see also Geological Survey
see also Minerals Management Service
see also National Park Service
see also Office of Surface Mining Reclamation and Enforcement
see also Office of Territorial and International Affairs
see also under By Federal Agency in the "Index by Categories"

Department of Justice
Activities of DOJ, FY91, annual rpt, 6004–1
Antitrust criminal enforcement activities of Justice Dept by industry div and offense, sentencing, and labor costs, FY90, GAO rpt, 26119–375
Asset Forfeiture Program of Justice Dept, seizures, finances, and disbursements, FY85-91, annual rpt, 6004–21

Banks and thrifts fraud cases, Justice Dept investigation and prosecution activities, 1989-92, GAO rpt, 26119–426
Budget of US, authoritative financial statements with appropriations, outlays, and receipts, by category and agency, FY91, annual rpt, 8104–2.2
Budget of US, obligations and authority by function, agency, and program, with summaries and analyses, FY93, annual rpt, 104–2
Corrupt govt officials prosecuted and convicted, by judicial district and level of govt, 1970-90, annual rpt, 6004–13
Debt delinquent on Federal accounts, cases and collections of DOJ and private law firms, pilot project results, FY91, annual rpt, 6004–20
Education funding by Federal agency, program, and recipient type, and instn spending, 1960s-91, annual rpt, 4824–8
Employee misconduct investigations of Justice Dept, by type of allegation and penalty, 1988-90, GAO rpt, 26119–380
Environmental laws enforcement activities of EPA and State govts, FY91, annual rpt, 9184–21
Environmental laws enforcement activities of Justice Dept, FY83-91, press release, 6008–37
Environmental laws enforcement activities of Justice Dept, FY83-92, annual press release, 6004–22
Executions by whether habeas corpus used to appeal conviction, and time from crime to execution, with data by race and State, 1977-91, 6008–34
Expenditures of Fed Govt in States, by type, program, agency, and State, FY91, annual rpt, 2464–2
Financial instns fraud and abuse, Justice Dept enforcement activity, staff, and case dispositions by instn type, 1988-92, 6008–35
Labor unions recognized in Fed Govt, agreements and membership by agency and facility, as of Jan 1991, biennial listing, 9844–14
Savings instns fraud and abuse, Federal indictments and case dispositions, periodic press release, 6002–3; 6008–33
US attorneys case processing and collections, by case type and Federal district, FY91, annual rpt, 6004–2
see also Bureau of Justice Assistance
see also Bureau of Justice Statistics
see also Bureau of Prisons
see also Community Relations Service
see also Drug Enforcement Administration
see also Federal Bureau of Investigation
see also Immigration and Naturalization Service
see also National Institute of Justice
see also Office for Victims of Crime
see also Office of Justice Programs
see also Office of Juvenile Justice and Delinquency Prevention
see also U.S. Marshals Service
see also U.S. Parole Commission
see also under By Federal Agency in the "Index by Categories"

Department of Labor

Activities and funding of DOL, by program and State, FY91, annual rpt, 6304–1
Budget of US, authoritative financial statements with appropriations, outlays, and receipts, by category and agency, FY91, annual rpt, 8104–2.2
Budget of US, obligations and authority by function, agency, and program, with summaries and analyses, FY93, annual rpt, 104–2
Displaced worker training programs spending, participation, and placements by State, 1990, GAO rpt, 26121–481
Education funding by Federal agency, program, and recipient type, and instn spending, 1960s-91, annual rpt, 4824–8
Expenditures of Fed Govt in States, by type, program, agency, and State, FY91, annual rpt, 2464–2
Fraud and abuse in DOL programs, audits and investigations, 2nd half FY92, semiannual rpt, 6302–2
Job Training Partnership Act State and local admin, funding, effectiveness, and participants, GAO rpt series, 26106–8
Labor unions recognized in Fed Govt, agreements and membership by agency and facility, as of Jan 1991, biennial listing, 9844–14
R&D and related funding of Fed Govt to higher education and nonprofit instns, by field, instn, agency, and State, FY90, annual rpt, 9627–17
see also Bureau of International Labor Affairs
see also Bureau of Labor Statistics
see also Employment and Training Administration
see also Employment Standards Administration
see also Mine Safety and Health Administration
see also Occupational Safety and Health Administration
see also Pension and Welfare Benefits Administration
see also Women's Bureau
see also under By Federal Agency in the "Index by Categories"

Department of Navy

Base construction, renovation, and closure, DOD budget requests by project, service branch, State, and country, FY93, annual rpt, 3544–15
Base support costs by function, and personnel and acreage by installation, by service branch, FY93, annual rpt, 3504–11
Budget of DOD, base construction and family housing appropriations by facility, service branch, and location, FY91-93, annual rpt, 3544–39
Budget of DOD, procurement appropriations by item, service branch, and defense agency, FY91-93, annual rpt, 3544–32
Budget of DOD, programs, policies, and operations, FY91, annual rpt, 3544–2
Budget of DOD, R&D appropriations by item, service branch, and defense agency, FY91-93, annual rpt, 3544–33
Budget of DOD, weapons acquisition costs by system and service branch, FY91-93, annual rpt, 3504–2
Budget of US, Bush Admin proposals, with detail for defense budgets, and historical data from FY34, FY93, 108–46.2
Commercial activities of DOD performed in-house, and work-years, by service branch, installation, and State, FY91, annual rpt, 3544–25
Courts (military) cases and actions, FY91, annual rpt, 3504–3
Expenditures and obligations of DOD, by function and service branch, quarterly rpt, 3542–3
Hazardous waste site remedial action at military installations, activities and funding by site and State, FY91, annual rpt, 3544–36
Health care personnel, and accessions by training source, by occupation, specialty, and service branch, FY90, annual rpt, 3544–24
Labor unions recognized in Fed Govt, agreements and membership by agency and facility, as of Jan 1991, biennial listing, 9844–14
Military Sealift Command shipping operations, finances, and personnel, FY91, annual rpt, 3804–14
Personnel (civilian) of DOD, by service branch and defense agency, with summary military employment data, quarterly rpt, 3542–16
Personnel (civilian and military) of DOD, by service branch, major installation, and State, as of Sept 1991, annual rpt, 3544–7
Personnel strengths, accessions, and attrition, detailed statistics for Navy and Naval Reserve, quarterly rpt, 3802–4
Physicians, by specialty, age, sex, and location of training and practice, 1990, State rpt series, 4116–6
Procurement, contractor debts owed to Fed Govt and deferred, status by service branch and firm, 1980-91, GAO rpt, 26123–400
Procurement, DOD prime contract awards by category, contract and contractor type, and service branch, FY82-1st half FY92, semiannual rpt, 3542–1
Procurement, DOD prime contract awards by contractor, service branch, State, and city, FY91, annual rpt, 3544–22
Procurement, DOD prime contract awards by detailed procurement category, FY88-91, annual rpt, 3544–18
Procurement, DOD prime contract awards by service branch and State, 1st half FY92, semiannual rpt, 3542–5
Procurement, DOD prime contract awards by size and type of contract, service branch, competitive status, category, and labor standard, FY91, annual rpt, 3544–19
Procurement, DOD prime contract awards in labor surplus areas, by service branch, State, and area, 1st half FY92, semiannual rpt, 3542–19
Procurement, subcontract awards by DOD contractors to small and disadvantaged business, by firm and service branch, quarterly rpt, 3542–17
Radiation exposure of Navy personnel on nuclear-powered vessels and at support facilities, and injury claims, 1950s-91, annual rpt, 3804–10
Radioactive waste from Navy nuclear-powered vessels and support facilities, releases in harbors, and public exposure, 1970s-91, annual rpt, 3804–11

Shipments by DOD of military and personal property, passenger traffic, and costs, by service branch and mode of transport, FY91, annual rpt, 3704–15
see also Marine Corps
see also Marine Reserve
see also Naval Oceanography Command
see also Navy
see also U.S. Naval Observatory
see also terms beginning with Defense and with Military

Department of State

Africa (sub-Saharan) economic, social, and political conditions, with US aid by program and country, 1991 rpt, 7008–58
Budget of US, authoritative financial statements with appropriations, outlays, and receipts, by category and agency, FY91, annual rpt, 8104–2.2
Budget of US, obligations and authority by function, agency, and program, with summaries and analyses, FY93, annual rpt, 104–2
Drug (illegal) production, eradication, and seizures, by substance, with US aid, by country, 1988-92, annual rpt, 7004–17
Economic conditions, policy, and trade practices, by country, 1989-91, annual rpt, 21384–5
Education funding by Federal agency, program, and recipient type, and instn spending, 1960s-91, annual rpt, 4824–8
Fish catch quotas for US 200 mile zone, allocations by species and country, periodic coastal area rpt series, discontinued, 7006–5
Foreign countries *Background Notes*, summary social, political, and economic data, series, 7006–2
Fraud and abuse in State Dept programs, audits and investigations, 2nd half FY92, semiannual rpt, 7002–6
Human rights conditions in 170 countries, and US economic and military aid, 1991, annual rpt, 21384–3
Labor unions recognized in Fed Govt, agreements and membership by agency and facility, as of Jan 1991, biennial listing, 9844–14
Living costs abroad, State Dept indexes, housing allowances, and hardship differentials by country and major city, quarterly rpt, 7002–7
Loan repayment status and terms by program and country, AID and predecessor agencies, quarterly rpt, 9912–3
Maritime claims and boundary agreements of coastal countries, series, 7006–8
Pacific territories admin, and Palau social, economic, and govtl data, FY91, annual rpt, 7004–6
Research on foreign policy devs and world areas, discontinued series, 7006–7
Soviet Union former Republics and Baltic States, US embassy positions planned by function, and filled, 1992, GAO rpt, 26123–403
Terrorism (intl) incidents, casualties, and attacks on US targets, by attack type and world area, 1991, annual rpt, 7004–13
Treaties and other bilateral and multilateral agreements of US in force, by country, as of Jan 1992, annual listing, 7004–1
UN participation of US, and member and nonmember shares of UN budget by country, FY89-91, annual rpt, 7004–5
UN voting record and share of votes in agreement with US, by issue, country, and world area, 1991, annual rpt, 7004–18
see also Bureau for Refugee Programs, State Department
see also Bureau of Consular Affairs, State Department
see also Bureau of Diplomatic Security, State Department
see also Bureau of Intelligence and Research, State Department
see also under By Federal Agency in the "Index by Categories"

Department of Transportation

Activities of DOT by subagency, budget, and summary accident data, FY89, annual rpt, 7304–1
Air traffic, capacity, and performance, by carrier and type of operation, monthly rpt, 7302–6
Air traffic, capacity, and performance for medium regionals, by carrier, quarterly rpt, 7302–8
Air travel to and from US on US and foreign flag carriers, by country, world area, and US port, monthly rpt, 7302–2
Airline consumer complaints by reason, passengers denied boarding, and late flights, by reporting carrier and airport, monthly rpt, 7302–11
Airline finances, by carrier, carrier group, and for total certificated system, quarterly rpt, 7302–7
Budget of US, authoritative financial statements with appropriations, outlays, and receipts, by category and agency, FY91, annual rpt, 8104–2.2
Budget of US, Bush Admin proposals, with detail for defense budgets, and historical data from FY34, FY93, 108–46.3
Budget of US, obligations and authority by function, agency, and program, with summaries and analyses, FY93, annual rpt, 104–2
Carpool high occupancy vehicle lanes design, enforcement, and use in selected cities, 1991 conf, 7308–204
Education funding by Federal agency, program, and recipient type, and instn spending, 1960s-91, annual rpt, 4824–8
Employment of DOT, by subagency, occupation, and selected personnel characteristics, FY91, annual rpt, 7304–18
Expenditures of Fed Govt in States and local areas, by type, State, county, and city, FY91, annual rpt, 2464–3.2
Expenditures of Fed Govt in States, by type, program, agency, and State, FY91, annual rpt, 2464–2
Finances and staff of DOT, by subagency, FY91-93, annual rpt, 7304–10
Fraud and abuse in DOT programs, audit resolution activities, 1st half FY92, semiannual rpt, 7302–12
Fraud and abuse in DOT programs, audits and investigations, 1st half FY92, semiannual rpt, 7302–4
Grants of DOT for planning and safety, by program, State, and for 40 SMSAs, FY89, annual rpt, 7304–7
Hazardous material transport accidents, casualties, and damage, by mode of transport, with DOT control activities, 1990, annual rpt, 7304–4
Labor unions recognized in Fed Govt, agreements and membership by agency and facility, as of Jan 1991, biennial listing, 9844–14
Philadelphia metro area transit service operations, costs and benefits, and local economic and air pollution impacts, 1970s-90 and projected to 2020, 7308–205
R&D and related funding of Fed Govt to higher education and nonprofit instns, by field, instn, agency, and State, FY90, annual rpt, 9627–17
Safety monitoring activities of DOT, press release series, 7306–10
see also Coast Guard
see also Coast Guard Reserve
see also Federal Aviation Administration
see also Federal Highway Administration
see also Federal Railroad Administration
see also Federal Transit Administration
see also Maritime Administration
see also National Highway Traffic Safety Administration
see also St. Lawrence Seaway Development Corp.
see also Urban Mass Transportation Administration
see also under By Federal Agency in the "Index by Categories"

Department of Treasury

Activities and finances of Treasury accounting offices, historic administrative records and other materials, Natl Archives final inventory, 1987 rpt, 9516–2.2
Bill offerings, auction results by Fed Reserve District, and terms, periodic press release series, 8002–7
Budget of US, authoritative financial statements with appropriations, outlays, and receipts, by category and agency, FY91, annual rpt, 8104–2.2
Budget of US, obligations and authority by function, agency, and program, with summaries and analyses, FY93, annual rpt, 104–2
Education funding by Federal agency, program, and recipient type, and instn spending, 1960s-91, annual rpt, 4824–8
Expenditures of Fed Govt in States, by type, program, agency, and State, FY91, annual rpt, 2464–2
Fed Govt contingent liabilities and claims paid on insured and guaranteed contracts with foreign obligors, by country and program, periodic rpt, 8002–12
Fed Govt financial operations, detailed data, *Treasury Bulletin*, quarterly rpt, 8002–4
Financial and economic analysis, technical paper series, 8006–6
Financial instns loan loss computations for tax returns under alternative methods, 1991 rpt, 8008–157
Foreign and US economic indicators, trade balances, and exchange rates, for selected OECD and Asian countries, 1992 semiannual rpt, 8002–14
Foreign govts and private obligors debt to US, by country and program, periodic rpt, 8002–6

Govt securities market performance, regulation, and reform issues, with auction results, 1990-91, 8008–154
Income (household) transition between higher and lower income levels, 1979-88, 8008–156
Labor unions recognized in Fed Govt, agreements and membership by agency and facility, as of Jan 1991, biennial listing, 9844–14
Loans of Treasury Dept and Federal Financing Bank to Govt corporations and agencies, outstanding amounts, 1987-91, GAO rpt, 26111–79
Money laundering investigations by Treasury Dept, civil penalty cases workload, processing, and disposition, 1985-91, GAO rpt, 26119–390
Multinatl firms US affiliates income tax compliance issues, with income and tax data by industry group, 1987-89, press release, 8008–155
Tax and loan account deposits, Fed Reserve Banks mgmt of securities held as collateral, 1991, GAO rpt, 26111–80
see also Bureau of Alcohol, Tobacco and Firearms
see also Bureau of Engraving and Printing
see also Bureau of the Public Debt
see also Federal Open Market Committee
see also Financial Management Service
see also Internal Revenue Service
see also Office of the Comptroller of Currency
see also Office of Thrift Supervision
see also U.S. Customs Service
see also U.S. Mint
see also U.S. Savings Bonds Division
see also U.S. Secret Service
see also under By Federal Agency in the "Index by Categories"

Department of Veterans Affairs
Activities and programs of VA, and veterans characteristics, FY91, annual rpt, 8604–3
Benefits overpayment and home loan debts, VA repayment waiver cases and dispositions, FY88-91, hearing, 21768–67
Budget of US, authoritative financial statements with appropriations, outlays, and receipts, by category and agency, FY91, annual rpt, 8104–2.2
Budget of US, obligations and authority by function, agency, and program, with summaries and analyses, FY93, annual rpt, 104–2
Compensation and pension cases of VA, by type of entitlement and period of service, monthly rpt, 8602–5
Disability and death compensation cases of VA, by entitlement type, period of service, and sex, as of Mar 1992, annual rpt, 8604–13
Disability and death compensation cases of VA, by entitlement type, period of service, sex, age, and State, FY90, annual rpt, 8604–7
Disability and death compensation cases of VA, semiannual rpt, periodicity change, 8602–8
Education aid under GI Bill and other programs, and participation by period of service and State, annual rpt, discontinued, 8604–9
Education funding by Federal agency, program, and recipient type, and instn spending, 1960s-91, annual rpt, 4824–8
Expenditures and beneficiaries of VA compensation, health, and rehabilitation programs, FY67-91, annual rpt, 8604–5
Expenditures for VA programs, by State, county, and congressional district, FY91, annual rpt, 8604–6
Expenditures of Fed Govt in States, by type, program, agency, and State, FY91, annual rpt, 2464–2
Fraud and abuse in VA programs, audits and investigations, 2nd half FY92, semiannual rpt, 8602–1
Health care facilities energy use and conservation, by VA facility, quarterly rpt, 8602–9
Health care for veterans, patients, visits, costs, and operating beds, by VA and contract facility, and region, quarterly rpt, 8602–4
Health care professionals of VA, by selected employment characteristics and VA district, quarterly rpt, 8602–6
Health care services of VA, needs, availability, structure, and funding, findings and recommendations, 1991 rpt, 8608–8
Health care services of VA, needs, availability, structure, and funding, 1991 compilation of papers, 8608–9
Health care staff of VA, and turnover, by occupation and location, 1991, annual rpt, 8604–8
Health care staff of VA, work-years, pay rates, and benefits use and costs, FY90, annual rpt, 9844–31
Insurance (life) for veterans and servicepersons, actuarial analyses of VA programs, 1991, annual rpt, 8604–1
Insurance (life) for veterans and servicepersons, finances and coverage by program and State, 1991, annual rpt, 8604–4
Labor unions recognized in Fed Govt, agreements and membership by agency and facility, as of Jan 1991, biennial listing, 9844–14
Physicians, by specialty, age, sex, and location of training and practice, 1990, State rpt series, 4116–6
War participants, deaths, veterans living, and compensation and pension recipients, for each US war, 1775-1991, annual rpt, 8604–2
see also Veterans Administration
see also Veterans Benefits Administration
see also Veterans Health Administration
see also Veterans Health Services and Research Administration
see also under By Federal Agency in the "Index by Categories"

Department stores
Advertised sale prices of dept stores and references to competitors prices, and actual consumer savings, 1990-91 local area study, 9408–57
Business statistics, detailed data for major industries and economic indicators, 1960-91, *Survey of Current Business* biennial supplement, 2704–1
Collective bargaining agreements expiring during year, and workers covered, by firm, union, industry group, and State, 1992, annual rpt, 6784–9
Construction authorized by building permits, by type of construction, region, State, and MSA, quarterly rpt, 2042–1.3
County Business Patterns, 1989: employment, establishments, and payroll, by SIC 2- to 4-digit industry and county, annual State rpt series, 2326–8
County Business Patterns, 1990: employment, establishments, and payroll, by SIC 2- to 4-digit industry and county, annual State rpt series, 2326–6
Employment, earnings, and hours, by selected SIC 1- to 4-digit industry, State, and for 275 MSAs, 1987-92, 6748–81
Employment, earnings, and hours, by SIC 1- to 4-digit industry, monthly 1989-Feb 1992, annual rpt, 6744–4
Employment of minorities and women, by occupation, SIC 1- to 3-digit industry, State, and MSA, 1991, annual rpt, 9244–1
Financial statements for manufacturing, mining, and trade corporations, by selected SIC 2- to 3-digit industry, quarterly rpt, 2502–1
Inventory price indexes for department stores, by class of item, monthly table, 6762–7
Labor productivity, indexes of output, hours, and employment by SIC 2- to 4-digit industry, 1967-90, annual rpt, 6824–1.4
Mail volume to and from households, use, and views, by class, source, content, and household characteristics, FY87-90, annual rpt, 9864–10
Occupational injury and illness rates, by SIC 2- to 4-digit industry, 1989-90, annual rpt, 6844–7
Occupational injury and illness rates, by SIC 2- to 4-digit industry, 1990, annual rpt, 6844–1
Sales and inventories, by kind of retail business, region, and selected State, MSA, and city, monthly rpt, 2413–3
Sales, inventories, purchases, gross margin, and accounts receivable, by SIC 2- to 4-digit kind of business and form of ownership, 1990, annual rpt, 2413–5
Sales of retailers, by kind of business, advance monthly rpt, 2413–2
Tax (income) returns of corporations, income and tax items by asset size and detailed industry, 1989, annual rpt, 8304–4; 8304–21
Tax (income) returns of partnerships, income statement and balance sheet items, by industry group, 1990, annual article, 8302–2.314
Tax (income) returns of sole proprietorships, income statement items, by industry group, 1990, annual article, 8302–2.317; 8302–2.320

Deportation
Aliens (illegal) held in Immigration and Naturalization Service detention facilities pending hearings, and legal aid requests, 1980s-91, GAO rpt, 26119–409
Cases and reviews in Federal district courts, 1991, annual rpt, 18204–8.18
Cases of deportation and exclusion, FY83-91, annual rpt, 6264–2.5
Cases of deportation and exclusion, FY91, annual summary rpt, 6264–7
Cases of deportation, by reason, data compilation, 1992 annual rpt, 6064–6.4
Immigrant and nonimmigrant visa applicants refused, and refusals overcome, by reason, FY90, annual rpt, 7184–1.3

Deposit insurance
Banking system reform issues, with top instn finances, fiscal impacts, and views of depositors, bankers, and regulators on deposit insurance, 1991 hearings, 21248–168
Banks financial performance, risk assessment, and regulation, 1991 annual conf papers, 9375–7
Budget deficit forecasting accuracy, contributing factors, and analysis of major programs, FY91, annual GAO rpt, 26104–23
Budget of US, CBO analysis of revenue and spending alternatives and projections of economic indicators, FY93-97, annual rpt, 26304–3
Budget of US, conversion of deposit insurance and Pension Benefit Guarantee Corp budget authority and outlays from cash to accrual accounting basis, FY93, 108–46.1
Budget of US, House concurrent resolution, with spending and revenue targets, FY93 and projected to FY97, annual rpt, 21264–2
Budget of US, midsession review of FY93 budget, by function, annual rpt, 104–7
Budget of US, obligations and authority by function, agency, and program, with summaries and analyses, FY93, annual rpt, 104–2
Coverage of deposits, for commercial and savings banks by State, 1990, annual rpt, 9294–4
Coverage of deposits in insured commercial and savings banks, by instn, State, MSA, and county, as of June 1991, annual regional rpt series, 9295–3
Coverage of household and small business deposits, and value of insurance to banks by instn, 1970s-90, hearing, 21408–126
Credit unions failures, assets and losses to Natl Credit Union Share Insurance Fund by asset size and charter, and for largest failures by instn, FY86-91, 9536–1.7
Credit unions federally insured, finances by instn characteristics and State, as of June 1992, semiannual rpt, 9532–6
Credit unions federally insured, finances, mergers, closings, and insurance fund losses and financial statements, FY91, annual rpt, 9534–7
Credit unions federally insured, finances, 1990-91, annual rpt, 9534–1
Credit unions financial performance and regulation, with background data, 1960s-90, GAO rpt, 26119–364
EC economic integration impacts on financial services, 1992 article, 9391–1.308
Failures of banks, undercapitalization duration relation to Bank Insurance Fund losses, 1985-90, article, 9391–1.312
FDIC finances and operations, insured deposits, and finances of banks needing FDIC aid, 1991 and trends from 1934, annual rpt, 9294–1
Fed Reserve banks expenses and operations, itemized by service, office, and district, 1991, annual rpt, 9364–11
Natl income and product accounts, comprehensive accounts and components, benchmark revisions, 1929-88, 2708–5
Natl income and product accounts, comprehensive accounts and components, *Survey of Current Business*, monthly rpt, 2702–1.26
Reform of financial system, issues, with finances, impacts of deposit insurance changes, and views of depositors and bankers, 1991 hearings, 25248–129
Regulation of banks and related issues, quarterly journal, 9292–4
Savings instns failure resolution activity of Resolution Trust Corp, assets, deposits, and assets availability and sales, periodic press release, 9722–1
Savings instns failures, costs and budget deficit and economic impacts, 1980s and projected to 2010, 26306–6.165
Savings instns financial statements, for instns insured by Savings Assn Insurance Fund by FHLB district and State, and for FDIC-insured savings banks, 1989, annual rpt, 8434–1
Uninsured bank deposits by type and bank size, and relation to bank size and selected operating ratios, 1980s-91, technical paper, 9385–8.126

Deposits
see Bank deposits
see Certificates of deposit
see Negotiable orders of withdrawal accounts
see Savings

Depreciation
Airline finances, by carrier, carrier group, and for total certificated system, quarterly rpt, 7302–7
Airline operations and passenger, cargo, and mail traffic, by type of service, air carrier, State, and country, 1981-90, annual rpt, 7504–1.6
Assets and debts of private sector, balance sheets by segment, 1960-91, semiannual rpt, 9365–4.1
Auto, van, and light truck ownership and operating costs, by vehicle size and year of operation, 1991 model year, biennial rpt, 7554–21
Banks in Fed Reserve System, expenses and operations itemized by service, office, and district, 1991, annual rpt, 9364–11
Budget of US, obligations and authority by function, agency, and program, with summaries and analyses, FY93, annual rpt, 104–2
Communications services revenue and expenses, itemized by SIC 2- to 4-digit kind of business, 1990, annual rpt, 2413–15
Electric power plants production and capital costs, operations, and fuel use, by fuel type, plant, utility, and location, 1990, annual rpt, 3164–9
Electric utilities finances and operations, detailed data for publicly and privately owned firms, 1990, annual rpt, 3164–11.4
Electric utilities finances and operations, detailed data for publicly owned firms, 1990, annual rpt, 3164–24
Electric utilities privately owned, finances and operations, detailed data, 1990, annual rpt, 3164–23
Energy producers finances and operations, by energy type for US firms domestic and foreign operations, 1990, annual rpt, 3164–44.1
Multinatl firms US affiliates, finances, and operations, by industry, world area of parent firm, and State, 1989-90, annual rpt, 2704–4
Multinatl firms US affiliates gross product, by component, industry, and country of parent firm, 1987-90, article, 2702–1.342
Multinatl US firms and foreign affiliates finances and operations, by industry and country, 1989 benchmark survey, annual rpt, 2704–5
Natl income and product accounts and components, *Survey of Current Business*, monthly rpt, 2702–1.23
Natural gas interstate pipeline company detailed financial and operating data, by firm, 1990, annual rpt, 3164–38
Nonprofit charitable organizations finances, summary data by asset size, 1989, article, 8302–2.325
Nonprofit charitable organizations finances, with data by State and for top 10 instns, 1988, article, 8302–2.302
Railroad (Class I) finances and operations, detailed data by firm, class of service, and district, 1990, annual rpt, 9486–5.1
Railroad (Class I) finances and operations, detailed data by firm, class of service, and district, 1991, annual rpt, 9486–6.1
Rice production, practices, costs, and land tenure, by production area, 1988, 1568–309
Tax (income) returns filed, by type of filer, selected income items, quarterly rpt, 8302–2.1
Tax (income) returns of corporations, income and tax items by asset size and detailed industry, 1989, annual rpt, 8304–4; 8304–21
Tax (income) returns of corporations, summary data by asset size and industry div, 1989, annual article, 8302–2.321
Tax (income) returns of individuals, by filing status, tax item, and income level, 1991, annual article, 8302–2.319
Tax (income) returns of partnerships, income statement and balance sheet items, by industry group, 1990, annual article, 8302–2.314
Tax (income) returns of sole proprietorships, income statement items, by industry group, 1990, annual article, 8302–2.317; 8302–2.320
Tax deductions for amortization of intangible assets from acquired businesses, IRS unresolved audits, and claims allowed, 1991 GAO rpt, 26119–365
Tax exempt organizations finances, with data by type, size, State, and for largest organizations, late 1940s-80s, compilation of papers, 8308–35
Tax exempt organizations with unrelated business income, finances by organization type, 1987, article, 8302–2.306
Telephone and telegraph firms detailed finances and operations, 1990, annual rpt, 9284–6
Telephone firms borrowing under Rural Telephone Program, and financial and operating data, by State, 1991, annual rpt, 1244–2
Truck and warehouse services finances and inventory, by SIC 2- to 4-digit industry, 1990 survey, annual rpt, 2413–14

Truck interstate carriers finances and operations, by district, 1990, annual rpt, 9486–5.2
Truck itemized costs per mile, finances, and operations, for agricultural carriers, 1991, annual rpt, 1311–15
Truck rates for fruit and vegetables paid by shippers and receivers, by commodity and city, and fleet itemized costs per mile, weekly rpt, 1311–22
TVA finances and operations by program and facility, FY91, annual rpt, 9804–32

Depressions
see Business cycles

Deregulation
see Government and business
see Price regulation

Des Moines, Iowa
see also under By City and By SMSA or MSA in the "Index by Categories"

DeSapio, Vincent
"Fluorspar and Certain Other Mineral Substances, Industry and Trade Summary", 9885–13.1

Deserts and desertification
see Arid zones

Desmeules, Marie
"Increasing Incidence of Primary Malignant Brain Tumors: Influence of Diagnostic Methods", 4472–1.309

Detective and protective services
Banks in Fed Reserve System, expenses and operations itemized by service, office, and district, 1991, annual rpt, 9364–11
County Business Patterns, 1989: employment, establishments, and payroll, by SIC 2- to 4-digit industry and county, annual State rpt series, 2326–8
County Business Patterns, 1990: employment, establishments, and payroll, by SIC 2- to 4-digit industry and county, annual State rpt series, 2326–6
Drug testing and results for airline and aviation safety employees, by drug type and occupational group, 1991, semiannual rpt, 7502–17
Employment and economic conditions, alternative BLS projections to 2005 and trends 1975-90, biennial rpt, 6744–19
Employment, earnings, and hours, by SIC 1- to 4-digit industry, monthly 1989-Feb 1992, annual rpt, 6744–4
Employment, unemployment, and labor force characteristics, by region and census div, 1991, annual rpt, 6744–7.1
House of Representatives salaries, expenses, and contingent fund disbursement, detailed listings, quarterly rpt, 21942–1
Input-output structure of US economy, detailed interindustry transactions for 541 industries, and components of final demand, 1982 benchmark data, 2708–17
Labor demand, turnover, and training completions, by detailed occupation, 1990 and projected to 2005, biennial rpt, 6744–3
Marshals Service activities, FY91, annual rpt, 6294–1
Nuclear weapons facilities of DOE, security deficiencies by type and facility, 1989-90, GAO rpt, 26113–557
Occupational Outlook Handbook, 1992-93, biennial rpt, 6744–1
Pacific territories population and housing detailed characteristics, by location, 1990 Census of Population and Housing, series, 2551–8
Senate receipts, itemized expenses by payee, and balances, 1st half FY92, semiannual listing, 25922–1
State and local govt employment of minorities and women, by occupation, function, pay level, and State, 1991, annual rpt, 9244–6
see also Campus security
see also Security devices

Detention
see Arrest
see Correctional institutions
see Habeas corpus
see Juvenile detention and correctional institutions
see Pretrial detention and release
see Prisoners

Detergent industry
see Soap and detergent industry

Dethier, Megan N.
"Effects of an Oil Spill and Freeze Event on Intertidal Community Structure in Washington", 5738–38.2

Detroit, Mich.
Auto alternative fuels use in Federal fleet, energy economy performance at 4 sites, FY91, annual rpt, 3304–28
Commuters, by county of residence and work, for top 10 metro areas, 1990 Census of Population, press release, 2328–84
CPI by component for US city average, and by region, population size, and for 15 metro areas, monthly rpt, 6762–1
CPI by component for US city average, and by selected metro area, region, and population size, monthly rpt, 6762–2
Drug abuse indicators for selected metro areas, research results, data collection, and policy issues, 1992 semiannual conf, 4492–5
Drug test results at arrest, by drug type, offense, and sex, for selected urban areas, quarterly rpt, 6062–3
Freight (waterborne domestic and foreign) by commodity, traffic, and passengers, by port and waterway, 1989, annual rpt, 3754–3.3
Fruit and vegetable shipments, and arrivals by city, by mode of transport and State and country of origin, 1991, annual rpt, 1311–4.1
Heroin prices and purity in 19 metro areas and Puerto Rico, by world area of origin, quarterly rpt, 6282–2
Housing and households characteristics, unit and neighborhood quality, and journey to work by MSA location, for 11 MSAs, 1985 survey, supplement, 2485–8
Housing and households characteristics, 1989 survey, MSA fact sheet, 2485–11.9
Housing and households detailed characteristics, and unit and neighborhood quality, by location, 1989 survey, MSA rpt, 2485–6.2
Pollution (air) levels in Detroit area, by pollutant and site, 1970s-90, 14648–28
Wages by occupation, and benefits, for office and plant workers, 1991 survey, periodic MSA rpt, 6785–16.4
see also under By City and By SMSA or MSA in the "Index by Categories"

Devaney, F. John
"Housing in America, 1989/90", 2486–2.1

Developing countries
Agricultural trade of US, by commodity and country, bimonthly rpt, 1522–1
Agricultural trade of US, by detailed commodity and country, 1991, annual rpt, 1524–8
Agricultural trade of US, by detailed commodity and country, 1991, semiannual rpt, 1522–4
AID activities, finances, and staff, by program and country, FY90, GAO rpt, 26123–382
AID dev projects and socioeconomic impacts, evaluation rpt series, 9916–1
AID economic aid to developing countries, obligations and disbursements by country, quarterly rpt, 9912–4
AID loans repayment status and terms by program and country, and status of predecessor agency loans, quarterly rpt, 9912–3
Debt burden indicators, conversion agreement terms, and swaps for conservation funds, by selected developing country, 1987-90, hearing, 25368–181
Debt burden indicators for 8 developing countries, alternative projections 1991-2000 and trends from 1974, technical paper, 9366–7.271
Debt burden of developing countries and relation to investment decline, with background data, 1960s-80s, technical paper, 9366–7.272
Debt conversions of highly indebted developing countries, impact on debt burden and secondary market debt, 1985-87, technical paper, 9366–6.294
Debt of developing countries, and IMF credit outstanding, by world area and country, 1985-91, annual rpt, 9114–7
Debt securities of developing countries, prices on secondary market relation to stock price indexes and other factors, model description and results, 1980s-90, technical paper, 9385–8.132
Disaster preparedness and economic, population, and political data, discontinued series, 9916–2
EC economic integration impacts on domestic and intl agricultural conditions, 1990 conf, 1528–325
Economic and military aid and loans from US and intl agencies, by program and country, FY46-91, annual rpt, 9914–5
Economic and social conditions of developing countries from 1960s, and Intl Dev Cooperation Agency and AID activities and funding, FY91-93, annual rpt, 9904–4
Economic, population, and agricultural data, US and other aid sources, and AID activity, country rpt series, 9916–12
Energy efficiency improvement issues and devs for developing countries, with data by end use and country, 1980s-90, 26358–260
Energy supply and demand, by fuel and end-use sector, 1950s-87 and forecast to 1995, 3166–6.58
Energy use and aid for developing countries, 1991 hearings, 25318–83
Exports and imports of US, by selected country, country group, and commodity group, 1991, annual rpt, 2044–37

Exports and imports of US, by world area, quarterly pamphlet, 2042–25
Exports, imports, and balances of US for manufactured goods, by SITC 2-digit commodity and country, quarterly rpt, 2042–35
Family planning and population activities of AID, grants by project and recipient, and contraceptive shipments, by country, FY91, annual rpt series, 9914–13
Food supply, needs, and aid for developing countries, status and alternative forecasts, world area rpt series, 1526–8
Imports of US given duty-free treatment for value of US material sent abroad, by commodity and country, 1987-90, annual rpt, 9884–14
Injury surveillance in developing countries, activities and CDC recommendations, 1992 narrative article, 4202–7.308
Intl Monetary Fund financial statements, and proposed funding quotas by member country, 1991 hearing, 21248–169
Investment (foreign direct) of US, by industry group and world area, 1989-91, annual article, 2702–1.332
Loans and other funding from intl financial instns by source and disbursements by purpose, by country, with US policy review, FY90, annual rpt, 15344–1
Loans of US banks to foreigners at all US and foreign offices, by country group and country, quarterly rpt, 13002–1
Military spending, arms trade, and force strengths, with govt spending and population, by country, 1979-89, annual rpt, 9824–1
Multinatl US firms and foreign affiliates finances and operations, by industry and country, 1989 benchmark survey, annual rpt, 2704–5
Multinatl US firms and foreign affiliates finances and operations, by industry and world area, 1988, annual article, 2702–1.329
Older persons in developing countries, population and selected characteristics, 1980s and projected to 2020, country rpt series, 2326–19
Older population and characteristics, by country, 1991 and projected to 2020, wallchart, 2328–82
Peace Corps activities, funding by program, and volunteers, by country, FY93, annual rpt, 9654–1
Population size, growth rates, and components of change, by country, projected 1990-2020 and trends from 1950, biennial rpt, 2324–9
Population size, life expectancy, and fertility, trends and projections, country rpt series, 2326–24
Statistical Abstract of US, 1992 annual data compilation, 2324–1.31
UN voting record and share of votes in agreement with US, by issue, country, and world area, 1991, annual rpt, 7004–18
see also under By Foreign Country in the "Index by Categories"
see also under names of individual countries

DeWeese, Richard
"Evaluation of Head Impact Kinematics for Passengers Seated Behind Interior Walls", 7506–10.120

DeWhitt, Ben
"Records Relating to Personal Participation in World War II: "The American Soldier" Surveys", 9516–1.10

DeWind, Josh
"Employment Obstacles Experienced by Foreign-Born Workers in New York City Because of the Employer Sanctions Provisions of the Immigration Reform and Control Act of 1986", 6366–6.7

Diabetes
Cases of acute and chronic conditions, disability, absenteeism, and health services use, by selected characteristics, 1990, annual rpt, 4147–10.182; 4147–10.183
Deaths and rates, by cause, age, sex, marital status, race, and State, 1989, US Vital Statistics advance annual rpt, 4146–5.124
Deaths and rates, by cause and age, preliminary 1990-91, US Vital Statistics annual rpt, 4144–7
Deaths and rates, by cause and selected social, demographic, and employment characteristics, 1979-85, natl longitudinal study, 4478–186
Deaths and rates, by cause, provisional data, monthly rpt, 4142–1.2
Deaths and rates, by detailed location, cause, and demographic characteristics, 1989, US Vital Statistics annual rpt, 4144–3
Deaths during 1986, decedents health condition, services use, habits, and social, employment, and other characteristics, 4147–20.19
Disability and work limitations of persons with chronic health conditions, by condition, age, and sex, 1983-86, 4946–1.2
Health condition and care indicators, 1950s-90 with health improvement and disease prevention goals for 1990, annual data compilation, 4144–11
HHS financial aid, by program, recipient, State, and city, FY91, annual regional listings, 4004–3
Hospital deaths of Medicare patients, actual and expected rates by diagnosis, with hospital characteristics, by instn, FY90, annual State rpt series, 4654–14
Indian (Navajo) diabetics and nondiabetics cholesterol and triglyceride levels, by age and sex, 1989-90 local area study, article, 4042–3.309
Indian Health Service and tribal facilities and use, and Indians health and other characteristics, by IHS region, 1980s-90, annual chartbook, 4084–7
Indian Health Service facilities, funding, operations, and Indian health and other characteristics, 1950s-91, annual chartbook, 4084–1
Insurance (health) denial by private carriers because of poor health, by selected characteristics, 1987, 4186–8.23
Kidney end-stage disease treatment facilities, Medicare enrollment and reimbursement, survival, and patient characteristics, 1984-90, annual rpt, 4654–16
Medicare payment of physicians, reforms impacts on services, and monitoring methods, 1992 annual rpt, 4004–34
OECD members health care costs, hospital use, resources, and economic and health indicators, by country, 1960s-90, article, 4652–1.322
Physicians office visits for diabetes, by characteristics of patient, physician, and visit, 1989, 4146–8.212

Diaz-Gimenez, Javier
"Banking in Computable General Equilibrium Economies", 9383–20.23
"Liquidity Constraints in Economies with Aggregate Fluctuations: A Quantitative Exploration", 9383–20.19

Dickey, Lynn E.
"Composition of Foods. 1991 Supplement: Raw, Processed, Prepared", 1356–3.17

Dictionaries
see Glossaries

Diesel fuel
Auto fuel economy test results for US and foreign makes, 1993 model year, annual rpt, 3304–11
Consumption of energy by fuel type, and miles traveled, by transport mode, projected 1990-2010 and trends from 1960s, 3008–124
Consumption of gasoline and other motor fuel by State, and tax rates by jurisdiction, monthly rpt, 7552–1
DOE Oak Ridge Natl Lab contractors excise tax refunds due from off-highway motor fuel use, 1988-90, 3006–5.26
Electric power supply, demand, and trade of Mexico and US, with data by fuel source, utility, and region, 1970s-89 and projected to 2000, 3408–2
Farm prices received and paid, by commodity and State, monthly rpt, 1629–1
Farm prices received and paid, by commodity and State, 1991, annual rpt, 1629–5
Farm production inputs supply, demand, and prices, 1970s-91 and projected to 1996, article, 1561–16.301
Farm production inputs supply, demand, and prices, 1980s-92, article, 1561–16.304
Farm production itemized costs, by farm sales size and region, 1991, annual rpt, 1614–3
Foreign and US energy production, trade, use, and reserves, and oil and refined products supply and prices, by country, 1981-90, annual rpt, 3164–50
Injuries from use of consumer products, by severity, victim age, and detailed product, 1991, annual rpt, 9164–6
Mines (underground) diesel engine exhaust emissions measurement and control, 1992 conf, 5608–177
Pacific basin countries energy supply and demand, and implications for US trade, country rpt series, 3406–6
Price indexes (producer), by stage of processing and detailed commodity, monthly rpt, 6762–6
Price indexes (producer), by stage of processing and detailed commodity, monthly 1991, annual rpt, 6764–2
Prices and spending for fuel, by type, end-use sector, and State, 1990, annual rpt, 3164–64
Prices and volume of oil products sold and purchased by refiners, processors, and distributors, by product, end-use sector, PAD district, and State, monthly rpt, 3162–11; 3164–85
Prices of wholesale and retail No 2 diesel oil, monthly rpt, 3162–24.9

Prices of wholesale and retail No 2 diesel oil, monthly 1975-88, 3168–123.9
Prices, supply, and demand, by fuel type and end-use sector, with foreign comparisons, 1981-90, annual fact book, 3164–76
Sales and deliveries of fuel oil and kerosene, by end-use, PAD district, and State, 1990, annual rpt, 3164–94
Tax (excise) collections of IRS, by source, quarterly rpt, 8302–1
Tax (excise) rates for motor fuels, by State, 1981-91, annual table, 7554–32
Tax rates for motor fuels, Federal and State, monthly rpt, 3162–11
Transit systems finances and operations, by mode, size of fleet and urban area, region, and for 518 systems, 1990, annual rpt, 7884–4
Transportation energy use by mode, fuel supply, and demographic and economic factors of vehicle use, 1970s-90, annual rpt, 3304–5

Diet
see Food consumption
see Nutrition and malnutrition
see Vitamins and nutrients

Dietitians and nutritionists
Education in science and engineering, grad programs enrollment by field, source of funds, and characteristics of student and instn, 1990, annual rpt, 9627–7
Hospital employment and job vacancy rate, by occupation, and instn size and control, 1981-88, annual rpt, 4114–12
Indian Health Service facilities, funding, operations, and Indian health and other characteristics, 1950s-91, annual chartbook, 4084–1
Labor demand, turnover, and training completions, by detailed occupation, 1990 and projected to 2005, biennial rpt, 6744–3
Labor supply and education of health professionals, by professional and other characteristics, and location, 1960s-92 and projected to 2020, biennial rpt, 4114–8
Military health care personnel, and accessions by training source, by occupation, specialty, and service branch, FY90, annual rpt, 3544–24
Occupational Outlook Handbook, 1992-93, biennial rpt, 6744–1
VA health care facilities trainees, by detailed program and city, FY91, annual rpt, 8704–4
VA health care services, needs, availability, structure, and funding, 1991 compilation of papers, 8608–9
VA health care staff and turnover, by occupation, physician specialty, and location, 1991, annual rpt, 8604–8

Digestive diseases
Cancer (colon) risk for men relation to weight-height index at college entrance and in middle age, and level of physical exercise, 1962-88 study, article, 4472–1.339
Cancer (colon) risk relation to diet, aspirin use, exercise, and other factors, 1982-88, article, 4472–1.346
Cancer (colon) risk relation to genetic mutation, 1925-65 British study, article, 4472–1.311
Cancer (colorectal) deaths relation to cancer screening use, 1979-88 local area study, article, 4472–1.349
Cancer (colorectal) early detection screening program effectiveness, 1984-88 study, article, 4042–3.333
Cancer (colorectal) mortality risk related to presence of intestinal polyps, 1959-86, article, 4472–1.325
Cancer (colorectal) risk relation to diet, for men, 1986-88, article, 4472–1.302
Cancer (colorectal) risk relation to dietary fiber, vitamin C, and beta carotene, 1992 article, 4472–1.358
Cancer (colorectal) risk relation to serum a-tocopherol levels, 1960s-82, article, 4472–1.308
Cancer (liver) patients with tumor suppression gene p53 mutations, by hepatitis B virus seropositivity, for US, Hawaii, and PRC, 1992 article, 4472–1.353
Cancer (liver) risk for women relation to parity and oral contraceptives use, 1985-86, article, 4472–1.331
Cancer (pancreatic) death risk relation to occupational DDT exposure and other characteristics, 1982 article, 4472–1.314
Cancer (stomach) risk relation to smoking and alcohol use, 1989-90 local area study, article, 4472–1.334
Cancer deaths and rates, by body site and selected social, demographic, and employment characteristics, 1979-85, natl longitudinal study, 4478–186
Cancer deaths and rates, by body site, provisional data, monthly rpt, 4142–1.2
Cases of acute and chronic conditions, disability, absenteeism, and health services use, by selected characteristics, 1990, annual rpt, 4147–10.182; 4147–10.183
Child infectious disease cases, and related disability and health care, by disease, health insurance status, and other characteristics, 1988, 4147–10.181
Chronic digestive disease prevalence, and procedures performed, by disease and patient characteristics, 1989, 4146–8.213
Cirrhosis of liver and other alcohol related disorders, hospital discharges, by sex, race, and age, 1979-89, 4486–1.16
Cirrhosis of liver deaths, by age, sex, race, and whether alcohol involved, 1988 and trends from 1910, annual rpt, 4486–1.13
Cirrhosis of liver deaths, by State and county, annual averages 1979-80 and 1983-85, 4488–10.4
Cirrhosis of liver hospital discharges and length of stay, by age, sex, and region, 1979-85, 4488–10.5
Cirrhosis of liver male patients sexual dysfunction indicators, 1992 article, 4482–1.307
Deaths and rates, by cause, age, sex, marital status, race, and State, 1989, US Vital Statistics advance annual rpt, 4146–5.124
Deaths and rates, by cause and age, preliminary 1990-91, US Vital Statistics annual rpt, 4144–7
Deaths and rates, by cause and selected social, demographic, and employment characteristics, 1979-85, natl longitudinal study, 4478–186
Deaths and rates, by cause, provisional data, monthly rpt, 4142–1.2
Deaths and rates, by detailed location, cause, and demographic characteristics, 1989, US Vital Statistics annual rpt, 4144–3
Deaths during 1986, decedents health condition, services use, habits, and social, employment, and other characteristics, 4147–20.19
Disability and work limitations of persons with chronic health conditions, by condition, age, and sex, 1983-86, 4946–1.2
Health condition and care indicators, 1950s-90 with health improvement and disease prevention goals for 1990, annual data compilation, 4144–11
HHS financial aid, by program, recipient, State, and city, FY91, annual regional listings, 4004–3
Hospital deaths of Medicare patients, actual and expected rates by diagnosis, with hospital characteristics, by instn, FY90, annual State rpt series, 4654–14
Hospital discharges and length of stay, by diagnosis, patient and instn characteristics, procedure performed, and payment source, 1990, annual rpt, 4147–13.112
Hospital discharges and length of stay by region and diagnosis, and procedures performed, by age and sex, 1990, annual rpt, 4146–8.211
Hospital discharges and length of stay under old and new survey designs, by diagnosis, patient and instn characteristics, and procedure, Jan-Mar 1988, 4147–13.110
Hospital discharges by detailed diagnostic and procedure category, primary diagnosis, and length of stay, by age, sex, and region, 1990, annual rpt, 4147–13.111
Indian Health Service and tribal facilities and use, and Indians health and other characteristics, by IHS region, 1980s-90, annual chartbook, 4084–7
Indian Health Service facilities, funding, operations, and Indian health and other characteristics, 1950s-91, annual chartbook, 4084–1
Indian Health Service, tribal, and contract facilities hospitalization, by diagnosis, age, sex, and service area, FY91, annual rpt, 4084–5
Intestinal parasites lab isolations, by State and organism, 1987, article, 4202–7.306
Liver transplants, failures, deaths, and survival rates, by hospital, 1987-89, annual rpt, 4104–17.3
OECD members health care costs, hospital use, resources, and economic and health indicators, by country, 1960s-90, article, 4652–1.322
Pancreas transplants, failures, deaths, and survival rates, by hospital, 1987-89, annual rpt, 4104–17.4
Physicians visits, by patient and practice characteristics, diagnosis, and services provided, 1989, annual rpt, 4147–13.109
Rotavirus cases, by region, monthly 1989-May 1991, article, 4202–7.317
see also under By Disease in the "Index by Categories"

DiGiovanni, Dawn M.
"Forest Statistics for Maryland, 1976 and 1986", 1206–12.16

Dillard, Fay B.
"U.S. Natural Gas Imports and Exports, 1991", 3162–4.301
DiLullo, Anthony J.
"Reconciliation of the U.S.-Canadian Current Account", 2702–1.341
Dinkins, Julia M.
"Expenditures for Food Away from Home", 1702–1.308
"Perceptions of Well-Being Among Three Age Cohorts of Rural Southern Elders", 1504–9.1
Dioxins
Agent Orange exposure cases at VA health centers, and exemptions from copayment requirements, 1989, GAO rpt, 26121–464
Agent Orange exposure health effects, literature review, 1990, annual rpt series, 8706–1
Carcinogens chemistry, sources, environment and health risks, and regulation, by substance and brand, 1991 annual rpt, 4044–15
Great Lakes industrial water pollution emissions, comparison of State, EPA, Intl Joint Commission, and Ontario standards, 1991 rpt, 14648–29
Industrial hazardous substances releases and reduction methods under EPA regulation, by chemical, source, industry, and location, 1989, annual rpt, 9234–6
Industrial hazardous substances releases and reduction methods under EPA regulation, with chemical stocks and use, facility directory, 1987-89, annual CD-ROM, 9234–7
Pesticide applicators dioxin serum levels, by exposure duration, 1988 study, article, 4472–1.303
Diplomacy
see Diplomatic and consular service
see Foreign relations
Diplomatic and consular service
Developing countries economic and social conditions from 1960s, and Intl Dev Cooperation Agency and AID activities and funding, FY91-93, annual rpt, 9904–4
Employment (civilian) of Fed Govt, work-years, pay rates, and benefits use and costs, by agency, FY90, annual rpt, 9844–31
Employment and payroll (civilian) of Fed Govt, by pay system, agency, and location, 1991, annual rpt, 9844–6
Former US govt officials representing foreign interests, activities and individuals, FY86-91, GAO rpt, 26123–134
Geographic Notes, foreign countries boundaries, claims, nomenclature, and other devs, quarterly rpt, 7142–3
Living costs abroad, State Dept indexes, housing allowances, and hardship differentials by country and major city, quarterly rpt, 7002–7
Soviet Union former Republics and Baltic States, US embassy positions planned by function, and filled, 1992, GAO rpt, 26123–403
Terrorism (intl) incidents, casualties, and attacks on US targets, by attack type and country, 1991, annual rpt, 7004–22
Terrorism (intl) incidents, casualties, and attacks on US targets, by attack type and world area, 1991, annual rpt, 7004–13
UN participation of US, and member and nonmember shares of UN budget by country, FY89-91, annual rpt, 7004–5
Visa (immigrant) applicants on waiting lists at consular office, by preference class, world region, and for top countries, as of Jan 1992, 7188–1
Visas of US issued and refused to immigrants and nonimmigrants, by class, issuing office, and nationality, FY90, annual rpt, 7184–1
Dire Emergency Supplemental Appropriations Act
Nicaragua economic and dev aid of US by type, and foreign debt by creditor, FY90-91, GAO rpt, 26123–398
Direct marketing
Cigarette ad and promotion costs by media, and market shares, by cigarette type, with sales and use, 1963-89, annual rpt, 9404–4
County Business Patterns, 1989: employment, establishments, and payroll, by SIC 2- to 4-digit industry and county, annual State rpt series, 2326–8
County Business Patterns, 1990: employment, establishments, and payroll, by SIC 2- to 4-digit industry and county, annual State rpt series, 2326–6
Employment, earnings, and hours, by SIC 1- to 4-digit industry, monthly 1989-Feb 1992, annual rpt, 6744–4
Mail order catalog price changes, and relation to inflation, by item, 1953-87, working paper, 9375–13.76
Mail volume to and from households, use, and views, by class, source, content, and household characteristics, FY87-90, annual rpt, 9864–10
Medicaid-eligible child health screenings, rural physicians participation effects of promotional mailing, for North Carolina, 1990, article, 4042–3.358
Sales and inventories, by kind of retail business, region, and selected State, MSA, and city, monthly rpt, 2413–3
Sales, inventories, purchases, gross margin, and accounts receivable, by SIC 2- to 4-digit kind of business and form of ownership, 1990, annual rpt, 2413–5
Sales of retailers, by kind of business, advance monthly rpt, 2413–2
Tax (income) returns of sole proprietorships, income statement items, by industry group, 1990, annual article, 8302–2.317; 8302–2.320
Tax revenue losses from out-of-State mail order sales, by State, 1990-92, 10048–84
Directories
Advisory committees of Fed Govt, and members, staff, meetings, and costs by agency, FY91, annual rpt, 9454–18
Agricultural exports info and service sources, 1991 annual listing, 1924–11
Agricultural industries in US with full and partial Japanese ownership, listing, 1992 rpt, 1528–332
Agricultural research and education grants, USDA competitive awards by program and recipient, FY91, annual listing, 1764–1
Agricultural research grants of USDA, by program, subagency, and country, FY92, annual listing, 1954–3
AID contracts and grants for technical and support services, by instn, country, and State, FY91, annual listing, 9914–7
AID contracts, grants, and cooperative agreements with higher education instns, by project, instn, and country, FY91, annual listing, 9914–6
Airport planning and dev project grants of FAA, by airport and location, quarterly press release, 7502–14
Allergy and Infectious Diseases Natl Inst activities, grants by recipient and location, and disease cases, FY84-91, annual rpt, 4474–30
Aluminum plant ownership, capacity, energy and aluminum sources, and startup and closing dates, by US and foreign plant and location, 1990, annual listing, 5604–49
Appalachia local dev projects, and funding by source, by program and State, FY91, annual rpt, 9084–1
Army Corps of Engineers activities and projects, FY88 and trends from 1800s, annual rpt, 3754–1.1
Army Corps of Engineers activities and projects, FY89 and trends from 1800s, annual rpt, 3754–1.2
Army Corps of Engineers activities and projects, FY90 and trends from 1800s, annual rpt, 3754–1.3
Arts Natl Endowment activities and grants, FY91, annual rpt, 9564–3
Assistance (financial and nonfinancial) of Fed Govt, and agency regional and local offices, 1992 base edition, annual listing, 104–5
Astronomical tables, time conversion factors, and listing of observatories worldwide, 1993, annual rpt, 3804–7
Auto and auto equipment recalls for safety-related defects, by make, monthly listing, 7762–12
Auto and auto equipment recalls for safety-related defects, by make, quarterly listing, 7762–2
Banks (insured commercial), Fed Reserve 9th District members financial data, by State, quarterly journal, 9383–19
Boats (recreational) and engines recalls for safety-related defects, by make, periodic listing, 7402–5
Bridges over navigable waters, with type of bridge and use, owner, dimensions, and location, 1991 regional listing series, 7406–5
Business America, foreign and domestic commerce, and US investment and trade opportunities, biweekly journal, 2042–24
Caribbean Basin Initiative export and investment incentives, contact listing, bibl, and US imports country, 1983-91, annual rpt, 2044–36
Census Bur State data centers and support agencies, 1992 annual listing, 2304–2
Census of Population and Housing, 1990: data coverage, collection procedures, products and services availability, and uses, guide, 2555–1
Census of Population and Housing, 1990: industry and occupation classification codes, alphabetical index, 2628–1
Census of Population and Housing, 1990: industry and occupation classification codes, classified index, 2628–2

Chemicals (synthetic organic) production, sales, and manufacturer listing, by product, 1990, annual rpt, 9884–3
Child abductions, runaways, and missing and exploited children, and Office of Juvenile Justice and Delinquency Prevention activities, FY90, annual rpt, 6064–36
Child abuse and neglect prevention and treatment, and disabled infant protection, grants by State, FY91, annual listing, 4584–6
Child abuse and neglect prevention and treatment, discretionary grants, FY91, annual listing, 4584–9
Coal distribution firms and producing districts served, quarterly rpt, annual listing, 3162–8
Coastal areas environmental mgmt programs of States, activities and Federal funding, FY90-91, biennial rpt, 2174–8
Consumer Product Safety Commission activities, recalls by brand, and casualties and medical costs, by product type, FY90, annual rpt, 9164–2
Containers (intermodal) and equipment owned by shipping and leasing companies, inventory by type and size, 1991, annual rpt, 7704–10
Credit unions assets, members, and location, 1992 annual listing, 9534–6
Criminal justice research and evaluation grants of Natl Inst of Justice, by recipient, FY91, 6066–20.24
DC metro area land acquisition and dev projects of Fed Govt, characteristics and funding by agency and project, FY92-96, annual rpt, 15454–1
Dental Research Natl Inst research and training grants, by recipient, FY90, annual listing, 4474–19
DOE R&D projects and funding at natl labs, universities, and other instns, periodic summary rpt series, 3004–18
Drug abuse prevention programs in schools, Education Dept recognition program, 1989/90-1990/91, annual listing, 4814–2
Eastern Europe imports from US, and trade and dev opportunities, monthly rpt, 2042–33
Economic Dev Admin activities, and funding by program, recipient, State, and county, FY91 and cumulative from FY66, annual rpt, 2064–2
Education (early childhood) for handicapped children, project descriptions, 1991/92, annual listing, 4944–10
Education (special) programs and funding of States, project listing, 1990/91, annual rpt, 4944–4
Education Dept financial aid programs, 1992 annual listing, 4804–3
Education funding of Fed Govt, with enrollment, program grants, and fellowships by State, for Indians, 1980s-FY91, annual rpt, 14874–1
Education research field projects funding and descriptions, FY90-91, annual listing, 4884–1
Educational Resources Info Center (ERIC) data base, foreign and US providers, 1992 biennial listing, 4814–4
Electric power plants and capacity, by fuel used, owner, location, and operating status, 1991 and for units planned 1992-2001, annual listing, 3164–36
Electric power plants financed by REA, with location, capacity, and owner, as of Jan 1992, annual listing, 1244–6
Electric power plants production and capital costs, operations, and fuel use, by fuel type, plant, utility, and location, 1990, annual rpt, 3164–9
Energy conservation aid of Fed Govt to public and nonprofit private instns, by building type and State, 1991, annual rpt, 3304–15
Energy-related inventions recommended by Natl Inst of Standards and Technology for DOE support, awards, and evaluation status, 1991, annual listing, 2214–5
Engineering research and education grants of NSF, FY91, annual listing, 9624–24
EPA R&D programs and funding, FY91, annual listing, 9184–18
EPA R&D programs and funding, planned FY92, annual listing, 9184–17
Exports and imports of US, by Harmonized System 6-digit commodity and country, 1991, annual rpt, 2424–13
Fish and shellfish foreign market conditions for US products, country rpt series, 2166–19
Fish and Wildlife Service restoration programs funding, land purchases, and project listing, by State, FY90, annual rpt, 5504–1
Fish Hatchery Natl System activities and deliveries, by species, hatchery, and jurisdiction of waters stocked, FY91, annual rpt, 5504–10
Foreign govts Chiefs of State and Cabinet members, by country, bimonthly listing, 9112–4
Foreign trade zones (US) operations and movement of goods, by zone and commodity, FY90, annual rpt, 2044–30
Gemstone producers listing, 1991, Mineral Industry Surveys, advance annual rpt, 5614–5.5
Geothermal resources, power plant capacity and operating status, leases, and wells, by location, 1960s-95, 3308–87
Geothermal resources, power plant generation, capacity, and dev potential, by location, 1988-90 and projected to 2030, 3168–122
Hazardous substances industrial releases and reduction methods under EPA regulation, with chemical stocks and use, facility directory, 1987-89, annual CD-ROM, 9234–7
Hazardous waste site remedial action under Superfund, current and proposed sites descriptions and status, periodic listings, series, 9216–3
Hazardous waste site remedial action under Superfund, current and proposed sites priority ranking and status by location, series, 9216–5
Hazardous waste site remedial action under Superfund, EPA records of decision by site, FY90, annual rpt, 9214–5
Health Care Financing Admin research activities and grants, by program, FY91, annual listing, 4654–10
Health data collection and availability, by country, 1991, biennial listing, 4124–8
Heart, Lung, and Blood Natl Inst activities, and grants by recipient and location, FY91 and disease trends from 1940, annual rpt, 4474–15
HHS financial aid, by program, recipient, State, and city, FY91, annual regional listings, 4004–3
Higher education enrollment, tuition, control, location, and other instn characteristics, 1991/92, biennial listing, 4844–3
Higher education instn tuition and other charges, by public and private 2- and 4-year instn, and State, 1991/92, annual listing, 4844–10
Historic and natural natl landmarks damaged and threatened, with owner, location, damage type, and recommended remedial action, 1990, annual listing, 5544–16
Humanities Natl Endowment activities and grants, FY91, annual rpt, 9564–2
Hwy interstate mileage, by route and State, 1991 listing, 7558–111
Hydroelectric power plants retired, characteristics and location, as of 1992, annual listing, 3084–12
Japan economic conditions, US investment and export opportunities, and trade practices, forecast 1991-93 and trends from 1988, 2048–159
Kidney end-stage disease research of CDC and HCFA, project listing, 1991, annual rpt, 4654–16
Kidney end-stage disease treatment facilities approved by Medicare, dialysis and transplant services and ownership, 1991 annual listing, 4654–17
Labor Intl Affairs Bur research contracts, FY83-91, annual listing, 6364–1
Labor surplus areas eligible for preferential Fed Govt contracts, monthly listing, 6402–1
Labor unions and employer organizations in foreign countries, listing, annual country rpt series, 6366–4
Labor unions recognized in Fed Govt, agreements and membership by agency and facility, as of Jan 1991, biennial listing, 9844–14
Libraries (depository) for Federal publications, 1992 annual listing, 2214–1
Libraries (public) services for Indians and Hawaii Natives, project listing and funding by tribe and State, FY90, annual rpt, 4874–5
Libraries for blind and handicapped, readership, circulation, staff, funding, and holdings, FY91, annual listing, 26404–3
Library research and demonstration projects and funding, FY67-86, listing, 4878–5
Library science training grants for disadvantaged students, by instn and State, FY91, annual listing, 4874–1
Literacy and English as a second language programs for adults, Education Dept and State programs, enrollment, and funding, by State, 1988-91, 4808–41
Literacy program for preschoolers and parents, Even Start program activities and grants by recipient, FY90, annual listing, 4804–41
Literacy programs in workplaces, project descriptions and Education Dept funding, FY91, annual listing, 4804–40
Lumber and wood products export market dev, assn listing, FAS periodic circular, supplement, 1925–36

Marine mammals research, Federal funding by topic, recipient, and agency, FY91, annual rpt, 14734–2
Measurement systems calibration, standard reference materials specifications and availability, 1992 biennial listing, 2214–2
Meat plants inspected and certified for exporting to US, by country, 1991, annual listing, 1374–2
Military budget, organization, personnel, weapons, and property, by service branch, State, and country, 1992 annual summary rpt, 3504–13
Military contractor subcontract awards to small and disadvantaged business, by firm and service branch, quarterly rpt, 3542–17
Military post exchanges operations, listing by facility and location worldwide, 1991-92, annual rpt, 3504–10
Military prime contract awards for R&D, for top 500 contractors, FY91, annual listing, 3544–4
Military prime contract awards for R&D to US and foreign nonprofit instns and govt agencies, by instn and location, FY91, annual listing, 3544–17
Mineral Industry Surveys, commodity reviews of production, trade, use, and industry operations, advance annual rpt series, 5614–5
Museum Services Inst activities and finances, and grants by recipient, FY91, annual rpt, 9564–7
NASA R&D funding to higher education instns, by field, instn, and State, FY91, annual listing, 9504–7
Neighborhood Reinvestment Corp contracting practices and oversight of local grantees, with grantee listing, FY88-91, GAO rpt, 26113–587
NSF grants and contracts, by field, recipient, and State, FY90, annual rpt, 9624–26
NSF R&D grant awards, by div and program, periodic rpt series, 9626–7
Nuclear reactors for domestic use and export by function and operating status, with owner, operating characteristics, and location, 1991 annual listing, 3354–15
Occupational Outlook Handbook, 1992-93, biennial rpt, 6744–1
Ocean pollution research, monitoring, and resources dev activities of Fed Govt, funding and project descriptions, FY89, annual rpt, 2144–23
Oil and gas field codes and locations, 1991, annual listing, 3164–70
Oil enhanced recovery research contracts of DOE, project summaries, funding, and bibl, quarterly rpt, 3002–14
Older population data sources of Fed Govt, interagency forum activities, and contacts, 1989-90, annual rpt, 14324–1
Overseas Business Reports: economic conditions, investment and export opportunities, and trade practices, country market research rpt series, 2046–6
Park natl system sites acreage and descriptions, 1991, biennial listing, 5544–5
Peat producing firms, with operating data, 1991, Mineral Industry Surveys, annual listing, 5614–32
Population and reproduction research, Fed Govt funding by project, FY90, annual listing, 4474–9
Poultry Natl Improvement Plan participating hatcheries and birds, by species and disease program, 1992, annual listing, 1394–15
Prisons Bur admin offices and correctional instns, facility characteristics, 1992, annual listing, 6244–4
Real estate assets of failed thrifts, inventory of properties available from Resolution Trust Corp, semiannual listing series, 9722–2
Salt production capacity, by firm and facility, 1991, annual listing, 5614–30
Sand and gravel producers, listing, 1990, Mineral Industry Surveys, advance annual rpt, 5614–5.1; 5614–5.6
Sand and gravel producers, listing, 1991, Mineral Industry Surveys, advance annual rpt, 5614–5.18
Savings and loan assns, FHLB 8th District members, locations, assets, and savings, 1992, annual listing, 9304–9
Savings instns, FHLB 1st District members, financial condition, and locations, 1992, annual listing, 9304–26
Savings instns, FHLB 10th District members, locations, assets, and deposits, 1992, annual listing, 9304–17
Savings instns, FHLB 11th District shareholder instns, offices, and financial condition, 1992 annual listing, 9304–23
School agencies (public elementary and secondary), by enrollment size and location, fall 1990, annual listing, 4834–1
SEC registration, firms required to file annual rpts, as of Sept 1991, annual listing, 9734–5
Shipbuilding and repair facilities, capacity, and employment, by shipyard, 1991, annual rpt, 7704–9
Ships for oceanographic research, vessel characteristics by higher education instn and Federal agency, 1992, annual listing, 3804–6
Ships in US merchant fleet and Natl Defense Reserve Fleet, vessels, tonnage, and owner, as of July 1991, semiannual listing, 7702–2
Ships under foreign flag owned by US firms and foreign affiliates, by type, owner, and country of registry and construction, as of July 1991, semiannual rpt, 7702–3
Small Business Investment Companies capital holdings, SBA obligation, and ownership, as of July 1992, semiannual listing, 9762–4
Solar photovoltaic R&D sponsored by DOE, projects, funding, and rpts, FY91, annual listing, 3304–20
States criminal justice systems activities, employment, funding, and data collection, by State, 1970s-91, annual rpt, 6064–40
Student supplemental grants, loans, and work-study awards, Federal share by instn and State, 1992/93, annual listing, 4804–17
Textile and apparel foreign market conditions for US exports, with domestic industry operations, country rpt series, 2046–15
Transit systems finances and operations, by mode, size of fleet and urban area, region, and for 518 systems, 1990, annual rpt, 7884–4
Transit systems R&D projects and funding of Federal Transit Admin, FY91, annual listing, 7884–1
Transit systems research and training grants to higher education instns, by project, FY92, annual listing, 7884–7
Transplants of organs, failures, deaths, and survival rates, by hospital, 1987-89, annual rpt series, 4104–17
Treaties and other bilateral and multilateral agreements of US in force, by country, as of Jan 1992, annual listing, 7004–1
Voluntary agencies foreign aid programs, funding, and outlays, by agency, 1990, annual rpt, 9914–9
Water resources data collection and analysis activities of USGS Water Resources Div Districts, with project descriptions, series, 5666–26
Weather (marine) forecast areas, and broadcast schedules and stations worldwide, as of Sept 1992, annual rpt, 2184–3
Weather (marine) forecast broadcast schedules worldwide, periodic rpt, 2182–9
Workers compensation advisory and study commissions, and functions, by State, 1992 annual rpt, 6504–11
see also Bibliographies
see also CD-ROM catalogs and guides
see also Chronologies
see also Computer data file guides
see also Demonstration and pilot projects
see also Government publications lists

Disability benefits and insurance
Employee compensation costs, by component, occupation, industry group, union status, and location, 1975-92, annual rpt, 6744–20.2
Expenditures (private) for social welfare, by category, 1970s-90, annual article, 4742–1.323
Expenditures, coverage, and benefits for social welfare programs, late 1930s-90, annual rpt, 4744–3.1
Expenditures for public welfare by program, FY50s-89, annual article, 4742–1.319
Foreign countries social security programs coverage, funding, eligibility, and benefits, by country, 1991, biennial rpt, 4746–4.62
Govt pension plan benefits and beneficiaries, by type of plan and eligibility, and level of govt, 1960s-80s, annual article, 4742–1.318
Households composition, income, benefits, and labor force status, Survey of Income and Program Participation methodology, working paper series, 2626–10
Mental illness (serious) among adults, functional limitations, govt aid, drugs used, visits to professionals, and other characteristics, 1989, 4146–8.220
Military disability retirement cases, by disposition, tenure, and whether receiving VA benefits, 1980s-90, GAO rpt, 26121–470
Short-term disability insurance laws of States, comparison of provisions, as of Jan 1992, semiannual revisions to base edition, 6402–2
State and local govt employees benefit plan coverage and provisions, by plan type, 1990, biennial rpt, 6784–21

Statistical Abstract of US, 1992 annual data compilation, 2324–1.12
Temporary disability benefits under State laws and for railroad workers, since 1950, quarterly rpt, 4742–1.4
Transit systems finances and operations, by mode, size of fleet and urban area, region, and for 518 systems, 1990, annual rpt, 7884–4
Veterans and servicepersons life insurance, actuarial analyses of VA programs, 1991, annual rpt, 8604–1
Veterans disability and death compensation and pension cases, by type of entitlement and period of service, monthly rpt, 8602–5
Veterans disability and death compensation cases of VA, by entitlement type, period of service, and sex, as of Mar 1992, annual rpt, 8604–13
Veterans disability and death compensation cases of VA, by entitlement type, period of service, sex, age, and State, FY90, annual rpt, 8604–7
Veterans health care, patients, visits, costs, and operating beds, by VA and contract facility, and region, quarterly rpt, 8602–4
Working age persons with disability, labor force status, type and cause of disability, and other characteristics, 1970s-89, chartbook, 4948–11
see also Maternity benefits
see also Old-Age, Survivors, Disability, and Health Insurance
see also Workers compensation

Disabled and handicapped persons
Census of Population and Housing, 1990: population and housing characteristics, detailed geographic coverage, State CD-ROM series, 2551–10
Census of Population and Housing, 1990: summary characteristics, by county, subdiv, and place, State rpt series, 2551–7
Chronic fatigue syndrome physical and mental symptoms prevalence, by sex, 1981-84, article, 4042–3.354
Chronic health conditions causing disability, prevalence and services use and needs, series, 4946–1
Criminal justice systems activities, spending, and employment, by level of govt, data compilation, 1992 annual rpt, 6064–6.1
DOT employment, by subagency, occupation, and selected personnel characteristics, FY91, annual rpt, 7304–18
Education data compilation, 1992 annual rpt, 4824–2
Employment experience of disabled following OASDI benefit award, by selected characteristics, 1980s, article, 4742–1.312
Employment history of disabled before and after SSI application, by age, diagnosis, industry div, and sex, aggregate 1937-87, article, 4742–1.308
Fed Govt civilian employees demographic and employment characteristics, as of Sept 1991, annual article, 9842–1.301
Fed Govt employment of disabled, share of workforce, 1982 and 1990, chartbook, 9248–20
Fed Govt employment of minorities, disabled, and veterans, and years of service, by occupation, age, sex, and agency, as of Sept 1990, biennial rpt, 9844–27
Fed Govt employment of minorities, women, and disabled, by agency and occupation, FY90, annual rpt, 9244–10
Higher education PhD degree recipients, by field and selected characteristics, 1979, 1984, and 1989, 4848–44
Households composition, income, benefits, and labor force status, Survey of Income and Program Participation methodology, working paper series, 2626–10
Immigrant and nonimmigrant visa applicants refused, and refusals overcome, by reason, FY90, annual rpt, 7184–1.3
Institutionalized population and persons in group quarters, by sex, race, county, place, and urban-rural location, 1990 Census of Population, State rpt series, 2531–1
Insurance (health) denial by private carriers because of poor health, by selected characteristics, 1987, 4186–8.23
Libraries for blind and handicapped, readership, circulation, staff, funding, and holdings, FY91, annual listing, 26404–3
NASA staff characteristics and personnel actions, FY91, annual rpt, 9504–1
OASDI beneficiary data collection system design compared to earlier surveys, with summary results, 1992 article, 4742–1.313
Older persons care by family members and others, caregiver quit probability related to selected characteristics, 1982, article, 4652–1.305
Older persons socioeconomic characteristics, 1900s-90 and projected to 2050, biennial chartbook, 12904–1
Older population, and health, economic, and other characteristics, with foreign comparisons, 1980s-91 with trends and projections, Current Population Rpt, 2546–2.165
Pacific territories population and housing detailed characteristics, by location, 1990 Census of Population and Housing, series, 2551–8
Population economic well-being indicators, by selected characteristics and household income and income-to-poverty ratio, 1984, 2546–20.22
Poverty status of families, by detailed characteristics, 1980 and 1988, GAO rpt, 26131–102
Poverty status of population and families, by detailed characteristics, 1991, annual Current Population Rpt, 2546–6.77
Science and engineering employment and education of disabled persons, by field and handicap, mid 1980s, biennial rpt, 9624–20.3
SSA minority, handicapped, and women employees, by pay grade, FY91, annual rpt, 4704–6
Statistical Abstract of US, 1992 annual data compilation, 2324–1.12
VA employment characteristics and activities, FY91, annual rpt, 8604–3.4
VA health care services, needs, availability, structure, and funding, 1991 compilation of papers, 8608–9
Veterans (Vietnam) employment status, by whether served in Southeast Asia, presence and severity of disability, VA programs use, age, race, and occupation, 1991, biennial press release, 6726–1.49
Veterans (Vietnam) labor force status and earnings, by whether served in Southeast Asia, presence and severity of disability, and selected other characteristics, 1989, article, 6722–1.326
Veterans disability by type, and deaths, by period of service, and VA activities, FY91, annual rpt, 8604–3.3
Vietnam population size, components of change, and selected characteristics, 1979, 1989, and projected to 2050, 2326–18.65
Vocational education enrollment, student and teacher characteristics, and outcomes, for secondary and postsecondary instns, 1970s-90, 4828–42
Women with disabilities, employment by occupation, and earnings, by race, 1988, fact sheet, 6564–1.2
Working age persons with disability, labor force status, type and cause of disability, and other characteristics, 1970s-89, chartbook, 4948–11
see also Adult day care
see also Aid to blind
see also Aid to disabled and handicapped persons
see also Architectural barriers to the handicapped
see also Blind
see also Deaf
see also Disability benefits and insurance
see also Discrimination against the handicapped
see also Group homes for the handicapped
see also Handicapped children
see also Learning disabilities
see also Medicare
see also Mental retardation
see also Mobility limitations
see also Old-Age, Survivors, Disability, and Health Insurance
see also Rehabilitation of the disabled
see also Sheltered workshops
see also Special education
see also Supplemental Security Income
see also Vocational rehabilitation

Disadvantaged
see Compensatory education
see Disabled and handicapped persons
see Discrimination against the handicapped
see Discrimination in credit
see Discrimination in education
see Discrimination in employment
see Discrimination in housing
see Handicapped children
see Minority businesses
see Minority employment
see Minority groups
see Poverty
see Racial discrimination
see Sex discrimination

Disarmament
see Arms control and disarmament

Disaster relief
AFDC emergency aid cases and payments, by State, quarterly FY90, annual rpt, 4584–3.1; 4584–3.2
Agricultural Stabilization and Conservation Service producer payments, by program and State, 1991, annual table, 1804–12
AID economic aid to developing countries, obligations and disbursements by country, quarterly rpt, 9912–4

Army Corps of Engineers water resources dev projects, characteristics, and costs, 1950s-89, biennial State rpt series, 3756–1
Army Corps of Engineers water resources dev projects, characteristics, and costs, 1950s-91, biennial State rpt series, 3756–2
Assistance (block and categorical grants) programs for State and local govts, FY91, biennial listing, 10044–8
Assistance (financial and nonfinancial) of Fed Govt, 1992 base edition, annual listing, 104–5
Budget of US, obligations and authority by function, agency, and program, with summaries and analyses, FY93, annual rpt, 104–2
Developing countries economic and social conditions from 1960s, and Intl Dev Cooperation Agency and AID activities and funding, FY91-93, annual rpt, 9904–4
Drought aid of Reclamation Bur, by western State, 1992 press release, 5306–4.17
Economic Dev Admin activities, and funding by program, recipient, State, and county, FY91 and cumulative from FY66, annual rpt, 2064–2
Expenditures of Fed Govt in States, by type, program, agency, and State, FY91, annual rpt, 2464–2
Farm crop insurance participation, private insurers and Fed Crop Insurance Corp finances, and disaster aid costs by program, 1980s-92, GAO rpt, 26113–556
Farmland damaged by natural disaster, Emergency Conservation Program aid and participation by State, FY91, annual rpt, 1804–22
Farmland damaged by natural disaster, Emergency Conservation Program funding by region and State, monthly rpt, 1802–13
FmHA activities, and loans and grants by program and State, FY91 and trends from FY70, annual rpt, 1184–17
FmHA loans, by type, borrower race, and State, quarterly rpt, 1182–5
FmHA loans, delinquencies, and lending practices, by loan program, FY88-91, GAO rpt, 26113–569
Foreign countries disasters, casualties, damage, and aid by US and others, FY91 and trends from FY64, annual rpt, 9914–12
Group quarters for natural disaster victims, population by race and sex, 1990 Census of Population, State rpt series, 2531–1
HHS financial aid, by program, recipient, State, and city, FY91, annual regional listings, 4004–3
Hurricane Hugo disaster loan offices of SBA, staff and salary and support costs, for Puerto Rico and Virgin Islands, 1989-91, GAO rpt, 26113–576
Land Mgmt Bur activities and funding by State, FY90, annual rpt, 5724–13
Natl Guard activities, personnel, and facilities, FY91, annual rpt, 3504–22
Red Cross activities and finances, FY91, annual rpt, 29254–1
Small Business Admin disaster loans, FY87-91, annual rpt, 9764–1
Timber and orchard damage from natural disaster, USDA restoration aid and program participation by practice and State, FY91, annual rpt, 1804–24
see also Agricultural insurance
see also War relief

Disasters
Army Corps of Engineers activities and projects, FY88 and trends from 1800s, annual rpt, 3754–1.1
Army Corps of Engineers activities and projects, FY89 and trends from 1800s, annual rpt, 3754–1.2
Army Corps of Engineers activities and projects, FY90 and trends from 1800s, annual rpt, 3754–1.3
Developing countries disaster preparedness and economic, population, and political data, discontinued series, 9916–2
Explosions (accidental) and casualties, by place of occurrence, 1987-91, annual rpt, 8484–4.1
Famine-affected populations, refugees, and displaced persons, CDC recommendations for disease surveillance, control and prevention, with background data, 1978-91, 4206–2.63
Foreign countries disasters, casualties, damage, and aid by US and others, FY91 and trends from FY64, annual rpt, 9914–12
Housing (rental) total, HUD-assisted by program, and eligible for aid, recent movers by reason, selected characteristics, and location, 1989, biennial rpt, 5184–11
Incidents and mgmt of disasters and natl security threats, with data by major event and State, 1992 annual rpt, 9434–6
Natl historic and natural landmarks damaged and threatened, with owner, location, damage type, and recommended remedial action, 1990, annual listing, 5544–16
Presidential declarations of natl disasters, by event type, aggregate FY82-91, annual rpt, 9434–6
Unemployed displaced workers, layoffs and recalls by layoff reason, industry, firm size, and State, 2nd half 1988, 6406–6.36
see also Accidents and accident prevention
see also Avalanches
see also Disaster relief
see also Drought
see also Earthquakes
see also Fires and fire prevention
see also Floods
see also Forest fires
see also Nuclear accidents and safety
see also Storms
see also Tsunamis
see also Volcanoes

Discrimination
see Age discrimination
see Civil rights
see Discrimination against the handicapped
see Discrimination in credit
see Discrimination in education
see Discrimination in employment
see Discrimination in housing
see Racial discrimination
see Sex discrimination

Discrimination against the handicapped
Aliens excluded and deported from US by cause and country, 1892-1991, annual rpt, 6264–2.5
Fed Govt and State rehabilitation activities and funding, FY91, annual rpt, 4944–1
HHS financial aid, by program, recipient, State, and city, FY91, annual regional listings, 4004–3
Housing (public) for aged, placement of younger mentally disabled tenants, behavioral problems, and services, 1990 survey, GAO rpt, 26113–590
Labor laws enacted, by State, 1991, annual article, 6722–1.309
see also Architectural barriers to the handicapped

Discrimination in credit
Housing rental and sales, discrimination against blacks and Hispanics in selected metro areas, 1989 study, series, 5186–16
Low income and minority communities bank loan activity, 1991 hearing, 21248–176
Mortgage activity impact of lending program for low- and moderate-income neighborhoods in Philadelphia, with background data, 1980s, working paper, 9387–8.266
Mortgage applications, dispositions, and secondary loan market sales, by purpose, lender type, and applicant and neighborhood characteristics, 1991, article, 9362–1.307
Mortgage applications of minorities, for Boston by disposition and financial characteristics, with problems in analyzing lender disclosure statements, 1990, working paper, 9373–27.15

Discrimination in education
Digest of Education Statistics, 1992 annual data compilation, 4824–2
Minority group and sexual discrimination in education, natl survey participation and data coverage, school district administrators views, 1991 survey, 4826–1.33
Student aid targeted to minority groups, higher education instns with awards and funding sources, by instn level and control, 1989/90, hearings, 21408–130
Women's educational equity program grants and contracts, by project, type, and State, 1988-92, annual rpt, 4804–2

Discrimination in employment
Alien workers discrimination and other employment-related problems in NYC, hotline calls, 1988, 6366–6.7
Army personnel, promotion, and training by race and for women, discrimination issues, annual rpt, discontinued, 3704–10
Assistance (financial and nonfinancial) of Fed Govt, 1992 base edition, annual listing, 104–5
Civil Rights Act issues, EEOC cases by issue, damage awards, and sexual harassment complaints and company policies, late 1970s-91, hearing, 21348–120
Court civil and criminal caseloads for Federal district, appeals, and special courts, 1991, annual rpt, 18204–8
Disabled persons rehabilitation, Federal and State activities and funding, FY90, annual rpt, 4944–1
FAA employees job satisfaction, impacts of promotion and pay equity by sex, 1992 technical rpt, 7506–10.105
Fed Equal Opportunity Recruitment Program activity, and employment by sex, race, pay grade, and occupational group, FY91, annual rpt, 9844–33

Fed Govt employment discrimination complaint processing and counseling costs, by agency, FY91, GAO rpt, 26119–388
Fed Govt employment discrimination complaints, processing, and disposition, by complaint type and agency, FY90, annual rpt, 9244–11
Fed Govt employment of minorities, disabled, and veterans, and years of service, by occupation, age, sex, and agency, as of Sept 1990, biennial rpt, 9844–27
Fed Govt personnel action appeals, decisions of Merit Systems Protection Board by agency and region, FY91, annual rpt, 9494–2
Fed Govt spending in States, by type, program, agency, and State, FY91, annual rpt, 2464–2
Fed Govt violations of personnel practices, cases by type, FY91, annual rpt, 9894–1
Labor laws enacted, by State, 1991, annual article, 6722–1.309
Marshals Service activities, FY91, annual rpt, 6294–1
Small Business Admin minority and women employment, and hiring goals, FY91, annual rpt, 9764–9
Washington State govt employees comparable worth agreement, compliance costs and indicators of success, mid 1980s-93, GAO rpt, 26119–410

Discrimination in housing
Assistance (financial and nonfinancial) of Fed Govt, 1992 base edition, annual listing, 104–5
Homeownership values, reasons, and barriers, views by race and tenure, 1992 survey, 9478–1
Mentally ill younger tenants placement in public housing designed for aged, behavioral problems, and services, 1990 survey, GAO rpt, 26113–590
Racial discrimination in housing rental and sales, for blacks and Hispanics in selected metro areas, 1989 study, series, 5186–16
Urban areas fiscal, economic, and social conditions, as of FY92, biennial rpt, 5184–7

Diseases and disorders
Agent Orange exposure health effects, literature review, 1990, annual rpt series, 8706–1
Cases of acute and chronic conditions, disability, absenteeism, and health services use, by selected characteristics, 1990, annual rpt, 4147–10.182; 4147–10.183
Chronic fatigue syndrome physical and mental symptoms prevalence, by sex, 1981-84, article, 4042–3.354
Chronic health conditions causing activity and work limitations, prevalence by condition, age, and sex, 1983-86, 4946–1.2
Costa Rica and Guatemala life expectancy, and death rate by cause and age, by sex, 1984 and trends from 1900, working paper, 2326–18.64
Data on health condition and care, indicators, 1988 natl survey, CD-ROM, 4147–10.184
Educational attainment relation to health condition and care, indicators by selected characteristics, 1989, 4147–10.180
Foreign countries disasters, casualties, damage, and aid by US and others, FY91 and trends from FY64, annual rpt, 9914–12
Hospital discharges by detailed diagnostic and procedure category, primary diagnosis, and length of stay, by age, sex, and region, 1990, annual rpt, 4147–13.111
Hospital outpatient and inpatient leading diagnoses and procedures, and costs by setting, 1987, article, 4652–1.314
Indian and Alaska Native youth health condition and behavioral patterns, by sex and grade, 1988-90, 4088–3
Indian Health Service and tribal facilities and use, and Indians health and other characteristics, by IHS region, 1980s-90, annual chartbook, 4084–7
Indian Health Service facilities, funding, operations, and Indian health and other characteristics, 1950s-91, annual chartbook, 4084–1
Indian Health Service outpatient services provided, by reason for visit and age, FY90, annual rpt, 4084–2
Military deaths by cause, age, race, and rank, and personnel captured and missing, by service branch, FY91, annual rpt, 3544–40
NIH rpts, 1992 annual listing, 4434–2
Older persons socioeconomic characteristics, 1900s-90 and projected to 2050, biennial chartbook, 12904–1
Pain and pain-related conditions, data available from NCHS, with bibl, 1992 rpt, 4147–1.27
Palau admin, and social, economic, and govtl data, FY91, annual rpt, 7004–6
Pollutants health effects, concentrations in food and environment, sources, human intake, and regulation, series, 9186–8
Pollutants health effects for animals by species and for humans, and environmental levels, for selected substances, series, 5506–14
Statistical Abstract of US, 1992 annual data compilation, 2324–1.3
Youth health condition, risk factors, and preventive and treatment services use and availability, 1970s-80s, 26358–234.2
see also Accidents and accident prevention
see also Acquired immune deficiency syndrome
see also Alcohol abuse and treatment
see also Allergies
see also Alzheimer's disease
see also Animal diseases and zoonoses
see also Birth defects
see also Black lung disease
see also Blood diseases and disorders
see also Cardiovascular diseases
see also Cerebrovascular diseases
see also Circulatory diseases
see also Diabetes
see also Digestive diseases
see also Drug abuse and treatment
see also Ear diseases and infections
see also Epidemiology and epidemiologists
see also Eye diseases and defects
see also Food and waterborne diseases
see also Genetic defects and diseases
see also Health condition
see also Health risk behavior
see also Hearing and hearing disorders
see also Hereditary diseases
see also Hypertension
see also Immunity disorders
see also Infective and parasitic diseases
see also Learning disabilities
see also Mental health and illness
see also Mental retardation
see also Metabolic and endocrine diseases
see also Mobility limitations
see also Musculoskeletal diseases
see also Neoplasms
see also Neurological disorders
see also Nose and throat disorders
see also Nutrition and malnutrition
see also Obesity
see also Occupational health and safety
see also Pathology
see also Pneumonia and influenza
see also Poisoning and drug reaction
see also Rabies
see also Respiratory diseases
see also Septicemia
see also Sexually transmitted diseases
see also Skin diseases
see also Spinal cord injuries
see also Stress
see also Tuberculosis
see also Urogenital diseases
see also Vaccination and vaccines
see also under By Disease in the "Index by Categories"

Disposable income
see Personal and household income

Distillate fuels
see Diesel fuel
see Fuel oil
see Kerosene

Distribution of income
see Business income and expenses, general
see Earnings, general
see National income and product accounts
see Personal and household income
see Poverty
see Wealth

District courts
see Federal district courts

District of Columbia
see D.C.

Districts
see Central business districts
see Common markets and free trade areas
see Congressional districts
see Export processing zones
see School districts
see Special districts
see Wards, city

Ditton, Robert B.
"Understanding the Market for Charter and Headboat Fishing Services", 2162–1.301

Diuretics
see Drugs

Diversification of business
see Economic concentration and diversification

Divestiture
Energy producers finances and operations, by energy type for US firms domestic and foreign operations, 1990, annual rpt, 3164–44
Food marketing sector finances, operations, and merger activity, for processors and distributors, 1991, annual rpt, 1544–22

Division of Research Grants, NIH
Grants and contracts of NIH, by inst and type of recipient, FY82-91, annual rpt, 4434–9
Women awarded NIH research and training grants, by recipient characteristics, inst, and host instn, FY90, annual rpt, 4434–18
Divorce
see Domestic relations courts and cases
see Marriage and divorce
Dixit, Praveen M.
"Domestic Food Assistance Programs: Measuring Benefits to Producers", 1548–390
Djibouti
Agricultural trade of US, by detailed commodity and country, 1991, annual rpt, 1524–8
Agricultural trade of US, by detailed commodity and country, 1991, semiannual rpt, 1522–4
AID economic aid to developing countries, obligations and disbursements by country, quarterly rpt, 9912–4
Borders (maritime) of Djibouti, geographic coordinates, as of 1985, 7006–8.8
Economic and military aid and loans from US and intl agencies, by program and country, FY46-91, annual rpt, 9914–5
Economic and social conditions of developing countries from 1960s, and Intl Dev Cooperation Agency and AID activities and funding, FY91-93, annual rpt, 9904–4
Economic, social, political, and geographic summary data, by country, 1992, annual factbook, 9114–2
Exports and imports of US, by transport mode, country, and SITC 1- to 3-digit commodity, 1991, annual rpt, 2424–12
Exports of US, detailed Schedule B commodities with countries of destination, 1991, annual rpt, 2424–10
Human rights conditions in 170 countries, and US economic and military aid, 1991, annual rpt, 21384–3
Military aid of US, arms sales, and training programs costs and budget requests, by program, world region, and country, FY91-93, annual rpt, 7144–13
Minerals Yearbook, Vol 3, 1989: foreign country review of production, trade, and policy, by commodity, annual rpt, 5604–35.1
Population size, growth rates, and components of change, by country, projected 1990-2020 and trends from 1950, biennial rpt, 2324–9
Refugee migration, and intl aid programs, by world area and country of origin and asylum, 1991, annual rpt, 7004–15
UN voting record and share of votes in agreement with US, by issue, country, and world area, 1991, annual rpt, 7004–18
Dobbins, James G.
"Surveillance of Congenital Cytomegalovirus Disease, 1990-91", 4202–7.314
Dobbs, David T.
"Federal Budget Estimates, FY93", 2702–1.310
Dobson, Allen
"Evaluation of Winners and Losers Under Medicare's Prospective Payment System", 17206–2.38
"Examination of Winners and Losers Under Medicare's Prospective Payment System: A Synthesis of the Evidence", 17206–2.36
Doctors
see Physicians
Documents
see Bibliographies
see Environmental impact statements
see Government documents
see Government forms and paperwork
see Government publications lists
DOD
see Department of Defense
DOE
see Department of Energy
Doering, Otto
"Environmental Challenges and Opportunities", 1504–9.1
Dolan, Robert
"Rating Northeasters", 2152–8.301
Dolphins
see Marine mammals
Dolton, David D.
"Mourning Dove Breeding Population Status, 1992", 5504–15
Domestic International Sales Corporations
Boycotts (intl) by OPEC and other countries, US firms and individuals cooperation and tax benefits denied, 1990, article, 8302–2.323
Income tax returns of foreign corporations and individuals, and US entities abroad, detailed data compilation, 1970s-89, quinquennial rpt, 8308–31
Income tax returns of Interest Charge-DISCs, assets, and income and tax data, by detailed industry, 1987, article, 8302–2.312
Tax (income) returns filed, by type of filer, selected income items, quarterly rpt, 8302–2.1
Tax (income) returns of corporations, income and tax items by asset size and detailed industry, 1989, annual rpt, 8304–4; 8304–21
Tax (income) returns of corporations with foreign tax credit, income and tax items by industry group, 1988, biennial article, 8302–2.316
Tax (income) returns of individuals with foreign earned income, income and tax items by income level and occupation, 1987, article, 8302–2.301
Tax collection activity of IRS, by type of tax, FY91, annual rpt, 8304–3.1
see also Foreign Sales Corporations
Domestic relations
see Caregivers and caregiving
see Child abuse and neglect
see Domestic relations courts and cases
see Domestic violence
see Families and households
see Marriage and divorce
Domestic relations courts and cases
Federal district court caseloads, 1991, annual rpt, 18204–8.14; 18204–11
Federal district courts domestic relations caseloads, 1991, annual rpt, 18204–8.18
see also Child support and alimony
Domestic violence
Arrests, by offense, offender characteristics, and location, 1991, annual rpt, 6224–2.2
Crimes, arrests, and rates, by offense, offender characteristics, population size, and jurisdiction, 1991, annual rpt, 6224–2.1; 6224–2.2
Fed Govt financial and nonfinancial domestic aid, 1992 base edition, annual listing, 104–5
HHS financial aid, by program, recipient, State, and city, FY91, annual regional listings, 4004–3
Homicides and rate, by weapon, circumstances, and victim characteristics, and years of potential life lost, 1980s, article, 4202–7.315
Homicides, by circumstance, victim and offender relationship, and type of weapon, 1991, annual rpt, 6224–2.1
Juvenile arrests, by sex, race, disposition, and offense, 1990, 6066–27.8
Police response to disturbances, officers assaulted and killed, by circumstances, 1990, annual rpt, 6224–3
Shelters and support services for victims of domestic violence, HUD grants by community, 1992, press release, 5006–3.80
Urban, rural, and suburban crime victimizations, by offense, circumstances, and victim and offender characteristics, 1987-89, 6066–3.48
Victimization rates, by victim and offender characteristics, circumstances, and offense, 1990 survey, annual rpt, 6066–3.47
Victimizations and arrest, by offense, circumstances, and location, data compilation, 1992 annual rpt, 6064–6.3; 6064–6.4
Victims of crime, compensation and support service programs funding, by offense and State, FY88-90, biennial rpt, 6064–37
Women in jail, by criminal background and sociodemographic characteristics, with comparisons to men, 1989, 6066–19.66
Women prisoners in State instns, by whether abused, and other characteristics, data compilation, 1992 annual rpt, 6064–6.6
see also Child abuse and neglect
Domestic workers and services
Consumer spending, natl income and product account benchmark revisions, 1929-88, 2708–5
Consumer spending, natl income and product accounts, comprehensive accounts and components, *Survey of Current Business*, monthly rpt, 2702–1.25
CPI by component for US city average, and by selected metro area, region, and population size, monthly rpt, 6762–2
Deaths and rates, by cause and selected social, demographic, and employment characteristics, 1979-85, natl longitudinal study, 4478–186
Educational attainment, by social and demographic characteristics and location, 1991 and trends from 1940, biennial Current Population Rpt, 2546–1.460
Employment and Earnings, detailed data, monthly rpt, 6742–2
Employment and economic conditions, alternative BLS projections to 2005 and trends 1975-90, biennial rpt, 6744–19
Employment, earnings, and hours, monthly press release, 6742–5
Employment, unemployment, and labor force characteristics, by region and census div, 1991, annual rpt, 6744–7.1
Immigration Reform and Control Act employer sanctions impacts on labor markets, with data for selected industries and metro areas, 1980s, working paper, 6366–6.10

Input-output structure of US economy, detailed interindustry transactions for 541 industries, and components of final demand, 1982 benchmark data, 2708–17
Labor demand, turnover, and training completions, by detailed occupation, 1990 and projected to 2005, biennial rpt, 6744–3
Occupational Outlook Handbook, 1992-93, biennial rpt, 6744–1
Pacific territories population and housing detailed characteristics, by location, 1990 Census of Population and Housing, series, 2551–8
Training for job qualification and skill improvement, workers participating by training source, occupation, age, sex, and race, 1991, 6728–32
Workers compensation laws of States and Fed Govt, 1992 annual rpt, 6504–11
see also Homemaker services

Domiciliary care
see Group homes for the handicapped
see Home health services
see Homemaker services
see Nursing homes

Dominguez, Angela
"Timeliness of Notification in Infectious Disease Cases", 4042–3.349

Dominica
Agricultural trade of US, by detailed commodity and country, 1991, semiannual rpt, 1522–4
Economic and social conditions, resources, and trade, and aid, 1992, annual factbook, 9914–14
Economic, social, political, and geographic summary data, by country, 1992, annual factbook, 9114–2
Exports and imports of US, by transport mode, country, and SITC 1- to 3-digit commodity, 1991, annual rpt, 2424–12
Human rights conditions in 170 countries, and US economic and military aid, 1991, annual rpt, 21384–3
Military aid of US, arms sales, and training programs costs and budget requests, by program, world region, and country, FY91-93, annual rpt, 7144–13
Population size, growth rates, and components of change, by country, projected 1990-2020 and trends from 1950, biennial rpt, 2324–9
UN voting record and share of votes in agreement with US, by issue, country, and world area, 1991, annual rpt, 7004–18

Dominican Republic
Agricultural trade of US, by detailed commodity and country, 1991, annual rpt, 1524–8
Agricultural trade of US, by detailed commodity and country, 1991, semiannual rpt, 1522–4
AID economic aid to developing countries, obligations and disbursements by country, quarterly rpt, 9912–4
AID loans repayment status and terms by program and country, and status of predecessor agency loans, quarterly rpt, 9912–3
Aliens (illegal) enforcement activity of Coast Guard, by nationality, 1st half FY92, semiannual rpt, 7402–4
Background Notes, summary social, political, and economic data, 1991 rpt, 7006–2.8
Economic and military aid and loans from US and intl agencies, by program and country, FY46-91, annual rpt, 9914–5
Economic and social conditions of developing countries from 1960s, and Intl Dev Cooperation Agency and AID activities and funding, FY91-93, annual rpt, 9904–4
Economic and social conditions, resources, and trade, and aid, 1992, annual factbook, 9914–14
Economic conditions, policy, and trade practices, by country, 1989-91, annual rpt, 21384–5
Economic, population, and agricultural data, US and other aid sources, and AID activity, 1990 country rpt, 9916–12.48
Economic, social, political, and geographic summary data, by country, 1992, annual factbook, 9114–2
Exports and imports of US, by commodity and country, 1980-90, world area rpt, 9116–1.4
Exports and imports of US, by Harmonized System 6-digit commodity and country, 1991, annual rpt, 2424–13
Exports and imports of US, by selected country, country group, and commodity group, 1991, annual rpt, 2044–37
Exports and imports of US, by transport mode, country, and SITC 1- to 3-digit commodity, 1991, annual rpt, 2424–12
Exports, imports, and balances of US for manufactured goods, by SITC 2-digit commodity and country, quarterly rpt, 2042–35
Exports of US, detailed Schedule B commodities with countries of destination, 1991, annual rpt, 2424–10
Human rights conditions in 170 countries, and US economic and military aid, 1991, annual rpt, 21384–3
Imports of US given duty-free treatment for value of US material sent abroad, by commodity and country, 1987-90, annual rpt, 9884–14
Military aid of US, arms sales, and training programs costs and budget requests, by program, world region, and country, FY91-93, annual rpt, 7144–13
Military spending, arms trade, and force strengths, with govt spending and population, by country, 1979-89, annual rpt, 9824–1
Multinatl US firms and foreign affiliates finances and operations, by industry and country, 1989 benchmark survey, annual rpt, 2704–5
Multinatl US firms foreign affiliates, income statement items by asset size, industry, and country, 1988, biennial article, 8302–2.322
Population size, growth rates, and components of change, by country, projected 1990-2020 and trends from 1950, biennial rpt, 2324–9
Refugee migration, and intl aid programs, by world area and country of origin and asylum, 1991, annual rpt, 7004–15
Steel trade, by product, country, and customs district, with US industry operating data, 1989-June 1992, semiannual rpt, 9882–15
UN voting record and share of votes in agreement with US, by issue, country, and world area, 1991, annual rpt, 7004–18
see also under By Foreign Country in the "Index by Categories"

Donald, James R.
"World and U.S. Agricultural Outlook", 1504–9.1

Donoghue, Linda R.
"Status of Wildland Fire Prevention Evaluation in the U.S.", 1208–417

Doolittle, Larry
"Status of Wildland Fire Prevention Evaluation in the U.S.", 1208–417

DOT
see Department of Transportation

Dothan, Ala.
Wages by occupation, and benefits for office and plant workers, 1992 survey, periodic MSA rpt, 6785–3.4

Dotsey, Michael
"Oil Shocks, Monetary Policy, and Economic Activity", 9389–1.304

Douglas, Ariz.
Wages by occupation, and benefits, for office and plant workers, 1992 survey, periodic MSA rpt, 6785–3.3

Douglas, Carl
"Crewing the Merchant Marine for Mobilization", 7708–5

Douvelis, George
"Soybean Production Estimates: A Journey Through the Last 27 Years", 1561–3.306

Drabenstott, Mark
"Farm Economy Turns Down", 9381–1.303
"Realignment in Farm Lending: Strategic Issues for the 1990s", 9381–10.122

Dracunculiasis
see Infective and parasitic diseases

Draft
see Draft evasion and protest
see Selective service

Draft evasion and protest
Sentences for Federal offenses, guidelines by offense and circumstances, series, 17668–1
US attorneys civil and criminal cases by type and disposition, and collections, by Federal district, FY91, annual rpt, 6004–2.1

Drake, David E.
"Bottom and Near-Bottom Sediment Dynamics in Norton Sound, Alaska", 2176–1.40

Drake, Mary Anne
"Nutritional Status and Dietary Adequacy of Single Homeless Women and Their Children in Shelters", 4042–3.330

Dredging
Army Corps of Engineers activities and projects, FY88 and trends from 1800s, annual rpt, 3754–1.1
Army Corps of Engineers activities and projects, FY89 and trends from 1800s, annual rpt, 3754–1.2
Army Corps of Engineers activities and projects, FY90 and trends from 1800s, annual rpt, 3754–1.3
Army Corps of Engineers dredging contracts to small businesses, costs and bidding activity, FY90-92, GAO rpt, 26113–589
Army Corps of Engineers water resources dev projects, characteristics, and costs, 1950s-89, biennial State rpt series, 3756–1
Army Corps of Engineers water resources dev projects, characteristics, and costs, 1950s-91, biennial State rpt series, 3756–2

Coastal and riparian areas environmental conditions, fish, wildlife, use, and mgmt, for individual ecosystems, series, 5506–9
Panama Canal dredging operations, FY91, annual rpt, 9664–3.2

Drew, Craig P.
"Energy Management Annual Report, FY91", 9804–26

Drinking places
see Restaurants and drinking places

Drinking water
see Water fluoridation
see Water supply and use

Drivers licenses
Accidents (fatal), deaths, and rates, by circumstances, characteristics of persons and vehicles involved, and location, 1990, annual rpt, 7764–10
Admin and requirements for drivers licenses, by State and Canada Province, as of Jan 1992, biennial rpt, 7554–18
Govt finances, tax systems and revenue, and fiscal structure, by level of govt and State, 1992 with historical trends, annual rpt, 10044–1
Hwy Statistics, detailed data by State, 1991, annual rpt, 7554–1
Hwy Statistics, summary data by State, 1990-91, annual rpt, 7554–24
Hwy Statistics, summary data with trends and projections, 1992 chartbook, 7554–41
Licensed drivers, percent distribution and population share by age, 1989, article, 1702–1.306
Licenses issued and in force by age and sex, fees, and renewal, by license class and State, 1990, annual rpt, 7554–16
Revenue, by level of govt, type of tax, State, and selected large county, quarterly rpt, 2462–3
Revenue of State govts by detailed source, and tax rates, by State, FY91, annual rpt, 2466–2.7
State govt revenue by source, spending and debt by function, and holdings, FY91, annual rpt, 2466–2.6
Statistical Abstract of US, 1992 annual data compilation, 2324–1.21
Travel patterns, personal and household characteristics, and auto and public transport use, 1990 survey, series, 7556–6

Driving while intoxicated
Accident deaths involving alcohol, by driver and victim age and blood alcohol levels, weekly rpt, quarterly table, 4202–1
Accident deaths involving alcohol, by driver and victim blood alcohol levels, and other characteristics, 1977-88, annual rpt, 4486–1.12
Accident deaths involving alcohol, by driver and victim blood alcohol levels, and other characteristics, 1977-89, annual rpt, 4486–1.14
Accidents (fatal), alcohol levels of drivers and others involved, by circumstances and characteristics of persons and vehicles, 1990, annual rpt, 7764–16
Accidents (fatal), deaths, and rates, by circumstances, characteristics of persons and vehicles involved, and location, 1990, annual rpt, 7764–10
Accidents, casualties, circumstances, and characteristics of persons and vehicles involved, 1990, annual rpt, 7764–18
Arrests, by offense, offender characteristics, and location, 1991, annual rpt, 6224–2.2
Arrests for drunk driving, sentencing, and prisoner drinking patterns and other characteristics, 1989, 6066–19.69
Boat accidents, casualties, and damage, by cause, vessel and operator characteristics, and State, 1991, annual rpt, 7404–1.2
Boating while intoxicated enforcement cases of Coast Guard, 1st half FY92, semiannual rpt, 7402–4
Costs (direct and indirect) of alcohol abuse, 1985, article, 4482–1.311
Court civil and criminal caseloads for Federal district, appeals, and bankruptcy courts, by type of suit and offense, circuit, and district, 1991, annual rpt, 18204–11
Court civil and criminal caseloads for Federal district, appeals, and special courts, 1991, annual rpt, 18204–8
Crime, criminal justice admin and enforcement, and public opinion, data compilation, 1992 annual rpt, 6064–6
Drunk driving accidents and casualties, by alcohol level, data compilation, 1992 annual rpt, 6064–6.3
Enforcement of DWI laws, incentive grants of Natl Hwy Traffic Safety Admin by State, 1992 press release, 7306–10.4
Health risk behavior, prevalence of 7 habits, by age, State, and other characteristics, 1986-90, article, 4202–7.305
Indian and Alaska Native youth health condition and behavioral patterns, by sex and grade, 1988-90, 4088–3
Indian health risk behavior, by region and for Montana, mid 1980s, article, 4042–3.346
Juvenile arrests, by sex, race, disposition, and offense, 1990, 6066–27.8
Juvenile courts drug and alcohol offenses cases, by disposition and offender age, sex, and race, 1985-88, 6066–27.7
Natl Hwy Traffic Safety Admin activities and grants, and fatal traffic accident data, 1990, annual rpt, 7764–1
Prisoners on probation by offense, and prisoner characteristics, 1990, annual rpt, 6064–26.2
Sentences for Federal offenses, guidelines by offense and circumstances, series, 17668–1
Statistical Abstract of US, 1992 annual data compilation, 2324–1.21
Truck accidents, casualties, and damage, by circumstances and characteristics of persons and vehicles involved, 1989, annual rpt, 7554–9
Truck accidents, circumstances, and characteristics of vehicles and persons involved, 1979-86, 7768–124
Victims of crime, compensation and support service programs funding, by offense and State, FY88-90, biennial rpt, 6064–37
Women in jail, by criminal background and sociodemographic characteristics, with comparisons to men, 1989, 6066–19.66
Youth alcohol use, knowledge, attitudes, and info sources, series, 4006–10

Dropouts
see School dropouts

Drought
Assistance of Reclamation Bur for drought relief, by western State, 1992 press release, 5306–4.17
Farm water supply, crop moisture, and drought indexes, weekly rpt, seasonal data, 2182–7
Farmland damaged by natural disaster, Emergency Conservation Program aid and participation by State, FY91, annual rpt, 1804–22
Foreign countries disasters, casualties, damage, and aid by US and others, FY91 and trends from FY64, annual rpt, 9914–12
Incidents and mgmt of disasters and natl security threats, with data by major event and State, 1992 annual rpt, 9434–6
Timber and orchard damage from natural disaster, USDA restoration aid and program participation by practice and State, FY91, annual rpt, 1804–24
Weather events and anomalies, precipitation and temperature for US and foreign locations, weekly rpt, 2182–6

Drowning
Alaska occupational injury deaths, by cause, occupation, and industry, early 1980s, article, 4042–3.307
Boat registrations, and accidents, casualties, and damage by cause, by vessel characteristics and State, 1991, annual rpt, 7404–1
Diving (underwater) accidents, illnesses, and deaths, by circumstances, diver characteristics, and location, 1970-90, annual rpt, 2144–29
Fire fighter deaths, by cause, circumstances, and location, 1990, annual rpt, 9434–8
Floods in Mississippi River and Gulf of Mexico basins, precipitation and water levels by site, damage, and deaths, 1982-83, 5666–27.33
Foreign countries disasters, casualties, damage, and aid by US and others, FY91 and trends from FY64, annual rpt, 9914–12
Homicides, by circumstance, victim and offender relationship, and type of weapon, 1991, annual rpt, 6224–2.1
PHS Commissioned Corps members deaths, by cause, 1965-89, article, 4042–3.316
Prevention of accidental injury and death, and treatment, 1991 conf papers, 4208–35

Drug abuse and treatment
Abuse of drugs and alcohol, by selected characteristics, 1991 survey, annual rpt series, 4494–5
Abuse of drugs, indicators for selected metro areas, research results, data collection, and policy issues, 1992 semiannual conf, 4492–5
Abuse of drugs, prices, seizures, and supply by country of origin, by substance, 1991, annual rpt, 6284–2
Abuse, treatment, and enforcement issues, series, 236–1; 236–3
ACTION activities and funding, by program, FY91, annual rpt, 9024–2
AIDS cases at VA health care centers by sex, race, risk factor, and facility, and AIDS prevention and treatment issues, quarterly rpt, 8702–1
AIDS cases by risk group, race, sex, age, State, and MSA, and deaths, quarterly rpt, 4202–9
AIDS knowledge, attitudes, and risk behaviors of women in methadone

maintenance programs, effects of life skills training, 1988-89 local area study, article, 4042–3.353
AIDS prevention programs for drug abusers and their sexual partners, client characteristics, and outcomes, for selected metro areas, 1989 annual conf, 4494–12
AIDS virus infection among drug abusers, disease progression longitudinal studies, 1987 conf papers, 4498–79
AIDS virus-related Medicaid claims and payments, by sex, age, risk group, eligibility, and source of care, for Michigan, mid 1980s, article, 4042–3.348
Assistance (financial and nonfinancial) of Fed Govt, 1992 base edition, annual listing, 104–5
Bacterial infections among intravenous drug users, by pre-injection skin cleaning habits, 1988-89 local area study, article, 4042–3.361
Budget of US, obligations and authority by function, agency, and program, with summaries and analyses, FY93, annual rpt, 104–2
Crime, criminal justice admin and enforcement, and public opinion, data compilation, 1992 annual rpt, 6064–6
Crime relationship to drug abuse and trafficking, and enforcement data, series, 6066–29
Criminal case processing in Federal district courts, and dispositions, by offense, district, and offender characteristics, 1989, annual data compilation, 6064–29
Criminal sentences for Federal offenses, guidelines by offense and circumstances, series, 17668–1
DC metro area drug, alcohol, and tobacco use, user characteristics, and consequences, series, 4496–12
Deaths and rates, by cause, age, sex, marital status, race, and State, 1989, US Vital Statistics advance annual rpt, 4146–5.124
Diving (underwater) accidents, illnesses, and deaths, by circumstances, diver characteristics, and location, 1970-90, annual rpt, 2144–29
Education (elementary and secondary) schools, teachers, staff, and enrollment, by selected characteristics, 1987/88-1988/89, 4836–3.10
Education data compilation, 1992 annual rpt, 4824–2
Education data, detail for elementary, secondary, and higher education, 1920s-91 and projected to 2002, annual rpt, 4824–1
Education data, summary trends, 1970s-91, annual pamphlet, 4824–10
Education natl goals progress indicators, by State, 1992, annual rpt, 15914–1
Facilities for drug and alcohol treatment, group home population, for Native American, urban, and metro areas, series, 2531–2
Facilities for drug and alcohol treatment, instnl and group home population by sex, race, county, place, and urban-rural location, 1990 Census of Population, State rpt series, 2531–1
Facilities for mental health, partial care services and patient characteristics, by instn type and State, 1970s-88, 4506–3.51
Fed Govt drug abuse and trafficking reduction programs activities, funding, staff, and Bush Admin budget request, by Federal agency, FY91-93, annual rpt, 234–2
Fed Govt drug abuse and trafficking reduction programs funding, and Bush Admin budget request, by agency, FY91-93, annual rpt, 234–1
Fed Govt drug abuse treatment, prevention, and enforcement grants by State, and State allocations by program, FY87-90, 6068–252
Food stamp recipient household size, composition, income, and income and deductions allowed, summer 1989, annual rpt, 1364–8
Foreign countries drug use and enforcement activities, by country, 1988-92, annual rpt, 7004–17
Health condition and care indicators, 1950s-90 with health improvement and disease prevention goals for 1990, annual data compilation, 4144–11
Hepatitis cases by infection source, age, sex, race, and State, and deaths, by strain, 1989 and trends from 1966, 4205–2
HHS financial aid, by program, recipient, State, and city, FY91, annual regional listings, 4004–3
Homeless persons aid programs of Fed Govt, program descriptions and funding, by agency and State, FY87-91, annual GAO rpt, 26104–21
Homeless persons transitional housing and support services, HUD grants by community, 1991, press release, 5006–3.80
Homeless persons transitional housing and support services program, outcome relation to client characteristics and services, FY87-90, GAO rpt, 26113–549
Homeless youths health conditions and risk behaviors, 1990 local area study, article, 4042–3.344
Hospital deaths of Medicare patients, actual and expected rates by diagnosis, with hospital characteristics, by instn, FY90, annual State rpt series, 4654–14
Housing (public) drug treatment and anticrime programs, HUD grants by recipient, FY91, press release, 5006–3.81
Housing (public) drug treatment and anticrime programs, HUD grants by recipient, FY92, press release, 5006–3.99
Immigrant and nonimmigrant visa applicants refused, and refusals overcome, by reason, FY90, annual rpt, 7184–1.3
Indian and Alaska Native youth health condition and behavioral patterns, by sex and grade, 1988-90, 4088–3
Indian Health Service facilities, funding, operations, and Indian health and other characteristics, 1950s-91, annual chartbook, 4084–1
Insurance (health) coverage and provisions of employee benefit plans, by plan type, for State and local govt employees, 1990, biennial rpt, 6784–21
LSD trafficking, abuse, and enforcement, and DEA field div activities, 1980s-91, 6288–9
Mines drug abuse screening and employee aid programs activities and policies, by mineral and firm size, 1989, 6668–8
Mothers abusing drugs, treatment and other services use, referrals, needs, and barriers, for 13 NIDA-funded programs, 1990/91 survey, 4498–76
Netherlands, Amsterdam drug abuser needle sharing, by selected characteristics, 1989-90 survey, article, 4042–3.369
Parole and probation clients in program for drug- and alcohol-dependent Federal offenders, as of various dates 1987-91, annual rpt, 18204–8.8
Population and labor force characteristics, 1940s-90 and projected to 2000, 15496–1.16
Prevalence of mental illness among adults by diagnosis, and health services use, 1980-83, article, 4042–3.368
Prevention of drug abuse, evaluation of services, methodological issues, 1991 conf, 4498–78
Prison and community-based facilities, population, employment, spending, and other characteristics, by State and for Fed Govt, 1990, annual rpt, 6064–26.3
Prison drug smuggling interdiction, inmate and staff testing, and treatment programs, by instn characteristics, 1989-90, 6066–19.70
Prison treatment units, and clients by age, sex, and race, by State, data compilation, 1992 annual rpt, 6064–6.6
Prisoners and parolees drug abuse treatment and education programs, activities, costs, and outcomes, 1990 conf, 4498–77
Probation population, by offender characteristics, sentence conditions, whether rearrested, and offense, 1986-89, 6066–19.65
Research on drug abuse and trafficking reduction, Natl Inst on Drug Abuse and Office of Justice Programs funding, 1970s-91, GAO rpt, 26131–99
Research on drug abuse and treatment, biological and behavioral factors, and addiction potential of new drugs, 1991 annual conf, 4494–11
Research on drug abuse and treatment, summaries of findings, resource materials, and grant listings, bimonthly rpt, 4492–4
Research on drug abuse services availability, need, use, outcome, costs, funding sources, and cost-effectiveness, series, 4496–11
Schools crime victimization, drug availability, and preventive measures, with student views, 1989 survey, 6066–3.46
Schools drug abuse prevention programs, Education Dept recognition program, 1989/90-1990/91, annual listing, 4814–2
Schools safety, discipline, and student drug use, elementary and secondary school principals views, 1991 survey, 4826–1.32
States criminal justice systems activities, employment, funding, and data collection, by State, 1970s-91, annual rpt, 6064–40
Statistical Abstract of US, 1992 annual data compilation, 2324–1.3; 2324–1.5
Teenage boys AIDS risk behavior, sexual activity, and drug and condom use, 1988, article, 4042–3.313
Treatment facilities for mental health care, staff, patients, and finances, 1970s-91, biennial rpt, 4094–1
Treatment services for drug abuse, costs, effectiveness, and financing issues, 1991 conf papers, 4498–80

VA health care facilities physicians, dentists, and nurses, by selected employment characteristics and VA district, quarterly rpt, 8602–6
Veterans post-traumatic stress cases by period of service, and VA treatment and rehabilitation program operations and staff, by site, FY91, annual rpt, 8704–6
Women arrestees drug abuse history and selected other characteristics, for 4 cities, 1988-89, 6068–246
Women in jail, by criminal background and sociodemographic characteristics, with comparisons to men, 1989, 6066–19.66
Youth drug, alcohol, and cigarette use and attitudes, by substance type and selected characteristics, 1975-91 surveys, press release, 4008–116; 4494–4
Youth health condition, risk factors, and preventive and treatment services use and availability, 1970s-80s, 26358–234.2
see also Alcohol abuse and treatment
see also Cocaine
see also Drug and alcohol testing
see also Drug and narcotics offenses
see also Marijuana

Drug Abuse Warning Network
Emergency room admissions, for selected metro areas, 1992 semiannual conf, 4492–5
LSD trafficking, abuse, and enforcement, and DEA field div activities, 1980s-91, 6288–9

Drug and alcohol testing
Air traffic controller staff and job applicant drug testing, program operations and medical staff views, 1990 survey, technical rpt, 7506–10.115
Airline and aviation safety employees drug testing and results, by drug type and occupational group, 1991, semiannual rpt, 7502–17
Arrests, by offense, offender characteristics, and location, data compilation, 1992 annual rpt, 6064–6.4
Arrests for drug- and nondrug-related offenses, urine test results by drug type, offense, and sex, for selected urban areas, quarterly rpt, 6062–3
Criminal justice systems activities, spending, and employment, by level of govt, data compilation, 1992 annual rpt, 6064–6.1
Criminal justice systems of States, activities, employment, funding, and data collection, by State, 1970s-91, annual rpt, 6064–40
Criminal offenders drug testing, grants and program costs by State, FY92, 236–3.3
Drug abuse indicators for selected metro areas, research results, data collection, and policy issues, 1992 semiannual conf, 4492–5
Drunk driving arrests, sentencing, and prisoner drinking patterns and other characteristics, 1989, 6066–19.69
Ethanol in blood of accident victims, analysis of levels from drinking and postmortem microbial fermentation, 1992 technical rpt, 7506–10.111
Labor laws enacted, by State, 1991, annual article, 6722–1.309
Mines drug abuse screening and employee aid programs activities and policies, by mineral and firm size, 1989, 6668–8
Police and sheriff depts drug enforcement activities, and employee drug testing policies, 1990, 6066–19.67
Police employment, spending, and operations, for State, city, county, and special district agencies, 1990, annual rpt, 6064–39
Prison drug smuggling interdiction, inmate and staff testing, and treatment programs, by instn characteristics, 1989-90, 6066–19.70
Probation population, by offender characteristics, sentence conditions, whether rearrested, and offense, 1986-89, 6066–19.65
Public opinion on employer drug testing, by sex, data compilation, 1992 annual rpt, 6064–6.2
Traffic accident deaths involving alcohol, by driver and victim blood alcohol levels and other characteristics, 1977-88, annual rpt, 4486–1.12; 4486–1.14
Traffic accidents and casualties, alcohol levels of drivers, data compilation, 1992 annual rpt, 6064–6.3
Traffic fatal accidents, alcohol levels of drivers and others, by circumstances and characteristics of persons and vehicles, 1990, annual rpt, 7764–16
Urinalysis methods accuracy, by drug type, 1991, 6068–247
Women arrestees drug abuse history and selected other characteristics, for 4 cities, 1988-89, 6068–246

Drug and narcotics offenses
Abuse of drugs, indicators for selected metro areas, research results, data collection, and policy issues, 1992 semiannual conf, 4492–5
Aliens excluded and deported from US by cause, and Immigration and Naturalization Service narcotics control, FY84-91, annual rpt, 6264–2.5
Arrests and criminal case processing through sentencing, cases and duration by disposition and offense, for selected cities, 1988, annual rpt, 6064–27
Arrests, by offense, offender characteristics, and location, data compilation, 1992 annual rpt, 6064–6.4
Arrests, by offense, offender characteristics, and location, 1991, annual rpt, 6224–2.2
Arrests for drug- and nondrug-related offenses, urine test results by drug type, offense, and sex, for selected urban areas, quarterly rpt, 6062–3
Assaults and deaths of law enforcement officers, by circumstances, agency, victim and offender characteristics, and location, 1991, annual rpt, 6224–3
Coast Guard enforcement activities, 1st half FY92, semiannual rpt, 7402–4
Court civil and criminal caseloads for Federal district, appeals, and bankruptcy courts, by type of suit and offense, circuit, and district, 1991, annual rpt, 18204–11
Court civil and criminal caseloads for Federal district, appeals, and special courts, 1991, annual rpt, 18204–8
Court criminal case processing in Federal district courts, and dispositions, by offense, district, and offender characteristics, 1989, annual data compilation, 6064–29
Court criminal case processing in Federal district courts, and dispositions, by offense, 1980-91, annual rpt, 6064–31
Crime, criminal justice admin and enforcement, and public opinion, data compilation, 1992 annual rpt, 6064–6
Crime relationship to drug abuse and trafficking, and enforcement data, series, 6066–29
Crimes, arrests, and rates, by offense, offender characteristics, population size, and jurisdiction, 1991, annual rpt, 6224–2.1; 6224–2.2
Data on drug offenses, enforcement, and public opinion, summaries of BJS rpts, 1975-90, annual pamphlet, 6064–30
Enforcement, abuse, and treatment issues, series, 236–1; 236–3
Fed Govt drug abuse and trafficking reduction programs activities, funding, staff, and Bush Admin budget request, by Federal agency, FY91-93, annual rpt, 234–2
Fed Govt drug abuse and trafficking reduction programs funding, and Bush Admin budget request, by agency, FY91-93, annual rpt, 234–1
Fed Govt drug abuse treatment, prevention, and enforcement grants by State, and State allocations by program, FY87-90, 6068–252
Fed Govt drug enforcement communications network, funding for equipment and DOD support, FY88-91 and projected to FY87, GAO rpt, 26123–372
Fed Govt drug enforcement grants, and allocations to local govts, by State, FY91, annual rpt, 6064–38
Fed Govt financial and nonfinancial domestic aid, 1992 base edition, annual listing, 104–5
Foreign countries drug production, eradication, and seizures, by illegal substance, with US aid, by country, 1988-92, annual rpt, 7004–17
Foreign countries economic and military aid loans and grants from US and intl agencies, by program and country, FY46-91, annual rpt, 9914–5
Heroin prices and purity in 19 metro areas and Puerto Rico, by world area of origin, quarterly rpt, 6282–2
Heroin seizures by Federal agencies, with NYC street prices and purity, FY82-91, GAO rpt, 26119–404
Heroin trafficking indicators for US, and foreign opium production by country, 1991, annual rpt, 6284–6
Homicides and rate, by weapon, circumstances, and victim characteristics, and years of potential life lost, 1980s, article, 4202–7.315
Homicides, by circumstance, victim and offender relationship, and type of weapon, 1991, annual rpt, 6224–2.1
Housing (public) drug treatment and anticrime programs, HUD grants by recipient, FY91, press release, 5006–3.81
Housing (public) drug treatment and anticrime programs, HUD grants by recipient, FY92, press release, 5006–3.99
Immigrant and nonimmigrant visa applicants refused, and refusals overcome, by reason, FY90, annual rpt, 7184–1.3
Immigration and Naturalization Service illegal alien and narcotics activities, FY84-91, annual rpt, 6264–2.5

Immigration and Naturalization Service illegal alien and narcotics activities, FY91, annual summary rpt, 6264–7
Juvenile arrests, by sex, race, disposition, and offense, 1990, 6066–27.8
Juvenile courts drug and alcohol offenses cases, by disposition and offender age, sex, and race, 1985-88, 6066–27.7
Local areas drug control task forces street-level enforcement activities, impacts on crime, and resident perceptions, studies, 1992 rpt, 6068–251
LSD trafficking, abuse, and enforcement, and DEA field div activities, 1980s-91, 6288–9
Marijuana crop eradication activities of DEA and local agencies by State, and drug potency and prices, 1982-91, annual rpt, 6284–4
Marshals Service activities, FY91, annual rpt, 6294–1
Military drug enforcement activities, funding by purpose, FY89-91, GAO rpt, 26123–390
Natl Guard drug enforcement support, strengths by mission, and assisted seizures and arrests, FY91, annual rpt, 3504–22
Police and sheriff depts drug enforcement activities, and employee drug testing policies, 1990, 6066–19.67
Police employment, spending, and operations, for State, city, county, and special district agencies, 1990, annual rpt, 6064–39
Postal Service inspection activities, 2nd half FY92, semiannual rpt, 9862–2
Prices of illegal drugs by type and selected metro area, and cocaine and heroin purity, quarterly rpt, 6282–1
Prices of illegal drugs by type, stage of processing, and country of origin, 1991, annual rpt, 6284–7
Prison and parole admissions and releases, sentence length, and time served, by offense and offender characteristics, 1988, annual rpt, 6064–33
Prison drug smuggling interdiction, inmate and staff testing, and treatment programs, by instn characteristics, 1989-90, 6066–19.70
Prisoners in Federal and contract instns, by selected characteristics, region, and Federal instn, FY89, annual rpt, 6244–1.1
Prisoners in Federal and State instns by sex, admissions, and instn capacity and overcrowding, by State, 1980s-91, annual rpt, 6066–25.47
Probation population, by offender characteristics, sentence conditions, whether rearrested, and offense, 1986-89, 6066–19.65
Research on drug abuse and trafficking reduction, Natl Inst on Drug Abuse and Office of Justice Programs funding, 1970s-91, GAO rpt, 26131–99
Schools crime victimization, drug availability, and preventive measures, with student views, 1989 survey, 6066–3.46
Seizures of criminal assets, Justice Dept program holdings, finances, and disbursements, FY85-91, annual rpt, 6004–21
Sentences for Federal crimes, guidelines use and results by offense and district, and Sentencing Commission activities, 1991, annual rpt, 17664–1
Sentences for Federal crimes, guidelines use and results by offense, 1984-1990, 6066–19.68
Sentences for Federal offenses, guidelines by offense and circumstances, series, 17668–1
Sentences of drug abuse and trafficking offenders involving Federal benefits loss, by selected characteristics of offenders, 1990-91, GAO rpt, 26119–398
Sentences under Federal mandatory minimum provisions, by defendant characteristics, and views on justice system impacts, FY90, 17668–2
State and local drug enforcement programs, FY91, annual rpt, 6064–32
Statistical Abstract of US, 1992 annual data compilation, 2324–1.5
Supply of drugs in US by country of origin, abuse, prices, and seizures, by substance, 1991, annual rpt, 6284–2
Tax litigation and enforcement activity of IRS, FY91, annual rpt, 8304–3.1
US attorneys civil and criminal cases by type and disposition, and collections, by Federal district, FY91, annual rpt, 6004–2.1; 6004–2.7
Wiretaps authorized, costs, arrests, trials, and convictions, by offense and jurisdiction, 1991, annual rpt, 18204–7
Women arrestees drug abuse history and selected other characteristics, for 4 cities, 1988-89, 6068–246
Women in jail, by criminal background and sociodemographic characteristics, with comparisons to men, 1989, 6066–19.66

Drug Enforcement Administration
Budget of US, obligations and authority by function, agency, and program, with summaries and analyses, FY93, annual rpt, 104–2
Cocaine trafficking in US and foreign countries, with prices and purity, 1988-90, annual rpt, 6284–5
Foreign countries drug enforcement personnel training of US, enrollment in US and host countries by program, FY91, annual rpt, 7004–17
Heroin prices and purity in 19 metro areas and Puerto Rico, by world area of origin, quarterly rpt, 6282–2
Heroin seizures by Federal agencies, with NYC street prices and purity, FY82-91, GAO rpt, 26119–404
Heroin trafficking indicators for US, and foreign opium production by country, 1991, annual rpt, 6284–6
LSD trafficking, abuse, and enforcement, and DEA field div activities, 1980s-91, 6288–9
Marijuana crop eradication activities of DEA and local agencies by State, and drug potency and prices, 1982-91, annual rpt, 6284–4
Prices of illegal drugs by type and selected metro area, and cocaine and heroin purity, quarterly rpt, 6282–1
Prices of illegal drugs by type, stage of processing, and country of origin, 1991, annual rpt, 6284–7
Supply of drugs in US by country of origin, abuse, prices, and seizures, by substance, 1991, annual rpt, 6284–2

Drug industry
see Pharmaceutical industry

Drug Use Forecasting System
Drug test results at arrest, by drug type, offense, and sex, for selected urban areas, quarterly rpt, 6062–3

Drugs
Advertising of prescription drugs in medical journals, accuracy, info completeness, and violations of FDA regulations, 1990, 4008–119
AIDS and tuberculosis cases in prisons, test results, and control and treatment policies, by location, 1990 survey, annual rpt, 6064–22
AIDS patients costs and service use under Medicaid, and service needs, for New Jersey waiver program, 1987-89, article, 4652–1.317
AIDS patients costs and service use under Medicaid, for California, 1984-86, article, 4652–1.301
Antihypertensive drugs impacts on pilot performance, 1992 technical rpt, 7506–10.119
Board and care home violations of State drug handling and dispensing regulations, for 3 metro areas, 1990-91, GAO rpt, 26121–447
Cancer (colon) risk relation to diet, aspirin use, exercise, and other factors, 1982-88, article, 4472–1.346
Carcinogens chemistry, sources, environment and health risks, and regulation, by substance and brand, 1991 annual rpt, 4044–15
Child infectious disease cases, and related disability and health care, by disease, health insurance status, and other characteristics, 1988, 4147–10.181
Consumer spending, natl income and product account benchmark revisions, 1929-88, 2708–5
Consumer spending, natl income and product accounts, comprehensive accounts and components, *Survey of Current Business*, monthly rpt, 2702–1.25
CPI by component for US city average, and by selected metro area, region, and population size, monthly rpt, 6762–2
Diabetes patients physician office visits, by characteristics of patient, physician, and visit, 1989, 4146–8.212
Diuretics use during pregnancy, weight gain, and other maternal health behaviors, by age, race, and poverty status, 1988, 4478–197
Diving (underwater) accidents, illnesses, and deaths, by circumstances, diver characteristics, and location, 1970-90, annual rpt, 2144–29
Expenditures for health care by funding source, 1990, with trends and indexes by service type from 1960, article, 4652–1.323
Exports and imports (agricultural) of US, by commodity and country, bimonthly rpt, 1522–1
Exports and imports (agricultural) of US, by detailed commodity and country, 1991, semiannual rpt, 1522–4
Exports and imports between US and outlying areas, by detailed commodity and mode of transport, 1991, annual rpt, 2424–11

Exports and imports of US, by Harmonized System 6-digit commodity and country, 1991, annual rpt, 2424–13
Exports and imports of US, by selected country, country group, and commodity group, 1991, annual rpt, 2044–37
Exports and imports of US, by transport mode, country, and SITC 1- to 3-digit commodity, 1991, annual rpt, 2424–12
Exports, imports, and balances of US for manufactured goods, by SITC 2-digit commodity and country, quarterly rpt, 2042–35
Exports of US, detailed Schedule B commodities with countries of destination, 1991, annual rpt, 2424–10
FDA regulations dev timeliness, with status and processing time for selected regulations, 1991, GAO rpt, 26121–453
Freight (waterborne domestic and foreign) by commodity, traffic, and passengers, by port and waterway, 1989, annual rpt, 3754–3
Health Care Financing Review, provider prices, price inputs and indexes, and labor, quarterly journal, 4652–1.1
Health condition and care indicators, 1950s-90 with health improvement and disease prevention goals for 1990, annual data compilation, 4144–11
HHS financial aid, by program, recipient, State, and city, FY91, annual regional listings, 4004–3
Home drug infusion therapy use, equipment, industry finances, and Medicare coverage options, 1992 rpt, 26358–258
Hypertension cases, stroke and heart disease risk, and drug dosages, with diagnosis and treatment methods, 1992 quadrennial rpt, 4478–198
Imports detained by FDA, by reason, product, shipper, brand, and country, monthly listing, 4062–2
Indian Health Service outpatient services provided, by reason for visit and age, FY90, annual rpt, 4084–2
Input-output structure of US economy, detailed interindustry transactions for 84 industries, and components of final demand, 1987, annual article, 2702–1.316
Input-output structure of US economy, detailed interindustry transactions for 541 industries, and components of final demand, 1982 benchmark data, 2708–17
Insurance (health) coverage and provisions of employee benefit plans, by plan type, for State and local govt employees, 1990, biennial rpt, 6784–21
Internist office visits, by characteristics of patient, physician, and visit, 1989, 4146–8.214
Manufacturing annual survey, 1990: value of shipments, by SIC 4- to 5-digit product class, 2506–14.1
Marketing applications for drugs, FDA processing by drug, purpose, and producer, 1991, annual rpt, 4064–14
Medicaid beneficiaries and payments, by service type, FY72-90, annual rpt, 4744–3.6
Medicaid coverage, funding, and costs, with reform recommendations, mid 1960s-92, 10048–83
Medicaid outlay differentials among States, with data by service type and eligibility category, FY89, article, 9373–1.303
Medicare and Medicaid beneficiaries and program operations, 1992, annual fact book, 4654–18
Mental health care facilities, staff, patients, and finances, 1970s-91, biennial rpt, 4094–1
Mental health care of affective disorder patients, by patient and facility characteristics, 1986, 4506–3.49
Mental illness (serious) among adults, functional limitations, govt aid, drugs used, visits to professionals, and other characteristics, 1989, 4146–8.220
Mental illness biological factors, with cases, research funding, and treatment methods, for major disorders, 1980s-91, 26356–9.4
Multinatl US firms and foreign affiliates finances and operations, by industry and country, 1989 benchmark survey, annual rpt, 2704–5
OECD trade, total and for 4 major countries, and US trade by country, by commodity, 1980-90, world area rpt series, 9116–1
Older persons health education centers medication mgmt and other preventive health activities, and Federal funding, FY83-91, article, 4042–3.303
Orphan drug tax credit, corporate income tax returns by asset size and detailed industry, 1989, annual rpt, 8304–4; 8304–21
Orphan drug tax credit, corporate income tax returns, quarterly rpt, 8302–2.1
Otitis media patients physician office visits, by specialty and characteristics of patient and visit, 1975-90, 4146–8.217
Pediatrician office visits, by characteristics of patient and visit, 1989, 4146–8.210
Physicians visits, by patient and practice characteristics, diagnosis, and services provided, 1989, annual rpt, 4147–13.109
Physicians visits, by patient and practice characteristics, diagnosis, and services provided, 1990, advance rpt, 4146–8.215
Prescription drug prices in US and other countries, industry profits, and R&D and marketing spending, 1980s-91 and projected to 2000, 25148–44
Price indexes (producer), by stage of processing and detailed commodity, monthly rpt, 6762–6
Price indexes (producer), by stage of processing and detailed commodity, monthly 1991, annual rpt, 6764–2
Prices (wholesale) of prescription drugs in Canada and US, by brand and vendor, 1991, GAO rpt, 26121–482
Prices of prescription drugs prices charged to VA and Fed Govt, by manufacturer and drug, 1990-91, hearing, 21768–68
Prices of prescription drugs prices charged to wholesalers, retailers, VA, and Fed Govt, for 29 drugs, 1985-91, GAO rpt, 26121–472
Production and sales of synthetic organic chemicals, and manufacturer listing, by product, 1990, annual rpt, 9884–3
Production of synthetic organic chemicals, by detailed product, quarterly rpt, 9882–1
Regulatory and investigation activities of FDA, quarterly rpt, 4062–3
Reproduction and population research, Fed Govt funding by project, FY90, annual listing, 4474–9
Shipments, trade, and use of drugs, by product, 1991, annual Current Industrial Rpt, 2506–8.5
Stockpiling of strategic material by Fed Govt, activity, and inventory by commodity, as of Sept 1991, semiannual rpt, 3542–22
Stockpiling of strategic material, inventories and needs, by commodity, 1992, annual rpt, 3544–37
Tariff Schedule of US, classifications for pharmaceutical and intermediate chemical products, 1992 rpt, 9886–4.185
Tax (income) returns of individuals, detailed data, 1988, annual rpt, 8304–2
Veterans post-traumatic stress cases by period of service, and VA treatment and rehabilitation program operations and staff, by site, FY91, annual rpt, 8704–6
Women's representation in clinical drug trials, and FDA policy guidance, 1988-91, GAO rpt, 26121–486
see also Biologic drug products
see also Chemotherapy
see also Cocaine
see also Drug abuse and treatment
see also Drug and alcohol testing
see also Drug and narcotics offenses
see also Drugstores
see also Hormones
see also Marijuana
see also Pharmaceutical industry
see also Poisoning and drug reaction
see also Vaccination and vaccines
see also under By Commodity in the "Index by Categories"

Drugstores
Business statistics, detailed data for major industries and economic indicators, 1960-91, *Survey of Current Business* biennial supplement, 2704–1
County Business Patterns, 1989: employment, establishments, and payroll, by SIC 2- to 4-digit industry and county, annual State rpt series, 2326–8
County Business Patterns, 1990: employment, establishments, and payroll, by SIC 2- to 4-digit industry and county, annual State rpt series, 2326–6
Employment, earnings, and hours, by SIC 1- to 4-digit industry, monthly 1989-Feb 1992, annual rpt, 6744–4
Employment of minorities and women, by occupation, SIC 1- to 3-digit industry, State, and MSA, 1991, annual rpt, 9244–1
Labor productivity, indexes of output, hours, and employment by SIC 2- to 4-digit industry, 1967-90, annual rpt, 6824–1.4
Occupational injury and illness rates, by SIC 2- to 4-digit industry, 1989-90, annual rpt, 6844–7
Occupational injury and illness rates, by SIC 2- to 4-digit industry, 1990, annual rpt, 6844–1
Sales and inventories, by kind of retail business, region, and selected State, MSA, and city, monthly rpt, 2413–3
Sales, inventories, purchases, gross margin, and accounts receivable, by SIC 2- to 4-digit kind of business and form of ownership, 1990, annual rpt, 2413–5

Sales of retailers, by kind of business, advance monthly rpt, 2413–2
Tax (income) returns of corporations, income and tax items by asset size and detailed industry, 1989, annual rpt, 8304–4; 8304–21
Tax (income) returns of sole proprietorships, income statement items, by industry group, 1990, annual article, 8302–2.317; 8302–2.320

Drunk drivers
see Driving while intoxicated

Drunkenness
see Alcohol abuse and treatment

Drury, Thomas F.
"Inventory of Pain Data from the National Center for Health Statistics. Vital and Health Statistics Series 1", 4147–1.27

Du Page County, Ill.
Housing and households characteristics, and unit and neighborhood quality, by MSA location for 11 MSAs, 1987 survey, supplement, 2485–8

Dubai
see United Arab Emirates

Dubin, Elliott J.
"Medicaid Intergovernmental Trends and Options", 10048–83

Duca, John V.
"Case of the Missing M2", 9379–1.303; 9379–12.83
"Effects of Credit Availability, Nonbank Competition, and Tax Reform on Bank Consumer Lending", 9379–12.88

Duck stamps
see Hunting and fishing licenses

Due process of law
Court civil and criminal caseloads for Federal district, appeals, and special courts, 1991, annual rpt, 18204–8
Felony case processing from arrest to sentencing, cases and duration by disposition and offense, for selected cities, 1988, annual rpt, 6064–27
Foreign countries human rights conditions in 170 countries, 1991, annual rpt, 21384–3
US attorneys civil and criminal cases by type and disposition, and collections, by Federal district, FY91, annual rpt, 6004–2.1; 6004–2.7
see also Civil procedure
see also Criminal procedure

Dueker, Michael J.
"Response of Market Interest Rates to Discount Rate Changes", 9391–1.314

Duewer, Lawrence A.
"Nation's Changing Beef Cow Herd", 1561–7.301

Duffield, James
"Testing for Impacts of Immigration Reform on Farm Employment and Wages", 1561–16.304

Duggan, James E.
"Social Security and the Public Debt", 8006–6.6
"Some Economic Aspects of the U.S. Health Care System", 8006–6.1

Duke, John
"Multifactor Productivity in Railroad Transportation", 6722–1.337

Dumas, Mark W.
"Productivity Trends: Prepared Fish and Seafoods Industry", 6722–1.342

Dumping
Communist and transitional economy countries imports of US, status of dumping investigations by product, quarterly rpt with articles, 9882–2
Electronics and services trade, tariffs, and industry operating data, commodity rpt series, 9885–12
Export and import agreements, negotiations, and related legislation, 1991, annual rpt, 444–1
Import restrictions and trade protectionism measures of US, Australia, Canada, and EC, cases initiated, 1980-85, article, 9379–1.301
Imports injury to US industries from foreign subsidized products and sales at less than fair value, investigations with background financial and operating data, series, 9886–19
Imports injury to US industries from foreign subsidized products, investigations with background financial and operating data, series, 9886–15
Imports injury to US industries from sales at less than fair value, investigations with background financial and operating data, series, 9886–14
Minerals and metals trade, tariffs, and industry operating data, commodity rpt series, 9885–13
USITC activities, investigations, and rpts, FY91, annual rpt, 9884–1
see also Trade adjustment assistance

Dumps
see Landfills

Duncan, Douglas G.
"Agricultural Bank Credit Outlook", 1504–9.1
"Bank Reform?", 1541–1.310

Dunham, Denis
"Food Cost Review, 1991", 1544–9

Dunham, Rex A.
"Outlook for Genetics Research and Application in Aquaculture", 1504–9.1

Dunlop, George S.
"Public Policy Issues That Challenge the Fresh Fruit and Vegetable Industry for 1992", 1504–9.1

Dunworth, Terence
"State Strategic Planning Under the Drug Formula Grant Program", 6068–252

Dupont, Jacqueline
"Nutrient Content of Foods Important to Health", 1504–9.1

Durst, Ron
"IRS Estimates of the Aggregate Net Farm Profit (Loss) of Farm Sole Proprietors", 1541–1.320

Duties
see Tariffs and foreign trade controls

Dyck, John
"Future of Agriculture and Trade in the Pacific: An Overview", 1524–4.3

Dyckman, Zachary
"Physician Cost Experience Under Private Health Insurance Programs", 4652–1.320

Dyeing and coloring materials
County Business Patterns, 1989: employment, establishments, and payroll, by SIC 2- to 4-digit industry and county, annual State rpt series, 2326–8
County Business Patterns, 1990: employment, establishments, and payroll, by SIC 2- to 4-digit industry and county, annual State rpt series, 2326–6
Exports and imports of US, by Harmonized System 6-digit commodity and country, 1991, annual rpt, 2424–13
Exports and imports of US, by transport mode, country, and SITC 1- to 3-digit commodity, 1991, annual rpt, 2424–12
Exports, imports, tariffs, and industry operating data for paints and inks, 1992 rpt, 9885–11.3
Exports of US, detailed Schedule B commodities with countries of destination, 1991, annual rpt, 2424–10
Manufacturing annual survey, 1990: finances and operations, by SIC 2- to 4-digit industry, series, 2506–14
Manufacturing census, 1987: concentration of largest firms measured by value added, and for shipments by SIC 2- and 4-digit industry, subject rpt, 2497–6
Manufacturing census, 1987: shipments of manufacturers products, by customer class and SIC 2- and 4-digit industry, subject rpt, 2497–4
Manufacturing finances and operations, by SIC 2- to 4-digit industry, forecast 1992, annual rpt, 2044–28
Occupational injury and illness rates, by SIC 2- to 4-digit industry, 1989-90, annual rpt, 6844–7
Occupational injury and illness rates, by SIC 2- to 4-digit industry, 1990, annual rpt, 6844–1
Price indexes (producer), by stage of processing and detailed commodity, monthly 1991, annual rpt, 6764–2
Production and sales of synthetic organic chemicals, and manufacturer listing, by product, 1990, annual rpt, 9884–3
Production of synthetic organic chemicals, by detailed product, quarterly rpt, 9882–1
Shipments, trade, and use of paint and related products, quarterly Current Industrial Rpt, 2506–8.4
Sulfur dyes from 3 countries at less than fair value, injury to US industry, investigation with background financial and operating data, 1992 rpt, 9886–14.347

Dykacz, Janice M.
"Comparison of Individual Characteristics and Death Rates of Disabled-Worker Beneficiaries Entitled in 1972 and 1985", 4742–1.321

D2 Associates
"Southeastern Regional Biomass Energy Program. Six Year Report: 1983-89", 9806–9.11

Ear diseases and infections
Cases of acute and chronic conditions, disability, absenteeism, and health services use, by selected characteristics, 1990, annual rpt, 4147–10.182; 4147–10.183
Child infectious disease cases, and related disability and health care, by disease, health insurance status, and other characteristics, 1988, 4147–10.181
OECD members health care costs, hospital use, resources, and economic and health indicators, by country, 1960s-90, article, 4652–1.322
Otitis media patients physician office visits, by specialty and characteristics of patient and visit, 1975-90, 4146–8.217

Earls, Felton
"Prevention of Violence and Injuries Due to Violence", 4208–35
Earned income tax credit
see Tax incentives and shelters
Earnings, general
AFDC beneficiaries demographic and financial characteristics, by State, FY90, annual rpt, 4584–7
Age of workers relation to wages and productivity, by sex and occupation, model description and results, 1991 working paper, 9377–9.128
Apprenticeship programs regulation, participation of minorities and women, and earnings, by occupation, 1990, GAO rpt, 26121–446
Asian and Pacific Islands Americans social and economic characteristics, for West and total US, 1990-91, Current Population Report, 2546–1.462
Black Americans social and economic characteristics, for South and total US, 1991 and trends from 1950, annual Current Population Rpt, 2546–1.463
Black women's labor force status, earnings, and other economic status indicators, and compared to whites, various periods 1939-88, 11048–191
BLS data collection, analysis, and presentation methods, by program, 1992 rpt, 6888–1
Building materials industry finances and operations, by SIC 4-digit industry, selected years 1977-89, article, 2042–1.302
Business cycle relation to earnings, 1960s-80s, article, 9377–1.304
Business statistics, detailed data for major industries and economic indicators, 1960-91, *Survey of Current Business* biennial supplement, 2704–1
Child care arrangements of younger working mothers, and costs, by selected characteristics, 1988, 6726–2.1
Child support payment and visitation practices of absent fathers, and mothers with custody, by employment and other characteristics, 1988, article, 6722–1.329
Collective bargaining contract expirations, wage increases, and coverage, by major industry group, 1991, annual article, 6722–1.306
Collective bargaining wage and benefit changes, by industry div, monthly rpt, 6782–1
Collective bargaining wage and benefit changes, quarterly press release, 6782–2
Collective bargaining wage changes and coverage, by industry and whether contract includes escalator clause and lump sum payment, 1982-91, annual article, 6722–1.325
College grads labor force status, job degree requirements, and earnings, with data by occupation, 1960s-90, article, 6722–1.330
Data on labor turnover, job openings, and new hires and wages, pilot survey results, costs, and methodology, 1990-91, 6728–40
Disabled persons rehabilitation, Federal and State activities and funding, FY90, annual rpt, 4944–1
Disabled persons work history before and after SSI application, by age, diagnosis, industry div, and sex, aggregate 1937-87, article, 4742–1.308
Displaced workers losing job 1987-92, labor force status by employment and other characteristics, as of Jan 1992, biennial press release, 6726–1.48
Distribution and equity of income, tax, and transfer payments, analyses and alternative estimates, series, 4746–14
Distribution of earnings among and within selected groups, by demographic and employment characteristics, late 1960s-80s, article, 6722–1.328
Earnings and hours of production or nonsupervisory workers on nonagricultural payrolls, monthly rpt, 6742–2.6
Earnings by industry group, region, and State, 1989-91, annual article, 2702–1.328
Earnings, employment, and hours, and other BLS economic indicators, transcripts of BLS Commissioner's monthly testimony, periodic rpt, 23846–4
Earnings, employment, and hours, monthly press release, 6742–5
Earnings, employment, hours, and productivity, by industry div, selected years 1929-91, annual rpt, 204–1.2
Economic indicators and components, and Fed Reserve 4th District business and financial conditions, monthly chartbook, 9377–10
Economic indicators and components, current data and annual trends, monthly rpt, 23842–1.2
Economic indicators, prices, labor costs, and productivity, BLS econometric analyses and methodology, working paper series, 6886–6
Education data, detail for elementary, secondary, and higher education, 1920s-91 and projected to 2002, annual rpt, 4824–1
Educational attainment, by social and demographic characteristics and location, 1991 and trends from 1940, biennial Current Population Rpt, 2546–1.460
Employment, earnings, and hours, by selected SIC 1- to 4-digit industry, State, and for 275 MSAs, 1987-92, 6748–81
Employment, earnings, and hours, by SIC 1- to 4-digit industry, monthly 1989-Feb 1992, annual rpt, 6744–4
Executive officers and board members pay, bonuses, and performance indicators, by company, 1991 hearing, 25248–130
Family members labor force status and earnings, by family composition and race, quarterly press release, 6742–21
Food stamp eligibility and payment errors, by type, recipient characteristics, and State, FY90, annual rpt, 1364–15
Food stamp recipient household size, composition, income, and income and deductions allowed, summer 1989, annual rpt, 1364–8
Forecasts of economic conditions and employment, alternative BLS projections to 2005 and trends 1975-90, biennial rpt, 6744–19
Foreign direct investment by method and industry div, and affiliated firms R&D spending, pay, employment, and trade compared to US-owned firms, 1980-90, article, 9391–1.309
High school class of 1972: community college attendance, by selected characteristics, natl longitudinal study, 1970s-86, 4888–7
Higher education grads and advanced degree recipients, average salaries by field, 1992 edition, annual rpt, 4824–2.28
Households composition, income, benefits, and labor force status, Survey of Income and Program Participation methodology, working paper series, 2626–10
Housing (rental) units, total, with HUD assistance by program, and eligible for aid, by unit, household, and neighborhood characteristics, and location, 1989, biennial rpt, 5184–11
Hwy scenic routes impacts on local economic conditions, by State, county, and selected byway, late 1980s, 7556–8.1
Immigrants earnings relative to general population, selected factors, 1992 technical paper, 9385–8.143
Immigration reform provisions for alien legalization and employer sanctions, wage impacts, model results, 1987-89, working paper, 6366–6.8
Imports and tariff provisions effect on US industries and products, investigations with background financial and operating data, series, 9886–4
Imports injury to US industries from foreign subsidized products and sales at less than fair value, investigations with background financial and operating data, series, 9886–19
Imports injury to US industries from foreign subsidized products, investigations with background financial and operating data, series, 9886–15
Imports injury to US industries from sales at less than fair value, investigations with background financial and operating data, series, 9886–14
Income (household, family, and personal), by source, detailed characteristics, and region, 1991, annual Current Population Rpt, 2546–6.76
Income (personal) per capita and by source, and employment, by industry div, State, MSA, and county, 1969-90, annual CD-ROM, 2704–7
Income (personal) per capita, by region compared to total US, alternative model results, 1929-87, working paper, 9387–8.257
Income tax returns of foreign corporations and individuals, and US entities abroad, detailed data compilation, 1970s-89, quinquennial rpt, 8308–31
Industry finances and operations, by SIC 2- to 4-digit industry, forecast 1992, annual rpt, 2044–28
Input-output structure of US economy, detailed interindustry transactions for 541 industries, and components of final demand, 1982 benchmark data, 2708–17
Labor force, wages, hours, and payroll costs, by major industry group and demographic characteristics, *Survey of Current Business*, monthly rpt, 2702–1.7
Labor laws enacted, by State, 1991, annual article, 6722–1.309
Labor productivity relation to wages, model description and results, late 1940s-90, working paper, 9393–10.20
Manufacturing annual survey, 1990: establishments, employment, finances, inventories, and energy use, by SIC 2- to 4-digit industry, 2506–14.2

Manufacturing census, 1987: concentration of largest firms measured by value added, and for shipments by SIC 2- and 4-digit industry, subject rpt, 2497–6
Monthly Labor Review, current statistics and articles, 6722–1
Multinatl US firms and foreign affiliates finances and operations, by industry and country, 1989 benchmark survey, annual rpt, 2704–5
Natl income and product accounts and components, *Survey of Current Business*, monthly rpt, 2702–1.23
Natl income and product accounts benchmark revisions of GDP and natl income, various periods 1959-80, tables, 2702–1.307
Natl income and product accounts, comprehensive accounts and components, benchmark revisions, 1929-88, 2708–5
Natl income and product accounts, comprehensive accounts and components, *Survey of Current Business*, monthly rpt, 2702–1.29
OASDHI coverage of employment and earnings, and social security contributions, by age, sex, race, State, and county, 1988, annual rpt, 4744–29
OASDHI coverage of employment and earnings, late 1930s-90, annual rpt, 4744–3.1; 4744–3.2; 4744–3.3
OASDI benefit determination, methodology for calculating average wage, with background data, mid 1970s-92, 4706–2.133
OASI benefits, earnings, and tax revenues under alternative eligibility criteria, 1990, technical paper, 4746–26.15
Occupational Outlook Handbook, 1992-93, biennial rpt, 6744–1
Occupational Outlook Quarterly, journal, 6742–1
Older persons and younger adults household income, by source, household composition, and age group, 1984 and 1989, article, 4742–1.304
Older persons and younger adults household income, by source, household composition, race, and age group, 1984-89, 4746–26.20
Older persons earnings impacts of 1983 OASI earnings test repeal, 1970-85, technical paper, 4746–26.13
Older persons income and sources, by OASDI beneficiary and poverty status, and other characteristics, 1990, biennial chartbook, 4744–25
Older persons income and sources, by whether OASDI beneficiary, poverty status, and other characteristics, 1990, biennial rpt, 4744–26
Older persons income by source, for married OASI beneficiaries by work and eligibility pattern of wife, 1982, article, 4746–26.12
Older persons socioeconomic characteristics, 1900s-90 and projected to 2050, biennial chartbook, 12904–1
Pacific territories population and housing detailed characteristics, by location, 1990 Census of Population and Housing, series, 2551–8
Population and labor force characteristics, 1940s-90 and projected to 2000, 15496–1.16
Poverty relation to low earnings, by work experience during year, household relationship, sex, race, age, and education, 1960s-90, Current Population Rpt, 2546–6.74
Poverty status of families, by detailed characteristics, 1980 and 1988, GAO rpt, 26131–102
Poverty status of population and families, by detailed characteristics, 1991, annual Current Population Rpt, 2546–6.77
Rural areas economic and social conditions, dev, and problems, periodic journal, 1502–7
Rural areas economic conditions and dev, quarterly journal, 1502–8
Rural areas employment and population characteristics, and role of education and training in economic dev, 1960s-80s, compilation of papers, 1598–277
Science and engineering employment characteristics of minorities, women, and disabled, by field, 1970s-91, biennial rpt, 9624–20.1
Science and engineering labor force, Federal and university research funding, and educational data, series, 9626–6
SSA and IRS reconciliation of employer wage report records, late 1970s-80s, GAO rpt, 26121–477
Statistical Abstract of US, 1992 annual data compilation, 2324–1.13; 2324–1.27
Student aid Pell grants and applicants, by tuition, income level, instn type and control, and State, 1990/91, annual rpt, 4804–1
Survey of Current Business, detailed financial and business data, and economic indicators, monthly rpt, 2702–1.3
Survey of Current Business, earnings and compensation indexes, monthly rpt, 2702–1.1
Tax (income) returns filed, by type of filer, selected income items, quarterly rpt, 8302–2.1
Tax (income) returns of individuals, by filing status, tax item, and income level, 1991, annual article, 8302–2.319
Tax (income) returns of individuals, detailed data, 1988, annual rpt, 8304–2
Tax (income) returns of individuals, selected income and tax items by income level, preliminary 1990, annual article, 8302–2.307
Tax (income) returns of individuals with foreign earned income, income and tax items by income level and occupation, 1987, article, 8302–2.301
Travel-related industries employment and receipts, for businesses near Blue Ridge Parkway, 1987, 7556–8.4
Unemployed displaced workers job search and placement aid effectiveness, relation to previous employment and other characteristics, 1979-87 studies, 15496–1.14
Unemployed persons finding work, by characteristics of worker and new job, aggregate 1986-89, 2546–20.20
Unemployed persons finding work by industry div, and earnings, by sector and sex, aggregate 1987-89, fact sheet, 2326–17.47
Unemployment insurance coverage of wages, by industry div, State, and MSA, 1990-91, annual press releases, 6784–17
Unemployment insurance programs of States and Fed Govt, benefits adequacy, and work disincentives, series, 6406–6
Unemployment insurance programs of States, benefits, coverage, exhaustions, and finances, 1990, annual tables, 6404–10
Union coverage of workers and earnings, by age, sex, race, occupational group, and industry div, 1990-91, annual press release, 6726–1.44
Veterans (Vietnam) labor force status and earnings, by whether served in Southeast Asia, presence and severity of disability, and selected other characteristics, 1989, article, 6722–1.326
Wage differentials among cities related to city size and worker characteristics, 1977-88, article, 9377–1.301
Wage differentials relation to worker occupation and employer, model description and results, 1991 working paper, 9377–9.130
Wage inequalities among income classes, regional and other factors, late 1970s-80s, article, 9379–1.307
Wages, hourly and weekly averages by industry div, monthly press release, 6742–3
Wages of full- and part-time workers, by selected characteristics, quarterly press release, 6742–20
White collar wages in private industry, by occupation and salary level, 1991, 6787–6.254
Women's labor force status and characteristics, 1960s-90, chartbook, 6748–85
Women's labor force status, earnings, and other characteristics, with comparisons to men, fact sheet series, 6564–1
Women's training on job, duration, costs, and impacts on gender differences in wages, model description and results, 1992 working paper, 6886–6.93
see also Agricultural wages
see also Area wage surveys
see also Earnings, local and regional
see also Earnings, specific industry
see also Educational employees pay
see also Employee benefits
see also Employee bonuses and work incentives
see also Employee ownership
see also Escalator clauses
see also Farm income
see also Federal pay
see also Foreign labor conditions
see also Government pay
see also Industry wage surveys
see also Labor costs and cost indexes
see also Military pay
see also Minimum wage
see also Payroll
see also Professionals' fees
see also State and local employees pay
see also Tips and tipping
see also Wage deductions

Earnings, local and regional
Appalachia food processing firms, employment, and shipments, and farm production, by commodity and State, 1960s-90, 9088–37
Dallas-Fort Worth metro area employment, earnings, hours, and CPI changes, late 1970s-91, annual rpt, 6964–2

Houston metro area employment, earnings, hours, and CPI changes, 1970s-91, annual rpt, 6964–1
Los Angeles wages and working conditions impacts of Immigration Reform and Control Act, 1980s-91, working paper, 6366–6.9
New England States economic indicators, Fed Reserve 1st District, monthly rpt, 9373–2
New England States employment growth after recessions, relation to selected economic factors, various periods 1969-90, article, 9373–1.315
North Central States business and economic conditions, Fed Reserve 9th District, quarterly journal, 9383–19
Southeastern US high technology employment and pay, by industry and State, 1990, press release, 6946–3.23
Southeastern US manufacturing hours and earnings, for 8 States, quarterly press release, 6942–7
Southwestern US employment by industry div, earnings, and hours, by State, monthly rpt, 6962–2
Washington and Oregon coastal areas tourism and recreation facilities and economic impacts, by county, 1983-88, 5738–40.3
see also Area wage surveys
see also under By Census Division, By City, By County, By Region, By SMSA or MSA, and By State in the "Index by Categories"

Earnings, specific industry
Auto and auto parts trade, production, and labor conditions, for US and compared to Canada and Mexico, 1950s-90, 6366–3.28
Construction employment, earnings, and hours, by selected SIC 2- to 3-digit industry, quarterly rpt, 2042–1.7
Food marketing sector hourly and weekly earnings, selected years 1963-90, annual rpt, 1544–22.3
Food prices (farm-retail), marketing cost components, and industry finances and productivity, 1960s-91, annual rpt, 1544–9.3
Food processing firms, employment, and shipments, and farm production, by commodity and State, for Appalachia, 1960s-90, 9088–37
Health Care Financing Review, provider prices, price inputs and indexes, and labor, quarterly journal, 4652–1.1
Minerals production, prices, trade, use, employment, tariffs, and stockpiles, by mineral, with foreign comparisons, 1987-91, annual rpt, 5604–18
Petrochemicals industries contract labor accidents, injuries, safety programs operations, and employee characteristics, 1986-91, 6608–6
Physicians income, practice revenue, hours worked, and malpractice insurance premiums paid, late 1970s-90, technical paper, 9366–6.296
Railroad employment and compensation, by age, sex, occupation, and years of service, 1985, annual rpt, 9704–2.4
Railroad employment, earnings, and hours, by occupation for Class I railroads, 1991, annual table, 9484–5
Textile mill employment, earnings, and hours, for 8 Southeastern States, quarterly press release, 6942–1
Timber industry impacts of northern spotted owl conservation methods in Pacific Northwest, and Federal and State spending, 1980s-95, 1208–388
Vending facilities run by blind on Federal and non-Federal property, finances and operations by agency and State, FY91, annual rpt, 4944–2
see also Agricultural wages
see also Educational employees pay
see also Farm income
see also Federal pay
see also Government pay
see also Industry wage surveys
see also Military pay
see also Payroll
see also State and local employees pay
see also under By Industry in the "Index by Categories"

Earth sciences
DOE R&D projects and funding at natl labs, universities, and other instns, FY91, annual summary rpt, 3004–18.1
Fed Govt aid to higher education and nonprofit instns for R&D and related activities, by field, instn, agency, and State, FY90, annual rpt, 9627–17
Higher education grad programs enrollment in science and engineering, by field, source of funds, and characteristics of student and instn, 1990, annual rpt, 9627–7
Military budget, manpower needs, costs, and force readiness by service branch, FY93, annual rpt, 3504–1
NASA project launch schedules and technical descriptions, press release series, 9506–2
NASA R&D funding to higher education instns, by field, instn, and State, FY91, annual listing, 9504–7
R&D funding by higher education instns and federally funded centers, by field, instn, and State, FY90, annual rpt, 9627–13
Science and Engineering Indicators, employment, education, R&D funding, and industry impacts, with foreign comparisons, 1960s-91, biennial rpt, 9624–10
see also Geography
see also Geology
see also Hydrology
see also Oceanography

Earthquakes
Alaska minerals resources and geologic characteristics, compilation of papers, 1990, annual rpt, 5664–15
Alaska OCS environmental conditions and oil dev impacts, compilation of papers, series, 2176–1
Fed Govt buildings and employees earthquake risk by agency and region, 1989, with location and size of major events from 1600s, GAO rpt, 26119–399
Foreign countries disasters, casualties, damage, and aid by US and others, FY91 and trends from FY64, annual rpt, 9914–12
Incidents and mgmt of disasters and natl security threats, with data by major event and State, 1992 annual rpt, 9434–6
Intensity of ground motion by station, 1990, annual rpt, 5664–14
Minerals offshore lease sales environmental and economic impacts in coastal areas, final statement series, 5736–7

East Pakistan
see Bangladesh

East-West trade
Agricultural trade of US, by detailed commodity and country, 1991, annual rpt, 1524–8
Agricultural trade of US, by detailed commodity and country, 1991, semiannual rpt, 1522–4
Agricultural trade of US with Eastern Europe, by commodity group and country, 1988-91, 1928–11
China economic performance and trade, 1980-91, annual rpt, 9114–5
China trade with NATO members, by country, annual rpt, discontinued, 7144–14
Eastern Europe export industries dev potential, with trade and industry finances and operations, for 5 countries, 1985-90, 9886–4.179
Eastern Europe imports from US, and trade and dev opportunities, monthly rpt, 2042–33
Eastern Europe trade with US, by commodity and country, 1987-91 and outlook for 1992, 2048–158
Export licensing, monitoring, and enforcement activities, FY91, annual rpt, 2024–1
Exports and imports of US, by Harmonized System 6-digit commodity and country, 1991, annual rpt, 2424–13
Exports and imports of US, by selected country, country group, and commodity group, 1991, annual rpt, 2044–37
Exports and imports of US, by transport mode, country, and SITC 1- to 3-digit commodity, 1991, annual rpt, 2424–12
Exports and imports of US, by world area, quarterly pamphlet, 2042–25
Exports and imports of US with Communist and transitional economy countries, by detailed commodity and country, quarterly rpt with articles, 9882–2
Imports of goods, services, and investment from US, trade barriers, impacts, and US actions, by country, 1991, annual rpt, 444–2
NATO members trade with Council for Mutual Economic Assistance Europe members, by country, annual rpt, discontinued, 7144–5
Oil exports to centrally planned economies from market economy countries, monthly rpt, 3162–42.2
Romania trade with US, and US import tariff rates, by commodity, 1985-91, GAO rpt, 26119–414
Services trade of US, direct and among multinatl firms affiliates, by industry and world area, 1986-91, article, 2702–1.336

Eastern Europe
Agricultural exports of US, for grains, oilseed products, hides, skins, and cotton, by country, weekly rpt, 1922–3
Agricultural trade by commodity and country, prices, and world market devs, monthly rpt, 1922–12

Agricultural trade of US, by commodity and country, bimonthly rpt, 1522–1
Agricultural trade of US, by detailed commodity and country, 1991, annual rpt, 1524–8
Agricultural trade of US, by detailed commodity and country, 1991, semiannual rpt, 1522–4
Agricultural trade of US with Eastern Europe, by commodity group and country, 1988-91, 1928–11
Cancer death rates, by body site, sex, and world area, 1969 and annual percent change 1969-86, article, 4472–1.306
EC economic integration impacts on domestic and intl agricultural conditions, 1990 conf, 1528–325
Economic aid to Eastern Europe by donor country, and Poland and Hungary exports by world area, 1988-91, GAO rpt, 26123–386
Economic and military aid and loans from US and intl agencies, by program and country, FY46-91, annual rpt, 9914–5
Economic and social conditions of developing countries from 1960s, and Intl Dev Cooperation Agency and AID activities and funding, FY91-93, annual rpt, 9904–4
Environmental remediation costs, and aid by donor, by Eastern European country, 1991 hearing, 25368–181
Export industries dev potential, with trade and industry finances and operations, for 5 Eastern Europe countries, 1985-90, 9886–4.179
Export licensing, monitoring, and enforcement activities, FY91, annual rpt, 2024–1
Exports and imports (waterborne) of US, by type of service, customs district, port, and world area, monthly rpt, 2422–7
Exports and imports of OECD, total and for 4 major countries, and US trade by country, by commodity, 1980-90, world area rpt, 9116–1.1
Exports and imports of US by country, and trade shifts by commodity, 1991, annual rpt, 9884–25
Exports and imports of US, by Harmonized System 6-digit commodity and country, 1991, annual rpt, 2424–13
Exports and imports of US, by selected country, country group, and commodity group, 1991, annual rpt, 2044–37
Exports and imports of US, by transport mode, country, and SITC 1- to 3-digit commodity, 1991, annual rpt, 2424–12
Exports and imports of US with Communist and transitional economy countries, by detailed commodity and country, quarterly rpt with articles, 9882–2
Exports and imports of US with Eastern Europe, by commodity and country, 1987-91 and outlook for 1992, 2048–158
Imports from US, and trade and dev opportunities, for Eastern Europe, monthly rpt, 2042–33
Loans of US banks to foreigners at all US and foreign offices, by country group and country, quarterly rpt, 13002–1
Market economy transition of Eastern Europe countries, economic conditions, trade, and foreign investment, by country, 1990-91, 9118–13
Multinatl US firms and foreign affiliates finances and operations, by industry and country, 1989 benchmark survey, annual rpt, 2704–5
NATO members and Japan economic aid to developing countries and Eastern Europe, 1980-91, annual rpt, 3544–28
Oil and gas production, use, and trade by country, centrally planned economy countries, monthly rpt, 9112–2
Peace Corps activities, funding by program, and volunteers, by country, FY93, annual rpt, 9654–1
Radio Free Europe and Radio Liberty broadcast and financial data, FY91, annual rpt, 10314–1
Refugee arrivals in US by world area and country of origin, and quotas, monthly rpt, 7002–4
Refugee arrivals in US by world area of origin and State of settlement, and Federal aid, FY91-92 and proposed FY93 allocations, annual rpt, 7004–16
Refugee migration, and intl aid programs, by world area and country of origin and asylum, 1991, annual rpt, 7004–15
Services trade of US, direct and among multinatl firms affiliates, by industry and world area, 1986-91, article, 2702–1.336
Steel trade, by product, country, and customs district, with US industry operating data, 1989-June 1992, semiannual rpt, 9882–15
Tax reform issues in transition to market economy, with tax rates, revenue, and govt spending compared to EC, by selected country, late 1960s-91, technical paper, 9366–7.278
Terrorism (intl) incidents, casualties, and attacks on US targets, by attack type and world area, 1991, annual rpt, 7004–13
Tobacco and cigarette production, consumption, and trade, by Eastern European country, 1985-91, article, 1561–10.303
Travel to US, by characteristics of visit and traveler, country, port city, and State of destination, quarterly rpt, 2902–1
UN voting record and share of votes in agreement with US, by issue, country, and world area, 1991, annual rpt, 7004–18
US military and civilian personnel and dependents, by service branch, world area, and country, quarterly rpt, 3542–20
see also Albania
see also Armenia
see also Azerbaijan
see also Bulgaria
see also Byelarus
see also Commonwealth of Independent States
see also Council for Mutual Economic Assistance
see also Czechoslovakia
see also Estonia
see also Georgia, Republic of
see also Germany, East
see also Hungary
see also Latvia
see also Lithuania
see also Moldova
see also Poland
see also Romania
see also Russia
see also Soviet Union
see also Ukraine
see also Warsaw Pact
see also Yugoslavia
see also under By Foreign Country in the "Index by Categories"

Eastman, A. Brent
"Trauma Care Systems", 4208–35

Eavesdropping
see Electronic surveillance

Eberts, Randall W.
"Causes and Consequences of Structural Changes in U.S. Labor Markets: A Review", 9377–1.304
"Wagner's Hypothesis: A Local Perspective", 9377–9.133

Eckard, Eugenia
"Wanted and Unwanted Births Reported by Mothers 15-44 Years of Age: U.S., 1976", 4147–16.6

Ecology
see Conservation of natural resources
see Environmental pollution and control
see Environmental sciences
see Marine pollution
see Marine resources conservation
see State funding for natural resources and conservation
see Wildlife and wildlife conservation

Economic and econometric models
Agricultural Economics Research, quarterly journal, 1502–3
Banks failures forecasting performance of asset risk indicators and other factors, 1980s-91, article, 9379–15.302
BLS data collection, analysis, and presentation methods, by program, 1992 rpt, 6888–1
BLS econometric analyses and methodology, for economic indicators, prices, labor costs, and productivity, working paper series, 6886–6
Energy Info Admin forecasting and data analysis models, 1992, annual listing, 3164–87
Energy supply, demand, and prices, by fuel type and end-use sector, alternative projections 1990-2010, annual rpt, 3164–75
Energy supply, demand, distribution, and regulatory impacts, series, 3166–6
Exports and imports of US, relation to trade composition and domestic and foreign capital investment, model description and results, late 1960s-89, article, 9385–1.302
Finance (intl) and financial policy, and external factors affecting US economy, technical paper series, 9366–7
Financial and banking devs in southeastern States, working paper series, 9371–10
Financial and economic analysis, and economic issues affecting North Central States, working paper series, 9375–13
Financial and economic analysis, and economic issues affecting Northeast States, working paper series, 9373–27
Financial and economic analysis and forecasting methodology, technical paper series, 9366–6; 9377–9
Financial and economic analysis of banking and nonbanking sectors, working paper series, 9381–10
Financial and economic analysis, technical paper series, 8006–6; 9379–12; 9383–20; 9385–8; 9389–19; 9393–10

Financial and economic devs, Fed Reserve Bank of Richmond bimonthly journal, 9389–1
Financial and monetary research and econometric analyses, working paper series, 9387–8
Food assistance programs impacts on farm income, by commodity, model description and results, 1989-90, 1548–390
Forecasts of economic indicators, performance of alternative models, 1992 article, 9391–1.316
Foreign countries economic and social conditions, working paper series, 2326–18
Housing finance studies, technical paper series, 8436–1
Inflation forecasting performance of expected long run inflation rate and commodity price indexes, 1960s-90, article, 9377–1.303
Input-output model of BEA, regional multipliers by industry and State, and methodology, 1992 guide, 2708–47
Inventories related to sales, by industry sector, model description and results, late 1960s-91, article, 9389–1.302
Labor productivity over business cycle relation to hours worked, model descriptions and results, 1940s-91, article, 9383–6.302
Mail volume and employment of USPS, impacts of competition and rate increases, with evaluation of alternative forecast models, 1970s-80s and forecast to 1995, GAO rpt, 26119–384
Manufacturing industries operations and performance, analytical rpt series, 2506–16
Middle Atlantic States economic indicators, forecasting performance of vector autoregression models, 1992 working paper, 9387–8.282
Monetary policy impacts on economic indicators, alternative model results, mid 1970s-91, technical paper, 9385–1.306; 9385–8.135
North American Free Trade Agreement proposal for Canada, US, and Mexico, economic impacts, alternative model descriptions, 1992 conf, 9886–4.182
Poverty population impact of inflation, alternative models assessment, 1992 article, 9377–1.306
Savings instns financial condition and devs, working paper series, 9379–14
Survey of Income and Program Participation, household composition, income, benefits, and labor force status, methodology, working paper series, 2626–10
see also Input-output analysis
see also Mathematic models and modeling

Economic assistance
see Economic policy
see International assistance
see Military assistance
see State funding for economic development

Economic censuses
Data collection and statistical program plans of Census Bur, advisory committees findings and recommendations, 1992 conf, 2628–35
Data collection, coverage, availability, and procedural history, 1987 economic censuses, 2628–16
Data coverage and availability for economic censuses and related statistics, 1992 preliminary guide, 2308–5
Data coverage and availability of Census Bur rpts and data files, 1992 annual listing, 2304–2
Data coverage by geographic level, maps, and reference products from Census Bur, 1992 rpt, 2308–67
Data from economic censuses of 1987 and related programs, CD-ROM series, 2326–22
Data from economic censuses of 1987 and related programs, CD-ROM series, user guides, 2306–8
Energy-related data coverage and availability from Census Bur, 1991 pamphlet, 2326–7.84
see also Census of Construction Industries
see also Census of Financial, Insurance, and Real Estate Industries
see also Census of Manufactures
see also Census of Mineral Industries
see also Census of Outlying Areas
see also Census of Retail Trade
see also Census of Service Industries
see also Census of Transportation
see also Census of Transportation, Communications, and Utilities Industries
see also Census of Wholesale Trade
see also Characteristics of Business Owners Survey
see also Enterprise Statistics Program
see also Survey of Characteristics of Business Owners
see also Survey of Minority-Owned Business Enterprises
see also Survey of Women-Owned Businesses

Economic concentration and diversification
Agricultural, fishery, and forest products trade, tariffs, and industry operating data, commodity rpt series, 9885–8
Bank deposits interest rates relation to market concentration, regulation, migration, and other factors, 1980s, technical paper, 9366–6.297
Banking industry structure, performance, and financial devs, for Fed Reserve 10th District, 1991, annual rpt, 9381–14
Banks (commercial) and trust companies, assets and liabilities of 10 largest organizations by State, 1990, annual rpt, 9364–5.11
Banks (natl) charters, mergers, liquidations, enforcement cases, and financial performance, with data by instn and State, quarterly rpt, 8402–3
Banks acquisitions of failed and other banks, financial performance relation to asset mix, market concentration, and other factors, 1984-90, article, 9292–4.304
Banks agricultural loans share of all loans, with market shares and returns on assets, by bank size, 1970s-80s, working paper, 9381–10.122
Banks and thrifts financial performance relation to market concentration, 1992 working paper, 9371–10.88
Banks checking account and commercial loan activity by bank size, and loan sales and assets for top banks, 1970s-90, working paper, 9387–8.264
Banks financial performance, risk assessment, and regulation, 1991 annual conf papers, 9375–7
Banks market conditions relation to mortgage interest rates, model results, 1987-88, technical paper, 9366–1.162
Banks profitability relation to market concentration, efficiency indicators, and regulation, model description and results, 1980s, technical paper, 9366–6.290
Cigarette ad and promotion costs by media, and market shares, by cigarette type, with sales and use, 1963-89, annual rpt, 9404–4
Farm production diversification measures, with data by commodity, 1990, article, 1541–1.314
Financial markets (intl) performance of foreign and US bank and securities firms, finances and competitiveness issues, 1980s, compilation of papers, 9385–10
Financial services use by households, by account type and instn type and location, 1989, article, 9362–1.303
Food marketing sector finances, operations, and merger activity, for processors and distributors, 1991, annual rpt, 1544–22
Grocery store profits and prices relation to market concentration, literature review, 1990 rpt, 9408–56
Hospital reimbursement by Medicare under prospective payment system, impacts on costs, industry structure and operations, and quality of care, series, 17206–2
Imports from Communist and transitional economy countries, market share by selected commodity, quarterly rpt, 9882–2
Imports injury to US industries from sales at less than fair value, investigations with background financial and operating data, series, 9886–14
Insurance company finances, by insurance type and firm, with some intl comparisons, 1991 conf, 9373–3.35
Japan *keiretsu* and independent corporations ownership and concentration indicators, 1984, technical paper, 9366–6.288
Manufacturing census, 1987: concentration of largest firms measured by value added, and for shipments by SIC 2- and 4-digit industry, subject rpt, 2497–6
Militarily strategic manufacturing industries finances, operations, and intl competitiveness, series, 2026–1
Oil company profits, refinery capacity, gasoline prices, and market share, by firm, 1991 hearing, 25528–120
Oil production disruption after Iraq invasion of Kuwait, impacts on futures prices, family budgets, and oil firms, 1990 hearings, 25408–116
Semiconductor industry (US) intl competitiveness, indicators and comparisons to Japan and Europe, 1980s and projected to 1994, working paper, 15036–1.1
Services (producer) industries in Midwest, employment concentration by industry group, MSA, and urban-rural location, 1970s-89, article, 9375–1.305
Telecommunications finances, rates, and traffic for US carriers intl operations, by service type, firm, and country, 1975-90, annual rpt, 9284–17
Telephone service subscribership, charges, and local and long distance firm finances and operations, late 1970s-92, semiannual rpt, 9282–7

Textile and apparel foreign market conditions for US exports, with domestic industry operations, country rpt series, 2046–15
see also Antitrust law
see also Business acquisitions and mergers
see also Competition
see also Holding companies
see also Monopolies and cartels
see also Ownership of enterprise

Economic crises and depressions
see Business cycles

Economic development
Assistance (block and categorical grants) programs for State and local govts, FY91, biennial listing, 10044–8
Black colleges grants from HUD for economic and community dev programs, by recipient, 1991, press release, 5006–3.85
Budget of US, House concurrent resolution, with spending and revenue targets, FY93 and projected to FY97, annual rpt, 21264–2
Budget of US, obligations and authority by function, agency, and program, with summaries and analyses, FY93, annual rpt, 104–2
Coastal areas environmental and economic impacts of offshore minerals lease sales, final statement series, 5736–7
Coastal areas environmental impacts of economic dev and population growth, 1960-80s and projected to 2010, series, 2176–8
Economic Dev Admin activities, and funding by program, recipient, State, and county, FY91 and cumulative from FY66, annual rpt, 2064–2
Economies of scale in output, technology, and trade, model description and results, 1992 technical paper, 9383–20.22
Expenditures of Fed Govt in States, by type, program, agency, and State, FY91, annual rpt, 2464–2
Fed Govt agencies and program operations investigations, summaries of findings, as of 1991, annual GAO rpt, 26104–5.2
Fed Govt financial and nonfinancial domestic aid, 1992 base edition, annual listing, 104–5
Labor laws enacted, by State, 1991, annual article, 6722–1.309
Natl income and product accounts, comprehensive accounts and components, benchmark revisions, 1929-88, 2708–5
Natl income and product accounts, comprehensive accounts and components, *Survey of Current Business*, monthly rpt, 2702–1.26
R&D funding by Fed Govt, by detailed function, program, and agency, FY91-93, annual rpt, 9627–9
Rural areas dev aid by Fed Govt, Bush Admin programs and initiatives, FY91, annual rpt, 1004–17
Rural areas economic and social conditions, dev, and problems, periodic journal, 1502–7
Rural areas economic conditions and dev, quarterly journal, 1502–8
Rural areas employment and population characteristics, and role of education and training in economic dev, 1960s-80s, compilation of papers, 1598–277
Rural Electrification Admin activities and finances, and loans by State, FY91 and trends from FY36, annual rpt, 1244–3
TVA finances and operations by program and facility, FY91, annual rpt, 9804–32
see also Business cycles
see also Community development
see also Community Development Block Grants
see also Developing countries
see also Economic indicators
see also Job creation
see also Regional planning
see also State funding for economic development
see also Urban Development Action Grants
see also Urban renewal

Economic Development Administration
Activities of EDA, and funding by program, recipient, State, and county, FY91 and cumulative from FY66, annual rpt, 2064–2
Budget of US, obligations and authority by function, agency, and program, with summaries and analyses, FY93, annual rpt, 104–2
Expenditures of Fed Govt in States, by type, program, agency, and State, FY91, annual rpt, 2464–2

Economic indicators
Agricultural Outlook, production, prices, marketing, and trade, by commodity, forecast and current situation, monthly rpt with articles, 1502–4
Banking and financial conditions, 1990, annual rpt, 9364–5
Banks in Texas, loans and financial ratios relation to economic indicators, 1970s-90, working paper, 9379–14.16
BEA rpts data coverage and availability, 1992 annual rpt, 2704–6
Budget deficit forecasting accuracy, contributing factors, and analysis of major programs, FY91, annual GAO rpt, 26104–23
Budget of US, CBO analysis and review of FY93 budget by function, annual rpt, 26304–2
Budget of US, CBO analysis of revenue and spending alternatives and projections of economic indicators, FY93-97, annual rpt, 26304–3
Budget of US, House Budget Committee analysis of Bush Admin proposals and economic assumptions, FY93, 21268–42
Budget of US, House concurrent resolution, with spending and revenue targets, FY93 and projected to FY97, annual rpt, 21264–2
Budget of US, midsession review of FY93 budget, by function, annual rpt, 104–7
Budget of US, obligations and authority by function, agency, and program, with summaries and analyses, FY93, annual rpt, 104–2
Business America, foreign and domestic commerce, and US investment and trade opportunities, biweekly journal, 2042–24
Business cycle (intl) impacts on economic indicators, for industrialized countries, 1950s-80s, working paper, 9383–20.16
Business cycle duration and strength indicators, late 1940s-91, article, 9373–1.301
Business cycle recession and expansion duration indicators, 1850s-1990, working paper, 9375–13.83
Business natl and local outlook, North Central States business leaders views, 1992 survey, article, 9383–19.303
Central America economic indicators, by country, 1969-89, working paper, 9916–13.4
China economic performance and trade, 1980-91, annual rpt, 9114–5
Communist and OECD countries economic conditions, annual rpt, discontinued, 7144–11
Consumer spending forecast performance of consumer sentiment index and other economic indicators, 1950s-90, article, 9393–8.304
Costa Rica economic indicators and reform issues, mid 1970s-90, working paper, 9916–13.5
Developing countries economic and social conditions from 1960s, and Intl Dev Cooperation Agency and AID activities and funding, FY91-93, annual rpt, 9904–4
Developing countries economic, population, and agricultural data, US and other aid sources, and AID activity, country rpt series, 9916–12
Eastern Europe transition to market economies, economic conditions, trade, and foreign investment, by country, 1990-91, 9118–13
Economic and financial devs, Fed Reserve Bank of Boston quarterly journal, 9373–25
Economic indicators and components, and Fed Reserve 4th District business and financial conditions, monthly chartbook, 9377–10
Economic indicators and components, current data and annual trends, monthly rpt, 23842–1
Economic indicators and cyclical devs and outlook, by Fed Reserve Bank District, periodic rpt, 9362–8
Economic indicators compounded annual rates of change, monthly rpt, 9391–3
Economic indicators performance, and Fed Reserve monetary policy objectives, as of July 1992, semiannual rpt, 9362–4
Economic indicators performance from 1961, and Commerce Dept rpts, biweekly listing, 2002–1
Economic indicators summary, monthly rpt, 2302–3
Economic Report of the President for 1991, economic effects of budget proposals, and trends and projections, 1940s-95, annual hearings, 23844–4
Economic Report of the President for 1992, Joint Economic Committee critique and policy recommendations, annual rpt, 23844–2
Economic Report of the President for 1992, with economic trends from 1929, annual rpt, 204–1
Economic review and outlook for US, analysis of Bush Admin and private projections, with small business views, 1991 hearings, 23848–230
Employment over business cycles, relation to regional and industrial economic factors, model description and results, 1992 working paper, 9381–10.134

Energy natl strategy plans for conservation, R&D, security, and pollution reduction, technical rpt series, 3006–13
Energy supply, demand, and price forecasts, economic and weather assumptions, quarterly rpt, 3162–34
Energy supply, demand, and prices, by fuel type and end-use sector, projections and underlying assumptions, 1995-2010, annual rpt, 3164–90
Energy supply, demand, distribution, and regulatory impacts, series, 3166–6
European Monetary Union fiscal policy impact on EC govts, with background data, mid 1970s-90, technical paper, 9393–10.18
Fed Reserve Bd and Reserve banks finances, staff, and review of monetary policy and economic devs, 1991, annual rpt, 9364–1
Financial and business detailed statistics, *Fed Reserve Bulletin*, monthly rpt with articles, 9362–1
Financial and economic analysis, technical paper series, 8006–6; 9379–12; 9383–20; 9385–8; 9389–19; 9393–10
Financial and economic devs, Fed Reserve Bank of New York quarterly journal, 9385–1
Financial and monetary conditions, selected US summary data, weekly rpt, 9391–4
Fiscal policy (supply side) of Reagan Admin, economic impacts, 1980s and trends from 1960s, technical paper, 9385–1.304; 9385–8.125
Forecasts of economic conditions and employment, alternative BLS projections to 2005 and trends 1975-90, biennial rpt, 6744–19
Forecasts of economic indicators, and errors, for Fed Reserve 3rd District by State, 1980s-93, article, 9387–1.303
Forecasts of economic indicators, performance of alternative models, 1992 article, 9391–1.316
Forecasts of economic indicators, performance of interest rate spreads, 1950s-90, working paper, 9375–13.67
Forecasts of economic indicators, performance of selected forecasters by indicator, 1950s-92, article, 9373–1.313
Forecasts of economic indicators, 1992-93 and trends from 1948, annual article, 9383–6.301
Forecasts of economic indicators, 1993-94 and trends from 1948, annual article, 9383–6.303
Foreign and US economic conditions, and trade devs and balances, with data by selected country and country group, monthly rpt, 9882–14
Foreign and US economic conditions, for major industrial countries, monthly rpt, 9112–1
Foreign and US economic indicators, trade balances, and exchange rates, for selected OECD and Asian countries, 1992 semiannual rpt, 8002–14
Foreign countries *Background Notes*, summary social, political, and economic data, series, 7006–2
Foreign countries economic and monetary trends, compounded annual rates of change and quarterly indicators for US and 7 major industrialized countries, quarterly rpt, 9391–7
Foreign countries economic conditions and implications for US, periodic country rpt series, 2046–4
Foreign countries economic conditions, policy, and trade practices, by country, 1989-91, annual rpt, 21384–5
Foreign countries economic indicators, and trade and investment flows, for selected countries and country groups, selected years 1946-91, annual rpt, 204–1.9
Foreign countries economic indicators, and trade and trade flows by commodity, by country, data compilation, monthly CD-ROM, 2002–6
Foreign countries economic, social, political, and geographic summary data, by country, 1992, annual factbook, 9114–2
GDP forecasting performance of selected economic indicators over selected forecast periods and business cycles, 1960s-91, article, 9375–1.307
Germany unification economic impacts for Germany, US, Japan, and worldwide, alternative projections 1991-99, technical paper, 9366–7.275
Haiti economic conditions, 1985-91, working paper, 9916–13.3
Housing prices and adjustments for quality changes, analysis of factors, 1950s-80s, working paper, 9373–27.7
Imports of US, relation to domestic and foreign economic indicators, model description and results, 1980s, technical paper, 9385–8.138
Israel economic conditions, US investment and export opportunities, and trade practices, 1992 rpt, 2008–32
Japan economic conditions, US investment and export opportunities, and trade practices, forecast 1991-93 and trends from 1988, 2048–159
Latin America economic and social conditions, resources, trade, and aid, 1992, annual factbook, 9914–14
Latin America economic conditions, trade, and foreign aid, working paper series, 9916–13
Michigan local areas economic conditions and public services impacts of reductions in Federal aid, with background data, 1970s-91, GAO rpt, 26121–483
Military spending reductions, economic impacts by defense contractor, industry, State, and congressional district, 1989-90 hearings, 23848–224
Military spending reductions, economic impacts of Bush Admin plans by industry and State, FY92-97, 26306–6.167
Monetary policy objectives of Fed Reserve, analysis and economic performance, 1950s-90 and projected to FY95, hearings, 21248–160
Monetary policy shocks impact on economic indicators, model description and results, 1970s-92, working paper, 9371–10.89
Municipal bond interest tax exemption economic impacts, 1980s-90, article, 9373–1.310
New England States economic indicators, Fed Reserve 1st District, monthly rpt, 9373–2
North Central States business and economic conditions, Fed Reserve 9th District, quarterly journal, 9383–19
Oil price increases economic impacts, 1970s-91, article, 9391–1.301
Overseas Business Reports: economic conditions, investment and export opportunities, and trade practices, country market research rpt series, 2046–6
Pollution (air) regulation under Clean Air Act 1990 amendments, economic impacts with background data for Midwest and US, 1992 article, 9375–1.304
Puerto Rico statehood referendum proposal, with background data on Federal outlays, economic conditions, and finances of corporations with tax-favored status, 1940s-88, hearing, 21448–46
Rural areas economic conditions and dev, quarterly journal, 1502–8
Savings instns failures, costs and budget deficit and economic impacts, 1980s and projected to 2010, 26306–6.165
Seasonal variations impact on economic indicators, model description and results, 1940s-80s, working paper, 9387–8.262
Singapore economic conditions and monetary policy, with exchange rate and money supply related to foreign prices and other factors, 1960s-90, article, 9379–1.304
Southeastern States, Fed Reserve 5th District, economic indicators by State, quarterly rpt, 9389–16
Southeastern States, Fed Reserve 8th District banking and economic conditions, quarterly rpt with articles, 9391–16
Soviet Union former Republics and Baltic States energy supply and use, and social, economic, and political indicators, 1989-90, 3168–126
Soviet Union former Republics and Baltic States population size and characteristics, 1989-92, 9118–19
Soviet Union trade and investment opportunities for US firms, contact listing, bibl, and background economic data, 1991 rpt, 2048–157
Statistical programs of Fed Govt, funding by agency, and BLS programs improvement spending, 1991 hearing, 23848–227
Survey of Current Business, detailed data for major industries and economic indicators, monthly rpt, 2702–1
Survey of Current Business, detailed data for major industries and economic indicators, 1960-91, biennial supplement, 2704–1
Tax policy impacts on economic performance and income distribution, issues and background data, with foreign comparisons, 1991 and trends, 21788–211
Tennessee Valley economic conditions, and compared to US, alternative projections 1992-2010 and trends from 1929, annual rpt, 9804–27
West Central States financial and economic devs, Fed Reserve 10th District, quarterly rpt, 9381–16
see also Business and industry
see also Business assets and liabilities, general
see also Business cycles
see also Business income and expenses, general
see also Business inventories
see also Capital investments, general

see also Consumer Price Index
see also Credit
see also Earnings, general
see also Economic and econometric models
see also Employment and unemployment, general
see also Flow-of-funds accounts
see also Gross Domestic Product
see also Gross National Product
see also Housing costs and financing
see also Housing sales
see also Industrial capacity and utilization
see also Industrial production
see also Industrial production indexes
see also Inflation
see also Job creation
see also Job vacancy
see also Labor productivity
see also Labor turnover
see also Money supply
see also National income and product accounts
see also Personal and household income
see also Personal consumption
see also Prices
see also Producer Price Index

Economic policy

Banks in Fed Reserve System, expenses and operations itemized by service, office, and district, 1991, annual rpt, 9364–11
Budget of US, CBO analysis of revenue and spending alternatives and projections of economic indicators, FY93-97, annual rpt, 26304–3
Budget of US, midsession review of FY93 budget, by function, annual rpt, 104–7
Dollar exchange rates of mark and yen, impact of central bank policy interventions, 1985-89, article, 9391–1.310
Dollar exchange rates of mark and yen, spot and forward market bid-ask spreads impacts of central bank intervention, mid 1980s-91, article, 9377–1.305
Dollar exchange rates of yen and mark, impact of central bank policy interventions and other factors, various periods 1983-90, working paper, 9377–9.138
Dollar exchange rates of yen and mark, impact of central bank policy interventions, 1987-90, working paper, 9377–9.134
Economic Report of the President for 1991, economic effects of budget proposals, and trends and projections, 1940s-95, annual hearings, 23844–4
Economic Report of the President for 1992, Joint Economic Committee critique and policy recommendations, annual rpt, 23844–2
Economic Report of the President for 1992, with economic trends from 1929, annual rpt, 204–1
Economic review and outlook for US, analysis of Bush Admin and private projections, with small business views, 1991 hearings, 23848–230
Financial and economic analysis, technical paper series, 8006–6; 9379–12; 9389–19
Financial and economic devs, Fed Reserve Bank of Atlanta bimonthly rpt with articles, 9371–1
Financial and economic devs, Fed Reserve Bank of Chicago bimonthly journal, 9375–1
Financial and economic devs, Fed Reserve Bank of Dallas quarterly journal, 9379–1
Financial and economic devs, Fed Reserve Bank of Kansas City quarterly journal, 9381–1
Financial and economic devs, Fed Reserve Bank of Minneapolis quarterly journal, 9383–6
Financial and economic devs, Fed Reserve Bank of New York quarterly journal, 9385–1
Financial and economic devs, Fed Reserve Bank of Philadelphia bimonthly journal, 9387–1
Financial and economic devs, Fed Reserve Bank of Richmond bimonthly journal, 9389–1
Financial and economic devs, Fed Reserve Bank of San Francisco periodic journal, 9393–8
Financial and economic devs, Fed Reserve Bank of St Louis bimonthly journal, 9391–1
Foreign countries economic conditions and implications for US, periodic country rpt series, 2046–4
Foreign countries economic conditions, policy, and trade practices, by country, 1989-91, annual rpt, 21384–5
Overseas Business Reports: economic conditions, investment and export opportunities, and trade practices, country market research rpt series, 2046–6
see also Business cycles
see also Defense expenditures
see also Economic development
see also Employment and unemployment, general
see also Fiscal policy
see also Foreign economic relations
see also Foreign trade
see also Foreign trade promotion
see also Government spending
see also Health care reform
see also Inflation
see also Interest rates
see also International assistance
see also International sanctions
see also Land reform
see also Military assistance
see also Monetary policy
see also Price regulation
see also Prices
see also State funding for economic development
see also Subsidies
see also Tariffs and foreign trade controls
see also terms beginning with Federal aid

Economic relations

see Foreign economic relations

Economic Research Service

Activities, funding, and staff of ERS, by branch, planned FY92, annual rpt, 1504–6
Agricultural Economics Research, quarterly journal, 1502–3
Agricultural Outlook, production, prices, marketing, and trade, by commodity, forecast and current situation, monthly rpt with articles, 1502–4
Agricultural situation and farm-related topics, monthly rpt, 1502–6
Apple (processed) demand and impacts of selected market factors, 1980s-91, 1548–392
Assets of farm sector by type, and real and nonreal estate debt, including and excluding operator households, by sales size, 1960-89, 1548–387
Brazil agricultural productivity indicators, 1968-87, 1528–331
Budget of US, obligations and authority by function, agency, and program, with summaries and analyses, FY93, annual rpt, 104–2
Businesses in rural areas, Fed Govt credit assistance by program and county characteristics, 1983-89, 1548–389
Cattle and calves for beef, ranches, inventory, producers, and returns, by herd size and region, mid 1940s-91, 1568–251
Cotton, wool, and synthetic fiber production, prices, trade, and use, periodic situation rpt with articles, 1561–1
Dairy production, prices, trade, and use, periodic situation rpt with articles, 1561–2
Data on agriculture, collection, methodology, and use for major time series of USDA, series, 1506–1
Developing countries food supply, needs, and aid, status and alternative forecasts, world area rpt series, 1526–8
EC economic integration impacts on domestic and intl agricultural conditions, 1990 conf, 1528–325
Economic Indicators of the Farm Sector, balance sheets, and receipts by detailed commodity, by State, 1986-90, annual rpt, 1544–18
Economic Indicators of the Farm Sector, itemized production costs, receipts, and returns, by commodity and region, 1975-90, annual rpt, 1544–20
Economic Indicators of the Farm Sector, production inputs, output, and productivity, by commodity and region, 1947-90, annual rpt, 1544–17
Employment of farm hired workers, and earnings, by selected characteristics, 1990, 1598–278
Exports and imports (agricultural) of US, by commodity and country, bimonthly rpt, 1522–1
Exports and imports (agricultural) of US, by detailed commodity and country, 1991, annual rpt, 1524–8
Exports and imports (agricultural) of US, by detailed commodity and country, 1991, semiannual rpt, 1522–4
Exports and imports (agricultural) of US, outlook and current situation, quarterly rpt, 1542–4
Exports and imports among US, Canada, and Mexico, intraindustry trade indexes by commodity, 1962-87, 1528–327
Exports and imports dependency indexes for total, merchandise, and agricultural products, by country, 1960s-88, 1528–328
Family farms financial condition, 1970s-88, annual rpt, 1504–4
Farm financial and marketing conditions, forecast 1992, annual conf, 1504–9
Farmland in US owned by foreigners, holdings, acquisitions, and disposals by land use, owner type and country, and State, 1991, annual rpt, 1584–2

Farmland in US owned by foreigners, holdings, acreage, and value by land use, owner country, State, and county, 1991, annual rpt, 1584–3
Feed and feed additives production, use, and prices, by commodity, State, and country, various periods 1949-92, 1568–308
Feed production, acreage, stocks, use, trade, prices, and price supports, periodic situation rpt with articles, 1561–4
Finances of farms, assets, liabilities, and debt by lender type, by State, 1960-89, 1548–384
Finances of farms, debts, assets, and receipts, and lenders financial condition, quarterly rpt with articles, 1541–1
Financial and marketing conditions of farms, forecast 1992, annual chartbook, 1504–8
Fish hatcheries and farms, production, costs, prices, and sales, for catfish and trout, 1970s-92, semiannual situation rpt, 1561–15
FmHA guaranteed loan program, characteristics of borrowers, lenders, and loans, FY88, 1548–386
Food assistance programs impacts on farm income, by commodity, model description and results, 1989-90, 1548–390
Food consumer research, marketing, legislation, and regulation devs, and consumption and price trends, quarterly journal, 1541–7
Food consumption, supply, trade, prices, spending, and indexes, by commodity, 1990, annual rpt, 1544–4
Food marketing sector finances, operations, and merger activity, for processors and distributors, 1991, annual rpt, 1544–22
Food prices (farm-retail), marketing cost components, and industry finances and productivity, 1920s-91, annual rpt, 1544–9
Foreign and US agricultural production, prices, trade, and use, periodic rpt, discontinued, 1522–3
Foreign and US agricultural supply and demand indicators, by selected crop, monthly rpt, 1522–5
Foreign countries agricultural production, prices, and trade, by country, 1980-91 and forecast 1992, annual world area rpt series, 1524–4
Fruit and nut production, prices, trade, stocks, and use, by selected crop, periodic situation rpt with articles, 1561–6
Fruit and vegetable imports under quarantine, by crop, country, and port of entry, FY89, annual rpt, 1524–7
Global climate change impacts on agricultural production and GDP, with data by crop and world area, mid 1970s-86, 1528–326
Income of farms, cash marketing receipts ranked by commodity and State, 1990, 1548–385
Irrigated farmland, farm characteristics, and water and fuel sources, by State and leading county, 1950s-88, 1588–122
Japan investment in US farmland and agricultural industries, with data by State and county, late 1960s-90, 1528–332
Livestock, meat, poultry, and egg production, prices, trade, and stocks, monthly rpt, 1561–17
Livestock, meat, poultry, and egg production, prices, trade, stocks, and use, periodic situation rpt with articles, 1561–7
Loans (farm) at risk of default, lender losses, and selected farm financial indicators, by type of farm and lender, 1984-89, 1548–383
Mexico agricultural trade with US and Canada, and impacts of North American Free Trade Agreement, 1980s-90, 1528–330
Morocco agricultural subsidies to producers and consumers, by selected commodity, 1970s-90, 1528–329
Oils, oilseeds, and fats production, prices, trade, and use, periodic situation rpt with articles, 1561–3
Population on farms, by employment, social, and economic characteristics, and region, 1990, annual Current Population Rpt, 2546–1.458
Poultry and egg production, prices, receipts, trade, and disposition, by species, 1960-90, annual rpt, 1564–13
Production inputs, finances, mgmt, and land value and transfers, periodic situation rpt with articles, 1561–16
Production itemized costs, receipts, and returns, by crop and State, 1987-89, annual rpt, 1544–24
Rice foreign and US production, prices, trade, stocks, and use, periodic situation rpt, 1561–8
Rice production, practices, costs, and land tenure, by production area, 1988, 1568–309
Rice shipments, by end use, package size, and State of origin and destination, 1960s-89, biennial rpt, 1564–11
Rural areas economic and social conditions, dev, and problems, periodic journal, 1502–7
Rural areas economic conditions and dev, quarterly journal, 1502–8
Rural areas employment and population characteristics, and role of education and training in economic dev, 1960s-80s, compilation of papers, 1598–277
Seed varieties patent protection, and wheat farmer profitability of using purchased seed, 1986-89, 1548–388
Sheep and wool production, use, and prices, and operations costs and returns, for western US, 1920s-90, 1548–382
Sugar and sweeteners production, prices, trade, supply, and use, quarterly situation rpt with articles, 1561–14
Tobacco (flue-cured) farms and farm operators, by region and selected characteristics, 1970s-87, 1568–307
Tobacco production, marketing, use, price supports, and trade, quarterly situation rpt with articles, 1561–10
Tomato production, acreage, and yield by State, trade and production by country, stocks, shipments, and prices, 1960s-91, 1568–310
Vegetable production, prices, trade, stocks, and use, for selected fresh and processing crops, periodic situation rpt with articles, 1561–11
Weather data for farmland, average precipitation and temperature by State, monthly 1950-90, biennial rpt, 1544–28
Weight and volume conversion factors for agricultural commodities and products, 1992 rpt, 1508–3
Wheat and rye foreign and US production, prices, trade, stocks, and use, quarterly situation rpt with articles, 1561–12
Women-headed households food spending, by item and selected characteristics, and compared to other households, 1970s-88, 1548–391

Economics

Agricultural Economics Research, quarterly journal, 1502–3
Agricultural research funding and staffing for USDA, State agencies, and other instns, by topic, FY91, annual rpt, 1744–2
Education data compilation, 1992 annual rpt, 4824–2
Fed Govt aid to higher education and nonprofit instns for R&D and related activities, by field, instn, agency, and State, FY90, annual rpt, 9627–17
Higher education grad programs enrollment in science and engineering, by field, source of funds, and characteristics of student and instn, 1990, annual rpt, 9627–7
Labor demand, turnover, and training completions, by detailed occupation, 1990 and projected to 2005, biennial rpt, 6744–3
Occupational Outlook Handbook, 1992-93, biennial rpt, 6744–1
R&D funding by higher education instns and federally funded centers, by field, instn, and State, FY90, annual rpt, 9627–13
see also Economic and econometric models
see also Economic policy
see also Medical costs

Ecuador

Agricultural trade of US, by detailed commodity and country, 1991, annual rpt, 1524–8
Agricultural trade of US, by detailed commodity and country, 1991, semiannual rpt, 1522–4
AID economic aid to developing countries, obligations and disbursements by country, quarterly rpt, 9912–4
AID loans repayment status and terms by program and country, and status of predecessor agency loans, quarterly rpt, 9912–3
Cuba trade, by commodity and country, mid 1980s-91, 9118–8
Economic and military aid and loans from US and intl agencies, by program and country, FY46-91, annual rpt, 9914–5
Economic and social conditions of developing countries from 1960s, and Intl Dev Cooperation Agency and AID activities and funding, FY91-93, annual rpt, 9904–4
Economic and social conditions, resources, and trade, and aid, 1992, annual factbook, 9914–14
Economic conditions, policy, and trade practices, by country, 1989-91, annual rpt, 21384–5
Economic, population, and agricultural data, US and other aid sources, and AID activity, 1991 country rpt, 9916–12.51

Economic, social, political, and geographic summary data, by country, 1992, annual factbook, 9114–2
Exports (duty free) under Andean Trade Preference Act from 4 countries to US, and business opportunities, 1989-91, 2048–161
Exports and imports of US, by commodity and country, 1980-90, world area rpt, 9116–1.7
Exports and imports of US, by Harmonized System 6-digit commodity and country, 1991, annual rpt, 2424–13
Exports and imports of US, by selected country, country group, and commodity group, 1991, annual rpt, 2044–37
Exports and imports of US, by transport mode, country, and SITC 1- to 3-digit commodity, 1991, annual rpt, 2424–12
Exports, imports, and balances of US for manufactured goods, by SITC 2-digit commodity and country, quarterly rpt, 2042–35
Exports of US, detailed Schedule B commodities with countries of destination, 1991, annual rpt, 2424–10
Fruit, vegetable, nut, and cut flower imports of US from Andean countries, 1989 and 1991, article, 1925–34.317
Human rights conditions in 170 countries, and US economic and military aid, 1991, annual rpt, 21384–3
Imports of goods, services, and investment from US, trade barriers, impacts, and US actions, by country, 1991, annual rpt, 444–2
Military aid of US, arms sales, and training programs costs and budget requests, by program, world region, and country, FY91-93, annual rpt, 7144–13
Military spending, arms trade, and force strengths, with govt spending and population, by country, 1979-89, annual rpt, 9824–1
Multinatl US firms and foreign affiliates finances and operations, by industry and country, 1989 benchmark survey, annual rpt, 2704–5
Oil exports to US by OPEC and non-OPEC countries, monthly rpt, 3162–24.3
Oil exports to US by OPEC and non-OPEC countries, monthly 1973-88, 3168–123.3
Oil production, investment needs, and exports, for 8 South America countries, 1980s-90 and projected to 2010, GAO rpt, 26123–396
Oil production, stocks, use, and trade, by selected country and country group, monthly rpt, 3162–42
Population size, growth rates, and components of change, by country, projected 1990-2020 and trends from 1950, biennial rpt, 2324–9
Refugee migration, and intl aid programs, by world area and country of origin and asylum, 1991, annual rpt, 7004–15
Steel trade, by product, country, and customs district, with US industry operating data, 1989-June 1992, semiannual rpt, 9882–15
Tax (estate) returns for nonresident aliens, property and tax data, by estate size and decedent country of residence, 1986, article, 8302–2.310
UN voting record and share of votes in agreement with US, by issue, country, and world area, 1991, annual rpt, 7004–18
see also under By Foreign Country in the "Index by Categories"

Edelmann, Patrick
"Water Quality of Fountain and Monument Creeks, South-Central Colorado, with Emphasis on Relation of Water Quality to Stream Classifications", 5666–27.25

Edison, Hali J.
"Purchasing Power Parity and Uncovered Interest Rate Parity: The U.S. 1974-90", 9366–7.279

Editorial occupations
see Journalism
see Writers and writing

Edlow, M. Dianna
"Expenditures for Food Away from Home", 1702–1.308

Education
Condition of Education, detail for elementary, secondary, and higher education, 1920s-91 and projected to 2002, annual rpt, 4824–1
Data on education, collection, processing, and reporting standards, 1991 narrative rpt, 4828–41
Digest of Education Statistics, 1992 annual data compilation, 4824–2
Foreign countries *Background Notes*, summary social, political, and economic data, series, 7006–2
Statistical Abstract of US, 1992 annual data compilation, 2324–1.4
see also Adult education
see also Agricultural education
see also American Schools and Hospitals Abroad
see also Area studies
see also Bilingual education
see also Black colleges
see also Black students
see also Business education
see also Campus security
see also Compensatory education
see also Correspondence courses
see also Curricula
see also Degrees, higher education
see also Discrimination in education
see also Educational attainment
see also Educational broadcasting
see also Educational employees pay
see also Educational enrollment
see also Educational exchanges
see also Educational facilities
see also Educational finance
see also Educational materials
see also Educational performance
see also Educational reform
see also Educational research
see also Educational retention rates
see also Educational technology
see also Educational tests
see also Elementary and secondary education
see also Federal aid to education
see also Federal aid to higher education
see also Federal aid to medical education
see also Federal aid to vocational education
see also Head Start Project
see also Health education
see also Higher education
see also Learning disabilities
see also Legal education
see also Libraries
see also Medical education
see also Military education
see also National Assessment of Educational Progress
see also Physical education and training
see also Preschool education
see also Private schools
see also Remedial education
see also School administration and staff
see also School boards
see also School busing
see also School districts
see also School dropouts
see also School lunch and breakfast programs
see also Scientific education
see also Sex education
see also Special education
see also Student aid
see also Student discipline
see also Students
see also Teacher education
see also Teachers
see also Tuition and fees
see also Veterans education
see also Vocational education and training
see also Work-study programs

Education Commission of the States
see National Assessment of Educational Progress

Education of handicapped children
see Special education

Educational attainment
Asian and Pacific Islands Americans social and economic characteristics, for West and total US, 1990-91, Current Population Report, 2546–1.462
Black Americans social and economic characteristics, for South and total US, 1991 and trends from 1950, annual Current Population Rpt, 2546–1.463
Black women's labor force status, earnings, and other economic status indicators, and compared to whites, various periods 1939-88, 11048–191
Business owner and business characteristics, for minority- and women-owned firms, by industry, employment and sales size, and form of ownership, 1987 survey, 2328–59
Census of Population and Housing, 1990: population and housing characteristics, detailed geographic coverage, State CD-ROM series, 2551–10
Census of Population and Housing, 1990: summary characteristics, by county, subdiv, and place, State rpt series, 2551–7
Condition of Education, detail for elementary, secondary, and higher education, 1920s-91 and projected to 2002, annual rpt, 4824–1
Consumer Income, socioeconomic characteristics of persons, families, and households, detailed cross-tabulations, Current Population Rpt series, 2546–6
Costa Rica economic indicators and reform issues, mid 1970s-90, working paper, 9916–13.5
Credit availability relation to college attainment, model description and results, 1991 working paper, 6886–6.92
Data on education, 1940s-95, pamphlet, 4828–35

Data on education, 1960s-91, annual pamphlet, 4824–3
Deaths and rates, by cause and selected social, demographic, and employment characteristics, 1979-85, natl longitudinal study, 4478–186
Digest of Education Statistics, 1992 annual data compilation, 4824–2
Earnings distribution among and within selected groups, by demographic and employment characteristics, late 1960s-80s, article, 6722–1.328
Earnings impacts of family economic background and educational attainment, model description and results, 1992 working paper, 6886–6.94
Fed Govt procurement operations employees job performance, and views on policies and practices, 1991 survey, 9498–17
Health condition and care relation to education, indicators by selected characteristics, 1989, 4147–10.180
Higher education noncollegiate instns enrollment and program completions, by sex and instn level and control, fall 1990, annual rpt, 4844–19
Households and family characteristics, by location, 1991, annual Current Population Rpt, 2546–1.457
Income (household) and poverty status under alternative income definitions, by recipient characteristics, 1979-91, annual Current Population Rpt, 2546–6.78
Income (personal) relative to median, by race and selected other characteristics, mid 1960s-89, Current Population Rpt, 2546–6.73
Job Training Partnership Act education and worker training program participants, by selected characteristics, 1986-88, 15496–1.15
Migration, immigration, and mover characteristics compared to nonmovers, 1987-90, annual Current Population Rpt, 2546–1.456
Migration since 1990, mover characteristics by same or different area, and compared to nonmovers, 1991, annual Current Population Rpt, 2546–1.464
Military recruits, share with high school diploma by sex and service branch, quarterly press release, 3542–7
Occupation training completions, and labor demand and turnover, by detailed occupation, 1990 and projected to 2005, biennial rpt, 6744–3
Older persons socioeconomic characteristics, 1900s-90 and projected to 2050, biennial chartbook, 12904–1
Older population, and health, economic, and other characteristics, with foreign comparisons, 1980s-91 with trends and projections, Current Population Rpt, 2546–2.165
Pacific territories population and housing detailed characteristics, by location, 1990 Census of Population and Housing, series, 2551–8
Police agencies employment, spending, and operations, FY90, 6066–25.44
Population and labor force characteristics, 1940s-90 and projected to 2000, 15496–1.16
Population economic well-being indicators, by selected characteristics and household income and income-to-poverty ratio, 1984, 2546–20.22
Population educational attainment, by social and demographic characteristics and location, 1991 and trends from 1940, biennial Current Population Rpt, 2546–1.460
Population educational enrollment status and attainment, by selected characteristics, 1990 and trends from 1947, annual Current Population Rpt, 2546–1.459
Public housing residents educational attainment, by selected characteristics, 1980s, 5188–132
Rural areas employment and population characteristics, and role of education and training in economic dev, 1960s-80s, compilation of papers, 1598–277
Rural areas job skill and educational requirements, impacts of industrial and occupational shifts, 1970s-80s and projected to 2000, article, 1502–7.302
Science and engineering enrollment, performance, curricula, student aid sources, and career plans, by sex and race, 1970s-91, biennial rpt, 9624–20.2
Sheriffs' agencies employment, spending, and operations, FY90, 6066–25.45
Single parent families in own and others homes, by financial, housing, and other characteristics, 1989, 2486–1.14
Soviet Union and US economic and sociodemographic indicators, selected years 1970-90, handbook, 2328–80
Statistical Abstract of US, 1992 annual data compilation, 2324–1.4; 2324–1.13
Unemployed displaced workers job search and placement aid effectiveness, relation to previous employment and other characteristics, 1979-87 studies, 15496–1.14
Vietnam population size, components of change, and selected characteristics, 1979, 1989, and projected to 2050, 2326–18.65
Women's labor force status, earnings, and other characteristics, with comparisons to men, fact sheet series, 6564–1
see also Degrees, higher education
see also Educational retention rates
see also National Assessment of Educational Progress
see also School dropouts
see also under By Educational Attainment in the "Index by Categories"

Educational broadcasting
Humanities Natl Endowment activities and grants, FY91, annual rpt, 9564–2
TV and radio stations on the air, by class of operation, monthly press release, 9282–4

Educational development
see Educational reform

Educational employees pay
Athletic depts at NCAA Div I schools, staff by race, and income, by sex and position, 1990/91, GAO rpt, 26121–476
Black higher education instns enrollment, finances, staff, and degrees, by instn and selected student characteristics, 1970s-90, 4848–46
Child day care and early childhood education programs availability, demand, use, costs, and provider and enrollee characteristics, 1990 survey, 4808–39
Collective bargaining wage and benefit changes and coverage, monthly rpt, 6782–1
Collective bargaining wage and benefit changes and coverage, 1st half 1992, semiannual press release, 6782–6
Condition of Education, detail for elementary, secondary, and higher education, 1920s-91 and projected to 2002, annual rpt, 4824–1
County Business Patterns, 1989: employment, establishments, and payroll, by SIC 2- to 4-digit industry and county, annual State rpt series, 2326–8
County Business Patterns, 1990: employment, establishments, and payroll, by SIC 2- to 4-digit industry and county, annual State rpt series, 2326–6
Data on education, enrollment, finances, teachers, and other characteristics, by State, 1969-89, 4828–33
Digest of Education Statistics, 1992 annual data compilation, 4824–2
Elementary and secondary education enrollment, staff, finances, operations, programs, and policies, 1987/88 biennial survey, series, 4836–3
Elementary and secondary public school systems enrollment, finances, staff, and high school grads, by State, FY89-90, annual rpt, 4834–6
Employee benefit plan coverage and provisions, by plan type, for State and local govt employees, 1990, biennial rpt, 6784–21
Employment Cost Index and alternative measure of compensation costs, by component, occupation, industry group, union status, and location, 1975-92, annual rpt, 6744–20
Employment, earnings, and hours, by SIC 1- to 4-digit industry, monthly 1989-Feb 1992, annual rpt, 6744–4
Govt employment and payroll, by function, level of govt, and jurisdiction, annual rpt series, 2466–1
Higher education enrollment, faculty, finances, and degrees, by instn level and control, and State, FY88, annual rpt, 4844–13
Higher education faculty and salaries, by rank, sex, instn type and control, and State, 1990/91, annual rpt, 4844–8
Labor hourly costs, by component, occupational group, industry div, union coverage, and region, 1992, annual rpt, 6744–21
Occupational Outlook Handbook, 1992-93, biennial rpt, 6744–1
Pacific territories population and housing detailed characteristics, by location, 1990 Census of Population and Housing, series, 2551–8
Payroll and employment of State and local govts, monthly rpt, 6742–4
Pension systems of State and local govts, finances, coverage, and benefits, by system, FY90, annual rpt, 2466–2.4
Private elementary and secondary schools, students, and staff characteristics, by school type and affiliation, 1987/88, 4836–3.8
Public schools teachers salaries, 1977/78-1990/91 and alternative projections to 2002/2003, annual rpt, 4824–4

School districts efficient use of staff, model description and results for Texas, 1987-89, technical paper, 9379–12.80
Statistical Abstract of US, 1992 annual data compilation, 2324–1.4
Teachers salaries, 1980s-93, annual press release, 4804–19
Vocational education enrollment, student and teacher characteristics, and outcomes, for secondary and postsecondary instns, 1970s-90, 4828–42

Educational enrollment
Adult education and literacy programs funding, enrollment, and activities, fact sheet series, 4806–4
Bilingual education enrollment, and eligible students not enrolled, by State, 1990-91, annual rpt, 4804–14
Black higher education instns enrollment, finances, staff, and degrees, by instn and selected student characteristics, 1970s-90, 4848–46
Census of Population and Housing, 1990: population and housing characteristics, detailed geographic coverage, State CD-ROM series, 2551–10
Census of Population and Housing, 1990: summary characteristics, by county, subdiv, and place, State rpt series, 2551–7
Compulsory school attendance laws enacted, by State, 1991, annual article, 6722–1.309
Condition of Education, detail for elementary, secondary, and higher education, 1920s-91 and projected to 2002, annual rpt, 4824–1
Condition of Education, summary trends, 1970s-91, annual pamphlet, 4824–10
Costa Rica economic indicators and reform issues, mid 1970s-90, working paper, 9916–13.5
Data on education, enrollment, degrees, teachers, and spending, 1977/78-1990/91 and alternative projections to 2002/2003, annual rpt, 4824–4
Data on education, enrollment, finances, teachers, and other characteristics, by State, 1969-89, 4828–33
Data on education, selected trends and projections 1979-2002, annual pamphlet, 4824–9
Data on education, 1940s-95, pamphlet, 4828–35
Data on education, 1960s-91, annual pamphlet, 4824–3
Developing countries economic and social conditions from 1960s, and Intl Dev Cooperation Agency and AID activities and funding, FY91-93, annual rpt, 9904–4.1
Digest of Education Statistics, 1992 annual data compilation, 4824–2
Elementary and secondary education enrollment, staff, finances, operations, programs, and policies, 1987/88 biennial survey, series, 4836–3
Elementary and secondary education enrollment, teachers, high school grads, and spending, by instn control and State, 1992/93, annual rpt, 4834–19
Elementary and secondary public school agencies, by enrollment size and location, fall 1990, annual listing, 4834–1
Elementary and secondary public school systems enrollment, finances, staff, and high school grads, by State, FY89-90, annual rpt, 4834–6
Elementary and secondary public schools and enrollment, by State, 1990/91, annual rpt, 4834–17
Elementary and secondary school system mgmt by higher education instn, Chelsea, Mass and Boston University demonstration program operations and results, 1988-90, 4808–38
Enrollment, by grade, instn type and control, and student characteristics, 1989 and trends from 1947, annual Current Population Rpt, 2546–1.459
Enrollment, staff, and spending, by instn level and control, and teacher salaries, 1980s-93, annual press release, 4804–19
Foreign and US compulsory attendance and testing policies, and enrollment, by selected country, 1970s-91, 26358–255
Head Start enrollment, funding, and staff, FY91, annual rpt, 4584–5
Head Start handicapped enrollment, by handicap, State, and for Indian and migrant programs, 1988/89, annual rpt, 4584–4
Health care professionals supply and education, by professional and other characteristics, and location, 1960s-92 and projected to 2020, biennial rpt, 4114–8
High school class of 1972: community college attendance, by selected characteristics, natl longitudinal study, 1970s-86, 4888–7
High school class of 1991: college enrollment, and labor force participation of grads and dropouts, by race and sex, annual press release, 6726–1.46
Higher education enrollment and degrees awarded, by sex, full- and part-time status, and instn level and control, fall 1991, annual rpt, 4844–16
Higher education enrollment, by level, race, and sex, fall 1980-90, biennial rpt, 4844–15
Higher education enrollment, faculty, finances, and degrees, by instn level and control, and State, FY88, annual rpt, 4844–13
Higher education enrollment, tuition, control, location, and other instn characteristics, 1991/92, biennial listing, 4844–3
Higher education instn student aid and other sources of support, with student expenses and characteristics, by instn type and control, 1987 triennial study, series, 4846–3; 4846–5
Higher education noncollegiate instns enrollment and program completions, by sex and instn level and control, fall 1990, annual rpt, 4844–19
Housing and households detailed characteristics, and unit and neighborhood quality, by location, 1989, biennial rpt supplement, 2485–13
Indian education funding of Fed Govt, with enrollment, program grants, and fellowships by State, 1980s-FY91, annual rpt, 14874–1
Indians and Alaska Natives education condition, indicators and comparisons to other groups, 1980s-90, 4808–42
Juvenile facilities compensatory education programs activities, participant and staff characteristics, and outcomes, 1991 rpts, 4808–40
Latin America economic and social conditions, resources, trade, and aid, 1992, annual factbook, 9914–14
Minority group higher education enrollment, completion, and degrees, by race, sex, and type of instn, 1970s-90, 26306–3.122
Natl Education Goals progress indicators, by State, 1992, annual rpt, 15914–1
Nuclear engineering enrollment and degrees granted by instn and State, and grad placement, by student characteristics, 1991, annual rpt, 3004–5
Pacific territories population and housing detailed characteristics, by location, 1990 Census of Population and Housing, series, 2551–8
Palau admin, and social, economic, and govtl data, FY91, annual rpt, 7004–6
Pell grants and applicants, by tuition, family and student income, instn type and control, and State, 1990/91, annual rpt, 4804–1
Radiation protection and health physics enrollment and degrees granted by instn and State, and grad placement, by student characteristics, 1991, annual rpt, 3004–7
Radiation protection and health physics enrollment and degrees granted by instn and State, and women grads plans and employment, 1991, annual rpt, 3006–8.19
Science and engineering grad enrollment, by field, source of funds, and characteristics of student and instn, 1990, annual rpt, 9626–8.3; 9627–7
Science and Engineering Indicators, employment, education, R&D funding, and industry impacts, with foreign comparisons, 1960s-91, biennial rpt, 9624–10
Science and engineering labor force, Federal and university research funding, and educational data, series, 9626–6
Soviet Union and US economic and sociodemographic indicators, selected years 1970-90, handbook, 2328–80
Special education programs, enrollment by age, staff, funding, and needs, by type of handicap and State, 1990/91, annual rpt, 4944–4
States elementary and secondary curricula, competency, and attendance requirements, with background data, 1970s-90, 4838–52
Statistical Abstract of US, 1992 annual data compilation, 2324–1.4
Vocational education enrollment, and academic and other credits earned, by subject and student characteristics, high school classes of 1982 and 1987, 4838–50
Vocational education enrollment, student and teacher characteristics, and outcomes, for secondary and postsecondary instns, 1970s-90, 4828–42
see also Black students
see also Educational retention rates
see also Foreign students
see also School dropouts
see also Students

Educational exchanges

Fulbright-Hays academic exchanges, grants by purpose, and foreign govt share of costs, by country, FY91, annual rpt, 10324–1

Japan and US technological info transfer activities, and researcher and student exchanges, 1988-89, GAO rpt, 26123–379

Educational facilities

Alteration and repair spending for commercial and public buildings, by type, size, age, and region, 1989, 2388–4

Asbestos in schools, abatement funding and costs by selected State, 1988-91, GAO rpt, 26113–560

Asbestos in schools, inspection and abatement effectiveness, staff and parental notification, and inspector and janitorial training, as of 1990, 9238–71

Assistance (financial and nonfinancial) of Fed Govt, 1992 base edition, annual listing, 104–5

Bombing incidents and casualties, by target, circumstances, and State, 1987-91, annual rpt, 8484–4.1

Child day care and early childhood education programs availability, demand, use, costs, and provider and enrollee characteristics, 1990 survey, 4808–39

Construction put in place, permits, housing sales, costs, material prices, and employment, quarterly rpt with articles, 2042–1

Construction put in place, value of new public and private structures, by type, monthly rpt, 2382–4

County Business Patterns, 1989: employment, establishments, and payroll, by SIC 2- to 4-digit industry and county, annual State rpt series, 2326–8

County Business Patterns, 1990: employment, establishments, and payroll, by SIC 2- to 4-digit industry and county, annual State rpt series, 2326–6

Crime victimization in schools, drug availability, and preventive measures, with student views, 1989 survey, 6066–3.46

Digest of Education Statistics, 1992 annual data compilation, 4824–2

Elementary and secondary education enrollment, staff, finances, operations, programs, and policies, 1987/88 biennial survey, series, 4836–3

Elementary and secondary public school systems spending for facilities, maintenance, acquisition, and community services, by State FY90, annual rpt, 4834–6

Elementary and secondary public schools and enrollment, by State, 1990/91, annual rpt, 4834–17

Energy conservation aid of Fed Govt to public and nonprofit private instns, by building type and State, 1991, annual rpt, 3304–15

Energy use in commercial buildings, costs, and conservation, by building characteristics, survey rpt series, 3166–8

Expenditures for public welfare by program, FY50s-89, annual article, 4742–1.319

Food and alcoholic beverage spending, by place of purchase, 1970-91, annual rpt, 1544–4.5

Head Start enrollment, funding, and staff, FY91, annual rpt, 4584–5

Health care system and OASDHI operations and reform issues, public opinion, 1991 surveys, 10176–2.2

Health clinics in schools under Indian Health Service and tribal admin, by IHS region, 1991, annual chartbook, 4084–7

Higher education instn physical plant inventory and classification methods, 1992 guidelines, 4848–48

Higher education instn revenue by source and spending by function, by State and instn control, FY82-90, annual rpt, 4844–6

Housing (rental) total, HUD-assisted by program, and eligible for aid, recent movers by reason, selected characteristics, and location, 1989, biennial rpt, 5184–11

Housing and households characteristics, and unit and neighborhood quality, by MSA location for 11 MSAs, 1987 survey, supplement, 2485–8

Housing and households detailed characteristics, and unit and neighborhood quality, by location, 1989, biennial rpt supplement, 2485–13

Military training and education programs funding, staff, students, and facilities, by service branch, FY93, annual rpt, 3504–5

Natl income and product accounts, comprehensive accounts and components, benchmark revisions, 1929-88, 2708–5

Natl income and product accounts, comprehensive accounts and components, *Survey of Current Business*, monthly rpt, 2702–1.28

Nuclear reactors for domestic use and export by function and operating status, with owner, operating characteristics, and location, 1991 annual listing, 3354–15

R&D facilities of higher education instns, space and equipment adequacy, needs, and funding by source, by instn type and control, 1992, biennial rpt, 9624–25

R&D funding by higher education instns and federally funded centers, by field, instn, and State, FY90, annual rpt, 9627–13

Science and Engineering Indicators, employment, education, R&D funding, and industry impacts, with foreign comparisons, 1960s-91, biennial rpt, 9624–10.5

Ships for oceanographic research, vessel characteristics by higher education instn and Federal agency, 1992, annual listing, 3804–6

Statistical Abstract of US, 1992 annual data compilation, 2324–1.4

see also Campus security

see also Libraries

Educational finance

Black higher education instns enrollment, finances, staff, and degrees, by instn and selected student characteristics, 1970s-90, 4848–46

Businesses aid to public schools, and business leaders views on education quality and reform, 1991 survey, article, 9383–19.301

Condition of Education, detail for elementary, secondary, and higher education, 1920s-91 and projected to 2002, annual rpt, 4824–1

Data on education, enrollment, degrees, teachers, and spending, 1977/78-1990/91 and alternative projections to 2002/2003, annual rpt, 4824–4

Data on education, enrollment, finances, teachers, and other characteristics, by State, 1969-89, 4828–33

Data on education, selected trends and projections 1979-2002, annual pamphlet, 4824–9

Data on education, 1940s-95, pamphlet, 4828–35

Data on education, 1960s-91, annual pamphlet, 4824–3

Developing countries economic and social conditions from 1960s, and Intl Dev Cooperation Agency and AID activities and funding, FY91-93, annual rpt, 9904–4

Digest of Education Statistics, 1992 annual data compilation, 4824–2

Elementary and secondary education enrollment, teachers, high school grads, and spending, by instn control and State, 1992/93, annual rpt, 4834–19

Elementary and secondary public school systems enrollment, finances, staff, and high school grads, by State, FY89-90, annual rpt, 4834–6

Elementary and secondary school system mgmt by higher education instn, Chelsea, Mass and Boston University demonstration program operations and results, 1988-90, 4808–38

Expenditures (private) for social welfare, by category, 1970s-90, annual article, 4742–1.323

Expenditures, coverage, and benefits for social welfare programs, late 1930s-90, annual rpt, 4744–3.1

Expenditures, enrollment, and spending, by instn level and control, and teachers salaries, 1980s-93, annual press release, 4804–19

Expenditures for public welfare by program, FY50s-89, annual article, 4742–1.319

Expenditures for public welfare programs, by program type and level of govt, FY65-89, annual article, 4742–1.302

Exports and imports of services, direct and among multinatl firms affiliates, by industry and world area, 1986-91, article, 2702–1.336

Govt direct spending and employment, by function and level of govt, selected years 1962-87, 10048–53

Govt finances, by level of govt, State, and for large cities and counties, annual rpt series, 2466–2

Govt finances, structure, and service delivery in large metro areas, local area rpt series, 10046–9

Health care professionals supply and education, by professional and other characteristics, and location, 1960s-92 and projected to 2020, biennial rpt, 4114–8

High school grads in- and out-migration impacts on local education spending, model description and results, 1980s, technical paper, 9379–12.81

Higher education enrollment, faculty, finances, and degrees, by instn level and control, and State, FY88, annual rpt, 4844–13

Higher education instn revenue by source and spending by function, by State and instn control, FY82-90, annual rpt, 4844-6
Input-output structure of US economy, detailed interindustry transactions for 84 industries, and components of final demand, 1987, annual article, 2702-1.316
Input-output structure of US economy, detailed interindustry transactions for 541 industries, and components of final demand, 1982 benchmark data, 2708-17
Juvenile facilities compensatory education programs activities, participant and staff characteristics, and outcomes, 1991 rpt, 4808-40.4
Libraries (public) finances, staff, and operations, by State and population size, 1990, annual rpt, 4824-6
Multinatl US firms and foreign affiliates finances and operations, by industry and country, 1989 benchmark survey, annual rpt, 2704-5
Natl Education Goals progress indicators, by State, 1992, annual rpt, 15914-1
Natl income and product accounts, comprehensive accounts and components, benchmark revisions, 1929-88, 2708-5
Natl income and product accounts, comprehensive accounts and components, *Survey of Current Business*, monthly rpt, 2702-1.29
Nonprofit charitable and other tax exempt organizations finances, by category and size of assets and contributions, 1988, annual article, 8302-2.315
Physicians recently graduating, specialties, school debt, and practice settings, and medical school funding sources, 1970s-91, hearing, 21368-135
R&D facilities of higher education instns, space and equipment adequacy, needs, and funding by source, by instn type and control, 1992, biennial rpt, 9624-25
R&D funding by higher education instns and federally funded centers, by field, instn, and State, FY90, annual rpt, 9627-13
Rural areas employment and population characteristics, and role of education and training in economic dev, 1960s-80s, compilation of papers, 1598-277
School districts budget efficiency measures, model description and results, 1992 technical paper, 9379-12.87
Science and Engineering Indicators, employment, education, R&D funding, and industry impacts, with foreign comparisons, 1960s-91, biennial rpt, 9624-10
Science and engineering labor force, Federal and university research funding, and educational data, series, 9626-6
Science and math achievement relation to selected school characteristics, natl assessment of elementary and high school students, 1985/86, 4896-6.7
Special education programs, enrollment by age, staff, funding, and needs, by type of handicap and State, 1990/91, annual rpt, 4944-4
Statistical Abstract of US, 1992 annual data compilation, 2324-1.4
Tax (income) returns of corporations, income and tax items by asset size and detailed industry, 1989, annual rpt, 8304-4; 8304-21
Tax (income) returns of sole proprietorships, income statement items, by industry group, 1990, annual article, 8302-2.317; 8302-2.320
Tax exempt organizations finances, with data by type, size, State, and for largest organizations, late 1940s-80s, compilation of papers, 8308-35
Tax exempt organizations with unrelated business income, finances by organization type, 1987, article, 8302-2.306
Testing costs, achievement scores by selected State, and attendance and testing policies, with foreign comparisons, 1970s-91, 26358-255
see also Educational employees pay
see also Federal aid to education
see also Federal aid to higher education
see also Federal aid to medical education
see also Federal aid to vocational education
see also State funding for education
see also State funding for higher education
see also Student aid
see also Tuition and fees

Educational materials
Agricultural summary data, young readers pamphlet series, 2346-1
Assistance (financial and nonfinancial) of Fed Govt, 1992 base edition, annual listing, 104-5
CPI by component for US city average, and by selected metro area, region, and population size, monthly rpt, 6762-2
Drug abuse and treatment research summaries, and resource materials and grant listings, bimonthly rpt, 4492-4
Elementary and secondary students educational performance, and factors affecting proficiency, by selected characteristics, 1990 natl assessments, subject rpt series, 4896-8
Elementary and secondary students educational performance in math, science, reading, and writing, 1969-90, 4898-32
Exports and imports between US and outlying areas, by detailed commodity and mode of transport, 1991, annual rpt, 2424-11
Exports and imports of US, by Harmonized System 6-digit commodity and country, 1991, annual rpt, 2424-13
Exports of US, detailed Schedule B commodities with countries of destination, 1991, annual rpt, 2424-10
Humanities Natl Endowment activities and grants, FY91, annual rpt, 9564-2
Juvenile facilities compensatory education programs activities, participant and staff characteristics, and outcomes, 1991 rpt, 4808-40.4
Mail revenue and subsidy for revenue forgone, by class of mail, FY91, and volume from FY87, annual rpt, 9864-1
Mail revenue, costs, and volume, by class of mail, FY91, annual rpt, 9864-2
Mail volume, revenues, and subsidies for revenue forgone, by class of mail, FY91, annual rpt, 9864-5.3
Mail volume to and from households, use, and views, by class, source, content, and household characteristics, FY87-90, annual rpt, 9864-10
NSF R&D grant awards, by div and program, FY87-90, periodic rpt, 9626-7.9
Price indexes (producer), by stage of processing and detailed commodity, monthly rpt, 6762-6
Price indexes (producer), by stage of processing and detailed commodity, monthly 1991, annual rpt, 6764-2
Reading performance and factors affecting proficiency, for elementary and secondary students, 1988 and 1990 natl assessments, 4898-33
Science and math achievement relation to selected school characteristics, natl assessment of elementary and high school students, 1985/86, 4896-6.7

Educational performance
Condition of Education, detail for elementary, secondary, and higher education, 1920s-91 and projected to 2002, annual rpt, 4824-1
Eighth grade class of 1988: educational performance and conditions, characteristics, attitudes, activities, and plans, natl longitudinal survey, series, 4826-9
Elementary and secondary students reading and math proficiency, and dropouts, by race, 1970s-90, 4838-52
Foreign and US students science and math proficiency, intl assessment results and other indicators by selected country, 1960s-80s, 4838-51
Higher education student performance, instns data collection activities, by instn level and control, 1991, 4848-45
Juvenile facilities compensatory education programs activities, participant and staff characteristics, and outcomes, 1991 rpts, 4808-40
Natl Education Goals progress indicators, by State, 1992, annual rpt, 15914-1
see also Degrees, higher education
see also Educational attainment
see also Educational retention rates
see also Educational tests
see also Learning disabilities
see also National Assessment of Educational Progress
see also School dropouts

Educational reform
Businesses aid to public schools, and business leaders views on education quality and reform, 1991 survey, article, 9383-19.301
Digest of Education Statistics, 1992 annual data compilation, 4824-2
Elementary and secondary school system mgmt by higher education instn, Chelsea, Mass and Boston University demonstration program operations and results, 1988-90, 4808-38
Elementary and secondary students educational performance, and factors affecting proficiency, by selected characteristics, 1990 natl assessments, subject rpt series, 4896-8
Indians and Alaska Natives education condition, indicators and comparisons to other groups, 1980s-90, 4808-42
NASA and contractor cooperative education programs activities, 1991, 9508-41
Natl Education Goals progress indicators, by State, 1992, annual rpt, 15914-1

Preschool students transition to kindergarten, programs and factors affecting activities, 1989-90 study, 4808–44
States elementary and secondary curricula, competency, and attendance requirements, with background data, 1970s-90, 4838–52

Educational research
Assistance (financial and nonfinancial) of Fed Govt, 1992 base edition, annual listing, 104–5
Educational Resources Info Center (ERIC) data base, foreign and US providers, 1992 biennial listing, 4814–4
Fast Response Survey System, estimates for education data, series, 4826–1
Fed Govt R&D funding, by detailed function, program, and agency, FY91-93, annual rpt, 9627–9
Field projects funding and descriptions, FY90-91, annual listing, 4884–1
Handicapped children early education project descriptions, 1991/92, annual listing, 4944–10
NSF R&D grant awards, by div and program, FY87-90, periodic rpt, 9626–7.9
Office of Educational Research and Improvement activities, FY91, annual narrative rpt, 4814–1
Tax (income) returns of corporations, income and tax items by asset size and detailed industry, 1989, annual rpt, 8304–4
Women's educational equity program grants and contracts, by project, type, and State, 1988-92, annual rpt, 4804–2
see also National Assessment of Educational Progress

Educational Resources Information Center
"Directory of ERIC Information Service Providers", 4814–4
"Recent Department of Education Publications in ERIC", 4812–1

Educational retention rates
Condition of Education, detail for elementary, secondary, and higher education, 1920s-91 and projected to 2002, annual rpt, 4824–1
Condition of Education, summary trends, 1970s-91, annual pamphlet, 4824–10
Data on education, enrollment, degrees, teachers, and spending, 1977/78-1990/91 and alternative projections to 2002/2003, annual rpt, 4824–4
Data on education, selected trends and projections 1979-2002, annual pamphlet, 4824–9
Data on education, 1940s-95, pamphlet, 4828–35
Digest of Education Statistics, 1992 annual data compilation, 4824–2
Eighth grade class of 1988: educational performance and conditions, characteristics, attitudes, activities, and plans, natl longitudinal survey, series, 4826–9
Elementary and secondary education enrollment, staff, finances, operations, programs, and policies, 1987/88 biennial survey, series, 4836–3
Elementary and secondary education enrollment, teachers, high school grads, and spending, by instn control and State, 1992/93, annual rpt, 4834–19
Elementary and secondary public school agencies, by enrollment size and location, fall 1990, annual listing, 4834–1
Elementary and secondary school system mgmt by higher education instn, Chelsea, Mass and Boston University demonstration program operations and results, 1988-90, 4808–38
High school class of 1972: community college attendance, by selected characteristics, natl longitudinal study, 1970s-86, 4888–7
High school dropout rates, and subsequent completion, by student and school characteristics, alternative estimates, 1991, annual rpt, 4834–23
High school dropouts and transfers between public and private schools, by instn control, income level, and race, 1990 survey, 4826–10.4
High school grads by instn control, and higher education completions by level, 1980s-93, annual press release, 4804–19
High school grads, other completions, and 12th and 9th grade enrollment, by State, classes of FY89 and FY90, annual rpt, 4834–6
Higher education student performance, instns data collection activities, by instn level and control, 1991, 4848–45
Latin America economic and social conditions, resources, trade, and aid, 1992, annual factbook, 9914–14
Minority group higher education enrollment, completion, and degrees, by race, sex, and type of instn, 1970s-90, 26306–3.122
Natl Education Goals progress indicators, by State, 1992, annual rpt, 15914–1
Special education programs, enrollment by age, staff, funding, and needs, by type of handicap and State, 1990/91, annual rpt, 4944–4
Statistical Abstract of US, 1992 annual data compilation, 2324–1.4
see also School dropouts

Educational technology
Computer use in elementary and secondary schools, by grade level, 1992 edition, annual rpt, 4824–2.30
see also Educational broadcasting

Educational television
see Educational broadcasting

Educational tests
Adult education and literacy programs funding, enrollment, and student characteristics and benefits, 1987-90, fact sheet, 4806–4.1; 4806–4.4
Adult education and literacy programs funding, enrollment by State, and student characteristics and benefits, 1987-90, fact sheet, 4806–4.2
Condition of Education, detail for elementary, secondary, and higher education, 1920s-91 and projected to 2002, annual rpt, 4824–1
Digest of Education Statistics, 1992 annual data compilation, 4824–2
DOD Dependents Schools basic skills and college entrance test scores, 1991-92, annual rpt, 3504–16
Eighth grade class of 1988: educational performance and conditions, characteristics, attitudes, activities, and plans, natl longitudinal survey, series, 4826–9
Elementary and secondary school system mgmt by higher education instn, Chelsea, Mass and Boston University demonstration program operations and results, 1988-90, 4808–38
High school class of 1972: community college attendance, by selected characteristics, natl longitudinal study, 1970s-86, 4888–7
High school classes of 1980 and 1982: education, employment, and family characteristics, activities, and attitudes, natl longitudinal study, series, 4826–2
Juvenile facilities compensatory education programs activities, participant and staff characteristics, and outcomes, 1991 rpt, 4808–40.4
Policies for testing and attendance, testing costs, and achievement scores by selected State, with foreign comparisons, 1970s-91, 26358–255
Public housing residents educational attainment, by selected characteristics, 1980s, 5188–132
Science and engineering enrollment, performance, curricula, student aid sources, and career plans, by sex and race, 1970s-91, biennial rpt, 9624–20.2
Science and Engineering Indicators, employment, education, R&D funding, and industry impacts, with foreign comparisons, 1960s-91, biennial rpt, 9624–10.1
States elementary and secondary curricula, competency, and attendance requirements, with background data, 1970s-90, 4838–52
Statistical Abstract of US, 1992 annual data compilation, 2324–1.4
see also National Assessment of Educational Progress

Edwards, Robert D.
"Estimated Oil and Gas Reserves: Pacific Outer Continental Shelf (as of Dec. 31, 1990)", 5734–7

Eggs
see Poultry industry and products

Egypt
Agricultural trade by commodity and country, prices, and world market devs, monthly rpt, 1922–12
Agricultural trade of US, by detailed commodity and country, 1991, annual rpt, 1524–8
Agricultural trade of US, by detailed commodity and country, 1991, semiannual rpt, 1522–4
AID economic aid to developing countries, obligations and disbursements by country, quarterly rpt, 9912–4
AID loans repayment status and terms by program and country, and status of predecessor agency loans, quarterly rpt, 9912–3
Cuba trade, by commodity and country, mid 1980s-91, 9118–8
Economic and military aid and loans from US and intl agencies, by program and country, FY46-91, annual rpt, 9914–5
Economic and social conditions of developing countries from 1960s, and Intl Dev Cooperation Agency and AID activities and funding, FY91-93, annual rpt, 9904–4

Economic conditions, policy, and trade practices, by country, 1989-91, annual rpt, 21384-5
Economic, social, political, and geographic summary data, by country, 1992, annual factbook, 9114-2
Exports and imports of US, by commodity and country, 1980-90, world area rpt, 9116-1.6
Exports and imports of US, by Harmonized System 6-digit commodity and country, 1991, annual rpt, 2424-13
Exports and imports of US, by selected country, country group, and commodity group, 1991, annual rpt, 2044-37
Exports and imports of US, by transport mode, country, and SITC 1- to 3-digit commodity, 1991, annual rpt, 2424-12
Exports, imports, and balances of US for manufactured goods, by SITC 2-digit commodity and country, quarterly rpt, 2042-35
Exports of US, detailed Schedule B commodities with countries of destination, 1991, annual rpt, 2424-10
Food supply, needs, and aid for developing countries, status and alternative forecasts, 1992 world area rpt, 1526-8.2
Human rights conditions in 170 countries, and US economic and military aid, 1991, annual rpt, 21384-3
Imports of goods, services, and investment from US, trade barriers, impacts, and US actions, by country, 1991, annual rpt, 444-2
Labor conditions, union coverage, and work accidents, 1992 annual country rpt, 6366-4.26
Military aid of US, arms sales, and training programs costs and budget requests, by program, world region, and country, FY91-93, annual rpt, 7144-13
Military spending, arms trade, and force strengths, with govt spending and population, by country, 1979-89, annual rpt, 9824-1
Minerals Yearbook, Vol 3, 1989: foreign country review of production, trade, and policy, by commodity, annual rpt, 5604-35.1
Multinatl US firms and foreign affiliates finances and operations, by industry and country, 1989 benchmark survey, annual rpt, 2704-5
Multinatl US firms foreign affiliates, income statement items by asset size, industry, and country, 1988, biennial article, 8302-2.322
Population size, growth rates, and components of change, by country, projected 1990-2020 and trends from 1950, biennial rpt, 2324-9
Refugee migration, and intl aid programs, by world area and country of origin and asylum, 1991, annual rpt, 7004-15
Steel trade, by product, country, and customs district, with US industry operating data, 1989-June 1992, semiannual rpt, 9882-15
UN voting record and share of votes in agreement with US, by issue, country, and world area, 1991, annual rpt, 7004-18
see also under By Foreign Country in the "Index by Categories"

Ehrenberg, Ralph E.
"Cartographic Records in the National Archives of the U.S. Useful for Urban Studies", 9516-1.1

Eichenbaum, Martin
"Liquidity Effects and the Monetary Transmission Mechanism", 9383-20.20

Eichorn, Ann
"Method for Assessing the Outcomes of Nursing Home Care Using Administrative Databases", 4164-2

Eisenberg, Laurence K.
"Generalized Put-Call Parity", 9371-10.67
"Option Pricing with Random Volatilities in Complete Markets", 9371-10.74
"Quantity-Adjusting Options and Forward Contracts", 9371-10.73

Eisler, Ronald
"Cyanide Hazards to Fish, Wildlife, and Invertebrates: A Synoptic Review", 5506-14.4
"Fenvalerate Hazards to Fish, Wildlife, and Invertebrates: A Synoptic Review", 5506-14.5

El-Bassel, Nabila
"15-Month Followup of Women Methadone Patients Taught Skills To Reduce Heterosexual HIV Transmission", 4042-3.353

El Paso. Tex.
see also under By City and By SMSA or MSA in the "Index by Categories"

El Salvador
Agricultural trade of US, by detailed commodity and country, 1991, annual rpt, 1524-8
Agricultural trade of US, by detailed commodity and country, 1991, semiannual rpt, 1522-4
AID economic aid to developing countries, obligations and disbursements by country, quarterly rpt, 9912-4
AID loans repayment status and terms by program and country, and status of predecessor agency loans, quarterly rpt, 9912-3
Economic and military aid and loans from US and intl agencies, by program and country, FY46-91, annual rpt, 9914-5
Economic and social conditions of developing countries from 1960s, and Intl Dev Cooperation Agency and AID activities and funding, FY91-93, annual rpt, 9904-4
Economic and social conditions, resources, and trade, and aid, 1992, annual factbook, 9914-14
Economic conditions, policy, and trade practices, by country, 1989-91, annual rpt, 21384-5
Economic indicators for Central America by country, 1969-89, working paper, 9916-13.4
Economic, population, and agricultural data, US and other aid sources, and AID activity, 1992 country rpt, 9916-12.66
Economic, social, political, and geographic summary data, by country, 1992, annual factbook, 9114-2
Exports and imports of US, by commodity and country, 1980-90, world area rpt, 9116-1.5
Exports and imports of US, by transport mode, country, and SITC 1- to 3-digit commodity, 1991, annual rpt, 2424-12
Exports, imports, and balances of US for manufactured goods, by SITC 2-digit commodity and country, quarterly rpt, 2042-35
Exports of US, detailed Schedule B commodities with countries of destination, 1991, annual rpt, 2424-10
Hostages kidnapped in El Salvador, listing as of 1991, 7004-22
Human rights conditions in 170 countries, and US economic and military aid, 1991, annual rpt, 21384-3
Imports of goods, services, and investment from US, trade barriers, impacts, and US actions, by country, 1991, annual rpt, 444-2
Military aid of US, arms sales, and training programs costs and budget requests, by program, world region, and country, FY91-93, annual rpt, 7144-13
Military spending, arms trade, and force strengths, with govt spending and population, by country, 1979-89, annual rpt, 9824-1
Population size, growth rates, and components of change, by country, projected 1990-2020 and trends from 1950, biennial rpt, 2324-9
Refugee migration, and intl aid programs, by world area and country of origin and asylum, 1991, annual rpt, 7004-15
UN voting record and share of votes in agreement with US, by issue, country, and world area, 1991, annual rpt, 7004-18

Elderly
see Aged and aging

Elections
Computer systems for voter registration and verification data storage and retrieval, use and characteristics, for selected counties, 1992 rpt, 9278-8
Criminal cases by type and disposition, and collections, for US attorneys, by Federal district, FY91, annual rpt, 6004-2.1
Criminal sentences for Federal offenses, guidelines by offense and circumstances, series, 17668-1
Fed Election Commission activities, campaign finances, elections, and procedures, press release series, 9276-1
Foreign countries economic, social, political, and geographic summary data, by country, 1992, annual factbook, 9114-2
Labor Relations Natl Board-conducted representation elections, by major industry group and location, FY90, annual rpt, 9584-1.2
Labor union representation elections conducted by NLRB, results, monthly rpt, 9582-2
Mail volume to and from households, use, and views, by class, source, content, and household characteristics, FY87-90, annual rpt, 9864-10
Older persons socioeconomic characteristics, 1900s-90 and projected to 2050, biennial chartbook, 12904-1
Older population, and health, economic, and other characteristics, with foreign comparisons, 1980s-91 with trends and projections, Current Population Rpt, 2546-2.165
Polling places access and services availability for aged and disabled, by State, 1990 natl elections, hearing, 21428-11

Puerto Rico statehood referendum proposal, with background data on Federal outlays, economic conditions, and finances of corporations with tax-favored status, 1940s-88, hearing, 21448–46
Statistical Abstract of US, 1992 annual data compilation, 2324–1.8
UN voting record and share of votes in agreement with US, by issue, country, and world area, 1991, annual rpt, 7004–18
Voter turnout by age and sex, 1990 congressional elections, with trends from 1964, fact sheet, 2326–17.39
Votes cast by party, candidate, and State, 1990 natl elections, biennial rpt, 21944–3
Voting age population, by sex, age, race, and State, forecast 1992 general elections, with votes cast from 1930, Current Population Rpt, 2546–3.170
Voting participation rates, by education level, 1964-90 elections, annual rpt, 4824–1
see also Campaign funds
see also Political action committees
see also Political conventions

Electric Consumers Protection Act
Hydroelectric power plants licensing by FERC, impacts of environmental laws, with staffing and plant safety incidents, 1980s-90s, GAO rpt, 26113–599

Electric power
Auto (electric-powered) R&D activity and DOE funding shares, FY91, annual rpt, 3304–2
Auto alternative fuels pollutant emissions by fuel type, and alcohol fuel production and inputs, 1991 hearing, 25318–82
Bonneville Power Admin mgmt of Fed Columbia River Power System, finances and sales, summary data, quarterly rpt, 3222–2
Bonneville Power Admin mgmt of Fed Columbia River Power System, finances, operations, and sales by customer, FY91, annual rpt, 3224–1
Bonneville Power Admin sales, revenues, and rates, by customer and customer type, 1991, semiannual rpt, 3222–1
Business electric power demand, and industrial and employment impacts of capacity shortfalls and new power plants, by selected State, 1960s-80s and projected to 2000, hearing, 21248–163
Business statistics, detailed data for major industries and economic indicators, *Survey of Current Business*, monthly rpt, 2702–1.12
Business statistics, detailed data for major industries and economic indicators, 1960-91, *Survey of Current Business* biennial supplement, 2704–1
Capital expenditures for plant and equipment, by major industry group, quarterly rpt, 2502–2
Census of Population and Housing, 1990: summary characteristics, by county, subdiv, and place, State rpt series, 2551–7
Coal-fired power plants generating capacity and replacement of energy imports, with background data, alternative forecasts 1990-2000, 3166–6.63
Coal production, reserves, use, and prices by State, exports by country, and employment, 1900s-90, biennial rpt, 3164–79
Commercial buildings energy use, costs, and conservation, by building characteristics, survey rpt series, 3166–8
Conservation programs of electric utilities, alternative planning strategies cost effectiveness, model results, 1991 rpt, 3308–100
Conservation programs of electric utilities, collaboration between utilities and interest groups, and effects on costs, 1992 rpt, 3308–104
Conservation programs of electric utilities, data reporting guidelines, with background data, 1991 rpt, 3308–101
Conservation programs of electric utilities, energy savings and spending, with data for top 25 firms, 1990, 3308–106
Conservation programs of electric utilities, energy savings measurement methodology, 1991, compilation of papers, 3308–102
Conservation programs of electric utilities, impacts on electric power prices and revenue requirements, alternative projections 1990-2010, 3308–105
Conservation programs of electric utilities, peak load reductions, energy savings, and costs, by region, 1989-90 and projected to 2000, article, 3162–35.302
Consumer spending, natl income and product account benchmark revisions, 1929-88, 2708–5
Consumer spending, natl income and product accounts, comprehensive accounts and components, *Survey of Current Business*, monthly rpt, 2702–1.25
Consumption of energy, by detailed fuel type, end-use sector, and State, 1960-90, State Energy Data System annual rpt, 3164–39
County Business Patterns, 1989: employment, establishments, and payroll, by SIC 2- to 4-digit industry and county, annual State rpt series, 2326–8
County Business Patterns, 1990: employment, establishments, and payroll, by SIC 2- to 4-digit industry and county, annual State rpt series, 2326–6
Demand (seasonal peak) for electricity and generating capacity, by region, annual rpt, suspended, 3404–6
Employment, earnings, and hours, by SIC 1- to 4-digit industry, monthly 1989-Feb 1992, annual rpt, 6744–4
Employment of minorities and women, by occupation, SIC 1- to 3-digit industry, State, and MSA, 1991, annual rpt, 9244–1
Exports and imports between US and outlying areas, by detailed commodity and mode of transport, 1991, annual rpt, 2424–11
Exports and imports of US, by country and detailed commodity, monthly rpt, 2422–12
Exports and imports of US, by Harmonized System 6-digit commodity and country, 1991, annual rpt, 2424–13
Exports and imports of US, by selected country, country group, and commodity group, 1991, annual rpt, 2044–37
Exports and imports of US, by transport mode, country, and SITC 1- to 3-digit commodity, 1991, annual rpt, 2424–12
Exports of US, detailed Schedule B commodities with countries of destination, 1991, annual rpt, 2424–10
Farm production inputs supply, demand, and prices, 1970s-91 and projected to 1996, article, 1561–16.301
Farm production inputs supply, demand, and prices, 1980s-92, article, 1561–16.304
Farm production itemized costs, by farm sales size and region, 1991, annual rpt, 1614–3
Foreign and US energy production and use, by energy type and country, 1981-90, annual rpt, 3164–50.5
Foreign and US energy production, trade, use, and reserves, and oil and refined products supply and prices, by country, 1981-90, annual rpt, 3164–50
Foreign and US energy supply and demand, by major fuel and end-use sector, 1950s-87 and forecast to 1995, 3166–6.58
Foreign countries economic conditions and implications for US, periodic country rpt series, 2046–4
Foreign countries economic, social, political, and geographic summary data, by country, 1992, annual factbook, 9114–2
Govt employment and payroll, by function, level of govt, and jurisdiction, annual rpt series, 2466–1
Govt labor productivity, indexes of output and labor costs by function, FY67-90, annual rpt, 6824–1.6
Housing (low income) energy aid, funding sources, costs, and participation, by State, FY90, annual rpt, 4584–1
Housing (rental) market absorption rates, by whether utilities included in rent, 1990, annual Current Housing Rpt, 2484–2
Housing (rental) units, total, with HUD assistance by program, and eligible for aid, by unit, household, and neighborhood characteristics, and location, 1989, biennial rpt, 5184–11
Housing and households characteristics, and unit and neighborhood quality, by MSA location for 11 MSAs, 1987 survey, supplement, 2485–8
Housing and households detailed characteristics, and unit and neighborhood quality, by location, 1989, biennial rpt supplement, 2485–13
Housing and households detailed characteristics, and unit and neighborhood quality, MSA surveys, series, 2485–6
Housing energy use, costs, and conservation, and household and housing characteristics, survey rpt series, 3166–7
Housing heating and air conditioning equipment shipments by type of fuel used, quarterly rpt, 2042–1.6
Housing units completed, single and multifamily units by structural and financial characteristics, and location, 1987-91, annual rpt, 2384–1
Industrial electricity use indexes, by SIC 2- to 4-digit industry, monthly rpt, 9365–2.24
Input-output structure of US economy, detailed interindustry transactions for 541 industries, and components of final demand, 1982 benchmark data, 2708–17
Labor productivity, indexes of output, hours, and employment by SIC 2- to 4-digit industry, 1967-90, annual rpt, 6824–1.4
Manufacturing annual survey, 1990: establishments, employment, finances, inventories, and energy use, by SIC 2- to 4-digit industry, 2506–14.2

Manufacturing annual survey, 1990: finances and operations, by SIC 2- and 3-digit industry and State, 2506–14.3
Manufacturing energy use and prices, by fuel type and industry, 1974-88, 3166–15.3
Manufacturing energy use and prices, 1988 survey, series, 3166–13
Mexico and US electric power supply, demand, and trade, with data by fuel source, utility, and region, 1970s-89 and projected to 2000, 3408–2
Natl Energy Strategy fossil fuel, electric power, conservation, and pollution reduction issues, 1991 hearings, 21368–136
Natl Energy Strategy plans for conservation, R&D, security, and pollution reduction, technical rpt series, 3006–13
New England States electric power sales, Fed Reserve 1st District, monthly rpt, 9373–2
Occupational injury and illness rates, by SIC 2- to 4-digit industry, 1989-90, annual rpt, 6844–7
Occupational injury and illness rates, by SIC 2- to 4-digit industry, 1990, annual rpt, 6844–1
Pacific Northwest electric power capacity and use, by end-use sector, projected under alternative fuel price cases, annual rpt, suspended, 3224–4
Pacific Northwest electric power capacity and use, by energy source, forecast under alternative load and demand cases, 1991-2012, annual rpt, 3224–3
Pacific territories population and housing detailed characteristics, by location, 1990 Census of Population and Housing, series, 2551–8
Panama Canal electric power generated, purchased, and sold, FY90-91, annual rpt, 9664–3.2
Production, dev, and distribution firms revenues and income, quarterly rpt, 3162–38
Production of electric power, and utility fuel use, stocks, and costs by fuel type, and sales, by State, monthly rpt, 3162–35
Production, sales, plant capacity, and fuel stocks, use, and costs, by State, 1986-90, annual rpt, 3164–11
Romania energy production and trade, 1970s-91, with capital investment projected to 2000, GAO rpt, 26123–402
Southeastern Power Admin sales by customer, plants, capacity, and Southeastern Fed Power Program financial statements, FY91, annual rpt, 3234–1
Southwestern Fed Power System financial statements, sales by customer, and operations and costs by project, FY91, annual rpt, 3244–1
Statistical Abstract of US, 1992 annual data compilation, 2324–1.19
Supply, demand, and distribution of energy, and regulatory impacts, series, 3166–6
Supply, demand, and prices, by fuel type and end-use sector, alternative projections by region, 1990-2010, annual rpt, 3164–96
Supply, demand, and prices, by fuel type and end-use sector, alternative projections 1990-2010, annual rpt, 3164–75
Supply, demand, and prices, by fuel type and end-use sector, projections and underlying assumptions, 1995-2010, annual rpt, 3164–90
Supply, demand, and prices, by fuel type and end-use sector, with foreign comparisons, 1981-90, annual fact book, 3164–76
Supply, demand, and prices, by fuel type and end-use sector, with foreign comparisons, 1991 and trends from 1949, annual rpt, 3164–74
Supply, demand, and prices, by fuel type, end-use sector, and country, detailed data, monthly rpt with articles, 3162–24
Supply, demand, and prices, by fuel type, end-use sector, and country, detailed data, monthly 1973-88, 3168–123
Supply, demand, and prices of energy, forecasts by resource type, quarterly rpt, 3162–34
Supply of electric power, production and capacity by fuel type, prices, demand, and air pollution law impacts, by region, projections, annual rpt, discontinued, 3164–81
Tax (income) returns of corporations, income and tax items by asset size and detailed industry, 1989, annual rpt, 8304–4; 8304–21
Transit systems finances and operations, by mode, size of fleet and urban area, region, and for 518 systems, 1990, annual rpt, 7884–4
Transportation energy use by mode, fuel supply, and demographic and economic factors of vehicle use, 1970s-90, annual rpt, 3304–5
TVA electric power purchases and resales, with electricity use, average bills, and rates by customer class, by distributor, 1991, annual tables, 9804–14
TVA electric power purchases of municipal and cooperative distributors, and prices and use by distributor and consumer sector, monthly rpt, 9802–1
TVA finances and electric power sales, FY91, annual rpt, 9804–1
TVA finances and operations by program and facility, FY91, annual rpt, 9804–32
Utilities finances and operations, detailed data for privately owned firms, 1990, annual rpt, 3164–23
Utilities finances and operations, detailed data for publicly and privately owned firms, 1990, annual rpt, 3164–11.4
Utilities finances and operations, detailed data for publicly owned firms, 1990, annual rpt, 3164–24
VA health care facilities energy use and conservation, by facility, quarterly rpt, 8602–9
Western Area Power Admin activities by plant, financial statements, and sales by customer, FY91, annual rpt, 3254–1
see also Electric power and heat cogeneration
see also Electric power plants and equipment
see also Electric power prices
see also Electrical machinery and equipment
see also Hydroelectric power
see also Nuclear power
see also Rural electrification
see also Solar energy
see also Wind energy

Electric power and heat cogeneration
Certification applications filed with FERC, for small power production and cogeneration facilities, FY80-91, annual listing, 3084–13
Consumption of electric power, indexes by SIC 2- to 4-digit industry, monthly rpt, 9365–2.24
Industrial electric power producers capacity, generation, and sales by industry div and State, and emissions, by census div, 1989-90, article, 3162–35.301
Manufacturing annual survey, 1990: establishments, employment, finances, inventories, and energy use, by SIC 2- to 4-digit industry, 2506–14.2
Manufacturing annual survey, 1990: finances and operations, by SIC 2- and 3-digit industry and State, 2506–14.3
Manufacturing energy use and prices, 1988 survey, series, 3166–13
Natl Energy Strategy Strategic Petroleum Reserve and energy efficiency issues, 1991 hearings, 21368–142
Pacific Northwest nonutility electric power generation and capacity, by energy source, purchasing utility, and facility, forecasts 1991-2012, annual rpt, 3224–3.4
Supply, demand, and prices, by fuel type and end-use sector, alternative projections by region, 1990-2010, annual rpt, 3164–96

Electric power plants and equipment
Acid rain environmental, economic, and health effects, and pollutant emissions, 1985-89 and alternative projections to 2030, 14358–4
Army Corps of Engineers activities and projects, FY88 and trends from 1800s, annual rpt, 3754–1.1
Army Corps of Engineers activities and projects, FY89 and trends from 1800s, annual rpt, 3754–1.2
Army Corps of Engineers activities and projects, FY90 and trends from 1800s, annual rpt, 3754–1.3
Birds of prey, rodent, and vegetation distribution and characteristics, for Idaho Snake River area, research results, 1991, annual rpt, 5724–14
Bonneville Power Admin mgmt of Fed Columbia River Power System, finances, operations, and sales by customer, FY91, annual rpt, 3224–1
Business statistics, detailed data for major industries and economic indicators, *Survey of Current Business*, monthly rpt, 2702–1.12; 2702–1.17
Business statistics, detailed data for major industries and economic indicators, 1960-91, *Survey of Current Business* biennial supplement, 2704–1
Cable (underground) from Canada at less than fair value, injury to US industry, investigation with background financial and operating data, 1992 rpt, 9886–14.341
Capacity and investment in power plants by fuel type, and industrial and employment impacts of new power plants, by selected State, 1960s-80s and projected to 2000, hearing, 21248–163
Capacity and plants, by fuel used, owner, location, and operating status, 1991, and for units planned 1992-2001, annual listing, 3164–36

Capacity and production of electric power by fuel type, prices, demand, and air pollution law impacts, by region, projections, annual rpt, discontinued, 3164–81
Capacity of power plants, production, sales, and fuel stocks, use, and costs, by State, 1986-90, annual rpt, 3164–11
Capital and production costs, operations, and fuel use, by fuel type, plant, utility, and location, 1990, annual rpt, 3164–9
Certification applications filed with FERC, for small power production and cogeneration facilities, FY80-91, annual listing, 3084–13
China biomass-fired electric power plant feasibility assessment, 1991 rpt, 3308–103
Coal and coke supply, demand, movements, prices, and stocks, by end-use sector and State, quarterly rpt, 3162–37
Coal-fired power plants air pollutant reduction technology funding, and impacts on energy costs and emissions, 1950s-87 and projected to 2010, annual rpt, 3334–5; 3338–4
Coal-fired power plants air pollutant reduction technology funding, and project descriptions, 1991, annual rpt, 3334–4
Coal-fired power plants generating capacity and replacement of energy imports, with background data, alternative forecasts 1990-2000, 3166–6.63
Coal mining restrictions on public land, impacts on production, costs, and demand, by region, 1985-88 and projected to 2075, 5668–125
Coal production and mines by county, prices, productivity, miners, and reserves, by mining method and State, 1990-91, annual rpt, 3164–25
Coal production, stocks, and shipments, by State of origin and destination, end-use sector, and mode of transport, quarterly rpt, 3162–8
Colorado River Basin Federal reservoir and power operations and revenues, 1991-92, annual rpt, 5824–6
Colorado River Storage Project finances and activities in western States, FY91, annual rpt, 5824–3
Construction put in place, permits, housing sales, costs, material prices, and employment, quarterly rpt with articles, 2042–1
Construction put in place, private and public, by type and region, monthly rpt, annual tables, 2382–4
Construction put in place, value of new public and private structures, by type, monthly rpt, 2382–4
County Business Patterns, 1989: employment, establishments, and payroll, by SIC 2- to 4-digit industry and county, annual State rpt series, 2326–8
County Business Patterns, 1990: employment, establishments, and payroll, by SIC 2- to 4-digit industry and county, annual State rpt series, 2326–6
Developing countries energy efficiency improvement issues and devs, with data by end use and country, 1980s-90, 26358–260
Employment, earnings, and hours, by SIC 1- to 4-digit industry, monthly 1989-Feb 1992, annual rpt, 6744–4
Employment of minorities and women, by occupation, SIC 1- to 3-digit industry, State, and MSA, 1991, annual rpt, 9244–1
Energy prices and spending, by fuel type, end-use sector, and State, 1990, annual rpt, 3164–64
Energy supply, demand, and prices, by fuel type and end-use sector, alternative projections by region, 1990-2010, annual rpt, 3164–96
Energy supply, demand, and prices, by fuel type and end-use sector, alternative projections 1990-2010, annual rpt, 3164–75
Energy supply, demand, and prices, by fuel type and end-use sector, projections and underlying assumptions, 1995-2010, annual rpt, 3164–90
Energy supply, demand, and prices, by fuel type and end-use sector, with foreign comparisons, 1991 and trends from 1949, annual rpt, 3164–74
Energy supply, demand, and prices, by fuel type, end-use sector, and country, detailed data, monthly rpt with articles, 3162–24
Energy supply, demand, and prices, by fuel type, end-use sector, and country, detailed data, monthly 1973-88, 3168–123
Energy supply, demand, and prices, forecasts by resource type, quarterly rpt, 3162–34
Energy use, by detailed fuel type, end-use sector, and State, 1960-90, State Energy Data System annual rpt, 3164–39
Energy use in transportation and other sectors, by fuel type, 1970s-90, annual rpt, 3304–5
Energy use of power plants, production, stocks, and costs by fuel type, and sales, by State, monthly rpt, 3162–35
Environmental Quality, status of problems, protection programs, research, and intl issues, 1991 annual rpt, 484–1
Eximbank loans for energy-related products and services, by country and firm, 1990, annual rpt, 9254–3
Export markets, competitiveness, and promotion, for US energy technology industries, 1992 technical rpt, 3006–13.5
Exports and imports between US and outlying areas, by detailed commodity and mode of transport, 1991, annual rpt, 2424–11
Exports and imports of US, by country and detailed commodity, monthly rpt, 2422–12
Exports and imports of US, by Harmonized System 6-digit commodity and country, 1991, annual rpt, 2424–13
Exports and imports of US, by transport mode, country, and SITC 1- to 3-digit commodity, 1991, annual rpt, 2424–12
Exports of US, detailed Schedule B commodities with countries of destination, 1991, annual rpt, 2424–10
Fed Govt power plants conversion to alternative fuels, 1992, annual rpt, 3334–2
Foreign and US energy supply and demand, by major fuel and end-use sector, 1950s-87 and forecast to 1995, 3166–6.58
Fuel oil and kerosene sales and deliveries, by end-use, PAD district, and State, 1990, annual rpt, 3164–94
Geothermal resources, power plant generation, capacity, and dev potential, by location, 1988-90 and projected to 2030, 3168–122
Hydroelectric power generation and capacity, for TVA projects, 1990, annual rpt, 9804–7
Hydroelectric power plants, generation, and capacity, for Reclamation Bur projects, 1978-90 and projected to 1995, 5828–14
Hydroelectric power plants licensing by FERC, impacts of environmental laws, with staffing and plant safety incidents, 1980s-90s, GAO rpt, 26113–599
Hydroelectric power plants retired, characteristics and location, as of 1992, annual listing, 3084–12
Imports of US given duty-free treatment for value of US material sent abroad, by commodity and country, 1987-90, annual rpt, 9884–14
Industrial electric power producers capacity, generation, and sales by industry div and State, and emissions, by census div, 1989-90, article, 3162–35.301
Input-output structure of US economy, detailed interindustry transactions for 541 industries, and components of final demand, 1982 benchmark data, 2708–17
Jordan oil shale-fired electric power plants, feasibility assessment with background data, 1990 rpt, 3008–127
Labor productivity, indexes of output, hours, and employment by SIC 2- to 4-digit industry, 1967-90, annual rpt, 6824–1.3
Manufacturing annual survey, 1990: finances and operations, by SIC 2- to 4-digit industry, series, 2506–14
Manufacturing census, 1987: concentration of largest firms measured by value added, and for shipments by SIC 2- and 4-digit industry, subject rpt, 2497–6
Manufacturing finances and operations, by SIC 2- to 4-digit industry, forecast 1992, annual rpt, 2044–28
Mexico and US electric power supply, demand, and trade, with data by fuel source, utility, and region, 1970s-89 and projected to 2000, 3408–2
Natl Energy Strategy plans for conservation, R&D, security, and pollution reduction, technical rpt series, 3006–13
Natl forests revenue, by source, forest, and State, FY91, annual rpt, 1204–34
Natural and supplemental gas production, prices, trade, use, reserves, and pipeline company finances, by firm and State, monthly rpt with articles, 3162–4
Natural gas supply, demand, prices, and distribution, by State, 1986-90 annual rpt, 3164–4
Natural gas use, by end-use sector and PAD district, seasonal weekly rpt, 3162–45
Nuclear power plant capacity and uranium needs, projected 1990-2005, annual rpt, 3164–82
Nuclear power plant capacity, availability, and load factors, by plant and foreign country, quarterly journal, annual tables, 3352–4.3
Nuclear power plant construction costs and status, and capacity, by plant, annual rpt, discontinued, 3164–69
Nuclear power plant safety standards and research, design, licensing, construction, operation, and finances, with data by reactor, quarterly journal, 3352–4

Nuclear power plant spent fuel and waste generation, inventory, and disposal, 1960s-90 and projected to 2020, annual rpt, 3364–2
Nuclear power plant spent fuel deliveries to DOE for disposal, by utility and reactor, projected 1998-2007, annual rpt, 3364–5
Nuclear power plant spent fuel discharges and additional storage capacity needed, by reactor, projected 1991-2040, annual rpt, 3354–2
Nuclear power plant spent fuel discharges, storage capacity, and inventories, by reactor, 1968-89, 3166–6.62
Nuclear power plant spent fuel storage capacity and inventories, by reactor, as of 1987, 3166–6.59
Nuclear reactor and other low-level radioactive disposal activities of States and interstate compacts, with data by disposal facility and reactor, 1990, annual rpt, 3004–36
Nuclear reactors for domestic use and export by function and operating status, with owner, operating characteristics, and location, 1991 annual listing, 3354–15
Nuclear reactors trade of OECD, total and for 4 major countries, and US trade by country, 1980-90, world area rpt series, 9116–1
Nuclear Regulatory Commission activities, finances, and staff, with data for individual power plants, FY91, annual rpt, 9634–2
Occupational injury and illness rates, by SIC 2- to 4-digit industry, 1989-90, annual rpt, 6844–7
Occupational injury and illness rates, by SIC 2- to 4-digit industry, 1990, annual rpt, 6844–1
OECD trade, total and for 4 major countries, and US trade by country, by commodity, 1980-90, world area rpt series, 9116–1
Oil and gas primary use prohibited for power and industrial plants, exemptions, and gas use by State, 1980-91, annual rpt, 3334–1
Pacific basin countries energy supply and demand, and implications for US trade, country rpt series, 3406–6
Pacific Northwest electric power capacity and use, by energy source, forecast under alternative load and demand cases, 1991-2012, annual rpt, 3224–3
Pacific Northwest nonutility electric power generation and capacity, by energy source, purchasing utility, and facility, forecasts 1991-2012, annual rpt, 3224–3.4
Pollution (air) abatement equipment shipments by industry, and new and backlog orders, by product, 1991, annual Current Industrial Rpt, 2506–12.5
Pollution (air) emissions and abatement equipment, for privately owned electric utilities by fuel type and State, 1986-90, annual rpt, 3164–11.5
Pollution (air) levels for 3 pollutants, and capacity of plants with abatement equipment, by type, 1985-90, annual rpt, 3164–74.5
Pollution abatement capital spending, for mining, petroleum refining, and electric utilities, 1990, annual Current Industrial Rpt, 2506–3.6
Price indexes (producer), by stage of processing and detailed commodity, monthly rpt, 6762–6
Prices paid by utilities for fossil fuels, FY90-91, annual rpt, 3084–9
Production and capacity use indexes, by SIC 2- to 4-digit industry, monthly rpt, 9365–2.24
R&D facilities of higher education instns, space and equipment adequacy, needs, and funding by source, by instn type and control, 1992, biennial rpt, 9624–25
Reclamation Bur irrigation activities, finances, and project impacts in western US, 1990, annual rpt, 5824–12
Replacement and renewal of aging steam power plants, costs and benefits for selected units, projected 1991-2000, article, 3162–35.303
Rural Electrification Admin financed electric power plants, with location, capacity, and owner, as of Jan 1992, annual listing, 1244–6
Rural Electrification Admin loans, and borrower operating and financial data, by distribution firm and State, 1991, annual rpt, 1244–1
Science, engineering, and technical employment in manufacturing, by field and industry, 1989, triennial rpt, 9627–23
Southeastern Power Admin sales by customer, plants, capacity, and Southeastern Fed Power Program financial statements, FY91, annual rpt, 3234–1
Southwestern Fed Power System financial statements, sales by customer, and operations and costs by project, FY91, annual rpt, 3244–1
Soviet Union and US economic and sociodemographic indicators, selected years 1970-90, handbook, 2328–80
Soviet Union former Republics and Baltic States energy supply and use, and social, economic, and political indicators, 1989-90, 3168–126
Steam-driven power plants fuel receipts, costs, and quality, by fuel, plant, utility, and State, 1991, annual rpt, 3164–42
TVA finances and operations by program and facility, FY91, annual rpt, 9804–32
Utilities finances and operations, detailed data for privately owned firms, 1990, annual rpt, 3164–23
Utilities finances and operations, detailed data for publicly and privately owned firms, 1990, annual rpt, 3164–11.4
Utilities finances and operations, detailed data for publicly owned firms, 1990, annual rpt, 3164–24
Water use by end use, well withdrawals, and public supply deliveries, by county, State rpt series, 5666–24
Western Area Power Admin activities by plant, financial statements, and sales by customer, FY91, annual rpt, 3254–1
Wiring devices and supplies shipments, trade, use, and firms, by product, 1991, annual Current Industrial Rpt, 2506–12.18
Wood, waste, and alcohol fuel use, by end-use sector and region, 1990, annual rpt, 3164–97
see also Electric power and heat cogeneration
see also Nuclear accidents and safety

Electric power prices
Bonneville Power Admin sales, revenues, and rates, by customer and customer type, 1991, semiannual rpt, 3222–1
Coal-fired power plants air pollutant reduction technology funding, and impacts on energy costs and emissions, 1950s-87 and projected to 2010, annual rpt, 3334–5; 3338–4
Coal-fired power plants generating capacity and replacement of energy imports, with background data, alternative forecasts 1990-2000, 3166–6.63
Conservation programs of electric utilities, collaboration between utilities and interest groups, and effects on costs, 1992 rpt, 3308–104
Conservation programs of electric utilities, impacts on electric power prices and revenue requirements, alternative projections 1990-2010, 3308–105
CPI by component for US city average, and by selected metro area, region, and population size, monthly rpt, 6762–2
Farm electric power use and average monthly bill, monthly rpt, annual table, 1629–1
Food marketing cost indexes, by expense category, monthly rpt with articles, 1502–4
Housing electric power bills, and rankings, by State, as of Jan 1991, annual rpt, 1244–1.6
Housing energy prices, by fuel type and State, 1990 and forecast 1991-92, 3166–6.61
Import price indexes for electric power, quarterly press release, 6762–13
Manufacturing energy use and prices, by fuel type and industry, 1974-88, 3166–15.3
New England States employment growth after recessions, relation to selected economic factors, various periods 1969-90, article, 9373–1.315
Pacific basin countries energy supply and demand, and implications for US trade, country rpt series, 3406–6
Prices and spending for fuel, by type, end-use sector, and State, 1990, annual rpt, 3164–64
Prices of fuel, by type, end-use sector, and region, projected 1991-2030, 3166–6.60
Prices, supply, and demand, by fuel type and end-use sector, alternative projections by region, 1990-2010, annual rpt, 3164–96
Prices, supply, and demand, by fuel type and end-use sector, alternative projections 1990-2010, annual rpt, 3164–75
Prices, supply, and demand, by fuel type and end-use sector, projections and underlying assumptions, 1995-2010, annual rpt, 3164–90
Prices, supply, and demand, by fuel type and end-use sector, with foreign comparisons, 1981-90, annual fact book, 3164–76
Prices, supply, and demand, by fuel type and end-use sector, with foreign comparisons, 1991 and trends from 1949, annual rpt, 3164–74
Prices, supply, and demand of energy, forecasts by resource type, quarterly rpt, 3162–34

Producer price indexes, by stage of processing and detailed commodity, monthly rpt, 6762–6
Producer price indexes, by stage of processing and detailed commodity, monthly 1991, annual rpt, 6764–2
Retail electric power prices, by end-use sector, monthly rpt, 3162–24.9; 3162–35
Retail electric power prices, by end-use sector, monthly 1973-88, 3168–123.9
Retail electric power sales and revenue, by end-use sector, 1986-90, annual rpt, 3164–11.3
Statistical Abstract of US, 1992 annual data compilation, 2324–1.15
TVA electric power purchases and resales, with electricity use, average bills, and rates by customer class, by distributor, 1991, annual tables, 9804–14
TVA electric power purchases of municipal and cooperative distributors, and prices and use by distributor and consumer sector, monthly rpt, 9802–1
VA health care facilities energy use and conservation, by facility, quarterly rpt, 8602–9

Electric utilities
see Electric power
see Electric power plants and equipment
see Electric power prices
see Rural electrification

Electrical machinery and equipment
Building materials PPI, by type, quarterly rpt, 2042–1.5
Business statistics, detailed data for major industries and economic indicators, *Survey of Current Business*, monthly rpt, 2702–1.16
Business statistics, detailed data for major industries and economic indicators, 1960-91, *Survey of Current Business* biennial supplement, 2704–1
Capital expenditures for plant and equipment, by major industry group, quarterly rpt, 2502–2
Collective bargaining agreements expiring during year, and workers covered, by firm, union, industry group, and State, 1992, annual rpt, 6784–9
County Business Patterns, 1989: employment, establishments, and payroll, by SIC 2- to 4-digit industry and county, annual State rpt series, 2326–8
County Business Patterns, 1990: employment, establishments, and payroll, by SIC 2- to 4-digit industry and county, annual State rpt series, 2326–6
Employment, earnings, and hours, by SIC 1- to 4-digit industry, monthly 1989-Feb 1992, annual rpt, 6744–4
Employment of minorities and women, by occupation, SIC 1- to 3-digit industry, State, and MSA, 1991, annual rpt, 9244–1
Employment, unemployment, and labor force characteristics, by region and census div, 1991, annual rpt, 6744–7.1
Energy use and prices, by fuel type and manufacturing industry, 1974-88, 3166–15.3
Energy use and prices for manufacturing industries, 1988 survey, series, 3166–13
Exports and imports between US and outlying areas, by detailed commodity and mode of transport, 1991, annual rpt, 2424–11
Exports and imports of US, by country and detailed commodity, monthly rpt, 2422–12
Exports and imports of US, by Harmonized System 6-digit commodity and country, 1991, annual rpt, 2424–13
Exports and imports of US, by selected country, country group, and commodity group, 1991, annual rpt, 2044–37
Exports and imports of US, by transport mode, country, and SITC 1- to 3-digit commodity, 1991, annual rpt, 2424–12
Exports, imports, and balances of US for manufactured goods, by SITC 2-digit commodity and country, quarterly rpt, 2042–35
Exports of US, detailed commodities by country, monthly CD-ROM, 2422–13
Exports of US, detailed Schedule B commodities with countries of destination, 1991, annual rpt, 2424–10
Foreign direct investment of US, by industry group and world area, 1989-91, annual article, 2702–1.332
Freight (waterborne domestic and foreign) by commodity, traffic, and passengers, by port and waterway, 1989, annual rpt, 3754–3
Hazardous substances industrial releases and reduction methods under EPA regulation, by chemical, source, industry, and location, 1989, annual rpt, 9234–6
Hazardous substances industrial releases and reduction methods under EPA regulation, with chemical stocks and use, facility directory, 1987-89, annual CD-ROM, 9234–7
Housing alteration and repair for owner-occupied units, costs and structural, household, financial, and project characteristics, 1987, 2486–1.13
Imports, exports, and employment impacts, by SIC 2- to 4-digit industry and commodity, quarterly rpt, 2322–2
Imports of US, detailed commodities by country, monthly CD-ROM, 2422–14
Imports of US given duty-free treatment for value of US material sent abroad, by commodity and country, 1987-90, annual rpt, 9884–14
Injuries from use of consumer products, by severity, victim age, and detailed product, 1991, annual rpt, 9164–6
Input-output structure of US economy, detailed interindustry transactions for 84 industries, and components of final demand, 1987, annual article, 2702–1.316
Input-output structure of US economy, detailed interindustry transactions for 541 industries, and components of final demand, 1982 benchmark data, 2708–17
Labor productivity, indexes of output, hours, and employment by SIC 2- to 4-digit industry, 1967-90, annual rpt, 6824–1.3
Manufacturing annual survey, 1990: finances and operations, by SIC 2- to 4-digit industry, series, 2506–14
Manufacturing census, 1987: concentration of largest firms measured by value added, and for shipments by SIC 2- and 4-digit industry, subject rpt, 2497–6
Manufacturing census, 1987: shipments of manufacturers products, by customer class and SIC 2- and 4-digit industry, subject rpt, 2497–4
Manufacturing corporations financial statements, by selected SIC 2- to 3-digit industry, quarterly rpt, 2502–1
Manufacturing finances and operations, by SIC 2- to 4-digit industry, forecast 1992, annual rpt, 2044–28
Manufacturing industries operations and performance, analytical rpt series, 2506–16
Manufacturing production, shipments, inventories, orders, and pollution control costs, periodic Current Industrial Rpt series, 2506–3
Mexico imports from US, by industry and State, 1987-91, 2048–154
Military and personal property shipments, passenger traffic, and costs, by service branch and mode of transport, FY91, annual rpt, 3704–15
Military prime contract awards, by detailed procurement category, FY88-91, annual rpt, 3544–18
Multinatl firms US affiliates finances and operations, by industry, country of parent firm, and State, 1987, 2708–48
Multinatl firms US affiliates, finances, and operations, by industry, world area of parent firm, and State, 1989-90, annual rpt, 2704–4
Multinatl US firms and foreign affiliates finances and operations, by industry and country, 1989 benchmark survey, annual rpt, 2704–5
Multinatl US firms foreign affiliates, income statement items by asset size, industry, and country, 1988, biennial article, 8302–2.322
Natl income and product accounts, comprehensive accounts and components, benchmark revisions, 1929-88, 2708–5
Natl income and product accounts, comprehensive accounts and components, *Survey of Current Business*, monthly rpt, 2702–1.29
Occupational injury and illness rates, by SIC 2- to 4-digit industry, 1989-90, annual rpt, 6844–7
Occupational injury and illness rates, by SIC 2- to 4-digit industry, 1990, annual rpt, 6844–1
OECD trade, total and for 4 major countries, and US trade by country, by commodity, 1980-90, world area rpt series, 9116–1
Pollution abatement capital and operating costs, by SIC 2- to 4-digit industry and State, 1990, annual Current Industrial Rpt, 2506–3.6
Price indexes (producer), by stage of processing and detailed commodity, monthly rpt, 6762–6
Price indexes (producer), by stage of processing and detailed commodity, monthly 1991, annual rpt, 6764–2
Puerto Rico and other US possessions corporations income tax returns, income and tax items, and employment, by selected industry, 1989, article, 8302–2.326
Science, engineering, and technical employment in manufacturing, by field and industry, 1989, triennial rpt, 9627–23
Switchgear, switchboard apparatus, relays, and other equipment shipments, trade, use, and firms, by product, 1991, annual Current Industrial Rpt, 2506–12.11

Tax (income) returns of corporations, income and tax items by asset size and detailed industry, 1989, annual rpt, 8304–4; 8304–21
Tax (income) returns of corporations with foreign tax credit, income and tax items by industry group, 1988, biennial article, 8302–2.316
Tax (income) returns of sole proprietorships, income statement items, by industry group, 1990, annual article, 8302–2.317; 8302–2.320
Wholesale trade sales and inventories, by SIC 2- to 3-digit kind of business, monthly rpt, 2413–7
Wire and cable (insulated) shipments, trade, use, and firms, by product, 1991, annual Current Industrial Rpt, 2506–10.8
Wiring devices and supplies shipments, trade, use, and firms, by product, 1991, annual Current Industrial Rpt, 2506–12.18
see also Batteries
see also Electric power plants and equipment
see also Electronics industry and products
see also Engines and motors
see also Household appliances and equipment
see also Lighting equipment
see also under By Commodity in the "Index by Categories"
see also under By Industry in the "Index by Categories"

Electronic data processing
see Computer industry and products
see Computer sciences
see Computer use
see Electronic funds transfer
see Information storage and retrieval systems

Electronic funds transfer
Bank deposits, account debits, and deposit turnover, for commercial banks by type of account, monthly rpt, 9365–2.5
Banks in Fed Reserve System, expenses and operations itemized by service, office, and district, 1991, annual rpt, 9364–11
Budget of US, authoritative financial statements with appropriations, outlays, and receipts, by category and agency, FY91, annual rpt, 8104–2.2
Fed Govt finances, cash and debt transactions, daily tables, 8102–4
Fed Reserve System, Bd of Governors, and district banks financial statements, performance, and fiscal services, 1991-92, annual rpt, 9364–10
Households bill payment transactions, by method, FY87-90, annual rpt, 9864–10
OASDI beneficiaries using direct deposit, and benefits, by State, 1990, annual rpt, 4744–3.3
Telegraph firms money order operations and revenue, 1990, annual rpt, 9284–6.3
see also Automated tellers

Electronic surveillance
Criminal releases electronically monitored, by offense and State, data compilation, 1992 annual rpt, 6064–6.6
Criminal releases electronically monitored, by region and State, 1990, annual rpt, 6064–26.2; 6064–26.5
Criminal releases electronically monitored by State, completions, violations, and new offenses, 1989, 6066–20.23
Criminal sentences for Federal offenses, guidelines by offense and circumstances, series, 17668–1
Employee electronic monitoring effects on mental and physical health and job satisfaction, for local telephone company workers, 1989, hearings, 21348–122
Equipment shipments, trade, use, and firms, for electronic communications systems and related products, 1991, annual Current Industrial Rpt, 2506–12.35
Hwy traffic mgmt and info electronic system, demonstration program results, late 1980s, 7558–119
Instruments and related products shipments, trade, use, and firms, by detailed type, 1991, annual Current Industrial Rpt, 2506–12.26
Parole and probation population, entries, and exits, by State, 1990, annual rpt, 6066–25.43
Statistical Abstract of US, 1992 annual data compilation, 2324–1.5
Wiretaps and results by offense and location, and public opinion, data compilation, 1992 annual rpt, 6064–6.2; 6064–6.5
Wiretaps authorized, costs, arrests, trials, and convictions, by offense and jurisdiction, 1991, annual rpt, 18204–7
see also Radar

Electronics industry and products
Communications and related electronic equipment shipments, trade, use, and firms, 1991, annual Current Industrial Rpt, 2506–12.35
Communications and security equipment authorizations of FCC, by type, FY91, annual rpt, 9284–4
Competitiveness (intl) of US high technology industries, with background data by industry and foreign comparisons, 1960s-91, GAO rpt, 26123–406
County Business Patterns, 1989: employment, establishments, and payroll, by SIC 2- to 4-digit industry and county, annual State rpt series, 2326–8
County Business Patterns, 1990: employment, establishments, and payroll, by SIC 2- to 4-digit industry and county, annual State rpt series, 2326–6
Employment, earnings, and hours, by SIC 1- to 4-digit industry, monthly 1989-Feb 1992, annual rpt, 6744–4
Employment of minorities and women, by occupation, SIC 1- to 3-digit industry, State, and MSA, 1991, annual rpt, 9244–1
Exports and imports between US and outlying areas, by detailed commodity and mode of transport, 1991, annual rpt, 2424–11
Exports and imports of US, by country and detailed commodity, monthly rpt, 2422–12
Exports and imports of US by country, and trade shifts by commodity, 1991, annual rpt, 9884–25
Exports and imports of US, by Harmonized System 6-digit commodity and country, 1991, annual rpt, 2424–13
Exports and imports of US, by transport mode, country, and SITC 1- to 3-digit commodity, 1991, annual rpt, 2424–12
Exports, imports, tariffs, and industry operating data for electronics and service industries, commodity rpt series, 9885–12
Exports of US, detailed commodities by country, monthly CD-ROM, 2422–13
Exports of US, detailed Schedule B commodities with countries of destination, 1991, annual rpt, 2424–10
Foreign direct investment of US, by industry group and world area, 1989-91, annual article, 2702–1.332
Health care electronic equipment shipments, trade, use, and firms, by product, 1991, annual Current Industrial Rpt, 2506–12.34
Imports detained by FDA, by reason, product, shipper, brand, and country, monthly listing, 4062–2
Imports of US, detailed commodities by country, monthly CD-ROM, 2422–14
Imports of US given duty-free treatment for value of US material sent abroad, by commodity and country, 1987-90, annual rpt, 9884–14
Input-output structure of US economy, detailed interindustry transactions for 84 industries, and components of final demand, 1987, annual article, 2702–1.316
Input-output structure of US economy, detailed interindustry transactions for 541 industries, and components of final demand, 1982 benchmark data, 2708–17
Labor productivity, indexes of output, hours, and employment by SIC 2- to 4-digit industry, 1967-90, annual rpt, 6824–1.3
Manufacturing annual survey, 1990: finances and operations, by SIC 2- to 4-digit industry, series, 2506–14
Manufacturing census, 1987: concentration of largest firms measured by value added, and for shipments by SIC 2- and 4-digit industry, subject rpt, 2497–6
Manufacturing census, 1987: shipments of manufacturers products, by customer class and SIC 2- and 4-digit industry, subject rpt, 2497–4
Manufacturing corporations financial statements, by selected SIC 2- to 3-digit industry, quarterly rpt, 2502–1
Manufacturing finances and operations, by SIC 2- to 4-digit industry, forecast 1992, annual rpt, 2044–28
Military prime contract awards, by category, contract and contractor type, and service branch, FY82-1st half FY92, semiannual rpt, 3542–1
Military prime contract awards, by category, contractor type, and State, FY89-91, annual rpt, 3544–11
Military prime contract awards, by detailed procurement category, FY88-91, annual rpt, 3544–18
Military prime contract awards, by size and type of contract, service branch, competitive status, category, and labor standard, FY91, annual rpt, 3544–19
Multinatl firms US affiliates finances and operations, by industry, country of parent firm, and State, 1987, 2708–48
Multinatl US firms and foreign affiliates finances and operations, by industry and country, 1989 benchmark survey, annual rpt, 2704–5
Occupational injury and illness rates, by SIC 2- to 4-digit industry, 1989-90, annual rpt, 6844–7

Occupational injury and illness rates, by SIC 2- to 4-digit industry, 1990, annual rpt, 6844–1
OECD trade, total and for 4 major countries, and US trade by country, by commodity, 1980-90, world area rpt series, 9116–1
Price indexes (producer), by stage of processing and detailed commodity, monthly rpt, 6762–6
Price indexes (producer), by stage of processing and detailed commodity, monthly 1991, annual rpt, 6764–2
Production and labor conditions of electronics industry, in 10 MSAs, EC, and top producer countries, late 1970s-80s, article, 9393–8.307
Puerto Rico and other US possessions corporations income tax returns, income and tax items, and employment, by selected industry, 1989, article, 8302–2.326
Radiation from electronic devices, incidents by type of device, and FDA control activities, 1991, annual rpt, 4064–13
Science, engineering, and technical employment in manufacturing, by field and industry, 1989, triennial rpt, 9627–23
Shipments, trade, use, and firms, for consumer electronics by product, 1991, annual Current Industrial Rpt, 2506–12.20
Small business R&D grants of Fed Govt, by program area, agency, MSA, and State, FY90, annual rpt, 9764–7
Statistical Abstract of US, 1992 annual data compilation, 2324–1.27
Switchgear, switchboard apparatus, relays, and other equipment shipments, trade, use, and firms, by product, 1991, annual Current Industrial Rpt, 2506–12.11
Tariff Schedule of US, classifications and rates of duty by detailed imported commodity, 1993 base edition, 9886–13
Tax (income) returns of corporations, income and tax items by asset size and detailed industry, 1989, annual rpt, 8304–4; 8304–21
see also Automated tellers
see also CD-ROM technology and use
see also Computer industry and products
see also Electronic funds transfer
see also Electronic surveillance
see also Home video and audio equipment
see also Lasers
see also Radio
see also Semiconductors
see also Television
see also Video recordings and equipment
see also under By Industry in the "Index by Categories"

Elementary and secondary education
Assistance (financial and nonfinancial) of Fed Govt, 1992 base edition, annual listing, 104–5
Condition of Education, detail for elementary, secondary, and higher education, 1920s-91 and projected to 2002, annual rpt, 4824–1
Data on education, enrollment, finances, teachers, and other characteristics, by State, 1969-89, 4828–33
Data on education, estimates from Fast Response Survey System, series, 4826–1
Data on education, selected trends and projections 1979-2002, annual pamphlet, 4824–9
Data on education, special topics, series, 4826–10
Data on education, 1940s-95, pamphlet, 4828–35
Data on education, 1960s-91, annual pamphlet, 4824–3
Data on elementary and secondary education, enrollment, staff, finances, operations, programs, and policies, 1987/88 biennial survey, series, 4836–3
Digest of Education Statistics, 1992 annual data compilation, 4824–2
Drug abuse prevention programs in schools, Education Dept recognition program, 1989/90-1990/91, annual listing, 4814–2
Eighth grade class of 1988: educational performance and conditions, characteristics, attitudes, activities, and plans, natl longitudinal survey, series, 4826–9
High school classes of 1980 and 1982: education, employment, and family characteristics, activities, and attitudes, natl longitudinal study, series, 4826–2
Indians and Alaska Natives education condition, indicators and comparisons to other groups, 1980s-90, 4808–42
Natl Education Goals progress indicators, by State, 1992, annual rpt, 15914–1
Science and Engineering Indicators, employment, education, R&D funding, and industry impacts, with foreign comparisons, 1960s-91, biennial rpt, 9624–10.1
States elementary and secondary curricula, competency, and attendance requirements, with background data, 1970s-90, 4838–52
Statistical Abstract of US, 1992 annual data compilation, 2324–1.4
see also Bilingual education
see also Compensatory education
see also Curricula
see also Discrimination in education
see also Educational attainment
see also Educational broadcasting
see also Educational enrollment
see also Educational exchanges
see also Educational facilities
see also Educational finance
see also Educational materials
see also Educational performance
see also Educational reform
see also Educational research
see also Educational retention rates
see also Educational technology
see also Educational tests
see also Federal aid to education
see also Head Start Project
see also National Assessment of Educational Progress
see also Preschool education
see also Private schools
see also Remedial education
see also School administration and staff
see also School districts
see also School dropouts
see also School lunch and breakfast programs
see also Special education
see also State funding for education
see also Students
see also Teacher education
see also Teachers
see also Vocational education and training

Elementary and Secondary School Civil Rights Survey
Participation and data coverage of survey, school district administrators views, 1991 survey, 4826–1.33

Elevators
County Business Patterns, 1989: employment, establishments, and payroll, by SIC 2- to 4-digit industry and county, annual State rpt series, 2326–8
County Business Patterns, 1990: employment, establishments, and payroll, by SIC 2- to 4-digit industry and county, annual State rpt series, 2326–6
Exports and imports between US and outlying areas, by detailed commodity and mode of transport, 1991, annual rpt, 2424–11
Exports and imports of US, by country and detailed commodity, monthly rpt, 2422–12
Exports and imports of US, by Harmonized System 6-digit commodity and country, 1991, annual rpt, 2424–13
Exports and imports of US, by transport mode, country, and SITC 1- to 3-digit commodity, 1991, annual rpt, 2424–12
Exports of US, detailed Schedule B commodities with countries of destination, 1991, annual rpt, 2424–10
Housing (rental) units, total, with HUD assistance by program, and eligible for aid, by unit, household, and neighborhood characteristics, and location, 1989, biennial rpt, 5184–11
Housing and households detailed characteristics, and unit and neighborhood quality, MSA surveys, series, 2485–6
Injuries from use of consumer products and related activities, by severity and victim age and sex, 1990, annual rpt, 9164–7
Injuries from use of consumer products, by severity, victim age, and detailed product, 1991, annual rpt, 9164–6
Input-output structure of US economy, detailed interindustry transactions for 541 industries, and components of final demand, 1982 benchmark data, 2708–17
Manufacturing annual survey, 1990: finances and operations, by SIC 2- to 4-digit industry, series, 2506–14
Manufacturing census, 1987: concentration of largest firms measured by value added, and for shipments by SIC 2- and 4-digit industry, subject rpt, 2497–6
Manufacturing census, 1987: shipments of manufacturers products, by customer class and SIC 2- and 4-digit industry, subject rpt, 2497–4
NYC housing supply, occupancy, condition, and household characteristics, by tenure and borough, 1991 triennial survey, 2488–3
Occupational injury and illness rates, by SIC 2- to 4-digit industry, 1989-90, annual rpt, 6844–7
Occupational injury and illness rates, by SIC 2- to 4-digit industry, 1990, annual rpt, 6844–1
Price indexes (producer), by stage of processing and detailed commodity, monthly rpt, 6762–6

Price indexes (producer), by stage of processing and detailed commodity, monthly 1991, annual rpt, 6764–2
Transit systems accidents and casualties by circumstances, damage, and ridership, by mode, 1990, annual rpt, 7884–13
see also Grain storage and facilities

Elkhart, Ind.
Wages by occupation, and benefits, for office and plant workers, 1991 survey, periodic MSA rpt, 6785–16.5

Ellice Islands
see Tuvalu

Elliehausen, Gregory E.
"Banking Markets and the Use of Financial Services by Households", 9362–1.303

Ellis, Gregory M.
"Assessing Economic Impacts to Coastal Recreation and Tourism from Oil and Gas Development in the Oregon and Washington Outer Continental Shelf", 5738–40.2

Ellis, Walter
"Payments of Child Support and Alimony", 1702–1.305

Elmi, Amina H.
"Housing Discrimination Study: Replication of 1977 Study Measures with Current Data", 5186–16.6

Elms, Joe D.
"Where Have All the Data Gone?", 2152–8.302

Embargo
see International sanctions

Emergency medical service
Accident deaths and injuries prevention, and treatment, 1991 conf papers, 4208–35
Ambulances PPI, monthly 1991, annual rpt, 6764–2
Cocaine-related emergency room episodes, by age, sex, race, and Hispanic origin, 1985-90, annual data compilation, 4144–11
Consumer Product Safety Commission activities, recalls by brand, and casualties and medical costs, by product type, FY90, annual rpt, 9164–2
Consumer products use, injuries by severity, victim age, and detailed product, 1991, annual rpt, 9164–6
Crime victimization rates, by victim and offender characteristics, circumstances, and offense, 1990 survey, annual rpt, 6066–3.47
Deaths during 1986, decedents health condition, services use, habits, and social, employment, and other characteristics, 4147–20.19
Drug abuse indicators for selected metro areas, research results, data collection, and policy issues, 1992 semiannual conf, 4492–5
Fed Govt financial and nonfinancial domestic aid, 1992 base edition, annual listing, 104–5
Fire-related injuries by severity, and deaths, by ignition source, victim age, and treatment location, 1984-85 local area study, article, 4042–3.340
Heroin trafficking indicators for US, 1990, annual rpt, 6284–6
Hospital deaths of Medicare patients, actual and expected rates by diagnosis, with hospital characteristics, by instn, FY90, annual State rpt series, 4654–14
Hospital trauma center cases and deaths by injury type, costs, and payment sources, with data for selected areas, 1991 hearing, 21348–123
Hospital trauma units, and other characteristics of Medicare hospital providers, by instn, 1990, annual State rpt series, 4654–14
Injuries from use of consumer products and related activities, by severity and victim age and sex, 1990, annual rpt, 9164–7
Labor demand, turnover, and training completions, by detailed occupation, 1990 and projected to 2005, biennial rpt, 6744–3
LSD trafficking, abuse, and enforcement, and DEA field div activities, 1980s-91, 6288–9
Medicaid payment and participation by service type, and cost compared to Medicare, by State, FY89, 17266–1.4
Medicare payment of physicians, vulnerable beneficiaries services use prior to fee schedule implementation, 1986-90, annual rpt, 17266–1.8
Military health care personnel, and accessions by training source, by occupation, specialty, and service branch, FY90, annual rpt, 3544–24
Occupational Outlook Handbook, 1992-93, biennial rpt, 6744–1
Physicians, by specialty, age, sex, and location of training and practice, 1990, State rpt series, 4116–6
Rural areas health care access for counties without hospitals and in which the only hospital closed, 1987-89, 17206–2.30
Traffic accidents direct and indirect costs, by cost type, payment source, and severity, 1980s, 7558–114
Traffic fatal accidents, emergency medical service involvement and response time, 1990, annual rpt, 7764–10
Youth health condition, risk factors, and preventive and treatment services use and availability, 1970s-80s, 26358–234.2

Emergency relief
see Disaster relief

Emergency 911 systems
see Telephones and telephone industry

Emery, Kenneth M.
"Do Interest Rates Help Predict Inflation?", 9379–1.306
"Forecasting Turning Points: Is a Two-State Characterization of the Business Cycle Appropriate?", 9379–12.95
"Inflation and Its Variability: A Note?", 9379–12.86

Emery, Robert F.
"Central Banks' Use in East Asia of Money Market Instruments in the Conduct of Monetary Policy", 9366–7.280

Emigration
see Immigration and emigration
see Refugees

Eminent domain
see Property condemnation

Emissions
see Air pollution
see Global climate change
see Motor vehicle exhaust

Employee benefits
AFDC beneficiaries demographic and financial characteristics, by State, FY90, annual rpt, 4584–7
Alien nonresidents income from US sources and tax withheld by country and US tax treaty status, detailed data compilation for income tax returns, 1984-88, quinquennial rpt, 8308–31
Alien nonresidents income from US sources and tax withheld by country and US tax treaty status, 1989, annual article, 8302–2.308
Applications to IRS for employee benefit plans, and coverage, by disposition and plan type, FY91, annual rpt, 8304–23
Banks in Fed Reserve System, expenses and operations itemized by service, office, and district, 1991, annual rpt, 9364–11
BLS data collection, analysis, and presentation methods, by program, 1992 rpt, 6888–1
Budget of US, obligations and authority by function, agency, and program, with summaries and analyses, FY93, annual rpt, 104–2
Collective bargaining wage and benefit changes, quarterly press release, 6782–2
Collective bargaining wage changes and coverage, by industry and whether contract includes escalator clause and lump sum payment, 1982-91, annual article, 6722–1.325
Communications services revenue and expenses, itemized by SIC 2- to 4-digit kind of business, 1990, annual rpt, 2413–15
Costs (hourly) of labor, by component, industry and occupational group, worker class, and firm size, monthly rpt, annual tables, 6782–1.2
Costs (hourly) of labor, by component, occupational group, industry div, union coverage, and region, 1992, annual rpt, 6744–21
Costs of employee compensation, alternative measures by component, occupation, industry group, union status, and location, 1975-92, annual rpt, 6744–20
Criminal sentences for Federal offenses, guidelines by offense and circumstances, series, 17668–1
Education (elementary and secondary) schools, teachers, staff, and enrollment, by selected characteristics, 1987/88-1988/89, 4836–3.10
Educational enrollment, finances, staff, and high school grads, for elementary and secondary public school systems by State, FY89-90, annual rpt, 4834–6
Electric utilities privately owned, finances and operations, detailed data, 1990, annual rpt, 3164–23
Expenditures (private) for social welfare, by category, 1970s-90, annual article, 4742–1.323
Farm labor, wages, hours, and perquisites, by State, monthly rpt, 1631–1
Farm production itemized costs, by farm sales size and region, 1991, annual rpt, 1614–3
Fed Govt civilian employees work-years by schedule, overtime, holidays, and personnel cost components, FY90-91, annual article, 9842–1.303
Fed Govt civilian employees work-years, pay rates, and benefits use and costs, by agency, FY90, annual rpt, 9844–31

Fed Govt employees physical fitness clubs memberships, agency costs, and personnel directors views on OPM guidelines and admin leave use, 1991-92, GAO rpt, 26119-393
Fed Govt employees transit subsidies, costs and participation by agency, 1992, GAO rpt, 26113-601
Fed Govt spending in States, by type, program, agency, and State, FY91, annual rpt, 2464-2
Fed Govt white collar employees views on work conditions and schedules, 1992 survey, 9848-41
Govt finances, by level of govt, State, and for large cities and counties, annual rpt series, 2466-2
Health Care Financing Review, provider prices, price inputs and indexes, and labor, quarterly journal, 4652-1.1
House of Representatives salaries, expenses, and contingent fund disbursement, detailed listings, quarterly rpt, 21942-1
Investment funds (collective) assets, instns involved, and accounts, by type of fund and holding, 1991, annual rpt, 13004-1.3
Labor laws enacted, by State, 1991, annual article, 6722-1.309
Leave benefits in small business compared to larger firms and govts, by occupational group, 1989-90, article, 6722-1.315
Leave for family reasons, State law provisions and employer compliance, for 4 States, 1987-91, hearing, 25548-105
Manufacturing annual survey, 1990: establishments, employment, finances, inventories, and energy use, by SIC 2- to 4-digit industry, 2506-14.2
Manufacturing annual survey, 1990: finances and operations, by SIC 2- and 3-digit industry and State, 2506-14.3
Multinatl firms US affiliates, finances, and operations, by industry, world area of parent firm, and State, 1989-90, annual rpt, 2704-4
Multinatl US firms and foreign affiliates finances and operations, by industry and country, 1989 benchmark survey, annual rpt, 2704-5
Natl income and product accounts, comprehensive accounts and components, benchmark revisions, 1929-88, 2708-5
Natl income and product accounts, comprehensive accounts and components, *Survey of Current Business*, monthly rpt, 2702-1.29; 2702-1.31
Natural gas interstate pipeline company detailed financial and operating data, by firm, 1990, annual rpt, 3164-38
Nonprofit charitable and other tax exempt organizations finances, by category and size of assets and contributions, 1988, annual article, 8302-2.315
Nonprofit charitable organizations finances, with data by State and for top 10 instns, 1988, article, 8302-2.302
Population economic well-being indicators, by selected characteristics and household income and income-to-poverty ratio, 1984, 2546-20.22
Postal Service employment and related expenses, FY91, annual rpt, 9864-5.3
Postal Service operating costs, itemized by class of mail, FY91, annual rpt, 9864-4
Railroad employee benefits and beneficiaries by type, and railroad employment and payroll, FY90, annual rpt, 9704-2
Railroad employee benefits program finances and beneficiaries, FY91, annual rpt, 9704-1
Railroad employment, earnings, and hours, by occupation for Class I railroads, 1991, annual table, 9484-5
Railroad retirement, survivors, unemployment, and health insurance programs, monthly rpt, 9702-2
Senate receipts, itemized expenses by payee, and balances, 1st half FY92, semiannual listing, 25922-1
State and local govt employees benefit plan coverage and provisions, by plan type, 1990, biennial rpt, 6784-21
Statistical Abstract of US, 1992 annual data compilation, 2324-1.9; 2324-1.13
Tax (excise) collections of IRS, by source, quarterly rpt, 8302-1
Tax (income) returns and supplemental documents filed, by type, FY91 and projected to FY2000, semiannual rpt, 8302-4
Tax (income) returns filed, by type of filer, selected income items, quarterly rpt, 8302-2.1
Tax (income) returns of corporations, income and tax items by asset size and detailed industry, 1989, annual rpt, 8304-4; 8304-21
Tax (income) returns of partnerships, income statement and balance sheet items, by industry group, 1990, annual article, 8302-2.314
Tax (income) returns of sole proprietorships, income statement items, by industry group, 1990, annual article, 8302-2.317
Tax collection, enforcement, and litigation activity of IRS, with data by type of tax, region, and State, FY91, annual rpt, 8304-3
Tax exclusion for employee benefits, Federal revenue forgone and coverage indicators, by benefit type, 1950s-80s and projected to 1995, GAO rpt, 26119-389
Tax exempt organizations and employee plans listed on IRS masterfile, determinations, applications, and rulings, FY91, annual rpt, 8304-3.2
Tax exempt organizations finances, with data by type, size, State, and for largest organizations, late 1940s-80s, compilation of papers, 8308-35
Tax exempt organizations with unrelated business income, finances by organization type, 1987, article, 8302-2.306
Tax returns and supplemental documents filed, by type, 1990 and projected to 1999, annual article, 8302-2.304
Tax returns filed, by type of tax and IRS district, 1990 and projected 1991-98, annual rpt, 8304-24
Tax returns filed, by type of tax and IRS region and service center, projected 1991-98 and trends from 1978, annual rpt, 8304-9
Teachers and administrators in private schools, pay, work conditions, and selected characteristics, by school type and affiliation, 1987/88, 4836-3.8
Teachers in higher education, and salaries, by faculty rank, sex, instn type and control, and State, 1990/91, annual rpt, 4844-8
Telephone and telegraph firms detailed finances and operations, 1990, annual rpt, 9284-6.2; 9284-6.3
Transit fare subsidies by employers, participation, and parking costs, by selected city, 1985-92, GAO rpt, 26113-597
Transit systems finances and operations, by mode, size of fleet and urban area, region, and for 518 systems, 1990, annual rpt, 7884-4
Truck and warehouse services finances and inventory, by SIC 2- to 4-digit industry, 1990 survey, annual rpt, 2413-14
Truck interstate carriers finances and operations, by district, 1990, annual rpt, 9486-5.2
Trust assets of banks, trust companies, and S&Ls, by type of asset and fund, selected firm, and State, 1991, annual rpt, 13004-1
VA health care facilities nonveteran outpatient visits, by eligibility type, facility, and region, quarterly rpt, 8602-4
Wage and benefit changes from collective bargaining and mgmt decisions, by industry div, monthly rpt, 6782-1
see also Area wage surveys
see also Civil service pensions
see also Disability benefits and insurance
see also Employee bonuses and work incentives
see also Employee ownership
see also Health insurance
see also Industry wage surveys
see also Labor costs and cost indexes
see also Life insurance
see also Military benefits and pensions
see also Pensions and pension funds
see also Vacations and holidays
see also Wage deductions

Employee bonuses and work incentives
Costs (hourly) of labor, by component, industry and occupational group, worker class, and firm size, monthly rpt, annual tables, 6782-1.2
Costs (hourly) of labor, by component, occupational group, industry div, union coverage, and region, 1992, annual rpt, 6744-21
Costs of employee compensation, by component, occupation, industry group, union status, and location, 1975-92, annual rpt, 6744-20.2
Executive officers and board members pay, bonuses, and performance indicators, by company, 1991 hearing, 25248-130
Fed Govt civilian employees work-years by schedule, overtime, holidays, and personnel cost components, FY90-91, annual article, 9842-1.303
Fed Govt employee incentive awards, costs, and benefits, by award type and agency, FY90, annual rpt, 9844-20
Fed Govt procurement operations employees job performance, and views on policies and practices, 1991 survey, 9498-17
Fed Govt Senior Executive Service members characteristics, entries, exits, and awards, FY79-91, annual rpt, 9844-36
NASA staff characteristics and personnel actions, FY91, annual rpt, 9504-1
Police employment, spending, and operations, for State, city, county, and special district agencies, 1990, annual rpt, 6064-39

State and local govt employees benefit plan coverage and provisions, by plan type, 1990, biennial rpt, 6784–21
Teachers and administrators in private schools, pay, work conditions, and selected characteristics, by school type and affiliation, 1987/88, 4836–3.8

Employee development
Air Force fiscal mgmt system operations and techniques, quarterly rpt, 3602–1
Air traffic control supervisor selection, relation to screening test and technical training performance, 1980s, technical rpt, 7506–10.116
Air traffic controller academy grads and military hires, training performance, facility assignments, and selected characteristics, 1988, 7506–10.101
Air traffic controller job performance and satisfaction impacts of training program, 1984-90, technical rpt, 7506–10.96
Banks in Fed Reserve System, expenses and operations itemized by service, office, and district, 1991, annual rpt, 9364–11
Criminal justice systems activities, spending, and employment, by level of govt, data compilation, 1992 annual rpt, 6064–6.1
Criminal justice systems of States, activities, employment, funding, and data collection, by State, 1970s-91, annual rpt, 6064–40
Customs Service mgmt and trade law enforcement effectiveness, staff and broker survey results, 1992 GAO rpt, 26119–420
Displaced worker employment and training services, and layoff alternatives, indicators of effectiveness, 1980s, 15498–28
Drug abuse and trafficking reduction programs activities, funding, staff, and Bush Admin budget request, by Federal agency, FY91-93, annual rpt, 234–2
Fed Govt agencies ethics regulation, activities, and staff, 1991, biennial rpt, 9834–1
Fed Govt procurement operations employees job performance, and views on policies and practices, 1991 survey, 9498–17
Fed Govt Senior Executive Service members characteristics, entries, exits, and awards, FY79-91, annual rpt, 9844–36
Fire fighter deaths, by cause, circumstances, and location, 1990, annual rpt, 9434–8
Fires, casualties, losses, and US Fire Admin activities, funding, and training programs, FY91, annual rpt, 9434–7
Foreign countries industrial trainees admitted to US, by country, FY81-91, annual rpt, 6264–2.3
Hazardous material transport accidents, casualties, and damage, by mode of transport, with DOT control activities, 1990, annual rpt, 7304–4
Hazardous substances occupational exposure, employer compliance with info and training regulations, employer views by firm size and industry div, 1989-91, GAO rpt, 26121–456
Hazardous substances occupational exposure, employer compliance with info and training regulations, inspections, and fines, by firm size and industry div, 1989-91, GAO rpt, 26121–439
Indian Health Service employment of Indians and non-Indians, training, hires, and quits, by occupation, FY90, annual rpt, 4084–6
Labor demand, turnover, and training completions, by detailed occupation, 1990 and projected to 2005, biennial rpt, 6744–3
Literacy programs in workplaces, demonstration projects funding and participants, FY88-90, 4808–43
Literacy programs in workplaces, project descriptions and Education Dept funding, FY91, annual listing, 4804–40
Marshals Service activities, FY91, annual rpt, 6294–1
Military training and education programs funding, staff, students, and facilities, by service branch, FY93, annual rpt, 3504–5
NASA staff characteristics and personnel actions, FY91, annual rpt, 9504–1
Occupational qualification and skill improvement training, workers participating by training source, occupation, age, sex, and race, 1991, 6728–32
Petrochemicals industries contract labor accidents, injuries, safety programs operations, and employee characteristics, 1986-91, 6608–6
Police agencies employment, spending, and operations, FY90, 6066–25.44
Sheriffs' agencies employment, spending, and operations, FY90, 6066–25.45
Teachers of science and math, professional dev project of Education Dept, school district participation by State, 1989/90, GAO rpt, 26121–488
Women's training on job, duration, costs, and impacts on gender differences in wages, model description and results, 1992 working paper, 6886–6.93

Employee-management relations
see Labor-management relations, general
see Labor-management relations in government

Employee ownership
Displaced worker employment and training services, and layoff alternatives, indicators of effectiveness, 1980s, 15498–28

Employee performance and appraisal
Air traffic controller job performance and satisfaction impacts of training program, 1984-90, technical rpt, 7506–10.96
Education (elementary and secondary) schools, teachers, staff, and enrollment, by selected characteristics, 1987/88-1988/89, 4836–3.10
Electronic monitoring of employees, effects on mental and physical health and job satisfaction, for local telephone company workers, 1989, hearings, 21348–122
Fed Govt agencies programs and services performance evaluation measures use, dev, and effectiveness, 1991 survey, GAO rpt, 26119–396
Fed Govt first-line supervisors performance ratings by self, superiors, and subordinates, 1991 survey, 9498–15
Fed Govt merit system oversight and enforcement activities of OPM, series, 9496–2
Fed Govt procurement operations employees job performance, and views on policies and practices, 1991 survey, 9498–17
Fed Govt Senior Executive Service members characteristics, entries, exits, and awards, FY79-91, annual rpt, 9844–36
Fed Govt violations of personnel practices, cases by type, FY91, annual rpt, 9894–1
Teachers and administrators in private schools, pay, work conditions, and selected characteristics, by school type and affiliation, 1987/88, 4836–3.8
see also Employee bonuses and work incentives

Employment and Training Administration
Activities of ETA, funding, and participant characteristics, by program, FY86-88, annual rpt, 6404–17
Budget of US, obligations and authority by function, agency, and program, with summaries and analyses, FY93, annual rpt, 104–2
Expenditures of Fed Govt in States, by type, program, agency, and State, FY91, annual rpt, 2464–2
Labor surplus areas eligible for preferential Fed Govt contracts, monthly listing, 6402–1
Trade adjustment aid for workers, petitions by disposition, selected industry, union, and State, monthly rpt, 6402–13
Unemployment insurance claims and covered unemployment by program, and extended benefit triggers, by State, weekly rpt, 6402–15
Unemployment insurance claims, by program, weekly press release, 6402–14
Unemployment insurance programs of States and Fed Govt, benefits adequacy, and work disincentives, series, 6406–6
Unemployment insurance programs of States, benefits, coverage, and tax provisions, as of July 1992, semiannual listing, 6402–7
Unemployment insurance programs of States, benefits, coverage, exhaustions, and finances, 1990, annual tables, 6404–10
Unemployment insurance programs of States, comparison of law provisions, as of Jan 1992, semiannual revisions to base edition, 6402–2
Unemployment insurance programs of States, quality appraisal results, FY91, annual rpt, 6404–16

Employment and unemployment, general
AFDC beneficiaries demographic and financial characteristics, by State, FY90, annual rpt, 4584–7
AFDC unemployed parent cases and payments, by State, quarterly FY90, annual rpt, 4584–3.1
BLS data collection, analysis, and presentation methods, by program, 1992 rpt, 6888–1
Budget of US, CBO analysis of revenue and spending alternatives and projections of economic indicators, FY93-97, annual rpt, 26304–3
Building materials industry finances and operations, by SIC 4-digit industry, selected years 1977-89, article, 2042–1.302
Business activity indicators, 1990, annual rpt, 9364–5.9
Business cycle duration and strength indicators, late 1940s-91, article, 9373–1.301
Business cycle recession and expansion duration indicators, 1850s-1990, working paper, 9375–13.83

Business statistics, detailed data for major industries and economic indicators, 1960-91, *Survey of Current Business* biennial supplement, 2704–1
Census of Population and Housing, 1990: population and housing characteristics, detailed geographic coverage, State CD-ROM series, 2551–10
Census of Population and Housing, 1990: summary characteristics, by county, subdiv, and place, State rpt series, 2551–7
Child support payment and visitation practices of absent fathers, and mothers with custody, by employment and other characteristics, 1988, article, 6722–1.329
College grads labor force status, job degree requirements, and earnings, with data by occupation, 1960s-90, article, 6722–1.330
Commuting to work, by mode, trip duration, and work location, 1980 and 1990, 7558–120
Consumer Income, socioeconomic characteristics of persons, families, and households, detailed cross-tabulations, Current Population Rpt series, 2546–6
County Business Patterns, 1989: employment, establishments, and payroll, by SIC 2- to 4-digit industry and county, annual State rpt series, 2326–8
County Business Patterns, 1990: employment, establishments, and payroll, by SIC 2- to 4-digit industry and county, annual State rpt series, 2326–6
Criminal case processing in Federal district courts, and dispositions, by offense, district, and offender characteristics, 1989, annual data compilation, 6064–29
Deaths and rates, by cause and selected social, demographic, and employment characteristics, 1979-85, natl longitudinal study, 4478–186
Deaths during 1986, decedents health condition, services use, habits, and social, employment, and other characteristics, 4147–20.19
Disabled persons rehabilitation, Federal and State activities and funding, FY90, annual rpt, 4944–1
Disabled persons work experience following OASDI benefit award, by selected characteristics, 1980s, article, 4742–1.312
Disabled persons work history before and after SSI application, by age, diagnosis, industry div, and sex, aggregate 1937-87, article, 4742–1.308
Disabled workers labor force status, type and cause of disability, and other characteristics, 1970s-89, chartbook, 4948–11
Drug, alcohol, and cigarette use, by selected characteristics, 1991 survey, annual rpt series, 4494–5
Drunk driving arrests, sentencing, and prisoner drinking patterns and other characteristics, 1989, 6066–19.69
Economic and monetary trends, compounded annual rates of change and quarterly indicators for US and 7 major industrialized countries, quarterly rpt, 9391–7
Economic conditions, and oil supply and demand, for major industrial countries, monthly rpt, 9112–1
Economic indicators and components, and Fed Reserve 4th District business and financial conditions, monthly chartbook, 9377–10
Economic indicators and components, current data and annual trends, monthly rpt, 23842–1.2
Economic indicators compounded annual rates of change, monthly rpt, 9391–3
Economic indicators, monthly rpt, 9362–1.2
Economic indicators performance, and Fed Reserve monetary policy objectives, as of July 1992, semiannual rpt, 9362–4
Education (adult) participation, by selected characteristics, 1991 survey, 4826–10.5
Education data, detail for elementary, secondary, and higher education, 1920s-91 and projected to 2002, annual rpt, 4824–1
Education data, summary trends, 1970s-91, annual pamphlet, 4824–10
Educational attainment, by social and demographic characteristics and location, 1991 and trends from 1940, biennial Current Population Rpt, 2546–1.460
Educational attainment of public housing residents, by selected characteristics, 1980s, 5188–132
Educational enrollment, by grade, instn type and control, and student characteristics, 1990 and trends from 1947, annual Current Population Rpt, 2546–1.459
Electric power demand, and industrial and employment impacts of capacity shortfalls and new power plants, by selected State, 1960s-80s and projected to 2000, hearing, 21248–163
Employment and earnings by industry div, and personal income per capita and by source, by industry div, State, MSA, and county, 1969-90, annual CD-ROM, 2704–7
Employment and Earnings, detailed data, monthly rpt, 6742–2
Employment, earnings, and hours, by selected SIC 1- to 4-digit industry, State, and for 275 MSAs, 1987-92, 6748–81
Employment, earnings, and hours, by SIC 1- to 4-digit industry, monthly 1989-Feb 1992, annual rpt, 6744–4
Employment, earnings, and hours, monthly press release, 6742–5
Employment in manufacturing and nonagricultural industries, by MSA, 1990-91, annual press release, 6946–3.24
Employment situation, earnings, hours, and other BLS economic indicators, transcripts of BLS Commissioner's monthly testimony, periodic rpt, 23846–4
Employment, unemployment, and labor force characteristics, by region, State, and selected metro area, 1991, annual rpt, 6744–7
Exports and imports impacts on US industries and employment, series, 6366–3
Exports, imports, balances, US consumption, and operations of industries affected, by industry, 1989-91, annual rpt, 9884–25
Family members labor force status and earnings, by family composition and race, quarterly press release, 6742–21
Family members labor force status, impacts on household, series, 6726–2
Family members supporting others outside household, by relationship, recipient living arrangements, and provider characteristics, 1988, Current Population Rpt, 2546–20.21
Farm population, by employment, social, and economic characteristics, and region, 1990, annual Current Population Rpt, 2546–1.458
Fiscal policy (supply side) of Reagan Admin, economic impacts, 1980s and trends from 1960s, technical paper, 9385–1.304; 9385–8.125
Food stamp eligibility and payment errors, by type, recipient characteristics, and State, FY90, annual rpt, 1364–15
Food stamp recipient household size, composition, income, and income and deductions allowed, summer 1989, annual rpt, 1364–8
Forecasts of economic conditions and employment, alternative BLS projections to 2005 and trends 1975-90, biennial rpt, 6744–19
Forecasts of economic indicators, 1992-93 and trends from 1948, annual article, 9383–6.301
Forecasts of economic indicators, 1993-94 and trends from 1948, annual article, 9383–6.303
Forecasts of employment and GNP, accuracy of BLS forecasts made late 1970s-85, as of 1990, article, 6722–1.335
Forecasts of employment by occupation, accuracy of BLS forecasts for 1990 made 1980, article, 6722–1.336
Forecasts of employment by occupation, accuracy of BLS forecasts for 1990 made 1982, article, 6742–1.302
Forecasts of industrial production and unemployment, performance of consumer sentiment surveys, 1991 working paper, 9371–10.69
Foreign-controlled US firms employment and trade compared to US multinatl firms, 1988, article, 9391–1.309
Foreign direct investment in US by country, and finances, employment, and acreage owned, by industry group of business acquired or established, 1985-91, annual article, 2702–1.320
Foreign travelers to US, spending by world area of residence, and economic impacts, by spending category and State, 1989, 2908–28
GDP forecasts for current quarter, performance of monthly advance indicators, 1981-91, article, 9393–8.305
Health condition and care relation to education, indicators by selected characteristics, 1989, 4147–10.180
High school and college grads and dropouts employment status and income, 1992 edition, annual rpt, 4824–2.28
High school class of 1991: college enrollment, and labor force participation of grads and dropouts, by race and sex, annual press release, 6726–1.46
Higher education grads labor force status, job degree requirements, and outlook, 1980s-90 and projected to 2005, article, 6722–1.331
Higher education instn student financial support by parents, by type and funding sources, and student, parent, and instn characteristics, fall 1986, 4846–3.11

Homeless persons transitional housing and support services program, outcome relation to client characteristics and services, FY87-90, GAO rpt, 26113–549
Households and family characteristics, by location, 1991, annual Current Population Rpt, 2546–1.457
Households composition, income, benefits, and labor force status, Survey of Income and Program Participation methodology, working paper series, 2626–10
Hwy scenic routes impacts on local economic conditions, by State, county, and selected byway, late 1980s, 7556–8.1
Immigration impacts on US labor force and employment, working paper series, 6366–6
Imports (duty-free) from Caribbean area, impact on US employment by industry, 1991, annual rpt, 6364–2
Imports and tariff provisions effect on US industries and products, investigations with background financial and operating data, series, 9886–4
Imports, exports, and employment impacts, by SIC 2- to 4-digit industry and commodity, quarterly rpt, 2322–2
Imports injury to US industries from foreign subsidized products and sales at less than fair value, investigations with background financial and operating data, series, 9886–19
Imports under Generalized System of Preferences, status, and US tariffs, with trade by country and US economic impacts, for selected commodities, 1987-91, annual rpt, 9884–23
Income (household) and poverty status under alternative income definitions, by recipient characteristics, 1979-91, annual Current Population Rpt, 2546–6.78
Income (personal) relative to median, by race and selected other characteristics, mid 1960s-89, Current Population Rpt, 2546–6.73
Income and consumer spending of households, for selected population groups, quarterly journal, 1702–1
Industry (US) intl competitiveness, with selected foreign and US operating data by major firm and product, series, 2046–12
Industry finances and operations, by SIC 2- to 4-digit industry, forecast 1992, annual rpt, 2044–28
Insurance (health) coverage of persons, by insurance type and selected characteristics, 1985-90, 2546–20.23
Insurance (health) denial by private carriers because of poor health, by selected characteristics, 1987, 4186–8.23
Interest rate spreads impacts on GNP and employment, various periods 1959-91, technical paper, 9385–8.131
Labor demand, turnover, and training completions, by detailed occupation, 1990 and projected to 2005, biennial rpt, 6744–3
Labor force characteristics, press release series, 6726–1
Labor force status by race and sex, employment by industry div, and unemployment duration and reason, selected years 1929-91, annual rpt, 204–1.2
Labor force, wages, hours, and payroll costs, by major industry group and demographic characteristics, *Survey of Current Business*, monthly rpt, 2702–1.7
Life expectancy, by sex, income, education, and labor force status, for whites, 1979-85, article, 4042–3.347
Living arrangements, family relationships, and marital status, by selected characteristics, 1991, annual Current Population Rpt, 2546–1.461
Local areas with labor surplus and eligible for preferential Fed Govt contracts, monthly listing, 6402–1
Manufacturing annual survey, 1990: establishments, employment, finances, inventories, and energy use, by SIC 2- to 4-digit industry, 2506–14.2
Manufacturing annual survey, 1990: finances and operations, by SIC 2- and 3-digit industry and State, 2506–14.3
Manufacturing census, 1987: concentration of largest firms measured by value added, and for shipments by SIC 2- and 4-digit industry, subject rpt, 2497–6
Manufacturing census, 1987: exporting establishments, shipments, and employment, by SIC 2-digit industry and State, 2506–16.2
Manufacturing debt/asset ratios impact on employment changes over the business cycle, 1960s-84, technical paper, 9366–6.286
Manufacturing trade, tariffs, and industry operating data, commodity rpt series, 9885–10
Married-couple families income, and spouses labor force participation and hours worked, by income class, 1979 and 1989, 23848–225
Mental illness (serious) among adults, functional limitations, govt aid, drugs used, visits to professionals, and other characteristics, 1989, 4146–8.220
Migration, immigration, and mover characteristics compared to nonmovers, 1987-90, annual Current Population Rpt, 2546–1.456
Migration since 1990, mover characteristics by same or different area, and compared to nonmovers, 1991, annual Current Population Rpt, 2546–1.464
Militarily strategic manufacturing industries finances, operations, and intl competitiveness, series, 2026–1
Military prime contract awards in labor surplus areas, by service branch, State, and area, 1st half FY92, semiannual rpt, 3542–19
Military spending reductions, economic impacts by defense contractor, industry, State, and congressional district, 1989-90 hearings, 23848–224
Military spending reductions, economic impacts of alternative plans, with data by industry and State, various periods 1949-87, article, 9385–1.313
Military spending reductions, economic impacts of Bush Admin plans by industry and State, FY92-97, 26306–6.167
Minority- and woman-owned businesses and owner characteristics, by industry, employment and sales size, and form of ownership, 1987 survey, 2328–59
Minority Business Dev Centers mgmt and financial aid, and characteristics of businesses, by region and State, FY91, annual rpt, 2104–6
Monthly Labor Review, current statistics and articles, 6722–1
Multinatl firms US affiliates finances and operations, by industry, country of parent firm, and State, 1987, 2702–1.340; 2708–48
Multinatl firms US affiliates finances and operations, by industry div, country of parent firm, and State, 1989-90, annual article, 2702–1.319; 2702–1.337
Multinatl firms US affiliates, finances, and operations, by industry, world area of parent firm, and State, 1989-90, annual rpt, 2704–4
Multinatl US firms and foreign affiliates finances and operations, by industry and country, 1989 benchmark survey, annual rpt, 2704–5
Multinatl US firms and foreign affiliates finances and operations, by industry and world area, 1988, annual article, 2702–1.329
Natl Commission for Employment Policy activities and rpts, 1991 annual rpt, 15494–1
Natl income and product accounts, comprehensive accounts and components, benchmark revisions, 1929-88, 2708–5
Natl income and product accounts, comprehensive accounts and components, *Survey of Current Business*, monthly rpt, 2702–1.29
OASDHI coverage of employment and earnings, and social security contributions, by age, sex, race, State, and county, 1988, annual rpt, 4744–29
OASDHI coverage of employment and earnings, late 1930s-90, annual rpt, 4744–3.1; 4744–3.2
OASDI beneficiary data collection system design compared to earlier surveys, with summary results, 1992 article, 4742–1.313
Occupational Outlook Quarterly, journal, 6742–1
Oil prices and interest rates related to GNP and employment, late 1940s-91, article, 9389–1.304
Older persons labor force status, income sources, and reasons for not working, with data by occupation, sex, and race, 1989-90 and projected to 2050, 21148–65
Older persons socioeconomic characteristics, 1900s-90 and projected to 2050, biennial chartbook, 12904–1
Older population, and health, economic, and other characteristics, with foreign comparisons, 1980s-91 with trends and projections, Current Population Rpt, 2546–2.165
Population and labor force characteristics, 1940s-90 and projected to 2000, 15496–1.16
Population economic well-being indicators, by selected characteristics and household income and income-to-poverty ratio, 1984, 2546–20.22
Population size and demographic changes impacts on economic conditions, with background data, 1950s-80s and projected to 2010, 23848–226

Poverty relation to low earnings, by work experience during year, household relationship, sex, race, age, and education, 1960s-90, Current Population Rpt, 2546–6.74
Poverty status of families, by detailed characteristics, 1980 and 1988, GAO rpt, 26131–102
Poverty status of population and families, by detailed characteristics, 1991, annual Current Population Rpt, 2546–6.77
Prisoners and movements, by offense, location, and selected other characteristics, data compilation, 1992 annual rpt, 6064–6.6
Public assistance benefits, beneficiaries, and spells of participation, by aid program and recipient characteristics, 1987-88, Current Population Rpt, 2546–20.25
Regional and industrial economic factors relation to employment over business cycles, model description and results, 1992 working paper, 9381–10.134
Research on employment and retirement, bibl, 1990 listing, 4746–26.14
Rural areas economic and social conditions, dev, and problems, periodic journal, 1502–7
Rural areas economic conditions and dev, quarterly journal, 1502–8
Rural areas employment and population characteristics, and role of education and training in economic dev, 1960s-80s, compilation of papers, 1598–277
Small Business Admin loan guarantee program participants finances, operations, characteristics, and views, 1991 survey, 9768–25
Small business finances, operations, owner characteristics, and Federal contracts, 1980s-90, annual rpt, 9764–6
Small Business Investment Company funding of selected firms, employment at start of investment and as of 1990, 9768–24
Statistical Abstract of US, 1992 annual data compilation, 2324–1; 2324–1.13
Taxes, spending, and govt efficiency, public opinion by respondent characteristics, 1992 survey, annual rpt, 10044–2
Technological devs effect on labor force, composition, and productivity, 1970s-90 and projected to 2005, industry rpt series, 6826–2
Trade adjustment aid for workers, petitions by disposition, selected industry, union, and State, monthly rpt, 6402–13
Travel patterns, personal and household characteristics, and auto and public transport use, 1990 survey, series, 7556–6
Unemployed persons finding work, by characteristics of worker and new job, aggregate 1986-89, 2546–20.20
Unemployed workers methods of seeking jobs, by sex, age, and race, monthly rpt, 6742–2.2
Unemployment by selected characteristics, health insurance coverage, and unemployment insurance benefits exhaustion, 1988-91 and projected to 1996, hearing, 21788–209
Unemployment, by State and metro area, monthly press release, 6742–12
Unemployment, employment, and labor force, by region and State, 1990-91, annual press release, 6726–1.45
Unemployment, employment, and labor force, by State, MSA, and city, monthly rpt, 6742–22
Unemployment rates and discouraged workers, quarterly 1980-83 and 1990-91, article, 9391–16.304
Union coverage of workers and earnings, by age, sex, race, occupational group, and industry div, 1990-91, annual press release, 6726–1.44
Vocational education enrollment, student and teacher characteristics, and outcomes, for secondary and postsecondary instns, 1970s-90, 4828–42
see also Absenteeism
see also Agricultural labor
see also Alien workers
see also Apprenticeship
see also Area wage surveys
see also Blue collar workers
see also Child labor
see also Clerical workers
see also Discrimination in employment
see also Domestic workers and services
see also Earnings, general
see also Employee benefits
see also Employee development
see also Employee performance and appraisal
see also Employment and unemployment, local and regional
see also Employment and unemployment, specific industry
see also Employment services
see also Engineers and engineering
see also Executives and managers
see also Foreign labor conditions
see also Government employees
see also Health occupations
see also Home-based offices and workers
see also Hours of labor
see also Industry wage surveys
see also Job creation
see also Job tenure
see also Job vacancy
see also Labor costs and cost indexes
see also Labor law
see also Labor-management relations, general
see also Labor-management relations in government
see also Labor productivity
see also Labor supply and demand
see also Labor turnover
see also Manpower training programs
see also Migrant workers
see also Military personnel
see also Minority employment
see also Moonlighting
see also Occupational health and safety
see also Occupational testing and certification
see also Occupations
see also Overtime
see also Paraprofessionals
see also Part-time employment
see also Payroll
see also Pensions and pension funds
see also Personnel management
see also Prison work programs
see also Production workers
see also Professional and technical workers
see also Public service employment
see also Retirement
see also Scientists and technicians
see also Self-employment
see also Sheltered workshops
see also Temporary and seasonal employment
see also Underemployment
see also Unemployment insurance
see also Unpaid family workers
see also Vacations and holidays
see also Veterans employment
see also Vocational rehabilitation
see also Volunteers
see also Wage deductions
see also Women's employment
see also Work conditions
see also Work incentive programs
see also Work stoppages
see also Workers compensation
see also Worksharing
see also Youth employment

Employment and unemployment, local and regional

Alaska rural areas population characteristics, and energy resources dev effects, series, 5736–5
American Samoa govt finances, with data on health and farm spending and employment, mid 1980s-91, GAO rpt, 26123–385
Appalachia food processing firms, employment, and shipments, and farm production, by commodity and State, 1960s-90, 9088–37
California employment changes impacts on employment in nearby States, regression results, 1992 article, 9393–8.306
Chicago airport employment, air cargo shipments by industry, and convention attendance, compared to other locations, mid 1970s-90, working paper, 9375–13.78
Dallas-Fort Worth metro area employment, earnings, hours, and CPI changes, late 1970s-91, annual rpt, 6964–2
DC immigrants from Central America, by selected employment and other characteristics, and reasons for migration, 1985-88, working paper, 6366–6.3
DC metro area drug, alcohol, and tobacco use, user characteristics, and consequences, series, 4496–12
Houston metro area employment, earnings, hours, and CPI changes, 1970s-91, annual rpt, 6964–1
Los Angeles wages and working conditions impacts of Immigration Reform and Control Act, 1980s-91, working paper, 6366–6.9
Middle Atlantic States economic conditions, Fed Reserve 3rd District, quarterly rpt, 9387–10
Middle Atlantic States manufacturing business outlook, monthly survey rpt, 9387–11
Midwest US producer services industries employment concentration, by industry group, MSA, and urban-rural location, 1970s-89, article, 9375–1.305
New England construction, real estate, and other economic performance indicators, compared to Texas and other areas, 1970s-91, article, 9373–1.302

New England States economic indicators, Fed Reserve 1st District, monthly rpt, 9373–2
New England States employment growth after recessions, relation to selected economic factors, various periods 1969-90, article, 9373–1.315
New England textile industry employment of Colombian immigrants, by selected characteristics, 1960s-80s, working paper, 6366–6.4
North Central States business and economic conditions, Fed Reserve 9th District, quarterly journal, 9383–19
Northwestern US and British Columbia forest industry production, prices, trade, and employment, quarterly rpt, 1202–3
NYC housing supply, occupancy, condition, and household characteristics, by tenure and borough, 1991 triennial survey, 2488–3
Ohio poverty, hunger, and public welfare program operations and indicators of need, by county, 1991 hearing, 21968–58
Pacific Northwest Indian tribes environmental, economic, and cultural impacts of OCS oil and gas lease and dev, with background data, 1970s-92, 5738–35
Pacific Northwest population, households, employment, income, fuel prices, and electricity demand, alternative forecasts 1991-2010, annual rpt, 3224–3.3
Pacific territories population and housing detailed characteristics, by location, 1990 Census of Population and Housing, series, 2551–8
Palau admin, and social, economic, and govtl data, FY91, annual rpt, 7004–6
Philadelphia metro area transit service operations, costs and benefits, and local economic and air pollution impacts, 1970s-90 and projected to 2020, 7308–205
Puerto Rico and other US possessions corporations income tax returns, income and tax items, and employment, by selected industry, 1989, article, 8302–2.326
Southeastern States, Fed Reserve 5th District, economic indicators by State, quarterly rpt, 9389–16
Southeastern States, Fed Reserve 6th District, economic indicators by State and MSA, quarterly rpt, 9371–14
Southeastern States, Fed Reserve 8th District banking and economic conditions, quarterly rpt with articles, 9391–16
Southeastern States, FHLB 4th District, employment and housing indicators by State, quarterly rpt, 9302–36
Southeastern US employment by industry div, earnings, and hours, for 8 States, quarterly press release, 6942–7
Southeastern US employment conditions, with comparisons to other regions, press release series, 6946–3
Southeastern US employment in multinatl firms US affiliates, by State, 1977 and 1988, article, 9391–16.302
Southeastern US manufacturing conditions, survey methodology and selected results, Dec 1991-July 1992, article, 9371–1.307
Southeastern US textile mill employment, earnings, and hours, for 8 States, quarterly press release, 6942–1
Southern US textile mill employment, 1951-91, annual rpt, 6944–1
Southwestern US employment by industry div, earnings, and hours, by State, monthly rpt, 6962–2
Tennessee Valley economic conditions, and compared to US, alternative projections 1992-2010 and trends from 1929, annual rpt, 9804–27
Texas banks loan losses relation to loan volume growth and other factors, mid 1970s-90, article, 9379–1.305
Texas construction, real estate, and other economic performance indicators, compared to New England and other areas, 1970s-91, article, 9373–1.302
Washington and Oregon coastal areas tourism and recreation facilities and economic impacts, by county, 1983-88, 5738–40.3
West Central States economic indicators, Fed Reserve 10th District, quarterly rpt, 9381–16.2
Western US employment growth by industry div and manufacturing group, Fed Reserve 10th District, 1990-91, annual article, 9381–1.302
see also Area wage surveys
see also Earnings, local and regional
see also under By Census Division, By City, By County, By Region, By SMSA or MSA, and By State in the "Index by Categories"

Employment and unemployment, specific industry
Advertising employment, by detailed occupation, 1990, article, 6722–1.341
Agricultural, fishery, and forest products trade, tariffs, and industry operating data, commodity rpt series, 9885–8
Airports employment, air cargo shipments by industry, and convention attendance, for Chicago and other locations, mid 1970s-90, working paper, 9375–13.78
Auto and auto parts trade, production, and labor conditions, for US and compared to Canada and Mexico, 1950s-90, 6366–3.28
Auto assembly plant productivity and relation to labor reserves, model description and results, 1991 working paper, 6886–6.89
Auto industry finances and operations, trade by country, and prices of selected US and foreign models, monthly rpt, 9882–8
Banks (Fed Reserve) and branch officers, staff, and salary, 1991, annual rpt, 9364–1.1
Banks (insured commercial) employment, by asset size and State, 1990, annual rpt, 9294–4
Banks (insured commercial), Fed Reserve 5th District members financial statements, by State, quarterly rpt, 9389–18
Banks (insured commercial) financial condition and performance, by asset size and region, quarterly rpt, 9292–1.1
Banks and thrifts finances and operations by deposit size, Fed Reserve functional cost analysis, 1991, annual rpt, 9364–6
Banks in Fed Reserve System, expenses and operations itemized by service, office, and district, 1991, annual rpt, 9364–11
Chemical and energy products trade, tariffs, and industry operating data, commodity rpt series, 9885–11
Clothing and other industries employment of aliens, and impacts on local economies, with background data, 1990 working paper, 6366–6.6
Coal production and mines by county, prices, productivity, miners, and reserves, by mining method and State, 1990-91, annual rpt, 3164–25
Coal production, reserves, use, and prices by State, exports by country, and employment, 1900s-90, biennial rpt, 3164–79
Construction employment, earnings, and hours, by selected SIC 2- to 3-digit industry, quarterly rpt, 2042–1.7
Containers (wood) industry productivity trends and technological devs, 1977-89, article, 6722–1.344
Credit unions federally insured, finances by instn characteristics and State, as of June 1992, semiannual rpt, 9532–6
Electric power distribution loans from REA, and borrower operating and financial data, by firm and State, 1991, annual rpt, 1244–1
Electric power plants production and capital costs, operations, and fuel use, by fuel type, plant, utility, and location, 1990, annual rpt, 3164–9
Electric utilities privately owned, finances and operations, detailed data, 1990, annual rpt, 3164–23
Electronics and services trade, tariffs, and industry operating data, commodity rpt series, 9885–12
Electronics industry production and labor conditions, in 10 MSAs, EC, and top producer countries, late 1970s-80s, article, 9393–8.307
Energy-related fields manpower studies and devs, series, 3006–8
Fed Reserve System, Bd of Governors, and district banks financial statements, performance, and fiscal services, 1991-92, annual rpt, 9364–10
Fish fresh and frozen products industry productivity trends and technological devs, 1972-90, article, 6722–1.342
Fish processing and wholesale plants and employment, by region, 1988, annual rpt, 2166–6.2
Fishery employment, vessels, plants, and cooperatives, by State, 1990, annual rpt, 2164–1.10
Food marketing sector finances, operations, and merger activity, for processors and distributors, 1991, annual rpt, 1544–22
Food processing firms, employment, and shipments, and farm production, by commodity and State, for Appalachia, 1960s-90, 9088–37
Footwear production, employment, use, prices, and US trade by country, quarterly rpt, 9882–6
Health Care Financing Review, provider prices, price inputs and indexes, and labor, quarterly journal, 4652–1.1
Health care services employment, compared to other industries, 1960s-91, article, 6722–1.347
Insurance industry financial condition, operations, assets, junk bond holdings, and State regulation, with intl comparisons, 1991 hearings, 25268–79

Lumber (hardwood) production, prices, employment, and trade, quarterly rpt, 1202–4
Machinery and equipment trade, tariffs, and industry operating data, commodity rpt series, 9885–9
Military budget and outlays, contracts, active-duty and civilian personnel, and defense industry employment, FY85-93, GAO rpt, 26123–399
Mineral Industry Surveys, commodity reviews of production, trade, use, and industry operations, advance annual rpt series, 5614–5
Minerals and metals trade, tariffs, and industry operating data, commodity rpt series, 9885–13
Minerals production, prices, trade, use, employment, tariffs, and stockpiles, by mineral, with foreign comparisons, 1987-91, annual rpt, 5604–18
Mines (coal) and related operations occupational injuries and incidence, employment, and hours, 1990, annual rpt, 6664–4
Mines (metal) and related operations occupational injuries and incidence, employment, and hours, 1990, annual rpt, 6664–3
Mines (nonmetallic minerals) and related operations occupational injuries and incidence, employment, and hours, 1990, annual rpt, 6664–1
Mines (sand and gravel) and related operations occupational injuries and incidence, employment, and hours, 1990, annual rpt, 6664–2
Mines (stone) and related operations occupational injuries and incidence, employment, and hours, 1990, annual rpt, 6664–5
Mines and mills injuries by circumstances, employment, and hours, by type of operation and State, quarterly rpt, 6662–1
Natural gas interstate pipeline company detailed financial and operating data, by firm, 1990, annual rpt, 3164–38
Nuts and bolts industry productivity trends and technological devs, 1958-90, article, 6722–1.343
Oil and gas exploratory rigs in operation, wells and footage drilled, and seismic exploration crews, monthly rpt, 3162–24.5
Oil and gas exploratory rigs in operation, wells and footage drilled, and seismic exploration crews, monthly 1973-88, 3168–123.5
Oil and gas industry labor productivity, 1959-87, article, 6722–1.316
Petrochemicals industries contract labor accidents, injuries, safety programs operations, and employee characteristics, 1986-91, 6608–6
Rail rapid transit systems safety, operating, and funding characteristics, 1988-89, 9618–19
Railroad (Amtrak) finances, executive office travel expenses and staff years, and membership dues by assn, FY88-92, GAO rpt, 26113–573
Railroad employee benefits program finances and beneficiaries, FY91, annual rpt, 9704–1
Railroad employment and compensation, by age, sex, occupation, and years of service, 1985, annual rpt, 9704–2.4
Railroad employment and finances, for ICC-regulated carriers, as of FY91, annual rpt, 9484–1
Railroad employment by occupational group, for Class I line-haul railroads, monthly rpt, 9482–3
Railroad employment, earnings, and hours, by occupation for Class I railroads, 1991, annual table, 9484–5
Railroad industry productivity measures, late 1950s-80s, article, 6722–1.337
Ship-related employment, FY90-91, annual rpt, 7704–14.3
Shipbuilding and repair facilities, capacity, and employment, by shipyard, 1991, annual rpt, 7704–9
Shipbuilding and repair subsidy elimination proposals of US and OECD, impacts on industry and trade, with data on US-flag vessels, 1980s-91, 9886–4.183
Ships in US merchant fleet, operating subsidies, construction, and ship-related employment, monthly rpt, 7702–1
Steel imports of US under voluntary restraint agreement, by product, customs district, and country, with US industry operating data, quarterly rpt, 9882–13
Steel trade, by product, country, and customs district, with US industry operating data, 1989-June 1992, semiannual rpt, 9882–15
Telephone and telegraph firms detailed finances and operations, 1990, annual rpt, 9284–6
Telephone firms borrowing under Rural Telephone Program, and financial and operating data, by State, 1991, annual rpt, 1244–2
Textile industry in New England, employment of Colombian immigrants by selected characteristics, 1960s-80s, working paper, 6366–6.4
Textile mill employment, earnings, and hours, for 8 Southeastern States, quarterly press release, 6942–1
Textile mill employment in southern US, 1951-91, annual rpt, 6944–1
Timber in northwestern US and British Columbia, production, prices, trade, and employment, quarterly rpt, 1202–3
Timber industry impacts of northern spotted owl conservation methods in Pacific Northwest, and Federal and State spending, 1980s-95, 1208–388
Timber sales of Forest Service, expenses, and operations, by region, State, and natl forest, FY91, annual rpts, 1204–36
Travel-related industries employment and receipts, for businesses near Blue Ridge Parkway, 1987, 7556–8.4
Travel-related industries employment and receipts, 1988, 7556–8.3
Truck and bus interstate carriers finances and operations, by district, 1990, annual rpt, 9486–5.3
Truck, bus, and rail carriers regulated by ICC, employment and finances, as of FY91, annual rpt, 9484–1
Truck interstate carriers finances and operations, by district, 1990, annual rpt, 9486–5.2
Uranium mining and milling industries finances and operations, with selected foreign comparisons, 1970s-90 and projected to 2005, annual rpt, 3164–82
Uranium reserves and industry operations, by region and State, various periods 1966-91, annual rpt, 3164–65.1
Uranium tailings at inactive mills, remedial action proposals, costs, site characteristics, and environmental, socioeconomic, and health impacts, series, 3356–4
see also Agricultural labor
see also Earnings, specific industry
see also Federal employees
see also Government employees
see also Health occupations
see also Industry wage surveys
see also Military personnel
see also State and local employees
see also Teachers
see also under By Industry in the "Index by Categories"
see also under By Occupation in the "Index by Categories"

Employment Cost Index
see Labor costs and cost indexes

Employment services
Assistance (block and categorical grants) programs for State and local govts, FY91, biennial listing, 10044–8
Assistance (financial and nonfinancial) of Fed Govt, 1992 base edition, annual listing, 104–5
Assistance programs of Fed Govt for public welfare, employment, and training, coordination issues with background data, 1991 rpt, 15498–29
Budget of US, obligations and authority by function, agency, and program, with summaries and analyses, FY93, annual rpt, 104–2
County Business Patterns, 1989: employment, establishments, and payroll, by SIC 2- to 4-digit industry and county, annual State rpt series, 2326–8
County Business Patterns, 1990: employment, establishments, and payroll, by SIC 2- to 4-digit industry and county, annual State rpt series, 2326–6
Disabled persons workshops finances, operations, and Federal procurement, FY82-91, annual rpt, 11714–1
Displaced worker employment and training services, and layoff alternatives, indicators of effectiveness, 1980s, 15498–28
Displaced worker training programs spending, participation, and placements by State, 1990, GAO rpt, 26121–481
Employment and Training Admin activities, funding, and participant characteristics, by program, FY86-88, annual rpt, 6404–17
Employment, earnings, and hours, by SIC 1- to 4-digit industry, monthly 1989-Feb 1992, annual rpt, 6744–4
Finances and operations, by SIC 2- to 4-digit industry, forecast 1992, annual rpt, 2044–28
Homeless persons transitional housing and support services, HUD grants by community, 1991, press release, 5006–3.80
Input-output structure of US economy, detailed interindustry transactions for 541 industries, and components of final demand, 1982 benchmark data, 2708–17

Labor Dept activities and funding, by program and State, FY91, annual rpt, 6304–1
Labor laws enacted, by State, 1991, annual article, 6722–1.309
Occupational injury and illness rates, by SIC 2- to 4-digit industry, 1989-90, annual rpt, 6844–7
Occupational injury and illness rates, by SIC 2- to 4-digit industry, 1990, annual rpt, 6844–1
Occupational Outlook Handbook, 1992-93, biennial rpt, 6744–1
Prison and community-based facilities, population, employment, spending, and other characteristics, by State and for Fed Govt, 1990, annual rpt, 6064–26.3
State and local govt employment of minorities and women, by occupation, function, and pay level, 1991, annual rpt, 9244–6.4
Unemployed displaced workers job search and placement aid effectiveness, relation to previous employment and other characteristics, 1979-87 studies, 15496–1.14

Employment Standards Administration
Black lung benefits and claims by State, trust fund receipts by source, and disbursements, 1991, annual rpt, 6504–3
Budget of US, obligations and authority by function, agency, and program, with summaries and analyses, FY93, annual rpt, 104–2
Workers compensation laws of States and Fed Govt, semiannual rpt, periodicity change, 6502–1
Workers compensation laws of States and Fed Govt, 1992 annual rpt, 6504–11
Workers compensation programs of States, admin, coverage, benefits, finances, processing, and staff, 1988-91, annual rpt, 6504–9
Workers compensation programs under Federal admin, finances and operations, FY91, annual rpt, 6504–10
see also Women's Bureau

Endangered species
Birds (least tern and piping plover) and habitat levels of selenium and other pollutants, for Missouri River in South Dakota, 1988-90, 5508–118
Coastal and riparian areas environmental conditions, fish, wildlife, use, and mgmt, for individual ecosystems, series, 5506–9
Desert areas public grazing acreage, use, fees, and endangered species, 1988-90, GAO rpt, 26113–552
Environmental Quality, status of problems, protection programs, research, and intl issues, 1991 annual rpt, 484–1
Fish and Wildlife Service conservation and habitat mgmt activities, FY91, annual narrative rpt, 5504–20
Fish Hatchery Natl System activities and deliveries, by species, hatchery, and jurisdiction of waters stocked, FY91, annual rpt, 5504–10
Forest Service activities and finances, by region and State, FY91, annual rpt, 1204–1.1
Listing and mgmt of endangered species, Fish and Wildlife Service and Natl Marine Fisheries Service activities, FY74-91, GAO rpt, 26113–578
Marine Mammal Protection Act admin, and populations, strandings, and catch permits by species and location, 1988-89, annual rpt, 2164–11
Marine mammals and birds incidental catch in California net fishing operations, 1984-85, 14738–13
Marine mammals and sea turtles population and mgmt, by species and region, 1988-90, annual rpt, 2164–22
Marine mammals incidental catch by fishing trawl vessels, by species, vessel flag and type, and North Pacific location, 1965-88, 2168–129
Marine mammals protection activities and funding, populations, and harvests, by species, 1990, annual rpt, 5504–12
Marine mammals protection, Federal and intl regulatory and research activities, 1991, annual rpt, 14734–1
Marine mammals tissue pollutant concentrations, by species and pollutant type, for Alaska, 1987-91, 2218–87
Minerals offshore lease sales environmental and economic impacts in coastal areas, final statement series, 5736–7
Owl (northern spotted) conservation methods in Pacific Northwest, findings and recommendations, 1990 rpt, 1208–385
Owl (northern spotted) conservation methods in Pacific Northwest, timber industry impacts, and Federal and State spending, 1980s-95, 1208–388
Pacific Northwest old-growth forests plant and wildlife population and species diversity, 1991 compilation of papers, 1208–386
Public lands acreage, grants, use, revenues, and allocations, by State, FY91, annual rpt, 5724–1.2
Research on fish and wildlife population, habitat, and mgmt, technical rpt series, 5506–12
Salmon conservation spending by organization, and population, for Columbia River basin, 1970-91, GAO rpt, 26113–577
Statistical Abstract of US, 1992 annual data compilation, 2324–1.6
Turtles (sea) excluder device use impacts on shrimp catch, by device type, for Texas fishery, 1983-87 and projected to 1997, article, 2162–1.302
Turtles (sea) population and mgmt, by species and region, 1988-90, annual rpt, 2164–22
Turtles (sea) sightings, strandings, and incidental catch, for Kemp's ridley turtles on Texas coast, late 1940s-90, 2168–132
Whales (humpback) habitat impacts of human activities in Hawaii, with data on shipping, whale watching, coastal construction, and aircraft, 1980s-90, 14738–14
Whales population and behavior in Chukchi and Beaufort Seas, by endangered species, 1982-91, 5738–32
Whales population and behavior in Chukchi and Beaufort Seas, by endangered species, 1990, 5738–36
Wolf (gray) kills of livestock, and farmer compensation claims and payments, for Minnesota, late 1970s-80s, 5508–115

Endangered Species Act
Listing and mgmt of endangered species, Fish and Wildlife Service and Natl Marine Fisheries Service activities, FY74-91, GAO rpt, 26113–578

Endocrine diseases
see Metabolic and endocrine diseases

Endter-Wada, Joanna
"Social Indicators Study of Alaskan Coastal Villages I. Key Informant Summaries, Volume 2: Schedule B Regions", 5736–5.17

Energy
see terms listed under Energy resources and consumption

Energy assistance
see Low-income energy assistance

Energy conservation
Auto and light truck fuel economy performance by make, standards, and enforcement, 1978-94 model years, annual rpt, 7764–9
Auto and light truck fuel use, economy, and miles traveled, projected 1990-2010 and trends from 1960s, 3008–124
Auto engine and power train R&D projects, DOE contracts and funding by recipient, FY91, annual rpt, 3304–17
Auto fuel economy improvements from new technologies, 1987-90 and alternative projections to 2010, 26358–251
Auto fuel economy test results for US and foreign makes, 1993 model year, annual rpt, 3304–11
Buildings (commercial and residential) energy conservation technologies use, costs, efficiency, and residential tax credits, 1970s-90 and projected to 2010, 26358–259
Commercial buildings energy use, costs, and conservation, by building characteristics, survey rpt series, 3166–8
Conservation and energy efficiency measures, use, and prices, by fuel type, end-use sector, selected industry, and region, annual rpt, discontinued, 3164–73
Consumption and conservation of energy, survey results and methodology, series, 3166–15
Developing countries energy efficiency improvement issues and devs, with data by end use and country, 1980s-90, 26358–260
DOE activities and finances, summary energy supply and demand data, and bibl, 1990, annual rpt, 3024–2
DOE energy use, costs, and conservation, by end use, fuel type, and field office, FY91, annual rpt, 3004–27
Electric utilities conservation programs alternative planning strategies cost effectiveness, model results, 1991 rpt, 3308–100
Electric utilities conservation programs, collaboration between utilities and interest groups, and effects on costs, 1992 rpt, 3308–104
Electric utilities conservation programs data reporting guidelines, with background data, 1991 rpt, 3308–101
Electric utilities conservation programs energy savings and spending, with data for top 25 firms, 1990, 3308–106
Electric utilities conservation programs, energy savings measurement methodology, 1991, compilation of papers, 3308–102

Electric utilities conservation programs, impacts on prices and revenue requirements, alternative projections 1990-2010, 3308–105
Electric utilities conservation programs, peak load reductions, energy savings, and costs, by region, 1989-90 and projected to 2000, article, 3162–35.302
Export markets, competitiveness, and promotion, for US energy technology industries, 1992 technical rpt, 3006–13.5
Fed Govt financial and nonfinancial domestic aid, 1992 base edition, annual listing, 104–5
Foreign and US oil dependency, energy demand, and efficiency measures, for 6 OECD countries, 1970s-80s, working paper, 9375–13.79
Housing (low income) energy aid, funding sources, costs, and participation, by State, FY90, annual rpt, 4584–1
Housing energy use, costs, and conservation, and household and housing characteristics, survey rpt series, 3166–7
Manufacturing energy use and prices, 1988 survey, series, 3166–13
Natl Energy Strategy auto fuel economy standards and alternative fuels issues, 1991 hearings, 21368–138
Natl Energy Strategy fossil fuel, electric power, conservation, and pollution reduction issues, 1991 hearings, 21368–136
Natl Energy Strategy plans for conservation, R&D, security, and pollution reduction, technical rpt series, 3006–13
Natl Energy Strategy Strategic Petroleum Reserve and energy efficiency issues, 1991 hearings, 21368–142
Oil and gas primary use prohibited for power and industrial plants, exemptions, and gas use by State, 1980-91, annual rpt, 3334–1
Oil company overcharge settlements funds received, and conservation and energy aid spending, by outlying area, 1990, GAO rpt, 26113–564
Public and nonprofit private instns conservation grants of Fed Govt, by building type and State, 1991, annual rpt, 3304–15
Recycling in manufacturing industries, fuel savings, and CO2 emissions reductions, 1988 and projected to 1995, hearing, 21368–140
State govt energy conservation programs, Federal aid and savings, by State, 1990, annual rpt, 3304–1
Supply, demand, and distribution of energy, and regulatory impacts, series, 3166–6
Supply, demand, and prices, by fuel type and end-use sector, projections and underlying assumptions, 1995-2010, annual rpt, 3164–90
Tax (income) returns of individuals, by filing status, tax item, and income level, 1991, annual article, 8302–2.319
Transportation energy use by mode, fuel supply, and demographic and economic factors of vehicle use, 1970s-90, annual rpt, 3304–5
TVA energy use by fuel type, and conservation costs and savings, FY91, annual rpt, 9804–26
VA health care facilities energy use and conservation, by facility, quarterly rpt, 8602–9
see also Alcohol fuels
see also Biomass energy
see also Electric power and heat cogeneration
see also Geothermal resources
see also Insulation
see also Solar energy
see also Synthetic fuels
see also Wind energy

Energy consumption
see Agricultural energy use
see Energy conservation
see Energy resources and consumption
see Government energy use
see Housing energy use
see Industrial and commercial energy use
see Transportation energy use
see under names of specific types of energy (listed under Energy resources and consumption)

Energy exploration and drilling
Alaska Arctic Natl Wildlife Refuge oil reserves and production, alternative forecasts 1985-2015, 3166–6.64
Alaska Beaufort Sea pollutant concentrations in sediment and marine life, by contaminant and site, 1985-89, 5738–33
Alaska minerals resources and geologic characteristics, compilation of papers, 1990, annual rpt, 5664–15
Alaska minerals resources, production, oil and gas leases, reserves, and exploratory wells, with maps and bibl, 1990, annual rpt, 5664–11
Alaska OCS environmental conditions and oil dev impacts, compilation of papers, series, 2176–1
Alaska rural areas population characteristics, and energy resources dev effects, series, 5736–5
Business statistics, detailed data for major industries and economic indicators, 1960-91, *Survey of Current Business* biennial supplement, 2704–1
Coastal and riparian areas environmental conditions, fish, wildlife, use, and mgmt, for individual ecosystems, series, 5506–9
County Business Patterns, 1989: employment, establishments, and payroll, by SIC 2- to 4-digit industry and county, annual State rpt series, 2326–8
County Business Patterns, 1990: employment, establishments, and payroll, by SIC 2- to 4-digit industry and county, annual State rpt series, 2326–6
Employment, earnings, and hours, by SIC 1- to 4-digit industry, monthly 1989-Feb 1992, annual rpt, 6744–4
Environmental regulation impacts on oil resources recovery, under alternative oil price, technology, and regulatory assumptions, projected 1990-2015, 3338–2
Equipment for drilling and transport, exports of US by country, 1991, annual rpt, 2424–10
Eximbank loans for energy-related products and services, by country and firm, 1990, annual rpt, 9254–3
Export markets, competitiveness, and promotion, for US energy technology industries, 1992 technical rpt, 3006–13.5
Foreign countries oil and gas reserves and discoveries, by country and country group, quarterly rpt, suspended, 3162–43
Geothermal resources, power plant capacity and operating status, leases, and wells, by location, 1960s-95, 3308–87
Geothermal resources, power plant generation, capacity, and dev potential, by location, 1988-90 and projected to 2030, 3168–122
Gulf of Mexico oil and gas reserves, production, and leasing status, by location, 1990, annual rpt, 5734–6
Imports, exports, and employment impacts, by SIC 2- to 4-digit industry and commodity, quarterly rpt, 2322–2
Income and revenue of oil drilling firms, quarterly rpt, 3162–38
Input-output structure of US economy, detailed interindustry transactions for 541 industries, and components of final demand, 1982 benchmark data, 2708–17
Kuwait oil fires set by Iraq, pollution levels, disease cases, and US remediation and monitoring spending, 1991 rpt, 9188–117
Multinatl firms US affiliates finances and operations, by industry, country of parent firm, and State, 1987, 2708–48
Multinatl firms US affiliates, finances, and operations, by industry, world area of parent firm, and State, 1989-90, annual rpt, 2704–4
Multinatl US firms and foreign affiliates finances and operations, by industry and country, 1989 benchmark survey, annual rpt, 2704–5
Natl historic and natural landmarks damaged and threatened, with owner, location, damage type, and recommended remedial action, 1990, annual listing, 5544–16
Natural gas interstate pipeline company detailed financial and operating data, by firm, 1990, annual rpt, 3164–38
Naval Petroleum and Oil Shale Reserves production and revenue by fuel type, sales by purchaser, and wells, by reserve, FY91, annual rpt, 3334–3
North Central States business and economic conditions, Fed Reserve 9th District, quarterly journal, 9383–19
Occupational injury and illness rates, by SIC 2- to 4-digit industry, 1989-90, annual rpt, 6844–7
Occupational injury and illness rates, by SIC 2- to 4-digit industry, 1990, annual rpt, 6844–1
Offshore oil and gas leasing and exploration activity, production, revenue, and environmental studies, by location, quarterly rpt, 5732–1
Offshore oil and gas reserves of Fed Govt, production, leasing and exploration activity, revenue, and costs, by ocean area, FY91, annual rpt, 5734–4
Oil and gas exploratory rigs in operation, wells and footage drilled, and seismic exploration crews, monthly rpt, 3162–24.5
Oil and gas exploratory rigs in operation, wells and footage drilled, and seismic exploration crews, monthly 1973-88, 3168–123.5
Oil and gas OCS production water discharges, treatment costs by method, 1992 rpt, 3166–6.66

Oil enhanced recovery research contracts of DOE, project summaries, funding, and bibl, quarterly rpt, 3002–14
Oil, gas, and gas liquids reserves and production, by State and substate area, 1991, annual rpt, 3164–46
Pacific basin countries energy supply and demand, and implications for US trade, country rpt series, 3406–6
Pacific Ocean OCS oil and gas production, and wells, by drilling platform under Federal lease, 1960s-90, annual rpt, 5734–9
Pacific Ocean OCS oil and gas production, reserves, and wells drilled by location, 1990, annual rpt, 5734–7
Partnership income and losses impact of 1986 Tax Reform Act, by profit status and selected industry, 1980s, article, 8302–2.313
Price indexes (producer), by stage of processing and detailed commodity, monthly 1991, annual rpt, 6764–2
Price indexes for producers of oil and gas drilling and production machinery and equipment, by detailed type, monthly rpt, 6762–6
Producers finances and operations, by energy type for US firms domestic and foreign operations, 1990, annual rpt, 3164–44.2
Public lands acreage and use, and Land Mgmt Bur activities and finances, annual State rpt series, 5724–11
Public lands acreage, grants, use, revenues, and allocations, by State, FY91, annual rpt, 5724–1.2
Public lands minerals resources and availability, State rpt series, 5606–7
Soviet Union and US economic and sociodemographic indicators, selected years 1970-90, handbook, 2328–80
Statistical Abstract of US, 1992 annual data compilation, 2324–1.25
Supply, demand, and prices, by fuel type and end-use sector, with foreign comparisons, 1981-90, annual fact book, 3164–76
Supply, demand, and prices, by fuel type and end-use sector, with foreign comparisons, 1991 and trends from 1949, annual rpt, 3164–74
Tax (income) returns of corporations, income and tax items by asset size and detailed industry, 1989, annual rpt, 8304–4; 8304–21
Tax (income) returns of corporations with foreign tax credit, income and tax items by industry group, 1988, biennial article, 8302–2.316
Tax (income) returns of partnerships, income statement and balance sheet items, by industry group, 1990, annual article, 8302–2.314
Tax (income) returns of sole proprietorships, income statement items, by industry group, 1990, annual article, 8302–2.317; 8302–2.320
Uranium mining and milling industries finances and operations, with selected foreign comparisons, 1970s-90 and projected to 2005, annual rpt, 3164–82
Uranium reserves and industry operations, by region and State, various periods 1966-91, annual rpt, 3164–65.1
Waste (industrial) generation, disposal, and regulation, by industry and State, mid 1980s-90, 26358–256
West Central States economic indicators, Fed Reserve 10th District, quarterly rpt, 9381–16.2
Whales (bowhead and white) migration through Beaufort Sea, behavior impacts of oil drilling and aircraft noise, spring 1990, 5738–27

Energy exports and imports
China minerals production and trade, by commodity, 1989-90, annual rpt, 5604–38
Cuba trade, by commodity and country, mid 1980s-91, 9118–8
Developing countries energy efficiency improvement issues and devs, with data by end use and country, 1980s-90, 26358–260
Electric power capacity and use in Pacific Northwest, by energy source, forecast under alternative load and demand cases, 1991-2012, annual rpt, 3224–3
Electric power import price indexes, quarterly press release, 6762–13
Electric power imports of US, by region, 1986-90, annual rpt, 3164–11.6
Electric power plants (coal-fired) generating capacity and replacement of energy imports, with background data, alternative forecasts 1990-2000, 3166–6.63
Electric power supply, demand, and trade of Mexico and US, with data by fuel source, utility, and region, 1970s-89 and projected to 2000, 3408–2
Environmental Quality, status of problems, protection programs, research, and intl issues, 1991 annual rpt, 484–1
Exports and imports of US, by country and detailed commodity, monthly rpt, 2422–12
Exports and imports of US by country, and trade shifts by commodity, 1991, annual rpt, 9884–25
Exports and imports of US, by selected country, country group, and commodity group, 1991, annual rpt, 2044–37
Exports and imports of US, by transport mode, country, and SITC 1- to 3-digit commodity, 1991, annual rpt, 2424–12
Exports, imports, and balances of US, by selected country, country group, and commodity group, preliminary data, monthly rpt, 2042–34
Exports, imports, and balances of US for manufactured goods, by SITC 2-digit commodity and country, quarterly rpt, 2042–35
Exports, imports, and trade flows, by country and commodity, with background economic indicators, data compilation, monthly CD-ROM, 2002–6
Exports, imports, tariffs, and industry operating data for energy and chemical products, commodity rpt series, 9885–11
Exports of US, detailed commodities by country, monthly CD-ROM, 2422–13
Foreign and US energy production, trade, use, and reserves, and oil and refined products supply and prices, by country, 1981-90, annual rpt, 3164–50
Imports of US, detailed commodities by country, monthly CD-ROM, 2422–14
Japan energy use and imports by fuel type, and gasoline prices, 1970s-80s, hearing, 21448–45
Mexico imports from US, by industry and State, 1987-91, 2048–154
Natl Energy Strategy plans for conservation, R&D, security, and pollution reduction, technical rpt series, 3006–13
OECD trade, total and for 4 major countries, and US trade by country, by commodity, 1980-90, world area rpt series, 9116–1
Pacific basin countries energy supply and demand, and implications for US trade, country rpt series, 3406–6
Romania energy production and trade, 1970s-91, with capital investment projected to 2000, GAO rpt, 26123–402
Solar collector and photovoltaic cell shipments by end-use sector and State, and trade, 1990, annual rpt, 3164–62
Soviet Union and US economic and sociodemographic indicators, selected years 1970-90, handbook, 2328–80
Soviet Union minerals production and exports, by commodity and Republic, 1975-90, annual rpt, 5604–39
Soviet Union oil production, and exports by country or world region of destination, 1980s-89, annual rpt, 23844–2
Statistical Abstract of US, 1992 annual data compilation, 2324–1.19
Supply and demand summary data, DOE activities and finances, and bibl, 1990, annual rpt, 3024–2
Supply, demand, and prices, by fuel type and end-use sector, alternative projections by region, 1990-2010, annual rpt, 3164–96
Supply, demand, and prices, by fuel type and end-use sector, alternative projections 1990-2010, annual rpt, 3164–75
Supply, demand, and prices, by fuel type and end-use sector, projections and underlying assumptions, 1995-2010, annual rpt, 3164–90
Supply, demand, and prices, by fuel type and end-use sector, with foreign comparisons, 1981-90, annual fact book, 3164–76
Supply, demand, and prices, by fuel type and end-use sector, with foreign comparisons, 1991 and trends from 1949, annual rpt, 3164–74
Supply, demand, and prices of energy, forecasts by resource type, quarterly rpt, 3162–34
Uranium imports impacts on US industry, with data on DOE enrichment program and stocks, 1980s-92, GAO rpt, 26113–584
Uranium marketing, contracts, prices, utility shipments, and trade, 1982-91 and projected to 2001, annual rpt, 3164–65.2
Uranium mining and milling industries finances and operations, with selected foreign comparisons, 1970s-90 and projected to 2005, annual rpt, 3164–82
see also Coal exports and imports
see also Natural gas exports and imports
see also Petroleum exports and imports

Energy Information Administration
Activities of EIA, 1991, annual rpt, 3164–29

Building (commercial) energy use, costs, and conservation, by building characteristics, survey rpt series, 3166–8
Coal and coke supply, demand, movements, prices, and stocks, by end-use sector and State, quarterly rpt, 3162–37
Coal production and mines by county, prices, productivity, miners, and reserves, by mining method and State, 1990-91, annual rpt, 3164–25
Coal production by State and region, weekly rpt, 3162–1
Coal production, prices, exports, and use by sector, with data by region, projections, annual rpt, discontinued, 3164–68
Coal production, reserves, use, and prices by State, exports by country, and employment, 1900s-90, biennial rpt, 3164–79
Coal production, stocks, and shipments, by State of origin and destination, end-use sector, and mode of transport, quarterly rpt, 3162–8
Coal trade flows and reserves, by country, annual rpt, discontinued, 3164–77
Data analysis and forecasting models of EIA, 1992, annual listing, 3164–87
Data collection forms of DOE and related rpts, 1991, annual listing, 3164–86
Data on energy resources, EIA rpts and data files, 1990, annual listing, 3164–98
Electric power plants (steam) fuel receipts, costs, and quality, by fuel, plant, utility, and State, 1991, annual rpt, 3164–42
Electric power plants and capacity, by fuel used, owner, location, and operating status, 1991 and for units planned 1992-2001, annual listing, 3164–36
Electric power plants production and capacity by fuel type, prices, demand, and air pollution law impacts, by region, projections, annual rpt, discontinued, 3164–81
Electric power plants production and capital costs, operations, and fuel use, by fuel type, plant, utility, and location, 1990, annual rpt, 3164–9
Electric power plants production, capacity, sales, and fuel stocks, use, and costs, by State, 1986-90, annual rpt, 3164–11
Electric power plants production, fuel use, stocks, and costs by fuel type, and sales, by State, monthly rpt, with articles, 3162–35
Electric power sales and revenue, by end-use sector, consumption level, and utility, 1990, annual rpt, 3164–91
Electric utilities finances and operations, detailed data for publicly owned firms, 1990, annual rpt, 3164–24
Electric utilities privately owned, finances and operations, detailed data, 1990, annual rpt, 3164–23
Energy producers finances and operations, by energy type for US firms domestic and foreign operations, 1990, annual rpt, 3164–44
Energy production, dev, and distribution firms revenues and income, quarterly rpt, 3162–38
Energy supply, demand, and prices, by fuel type and end-use sector, alternative projections by region, 1990-2010, annual rpt, 3164–96
Energy supply, demand, and prices, by fuel type and end-use sector, alternative projections 1990-2010, annual rpt, 3164–75
Energy supply, demand, and prices, by fuel type and end-use sector, projections and underlying assumptions, 1995-2010, annual rpt, 3164–90
Energy supply, demand, and prices, by fuel type and end-use sector, with foreign comparisons, 1981-90, annual fact book, 3164–76
Energy supply, demand, and prices, by fuel type and end-use sector, with foreign comparisons, 1991 and trends from 1949, annual rpt, 3164–74
Energy supply, demand, and prices, by fuel type, end-use sector, and country, detailed data, monthly rpt with articles, 3162–24
Energy supply, demand, and prices, by fuel type, end-use sector, and country, detailed data, monthly 1973-88, 3168–123
Energy supply, demand, and prices, forecasts by resource type, quarterly rpt, 3162–34
Energy supply, demand, distribution, and regulatory impacts, series, 3166–6
Energy use and conservation, survey results and methodology, series, 3166–15
Energy use, by detailed fuel type, end-use sector, and State, 1960-90, State Energy Data System annual rpt, 3164–39
Energy use, prices, and conservation and efficiency measures, by fuel type, end-use sector, selected industry, and region, annual rpt, discontinued, 3164–73
Foreign and US energy production, trade, use, and reserves, and oil and refined products supply and prices, by country, 1981-90, annual rpt, 3164–50
Foreign and US energy use and production, by fuel type, country, and country group, projected 1995-2010 and trends from 1970, annual rpt, 3164–84
Foreign countries oil and gas reserves and discoveries, by country and country group, quarterly rpt, suspended, 3162–43
Foreign countries oil reserves, production, and resource lifespan under alternative production rates, trends and projections, discontinued series, 3166–9
Foreign direct investment in US energy sources by type and firm, and US affiliates operations, as of 1990, annual rpt, 3164–80
Fuel oil and kerosene sales and deliveries, by end-use, PAD district, and State, 1990, annual rpt, 3164–94
Geothermal resources, power plant generation, capacity, and dev potential, by location, 1988-90 and projected to 2030, 3168–122
Heating fuels production, imports, stocks, and prices, by selected PAD district and State, seasonal weekly rpt, 3162–45
Housing energy use, costs, and conservation, and household and housing characteristics, survey rpt series, 3166–7
Manufacturing energy use and prices, 1988 survey, series, 3166–13
Natural and supplemental gas production, prices, trade, use, reserves, and pipeline company finances, by firm and State, monthly rpt with articles, 3162–4
Natural gas interstate pipeline capacity, use, contract deliveries, and prices, by region, State, and firm, 1990, 3168–125
Natural gas interstate pipeline company detailed financial and operating data, by firm, 1990, annual rpt, 3164–38
Natural gas interstate pipeline company reserves and production, by firm, 1963-91 and deliverability projected to 2011, last issue of annual rpt, 3164–33
Natural gas supply, demand, prices, and distribution, by State, 1986-90 annual rpt, 3164–4
Nuclear power plant construction costs and status, and capacity, by plant, annual rpt, discontinued, 3164–69
Oil and gas field codes and locations, 1991, annual listing, 3164–70
Oil and gas reserves, production, and ultimate recovery, by location, with field technical characteristics, series, 3166–14
Oil and gas supply, demand, and prices, alternative projections, annual rpt, discontinued, 3164–89
Oil and refined products supply and demand, refinery capacity and use, and prices, weekly rpt, 3162–32
Oil company effective income tax rates, with background income and tax data for domestic and foreign operations, 1977-89, 3168–124
Oil crude, gas liquids, and refined products supply, demand, and movement, by PAD district and State, 1991, annual rpt, 3164–2
Oil, gas, and gas liquids reserves and production, by State and substate area, 1991, annual rpt, 3164–46
Oil production, stocks, use, and trade, by selected country and country group, monthly rpt, 3162–42
Oil products prices, sales, and purchases of refiners, processors, and distributors, by product, end-use sector, PAD district, and State, 1991, annual rpt, 3164–85
Oil products sales and purchases of refiners, processors, and distributors, by product, end-use sector, PAD district, and State, monthly rpt, 3162–11
Oil, refined products, and gas liquids supply, demand, trade, stocks, and refining, by detailed product, State, and PAD district, monthly rpt with articles, 3162–6
Prices and spending for fuel, by type, end-use sector, and State, 1990, annual rpt, 3164–64
Solar collector and photovoltaic cell shipments by end-use sector and State, and trade, 1990, annual rpt, 3164–62
Soviet Union former Republics and Baltic States energy supply and use, and social, economic, and political indicators, 1989-90, 3168–126
Uranium mining and milling industries finances and operations, with selected foreign comparisons, 1970s-90 and projected to 2005, annual rpt, 3164–82
Uranium supply and industry operations, various periods 1947-91 and projected to 2001, annual rpt, 3164–65
Wood, waste, and alcohol fuel use, by end-use sector and region, 1990, annual rpt, 3164–97

Energy prices
Biomass energy program of TVA, operations, finances, and technological characteristics, series, 9806–9
Business statistics, detailed data for major industries and economic indicators, 1960-91, *Survey of Current Business* biennial supplement, 2704–1
Commercial buildings energy use, costs, and conservation, by building characteristics, survey rpt series, 3166–8
CPI by component for US city average, and by selected metro area, region, and population size, monthly rpt, 6762–2
CPI changes for selected items, 1982-91, annual article, 6722–1.322
Economic indicators and components, current data and annual trends, monthly rpt, 23842–1.4
Economic indicators compounded annual rates of change, monthly rpt, 9391–3
Electric power plants (coal-fired) generating capacity and replacement of energy imports, with background data, alternative forecasts 1990-2000, 3166–6.63
Farm prices received and paid, by commodity and State, monthly rpt, 1629–1
Food prices (farm-retail), marketing cost components, and industry finances and productivity, 1920s-91, annual rpt, 1544–9
Housing energy prices, by fuel type and State, 1990 and forecast 1991-92, 3166–6.61
Housing energy use, costs, and conservation, and household and housing characteristics, survey rpt series, 3166–7
Manufacturing energy use and prices, 1988 survey, series, 3166–13
Natl Energy Strategy plans for conservation, R&D, security, and pollution reduction, technical rpt series, 3006–13
Prices and spending for fuel, by type, end-use sector, and State, 1990, annual rpt, 3164–64
Prices of fuel, by type, end-use sector, and region, projected 1991-2030, 3166–6.60
Prices, supply, and demand, by fuel type and end-use sector, alternative projections by region, 1990-2010, annual rpt, 3164–96
Prices, supply, and demand, by fuel type and end-use sector, alternative projections 1990-2010, annual rpt, 3164–75
Prices, supply, and demand, by fuel type and end-use sector, projections and underlying assumptions, 1995-2010, annual rpt, 3164–90
Prices, supply, and demand, by fuel type and end-use sector, with foreign comparisons, 1981-90, annual fact book, 3164–76
Prices, supply, and demand, by fuel type and end-use sector, with foreign comparisons, 1991 and trends from 1949, annual rpt, 3164–74
Prices, supply, and demand of energy, forecasts by resource type, quarterly rpt, 3162–34
Producer Price Index, by major commodity group and subgroup, and processing stage, monthly press release, 6762–5
Producer price indexes, by stage of processing and detailed commodity, monthly rpt, 6762–6
Producer price indexes, by stage of processing and detailed commodity, monthly 1991, annual rpt, 6764–2
Producer price indexes, changes for selected items by stage of processing, 1987-91, article, 6722–1.323
Statistical Abstract of US, 1992 annual data compilation, 2324–1.15; 2324–1.19
Tennessee Valley economic conditions, and compared to US, alternative projections 1992-2010 and trends from 1929, annual rpt, 9804–27
Uranium marketing, contracts, prices, utility shipments, and trade, 1982-91 and projected to 2001, annual rpt, 3164–65.2
Uranium mining and milling industries finances and operations, with selected foreign comparisons, 1970s-90 and projected to 2005, annual rpt, 3164–82
see also Coal prices
see also Electric power prices
see also Natural gas prices
see also Petroleum prices

Energy production
see Energy production costs
see under Energy resources and consumption (for data on total production)
see under names of specific types of energy

Energy production costs
Biomass energy program of TVA, operations, finances, and technological characteristics, series, 9806–9
China biomass-fired electric power plant feasibility assessment, 1991 rpt, 3308–103
Coal-fired power plants air pollutant reduction technology funding, and impacts on energy costs and emissions, 1950s-87 and projected to 2010, annual rpt, 3334–5; 3338–4
Coal mining restrictions on public land, impacts on production, costs, and demand, by region, 1985-88 and projected to 2075, 5668–125
Developing countries energy efficiency improvement issues and devs, with data by end use and country, 1980s-90, 26358–260
Electric power distribution loans from REA, and borrower operating and financial data, by firm and State, 1991, annual rpt, 1244–1
Electric power plants (coal-fired) generating capacity and replacement of energy imports, with background data, alternative forecasts 1990-2000, 3166–6.63
Electric power plants (steam), delivered cost of coal, residual oil, and natural gas, monthly rpt, 3162–24.9
Electric power plants (steam), delivered cost of coal, residual oil, and natural gas, monthly 1973-88, 3168–123.9
Electric power plants production and capital costs, operations, and fuel use, by fuel type, plant, utility, and location, 1990, annual rpt, 3164–9
Electric power plants production, capacity, sales, and fuel stocks, use, and costs, by State, 1986-90, annual rpt, 3164–11
Electric power plants production, fuel use, stocks, and costs by fuel type, and sales, by State, monthly rpt, with articles, 3162–35
Electric power price components, alternative projections by region, 1990-2010, annual rpt, 3164–96
Electric power supply, demand, and trade of Mexico and US, with data by fuel source, utility, and region, 1970s-89 and projected to 2000, 3408–2
Electric utilities finances and operations, detailed data for publicly and privately owned firms, 1990, annual rpt, 3164–11.4
Electric utilities finances and operations, detailed data for publicly owned firms, 1990, annual rpt, 3164–24
Electric utilities operation under Public Utility Holding Company Act, with capacity and construction costs, late 1960s-80s, 3006–13.1
Electric utilities privately owned, finances and operations, detailed data, 1990, annual rpt, 3164–23
Energy supply, demand, and prices, by fuel type and end-use sector, with foreign comparisons, 1991 and trends from 1949, annual rpt, 3164–74
Environmental regulation impacts on oil resources recovery, under alternative oil price, technology, and regulatory assumptions, projected 1990-2015, 3338–2
Jordan oil shale-fired electric power plants, feasibility assessment with background data, 1990 rpt, 3008–127
Natural gas interstate pipeline company detailed financial and operating data, by firm, 1990, annual rpt, 3164–38
Natural gas supply, demand, prices, and distribution, by State, 1986-90 annual rpt, 3164–4
Prices, supply, and demand, by fuel type and end-use sector, with foreign comparisons, 1981-90, annual fact book, 3164–76
Producers finances and operations, by energy type for US firms domestic and foreign operations, 1990, annual rpt, 3164–44
Southwestern Fed Power System financial statements, sales by customer, and operations and costs by project, FY91, annual rpt, 3244–1
Tax (income) returns of corporations, income and tax items by asset size and detailed industry, 1989, annual rpt, 8304–4; 8304–21
Uranium enrichment facilities of DOE, financial statements, FY90-91, annual rpt, 3354–7
Uranium imports impacts on US industry, with data on DOE enrichment program and stocks, 1980s-92, GAO rpt, 26113–584
Uranium mining and milling industries finances and operations, with selected foreign comparisons, 1970s-90 and projected to 2005, annual rpt, 3164–82
Uranium reserves and industry operations, by region and State, various periods 1966-91, annual rpt, 3164–65.1

Energy projections
Alaska Arctic Natl Wildlife Refuge oil reserves and production, alternative forecasts 1985-2015, 3166–6.64
Auto fuel economy improvements from new technologies, 1987-90 and alternative projections to 2010, 26358–251
Coal coke use and costs in steel industry, effects of Clean Air Act, 1985-91 and projected to 2003, 5606–5.10

Coal-fired power plants air pollutant reduction technology funding, and impacts on energy costs and emissions, 1950s-87 and projected to 2010, annual rpt, 3334–5; 3338–4
Coal mining restrictions on public land, impacts on production, costs, and demand, by region, 1985-88 and projected to 2075, 5668–125
Coal production, prices, exports, and use by sector, with data by region, projections, annual rpt, discontinued, 3164–68
Data analysis and forecasting models of EIA, 1992, annual listing, 3164–87
Electric power demand, and industrial and employment impacts of capacity shortfalls and new power plants, by selected State, 1960s-80s and projected to 2000, hearing, 21248–163
Electric power plants (coal-fired) generating capacity and replacement of energy imports, with background data, alternative forecasts 1990-2000, 3166–6.63
Electric power plants and capacity, by fuel used, owner, location, and operating status, 1991 and for units planned 1992-2001, annual listing, 3164–36
Electric power plants production and capacity by fuel type, prices, demand, and air pollution law impacts, by region, projections, annual rpt, discontinued, 3164–81
Electric power plants sales, imports, nonutility purchases, capacity, production, fuel use and costs, and prices, 1995-2010, annual rpt, 3164–11
Electric power seasonal peak demand and generating capacity, by region, annual rpt, suspended, 3404–6
Electric power supply, demand, and trade of Mexico and US, with data by fuel source, utility, and region, 1970s-89 and projected to 2000, 3408–2
Electric utilities conservation programs alternative planning strategies cost effectiveness, model results, 1991 rpt, 3308–100
Electric utilities conservation programs data reporting guidelines, with background data, 1991 rpt, 3308–101
Electric utilities conservation programs, impacts on prices and revenue requirements, alternative projections 1990-2010, 3308–105
Electric utilities conservation programs, peak load reductions, energy savings, and costs, by region, 1989-90 and projected to 2000, article, 3162–35.302
Foreign and US energy supply and demand, by major fuel and end-use sector, 1950s-87 and forecast to 1995, 3166–6.58
Foreign and US energy use and production, by fuel type, country, and country group, projected 1995-2010 and trends from 1970, annual rpt, 3164–84
Geothermal resources, power plant generation, capacity, and dev potential, by location, 1988-90 and projected to 2030, 3168–122
Hydroelectric power plants, generation, and capacity, for Reclamation Bur projects, 1978-90 and projected to 1995, 5828–14
Natl Energy Strategy fossil fuel, electric power, conservation, and pollution reduction issues, 1991 hearings, 21368–136
Natl Energy Strategy plans for conservation, R&D, security, and pollution reduction, technical rpt series, 3006–13
Natural gas interstate pipeline company reserves and production, by firm, 1963-91 and deliverability projected to 2011, last issue of annual rpt, 3164–33
Nuclear power plant spent fuel and waste generation, inventory, and disposal, 1960s-90 and projected to 2020, annual rpt, 3364–2
Nuclear power plant spent fuel deliveries to DOE for disposal, by utility and reactor, projected 1998-2007, annual rpt, 3364–5
Nuclear power plant spent fuel discharges and additional storage capacity needed, by reactor, projected 1991-2040, annual rpt, 3354–2
Nuclear waste repository research, transport, and disposal costs under alternative systems, 1983-89 and projected to 2094, 3368–5
Oil and gas supply, demand, and prices, alternative projections, annual rpt, discontinued, 3164–89
Oil resources recovery impacts of environmental regulation, under alternative oil price, technology, and regulatory assumptions, projected 1990-2015, 3338–2
Pacific basin countries energy supply and demand, and implications for US trade, country rpt series, 3406–6
Pacific Northwest electric power capacity and use, by end-use sector, projected under alternative fuel price cases, annual rpt, suspended, 3224–4
Pacific Northwest electric power capacity and use, by energy source, forecast under alternative load and demand cases, 1991-2012, annual rpt, 3224–3
Pacific Northwest nonutility electric power generation and capacity, by energy source, purchasing utility, and facility, forecasts 1991-2012, annual rpt, 3224–3.4
Pacific Northwest population, households, employment, income, fuel prices, and electricity demand, alternative forecasts 1991-2010, annual rpt, 3224–3.3
Prices of fuel, by type, end-use sector, and region, projected 1991-2030, 3166–6.60
South America oil production, investment needs, and exports, for 8 countries, 1980s-90 and projected to 2010, GAO rpt, 26123–396
Strategic Petroleum Reserve capacity, inventory, fill rate, and finances, quarterly rpt, 3002–13
Supply, demand, and distribution of energy, and regulatory impacts, series, 3166–6
Supply, demand, and price projections, by fuel type and end-use sector, biennial rpt, discontinued, 3004–13
Supply, demand, and prices, by fuel type and end-use sector, alternative projections by region, 1990-2010, annual rpt, 3164–96
Supply, demand, and prices, by fuel type and end-use sector, alternative projections 1990-2010, annual rpt, 3164–75
Supply, demand, and prices, by fuel type and end-use sector, projections and underlying assumptions, 1995-2010, annual rpt, 3164–90
Supply, demand, and prices of energy, forecasts by resource type, quarterly rpt, 3162–34
Transportation energy use by fuel type, and miles traveled, by mode, projected 1990-2010 and trends from 1960s, 3008–124
Uranium marketing, contracts, prices, utility shipments, and trade, 1982-91 and projected to 2001, annual rpt, 3164–65.2
Uranium mining and milling industries finances and operations, with selected foreign comparisons, 1970s-90 and projected to 2005, annual rpt, 3164–82

Energy research and development
Auto (electric-powered) R&D activity and DOE funding shares, FY91, annual rpt, 3304–2
Buildings (commercial and residential) energy conservation technologies use, costs, efficiency, and residential tax credits, 1970s-90 and projected to 2010, 26358–259
Developing countries energy efficiency improvement issues and devs, with data by end use and country, 1980s-90, 26358–260
DOE real property owned and leased, by type, subagency, contractor, and site, FY91, annual rpt, 3004–28
Electric utilities privately owned, finances and operations, detailed data, 1990, annual rpt, 3164–23
Inventions recommended by Natl Inst of Standards and Technology for DOE support, awards, and evaluation status, 1991, annual listing, 2214–5
Natl Energy Strategy plans for conservation and pollution reduction, funding for R&D and basic science activities, FY91-93, 3008–128
Natl Energy Strategy plans for conservation, R&D, security, and pollution reduction, technical rpt series, 3006–13
Natural gas interstate pipeline company detailed financial and operating data, by firm, 1990, annual rpt, 3164–38
Nuclear power plant safety standards and research, design, licensing, construction, operation, and finances, with data by reactor, quarterly journal, 3352–4
Nuclear reactors for domestic use and export by function and operating status, with owner, operating characteristics, and location, 1991 annual listing, 3354–15
Nuclear-related employment of scientists and engineers, by industry sector and occupation, 1983-91, 3006–8.20
Producers finances and operations, by energy type for US firms domestic and foreign operations, 1990, annual rpt, 3164–44.5
Radioactive waste and spent fuel generation, inventory, and disposal, 1960s-90 and projected to 2020, annual rpt, 3364–2
Science and Engineering Indicators, employment, education, R&D funding, and industry impacts, with foreign comparisons, 1960s-91, biennial rpt, 9624–10
Solar collector and photovoltaic cell shipments by end-use sector and State, and trade, 1990, annual rpt, 3164–62
Superconducting Super Collider particle accelerator program of DOE, conventional facility construction funding and estimated and actual costs, 1988-99, 3006–5.32

Tax (income) returns of corporations, income and tax items by asset size and detailed industry, 1989, annual rpt, 8304–4; 8304–21
see also Department of Energy National Laboratories
see also Energy exploration and drilling
see also Federal funding for energy programs

Energy reserves
Foreign countries mineral production, reserves, and industry role in domestic economy and world supply, world area and country rpt series, 5606–1
Pacific basin countries energy supply and demand, and implications for US trade, country rpt series, 3406–6
Uranium mining and milling industries finances and operations, with selected foreign comparisons, 1970s-90 and projected to 2005, annual rpt, 3164–82
Uranium reserves and industry operations, by region and State, various periods 1966-91, annual rpt, 3164–65.1
see also Coal reserves
see also Natural gas reserves
see also Petroleum reserves

Energy resources and consumption
Census Bur energy-related data coverage and availability, 1991 pamphlet, 2326–7.84
China minerals production and trade, by commodity, 1989-90, annual rpt, 5604–38
Consumer spending, natl income and product account benchmark revisions, 1929-88, 2708–5
Consumer spending, natl income and product accounts, comprehensive accounts and components, *Survey of Current Business*, monthly rpt, 2702–1.25
Consumption and conservation of energy, survey results and methodology, series, 3166–15
Consumption of energy, by detailed fuel type, end-use sector, and State, 1960-90, State Energy Data System annual rpt, 3164–39
Data analysis and forecasting models of EIA, 1992, annual listing, 3164–87
Data on energy resources, EIA rpts and data files, 1990, annual listing, 3164–98
Developing countries economic and social conditions from 1960s, and Intl Dev Cooperation Agency and AID activities and funding, FY91-93, annual rpt, 9904–4
Developing countries energy use and aid, 1991 hearings, 25318–83
Employment in energy-related fields, manpower studies and devs, series, 3006–8
Environmental Quality, status of problems, protection programs, research, and intl issues, 1991 annual rpt, 484–1
Foreign and US energy production, trade, use, and reserves, and oil and refined products supply and prices, by country, 1981-90, annual rpt, 3164–50
Foreign and US energy supply and demand, by major fuel and end-use sector, 1950s-87 and forecast to 1995, 3166–6.58
Foreign and US energy use and production, by fuel type, country, and country group, projected 1995-2010 and trends from 1970, annual rpt, 3164–84
Foreign countries economic indicators, and trade and trade flows by commodity, by country, data compilation, monthly CD-ROM, 2002–6
Input-output structure of US economy, detailed interindustry transactions for 84 industries, and components of final demand, 1987, annual article, 2702–1.316
Investigations of GAO, 1991, listing, 26106–10.6
Japan energy use and imports by fuel type, and gasoline prices, 1970s-80s, hearing, 21448–45
Jordan oil shale-fired electric power plants, feasibility assessment with background data, 1990 rpt, 3008–127
Natl Energy Strategy plans for conservation, R&D, security, and pollution reduction, technical rpt series, 3006–13
Natl income and product accounts and components, *Survey of Current Business*, monthly rpt, 2702–1.23
Pacific basin countries energy supply and demand, and implications for US trade, country rpt series, 3406–6
Pacific territories population and housing detailed characteristics, by location, 1990 Census of Population and Housing, series, 2551–8
Producer operations, trade, and tariffs, for energy and chemical products, commodity rpt series, 9885–11
Production and capacity use indexes, by SIC 2- to 4-digit industry, monthly rpt, 9365–2.24
Soviet Union former Republics and Baltic States energy supply and use, and social, economic, and political indicators, 1989-90, 3168–126
Soviet Union minerals production and exports, by commodity and Republic, 1975-90, annual rpt, 5604–39
Statistical Abstract of US, 1992 annual data compilation, 2324–1.19
Supply and demand summary data, DOE activities and finances, and bibl, 1990, annual rpt, 3024–2
Supply, demand, and distribution of energy, and regulatory impacts, series, 3166–6
Supply, demand, and prices, by fuel type and end-use sector, with foreign comparisons, 1981-90, annual fact book, 3164–76
Supply, demand, and prices, by fuel type and end-use sector, with foreign comparisons, 1991 and trends from 1949, annual rpt, 3164–74
see also Agricultural energy use
see also Alcohol fuels
see also Aviation fuels
see also Biomass energy
see also Coal and coal mining
see also Coal exports and imports
see also Coal prices
see also Coal reserves
see also Coal stocks
see also Department of Energy National Laboratories
see also Diesel fuel
see also Electric power
see also Electric power and heat cogeneration
see also Electric power plants and equipment
see also Electric power prices
see also Energy conservation
see also Energy exploration and drilling
see also Energy exports and imports
see also Energy prices
see also Energy production costs
see also Energy projections
see also Energy research and development
see also Energy reserves
see also Energy stocks and inventories
see also Energy supply disruptions
see also Federal funding for energy programs
see also Fuel oil
see also Fuel tax
see also Gasohol
see also Gasoline
see also Geothermal resources
see also Government energy use
see also Housing energy use
see also Hydroelectric power
see also Industrial and commercial energy use
see also Kerosene
see also Liquefied petroleum gas
see also Low-income energy assistance
see also Motor fuels
see also Natural gas and gas industry
see also Natural gas exports and imports
see also Natural gas liquids
see also Natural gas prices
see also Natural gas reserves
see also Nuclear power
see also Offshore oil and gas
see also Oil shale
see also Oil spills
see also Petrochemicals
see also Petroleum and petroleum industry
see also Petroleum exports and imports
see also Petroleum prices
see also Petroleum reserves
see also Petroleum stocks
see also Solar energy
see also Synthetic fuels
see also Transportation energy use
see also Uranium
see also Water power
see also Wind energy
see also Wood fuel

Energy stocks and inventories
Electric utilities fuel use and end of month stocks, by prime mover and energy resource, monthly rpt, 3162–24.7
Electric utilities fuel use and end of month stocks, by prime mover and energy resource, monthly 1973-88, 3168–123.7
Natural and supplemental gas production, prices, trade, use, reserves, and pipeline company finances, by firm and State, monthly rpt with articles, 3162–4
Natural gas interstate pipeline company detailed financial and operating data, by firm, 1990, annual rpt, 3164–38
Natural gas liquids supply, demand, and movement, by PAD district and State, 1991, annual rpt, 3164–2
Natural gas liquids supply, demand, trade, stocks, and refining, by detailed product and PAD district, monthly rpt with articles, 3162–6
Natural gas supply, demand, prices, and distribution, by State, 1986-90 annual rpt, 3164–4
Supply, demand, and prices, by fuel type and end-use sector, with foreign comparisons, 1981-90, annual fact book, 3164–76

Supply, demand, and prices, by fuel type and end-use sector, with foreign comparisons, 1991 and trends from 1949, annual rpt, 3164–74
Supply, demand, and prices of energy, forecasts by resource type, quarterly rpt, 3162–34
Tax (income) returns of corporations, income and tax items by asset size and detailed industry, 1989, annual rpt, 8304–4
Uranium enrichment facilities of DOE, financial statements, FY90-91, annual rpt, 3354–7
Uranium imports impacts on US industry, with data on DOE enrichment program and stocks, 1980s-92, GAO rpt, 26113–584
Uranium marketing, contracts, prices, utility shipments, and trade, 1982-91 and projected to 2001, annual rpt, 3164–65.2
Uranium mining and milling industries finances and operations, with selected foreign comparisons, 1970s-90 and projected to 2005, annual rpt, 3164–82
see also Coal stocks
see also Naval Petroleum Reserves
see also Petroleum stocks
see also Strategic Petroleum Reserve

Energy supply disruptions
Electric power demand, and industrial and employment impacts of capacity shortfalls and new power plants, by selected State, 1960s-80s and projected to 2000, hearing, 21248–163
Electric power disturbances, utility, location, customers affected, power losses, cause, and restoration time involved, listing, monthly rpt, 3162–35
Electric power disturbances, utility, location, customers affected, power losses, cause, and restoration time involved, listing, 1990, annual rpt, 3164–11
Industrial plants energy supply disruptions, related worker displacement and unemployment insurance claims, quarterly press release, 6742–23
Industrial plants energy supply disruptions, related worker displacement, 1990, annual rpt, 6744–18
Iraq invasion of Kuwait, oil production disruption impacts on futures prices, family budgets, and oil firms, 1990 hearings, 25408–116
Mgmt of disasters and natl security threats, with data by major event and State, 1992 annual rpt, 9434–6
Oil imports from Persian Gulf, US and OECD dependence indicators, and US military supply, late 1970s-80s and supply disruptions from 1951, 3166–6.65
Oil supply disruptions, shortfalls and share of world consumption disrupted, for major events, 1951-89, hearings, 21368–142
Supply, demand, and prices of energy, forecasts by resource type, quarterly rpt, 3162–34
Uranium mining and milling industries finances and operations, with selected foreign comparisons, 1970s-90 and projected to 2005, annual rpt, 3164–82

Energy use
see Agricultural energy use
see Energy conservation
see Energy resources and consumption
see Government energy use
see Housing energy use
see Industrial and commercial energy use
see Transportation energy use
see under names of specific types of energy (listed under Energy resources and consumption)

Engel, Charles M.
"Can the Markov Switching Model Forecast Exchange Rates?", 9381–10.125
"Is Real Exchange Rate Variability Caused by Relative Price Changes? An Empirical Investigation", 9381–10.123
"Tests of Mean-Variance Efficiency of International Equity Markets", 9385–8.137

Engineered materials
see Advanced materials
see Biotechnology
see Polymers

Engineers and engineering
Air traffic control and airway facilities staff, by employment and other characteristics, FY90, annual rpt, 7504–41
Army Corps of Engineers activities, FY90, annual rpt, 3754–1
County Business Patterns, 1989: employment, establishments, and payroll, by SIC 2- to 4-digit industry and county, annual State rpt series, 2326–8
County Business Patterns, 1990: employment, establishments, and payroll, by SIC 2- to 4-digit industry and county, annual State rpt series, 2326–6
Degree (PhD) recipients in higher education, by field and selected characteristics, 1979, 1984, and 1989, 4848–44
Degrees awarded in higher education, by level, field, race, and sex, 1989/90 and trends from 1980/81, annual rpt, 4844–17
DOE R&D projects and funding at natl labs, universities, and other instns, FY91, annual summary rpt, 3004–18.2
DOT employment, by subagency, occupation, and selected personnel characteristics, FY91, annual rpt, 7304–18
Education data compilation, 1992 annual rpt, 4824–2
Education in science and engineering, grad programs enrollment by field, source of funds, and characteristics of student and instn, 1990, annual rpt, 9627–7
Employment and economic conditions, alternative BLS projections to 2005 and trends 1975-90, biennial rpt, 6744–19
Employment, earnings, and hours, by SIC 1- to 4-digit industry, monthly 1989-Feb 1992, annual rpt, 6744–4
Employment of scientists and engineers, and related topics, advance rpt series, 9626–8
Employment of scientists, engineers, and technicians by industry and occupation, and degrees awarded, 1970s-90 and projected to 2005, article, 6722–1.314
Employment, unemployment, and labor force characteristics, by region and census div, 1991, annual rpt, 6744–7.1
Environmental Quality, status of problems, protection programs, research, and intl issues, 1991 annual rpt, 484–1
Exports and imports of services, direct and among multinatl firms affiliates, by industry and world area, 1986-91, article, 2702–1.336
Fed Govt aid to higher education and nonprofit instns for R&D and related activities, by field, instn, agency, and State, FY90, annual rpt, 9627–17
Flight engineers certified by FAA, by age, sex, region, and State, 1991, annual rpt, 7504–2
Input-output structure of US economy, detailed interindustry transactions for 541 industries, and components of final demand, 1982 benchmark data, 2708–17
Japan R&D activities of US firms, employee characteristics, and mgmt views on benefits and drawbacks, 1991 rpt, 9628–88
Labor demand, turnover, and training completions, by detailed occupation, 1990 and projected to 2005, biennial rpt, 6744–3
Labor force, Federal and university research funding, and educational data, for science and engineering, series, 9626–6
Manufacturing employment of scientists, engineers, and technicians, by field and industry, 1989, triennial rpt, 9627–23
Military budget, R&D appropriations by item, service branch, and defense agency, FY91-93, annual rpt, 3544–33
Minority group, women, and disabled persons employment and education in science and engineering, by field, mid 1970s-91, biennial rpt, 9624–20
Multinatl US firms and foreign affiliates finances and operations, by industry and country, 1989 benchmark survey, annual rpt, 2704–5
NASA Apollo era science and engineering staff background and characteristics, 1958-70, 9508–39
NASA R&D funding to higher education instns, by field, instn, and State, FY91, annual listing, 9504–7
Navy personnel strengths, accessions, and attrition, detailed statistics, quarterly rpt, 3802–4
NSF activities, finances, and funding by program, FY91, annual rpt, 9624–6
NSF R&D grant awards, by div and program, periodic rpt series, 9626–7
Nuclear engineering enrollment and degrees by instn and State, and women grads plans and employment, 1991, annual rpt, 3006–8.18
Nuclear engineering enrollment and degrees granted by instn and State, and grad placement, by student characteristics, 1991, annual rpt, 3004–5
Nuclear-related employment of scientists and engineers, by industry sector and occupation, 1983-91, 3006–8.20
Occupational injury and illness rates, by SIC 2- to 4-digit industry, 1989-90, annual rpt, 6844–7
Occupational injury and illness rates, by SIC 2- to 4-digit industry, 1990, annual rpt, 6844–1
Occupational Outlook Handbook, 1992-93, biennial rpt, 6744–1
Pacific territories population and housing detailed characteristics, by location, 1990 Census of Population and Housing, series, 2551–8

R&D facilities of higher education instns, space and equipment adequacy, needs, and funding by source, by instn type and control, 1992, biennial rpt, 9624–25
R&D funding by higher education instns and federally funded centers, by field, instn, and State, FY90, annual rpt, 9627–13
Research and education grants of NSF for engineering, FY91, annual listing, 9624–24
Science and Engineering Indicators, employment, education, R&D funding, and industry impacts, with foreign comparisons, 1960s-91, biennial rpt, 9624–10
Small business R&D grants of Fed Govt, by program area, agency, MSA, and State, FY90, annual rpt, 9764–7
Statistical Abstract of US, 1992 annual data compilation, 2324–1.20
Tax (income) returns of corporations, income and tax items by asset size and detailed industry, 1989, annual rpt, 8304–4; 8304–21
Tax (income) returns of partnerships, income statement and balance sheet items, by industry group, 1990, annual article, 8302–2.314
Tax (income) returns of sole proprietorships, income statement items, by industry group, 1990, annual article, 8302–2.317; 8302–2.320
Telecommunications and Info Natl Admin rpts, FY91, annual listing, 2804–3
Uranium tailings at inactive mills, remedial action proposals, costs, site characteristics, and environmental, socioeconomic, and health impacts, series, 3356–4
see also Architecture
see also Biotechnology
see also Technological innovations
see also Traffic engineering

Engines and motors
Aircraft engine rotor failures, by carrier and incident characteristics, 1988, annual rpt, 7504–50
Aircraft engine shipments, trade, use, and firms, by type, monthly Current Industrial Rpt, 2506–12.24
Airline flight and engine hours, and shutdown rates, by aircraft and engine model, and air carrier, monthly rpt, 7502–13
Auto (electric-powered) R&D activity and DOE funding shares, FY91, annual rpt, 3304–2
Auto engine and power train R&D projects, DOE contracts and funding by recipient, FY91, annual rpt, 3304–17
Auto parts trade with Japan and other countries, 1985-90 and forecast to 1994, annual rpt, 2004–10
County Business Patterns, 1989: employment, establishments, and payroll, by SIC 2- to 4-digit industry and county, annual State rpt series, 2326–8
County Business Patterns, 1990: employment, establishments, and payroll, by SIC 2- to 4-digit industry and county, annual State rpt series, 2326–6
Employment, earnings, and hours, by SIC 1- to 4-digit industry, monthly 1989-Feb 1992, annual rpt, 6744–4
Exports and imports between US and outlying areas, by detailed commodity and mode of transport, 1991, annual rpt, 2424–11
Exports and imports of US, by country and detailed commodity, monthly rpt, 2422–12
Exports and imports of US, by Harmonized System 6-digit commodity and country, 1991, annual rpt, 2424–13
Exports and imports of US, by transport mode, country, and SITC 1- to 3-digit commodity, 1991, annual rpt, 2424–12
Exports of US, detailed Schedule B commodities with countries of destination, 1991, annual rpt, 2424–10
Fluid power products shipments and firms, by product, 1991, annual Current Industrial Rpt, 2506–12.31
Imports of US given duty-free treatment for value of US material sent abroad, by commodity and country, 1987-90, annual rpt, 9884–14
Injuries from use of consumer products, by severity, victim age, and detailed product, 1991, annual rpt, 9164–6
Input-output structure of US economy, detailed interindustry transactions for 84 industries, and components of final demand, 1987, annual article, 2702–1.316
Input-output structure of US economy, detailed interindustry transactions for 541 industries, and components of final demand, 1982 benchmark data, 2708–17
Labor productivity, indexes of output, hours, and employment by SIC 2- to 4-digit industry, 1967-90, annual rpt, 6824–1.3
Manufacturing annual survey, 1990: finances and operations, by SIC 2- to 4-digit industry, series, 2506–14
Manufacturing census, 1987: concentration of largest firms measured by value added, and for shipments by SIC 2- and 4-digit industry, subject rpt, 2497–6
Manufacturing census, 1987: shipments of manufacturers products, by customer class and SIC 2- and 4-digit industry, subject rpt, 2497–4
Manufacturing finances and operations, by SIC 2- to 4-digit industry, forecast 1992, annual rpt, 2044–28
Mexico auto engine exports, by firm and plant location, 1982-91, 6366–3.28
Military and personal property shipments, passenger traffic, and costs, by service branch and mode of transport, FY91, annual rpt, 3704–15
Military prime contract awards, by detailed procurement category, FY88-91, annual rpt, 3544–18
Mines (underground) diesel engine exhaust emissions measurement and control, 1992 conf, 5608–177
Multinatl US firms and foreign affiliates finances and operations, by industry and country, 1989 benchmark survey, annual rpt, 2704–5
Natl income and product accounts, comprehensive accounts and components, benchmark revisions, 1929-88, 2708–5
Natl income and product accounts, comprehensive accounts and components, *Survey of Current Business*, monthly rpt, 2702–1.28
Occupational injury and illness rates, by SIC 2- to 4-digit industry, 1989-90, annual rpt, 6844–7
Occupational injury and illness rates, by SIC 2- to 4-digit industry, 1990, annual rpt, 6844–1
OECD trade, total and for 4 major countries, and US trade by country, by commodity, 1980-90, world area rpt series, 9116–1
Price indexes (producer), by stage of processing and detailed commodity, monthly rpt, 6762–6
Price indexes (producer), by stage of processing and detailed commodity, monthly 1991, annual rpt, 6764–2
Recalls of motor vehicles and equipment with safety-related defects, by make, monthly listing, 7762–12
Recalls of motor vehicles and equipment with safety-related defects, by make, quarterly listing, 7762–2
Recalls of recreational boats and engines with safety-related defects, by make, periodic listing, 7402–5
Science, engineering, and technical employment in manufacturing, by field and industry, 1989, triennial rpt, 9627–23
Shipments of motors and generators, trade, use, and firms, by product, 1991, annual Current Industrial Rpt, 2506–12.17
Shipments, trade, use, and firms, for internal combustion engines by product, 1991, annual Current Industrial Rpt, 2506–12.6
see also Electric power plants and equipment
see also under By Commodity in the "Index by Categories"

England
see United Kingdom

England, Harvey M., Jr.
"Comparisons of Molecular Sieve Oxygen Concentrators for Potential Medical Use Aboard Commercial Aircraft", 7506–10.109

English language
see Language arts
see Language use and ability

Enlistment
see Voluntary military service

Enrollment
see Educational enrollment

Enterprise Statistics Program
Data collection, coverage, availability, and procedural history, 1987 economic censuses, 2628–16
Data coverage and availability for economic censuses and related statistics, 1992 preliminary guide, 2308–5

Enterprise zones
see Community development
see Export processing zones

Entertainment
see Performing arts
see Recreation

Environmental assessments
see Environmental impact statements

Environmental Data and Information Service
see National Environmental Satellite, Data, and Information Service

Environmental impact statements
Alaska OCS environmental conditions and oil dev impacts, compilation of papers, series, 2176–1

California OCS oil and gas dev impacts on water quality, marine life, and sediments, by site, 1986-90, annual rpt, 5734–11
Environmental Quality, status of problems, protection programs, research, and intl issues, 1991 annual rpt, 484–1
Forest Service activities and finances, by region and State, FY91, annual rpt, 1204–1.1
Minerals offshore lease sales environmental and economic impacts in coastal areas, final statement series, 5736–7
New Mexico Caballo Resource Area public land mgmt, and grazing, environmental, and leasing activities, FY90-91, annual rpt, 5724–17
Nuclear weapons test areas in Nevada and other sites, radionuclide concentrations in air, water, humans, animals, and milk, 1990, annual rpt, 9194–17
Oil and gas OCS leasing and exploration activity, production, revenue, and environmental studies, by location, quarterly rpt, 5732–1
Owl (northern spotted) conservation methods in Pacific Northwest, timber industry impacts, and Federal and State spending, 1980s-95, 1208–388
Pacific Northwest Indian tribes environmental, economic, and cultural impacts of OCS oil and gas lease and dev, with background data, 1970s-92, 5738–35
Public lands acreage and use, and Land Mgmt Bur activities and finances, annual State rpt series, 5724–11
Uranium tailings at inactive mills, remedial action proposals, costs, site characteristics, and environmental, socioeconomic, and health impacts, series, 3356–4

Environmental pollution and control
Abatement and control equipment and other industries concentration measured by shipments, 1987 Census of Manufactures, subject rpt, 2497–6
Abatement and control equipment manufacturers shipments by customer class and SIC 2- and 4-digit industry, 1987 Census of Manufactures, subject rpt, 2497–4
Abatement spending by govts, business, and consumers, 1972-90, annual article, 2702–1.321
Abatement spending, capital and operating costs by SIC 2- to 4-digit industry and State, 1990, annual Current Industrial Rpt, 2506–3.6
Abatement spending, capital and operating costs by SIC 2-digit manufacturing industry, 1991, advance annual Current Industrial Rpt, 2506–3.6
Agricultural Conservation Program acreage and projects, by State, 1936-90, quinquennial rpt, 1808–1
Agricultural Conservation Program participation and payments, by practice and State, FY91, annual rpt, 1804–7
Alaska OCS environmental conditions and oil dev impacts, compilation of papers, series, 2176–1
Assistance (block and categorical grants) programs for State and local govts, FY91, biennial listing, 10044–8
Assistance (financial and nonfinancial) of Fed Govt, 1992 base edition, annual listing, 104–5
Budget of US, obligations and authority by function, agency, and program, with summaries and analyses, FY93, annual rpt, 104–2
Disasters and natl security incidents and mgmt, with data by major event and State, 1992 annual rpt, 9434–6
Eastern Europe environmental remediation costs, and aid by donor, by country, 1991 hearing, 25368–181
Electric utilities privately owned, pollution abatement outlays by type of pollutant and equipment, and firm, 1990, annual rpt, 3164–23
Energy natl strategy plans for conservation and pollution reduction, funding for R&D and basic science activities, FY91-93, 3008–128
Environmental quality, pollutant discharge by type, and EPA protection activities, biennial summary rpt, discontinued, 9184–16
Environmental Quality, status of problems, protection programs, research, and intl issues, 1991 annual rpt, 484–1
EPA pollution control grant program activities, monthly rpt, 9182–8
EPA R&D programs and funding, FY91, annual listing, 9184–18
EPA R&D programs and funding, planned FY92, annual listing, 9184–17
EPA rpts in NTIS collection, quarterly listing, 9182–5
Fed Govt spending in States, by type, program, agency, and State, FY91, annual rpt, 2464–2
Foreign countries *Geographic Notes*, boundaries, claims, nomenclature, and other devs, quarterly rpt, 7142–3
Health care professionals supply and education, by professional and other characteristics, and location, 1960s-92 and projected to 2020, biennial rpt, 4114–8
Health effects of selected pollutants, concentrations in food and environment, sources, human intake, and regulation, series, 9186–8
Health effects of selected pollutants on animals by species and on humans, and environmental levels, series, 5506–14
HHS financial aid, by program, recipient, State, and city, FY91, annual regional listings, 4004–3
Historic and natural natl landmarks damaged and threatened, with owner, location, damage type, and recommended remedial action, 1990, annual listing, 5544–16
Investigations of GAO, 1991, listing, 26106–10.6
Recycling of municipal and industrial waste, costs, revenues, and secondary products trade and related energy use and pollution reductions, 1991 hearings, 21368–139
Statistical Abstract of US, 1992 annual data compilation, 2324–1.6
Tax (excise) collections of IRS, by source, quarterly rpt, 8302–2.1
Timber in southeastern US, resources mgmt and research, 1990 biennial conf papers, 1204–35
see also Acid rain
see also Air pollution
see also Asbestos contamination
see also Dioxins
see also Environmental impact statements
see also Environmental regulation
see also Global climate change
see also Hazardous waste and disposal
see also International cooperation in environmental sciences
see also Landfills
see also Lead poisoning and pollution
see also Marine pollution
see also Mercury pollution
see also Motor vehicle exhaust
see also Noise
see also Oil spills
see also Pesticides
see also Radiation
see also Radioactive waste and disposal
see also Radon
see also Reclamation of land
see also Recycling of waste materials
see also Refuse and refuse disposal
see also Soil pollution
see also State funding for natural resources and conservation
see also Trace metals
see also Water pollution

Environmental Protection Agency
Acid rain distribution, pH levels, and composition, monitoring results by site, 1989, annual rpt, 9194–20
Activities and finances of EPA, annual rpt, discontinued, 9184–20
Activities and progress for EPA regulatory and protection programs operations and mgmt goals, by office, quarterly rpt, 9182–11
Activities of EPA, biennial summary rpt, discontinued, 9184–16
Air pollution abatement activity of EPA, compliance, and monitoring stations operating status, annual rpt, discontinued, 9194–4
Air pollution levels for 6 pollutants, and measurements exceeding natl standards, by site, 1990-91, annual rpt, 9194–5
Air pollution levels for 6 pollutants, by source and selected MSA, 1982-91, annual rpt, 9194–1
Asbestos in schools, abatement funding and costs by selected State, 1988-91, GAO rpt, 26113–560
Asbestos in schools, inspection and abatement effectiveness, staff and parental notification, and inspector and janitorial training, as of 1990, 9238–71
Auto fuel economy test results for US and foreign makes, 1993 model year, annual rpt, 3304–11
Budget of US, authoritative financial statements with appropriations, outlays, and receipts, by category and agency, FY91, annual rpt, 8104–2.2
Budget of US, obligations and authority by function, agency, and program, with summaries and analyses, FY93, annual rpt, 104–2
Education funding by Federal agency, program, and recipient type, and instn spending, 1960s-91, annual rpt, 4824–8
Enforcement of environmental laws by EPA and State govts, activities, FY91, annual rpt, 9184–21
Expenditures of Fed Govt in States, by type, program, agency, and State, FY91, annual rpt, 2464–2

Fraud and abuse in EPA programs, audits and investigations, 1st half FY92, semiannual rpt, 9182–10
Grants for pollution control, EPA program activities, monthly rpt, 9182–8
Great Lakes industrial water pollution emissions, comparison of State, EPA, Intl Joint Commission, and Ontario standards, 1991 rpt, 14648–29
Hazardous substances industrial releases and reduction methods under EPA regulation, by chemical, source, industry, and location, 1989, annual rpt, 9234–6
Hazardous substances industrial releases and reduction methods under EPA regulation, with chemical stocks and use, facility directory, 1987-89, annual CD-ROM, 9234–7
Hazardous substances industrial releases and reduction methods under EPA regulation, with chemical stocks and use, facility directory, 1991 CD-ROM user guide, 9238–70
Hazardous waste generation reduction, accuracy of voluntary industry programs rpts to EPA, 1992 GAO rpt, 26131–98
Health effects of selected pollutants, concentrations in food and environment, sources, human intake, and regulation, series, 9186–8
Industrial pollutant concentrations and costs by process and waste prevention or treatment method, biennial conf, suspended, 9184–22
Kuwait oil fires set by Iraq, pollution levels, disease cases, and US remediation and monitoring spending, 1991 rpt, 9188–117
Kuwait oil fires set by Iraqi forces, air pollution levels by substance and site, as of Mar 1991, 9188–116
Labor unions recognized in Fed Govt, agreements and membership by agency and facility, as of Jan 1991, biennial listing, 9844–14
Publications of EPA in NTIS collection, quarterly listing, 9182–5
R&D and related funding of Fed Govt to higher education and nonprofit instns, by field, instn, agency, and State, FY90, annual rpt, 9627–17
R&D programs and funding of EPA, FY91, annual listing, 9184–18
R&D programs and funding of EPA, planned FY92, annual listing, 9184–17
Radiation and radionuclide concentrations in air, water, and milk, monitoring results by site, quarterly rpt, 9192–5
Radionuclide concentrations in air, water, humans, animals, and milk near Nevada and other nuclear test sites, 1990, annual rpt, 9194–17
Radon indoor air pollution levels, by county and State, annual rpt, discontinued, 9194–19
Superfund hazardous waste site remedial action, current and proposed sites descriptions and status, periodic listings, series, 9216–3
Superfund hazardous waste site remedial action, current and proposed sites priority ranking and status by location, series, 9216–5
Superfund hazardous waste site remedial action, EPA records of decision by site, FY90, annual rpt, 9214–5
Toxicology Natl Program research and testing activities, FY90 and planned FY91, annual rpt, 4044–16
Wastewater treatment and collection facility construction funding needs and Fed Govt grants, by State, 1990 and projected to 2010, biennial rpt, 9204–7
Wastewater treatment facilities construction grants of EPA to State and local govts, monthly listing, discontinued, 9202–3
Water pollution discharge permits, and EPA info system coverage and costs, 1991-92, GAO rpt, 26125–46

Environmental regulation
Acid rain environmental, economic, and health effects, and pollutant emissions, 1985-89 and alternative projections to 2030, 14358–4
Agricultural Conservation Program participation and payments, by practice and State, FY91, annual rpt, 1804–7
Air pollution levels for 6 pollutants, and measurements exceeding natl standards, by site, 1990-91, annual rpt, 9194–5
Asbestos in schools, inspection and abatement effectiveness, staff and parental notification, and inspector and janitorial training, as of 1990, 9238–71
Bonneville Power Admin hazardous waste mgmt and environmental protection standards compliance activities, 1991, annual rpt, 3224–6
Carcinogens chemistry, sources, environment and health risks, and regulation, by substance and brand, 1991 annual rpt, 4044–15
Clean Air Act 1990 amendments economic impacts with background data for Midwest and US, 1992 article, 9375–1.304
Coal coke use and costs in steel industry, effects of Clean Air Act, 1985-91 and projected to 2003, 5606–5.10
Coal mining restrictions on public land, impacts on production, costs, and demand, by region, 1985-88 and projected to 2075, 5668–125
Coal Surface Mining Reclamation and Enforcement Office activities and funding, by State and Indian tribe, FY91, annual rpt, 5644–1
Court civil and criminal caseloads for Federal district, appeals, and bankruptcy courts, by type of suit and offense, circuit, and district, 1991, annual rpt, 18204–11
Court civil and criminal caseloads for Federal district, appeals, and special courts, 1991, annual rpt, 18204–8
Criminal sentences for Federal offenses, guidelines by offense and circumstances, series, 17668–1
Dolphin protection embargo impacts on US tuna imports, by country, 1989-92, article, 9882–16.303
Electric power and industrial plants prohibited from oil and gas primary use, exemptions, and gas use by State, 1980-91, annual rpt, 3334–1
Energy natl strategy plans for conservation, R&D, security, and pollution reduction, technical rpt series, 3006–13
Energy supply, demand, distribution, and regulatory impacts, series, 3166–6
Environmental Quality, status of problems, protection programs, research, and intl issues, 1991 annual rpt, 484–1
EPA and State govt enforcement of environmental laws, activities, FY91, annual rpt, 9184–21
EPA programs fraud and abuse, audits and investigations, 1st half FY92, semiannual rpt, 9182–10
EPA regulatory and protection programs operations and mgmt goals, progress and activities, by office, quarterly rpt, 9182–11
Farm financial and marketing conditions, forecast 1992, annual conf, 1504–9
Great Lakes industrial water pollution emissions, comparison of State, EPA, Intl Joint Commission, and Ontario standards, 1991 rpt, 14648–29
Hazardous material transport accidents, casualties, and damage, by mode of transport, with DOT control activities, 1990, annual rpt, 7304–4
Hazardous substances industrial releases and reduction methods under EPA regulation, with chemical stocks and use, facility directory, 1987-89, annual CD-ROM, 9234–7
Hazardous substances industrial releases and reduction methods under EPA regulation, with chemical stocks and use, facility directory, 1991 CD-ROM user guide, 9238–70
Hazardous waste generated, and treated by process, by State, 1987-89 and projected to 2009, hearing, 21408–132
Hazardous waste generation reduction, accuracy of voluntary industry programs rpts to EPA, 1992 GAO rpt, 26131–98
Hazardous waste site remedial action under Superfund, current and proposed sites descriptions and status, periodic listings, series, 9216–3
Hazardous waste site remedial action under Superfund, current and proposed sites priority ranking and status by location, series, 9216–5
Health effects of selected pollutants, concentrations in food and environment, sources, human intake, and regulation, series, 9186–8
Housing affordability and availability, impacts of govt land use regulations and rent control, and low income housing condition, 1991 hearing, 21248–174
Hydroelectric power plants licensing by FERC, impacts of environmental laws, with staffing and plant safety incidents, 1980s-90s, GAO rpt, 26113–599
Industrial hazardous substances releases and reduction methods under EPA regulation, by chemical, source, industry, and location, 1989, annual rpt, 9234–6
Industrial waste generation, disposal, and regulation, by industry and State, mid 1980s-90, 26358–256
Investigations of Federal agency and program operations, summaries of findings, as of 1991, annual GAO rpt, 26104–5.2
Justice Dept enforcement of environmental laws, activities, FY83-91, press release, 6008–37
Justice Dept enforcement of environmental laws, activities, FY83-92, annual press release, 6004–22
Lead paint abatement costs and results, demonstration project design and findings, 1991 rpt, 5188–131

Mexico maquiladora plants environmental regulation enforcement activities, staff, and funding, 1989-92, GAO rpt, 26119–416
Military base construction, renovation, and closure, budget requests by project, service branch, State, and country, FY93, annual rpt, 3544–15
Military bases underground storage tanks for hazardous substances, DOD compliance with EPA regulations, 1988-91, GAO rpt, 26123–395
Military reserves facilities environmental remediation required, sites and costs, FY91-92, annual rpt, 3544–31.2
Nuclear Regulatory Commission activities, finances, and staff, with data for individual power plants, FY91, annual rpt, 9634–2
Nuclear Regulatory Commission budget, staff, and activities, by program, FY91-93, annual rpt, 9634–9
Nuclear Waste Fund utility payments and liabilities by State, and uranium enrichment customers costs of regulation and waste mgmt, 1991 hearings, 21368–137
Nuclear weapons facilities of DOE, contractor fees, environmental and safety enforcement activity, and salaries, by contractor and facility, 1987-88, hearing, 21408–127
Oil resources recovery impacts of environmental regulation, under alternative oil price, technology, and regulatory assumptions, projected 1990-2015, 3338–2
Oil underground storage, Federal trust fund for leaking tanks, financial condition, monthly rpt, 8102–9.11
Pesticide residue on Mexico fruit and vegetable exports to US, US and Mexico standards and violations, FY79-91, GAO rpt, 26113–585
Pollution abatement spending by govts, business, and consumers, 1972-90, annual article, 2702–1.321
Public lands acreage, grants, use, revenues, and allocations, by State, FY91 and trends, annual rpt, 5724–1
Radioactive materials shipments on US hwys, by material type, carrier, and shipper, 1985-90, 3008–129
Tax (excise) collections of IRS, by source, quarterly rpt, 8302–1
Tax (excise) on hazardous waste generation and disposal, rates, and firms filing returns, by substance type, 1989, annual article, 8302–2.303
Unemployed displaced workers, layoffs and recalls by layoff reason, industry, firm size, and State, 2nd half 1988, 6406–6.36
Unemployed displaced workers, layoffs and unemployment insurance claims by reason, industry, selected characteristics, and State, quarterly press release, 6742–23
Unemployed displaced workers, layoffs and unemployment insurance claims by reason, industry, selected characteristics, MSA, and State, 1990, annual rpt, 6744–18
US attorneys civil and criminal cases by type and disposition, and collections, by Federal district, FY91, annual rpt, 6004–2.1
Wastewater treatment plants construction loan funds for local govts, costs and State officials views by State, projected 1991-2000, GAO rpt, 26113–561
Water pollution discharge permits, and EPA info system coverage and costs, 1991-92, GAO rpt, 26125–46
see also Environmental impact statements
see also Hunting and fishing licenses

Environmental sciences
Alaska OCS environmental conditions and oil dev impacts, compilation of papers, series, 2176–1
Environmental Quality, status of problems, protection programs, research, and intl issues, 1991 annual rpt, 484–1
Fed Govt aid to higher education and nonprofit instns for R&D and related activities, by field, instn, agency, and State, FY90, annual rpt, 9627–17
Higher education grad programs enrollment in science and engineering, by field, source of funds, and characteristics of student and instn, 1990, annual rpt, 9627–7
Minority group, women, and disabled persons employment and education in science and engineering, by field, mid 1970s-91, biennial rpt, 9624–20
NASA R&D funding to higher education instns, by field, instn, and State, FY91, annual listing, 9504–7
NOAA Environmental Research Labs rpts, FY91, annual listing, 2144–25
NSF activities, finances, and funding by program, FY91, annual rpt, 9624–6
NSF R&D grant awards, by div and program, FY90, periodic rpt, 9626–7.6
R&D facilities of higher education instns, space and equipment adequacy, needs, and funding by source, by instn type and control, 1992, biennial rpt, 9624–25
R&D funding by higher education instns and federally funded centers, by field, instn, and State, FY90, annual rpt, 9627–13
Science and Engineering Indicators, employment, education, R&D funding, and industry impacts, with foreign comparisons, 1960s-91, biennial rpt, 9624–10
Small business R&D grants of Fed Govt, by program area, agency, MSA, and State, FY90, annual rpt, 9764–7
see also Astronomy
see also Atmospheric sciences
see also Earth sciences
see also Energy research and development
see also International cooperation in environmental sciences
see also Meteorology
see also Oceanography

Epidemiology and epidemiologists
AIDS case definitions of CDC proposed for 1992, compared to 1982-87 definitions, 1992 rpt, 26356–6.6
Animal disease outbreaks in US and foreign countries, quarterly rpt, 1392–3
Cancer Natl Inst epidemiology and biometry activities, FY91, annual rpt, 4474–29
Education in science and engineering, grad programs enrollment by field, source of funds, and characteristics of student and instn, 1990, annual rpt, 9627–7
HHS financial aid, by program, recipient, State, and city, FY91, annual regional listings, 4004–3
Lyme disease surveillance activities of State health depts, 1992 article, 4042–3.364
Minority grads of CDC Epidemic Intelligence Service, by race and current employer, 1950s-80s, article, 4042–3.374
Morbidity and Mortality Weekly Report, infectious notifiable disease cases by age, race, and State, and deaths, 1940s-91, annual rpt, 4204–1
Morbidity and Mortality Weekly Report, infectious notifiable disease cases by State, and public health issues, 4202–1
Morbidity and Mortality Weekly Report, special supplements, series, 4206–2
Public Health Reports, bimonthly journal, 4042–3
Refugees, displaced persons, and population affected by famine, CDC recommendations for disease surveillance, control, and prevention, with background data, 1978-91, 4206–2.63
Spain, Catalonia infectious disease surveillance, interval between onset and public health agency notification, 1982-86, article, 4042–3.349
Togo health surveillance system dev, 1986-91, article, 4202–7.322
see also Diseases and disorders
see also Public health

Epstein, Seth
"Resolution Costs of Bank Failures: An Update of the FDIC Historical Loss Model", 9292–4.303

Equal employment opportunity
see Discrimination in employment

Equal Employment Opportunity Commission
Budget of US, authoritative financial statements with appropriations, outlays, and receipts, by category and agency, FY91, annual rpt, 8104–2.2
Budget of US, obligations and authority by function, agency, and program, with summaries and analyses, FY93, annual rpt, 104–2
Cases of discrimination filed with EEOC, by issue, 1991, hearing, 21348–120
Expenditures of Fed Govt in States, by type, program, agency, and State, FY91, annual rpt, 2464–2
Fed Govt employment discrimination complaint processing and counseling costs, by agency, FY91, GAO rpt, 26119–388
Fed Govt employment discrimination complaints, processing, and disposition, by complaint type and agency, FY90, annual rpt, 9244–11
Fed Govt employment of minorities, women, and disabled, by agency and occupation, FY90, annual rpt, 9244–10
Labor unions recognized in Fed Govt, agreements and membership by agency and facility, as of Jan 1991, biennial listing, 9844–14
Minority group and women employment by industry sector, and govt salaries, by occupation, mid 1960s-90, chartbook, 9248–20
Minority group and women employment, by occupation, SIC 1- to 3- digit industry, State, and MSA, 1991, annual rpt, 9244–1

State and local govt employment of minorities and women, by occupation, function, pay level, and State, 1991, annual rpt, 9244–6

Equatorial Guinea

Agricultural trade of US, by detailed commodity and country, 1991, annual rpt, 1524–8

Agricultural trade of US, by detailed commodity and country, 1991, semiannual rpt, 1522–4

AID economic aid to developing countries, obligations and disbursements by country, quarterly rpt, 9912–4

Economic and military aid and loans from US and intl agencies, by program and country, FY46-91, annual rpt, 9914–5

Economic and social conditions of developing countries from 1960s, and Intl Dev Cooperation Agency and AID activities and funding, FY91-93, annual rpt, 9904–4

Economic, social, political, and geographic summary data, by country, 1992, annual factbook, 9114–2

Exports and imports of US, by transport mode, country, and SITC 1- to 3-digit commodity, 1991, annual rpt, 2424–12

Human rights conditions in 170 countries, and US economic and military aid, 1991, annual rpt, 21384–3

Military aid of US, arms sales, and training programs costs and budget requests, by program, world region, and country, FY91-93, annual rpt, 7144–13

Military spending, arms trade, and force strengths, with govt spending and population, by country, 1979-89, annual rpt, 9824–1

Minerals Yearbook, Vol 3, 1989: foreign country review of production, trade, and policy, by commodity, annual rpt, 5604–35.1

Population size, growth rates, and components of change, by country, projected 1990-2020 and trends from 1950, biennial rpt, 2324–9

UN voting record and share of votes in agreement with US, by issue, country, and world area, 1991, annual rpt, 7004–18

Erickson, Kenneth

"Balance Sheet Outlook for the Farm Sector in 1992", 1504–9.1

"Farm Equity by State, Ranked Three Ways", 1541–1.303

"Farm Financial Performance by Farm Credit District, 1980, 1985, and 1990", 1541–1.317

"Farm Sector Balance Sheet, Including Operator Households, 1960-89, and Excluding Operator Households, 1974-89: By Sales Class", 1548–387

"Farm Sector Balance Sheet, Including Operator Households, 1960-89: U.S. and by State", 1548–384

Erickson, Timothy

"Restricting Regression Slopes in the Errors-in-Variables Model by Bounding the Error Correlation", 6886–6.96

Erie, Pa.

see also under By City and By SMSA or MSA in the "Index by Categories"

Erosion

see Soils and soil conservation

Escalator clauses

Budget of US, obligations and authority by function, agency, and program, with summaries and analyses, FY93, annual rpt, 104–2

Collective bargaining contract expirations, wage increases, and coverage, by major industry group, 1991, annual article, 6722–1.306

Collective bargaining wage and benefit changes, quarterly press release, 6782–2

Collective bargaining wage changes and coverage, by industry and whether contract includes escalator clause and lump sum payment, 1982-91, annual article, 6722–1.325

Pension plan finances, participation, and benefits, for 9 OECD countries, with data by firm and worker characteristics, 1990 conf, 6688–2

Sales contract escalation clauses, use of Producer Price Index, methodology, 1991 rpt, 6888–23

State and local govt collective bargaining, wage and benefit changes and coverage, 1st half 1992, semiannual press release, 6782–6

Supplemental Security Income and Medicaid eligibility and payment provisions, and beneficiaries living arrangements, by State, 1992, annual rpt, 4704–13

Wage adjustments in collective bargaining, Monthly Labor Review, 6722–1.3

Wage and benefit changes from collective bargaining and mgmt decisions, by industry div, monthly rpt, 6782–1

Eskimos

see Alaska Natives

Espinosa, Marco

"Multiple Reserve Requirements: The Case of Small Open Economies", 9371–10.70

Espionage

Fed Govt and military agencies espionage cases, US natls convicted by selected personal, employment, and espionage characteristics, 1945-89, hearings, 25428–2

Sentences for Federal offenses, guidelines by offense and circumstances, series, 17668–1

Essey, Mitchell A.

"Status of the State-Federal Bovine Tuberculosis Eradication Program, FY91", 1394–13.2

Estate tax

Alien nonresidents estate tax returns, property and tax data, by estate size and decedent country of residence, 1986, article, 8302–2.310

Budget of US, authoritative financial statements with appropriations, outlays, and receipts, by category and agency, FY91, annual rpt, 8104–2.2

Budget of US, CBO analysis of revenue and spending alternatives and projections of economic indicators, FY93-97, annual rpt, 26304–3

Budget of US, historical data, selected years FY34-91 and projected to FY97, 108–46.5

Budget of US, obligations and authority by function, agency, and program, with summaries and analyses, FY93, annual rpt, 104–2

Budget of US, receipts by source, outlays by agency and program, and balances, monthly rpt, 8102–3

Collections, enforcement, and litigation activity of IRS, with data by type of tax, region, and State, FY91, annual rpt, 8304–3

Fed Govt finances, cash and debt transactions, daily tables, 8102–4

Fed Govt internal revenue and refunds, by type of tax, quarterly rpt, 8302–2.1

Fed Govt receipts by source and outlays by agency, *Treasury Bulletin*, quarterly rpt, 8002–4.1

Finances of govts, tax systems and revenue, and fiscal structure, by level of govt and State, 1992 and historical trends, annual rpt, 10044–1

Foreign and US income and capital tax policies, with background data for EC, Japan, and US, mid 1960s-91, article, 9373–1.316

Income tax returns of foreign corporations and individuals, and US entities abroad, detailed data compilation, 1970s-89, quinquennial rpt, 8308–31

Natl income and product accounts, comprehensive accounts and components, benchmark revisions, 1929-88, 2708–5

Natl income and product accounts, comprehensive accounts and components, *Survey of Current Business*, monthly rpt, 2702–1.26

Returns and supplemental documents filed, by type, FY91 and projected to FY2000, semiannual rpt, 8302–4

Returns and supplemental documents filed, by type, 1990 and projected to 1999, annual article, 8302–2.304

Returns filed, by type of tax and IRS district, 1990 and projected 1991-98, annual rpt, 8304–24

Returns filed, by type of tax, region, and IRS service center, projected 1991-98 and trends from 1978, annual rpt, 8304–9

Returns for estate tax, property and tax data by size of gross estate and State, 1989-90, article, 8302–2.305

State govt revenue by source, spending and debt by function, and holdings, FY91, annual rpt, 2466–2.6

State govt tax collections by detailed type of tax, and tax rates, by State, FY91, annual rpt, 2466–2.7

see also Gift tax

Estonia

Agricultural production, prices, and trade, for former USSR republics, 1960s-91 and forecast 1992, annual rpt, 1524–4.1

Agricultural trade of US with Eastern Europe, by commodity group and country, 1988-91, 1928–11

Economic conditions, policy, and trade practices, by country, 1989-91, annual rpt, 21384–5

Economic, social, political, and geographic summary data, by country, 1992, annual factbook, 9114–2

Embassies of US in former Soviet republics and Baltic States, positions planned by function, and filled, 1992, GAO rpt, 26123–403

Energy supply and use, and social, economic, and political indicators for former Soviet Republics and Baltic States, 1989-90, 3168–126

Energy use and production of former USSR Republics, by fuel type, 1990, annual rpt, 3164–84.2
Human rights conditions in 170 countries, and US economic and military aid, 1991, annual rpt, 21384–3
Livestock and meat inventories, use, and imports, by former USSR republic, 1986-93, semiannual rpt, 1925–33.2
Military aid of US, arms sales, and training programs costs and budget requests, by program, world region, and country, FY91-93, annual rpt, 7144–13
Older population and selected characteristics, 1980s and projected to 2020, country rpt, 2326–19.8
Population size and characteristics of former Soviet Republics and Baltic States, 1989-92, 9118–19
Refugee migration, and intl aid programs, by world area and country of origin and asylum, 1991, annual rpt, 7004–15
UN voting record and share of votes in agreement with US, by issue, country, and world area, 1991, annual rpt, 7004–18

Estuaries
Alaska OCS environmental conditions and oil dev impacts, compilation of papers, series, 2176–1
Army Corps of Engineers activities and projects, FY88 and trends from 1800s, annual rpt, 3754–1.1
Army Corps of Engineers activities and projects, FY89 and trends from 1800s, annual rpt, 3754–1.2
Army Corps of Engineers activities and projects, FY90 and trends from 1800s, annual rpt, 3754–1.3
Environmental conditions and mgmt, for individual estuaries, conf series, discontinued, 2146–6
Environmental conditions, fish, wildlife, use, and mgmt, for individual coastal and riparian ecosystems, series, 5506–9
Environmental conditions of estuaries, research results and methodology, series, 2176–7
Environmental mgmt of coastal areas, State activities and Federal funding, FY90-91, biennial rpt, 2174–8
NOAA activities and funding for ocean pollution, estuary, and coastal waters monitoring and assessment, FY90, annual rpt, 2174–9
Pollutant concentrations in coastal and estuarine fish, shellfish, and environment, series, 2176–3
Shellfish harvest in estuaries, approved and restricted areas, and pollution sources, by estuary, State, and coastal region, 1990, quinquennial rpt, 2178–33
Water quality, chemistry, hydrology, and other characteristics, local area studies, series, 5666–27
see also Wetlands

Ethanol
see Alcohol fuels

Ethics and morality
Tax (income) admin and compliance issues, and taxpayer views, 1991 conf, 8304–25
see also Business ethics
see also Conflict of interests
see also Financial disclosure
see also Judicial ethics
see also Legal ethics
see also Medical ethics
see also Political ethics
see also Scientific ethics

Ethiopia
Agricultural trade of US, by detailed commodity and country, 1991, annual rpt, 1524–8
Agricultural trade of US, by detailed commodity and country, 1991, semiannual rpt, 1522–4
AID economic aid to developing countries, obligations and disbursements by country, quarterly rpt, 9912–4
AID loans repayment status and terms by program and country, and status of predecessor agency loans, quarterly rpt, 9912–3
Economic and military aid and loans from US and intl agencies, by program and country, FY46-91, annual rpt, 9914–5
Economic and social conditions of developing countries from 1960s, and Intl Dev Cooperation Agency and AID activities and funding, FY91-93, annual rpt, 9904–4
Economic, social, political, and geographic summary data, by country, 1992, annual factbook, 9114–2
Exports and imports of US, by commodity and country, 1980-90, world area rpt, 9116–1.2
Exports and imports of US, by transport mode, country, and SITC 1- to 3-digit commodity, 1991, annual rpt, 2424–12
Exports of US, detailed Schedule B commodities with countries of destination, 1991, annual rpt, 2424–10
Food supply, needs, and aid for developing countries, status and alternative forecasts, 1992 world area rpt, 1526–8.2
Human rights conditions in 170 countries, and US economic and military aid, 1991, annual rpt, 21384–3
Military aid of US, arms sales, and training programs costs and budget requests, by program, world region, and country, FY91-93, annual rpt, 7144–13
Military spending, arms trade, and force strengths, with govt spending and population, by country, 1979-89, annual rpt, 9824–1
Minerals Yearbook, Vol 3, 1989: foreign country review of production, trade, and policy, by commodity, annual rpt, 5604–35.1
Population size, growth rates, and components of change, by country, projected 1990-2020 and trends from 1950, biennial rpt, 2324–9
Refugee migration, and intl aid programs, by world area and country of origin and asylum, 1991, annual rpt, 7004–15
UN voting record and share of votes in agreement with US, by issue, country, and world area, 1991, annual rpt, 7004–18

Ethnic groups
see Ancestry
see Hispanic Americans
see Minority employment
see Minority groups
see under By Race and Ethnic Group in the "Index by Categories"

Eugene, Oreg.
see also under By City and By SMSA or MSA in the "Index by Categories"

Eugeni, Francesca
"Making Sense of Economic Indicators: A Consumers' Guide to Indicators of Real Economic Activity", 9375–1.307

Eurocurrency
Eurodollar deposit rates, weekly chartbook, 9365–1.5
Financial markets (intl) performance of foreign and US bank and securities firms, finances and competitiveness issues, 1980s, compilation of papers, 9385–10
Futures and options trading volume, by commodity and exchange, FY91, annual rpt, 11924–2
Futures trading in selected commodities and financial instruments and indexes, for NYC, Chicago, and other markets activity, biweekly rpt, 11922–5
Germany unification economic impacts for Germany, US, Japan, and worldwide, alternative projections 1991-99, technical paper, 9366–7.275
Interest rates for commercial paper, govt securities, other financial instruments, and home mortgages, monthly rpt, 9365–2.14

Europe
Agricultural exports of US, for grains, oilseed products, hides, skins, and cotton, by country, weekly rpt, 1922–3
Agricultural trade by commodity and country, prices, and world market devs, monthly rpt, 1922–12
Agricultural trade of US, by commodity and country, bimonthly rpt, 1522–1
Agricultural trade of US, by detailed commodity and country, 1991, annual rpt, 1524–8
Agricultural trade of US, by detailed commodity and country, 1991, semiannual rpt, 1522–4
AID contracts and grants for technical and support services, by instn, country, and State, FY91, annual listing, 9914–7
AID economic aid to developing countries, obligations and disbursements by country, quarterly rpt, 9912–4
Air traffic and passengers, for intl routes over north Atlantic, by aviation type and route, alternative forecasts 1992-2010 and trends from 1982, annual rpt, 7504–44
Cancer death rates, by body site, sex, and world area, 1969 and annual percent change 1969-86, article, 4472–1.306
Construction contract awards and billings, by country of contractor and world area of award, 1990, annual article, 2042–1.304
Dollar exchange rate trade-weighted index of Fed Reserve Bank of Atlanta, by world area, quarterly rpt, 9371–15
Dollar exchange rate trade-weighted index of Fed Reserve Bank of Dallas, by world area, monthly rpt, 9379–13
Economic and military aid and loans from US and intl agencies, by program and country, FY46-91, annual rpt, 9914–5
Energy producers finances and operations, by energy type for US firms domestic and foreign operations, 1990, annual rpt, 3164–44.2
Energy production by type, and oil trade, and use, by country group and selected country, monthly rpt, 9112–2

Energy supply and demand, by fuel and end-use sector, 1950s-87 and forecast to 1995, 3166–6.58
Energy use and production, by fuel type, country, and country group, projected 1995-2010 and trends from 1970, annual rpt, 3164–84
Exports and imports (waterborne) of US, by type of service, customs district, port, and world area, monthly rpt, 2422–7
Exports and imports of US, by Harmonized System 6-digit commodity and country, 1991, annual rpt, 2424–13
Exports and imports of US, by selected country, country group, and commodity group, 1991, annual rpt, 2044–37
Exports and imports of US, by transport mode, country, and SITC 1- to 3-digit commodity, 1991, annual rpt, 2424–12
Farm household members off-farm employment, for Europe, 1987, article, 1502–7.301
Immigrant and nonimmigrant visas of US issued and refused, by class, issuing office, and nationality, FY90, annual rpt, 7184–1
Immigrants admitted to US, by class of admission, country of birth, and MSA of destination, FY91, advance annual rpt, 6264–4
Immigrants and legalized aliens, by occupational group and country of birth, preliminary FY91, annual tables, 6264–1
Immigrants and nonimmigrants admitted to US, alien workers, visitors, deportations, and naturalizations, FY91, annual summary rpt, 6264–7
Immigration to US, alien workers, visitors, deportations, and naturalizations, by country, FY91 and trends from 1820, annual rpt, 6264–2
Income tax returns of foreign corporations and individuals, and US entities abroad, detailed data compilation, 1970s-89, quinquennial rpt, 8308–31
Investment (foreign direct) in US, by industry group and world area, 1989-91, annual article, 2702–1.331
Investment (foreign direct) of US, by industry group and world area, 1989-91, annual article, 2702–1.332
Labor costs (manufacturing) and productivity, by selected country, 1950s-91, press release, 6726–1.55
Labor costs and indexes, by selected country, 1991, semiannual rpt, 6822–3
Loans of US banks to foreigners at all US and foreign offices, by country group and country, quarterly rpt, 13002–1
Lumber (hardwood) exports of US to Europe and Asia, by species and country, 1981-90, 1208–373
Military aid of US, arms sales, and training, by country, FY50-91, annual rpt, 3904–3
Military aid of US, arms sales, and training programs costs and budget requests, by program, world region, and country, FY91-93, annual rpt, 7144–13
Military spending, arms trade, and force strengths, with govt spending and population, by country, 1979-89, annual rpt, 9824–1
Multinatl firms US affiliates finances and operations, by industry, country of parent firm, and State, 1987, 2708–48
Multinatl firms US affiliates, finances, and operations, by industry, world area of parent firm, and State, 1989-90, annual rpt, 2704–4
Multinatl US firms and foreign affiliates finances and operations, by industry and country, 1989 benchmark survey, annual rpt, 2704–5
Multinatl US firms foreign affiliates, income statement items by asset size, industry, and country, 1988, biennial article, 8302–2.322
NATO and Warsaw Pact military forces reductions and ceilings under CFE treaty, as of Nov 1990, 9828–1
Oil supply, demand, and stock forecasts, by world area, quarterly rpt, 3162–34
Persian Gulf War allied and other countries cash and in-kind contributions, by type and country, 1990-91, GAO rpt, 26123–371
Population size, growth rates, and components of change, by country, projected 1990-2020 and trends from 1950, biennial rpt, 2324–9
Refugee migration, and intl aid programs, by world area and country of origin and asylum, 1991, annual rpt, 7004–15
Semiconductor industry (US) intl competitiveness, indicators and comparisons to Japan and Europe, 1980s and projected to 1994, working paper, 15036–1.1
Tax (income) returns for foreign corporate activity in US, selected income and tax items, by industry div and selected country, 1988, article, 8302–2.309
Terrorism (intl) incidents, casualties, and attacks on US targets, by attack type and country, 1991, annual rpt, 7004–22
Terrorism (intl) incidents, casualties, and attacks on US targets, by attack type and world area, 1991, annual rpt, 7004–13
Tide height and time daily at coastal points, forecast 1993, annual rpt, 2174–2.4
Timber in northwestern US and British Columbia, production, prices, trade, and employment, quarterly rpt, 1202–3
Travel to and from US, and travel receipts and payments, by world area, with data by country, 1985-90, annual rpt, 2904–10
Travel to and from US on US and foreign flag air carriers, by country, world area, and US port, monthly rpt, 7302–2
Travel to US, by characteristics of visit and traveler, country, port city, and State of destination, quarterly rpt, 2902–1
Travel to US, spending by world area of residence, and economic impact, by spending category and State, 1989, 2908–28
UN voting record and share of votes in agreement with US, by issue, country, and world area, 1991, annual rpt, 7004–18
US military and civilian personnel and dependents, by service branch, world area, and country, quarterly rpt, 3542–20
Weather conditions and effect on agriculture, by US region, State, and city, and world area, weekly rpt, 2182–7
Weather events and anomalies, precipitation and temperature for US and foreign locations, weekly rpt, 2182–6
Weather forecasts accuracy evaluations, for US, UK, and European systems, quarterly rpt, 2182–8
Weather forecasts for US and Northern Hemisphere, precipitation and temperature by location, semimonthly rpt, 2182–1
see also Albania
see also Andorra
see also Armenia
see also Austria
see also Azerbaijan
see also Belgium
see also Bulgaria
see also Byelarus
see also Central Treaty Organization
see also Commonwealth of Independent States
see also Cyprus
see also Czechoslovakia
see also Denmark
see also Eastern Europe
see also Estonia
see also Eurocurrency
see also European Community
see also European Free Trade Association
see also European Space Agency
see also Finland
see also France
see also Georgia, Republic of
see also Germany
see also Germany, East
see also Germany, West
see also Gibraltar
see also Greece
see also Hungary
see also Iceland
see also Ireland
see also Italy
see also Latvia
see also Liechtenstein
see also Lithuania
see also Luxembourg
see also Malta
see also Moldova
see also Monaco
see also Netherlands
see also North Atlantic Treaty Organization
see also Norway
see also Organization for Economic Cooperation and Development
see also Poland
see also Portugal
see also Romania
see also Russia
see also San Marino
see also Soviet Union
see also Spain
see also Sweden
see also Switzerland
see also Ukraine
see also United Kingdom
see also Yugoslavia
see also under By Foreign Country in the "Index by Categories"

European Coal and Steel Community
AID loans repayment status and terms by program and country, and status of predecessor agency loans, quarterly rpt, 9912–3

European Community
Agricultural export subsidies of EC by commodity and destination, FAS monthly circular, 1925–32
Agricultural exports of US, for grains, oilseed products, hides, skins, and cotton, by country, weekly rpt, 1922–3
Agricultural production, acreage, and yield for selected crops, forecasts by selected world region and country, FAS monthly circular, 1925–28

Agricultural trade by commodity and country, prices, and world market devs, monthly rpt, 1922–12
Agricultural trade of US, by commodity and country, bimonthly rpt, 1522–1
Agricultural trade of US, by detailed commodity and country, 1991, annual rpt, 1524–8
Agricultural trade of US, by detailed commodity and country, 1991, semiannual rpt, 1522–4
AID loans repayment status and terms by program and country, and status of predecessor agency loans, quarterly rpt, 9912–3
Almond production, trade, use, and stocks, for 6 countries and US, 1990-93, annual article, 1925–34.337
Dairy imports under quota by commodity, by country of origin, FAS monthly rpt, 1925–31
Drug abuse indicators, by world region and selected country, 1992 semiannual conf, 4492–5.2
Economic conditions, policy, and trade practices, by country, 1989-91, annual rpt, 21384–5
Economic integration of EC, fiscal policy impact of European Monetary Union on member govts, with background data, mid 1970s-90, technical paper, 9393–10.18
Economic integration of EC, impacts on domestic and intl agricultural conditions, 1990 conf, 1528–325
Economic integration of EC impacts on domestic economic conditions and US trade, with background data, 1986-91, 9886–4.181
Economic integration of EC, impacts on financial services industry, 1992 article, 9391–1.308
Economic integration of EC, monetary union impacts on France, Germany, and Italy monetary policies, 1992 technical paper, 9385–8.145
Electronics industry production and labor conditions, in 10 MSAs, EC, and top producer countries, late 1970s-80s, article, 9393–8.307
Exports and imports of US by country, and trade shifts by commodity, 1991, annual rpt, 9884–25
Exports and imports of US, by selected country, country group, and commodity group, 1991, annual rpt, 2044–37
Exports and imports of US with EC by country, and total agricultural trade, annual rpt, discontinued, 7144–7
Exports and imports, trade agreements and relations, and USITC investigations, 1991, annual rpt, 9884–5
Exports, imports, and balances of US, by selected country, country group, and commodity group, preliminary data, monthly rpt, 2042–34
Exports, imports, and balances of US for manufactured goods, by SITC 2-digit commodity and country, quarterly rpt, 2042–35
Exports, imports, and balances of US with major trading partners, by product category, 1987-91, annual chartbook, 9884–21
Exports, imports, and tariffs between Mexico and US, by commodity, impacts of North American Free Trade Agreement and compared to EC expansion to Mediterranean, 1970s-80s, 6366–3.29
Exports, imports, membership, and trade impacts of regional preferential trading arrangements, by group, late 1940s-91, article, 9373–1.308
Grain production, supply, trade, and use, by country and world region, forecasts and trends, FAS monthly circular, 1925–2.1
Import restrictions and trade protectionism measures of US, Australia, Canada, and EC, cases initiated, 1980-85, article, 9379–1.301
Imports of goods, services, and investment from US, trade barriers, impacts, and US actions, by country, 1991, annual rpt, 444–2
Insurance company finances, by insurance type and firm, with some intl comparisons, 1991 conf, 9373–3.35
Interest rate forecasting performance of short- and long-term rate spreads, for US and 6 EC countries, 1950s-91, technical paper, 9385–8.136
Investment (foreign direct) in US, by industry group and world area, 1989-91, annual article, 2702–1.331
Investment (foreign direct) of US, by industry group and world area, 1989-91, annual article, 2702–1.332
Loans and grants for economic and military aid from US and intl agencies, by program and country, FY46-91, annual rpt, 9914–5
Manufacturing industry (US) intl competitiveness, trade and economic policies with background data and foreign comparisons, 1991 rpt, 26358–252
Meat (beef and pork) supply and use of EC, by country, 1988-92, semiannual rpt, 1925–33.2
Multinatl firms US affiliates, finances, and operations, by industry, world area of parent firm, and State, 1989-90, annual rpt, 2704–4
Multinatl US firms and foreign affiliates finances and operations, by industry and country, 1989 benchmark survey, annual rpt, 2704–5
Multinatl US firms foreign affiliates capital expenditures, by major industry group, world area, and country, 1987-92, semiannual article, 2702–1.312
Multinatl US firms foreign affiliates capital expenditures, by major industry group, world area, and country, 1988-92, semiannual article, 2702–1.335
Multinatl US firms foreign affiliates, income statement items by asset size, industry, and country, 1988, biennial article, 8302–2.322
Public interest and expectations for science and technology, 1990 survey, biennial rpt, 9624–10.7
Raisin imports of EC member countries and Canada, and Turkey exports, by country, 1989-93, semiannual article, 1925–34.348
Refugee migration, and intl aid programs, by world area and country of origin and asylum, 1991, annual rpt, 7004–15
Seed exports, by type, world region, and country, FAS quarterly rpt, 1925–13
Services trade of US, direct and among multinatl firms affiliates, by industry and world area, 1986-91, article, 2702–1.336
Standards for production, controls, and processes, domestic and intl dev in US and EC, 1980s-91, 26358–257
Steel imports of US under voluntary restraint agreement, by product, customs district, and country, with US industry operating data, quarterly rpt, 9882–13
Steel trade, by product, country, and customs district, with US industry operating data, 1989-June 1992, semiannual rpt, 9882–15
Subsidies of EC govts, by industry sector and for Airbus Industrie, by country, 1980s-91, hearing, 21708–132
Tax (income and capital) policies, with background data, for EC, Japan, and US, mid 1960s-91, article, 9373–1.316
Textile imports under Multifiber Arrangement by product and country, and status of bilateral agreements, 1988-91, annual rpt, 9884–18
Tobacco and cigarette production, use, trade, and subsidies, by EC member country, 1991, article, 1925–16.306
Tobacco trade of EC members, by country of origin and destination, 1990-91, annual article, 1925–16.314
Tomato (paste and canned) minimum grower price and processor subsidy, by EC country, 1985/86-1992/93, article, 1925–34.336
Wine production, trade, use, and stocks for EC, and Australia and US exports by country, 1985-92, article, 1925–34.325
Wine trade of EC, with exports by country, 1988-91, article, 1925–34.324

European Free Trade Association
Exports, imports, membership, and trade impacts of regional preferential trading arrangements, by group, late 1940s-91, article, 9373–1.308

European Space Agency
Launchings of satellites and other space objects since 1957, quarterly listing, 9502–2

Eutrophication
Coastal areas environmental conditions and mgmt, for individual areas, conf series, 2146–8
Estuary environmental conditions, research results and methodology, series, 2176–7

Evans, Charles L.
"Productivity Shocks and Real Business Cycles", 9375–13.73
"Seasonal Solow Residuals and Christmas: A Case for Labor Hoarding and Increasing Returns", 9375–13.71
"Seasonality and Equilibrium Business Cycle Theories", 9375–13.74

Evansville, Ind.
Wages by occupation, for office and plant workers, 1992 survey, periodic MSA rpt, 6785–17.2
see also under By City and By SMSA or MSA in the "Index by Categories"

Evidence
Felony case processing from arrest to sentencing, cases and duration by disposition and offense, for selected cities, 1988, annual rpt, 6064–27
Wiretaps authorized, costs, arrests, trials, and convictions, by offense and jurisdiction, 1991, annual rpt, 18204–7

Exceptional children
see Handicapped children
see Special education
Exchange of persons programs
Admissions to US of aliens, by country, FY81-91, annual rpt, 6264–2.3
Japan and US technological info transfer activities, and researcher and student exchanges, 1988-89, GAO rpt, 26123–379
see also Educational exchanges
Exchange rates
see Foreign exchange
Excise tax
Alcohol, Tobacco, and Firearms Bur and IRS tax enforcement activities and collections, 1991 hearing, 21788–217
Alcoholic beverages and tobacco production, removals, stocks, and material used, by State, monthly rpt series, 8486–1
Auto equipment excise taxes of Fed Govt and States, 1991, annual rpt, 7554–1
Auto, van, and light truck ownership and operating costs, by vehicle size and year of operation, 1991 model year, biennial rpt, 7554–21
Autos with low gas mileage, Federal excise tax rates by model, and revenues, 1980s-91, annual rpt, 3304–5.3
Budget of US, authoritative financial statements with appropriations, outlays, and receipts, by category and agency, FY91, annual rpt, 8104–2.2
Budget of US, CBO analysis and review of FY93 budget by function, annual rpt, 26304–2
Budget of US, CBO analysis of revenue and spending alternatives and projections of economic indicators, FY93-97, annual rpt, 26304–3
Budget of US, historical data, selected years FY34-91 and projected to FY97, 108–46.5
Budget of US, obligations and authority by function, agency, and program, with summaries and analyses, FY93, annual rpt, 104–2
Budget of US, receipts by source, outlays by agency and program, and balances, monthly rpt, 8102–3
Coal excise tax and other black lung trust fund receipts, fund disbursements, and claims and benefits by State, 1991, annual rpt, 6504–3
Coal Surface Mining Reclamation and Enforcement Office activities and funding, by State and Indian tribe, FY91, annual rpt, 5644–1
Collections, enforcement, and litigation activity of IRS, with data by type of tax, region, and State, FY91, annual rpt, 8304–3
DOE Oak Ridge Natl Lab contractors excise tax refunds due from off-highway motor fuel use, 1988-90, 3006–5.26
Energy producers finances and operations, by energy type for US firms domestic and foreign operations, 1990, annual rpt, 3164–44.1
Fed Govt finances, cash and debt transactions, daily tables, 8102–4
Fed Govt internal revenue and refunds, by type of tax, quarterly rpt, 8302–2.1
Fed Govt receipts by source and outlays by agency, *Treasury Bulletin*, quarterly rpt, 8002–4.1
Finances of govts, by level of govt, State, and for large cities and counties, annual rpt series, 2466–2
Finances of govts, tax systems and revenue, and fiscal structure, by level of govt and State, 1992 and historical trends, annual rpt, 10044–1
Hazardous waste generation and disposal taxes, rates, and firms filing returns, by substance type, 1989, annual article, 8302–2.303
Hwy funding and allocation methods, for Federal-aid system, FY92-97, 7558–107
Income tax returns of individuals, by filing status, tax item, and income level, 1991, annual article, 8302–2.319
IRS collections, by excise tax source, quarterly rpt, 8302–1
Latin America, Canada, and US tobacco production and use, and related economic, health, and social issues, 1950s-92, annual rpt, 4204–18
Luxury tax revenue, and related IRS administrative costs, FY91 and projected to FY95, GAO rpt, 26119–385
Natl income and product accounts and components, *Survey of Current Business*, monthly rpt, 2702–1.23
Natl income and product accounts, comprehensive accounts and components, benchmark revisions, 1929-88, 2708–5
Natl income and product accounts, comprehensive accounts and components, *Survey of Current Business*, monthly rpt, 2702–1.26
New England States economic indicators, Fed Reserve 1st District, monthly rpt, 9373–2
Nonprofit charitable organizations finances, summary data by asset size, 1989, article, 8302–2.325
Nonprofit charitable organizations finances, with data by State and for top 10 instns, 1988, article, 8302–2.302
Oil imports from OPEC, economic impacts of tariffs and excise taxes, model description and results, 1992 technical paper, 9379–12.96
Returns and supplemental documents filed, by type, FY91 and projected to FY2000, semiannual rpt, 8302–4
Returns and supplemental documents filed, by type, 1990 and projected to 1999, annual article, 8302–2.304
Returns filed, by type of tax and IRS district, 1990 and projected 1991-98, annual rpt, 8304–24
Returns filed, by type of tax, region, and IRS service center, projected 1991-98 and trends from 1978, annual rpt, 8304–9
Smoking control strategies effectiveness, with data on research funding, smoking prevalence, cancer deaths, and taxation, 1900s-91, 4476–7.1
Statistical Abstract of US, 1992 annual data compilation, 2324–1.9
Tax exempt organizations finances, with data by type, size, State, and for largest organizations, late 1940s-80s, compilation of papers, 8308–35
Tobacco production, marketing, use, price supports, and trade, quarterly situation rpt with articles, 1561–10
Tobacco tax rates and receipts of Fed Govt and States, FY86-91, annual rpt, 1319–1.4
Transit systems finances and operations, by mode, size of fleet and urban area, region, and for 518 systems, 1990, annual rpt, 7884–4
Transportation infrastructure financing through user fees, with data on hwys, airports, and waterways, 1985-91, 26306–6.170
see also Fuel tax
see also Sales tax
see also Tolls
see also Windfall profit tax
Executive agreements
Bilateral and multilateral treaties and other agreements in force, by country, as of Jan 1992, annual listing, 7004–1
Executive clemency
see Pardons
Executive-congressional relations
see Congressional-executive relations
Executive departments
see Federal executive departments
Executive impoundment of appropriated funds
Rescissions and deferrals of budget authority, monthly rpt, 102–2
Executive Office of the President
Budget of US, authoritative financial statements with appropriations, outlays, and receipts, by category and agency, FY91, annual rpt, 8104–2.2
Budget of US, obligations and authority by function, agency, and program, with summaries and analyses, FY93, annual rpt, 104–2
Budget of US, receipts by source, outlays by agency and program, and balances, monthly rpt, 8102–3
see also Council of Economic Advisers
see also Council on Environmental Quality
see also National Security Council
see also Office of Management and Budget
see also Office of National Drug Control Policy
see also Office of Policy Development
see also Office of Science and Technology Policy
see also Office of the U.S. Trade Representative
see also Office of the Vice President
see also under names of individual Presidential commissions (starting with Presidential or President's)
Executives and managers
Air traffic control supervisor selection, relation to screening test and technical training performance, 1980s, technical rpt, 7506–10.116
Banks (Fed Reserve) and branch officers, staff, and salary, 1991, annual rpt, 9364–1.1
Corporations securities holdings by shareholder type, and mgmt and executive pay issues, with data by company, 1991 hearing, 25248–130
Deaths and rates, by cause and selected social, demographic, and employment characteristics, 1979-85, natl longitudinal study, 4478–186
Educational attainment, by social and demographic characteristics and location, 1991 and trends from 1940, biennial Current Population Rpt, 2546–1.460
Employment and economic conditions, alternative BLS projections to 2005 and trends 1975-90, biennial rpt, 6744–19

Employment Cost Index and alternative measure of compensation costs, by component, occupation, industry group, union status, and location, 1975-92, annual rpt, 6744–20
Employment, unemployment, and labor force characteristics, by region, State, and selected metro area, 1991, annual rpt, 6744–7
Fed Govt civilian employment and payroll, by pay system, agency, and location, 1991, annual rpt, 9844–6
Fed Govt employment of minorities, women, and disabled, by agency and occupation, FY90, annual rpt, 9244–10
Fed Govt first-line supervisors performance ratings by self, superiors, and subordinates, 1991 survey, 9498–15
Fed Govt procurement operations employees job performance, and views on policies and practices, 1991 survey, 9498–17
Fed Govt Senior Executive Service members characteristics, entries, exits, and awards, FY79-91, annual rpt, 9844–36
Fed Govt Senior Executive Service members views on work environment, 1989 and 1991 surveys, GAO rpt, 26119–402
Fed Govt Senior Executive Service noncareer and Schedule C appointments, by agency, 1990-91, GAO rpt, 26119–412
Financial instns fraud and abuse, Justice Dept enforcement activity, staff, and case dispositions by instn type, 1988-92, 6008–35
Higher education faculty and staff, by occupation, full- and part-time status, sex, and instn type and control, fall 1989, biennial rpt, 4844–18
Immigrants and legalized aliens, by occupational group and country of birth, preliminary FY91, annual tables, 6264–1
Immigration to US, alien workers, visitors, deportations, and naturalizations, by country, FY91 and trends from 1820, annual rpt, 6264–2
Income (household, family, and personal), by source, detailed characteristics, and region, 1991, annual Current Population Rpt, 2546–6.76
Labor demand, turnover, and training completions, by detailed occupation, 1990 and projected to 2005, biennial rpt, 6744–3
Labor hourly costs, by component, occupational group, industry div, union coverage, and region, 1992, annual rpt, 6744–21
Minority group and women employment, by occupation, SIC 1- to 3- digit industry, State, and MSA, 1991, annual rpt, 9244–1
Occupational Outlook Handbook, 1992-93, biennial rpt, 6744–1
Pacific territories population and housing detailed characteristics, by location, 1990 Census of Population and Housing, series, 2551–8
Prison staff in Federal instns, by selected characteristics, region, and instn, FY89, annual rpt, 6244–1.2
Railroad (Amtrak) finances, executive office travel expenses and staff years, and membership dues by assn, FY88-92, GAO rpt, 26113–573
Savings instns conversion from mutual to stock ownership, chief executive stock holdings and stock price changes, 1986-87, article, 9373–1.307
Savings instns fraud and abuse, Federal indictments and case dispositions, periodic press release, 6002–3; 6008–33
Science and engineering employment characteristics of minorities, women, and disabled, by field, 1970s-91, biennial rpt, 9624–20.1
Science and engineering labor force, Federal and university research funding, and educational data, series, 9626–6
Science, engineering, and technical employment in manufacturing, by field and industry, 1989, triennial rpt, 9627–23
Small Business Admin minority and women employment, and hiring goals, FY91, annual rpt, 9764–9
Training for job qualification and skill improvement, workers participating by training source, occupation, age, sex, and race, 1991, 6728–32
see also Business management
see also Officials

Exercise
see Physical exercise
see Sports and athletics

Exhibitions and trade fairs
Business America, foreign and domestic commerce, and US investment and trade opportunities, biweekly journal, 2042–24
Caribbean Basin Initiative export and investment incentives, contact listing, bibl, and US imports country, 1983-91, annual rpt, 2044–36
Conventions and attendance in Great Lakes cities, 1987, and for Chicago, 1983-90, working paper, 9375–13.78
Eastern Europe imports from US, and trade and dev opportunities, monthly rpt, 2042–33
Soviet Union trade and investment opportunities for US firms, contact listing, bibl, and background economic data, 1991 rpt, 2048–157

Eximbank
see Export-Import Bank

Expedited Funds Availability Act
Bank deposits availability policies, with background data, 1980s-90, last issue of annual report, 9364–13

Exploration, natural resources
see Energy exploration and drilling
see Mines and mineral resources

Explosives
Accidents (occupational) injury and illness rates by SIC 2- to 4-digit industry, and deaths by cause and industry div, 1990, annual rpt, 6844–1
Accidents involving consumer products and related activities, injuries by severity and victim age and sex, 1990, annual rpt, 9164–7
Accidents involving consumer products, injuries by severity, victim age, and detailed product, 1991, annual rpt, 9164–6
Consumption of explosives and blasting agents, by type, industry, and State, 1991, Mineral Industry Surveys, annual rpt, 5614–22
County Business Patterns, 1989: employment, establishments, and payroll, by SIC 2- to 4-digit industry and county, annual State rpt series, 2326–8
County Business Patterns, 1990: employment, establishments, and payroll, by SIC 2- to 4-digit industry and county, annual State rpt series, 2326–6
Court civil and criminal caseloads for Federal district, appeals, and special courts, 1991, annual rpt, 18204–8
Criminal sentences for Federal offenses, guidelines by offense and circumstances, series, 17668–1
Exports and imports between US and outlying areas, by detailed commodity and mode of transport, 1991, annual rpt, 2424–11
Exports and imports of US, by country and detailed commodity, monthly rpt, 2422–12
Exports and imports of US, by Harmonized System 6-digit commodity and country, 1991, annual rpt, 2424–13
Exports and imports of US, by transport mode, country, and SITC 1- to 3-digit commodity, 1991, annual rpt, 2424–12
Exports of US, detailed Schedule B commodities with countries of destination, 1991, annual rpt, 2424–10
Fireworks explosions, casualties, and damages, for legal and illegal fireworks, 1987-91, annual rpt, 8484–4.1
Input-output structure of US economy, detailed interindustry transactions for 541 industries, and components of final demand, 1982 benchmark data, 2708–17
Manufacturing annual survey, 1990: finances and operations, by SIC 2- to 4-digit industry, series, 2506–14
Manufacturing census, 1987: concentration of largest firms measured by value added, and for shipments by SIC 2- and 4-digit industry, subject rpt, 2497–6
Manufacturing census, 1987: shipments of manufacturers products, by customer class and SIC 2- and 4-digit industry, subject rpt, 2497–4
Military and personal property shipments, passenger traffic, and costs, by service branch and mode of transport, FY91, annual rpt, 3704–15
Minerals Yearbook, Vol 1, 1989: commodity reviews of production, use, trade, prices, and mining operations, annual rpt, 5604–33
Occupational injury and illness rates, by SIC 2- to 4-digit industry, 1989-90, annual rpt, 6844–7
OECD trade, total and for 4 major countries, and US trade by country, by commodity, 1980-90, world area rpt series, 9116–1
Price indexes (producer), by stage of processing and detailed commodity, monthly rpt, 6762–6
Price indexes (producer), by stage of processing and detailed commodity, monthly 1991, annual rpt, 6764–2
Thefts and recoveries of explosives by State, and accidental detonations by place of occurrence, 1987-91, annual rpt, 8484–4
Transport of hazardous material, accidents, casualties, and damage, by mode of transport, with DOT control activities, 1990, annual rpt, 7304–4

see also Ammunition
see also Bombs
see also Nuclear explosives and explosions

Export-Import Bank
Budget of US, authoritative financial statements with appropriations, outlays, and receipts, by category and agency, FY91, annual rpt, 8104–2.2
Budget of US, obligations and authority by function, agency, and program, with summaries and analyses, FY93, annual rpt, 104–2
Credit programs for exports, activities of Eximbank and 6 OECD countries, 1990, annual rpt, 9254–3
Debt to US of foreign govts and private obligors, by country and program, periodic rpt, 8002–6
Labor unions recognized in Fed Govt, agreements and membership by agency and facility, as of Jan 1991, biennial listing, 9844–14
Latin America economic and social conditions, resources, trade, and aid, 1992, annual factbook, 9914–14
Liabilities (contingent) and claims paid by Fed Govt on federally insured and guaranteed contracts with foreign obligors, by country and program, periodic rpt, 8002–12
Loans and grants for economic and military aid from US and intl agencies, by program and country, FY46-91, annual rpt, 9914–5
Loans of Eximbank, guarantees, and insurance authorizations, by country, FY90, annual rpt, 15344–1.12

Export processing zones
Clothing exports to US, and domestic and US-owned industry production costs and operations, for Caribbean area and Mexico, impacts of North American Free Trade Agreement, 1992 rpt, 9886–4.186
Mexico and US economic and trade impacts of proposed North American Free Trade Agreement, with data on maquiladora plants, 1980s-90, hearings, 21788–210
Mexico maquiladora plants environmental regulation enforcement activities, staff, and funding, 1989-92, GAO rpt, 26119–416
Mexico trade with US and other countries, foreign investment, and maquiladoras operations, 1980s-91, GAO rpt, 26119–417
Shipments through US foreign trade zones, articles with foreign content by product, 1989, working paper, 9375–13.86
US foreign trade zone operations and movement of goods, by zone and commodity, FY90, annual rpt, 2044–30

Exports and imports
see Agricultural exports and imports
see Balance of payments
see Coal exports and imports
see Common markets and free trade areas
see East-West trade
see Energy exports and imports
see Export processing zones
see Foreign trade
see Foreign trade promotion
see Motor vehicle exports and imports
see Natural gas exports and imports
see Petroleum exports and imports
see Tariffs and foreign trade controls
see under names of specific commodities or commodity groups

Expositions
see Exhibitions and trade fairs

Extension work
see Agricultural extension work

Extradition
Criminal cases by type and disposition, and collections, for US attorneys, by Federal district, FY91, annual rpt, 6004–2.1
Marshals Service activities, FY91, annual rpt, 6294–1

Exxon Corp.
Alaska oil spill from tanker Exxon Valdez, impacts on marine mammals, and resulting legislation, 1991 annual rpt, 14734–1
Overcharge settlements of oil companies, funds received, and conservation and energy aid spending, by outlying area, 1990, GAO rpt, 26113–564

Eye diseases and defects
Air traffic controller color blindness impacts on performance, 1992 rpt, 7506–10.102
Cases of acute and chronic conditions, disability, absenteeism, and health services use, by selected characteristics, 1990, annual rpt, 4147–10.182; 4147–10.183
Cataract surgery reimbursement by Medicare, savings from denial of claims for unnecessary and poor service, 1988, 4006–11.2; 4006–11.3
Color blindness of air traffic controllers, impacts on performance, 1992 technical rpt, 7506–10.123; 7506–10.125
Diabetes patients physician office visits, by characteristics of patient, physician, and visit, 1989, 4146–8.212
Disability and work limitations of persons with chronic health conditions, by condition, age, and sex, 1983-86, 4946–1.2
Head Start handicapped enrollment, by handicap, State, and for Indian and migrant programs, 1988/89, annual rpt, 4584–4
HHS financial aid, by program, recipient, State, and city, FY91, annual regional listings, 4004–3
Medicaid payment and participation by service type, and cost compared to Medicare, by State, FY89, 17266–1.4
OECD members health care costs, hospital use, resources, and economic and health indicators, by country, 1960s-90, article, 4652–1.322
Pilots with aphakia and artificial lens implants, by sex and class of medical certificate, 1982-85, technical rpt, 7506–10.114
see also Blind
see also Optometry

Ezzati, Trena M.
"Office Visits for Diabetes Mellitus, National Ambulatory Medical Care Survey: U.S., 1977", 4147–16.6
"Sample Design: Third National Health and Nutrition Examination Survey. Vital and Health Statistics Series 2", 4147–2.115

FAA
see Federal Aviation Administration

Fabrics
see Synthetic fibers and fabrics
see Textile industry and fabrics

Factories
see Industrial plants and equipment

Factory workers
see Production workers

Faculty
see Educational employees pay
see School administration and staff
see Teachers

Faeroes
Exports and imports of US, by transport mode, country, and SITC 1- to 3-digit commodity, 1991, annual rpt, 2424–12

Fahey, Thomas D.
"Lumber and Veneer Recovery from Intensively Managed Young-Growth Douglas-Fir", 1208–413
"Veneer Recovery of Douglas-Fir from the Coast and Cascade Ranges of Oregon and Washington", 1208–396

Fahim-Nader, Mahnaz
"Capital Expenditures by Majority-Owned Foreign Affiliates of U.S. Companies, Latest Plans for 1992", 2702–1.335
"Capital Expenditures by Majority-Owned Foreign Affiliates of U.S. Companies, Plans for 1992", 2702–1.312
"U.S. Business Enterprises Acquired or Established by Foreign Direct Investors in 1991", 2702–1.320

Fair employment practices
see Discrimination in employment

Fair housing
see Discrimination in housing

Fair Labor Standards Act
Child labor certification and injury reporting procedures of States, relation to proposed Federal guidelines, 1991, GAO rpt, 26121–451
Los Angeles wages and working conditions impacts of Immigration Reform and Control Act, 1980s-91, working paper, 6366–6.9
Minimum wage rates, 1938-91, annual rpt, 4744–3.1

Fairfax County, Va.
Fed Govt land acquisition and dev projects in DC metro area, characteristics and funding by agency and project, FY92-96, annual rpt, 15454–1
Housing and households characteristics, unit and neighborhood quality, and journey to work by MSA location, for 11 MSAs, 1985 survey, supplement, 2485–8
Housing and households detailed characteristics, and unit and neighborhood quality, by location, 1989 survey, MSA rpt, 2485–6.1

Fairfield, Calif.
Wages by occupation, and benefits, for office and plant workers, 1992 survey, periodic MSA rpt, 6785–3.3

Fairs
see Exhibitions and trade fairs

Fairweather, Mary Lou
"Annual Southwestern Region Pest Conditions Report, 1991", 1206–11.2

Faith
see Clergy
see Missions and missionaries

see Religion
see Religious liberty
see Religious organizations

Falkland Islands (Malvinas)
Economic and social conditions, resources, and trade, and aid, 1992, annual factbook, 9914–14
Exports and imports of US, by transport mode, country, and SITC 1- to 3-digit commodity, 1991, annual rpt, 2424–12

Fallout
see Nuclear explosives and explosions

Fama, Teresa
"Effect of the OBRA 1989 Payment Provision for Small Rural Medicare-Dependent Hospitals", 17206–2.42

Families and households
Alcohol use, knowledge, attitudes, and info sources of youth, series, 4006–10
Alteration and repair of owner-occupied homes, costs and structural, household, financial, and project characteristics, 1987, 2486–1.13
American Housing Survey: unit and household characteristics of recent movers, and reason for move, by tenure, 1989, 2486–1.12
American Housing Survey: unit and households characteristics, and unit and neighborhood quality, by MSA location for 11 MSAs, 1987 survey, supplement, 2485–8
American Housing Survey: unit and households characteristics, MSA fact sheet series, 2485–11
American Housing Survey: unit and households detailed characteristics, and unit and neighborhood quality, MSA rpt series, 2485–6
American Housing Survey: unit and households detailed characteristics, and unit and neighborhood quality, 1989, biennial rpt supplement, 2485–13
American Housing Survey: unit and households detailed characteristics, and unit and neighborhood quality, 1989, wallchart, 2485–12
Asian and Pacific Islands Americans social and economic characteristics, for West and total US, 1990-91, Current Population Report, 2546–1.462
Black Americans social and economic characteristics, for South and total US, 1991 and trends from 1950, annual Current Population Rpt, 2546–1.463
Cancer (lung) risk relation to environmental smoke exposure, for nonsmoking women, local area study, 1992 article, 4472–1.342
Census of Housing, 1990: summary unit characteristics, by householder race and age, county, place, and urban-rural location, State rpt series, 2471–1
Census of Population and Housing, 1990: detailed geographic coverage, State CD-ROM series, 2551–9
Census of Population and Housing, 1990: population and housing characteristics, detailed geographic coverage, State CD-ROM series, 2551–10
Census of Population and Housing, 1990: summary characteristics, by county, subdiv, and place, State rpt series, 2551–7
Census of Population and Housing, 1990: summary characteristics, households, and land area, by county, subdiv, and place, State rpt series, 2551–1
Census of Population, 1990: population characteristics and living arrangements, by county, place, and urban-rural location, State rpt series, 2531–1
Census of Population, 1990: population characteristics and living arrangements, for Native American, urban, and metro areas, series, 2531–2
Child care arrangements prior to 1st grade, by setting and parents' educational level, 1991 survey, 4826–10.2
Consumer Income, socioeconomic characteristics of persons, families, and households, detailed cross-tabulations, Current Population Rpt series, 2546–6
Crime victimization of households, by offense, household characteristics, and location, 1975-91, annual rpt, 6066–25.49
Crime victimization rates, by victim and offender characteristics, circumstances, and offense, 1990 survey, annual rpt, 6066–3.47
Current Housing Reports, unit and household characteristics, subject rpt series, 2486–1; 2486–2
Deaths and rates, by cause and selected social, demographic, and employment characteristics, 1979-85, natl longitudinal study, 4478–186
Economic well-being indicators, by selected population characteristics and household income and income-to-poverty ratio, 1984, 2546–20.22
Educational attainment, by social and demographic characteristics and location, 1991 and trends from 1940, biennial Current Population Rpt, 2546–1.460
Educational performance and conditions, characteristics, attitudes, activities, and plans, 1988 8th grade class, natl longitudinal survey, series, 4826–9
Employment and Earnings, detailed data, monthly rpt, 6742–2.9
Employment and unemployment, by age, sex, race, marital and family status, industry div, and State, Monthly Labor Review, 6722–1.2
Enrollment, by grade, instn type and control, and student characteristics, 1989 and trends from 1947, annual Current Population Rpt, 2546–1.459
Family Economics Review, consumer goods prices and supply, and home economics, quarterly journal, 1702–1
Family relationships, living arrangements, and marital status, by selected characteristics, 1991, annual Current Population Rpt, 2546–1.461
Farm population, by employment, social, and economic characteristics, and region, 1990, annual Current Population Rpt, 2546–1.458
Financial services use by households, by account type and instn type and location, 1989, article, 9362–1.303
Flow-of-funds accounts, savings, investments, and credit statements, quarterly rpt, 9365–3.3
Food stamp eligibility and payment errors, by type, recipient characteristics, and State, FY90, annual rpt, 1364–15
Food stamp recipient household size, composition, income, and income and deductions allowed, summer 1989, annual rpt, 1364–8
Foreign travel to US and Canada, market analyses with detailed trip and traveler characteristics, country rpt series, 2906–2
Grandchildren in households, and families with grandchildren present, by presence of parents and race, 1991, annual Current Population Rpt, 2546–1.461
Health condition and care indicators, 1988 natl survey, CD-ROM, 4147–10.184
High school classes of 1980 and 1982: education, employment, and family characteristics, activities, and attitudes, natl longitudinal study, series, 4826–2
Home mortgages FHA-insured, financial, property, and borrower characteristics, by metro area, 1991, annual rpt, 5144–24
Home mortgages FHA-insured, financial, property, and borrower characteristics, by State, 1991, annual rpt, 5144–1; 5144–25
Home mortgages FHA-insured, financial, property, and borrower characteristics, 1991, annual rpt, 5144–17; 5144–23
Homeless families in transitional housing, HUD support services grants by recipient, 1991, press release, 5006–3.87
Homeless persons transitional housing and support services, HUD grants by community, 1991, press release, 5006–3.80
Homeless persons transitional housing and support services program, outcome relation to client characteristics and services, FY87-90, GAO rpt, 26113–549
Homeownership rates, by household type, householder age and sex, and location, 1960s-91, annual rpt, 2484–1.3
Households and family characteristics, by location, 1991, annual Current Population Rpt, 2546–1.457
Households and housing unit summary characteristics, 1989 and trends, chartbook, 2486–2.1
Immigrant and nonimmigrant visas of US issued and refused, by class, issuing office, and nationality, FY90, annual rpt, 7184–1
Immigrant visa applicants on waiting lists at consular office, by preference class, world region, and for top countries, as of Jan 1992, 7188–1
Immigrants admitted to US, by class of admission, country of birth, and MSA of destination, FY91, advance annual rpt, 6264–4
Immigrants and nonimmigrants admitted to US, alien workers, visitors, deportations, and naturalizations, FY91, annual summary rpt, 6264–7
Immigrants from Central America in DC, by selected employment and other characteristics, and reasons for migration, 1985-88, working paper, 6366–6.3
Immigrants from Colombia employed in New England textile industry, by selected characteristics, 1960s-80s, working paper, 6366–6.4
Immigration to US, alien workers, visitors, deportations, and naturalizations, by country, FY91 and trends from 1820, annual rpt, 6264–2

Indian and Alaska Native youth health condition and behavioral patterns, by sex and grade, 1988-90, 4088-3
Labor force status effects on families, series, 6726-2
Labor force status of family members and earnings, by family composition and race, quarterly press release, 6742-21
Labor force status of family members, monthly rpt, 6742-2.1
Mail volume to and from households, use, and views, by class, source, content, and household characteristics, FY87-90, annual rpt, 9864-10
Migration, immigration, and mover characteristics compared to nonmovers, 1987-90, annual Current Population Rpt, 2546-1.456
Migration of households, moving rates by tenure and age, and housing value by mobility status and region, 1989, fact sheet, 2326-17.38
Migration since 1990, mover characteristics by same or different area, and compared to nonmovers, 1991, annual Current Population Rpt, 2546-1.464
Mortgage applications, dispositions, and secondary loan market sales, by purpose, lender type, and applicant and neighborhood characteristics, 1991, article, 9362-1.307
Natl income and product accounts, comprehensive accounts and components, benchmark revisions, 1929-88, 2708-5
Natl income and product accounts, comprehensive accounts and components, *Survey of Current Business*, monthly rpt, 2702-1.24
NYC housing supply, occupancy, condition, and household characteristics, by tenure and borough, 1991 triennial survey, 2488-3
Older persons income and sources, by OASDI beneficiary and poverty status, and other characteristics, 1990, biennial chartbook, 4744-25
Older persons socioeconomic characteristics, 1900s-90 and projected to 2050, biennial chartbook, 12904-1
Older population, and health, economic, and other characteristics, with foreign comparisons, 1980s-91 with trends and projections, Current Population Rpt, 2546-2.165
Pacific Northwest population, households, employment, income, fuel prices, and electricity demand, alternative forecasts 1991-2010, annual rpt, 3224-3.3
Pacific territories population and housing detailed characteristics, by location, 1990 Census of Population and Housing, series, 2551-8
Population and housing summary data and trends, 1970s-91, Current Population Rpt, fact sheet, 2546-2.163
Population size and demographic changes impacts on economic conditions, with background data, 1950s-80s and projected to 2010, 23848-226
Poverty relation to low earnings, by work experience during year, household relationship, sex, race, age, and education, 1960s-90, Current Population Rpt, 2546-6.74
Poverty status by age group and living arrangements, and family poverty threshold, late 1930s-91, annual rpt, 4744-3.1
Poverty status of families, by detailed characteristics, 1980 and 1988, GAO rpt, 26131-102
Poverty status of population and families, by detailed characteristics, 1991, annual Current Population Rpt, 2546-6.77
Public assistance benefits, beneficiaries, and spells of participation, by aid program and recipient characteristics, 1987-88, Current Population Rpt, 2546-20.25
Quality of family life and relationships, and other issues, views of parents and children, 1990 survey, 15528-2
Rental housing units, total, with HUD assistance by program, and eligible for aid, by unit, household, and neighborhood characteristics, and location, 1989, biennial rpt, 5184-11
Research on population and reproduction, Federal funding by project, FY90, annual listing, 4474-9
Research on population and reproduction, Natl Inst of Child Health and Human Dev funding and activities, 1991, annual rpt, 4474-33
Single person and nonfamily households social, economic and housing characteristics, by tenure, 1989, 2486-1.15
Statistical Abstract of US, 1992 annual data compilation, 2324-1.1; 2324-1.16
Survey of Income and Program Participation, data collection, methodology, and availability, 1991 users guide, 2628-24
Survey of Income and Program Participation, household composition, income, benefits, and labor force status, methodology, working paper series, 2626-10
Survey of Income and Program Participation, household income and socioeconomic characteristics, special study series, 2546-20
Telecommunications industry intl competitiveness, structure, and devs, with background data and foreign comparisons, 1991 rpt, 2808-30
Telephone service subscribership, charges, and local and long distance firm finances and operations, late 1970s-92, semiannual rpt, 9282-7
Tennessee Valley economic conditions, and compared to US, alternative projections 1992-2010 and trends from 1929, annual rpt, 9804-27
Travel patterns, personal and household characteristics, and auto and public transport use, 1990 survey, series, 7556-6
Travel patterns, personal and household characteristics, and auto use, 1950-90, annual rpt, 3304-5.4
Travel patterns, personal and household characteristics, and auto use, 1990 survey, annual rpt, 7554-1.6
Wages of full- and part-time workers, by selected characteristics, quarterly press release, 6742-20
Women in jail, by criminal background and sociodemographic characteristics, with comparisons to men, 1989, 6066-19.66
Women's labor force status and characteristics, 1960s-90, chartbook, 6748-85
Women's labor force status, by age, race, and family status, quarterly rpt, 6742-17
Women's labor force status, earnings, and other characteristics, with comparisons to men, fact sheet series, 6564-1
see also Adoption
see also Aid to Families with Dependent Children
see also Caregivers and caregiving
see also Child abuse and neglect
see also Child support and alimony
see also Child welfare
see also Children
see also Domestic relations courts and cases
see also Domestic violence
see also Family budgets
see also Family planning
see also Group quarters
see also Housing energy use
see also Living arrangements
see also Marriage and divorce
see also Maternity benefits
see also Military dependents
see also Parents
see also Personal and household income
see also Single parents
see also Unpaid family workers
see also Widows and widowers

Family budgets

Assets and debts of private sector, balance sheets by segment, 1960-91, semiannual rpt, 9365-4.1
Assets of households, net worth distribution under alternative sample weighting systems to account for inconsistency in survey design and response rates, 1992 rpt, 9368-91
Bank deposit insurance coverage of households and small businesses, and value of insurance to banks by instn, 1970s-90, hearing, 21408-126
Black women's labor force status, earnings, and other economic status indicators, and compared to whites, various periods 1939-88, 11048-191
Child care arrangements of mothers employed and in school, and costs, by age of child and characteristics of mother, 1988, Current Population Rpt, 2546-20.24
Credit cards held by household income, age, and card type, and debt outstanding, with issuer costs and revenue, 1970s-80, article, 9362-1.306
Economic indicators, prices, labor costs, and productivity, BLS econometric analyses and methodology, working paper series, 6886-6
Energy aid for low income households, coverage and impacts on energy use and costs, selected years FY79-89, 4588-2
Entertainment spending by households, recreation participation by activity, and video product and pet ownership, 1970s-90, article, 1702-1.303
Family Economics Review, consumer goods prices and supply, and home economics, quarterly journal, 1702-1
Financial status of families, income, net worth, and assets and debt by type, by income and selected characteristics, 1983 and 1989, article, 9362-1.301

Food spending at and away from home, by selected characteristics, 1989, article, 1702–1.308
Food spending of women-headed households, by item and selected characteristics, and compared to other households, 1970s-88, 1548–391
Handicapped children's formal and informal care, outlays and time spent relation to diagnosis and other characteristics, 1988, article, 4042–3.329
Health care spending by businesses, households, and govts, 1965-90, annual article, 4652–1.309
Higher education instn student aid and other sources of support, with student expenses and characteristics, by instn type and control, 1987 triennial study, series, 4846–3; 4846–5
Higher education instn student financial support by parents, by type and funding sources, and student, parent, and instn characteristics, fall 1986, 4846–3.11
Housing alteration and repair for owner-occupied units, with housing costs as share of income, 1987, 2486–1.13
Housing costs exceeding 28% of gross income, families income by source and expenses by type, by tenure and other characteristics, 1989, article, 1702–1.304
Married couples aged 18-25, income and expenses by wife's employment status and family size, 1988-89, article, 1702–1.302
Oil production disruption after Iraq invasion of Kuwait, impacts on futures prices, family budgets, and oil firms, 1990 hearings, 25408–116
Older persons ability to pay out of pocket health care costs, indicators by selected characteristics, 1984, article, 4742–1.307
Older persons income sources, assets, and health care financing issues, 1991 rpt, 10176–3.3; 10176–3.4
Population economic well-being indicators, by selected characteristics and household income and income-to-poverty ratio, 1984, 2546–20.22
Telephone local service charges and low-income subsidies, by region, company, and city, 1980s-91, semiannual rpt, 9282–8
Telephone service subscribership, charges, and local and long distance firm finances and operations, late 1970s-92, semiannual rpt, 9282–7
Wealth, income, and poverty measures for households, families, and individuals, 1960s-90, Current Population Rpt, chartbook, 2546–6.75
Women (older) living alone, income by source, and expenses by type, by marital status, 1988-89, article, 1702–1.301
see also Personal consumption

Family courts
see Domestic relations courts and cases

Family income
see Personal and household income
see under By Income in the "Index by Categories"

Family planning
Developing countries economic and social conditions from 1960s, and Intl Dev Cooperation Agency and AID activities and funding, FY91-93, annual rpt, 9904–4
Developing countries family planning and population activities of AID, grants by project and recipient, and contraceptive shipments, by country, FY91, annual rpt series, 9914–13
Drug abuse by mothers, treatment and other services use, referrals, needs, and barriers, for 13 NIDA-funded programs, 1990/91 survey, 4498–76
Drug abuse treatment programs family planning services, 1992 conf, 4492–5.2
Foreign countries contraception use by women, by age and country, 1991 biennial rpt, 2324–9
Health condition and care indicators, 1950s-90 with health improvement and disease prevention goals for 1990, annual data compilation, 4144–11
HHS financial aid, by program, recipient, State, and city, FY91, annual regional listings, 4004–3
Medicaid beneficiaries and payments, by service type, FY72-90, annual rpt, 4744–3.6
Medicare and Medicaid beneficiaries and program operations, 1992, annual fact book, 4654–18
Research on population and reproduction, Federal funding by project, FY90, annual listing, 4474–9
Research on population and reproduction, Natl Inst of Child Health and Human Dev funding and activities, 1991, annual rpt, 4474–33
see also Abortion
see also Contraceptives
see also Sex education
see also Sexual sterilization

Family Support Act
Dependent care tax credit impacts of Act, Federal revenue losses and gains, FY88-93, 21788–212

Family Support Administration
AFDC beneficiaries by county, payments, application processing and disposition, hearings, and fraud cases, by State, annual rpt, issuing agency change, 4694–7
AFDC beneficiaries demographic and financial characteristics, by State, annual rpt, issuing agency transfer, 4694–1
AFDC provisions, by State, annual rpt, issuing agency change, 4694–4
Energy aid for low income households, funding sources, costs, and participation, by State, annual rpt, issuing agency change, 4694–8
Energy aid for low income households, program characteristics by State, annual rpt, issuing agency change, 4694–9
Refugee arrivals and resettlement in US, by age, sex, sponsoring agency, State, and country, monthly rpt, 4592–1
Refugee arrivals and resettlement in US, by age, sex, sponsoring agency, State, and country, monthly rpt, issuing agency transfer, 4692–2
see also Administration for Children and Families

Famine
see Disasters

Famulari, Melissa
"Household-Based, Nonparametric Test of Demand Theory", 6886–6.88

Fannie Mae
see Federal National Mortgage Association

Fant, Mary L.
"Foreign Agricultural Trade of the U.S., 1991: Supplementary Tables", 1524–8

Farley, Donna O.
"Longitudinal Comparison of Charge-Based Weights and Cost-Based Weights", 4652–1.318

Farm costs
see Agricultural finance
see Agricultural production costs

Farm Costs and Returns Survey
Economic Indicators of the Farm Sector, itemized production costs, receipts, and returns, by commodity and region, 1975-90, annual rpt, 1544–20
Production itemized costs, receipts, and returns, by crop and State, 1987-89, annual rpt, 1544–24
Tobacco (flue-cured) farms and farm operators, by region and selected characteristics, 1970s-87, 1568–307

Farm Credit Administration
Budget of US, authoritative financial statements with appropriations, outlays, and receipts, by category and agency, FY91, annual rpt, 8104–2.2
Budget of US, obligations and authority by function, agency, and program, with summaries and analyses, FY93, annual rpt, 104–2
Farm Credit System financial statements and loan activity by lender type, and borrower characteristics, 1991, annual rpt, 9264–2
Financial condition of Farm Credit System, quarterly rpt, 9262–2
Financial condition of Farm Credit System, 1991, annual rpt, 9264–5

Farm Credit Banks
see Farm Credit System

Farm Credit System
Budget of US, financial statements of federally sponsored enterprises, FY93, annual rpt, 104–2.6
Business statistics, detailed data for major industries and economic indicators, *Survey of Current Business*, monthly rpt, 2702–1.8
Business statistics, detailed data for major industries and economic indicators, 1960-91, *Survey of Current Business* biennial supplement, 2704–1
Cooperatives loans, assets, net worth, and assns, for FCS by district, 1990, annual rpt, 1124–1
Economic Indicators of the Farm Sector, balance sheets, and receipts by detailed commodity, by State, 1986-90, annual rpt, 1544–18
Financial and marketing conditions of farms, forecast 1992, annual chartbook, 1504–8
Financial condition of FCS, quarterly rpt, 9262–2
Financial condition of FCS, 1990-91, article, 1122–1.301
Financial condition of FCS, 1991, annual rpt, 9264–5
Financial statements and loan activity by lender type, and borrower characteristics, 1991, annual rpt, 9264–2
Flow-of-funds accounts, savings, investments, and credit statements, quarterly rpt, 9365–3.3

Land transfers, by source of credit financing and region, 1982-92, article, 1561–16.302
Loans (farm) at risk of default, lender losses, and selected farm financial indicators, by type of farm and lender, 1984-89, 1548–383
Loans (farm) by purpose and source, quarterly rpt, 9365–3.10
Loans (farm) guaranteed by FmHA, characteristics of borrowers, lenders, and loans, FY88, 1548–386
Loans (farm) outstanding, and lenders financial condition, quarterly rpt with articles, 1541–1
Loans (farm) outstanding, by lender type and State, 1960-89, 1548–384
Member assns of FCS, by instn type and district, 1992 article, 1541–1.311
North Central States farm credit conditions and economic devs, Fed Reserve 7th District, monthly rpt, 9375–10
see also Federal Agricultural Mortgage Corp.

Farm debt
see Agricultural credit
see Agricultural finance

Farm income
Acreage of farmland, and operations, by sales size, region, and State, 1990-92, annual rpt, 1614–4
Agricultural Outlook, production, prices, marketing, and trade, by commodity, forecast and current situation, monthly rpt with articles, 1502–4
Agricultural situation and farm-related topics, monthly rpt, 1502–6
Agricultural Statistics, 1991, annual rpt, 1004–1
Appalachia food processing firms, employment, and shipments, and farm production, by commodity and State, 1960s-90, 9088–37
Business statistics, detailed data for major industries and economic indicators, *Survey of Current Business*, monthly rpt, 2702–1.3
Business statistics, detailed data for major industries and economic indicators, 1960-91, *Survey of Current Business* biennial supplement, 2704–1
Economic and social conditions, dev, and problems in rural areas, periodic journal, 1502–7
Economic Indicators of the Farm Sector, balance sheets, and receipts by detailed commodity, by State, 1986-90, annual rpt, 1544–18
Economic Indicators of the Farm Sector, itemized production costs, receipts, and returns, by commodity and region, 1975-90, annual rpt, 1544–20
Family farms financial condition, 1970s-88, annual rpt, 1504–4
Farm operators nonfarm self-employment income by source and farm profit and loss, and tax burden, 1987, article, 1541–1.320
Finances of farms, debts, assets, and receipts, and lenders financial condition, quarterly rpt with articles, 1541–1
Financial and marketing conditions of farms, forecast 1992, annual chartbook, 1504–8
Financial and marketing conditions of farms, forecast 1992, annual conf, 1504–9
Financial condition of farms, selected years 1939-91, annual rpt, 204–1.8
Fish (catfish) raised on farms, production, inventory, sales, prices, and imports, monthly release, 1631–14
Fish (trout) raised on farms, production, sales, prices, and losses, 1991-92, annual rpt, 1631–16
Fish hatcheries and farms, production, costs, prices, and sales, for catfish and trout, 1970s-92, semiannual situation rpt, 1561–15
Flower and foliage production, sales, prices, and growers, by crop and State, 1990-91 and planting planned 1992, annual rpt, 1631–8
Food assistance programs impacts on farm income, by commodity, model description and results, 1989-90, 1548–390
Fruit, nut, and berry farm income, acreage, prices received, and production costs, by commodity and region, 1987, article, 1561–6.301
Households (farm), by income level, 1989, annual Current Population Rpt, 2546–1.458
Income (household, family, and personal), by source, detailed characteristics, and region, 1991, annual Current Population Rpt, 2546–6.76
Income (personal) per capita and by source, and employment, by industry div, State, MSA, and county, 1969-90, annual CD-ROM, 2704–7
Income of farms, cash marketing receipts ranked by commodity and State, 1990, 1548–385
Irrigated farmland, farm characteristics, and water and fuel sources, by State and leading county, 1950s-88, 1588–122
Livestock grazing forage demand, and meat supply and demand, indicators, 1960s-90 and projected to 2030, 1208–404
Loans (farm) at risk of default, lender losses, and selected farm financial indicators, by type of farm and lender, 1984-89, 1548–383
Loans (farm) guaranteed by FmHA, characteristics of borrowers, lenders, and loans, FY88, 1548–386
Meat animal production, prices, receipts, and disposition, by species and State, 1990-91, annual rpt, 1623–8
Milk of manufacturing grade, fat content and prices received by farmers in Minnesota and Wisconsin, 1989-91, annual rpt, 1629–2
Milk production, use, and receipts, and milk cow inventory, by State, 1989-91, annual rpt, 1627–4
Mint oil production, yield, and farm prices by State, and NYC spot prices, 1989-92, FAS annual circular, 1925–15.2
Mushroom production, sales, and prices, by State, 1966/67-1991/92 and planned 1992/93, annual rpt, 1631–9
Natl income and product accounts and components, *Survey of Current Business*, monthly rpt, 2702–1.23
Natl income and product accounts, comprehensive accounts and components, benchmark revisions, 1929-88, 2708–5
Natl income and product accounts, comprehensive accounts and components, *Survey of Current Business*, monthly rpt, 2702–1.24
North Central States farm credit conditions and economic devs, Fed Reserve 7th District, monthly rpt, 9375–10
North Central States farm credit conditions, earnings, and expenses, Fed Reserve 9th District, quarterly rpt, 9383–11
Potato production, prices, stocks, and use, by State, 1980s-91, annual rpt, 1621–11
Poultry (chicken, egg, and turkey) production and prices, by State, 1990-91, annual rpt, 1625–5
Poultry and egg prices and marketing, by selected region, State, and city, monthly and weekly 1991, annual rpt, 1317–2
Poultry and egg production, prices, receipts, trade, and disposition, by species, 1960-90, annual rpt, 1564–13
Poverty status of population and families, by detailed characteristics, 1991, annual Current Population Rpt, 2546–6.77
Prices (farm-retail) for food, marketing cost components, and industry finances and productivity, 1920s-91, annual rpt, 1544–9
Prices received and paid by farmers, by commodity and State, monthly rpt, 1629–1
Prices received and paid by farmers, by commodity and State, 1991, annual rpt, 1629–5
Receipts, returns, itemized production costs, by crop and State, 1987-89, annual rpt, 1544–24
Rice foreign and US production, prices, trade, stocks, and use, periodic situation rpt, 1561–8
Rice production, practices, costs, and land tenure, by production area, 1988, 1568–309
Self-employed persons farm and nonfarm business income, 1989, article, 1541–1.301
Sheep and wool production, use, and prices, and operations costs and returns, for western US, 1920s-90, 1548–382
Southeastern States, Fed Reserve 5th District, economic indicators by State, quarterly rpt, 9389–16
Statistical Abstract of US, 1992 annual data compilation, 2324–1.23
Survey of Current Business, detailed data for major industries and economic indicators, monthly rpt, 2702–1.4
Tax (income) returns filed, by type of filer, selected income items, quarterly rpt, 8302–2.1
Tax (income) returns of corporations, income and tax items by asset size and detailed industry, 1989, annual rpt, 8304–4; 8304–21
Tax (income) returns of individuals, detailed data, 1988, annual rpt, 8304–2
Tax (income) returns of individuals, selected income and tax items by income level, preliminary 1990, annual article, 8302–2.307
Tax (income) returns of partnerships, income statement and balance sheet items, by industry group, 1990, annual article, 8302–2.314
Tobacco marketing activity, prices, and sales, by grade, type, market, and State, 1991, annual rpt series, 1319–5
Tobacco production, prices, stocks, taxes by State, and trade and production by country, 1991, annual rpt, 1319–1

Vegetable production, prices, trade, stocks, and use, for selected fresh and processing crops, periodic situation rpt with articles, 1561–11
West Central States economic indicators, Fed Reserve 10th District, quarterly rpt, 9381–16.2
see also Agricultural production quotas and price supports
see also Agricultural subsidies
see also Agricultural wages

Farm labor
see Agricultural labor
see Agricultural wages
see Farm operators
see Migrant workers

Farm machinery
see Agricultural machinery and equipment

Farm operators
Assets of farm sector by type, and real and nonreal estate debt, including and excluding operator households, by sales size, 1960-89, 1548–387
Crop subsidies of USDA, deficiency payments by payment size and producer form of organization, 1990, GAO rpt, 26113–574
Deaths and rates, by cause and selected social, demographic, and employment characteristics, 1979-85, natl longitudinal study, 4478–186
Educational attainment of farm operators, by age, 1890s-1990, article, 1541–1.316
Family farms financial condition, 1970s-88, annual rpt, 1504–4
Income of farm operators from nonfarm self-employment sources, and farm profit and loss, and tax burden, 1987, article, 1541–1.320
Insurance (health) coverage of farm operators, by source of insurance, 1989, article, 1541–1.318
Loans (farm) guaranteed by FmHA, characteristics of borrowers, lenders, and loans, FY88, 1548–386
Occupational Outlook Handbook, 1992-93, biennial rpt, 6744–1
Part-time farming, selected characteristics of operation, 1987, young readers pamphlet, 2346–1.6
Population on farms, by employment, social, and economic characteristics, and region, 1990, annual Current Population Rpt, 2546–1.458
Small business finances, operations, owner characteristics, and Federal contracts, 1980s-90, annual rpt, 9764–6
Statistical Abstract of US, 1992 annual data compilation, 2324–1.23
Tobacco (flue-cured) farms and farm operators, by region and selected characteristics, 1970s-87, 1568–307
Young farm operators acreage owned and rented by region, and method of acquisition of owned acreage, 1992 article, 1541–1.319

Farm population
Agricultural Statistics, 1991, annual rpt, 1004–1
Black Americans social and economic characteristics, for South and total US, 1991 and trends from 1950, annual Current Population Rpt, 2546–1.463
Data on agriculture, young readers pamphlet series, 2346–1
Europe farm household members off-farm employment, 1987, article, 1502–7.301
Financial condition of farm households, by farm sales size and region, 1990, article, 1541–1.315
Food produced and consumed on farms, natl income and product account benchmark revisions, 1929-88, 2708–5
Food produced and consumed on farms, natl income and product accounts, comprehensive accounts and components, *Survey of Current Business*, monthly rpt, 2702–1.25
Housing (rental) units, total, with HUD assistance by program, and eligible for aid, by unit, household, and neighborhood characteristics, and location, 1989, biennial rpt, 5184–11
Housing and households detailed characteristics, and unit and neighborhood quality, by location, 1989, biennial rpt supplement, 2485–13
Population on farms, by employment, social, and economic characteristics, and region, 1990, annual Current Population Rpt, 2546–1.458
Population on farms, employment, and labor productivity, 1947-90, annual rpt, 204–1.8
Rural areas economic and social conditions, dev, and problems, periodic journal, 1502–7
Statistical Abstract of US, 1992 annual data compilation, 2324–1.23
Western US activities of Reclamation Bur, land and population served, and recreation areas, by location, 1990, annual rpt, 5824–12
see also Farm operators

Farm prices
see Agricultural prices
see Food prices

Farmer Mac
see Federal Agricultural Mortgage Corp.

Farmers Home Administration
Activities of FmHA, and loans and grants by program and State, FY91 and trends from FY70, annual rpt, 1184–17
American Housing Survey: unit and households detailed characteristics, and unit and neighborhood quality, MSA rpt series, 2485–6
Borrowers, by loan type, borrower characteristics, and State, quarterly rpt, discontinued, 1182–8
Borrowers, by loan type, race, and State, quarterly rpt, 1182–5
Budget of US, obligations and authority by function, agency, and program, with summaries and analyses, FY93, annual rpt, 104–2
Disaster relief to farmers, Fed Govt costs by program, 1980s-92, GAO rpt, 26113–556
Economic Indicators of the Farm Sector, balance sheets, and receipts by detailed commodity, by State, 1986-90, annual rpt, 1544–18
Expenditures of Fed Govt in States, by type, program, agency, and State, FY91, annual rpt, 2464–2
Housing units (1-family) sold and sales price by type of financing, monthly rpt, quarterly tables, 2382–3.2
Housing units completed, single and multifamily units by structural and financial characteristics, and location, 1987-91, annual rpt, 2384–1
Loan guarantees of FmHA to business and industry in rural areas, by State and industry, and closures and defaults, FY74-91, GAO rpt, 26113–591
Loans (farm) at risk of default, lender losses, and selected farm financial indicators, by type of farm and lender, 1984-89, 1548–383
Loans (farm) by purpose and source, quarterly rpt, 9365–3.10
Loans (farm) guaranteed by FmHA, characteristics of borrowers, lenders, and loans, FY88, 1548–386
Loans (farm) outstanding, and lenders financial condition, quarterly rpt with articles, 1541–1
Loans (farm) outstanding, by lender type and State, 1960-89, 1548–384
Loans (farm and home) and borrower supervision activities, for FmHA programs, by State, monthly rpt, 1182–1
Loans (home) of FmHA for low income rental units in rural areas, and impacts of programs to maintain supply and to deter mortgage prepayment, 1988-91, GAO rpt, 26113–586
Loans of FmHA outstanding and delinquent, and lending practices, FY88-91, GAO rpt, 26113–569
Mortgage applications, dispositions, and secondary loan market sales, by purpose, lender type, and applicant and neighborhood characteristics, 1991, article, 9362–1.307
Property acquired by FmHA through foreclosure, acreage, value, and sales, for farm and nonfarm property by State, monthly rpt, 1182–6
Property acquired by FmHA through foreclosure, 1-family homes, value, sales, and leases, by State, monthly rpt, 1182–7

Farming
see Farm income
see Farm operators
see Farm population
see Farms and farmland
see under Agriculture and terms beginning with Agricultural
see under By Industry in the "Index by Categories"
see under By Occupation in the "Index by Categories"

Farms and farmland
Acreage of farmland, and operations, by sales size, region, and State, 1990-92, annual rpt, 1614–4
Acreage planted and harvested, by crop and State, 1990-91 and planned as of June 1992, annual rpt, 1621–23
Acreage planted, by selected crop and State, 1983-91 and planned 1992, annual rpt, 1621–22
Acreage, production, and related data, by selected crop and State, monthly rpt, 1621–1
Agricultural Economics Research, quarterly journal, 1502–3
Agricultural Outlook, production, prices, marketing, and trade, by commodity, forecast and current situation, monthly rpt with articles, 1502–4
Agricultural Statistics, 1991, annual rpt, 1004–1
Capital (fixed), govt and private nonresidential structures and equipment,

residential capital, and consumer-owned durable goods, 1925-90, annual article, 2702–1.305; 2702–1.327
Cattle and calves for beef, ranches, inventory, producers, and returns, by herd size and region, mid 1940s-91, 1568–251
Coastal and riparian areas environmental conditions, fish, wildlife, use, and mgmt, for individual ecosystems, series, 5506–9
Coastal areas and watersheds pollution indicators, by location, 1980s-90, 2178–35
Conservation program of USDA, acreage, projects, participation, and funding, by State, 1936-90, quinquennial rpt, 1808–1
Conservation program of USDA, participation and payments by practice and State, FY91, annual rpt, 1804–7
Construction put in place (public and private), by type, quarterly rpt, 2042–1.1
Construction put in place, value of new public and private structures, by type, monthly rpt, 2382–4
Data on agriculture, collection, methodology, and use for major time series of USDA, series, 1506–1
Data on agriculture, young readers pamphlet series, 2346–1
Economic and social conditions, dev, and problems in rural areas, periodic journal, 1502–7
Economic Indicators of the Farm Sector, balance sheets, and receipts by detailed commodity, by State, 1986-90, annual rpt, 1544–18
Economic Indicators of the Farm Sector, production inputs, output, and productivity, by commodity and region, 1947-90, annual rpt, 1544–17
Environmental Quality, status of problems, protection programs, research, and intl issues, 1991 annual rpt, 484–1
Family farms financial condition, 1970s-88, annual rpt, 1504–4
Flower and foliage production, sales, prices, and growers, by crop and State, 1990-91 and planting planned 1992, annual rpt, 1631–8
Foreign countries agricultural production, prices, and trade, by country, 1980-91 and forecast 1992, annual world area rpt series, 1524–4
Foreign countries economic, social, political, and geographic summary data, by country, 1992, annual factbook, 9114–2
Foreign ownership of US farmland, holdings, acquisitions, and disposals by land use, owner type and country, and State, 1991, annual rpt, 1584–2
Foreign ownership of US farmland, holdings, acreage, and value by land use, owner country, State, and county, 1991, annual rpt, 1584–3
Indian and govt lands under Bur of Indian Affairs mgmt, acreage, leases, and use, 1989, annual rpt, 5704–12
Japan investment in US farmland and agricultural industries, with data by State and county, late 1960s-90, 1528–332
Mink and pelt production, prices, and farms, selected years 1969-92, annual rpt, 1631–7
North Central States farm credit conditions and farmland market values, Fed Reserve 9th District, quarterly rpt, 9383–11
Real estate assets of failed thrifts, inventory of properties available from Resolution Trust Corp, 1991, semiannual listing, 9722–2.7
Real estate assets of failed thrifts, inventory of properties available from Resolution Trust Corp, 1992, semiannual listing, 9722–2.14
Research (agricultural) funding and staffing for USDA, State agencies, and other instns, by topic, FY91, annual rpt, 1744–2
Sheep and wool production, use, and prices, and operations costs and returns, for western US, 1920s-90, 1548–382
Southwestern US farm credit conditions and real estate values, Fed Reserve 11th District, quarterly rpt, 9379–11
Statistical Abstract of US, 1992 annual data compilation, 2324–1.23
Storage facility and equipment loans to farmers under CCC grain program, by State, monthly table, 1802–9
Swine inventory, value, farrowings, and farms, by State, quarterly release, 1623–3
Tobacco (flue-cured) farms and farm operators, by region and selected characteristics, 1970s-87, 1568–307
Value and transfers of farmland, production inputs, finances, and mgmt, periodic situation rpt with articles, 1561–16
Water pollution from farming, funding for control under Rural Clean Water Program by region and State, monthly rpt, 1802–14
Weather data for farmland, average precipitation and temperature by State, monthly 1950-90, biennial rpt, 1544–28
West Central States farm real estate values, farm loan trends, and regional farm price index, Fed Reserve 10th District, quarterly rpt, 9381–16.1
Wisconsin timber resources and removals, by species, forest type, ownership, and county, series, 1206–34
see also Agricultural accidents and safety
see also Agricultural credit
see also Agricultural education
see also Agricultural energy use
see also Agricultural exports and imports
see also Agricultural extension work
see also Agricultural finance
see also Agricultural forecasts
see also Agricultural insurance
see also Agricultural labor
see also Agricultural machinery and equipment
see also Agricultural marketing
see also Agricultural policy
see also Agricultural prices
see also Agricultural production
see also Agricultural production costs
see also Agricultural production quotas and price supports
see also Agricultural productivity
see also Agricultural sciences and research
see also Agricultural stocks
see also Agricultural subsidies
see also Agricultural surpluses
see also Agricultural wages
see also Farm income
see also Farm operators
see also Farm population
see also Farmers Home Administration
see also Fertilizers
see also Irrigation
see also Pasture and rangeland
see also Pesticides
see also Soil pollution
see also Soils and soil conservation

Faroe Islands
see Faeroes

Farris, Elizabeth
"Public School Principal Survey on Safe, Disciplined, and Drug-Free Schools", 4826–1.32

Fast food
see Restaurants and drinking places

Fast Response Survey System
Data on education, estimates from Fast Response Survey System, series, 4826–1

Fats and oils
see Oils, oilseeds, and fats

Fayetteville, N.C.
see also under By City and By SMSA or MSA in the "Index by Categories"

FBI
see Federal Bureau of Investigation

FCC
see Federal Communications Commission

FDA
see Food and Drug Administration

Federal advisory bodies
see Federal boards, committees, and commissions

Federal agencies
see Federal boards, committees, and commissions
see Federal executive departments
see Federal independent agencies
see under By Federal Agency in the "Index by Categories"

Federal agencies fraud, waste, and abuse investigations
see Federal Inspectors General reports

Federal Agricultural Mortgage Corp.
Credit availability and farms eligibility, for Farmer Mac, 1989, article, 1541–1.304

Federal aid programs
Assistance (financial and nonfinancial) of Fed Govt, 1992 base edition, annual listing, 104–5
Budget deficit reduction under Gramm-Rudman Act, CBO sequestration estimates, FY93, annual rpt, 26304–6
Budget of US, authoritative financial statements with appropriations, outlays, and receipts, by category and agency, FY91, annual rpt, 8104–2.2
Budget of US, balances of budget authority obligated and unobligated, by function and agency, FY90-93, annual rpt, 104–8
Budget of US, CBO analysis and review of FY93 budget by function, annual rpt, 26304–2
Budget of US, CBO analysis of revenue and spending alternatives and projections of economic indicators, FY93-97, annual rpt, 26304–3
Budget of US, House Budget Committee analysis of Bush Admin proposals and economic assumptions, FY93, 21268–42
Budget of US, House concurrent resolution, with spending and revenue targets, FY93 and projected to FY97, annual rpt, 21264–2
Budget of US, midsession review of FY93 budget, by function, annual rpt, 104–7

Budget of US, obligations and authority by function, agency, and program, with summaries and analyses, FY93, annual rpt, 104–2
Budget of US, receipts by source, outlays by agency and program, and balances, monthly rpt, 8102–3
Criminal cases by type and disposition, and collections, for US attorneys, by Federal district, FY91, annual rpt, 6004–2.1
Drug abuse and trafficking offenders losing Federal benefits under new sentencing guidelines, by selected characteristics, 1990-91, GAO rpt, 26119–398
Economic Report of the President for 1992, with economic trends from 1929, annual rpt, 204–1
Expenditures (direct) and employment, by function and level of govt, selected years 1962-87, 10048–53
Expenditures of Fed Govt, by function, FY90, annual rpt, 2466–2.2
Expenditures of Fed Govt in States and local areas, by type, State, county, and city, FY91, annual rpt, 2464–3
Expenditures of Fed Govt in States, by type, program, agency, and State, FY91, annual rpt, 2464–2
Finances of Fed Govt, cash and debt transactions, daily tables, 8102–4
Fiscal policy (supply side) of Reagan Admin, economic impacts, 1980s and trends from 1960s, technical paper, 9385–1.304; 9385–8.125
Investigations of Federal agency and program operations, summaries of findings, as of 1991, annual GAO rpt, 26104–5
Labor productivity of Federal employees, indexes of output and labor costs by function, FY67-90, annual rpt, 6824–1.6
Loans and loan guarantees of Fed Govt, outstanding amounts by agency and program, *Treasury Bulletin*, quarterly rpt, 8002–4.11
Loans, loan guarantees, and grants of Fed Govt, administrative costs budget accounting, by program and agency, 1992 rpt, 26306–6.166
Natl income and product accounts, comprehensive accounts and components, benchmark revisions, 1929-88, 2708–5
Natl income and product accounts, comprehensive accounts and components, *Survey of Current Business*, monthly rpt, 2702–1.26
Statistical Abstract of US, 1992 annual data compilation, 2324–1.9
see also Agricultural credit
see also Agricultural production quotas and price supports
see also Agricultural subsidies
see also Agricultural surpluses
see also Aid to Families with Dependent Children
see also Child welfare
see also Community Development Block Grants
see also Federal aid to arts and humanities
see also Federal aid to education
see also Federal aid to higher education
see also Federal aid to highways
see also Federal aid to housing
see also Federal aid to law enforcement
see also Federal aid to libraries
see also Federal aid to local areas
see also Federal aid to medical education
see also Federal aid to medicine
see also Federal aid to railroads
see also Federal aid to rural areas
see also Federal aid to States
see also Federal aid to transportation
see also Federal aid to vocational education
see also Federal funding for energy programs
see also Federal funding for research and development
see also Federally Funded R&D Centers
see also Food assistance
see also Food stamp programs
see also Government and business
see also Head Start Project
see also Income maintenance
see also Legal aid
see also Manpower training programs
see also Medicaid
see also Medical assistance
see also Medicare
see also Old-Age, Survivors, Disability, and Health Insurance
see also Public housing
see also Public service employment
see also Public welfare programs
see also Rent supplements
see also Revenue sharing
see also School lunch and breakfast programs
see also Shipbuilding and operating subsidies
see also Social security
see also Student aid
see also Subsidies
see also Supplemental Security Income
see also Tax expenditures
see also Unemployment insurance
see also Urban Development Action Grants
see also Veterans benefits and pensions
see also Veterans health facilities and services
see also Veterans housing

Federal aid to agriculture
see Agricultural credit
see Agricultural production quotas and price supports
see Agricultural subsidies
see Agricultural surpluses
see Federal aid to rural areas

Federal aid to arts and humanities
Assistance (financial and nonfinancial) of Fed Govt, 1992 base edition, annual listing, 104–5
Budget of US, obligations and authority by function, agency, and program, with summaries and analyses, FY93, annual rpt, 104–2
Expenditures for arts, by level of govt, State, and selected city, FY86-92, GAO rpt, 26119–371
Expenditures of Fed Govt in States, by type, program, agency, and State, FY91, annual rpt, 2464–2
Museum Services Inst activities and finances, and grants by recipient, FY91, annual rpt, 9564–7
Museum Services Inst grants, by recipient, annual press release series, discontinued, 9564–6
Natl Endowment for Arts activities and grants, FY91, annual rpt, 9564–3
Natl Endowment for Humanities activities and grants, FY91, annual rpt, 9564–2
Smithsonian Instn activities and finances, FY91, annual rpt, 29574–1
Statistical Abstract of US, 1992 annual data compilation, 2324–1.7

Federal aid to business
see Government and business
see Subsidies

Federal aid to cities
see Federal aid to local areas

Federal aid to education
Adult education and literacy programs funding, enrollment, and activities, fact sheet series, 4806–4
Appalachia local dev projects, and funding by source, by program and State, FY91, annual rpt, 9084–1
Arts Natl Endowment activities and grants, FY91, annual rpt, 9564–3
Asbestos in schools, abatement funding and costs by selected State, 1988-91, GAO rpt, 26113–560
Assistance (block and categorical grants) programs for State and local govts, FY91, biennial listing, 10044–8
Assistance (financial and nonfinancial) of Fed Govt, 1992 base edition, annual listing, 104–5
Bilingual education enrollment, and eligible students not enrolled, by State, 1990-91, annual rpt, 4804–14
Budget of US, balances of budget authority obligated and unobligated, by function and agency, FY90-93, annual rpt, 104–8
Budget of US, Bush Admin proposals, with detail for defense budgets, and historical data from FY34, FY93, 108–46
Budget of US, CBO analysis and review of FY93 budget by function, annual rpt, 26304–2
Budget of US, CBO analysis of revenue and spending alternatives and projections of economic indicators, FY93-97, annual rpt, 26304–3
Budget of US, House concurrent resolution, with spending and revenue targets, FY93 and projected to FY97, annual rpt, 21264–2
Budget of US, midsession review of FY93 budget, by function, annual rpt, 104–7
Budget of US, obligations and authority by function, agency, and program, with summaries and analyses, FY93, annual rpt, 104–2
Budget of US, receipts by source, outlays by agency and program, and balances, monthly rpt, 8102–3
Compensatory education grants, and allocation by function, for 8 school districts, 1990/91, GAO rpt, 26121–478
Condition of Education, detail for elementary, secondary, and higher education, 1920s-91 and projected to 2002, annual rpt, 4824–1
Construction put in place, by type of construction, quarterly rpt, 2042–1.1
Digest of Education Statistics, 1992 annual data compilation, 4824–2
Drug abuse and trafficking reduction programs activities, funding, staff, and Bush Admin budget request, by Federal agency, FY91-93, annual rpt, 234–2
Education Dept financial aid programs, 1992 annual listing, 4804–3
Elementary and secondary public school systems enrollment, finances, staff, and high school grads, by State, FY89-90, annual rpt, 4834–6

Expenditures (direct) and employment, by function and level of govt, selected years 1962-87, 10048–53
Expenditures for education by Federal agency, program, and recipient type, and instn spending, 1960s-91, annual rpt, 4824–8
Expenditures for public welfare by program, FY50s-89, annual article, 4742–1.319
Expenditures for public welfare programs, by program type and level of govt, FY65-89, annual article, 4742–1.302
Expenditures of Fed Govt in States, by type, program, agency, and State, FY91, annual rpt, 2464–2
Finances of Fed Govt, cash and debt transactions, daily tables, 8102–4
Finances of govts, by level of govt, State, and for large cities and counties, annual rpt series, 2466–2
Finances of govts, tax systems and revenue, and fiscal structure, by level of govt and State, 1992 and historical trends, annual rpt, 10044–1
Fiscal policy (supply side) of Reagan Admin, economic impacts, 1980s and trends from 1960s, technical paper, 9385–1.304; 9385–8.125
Fraud and abuse in Education Dept programs, audits and investigations, 2nd half FY92, semiannual rpt, 4802–1
Handicapped children early education project descriptions, 1991/92, annual listing, 4944–10
Homeless persons aid by program and Federal agency, and indicators of need, 1990, annual rpt, 14364–1
Homeless persons aid programs of Fed Govt, program descriptions and funding, by agency and State, FY87-91, annual GAO rpt, 26104–21
Humanities Natl Endowment activities and grants, FY91, annual rpt, 9564–2
Indian education funding of Fed Govt, with enrollment, program grants, and fellowships by State, 1980s-FY91, annual rpt, 14874–1
Investigations of Federal agency and program operations, summaries of findings, as of 1991, annual GAO rpt, 26104–5.3
Juvenile facilities compensatory education programs activities, participant and staff characteristics, and outcomes, 1991 rpts, 4808–40
Labor productivity of Federal employees, indexes of output and labor costs by function, FY67-90, annual rpt, 6824–1.6
Lands (public) acreage and grants, by State, FY91 and trends, annual rpt, 5724–1.1
Literacy program for preschoolers and parents, Even Start program activities and grants by recipient, FY90, annual listing, 4804–41
Literacy programs in workplaces, demonstration projects funding and participants, FY88-90, 4808–43
Literacy programs in workplaces, project descriptions and Education Dept funding, FY91, annual listing, 4804–40
Mail operating costs of USPS, itemized by class of mail, FY91, annual rpt, 9864–4
Mail revenue, costs, and volume, by class of mail, FY91, annual rpt, 9864–2
Mail volume, revenues, and subsidies for revenue forgone, by class of mail, FY91, annual rpt, 9864–5.3
Military service academies prep schools costs and student performance indicators, 1988-90, GAO rpt, 26123–380
Minority business funding, by program and Federal agency, FY91, annual rpt, 2104–5
NASA and contractor cooperative education programs activities, 1991, 9508–41
Natl Education Goals progress indicators, by State, 1992, annual rpt, 15914–1
Natl income and product accounts, comprehensive accounts and components, benchmark revisions, 1929-88, 2708–5
Natl income and product accounts, comprehensive accounts and components, *Survey of Current Business*, monthly rpt, 2702–1.26
NSF activities, finances, and funding by program, FY91, annual rpt, 9624–6
R&D funding by Fed Govt, by detailed function, program, and agency, FY91-93, annual rpt, 9627–9
Research on education, field projects funding and descriptions, FY90-91, annual listing, 4884–1
Science and math teacher dev project of Education Dept, school district participation by State, 1989/90, GAO rpt, 26121–488
Special education programs, enrollment by age, staff, funding, and needs, by type of handicap and State, 1990/91, annual rpt, 4944–4
Statistical Abstract of US, 1992 annual data compilation, 2324–1.4
Women's educational equity program grants and contracts, by project, type, and State, 1988-92, annual rpt, 4804–2
see also Federal aid to higher education
see also Federal aid to medical education
see also Federal aid to vocational education
see also Head Start Project
see also School lunch and breakfast programs
see also Student aid
see also Veterans education

Federal aid to energy programs
see Federal funding for energy programs

Federal aid to higher education
Agricultural research funding and staffing for USDA, State agencies, and other instns, by topic, FY91, annual rpt, 1744–2
AID contracts and grants for technical and support services, by instn, country, and State, FY91, annual listing, 9914–7
AID contracts, grants, and cooperative agreements with higher education instns, by project, instn, and country, FY91, annual listing, 9914–6
Arkansas govt science agency research grants and industry sponsors matching funds, and Federal R&D aid to higher education instns, mid 1980s-90, hearing, 21708–131
Assistance (block and categorical grants) programs for State and local govts, FY91, biennial listing, 10044–8
Assistance (financial and nonfinancial) of Fed Govt, 1992 base edition, annual listing, 104–5
Black higher education instns enrollment, finances, staff, and degrees, by instn and selected student characteristics, 1970s-90, 4848–46
Budget of US, obligations and authority by function, agency, and program, with summaries and analyses, FY93, annual rpt, 104–2
Digest of Education Statistics, 1992 annual data compilation, 4824–2
DOE contracts and grants, by category, State, and for top contractors, FY91, annual rpt, 3004–21
DOE R&D projects and funding at natl labs, universities, and other instns, periodic summary rpt series, 3004–18
Engineering research and education grants of NSF, FY91, annual listing, 9624–24
Expenditures for education by Federal agency, program, and recipient type, and instn spending, 1960s-91, annual rpt, 4824–8
Expenditures of Fed Govt in States, by type, program, agency, and State, FY91, annual rpt, 2464–2
Finances, enrollment, faculty, and degrees in higher education, by instn level and control, and State, FY88, annual rpt, 4844–13
Finances of higher education instns, revenue by source and spending by function, by State and instn control, FY82-90, annual rpt, 4844–6
Forest Service activities and finances, by region and State, FY91, annual rpt, 1204–1.3
HHS financial aid, by program, recipient, State, and city, FY91, annual regional listings, 4004–3
Humanities Natl Endowment activities and grants, FY91, annual rpt, 9564–2
Libraries (research) funding of Education Dept, by project, instn, and State, FY90, annual listing, 4874–2
Military prime contract awards, by category, contract and contractor type, and service branch, FY82-1st half FY92, semiannual rpt, 3542–1
Military prime contract awards, by category, contractor type, and State, FY89-91, annual rpt, 3544–11
Military prime contract awards for R&D, for top 500 contractors, FY91, annual listing, 3544–4
Military prime contract awards for R&D to US and foreign nonprofit instns and govt agencies, by instn and location, FY91, annual listing, 3544–17
NASA funding by program and type of performer, and contract awards by State, FY91, annual rpt, 9504–6.2
NASA procurement contract awards, by type, contractor, State, and country, FY92 with trends from 1961, semiannual rpt, 9502–6
NASA R&D funding to higher education instns, by field, instn, and State, FY91, annual listing, 9504–7
Natl income and product accounts, comprehensive accounts and components, benchmark revisions, 1929-88, 2708–5
Natl income and product accounts, comprehensive accounts and components, *Survey of Current Business*, monthly rpt, 2702–1.26

NIH grants and contracts, by inst and type of recipient, FY82-91, annual rpt, 4434–9
NSF grants and contracts, by field, recipient, and State, FY90, annual rpt, 9624–26
NSF R&D grant awards, by div and program, periodic rpt series, 9626–7
Oil enhanced recovery research contracts of DOE, project summaries, funding, and bibl, quarterly rpt, 3002–14
R&D and related funding of Fed Govt to higher education and nonprofit instns, by field, instn, agency, and State, FY89, advance annual rpt, 9626–8.2; 9627–17
R&D and related funding of Fed Govt to higher education, by field, instn, agency, and State, FY90, advance annual rpt, 9626–8.6
R&D facilities of higher education instns, space and equipment adequacy, needs, and funding by source, by instn type and control, 1992, biennial rpt, 9624–25
R&D funding by Fed Govt for higher education instns, indirect costs and effects of alternative reimbursement policies, FY89, GAO rpt, 26113–592
R&D funding by higher education instns and federally funded centers, by field, instn, and State, FY90, advance annual rpt, 9626–8.5
R&D funding by higher education instns and federally funded centers, by field, instn, and State, FY90, annual rpt, 9627–13
R&D funding by higher education instns and federally funded centers, by field, instn, and State, FY91, advance annual rpt, 9626–8.7
R&D grants of NSF for undergrads, administrator and recipient characteristics and views, 1987-89, 9628–86
R&D licenses for university activities supported by NSF and NIH, transfer to private firms, related income, and scientists associated with licensees, FY89-90, GAO rpt, 26113–575
Science and engineering curricula improvement grants of NSF for higher education instns, recipient characteristics and views, 1985-87, 9628–87
Science and Engineering Indicators, employment, education, R&D funding, and industry impacts, with foreign comparisons, 1960s-91, biennial rpt, 9624–10
Science and engineering labor force, Federal and university research funding, and educational data, series, 9626–6
Transit systems research and training grants to higher education instns, by project, FY92, annual listing, 7884–7
see also Federal aid to medical education
see also Student aid
see also Veterans education
see also Work-study programs

Federal aid to highways
Appalachia hwy system and access roads funding and completion status, by State, quarterly tables, 9082–1
Appalachia local dev projects, and funding by source, by program and State, FY91, annual rpt, 9084–1
Assistance (financial and nonfinancial) of Fed Govt, 1992 base edition, annual listing, 104–5
Bridge replacement and repair program funding by bridge, and bridge status, by State, 1990, biennial rpt, 7554–27
Census of Population and intercensal data use in Federal formula grant allocation, with data by program and State, FY91, 25408–120
Colorado River Storage Project finances and activities in western States, FY91, annual rpt, 5824–3
Construction (hwy) minority contractor training, funding by region, FY92, annual release, 7554–40
Construction bids and contracts for Federal-aid hwys, by State, 1st half 1992, semiannual rpt, 7552–12
Construction material prices and indexes for Federal-aid hwy system, by type of material and urban-rural location, quarterly rpt, 7552–7
Construction material prices and indexes for Federal-aid hwy system, by type of material, quarterly press release, 7552–16
Construction material use by type, and spending for hwys, by State, 1940s-91, annual rpt, 7554–29
Construction put in place, by type of construction, quarterly rpt, 2042–1.1
Construction spending by Fed Govt, by type of structure, FY85-92, annual article, 2042–1.303
DOT planning and safety grants, by program, State, and for 40 SMSAs, FY89, annual rpt, 7304–7
Expenditures and allocation methods, for Federal-aid hwy system, FY92-97, 7558–107
Expenditures, costs for completion, and mileage of Federal-aid hwy system, by State, 1989-91 and projected to FY93, 21648–66
Expenditures for hwy and transit system programs, proposed FY92-97, 7558–117
Expenditures of Fed Govt, by function, FY90, annual rpt, 2466–2.2
Expenditures of Fed Govt in States, by type, program, agency, and State, FY91, annual rpt, 2464–2
FHwA funding for hwys, FY79-89, annual rpt, 7304–1
Finances of govts, tax systems and revenue, and fiscal structure, by level of govt and State, 1992 and historical trends, annual rpt, 10044–1
Forest Service activities and finances, by region and State, FY91, annual rpt, 1204–1.1
Forests (natl) timber sales, expenses, and operations, by region, State, and natl forest, FY91, annual rpts, 1204–36
Hwy Statistics, detailed data by State, 1991, annual rpt, 7554–1
Hwy Statistics, summary data by State, 1990-91, annual rpt, 7554–24
Hwy Statistics, summary data with trends and projections, 1992 chartbook, 7554–41
Interstate hwy mileage, by completion status and State, as of June 1992, semiannual rpt, 7552–5
R&D for hwy design and construction, quarterly journal, 7552–3
Safety program funding by State, and accident and death reductions, FY91, annual rpt, 7554–26
Scenic byway routes and mileage, by govt ownership, land use and usage restrictions, and other characteristics, 1990, 7558–112
State govt revenue by source, spending and debt by function, and holdings, FY91, annual rpt, 2466–2.6
Traffic safety grants and activities of Natl Hwy Traffic Safety Admin, and fatal traffic accident data, 1990, annual rpt, 7764–1
Trust funds financial condition, for hwys, monthly rpt, 8102–9.7
Urban areas transit systems and hwys, Federal aid by selected State, aggregate FY76-91, GAO rpt, 26113–570

Federal aid to housing
AID housing and urban dev program, FY91, annual rpt, 9914–4
Apartment units completed, by type and for units under Federal subsidy, 1970-90, annual rpt, 2484–2
Apartment units completed under Federal subsidy, 1970-91, annual rpt, 2484–3
Appalachia local dev projects, and funding by source, by program and State, FY91, annual rpt, 9084–1
Assistance (block and categorical grants) programs for State and local govts, FY91, biennial listing, 10044–8
Assistance (financial and nonfinancial) of Fed Govt, 1992 base edition, annual listing, 104–5
Assistance for housing and community dev programs of HUD, press release series, 5006–3
Assistance programs under Ways and Means Committee jurisdiction, finances, operations, and participant characteristics, FY70s-91, annual rpt, 21784–11
Budget of US, balances of budget authority obligated and unobligated, by function and agency, FY90-93, annual rpt, 104–8
Budget of US, CBO analysis and review of FY93 budget by function, annual rpt, 26304–2
Budget of US, CBO analysis of revenue and spending alternatives and projections of economic indicators, FY93-97, annual rpt, 26304–3
Budget of US, House concurrent resolution, with spending and revenue targets, FY93 and projected to FY97, annual rpt, 21264–2
Budget of US, midsession review of FY93 budget, by function, annual rpt, 104–7
Budget of US, obligations and authority by function, agency, and program, with summaries and analyses, FY93, annual rpt, 104–2
Community Dev Block Grant activities and funding, by program, FY75-91, annual rpt, 5124–8
Construction put in place, by type of construction, quarterly rpt, 2042–1.1
Construction spending by Fed Govt, by type of structure, FY85-92, annual article, 2042–1.303
Expenditures for public welfare by program, FY50s-89, annual article, 4742–1.319
Expenditures for public welfare programs, by program type and level of govt, FY65-89, annual article, 4742–1.302
Expenditures of Fed Govt in States, by type, program, agency, and State, FY91, annual rpt, 2464–2

Fed Home Loan Banks affordable housing program operations, 1990, hearing, 21248–170
Finances of govts, by level of govt, State, and for large cities and counties, annual rpt series, 2466–2
Fraud and abuse in HUD programs, audits and investigations, FY92, semiannual rpt, 5002–8; 5002–11
Fraud and abuse in HUD programs, financial and program mgmt improvement activities, FY91, annual rpt, 5004–9
Govt Natl Mortgage Assn finances, and mortgage-backed securities program, FY91, annual rpt, 5144–6
Homeless persons aid by program and Federal agency, and indicators of need, 1990, annual rpt, 14364–1
Homeless persons aid programs of Fed Govt, program descriptions and funding, by agency and State, FY87-91, annual GAO rpt, 26104–21
Homeless persons housing and support services projects, funding, and clients, by organization, FY87 and FY90, GAO rpt, 26113–593
HUD activities, and housing programs operations and funding, 1990, annual rpt, 5004–10
Indian (Navajo and Hopi) relocation program activities and caseloads, monthly rpt, 16002–1
Loans and loan guarantees of Fed Govt, outstanding amounts by agency and program, *Treasury Bulletin*, quarterly rpt, 8002–4.11
Low income housing developers tax credits, subsidies, project and tenant characteristics, and investor returns, 1987-88, 5188–133
Natl income and product accounts, comprehensive accounts and components, benchmark revisions, 1929-88, 2708–5
Natl income and product accounts, comprehensive accounts and components, *Survey of Current Business*, monthly rpt, 2702–1.26
Rehabilitation of rental housing, HUD funding and activities by program and region, FY91, annual rpt, 5124–7
Tax (income) returns of individuals, detailed data, 1988, annual rpt, 8304–2
see also Farmers Home Administration
see also Housing (FHA), HUD
see also Mortgages
see also Public housing
see also Rent supplements
see also Veterans housing

Federal aid to law enforcement
Activities of Justice Dept, FY91, annual rpt, 6004–1
Asset Forfeiture Program of Justice Dept, seizures, finances, and disbursements, FY85-91, annual rpt, 6004–21
Assistance (block and categorical grants) programs for State and local govts, FY91, biennial listing, 10044–8
Assistance (financial and nonfinancial) of Fed Govt, 1992 base edition, annual listing, 104–5
Budget of US, Bush Admin proposals, with detail for defense budgets, and historical data from FY34, FY93, 108–46
Budget of US, CBO analysis and review of FY93 budget by function, annual rpt, 26304–2
Budget of US, CBO analysis of revenue and spending alternatives and projections of economic indicators, FY93-97, annual rpt, 26304–3
Budget of US, House concurrent resolution, with spending and revenue targets, FY93 and projected to FY97, annual rpt, 21264–2
Budget of US, midsession review of FY93 budget, by function, annual rpt, 104–7
Budget of US, obligations and authority by function, agency, and program, with summaries and analyses, FY93, annual rpt, 104–2
Budget of US, receipts by source, outlays by agency and program, and balances, monthly rpt, 8102–3
Driving while intoxicated enforcement incentive grants of Natl Hwy Traffic Safety Admin, by State, 1992 press release, 7306–10.4
Drug abuse and trafficking reduction programs activities, funding, staff, and Bush Admin budget request, by Federal agency, FY91-93, annual rpt, 234–2
Drug abuse and trafficking reduction programs funding, and Bush Admin budget request, by Federal agency, FY91-93, annual rpt, 234–1
Drug abuse and trafficking reduction research funding by Natl Inst on Drug Abuse and Office of Justice Programs, 1970s-91, GAO rpt, 26131–99
Drug abuse, treatment, and enforcement issues, series, 236–3
Drug abuse treatment, prevention, and enforcement grants by State, and State allocations by program, FY87-90, 6068–252
Drug enforcement activities of DOD, funding by purpose, FY89-91, GAO rpt, 26123–390
Drug enforcement grants of Fed Govt, and allocations to local govts, by State, FY91, annual rpt, 6064–38
Expenditures (direct) and employment, by function and level of govt, selected years 1962-87, 10048–53
Expenditures and employment for law enforcement, by activity and level of govt, data compilation, 1992 annual rpt, 6064–6.1
Expenditures, employment, and payroll, by activity, level of govt, and State, FY90, annual rpt, 6066–25.50
Expenditures of Fed Govt in States, by type, program, agency, and State, FY91, annual rpt, 2464–2
Fingerprint identification system of FBI, automation costs, staff, and workload, FY90 and projected to FY2000, 26358–253
Marijuana crop eradication activities of DEA and local agencies by State, and drug potency and prices, 1982-91, annual rpt, 6284–4
Marine mammals protection activities and funding, populations, and harvests, by species, 1990, annual rpt, 5504–12
Marshals Service activities, FY91, annual rpt, 6294–1
Money laundering investigation activities of States and Fed Govt, and use of IRS large cash transaction rpts, by State, 1985-91, GAO rpt, 26119–430
Natl income and product accounts, comprehensive accounts and components, benchmark revisions, 1929-88, 2708–5
Natl income and product accounts, comprehensive accounts and components, *Survey of Current Business*, monthly rpt, 2702–1.26
Office of Justice Programs activities and funding, FY91, annual rpt, 6064–18
Prison and community-based facilities, population, employment, spending, and other characteristics, by State and for Fed Govt, 1990, annual rpt, 6064–26.3; 6068–218
Prison construction and operating costs, capacity, and inmates, for Federal and State facilities, 1985-89, GAO rpt, 26119–407
R&D funding by Fed Govt, by detailed function, program, and agency, FY91-93, annual rpt, 9627–9
Research and program evaluation for criminal justice, Natl Inst of Justice grants by recipient, FY91, 6066–20.24
Victims of crime, compensation and support service programs funding, by offense and State, FY88-90, biennial rpt, 6064–37
Victims of crime, compensation and support service programs operations, series, 6066–31

Federal aid to libraries
Agricultural research and education appropriations of USDA, by program and subagency, FY83-91, annual rpt, 1004–19
Assistance (financial and nonfinancial) of Fed Govt, 1992 base edition, annual listing, 104–5
Blind and disabled persons library services, readership, circulation, staff, funding, and holdings, FY91, annual listing, 26404–3
Expenditures (direct) and employment, by function and level of govt, selected years 1962-87, 10048–53
Expenditures for education by Federal agency, program, and recipient type, and instn spending, 1960s-91, annual rpt, 4824–8
Expenditures of Fed Govt in States, by type, program, agency, and State, FY91, annual rpt, 2464–2
Humanities Natl Endowment activities and grants, FY91, annual rpt, 9564–2
Indian and Hawaii Native public libraries services, project listing and funding by tribe and State, FY90, annual rpt, 4874–5
Mail operating costs of USPS, itemized by class of mail, FY91, annual rpt, 9864–4
Mail revenue and subsidy for revenue forgone, by class of mail, FY91, and volume from FY87, annual rpt, 9864–1
Mail revenue, costs, and volume, by class of mail, FY91, annual rpt, 9864–2
Mail volume, revenues, and subsidies for revenue forgone, by class of mail, FY91, annual rpt, 9864–5
Natl Archives and Records Admin activities, finances, holdings, and staff, FY91, annual rpt, 9514–2
Natl Commission on Libraries and Info Science activities, FY91, annual rpt, 15634–1
NIH grants and contracts, quarterly listing, 4432–1

Public libraries finances, staff, and operations, by State and population size, 1990, annual rpt, 4824–6
Research and demonstration projects for libraries, and funding, FY67-86, listing, 4878–5
Research library funding of Education Dept, by project, instn, and State, FY90, annual listing, 4874–2
Training in library science, grants for disadvantaged students, by instn and State, FY91, annual listing, 4874–1

Federal aid to local areas
AIDS patients health care and support services funding under Ryan White CARE Act, and Federal grants by metro area, 1991, article, 4042–3.352
Appalachian Regional Commission funding, by project and State, planned FY92, annual rpt, 9084–3
Arts Natl Endowment activities and grants, FY91, annual rpt, 9564–3
Assistance (block and categorical grants) programs for State and local govts, FY91, biennial listing, 10044–8
Assistance (financial and nonfinancial) of Fed Govt, 1992 base edition, annual listing, 104–5
Birds (northern spotted owl) conservation methods in Pacific Northwest, timber industry impacts, and Federal and State spending, 1980s-95, 1208–388
Block grants discretionary spending, congressional changes to set-aside and cost-ceiling requirements for 11 programs, FY82-91, GAO rpt, 26121–466
Budget of US, House Budget Committee analysis of Bush Admin proposals and economic assumptions, FY93, 21268–42
Budget of US, midsession review of FY93 budget, by function, annual rpt, 104–7
Budget of US, obligations and authority by function, agency, and program, with summaries and analyses, FY93, annual rpt, 104–2
DOT planning and safety grants, by program, State, and for 40 SMSAs, FY89, annual rpt, 7304–7
Drug abuse and trafficking reduction programs activities, funding, staff, and Bush Admin budget request, by Federal agency, FY91-93, annual rpt, 234–2
Economic Dev Admin activities, and funding by program, recipient, State, and county, FY91 and cumulative from FY66, annual rpt, 2064–2
Economic indicators and components, current data and annual trends, monthly rpt, 23842–1.6
Education funding by Federal agency, program, and recipient type, and instn spending, 1960s-91, annual rpt, 4824–8
EPA pollution control grant program activities, monthly rpt, 9182–8
Expenditures (direct) and employment, by function and level of govt, selected years 1962-87, 10048–53
Expenditures of Fed Govt in States and local areas, by type, State, county, and city, FY91, annual rpt, 2464–3
Expenditures of Fed Govt in States, by type, program, agency, and State, FY91, annual rpt, 2464–2
Finances of govts, by level of govt, State, and for large cities and counties, annual rpt series, 2466–2
HHS financial aid, by program, recipient, State, and city, FY91, annual regional listings, 4004–3
Homeless persons aid programs of Fed Govt, program descriptions and funding, by agency and State, FY87-91, annual GAO rpt, 26104–21
Housing (rental) rehabilitation funding and activities of HUD, by program and region, FY91, annual rpt, 5124–7
Indian (Navajo and Hopi) relocation program activities and caseloads, monthly rpt, 16002–1
Indian crime victim compensation and support service programs operations, 1988-90, 6066–31.1
Indian education funding of Fed Govt, with enrollment, program grants, and fellowships by State, 1980s-FY91, annual rpt, 14874–1
Jails providing housing to Marshals Service prisoners, funding and surplus property awards, FY91, annual rpt, 6294–1
Labor surplus areas eligible for preferential Fed Govt contracts, monthly listing, 6402–1
Land and Water Conservation Fund allocations for outdoor recreation area dev, by State, FY93, annual table, 5544–15
Lands (public) acreage, grants, use, revenues, and allocations, by State, FY91, annual rpt, 5724–1.3
Literacy program for preschoolers and parents, Even Start program activities and grants by recipient, FY90, annual listing, 4804–41
Loans and loan guarantees of Fed Govt, outstanding amounts by agency and program, *Treasury Bulletin*, quarterly rpt, 8002–4.11
Michigan local areas economic conditions and public services impacts of reductions in Federal aid, with background data, 1970s-91, GAO rpt, 26121–483
Neighborhood Dev Demonstration program evaluation, grantee organization characteristics, activities, finances, and private sector support, 1984-89, 5188–119
Public works financing, use, and condition, 1990 hearing, 21648–67
Railroad (commuter) and other transit systems grants of Fed Transit Admin, FY93, annual rpt, 7884–12
San Antonio, Tex, govt funding for public housing and health, with background data, 1989-91, hearing, 21248–172
Transit systems finances and operations, by mode, size of fleet and urban area, region, and for 518 systems, 1990, annual rpt, 7884–4
Transit systems grants of Federal Transit Admin, by city and State, FY91, annual rpt, 7884–10
see also Community Development Block Grants
see also Federal aid to rural areas
see also Revenue sharing
see also Urban Development Action Grants

Federal aid to medical education
Allergy and Infectious Diseases Natl Inst activities, grants by recipient and location, and disease cases, FY84-91, annual rpt, 4474–30
Assistance (financial and nonfinancial) of Fed Govt, 1992 base edition, annual listing, 104–5
Budget of US, obligations and authority by function, agency, and program, with summaries and analyses, FY93, annual rpt, 104–2
Dental Research Natl Inst research and training grants, by recipient, FY90, annual listing, 4474–19
General Medical Sciences Natl Inst activities, budget, and research and training funding by program, FY91, annual rpt, 4474–38
Health care professionals supply and education, by professional and other characteristics, and location, 1960s-92 and projected to 2020, biennial rpt, 4114–8
Heart, Lung, and Blood Natl Inst activities, and grants by recipient and location, FY91 and disease trends from 1940, annual rpt, 4474–15
HHS financial aid, by program, recipient, State, and city, FY91, annual regional listings, 4004–3
Military health care personnel, and accessions by training source, by occupation, specialty, and service branch, FY90, annual rpt, 3544–24
Neurological Disorders and Stroke Natl Inst activities, and disorder cases, FY91, annual rpt, 4474–25
NIH activities, staff, funding, and facilities, historical data, 1991 annual rpt, 4434–1
NIH grants and contracts, by inst and type of recipient, FY82-91, annual rpt, 4434–9
Nutrition biomedical and behavioral research and training, NIH activities and funding by inst, FY90, annual rpt, 4434–15
Physicians recently graduating, specialties, school debt, and practice settings, and medical school funding sources, 1970s-91, hearing, 21368–135
R&D and related funding of Fed Govt to higher education and nonprofit instns, by field, instn, agency, and State, FY90, annual rpt, 9627–17
Science and engineering grad enrollment, by field, source of funds, and characteristics of student and instn, 1990, annual rpt, 9627–7
Women awarded NIH research and training grants, by recipient characteristics, inst, and host instn, FY90, annual rpt, 4434–18

Federal aid to medicine
AIDS patients health care and support services funding under Ryan White CARE Act, and Federal grants by metro area, 1991, article, 4042–3.352
AIDS prevention and control plans, cases, and Federal funding, 1980s-94, 4048–22
Alcohol abuse direct and indirect costs, 1985, article, 4482–1.311
Alcohol abuse research, treatment programs, and patient characteristics and health effects, quarterly journal, 4482–1
Allergy and Infectious Diseases Natl Inst activities, grants by recipient and location, and disease cases, FY84-91, annual rpt, 4474–30
Assistance (block and categorical grants) programs for State and local govts, FY91, biennial listing, 10044–8

Assistance (financial and nonfinancial) of Fed Govt, 1992 base edition, annual listing, 104–5
Bone marrow donors, minority recruitment, Federal aid, transplants, costs, payment sources, 1987-92, GAO rpt, 26121–487
Budget of US, CBO analysis and review of FY93 budget by function, annual rpt, 26304–2
Budget of US, CBO analysis of revenue and spending alternatives and projections of economic indicators, FY93-97, annual rpt, 26304–3
Budget of US, House concurrent resolution, with spending and revenue targets, FY93 and projected to FY97, annual rpt, 21264–2
Budget of US, obligations and authority by function, agency, and program, with summaries and analyses, FY93, annual rpt, 104–2
Budget of US, receipts by source, outlays by agency and program, and balances, monthly rpt, 8102–3
Cancer (breast) research funding, cases, and deaths, 1970s-90, GAO rpt, 26131–92
Cancer Natl Inst activities, grants by recipient, and cancer deaths and cases, FY91 and trends, annual rpt, 4474–13
Cancer Natl Inst contracts and grants, by recipient and location, annual listing, discontinued, 4474–28
Cancer Natl Inst epidemiology and biometry activities, FY91, annual rpt, 4474–29
Construction put in place, by type of construction, quarterly rpt, 2042–1.1
Construction spending by Fed Govt, by type of structure, FY85-92, annual article, 2042–1.303
Costs, use, and structure of private and public health care delivery, indicators, issues, and foreign comparisons, 1960s-80s, technical paper, 8006–6.1
Dental Research Natl Inst research and training grants, by recipient, FY90, annual listing, 4474–19
Developing countries family planning and population activities of AID, grants by project and recipient, and contraceptive shipments, by country, FY91, annual rpt series, 9914–13
Disabled persons rehabilitation, Federal and State activities and funding, FY90, annual rpt, 4944–1
Drug abuse and trafficking reduction research funding by Natl Inst on Drug Abuse and Office of Justice Programs, 1970s-91, GAO rpt, 26131–99
Drug abuse and treatment research summaries, and resource materials and grant listings, bimonthly rpt, 4492–4
Drug abuse services availability, need, use, outcome, costs, funding sources, and cost-effectiveness, series, 4496–11
Drug abuse, treatment, and enforcement issues, series, 236–3
Drug abuse treatment, prevention, and enforcement grants by State, and State allocations by program, FY87-90, 6068–252
Expenditures (direct) and employment, by function and level of govt, selected years 1962-87, 10048–53
Expenditures for health care and factors in costs, with data by payment source and service type, 1960s-90 and projected to 2000, 26306–6.175
Expenditures for health care by businesses, households, and govts, 1965-90, annual article, 4652–1.309
Expenditures for health care by funding source, 1990, with trends and indexes by service type from 1960, article, 4652–1.323
Expenditures for public welfare by program, FY50s-89, annual article, 4742–1.319
Expenditures of Fed Govt in States, by type, program, agency, and State, FY91, annual rpt, 2464–2
Finances of govts, by level of govt, State, and for large cities and counties, annual rpt series, 2466–2
Fraud and abuse in HHS programs, audits and investigations, 1st half FY92, semiannual rpt, 4002–6
General Medical Sciences Natl Inst activities, budget, and research and training funding by program, FY91, annual rpt, 4474–38
Health Care Financing Admin research activities and grants, by program, FY91, annual listing, 4654–10
Health condition and care indicators, 1950s-90 with health improvement and disease prevention goals for 1990, annual data compilation, 4144–11
Heart, Lung, and Blood Natl Inst activities and Advisory Council recommendations, 1991 narrative rpt, 4474–22
Heart, Lung, and Blood Natl Inst activities, and grants by recipient and location, FY91 and disease trends from 1940, annual rpt, 4474–15
HHS financial aid, by program, recipient, State, and city, FY91, annual regional listings, 4004–3
Investigations of Federal agency and program operations, summaries of findings, as of 1991, annual GAO rpt, 26104–5.3
Kidney end-stage disease research of CDC and HCFA, project listing, 1991, annual rpt, 4654–16
Loans and loan guarantees of Fed Govt, outstanding amounts by agency and program, *Treasury Bulletin*, quarterly rpt, 8002–4.11
Maternal and child health services block grant beneficiary and taxpayer equity among States, issues, alternative allocation formulas, and background data, 1992 GAO rpt, 26121–454
Mental health care facilities, staff, patients, and finances, 1970s-91, biennial rpt, 4094–1
Mental illness (post-traumatic stress) among veterans by period of service, and VA treatment and rehabilitation program operations and staff, FY91, annual rpt, 8704–6
NASA R&D funding to higher education instns, by field, instn, and State, FY91, annual listing, 9504–7
Natl income and product accounts, comprehensive accounts and components, benchmark revisions, 1929-88, 2708–5
Natl income and product accounts, comprehensive accounts and components, *Survey of Current Business*, monthly rpt, 2702–1.26
Neurological Disorders and Stroke Natl Inst activities, and disorder cases, FY91, annual rpt, 4474–25
Neurosciences research and public policy issues, series, 26356–9
NIH activities, staff, funding, and facilities, historical data, 1991 annual rpt, 4434–1
NIH grants and contracts, by inst and type of recipient, FY82-91, annual rpt, 4434–9
NIH grants and contracts, quarterly listing, 4432–1
Nutrition biomedical and behavioral research and training, NIH activities and funding by inst, FY90, annual rpt, 4434–15
Older persons health education centers medication mgmt and other preventive health activities, and Federal funding, FY83-91, article, 4042–3.303
R&D and related funding of Fed Govt to higher education and nonprofit instns, by field, instn, agency, and State, FY90, annual rpt, 9627–17
R&D funding by Fed Govt, by detailed function, program, and agency, FY91-93, annual rpt, 9627–9
Radiation from electronic devices, and FDA control activities and R&D grants, contracts, and interagency agreements, 1991, annual rpt, 4064–13
Reproduction and population research, Fed Govt funding by project, FY90, annual listing, 4474–9
Reproduction and population research, Natl Inst of Child Health and Human Dev funding and activities, 1991, annual rpt, 4474–33
Science and Engineering Indicators, employment, education, R&D funding, and industry impacts, with foreign comparisons, 1960s-91, biennial rpt, 9624–10.4
Smoking prevalence, health effects, and control strategies effectiveness, research results, series, 4476–7
Toxicology Natl Program research and testing activities, FY90 and planned FY91, annual rpt, 4044–16
Women awarded NIH research and training grants, by recipient characteristics, inst, and host instn, FY90, annual rpt, 4434–18
Youth health promotion and adolescent health training funding by Federal agencies, FY88-90, 26358–234.3
see also Civilian Health and Medical Program of the Uniformed Services
see also Federal aid to medical education
see also Medicaid
see also Medicare
see also Military health facilities and services
see also Supplemental Security Income
see also Veterans health facilities and services

Federal aid to railroads
Amtrak finances and operations, FY91, annual rpt, 29524–1
Assistance (financial and nonfinancial) of Fed Govt, 1992 base edition, annual listing, 104–5
Budget of US, obligations and authority by function, agency, and program, with summaries and analyses, FY93, annual rpt, 104–2
Commuter railroad and other transit systems grants of Fed Transit Admin, FY93, annual rpt, 7884–12

DOT planning and safety grants, by program, State, and for 40 SMSAs, FY89, annual rpt, 7304–7
Expenditures of Fed Govt in States, by type, program, agency, and State, FY91, annual rpt, 2464–2
Lands (public) acreage and grants, by State, FY91 and trends, annual rpt, 5724–1.1
Safety, operating, and funding characteristics of rail rapid transit systems, 1988-89, 9618–19
Urban areas transit systems grants of Federal Transit Admin, by city and State, FY91, annual rpt, 7884–10

Federal aid to research and development
see Federal funding for research and development

Federal aid to rural areas
Appalachia hwy system and access roads funding and completion status, by State, quarterly tables, 9082–1
Appalachia local dev projects, and funding by source, by program and State, FY91, annual rpt, 9084–1
Appalachian Regional Commission funding, by project and State, planned FY92, annual rpt, 9084–3
Assistance (block and categorical grants) programs for State and local govts, FY91, biennial listing, 10044–8
Assistance (financial and nonfinancial) of Fed Govt, 1992 base edition, annual listing, 104–5
Assistance of Fed Govt to rural areas, Bush Admin programs and initiatives, FY91, annual rpt, 1004–17
Budget of US, House Budget Committee analysis of Bush Admin proposals and economic assumptions, FY93, 21268–42
Businesses in rural areas, Fed Govt credit assistance by program and county characteristics, 1983-89, 1548–389
Colorado River Salinity Control Program participation and payments, FY87-91, annual rpt, 1804–23
Conservation program of USDA, acreage, projects, participation, and funding, by State, 1936-90, quinquennial rpt, 1808–1
Conservation program of USDA, funding by practice, region and State, monthly rpt, 1802–15
Conservation program of USDA, participation and payments by practice and State, FY91, annual rpt, 1804–7
Economic and social conditions, dev, and problems in rural areas, periodic journal, 1502–7
Economic dev and other REA loans by State, and REA activities and finances, FY91 and trends from FY36, annual rpt, 1244–3
Expenditures of Fed Govt in States, by type, program, agency, and State, FY91, annual rpt, 2464–2
Small Business Admin loans to tourism-related and other small businesses in rural areas, FY86-1st half FY91, hearing, 21728–79
Timber improvement program for private land, Fed Govt cost-sharing funds by region and State, monthly rpt, 1802–11
Water pollution from farming, funding for control under Rural Clean Water Program by region and State, monthly rpt, 1802–14
see also Agricultural production quotas and price supports
see also Agricultural subsidies
see also Farm Credit Administration
see also Farm Credit System
see also Farmers Home Administration
see also Rural Electrification Administration
see also Rural Telephone Bank

Federal aid to States
Agricultural research funding and staffing for USDA, State agencies, and other instns, by topic, FY91, annual rpt, 1744–2
American Samoa govt finances, with data on health and farm spending and employment, mid 1980s-91, GAO rpt, 26123–385
Arts funding, by level of govt, State, and selected city, FY86-92, GAO rpt, 26119–371
Arts Natl Endowment activities and grants, FY91, annual rpt, 9564–3
Assistance (block and categorical grants) programs for State and local govts, FY91, biennial listing, 10044–8
Assistance (financial and nonfinancial) of Fed Govt, 1992 base edition, annual listing, 104–5
Block grants discretionary spending, congressional changes to set-aside and cost-ceiling requirements for 11 programs, FY82-91, GAO rpt, 26121–466
Budget of US, historical data, selected years FY34-91 and projected to FY97, 108–46.5
Budget of US, House Budget Committee analysis of Bush Admin proposals and economic assumptions, FY93, 21268–42
Budget of US, obligations and authority by function, agency, and program, with summaries and analyses, FY93, annual rpt, 104–2
Bus (intercity) deregulation in 1982, impacts on service, ridership, and State and Federal funding, with background data, 1980s-92, GAO rpt, 26113–583
Child abuse and neglect prevention and treatment, and disabled infant protection, grants by State, FY91, annual listing, 4584–6
Child abuse and neglect prevention and treatment, discretionary grants, FY91, annual listing, 4584–9
Child Support Enforcement Program collections for non-AFDC clients, administrative costs, and user fees, by State, with Federal shares of costs, 1990, GAO rpt, 26121–463
Coal Surface Mining Reclamation and Enforcement Office activities and funding, by State and Indian tribe, FY91, annual rpt, 5644–1
Coastal areas environmental mgmt programs of States, activities and Federal funding, FY90-91, biennial rpt, 2174–8
Community Dev Block Grant activities and funding, by program, FY75-91, annual rpt, 5124–8
Consumer Product Safety Commission activities, recalls by brand, and casualties and medical costs, by product type, FY90, annual rpt, 9164–2
Crime victim compensation and support service programs funding, by offense and State, FY88-90, biennial rpt, 6064–37
Crime victim compensation and support service programs operations, series, 6066–31
Disabled persons rehabilitation, Federal and State activities and funding, FY90, annual rpt, 4944–1
Disasters and natl security incidents and mgmt, with data by major event and State, 1992 annual rpt, 9434–6
DOT planning and safety grants, by program, State, and for 40 SMSAs, FY89, annual rpt, 7304–7
Driving while intoxicated enforcement incentive grants of Natl Hwy Traffic Safety Admin, by State, 1992 press release, 7306–10.4
Drug abuse and trafficking reduction programs activities, funding, staff, and Bush Admin budget request, by Federal agency, FY91-93, annual rpt, 234–2
Drug abuse, treatment, and enforcement issues, series, 236–3
Drug abuse treatment, prevention, and enforcement grants by State, and State allocations by program, FY87-90, 6068–252
Drug enforcement grants of Fed Govt, and allocations to local govts, by State, FY91, annual rpt, 6064–38
Economic Dev Admin activities, and funding by program, recipient, State, and county, FY91 and cumulative from FY66, annual rpt, 2064–2
Economic indicators and components, current data and annual trends, monthly rpt, 23842–1.6
Education (early childhood) for handicapped children, project descriptions, 1991/92, annual listing, 4944–10
Education funding by Federal agency, program, and recipient type, and instn spending, 1960s-91, annual rpt, 4824–8
Energy conservation programs of States, Federal aid and savings, by State, 1990, annual rpt, 3304–1
EPA pollution control grant program activities, monthly rpt, 9182–8
Expenditures of Fed Govt in States and local areas, by type, State, county, and city, FY91, annual rpt, 2464–3
Expenditures of Fed Govt in States, by type, program, agency, and State, FY91, annual rpt, 2464–2
Finances of govts, by level of govt, State, and for large cities and counties, annual rpt series, 2466–2
Finances of govts, tax systems and revenue, and fiscal structure, by level of govt and State, 1992 and historical trends, annual rpt, 10044–1
Fish and Wildlife Service restoration and hunter safety funding, by State, FY92, semiannual press release, 5502–1
Fish and Wildlife Service restoration programs funding, land purchases, and project listing, by State, FY90, annual rpt, 5504–1
Fish Hatchery Natl System activities and deliveries, by species, hatchery, and jurisdiction of waters stocked, FY91, annual rpt, 5504–10
Forest Service activities and finances, by region and State, FY91, annual rpt, 1204–1

Forests (natl) timber sales, expenses, and operations, by region, State, and natl forest, FY91, annual rpts, 1204–36
Formula grants of Fed Govt, use of adjusted census and intercensal data for allocation, with data by program and State, FY91, 25408–120
Foster care programs of States, Federal funding and children served, by State, 1981-89, hearing, 21788–208
HHS financial aid, by program, recipient, State, and city, FY91, annual regional listings, 4004–3
Historic Preservation Fund grants, by State, FY93, annual press release, 5544–9
Homeless persons aid programs of Fed Govt, program descriptions and funding, by agency and State, FY87-91, annual GAO rpt, 26104–21
Housing (rental) rehabilitation funding and activities of HUD, by program and region, FY91, annual rpt, 5124–7
Humanities Natl Endowment activities and grants, FY91, annual rpt, 9564–2
Hwy funding and allocation methods, for Federal-aid system, FY92-97, 7558–107
Hwy Statistics, detailed data by State, 1991, annual rpt, 7554–1
Land and Water Conservation Fund allocations for outdoor recreation area dev, by State, FY93, annual table, 5544–15
Land Mgmt Bur activities and funding by State, FY90, annual rpt, 5724–13
Lands (public) acreage, grants, use, revenues, and allocations, by State, FY91 and trends, annual rpt, 5724–1
Marine mammals protection activities and funding, populations, and harvests, by species, 1990, annual rpt, 5504–12
Maternal and child health services block grant beneficiary and taxpayer equity among States, issues, alternative allocation formulas, and background data, 1992 GAO rpt, 26121–454
Money laundering investigation activities of States and Fed Govt, and use of IRS large cash transaction rpts, by State, 1985-91, GAO rpt, 26119–430
OASDI Disability Insurance eligibility determinations by States, caseloads, Federal funding, and State directors views, 1980s-91, hearing, 21148–63
Public works financing, use, and condition, 1990 hearing, 21648–67
Puerto Rico statehood referendum proposal, with background data on Federal outlays, economic conditions, and finances of corporations with tax-favored status, 1940s-88, hearing, 21448–46
Technology transfer by Federal R&D labs to small manufacturers, promotional programs activities and grants to States, late 1980s-91, GAO rpt, 26113–551
Tree planting on govt land contracted to small businesses, Federal grants, State funding, and projects, by State, FY91, annual rpt, 9764–10
Wastewater treatment and collection facility construction funding needs and Fed Govt grants, by State, 1990 and projected to 2010, biennial rpt, 9204–7
Wastewater treatment plants construction loan funds for local govts, costs and State officials views by State, projected 1991-2000, GAO rpt, 26113–561
Water resources data collection and analysis activities of USGS Water Resources Div Districts, with project descriptions, series, 5666–26
Wetlands (coastal) conservation funding by project, 1992 press release, 5306–4.12
see also Medicaid
see also Revenue sharing
see also Supplemental Security Income
see also Unemployment insurance

Federal aid to transportation
Air traffic control and airway facilities and services, finances and operations, FY86-90, annual rpt, 7504–37
Air traffic control and airway facilities improvement activities under Aviation System Capital Investment Plan, 1981-91 and projected to 2006, annual rpt, 7504–12
Airport and Airway Trust Fund financial condition, monthly rpt, 8102–9.5
Airport and Airway Trust Fund improvement spending, by airport and State, FY92, annual rpt, 7504–48
Airport capacity improvement projects and funding, traffic, and delays, by major airport, 1988-90 and forecast to 2000, annual rpt, 7504–43
Airport dev program grants and projects, by FAA region and State, FY90, annual rpt, 7504–1.3
Airport improvement program of FAA, activities and grants by State and airport, FY91, annual rpt, 7504–38
Airport planning and dev project grants of FAA, by airport and location, quarterly press release, 7502–14
Assistance (block and categorical grants) programs for State and local govts, FY91, biennial listing, 10044–8
Assistance (financial and nonfinancial) of Fed Govt, 1992 base edition, annual listing, 104–5
Budget of US, balances of budget authority obligated and unobligated, by function and agency, FY90-93, annual rpt, 104–8
Budget of US, CBO analysis and review of FY93 budget by function, annual rpt, 26304–2
Budget of US, CBO analysis of revenue and spending alternatives and projections of economic indicators, FY93-97, annual rpt, 26304–3
Budget of US, House concurrent resolution, with spending and revenue targets, FY93 and projected to FY97, annual rpt, 21264–2
Budget of US, midsession review of FY93 budget, by function, annual rpt, 104–7
Budget of US, obligations and authority by function, agency, and program, with summaries and analyses, FY93, annual rpt, 104–2
Budget of US, receipts by source, outlays by agency and program, and balances, monthly rpt, 8102–3
Bus (intercity) deregulation in 1982, impacts on service, ridership, and State and Federal funding, with background data, 1980s-92, GAO rpt, 26113–583
Bus exhaust emissions reduction programs, funding, and alternative fuel bus dev, periodic rpt, 7882–3
DOT activities by subagency, budget, and summary accident data, FY89, annual rpt, 7304–1
DOT finances and staff, by subagency, FY91-93, annual rpt, 7304–10
DOT planning and safety grants, by program, State, and for 40 SMSAs, FY89, annual rpt, 7304–7
Electric-powered autos, R&D activity and DOE funding shares, FY91, annual rpt, 3304–2
Expenditures (direct) and employment, by function and level of govt, selected years 1962-87, 10048–53
Expenditures for hwy and transit system programs, proposed FY92-97, 7558–117
Expenditures of Fed Govt in States, by type, program, agency, and State, FY91, annual rpt, 2464–2
FAA activities and finances, and staff by region, FY90-91, annual rpt, 7504–10
FAA research funding and staff, by research area and project, FY88-91, GAO rpt, 26113–565
Fed Transit Admin grants by State, and oversight, 1988-92, GAO rpt, 26113–600
Fraud and abuse in DOT programs, audit resolution activities, 1st half FY92, semiannual rpt, 7302–12
Fraud and abuse in DOT programs, audits and investigations, 1st half FY92, semiannual rpt, 7302–4
Inland waterways trust funds financial condition, monthly rpt, 8102–9.8
Investigations of Federal agency and program operations, summaries of findings, as of 1991, annual GAO rpt, 26104–5.2
Lands (public) acreage and grants, by State, FY91 and trends, annual rpt, 5724–1.1
Loans and loan guarantees of Fed Govt, outstanding amounts by agency and program, *Treasury Bulletin*, quarterly rpt, 8002–4.11
Natl income and product accounts, comprehensive accounts and components, benchmark revisions, 1929-88, 2708–5
Natl income and product accounts, comprehensive accounts and components, *Survey of Current Business*, monthly rpt, 2702–1.26
Port improvement capital expenditures and financing methods, by region and selected port, 1946-89, 7708–6
R&D funding by Fed Govt, by detailed function, program, and agency, FY91-93, annual rpt, 9627–9
Railroad (commuter) and other transit systems grants of Fed Transit Admin, FY93, annual rpt, 7884–12
Statistical Abstract of US, 1992 annual data compilation, 2324–1.21
Transit systems finances and operations, by mode, size of fleet and urban area, region, and for 518 systems, 1990, annual rpt, 7884–4
Transit systems finances, equipment, and ridership characteristics, 1985-90, biennial rpt, 7884–8
Transit systems R&D projects and funding of Federal Transit Admin, FY91, annual listing, 7884–1
Transit systems research and training grants to higher education instns, by project, FY92, annual listing, 7884–7
Urban areas transit systems and hwys, Federal aid by selected State, aggregate FY76-91, GAO rpt, 26113–570

Urban areas transit systems grants of Federal Transit Admin, by city and State, FY91, annual rpt, 7884–10
User fees financing of transportation infrastructure, with data on hwys, airports, and waterways, 1985-91, 26306–6.170
see also Federal aid to highways
see also Federal aid to railroads
see also Shipbuilding and operating subsidies

Federal aid to vocational education
Assistance (block and categorical grants) programs for State and local govts, FY91, biennial listing, 10044–8
Assistance (financial and nonfinancial) of Fed Govt, 1992 base edition, annual listing, 104–5
Expenditures for education by Federal agency, program, and recipient type, and instn spending, 1960s-91, annual rpt, 4824–8
Expenditures for education, by Federal agency, program, and State, FY65-92, annual rpt, 4824–2.27
Expenditures of Fed Govt in States, by type, program, agency, and State, FY91, annual rpt, 2464–2
HHS financial aid, by program, recipient, State, and city, FY91, annual regional listings, 4004–3

Federal Aviation Administration
Activities and finances of FAA, and staff by region, FY90-91, annual rpt, 7504–10
Activities of FAA, and detailed data on aircraft, traffic, carriers, and airports, 1981-90, annual rpt, 7504–1
Air traffic control and airway facilities and services, finances and operations, FY86-90, annual rpt, 7504–37
Air traffic control and airway facilities improvement activities under Aviation System Capital Investment Plan, 1981-91 and projected to 2006, annual rpt, 7504–12
Air traffic control and airway facilities staff, by employment and other characteristics, FY90, annual rpt, 7504–41
Air traffic control and pilot errors, runway incursions, and near collisions, monthly rpt, 7502–15
Aircraft engine rotor failures, by carrier and incident characteristics, 1988, annual rpt, 7504–50
Aircraft registered with FAA, by type and characteristics of aircraft, make, carrier, State, and county, 1991, annual rpt, 7504–3
Airline finances and operations, summary data, quarterly rpt, 7502–16
Airport capacity improvement projects and funding, traffic, and delays, by major airport, 1988-90 and forecast to 2000, annual rpt, 7504–43
Airport improvement program of FAA, activities and grants by State and airport, FY91, annual rpt, 7504–38
Airport planning and dev project grants of FAA, by airport and location, quarterly press release, 7502–14
Airport security operations to prevent hijacking, screening results, enforcement actions, and hijacking attempts, semiannual rpt, periodicity change, 7502–5; 7504–49
Alaska airport dev plans, annual rpt, discontinued, 7504–36
Atlantic Ocean intl air traffic and passengers, by aviation type and route, alternative forecasts 1992-2010 and trends from 1982, annual rpt, 7504–44
Budget of US, obligations and authority by function, agency, and program, with summaries and analyses, FY93, annual rpt, 104–2
Collisions (mid-air) and near collisions, and relation to air traffic density, 1981-86, 7508–76
Drug testing and results for airline and aviation safety employees, by drug type and occupational group, 1991, semiannual rpt, 7502–17
Employment of DOT, by subagency, occupation, and selected personnel characteristics, FY91, annual rpt, 7304–18
Expenditures of Fed Govt in States, by type, program, agency, and State, FY91, annual rpt, 2464–2
Flight and engine hours, and shutdown rates, by aircraft and engine model, and air carrier, monthly rpt, 7502–13
Flight service station workload of FAA, pilot briefs, contacts, and flight plans by facility, projected FY92-2002 and trends from FY83, annual rpt, 7504–39
Hijackings, on-board explosions, and other crime, US and foreign incidents, 1986-90, annual rpt, 7504–31
Instrument flight rule aircraft handled, by user type, FAA traffic control center, and region, FY85-91 and projected to FY2005, annual rpt, 7504–15
Medical research and test results for aviation, technical rpt series, 7506–10
Pacific Ocean intl air traffic and passengers, by route, alternative forecasts 1992-2010 and trends from 1980, annual rpt, 7504–51
Pilots and nonpilots certified by FAA, by certificate type, age, sex, region, and State, 1991, annual rpt, 7504–2
Research funding and staff of FAA, by research area and project, FY88-91, GAO rpt, 26113–565
Traffic (passenger and cargo), and departures by aircraft type, by carrier and airport, 1991, annual rpt, 7504–35
Traffic (passenger and cargo), carrier enplanement shares, and FAA airport improvement program grants, by airport and State, 1990, annual rpt, 7504–48
Traffic, aircraft, pilots, airports, and fuel use, forecast FY92-2003 and trends from FY82, annual rpt, 7504–6
Traffic and other aviation activity forecasts of FAA, 1992 annual conf, 7504–28
Traffic and passenger and freight enplanements, by airport, 1960s-91 and projected to 2010, hub area rpt series, 7506–7
Traffic and passenger enplanements, by airport, region, and State, projected FY92-2005 and trends from FY83, annual rpt, 7504–7
Traffic levels at FAA air traffic control facilities, by airport and State, FY91, annual rpt, 7504–27
User fees financing of transportation infrastructure, with data on hwys, airports, and waterways, 1985-91, 26306–6.170

Federal bankruptcy courts
Admin of Federal bankruptcy cases, costs and efficiency of 2 programs, 1990-91, GAO rpt, 26119–421
Caseloads (civil and criminal) for Federal district, appeals, and bankruptcy courts, by offense, circuit, and district, 1991, annual rpt, 18204–11
Caseloads (civil and criminal) for Federal district, appeals, and special courts, by offense, circuit, and district, 1991, annual rpt, 18204–8
Judicial Conf proceedings and findings, spring 1992, semiannual rpt, 18202–2
US attorneys work hours, by type of court and Federal district, FY91, annual rpt, 6004–2.6

Federal boards, committees, and commissions
Advisory committees of Fed Govt, and members, staff, meetings, and costs by agency, FY91, annual rpt, 9454–18
Budget of US, authoritative financial statements with appropriations, outlays, and receipts, by category and agency, FY91, annual rpt, 8104–2.2
Budget of US, obligations and authority by function, agency, and program, with summaries and analyses, FY93, annual rpt, 104–2
Budget of US, receipts by source, outlays by agency and program, and balances, monthly rpt, 8102–3
Education funding by Federal agency, program, and recipient type, and instn spending, 1960s-91, annual rpt, 4824–8
Employment and payroll (civilian) of Fed Govt, by agency in DC metro area, total US, and abroad, bimonthly rpt, 9842–1
Financial operations of Fed Govt, detailed data, *Treasury Bulletin*, quarterly rpt, 8002–4
Labor unions recognized in Fed Govt, agreements and membership by agency and facility, as of Jan 1991, biennial listing, 9844–14
see also Advisory Commission on Intergovernmental Relations
see also Advisory Commission on Regulatory Barriers to Affordable Housing
see also Advisory Committee on Federal Pay
see also Advisory Council on Social Security
see also Board for International Broadcasting
see also Commission on Civil Rights
see also Commission on the Future Structure of Veterans Health Care
see also Committee for Purchase from the Blind and Other Severely Handicapped
see also Commodity Futures Trading Commission
see also Delaware River Basin Commission
see also Federal Council on the Aging
see also Federal Election Commission
see also Federal Financial Institutions Examination Council
see also Federal Financing Bank
see also Federal independent agencies
see also Federal Labor Relations Authority
see also Federal Mine Safety and Health Review Commission
see also Fulbright, J. William, Foreign Scholarship Board
see also Goldwater, Barry, Scholarship and Excellence in Education Foundation

see also Indian Nations at Risk Task Force
see also Institute of American Indian and Alaska Native Culture and Arts Development
see also Interagency Council on the Homeless
see also Interagency Forum on Aging-Related Statistics
see also Interagency Scientific Committee to Address the Conservation of the Northern Spotted Owl
see also Interagency Task Force on Acid Precipitation
see also Interdepartment Radio Advisory Committee
see also International Boundary and Water Commission, U.S. and Mexico
see also International Joint Commission, U.S. and Canada
see also Interstate Commission on the Potomac River Basin
see also Investment Advisory Council
see also Japan-U.S. Friendship Commission
see also Madison, James, Memorial Fellowship Foundation
see also Marine Mammal Commission
see also Migratory Bird Conservation Commission
see also National Advisory Committee on Semiconductors
see also National Advisory Council on Educational Research and Improvement
see also National Advisory Council on Indian Education
see also National Advisory Council on International Monetary and Financial Policies
see also National Capital Planning Commission
see also National Commission for Employment Policy
see also National Commission on Children
see also National Commission on Libraries and Information Science
see also National Education Goals Panel
see also National Narcotics Intelligence Consumers Committee
see also Navajo and Hopi Indian Relocation Commission
see also Office of Navajo and Hopi Indian Relocation
see also Physician Payment Review Commission
see also Prospective Payment Assessment Commission
see also Susquehanna River Basin Commission
see also Truman, Harry S., Scholarship Foundation
see also U.S. Architectural and Transportation Barriers Compliance Board
see also U.S. Holocaust Memorial Council
see also U.S. Sentencing Commission
see also Water Resources Council
see also under By Federal Agency in the "Index by Categories"
see also under names of individual Presidential commissions (starting with Presidential or President's)

Federal budget
see Budget of the U.S.

Federal buildings
see Public buildings

Federal Bureau of Investigation
Assaults and deaths of law enforcement officers, by circumstances, agency, victim and offender characteristics, and location, 1991, annual rpt, 6224–3
Bombing incidents, casualties, and damage, by target, circumstances, and State, 1991, annual rpt, 6224–5
Budget of US, obligations and authority by function, agency, and program, with summaries and analyses, FY93, annual rpt, 104–2
Crime Index by population size and region, and offenses by large city, 1st half 1992, semiannual rpt, 6222–1
Crimes, arrests by offender characteristics, and rates, by offense, and law enforcement employees, by population size and jurisdiction, 1991, annual rpt, 6224–2
Fingerprint identification system of FBI, automation costs, staff, and workload, FY90 and projected to FY2000, 26358–253
Terrorism incidents in US, related activity, and casualties, by attack type, target, group, and location, 1991, annual rpt, 6224–6

Federal Bureau of Prisons
see Bureau of Prisons

Federal Communications Commission
Budget of US, authoritative financial statements with appropriations, outlays, and receipts, by category and agency, FY91, annual rpt, 8104–2.2
Budget of US, obligations and authority by function, agency, and program, with summaries and analyses, FY93, annual rpt, 104–2
Fiber optics and copper wire mileage and access lines, and fiber systems investment, by telecommunications firm, 1985-91, annual rpt, 9284–18
Intl telecommunications operations of US carriers, finances, rates, and traffic by service type, firm, and country, 1975-90, annual rpt, 9284–17
Labor unions recognized in Fed Govt, agreements and membership by agency and facility, as of Jan 1991, biennial listing, 9844–14
Licensing activities of FCC, by class of operation, FY91, annual rpt, 9284–4
Radio frequency assignments for mobile communications, effects of auctioning frequencies, 1990, 26306–6.169
Telephone and telegraph firms detailed finances and operations, 1990, annual rpt, 9284–6
Telephone local service charges and low-income subsidies, by region, company, and city, 1980s-91, semiannual rpt, 9282–8
Telephone service subscribership, charges, and local and long distance firm finances and operations, late 1970s-92, semiannual rpt, 9282–7
TV and radio stations on the air, by class of operation, monthly press release, 9282–4
TV channel allocation and license status, for commercial and noncommercial UHF and VHF stations by market, as of June 1992, semiannual rpt, 9282–6

Federal contracts
see Government contracts and procurement

Federal corporations
see Government corporations and enterprises

Federal Council on the Aging
Older persons socioeconomic characteristics, 1900s-90 and projected to 2050, biennial chartbook, 12904–1

Federal courts
see Administrative Office of the U.S. Courts
see Court of International Trade
see Court of Military Appeals
see Courts
see Federal bankruptcy courts
see Federal courts of appeals
see Federal district courts
see Supreme Court
see Tax Court of the U.S.
see U.S. Claims Court
see U.S. Court of Appeals for the Federal Circuit

Federal courts of appeals
Budget of US, authoritative financial statements with appropriations, outlays, and receipts, by category and agency, FY91, annual rpt, 8104–2.2
Budget of US, obligations and authority by function, agency, and program, with summaries and analyses, FY93, annual rpt, 104–2
Caseloads (civil and criminal) for Federal district, appeals, and bankruptcy courts, by offense, circuit, and district, 1991, annual rpt, 18204–11
Caseloads (civil and criminal) for Federal district, appeals, and special courts, by offense, circuit, and district, 1991, annual rpt, 18204–8
Criminal case processing in Federal courts, by offense, disposition, and jurisdiction, data compilation, 1992 annual rpt, 6064–6.5
Judicial Conf proceedings and findings, spring 1992, semiannual rpt, 18202–2
Labor Relations Natl Board activities, cases, elections conducted, and litigation, FY90, annual rpt, 9584–1
Statistical Abstract of US, 1992 annual data compilation, 2324–1.5
US attorneys work hours, by type of court and Federal district, FY91, annual rpt, 6004–2.6
see also U.S. Court of Appeals for the Federal Circuit

Federal Crop Insurance Corp.
Budget of US, obligations and authority by function, agency, and program, with summaries and analyses, FY93, annual rpt, 104–2
Expenditures of Fed Govt for disaster aid by program, with farm crop insurance participation and finances of private insurers and FCIC, 1980s-92, GAO rpt, 26113–556
Financial performance of FCIC, and effect of alternative price forecasts on program costs, 1983-89, GAO rpt, 26131–95

Federal Deposit Insurance Corp.
Banks (insured commercial and savings) finances, by State, 1990, annual rpt, 9294–4
Banks (insured commercial and savings) financial condition and performance, by asset size and region, quarterly rpt, 9292–1

Budget of US, authoritative financial statements with appropriations, outlays, and receipts, by category and agency, FY91, annual rpt, 8104–2.2
Budget of US, obligations and authority by function, agency, and program, with summaries and analyses, FY93, annual rpt, 104–2
Deposits in insured commercial and savings banks, by instn, State, MSA, and county, as of June 1991, annual regional rpt series, 9295–3
Employee pay comparability among Federal bank regulatory agencies, and turnover, by occupation, 1991, GAO rpt, 26119–368
Finances and operations of FDIC, insured deposits, and finances of banks needing FDIC aid, 1991 and trends from 1934, annual rpt, 9294–1
Labor unions recognized in Fed Govt, agreements and membership by agency and facility, as of Jan 1991, biennial listing, 9844–14
Merger applications approved, and assets and offices involved, by bank, 1990, annual rpt, 9294–5
Real estate supply and demand, housing and commercial property market activity indicators by region, quarterly rpt, 9292–6
Regulation of banks and related issues, quarterly journal, 9292–4
Savings instns financial statements, for instns insured by Savings Assn Insurance Fund by FHLB district and State, and for FDIC-insured savings banks, 1989, annual rpt, 8434–1

Federal district courts
Budget of US, obligations and authority by function, agency, and program, with summaries and analyses, FY93, annual rpt, 104–2
Caseloads (civil and criminal) for Federal district, appeals, and bankruptcy courts, by offense, circuit, and district, 1991, annual rpt, 18204–11
Caseloads (civil and criminal) for Federal district, appeals, and special courts, by offense, circuit, and district, 1991, annual rpt, 18204–8
Corrupt govt officials prosecuted and convicted, by judicial district and level of govt, 1970-90, annual rpt, 6004–13
Criminal case processing in Federal district courts, and dispositions, by offense, district, and offender characteristics, 1989, annual data compilation, 6064–29
Criminal case processing in Federal district courts, and dispositions, by offense, 1980-91, annual rpt, 6064–31
Criminal caseload of Federal district courts, by district, data compilation, 1992 annual rpt, 6064–6.5
Criminal justice systems activities, spending, and employment, by level of govt, data compilation, 1992 annual rpt, 6064–6.1
Executions by whether habeas corpus used to appeal conviction, and time from crime to execution, with data by race and State, 1977-91, 6008–34
Judicial Conf proceedings and findings, spring 1992, semiannual rpt, 18202–2
Juror (grand and petit) use and costs, trials, and trial days, by Federal district court, annual rpt, discontinued, 18204–4
Sentences for Federal crimes, guidelines use and results by offense and district, and Sentencing Commission activities, 1991, annual rpt, 17664–1
Sentences for Federal crimes, guidelines use and results by offense, 1984-1990, 6066–19.68
Statistical Abstract of US, 1992 annual data compilation, 2324–1.5
US attorneys case processing and collections, by case type and Federal district, FY91, annual rpt, 6004–2
Wiretaps authorized, costs, arrests, trials, and convictions, by offense and jurisdiction, 1991, annual rpt, 18204–7
see also Federal bankruptcy courts

Federal Election Commission
Activities of FEC, and election campaign finances, various periods 1975-91, annual rpt, 9274–1
Activities of FEC, elections, procedures, and campaign finances, press release series, 9276–1
Budget of US, authoritative financial statements with appropriations, outlays, and receipts, by category and agency, FY91, annual rpt, 8104–2.2
Budget of US, obligations and authority by function, agency, and program, with summaries and analyses, FY93, annual rpt, 104–2
Campaign finances reported to FEC, by type of filer, 1990 natl elections, biennial rpt series, 9276–2
Computer systems for voter registration and verification data storage and retrieval, use and characteristics, for selected counties, 1992 rpt, 9278–8
Independent expenditures of firms and assns for campaign-related internal communications, by organization, location, and candidate, 1991-92, biennial rpt, 9274–3
Labor unions recognized in Fed Govt, agreements and membership by agency and facility, as of Jan 1991, biennial listing, 9844–14
Polling places access and services availability for aged and disabled, by State, 1990 natl elections, hearing, 21428–11
Tax (income) return checkoff for contribution to presidential campaign fund, receipts and outlays, mid 1970s-91 and alternative projections to 1993, hearing, 21428–10

Federal Emergency Management Agency
Arson cases, civilian and fire fighter casualties, and property damage, 1986-89, 9438–14
Budget of US, authoritative financial statements with appropriations, outlays, and receipts, by category and agency, FY91, annual rpt, 8104–2.2
Budget of US, obligations and authority by function, agency, and program, with summaries and analyses, FY93, annual rpt, 104–2
Disasters and natl security incidents and mgmt, with data by major event and State, 1992 annual rpt, 9434–6
Education funding by Federal agency, program, and recipient type, and instn spending, 1960s-91, annual rpt, 4824–8
Expenditures of Fed Govt in States, by type, program, agency, and State, FY91, annual rpt, 2464–2
Fire fighter deaths, by cause, circumstances, and location, 1990, annual rpt, 9434–8
Labor unions recognized in Fed Govt, agreements and membership by agency and facility, as of Jan 1991, biennial listing, 9844–14
see also U.S. Fire Administration

Federal employees
Advisory committees of Fed Govt, and members, staff, meetings, and costs by agency, FY91, annual rpt, 9454–18
Air traffic control and airway facilities staff, by employment and other characteristics, FY90, annual rpt, 7504–41
Air traffic controller job performance and satisfaction impacts of training program, 1984-90, technical rpt, 7506–10.96
Air traffic controller job satisfaction, relation to work conditions and worker characteristics, 1992 technical rpt, 7506–10.117
Air travel by Federal officials aboard military aircraft, trips of 11 officials by reason, with costs and reimbursements, 1989-91, GAO rpt, 26111–78
Air travel by Federal officials and Congress aboard military aircraft, and aircraft inventory characteristics, 1989-91, GAO rpt, 26123–384
Asian and Pacific Islands Americans social and economic characteristics, for West and total US, 1990-91, Current Population Report, 2546–1.462
Assaults and deaths of law enforcement officers, by circumstances, agency, victim and offender characteristics, and location, 1991, annual rpt, 6224–3
Assets of Fed Govt targeted for disposition, inventories by type, and related employment and contracts, by agency, FY90, GAO rpt, 26119–369
Black Americans social and economic characteristics, for South and total US, 1991 and trends from 1950, annual Current Population Rpt, 2546–1.463
Business statistics, detailed data for major industries and economic indicators, 1960-91, *Survey of Current Business* biennial supplement, 2704–1
Corrupt govt officials prosecuted and convicted, by judicial district and level of govt, 1970-90, annual rpt, 6004–13
Criminal justice systems activities, spending, and employment, by level of govt, data compilation, 1992 annual rpt, 6064–6.1
Earthquake risk for Federal buildings and employees, by agency and region, 1989, with location and size of major events from 1600s, GAO rpt, 26119–399
Employment (civilian) of Fed Govt, by demographic characteristics and agency, 1990, GAO rpt, 26119–383
Employment (civilian) of Fed Govt, work-years, pay rates, and benefits use and costs, by agency, FY90, annual rpt, 9844–31
Employment and direct spending, by function and level of govt, selected years 1967-87, 10048–53
Employment and payroll (civilian) of Fed Govt, by agency in DC metro area, total US, and abroad, bimonthly rpt, 9842–1

Employment and payroll (civilian) of Fed Govt, by pay system, agency, and location, 1991, annual rpt, 9844–6
Employment and payroll, by function, level of govt, and State, 1991, annual rpt, 2466–1.1
Employment, earnings, and hours, by selected SIC 1- to 4-digit industry, State, and for 275 MSAs, 1987-92, 6748–81
Employment, earnings, and hours, by SIC 1- to 4-digit industry, monthly 1989-Feb 1992, annual rpt, 6744–4
Employment situation, earnings, hours, and other BLS economic indicators, transcripts of BLS Commissioner's monthly testimony, periodic rpt, 23846–4
Espionage against Federal and military agencies, US natls convicted by selected personal, employment, and espionage characteristics, 1945-89, hearings, 25428–2
Ethics regulation, activities, and staff of Federal agencies, 1991, biennial rpt, 9834–1
Health Care Financing Review, provider prices, price inputs and indexes, and labor, quarterly journal, 4652–1.1
Health care professionals supply and education, by professional and other characteristics, and location, 1960s-92 and projected to 2020, biennial rpt, 4114–8
Higher education PhD degree recipients employment plans, by employer type, work activity, and field, 1979, 1984, and 1989, 4848–44
Immigrants admitted to US, by class and country, FY85-91, annual rpt, 6264–2.1
Insurance (health and life) programs of Fed Govt, coverage and finances, annual rpt, discontinued, 9844–35
Judicial personnel, by position, June 1990-91, annual rpt, 18204–8.11
Law enforcement spending, employment, and payroll, by activity, level of govt, and State, FY90, annual rpt, 6066–25.50
Minority group and women employment by industry sector, and govt salaries, by occupation, mid 1960s-90, chartbook, 9248–20
Minority group, disabled, and veteran employment in Fed Govt, and years of service, by occupation, age, sex, and agency, as of Sept 1990, biennial rpt, 9844–27
Minority group, women, and disabled employment of Fed Govt, by agency and occupation, FY90, annual rpt, 9244–10
Moonlighting by Federal employees, selected characteristics of 2nd job and Federal position, FY88-90, GAO rpt, 26119–386
Occupational Outlook Handbook, 1992-93, biennial rpt, 6744–1
Pacific territories population and housing detailed characteristics, by location, 1990 Census of Population and Housing, series, 2551–8
Physical fitness clubs memberships for Federal employees, agency costs, and personnel directors views on OPM guidelines and admin leave use, 1991-92, GAO rpt, 26119–393
Physicians, by specialty, age, sex, and location of training and practice, 1990, State rpt series, 4116–6
Prison and community-based facilities, population, employment, spending, and other characteristics, by State and for Fed Govt, 1990, annual rpt, 6064–26.3; 6068–218
Prison drug smuggling interdiction, inmate and staff testing, and treatment programs, by instn characteristics, 1989-90, 6066–19.70
Procurement operations of Fed Govt, employees job performance, and views on policies and practices, 1991 survey, 9498–17
Productivity of Federal employees, indexes of output and labor costs by function, FY67-90, annual rpt, 6824–1.6
Recruitment for Federal entry-level professional positions, reasons for accepting or declining offer, 1990 surveys, GAO rpt, 26119–387
Recruitment visits at colleges by Federal agencies and private companies, and school officials views, 1991, GAO rpt, 26119–377
Science and engineering labor force, Federal and university research funding, and educational data, series, 9626–6
Senior Executive Service members characteristics, entries, exits, and awards, FY79-91, annual rpt, 9844–36
Senior Executive Service members views on work environment, 1989 and 1991 surveys, GAO rpt, 26119–402
Senior Executive Service noncareer and Schedule C appointments, by agency, 1990-91, GAO rpt, 26119–412
Southwestern US employment by industry div, earnings, and hours, by State, monthly rpt, 6962–2
Statistical Abstract of US, 1992 annual data compilation, 2324–1.10
Supervisors (first-line) in Fed Govt, performance ratings by self, superiors, and subordinates, 1991 survey, 9498–15
Training for job qualification and skill improvement, workers participating by training source, occupation, age, sex, and race, 1991, 6728–32
Unemployment insurance claims and covered unemployment by program, and extended benefit triggers, by State, weekly rpt, 6402–15
Unemployment insurance claims, by program, weekly press release, 6402–14
VA health care facilities nonveteran outpatient visits, by eligibility type, facility, and region, quarterly rpt, 8602–4
Veterans (Vietnam) labor force status and earnings, by whether served in Southeast Asia, presence and severity of disability, and selected other characteristics, 1989, article, 6722–1.326
Veterans employment by Federal agency, and hiring practices, 1988-91, GAO rpt, 26119–391
Vietnam Orderly Departure Program, former Fed Govt employees arrivals in US and refugee camps, monthly rpt, 7002–4
Weather services activities and funding, by Federal agency, planned FY92-93, annual rpt, 2144–2
White collar employees of Fed Govt, views on work conditions and schedules, 1992 survey, 9848–41
Work conditions in Fed Govt, employee views, 1991 survey, GAO rpt, 26119–406
Workers compensation benefits, by type of program and insurer, and State, 1988-89, annual article, 4742–1.311
Workers compensation costs of Fed Govt, and vocational rehabilitation costs and workload, FY82-90, GAO rpt, 26119–381
Workers compensation laws of States and Fed Govt, 1992 annual rpt, 6504–11
see also Civil service pensions
see also Civil service system
see also Congressional employees
see also Diplomatic and consular service
see also Federal pay
see also Labor-management relations in government
see also Military personnel
see also Postal employees
see also Presidential appointments
see also under names of individual Federal departments and agencies

Federal Energy Administration
see Department of Energy

Federal Energy Regulatory Commission
Activities of FERC, hydroelectric project licensing, and rate regulation, FY91, annual rpt, 3084–9
Electric power plants certification applications filed with FERC, for small production and cogeneration facilities, FY80-91, annual listing, 3084–13
Hydroelectric power plants licensing by FERC, impacts of environmental laws, with staffing and plant safety incidents, 1980s-90s, GAO rpt, 26113–599
Hydroelectric power plants retired, characteristics and location, as of 1992, annual listing, 3084–12
Labor unions recognized in Fed Govt, agreements and membership by agency and facility, as of Jan 1991, biennial listing, 9844–14
Natural gas pipelines and owners, and fields, as of Sept 1990, map, 3088–21

Federal executive departments
Budget of US, obligations and authority by function, agency, and program, with summaries and analyses, FY93, annual rpt, 104–2
Budget of US, receipts by source, outlays by agency and program, and balances, monthly rpt, 8102–3
Employment (civilian) of Fed Govt, work-years, pay rates, and benefits use and costs, by agency, FY90, annual rpt, 9844–31
Employment and payroll (civilian) of Fed Govt, by agency in DC metro area, total US, and abroad, bimonthly rpt, 9842–1
Ethics regulation, activities, and staff of Federal agencies, 1991, biennial rpt, 9834–1
Financial operations of Fed Govt, detailed data, *Treasury Bulletin*, quarterly rpt, 8002–4
Investigations of Federal agency and program operations, summaries of findings, as of 1991, annual GAO rpt, 26104–5
Labor unions recognized in Fed Govt, agreements and membership by agency and facility, as of Jan 1991, biennial listing, 9844–14

Natl Archives holdings of Federal agencies administrative records and other materials, final inventories, series, 9516–2
see also Federal boards, committees, and commissions
see also Federal independent agencies
see also under By Federal Agency in the "Index by Categories"
see also under names of individual Federal departments and agencies

Federal expenditures
see Budget of the U.S.
see Defense expenditures
see Government contracts and procurement
see Government spending
see terms beginning with Federal aid and Federal funding

Federal Financial Institutions Examination Council
Banks (insured commercial and FDIC-insured savings) assets, income, and financial ratios, by asset size and State, quarterly rpt, 13002–3
Budget of US, obligations and authority by function, agency, and program, with summaries and analyses, FY93, annual rpt, 104–2
Financial statements of FFIEC, and bank and thrift finances by instn type, 1991, annual rpt, 13004–2
Loans of US banks to foreigners at all US and foreign offices, by country group and country, quarterly rpt, 13002–1
Trust assets of banks, trust companies, and S&Ls, by type of asset and fund, selected firm, and State, 1991, annual rpt, 13004–1

Federal Financing Bank
Budget of US, obligations and authority by function, agency, and program, with summaries and analyses, FY93, annual rpt, 104–2
Holdings and transactions of Fed Financing Bank, by borrower, monthly press release, 12802–1
Liabilities (contingent) and claims paid by Fed Govt on federally insured and guaranteed contracts with foreign obligors, by country and program, periodic rpt, 8002–12
Loans of Treasury Dept and FFB to govt corporations and agencies, outstanding amounts, 1987-91, GAO rpt, 26111–79
Rural Electrification Admin activities and finances, and loans by State, FY91 and trends from FY36, annual rpt, 1244–3
Small Business Admin dev company loan program and debenture sale activity, with data by firm, industry div, State, and region, quarterly rpt, 9762–6

Federal funding for energy programs
Agricultural research and education grants, USDA competitive awards by program and recipient, FY91, annual listing, 1764–1
Assistance (block and categorical grants) programs for State and local govts, FY91, biennial listing, 10044–8
Assistance (financial and nonfinancial) of Fed Govt, 1992 base edition, annual listing, 104–5
Auto (electric-powered) R&D activity and DOE funding shares, FY91, annual rpt, 3304–2
Auto engine and power train R&D projects, DOE contracts and funding by recipient, FY91, annual rpt, 3304–17
Biomass energy program of TVA, operations, finances, and technological characteristics, series, 9806–9
Budget of US, balances of budget authority obligated and unobligated, by function and agency, FY90-93, annual rpt, 104–8
Budget of US, Bush Admin proposals, with detail for defense budgets, and historical data from FY34, FY93, 108–46
Budget of US, CBO analysis and review of FY93 budget by function, annual rpt, 26304–2
Budget of US, CBO analysis of revenue and spending alternatives and projections of economic indicators, FY93-97, annual rpt, 26304–3
Budget of US, House concurrent resolution, with spending and revenue targets, FY93 and projected to FY97, annual rpt, 21264–2
Budget of US, midsession review of FY93 budget, by function, annual rpt, 104–7
Budget of US, obligations and authority by function, agency, and program, with summaries and analyses, FY93, annual rpt, 104–2
Budget of US, receipts by source, outlays by agency and program, and balances, monthly rpt, 8102–3
Conservation aid of Fed Govt to public and nonprofit private instns, by building type and State, 1991, annual rpt, 3304–15
Conservation of energy for housing and commercial buildings, technologies use, costs, efficiency, and residential tax credits, 1970s-90 and projected to 2010, 26358–259
Conservation of energy, State programs aid from Fed Govt, and energy savings, by State, 1990, annual rpt, 3304–1
DOE activities and finances, summary energy supply and demand data, and bibl, 1990, annual rpt, 3024–2
DOE budget authority, by program and subagency, FY92, annual rpt, 3024–5
DOE contracts and grants, by category, State, and for top contractors, FY91, annual rpt, 3004–21
DOE programs finances and mgmt, audits and investigations, series, 3006–5
DOE R&D field offices and facilities, activities, staff, and finances, FY91, biennial rpt, 3004–4
Expenditures of Fed Govt in States, by type, program, agency, and State, FY91, annual rpt, 2464–2
Finances of Fed Govt, cash and debt transactions, daily tables, 8102–4
Fraud and abuse in DOE programs, audit resolution activities, 2nd half FY92, semiannual rpt, 3002–15
Fraud and abuse in DOE programs, audits and investigations, 2nd half FY92, semiannual rpt, 3002–12
Inventions recommended by Natl Inst of Standards and Technology for DOE support, awards, and evaluation status, 1991, annual listing, 2214–5
Investigations of Federal agency and program operations, summaries of findings, as of 1991, annual GAO rpt, 26104–5.2
Loans and loan guarantees of Fed Govt, outstanding amounts by agency and program, *Treasury Bulletin*, quarterly rpt, 8002–4.11
Natl Energy Strategy plans for conservation, R&D, security, and pollution reduction, technical rpt series, 3006–13
Natl income and product accounts, comprehensive accounts and components, benchmark revisions, 1929-88, 2708–5
Natl income and product accounts, comprehensive accounts and components, *Survey of Current Business*, monthly rpt, 2702–1.26
Oil enhanced recovery research contracts of DOE, project summaries, funding, and bibl, quarterly rpt, 3002–14
R&D funding by Fed Govt, by detailed function, program, and agency, FY91-93, annual rpt, 9627–9
R&D projects and funding of DOE at natl labs, universities, and other instns, periodic summary rpt series, 3004–18
Rural Electrification Admin loans, and borrower operating and financial data, by distribution firm and State, 1991, annual rpt, 1244–1
Science and Engineering Indicators, employment, education, R&D funding, and industry impacts, with foreign comparisons, 1960s-91, biennial rpt, 9624–10.4
Small business procurement contract awards of DOE, by business type and subagency, FY90, annual rpt, 3004–35
Small business R&D grants of Fed Govt, by program area, agency, MSA, and State, FY90, annual rpt, 9764–7
Solar photovoltaic R&D sponsored by DOE, projects, funding, and rpts, FY91, annual listing, 3304–20
Southeastern Power Admin sales by customer, plants, capacity, and Southeastern Fed Power Program financial statements, FY91, annual rpt, 3234–1
Strategic Petroleum Reserve capacity, inventory, fill rate, and finances, quarterly rpt, 3002–13
TVA energy use by fuel type, and conservation costs and savings, FY91, annual rpt, 9804–26
TVA finances and operations by program and facility, FY91, annual rpt, 9804–32
Uranium enrichment facilities of DOE, financial statements, FY90-91, annual rpt, 3354–7
see also Department of Energy National Laboratories
see also Low-income energy assistance

Federal funding for research and development
Acid rain research activities and funding, by Federal agency, projected FY91-92, 14358–3
Agricultural research and education appropriations of USDA, by program and subagency, FY83-91, annual rpt, 1004–19
Agricultural research and education grants, USDA competitive awards by program and recipient, FY91, annual listing, 1764–1
Agricultural research funding and staffing for USDA, State agencies, and other instns, by topic, FY91, annual rpt, 1744–2

Agricultural research grants of USDA, by program, subagency, and country, FY92, annual listing, 1954–3
AID contracts and grants for technical and support services, by instn, country, and State, FY91, annual listing, 9914–7
AID contracts, grants, and cooperative agreements with higher education instns, by project, instn, and country, FY91, annual listing, 9914–6
Air traffic control and airway facilities improvement activities under Aviation System Capital Investment Plan, 1981-91 and projected to 2006, annual rpt, 7504–12
Arkansas govt science agency research grants and industry sponsors matching funds, and Federal R&D aid to higher education instns, mid 1980s-90, hearing, 21708–131
Assistance (block and categorical grants) programs for State and local govts, FY91, biennial listing, 10044–8
Assistance (financial and nonfinancial) of Fed Govt, 1992 base edition, annual listing, 104–5
Budget of US, Bush Admin proposals, with detail for defense budgets, and historical data from FY34, FY93, 108–46
Budget of US, House Budget Committee analysis of Bush Admin proposals and economic assumptions, FY93, 21268–42
Budget of US, House concurrent resolution, with spending and revenue targets, FY93 and projected to FY97, annual rpt, 21264–2
Budget of US, midsession review of FY93 budget, by function, annual rpt, 104–7
Budget of US, obligations and authority by function, agency, and program, with summaries and analyses, FY93, annual rpt, 104–2
Budget of US, receipts by source, outlays by agency and program, and balances, monthly rpt, 8102–3
Coal-fired power plants air pollutant reduction technology funding, and impacts on energy costs and emissions, 1950s-87 and projected to 2010, annual rpt, 3334–5; 3338–4
Coal-fired power plants air pollutant reduction technology funding, and project descriptions, 1991, annual rpt, 3334–4
Coal Surface Mining Reclamation and Enforcement Office activities and funding, by State and Indian tribe, FY91, annual rpt, 5644–1
DOE Superconducting Super Collider particle accelerator program, conventional facility construction funding and estimated and actual costs, 1988-99, 3006–5.32
Drug abuse and trafficking reduction programs activities, funding, staff, and Bush Admin budget request, by Federal agency, FY91-93, annual rpt, 234–2
Drug abuse and trafficking reduction research funding by Natl Inst on Drug Abuse and Office of Justice Programs, 1970s-91, GAO rpt, 26131–99
Economic Dev Admin activities, and funding by program, recipient, State, and county, FY91 and cumulative from FY66, annual rpt, 2064–2
Engineering research and education grants of NSF, FY91, annual listing, 9624–24
EPA pollution control grant program activities, monthly rpt, 9182–8
EPA R&D programs and funding, FY91, annual listing, 9184–18
EPA R&D programs and funding, planned FY92, annual listing, 9184–17
Expenditures for education by Federal agency, program, and recipient type, and instn spending, 1960s-91, annual rpt, 4824–8
Expenditures for education, by Federal agency, program, and State, FY65-92, annual rpt, 4824–2.27
Expenditures for R&D by Fed Govt and higher education instns, labor force, and educational data, for science and engineering, series, 9626–6
Expenditures for R&D by Fed Govt, and related topics, advance rpt series, 9626–8
Expenditures for R&D by Fed Govt, by detailed function, program, and agency, FY91-93, annual rpt, 9627–9
Expenditures of Fed Govt for large-scale R&D projects, issues and impacts on other research, with data for space station and super collider, 1991 hearings, 21268–43
Expenditures of Fed Govt in States, by type, program, agency, and State, FY91, annual rpt, 2464–2
FAA research funding and staff, by research area and project, FY88-91, GAO rpt, 26113–565
Fiscal policy (supply side) of Reagan Admin, economic impacts, 1980s and trends from 1960s, technical paper, 9385–1.304; 9385–8.125
Fish and Wildlife Service restoration programs funding, land purchases, and project listing, by State, FY90, annual rpt, 5504–1
Fishery research of State fish and wildlife agencies, federally funded projects and costs, annual listing, discontinued, 5504–23
Forest Service activities and finances, by region and State, FY91, annual rpt, 1204–1
Geological Survey activities and funding, FY91, annual rpt, 5664–8
Great Lakes Science Advisory Board research activities and water quality goals, FY91, biennial rpt, 14644–6
Higher education and nonprofit instns R&D and related activities funding by Fed Govt, by field, instn, agency, and State, FY90, annual rpt, 9627–17
Higher education instn and federally funded center R&D funding, by field, instn, and State, FY90, annual rpt, 9627–13
Higher education instn R&D facilities space and equipment adequacy, needs, and funding by source, by instn type and control, 1992, biennial rpt, 9624–25
Higher education instn R&D funding by Fed Govt, indirect costs and effects of alternative reimbursement policies, FY89, GAO rpt, 26113–592
Higher education instn R&D supported by NSF and NIH, license transfer to private firms, related income, and scientists associated with licensees, FY89-90, GAO rpt, 26113–575
Higher education instn undergrad research grants of NSF, administrator and recipient characteristics and views, 1987-89, 9628–86
Hwy construction and design R&D, quarterly journal, 7552–3
Industry (US) intl competitiveness, with selected foreign and US operating data by major firm and product, series, 2046–12
Labor Intl Affairs Bur research contracts, FY83-91, annual listing, 6364–1
MarAd activities, finances, subsidies, and world merchant fleet operations, FY91, annual rpt, 7704–14
Marine mammals protection activities and funding, populations, and harvests, by species, 1990, annual rpt, 5504–12
Militarily strategic manufacturing industries finances, operations, and intl competitiveness, series, 2026–1
NASA funding by program and type of performer, and contract awards by State, FY91, annual rpt, 9504–6.2
NASA procurement contract awards, by type, contractor, State, and country, FY92 with trends from 1961, semiannual rpt, 9502–6
NASA R&D funding to higher education instns, by field, instn, and State, FY91, annual listing, 9504–7
Natl Energy Strategy plans for conservation and pollution reduction, funding for R&D and basic science activities, FY91-93, 3008–128
NSF activities, finances, and funding by program, FY91, annual rpt, 9624–6
NSF grants and contracts, by field, recipient, and State, FY90, annual rpt, 9624–26
NSF programs fraud and abuse, audits and investigations, 2nd half FY92, semiannual rpt, 9622–1
NSF R&D grant awards, by div and program, periodic rpt series, 9626–7
NSF Science Resources Studies Div project descriptions and rpts, annual listing, suspended, 9624–21
Nuclear power plant safety standards and research, design, licensing, construction, operation, and finances, with data by reactor, quarterly journal, 3352–4
Nuclear Regulatory Commission budget, staff, and activities, by program, FY91-93, annual rpt, 9634–9
Nuclear Waste Fund finances, and DOE Civilian Radioactive Waste Mgmt Office R&D costs, FY90-91, annual rpt, 3364–1
Nuclear Waste Fund finances, and DOE Civilian Radioactive Waste Mgmt Program costs, quarterly rpt, 3362–1
Nuclear waste repository research, transport, and disposal costs under alternative systems, 1983-89 and projected to 2094, 3368–5
Ocean pollution, estuary, and coastal waters monitoring and assessment, NOAA activities and funding, FY90, annual rpt, 2174–9
Ocean pollution research, monitoring, and resources dev activities of Fed Govt, funding and project descriptions, FY89, annual rpt, 2144–23
Ocean pollution research, monitoring, and resources dev activities of Fed Govt, 5-year plan and funding by agency, FY87-92, triennial rpt, 2148–56
Peace Inst activities and finances, FY90-91, biennial rpt, 29594–1

Population and reproduction research, Fed Govt funding by project, FY90, annual listing, 4474–9
Science and engineering grad enrollment, by field, source of funds, and characteristics of student and instn, 1990, annual rpt, 9627–7
Science and Engineering Indicators, employment, education, R&D funding, and industry impacts, with foreign comparisons, 1960s-91, biennial rpt, 9624–10
Semiconductor industry R&D consortium funding, outlays, and effectiveness in improving US competitive position, 1980s-92, GAO rpt, 26113–588
Small business product and service R&D grants of Fed Govt, indicators of commercial success, FY88-90, chartbook, 9768–23
Small business R&D grants of Fed Govt, by program area, agency, MSA, and State, FY90, annual rpt, 9764–7
Small business R&D grants of Fed Govt, project sales by type and dev funding by source, by agency and selected firm, 1984-91, GAO rpt, 26113–393
Smithsonian Instn activities and finances, FY91, annual rpt, 29574–1
Space and aeronautics activities and budgets, by Federal agency, FY59-91, annual rpt, 9504–9.2
Statistical Abstract of US, 1992 annual data compilation, 2324–1.20
Superconducting super collider and other large-scale R&D projects of Fed Govt, issues and impacts on other research, 1991 hearings, 21268–43
Superconducting super collider construction costs, and funding by source, FY88-91 and projected to FY99, 3006–5.28
Superconducting Super Collider particle accelerator program of DOE, conventional facility construction funding and estimated and actual costs, 1988-99, 3006–5.32
Technology Assessment Office activities and rpts, FY91, annual rpt, 26354–3
Technology transfer by Federal R&D labs to small manufacturers, promotional programs activities and grants to States, late 1980s-91, GAO rpt, 26113–551
Telecommunications and Info Natl Admin rpts, FY91, annual listing, 2804–3
Traffic safety grants and activities of Natl Hwy Traffic Safety Admin, and fatal traffic accident data, 1990, annual rpt, 7764–1
Transit systems R&D projects and funding of Federal Transit Admin, FY91, annual listing, 7884–1
Transit systems research and training grants to higher education instns, by project, FY92, annual listing, 7884–7
Weather services activities and funding, by Federal agency, planned FY92-93, annual rpt, 2144–2
see also Defense research
see also Department of Energy National Laboratories
see also Federal aid to medicine
see also Federal funding for energy programs
see also Federally Funded R&D Centers

Federal Grain Inspection Service
Activities and finances of FGIS, domestic and export inspections, foreign buyers complaints, and handling facilities explosions, FY92, annual rpt, 1294–1
Budget of US, obligations and authority by function, agency, and program, with summaries and analyses, FY93, annual rpt, 104–2
Revenue of USDA, by source and subagency, FY88-92, GAO rpt, 26113–602

Federal grants
see terms beginning with Federal aid and Federal funding

Federal Highway Administration
Accidents direct and indirect costs, by cost type, payment source, and severity, 1980s, 7558–114
Auto, van, and light truck ownership and operating costs, by vehicle size and year of operation, 1991 model year, biennial rpt, 7554–21
Bridge replacement and repair program funding by bridge, and bridge status, by State, 1990, biennial rpt, 7554–27
Budget of US, obligations and authority by function, agency, and program, with summaries and analyses, FY93, annual rpt, 104–2
Commuting to work, by mode, trip duration, and work location, 1980 and 1990, 7558–120
Construction (hwy) minority contractor training, funding by region, FY92, annual release, 7554–40
Construction bids and contracts for Federal-aid hwys, by State, 1st half 1992, semiannual rpt, 7552–12
Construction material prices and indexes for Federal-aid hwy system, by type of material and urban-rural location, quarterly rpt, 7552–7
Construction material prices and indexes for Federal-aid hwy system, by type of material, quarterly press release, 7552–16
Construction material use by type, and spending for hwys, by State, 1940s-91, annual rpt, 7554–29
Construction zones temporary pavement markings impacts on driver performance, 1992 rpt, 7558–116
Construction zones traffic control and safety procedures and equipment, 1991 conf, 7558–115
Drivers licenses issued and in force by age and sex, fees, and renewal, by license class and State, 1990, annual rpt, 7554–16
Drivers licenses requirements and admin, by State and Canada Province, as of Jan 1992, biennial rpt, 7554–18
Electronic traffic mgmt and info system, demonstration program results, late 1980s, 7558–119
Employment of DOT, by subagency, occupation, and selected personnel characteristics, FY91, annual rpt, 7304–18
Expenditures and allocation methods, for Federal-aid hwy system, FY92-97, 7558–107
Expenditures for hwy and transit system programs, proposed FY92-97, 7558–117
Expenditures for traffic safety programs of FHwA, by State, FY90, annual rpt, 7764–1.1
Expenditures of Fed Govt in States, by type, program, agency, and State, FY91, annual rpt, 2464–2
Expenditures of FHwA for hwys, FY79-89, annual rpt, 7304–1
Gasoline and other motor fuel tax rates, by State, 1981-91, annual table, 7554–32
Gasoline and other motor fuel use by State, and tax rates by jurisdiction, monthly rpt, 7552–1
Hwy Statistics, detailed data by State, 1991, annual rpt, 7554–1
Hwy Statistics, summary data by State, 1990-91, annual rpt, 7554–24
Hwy Statistics, summary data with trends and projections, 1992 chartbook, 7554–41
Interstate hwy mileage, by completion status and State, as of June 1992, semiannual rpt, 7552–5
Interstate hwy mileage, by route and State, 1991 listing, 7558–111
Lighting of roadways, impacts on traffic accidents by circumstances, 1991 rpt, 7558–118
R&D for hwy design and construction, quarterly journal, 7552–3
Research on traffic safety, literature review, with data on accidents and impact of safety measures, 1961-90, 7558–98
Safety program funding by State, and accident and death reductions, FY91, annual rpt, 7554–26
Scenic byway routes and mileage, by govt ownership, land use and usage restrictions, and other characteristics, 1990, 7558–112
Scenic byways economic, safety, and other issues, series, 7556–8
Speed averages and vehicles exceeding 55 mph, by State, quarterly rpt, 7552–14
Traffic accidents, casualties, and rates, by hwy type and State, 1989, annual rpt, 7554–2
Traffic volume on rural roads and city streets, monthly rpt, 7552–8
Travel patterns, personal and household characteristics, and auto and public transport use, 1990 survey, series, 7556–6
Truck accidents, casualties, and damage, by circumstances and characteristics of persons and vehicles involved, 1989, annual rpt, 7554–9
Trucks (wide) on narrow hwys, lane location characteristics and effects on other traffic, 1991 rpt, 7558–113

Federal Home Loan Bank Board
Budget of US, authoritative financial statements with appropriations, outlays, and receipts, by category and agency, FY91, annual rpt, 8104–2.2
Labor unions recognized in Fed Govt, agreements and membership by agency and facility, as of Jan 1991, biennial listing, 9844–14
Members of Fed Home Loan Bank System, and assets, annual listing, discontinued, 9314–5
see also Office of Thrift Supervision

Federal Home Loan Bank of Atlanta
Financial statements of Bank, quarterly rpt, 9302–37
Financial statements of Bank, 1990-91, annual rpt, 9304–1
Savings instns, FHLB 4th District members finances, by State, 1985-89, discontinued annual rpt series, 9304–29
Southeastern States, FHLB 4th District, employment and housing indicators by State, quarterly rpt, 9302–36
Federal Home Loan Bank of Boston
Financial statements of Bank, and members by type of instn and State, 1990-91, annual rpt, 9304–2
Financial statements of Bank, quarterly rpt, 9302–35
Savings instns, FHLB 1st District members, financial condition, and locations, 1992, annual listing, 9304–26
Savings instns, FHLB 1st District members financial operations compared to banks, and related economic and housing indicators, bimonthly rpt with articles, suspended, 9302–4
Federal Home Loan Bank of Chicago
Financial statements of Bank, 1989-91, annual rpt, 9304–4
Housing vacancy rates for single and multifamily units and mobile homes in FHLB 7th District, by ZIP code, annual MSA rpt series, 9304–18
Mortgage interest fixed and adjustable rates and fees offered by Illinois S&Ls, monthly rpt, discontinued, 9302–6
Mortgage interest fixed and adjustable rates and fees offered by Wisconsin S&Ls, monthly rpt, discontinued, 9302–7
Savings instns, FHLB 7th District and natl cost of funds indexes, and mortgage rates, monthly rpt, 9302–30
Savings instns, FHLB 7th District members assets and deposits by instn and market area, annual rpt, discontinued, 9304–28
Federal Home Loan Bank of Cincinnati
Financial statements of Bank, 1989-91, annual rpt, 9304–6
Housing vacancy rates for single and multifamily units and mobile homes in FHLB 5th District, discontinued annual MSA rpt series, 9304–27
Federal Home Loan Bank of Dallas
Financial statements of Bank, 1989-91, annual rpt, 9304–11
Housing vacancy rates for single and multifamily units and mobile homes in FHLB 9th District, discontinued annual MSA rpt series, 9304–19
Federal Home Loan Bank of Des Moines
Financial statements of Bank, 1989-91, annual rpt, 9304–7
Savings and loan assns, FHLB 8th District members, locations, assets, and savings, 1992, annual listing, 9304–9
Federal Home Loan Bank of Indianapolis
Savings and loan assns, FHLB 6th District insured members financial condition and operations by State, quarterly rpt, 9302–23
Savings instns, FHLB 6th and 11th District and natl cost of funds indexes, and mortgage and Treasury bill rates, monthly rpt, 9302–38
Federal Home Loan Bank of New York
Financial statements of Bank, 1989-91, annual rpt, 9304–12
Federal Home Loan Bank of Pittsburgh
Financial statements of Bank, 1989-91, annual rpt, 9304–13
Federal Home Loan Bank of San Francisco
Financial statements of Bank, 1989-91, annual rpt, 9304–14
Savings instns, FHLB 11th District shareholder instns, offices, and financial condition, 1992 annual listing, 9304–23
Savings instns regulatory issues, 1989 annual conf, 9304–24
Federal Home Loan Bank of Seattle
Financial statements of Bank, 1989-91, annual rpt, 9304–15
Housing vacancy rates for single and multifamily units and mobile homes in FHLB 12th District, by ZIP code, annual MSA rpt series, 9304–21
Federal Home Loan Bank of Topeka
Financial statements of Bank, 1989-91, annual rpt, 9304–16
Housing vacancy rates for single and multifamily units and mobile homes in FHLB 10th District, by ZIP code, annual MSA rpt series, 9304–22
Savings instns, FHLB 10th District members, locations, assets, and deposits, 1992, annual listing, 9304–17
Federal Home Loan Banks
Budget of US, financial statements of federally sponsored enterprises, FY93, annual rpt, 104–2.6
Finances of FHLBs, and affordable housing programs, 1991 hearings, 21248–170
Financial statements of FHLBs, monthly rpt, 9442–1
Financial statements of FHLBs, 1989-91, annual rpt, 9444–1
see also Federal Home Loan Bank Board
see also Federal Home Loan Bank of Atlanta
see also Federal Home Loan Bank of Boston
see also Federal Home Loan Bank of Chicago
see also Federal Home Loan Bank of Cincinnati
see also Federal Home Loan Bank of Dallas
see also Federal Home Loan Bank of Des Moines
see also Federal Home Loan Bank of Indianapolis
see also Federal Home Loan Bank of New York
see also Federal Home Loan Bank of Pittsburgh
see also Federal Home Loan Bank of San Francisco
see also Federal Home Loan Bank of Seattle
see also Federal Home Loan Bank of Topeka
Federal Home Loan Mortgage Corp.
Budget of US, financial statements of federally sponsored enterprises, FY93, annual rpt, 104–2.6
Finances of FHLMC, 1991 hearings, 21248–170
Financial condition and capital adequacy of Freddie Mac, 1990, annual rpt, 5184–8
Financial statements and activities of FHLMC, 1991, annual rpt, 9414–1
Home mortgage market activity and debt outstanding, 1987-90, annual rpt, 9364–5.7
Mortgage applications, dispositions, and secondary loan market sales, by purpose, lender type, and applicant and neighborhood characteristics, 1991, article, 9362–1.307
Mortgage interest fixed and adjustable rates and fees offered, by region, weekly rpt, 9412–3
Federal Housing Administration
see Housing (FHA), HUD
Federal Housing Finance Board
Budget of US, authoritative financial statements with appropriations, outlays, and receipts, by category and agency, FY91, annual rpt, 8104–2.2
Budget of US, obligations and authority by function, agency, and program, with summaries and analyses, FY93, annual rpt, 104–2
Fed Home Loan Banks financial statements, 1989-91, annual rpt, 9444–1
Financial statements of FHLBs, monthly rpt, 9442–1
Mortgages (conventional) terms at closing, by lender type, with periodic data by district, State, and for 32 MSAs, monthly rpt, 9442–2
Mortgages (conventional) terms at closing, for fixed- and adjustable-rate loans by purpose, FHLB district, State, and selected MSA, 1960s-91, annual rpt, 9444–2
Federal independent agencies
Budget of US, authoritative financial statements with appropriations, outlays, and receipts, by category and agency, FY91, annual rpt, 8104–2.2
Budget of US, obligations and authority by function, agency, and program, with summaries and analyses, FY93, annual rpt, 104–2
Budget of US, receipts by source, outlays by agency and program, and balances, monthly rpt, 8102–3
Education funding by Federal agency, program, and recipient type, and instn spending, 1960s-91, annual rpt, 4824–8
Employment (civilian) of Fed Govt, work-years, pay rates, and benefits use and costs, by agency, FY90, annual rpt, 9844–31
Employment and payroll (civilian) of Fed Govt, by agency in DC metro area, total US, and abroad, bimonthly rpt, 9842–1
Financial operations of Fed Govt, detailed data, *Treasury Bulletin*, quarterly rpt, 8002–4
Flow-of-funds accounts, savings, investments, and credit statements, quarterly rpt, 9365–3.3
Investigations of Federal agency and program operations, summaries of findings, as of 1991, annual GAO rpt, 26104–5
Labor unions recognized in Fed Govt, agreements and membership by agency and facility, as of Jan 1991, biennial listing, 9844–14
see also ACTION
see also Administrative Conference of the U.S.
see also Advisory Council on Historic Preservation
see also African Development Foundation

see also American Battle Monuments Commission
see also Appalachian Regional Commission
see also Central Intelligence Agency
see also Commission of Fine Arts
see also Consumer Product Safety Commission
see also Environmental Protection Agency
see also Equal Employment Opportunity Commission
see also Export-Import Bank
see also Farm Credit Administration
see also Federal boards, committees, and commissions
see also Federal Communications Commission
see also Federal Deposit Insurance Corp.
see also Federal Emergency Management Agency
see also Federal Home Loan Bank Board
see also Federal Housing Finance Board
see also Federal Maritime Commission
see also Federal Mediation and Conciliation Service
see also Federal National Mortgage Association
see also Federal Reserve System
see also Federal Trade Commission
see also General Services Administration
see also Government corporations and enterprises
see also Interstate Commerce Commission
see also Merit Systems Protection Board
see also National Aeronautics and Space Administration
see also National Archives and Records Administration
see also National Credit Union Administration
see also National Foundation on the Arts and the Humanities
see also National Labor Relations Board
see also National Mediation Board
see also National Railroad Adjustment Board
see also National Science Foundation
see also National Transportation Safety Board
see also Neighborhood Reinvestment Corp.
see also Nuclear Regulatory Commission
see also Occupational Safety and Health Review Commission
see also Office of Government Ethics
see also Office of Personnel Management
see also Panama Canal Commission
see also Peace Corps
see also Postal Rate Commission
see also Railroad Retirement Board
see also Resolution Trust Corp.
see also Securities and Exchange Commission
see also Selective Service System
see also Small Business Administration
see also Student Loan Marketing Association
see also Tennessee Valley Authority
see also U.S. Arms Control and Disarmament Agency
see also U.S. Information Agency
see also U.S. International Development Cooperation Agency
see also U.S. International Trade Commission
see also U.S. Office of Special Counsel
see also U.S. Postal Service
see also Veterans Administration
see also under By Federal Agency in the "Index by Categories"

Federal Inspectors General reports

Activities of Inspectors General, and fraud and abuse audits and investigations by agency, FY91, annual rpt, 104–29
Alcohol use, knowledge, attitudes, and info sources of youth, series, 4006–10
Commerce Dept programs fraud and abuse, audits and investigations, 2nd half FY92, semiannual rpt, 2002–5
DOD programs fraud and abuse, audits and investigations, 2nd half FY92, semiannual rpt, 3542–18
DOE programs finances and mgmt, audits and investigations, series, 3006–5
DOE programs fraud and abuse, audit resolution activities, 2nd half FY92, semiannual rpt, 3002–15
DOE programs fraud and abuse, audits and investigations, 2nd half FY92, semiannual rpt, 3002–12
DOT programs fraud and abuse, audit resolution activities, 1st half FY92, semiannual rpt, 7302–12
DOT programs fraud and abuse, audits and investigations, FY80-89, annual rpt, 7304–1
DOT programs fraud and abuse, audits and investigations, 1st half FY92, semiannual rpt, 7302–4
Education Dept programs fraud and abuse, audits and investigations, 2nd half FY92, semiannual rpt, 4802–1
EPA programs fraud and abuse, audits and investigations, 1st half FY92, semiannual rpt, 9182–10
GSA programs fraud and abuse, audits and investigations, 1st half FY92, semiannual rpt, 9452–8
Health care professionals licensing and disciplinary actions of State medical boards, 1950s-88, series, 4006–8
HHS programs fraud and abuse, audits and investigations, 1st half FY92, semiannual rpt, 4002–6
Hospital closures in 1990, operating characteristics, current use, and location, annual rpt, 4004–35
HUD programs fraud and abuse, audits and investigations, FY92, semiannual rpt, 5002–8; 5002–11
Interior Dept programs fraud and abuse, audits and investigations, 2nd half FY92, semiannual rpt, 5302–2
Labor Dept programs fraud and abuse, audits and investigations, 2nd half FY92, semiannual rpt, 6302–2
Medicare beneficiaries multiple hospital admissions, by reason and characteristics of instn and patient, 1985, 4008–117
Medicare financial and admin issues, Inspector General rpts, series, 4006–11
Medicare reimbursement of hospitals under prospective payment system, diagnosis related group code assignment and effects on care and instn finances, series, 4006–7
NASA programs fraud and abuse, audits and investigations, 2nd half FY92, semiannual rpt, 9502–9
NSF programs fraud and abuse, audits and investigations, 2nd half FY92, semiannual rpt, 9622–1
Resolution Trust Corp programs fraud and abuse, audits and investigations, 2nd half FY92, semiannual rpt, 9722–6
Small Business Admin programs fraud and abuse, audits and investigations, 1st half FY92, semiannual rpt, 9762–5
State Dept programs fraud and abuse, audits and investigations, 2nd half FY92, semiannual rpt, 7002–6
USDA programs fraud and abuse, audits and investigations, FY92, semiannual rpt, 1002–4
USIA programs fraud and abuse, audits and investigations, 1st half FY92, semiannual rpt, 9852–2
VA programs fraud and abuse, audits and investigations, 2nd half FY92, semiannual rpt, 8602–1

Federal Intermediate Credit Banks

see Farm Credit System

Federal Judicial Center

Budget of US, authoritative financial statements with appropriations, outlays, and receipts, by category and agency, FY91, annual rpt, 8104–2.2
Budget of US, obligations and authority by function, agency, and program, with summaries and analyses, FY93, annual rpt, 104–2

Federal Labor Relations Authority

Activities of FLRA and Fed Service Impasses Panel, and cases by union, agency, and disposition, FY86-91, annual rpt, 13364–1
Budget of US, authoritative financial statements with appropriations, outlays, and receipts, by category and agency, FY91, annual rpt, 8104–2.2
Budget of US, obligations and authority by function, agency, and program, with summaries and analyses, FY93, annual rpt, 104–2

Federal land banks

see Farm Credit System

Federal lands

see Government supplies and property
see Military bases, posts, and reservations
see Public lands

Federal-local relations

Army Corps of Engineers activities and projects, FY88 and trends from 1800s, annual rpt, 3754–1.1
Army Corps of Engineers activities and projects, FY89 and trends from 1800s, annual rpt, 3754–1.2
Army Corps of Engineers activities and projects, FY90 and trends from 1800s, annual rpt, 3754–1.3
Army Corps of Engineers water resources dev projects, characteristics, and costs, 1950s-89, biennial State rpt series, 3756–1
Army Corps of Engineers water resources dev projects, characteristics, and costs, 1950s-91, biennial State rpt series, 3756–2
Army Corps of Engineers water resources dev projects, local sponsors views on cooperation and cost sharing, 1991 survey, GAO rpt, 26113–548
Historic and natural natl landmarks damaged and threatened, with owner, location, damage type, and recommended remedial action, 1990, annual listing, 5544–16

see also Federal aid to local areas
see also Indian claims
see also Revenue sharing
Federal Maritime Commission
Activities of FMC, case filings by type and disposition, and civil penalties by shipper, FY91, annual rpt, 9334–1
Budget of US, authoritative financial statements with appropriations, outlays, and receipts, by category and agency, FY91, annual rpt, 8104–2.2
Budget of US, obligations and authority by function, agency, and program, with summaries and analyses, FY93, annual rpt, 104–2
Federal Mediation and Conciliation Service
Activities of FMCS, and cases by issue, region, and State, FY85-90, annual rpt, 9344–1
Budget of US, authoritative financial statements with appropriations, outlays, and receipts, by category and agency, FY91, annual rpt, 8104–2.2
Budget of US, obligations and authority by function, agency, and program, with summaries and analyses, FY93, annual rpt, 104–2
Labor unions recognized in Fed Govt, agreements and membership by agency and facility, as of Jan 1991, biennial listing, 9844–14
Federal Mine Safety and Health Review Commission
Budget of US, authoritative financial statements with appropriations, outlays, and receipts, by category and agency, FY91, annual rpt, 8104–2.2
Budget of US, obligations and authority by function, agency, and program, with summaries and analyses, FY93, annual rpt, 104–2
Federal National Mortgage Association
Activities and finances of Fannie Mae, 1991, annual rpt, 5184–9; 9474–1
Budget of US, financial statements of federally sponsored enterprises, FY93, annual rpt, 104–2.6
Finances of FNMA, 1991 hearings, 21248–170
Home mortgage market activity and debt outstanding, 1987-90, annual rpt, 9364–5.7
Homeownership values, reasons, and barriers, views by race and tenure, 1992 survey, 9478–1
Mortgage applications, dispositions, and secondary loan market sales, by purpose, lender type, and applicant and neighborhood characteristics, 1991, article, 9362–1.307
Federal officials
see Officials
Federal Open Market Committee
Fed Reserve Bd and Reserve banks finances, staff, and review of monetary policy and economic devs, 1991, annual rpt, 9364–1
Monetary aggregates growth and related devs, and FOMC activity, annual article, 9385–1
Policies and transactions, *Fed Reserve Bulletin*, monthly rpt with articles, 9362–1
Federal pay
Advisory committees of Fed Govt, and members, staff, meetings, and costs by agency, FY91, annual rpt, 9454–18
Banks regulatory agencies of Fed Govt, pay comparability and turnover, by occupation, 1991, GAO rpt, 26119–368
Benefits for Federal employee retirement, health, and life insurance, coverage and finances of 4 programs, FY86-90, annual rpt, 9844–37
Budget of US, authoritative financial statements with appropriations, outlays, and receipts, by category and agency, FY91, annual rpt, 8104–2.2
Budget of US, obligations and authority by function, agency, and program, with summaries and analyses, FY93, annual rpt, 104–2
Civil service merit systems operations, pay, appointments, and promotions, for Canada and US, late 1980s-91, 9498–16
Claims Court caseload by type of suit, and judgments, FY92, annual rpt, 18224–1
Criminal justice systems activities, spending, and employment, by level of govt, data compilation, 1992 annual rpt, 6064–6.1
FAA employees job satisfaction, impacts of promotion and pay equity by sex, 1992 technical rpt, 7506–10.105
Finances of Fed Govt, cash and debt transactions, daily tables, 8102–4
House of Representatives salaries, expenses, and contingent fund disbursement, detailed listings, quarterly rpt, 21942–1
Incentive awards to Federal employees, costs, and benefits, by award type and agency, FY90, annual rpt, 9844–20
Income (household, family, and personal), by source, detailed characteristics, and region, 1991, annual Current Population Rpt, 2546–6.76
Income (personal) per capita and by source, and employment, by industry div, State, MSA, and county, 1969-90, annual CD-ROM, 2704–7
Insurance (health) programs for Federal civilian employees, enrollment, profits, and administrative costs, by plan, 1984-90, GAO rpt, 26119–376
Law enforcement spending, employment, and payroll, by activity, level of govt, and State, FY90, annual rpt, 6066–25.50
Merit system oversight and enforcement activities of OPM, series, 9496–2
Natl income and product accounts and components, *Survey of Current Business*, monthly rpt, 2702–1.23
Occupational Outlook Handbook, 1992-93, biennial rpt, 6744–1
Pacific territories population and housing detailed characteristics, by location, 1990 Census of Population and Housing, series, 2551–8
Pay comparability of Fed Govt with private industry, and recommended and actual pay adjustments, annual rpt, discontinued, 10104–1
Pay rates, employment, work-years, and benefits use and costs, by agency, FY90, annual rpt, 9844–31
Payroll and employment (civilian) of Fed Govt, by agency in DC metro area, total US, and abroad, bimonthly rpt, 9842–1
Payroll and employment (civilian) of Fed Govt, by pay system, agency, and location, 1991, annual rpt, 9844–6
Payroll and employment, by function, level of govt, and State, 1991, annual rpt, 2466–1.1
Payroll of Fed Govt, by State and county, FY91, annual rpt, 2464–3.1
Payroll of Fed Govt, spending for civilian, military, and postal workers by State, FY91, annual rpt, 2464–2
Postal Service employment and related expenses, FY91, annual rpt, 9864–5
Postal Service operating costs, itemized by class of mail, FY91, annual rpt, 9864–4
Postal Service personnel costs, by segment and occupation, FY91, annual rpt, 9864–2
Senate receipts, itemized expenses by payee, and balances, 1st half FY92, semiannual listing, 25922–1
Senior Executive Service members characteristics, entries, exits, and awards, FY79-91, annual rpt, 9844–36
Statistical Abstract of US, 1992 annual data compilation, 2324–1.10
Tax (withholding) delinquent accounts of Federal agencies, and compared to other taxpayers, 1990, hearing, 21788–206
Transit fare subsidies for Federal employees, costs and participation by agency, 1992, GAO rpt, 26113–601
VA health care facilities physicians, dentists, and nurses, by selected employment characteristics and VA district, quarterly rpt, 8602–6
White collar employees of Fed Govt, views on work conditions and schedules, 1992 survey, 9848–41
see also Civil service pensions
see also Military benefits and pensions
see also Military pay
Federal Power Marketing Administrations
see Alaska Power Administration
see Bonneville Power Administration
see Southeastern Power Administration
see Southwestern Power Administration
see Western Area Power Administration
Federal Prison Industries
Finances and operations of FPI, FY91, annual rpt, 6244–3
Sales, by commodity and Federal agency, FY91, annual rpt, 6244–5
Federal publications lists
see Government publications lists
Federal Railroad Administration
Accidents, casualties, and damage, by cause, railroad, and State, 1991, annual rpt, 7604–1
Accidents, casualties, damage, and circumstances, by incident, 1988, annual rpt, 7604–3
Activities of FRA, safety inspectors by State, and accidents, casualties, and damage, 1990, annual rpt, 7604–12
Budget of US, obligations and authority by function, agency, and program, with summaries and analyses, FY93, annual rpt, 104–2
Employment of DOT, by subagency, occupation, and selected personnel characteristics, FY91, annual rpt, 7304–18
Expenditures of Fed Govt in States, by type, program, agency, and State, FY91, annual rpt, 2464–2

Freight shipped by rail, by commodity and region of origin and destination, 1989, annual rpt, 7604–6
Hwy-railroad grade-crossing accidents, detailed data by State and railroad, 1991, annual rpt, 7604–2
Safety violation claims settled, by rail carrier, FY91, annual rpt, 7604–10

Federal Republic of Germany
see Germany
see Germany, West

Federal Reserve Bank of Atlanta
Dollar exchange rate trade-weighted index of Bank, by world area, quarterly rpt, 9371–15
Economic indicators by State and MSA, Fed Reserve 6th District, quarterly rpt, added data, 9371–14
Financial and banking devs in southeastern States, working paper series, 9371–10
Financial and economic devs, bimonthly journal, 9371–1
Financial statements of Bank, 1990-91, annual rpt, 9371–4

Federal Reserve Bank of Boston
Economic and financial devs, quarterly journal, 9373–25
Economic indicators for New England States, Fed Reserve 1st District, monthly rpt, 9373–2
Financial and economic analysis, and economic issues affecting Northeast States, working paper series, 9373–27
Financial and economic devs, bimonthly journal, 9373–1
Financial and monetary studies, conf series, 9373–3
Financial statements of Bank, 1990-91, annual rpt, 9373–26

Federal Reserve Bank of Chicago
Banks financial performance, risk assessment, and regulation, 1991 annual conf papers, 9375–7
Farm credit conditions and economic devs, Fed Reserve 7th District, monthly rpt, 9375–10
Financial and economic analysis, and economic issues affecting North Central States, working paper series, 9375–13
Financial and economic devs, bimonthly journal, 9375–1
Financial statements of Bank, 1990-91, annual rpt, 9375–5

Federal Reserve Bank of Cleveland
Economic indicators and components, and Fed Reserve 4th District business and financial conditions, monthly chartbook, 9377–10
Financial and economic analysis and forecasting methodology, technical paper series, 9377–9
Financial and economic devs, quarterly journal, 9377–1
Financial statements of Bank, 1990-91, annual rpt, 9377–5

Federal Reserve Bank of Dallas
Dollar exchange rate trade-weighted index of Bank, by world area, monthly rpt, 9379–13
Farm credit conditions and real estate values, Fed Reserve 11th District, quarterly rpt, 9379–11
Financial and economic analysis, technical paper series, 9379–12
Financial and economic devs, quarterly journal, 9379–1
Financial instns in Texas and Federal Reserve 11th District, financial condition and devs, periodic journal, 9379–15
Financial statements of Bank, 1990-91, annual rpt, 9379–2
Savings instns financial condition and devs, working paper series, 9379–14

Federal Reserve Bank of Kansas City
Banking industry structure, performance, and financial devs, for Fed Reserve 10th District, 1991, annual rpt, 9381–14
Financial and economic analysis of banking and nonbanking sectors, working paper series, 9381–10
Financial and economic devs, Fed Reserve 10th District, quarterly rpt, 9381–16
Financial and economic devs, quarterly journal, 9381–1
Financial and monetary studies, conf series, 9381–13
Financial statements of Bank, 1990-91, annual rpt, 9381–3

Federal Reserve Bank of Minneapolis
Business and economic conditions, Fed Reserve 9th District, quarterly journal, 9383–19
Farm credit conditions, earnings, and expenses, Fed Reserve 9th District, quarterly rpt, 9383–11
Financial and economic analysis, technical paper series, 9383–20
Financial and economic devs, quarterly journal, 9383–6
Financial statements of Bank, 1990-91, annual rpt, 9383–2

Federal Reserve Bank of New York
Financial and economic analysis, technical paper series, 9385–8
Financial and economic devs, quarterly journal, 9385–1
Financial statements of Bank, 1990-91, annual rpt, 9385–2
Intl financial markets performance of foreign and US bank and securities firms, finances and competitiveness issues, 1980s, compilation of papers, 9385–10

Federal Reserve Bank of Philadelphia
Economic conditions, Fed Reserve 3rd District, quarterly rpt, 9387–10
Financial and economic devs, bimonthly journal, 9387–1
Financial and monetary research and econometric analyses, working paper series, 9387–8
Financial statements of Bank, 1990-91, annual rpt, 9387–3
Manufacturing business outlook, for Fed Reserve 3rd District, monthly survey rpt, 9387–11
Middle Atlantic States manufacturing output index, monthly rpt, 9387–12

Federal Reserve Bank of Richmond
Banks (insured commercial), Fed Reserve 5th District members financial statements, by State, quarterly rpt, 9389–18
Economic indicators by State, Fed Reserve 5th District, quarterly rpt, 9389–16
Financial and economic analysis, technical paper series, 9389–19
Financial and economic devs, bimonthly journal, 9389–1
Financial statements of Bank, 1990-91, annual rpt, 9389–2

Federal Reserve Bank of San Francisco
Financial and economic analysis, technical paper series, 9393–10
Financial and economic devs, periodic journal, 9393–8
Financial statements of Bank, 1990-91, annual rpt, 9393–2

Federal Reserve Bank of St. Louis
Economic and banking conditions, for Fed Reserve 8th District, quarterly rpt with articles, 9391–16
Economic indicators compounded annual rates of change, monthly rpt, 9391–3
Financial and economic devs, bimonthly journal, 9391–1
Financial and monetary conditions, selected US summary data, weekly rpt, 9391–4
Financial statements of Bank, 1990-91, annual rpt, 9391–17
Intl transactions of US, and economic and monetary trends for US and 7 major industrialized countries, quarterly rpt, 9391–7
Monetary trends, monthly rpt, 9391–2

Federal Reserve Board of Governors
Assets and debts of private sector, balance sheets by segment, 1960-91, semiannual rpt series, 9365–4
Bank deposits availability policies, with background data, 1980s-90, last issue of annual report, 9364–13
Banking and financial conditions, 1990, annual rpt, 9364–5
Banks and thrifts finances and operations by deposit size, Fed Reserve functional cost analysis, 1991, annual rpt, 9364–6
Budget of US, financial statements of federally sponsored enterprises, FY93, annual rpt, 104–2.6
Credit, interest rates, banking activity, and industrial production, monthly rpt series, 9365–2
Data concordance for *Federal Reserve Bulletin* and *Annual Statistical Digest*, 1990 annual rpt, 9364–8
Economic indicators and cyclical devs and outlook, by Fed Reserve Bank District, periodic rpt, 9362–8
Economic policy and banking practices, technical paper series, 9366–1
Expenses and operations of Fed Reserve banks, itemized by service, office, and district, 1991, annual rpt, 9364–11
Finance (intl) and financial policy, and external factors affecting US economy, technical paper series, 9366–7
Finances and staff of Fed Reserve Bd and Reserve banks, and review of monetary policy and economic devs, 1991, annual rpt, 9364–1
Financial and business detailed statistics, *Fed Reserve Bulletin*, monthly rpt with articles, 9362–1
Financial and economic analysis and forecasting methodology, technical paper series, 9366–6
Financial, banking, and mortgage market activity, weekly rpt series, 9365–1
Financial statements, performance, and fiscal services, for Fed Reserve System, Bd of Governors, and district banks, 1990-92, annual rpt, 9364–10
Flow-of-funds accounts, assets and liabilities by type and economic sector, annual rpt, suspended, 9364–3

Flow-of-funds accounts, US banks foreign branches assets and liabilities, and agricultural credit, quarterly rpt series, 9365–3
Households net worth distribution under alternative sample weighting systems to account for inconsistency in survey design and response rates, 1992 rpt, 9368–91
Monetary policy objectives of Fed Reserve, and performance of major economic indicators, as of July 1992, semiannual rpt, 9362–4
Securities credit issues of stockbrokers and other nonbank lenders, as of June 1991, annual rpt series, 9365–5
Service fees, minimum balances, and services offered by banks and thrifts, by service type, 1991, annual rpt, 9364–12

Federal Reserve System
Banking and financial conditions, 1990, annual rpt, 9364–5
Banks seasonal borrowing from Fed Reserve, participants financial and other characteristics, Fed Reserve 8th District, 1984-90, article, 9391–1.311
Budget of US, historical data, selected years FY34-91 and projected to FY97, 108–46.5
Business statistics, detailed data for major industries and economic indicators, *Survey of Current Business*, monthly rpt, 2702–1.8
Business statistics, detailed data for major industries and economic indicators, 1960-91, *Survey of Current Business* biennial supplement, 2704–1
County Business Patterns, 1989: employment, establishments, and payroll, by SIC 2- to 4-digit industry and county, annual State rpt series, 2326–8
County Business Patterns, 1990: employment, establishments, and payroll, by SIC 2- to 4-digit industry and county, annual State rpt series, 2326–6
Credit and reserves of depository instns, 1959-91, annual rpt, 204–1.5
Discount rates of Fed Reserve, relation to monetary and fiscal policy, model description and results, 1970s-91, working paper, 9379–14.20
Expenses and operations of Fed Reserve banks, itemized by service, office, and district, 1991, annual rpt, 9364–11
Finances and operations of banks and thrifts by deposit size, Fed Reserve functional cost analysis, 1991, annual rpt, 9364–6
Finances and staff of Fed Reserve Bd and Reserve banks, and review of monetary policy and economic devs, 1991, annual rpt, 9364–1
Financial, banking, and mortgage market activity, weekly rpt series, 9365–1
Financial operations of Fed Govt, detailed data, *Treasury Bulletin*, quarterly rpt, 8002–4
Financial statements for Fed Reserve services, monthly rpt, periodic data, 9362–1.4
Financial statements, performance, and fiscal services, for Fed Reserve System, Bd of Governors, and district banks, 1990-92, annual rpt, 9364–10
Govt securities market performance, regulation, and reform issues, with auction results, 1990-91, 8008–154
Great Depression monetary policy conduct of Fed Reserve, with discount rate and other policy indicators, selected qtrs 1923-31, article, 9391–1.306
Monetary policy objectives of Fed Reserve, analysis and economic performance, 1950s-90 and projected to FY95, hearings, 21248–160
Monetary policy objectives of Fed Reserve, and performance of major economic indicators, as of July 1992, semiannual rpt, 9362–4
Natl income and product accounts, comprehensive accounts and components, benchmark revisions, 1929-88, 2708–5
Natl income and product accounts, comprehensive accounts and components, *Survey of Current Business*, monthly rpt, 2702–1.26
Reserve and overdraft requirements of Fed Reserve and 3 foreign central banks, with balance sheets and deposit balances, 1989-90, article, 9377–1.307
Reserves and borrowings of all member banks, monthly rpt, 23842–1.5
Reserves of depository instns, reserve and margin requirements, and borrowings from Fed Reserve, monthly rpt, 9362–1.1
Transactions of US Treasury with Fed Reserve Banks, daily tables, 8102–4
Treasury tax and loan account deposits, Fed Reserve Banks mgmt of securities held as collateral, 1991, GAO rpt, 26111–80
see also Federal Open Market Committee
see also Federal Reserve Bank of Atlanta
see also Federal Reserve Bank of Boston
see also Federal Reserve Bank of Chicago
see also Federal Reserve Bank of Cleveland
see also Federal Reserve Bank of Dallas
see also Federal Reserve Bank of Kansas City
see also Federal Reserve Bank of Minneapolis
see also Federal Reserve Bank of New York
see also Federal Reserve Bank of Philadelphia
see also Federal Reserve Bank of Richmond
see also Federal Reserve Bank of San Francisco
see also Federal Reserve Bank of St. Louis
see also Federal Reserve Board of Governors

Federal Savings and Loan Insurance Corp
Finances and operations of FDIC, insured deposits, and finances of banks needing FDIC aid, 1991 and trends from 1934, annual rpt, 9294–1

Federal Service Impasses Panel
see Federal Labor Relations Authority

Federal-State relations
Army Corps of Engineers recreation facilities mgmt, acreage, visits, and non-Federal public and private dev alternatives, 1980s-90, 3758–8
Cattle tuberculosis cases and cooperative Federal-State eradication activities, by State, FY90-91, annual rpt, 1394–13
Coal Surface Mining Reclamation and Enforcement Office activities and funding, by State and Indian tribe, FY91, annual rpt, 5644–1
Coastal areas environmental mgmt programs of States, activities and Federal funding, FY90-91, biennial rpt, 2174–8
EPA regulatory and protection programs operations and mgmt goals, progress and activities, by office, quarterly rpt, 9182–11
FDA investigations and regulatory activities, quarterly rpt, 4062–3
Geological Survey activities and funding, FY91, annual rpt, 5664–8
Historic and natural natl landmarks damaged and threatened, with owner, location, damage type, and recommended remedial action, 1990, annual listing, 5544–16
OASDI coverage of State and local govt employees under voluntary Federal-State agreements, 1987, article, 4742–1.315
Unemployment insurance programs of States and Fed Govt, benefits adequacy, and work disincentives, series, 6406–6
Unemployment insurance programs of States, benefits, coverage, exhaustions, and finances, 1990, annual tables, 6404–10
Wetlands (coastal) mapping projects status, costs, and methods, 1990 conf, 5508–116
see also Federal aid to States

Federal stockpiles
see Stockpiling

Federal Trade Commission
Activities of FTC, FY90, annual narrative rpt, 9404–1
Budget of US, authoritative financial statements with appropriations, outlays, and receipts, by category and agency, FY91, annual rpt, 8104–2.2
Budget of US, obligations and authority by function, agency, and program, with summaries and analyses, FY93, annual rpt, 104–2
Cigarette ad and promotion costs by media, and market shares, by cigarette type, with sales and use, 1963-89, annual rpt, 9404–4
Cigarette smoke tar, nicotine, and carbon monoxide content, by brand, 1990, 9408–53
Department store advertised sale prices and references to competitors prices, and actual consumer savings, 1990-91 local area study, 9408–57
Grocery store profits and prices relation to market concentration, literature review, 1990 rpt, 9408–56
Labor unions recognized in Fed Govt, agreements and membership by agency and facility, as of Jan 1991, biennial listing, 9844–14
Merger announcements and antitrust challenges impact on stock returns of rival firms, 1980s, 9408–55
Shipping industry structure, rates, and effects of Shipping Act, by route, 1980s, 9408–54

Federal Transit Administration
Accidents and casualties on transit systems by circumstances, damage, and ridership, by mode, 1990, annual rpt, 7884–13
Budget of US, obligations and authority by function, agency, and program, with summaries and analyses, FY93, annual rpt, 104–2
Bus exhaust emissions reduction programs, funding, and alternative fuel bus dev, periodic rpt, 7882–3
Finances, equipment, and ridership characteristics of transit systems, 1985-90, biennial rpt, 7884–8
Grants of FTA by State, and oversight, 1988-92, GAO rpt, 26113–600

Grants of FTA for commuter railroad and other transit systems, FY93, annual rpt, 7884–12
Grants of FTA for transit systems, by city and State, FY91, annual rpt, 7884–10
Grants to higher education instns for transit research and training, by project, FY92, annual listing, 7884–7
R&D projects and funding of FTA, FY91, annual listing, 7884–1
Research on transit systems, rpts, 1991, annual listing, 7884–11
Transit systems finances and operations, by mode, size of fleet and urban area, region, and for 518 systems, 1990, annual rpt, 7884–4
see also Urban Mass Transportation Administration

Federally Funded R&D Centers
DOE R&D field offices and facilities, activities, staff, and finances, FY91, biennial rpt, 3004–4
Expenditures for R&D by higher education instns and federally funded centers, by field, instn, and State, FY90, annual rpt, 9627–13
Expenditures of Fed Govt for higher education instns R&D and federally funded centers, by field, instn, and State, FY90, advance annual rpt, 9626–8.5; 9626–8.7
Japan and US technological info transfer activities, and researcher and student exchanges, 1988-89, GAO rpt, 26123–379
Market potential of industrial and Federal labs technological innovations, results of annual *R&D 100* awards competition, 1960s-90, 2218–86
NASA procurement contract awards, by type, contractor, State, and country, FY92 with trends from 1961, semiannual rpt, 9502–6
Science and Engineering Indicators, employment, education, R&D funding, and industry impacts, with foreign comparisons, 1960s-91, biennial rpt, 9624–10
see also Department of Energy National Laboratories

Federally impacted areas
see Impacted areas

Federated States of Micronesia
see Micronesia Federated States

Federer, C. Anthony
"Thirty Years of Hydrometeorologic Data at the Hubbard Brook Experimental Forest, New Hampshire", 1208–410

Feeds
see Animal feed

Feedstocks, petrochemical
see Petrochemicals

Feliz, Raul A.
"Cointegration and Tests of a Classical Model of Inflation in Argentina, Bolivia, Brazil, Mexico, and Peru", 9379–12.91

Fellowships
see Student aid

Fernandez, Rosa
"Fall Staff in Postsecondary Institutions, 1989", 4844–18

Fernelius, Leonard W.
"Dichotomy Becomes Reality: Ten Years of the Federal Reserve as Regulator and Competitor", 9383–2

Ferries
Commuting to work, by mode, trip duration, and work location, 1980 and 1990, 7558–120
County Business Patterns, 1989: employment, establishments, and payroll, by SIC 2- to 4-digit industry and county, annual State rpt series, 2326–8
County Business Patterns, 1990: employment, establishments, and payroll, by SIC 2- to 4-digit industry and county, annual State rpt series, 2326–6
Finances and operations of transit systems, by mode, size of fleet and urban area, region, and for 518 systems, 1990, annual rpt, 7884–4
Urban areas transit systems grants of Federal Transit Admin, by city and State, FY91, annual rpt, 7884–10

Ferrosilicon
see Iron and steel industry

Fertility
Birth expectations, 1990, and immigrant fertility, 1988, fact sheet, 2326–17.41
Developing countries economic and social conditions from 1960s, and Intl Dev Cooperation Agency and AID activities and funding, FY91-93, annual rpt, 9904–4
Developing countries family planning and population activities of AID, grants by project and recipient, and contraceptive shipments, by country, FY91, annual rpt series, 9914–13
Developing countries population size, life expectancy, and fertility, trends and forecasts, country rpt series, 2326–24
Farm population, by employment, social, and economic characteristics, and region, 1990, annual Current Population Rpt, 2546–1.458
Foreign countries population size, growth rates, and components of change, by country, projected 1990-2020 and trends from 1950, biennial rpt, 2324–9
Health condition and care indicators, 1950s-90 with health improvement and disease prevention goals for 1990, annual data compilation, 4144–11
Latin America economic and social conditions, resources, trade, and aid, 1992, annual factbook, 9914–14
Pacific territories population and housing detailed characteristics, by location, 1990 Census of Population and Housing, series, 2551–8
Population size and components of change, alternative projections 1990-2080 and trends from 1900, annual actuarial rpt, 4706–1.106
Research on population and reproduction, Federal funding by project, FY90, annual listing, 4474–9
Research on population and reproduction, Natl Inst of Child Health and Human Dev funding and activities, 1991, annual rpt, 4474–33
Soviet Union and US economic and sociodemographic indicators, selected years 1970-90, handbook, 2328–80
Soviet Union former Republics and Baltic States population size and characteristics, 1989-92, 9118–19
Statistical Abstract of US, 1992 annual data compilation, 2324–1.2
Vietnam population size, components of change, and selected characteristics, 1979, 1989, and projected to 2050, 2326–18.65
see also Abortion
see also Births
see also Family planning
see also Population size

Fertilizers
Agricultural Outlook, production, prices, marketing, and trade, by commodity, forecast and current situation, monthly rpt with articles, 1502–4
Business statistics, detailed data for major industries and economic indicators, *Survey of Current Business*, monthly rpt, 2702–1.11
Business statistics, detailed data for major industries and economic indicators, 1960-91, *Survey of Current Business* biennial supplement, 2704–1
Cameroon fertilizer producer subsidy elimination, effectiveness of AID support of govt reforms, 1987-92, 9916–1.76
Canada-US trade agreement issues, with data on Canada fertilizer and agricultural production and trade, 1960s-90s, hearing, 25368–179
China minerals production and trade, by commodity, 1989-90, annual rpt, 5604–38
Coastal areas and watersheds pollution indicators, by location, 1980s-90, 2178–35
Consumption of fertilizer, by type and region, 1947-90, annual rpt, 1544–17.2
Consumption of fertilizer, by type and State, 1991-92, annual rpt, 9804–30
County Business Patterns, 1989: employment, establishments, and payroll, by SIC 2- to 4-digit industry and county, annual State rpt series, 2326–8
County Business Patterns, 1990: employment, establishments, and payroll, by SIC 2- to 4-digit industry and county, annual State rpt series, 2326–6
Eastern Europe export industries dev potential, with trade and industry finances and operations, for 5 countries, 1985-90, 9886–4.179
Employment, earnings, and hours, by SIC 1- to 4-digit industry, monthly 1989-Feb 1992, annual rpt, 6744–4
Energy use and prices for manufacturing industries, 1988 survey, series, 3166–13
Environmental Quality, status of problems, protection programs, research, and intl issues, 1991 annual rpt, 484–1
Exports and imports (agricultural) of US, by commodity and country, bimonthly rpt, 1522–1
Exports and imports (agricultural) of US, by detailed commodity and country, 1991, annual rpt, 1524–8
Exports and imports (agricultural) of US, by detailed commodity and country, 1991, semiannual rpt, 1522–4
Exports and imports between US and outlying areas, by detailed commodity and mode of transport, 1991, annual rpt, 2424–11
Exports and imports of US, by country and detailed commodity, monthly rpt, 2422–12
Exports and imports of US, by Harmonized System 6-digit commodity and country, 1991, annual rpt, 2424–13

Exports and imports of US, by selected country, country group, and commodity group, 1991, annual rpt, 2044–37
Exports and imports of US, by transport mode, country, and SITC 1- to 3-digit commodity, 1991, annual rpt, 2424–12
Exports, imports, and balances of US for manufactured goods, by SITC 2-digit commodity and country, quarterly rpt, 2042–35
Exports of US, detailed Schedule B commodities with countries of destination, 1991, annual rpt, 2424–10
Farm fertilizer and pesticide use, and application rates, by type, crop, and State, series, 1616–1
Farm prices received and paid, by commodity and State, monthly rpt, 1629–1
Farm production inputs, finances, mgmt, and land value and transfers, periodic situation rpt with articles, 1561–16
Farm production itemized costs, by farm sales size and region, 1991, annual rpt, 1614–3
Farm production itemized costs, receipts, and returns, by commodity and region, 1975-90, annual rpt, 1544–20
Farm production itemized costs, receipts, and returns, by crop and State, 1987-89, annual rpt, 1544–24
Farm sector balance sheet, and marketing receipts by detailed commodity, by State, 1986-90, annual rpt, 1544–18
Foreign countries agricultural production, prices, and trade, by country, 1980-91 and forecast 1992, annual world area rpt series, 1524–4
Freight (waterborne domestic and foreign) by commodity, traffic, and passengers, by port and waterway, 1989, annual rpt, 3754–3
Futures trading in selected commodities and financial instruments and indexes, for NYC, Chicago, and other markets activity, biweekly rpt, 11922–5
Hazardous substances industrial releases and reduction methods under EPA regulation, with chemical stocks and use, facility directory, 1987-89, annual CD-ROM, 9234–7
Injuries from use of consumer products, by severity, victim age, and detailed product, 1991, annual rpt, 9164–6
Input-output structure of US economy, detailed interindustry transactions for 541 industries, and components of final demand, 1982 benchmark data, 2708–17
Irrigated farmland, farm characteristics, and water and fuel sources, by State and leading county, 1950s-88, 1588–122
Labor productivity, indexes of output, hours, and employment by SIC 2- to 4-digit industry, 1967-90, annual rpt, 6824–1.3
Manufacturing annual survey, 1990: finances and operations, by SIC 2- to 4-digit industry, series, 2506–14
Manufacturing census, 1987: concentration of largest firms measured by value added, and for shipments by SIC 2- and 4-digit industry, subject rpt, 2497–6
Manufacturing census, 1987: shipments of manufacturers products, by customer class and SIC 2- and 4-digit industry, subject rpt, 2497–4
Manufacturing finances and operations, by SIC 2- to 4-digit industry, forecast 1992, annual rpt, 2044–28
Minerals Yearbook, Vol 1, 1989: commodity reviews of production, use, trade, prices, and mining operations, annual rpt, 5604–33
Minerals Yearbook, Vol 2, 1989: State reviews of production and sales by commodity, and business activity, annual rpt series, 5604–16
Minerals Yearbook, Vol 2, 1990: State reviews of production and sales by commodity, and business activity, annual rpt series, 5604–22
Occupational injury and illness rates, by SIC 2- to 4-digit industry, 1989-90, annual rpt, 6844–7
Occupational injury and illness rates, by SIC 2- to 4-digit industry, 1990, annual rpt, 6844–1
OECD trade, total and for 4 major countries, and US trade by country, by commodity, 1980-90, world area rpt series, 9116–1
Price indexes (producer), by stage of processing and detailed commodity, monthly rpt, 6762–6
Price indexes (producer), by stage of processing and detailed commodity, monthly 1991, annual rpt, 6764–2
Prices received and paid by farmers, by commodity and State, 1991, annual rpt, 1629–5
Production of inorganic fertilizer by State, stocks, trade, and use, by product, quarterly Current Industrial Rpt, 2506–8.2
Production, trade, use, and foreign investment in US industry, for minerals, 1985-90 and projected to 2000, annual rpt, 5304–5
Rice production, practices, costs, and land tenure, by production area, 1988, 1568–309
Shipments, trade, use, and firms, by product and State, with stocks, for inorganic fertilizers, 1991, annual Current Industrial Rpt, 2506–8.13; 2506–8.14
Soviet Union and US economic and sociodemographic indicators, selected years 1970-90, handbook, 2328–80
Soybean tillage systems impacts on yield and inputs use and costs, 1990, article, 1561–3.304
TVA agriculture and fertilizer rpts, 1970-90, annual listing, 9804–28
TVA finances and operations by program and facility, FY91, annual rpt, 9804–32
Water (groundwater) supply, quality, chemistry, and use, State and local area rpt series, 5666–28
Water supply and quality in streams and lakes, and groundwater levels in wells, by drainage basin, 1990, annual State rpt series, 5666–10
Water supply and quality in streams and lakes, and groundwater levels in wells, by drainage basin, 1990-91, annual CD-ROM, 5664–18
Water supply and quality in streams and lakes, and groundwater levels in wells, by drainage basin, 1991, annual State rpt series, 5666–12
see also under By Commodity in the "Index by Categories"

Fetal alcohol syndrome
see Birth defects

Fetal deaths
Deaths and rates, by detailed location, cause, and demographic characteristics, 1989, US Vital Statistics annual rpt, 4144–3
Health condition and care indicators, 1950s-90 with health improvement and disease prevention goals for 1990, annual data compilation, 4144–11
Maternal deaths related to spontaneous abortion, 1972-87, annual article, 4202–7.324
Pregnancy outcome probabilities, by gestation week, 1980, article, 4042–3.324
Statistical Abstract of US, 1992 annual data compilation, 2324–1.2
Youth health condition, risk factors, and preventive and treatment services use and availability, 1970s-80s, 26358–234.2
see also Abortion
see also Infant mortality

Fettig, David
"American Indian Economic Development", 9383–19.304
"Dichotomy Becomes Reality: Ten Years of the Federal Reserve as Regulator and Competitor", 9383–2

FHA
see Housing (FHA), HUD

FHwA
see Federal Highway Administration

Fiber optics
Competitiveness (intl) of US high technology industries, with background data by industry and foreign comparisons, 1960s-91, GAO rpt, 26123–406
Exports and imports between US and outlying areas, by detailed commodity and mode of transport, 1991, annual rpt, 2424–11
Exports and imports of US, by country and detailed commodity, monthly rpt, 2422–12
Exports and imports of US, by Harmonized System 6-digit commodity and country, 1991, annual rpt, 2424–13
Exports of US, detailed Schedule B commodities with countries of destination, 1991, annual rpt, 2424–10
Manufacturing finances and operations, by SIC 2- to 4-digit industry, forecast 1992, annual rpt, 2044–28
Military prime contract awards, by detailed procurement category, FY88-91, annual rpt, 3544–18
Shipments, trade, use, and firms, for electronic communications systems and related products, 1991, annual Current Industrial Rpt, 2506–12.35
Telecommunications fiber optics and copper wire mileage and access lines, and fiber systems investment, by firm, 1985-91, annual rpt, 9284–18
Telecommunications industry intl competitiveness, structure, and devs, with background data and foreign comparisons, 1991 rpt, 2808–30
Wire and cable (insulated) shipments, trade, use, and firms, by product, 1991, annual Current Industrial Rpt, 2506–10.8

Fibers
see Cotton
see Natural fibers
see Silk
see Synthetic fibers and fabrics
see Wool and wool trade
FICA
see Social security tax
Fieleke, Norman S.
"One Trading World, or Many: The Issue of Regional Trading Blocs", 9373–1.308
Fight, Roger D.
"Price Projections for Selected Grades of Douglas-Fir, Coast Hem-Fir, Inland Hem-Fir, and Ponderosa Pine Lumber", 1208–424
Fiji
AID economic aid to developing countries, obligations and disbursements by country, quarterly rpt, 9912–4
Economic and social conditions of developing countries from 1960s, and Intl Dev Cooperation Agency and AID activities and funding, FY91-93, annual rpt, 9904–4
Economic, social, political, and geographic summary data, by country, 1992, annual factbook, 9114–2
Exports and imports of US, by transport mode, country, and SITC 1- to 3-digit commodity, 1991, annual rpt, 2424–12
Exports of US, detailed Schedule B commodities with countries of destination, 1991, annual rpt, 2424–10
Human rights conditions in 170 countries, and US economic and military aid, 1991, annual rpt, 21384–3
Military aid of US, arms sales, and training programs costs and budget requests, by program, world region, and country, FY91-93, annual rpt, 7144–13
Military spending, arms trade, and force strengths, with govt spending and population, by country, 1979-89, annual rpt, 9824–1
Minerals Yearbook, Vol 3, 1989: foreign country review of production, trade, and policy, by commodity, annual rpt, 5604–35.2
Population size, growth rates, and components of change, by country, projected 1990-2020 and trends from 1950, biennial rpt, 2324–9
UN voting record and share of votes in agreement with US, by issue, country, and world area, 1991, annual rpt, 7004–18
Films
see Motion pictures
Finance
Business statistics, detailed data for major industries and economic indicators, 1960-91, *Survey of Current Business* biennial supplement, 2704–1
Fed Govt financial operations, detailed data, *Treasury Bulletin*, quarterly rpt, 8002–4
Federal Reserve Bulletin, detailed financial statistics, monthly rpt with articles, 9362–1
Financial and banking devs in southeastern States, working paper series, 9371–10
Financial and economic analysis, and economic issues affecting North Central States, working paper series, 9375–13
Financial and economic analysis, and economic issues affecting Northeast States, working paper series, 9373–27
Financial and economic analysis and forecasting methodology, technical paper series, 9377–9
Financial and economic analysis of banking and nonbanking sectors, working paper series, 9381–10
Financial and economic analysis, technical paper series, 9379–12; 9383–20; 9385–8; 9389–19; 9393–10
Financial and economic devs, Fed Reserve Bank of Atlanta bimonthly journal, 9371–1
Financial and economic devs, Fed Reserve Bank of Chicago bimonthly journal, 9375–1
Financial and economic devs, Fed Reserve Bank of Cleveland quarterly journal, 9377–1
Financial and economic devs, Fed Reserve Bank of Dallas quarterly journal, 9379–1
Financial and economic devs, Fed Reserve Bank of Kansas City quarterly journal, 9381–1
Financial and economic devs, Fed Reserve Bank of Minneapolis quarterly journal, 9383–6
Financial and economic devs, Fed Reserve Bank of New York quarterly journal, 9385–1
Financial and economic devs, Fed Reserve Bank of Philadelphia bimonthly journal, 9387–1
Financial and economic devs, Fed Reserve Bank of Richmond bimonthly journal, 9389–1
Financial and economic devs, Fed Reserve Bank of San Francisco periodic journal, 9393–8
Financial and economic devs, Fed Reserve Bank of St Louis bimonthly journal, 9391–1
Financial and monetary research and econometric analyses, working paper series, 9387–8
Financial and monetary studies, Fed Reserve Bank of Boston conf series, 9373–3
Financial and monetary studies, Fed Reserve Bank of Kansas City conf series, 9381–13
see also Agricultural credit
see also Agricultural finance
see also Bankruptcy
see also Banks and banking
see also Certificates of deposit
see also Commercial credit
see also Consumer credit
see also Credit
see also Educational finance
see also Financial institutions
see also Financial institutions regulation
see also Fiscal policy
see also Flow-of-funds accounts
see also Foreign exchange
see also Futures trading
see also Government securities
see also Gross Domestic Product
see also Gross National Product
see also Housing costs and financing
see also Individual retirement arrangements
see also Inflation
see also Input-output analysis
see also Insurance and insurance industry
see also Interest rates
see also International finance
see also International reserves
see also Investments
see also Loans
see also Monetary policy
see also Money supply
see also Municipal bonds
see also National income and product accounts
see also New York Stock Exchange
see also Prices
see also Securities
see also Stock exchanges
Finance companies
Assets by type of financial instn, and for top 10 finance companies by firm, 1970 and 1990, article, 9391–16.305
Assets, liabilities, and business loans of finance companies, monthly rpt, 9362–1.1
Assets, liabilities, and credit activities, monthly rpt series, 9365–2
Assets, operating ratios, and growth indicators, for top 20 finance companies, 1980s-90, article, 9385–1.309
Business credit outstanding, for finance companies, 1990, annual rpt, 9364–5.7
Business statistics, detailed data for major industries and economic indicators, 1960-91, *Survey of Current Business* biennial supplement, 2704–1
Credit (installment) outstanding and terms, by lender and credit type, monthly rpt, 9365–2.6
Credit outstanding and leasing activities of finance companies, by credit type, monthly rpt, 9365–2.7
Employment, earnings, and hours, by SIC 1- to 4-digit industry, monthly 1989-Feb 1992, annual rpt, 6744–4
Flow-of-funds accounts, savings, investments, and credit statements, quarterly rpt, 9365–3.3
Households financial services use, by account type and instn type and location, 1989 survey, article, 9362–1.303
Input-output structure of US economy, detailed interindustry transactions for 541 industries, and components of final demand, 1982 benchmark data, 2708–17
Loans (consumer) of banks, relation to bank-auto finance company interest rate spread, tax reform, and other factors, 1970s-91, working paper, 9379–12.88
Mortgage loan activity, by type of lender, loan, and mortgaged property, monthly press release, 5142–18
Mortgage loan activity, by type of lender, loan, and mortgaged property, quarterly press release, 5142–30
Mortgages (conventional) terms at closing, by lender type, with periodic data by district, State, and for 32 MSAs, monthly rpt, 9442–2
Small business financing sources, and business financial data by size, type, and industry, 1980s-90, annual rpt, 9764–6.2
Tax (income) returns of corporations, income and tax items by asset size and detailed industry, 1989, annual rpt, 8304–4; 8304–21
Financial crises and depressions
see Business cycles

Financial disclosure
Election campaign finances and FEC activities, various periods 1975-91, annual rpt, 9274-1
Election campaign finances to FEC, by type of filer, 1990 natl elections, biennial rpt series, 9276-2
Election campaign-related internal communications of firms and assns, spending by organization, location, and candidate, 1991-92, biennial rpt, 9274-3
Elections, procedures, campaign finances, and Fed Election Commission activities, press release series, 9276-1
Fed Govt agencies ethics regulation, activities, and staff, 1991, biennial rpt, 9834-1
Mortgage applications of minorities, for Boston by disposition and financial characteristics, with problems in analyzing lender disclosure statements, 1990, working paper, 9373-27.15
SEC registration, firms required to file annual rpts, as of Sept 1991, annual listing, 9734-5
Unemployment insurance programs of States, quality appraisal results, FY91, annual rpt, 6404-16

Financial institutions
AID loans repayment status and terms by program and country, and status of predecessor agency loans, quarterly rpt, 9912-3
Assets and debts of private sector, balance sheets by segment, 1960-91, semiannual rpt, 9365-4.1
Assets by type of financial instn, and for top 10 finance companies by firm, 1970 and 1990, article, 9391-16.305
Bombing incidents, casualties, and damage, by target, circumstances, and State, 1991, annual rpt, 6224-5
Business cycle recession and expansion duration indicators, 1850s-1990, working paper, 9375-13.83
Business statistics, detailed data for major industries and economic indicators, *Survey of Current Business*, monthly rpt, 2702-1.8
Business statistics, detailed data for major industries and economic indicators, 1960-91, *Survey of Current Business* biennial supplement, 2704-1
Capital expenditures for plant and equipment, by major industry group, quarterly rpt, 2502-2
Collective bargaining agreements expiring during year, and workers covered, by firm, union, industry group, and State, 1992, annual rpt, 6784-9
Commercial paper outstanding, by issuer and holder type, and foreign firms paper issued by US subsidiaries and foreign offices, 1980s-91, article, 9362-1.308
County Business Patterns, 1989: employment, establishments, and payroll, by SIC 2- to 4-digit industry and county, annual State rpt series, 2326-8
County Business Patterns, 1990: employment, establishments, and payroll, by SIC 2- to 4-digit industry and county, annual State rpt series, 2326-6
Credit card issuers, and banks credit operations, costs and revenue, mid 1970s-91, article, 9362-1.306
Deaths and rates, by cause and selected social, demographic, and employment characteristics, 1979-85, natl longitudinal study, 4478-186
EC economic integration impacts on financial services, 1992 article, 9391-1.308
Employment and Earnings, detailed data, monthly rpt, 6742-2.5
Employment Cost Index and alternative measure of compensation costs, by component, occupation, industry group, union status, and location, 1975-92, annual rpt, 6744-20
Employment, earnings, and hours, by selected SIC 1- to 4-digit industry, State, and for 275 MSAs, 1987-92, 6748-81
Employment, earnings, and hours, by SIC 1- to 4-digit industry, monthly 1989-Feb 1992, annual rpt, 6744-4
Employment, earnings, and hours, monthly press release, 6742-5
Employment of minorities and women, by occupation, SIC 1- to 3-digit industry, State, and MSA, 1991, annual rpt, 9244-1
Employment situation, earnings, hours, and other BLS economic indicators, transcripts of BLS Commissioner's monthly testimony, periodic rpt, 23846-4
Employment, unemployment, and labor force characteristics, by region, State, and selected metro area, 1991, annual rpt, 6744-7
Federal Reserve Bulletin, detailed financial statistics, monthly rpt with articles, 9362-1
Finances and operations of banks and thrifts by deposit size, Fed Reserve functional cost analysis, 1991, annual rpt, 9364-6
Financial and economic analysis of banking and nonbanking sectors, working paper series, 9381-10
Financial condition of banks and thrifts, and devs, periodic journal, 9379-15
Foreign direct investment in US, by industry group and world area, 1989-91, annual article, 2702-1.331
Foreign direct investment in US, major transactions by type, industry, country, and US location, 1990, annual rpt, 2044-20
Foreign direct investment of US, by industry group and world area, 1989-91, annual article, 2702-1.332
Gross State Product by component, industry div, and State, 1977-89, article, 2702-1.303
Income tax returns of foreign corporations and individuals, and US entities abroad, detailed data compilation, 1970s-89, quinquennial rpt, 8308-31
Input-output structure of US economy, detailed interindustry transactions for 84 industries, and components of final demand, 1987, annual article, 2702-1.316
Input-output structure of US economy, detailed interindustry transactions for 541 industries, and components of final demand, 1982 benchmark data, 2708-17
Intl financial markets performance of foreign and US bank and securities firms, finances and competitiveness issues, 1980s, compilation of papers, 9385-10
Mail volume to and from households, use, and views, by class, source, content, and household characteristics, FY87-90, annual rpt, 9864-10
Minority- and woman-owned businesses and owner characteristics, by industry, employment and sales size, and form of ownership, 1987 survey, 2328-59
Multinatl firms US affiliates finances and operations, by industry, country of parent firm, and State, 1987, 2708-48
Multinatl firms US affiliates, finances, and operations, by industry, world area of parent firm, and State, 1989-90, annual rpt, 2704-4
Multinatl US firms and foreign affiliates finances and operations, by industry and country, 1989 benchmark survey, annual rpt, 2704-5
Multinatl US firms foreign affiliates, income statement items by asset size, industry, and country, 1988, biennial article, 8302-2.322
Natl income and product accounts, comprehensive accounts and components, benchmark revisions, 1929-88, 2708-5
Natl income and product accounts, comprehensive accounts and components, *Survey of Current Business*, monthly rpt, 2702-1.29
New England States economic indicators, Fed Reserve 1st District, monthly rpt, 9373-2
Occupational injuries, illnesses, and lost workdays, by SIC 2-digit industry, 1990-91, annual press release, 6844-3
Occupational injury and illness rates, by SIC 2- to 4-digit industry, 1989-90, annual rpt, 6844-7
Occupational injury and illness rates, by SIC 2- to 4-digit industry, 1990, annual rpt, 6844-1
Pacific territories population and housing detailed characteristics, by location, 1990 Census of Population and Housing, series, 2551-8
Puerto Rico and other US possessions corporations income tax returns, income and tax items, and employment, by selected industry, 1989, article, 8302-2.326
Small business finances, operations, owner characteristics, and Federal contracts, 1980s-90, annual rpt, 9764-6
Southeastern US employment by industry div, earnings, and hours, for 8 States, quarterly press release, 6942-7
Statistical Abstract of US, 1992 annual data compilation, 2324-1.16
Tax (income) returns filed, by type of filer, selected income items, quarterly rpt, 8302-2.1
Tax (income) returns for foreign corporate activity in US, selected income and tax items, by industry div and selected country, 1988, article, 8302-2.309
Tax (income) returns of corporations, income and tax items by asset size and detailed industry, 1989, annual rpt, 8304-4; 8304-21
Tax (income) returns of corporations with foreign tax credit, income and tax items by industry group, 1988, biennial article, 8302-2.316

Tax (income) returns of financial instns, loan loss computations alternative methods, 1991 rpt, 8008–157
Tax (income) returns of partnerships, income statement and balance sheet items, by industry group, 1990, annual article, 8302–2.314
Tax (income) returns of sole proprietorships, income statement items, by industry group, 1990, annual article, 8302–2.317; 8302–2.320
Wage and benefit changes from collective bargaining and mgmt decisions, by industry div, monthly rpt, 6782–1
Wages by occupation, and benefits for office and plant workers, periodic MSA survey rpt series, 6785–12; 6785–16; 6785–17
see also Automated tellers
see also Bank holding companies
see also Banks and banking
see also Census of Financial, Insurance, and Real Estate Industries
see also Credit unions
see also Deposit insurance
see also Farm Credit System
see also Federal Reserve System
see also Finance companies
see also Financial institutions regulation
see also Insurance and insurance industry
see also Mutual funds
see also Savings institutions
see also Stockbrokers
see also under By Industry in the "Index by Categories"

Financial Institutions Reform, Recovery, and Enforcement Act
Employee pay comparability among Federal bank regulatory agencies, and turnover, by occupation, 1991, GAO rpt, 26119–368

Financial institutions regulation
Bank deposits availability policies, with background data, 1980s-90, last issue of annual report, 9364–13
Bank deposits interest rates relation to market concentration, regulation, migration, and other factors, 1980s, technical paper, 9366–6.297
Bank holding companies capital requirements impacts on asset growth, 1989-91, working paper, 9375–13.88
Bank holding companies, financial ratios, banks held, and equity financing relation to regulatory capital standards, 1970s-90, technical paper, 9366–6.291
Bank of Credit and Commerce Intl DC office financial statements, 1984-90, GAO rpt, 26119–427
Banking system reform impacts on consumers, with background data, 1991 hearing, 21248–167
Banking system reform issues, with top instn finances, fiscal impacts, and views of depositors, bankers, and regulators on deposit insurance, 1991 hearings, 21248–168
Banks (natl) charters, mergers, liquidations, enforcement cases, and financial performance, with data by instn and State, quarterly rpt, 8402–3
Banks financial performance, risk assessment, and regulation, 1991 annual conf papers, 9375–7
Banks profitability relation to market concentration, efficiency indicators, and regulation, model description and results, 1980s, technical paper, 9366–6.290
Banks regulation and related issues, North Central States business leaders views, 1992 survey, article, 9383–19.305
Banks regulation and related issues, quarterly journal, 9292–4
Banks reserve requirements of Fed Reserve Bd relation to GNP and investment, 1991 working paper, 9375–13.72
Banks securities new issues by type of instrument, relation to primary capital ratio and other factors, 1983-86, working paper, 9371–10.79
Budget of US, obligations and authority by function, agency, and program, with summaries and analyses, FY93, annual rpt, 104–2
Check-cashing outlets fees by type of check, and legal maximum in regulated States, 1991 article, 9381–1.301
Computer data processing vendors contracts with banks and thrifts, involvement of illegal business transactions, and instn and vendor views, 1985-90, GAO rpt, 26119–374
Credit unions federally insured, finances, 1990-91, annual rpt, 9534–1
Credit unions finances, operations, and regulation, series, 9536–1
Credit unions financial performance and regulation, with background data, 1960s-90, GAO rpt, 26119–364
Crimes, by characteristics of victim and offender, circumstances, and location, data compilation, 1992 annual rpt, 6064–6.3
Deposit interest rate deregulation impacts on bank asset risk, alternative model descriptions and results, 1970s-80s, working paper, 9379–14.15
EC economic integration impacts on financial services, 1992 article, 9391–1.308
Exports of goods, services, and investment, trade barriers, impacts, and US actions, by country, 1991, annual rpt, 444–2
FDIC regulatory enforcement activities, 1991, annual rpt, 9294–1
Fed Govt bank regulatory agencies pay comparability and turnover, by occupation, 1991, GAO rpt, 26119–368
Fed Home Loan Mortgage Corp financial condition and capital adequacy, 1990, annual rpt, 5184–8
Fed Reserve Bd and Reserve banks finances, staff, and review of monetary policy and economic devs, 1991, annual rpt, 9364–1
Fed Reserve Bd reserve requirements and other policy actions impacts on M1 and M2 growth, 1959-92, article, 9391–1.313
Fed Reserve System, Bd of Governors, and district banks financial statements, performance, and fiscal services, 1991-92, annual rpt, 9364–10
Foreign and US monetary policy and central bank regulation, for 6 countries, 1980-90, article, 9385–1.308
Foreign bank loans to US businesses by location of issuer, with impact of change in Fed Reserve Bd reserve requirements, 1980s-91, article, 9385–1.307
Fraud and abuse in financial instns, Justice Dept enforcement activity, staff, and case dispositions by instn type, 1988-92, 6008–35
Fraud and abuse in thrifts, Federal indictments and case dispositions, periodic press release, 6002–3; 6008–33
Fraud in banks and thrifts, Justice Dept investigation and prosecution activities, 1989-92, GAO rpt, 26119–426
Futures contracts margin requirements for metals and stock index futures, impact on prices, volatility, and trading activity, 1970s-90, technical paper, 9385–8.127
Futures margin requirements impacts on contract price volatility, 1970s-89, article, 9375–1.302
Govt securities market performance, regulation, and reform issues, with auction results, 1990-91, 8008–154
Insurance (health) coverage and availability, and other health care system reform issues, 1991 hearing, 21788–216
Insurance (health) coverage of selected services, State mandates, 1990, 10176–3.2
Insurance (health) private plans to supplement Medicare, loss ratio performance, by firm, 1988-89, GAO rpt, 26121–452
Insurance (health) reforms of States to improve small business access, provisions with background data by State, 1991, GAO rpt, 26121–462
Insurance (health) under multiple employer welfare arrangements, coverage, unpaid claims, and regulation, by State, 1988-91, GAO rpt, 26121–443
Insurance (life) industry assets by type, and South Central States guaranty fund limits, 1992 article, 9391–16.310
Insurance (life and health) company failures, and State guaranty fund assessments, by State, 1975-90, GAO rpt, 26119–392
Insurance industry finances, failures, and regulation, with data by firm and State, 1990 hearing, 25528–119
Insurance industry financial condition, operations, assets, junk bond holdings, and State regulation, with intl comparisons, 1991 hearings, 25268–79
Merger applications approved, and assets and offices involved, by bank, 1990, annual rpt, 9294–5
Money laundering investigation activities of States and Fed Govt, and use of IRS large cash transaction rpts, by State, 1985-91, GAO rpt, 26119–430
Money laundering investigations by Treasury Dept, civil penalty cases workload, processing, and disposition, 1985-91, GAO rpt, 26119–390
Mortgage applications of minorities, for Boston by disposition and financial characteristics, with problems in analyzing lender disclosure statements, 1990, working paper, 9373–27.15
Public opinion on taxes, spending, and govt efficiency, by respondent characteristics, 1992 survey, annual rpt, 10044–2
Reconstruction Finance Corp capital aid to banks, impact on solvency status and financial ratios, 1920s-40, article, 9381–1.304
Reform of financial system, issues, with finances, impacts of deposit insurance changes, and views of depositors and bankers, 1991 hearings, 25248–129
Reserve and overdraft requirements of Fed Reserve and 3 foreign central banks, with balance sheets and deposit balances, 1989-90, article, 9377–1.307

Resolution Trust Corp obligation limits compliance, and balance sheet, quarterly GAO rpt, 26102-6
Resolution Trust Corp programs fraud and abuse, audits and investigations, 2nd half FY92, semiannual rpt, 9722-6
Savings instns failure resolution activity and finances of Resolution Trust Corp, with data by asset type, State, region, and instn, monthly rpt, 9722-3
Savings instns failure resolution activity of Resolution Trust Corp, assets, deposits, and assets availability and sales, periodic press release, 9722-1
Savings instns failure resolution activity of Resolution Trust Corp, with data by State and instn, and RTC finances, 1990, annual rpt, 9724-1
Savings instns failure resolution costs, impacts of capital standards relaxation, 1979-92, working paper, 9377-9.140
Savings instns failures, costs and budget deficit and economic impacts, 1980s and projected to 2010, 26306-6.165
Savings instns failures, financial performance of instns under Resolution Trust Corp conservatorship, quarterly rpt, 9722-5
Savings instns insured by Savings Assn Insurance Fund, assets, liabilities, and deposit and loan activity, by conservatorship status, monthly rpt, 8432-1
Savings instns regulatory issues, 1989 annual conf, 9304-24
SEC activities, securities industry finances, and exchange activity, selected years 1938-FY91, annual rpt, 9734-2
SEC registration, firms required to file annual rpts, as of Sept 1991, annual listing, 9734-5
Securities dispute arbitration between brokers and investors, outcomes related to forum type and other factors, 1992 GAO rpt, 26119-401
Securities Investor Protection Corp regulatory activity and finances, 1970s-91, GAO rpt, 26119-419
Service fees, minimum balances, and services offered by banks and thrifts, by service type, 1991, annual rpt, 9364-12
Small Business Admin guaranteed loans issued under regular, certified, and preferred lender programs, selected characteristics, FY83-90, GAO rpt, 26113-581
Small business capital formation sources and issues, 1991 annual conf, 9734-4
Statistical Abstract of US, 1992 annual data compilation, 2324-1.16
Taiwan monetary and foreign exchange policies, with money supply, interest rates, and other economic indicators, 1980s, article, 9393-8.303
see also Deposit insurance

Financial Management Service
Budget of US, authoritative financial statements with appropriations, outlays, and receipts, by agency, FY91, annual rpt, 8104-2
Budget of US, obligations and authority by function, agency, and program, with summaries and analyses, FY93, annual rpt, 104-2
Budget of US, receipts by source, outlays by agency and program, and balances, monthly rpt, 8102-3
Currency (foreign) holdings of US, transactions and balances by program and country, 1st half FY92, semiannual rpt, 8102-7
Currency (foreign) purchases of US with dollars, by country, 1st half FY92, semiannual rpt, 8102-5
Finances of Fed Govt, cash and debt transactions, daily tables, 8102-4
Foreign countries currency exchange rates offered by US disbursing offices, by country, quarterly rpt, 8102-6
Trust funds of Fed Govt, financial condition, periodic rpt series, 8102-9

Financial ratios
see Operating ratios

Financial statements
see Business assets and liabilities, general
see Business assets and liabilities, specific industry
see Business income and expenses, general
see Business income and expenses, specific industry
see Government assets and liabilities
see Operating ratios

Financing Corp.
Budget of US, financial statements of federally sponsored enterprises, FY93, annual rpt, 104-2.6

Fine arts
see Art
see Arts and the humanities

Fines and settlements
Airport security operations to prevent hijacking, screening results, enforcement actions, and hijacking attempts, 1990, annual rpt, 7504-49
Alcohol sale permits revoked and suspended, fines, and inspections, for Bur of Alcohol, Tobacco, and Firearms, FY78-90, hearing, 21788-217
Auto and light truck fuel economy performance by make, standards, and enforcement, 1978-94 model years, annual rpt, 7764-9
Banks and thrifts fraud cases, Justice Dept investigation and prosecution activities, 1989-92, GAO rpt, 26119-426
Budget of US, authoritative financial statements with appropriations, outlays, and receipts, by category and agency, FY91, annual rpt, 8104-2.2
Coal Surface Mining Reclamation and Enforcement Office activities and funding, by State and Indian tribe, FY91, annual rpt, 5644-1
Coast Guard enforcement activities, 1st half FY92, semiannual rpt, 7402-4
Environmental laws enforcement activities of EPA and State govts, FY91, annual rpt, 9184-21
Environmental laws enforcement activities of Justice Dept, FY83-91, press release, 6008-37
Environmental laws enforcement activities of Justice Dept, FY83-92, annual press release, 6004-22
Exporters (US) antiboycott law violations and fines by firm, and invitations to boycott by country, FY91, annual rpt, 2024-1
Fed Govt accounts receivable, delinquent debt cases and collections of Justice Dept and private law firms, pilot project results, FY91, annual rpt, 6004-20
Federal criminal sentencing, guidelines by offense and circumstances, series, 17668-1
Federal criminal sentencing, guidelines use and results by offense and district, and Sentencing Commission activities, 1991, annual rpt, 17664-1
Financial instns fraud and abuse, Justice Dept enforcement activity, staff, and case dispositions by instn type, 1988-92, 6008-35
FTC activities, FY90, annual narrative rpt, 9404-1
GSA programs fraud and abuse, audits and investigations, 1st half FY92, semiannual rpt, 9452-8
Hazardous materials transport violations and DOT penalties assessed, by company, 1990, annual rpt, 7304-4
Immigration and nationality violations, prosecutions, fines, imprisonment, and convictions, and deportation and exclusion cases, FY85-91, annual rpt, 6264-2.5
Maritime Commission activities, case filings by type and disposition, and civil penalties by shipper, FY91, annual rpt, 9334-1
Military procurement fraud cases dispositions, fines, and settlements, for top 100 firms, 1981-92, GAO rpt, 26119-423
Natl income and product accounts, comprehensive accounts and components, benchmark revisions, 1929-88, 2708-5
Natl income and product accounts, comprehensive accounts and components, *Survey of Current Business*, monthly rpt, 2702-1.26
Northern Mariana Islands, Saipan garment factories occupational health and safety violations and penalties assessed by OSHA, Mar 1992, press release, 6606-3.10
Nuclear weapons facilities of DOE, contractor fees, environmental and safety enforcement activity, and salaries, by contractor and facility, 1987-88, hearing, 21408-127
Occupational exposure to hazardous substances, employer compliance with info and training regulations, inspections, and fines, by firm size and industry div, 1989-91, GAO rpt, 26121-439
Occupational Safety and Health Admin penalties assessed compared to maximum allowable, by firm size and region, FY89, GAO rpt, 26121-455
Oil company overcharge settlements funds received, and conservation and energy aid spending, by outlying area, 1990, GAO rpt, 26113-564
Oil industry overcharge settlements, use in low income energy assistance, by State, FY90, annual rpt, 4584-1
Probation population, by offender characteristics, sentence conditions, whether rearrested, and offense, 1986-89, 6066-19.65
Railroad safety violation claims settled, by carrier, FY91, annual rpt, 7604-10
Savings instns failure resolution activity of Resolution Trust Corp, with fraud and abuse Federal indictments and case dispositions, 1990, annual rpt, 9724-1
Savings instns fraud and abuse, Federal indictments and case dispositions, periodic press release, 6002-3; 6008-33

Securities dispute arbitration between brokers and investors, outcomes related to forum type and other factors, 1992 GAO rpt, 26119–401
Tax (income) compliance of corporations, and IRS enforcement activities, 1970s-92, hearing, 25408–118
Tax litigation and enforcement activity of IRS, FY91, annual rpt, 8304–3.1
VA programs fraud and abuse, audits and investigations, 2nd half FY92, semiannual rpt, 8602–1
see also Crime victim compensation
see also Judgments, civil procedure
see also Torts

Fingerprints
see Forensic sciences

Fink, Raymond
"Trends in Health and Health Care Among Blacks and Hispanics in New York City During the 1980s", 4164–2

Finland
Agricultural trade of US, by detailed commodity and country, 1991, annual rpt, 1524–8
Agricultural trade of US, by detailed commodity and country, 1991, semiannual rpt, 1522–4
AID loans repayment status and terms by program and country, and status of predecessor agency loans, quarterly rpt, 9912–3
Cuba trade, by commodity and country, mid 1980s-91, 9118–8
Economic and military aid and loans from US and intl agencies, by program and country, FY46-91, annual rpt, 9914–5
Economic conditions, income, production, prices, employment, and trade, 1992 periodic country rpt, 2046–4.31
Economic conditions, policy, and trade practices, by country, 1989-91, annual rpt, 21384–5
Economic, social, political, and geographic summary data, by country, 1992, annual factbook, 9114–2
Exports and imports of US, by Harmonized System 6-digit commodity and country, 1991, annual rpt, 2424–13
Exports and imports of US, by selected country, country group, and commodity group, 1991, annual rpt, 2044–37
Exports and imports of US, by transport mode, country, and SITC 1- to 3-digit commodity, 1991, annual rpt, 2424–12
Exports, imports, and balances of US for manufactured goods, by SITC 2-digit commodity and country, quarterly rpt, 2042–35
Exports of US, detailed Schedule B commodities with countries of destination, 1991, annual rpt, 2424–10
Health care costs and components, services use, resources, and economic indicators, by OECD country, 1960s-90, article, 4652–1.322
Human rights conditions in 170 countries, and US economic and military aid, 1991, annual rpt, 21384–3
Imports of goods, services, and investment from US, trade barriers, impacts, and US actions, by country, 1991, annual rpt, 444–2
Labor conditions, union coverage, and work accidents, 1991 annual country rpt, 6366–4.14
Military spending, arms trade, and force strengths, with govt spending and population, by country, 1979-89, annual rpt, 9824–1
Multinatl US firms and foreign affiliates finances and operations, by industry and country, 1989 benchmark survey, annual rpt, 2704–5
Multinatl US firms foreign affiliates, income statement items by asset size, industry, and country, 1988, biennial article, 8302–2.322
Nuclear power generation in US and 20 countries, monthly rpt, 3162–24.10
Nuclear power generation in US and 20 countries, monthly 1973-88, 3168–123.10
Oil production, stocks, use, and trade, by selected country and country group, monthly rpt, 3162–42
Population size, growth rates, and components of change, by country, projected 1990-2020 and trends from 1950, biennial rpt, 2324–9
Refugee migration, and intl aid programs, by world area and country of origin and asylum, 1991, annual rpt, 7004–15
Steel (carbon flat-rolled) products from 21 countries, injury to US industry from foreign subsidized and less than fair value imports, investigation with background financial and operating data, 1992 rpt, 9886–19.85
Steel imports of US under voluntary restraint agreement, by product, customs district, and country, with US industry operating data, quarterly rpt, 9882–13
Steel trade, by product, country, and customs district, with US industry operating data, 1989-June 1992, semiannual rpt, 9882–15
Tax revenue, by level of govt and type of tax, for OECD countries, mid 1960s-90, annual rpt, 10044–1.2
UN voting record and share of votes in agreement with US, by issue, country, and world area, 1991, annual rpt, 7004–18
see also under By Foreign Country in the "Index by Categories"

Fire departments
Arson cases, civilian and fire fighter casualties, and property damage, 1986-89, 9438–14
Deaths of fire fighters, by cause, circumstances, and location, 1990, annual rpt, 9434–8
Employee benefit plan coverage and provisions, by plan type, for State and local govt employees, 1990, biennial rpt, 6784–21
Employment and payroll, by function and level of govt, annual rpt series, 2466–1
Expenditures (direct) and employment, by function and level of govt, selected years 1962-87, 10048–53
Expenditures by function, and revenues by source, natl income and product account benchmark revisions, 1929-88, 2708–5
Expenditures by function, and revenues by source, natl income and product accounts, *Survey of Current Business*, monthly rpt, 2702–1.26
Finances of govts, by level of govt, State, and for large cities and counties, annual rpt series, 2466–2
Finances of govts, tax systems and revenue, and fiscal structure, by level of govt and State, 1992 and historical trends, annual rpt, 10044–1
Labor demand, turnover, and training completions, by detailed occupation, 1990 and projected to 2005, biennial rpt, 6744–3
Occupational Outlook Handbook, 1992-93, biennial rpt, 6744–1
Pension plans for police and firefighters, participation requirements, and earnings replacement, 1990, article, 6722–1.350
State and local govt employment of minorities and women, by occupation, function, and pay level, 1991, annual rpt, 9244–6.4
Traffic fatal accidents, deaths, and rates, by circumstances, characteristics of persons and vehicles involved, and location, 1990, annual rpt, 7764–10
Trucks PPI, monthly 1991, annual rpt, 6764–2
US Fire Admin activities, funding, and training programs, with fires, casualties, and losses, FY91, annual rpt, 9434–7

Firearms
Aircraft hijackings, on-board explosions, and other crimes, US and foreign incidents, 1986-90, annual rpt, 7504–31
Airport security operations to prevent hijacking, screening results, enforcement actions, and hijacking attempts, 1990, annual rpt, 7504–49
County Business Patterns, 1989: employment, establishments, and payroll, by SIC 2- to 4-digit industry and county, annual State rpt series, 2326–8
County Business Patterns, 1990: employment, establishments, and payroll, by SIC 2- to 4-digit industry and county, annual State rpt series, 2326–6
Court civil and criminal caseloads for Federal district, appeals, and bankruptcy courts, by type of suit and offense, circuit, and district, 1991, annual rpt, 18204–11
Court civil and criminal caseloads for Federal district, appeals, and special courts, 1991, annual rpt, 18204–8
Crime, criminal justice admin and enforcement, and public opinion, data compilation, 1992 annual rpt, 6064–6
Crime victimization in cities, suburbs, and rural areas, by offense, circumstances, and victim and offender characteristics, 1987-89, 6066–3.48
Crime victimization rates, by victim and offender characteristics, circumstances, and offense, 1990 survey, annual rpt, 6066–3.47
Criminal cases by type and disposition, and collections, for US attorneys, by Federal district, FY91, annual rpt, 6004–2.1
Criminal sentences for Federal offenses, guidelines by offense and circumstances, series, 17668–1
Dealers of firearms licensed by Bur of Alcohol, Tobacco, and Firearms, views on regulatory inspections, 1992 survey, GAO rpt, 26119–429
Exports and imports between US and outlying areas, by detailed commodity and mode of transport, 1991, annual rpt, 2424–11

Exports and imports of US, by country and detailed commodity, monthly rpt, 2422–12
Exports and imports of US, by Harmonized System 6-digit commodity and country, 1991, annual rpt, 2424–13
Exports and imports of US, by transport mode, country, and SITC 1- to 3-digit commodity, 1991, annual rpt, 2424–12
Exports of US, detailed Schedule B commodities with countries of destination, 1991, annual rpt, 2424–10
Homicides and rate, by weapon, circumstances, and victim characteristics, and years of potential life lost, 1980s, article, 4202–7.315
Homicides, by circumstance, victim and offender relationship, and type of weapon, 1991, annual rpt, 6224–2.1
Imports of US given duty-free treatment for value of US material sent abroad, by commodity and country, 1987-90, annual rpt, 9884–14
Injuries from use of consumer products and related activities, by severity and victim age and sex, 1990, annual rpt, 9164–7
Injuries from use of consumer products, by severity, victim age, and detailed product, 1991, annual rpt, 9164–6
Law enforcement officer assaults and deaths by circumstances, agency, victim and offender characteristics, and location, 1990, annual rpt, 6224–3
Manufacturing annual survey, 1990: finances and operations, by SIC 2- to 4-digit industry, series, 2506–14
Manufacturing census, 1987: concentration of largest firms measured by value added, and for shipments by SIC 2- and 4-digit industry, subject rpt, 2497–6
Manufacturing census, 1987: shipments of manufacturers products, by customer class and SIC 2- and 4-digit industry, subject rpt, 2497–4
Occupational injury and illness rates, by SIC 2- to 4-digit industry, 1989-90, annual rpt, 6844–7
Occupational injury and illness rates, by SIC 2- to 4-digit industry, 1990, annual rpt, 6844–1
OECD trade, total and for 4 major countries, and US trade by country, by commodity, 1980-90, world area rpt series, 9116–1
Police agencies employment, spending, and operations, FY90, 6066–25.44
Police employment, spending, and operations, for State, city, county, and special district agencies, 1990, annual rpt, 6064–39
Price indexes (producer), by stage of processing and detailed commodity, monthly rpt, 6762–6
Price indexes (producer), by stage of processing and detailed commodity, monthly 1991, annual rpt, 6764–2
Prisoners in Federal and contract instns, by selected characteristics, region, and Federal instn, FY89, annual rpt, 6244–1.1
Public opinion on crime and crime-related issues, by respondent characteristics, data compilation, 1992 annual rpt, 6064–6.2
Sentences for Federal crimes, guidelines use and results by offense and district, and Sentencing Commission activities, 1991, annual rpt, 17664–1
Sentences under Federal mandatory minimum provisions, by defendant characteristics, and views on justice system impacts, FY90, 17668–2
Sheriffs' agencies employment, spending, and operations, FY90, 6066–25.45
Statistical Abstract of US, 1992 annual data compilation, 2324–1.2; 2324–1.5
Tariff Schedule of US, classifications and rates of duty by detailed imported commodity, 1993 base edition, 9886–13
Tax (excise) collections of IRS, by source, quarterly rpt, 8302–1
see also Ammunition
see also Military weapons

Fires and fire prevention
Aircraft accidents and circumstances, for US operations of domestic and foreign airlines and general aviation, periodic rpt, 9612–1
Aircraft accidents, casualties, and damage, for commercial operations by detailed circumstances, 1988, annual rpt, 9614–2
Boat registrations, and accidents, casualties, and damage by cause, by vessel characteristics and State, 1991, annual rpt, 7404–1
Burn units, and other characteristics of Medicare hospital providers, by instn, 1990, annual State rpt series, 4654–14
Extinguishers and fire fighting vehicles, exports of US by country, 1991, annual rpt, 2424–11
Extinguishers and smoke detectors, exports and imports of US by country, 1991, annual rpt, 2424–13
Extinguishers and smoke detectors, exports of US by country, 1991, annual rpt, 2424–10
Extinguishers PPI, monthly rpt, 6762–6
Extinguishers PPI, monthly 1991, annual rpt, 6764–2
Fatal and nonfatal fire injuries, by ignition source, victim age, and injury severity and treatment location, 1984-85 local area study, article, 4042–3.340
Fed Govt financial and nonfinancial domestic aid, 1992 base edition, annual listing, 104–5
Foreign countries disasters, casualties, damage, and aid by US and others, FY91 and trends from FY64, annual rpt, 9914–12
Incidents and mgmt of disasters and natl security threats, with data by major event and State, 1992 annual rpt, 9434–6
Injury and accidental death prevention, and treatment, 1991 conf papers, 4208–35
Kuwait oil fires set by Iraq, pollution levels, disease cases, and US remediation and monitoring spending, 1991 rpt, 9188–117
Kuwait oil fires set by Iraqi forces, air pollution levels by substance and site, as of Mar 1991, 9188–116
Kuwait oil fires set by Iraqi forces, air pollution levels, health effects, intl monitoring activities, and wells affected, 1991, GAO rpt, 26113–566
Military prime contract awards, by detailed procurement category, FY88-91, annual rpt, 3544–18
NASA accidents, casualties, damage, and safety activities, FY91, annual rpt, 9504–4
Panama Canal fires, and related property loss, FY90-91, annual rpt, 9664–3.2
Petrochemicals industries contract labor accidents, injuries, safety programs operations, and employee characteristics, 1986-91, 6608–6
Prisoners in State and Federal instns, violations by type, 1990, quinquennial rpt, 6068–218
Public lands acreage, grants, use, revenues, and allocations, by State, FY91, annual rpt, 5724–1.3
Railroad accidents, casualties, and damage, by cause, railroad, and State, 1991, annual rpt, 7604–1
Railroad accidents, casualties, circumstances, and railroad involved, 1988, annual rpt, 9614–8
Statistical Abstract of US, 1992 annual data compilation, 2324–1.5
Traffic fatal accidents, deaths, and rates, by circumstances, characteristics of persons and vehicles involved, and location, 1990, annual rpt, 7764–10
Transit systems accidents and casualties by circumstances, damage, and ridership, by mode, 1990, annual rpt, 7884–13
US Fire Admin activities, funding, and training programs, with fires, casualties, and losses, FY91, annual rpt, 9434–7
Wildfires and acreage burned, by type of land, ownership, cause, region, and State, 1984-90, annual rpt, 1204–4
see also Arson
see also Fire departments
see also Forest fires
see also Inflammable materials

Fireworks
see Explosives

Fiscal policy
Budget deficits impacts on GNP and public and foreign debt, projected under alternative reduction policies, 1990-2020 with intl comparisons from 1981, GAO rpt, 26109–5
Budget of US, Bush Admin proposals, with detail for defense budgets, and historical data from FY34, FY93, 108–46
Budget of US, CBO analysis of revenue and spending alternatives and projections of economic indicators, FY93-97, annual rpt, 26304–3
Costs of raising funds for aggregate govt spending, measurement of marginal benefits, model description and results, 1992 working paper, 9387–8.265
Economic performance and income distribution impacts of tax policy, issues and background data, with foreign comparisons, 1991 and trends, 21788–211
Economic policy and banking practices, technical paper series, 9366–1
Economic Report of the President for 1991, economic effects of budget proposals, and trends and projections, 1940s-95, annual hearings, 23844–4
Economic Report of the President for 1992, Joint Economic Committee critique and policy recommendations, annual rpt, 23844–2
Economic Report of the President for 1992, with economic trends from 1929, annual rpt, 204–1

Fed Govt financial operations, detailed data, *Treasury Bulletin*, quarterly rpt, 8002–4
Fed Reserve discount rates relation to monetary and fiscal policy, model description and results, 1970s-91, working paper, 9379–14.20
Financial and economic analysis, technical paper series, 8006–6; 9379–12
GNP seasonal growth relation to monetary, fiscal, and demand indicators, 1991 working paper, 9375–13.74
Govt finances, by level of govt, State, and for large cities and counties, annual rpt series, 2466–2
Govt finances, tax systems and revenue, and fiscal structure, by level of govt and State, 1992 with historical trends, annual rpt, 10044–1
Local govts in metro areas, finances, structure, and service delivery, local area rpt series, 10046–9
Productivity shocks impacts on business cycles, and relation to monetary, fiscal, and demand indicators, 1991 working paper, 9375–13.73
Public debt burden on future generations forecast under alternative tax, OASDI, and Medicare policies, 1992 working paper, 9377–9.137
Reagan Admin supply-side fiscal policy, economic impacts, 1980s and trends from 1960s, technical paper, 9385–1.304; 9385–8.125
State and local govt fiscal condition, with data by State and selected city, 1991 hearing, 21268–44
see also Budget of the U.S.
see also Economic policy
see also Foreign budgets
see also Government assets and liabilities
see also Government spending
see also Income taxes
see also Monetary policy
see also Public debt
see also Subsidies
see also Tax expenditures
see also Tax incentives and shelters
see also Tax laws and courts
see also Tax reform
see also Taxation
see also terms beginning with Federal aid

Fischer, John W.
"Airbus Industrie: An Economic and Trade Perspective", 21708–132

Fish and fishing industry
Acid rain environmental, economic, and health effects, and pollutant emissions, 1985-89 and alternative projections to 2030, 14358–4
Agricultural Statistics, 1991, annual rpt, 1004–1
Alaska Beaufort Sea coastal anadromous fish population, migration, and habitat conditions, summer 1990, 5738–37
Alaska Copper River Delta wetland environmental conditions, 1987, 1208–401
Alaska OCS environmental conditions and oil dev impacts, compilation of papers, series, 2176–1
Alaska rural areas population characteristics, and energy resources dev effects, series, 5736–5
Appalachia food processing firms, employment, and shipments, and farm production, by commodity and State, 1960s-90, 9088–37
Atlantic Ocean fish and shellfish catch and stocks, by species and northwest location, 1887-1991 and forecast to 1993, semiannual conf, 2162–9
Atlantic Ocean fish and shellfish distribution, bottom trawl survey results by species and location, periodic rpt series, 2164–18
Bass (striped) stocks status on Atlantic coast, and sport and commercial catch by State, 1979-90, annual rpt, 5504–29
Billfish tagged and recovered by location, and Japan catch in US waters, 1950-90, annual rpt, 2164–7
Business statistics, detailed data for major industries and economic indicators, *Survey of Current Business*, monthly rpt, 2702–1.13
Business statistics, detailed data for major industries and economic indicators, 1960-91, *Survey of Current Business* biennial supplement, 2704–1
Coast Guard enforcement activities, 1st half FY92, semiannual rpt, 7402–4
Coastal and riparian areas environmental conditions, fish, wildlife, use, and mgmt, for individual ecosystems, series, 5506–9
Coastal areas environmental conditions and mgmt, for individual areas, conf series, 2146–8
Cold storage holdings of fish and shellfish, by product and species, preliminary data, monthly press release, 2162–2
Consumption, supply, trade, prices, spending, and indexes, by food commodity, 1990, annual rpt, 1544–4
County Business Patterns, 1989: employment, establishments, and payroll, by SIC 2- to 4-digit industry and county, annual State rpt series, 2326–8
County Business Patterns, 1990: employment, establishments, and payroll, by SIC 2- to 4-digit industry and county, annual State rpt series, 2326–6
CPI by component for US city average, and by selected metro area, region, and population size, monthly rpt, 6762–2
Cuba trade, by commodity and country, mid 1980s-91, 9118–8
Disease cases and outbreaks related to fish and shellfish consumption, by species, cause, and State, 1969-87, hearing, 21568–51
Environmental quality indicators, NOAA monitoring results, 1991 annual summary rpt, 2144–27
Environmental Quality, status of problems, protection programs, research, and intl issues, 1991 annual rpt, 484–1
Estuary environmental conditions, research results and methodology, series, 2176–7
Exports and imports (agricultural) of US, by commodity and country, bimonthly rpt, 1522–1
Exports and imports (agricultural) of US, by detailed commodity and country, 1991, annual rpt, 1524–8
Exports and imports (agricultural) of US, by detailed commodity and country, 1991, semiannual rpt, 1522–4
Exports and imports between US and outlying areas, by detailed commodity and mode of transport, 1991, annual rpt, 2424–11
Exports and imports of US, by country and detailed commodity, monthly rpt, 2422–12
Exports and imports of US, by Harmonized System 6-digit commodity and country, 1991, annual rpt, 2424–13
Exports and imports of US, by selected country, country group, and commodity group, 1991, annual rpt, 2044–37
Exports and imports of US, by transport mode, country, and SITC 1- to 3-digit commodity, 1991, annual rpt, 2424–12
Exports, imports, tariffs, and industry operating data for agricultural, fishery, and forest products, commodity rpt series, 9885–8
Exports, imports, tariffs, and industry operating data for fish, 1992 rpt, 9885–8.7
Exports of US, detailed commodities by country, monthly CD-ROM, 2422–13
Exports of US, detailed Schedule B commodities with countries of destination, 1991, annual rpt, 2424–10
Fed Govt financial and nonfinancial domestic aid, 1992 base edition, annual listing, 104–5
Fishing (net) operations off California, marine mammals and birds incidental catch, 1984-85, 14738–13
Foreign and US oils, oilseeds, and fats production and trade, FAS periodic circular series, 1925–1
Foreign countries economic, social, political, and geographic summary data, by country, 1992, annual factbook, 9114–2
Foreign countries maritime claims and boundary agreements, series, 7006–8
Foreign countries market conditions for US fish and shellfish products, country rpt series, 2166–19
Forest Service activities and finances, by region and State, FY91, annual rpt, 1204–1.1
Freight (waterborne domestic and foreign) by commodity, traffic, and passengers, by port and waterway, 1989, annual rpt, 3754–3
Great Lakes Science Advisory Board research activities and water quality goals, FY91, biennial rpt, 14644–6
Hatcheries and research stations under Fish and Wildlife Service mgmt, acreage by site and State, as of Sept 1992, annual rpt, 5504–8
Imports of US, detailed commodities by country, monthly CD-ROM, 2422–14
Input-output structure of US economy, detailed interindustry transactions for 541 industries, and components of final demand, 1982 benchmark data, 2708–17
Labor demand, turnover, and training completions, by detailed occupation, 1990 and projected to 2005, biennial rpt, 6744–3
Landings and trade of commercial fisheries, by species, 1980-91, semiannual rpt, 1561–15.1
Landings, resources, and mgmt, for fish and shellfish species and region, 1988-90, annual rpt, 2164–22
Landings, trade, use, and fishery operations, with selected foreign data, by species, 1980s-91, annual rpt, 2164–1

Latin America economic and social conditions, resources, trade, and aid, 1992, annual factbook, 9914–14
Manufacturing annual survey, 1990: finances and operations, by SIC 2- to 4-digit industry, series, 2506–14
Manufacturing census, 1987: concentration of largest firms measured by value added, and for shipments by SIC 2- and 4-digit industry, subject rpt, 2497–6
Manufacturing census, 1987: shipments of manufacturers products, by customer class and SIC 2- and 4-digit industry, subject rpt, 2497–4
Manufacturing finances and operations, by SIC 2- to 4-digit industry, forecast 1992, annual rpt, 2044–28
Marine Fisheries Review, US and foreign fisheries resources, dev, mgmt, and research, quarterly journal, 2162–1
Marine Mammal Protection Act admin, and populations, strandings, and catch permits by species and location, 1988-89, annual rpt, 2164–11
Marine mammals incidental catch by fishing trawl vessels, by species, vessel flag and type, and North Pacific location, 1965-88, 2168–129
Minerals offshore lease sales environmental and economic impacts in coastal areas, final statement series, 5736–7
Multinatl firms US affiliates finances and operations, by industry, country of parent firm, and State, 1987, 2708–48
Nutrient, caloric, and waste composition, detailed data for raw, processed, and prepared foods, 1992 rpt, 1356–3.17
Occupational injury and illness rates, by SIC 2- to 4-digit industry, 1989-90, annual rpt, 6844–7
Occupational injury and illness rates, by SIC 2- to 4-digit industry, 1990, annual rpt, 6844–1
Occupational Outlook Handbook, 1992-93, biennial rpt, 6744–1
OECD trade, total and for 4 major countries, and US trade by country, by commodity, 1980-90, world area rpt series, 9116–1
Oil and fat production, consumption by end use, and stocks, by type, monthly Current Industrial Rpt, 2506–4.4
Oil and meal (fish) production and trade, quarterly tables, 2162–3
Oregon OCS rocky banks fish and invertebrate population and habitats, 1988-90, 5738–39
Pacific Northwest Indian tribes environmental, economic, and cultural impacts of OCS oil and gas lease and dev, with background data, 1970s-92, 5738–35
Pacific Ocean (northern) fish catch, driftnet fishing impacts, and fish feeding, habitat, and other characteristics, 1988 conf, 2168–131
Palau admin, and social, economic, and govtl data, FY91, annual rpt, 7004–6
Pollutant concentrations in coastal and estuarine fish, shellfish, and environment, series, 2176–3
Pollutants health effects for animals by species and for humans, and environmental levels, for selected substances, series, 5506–14
Price indexes (producer), by stage of processing and detailed commodity, monthly rpt, 6762–6
Price indexes (producer), by stage of processing and detailed commodity, monthly 1991, annual rpt, 6764–2
Production of processed fish by location, and trade, by species and product, 1988-91, annual rpts, 2166–6
Productivity trends and technological devs in fresh or frozen fish products industry, 1972-90, article, 6722–1.342
Quotas for US 200 mile fishing zone, allocations by species and country, periodic coastal area rpt series, discontinued, 7006–5
Radiation exposure of population near commercial reactors, by body site, age group, and selected plant, 1988, annual rpt, 9634–7
Radiation exposure of population near Hanford, Wash, nuclear plant, with methodology, 1944-91, series, 3356–5
Research of State fish and wildlife agencies, federally funded fishery projects and costs, annual listing, discontinued, 5504–23
Research on fish and wildlife population, habitat, and mgmt, technical rpt series, 5506–12
Restoration programs of Fish and Wildlife Service, funding, land purchases, and project listing, by State, FY90, annual rpt, 5504–1
Salmon conservation spending by organization, and population, for Columbia River basin, 1970-91, GAO rpt, 26113–577
Sharks and other fish tagged and recovered, by species, 1991, annual rpt, 2164–21
Southwestern US streams water quality and fish population impacts of land mgmt and forest fires, 1980s-91, 1208–390
Statistical Abstract of US, 1992 annual data compilation, 2324–1.24
Tax (income) returns of sole proprietorships, income statement items, by industry group, 1990, annual article, 8302–2.317; 8302–2.320
Tuna fishery porpoise kill, and Federal and intl marine mammal protection activity, with bibl, 1991, annual rpt, 14734–1
Tuna industry competitiveness and dolphin protection issues, investigation with background financial and operating data and foreign comparisons, 1992 rpt, 9886–4.187
Tuna production, consumption, trade, and impacts of US dolphin protection embargo, 1989-92, article, 9882–16.303
Turtles (sea) sightings, strandings, and incidental catch, for Kemp's ridley turtles on Texas coast, late 1940s-90, 2168–132
Weight and volume conversion factors for agricultural commodities and products, 1992 rpt, 1508–3
see also Aquaculture
see also Fishing, sport
see also Marine mammals
see also Marine resources conservation
see also Shellfish
see also under By Commodity in the "Index by Categories"

Fish and Wildlife Service
Acreage of refuges and other land under FWS mgmt, by site and State, as of Sept 1992, annual rpt, 5504–8
Activities of FWS in conservation and habitat mgmt, FY91, annual narrative rpt, 5504–20
Bass (striped) stocks status on Atlantic coast, and sport and commercial catch by State, 1979-90, annual rpt, 5504–29
Birds (least tern and piping plover) and habitat levels of selenium and other pollutants, for Missouri River in South Dakota, 1988-90, 5508–118
Budget of US, obligations and authority by function, agency, and program, with summaries and analyses, FY93, annual rpt, 104–2
Coastal and riparian areas environmental conditions, fish, wildlife, use, and mgmt, for individual ecosystems, series, 5506–9
Crane (sandhill) hunting activity and permits, by State and county, 1990/91-1991/92, annual rpt, 5504–31
Duck breeding population, by species, State, and Canada Province, 1991-92 with trends from 1955, annual rpt, 5504–30
Duck hunting stamps philatelic and sales info, 1992/93, annual supplement, 5504–25
Ducks population and nesting success in south-central North Dakota, by species, with habitat conditions, 1960s-81, 5508–120
Endangered species listing and mgmt activities of FWS and Natl Marine Fisheries Service, FY74-91, GAO rpt, 26113–578
Expenditures of Fed Govt in States, by type, program, agency, and State, FY91, annual rpt, 2464–2
Fishery research of State fish and wildlife agencies, federally funded projects and costs, annual listing, discontinued, 5504–23
Hatchery Natl System activities and deliveries, by species, hatchery, and jurisdiction of waters stocked, FY91, annual rpt, 5504–10
Licenses for fishing and hunting issued, and costs, by State, FY91, annual tables, 5504–16
Marine mammals protection activities and funding, populations, and harvests, by species, 1990, annual rpt, 5504–12
Mourning dove population, by hunting and nonhunting State, 1966-92, annual rpt, 5504–15
Owl (northern spotted) conservation methods in Pacific Northwest, findings and recommendations, 1990 rpt, 1208–385
Pesticide levels and water toxicity indicators, for natl wildlife refuge wetlands in South Dakota, 1990, 5508–117
Pollutants health effects for animals by species and for humans, and environmental levels, for selected substances, series, 5506–14
Research on fish and wildlife population, habitat, and mgmt, technical rpt series, 5506–12
Restoration and hunter safety funding of FWS, by State, FY92, semiannual press release, 5502–1

Restoration programs of FWS, funding, land purchases, and project listing, by State, FY90, annual rpt, 5504–1
Salmon aquaculture activities of Little White Salmon National Fish Hatchery, by species and river, late 1890s-1980s, 5508–114
Waterfowl (migratory) hunter harvest, age and sex ratios by species, State, and flyway, 1987-91, annual rpt, 5504–32
Waterfowl (migratory) hunter harvest and unretrieved kills, and duck stamps sold, by species, State, Canada Province, and flyway, 1990-91, annual rpt, 5504–28
Waterfowl (migratory) population, habitat conditions, and flight forecasts, for Canada and US by region, 1992 and trends from 1955, annual rpt, 5504–27
Wetlands (coastal) conservation funding by project, 1992 press release, 5306–4.12
Wetlands (coastal) mapping projects status, costs, and methods, 1990 conf, 5508–116
Wetlands acreage and losses, by wetland type, 1970s-80s, 5508–89
Wetlands acreage in Florida, by wetland type, 1970s-80s, 5508–119
Wetlands and riparian soil and plant characteristics, series, 5506–10
Wetlands wildlife and migratory bird habitat acquisition, funding by State, 1992, press release, 5306–4.13; 5306–4.16
Wolf (gray) kills of livestock, and farmer compensation claims and payments, for Minnesota, late 1970s-80s, 5508–115
Woodcock population from 1968, and hunter harvest, by State, 1992, annual rpt, 5504–11

Fisher, Brian S.
"World Grain Trade Prospects: an Australian Perspective", 1504–9.1

Fisher, Charles R.
"Trends in Total Hospital Financial Performance Under the Prospective Payment System", 4652–1.315

Fisher, Gordon M.
"Poverty Guidelines for 1992", 4742–1.310

Fisheries
see Fish and fishing industry

Fishing, sport
Acid rain environmental, economic, and health effects, and pollutant emissions, 1985-89 and alternative projections to 2030, 14358–4
Bass (striped) stocks status on Atlantic coast, and sport and commercial catch by State, 1979-90, annual rpt, 5504–29
Billfish catch in northern Gulf of Mexico, by species and location, 1990, annual rpt, 2164–23
Billfish tagged and recovered by location, and Japan catch in US waters, 1950-90, annual rpt, 2164–7
Coastal areas environmental conditions and mgmt, for individual areas, conf series, 2146–8
Colorado River Storage Project power sales, and Glen Canyon Dam operations, 1960s-80s, hearing, 21448–47
Environmental Quality, status of problems, protection programs, research, and intl issues, 1991 annual rpt, 484–1
Forests (natl) recreational use, by type of activity and State, 1991, annual rpt, 1204–17
Hatcheries and research stations under Fish and Wildlife Service mgmt, acreage by site and State, as of Sept 1992, annual rpt, 5504–8
Hatchery Natl System activities and deliveries, by species, hatchery, and jurisdiction of waters stocked, FY91, annual rpt, 5504–10
Injuries from use of consumer products and related activities, by severity and victim age and sex, 1990, annual rpt, 9164–7
Injuries from use of consumer products, by severity, victim age, and detailed product, 1991, annual rpt, 9164–6
Ocean sport anglers, fishing activities, and catch by species, by angler characteristics and State, annual coastal area rpt series, 2166–17
Ocean sport anglers using charter and partyboat services, age, income, and sources of advertising influencing vessel choice, 1974-86, article, 2162–1.301
Ocean sport fishing catch, by species, mode of fishing, and coastal region, 1991, annual rpt, 2164–1.2
Public lands acreage and use, and Land Mgmt Bur activities and finances, annual State rpt series, 5724–11
Public lands acreage, grants, use, revenues, and allocations, by State, FY91, annual rpt, 5724–1.2
Research and tagging activities, by game fish species, 1990, annual rpt, 2164–24
Restoration and hunter safety funding of Fish and Wildlife Service, by State, FY92, semiannual press release, 5502–1
Restoration programs of Fish and Wildlife Service, funding, land purchases, and project listing, by State, FY90, annual rpt, 5504–1
Vermont White River basin stream recreation use by activity, time, and location, 1987, 1208–400
see also Hunting and fishing licenses

Fissionable materials
see Radioactive materials
see Uranium

Fitzgerald, Hiram E.
"Early Developmental Factors and Risk for Alcohol Problems", 4482–1.303

Fitzgerald, John
"Alternative Samples for Welfare Duration in SIPP: Does Attrition Matter?", 2626–10.148

Fitzgerald, Terry
"Banking in Computable General Equilibrium Economies: Technical Appendices I and II", 9383–20.25

Fitzsimmons, Stephen J.
"Research Experiences for Undergraduates (REU) Program of the National Science Foundation", 9628–86

Fixed investment
see Capital investments, general
see Capital investments, specific industry

Fixler, Dennis J.
"Measuring Financial Service Output and Prices in Commercial Banking", 6886–6.91

Flammable materials
see Inflammable materials

Fleskes, Joseph P.
"Dabbling Duck Recruitment in Relation to Habitat and Predators at Union Slough National Wildlife Refuge, Iowa", 5506–12.5

Flint, Mich.
see also under By City and By SMSA or MSA in the "Index by Categories"

Flood control
Agricultural Conservation Program acreage and projects, by State, 1936-90, quinquennial rpt, 1808–1
Army Corps of Engineers activities and projects, FY88 and trends from 1800s, annual rpt, 3754–1.1
Army Corps of Engineers activities and projects, FY89 and trends from 1800s, annual rpt, 3754–1.2
Army Corps of Engineers activities and projects, FY90 and trends from 1800s, annual rpt, 3754–1.3
Army Corps of Engineers water resources dev projects, characteristics, and costs, 1950s-89, biennial State rpt series, 3756–1
Army Corps of Engineers water resources dev projects, characteristics, and costs, 1950s-91, biennial State rpt series, 3756–2
Assistance (financial and nonfinancial) of Fed Govt, 1992 base edition, annual listing, 104–5
Colorado River Basin Federal reservoir and power operations and revenues, 1991-92, annual rpt, 5824–6
Colorado River Storage Project finances and activities in western States, FY91, annual rpt, 5824–3
Expenditures of Fed Govt in States, by type, program, agency, and State, FY91, annual rpt, 2464–2
FmHA activities, and loans and grants by program and State, FY91 and trends from FY70, annual rpt, 1184–17
Forest Service activities and finances, by region and State, FY91, annual rpt, 1204–1.2
Great Lakes flood prevention activities of Army Corps of Engineers and Intl Joint Commission, monthly rpt and supplements, 3752–1
Reclamation Bur water storage and carriage facilities, capacity, and operating status, as of Sept 1990, biennial listing, 5824–7
Research on water resources, data collection and analysis activities of USGS Water Resources Div Districts, with project descriptions, series, 5666–26
Tennessee Valley river control activities, and hydroelectric power generation and capacity, 1990, annual rpt, 9804–7
TVA finances and operations by program and facility, FY91, annual rpt, 9804–32
Water quality, chemistry, hydrology, and other characteristics, local area studies, series, 5666–27
Water supply and quality in streams and lakes, and groundwater levels in wells, by drainage basin, 1990, annual State rpt series, 5666–10
Water supply and quality in streams and lakes, and groundwater levels in wells, by drainage basin, 1990-91, annual CD-ROM, 5664–18
Water supply and quality in streams and lakes, and groundwater levels in wells, by drainage basin, 1991, annual State rpt series, 5666–12
Water supply in US and southern Canada, streamflow, surface and groundwater conditions, and reservoir levels, by location, monthly rpt, 5662–3

see also Dams
see also Dredging
see also Reservoirs
see also Watershed projects

Floods
Army Corps of Engineers activities and projects, FY88 and trends from 1800s, annual rpt, 3754–1.1
Army Corps of Engineers activities and projects, FY89 and trends from 1800s, annual rpt, 3754–1.2
Army Corps of Engineers activities and projects, FY90 and trends from 1800s, annual rpt, 3754–1.3
Army Corps of Engineers water resources dev projects, characteristics, and costs, 1950s-89, biennial State rpt series, 3756–1
Army Corps of Engineers water resources dev projects, characteristics, and costs, 1950s-91, biennial State rpt series, 3756–2
Farm water supply, crop moisture, and drought indexes, weekly rpt, seasonal data, 2182–7
Farmland damaged by natural disaster, Emergency Conservation Program aid and participation by State, FY91, annual rpt, 1804–22
Foreign countries disasters, casualties, damage, and aid by US and others, FY91 and trends from FY64, annual rpt, 9914–12
Incidents and mgmt of disasters and natl security threats, with data by major event and State, 1992 annual rpt, 9434–6
Mississippi River and Gulf of Mexico basins floods, precipitation and water levels by site, damage, and deaths, 1982-83, 5666–27.33
Research on water resources, data collection and analysis activities of USGS Water Resources Div Districts, with project descriptions, series, 5666–26
Statistical Abstract of US, 1992 annual data compilation, 2324–1.6
Water supply in US and southern Canada, streamflow, surface and groundwater conditions, and reservoir levels, by location, monthly rpt, 5662–3
Weather events and anomalies, precipitation and temperature for US and foreign locations, weekly rpt, 2182–6
Weather trends and deviations, by world region, 1880s-1990, annual chartbook, 2184–9
see also Flood control
see also Tsunamis

Floor coverings
Ceramic floor and wall tiles trade, tariffs, and industry operating data, 1992 rpt, 9885–13.2
Exports and imports between US and outlying areas, by detailed commodity and mode of transport, 1991, annual rpt, 2424–11
Exports and imports of US, by country and detailed commodity, monthly rpt, 2422–12
Exports and imports of US, by Harmonized System 6-digit commodity and country, 1991, annual rpt, 2424–13
Exports and imports of US, by transport mode, country, and SITC 1- to 3-digit commodity, 1991, annual rpt, 2424–12
Exports of US, detailed Schedule B commodities with countries of destination, 1991, annual rpt, 2424–10
Foreign countries market conditions for US textile and apparel exports, with domestic industry operations, country rpt series, 2046–15
Input-output structure of US economy, detailed interindustry transactions for 541 industries, and components of final demand, 1982 benchmark data, 2708–17
Manufacturing census, 1987: concentration of largest firms measured by value added, and for shipments by SIC 2- and 4-digit industry, subject rpt, 2497–6
Manufacturing finances and operations, by SIC 2- to 4-digit industry, forecast 1992, annual rpt, 2044–28
Price indexes (producer), by stage of processing and detailed commodity, monthly 1991, annual rpt, 6764–2
Price indexes (producer) for building materials, by type, quarterly rpt, 2042–1.5
Retail trade sales and inventories, by kind of business, region, and selected State, MSA, and city, monthly rpt, 2413–3
Retail trade sales, inventories, purchases, gross margin, and accounts receivable, by SIC 2- to 4-digit kind of business and form of ownership, 1990, annual rpt, 2413–5
Textile and apparel exports of US, by product group and country, quarterly rpt, 2042–36
see also Carpets and rugs

Florence, S.C.
Wages by occupation, and benefits for office and plant workers, 1992 survey, periodic MSA rpt, 6785–3.5

Florida
Banks (insured commercial and savings) deposits by instn, State, MSA, and county, as of June 1991, annual regional rpt, 9295–3.2
Cancer incidence impacts of migration, and treatment resources availability, for Florida by county, 1980, article, 4042–3.339
Celery acreage planted and growing, by growing area, monthly rpt, 1621–14
County Business Patterns, 1990: employment, establishments, and payroll, by SIC 2- to 4-digit industry and county, annual State rpt, 2326–6.11
Deaths and rates, by detailed location, cause, and demographic characteristics, 1989, US Vital Statistics annual rpt, 4144–3.1
Economic indicators by State and MSA, Fed Reserve 6th District, quarterly rpt, 9371–14
Electric power demand, and industrial and employment impacts of capacity shortfalls and new power plants, by selected State, 1960s-80s and projected to 2000, hearing, 21248–163
Employment and housing indicators by State, FHLB 4th District, quarterly rpt, 9302–36
Employment by industry div, earnings, and hours, for 8 southeastern States, quarterly press release, 6942–7
Employment, earnings, and hours, by selected SIC 1- to 4-digit industry, State, and for 275 MSAs, 1987-92, 6748–81
Estuary environmental and fishery conditions, research results and methodology, 1992 rpt, 2176–7.28
Fed Govt spending in States and local areas, by type, State, county, and city, FY91, annual rpt, 2464–3
Fed Govt spending in States, by type, program, agency, and State, FY91, annual rpt, 2464–2
Flower and foliage shipments from Florida by State and mode of transport, US imports by country, and prices, by variety, mid 1980s-91, annual rpt, 1311–24
Fruit shipments, production, and marketing, for Florida, with US trade and prices, by commodity, 1970s-91, annual rpt, 1311–23
HHS financial aid, by program, recipient, State, and city, FY91, annual regional listing, 4004–3.4
Hospital deaths of Medicare patients, actual and expected rates by diagnosis, and hospital characteristics, by instn, FY90 annual State rpt, 4654–14.10
Housing census, 1990: summary unit characteristics, by householder race and age, county, place, and urban-rural location, State rpt, 2471–1.11
Hurricanes in northwest Atlantic Ocean, correlation with Sahel Africa rainfall, 1947-90, 2148–61
Manatees killed in Florida and other US waters, by cause, 1978-91, annual rpt, 14734–1
Military prime contract awards, by contractor, service branch, State, and city, FY91, annual rpt, 3544–22
Mineral Industry Surveys, State reviews of production, 1991, preliminary annual rpt, 5614–6
Minerals Yearbook, Vol 2, 1990: State review of production and sales by commodity, and business activity, annual rpt, 5604–22.10
Multinatl firms US affiliates finances and operations, by industry, country of parent firm, and State, 1987, 2708–48
Peaches production, marketing, and prices in 3 southeastern States and Appalachia, 1991, annual rpt, 1311–12
Physicians, by specialty, age, sex, and location of training and practice, 1990, State rpt, 4116–6.10
Population and housing census, 1990: detailed geographic coverage, State CD-ROM, 2551–9.5
Population and housing census, 1990: population and housing characteristics, detailed geographic coverage, State CD-ROM, 2551–10.12; 2551–10.13
Population and housing census, 1990: summary characteristics, by county, subdiv, and place, State rpt, 2551–7.11
Population census, 1990: population characteristics and living arrangements, by county, place, and urban-rural location, State rpt, 2531–1.11
Radiation and other pollutant releases from DOE contractor research lab and nuclear weapons facilities, monitoring results, 1992 annual site rpt, 3324–2.12
Statistical Abstract of US, 1992 annual data compilation, 2324–1
Textile mill employment, earnings, and hours, for 8 Southeastern States, quarterly press release, 6942–1

Timber in Florida, industrial roundwood production, by product and county, 1987 and 1989, 1208–352
Wages by occupation, for office and plant workers, 1992 survey, periodic labor market rpt, 6785–3.5
Water quality, chemistry, hydrology, and other characteristics, 1990 local area study, 5666–27.28
Water resources data collection and analysis activities of USGS Water Resources Div District, with project descriptions, 1991 rpt, 5666–26.18
Water use by end use, well withdrawals, and public supply deliveries, by county, 1987, State rpt, 5666–24.13
Wetlands acreage in Florida, by wetland type, 1970s-80s, 5508–119
see also Boca Raton, Fla.
see also Clearwater, Fla.
see also Dade County, Fla.
see also Delray Beach, Fla.
see also Fort Lauderdale, Fla.
see also Hialeah, Fla.
see also Hollywood, Fla.
see also Jacksonville, Fla.
see also Miami, Fla.
see also Orlando, Fla.
see also Pinellas County, Fla.
see also Pompano Beach, Fla.
see also St. Petersburg, Fla.
see also Tampa, Fla.
see also West Palm Beach, Fla.
see also under By State in the "Index by Categories"

Flow-of-funds accounts
Assets and debts of private sector, balance sheets by segment, 1960-91, semiannual rpt, 9365–4.1
Assets and liabilities in flow-of-funds accounts, by type and economic sector, annual rpt, suspended, 9364–3
Credit market debt outstanding, and statements of assets and liabilities, by sector, 1989-90, annual rpt, 9364–5.8
Credit markets, direct and indirect sources of funds, monthly rpt, 9362–1.1
Flow-of-funds accounts, savings, investments, and credit statements, quarterly rpt, 9365–3.3
Foreign countries economic indicators, and trade and investment flows, for selected countries and country groups, selected years 1946-91, annual rpt, 204–1.9
Foreign direct investment of US, by industry group and world area, 1989-91, annual article, 2702–1.332
Intl investment position of US, by component, industry, world region, and country, 1990-91, annual article, 2702–1.323
Medicare contributions and disbursements, by State, 1985, 4006–11.4
Statistical Abstract of US, 1992 annual data compilation, 2324–1.16

Flowers and nursery products
Agricultural Statistics, 1991, annual rpt, 1004–1
Consumer spending, natl income and product account benchmark revisions, 1929-88, 2708–5
Consumer spending, natl income and product accounts, comprehensive accounts and components, *Survey of Current Business*, monthly rpt, 2702–1.25
CPI by component for US city average, and by selected metro area, region, and population size, monthly rpt, 6762–2
Exports and imports (agricultural) of US, by commodity and country, bimonthly rpt, 1522–1
Exports and imports (agricultural) of US, by detailed commodity and country, 1991, annual rpt, 1524–8
Exports and imports (agricultural) of US, by detailed commodity and country, 1991, semiannual rpt, 1522–4
Exports and imports between US and outlying areas, by detailed commodity and mode of transport, 1991, annual rpt, 2424–11
Exports and imports of US, by country and detailed commodity, monthly rpt, 2422–12
Exports and imports of US, by Harmonized System 6-digit commodity and country, 1991, annual rpt, 2424–13
Exports of US, detailed Schedule B commodities with countries of destination, 1991, annual rpt, 2424–10
Farm financial and marketing conditions, forecast 1992, annual chartbook, 1504–8
Farm income, cash marketing receipts ranked by commodity and State, 1990, 1548–385
Farm sector balance sheet, and receipts by detailed commodity, by State, 1986-90, annual rpt, 1544–18
Imports of cut flowers, by type and country, FAS monthly circular with articles, 1925–34
Injuries from use of consumer products, by severity, victim age, and detailed product, 1991, annual rpt, 9164–6
Input-output structure of US economy, detailed interindustry transactions for 541 industries, and components of final demand, 1982 benchmark data, 2708–17
Latin America economic and social conditions, resources, trade, and aid, 1992, annual factbook, 9914–14
Production, sales, prices, and growers, by flower and foliage crop and State, 1990-91 and planting planned 1992, annual rpt, 1631–8
Shipments of domestic and imported cut flowers and decorative greens, by State and country of origin, weekly rpt, 1311–3
Shipments of flowers and foliage from Florida by State and mode of transport, US imports by country, and prices, by variety, mid 1980s-91, annual rpt, 1311–24
Tree planting on govt land contracted to small businesses, Federal grants, State funding, and projects, by State, FY91, annual rpt, 9764–10
Tree seedlings produced for forest planting, by nursery ownership and State, FY91, annual rpt, 1204–7.2
see also Seeds

Floyd, Dale E.
"Southeast During the Civil War: Selected War Department Records in the National Archives of the U.S.", 9516–1.2

Flu
see Pneumonia and influenza

Fluoridation
see Water fluoridation

Fluoride dental products
see Personal care products

Fluorspar
see Nonmetallic minerals and mines

FNMA
see Federal National Mortgage Association

Foertsch, Mary A.
"Reading In and Out of School: Factors Influencing the Literacy Achievement of American Students in Grades 4, 8, and 12, in 1988 and 1990", 4898–33

Folic acid
see Vitamins and nutrients

Fomby, Thomas B.
"Threshold Cointegration", 9379–12.90

Fontana, Alan
"Age and Cohort Effects in PTSD", 8704–6
"Causal Model of the Etiology of PTSD", 8704–6
"Long Journey Home II: The Second Progress Report on the Department of Veterans Affairs PTSD Clinical Teams Program", 8704–6
"Long-Term Sequelae of Combat in World War II, Korea and Vietnam: A Comparative Study", 8704–6
"War Zone Traumas and PTSD Symptomatology", 8704–6

Food and Drug Administration
Activities of FDA, quarterly rpt, 4062–3
Assistance (financial) of HHS, by program, recipient, State, and city, FY91, annual regional listings, 4004–3
Blood banks safety violations, FDA enforcement, disease transmittal, and Houston regional center activities and finances, 1970s-91, hearings, 21368–134
Bovine somatotropin (bST) dairy industry use, effectiveness of FDA testing for human and animal safety, 1991, GAO rpt, 26131–101
Budget of US, obligations and authority by function, agency, and program, with summaries and analyses, FY93, annual rpt, 104–2
Drug (prescription) advertising in medical journals, accuracy, info completeness, and violations of FDA regulations, 1990, 4008–119
Drug (prescription) clinical trials representation of women, and FDA policy guidance, 1988-91, GAO rpt, 26121–486
Drug approvals of FDA, by firm, 1985-90, 25148–44
Drug marketing application processing of FDA, by drug, purpose, and producer, 1991, annual rpt, 4064–14
Imports detained by FDA, by reason, product, shipper, brand, and country, monthly listing, 4062–2
Pesticide residue in food imports, FDA enforcement, with contaminated shipments distributed, damages assessed and paid, and repeat offenders, FY88-90, GAO rpt, 26113–598
Radiation from electronic devices, incidents by type of device, and FDA control activities, 1991, annual rpt, 4064–13
Regulations dev by FDA, timeliness, with status and processing time for selected regulations, 1991, GAO rpt, 26121–453

Shellfish harvest in estuaries, approved and restricted areas, and pollution sources, by estuary, State, and coastal region, 1990, quinquennial rpt, 2178–33
Toxicology Natl Program research and testing activities, FY90 and planned FY91, annual rpt, 4044–16

Food and food industry
Agricultural Statistics, 1991, annual rpt, 1004–1
Appalachia food processing firms, employment, and shipments, and farm production, by commodity and State, 1960s-90, 9088–37
Business statistics, detailed data for major industries and economic indicators, *Survey of Current Business*, monthly rpt, 2702–1.13
Business statistics, detailed data for major industries and economic indicators, 1960-91, *Survey of Current Business* biennial supplement, 2704–1
Capital expenditures for plant and equipment, by major industry group, quarterly rpt, 2502–2
Collective bargaining agreements expiring during year, and workers covered, by firm, union, industry group, and State, 1992, annual rpt, 6784–9
Cooperatives (food marketing) exports under intl business arrangements, 1985-88, 1128–69
County Business Patterns, 1989: employment, establishments, and payroll, by SIC 2- to 4-digit industry and county, annual State rpt series, 2326–8
County Business Patterns, 1990: employment, establishments, and payroll, by SIC 2- to 4-digit industry and county, annual State rpt series, 2326–6
Cuba trade, by commodity and country, mid 1980s-91, 9118–8
EC economic integration impacts on domestic and intl agricultural conditions, 1990 conf, 1528–325
Employment, earnings, and hours, by SIC 1- to 4-digit industry, monthly 1989-Feb 1992, annual rpt, 6744–4
Employment, unemployment, and labor force characteristics, by region and census div, 1991, annual rpt, 6744–7.1
Energy use and prices, by fuel type and manufacturing industry, 1974-88, 3166–15.3
Energy use and prices for manufacturing industries, 1988 survey, series, 3166–13
Exports and imports (agricultural) of US, by detailed commodity and country, 1991, annual rpt, 1524–8
Exports and imports (agricultural) of US, by detailed commodity and country, 1991, semiannual rpt, 1522–4
Exports and imports between US and outlying areas, by detailed commodity and mode of transport, 1991, annual rpt, 2424–11
Exports and imports of US, by country and detailed commodity, monthly rpt, 2422–12
Exports and imports of US, by Harmonized System 6-digit commodity and country, 1991, annual rpt, 2424–13
Exports and imports of US, by transport mode, country, and SITC 1- to 3-digit commodity, 1991, annual rpt, 2424–12
Exports of US, detailed commodities by country, monthly CD-ROM, 2422–13
Exports of US, detailed Schedule B commodities with countries of destination, 1991, annual rpt, 2424–10
Finances and productivity of food industry, marketing cost components, and farm-retail food prices, 1920s-91, annual rpt, 1544–9
Finances, operations, and merger activity, for food processors and distributors, 1991, annual rpt, 1544–22
Foreign countries agricultural production, consumption, and policies, and US export dev and promotion, monthly journal, 1922–2
Foreign direct investment in US, by industry group and world area, 1989-91, annual article, 2702–1.331
Foreign direct investment of US, by industry group and world area, 1989-91, annual article, 2702–1.332
Freight (waterborne domestic and foreign) by commodity, traffic, and passengers, by port and waterway, 1989, annual rpt, 3754–3
Hazardous substances industrial releases and reduction methods under EPA regulation, by chemical, source, industry, and location, 1989, annual rpt, 9234–6
Hazardous substances industrial releases and reduction methods under EPA regulation, with chemical stocks and use, facility directory, 1987-89, annual CD-ROM, 9234–7
Imports detained by FDA, by reason, product, shipper, brand, and country, monthly listing, 4062–2
Imports, exports, and employment impacts, by SIC 2- to 4-digit industry and commodity, quarterly rpt, 2322–2
Imports of US, detailed commodities by country, monthly CD-ROM, 2422–14
Input-output structure of US economy, detailed interindustry transactions for 84 industries, and components of final demand, 1987, annual article, 2702–1.316
Input-output structure of US economy, detailed interindustry transactions for 541 industries, and components of final demand, 1982 benchmark data, 2708–17
Japan investment in US farmland and agricultural industries, with data by State and county, late 1960s-90, 1528–332
Labor productivity, indexes of output, hours, and employment by SIC 2- to 4-digit industry, 1967-90, annual rpt, 6824–1.3
Manufacturing annual survey, 1990: finances and operations, by SIC 2- to 4-digit industry, series, 2506–14
Manufacturing census, 1987: concentration of largest firms measured by value added, and for shipments by SIC 2- and 4-digit industry, subject rpt, 2497–6
Manufacturing census, 1987: shipments of manufacturers products, by customer class and SIC 2- and 4-digit industry, subject rpt, 2497–4
Manufacturing corporations financial statements, by selected SIC 2- to 3-digit industry, quarterly rpt, 2502–1
Manufacturing finances and operations, by SIC 2- to 4-digit industry, forecast 1992, annual rpt, 2044–28
Manufacturing industries operations and performance, analytical rpt series, 2506–16
Manufacturing production, shipments, inventories, orders, and pollution control costs, periodic Current Industrial Rpt series, 2506–3
Marketing, consumer research, legislation, and regulation devs, and consumption and price trends, quarterly journal, 1541–7
Mexico imports from US, by industry and State, 1987-91, 2048–154
Multinatl firms US affiliates finances and operations, by industry, country of parent firm, and State, 1987, 2708–48
Multinatl firms US affiliates, finances, and operations, by industry, world area of parent firm, and State, 1989-90, annual rpt, 2704–4
Multinatl US firms and foreign affiliates finances and operations, by industry and country, 1989 benchmark survey, annual rpt, 2704–5
Multinatl US firms foreign affiliates, income statement items by asset size, industry, and country, 1988, biennial article, 8302–2.322
Natl income and product accounts, comprehensive accounts and components, benchmark revisions, 1929-88, 2708–5
Natl income and product accounts, comprehensive accounts and components, *Survey of Current Business*, monthly rpt, 2702–1.29
Nutrient, caloric, and waste composition of food, detailed data for raw, processed, and prepared foods, series, 1356–3
Occupational injury and illness rates, by SIC 2- to 4-digit industry, 1989-90, annual rpt, 6844–7
Occupational injury and illness rates, by SIC 2- to 4-digit industry, 1990, annual rpt, 6844–1
Pacific Northwest population, households, employment, income, fuel prices, and electricity demand, alternative forecasts 1991-2010, annual rpt, 3224–3.3
Pacific territories population and housing detailed characteristics, by location, 1990 Census of Population and Housing, series, 2551–8
Pollutants health effects, concentrations in food and environment, sources, human intake, and regulation, series, 9186–8
Pollution abatement capital and operating costs, by SIC 2- to 4-digit industry and State, 1990, annual Current Industrial Rpt, 2506–3.6
Processed food production and stocks by State, shipments, exports, ingredients, and use, periodic Current Industrial Rpt series, 2506–4
Puerto Rico and other US possessions corporations income tax returns, income and tax items, and employment, by selected industry, 1989, article, 8302–2.326
Research (agricultural) funding and staffing for USDA, State agencies, and other instns, by topic, FY91, annual rpt, 1744–2
Sales of farm products by stage of processing and marketing, and trade, by selected commodity, 1987, young readers pamphlet, 2346–1.5

School lunch programs food donations processing, contracts, and processors problems with State reporting requirements, with data by State, 1989-91, GAO rpt, 26113–555
Science, engineering, and technical employment in manufacturing, by field and industry, 1989, triennial rpt, 9627–23
Snack foods and sweets nutrient, caloric, and waste composition, 1992 rpt, 1356–3.17
Soviet Union and US economic and sociodemographic indicators, selected years 1970-90, handbook, 2328–80
Supply, consumption, trade, prices, spending, and indexes, by food commodity, 1990, annual rpt, 1544–4
Tax (income) returns of corporations, income and tax items by asset size and detailed industry, 1989, annual rpt, 8304–4; 8304–21
Tax (income) returns of corporations with foreign tax credit, income and tax items by industry group, 1988, biennial article, 8302–2.316
Tax (income) returns of sole proprietorships, income statement items, by industry group, 1990, annual article, 8302–2.317; 8302–2.320
Vending machine shipments by product, trade, and use, 1991, Current Industrial Rpt, 2506–12.10
Weight and volume conversion factors for agricultural commodities and products, 1992 rpt, 1508–3
Wholesale trade sales and inventories, by SIC 2- to 3-digit kind of business, monthly rpt, 2413–7
see also Animal feed
see also Aquaculture
see also Baking and bakery products
see also Beer and breweries
see also Beverages
see also Candy and confectionery products
see also Cocoa and chocolate
see also Coffee
see also Cold storage and refrigeration
see also Dairy industry and products
see also Fish and fishing industry
see also Food and waterborne diseases
see also Food assistance
see also Food consumption
see also Food ingredients and additives
see also Food inspection
see also Food prices
see also Food stamp programs
see also Food stores
see also Food supply
see also Fruit and fruit products
see also Grains and grain products
see also Honey and beekeeping
see also Ice, manufactured
see also Liquor and liquor industry
see also Livestock and livestock industry
see also Meat and meat products
see also Nuts
see also Oils, oilseeds, and fats
see also Packaging and containers
see also Peanuts
see also Pet food and supplies
see also Poultry industry and products
see also Restaurants and drinking places
see also Shellfish
see also Soft drink industry and products
see also Spices and herbs
see also Sugar industry and products
see also Synthetic food products
see also Syrups and sweeteners
see also Tea
see also Vegetables and vegetable products
see also Wine and winemaking
see also under By Commodity in the "Index by Categories"
see also under By Industry in the "Index by Categories"

Food and Nutrition Service
Budget of US, obligations and authority by function, agency, and program, with summaries and analyses, FY93, annual rpt, 104–2
Expenditures of Fed Govt in States, by type, program, agency, and State, FY91, annual rpt, 2464–2
Food aid programs of USDA, costs and participation by program, annual rpt, suspended, 1364–9
Food stamp eligibility and payment errors, by type, recipient characteristics, and State, FY90, annual rpt, 1364–15
Food stamp recipient household size, composition, income, and income and deductions allowed, summer 1989, annual rpt, 1364–8
Women, infants, and children food aid program of USDA, participants and costs by State and Indian agency, FY90, annual tables, 1364–12
Women, infants, and children food aid program of USDA, participants by race, State, and Indian agency, Apr 1991, annual rpt, 1364–16
Women, infants, and children food aid program of USDA, participants, clinics, and costs, by State and Indian agency, monthly tables, 1362–16
Women, infants, and children food aid program of USDA, State contract awards and bid prices for infant formula, late 1980s-91, hearing, 25528–118

Food and waterborne diseases
Bacillus cereus food poisoning outbreak at a catered event, 1989 local area study, article, 4042–3.350
Cases and outbreaks of waterborne disease, by type, source, and location, 1989-90, article, 4202–7.301
Cholera surveillance in Latin America, activities and CDC recommendations, 1992 narrative article, 4202–7.310
Deaths and rates, by cause, provisional data, monthly rpt, 4142–1.2
Deaths and rates, by detailed location, cause, and demographic characteristics, 1989, US Vital Statistics annual rpt, 4144–3
Farm financial and marketing conditions, forecast 1992, annual conf, 1504–9
Fish and shellfish-related disease cases and outbreaks, by cause, species, and State, 1969-87, hearing, 21568–51
Foreign travel vaccination needs by country, and disease prevention recommendations, 1992 annual rpt, 4204–11
Health condition and care indicators, 1950s-90 with health improvement and disease prevention goals for 1990, annual data compilation, 4144–11
Hepatitis cases by infection source, age, sex, race, and State, and deaths, by strain, 1989 and trends from 1966, 4205–2
HHS financial aid, by program, recipient, State, and city, FY91, annual regional listings, 4004–3
Kuwait oil fires set by Iraq, pollution levels, disease cases, and US remediation and monitoring spending, 1991 rpt, 9188–117
Morbidity and Mortality Weekly Report, infectious notifiable disease cases by age, race, and State, and deaths, 1940s-91, annual rpt, 4204–1
Morbidity and Mortality Weekly Report, infectious notifiable disease cases by State, and public health issues, 4202–1
Trichinosis cases in US, by type of meat and State, 1987-90, article, 4202–7.304
Water supply and quality in streams and lakes, and groundwater levels in wells, by drainage basin, 1990, annual State rpt series, 5666–10
Water supply and quality in streams and lakes, and groundwater levels in wells, by drainage basin, 1990-91, annual CD-ROM, 5664–18
Water supply and quality in streams and lakes, and groundwater levels in wells, by drainage basin, 1991, annual State rpt series, 5666–12
see also Food inspection
see also under By Disease in the "Index by Categories"

Food assistance
Agricultural Statistics, 1991, annual rpt, 1004–1
Assistance (block and categorical grants) programs for State and local govts, FY91, biennial listing, 10044–8
Assistance (financial and nonfinancial) of Fed Govt, 1992 base edition, annual listing, 104–5
Bean (dried) prices by State, market activity, and foreign and US production, use, stocks, and trade, weekly rpt, 1311–17
Bean (dried) production and prices by State, exports and foreign production by country, and USDA food aid purchases, by bean type, 1986-91, annual rpt, 1311–18
Budget of US, obligations and authority by function, agency, and program, with summaries and analyses, FY93, annual rpt, 104–2
CCC dairy price support program foreign donations and domestic donations to poor, schools, Prisons Bur, and VA, monthly rpt, 1802–2
Child nutrition programs of USDA, funding by program and State, FY90-91, annual rpt, 4824–2.27
Consumer research, food marketing, legislation, and regulation devs, and consumption and price trends, quarterly journal, 1541–7
Debt to US of foreign govts and private obligors, by country and program, periodic rpt, 8002–6
Developing countries economic and social conditions from 1960s, and Intl Dev Cooperation Agency and AID activities and funding, FY91-93, annual rpt, 9904–4
Developing countries food supply, needs, and aid, status and alternative forecasts, world area rpt series, 1526–8

Expenditures for public welfare by program, FY50s-89, annual article, 4742–1.319
Expenditures of Fed Govt in States, by type, program, agency, and State, FY91, annual rpt, 2464–2
Exports and imports between US and outlying areas, by detailed commodity and mode of transport, 1991, annual rpt, 2424–11
Exports and imports of US, by Harmonized System 6-digit commodity and country, 1991, annual rpt, 2424–13
Exports of US, detailed Schedule B commodities with countries of destination, 1991, annual rpt, 2424–10
Farm income impacts of food assistance programs, by commodity, model description and results, 1989-90, 1548–390
Fed Govt finances, cash and debt transactions, daily tables, 8102–4
Foreign countries disasters, casualties, damage, and aid by US and others, FY91 and trends from FY64, annual rpt, 9914–12
HHS financial aid, by program, recipient, State, and city, FY91, annual regional listings, 4004–3
Homeless persons aid by program and Federal agency, and indicators of need, 1990, annual rpt, 14364–1
Homeless persons aid programs of Fed Govt, program descriptions and funding, by agency and State, FY87-91, annual GAO rpt, 26104–21
Honey production, prices, trade, stocks, marketing, and CCC honey loan and distribution activities, monthly rpt, 1311–2
Households composition, income, benefits, and labor force status, Survey of Income and Program Participation methodology, working paper series, 2626–10
Mississippi poverty, hunger, and public welfare program operations and indicators of need, 1991 hearing, 21968–57
Ohio poverty, hunger, and public welfare program operations and indicators of need, by county, 1991 hearing, 21968–58
Population economic well-being indicators, by selected characteristics and household income and income-to-poverty ratio, 1984, 2546–20.22
Puerto Rico food assistance program funding and restrictions, FY90-91, GAO rpt, 26113–580
Purchases by food aid programs, by commodity, firm, and shipping point or destination, weekly rpt, 1302–3
Rice exports under Federal programs, periodic situation rpt, 1561–8
Statistical Abstract of US, 1992 annual data compilation, 2324–1.12
USDA food aid programs costs and participation, by program, annual rpt, suspended, 1364–9
Women, infants, and children food aid program of USDA, participant referrals to social service programs, by type and reason, 1990 local area study, article, 4042–3.318
Women, infants, and children food aid program of USDA, participants and costs by State and Indian agency, FY90, annual tables, 1364–12
Women, infants, and children food aid program of USDA, participants by race, State, and Indian agency, Apr 1991, annual rpt, 1364–16
Women, infants, and children food aid program of USDA, participants, clinics, and costs, by State and Indian agency, monthly tables, 1362–16
Women, infants, and children food aid program of USDA, prenatal enrollment, by selected maternal and prenatal care characteristics, 1988-89 local area study, article, 4042–3.305
Women, infants, and children food aid program of USDA, prenatal participation effects on birthweight and health and social welfare costs, 1960s-90, GAO rpt, 26121–458
Women, infants, and children food aid program of USDA, State contract awards and bid prices for infant formula, late 1980s-91, hearing, 25528–118
see also Food stamp programs
see also Public Law 480
see also School lunch and breakfast programs

Food consumption

Agricultural Outlook, production, prices, marketing, and trade, by commodity, forecast and current situation, monthly rpt with articles, 1502–4
Agricultural Statistics, 1991, annual rpt, 1004–1
Apple (processed) demand and impacts of selected market factors, 1980s-91, 1548–392
Bean (dried) prices by State, market activity, and foreign and US production, use, stocks, and trade, weekly rpt, 1311–17
Cancer (colon) risk relation to diet, aspirin use, exercise, and other factors, 1982-88, article, 4472–1.346
Cancer (colorectal) risk relation to diet, for men, 1986-88, article, 4472–1.302
Confectionery products shipments and per capita consumption, 1981-91, semiannual rpt, 1925–9.2
Consumer spending, natl income and product account benchmark revisions, 1929-88, 2708–5
Consumer spending, natl income and product accounts, comprehensive accounts and components, *Survey of Current Business*, monthly rpt, 2702–1.25
Consumption of food, dietary composition, and nutrient intake, natl survey methodology changes and sample results, 1990 rpt, 1358–6
Consumption, supply, trade, prices, spending, and indexes, by food commodity, 1990, annual rpt, 1544–4
Dairy production, prices, trade, and use, periodic situation rpt with articles, 1561–2
Dairy production, trade, use, and prices, for US and selected countries, forecast 1992 and trends from 1987, FAS semiannual circular, 1925–10
Developing countries food supply, needs, and aid, status and alternative forecasts, world area rpt series, 1526–8
Expenditures by category, and income, by selected household characteristics, 1991 survey, annual press release, 6726–1.53
Expenditures by category, selected household characteristics, and region, Consumer Expenditure Survey, quarterly rpt, 6762–14
Expenditures for food at and away from home, by selected characteristics, 1989, article, 1702–1.308
Expenditures for food, 1975-91, annual rpt, 1544–9
Exports, imports, tariffs, and industry operating data for agricultural, fishery, and forest products, commodity rpt series, 9885–8
Farm financial and marketing conditions, forecast 1992, annual chartbook, 1504–8
Farm home consumption of meat raised on premises, by species and State, 1990-91, annual rpt, 1623–8
Fish and fish products per capita use for US, 1909-91, and by country, average 1987-89, annual rpt, 2164–1.8
Foreign and US agricultural supply and demand indicators, by selected crop, monthly rpt, 1522–5
Foreign countries agricultural production, prices, and trade, by country, 1980-91 and forecast 1992, annual world area rpt series, 1524–4
Fruit and nut production, prices, trade, stocks, and use, by selected crop, periodic situation rpt with articles, 1561–6
Germany fresh fruit production, EC and non-EC imports, and consumption, by commodity, 1990-92, article, 1925–34.340
Indian and Alaska Native youth health condition and behavioral patterns, by sex and grade, 1988-90, 4088–3
Input-output structure of US economy, detailed interindustry transactions for 541 industries, and components of final demand, 1982 benchmark data, 2708–17
Japan fish consumption, by species, 1977-90, 2166–19.11
Maternal and child health indicators and services use, by age, race, and poverty status, 1988, 4478–197
Meat and poultry foreign and US production, trade, and use, by selected country, FAS semiannual circular series, 1925–33
Meat, poultry, and egg consumption per capita, periodic situation rpt with articles, 1561–7
Natl income and product accounts and components, *Survey of Current Business*, monthly rpt, 2702–1.23
Oils, oilseeds, and fats foreign and US production and trade, FAS periodic circular series, 1925–1
Oils, oilseeds, and fats production, prices, trade, and use, periodic situation rpt with articles, 1561–3
Poultry and egg production, prices, receipts, trade, and disposition, by species, 1960-90, annual rpt, 1564–13
Processed food production and stocks by State, shipments, exports, ingredients, and use, periodic Current Industrial Rpt series, 2506–4
Radiation exposure of population near commercial reactors, by body site, age group, and selected plant, 1988, annual rpt, 9634–7

Research (agricultural) funding and staffing for USDA, State agencies, and other instns, by topic, FY91, annual rpt, 1744–2
Research on food consumption, marketing, legislation, and regulation devs, and consumption and price trends, quarterly journal, 1541–7
Rice foreign and US production, prices, trade, stocks, and use, periodic situation rpt, 1561–8
Rice shipments, by end use, package size, and State of origin and destination, 1960s-89, biennial rpt, 1564–11
Soviet Union and US economic and sociodemographic indicators, selected years 1970-90, handbook, 2328–80
Statistical Abstract of US, 1992 annual data compilation, 2324–1.3
Sugar and honey foreign and US production, prices, trade, and use, FAS periodic circular series, 1925–14
Sugar and sweeteners production, prices, trade, supply, and use, quarterly situation rpt with articles, 1561–14
Travel to US, by characteristics of visit and traveler, world area of origin, and US destination, 1991 survey, annual rpt, 2904–12
Vegetable production, prices, trade, stocks, and use, for selected fresh and processing crops, periodic situation rpt with articles, 1561–11
Wheat and rye foreign and US production, prices, trade, stocks, and use, quarterly situation rpt with articles, 1561–12
Women-headed households food spending, by item and selected characteristics, and compared to other households, 1970s-88, 1548–391
see also Alcohol use
see also Food assistance
see also Food stamp programs
see also Nutrition and malnutrition
see also Vitamins and nutrients

Food for Peace Program
see Public Law 480

Food ingredients and additives
Carcinogens chemistry, sources, environment and health risks, and regulation, by substance and brand, 1991 annual rpt, 4044–15
Confectionery shipments, trade, use, and ingredients used, by product, 1991, annual Current Industrial Rpt, 2506–4.5
Consumption, supply, trade, prices, spending, and indexes, by food commodity, 1990, annual rpt, 1544–4
Egg (processed) production, and ingredients added, 1971-90, annual rpt, 1564–13.2
Egg production by type of product, and eggs broken under Federal inspection by region, monthly rpt, 1625–2
Exports and imports between US and outlying areas, by detailed commodity and mode of transport, 1991, annual rpt, 2424–11
Exports and imports of US, by country and detailed commodity, monthly rpt, 2422–12
Exports and imports of US, by Harmonized System 6-digit commodity and country, 1991, annual rpt, 2424–13
Exports and imports of US, by transport mode, country, and SITC 1- to 3-digit commodity, 1991, annual rpt, 2424–12
Exports of US, detailed Schedule B commodities with countries of destination, 1991, annual rpt, 2424–10
FDA investigations and regulatory activities, quarterly rpt, 4062–3
Feed and feed additives production, use, and prices, by commodity, State, and country, various periods 1949-92, 1568–308
Hazardous substances industrial releases and reduction methods under EPA regulation, by chemical, source, industry, and location, 1989, annual rpt, 9234–6
Hazardous substances industrial releases and reduction methods under EPA regulation, with chemical stocks and use, facility directory, 1987-89, annual CD-ROM, 9234–7
Manufacturing annual survey, 1990: value of shipments, by SIC 4- to 5-digit product class, 2506–14.1
Nutrient, caloric, and waste composition of food, detailed data for raw, processed, and prepared foods, series, 1356–3
Price indexes (producer), by stage of processing and detailed commodity, monthly rpt, 6762–6
Price indexes (producer), by stage of processing and detailed commodity, monthly 1991, annual rpt, 6764–2
Production and sales of synthetic organic chemicals, and manufacturer listing, by product, 1990, annual rpt, 9884–3
Production of processed food and stocks by State, shipments, exports, ingredients, and use, periodic Current Industrial Rpt series, 2506–4
Production of synthetic organic chemicals, by detailed product, quarterly rpt, 9882–1
Rice shipments, by end use, package size, and State of origin and destination, 1960s-89, biennial rpt, 1564–11
Toxicology Natl Program research and testing activities, FY90 and planned FY91, annual rpt, 4044–16
Weight and volume conversion factors for agricultural commodities and products, 1992 rpt, 1508–3
see also Cholesterol
see also Cocoa and chocolate
see also Spices and herbs
see also Sugar industry and products
see also Syrups and sweeteners
see also Vitamins and nutrients

Food inspection
Assistance (block and categorical grants) programs for State and local govts, FY91, biennial listing, 10044–8
Assistance (financial and nonfinancial) of Fed Govt, 1992 base edition, annual listing, 104–5
Cattle (dairy) slaughtered under Federal inspection, 1991, annual rpt, 1317–1.6
Egg production by type of product, and eggs broken under Federal inspection by region, monthly rpt, 1625–2
Expenditures of Fed Govt in States, by type, program, agency, and State, FY91, annual rpt, 2464–2
FDA investigations and regulatory activities, quarterly rpt, 4062–3
Fishery products and establishments inspected, 1991, annual rpt, 2164–1.10
Grain inspected for domestic use and export, foreign buyers complaints, and handling facilities explosions, FY92, annual rpt, 1294–1
Grain inspected for export, weekly rpt, 1313–4
Grain production, prices, trade, and export inspections by US port and country of destination, by grain type, weekly rpt, 1313–2
Imports detained by FDA, by reason, product, shipper, brand, and country, monthly listing, 4062–2
Livestock inspected by Fed Govt, by type, weekly rpt, 1315–1
Livestock slaughter, meat production, and slaughter plants, by species and State, 1991, annual rpt, 1623–10
Livestock slaughter under Fed Govt inspection, by livestock type and region, monthly rpt, 1623–9
Meat and poultry inspection for domestic use and export, and rejections by cause, by type of animal and product, FY90, annual rpt, 1374–3
Meat from Canada inspected and rejected, by US port of entry, 1989-91, hearing, 21368–141
Meat plants inspected and certified for exporting to US, by country, 1991, annual listing, 1374–2
Meat trade of US and Canada, inspection activity, 1989-91, GAO rpt, 26113–595
Peanut production, prices, stocks, exports, use, inspection, and quality, by region and State, 1982-91, annual rpt, 1311–5
Pesticide residue in food imports, FDA enforcement, with contaminated shipments distributed, damages assessed and paid, and repeat offenders, FY88-90, GAO rpt, 26113–598
Pesticide residue on Mexico fruit and vegetable exports to US, US and Mexico standards and violations, FY79-91, GAO rpt, 26113–585
Poultry and egg prices and marketing, by selected region, State, and city, monthly and weekly 1991, annual rpt, 1317–2
Poultry and egg production, prices, receipts, trade, and disposition, by species, 1960-90, annual rpt, 1564–13
Poultry Natl Improvement Plan participating hatcheries and birds, by species and disease program, 1992, annual listing, 1394–15
Poultry slaughtered under Fed Govt inspection, pounds certified, and condemnations by cause, by State, monthly rpt, 1625–3
Rice market activities, prices, inspections, sales, trade, supply, and use, for US and selected foreign markets, weekly rpt, 1313–8
Ship (passenger) sanitary inspection scores, biweekly rpt, 4202–10
Tea imports inspected by FDA, by type and country, 1985-91, FAS annual circular, 1925–15.3
USDA revenue, by source and subagency, FY88-92, GAO rpt, 26113–602
see also Food and waterborne diseases

Food poisoning
see Food and waterborne diseases

Food prices
Agricultural Outlook, production, prices, marketing, and trade, by commodity, forecast and current situation, monthly rpt with articles, 1502–4

Agricultural Statistics, 1991, annual rpt, 1004–1
Apple (processed) demand and impacts of selected market factors, 1980s-91, 1548–392
Assistance programs purchases of food, by commodity, firm, and shipping point or destination, weekly rpt, 1302–3
Business statistics, detailed data for major industries and economic indicators, *Survey of Current Business*, monthly rpt, 2702–1.13
Business statistics, detailed data for major industries and economic indicators, 1960-91, *Survey of Current Business* biennial supplement, 2704–1
Consumer research, food marketing, legislation, and regulation devs, and consumption and price trends, quarterly journal, 1541–7
CPI by component for US city average, and by selected metro area, region, and population size, monthly rpt, 6762–2
CPI changes for selected items, 1982-91, annual article, 6722–1.322
Dairy prices, by product and selected area, with related marketing data, 1991, annual rpt, 1317–1
Dairy production by State, stocks, prices, and CCC price support activities, by product type, monthly rpt, 1627–3
Dairy production, prices, trade, and use, periodic situation rpt with articles, 1561–2
Dairy production, trade, use, and prices, for US and selected countries, forecast 1992 and trends from 1987, FAS semiannual circular, 1925–10
Developing countries food supply, needs, and aid, status and alternative forecasts, world area rpt series, 1526–8
Economic indicators and components, current data and annual trends, monthly rpt, 23842–1.4
Economic indicators compounded annual rates of change, monthly rpt, 9391–3
Export and import price indexes for goods and services, and dollar exchange rate indexes, quarterly press release, 6762–13
Family Economics Review, consumer goods prices and supply, and home economics, quarterly journal, 1702–1
Farm financial and marketing conditions, forecast 1992, annual chartbook, 1504–8
Farm financial and marketing conditions, forecast 1992, annual conf, 1504–9
Farm-retail food prices, marketing cost components, and industry finances and productivity, 1920s-91, annual rpt, 1544–9
Fish exvessel prices, value added, and consumer spending, 1985-91, annual rpt, 2164–1.9
Foreign and US economic conditions, for major industrial countries, monthly rpt, 9112–1
Foreign and US food prices in selected world capitals, monthly rpt, semiannual data, 1922–12
Fruit and nut production, prices, and use, annual rpt series, 1621–18
Fruit and nut production, prices, trade, stocks, and use, by selected crop, periodic situation rpt with articles, 1561–6
Fruit and vegetable wholesale prices in NYC by State, and shipments and arrivals by mode of transport, by commodity, weekly rpt, 1311–20
Fruit and vegetable wholesale prices in NYC, Chicago, and selected shipping points, by crop, 1991, annual rpt, 1311–8
Fruit and vegetable wholesale prices in NYC-Newark, and arrivals by mode of transport, by commodity and State, 1990, annual rpt, 1311–21
Infant formula bid prices and contracts awarded by States under USDA food aid program for women, infants, and children, late 1980s-91, hearing, 25528–118
Meat and fish retail and producer prices, 1987-92, semiannual situation rpt, 1561–15.3
Meat, poultry, and egg production, prices, trade, and stocks, monthly rpt, 1561–17
Meat, poultry, and egg production, prices, trade, stocks, and use, periodic situation rpt with articles, 1561–7
Milk order market prices and detailed operations, by State and market area, 1990-91, annual rpt, 1317–3
Milk order market prices and detailed operations, monthly rpt with articles, 1317–4
Mint oil production, yield, and farm prices by State, and NYC spot prices, 1989-92, FAS annual circular, 1925–15.2
North Central States farm credit conditions and economic devs, Fed Reserve 7th District, monthly rpt, 9375–10
Poultry and egg prices and marketing, by selected region, State, and city, monthly and weekly 1991, annual rpt, 1317–2
Poultry and egg production, prices, receipts, trade, and disposition, by species, 1960-90, annual rpt, 1564–13
Prices, supply, demand, trade, spending, and indexes, by food commodity, 1990, annual rpt, 1544–4
Producer Price Index, by major commodity group and subgroup, and processing stage, monthly press release, 6762–5
Producer price indexes, by stage of processing and detailed commodity, monthly rpt, 6762–6
Producer price indexes, by stage of processing and detailed commodity, monthly 1991, annual rpt, 6764–2
Producer price indexes, changes for selected items by stage of processing, 1987-91, article, 6722–1.323
Spice and pepper spot prices in NYC, 1980s-92, FAS annual circular, 1925–15.1
Statistical Abstract of US, 1992 annual data compilation, 2324–1.15
Sugar and sweeteners production, prices, trade, supply, and use, quarterly situation rpt with articles, 1561–14
Sugar prices in NYC, by grade, monthly 1986-May 1992, FAS semiannual circular, 1925–14.2
Sugar prices in NYC, by grade, monthly 1986-Oct 1992, FAS semiannual circular, 1925–14.3
Tomato production, acreage, and yield by State, trade and production by country, stocks, shipments, and prices, 1960s-91, 1568–310
Vegetable production, prices, trade, stocks, and use, for selected fresh and processing crops, periodic situation rpt with articles, 1561–11
see also Agricultural prices

Food Safety and Inspection Service
Budget of US, obligations and authority by function, agency, and program, with summaries and analyses, FY93, annual rpt, 104–2
Expenditures of Fed Govt in States, by type, program, agency, and State, FY91, annual rpt, 2464–2
Meat and poultry inspection for domestic use and export, and rejections by cause, by type of animal and product, FY90, annual rpt, 1374–3
Meat from Canada inspected and rejected, by US port of entry, 1989-91, hearing, 21368–141
Meat plants inspected and certified for exporting to US, by country, 1991, annual listing, 1374–2
Revenue of USDA, by source and subagency, FY88-92, GAO rpt, 26113–602

Food shortage
see Food supply
see Nutrition and malnutrition

Food stamp programs
Assistance (financial and nonfinancial) of Fed Govt, 1992 base edition, annual listing, 104–5
Banks in Fed Reserve System, expenses and operations itemized by service, office, and district, 1991, annual rpt, 9364–11
Beneficiaries of food stamps, household size, composition, income, and income and deductions allowed, summer 1989, annual rpt, 1364–8
Benefits, beneficiaries, and spells of participation, by aid program and recipient characteristics, 1987-88, Current Population Rpt, 2546–20.25
Benefits payment and eligibility errors, by type, recipient characteristics, and State, FY90, annual rpt, 1364–15
Budget of US, obligations and authority by function, agency, and program, with summaries and analyses, FY93, annual rpt, 104–2
Consumer research, food marketing, legislation, and regulation devs, and consumption and price trends, quarterly journal, 1541–7
Expenditures, coverage, and benefits for social welfare programs, late 1930s-90, annual rpt, 4744–3.1; 4744–3.3; 4744–3.9
Expenditures of Fed Govt in States, by type, program, agency, and State, FY91, annual rpt, 2464–2
Fed Reserve banks finances and staff, 1991, annual rpt, 9364–1.1
Finances of Fed Govt, cash and debt transactions, daily tables, 8102–4
Households (single person and nonfamily) social, economic and housing characteristics, by tenure, 1989, 2486–1.15
Households composition, income, benefits, and labor force status, Survey of Income and Program Participation methodology, working paper series, 2626–10

Housing (rental) units, total, with HUD assistance by program, and eligible for aid, by unit, household, and neighborhood characteristics, and location, 1989, biennial rpt, 5184–11
Housing and households detailed characteristics, and unit and neighborhood quality, MSA surveys, series, 2485–6
Income (household) and poverty status under alternative income definitions, by recipient characteristics, 1979-91, annual Current Population Rpt, 2546–6.78
Natl income and product accounts, comprehensive accounts and components, benchmark revisions, 1929-88, 2708–5
Natl income and product accounts, comprehensive accounts and components, *Survey of Current Business*, monthly rpt, 2702–1.26
Ohio poverty, hunger, and public welfare program operations and indicators of need, by county, 1991 hearing, 21968–58
Population economic well-being indicators, by selected characteristics and household income and income-to-poverty ratio, 1984, 2546–20.22
Poverty status of population and families, by detailed characteristics, 1991, annual Current Population Rpt, 2546–6.77
Puerto Rico statehood referendum proposal, with background data on Federal outlays, economic conditions, and finances of corporations with tax-favored status, 1940s-88, hearing, 21448–46
Single mothers family income, and impacts of child care, govt and child support payments, taxes, and marriage, with data by State, 1970s-91, 21788–212
Single parent families in own and others homes, by financial, housing, and other characteristics, 1989, 2486–1.14
Statistical Abstract of US, 1992 annual data compilation, 2324–1.12
Women-headed households food spending, by item and selected characteristics, and compared to other households, 1970s-88, 1548–391

Food stocks
see Agricultural stocks
see Food supply

Food stores
Alteration and repair spending for commercial and public buildings, by type, size, age, and region, 1989, 2388–4
Business statistics, detailed data for major industries and economic indicators, 1960-91, *Survey of Current Business* biennial supplement, 2704–1
Collective bargaining agreements expiring during year, and workers covered, by firm, union, industry group, and State, 1992, annual rpt, 6784–9
County Business Patterns, 1989: employment, establishments, and payroll, by SIC 2- to 4-digit industry and county, annual State rpt series, 2326–8
County Business Patterns, 1990: employment, establishments, and payroll, by SIC 2- to 4-digit industry and county, annual State rpt series, 2326–6
Employment, earnings, and hours, by SIC 1- to 4-digit industry, monthly 1989-Feb 1992, annual rpt, 6744–4
Employment of minorities and women, by occupation, SIC 1- to 3-digit industry, State, and MSA, 1991, annual rpt, 9244–1
Energy use in commercial buildings, costs, and conservation, by building characteristics, survey rpt series, 3166–8
Expenditures for food and alcoholic beverages, by place of purchase, 1970-91, annual rpt, 1544–4.5
Finances and operations, by SIC 2- to 4-digit industry, forecast 1992, annual rpt, 2044–28
Finances, operations, and merger activity, for food processors and distributors, 1991, annual rpt, 1544–22
Financial statements for manufacturing, mining, and trade corporations, by selected SIC 2- to 3-digit industry, quarterly rpt, 2502–1
Labor productivity, indexes of output, hours, and employment by SIC 2- to 4-digit industry, 1967-90, annual rpt, 6824–1.4
Mail volume to and from households, use, and views, by class, source, content, and household characteristics, FY87-90, annual rpt, 9864–10
Market concentration relation to profits and prices, for grocery stores, literature review, 1990 rpt, 9408–56
Multinatl firms US affiliates finances and operations, by industry, country of parent firm, and State, 1987, 2708–48
Occupational injury and illness rates, and lost workdays by State, for grocery stores, 1990, article, 6722–1.339
Occupational injury and illness rates, by SIC 2- to 4-digit industry, 1989-90, annual rpt, 6844–7
Occupational injury and illness rates, by SIC 2- to 4-digit industry, 1990, annual rpt, 6844–1
Prices (farm-retail) for food, marketing cost components, and industry finances and productivity, 1920s-91, annual rpt, 1544–9
Public service announcements on nutrition displayed in supermarkets, effectiveness, local area study, 1992 article, 4042–3.371
Robberies, by type of premises, population size, and region, 1991, annual rpt, 6224–2.1
Sales and inventories, by kind of retail business, region, and selected State, MSA, and city, monthly rpt, 2413–3
Sales, inventories, purchases, gross margin, and accounts receivable, by SIC 2- to 4-digit kind of business and form of ownership, 1990, annual rpt, 2413–5
Sales of retailers, by kind of business, advance monthly rpt, 2413–2
Statistical Abstract of US, 1992 annual data compilation, 2324–1.28
Tax (income) returns of corporations, income and tax items by asset size and detailed industry, 1989, annual rpt, 8304–4; 8304–21
Tax (income) returns of partnerships, income statement and balance sheet items, by industry group, 1990, annual article, 8302–2.314
Tax (income) returns of sole proprietorships, income statement items, by industry group, 1990, annual article, 8302–2.317; 8302–2.320

Food supply
Agricultural Outlook, production, prices, marketing, and trade, by commodity, forecast and current situation, monthly rpt with articles, 1502–4
Agricultural Statistics, 1991, annual rpt, 1004–1
Business statistics, detailed data for major industries and economic indicators, *Survey of Current Business*, monthly rpt, 2702–1.13
Developing countries economic, population, and agricultural data, US and other aid sources, and AID activity, country rpt series, 9916–12
Developing countries food supply, needs, and aid, status and alternative forecasts, world area rpt series, 1526–8
Foreign and US agricultural supply and demand indicators, by selected crop, monthly rpt, 1522–5
Foreign countries agricultural production, prices, and trade, by country, 1980-91 and forecast 1992, annual world area rpt series, 1524–4
Marketing, consumer research, legislation, and regulation devs, and consumption and price trends, quarterly journal, 1541–7
Research (agricultural) funding and staffing for USDA, State agencies, and other instns, by topic, FY91, annual rpt, 1744–2
Supply, consumption, trade, prices, spending, and indexes, by food commodity, 1990, annual rpt, 1544–4
see also Agricultural production
see also Agricultural stocks
see also Nutrition and malnutrition
see also under names of specific agricultural commodities (for data on production and stocks)

Foot health and diseases
see Podiatry

Football
Injuries from use of consumer products and related activities, by severity and victim age and sex, 1990, annual rpt, 9164–7
Injuries from use of consumer products, by severity, victim age, and detailed product, 1991, annual rpt, 9164–6
NCAA Div I athletic depts staff by race, and income, by sex and position, 1990/91, GAO rpt, 26121–476

Footwear
see Shoes and shoe industry

Forage
see Animal feed
see Pasture and rangeland

Foran, Jeffery A.
"Control of Discharges of Toxic Pollutants into the Great Lakes and Their Tributaries: Development of Benchmarks", 14648–29

Forced labor
Foreign countries human rights conditions in 170 countries, 1991, annual rpt, 21384–3
Sentences for Federal offenses, guidelines by offense and circumstances, series, 17668–1

Ford Motor Co.
Employee health care costs of Ford Motor Co and foreign subsidiaries, with data on foreign and US health care systems, 1987-90, article, 9882–16.302

Energy economy test results, 1993 model year, annual rpt, 3304–11
Safety of domestic and foreign autos, crash test results by model, model years 1987-91, 7768–111
Safety of domestic and foreign autos, crash test results by model, press release series, 7766–7
Stock prices relation to corporate earnings, model results with data for Ford Motor Co, 1950s-90, article, 9373–1.306

Forecasts
see Agricultural forecasts
see Energy projections
see Population projections
see Projections and forecasts

Foreign affairs
see Foreign relations

Foreign Agricultural Service
AgExporter, production, consumption, and policies for selected countries, and US export dev and promotion, monthly journal, 1922–2
Budget of US, obligations and authority by function, agency, and program, with summaries and analyses, FY93, annual rpt, 104–2
Cocoa and cocoa products foreign and US production, prices, and trade, 1980s-93, FAS semiannual circular, 1925–9
Coffee production, trade, and use, by country, with US and intl prices, FAS periodic circular, 1925–5
Cotton production and trade for US and selected countries, FAS periodic circular series, 1925–4
Dairy imports under quota by commodity, by country of origin, FAS monthly rpt, 1925–31
Dairy production, trade, use, and prices, for US and selected countries, forecast 1992 and trends from 1987, FAS semiannual circular, 1925–10
Eastern Europe agricultural trade with US, by commodity group and country, 1988-91, 1928–11
Export promotion activities of FAS trade offices, operating costs, and funding by program, by country, 1989-90, GAO rpt, 26123–370
Exports (agricultural) info and service sources, 1991 annual listing, 1924–11
Exports and imports (agricultural) commodity and country, prices, and world market devs, monthly rpt, 1922–12
Exports of grains, oilseed products, hides, skins, and cotton, by country, weekly rpt, dropped data, 1922–3
Fruit, vegetable, and nut (fresh and processed) foreign and US production and trade, FAS monthly circular with articles, 1925–34
Grain foreign and US production, prices, trade, stocks, and use, FAS periodic circular series, 1925–2
Livestock, poultry, and dairy products foreign and US production, trade, and use, by selected country, FAS semiannual circular series, 1925–33
Livestock, poultry, and dairy trade, by commodity and country, FAS monthly circular, 1925–32
Lumber and wood products trade and export promotion of US by country, and trade balance, by commodity, FAS periodic circular, 1925–36
Oils, oilseeds, and fats foreign and US production and trade, FAS periodic circular series, 1925–1
PL 480 concessional sales agreements, market value, and shipping costs, by country, annual rpt, discontinued, 1924–6
PL 480 long-term credit sales allocations, periodic press release, discontinued, 1922–7
Production, acreage, and yield for selected crops, forecasts by selected world region and country, FAS monthly circular, 1925–28
Seed exports, by type, world region, and country, FAS quarterly rpt, 1925–13
Spice, essential oil, and tea foreign and US production, prices, and trade, FAS annual circular series, 1925–15
Sugar and honey foreign and US production, prices, trade, and use, FAS periodic circular series, 1925–14
Sugar and sugar product imports of US under quota, by country, weekly rpt, 1922–9
Tobacco and products foreign and US industry review, FAS monthly circular with articles, 1925–16

Foreign agriculture
AgExporter, production, consumption, and policies for selected countries, and US export dev and promotion, monthly journal, 1922–2
Agricultural Outlook, production, prices, marketing, and trade, by commodity, forecast and current situation, monthly rpt with articles, 1502–4
Agricultural Statistics, 1991, annual rpt, 1004–1
AID dev projects and socioeconomic impacts, evaluation rpt series, 9916–1
Animal disease outbreaks in US and foreign countries, quarterly rpt, 1392–3
Background Notes, foreign countries summary social, political, and economic data, series, 7006–2
Bean (dried) prices by State, market activity, and foreign and US production, use, stocks, and trade, weekly rpt, 1311–17
Bean (dried) production and prices by State, exports and foreign production by country, and USDA food aid purchases, by bean type, 1986-91, annual rpt, 1311–18
Brazil agricultural productivity indicators, 1968-87, 1528–331
Chile fruit exports to US, sales by port of entry, and prices in 5 terminal cities, by commodity, 1990/91, annual rpt, 1311–27
China economic performance and trade, 1980-91, annual rpt, 9114–5
Cocoa and cocoa products foreign and US production, prices, and trade, 1980s-93, FAS semiannual circular, 1925–9
Coffee production, trade, and use, by country, with US and intl prices, FAS periodic circular, 1925–5
Cotton production and trade for US and selected countries, FAS periodic circular series, 1925–4
Cotton, wool, and synthetic fiber production, prices, trade, and use, periodic situation rpt with articles, 1561–1
Dairy production, trade, use, and prices, for US and selected countries, forecast 1992 and trends from 1987, FAS semiannual circular, 1925–10
Developing countries economic and social conditions from 1960s, and Intl Dev Cooperation Agency and AID activities and funding, FY91-93, annual rpt, 9904–4
Developing countries economic, population, and agricultural data, US and other aid sources, and AID activity, country rpt series, 9916–12
Developing countries energy efficiency improvement issues and devs, with data by end use and country, 1980s-90, 26358–260
Developing countries food supply, needs, and aid, status and alternative forecasts, world area rpt series, 1526–8
Drug (illegal) production, eradication, and seizures, by substance, with US aid, by country, 1988-92, annual rpt, 7004–17
EC economic integration impacts on domestic and intl agricultural conditions, 1990 conf, 1528–325
Economic conditions in foreign countries and implications for US, periodic country rpt series, 2046–4
Economic indicators, and trade and trade flows by commodity, by country, data compilation, monthly CD-ROM, 2002–6
Economic, social, political, and geographic summary data, by country, 1992, annual factbook, 9114–2
Europe farm household members off-farm employment, 1987, article, 1502–7.301
Farm financial and marketing conditions, forecast 1992, annual chartbook, 1504–8
Farm financial and marketing conditions, forecast 1992, annual conf, 1504–9
Fish catch by world region, processing, and US trade, 1980-91, semiannual rpt, 1561–15.1
Fish catch, trade, use, and fishery operations, with selected foreign data, by species, 1980s-91, annual rpt, 2164–1
Fruit, vegetable, and nut (fresh and processed) foreign and US production and trade, FAS monthly circular with articles, 1925–34
Global climate change impacts on agricultural production and GDP, with data by crop and world area, mid 1970s-86, 1528–326
Grain foreign and US production, prices, trade, stocks, and use, FAS periodic circular series, 1925–2
Latin America economic and social conditions, resources, trade, and aid, 1992, annual factbook, 9914–14
Livestock, poultry, and dairy products foreign and US production, trade, and use, by selected country, FAS semiannual circular series, 1925–33
Mexico agricultural trade with US and Canada, and impacts of North American Free Trade Agreement, 1980s-90, 1528–330
Molasses supply, use, wholesale prices by market, and imports by country, 1986-91, annual rpt, 1311–19
Morocco agricultural subsidies to producers and consumers, by selected commodity, 1970s-90, 1528–329

Oils, oilseeds, and fats foreign and US production and trade, FAS periodic circular series, 1925–1
Opium production and acreage under cultivation, by country, 1990, 6284–6
Overseas Business Reports: economic conditions, investment and export opportunities, and trade practices, country market research rpt series, 2046–6
Peanut and peanut oil exports of US, and foreign production, by country, 1986-92 and forecast 1993, annual rpt, 1311–5.2
Pesticide residue on Mexico fruit and vegetable exports to US, US and Mexico standards and violations, FY79-91, GAO rpt, 26113–585
Production, acreage, and yield for selected crops, forecasts by selected world region and country, FAS monthly circular, 1925–28
Production inputs supply, demand, and prices, 1970s-91 and projected to 1996, article, 1561–16.301
Production inputs supply, demand, and prices, 1980s-92, article, 1561–16.304
Production, prices, and trade of agricultural commodities, by country, 1980-91 and forecast 1992, annual world area rpt series, 1524–4
Production, prices, trade, and use, for foreign and US agriculture, periodic rpt, discontinued, 1522–3
Research (agricultural) funding and staffing for USDA, State agencies, and other instns, by topic, FY91, annual rpt, 1744–2
Research grants of USDA, by program, subagency, and country, FY92, annual listing, 1954–3
Rice foreign and US production, prices, trade, stocks, and use, periodic situation rpt, 1561–8
Rice market activities, prices, inspections, sales, trade, supply, and use, for US and selected foreign markets, weekly rpt, 1313–8
Soviet Union agricultural production indicators, by region and selected former Republic, 1980s-90, annual rpt, 23844–2
Soviet Union and US economic and sociodemographic indicators, selected years 1970-90, handbook, 2328–80
Spice, essential oil, and tea foreign and US production, prices, and trade, FAS annual circular series, 1925–15
Statistical Abstract of US, 1992 annual data compilation, 2324–1.31
Sugar and honey foreign and US production, prices, trade, and use, FAS periodic circular series, 1925–14
Supply and demand indicators for selected foreign and US crops, monthly rpt, 1522–5
Tobacco and products foreign and US industry review, FAS monthly circular with articles, 1925–16
Tobacco production, prices, stocks, taxes by State, and trade and production by country, 1991, annual rpt, 1319–1
Tomato production, acreage, and yield by State, trade and production by country, stocks, shipments, and prices, 1960s-91, 1568–310
Uganda cash transfers from AID linked to nontraditional crop export programs, 1988-90, 9916–1.77
Weather conditions and effect on agriculture, by US region, State, and city, and world area, weekly rpt, 2182–7
Wheat and rye foreign and US production, prices, trade, stocks, and use, quarterly situation rpt with articles, 1561–12

Foreign area studies
see Area studies

Foreign assistance
see International assistance

Foreign budgets
AID dev projects and socioeconomic impacts, evaluation rpt series, 9916–1
Assets and liabilities of foreign govts, and transactions in securities, monthly rpt, 9362–1.3
Central America economic indicators, by country, 1969-89, working paper, 9916–13.4
Costa Rica economic indicators and reform issues, mid 1970s-90, working paper, 9916–13.5
Current account balance and net assets, relation to inflation, unemployment rate, and govt lending, for OECD countries, 1970s-89, technical paper, 9366–7.274
Deficits share of GDP, for US and 4 OECD countries, 1981 and 1989, GAO rpt, 26109–5
Developing countries economic and social conditions from 1960s, and Intl Dev Cooperation Agency and AID activities and funding, FY91-93, annual rpt, 9904–4
Developing countries economic, population, and agricultural data, US and other aid sources, and AID activity, country rpt series, 9916–12
Eastern Europe transition to market economies, tax reform issues, with tax rates, revenue, and govt spending compared to EC, by selected country, late 1960s-91, technical paper, 9366–7.278
EC economic integration impacts on domestic and intl agricultural conditions, 1990 conf, 1528–325
Economic conditions in foreign countries and implications for US, periodic country rpt series, 2046–4
Economic, social, political, and geographic summary data, by country, 1992, annual factbook, 9114–2
European Monetary Union fiscal policy impact on EC govts, with background data, mid 1970s-90, technical paper, 9393–10.18
Haiti economic conditions, 1985-91, working paper, 9916–13.3
Interest rates (long term) relation to rates of return to capital, economic policies, and other factors, US and 4 countries, 1960s-90, article, 9385–1.301
Intl Monetary Fund financial statements, and proposed funding quotas by member country, 1991 hearing, 21248–169
Israel economic conditions, US investment and export opportunities, and trade practices, 1992 rpt, 2008–32
Italy public debt burden on future generations, alternative forecasts, 1992 working paper, 9377–9.139
Military spending, arms trade, and force strengths, with govt spending and population, by country, 1979-89, annual rpt, 9824–1
NATO, Japan, and South Korea military spending and indicators of ability to support common defense, by country, 1970s-90, annual rpt, 3544–28
OECD members govt budget surplus and deficit, and govt debt privately held, turnover, and selling procedures, FY91, 8008–154
Overseas Business Reports: economic conditions, investment and export opportunities, and trade practices, country market research rpt series, 2046–6
Science and Engineering Indicators, employment, education, R&D funding, and industry impacts, with foreign comparisons, 1960s-91, biennial rpt, 9624–10
Tax (value added) alternative proposals revenue impacts, with background data and intl comparisons, 1992 rpt, 26306–6.168
UN participation of US, and member and nonmember shares of UN budget by country, FY89-91, annual rpt, 7004–5
see also International reserves

Foreign competition
Agricultural, fishery, and forest products trade, tariffs, and industry operating data, commodity rpt series, 9885–8
Agricultural imports of US, competitive and noncompetitive, by commodity and country, bimonthly rpt, 1522–1.2
Budget of US, House concurrent resolution, with spending and revenue targets, FY93 and projected to FY97, annual rpt, 21264–2
Caribbean area duty-free exports to US, and imports from US, by country, and impact on US employment, by commodity, 1991, annual rpt, 6364–2
Chemical and energy products trade, tariffs, and industry operating data, commodity rpt series, 9885–11
Construction contract awards and billings, by country of contractor and world area of award, 1990, annual article, 2042–1.304
Credit programs for exports, activities of Eximbank and 6 OECD countries, 1990, annual rpt, 9254–3
Electronics and services trade, tariffs, and industry operating data, commodity rpt series, 9885–12
Employment and industry impacts of trade, series, 6366–3
Energy technologies export markets, competitiveness, and promotion, for US industries, 1992 technical rpt, 3006–13.5
Export and import agreements, negotiations, and related legislation, 1991, annual rpt, 444–1
Exports, imports, and intl competitiveness of US industries, trends and outlook, quarterly rpt with articles, 9882–16
Exports of manufactured goods, total and for US and major competitors, by country of destination, annual commodity market share rpt series, discontinued, 2046–13
Exports of manufactured goods, total and for US and major competitors, by SITC 1- to 5-digit commodity, annual country market share rpt series, discontinued, 2046–2
Financial markets (intl) performance of foreign and US bank and securities firms, finances and competitiveness issues, 1980s, compilation of papers, 9385–10

Imports and tariff provisions effect on US industries and products, investigations with background financial and operating data, series, 9886–4
Imports injury to US industries from foreign subsidized products and sales at less than fair value, investigations with background financial and operating data, series, 9886–19
Imports injury to US industries from foreign subsidized products, investigations with background financial and operating data, series, 9886–15
Imports injury to US industries from sales at less than fair value, investigations with background financial and operating data, series, 9886–14
Imports under Generalized System of Preferences, status, and US tariffs, with trade by country and US economic impacts, for selected commodities, 1987-91, annual rpt, 9884–23
Indexes of trade dependency for total, merchandise, and agricultural products, by country, 1960s-88, 1528–328
Industry (US) intl competitiveness, with selected foreign and US operating data by major firm and product, series, 2046–12
Lumber (softwood) from Canada, costs and production compared to US, 1970s-91, hearing, 21728–78
Machinery and equipment trade, tariffs, and industry operating data, commodity rpt series, 9885–9
Manufacturing industry (US) intl competitiveness, trade and economic policies with background data and foreign comparisons, 1991 rpt, 26358–252
Manufacturing trade, tariffs, and industry operating data, commodity rpt series, 9885–10
Materials (critical) industry status and intl competitiveness, with data on semiconductors and advanced ceramics, 1991 hearing, 21708–130
Militarily strategic manufacturing industries finances, operations, and intl competitiveness, series, 2026–1
Minerals and metals trade, tariffs, and industry operating data, commodity rpt series, 9885–13
North America intraindustry trade indexes, for US, Canada, and Mexico, by commodity, 1962-87, 1528–327
OECD intl trade position for US and 4 countries, and factors affecting US competition, quarterly pamphlet, 2042–25
Semiconductor industry (US) intl competitiveness, indicators and comparisons to Japan and Europe, 1980s and projected to 1994, working paper, 15036–1.1
Semiconductor industry (US) intl competitiveness, status, outlook, and Federal policy, 1980s, annual rpt, 15034–1
Semiconductor industry R&D consortium funding, outlays, and effectiveness in improving US competitive position, 1980s-92, GAO rpt, 26113–588
Steel imports of US under voluntary restraint agreement, by product, customs district, and country, with US industry operating data, quarterly rpt, 9882–13
Steel trade, by product, country, and customs district, with US industry operating data, 1989-June 1992, semiannual rpt, 9882–15
Technology-intensive industries intl competitiveness, with background data by industry and foreign comparisons, 1960s-91, GAO rpt, 26123–406
Textile and apparel foreign market conditions for US exports, with domestic industry operations, country rpt series, 2046–15
Unemployed displaced workers, layoffs and recalls by layoff reason, industry, firm size, and State, 2nd half 1988, 6406–6.36
Unemployed displaced workers, layoffs and unemployment insurance claims by reason, industry, selected characteristics, and State, quarterly press release, 6742–23
Unemployed displaced workers, layoffs and unemployment insurance claims by reason, industry, selected characteristics, MSA, and State, 1990, annual rpt, 6744–18
USITC activities, investigations, and rpts, FY91, annual rpt, 9884–1
see also Dumping
see also Foreign trade

Foreign corporations
Airport security operations to prevent hijacking, screening results, enforcement actions, and hijacking attempts, 1990, annual rpt, 7504–49
Aluminum plant ownership, capacity, energy and aluminum sources, and startup and closing dates, by US and foreign plant and location, 1990, annual listing, 5604–49
Background Notes, foreign countries summary social, political, and economic data, series, 7006–2
Banks branches and agencies of foreign banks, assets and liabilities, monthly rpt, 9362–1.1
Banks branches and agencies of foreign banks, assets and liabilities, monthly rpt, quarterly data, 9362–1.4
Boycotts (intl) by OPEC and other countries, US firms and individuals cooperation and tax benefits denied, 1990, article, 8302–2.323
Business America, foreign and domestic commerce, and US investment and trade opportunities, biweekly journal, 2042–24
China and other Asia countries trade with US, composition and trends, 1980s-91, article, 9385–1.303
Commercial paper outstanding, by issuer and holder type, and foreign firms paper issued by US subsidiaries and foreign offices, 1980s-91, article, 9362–1.308
Competitiveness (intl) of US industries, with selected foreign and US operating data by major firm and product, series, 2046–12
Farmland in US owned by foreigners, holdings, acquisitions, and disposals by land use, owner type and country, and State, 1991, annual rpt, 1584–2
Imports and tariff provisions effect on US industries and products, investigations with background financial and operating data, series, 9886–4
Imports injury to US industries from foreign subsidized products and sales at less than fair value, investigations with background financial and operating data, series, 9886–19
Income from US sources and tax withheld for foreign natls not residing in US, by country and tax treaty status, 1989, annual article, 8302–2.308
Income tax returns of foreign corporations and individuals, and US entities abroad, detailed data compilation, 1970s-89, quinquennial rpt, 8308–31
Insurance industry financial condition, operations, assets, junk bond holdings, and State regulation, with intl comparisons, 1991 hearings, 25268–79
Iraq loans from Banca Nazionale del Lavoro Atlanta office, with purpose and exporting country and company involved, 1991 hearing, 21248–165
Military prime contract awards, by category, contract and contractor type, and service branch, FY82-1st half FY92, semiannual rpt, 3542–1
Military prime contract awards for R&D, for top 500 contractors, FY91, annual listing, 3544–4
Minerals foreign and US supply under alternative market conditions, reserves, and background industry data, series, 5606–4
Minerals production, reserves, and industry role in domestic economy and world supply, world area and country rpt, series, 5606–1
Overseas Business Reports: economic conditions, investment and export opportunities, and trade practices, country market research rpt series, 2046–6
Patents (US) granted to US and foreign applicants, by applicant and country, 1960s-91, annual rpt, 2244–3
Pension plan finances, participation, and benefits, for 9 OECD countries, with data by firm and worker characteristics, 1990 conf, 6688–2
R&D licenses for university activities supported by NSF and NIH, transfer to private firms, related income, and scientists associated with licensees, FY89-90, GAO rpt, 26113–575
Services trade of US, direct and among multinatl firms affiliates, by industry and world area, 1986-91, article, 2702–1.336
Tax (income) returns filed, by type of return and IRS district, 1990 and projected 1991-98, annual rpt, 8304–24
Tax (income) returns filed, by type of tax and IRS region and service center, projected 1991-98 and trends from 1978, annual rpt, 8304–9
Tax (income) returns of corporations, income and tax items by asset size and detailed industry, 1989, annual rpt, 8304–4; 8304–21
Tax (income and capital) policies, with background data, for EC, Japan, and US, mid 1960s-91, article, 9373–1.316
Textile and apparel foreign market conditions for US exports, with domestic industry operations, country rpt series, 2046–15
see also Multinational corporations

Foreign countries
Aircraft hijackings, on-board explosions, and other crimes, US and foreign incidents, 1986-90, annual rpt, 7504–31
American Battle Monuments Commission activities, expenses, and visitors by site, FY87, annual rpt, 9064–1

Background Notes, foreign countries summary social, political, and economic data, series, 7006–2
Census Bur data files and rpts, coverage and availability, 1992 annual listing, 2304–2
Chiefs of State and Cabinet members, by country, bimonthly listing, 9112–4
Classification codes for countries and ports under Tariff Schedule of US, 1992 base edition supplement, 9886–13
Classification codes for countries, commodities, and customs districts for Census Bur export statistics, 1990 base edition and supplements, 2428–5
Economic and monetary trends, compounded annual rates of change and quarterly indicators for US and 7 major industrialized countries, quarterly rpt, 9391–7
Economic and social conditions of foreign countries, working paper series, 2326–18
Economic, social, political, and geographic summary data, by country, 1992, annual factbook, 9114–2
Education data, detail for elementary, secondary, and higher education, 1920s-91 and projected to 2002, annual rpt, 4824–1
Education data for foreign countries, and students enrolled in US higher education instns, 1992 edition, annual rpt, 4824–2.29
Educational Resources Info Center (ERIC) data base, foreign and US providers, 1992 biennial listing, 4814–4
Geographic Notes, foreign countries boundaries, claims, nomenclature, and other devs, quarterly rpt, 7142–3
Health care services use, spending, payment sources, and admin, with foreign comparisons, 1970s-90, chartbook, 21788–213
Health condition and care indicators, 1950s-90 with health improvement and disease prevention goals for 1990, annual data compilation, 4144–11
Health data collection and availability, by country, 1991, biennial listing, 4124–8
Health, welfare, and research aid from HHS, by program, recipient, and country, FY91, annual listing, 4004–3.10
Living costs abroad, State Dept indexes, housing allowances, and hardship differentials by country and major city, quarterly rpt, 7002–7
Mail (US) revenue, FY91, and volume from FY87, annual rpt, 9864–1
Mail (US) to foreign countries, USPS itemized operating costs, FY91, annual rpt, 9864–4
Mail (US) to foreign countries, USPS revenue, and costs by class of mail, FY91, annual rpt, 9864–2
Mail (US) to foreign countries, USPS revenue and volume, quarterly rpt, 9862–1
Mail (US) to foreign countries, USPS revenues, and postal rates by country, FY91, annual rpt, 9864–5
Mail to and from US households, FY87-90, annual rpt, 9864–10
Minerals foreign and US supply under alternative market conditions, reserves, and background industry data, series, 5606–4
Minerals industry operations, trends, and projections for selected countries, series, 5606–5
Minerals production, prices, trade, use, employment, tariffs, and stockpiles, by mineral, with foreign comparisons, 1987-91, annual rpt, 5604–18
Minerals production, reserves, and industry role in domestic economy and world supply, world area and country rpt, series, 5606–1
Minerals Yearbook, Vol 1, 1990: commodity reviews of production, reserves, supply, use, and trade, annual rpt series, 5604–20
Minerals Yearbook, Vol 1, 1991: commodity reviews of production, reserves, supply, use, and trade, annual rpt series, 5604–15
Minerals Yearbook, Vol 3: foreign country reviews of production, trade, and policy, by commodity, annual rpt series, suspended, 5604–17
Minerals Yearbook, Vol 3, 1989: foreign country reviews of production, trade, and policy, by commodity, annual rpt, 5604–35
Nuclear power plant capacity, availability, and load factors, by plant and foreign country, quarterly journal, annual tables, 3352–4.3
Oil reserves, production, and resource lifespan under alternative production rates, trends and projections, discontinued series, 3166–9
Older population and characteristics, by country, 1991 and projected to 2020, wallchart, 2328–82
Patents (US) granted to US and foreign applicants, by applicant and country, 1960s-91, annual rpt, 2244–3
Population density for selected cities and countries, and distribution, life expectancy, and infant mortality by world region, 1991, fact sheet, 2326–17.50
Population size, growth rates, and components of change, by country, projected 1990-2020 and trends from 1950, biennial rpt, 2324–9
Science and Engineering Indicators, employment, education, R&D funding, and industry impacts, with foreign comparisons, 1960s-91, biennial rpt, 9624–10
Social security programs coverage, funding, eligibility, and benefits, by country, 1991, biennial rpt, 4746–4.62
Space launchings and characteristics of craft and flight, by country, 1957-91, annual rpt, 9504–9.1
Statistical Abstract of US, 1992 annual data compilation, 2324–1; 2324–1.31
Travel to and from US, and travel receipts and payments, by world area, with data by country, 1985-90, annual rpt, 2904–10
Travel to and from US on US and foreign flag air carriers, by country, world area, and US port, monthly rpt, 7302–2
Travel to US and Canada, market analysis with detailed trip and traveler characteristics, country rpt series, 2906–2
Travel to US, by characteristics of visit and traveler, world area of origin, and US destination, 1991 survey, annual rpt, 2904–12
Travel to US, spending by world area of residence, and economic impact, by spending category and State, 1989, 2908–28
US citizens deaths abroad, by selected cause, 1975 and 1984, article, 4042–3.315
US govt civilian employment and payroll abroad, by agency, bimonthly rpt, 9842–1
US govt civilian employment and payroll, by pay system and location, 1991, annual rpt, 9844–6.1
US Medicare enrollees living overseas, by eligibility and coverage type, FY87, annual rpt, 4654–5
US military and civilian personnel and dependents, by service branch, world area, and country, quarterly rpt, 3542–20
US military base support costs by function, and personnel and acreage by installation, by service branch, FY93, annual rpt, 3504–11
US military draft registrants residing abroad, FY91, annual rpt, 9744–1
US military hospitals abroad, admissions, beds, outpatient visits, and births, by service branch, quarterly rpt, 3542–15
US military personnel abroad, by service branch, world area, and country, quarterly press release, 3542–9
US military prime contract awards for R&D to US and foreign nonprofit instns and govt agencies, by instn and location, FY91, annual listing, 3544–17
US personal transfer payments to foreigners, *Survey of Current Business*, monthly rpt, 2702–1.3; 2702–1.23
US veterans living abroad, VA expenses by type and location, FY91, annual rpt, 8604–3.4
US veterans programs spending, by US and foreign location, FY91, annual rpt, 8604–6
Vaccination needs for intl travel by country, and disease prevention recommendations, 1992 annual rpt, 4204–11
Weather data for surface and upper air, averages by foreign and US station, monthly rpt, 2152–4
Weather events and anomalies, precipitation and temperature for US and foreign locations, weekly rpt, 2182–6
see also Africa
see also Agricultural exports and imports
see also Alien workers
see also Aliens
see also Asia
see also Balance of payments
see also Caribbean area
see also Central America
see also Centrally planned economies
see also Citizenship
see also Deportation
see also Developing countries
see also Diplomatic and consular service
see also East-West trade
see also Eastern Europe
see also Educational exchanges
see also Europe
see also Foreign agriculture
see also Foreign budgets
see also Foreign competition
see also Foreign corporations

see also Foreign debts
see also Foreign economic relations
see also Foreign exchange
see also Foreign investments
see also Foreign labor conditions
see also Foreign languages
see also Foreign medical graduates
see also Foreign opinion of U.S.
see also Foreign relations
see also Foreign students
see also Foreign trade
see also Foreign trade promotion
see also Immigration and emigration
see also International assistance
see also International cooperation in conservation
see also International cooperation in cultural activities
see also International cooperation in environmental sciences
see also International cooperation in law enforcement
see also International cooperation in science and technology
see also International crime
see also International finance
see also International military forces
see also International reserves
see also International sanctions
see also Latin America
see also Middle East
see also Military assistance
see also North America
see also Oceania
see also Refugees
see also South America
see also Southeast Asia
see also Tariffs and foreign trade controls
see also Trade agreements
see also Treaties and conventions
see also under By Foreign Country in the "Index by Categories"
see also under names of individual countries

Foreign currency programs
see Special foreign currency programs

Foreign debts
AID loans repayment status and terms by program and country, and status of predecessor agency loans, quarterly rpt, 9912–3
Assets and debts of private sector, balance sheets by segment, 1960-91, semiannual rpt, 9365–4.1
Assistance (financial and nonfinancial) of Fed Govt, 1992 base edition, annual listing, 104–5
Banks (foreign) loans to US business by location of issuer, with impact of change in Fed Reserve Bd reserve requirements, 1980s-91, article, 9385–1.307
Banks (natl) charters, mergers, liquidations, enforcement cases, and financial performance, with data by instn and State, quarterly rpt, 8402–3
Banks (US) and nonbanking firms liabilities to and claims on foreigners, by country, 1989-90, annual rpt, 9364–5.10
Banks (US) foreign lending at all US and foreign offices, by country group and country, quarterly rpt, 13002–1
Banks and nonbank liabilities to and claims on foreigners, by type and world area, monthly rpt, 9362–1.3
Budget deficits impacts on GNP and public and foreign debt, projected under alternative reduction policies, 1990-2020 with intl comparisons from 1981, GAO rpt, 26109–5
Budget of US, analysis of Federal debt held by foreigners, FY65-91, annual rpt, 104–2.2
Currency (foreign) positions of US firms and foreign branches or affiliates, *Treasury Bulletin*, quarterly rpt, 8002–4.14
Developing countries debt burden indicators, conversion agreement terms, and swaps for conservation funds, by selected country, 1987-90, hearing, 25368–181
Developing countries debt burden indicators, for 8 countries, alternative projections 1991-2000 and trends from 1974, technical paper, 9366–7.271
Developing countries debt burden relation to investment decline, with background data, 1960s-80s, technical paper, 9366–7.272
Developing countries debt securities prices on secondary market, relation to stock price indexes and other factors, model description and results, 1980s-90, technical paper, 9385–8.132
Developing countries debt to foreign lenders, and IMF credit outstanding, by country, 1985-91, annual rpt, 9114–7
Developing countries economic and social conditions from 1960s, and Intl Dev Cooperation Agency and AID activities and funding, FY91-93, annual rpt, 9904–4
Developing countries with heavy debts, debt conversions impact on debt burden and secondary market debt, 1985-87, technical paper, 9366–6.294
Economic and military aid and loans from US and intl agencies, by program and country, FY46-91, annual rpt, 9914–5
Fed Govt finances, cash and debt transactions, daily tables, 8102–4
Haiti economic conditions, 1985-91, working paper, 9916–13.3
Investment (intl) position of US, by component, industry, world region, and country, 1990-91, annual article, 2702–1.323
Iraq loans from Banca Nazionale del Lavoro Atlanta office, with purpose and exporting country and company involved, 1991 hearing, 21248–165
Israel economic conditions, US investment and export opportunities, and trade practices, 1992 rpt, 2008–32
Latin America economic and social conditions, resources, trade, and aid, 1992, annual factbook, 9914–14
Latin America economic conditions, trade, and foreign aid, working paper series, 9916–13
Latin America exports, investment, debt, and tariffs for 7 countries, and trade and investment policy liberalization issues, mid 1960s-91, 9886–4.184
Nicaragua economic and dev aid of US by type, and foreign debt by creditor, FY90-91, GAO rpt, 26123–398
Outstanding debt on US credit, by program, world area, and country, selected years 1940-89, annual rpt, 15344–1.1
Outstanding debt to US of foreign govts and private obligors, by country and program, periodic rpt, 8002–6
Statistical Abstract of US, 1992 annual data compilation, 2324–1.16; 2324–1.31
Survey of Current Business, monthly rpt, quarterly tables, 2702–1.33
US govt contingent liabilities and claims paid on federally insured and guaranteed contracts with foreign obligors, by country and program, periodic rpt, 8002–12
US govt liabilities to foreigners and foreign official instns, *Treasury Bulletin*, quarterly rpt, 8002–4.12
see also Balance of payments
see also International reserves
see also Public debt

Foreign economic relations
Assistance (financial and nonfinancial) of Fed Govt, 1992 base edition, annual listing, 104–5
Background Notes, foreign countries summary social, political, and economic data, series, 7006–2
Economic conditions in foreign countries and implications for US, periodic country rpt series, 2046–4
Economic indicators, and trade and investment flows, for selected countries and country groups, selected years 1946-91, annual rpt, 204–1.9
Overseas Business Reports: economic conditions, investment and export opportunities, and trade practices, country market research rpt series, 2046–6
Tax (income and capital) policies, with background data, for EC, Japan, and US, mid 1960s-91, article, 9373–1.316
see also Agricultural exports and imports
see also Arms trade
see also Balance of payments
see also Dumping
see also East-West trade
see also Foreign competition
see also Foreign corporations
see also Foreign debts
see also Foreign exchange
see also Foreign investments
see also Foreign trade
see also Foreign trade promotion
see also International assistance
see also International finance
see also International sanctions
see also Military assistance
see also Multinational corporations
see also Tariffs and foreign trade controls
see also Trade agreements
see also Treaties and conventions

Foreign exchange
Background Notes, foreign countries summary social, political, and economic data, series, 7006–2
Banks (insured commercial and savings) finances, for foreign and domestic offices, by asset size, 1990, annual rpt, 9294–4.2
Currency (foreign) accounts owned by US under AID admin and by foreign govts with joint AID control, status by program and country, quarterly rpt, 9912–1
Currency (foreign) holdings of US, transactions and balances by program and country, 1st half FY92, semiannual rpt, 8102–7
Currency (foreign) positions of US firms and foreign branches or affiliates, *Treasury Bulletin*, quarterly rpt, 8002–4.14
Currency (foreign) purchases of US with dollars, by country, 1st half FY92, semiannual rpt, 8102–5

Currency (foreign and US) shares of intl transactions, with background data, for 5 countries, 1960s-80s, 9381–10.129
Dollar exchange and money rates, for 31 countries, 1990, annual rpt, 9364–5.10
Dollar exchange rate forecasting performance of forward rates, 1991 working paper, 9371–10.68
Dollar exchange rate relation to interest rates and inflation, model description and results, 1974-90, technical paper, 9366–7.279
Dollar exchange rate trade-weighted index, for agricultural commodities, monthly rpt with articles, 1502–4
Dollar exchange rate trade-weighted index of Fed Reserve Bank of Atlanta, by world area, quarterly rpt, 9371–15
Dollar exchange rate trade-weighted index of Fed Reserve Bank of Dallas, by world area, monthly rpt, 9379–13
Dollar exchange rate trade-weighted index of Fed Reserve, weekly rpt, 9391–4
Dollar exchange rate trade-weighted index, *Treasury Bulletin*, quarterly rpt, 8002–4.12
Dollar exchange rates, and State Dept indexes of living costs abroad and allowances, by country and major city, quarterly rpt, 7002–7
Dollar exchange rates of mark and yen, impact of central bank policy interventions, 1985-89, article, 9391–1.310
Dollar exchange rates of mark and yen, spot and forward market bid-ask spreads impacts of central bank intervention, mid 1980s-91, article, 9377–1.305
Dollar exchange rates of OECD and Asian currencies, 1992 semiannual rpt, 8002–14
Dollar exchange rates of yen and mark, impact of central bank policy interventions and other factors, various periods 1983-90, working paper, 9377–9.138
Dollar exchange rates of yen and mark, impact of central bank policy interventions, 1987-90, working paper, 9377–9.134
Dollar exchange rates of 5 OECD countries, bimonthly rpt, 1522–1.3
Dollar exchange rates of 9 countries, *Survey of Current Business*, monthly rpt, quarterly tables, 2702–1.33
Dollar exchange rates of 10 currencies, 1967-91, annual rpt, 204–1.9
Dollar exchange rates of 13 currencies, monthly rpt, 1922–12
Dollar exchange rates of 13 currencies, 1960s-90, article, 6722–1.304
Dollar exchange rates of 13 currencies, 1991, press release, 6726–1.55
Dollar exchange rates of 29 currencies, 1991, semiannual rpt, 6822–3
Dollar exchange rates of 31 currencies, and trade-weighted US index, monthly rpt, 9362–1.3
Dollar exchange rates of 35 currencies, weekly chartbook, 9365–1.5
Dollar exchange rates offered by US disbursing offices, by country, quarterly rpt, 8102–6
Economic and monetary trends, compounded annual rates of change and quarterly indicators for US and 7 major industrialized countries, quarterly rpt, 9391–7
Economic conditions, and trade devs and balances, with data by selected country and country group, monthly rpt, 9882–14
Economic conditions in foreign countries and implications for US, periodic country rpt series, 2046–4
Economic conditions, policy, and trade practices, by country, 1989-91, annual rpt, 21384–5
Economic indicators and components, and Fed Reserve 4th District business and financial conditions, monthly chartbook, 9377–10
Economic, social, political, and geographic summary data, by country, 1992, annual factbook, 9114–2
Exchange rate variability and other factors, relation to inter- and intra-industry foreign trade for US, Germany, and Japan, 1960s-88, working paper, 9371–10.81
Exchange settlement daily transactions, by country, 1989 trends from 1986, article, 9391–1.304
Exchange Stabilization Fund balance sheet and income and expenses, *Treasury Bulletin*, quarterly rpt, 8002–4.15
Export and import price indexes for goods and services, and dollar exchange rate indexes, quarterly press release, 6762–13
Fed Reserve Bd and Reserve banks finances, staff, and review of monetary policy and economic devs, 1991, annual rpt, 9364–1
Finance (intl) and financial policy, and external factors affecting US economy, technical paper series, 9366–7
Financial markets (intl) performance of foreign and US bank and securities firms, finances and competitiveness issues, 1980s, compilation of papers, 9385–10
Flow-of-funds accounts, savings, investments, and credit statements, quarterly rpt, 9365–3.3
Forecasts of exchange rates, performance of alternative models, 1970s-91, working paper, 9381–10.125
Free trade and currency zones devs, and impacts on monetary policy, 1991 conf, 9381–13.1
Futures and options trading volume, by commodity and exchange, FY91, annual rpt, 11924–2
Futures trading in selected commodities and financial instruments and indexes, for NYC, Chicago, and other markets activity, biweekly rpt, 11922–5
Interest rates, productivity, and other factors relation to foreign exchange rates, for US and 3 OECD countries, 1970s-90, working paper, 9393–10.21
Investment (foreign direct) in US, relation to exchange rate and relative labor costs and wealth indicators, for 7 countries, 1980s, working paper, 9373–27.10
Investment (intl) position of US, by component, industry, world region, and country, 1990-91, annual article, 2702–1.323
Manufacturing profits relation to real exchange rate, model description and results, 1992 technical paper, 9385–8.142
OECD and US exchange rate indexes, 1980s-90, annual rpt, 9254–3
OECD intl trade position for US and 4 countries, and factors affecting US competition, quarterly pamphlet, 2042–25
OECD members exchange rate variability indicators, by selected country, various periods 1959-90, article, 9371–1.304
OECD members health care costs, hospital use, resources, and economic and health indicators, by country, 1960s-90, article, 4652–1.322
Prices (relative domestic and foreign), relation to foreign exchange rates, for US and 7 other countries, model description and results 1970s-90, working paper, 9381–10.123
Risk premiums in foreign exchange markets, impacts of unconventional preferences, model description and results, 1992 working paper, 9381–10.131
Singapore economic conditions and monetary policy, with exchange rate and money supply related to foreign prices and other factors, 1960s-90, article, 9379–1.304
Statistical Abstract of US, 1992 annual data compilation, 2324–1.31
Taiwan monetary and foreign exchange policies, with money supply, interest rates, and other economic indicators, 1980s, article, 9393–8.303
Treasury and Fed Reserve foreign exchange operations, *Fed Reserve Bulletin*, monthly rpt, quarterly article, 9362–1
Treasury and Fed Reserve foreign exchange operations, quarterly journal, 9385–1
see also Balance of payments
see also Eurocurrency
see also International reserves

Foreign investments
Andean Trade Preference Act duty-free exports from 4 countries to US, and business opportunities, 1989-91, 2048–161
Assets and debts of private sector, balance sheets by segment, 1960-91, semiannual rpt, 9365–4.1
Banks (insured commercial and savings) finances, for foreign and domestic offices, by asset size, 1990, annual rpt, 9294–4.2
Banks (US) and nonbanking firms liabilities to and claims on foreigners, by country, 1989-90, annual rpt, 9364–5.10
Business America, foreign and domestic commerce, and US investment and trade opportunities, biweekly journal, 2042–24
Canada and US current accounts balance reconciliation adjustment methodology, with background data, 1990-91, article, 2702–1.341
Caribbean area duty-free exports to US, by commodity and country, with consumer and industry impacts, 1984-91, annual rpt, 9884–20
Caribbean Basin Initiative export and investment incentives, contact listing, bibl, and US imports country, 1983-91, annual rpt, 2044–36
Chile trade and investment policies, foreign direct investment, and US agricultural trade and tariffs, 1985-91, GAO rpt, 26119–408
Corporations and govt securities of US, foreign transactions, monthly rpt, 9362–1.3
Currency (foreign) positions of US firms and foreign branches or affiliates, *Treasury Bulletin*, quarterly rpt, 8002–4.14

Current account balance and net capital flows, 1989-91, semiannual rpt, 8002–14
Developing countries debt burden relation to investment decline, with background data, 1960s-80s, technical paper, 9366–7.272
Direct foreign investment and trade of US, barriers, impacts, and US actions, by country, 1990, annual rpt, 444–2
Direct foreign investment in US by country, and finances, employment, and acreage owned, by industry group of business acquired or established, 1985-91, annual article, 2702–1.320
Direct foreign investment in US, by industry group and world area, 1989-91, annual article, 2702–1.331
Direct foreign investment in US by top 10 countries, factors affecting rate of return, and compared to returns for US firms, 1980s-91, article, 2702–1.330
Direct foreign investment in US by type and industry div, and affiliated firms R&D spending, pay, employment, and trade compared to US-owned firms, 1980-90, article, 9391–1.309
Direct foreign investment in US, major transactions by type, industry, country, and US location, 1990, annual rpt, 2044–20
Direct foreign investment in US, relation to exchange rate and relative labor costs and wealth indicators, for 7 countries, 1980s, working paper, 9373–27.10
Direct foreign investment of US, by industry group and world area, 1989-91, annual article, 2702–1.332
Eastern Europe transition to market economies, economic conditions, trade, and foreign investment, by country, 1990-91, 9118–13
EC economic integration impacts on domestic and intl agricultural conditions, 1990 conf, 1528–325
EC economic integration impacts on domestic economic conditions and US trade, with background data, 1986-91, 9886–4.181
Economic conditions, policy, and trade practices, by country, 1989-91, annual rpt, 21384–5
Economic indicators and components, current data and annual trends, monthly rpt, 23842–1.7
Energy producers finances and operations, by energy type for US firms domestic and foreign operations, 1990, annual rpt, 3164–44
Energy resources of US, foreign direct investment by energy type and firm, US affiliates operations, and acquisitions, as of 1990, annual rpt, 3164–80
Exports, imports, and trade flows, by country and commodity, with background economic indicators, data compilation, monthly CD-ROM, 2002–6
Exports of US, impacts of variation in foreign investment demand, 1991 technical paper, 9366–7.277
Farmland (US) owned by foreigners, by owner country and State, as of Dec 1991, article, 1561–16.302
Farmland in US owned by foreigners, holdings, acquisitions, and disposals by land use, owner type and country, and State, 1991, annual rpt, 1584–2
Farmland in US owned by foreigners, holdings, acreage, and value by land use, owner country, State, and county, 1991, annual rpt, 1584–3
Financial markets (intl) performance of foreign and US bank and securities firms, finances and competitiveness issues, 1980s, compilation of papers, 9385–10
Flow-of-funds accounts, savings, investments, and credit statements, quarterly rpt, 9365–3.3
Flows of trade and investment, and economic indicators, for selected countries and country groups, selected years 1946-91, annual rpt, 204–1.1; 204–1.9
Food processing and distribution firms, foreign ownership by country, 1980s-90, annual rpt, 1544–22.4
Futures contracts held by foreigners, by type and country, 1989, article, 8002–4.301
Income from US sources and tax withheld for foreign natls not residing in US, by country and tax treaty status, 1989, annual article, 8302–2.308
Income tax returns of foreign corporations and individuals, and US entities abroad, detailed data compilation, 1970s-89, quinquennial rpt, 8308–31
Intl investment position of US, by component, industry, world region, and country, 1990-91, annual article, 2702–1.323
Intl transactions summary, 1980s-91, annual article, 9362–1.304
Israel economic conditions, US investment and export opportunities, and trade practices, 1992 rpt, 2008–32
Japan economic conditions, US investment and export opportunities, and trade practices, forecast 1991-93 and trends from 1988, 2048–159
Japan investment in US farmland and agricultural industries, with data by State and county, late 1960s-90, 1528–332
Japan R&D activities of US firms, employee characteristics, and mgmt views on benefits and drawbacks, 1991 rpt, 9628–88
Latin America economic and social conditions, resources, trade, and aid, 1992, annual factbook, 9914–14
Liabilities (contingent) and claims paid by Fed Govt on federally insured and guaranteed contracts with foreign obligors, by country and program, periodic rpt, 8002–12
Manufacturing industry (US) intl competitiveness, trade and economic policies with background data and foreign comparisons, 1991 rpt, 26358–252
Mexico trade with US and other countries, foreign investment, and maquiladoras operations, 1980s-91, GAO rpt, 26119–417
Minerals production, trade, use, and foreign investment in US industry, 1985-90 and projected to 2000, annual rpt, 5304–5
Multinatl firms US affiliates, royalties and fees received and paid, and nonbank and manufacturing employment in Fed Reserve 8th District, 1970s-90, article, 9391–16.302
Natl income and product accounts, comprehensive accounts and components, benchmark revisions, 1929-88, 2708–5
Natl income and product accounts, comprehensive accounts and components, *Survey of Current Business*, monthly rpt, 2702–1.27
OECD intl trade position for US and 4 countries, and factors affecting US competition, quarterly pamphlet, 2042–25
Overseas Business Reports: economic conditions, investment and export opportunities, and trade practices, country market research rpt series, 2046–6
Science and Engineering Indicators, employment, education, R&D funding, and industry impacts, with foreign comparisons, 1960s-91, biennial rpt, 9624–10.4; 9624–10.6
Securities (intl) returns, relation to interest rates and other factors, model description, 1992 technical paper, 9385–8.137
Southeastern States, Fed Reserve 5th District insured commercial banks financial statements, by State, quarterly rpt, 9389–18
Soviet Union trade and investment opportunities for US firms, contact listing, bibl, and background economic data, 1991 rpt, 2048–157
Statistical Abstract of US, 1992 annual data compilation, 2324–1.16; 2324–1.27; 2324–1.29
Survey of Current Business, monthly rpt, quarterly tables, 2702–1.33
Tax (income) returns filed, by type of filer, selected income items, quarterly rpt, 8302–2.1
Tax (income) returns for foreign corporate activity in US, selected income and tax items, by industry div and selected country, 1988, article, 8302–2.309
Tax (income) returns of corporations, income and tax items by asset size and detailed industry, 1989, annual rpt, 8304–4; 8304–21
Tax (income) returns of corporations with foreign tax credit, income and tax items by industry group, 1988, biennial article, 8302–2.316
Tax (income) returns of individuals, by filing status, tax item, and income level, 1991, annual article, 8302–2.319
Tax (income) returns of individuals, detailed data, 1988, annual rpt, 8304–2
Tax (income) returns of individuals with foreign earned income, income and tax items by income level and occupation, 1987, article, 8302–2.301
Tax (income) withholding and related documents filed, by type and IRS service center, 1991 and projected 1992-99, annual rpt, 8304–22
Treasury bill offerings, auction results by Fed Reserve District, and terms, periodic press release series, 8002–7
Trust assets of banks, trust companies, and S&Ls, by type of asset and fund, selected firm, and State, 1991, annual rpt, 13004–1
Uranium reserves and industry operations, by region and State, various periods 1966-91, annual rpt, 3164–65.1
see also Foreign corporations
see also Multinational corporations

Foreign labor conditions
Background Notes, foreign countries summary social, political, and economic data, series, 7006–2
BLS data collection, analysis, and presentation methods, by program, 1992 rpt, 6888–1
Caribbean area duty-free exports to US, by commodity and country, with consumer and industry impacts, 1984-91, annual rpt, 9884–20
China rural areas labor force conditions, with farm labor productivity, late 1970s-91, article, 1524–4.2
Competitiveness (intl) of US industries, with selected foreign and US operating data by major firm and product, series, 2046–12
Costa Rica economic indicators and reform issues, mid 1970s-90, working paper, 9916–13.5
Current account balance and net assets, relation to inflation, unemployment rate, and govt lending, for OECD countries, 1970s-89, technical paper, 9366–7.274
Developing countries aged population and selected characteristics, 1980s and projected to 2020, country rpt series, 2326–19
Developing countries economic and social conditions from 1960s, and Intl Dev Cooperation Agency and AID activities and funding, FY91-93, annual rpt, 9904–4
Eastern Europe pension systems finances and provisions, 1950s-90 and alternative projections to 2025, technical paper, 8006–6.7
EC economic integration impacts on domestic and intl agricultural conditions, 1990 conf, 1528–325
Economic and monetary trends, compounded annual rates of change and quarterly indicators for US and 7 major industrialized countries, quarterly rpt, 9391–7
Economic and social conditions of foreign countries, working paper series, 2326–18
Economic conditions, and oil supply and demand, for major industrial countries, monthly rpt, 9112–1
Economic conditions, and trade devs and balances, with data by selected country and country group, monthly rpt, 9882–14
Economic conditions in foreign countries and implications for US, periodic country rpt series, 2046–4
Economic conditions, policy, and trade practices, by country, 1989-91, annual rpt, 21384–5
Economic indicators, and trade and investment flows, for selected countries and country groups, selected years 1946-91, annual rpt, 204–1.9
Economic, social, political, and geographic summary data, by country, 1992, annual factbook, 9114–2
Employment and unemployment current statistics and articles, Monthly Labor Review, 6722–1
Employment, unemployment, and productivity indexes, for US and selected OECD countries, Monthly Labor Review, 6722–1.6
Export and import balances relation to productivity and capital investment, for selected countries, 1960s-90, working paper, 9393–10.22
Ford Motor Co and foreign subsidiaries employee health care costs, with data on foreign and US health care systems, 1987-90, article, 9882–16.302
Human rights conditions in 170 countries, and US economic and military aid, 1991, annual rpt, 21384–3
Intl transactions summary, 1980s-91, annual article, 9362–1.304
Investment (foreign direct) in US, relation to exchange rate and relative labor costs and wealth indicators, for 7 countries, 1980s, working paper, 9373–27.10
Israel economic conditions, US investment and export opportunities, and trade practices, 1992 rpt, 2008–32
Japan R&D activities of US firms, employee characteristics, and mgmt views on benefits and drawbacks, 1991 rpt, 9628–88
Labor conditions, union coverage, and work accidents in foreign countries, annual country rpt series, 6366–4
Latin America, Canada, and US tobacco production and use, and related economic, health, and social issues, 1950s-92, annual rpt, 4204–18
Latin America economic and social conditions, resources, trade, and aid, 1992, annual factbook, 9914–14
Manufacturing hourly compensation costs, by industry and country, series, 6826–3
Manufacturing hourly wage, US, China, and 5 Asia countries, 1980s-89, article, 9385–1.303
Manufacturing labor costs and indexes, by selected country, 1991, semiannual rpt, 6822–3
Manufacturing labor productivity and costs, by selected country, 1950s-91, press release, 6726–1.55
Manufacturing labor productivity and unit costs for 14 countries, 1960s-90, article, 6722–1.304
Mexico and US economic and trade impacts of proposed North American Free Trade Agreement, with data on maquiladora plants, 1980s-90, hearings, 21788–210
Minerals production, reserves, and industry role in domestic economy and world supply, world area and country rpt, series, 5606–1
Multinatl US firms and foreign affiliates finances and operations, by industry and country, 1989 benchmark survey, annual rpt, 2704–5
Multinatl US firms and foreign affiliates finances and operations, by industry and world area, 1988, annual article, 2702–1.329
NATO, Japan, and South Korea military spending and indicators of ability to support common defense, by country, 1970s-90, annual rpt, 3544–28
OECD members health care costs, hospital use, resources, and economic and health indicators, by country, 1960s-90, article, 4652–1.322
Overseas Business Reports: economic conditions, investment and export opportunities, and trade practices, country market research rpt series, 2046–6
Pension plan finances, participation, and benefits, for 9 OECD countries, with data by firm and worker characteristics, 1990 conf, 6688–2
Research contracts of Bur of Intl Labor Affairs, FY83-91, annual listing, 6364–1
Singapore economic conditions and monetary policy, with exchange rate and money supply related to foreign prices and other factors, 1960s-90, article, 9379–1.304
Soviet Union former Republics and Baltic States population size and characteristics, 1989-92, 9118–19
Statistical Abstract of US, 1992 annual data compilation, 2324–1.31
Textile and apparel foreign market conditions for US exports, with domestic industry operations, country rpt series, 2046–15
Union membership for 12 countries, 1955-90, article, 6722–1.305
Vietnam population size, components of change, and selected characteristics, 1979, 1989, and projected to 2050, 2326–18.65
Women's labor force status in 9 OECD countries, 1990, chartbook, 6748–85

Foreign languages
Background Notes, foreign countries summary social, political, and economic data, series, 7006–2
Census of Population and Housing, 1990: population and housing characteristics, detailed geographic coverage, State CD-ROM series, 2551–10
Census of Population and Housing, 1990: summary characteristics, by county, subdiv, and place, State rpt series, 2551–7
Degrees awarded in higher education, by level, field, race, and sex, 1989/90 and trends from 1980/81, annual rpt, 4844–17
Education data compilation, 1992 annual rpt, 4824–2
Education data, detail for elementary, secondary, and higher education, 1920s-91 and projected to 2002, annual rpt, 4824–1
Eighth grade class of 1988: Asian and Hispanic students proficiency in English and language at home, by selected characteristics, natl longitudinal survey, 1992 rpt, 4826–9.12
Foreign countries economic, social, political, and geographic summary data, by country, 1992, annual factbook, 9114–2
Natl Education Goals progress indicators, by State, 1992, annual rpt, 15914–1
Pacific territories population and housing detailed characteristics, by location, 1990 Census of Population and Housing, series, 2551–8
Radio Free Europe and Radio Liberty broadcast and financial data, FY91, annual rpt, 10314–1
Statistical Abstract of US, 1992 annual data compilation, 2324–1.4
Vocational education enrollment, and academic and other credits earned, by subject and student characteristics, high school classes of 1982 and 1987, 4838–50
see also Bilingual education
see also Language use and ability

Foreign loans
see Export-Import Bank
see Foreign debts

see International assistance
see Military assistance

Foreign medical graduates

Admissions to US of immigrants, alien workers, and visitors, deportations, and naturalizations, by country, FY91 and trends from 1820, annual rpt, 6264–2

Employment of foreign medical grads in US by age, sex, professional characteristics, State, and country, with US medical school foreign students, 1960s-80s, working paper, 6366–6.2

Enrollment in science and engineering grad programs, by field, source of funds, and characteristics of student and instn, 1990, annual rpt, 9627–7

Health condition and care indicators, 1950s-90 with health improvement and disease prevention goals for 1990, annual data compilation, 4144–11

Labor supply and education of health professionals, by professional and other characteristics, and location, 1960s-92 and projected to 2020, biennial rpt, 4114–8

Military health care personnel, and accessions by training source, by occupation, specialty, and service branch, FY90, annual rpt, 3544–24

Physicians, by specialty, age, sex, and location of training and practice, 1990, State rpt series, 4116–6

Foreign military sales

see Arms trade
see Military assistance

Foreign opinion of U.S.

Science and technology public knowledge, interest, and expectations, 1990 survey, biennial rpt, 9624–10.7

Travel to US and Canada, market analysis with detailed trip and traveler characteristics, country rpt series, 2906–2

Foreign relations

Agents of foreign interests, former US govt officials and activities, FY86-91, GAO rpt, 26123–134

Background Notes, foreign countries summary social, political, and economic data, series, 7006–2

Budget deficit reduction under Gramm-Rudman Act, CBO sequestration estimates, FY93, annual rpt, 26304–6

Budget deficit reduction under Gramm-Rudman Act, OMB sequestration estimates, by category, FY92, annual rpt, 104–27

Budget of US, Bush Admin proposals, with detail for defense budgets, and historical data from FY34, FY93, 108–46

Budget of US, CBO analysis and review of FY93 budget by function, annual rpt, 26304–2

Budget of US, CBO analysis of revenue and spending alternatives and projections of economic indicators, FY93-97, annual rpt, 26304–3

Budget of US, midsession review of FY93 budget, by function, annual rpt, 104–7

Budget of US, obligations and authority by function, agency, and program, with summaries and analyses, FY93, annual rpt, 104–2

Criminal cases by type and disposition, and collections, for US attorneys, by Federal district, FY91, annual rpt, 6004–2.1

FDA investigations and regulatory activities, quarterly rpt, 4062–3

Fed Govt agencies and program operations investigations, summaries of findings, as of 1991, annual GAO rpt, 26104–5.1

Loans and loan guarantees of Fed Govt, outstanding amounts by agency and program, *Treasury Bulletin*, quarterly rpt, 8002–4.11

Natl income and product accounts, comprehensive accounts and components, benchmark revisions, 1929-88, 2708–5

Natl income and product accounts, comprehensive accounts and components, *Survey of Current Business*, monthly rpt, 2702–1.26

Research on foreign policy devs and world areas, discontinued series, 7006–7

State Dept programs fraud and abuse, audits and investigations, 2nd half FY92, semiannual rpt, 7002–6

UN voting record and share of votes in agreement with US, by issue, country, and world area, 1991, annual rpt, 7004–18

see also Arms trade
see also Diplomatic and consular service
see also East-West trade
see also Educational exchanges
see also Exchange of persons programs
see also Executive agreements
see also Foreign countries
see also Foreign debts
see also Foreign economic relations
see also Foreign opinion of U.S.
see also Foreign students
see also Foreign trade
see also Foreign trade promotion
see also International assistance
see also International cooperation in conservation
see also International cooperation in cultural activities
see also International cooperation in environmental sciences
see also International cooperation in law enforcement
see also International cooperation in science and technology
see also International military forces
see also International reserves
see also International sanctions
see also Military assistance
see also Military intervention
see also Military invasion and occupation
see also Treaties and conventions
see also War

Foreign Sales Corporations

Income tax returns of foreign corporations and individuals, and US entities abroad, detailed data compilation, 1970s-89, quinquennial rpt, 8308–31

Income tax returns of FSCs, assets, and income and tax items, by industry, country of incorporation, and transaction pricing method, 1987, article, 8302–2.311

Tax (income) returns filed, by type of return and IRS district, 1990 and projected 1991-98, annual rpt, 8304–24

Tax (income) returns filed, by type of tax and IRS region and service center, projected 1991-98 and trends from 1978, annual rpt, 8304–9

Tax (income) returns of corporations, income and tax items by asset size and detailed industry, 1989, annual rpt, 8304–4; 8304–21

Tax (income) returns of corporations with foreign tax credit, income and tax items by industry group, 1988, biennial article, 8302–2.316

see also Domestic International Sales Corporations

Foreign Service

see Diplomatic and consular service

Foreign students

Admissions to US of immigrants, alien workers, and visitors, deportations, and naturalizations, by country, FY91 and trends from 1820, annual rpt, 6264–2

Admissions to US of immigrants and nonimmigrants, alien workers, deportations, and naturalizations, FY91, annual summary rpt, 6264–7

Black higher education instns enrollment, finances, staff, and degrees, by instn and selected student characteristics, 1970s-90, 4848–46

Condition of Education, detail for elementary, secondary, and higher education, 1920s-91 and projected to 2002, annual rpt, 4824–1

Degree (PhD) recipients in higher education, by field and selected characteristics, 1979, 1984, and 1989, 4848–44

Degrees awarded in higher education, by level, field, race, and sex, 1989/90 and trends from 1980/81, annual rpt, 4844–17

Digest of Education Statistics, 1992 annual data compilation, 4824–2

Enrollment in higher education, by level, race, and sex, fall 1980-90, biennial rpt, 4844–15

Expenditures of foreign visitors to US, by trip purpose and world area of residence, 1989, 2908–28

Health care professionals supply and education, by professional and other characteristics, and location, 1960s-92 and projected to 2020, biennial rpt, 4114–8

Japan students in US, by field, 1988-89, GAO rpt, 26123–379

Latin America dev grants of Inter-American Foundation by program area, and fellowships by field and instn, by country, FY72-91, annual rpt, 14424–2

Latin America dev grants of Inter-American Foundation by recipient, and fellowships, by country, FY91, annual rpt, 14424–1

Nuclear engineering enrollment and degrees granted by instn and State, and grad placement, by student characteristics, 1991, annual rpt, 3004–5

Radiation protection and health physics enrollment and degrees granted by instn and State, and grad placement, by student characteristics, 1991, annual rpt, 3004–7

Science and engineering enrollment, performance, curricula, student aid sources, and career plans, by sex and race, 1970s-91, biennial rpt, 9624–20.2

Science and engineering grad enrollment, by field, source of funds, and characteristics of student and instn, 1990, annual rpt, 9627–7

Science and engineering labor force, Federal and university research funding, and educational data, series, 9626–6

Soviet Union and US economic and sociodemographic indicators, selected years 1970-90, handbook, 2328–80

Statistical Abstract of US, 1992 annual data compilation, 2324–1.4
Travel to US, by characteristics of visit and traveler, country, port city, and State of destination, quarterly rpt, 2902–1
Travel to US, by characteristics of visit and traveler, world area of origin, and US destination, 1991 survey, annual rpt, 2904–12
see also Educational exchanges
see also Foreign medical graduates

Foreign trade
Africa (sub-Saharan) economic, social, and political conditions, with US aid by program and country, 1991 rpt, 7008–58
Andean Trade Preference Act duty-free exports from 4 countries to US, and business opportunities, 1989-91, 2048–161
Background Notes, foreign countries summary social, political, and economic data, series, 7006–2
BLS data collection, analysis, and presentation methods, by program, 1992 rpt, 6888–1
Business America, foreign and domestic commerce, and US investment and trade opportunities, biweekly journal, 2042–24
Business cycle recession and expansion duration indicators, 1850s-1990, working paper, 9375–13.83
Business statistics, detailed data for major industries and economic indicators, *Survey of Current Business*, monthly rpt, 2702–1
Business statistics, detailed data for major industries and economic indicators, 1960-91, *Survey of Current Business* biennial supplement, 2704–1
Canada and US trade over Great Lakes, and other foreign trade, by type of vessel, 1987-89, annual rpt, 7704–7.3
Caribbean area duty-free exports to US, and imports from US, by country, and impact on US employment, by commodity, 1991, annual rpt, 6364–2
Caribbean area duty-free exports to US, by commodity and country, with consumer and industry impacts, 1984-91, annual rpt, 9884–20
Caribbean Basin Initiative export and investment incentives, contact listing, bibl, and US imports country, 1983-91, annual rpt, 2044–36
Census Bur data collection and statistical program plans, advisory committees findings and recommendations, 1992 conf, 2628–35
Census Bur data files and rpts, coverage and availability, 1992 annual listing, 2304–2
Central America economic indicators, by country, 1969-89, working paper, 9916–13.4
China and other Asia countries trade with US, composition and trends, 1980s-91, article, 9385–1.303
Classification codes for countries, commodities, and customs districts for Census Bur export statistics, 1990 base edition and supplements, 2428–5
Cuba trade, by commodity and country, mid 1980s-91, 9118–8
Developing countries economic and social conditions from 1960s, and Intl Dev Cooperation Agency and AID activities and funding, FY91-93, annual rpt, 9904–4
Developing countries economic, population, and agricultural data, US and other aid sources, and AID activity, country rpt series, 9916–12
Dollar exchange rate trade-weighted index of Fed Reserve Bank of Atlanta, by world area, quarterly rpt, 9371–15
Dollar exchange rate trade-weighted index of Fed Reserve Bank of Dallas, by world area, monthly rpt, 9379–13
Eastern Europe trade with US, by commodity and country, 1987-91 and outlook for 1992, 2048–158
Eastern Europe transition to market economies, economic conditions, trade, and foreign investment, by country, 1990-91, 9118–13
EC economic integration impacts on domestic economic conditions and US trade, with background data, 1986-91, 9886–4.181
EC trade with US by country, and total agricultural trade, annual rpt, discontinued, 7144–7
Economic and monetary trends, compounded annual rates of change and quarterly indicators for US and 7 major industrialized countries, quarterly rpt, 9391–7
Economic conditions, and oil supply and demand, for major industrial countries, monthly rpt, 9112–1
Economic conditions, and trade devs and balances, with data by selected country and country group, monthly rpt, 9882–14
Economic conditions in foreign countries and implications for US, periodic country rpt series, 2046–4
Economic conditions, policy, and trade practices, by country, 1989-91, annual rpt, 21384–5
Economic indicators and components, and Fed Reserve 4th District business and financial conditions, monthly chartbook, 9377–10
Economic indicators and components, current data and annual trends, monthly rpt, 23842–1.7
Economic indicators compounded annual rates of change, monthly rpt, 9391–3
Economic, social, political, and geographic summary data, by country, 1992, annual factbook, 9114–2
Economies of scale in output, technology, and trade, model description and results, 1992 technical paper, 9383–20.22
Employment and industry impacts of trade, series, 6366–3
Exchange rate variability and other factors, relation to inter- and intra-industry foreign trade for US, Germany, and Japan, 1960s-88, working paper, 9371–10.81
Exports and imports among US, Canada, and Japan related to domestic and foreign prices and income, 1965-87, technical paper, 9366–7.276
Exports and imports dependency indexes for total, merchandise, and agricultural products, by country, 1960s-88, 1528–328
Exports and imports of US, by country and detailed commodity, monthly rpt, 2422–12
Exports and imports of US by country, and trade shifts by commodity, 1991, annual rpt, 9884–25
Exports and imports of US, by Harmonized System 6-digit commodity and country, 1991, annual rpt, 2424–13
Exports and imports of US, by selected country, country group, and commodity group, 1991, annual rpt, 2044–37
Exports and imports of US, by transport mode, country, and SITC 1- to 3-digit commodity, 1991, annual rpt, 2424–12
Exports and imports of US, relation to trade composition and domestic and foreign capital investment, model description and results, late 1960s-89, article, 9385–1.302
Exports and imports relation to balance of trade, model description and results, 1950s-90, working paper, 9377–9.142
Exports and imports relation to terms of trade and GNP, alternative models description and results, 1992 working paper, 9377–9.144
Exports and imports, trade agreements and relations, and USITC investigations, 1991, annual rpt, 9884–5
Exports, imports, and balances, monthly rpt, 9362–1.3
Exports, imports, and balances of US, by selected country, country group, and commodity group, preliminary data, monthly rpt, 2042–34
Exports, imports, and balances of US with major trading partners, by product category, 1987-91, annual chartbook, 9884–21
Exports, imports, and employment of US multinatl firms compared to foreign-controlled US firms, 1988, article, 9391–1.309
Exports, imports, and intl competitiveness of US industries, trends and outlook, quarterly rpt with articles, 9882–16
Exports, imports, and trade flows, by country and commodity, with background economic indicators, data compilation, monthly CD-ROM, 2002–6
Exports of manufactured goods for US and major competitors, market share rpts, annual listing, discontinued, 2044–6
Exports of manufactured goods, total and for US and major competitors, by country of destination, annual commodity market share rpt series, discontinued, 2046–13
Exports of manufactured goods, total and for US and major competitors, by SITC 1- to 5-digit commodity, annual country market share rpt series, discontinued, 2046–2
Exports of US, detailed commodities by country, monthly CD-ROM, 2422–13
Exports of US, detailed Schedule B commodities with countries of destination, 1991, annual rpt, 2424–10
Exports of US, impacts of variation in foreign investment demand, 1991 technical paper, 9366–7.277
Finance (intl) and financial policy, and external factors affecting US economy, technical paper series, 9366–7
Flows of trade and investment, and economic indicators, for selected countries and country groups, selected years 1946-91, annual rpt, 204–1.1; 204–1.9

Forecasts of economic conditions and employment, alternative BLS projections to 2005 and trends 1975-90, biennial rpt, 6744–19
Forecasts of economic indicators, 1992-93 and trends from 1948, annual article, 9383–6.301
Forecasts of economic indicators, 1993-94 and trends from 1948, annual article, 9383–6.303
Generalized System of Preferences status, and US tariffs, with trade by country and US economic impacts, for selected commodities, 1987-91, annual rpt, 9884–23
Haiti economic conditions, 1985-91, working paper, 9916–13.3
Import price indexes for manufactured and nonmanufactured goods, changes by world area, 1991-92, article, 6722–1.327
Imports and tariff provisions effect on US industries and products, investigations with background financial and operating data, series, 9886–4
Imports demand relation to prices and household income, model description and results, 1992 technical paper, 9385–8.141
Imports, exports, and employment impacts, by SIC 2- to 4-digit industry and commodity, quarterly rpt, 2322–2
Imports injury to US industries from foreign subsidized products, investigations with background financial and operating data, series, 9886–15
Imports injury to US industries from sales at less than fair value, investigations with background financial and operating data, series, 9886–14
Imports injury to US industries, USITC rpts, 1984-91, annual listing, 9884–12
Imports of US, detailed commodities by country, monthly CD-ROM, 2422–14
Imports of US given duty-free treatment for value of US material sent abroad, by commodity and country, 1987-90, annual rpt, 9884–14
Imports of US, relation to domestic and foreign economic indicators, model description and results, 1980s, technical paper, 9385–8.138
Income tax returns of foreign corporations and individuals, and US entities abroad, detailed data compilation, 1970s-89, quinquennial rpt, 8308–31
Industry finances and operations, by SIC 2- to 4-digit industry, forecast 1992, annual rpt, 2044–28
Input-output structure of US economy, detailed interindustry transactions for 84 industries, and components of final demand, 1987, annual article, 2702–1.316
Input-output structure of US economy, detailed interindustry transactions for 541 industries, and components of final demand, 1982 benchmark data, 2708–17
Intl transactions summary, 1980s-91, annual article, 9362–1.304
Israel economic conditions, US investment and export opportunities, and trade practices, 1992 rpt, 2008–32
Japan economic conditions, US investment and export opportunities, and trade practices, forecast 1991-93 and trends from 1988, 2048–159
Latin America and Caribbean country imports from US, by State of origin and country, 1987 and 1990, 2048–160
Latin America economic and social conditions, resources, trade, and aid, 1992, annual factbook, 9914–14
Latin America economic conditions, trade, and foreign aid, working paper series, 9916–13
Latin America trade, and balance of trade with US, by country, annual rpt, suspended, 2044–34
Manufacturing census, 1987: exporting establishments, shipments, and employment, by SIC 2-digit industry and State, 2506–16.2
Manufacturing exports, imports, and balances of US, by SITC 2-digit commodity and country, quarterly rpt, 2042–35
Mexico imports from US, by industry and State, 1987-91, 2048–154
Mexico trade with US and other countries, foreign investment, and maquiladoras operations, 1980s-91, GAO rpt, 26119–417
Minority- and woman-owned businesses and owner characteristics, by industry, employment and sales size, and form of ownership, 1987 survey, 2328–59
Multinatl firms US affiliates finances and operations, by industry div, country of parent firm, and State, 1989-90, annual article, 2702–1.319
Multinatl firms US affiliates, finances, and operations, by industry, world area of parent firm, and State, 1989-90, annual rpt, 2704–4
Multinatl US firms and foreign affiliates finances and operations, by industry and country, 1989 benchmark survey, annual rpt, 2704–5
Multinatl US firms and foreign affiliates finances and operations, by industry and world area, 1988, annual article, 2702–1.329
Multinatl US firms foreign affiliates, income statement items by asset size, industry, and country, 1988, biennial article, 8302–2.322
Natl income and product accounts and components, *Survey of Current Business*, monthly rpt, 2702–1.23
Natl income and product accounts benchmark revisions, methodological changes and revised summary tables, 1959-91, article, 2702–1.302
Natl income and product accounts benchmark revisions of GDP and natl income, various periods 1959-80, tables, 2702–1.307
Natl income and product accounts, comprehensive accounts and components, benchmark revisions, 1929-88, 2708–5
Natl income and product accounts, comprehensive accounts and components, *Survey of Current Business*, monthly rpt, 2702–1.27
North America intraindustry trade indexes, for US, Canada, and Mexico, by commodity, 1962-87, 1528–327
OECD intl trade position for US and 4 countries, and factors affecting US competition, quarterly pamphlet, 2042–25
OECD trade, by country, annual rpt, discontinued, 7144–10
OECD trade, total and for 4 major countries, and US trade by country, by commodity, 1980-90, world area rpt series, 9116–1
OPEC and other countries intl boycotts, US firms and individuals cooperation and tax benefits denied, 1990, article, 8302–2.323
Outlying areas trade with US, by detailed commodity and mode of transport, 1991, annual rpt, 2424–11
Overseas Business Reports: economic conditions, investment and export opportunities, and trade practices, country market research rpt series, 2046–6
Palau admin, and social, economic, and govtl data, FY91, annual rpt, 7004–6
Poland and Hungary exports, by world area, 1988-91, GAO rpt, 26123–386
Price indexes for exports and imports, by selected end-use category, monthly press release, 6762–15
Price indexes for exports and imports of goods and services, and dollar exchange rate indexes, quarterly press release, 6762–13
Price indexes for exports and imports of US, by SITC commodity, end-use, and SIC industry, Monthly Labor Review, 6722–1.4
Science and Engineering Indicators, employment, education, R&D funding, and industry impacts, with foreign comparisons, 1960s-91, biennial rpt, 9624–10.6
Services trade of US, direct and among multinatl firms affiliates, by industry and world area, 1986-91, article, 2702–1.336
Small business R&D grants of Fed Govt, project sales by type and dev funding by source, by agency and selected firm, 1984-91, GAO rpt, 26113–393
Statistical Abstract of US, 1992 annual data compilation, 2324–1.15; 2324–1.22; 2324–1.27; 2324–1.29; 2324–1.31
Tax (income) returns of Foreign Sales Corps, assets, and income and tax items, by industry, country of incorporation, and transaction pricing method, 1987, article, 8302–2.311
Technology-intensive industries intl competitiveness, with background data by industry and foreign comparisons, 1960s-91, GAO rpt, 26123–406
USITC activities, investigations, and rpts, FY91, annual rpt, 9884–1
see also Agricultural exports and imports
see also Arms trade
see also Balance of payments
see also Coal exports and imports
see also Common markets and free trade areas
see also Customs administration
see also Domestic International Sales Corporations
see also Dumping
see also East-West trade
see also Energy exports and imports
see also Export-Import Bank
see also Export processing zones
see also Foreign competition
see also Foreign exchange
see also Foreign investments

see also Foreign Sales Corporations
see also Foreign trade promotion
see also General Agreement on Tariffs and Trade
see also International assistance
see also Maritime law
see also Military assistance
see also Motor vehicle exports and imports
see also Natural gas exports and imports
see also North American Free Trade Agreement
see also Petroleum exports and imports
see also Ships and shipping
see also Tariffs and foreign trade controls
see also Technology transfer
see also Trade adjustment assistance
see also Trade agreements
see also under names of specific commodities or commodity groups

Foreign trade promotion

Agricultural export promotion activities of FAS trade offices, operating costs, and funding by program, by country, 1989-90, GAO rpt, 26123-370
Agricultural exports info and service sources, 1991 annual listing, 1924-11
Agricultural exports under federally financed programs, by commodity and country, bimonthly rpt, periodic data, 1522-1
Agricultural production, consumption, and policies for selected countries, and US export dev and promotion, monthly journal, 1922-2
Andean Trade Preference Act duty-free exports from 4 countries to US, and business opportunities, 1989-91, 2048-161
Assistance (financial and nonfinancial) of Fed Govt, 1992 base edition, annual listing, 104-5
Budget of US, obligations and authority by function, agency, and program, with summaries and analyses, FY93, annual rpt, 104-2
Business America, foreign and domestic commerce, and US investment and trade opportunities, biweekly journal, 2042-24
Caribbean area duty-free exports to US, by commodity and country, with consumer and industry impacts, 1984-91, annual rpt, 9884-20
Caribbean Basin Initiative export and investment incentives, contact listing, bibl, and US imports country, 1983-91, annual rpt, 2044-36
Cotton production, trade, and use, for selected countries, FAS monthly circular, 1925-4.2
Credit programs for exports, activities of Eximbank and 6 OECD countries, 1990, annual rpt, 9254-3
Credit sales agreement terms, by commodity and country, FY90, annual rpt, 15344-1.11
Developing countries economic and social conditions from 1960s, and Intl Dev Cooperation Agency and AID activities and funding, FY91-93, annual rpt, 9904-4
Domestic Intl Sales Corps (Interest Charge) income tax returns, assets, and income and tax items, by detailed industry, 1987, article, 8302-2.312
Eastern Europe imports from US, and trade and dev opportunities, monthly rpt, 2042-33
Energy technologies export markets, competitiveness, and promotion, for US industries, 1992 technical rpt, 3006-13.5
Exports, imports, and trade flows, by country and commodity, with background economic indicators, data compilation, monthly CD-ROM, 2002-6
Fed Govt contingent liabilities and claims paid on insured and guaranteed contracts with foreign obligors, by country and program, periodic rpt, 8002-12
Fish and shellfish foreign market conditions for US products, country rpt series, 2166-19
Foreign countries economic conditions, policy, and trade practices, by country, 1989-91, annual rpt, 21384-5
Grain and feed trade policy impacts on importing and exporting countries, FAS monthly circular, 1925-2.4
Israel economic conditions, US investment and export opportunities, and trade practices, 1992 rpt, 2008-32
Japan economic conditions, US investment and export opportunities, and trade practices, forecast 1991-93 and trends from 1988, 2048-159
Lumber and wood products trade and export promotion of US by country, and trade balance, by commodity, FAS periodic circular, 1925-36
Manufacturing industry (US) intl competitiveness, trade and economic policies with background data and foreign comparisons, 1991 rpt, 26358-252
Minority Business Dev Centers mgmt and financial aid, and characteristics of businesses, by region and State, FY91, annual rpt, 2104-6
Oils, oilseeds, and fats foreign and US production and trade, FAS periodic circular series, 1925-1
Overseas Business Reports: economic conditions, investment and export opportunities, and trade practices, country market research rpt series, 2046-6
Poultry and products foreign and US production, trade, and use, by selected country, FAS semiannual circular series, 1925-33
Seed exports, by type, world region, and country, FAS quarterly rpt, 1925-13
Soviet Union trade and investment opportunities for US firms, contact listing, bibl, and background economic data, 1991 rpt, 2048-157
Textile and apparel exports of US, by product group and country, quarterly rpt, 2042-36
Travel to US, market research data available from US Travel and Tourism Admin, 1992, annual rpt, 2904-15
Uganda cash transfers from AID linked to nontraditional crop export programs, 1988-90, 9916-1.77
see also Exhibitions and trade fairs

Foreign Trade Zones Board

Trade zones (US) operations and movement of goods, by zone and commodity, FY90, annual rpt, 2044-30

Forensic sciences

Fingerprint identification system of FBI, automation costs, staff, and workload, FY90 and projected to FY2000, 26358-253
Military reserves dental panoral radiographs on file, share of forces covered by component, 1991, annual rpt, 3544-31.1
Physicians, by specialty, age, sex, and location of training and practice, 1990, State rpt series, 4116-6

Foreso, Cynthia B.

"Crude Petroleum, Industry and Trade Summary", 9885-11.4

Forest fires

Environmental Quality, status of problems, protection programs, research, and intl issues, 1991 annual rpt, 484-1
Fire fighter deaths, by cause, circumstances, and location, 1990, annual rpt, 9434-8
Foreign countries disasters, casualties, damage, and aid by US and others, FY91 and trends from FY64, annual rpt, 9914-12
Forest Service activities and finances, by region and State, FY91, annual rpt, 1204-1
Incidents and mgmt of disasters and natl security threats, with data by major event and State, 1992 annual rpt, 9434-6
Old-growth forests ecology, mgmt, and research methods, for Rocky Mountains and southwest US, 1992 conf, 1208-421
Prevention of fire on public lands, evaluation of activities, methods and effectiveness, 1989 survey, 1208-417
Public lands acreage and use, and Land Mgmt Bur activities and finances, annual State rpt series, 5724-11
Public lands acreage, grants, use, revenues, and allocations, by State, FY91, annual rpt, 5724-1.3
Recreational choices of wilderness visitors, impacts of fires, 1989 local area survey, 1208-422
Utah forest habitats impacts of fires, 1992 rpt, 1208-420
Water quality and fish population in southwestern US streams, impacts of land mgmt and forest fires, 1980s-91, 1208-390
Wilderness areas fires ecology, mgmt, cultural impacts, and historic patterns, 1990 conf, 1208-415
Wildfires and acreage burned, by type of land, ownership, cause, region, and State, 1984-90, annual rpt, 1204-4

Forest Service

Acreage of land under Forest Service mgmt, by forest and location, 1991 and historic trends, annual rpt, 1204-2
Activities and finances of Forest Service, by region and State, FY91, annual rpt, 1204-1
Alabama timber acreage and value, by species, forest type, ownership, and county, 1990, series, 1206-30
Alabama timber acreage converted from nonforest use, reforested, and harvested, for pine, 1950s-90, 1208-409
Alaska Copper River Delta wetland environmental conditions, 1987, 1208-401
Alaska timber acreage and resources, by species, ownership class, and inventory unit, series, 1206-9
Aspen forest vegetation, climate, and other environmental characteristics, for upper Great Lakes area, 1991 rpt, 1208-418

Birds in western US Great Basin sagebrush habitat, population density by species, 1978-83 studies, 1208–402
Budget of US, obligations and authority by function, agency, and program, with summaries and analyses, FY93, annual rpt, 104–2
California lumber mills, operations, timber use by species and origin, and residue use, by product and county, 1988, 1208–108
Camping in wilderness areas, impacts on plants and soils, 1979-90 studies, 1208–395
Expenditures of Fed Govt in States, by type, program, agency, and State, FY91, annual rpt, 2464–2
Expenditures of Forest Service recreation uses fund by purpose, and wilderness mgmt funds reprogrammed to other activities, FY88-90, GAO rpt, 26113–550
Fires (wild) and acreage burned, by type of land, ownership, cause, region, and State, 1984-90, annual rpt, 1204–4
Fires effects on selected forest habitats, for Utah, 1992 rpt, 1208–420
Fires effects on wilderness visitors recreation choices, 1989 local area survey, 1208–422
Fires on public lands, prevention activities evaluation methods and effectiveness, 1989 survey, 1208–417
Fires on wildlands, ecology, mgmt, cultural impacts, and historic patterns, 1990 conf, 1208–415
Florida industrial roundwood lumber production, by product and county, 1967-89, 1208–352
Georgia industrial roundwood lumber production, by product, 1986 and 1989, 1208–393
Global climate change impacts on mountain grassland vegetation, monitoring study results, 1969 and 1988, 1208–425
Grazing of livestock, indicators of grazing forage demand and meat supply and demand, 1960s-90 and projected to 2030, 1208–404
Hydrology and climate data for Hubbard Brook Experimental Forest NH, 1956-89, 1208–410
Insect (mountain pine beetle) infestation in the Black Hills Natl Forest, and ponderosa pine kills, 1989-91, 1208–408
Insect and disease incidence and damage in forests, and control activities, State rpt series, 1206–49
Insect and disease incidence and damage in forests, annual regional rpt series, 1206–11
Insect and disease incidence and damage in forests, by State, 1990, annual rpt, 1204–8
Insect and disease infestation in western US timber from lumber imports from USSR, economic and environmental impacts, 1991 and projected to 2040, 1208–389
Iowa timber resources and removals, by species, forest and tree characteristics, ownership, and county, 1988-90 and trends from 1973-74, 1208–75
Labor demand elasticities for lumber and paper products industries, 1992 rpt, 1208–416
Louisiana timber resources, by ownership, forest and tree characteristics, and parish, 1991, series, 1206–35
Lumber (hardwood) exports of US to Europe and Asia, by species and country, 1981-90, 1208–373
Lumber (hardwood) production, prices, employment, and trade, quarterly rpt, 1202–4
Lumber (veneer) recovered from Douglas-fir logs and blocks at Oregon and Washington mills, by grade and type, 1981-83 study, 1208–396
Lumber and veneer recovery and quality from young growth Douglas fir, effects of timber stand and log characteristics, model description and results, 1991 rpt, 1208–413
Lumber preservatives performance test results, by type, late 1930s-80s, 1208–391
Lumber prices, by grade and Pacific Northwest species, 1971-90 and projected to 2040, 1208–424
Michigan fuelwood production, by species, land ownership, survey region, county, and location, 1986, 1208–412
Minnesota fuelwood production, by species, land ownership, and location, 1988, 1208–398
Minnesota timber acreage, resources, and removals, by ownership, forest and tree characteristics, and county, 1990, series, 1206–24
Missouri fuelwood production, by species, land ownership, and location, 1987, 1208–399
Missouri timber resources and removals, by species, forest and tree characteristics, ownership, and county, 1987-89 and trends from 1959, 1208–76
Missouri timber resources and removals by species, land ownership, and county, 1988-89, series, 1206–3
Montana timber outside natl forests, acreage, resources, and mortality, by species and ownership class, 1988-89, 1206–25
North Central States pulpwood production and mill receipts, by species, mill, State, and county, 1990, annual rpt, 1204–19
North Central States pulpwood production in 3 States, by species and county, 1990, 1208–397
North Central States timber harvest and industrial roundwood production, by product and county, State rpt series, 1206–10
North Central States timber harvest, estimation methodology, 1991 rpt, 1208–419
Northeastern US hardwood forests ecology and mgmt, 1992, 1208–405
Northeastern US industrial roundwood production by product, State rpt series, 1206–15
Northeastern US pulpwood production by species and county, and shipments, by State, 1990, annual rpt, 1204–18
Northeastern US timber resources and removals, by species, ownership, and county, State rpt series, 1206–12
Northwestern US and British Columbia forest industry production, prices, trade, and employment, quarterly rpt, 1202–3
Oak decline disease incidence and losses, for western Virginia, 1986, 1208–384
Old-growth forests ecology, mgmt, and research methods, for Rocky Mountains and southwest US, 1992 conf, 1208–421
Oregon lumber production, and industry operations, by county, 1988, 1208–280
Owl (northern spotted) conservation methods in Pacific Northwest, findings and recommendations, 1990 rpt, 1208–385
Owl (northern spotted) conservation methods in Pacific Northwest, timber industry impacts, and Federal and State spending, 1980s-95, 1208–388
Pacific Northwest old-growth forests plant and wildlife population and species diversity, 1991 compilation of papers, 1208–386
Pine (ponderosa) fenceposts service life and costs, by preservative treatment method and site, 1992 rpt, 1208–406
Planting and stand improvement, by ownership and State, FY91, annual rpt, 1204–7
Private landowners restriction of access to public lands, reasons and impacts on recreation and land mgmt activities, 1991-92 surveys, GAO rpt, 26113–571
Publications of Rocky Mountain Forest and Range Experiment Station, 1980-89 listing, 1208–403
Recreational use of natl forests, by type of activity and State, 1991, annual rpt, 1204–17
Recreational use of natl forests, factors affecting regional growth, shift-share analysis, 1992 rpt, 1208–423
Research and mgmt of timber resources, for southeast US, 1990 biennial conf papers, 1204–35
Research on forestry, activities and bibl, annual rpt, suspended, 1204–14
Revenue of natl forest land, by source, forest, and State, FY91, annual rpt, 1204–34
Revenue of natl forest land, share paid to States, and acreage, by forest, county, and congressional district, FY92, annual rpt, 1204–33
Revenue of USDA, by source and subagency, FY88-92, GAO rpt, 26113–602
Rocky Mountain States timber and mill residue production, by species, ownership, and county, series, 1206–17
South Carolina timber resources damage from Hurricane Hugo, by species, damage class, and county, as of 1990, 1208–411
Southeastern US pulpwood and residue prices, spending, and transport shares by mode, 1989-90, annual rpt, 1204–22
Southern US timber resources and removals, by species, ownership, State, and county, series, 1206–8
Southern US veneer log receipts, production, and shipments, by species and State, with residue use, 1988, 1208–407
Tennessee timber acreage and resources, by species, ownership class, and county, 1989, series, 1206–27
Timber sales of Forest Service, expenses, and operations, by region, State, and natl forest, FY91, annual rpts, 1204–36

Timber stumpage prices, for sawtimber sold from natl forests in Pacific Northwest, monthly 1975-89, 1208–387
Tropical woods kiln drying time relation to moisture content and other properties, for 650 species, 1991 rpt, 1208–392
Vermont White River basin stream recreation use by activity, time, and location, 1987, 1208–400
Virginia industrial roundwood production, shipments, and residue volume, by species, product, and location, 1987-89, 1208–138
Virginia timber resources, growth, and removals, by species, ownership, treatment, and county, 1990-92, series, 1206–6
Washington State timber acreage and resources, by species, ownership class, and county, 1988-89 with harvest trends from 1955, series, 1206–28
Water quality and fish population in southwestern US streams, impacts of land mgmt and forest fires, 1980s-91, 1208–390
West Virginia timber, hardwood stands single-tree selection mgmt methods, tree density and growth by species, 1950s-83, 1208–394
Wildlife habitats assessment use of forest inventories, with data for northern coastal California, as of 1985, 1208–414
Wisconsin timber resources and removals, by species, forest type, ownership, and county, series, 1206–34

Forests and forestry

Agricultural Conservation Program acreage and projects, by State, 1936-90, quinquennial rpt, 1808–1
Agricultural Conservation Program participation and payments, by practice and State, FY91, annual rpt, 1804–7
Agricultural Stabilization and Conservation Service producer payments, by program and State, 1991, annual table, 1804–12
Agricultural Statistics, 1991, annual rpt, 1004–1
Alabama timber acreage and value, by species, forest type, ownership, and county, 1990, series, 1206–30
Alabama timber acreage converted from nonforest use, reforested, and harvested, for pine, 1950s-90, 1208–409
Alaska timber acreage and resources, by species, ownership class, and inventory unit, series, 1206–9
Aspen forest vegetation, climate, and other environmental characteristics, for upper Great Lakes area, 1991 rpt, 1208–418
County Business Patterns, 1989: employment, establishments, and payroll, by SIC 2- to 4-digit industry and county, annual State rpt series, 2326–8
County Business Patterns, 1990: employment, establishments, and payroll, by SIC 2- to 4-digit industry and county, annual State rpt series, 2326–6
Disaster damage to timber and orchards, USDA restoration aid and program participation by practice and State, FY91, annual rpt, 1804–24
Environmental Quality, status of problems, protection programs, research, and intl issues, 1991 annual rpt, 484–1
Farmland value, rent, taxes, foreign ownership, and transfers by probable use and lender type, with data by region and State, 1981-92, article, 1561–16.302
Fed Govt financial and nonfinancial domestic aid, 1992 base edition, annual listing, 104–5
Fed Govt spending in States, by type, program, agency, and State, FY91, annual rpt, 2464–2
Foreign countries agricultural research grants of USDA, by program, subagency, and country, FY92, annual listing, 1954–3
Foreign countries economic, social, political, and geographic summary data, by country, 1992, annual factbook, 9114–2
Foreign ownership of US farmland, holdings, acquisitions, and disposals by land use, owner type and country, and State, 1991, annual rpt, 1584–2
Foreign ownership of US farmland, holdings, acreage, and value by land use, owner country, State, and county, 1991, annual rpt, 1584–3
Forest Service activities and finances, by region and State, FY91, annual rpt, 1204–1
Hydrology and climate data for Hubbard Brook Experimental Forest NH, 1956-89, 1208–410
Improvement program for private timberland, Fed Govt cost-sharing funds by region and State, monthly rpt, 1802–11
Improvement program for private timberland, participation and payments by State, FY91, annual rpt, 1804–20
Indian and govt lands under Bur of Indian Affairs mgmt, acreage, leases, and use, 1989, annual rpt, 5704–12
Input-output structure of US economy, detailed interindustry transactions for 541 industries, and components of final demand, 1982 benchmark data, 2708–17
Insect (mountain pine beetle) infestation in the Black Hills Natl Forest, and ponderosa pine kills, 1989-91, 1208–408
Insect and disease incidence and damage in forests, and control activities, State rpt series, 1206–49
Insect and disease incidence and damage in forests, annual regional rpt series, 1206–11
Insect and disease incidence and damage in forests, by State, 1990, annual rpt, 1204–8
Insect and disease infestation in western US timber from lumber imports from USSR, economic and environmental impacts, 1991 and projected to 2040, 1208–389
Iowa timber resources and removals, by species, forest and tree characteristics, ownership, and county, 1988-90 and trends from 1973-74, 1208–75
Latin America economic and social conditions, resources, trade, and aid, 1992, annual factbook, 9914–14
Louisiana timber resources, by ownership, forest and tree characteristics, and parish, 1991, series, 1206–35
Minnesota timber acreage, resources, and removals, by ownership, forest and tree characteristics, and county, 1990, series, 1206–24
Missouri timber resources and removals, by species, forest and tree characteristics, ownership, and county, 1987-89 and trends from 1959, 1208–76
Missouri timber resources and removals by species, land ownership, and county, 1988-89, series, 1206–3
Montana timber outside natl forests, acreage, resources, and mortality, by species and ownership class, 1988-89, 1206–25
Multinatl firms US affiliates finances and operations, by industry, country of parent firm, and State, 1987, 2708–48
North Central States timber harvest, estimation methodology, 1991 rpt, 1208–419
Northeastern US hardwood forests ecology and mgmt, 1992, 1208–405
Northeastern US timber resources and removals, by species, ownership, and county, State rpt series, 1206–12
Northwestern US and British Columbia forest industry production, prices, trade, and employment, quarterly rpt, 1202–3
Oak decline disease incidence and losses, for western Virginia, 1986, 1208–384
Occupational injury and illness rates, by SIC 2- to 4-digit industry, 1989-90, annual rpt, 6844–7
Occupational injury and illness rates, by SIC 2- to 4-digit industry, 1990, annual rpt, 6844–1
Occupational Outlook Handbook, 1992-93, biennial rpt, 6744–1
Old-growth forests ecology, mgmt, and research methods, for Rocky Mountains and southwest US, 1992 conf, 1208–421
Pacific Northwest Indian tribes environmental, economic, and cultural impacts of OCS oil and gas lease and dev, with background data, 1970s-92, 5738–35
Pacific Northwest old-growth forests plant and wildlife population and species diversity, 1991 compilation of papers, 1208–386
Planting and stand improvement, by ownership and State, FY91, annual rpt, 1204–7
Public lands acreage, grants, use, revenues, and allocations, by State, FY91, annual rpt, 5724–1.2
Publications of Rocky Mountain Forest and Range Experiment Station, 1980-89 listing, 1208–403
Research (agricultural) funding and staffing for USDA, State agencies, and other instns, by topic, FY91, annual rpt, 1744–2
Research and education grants, USDA competitive awards by program and recipient, FY91, annual listing, 1764–1
Research and mgmt of timber resources, for southeast US, 1990 biennial conf papers, 1204–35
Research on forestry, activities and bibl, annual rpt, suspended, 1204–14
Rocky Mountain States timber and mill residue production, by species, ownership, and county, series, 1206–17
South Carolina timber resources damage from Hurricane Hugo, by species, damage class, and county, as of 1990, 1208–411

Southern US timber resources and removals, by species, ownership, State, and county, series, 1206–8
Statistical Abstract of US, 1992 annual data compilation, 2324–1.24
Tax (income) returns of sole proprietorships, income statement items, by industry group, 1990, annual article, 8302–2.317; 8302–2.320
Tennessee timber acreage and resources, by species, ownership class, and county, 1989, series, 1206–27
Tropical forests condition, conservation methods, and biological diversity issues, 1992 rpt, 26358–262
Virginia timber resources, growth, and removals, by species, ownership, treatment, and county, 1990-92, series, 1206–6
Washington State timber acreage and resources, by species, ownership class, and county, 1988-89 with harvest trends from 1955, series, 1206–28
West Virginia timber, hardwood stands single-tree selection mgmt methods, tree density and growth by species, 1950s-83, 1208–394
Wildlife habitats assessment use of forest inventories, with data for northern coastal California, as of 1985, 1208–414
Wisconsin timber resources and removals, by species, forest type, ownership, and county, series, 1206–34
see also Forest fires
see also Gum and wood chemicals
see also Lumber industry and products
see also National forests
see also National parks
see also State forests
see also Wood fuel

Forgery
see Counterfeiting and forgery

Forrestal, Robert P.
"CRA and the 1990 HMDA Data: Moving Beyond the Impasse", 9371–4

Fort Lauderdale, Fla.
CPI by component for US city average, and by region, population size, and for 15 metro areas, monthly rpt, 6762–1
CPI by component for US city average, and by selected metro area, region, and population size, monthly rpt, 6762–2
Drug test results at arrest, by drug type, offense, and sex, for selected urban areas, quarterly rpt, 6062–3
Housing and households characteristics, and unit and neighborhood quality, by MSA location for 11 MSAs, 1986 survey, supplement, 2485–8
Housing starts and completions authorized by building permits in 40 MSAs, quarterly rpt, 2382–9
Wages by occupation, and benefits for office and plant workers, 1991 survey, periodic MSA rpt, 6785–3.1
see also under By City and By SMSA or MSA in the "Index by Categories"

Fort Myers, Fla.
see also under By City and By SMSA or MSA in the "Index by Categories"

Fort Pierce, Fla.
see also under By City and By SMSA or MSA in the "Index by Categories"

Fort Wayne, Ind.
see also under By City and By SMSA or MSA in the "Index by Categories"

Fort Worth, Tex.
Commuters, by county of residence and work, for top 10 metro areas, 1990 Census of Population, press release, 2328–84
CPI by component for US city average, and by region, population size, and for 15 metro areas, monthly rpt, 6762–1
CPI by component for US city average, and by selected metro area, region, and population size, monthly rpt, 6762–2
CPI by major component for 2 Texas MSAs, monthly rpt, 6962–2
Employment, earnings, hours, and CPI changes, for Dallas-Fort Worth metro area, late 1970s-91, annual rpt, 6964–2
Housing and households characteristics, unit and neighborhood quality, and journey to work by MSA location, for 11 MSAs, 1985 survey, supplement, 2485–8
Housing and households characteristics, 1989 survey, MSA fact sheet, 2485–11.10
Housing and households detailed characteristics, and unit and neighborhood quality, by location, 1989 survey, MSA rpt, 2485–6.6
Housing starts and completions authorized by building permits in 40 MSAs, quarterly rpt, 2382–9
see also under By City and By SMSA or MSA in the "Index by Categories"

Fortune, Peter
"Municipal Bond Market, Part II: Problems and Policies", 9373–1.310

Foster Grandparent Program
Activities and funding of ACTION, by program, FY91, annual rpt, 9024–2

Foster home care
AIDS patients costs and service use under Medicaid, and service needs, for New Jersey waiver program, 1987-89, article, 4652–1.317
Assistance for foster care programs of States, Federal funding and children served, by State, 1981-89, hearing, 21788–208
Assistance programs under Ways and Means Committee jurisdiction, finances, operations, and participant characteristics, FY70s-91, annual rpt, 21784–11
HHS financial aid, by program, recipient, State, and city, FY91, annual regional listings, 4004–3
Living arrangements, family relationships, and marital status, by selected characteristics, 1991, annual Current Population Rpt, 2546–1.461
Population economic well-being indicators, by selected characteristics and household income and income-to-poverty ratio, 1984, 2546–20.22
Supplemental Security Income and Medicaid eligibility and payment provisions, and beneficiaries living arrangements, by State, 1992, annual rpt, 4704–13

Foster, Russell J.
"Byproduct Output from the Domestic Primary Copper, Lead, and Zinc Industries", 5608–170

Foundations
see Nonprofit organizations and foundations

Foundries
Aluminum plant ownership, capacity, energy and aluminum sources, and startup and closing dates, by US and foreign plant and location, 1990, annual listing, 5604–49
Capital expenditures for plant and equipment, by major industry group, quarterly rpt, 2502–2
County Business Patterns, 1989: employment, establishments, and payroll, by SIC 2- to 4-digit industry and county, annual State rpt series, 2326–8
County Business Patterns, 1990: employment, establishments, and payroll, by SIC 2- to 4-digit industry and county, annual State rpt series, 2326–6
Employment of minorities and women, by occupation, SIC 1- to 3-digit industry, State, and MSA, 1991, annual rpt, 9244–1
Hazardous substances industrial releases and reduction methods under EPA regulation, by chemical, source, industry, and location, 1989, annual rpt, 9234–6
Manufacturing annual survey, 1990: finances and operations, by SIC 2- to 4-digit industry, series, 2506–14
Manufacturing census, 1987: concentration of largest firms measured by value added, and for shipments by SIC 2- and 4-digit industry, subject rpt, 2497–6
Manufacturing census, 1987: shipments of manufacturers products, by customer class and SIC 2- and 4-digit industry, subject rpt, 2497–4
Manufacturing finances and operations, by SIC 2- to 4-digit industry, forecast 1992, annual rpt, 2044–28
Manufacturing industries operations and performance, analytical rpt series, 2506–16
Occupational injury and illness rates, by SIC 2- to 4-digit industry, 1989-90, annual rpt, 6844–7
Occupational injury and illness rates, by SIC 2- to 4-digit industry, 1990, annual rpt, 6844–1
Pollution (air) abatement equipment shipments by industry, and new and backlog orders, by product, 1991, annual Current Industrial Rpt, 2506–12.5
Pollution abatement capital and operating costs, by SIC 2- to 4-digit industry and State, 1990, annual Current Industrial Rpt, 2506–3.6
Price indexes (producer), by stage of processing and detailed commodity, monthly 1991, annual rpt, 6764–2
Steel mills coke batteries and capacity by age, 1991 and projected to 1998, 5606–5.10

Fox, James W.
"Feedback Loops and Economics of Scale: Achieving Export-Led Growth in the Caribbean Basin", 9916–13.2

France
Agricultural trade of US, by detailed commodity and country, 1991, annual rpt, 1524–8
Agricultural trade of US, by detailed commodity and country, 1991, semiannual rpt, 1522–4

AID loans repayment status and terms by program and country, and status of predecessor agency loans, quarterly rpt, 9912–3
Cuba trade, by commodity and country, mid 1980s-91, 9118–8
Currency (foreign and US) shares of intl transactions, with background data, for 5 countries, 1960s-80s, 9381–10.129
Economic and military aid and loans from US and intl agencies, by program and country, FY46-91, annual rpt, 9914–5
Economic and monetary trends, compounded annual rates of change and quarterly indicators for US and 7 major industrialized countries, quarterly rpt, 9391–7
Economic conditions, and oil supply and demand, for major industrial countries, monthly rpt, 9112–1
Economic conditions, consumer and stock prices and production indexes, for 7 OECD countries, *Survey of Current Business*, monthly rpt, 2702–1.1
Economic conditions, income, production, prices, employment, and trade, 1992 periodic country rpt, 2046–4.38
Economic conditions, policy, and trade practices, by country, 1989-91, annual rpt, 21384–5
Economic indicators, and dollar exchange rates, for selected OECD countries, 1992 semiannual rpt, 8002–14
Economic, social, political, and geographic summary data, by country, 1992, annual factbook, 9114–2
Energy production by type, and oil trade, and use, by country group and selected country, monthly rpt, 9112–2
European Monetary Union impacts on France, Germany, and Italy monetary policies, 1992 technical paper, 9385–8.145
Export credit activity of Eximbank and 6 OECD countries, 1990, annual rpt, 9254–3
Exports and imports, intl position of US and 4 OECD countries, and factors affecting US competition, quarterly pamphlet, 2042–25
Exports and imports of OECD, total and for 4 major countries, and US trade by country, by commodity, 1980-90, world area rpt series, 9116–1
Exports and imports of US by country, and trade shifts by commodity, 1991, annual rpt, 9884–25
Exports and imports of US, by Harmonized System 6-digit commodity and country, 1991, annual rpt, 2424–13
Exports and imports of US, by selected country, country group, and commodity group, 1991, annual rpt, 2044–37
Exports and imports of US, by transport mode, country, and SITC 1- to 3-digit commodity, 1991, annual rpt, 2424–12
Exports, imports, and balances of US for manufactured goods, by SITC 2-digit commodity and country, quarterly rpt, 2042–35
Exports, imports, and balances of US with major trading partners, by product category, 1987-91, annual chartbook, 9884–21
Exports of US, detailed Schedule B commodities with countries of destination, 1991, annual rpt, 2424–10
Farmland in US owned by foreigners, holdings, acreage, and value by land use, owner country, State, and county, 1991, annual rpt, 1584–3
Financial markets (intl) performance of foreign and US bank and securities firms, finances and competitiveness issues, 1980s, compilation of papers, 9385–10
Gold standard relation to inflation, with background data for UK, US, France, and Italy, 1730s-1930s, working paper, 9377–9.136
Health care costs and components, services use, resources, and economic indicators, by OECD country, 1960s-90, article, 4652–1.322
Human rights conditions in 170 countries, and US economic and military aid, 1991, annual rpt, 21384–3
Imports of goods, services, and investment from US, trade barriers, impacts, and US actions, by country, 1991, annual rpt, 444–2
Imports of US given duty-free treatment for value of US material sent abroad, by commodity and country, 1987-90, annual rpt, 9884–14
Interest and exchange rates, security yields, and stock indexes, for selected foreign countries, weekly chartbook, 9365–1.5
Interest rates (long term) relation to rates of return to capital, economic policies, and other factors, US and 4 countries, 1960s-90, article, 9385–1.301
Intl transactions of US with 9 countries, 1989-91, *Survey of Current Business*, monthly rpt, annual table, 2702–1.33
Investment (foreign direct) in US, major transactions by type, industry, country, and US location, 1990, annual rpt, 2044–20
Labor conditions, union coverage, and work accidents, 1992 annual country rpt, 6366–4.49
Manufacturing industry (US) intl competitiveness, trade and economic policies with background data and foreign comparisons, 1991 rpt, 26358–252
Military spending, arms trade, and force strengths, with govt spending and population, by country, 1979-89, annual rpt, 9824–1
Multinatl firms US affiliates finances and operations, by industry, country of parent firm, and State, 1987, 2708–48
Multinatl firms US affiliates, finances, and operations, by industry, world area of parent firm, and State, 1989-90, annual rpt, 2704–4
Multinatl US firms and foreign affiliates finances and operations, by industry and country, 1989 benchmark survey, annual rpt, 2704–5
Multinatl US firms foreign affiliates, income statement items by asset size, industry, and country, 1988, biennial article, 8302–2.322
Nuclear power generation in US and 20 countries, monthly rpt, 3162–24.10
Nuclear power generation in US and 20 countries, monthly 1973-88, 3168–123.10
Oil production, stocks, use, and trade, by selected country and country group, monthly rpt, 3162–42
Oil use and stocks for selected OECD countries, monthly rpt, 3162–24.10
Oil use and stocks for selected OECD countries, 1973-88, 3168–123.10
Pollution (air) contributing to global warming, emissions by monitoring site and country, and temperature change by world area and US region, 1860s-1990, annual rpt, 3004–33
Population size, growth rates, and components of change, by country, projected 1990-2020 and trends from 1950, biennial rpt, 2324–9
Refugee migration, and intl aid programs, by world area and country of origin and asylum, 1991, annual rpt, 7004–15
Science and Engineering Indicators, employment, education, R&D funding, and industry impacts, with foreign comparisons, 1960s-91, biennial rpt, 9624–10
Spacecraft and satellite launches since 1957, quarterly listing, 9502–2
Steel (carbon flat-rolled) products from 21 countries, injury to US industry from foreign subsidized and less than fair value imports, investigation with background financial and operating data, 1992 rpt, 9886–19.85
Steel (hot-rolled) products containing lead or bismuth from 4 countries, injury to US industry from foreign subsidized and less than fair value imports, investigation with background financial and operating data, 1992 rpt, 9886–19.82
Steel trade, by product, country, and customs district, with US industry operating data, 1989-June 1992, semiannual rpt, 9882–15
Tax (estate) returns for nonresident aliens, property and tax data, by estate size and decedent country of residence, 1986, article, 8302–2.310
Tax (income) returns for foreign corporate activity in US, selected income and tax items, by industry div and selected country, 1988, article, 8302–2.309
Tax (income) returns, income, and tax withheld for foreign partners of US partnerships, by country, 1990, article, 8302–2.324
Tax revenue, by level of govt and type of tax, for OECD countries, mid 1960s-90, annual rpt, 10044–1.2
Telecommunications industry intl competitiveness, structure, and devs, with background data and foreign comparisons, 1991 rpt, 2808–30
Transportation energy use, fuel prices, vehicle registrations, and mileage, by selected country, 1950-89, annual rpt, 3304–5.1
Travel to US and Canada, market analysis with trip and traveler characteristics, 1989, country rpt, 2906–2.15
UN voting record and share of votes in agreement with US, by issue, country, and world area, 1991, annual rpt, 7004–18
see also French Guiana
see also Monaco
see also New Caledonia

see also St. Pierre and Miquelon
see also under By Foreign Country in the "Index by Categories"
Franchises
Child day care and early childhood education programs availability, demand, use, costs, and provider and enrollee characteristics, 1990 survey, 4808–39
Exports and imports of services, direct and among multinatl firms affiliates, by industry and world area, 1986-91, article, 2702–1.336
Food marketing sector finances, operations, and merger activity, for processors and distributors, 1991, annual rpt, 1544–22
Minority- and woman-owned businesses and owner characteristics, by industry, employment and sales size, and form of ownership, 1987 survey, 2328–59
Multinatl US firms and foreign affiliates finances and operations, by industry and country, 1989 benchmark survey, annual rpt, 2704–5
Small Business Admin loan guarantee program participants finances, operations, characteristics, and views, 1991 survey, 9768–25
Statistical Abstract of US, 1992 annual data compilation, 2324–1.28
Franco, Daniele
"General Accounting: The Case of Italy", 9377–9.139
Frank, Michelle S.
"Annual Southwestern Region Pest Conditions Report, 1991", 1206–11.2
Frankel, Allen B.
"Primer on the Japanese Banking System", 9366–7.273
Franklin County, Ohio
Housing and households characteristics, and unit and neighborhood quality, by MSA location for 11 MSAs, 1987 survey, supplement, 2485–8
Franklin, James C.
"Industry Output and Job Growth Continues Slow into Next Century", 6744–19
Fraser, Alexa
"Evaluation of the Asbestos Hazard Emergency Response Act (AHERA): Final Report", 9238–71
Fraud
AFDC fraud cases, referrals, and disposition, by State, FY90, annual rpt, 4584–3.5
Arrests and criminal case processing through sentencing, cases and duration by disposition and offense, for selected cities, 1988, annual rpt, 6064–27
Arrests, by offense, offender characteristics, and location, 1991, annual rpt, 6224–2.2
Arrests for fraud and forgery, case dispositions, and sentencing, by age, sex, race, and offense type, 1983-88, 6066–19.64
Bank deposits availability policies, and related fraud, 1984-90, annual rpt, 9364–13
Banks and thrifts fraud cases, Justice Dept investigation and prosecution activities, 1989-92, GAO rpt, 26119–426
Bombings with insurance fraud motive, 1987-91, annual rpt, 8484–4.1
Court civil and criminal caseloads for Federal district, appeals, and bankruptcy courts, by type of suit and offense, circuit, and district, 1991, annual rpt, 18204–11
Court civil and criminal caseloads for Federal district, appeals, and special courts, 1991, annual rpt, 18204–8
Court criminal case processing in Federal district courts, and dispositions, by offense, district, and offender characteristics, 1989, annual data compilation, 6064–29
Court criminal case processing in Federal district courts, and dispositions, by offense, 1980-91, annual rpt, 6064–31
Crime, criminal justice admin and enforcement, and public opinion, data compilation, 1992 annual rpt, 6064–6
DOD Civilian Health and Medical Program of Uniformed Services fraud and abuse cases and referrals, FY89-90, annual chartbook, 3504–23.4
Fed Govt employees misconduct reporting, awareness of protection and other factors influencing reporting, 1992 survey, GAO rpt, 26119–413
HUD programs fraud and abuse, financial and program mgmt improvement activities, FY91, annual rpt, 5004–9
Immigrant and nonimmigrant visa applicants refused, and refusals overcome, by reason, FY90, annual rpt, 7184–1.3
Immigration and Naturalization Service illegal alien and narcotics activities, FY84-91, annual rpt, 6264–2.5
Income tax fraudulent returns filed in paper and electronic format, and refunds involved, 1988-92, GAO rpt, 26119–400
IRS internal audits, and employee and nonemployee violations, FY91, annual rpt, 8304–3.1
IRS undercover criminal investigations and costs by criminal activity, and success rates, by region, mid 1980s-90, GAO rpt, 26119–394
Juvenile arrests, by sex, race, disposition, and offense, 1990, 6066–27.8
Medicaid fraud, funding for remediation by State, FY91, annual regional listings, 4004–3
Military procurement fraud cases dispositions, fines, and settlements, for top 100 firms, 1981-92, GAO rpt, 26119–423
Military supplies theft and fraud losses, and inventory control measures adequacy, 1988-91, GAO rpt, 26123–377
Postal Service inspection activities, 2nd half FY92, semiannual rpt, 9862–2
Prison and parole admissions and releases, sentence length, and time served, by offense and offender characteristics, 1988, annual rpt, 6064–33
Prisoners in Federal and contract instns, by selected characteristics, region, and Federal instn, FY89, annual rpt, 6244–1.1
Probation population, by offender characteristics, sentence conditions, whether rearrested, and offense, 1986-89, 6066–19.65
Savings instns fraud and abuse, Federal indictments and case dispositions, periodic press release, 6002–3; 6008–33
Secret Service counterfeiting and other investigations and arrests by type, and disposition, FY91 and trends from FY82, annual rpt, 8464–1
Securities law enforcement activities of SEC, FY91, annual rpt, 9734–2.3
Sentences for Federal crimes, guidelines use and results by offense and district, and Sentencing Commission activities, 1991, annual rpt, 17664–1
Sentences for Federal crimes, guidelines use and results by offense, 1984-1990, 6066–19.68
Sentences for Federal offenses, guidelines by offense and circumstances, series, 17668–1
Unemployment insurance programs of States, quality appraisal results, FY91, annual rpt, 6404–16
US attorneys case processing and collections, by case type and Federal district, FY91, annual rpt, 6004–2
Wiretaps authorized, costs, arrests, trials, and convictions, by offense and jurisdiction, 1991, annual rpt, 18204–7
Women in jail, by criminal background and sociodemographic characteristics, with comparisons to men, 1989, 6066–19.66
see also Counterfeiting and forgery
see also Federal Inspectors General reports
see also Money laundering
Fravel, Dennis A.
"Agricultural and Horticultural Machinery, Industry and Trade Summary", 9885–9.3
Frayer, W. E.
"Florida Wetlands, Status and Trends, 1970's-80's", 5508–119
Frazao, Elizabeth
"Food Spending by Female-Headed Households", 1548–391
Frazis, Harley J.
"Selection Bias and the Diploma Effect", 6886–6.81
"Wages, Family Background, and Endogenous Schooling", 6886–6.94
"What Researchers Have Learned from the National Longitudinal Surveys About Youth Unemployment", 6728–42
Freddie Mac
see Federal Home Loan Mortgage Corp.
Freedom of information
Court civil and criminal caseloads for Federal district, appeals, and bankruptcy courts, by type of suit and offense, circuit, and district, 1991, annual rpt, 18204–11
Court civil and criminal caseloads for Federal district, appeals, and special courts, 1991, annual rpt, 18204–8
Fed Govt info security measures and classification actions monitored by Info Security Oversight Office, FY91, annual rpt, 9454–21
HHS Freedom of Info Act requests, disposition, costs, and fees, 1991, annual rpt, 4004–21
USDA programs fraud and abuse, audits and investigations, FY92, semiannual rpt, 1002–4
see also Censorship
see also Freedom of the press
Freedom of the press
Foreign countries human rights conditions in 170 countries, 1991, annual rpt, 21384–3
Freight
Animal protection, licensing, and inspection activities of USDA, and animals used in research, by State, FY90, annual rpt, 1394–10

Apple production, marketing, and prices, for Appalachia and compared to other States, 1989-92, annual rpt, 1311–13
Business statistics, detailed data for major industries and economic indicators, *Survey of Current Business*, monthly rpt, 2702–1.10
Business statistics, detailed data for major industries and economic indicators, 1960-91, *Survey of Current Business* biennial supplement, 2704–1
Coal and coke production, shipments, and trade, by State of origin and destination, end-use sector, and mode of transport, quarterly rpt, 3162–37.1
Coal production, stocks, and shipments, by State of origin and destination, end-use sector, and mode of transport, quarterly rpt, 3162–8
County Business Patterns, 1989: employment, establishments, and payroll, by SIC 2- to 4-digit industry and county, annual State rpt series, 2326–8
County Business Patterns, 1990: employment, establishments, and payroll, by SIC 2- to 4-digit industry and county, annual State rpt series, 2326–6
Employment, earnings, and hours, by SIC 1- to 4-digit industry, monthly 1989-Feb 1992, annual rpt, 6744–4
Energy use by fuel type, and miles traveled, by transport mode, projected 1990-2010 and trends from 1960s, 3008–124
Energy use by mode of transport, fuel supply, and demographic and economic factors of vehicle use, 1970s-90, annual rpt, 3304–5
Exports and imports of services, direct and among multinatl firms affiliates, by industry and world area, 1986-91, article, 2702–1.336
Exports and imports of US, by transport mode, country, and SITC 1- to 3-digit commodity, 1991, annual rpt, 2424–12
Farm, food, grain, and all products rail freight index, and selected shipments by mode, monthly rpt with articles, 1502–4
Farm production itemized costs, by farm sales size and region, 1991, annual rpt, 1614–3
Flower and foliage shipments from Florida by State and mode of transport, US imports by country, and prices, by variety, mid 1980s-91, annual rpt, 1311–24
Food marketing cost indexes, by expense category, monthly rpt with articles, 1502–4
Food prices (farm-retail), marketing cost components, and industry finances and productivity, 1920s-91, annual rpt, 1544–9
Foreign trade zones (US) operations and movement of goods, by zone and commodity, FY90, annual rpt, 2044–30
Fruit and vegetable shipments, and arrivals by city, by mode of transport and State and country of origin, 1991, annual rpt series, 1311–4
Fruit and vegetable shipments by mode of transport, arrivals, and imports, by commodity and State and country of origin, weekly rpt, 1311–3
Fruit and vegetable shipments by truck, monthly by State and country of origin, and rates weekly by growing area and market, 1991, annual rpt, 1311–15
Fruit and vegetable wholesale prices in NYC by State, and shipments and arrivals by mode of transport, by commodity, weekly rpt, 1311–20
Fruit and vegetable wholesale prices in NYC-Newark, and arrivals by mode of transport, by commodity and State, 1990, annual rpt, 1311–21
Fruit shipments, production, and marketing, for Florida, with US trade and prices, by commodity, 1970s-91, annual rpt, 1311–23
Grain shipments and rates for barge and rail loadings, periodic situation rpt with articles, 1561–4
Grape shipments from California and arrivals by city by mode of transport, prices, and production, by variety, 1970s-90, annual rpt, 1311–25
Household goods carriers financial and operating data by firm, quarterly rpt, 9482–14
Input-output structure of US economy, detailed interindustry transactions for 541 industries, and components of final demand, 1982 benchmark data, 2708–17
Lumber (pulpwood and residue) prices, spending, and transport shares by mode, for southeast US, 1989-90, annual rpt, 1204–22
Military and personal property shipments by commercial cariers, and cost savings from bill audits and rate negotiations, FY99-91, GAO rpt, 26123–369
Military and personal property shipments, passenger traffic, and costs, by service branch and mode of transport, FY91, annual rpt, 3704–15
Military Sealift Command shipping operations, finances, and personnel, FY91, annual rpt, 3804–14
Occupational injury and illness rates, by SIC 2- to 4-digit industry, 1989-90, annual rpt, 6844–7
Occupational injury and illness rates, by SIC 2- to 4-digit industry, 1990, annual rpt, 6844–1
Ohio River basin waterway facilities, freight by commodity and port, and recreation, by waterway, 1988-89, annual rpt, 3754–6
Potato production, acreage, prices, and shipments, for 7 major producer States, and compared to other States, 1970s-92, annual rpt, 1311–29
Potato production, acreage, shipments, and arrivals, for Maine by variety, and compared to other States and Canada, 1991-92, annual rpt, 1311–26
Price indexes (producer), by stage of processing and detailed commodity, monthly 1991, annual rpt, 6764–2
Railroad (Class I) finances and operations, detailed data by firm, class of service, and district, 1990, annual rpt, 9486–5.1
Railroad (Class I) finances and operations, detailed data by firm, class of service, and district, 1991, annual rpt, 9486–6.1
Railroad freight, by commodity and region of origin and destination, 1989, annual rpt, 7604–6
Railroad revenue, income, freight, and rate of return, by Class I freight railroad and district, quarterly rpt, 9482–2
Rate setting disputes with Fed Govt, US Claims Court caseloads by disposition, FY92, annual rpt, 18224–1
Shipborne commerce (domestic) of US, freight by major commodity group, vessel type, and port, 1987-89, annual rpt, 7704–7
Shipborne commerce (domestic and foreign) of US, freight by port, 1990, annual rpt, 3754–7
Shipborne trade of US, and Fed Govt sponsored cargo by agency, total and US-flag share by vessel type, selected years 1981-90, annual rpt, 7704–14.2; 7704–14.3
Shipping industry structure, rates, and effects of Shipping Act, by route, 1980s, 9408–54
Soviet Union and US economic and sociodemographic indicators, selected years 1970-90, handbook, 2328–80
St Lawrence Seaway ship, cargo, and passenger traffic, and toll revenue, 1991 and trends from 1959, annual rpt, 7744–2
Statistical Abstract of US, 1992 annual data compilation, 2324–1.21; 2324–1.22
Truck and bus interstate carriers finances and operations, by district, 1990, annual rpt, 9486–5.3
Truck and warehouse services finances and inventory, by SIC 2- to 4-digit industry, 1990 survey, annual rpt, 2413–14
Truck interstate carriers finances and operations, by district, 1990, annual rpt, 9486–5.2
Truck rates for fruit and vegetables paid by shippers and receivers, by commodity and city, and fleet itemized costs per mile, weekly rpt, 1311–22
Truck transport of property, financial and operating data by region and firm, quarterly rpt, 9482–5
Vegetable truck rates, by crop, growing area, and market, periodic situation rpt with articles, 1561–11
Waterborne commerce (domestic and foreign) of US, freight by commodity, traffic, and passengers, by port and waterway, 1989, annual rpt, 3754–3
see also Air cargo
see also Containerization
see also Hazardous substances transport

Freitag, H. Paul
"Equatorial Wind, Current and Temperature Data: 108 Degrees West to 140 Degrees West; Apr. 1983-Oct. 1987", 2148–62

French, George E.
"Early Corrective Action for Troubled Banks", 9292–4.301

French Guiana
Agricultural trade of US, by detailed commodity and country, 1991, annual rpt, 1524–8
Agricultural trade of US, by detailed commodity and country, 1991, semiannual rpt, 1522–4
Economic and social conditions, resources, and trade, and aid, 1992, annual factbook, 9914–14
Economic, social, political, and geographic summary data, by country, 1992, annual factbook, 9114–2
Exports and imports of US, by transport mode, country, and SITC 1- to 3-digit commodity, 1991, annual rpt, 2424–12

Exports of US, detailed Schedule B commodities with countries of destination, 1991, annual rpt, 2424–10
Population size, growth rates, and components of change, by country, projected 1990-2020 and trends from 1950, biennial rpt, 2324–9
Refugee migration, and intl aid programs, by world area and country of origin and asylum, 1991, annual rpt, 7004–15

French Polynesia
Exports and imports of US, by transport mode, country, and SITC 1- to 3-digit commodity, 1991, annual rpt, 2424–12

Frenkel, Jacob A.
"Macroeconomic Policy Implications of Trade and Currency Zones", 9381–13.1

Frenzen, Paul D.
"Rural Areas Gained Doctors During the 1980's", 1502–7.304

Freshley, M. D.
"Hanford Environmental Dose Reconstruction Project, Ground-Water Contribution to Dose from Past Hanford Operations", 3356–5.7

Fresno, Calif.
see also under By City and By SMSA or MSA in the "Index by Categories"

Frey, Carolin M.
"Representativeness of the Surveillance, Epidemiology, and End Results Program Data: Recent Trends in Cancer Mortality Rates", 4472–1.320

Fribush, Lillian A.
"Earnings and Employment Data for Wage and Salary Workers Covered Under Social Security by State and County, 1988", 4744–29

Friedberg, Wallace
"Radiation Exposure of Air Carrier Crewmembers II", 7506–10.98

Friedell, Gilbert H.
"Incidence of Dysplasia and Carcinoma of the Uterine Cervix in an Appalachian Population", 4472–1.327

Friedenberg, Howard L.
"Regional Multipliers: A User Handbook for the Regional Input-Output Modeling System (RIMS II)", 2708–47

Friedman, Benjamin M.
"Why Does the Paper-Bill Spread Predict Real Economic Activity?", 9375–13.67

Friedman, Brian L.
"Productivity in Crude Oil and Natural Gas Production", 6722–1.316

Fries, Sylvia D.
"NASA Engineers and the Age of Apollo", 9508–39

Frieswyk, Thomas S.
"Forest Statistics for Maryland, 1976 and 1986", 1206–12.16

Fringe benefits
see Employee benefits

Fritts, Steven H.
"Trends and Management of Wolf-Livestock Conflicts in Minnesota", 5508–115

Frost, Floyd
"Racial Misclassification of Native Americans in a Surveillance, Epidemiology, and End Results Cancer Registry", 4472–1.324

Fruit and fruit products
Agricultural Statistics, 1991, annual rpt, 1004–1
Appalachia food processing firms, employment, and shipments, and farm production, by commodity and State, 1960s-90, 9088–37
Apple (processed) demand and impacts of selected market factors, 1980s-91, 1548–392
Apple imports of 5 Persian Gulf countries, by country of origin, 1981-90, article, 1925–34.322
Apple production, marketing, and prices, for Appalachia and compared to other States, 1989-92, annual rpt, 1311–13
Apple seasonal price forecasts based on production, price, and stocks, 1970s-91, article, 1561–6.303
California fruit and vegetable processing industry, workers affected by plant closures, 1977-86, working paper, 6366–6.5
Cherry production, by State, 1990-92, annual rpt, 1621–18.2
Cherry production, imports from US, and prices, for Japan, 1988-92, article, 1925–34.339
Chile fruit exports to US, sales by port of entry, and prices in 5 terminal cities, by commodity, 1990/91, annual rpt, 1311–27
Cold storage food stocks by commodity and census div, and warehouse space use, by State, monthly rpt, 1631–5
Cold storage food stocks by commodity, and warehouse space use, by census div, 1991, annual rpt, 1631–11
Cold storage warehouses and capacity, by State, as of Oct 1991, biennial rpt, 1614–2
Consumption, supply, trade, prices, spending, and indexes, by food commodity, 1990, annual rpt, 1544–4
County Business Patterns, 1989: employment, establishments, and payroll, by SIC 2- to 4-digit industry and county, annual State rpt series, 2326–8
County Business Patterns, 1990: employment, establishments, and payroll, by SIC 2- to 4-digit industry and county, annual State rpt series, 2326–6
CPI by component for US city average, and by selected metro area, region, and population size, monthly rpt, 6762–2
Cranberry production, prices, use, and acreage, for selected States, 1990-91 and forecast 1992, annual rpt, 1621–18.5
Cuba trade, by commodity and country, mid 1980s-91, 9118–8
Disaster damage to timber and orchards, USDA restoration aid and program participation by practice and State, FY91, annual rpt, 1804–24
Employment, earnings, and hours, by SIC 1- to 4-digit industry, monthly 1989-Feb 1992, annual rpt, 6744–4
Employment of minorities and women, by occupation, SIC 1- to 3-digit industry, State, and MSA, 1991, annual rpt, 9244–1
Exports and imports (agricultural) of US, by commodity and country, bimonthly rpt, 1522–1
Exports and imports (agricultural) of US, by detailed commodity and country, 1991, annual rpt, 1524–8
Exports and imports (agricultural) of US, by detailed commodity and country, 1991, semiannual rpt, 1522–4
Exports and imports between US and outlying areas, by detailed commodity and mode of transport, 1991, annual rpt, 2424–11
Exports and imports of US, by country and detailed commodity, monthly rpt, 2422–12
Exports and imports of US, by Harmonized System 6-digit commodity and country, 1991, annual rpt, 2424–13
Exports and imports of US, by selected country, country group, and commodity group, 1991, annual rpt, 2044–37
Exports and imports of US, by transport mode, country, and SITC 1- to 3-digit commodity, 1991, annual rpt, 2424–12
Exports of US, detailed Schedule B commodities with countries of destination, 1991, annual rpt, 2424–10
Farm financial and marketing conditions, forecast 1992, annual chartbook, 1504–8
Farm financial and marketing conditions, forecast 1992, annual conf, 1504–9
Farm income, acreage, prices received, and production costs, for fruit, nut, and berry operations by commodity and region, 1987, article, 1561–6.301
Farm income, cash marketing receipts ranked by commodity and State, 1990, 1548–385
Farm sector balance sheet, and receipts by detailed commodity, by State, 1986-90, annual rpt, 1544–18
Fertilizer and pesticide use and application rates, by type, crop, and State, 1991, 1616–1.3
Fertilizer use and application rates, by type and crop, for California, 1990, 1616–1.2
Foreign and US fresh and processed fruit, vegetable, and nut production and trade, FAS monthly circular with articles, 1925–34
Foreign countries agricultural production, prices, and trade, by country, 1980-91 and forecast 1992, annual world area rpt series, 1524–4
Freight (waterborne domestic and foreign) by commodity, traffic, and passengers, by port and waterway, 1989, annual rpt, 3754–3
Grape (table and wine) production by variety, and wine exports and imports by country, for Brazil, 1991-92, article, 1925–34.341
Grape shipments from California and arrivals by city by mode of transport, prices, and production, by variety, 1970s-90, annual rpt, 1311–25
Grapes crushed and purchased, and grower prices and returns, for California, by type and variety, 1990-91, annual rpt, 1311–30
Imports of fruits and vegetables under quarantine, by crop, country, and port of entry, FY89, annual rpt, 1524–7
Input-output structure of US economy, detailed interindustry transactions for 541 industries, and components of final demand, 1982 benchmark data, 2708–17
Irrigation projects of Reclamation Bur in western US, crop production and acreage by commodity, State, and project, 1990, annual rpt, 5824–12

Kiwifruit acreage, production, and trade, by country, 1985-92, article, 1925–34.314
Kiwifruit from New Zealand at less than fair value, injury to US industry, investigation with background financial and operating data, 1992 rpt, 9886–14.345
Labor productivity, indexes of output, hours, and employment by SIC 2- to 4-digit industry, 1967-90, annual rpt, 6824–1.3
Latin America economic and social conditions, resources, trade, and aid, 1992, annual factbook, 9914–14
Liquor production, stocks, materials used, and taxable and tax-free removals, by State, monthly rpt, 8486–1.3
Manufacturing annual survey, 1990: finances and operations, by SIC 2- to 4-digit industry, series, 2506–14
Manufacturing census, 1987: concentration of largest firms measured by value added, and for shipments by SIC 2- and 4-digit industry, subject rpt, 2497–6
Manufacturing census, 1987: shipments of manufacturers products, by customer class and SIC 2- and 4-digit industry, subject rpt, 2497–4
Manufacturing finances and operations, by SIC 2- to 4-digit industry, forecast 1992, annual rpt, 2044–28
Melon production, acreage, and yield, current and forecast by State, periodic rpt, 1621–12
Melons production, value, and acreage, by State, 1989-91, annual rpts, 1621–25
Mexico fruit trade with US, 1989-91, and US tariffs under proposed North American Free Trade Agreement, 1992, by commodity, article, 1561–6.304
Multinatl US firms and foreign affiliates finances and operations, by industry and country, 1989 benchmark survey, annual rpt, 2704–5
Nutrient, caloric, and waste composition, detailed data for raw, processed, and prepared foods, 1992 rpt, 1356–3.17
Occupational injury and illness rates, by SIC 2- to 4-digit industry, 1989-90, annual rpt, 6844–7
Occupational injury and illness rates, by SIC 2- to 4-digit industry, 1990, annual rpt, 6844–1
OECD trade, total and for 4 major countries, and US trade by country, by commodity, 1980-90, world area rpt series, 9116–1
Peaches production, marketing, and prices in 3 southeastern States and Appalachia, 1991, annual rpt, 1311–12
Pineapple (canned fruit and juice) production and exports, by country, and Mexico export prices, selected years 1987-92, annual article, 1925–34.327
Pineapple (canned fruit and juice) production and exports, for 2 countries, forecast 1992, semiannual article, 1925–34.346
Price indexes (producer), by stage of processing and detailed commodity, monthly rpt, 6762–6
Price indexes (producer), by stage of processing and detailed commodity, monthly 1991, annual rpt, 6764–2
Prices (farm-retail) for food, marketing cost components, and industry finances and productivity, 1920s-91, annual rpt, 1544–9
Prices (wholesale) for fresh fruit and vegetables in NYC, Chicago, and selected shipping points, by crop, 1991, annual rpt, 1311–8
Prices (wholesale) of fruit and vegetables in NYC by State, and shipments and arrivals by mode of transport, by commodity, weekly rpt, 1311–20
Prices (wholesale) of fruit and vegetables in NYC-Newark, and arrivals by mode of transport, by commodity and State, 1990, annual rpt, 1311–21
Prices received and paid by farmers, by commodity and State, monthly rpt, 1629–1
Prices received and paid by farmers, by commodity and State, 1991, annual rpt, 1629–5
Prices received by farmers and production value, by detailed crop and State, 1989-91, annual rpt, 1621–2
Production, farms, acreage, and related data, by selected crop and State, monthly rpt, 1621–1
Production inputs, output, and productivity for farms, by commodity and region, 1947-90, annual rpt, 1544–17
Production, prices, and use of fruit and nuts, annual rpt series, 1621–18
Production, prices, trade, and marketing, by commodity, current situation and forecast, monthly rpt with articles, 1502–4
Production, prices, trade, stocks, and use, by selected crop, periodic situation rpt with articles, 1561–6
Radiation exposure of population near Hanford, Wash, nuclear plant, with methodology, 1944-91, series, 3356–5
Raisin and prune production, trade, use, and stocks, by country, and South Africa production by raisin type, 1988-92, semiannual article, 1925–34.321
Raisin and prune production, trade, use, and stocks, by country, 1989-93, semiannual article, 1925–34.348
Science, engineering, and technical employment in manufacturing, by field and industry, 1989, triennial rpt, 9627–23
Shipments by mode of transport, arrivals, and imports, for fruit and vegetables by commodity and State and country of origin, weekly rpt, 1311–3
Shipments of fruit and vegetables, and arrivals by city, by mode of transport and State and country of origin, 1991, annual rpt series, 1311–4
Shipments, production, and marketing of fruit and vegetables, for Florida, with US trade and prices, by commodity, 1970s-91, annual rpt, 1311–23
Soviet Union and US economic and sociodemographic indicators, selected years 1970-90, handbook, 2328–80
Statistical Abstract of US, 1992 annual data compilation, 2324–1.3; 2324–1.23
Strawberries production, value, and acreage, by State, 1989-91, annual rpts, 1621–25
Strawberry production, acreage, and yield, current and forecast by State, periodic rpt, 1621–12
Strawberry trade of US and Mexico, and Mexico and Chile supply and use, 1987-92, annual article, 1925–34.315
Tax (income) returns of corporations, income and tax items by asset size and detailed industry, 1989, annual rpt, 8304–21
Tax (income) returns of partnerships, income statement and balance sheet items, by industry group, 1990, annual article, 8302–2.314
Truck rates for fruit and vegetables paid by shippers and receivers, by commodity and city, and fleet itemized costs per mile, weekly rpt, 1311–22
Truck rates for fruit and vegetables weekly by growing area and market, and shipments monthly by State and country of origin, 1991, annual rpt, 1311–15
Weight and volume conversion factors for agricultural commodities and products, 1992 rpt, 1508–3
see also Citrus fruits
see also Nuts
see also Vegetables and vegetable products
see also under By Commodity in the "Index by Categories"

Frydl, Edward J.
"Overhangs and Hangovers: Coping with the Imbalances of the 1980s", 9385–2

FTC
see Federal Trade Commission

FTC Communications
Finances and operations, detail for telegraph firms, 1990, annual rpt, 9284–6.3

Fu Associates Ltd.
"Demographic Profiles of the Airway Facilities Work Force, Annual Report, FY90 Year-End Data", 7504–41

Fuel
see terms listed under Energy resources and consumption

Fuel oil
Business statistics, detailed data for major industries and economic indicators, *Survey of Current Business*, monthly rpt, 2702–1.17
Business statistics, detailed data for major industries and economic indicators, 1960-91, *Survey of Current Business* biennial supplement, 2704–1
Commercial buildings energy use, costs, and conservation, by building characteristics, survey rpt series, 3166–8
Consumption of energy, by detailed fuel type, end-use sector, and State, 1960-90, State Energy Data System annual rpt, 3164–39
CPI by component for US city average, and by selected metro area, region, and population size, monthly rpt, 6762–2
Electric power plants and capacity, by fuel used, owner, location, and operating status, 1991 and for units planned 1992-2001, annual listing, 3164–36
Exports and imports between US and outlying areas, by detailed commodity and mode of transport, 1991, annual rpt, 2424–11
Exports and imports of US, by country and detailed commodity, monthly rpt, 2422–12
Exports and imports of US, by Harmonized System 6-digit commodity and country, 1991, annual rpt, 2424–13
Exports of US, detailed Schedule B commodities with countries of destination, 1991, annual rpt, 2424–10

Foreign and US energy production, trade, use, and reserves, and oil and refined products supply and prices, by country, 1981-90, annual rpt, 3164–50
Freight (waterborne domestic and foreign) by commodity, traffic, and passengers, by port and waterway, 1989, annual rpt, 3754–3
Futures and options trading volume, by commodity and exchange, FY91, annual rpt, 11924–2
Futures trading in selected commodities and financial instruments and indexes, for NYC, Chicago, and other markets activity, biweekly rpt, 11922–5
Heating fuels production, imports, stocks, and prices, by selected PAD district and State, seasonal weekly rpt, 3162–45
Housing (low income) energy aid, funding sources, costs, and participation, by State, FY90, annual rpt, 4584–1
Housing (rental) units, total, with HUD assistance by program, and eligible for aid, by unit, household, and neighborhood characteristics, and location, 1989, biennial rpt, 5184–11
Housing and households detailed characteristics, and unit and neighborhood quality, MSA surveys, series, 2485–6
Housing energy prices, by fuel type and State, 1990 and forecast 1991-92, 3166–6.61
Housing energy use, costs, and conservation, and household and housing characteristics, survey rpt series, 3166–7
Housing heating and air conditioning equipment shipments by type of fuel used, quarterly rpt, 2042–1.6
Housing units completed, single and multifamily units by structural and financial characteristics, and location, 1987-91, annual rpt, 2384–1
Manufacturing energy use and prices, by fuel type and industry, 1974-88, 3166–15.3
Pacific basin countries energy supply and demand, and implications for US trade, country rpt series, 3406–6
Pacific Northwest population, households, employment, income, fuel prices, and electricity demand, alternative forecasts 1991-2010, annual rpt, 3224–3.3
Price indexes (producer), by stage of processing and detailed commodity, monthly 1991, annual rpt, 6764–2
Prices and spending for fuel, by type, end-use sector, and State, 1990, annual rpt, 3164–64
Prices and volume of oil products sold and purchased by refiners, processors, and distributors, by product, end-use sector, PAD district, and State, monthly rpt, 3162–11; 3164–85
Prices of fuel, by type, end-use sector, and region, projected 1991-2030, 3166–6.60
Sales and deliveries of fuel oil and kerosene, by end-use, PAD district, and State, 1990, annual rpt, 3164–94
Supply and demand of oil and refined products, refinery capacity and use, and prices, weekly rpt, 3162–32
Supply, demand, and movement of crude oil, gas liquids, and refined products, by PAD district and State, 1991, annual rpt, 3164–2
Supply, demand, and prices, by fuel type and end-use sector, alternative projections by region, 1990-2010, annual rpt, 3164–96
Supply, demand, and prices, by fuel type and end-use sector, alternative projections 1990-2010, annual rpt, 3164–75
Supply, demand, and prices, by fuel type and end-use sector, projections and underlying assumptions, 1995-2010, annual rpt, 3164–90
Supply, demand, and prices, by fuel type and end-use sector, with foreign comparisons, 1991 and trends from 1949, annual rpt, 3164–74.2
Supply, demand, and prices, by fuel type, end-use sector, and country, detailed data, monthly rpt with articles, 3162–24
Supply, demand, and prices, by fuel type, end-use sector, and country, detailed data, monthly 1973-88, 3168–123
Supply, demand, and prices of energy, forecasts by resource type, quarterly rpt, 3162–34
Supply, demand, trade, stocks, and refining of oil and gas liquids, by detailed product, State, and PAD district, monthly rpt with articles, 3162–6
Supply of oil products, EIA and alternative estimates, 1981-90, annual article, 3162–6.302
Transportation energy use by mode, fuel supply, and demographic and economic factors of vehicle use, 1970s-90, annual rpt, 3304–5
VA health care facilities energy use and conservation, by facility, quarterly rpt, 8602–9
Washington State oil spill off northern coast in 1988, pollutant levels and impacts on marine biota, by site, as of 1990, 5738–38

Fuel tax
Budget of US, authoritative financial statements with appropriations, outlays, and receipts, by category and agency, FY91, annual rpt, 8104–2.2
Budget of US, CBO analysis of revenue and spending alternatives and projections of economic indicators, FY93-97, annual rpt, 26304–3
Collections of taxes, by level of govt, type of tax, State, and selected counties, quarterly rpt, 2462–3
DOE Oak Ridge Natl Lab contractors excise tax refunds due from off-highway motor fuel use, 1988-90, 3006–5.26
Energy use by mode of transport, fuel supply, and demographic and economic factors of vehicle use, 1970s-90, annual rpt, 3304–5
Finances of govts, tax systems and revenue, and fiscal structure, by level of govt and State, 1992 and historical trends, annual rpt, 10044–1
Gasoline and diesel fuel Federal and State tax rates, by State, 1991, annual rpt, 3164–85
Gasoline, gasohol, and diesel fuel Federal and State tax rates, monthly rpt, 3162–11
Hwy funding and allocation methods, for Federal-aid system, FY92-97, 7558–107
Hwy Statistics, summary data by State, 1990-91, annual rpt, 7554–24
Income tax returns of individuals, detailed data, 1988, annual rpt, 8304–2
IRS collections, by excise tax source, quarterly rpt, 8302–1
Natl income and product accounts, comprehensive accounts and components, benchmark revisions, 1929-88, 2708–5
Natl income and product accounts, comprehensive accounts and components, *Survey of Current Business*, monthly rpt, 2702–1.26
OPEC oil imports of US, economic impacts of tariffs and excise taxes, model description and results, 1992 technical paper, 9379–12.96
State and local govt tax rates on gasoline and other motor fuel, by jurisdiction, monthly rpt, 7552–1
State govt tax collections by detailed type of tax, and tax rates, by State, FY91, annual rpt, 2466–2.7
State govt tax rates on motor fuel, and gallons taxed, by State, 1991, annual rpt, 7554–1
State govt tax rates on motor fuel, by State, 1981-91, annual table, 7554–32
Statistical Abstract of US, 1992 annual data compilation, 2324–1.21
Tax (excise) collections of IRS, by source, quarterly rpt, 8302–2.1
Transportation infrastructure financing through user fees, with data on hwys, airports, and waterways, 1985-91, 26306–6.170

Fujairah
see United Arab Emirates

Fulbright, J. William, Foreign Scholarship Board
Exchanges under Fulbright-Hays program, grants by purpose, and foreign govt share of costs, by country, FY91, annual rpt, 10324–1

Fulcher, Nancy
"Steel: Semiannual Monitoring Report. Special Focus: Privatization in the Latin American Steel Industry. Report to the Committee on Ways and Means on Investigation No. 332-327 Under Section 332 of the Tariff Act of 1930", 9882–15

Fuldner, Art
"Performance Optimization and Repowering of Generating Units", 3162–35.303

Fullenkamp, Connel R.
"Returns on Capital Assets and Variations in Economic Growth and Volatility: A Model of Bayesian Learning", 9385–8.124

Fuller, Suzanne M.
"Breast Cancer Beliefs of Women Participating in a Television-Promoted Mammography Screening Project", 4042–3.370

Fullerton, Howard N., Jr.
"Evaluation of Labor Force Projections to 1990", 6722–1.334
"Labor Force Projections: The Baby Boom Moves On", 6744–19

Functional limitations
see Mobility limitations

Funerals
see Cemeteries and funerals
see Military cemeteries and funerals

Fungicides
see Pesticides
Furniture and furnishings
Collective bargaining agreements expiring during year, and workers covered, by firm, union, industry group, and State, 1992, annual rpt, 6784–9
Consumer Expenditure Survey, spending by category, selected household characteristics, and region, quarterly rpt, 6762–14
Consumer holdings of durable goods, by type, in current and constant dollars, 1925-90, annual article, 2702–1.305
Consumer holdings of durable goods, by type, in current and constant dollars, 1988-91, annual article, 2702–1.327
Consumer spending, natl income and product account benchmark revisions, 1929-88, 2708–5
Consumer spending, natl income and product accounts, comprehensive accounts and components, *Survey of Current Business*, monthly rpt, 2702–1.25
County Business Patterns, 1989: employment, establishments, and payroll, by SIC 2- to 4-digit industry and county, annual State rpt series, 2326–8
County Business Patterns, 1990: employment, establishments, and payroll, by SIC 2- to 4-digit industry and county, annual State rpt series, 2326–6
CPI by component for US city average, and by selected metro area, region, and population size, monthly rpt, 6762–2
Employment, earnings, and hours, by SIC 1- to 4-digit industry, monthly 1989-Feb 1992, annual rpt, 6744–4
Employment of minorities and women, by occupation, SIC 1- to 3-digit industry, State, and MSA, 1991, annual rpt, 9244–1
Employment, unemployment, and labor force characteristics, by region and census div, 1991, annual rpt, 6744–7.1
Energy use and prices, by fuel type and manufacturing industry, 1974-88, 3166–15.3
Energy use and prices for manufacturing industries, 1988 survey, series, 3166–13
Exports and imports between US and outlying areas, by detailed commodity and mode of transport, 1991, annual rpt, 2424–11
Exports and imports of US, by country and detailed commodity, monthly rpt, 2422–12
Exports and imports of US, by Harmonized System 6-digit commodity and country, 1991, annual rpt, 2424–13
Exports and imports of US, by selected country, country group, and commodity group, 1991, annual rpt, 2044–37
Exports and imports of US, by transport mode, country, and SITC 1- to 3-digit commodity, 1991, annual rpt, 2424–12
Exports, imports, and balances of US for manufactured goods, by SITC 2-digit commodity and country, quarterly rpt, 2042–35
Exports of US, detailed commodities by country, monthly CD-ROM, 2422–13
Exports of US, detailed Schedule B commodities with countries of destination, 1991, annual rpt, 2424–10
Farm finances, assets, liabilities, and debt by lender type, by State, 1960-89, 1548–384
Farm sector balance sheet, and marketing receipts by detailed commodity, by State, 1986-90, annual rpt, 1544–18
Foreign countries market conditions for US textile and apparel exports, with domestic industry operations, country rpt series, 2046–15
Freight (waterborne domestic and foreign) by commodity, traffic, and passengers, by port and waterway, 1989, annual rpt, 3754–3
Hazardous substances industrial releases and reduction methods under EPA regulation, by chemical, source, industry, and location, 1989, annual rpt, 9234–6
Hazardous substances industrial releases and reduction methods under EPA regulation, with chemical stocks and use, facility directory, 1987-89, annual CD-ROM, 9234–7
House of Representatives salaries, expenses, and contingent fund disbursement, detailed listings, quarterly rpt, 21942–1
Imports, exports, and employment impacts, by SIC 2- to 4-digit industry and commodity, quarterly rpt, 2322–2
Imports of textiles under Multifiber Arrangement by product and country, and status of bilateral agreements, 1988-91, annual rpt, 9884–18
Imports of US, detailed commodities by country, monthly CD-ROM, 2422–14
Imports of US given duty-free treatment for value of US material sent abroad, by commodity and country, 1987-90, annual rpt, 9884–14
Injuries from use of consumer products and related activities, by severity and victim age and sex, 1990, annual rpt, 9164–7
Injuries from use of consumer products, by severity, victim age, and detailed product, 1991, annual rpt, 9164–6
Injuries from use of consumer products, related deaths and costs, and recalls by brand, by product type, FY90, annual rpt, 9164–2
Input-output structure of US economy, detailed interindustry transactions for 84 industries, and components of final demand, 1987, annual article, 2702–1.316
Input-output structure of US economy, detailed interindustry transactions for 541 industries, and components of final demand, 1982 benchmark data, 2708–17
Labor productivity, indexes of output, hours, and employment by SIC 2- to 4-digit industry, 1967-90, annual rpt, 6824–1.3
Manufacturing annual survey, 1990: finances and operations, by SIC 2- to 4-digit industry, series, 2506–14
Manufacturing census, 1987: concentration of largest firms measured by value added, and for shipments by SIC 2- and 4-digit industry, subject rpt, 2497–6
Manufacturing census, 1987: shipments of manufacturers products, by customer class and SIC 2- and 4-digit industry, subject rpt, 2497–4
Manufacturing finances and operations, by SIC 2- to 4-digit industry, forecast 1992, annual rpt, 2044–28
Manufacturing industries operations and performance, analytical rpt series, 2506–16
Manufacturing production, shipments, inventories, orders, and pollution control costs, periodic Current Industrial Rpt series, 2506–3
Mexico imports from US, by industry and State, 1987-91, 2048–154
Military and personal property shipments, passenger traffic, and costs, by service branch and mode of transport, FY91, annual rpt, 3704–15
Military prime contract awards, by detailed procurement category, FY88-91, annual rpt, 3544–18
Military Sealift Command shipping operations, finances, and personnel, FY91, annual rpt, 3804–14
Multinatl firms US affiliates finances and operations, by industry, country of parent firm, and State, 1987, 2708–48
Natl income and product accounts and components, *Survey of Current Business*, monthly rpt, 2702–1.23
Occupational injury and illness rates, by SIC 2- to 4-digit industry, 1989-90, annual rpt, 6844–7
Occupational injury and illness rates, by SIC 2- to 4-digit industry, 1990, annual rpt, 6844–1
OECD trade, total and for 4 major countries, and US trade by country, by commodity, 1980-90, world area rpt series, 9116–1
Pollution abatement capital and operating costs, by SIC 2- to 4-digit industry and State, 1990, annual Current Industrial Rpt, 2506–3.6
Price indexes (producer), by stage of processing and detailed commodity, monthly rpt, 6762–6
Price indexes (producer), by stage of processing and detailed commodity, monthly 1991, annual rpt, 6764–2
Price indexes for department store inventories, by class of item, monthly table, 6762–7
Production, prices, employment, and trade, for hardwood lumber and products, quarterly rpt, 1202–4
Retail trade sales and inventories, by kind of business, region, and selected State, MSA, and city, monthly rpt, 2413–3
Retail trade sales, by kind of business, advance monthly rpt, 2413–2
Retail trade sales, inventories, purchases, gross margin, and accounts receivable, by SIC 2- to 4-digit kind of business and form of ownership, 1990, annual rpt, 2413–5
Science, engineering, and technical employment in manufacturing, by field and industry, 1989, triennial rpt, 9627–23
Tax (income) returns of corporations, income and tax items by asset size and detailed industry, 1989, annual rpt, 8304–4; 8304–21
Tax (income) returns of sole proprietorships, income statement items, by industry group, 1990, annual article, 8302–2.317; 8302–2.320
Textile and apparel exports of US, by product group and country, quarterly rpt, 2042–36

Truck transport of household goods, financial and operating data by firm, quarterly rpt, 9482–14
Truck transport of household goods, performance and disposition of damage claims, for selected carriers, 1991, annual rpt, 9484–11
Warehouse services finances, by SIC 3- to 4-digit industry, 1990 survey, annual rpt, 2413–14
Wholesale trade sales and inventories, by SIC 2- to 3-digit kind of business, monthly rpt, 2413–7
see also Antiques
see also Carpets and rugs
see also Floor coverings
see also Household appliances and equipment
see also Household supplies and utensils
see also Wall coverings
see also under By Commodity in the "Index by Categories"
see also under By Industry in the "Index by Categories"

Furry, Marilyn M.
"Overview of Home-Based Work: Results from a Regional Research Project", 1702–1.307

Furs and fur industry
County Business Patterns, 1989: employment, establishments, and payroll, by SIC 2- to 4-digit industry and county, annual State rpt series, 2326–8
County Business Patterns, 1990: employment, establishments, and payroll, by SIC 2- to 4-digit industry and county, annual State rpt series, 2326–6
Exports and imports (agricultural) of US, by commodity and country, bimonthly rpt, 1522–1
Exports and imports (agricultural) of US, by detailed commodity and country, 1991, annual rpt, 1524–8
Exports and imports (agricultural) of US, by detailed commodity and country, 1991, semiannual rpt, 1522–4
Exports and imports between US and outlying areas, by detailed commodity and mode of transport, 1991, annual rpt, 2424–11
Exports and imports of dairy, livestock, and poultry products, by commodity and country, FAS monthly circular, 1925–32
Exports and imports of US, by country and detailed commodity, monthly rpt, 2422–12
Exports and imports of US, by Harmonized System 6-digit commodity and country, 1991, annual rpt, 2424–13
Exports and imports of US, by transport mode, country, and SITC 1- to 3-digit commodity, 1991, annual rpt, 2424–12
Exports of US, detailed Schedule B commodities with countries of destination, 1991, annual rpt, 2424–10
Manufacturing annual survey, 1990: finances and operations, by SIC 2- to 4-digit industry, series, 2506–14
Manufacturing census, 1987: concentration of largest firms measured by value added, and for shipments by SIC 2- and 4-digit industry, subject rpt, 2497–6
Manufacturing census, 1987: shipments of manufacturers products, by customer class and SIC 2- and 4-digit industry, subject rpt, 2497–4
Mink and pelt production, prices, and farms, selected years 1969-92, annual rpt, 1631–7
Price indexes (producer), by stage of processing and detailed commodity, monthly rpt, 6762–6
Price indexes (producer), by stage of processing and detailed commodity, monthly 1991, annual rpt, 6764–2
Tax (luxury) revenue, and related IRS administrative costs, FY91 and projected to FY95, GAO rpt, 26119–385
see also Hides and skins

Future
see Projections and forecasts

Futures trading
Banks (insured commercial and savings) finances, for foreign and domestic offices, by asset size, 1990, annual rpt, 9294–4.2
Cocoa bean futures prices at NYC exchange, 1980s-93, FAS semiannual circular, 1925–9
Cotton prices at selected spot markets, NYC futures prices, and CCC loan rates, 1991/92 and trends from 1944, annual rpt, 1309–2
Cotton prices in 7 spot markets, futures prices at NYC exchange, farm prices, and CCC loan stocks, monthly rpt, 1309–1
Dairy prices, by product and selected area, with related marketing data, 1991, annual rpt, 1317–1
Exchange activity in selected commodities and financial instruments and indexes, for NYC, Chicago, and other markets, biweekly rpt, 11922–5
Fertilizer futures contract price changes, 1980s-91, article, 1561–16.301
Foreign holdings of US futures contracts, by type and country, 1989, article, 8002–4.301
Gold and silver futures trading, Mineral Industry Surveys, monthly rpt, 5612–1.10
Grain futures contracts, stocks in deliverable position by type, weekly tables, 11922–4
Grain futures settlement prices, by commodity and exchange, weekly rpt, 1313–2
Margin requirements for futures contracts, impacts on price volatility, 1970s-89, article, 9375–1.302
Margin requirements on metal and stock index futures contracts, impact on prices, volatility, and trading activity, 1970s-90, technical paper, 9385–8.127
Market decline of Nov 1991, impacts of trading related to option and futures expirations, 9738–22
Metals industries economic performance indicators and indexes, by commodity, monthly rpt, 5602–5
Natural gas futures market, prices and contract activity, 1990-92, article, 3162–4.302
Oil production disruption after Iraq invasion of Kuwait, impacts on futures prices, family budgets, and oil firms, 1990 hearings, 25408–116
Rice market activities, prices, inspections, sales, trade, supply, and use, for US and selected foreign markets, weekly rpt, 1313–8
Rice season average price forecasts using futures settlement prices, 1990-92, article, 1561–8.301
Soybean season average price forecasts using futures settlement prices, 1986-92, article, 1561–3.303
Statistical Abstract of US, 1992 annual data compilation, 2324–1.15; 2324–1.16
Trading activity by commodity and exchange, and Commodity Futures Trading Commission oversight, FY91, annual rpt, 11924–2
Wheat season average price forecasts using futures settlement prices, 1986-92, article, 1561–12.301
see also Options trading

Gabon
Agricultural trade of US, by detailed commodity and country, 1991, annual rpt, 1524–8
Agricultural trade of US, by detailed commodity and country, 1991, semiannual rpt, 1522–4
AID economic aid to developing countries, obligations and disbursements by country, quarterly rpt, 9912–4
Background Notes, summary social, political, and economic data, 1991 rpt, 7006–2.1
Economic and military aid and loans from US and intl agencies, by program and country, FY46-91, annual rpt, 9914–5
Economic conditions, income, production, prices, employment, and trade, 1992 periodic country rpt, 2046–4.36
Economic conditions, policy, and trade practices, by country, 1989-91, annual rpt, 21384–5
Economic, social, political, and geographic summary data, by country, 1992, annual factbook, 9114–2
Exports and imports of US, by commodity and country, 1980-90, world area rpt, 9116–1.2
Exports and imports of US, by transport mode, country, and SITC 1- to 3-digit commodity, 1991, annual rpt, 2424–12
Exports of US, detailed Schedule B commodities with countries of destination, 1991, annual rpt, 2424–10
Human rights conditions in 170 countries, and US economic and military aid, 1991, annual rpt, 21384–3
Military aid of US, arms sales, and training programs costs and budget requests, by program, world region, and country, FY91-93, annual rpt, 7144–13
Military spending, arms trade, and force strengths, with govt spending and population, by country, 1979-89, annual rpt, 9824–1
Minerals Yearbook, Vol 3, 1989: foreign country review of production, trade, and policy, by commodity, annual rpt, 5604–35.1
Oil exports to US by OPEC and non-OPEC countries, monthly rpt, 3162–24.3
Oil exports to US by OPEC and non-OPEC countries, monthly 1973-88, 3168–123.3
Oil production, stocks, use, and trade, by selected country and country group, monthly rpt, 3162–42
Population size, growth rates, and components of change, by country, projected 1990-2020 and trends from 1950, biennial rpt, 2324–9

Refugee migration, and intl aid programs, by world area and country of origin and asylum, 1991, annual rpt, 7004–15
UN voting record and share of votes in agreement with US, by issue, country, and world area, 1991, annual rpt, 7004–18

Gage, B. D.
"Analyses of Natural Gases, 1991", 5604–2

Gagnon, Joseph
"Taxation and Inflation: A New Explanation for Current Account Imbalances", 9366–7.274

Gagnon, Raymond O.
"Office Visits Involving X-rays, National Ambulatory Medical Care Survey: U.S., 1977", 4147–16.6

Gaibler, Floyd D.
"U.S. Dairy Prospects and Programs", 1504–9.1

Gale, Fred
"How Young Farmers Accumulate Farmland", 1541–1.319
"Structural Change in the U.S. Farm Sector, 1974-87: Thirteenth Annual Family Farm Report to Congress", 1504–4

Galloway, Yvonne
"Surveillance for Measles—New Zealand, 1991", 4202–7.321

Gallup Organization
"Residential Fuelwood Consumption in the Southeastern U.S.", 9806–9.12

Galveston, Tex.
CPI by component for US city average, and by region, population size, and for 15 metro areas, monthly rpt, 6762–1
CPI by component for US city average, and by selected metro area, region, and population size, monthly rpt, 6762–2
Freight (waterborne domestic and foreign) by commodity, traffic, and passengers, by port and waterway, 1989, annual rpt, 3754–3.2
Housing starts and completions authorized by building permits in 40 MSAs, quarterly rpt, 2382–9

Gambia
Agricultural trade of US, by detailed commodity and country, 1991, annual rpt, 1524–8
Agricultural trade of US, by detailed commodity and country, 1991, semiannual rpt, 1522–4
AID economic aid to developing countries, obligations and disbursements by country, quarterly rpt, 9912–4
Economic and military aid and loans from US and intl agencies, by program and country, FY46-91, annual rpt, 9914–5
Economic and social conditions of developing countries from 1960s, and Intl Dev Cooperation Agency and AID activities and funding, FY91-93, annual rpt, 9904–4
Economic, social, political, and geographic summary data, by country, 1992, annual factbook, 9114–2
Exports and imports of US, by transport mode, country, and SITC 1- to 3-digit commodity, 1991, annual rpt, 2424–12
Human rights conditions in 170 countries, and US economic and military aid, 1991, annual rpt, 21384–3
Military aid of US, arms sales, and training programs costs and budget requests, by program, world region, and country, FY91-93, annual rpt, 7144–13
Military spending, arms trade, and force strengths, with govt spending and population, by country, 1979-89, annual rpt, 9824–1
Minerals Yearbook, Vol 3, 1989: foreign country review of production, trade, and policy, by commodity, annual rpt, 5604–35.1
Population size, growth rates, and components of change, by country, projected 1990-2020 and trends from 1950, biennial rpt, 2324–9
Refugee migration, and intl aid programs, by world area and country of origin and asylum, 1991, annual rpt, 7004–15
UN voting record and share of votes in agreement with US, by issue, country, and world area, 1991, annual rpt, 7004–18

Gambling
Arrests, by offense, offender characteristics, and location, data compilation, 1992 annual rpt, 6064–6.4
Arrests, by offense, offender characteristics, and location, 1991, annual rpt, 6224–2.2
Court civil and criminal caseloads for Federal district, appeals, and bankruptcy courts, by type of suit and offense, circuit, and district, 1991, annual rpt, 18204–11
Court civil and criminal caseloads for Federal district, appeals, and special courts, 1991, annual rpt, 18204–8
Court criminal case processing in Federal district courts, and dispositions, by offense, district, and offender characteristics, 1989, annual data compilation, 6064–29
Court criminal case processing in Federal district courts, and dispositions, by offense, 1980-91, annual rpt, 6064–31
Drug abuse and treatment among special populations, 1992 conf, 4492–5.2
Juvenile arrests, by sex, race, disposition, and offense, 1990, 6066–27.8
Sentences for Federal crimes, guidelines use and results by offense and district, and Sentencing Commission activities, 1991, annual rpt, 17664–1
Sentences for Federal offenses, guidelines by offense and circumstances, series, 17668–1
Tax (excise) collections of IRS, by source, quarterly rpt, 8302–1
Tax (excise) returns filed, by type of return and IRS district, 1990 and projected 1991-98, annual rpt, 8304–24
Tax (excise) returns filed, by type of tax and IRS region and service center, projected 1991-98 and trends from 1978, annual rpt, 8304–9
Tax (income) withholding and related documents filed, by type and IRS service center, 1991 and projected 1992-99, annual rpt, 8304–22
US attorneys civil and criminal cases by type and disposition, and collections, by Federal district, FY91, annual rpt, 6004–2.1
Wiretaps authorized, costs, arrests, trials, and convictions, by offense and jurisdiction, 1991, annual rpt, 18204–7
see also Horse racing
see also Lotteries
see also Pari-mutuel wagering

Game
see Birds and bird conservation
see Hunting and fishing licenses
see Hunting and trapping
see Wildlife and wildlife conservation

GAO
see General Accounting Office

Garabrant, David H.
"DDT and Related Compounds and Risk of Pancreatic Cancer", 4472–1.314

Garbage
see Landfills
see Refuse and refuse disposal

Garden Grove, Calif.
Housing and households characteristics, and unit and neighborhood quality, by MSA location for 11 MSAs, 1986 survey, supplement, 2485–8

Gardening
see Flowers and nursery products
see Lawn and garden equipment

Gardner, Bruce
"New Demands for Biofuels and Alternative Products", 1504–9.1

Garfinkel, Michelle R.
"Alternative Measures of the Monetary Base: What Are the Differences and Are They Important?", 9391–1.302

Garment industry
see Clothing and clothing industry

Garner, C. Alan
"Will the Real Price of Housing Drop Sharply in the 1990s?", 9381–1.305

Garner, Thesia I.
"Economic Dimensions of Household Gift-Giving", 6886–6.90
"Evaluation of Subjective Poverty Definitions Comparing Results from the U.S. and the Netherlands", 6886–6.84

Garrett, Bonnie
"Effects of Credit Availability, Nonbank Competition, and Tax Reform on Bank Consumer Lending", 9379–12.88

Garrison, Howard H.
"Planned R&D Expenditures of Major U.S. Firms: 1990-91", 9626–6.38

Gary, Ind.
CPI by component for US city average, and by region, population size, and for 15 metro areas, monthly rpt, 6762–1
CPI by component for US city average, and by selected metro area, region, and population size, monthly rpt, 6762–2
Housing starts and completions authorized by building permits in 40 MSAs, quarterly rpt, 2382–9
Wages by occupation, and benefits, for office and plant workers, 1992 survey, periodic MSA rpt, 6785–17.1
see also under By City and By SMSA or MSA in the "Index by Categories"

Gas appliances
see Household appliances and equipment

Gas utilities
see Natural gas and gas industry

Gas wells
see Energy exploration and drilling

Gases
Accidents (occupational) injury and illness rates by SIC 2- to 4-digit industry, and deaths by cause and industry div, 1990, annual rpt, 6844–1
Business statistics, detailed data for major industries and economic indicators, *Survey of Current Business*, monthly rpt, 2702–1.11

Business statistics, detailed data for major industries and economic indicators, 1960-91, *Survey of Current Business* biennial supplement, 2704–1
County Business Patterns, 1989: employment, establishments, and payroll, by SIC 2- to 4-digit industry and county, annual State rpt series, 2326–8
County Business Patterns, 1990: employment, establishments, and payroll, by SIC 2- to 4-digit industry and county, annual State rpt series, 2326–6
Exports and imports between US and outlying areas, by detailed commodity and mode of transport, 1991, annual rpt, 2424–11
Exports and imports of US, by country and detailed commodity, monthly rpt, 2422–12
Exports and imports of US, by Harmonized System 6-digit commodity and country, 1991, annual rpt, 2424–13
Exports and imports of US, by transport mode, country, and SITC 1- to 3-digit commodity, 1991, annual rpt, 2424–12
Exports of US, detailed Schedule B commodities with countries of destination, 1991, annual rpt, 2424–10
Foreign countries mineral production, reserves, and industry role in domestic economy and world supply, world area and country rpt series, 5606–1
Helium and other components of natural gas, analyses of individual wells and pipelines, 1985-91, annual rpt, 5604–2
Helium and other components of natural gas, analyses of individual wells and pipelines, 1986-90, 5608–132
Manufacturing annual survey, 1990: finances and operations, by SIC 2- to 4-digit industry, series, 2506–14
Manufacturing census, 1987: concentration of largest firms measured by value added, and for shipments by SIC 2- and 4-digit industry, subject rpt, 2497–6
Manufacturing census, 1987: shipments of manufacturers products, by customer class and SIC 2- and 4-digit industry, subject rpt, 2497–4
Manufacturing finances and operations, by SIC 2- to 4-digit industry, forecast 1992, annual rpt, 2044–28
Minerals Yearbook, Vol 1, 1989: commodity reviews of production, use, trade, prices, and mining operations, annual rpt, 5604–33
Minerals Yearbook, Vol 1, 1990: commodity reviews of production, reserves, supply, use, and trade, annual rpt series, 5604–20
Minerals Yearbook, Vol 1, 1991: commodity reviews of production, reserves, supply, use, and trade, annual rpt series, 5604–15
Minerals Yearbook, Vol 2, 1989: State reviews of production and sales by commodity, and business activity, annual rpt series, 5604–16
Minerals Yearbook, Vol 2, 1990: State reviews of production and sales by commodity, and business activity, annual rpt series, 5604–22
Minerals Yearbook, Vol 3, 1989: foreign country reviews of production, trade, and policy, by commodity, annual rpt, 5604–35
Price indexes (producer), by stage of processing and detailed commodity, monthly rpt, 6762–6
Price indexes (producer), by stage of processing and detailed commodity, monthly 1991, annual rpt, 6764–2
Production and shipments of industrial gases, by product and State, 1991, annual Current Industrial Rpt, 2506–8.15
Production by State, shipments, trade, and use, by product for inorganic chemicals, 1991, annual Current Industrial Rpt, 2506–8.14
Production of industrial gases, by product, quarterly Current Industrial Rpt, 2506–8.3
Production, prices, trade, use, employment, tariffs, and stockpiles, by mineral, with foreign comparisons, 1987-91, annual rpt, 5604–18
see also Air pollution
see also Liquefied petroleum gas
see also Natural gas and gas industry
see also Natural gas liquids
see also Radon

Gasohol
Consumption of gasohol, and fuel tax exemptions, by State, 1980-91, annual rpt, 3304–5.5
Consumption of gasohol, by State, 1991, annual rpt, 7554–1.1
Consumption of gasoline and other motor fuel by State, and tax rates by jurisdiction, monthly rpt, 7552–1
Consumption of wood, waste, and alcohol fuels, by end-use sector and region, 1990, annual rpt, 3164–97
DOE Oak Ridge Natl Lab contractors excise tax refunds due from off-highway motor fuel use, 1988-90, 3006–5.26
Energy use by mode of transport, fuel supply, and demographic and economic factors of vehicle use, 1970s-90, annual rpt, 3304–5
Oxygenate supply and blending in gasoline, by PAD district, monthly data, weekly rpt, 3162–32.3
Oxygenate supply, blending in gasoline, and plant capacity and use, by PAD district, monthly rpt, 3162–6.4
Pollution (air) emissions of alternative fuels by fuel type, and alcohol fuel production and inputs, 1991 hearing, 25318–82
Tax (excise) rates for motor fuels, by State, 1981-91, annual table, 7554–32
Tax rates for motor fuels, Federal and State, monthly rpt, 3162–11

Gasoline
Auto fuel economy test results for US and foreign makes, 1993 model year, annual rpt, 3304–11
Auto, van, and light truck ownership and operating costs, by vehicle size and year of operation, 1991 model year, biennial rpt, 7554–21
Business statistics, detailed data for major industries and economic indicators, *Survey of Current Business*, monthly rpt, 2702–1.17
Business statistics, detailed data for major industries and economic indicators, 1960-91, *Survey of Current Business* biennial supplement, 2704–1
Consumption of energy, by detailed fuel type, end-use sector, and State, 1960-90, State Energy Data System annual rpt, 3164–39
Consumption of energy by fuel type, and miles traveled, by transport mode, projected 1990-2010 and trends from 1960s, 3008–124
Consumption of gasoline and other motor fuel by State, and tax rates by jurisdiction, monthly rpt, 7552–1
Consumption of gasoline, and taxes, by State, 1990-91, annual rpt, 7554–24
Consumption of motor fuel, by consuming sector and State, 1991, annual rpt, 7554–1.1
CPI by component for US city average, and by selected metro area, region, and population size, monthly rpt, 6762–2
DOE Oak Ridge Natl Lab contractors excise tax refunds due from off-highway motor fuel use, 1988-90, 3006–5.26
Exports and imports between US and outlying areas, by detailed commodity and mode of transport, 1991, annual rpt, 2424–11
Exports and imports of US, by country and detailed commodity, monthly rpt, 2422–12
Exports and imports of US, by Harmonized System 6-digit commodity and country, 1991, annual rpt, 2424–13
Exports of US, detailed Schedule B commodities with countries of destination, 1991, annual rpt, 2424–10
Farm prices received and paid, by commodity and State, monthly rpt, 1629–1
Farm prices received and paid, by commodity and State, 1991, annual rpt, 1629–5
Farm production inputs supply, demand, and prices, 1970s-91 and projected to 1996, article, 1561–16.301
Farm production inputs supply, demand, and prices, 1980s-92, article, 1561–16.304
Farm production itemized costs, by farm sales size and region, 1991, annual rpt, 1614–3
Foreign and US energy production, trade, use, and reserves, and oil and refined products supply and prices, by country, 1981-90, annual rpt, 3164–50
Foreign and US oil production, trade, stocks, and prices, by refined product and country, 1987-90, annual rpt, 3164–50.2
Foreign direct investment in US energy sources by type and firm, and US affiliates operations, as of 1990, annual rpt, 3164–80
Freight (waterborne domestic and foreign) by commodity, traffic, and passengers, by port and waterway, 1989, annual rpt, 3754–3
Futures and options trading volume, by commodity and exchange, FY91, annual rpt, 11924–2
Futures trading in selected commodities and financial instruments and indexes, for NYC, Chicago, and other markets activity, biweekly rpt, 11922–5
Injuries from use of consumer products, by severity, victim age, and detailed product, 1991, annual rpt, 9164–6
Iraq invasion of Kuwait, oil production disruption impacts on futures prices, family budgets, and oil firms, 1990 hearings, 25408–116

Manufacturing annual survey, 1990: finances and operations, by SIC 2- to 4-digit industry, series, 2506–14
Naval Petroleum and Oil Shale Reserves production and revenue by fuel type, sales by purchaser, and wells, by reserve, FY91, annual rpt, 3334–3
Pacific basin countries energy supply and demand, and implications for US trade, country rpt series, 3406–6
Price indexes (producer), by stage of processing and detailed commodity, monthly rpt, 6762–6
Price indexes (producer), by stage of processing and detailed commodity, monthly 1991, annual rpt, 6764–2
Prices and spending for fuel, by type, end-use sector, and State, 1990, annual rpt, 3164–64
Prices and volume of oil products sold and purchased by refiners, processors, and distributors, by product, end-use sector, PAD district, and State, monthly rpt, 3162–11; 3164–85
Prices of fuel, by type, end-use sector, and region, projected 1991-2030, 3166–6.60
Prices, supply, and demand, by fuel type and end-use sector, with foreign comparisons, 1981-90, annual fact book, 3164–76
Statistical Abstract of US, 1992 annual data compilation, 2324–1.15; 2324–1.25
Supply and demand of oil and refined products, refinery capacity and use, and prices, weekly rpt, 3162–32
Supply and demand of oxygenated gasoline in carbon monoxide nonattainment areas, forecast winter 1992/93, article, 3162–24.301
Supply, demand, and movement of crude oil, gas liquids, and refined products, by PAD district and State, 1991, annual rpt, 3164–2
Supply, demand, and prices, by fuel type and end-use sector, alternative projections by region, 1990-2010, annual rpt, 3164–96
Supply, demand, and prices, by fuel type and end-use sector, alternative projections 1990-2010, annual rpt, 3164–75
Supply, demand, and prices, by fuel type and end-use sector, projections and underlying assumptions, 1995-2010, annual rpt, 3164–90
Supply, demand, and prices, by fuel type and end-use sector, with foreign comparisons, 1991 and trends from 1949, annual rpt, 3164–74.1; 3164–74.2
Supply, demand, and prices, by fuel type, end-use sector, and country, detailed data, monthly rpt with articles, 3162–24
Supply, demand, and prices, by fuel type, end-use sector, and country, detailed data, monthly 1973-88, 3168–123
Supply, demand, and prices of energy, forecasts by resource type, quarterly rpt, 3162–34
Supply, demand, trade, stocks, and refining of oil and gas liquids, by detailed product, State, and PAD district, monthly rpt with articles, 3162–6
Supply of oil products, EIA and alternative estimates, 1981-90, annual article, 3162–6.302
Tax rates for motor fuels, Federal and State, monthly rpt, 3162–11
Transit systems finances and operations, by mode, size of fleet and urban area, region, and for 518 systems, 1990, annual rpt, 7884–4
Transportation energy use by mode, fuel supply, and demographic and economic factors of vehicle use, 1970s-90, annual rpt, 3304–5
see also Aviation fuels
see also Diesel fuel
see also Fuel tax
see also Gasohol
see also Gasoline service stations

Gasoline service stations
Business statistics, detailed data for major industries and economic indicators, 1960-91, *Survey of Current Business* biennial supplement, 2704–1
Construction authorized by building permits, by type of construction, region, State, and MSA, quarterly rpt, 2042–1.3
County Business Patterns, 1989: employment, establishments, and payroll, by SIC 2- to 4-digit industry and county, annual State rpt series, 2326–8
County Business Patterns, 1990: employment, establishments, and payroll, by SIC 2- to 4-digit industry and county, annual State rpt series, 2326–6
Credit (installment) outstanding and terms, by lender and credit type, monthly rpt, 9365–2.6
Credit cards held by household income, age, and card type, and debt outstanding, with issuer costs and revenue, 1970s-80, article, 9362–1.306
Employment, earnings, and hours, by SIC 1- to 4-digit industry, monthly 1989-Feb 1992, annual rpt, 6744–4
Foreign direct investment in US energy sources by type and firm, and US affiliates operations, as of 1990, annual rpt, 3164–80
Labor productivity, indexes of output, hours, and employment by SIC 2- to 4-digit industry, 1967-90, annual rpt, 6824–1.4
Mail volume to and from households, use, and views, by class, source, content, and household characteristics, FY87-90, annual rpt, 9864–10
Multinatl firms US affiliates finances and operations, by industry, country of parent firm, and State, 1987, 2708–48
Multinatl US firms and foreign affiliates finances and operations, by industry and country, 1989 benchmark survey, annual rpt, 2704–5
Occupational injury and illness rates, by SIC 2- to 4-digit industry, 1989-90, annual rpt, 6844–7
Occupational injury and illness rates, by SIC 2- to 4-digit industry, 1990, annual rpt, 6844–1
Price competition among gasoline service stations, and divorcement from oil companies, issues with data by firm, city, and State, 1991 hearing, 25528–120
Robberies, by type of premises, population size, and region, 1991, annual rpt, 6224–2.1
Sales and inventories, by kind of retail business, region, and selected State, MSA, and city, monthly rpt, 2413–3
Sales, inventories, purchases, gross margin, and accounts receivable, by SIC 2- to 4-digit kind of business and form of ownership, 1990, annual rpt, 2413–5
Sales of retailers, by kind of business, advance monthly rpt, 2413–2
Tax (income) returns of corporations, income and tax items by asset size and detailed industry, 1989, annual rpt, 8304–4; 8304–21
Tax (income) returns of partnerships, income statement and balance sheet items, by industry group, 1990, annual article, 8302–2.314
Tax (income) returns of sole proprietorships, income statement items, by industry group, 1990, annual article, 8302–2.317; 8302–2.320
see also Automobile repair and maintenance

Gasoline tax
see Fuel tax

Gastonia, N.C.
Housing starts and completions authorized by building permits in 40 MSAs, quarterly rpt, 2382–9

Gastrointestinal diseases
see Digestive diseases

GATT
see General Agreement on Tariffs and Trade

Gatton, David E.
"U.S. Petroleum Supply", 3164–2.1

Gaumer, Gary L.
"Medicare's Prospective Payment System: A Critical Appraisal", 4652–1.312

Gavett, Earle E.
"Alternative Diesel Fuels from Oilseeds", 1504–9.1

Gavin, William T.
"Different Kind of Money Illusion: The Case of Long and Variable Lags", 9377–9.131

Gawalt, John R.
"Planned R&D Expenditures of Major U.S. Firms: 1990-91", 9626–6.38

Gazdar, M. Nasir
"India: Asia Pacific Energy Series Country Report", 3406–6.10
"Pakistan: Asia-Pacific Energy Series Country Report", 3406–6.11

GDP
see Gross Domestic Product

Gee, C. Kerry
"Factors Affecting the Demand for Grazed Forage in the U.S.", 1208–404

Gemstones
Exports and imports between US and outlying areas, by detailed commodity and mode of transport, 1991, annual rpt, 2424–11
Exports and imports of US, by country and detailed commodity, monthly rpt, 2422–12
Exports and imports of US, by Harmonized System 6-digit commodity and country, 1991, annual rpt, 2424–13
Exports of US, detailed Schedule B commodities with countries of destination, 1991, annual rpt, 2424–10
Mineral Industry Surveys, State reviews of production, 1991, preliminary annual rpt, 5614–6
Minerals Yearbook, Vol 1, 1989: commodity reviews of production, use, trade, prices, and mining operations, annual rpt, 5604–33

Minerals Yearbook, Vol 2, 1989: State reviews of production and sales by commodity, and business activity, annual rpt series, 5604–16
Minerals Yearbook, Vol 2, 1990: State reviews of production and sales by commodity, and business activity, annual rpt series, 5604–22
Minerals Yearbook, Vol 3, 1989: foreign country reviews of production, trade, and policy, by commodity, annual rpt, 5604–35
Occupational injuries and incidence, employment, and hours in nonmetallic minerals mines and related operations, 1990, annual rpt, 6664–1
Producers of gemstones, listing, 1991, Mineral Industry Surveys, advance annual rpt, 5614–5.5
Production, prices, trade, use, employment, tariffs, and stockpiles, by mineral, with foreign comparisons, 1987-91, annual rpt, 5604–18
Stockpiling of strategic material by Fed Govt, activity, and inventory by commodity, as of Sept 1991, semiannual rpt, 3542–22
Stockpiling of strategic material, inventories and needs, by commodity, 1992, annual rpt, 3544–37
see also Jewelry

Gendell, Murray
"Trends in Retirement Age by Sex, 1950-2005", 6722–1.332

General Accounting Office
Activities and operations of GAO, and resulting cost savings to Fed Govt, FY91, annual rpt, 26104–1
Administrative law judges views toward establishment of separate ALJ agency, 1992, GAO report, 26119–428
AFDC Job Opportunities and Basic Skills Training program high-risk participants, by State and services received, FY91, GAO rpt, 26121–489
AFDC Job Opportunities and Basic Skills Training program State admin, and Unemployed Parent program caseloads and payments by State, 1991 GAO rpt, 26131–96
Agent Orange exposure cases at VA health centers, and exemptions from copayment requirements, 1989, GAO rpt, 26121–464
Agricultural and water conservation programs of USDA, cost sharing payments and eligibility requirements, FY88-92, GAO rpt, 26113–572
Agricultural export promotion activities of FAS trade offices, operating costs, and funding by program, by country, 1989-90, GAO rpt, 26123–370
AID activities, finances, and staff, by program and country, FY90, GAO rpt, 26123–382
Air travel by Federal officials aboard military aircraft, trips of 11 officials by reason, with costs and reimbursements, 1989-91, GAO rpt, 26111–78
Air travel by Federal officials and Congress aboard military aircraft, and aircraft inventory characteristics, 1989-91, GAO rpt, 26123–384
Aliens (illegal) held in Immigration and Naturalization Service detention facilities pending hearings, and legal aid requests, 1980s-91, GAO rpt, 26119–409
American Samoa govt finances, with data on health and farm spending and employment, mid 1980s-91, GAO rpt, 26123–385
Antitrust criminal enforcement activities of Justice Dept by industry div and offense, sentencing, and labor costs, FY90, GAO rpt, 26119–375
Apprenticeship programs regulation, participation of minorities and women, and earnings, by occupation, 1990, GAO rpt, 26121–446
Arbitration of securities disputes between brokers and investors, outcomes related to forum type and other factors, 1992 GAO rpt, 26119–401
Army Apache helicopter use and performance during Persian Gulf War, 1991, GAO rpt, 26123–378
Army Corps of Engineers dredging contracts to small businesses, costs and bidding activity, FY90-92, GAO rpt, 26113–589
Army Corps of Engineers water resources dev projects, local sponsors views on cooperation and cost sharing, 1991 survey, GAO rpt, 26113–548
Arts funding, by level of govt, State, and selected city, FY86-92, GAO rpt, 26119–371
Asbestos in schools, abatement funding and costs by selected State, 1988-91, GAO rpt, 26113–560
Assets of Fed Govt targeted for disposition, inventories by type, and related employment and contracts, by agency, FY90, GAO rpt, 26119–369
Athletic depts at NCAA Div I schools, staff by race, and income, by sex and position, 1990/91, GAO rpt, 26121–476
Auto rental age restrictions impacts on military personnel, with personnel by age, and rental receipts by company, 1991, GAO rpt, 26123–391
Bank of Credit and Commerce Intl DC office financial statements, 1984-90, GAO rpt, 26119–427
Bankruptcy case admin of Fed Govt, costs and efficiency of 2 programs, 1990-91, GAO rpt, 26119–421
Banks and thrifts contracts with computer data processing vendors, involvement of illegal business transactions, and instn and vendor views, 1985-90, GAO rpt, 26119–374
Banks and thrifts fraud cases, Justice Dept investigation and prosecution activities, 1989-92, GAO rpt, 26119–426
Banks assets valuation impact of market value accounting for debt securities, by bank asset size, 1990, GAO rpt, 26111–77
Banks regulatory agencies of Fed Govt, pay comparability and turnover, by occupation, 1991, GAO rpt, 26119–368
Block grants discretionary spending, congressional changes to set-aside and cost-ceiling requirements for 11 programs, FY82-91, GAO rpt, 26121–466
Board and care home violations of State drug handling and dispensing regulations, for 3 metro areas, 1990-91, GAO rpt, 26121–447
Bone marrow donors, minority recruitment, Federal aid, transplants, costs, payment sources, 1987-92, GAO rpt, 26121–487
Bovine somatotropin (bST) dairy industry use, effectiveness of FDA testing for human and animal safety, 1991, GAO rpt, 26131–101
Budget deficit forecasting accuracy, contributing factors, and analysis of major programs, FY91, annual GAO rpt, 26104–23
Budget deficits impacts on GNP and public and foreign debt, projected under alternative reduction policies, 1990-2020 with intl comparisons from 1981, GAO rpt, 26109–5
Budget of US, authoritative financial statements with appropriations, outlays, and receipts, by category and agency, FY91, annual rpt, 8104–2.2
Budget of US, obligations and authority by function, agency, and program, with summaries and analyses, FY93, annual rpt, 104–2
Bus (intercity) deregulation in 1982, impacts on service, ridership, and State and Federal funding, with background data, 1980s-92, GAO rpt, 26113–583
Cancer (breast) research funding, cases, and deaths, 1970s-90, GAO rpt, 26131–92
Census of Population, 1990: homeless shelter and on-street population counts, assessment of methodology and procedures, GAO rpt, 26119–370
Census of Population, 1990: post-enumeration review of planning and conduct of census, and recommendations for improvement, GAO rpt, 26119–403
Child labor certification and injury reporting procedures of States, relation to proposed Federal guidelines, 1991, GAO rpt, 26121–451
Child support awards, payment status, reasons for nonpayment, and mothers characteristics, by fathers residence in and out of State, 1990, GAO rpt, 26121–442
Child Support Enforcement Program collections for non-AFDC clients, administrative costs, and user fees, by State, with Federal shares of costs, 1990, GAO rpt, 26121–463
Child support overdue payments deducted from wages, interstate enforcement effectiveness, 1991, GAO rpt, 26121–445
Chile trade and investment policies, foreign direct investment, and US agricultural trade and tariffs, 1985-91, GAO rpt, 26119–408
Coal industry retirees pension and health trust funds financial condition, employer contributions, and beneficiaries, late 1970s-92, GAO rpt, 26121–469; 26121–471
Corporations income taxes and effective rates on US, foreign, and worldwide income, by company and industry, 1980s, GAO rpt, 26119–289
Corporations under domestic and foreign control, finances and tax burdens, 1983-87, GAO rpt, 26119–411
Credit unions financial performance and regulation, with background data, 1960s-90, GAO rpt, 26119–364
Customs Service mgmt and trade law enforcement effectiveness, staff and broker survey results, 1992 GAO rpt, 26119–420

Desert areas public grazing acreage, use, fees, and endangered species, 1988-90, GAO rpt, 26113–552
Disability benefit applications under OASDI and SSI, dispositions, awards, and administrative law judge hearing outcomes, by race, 1988, GAO rpt, 26121–459
Drug (heroin) seizures by Federal agencies, with NYC street prices and purity, FY82-91, GAO rpt, 26119–404
Drug (prescription) clinical trials representation of women, and FDA policy guidance, 1988-91, GAO rpt, 26121–486
Drug (prescription) prices charged to wholesalers, retailers, VA, and Fed Govt, for 29 drugs, 1985-91, GAO rpt, 26121–472
Drug (prescription) prices in Canada and US, by brand and vendor, 1991, GAO rpt, 26121–482
Drug abuse and trafficking offenders losing Federal benefits under new sentencing guidelines, by selected characteristics, 1990-91, GAO rpt, 26119–398
Drug abuse and trafficking reduction research funding by Natl Inst on Drug Abuse and Office of Justice Programs, 1970s-91, GAO rpt, 26131–99
Drug enforcement activities of DOD, funding by purpose, FY89-91, GAO rpt, 26123–390
Drug enforcement communications network for Federal agencies, funding for equipment and DOD support, FY88-91 and projected to FY87, GAO rpt, 26123–372
Earthquake risk for Federal buildings and employees, by agency and region, 1989, with location and size of major events from 1600s, GAO rpt, 26119–399
Eastern Europe economic aid by donor country, and Poland and Hungary exports by world area, 1988-91, GAO rpt, 26123–386
Education (compensatory) grants, and allocation by function, for 8 school districts, 1990/91, GAO rpt, 26121–478
Education in science and math, teacher dev project of Education Dept, school district participation by State, 1989/90, GAO rpt, 26121–488
Employee benefits tax exclusion, Federal revenue forgone and coverage indicators, by benefit type, 1950s-80s and projected to 1995, GAO rpt, 26119–389
Employee-mgmt relations in Fed Govt, program operations and effectiveness, agency and union representatives views, 1990-91 surveys, GAO rpt, 26119–367
Employee recruitment for Federal entry-level professional positions, reasons for accepting or declining offer, 1990 surveys, GAO rpt, 26119–387
Employees and hirees background checks by OPM, efficiency, and Federal agency managers views on timeliness and quality, FY90, GAO rpt, 26119–373
Employees of Fed Govt moonlighting, selected characteristics of 2nd job and Federal position, FY88-90, GAO rpt, 26119–386
Employees reporting misconduct in Fed Govt, awareness of protection and other factors influencing reporting, 1992 survey, GAO rpt, 26119–413
Employment (civilian) of Fed Govt, by demographic characteristics and agency, 1990, GAO rpt, 26119–383
Employment (noncareer) of Fed Govt, conversions to career appointments, by pay grade and agency, 1988-89, GAO rpt, 26119–382
Employment discrimination complaints, processing and counseling costs, by agency, FY91, GAO rpt, 26119–388
Employment of veterans by Federal agency, and hiring practices, 1988-91, GAO rpt, 26119–391
Employment recruitment visits at colleges by Federal agencies and private companies, and school officials views, 1991, GAO rpt, 26119–377
Endangered species listing and mgmt activities of Fish and Wildlife Service and Natl Marine Fisheries Service, FY74-91, GAO rpt, 26113–578
FAA research funding and staff, by research area and project, FY88-91, GAO rpt, 26113–565
Farm crop insurance participation, private insurers and Fed Crop Insurance Corp finances, and disaster aid costs by program, 1980s-92, GAO rpt, 26113–556
Farm crop subsidies of USDA, deficiency payments by payment size and producer form of organization, 1990, GAO rpt, 26113–574
Farm price, production, and supply forecasts used for USDA commodity program outlays, accuracy, 1975-88, GAO rpt, 26131–94
FDA regulations dev timeliness, with status and processing time for selected regulations, 1991, GAO rpt, 26121–453
Fed Crop Insurance Corp financial performance, and effect of alternative price forecasts on program costs, 1983-89, GAO rpt, 26131–95
Fed Govt agencies programs and services performance evaluation measures use, dev, and effectiveness, 1991 survey, GAO rpt, 26119–396
Fed Govt employees views on work condition, 1991 survey, GAO rpt, 26119–406
Fed Transit Admin grants by State, and oversight, 1988-92, GAO rpt, 26113–600
Firearms dealers licensed by Bur of Alcohol, Tobacco and Firearms, views on regulatory inspections, 1992 survey, GAO rpt, 26119–429
Fish (salmon) conservation spending by organization, and population, for Columbia River basin, 1970-91, GAO rpt, 26113–577
FmHA loan guarantees to business and industry in rural areas, by State and industry, and closures and defaults, FY74-91, GAO rpt, 26113–591
FmHA loans, delinquencies, and lending practices, by loan program, FY88-91, GAO rpt, 26113–569
Food aid program of USDA for women, infants, and children, prenatal participation effects on birthweight and health and social welfare costs, 1960s-90, GAO rpt, 26121–458
Food assistance program in Puerto Rico, funding and restrictions, FY90-91, GAO rpt, 26113–580
Foreign countries interests represented by former US govt officials, activities and individuals, FY86-91, GAO rpt, 26123–134
Forest Service recreation uses fund outlays by purpose, and wilderness mgmt funds reprogrammed to other activities, FY88-90, GAO rpt, 26113–550
Hazardous waste generation reduction, accuracy of voluntary industry programs rpts to EPA, 1992 GAO rpt, 26131–98
Health care services assessment for insurance firms, utilization review organizations finances, operations, and staff, 1990, GAO rpt, 26121–490
Health care spending per capita by State, 1990, and relation to income, services availability, rate control, and other factors, 1982, GAO rpt, 26121–444
Health insurance programs for Federal civilian employees, enrollment, profits, and administrative costs, by plan, 1984-90, GAO rpt, 26119–376
Hispanic Americans health insurance coverage, by source, employment and poverty status, and origin, 1987-90, GAO rpt, 26131–97
Homeless persons aid programs of Fed Govt, program descriptions and funding, by agency and State, FY87-91, annual GAO rpt, 26104–21
Homeless persons housing and support services projects, funding, and clients, by organization, FY87 and FY90, GAO rpt, 26113–593
Homeless persons housing in rehabilitated single occupancy units, funding and characteristics, by city, FY87-91, GAO rpt, 26113–596
Homeless persons transitional housing and support services program, outcome relation to client characteristics and services, FY87-90, GAO rpt, 26113–549
Housing (low income) eligibility, tenants reported income agreement with tax records, 1989-90, GAO rpt, 26121–468
Housing (low income rental) in rural areas, FmHA loans and impacts of programs to maintain supply and to deter mortgage prepayment, 1988-91, GAO rpt, 26113–586
Housing (public) for aged, placement of younger mentally disabled tenants, behavioral problems, and services, 1990 survey, GAO rpt, 26113–590
Hurricane Hugo disaster loan offices of SBA, staff and salary and support costs, for Puerto Rico and Virgin Islands, 1989-91, GAO rpt, 26113–576
Hydroelectric power plants licensing by FERC, impacts of environmental laws, with staffing and plant safety incidents, 1980s-90s, GAO rpt, 26113–599
Indian land ownership, multiple ownership, and Bur of Indian Affairs records maintenance, for 12 reservations, 1991, GAO rpt, 26113–559
Indian reservations dams with safety problems, Bur of Indian Affairs and tribal mgmt, and Interior Dept funding, 1980s-91, GAO rpt, 26113–558
Indians and Alaska Natives organizations AFDC Job Opportunities and Basic Skills Training programs, funding and eligibility, FY91, GAO rpt, 26121–460

Info storage and transmission on electronic formats, costs and revenues for 4 Federal agencies, FY85-91, GAO rpt, 26125–47
Insurance (health) provided by employer, costs and cost factors by industry div and firm size, 1987-91, GAO rpt, 26121–485
Insurance (health) reforms of States to improve small business access, provisions with background data by State, 1991, GAO rpt, 26121–462
Insurance (health) under multiple employer welfare arrangements, coverage, unpaid claims, and regulation, by State, 1988-91, GAO rpt, 26121–443
Insurance (life and health) company failures, and State guaranty fund assessments, by State, 1975-90, GAO rpt, 26119–392
Investigations of Federal agency and program operations, summaries of findings, as of 1991, annual GAO rpt, 26104–5
IRS ethical climate, misconduct, reporting and retaliation, and staff and mgmt integrity, employees views, 1991 GAO rpt, 26119–366
IRS undercover criminal investigations and costs by criminal activity, and success rates, by region, mid 1980s-90, GAO rpt, 26119–394
Japan and US technological info transfer activities, and researcher and student exchanges, 1988-89, GAO rpt, 26123–379
Job Training Partnership Act State and local admin, funding, effectiveness, and participants, GAO rpt series, 26106–8
Justice Dept employee misconduct investigations, by type of allegation and penalty, 1988-90, GAO rpt, 26119–380
Kuwait oil fires set by Iraqi forces, air pollution levels, health effects, intl monitoring activities, and wells affected, 1991, GAO rpt, 26113–566
Labs of Fed Govt, technology transfer to small manufacturers, promotional programs activities and grants to States, late 1980s-91, GAO rpt, 26113–551
Livestock grazing on natl rangeland, BLM mgmt, officials views, 1980s-90, GAO rpt, 26113–567
Loans of Treasury Dept and Federal Financing Bank to Govt corporations and agencies, outstanding amounts, 1987-91, GAO rpt, 26111–79
Mail volume and employment of USPS, impacts of competition and rate increases, with evaluation of alternative forecast models, 1970s-80s and forecast to 1995, GAO rpt, 26119–384
Marshall Islands Nuclear Claims Trust Fund financial condition, and health care benefits and enrollment, 1987-92, GAO rpt, 26123–405
Maternal and child health services block grant beneficiary and taxpayer equity among States, issues, alternative allocation formulas, and background data, 1992 GAO rpt, 26121–454
Meat production, inventory, and price forecasts of USDA, accuracy, 1980s, GAO rpt, 26131–93
Meat trade of US and Canada, inspection activity, 1989-91, GAO rpt, 26113–595
Medicare supplemental private insurance loss ratio performance, by firm, 1988-89, GAO rpt, 26121–452
Mexico maquiladora plants environmental regulation enforcement activities, staff, and funding, 1989-92, GAO rpt, 26119–416
Mexico trade with US and other countries, foreign investment, and maquiladoras operations, 1980s-91, GAO rpt, 26119–417
Mexico-US trade agreement impacts on truck traffic at border crossings, Customs Service staff needs, and hwy improvement costs, projected to 2000 with trends from 1986, GAO rpt, 26123–368
Michigan local areas economic conditions and public services impacts of reductions in Federal aid, with background data, 1970s-91, GAO rpt, 26121–483
Military and personal property shipments by commercial cariers, and cost savings from bill audits and rate negotiations, FY99-91, GAO rpt, 26123–369
Military base closings in Germany, US liability for local natl employee severance pay, projected FY91-95, GAO rpt, 26123–383
Military bases underground storage tanks for hazardous substances, DOD compliance with EPA regulations, 1988-91, GAO rpt, 26123–395
Military biological warfare agent vaccine dev and production of Salk Inst, and Army contract costs by component, late 1970s-91, GAO rpt, 26123–374
Military budget and outlays, contracts, active-duty and civilian personnel, and defense industry employment, FY85-93, GAO rpt, 26123–399
Military contractor debts owed to Fed Govt and deferred, status by service branch and firm, 1980-91, GAO rpt, 26123–400
Military disability retirement cases, by disposition, tenure, and whether receiving VA benefits, 1980s-90, GAO rpt, 26121–470
Military homosexual personnel discharges by pay grade, tenure, race, sex, and occupation, and investigations, by service branch, 1980s-90, GAO rpt, 26123–392
Military officers newly commissioned, share from service academies, and academy attrition, 1970s-91 and projected to FY97, GAO rpt, 26123–389
Military personnel occupational distribution, by race, sex, and service branch, FY90, GAO rpt, 26123–381
Military personnel reductions planned by service branch, and women and minorities affected by Army and Air Force plans, FY90-91, GAO rpt, 26123–373
Military procurement fraud cases dispositions, fines, and settlements, for top 100 firms, 1981-92, GAO rpt, 26119–423
Military service academies prep schools costs and student performance indicators, 1988-90, GAO rpt, 26123–380
Military supplies theft and fraud losses, and inventory control measures adequacy, 1988-91, GAO rpt, 26123–377
Military training accidents, and deaths by cause, by service branch, FY88-91, GAO rpt, 26123–397
Minority business Federal procurement set-aside contracts, by State, FY90, GAO rpt, 26113–563
Money laundering investigation activities of States and Fed Govt, and use of IRS large cash transaction rpts, by State, 1985-91, GAO rpt, 26119–430
Money laundering investigations by Treasury Dept, civil penalty cases workload, processing, and disposition, 1985-91, GAO rpt, 26119–390
NATO military base construction projects, and US funding, by project status, 1985-93, GAO rpt, 26123–388
Navy ship construction contract costs and funding, FY83-91, GAO rpt, 26123–401
Neighborhood Reinvestment Corp contracting practices and oversight of local grantees, with grantee listing, FY88-91, GAO rpt, 26113–587
Nicaragua economic and dev aid of US by type, and foreign debt by creditor, FY90-91, GAO rpt, 26123–398
Nuclear power plant safety inspection activities and emergency response procedures of Intl Atomic Energy Agency since 1986 Chernobyl accident, 1991, GAO rpt, 26123–367
Nuclear weapons facilities of DOE, security deficiencies by type and facility, 1989-90, GAO rpt, 26113–557
OASDI and SSI benefit overpayments, and overpaid beneficiaries characteristics, late 1970s-90, GAO rpt, 26121–484
Occupational exposure to hazardous substances, employer compliance with info and training regulations, employer views by firm size and industry div, 1989-91, GAO rpt, 26121–456
Occupational exposure to hazardous substances, employer compliance with info and training regulations, inspections, and fines, by firm size and industry div, 1989-91, GAO rpt, 26121–439
Occupational Safety and Health Admin penalties assessed compared to maximum allowable, by firm size and region, FY89, GAO rpt, 26121–455
Occupational safety enforcement activities of Federal and State agencies, inspections, closure orders, and violations contested and upheld, FY91, GAO rpt, 26121–461
Oil company overcharge settlements funds received, and conservation and energy aid spending, by outlying area, 1990, GAO rpt, 26113–564
Older persons in poverty, by health, nutrition, assistance, and other characteristics, 1990, GAO rpt, 26131–100
Pacemaker lead implants, failures, and costs, by model, 1992 GAO rpt, 26131–103
Pension plan survivor benefits and coverage of spouses, by income level, age, and sex, 1989, GAO rpt, 26121–450
Persian Gulf War aircraft, tank, and personnel carrier deployment and operating capability, and spare parts availability, 1990-91, GAO rpt, 26123–375
Persian Gulf War allied and other countries cash and in-kind contributions, by type and country, 1990-91, GAO rpt, 26123–371
Persian Gulf War allied countries cash and in-kind contributions, by type and country, and status of DOD accounts, as of Sept 1991, annual GAO rpt, 26104–24

Persian Gulf War chemical protective suits and masks contractor deliveries and field inspections, 1990-91, GAO rpt, 26123–387
Persian Gulf War Operation Desert Storm deployment, by sex, race, rank, and service branch, 1990-91, GAO rpt, 26123–394
Pesticide residue in food imports, FDA enforcement, with contaminated shipments distributed, damages assessed and paid, and repeat offenders, FY88-90, GAO rpt, 26113–598
Pesticide residue on Mexico fruit and vegetable exports to US, US and Mexico standards and violations, FY79-91, GAO rpt, 26113–585
Physical fitness clubs memberships for Federal employees, agency costs, and personnel directors views on OPM guidelines and admin leave use, 1991-92, GAO rpt, 26119–393
Physicians in community and migrant health centers, hospital admitting privileges status and issues, 1991, GAO rpt, 26121–465
Pipelines inspections using internal electronic devices, costs and effectiveness, 1985-91, GAO rpt, 26113–594
Pollution (air) emissions of aircraft compared to other sources, by pollutant, 1989, GAO rpt, 26113–562
Pollution (water) discharge permits, and EPA info system coverage and costs, 1991-92, GAO rpt, 26125–46
Postal employees work hour allocations in offices with high and low workloads, effectiveness, FY89-90, GAO rpt, 26119–379
Postal Service automation impacts on labor hours, by task, 1990-91 with projected use of selected equipment to 1995, GAO rpt, 26119–395
Postal Service on-time delivery of 1st class mail, impacts of standards revisions, 1990-91, GAO rpt, 26119–431
Poverty status of families, by detailed characteristics, 1980 and 1988, GAO rpt, 26131–102
Prison construction and operating costs, capacity, and inmates, for Federal and State facilities, 1985-89, GAO rpt, 26119–407
Prison employment requirements for new and expanded Federal facilities, by occupation, FY87-95, GAO rpt, 26119–397
Public lands access restricted by private landowners, reasons and impacts on recreation and land mgmt activities, 1991-92 surveys, GAO rpt, 26113–571
Public rangeland livestock grazing allotments, permits, acreage, and stocking rates, by BLM State office, as of Sept 1991, GAO rpt, 26113–582
Publications of GAO, FY91, annual listing, 26104–17
Publications of GAO, topical listings, series, 26106–10
Quality mgmt practices of Fed Govt, employee views, 1992 survey, GAO rpt, 26119–425
R&D funding by Fed Govt for higher education instns, indirect costs and effects of alternative reimbursement policies, FY89, GAO rpt, 26113–592
R&D licenses for university activities supported by NSF and NIH, transfer to private firms, related income, and scientists associated with licensees, FY89-90, GAO rpt, 26113–575
Railroad (Amtrak) finances, executive office travel expenses and staff years, and membership dues by assn, FY88-92, GAO rpt, 26113–573
Railroad accidents caused by human factors, and safety impacts of engineer work scheduling, 1989-90, GAO rpt, 26113–579
Resolution Trust Corp assets disposition, use of private contractors, fees paid, and location of assets, 1990-91, GAO rpt, 26119–424
Resolution Trust Corp obligation limits compliance, and balance sheet, quarterly GAO rpt, 26102–6
Resolution Trust Corp real estate assets marketing activities, real estate industry views, 1991 survey, GAO rpt, 26119–422
Romania energy production and trade, 1970s-91, with capital investment projected to 2000, GAO rpt, 26123–402
Romania trade with US, and US import tariff rates, by commodity, 1985-91, GAO rpt, 26119–414
Savings instns failures, Resolution Trust Corp sales of real estate and other assets, 1990-91, GAO rpt, 26119–372
School lunch programs food donations processing, contracts, and processors problems with State reporting requirements, with data by State, 1989-91, GAO rpt, 26113–555
Securities Investor Protection Corp regulatory activity and finances, 1970s-91, GAO rpt, 26119–419
Semiconductor industry R&D consortium funding, outlays, and effectiveness in improving US competitive position, 1980s-92, GAO rpt, 26113–588
Senior Executive Service members views on work environment, 1989 and 1991 surveys, GAO rpt, 26119–402
Senior Executive Service noncareer and Schedule C appointments, by agency, 1990-91, GAO rpt, 26119–412
Sentences for Federal offenses, guidelines impacts on sentence disparity by offender race and other characteristics, 1985-90, GAO rpt, 26119–415
Ships in Natl Defense Reserve Fleet, use in Persian Gulf War, and revenue from scrap sales, 1987-91, GAO rpt, 26123–376
Small Business Admin direct and guaranteed loans, principal outstanding, and losses, by program, borrower race and sex, and State, 1950s-90, GAO rpt, 26113–554
Small Business Admin guaranteed loans issued under regular, certified, and preferred lender programs, selected characteristics, FY83-90, GAO rpt, 26113–581
Small business loan collateral adequacy for failed firms, with loan liquidation recoveries and losses, FY89, GAO rpt, 26113–553
Small business R&D grants of Fed Govt, project sales by type and dev funding by source, by agency and selected firm, 1984-91, GAO rpt, 26113–393
South America oil production, investment needs, and exports, for 8 countries, 1980s-90 and projected to 2010, GAO rpt, 26123–396
Soviet Union former Republics and Baltic States, US embassy positions planned by function, and filled, 1992, GAO rpt, 26123–403
SSA and IRS reconciliation of employer wage report records, late 1970s-80s, GAO rpt, 26121–477
State and local govt finances, obligations and resources compared to Fed Govt, 1960s-90, GAO rpt, 26121–457
Student Community Service Learning work-study program, earnings and operations, 1986-90, GAO rpt, 26121–449
Student guaranteed loan participation and default rates, for correspondence schools, FY87-89, GAO rpt, 26121–448
Student guaranteed loan Stafford program, Education Dept collection of lender origination fees, 1980s-91, GAO rpt, 26121–467
Student loan Perkins program income, losses, and Federal and school contributions, late 1950s-89, GAO rpt, 26121–440
Student supplemental and parent loans and defaults, for freshmen and other students, by whether proprietary instn, FY89-91, GAO rpt, 26121–473
Tax (income) aid telephone system of IRS, improvements in accuracy, 1989-91, GAO rpt, 26119–418
Tax (income) compliance issues for large firms, with income, taxes paid, and tax credits, 1988, GAO rpt, 26119–405
Tax (income) earned income credit advance payment option, participation, taxpayer awareness, employer burden, and IRS admin, 1989-90, GAO rpt, 26119–378
Tax (income) returns filed using alternative methods, with fraud, and conventional form preparation time and processing costs, 1986-92, GAO rpt, 26119–400
Tax (luxury) revenue, and related IRS administrative costs, FY91 and projected to FY95, GAO rpt, 26119–385
Tax deductions for amortization of intangible assets from acquired businesses, IRS unresolved audits, and claims allowed, 1991 GAO rpt, 26119–365
Technology-intensive industries intl competitiveness, with background data by industry and foreign comparisons, 1960s-91, GAO rpt, 26123–406
Transit fare subsidies by employers, participation, and parking costs, by selected city, 1985-92, GAO rpt, 26113–597
Transit fare subsidies for Federal employees, costs and participation by agency, 1992, GAO rpt, 26113–601
Transit systems and hwys in urban areas, Federal aid by selected State, aggregate FY76-91, GAO rpt, 26113–570
Treasury tax and loan account deposits, Fed Reserve Banks mgmt of securities held as collateral, 1991, GAO rpt, 26111–80
Trucks (long combination) hwy use and size restrictions, and accidents, by State, 1980s-90, GAO rpt, 26113–568

UN peacekeeping operations costs by mission, and assessment rates by country, 1948-92, GAO rpt, 26123–404
Unemployed displaced worker training programs spending, participation, and placements by State, 1990, GAO rpt, 26121–481
UNESCO fiscal mgmt, spending, staff, and funding sources, mid 1970s-92, GAO rpt, 26123–84
Uranium imports impacts on US industry, with data on DOE enrichment program and stocks, 1980s-92, GAO rpt, 26113–584
USDA revenue, by source and subagency, FY88-92, GAO rpt, 26113–602
VA health care services income eligibility and copayment enforcement, and revenue forgone from unreported income, 1987-91, GAO rpt, 26121–479
VA hospitals compliance with accreditation commission quality assurance standards, by facility and region, 1989-90, GAO rpt, 26121–441
VA payments to private health care providers, by VA clinic, FY90, GAO rpt, 26121–474
Washington State govt employees comparable worth agreement, compliance costs and indicators of success, mid 1980s-93, GAO rpt, 26119–410
Wastewater treatment plants construction loan funds for local govts, costs and State officials views by State, projected 1991-2000, GAO rpt, 26113–561
Water (groundwater) pesticide contamination, vulnerability indicators by State and county, 1987-89, GAO rpt, 26131–91
Workers compensation costs of Fed Govt, and vocational rehabilitation costs and workload, FY82-90, GAO rpt, 26119–381

General Agreement on Tariffs and Trade
Export and import product standards under GATT, Natl Inst of Standards and Technology info activities, and proposed standards by agency and country, 1991, annual rpt, 2214–6
Exports and imports, trade agreements and relations, and USITC investigations, 1991, annual rpt, 9884–5

General aviation
Accidents and circumstances, for US operations of domestic and foreign airlines and general aviation, periodic rpt, 9612–1
Accidents, deaths, and circumstances, by carrier and carrier type, preliminary 1991, annual press release, 9614–9
Air traffic control and airway facilities improvement activities under Aviation System Capital Investment Plan, 1981-91 and projected to 2006, annual rpt, 7504–12
Aircraft registered with FAA, by type and characteristics of aircraft, make, carrier, State, and county, 1991, annual rpt, 7504–3
Atlantic Ocean intl air traffic and passengers, by aviation type and route, alternative forecasts 1992-2010 and trends from 1982, annual rpt, 7504–44
Hijacking attempts and airport security operations, screening results, and enforcement actions, 1990, annual rpt, 7504–49
Hijackings, on-board explosions, and other crime, US and foreign incidents, 1986-90, annual rpt, 7504–31
Instrument flight rule aircraft handled, by user type, FAA traffic control center, and region, FY85-91 and projected to FY2005, annual rpt, 7504–15
Pilots and nonpilots certified by FAA, by certificate type, age, sex, region, and State, 1991, annual rpt, 7504–2
Traffic, aircraft, carriers, airports, and FAA activities, detailed data, 1981-90, annual rpt, 7504–1
Traffic, aircraft, pilots, airports, and fuel use, forecast FY92-2003 and trends from FY82, annual rpt, 7504–6
Traffic and other aviation activity forecasts of FAA, 1992 annual conf, 7504–28
Traffic and passenger and freight enplanements, by airport, 1960s-91 and projected to 2010, hub area rpt series, 7506–7
Traffic and passenger enplanements, by airport, region, and State, projected FY92-2005 and trends from FY83, annual rpt, 7504–7
Traffic levels at FAA air traffic control facilities, by airport and State, FY91, annual rpt, 7504–27

General Motors Corp.
Energy economy test results, 1993 model year, annual rpt, 3304–11
Production and inventory control system efficiency at GMC, model description and results, 1992 working paper, 9375–13.87
Safety of domestic and foreign autos, crash test results by model, model years 1987-91, 7768–111
Safety of domestic and foreign autos, crash test results by model, press release series, 7766–7

General Services Administration
Activities and finances of GSA, FY91, annual rpt, 9454–1
Advisory committees of Fed Govt, and members, staff, meetings, and costs by agency, FY91, annual rpt, 9454–18
Assistance (financial and nonfinancial) of Fed Govt, 1992 base edition, annual listing, 104–5
Budget of US, authoritative financial statements with appropriations, outlays, and receipts, by category and agency, FY91, annual rpt, 8104–2.2
Budget of US, obligations and authority by function, agency, and program, with summaries and analyses, FY93, annual rpt, 104–2
Education funding by Federal agency, program, and recipient type, and instn spending, 1960s-91, annual rpt, 4824–8
Fraud and abuse in GSA programs, audits and investigations, 1st half FY92, semiannual rpt, 9452–8
Info Security Oversight Office monitoring of Federal security measures and classification actions, FY91, annual rpt, 9454–21
Labor unions recognized in Fed Govt, agreements and membership by agency and facility, as of Jan 1991, biennial listing, 9844–14
Natl Archives historical materials, final inventories, series, issuing agency transfer, 9456–3
Natl Archives historical statistical materials, special collections, series, issuing agency transfer, 9456–1

Generalized System of Preferences
see Tariffs and foreign trade controls

Generating plants
see Electric power plants and equipment

Generic products
Fruit and vegetable processing industry in California, workers affected by plant closings, 1977-86, working paper, 6366–6.5

Genetic defects and diseases
Cancer (breast) death risk by presence of genetic mutations, and family breast cancer history, 1977-82, article, 4472–1.317
Cancer (breast) progression relation to loss of chromosomal heterozygosity, 1984-91 local area study, article, 4472–1.310
Cancer (breast) risk for women relation to incidence among male relatives, 1978-79, article, 4472–1.330
Cancer (breast) severity relation to HER-2/neu gene amplification and overexpression, 1992 study, 4472–1.337
Cancer (breast) tumor genetic mutations, and presence relation to patient survival, 1992 article, 4472–1.329
Cancer (breast) tumors with genetic mutations, 1992 article, 4472–1.305
Cancer (cervical) relapse and metastasis risk related to c-myc gene overexpression and human papillomavirus infection, 1984-88 study, article, 4472–1.348
Cancer (colon) risk relation to genetic mutation, 1925-65 British study, article, 4472–1.311
Cancer (esophageal) risk for relatives of cases in Yaocun Commune, Linxian, PRC, 1989, article, 4472–1.315
Cancer (leukemia) patients ras oncogene activation risk from occupational dust and chemical exposure, 1992 article, 4472–1.352
Cancer (liver) patients with tumor suppression gene p53 mutations, by hepatitis B virus seropositivity, for US, Hawaii, and PRC, 1992 article, 4472–1.353
Cancer (ovarian and lung) MDR1 gene levels, by type of treatment, 1992 article, 4472–1.345
Cancer (prostate) risk relation to presence of genetic mutations, 1992 article, 4472–1.322
Cancer (Wilms' tumor) patients with WT1 gene in kidney tissue, 1992 article, 4472–1.304
HHS financial aid, by program, recipient, State, and city, FY91, annual regional listings, 4004–3
Mental illness biological factors, with cases, research funding, and treatment methods, for major disorders, 1980s-91, 26356–9.4
Research on population and reproduction, Natl Inst of Child Health and Human Dev funding and activities, 1991, annual rpt, 4474–33
see also Hereditary diseases

Genetic engineering
see Biotechnology

Genetics
Fish and shellfish aquaculture in US and Japan, mgmt, methods, and biological data for selected species, 1989 conf, annual rpt, 2164–15
HHS financial aid, by program, recipient, State, and city, FY91, annual regional listings, 4004–3
Higher education grad programs enrollment in science and engineering, by field, source of funds, and characteristics of student and instn, 1990, annual rpt, 9627–7
Natl Inst of General Medical Sciences activities, budget, and research and training funding by program, FY91, annual rpt, 4474–38
Research on population and reproduction, Natl Inst of Child Health and Human Dev funding and activities, 1991, annual rpt, 4474–33
see also Biotechnology
see also Genetic defects and diseases
see also Hereditary diseases

Genito-urinary diseases
see Sexually transmitted diseases
see Urogenital diseases

Gentile, Claudia
"Exploring New Methods for Collecting Students' School-Based Writing. NAEP's 1990 Portfolio Study", 4896–8.4

Geography
Alaska minerals resources and geologic characteristics, compilation of papers, 1990, annual rpt, 5664–15
Census Bur data files and rpts, coverage and availability, 1992 annual listing, 2304–2
Census of Population and Housing, 1990: data coverage, collection procedures, products and services availability, and uses, guide, 2555–1
Education in science and engineering, grad programs enrollment by field, source of funds, and characteristics of student and instn, 1990, annual rpt, 9627–7
Educational performance by subject and selected student characteristics, standard test results and credits, 1992 edition, annual rpt, 4824–2.12
Foreign countries *Geographic Notes*, boundaries, claims, nomenclature, and other devs, quarterly rpt, 7142–3
Statistical Abstract of US, 1992 annual data compilation, 2324–1.6
see also Cartography
see also Topography

Geological phenomena
see Earthquakes
see Volcanoes

Geological Survey
Activities and funding of USGS, FY91, annual rpt, 5664–8
Alaska minerals resources and geologic characteristics, compilation of papers, 1990, annual rpt, 5664–15
Alaska minerals resources, production, oil and gas leases, reserves, and exploratory wells, with maps and bibl, 1990, annual rpt, 5664–11
Budget of US, obligations and authority by function, agency, and program, with summaries and analyses, FY93, annual rpt, 104–2
Coal mining restrictions on public land, impacts on production, costs, and demand, by region, 1985-88 and projected to 2075, 5668–125
Earthquakes and other ground motion, intensity by station, 1990, annual rpt, 5664–14
Groundwater supply, quality, chemistry, and use, State and local area rpt series, 5666–28
Groundwater supply, quality, chemistry, other characteristics, and use, regional rpt series, 5666–25
Minerals (strategic) supply and characteristics of individual deposits, by country, commodity rpt series, 5666–21
North Central States strategic minerals deposits, characteristics, 1992 compilation of papers, 5668–127
Publications of USGS, monthly listing, 5662–1
Publications of USGS, 1991, annual listing, 5664–4
Radon and other radionuclide levels in air, water, soil, and uranium mill tailings, by site and region, 1950s-80s, compilation of papers, 5668–126
Water quality, chemistry, hydrology, and other characteristics, local area studies, series, 5666–27
Water resources data collection and analysis activities of USGS Water Resources Div Districts, with project descriptions, series, 5666–26
Water supply and quality in streams and lakes, and groundwater levels in wells, by drainage basin, 1990, annual State rpt series, 5666–10
Water supply and quality in streams and lakes, and groundwater levels in wells, by drainage basin, 1990-91, annual CD-ROM, 5664–18
Water supply and quality in streams and lakes, and groundwater levels in wells, by drainage basin, 1991, annual State rpt series, 5666–12
Water supply in US and southern Canada, streamflow, surface and groundwater conditions, and reservoir levels, by location, monthly rpt, 5662–3
Water use by end use, well withdrawals, and public supply deliveries, by county, State rpt series, 5666–24

Geology
Alaska minerals resources and geologic characteristics, compilation of papers, 1990, annual rpt, 5664–15
Alaska OCS environmental conditions and oil dev impacts, compilation of papers, series, 2176–1
Coastal and riparian areas environmental conditions, fish, wildlife, use, and mgmt, for individual ecosystems, series, 5506–9
Coastal areas environmental conditions and mgmt, for individual areas, conf series, 2146–8
DOE R&D projects and funding at natl labs, universities, and other instns, FY91, annual summary rpt, 3004–18.1
Geological Survey activities and funding, FY91, annual rpt, 5664–8
Geological Survey rpts, 1991, annual listing, 5664–4
Groundwater supply, quality, chemistry, and use, State and local area rpt series, 5666–28
Groundwater supply, quality, chemistry, other characteristics, and use, regional rpt series, 5666–25
Labor demand, turnover, and training completions, by detailed occupation, 1990 and projected to 2005, biennial rpt, 6744–3
Minerals offshore lease sales environmental and economic impacts in coastal areas, final statement series, 5736–7
Occupational Outlook Handbook, 1992-93, biennial rpt, 6744–1
Oceanographic research and distribution activities of World Data Center A by country, and cruises by ship, 1990, annual rpt, 2144–15
Oil and gas OCS reserves, geophysical data collection activities and costs, by region, 1976-90, 5738–41
Uranium tailings at inactive mills, remedial action proposals, costs, site characteristics, and environmental, socioeconomic, and health impacts, series, 3356–4
Water quality, chemistry, hydrology, and other characteristics, local area studies, series, 5666–27

Georgia
Appalachian Regional Commission funding, by project and State, planned FY92, annual rpt, 9084–3
Banks (insured commercial and savings) deposits by instn, State, MSA, and county, as of June 1991, annual regional rpt, 9295–3.2
Deaths and rates, by detailed location, cause, and demographic characteristics, 1989, US Vital Statistics annual rpt, 4144–3.1
Economic indicators by State and MSA, Fed Reserve 6th District, quarterly rpt, 9371–14
Electric power demand, and industrial and employment impacts of capacity shortfalls and new power plants, by selected State, 1960s-80s and projected to 2000, hearing, 21248–163
Employment and housing indicators by State, FHLB 4th District, quarterly rpt, 9302–36
Employment by industry div, earnings, and hours, for 8 southeastern States, quarterly press release, 6942–7
Employment, earnings, and hours, by selected SIC 1- to 4-digit industry, State, and for 275 MSAs, 1987-92, 6748–81
Fed Govt spending in States and local areas, by type, State, county, and city, FY91, annual rpt, 2464–3
Fed Govt spending in States, by type, program, agency, and State, FY91, annual rpt, 2464–2
HHS financial aid, by program, recipient, State, and city, FY91, annual regional listing, 4004–3.4
Hospital deaths of Medicare patients, actual and expected rates by diagnosis, and hospital characteristics, by instn, FY90 annual State rpt, 4654–14.11
Housing census, 1990: inventory, occupancy, and costs, State fact sheet, 2326–21.12
Housing census, 1990: summary unit characteristics, by householder race and age, county, place, and urban-rural location, State rpt, 2471–1.12
Lumber (industrial roundwood) production, by product, for Georgia, 1986 and 1989, 1208–393

Military prime contract awards, by contractor, service branch, State, and city, FY91, annual rpt, 3544–22
Mineral Industry Surveys, State reviews of production, 1991, preliminary annual rpt, 5614–6
Multinatl firms US affiliates finances and operations, by industry, country of parent firm, and State, 1987, 2708–48
Peaches production, marketing, and prices in 3 southeastern States and Appalachia, 1991, annual rpt, 1311–12
Physicians, by specialty, age, sex, and location of training and practice, 1990, State rpt, 4116–6.11
Population and housing census, 1990: detailed geographic coverage, State CD-ROM, 2551–9.5
Population and housing census, 1990: population and housing characteristics, detailed geographic coverage, State CD-ROM, 2551–10.14
Population and housing census, 1990: summary characteristics, by county, subdiv, and place, State rpt, 2551–7.12
Population census, 1990: population characteristics and living arrangements, by county, place, and urban-rural location, State rpt, 2531–1.12
Statistical Abstract of US, 1992 annual data compilation, 2324–1
Textile mill employment, earnings, and hours, for 8 Southeastern States, quarterly press release, 6942–1
Water resources dev projects of Army Corps of Engineers, characteristics, and costs, 1950s-91, biennial State rpt, 3756–2.11
see also Atlanta, Ga.
see also Cobb County, Ga.
see also Columbus, Ga.
see also DeKalb County, Ga.
see also Savannah, Ga.
see also under By State in the "Index by Categories"

Georgia, Republic of
Agricultural production, prices, and trade, for former USSR republics, 1960s-91 and forecast 1992, annual rpt, 1524–4.1
Economic, social, political, and geographic summary data, by country, 1992, annual factbook, 9114–2
Embassies of US in former Soviet republics and Baltic States, positions planned by function, and filled, 1992, GAO rpt, 26123–403
Energy supply and use, and social, economic, and political indicators for former Soviet Republics and Baltic States, 1989-90, 3168–126
Energy use and production of former USSR Republics, by fuel type, 1990, annual rpt, 3164–84.2
Exports and imports of US with Communist and transitional economy countries, by detailed commodity and country, quarterly rpt with articles, 9882–2
Livestock and meat inventories, use, and imports, by former USSR republic, 1986-93, semiannual rpt, 1925–33.2
Population size and characteristics of former Soviet Republics and Baltic States, 1989-92, 9118–19

Geothermal resources
Consumption of energy, by detailed fuel type, end-use sector, and State, 1960-90, State Energy Data System annual rpt, 3164–39
Electric power plants (geothermal) capacity and operating status, wells, and leases, by location, 1960s-95, 3308–87
Electric power plants (geothermal), generation, capacity, and dev potential, by location, 1988-90 and projected to 2030, 3168–122
Electric power plants and capacity, by fuel used, owner, location, and operating status, 1991 and for units planned 1992-2001, annual listing, 3164–36
Electric power plants certification applications filed with FERC, for small production and cogeneration facilities, FY80-91, annual listing, 3084–13
Foreign and US energy production and use, by energy type and country, 1981-90, annual rpt, 3164–50.5
Mexico and US electric power supply, demand, and trade, with data by fuel source, utility, and region, 1970s-89 and projected to 2000, 3408–2
Pacific basin countries energy supply and demand, and implications for US trade, country rpt series, 3406–6
Pacific Northwest electric power capacity and use, by energy source, forecast under alternative load and demand cases, 1991-2012, annual rpt, 3224–3
Pacific Northwest nonutility electric power generation and capacity, by energy source, purchasing utility, and facility, forecasts 1991-2012, annual rpt, 3224–3.4
Public lands acreage and use, and Land Mgmt Bur activities and finances, annual State rpt series, 5724–11
Public lands acreage, grants, use, revenues, and allocations, by State, FY91, annual rpt, 5724–1.2
Public lands minerals resources and availability, State rpt series, 5606–7
Supply, demand, and prices, by fuel type and end-use sector, alternative projections 1990-2010, annual rpt, 3164–75
Supply, demand, and prices, by fuel type and end-use sector, projections and underlying assumptions, 1995-2010, annual rpt, 3164–90
Supply, demand, and prices, by fuel type and end-use sector, with foreign comparisons, 1981-90, annual fact book, 3164–76
Supply, demand, and prices, by fuel type and end-use sector, with foreign comparisons, 1991 and trends from 1949, annual rpt, 3164–74

Gerald, Debra E.
"Projections of Education Statistics to 2003", 4824–4

Geriatrics
Education (health) centers for aged, medication mgmt and other preventive health activities, and Federal funding, FY83-91, article, 4042–3.303
HHS financial aid, by program, recipient, State, and city, FY91, annual regional listings, 4004–3
Hospital deaths of Medicare patients, actual and expected rates by diagnosis, with hospital characteristics, by instn, FY90, annual State rpt series, 4654–14
Labor supply and education of health professionals, by professional and other characteristics, and location, 1960s-92 and projected to 2020, biennial rpt, 4114–8
VA Geriatric Research, Education and Clinical Centers activities and finances, FY88, annual rpt, 8704–8
VA health care facilities physicians, dentists, and nurses, by selected employment characteristics and VA district, quarterly rpt, 8602–6
VA health care facilities trainees, by detailed program and city, FY91, annual rpt, 8704–4
VA health care services, needs, availability, structure, and funding, 1991 compilation of papers, 8608–9
VA health care staff and turnover, by occupation, physician specialty, and location, 1991, annual rpt, 8604–8

German Democratic Republic
see Germany, East

Germany
Agricultural trade of US, by detailed commodity and country, 1991, annual rpt, 1524–8
Agricultural trade of US, by detailed commodity and country, 1991, semiannual rpt, 1522–4
AID loans repayment status and terms by program and country, and status of predecessor agency loans, quarterly rpt, 9912–3
Banks reserve and overdraft requirements of Fed Reserve and 3 foreign central banks, with balance sheets and deposit balances, 1989-90, article, 9377–1.307
Construction activity in former East and West regions of Germany, 1991, article, 2042–1.306
Cuba trade, by commodity and country, mid 1980s-91, 9118–8
Currency (foreign and US) shares of intl transactions, with background data, for 5 countries, 1960s-80s, 9381–10.129
Dollar exchange rates of mark and yen, impact of central bank policy interventions, 1985-89, article, 9391–1.310
Dollar exchange rates of mark and yen, spot and forward market bid-ask spreads impacts of central bank intervention, mid 1980s-91, article, 9377–1.305
Drug abuse indicators, by world region and selected country, 1992 semiannual conf, 4492–5.2
Economic and monetary trends, compounded annual rates of change and quarterly indicators for US and 7 major industrialized countries, quarterly rpt, 9391–7
Economic conditions, income, production, prices, employment, and trade, 1992 periodic country rpt, 2046–4.24
Economic conditions, policy, and trade practices, by country, 1989-91, annual rpt, 21384–5
Economic indicators, and dollar exchange rates, for selected OECD countries, 1992 semiannual rpt, 8002–14
Economic, social, political, and geographic summary data, by country, 1992, annual factbook, 9114–2
European Monetary Union impacts on France, Germany, and Italy monetary policies, 1992 technical paper, 9385–8.145

Export credit activity of Eximbank and 6 OECD countries, 1990, annual rpt, 9254–3
Exports and imports among US, Canada, and Japan related to domestic and foreign prices and income, 1965-87, technical paper, 9366–7.276
Exports and imports, intl position of US and 4 OECD countries, and factors affecting US competition, quarterly pamphlet, 2042–25
Exports and imports of US by country, and trade shifts by commodity, 1991, annual rpt, 9884–25
Exports and imports of US, by Harmonized System 6-digit commodity and country, 1991, annual rpt, 2424–13
Exports and imports of US, by selected country, country group, and commodity group, 1991, annual rpt, 2044–37
Exports and imports of US, by transport mode, country, and SITC 1- to 3-digit commodity, 1991, annual rpt, 2424–12
Exports, imports, and balances of US, by selected country, country group, and commodity group, preliminary data, monthly rpt, 2042–34
Exports, imports, and balances of US for manufactured goods, by SITC 2-digit commodity and country, quarterly rpt, 2042–35
Exports, imports, and balances of US with major trading partners, by product category, 1987-91, annual chartbook, 9884–21
Exports of US, detailed Schedule B commodities with countries of destination, 1991, annual rpt, 2424–10
Farmland in US owned by foreigners, holdings, acreage, and value by land use, owner country, State, and county, 1991, annual rpt, 1584–3
Fruit (fresh) production, EC and non-EC imports, and consumption, by commodity, for Germany, 1990-92, article, 1925–34.340
Health care costs and components, services use, resources, and economic indicators, by OECD country, 1960s-90, article, 4652–1.322
Human rights conditions in 170 countries, and US economic and military aid, 1991, annual rpt, 21384–3
Imports of goods, services, and investment from US, trade barriers, impacts, and US actions, by country, 1991, annual rpt, 444–2
Imports of US given duty-free treatment for value of US material sent abroad, by commodity and country, 1987-90, annual rpt, 9884–14
Inflationary periods relative price changes and money demand behavior, for Germany, 1920-23, and for PRC, 1946-49, working paper, 9371–10.86
Interest and exchange rates, security yields, and stock indexes, for selected foreign countries, weekly chartbook, 9365–1.5
Interest rates (long term) relation to rates of return to capital, economic policies, and other factors, US and 4 countries, 1960s-90, article, 9385–1.301
Intl transactions of US with 9 countries, 1989-91, *Survey of Current Business*, monthly rpt, annual table, 2702–1.33
Labor conditions, union coverage, and work accidents, 1991 annual country rpt, 6366–4.5
Manufacturing industry (US) intl competitiveness, trade and economic policies with background data and foreign comparisons, 1991 rpt, 26358–252
Mexico trade with US and other countries, foreign investment, and maquiladoras operations, 1980s-91, GAO rpt, 26119–417
Monetary policies and central bank regulation in US and 5 countries, 1980-91, article, 9385–1.308
Nuclear power generation in US and 20 countries, monthly rpt, 3162–24.10
Nuclear power generation in US and 20 countries, monthly 1973-88, 3168–123.10
Oil production, stocks, use, and trade, by selected country and country group, monthly rpt, 3162–42
Oil use and stocks for selected OECD countries, monthly rpt, 3162–24.10
Oil use and stocks for selected OECD countries, 1973-88, 3168–123.10
Persian Gulf War allied and other countries cash and in-kind contributions, by type and country, 1990-91, GAO rpt, 26123–371
Persian Gulf War allied countries cash and in-kind contributions, by type and country, and status of DOD accounts, as of Sept 1991, annual GAO rpt, 26104–24
Population size, growth rates, and components of change, by country, projected 1990-2020 and trends from 1950, biennial rpt, 2324–9
Rayon yarn (high-tenacity filament) from Germany at less than fair value, injury to US industry, investigation with background financial and operating data, 1992 rpt, 9886–14.350
Refugee migration, and intl aid programs, by world area and country of origin and asylum, 1991, annual rpt, 7004–15
Spacecraft and satellite launches since 1957, quarterly listing, 9502–2
Steel (carbon flat-rolled) products from 21 countries, injury to US industry from foreign subsidized and less than fair value imports, investigation with background financial and operating data, 1992 rpt, 9886–19.85
Steel (hot-rolled) products containing lead or bismuth from 4 countries, injury to US industry from foreign subsidized and less than fair value imports, investigation with background financial and operating data, 1992 rpt, 9886–19.82
Steel trade, by product, country, and customs district, with US industry operating data, 1989-June 1992, semiannual rpt, 9882–15
Tax (income) final withholding systems use in 4 countries, and feasibility of US adoption, with background data, 1986-92, GAO rpt, 26119–400
Tax revenue, by level of govt and type of tax, for OECD countries, mid 1960s-90, annual rpt, 10044–1.2
Technology-intensive industries intl competitiveness, with background data by industry and foreign comparisons, 1960s-91, GAO rpt, 26123–406
Telecommunications industry intl competitiveness, structure, and devs, with background data and foreign comparisons, 1991 rpt, 2808–30
UN voting record and share of votes in agreement with US, by issue, country, and world area, 1991, annual rpt, 7004–18
Unification of Germany, economic impacts for Germany, US, Japan, and worldwide, alternative projections 1991-99, technical paper, 9366–7.275
US military base closings in Germany, US liability for local natl employee severance pay, projected FY91-95, GAO rpt, 26123–383
see also Germany, East
see also Germany, West
see also under By Foreign Country in the "Index by Categories"

Germany, East

Economic and military aid and loans from US and intl agencies, by program and country, FY46-91, annual rpt, 9914–5
Energy production by type, and oil trade, and use, by country group and selected country, monthly rpt, 9112–2
Export licensing, monitoring, and enforcement activities, FY91, annual rpt, 2024–1
Exports and imports of US, by commodity and country, 1980-90, world area rpt, 9116–1.1
Labor conditions, union coverage, and work accidents, 1991 annual country rpt, 6366–4.5
Military spending, arms trade, and force strengths, with govt spending and population, by country, 1979-89, annual rpt, 9824–1
Pollution (air) contributing to global warming, emissions by monitoring site and country, and temperature change by world area and US region, 1860s-1990, annual rpt, 3004–33
Steel imports of US under voluntary restraint agreement, by product, customs district, and country, with US industry operating data, quarterly rpt, 9882–13

Germany, West

Dollar exchange rates of yen and mark, impact of central bank policy interventions and other factors, various periods 1983-90, working paper, 9377–9.138
Dollar exchange rates of yen and mark, impact of central bank policy interventions, 1987-90, working paper, 9377–9.134
Economic and military aid and loans from US and intl agencies, by program and country, FY46-91, annual rpt, 9914–5
Economic conditions, and oil supply and demand, for major industrial countries, monthly rpt, 9112–1
Economic conditions, consumer and stock prices and production indexes, for 7 OECD countries, *Survey of Current Business*, monthly rpt, 2702–1.1
Energy production by type, and oil trade, and use, by country group and selected country, monthly rpt, 9112–2
Exchange rate variability and other factors, relation to inter- and intra-industry foreign trade for US, Germany, and Japan, 1960s-88, working paper, 9371–10.81

Exports and imports of OECD, total and for 4 major countries, and US trade by country, by commodity, 1980-90, world area rpt series, 9116–1
Exports, imports, and balances of US with major trading partners, by product category, 1987-91, annual chartbook, 9884–21
Financial markets (intl) performance of foreign and US bank and securities firms, finances and competitiveness issues, 1980s, compilation of papers, 9385–10
Income (household) and wealth distribution by selected characteristics, with foreign comparisons, 1992 compilation of papers, Current Population Rpt, 2546–6.79
Investment (foreign direct) in US, major transactions by type, industry, country, and US location, 1990, annual rpt, 2044–20
Labor conditions, union coverage, and work accidents, 1991 annual country rpt, 6366–4.5
Military spending, arms trade, and force strengths, with govt spending and population, by country, 1979-89, annual rpt, 9824–1
Multinatl firms US affiliates finances and operations, by industry, country of parent firm, and State, 1987, 2708–48
Multinatl firms US affiliates, finances, and operations, by industry, world area of parent firm, and State, 1989-90, annual rpt, 2704–4
Multinatl US firms and foreign affiliates finances and operations, by industry and country, 1989 benchmark survey, annual rpt, 2704–5
Multinatl US firms foreign affiliates, income statement items by asset size, industry, and country, 1988, biennial article, 8302–2.322
Nuclear power generation in US and 20 countries, monthly rpt, 3162–24.10
Nuclear power generation in US and 20 countries, monthly 1973-88, 3168–123.10
Oil use and stocks for selected OECD countries, monthly rpt, 3162–24.10
Oil use and stocks for selected OECD countries, 1973-88, 3168–123.10
Pollution (air) contributing to global warming, emissions by monitoring site and country, and temperature change by world area and US region, 1860s-1990, annual rpt, 3004–33
Refugee migration, and intl aid programs, by world area and country of origin and asylum, 1991, annual rpt, 7004–15
Savings rates, and ratio of aged to working age population, for US, Japan, and West Germany, 1980s-90, article, 9387–1.302
Science and Engineering Indicators, employment, education, R&D funding, and industry impacts, with foreign comparisons, 1960s-91, biennial rpt, 9624–10
Tax (estate) returns for nonresident aliens, property and tax data, by estate size and decedent country of residence, 1986, article, 8302–2.310
Tax (income) returns for foreign corporate activity in US, selected income and tax items, by industry div and selected country, 1988, article, 8302–2.309
Tax (income) returns, income, and tax withheld for foreign partners of US partnerships, by country, 1990, article, 8302–2.324
Transportation energy use, fuel prices, vehicle registrations, and mileage, by selected country, 1950-89, annual rpt, 3304–5.1
Travel to US and Canada, market analysis with trip and traveler characteristics, 1989, country rpt, 2906–2.15

Gertel, Karl
"Farmland Prices, Past and Prospective", 1561–16.302

Getz, Patricia M.
"BLS Establishment Estimates Revised to March 1991 Benchmarks", 6742–2.306

Geweke, John
"Evaluating the Accuracy of Sampling-Based Approaches to the Calculation of Posterior Moments", 9383–20.18

Ghana
Agricultural trade of US, by detailed commodity and country, 1991, annual rpt, 1524–8
Agricultural trade of US, by detailed commodity and country, 1991, semiannual rpt, 1522–4
AID economic aid to developing countries, obligations and disbursements by country, quarterly rpt, 9912–4
AID loans repayment status and terms by program and country, and status of predecessor agency loans, quarterly rpt, 9912–3
Economic and military aid and loans from US and intl agencies, by program and country, FY46-91, annual rpt, 9914–5
Economic and social conditions of developing countries from 1960s, and Intl Dev Cooperation Agency and AID activities and funding, FY91-93, annual rpt, 9904–4
Economic conditions, policy, and trade practices, by country, 1989-91, annual rpt, 21384–5
Economic, social, political, and geographic summary data, by country, 1992, annual factbook, 9114–2
Exports and imports of US, by commodity and country, 1980-90, world area rpt, 9116–1.2
Exports and imports of US, by transport mode, country, and SITC 1- to 3-digit commodity, 1991, annual rpt, 2424–12
Exports of US, detailed Schedule B commodities with countries of destination, 1991, annual rpt, 2424–10
Food supply, needs, and aid for developing countries, status and alternative forecasts, 1992 world area rpt, 1526–8.2
Human rights conditions in 170 countries, and US economic and military aid, 1991, annual rpt, 21384–3
Military aid of US, arms sales, and training programs costs and budget requests, by program, world region, and country, FY91-93, annual rpt, 7144–13
Military spending, arms trade, and force strengths, with govt spending and population, by country, 1979-89, annual rpt, 9824–1
Minerals Yearbook, Vol 3, 1989: foreign country review of production, trade, and policy, by commodity, annual rpt, 5604–35.1
Population size, growth rates, and components of change, by country, projected 1990-2020 and trends from 1950, biennial rpt, 2324–9
Refugee migration, and intl aid programs, by world area and country of origin and asylum, 1991, annual rpt, 7004–15
UN voting record and share of votes in agreement with US, by issue, country, and world area, 1991, annual rpt, 7004–18

GI Bill
see Veterans education

Gianessi, Leonard P.
"Reregistration of Minor Use Pesticides: Some Observations and Implications", 1561–16.301

Gibraltar
Agricultural trade of US, by detailed commodity and country, 1991, annual rpt, 1524–8
Agricultural trade of US, by detailed commodity and country, 1991, semiannual rpt, 1522–4
Economic, social, political, and geographic summary data, by country, 1992, annual factbook, 9114–2
Exports and imports of US, by transport mode, country, and SITC 1- to 3-digit commodity, 1991, annual rpt, 2424–12
Exports of US, detailed Schedule B commodities with countries of destination, 1991, annual rpt, 2424–10
Population size, growth rates, and components of change, by country, projected 1990-2020 and trends from 1950, biennial rpt, 2324–9

Gift tax
Budget of US, CBO analysis of revenue and spending alternatives and projections of economic indicators, FY93-97, annual rpt, 26304–3
Budget of US, receipts by source, outlays by agency and program, and balances, monthly rpt, 8102–3
Collections, enforcement, and litigation activity of IRS, with data by type of tax, region, and State, FY91, annual rpt, 8304–3
Fed Govt internal revenue and refunds, by type of tax, quarterly rpt, 8302–2.1
Fed Govt receipts by source and outlays by agency, *Treasury Bulletin*, quarterly rpt, 8002–4.1
Fed Govt tax revenues, by type of tax, quarterly rpt, 2462–3
Finances of govts, tax systems and revenue, and fiscal structure, by level of govt and State, 1992 and historical trends, annual rpt, 10044–1
Foreign and US income and capital tax policies, with background data for EC, Japan, and US, mid 1960s-91, article, 9373–1.316
Returns and supplemental documents filed, by type, FY91 and projected to FY2000, semiannual rpt, 8302–4
Returns and supplemental documents filed, by type, 1990 and projected to 1999, annual article, 8302–2.304
Returns filed, by type of tax and IRS district, 1990 and projected 1991-98, annual rpt, 8304–24
Returns filed, by type of tax, region, and IRS service center, projected 1991-98 and trends from 1978, annual rpt, 8304–9

State govt revenue by source, spending and debt by function, and holdings, FY91, annual rpt, 2466–2.6
State govt tax collections by detailed type of tax, and tax rates, by State, FY91, annual rpt, 2466–2.7

Gifts and private contributions
Black higher education instns enrollment, finances, staff, and degrees, by instn and selected student characteristics, 1970s-90, 4848–46
Budget of US, authoritative financial statements with appropriations, outlays, and receipts, by category and agency, FY91, annual rpt, 8104–2.2
Education data compilation, 1992 annual rpt, 4824–2
Exports and imports between US and outlying areas, by detailed commodity and mode of transport, 1991, annual rpt, 2424–11
Exports and imports of US, by Harmonized System 6-digit commodity and country, 1991, annual rpt, 2424–13
Exports of US, detailed Schedule B commodities with countries of destination, 1991, annual rpt, 2424–10
Family members supporting others outside household, by relationship and provider characteristics, 1988, fact sheet, 2326–17.48
Family members supporting others outside household, by relationship, recipient living arrangements, and provider characteristics, 1988, Current Population Rpt, 2546–20.21
Foreign countries aid programs of private voluntary agencies, funding, and outlays, by agency, 1990, annual rpt, 9914–9
Forest Service activities and finances, by region and State, FY91, annual rpt, 1204–1
Higher education enrollment, faculty, finances, and degrees, by instn level and control, and State, FY88, annual rpt, 4844–13
Higher education instn revenue by source and spending by function, by State and instn control, FY82-90, annual rpt, 4844–6
Higher education instn student financial support by parents, by type and funding sources, and student, parent, and instn characteristics, fall 1986, 4846–3.11
House of Representatives members gifts for reduction of US public debt, quarterly rpt, 21942–1
Households charitable contribution probability and value relation to household composition and other factors, model results, 1991 working paper, 6886–6.90
Library of Congress gift, trust, and service fee funds, FY91, annual rpt, 26404–1
Mail volume to and from households, use, and views, by class, source, content, and household characteristics, FY87-90, annual rpt, 9864–10
Neighborhood Dev Demonstration program evaluation, grantee organization characteristics, activities, finances, and private sector support, 1984-89, 5188–119
Nonprofit charitable and other tax exempt organizations finances, by category and size of assets and contributions, 1988, annual article, 8302–2.315
Nonprofit charitable organizations finances, with data by State and for top 10 instns, 1988, article, 8302–2.302
Older persons income and sources, by whether OASDI beneficiary, poverty status, and other characteristics, 1990, biennial rpt, 4744–26
Public debt issued, redeemed, and outstanding, by series and source, and gifts to reduce debt, monthly rpt, 8242–2
R&D facilities of higher education instns, space and equipment adequacy, needs, and funding by source, by instn type and control, 1992, biennial rpt, 9624–25
Red Cross activities and finances, FY91, annual rpt, 29254–1
Refugee migration, and intl aid programs, by world area and country of origin and asylum, 1991, annual rpt, 7004–15
Smithsonian Instn activities and finances, FY91, annual rpt, 29574–1
Statistical Abstract of US, 1992 annual data compilation, 2324–1.12
Tax (estate) returns property and tax data, by size of gross estate and State, 1989-90, article, 8302–2.305
Tax (income) policy impacts on charitable contributions, model description and results, 1991 working paper, 6886–6.83
Tax (income) returns filed, by type of filer, selected income items, quarterly rpt, 8302–2.1
Tax (income) returns of corporations, income and tax items by asset size and detailed industry, 1989, annual rpt, 8304–4; 8304–21
Tax (income) returns of individuals, by filing status, tax item, and income level, 1991, annual article, 8302–2.319
Tax (income) returns of individuals, detailed data, 1988, annual rpt, 8304–2
Tax (income) returns of individuals, selected income and tax items by income level, preliminary 1990, annual article, 8302–2.307
Tax exempt organizations finances, with data by type, size, State, and for largest organizations, late 1940s-80s, compilation of papers, 8308–35
Tax exempt organizations with unrelated business income, finances by organization type, 1987, article, 8302–2.306
Truman, Harry S, Scholarship Fund receipts by source, transfers, and investment holdings and transactions, monthly rpt, 14312–1
see also Campaign funds
see also Gift tax

Gilbert Islands
see Kiribati

Gilbert, M. Jean
"Acculturation and Changes in Drinking Patterns Among Mexican-American Women: Implications for Prevention", 4482–1.309

Gilbert, R. Alton
"Effects of Legislating Prompt Corrective Action on the Bank Insurance Fund", 9391–1.312
"Implications of Netting Arrangements for Bank Risk in Foreign Exchange Transactions", 9391–1.304

Gilkeson, James H.
"Convexity Trap: Pitfalls in Financing Mortgage Portfolios and Related Securities", 9371–1.308

Gill, Mohinder
"Sorghum Production Practices and Input Use: 1991", 1561–16.304

Gilliard, Darrell K.
"National Corrections Reporting Program, 1988", 6064–33

Gillingham, Robert
"Econometric Model of Capital Gains Realization Behavior", 8006–6.4
"Effect of Marginal Tax Rates on Capital Gains Revenue: Another Look at the Evidence", 8006–6.3
"Historical Trends in the U.S. Cost of Capital", 8006–6.2

Gillum, Richard F.
"Epidemiology of Resting Pulse Rate of Persons Ages 25-74—Data from NHANES 1971-74", 4042–3.321

Ginzel, John
"Outlook for Red Meats", 1504–9.1

Giovannucci, Edward
"Relationship of Diet to Risk of Colorectal Adenoma in Men", 4472–1.302

Girl Scouts of U.S.A.
Statistical Abstract of US, 1992 annual data compilation, 2324–1.7

Gjovik, Lee R.
"Service Life of Treated and Untreated Black Hills Ponderosa Pine Fenceposts", 1208–406

Glaciers
Alaska minerals resources and geologic characteristics, compilation of papers, 1990, annual rpt, 5664–15
Research (intl) in glaciology, summaries, methodology, and bibls, series, 2156–18

Glaessel-Brown, Eleanor E.
"Immigration Policy and Colombian Textile Workers in New England", 6366–6.4

Glass and glass industry
Business statistics, detailed data for major industries and economic indicators, *Survey of Current Business*, monthly rpt, 2702–1.20
Business statistics, detailed data for major industries and economic indicators, 1960-91, *Survey of Current Business* biennial supplement, 2704–1
County Business Patterns, 1989: employment, establishments, and payroll, by SIC 2- to 4-digit industry and county, annual State rpt series, 2326–8
County Business Patterns, 1990: employment, establishments, and payroll, by SIC 2- to 4-digit industry and county, annual State rpt series, 2326–6
Employment, earnings, and hours, by SIC 1- to 4-digit industry, monthly 1989-Feb 1992, annual rpt, 6744–4
Employment of minorities and women, by occupation, SIC 1- to 3-digit industry, State, and MSA, 1991, annual rpt, 9244–1
Exports and imports between US and outlying areas, by detailed commodity and mode of transport, 1991, annual rpt, 2424–11
Exports and imports of US, by country and detailed commodity, monthly rpt, 2422–12

Exports and imports of US, by Harmonized System 6-digit commodity and country, 1991, annual rpt, 2424–13
Exports and imports of US, by transport mode, country, and SITC 1- to 3-digit commodity, 1991, annual rpt, 2424–12
Exports of US, detailed commodities by country, monthly CD-ROM, 2422–13
Exports of US, detailed Schedule B commodities with countries of destination, 1991, annual rpt, 2424–10
Freight (waterborne domestic and foreign) by commodity, traffic, and passengers, by port and waterway, 1989, annual rpt, 3754–3
Imports, exports, and employment impacts, by SIC 2- to 4-digit industry and commodity, quarterly rpt, 2322–2
Imports of US, detailed commodities by country, monthly CD-ROM, 2422–14
Injuries from use of consumer products and related activities, by severity and victim age and sex, 1990, annual rpt, 9164–7
Injuries from use of consumer products, by severity, victim age, and detailed product, 1991, annual rpt, 9164–6
Input-output structure of US economy, detailed interindustry transactions for 84 industries, and components of final demand, 1987, annual article, 2702–1.316
Input-output structure of US economy, detailed interindustry transactions for 541 industries, and components of final demand, 1982 benchmark data, 2708–17
Labor productivity, indexes of output, hours, and employment by SIC 2- to 4-digit industry, 1967-90, annual rpt, 6824–1.3
Manufacturing annual survey, 1990: finances and operations, by SIC 2- to 4-digit industry, series, 2506–14
Manufacturing census, 1987: concentration of largest firms measured by value added, and for shipments by SIC 2- and 4-digit industry, subject rpt, 2497–6
Manufacturing census, 1987: shipments of manufacturers products, by customer class and SIC 2- and 4-digit industry, subject rpt, 2497–4
Manufacturing finances and operations, by SIC 2- to 4-digit industry, forecast 1992, annual rpt, 2044–28
Multinatl firms US affiliates finances and operations, by industry, country of parent firm, and State, 1987, 2708–48
Multinatl US firms and foreign affiliates finances and operations, by industry and country, 1989 benchmark survey, annual rpt, 2704–5
Occupational injury and illness rates, by SIC 2- to 4-digit industry, 1989-90, annual rpt, 6844–7
Occupational injury and illness rates, by SIC 2- to 4-digit industry, 1990, annual rpt, 6844–1
OECD trade, total and for 4 major countries, and US trade by country, by commodity, 1980-90, world area rpt series, 9116–1
Price indexes (producer), by stage of processing and detailed commodity, monthly rpt, 6762–6
Price indexes (producer), by stage of processing and detailed commodity, monthly 1991, annual rpt, 6764–2
Production, shipments, trade, and stocks, by glass product, periodic Current Industrial Rpt series, 2506–9
Recycling of municipal and industrial waste, costs, revenues, and secondary products trade and related energy use and pollution reductions, 1991 hearings, 21368–139
Science, engineering, and technical employment in manufacturing, by field and industry, 1989, triennial rpt, 9627–23
Tax (income) returns of corporations, income and tax items by asset size and detailed industry, 1989, annual rpt, 8304–4; 8304–21
see also under By Industry in the "Index by Categories"

Glass, Ronald J.
"Estimates of Recreation Use in the White River Drainage, Vermont", 1208–400

Glassware
see Household supplies and utensils

Glavin, Margaret O'K.
"Nutrition Labeling: Phase Two", 1504–9.1

Glaz, B.
"Evaluation of New Canal Point Sugarcane Clones, 1991-92 Harvest Season", 1704–2

Gleason, Philip M.
"Using SIPP To Analyze Black-White Differences in Youth Employment", 2626–10.146

Glick, Reuven
"Fiscal Policy in Monetary Unions: Implications for Europe", 9393–10.18
"Global Versus Country-Specific Productivity Shocks and the Current Account", 9393–10.22

Global climate change
Agricultural production and GDP impacts of global climate change, with data by crop and world area, mid 1970s-86, 1528–326
Auto alternative fuels pollutant emissions by fuel type, and alcohol fuel production and inputs, 1991 hearing, 25318–82
Budget of US, analysis of specific proposals, FY93, annual rpt, 104–2.2
Carbon dioxide in atmosphere, DOE R&D programs and funding at natl labs, universities, and other instns, FY92, annual summary rpt, 3004–18.10
Developing countries energy efficiency improvement issues and devs, with data by end use and country, 1980s-90, 26358–260
Emissions and concentrations of pollutants contributing to global warming, by monitoring site, source, and country, and temperature change by world area and US region, 1860s-1990, annual rpt, 3004–33
Emissions of pollutants contributing to climate change, atmospheric concentrations by location, and monitoring activities, 1990, annual rpt, 2144–28
Emissions of pollutants contributing to greenhouse effect and climate impacts, literature review, 1980s and projected to 2075, 3338–3
Energy natl strategy fossil fuel, electric power, conservation, and pollution reduction issues, 1991 hearings, 21368–136
Energy natl strategy plans for conservation, R&D, security, and pollution reduction, technical rpt series, 3006–13
Environmental quality indicators, NOAA monitoring results, 1991 annual summary rpt, 2144–27
Environmental Quality, status of problems, protection programs, research, and intl issues, 1991 annual rpt, 484–1
EPA R&D programs and funding, planned FY92, annual listing, 9184–17
Plants in mountain grassland areas, impacts of global climate change, monitoring study results, 1969 and 1988, 1208–425
Weather conditions and forecasts, data collection and analysis issues, 1991 annual conf, 2184–10
Weather trends and deviations, by world region, 1880s-1990, annual chartbook, 2184–9

Global Competitiveness Corp.
"Survey of Direct U.S. Private Capital Investment in Research and Development Facilities in Japan", 9628–88

Global Geochemistry Corp.
"Analysis of Acid Precipitation Samples Collected by State Agencies: January-December 1989", 9194–20

Glossaries
Astronomical tables, time conversion factors, and listing of observatories worldwide, 1993, annual rpt, 3804–7
Computer systems purchase and use, and data recording, processing, and transfer, Fed Govt standards, series, 2216–2
Consumption of energy, by detailed fuel type, end-use sector, and State, 1960-90, State Energy Data System annual rpt, 3164–39
Electric power plants production and capital costs, operations, and fuel use, by fuel type, plant, utility, and location, 1990, annual rpt, 3164–9
Electric power plants production, capacity, sales, and fuel stocks, use, and costs, by State, 1986-90, annual rpt, 3164–11
Electric power plants production, fuel use, stocks, and costs by fuel type, and sales, by State, monthly rpt, with articles, 3162–35
Electric utilities finances and operations, detailed data for publicly owned firms, 1990, annual rpt, 3164–24
Electric utilities privately owned, finances and operations, detailed data, 1990, annual rpt, 3164–23
Energy use, costs, and conservation, and household and housing characteristics, survey rpt series, 3166–7
Higher education data collection system, glossary, 1992 rpt, 4848–47
Medicaid reimbursement of hospitals, provisions by State, 1991, 17206–2.35
Natural and supplemental gas production, prices, trade, use, reserves, and pipeline company finances, by firm and State, monthly rpt with articles, 3162–4
Radioactive waste and spent fuel generation, inventory, and disposal, 1960s-90 and projected to 2020, annual rpt, 3364–2
Semiconductor industry R&D consortium funding, outlays, and effectiveness in improving US competitive position, 1980s-92, GAO rpt, 26113–588
Supply, demand, trade, stocks, and refining of oil and gas liquids, by detailed product, State, and PAD district, monthly rpt with articles, 3162–6

Tidal currents, daily time and velocity by station for North America and Asia coasts, forecast 1993, annual rpts, 2174–1
Transit systems finances and operations, by mode, size of fleet and urban area, region, and for 518 systems, 1990, annual rpt, 7884–4

GNMA
see Government National Mortgage Association

GNP
see Gross National Product

Gokhale, Jagadeesh
"Estimating a Firm's Age-Productivity Profile Using the Present Value of Workers' Earnings", 9377–9.128

Gold
Budget of US, authoritative financial statements with appropriations, outlays, and receipts, by category and agency, FY91, annual rpt, 8104–2.2
Business statistics, detailed data for major industries and economic indicators, *Survey of Current Business*, monthly rpt, 2702–1.8
Business statistics, detailed data for major industries and economic indicators, 1960-91, *Survey of Current Business* biennial supplement, 2704–1
Coin production and monetary metals use and holdings of US Mint, by metal type, FY91, annual rpt, 8204–1
County Business Patterns, 1989: employment, establishments, and payroll, by SIC 2- to 4-digit industry and county, annual State rpt series, 2326–8
County Business Patterns, 1990: employment, establishments, and payroll, by SIC 2- to 4-digit industry and county, annual State rpt series, 2326–6
Exports and imports between US and outlying areas, by detailed commodity and mode of transport, 1991, annual rpt, 2424–11
Exports and imports of US, by country and detailed commodity, monthly rpt, 2422–12
Exports and imports of US, by Harmonized System 6-digit commodity and country, 1991, annual rpt, 2424–13
Exports and imports of US, by selected country, country group, and commodity group, 1991, annual rpt, 2044–37
Exports and imports of US, by transport mode, country, and SITC 1- to 3-digit commodity, 1991, annual rpt, 2424–12
Exports, imports, and balances of US for manufactured goods, by SITC 2-digit commodity and country, quarterly rpt, 2042–35
Exports of US, detailed Schedule B commodities with countries of destination, 1991, annual rpt, 2424–10
Fed Reserve banks finances and staff, 1991, annual rpt, 9364–1.1
Flow-of-funds accounts, savings, investments, and credit statements, quarterly rpt, 9365–3.3
Foreign countries economic conditions and implications for US, periodic country rpt series, 2046–4
Foreign countries mineral production, reserves, and industry role in domestic economy and world supply, world area and country rpt series, 5606–1
Futures and options trading volume, by commodity and exchange, FY91, annual rpt, 11924–2
Futures trading in selected commodities and financial instruments and indexes, for NYC, Chicago, and other markets activity, biweekly rpt, 11922–5
Inflation relation to gold standard, with background data for UK, US, France, and Italy, 1730s-1930s, working paper, 9377–9.136
Investment (intl) position of US, by component, industry, world region, and country, 1990-91, annual article, 2702–1.323
Mineral Industry Surveys, commodity review of production, trade, stocks, and use, monthly rpt, 5612–1.10
Mineral Industry Surveys, State reviews of production, 1991, preliminary annual rpt, 5614–6
Minerals Yearbook, Vol 1, 1989: commodity reviews of production, use, trade, prices, and mining operations, annual rpt, 5604–33
Minerals Yearbook, Vol 1, 1990: commodity review of production, reserves, supply, use, and trade, annual rpt, 5604–20.24
Minerals Yearbook, Vol 2, 1989: State reviews of production and sales by commodity, and business activity, annual rpt series, 5604–16
Minerals Yearbook, Vol 2, 1990: State reviews of production and sales by commodity, and business activity, annual rpt series, 5604–22
Minerals Yearbook, Vol 3, 1989: foreign country reviews of production, trade, and policy, by commodity, annual rpt, 5604–35
Mines (metal) and related operations occupational injuries and incidence, employment, and hours, 1990, annual rpt, 6664–3
Price indexes (producer), by stage of processing and detailed commodity, monthly rpt, 6762–6
Price indexes (producer), by stage of processing and detailed commodity, monthly 1991, annual rpt, 6764–2
Prices in London, current and 4-year trends, weekly chartbook, 9365–1.5
Production and prices of primary metals mining byproducts, by commodity, 1965-90, 5608–170
Production in 5 western States, and prices, for 5 nonferrous metals, 1848-1990, 5608–178
Production, prices, trade, and foreign and US industry devs, by commodity, bimonthly rpt, 5602–4
Production, prices, trade, use, employment, tariffs, and stockpiles, by mineral, with foreign comparisons, 1987-91, annual rpt, 5604–18
Production, trade, use, and foreign investment in US industry, for minerals, 1985-90 and projected to 2000, annual rpt, 5304–5
Reserve assets of US by type, *Treasury Bulletin*, quarterly rpt, 8002–4.12
Reserve assets of US, monthly rpt, 9362–1.3

Goldberg, I.
"International Strategic Minerals Inventory Summary Report: Vanadium", 5666–21.11

Goldberg, Miriam L.
"Derived Annual Estimates of Manufacturing Energy Consumption, 1974-88. Energy Consumption Series", 3166–15.3
"Lighting in Commercial Buildings. Energy Consumption Series", 3166–15.1

Goldstein, Morris
"Macroeconomic Policy Implications of Trade and Currency Zones", 9381–13.1

Goldwater, Barry, Scholarship and Excellence in Education Foundation
Awards and finances, FY87-91, annual rpt, 10404–1
Expenditures for education by Federal agency, program, and recipient type, and instn spending, 1960s-91, annual rpt, 4824–8

Golf
County Business Patterns, 1989: employment, establishments, and payroll, by SIC 2- to 4-digit industry and county, annual State rpt series, 2326–8
County Business Patterns, 1990: employment, establishments, and payroll, by SIC 2- to 4-digit industry and county, annual State rpt series, 2326–6
Injuries from use of consumer products and related activities, by severity and victim age and sex, 1990, annual rpt, 9164–7

Golob, John E.
"Allais Theory Suggests a Solution and an Explanation for the Equity Premium Puzzle", 9381–10.133

Gomme, Frank
"World Grain Outlook", 1504–9.1

Goolsby, D. A.
"Distribution of Selected Herbicides and Nitrate in the Mississippi River and Its Major Tributaries, April Through June 1991", 5666–27.34

Gordon, Dan
"Source of Losses to the National Credit Union Share Insurance Fund", 9536–1.7

Gordon, David B.
"Dynamic Impacts of Monetary Policy: An Exercise in Tentative Identification", 9371–10.89
"In Search of the Liquidity Effect", 9371–10.75

Goshen, Ind.
Wages by occupation, and benefits, for office and plant workers, 1991 survey, periodic MSA rpt, 6785–16.5

Gottholm, B. William
"Toxic Contaminants in the Gulf of Maine", 2176–3.17

Goudreau, Robert E.
"Commercial Bank Profitability Rises as Interest Margins and Securities Sales Increase", 9371–1.305

Gould, David M.
"Free Trade Agreements and the Credibility of Trade Reforms", 9379–1.301
"Immigrant Links to the Home Country: Implications for Trade, Welfare and Factor Rewards", 9379–12.84

Government agencies
see Government corporations and enterprises
see Local government

see State government
see under By Federal Agency in the "Index by Categories"
see under Federal boards, committees, and commissions
see under Federal executive departments
see under Federal independent agencies

Government and business

Appalachia local dev projects, and funding by source, by program and State, FY91, annual rpt, 9084–1
Assistance (block and categorical grants) programs for State and local govts, FY91, biennial listing, 10044–8
Assistance (financial and nonfinancial) of Fed Govt, 1992 base edition, annual listing, 104–5
Auto fuel economy improvements from new technologies, 1987-90 and alternative projections to 2010, 26358–251
Blind-operated vending facilities on Federal and non-Federal property, finances and operations by agency and State, FY91, annual rpt, 4944–2
Budget of US, House concurrent resolution, with spending and revenue targets, FY93 and projected to FY97, annual rpt, 21264–2
Budget of US, midsession review of FY93 budget, by function, annual rpt, 104–7
Budget of US, obligations and authority by function, agency, and program, with summaries and analyses, FY93, annual rpt, 104–2
Budget of US, receipts by source, outlays by agency and program, and balances, monthly rpt, 8102–3
Businesses aid to public schools, and business leaders views on education quality and reform, 1991 survey, article, 9383–19.301
Computer systems purchase and use, and data recording, processing, and transfer, Fed Govt standards, series, 2216–2
Export and import product standards under GATT, Natl Inst of Standards and Technology info activities, and proposed standards by agency and country, 1991, annual rpt, 2214–6
Export credit activity of Eximbank and 6 OECD countries, 1990, annual rpt, 9254–3
Food consumer research, marketing, legislation, and regulation devs, and consumption and price trends, quarterly journal, 1541–7
Israel economic conditions, US investment and export opportunities, and trade practices, 1992 rpt, 2008–32
Labs of Fed Govt, technology transfer to small manufacturers, promotional programs activities and grants to States, late 1980s-91, GAO rpt, 26113–551
Lands (public) acreage and grants, by State, FY91 and trends, annual rpt, 5724–1.1
Loans and loan guarantees of Fed Govt, outstanding amounts by agency and program, *Treasury Bulletin*, quarterly rpt, 8002–4.11
Manufacturing industry (US) intl competitiveness, trade and economic policies with background data and foreign comparisons, 1991 rpt, 26358–252
Minority Business Dev Centers mgmt and financial aid, and characteristics of businesses, by region and State, FY91, annual rpt, 2104–6
Natl income and product accounts, comprehensive accounts and components, benchmark revisions, 1929-88, 2708–5
Natl income and product accounts, comprehensive accounts and components, *Survey of Current Business*, monthly rpt, 2702–1.26
Oil and gas primary use prohibited for power and industrial plants, exemptions, and gas use by State, 1980-91, annual rpt, 3334–1
Overseas Business Reports: economic conditions, investment and export opportunities, and trade practices, country market research rpt series, 2046–6
Public opinion on taxes, spending, and govt efficiency, by respondent characteristics, 1992 survey, annual rpt, 10044–2
Rural areas businesses credit assistance of Fed Govt, by program and county characteristics, 1983-89, 1548–389
Semiconductor industry (US) intl competitiveness, status, outlook, and Federal policy, 1980s, annual rpt, 15034–1
Shipping industry structure, rates, and effects of Shipping Act, by route, 1980s, 9408–54
Spacecraft launches and other activities of NASA and USSR, with flight data, 1957-91, annual rpt, 9504–6.1
Standards for production, controls, and processes, domestic and intl dev in US and EC, 1980s-91, 26358–257
Telecommunications industry intl competitiveness, structure, and devs, with background data and foreign comparisons, 1991 rpt, 2808–30
Telephone firms borrowing under Rural Telephone Program, loan activity by State, FY91, annual tables, 1244–8
Telephone revenue increases requested, ordered, and pending, 1984-90, annual rpt, 9284–6.8
Weights, measures, and performance standards dev, proposals, and policies, 1992 annual conf, 2214–7
see also Administrative law and procedure
see also Agricultural production quotas and price supports
see also Agricultural subsidies
see also Commercial law
see also Consumer protection
see also Defense contracts and procurement
see also Defense industries
see also Environmental regulation
see also Federal aid to railroads
see also Federal funding for research and development
see also Financial institutions regulation
see also Food inspection
see also Government contracts and procurement
see also Government corporations and enterprises
see also Government inspections
see also Health care reform
see also Labor law
see also Lobbying and lobbying groups
see also Medical regulation
see also Mineral leases
see also Oil and gas leases
see also Price regulation
see also Subsidies
see also Tax exempt securities
see also Tax expenditures
see also Tax incentives and shelters
see also Trade adjustment assistance
see also under names of individual Federal agencies and commissions

Government and the press

see also Freedom of the press

Government assets and liabilities

Army and Air Force Exchange Service financial statements, 1990, annual rpt, 3504–21
Assets and debts of private sector, balance sheets by segment, 1960-91, semiannual rpt, 9365–4.1
Bank Insurance Fund finances projected under alternative assumptions about bank failures and assets involved, 1991-93, hearing, 21248–166
Bank Insurance Fund losses relation to duration of failed bank undercapitalization, 1985-90, article, 9391–1.312
Bond (junk) holdings of Resolution Trust Corp, quarterly press release, 9722–4
Bonneville Power Admin mgmt of Fed Columbia River Power System, finances and sales, summary data, quarterly rpt, 3222–2
Bonneville Power Admin mgmt of Fed Columbia River Power System, finances, operations, and sales by customer, FY91, annual rpt, 3224–1
Budget of US, authoritative financial statements with appropriations, outlays, and receipts, by category and agency, FY91, annual rpt, 8104–2.2
Budget of US, House concurrent resolution, with spending and revenue targets, FY93 and projected to FY97, annual rpt, 21264–2
Budget of US, obligations and authority by function, agency, and program, with summaries and analyses, FY93, annual rpt, 104–2
Colorado River Storage Project finances and activities in western States, FY91, annual rpt, 5824–3
Credit Union Natl Admin Central Liquidity Facility financial statements, FY91, annual rpt, 9534–5
Credit Union Natl Share Insurance Fund losses from failed credit unions, by asset size and charter, and for largest failures by instn, FY86-91, 9536–1.7
DC govt finances, revenue by source, financial statements, and employment, with income in central city and suburbs compared to other cities, 1991 hearings, 21308–28
Economic Report of the President for 1992, with economic trends from 1929, annual rpt, 204–1.10
Farm Credit System financial condition, quarterly rpt, 9262–2
Farm Credit System financial statements and loan activity by lender type, and borrower characteristics, 1991, annual rpt, 9264–2
Farm Credit System financial statements, 1991, annual rpt, 9264–5
FDIC finances and operations, insured deposits, and finances of banks needing FDIC aid, 1991 and trends from 1934, annual rpt, 9294–1

Fed Financing Bank holdings and transactions, by borrower, monthly press release, 12802–1
Fed Govt assets targeted for disposition, inventories by type, and related employment and contracts, by agency, FY90, GAO rpt, 26119–369
Fed Govt liabilities and other financial commitments, by type, *Treasury Bulletin*, quarterly rpt, 8002–4.3
Fed Govt receipts by source and outlays by agency, *Treasury Bulletin*, quarterly rpt, 8002–4.1
Fed Home Loan Bank of Atlanta financial statements, quarterly rpt, 9302–37
Fed Home Loan Bank of Atlanta financial statements, 1989-91, annual rpt, 9304–1
Fed Home Loan Bank of Boston financial statements, quarterly rpt, 9302–35
Fed Home Loan Bank of Boston financial statements, 1990-91, annual rpt, 9304–2
Fed Home Loan Bank of Chicago financial statements, 1989-91, annual rpt, 9304–4
Fed Home Loan Bank of Cincinnati financial statements, 1989-91, annual rpt, 9304–6
Fed Home Loan Bank of Dallas financial statements, 1989-91, annual rpt, 9304–11
Fed Home Loan Bank of Des Moines financial statements, 1989-91, annual rpt, 9304–7
Fed Home Loan Bank of New York financial statements, 1989-91, annual rpt, 9304–12
Fed Home Loan Bank of Pittsburgh financial statements, 1989-91, annual rpt, 9304–13
Fed Home Loan Bank of San Francisco financial statements, 1989-91, annual rpt, 9304–14
Fed Home Loan Bank of Seattle financial statements, 1989-91, annual rpt, 9304–15
Fed Home Loan Bank of Topeka financial statements, 1989-91, annual rpt, 9304–16
Fed Home Loan Banks financial statements, monthly tables, 9442–1
Fed Home Loan Banks financial statements, 1989-91, annual rpt, 9444–1
Fed Home Loan Mortgage Corp activities and financial statements, 1991, annual rpt, 9414–1
Fed Home Loan Mortgage Corp financial condition and capital adequacy, 1990, annual rpt, 5184–8
Fed Natl Mortgage Assn activities and finances, 1991, annual rpt, 5184–9; 9474–1
Fed Natl Mortgage Assn, Fed Home Loan Mortgage Corp, and FHLBs finances, 1991 hearings, 21248–170
Fed Reserve Bank of Atlanta financial statements, 1990-91, annual rpt, 9371–4
Fed Reserve Bank of Boston financial statements, 1990-91, annual rpt, 9373–26
Fed Reserve Bank of Chicago financial statements, 1990-91, annual rpt, 9375–5
Fed Reserve Bank of Cleveland financial statements, 1990-91, annual rpt, 9377–5
Fed Reserve Bank of Dallas financial statements, 1990-91, annual rpt, 9379–2
Fed Reserve Bank of Kansas City financial statements, 1990-91, annual rpt, 9381–3
Fed Reserve Bank of Minneapolis financial statements, 1990-91, annual rpt, 9383–2
Fed Reserve Bank of New York financial statements, 1990-91, annual rpt, 9385–2
Fed Reserve Bank of Philadelphia financial statements, 1990-91, annual rpt, 9387–3
Fed Reserve Bank of Richmond financial statements, 1990-91, annual rpt, 9389–2
Fed Reserve Bank of San Francisco financial statements, 1990-91, annual rpt, 9393–2
Fed Reserve Bank of St Louis financial statements, 1990-91, annual rpt, 9391–17
Fed Reserve Bd and Reserve banks finances, staff, and review of monetary policy and economic devs, 1991, annual rpt, 9364–1
FHA-insured mortgage activities, audits, and financial statements, FY90-91, annual rpt, 5144–26
Govt Natl Mortgage Assn finances, and mortgage-backed securities program, FY91, annual rpt, 5144–6
GPO activities, finances, and production, FY91, annual rpt, 26204–1
GSA activities and finances, FY91, annual rpt, 9454–1
Immigration and Naturalization Service activities and finances, FY91, annual summary rpt, 6264–7
Justice Dept Asset Forfeiture Program seizures, finances, and disbursements, FY85-91, annual rpt, 6004–21
Loans, loan guarantees, and grants of Fed Govt, administrative costs budget accounting, by program and agency, 1992 rpt, 26306–6.166
Loans of Treasury Dept and Federal Financing Bank to Govt corporations and agencies, outstanding amounts, 1987-91, GAO rpt, 26111–79
Merit Systems Protection Board activities, staff, and finances, FY91, annual rpt, 9494–5
Mint (US) activities, finances, coin and medals production and holdings, and gold and silver transactions, by facility, FY91, annual rpt, 8204–1
Natl income and product accounts, comprehensive accounts and components, benchmark revisions, 1929-88, 2708–5
Natl income and product accounts, comprehensive accounts and components, *Survey of Current Business*, monthly rpt, 2702–1.26
New England States govt retirement systems investment policy assessment, with system assets and liabilities, by State, 1992 article, 9373–25.301
Panama Canal Commission finances and activities, with Canal traffic and local govt operations, FY91, annual rpt, 9664–3
Pension Benefit Guaranty Corp activities and finances, FY91, annual rpt, 9674–1
Pension Benefit Guaranty Corp single- and multi-employer funds balances, FY91, article, 9391–16.309
Pension plans terminated, liabilities, assets, and Pension Benefit Guarantee Corp recoveries and losses, with top 50 underfunded plans, mid 1970s-91, article, 9371–1.302
Postal Service activities, finances, and mail volume and subsidies, FY91, annual rpt, 9864–5.3
Postal Service activities, financial statements, and employment, FY87-91, annual rpt, 9864–1
Prison Industries (Federal) finances and operations, FY91, annual rpt, 6244–3
Radio Free Europe and Radio Liberty broadcast and financial data, FY91, annual rpt, 10314–1
Railroad (Amtrak) finances and operations, FY91, annual rpt, 29524–1
Railroad (Amtrak) finances, executive office travel expenses and staff years, and membership dues by assn, FY88-92, GAO rpt, 26113–573
Railroad Retirement Accounts financial statements, FY91, annual rpt, 9704–1
Real estate assets of failed thrifts, sales by Resolution Trust Corp, and disposition of other assets, 1990-91, GAO rpt, 26119–372
Red Cross activities and finances, FY91, annual rpt, 29254–1
Resolution Trust Corp activities and finances, with data on savings instns conservatorships by State and instn, 1990, annual rpt, 9724–1
Resolution Trust Corp assets disposition, use of private contractors, fees paid, and location of assets, 1990-91, GAO rpt, 26119–424
Resolution Trust Corp obligation limits compliance, and balance sheet, quarterly GAO rpt, 26102–6
Resolution Trust Corp real estate assets from failed thrifts, availability, semiannual listing series, 9722–2
Resolution Trust Corp real estate assets marketing activities, real estate industry views, 1991 survey, GAO rpt, 26119–422
Rural Telephone Bank financial statements, FY91, annual rpt, 1244–4
Savings instns failures, financial performance of instns under Resolution Trust Corp conservatorship, quarterly rpt, 9722–5
Small Business Admin loan and contract activity by program and firm, and financial condition, FY91, annual rpt, 9764–1
Southwestern Fed Power System financial statements, sales by customer, and operations and costs by project, FY91, annual rpt, 3244–1
St Lawrence Seaway Dev Corp finances and activities, with Seaway cargo tonnage, and shipping costs compared to other US ports, 1990, annual rpt, 7744–1
State and local govt employees pension system cash and security holdings and finances, quarterly rpt, 2462–2
Student Loan Marketing Assn activities and finances, 1991, annual rpt, 9784–1
TVA finances and electric power sales, FY91, annual rpt, 9804–1
TVA finances and operations by program and facility, FY91, annual rpt, 9804–32
Uranium enrichment facilities of DOE, financial statements, FY90-91, annual rpt, 3354–7
Western Area Power Admin activities by plant, financial statements, and sales by customer, FY91, annual rpt, 3254–1
Workers compensation programs under Federal admin, finances and operations, FY91, annual rpt, 6504–10
see also Defense budgets and appropriations
see also Foreign budgets

see also Foreign debts
see also Government revenues
see also Government securities
see also Government spending
see also Government supplies and property
see also Government trust funds
see also International reserves
see also Military supplies and property
see also Municipal bonds
see also Public debt
see also State government spending
see also U.S. savings bonds
Government bonds
see Government securities
see Municipal bonds
see Tax exempt securities
see U.S. savings bonds
Government buildings
see Public buildings
Government census
see Census of Governments
Government-citizen lawsuits
Claims Court caseload by type of suit, and judgments, FY92, annual rpt, 18224–1
Court civil and criminal caseloads for Federal district, appeals, and bankruptcy courts, by type of suit and offense, circuit, and district, 1991, annual rpt, 18204–11
Court civil and criminal caseloads for Federal district, appeals, and special courts, 1991, annual rpt, 18204–8
US attorneys case processing and collections, by case type and Federal district, FY91, annual rpt, 6004–2
Government-citizen relations
Asbestos in schools, inspection and abatement effectiveness, staff and parental notification, and inspector and janitorial training, as of 1990, 9238–71
Census of Population, 1990: minority group participation in census, effectiveness and quality of outreach and promotional programs, hearing, 21628–103
FDA investigations and regulatory activities, quarterly rpt, 4062–3
Historic and natural natl landmarks damaged and threatened, with owner, location, damage type, and recommended remedial action, 1990, annual listing, 5544–16
IRS collections, enforcement, and litigation activity, with data by type of tax, region, and State, FY91, annual rpt, 8304–3
IRS individual income tax returns processing and taxpayer info activity, electronic and experimental filings, and refunds, periodic press release, 8302–6
IRS taxpayer assistance and education programs performance indicators, FY91, annual rpt, 8304–3.1
IRS telephone system for income tax aid, improvements in accuracy, 1989-91, GAO rpt, 26119–418
Mail (penalty) to households, by content, FY87-90, annual rpt, 9864–10
OASDHI and SSI admin, case processing, staff, and client problems with contacting SSA offices, 1980s-90, hearing, 25148–45
Public lands access restricted by private landowners, reasons and impacts on recreation and land mgmt activities, 1991-92 surveys, GAO rpt, 26113–571
Public opinion on taxes, spending, and govt efficiency, by respondent characteristics, 1992 survey, annual rpt, 10044–2
SSA public contact experience and satisfaction, and other OASDHI issues, public opinion, 1991 survey, 10176–2.2
Tax (income) earned income credit advance payment option, participation, taxpayer awareness, employer burden, and IRS admin, 1989-90, GAO rpt, 26119–378
see also Civil rights
see also Elections
see also Government and business
see also Government-citizen lawsuits
see also Impacted areas
see also Lobbying and lobbying groups
see also Taxation
Government contracts and procurement
Aerospace industry sales, orders, backlog, and firms, by product for govt, military, and other customers, 1991, annual Current Industrial Rpt, 2506–12.22
AID and Intl Dev Cooperation Agency activities and funding, FY91-93, with developing countries economic and social conditions from 1960s, annual rpt, 9904–4
AID contracts and grants for technical and support services, by instn, country, and State, FY91, annual listing, 9914–7
AID contracts, grants, and cooperative agreements with higher education instns, by project, instn, and country, FY91, annual listing, 9914–6
Argonne Natl Lab procurement from govt supply sources, FY91, 3006–5.29
Army Corps of Engineers recreation facilities mgmt, acreage, visits, and non-Federal public and private dev alternatives, 1980s-90, 3758–8
Audiovisual activities and spending of Fed Govt, by whether performed in-house and agency, FY91, annual rpt, 9514–1
Budget of US, authoritative financial statements with appropriations, outlays, and receipts, by category and agency, FY91, annual rpt, 8104–2.2
Cancer Natl Inst contracts and grants, by recipient and location, annual listing, discontinued, 4474–28
Capitol Architect activities, funding, costs, and contracts, FY89, annual rpt, 25944–1
Capitol Architect outlays for salaries, supplies, and services, itemized by payee and function, 2nd half FY91, semiannual rpt, 25922–2
Claims Court caseload by type of suit, and judgments, FY92, annual rpt, 18224–1
Commerce Dept programs fraud and abuse, audits and investigations, 2nd half FY92, semiannual rpt, 2002–5
DC metro area land acquisition and dev projects of Fed Govt, characteristics and funding by agency and project, FY92-96, annual rpt, 15454–1
Disabled persons workshops finances, operations, and Federal procurement, FY82-91, annual rpt, 11714–1
DOE contractor computer system security and controls at Strategic Petroleum Reserve offices, 1991, 3006–5.27
DOE contractor research lab and nuclear weapons facilities radiation and other pollutant releases, monitoring results, annual site rpt series, 3324–2
DOE mgmt and operating contract admin at Nevada Field Office, funding, property value, and staff, FY88-90, 3006–5.31
DOE Oak Ridge Natl Lab contractors excise tax refunds due from off-highway motor fuel use, 1988-90, 3006–5.26
DOE procurement contract awards to small businesses, by business type and subagency, FY90, annual rpt, 3004–35
DOE R&D field offices and facilities, activities, staff, and finances, FY91, biennial rpt, 3004–4
DOE real property owned and leased, by type, subagency, contractor, and site, FY91, annual rpt, 3004–28
DOT programs fraud and abuse, audit resolution activities, 1st half FY92, semiannual rpt, 7302–12
DOT programs fraud and abuse, audits and investigations, 1st half FY92, semiannual rpt, 7302–4
Drug (prescription) prices charged to VA and Fed Govt, by manufacturer and drug, 1990-91, hearing, 21768–68
Drug (prescription) prices charged to wholesalers, retailers, VA, and Fed Govt, for 29 drugs, 1985-91, GAO rpt, 26121–472
Electric power capacity and use in Pacific Northwest, by energy source, forecast under alternative load and demand cases, 1991-2012, annual rpt, 3224–3
Employees in Fed Govt procurement operations, job performance, and views on policies and practices, 1991 survey, 9498–17
EPA programs fraud and abuse, audits and investigations, 1st half FY92, semiannual rpt, 9182–10
Expenditures of Fed Govt in States and local areas, by type, State, county, and city, FY91, annual rpt, 2464–3
Expenditures of Fed Govt in States, by type, program, agency, and State, FY91, annual rpt, 2464–2
Fed Govt agencies administrative records and other holdings of Natl Archives, final inventories, series, 9516–2
Fed Govt assets targeted for disposition, inventories by type, and related employment and contracts, by agency, FY90, GAO rpt, 26119–369
Fed Govt obligations by function and agency, *Treasury Bulletin*, quarterly rpt, 8002–4.2
Fed Transit Admin grants by State, and oversight, 1988-92, GAO rpt, 26113–600
Finances of govts, tax systems and revenue, and fiscal structure, by level of govt and State, 1992 and historical trends, annual rpt, 10044–1
Food aid programs purchases, by commodity, firm, and shipping point or destination, weekly rpt, 1302–3
Fraud and abuse in Fed Govt, audits and investigations by agency, FY91, annual rpt, 104–29
GPO activities, finances, and production, FY91, annual rpt, 26204–1
GSA programs fraud and abuse, audits and investigations, 1st half FY92, semiannual rpt, 9452–8
Health Care Financing Admin procurement contracts, by business category, FY87, annual rpt, 4654–5
HHS financial aid, by program, recipient, State, and city, FY91, annual regional listings, 4004–3

HHS programs fraud and abuse, audits and investigations, 1st half FY92, semiannual rpt, 4002–6
Higher education enrollment, faculty, finances, and degrees, by instn level and control, and State, FY88, annual rpt, 4844–13
HUD programs fraud and abuse, audits and investigations, FY92, semiannual rpt, 5002–8; 5002–11
Hwy construction bids and contracts for Federal-aid hwys, by State, 1st half 1992, semiannual rpt, 7552–12
Indian Health Service, tribal, and contract facilities hospitalization, by diagnosis, age, sex, and service area, FY91, annual rpt, 4084–5
Infant formula bid prices and contracts awarded by States under USDA food aid program for women, infants, and children, late 1980s-91, hearing, 25528–118
Input-output structure of US economy, detailed interindustry transactions for 84 industries, and components of final demand, 1987, annual article, 2702–1.316
Input-output structure of US economy, detailed interindustry transactions for 541 industries, and components of final demand, 1982 benchmark data, 2708–17
Interior Dept programs fraud and abuse, audits and investigations, 2nd half FY92, semiannual rpt, 5302–2
Investigations of Federal agency and program operations, summaries of findings, as of 1991, annual GAO rpt, 26104–5
Labor laws enacted, by State, 1991, annual article, 6722–1.309
Labor productivity of Federal employees, indexes of output and labor costs by function, FY67-90, annual rpt, 6824–1.6
Labor surplus areas eligible for preferential Fed Govt contracts, monthly listing, 6402–1
Lead paint abatement costs and results, demonstration project design and findings, 1991 rpt, 5188–131
Manufacturing census, 1987: shipments of manufacturers products, by customer class and SIC 2- and 4-digit industry, subject rpt, 2497–4
Minority Business Dev Centers mgmt and financial aid, and characteristics of businesses, by region and State, FY91, annual rpt, 2104–6
Minority business Federal procurement set-aside contracts, by participant race and sex, industry, firm, and State, FY90, annual rpt, 9764–8
Minority business Federal procurement set-aside contracts, by State, FY90, GAO rpt, 26113–563
Minority business funding, by program and Federal agency, FY91, annual rpt, 2104–5
NASA accidents, casualties, damage, and safety activities, FY91, annual rpt, 9504–4
NASA and contractor cooperative education programs activities, 1991, 9508–41
NASA funding by program and type of performer, and contract awards by State, FY91, annual rpt, 9504–6.2
NASA programs fraud and abuse, audits and investigations, 2nd half FY92, semiannual rpt, 9502–9
NASA space station *Freedom* technical characteristics, funding, and contracts by State, 1985-92 and projected 1997-2002, 9508–40
Natl income and product accounts and components, *Survey of Current Business*, monthly rpt, 2702–1.23
Natl income and product accounts benchmark revisions of GDP and natl income, various periods 1959-80, tables, 2702–1.307
Natl income and product accounts, comprehensive accounts and components, benchmark revisions, 1929-88, 2708–5
Natl income and product accounts, comprehensive accounts and components, *Survey of Current Business*, monthly rpt, 2702–1.26
Neighborhood Reinvestment Corp contracting practices and oversight of local grantees, with grantee listing, FY88-91, GAO rpt, 26113–587
NIH grants and contracts, by inst and type of recipient, FY82-91, annual rpt, 4434–9
NSF programs fraud and abuse, audits and investigations, 2nd half FY92, semiannual rpt, 9622–1
Nuclear weapons facilities of DOE, contractor fees, environmental and safety enforcement activity, and salaries, by contractor and facility, 1987-88, hearing, 21408–127
Postal Service inspection activities, 2nd half FY92, semiannual rpt, 9862–2
Prison and community-based facilities, population, employment, spending, and other characteristics, by State and for Fed Govt, 1990, quinquennial rpt, 6068–218
Prison Industries (Federal) finances and operations, FY91, annual rpt, 6244–3
Prison Industries (Federal) sales, by commodity and Federal agency, FY91, annual rpt, 6244–5
Prisoners in Federal and contract instns, by selected characteristics and region, FY89, annual rpt, 6244–1.1
Resolution Trust Corp assets disposition, use of private contractors, fees paid, and location of assets, 1990-91, GAO rpt, 26119–424
Savings instns failure resolution activity and finances of Resolution Trust Corp, with data by asset type, State, region, and instn, monthly rpt, 9722–3
School lunch programs food donations processing, contracts, and processors problems with State reporting requirements, with data by State, 1989-91, GAO rpt, 26113–555
Small Business Admin loan and contract activity by program and firm, and financial condition, FY91, annual rpt, 9764–1
Small Business Admin programs fraud and abuse, audits and investigations, 1st half FY92, semiannual rpt, 9762–5
Small business finances, operations, owner characteristics, and Federal contracts, 1980s-90, annual rpt, 9764–6
Small business R&D grants of Fed Govt, project sales by type and dev funding by source, by agency and selected firm, 1984-91, GAO rpt, 26113–393
Space programs procurement contract awards of NASA, by type, contractor, State, and country, FY92 with trends from 1961, semiannual rpt, 9502–6
State Dept programs fraud and abuse, audits and investigations, 2nd half FY92, semiannual rpt, 7002–6
Tree planting on govt land contracted to small businesses, Federal grants, State funding, and projects, by State, FY91, annual rpt, 9764–10
TVA finances and operations by program and facility, FY91, annual rpt, 9804–32
US attorneys civil and criminal cases by type and disposition, and collections, by Federal district, FY91, annual rpt, 6004–2.1; 6004–2.5
USDA programs fraud and abuse, audits and investigations, FY92, semiannual rpt, 1002–4
USIA programs fraud and abuse, audits and investigations, 1st half FY92, semiannual rpt, 9852–2
VA and non-VA facilities health services sharing contracts, by service type and region, FY91, annual rpt, 8704–5
VA and non-VA facilities health services sharing contracts, by service type, FY80-90, compilation of papers, 8608–9
VA programs fraud and abuse, audits and investigations, 2nd half FY92, semiannual rpt, 8602–1
see also Defense contracts and procurement
see also Federal funding for energy programs
see also Federal funding for research and development

Government corporations and enterprises
Assets and debts of private sector, balance sheets by segment, 1960-91, semiannual rpt, 9365–4.1
Budget of US, obligations and authority by function, agency, and program, with summaries and analyses, FY93, annual rpt, 104–2
Budget of US, receipts by source, outlays by agency and program, and balances, monthly rpt, 8102–3
Financial operations of Fed Govt, detailed data, *Treasury Bulletin*, quarterly rpt, 8002–4
Input-output structure of US economy, detailed interindustry transactions for 84 industries, and components of final demand, 1987, annual article, 2702–1.316
Input-output structure of US economy, detailed interindustry transactions for 541 industries, and components of final demand, 1982 benchmark data, 2708–17
Investigations of Federal agency and program operations, summaries of findings, as of 1991, annual GAO rpt, 26104–5
Israel economic conditions, US investment and export opportunities, and trade practices, 1992 rpt, 2008–32
Loans of Treasury Dept and Federal Financing Bank to Govt corporations and agencies, outstanding amounts, 1987-91, GAO rpt, 26111–79
Mortgage loan activity, by type of lender, loan, and mortgaged property, monthly press release, 5142–18
Mortgage loan activity, by type of lender, loan, and mortgaged property, quarterly press release, 5142–30

Natl income and product accounts, comprehensive accounts and components, benchmark revisions, 1929-88, 2708–5
Natl income and product accounts, comprehensive accounts and components, *Survey of Current Business*, monthly rpt, 2702–1.24
Statistical Abstract of US, 1992 annual data compilation, 2324–1.10
see also Commodity Credit Corp.
see also Communications Satellite Corp.
see also Corporation for Public Broadcasting
see also Export-Import Bank
see also Federal Agricultural Mortgage Corp.
see also Federal Crop Insurance Corp.
see also Federal Deposit Insurance Corp.
see also Federal Home Loan Mortgage Corp.
see also Federal Housing Finance Board
see also Federal National Mortgage Association
see also Federal Prison Industries
see also Federal Savings and Loan Insurance Corp.
see also Financing Corp.
see also Government National Mortgage Association
see also Inter-American Foundation
see also Legal Services Corp.
see also National Railroad Passenger Corp.
see also Neighborhood Reinvestment Corp.
see also Overseas Private Investment Corp.
see also Pennsylvania Avenue Development Corp.
see also Pension Benefit Guaranty Corp.
see also Reconstruction Finance Corp.
see also Resolution Trust Corp.
see also Rural Telephone Bank
see also Securities Investor Protection Corp.
see also St. Lawrence Seaway Development Corp.
see also Student Loan Marketing Association
see also Tennessee Valley Authority
see also U.S. Postal Service

Government debt
see Public debt

Government documents
Forest Service activities and finances, by region and State, FY91, annual rpt, 1204–1.3
GPO activities, finances, and production, FY91, annual rpt, 26204–1
GPO activities, staff, and productivity, 1970s-90 and projected to 2000, 26208–4
Labor productivity of Federal employees, indexes of output and labor costs by function, FY67-90, annual rpt, 6824–1.6
Natl Archives and Records Admin activities, finances, holdings, and staff, FY91, annual rpt, 9514–2
Natl Archives holdings of Federal agencies administrative records and other materials, final inventories, series, 9516–2
Natl Archives holdings of Federal publications and other material, special collections, series, 9516–1
see also CD-ROM catalogs and guides
see also CD-ROM releases
see also Environmental impact statements
see also Federal Inspectors General reports
see also Government forms and paperwork
see also Government publications lists

Government efficiency
AFDC application processing duration, and time from hearing requests to decision, by State, FY90, annual rpt, 4584–3.3; 4584–3.4
Air Force fiscal mgmt system operations and techniques, quarterly rpt, 3602–1
Banks in Fed Reserve System, expenses and operations itemized by service, office, and district, 1991, annual rpt, 9364–11
Budget of US, Bush Admin mgmt proposals, by function, FY93, annual rpt, 104–2.2
Court civil and criminal case dispositions and trials, and time to trial and case disposition, for Federal district courts, 1991, annual rpt, 18204–8.18
Drug marketing application processing of FDA, by drug, purpose, and producer, 1991, annual rpt, 4064–14
Employment discrimination complaints, processing, and disposition, by complaint type and Federal agency, FY90, annual rpt, 9244–11
EPA regulatory and protection programs operations and mgmt goals, progress and activities, by office, quarterly rpt, 9182–11
Fed Govt agencies and program operations investigations, summaries of findings, as of 1991, annual GAO rpt, 26104–5
Fed Govt agencies programs and services performance evaluation measures use, dev, and effectiveness, 1991 survey, GAO rpt, 26119–396
FmHA activities, and loans and grants by program and State, FY91 and trends from FY70, annual rpt, 1184–17
Food stamp eligibility and payment errors, by type, recipient characteristics, and State, FY90, annual rpt, 1364–15
GPO activities, staff, and productivity, 1970s-90 and projected to 2000, 26208–4
Incentive awards to Federal employees, costs, and benefits, by award type and agency, FY90, annual rpt, 9844–20
Info collection of Fed Govt under Paperwork Reduction Act, respondent burden, OMB reviews, violations, and major info systems proposals, 1981-92, annual rpt, 104–26
IRS individual income tax returns processing and taxpayer info activity, electronic and experimental filings, and refunds, periodic press release, 8302–6
IRS operating costs, collections, and ratios, FY91, annual rpt, 8304–3.2
Labor productivity of Federal employees, indexes of output and labor costs by function, FY67-90, annual rpt, 6824–4
Labor productivity of govt employees, indexes of output and labor costs by function, FY67-90, annual rpt, 6824–1.6
Medicare admin and research, and HCFA affirmative action and accreditation programs, FY87, annual rpt, 4654–5
Merit system oversight and enforcement activities of OPM, series, 9496–2
Merit Systems Protection Board decisions on appeals of Fed Govt personnel actions, by agency and region, FY91, annual rpt, 9494–2
OASDHI and SSI admin, case processing, staff, and client problems with contacting SSA offices, 1980s-90, hearing, 25148–45
Postal Service activities, finances, and mail volume and subsidies, FY91, annual rpt, 9864–5
Postal Service activities, financial statements, and employment, FY87-91, annual rpt, 9864–1
Procurement operations of Fed Govt, employees job performance, and views on policies and practices, 1991 survey, 9498–17
Public opinion on taxes, spending, and govt efficiency, by respondent characteristics, 1992 survey, annual rpt, 10044–2
Quality mgmt practices of Fed Govt, employee views, 1992 survey, GAO rpt, 26119–425
SSA activities, litigation, finances, and staff, FY91, annual rpt, 4704–6
Supervisors (first-line) in Fed Govt, performance ratings by self, superiors, and subordinates, 1991 survey, 9498–15
Unemployment insurance programs of States, quality appraisal results, FY91, annual rpt, 6404–16
see also Federal Inspectors General reports
see also General Accounting Office

Government employees
Business statistics, detailed data for major industries and economic indicators, 1960-91, *Survey of Current Business* biennial supplement, 2704–1
Employment and direct spending, by function and level of govt, selected years 1967-87, 10048–53
Employment and Earnings, detailed data, monthly rpt, 6742–2.5
Employment and payroll, by function and level of govt, annual rpt series, 2466–1
Employment Cost Index and alternative measure of compensation costs, by component, occupation, industry group, union status, and location, 1975-92, annual rpt, 6744–20
Employment, earnings, and hours, by selected SIC 1- to 4-digit industry, State, and for 275 MSAs, 1987-92, 6748–81
Employment, earnings, and hours, by SIC 1- to 4-digit industry, monthly 1989-Feb 1992, annual rpt, 6744–4
Employment, earnings, and hours, monthly press release, 6742–5
Employment, unemployment, and labor force characteristics, by State, MSA, and selected city, 1991, annual rpt, 6744–7.2; 6744–7.3
New England States economic indicators, Fed Reserve 1st District, monthly rpt, 9373–2
NYC housing supply, occupancy, condition, and household characteristics, by tenure and borough, 1991 triennial survey, 2488–3
Pacific territories population and housing detailed characteristics, by location, 1990 Census of Population and Housing, series, 2551–8
Palau admin, and social, economic, and govtl data, FY91, annual rpt, 7004–6
Southeastern US employment by industry div, earnings, and hours, for 8 States, quarterly press release, 6942–7
Statistical Abstract of US, 1992 annual data compilation, 2324–1.9
Tennessee Valley economic conditions, and compared to US, alternative projections 1992-2010 and trends from 1929, annual rpt, 9804–27

Terrorism (intl) incidents, casualties, and attacks on US targets, by attack type and country, 1991, annual rpt, 7004–22
Terrorism (intl) incidents, casualties, and attacks on US targets, by attack type and world area, 1991, annual rpt, 7004–13
Youth labor force status, by sex, race, and industry div, summer 1988-92, annual press release, 6744–14
see also Civil service pensions
see also Civil service system
see also Congressional employees
see also Corruption and bribery
see also Federal employees
see also Federal pay
see also Government pay
see also International employees
see also Labor-management relations in government
see also Military pay
see also Military personnel
see also Officials
see also Police
see also Political ethics
see also Postal employees
see also Public service employment
see also State and local employees
see also State and local employees pay
see also State police

Government energy use
Auto alternative fuels use in Federal fleet, energy economy performance at 4 sites, FY91, annual rpt, 3304–28
Auto fleet size, trip characteristics, and energy use, by fleet type, 1970s-90, annual rpt, 3304–5.3
Bonneville Power Admin mgmt of Fed Columbia River Power System, finances, operations, and sales by customer, FY91, annual rpt, 3224–1
Bonneville Power Admin sales, revenues, and rates, by customer and customer type, 1991, semiannual rpt, 3222–1
Building (commercial) energy use, costs, and conservation, by building characteristics, survey rpt series, 3166–8
Business statistics, detailed data for major industries and economic indicators, *Survey of Current Business*, monthly rpt, 2702–1.12
Conservation aid of Fed Govt to public and nonprofit private instns, by building type and State, 1991, annual rpt, 3304–15
Conservation of energy, State programs aid from Fed Govt, and energy savings, by State, 1990, annual rpt, 3304–1
DOE energy use, costs, and conservation, by end use, fuel type, and field office, FY91, annual rpt, 3004–27
Electric utilities privately owned, finances and operations, detailed data, 1990, annual rpt, 3164–23
Fed Govt energy use, by agency and fuel type, FY78-91, annual rpt, 3164–74.1
Fed Govt power plants conversion to alternative fuels, 1992, annual rpt, 3334–2
Gasoline and other motor fuel use, by consuming sector and State, 1991, annual rpt, 7554–1.1
Military oil supply, by world region of origin, FY85-87, 3166–6.65
Military prime contract awards, by category, contract and contractor type, and service branch, FY82-1st half FY92, semiannual rpt, 3542–1
Military prime contract awards, by category, contractor type, and State, FY89-91, annual rpt, 3544–11
Military prime contract awards, by detailed procurement category, FY88-91, annual rpt, 3544–18
Natl income and product accounts, comprehensive accounts and components, benchmark revisions, 1929-88, 2708–5
Natl income and product accounts, comprehensive accounts and components, *Survey of Current Business*, monthly rpt, 2702–1.26
Natural gas interstate pipeline company detailed financial and operating data, by firm, 1990, annual rpt, 3164–38
Pacific Northwest electric power capacity and use, by energy source, forecast under alternative load and demand cases, 1991-2012, annual rpt, 3224–3
Persian Gulf War costs to US by category and service branch, and offsetting contributions by allied country, monthly rpt, 102–3
Southwestern Fed Power System financial statements, sales by customer, and operations and costs by project, FY91, annual rpt, 3244–1
TVA energy use by fuel type, and conservation costs and savings, FY91, annual rpt, 9804–26
VA health care facilities energy use and conservation, by facility, quarterly rpt, 8602–9

Government forms and paperwork
Criminal sentences for Federal offenses, guidelines by offense and circumstances, series, 17668–1
DOE data collection forms and related rpts, 1991, annual listing, 3164–86
Energy Info Admin activities, 1991, annual rpt, 3164–29
Fed Govt agencies administrative records and other holdings of Natl Archives, final inventories, series, 9516–2
Hazardous waste generation reduction, accuracy of voluntary industry programs rpts to EPA, 1992 GAO rpt, 26131–98
Identification cards issued for nondrivers, characteristics and fees by State, as of Jan 1992, biennial rpt, 7554–18
Mail volume to and from households, use, and views, by class, source, content, and household characteristics, FY87-90, annual rpt, 9864–10
Medicare beneficiaries knowledge of and experience with physician billing and payment under Medicare, by selected characteristics, 1988-89, 17266–2.1
Medicare providers identification number assignment by carriers, operations, 1989-90, 4006–11.1
Money laundering investigation activities of States and Fed Govt, and use of IRS large cash transaction rpts, by State, 1985-91, GAO rpt, 26119–430
NIH research and training grants awarded to women, by recipient characteristics, inst, and host instn, FY90, annual rpt, 4434–18
Occupational deaths data collection program of BLS and States, with results by selected worker characteristics, 1991, article, 6722–1.338
Paperwork Reduction Act effects on Fed Govt info collection, with respondent burden, OMB reviews, violations, and major info systems proposals, 1981-92, annual rpt, 104–26
Railroad safety violation claims settled, by carrier, FY91, annual rpt, 7604–10
School lunch programs food donations processing, contracts, and processors problems with State reporting requirements, with data by State, 1989-91, GAO rpt, 26113–555
Social security number issues, 1937-90, annual rpt, 4744–3.2
Tax (income) earned income credit advance payment option, participation, taxpayer awareness, employer burden, and IRS admin, 1989-90, GAO rpt, 26119–378
Tax (income) return checkoff for contribution to presidential campaign fund, receipts and outlays, mid 1970s-91 and alternative projections to 1993, hearing, 21428–10
Tax (income) returns and supplemental documents filed, by type, FY91 and projected to FY2000, semiannual rpt, 8302–4
Tax (income) returns filed, by type, IRS service center, and whether full-paid, refund, and electronically filed, 1990 and projected to 1998, semiannual rpt, 8302–7
Tax (income) returns filed, by type of filer, selected income items, quarterly rpt, 8302–2.1
Tax (income) returns filed using alternative methods, with fraud, and conventional form preparation time and processing costs, 1986-92, GAO rpt, 26119–400
Tax (income) returns of individuals, by filing status, tax item, and income level, 1991, annual article, 8302–2.319
Tax (income) returns of individuals, IRS processing and taxpayer info activity, electronic and experimental filings, and refunds, periodic press release, 8302–6
Tax (income) withholding and related documents filed, by type and IRS service center, 1991 and projected 1992-99, annual rpt, 8304–22
Tax collection, enforcement, and litigation activity of IRS, with data by type of tax, region, and State, FY91, annual rpt, 8304–3
Tax returns and supplemental documents filed, by type, 1990 and projected to 1999, annual article, 8302–2.304
Tax returns filed, by type of tax and IRS district, 1990 and projected 1991-98, annual rpt, 8304–24
Tax returns filed, by type of tax and IRS region and service center, projected 1991-98 and trends from 1978, annual rpt, 8304–9
Wage reporting by employers, SSA and IRS reconciliation of records, late 1970s-80s, GAO rpt, 26121–477
see also Licenses and permits

Government grants
see Community Development Block Grants
see Federal aid programs
see Federal funding for research and development
see Revenue sharing

see Urban Development Action Grants
see terms beginning with Federal aid

Government housing
see Public housing

Government information
Advisory committees of Fed Govt, and members, staff, meetings, and costs by agency, FY91, annual rpt, 9454–18
Assistance (financial and nonfinancial) of Fed Govt, 1992 base edition, annual listing, 104–5
BEA rpts data coverage and availability, 1992 annual article, 2702–1.308
Electronic info storage and transmission costs and revenues for 4 Federal agencies, FY85-91, GAO rpt, 26125–47
Environmental quality indicators, NOAA monitoring results, 1991 annual summary rpt, 2144–27
Export and import product standards under GATT, Natl Inst of Standards and Technology info activities, and proposed standards by agency and country, 1991, annual rpt, 2214–6
FBI fingerprint identification system automation costs, staff, and workload, FY90 and projected to FY2000, 26358–253
Fed Govt agencies and program operations investigations, summaries of findings, as of 1991, annual GAO rpt, 26104–5.4
Fed Reserve data concordance for *Federal Reserve Bulletin* and *Annual Statistical Digest*, 1990 annual rpt, 9364–8
Fishery info and rpts of Natl Marine Fisheries Service, 1991, annual rpt, 2164–1
Geological Survey activities and funding, FY91, annual rpt, 5664–8
Indian land ownership, multiple ownership, and Bur of Indian Affairs records maintenance, for 12 reservations, 1991, GAO rpt, 26113–559
Labor productivity of Federal employees, indexes of output and labor costs by function, FY67-90, annual rpt, 6824–1.6
Land Mgmt Bur activities and finances, and public land acreage and use, annual State rpt series, 5724–11
Oceanographic research and distribution activities of World Data Center A by country, and cruises by ship, 1990, annual rpt, 2144–15
Security measures and classification actions of Fed Govt monitored by Info Security Oversight Office, FY91, annual rpt, 9454–21
Technology transfer by Federal R&D labs to small manufacturers, promotional programs activities and grants to States, late 1980s-91, GAO rpt, 26113–551
Weather services activities and funding, by Federal agency, planned FY92-93, annual rpt, 2144–2
see also CD-ROM catalogs and guides
see also CD-ROM releases
see also Computer data file guides
see also Freedom of information
see also Government documents
see also Government forms and paperwork
see also Government publications lists
see also Statistical programs and activities

Government inspections
Alcohol sale permits revoked and suspended, fines, and inspections, for Bur of Alcohol, Tobacco, and Firearms, FY78-90, hearing, 21788–217
Animal protection, licensing, and inspection activities of USDA, and animals used in research, by State, FY90, annual rpt, 1394–10
Asbestos in schools, inspection and abatement effectiveness, staff and parental notification, and inspector and janitorial training, as of 1990, 9238–71
Assistance (financial and nonfinancial) of Fed Govt, 1992 base edition, annual listing, 104–5
Auto safety, crash test results by domestic and foreign model, model years 1987-91, 7768–111
Auto safety crash test results, by domestic and foreign model, press release series, 7766–7
Auto safety crash test results, by model, FY89, annual rpt, 7304–1.2
Banks in Fed Reserve System, expenses and operations itemized by service, office, and district, 1991, annual rpt, 9364–11
Blood banks safety violations, FDA enforcement, disease transmittal, and Houston regional center activities and finances, 1970s-91, hearings, 21368–134
Board and care home violations of State drug handling and dispensing regulations, for 3 metro areas, 1990-91, GAO rpt, 26121–447
Coal Surface Mining Reclamation and Enforcement Office activities and funding, by State and Indian tribe, FY91, annual rpt, 5644–1
Customs Service mgmt and trade law enforcement effectiveness, staff and broker survey results, 1992 GAO rpt, 26119–420
DOT employment, by subagency, occupation, and selected personnel characteristics, FY91, annual rpt, 7304–18
Expenditures (direct) and employment, by function and level of govt, selected years 1962-87, 10048–53
FDA investigations and regulatory activities, quarterly rpt, 4062–3
Fed Govt agencies programs and services performance evaluation measures use, dev, and effectiveness, 1991 survey, GAO rpt, 26119–396
Firearms dealers licensed by Bur of Alcohol, Tobacco and Firearms, views on regulatory inspections, 1992 survey, GAO rpt, 26119–429
Hazardous material transport accidents, casualties, and damage, by mode of transport, with DOT control activities, 1990, annual rpt, 7304–4
Health care facilities excluded from Medicare prospective payment system, quality standards and review, certification, accreditation, and licensing, 1991 survey, 17206–2.41
Hearing aid performance test results, by make and model, 1992 annual rpt, 8704–3
Imports detained by FDA, by reason, product, shipper, brand, and country, monthly listing, 4062–2
Info Security Oversight Office monitoring of Federal security measures and classification actions, FY91, annual rpt, 9454–21
Labor productivity of Federal employees, indexes of output and labor costs by function, FY67-90, annual rpt, 6824–1.6
Labs (clinical) test performance standards and proficiency testing, HHS regulations, 1992 rpt, 4206–2.52
Natl Hwy Traffic Safety Admin activities and grants, and fatal traffic accident data, 1990, annual rpt, 7764–1
NATO and Warsaw Pact military forces reductions and ceilings under CFE treaty, inspections, and US compliance costs and savings, 1991 hearings, 25388–59
Northern Mariana Islands, Saipan garment factories occupational health and safety violations and penalties assessed by OSHA, Mar 1992, press release, 6606–3.10
Nuclear Regulatory Commission activities, finances, and staff, with data for individual power plants, FY91, annual rpt, 9634–2
Nuclear Regulatory Commission budget, staff, and activities, by program, FY91-93, annual rpt, 9634–9
Nuclear weapons facilities of DOE, contractor fees, environmental and safety enforcement activity, and salaries, by contractor and facility, 1987-88, hearing, 21408–127
Occupational exposure to hazardous substances, employer compliance with info and training regulations, inspections, and fines, by firm size and industry div, 1989-91, GAO rpt, 26121–439
Occupational safety enforcement activities of Federal and State agencies, inspections, closure orders, and violations contested and upheld, FY91, GAO rpt, 26121–461
Oil and gas OCS leasing and exploration activity, production, revenue, and environmental studies, by location, quarterly rpt, 5732–1
Postal Service inspection activities, FY91, annual rpt, 9864–9
Postal Service inspection activities, 2nd half FY92, semiannual rpt, 9862–2
Railroad accidents, casualties, and damage, Fed Railroad Admin activities, and safety inspectors by State, 1990, annual rpt, 7604–12
Truck and bus safety inspections of States, and vehicles and drivers ordered out of service, FY85-89, annual rpt, 7304–1.2
see also Federal Inspectors General reports
see also Food inspection
see also Government investigations

Government investigations
Airport security operations to prevent hijacking, screening results, enforcement actions, and hijacking attempts, 1990, annual rpt, 7504–49
Assistance (financial and nonfinancial) of Fed Govt, 1992 base edition, annual listing, 104–5
Communist and transitional economy countries trade with US, by detailed commodity and country, quarterly rpt with articles, 9882–2
Community Relations Service investigation and mediation of minority discrimination disputes, activities and funding, FY91, annual rpt, 6004–9

Election campaign finances and FEC activities, various periods 1975-91, annual rpt, 9274–1
Exports and imports, trade agreements and relations, and USITC investigations, 1991, annual rpt, 9884–5
Fed Govt employees and hirees background checks by OPM, efficiency, and agency managers views on timeliness and quality, FY90, GAO rpt, 26119–373
Imports and tariff provisions effect on US industries and products, investigations with background financial and operating data, series, 9886–4
Imports injury to US industries from foreign subsidized products and sales at less than fair value, investigations with background financial and operating data, series, 9886–19
Imports injury to US industries from foreign subsidized products, investigations with background financial and operating data, series, 9886–15
Imports injury to US industries from sales at less than fair value, investigations with background financial and operating data, series, 9886–14
Imports injury to US industries, USITC activities, investigations, and rpts, FY91, annual rpt, 9884–1
Imports injury to US industries, USITC rpts, 1984-91, annual listing, 9884–12
Imports under Generalized System of Preferences, status, and US tariffs, with trade by country and US economic impacts, for selected commodities, 1987-91, annual rpt, 9884–23
Maritime Commission activities, case filings by type and disposition, and civil penalties by shipper, FY91, annual rpt, 9334–1
Medicare admin and research, and HCFA affirmative action and accreditation programs, FY87, annual rpt, 4654–5
Nuclear material inventory discrepancies at DOE and contractor facilities, 1990/91, annual rpt, 3344–2
Occupational deaths, by equipment type, circumstances, and OSHA standards violated, series, 6606–2
Railroad accidents, casualties, damage, and circumstances, by incident, 1988, annual rpt, 7604–3
Securities law enforcement activities of SEC, FY91, annual rpt, 9734–2.3
Toxicology Natl Program research and testing activities, FY90 and planned FY91, annual rpt, 4044–16
Transportation Natl Safety Board investigations and recommendations, and accidents and casualties by mode, 1990, annual rpt, 9614–1
see also Congressional investigations
see also Criminal investigations
see also Environmental impact statements
see also Federal Inspectors General reports
see also General Accounting Office
see also Government inspections

Government lands
see Public lands

Government loans and grants
see Federal aid programs
see Federal funding for research and development
see terms beginning with Federal aid

Government National Mortgage Association
Budget of US, obligations and authority by function, agency, and program, with summaries and analyses, FY93, annual rpt, 104–2
Finances and mortgage-backed securities program of GNMA, FY91, annual rpt, 5144–6
Mortgage applications, dispositions, and secondary loan market sales, by purpose, lender type, and applicant and neighborhood characteristics, 1991, article, 9362–1.307

Government ownership
Electric power plants of Fed Govt, conversion to alternative fuels, 1992, annual rpt, 3334–2
Electric utilities publicly owned, finances and operations, 1990, annual rpt, 3164–24.1
Hospital deaths of Medicare patients, actual and expected rates by diagnosis, with hospital characteristics, by instn, FY90, annual State rpt series, 4654–14
Mental health care facilities, staff, and patient characteristics, *Statistical Notes* series, 4506–3
Uranium supply and industry operations, various periods 1947-91 and projected to 2001, annual rpt, 3164–65
see also Government assets and liabilities
see also Government corporations and enterprises
see also Government supplies and property
see also Military bases, posts, and reservations
see also Military health facilities and services
see also Military supplies and property
see also Public buildings
see also Public lands
see also Public works
see also Surplus government property
see also Veterans health facilities and services

Government pay
Canada and US civil service merit systems operations, pay, appointments, and promotions, late 1980s-91, 9498–16
Natl income and product accounts, comprehensive accounts and components, benchmark revisions, 1929-88, 2708–5
Natl income and product accounts, comprehensive accounts and components, *Survey of Current Business*, monthly rpt, 2702–1.29
Pacific territories population and housing detailed characteristics, by location, 1990 Census of Population and Housing, series, 2551–8
Statistical Abstract of US, 1992 annual data compilation, 2324–1.9
see also Civil service pensions
see also Educational employees pay
see also Federal pay
see also Military benefits and pensions
see also Military pay
see also State and local employees pay

Government price control
see Price regulation

Government Printing Office
Activities, finances, and production of GPO, FY91, annual rpt, 26204–1
Activities, staff, and productivity of GPO, 1970s-90 and projected to 2000, 26208–4
Bookstores of GPO, 1992 annual listing, 2304–2
Budget of US, authoritative financial statements with appropriations, outlays, and receipts, by category and agency, FY91, annual rpt, 8104–2.2
Budget of US, obligations and authority by function, agency, and program, with summaries and analyses, FY93, annual rpt, 104–2
Labor unions recognized in Fed Govt, agreements and membership by agency and facility, as of Jan 1991, biennial listing, 9844–14

Government publications
see Government documents
see Government publications lists

Government publications lists
Agricultural data collection, methodology, and use, for major time series of USDA, series, 1506–1
Agricultural Statistics Board releases planned 1992, annual listing, 1614–1
American Housing Survey, data coverage, products, and metro areas surveyed 1974-94, 2328–89
Aviation medicine research rpts, 1991 listing, 7506–10.97
BEA rpts data coverage and availability, 1992 annual article, 2702–1.308
BEA rpts data coverage and availability, 1992 annual rpt, 2704–6
Census Bur activities, rpts, and user services, monthly rpt, 2302–3
Census Bur data files and rpts, coverage and availability, 1992 annual listing, 2304–2
Census Bur geographic levels of data coverage, maps, and reference products, 1992 rpt, 2308–67
Census Bur rpts and data files, coverage, availability, and use, series, 2326–7
Census Bur rpts and data files, monthly listing, 2302–6
Census of Population and Housing, 1990: data coverage, collection procedures, products and services availability, and uses, guide, 2555–1
Census of Population and Housing, 1990: data summary, use, and availability, for selected long form questions, fact sheet series, 2326–23
Census of Population and Housing, 1990: detailed geographic coverage, CD-ROM user guide, 2308–65
Census of Population and Housing, 1990: maps and cartographic products availability, listing, 2308–66
Child abductions, runaways, and missing and exploited children, and Office of Juvenile Justice and Delinquency Prevention activities, FY90, annual rpt, 6064–36
Commerce Dept rpts, biweekly listing, 2002–1
Computer data processing standards of Fed Govt, rpts, 1991 listing, 2216–2.202
Criminal justice systems of States, activities, employment, funding, and data collection, by State, 1970s-91, annual rpt, 6064–40
DOD Directorate for Info Operations and Rpts publications, 1991 listing, 3548–21
DOE data collection forms and related rpts, 1991, annual listing, 3164–86
Drug abuse and treatment research summaries, and resource materials and grant listings, bimonthly rpt, 4492–4

Drug enforcement, offenses, and public opinion, summaries of BJS rpts, 1975-90, annual pamphlet, 6064–30
Economic censuses, 1987: data collection, coverage, availability, and procedural history, 2628–16
Education Dept rpts, 1992 semiannual listing, 4812–1
Education Statistics Natl Center rpts, periodic listing, 4822–1
Employment Policy Natl Commission activities and rpts, 1991 annual rpt, 15494–1
Energy Info Admin activities, 1991, annual rpt, 3164–29
Energy Info Admin rpts and data files, 1991, annual listing, 3164–98
Energy use, costs, and conservation, and household and housing characteristics, survey rpt series, 3166–7
Environmental quality indicators, NOAA monitoring results, 1991 annual summary rpt, 2144–27
EPA rpts in NTIS collection, quarterly listing, 9182–5
Exports of manufactured goods for US and major competitors, market share rpts, annual listing, discontinued, 2044–6
FDA investigations and regulatory activities, quarterly rpt, 4062–3
Fires, casualties, losses, and US Fire Admin activities, funding, and training programs, FY91, annual rpt, 9434–7
Fishery info and rpts of Natl Marine Fisheries Service, 1991, annual rpt, 2164–1
Foreign countries *Background Notes*, summary social, political, and economic data, 1991 listing, 7006–2.9
Foreign countries *Background Notes*, summary social, political, and economic data, 1992 listing, 7006–2.10; 7006–2.24; 7006–2.28
Forest Service Rocky Mountain Forest and Range Experiment Station rpts, 1980-89, listing, 1208–403
FTC activities, FY90, annual narrative rpt, 9404–1
GAO activities, operations, and resulting cost savings to Fed Govt, FY91, annual rpt, 26104–1
GAO rpts, FY91, annual listing, 26104–17
GAO rpts, topical listings, series, 26106–10
Geological Survey rpts and research journal articles, monthly listing, 5662–1
Geological Survey rpts, 1991, annual listing, 5664–4
Health Statistics Natl Center rpts, quarterly listing, 4122–2
Hwy construction and design R&D, quarterly journal, 7552–3
Hwy Traffic Safety Natl Admin and Fed Hwy Admin activities, 1990, annual rpt, 7764–1
Intl Trade Admin rpts, biweekly rpt, annual listing, 2042–24
Investigations of Federal agency and program operations, summaries of findings, as of 1991, annual GAO rpt, 26104–5
Libraries and Info Science Natl Commission activities, FY91, annual rpt, 15634–1
Library of Congress rpts and products, 1992-93, biennial listing, 26404–6
MarAd activities, finances, subsidies, and world merchant fleet operations, FY91, annual rpt, 7704–14
Measurement systems calibration, standard reference materials specifications and availability, 1992 biennial listing, 2214–2
Medicare admin and research, and HCFA affirmative action and accreditation programs, FY87, annual rpt, 4654–5
Medicare reimbursement of hospitals under prospective payment system, methodology, inputs, and data by diagnostic group, 1992 annual rpt, 17204–1
Minerals resources of Alaska, production, oil and gas leases, reserves, and exploratory wells, with maps and bibl, 1990, annual rpt, 5664–11
Mines Bur rpts and patents, monthly listing, 5602–2
Natl Archives and Records Admin activities, finances, holdings, and staff, FY91, annual rpt, 9514–2
Natl Archives holdings of Federal agencies administrative records and other materials, final inventories, series, 9516–2
Natl Archives holdings of Federal publications and other material, special collections, series, 9516–1
Natl Inst of Standards and Technology rpts, 1991, annual listing, 2214–1
NIH rpts, 1992 annual listing, 4434–2
NOAA Environmental Research Labs rpts, FY91, annual listing, 2144–25
NSF activities, finances, and funding by program, FY91, annual rpt, 9624–6
NSF rpts, 1992 annual listing, 9624–16
Ocean pollution research projects, rpts and data files, FY84-87, listing, 2158–51
Oil enhanced recovery research contracts of DOE, project summaries, funding, and bibl, quarterly rpt, 3002–14
Older population data sources of Fed Govt, interagency forum activities, and contacts, 1989-90, annual rpt, 14324–1
Radiation exposure of population near Hanford, Wash, nuclear plant, with methodology, 1944-91, series, 3356–5
Smithsonian Instn activities, rpts, and funding by donor, FY91, annual rpt, 29574–1.2
Soil surveys and maps for counties, 1899-1991, annual listing, 1264–11
SSA activities, litigation, finances, and staff, FY91, annual rpt, 4704–6
Statistical Abstract of US, guide to sources, 1992 annual rpt, 2324–1
Survey of Income and Program Participation, data collection, methodology, and availability, 1991 users guide, 2628–24
Technology Assessment Office activities and rpts, FY91, annual rpt, 26354–3
Telecommunications and Info Natl Admin rpts, FY91, annual listing, 2804–3
Toxicology Natl Program research and testing activities, FY90 and planned FY91, annual rpt, 4044–16
Travel to US, market research data available from US Travel and Tourism Admin, 1992, annual rpt, 2904–15
TVA agriculture and fertilizer rpts, 1970-90, annual listing, 9804–28
USITC activities, investigations, and rpts, FY91, annual rpt, 9884–1
USITC rpts, 1984-91, annual listing, 9884–12
Vital and Health Statistics series and other NCHS rpts, 1990-91, annual listing, 4124–1
see also CD-ROM catalogs and guides

Government regulation
see Administrative law and procedure
see Antitrust law
see Environmental regulation
see Financial institutions regulation
see Government and business
see Government forms and paperwork
see Government inspections
see Health care reform
see Interstate commerce
see Licenses and permits
see Medical regulation
see Price regulation

Government reorganization
Administrative law judges views toward establishment of separate ALJ agency, 1992, GAO report, 26119–428
Army line officer accessions, involuntary separations, and strengths under alternative force reduction plans, FY90-95, 26306–3.121
Budget of US, Bush Admin mgmt proposals, by function, FY93, annual rpt, 104–2.2
Military personnel reductions planned by service branch, and women and minorities affected by Army and Air Force plans, FY90-91, GAO rpt, 26123–373

Government revenues
American Samoa govt finances, with data on health and farm spending and employment, mid 1980s-91, GAO rpt, 26123–385
Business cycle contractions and expansions, changes in State and local govt finances, late 1940s-91, article, 9375–1.303
Business statistics, detailed data for major industries and economic indicators, 1960-91, *Survey of Current Business* biennial supplement, 2704–1
DC govt finances, revenue by source, financial statements, and employment, with income in central city and suburbs compared to other cities, 1991 hearings, 21308–28
Fed Govt finances, cash and debt transactions, daily tables, 8102–4
Fed Govt financial transactions, *Survey of Current Business*, monthly rpt, 2702–1.8
Fed Govt receipts by source and outlays by agency, *Treasury Bulletin*, quarterly rpt, 8002–4.1
Finances of govts, by level of govt, State, and for large cities and counties, annual rpt series, 2466–2
Finances of govts, revenue and spending by level of govt, natl income and product accounts, 1959-91, annual rpt, 204–1.6
Finances of govts, tax systems and revenue, and fiscal structure, by level of govt and State, 1992 and historical trends, annual rpt, 10044–1
Forecasts of economic conditions and employment, alternative BLS projections to 2005 and trends 1975-90, biennial rpt, 6744–19
Hwy receipts by source, and spending by function, by level of govt and State, 1991, annual rpt, 7554–1.3

Local govts in metro areas, finances, structure, and service delivery, local area rpt series, 10046–9
Natl income and product accounts and components, *Survey of Current Business*, monthly rpt, 2702–1.23
Natl income and product accounts, comprehensive accounts and components, benchmark revisions, 1929-88, 2708–5
Natl income and product accounts, comprehensive accounts and components, *Survey of Current Business*, monthly rpt, 2702–1.26
Palau admin, and social, economic, and govtl data, FY91, annual rpt, 7004–6
Public lands acreage and use, and Land Mgmt Bur activities and finances, annual State rpt series, 5724–11
State and local govt fiscal condition, with data by State and selected city, 1991 hearing, 21268–44
State and local govt revenue by source and outlays by type, 1987-91, annual article, 2702–1.311
Statistical Abstract of US, 1992 annual data compilation, 2324–1.9; 2324–1.10
Timber sales of Forest Service, expenses, and operations, by region, State, and natl forest, FY91, annual rpts, 1204–36
USDA revenue, by source and subagency, FY88-92, GAO rpt, 26113–602
see also Budget of the U.S.
see also Estate tax
see also Excise tax
see also Foreign budgets
see also Gift tax
see also Government assets and liabilities
see also Income taxes
see also Mineral leases
see also Oil and gas leases
see also Property tax
see also Sales tax
see also Severance taxes
see also Social security tax
see also State and local taxes
see also Tariffs and foreign trade controls
see also Tax expenditures
see also Taxation
see also Tolls
see also Unemployment insurance tax
see also User fees
see also Value added tax

Government securities

Assets and debts of private sector, balance sheets by segment, 1960-91, semiannual rpt, 9365–4.1
Banks (insured commercial and savings) finances, for foreign and domestic offices, by asset size, 1990, annual rpt, 9294–4.2
Banks (natl) charters, mergers, liquidations, enforcement cases, and financial performance, with data by instn and State, quarterly rpt, 8402–3
Banks in Fed Reserve System, expenses and operations itemized by service, office, and district, 1991, annual rpt, 9364–11
Budget of US, authoritative financial statements with appropriations, outlays, and receipts, by category and agency, FY91, annual rpt, 8104–2.2
Budget of US, CBO analysis of revenue and spending alternatives and projections of economic indicators, FY93-97, annual rpt, 26304–3
Budget of US, obligations and authority by function, agency, and program, with summaries and analyses, FY93, annual rpt, 104–2
Budget of US, receipts by source, outlays by agency and program, and balances, monthly rpt, 8102–3
Business statistics, detailed data for major industries and economic indicators, *Survey of Current Business*, monthly rpt, 2702–1.8
Business statistics, detailed data for major industries and economic indicators, 1960-91, *Survey of Current Business* biennial supplement, 2704–1
Credit unions federally insured, finances by instn characteristics and State, as of June 1992, semiannual rpt, 9532–6
Economic indicators and components, and Fed Reserve 4th District business and financial conditions, monthly chartbook, 9377–10
Fed Govt finances, cash and debt transactions, daily tables, 8102–4
Fed Govt trust funds financial condition, by fund, periodic rpt series, 8102–9
Fed Home Loan Mortgage Corp activities and financial statements, 1991, annual rpt, 9414–1
Fed Reserve banks finances and staff, 1991, annual rpt, 9364–1.1
Fed Reserve Bd discount rate changes relation to Treasury bill rates, alternative estimates, 1970s-80s, article, 9391–1.314
Finances of govts, by level of govt, State, and for large cities and counties, annual rpt series, 2466–2
Finances of govts, tax systems and revenue, and fiscal structure, by level of govt and State, 1992 and historical trends, annual rpt, 10044–1
Financial and business detailed statistics, *Fed Reserve Bulletin*, monthly rpt with articles, 9362–1
Financial operations of Fed Govt, detailed data, *Treasury Bulletin*, quarterly rpt, 8002–4
Flow-of-funds accounts, savings, investments, and credit statements, quarterly rpt, 9365–3.3
Foreign and US industrial stock indexes and long-term govt bond yields, for selected countries, weekly chartbook, 9365–1.5
Foreign govts assets and liabilities, and transactions in securities, monthly rpt, 9362–1.3
Forgery of checks and bonds, Secret Service investigations and arrests, FY91 and trends from FY82, annual rpt, 8464–1
Futures and options trading volume, by commodity and exchange, FY91, annual rpt, 11924–2
Futures trading in selected commodities and financial instruments and indexes, for NYC, Chicago, and other markets activity, biweekly rpt, 11922–5
Govt Natl Mortgage Assn finances, and mortgage-backed securities program, FY91, annual rpt, 5144–6
Hwy receipts by source, and spending by function, by level of govt and State, 1991, annual rpt, 7554–1.3
Interest rates for commercial paper, govt securities, other financial instruments, and home mortgages, monthly rpt, 9365–2.14
Interest rates in money and capital markets, weekly averages by instrument, 1990, annual rpt, 9364–5.3
Intl financial markets performance of foreign and US bank and securities firms, finances and competitiveness issues, 1980s, compilation of papers, 9385–10
Intl investment position of US, by component, industry, world region, and country, 1990-91, annual article, 2702–1.323
Issues, redemptions, and bonds outstanding, monthly rpt, 8242–2
Market performance, regulation, and reform issues for govt securities, with auction results, 1990-91, 8008–154
Medicare Hospital Insurance trust fund finances, mid 1960s-91 and alternative projections to 2066, annual rpt, 4654–11
Medicare Supplementary Medical Insurance trust fund finances, mid 1960s-91 and projected to 2065, annual rpt, 4654–12
Mortgage-backed securities transactions, and other activity of Fed Natl Mortgage Assn, 1991, annual rpt, 5184–9; 9474–1
OASDI trust funds finances, since 1940, quarterly rpt, 4742–1.1
OASDI trust funds finances, 1937-FY91 and alternative projections to 2070, annual rpt, 4704–4
Ownership of govt securities, dealer transactions and financing sources, and new State and local issues, monthly rpt, 9362–1.1
Ownership of govt securities, dealer transactions and financing sources, and new State and local issues, 1990, annual rpt, 9364–5.5; 9364–5.10
Pension funds (public) investment in housing, and public and private funds holdings of mortgages, mortgage-backed securities, and govt securities, 1986-90, 5188–134
Port improvement capital expenditures and financing methods, by region and selected port, 1946-89, 7708–6
Rural Electrification Admin activities and finances, and loans by State, FY91 and trends from FY36, annual rpt, 1244–3
Rural Telephone Bank financial statements, FY91, annual rpt, 1244–4
Southeastern States, Fed Reserve 5th District insured commercial banks financial statements, by State, quarterly rpt, 9389–18
Southeastern States, Fed Reserve 8th District banking and economic conditions, quarterly rpt with articles, 9391–16
State and local govt employees pension system cash and security holdings and finances, quarterly rpt, 2462–2
Statistical Abstract of US, 1992 annual data compilation, 2324–1.9; 2324–1.10
Tax (estate) returns for nonresident aliens, property and tax data, by estate size and decedent country of residence, 1986, article, 8302–2.310
Tax (estate) returns property and tax data, by size of gross estate and State, 1989-90, article, 8302–2.305
Tax (income) returns filed, by type of filer, selected income items, quarterly rpt, 8302–2.1
Tax (income) returns of corporations, income and tax items by asset size and detailed industry, 1989, annual rpt, 8304–4; 8304–21

Tax exempt organizations finances, with data by type, size, State, and for largest organizations, late 1940s-80s, compilation of papers, 8308–35
Treasury bill interest rates, factors affecting before- and after-tax real rates, model description and results, 1960s-89, working paper, 9373–27.6
Treasury bill offerings, auction results by Fed Reserve District, and terms, periodic press release series, 8002–7
Truman, Harry S, Scholarship Fund receipts by source, transfers, and investment holdings and transactions, monthly rpt, 14312–1
Trust assets of banks, trust companies, and S&Ls, by type of asset and fund, selected firm, and State, 1991, annual rpt, 13004–1
Yields and interest rates for Treasury bills and US and municipal bonds, monthly rpt, 23842–1.5
Yields and interest rates on govt issues, weekly rpt, 9391–4
Yields, interest rates, issues, offerings, and ownership of govt securities, by type, selected years 1929-91, annual rpt, 204–1.5; 204–1.6
Yields on corporate, Treasury, and municipal long-term bonds, *Treasury Bulletin*, quarterly rpt, 8002–4.9
Yields, *Survey of Current Business*, cyclical indicators, monthly rpt, 2702–1.1
see also Municipal bonds
see also Tax exempt securities
see also U.S. savings bonds

Government services
see Public services

Government spending
Advisory committees of Fed Govt, and members, staff, meetings, and costs by agency, FY91, annual rpt, 9454–18
Business cycle contractions and expansions, changes in State and local govt finances, late 1940s-91, article, 9375–1.303
Business statistics, detailed data for major industries and economic indicators, *Survey of Current Business*, monthly rpt, 2702–1.8
Business statistics, detailed data for major industries and economic indicators, 1960-91, *Survey of Current Business* biennial supplement, 2704–1
Construction spending by Fed Govt, by type of structure, FY85-92, annual article, 2042–1.303
Economic indicators and components, current data and annual trends, monthly rpt, 23842–1.6
Economic indicators compounded annual rates of change, monthly rpt, 9391–3
Economic indicators impacts of govt spending, model description and results, 1992 technical paper, 9379–12.93
Expenditures (direct) and employment, by function and level of govt, selected years 1962-87, 10048–53
Fed Govt finances, cash and debt transactions, daily tables, 8102–4
Fed Govt financial operations, detailed data, *Treasury Bulletin*, quarterly rpt, 8002–4
Fed Govt financial transactions, *Survey of Current Business*, monthly rpt, 2702–1.8
Finances of govts, by level of govt, State, and for large cities and counties, annual rpt series, 2466–2
Finances of State and local govts, obligations and resources compared to Fed Govt, 1960s-90, GAO rpt, 26121–457
Finances of State and local govts, revenue by source and outlays by type, 1987-91, annual article, 2702–1.311
Fiscal condition of State and local govts, with data by State and selected city, 1991 hearing, 21268–44
Fiscal policy (supply side) of Reagan Admin, economic impacts, 1980s and trends from 1960s, technical paper, 9385–1.304; 9385–8.125
Flow-of-funds accounts, savings, investments, and credit statements, quarterly rpt, 9365–3.3
Forecasts of economic conditions and employment, alternative BLS projections to 2005 and trends 1975-90, biennial rpt, 6744–19
Gross State Product by component, industry div, and State, 1977-89, article, 2702–1.303
Health condition and care indicators, 1950s-90 with health improvement and disease prevention goals for 1990, annual data compilation, 4144–11
Input-output structure of US economy, detailed interindustry transactions for 541 industries, and components of final demand, 1982 benchmark data, 2708–17
Investigations of Federal agency and program operations, summaries of findings, as of 1991, annual GAO rpt, 26104–5
Local govts in metro areas, finances, structure, and service delivery, local area rpt series, 10046–9
Mail (franked and penalty) revenue and volume, FY87, annual rpt, 9864–1
Mail (penalty) for Federal agencies, USPS itemized operating costs, FY91, annual rpt, 9864–4
Natl income and product accounts and components, *Survey of Current Business*, monthly rpt, 2702–1.23
Natl income and product accounts benchmark revisions, methodological changes and revised summary tables, 1959-91, article, 2702–1.302
Natl income and product accounts, comprehensive accounts and components, benchmark revisions, 1929-88, 2708–5
Natl income and product accounts, comprehensive accounts and components, *Survey of Current Business*, monthly rpt, 2702–1.26
New England States employment growth after recessions, relation to selected economic factors, various periods 1969-90, article, 9373–1.315
Pollution abatement spending by govts, business, and consumers, 1972-90, annual article, 2702–1.321
Public opinion on taxes, spending, and govt efficiency, by respondent characteristics, 1992 survey, annual rpt, 10044–2
Statistical Abstract of US, 1992 annual data compilation, 2324–1.9; 2324–1.10
Statistical programs of Fed Govt, funding by agency, and BLS programs improvement spending, 1991 hearing, 23848–227
UN participation of US, and member and nonmember shares of UN budget by country, FY89-91, annual rpt, 7004–5
see also Agricultural production quotas and price supports
see also Agricultural subsidies
see also Budget of the U.S.
see also Civil service pensions
see also Defense expenditures
see also Executive impoundment of appropriated funds
see also Federal aid programs
see also Federal aid to arts and humanities
see also Federal aid to education
see also Federal aid to higher education
see also Federal aid to highways
see also Federal aid to housing
see also Federal aid to law enforcement
see also Federal aid to libraries
see also Federal aid to local areas
see also Federal aid to medical education
see also Federal aid to medicine
see also Federal aid to railroads
see also Federal aid to rural areas
see also Federal aid to States
see also Federal aid to transportation
see also Federal aid to vocational education
see also Federal funding for energy programs
see also Federal funding for research and development
see also Federal pay
see also Foreign budgets
see also Government assets and liabilities
see also Government contracts and procurement
see also Government energy use
see also Government pay
see also Military benefits and pensions
see also Military pay
see also Nonappropriated funds
see also Public services
see also Public welfare programs
see also Revenue sharing
see also State and local employees pay
see also State funding for economic development
see also State funding for education
see also State funding for health and hospitals
see also State funding for higher education
see also State funding for local areas
see also State funding for natural resources and conservation
see also State funding for public safety
see also State funding for social welfare
see also State funding for transportation
see also State government spending
see also Subsidies
see also Veterans benefits and pensions
see also under names of individual Federal departments and agencies

Government supplies and property
Assistance (financial and nonfinancial) of Fed Govt, 1992 base edition, annual listing, 104–5
Auto alternative fuels use in Federal fleet, energy economy performance at 4 sites, FY91, annual rpt, 3304–28
Auto fleet size, trip characteristics, and energy use, by fleet type, 1970s-90, annual rpt, 3304–5.3
Bombing incidents and casualties, by target, circumstances, and State, 1987-91, annual rpt, 8484–4.1
Bombing incidents, casualties, and damage, by target, circumstances, and State, 1991, annual rpt, 6224–5

Bridges over navigable waters, with type of bridge and use, owner, dimensions, and location, 1991 regional listing series, 7406–5
Budget of US, obligations and authority by function, agency, and program, with summaries and analyses, FY93, annual rpt, 104–2
Capital (fixed), govt and private nonresidential structures and equipment, residential capital, and consumer-owned durable goods, 1925-90, annual article, 2702–1.305; 2702–1.306; 2702–1.327; 2702–1.338
Colorado River Storage Project finances and activities in western States, FY91, annual rpt, 5824–3
Construction put in place, value of new public and private structures, by type, monthly rpt, 2382–4
Criminal cases by type and disposition, and collections, for US attorneys, by Federal district, FY91, annual rpt, 6004–2.1; 6004–2.7
DOE energy use, costs, and conservation, by end use, fuel type, and field office, FY91, annual rpt, 3004–27
DOE real property owned and leased, by type, subagency, contractor, and site, FY91, annual rpt, 3004–28
Fed Govt obligations by function and agency, *Treasury Bulletin*, quarterly rpt, 8002–4.2
FmHA property acquired through foreclosure, acreage, value, and sales, for farm and nonfarm property by State, monthly rpt, 1182–6
FmHA property acquired through foreclosure, 1-family homes, value, sales, and leases, by State, monthly rpt, 1182–7
Freight (waterborne domestic and foreign) by commodity, traffic, and passengers, by port and waterway, 1989, annual rpt, 3754–3
GSA activities and finances, FY91, annual rpt, 9454–1
GSA programs fraud and abuse, audits and investigations, 1st half FY92, semiannual rpt, 9452–8
Hazardous waste site remedial action under Superfund, current and proposed sites priority ranking and status by location, series, 9216–5
Labor productivity of Federal employees, indexes of output and labor costs by function, FY67-90, annual rpt, 6824–1.6
Loans and loan guarantees of Fed Govt, outstanding amounts by agency and program, *Treasury Bulletin*, quarterly rpt, 8002–4.11
Motor vehicle registrations, by public and private ownership, vehicle type, and State, 1991, annual rpt, 7554–1.2
NASA accidents, casualties, damage, and safety activities, FY91, annual rpt, 9504–4
Patents (US) granted to US and foreign applicants, by applicant and country, 1960s-91, annual rpt, 2244–3
Patents granted to Federal agencies, FY82-91, annual rpt, 2244–1.2
Postal Service activities, finances, and mail volume and subsidies, FY91, annual rpt, 9864–5
Prison Industries (Federal) sales, by commodity and Federal agency, FY91, annual rpt, 6244–5
Radio frequency assignments for Federal use, by agency, 1st half 1992, semiannual rpt, 2802–1
Ships in US merchant fleet, operating subsidies, construction, and ship-related employment, monthly rpt, 7702–1
Terrorism (intl) incidents, casualties, and attacks on US targets, by attack type and country, 1991, annual rpt, 7004–22
Terrorism (intl) incidents, casualties, and attacks on US targets, by attack type and world area, 1991, annual rpt, 7004–13
Terrorism incidents in US, related activity, and casualties, by attack type, target, group, and location, 1991, annual rpt, 6224–6
Truck transport of household goods, performance and disposition of damage claims, for selected carriers, 1991, annual rpt, 9484–11
VA mortgage loan activity, defaults, and property acquired, FY67-91, annual rpt, 8604–5.3
Westinghouse Co procurement from govt supply sources, for Savannah River nuclear weapons plant operations, 1990-91, 3006–5.33
see also Military bases, posts, and reservations
see also Military supplies and property
see also Public buildings
see also Public lands
see also Surplus government property

Government trust funds

Abandoned Mine Reclamation Fund financial status, FY91, annual rpt, 5644–1
Airport and Airway Trust Fund improvement spending, by airport and State, FY92, annual rpt, 7504–48
Airport and Airway Trust Fund receipts and outlays, FY90, annual rpt, 7504–37
Airport and Airway Trust Fund receipts and outlays, FY90-91, annual rpt, 7504–10
Birds (waterfowl) refuge and breeding area acreage acquired by Fed Govt, and costs, by site and State, FY92, annual rpt, 14784–1
Black lung benefits and claims by State, trust fund receipts by source, and disbursements, 1991, annual rpt, 6504–3
Budget of US, authoritative financial statements with appropriations, outlays, and receipts, by agency, FY91, annual rpt, 8104–2
Budget of US, balances of budget authority obligated and unobligated, by function and agency, FY90-93, annual rpt, 104–8
Budget of US, Bush Admin proposals, with detail for defense budgets, and historical data from FY34, FY93, 108–46.2
Budget of US, CBO analysis of revenue and spending alternatives and projections of economic indicators, FY93-97, annual rpt, 26304–3
Budget of US, obligations and authority by function, agency, and program, with summaries and analyses, FY93, annual rpt, 104–2
Budget of US, receipts by source, outlays by agency and program, and balances, monthly rpt, 8102–3
Civil service retirement system actuarial valuation, FY79-91 and projected to FY2065, annual rpt, 9844–34
Credit unions federally insured, finances, mergers, closings, and insurance fund losses and financial statements, FY91, annual rpt, 9534–7
Crime victim compensation and support service programs funding, by offense and State, FY88-90, biennial rpt, 6064–37
Currency (foreign) accounts owned by US under AID admin and by foreign govts with joint AID control, status by program and country, quarterly rpt, 9912–1
Currency (foreign) holdings of US, transactions and balances by program and country, 1st half FY92, semiannual rpt, 8102–7
Education funding by Federal agency, program, and recipient type, and instn spending, 1960s-91, annual rpt, 4824–8
EPA pollution control grant program activities, monthly rpt, 9182–8
Fed Govt civilian employees retirement, health, and life insurance benefits, coverage and finances of 4 programs, FY86-90, annual rpt, 9844–37
Fed Govt spending in States, by type, program, agency, and State, FY91, annual rpt, 2464–2
Fed Govt trust funds financial condition, by fund, periodic rpt series, 8102–9
Finances and operations of programs under Ways and Means Committee jurisdiction, FY70s-91, annual rpt, 21784–11
Finances of govts, by level of govt, State, and for large cities and counties, annual rpt series, 2466–2
Finances of govts, tax systems and revenue, and fiscal structure, by level of govt and State, 1992 and historical trends, annual rpt, 10044–1
Forest Service activities and finances, by region and State, FY91, annual rpt, 1204–1
Historic Preservation Fund grants, by State, FY93, annual press release, 5544–9
Hwy funding and allocation methods, for Federal-aid system, FY92-97, 7558–107
Hwy Trust Fund receipts by source, and apportionments, by State, 1991, annual rpt, 7554–1.3
Hwy Trust Fund status and net revenues, FY57-90, annual rpt, 7554–24
Indian trust fund overpayments and shortages, by account, 1970s-91, hearing, 21408–131
Inter-American Foundation dev grants by program area, and fellowships by field and instn, by country, FY72-91, annual rpt, 14424–2
Judicial Survivors Annuity Fund financial condition and annuitants, June 1987-91, annual rpt, 18204–8.12
Labor Dept activities and funding, by program and State, FY91, annual rpt, 6304–1
Land and Water Conservation Fund allocations for outdoor recreation area dev, by State, FY93, annual table, 5544–15
Lands (public) acreage, grants, use, revenues, and allocations, by State, FY91, annual rpt, 5724–1.3

Library of Congress activities, acquisitions, services, and financial statements, FY91, annual rpt, 26404–1
Marshall Islands Nuclear Claims Trust Fund financial condition, and health care benefits and enrollment, 1987-92, GAO rpt, 26123–405
Medicare and Medicaid beneficiaries and program operations, 1992, annual fact book, 4654–18
Medicare Hospital Insurance trust fund finances, mid 1960s-91 and alternative projections to 2066, annual rpt, 4654–11
Medicare Supplementary Medical Insurance trust fund finances, mid 1960s-91 and projected to 2065, annual rpt, 4654–12
Military outlays and obligations, by function and service branch, quarterly rpt, 3542–3
Natl Archives and Records Admin activities, finances, holdings, and staff, FY91, annual rpt, 9514–2
Natl income and product accounts, comprehensive accounts and components, benchmark revisions, 1929-88, 2708–5
Natl income and product accounts, comprehensive accounts and components, *Survey of Current Business*, monthly rpt, 2702–1.26
Nuclear Waste Fund finances, and DOE Civilian Radioactive Waste Mgmt Office R&D costs, FY90-91, annual rpt, 3364–1
Nuclear Waste Fund finances, and DOE Civilian Radioactive Waste Mgmt Program costs, quarterly rpt, 3362–1
Nuclear Waste Fund utility payments and liabilities by State, and uranium enrichment customers costs of regulation and waste mgmt, 1991 hearings, 21368–137
OASDHI and health care system status and reform, Advisory Commission on Social Security findings and recommendations, 1991 quadrennial rpt, 10178–1
OASDHI, Medicaid, SSI, and related programs benefits, beneficiary characteristics, and trust funds, selected years 1937-90, annual rpt, 4744–3
OASDHI trust funds finances, FY91 and projected to 2066, annual rpt, 4654–8
OASDHI trust funds finances, FY91 with projections, annual article, 4742–1.314
OASDHI trust funds finances impacts of Federal debt, with background data, 1990-2065, technical paper, 8006–6.6
OASDI and Medicare trust fund finances, economic assumptions, outlook, and health care system reform issues, series, 10176–1
OASDI trust funds finances, since 1940, quarterly rpt, 4742–1.1
OASDI trust funds finances, 1937-FY91 and alternative projections to 2070, annual rpt, 4704–4
OASDI trust funds income and outlays, FY91, annual rpt, 4704–6
Pension Benefit Guaranty Corp activities and finances, FY91, annual rpt, 9674–1
Pension plans assets, for public and private funds, 1981-90, annual rpt, 9364–5.12
Public debt issued, redeemed, and outstanding, by series and source, and gifts to reduce debt, monthly rpt, 8242–2
Railroad employee benefits program finances and beneficiaries, FY91, annual rpt, 9704–1
Railroad retirement and unemployment insurance accounts status, and interchange with OASDHI fund, FY90, annual rpt, 9704–2.1
Receipts, outlays, debt, and assets, by fund, *Treasury Bulletin*, quarterly rpt, 8002–4.1; 8002–4.5; 8002–4.16
Red Cross activities and finances, FY91, annual rpt, 29254–1
Rural Electrification Admin activities and finances, and loans by State, FY91 and trends from FY36, annual rpt, 1244–3
Small Business Admin loan and contract activity by program and firm, and financial condition, FY91, annual rpt, 9764–1
Smithsonian Instn activities and finances, FY91, annual rpt, 29574–1
State and local govt employees pension system cash and security holdings and finances, quarterly rpt, 2462–2
Statistical Abstract of US, 1992 annual data compilation, 2324–1.10
Truman, Harry S, Scholarship Fund receipts by source, transfers, and investment holdings and transactions, monthly rpt, 14312–1
VA health care services, needs, availability, structure, and funding, 1991 compilation of papers, 8608–9
Veterans and servicepersons life insurance, actuarial analyses of VA programs, 1991, annual rpt, 8604–1
Veterans and servicepersons life insurance of VA, finances and coverage by program and State, 1991, annual rpt, 8604–4
Workers compensation programs under Federal admin, finances and operations, FY91, annual rpt, 6504–10
see also Unemployment trust funds

Government workers
see Congressional employees
see Federal employees
see Government employees
see Government pay
see Military personnel
see Postal employees
see State and local employees

Gowdy, Van
"Evaluation of Head Impact Kinematics for Passengers Seated Behind Interior Walls", 7506–10.120

Grad, Susan
"Income of the Population 55 and Over, 1990", 4744–26

Graduates
see Degrees, higher education
see Educational attainment

Grady, William R.
"Remarriages of Women 15-44 Years of Age Whose First Marriage Ended in Divorce: U.S., 1976", 4147–16.6

Graham, John
"Motor Vehicle Injury Prevention", 4208–35

Grain storage and facilities
Explosions and casualties in grain handling facilities, by firm, FY92, annual rpt, 1294–1
Feed production, acreage, stocks, use, trade, prices, and price supports, periodic situation rpt with articles, 1561–4
Foreign and US grain production, prices, trade, stocks, and use, FAS periodic circular series, 1925–2
Hops stocks held by growers, dealers, and brewers, 1990-92, semiannual press release, 1621–8
Loan support programs of USDA for grains, activity and status by grain and State, monthly rpt, 1802–3
Loans to farmers under CCC program for grain storage facilities and equipment, by State, monthly table, 1802–9
Rice stocks on and off farms and total in all positions, periodic rpt, 1621–7
Soybean storage in commercial elevators, foreign material removal methods and costs, 1991, article, 1561–3.302
Stocks of grain by region and market city, and grain inspected for export, by type, weekly rpt, 1313–4
Stocks of grain on and off farms, by crop, quarterly rpt, 1621–4

Grains and grain products
Acreage planted and harvested, by crop and State, 1990-91 and planned as of June 1992, annual rpt, 1621–23
Acreage planted, by selected crop and State, 1983-91 and planned 1992, annual rpt, 1621–22
Acreage reduction program compliance, enrollment, and yield on planted acreage, by commodity and State, annual press release series, 1004–20
Agricultural Stabilization and Conservation Service rye programs, 1955-92, annual fact sheet, 1806–4.10
Agricultural Statistics, 1991, annual rpt, 1004–1
Alcoholic beverages production, stocks, materials used, and taxable and tax-free removals, for beer and distilled spirits by State, monthly rpt, 8486–1.1; 8486–1.3
Barley and corn feed and industrial use, revised estimates 1980s-91, article, 1561–4.301
Business statistics, detailed data for major industries and economic indicators, *Survey of Current Business*, monthly rpt, 2702–1.13
Business statistics, detailed data for major industries and economic indicators, 1960-91, *Survey of Current Business* biennial supplement, 2704–1
CCC certificate exchange activity, by commodity, biweekly press release, 1802–16
CCC financial condition and major commodity program operations, FY63-88, annual chartbook, 1824–2
Consumption, supply, trade, prices, spending, and indexes, by food commodity, 1990, annual rpt, 1544–4
County Business Patterns, 1989: employment, establishments, and payroll, by SIC 2- to 4-digit industry and county, annual State rpt series, 2326–8
County Business Patterns, 1990: employment, establishments, and payroll, by SIC 2- to 4-digit industry and county, annual State rpt series, 2326–6
CPI by component for US city average, and by selected metro area, region, and population size, monthly rpt, 6762–2
Developing countries food supply, needs, and aid, status and alternative forecasts, world area rpt series, 1526–8
Employment, earnings, and hours, by SIC 1- to 4-digit industry, monthly 1989-Feb 1992, annual rpt, 6744–4

Employment of minorities and women, by occupation, SIC 1- to 3-digit industry, State, and MSA, 1991, annual rpt, 9244–1
Export licensing, monitoring, and enforcement activities, FY91, annual rpt, 2024–1
Exports and imports (agricultural) commodity and country, prices, and world market devs, monthly rpt, 1922–12
Exports and imports (agricultural) of US, by commodity and country, bimonthly rpt, 1522–1
Exports and imports (agricultural) of US, by detailed commodity and country, 1991, annual rpt, 1524–8
Exports and imports (agricultural) of US, by detailed commodity and country, 1991, semiannual rpt, 1522–4
Exports and imports between US and outlying areas, by detailed commodity and mode of transport, 1991, annual rpt, 2424–11
Exports and imports of US, by country and detailed commodity, monthly rpt, 2422–12
Exports and imports of US, by Harmonized System 6-digit commodity and country, 1991, annual rpt, 2424–13
Exports and imports of US, by selected country, country group, and commodity group, 1991, annual rpt, 2044–37
Exports and imports of US, by transport mode, country, and SITC 1- to 3-digit commodity, 1991, annual rpt, 2424–12
Exports of grains, oilseed products, hides, skins, and cotton, by country, weekly rpt, dropped data, 1922–3
Exports of US, detailed Schedule B commodities with countries of destination, 1991, annual rpt, 2424–10
Farm financial and marketing conditions, forecast 1992, annual chartbook, 1504–8
Farm financial and marketing conditions, forecast 1992, annual conf, 1504–9
Farm sector balance sheet, and receipts by detailed commodity, by State, 1986-90, annual rpt, 1544–18
Fertilizer and pesticide use and application rates, by type, crop, and State, 1991, 1616–1.1
Flour milling production by State, stocks, daily capacity, and exports by country, monthly Current Industrial Rpt, 2506–4.1
Foreign and US agricultural production, acreage, and yield for selected crops, forecasts by selected world region and country, FAS monthly circular, 1925–28
Foreign and US agricultural supply and demand indicators, by selected crop, monthly rpt, 1522–5
Foreign and US grain production, prices, trade, stocks, and use, FAS periodic circular series, 1925–2
Foreign countries agricultural production, prices, and trade, by country, 1980-91 and forecast 1992, annual world area rpt series, 1524–4
Freight (waterborne domestic and foreign) by commodity, traffic, and passengers, by port and waterway, 1989, annual rpt, 3754–3
Futures and options trading volume, by commodity and exchange, FY91, annual rpt, 11924–2
Futures contracts, stocks in deliverable position by type, weekly tables, 11922–4
Futures trading in selected commodities and financial instruments and indexes, for NYC, Chicago, and other markets activity, biweekly rpt, 11922–5
Input-output structure of US economy, detailed interindustry transactions for 541 industries, and components of final demand, 1982 benchmark data, 2708–17
Inspections of grain for domestic use and export, foreign buyers complaints, and handling facilities explosions, FY92, annual rpt, 1294–1
Inspections of grain for export, and stocks by region and market city, by type, weekly rpt, 1313–4
Irrigation projects of Reclamation Bur in western US, crop production and acreage by commodity, State, and project, 1990, annual rpt, 5824–12
Labor productivity, indexes of output, hours, and employment by SIC 2- to 4-digit industry, 1967-90, annual rpt, 6824–1.3
Loan support programs of USDA for grains, activity and status by grain and State, monthly rpt, 1802–3
Manufacturing annual survey, 1990: finances and operations, by SIC 2- to 4-digit industry, series, 2506–14
Manufacturing census, 1987: concentration of largest firms measured by value added, and for shipments by SIC 2- and 4-digit industry, subject rpt, 2497–6
Manufacturing census, 1987: shipments of manufacturers products, by customer class and SIC 2- and 4-digit industry, subject rpt, 2497–4
Manufacturing finances and operations, by SIC 2- to 4-digit industry, forecast 1992, annual rpt, 2044–28
Multinatl US firms and foreign affiliates finances and operations, by industry and country, 1989 benchmark survey, annual rpt, 2704–5
Nutrient, caloric, and waste composition, detailed data for raw, processed, and prepared foods, 1992 rpt, 1356–3.17
Occupational injury and illness rates, by SIC 2- to 4-digit industry, 1989-90, annual rpt, 6844–7
Occupational injury and illness rates, by SIC 2- to 4-digit industry, 1990, annual rpt, 6844–1
OECD trade, total and for 4 major countries, and US trade by country, by commodity, 1980-90, world area rpt series, 9116–1
Ohio River basin waterway facilities, freight by commodity and port, and recreation, by waterway, 1988-89, annual rpt, 3754–6
Pollution (air) abatement equipment shipments by industry, and new and backlog orders, by product, 1991, annual Current Industrial Rpt, 2506–12.5
Price indexes (producer), by stage of processing and detailed commodity, monthly rpt, 6762–6
Price indexes (producer), by stage of processing and detailed commodity, monthly 1991, annual rpt, 6764–2
Prices (farm-retail) for food, marketing cost components, and industry finances and productivity, 1920s-91, annual rpt, 1544–9
Prices received and paid by farmers, by commodity and State, monthly rpt, 1629–1
Prices received and paid by farmers, by commodity and State, 1991, annual rpt, 1629–5
Prices received by farmers and production value, by detailed crop and State, 1989-91, annual rpt, 1621–2
Production, farms, acreage, and related data, by selected crop and State, monthly rpt, 1621–1
Production inputs, output, and productivity for farms, by commodity and region, 1947-90, annual rpt, 1544–17
Production itemized costs, receipts, and returns, by commodity and region, 1975-90, annual rpt, 1544–20
Production itemized costs, receipts, and returns, by crop and State, 1987-89, annual rpt, 1544–24
Production, prices, trade, and export inspections by US port and country of destination, by grain type, weekly rpt, 1313–2
Production, prices, trade, and marketing, by commodity, current situation and forecast, monthly rpt with articles, 1502–4
Rye and wheat acreage seeded, by State, 1990-92, annual rpt, 1621–30
Rye foreign and US production, prices, trade, stocks, and use, quarterly situation rpt with articles, 1561–12
Science, engineering, and technical employment in manufacturing, by field and industry, 1989, triennial rpt, 9627–23
Seed exports, by type, world region, and country, FAS quarterly rpt, 1925–13
Soviet Union and US economic and sociodemographic indicators, selected years 1970-90, handbook, 2328–80
Stocks of grain on and off farms, by crop, quarterly rpt, 1621–4
Tax (income) returns of corporations, income and tax items by asset size and detailed industry, 1989, annual rpt, 8304–4; 8304–21
Weight and volume conversion factors for agricultural commodities and products, 1992 rpt, 1508–3
see also Alcohol fuels
see also Animal feed
see also Baking and bakery products
see also Corn
see also Gasohol
see also Grain storage and facilities
see also Hops
see also Oils, oilseeds, and fats
see also Rice
see also Soybeans
see also Wheat
see also under By Commodity in the "Index by Categories"

Graitcer, Philip L.
"Injury Surveillance in Developing Countries", 4202–7.308

Grall, Timothy S.
"Housing Characteristics of One-Parent Households: 1989", 2486–1.14

Gramm-Rudman Act
see Balanced Budget and Emergency Deficit Control Act

Grand Rapids, Mich.
see also under By City and By SMSA or MSA in the "Index by Categories"

Grandjean, Philippe
"Cancer Incidence and Mortality in Workers Exposed to Fluoride", 4472–1.359

Grant, Bridget F.
"Liver Cirrhosis Mortality in the U.S., 1973-88", 4486–1.13
"Prevalence of DSM-III-R Alcohol Abuse and Dependence, U.S., 1988", 4482–1.306

Grant, Robert B.
"Outpatient Surgery: Helping To Contain Health Care Costs", 6722–1.349

Grants and grants-in-aid
see State funding for economic development
see State funding for education
see State funding for health and hospitals
see State funding for higher education
see State funding for local areas
see State funding for public safety
see State funding for social welfare
see State government spending
see terms beginning with Federal aid

Grapes
see Fruit and fruit products

Graphics
see Advertising
see Art
see Cartography
see Chartbooks
see Maps
see Photography and photographic equipment
see Printing and publishing industry

Gravel
see Sand and gravel

Graves, Edmund J.
"Detailed Diagnoses and Procedures, National Hospital Discharge Survey, 1990. Vital and Health Statistics Series 13", 4147–13.111
"Expected Principal Source of Payment for Hospital Discharges: U.S., 1990", 4146–8.221
"National Hospital Discharge Survey: Annual Summary, 1990. Vital and Health Statistics Series 13", 4147–13.112
"1990 Summary: National Hospital Discharge Survey", 4146–8.211

Gray, Maureen B.
"Consumer Spending on Durables and Services in the 1980's", 6722–1.324

Gray wolf
see Endangered species

Grazing
see Pasture and rangeland

Great Britain
see United Kingdom

Great Lakes
Army Corps of Engineers water resources dev projects, characteristics, and costs, 1950s-89, biennial State rpt series, 3756–1
Army Corps of Engineers water resources dev projects, characteristics, and costs, 1950s-91, biennial State rpt series, 3756–2
Coal and coke production, shipments, and trade, by State of origin and destination, end-use sector, and mode of transport, quarterly rpt, 3162–37.1
Coal production, stocks, and shipments, by State of origin and destination, end-use sector, and mode of transport, quarterly rpt, 3162–8
Environmental Quality, status of problems, protection programs, research, and intl issues, 1991 annual rpt, 484–1
Environmental research lab for Great Lakes, activities, FY91 annual rpt, 2144–26
Fish catch, trade, use, and fishery operations, with selected foreign data, by species, 1980s-91, annual rpt, 2164–1
Fish Hatchery Natl System activities and deliveries, by species, hatchery, and jurisdiction of waters stocked, FY91, annual rpt, 5504–10
Freight (shipborne domestic), by major commodity group, vessel type, and port, 1987-89, annual rpt, 7704–7
Freight (waterborne domestic and foreign) by commodity, traffic, and passengers, by port and waterway, 1989, annual rpt, 3754–3.3
Mink and otter population, breeding, trapping, pollutant levels, and research status, for Great Lakes area, 1991 conf, 14648–27
NOAA oceanographic and other research activities, FY87-88, biennial rpt, 2144–6
Pollution (water) industrial emissions in Great Lakes, comparison of State, EPA, Intl Joint Commission, and Ontario standards, 1991 rpt, 14648–29
Pollution control policy and activities, and water quality, for Great Lakes Basin, 1991, biennial rpt, 14644–1
Port improvement capital expenditures and financing methods, by region and selected port, 1946-89, 7708–6
Research activities and water quality goals of Great Lakes Science Advisory Board, FY91, biennial rpt, 14644–6
Ships in Great Lakes fleet, and tonnage, by activity status and vessel type, FY91, annual rpt, 7704–14.2
Ships in US merchant fleet, operating subsidies, construction, and ship-related employment, monthly rpt, 7702–1
St Lawrence Seaway Dev Corp finances and activities, with Seaway cargo tonnage, and shipping costs compared to other US ports, 1990, annual rpt, 7744–1
Water level benchmarks, for Intl Great Lakes Datum 1985, 2178–34
Water levels in Great Lakes, monthly and annual averages by station, 1860-1990, quinquennial rpt, 2178–1
Water levels of Great Lakes and connecting channels, and forecasts, semimonthly rpt, 3752–2
Water levels of Great Lakes, and forecasts, monthly rpt and supplements, 3752–1
Water levels of Great Lakes, daily and monthly averages by site, 1991 and cumulative from 1900, annual rpt, 2174–3
Water supply and quality in streams and lakes, and groundwater levels in wells, by drainage basin, 1990, annual State rpt series, 5666–10
Water supply and quality in streams and lakes, and groundwater levels in wells, by drainage basin, 1991, annual State rpt series, 5666–12
Water supply in northeastern US, precipitation and stream runoff by station, monthly rpt, 2182–3
Weather (marine) forecast areas, and broadcast schedules and stations worldwide, as of Sept 1992, annual rpt, 2184–3
Weather (marine) forecast broadcast schedules worldwide, periodic rpt, 2182–9

Great Lakes Environmental Research Laboratory
see National Oceanic and Atmospheric Administration

Great Plains
see North Central States
see under By Region in the "Index by Categories"

Greece
Agricultural trade of US, by detailed commodity and country, 1991, annual rpt, 1524–8
Agricultural trade of US, by detailed commodity and country, 1991, semiannual rpt, 1522–4
AID loans repayment status and terms by program and country, and status of predecessor agency loans, quarterly rpt, 9912–3
Cuba trade, by commodity and country, mid 1980s-91, 9118–8
Drug abuse indicators, by world region and selected country, 1991 semiannual conf, 4492–5.1
Economic and military aid and loans from US and intl agencies, by program and country, FY46-91, annual rpt, 9914–5
Economic and social conditions of developing countries from 1960s, and Intl Dev Cooperation Agency and AID activities and funding, FY91-93, annual rpt, 9904–4
Economic conditions, income, production, prices, employment, and trade, 1992 periodic country rpt, 2046–4.18
Economic conditions, investment and export opportunities, and trade practices, 1992 country market research rpt, 2046–6.6
Economic conditions, policy, and trade practices, by country, 1989-91, annual rpt, 21384–5
Economic, social, political, and geographic summary data, by country, 1992, annual factbook, 9114–2
Exports and imports of US, by transport mode, country, and SITC 1- to 3-digit commodity, 1991, annual rpt, 2424–12
Exports, imports, and balances of US for manufactured goods, by SITC 2-digit commodity and country, quarterly rpt, 2042–35
Exports of US, detailed Schedule B commodities with countries of destination, 1991, annual rpt, 2424–10
Health care costs and components, services use, resources, and economic indicators, by OECD country, 1960s-90, article, 4652–1.322
Human rights conditions in 170 countries, and US economic and military aid, 1991, annual rpt, 21384–3
Imports of goods, services, and investment from US, trade barriers, impacts, and US actions, by country, 1991, annual rpt, 444–2

Imports of US given duty-free treatment for value of US material sent abroad, by commodity and country, 1987-90, annual rpt, 9884–14
Labor conditions, union coverage, and work accidents, 1992 annual country rpt, 6366–4.35
Military aid of US, arms sales, and training programs costs and budget requests, by program, world region, and country, FY91-93, annual rpt, 7144–13
Military spending, arms trade, and force strengths, with govt spending and population, by country, 1979-89, annual rpt, 9824–1
Multinatl US firms and foreign affiliates finances and operations, by industry and country, 1989 benchmark survey, annual rpt, 2704–5
Multinatl US firms foreign affiliates, income statement items by asset size, industry, and country, 1988, biennial article, 8302–2.322
Oil production, stocks, use, and trade, by selected country and country group, monthly rpt, 3162–42
Population size, growth rates, and components of change, by country, projected 1990-2020 and trends from 1950, biennial rpt, 2324–9
Refugee migration, and intl aid programs, by world area and country of origin and asylum, 1991, annual rpt, 7004–15
Ships in world merchant fleet, tonnage, and new ship construction and deliveries, by vessel type and country, as of Jan 1992, annual rpt, 7704–3
Steel trade, by product, country, and customs district, with US industry operating data, 1989-June 1992, semiannual rpt, 9882–15
Tax revenue, by level of govt and type of tax, for OECD countries, mid 1960s-90, annual rpt, 10044–1.2
UN voting record and share of votes in agreement with US, by issue, country, and world area, 1991, annual rpt, 7004–18
see also under By Foreign Country in the "Index by Categories"

Green, George R.
"Composite Index of Coincident Indicators and Alternative Coincident Indexes", 2702–1.322

Green, Gordon
"Factors Affecting Black-White Income Differentials: A Decomposition", 2546–6.79
"International Comparisons of Earnings Inequality for Men in the 1980's", 2546–6.79

Green, Ira
"Hyperthermia in Conjunction with Cancer Chemotherapy. Health Technology Assessment Report, 1991", 4186–10.7
"Polysomnography and Sleep Disorder Centers. Health Technology Assessment Report, 1991", 4186–10.9

Greenberg, Michael
"Blue Thursday? Homicide and Suicide Among Urban 15—24-Year-Old Black Male Americans", 4042–3.323

Greenfeld, Lawrence A.
"Prisons and Prisoners in the U.S.", 6068–248

Greenfield, Victoria A.
"Auctioning Radio Spectrum Licenses", 26306–6.169

Greenhorne and O'Mara, Inc.
"Analysis and Summary of the 1990 National Scenic Byways Study Inventory", 7558–112
"Final Case Study for the National Scenic Byways Study: Safety, Traffic and Cost Considerations on Scenic Byways", 7556–8.5

Greenhouse effect
see Global climate change

Greenland
Agricultural trade of US, by detailed commodity and country, 1991, annual rpt, 1524–8
Agricultural trade of US, by detailed commodity and country, 1991, semiannual rpt, 1522–4
Economic, social, political, and geographic summary data, by country, 1992, annual factbook, 9114–2
Exports and imports of US, by transport mode, country, and SITC 1- to 3-digit commodity, 1991, annual rpt, 2424–12
Exports of US, detailed Schedule B commodities with countries of destination, 1991, annual rpt, 2424–10
Population size, growth rates, and components of change, by country, projected 1990-2020 and trends from 1950, biennial rpt, 2324–9
Tide height and time daily at coastal points, forecast 1993, annual rpt, 2174–2.3

Greenlees, John S.
"Effect of Marginal Tax Rates on Capital Gains Revenue: Another Look at the Evidence", 8006–6.3
"Historical Trends in the U.S. Cost of Capital", 8006–6.2

Greensboro, N.C.
Wages by occupation, and benefits for office and plant workers, 1992 survey, periodic MSA rpt, 6785–3.5
see also under By City and By SMSA or MSA in the "Index by Categories"

Greenville, S.C.
see also under By City and By SMSA or MSA in the "Index by Categories"

Greenwood, Jeremy
"On the Existence and Uniqueness of Nonoptimal Equilibria in Dynamic Stochastic Economies", 9383–20.21

Greenwood, Michael J.
"Economic Effects of Immigrants on Native and Foreign-Born Workers: Complementarity, Substitutability, and Other Channels of Influence", 6366–6.12
"Labor Market Consequences of U.S. Immigration: A Survey", 6366–6.1

Gregorio, David I.
"Detecting Colorectal Cancer with a Large Scale Fecal Occult Blood Testing Program", 4042–3.333

Grenada
Agricultural trade of US, by detailed commodity and country, 1991, semiannual rpt, 1522–4
AID economic aid to developing countries, obligations and disbursements by country, quarterly rpt, 9912–4
Economic and military aid and loans from US and intl agencies, by program and country, FY46-91, annual rpt, 9914–5
Economic and social conditions of developing countries from 1960s, and Intl Dev Cooperation Agency and AID activities and funding, FY91-93, annual rpt, 9904–4
Economic and social conditions, resources, and trade, and aid, 1992, annual factbook, 9914–14
Economic, social, political, and geographic summary data, by country, 1992, annual factbook, 9114–2
Exports and imports of US, by transport mode, country, and SITC 1- to 3-digit commodity, 1991, annual rpt, 2424–12
Exports of US, detailed Schedule B commodities with countries of destination, 1991, annual rpt, 2424–10
Human rights conditions in 170 countries, and US economic and military aid, 1991, annual rpt, 21384–3
Military aid of US, arms sales, and training programs costs and budget requests, by program, world region, and country, FY91-93, annual rpt, 7144–13
Nutmeg and mace production in Grenada, 1970s-91, FAS annual circular, 1925–15.1
Population size, growth rates, and components of change, by country, projected 1990-2020 and trends from 1950, biennial rpt, 2324–9
UN voting record and share of votes in agreement with US, by issue, country, and world area, 1991, annual rpt, 7004–18

Greyhound Lines, Inc.
Finances and operations of interstate carriers, 1990, annual rpt, 9486–5.3

Griffith, Jeanne E.
"International Mathematics and Science Assessments: What Have We Learned?", 4838–51

Griffith, Patricia A.
"Summary of Water Resources Activities of the USGS in Colorado, FY91", 5666–26.24

Grise, Verner N.
"Changing Tobacco User's Dollar", 1561–10.304
"Nonfarm Tobacco Industry Regulations", 1561–10.302
"Outlook for Tobacco", 1504–9.1
"U.S. Tobacco Imports", 1561–10.306

Grocery stores
see Food stores

Gronberg, Jo Ann M.
"Estimation of a Water Budget for the Central Part of the Western San Joaquin Valley, California. Regional Aquifer-System Analysis ", 5666–25.14

Gronberg, Timothy J.
"Wagner's Hypothesis: A Local Perspective", 9377–9.133

Groshen, Erica L.
"Causes and Consequences of Structural Changes in U.S. Labor Markets: A Review", 9377–1.304
"Components of City-Size Wage Differentials, 1973-88", 9377–1.301
"Rising Inequality in a Salary Survey: Another Piece of the Puzzle", 9377–9.130

Gross Domestic Product
Agricultural Outlook, production, prices, marketing, and trade, by commodity, forecast and current situation, monthly rpt with articles, 1502–4

Andean Trade Preference Act duty-free exports from 4 countries to US, and business opportunities, 1989-91, 2048–161
Banks loan interest rates and default risk relation to GDP and money supply, model description and results, 1992 working paper, 9387–8.283
Budget of US, CBO analysis of revenue and spending alternatives and projections of economic indicators, FY93-97, annual rpt, 26304–3
Budget of US, historical data, selected years FY34-91 and projected to FY97, 108–46.5
Business statistics, detailed data for major industries and economic indicators, *Survey of Current Business*, monthly rpt, 2702–1
Business statistics, detailed data for major industries and economic indicators, 1960-91, *Survey of Current Business* biennial supplement, 2704–1
Central America economic indicators, by country, 1969-89, working paper, 9916–13.4
Developing countries economic and social conditions from 1960s, and Intl Dev Cooperation Agency and AID activities and funding, FY91-93, annual rpt, 9904–4
Eastern Europe transition to market economies, economic conditions, trade, and foreign investment, by country, 1990-91, 9118–13
Economic indicators and components, and Fed Reserve 4th District business and financial conditions, monthly chartbook, 9377–10
Economic indicators and components, current data and annual trends, monthly rpt, 23842–1.1
Economic indicators compounded annual rates of change, monthly rpt, 9391–3
Economic indicators, monthly rpt, 9362–1.2
Economic indicators performance, and Fed Reserve monetary policy objectives, as of July 1992, semiannual rpt, 9362–4
Economic Report of the President for 1992, with economic trends from 1929, annual rpt, 204–1
Economies of scale in output, technology, and trade, model description and results, 1992 technical paper, 9383–20.22
Forecasts of GDP for current quarter, performance of monthly advance indicators, 1981-91, article, 9393–8.305
Forecasts of GDP, performance of selected economic indicators over selected forecast periods and business cycles, 1960s-91, article, 9375–1.307
Foreign and US economic conditions, for major industrial countries, monthly rpt, 9112–1
Foreign and US energy use and production, by fuel type, country, and country group, projected 1995-2010 and trends from 1970, annual rpt, 3164–84
Foreign countries economic and monetary trends, compounded annual rates of change and quarterly indicators for US and 7 major industrialized countries, quarterly rpt, 9391–7
Foreign countries economic conditions and implications for US, periodic country rpt series, 2046–4
Foreign countries economic conditions, policy, and trade practices, by country, 1989-91, annual rpt, 21384–5
Foreign countries economic indicators, and trade and investment flows, for selected countries and country groups, selected years 1946-91, annual rpt, 204–1.9
Foreign countries economic, social, political, and geographic summary data, by country, 1992, annual factbook, 9114–2
GDP use to measure real output, and effect of alternative price weights, 1959-90, article, 2702–1.314
Germany unification economic impacts for Germany, US, Japan, and worldwide, alternative projections 1991-99, technical paper, 9366–7.275
Global climate change impacts on agricultural production and GDP, with data by crop and world area, mid 1970s-86, 1528–326
Haiti economic conditions, 1985-91, working paper, 9916–13.3
Health care spending and factors in increase, with background data and foreign comparisons, various periods 1929-90, technical paper, 9366–6.296
Israel economic conditions, US investment and export opportunities, and trade practices, 1992 rpt, 2008–32
Latin America economic and social conditions, resources, trade, and aid, 1992, annual factbook, 9914–14
Latin America exports, investment, debt, and tariffs for 7 countries, and trade and investment policy liberalization issues, mid 1960s-91, 9886–4.184
Medicare contributions and disbursements, by State, 1985, 4006–11.4
Multinatl firms US affiliates gross product, by component, industry, and country of parent firm, 1987-90, article, 2702–1.342
Natl income and product accounts and components, summary data 1959-91, tables, 2702–1.334
Natl income and product accounts and components, *Survey of Current Business*, monthly rpt, 2702–1.23
Natl income and product accounts benchmark revisions of GDP and natl income, various periods 1959-80, tables, 2702–1.307
Natl income and product accounts, comprehensive accounts and components, benchmark revisions, 1929-88, 2708–5
Natl income and product accounts, comprehensive accounts and components, *Survey of Current Business*, monthly rpt, 2702–1.24
Natl income and product accounts revisions to GDP, personal income, and selected foreign transactions, various periods 1959-90, tables, 2702–1.313
NATO, Japan, and South Korea military spending and indicators of ability to support common defense, by country, 1970s-90, annual rpt, 3544–28
OECD members health care costs, hospital use, resources, and economic and health indicators, by country, 1960s-90, article, 4652–1.322
State govt spending impacts of gross product, with data by industry div and State, 1960s-86, working paper, 9377–9.133
State gross product by component, industry div, and State, 1977-89, article, 2702–1.303
Statistical Abstract of US, 1992 annual data compilation, 2324–1.14
Tax policy impacts on economic performance and income distribution, issues and background data, with foreign comparisons, 1991 and trends, 21788–211
Tennessee Valley economic conditions, and compared to US, alternative projections 1992-2010 and trends from 1929, annual rpt, 9804–27
West Central States, gross State product and growth rates by industry div and State, 1979-89, article, 9381–1.306
see also Gross National Product

Gross, Edward B., Jr.
"Individual Income Tax Returns, Preliminary Data, 1990", 8302–2.307

Gross National Product
Banks reserve requirements of Fed Reserve Bd relation to GNP and investment, 1991 working paper, 9375–13.72
Budget deficits impacts on GNP and public and foreign debt, projected under alternative reduction policies, 1990-2020 with intl comparisons from 1981, GAO rpt, 26109–5
Budget of US, CBO analysis of revenue and spending alternatives and projections of economic indicators, FY93-97, annual rpt, 26304–3
Budget of US, obligations and authority by function, agency, and program, with summaries and analyses, FY93, annual rpt, 104–2
Business cycle (intl) impacts on economic indicators, for industrialized countries, 1950s-80s, working paper, 9383–20.16
Business cycle duration and strength indicators, late 1940s-91, article, 9373–1.301
Business cycle patterns of GNP growth, alternative model descriptions and results, 1950s-80s, technical paper, 9385–8.139
Business cycle recession and expansion duration indicators, 1850s-1990, working paper, 9375–13.83
Business statistics, detailed data for major industries and economic indicators, *Survey of Current Business*, monthly rpt, 2702–1
Developing countries economic and social conditions from 1960s, and Intl Dev Cooperation Agency and AID activities and funding, FY91-93, annual rpt, 9904–4
Economic indicators and relation to govt finances by level of govt, selected years 1929-91, annual rpt, 10044–1
Exports and imports relation to terms of trade and GNP, alternative models description and results, 1992 working paper, 9377–9.144
Financial and economic analysis and forecasting methodology, technical paper series, 9366–6
Fiscal policy (supply side) of Reagan Admin, economic impacts, 1980s and trends from 1960s, technical paper, 9385–1.304; 9385–8.125
Forecasts of economic conditions and employment, alternative BLS projections to 2005 and trends 1975-90, biennial rpt, 6744–19

Forecasts of economic indicators, 1992-93 and trends from 1948, annual article, 9383–6.301
Forecasts of economic indicators, 1993-94 and trends from 1948, annual article, 9383–6.303
Forecasts of employment and GNP, accuracy of BLS forecasts made late 1970s-85, as of 1990, article, 6722–1.335
Foreign and US economic indicators, trade balances, and exchange rates, for selected OECD and Asian countries, 1992 semiannual rpt, 8002–14
Foreign countries *Background Notes*, summary social, political, and economic data, series, 7006–2
Foreign countries economic conditions and implications for US, periodic country rpt series, 2046–4
Foreign countries economic, social, political, and geographic summary data, by country, 1992, annual factbook, 9114–2
Foreign countries military spending, arms trade, and force strengths, with govt spending and population, by country, 1979-89, annual rpt, 9824–1
Interest rate spreads impacts on GNP and employment, various periods 1959-91, technical paper, 9385–8.131
Monetary and fiscal policies relation to GNP variability, 1950s-91, working paper, 9381–10.132
Natl income and product accounts and components, *Survey of Current Business*, monthly rpt, 2702–1.23
Natl income and product accounts, comprehensive accounts and components, benchmark revisions, 1929-88, 2708–5
Natl income and product accounts, comprehensive accounts and components, *Survey of Current Business*, monthly rpt, 2702–1.24
OECD members GNP and GNP growth, by country, annual rpt, discontinued, 7144–8
Oil prices and interest rates related to GNP and employment, late 1940s-91, article, 9389–1.304
Overseas Business Reports: economic conditions, investment and export opportunities, and trade practices, country market research rpt series, 2046–6
Palau admin, and social, economic, and govtl data, FY91, annual rpt, 7004–6
Seasonal growth of GNP relation to monetary, fiscal, and demand indicators, 1991 working paper, 9375–13.74
Seasonal variations in GNP, relation to labor hoarding and returns to scale, 1991 working paper, 9375–13.71
Statistical Abstract of US, 1992 annual data compilation, 2324–1.14
Transportation energy use by mode, fuel supply, and demographic and economic factors of vehicle use, 1970s-90, annual rpt, 3304–5.2
see also Gross Domestic Product

Grosskopf, Shawna
"Allocative Inefficiency in Education", 9379–12.80
"Budget Constrained Frontier Measures of Fiscal Equality and Efficiency in Schooling", 9379–12.87

Grossman, Glenn M.
"Life Insurance Benefits in Small Establishments and Government", 6722–1.346

Groundwater
see Hydrology
see Rivers and waterways
see Water supply and use

Group health
see Blue Cross-Blue Shield
see Health insurance
see Health maintenance organizations

Group homes for the handicapped
Census of Population, 1990: population characteristics and living arrangements, by county, place, and urban-rural location, State rpt series, 2531–1
Drug handling and dispensing in board and care homes, violations of State regulations, for 3 metro areas, 1990-91, GAO rpt, 26121–447
Homeless persons with handicaps, HUD group housing grants by recipient, 1991, press release, 5006–3.79
Homeless persons with handicaps, HUD group housing grants by recipient, 1992, press release, 5006–3.96
Supplemental Security Income and Medicaid eligibility and payment provisions, and beneficiaries living arrangements, by State, 1992, annual rpt, 4704–13

Group quarters
AFDC beneficiaries demographic and financial characteristics, by State, FY90, annual rpt, 4584–7
Census of Population and Housing, 1990: detailed geographic coverage, State CD-ROM series, 2551–9
Census of Population and Housing, 1990: population and housing characteristics, detailed geographic coverage, State CD-ROM series, 2551–10
Census of Population and Housing, 1990: summary characteristics, households, and land area, by county, subdiv, and place, State rpt series, 2551–1
Census of Population, 1990: population characteristics and living arrangements, by county, place, and urban-rural location, State rpt series, 2531–1
Census of Population, 1990: population characteristics and living arrangements, for Native American, urban, and metro areas, series, 2531–2
County Business Patterns, 1989: employment, establishments, and payroll, by SIC 2- to 4-digit industry and county, annual State rpt series, 2326–8
County Business Patterns, 1990: employment, establishments, and payroll, by SIC 2- to 4-digit industry and county, annual State rpt series, 2326–6
Deaths and rates, by cause and selected social, demographic, and employment characteristics, 1979-85, natl longitudinal study, 4478–186
Higher education instn student aid and other sources of support, with student expenses and characteristics, by instn type and control, 1987 triennial study, series, 4846–3; 4846–5
Higher education instn tuition and other charges, by public and private 2- and 4-year instn, and State, 1991/92, annual listing, 4844–10
Input-output structure of US economy, detailed interindustry transactions for 541 industries, and components of final demand, 1982 benchmark data, 2708–17
Living arrangements, family relationships, and marital status, by selected characteristics, 1991, annual Current Population Rpt, 2546–1.461
Pacific territories population and housing detailed characteristics, by location, 1990 Census of Population and Housing, series, 2551–8
Statistical Abstract of US, 1992 annual data compilation, 2324–1.1
Supplemental Security Income and Medicaid eligibility and payment provisions, and beneficiaries living arrangements, by State, 1992, annual rpt, 4704–13
see also Group homes for the handicapped
see also Transient housing

Grubb, W. Norton
"Trends in Wage and Salary Inequality, 1967-88", 6722–1.328

Gruben, William C.
"Economic Liberalization in the Americas", 9379–2
"On the Future Erosion of the North American Free Trade Agreement", 9379–12.89

Grymes, John A.
"Historical Trends: State Education Facts, 1969-89", 4828–33

GSA
see General Services Administration

Guadagno, Mary Ann
"Families with High Housing Expenditures: A Comparison of Homeowners and Renters", 1702–1.304

Guadalupe County, Tex.
Housing and households characteristics, and unit and neighborhood quality, by MSA location for 11 MSAs, 1986 survey, supplement, 2485–8

Guadeloupe
Economic and social conditions, resources, and trade, and aid, 1992, annual factbook, 9914–14
Exports and imports of US, by transport mode, country, and SITC 1- to 3-digit commodity, 1991, annual rpt, 2424–12
Exports of US, detailed Schedule B commodities with countries of destination, 1991, annual rpt, 2424–10

Guam
Banks (insured commercial and savings) deposits by instn, State, MSA, and county, as of June 1991, annual regional rpt, 9295–3.6
Deaths and rates, by detailed location, cause, and demographic characteristics, 1989, US Vital Statistics annual rpt, 4144–3.2
Economic, social, political, and geographic summary data, by country, 1992, annual factbook, 9114–2
Exports and imports between US and outlying areas, by detailed commodity and mode of transport, 1991, annual rpt, 2424–11
Fed Govt spending in States and local areas, by type, State, county, and city, FY91, annual rpt, 2464–3
Fed Govt spending in States, by type, program, agency, and State, FY91, annual rpt, 2464–2

Fires (wild) and acreage burned, by type of land, ownership, cause, region, and State, 1984-90, annual rpt, 1204–4
HHS financial aid, by program, recipient, State, and city, FY91, annual regional listing, 4004–3.9
Hospital deaths of Medicare patients, actual and expected rates by diagnosis, and hospital characteristics, by instn, FY90 annual State rpt, 4654–14.12
Oil company overcharge settlements funds received, and conservation and energy aid spending, by outlying area, 1990, GAO rpt, 26113–564
Physicians, by specialty, age, sex, and location of training and practice, 1990, State rpt, 4116–6.53
Population and housing census, 1990: detailed characteristics, by location, outlying area rpt, 2551–8.3
Population size, growth rates, and components of change, by country, projected 1990-2020 and trends from 1950, biennial rpt, 2324–9
Statistical Abstract of US, 1992 annual data compilation, 2324–1.30
Tax (income) returns of Foreign Sales Corps, assets, and income and tax items, by industry, country of incorporation, and transaction pricing method, 1987, article, 8302–2.311
see also under By Outlying Area in the "Index by Categories"

Guaranteed income
see Income maintenance

Guarantees and warranties
see also Surety bonds

Guardianship
OASDI and SSI recipients with representative payee, by beneficiary type, 1990, annual rpt, 4744–3.3; 4744–3.8
Supplemental Security Income and Medicaid eligibility and payment provisions, and beneficiaries living arrangements, by State, 1992, annual rpt, 4704–13
Veterans benefits under guardianship, for incompetent and minor recipients, 1967-91, annual rpt, 8604–5.2
see also Foster home care
see also Parents

Guatemala
Agricultural trade of US, by detailed commodity and country, 1991, annual rpt, 1524–8
Agricultural trade of US, by detailed commodity and country, 1991, semiannual rpt, 1522–4
AID economic aid to developing countries, obligations and disbursements by country, quarterly rpt, 9912–4
AID loans repayment status and terms by program and country, and status of predecessor agency loans, quarterly rpt, 9912–3
Background Notes, summary social, political, and economic data, 1992 rpt, 7006–2.14
Death rates by cause and age, and life expectancy, by sex, for Costa Rica and Guatemala, 1984 and trends from 1900, working paper, 2326–18.64
Economic and military aid and loans from US and intl agencies, by program and country, FY46-91, annual rpt, 9914–5
Economic and social conditions of developing countries from 1960s, and Intl Dev Cooperation Agency and AID activities and funding, FY91-93, annual rpt, 9904–4
Economic and social conditions, resources, and trade, and aid, 1992, annual factbook, 9914–14
Economic conditions, policy, and trade practices, by country, 1989-91, annual rpt, 21384–5
Economic indicators for Central America by country, 1969-89, working paper, 9916–13.4
Economic, population, and agricultural data, US and other aid sources, and AID activity, 1992 country rpt, 9916–12.60
Economic, social, political, and geographic summary data, by country, 1992, annual factbook, 9114–2
Exports and imports of US, by commodity and country, 1980-90, world area rpt, 9116–1.5
Exports and imports of US, by Harmonized System 6-digit commodity and country, 1991, annual rpt, 2424–13
Exports and imports of US, by selected country, country group, and commodity group, 1991, annual rpt, 2044–37
Exports and imports of US, by transport mode, country, and SITC 1- to 3-digit commodity, 1991, annual rpt, 2424–12
Exports, imports, and balances of US for manufactured goods, by SITC 2-digit commodity and country, quarterly rpt, 2042–35
Exports of US, detailed Schedule B commodities with countries of destination, 1991, annual rpt, 2424–10
Human rights conditions in 170 countries, and US economic and military aid, 1991, annual rpt, 21384–3
Imports of goods, services, and investment from US, trade barriers, impacts, and US actions, by country, 1991, annual rpt, 444–2
Military aid of US, arms sales, and training programs costs and budget requests, by program, world region, and country, FY91-93, annual rpt, 7144–13
Military spending, arms trade, and force strengths, with govt spending and population, by country, 1979-89, annual rpt, 9824–1
Multinatl US firms and foreign affiliates finances and operations, by industry and country, 1989 benchmark survey, annual rpt, 2704–5
Multinatl US firms foreign affiliates, income statement items by asset size, industry, and country, 1988, biennial article, 8302–2.322
Population size, growth rates, and components of change, by country, projected 1990-2020 and trends from 1950, biennial rpt, 2324–9
Refugee migration, and intl aid programs, by world area and country of origin and asylum, 1991, annual rpt, 7004–15
Steel trade, by product, country, and customs district, with US industry operating data, 1989-June 1992, semiannual rpt, 9882–15
UN voting record and share of votes in agreement with US, by issue, country, and world area, 1991, annual rpt, 7004–18
see also under By Foreign Country in the "Index by Categories"

Guenther, Patricia M.
"Effects of Procedural Differences Between 1977 and 1987 in the Nationwide Food Consumption Survey on Estimates of Food and Nutrient Intakes: Results of the USDA 1988 Bridging Study", 1358–6

Guinea
Agricultural trade of US, by detailed commodity and country, 1991, annual rpt, 1524–8
Agricultural trade of US, by detailed commodity and country, 1991, semiannual rpt, 1522–4
AID economic aid to developing countries, obligations and disbursements by country, quarterly rpt, 9912–4
AID loans repayment status and terms by program and country, and status of predecessor agency loans, quarterly rpt, 9912–3
Economic and military aid and loans from US and intl agencies, by program and country, FY46-91, annual rpt, 9914–5
Economic and social conditions of developing countries from 1960s, and Intl Dev Cooperation Agency and AID activities and funding, FY91-93, annual rpt, 9904–4
Economic conditions, income, production, prices, employment, and trade, 1991 periodic country rpt, 2046–4.7
Economic, population, and agricultural data, US and other aid sources, and AID activity, 1991 country rpt, 9916–12.57
Economic, social, political, and geographic summary data, by country, 1992, annual factbook, 9114–2
Exports and imports of US, by transport mode, country, and SITC 1- to 3-digit commodity, 1991, annual rpt, 2424–12
Exports of US, detailed Schedule B commodities with countries of destination, 1991, annual rpt, 2424–10
Human rights conditions in 170 countries, and US economic and military aid, 1991, annual rpt, 21384–3
Military aid of US, arms sales, and training programs costs and budget requests, by program, world region, and country, FY91-93, annual rpt, 7144–13
Military spending, arms trade, and force strengths, with govt spending and population, by country, 1979-89, annual rpt, 9824–1
Minerals production, reserves, and industry role in domestic economy and world supply, 1992 country rpt, 5606–1.20
Minerals Yearbook, Vol 3, 1989: foreign country review of production, trade, and policy, by commodity, annual rpt, 5604–35.1
Population size, growth rates, and components of change, by country, projected 1990-2020 and trends from 1950, biennial rpt, 2324–9
Steel trade, by product, country, and customs district, with US industry operating data, 1989-June 1992, semiannual rpt, 9882–15
UN voting record and share of votes in agreement with US, by issue, country, and world area, 1991, annual rpt, 7004–18

Guinea-Bissau
Agricultural trade of US, by detailed commodity and country, 1991, annual rpt, 1524–8
Agricultural trade of US, by detailed commodity and country, 1991, semiannual rpt, 1522–4
AID economic aid to developing countries, obligations and disbursements by country, quarterly rpt, 9912–4
Economic and military aid and loans from US and intl agencies, by program and country, FY46-91, annual rpt, 9914–5
Economic and social conditions of developing countries from 1960s, and Intl Dev Cooperation Agency and AID activities and funding, FY91-93, annual rpt, 9904–4
Economic, social, political, and geographic summary data, by country, 1992, annual factbook, 9114–2
Exports and imports of US, by transport mode, country, and SITC 1- to 3-digit commodity, 1991, annual rpt, 2424–12
Human rights conditions in 170 countries, and US economic and military aid, 1991, annual rpt, 21384–3
Military aid of US, arms sales, and training programs costs and budget requests, by program, world region, and country, FY91-93, annual rpt, 7144–13
Military spending, arms trade, and force strengths, with govt spending and population, by country, 1979-89, annual rpt, 9824–1
Minerals Yearbook, Vol 3, 1989: foreign country review of production, trade, and policy, by commodity, annual rpt, 5604–35.1
Population size, growth rates, and components of change, by country, projected 1990-2020 and trends from 1950, biennial rpt, 2324–9
Refugee migration, and intl aid programs, by world area and country of origin and asylum, 1991, annual rpt, 7004–15
UN voting record and share of votes in agreement with US, by issue, country, and world area, 1991, annual rpt, 7004–18

Guinivan, Phyllis
"Review of Literature on Herbicides, Including Phenoxy Herbicides and Associated Dioxins: Volume XIX Analysis of Recent Literature on Health Effects and Volume XX Annotated Bibliography of Recent Literature on Health Effects", 8706–1.5

Gulf Coast Regional Blood Center
Blood banks safety violations, FDA enforcement, disease transmittal, and Houston regional center activities and finances, 1970s-91, hearings, 21368–134

Gulf of Alaska
Army Corps of Engineers water resources dev projects, characteristics, and costs, 1950s-89, biennial State rpt series, 3756–1
Army Corps of Engineers water resources dev projects, characteristics, and costs, 1950s-91, biennial State rpt series, 3756–2
Environmental conditions and oil dev impacts for Alaska OCS, compilation of papers, series, 2176–1
Fish catch, trade, use, and fishery operations, with selected foreign data, by species, 1980s-91, annual rpt, 2164–1
Marine mammals incidental catch by fishing trawl vessels, by species, vessel flag and type, and North Pacific location, 1965-88, 2168–129
see also Cook Inlet, Alaska
see also Prince William Sound, Alaska

Gulf of Mexico
Coastal areas environmental conditions and mgmt, for individual areas, conf series, 2146–8
Estuary environmental and fishery conditions, research results and methodology, 1992 rpt, 2176–7.28
Estuary environmental conditions, research results and methodology, 1991 local area rpt, 2176–7.26
Estuary environmental conditions, research results and methodology, 1992 local area rpt, 2176–7.27
Fish (billfish) catch in Gulf of Mexico, by species and location, 1990, annual rpt, 2164–23
Fish (billfish) tagged and recovered by location, and Japan catch in US waters, 1950-90, annual rpt, 2164–7
Fish (game) tagging and research activities, by species, 1990, annual rpt, 2164–24
Fish and shellfish resources and catch, marine mammal and sea turtle population, and mgmt, by species and region, 1988-90, annual rpt, 2164–22
Fish catch, trade, use, and fishery operations, with selected foreign data, by species, 1980s-91, annual rpt, 2164–1
Fishing (ocean sport) activities, and catch by species, by angler characteristics and State, 1990-91, annual coastal area rpt, 2166–17.1
Freight (shipborne domestic), by major commodity group, vessel type, and port, 1987-89, annual rpt, 7704–7
Freight (waterborne domestic and foreign) by commodity, traffic, and passengers, by port and waterway, 1989, annual rpt, 3754–3.2
Marine Fisheries Review, US and foreign fisheries resources, dev, mgmt, and research, quarterly journal, 2162–1
Oil and gas OCS lease sales in Gulf of Mexico, by company and tract, 1990, annual rpt, 5734–8
Oil and gas OCS reserves of Fed Govt, leasing and exploration activity, production, revenue, and costs, by ocean area, FY91, annual rpt, 5734–4
Oil and gas OCS reserves, production, and leasing status, for Gulf of Mexico by location, 1990, annual rpt, 5734–6
Oil and gas reserves, production, and ultimate recovery, by location, with field technical characteristics, series, 3166–14
Port improvement capital expenditures and financing methods, by region and selected port, 1946-89, 7708–6
Sharks and other fish tagged and recovered, by species, 1991, annual rpt, 2164–21
Shellfish harvest in estuaries, approved and restricted areas, and pollution sources, by estuary, State, and coastal region, 1990, quinquennial rpt, 2178–33
Temperature of sea surface by ocean and for US coastal areas, and Bering Sea ice conditions, monthly rpt, 2182–5
Tidal currents, daily time and velocity by station for North America coasts, forecast 1993, annual rpt, 2174–1.1
Tide height and time daily at coastal points, forecast 1993, annual rpt, 2174–2.3
Water supply and quality in streams and lakes, and groundwater levels in wells, by drainage basin, 1990, annual State rpt series, 5666–10
Water supply and quality in streams and lakes, and groundwater levels in wells, by drainage basin, 1991, annual State rpt series, 5666–12
Weather (marine) forecast areas, and broadcast schedules and stations worldwide, as of Sept 1992, annual rpt, 2184–3
Weather (marine) forecast broadcast schedules worldwide, periodic rpt, 2182–9

Gullickson, William
"Multifactor Productivity in Manufacturing Industries", 6722–1.345

Gum and wood chemicals
County Business Patterns, 1989: employment, establishments, and payroll, by SIC 2- to 4-digit industry and county, annual State rpt series, 2326–8
County Business Patterns, 1990: employment, establishments, and payroll, by SIC 2- to 4-digit industry and county, annual State rpt series, 2326–6
Employment, earnings, and hours, by SIC 1- to 4-digit industry, monthly 1989-Feb 1992, annual rpt, 6744–4
Exports and imports between US and outlying areas, by detailed commodity and mode of transport, 1991, annual rpt, 2424–11
Exports and imports of US, by country and detailed commodity, monthly rpt, 2422–12
Exports and imports of US, by Harmonized System 6-digit commodity and country, 1991, annual rpt, 2424–13
Exports of US, detailed Schedule B commodities with countries of destination, 1991, annual rpt, 2424–10
Freight (waterborne domestic and foreign) by commodity, traffic, and passengers, by port and waterway, 1989, annual rpt, 3754–3
Input-output structure of US economy, detailed interindustry transactions for 541 industries, and components of final demand, 1982 benchmark data, 2708–17
Manufacturing annual survey, 1990: finances and operations, by SIC 2- to 4-digit industry, series, 2506–14
Manufacturing census, 1987: concentration of largest firms measured by value added, and for shipments by SIC 2- and 4-digit industry, subject rpt, 2497–6
Manufacturing census, 1987: shipments of manufacturers products, by customer class and SIC 2- and 4-digit industry, subject rpt, 2497–4
Occupational injury and illness rates, by SIC 2- to 4-digit industry, 1989-90, annual rpt, 6844–7
Occupational injury and illness rates, by SIC 2- to 4-digit industry, 1990, annual rpt, 6844–1
Price indexes (producer), by stage of processing and detailed commodity, monthly rpt, 6762–6

Price indexes (producer), by stage of processing and detailed commodity, monthly 1991, annual rpt, 6764–2
Stockpiling of strategic material, inventories and needs, by commodity, 1992, annual rpt, 3544–37

Guns
see Firearms
see Military weapons

Gunther, Jeffery W.
"Bank Credit and Economic Activity: Evidence from the Texas Banking Decline", 9379–14.16
"Friction Model of Discount Rate Changes", 9379–14.20

Guntheroth, Warren G.
"Seasonal Association Between SIDS Deaths and Kindergarten Absences", 4042–3.331

Guterman, Stuart
"Effect of the OBRA 1989 Payment Provision for Small Rural Medicare-Dependent Hospitals", 17206–2.42

Gutzmer, D. I.
"Comparison of Wood Preservatives in Stake Tests: 1991 Progress Report", 1208–391

Guyana
Agricultural trade of US, by detailed commodity and country, 1991, annual rpt, 1524–8
Agricultural trade of US, by detailed commodity and country, 1991, semiannual rpt, 1522–4
AID economic aid to developing countries, obligations and disbursements by country, quarterly rpt, 9912–4
AID loans repayment status and terms by program and country, and status of predecessor agency loans, quarterly rpt, 9912–3
Economic and military aid and loans from US and intl agencies, by program and country, FY46-91, annual rpt, 9914–5
Economic and social conditions of developing countries from 1960s, and Intl Dev Cooperation Agency and AID activities and funding, FY91-93, annual rpt, 9904–4
Economic and social conditions, resources, and trade, and aid, 1992, annual factbook, 9914–14
Economic, social, political, and geographic summary data, by country, 1992, annual factbook, 9114–2
Exports and imports of US, by transport mode, country, and SITC 1- to 3-digit commodity, 1991, annual rpt, 2424–12
Exports of US, detailed Schedule B commodities with countries of destination, 1991, annual rpt, 2424–10
Human rights conditions in 170 countries, and US economic and military aid, 1991, annual rpt, 21384–3
Labor conditions, union coverage, and work accidents, 1992 annual country rpt, 6366–4.39
Military aid of US, arms sales, and training programs costs and budget requests, by program, world region, and country, FY91-93, annual rpt, 7144–13
Military spending, arms trade, and force strengths, with govt spending and population, by country, 1979-89, annual rpt, 9824–1
Population size, growth rates, and components of change, by country, projected 1990-2020 and trends from 1950, biennial rpt, 2324–9
Refugee migration, and intl aid programs, by world area and country of origin and asylum, 1991, annual rpt, 7004–15
UN voting record and share of votes in agreement with US, by issue, country, and world area, 1991, annual rpt, 7004–18

Gyourko, Joseph
"Leasing as a Lottery: Implications for Rational Building Surges and Increasing Vacancies", 9387–8.273

Ha, Jiming
"Strategic Capital Taxation in Large, Open Economies with Mobile Capital", 9381–10.130

Habeas corpus
Court civil and criminal caseloads for Federal district, appeals, and special courts, 1991, annual rpt, 18204–8
Deportation and exclusion cases, writs of habeas corpus, judicial review, and declaratory judgments, FY84-91, annual rpt, 6264–2.5
Executions by whether habeas corpus used to appeal conviction, and time from crime to execution, with data by race and State, 1977-91, 6008–34
Prisoners petitions filed in Federal courts of appeals and district courts, by type of petition, circuit, and district, 1991, annual rpt, 18204–11
US attorneys case processing and collections, by case type and Federal district, FY91, annual rpt, 6004–2

Hackett, Ronald L.
"Pulpwood Production in the Lake States, 1990", 1208–397
"Pulpwood Production in the North-Central Region, 1990", 1204–19
"Residential Fuelwood Production and Sources from Roundwood in Minnesota, 1988", 1208–398
"Residential Fuelwood Production and Sources from Roundwood in Missouri, 1987", 1208–399

Hacklander, Duane
"Farm Equity by State, Ranked Three Ways", 1541–1.303

Hagemeyer, D.
"Occupational Radiation Exposure at Commercial Nuclear Power Reactors and Other Facilities, 1989", 9634–3

Hahn, Jerold T.
"Timber Resource of Missouri, Statistical Report, 1989", 1208–76

Haiti
Agricultural trade of US, by detailed commodity and country, 1991, annual rpt, 1524–8
Agricultural trade of US, by detailed commodity and country, 1991, semiannual rpt, 1522–4
AID economic aid to developing countries, obligations and disbursements by country, quarterly rpt, 9912–4
AID loans repayment status and terms by program and country, and status of predecessor agency loans, quarterly rpt, 9912–3
Aliens (illegal) enforcement activity of Coast Guard, by nationality, 1st half FY92, semiannual rpt, 7402–4
Aliens (illegal) held in Immigration and Naturalization Service detention facilities pending hearings, and legal aid requests, 1980s-91, GAO rpt, 26119–409
Economic and military aid and loans from US and intl agencies, by program and country, FY46-91, annual rpt, 9914–5
Economic and social conditions of developing countries from 1960s, and Intl Dev Cooperation Agency and AID activities and funding, FY91-93, annual rpt, 9904–4
Economic and social conditions, resources, and trade, and aid, 1992, annual factbook, 9914–14
Economic conditions in Haiti, 1985-91, working paper, 9916–13.3
Economic conditions, policy, and trade practices, by country, 1989-91, annual rpt, 21384–5
Economic, social, political, and geographic summary data, by country, 1992, annual factbook, 9114–2
Exports and imports of US, by commodity and country, 1980-90, world area rpt, 9116–1.4
Exports and imports of US, by transport mode, country, and SITC 1- to 3-digit commodity, 1991, annual rpt, 2424–12
Exports, imports, and balances of US for manufactured goods, by SITC 2-digit commodity and country, quarterly rpt, 2042–35
Exports of US, detailed Schedule B commodities with countries of destination, 1991, annual rpt, 2424–10
Food supply, needs, and aid for developing countries, status and alternative forecasts, 1992 world area rpt, 1526–8.2
Human rights conditions in 170 countries, and US economic and military aid, 1991, annual rpt, 21384–3
Military aid of US, arms sales, and training programs costs and budget requests, by program, world region, and country, FY91-93, annual rpt, 7144–13
Military spending, arms trade, and force strengths, with govt spending and population, by country, 1979-89, annual rpt, 9824–1
Population size, growth rates, and components of change, by country, projected 1990-2020 and trends from 1950, biennial rpt, 2324–9
Refugee migration, and intl aid programs, by world area and country of origin and asylum, 1991, annual rpt, 7004–15
UN voting record and share of votes in agreement with US, by issue, country, and world area, 1991, annual rpt, 7004–18

Hajjar, Moufid
"Non-Acquired Immune Deficiency Syndrome-Defining Malignancies in a Hospital-Based Cohort of Human Immunodeficiency Virus-Infected Patients: Bordeaux, France, 1985-91", 4472–1.351

Hakken, Jon
"Effects of Adopting a Value-Added Tax", 26306–6.168

Hakkio, Craig S.
"Comment on William Poole's Paper 'Exchange Rate Management and Monetary Policy Mismanagement: A Study of Germany, Japan, UK, and U.S. After Plaza' ", 9381–10.124
"International Role of the Dollar", 9381–10.129

Haldorson, Lewis
"Maturity and Fecundity in the Rockfishes, *Sebastes* spp., a Review", 2162–1.302

Hales, Thomas
"Health Hazard Evaluation Report: U.S. West Communications, Phoenix, Ariz.; Minneapolis, Minn.; Denver, Colo.", 4248–93

Halfway houses
see Community-based correctional programs
see Group homes for the handicapped
see Sheltered workshops

Hall, Jolene
"Hospital Closures: 1985-88", 17206–2.27

Hall, Troy E.
"Trends in Campsite Condition: Eagle Cap Wilderness, Bob Marshall Wilderness, and Grand Canyon National Park", 1208–395

Hallman, Jeffrey J.
"Commodity Prices and P-Star", 9377–1.303

Hamak, John E.
"Analyses of Natural Gases, 1986-90", 5608–132
"Analyses of Natural Gases, 1991", 5604–2

Hambleton, Ronald K.
"Levels of Mathematics Achievement: Initial Performance Standards for the 1990 NAEP Mathematics Assessment. Volume III, Technical Report", 4896–8.6

Hambor, John C.
"Issues in Eastern European Social Security Reform", 8006–6.7

Hamilton, Douglas R.
"Economic Implications of Rising Health Care Costs", 26306–6.174

Hamilton, Ohio
CPI by component for US city average, and by selected metro area, region, and population size, monthly rpt, 6762–2
Housing and households characteristics, and unit and neighborhood quality, by MSA location for 11 MSAs, 1986 survey, supplement, 2485–8
see also under By City and By SMSA or MSA in the "Index by Categories"

Hamm, Shannon R.
"Mushroom Supply and Utilization in the U.S.", 1561–11.303

Hammerslough, Charles R.
"Estimating the Probability of Spontaneous Abortion in the Presence of Induced Abortion and Vice Versa", 4042–3.324

Hammett, Marcella
"Homicide Surveillance—U.S., 1979-88", 4202–7.315

Hammett, Theodore M.
"1990 Update: AIDS in Correctional Facilities", 6064–22

Hammond, Ind.
Wages by occupation, and benefits, for office and plant workers, 1992 survey, periodic MSA rpt, 6785–17.1

Hammonds, Tim
"State of the Supermarket Industry", 1504–9.1

Handelsman, Harry
"Intermittent Positive Pressure Breathing (IPPB) Therapy. Health Technology Assessment Report, 1991", 4186–10.6

Handicapped
see Aid to blind
see Aid to disabled and handicapped persons
see Architectural barriers to the handicapped
see Blind
see Deaf
see Disabled and handicapped persons
see Discrimination against the handicapped
see Group homes for the handicapped
see Handicapped children
see Learning disabilities
see Mental retardation
see Mobility limitations
see Rehabilitation of the disabled
see Supplemental Security Income

Handicapped children
Cases, insurance coverage, and health care services use, for handicapped children with special needs, by selected characteristics, 1988, 4146–8.216
Child and maternal health condition and services use, indicators by age, race, and poverty status, 1988, 4478–197
Child day care and early childhood education programs availability, demand, use, costs, and provider and enrollee characteristics, 1990 survey, 4808–39
Education data compilation, 1992 annual rpt, 4824–2
Family outlays for formal and informal care of handicapped children, and time spent, relation to diagnosis and other characteristics, 1988, article, 4042–3.329
Food aid program of USDA for women, infants, and children, prenatal participation effects on birthweight and health and social welfare costs, 1960s-90, GAO rpt, 26121–458
Functional disability prevalence and severity, by type of activity needing assistance, age, and sex, 1979-80, 4946–1.1
Head Start handicapped enrollment, by handicap, State, and for Indian and migrant programs, 1988/89, annual rpt, 4584–4
HHS financial aid, by program, recipient, State, and city, FY91, annual regional listings, 4004–3
Infants born with severe disabilities, protective and parental services programs grants by State, FY91, annual listing, 4584–6
Mental health care facilities, staff, and patient characteristics, *Statistical Notes* series, 4506–3
Mental health care facilities, staff, patients, and finances, 1970s-91, biennial rpt, 4094–1
OASDI benefits and beneficiaries, by category, age, and sex, quarterly rpt, 4742–1.1
see also Birth defects
see also Learning disabilities
see also Old-Age, Survivors, Disability, and Health Insurance
see also Special education
see also Supplemental Security Income

Handy, Charles R.
"Implications of a Single EC Market for the U.S. Food Manufacturing Sector", 1528–325

Hanemann, Patrick
"U.S. Produce Industry and the North American Free Trade Agreement", 1504–9.1

Hanford Engineering Development Laboratory
see also Department of Energy National Laboratories

Hanford Environmental Dose Reconstruction Project
Radiation exposure of population near Hanford, Wash, nuclear plant, with methodology, 1944-91, series, 3356–5

Hanford Site, Wash.
Radiation and other pollutant releases from DOE contractor research lab and nuclear weapons facilities, monitoring results, 1991 annual site rpt, 3324–2.8
Radiation exposure of population near Hanford, Wash, nuclear plant, with methodology, 1944-91, series, 3356–5

Hankey, Ron
"Performance Optimization and Repowering of Generating Units", 3162–35.303

Hannah, A. C.
"World View on Sugar Trade and Prices", 1504–9.1; 1561–14.301

Hansen, Gary D.
"Labor Market in Real Business Cycle Theory", 9383–6.302

Hansen, LeRoy
"Farmer Response to Changes in Climate: The Case of Corn Production", 1502–3.302
"Intellectual Property Rights and the Private Seed Industry", 1548–388

Hansen, Mark H.
"Timber Resource of Missouri's Riverborder, 1989", 1206–3.8

Hanson, Donald A.
"1990 Clean Air Act: A Tougher Regulatory Challenge Facing Midwest Industry", 9375–1.304

Hanson, Gregory D.
"Loan Payment Problems of Farmers in the Mid-1980's", 1548–383

Hanzlick, Dennis
"Integration of Circulation Data in the Beaufort Sea", 2176–1.40

Harbaugh, Christina W.
"Rural Labor Force Trends in China", 1524–4.2

Harbors and ports
Army Corps of Engineers activities and projects, FY88 and trends from 1800s, annual rpt, 3754–1.1
Army Corps of Engineers activities and projects, FY89 and trends from 1800s, annual rpt, 3754–1.2
Army Corps of Engineers activities and projects, FY90 and trends from 1800s, annual rpt, 3754–1.3
Army Corps of Engineers water resources dev projects, characteristics, and costs, 1950s-89, biennial State rpt series, 3756–1
Army Corps of Engineers water resources dev projects, characteristics, and costs, 1950s-91, biennial State rpt series, 3756–2

Bridges over navigable waters, with type of bridge and use, owner, dimensions, and location, 1991 regional listing series, 7406–5
Capital expenditures for facility improvement, and financing methods, by region and selected port, 1946-89, 7708–6
Classification codes for countries and ports under Tariff Schedule of US, 1992 base edition supplement, 9886–13
Coal and coke production, shipments, and trade, by State of origin and destination, end-use sector, and mode of transport, quarterly rpt, 3162–37.1
Coal production, stocks, and shipments, by State of origin and destination, end-use sector, and mode of transport, quarterly rpt, 3162–8
Coastal areas environmental conditions and mgmt, for individual areas, conf series, 2146–8
Environmental mgmt of coastal areas, State activities and Federal funding, FY90-91, biennial rpt, 2174–8
Export statistics classification codes of Census Bur for countries, commodities, and customs districts, 1990 base edition and supplements, 2428–5
Exports and imports (waterborne) of US, by type of service, customs district, port, and world area, monthly rpt, 2422–7
Exports of US, detailed commodities by country, monthly CD-ROM, 2422–13
Fed Govt Harbor Maintenance Trust Fund financial condition, monthly rpt, 8102–9.12
Fish catch, by species, use, region, State, and major port, 1980s-91, annual rpt, 2164–1.1
Foreign countries economic, social, political, and geographic summary data, by country, 1992, annual factbook, 9114–2
Freight (shipborne domestic), by major commodity group, vessel type, and port, 1987-89, annual rpt, 7704–7
Freight (waterborne domestic and foreign) by commodity, traffic, and passengers, by port and waterway, 1989, annual rpt, 3754–3
Freight (waterborne domestic and foreign), by port, 1990, annual rpt, 3754–7
Govt employment and payroll, by function, level of govt, and jurisdiction, annual rpt series, 2466–1
Imports of US, detailed commodities by country, monthly CD-ROM, 2422–14
Middle Atlantic States tide height and tidal current velocity daily at selected coastal stations, forecast 1993, annual rpt, 2174–11
Military and personal property shipments, passenger traffic, and costs, by service branch and mode of transport, FY91, annual rpt, 3704–15
Minerals offshore lease sales environmental and economic impacts in coastal areas, final statement series, 5736–7
Navy nuclear-powered vessels and support facilities radioactive waste, releases in harbors, and public exposure, 1970s-91, annual rpt, 3804–11
Ohio River basin waterway facilities, freight by commodity and port, and recreation, by waterway, 1988-89, annual rpt, 3754–6
St Lawrence Seaway ship, cargo, and passenger traffic, and toll revenue, 1991 and trends from 1959, annual rpt, 7744–2
Tidal currents, daily time and velocity by station for North America and Asia coasts, forecast 1993, annual rpts, 2174–1
Tide height and time daily at coastal points worldwide, forecast 1993, annual rpt series, 2174–2
Water quality, chemistry, hydrology, and other characteristics, local area studies, series, 5666–27
Workers compensation programs under Federal admin, finances and operations, FY91, annual rpt, 6504–10
see also Dredging

Harden, Stephen D.
"Physician Customary Charges and Medicare Payment Experience: Study Findings", 4652–1.307

Hardouvelis, Gikas A.
"Intertemporal Asset Pricing Models and the Cross Section of Expected Stock Returns", 9385–8.146
"Margin Requirements, Price Fluctuations, and Market Participation in Metal and Stock Index Futures", 9385–8.127
"Relative Cost of Capital for Marginal Firms over the Business Cycle", 9385–1.312
"Term Structure Spread and Future Changes in Long and Short Rates: Is There a Puzzle?", 9385–8.136

Hardware
Business statistics, detailed data for major industries and economic indicators, 1960-91, *Survey of Current Business* biennial supplement, 2704–1
County Business Patterns, 1989: employment, establishments, and payroll, by SIC 2- to 4-digit industry and county, annual State rpt series, 2326–8
County Business Patterns, 1990: employment, establishments, and payroll, by SIC 2- to 4-digit industry and county, annual State rpt series, 2326–6
CPI by component for US city average, and by selected metro area, region, and population size, monthly rpt, 6762–2
Employment, earnings, and hours, by SIC 1- to 4-digit industry, monthly 1989-Feb 1992, annual rpt, 6744–4
Exports and imports between US and outlying areas, by detailed commodity and mode of transport, 1991, annual rpt, 2424–11
Exports and imports of US, by country and detailed commodity, monthly rpt, 2422–12
Exports and imports of US, by Harmonized System 6-digit commodity and country, 1991, annual rpt, 2424–13
Exports and imports of US, by transport mode, country, and SITC 1- to 3-digit commodity, 1991, annual rpt, 2424–12
Exports of US, detailed Schedule B commodities with countries of destination, 1991, annual rpt, 2424–10
Injuries from use of consumer products and related activities, by severity and victim age and sex, 1990, annual rpt, 9164–7
Injuries from use of consumer products, by severity, victim age, and detailed product, 1991, annual rpt, 9164–6
Input-output structure of US economy, detailed interindustry transactions for 541 industries, and components of final demand, 1982 benchmark data, 2708–17
Lockwashers (helical spring) from PRC and Taiwan at less than fair value, injury to US industry, investigation with background financial and operating data, 1992 rpt, 9886–14.362
Manufacturing annual survey, 1990: finances and operations, by SIC 2- to 4-digit industry, series, 2506–14
Manufacturing census, 1987: concentration of largest firms measured by value added, and for shipments by SIC 2- and 4-digit industry, subject rpt, 2497–6
Manufacturing census, 1987: shipments of manufacturers products, by customer class and SIC 2- and 4-digit industry, subject rpt, 2497–4
Manufacturing finances and operations, by SIC 2- to 4-digit industry, forecast 1992, annual rpt, 2044–28
Military prime contract awards, by detailed procurement category, FY88-91, annual rpt, 3544–18
Nuts and bolts industry productivity trends and technological devs, 1958-90, article, 6722–1.343
Occupational injury and illness rates, by SIC 2- to 4-digit industry, 1989-90, annual rpt, 6844–7
Occupational injury and illness rates, by SIC 2- to 4-digit industry, 1990, annual rpt, 6844–1
Price indexes (producer), by stage of processing and detailed commodity, monthly rpt, 6762–6
Price indexes (producer), by stage of processing and detailed commodity, monthly 1991, annual rpt, 6764–2
Retail trade sales and inventories, by kind of business, region, and selected State, MSA, and city, monthly rpt, 2413–3
Retail trade sales, by kind of business, advance monthly rpt, 2413–2
Retail trade sales, inventories, purchases, gross margin, and accounts receivable, by SIC 2- to 4-digit kind of business and form of ownership, 1990, annual rpt, 2413–5
Science, engineering, and technical employment in manufacturing, by field and industry, 1989, triennial rpt, 9627–23
Shipments and PPI for building materials, by type, quarterly rpt, 2042–1.5; 2042–1.6
Tax (income) returns of corporations, income and tax items by asset size and detailed industry, 1989, annual rpt, 8304–4
Wholesale trade sales and inventories, by SIC 2- to 3-digit kind of business, monthly rpt, 2413–7
see also Lawn and garden equipment
see also Tools

Hardy, Ann M.
"AIDS Knowledge and Attitudes. Provisional Data from the National Health Interview Survey", 4146–8.218
"Incidence and Impact of Selected Infectious Diseases in Childhood", 4147–10.181

Harkey, D. L.
"Operational Impacts of Wider Trucks on Narrow Roadways", 7558–113

Harkey, David L.
"Non-Permanent Pavement Markings in Work Zones", 7558–116

Harksen, C. J.
"Water Resources Activities of the USGS in Montana, Oct. 1989-Sept. 1991", 5666–26.21

Harlow, Caroline W.
"Drug Enforcement and Treatment in Prisons, 1990", 6066–19.70

Harper, Dennis C.
"Improving Health Care Communication for Persons with Mental Retardation", 4042–3.328

Harper, Robert G., III
"Comparisons of Independent Statistics on Petroleum Supply", 3162–6.302

Harris County, Tex.
Housing and households characteristics, and unit and neighborhood quality, by MSA location for 11 MSAs, 1987 survey, supplement, 2485–8

Harris, Ethan S.
"Supply-Side Consequences of U.S. Fiscal Policy in the 1980s", 9385–1.304; 9385–8.125

Harris, J. Michael
"Processed Apple Sales, 1986-90: The Effects of Market Factors", 1548–392

Harris, Joan S.
"Source of Payment for the Medical Cost of Motor Vehicle Injuries in the U.S.", 7768–122

Harris, Randall E.
"Breast Cancer Risk: Effects of Estrogen Replacement Therapy and Body Mass", 4472–1.350

Harrisburg, Pa.
Wages by occupation, and benefits for office and plant workers, 1992 survey, periodic MSA rpt, 6785–3.4
see also under By City and By SMSA or MSA in the "Index by Categories"

Harry S. Truman Scholarship Foundation
see Truman, Harry S., Scholarship Foundation

Hart, Tracy
"Intra-Industry Trade Indexes for Canada, Mexico, and the U.S., 1962-87", 1528–327

Hartford, Conn.
Housing and households characteristics, and unit and neighborhood quality, by MSA location for 11 MSAs, 1987 survey, supplement, 2485–8
see also under By City and By SMSA or MSA in the "Index by Categories"

Hartgers, C.
"Needle Sharing and Participation in the Amsterdam Syringe Exchange Program Among HIV-Seronegative Injecting Drug Users", 4042–3.369

Harthun, Laura A.
"Profiles in Safety and Health: The Soft Drink Industry", 6722–1.319; 6728–41

Harvey, David J.
"Farm-Raised Shrimp: Impacts on U.S. Seafood Trade", 1561–15.301
"Outlook for U.S. Aquaculture", 1504–9.1

Harvey, James
"Commercial Bank Performance, 1991", 9381–14
"Thrift Industry Performance, 1991", 9381–14

Harwarth, Irene B.
"Historical Trends: State Education Facts, 1969-89", 4828–33

Harwell, Debra
"Index of Bank Control Share Prices", 9381–14

Hasan, Iftekhar
"Note on Competition, Fixed Costs, and the Profitability of Depository Intermediaries", 9371–10.88

Hatchl, Barbara L.
"Maps and More: Your Guide to Census Bureau Geography", 2308–67

Hatfield, Brian B.
"Summary Report of Observations of Coastal Gill and Trammel Net Fisheries in Central California—Oct. 1, 1984-Mar. 31, 1985", 14738–13

Haubrich, Joseph G.
"Financial Efficiency and Aggregate Fluctuations: An Exploration", 9377–1.302
"Risk Aversion, Performance Pay, and the Principal-Agent Problem", 9377–9.127
"Sources and Nature of Long-Term Memory in the Business Cycle", 9377–9.125

Haupt, Barbara J.
"Estimates from Two Survey Designs: National Hospital Discharge Survey. Vital and Health Statistics Series 13", 4147–13.110

Haverhill, Mass.
Wages by occupation, and benefits, for office and plant workers, 1991 survey, periodic MSA rpt, 6785–16.3

Hawaii
Banks (insured commercial and savings) deposits by instn, State, MSA, and county, as of June 1991, annual regional rpt, 9295–3.6
Cancer (liver) patients with tumor suppression gene p53 mutations, by hepatitis B virus seropositivity, for US, Hawaii, and PRC, 1992 article, 4472–1.353
Coffee production for Puerto Rico and Hawaii, 1950s-91, FAS periodic circular, 1925–5
Deaths and rates, by detailed location, cause, and demographic characteristics, 1989, US Vital Statistics annual rpt, 4144–3.1
Employment, earnings, and hours, by selected SIC 1- to 4-digit industry, State, and for 275 MSAs, 1987-92, 6748–81
Fed Govt spending in States and local areas, by type, State, county, and city, FY91, annual rpt, 2464–3
Fed Govt spending in States, by type, program, agency, and State, FY91, annual rpt, 2464–2
Freight (waterborne domestic and foreign) by commodity, traffic, and passengers, by port and waterway, 1989, annual rpt, 3754–3.4
Geothermal resources, power plant generation, capacity, and dev potential, by location, 1988-90 and projected to 2030, 3168–122
Ginger acreage and production in Hawaii, 1977-91, FAS annual circular, 1925–15.1
HHS financial aid, by program, recipient, State, and city, FY91, annual regional listing, 4004–3.9
Hospital deaths of Medicare patients, actual and expected rates by diagnosis, and hospital characteristics, by instn, FY90 annual State rpt, 4654–14.12
Housing census, 1990: summary unit characteristics, by householder race and age, county, place, and urban-rural location, State rpt, 2471–1.13
Libraries (public) services for Indians and Hawaii Natives, project listing and funding by tribe and State, FY90, annual rpt, 4874–5
Military and DOD civilian personnel and dependents, by service branch and US and foreign location, quarterly rpt, 3542–20
Military prime contract awards, by contractor, service branch, State, and city, FY91, annual rpt, 3544–22
Mineral Industry Surveys, State reviews of production, 1991, preliminary annual rpt, 5614–6
Minerals offshore lease sales environmental and economic impacts in coastal areas, 1990 final statement, 5736–7.1
Multinatl firms US affiliates finances and operations, by industry, country of parent firm, and State, 1987, 2708–48
Native Hawaiian students enrolled in special education, by handicapping condition, and compared to other groups, 1986/87, annual rpt, 4944–4
Physicians, by specialty, age, sex, and location of training and practice, 1990, State rpt, 4116–6.12
Pollution (air) contributing to global warming, emissions by monitoring site and country, and temperature change by world area and US region, 1860s-1990, annual rpt, 3004–33
Population and housing census, 1990: detailed geographic coverage, State CD-ROM, 2551–9.9
Population and housing census, 1990: population and housing characteristics, detailed geographic coverage, State CD-ROM, 2551–10.2
Population and housing census, 1990: summary characteristics, by county, subdiv, and place, State rpt, 2551–7.13
Population census, 1990: population characteristics and living arrangements, by county, place, and urban-rural location, State rpt, 2531–1.13
Prenatal care adequacy relation to mothers ethnic group and other characteristics, for Hawaii, 1992 article, 4042–3.366
Shipborne commerce (domestic) of US, freight by major commodity group, vessel type, and port, 1987-89, annual rpt, 7704–7
Statistical Abstract of US, 1992 annual data compilation, 2324–1
Telecommunications domestic and intl rates, by type of service and area served, 1990, annual rpt, 9284–6.6
Tide height and time daily at coastal points, forecast 1993, annual rpt, 2174–2.2
Water supply and quality in streams and lakes, and groundwater levels in wells, by drainage basin, 1990, annual State rpt, 5666–10.10

Whales (humpback) habitat impacts of human activities in Hawaii, with data on shipping, whale watching, coastal construction, and aircraft, 1980s-90, 14738–14
see also Honolulu, Hawaii
see also under By State in the "Index by Categories"

Hawaiian Telephone Co.
Finances, rates, and traffic for US telecommunications carriers intl operations, by service type, firm, and country, 1975-90, annual rpt, 9284–17

Hay
see Animal feed
see Pasture and rangeland

Hay, Lauren E.
"Water-Quality Trends in New Jersey Streams", 5666–27.27

Haynes, Richard W.
"Monthly Stumpage Prices for the Pacific Northwest", 1208–387
"Price Projections for Selected Grades of Douglas-Fir, Coast Hem-Fir, Inland Hem-Fir, and Ponderosa Pine Lumber", 1208–424

Hazardous substances
Criminal cases by type and disposition, and collections, for US attorneys, by Federal district, FY91, annual rpt, 6004–2.1
Criminal sentences for Federal offenses, guidelines by offense and circumstances, series, 17668–1
Disasters and natl security incidents and mgmt, with data by major event and State, 1992 annual rpt, 9434–6
EPA R&D programs and funding, planned FY92, annual listing, 9184–17
Fed Govt spending in States, by type, program, agency, and State, FY91, annual rpt, 2464–2
Health effects of selected pollutants, concentrations in food and environment, sources, human intake, and regulation, series, 9186–8
Health effects of selected pollutants on animals by species and on humans, and environmental levels, series, 5506–14
HHS financial aid, by program, recipient, State, and city, FY91, annual regional listings, 4004–3
Industrial hazardous substances releases and reduction methods under EPA regulation, by chemical, source, industry, and location, 1989, annual rpt, 9234–6
Industrial hazardous substances releases and reduction methods under EPA regulation, with chemical stocks and use, facility directory, 1987-89, annual CD-ROM, 9234–7
Industrial hazardous substances releases and reduction methods under EPA regulation, with chemical stocks and use, facility directory, 1991 CD-ROM user guide, 9238–70
Injuries from use of consumer products and related activities, by severity and victim age and sex, 1990, annual rpt, 9164–7
Marine mammals tissue pollutant concentrations, by species and pollutant type, for Alaska, 1987-91, 2218–87
Military bases underground storage tanks for hazardous substances, DOD compliance with EPA regulations, 1988-91, GAO rpt, 26123–395
Nicotine, tar, and carbon monoxide content of cigarettes, by brand, 1990, 9408–53
Occupational exposure to hazardous substances, employer compliance with info and training regulations, employer views by firm size and industry div, 1989-91, GAO rpt, 26121–456
Occupational exposure to hazardous substances, employer compliance with info and training regulations, inspections, and fines, by firm size and industry div, 1989-91, GAO rpt, 26121–439
Occupational illness rates, by cause and SIC 2- to 3-digit industry, 1990, annual rpt, 6844–1
Research and testing activities under Natl Toxicology Program, FY90 and planned FY91, annual rpt, 4044–16
Tax (excise) collections of IRS, by source, quarterly rpt, 8302–1
see also Air pollution
see also Asbestos contamination
see also Carcinogens
see also Dioxins
see also Hazardous substances transport
see also Hazardous waste and disposal
see also Inflammable materials
see also Lead poisoning and pollution
see also Marine pollution
see also Mercury pollution
see also Motor vehicle exhaust
see also Pesticides
see also Poisoning and drug reaction
see also Product safety
see also Radiation
see also Radioactive materials
see also Radioactive waste and disposal
see also Radon
see also Soil pollution
see also Trace metals
see also Water pollution

Hazardous substances transport
Accidents, and mgmt of disasters and natl security threats, with data by major event and State, 1992 annual rpt, 9434–6
Accidents, casualties, and damage involving hazardous substances, by mode of transport, with DOT control activities, 1990, annual rpt, 7304–4
Airport security inspections of hazardous cargo, compliance and enforcement actions, 1990, annual rpt, 7504–49
Bonneville Power Admin hazardous waste mgmt and environmental protection standards compliance activities, 1991, annual rpt, 3224–6
DOT activities by subagency, budget, and summary accident data, FY89, annual rpt, 7304–1
Industrial hazardous substances releases and reduction methods under EPA regulation, by chemical, source, industry, and location, 1989, annual rpt, 9234–6
Industrial hazardous substances releases and reduction methods under EPA regulation, with chemical stocks and use, facility directory, 1987-89, annual CD-ROM, 9234–7
Radioactive low-level waste disposal activities of States and interstate compacts, with data by disposal facility and reactor, 1990, annual rpt, 3004–36
Radioactive low-level waste from DOE military activities, disposal methods and costs, 1991, 3006–5.30
Radioactive materials shipments on US hwys, by material type, carrier, and shipper, 1985-90, 3008–129
Radioactive waste repository research, transport, and disposal costs under alternative systems, 1983-89 and projected to 2094, 3368–5
Railroad accidents, casualties, and damage, Fed Railroad Admin activities, and safety inspectors by State, 1990, annual rpt, 7604–12
Railroad accidents, casualties, circumstances, and railroad involved, 1988, annual rpt, 9614–8
Railroad accidents involving hazardous materials, casualties, and circumstances, 1984-89, 9618–18
Railroad accidents involving hazardous materials, damage, and persons evacuated, by cause, railroad, and State, 1991, annual rpt, 7604–1
Railroad accidents involving hazardous materials, damage, and persons evacuated, by incident, 1988, annual rpt, 7604–3
Railroad freight, by commodity and region of origin and destination, 1989, annual rpt, 7604–6
Railroad safety violation claims settled, by carrier, FY91, annual rpt, 7604–10
Traffic fatal accidents, deaths, and rates, by circumstances, characteristics of persons and vehicles involved, and location, 1990, annual rpt, 7764–10
Truck accidents, casualties, and damage, by circumstances and characteristics of persons and vehicles involved, 1989, annual rpt, 7554–9
Waterborne commerce (domestic and foreign) of US, freight by commodity, traffic, and passengers, by port and waterway, 1989, annual rpt, 3754–3

Hazardous waste and disposal
Bonneville Power Admin hazardous waste mgmt and environmental protection standards compliance activities, 1991, annual rpt, 3224–6
Budget of US, obligations and authority by function, agency, and program, with summaries and analyses, FY93, annual rpt, 104–2
Environmental Quality, status of problems, protection programs, research, and intl issues, 1991 annual rpt, 484–1
EPA and State govt enforcement of environmental laws, activities, FY91, annual rpt, 9184–21
EPA pollution control grant program activities, monthly rpt, 9182–8
Fed Govt financial and nonfinancial domestic aid, 1992 base edition, annual listing, 104–5
HHS financial aid, by program, recipient, State, and city, FY91, annual regional listings, 4004–3
Industrial hazardous substances releases and reduction methods under EPA regulation, by chemical, source, industry, and location, 1989, annual rpt, 9234–6
Industrial hazardous substances releases and reduction methods under EPA regulation, with chemical stocks and use, facility directory, 1987-89, annual CD-ROM, 9234–7
Industrial hazardous substances releases and reduction methods under EPA regulation,

with chemical stocks and use, facility directory, 1991 CD-ROM user guide, 9238–70
Industrial pollutant concentrations and costs by process and waste prevention or treatment method, biennial conf, suspended, 9184–22
Industrial reduction of hazardous waste generation, accuracy of voluntary programs rpts to EPA, 1992 GAO rpt, 26131–98
Justice Dept enforcement of environmental laws, activities, FY83-92, annual press release, 6004–22
Manufacturing pollution abatement capital and operating costs, by SIC 2- to 4-digit industry and State, 1990, annual Current Industrial Rpt, 2506–3.6
Military installations hazardous waste site remedial action, activities and funding by site and State, FY91, annual rpt, 3544–36
Minerals offshore lease sales environmental and economic impacts in coastal areas, final statement series, 5736–7
Oil resources recovery impacts of environmental regulation, under alternative oil price, technology, and regulatory assumptions, projected 1990-2015, 3338–2
R&D facilities of higher education instns, space and equipment adequacy, needs, and funding by source, by instn type and control, 1992, biennial rpt, 9624–25
R&D programs and funding of EPA, planned FY92, annual listing, 9184–17
Statistical Abstract of US, 1992 annual data compilation, 2324–1.6
Superfund financial condition, monthly rpt, 8102–9.6
Superfund hazardous waste site remedial action, current and proposed sites descriptions and status, periodic listings, series, 9216–3
Superfund hazardous waste site remedial action, current and proposed sites priority ranking and status by location, series, 9216–5
Superfund hazardous waste site remedial action, EPA records of decision by site, FY90, annual rpt, 9214–5
Superfund R&D projects and funding, FY91, annual listing, 9184–18
Tax (excise) on hazardous waste generation and disposal, rates, and firms filing returns, by substance type, 1989, annual article, 8302–2.303
Treatment of hazardous waste by process, and waste generated, by State, 1987-89 and projected to 2009, hearing, 21408–132
see also Radioactive waste and disposal

Hazelnuts
see Nuts

Head Start Project
Child day care and early childhood education programs availability, demand, use, costs, and provider and enrollee characteristics, 1990 survey, 4808–39
Drug abuse by mothers, treatment and other services use, referrals, needs, and barriers, for 13 NIDA-funded programs, 1990/91 survey, 4498–76
Enrollment, funding, and staff for Head Start, FY91, annual rpt, 4584–5
Handicapped children enrollment in Head Start, by handicap, State, and for Indian and migrant programs, 1988/89, annual rpt, 4584–4
HHS financial aid, by program, recipient, State, and city, FY91, annual regional listings, 4004–3
Ohio poverty, hunger, and public welfare program operations and indicators of need, by county, 1991 hearing, 21968–58
Poor families self-sufficiency aid and Head Start programs, HUD and HHS joint funding by recipient, 1991, press release, 5006–3.83

Health care costs
see Medical costs

Health Care Financing Administration
Assistance (financial) of HHS, by program, recipient, State, and city, FY91, annual regional listings, 4004–3
Budget of US, obligations and authority by function, agency, and program, with summaries and analyses, FY93, annual rpt, 104–2
Health Care Financing Review, quarterly journal, 4652–1
Hospital deaths of Medicare patients, actual and expected rates by diagnosis, with hospital characteristics, by instn, FY90, annual State rpt series, 4654–14
Kidney end-stage disease treatment facilities approved by Medicare, dialysis and transplant services and ownership, 1991 annual listing, 4654–17
Kidney end-stage disease treatment facilities, Medicare enrollment and reimbursement, survival, and patient characteristics, 1984-90, annual rpt, 4654–16
Medicaid coverage, eligibility, and payment provisions of States, as of March 1992, annual rpt, 4654–19
Medicare admin and research, and HCFA affirmative action and accreditation programs, FY87, annual rpt, 4654–5
Medicare and Medicaid beneficiaries and program operations, 1992, annual fact book, 4654–18
Medicare Hospital Insurance trust fund finances, mid 1960s-91 and alternative projections to 2066, annual rpt, 4654–11
Medicare Supplementary Medical Insurance trust fund finances, mid 1960s-91 and projected to 2065, annual rpt, 4654–12
Nursing home compliance with Medicare and Medicaid regulations, and patient characteristics, by facility, suspended annual State rpt series, 4654–15
OASDHI trust funds finances, FY91 and projected to 2066, annual rpt, 4654–8
Research activities and grants of HCFA, by program, FY91, annual listing, 4654–10

Health care reform
Advisory Commission on Social Security findings and recommendations on OASDHI and health care system status and reform, series, 10176–3
Insurance (health) administrative and employer costs, coverage, public views, Canada and UK systems, and other reform issues, 1950s-91, hearings, 25368–180
Insurance (health) coverage and availability, and other health care system reform issues, 1991 hearing, 21788–216
Long term health care financing reform issues, 1991 rpt, 10176–3.7
OASDHI and health care system status and reform, Advisory Commission on Social Security findings and recommendations, 1991 quadrennial rpt, 10178–1
OASDI and Medicare trust fund finances, economic assumptions, outlook, and health care system reform issues, series, 10176–1
Public opinion on OASDHI and health care system operations and reform issues, 1991 surveys, 10176–2.2
Small business access to health insurance, States reform provisions with background data, 1991, GAO rpt, 26121–462
States health care system reform proposals, with background data, 1970s-80s, article, 9375–1.308
Universal coverage for health care, costs of alternative funding proposals, with background data, 1991 rpt, 26306–6.163

Health condition
Aviation medicine research and test results, technical rpt series, 7506–10
Czechoslovakia health care system, spending, and population health condition indicators, 1988-89, article, 4042–3.363
Data collection for health and vital statistics, and use for planning and evaluation, 1991 biennial conf, 4164–2
Data on health condition and care, indicators, 1988 natl survey, CD-ROM, 4147–10.184
Data on health condition and health care resources, use, and spending, 1950s-90, with health improvement and disease prevention goals for 1990, annual data compilation, 4144–11
Data on health condition and quality of life measures, rpts and other info sources, quarterly listing, 4122–1
Developing countries aged population and selected characteristics, 1980s and projected to 2020, country rpt series, 2326–19
Developing countries economic, population, and agricultural data, US and other aid sources, and AID activity, country rpt series, 9916–12
Diving (underwater) accidents, illnesses, and deaths, by circumstances, diver characteristics, and location, 1970-90, annual rpt, 2144–29
Educational attainment relation to health condition and care, indicators by selected characteristics, 1989, 4147–10.180
Foreign and US health data collection and availability, by country, 1991, biennial listing, 4124–8
Homeless families health condition and access to care, indicators, local area study, 1991 conf paper, 4164–2
Indian and Alaska Native youth health condition and behavioral patterns, by sex and grade, 1988-90, 4088–3
Indian Health Service and tribal facilities and use, and Indians health and other characteristics, by IHS region, 1980s-90, annual chartbook, 4084–7
Indian Health Service facilities, funding, operations, and Indian health and other characteristics, 1950s-91, annual chartbook, 4084–1

Insurance (health) denial by private carriers because of poor health, by selected characteristics, 1987, 4186–8.23
Medicare beneficiaries knowledge of and experience with physician billing and payment under Medicare, by selected characteristics, 1988-89, 17266–2.1
NYC black and Hispanic health condition and care indicators, 1980s, conf paper, 4164–2
OASDI beneficiary data collection system design compared to earlier surveys, with summary results, 1992 article, 4742–1.313
Older persons ability to pay out of pocket health care costs, indicators by selected characteristics, 1984, article, 4742–1.307
Older persons in poverty, by health, nutrition, assistance, and other characteristics, 1990, GAO rpt, 26131–100
Older persons socioeconomic characteristics, 1900s-90 and projected to 2050, biennial chartbook, 12904–1
Population economic well-being indicators, by selected characteristics and household income and income-to-poverty ratio, 1984, 2546–20.22
Public Health Reports, bimonthly journal, 4042–3
Retirees health and other characteristics related to Medicare use and charges 2 years later, 1984, article, 4652–1.319
Statistical Abstract of US, 1992 annual data compilation, 2324–1.3
Uranium tailings at inactive mills, remedial action proposals, costs, site characteristics, and environmental, socioeconomic, and health impacts, series, 3356–4
Vital and Health Statistics series: advance data rpts, 4146–8
Vital and Health Statistics series and other NCHS rpts, 1990-91, annual listing, 4124–1
Vital and Health Statistics series: health condition, medical costs, and use of facilities and services, 4147–10
Vital and Health Statistics series: reprints of advance data rpts, 4147–16
Vitamin supplement use correlation to health condition and behaviors, local area study, 1992 article, 4042–3.373
Youth health condition, risk factors, and preventive and treatment services use and availability, 1970s-80s, 26358–234
see also Absenteeism
see also Dental condition
see also Disabled and handicapped persons
see also Diseases and disorders
see also Handicapped children
see also Health risk behavior
see also Hospitalization
see also Medical examinations and tests
see also Mental health and illness
see also Mobility limitations
see also Nutrition and malnutrition
see also Obesity
see also Occupational health and safety
see also Stress
see also Vital statistics

Health education
AIDS and tuberculosis cases in prisons, test results, and control and treatment policies, by location, 1990 survey, annual rpt, 6064–22
AIDS knowledge, attitudes, and risk behaviors of women in methadone maintenance programs, effects of life skills training, 1988-89 local area study, article, 4042–3.353
AIDS prevention program for minority youth, interactive videodisc presentation effectiveness, 1992 article, 4042–3.332
AIDS prevention programs for drug abusers and their sexual partners, client characteristics, and outcomes, for selected metro areas, 1989 annual conf, 4494–12
AIDS public knowledge, attitudes, info sources, and testing, 1991 survey, 4146–8.218
Assistance (financial and nonfinancial) of Fed Govt, 1992 base edition, annual listing, 104–5
Cancer (cervical and breast) screening among poor black women, effects of in-home promotion program, 1989-92, article, 4042–3.338
Cancer info telephone helpline of Natl Cancer Inst, calls by caller type, 1983-90, article, 4042–3.325
Condom use promotion effectiveness in prevention of sexually transmitted disease reinfection, 1988 local area study, article, 4042–3.376
Developing countries family planning and population activities of AID, grants by project and recipient, and contraceptive shipments, by country, FY91, annual rpt series, 9914–13
Drug abuse prevention programs in schools, Education Dept recognition program, 1989/90-1990/91, annual listing, 4814–2
Drug abuse prevention services evaluation, methodological issues, 1991 conf, 4498–78
HHS financial aid, by program, recipient, State, and city, FY91, annual regional listings, 4004–3
Kidney end-stage disease treatment facilities, Medicare enrollment and reimbursement, survival, and patient characteristics, 1984-90, annual rpt, 4654–16
Mammography use by older women, relation to views and participation in promotional workshop, local area study, 1992 article, 4042–3.337
Mexican American obese women participation in weight loss and nutrition education programs, effectiveness, local area study, 1992 article, 4042–3.356
Morbidity and Mortality Weekly Report, infectious notifiable disease cases by State, and public health issues, 4202–1
Older persons health education centers medication mgmt and other preventive health activities, and Federal funding, FY83-91, article, 4042–3.303
Older persons health promotion program, costs and effectiveness of case mgmt and health education, 1980-83 local area study, article, 4042–3.342
Prisoners and parolees drug abuse treatment and education programs, activities, costs, and outcomes, 1990 conf, 4498–77
Smoking, tobacco, and health impacts research rpts, 1991 annual report, 4204–19
VA health care facilities trainees, by detailed program and city, FY91, annual rpt, 8704–4
see also Sex education

Health, Education and Welfare Department
see Department of Education
see Department of Health and Human Services

Health facilities administration
Blood banks safety violations, FDA enforcement, disease transmittal, and Houston regional center activities and finances, 1970s-91, hearings, 21368–134
Board and care home violations of State drug handling and dispensing regulations, for 3 metro areas, 1990-91, GAO rpt, 26121–447
Expenditures, use, payment sources, and admin of health care services, with foreign comparisons, 1970s-90, chartbook, 21788–213
Foreign and US health care administrative costs for all and public programs, by selected OECD country, mid 1970s-90, article, 4652–1.325
Govt employment and payroll, by function, level of govt, and jurisdiction, annual rpt series, 2466–1
HHS financial aid, by program, recipient, State, and city, FY91, annual regional listings, 4004–3
Hospital costs and use, data compilation project analyses, series, 4186–6
Hospital employment and job vacancy rate, by occupation, and instn size and control, 1981-88, annual rpt, 4114–12
Indian Health Service employment of Indians and non-Indians, training, hires, and quits, by occupation, FY90, annual rpt, 4084–6
Labor supply and education of health professionals, by professional and other characteristics, and location, 1960s-92 and projected to 2020, biennial rpt, 4114–8
Mental health care facilities, staff, and patient characteristics, *Statistical Notes* series, 4506–3
Mental health care facilities, staff, patients, and finances, 1970s-91, biennial rpt, 4094–1
Military health care personnel, and accessions by training source, by occupation, specialty, and service branch, FY90, annual rpt, 3544–24
Occupational Outlook Handbook, 1992-93, biennial rpt, 6744–1
Physicians, by specialty, age, sex, and location of training and practice, 1990, State rpt series, 4116–6
Public confidence in people running selected social instns, 1972-88 surveys, biennial rpt, 9624–10.7
VA health care facilities physicians, dentists, and nurses, by selected employment characteristics and VA district, quarterly rpt, 8602–6
VA health care facilities trainees, by detailed program and city, FY91, annual rpt, 8704–4
VA health care staff and turnover, by occupation, physician specialty, and location, 1991, annual rpt, 8604–8
Veterans post-traumatic stress cases by period of service, and VA treatment and rehabilitation program operations and staff, by site, FY91, annual rpt, 8704–6
see also Health care reform

see also Health planning and evaluation
Health facilities and services
AIDS patients costs and service use under Medicaid, and service needs, for New Jersey waiver program, 1987-89, article, 4652–1.317
Alteration and repair spending for commercial and public buildings, by type, size, age, and region, 1989, 2388–4
Assistance (financial and nonfinancial) of Fed Govt, 1992 base edition, annual listing, 104–5
Bombing incidents, casualties, and damage, by target, circumstances, and State, 1991, annual rpt, 6224–5
Cancer incidence impacts of migration, and treatment resources availability, for Florida by county, 1980, article, 4042–3.339
Contracts for sharing health services among VA and non-VA facilities, by service type and region, FY91, annual rpt, 8704–5
County Business Patterns, 1989: employment, establishments, and payroll, by SIC 2- to 4-digit industry and county, annual State rpt series, 2326–8
County Business Patterns, 1990: employment, establishments, and payroll, by SIC 2- to 4-digit industry and county, annual State rpt series, 2326–6
Data on health condition and care, indicators, 1950s-90, with health improvement and disease prevention goals for 1990, annual data compilation, 4144–11
Developing countries economic and social conditions from 1960s, and Intl Dev Cooperation Agency and AID activities and funding, FY91-93, annual rpt, 9904–4
Education natl goals progress indicators, by State, 1992, annual rpt, 15914–1
Employment, earnings, and hours, by SIC 1- to 4-digit industry, monthly 1989-Feb 1992, annual rpt, 6744–4
Energy use in commercial buildings, costs, and conservation, by building characteristics, survey rpt series, 3166–8
Fed Govt labor productivity, indexes of output and labor costs by function, FY67-90, annual rpt, 6824–1.6
Finances and operations, by SIC 2- to 4-digit industry, forecast 1992, annual rpt, 2044–28
Foreign and US health data collection and availability, by country, 1991, biennial listing, 4124–8
Health Care Financing Review, quarterly journal, 4652–1
HHS financial aid, by program, recipient, State, and city, FY91, annual regional listings, 4004–3
Homeless families health condition and access to care, indicators, local area study, 1991 conf paper, 4164–2
Homeless persons transitional housing and support services program, outcome relation to client characteristics and services, FY87-90, GAO rpt, 26113–549
Housing units with nonresidential activities on premises, MSA surveys, series, 2485–6
Indian Health Service and tribal facilities and use, and Indians health and other characteristics, by IHS region, 1980s-90, annual chartbook, 4084–7
Indian Health Service and tribal facility outpatient visits, by type of provider, selected hospital, and service area, FY91, annual rpt, 4084–3
Indian Health Service facilities, funding, operations, and Indian health and other characteristics, 1950s-91, annual chartbook, 4084–1
Indian Health Service outpatient services provided, by reason for visit and age, FY90, annual rpt, 4084–2
Input-output structure of US economy, detailed interindustry transactions for 541 industries, and components of final demand, 1982 benchmark data, 2708–17
Kidney dialysis facilities distribution related to area characteristics and facility ownership, 1982, article, 4652–1.306
Kidney end-stage disease treatment facilities approved by Medicare, dialysis and transplant services and ownership, 1991 annual listing, 4654–17
Labor hourly costs, by component, occupational group, industry div, union coverage, and region, 1992, annual rpt, 6744–21
Mail volume to and from households, use, and views, by class, source, content, and household characteristics, FY87-90, annual rpt, 9864–10
Medicare coverage of new health care technologies, risks and benefit evaluations, series, 4186–10
Multinatl firms US affiliates finances and operations, by industry, country of parent firm, and State, 1987, 2708–48
Multinatl US firms and foreign affiliates finances and operations, by industry and country, 1989 benchmark survey, annual rpt, 2704–5
Natl income and product accounts, comprehensive accounts and components, benchmark revisions, 1929-88, 2708–5
Natl income and product accounts, comprehensive accounts and components, *Survey of Current Business*, monthly rpt, 2702–1.29
Neighborhood and housing quality, indicators and attitudes, by householder type and location, for 11 MSAs, 1987 survey, supplement, 2485–8
NIH activities, staff, funding, and facilities, historical data, 1991 annual rpt, 4434–1
NYC black and Hispanic health condition and care indicators, 1980s, conf paper, 4164–2
Occupational injury and illness rates, by SIC 2- to 4-digit industry, 1989-90, annual rpt, 6844–7
Occupational injury and illness rates, by SIC 2- to 4-digit industry, 1990, annual rpt, 6844–1
Pacific territories population and housing detailed characteristics, by location, 1990 Census of Population and Housing, series, 2551–8
Palau admin, and social, economic, and govtl data, FY91, annual rpt, 7004–6
Prison and community-based facilities, population, employment, spending, and other characteristics, by State and for Fed Govt, 1990, quinquennial rpt, 6068–218
Prisons Bur admin offices and correctional instns, facility characteristics, 1992, annual listing, 6244–4
Reform of health care system, issues, insurance coverage and availability, and foreign comparisons, 1991 hearing, 21788–216
Tax (income) returns of corporations, income and tax items by asset size and detailed industry, 1989, annual rpt, 8304–4; 8304–21
Tax (income) returns of partnerships, income statement and balance sheet items, by industry group, 1990, annual article, 8302–2.314
Tax (income) returns of sole proprietorships, income statement items, by industry group, 1990, annual article, 8302–2.317; 8302–2.320
Use of health services and total and out-of-pocket spending, by type of insurance coverage and selected characteristics, 1987, 4186–8.24
Use, spending, payment sources, and admin of health care services, with foreign comparisons, 1970s-90, chartbook, 21788–213
Vital and Health Statistics series and other NCHS rpts, 1990-91, annual listing, 4124–1
Vital and Health Statistics series: health care facilities use and labor force, 4147–13
Vital and Health Statistics series: health condition, medical costs, and use of facilities and services, 4147–10
Youth health condition, risk factors, and preventive and treatment services use and availability, 1970s-80s, 26358–234
see also Abortion
see also Alcohol abuse and treatment
see also Chemotherapy
see also Civilian Health and Medical Program of the Uniformed Services
see also Clinics
see also Community health services
see also Dentists and dentistry
see also Drug abuse and treatment
see also Emergency medical service
see also Family planning
see also Group homes for the handicapped
see also Health care reform
see also Health facilities administration
see also Health insurance
see also Health maintenance organizations
see also Health occupations
see also Health planning and evaluation
see also Home health services
see also Hospices
see also Hospitalization
see also Hospitals
see also Laboratories
see also Mammography
see also Maternity homes
see also Medical costs
see also Medical examinations and tests
see also Medical regulation
see also Medical supplies and equipment
see also Medical transplants
see also Mental health facilities and services
see also Military health facilities and services
see also Nursing homes
see also Occupational therapy
see also Physical therapy
see also Public health
see also Regional medical programs
see also Rehabilitation of the disabled

see also Respiratory therapy
see also Speech pathology and audiology
see also State funding for health and hospitals
see also Vaccination and vaccines
see also Veterans health facilities and services
see also terms listed under Health occupations
see also under Medicine and terms beginning with Medical

Health insurance

AIDS cases among children, hospital use and charges by instn and patient characteristics, and payment source, 1986-87, 4186–6.16
Assistance programs under Ways and Means Committee jurisdiction, finances, operations, and participant characteristics, FY70s-91, annual rpt, 21784–11
Bone marrow donors, minority recruitment, Federal aid, transplants, costs, payment sources, 1987-92, GAO rpt, 26121–487
Child and maternal health condition and services use, indicators by age, race, and poverty status, 1988, 4478–197
Child infectious disease cases, and related disability and health care, by disease, health insurance status, and other characteristics, 1988, 4147–10.181
Child support awards, payment status, reasons for nonpayment, and mothers characteristics, by fathers residence in and out of State, 1990, GAO rpt, 26121–442
Children (handicapped) formal and informal care, outlays and time spent relation to diagnosis and other characteristics, 1988, article, 4042–3.329
Children (handicapped) with special needs, insurance coverage, and health care services use, by selected characteristics, 1988, 4146–8.216
Costs, use, and structure of private and public health care delivery, indicators, issues, and foreign comparisons, 1960s-80s, technical paper, 8006–6.1
County Business Patterns, 1989: employment, establishments, and payroll, by SIC 2- to 4-digit industry and county, annual State rpt series, 2326–8
County Business Patterns, 1990: employment, establishments, and payroll, by SIC 2- to 4-digit industry and county, annual State rpt series, 2326–6
Coverage under health insurance and govt aid, with background data 1960s-91 and govt fiscal impacts projected to 2002, 26306–6.174
Coverage under health insurance, by insurance type and selected characteristics, 1985-90, 2546–20.23
Coverage under health insurance, fall 1990, and persons with lapses in coverage by race, age, education, and poverty and marital status, 1987-89, fact sheet, 2326–17.49
Crime victimization rates, by victim and offender characteristics, circumstances, and offense, 1990 survey, annual rpt, 6066–3.47
Denial of health insurance by private carriers because of poor health, by selected characteristics, 1987, 4186–8.23
Diabetes patients physician office visits, by characteristics of patient, physician, and visit, 1989, 4146–8.212
Disabled persons assistive technology equipment and home accessibility features, use, payment sources, and unmet needs, by age, 1990, 4146–8.219
Employer-provided health insurance, and employee share of costs, by plan type and level of service use, 1989-90, article, 6722–1.348
Employer-provided health insurance costs and cost factors by industry div and firm size, 1987-91, GAO rpt, 26121–485
Employer-provided health insurance for inpatient and outpatient surgery, 1989-90, article, 6722–1.349
Employer-provided health insurance under multiple employer welfare arrangements, coverage, unpaid claims, and regulation, by State, 1988-91, GAO rpt, 26121–443
Employer-provided HMO and fee-for-service plan coverage of hospital care alternatives, 1989, article, 6722–1.302
Employment, earnings, and hours, by SIC 1- to 4-digit industry, monthly 1989-Feb 1992, annual rpt, 6744–4
Expenditures, coverage, and benefits for social welfare programs, late 1930s-90, annual rpt, 4744–3.1
Expenditures for health care and factors in costs, with data by payment source and service type, 1960s-90 and projected to 2000, 26306–6.175
Expenditures for health care by businesses, households, and govts, 1965-90, annual article, 4652–1.309
Expenditures for health care by funding source, 1990, with trends and indexes by service type from 1960, article, 4652–1.323
Failures of life and health insurance companies, and State guaranty fund assessments, by State, 1975-90, GAO rpt, 26119–392
Farm operators coverage under health insurance, by source of insurance, 1989, article, 1541–1.318
Fed Govt civilian employee health insurance programs enrollment, profits, and administrative costs, by plan, 1984-90, GAO rpt, 26119–376
Fed Govt civilian employees health and life insurance program coverage and finances, annual rpt, discontinued, 9844–35
Fed Govt civilian employees retirement, health, and life insurance benefits, coverage and finances of 4 programs, FY86-90, annual rpt, 9844–37
Fed Govt civilian employees work-years, pay rates, and benefits use and costs, by agency, FY90, annual rpt, 9844–31
Financial condition of insurance industry, operations, assets, junk bond holdings, and State regulation, with intl comparisons, 1991 hearings, 25268–79
Ford Motor Co and foreign subsidiaries employee health care costs, with data on foreign and US health care systems, 1987-90, article, 9882–16.302
Foreign countries social security programs coverage, funding, eligibility, and benefits, by country, 1991, biennial rpt, 4746–4.62
Health condition and care indicators, 1950s-90 with health improvement and disease prevention goals for 1990, annual data compilation, 4144–11
Hispanic Americans health insurance coverage, by source, employment and poverty status, and origin, 1987-90, GAO rpt, 26131–97
Homeless families health condition and access to care, indicators, local area study, 1991 conf paper, 4164–2
Hospital discharges and length of stay, by diagnosis, patient and instn characteristics, procedure performed, and payment source, 1990, annual rpt, 4147–13.112
Hospital discharges, by payment source, diagnosis, patient characteristics, and region, and procedures performed, 1990, 4146–8.221
Hospital reimbursement by private insurers, standard rates proposal with data on coverage, payments, and hospital uncompensated care, 1992 rpt, 17206–1.16
Hospital trauma center cases and deaths by injury type, costs, and payment sources, with data for selected areas, 1991 hearing, 21348–123
Households composition, income, benefits, and labor force status, Survey of Income and Program Participation methodology, working paper series, 2626–10
Income (household) and poverty status under alternative income definitions, by recipient characteristics, 1979-91, annual Current Population Rpt, 2546–6.78
Internist office visits, by characteristics of patient, physician, and visit, 1989, 4146–8.214
Labor hourly costs, by component, industry and occupational group, worker class, and firm size, monthly rpt, annual tables, 6782–1.2
Medicare supplemental private insurance loss ratio performance, by firm, 1988-89, GAO rpt, 26121–452
Medicare supplemental private insurance plans voluntary compliance with Federal standards, FY87, annual rpt, 4654–5
Mental health care of affective disorder patients, by patient and facility characteristics, 1986, 4506–3.49
Natl income and product accounts, comprehensive accounts and components, benchmark revisions, 1929-88, 2708–5
Natl income and product accounts, comprehensive accounts and components, *Survey of Current Business*, monthly rpt, 2702–1.25
OASDI beneficiary data collection system design compared to earlier surveys, with summary results, 1992 article, 4742–1.313
Occupational injury and illness rates, by SIC 2- to 4-digit industry, 1989-90, annual rpt, 6844–7
Occupational injury and illness rates, by SIC 2- to 4-digit industry, 1990, annual rpt, 6844–1
Older persons ability to pay out of pocket health care costs, indicators by selected characteristics, 1984, article, 4742–1.307
Older persons Medicare liability, other insurance coverage, and out-of-pocket expenses, 1991 and trends from 1961, annual rpt, 17204–2
Older persons socioeconomic characteristics, 1900s-90 and projected to 2050, biennial chartbook, 12904–1

Older population, and health, economic, and other characteristics, with foreign comparisons, 1980s-91 with trends and projections, Current Population Rpt, 2546–2.165
Pediatrician office visits, by characteristics of patient and visit, 1989, 4146–8.210
Pension plans health benefits accounting standards changes, and impacts on firm finances, with background data, 1986-89, technical paper, 9366–6.298
Physicians visits, by patient and practice characteristics, diagnosis, and services provided, 1989, annual rpt, 4147–13.109
Population economic well-being indicators, by selected characteristics and household income and income-to-poverty ratio, 1984, 2546–20.22
Poverty status of population and families, by detailed characteristics, 1991, annual Current Population Rpt, 2546–6.77
Railroad employee sickness benefits and beneficiaries, by age, occupation, and disease, 1989/90, annual rpt, 9704–2.3
Small business provision of health insurance, cost and access issues, 1991 hearings, 21788–218
State and local govt employees benefit plan coverage and provisions, by plan type, 1990, biennial rpt, 6784–21
Statistical Abstract of US, 1992 annual data compilation, 2324–1.3; 2324–1.16
Tax exclusion for employee benefits, Federal revenue forgone and coverage indicators, by benefit type, 1950s-80s and projected to 1995, GAO rpt, 26119–389
Traffic accident injury hospitalization, costs, and discharges, by payment source and State, mid 1980s-90, 7768–122
Traffic accidents direct and indirect costs, by cost type, payment source, and severity, 1980s, 7558–114
Transit systems finances and operations, by mode, size of fleet and urban area, region, and for 518 systems, 1990, annual rpt, 7884–4
Unemployment by selected characteristics, health insurance coverage, and unemployment insurance benefits exhaustion, 1988-91 and projected to 1996, hearing, 21788–209
Use of health services and total and out-of-pocket spending, by type of insurance coverage and selected characteristics, 1987, 4186–8.24
Utilization review organizations assessment of health services for insurance firms, with URO finances, operations, and staff, 1990, GAO rpt, 26121–490
VA health care services, needs, availability, structure, and funding, 1991 compilation of papers, 8608–9
Youth health condition, risk factors, and preventive and treatment services use and availability, 1970s-80s, 26358–234.3
see also Area wage surveys
see also Blue Cross-Blue Shield
see also Civilian Health and Medical Program of the Uniformed Services
see also Disability benefits and insurance
see also Health care reform
see also Health maintenance organizations
see also Industry wage surveys
see also Medicaid
see also Medicare
see also Old-Age, Survivors, Disability, and Health Insurance
see also Workers compensation

Health maintenance organizations
County Business Patterns, 1989: employment, establishments, and payroll, by SIC 2- to 4-digit industry and county, annual State rpt series, 2326–8
County Business Patterns, 1990: employment, establishments, and payroll, by SIC 2- to 4-digit industry and county, annual State rpt series, 2326–6
Diabetes patients physician office visits, by characteristics of patient, physician, and visit, 1989, 4146–8.212
Employer-provided health insurance, and employee share of costs, by plan type and level of service use, 1989-90, article, 6722–1.348
Employer-provided health insurance and HMO coverage, premiums paid, 1988-90, 10176–3.2
Employer-provided HMO and fee-for-service plan coverage of hospital care alternatives, 1989, article, 6722–1.302
Enrollment in HMOs in State with hospital ratesetting, as of 1990, article, 4652–1.311
Enrollment in HMOs, 1992, annual fact book, 4654–18
Fed Govt civilian employees retirement, health, and life insurance benefits, coverage and finances of 4 programs, FY86-90, annual rpt, 9844–37.2
Health Care Financing Admin research activities and grants, by program, FY91, annual listing, 4654–10
Health condition and care indicators, 1950s-90 with health improvement and disease prevention goals for 1990, annual data compilation, 4144–11
Hospital reimbursement by private insurers, standard rates proposal with data on coverage, payments, and hospital uncompensated care, 1992 rpt, 17206–1.16
Internist office visits, by characteristics of patient, physician, and visit, 1989, 4146–8.214
Medicare admin and research, and HCFA affirmative action and accreditation programs, FY87, annual rpt, 4654–5
Medicare reimbursement of HMOs under prospective payment system, alternative methods for determining local payment, 1991, article, 4652–1.321
Mental health care facilities, staff, patients, and finances, 1970s-91, biennial rpt, 4094–1
Physicians visits, by patient and practice characteristics, diagnosis, and services provided, 1989, annual rpt, 4147–13.109
State and local govt employees benefit plan coverage and provisions, by plan type, 1990, biennial rpt, 6784–21
Statistical Abstract of US, 1992 annual data compilation, 2324–1.3
Traffic accident injury hospitalization, costs, and discharges, by payment source and State, mid 1980s-90, 7768–122
Use, costs, and structure of private and public health care delivery, indicators, issues, and foreign comparisons, 1960s-80s, technical paper, 8006–6.1

Health occupations
AIDS cases by risk group, race, sex, age, State, and MSA, and deaths, quarterly rpt, 4202–9
Criminal justice systems activities, spending, and employment, by level of govt, data compilation, 1992 annual rpt, 6064–6.1
Data on health condition and care, indicators, 1950s-90, with health improvement and disease prevention goals for 1990, annual data compilation, 4144–11
Employment and economic conditions, alternative BLS projections to 2005 and trends 1975-90, biennial rpt, 6744–19
Employment Cost Index and alternative measure of compensation costs, by component, occupation, industry group, union status, and location, 1975-92, annual rpt, 6744–20
Employment in health care services, compared to other industries, 1960s-91, article, 6722–1.347
Employment, unemployment, and labor force characteristics, by region and census div, 1991, annual rpt, 6744–7.1
Foreign and US health data collection and availability, by country, 1991, biennial listing, 4124–8
Hepatitis cases by infection source, age, sex, race, and State, and deaths, by strain, 1989 and trends from 1966, 4205–2
HHS financial aid, by program, recipient, State, and city, FY91, annual regional listings, 4004–3
Hospital employment and job vacancy rate, by occupation, and instn size and control, 1981-88, annual rpt, 4114–12
Indian Health Service employment of Indians and non-Indians, training, hires, and quits, by occupation, FY90, annual rpt, 4084–6
Labor demand, turnover, and training completions, by detailed occupation, 1990 and projected to 2005, biennial rpt, 6744–3
Labor supply and education of health professionals, by professional and other characteristics, and location, 1960s-92 and projected to 2020, biennial rpt, 4114–8
Licensing and discipline of health professionals by State medical boards, 1950s-88, series, 4006–8
Medicare reimbursement of hospitals under prospective payment system, and effect on services, finances, and beneficiary payments, 1980-91, annual rpt, 17204–2
Mental health care facilities, staff, patients, and finances, 1970s-91, biennial rpt, 4094–1
Mentally retarded patients, training materials effectiveness in improving health care providers communication skills, 1992 article, 4042–3.328
Military budget, manpower needs, costs, and force readiness by service branch, FY93, annual rpt, 3504–1
Military health care personnel, and accessions by training source, by occupation, specialty, and service branch, FY90, annual rpt, 3544–24
Occupational Outlook Handbook, 1992-93, biennial rpt, 6744–1
OECD members health care costs, hospital use, resources, and economic and health indicators, by country, 1960s-90, article, 4652–1.322

Pacific territories population and housing detailed characteristics, by location, 1990 Census of Population and Housing, series, 2551–8
PHS Commissioned Corps members deaths, by cause, 1965-89, article, 4042–3.316
Smoking among hospital employees, patients views by smoking history, 1989 local area study, article, 4042–3.334
Technological devs effect on labor force, composition, and productivity, 1970s-90 and projected to 2005, industry rpt, 6826–2.8
VA health care facilities trainees, by detailed program and city, FY91, annual rpt, 8704–4
VA health care staff and turnover, by occupation, physician specialty, and location, 1991, annual rpt, 8604–8
VA health care staff, work-years, pay rates, and benefits use and costs, FY90, annual rpt, 9844–31
Veterans Health Services and Research Admin health care staff and salary, by pay system and occupational group, 1991, annual rpt, 9844–6.3
Vital and Health Statistics series: health care facilities use and labor force, 4147–13
see also Allied health personnel
see also Anesthesiology
see also Chiropractic and naturopathy
see also Clinical laboratory technicians
see also Dentists and dentistry
see also Dietitians and nutritionists
see also Epidemiology and epidemiologists
see also Foreign medical graduates
see also Geriatrics
see also Health facilities administration
see also Medical education
see also Midwives
see also Nuclear medicine and radiology
see also Nurses and nursing
see also Obstetrics and gynecology
see also Occupational therapy
see also Optometry
see also Orthopedics
see also Osteopathy
see also Pathology
see also Pediatrics
see also Pharmacists and pharmacy
see also Physical therapy
see also Physicians
see also Podiatry
see also Psychiatry
see also Respiratory therapy
see also Social work
see also Speech pathology and audiology
see also Surgeons and surgery
see also Veterinary medicine
see also under Medicine and terms beginning with Medical

Health of workers
see Absenteeism
see Occupational health and safety

Health planning and evaluation
AIDS and tuberculosis cases in prisons, test results, and control and treatment policies, by location, 1990 survey, annual rpt, 6064–22
AIDS prevention and control plans, cases, and Federal funding, 1980s-94, 4048–22
Assistance (financial and nonfinancial) of Fed Govt, 1992 base edition, annual listing, 104–5
Data collection for health and vital statistics, and use for planning and evaluation, 1991 biennial conf, 4164–2
Data on health condition and care, indicators, 1950s-90, with health improvement and disease prevention goals for 1990, annual data compilation, 4144–11
Disease and injury prevention activities effectiveness, evaluation methodologies, 1992 rpt, 4206–2.53
Drug abuse services availability, need, use, outcome, costs, funding sources, and cost-effectiveness, series, 4496–11
HHS financial aid, by program, recipient, State, and city, FY91, annual regional listings, 4004–3
Labor supply and education of health professionals, by professional and other characteristics, and location, 1960s-92 and projected to 2020, biennial rpt, 4114–8
OASDHI and health care system status and reform, Advisory Commission on Social Security findings and recommendations, 1991 quadrennial rpt, 10178–1
OASDI and Medicare trust fund finances, economic assumptions, outlook, and health care system reform issues, series, 10176–1
Oregon Medicaid waiver proposal for managed care, services priorities dev procedures and issues, with background data, 1992 rpt, 26358–254
Public Health Reports, bimonthly journal, 4042–3
Reform of health care system, issues, insurance coverage and availability, and foreign comparisons, 1991 hearing, 21788–216
Research activities and grants of HCFA, by program, FY91, annual listing, 4654–10
VA health care facilities trainees, by detailed program and city, FY91, annual rpt, 8704–4
see also Regional medical programs

Health Resources and Services Administration
Assistance (financial) of HHS, by program, recipient, State, and city, FY91, annual regional listings, 4004–3
Budget of US, obligations and authority by function, agency, and program, with summaries and analyses, FY93, annual rpt, 104–2
Expenditures of Fed Govt in States, by type, program, agency, and State, FY91, annual rpt, 2464–2
Transplants of organs, failures, deaths, and survival rates, by hospital, 1987-89, annual rpt series, 4104–17
see also Bureau of Health Professions
see also National Health Service Corps

Health risk behavior
AIDS cases at VA health care centers by sex, race, risk factor, and facility, and AIDS prevention and treatment issues, quarterly rpt, 8702–1
AIDS cases by risk group, race, sex, age, State, and MSA, and deaths, quarterly rpt, 4202–9
AIDS knowledge, attitudes, and risk behaviors of women in methadone maintenance programs, effects of life skills training, 1988-89 local area study, article, 4042–3.353
AIDS public knowledge, attitudes, info sources, and testing, 1991 survey, 4146–8.218
Deaths during 1986, decedents health condition, services use, habits, and social, employment, and other characteristics, 4147–20.19
Family life and relationships quality and other issues, views of parents and children, 1990 survey, 15528–2
Health condition and care indicators, 1950s-90 with health improvement and disease prevention goals for 1990, annual data compilation, 4144–11
Heart disease risk factors prevalence in Missouri, 1989-90, article, 4042–3.302
Homeless youths health conditions and risk behaviors, 1990 local area study, article, 4042–3.344
Indian and Alaska Native youth health condition and behavioral patterns, by sex and grade, 1988-90, 4088–3
Indian health risk behavior, by region and for Montana, mid 1980s, article, 4042–3.346
Prevalence of 7 habits, by age, State, and other characteristics, 1986-90, article, 4202–7.305
Teenage boys AIDS risk behavior, sexual activity, and drug and condom use, 1988, article, 4042–3.313
Vitamin supplement use correlation to health condition and behaviors, local area study, 1992 article, 4042–3.373
Youth health condition, risk factors, and preventive and treatment services use and availability, 1970s-80s, 26358–234
Youth risk behavior, by level of alcohol use and sex, 1987, article, 4482–1.308
see also Accidents and accident prevention
see also Alcohol abuse and treatment
see also Driving while intoxicated
see also Drug abuse and treatment
see also Motor vehicle safety devices
see also Nutrition and malnutrition
see also Obesity
see also Physical exercise
see also Preventive medicine
see also Sexual behavior
see also Smoking
see also Stress

Health surveys
see under names of individual surveys (listed under Surveys)

Hearing and hearing disorders
Air traffic controller and pilot hearing impacts of headset interference tones, 1992 technical rpt, 7506–10.100
Disability and work limitations of persons with chronic health conditions, by condition, age, and sex, 1983-86, 4946–1.2
Fed Govt employment of minorities, disabled, and veterans, and years of service, by occupation, age, sex, and agency, as of Sept 1990, biennial rpt, 9844–27
Head Start handicapped enrollment, by handicap, State, and for Indian and migrant programs, 1988/89, annual rpt, 4584–4
Hearing aid performance test results, by make and model, 1992 annual rpt, 8704–3

HHS financial aid, by program, recipient, State, and city, FY91, annual regional listings, 4004–3
Insurance (health) coverage and provisions of employee benefit plans, by plan type, for State and local govt employees, 1990, biennial rpt, 6784–21
Workers compensation laws of States and Fed Govt, 1992 annual rpt, 6504–11
see also Deaf
see also Ear diseases and infections
see also Speech pathology and audiology

Heart diseases
see Cardiovascular diseases

Heating
see Plumbing and heating

Heating oil
see Fuel oil

Hecht, Arthur
"Records and Policies of the Post Office Department Relating to Place-Names", 9516–1.5

Heckard, Robert
"Effect of the 65 MPH Speed Limit on Travel Speeds and Related Crashes", 7768–121

Heckbert, Susan R.
"Glutathione S-Transferase and Epoxide Hydrolase Activity in Human Leukocytes in Relation to Risk of Lung Cancer and Other Smoking-Related Cancers", 4472–1.307

Hecker, Daniel E.
"Reconciling Conflicting Data on Jobs for College Graduates", 6722–1.330

Hedging
see Futures trading

Hefner, J. M.
"Florida Wetlands, Status and Trends, 1970's-80's", 5508–119

Height
see Body measurements

Heikkila, Ralph C.
"Election Signature Retrieval Systems", 9278–8

Helicopters
Accidents and circumstances, for US operations of domestic and foreign airlines and general aviation, periodic rpt, 9612–1
Air traffic control and airway facilities improvement activities under Aviation System Capital Investment Plan, 1981-91 and projected to 2006, annual rpt, 7504–12
Army Apache helicopter use and performance during Persian Gulf War, 1991, GAO rpt, 26123–378
Exports and imports between US and outlying areas, by detailed commodity and mode of transport, 1991, annual rpt, 2424–11
Exports and imports of US, by country and detailed commodity, monthly rpt, 2422–12
Exports and imports of US, by Harmonized System 6-digit commodity and country, 1991, annual rpt, 2424–13
Exports of US, detailed Schedule B commodities with countries of destination, 1991, annual rpt, 2424–10
Flight and engine hours, and shutdown rates, by aircraft and engine model, and air carrier, monthly rpt, 7502–13
Foreign countries military spending, arms trade, and force strengths, with govt spending and population, by country, 1979-89, annual rpt, 9824–1
Military weapons acquisition costs by system and service branch, DOD budget, FY91-93, annual rpt, 3504–2
NATO and Warsaw Pact military forces reductions and ceilings under CFE treaty, inspections, and US compliance costs and savings, 1991 hearings, 25388–59
Pilots and nonpilots certified by FAA, by certificate type, age, sex, region, and State, 1991, annual rpt, 7504–2
Police employment, spending, and operations, for State, city, county, and special district agencies, 1990, annual rpt, 6064–39
Price indexes (producer), by stage of processing and detailed commodity, monthly rpt, 6762–6
Price indexes (producer), by stage of processing and detailed commodity, monthly 1991, annual rpt, 6764–2
Registration of aircraft with FAA, by type and characteristics of aircraft, make, carrier, State, and county, 1991, annual rpt, 7504–3
Shipments of general aviation aircraft, and commercial carriers orders and deliveries, by aircraft type, quarterly rpt, 7502–16
Shipments, trade, use, and firms, by type of craft and engine, monthly Current Industrial Rpt, 2506–12.24
Traffic, aircraft, carriers, airports, and FAA activities, detailed data, 1981-90, annual rpt, 7504–1
Traffic, aircraft, pilots, airports, and fuel use, forecast FY92-2003 and trends from FY82, annual rpt, 7504–6

Helium
see Gases

Helkie, William L.
"External Adjustment in Selected Developing Countries in the 1990s", 9366–7.271

Hellman, Chan
"Effects of Subordinate Feedback to the Supervisor and Participation in Decision-Making in the Prediction of Organizational Support", 7506–10.113

Hendershot, Gerry E.
"Trends in Breast Feeding", 4147–16.6

Hendershott, Patric H.
"Treasury Bill Rates in the 1970s and 1980s", 9373–27.6

Henderson, Dennis R.
"Implications of a Single EC Market for the U.S. Food Manufacturing Sector", 1528–325

Henderson, Yolanda K.
"Capital Costs, Industrial Mix, and the Composition of Business Investment", 9373–1.304

Henke, Robin R.
"Parental Financial Support for Undergraduate Education: 1987 National Postsecondary Student Aid Study", 4846–3.11

Hennepin County, Minn.
Housing and households characteristics, unit and neighborhood quality, and journey to work by MSA location, for 11 MSAs, 1985 survey, supplement, 2485–8
Housing and households detailed characteristics, and unit and neighborhood quality, by location, 1989 survey, MSA rpt, 2485–6.7

Hennessey, John C.
"Comparison of Individual Characteristics and Death Rates of Disabled-Worker Beneficiaries Entitled in 1972 and 1985", 4742–1.321

Hepatitis
see Infective and parasitic diseases
see Vaccination and vaccines

Herbert, John H.
"Natural Gas Futures Contract Market—The First 2 Years", 3162–4.302

Herbicides
see Pesticides

Herbs
see Spices and herbs

Hereditary diseases
Cancer (breast) death risk by presence of genetic mutations, and family breast cancer history, 1977-82, article, 4472–1.317
Cytomegalovirus (congenital) disease cases, by infant, mother, and birth characteristics, type of impairment, State, and Canada Province, 1990-91, 4202–7.314

Herruzo, A. Casimiro
"Developments in the Spanish Rice Market Since Joining the European Community: Implications for the U.S. Rice Industry", 1561–8.304

Hertzler, Glenn J., Jr.
"Status of FmHA Farmer Programs", 1504–9.1

Hervey, Jack L.
"Examination of Change in Energy Dependence and Efficiency in the Six Largest Energy Using Countries: 1970-88", 9375–13.79

Herwaldt, Barbara L.
"Waterborne-Disease Outbreaks, 1989-90", 4202–7.301

Herzenberg, Stephen A.
"North American Auto Industry at the Onset of Continental Free Trade Negotiations", 6366–3.28

Hetzel, Robert L.
"Indexed Bonds as an Aid to Monetary Policy", 9389–2

HEW
see Department of Education
see Department of Health and Human Services

Heynen, William J.
"Agricultural Maps in the National Archives of the U.S., circa 1860-1930", 9516–1.7
"Records and Policies of the Post Office Department Relating to Place-Names", 9516–1.5

Hialeah, Fla.
Housing starts and completions authorized by building permits in 40 MSAs, quarterly rpt, 2382–9
Wages by occupation, for office and plant workers, 1991 survey, periodic MSA rpt, 6785–16.3

Hickenbotham, Terry
"Minor Oilseeds: Outlook or Look Out?", 1504–9.1

Hickok, Susan
"Explaining the Persistence of the U.S. Trade Deficit in the Late 1980s", 9385-1.302
Hickory, N.C.
see also under By City and By SMSA or MSA in the "Index by Categories"
Hides and skins
Agricultural Statistics, 1991, annual rpt, 1004-1
Business statistics, detailed data for major industries and economic indicators, 1960-91, *Survey of Current Business* biennial supplement, 2704-1
Cold storage food stocks by commodity, and warehouse space use, by census div, 1991, annual rpt, 1631-11
Exports and imports (agricultural) of US, by commodity and country, bimonthly rpt, 1522-1
Exports and imports (agricultural) of US, by detailed commodity and country, 1991, annual rpt, 1524-8
Exports and imports (agricultural) of US, by detailed commodity and country, 1991, semiannual rpt, 1522-4
Exports and imports between US and outlying areas, by detailed commodity and mode of transport, 1991, annual rpt, 2424-11
Exports and imports of dairy, livestock, and poultry products, by commodity and country, FAS monthly circular, 1925-32
Exports and imports of US, by country and detailed commodity, monthly rpt, 2422-12
Exports and imports of US, by Harmonized System 6-digit commodity and country, 1991, annual rpt, 2424-13
Exports and imports of US, by selected country, country group, and commodity group, 1991, annual rpt, 2044-37
Exports and imports of US, by transport mode, country, and SITC 1- to 3-digit commodity, 1991, annual rpt, 2424-12
Exports of grains, oilseed products, hides, skins, and cotton, by country, weekly rpt, dropped data, 1922-3
Exports of US, detailed Schedule B commodities with countries of destination, 1991, annual rpt, 2424-10
Farm sector balance sheet, and receipts by detailed commodity, by State, 1986-90, annual rpt, 1544-18
Foreign and US livestock, poultry, and dairy production, trade, and use, by selected country, FAS semiannual circular series, 1925-33
Foreign countries agricultural production, prices, and trade, by country, 1980-91 and forecast 1992, annual world area rpt series, 1524-4
Manufacturing annual survey, 1990: finances and operations, by SIC 2- to 4-digit industry, series, 2506-14
Marketing data for livestock, meat, and wool, by species and market, weekly rpt, 1315-1
OECD trade, total and for 4 major countries, and US trade by country, by commodity, 1980-90, world area rpt series, 9116-1
Price indexes (producer), by stage of processing and detailed commodity, monthly rpt, 6762-6
Price indexes (producer), by stage of processing and detailed commodity, monthly 1991, annual rpt, 6764-2
see also Furs and fur industry
see also Leather industry and products
see also under By Commodity in the "Index by Categories"
Higgins, Kenneth F.
"Waterfowl Production on the Woodworth Station in South-central North Dakota, 1965-81", 5508-120
High Point, N.C.
Wages by occupation, and benefits for office and plant workers, 1992 survey, periodic MSA rpt, 6785-3.5
High School and Beyond Survey
Student education, employment, and family characteristics, activities, and attitudes, classes of 1980 and 1982, natl longitudinal study, series, 4826-2
Vocational education enrollment, and academic and other credits earned, by subject and student characteristics, high school classes of 1982 and 1987, 4838-50
High School Transcript Study
Vocational education enrollment, and academic and other credits earned, by subject and student characteristics, high school classes of 1982 and 1987, 4838-50
High schools
see Elementary and secondary education
High-speed ground transportation
Accidents and casualties on transit systems by circumstances, damage, and ridership, by mode, 1990, annual rpt, 7884-13
Finances and operations of transit systems, by mode, size of fleet and urban area, region, and for 518 systems, 1990, annual rpt, 7884-4
Safety, operating, and funding characteristics of rail rapid transit systems, 1988-89, 9618-19
Higher education
Condition of Education, detail for elementary, secondary, and higher education, 1920s-91 and projected to 2002, annual rpt, 4824-1
Data collection activities of higher education instns, for student performance by instn level and control, 1991, 4848-45
Data on education, enrollment, finances, teachers, and other characteristics, by State, 1969-89, 4828-33
Data on education, selected trends and projections 1979-2002, annual pamphlet, 4824-9
Data on education, 1940s-95, pamphlet, 4828-35
Data on education, 1960s-91, annual pamphlet, 4824-3
Data on higher education, data collection system glossary, 1992 rpt, 4848-47
Data on higher education, enrollment, faculty, finances, and degrees, by instn level and control, and State, FY88, annual rpt, 4844-13
Digest of Education Statistics, 1992 annual data compilation, 4824-2
Employment recruitment visits at colleges by Federal agencies and private companies, and school officials views, 1991, GAO rpt, 26119-377
Instns, enrollment, tuition, control, location, and other characteristics of higher education instns, 1991/92, biennial listing, 4844-3
Patents (US) granted to US and foreign applicants, by applicant and country, 1960s-91, annual rpt, 2244-3
R&D facilities of higher education instns, space and equipment adequacy, needs, and funding by source, by instn type and control, 1992, biennial rpt, 9624-25
Statistical Abstract of US, 1992 annual data compilation, 2324-1.4
see also Adult education
see also Agricultural education
see also Area studies
see also Black colleges
see also Business education
see also Campus security
see also Curricula
see also Degrees, higher education
see also Educational attainment
see also Educational broadcasting
see also Educational enrollment
see also Educational exchanges
see also Educational facilities
see also Educational finance
see also Educational materials
see also Educational performance
see also Educational research
see also Educational technology
see also Educational tests
see also Federal aid to higher education
see also Federal aid to medical education
see also Junior colleges
see also Legal education
see also Medical education
see also Reserve Officers Training Corps
see also School administration and staff
see also Scientific education
see also Service academies
see also State funding for higher education
see also Student aid
see also Students
see also Teacher education
see also Teachers
see also Veterans education
see also Vocational education and training
see also Work-study programs
Higher Education General Information Survey
see Integrated Postsecondary Education Data System
Highways, streets, and roads
Appalachia hwy system and access roads funding and completion status, by State, quarterly tables, 9082-1
Appalachia local dev projects, and funding by source, by program and State, FY91, annual rpt, 9084-1
Business statistics, detailed data for major industries and economic indicators, 1960-91, *Survey of Current Business* biennial supplement, 2704-1
Census of Population, 1990: homeless shelter and on-street population counts, assessment of methodology and procedures, GAO rpt, 26119-370
Conditions and funding of rural hwys and bridges, discontinued series, 1276-1
Construction material PPI, by construction industry, monthly rpt, 6762-6
Construction material prices and indexes for Federal-aid hwy system, by type of material and urban-rural location, quarterly rpt, 7552-7

Construction material prices and indexes for Federal-aid hwy system, by type of material, quarterly press release, 7552–16
Construction material use by type, and spending for hwys, by State, 1940s-91, annual rpt, 7554–29
Construction put in place and cost indexes, by type of construction, quarterly rpt, 2042–1.1; 2042–1.5
Construction put in place, value of new public and private structures, by type, monthly rpt, 2382–4
County Business Patterns, 1989: employment, establishments, and payroll, by SIC 2- to 4-digit industry and county, annual State rpt series, 2326–8
County Business Patterns, 1990: employment, establishments, and payroll, by SIC 2- to 4-digit industry and county, annual State rpt series, 2326–6
Crime victimization rates, by victim and offender characteristics, circumstances, and offense, 1990 survey, annual rpt, 6066–3.47
Energy use by mode of transport, fuel supply, and demographic and economic factors of vehicle use, 1970s-90, annual rpt, 3304–5
Foreign countries economic, social, political, and geographic summary data, by country, 1992, annual factbook, 9114–2
Govt direct spending and employment, by function and level of govt, selected years 1962-87, 10048–53
Govt employment and payroll, by function, level of govt, and jurisdiction, annual rpt series, 2466–1
Govt finances, by level of govt, State, and for large cities and counties, annual rpt series, 2466–2
Govt finances, structure, and service delivery in large metro areas, local area rpt series, 10046–9
Hwy Statistics, detailed data by State, 1991, annual rpt, 7554–1
Hwy Statistics, summary data by State, 1990-91, annual rpt, 7554–24
Hwy Statistics, summary data with trends and projections, 1992 chartbook, 7554–41
Input-output structure of US economy, detailed interindustry transactions for 541 industries, and components of final demand, 1982 benchmark data, 2708–17
Interstate hwy mileage, by route and State, 1991 listing, 7558–111
Mexico-US trade agreement impacts on truck traffic at border crossings, Customs Service staff needs, and hwy improvement costs, projected to 2000 with trends from 1986, GAO rpt, 26123–368
Natl Hwy Traffic Safety Admin and Fed Hwy Admin activities and grants, 1990, annual rpt, 7764–1
Natl income and product accounts, comprehensive accounts and components, benchmark revisions, 1929-88, 2708–5
Natl income and product accounts, comprehensive accounts and components, *Survey of Current Business*, monthly rpt, 2702–1.28
Neighborhood and housing quality, indicators and attitudes, by householder type and location, 1989, biennial rpt supplement, 2485–13
Neighborhood and housing quality, indicators and attitudes, MSA surveys, series, 2485–6
Neighborhood quality, indicators and attitudes of renter households, by whether receiving and eligible for HUD assistance, householder characteristics, and location, 1989, biennial rpt, 5184–11
Palau admin, and social, economic, and govtl data, FY91, annual rpt, 7004–6
Public lands acreage and use, and Land Mgmt Bur activities and finances, annual State rpt series, 5724–11
Public opinion on taxes, spending, and govt efficiency, by respondent characteristics, 1992 survey, annual rpt, 10044–2
R&D for hwy design and construction, quarterly journal, 7552–3
Radioactive materials shipments on US hwys, by material type, carrier, and shipper, 1985-90, 3008–129
Robberies, by type of premises, population size, and region, 1991, annual rpt, 6224–2.1
Scenic byway routes and mileage, by govt ownership, land use and usage restrictions, and other characteristics, 1990, 7558–112
Scenic byways economic, safety, and other issues, series, 7556–8
State and local govt employment of minorities and women, by occupation, function, and pay level, 1991, annual rpt, 9244–6.4
Statistical Abstract of US, 1992 annual data compilation, 2324–1.21
Traffic volume on rural roads and city streets, monthly rpt, 7552–8
User fees financing of transportation infrastructure, with data on hwys, airports, and waterways, 1985-91, 26306–6.170
see also Bridges and tunnels
see also Federal aid to highways
see also Traffic accident fatalities
see also Traffic accidents and safety
see also Traffic engineering
see also Traffic laws and courts

Hijacking of aircraft
see Air piracy

Hiles, David R.
"Health Services: The Real Jobs Machine", 6722–1.347

Hilgert, Cecelia
"Charities and Other Tax-Exempt Organizations, 1988", 8302–2.315

Hill, Barry R.
"Suspended-Sediment Budgets for Four Drainage Basins Tributary to Lake Tahoe, California and Nevada, 1984-87", 5666–27.32

Hill, Edward E.
"Records of the Department of the Interior, Record Group 48", 9516–2.1

Hill, Lawrence J.
"Assessment of Using Oil Shale for Power Production in the Hashemite Kingdom of Jordan", 3008–127
"Comparison of Methods To Integrate DSM and Supply Resources in Electric-Utility Planning", 3308–100

Hill, Walter E.
"Making Rural Policy for the 1990's and Beyond: A Federal Government View", 1504–9.1

Hills, Carla A.
"Uruguay Round Opportunities", 1504–9.1

Hilton, J.
"Heavy-Duty Trucks in Crashes, NASS, 1979-86", 7768–124

Himmelberg , Charles P.
"R&D and Internal Finance: A Panel Study of Small Firms in High-Tech Industries", 9375–13.75

Hindall, Steven M.
"Current Water Resources Activities in Ohio, 1991", 5666–26.23

Hinds, M. Ward
"Impact of a Local Ordinance Banning Tobacco Sales to Minors", 4042–3.336

Hinton, David
"U.S. Petroleum Developments: 1991", 3162–6.301

Hires
see Labor turnover

Hirst, Eric
"Effects of Utility DSM Programs on Risk", 3308–105
"Electric-Utility DSM Programs: Terminology and Reporting Formats", 3308–101
"Electric-Utility DSM Programs: 1990 Data and Forecasts to 2000", 3308–106

Hispanic Americans
AIDS cases by risk group, race, sex, age, State, and MSA, and deaths, quarterly rpt, 4202–9
Alcohol use among Mexican American women, by whether immigrant and occupational group, 1992 article, 4482–1.309
Births and rates, by characteristics of birth, infant, and mother, and presence of maternal risk factors and birth defects, 1989, 4146–5.125
Business mgmt and financial aid from Minority Business Dev Centers, and characteristics of businesses, by region and State, FY91, annual rpt, 2104–6
Business owner and business characteristics, for minority- and women-owned firms, by industry, employment and sales size, and form of ownership, 1987 survey, 2328–59
Census of Population and Housing, 1990: data summary, use, and availability, fact sheet, 2326–23.3
Census of Population and Housing, 1990: detailed geographic coverage, State CD-ROM series, 2551–9
Census of Population and Housing, 1990: population and housing characteristics, detailed geographic coverage, State CD-ROM series, 2551–10
Census of Population and Housing, 1990: summary characteristics, households, and land area, by county, subdiv, and place, State rpt series, 2551–1
Census of Population, 1990: ancestry of US population, by group and State, press release, 2328–87
Census of Population, 1990: minority group participation in census, effectiveness and quality of outreach and promotional programs, hearing, 21628–103
Census of Population, 1990: population characteristics and living arrangements, by county, place, and urban-rural location, State rpt series, 2531–1
Census of Population, 1990: population characteristics and living arrangements, for Native American, urban, and metro areas, series, 2531–2

Consumer Income, socioeconomic characteristics of persons, families, and households, detailed cross-tabulations, Current Population Rpt series, 2546–6
Crime, criminal justice admin and enforcement, and public opinion, data compilation, 1992 annual rpt, 6064–6
Crimes, arrests, and rates, by offense, offender characteristics, population size, and jurisdiction, 1991, annual rpt, 6224–2.1; 6224–2.2
Deaths and rates, by cause and selected social, demographic, and employment characteristics, 1979-85, natl longitudinal study, 4478–186
Drug, alcohol, and cigarette use, by selected characteristics, 1991 survey, annual rpt series, 4494–5
Education data compilation, 1992 annual rpt, 4824–2
Education data, detail for elementary, secondary, and higher education, 1920s-91 and projected to 2002, annual rpt, 4824–1
Education in science and math, natl assessment of elementary and high school students, 1985/86, series, 4896–6
Educational attainment, by social and demographic characteristics and location, 1991 and trends from 1940, biennial Current Population Rpt, 2546–1.460
Educational enrollment, by grade, instn type and control, and student characteristics, 1990 and trends from 1947, annual Current Population Rpt, 2546–1.459
Educational performance and conditions, characteristics, attitudes, activities, and plans, 1988 8th grade class, natl longitudinal survey, series, 4826–9
Educational performance of elementary and secondary students, and factors affecting proficiency, by selected characteristics, 1990 natl assessments, subject rpt series, 4896–8
Eighth grade class of 1988: Asian and Hispanic students proficiency in English and language at home, by selected characteristics, natl longitudinal survey, 1992 rpt, 4826–9.12
Employment and unemployment current statistics and articles, Monthly Labor Review, 6722–1
Employment, earnings, and hours, monthly press release, 6742–5
Employment of minorities and women, by occupation, SIC 1- to 3-digit industry, State, and MSA, 1991, annual rpt, 9244–1
Employment, unemployment, and labor force characteristics, by region, State, and selected metro area, 1991, annual rpt, 6744–7
Farm population, by employment, social, and economic characteristics, and region, 1990, annual Current Population Rpt, 2546–1.458
Fed Equal Opportunity Recruitment Program activity, and employment by sex, race, pay grade, and occupational group, FY91, annual rpt, 9844–33
Fed Govt employment of minorities, disabled, and veterans, and years of service, by occupation, age, sex, and agency, as of Sept 1990, biennial rpt, 9844–27
FmHA loans, by type, borrower race, and State, quarterly rpt, 1182–5
Food aid program of USDA for women, infants, and children, participants by race, State, and Indian agency, 1991, annual rpt, 1364–16
Health care professionals supply and education, by professional and other characteristics, and location, 1960s-92 and projected to 2020, biennial rpt, 4114–8
Health condition and care indicators, 1950s-90 with health improvement and disease prevention goals for 1990, annual data compilation, 4144–11
High school classes of 1980 and 1982: education, employment, and family characteristics, activities, and attitudes, natl longitudinal study, series, 4826–2
Higher education degrees awarded, by level, field, race, and sex, 1989/90 and trends from 1980/81, annual rpt, 4844–17
Higher education enrollment, by level, race, and sex, fall 1980-90, biennial rpt, 4844–15
Higher education enrollment, by sex and race, 1976-2000, annual rpt, 4824–4
Households and family characteristics, by location, 1991, annual Current Population Rpt, 2546–1.457
Households and housing characteristics, and unit and neighborhood quality, by MSA location for 11 MSAs, 1987 survey, supplement, 2485–8
Households and housing detailed characteristics, and unit and neighborhood quality, by location, 1989, biennial rpt supplement, 2485–13
Households and housing detailed characteristics, and unit and neighborhood quality, MSA surveys, series, 2485–6
Households composition, income, benefits, and labor force status, Survey of Income and Program Participation methodology, working paper series, 2626–10
Housing (rental) units, total, with HUD assistance by program, and eligible for aid, by unit, household, and neighborhood characteristics, and location, 1989, biennial rpt, 5184–11
Housing census, 1990: summary unit characteristics, by householder race and age, county, place, and urban-rural location, State rpt series, 2471–1
Housing rental and sales, discrimination against blacks and Hispanics in selected metro areas, 1989 study, series, 5186–16
Income (household) and poverty status under alternative income definitions, by recipient characteristics, 1979-91, annual Current Population Rpt, 2546–6.78
Income (personal) relative to median, by race and selected other characteristics, mid 1960s-89, Current Population Rpt, 2546–6.73
Insurance (health) coverage of Hispanics, by source, employment and poverty status, and origin, 1987-90, GAO rpt, 26131–97
Labor demand, turnover, and training completions, by detailed occupation, 1990 and projected to 2005, biennial rpt, 6744–3
Labor force status, by race, detailed Hispanic origin, and sex, quarterly rpt, 6742–18
Labor force, wages, hours, and payroll costs, by major industry group and demographic characteristics, *Survey of Current Business*, monthly rpt, 2702–1.7
Living arrangements, family relationships, and marital status, by selected characteristics, 1991, annual Current Population Rpt, 2546–1.461
Migration, immigration, and mover characteristics compared to nonmovers, 1987-90, annual Current Population Rpt, 2546–1.456
Migration since 1990, mover characteristics by same or different area, and compared to nonmovers, 1991, annual Current Population Rpt, 2546–1.464
Military personnel deployment in Operation Desert Storm, by sex, race, rank, and service branch, 1990-91, GAO rpt, 26123–394
Nuclear engineering enrollment and degrees granted by instn and State, and grad placement, by student characteristics, 1991, annual rpt, 3004–5
NYC black and Hispanic health condition and care indicators, 1980s, conf paper, 4164–2
NYC housing supply, occupancy, condition, and household characteristics, by tenure and borough, 1991 triennial survey, 2488–3
Obese Mexican American women participation in weight loss and nutrition education programs, effectiveness, local area study, 1992 article, 4042–3.356
Population economic well-being indicators, by selected characteristics and household income and income-to-poverty ratio, 1984, 2546–20.22
Population size, by race and Hispanic origin, 1992 and projected 2000-2050, press release, 2328–85
Poverty relation to low earnings, by work experience during year, household relationship, sex, race, age, and education, 1960s-90, Current Population Rpt, 2546–6.74
Prison and community-based facilities, population, employment, spending, and other characteristics, by State and for Fed Govt, 1990, quinquennial rpt, 6068–218
Prisoners, characteristics, and movements, by State, 1990, annual rpt, 6064–26
Prisoners in Federal and contract instns, by selected characteristics, region, and Federal instn, FY89, annual rpt, 6244–1.1
Radiation protection and health physics enrollment and degrees granted by instn and State, and grad placement, by student characteristics, 1991, annual rpt, 3004–7
Science and engineering employment and education of minorities, women, and disabled, by field, mid 1970s-91, biennial rpt, 9624–20
Science and engineering grad enrollment, by field, source of funds, and characteristics of student and instn, 1990, annual rpt, 9627–7
Science and Engineering Indicators, employment, education, R&D funding, and industry impacts, with foreign comparisons, 1960s-91, biennial rpt, 9624–10

State and local govt employment of minorities and women, by occupation, function, pay level, and State, 1991, annual rpt, 9244–6
Statistical Abstract of US, 1992 annual data compilation, 2324–1
Unemployed displaced workers, layoffs and unemployment insurance claims by reason, industry, selected characteristics, and State, quarterly press release, 6742–23
Unemployed displaced workers, layoffs and unemployment insurance claims by reason, industry, selected characteristics, MSA, and State, 1990, annual rpt, 6744–18
see also under By Race and Ethnic Group in the "Index by Categories"

Historic events
see Chronologies

Historic sites
Acreage and descriptions of natl park system sites, 1991, biennial listing, 5544–5
Acreage of land under Forest Service mgmt, by forest and location, 1991, annual rpt, 1204–2
Acreage of land under Natl Park Service mgmt, by site, ownership, and region, FY92, semiannual rpt, 5542–1
Assistance (financial and nonfinancial) of Fed Govt, 1992 base edition, annual listing, 104–5
Criminal cases by type and disposition, and collections, for US attorneys, by Federal district, FY91, annual rpt, 6004–2.1
Damaged and threatened natl historic and natural landmarks, with owner, location, damage type, and recommended remedial action, 1990, annual listing, 5544–16
DC metro area land acquisition and dev projects of Fed Govt, characteristics and funding by agency and project, FY92-96, annual rpt, 15454–1
Environmental Quality, status of problems, protection programs, research, and intl issues, 1991 annual rpt, 484–1
Fed Govt spending in States, by type, program, agency, and State, FY91, annual rpt, 2464–2
Minerals offshore lease sales environmental and economic impacts in coastal areas, final statement series, 5736–7
New Mexico Caballo Resource Area public land mgmt, and grazing, environmental, and leasing activities, FY90-91, annual rpt, 5724–17
Preservation Fund grants, by State, FY93, annual press release, 5544–9
Visits in natl park system, by park and State, monthly rpt, 5542–4
Visits in natl park system, by park and State, 1991, annual rpt, 5544–12
see also Monuments and memorials

History
American Historical Assn financial statements, and membership by State, 1990, annual rpt, 29574–2
Degree (PhD) recipients in higher education, by field and selected characteristics, 1979, 1984, and 1989, 4848–44
Educational performance by subject and selected student characteristics, standard test results and credits, 1992 edition, annual rpt, 4824–2.12
Fed Govt aid to higher education and nonprofit instns for R&D and related activities, by field, instn, agency, and State, FY90, annual rpt, 9627–17

Hitchner, Roger E.
"Outlook for Farm Commodity Program Spending, FY92-97", 26306–6.171

HIV virus group
see Acquired immune deficiency syndrome

Hixon, Mark A.
"Fish Assemblages of Rocky Banks of the Pacific Northwest, Final Report", 5738–39

Hoachlander, E. Gareth
"Participation in Secondary Vocational Education, 1982-87", 4838–50

Hoagland, N. Theresa
"U.S. Army Corps of Engineers Recreation Study: A Plan Prepared for the Assistant Secretary of the Army (Civil Works)", 3758–8

Hobbs, James R.
"Foreign Corporations with Income Effectively Connected with a U.S. Business, 1988", 8302–2.309
"Transactions Between Foreign Controlled Corporations and Related Foreign Persons, 1988: Data Release", 8302–2.318

Hoel, David G.
"Trends in Cancer Mortality in 15 Industrialized Countries, 1969-86", 4472–1.306

Hoffman, Charlene M.
"Digest of Education Statistics, 1992", 4824–2
"Federal Support for Education: FY80-91", 4824–8
"Historically Black Colleges and Universities, 1976-90", 4848–46

Hoffman, Keith L.
"Covariances for Estimated Totals When Comparing Between Years. Vital and Health Statistics Series 2", 4147–2.114

Hoffman, Linwood A.
"Forecasting Producer Prices of Rough Rice with Futures Prices", 1561–8.301
"Forecasting Season-Average Wheat Prices Using Futures Prices", 1561–12.301
"Forecasting U.S. Soybean Prices with Futures Prices", 1561–3.303

Hogan, Andrew J.
"HIV Infection Treatment Costs Under Medicaid in Michigan", 4042–3.348

Hogan, Christopher
"Fee Update and Medicare Volume Performance Standards for 1992", 17266–1.3
"Monitoring Access of Medicare Beneficiaries: Report to Congress", 17266–1.8
"Monitoring Access: Report to Congress", 17266–1.5

Holding companies
County Business Patterns, 1989: employment, establishments, and payroll, by SIC 2- to 4-digit industry and county, annual State rpt series, 2326–8
County Business Patterns, 1990: employment, establishments, and payroll, by SIC 2- to 4-digit industry and county, annual State rpt series, 2326–6
Employment, earnings, and hours, by SIC 1- to 4-digit industry, monthly 1989-Feb 1992, annual rpt, 6744–4
Multinatl firms US affiliates finances and operations, by industry, country of parent firm, and State, 1987, 2708–48
Multinatl US firms and foreign affiliates finances and operations, by industry and country, 1989 benchmark survey, annual rpt, 2704–5
Occupational injury and illness rates, by SIC 2- to 4-digit industry, 1989-90, annual rpt, 6844–7
Occupational injury and illness rates, by SIC 2- to 4-digit industry, 1990, annual rpt, 6844–1
Tax (income) returns filed, by type of return and IRS district, 1990 and projected 1991-98, annual rpt, 8304–24
Tax (income) returns filed, by type of tax and IRS region and service center, projected 1991-98 and trends from 1978, annual rpt, 8304–9
Tax (income) returns of corporations, income and tax items by asset size and detailed industry, 1989, annual rpt, 8304–4; 8304–21
Tax (income) returns of corporations with foreign tax credit, income and tax items by industry group, 1988, biennial article, 8302–2.316
Tax (income) returns of partnerships, income statement and balance sheet items, by industry group, 1990, annual article, 8302–2.314
Tax exempt organizations and employee plans listed on IRS masterfile, determinations, applications, and rulings, FY91, annual rpt, 8304–3.2
Telephone and telegraph corporate control and holding company finances and operations, 1990, annual rpt, 9284–6.1
Trust assets of banks, trust companies, and S&Ls, by type of asset and fund, selected firm, and State, 1991, annual rpt, 13004–1
see also Bank holding companies

Holidays
see Vacations and holidays

Holland
see Netherlands

Holloway, Edwin T.
"Small Business Administration's Small Business Investment Company Program: A Review of Selected Issues", 25728–44

Hollywood, Fla.
Housing starts and completions authorized by building permits in 40 MSAs, quarterly rpt, 2382–9
Wages by occupation, and benefits for office and plant workers, 1991 survey, periodic MSA rpt, 6785–3.1

Holmes, Howard J.
"Oceanos' Heroes", 2152–8.302

Holmes, Wendell
"Self Employed: How Do Farmers Stack Up?", 1541–1.301

Holy See
see Vatican City

Holzmayer, Tatyana A.
"Clinical Correlates of MDR1 (P-glycoprotein) Gene Expression in Ovarian and Small-Cell Lung Carcinomas", 4472–1.345

Home-based offices and workers
American Housing Survey: unit and households characteristics, unit and neighborhood quality, and journey to work by MSA location, for 11 MSAs, 1985 survey, supplement, 2485–8

American Housing Survey: unit and households detailed characteristics, and unit and neighborhood quality, 1989, biennial rpt supplement, 2485–13
Child day care and early childhood education programs availability, demand, use, costs, and provider and enrollee characteristics, 1990 survey, 4808–39
Employment and personal characteristics of home-based workers, and views, 1989, article, 1702–1.307
Pacific territories population and housing detailed characteristics, by location, 1990 Census of Population and Housing, series, 2551–8
Workers at home, and hours, by worker characteristics, occupational group and industry div, 1991, press release, 6726–1.52

Home economics
Degrees awarded in higher education, by level, field, race, and sex, 1989/90 and trends from 1980/81, annual rpt, 4844–17
Education data compilation, 1992 annual rpt, 4824–2
Enrollment in vocational education, and academic and other credits earned, by subject and student characteristics, high school classes of 1982 and 1987, 4838–50
Enrollment in vocational education, student and teacher characteristics, and outcomes, for secondary and postsecondary instns, 1970s-90, 4828–42
Farm financial and marketing conditions, forecast 1992, annual conf, 1504–9
Teachers of vocational education, by subject area and selected characteristics, for public high schools, 1987/88, 4836–3.9
see also Family budgets

Home health services
AIDS patients costs and service use under Medicaid, and service needs, for New Jersey waiver program, 1987-89, article, 4652–1.317
AIDS patients costs and service use under Medicaid, for California, 1984-86, article, 4652–1.301
AIDS virus-related Medicaid claims and payments, by sex, age, risk group, eligibility, and source of care, for Michigan, mid 1980s, article, 4042–3.348
Children (handicapped) formal and informal care, outlays and time spent relation to diagnosis and other characteristics, 1988, article, 4042–3.329
County Business Patterns, 1989: employment, establishments, and payroll, by SIC 2- to 4-digit industry and county, annual State rpt series, 2326–8
County Business Patterns, 1990: employment, establishments, and payroll, by SIC 2- to 4-digit industry and county, annual State rpt series, 2326–6
Deaths during 1986, decedents health condition, services use, habits, and social, employment, and other characteristics, 4147–20.19
Drug infusion therapy in home, use, equipment, industry finances, and Medicare coverage options, 1992 rpt, 26358–258
Employer-provided HMO and fee-for-service plan coverage of hospital care alternatives, 1989, article, 6722–1.302
Health Care Financing Review, provider prices, price inputs and indexes, and labor, quarterly journal, 4652–1.1
HHS financial aid, by program, recipient, State, and city, FY91, annual regional listings, 4004–3
Insurance (health) coverage and provisions of employee benefit plans, by plan type, for State and local govt employees, 1990, biennial rpt, 6784–21
Kidney end-stage disease treatment facilities, Medicare enrollment and reimbursement, survival, and patient characteristics, 1984-90, annual rpt, 4654–16
Long term health care financing reform issues, 1991 rpt, 10176–3.7
Medicaid coverage, funding, and costs, with reform recommendations, mid 1960s-92, 10048–83
Medicare admin and research, and HCFA affirmative action and accreditation programs, FY87, annual rpt, 4654–5
Medicare and Medicaid beneficiaries and program operations, 1992, annual fact book, 4654–18
Medicare and Medicaid enrollees, benefits, reimbursements, and services use, mid 1960s-90, annual rpt, 4744–3.5; 4744–3.6
Medicare and non-Medicare patients home health care services use and nursing visits, for Virginia, 1983-85, article, 4652–1.302
Medicare reimbursement of hospitals under prospective payment system, and effect on services, finances, and beneficiary payments, 1980-91, annual rpt, 17204–2
Medicare reimbursement of hospitals under prospective payment system, methodology, inputs, and data by diagnostic group, 1992 annual rpt, 17204–1
Occupational Outlook Handbook, 1992-93, biennial rpt, 6744–1
Older persons care by family members and others, caregiver quit probability related to selected characteristics, 1982, article, 4652–1.305
Quality standards and review for health care facilities excluded from Medicare prospective payment system, certification, accreditation, and licensing, 1991 survey, 17206–2.41
Retirees health and other characteristics related to Medicare use and charges 2 years later, 1984, article, 4652–1.319
VA health care services, needs, availability, structure, and funding, 1991 compilation of papers, 8608–9
Veterans disability and death compensation cases of VA, by entitlement type, period of service, and sex, as of Mar 1992, annual rpt, 8604–13
Veterans disability and death compensation cases of VA, by entitlement type, period of service, sex, age, and State, FY90, annual rpt, 8604–7
Veterans health care, patients, visits, costs, and operating beds, by VA and contract facility, and region, quarterly rpt, 8602–4

Home Mortgage Disclosure Act
Minority groups mortgage applications, for Boston by disposition and financial characteristics, with problems in analyzing lender disclosure statements, 1990, working paper, 9373–27.15

Home ownership
see Housing sales
see Housing tenure

Home video and audio equipment
Business statistics, detailed data for major industries and economic indicators, *Survey of Current Business*, monthly rpt, 2702–1.16
Business statistics, detailed data for major industries and economic indicators, 1960-91, *Survey of Current Business* biennial supplement, 2704–1
Consumer spending, natl income and product account benchmark revisions, 1929-88, 2708–5
Consumer spending, natl income and product accounts, comprehensive accounts and components, *Survey of Current Business*, monthly rpt, 2702–1.25
County Business Patterns, 1989: employment, establishments, and payroll, by SIC 2- to 4-digit industry and county, annual State rpt series, 2326–8
County Business Patterns, 1990: employment, establishments, and payroll, by SIC 2- to 4-digit industry and county, annual State rpt series, 2326–6
CPI by component for US city average, and by selected metro area, region, and population size, monthly rpt, 6762–2
Exports and imports between US and outlying areas, by detailed commodity and mode of transport, 1991, annual rpt, 2424–11
Exports and imports of US, by country and detailed commodity, monthly rpt, 2422–12
Exports and imports of US, by Harmonized System 6-digit commodity and country, 1991, annual rpt, 2424–13
Exports and imports of US, by transport mode, country, and SITC 1- to 3-digit commodity, 1991, annual rpt, 2424–12
Exports, imports, tariffs, and industry operating data for TV receivers and video monitors, 1992 rpt, 9885–12.1
Exports of US, detailed Schedule B commodities with countries of destination, 1991, annual rpt, 2424–10
Households entertainment spending, recreation participation by activity, and video product and pet ownership, 1970s-90, article, 1702–1.303
Imports of US given duty-free treatment for value of US material sent abroad, by commodity and country, 1987-90, annual rpt, 9884–14
Injuries from use of consumer products and related activities, by severity and victim age and sex, 1990, annual rpt, 9164–7
Injuries from use of consumer products, by severity, victim age, and detailed product, 1991, annual rpt, 9164–6
Input-output structure of US economy, detailed interindustry transactions for 541 industries, and components of final demand, 1982 benchmark data, 2708–17
Labor productivity, indexes of output, hours, and employment by SIC 2- to 4-digit industry, 1967-90, annual rpt, 6824–1.3
Manufacturing annual survey, 1990: value of shipments, by SIC 4- to 5-digit product class, 2506–14.1
Manufacturing census, 1987: concentration of largest firms measured by value added, and for shipments by SIC 2- and 4-digit industry, subject rpt, 2497–6

Manufacturing census, 1987: shipments of manufacturers products, by customer class and SIC 2- and 4-digit industry, subject rpt, 2497–4
Manufacturing finances and operations, by SIC 2- to 4-digit industry, forecast 1992, annual rpt, 2044–28
Occupational injury and illness rates, by SIC 2- to 4-digit industry, 1989-90, annual rpt, 6844–7
Occupational injury and illness rates, by SIC 2- to 4-digit industry, 1990, annual rpt, 6844–1
OECD trade, total and for 4 major countries, and US trade by country, by commodity, 1980-90, world area rpt series, 9116–1
Pacific territories population and housing detailed characteristics, by location, 1990 Census of Population and Housing, series, 2551–8
Population economic well-being indicators, by selected characteristics and household income and income-to-poverty ratio, 1984, 2546–20.22
Price indexes (producer), by stage of processing and detailed commodity, monthly rpt, 6762–6
Price indexes (producer), by stage of processing and detailed commodity, monthly 1991, annual rpt, 6764–2
Retail trade sales and inventories, by kind of business, region, and selected State, MSA, and city, monthly rpt, 2413–3
Retail trade sales, inventories, purchases, gross margin, and accounts receivable, by SIC 2- to 4-digit kind of business and form of ownership, 1990, annual rpt, 2413–5
Science, engineering, and technical employment in manufacturing, by field and industry, 1989, triennial rpt, 9627–23
Shipments, trade, use, and firms, for consumer electronics by product, 1991, annual Current Industrial Rpt, 2506–12.20
Shipments, trade, use, and firms, for electronic communications systems and related products, 1991, annual Current Industrial Rpt, 2506–12.35
Soviet Union and US economic and sociodemographic indicators, selected years 1970-90, handbook, 2328–80
Statistical Abstract of US, 1992 annual data compilation, 2324–1.27
Tax (income) returns of corporations, income and tax items by asset size and detailed industry, 1989, annual rpt, 8304–4; 8304–21
see also Video recordings and equipment
see also under By Commodity in the "Index by Categories"

Homeless population
Assistance (financial and nonfinancial) of Fed Govt, 1992 base edition, annual listing, 104–5
Assistance for homeless of Fed Govt by program and agency, and indicators of need, 1990, annual rpt, 14364–1
Assistance for homeless of Fed Govt, program descriptions and funding, by agency and State, FY91, annual GAO rpt, 26104–21
Budget of US, House Budget Committee analysis of Bush Admin proposals and economic assumptions, FY93, 21268–42
Census of Population, 1990: homeless shelter and on-street population counts, assessment of methodology and procedures, GAO rpt, 26119–370
Census of Population, 1990: population characteristics and living arrangements, by county, place, and urban-rural location, State rpt series, 2531–1
Disabled homeless persons group housing, HUD grants by recipient, 1991, press release, 5006–3.79
Disabled homeless persons group housing, HUD grants by recipient, 1992, press release, 5006–3.96
Education services for homeless adults, program activities, and participation, by State, FY88-89, annual rpt, 4804–39
Fed Govt spending in States, by type, program, agency, and State, FY91, annual rpt, 2464–2
Foreign countries disasters, casualties, damage, and aid by US and others, FY91 and trends from FY64, annual rpt, 9914–12
Health condition and access to care, indicators for homeless families, local area study, 1991 conf paper, 4164–2
HHS financial aid, by program, recipient, State, and city, FY91, annual regional listings, 4004–3
Housing (transitional) and support services for homeless persons, HUD grants by community, 1991, press release, 5006–3.80
Housing (transitional) and support services for homeless persons, HUD grants by community, 1992, press release, 5006–3.95
Housing and support services projects for homeless, funding, and clients, by organization, FY87 and FY90, GAO rpt, 26113–593
Housing for homeless persons in rehabilitated single occupancy units, funding and characteristics, by city, FY87-91, GAO rpt, 26113–596
Housing for homeless persons in rehabilitated single occupancy units, HUD grants by community, 1991, press release, 5006–3.82
Housing for homeless persons in rehabilitated single occupancy units, HUD grants by community, 1992, press release, 5006–3.90
HUD support services grants for homeless families in transitional housing, by recipient, 1991, press release, 5006–3.87
Mentally ill homeless persons, HUD rent assistance and support services grants, by recipient, 1992, press release, 5006–3.89
Nutrient intake, body measurements, and blood chemistry of homeless mothers and children, 1989-90 local area study, article, 4042–3.330
Transitional housing and support services for homeless, program outcome relation to client characteristics and services, FY87-90, GAO rpt, 26113–549
Tuberculosis prevention and control among at-risk minority and homeless populations, CDC recommendations, 1992 rpt, 4206–2.55
Urban areas fiscal, economic, and social conditions, as of FY92, biennial rpt, 5184–7
Youth homeless population, health conditions and risk behaviors, 1990 local area study, article, 4042–3.344
Youths entering runaway and homeless centers, by selected characteristics, data compilation, 1992 annual rpt, 6064–6.6

Homemaker services
Employment, earnings, and hours, by SIC 1- to 4-digit industry, monthly 1989-Feb 1992, annual rpt, 6744–4
Labor demand, turnover, and training completions, by detailed occupation, 1990 and projected to 2005, biennial rpt, 6744–3
Occupational Outlook Handbook, 1992-93, biennial rpt, 6744–1

Homesteads
Public lands acreage and grants, by State, FY91 and trends, annual rpt, 5724–1.1
Urban areas fiscal, economic, and social conditions, as of FY92, biennial rpt, 5184–7
Urban Homesteading Program properties, units, and rehabilitation costs by financing source, FY91, annual rpt, 5124–7

Homicide
Alaska occupational injury deaths, by cause, occupation, and industry, early 1980s, article, 4042–3.307
Alcohol-related deaths, by cause, State, and county, annual averages 1979-80 and 1983-85, 4488–10.4
Arrests and criminal case processing through sentencing, cases and duration by disposition and offense, for selected cities, 1988, annual rpt, 6064–27
Black young men homicide and suicide victims, by day of week, and compared to whites and women, 1979-85, article, 4042–3.323
Bombing incidents and casualties, by target, circumstances, and State, 1987-91, annual rpt, 8484–4.1
Court civil and criminal caseloads for Federal district, appeals, and bankruptcy courts, by type of suit and offense, circuit, and district, 1991, annual rpt, 18204–11
Court civil and criminal caseloads for Federal district, appeals, and special courts, 1991, annual rpt, 18204–8
Court criminal case processing in Federal district courts, and dispositions, by offense, district, and offender characteristics, 1989, annual data compilation, 6064–29
Court criminal case processing in Federal district courts, and dispositions, by offense, 1980-91, annual rpt, 6064–31
Crime, criminal justice admin and enforcement, and public opinion, data compilation, 1992 annual rpt, 6064–6
Crime Index by population size and region, and offenses by large city, 1st half 1992, semiannual rpt, 6222–1
Crimes, arrests by offender characteristics, and rates, by offense, and law enforcement employees, by population size and jurisdiction, 1991, annual rpt, 6224–2
Deaths and rates, by cause, age, sex, marital status, race, and State, 1989, US Vital Statistics advance annual rpt, 4146–5.124

Deaths and rates, by cause and age, preliminary 1990-91, US Vital Statistics annual rpt, 4144–7
Deaths and rates, by cause and selected social, demographic, and employment characteristics, 1979-85, natl longitudinal study, 4478–186
Deaths and rates, by cause, provisional data, monthly rpt, 4142–1.2
Deaths and rates, by detailed location, cause, and demographic characteristics, 1989, US Vital Statistics annual rpt, 4144–3
Deaths and rates for homicide, by weapon, circumstances, and victim characteristics, and years of potential life lost, 1980s, article, 4202–7.315
Deaths by cause, age, race, and sex, 1950s-90, with health improvement and disease prevention goals for 1990, annual data compilation, 4144–11
Drug control street-level task forces enforcement activities, impacts on crime, and residents views, local area studies, 1992 rpt, 6068–251
Drug test results at arrest, by drug type, offense, and sex, for selected urban areas, quarterly rpt, 6062–3
Executions of prisoners, by offense and race, 1930-90, annual rpt, 6064–26.6
Hospital trauma center cases and deaths by injury type, costs, and payment sources, with data for selected areas, 1991 hearing, 21348–123
Indian Health Service and tribal facilities and use, and Indians health and other characteristics, by IHS region, 1980s-90, annual chartbook, 4084–7
Indian Health Service facilities, funding, operations, and Indian health and other characteristics, 1950s-91, annual chartbook, 4084–1
Juvenile arrests, by sex, race, disposition, and offense, 1990, 6066–27.8
Military deaths by cause, age, race, and rank, and personnel captured and missing, by service branch, FY91, annual rpt, 3544–40
PHS Commissioned Corps members deaths, by cause, 1965-89, article, 4042–3.316
Prison and parole admissions and releases, sentence length, and time served, by offense and offender characteristics, 1988, annual rpt, 6064–33
Prison deaths in State and Fed Govt facilities, by cause, 1990, quinquennial rpt, 6068–218
Prisoners in Federal and contract instns, by selected characteristics, region, and Federal instn, FY89, annual rpt, 6244–1.1
Prisoners in Federal and State instns, deaths by cause, sex, and State, 1990, annual rpt, 6064–26.3; 6064–26.4
Prisoners in jails, deaths by cause, 1990-91, annual rpt, 6066–25.48
Probation population, by offender characteristics, sentence conditions, whether rearrested, and offense, 1986-89, 6066–19.65
Sentences for Federal crimes, guidelines use and results by offense and district, and Sentencing Commission activities, 1991, annual rpt, 17664–1
Sentences for Federal offenses, guidelines by offense and circumstances, series, 17668–1
States criminal justice systems activities, employment, funding, and data collection, by State, 1970s-91, annual rpt, 6064–40
Statistical Abstract of US, 1992 annual data compilation, 2324–1.5
Terrorism (intl) incidents, casualties, and attacks on US targets, by attack type and country, 1991, annual rpt, 7004–22
Terrorism (intl) incidents, casualties, and attacks on US targets, by attack type and world area, 1991, annual rpt, 7004–13
Victims of crime, compensation and support service programs funding, by offense and State, FY88-90, biennial rpt, 6064–37
Wiretaps authorized, costs, arrests, trials, and convictions, by offense and jurisdiction, 1991, annual rpt, 18204–7
Women in jail, by criminal background and sociodemographic characteristics, with comparisons to men, 1989, 6066–19.66
see also Assaults on police

Homosexuality

AIDS cases and deaths, by whether intravenous drug user and sexual orientation, for selected metro areas, 1992 semiannual conf, 4492–5
AIDS cases at VA health care centers by sex, race, risk factor, and facility, and AIDS prevention and treatment issues, quarterly rpt, 8702–1
AIDS cases by risk group, race, sex, age, State, and MSA, and deaths, quarterly rpt, 4202–9
AIDS virus-related Medicaid claims and payments, by sex, age, risk group, eligibility, and source of care, for Michigan, mid 1980s, article, 4042–3.348
Hepatitis cases by infection source, age, sex, race, and State, and deaths, by strain, 1989 and trends from 1966, 4205–2
Homeless youths health conditions and risk behaviors, 1990 local area study, article, 4042–3.344
Military homosexual personnel discharges by pay grade, tenure, race, sex, and occupation, and investigations, by service branch, 1980s-90, GAO rpt, 26123–392
Population sexual partners in lifetime and past year, by selected characteristics, 1988 local area study, article, 4042–3.311
Public opinion on homosexual relations legality, by respondent characteristics, data compilation, 1992 annual rpt, 6064–6.2
Public opinion on whether homosexuals should hold selected jobs, 1977-91 surveys, GAO rpt, 26123–392.1
Teenage boys AIDS risk behavior, sexual activity, and drug and condom use, 1988, article, 4042–3.313

Honduras

Agricultural trade of US, by detailed commodity and country, 1991, annual rpt, 1524–8
Agricultural trade of US, by detailed commodity and country, 1991, semiannual rpt, 1522–4
AID economic aid to developing countries, obligations and disbursements by country, quarterly rpt, 9912–4
AID loans repayment status and terms by program and country, and status of predecessor agency loans, quarterly rpt, 9912–3
Background Notes, summary social, political, and economic data, 1992 rpt, 7006–2.15
Economic and military aid and loans from US and intl agencies, by program and country, FY46-91, annual rpt, 9914–5
Economic and social conditions of developing countries from 1960s, and Intl Dev Cooperation Agency and AID activities and funding, FY91-93, annual rpt, 9904–4
Economic and social conditions, resources, and trade, and aid, 1992, annual factbook, 9914–14
Economic conditions, policy, and trade practices, by country, 1989-91, annual rpt, 21384–5
Economic indicators for Central America by country, 1969-89, working paper, 9916–13.4
Economic, population, and agricultural data, US and other aid sources, and AID activity, 1991 country rpt, 9916–12.54
Economic, social, political, and geographic summary data, by country, 1992, annual factbook, 9114–2
Exports and imports of US, by commodity and country, 1980-90, world area rpt, 9116–1.5
Exports and imports of US, by transport mode, country, and SITC 1- to 3-digit commodity, 1991, annual rpt, 2424–12
Exports, imports, and balances of US for manufactured goods, by SITC 2-digit commodity and country, quarterly rpt, 2042–35
Exports of US, detailed Schedule B commodities with countries of destination, 1991, annual rpt, 2424–10
Human rights conditions in 170 countries, and US economic and military aid, 1991, annual rpt, 21384–3
Labor conditions, union coverage, and work accidents, 1991 annual country rpt, 6366–4.12
Military aid of US, arms sales, and training programs costs and budget requests, by program, world region, and country, FY91-93, annual rpt, 7144–13
Military spending, arms trade, and force strengths, with govt spending and population, by country, 1979-89, annual rpt, 9824–1
Multinatl US firms and foreign affiliates finances and operations, by industry and country, 1989 benchmark survey, annual rpt, 2704–5
Multinatl US firms foreign affiliates, income statement items by asset size, industry, and country, 1988, biennial article, 8302–2.322
Population size, growth rates, and components of change, by country, projected 1990-2020 and trends from 1950, biennial rpt, 2324–9
Refugee migration, and intl aid programs, by world area and country of origin and asylum, 1991, annual rpt, 7004–15
UN voting record and share of votes in agreement with US, by issue, country, and world area, 1991, annual rpt, 7004–18

Honey and beekeeping

Agricultural Stabilization and Conservation Service honey programs, 1960-90, annual fact sheet, 1806–4.2

Agricultural Stabilization and Conservation Service honey programs, 1960-91, annual fact sheet, 1806-4.12
Agricultural Statistics, 1991, annual rpt, 1004-1
CCC certificate exchange activity, by commodity, biweekly press release, 1802-16
Colony rentals, and pollinated crop value, by crop, 1989, hearings, 25168-78
Exports and imports (agricultural) of US, by detailed commodity and country, 1991, semiannual rpt, 1522-4
Exports and imports between US and outlying areas, by detailed commodity and mode of transport, 1991, annual rpt, 2424-11
Exports and imports of US, by country and detailed commodity, monthly rpt, 2422-12
Exports and imports of US, by Harmonized System 6-digit commodity and country, 1991, annual rpt, 2424-13
Exports, imports, tariffs, and industry operating data for natural sweeteners, 1992 rpt, 9885-8.9
Exports of US, detailed Schedule B commodities with countries of destination, 1991, annual rpt, 2424-10
Farm sector balance sheet, and receipts by detailed commodity, by State, 1986-90, annual rpt, 1544-18
Foreign and US production, prices, trade, and use, FAS periodic circular series, 1925-14
Imports of honey, quarterly situation rpt, 1561-14.2
Production, prices, and stocks of honey, and bee colonies, by State, 1990-91, annual rpt, 1631-6
Production, prices, trade, stocks, and marketing of honey, and CCC loan and distribution activities, monthly rpt, 1311-2

Hong Kong
Agricultural production, prices, and trade, by country, 1980s and forecast 1992, annual world region rpt, 1524-4.3
Agricultural trade by commodity and country, prices, and world market devs, monthly rpt, 1922-12
Agricultural trade of US, by detailed commodity and country, 1991, annual rpt, 1524-8
Agricultural trade of US, by detailed commodity and country, 1991, semiannual rpt, 1522-4
Economic and military aid and loans from US and intl agencies, by program and country, FY46-91, annual rpt, 9914-5
Economic conditions, income, production, prices, employment, and trade, 1992 periodic country rpt, 2046-4.59
Economic conditions, policy, and trade practices, by country, 1989-91, annual rpt, 21384-5
Economic, social, political, and geographic summary data, by country, 1992, annual factbook, 9114-2
Export and import balances of US, and dollar exchange rates, with 5 Asian countries, 1992 semiannual rpt, 8002-14
Exports and imports of China and other Asia countries with US, composition and trends, 1980s-91, article, 9385-1.303
Exports and imports of US, by commodity and country, 1980-90, world area rpt, 9116-1.3
Exports and imports of US, by Harmonized System 6-digit commodity and country, 1991, annual rpt, 2424-13
Exports and imports of US, by selected country, country group, and commodity group, 1991, annual rpt, 2044-37
Exports and imports of US, by transport mode, country, and SITC 1- to 3-digit commodity, 1991, annual rpt, 2424-12
Exports, imports, and balances of US for manufactured goods, by SITC 2-digit commodity and country, quarterly rpt, 2042-35
Exports of US, detailed Schedule B commodities with countries of destination, 1991, annual rpt, 2424-10
Human rights conditions in 170 countries, and US economic and military aid, 1991, annual rpt, 21384-3
Labor conditions, union coverage, and work accidents, 1992 annual country rpt, 6366-4.40
Minerals Yearbook, Vol 3, 1989: foreign country review of production, trade, and policy, by commodity, annual rpt, 5604-35.2
Multinatl US firms and foreign affiliates finances and operations, by industry and country, 1989 benchmark survey, annual rpt, 2704-5
Multinatl US firms foreign affiliates, income statement items by asset size, industry, and country, 1988, biennial article, 8302-2.322
Population size, growth rates, and components of change, by country, projected 1990-2020 and trends from 1950, biennial rpt, 2324-9
Raisin imports of 3 countries, and Chile exports, by country of origin and destination, 1988-91, semiannual article, 1925-34.321
Refugee migration, and intl aid programs, by world area and country of origin and asylum, 1991, annual rpt, 7004-15
Steel trade, by product, country, and customs district, with US industry operating data, 1989-June 1992, semiannual rpt, 9882-15
Sweaters from 3 countries at less than fair value, injury to US industry, investigation supplement, 1992 rpt, 9886-14.363
Tax (estate) returns for nonresident aliens, property and tax data, by estate size and decedent country of residence, 1986, article, 8302-2.310
see also under By Foreign Country in the "Index by Categories"

Honolulu, Hawaii
CPI by component for US city average, and by selected metro area, region, and population size, monthly rpt, 6762-2
Drug abuse indicators for selected metro areas, research results, data collection, and policy issues, 1992 semiannual conf, 4492-5

Hooks, Linda M.
"Impact of Deposit Interest Rate Deregulation on Bank Riskiness", 9379-14.15
"Test of the Stability of Early Warning Models of Bank Failures", 9379-14.18
"What Do Early Warning Models Tell Us About Asset Risk and Bank Failures?", 9379-15.302

Hopkins, Donald R.
"Surveillance of Dracunculiasis, 1981-91", 4202-7.307

Hopkinsville, Ky.
Wages by occupation, and benefits for office and plant workers, 1992 survey, periodic MSA rpt, 6785-3.5

Hops
Agricultural Statistics, 1991, annual rpt, 1004-1
Beer production, stocks, material used, tax-free removals, and taxable removals by State, monthly rpt, 8486-1.1
Exports and imports (agricultural) of US, by commodity and country, bimonthly rpt, 1522-1
Exports and imports (agricultural) of US, by detailed commodity and country, 1991, annual rpt, 1524-8
Exports and imports (agricultural) of US, by detailed commodity and country, 1991, semiannual rpt, 1522-4
Exports and imports between US and outlying areas, by detailed commodity and mode of transport, 1991, annual rpt, 2424-11
Exports and imports of US, by Harmonized System 6-digit commodity and country, 1991, annual rpt, 2424-13
Exports of US, detailed Schedule B commodities with countries of destination, 1991, annual rpt, 2424-10
Farm sector balance sheet, and receipts by detailed commodity, by State, 1986-90, annual rpt, 1544-18
Foreign and US fresh and processed fruit, vegetable, and nut production and trade, FAS monthly circular with articles, 1925-34
Prices received and paid by farmers, by commodity and State, 1991, annual rpt, 1629-5
Prices received by farmers and production value, by detailed crop and State, 1989-91, annual rpt, 1621-2
Production, farms, acreage, and related data, by selected crop and State, monthly rpt, 1621-1
Production, stocks, and use of hops, and US trade by country, monthly rpt, 1313-7
Stocks held by growers, dealers, and brewers, 1990-92, semiannual press release, 1621-8

Hordinsky, Jerry R.
"Tolerance of Beta Blocked Hypertensives During Orthostatic and Altitude Stresses", 7506-10.119

Hormones
Alcohol abuse impacts on sexual function, for men with cirrhosis of liver, 1992 article, 4482-1.307
Bovine somatotropin (bST) dairy industry use, effectiveness of FDA testing for human and animal safety, 1991, GAO rpt, 26131-101
Cancer (breast) recurrence risk by thymidine kinase levels and estrogen receptor status, 1992 article, 4472-1.355
Cancer (breast) risk relation to estrogen replacement therapy use, body mass index, and other risk factors, 1987-89 NYC study, article, 4472-1.350

Carcinogens chemistry, sources, environment and health risks, and regulation, by substance and brand, 1991 annual rpt, 4044–15
Exports and imports of US, by country and detailed commodity, monthly rpt, 2422–12
Exports and imports of US, by Harmonized System 6-digit commodity and country, 1991, annual rpt, 2424–13
Fish and shellfish aquaculture in US and Japan, mgmt, methods, and biological data for selected species, 1989 conf, annual rpt, 2164–15
Menopause treatment with hormone replacement therapy, use, health risks, and research funding, 1992 rpt, 26358–261
Price indexes (producer), by stage of processing and detailed commodity, monthly 1991, annual rpt, 6764–2
Production and sales of synthetic organic chemicals, and manufacturer listing, by product, 1990, annual rpt, 9884–3
Research on population and reproduction, Federal funding by project, FY90, annual listing, 4474–9
Shipments, trade, and use of drugs, by product, 1991, annual Current Industrial Rpt, 2506–8.5
Steroids and other drug use and attitudes of youth, 1975-91 surveys, press release, 4008–116
Steroids use and attitudes of youth, by selected characteristics, 1975-91 surveys, annual rpt, 4494–4
Steroids use, by selected characteristics, 1991 survey, annual rpt series, 4494–5
see also Metabolic and endocrine diseases

Horn, Laura
"Profile of American Eighth-Grade Mathematics and Science Instruction. National Education Longitudinal Study of 1988", 4826–9.13
"Profile of Parents of Eighth Graders. National Education Longitudinal Study of 1988", 4826–9.15

Hornbeck, James W.
"Ecology and Management of Northern Hardwood Forests in New England", 1208–405

Horne, David K.
"Bank Dividend Patterns", 9292–4.302

Hornsby, Andrew P., Jr.
"Future Trends in the Food Stamp Program", 1504–9.1

Horse racing
County Business Patterns, 1989: employment, establishments, and payroll, by SIC 2- to 4-digit industry and county, annual State rpt series, 2326–8
County Business Patterns, 1990: employment, establishments, and payroll, by SIC 2- to 4-digit industry and county, annual State rpt series, 2326–6
Input-output structure of US economy, detailed interindustry transactions for 541 industries, and components of final demand, 1982 benchmark data, 2708–17

Horses
see Horse racing

Horses, wild
see Wildlife and wildlife conservation

Horticulture
Occupational Outlook Handbook, 1992-93, biennial rpt, 6744–1
see also Flowers and nursery products

Hospices
Deaths during 1986, decedents health condition, services use, habits, and social, employment, and other characteristics, 4147–20.19
Employer-provided HMO and fee-for-service plan coverage of hospital care alternatives, 1989, article, 6722–1.302
Hospital deaths of Medicare patients, actual and expected rates by diagnosis, with hospital characteristics, by instn, FY90, annual State rpt series, 4654–14
Insurance (health) coverage and provisions of employee benefit plans, by plan type, for State and local govt employees, 1990, biennial rpt, 6784–21
Medicare admin and research, and HCFA affirmative action and accreditation programs, FY87, annual rpt, 4654–5
Medicare and Medicaid beneficiaries and program operations, 1992, annual fact book, 4654–18
Medicare reimbursement of hospitals under prospective payment system, and effect on services, finances, and beneficiary payments, 1980-91, annual rpt, 17204–2
Medicare reimbursement of hospitals under prospective payment system, methodology, inputs, and data by diagnostic group, 1992 annual rpt, 17204–1

Hospital administration and staff
see Health facilities administration

Hospital Cost and Clinical Research Project
Costs and use of hospitals, data compilation project analyses, series, 4186–6

Hospital Cost and Utilization Project
Costs and use of hospitals, data compilation project analyses, series, 4186–6

Hospitalization
Acute and chronic health conditions, disability, absenteeism, and health services use, by selected characteristics, 1990, annual rpt, 4147–10.182; 4147–10.183
AIDS cases among children, hospital use and charges by instn and patient characteristics, and payment source, 1986-87, 4186–6.16
AIDS patients costs and service use under Medicaid, and service needs, for New Jersey waiver program, 1987-89, article, 4652–1.317
AIDS patients costs and service use under Medicaid, for California, 1984-86, article, 4652–1.301
AIDS virus-related Medicaid claims and payments, by sex, age, risk group, eligibility, and source of care, for Michigan, mid 1980s, article, 4042–3.348
Alcohol-related diagnoses hospital discharges and length of stay, by age, sex, race, and region, 1979-85, 4488–10.5
Alcohol-related disorder hospital discharges and length of stay, by diagnosis, sex, age, and race, 1979-89, 4486–1.16
Cancer patients hospitalized by purpose and body site, case classification effect on charges and length of stay, FY85, article, 4652–1.304
Children (handicapped) with special needs, insurance coverage, and health care services use, by selected characteristics, 1988, 4146–8.216
Consumer products use, injuries by severity, victim age, and detailed product, 1991, annual rpt, 9164–6
Consumer spending, natl income and product account benchmark revisions, 1929-88, 2708–5
Consumer spending, natl income and product accounts, comprehensive accounts and components, *Survey of Current Business*, monthly rpt, 2702–1.25
Crime victimization rates, by victim and offender characteristics, circumstances, and offense, 1990 survey, annual rpt, 6066–3.47
Czechoslovakia health care system, spending, and population health condition indicators, 1988-89, article, 4042–3.363
Data on health condition and care, indicators, 1988 natl survey, CD-ROM, 4147–10.184
Deaths during 1986, decedents health condition, services use, habits, and social, employment, and other characteristics, 4147–20.19
Deaths of Medicare patients, actual and expected rates by diagnosis, with hospital characteristics, by instn, FY90, annual State rpt series, 4654–14
Discharges and length of stay, by diagnosis, patient and instn characteristics, procedure performed, and payment source, 1990, annual rpt, 4147–13.112
Discharges and length of stay by region and diagnosis, and procedures performed, by age and sex, 1990, annual rpt, 4146–8.211
Discharges and length of stay under old and new survey designs, by diagnosis, patient and instn characteristics, and procedure, Jan-Mar 1988, 4147–13.110
Discharges by detailed diagnostic and procedure category, primary diagnosis, and length of stay, by age, sex, and region, 1990, annual rpt, 4147–13.111
Drug abuse indicators for selected metro areas, research results, data collection, and policy issues, 1992 semiannual conf, 4492–5
Drug abuse treatment services costs, effectiveness, and financing issues, 1991 conf papers, 4498–80
Educational attainment relation to health condition and care, indicators by selected characteristics, 1989, 4147–10.180
Expenditures for health care and factors in increase, with background data and foreign comparisons, various periods 1929-90, technical paper, 9366–6.296
Expenditures for health care by funding source, 1990, with trends and indexes by service type from 1960, article, 4652–1.323
Fire-related injuries by severity, and deaths, by ignition source, victim age, and treatment location, 1984-85 local area study, article, 4042–3.340
Foreign and US health data collection and availability, by country, 1991, biennial listing, 4124–8
Health Care Financing Review, provider prices, price inputs and indexes, and labor, quarterly journal, 4652–1.1

Health condition and care indicators, 1950s-90 with health improvement and disease prevention goals for 1990, annual data compilation, 4144–11
Health service areas, indicators of service use, and residents seeking care outside area, under alternative area definitions, 1988-89, 4147–2.113
Heart disease hospitalization and death risk related to alcohol use level, 1990 article, 4482–1.301
Hepatitis cases by infection source, age, sex, race, and State, and deaths, by strain, 1989 and trends from 1966, 4205–2
Hospital financial performance under Medicare, 1977-89, article, 4652–1.315
Indian Health Service and tribal facilities and use, and Indians health and other characteristics, by IHS region, 1980s-90, annual chartbook, 4084–7
Indian Health Service and tribal hospital admissions, length of stay, beds, and births, by facility and service area, FY90-91, annual rpt, 4084–4
Indian Health Service and tribal hospital capacity, use, and births, by area and facility, quarterly rpt, 4082–1
Indian Health Service facilities, funding, operations, and Indian health and other characteristics, 1950s-91, annual chartbook, 4084–1
Indian Health Service, tribal, and contract facilities hospitalization, by diagnosis, age, sex, and service area, FY91, annual rpt, 4084–5
Infant (newborn) intensive care, assessment of alternative case mix groupings intended to improve cost homogeneity, 1985, article, 4652–1.303
Injuries from use of consumer products and related activities, by severity and victim age and sex, 1990, annual rpt, 9164–7
Institutionalized population and persons in group quarters, by sex, race, county, place, and urban-rural location, 1990 Census of Population, State rpt series, 2531–1
Insurance (health) coverage and provisions of employee benefit plans, by plan type, for State and local govt employees, 1990, biennial rpt, 6784–21
Kidney end-stage disease treatment facilities, Medicare enrollment and reimbursement, survival, and patient characteristics, 1984-90, annual rpt, 4654–16
Maternal and child health indicators and services use, by age, race, and poverty status, 1988, 4478–197
Medicaid coverage, funding, and costs, with reform recommendations, mid 1960s-92, 10048–83
Medicaid reimbursement of hospitals, provisions by State, 1991, 17206–2.35
Medicare admin and research, and HCFA affirmative action and accreditation programs, FY87, annual rpt, 4654–5
Medicare and Medicaid beneficiaries and program operations, 1992, annual fact book, 4654–18
Medicare and Medicaid enrollees, benefits, reimbursements, and services use, mid 1960s-90, annual rpt, 4744–3.5; 4744–3.6
Medicare beneficiaries multiple hospital admissions, by reason and characteristics of instn and patient, 1985, 4008–117
Medicare payment of physicians, reforms impacts on services, and monitoring methods, 1992 annual rpt, 4004–34
Medicare payment of physicians, vulnerable beneficiaries services use prior to fee schedule implementation, 1986-90, annual rpt, 17266–1.8
Medicare reimbursement of hospitals under prospective payment system, and effect on services, finances, and beneficiary payments, 1980-91, annual rpt, 17204–2
Medicare reimbursement of hospitals under prospective payment system, diagnosis related group code assignment and effects on care and instn finances, series, 4006–7
Medicare reimbursement of hospitals under prospective payment system, impacts on costs, industry structure and operations, and quality of care, series, 17206–2
Mental health care facilities, staff, and patient characteristics, *Statistical Notes* series, 4506–3
Mental health care facilities, staff, patients, and finances, 1970s-91, biennial rpt, 4094–1
Mental illness (schizophrenia) cases, share by disposition 10 and 30 years after diagnosis, 1992 rpt, 26356–9.4
Mental illness prevalence among adults by diagnosis, and health services use, 1980-83, article, 4042–3.368
Military health care benefits and costs under Civilian Health and Medical Program of Uniformed Services, FY85-90, annual chartbook, 3504–23
Military health care facilities of DOD in US and abroad, admissions, beds, outpatient visits, and births, by service branch, quarterly rpt, 3542–15
OECD members health care costs, hospital use, resources, and economic and health indicators, by country, 1960s-90, article, 4652–1.322
Older persons ability to pay out of pocket health care costs, indicators by selected characteristics, 1984, article, 4742–1.307
Older persons health and long-term care needs, financial issues with background data, 1991 rpt, 10176–1.3
Older persons socioeconomic characteristics, 1900s-90 and projected to 2050, biennial chartbook, 12904–1
Oregon Medicaid waiver proposal for managed care, services priorities dev procedures and issues, with background data, 1992 rpt, 26358–254
Payment sources expected for hospital discharges, by diagnosis, patient characteristics, and region, and procedures performed, 1990, 4146–8.221
Physicians in community and migrant health centers, hospital admitting privileges status and issues, 1991, GAO rpt, 26121–465
Population economic well-being indicators, by selected characteristics and household income and income-to-poverty ratio, 1984, 2546–20.22
Retirees health and other characteristics related to Medicare use and charges 2 years later, 1984, article, 4652–1.319
Soviet Union and US economic and sociodemographic indicators, selected years 1970-90, handbook, 2328–80
Statistical Abstract of US, 1992 annual data compilation, 2324–1.3
Traffic accident injury hospitalization, costs, and discharges, by payment source and State, mid 1980s-90, 7768–122
Transplants of organs, failure and death risk by selected transplant and patient characteristics, 1987-89, annual rpt, 4104–17.1
Trauma center cases and deaths by injury type, costs, and payment sources, with data for selected areas, 1991 hearing, 21348–123
Use and costs of hospitals, data compilation project analyses, series, 4186–6
Use, costs, and structure of private and public health care delivery, indicators, issues, and foreign comparisons, 1960s-80s, technical paper, 8006–6.1
VA activities and programs, and veterans characteristics, FY91, annual rpt, 8604–3
VA health care services, needs, availability, structure, and funding, 1991 compilation of papers, 8608–9
Veterans health care, patients, visits, costs, and operating beds, by VA and contract facility, and region, quarterly rpt, 8602–4
Veterans in VA and non-VA health facilities, by type, FY67-91, annual rpt, 8604–5.3
Vital and Health Statistics series: health care facilities use and labor force, 4147–13
Youth health condition, risk factors, and preventive and treatment services use and availability, 1970s-80s, 26358–234.2; 26358–234.3

Hospitalization insurance
see Health insurance

Hospitals
Allergy and Infectious Diseases Natl Inst activities, grants by recipient and location, and disease cases, FY84-91, annual rpt, 4474–30
Appalachian Regional Commission health care services projects by State, and project listing, 1960s-80s, 9088–38
Closings of hospitals in 1990, operating characteristics, current use, and location, annual rpt, 4004–35
Closings of hospitals relation to hospital and community characteristics, by metro-nonmetro location, 1980-87, article, 4042–3.341
Construction put in place, permits, housing sales, costs, material prices, and employment, quarterly rpt with articles, 2042–1
Construction put in place, value of new public and private structures, by type, monthly rpt, 2382–4
Costs (operating, capital, and total) of hospitals, model estimates of factors affecting variation, 1985-89, article, 4652–1.313
Costs and use of hospitals, data compilation project analyses, series, 4186–6
County Business Patterns, 1989: employment, establishments, and payroll, by SIC 2- to 4-digit industry and county, annual State rpt series, 2326–8
County Business Patterns, 1990: employment, establishments, and payroll, by SIC 2- to 4-digit industry and county, annual State rpt series, 2326–6

CPI by component for US city average, and by selected metro area, region, and population size, monthly rpt, 6762–2
Deaths of Medicare patients, actual and expected rates by diagnosis, with hospital characteristics, by instn, FY90, annual State rpt series, 4654–14
Dental Research Natl Inst research and training grants, by recipient, FY90, annual listing, 4474–19
Employment, earnings, and hours, by SIC 1- to 4-digit industry, monthly 1989-Feb 1992, annual rpt, 6744–4
Employment for hospitals, by occupation, and instn size and control, 1981-88, annual rpt, 4114–12
Employment of minorities and women, by occupation, SIC 1- to 3-digit industry, State, and MSA, 1991, annual rpt, 9244–1
Energy conservation aid of Fed Govt to public and nonprofit private instns, by building type and State, 1991, annual rpt, 3304–15
Energy use in commercial buildings, costs, and conservation, by building characteristics, survey rpt series, 3166–8
Expenditures for health care and factors in costs, with data by payment source and service type, 1960s-90 and projected to 2000, 26306–6.175
Expenditures, use, payment sources, and admin of health care services, with foreign comparisons, 1970s-90, chartbook, 21788–213
Financial performance of hospitals under Medicare, 1977-89, article, 4652–1.315
Govt direct spending and employment, by function and level of govt, selected years 1962-87, 10048–53
Govt employment and payroll, by function, level of govt, and jurisdiction, annual rpt series, 2466–1
Govt finances, by level of govt, State, and for large cities and counties, annual rpt series, 2466–2
Group quarters for hospital nurses and interns, population by race and sex, 1990 Census of Population, State rpt series, 2531–1
Health Care Financing Review, provider prices, price inputs and indexes, and labor, quarterly journal, 4652–1.1
Health condition and care indicators, 1950s-90 with health improvement and disease prevention goals for 1990, annual data compilation, 4144–11
Higher education instn hospital operations, revenue and spending by State and instn control, FY82-90, annual rpt, 4844–6
Indian Health Service and tribal facilities and use, and Indians health and other characteristics, by IHS region, 1980s-90, annual chartbook, 4084–7
Indian Health Service and tribal hospital admissions, length of stay, beds, and births, by facility and service area, FY90-91, annual rpt, 4084–4
Indian Health Service and tribal hospital capacity, use, and births, by area and facility, quarterly rpt, 4082–1
Indian Health Service facilities, funding, operations, and Indian health and other characteristics, 1950s-91, annual chartbook, 4084–1
Input-output structure of US economy, detailed interindustry transactions for 541 industries, and components of final demand, 1982 benchmark data, 2708–17
Kidney end-stage disease treatment facilities approved by Medicare, dialysis and transplant services and ownership, 1991 annual listing, 4654–17
Kidney end-stage disease treatment facilities, Medicare enrollment and reimbursement, survival, and patient characteristics, 1984-90, annual rpt, 4654–16
Labor hourly costs, by component, occupational group, industry div, union coverage, and region, 1992, annual rpt, 6744–21
Labor supply and education of health professionals, by professional and other characteristics, and location, 1960s-92 and projected to 2020, biennial rpt, 4114–8
Medicaid coverage, eligibility, and payment provisions of States, as of March 1992, annual rpt, 4654–19
Medicaid coverage, funding, and costs, with reform recommendations, mid 1960s-92, 10048–83
Medicaid outlay differentials among States, with data by service type and eligibility category, FY89, article, 9373–1.303
Medicaid reimbursement of hospitals, and States rate-setting, adjustments for volume fluctuation, 1991, 17206–2.34
Medicaid reimbursement of hospitals, provisions by State, 1991, 17206–2.35
Medicare admin and research, and HCFA affirmative action and accreditation programs, FY87, annual rpt, 4654–5
Medicare and Medicaid beneficiaries and program operations, 1992, annual fact book, 4654–18
Medicare facilities and beds, from 1967, and by State, 1990, annual rpt, 4744–3.5
Medicare payment of physicians, vulnerable beneficiaries services use prior to fee schedule implementation, 1986-90, annual rpt, 17266–1.8
Medicare providers staffing, services available, and other characteristics, by hospital, FY90, annual State rpt series, 4654–14
Medicare reimbursement of hospitals under prospective payment and alternative systems, HCFA research activities and grants, FY91, annual listing, 4654–10
Medicare reimbursement of hospitals under prospective payment system, analyses of alternative payment plans, series, 17206–1
Medicare reimbursement of hospitals under prospective payment system, and effect on services, finances, and beneficiary payments, 1980-91, annual rpt, 17204–2
Medicare reimbursement of hospitals under prospective payment system, case mix index and payments impacts of cost and charge weights, FY85-87, article, 4652–1.318
Medicare reimbursement of hospitals under prospective payment system, diagnosis related group code assignment and effects on care and instn finances, series, 4006–7
Medicare reimbursement of hospitals under prospective payment system, impacts on costs, industry structure and operations, and quality of care, series, 17206–2
Medicare reimbursement of hospitals under prospective payment system, impacts on operating costs and margins, 1980s, article, 4652–1.312
Medicare reimbursement of hospitals under prospective payment system, methodology, inputs, and data by diagnostic group, 1992 annual rpt, 17204–1
Medicare reimbursement of hospitals under prospective payment system, omitted services impacts on hospital revenue, FY85, article, 4652–1.316
Medicare reimbursement of hospitals under prospective payment system, rural area instns financial performance and impacts of PPS policy changes, 1991 rpt, 26306–6.164
Nonprofit charitable and other tax exempt organizations finances, by category and size of assets and contributions, 1988, annual article, 8302–2.315
Occupational injury and illness rates, by SIC 2- to 4-digit industry, 1989-90, annual rpt, 6844–7
Occupational injury and illness rates, by SIC 2- to 4-digit industry, 1990, annual rpt, 6844–1
OECD members health care costs, hospital use, resources, and economic and health indicators, by country, 1960s-90, article, 4652–1.322
Oregon Medicaid waiver proposal for managed care, services priorities dev procedures and issues, with background data, 1992 rpt, 26358–254
Outpatient and inpatient leading diagnoses and procedures, and costs by setting, 1987, article, 4652–1.314
Outpatient depts and other facilities excluded from Medicare prospective payment system, quality standards and review, certification, accreditation, and licensing, 1991 survey, 17206–2.41
Physicians, by specialty, age, sex, and location of training and practice, 1990, State rpt series, 4116–6
R&D and related funding of Fed Govt to higher education and nonprofit instns, by field, instn, agency, and State, FY90, annual rpt, 9627–17.1
Soviet Union and US economic and sociodemographic indicators, selected years 1970-90, handbook, 2328–80
Statistical Abstract of US, 1992 annual data compilation, 2324–1.3
Tax (income) returns of corporations, income and tax items by asset size and detailed industry, 1989, annual rpt, 8304–4; 8304–21
Tax exempt organizations finances, with data by type, size, State, and for largest organizations, late 1940s-80s, compilation of papers, 8308–35
Tax exempt organizations with unrelated business income, finances by organization type, 1987, article, 8302–2.306
Technological devs effect on labor force, composition, and productivity, 1970s-90 and projected to 2005, industry rpt, 6826–2.8
Wages and employees of hospitals by occupation, and benefits, by region and selected MSA, 1991 survey, 6787–6.254

Workers compensation regulation of physician fees and hospital rates, provisions by State, 1992 annual rpt, 6504–11
see also American Schools and Hospitals Abroad
see also Clinics
see also Emergency medical service
see also Health facilities administration
see also Health maintenance organizations
see also Hospitalization
see also Mental health facilities and services
see also Military health facilities and services
see also Nursing homes
see also Veterans health facilities and services

Hostages
Aircraft hijackings, on-board explosions, and other crimes, US and foreign incidents, 1986-90, annual rpt, 7504–31
Banks robberies and related crimes by State, casualties, and hostages, data compilation, 1992 annual rpt, 6064–6.3
Terrorism (intl) incidents, casualties, and attacks on US targets, by attack type and world area, 1991, annual rpt, 7004–13
US hostages kidnapped overseas, listing as of 1991, annual rpt, 7004–22

Hotels and motels
Alteration and repair spending for commercial and public buildings, by type, size, age, and region, 1989, 2388–4
Business statistics, detailed data for major industries and economic indicators, *Survey of Current Business*, monthly rpt, 2702–1.10
Business statistics, detailed data for major industries and economic indicators, 1960-91, *Survey of Current Business* biennial supplement, 2704–1
Coastal areas construction authorized by permit, by building type, 1970-89, 2176–8.3
Construction put in place, and authorized by region, by type, quarterly rpt, 2042–1.1; 2042–1.3
Construction put in place, value of new public and private structures, by type, monthly rpt, 2382–4
County Business Patterns, 1989: employment, establishments, and payroll, by SIC 2- to 4-digit industry and county, annual State rpt series, 2326–8
County Business Patterns, 1990: employment, establishments, and payroll, by SIC 2- to 4-digit industry and county, annual State rpt series, 2326–6
CPI by component for US city average, and by selected metro area, region, and population size, monthly rpt, 6762–2
Employment and receipts of travel-related industries, 1988, 7556–8.3
Employment, earnings, and hours, by SIC 1- to 4-digit industry, monthly 1989-Feb 1992, annual rpt, 6744–4
Employment of minorities and women, by occupation, SIC 1- to 3-digit industry, State, and MSA, 1991, annual rpt, 9244–1
Energy use in commercial buildings, costs, and conservation, by building characteristics, survey rpt series, 3166–8
Food and alcoholic beverage spending, by place of purchase, 1970-91, annual rpt, 1544–4.5
Foreign travel to US and Canada, market analyses with detailed trip and traveler characteristics, country rpt series, 2906–2
Foreign travelers to US, spending by world area of residence, and economic impacts, by spending category and State, 1989, 2908–28
Forests (natl) recreational use, by type of activity and State, 1991, annual rpt, 1204–17
Homeless persons housing in rehabilitated single occupancy units, funding and characteristics, by city, FY87-91, GAO rpt, 26113–596
Homeless persons housing in rehabilitated single occupancy units, HUD grants by community, 1991, press release, 5006–3.82
Homeless persons housing in rehabilitated single occupancy units, HUD grants by community, 1992, press release, 5006–3.90
Input-output structure of US economy, detailed interindustry transactions for 541 industries, and components of final demand, 1982 benchmark data, 2708–17
Labor productivity, indexes of output, hours, and employment by SIC 2- to 4-digit industry, 1967-90, annual rpt, 6824–1.4
Multinatl firms US affiliates finances and operations, by industry, country of parent firm, and State, 1987, 2708–48
Multinatl US firms and foreign affiliates finances and operations, by industry and country, 1989 benchmark survey, annual rpt, 2704–5
Natl income and product accounts, comprehensive accounts and components, benchmark revisions, 1929-88, 2708–5
Natl income and product accounts, comprehensive accounts and components, *Survey of Current Business*, monthly rpt, 2702–1.29
Occupational injury and illness rates, by SIC 2- to 4-digit industry, 1989-90, annual rpt, 6844–7
Occupational injury and illness rates, by SIC 2- to 4-digit industry, 1990, annual rpt, 6844–1
Occupational Outlook Handbook, 1992-93, biennial rpt, 6744–1
Pacific territories population and housing detailed characteristics, by location, 1990 Census of Population and Housing, series, 2551–8
Palau admin, and social, economic, and govtl data, FY91, annual rpt, 7004–6
Park natl system visits and overnight stays, by park and State, monthly rpt, 5542–4
Park natl system visits and overnight stays, by park and State, 1991, annual rpt, 5544–12
Savings instns failures, inventory of real estate assets available from Resolution Trust Corp, 1991, semiannual listing, 9722–2.1
Savings instns failures, inventory of real estate assets available from Resolution Trust Corp, 1992, semiannual listing, 9722–2.8
Tax (income) returns of corporations, income and tax items by asset size and detailed industry, 1989, annual rpt, 8304–4; 8304–21
Tax (income) returns of partnerships, income statement and balance sheet items, by industry group, 1990, annual article, 8302–2.314
Tax (income) returns of sole proprietorships, income statement items, by industry group, 1990, annual article, 8302–2.317; 8302–2.320
Travel to US, by characteristics of visit and traveler, world area of origin, and US destination, 1991 survey, annual rpt, 2904–12
Washington and Oregon coastal areas tourism and recreation facilities and economic impacts, by county, 1983-88, 5738–40.3

Hotta, S. Steven
"Cardiac Rehabilitation Programs: Heart Transplant, Percutaneous Transluminal Coronary Angioplasty, and Heart Valve Surgery Patients. Health Technology Assessment Report, 1991", 4186–10.8

Houchens, Robert L.
"Within DRG Case Complexity Change in FY90", 17206–2.39

Hourani, Laurel L.
"Concordance of Hospital Cancer Registry- and Physician-Collected Data for Patients with Melanoma", 4472–1.354

Hours of labor
Aircraft flight attendant work hour limitation proposals, with emergency evacuations and related casualties by incident, 1975-89, hearing, 21648–68
Banks in Fed Reserve System, expenses and operations itemized by service, office, and district, 1991, annual rpt, 9364–11
Black women's labor force status, earnings, and other economic status indicators, and compared to whites, various periods 1939-88, 11048–191
Building materials industry finances and operations, by SIC 4-digit industry, selected years 1977-89, article, 2042–1.302
Business owner and business characteristics, for minority- and women-owned firms, by industry, employment and sales size, and form of ownership, 1987 survey, 2328–59
Business statistics, detailed data for major industries and economic indicators, 1960-91, *Survey of Current Business* biennial supplement, 2704–1
Child care arrangements of mothers employed and in school, and costs, by age of child and characteristics of mother, 1988, Current Population Rpt, 2546–20.24
Child care arrangements of younger working mothers, and costs, by selected characteristics, 1988, 6726–2.1
Child support payment and visitation practices of absent fathers, and mothers with custody, by employment and other characteristics, 1988, article, 6722–1.329
Construction employment, earnings, and hours, by selected SIC 2- to 3-digit industry, quarterly rpt, 2042–1.7
Containers (wood) industry productivity trends and technological devs, 1977-89, article, 6722–1.344
Dallas-Fort Worth metro area employment, earnings, hours, and CPI changes, late 1970s-91, annual rpt, 6964–2

Earnings distribution among and within selected groups, by demographic and employment characteristics, late 1960s-80s, article, 6722–1.328
Economic indicators and components, current data and annual trends, monthly rpt, 23842–1.2
Employment and Earnings, detailed data, monthly rpt, 6742–2.3; 6742–2.6
Employment and unemployment current statistics, Monthly Labor Review, 6722–1.1
Employment, earnings, and hours, by selected SIC 1- to 4-digit industry, State, and for 275 MSAs, 1987-92, 6748–81
Employment, unemployment, and labor force characteristics, by region and State, 1991, annual rpt, 6744–7.1; 6744–7.2
Farm hired workers and earnings, by selected characteristics, 1990, 1598–278
Farm labor, wages, hours, and perquisites, by State, monthly rpt, 1631–1
Farm production inputs, output, and productivity, by commodity and region, 1947-90, annual rpt, 1544–17
Fed Govt civilian employees work-years, pay rates, and benefits use and costs, by agency, FY90, annual rpt, 9844–31
Fish fresh and frozen products industry productivity trends and technological devs, 1972-90, article, 6722–1.342
Foreign and US manufacturing labor productivity and unit costs, for 14 countries, 1960s-90, article, 6722–1.304
Foreign countries labor conditions, union coverage, and work accidents, annual country rpt series, 6366–4
Health Care Financing Review, provider prices, price inputs and indexes, and labor, quarterly journal, 4652–1.1
Home-based workers and hours, by worker characteristics, occupational group and industry div, 1991, press release, 6726–1.52
Home-based workers by selected characteristics, and views, 1989, article, 1702–1.307
Hours and earnings, by industry div and major manufacturing group, Monthly Labor Review, 6722–1.2
Hours, employment, and earnings, and other BLS economic indicators, transcripts of BLS Commissioner's monthly testimony, periodic rpt, 23846–4
Hours, employment, and earnings, by SIC 1- to 4-digit industry, monthly 1989-Feb 1992, annual rpt, 6744–4
Hours, employment, and earnings, monthly press release, 6742–5
Hours, employment, earnings, and productivity, by industry div, 1955-91, annual rpt, 204–1.2
Houston metro area employment, earnings, hours, and CPI changes, 1970s-91, annual rpt, 6964–1
Imports and tariff provisions effect on US industries and products, investigations with background financial and operating data, series, 9886–4
Imports injury to US industries from foreign subsidized products and sales at less than fair value, investigations with background financial and operating data, series, 9886–19
Imports injury to US industries from foreign subsidized products, investigations with background financial and operating data, series, 9886–15
Imports injury to US industries from sales at less than fair value, investigations with background financial and operating data, series, 9886–14
Industrial production forecasting performance of Natl Assn of Purchasing Managers manufacturing activity index and production-worker hours, 1980s-91, article, 9371–1.301
Labor force, wages, hours, and payroll costs, by major industry group and demographic characteristics, *Survey of Current Business*, monthly rpt, 2702–1.7
Labor laws enacted, by State, 1991, annual article, 6722–1.309
Labor productivity over business cycle relation to hours worked, model descriptions and results, 1940s-91, article, 9383–6.302
Manufacturing annual survey, 1990: establishments, employment, finances, inventories, and energy use, by SIC 2- to 4-digit industry, 2506–14.2
Manufacturing annual survey, 1990: finances and operations, by SIC 2- and 3-digit industry and State, 2506–14.3
Manufacturing census, 1987: concentration of largest firms measured by value added, and for shipments by SIC 2- and 4-digit industry, subject rpt, 2497–6
Married-couple families income, and spouses labor force participation and hours worked, by income class, 1979 and 1989, 23848–225
Middle Atlantic States manufacturing business outlook, monthly survey rpt, 9387–11
Military in-house commercial activities work-years, by service branch, State, and installation, FY91, annual rpt, 3544–25
Mines (coal) and related operations occupational injuries and incidence, employment, and hours, 1990, annual rpt, 6664–4
Mines (metal) and related operations occupational injuries and incidence, employment, and hours, 1990, annual rpt, 6664–3
Mines (nonmetallic minerals) and related operations occupational injuries and incidence, employment, and hours, 1990, annual rpt, 6664–1
Mines (sand and gravel) and related operations occupational injuries and incidence, employment, and hours, 1990, annual rpt, 6664–2
Mines (stone) and related operations occupational injuries and incidence, employment, and hours, 1990, annual rpt, 6664–5
Mines and mills injuries by circumstances, employment, and hours, by type of operation and State, quarterly rpt, 6662–1
Multinatl US firms and foreign affiliates finances and operations, by industry and country, 1989 benchmark survey, annual rpt, 2704–5
Natl income and product accounts, comprehensive accounts and components, benchmark revisions, 1929-88, 2708–5
Natl income and product accounts, comprehensive accounts and components, *Survey of Current Business*, monthly rpt, 2702–1.29
New England States economic indicators, Fed Reserve 1st District, monthly rpt, 9373–2
Nuts and bolts industry productivity trends and technological devs, 1958-90, article, 6722–1.343
NYC housing supply, occupancy, condition, and household characteristics, by tenure and borough, 1991 triennial survey, 2488–3
OASDI beneficiary data collection system design compared to earlier surveys, with summary results, 1992 article, 4742–1.313
Occupational Outlook Handbook, 1992-93, biennial rpt, 6744–1
Oil and gas industry labor productivity, 1959-87, article, 6722–1.316
Pacific territories population and housing detailed characteristics, by location, 1990 Census of Population and Housing, series, 2551–8
Petrochemicals industries contract labor accidents, injuries, safety programs operations, and employee characteristics, 1986-91, 6608–6
Physicians income, practice revenue, hours worked, and malpractice insurance premiums paid, late 1970s-90, technical paper, 9366–6.296
Physicians time and effort in patient visits, office personnel services, and coding manual use in billing, by selected specialty, 1989 survey, 17266–2.5
Postal employees work hour allocations in offices with high and low workloads, effectiveness, FY89-90, GAO rpt, 26119–379
Railroad accidents caused by human factors, and safety impacts of engineer work scheduling, 1989-90, GAO rpt, 26113–579
Railroad employment, earnings, and hours, by occupation for Class I railroads, 1991, annual table, 9484–5
Railroad industry productivity measures, late 1950s-80s, article, 6722–1.337
Railroad safety violation claims settled, by carrier, FY91, annual rpt, 7604–10
Schedules of work, and workers with flexible hours and shift work by selected characteristics, 1991, press release, 6726–1.50
Southeastern US manufacturing hours and earnings, for 8 States, quarterly press release, 6942–7
Southwestern US employment by industry div, earnings, and hours, by State, monthly rpt, 6962–2
Statistical Abstract of US, 1992 annual data compilation, 2324–1.13
Surgeons preoperative and postoperative visits included in global fee, duration, and setting, for 160 procedures, 1990 survey, 17266–2.6
Survey of Current Business, detailed financial and business data, and economic indicators, monthly rpt, 2702–1.1
Teachers in public schools, demographic and employment characteristics, 1992 annual data compilation, 4824–2.9

Technological devs effect on labor force, composition, and productivity, 1970s-90 and projected to 2005, industry rpt series, 6826–2
Textile mill employment, earnings, and hours, for 8 Southeastern States, quarterly press release, 6942–1
Truck accidents, casualties, and damage, by circumstances and characteristics of persons and vehicles involved, 1989, annual rpt, 7554–9
Truck interstate carriers finances and operations, by district, 1990, annual rpt, 9486–5.2
US attorneys work hours, by type of court and Federal district, FY91, annual rpt, 6004–2.6
Women's labor force status, earnings, and other characteristics, with comparisons to men, fact sheet series, 6564–1
Work stoppages, workers involved, and days idle, 1991 and trends from 1947, annual press release, 6784–12
see also Absenteeism
see also Area wage surveys
see also Earnings, general
see also Earnings, local and regional
see also Earnings, specific industry
see also Industry wage surveys
see also Labor productivity
see also Moonlighting
see also Overtime
see also Part-time employment
see also Temporary and seasonal employment
see also Underemployment
see also Worksharing

Hours of Service Act
Railroad accidents caused by human factors, and safety impacts of engineer work scheduling, 1989-90, GAO rpt, 26113–579

House Administration Committee
Election (presidential) campaign fund contributions from income tax return checkoff, receipts and outlays, mid 1970s-91 and alternative projections to 1993, hearing, 21428–10
Election polling places accessibility and services availability for aged and disabled, by State, 1990 natl elections, hearing, 21428–11

House Aging Committee, Select
Blind persons by age, older blind persons by State, and State rehabilitation services, 1989, 21148–64
Medicare premiums and out-of-pocket costs paid by Medicaid, eligibility and participation, by State, 1991, hearing, 21148–67
OASDI Disability Insurance eligibility determinations by States, caseloads, Federal funding, and State directors views, 1980s-91, hearing, 21148–63
Older persons labor force status, income sources, and reasons for not working, with data by occupation, sex, and race, 1989-90 and projected to 2050, 21148–65
State govt pension funds use to balance budgets, with data for 2 States, 1991 hearing, 21148–66

House Banking, Finance and Urban Affairs Committee
Bank Insurance Fund finances projected under alternative assumptions about bank failures and assets involved, 1991-93, hearing, 21248–166
Banking system reform impacts on consumers, with background data, 1991 hearing, 21248–167
Banking system reform issues, with top instn finances, fiscal impacts, and views of depositors, bankers, and regulators on deposit insurance, 1991 hearings, 21248–168
Banks mergers antitrust issues, with background financial data by State and selected instn, 1991 hearing, 21248–176
Bond (municipal) insurer finances and capital adequacy indicators, by firm and sector, 1986-90, hearing, 21248–173
Coin and medal production by denomination, capacity, and facility improvement funding, by mint, with monetary metals purchases, projected FY92-96, hearing, 21248–164
Credit card issuers disclosure of terms and conditions to consumers, with finances and operations, 1991 hearing, 21248–175
Electric power demand, and industrial and employment impacts of capacity shortfalls and new power plants, by selected State, 1960s-80s and projected to 2000, hearing, 21248–163
Fed Natl Mortgage Assn, Fed Home Loan Mortgage Corp, and FHLBs finances, 1991 hearings, 21248–170
Housing affordability and availability, impacts of govt land use regulations and rent control, and low income housing condition, 1991 hearing, 21248–174
Intl Monetary Fund financial statements, and proposed funding quotas by member country, 1991 hearing, 21248–169
Iraq loans from Banca Nazionale del Lavoro Atlanta office, with purpose and exporting country and company involved, 1991 hearing, 21248–165
Monetary policy objectives of Fed Reserve, analysis and economic performance, 1950s-90 and projected to FY95, hearings, 21248–160
Mortgages FHA-insured by State, financing costs, and loans in force and claims by loan-to-value ratio, 1970s-80s, hearings, 21248–162
Real estate agent fees for mortgage banker referrals, and other issues, consumer views, 1989 survey, hearings, 21248–161
San Antonio, Tex, govt funding for public housing and health, with background data, 1989-91, hearing, 21248–172
Savings instns failure resolution activity of Resolution Trust Corp, brokered deposits, fees, and interest rates by instn and region, as of July 1991, hearing, 21248–171

House Budget Committee
Budget of US, House Budget Committee analysis of Bush Admin proposals and economic assumptions, FY93, 21268–42
Budget of US, House concurrent resolution, with spending and revenue targets, FY93 and projected to FY97, annual rpt, 21264–2
R&D funding of Fed Govt for large-scale projects, issues and impacts on other research, with data for space station and super collider, 1991 hearings, 21268–43
State and local govt fiscal condition, with data by State and selected city, 1991 hearing, 21268–44

House District of Columbia Committee
Govt finances, revenue by source, financial statements, and employment for DC, with income in central city and suburbs compared to other cities, 1991 hearings, 21308–28

House Education and Labor Committee
Discrimination in employment, Civil Rights Act issues, EEOC cases by issue, damage awards, and sexual harassment complaints and company policies, late 1970s-91, hearing, 21348–120
Electronic monitoring of employees, effects on mental and physical health and job satisfaction, for local telephone company workers, 1989, hearings, 21348–122
Hospital trauma center cases and deaths by injury type, costs, and payment sources, with data for selected areas, 1991 hearing, 21348–123
Strikes, replacement workers hired, and impacts on firm operating capacity, with data for NYC, 1984-88, hearing, 21348–121

House Energy and Commerce Committee
Blood banks safety violations, FDA enforcement, disease transmittal, and Houston regional center activities and finances, 1970s-91, hearings, 21368–134
Meat from Canada inspected and rejected, by US port of entry, 1989-91, hearing, 21368–141
Natl Energy Strategy auto fuel economy standards and alternative fuels issues, 1991 hearings, 21368–138
Natl Energy Strategy fossil fuel, electric power, conservation, and pollution reduction issues, 1991 hearings, 21368–136
Natl Energy Strategy nuclear power, waste mgmt, and uranium enrichment issues, 1991 hearings, 21368–137
Natl Energy Strategy Strategic Petroleum Reserve and energy efficiency issues, 1991 hearings, 21368–142
Physicians recently graduating, specialties, school debt, and practice settings, and medical school funding sources, 1970s-91, hearing, 21368–135
Recycling in manufacturing industries, fuel savings, and CO2 emissions reductions, 1988 and projected to 1995, hearing, 21368–140
Recycling of municipal and industrial waste, costs, revenues, and secondary products trade and related energy use and pollution reductions, 1991 hearings, 21368–139

House Foreign Affairs Committee
Economic conditions, policy, and trade practices, by country, 1989-91, annual rpt, 21384–5
Human rights conditions in 170 countries, and US economic and military aid, 1991, annual rpt, 21384–3

House Government Operations Committee
Bank deposit insurance coverage of households and small businesses, and value of insurance to banks by instn, 1970s-90, hearing, 21408–126

Hazardous waste generated, and treated by process, by State, 1987-89 and projected to 2009, hearing, 21408–132
Indian trust fund overpayments and shortages, by account, 1970s-91, hearing, 21408–131
Minority group targeted student aid, higher education instns with awards and funding sources, by instn level and control, 1989/90, hearings, 21408–130
Nuclear weapons facilities of DOE, contractor fees, environmental and safety enforcement activity, and salaries, by contractor and facility, 1987-88, hearing, 21408–127
Occupational repetitive motion injury rates by selected industry, with data for California, 1980s, hearing, 21408–128
State govt budget balances, balances as share of outlays, and costs of Medicaid coverage expansion, FY89-92, hearing, 21408–129

House Hunger Committee, Select
Mississippi poverty, hunger, and public welfare program operations and indicators of need, 1991 hearing, 21968–57
Ohio poverty, hunger, and public welfare program operations and indicators of need, by county, 1991 hearing, 21968–58

House Interior and Insular Affairs Committee
Colorado River Storage Project power sales, and Glen Canyon Dam operations, 1960s-80s, hearing, 21448–47
Japan energy use and imports by fuel type, and gasoline prices, 1970s-80s, hearing, 21448–45
Puerto Rico statehood referendum proposal, with background data on Federal outlays, economic conditions, and finances of corporations with tax-favored status, 1940s-88, hearing, 21448–46

House Merchant Marine and Fisheries Committee
Disease cases and outbreaks related to fish and shellfish consumption, by species, cause, and State, 1969-87, hearing, 21568–51

House of Representatives
Budget of US, authoritative financial statements with appropriations, outlays, and receipts, by category and agency, FY91, annual rpt, 8104–2.2
Budget of US, obligations and authority by function, agency, and program, with summaries and analyses, FY93, annual rpt, 104–2
Buildings and grounds under Capitol Architect supervision, itemized outlays by payee and function, 2nd half FY91, semiannual rpt, 25922–2
Election (general) Federal and non-Federal party transfers, by State, 1992 House and Senate elections, press release, 9276–1.111; 9276–1.113
Election campaign finances and FEC activities, various periods 1975-91, annual rpt, 9274–1
Election campaign finances to FEC, by type of filer, 1990 natl elections, biennial rpt series, 9276–2
Election campaign receipts and spending of congressional candidates, by candidate and State, late 1980s-92, press release, 9276–1.102; 9276–1.103; 9276–1.108; 9276–1.112
Election campaign-related internal communications of firms and assns, spending by organization, location, and candidate, 1991-92, biennial rpt, 9274–3
Election participation since 1930, and voting age population, by sex, age, race, and State, forecast 1992 general elections, Current Population Rpt, 2546–3.170
Former US govt officials representing foreign interests, activities and individuals, FY86-91, GAO rpt, 26123–134
Salaries, expenses, and contingent fund disbursement, detailed listings, quarterly rpt, 21942–1
Statistical Abstract of US, 1992 annual data compilation, 2324–1.8
Votes cast by party, candidate, and State, 1990 natl elections, biennial rpt, 21944–3
see also House Special Publications
see also under names of individual committees (starting with House or Joint)
see also under names of individual subcommittees (starting with Subcommittee)

House Post Office and Civil Service Committee
Census Bur planning for 2000 decennial census and economic statistics program improvement, FY92 budget proposals, hearing, 21628–98
Census of Population, local govts participation in 1990 census and plans for 2000 census, hearing, 21628–100
Census of Population, 1990: data accuracy and enumeration methodology issues, hearing, 21628–97
Census of Population, 1990: data accuracy, evaluation, and adjustment issues, hearing, 21628–99
Census of Population, 1990: data adjustment for undercounts, Commerce Dept decision against adjustment, hearing, 21628–101
Census of Population, 1990: data adjustment for undercounts, evaluation of advisability, with error rates by race and selected city, hearing, 21628–102
Census of Population, 1990: minority group participation in census, effectiveness and quality of outreach and promotional programs, hearing, 21628–103
Census of Population, 2000: planning activities, and review of 1990 census operations, hearing, 21628–104

House Public Works and Transportation Committee
Aircraft flight attendant work hour limitation proposals, with emergency evacuations and related casualties by incident, 1975-89, hearing, 21648–68
Container (intermodal) traffic by mode, use of containers over legal weight for hwy use, and California enforcement activity, 1960s-88, hearing, 21648–65
Hwy funding, costs for completion, and mileage of Federal-aid system, by State, 1989-91 and projected to FY93, 21648–66
Public works financing, use, and condition, 1990 hearing, 21648–67

House Science, Space, and Technology Committee
Arkansas govt science agency research grants and industry sponsors matching funds, and Federal R&D aid to higher education instns, mid 1980s-90, hearing, 21708–131
EC govt subsidies, by industry sector and for Airbus Industrie, by country, 1980s-91, hearing, 21708–132
Materials (critical) industry status and intl competitiveness, with data on semiconductors and advanced ceramics, 1991 hearing, 21708–130

House Small Business Committee
Lumber (softwood) from Canada, costs and production compared to US, 1970s-91, hearing, 21728–78
Rural areas tourism-related and other small businesses, SBA loans, FY86-1st half FY91, hearing, 21728–79

House Special Publications
House of Representatives salaries, expenses, and contingent fund disbursement, detailed listings, quarterly rpt, 21942–1
Votes cast by party, candidate, and State, 1990 natl elections, biennial rpt, 21944–3

House trailers
see Mobile homes

House Veterans' Affairs Committee
Drug (prescription) prices charged to VA and Fed Govt, by manufacturer and drug, 1990-91, hearing, 21768–68
VA benefit overpayment and home loan debt repayment waiver cases and dispositions, FY88-91, hearing, 21768–67

House Ways and Means Committee
AFDC applicants recently unemployed, characteristics of prior job and unemployment insurance eligibility, for Maryland, 1988-90, hearing, 21788–207
Customs inspectors overtime pay issues, 1991 hearing, 21788–214
Fed Govt programs under Committee jurisdiction, finances, operations, and participant characteristics, FY70s-91, annual rpt, 21784–11
Foreign countries economic conditions, policy, and trade practices, by country, 1989-91, annual rpt, 21384–5
Foster care programs of States, Federal funding and children served, by State, 1981-89, hearing, 21788–208
Health care services use, spending, payment sources, and admin, with foreign comparisons, 1970s-90, chartbook, 21788–213
Health care system reform issues, insurance coverage and availability, and foreign comparisons, 1991 hearing, 21788–216
Insurance (health) provided by small businesses, cost and access issues, 1991 hearings, 21788–218
Mexico and US economic and trade impacts of proposed North American Free Trade Agreement, with data on maquiladora plants, 1980s-90, hearings, 21788–210
OASI retirement earnings test, liberalization effect on beneficiaries and Federal revenue, 1991 hearing, 21788–215
Single mothers family income, and impacts of child care, govt and child support payments, taxes, and marriage, with data by State, 1970s-91, 21788–212
Tax (withholding) delinquent accounts of Federal agencies, and compared to other taxpayers, 1990, hearing, 21788–206
Tax enforcement activities and collections of Bur of Alcohol, Tobacco, and Firearms and IRS, 1991 hearing, 21788–217
Tax policy impacts on economic performance and income distribution,

issues and background data, with foreign comparisons, 1991 and trends, 21788–211
Unemployment by selected characteristics, health insurance coverage, and unemployment insurance benefits exhaustion, 1988-91 and projected to 1996, hearing, 21788–209

Household appliances and equipment

American Housing Survey: unit and households characteristics, and unit and neighborhood quality, by MSA location for 11 MSAs, 1987 survey, supplement, 2485–8
American Housing Survey: unit and households detailed characteristics, and unit and neighborhood quality, MSA rpt series, 2485–6
American Housing Survey: unit and households detailed characteristics, and unit and neighborhood quality, 1989, biennial rpt supplement, 2485–13
Apartment completions by region and metro-nonmetro location, and absorption rate, by size and rent class, preliminary 1991, annual Current Housing Rpt, 2484–3
Apartment market absorption rates and characteristics for nonsubsidized furnished and unfurnished units, 1990, annual Current Housing Rpt, 2484–2
Business statistics, detailed data for major industries and economic indicators, *Survey of Current Business*, monthly rpt, 2702–1.16
Business statistics, detailed data for major industries and economic indicators, 1960-91, *Survey of Current Business* biennial supplement, 2704–1
Census of Population and Housing, 1990: summary characteristics, by county, subdiv, and place, State rpt series, 2551–7
Consumer holdings of durable goods, by type, in current and constant dollars, 1925-90, annual article, 2702–1.305
Consumer holdings of durable goods, by type, in current and constant dollars, 1988-91, annual article, 2702–1.327
Consumer spending, natl income and product account benchmark revisions, 1929-88, 2708–5
Consumer spending, natl income and product accounts, comprehensive accounts and components, *Survey of Current Business*, monthly rpt, 2702–1.25
Consumer spending on selected durable goods and services, 1980-90, article, 6722–1.324
County Business Patterns, 1989: employment, establishments, and payroll, by SIC 2- to 4-digit industry and county, annual State rpt series, 2326–8
County Business Patterns, 1990: employment, establishments, and payroll, by SIC 2- to 4-digit industry and county, annual State rpt series, 2326–6
CPI by component for US city average, and by selected metro area, region, and population size, monthly rpt, 6762–2
Department store advertised sale prices and references to competitors prices, and actual consumer savings, 1990-91 local area study, 9408–57
Developing countries energy efficiency improvement issues and devs, with data by end use and country, 1980s-90, 26358–260
Employment, earnings, and hours, by SIC 1- to 4-digit industry, monthly 1989-Feb 1992, annual rpt, 6744–4
Employment of minorities and women, by occupation, SIC 1- to 3-digit industry, State, and MSA, 1991, annual rpt, 9244–1
Energy aid for low income households, coverage and impacts on energy use and costs, selected years FY79-89, 4588–2
Energy conservation technologies for housing and commercial buildings, use, costs, efficiency, and residential tax credits, 1970s-90 and projected to 2010, 26358–259
Energy supply, demand, and prices, by fuel type and end-use sector, projections and underlying assumptions, 1995-2010, annual rpt, 3164–90
Energy use, costs, and conservation, and household and housing characteristics, survey rpt series, 3166–7
Energy use of households, and availability of appliances by type, selected years 1978-90, annual rpt, 3164–74.1
Exports and imports between US and outlying areas, by detailed commodity and mode of transport, 1991, annual rpt, 2424–11
Exports and imports of US, by country and detailed commodity, monthly rpt, 2422–12
Exports and imports of US, by Harmonized System 6-digit commodity and country, 1991, annual rpt, 2424–13
Exports and imports of US, by transport mode, country, and SITC 1- to 3-digit commodity, 1991, annual rpt, 2424–12
Exports, imports, tariffs, and industry operating data for household appliances and heating equipment, 1992 rpt, 9885–9.4
Exports of US, detailed Schedule B commodities with countries of destination, 1991, annual rpt, 2424–10
Home mortgages FHA-insured, financial, property, and borrower characteristics, by metro area, 1991, annual rpt, 5144–24
Home mortgages FHA-insured, financial, property, and borrower characteristics, by State, 1991, annual rpt, 5144–1
Home mortgages FHA-insured, financial, property, and borrower characteristics, 1991, annual rpt, 5144–17; 5144–23
Housing and households summary characteristics, 1989 and trends, chartbook, 2486–2.1
Housing units completed, single and multifamily units by structural and financial characteristics, and location, 1987-91, annual rpt, 2384–1
Injuries from use of consumer products and related activities, by severity and victim age and sex, 1990, annual rpt, 9164–7
Injuries from use of consumer products, by severity, victim age, and detailed product, 1991, annual rpt, 9164–6
Injuries from use of consumer products, related deaths and costs, and recalls by brand, by product type, FY90, annual rpt, 9164–2
Input-output structure of US economy, detailed interindustry transactions for 84 industries, and components of final demand, 1987, annual article, 2702–1.316
Input-output structure of US economy, detailed interindustry transactions for 541 industries, and components of final demand, 1982 benchmark data, 2708–17
Labor productivity, indexes of output, hours, and employment by SIC 2- to 4-digit industry, 1967-90, annual rpt, 6824–1.3
Manufacturing annual survey, 1990: finances and operations, by SIC 2- to 4-digit industry, series, 2506–14
Manufacturing census, 1987: concentration of largest firms measured by value added, and for shipments by SIC 2- and 4-digit industry, subject rpt, 2497–6
Manufacturing census, 1987: shipments of manufacturers products, by customer class and SIC 2- and 4-digit industry, subject rpt, 2497–4
Manufacturing finances and operations, by SIC 2- to 4-digit industry, forecast 1992, annual rpt, 2044–28
Multinatl US firms and foreign affiliates finances and operations, by industry and country, 1989 benchmark survey, annual rpt, 2704–5
NYC housing supply, occupancy, condition, and household characteristics, by tenure and borough, 1991 triennial survey, 2488–3
Occupational injury and illness rates, by SIC 2- to 4-digit industry, 1989-90, annual rpt, 6844–7
Occupational injury and illness rates, by SIC 2- to 4-digit industry, 1990, annual rpt, 6844–1
Pacific territories population and housing detailed characteristics, by location, 1990 Census of Population and Housing, series, 2551–8
Population economic well-being indicators, by selected characteristics and household income and income-to-poverty ratio, 1984, 2546–20.22
Price indexes (producer), by stage of processing and detailed commodity, monthly rpt, 6762–6
Price indexes (producer), by stage of processing and detailed commodity, monthly 1991, annual rpt, 6764–2
Price indexes for department store inventories, by class of item, monthly table, 6762–7
Production of building materials, by type, quarterly rpt, 2042–1.6
Radiation from electronic devices, incidents by type of device, and FDA control activities, 1991, annual rpt, 4064–13
Rental housing units, total, with HUD assistance by program, and eligible for aid, by unit, household, and neighborhood characteristics, and location, 1989, biennial rpt, 5184–11
Retail trade sales and inventories, by kind of business, region, and selected State, MSA, and city, monthly rpt, 2413–3
Retail trade sales, by kind of business, advance monthly rpt, 2413–2
Retail trade sales, inventories, purchases, gross margin, and accounts receivable, by SIC 2- to 4-digit kind of business and form of ownership, 1990, annual rpt, 2413–5

Science, engineering, and technical employment in manufacturing, by field and industry, 1989, triennial rpt, 9627–23
Shipments, trade, use, and firms, for appliances by product, 1991, annual Current Industrial Rpt, 2506–12.16
Shipments, trade, use, and firms, for electric housewares and fans by product, 1991, annual Current Industrial Rpt, 2506–12.15
Single parent families in own and others homes, by financial, housing, and other characteristics, 1989, 2486–1.14
Soviet Union and US economic and sociodemographic indicators, selected years 1970-90, handbook, 2328–80
Statistical Abstract of US, 1992 annual data compilation, 2324–1.26; 2324–1.27
Tax (income) returns of corporations, income and tax items by asset size and detailed industry, 1989, annual rpt, 8304–4; 8304–21
Thefts, and value of property stolen and recovered, by property type, 1991, annual rpt, 6224–2.1
TVA electric power purchases of municipal and cooperative distributors, and prices and use by distributor and consumer sector, monthly rpt, 9802–1
see also Air conditioning
see also Furniture and furnishings
see also Hardware
see also Home video and audio equipment
see also Household supplies and utensils
see also Insulation
see also Lawn and garden equipment
see also Lighting equipment
see also Plumbing and heating
see also Security devices
see also Tools
see also Video recordings and equipment
see also Watches and clocks

Household income
see Personal and household income

Household supplies and utensils
Chemicals (inorganic) production by State, shipments, trade, and use, by product, 1991, annual Current Industrial Rpt, 2506–8.14
Consumer holdings of durable goods, by type, in current and constant dollars, 1925-90, annual article, 2702–1.305
Consumer holdings of durable goods, by type, in current and constant dollars, 1988-91, annual article, 2702–1.327
Consumer spending, natl income and product account benchmark revisions, 1929-88, 2708–5
Consumer spending, natl income and product accounts, comprehensive accounts and components, *Survey of Current Business*, monthly rpt, 2702–1.25
County Business Patterns, 1989: employment, establishments, and payroll, by SIC 2- to 4-digit industry and county, annual State rpt series, 2326–8
County Business Patterns, 1990: employment, establishments, and payroll, by SIC 2- to 4-digit industry and county, annual State rpt series, 2326–6
CPI by component for US city average, and by selected metro area, region, and population size, monthly rpt, 6762–2
Exports and imports between US and outlying areas, by detailed commodity and mode of transport, 1991, annual rpt, 2424–11
Exports and imports of US, by country and detailed commodity, monthly rpt, 2422–12
Exports and imports of US, by Harmonized System 6-digit commodity and country, 1991, annual rpt, 2424–13
Exports and imports of US, by transport mode, country, and SITC 1- to 3-digit commodity, 1991, annual rpt, 2424–12
Exports of US, detailed Schedule B commodities with countries of destination, 1991, annual rpt, 2424–10
Foreign countries market conditions for US textile and apparel exports, with domestic industry operations, country rpt series, 2046–15
Glassware shipments, trade, use, and firms, by product, 1991, annual Current Industrial Rpt, 2506–9.3
Imports detained by FDA, by reason, product, shipper, brand, and country, monthly listing, 4062–2
Injuries from use of consumer products and related activities, by severity and victim age and sex, 1990, annual rpt, 9164–7
Injuries from use of consumer products, by severity, victim age, and detailed product, 1991, annual rpt, 9164–6
Injuries from use of consumer products, related deaths and costs, and recalls by brand, by product type, FY90, annual rpt, 9164–2
Light bulb production, shipments, stocks, trade, and firms, by type, monthly and quarterly Current Industrial Rpts, 2506–12.13; 2506–12.33
Linens production, shipments, trade, inventories, and use, quarterly Current Industrial Rpt, 2506–6.6
Manufacturing annual survey, 1990: finances and operations, by SIC 2- to 4-digit industry, series, 2506–14
Manufacturing census, 1987: concentration of largest firms measured by value added, and for shipments by SIC 2- and 4-digit industry, subject rpt, 2497–6
Manufacturing census, 1987: shipments of manufacturers products, by customer class and SIC 2- and 4-digit industry, subject rpt, 2497–4
Manufacturing finances and operations, by SIC 2- to 4-digit industry, forecast 1992, annual rpt, 2044–28
Occupational injury and illness rates, by SIC 2- to 4-digit industry, 1989-90, annual rpt, 6844–7
Occupational injury and illness rates, by SIC 2- to 4-digit industry, 1990, annual rpt, 6844–1
OECD trade, total and for 4 major countries, and US trade by country, by commodity, 1980-90, world area rpt series, 9116–1
Price indexes (producer), by stage of processing and detailed commodity, monthly rpt, 6762–6
Price indexes (producer), by stage of processing and detailed commodity, monthly 1991, annual rpt, 6764–2
Price indexes for department store inventories, by class of item, monthly table, 6762–7
Textile and apparel exports of US, by product group and country, quarterly rpt, 2042–36
see also Adhesives
see also Hardware
see also Personal care products
see also under By Commodity in the "Index by Categories"

Household workers
see Domestic workers and services

Households
see Families and households

Housewares
see Furniture and furnishings
see Household appliances and equipment
see Household supplies and utensils

Housing
see Apartment houses
see Building permits
see Census of Housing
see Community-based correctional programs
see Condominiums and cooperatives
see Discrimination in housing
see Federal aid to housing
see Foster home care
see Group homes for the handicapped
see Group quarters
see Home-based offices and workers
see Homesteads
see Hotels and motels
see Household appliances and equipment
see Housing (FHA), HUD
see Housing condition and occupancy
see Housing construction
see Housing costs and financing
see Housing energy use
see Housing maintenance and repair
see Housing sales
see Housing supply and requirements
see Housing tenure
see Insulation
see Living arrangements
see Low-income housing
see Military housing
see Mobile homes
see Mortgages
see Prefabricated buildings
see Public housing
see Real estate business
see Relocation
see Rent
see Rent control
see Rent supplements
see Rooming and boarding houses
see Transient housing
see Urban renewal
see Veterans housing
see Wrecking and demolition

Housing (FHA), HUD
American Housing Survey: unit and households detailed characteristics, and unit and neighborhood quality, MSA rpt series, 2485–6
Applications to FHA for new and existing units, refinancings, and housing starts, monthly rpt, 5142–44
Financial statements, audits, and activities of FHA, FY90-91, annual rpt, 5144–26
Govt Natl Mortgage Assn finances, and mortgage-backed securities program, FY91, annual rpt, 5144–6
Home mortgages FHA-insured, and foreclosures, by State and county, 1991 and cumulative from 1934, annual rpt, 5144–15

Home mortgages FHA-insured, financial, property, and borrower characteristics, by State, 1991, annual rpt, 5144–1
Home mortgages FHA-insured, financial, property, and borrower characteristics, 1991, annual rpt, 5144–17; 5144–23
Housing units (1-family) sold and sales price by type of financing, monthly rpt, quarterly tables, 2382–3.2
Housing units completed, single and multifamily units by structural and financial characteristics, and location, 1987-91, annual rpt, 2384–1
Insured mortgages for 1-family units, by loan type and mortgage characteristics, quarterly rpt, 5142–45
Insured mortgages secondary market prices and yields, and interest rates on construction and conventional mortgage loans, by region, monthly press release, 5142–20
Mortgage applications, dispositions, and secondary loan market sales, by purpose, lender type, and applicant and neighborhood characteristics, 1991, article, 9362–1.307
Mortgage loan activity, by type of lender, loan, and mortgaged property, monthly press release, 5142–18
Mortgage loan activity, by type of lender, loan, and mortgaged property, quarterly press release, 5142–30
Mortgage originations, by State, 1982-90, annual press release, 5144–21
Mortgages FHA-insured by State, financing costs, and loans in force and claims by loan-to-value ratio, 1970s-80s, hearings, 21248–162
Mortgages FHA-insured, financial, property, and borrower characteristics, by metro area, 1991, annual rpt, 5144–24
Mortgages FHA-insured, financial, property, and borrower characteristics, by State, 1991, annual rpt, 5144–25
Mortgages FHA-insured, insurance fund financial condition with background housing and mortgage data, 1970s-90s, hearing, 25248–128
Natl income and product accounts, comprehensive accounts and components, benchmark revisions, 1929-88, 2708–5
Natl income and product accounts, comprehensive accounts and components, *Survey of Current Business*, monthly rpt, 2702–1.26
Rental housing units, total, with HUD assistance by program, and eligible for aid, by unit, household, and neighborhood characteristics, and location, 1989, biennial rpt, 5184–11

Housing and Urban Development Department
see Department of Housing and Urban Development

Housing census
see Census of Housing
see Census of Population and Housing

Housing condition and occupancy
American Housing Survey: unit and household characteristics of recent movers, and reason for move, by tenure, 1989, 2486–1.12
American Housing Survey: unit and households characteristics, and unit and neighborhood quality, by MSA location for 11 MSAs, 1987 survey, supplement, 2485–8
American Housing Survey: unit and households characteristics, MSA fact sheet series, 2485–11
American Housing Survey: unit and households detailed characteristics, and unit and neighborhood quality, MSA rpt series, 2485–6
American Housing Survey: unit and households detailed characteristics, and unit and neighborhood quality, 1989, biennial rpt supplement, 2485–13
American Housing Survey: unit and households detailed characteristics, and unit and neighborhood quality, 1989, wallchart, 2485–12
Apartment and condominium completions and absorption rates, by size and price class, preliminary 1991, annual Current Housing Rpt, 2484–3
Apartment market absorption rates and characteristics for nonsubsidized furnished and unfurnished units, 1990, annual Current Housing Rpt, 2484–2
Arson incidents by whether structure occupied, property value, and arrest rate, by property type, 1991, annual rpt, 6224–2.1
Bombing incidents and casualties, by target, circumstances, and State, 1987-91, annual rpt, 8484–4.1
Bombing incidents, casualties, and damage, by target, circumstances, and State, 1991, annual rpt, 6224–5
Census of Housing, 1990: inventory, occupancy, and costs, State fact sheet series, 2326–21
Census of Housing, 1990: summary unit characteristics, by householder race and age, county, place, and urban-rural location, State rpt series, 2471–1
Census of Population and Housing, 1990: detailed geographic coverage, State CD-ROM series, 2551–9
Census of Population and Housing, 1990: population and housing characteristics, detailed geographic coverage, State CD-ROM series, 2551–10
Census of Population and Housing, 1990: summary characteristics, by county, subdiv, and place, State rpt series, 2551–7
Census of Population and Housing, 1990: summary characteristics, households, and land area, by county, subdiv, and place, State rpt series, 2551–1
Crime victimization rates, by victim and offender characteristics, circumstances, and offense, 1990 survey, annual rpt, 6066–3.47
Data on population and housing, and policy issues, fact sheet series, 2326–17
Economic indicators and components, current data and annual trends, monthly rpt, 23842–1.3
Energy use, costs, and conservation, and household and housing characteristics, survey rpt series, 3166–7
Home mortgages FHA-insured, financial, property, and borrower characteristics, by metro area, 1991, annual rpt, 5144–24
Home mortgages FHA-insured, financial, property, and borrower characteristics, by State, 1991, annual rpt, 5144–1; 5144–25
Home mortgages FHA-insured, financial, property, and borrower characteristics, 1991, annual rpt, 5144–17; 5144–23
Households and family characteristics, by location, 1991, annual Current Population Rpt, 2546–1.457
Housing and households summary characteristics, 1989 and trends, chartbook, 2486–2.1
Low income housing condition, affordability and availability indicators, and impacts of govt land use regulations and rent control, 1991 hearing, 21248–174
New England construction, real estate, and other economic performance indicators, compared to Texas and other areas, 1970s-91, article, 9373–1.302
New single and multifamily units, by structural and financial characteristics, inside-outside MSAs, and region, 1987-91, annual rpt, 2384–1
North Central States, FHLB 7th District housing vacancy rates for single and multifamily units and mobile homes, by ZIP code, annual MSA rpt series, 9304–18
NYC housing supply, occupancy, condition, and household characteristics, by tenure and borough, 1991 triennial survey, 2488–3
Pacific territories population and housing detailed characteristics, by location, 1990 Census of Population and Housing, series, 2551–8
Paint (lead-based) abatement programs for low- and moderate-income housing, HUD grants to public agencies, 1992 press release, 5006–3.102
Population economic well-being indicators, by selected characteristics and household income and income-to-poverty ratio, 1984, 2546–20.22
Population size and demographic changes impacts on economic conditions, with background data, 1950s-80s and projected to 2010, 23848–226
Prices of housing and adjustments for quality changes, analysis of factors, 1950s-80s, working paper, 9373–27.7
Public housing for aged, placement of younger mentally disabled tenants, behavioral problems, and services, 1990 survey, GAO rpt, 26113–590
Radon and other radionuclide levels in air, water, soil, and uranium mill tailings, by site and region, 1950s-80s, compilation of papers, 5668–126
Rental housing units, total, with HUD assistance by program, and eligible for aid, by unit, household, and neighborhood characteristics, and location, 1989, biennial rpt, 5184–11
Savings instns failures, inventory of real estate assets available from Resolution Trust Corp, 1991, semiannual listing, 9722–2.2; 9722–2.3; 9722–2.4; 9722–2.5; 9722–2.6
Savings instns failures, inventory of real estate assets available from Resolution Trust Corp, 1992, semiannual listing, 9722–2.9; 9722–2.10; 9722–2.11; 9722–2.12; 9722–2.13
Single parent families in own and others homes, by financial, housing, and other characteristics, 1989, 2486–1.14

Single person and nonfamily households social, economic and housing characteristics, by tenure, 1989, 2486–1.15
Soviet Union and US economic and sociodemographic indicators, selected years 1970-90, handbook, 2328–80
Statistical Abstract of US, 1992 annual data compilation, 2324–1.26
Taxes, spending, and govt efficiency, public opinion by respondent characteristics, 1992 survey, annual rpt, 10044–2
Vacancy rates for metro areas with significant changes, by tenure, 1989 and 1991, fact sheet, 2326–17.51
Vacant housing characteristics and costs, and occupancy and vacancy rates, by region and metro-nonmetro location, quarterly rpt, 2482–1
Vacant housing characteristics, and occupancy and vacancy rates, by tenure and location, 1960s-91, annual rpt, 2484–1
West Central States, FHLB 10th District housing vacancy rates for single and multifamily units and mobile homes, by ZIP code, annual MSA rpt series, 9304–22
Western States, FHLB 12th District housing vacancy rates for single and multifamily units and mobile homes, by ZIP code, annual MSA rpt series, 9304–21
Wiretaps authorized, costs, arrests, trials, and convictions, by offense and jurisdiction, 1991, annual rpt, 18204–7
see also Families and households
see also Furniture and furnishings
see also Household appliances and equipment
see also Housing maintenance and repair
see also Housing tenure
see also Insulation
see also Plumbing and heating
see also Rent
see also Rent supplements
see also Transient housing

Housing construction

Apartment and condominium completions and absorption rates, by size and price class, preliminary 1991, annual Current Housing Rpt, 2484–3
Apartment and condominium completions by rent class and sales price, and market absorption rates, quarterly rpt, 2482–2
Apartment units completed, by type and for units under Federal subsidy, 1970-90, annual rpt, 2484–2
Business activity indicators, 1990, annual rpt, 9364–5.9
Business statistics, detailed data for major industries and economic indicators, *Survey of Current Business*, monthly rpt, 2702–1.5
Business statistics, detailed data for major industries and economic indicators, 1960-91, *Survey of Current Business* biennial supplement, 2704–1
Coastal areas construction authorized by permit, by building type, 1970-89, 2176–8.3
Economic indicators and components, and Fed Reserve 4th District business and financial conditions, monthly chartbook, 9377–10
Economic indicators and components, current data and annual trends, monthly rpt, 23842–1.3
Economic indicators, monthly rpt, 9362–1.2
Employment, earnings, and hours, by SIC 1- to 4-digit industry, monthly 1989-Feb 1992, annual rpt, 6744–4
Farmland value, rent, taxes, foreign ownership, and transfers by probable use and lender type, with data by region and State, 1981-92, article, 1561–16.302
Fed Govt financial and nonfinancial domestic aid, 1992 base edition, annual listing, 104–5
Finances and operations, by SIC 2- to 4-digit industry, forecast 1992, annual rpt, 2044–28
Germany construction activity in former East and West regions, 1991, article, 2042–1.306
Housing and households summary characteristics, 1989 and trends, chartbook, 2486–2.1
Indian (Navajo and Hopi) relocation program activities and caseloads, monthly rpt, 16002–1
Input-output structure of US economy, detailed interindustry transactions for 541 industries, and components of final demand, 1982 benchmark data, 2708–17
Japan construction activity, by type and region, selected years 1985-91, article, 2042–1.307
Loan rates for FHA and conventional construction loans by region, and builders with declining, stable, and advancing trends in new plans and unsold units, monthly press release, 5142–20
Low income housing developers tax credits, subsidies, project and tenant characteristics, and investor returns, 1987-88, 5188–133
Low income rental housing and homeownership assistance, HUD grants by recipient, FY92, press release, 5006–3.86
Mortgage applications to FHA for new and existing units, refinancings, and housing starts, monthly rpt, 5142–44
Mortgage loan activity, by type of lender, loan, and mortgaged property, monthly press release, 5142–18
Mortgage loan activity, by type of lender, loan, and mortgaged property, quarterly press release, 5142–30
Natl income and product accounts, comprehensive accounts and components, benchmark revisions, 1929-88, 2708–5
Natl income and product accounts, comprehensive accounts and components, *Survey of Current Business*, monthly rpt, 2702–1.24; 2702–1.31
New construction (public and private) put in place, value by type, monthly rpt, 2382–4
New England States economic indicators, Fed Reserve 1st District, monthly rpt, 9373–2
New housing construction and sales by region, permits by State and MSA, costs, and material prices, quarterly rpt with articles, 2042–1
New housing starts and authorizations, 1959-91 with trends from 1929, annual rpt, 204–1.3
New housing starts and completions authorized by building permits in 40 MSAs, quarterly rpt, 2382–9
New housing starts, by units per structure and metro-nonmetro location, and mobile home placements and prices, by region, monthly rpt, 2382–1
New housing units authorized, by region, State, selected MSA, and permit-issuing place, monthly rpt, 2382–5
New housing units authorized, by State, MSA, and permit-issuing place, 1991, annual rpt, 2384–2
New housing units completed and under construction, by units per structure, region, and inside-outside MSAs, monthly rpt, 2382–2
New single and multifamily units, by structural and financial characteristics, inside-outside MSAs, and region, 1987-91, annual rpt, 2384–1
New single-family houses sold and for sale, by price, stage of construction, months on market, and region, monthly rpt, 2382–3
North Central States, FHLB 7th District housing vacancy rates for single and multifamily units and mobile homes, by ZIP code, annual MSA rpt series, 9304–18
Occupational injury and illness rates and lost workdays, for selected industries, 1978-89, compilation of papers, 6728–41
Occupational injury and illness rates, by SIC 2- to 4-digit industry, 1989-90, annual rpt, 6844–7
Occupational injury and illness rates, by SIC 2- to 4-digit industry, 1990, annual rpt, 6844–1
Pacific Northwest population, households, employment, income, fuel prices, and electricity demand, alternative forecasts 1991-2010, annual rpt, 3224–3.3
Southeastern States, Fed Reserve 6th District, economic indicators by State and MSA, quarterly rpt, 9371–14
Southeastern States, FHLB 4th District, employment and housing indicators by State, quarterly rpt, 9302–36
Soviet Union construction activity and building materials production, 1985-92, article, 2042–1.301
Statistical Abstract of US, 1992 annual data compilation, 2324–1.26
Supply and demand for housing and commercial real estate, market activity indicators by region, quarterly rpt, 9292–6
West Central States, FHLB 10th District housing vacancy rates for single and multifamily units and mobile homes, by ZIP code, annual MSA rpt series, 9304–22
Western States, FHLB 12th District housing vacancy rates for single and multifamily units and mobile homes, by ZIP code, annual MSA rpt series, 9304–21
see also Building materials
see also Federal aid to housing
see also Housing condition and occupancy
see also Housing costs and financing
see also Housing maintenance and repair
see also Insulation
see also Prefabricated buildings
see also Property value

see also Public housing
see also Wrecking and demolition

Housing costs and financing

Affordability and availability of housing, impacts of govt land use regulations and rent control, and low income housing condition, 1991 hearing, 21248–174
Alteration and repair of owner-occupied homes, costs and structural, household, financial, and project characteristics, 1987, 2486–1.13
Alteration and repair spending for housing, by type, tenure, region, and other characteristics, quarterly rpt, 2382–7
American Housing Survey: unit and household characteristics of recent movers, and reason for move, by tenure, 1989, 2486–1.12
American Housing Survey: unit and households characteristics, and unit and neighborhood quality, by MSA location for 11 MSAs, 1987 survey, supplement, 2485–8
American Housing Survey: unit and households characteristics, MSA fact sheet series, 2485–11
American Housing Survey: unit and households detailed characteristics, and unit and neighborhood quality, MSA rpt series, 2485–6
American Housing Survey: unit and households detailed characteristics, and unit and neighborhood quality, 1989, biennial rpt supplement, 2485–13
American Housing Survey: unit and households detailed characteristics, and unit and neighborhood quality, 1989, wallchart, 2485–12
Appreciation rate of housing prices, alternative models description and results, 1992 working paper, 9387–8.284
Business statistics, detailed data for major industries and economic indicators, 1960-91, *Survey of Current Business* biennial supplement, 2704–1
Census of Housing, 1990: inventory, occupancy, and costs, State fact sheet series, 2326–21
Census of Housing, 1990: summary unit characteristics, by householder race and age, county, place, and urban-rural location, State rpt series, 2471–1
Census of Population and Housing, 1990: detailed geographic coverage, State CD-ROM series, 2551–9
Census of Population and Housing, 1990: population and housing characteristics, detailed geographic coverage, State CD-ROM series, 2551–10
Census of Population and Housing, 1990: summary characteristics, by county, subdiv, and place, State rpt series, 2551–7
Census of Population and Housing, 1990: summary characteristics, households, and land area, by county, subdiv, and place, State rpt series, 2551–1
Condominium completions and absorption rates, by size and price class, preliminary 1991, annual Current Housing Rpt, 2484–3
Condominium completions by rent class and sales price, and market absorption rates, quarterly rpt, 2482–2
Consumer Expenditure Survey, spending by category, and income, by selected household characteristics, 1991, annual press release, 6726–1.53
Consumer Expenditure Survey, spending by category, selected household characteristics, and region, quarterly rpt, 6762–14
Consumer spending, natl income and product account benchmark revisions, 1929-88, 2708–5
Consumer spending, natl income and product accounts, comprehensive accounts and components, *Survey of Current Business*, monthly rpt, 2702–1.25
Costs of housing exceeding 28% of gross income, families income by source and expenses by type, by tenure and other characteristics, 1989, article, 1702–1.304
CPI by component for US city average, and by selected metro area, region, and population size, monthly rpt, 6762–2
CPI changes for selected items, 1982-91, annual article, 6722–1.322
Developing countries economic and social conditions from 1960s, and Intl Dev Cooperation Agency and AID activities and funding, FY91-93, annual rpt, 9904–4
Discrimination in housing rental and sales, for blacks and Hispanics in selected metro areas, 1989 study, series, 5186–16
Economic indicators and components, and Fed Reserve 4th District business and financial conditions, monthly chartbook, 9377–10
Economic indicators and components, current data and annual trends, monthly rpt, 23842–1.4
Energy use, costs, and conservation, and household and housing characteristics, survey rpt series, 3166–7
Equity returns counted as income, and other income definitions effects on household income and poverty rate, by recipient characteristics, 1991, annual Current Population Rpt, 2546–6.78
Flow-of-funds accounts, savings, investments, and credit statements, quarterly rpt, 9365–3.3
FmHA activities, and loans and grants by program and State, FY91 and trends from FY70, annual rpt, 1184–17
FmHA loans and borrower supervision activities in farm and housing programs, by type and State, monthly rpt, 1182–1
Food stamp recipient household size, composition, income, and income and deductions allowed, summer 1989, annual rpt, 1364–8
Foreign countries living costs, State Dept indexes, housing allowances, and hardship differentials by country and major city, quarterly rpt, 7002–7
Govt spending, coverage, and benefits for social welfare programs, late 1930s-90, annual rpt, 4744–3.1
Govt spending for public welfare programs, by program type and level of govt, FY65-89, annual article, 4742–1.302
Home mortgages FHA-insured, financial, property, and borrower characteristics, by metro area, 1991, annual rpt, 5144–24
Home mortgages FHA-insured, financial, property, and borrower characteristics, by State, 1991, annual rpt, 5144–1; 5144–25
Home mortgages FHA-insured, financial, property, and borrower characteristics, 1991, annual rpt, 5144–17; 5144–23
Homeownership values, reasons, and barriers, views by race and tenure, 1992 survey, 9478–1
Housing and households summary characteristics, 1989 and trends, chartbook, 2486–2.1
Housing finance studies, technical paper series, 8436–1
Low income housing developers tax credits, subsidies, project and tenant characteristics, and investor returns, 1987-88, 5188–133
Mobile home placements and prices by State, and dealer inventories, by region, monthly rpt, 2382–1
Natl income and product accounts and components, *Survey of Current Business*, monthly rpt, 2702–1.23
New construction (public and private) put in place, value by type, monthly rpt, 2382–4
New England construction, real estate, and other economic performance indicators, compared to Texas and other areas, 1970s-91, article, 9373–1.302
New England States economic indicators, Fed Reserve 1st District, monthly rpt, 9373–2
New housing construction and sales by region, permits by State and MSA, costs, and material prices, quarterly rpt with articles, 2042–1
New single and multifamily units, by structural and financial characteristics, inside-outside MSAs, and region, 1987-91, annual rpt, 2384–1
New single-family houses sold and for sale, by price, stage of construction, months on market, and region, monthly rpt, 2382–3
NYC housing supply, occupancy, condition, and household characteristics, by tenure and borough, 1991 triennial survey, 2488–3
Older persons socioeconomic characteristics, 1900s-90 and projected to 2050, biennial chartbook, 12904–1
Pacific territories population and housing detailed characteristics, by location, 1990 Census of Population and Housing, series, 2551–8
Population and housing summary data and trends, 1970s-91, Current Population Rpt, fact sheet, 2546–2.163
Population size and demographic changes impacts on economic conditions, with background data, 1950s-80s and projected to 2010, 23848–226
Prices (median) of all and previously occupied 1-family homes, by region and State, 1989-91, annual rpt, 9444–2.3
Prices (real) of housing, projected under alternative population assumptions, 1991-2000, article, 9381–1.305
Prices of housing and adjustments for quality changes, analysis of factors, 1950s-80s, working paper, 9373–27.7
Savings instns failures, inventory of real estate assets available from Resolution Trust Corp, 1991, semiannual listing, 9722–2.2; 9722–2.3; 9722–2.4; 9722–2.5; 9722–2.6

Savings instns failures, inventory of real estate assets available from Resolution Trust Corp, 1992, semiannual listing, 9722–2.9; 9722–2.10; 9722–2.11; 9722–2.12; 9722–2.13
Single parent families in own and others homes, by financial, housing, and other characteristics, 1989, 2486–1.14
Single person and nonfamily households social, economic and housing characteristics, by tenure, 1989, 2486–1.15
Statistical Abstract of US, 1992 annual data compilation, 2324–1.26
Tax (income) returns of individuals with foreign earned income, income and tax items by income level and occupation, 1987, article, 8302–2.301
Vacant housing characteristics and costs, and occupancy and vacancy rates, by region and metro-nonmetro location, quarterly rpt, 2482–1
Vacant housing characteristics, and occupancy and vacancy rates, by tenure and location, 1960s-91, annual rpt, 2484–1
see also Federal aid to housing
see also Housing sales
see also Mortgages
see also Property value
see also Rent
see also Rent supplements

Housing Discrimination Study
Racial discrimination in housing rental and sales, for blacks and Hispanics in selected metro areas, 1989 study, series, 5186–16

Housing energy use
American Housing Survey: unit and households characteristics, MSA fact sheet series, 2485–11
American Housing Survey: unit and households detailed characteristics, and unit and neighborhood quality, MSA rpt series, 2485–6
American Housing Survey: unit and households detailed characteristics, and unit and neighborhood quality, 1989, wallchart, 2485–12
Apartment completions by region and metro-nonmetro location, and absorption rate, by size and rent class, preliminary 1991, annual Current Housing Rpt, 2484–3
Apartment market absorption rates, by whether utilities included in rent, 1990, annual Current Housing Rpt, 2484–2
Bonneville Power Admin mgmt of Fed Columbia River Power System, finances and sales, summary data, quarterly rpt, 3222–2
Business statistics, detailed data for major industries and economic indicators, *Survey of Current Business*, monthly rpt, 2702–1.12
Census of Population and Housing, 1990: population and housing characteristics, detailed geographic coverage, State CD-ROM series, 2551–10
Census of Population and Housing, 1990: summary characteristics, by county, subdiv, and place, State rpt series, 2551–7
Coal and coke supply, demand, movements, prices, and stocks, by end-use sector and State, quarterly rpt, 3162–37
Coal production, stocks, and shipments, by State of origin and destination, end-use sector, and mode of transport, quarterly rpt, 3162–8
Conservation of energy for housing and commercial buildings, technologies use, costs, efficiency, and residential tax credits, 1970s-90 and projected to 2010, 26358–259
Conservation programs of electric utilities, collaboration between utilities and interest groups, and effects on costs, 1992 rpt, 3308–104
Consumer spending, natl income and product account benchmark revisions, 1929-88, 2708–5
Consumer spending, natl income and product accounts, comprehensive accounts and components, *Survey of Current Business*, monthly rpt, 2702–1.25
CPI by component for US city average, and by selected metro area, region, and population size, monthly rpt, 6762–2
Developing countries energy efficiency improvement issues and devs, with data by end use and country, 1980s-90, 26358–260
Electric power billings for housing, and rankings, by State, as of Jan 1991, annual rpt, 1244–1.6
Electric power plants production, capacity, sales, and fuel stocks, use, and costs, by State, 1986-90, annual rpt, 3164–11
Electric power plants production, fuel use, stocks, and costs by fuel type, and sales, by State, monthly rpt, with articles, 3162–35
Electric power sales and revenue, by end-use sector, consumption level, and utility, 1990, annual rpt, 3164–91
Electric utilities finances and operations, detailed data for publicly owned firms, 1990, annual rpt, 3164–24
Electric utilities privately owned, finances and operations, detailed data, 1990, annual rpt, 3164–23
Energy supply, demand, and prices, by fuel type and end-use sector, alternative projections by region, 1990-2010, annual rpt, 3164–96
Energy supply, demand, and prices, by fuel type and end-use sector, alternative projections 1990-2010, annual rpt, 3164–75
Energy supply, demand, and prices, by fuel type and end-use sector, projections and underlying assumptions, 1995-2010, annual rpt, 3164–90
Energy supply, demand, and prices, by fuel type and end-use sector, with foreign comparisons, 1981-90, annual fact book, 3164–76
Energy supply, demand, and prices, by fuel type and end-use sector, with foreign comparisons, 1991 and trends from 1949, annual rpt, 3164–74
Energy supply, demand, and prices, by fuel type, end-use sector, and country, detailed data, monthly rpt with articles, 3162–24
Energy supply, demand, and prices, by fuel type, end-use sector, and country, detailed data, monthly 1973-88, 3168–123
Energy supply, demand, and prices, forecasts by resource type, quarterly rpt, 3162–34
Energy use, by detailed fuel type, end-use sector, and State, 1960-90, State Energy Data System annual rpt, 3164–39
Energy use, costs, and conservation, and household and housing characteristics, survey rpt series, 3166–7
Energy use in transportation and other sectors, by fuel type, 1970s-90, annual rpt, 3304–5
Foreign and US energy supply and demand, by major fuel and end-use sector, 1950s-87 and forecast to 1995, 3166–6.58
Fuel oil and kerosene sales and deliveries, by end-use, PAD district, and State, 1990, annual rpt, 3164–94
Heating fuels production, imports, stocks, and prices, by selected PAD district and State, seasonal weekly rpt, 3162–45
Home mortgages FHA-insured, financial, property, and borrower characteristics, by metro area, 1991, annual rpt, 5144–24
Home mortgages FHA-insured, financial, property, and borrower characteristics, by State, 1991, annual rpt, 5144–1
Home mortgages FHA-insured, financial, property, and borrower characteristics, 1991, annual rpt, 5144–23
Housing units completed, single and multifamily units by structural and financial characteristics, and location, 1987-91, annual rpt, 2384–1
Housing units completed, single and multifamily units by structural characteristics, monthly rpt, quarterly tables, 2382–2.2
Input-output structure of US economy, detailed interindustry transactions for 541 industries, and components of final demand, 1982 benchmark data, 2708–17
Natl Energy Strategy plans for conservation, R&D, security, and pollution reduction, technical rpt series, 3006–13
Natl income and product accounts and components, *Survey of Current Business*, monthly rpt, 2702–1.23
Natural and supplemental gas production, prices, trade, use, reserves, and pipeline company finances, by firm and State, monthly rpt with articles, 3162–4
Natural gas interstate pipeline company detailed financial and operating data, by firm, 1990, annual rpt, 3164–38
Natural gas supply, demand, prices, and distribution, by State, 1986-90 annual rpt, 3164–4
New England States electric power sales, Fed Reserve 1st District, monthly rpt, 9373–2
NYC housing supply, occupancy, condition, and household characteristics, by tenure and borough, 1991 triennial survey, 2488–3
Oil products prices, sales, and purchases of refiners, processors, and distributors, by product, end-use sector, PAD district, and State, 1991, annual rpt, 3164–85
Oil products sales and purchases of refiners, processors, and distributors, by product, end-use sector, PAD district, and State, monthly rpt, 3162–11
Pacific basin countries energy supply and demand, and implications for US trade, country rpt series, 3406–6

Pacific Northwest electric power capacity and use, by energy source, forecast under alternative load and demand cases, 1991-2012, annual rpt, 3224–3
Pacific territories population and housing detailed characteristics, by location, 1990 Census of Population and Housing, series, 2551–8
Prices and spending for fuel, by type, end-use sector, and State, 1990, annual rpt, 3164–64
Prices of energy for housing, by fuel type and State, 1990 and forecast 1991-92, 3166–6.61
Prices of fuel, by type, end-use sector, and region, projected 1991-2030, 3166–6.60
Rental housing units, total, with HUD assistance by program, and eligible for aid, by unit, household, and neighborhood characteristics, and location, 1989, biennial rpt, 5184–11
Solar collector and photovoltaic cell shipments by end-use sector and State, and trade, 1990, annual rpt, 3164–62
Statistical Abstract of US, 1992 annual data compilation, 2324–1.19
Tax (income) returns filed, by type of filer, selected income items, quarterly rpt, 8302–2.1
TVA electric power purchases and resales, with electricity use, average bills, and rates by customer class, by distributor, 1991, annual tables, 9804–14
TVA electric power purchases of municipal and cooperative distributors, and prices and use by distributor and consumer sector, monthly rpt, 9802–1
Wood, waste, and alcohol fuel use, by end-use sector and region, 1990, annual rpt, 3164–97
see also Low-income energy assistance

Housing insulation
see Insulation

Housing maintenance and repair
American Housing Survey: unit and households detailed characteristics, and unit and neighborhood quality, MSA rpt series, 2485–6
American Housing Survey: unit and households detailed characteristics, and unit and neighborhood quality, 1989, wallchart, 2485–12
Construction put in place, permits, housing sales, costs, material prices, and employment, quarterly rpt with articles, 2042–1
CPI by component for US city average, and by selected metro area, region, and population size, monthly rpt, 6762–2
Disabled persons assistive technology equipment and home accessibility features, use, payment sources, and unmet needs, by age, 1990, 4146–8.219
Energy conservation technologies for housing and commercial buildings, use, costs, efficiency, and residential tax credits, 1970s-90 and projected to 2010, 26358–259
Expenditures for housing alterations and repair, by type, tenure, region, and other characteristics, quarterly rpt, 2382–7
FmHA activities, and loans and grants by program and State, FY91 and trends from FY70, annual rpt, 1184–17
Home mortgages FHA-insured, financial, property, and borrower characteristics, by metro area, 1991, annual rpt, 5144–24
Home mortgages FHA-insured, financial, property, and borrower characteristics, by State, 1991, annual rpt, 5144–1
Home mortgages FHA-insured, financial, property, and borrower characteristics, 1991, annual rpt, 5144–17; 5144–23
Homeless persons housing in rehabilitated single occupancy units, funding and characteristics, by city, FY87-91, GAO rpt, 26113–596
Homeless persons housing in rehabilitated single occupancy units, HUD grants by community, 1991, press release, 5006–3.82
Homeless persons housing in rehabilitated single occupancy units, HUD grants by community, 1992, press release, 5006–3.90
Homeless persons transitional housing and support services, HUD grants by community, 1991, press release, 5006–3.80
Housing and households summary characteristics, 1989 and trends, chartbook, 2486–2.1
HUD activities, and housing programs operations and funding, 1990, annual rpt, 5004–10
Indian Health Service facilities, funding, operations, and Indian health and other characteristics, 1950s-91, annual chartbook, 4084–1
Input-output structure of US economy, detailed interindustry transactions for 541 industries, and components of final demand, 1982 benchmark data, 2708–17
Lead paint abatement costs and results, demonstration project design and findings, 1991 rpt, 5188–131
Loan activity of savings instns insured by Savings Assn Insurance Fund by FHLB district and State, and for FDIC-insured savings banks, 1989, annual rpt, 8434–1
Low income housing developers tax credits, subsidies, project and tenant characteristics, and investor returns, 1987-88, 5188–133
Low income housing energy aid, funding sources, costs, and participation, by State, FY90, annual rpt, 4584–1
Mortgages FHA-insured for 1-family units, by loan type and mortgage characteristics, quarterly rpt, 5142–45
Owner-occupied housing units alteration and repair, costs and structural, household, financial, and project characteristics, 1987, 2486–1.13
Owner-occupied housing units alteration and repair, owners doing own work by age and household income, 1986-87, fact sheet, 2326–17.45
Paint (lead-based) abatement programs for low- and moderate-income housing, HUD grants to public agencies, 1992 press release, 5006–3.102
Price indexes (producer) for material inputs, by construction industry, monthly rpt, 6762–6
Price indexes for department store inventories, by class of item, monthly table, 6762–7
Rental housing rehabilitation funding and activities of HUD, by program and region, FY91, annual rpt, 5124–7
Rental housing units, total, with HUD assistance by program, and eligible for aid, by unit, household, and neighborhood characteristics, and location, 1989, biennial rpt, 5184–11
Statistical Abstract of US, 1992 annual data compilation, 2324–1.26
see also Insulation

Housing rehabilitation
see Housing maintenance and repair
see Urban renewal

Housing sales
Business activity indicators, 1990, annual rpt, 9364–5.9
Condominium absorption rates, by sales class and size, 1990, annual Current Housing Rpt, 2484–2
Condominium completions and absorption rates, by size and price class, preliminary 1991, annual Current Housing Rpt, 2484–3
Discrimination in housing rental and sales, for blacks and Hispanics in selected metro areas, 1989 study, series, 5186–16
Economic indicators and components, current data and annual trends, monthly rpt, 23842–1.3
FmHA property acquired through foreclosure, 1-family homes, value, sales, and leases, by State, monthly rpt, 1182–7
Indian (Navajo and Hopi) relocation program activities and caseloads, monthly rpt, 16002–1
Inventory of unsold new units, share of builders reporting declining, stable, and advancing trends, monthly press release, 5142–20
Natl income and product accounts, comprehensive accounts and components, benchmark revisions, 1929-88, 2708–5
Natl income and product accounts, comprehensive accounts and components, *Survey of Current Business*, monthly rpt, 2702–1.28
New and existing housing units sold, and average price, by region, quarterly rpt, 2042–1.2
New single and multifamily units, by structural and financial characteristics, inside-outside MSAs, and region, 1987-91, annual rpt, 2384–1
New single-family houses sold and for sale, by price, stage of construction, months on market, and region, monthly rpt, 2382–3
Southeastern States, FHLB 4th District, employment and housing indicators by State, quarterly rpt, 9302–36
Statistical Abstract of US, 1992 annual data compilation, 2324–1.26
Supply and demand for housing and commercial real estate, market activity indicators by region, quarterly rpt, 9292–6

Housing starts
see Housing construction

Housing supply and requirements
Alaska rural areas population characteristics, and energy resources dev effects, series, 5736–5
American Housing Survey: unit and households detailed characteristics, and unit and neighborhood quality, MSA rpt series, 2485–6

American Housing Survey: unit and households detailed characteristics, and unit and neighborhood quality, 1989, wallchart, 2485–12
Apartment and condominium completions by rent class and sales price, and market absorption rates, quarterly rpt, 2482–2
Apartment market absorption rates and characteristics for nonsubsidized furnished and unfurnished units, 1990, annual Current Housing Rpt, 2484–2
Appalachian States, FHLB 5th District housing vacancy rates, discontinued annual MSA rpt series, 9304–27
Census Bur data files and rpts, coverage and availability, 1992 annual listing, 2304–2
Census of Housing, 1990: inventory, occupancy, and costs, State fact sheet series, 2326–21
Census of Housing, 1990: summary unit characteristics, by householder race and age, county, place, and urban-rural location, State rpt series, 2471–1
Census of Population and Housing, 1990: data summary, use, and availability, for selected long form questions, fact sheet series, 2326–23
Census of Population and Housing, 1990: detailed geographic coverage, State CD-ROM series, 2551–9
Census of Population and Housing, 1990: population and housing characteristics, detailed geographic coverage, State CD-ROM series, 2551–10
Census of Population and Housing, 1990: summary characteristics, by county, subdiv, and place, State rpt series, 2551–7
Current Housing Reports, unit and household characteristics, subject rpt series, 2486–1; 2486–2
Israel economic conditions, US investment and export opportunities, and trade practices, 1992 rpt, 2008–32
Low income rental housing in rural areas, FmHA loans and impacts of programs to maintain supply and to deter mortgage prepayment, 1988-91, GAO rpt, 26113–586
New single-family houses sold and for sale, by price, stage of construction, months on market, and region, monthly rpt, 2382–3
North Central States, FHLB 7th District housing vacancy rates for single and multifamily units and mobile homes, by ZIP code, annual MSA rpt series, 9304–18
NYC housing supply, occupancy, condition, and household characteristics, by tenure and borough, 1991 triennial survey, 2488–3
Pacific Northwest population, households, employment, income, fuel prices, and electricity demand, alternative forecasts 1991-2010, annual rpt, 3224–3.3
Pacific territories population and housing detailed characteristics, by location, 1990 Census of Population and Housing, series, 2551–8
South Central States, FHLB 9th District housing vacancy rates, discontinued annual MSA rpt series, 9304–19
Soviet Union and US economic and sociodemographic indicators, selected years 1970-90, handbook, 2328–80
Statistical Abstract of US, 1992 annual data compilation, 2324–1.26
Supply and demand for housing and commercial real estate, market activity indicators by region, quarterly rpt, 9292–6
Vacant housing characteristics and costs, and occupancy and vacancy rates, by region and metro-nonmetro location, quarterly rpt, 2482–1
Vacant housing characteristics, and occupancy and vacancy rates, by tenure and location, 1960s-91, annual rpt, 2484–1
West Central States, FHLB 10th District housing vacancy rates for single and multifamily units and mobile homes, by ZIP code, annual MSA rpt series, 9304–22
Western States, FHLB 12th District housing vacancy rates for single and multifamily units and mobile homes, by ZIP code, annual MSA rpt series, 9304–21
see also Building permits
see also Housing condition and occupancy
see also Housing construction
see also Housing costs and financing
see also Housing sales
see also Urban renewal
see also Wrecking and demolition

Housing tenure

Alteration and repair of owner-occupied homes, costs and structural, household, financial, and project characteristics, 1987, 2486–1.13
Alteration and repair spending for housing, by type, tenure, region, and other characteristics, quarterly rpt, 2382–7
American Housing Survey: unit and household characteristics of recent movers, and reason for move, by tenure, 1989, 2486–1.12
American Housing Survey: unit and households characteristics, and unit and neighborhood quality, by MSA location for 11 MSAs, 1987 survey, supplement, 2485–8
American Housing Survey: unit and households characteristics, MSA fact sheet series, 2485–11
American Housing Survey: unit and households detailed characteristics, and unit and neighborhood quality, MSA rpt series, 2485–6
American Housing Survey: unit and households detailed characteristics, and unit and neighborhood quality, 1989, biennial rpt supplement, 2485–13
Asian and Pacific Islands Americans social and economic characteristics, for West and total US, 1990-91, Current Population Report, 2546–1.462
Capital (fixed), govt and private nonresidential structures and equipment, residential capital, and consumer-owned durable goods, 1925-90, annual article, 2702–1.305; 2702–1.306; 2702–1.327; 2702–1.338
Census of Housing, 1990: inventory, occupancy, and costs, State fact sheet series, 2326–21
Census of Housing, 1990: summary unit characteristics, by householder race and age, county, place, and urban-rural location, State rpt series, 2471–1
Census of Population and Housing, 1990: detailed geographic coverage, State CD-ROM series, 2551–9
Census of Population and Housing, 1990: population and housing characteristics, detailed geographic coverage, State CD-ROM series, 2551–10
Census of Population and Housing, 1990: summary characteristics, by county, subdiv, and place, State rpt series, 2551–7
Census of Population and Housing, 1990: summary characteristics, households, and land area, by county, subdiv, and place, State rpt series, 2551–1
Consumer Income, socioeconomic characteristics of persons, families, and households, detailed cross-tabulations, Current Population Rpt series, 2546–6
Crime victimization rates, by victim and offender characteristics, circumstances, and offense, 1990 survey, annual rpt, 6066–3.47
Families financial status, income, net worth, and assets and debt by type, by income and selected characteristics, 1983 and 1989, article, 9362–1.301
Homeownership values, reasons, and barriers, views by race and tenure, 1992 survey, 9478–1
Households and family characteristics, by location, 1991, annual Current Population Rpt, 2546–1.457
Housing and households summary characteristics, 1989 and trends, chartbook, 2486–2.1
Housing energy use, costs, and conservation, and household and housing characteristics, survey rpt series, 3166–7
Income and consumer spending of households, for selected population groups, quarterly journal, 1702–1
Living arrangements, family relationships, and marital status, by selected characteristics, 1991, annual Current Population Rpt, 2546–1.461
Migration, immigration, and mover characteristics compared to nonmovers, 1987-90, annual Current Population Rpt, 2546–1.456
Migration of households, moving rates by tenure and age, and housing value by mobility status and region, 1989, fact sheet, 2326–17.38
Migration since 1990, mover characteristics by same or different area, and compared to nonmovers, 1991, annual Current Population Rpt, 2546–1.464
NYC housing supply, occupancy, condition, and household characteristics, by tenure and borough, 1991 triennial survey, 2488–3
Older persons socioeconomic characteristics, 1900s-90 and projected to 2050, biennial chartbook, 12904–1
Ownership of homes, rates by location and age of householder, quarterly rpt, 2482–1
Ownership rate, and change in housing tenure, by age, 1980s and projected to 2000, fact sheet, 2326–17.52
Ownership rate for 30 largest metro areas, and direction of change in rate by State, 1989-91, fact sheet, 2326–17.46
Pacific territories population and housing detailed characteristics, by location, 1990 Census of Population and Housing, series, 2551–8

Population economic well-being indicators, by selected characteristics and household income and income-to-poverty ratio, 1984, 2546–20.22
Rental housing units, total, with HUD assistance by program, and eligible for aid, by unit, household, and neighborhood characteristics, and location, 1989, biennial rpt, 5184–11
Single parent families in own and others homes, by financial, housing, and other characteristics, 1989, 2486–1.14
Single parent share of family households, and homeownership rate by marital status, by race, 1989, fact sheet, 2326–17.44
Single person and nonfamily households social, economic and housing characteristics, by tenure, 1989, 2486–1.15
Statistical Abstract of US, 1992 annual data compilation, 2324–1.26
Taxes, spending, and govt efficiency, public opinion by respondent characteristics, 1992 survey, annual rpt, 10044–2
Vacancy rates for metro areas with significant changes, by tenure, 1989 and 1991, fact sheet, 2326–17.51
Vacant housing characteristics and costs, and occupancy and vacancy rates, by region and metro-nonmetro location, quarterly rpt, 2482–1
Vacant housing characteristics, and occupancy and vacancy rates, by tenure and location, 1960s-91, annual rpt, 2484–1
see also Condominiums and cooperatives
see also Housing sales
see also Rent

Houston, Tex.
Commuters, by county of residence and work, for top 10 metro areas, 1990 Census of Population, press release, 2328–84
CPI by component for US city average, and by region, population size, and for 15 metro areas, monthly rpt, 6762–1
CPI by component for US city average, and by selected metro area, region, and population size, monthly rpt, 6762–2
CPI by major component for 2 Texas MSAs, monthly rpt, 6962–2
Drug test results at arrest, by drug type, offense, and sex, for selected urban areas, quarterly rpt, 6062–3
Employment, earnings, hours, and CPI changes, for Houston metro area, 1970s-91, annual rpt, 6964–1
Heroin prices and purity in 19 metro areas and Puerto Rico, by world area of origin, quarterly rpt, 6282–2
Housing and households characteristics, and unit and neighborhood quality, by MSA location for 11 MSAs, 1987 survey, supplement, 2485–8
Housing starts and completions authorized by building permits in 40 MSAs, quarterly rpt, 2382–9
Immigration Reform and Control Act employer sanctions impacts on labor markets, with data for selected industries and metro areas, 1980s, working paper, 6366–6.10
Oil prices by product, for 4 cities, seasonal weekly rpt, 3162–45
Wages by occupation, and benefits, for office and plant workers, 1992 survey, periodic MSA rpt, 6785–17.3
see also under By City and By SMSA or MSA in the "Index by Categories"

Howard, David H.
"External Adjustment in Selected Developing Countries in the 1990s", 9366–7.271

Howard, James O.
"California's Forest Products Industry: 1988", 1208–108
"Oregon's Forest Products Industry: 1988", 1208–280

Howe, David K.
"What Researchers Have Learned from the National Longitudinal Surveys About Youth Unemployment", 6728–42

Howe, Geoffrey R.
"Dietary Intake of Fiber and Decreased Risk of Cancers of the Colon and Rectum: Evidence from the Combined Analysis of 13 Case-Control Studies", 4472–1.358

Howe, Howard
"Determinants of Long-Term Interest Rates: An Empirical Study of Several Industrial Countries", 9385–1.301

Howell, Craig
"Recession, Energy Prices Ease Producer Price Inflation, 1991", 6722–1.323

Howenstine, Ned G.
"Foreign Direct Investment in the U.S.: Establishment Data for 1987", 2702–1.340

Hsia, Chu Chieh
"Mutations of p53 Gene in Hepatocellular Carcinoma: Roles of Hepatitis B Virus and Aflatoxin Contamination in the Diet", 4472–1.353

Hsia, David C.
"Good Quality Care Increases Hospital Profits Under Prospective Payment", 4652–1.316

Hsing, Ann W.
"Parity and Primary Liver Cancer Among Young Women", 4472–1.331

Hu, Patricia S.
"Summary of Travel Trends: 1990 Nationwide Personal Transportation Survey", 7556–6.2

Huang, Wen-Yuan
"Determination of a Variable Price Support Schedule as Applied to Agricultural Production Control", 1502–3.301

Hubbard, R. Glenn
"Household Income Mobility During the 1980s: A Statistical Assessment Based on Tax Return Data", 8008–156
"Internal Net Worth and the Investment Process: An Application to U.S. Agriculture", 9375–13.77

HUD
see Department of Housing and Urban Development

Hudson, Bettie L.
"Advance Report of Final Mortality Statistics, 1989", 4146–5.124

Hudson River
Freight (waterborne domestic and foreign) by commodity, traffic, and passengers, by port and waterway, 1989, annual rpt, 3754–3.1
Water supply and quality in streams and lakes, and groundwater levels in wells, by drainage basin, 1990, annual State rpt series, 5666–10
Water supply and quality in streams and lakes, and groundwater levels in wells, by drainage basin, 1991, annual State rpt series, 5666–12
Water supply in northeastern US, precipitation and stream runoff by station, monthly rpt, 2182–3
Water supply in US and southern Canada, streamflow, surface and groundwater conditions, and reservoir levels, by location, monthly rpt, 5662–3

Huffine, Edwin F.
"Enhancement of Drug Detection and Identification by Use of Various Derivatizing Reagents on GC-FTIR Analysis", 7506–10.112

Huffman, Gregory W.
"Analysis of the Impact of Two Fiscal Policies on the Behavior of a Dynamic Asset Market", 9379–12.97
"On the Existence and Uniqueness of Nonoptimal Equilibria in Dynamic Stochastic Economies", 9383–20.21

Hughes, Joseph P.
"Quality and Risk-Adjusted Cost Function for Banks: Evidence on the 'Too-Big-To-Fail' Doctrine", 9387–8.260

Hughes, Vergie
"Producer Milk Marketed Under Federal Milk Orders by State of Origin", 1317–4.301

Huh, Chan G.
"Causality and Correlations of Output and Nominal Variables in a Real Business Cycle Model", 9393–10.19
"Modelling the Time Series Behavior of the Aggregate Wage Rate", 9393–10.20

Hukill, Craig
"Labor and the Supreme Court: Significant Issues of 1991-92", 6722–1.308

Human experimentation
Drug (prescription) clinical trials representation of women, and FDA policy guidance, 1988-91, GAO rpt, 26121–486
HHS financial aid, by program, recipient, State, and city, FY91, annual regional listings, 4004–3
Reproduction and population research, Fed Govt funding by project, FY90, annual listing, 4474–9

Human immunodeficiency virus
see Acquired immune deficiency syndrome

Human Nutrition Information Service
Budget of US, obligations and authority by function, agency, and program, with summaries and analyses, FY93, annual rpt, 104–2
Food composition, detailed data on nutrients, calories, and waste, for raw, processed, and prepared foods, series, 1356–3
Food consumption, dietary composition, and nutrient intake, natl survey methodology changes and sample results, 1990 rpt, 1358–6

Human papillomavirus
see Infective and parasitic diseases

Human resources management
see Civil service system
see Employee development
see Employee performance and appraisal
see Employment services
see Personnel management

Human rights
see Civil rights
Humanities
see Arts and the humanities
Humpage, Owen F.
"New Results on the Impact of Central-Bank Intervention on Deviations from Uncovered Interest Parity", 9377–9.138
"Post-Louvre Intervention: Did Target Zones Stabilize the Dollar?", 9377–9.134
Hung, Juann
"Explaining the Persistence of the U.S. Trade Deficit in the Late 1980s", 9385–1.302
Hungary
Agricultural trade of US, by detailed commodity and country, 1991, annual rpt, 1524–8
Agricultural trade of US, by detailed commodity and country, 1991, semiannual rpt, 1522–4
Agricultural trade of US with Eastern Europe, by commodity group and country, 1988-91, 1928–11
Child respiratory disease cases, by type, age, and air pollution levels, for Sopron, Hungary, 1990, article, 4202–7.319
Drug abuse indicators, by world region and selected country, 1991 semiannual conf, 4492–5.1
Economic and military aid and loans from US and intl agencies, by program and country, FY46-91, annual rpt, 9914–5
Economic and social conditions of developing countries from 1960s, and Intl Dev Cooperation Agency and AID activities and funding, FY91-93, annual rpt, 9904–4
Economic conditions, policy, and trade practices, by country, 1989-91, annual rpt, 21384–5
Economic, social, political, and geographic summary data, by country, 1992, annual factbook, 9114–2
Export industries dev potential, with trade and industry finances and operations, for 5 Eastern Europe countries, 1985-90, 9886–4.179
Export licensing, monitoring, and enforcement activities, FY91, annual rpt, 2024–1
Exports and imports of US, by commodity and country, 1980-90, world area rpt, 9116–1.1
Exports and imports of US, by transport mode, country, and SITC 1- to 3-digit commodity, 1991, annual rpt, 2424–12
Exports and imports of US with Communist and transitional economy countries, by detailed commodity and country, quarterly rpt with articles, 9882–2
Exports and imports of US with Eastern Europe, by commodity and country, 1987-91 and outlook for 1992, 2048–158
Exports, imports, and balances of US for manufactured goods, by SITC 2-digit commodity and country, quarterly rpt, 2042–35
Exports of Poland and Hungary, by world area, 1988-91, GAO rpt, 26123–386
Exports of US, detailed Schedule B commodities with countries of destination, 1991, annual rpt, 2424–10
Human rights conditions in 170 countries, and US economic and military aid, 1991, annual rpt, 21384–3
Imports of goods, services, and investment from US, trade barriers, impacts, and US actions, by country, 1991, annual rpt, 444–2
Labor conditions, union coverage, and work accidents, 1992 annual country rpt, 6366–4.28
Market economy transition of Eastern Europe countries, trade, and foreign investment, by country, 1990-91, 9118–13
Military aid of US, arms sales, and training programs costs and budget requests, by program, world region, and country, FY91-93, annual rpt, 7144–13
Military spending, arms trade, and force strengths, with govt spending and population, by country, 1979-89, annual rpt, 9824–1
Older population and selected characteristics, 1980s and projected to 2020, country rpt, 2326–19.7
Pension systems finances and provisions in Eastern Europe, 1950s-90 and alternative projections to 2025, technical paper, 8006–6.7
Population size, growth rates, and components of change, by country, projected 1990-2020 and trends from 1950, biennial rpt, 2324–9
Refugee migration, and intl aid programs, by world area and country of origin and asylum, 1991, annual rpt, 7004–15
Steel imports of US under voluntary restraint agreement, by product, customs district, and country, with US industry operating data, quarterly rpt, 9882–13
Steel trade, by product, country, and customs district, with US industry operating data, 1989-June 1992, semiannual rpt, 9882–15
Sulfanilic acid from Hungary and India, injury to US industry from foreign subsidized and less than fair value imports, investigation with background financial and operating data, 1992 rpt, 9886–19.83
Tax reform issues in transition to market economy, with tax rates, revenue, and govt spending compared to EC, by selected country, late 1960s-91, technical paper, 9366–7.278
UN voting record and share of votes in agreement with US, by issue, country, and world area, 1991, annual rpt, 7004–18
Wine exports of Hungary by type and country, vineyard acreage, and grape production, 1988-90, article, 1925–34.331
Hunger
see Food assistance
see Food supply
see Nutrition and malnutrition
Hunley, Charles
"Cooperative Tobacco Warehouses Show Gain in Marketing Activity", 1122–1.304
Hunt, Gary L.
"Economic Effects of Immigrants on Native and Foreign-Born Workers: Complementarity, Substitutability, and Other Channels of Influence", 6366–6.12
Hunter, William C.
"Optimal Venture Capital Solicitation Under a Horizon Constraint", 9371–10.83
"Rational Expectations and Security Analysts' Earnings Forecasts", 9371–10.84
Hunterdon County, N.J.
Wages by occupation, for office and plant workers, 1991 survey, periodic MSA rpt, 6785–12.3
Hunting and fishing licenses
Birds (sandhill crane) hunting activity and permits, by State and county, 1990/91-1991/92, annual rpt, 5504–31
Duck hunting stamps philatelic and sales info, 1992/93, annual supplement, 5504–25
Duck stamps sold, by State and flyway, and permits by Canada Province, 1990-91, annual rpt, 5504–28
Issues of fishing and hunting licenses, and costs, by State, FY91, annual tables, 5504–16
State govt revenue by source, spending and debt by function, and holdings, FY91, annual rpt, 2466–2.6
Statistical Abstract of US, 1992 annual data compilation, 2324–1.7
Tax collections of State govts by detailed type of tax, and tax rates, by State, FY91, annual rpt, 2466–2.7
Hunting and trapping
Alaska rural areas population characteristics, and energy resources dev effects, series, 5736–5
Bears (grizzly) in Yellowstone Natl Park area, monitoring results, 1991, annual rpt, 5544–4
Birds (mourning dove) population, by hunting and nonhunting State, 1966-92, annual rpt, 5504–15
Birds (sandhill crane) hunting activity and permits, by State and county, 1990/91-1991/92, annual rpt, 5504–31
Birds (waterfowl) hunter harvest, age and sex ratios by species, State, and flyway, 1987-91, annual rpt, 5504–32
Birds (waterfowl) hunter harvest and unretrieved kills, and duck stamps sold, by species, State, and flyway, 1990-91, annual rpt, 5504–28
Birds (woodcock) population in US and Canada from 1968, and hunter harvest, by State, 1992, annual rpt, 5504–11
County Business Patterns, 1989: employment, establishments, and payroll, by SIC 2- to 4-digit industry and county, annual State rpt series, 2326–8
County Business Patterns, 1990: employment, establishments, and payroll, by SIC 2- to 4-digit industry and county, annual State rpt series, 2326–6
Environmental Quality, status of problems, protection programs, research, and intl issues, 1991 annual rpt, 484–1
Fish and Wildlife Service restoration and hunter safety funding, by State, FY92, semiannual press release, 5502–1
Fish and Wildlife Service restoration programs funding, land purchases, and project listing, by State, FY90, annual rpt, 5504–1
Forest Service activities and finances, by region and State, FY91, annual rpt, 1204–1.1

Forests (natl) recreational use, by type of activity and State, 1991, annual rpt, 1204–17
Marine mammals protection activities and funding, populations, and harvests, by species, 1990, annual rpt, 5504–12
Mink and otter population, breeding, trapping, pollutant levels, and research status, for Great Lakes area, 1991 conf, 14648–27
Occupational Outlook Handbook, 1992-93, biennial rpt, 6744–1
Public lands acreage, grants, use, revenues, and allocations, by State, FY91, annual rpt, 5724–1.2
Tax (income) returns of sole proprietorships, income statement items, by industry group, 1990, annual article, 8302–2.317; 8302–2.320
see also Fish and fishing industry
see also Fishing, sport
see also Hunting and fishing licenses

Huntington, Tex.
see also under By City and By SMSA or MSA in the "Index by Categories"

Huntington, W.Va.
Freight (waterborne domestic and foreign) by commodity, traffic, and passengers, by port and waterway, 1989, annual rpt, 3754–3.2

Huntsville, Ala.
Wages by occupation, and benefits, for office and plant workers, 1992 survey, periodic MSA rpt, 6785–17.1
see also under By City and By SMSA or MSA in the "Index by Categories"

Hurley, Susan F.
"Effectiveness, Costs, and Cost-Effectiveness of Recruitment Strategies for a Mammographic Screening Program To Detect Breast Cancer", 4472–1.318

Hussar, William J.
"Projections of Education Statistics to 2003", 4824–4

Hutchins, Cecil C., Jr.
"Changes in Output of Industrial Timber Products in Virginia, 1987-89", 1208–138

Hutchison, Michael
"Fiscal Policy in Monetary Unions: Implications for Europe", 9393–10.18

Hutson, Susan S.
"Ground-Water Use by Public Supply Systems in Tennessee, 1988", 5666–24.14

Hyberg, Bengt
"Determination of a Variable Price Support Schedule as Applied to Agricultural Production Control", 1502–3.301
"Soybean Quality Issues: Cleaning Practices at Commercial Elevators", 1561–3.302

Hydroelectric power
Army Corps of Engineers activities and projects, FY88 and trends from 1800s, annual rpt, 3754–1.1
Army Corps of Engineers activities and projects, FY89 and trends from 1800s, annual rpt, 3754–1.2
Army Corps of Engineers activities and projects, FY90 and trends from 1800s, annual rpt, 3754–1.3
Army Corps of Engineers water resources dev projects, characteristics, and costs, 1950s-89, biennial State rpt series, 3756–1
Army Corps of Engineers water resources dev projects, characteristics, and costs, 1950s-91, biennial State rpt series, 3756–2
Bonneville Power Admin mgmt of Fed Columbia River Power System, finances, operations, and sales by customer, FY91, annual rpt, 3224–1
Business statistics, detailed data for major industries and economic indicators, *Survey of Current Business*, monthly rpt, 2702–1.12
Business statistics, detailed data for major industries and economic indicators, 1960-91, *Survey of Current Business* biennial supplement, 2704–1
Certification applications filed with FERC, for small power production and cogeneration facilities, FY80-91, annual listing, 3084–13
Certification of hydroelectric projects, rate regulation, and other FERC activities, FY91, annual rpt, 3084–9
Colorado River Basin Federal reservoir and power operations and revenues, 1991-92, annual rpt, 5824–6
Colorado River Storage Project finances and activities in western States, FY91, annual rpt, 5824–3
Colorado River Storage Project power sales, and Glen Canyon Dam operations, 1960s-80s, hearing, 21448–47
Consumption of energy, by detailed fuel type, end-use sector, and State, 1960-90, State Energy Data System annual rpt, 3164–39
Environmental Quality, status of problems, protection programs, research, and intl issues, 1991 annual rpt, 484–1
Foreign and US energy production and use, by energy type and country, 1981-90, annual rpt, 3164–50.1; 3164–50.5; 3164–50.7
Japan energy use and imports by fuel type, and gasoline prices, 1970s-80s, hearing, 21448–45
Mexico and US electric power supply, demand, and trade, with data by fuel source, utility, and region, 1970s-89 and projected to 2000, 3408–2
Pacific basin countries energy supply and demand, and implications for US trade, country rpt series, 3406–6
Pacific Northwest electric power capacity and use, by energy source, forecast under alternative load and demand cases, 1991-2012, annual rpt, 3224–3
Pacific Northwest nonutility electric power generation and capacity, by energy source, purchasing utility, and facility, forecasts 1991-2012, annual rpt, 3224–3.4
Power plants (hydroelectric) licensing by FERC, impacts of environmental laws, with staffing and plant safety incidents, 1980s-90s, GAO rpt, 26113–599
Power plants (hydroelectric) retired, characteristics and location, as of 1992, annual listing, 3084–12
Power plants and capacity, by fuel used, owner, location, and operating status, 1991, and for units planned 1992-2001, annual listing, 3164–36
Power plants capacity and investment by fuel type, and industrial and employment impacts of new power plants, by selected State, 1960s-80s and projected to 2000, hearing, 21248–163
Power plants capital and production costs, operations, and fuel use, by fuel type, plant, utility, and location, 1990, annual rpt, 3164–9
Power plants production, fuel use, stocks, and costs by fuel type, and sales, by State, monthly rpt, 3162–35
Production, plant capacity, and fuel use, by fuel type, census div, and State, 1986-90, annual rpt, 3164–11.1
Reclamation Bur hydroelectric power plants, generation, and capacity, 1978-90 and projected to 1995, 5828–14
Reclamation Bur irrigation activities, finances, and project impacts in western US, 1990, annual rpt, 5824–12
Rural Electrification Admin financed electric power plants, with location, capacity, and owner, as of Jan 1992, annual listing, 1244–6
Southwestern Fed Power System financial statements, sales by customer, and operations and costs by project, FY91, annual rpt, 3244–1
Statistical Abstract of US, 1992 annual data compilation, 2324–1.19
Supply, demand, and prices, by fuel type and end-use sector, alternative projections by region, 1990-2010, annual rpt, 3164–96
Supply, demand, and prices, by fuel type and end-use sector, alternative projections 1990-2010, annual rpt, 3164–75
Supply, demand, and prices, by fuel type and end-use sector, projections and underlying assumptions, 1995-2010, annual rpt, 3164–90
Supply, demand, and prices, by fuel type and end-use sector, with foreign comparisons, 1991 and trends from 1949, annual rpt, 3164–74
Supply, demand, and prices, by fuel type, end-use sector, and country, detailed data, monthly rpt with articles, 3162–24
Supply, demand, and prices, by fuel type, end-use sector, and country, detailed data, monthly 1973-88, 3168–123
Supply, demand, and prices of energy, forecasts by resource type, quarterly rpt, 3162–34
Tennessee Valley river control activities, and hydroelectric power generation and capacity, 1990, annual rpt, 9804–7
TVA finances and operations by program and facility, FY91, annual rpt, 9804–32
Utilities finances and operations, detailed data for privately owned firms, 1990, annual rpt, 3164–23
Utilities finances and operations, detailed data for publicly owned firms, 1990, annual rpt, 3164–24
Water supply in US and southern Canada, streamflow, surface and groundwater conditions, and reservoir levels, by location, monthly rpt, 5662–3
Water use by end use, well withdrawals, and public supply deliveries, by county, State rpt series, 5666–24
Western Area Power Admin activities by plant, financial statements, and sales by customer, FY91, annual rpt, 3254–1

Hydrology
Alaska OCS environmental conditions and oil dev impacts, compilation of papers, series, 2176–1

California OCS oil and gas dev impacts on water quality, marine life, and sediments, by site, 1986-90, annual rpt, 5734–11
Coastal and riparian areas environmental conditions, fish, wildlife, use, and mgmt, for individual ecosystems, series, 5506–9
Coastal areas environmental conditions and mgmt, for individual areas, conf series, 2146–8
DOE R&D projects and funding at natl labs, universities, and other instns, FY91, annual summary rpt, 3004–18.1
Estuary environmental conditions, research results and methodology, series, 2176–7
Geological Survey activities and funding, FY91, annual rpt, 5664–8
Great Lakes Environmental Research Lab activities, FY91 annual rpt, 2144–26
Groundwater supply, quality, chemistry, and use, State and local area rpt series, 5666–28
Groundwater supply, quality, chemistry, other characteristics, and use, regional rpt series, 5666–25
New Hampshire Hubbard Brook Experimental Forest hydrology and climate data, 1956-89, 1208–410
Radon and other radionuclide levels in air, water, soil, and uranium mill tailings, by site and region, 1950s-80s, compilation of papers, 5668–126
Research on water resources, data collection and analysis activities of USGS Water Resources Div Districts, with project descriptions, series, 5666–26
Water quality, chemistry, hydrology, and other characteristics, local area studies, series, 5666–27
Water supply in US and southern Canada, streamflow, surface and groundwater conditions, and reservoir levels, by location, monthly rpt, 5662–3
Weather conditions and forecasts, data collection and analysis issues, 1991 annual conf, 2184–10
Wetlands acid neutralizing capability for mining runoff, with pollutant levels and site characteristics, for Pennsylvania, 1987-90, 5608–171
see also Oceanography
see also Water area
see also Water pollution
see also Water power
see also Water resources development
see also Water supply and use
see also Watershed projects

Hydrothermal power
see Geothermal resources

Hyman, David J.
"Cholesterol Treatment Practices of Primary Care Physicians", 4042–3.345

Hyndman, Paul C.
"Availability of Federally Owned Minerals for Exploration and Development in Western States: Idaho, 1988", 5606–7.7

Hypertension
Cases of acute and chronic conditions, disability, absenteeism, and health services use, by selected characteristics, 1990, annual rpt, 4147–10.182; 4147–10.183
Cases of hypertension, stroke and heart disease risk, and drug dosages, with diagnosis and treatment methods, 1992 quadrennial rpt, 4478–198
Deaths and rates, by cause, age, sex, marital status, race, and State, 1989, US Vital Statistics advance annual rpt, 4146–5.124
Deaths and rates, by cause and age, preliminary 1990-91, US Vital Statistics annual rpt, 4144–7
Deaths and rates, by cause and selected social, demographic, and employment characteristics, 1979-85, natl longitudinal study, 4478–186
Deaths and rates, by cause, provisional data, monthly rpt, 4142–1.2
Deaths and rates, by detailed location, cause, and demographic characteristics, 1989, US Vital Statistics annual rpt, 4144–3
Deaths during 1986, decedents health condition, services use, habits, and social, employment, and other characteristics, 4147–20.19
Developing countries aged population and selected characteristics, 1980s and projected to 2020, country rpt series, 2326–19
Diabetes patients physician office visits, by characteristics of patient, physician, and visit, 1989, 4146–8.212
Diet diversity relation to hypertension among Saba Islands residents, 1983-86 study, article, 4042–3.343
Disability and work limitations of persons with chronic health conditions, by condition, age, and sex, 1983-86, 4946–1.2
Drug (antihypertensive) impacts on pilot performance, 1992 technical rpt, 7506–10.119
Health condition and care indicators, 1950s-90 with health improvement and disease prevention goals for 1990, annual data compilation, 4144–11
Heart disease risk factors prevalence in Missouri, 1989-90, article, 4042–3.302
Indian health risk behavior, by region and for Montana, mid 1980s, article, 4042–3.346
Insurance (health) denial by private carriers because of poor health, by selected characteristics, 1987, 4186–8.23
Kidney end-stage disease treatment facilities, Medicare enrollment and reimbursement, survival, and patient characteristics, 1984-90, annual rpt, 4654–16
Medicare payment of physicians, reforms impacts on services, and monitoring methods, 1992 annual rpt, 4004–34
Natl Heart, Lung, and Blood Inst activities, and grants by recipient and location, FY91 and disease trends from 1940, annual rpt, 4474–15
OECD members health care costs, hospital use, resources, and economic and health indicators, by country, 1960s-90, article, 4652–1.322

IBRD
see International Bank for Reconstruction and Development

ICC
see Interstate Commerce Commission

Ice conditions
Alaska OCS environmental conditions and oil dev impacts, compilation of papers, series, 2176–1
Bering Sea and Alaska north coast ice conditions, monthly rpt, 2182–5
Diving (underwater) accidents, illnesses, and deaths, by circumstances, diver characteristics, and location, 1970-90, annual rpt, 2144–29
Environmental quality indicators, NOAA monitoring results, 1991 annual summary rpt, 2144–27
Icebergs sightings in North Atlantic Grand Banks area, by source, 1991, article, 2152–8.301
Research (intl) in glaciology, summaries, methodology, and bibls, series, 2156–18
Traffic safety research, literature review, with data on accidents and impact of safety measures, 1961-90, 7558–98
Weather (marine) forecast areas, and broadcast schedules and stations worldwide, as of Sept 1992, annual rpt, 2184–3
Weather (marine) forecast broadcast schedules worldwide, periodic rpt, 2182–9
Weather trends and deviations, by world region, 1880s-1990, annual chartbook, 2184–9
Whales (bowhead and white) migration through Beaufort Sea, behavior impacts of oil drilling and aircraft noise, spring 1990, 5738–27
Whales population and behavior in Chukchi and Beaufort Seas, by endangered species, 1982-91, 5738–32
Whales population and behavior in Chukchi and Beaufort Seas, by endangered species, 1990, 5738–36
see also Glaciers

Ice, manufactured
County Business Patterns, 1989: employment, establishments, and payroll, by SIC 2- to 4-digit industry and county, annual State rpt series, 2326–8
County Business Patterns, 1990: employment, establishments, and payroll, by SIC 2- to 4-digit industry and county, annual State rpt series, 2326–6
Freight (waterborne domestic and foreign) by commodity, traffic, and passengers, by port and waterway, 1989, annual rpt, 3754–3
Input-output structure of US economy, detailed interindustry transactions for 541 industries, and components of final demand, 1982 benchmark data, 2708–17
Manufacturing annual survey, 1990: finances and operations, by SIC 2- to 4-digit industry, series, 2506–14
Manufacturing census, 1987: concentration of largest firms measured by value added, and for shipments by SIC 2- and 4-digit industry, subject rpt, 2497–6
Manufacturing census, 1987: shipments of manufacturers products, by customer class and SIC 2- and 4-digit industry, subject rpt, 2497–4
Price indexes (producer), by stage of processing and detailed commodity, monthly rpt, 6762–6
Price indexes (producer), by stage of processing and detailed commodity, monthly 1991, annual rpt, 6764–2

Iceland
Agricultural trade of US, by detailed commodity and country, 1991, annual rpt, 1524–8
Agricultural trade of US, by detailed commodity and country, 1991, semiannual rpt, 1522–4
AID loans repayment status and terms by program and country, and status of predecessor agency loans, quarterly rpt, 9912–3
Economic and military aid and loans from US and intl agencies, by program and country, FY46-91, annual rpt, 9914–5
Economic conditions, income, production, prices, employment, and trade, 1992 periodic country rpt, 2046–4.49
Economic, social, political, and geographic summary data, by country, 1992, annual factbook, 9114–2
Exports and imports of US, by transport mode, country, and SITC 1- to 3-digit commodity, 1991, annual rpt, 2424–12
Exports of US, detailed Schedule B commodities with countries of destination, 1991, annual rpt, 2424–10
Health care costs and components, services use, resources, and economic indicators, by OECD country, 1960s-90, article, 4652–1.322
Human rights conditions in 170 countries, and US economic and military aid, 1991, annual rpt, 21384–3
Labor conditions, union coverage, and work accidents, 1992 annual country rpt, 6366–4.53
Military spending, arms trade, and force strengths, with govt spending and population, by country, 1979-89, annual rpt, 9824–1
Oil production, stocks, use, and trade, by selected country and country group, monthly rpt, 3162–42
Population size, growth rates, and components of change, by country, projected 1990-2020 and trends from 1950, biennial rpt, 2324–9
Refugee migration, and intl aid programs, by world area and country of origin and asylum, 1991, annual rpt, 7004–15
Tax revenue, by level of govt and type of tax, for OECD countries, mid 1960s-90, annual rpt, 10044–1.2
UN voting record and share of votes in agreement with US, by issue, country, and world area, 1991, annual rpt, 7004–18
see also under By Foreign Country in the "Index by Categories"

ICF, Inc.
"Evaluation of the Low-Income Housing Tax Credit, Final Report", 5188–133
"Policies, Procedures, and Organization of the Federal Home Loan Mortgage Corporation", 5184–8
"Policies, Procedures, and Organization of the Federal National Mortgage Association", 5184–9
"Potential Cumulative Impacts of Environmental Regulatory Initiatives on U.S. Crude Oil Exploration and Production", 3338–2

Idaho
Banks (insured commercial and savings) deposits by instn, State, MSA, and county, as of June 1991, annual regional rpt, 9295–3.6
Bears (grizzly) in Yellowstone Natl Park area, monitoring results, 1991, annual rpt, 5544–4
Birds of prey, rodent, and vegetation distribution and characteristics, for Idaho Snake River area, research results, 1991, annual rpt, 5724–14
County Business Patterns, 1990: employment, establishments, and payroll, by SIC 2- to 4-digit industry and county, annual State rpt, 2326–6.14
Deaths and rates, by detailed location, cause, and demographic characteristics, 1989, US Vital Statistics annual rpt, 4144–3.1
Employment, earnings, and hours, by selected SIC 1- to 4-digit industry, State, and for 275 MSAs, 1987-92, 6748–81
Fed Govt spending in States and local areas, by type, State, county, and city, FY91, annual rpt, 2464–3
Fed Govt spending in States, by type, program, agency, and State, FY91, annual rpt, 2464–2
HHS financial aid, by program, recipient, State, and city, FY91, annual regional listing, 4004–3.10
Hospital deaths of Medicare patients, actual and expected rates by diagnosis, and hospital characteristics, by instn, FY90 annual State rpt, 4654–14.13
Housing census, 1990: inventory, occupancy, and costs, State fact sheet, 2326–21.14
Housing census, 1990: summary unit characteristics, by householder race and age, county, place, and urban-rural location, State rpt, 2471–1.14
Metals (nonferrous) production in 5 western States, and prices, for 5 metals, 1848-1990, 5608–178
Military prime contract awards, by contractor, service branch, State, and city, FY91, annual rpt, 3544–22
Mineral Industry Surveys, State reviews of production, 1991, preliminary annual rpt, 5614–6
Minerals resources and availability on public lands, 1988, State rpt, 5606–7.7
Minerals Yearbook, Vol 2, 1990: State review of production and sales by commodity, and business activity, annual rpt, 5604–22.13
Multinatl firms US affiliates finances and operations, by industry, country of parent firm, and State, 1987, 2708–48
Physicians, by specialty, age, sex, and location of training and practice, 1990, State rpt, 4116–6.13
Population and housing census, 1990: detailed geographic coverage, State CD-ROM, 2551–9.8
Population and housing census, 1990: population and housing characteristics, detailed geographic coverage, State CD-ROM, 2551–10.15
Population and housing census, 1990: summary characteristics, by county, subdiv, and place, State rpt, 2551–7.14
Population census, 1990: population characteristics and living arrangements, by county, place, and urban-rural location, State rpt, 2531–1.14
Population, households, employment, income, fuel prices, and electricity demand for Pacific Northwest, alternative forecasts 1991-2010 with trends from 1980, annual rpt, 3224–3.3
Potato production, acreage, prices, and shipments, for 7 major producer States, and compared to other States, 1970s-92, annual rpt, 1311–29
Statistical Abstract of US, 1992 annual data compilation, 2324–1
Timber in northwestern US and British Columbia, production, prices, trade, and employment, quarterly rpt, 1202–3
Timber insect and disease incidence and damage, and control activities, 1990, State rpt, 1206–49.1
Timber insect and disease incidence and damage, and control activities, 1991, State rpt, 1206–49.4
Uranium tailings at inactive Lowman mill, remedial action proposals, costs, site characteristics, and environmental, socioeconomic, and health impacts, 1991 rpt, 3356–4.11
Water quality, chemistry, hydrology, and other characteristics, 1990 local area study, 5666–27.24
Water resources dev projects of Army Corps of Engineers, characteristics, and costs, 1950s-91, biennial State rpt, 3756–2.13
Water supply, and snow survey results, monthly State rpt, 1266–2.4
Water supply, and snow survey results, 1990, annual State rpt, 1264–14.3
see also under By State in the "Index by Categories"

Idaho National Engineering Laboratory
see also Department of Energy National Laboratories

Iden, George
"Economic Effects of the Savings and Loan Crisis", 26306–6.165
"Economic Implications of Rising Health Care Costs", 26306–6.174

Idiopathic CD4 T-lymphocytopenia
see Immunity disorders

Iezzoni, Lisa I.
"Purpose of Admission and Resource Use During Cancer Hospitalizations", 4652–1.304

Illegitimacy
see Births out of wedlock

Illinois
Banks (insured commercial and savings) deposits by instn, State, MSA, and county, as of June 1991, annual regional rpt, 9295–3.3
Banks (multinatl) US branches assets and liabilities, total and for 3 States, monthly rpt, quarterly data, 9362–1.4
Coal production and mines by county, prices, productivity, miners, and reserves, by mining method and State, 1990-91, annual rpt, 3164–25
County Business Patterns, 1990: employment, establishments, and payroll, by SIC 2- to 4-digit industry and county, annual State rpt, 2326–6.15
Deaths and rates, by detailed location, cause, and demographic characteristics, 1989, US Vital Statistics annual rpt, 4144–3.1
Electric power demand, and industrial and employment impacts of capacity shortfalls and new power plants, by selected State, 1960s-80s and projected to 2000, hearing, 21248–163
Employment, earnings, and hours, by selected SIC 1- to 4-digit industry, State, and for 275 MSAs, 1987-92, 6748–81

Fed Govt spending in States and local areas, by type, State, county, and city, FY91, annual rpt, 2464–3
Fed Govt spending in States, by type, program, agency, and State, FY91, annual rpt, 2464–2
Floods in Mississippi River and Gulf of Mexico basins, precipitation and water levels by site, damage, and deaths, 1982-83, 5666–27.33
HHS financial aid, by program, recipient, State, and city, FY91, annual regional listing, 4004–3.5
Hospital deaths of Medicare patients, actual and expected rates by diagnosis, and hospital characteristics, by instn, FY90 annual State rpt, 4654–14.14
Hospitals in rural areas, Medicare admission rates and charges, by instn, patient, and care characteristics, mid 1980s, 17206–2.33
Housing census, 1990: inventory, occupancy, and costs, State fact sheet, 2326–21.15
Housing census, 1990: summary unit characteristics, by householder race and age, county, place, and urban-rural location, State rpt, 2471–1.15
Housing vacancy rates for single and multifamily units and mobile homes in FHLB 7th District, by ZIP code, annual MSA rpt series, 9304–18
Military prime contract awards, by contractor, service branch, State, and city, FY91, annual rpt, 3544–22
Mineral Industry Surveys, State reviews of production, 1991, preliminary annual rpt, 5614–6
Minerals (strategic) deposits in North Central States, characteristics, 1992 compilation of papers, 5668–127
Minerals Yearbook, Vol 2, 1990: State review of production and sales by commodity, and business activity, annual rpt, 5604–22.14
Mortgage interest fixed and adjustable rates and fees offered by Illinois S&Ls, monthly rpt, discontinued, 9302–6
Multinatl firms US affiliates finances and operations, by industry, country of parent firm, and State, 1987, 2708–48
Physicians, by specialty, age, sex, and location of training and practice, 1990, State rpt, 4116–6.14
Population and housing census, 1990: detailed geographic coverage, State CD-ROM, 2551–9.3
Population and housing census, 1990: summary characteristics, by county, subdiv, and place, State rpt, 2551–7.15
Population census, 1990: population characteristics and living arrangements, by county, place, and urban-rural location, State rpt, 2531–1.15
Savings instns, FHLB 7th District and natl cost of funds indexes, and mortgage rates, monthly rpt, 9302–30
State govt pension funds use to balance budgets, with data for 2 States, 1991 hearing, 21148–66
Statistical Abstract of US, 1992 annual data compilation, 2324–1
Water quality, chemistry, hydrology, and other characteristics, 1991 local area study, 5666–27.34
Water resources dev projects of Army Corps of Engineers, characteristics, and costs, 1950s-91, biennial State rpt, 3756–2.14
see also Champaign, Ill.
see also Chicago, Ill.
see also Cook County, Ill.
see also Decatur, Ill.
see also Du Page County, Ill.
see also Joliet, Ill.
see also Lake County, Ill.
see also Moline, Ill.
see also Rantoul, Ill.
see also Rock Island, Ill.
see also St. Clair County, Ill.
see also Urbana, Ill.
see also under By State in the "Index by Categories"

Illinois River
Freight (waterborne domestic and foreign) by commodity, traffic, and passengers, by port and waterway, 1989, annual rpt, 3754–3.2; 3754–3.3
Water quality, chemistry, hydrology, and other characteristics, 1991 local area study, 5666–27.34
Water supply and quality in streams and lakes, and groundwater levels in wells, by drainage basin, 1990, annual State rpt series, 5666–10
Water supply and quality in streams and lakes, and groundwater levels in wells, by drainage basin, 1991, annual State rpt series, 5666–12

Illiteracy
see Literacy and illiteracy

Illness
see Disabled and handicapped persons
see Diseases and disorders
see Hospitalization

Imitation food products
see Synthetic food products

Immigration and emigration
Admissions to US of immigrants, alien workers, and visitors, deportations, and naturalizations, by country, FY91 and trends from 1820, annual rpt, 6264–2
Admissions to US of immigrants and legalized aliens, by occupational group and country of birth, preliminary FY91, annual table, 6264–1
Admissions to US of immigrants and nonimmigrants, alien workers, deportations, and naturalizations, FY91, annual summary rpt, 6264–7
Admissions to US of immigrants, by class of admission, country of birth, and MSA of destination, FY91, advance annual rpt, 6264–4
Adult literacy and English as a second language programs, Education Dept and State programs, enrollment, and funding, by State, 1988-91, 4808–41
Census of Population and Housing, 1990: immigrants, by period of entry, citizenship, State, birthplace, and for top cities and counties, press release, 2328–88
Census of Population and Housing, 1990: population and housing characteristics, detailed geographic coverage, State CD-ROM series, 2551–10
Census of Population and Housing, 1990: summary characteristics, by county, subdiv, and place, State rpt series, 2551–7
Central America immigrants in DC, by selected employment and other characteristics, and reasons for migration, 1985-88, working paper, 6366–6.3
Colombia immigrants employment in New England textile industry, by selected characteristics, 1960s-80s, working paper, 6366–6.4
Court civil and criminal caseloads for Federal district, appeals, and bankruptcy courts, by type of suit and offense, circuit, and district, 1991, annual rpt, 18204–11
Court civil and criminal caseloads for Federal district, appeals, and special courts, 1991, annual rpt, 18204–8
Crime, criminal justice admin and enforcement, and public opinion, data compilation, 1992 annual rpt, 6064–6
Criminal case processing in Federal district courts, and dispositions, by offense, district, and offender characteristics, 1989, annual data compilation, 6064–29
Criminal case processing in Federal district courts, and dispositions, by offense, 1980-91, annual rpt, 6064–31
Criminal cases by type and disposition, and collections, for US attorneys, by Federal district, FY91, annual rpt, 6004–2.1; 6004–2.7
Criminal offenders in Federal instns, by region and instn, FY89, annual rpt, 6244–1.1
Criminal sentences for Federal offenses, guidelines use and results by offense and district, and Sentencing Commission activities, 1991, annual rpt, 17664–1
Data on immigration enforcement, issues and trends, fact sheet series, 6266–2
Deaths and rates, by cause and selected social, demographic, and employment characteristics, 1979-85, natl longitudinal study, 4478–186
Earnings of immigrants relative to general population, selected factors, 1992 technical paper, 9385–8.143
Eighth grade class of 1988: Asian and Hispanic students proficiency in English and language at home, by selected characteristics, natl longitudinal survey, 1992 rpt, 4826–9.12
Fed Govt spending in States, by type, program, agency, and State, FY91, annual rpt, 2464–2
Foreign countries human rights conditions in 170 countries, 1991, annual rpt, 21384–3
Housing and households characteristics, and unit and neighborhood quality, by MSA location for 11 MSAs, 1987 survey, supplement, 2485–8
Illegal entry and smuggling of aliens, Federal sentencing guidelines by offense and circumstances, series, 17668–1
Israel economic conditions, US investment and export opportunities, and trade practices, 1992 rpt, 2008–32
Labor force and employment impacts of immigration, working paper series, 6366–6
NYC housing supply, occupancy, condition, and household characteristics, by tenure and borough, 1991 triennial survey, 2488–3
Older population, and health, economic, and other characteristics, with foreign comparisons, 1980s-91 with trends and projections, Current Population Rpt, 2546–2.165

Pacific territories population and housing detailed characteristics, by location, 1990 Census of Population and Housing, series, 2551–8
Population and labor force characteristics, 1940s-90 and projected to 2000, 15496–1.16
Population migration, immigration, and mover characteristics compared to nonmovers, 1987-90, annual Current Population Rpt, 2546–1.456
Population migration since 1990, mover characteristics by same or different area, and compared to nonmovers, 1991, annual Current Population Rpt, 2546–1.464
Population size and components of change, alternative projections 1990-2080 and trends from 1900, annual actuarial rpt, 4706–1.106
Population size, July 1991-92, by region, census div, and State, annual press release, 2324–10
Prison and parole admissions and releases, sentence length, and time served, by offense and offender characteristics, 1988, annual rpt, 6064–33
Research on population and reproduction, Federal funding by project, FY90, annual listing, 4474–9
Statistical Abstract of US, 1992 annual data compilation, 2324–1.1; 2324–1.5
Vietnam population size, components of change, and selected characteristics, 1979, 1989, and projected to 2050, 2326–18.65
Visas of US, immigrants on waiting list, by family and employment preference class and nationality, as of Jan 1992, 7188–1
Visas of US issued and refused to immigrants and nonimmigrants, by class, issuing office, and nationality, FY90, annual rpt, 7184–1
see also Alien workers
see also Aliens
see also Deportation
see also Foreign medical graduates
see also Foreign students
see also Mexicans in the U.S.
see also Passports and visas
see also Refugees

Immigration and Naturalization Service
Admissions to US of immigrants, alien workers, and visitors, deportations, and naturalizations, by country, FY91 and trends from 1820, annual rpt, 6264–2
Admissions to US of immigrants and legalized aliens, by occupational group and country of birth, preliminary FY91, annual table, 6264–1
Admissions to US of immigrants and nonimmigrants, alien workers, deportations, and naturalizations, FY91, annual summary rpt, 6264–7
Admissions to US of immigrants, by class of admission, country of birth, and MSA of destination, FY91, advance annual rpt, 6264–4
Applications for legal residence under Immigration Reform and Control Act, periodic rpt, discontinued, 6262–3
Border Patrol illegal alien apprehensions and agent shifts, mid 1980s-91, working paper, 6366–6.9
Budget of US, obligations and authority by function, agency, and program, with summaries and analyses, FY93, annual rpt, 104–2
Data on immigration enforcement, issues and trends, fact sheet series, 6266–2
Drug (heroin) seizures by Federal agencies, with NYC street prices and purity, FY82-91, GAO rpt, 26119–404
Illegal aliens held in INS detention facilities pending hearings, and legal aid requests, 1980s-91, GAO rpt, 26119–409
Mexico-US trade agreement impacts on truck traffic at border crossings, Customs Service staff needs, and hwy improvement costs, projected to 2000 with trends from 1986, GAO rpt, 26123–368

Immigration Reform and Control Act
Admissions to US of immigrants and legalized aliens, by occupational group and country of birth, preliminary FY91, annual table, 6264–1
Admissions to US of immigrants, by class of admission, country of birth, and MSA of destination, FY91, advance annual rpt, 6264–4
Applications for legal residence under IRCA, periodic rpt, discontinued, 6262–3
Applications for legalization under IRCA, by State and country of origin, FY91 annual summary rpt, 6264–7
Applications for legalization under IRCA, by State, MSA, and country of origin, FY90-91, annual rpt, 6264–2
Discrimination and other employment-related problems of alien workers in NYC, hotline calls, 1988, 6366–6.7
Employer sanctions impacts on labor markets, with data for selected industries and metro areas, 1980s, working paper, 6366–6.10
Los Angeles wages and working conditions impacts of Immigration Reform and Control Act, 1980s-91, working paper, 6366–6.9
Wages impacts of immigration reform provisions for alien legalization and employer sanctions, model results, 1987-89, working paper, 6366–6.8

Immunity disorders
Cancer deaths and rates, by body site, provisional data, monthly rpt, 4142–1.2
HHS financial aid, by program, recipient, State, and city, FY91, annual regional listings, 4004–3
Idiopathic CD4+ T-lymphocytopenia epidemiology and patient characteristics, 1992 conf, 4208–36
Natl Inst of Allergy and Infectious Diseases activities, grants by recipient and location, and disease cases, FY84-91, annual rpt, 4474–30
see also Acquired immune deficiency syndrome
see also Allergies

Immunity from prosecution
see Privileges and immunities

Immunology
see Vaccination and vaccines

Impacted areas
Birds (northern spotted owl) conservation methods in Pacific Northwest, timber industry impacts, and Federal and State spending, 1980s-95, 1208–388
Education funding by Federal agency, program, and recipient type, and instn spending, 1960s-91, annual rpt, 4824–8
Expenditures of Fed Govt in States, by type, program, agency, and State, FY91, annual rpt, 2464–2
Forests (natl) revenue share paid to States, and acreage, by forest, county, and congressional district, FY92, annual rpt, 1204–33
Home mortgages FHA-insured for 1-family units, by loan type and mortgage characteristics, quarterly rpt, 5142–45
Land Mgmt Bur activities in southwestern US, FY91, annual rpt, 5724–15
Public lands acreage and use, and Land Mgmt Bur activities and finances, annual State rpt series, 5724–11
Public lands, Fed Govt payments to local govts in lieu of property taxes, by State, FY92, annual press release, 5306–4.15
State govt payments to local govts in lieu of property taxes, by State, 1989, annual rpt, 10044–1

Imports
see Agricultural exports and imports
see Coal exports and imports
see East-West trade
see Energy exports and imports
see Foreign trade
see Motor vehicle exports and imports
see Natural gas exports and imports
see Petroleum exports and imports
see Tariffs and foreign trade controls

Impoundment
see Executive impoundment of appropriated funds

Imprisonment
see Correctional institutions
see Juvenile detention and correctional institutions
see Military prisons
see Prisoners
see Prisoners of war

Ince, Peter J.
"Wastepaper Recycling and the Future Timber Market", 1504–9.1

Income
see Business income and expenses, general
see Business income and expenses, specific industry
see Earnings, general
see Earnings, local and regional
see Farm income
see Income maintenance
see Income taxes
see National income and product accounts
see Personal and household income
see Poverty
see Professionals' fees
see Tips and tipping
see Underground economy
see under By Income in the "Index by Categories"

Income maintenance
Assistance (block and categorical grants) programs for State and local govts, FY91, biennial listing, 10044–8
Assistance (financial and nonfinancial) of Fed Govt, 1992 base edition, annual listing, 104–5
Assistance programs under Ways and Means Committee jurisdiction, finances, operations, and participant characteristics, FY70s-91, annual rpt, 21784–11
Beneficiaries and taxes collected for social insurance programs since 1940, quarterly rpt, 4742–1.4

Benefits, beneficiaries, and spells of participation, by aid program and recipient characteristics, 1987-88, Current Population Rpt, 2546-20.25
Benefits, beneficiary characteristics, and trust funds of OASDHI, Medicaid, SSI, and related programs, selected years 1937-90, annual rpt, 4744-3
Budget of US, CBO analysis and review of FY93 budget by function, annual rpt, 26304-2
Budget of US, CBO analysis of revenue and spending alternatives and projections of economic indicators, FY93-97, annual rpt, 26304-3
Budget of US, House concurrent resolution, with spending and revenue targets, FY93 and projected to FY97, annual rpt, 21264-2
Budget of US, midsession review of FY93 budget, by function, annual rpt, 104-7
Budget of US, obligations and authority by function, agency, and program, with summaries and analyses, FY93, annual rpt, 104-2
Chronology of income maintenance and health care financing, major private and public actions, 1636-1991, quadrennial rpt, 10178-1
Crime victim compensation and support service programs funding, by offense and State, FY88-90, biennial rpt, 6064-37
Distribution and equity of income, tax, and transfer payments, analyses and alternative estimates, series, 4746-14
Expenditures (direct) and employment, by function and level of govt, selected years 1962-87, 10048-53
Expenditures of Fed Govt in States and local areas, by type, State, and county, FY91, annual rpt, 2464-3.1
Expenditures of Fed Govt in States, by type, program, agency, and State, FY91, annual rpt, 2464-2
General assistance cases and beneficiaries, by State, MSA, and county, FY90, annual rpt, 4584-3.1; 4584-3.6
Govt finances, tax systems and revenue, and fiscal structure, by level of govt and State, 1992 with historical trends, annual rpt, 10044-1
HHS financial aid, by program, recipient, State, and city, FY91, annual regional listings, 4004-3
Households (single person and nonfamily) social, economic and housing characteristics, by tenure, 1989, 2486-1.15
Households, family, and personal income, by source, detailed characteristics, and region, 1991, annual Current Population Rpt, 2546-6.76
Households, family, and personal income, wealth, and poverty measures, 1960s-90, Current Population Rpt, chartbook, 2546-6.75
Income (household) and poverty status under alternative income definitions, by recipient characteristics, 1979-91, annual Current Population Rpt, 2546-6.78
Income (personal) per capita and by source, and employment, by industry div, State, MSA, and county, 1969-90, annual CD-ROM, 2704-7
Job Training Partnership Act support services and supplementary payments, and impact on single parent participation, 199091, 26106-8.15
Natl income and product accounts and components, *Survey of Current Business*, monthly rpt, 2702-1.23
Pacific territories population and housing detailed characteristics, by location, 1990 Census of Population and Housing, series, 2551-8
Population economic well-being indicators, by selected characteristics and household income and income-to-poverty ratio, 1984, 2546-20.22
Poverty status of population and families, by detailed characteristics, 1991, annual Current Population Rpt, 2546-6.77
Presidential approval rating and political party affiliation impact on defense spending and transfer payments, model description and results, 1950s-88, working paper, 9393-10.17
R&D funding by Fed Govt, by detailed function, program, and agency, FY91-93, annual rpt, 9627-9
Single parent families in own and others homes, by financial, housing, and other characteristics, 1989, 2486-1.14
Social Security Bulletin, OASDHI and other program operations and beneficiary characteristics, from 1940, quarterly journal, 4742-1
Statistical Abstract of US, 1992 annual data compilation, 2324-1.12
Survey of Current Business, detailed financial and business data, and economic indicators, monthly rpt, 2702-1.3
Survey of Income and Program Participation, data collection, methodology, and availability, 1991 users guide, 2628-24
Survey of Income and Program Participation, household composition, income, benefits, and labor force status, methodology, working paper series, 2626-10
see also Aid to Families with Dependent Children
see also Disability benefits and insurance
see also Food stamp programs
see also Low-income energy assistance
see also Maternity benefits
see also Medicaid
see also Medicare
see also Old-Age, Survivors, Disability, and Health Insurance
see also Public welfare programs
see also Rent supplements
see also Social security
see also State funding for social welfare
see also Supplemental Security Income
see also Transportation assistance
see also Unemployment insurance
see also Workers compensation

Income taxes
Admin and compliance issues, and taxpayer views, 1991 conf, 8304-25
Assets and debts of private sector, balance sheets by segment, 1960-91, semiannual rpt, 9365-4.1
Boycotts (intl) by OPEC and other countries, US firms and individuals cooperation and tax benefits denied, 1990, article, 8302-2.323
Brackets (income) simplification under tax reform in US and other countries, fiscal effects, late 1970s-92, working paper, 9377-9.143
Budget of US, authoritative financial statements with appropriations, outlays, and receipts, by category and agency, FY91, annual rpt, 8104-2.2
Budget of US, CBO analysis and review of FY93 budget by function, annual rpt, 26304-2
Budget of US, CBO analysis of revenue and spending alternatives and projections of economic indicators, FY93-97, annual rpt, 26304-3
Budget of US, historical data, selected years FY34-91 and projected to FY97, 108-46.5
Budget of US, obligations and authority by function, agency, and program, with summaries and analyses, FY93, annual rpt, 104-2
Budget of US, receipts by source, outlays by agency and program, and balances, monthly rpt, 8102-3
Business statistics, detailed data for major industries and economic indicators, 1960-91, *Survey of Current Business* biennial supplement, 2704-1
Capital gains tax rates impacts on taxpayer gains and long-term revenues, 1990 technical paper, 8006-6.4
Capital gains tax rates relation to tax revenues, mid 1950s-80s, technical paper, 8006-6.3
Capital investment in plant and equipment, tax rates, and rates of return, alternative estimates, 1950s-80s, technical paper, 8006-6.2
Collections, enforcement, and litigation activity of IRS, with data by type of tax, region, and State, FY91, annual rpt, 8304-3
Collections of taxes, by level of govt, type of tax, State, and selected counties, quarterly rpt, 2462-3
Corporations and individual income taxes, monthly rpt, quarterly and annual data, 23842-1.6
Corporations income tax compliance, and IRS enforcement activities, 1970s-92, hearing, 25408-118
Corporations income tax compliance issues for large firms, with income, taxes paid, and tax credits, 1988, GAO rpt, 26119-405
Corporations income tax returns, income and tax items by asset size and detailed industry, 1989, annual rpt, 8304-4; 8304-21
Corporations income tax returns, summary data by asset size and industry div, 1989, annual article, 8302-2.321
Corporations income taxes and effective rates on US, foreign, and worldwide income, by company and industry, 1980s, GAO rpt, 26119-289
Corporations under domestic and foreign control, finances and tax burdens, 1983-87, GAO rpt, 26119-411
Distribution and equity of income, tax, and transfer payments, analyses and alternative estimates, series, 4746-14
Domestic Intl Sales Corps (Interest Charge) income tax returns, assets, and income and tax items, by detailed industry, 1987, article, 8302-2.312

Economic performance and income distribution impacts of tax policy, issues and background data, with foreign comparisons, 1991 and trends, 21788–211
Economic Report of the President for 1992, Joint Economic Committee critique and policy recommendations, annual rpt, 23844–2
Election (presidential) campaign fund contributions from income tax return checkoff, receipts and outlays, mid 1970s-91 and alternative projections to 1993, hearing, 21428–10
Electric utilities finances and operations, detailed data for publicly owned firms, 1990, annual rpt, 3164–24
Electric utilities privately owned, finances and operations, detailed data, 1990, annual rpt, 3164–23
Employee benefits tax exclusion, Federal revenue forgone and coverage indicators, by benefit type, 1950s-80s and projected to 1995, GAO rpt, 26119–389
Energy producers finances and operations, by energy type for US firms domestic and foreign operations, 1990, annual rpt, 3164–44
Enforcement of tax payment activities of IRS, and related collections, FY88-92, hearing, 21788–217
Family income and Federal tax rates, by income level, late 1970s-94, 21788–212
Farm operators nonfarm self-employment income by source and farm profit and loss, and tax burden, 1987, article, 1541–1.320
Farm sector balance sheet, and marketing receipts by detailed commodity, by State, 1986-90, annual rpt, 1544–18
Fed Govt finances, cash and debt transactions, daily tables, 8102–4
Fed Govt internal revenue and refunds, by type of tax, quarterly rpt, 8302–2.1
Fed Govt receipts by source and outlays by agency, *Treasury Bulletin*, quarterly rpt, 8002–4.1
Finances of govts, by level of govt, State, and for large cities and counties, annual rpt series, 2466–2
Finances of govts, tax systems and revenue, and fiscal structure, by level of govt and State, 1992 and historical trends, annual rpt, 10044–1
Flow-of-funds accounts, savings, investments, and credit statements, quarterly rpt, 9365–3.3
Foreign and US income and capital tax policies, with background data for EC, Japan, and US, mid 1960s-91, article, 9373–1.316
Foreign corporations and individuals, and US entities abroad, detailed data compilation for income tax returns, 1970s-89, quinquennial rpt, 8308–31
Foreign direct investment in US by top 10 countries, factors affecting rate of return, and compared to returns for US firms, 1980s-91, article, 2702–1.330
Foreign-earned income on US individual returns, income and tax items by income level and occupation, 1987, article, 8302–2.301
Foreign-owned corporate activity in US, income tax returns and selected income and tax items, by industry div and selected country, 1988, article, 8302–2.309
Foreign partners of US partnerships, income and tax withheld, by country, 1990, article, 8302–2.324
Foreign Sales Corps income tax returns, assets, and income and tax items, by industry, country of incorporation, and transaction pricing method, 1987, article, 8302–2.311
Households income and poverty status under alternative income definitions, by recipient characteristics, 1991, annual Current Population Rpt, 2546–6.78
Individual income tax liability and payments, and total and taxable personal income, quarterly 1959-91, annual article, 2702–1.326
Individual income tax returns, detailed data, 1988, annual rpt, 8304–2
Individual income tax returns processing and taxpayer info activity, electronic and experimental filings, and refunds, periodic press release, 8302–6
Individual income tax returns, selected income and tax items by income level, preliminary 1990, annual article, 8302–2.307
Motor vehicle industry finances, and average fleet fuel economy, by selected firm, 1991 hearings, 21368–138
Multinatl firms US affiliates, finances, and operations, by industry, world area of parent firm, and State, 1989-90, annual rpt, 2704–4
Multinatl firms US affiliates gross product, by component, industry, and country of parent firm, 1987-90, article, 2702–1.342
Multinatl firms US affiliates income tax compliance issues, with income and tax data by industry group, 1987-89, press release, 8008–155
Multinatl US firms and foreign affiliates finances and operations, by industry and country, 1989 benchmark survey, annual rpt, 2704–5
Multinatl US firms foreign affiliates, income statement items by asset size, industry, and country, 1988, biennial article, 8302–2.322
Natl income and product accounts and components, *Survey of Current Business*, monthly rpt, 2702–1.23
Natl income and product accounts, comprehensive accounts and components, benchmark revisions, 1929-88, 2708–5
Natl income and product accounts, comprehensive accounts and components, *Survey of Current Business*, monthly rpt, 2702–1.26
Natural gas interstate pipeline company detailed financial and operating data, by firm, 1990, annual rpt, 3164–38
New England States economic indicators, Fed Reserve 1st District, monthly rpt, 9373–2
Nonprofit charitable organizations finances, summary data by asset size, 1989, article, 8302–2.325
Nonprofit charitable organizations finances, with data by State and for top 10 instns, 1988, article, 8302–2.302
North Central States, FHLB 6th District insured S&Ls financial condition and operations by State, quarterly rpt, 9302–23
OASI benefits, earnings, and tax revenues under alternative eligibility criteria, 1990, technical paper, 4746–26.15
OASI retirement earnings test, liberalization effect on beneficiaries and Federal revenue, 1991 hearing, 21788–215
Oil company effective income tax rates, with background income and tax data for domestic and foreign operations, 1977-89, 3168–124
Partnership income tax returns, income statement and balance sheet items by industry group, 1990, annual article, 8302–2.314
Partnership losses and total income of high-income individuals, by average tax rate, 1985-89, article, 8302–2.313
Pension plan earnings and contributions tax exclusions, cost and benefit issues with background data, 1970s-FY92, article, 9373–1.305
Public opinion on taxes, spending, and govt efficiency, by respondent characteristics, 1992 survey, annual rpt, 10044–2
Puerto Rico and other US possessions corporations income tax returns, income and tax items, and employment, by selected industry, 1989, article, 8302–2.326
Returns and supplemental documents filed, by type, FY91 and projected to FY2000, semiannual rpt, 8302–4
Returns filed, by type, IRS service center, and whether full-paid, refund, and electronically filed, 1990 and projected to 1998, semiannual rpt, 8302–7
Returns filed, by type of filer, detailed preliminary and supplementary data, quarterly rpt with articles, 8302–2
Returns filed, by type of tax and IRS district, 1990 and projected 1991-98, annual rpt, 8304–24
Returns filed, by type of tax, region, and IRS service center, projected 1991-98 and trends from 1978, annual rpt, 8304–9
Returns filed using alternative methods, with fraud, and conventional form preparation time and processing costs, 1986-92, GAO rpt, 26119–400
Savings instns financial statements, for instns insured by Savings Assn Insurance Fund by FHLB district and State, and for FDIC-insured savings banks, 1989, annual rpt, 8434–1
Savings instns insured by Savings Assn Insurance Fund, finances by profitability group, district, and State, quarterly rpt, 8432–4
Single mothers family income, and impacts of child care, govt and child support payments, taxes, and marriage, with data by State, 1970s-91, 21788–212
Sole proprietorship income tax returns, income statement items by industry group, 1990, annual article, 8302–2.317; 8302–2.320
Southeastern States, Fed Reserve 5th District insured commercial banks financial statements, by State, quarterly rpt, 9389–18
Statistical Abstract of US, 1992 annual data compilation, 2324–1.9; 2324–1.10; 2324–1.17
Telephone and telegraph firms detailed finances and operations, 1990, annual rpt, 9284–6

Telephone firms borrowing under Rural Telephone Program, and financial and operating data, by State, 1991, annual rpt, 1244–2
Telephone system of IRS for income tax questions, improvements in accuracy, 1989-91, GAO rpt, 26119–418
Timber sales of Forest Service, expenses, and operations, by region, State, and natl forest, FY91, annual rpts, 1204–36
Transit systems finances and operations, by mode, size of fleet and urban area, region, and for 518 systems, 1990, annual rpt, 7884–4
Truck and bus interstate carriers finances and operations, by district, 1990, annual rpt, 9486–5.3
Truck, bus, and rail carriers regulated by ICC, employment and finances, as of FY91, annual rpt, 9484–1
see also Tax delinquency and evasion
see also Tax incentives and shelters
see also Tax protests and appeals
see also Windfall profit tax
see also Withholding tax

Independent agencies
see Federal independent agencies

Indexes
see Bibliographies
see CD-ROM catalogs and guides
see Computer data file guides
see Consumer Price Index
see Cost of living
see Directories
see Government publications lists
see Industrial production indexes
see Labor costs and cost indexes
see Producer Price Index

India
Agricultural exports of US, for grains, oilseed products, hides, skins, and cotton, by country, weekly rpt, 1922–3
Agricultural trade of US, by detailed commodity and country, 1991, annual rpt, 1524–8
Agricultural trade of US, by detailed commodity and country, 1991, semiannual rpt, 1522–4
AID economic aid to developing countries, obligations and disbursements by country, quarterly rpt, 9912–4
AID loans repayment status and terms by program and country, and status of predecessor agency loans, quarterly rpt, 9912–3
Cuba trade, by commodity and country, mid 1980s-91, 9118–8
Dracunculiasis cases, and surveillance and eradication programs, for India, Pakistan, and Africa, 1980s-91, article, 4202–7.307
Dyes (sulfur) from 3 countries at less than fair value, injury to US industry, investigation with background financial and operating data, 1992 rpt, 9886–14.347
Economic and military aid and loans from US and intl agencies, by program and country, FY46-91, annual rpt, 9914–5
Economic and social conditions of developing countries from 1960s, and Intl Dev Cooperation Agency and AID activities and funding, FY91-93, annual rpt, 9904–4
Economic conditions, income, production, prices, employment, and trade, 1992 periodic country rpt, 2046–4.47
Economic conditions, policy, and trade practices, by country, 1989-91, annual rpt, 21384–5
Economic, social, political, and geographic summary data, by country, 1992, annual factbook, 9114–2
Energy supply and demand, and implications for US trade, 1992 country rpt, 3406–6.10
Exports and imports of US, by commodity and country, 1980-90, world area rpt, 9116–1.3
Exports and imports of US, by Harmonized System 6-digit commodity and country, 1991, annual rpt, 2424–13
Exports and imports of US, by selected country, country group, and commodity group, 1991, annual rpt, 2044–37
Exports and imports of US, by transport mode, country, and SITC 1- to 3-digit commodity, 1991, annual rpt, 2424–12
Exports, imports, and balances of US for manufactured goods, by SITC 2-digit commodity and country, quarterly rpt, 2042–35
Exports, imports, and balances of US with major trading partners, by product category, 1987-91, annual chartbook, 9884–21
Exports of US, detailed Schedule B commodities with countries of destination, 1991, annual rpt, 2424–10
Food supply, needs, and aid for developing countries, status and alternative forecasts, 1992 world area rpt, 1526–8.2
Human rights conditions in 170 countries, and US economic and military aid, 1991, annual rpt, 21384–3
Imports of goods, services, and investment from US, trade barriers, impacts, and US actions, by country, 1991, annual rpt, 444–2
Labor conditions, union coverage, and work accidents, 1992 annual country rpt, 6366–4.25
Military aid of US, arms sales, and training programs costs and budget requests, by program, world region, and country, FY91-93, annual rpt, 7144–13
Military spending, arms trade, and force strengths, with govt spending and population, by country, 1979-89, annual rpt, 9824–1
Minerals Yearbook, Vol 3, 1989: foreign country review of production, trade, and policy, by commodity, annual rpt, 5604–35.2
Multinatl US firms and foreign affiliates finances and operations, by industry and country, 1989 benchmark survey, annual rpt, 2704–5
Multinatl US firms foreign affiliates, income statement items by asset size, industry, and country, 1988, biennial article, 8302–2.322
Nuclear power generation in US and 20 countries, monthly rpt, 3162–24.10
Nuclear power generation in US and 20 countries, monthly 1973-88, 3168–123.10
Pollution (air) contributing to global warming, emissions by monitoring site and country, and temperature change by world area and US region, 1860s-1990, annual rpt, 3004–33
Population size, growth rates, and components of change, by country, projected 1990-2020 and trends from 1950, biennial rpt, 2324–9
Population size, life expectancy, and fertility, trends and projections, 1992 country rpt, 2326–24.3
Refugee migration, and intl aid programs, by world area and country of origin and asylum, 1991, annual rpt, 7004–15
Spacecraft and satellite launches since 1957, quarterly listing, 9502–2
Steel trade, by product, country, and customs district, with US industry operating data, 1989-June 1992, semiannual rpt, 9882–15
Sulfanilic acid from Hungary and India, injury to US industry from foreign subsidized and less than fair value imports, investigation with background financial and operating data, 1992 rpt, 9886–19.83
UN voting record and share of votes in agreement with US, by issue, country, and world area, 1991, annual rpt, 7004–18
see also under By Foreign Country in the "Index by Categories"

Indian claims
US Claims Court caseload by type of suit, and judgments, FY92, annual rpt, 18224–1

Indian Health Service
Assistance (financial) of HHS, by program, recipient, State, and city, FY91, annual regional listings, 4004–3
Budget of US, obligations and authority by function, agency, and program, with summaries and analyses, FY93, annual rpt, 104–2
Education funding of Fed Govt, with enrollment, program grants, and fellowships by State, for Indians, 1980s-FY91, annual rpt, 14874–1
Employment of Indians and non-Indians, training, hires, and quits, for IHS by occupation, FY90, annual rpt, 4084–6
Facilities, funding, and operations of IHS, and Indian health and other characteristics, 1950s-91, annual chartbook, 4084–1
Facilities of IHS, use, and Indian health and other characteristics, by IHS region, 1980s-90, annual chartbook, 4084–7
Hospital admissions, length of stay, beds, and births, by IHS and tribal facility and service area, FY90-91, annual rpt, 4084–4
Hospital capacity, use, and births, by area and IHS and tribal facility, quarterly rpt, 4082–1
Hospitalization in IHS, tribal, and contract facilities, by diagnosis, age, sex, and service area, FY91, annual rpt, 4084–5
Outpatient services provided at IHS facilities, by reason for visit and age, FY90, annual rpt, 4084–2
Outpatient visits to IHS and tribal facilities, by type of provider, selected hospital, and service area, FY91, annual rpt, 4084–3
Youth health condition and behavioral patterns, by sex and grade, for Indians and Alaska Natives, 1988-90, 4088–3

Indian Nations at Risk Task Force
Education condition of Indians and Alaska Natives, indicators and comparisons to other groups, 1980s-90, 4808–42
Indian Ocean
Environmental summary data, and intl claims and disputes, 1992 annual factbook, 9114–2
Fish (tuna) catch in Indian Ocean, by species and country of vessel origin, 1974-86, article, 2162–1.301
Hurricanes and tropical storms in Pacific and Indian Oceans, paths and surveillance, 1991, annual rpt, 3804–8
Mariners Weather Log, quarterly journal, 2152–8
Temperature of sea surface by ocean and for US coastal areas, and Bering Sea ice conditions, monthly rpt, 2182–5
Tide height and time daily at coastal points, forecast 1993, annual rpt, 2174–2.5
Weather (marine) forecast areas, and broadcast schedules and stations worldwide, as of Sept 1992, annual rpt, 2184–3
Weather (marine) forecast broadcast schedules worldwide, periodic rpt, 2182–9
Indiana
Banks (insured commercial and savings) deposits by instn, State, MSA, and county, as of June 1991, annual regional rpt, 9295–3.3
Coal production and mines by county, prices, productivity, miners, and reserves, by mining method and State, 1990-91, annual rpt, 3164–25
Deaths and rates, by detailed location, cause, and demographic characteristics, 1989, US Vital Statistics annual rpt, 4144–3.1
Electric power demand, and industrial and employment impacts of capacity shortfalls and new power plants, by selected State, 1960s-80s and projected to 2000, hearing, 21248–163
Employment, earnings, and hours, by selected SIC 1- to 4-digit industry, State, and for 275 MSAs, 1987-92, 6748–81
Fed Govt spending in States and local areas, by type, State, county, and city, FY91, annual rpt, 2464–3
Fed Govt spending in States, by type, program, agency, and State, FY91, annual rpt, 2464–2
HHS financial aid, by program, recipient, State, and city, FY91, annual regional listing, 4004–3.5
Hospital deaths of Medicare patients, actual and expected rates by diagnosis, and hospital characteristics, by instn, FY90 annual State rpt, 4654–14.15
Housing census, 1990: inventory, occupancy, and costs, State fact sheet, 2326–21.16
Housing census, 1990: summary unit characteristics, by householder race and age, county, place, and urban-rural location, State rpt, 2471–1.16
Medicaid impacts on State budgets, and program financing, cost control measures, enrollment, and services coverage, by selected State, 1960s-80s and projected to 1997, 10176–3.6
Military prime contract awards, by contractor, service branch, State, and city, FY91, annual rpt, 3544–22
Mineral Industry Surveys, State reviews of production, 1991, preliminary annual rpt, 5614–6
Minerals Yearbook, Vol 2, 1990: State review of production and sales by commodity, and business activity, annual rpt, 5604–22.15
Multinatl firms US affiliates finances and operations, by industry, country of parent firm, and State, 1987, 2708–48
Physicians, by specialty, age, sex, and location of training and practice, 1990, State rpt, 4116–6.15
Population and housing census, 1990: detailed geographic coverage, State CD-ROM, 2551–9.3
Population and housing census, 1990: summary characteristics, by county, subdiv, and place, State rpt, 2551–7.16
Population census, 1990: population characteristics and living arrangements, by county, place, and urban-rural location, State rpt, 2531–1.16
Savings and loan assns, FHLB 6th District insured members financial condition and operations by State, quarterly rpt, 9302–23
Statistical Abstract of US, 1992 annual data compilation, 2324–1
Water quality, chemistry, hydrology, and other characteristics, 1991 local area study, 5666–27.34
Water resources dev projects of Army Corps of Engineers, characteristics, and costs, 1950s-91, biennial State rpt, 3756–2.15
see also Bloomington, Ind.
see also Elkhart, Ind.
see also Evansville, Ind.
see also Gary, Ind.
see also Goshen, Ind.
see also Hammond, Ind.
see also Indianapolis, Ind.
see also Lake County, Ind.
see also Vincennes, Ind.
see also under By State in the "Index by Categories"
Indianapolis, Ind.
Drug test results at arrest, by drug type, offense, and sex, for selected urban areas, quarterly rpt, 6062–3
Wages by occupation, for office and plant workers, 1991 survey, periodic MSA rpt, 6785–12.1
see also under By City and By SMSA or MSA in the "Index by Categories"
Indians
AFDC Job Opportunities and Basic Skills Training programs operated by Indian and Alaska Native organizations, funding and persons eligible, FY91, GAO rpt, 26121–460
AIDS cases by risk group, race, sex, age, State, and MSA, and deaths, quarterly rpt, 4202–9
Arrests and prisoners, by offense, offender characteristics, and location, data compilation, 1992 annual rpt, 6064–6.4; 6064–6.6
Arrests, by offense, offender characteristics, and location, 1991, annual rpt, 6224–2.2
Assistance (financial and nonfinancial) of Fed Govt, 1992 base edition, annual listing, 104–5
Births of low birthweight to Indians, compared to whites and blacks, for New York, 1980s, article, 4042–3.359
Business mgmt and financial aid from Minority Business Dev Centers, and characteristics of businesses, by region and State, FY91, annual rpt, 2104–6
Cancer cases among Indians, and racial misclassification in Natl Cancer Inst registry, 1974-89, article, 4472–1.324
Cancer cases, and incidence and survival rates, for Indians with comparisons to whites, for 2 States, 1982-87, article, 4472–1.347
Census of Population and Housing, 1990: data summary, use, and availability, fact sheet, 2326–23.2
Census of Population and Housing, 1990: detailed geographic coverage, State CD-ROM series, 2551–9
Census of Population and Housing, 1990: Indian tribes population size, with data by State, press release, 2328–86
Census of Population and Housing, 1990: population and housing characteristics, detailed geographic coverage, State CD-ROM series, 2551–10
Census of Population and Housing, 1990: summary characteristics, by county, subdiv, and place, State rpt series, 2551–7
Census of Population and Housing, 1990: summary characteristics, households, and land area, by county, subdiv, and place, State rpt series, 2551–1
Census of Population, 1990: ancestry of US population, by group and State, press release, 2328–87
Census of Population, 1990: population characteristics and living arrangements, by county, place, and urban-rural location, State rpt series, 2531–1
Census of Population, 1990: population characteristics and living arrangements, for Native American, urban, and metro areas, series, 2531–2
Coal leasing activity on Federal and Indian lands, acreage, production, and revenues, by State, 1981-90, biennial rpt, 3164–79
Coal Surface Mining Reclamation and Enforcement Office activities and funding, by State and Indian tribe, FY91, annual rpt, 5644–1
Colorado River Storage Project finances and activities in western States, FY91, annual rpt, 5824–3
Community Dev Block Grant activities and funding, by program, FY75-91, annual rpt, 5124–8
Crime victim compensation and support service programs funding, by offense and State, FY88-90, biennial rpt, 6064–37
Crime victim compensation and support service programs operations, for Indians, 1988-90, 6066–31.1
Criminal cases by type and disposition, and collections, for US attorneys, by Federal district, FY91, annual rpt, 6004–2.1; 6004–2.7
Dams on Indian reservations, Bur of Indian Affairs and tribal mgmt of unsafe dams and Interior Dept funding, 1980s-91, GAO rpt, 26113–558
Diabetic and nondiabetic Navajo cholesterol and triglyceride levels, by age and sex, 1989-90 local area study, article, 4042–3.309

Education (special) enrollment by age, staff, funding, and needs, by type of handicap and State, 1990/91, annual rpt, 4944–4
Education condition of Indians and Alaska Natives, indicators and comparisons to other groups, 1980s-90, 4808–42
Education data compilation, 1992 annual rpt, 4824–2
Education data, detail for elementary, secondary, and higher education, 1920s-91 and projected to 2002, annual rpt, 4824–1
Education funding by Federal agency, program, and recipient type, and instn spending, 1960s-91, annual rpt, 4824–8
Education funding of Fed Govt, with enrollment, program grants, and fellowships by State, for Indians, 1980s-FY91, annual rpt, 14874–1
Education in Head Start programs, enrollment, funding, and staff, FY91, annual rpt, 4584–5
Educational performance and conditions, characteristics, attitudes, activities, and plans, 1988 8th grade class, natl longitudinal survey, series, 4826–9
Educational performance of elementary and secondary students, and factors affecting proficiency, by selected characteristics, 1990 natl assessments, subject rpt series, 4896–8
Electric power sales by customer, activities by plant, and financial statements of Western Area Power Admin, FY91, annual rpt, 3254–1
Employment of minorities and women, by occupation, SIC 1- to 3-digit industry, State, and MSA, 1991, annual rpt, 9244–1
Energy aid for low income households, funding sources, costs, and participation, by State, FY90, annual rpt, 4584–1
EPA pollution control grant program activities, monthly rpt, 9182–8
Fed Equal Opportunity Recruitment Program activity, and employment by sex, race, pay grade, and occupational group, FY91, annual rpt, 9844–33
Fed Govt employment of minorities, disabled, and veterans, and years of service, by occupation, age, sex, and agency, as of Sept 1990, biennial rpt, 9844–27
Fed Govt spending in States, by type, program, agency, and State, FY91, annual rpt, 2464–2
Fetal alcohol syndrome rates among Indians in Canada and Southwestern US, 1970s-80s, article, 4482–1.310
Fish Hatchery Natl System activities and deliveries, by species, hatchery, and jurisdiction of waters stocked, FY91, annual rpt, 5504–10
FmHA activities, and loans and grants by program and State, FY91 and trends from FY70, annual rpt, 1184–17
FmHA loans, by type, borrower race, and State, quarterly rpt, 1182–5
Food aid program of USDA for women, infants, and children, participants and costs by State and Indian agency, FY90, annual tables, 1364–12
Food aid program of USDA for women, infants, and children, participants by race, State, and Indian agency, 1991, annual rpt, 1364–16
Food aid program of USDA for women, infants, and children, participants, clinics, and costs, by State and Indian agency, monthly tables, 1362–16
Head Start handicapped enrollment, by handicap, State, and for Indian and migrant programs, 1988/89, annual rpt, 4584–4
Health care outpatient services provided at Indian Health Service facilities, by reason for visit and age, FY90, annual rpt, 4084–2
Health care outpatient visits to Indian Health Service and tribal facilities, by type of provider, selected hospital, and service area, FY91, annual rpt, 4084–3
Health care professionals supply and education, by professional and other characteristics, and location, 1960s-92 and projected to 2020, biennial rpt, 4114–8
Health care services employment of Indians and non-Indians by Indian Health Service, training, hires, and quits, by occupation, FY90, annual rpt, 4084–6
Health condition and care indicators, 1950s-90 with health improvement and disease prevention goals for 1990, annual data compilation, 4144–11
Health condition and other characteristics of Indians, and Indian Health Service facilities and use, by IHS region, 1980s-90, annual chartbook, 4084–7
Health condition and other characteristics of Indians, and Indian Health Service facilities, funding, and operations, 1950s-91, annual chartbook, 4084–1
Health risk behavior among Indians, by region and for Montana, mid 1980s, article, 4042–3.346
HHS financial aid, by program, recipient, State, and city, FY91, annual regional listings, 4004–3
Higher education degrees awarded, by level, field, race, and sex, 1989/90 and trends from 1980/81, annual rpt, 4844–17
Higher education enrollment, by level, race, and sex, fall 1980-90, biennial rpt, 4844–15
Higher education enrollment, by sex and race, 1976-2000, annual rpt, 4824–4
Hospital admissions, length of stay, beds, and births, by Indian Health Service and tribal facility and service area, FY90-91, annual rpt, 4084–4
Hospital capacity, use, and births, by area and Indian Health Service and tribal facility, quarterly rpt, 4082–1
Hospitalization in Indian Health Service, tribal, and contract facilities, by diagnosis, age, sex, and IHS service area, FY91, annual rpt, 4084–5
Housing (public) drug treatment and anticrime programs, HUD grants by recipient, FY91, press release, 5006–3.81
Housing (public) drug treatment and anticrime programs, HUD grants by recipient, FY92, press release, 5006–3.99
Housing (public and Indian) tenant assns, HUD project mgmt and operation training grants by recipient, FY91, press release, 5006–3.77
Housing (public and Indian) tenant assns, HUD project mgmt and operation training grants by recipient, FY92, press release, 5006–3.100
Housing census, 1990: summary unit characteristics, by householder race and age, county, place, and urban-rural location, State rpt series, 2471–1
Housing programs of HUD, operations and funding, 1990, annual rpt, 5004–10
Land ownership, multiple ownership, and Bur of Indian Affairs records maintenance, for 12 reservations, 1991, GAO rpt, 26113–559
Lands (Indian and govt) under BIA mgmt, acreage, leases, and use, 1989, annual rpt, 5704–12
Lands (public) acreage, grants, use, revenues, and allocations, by State, FY91, annual rpt, 5724–1.3
Libraries (public) services for Indians and Hawaii Natives, project listing and funding by tribe and State, FY90, annual rpt, 4874–5
Maps and other cartographic records of historic Indian territories and resources, Natl Archives special collection, 1981 rpt, 9516–1.4
Minerals resources and availability on public lands, State rpt series, 5606–7
North Central States Indian population and Indian-owned firms, by State, selected years 1987-90, article, 9383–19.304
Nuclear engineering enrollment and degrees granted by instn and State, and grad placement, by student characteristics, 1991, annual rpt, 3004–5
NYC housing supply, occupancy, condition, and household characteristics, by tenure and borough, 1991 triennial survey, 2488–3
Oil, gas, and minerals production and revenue on Federal and Indian land, by State, 1991 and trends from 1920, annual rpt, 5734–2
Pacific Northwest Indian tribes environmental, economic, and cultural impacts of OCS oil and gas lease and dev, with background data, 1970s-92, 5738–35
Population size, by race and Hispanic origin, 1992 and projected 2000-2050, press release, 2328–85
Pregnant women smoking, by age and marital status, for Indians in Washington State, mid 1980s, article, 4042–3.306
Prenatal care and adverse birth outcomes for Indians, relation to local services availability, 1980-85, conf paper, 4164–2
Prison and community-based facilities, population, employment, spending, and other characteristics, by State and for Fed Govt, 1990, quinquennial rpt, 6068–218
Prisoners, characteristics, and movements, by State, 1990, annual rpt, 6064–26
Radiation exposure of population near Hanford, Wash, nuclear plant, with methodology, 1944-91, series, 3356–5
Radiation protection and health physics enrollment and degrees granted by instn and State, and grad placement, by student characteristics, 1991, annual rpt, 3004–7
Relocation program for Navajo and Hopi, activities and caseloads, monthly rpt, 16002–1
Science and engineering employment and education of minorities, women, and disabled, by field, mid 1970s-91, biennial rpt, 9624–20

Science and engineering grad enrollment, by field, source of funds, and characteristics of student and instn, 1990, annual rpt, 9627–7
Science and Engineering Indicators, employment, education, R&D funding, and industry impacts, with foreign comparisons, 1960s-91, biennial rpt, 9624–10
State and local govt employment of minorities and women, by occupation, function, pay level, and State, 1991, annual rpt, 9244–6
Statistical Abstract of US, 1992 annual data compilation, 2324–1
Trust funds of Indians, Bur of Indian Affairs overpayments and shortages, by account, 1970s-91, hearing, 21408–131
Uranium reserves and industry operations, by region and State, various periods 1966-91, annual rpt, 3164–65.1
Wastewater treatment and collection facility construction funding needs and Fed Govt grants, by State, 1990 and projected to 2010, biennial rpt, 9204–7
Wisconsin timber resources and removals, by species, forest type, ownership, and county, series, 1206–34
Youth health condition and behavioral patterns, by sex and grade, for Indians and Alaska Natives, 1988-90, 4088–3
see also Alaska Natives
see also Indian claims
see also under By Race and Ethnic Group in the "Index by Categories"

Indigent defense
see Legal aid

Individual retirement arrangements
Assets of collective investment funds, instns involved, and accounts, by type of fund and holding, 1991, annual rpt, 13004–1.3
Banks (insured commercial) domestic and foreign office consolidated financial statements, monthly rpt, quarterly data, 9362–1.4
Banks (insured commercial and savings) finances, for foreign and domestic offices, by asset size, 1990, annual rpt, 9294–4.2
Banks and thrifts finances and operations by deposit size, Fed Reserve functional cost analysis, 1991, annual rpt, 9364–6
Credit unions federally insured, finances by instn characteristics and State, as of June 1992, semiannual rpt, 9532–6
Credit unions federally insured, finances, 1990-91, annual rpt, 9534–1
Families financial status, income, net worth, and assets and debt by type, by income and selected characteristics, 1983 and 1989, article, 9362–1.301
Households financial services use, by account type and instn type and location, 1989 survey, article, 9362–1.303
Savings impact of IRAs, 1979-84, working paper, 9381–10.126
Savings instns financial statements, for instns insured by Savings Assn Insurance Fund by FHLB district and State, and for FDIC-insured savings banks, 1989, annual rpt, 8434–1
Southeastern States, Fed Reserve 5th District insured commercial banks financial statements, by State, quarterly rpt, 9389–18
Statistical Abstract of US, 1992 annual data compilation, 2324–1.12
Tax (excise) collections of IRS, by source, quarterly rpt, 8302–1
Tax (income) returns filed, by type of filer, selected income items, quarterly rpt, 8302–2.1
Tax (income) returns of individuals, detailed data, 1988, annual rpt, 8304–2
Tax (income) returns of individuals, selected income and tax items by income level, preliminary 1990, annual article, 8302–2.307
Tax (income) withholding and related documents filed, by type and IRS service center, 1991 and projected 1992-99, annual rpt, 8304–22

Indochina
see Cambodia
see Laos
see Southeast Asia
see Vietnam

Indonesia
Agricultural trade of US, by detailed commodity and country, 1991, annual rpt, 1524–8
Agricultural trade of US, by detailed commodity and country, 1991, semiannual rpt, 1522–4
AID economic aid to developing countries, obligations and disbursements by country, quarterly rpt, 9912–4
AID loans repayment status and terms by program and country, and status of predecessor agency loans, quarterly rpt, 9912–3
Cuba trade, by commodity and country, mid 1980s-91, 9118–8
Economic and military aid and loans from US and intl agencies, by program and country, FY46-91, annual rpt, 9914–5
Economic and social conditions of developing countries from 1960s, and Intl Dev Cooperation Agency and AID activities and funding, FY91-93, annual rpt, 9904–4
Economic conditions, income, production, prices, employment, and trade, 1992 periodic country rpt, 2046–4.14; 2046–4.55
Economic conditions, investment and export opportunities, and trade practices, 1992 country market research rpt, 2046–6.4
Economic conditions, policy, and trade practices, by country, 1989-91, annual rpt, 21384–5
Economic, social, political, and geographic summary data, by country, 1992, annual factbook, 9114–2
Energy supply and demand, and implications for US trade, 1991 country rpt, 3406–6.9
Exports and imports of US, by commodity and country, 1980-90, world area rpt, 9116–1.3
Exports and imports of US, by Harmonized System 6-digit commodity and country, 1991, annual rpt, 2424–13
Exports and imports of US, by selected country, country group, and commodity group, 1991, annual rpt, 2044–37
Exports and imports of US, by transport mode, country, and SITC 1- to 3-digit commodity, 1991, annual rpt, 2424–12
Exports, imports, and balances of US for manufactured goods, by SITC 2-digit commodity and country, quarterly rpt, 2042–35
Exports of US, detailed Schedule B commodities with countries of destination, 1991, annual rpt, 2424–10
Food supply, needs, and aid for developing countries, status and alternative forecasts, 1992 world area rpt, 1526–8.2
Human rights conditions in 170 countries, and US economic and military aid, 1991, annual rpt, 21384–3
Imports of goods, services, and investment from US, trade barriers, impacts, and US actions, by country, 1991, annual rpt, 444–2
Military aid of US, arms sales, and training programs costs and budget requests, by program, world region, and country, FY91-93, annual rpt, 7144–13
Military spending, arms trade, and force strengths, with govt spending and population, by country, 1979-89, annual rpt, 9824–1
Minerals Yearbook, Vol 3, 1989: foreign country review of production, trade, and policy, by commodity, annual rpt, 5604–35.2
Multinatl US firms and foreign affiliates finances and operations, by industry and country, 1989 benchmark survey, annual rpt, 2704–5
Multinatl US firms foreign affiliates, income statement items by asset size, industry, and country, 1988, biennial article, 8302–2.322
Natural gas and liquefied gas trade of US with 5 countries, by US firm, 1955-91, annual article, 3162–4.301
Oil production, and exports and prices for US, by major exporting country, detailed data, monthly rpt with articles, 3162–24
Oil production, and exports and prices for US, by major exporting country, detailed data, monthly 1973-88, 3168–123
Oil production, stocks, use, and trade, by selected country and country group, monthly rpt, 3162–42
Population size, growth rates, and components of change, by country, projected 1990-2020 and trends from 1950, biennial rpt, 2324–9
Population size, life expectancy, and fertility, trends and projections, 1992 country rpt, 2326–24.2
Refugee migration, and intl aid programs, by world area and country of origin and asylum, 1991, annual rpt, 7004–15
Spacecraft and satellite launches since 1957, quarterly listing, 9502–2
Steel trade, by product, country, and customs district, with US industry operating data, 1989-June 1992, semiannual rpt, 9882–15
UN voting record and share of votes in agreement with US, by issue, country, and world area, 1991, annual rpt, 7004–18
see also under By Foreign Country in the "Index by Categories"

Industrial accidents and safety
see Hazardous substances
see Mine accidents and safety
see Occupational health and safety

see Railroad accidents and safety
see Transportation accidents and safety
Industrial and commercial energy use
Aluminum plant ownership, capacity, energy and aluminum sources, and startup and closing dates, by US and foreign plant and location, 1990, annual listing, 5604–49
Bonneville Power Admin mgmt of Fed Columbia River Power System, finances and sales, summary data, quarterly rpt, 3222–2
Bonneville Power Admin mgmt of Fed Columbia River Power System, finances, operations, and sales by customer, FY91, annual rpt, 3224–1
Bonneville Power Admin sales, revenues, and rates, by customer and customer type, 1991, semiannual rpt, 3222–1
Building (commercial) energy use, costs, and conservation, by building characteristics, survey rpt series, 3166–8
Buildings (commercial and residential) energy conservation technologies use, costs, efficiency, and residential tax credits, 1970s-90 and projected to 2010, 26358–259
Business statistics, detailed data for major industries and economic indicators, *Survey of Current Business*, monthly rpt, 2702–1.12; 2702–1.17
Business statistics, detailed data for major industries and economic indicators, 1960-91, *Survey of Current Business* biennial supplement, 2704–1
Coal and coke supply, demand, movements, prices, and stocks, by end-use sector and State, quarterly rpt, 3162–37
Coal mining restrictions on public land, impacts on production, costs, and demand, by region, 1985-88 and projected to 2075, 5668–125
Coal production and mines by county, prices, productivity, miners, and reserves, by mining method and State, 1990-91, annual rpt, 3164–25
Coal production, stocks, and shipments, by State of origin and destination, end-use sector, and mode of transport, quarterly rpt, 3162–8
Conservation of energy, State programs aid from Fed Govt, and energy savings, by State, 1990, annual rpt, 3304–1
Consumption and conservation of energy, survey results and methodology, series, 3166–15
Developing countries energy efficiency improvement issues and devs, with data by end use and country, 1980s-90, 26358–260
Disruption of energy supply to industrial plants, related worker displacement and unemployment insurance claims, quarterly press release, 6742–23
Disruption of energy supply to industrial plants, related worker displacement, 1990, annual rpt, 6744–18
Electric power demand, and industrial and employment impacts of capacity shortfalls and new power plants, by selected State, 1960s-80s and projected to 2000, hearing, 21248–163
Electric power plants production and capital costs, operations, and fuel use, by fuel type, plant, utility, and location, 1990, annual rpt, 3164–9
Electric power plants production, capacity, sales, and fuel stocks, use, and costs, by State, 1986-90, annual rpt, 3164–11
Electric power plants production, fuel use, stocks, and costs by fuel type, and sales, by State, monthly rpt, with articles, 3162–35
Electric power sales and revenue, by end-use sector, consumption level, and utility, 1990, annual rpt, 3164–91
Electric power use indexes, by SIC 2- to 4-digit industry, monthly rpt, 9365–2.24
Electric utilities finances and operations, detailed data for publicly owned firms, 1990, annual rpt, 3164–24
Electric utilities privately owned, finances and operations, detailed data, 1990, annual rpt, 3164–23
Energy supply, demand, and prices, by fuel type and end-use sector, alternative projections by region, 1990-2010, annual rpt, 3164–96
Energy supply, demand, and prices, by fuel type and end-use sector, alternative projections 1990-2010, annual rpt, 3164–75
Energy supply, demand, and prices, by fuel type and end-use sector, projections and underlying assumptions, 1995-2010, annual rpt, 3164–90
Energy supply, demand, and prices, by fuel type and end-use sector, with foreign comparisons, 1981-90, annual fact book, 3164–76
Energy supply, demand, and prices, by fuel type and end-use sector, with foreign comparisons, 1991 and trends from 1949, annual rpt, 3164–74
Energy supply, demand, and prices, by fuel type, end-use sector, and country, detailed data, monthly rpt with articles, 3162–24
Energy supply, demand, and prices, by fuel type, end-use sector, and country, detailed data, monthly 1973-88, 3168–123
Energy supply, demand, and prices, forecasts by resource type, quarterly rpt, 3162–34
Energy use, by detailed fuel type, end-use sector, and State, 1960-90, State Energy Data System annual rpt, 3164–39
Energy use in transportation and other sectors, by fuel type, 1970s-90, annual rpt, 3304–5
Environmental Quality, status of problems, protection programs, research, and intl issues, 1991 annual rpt, 484–1
Foreign and US energy supply and demand, by major fuel and end-use sector, 1950s-87 and forecast to 1995, 3166–6.58
Fuel oil and kerosene sales and deliveries, by end-use, PAD district, and State, 1990, annual rpt, 3164–94
Gasoline and other motor fuel use, by consuming sector and State, 1991, annual rpt, 7554–1.1
Health Care Financing Review, provider prices, price inputs and indexes, and labor, quarterly journal, 4652–1.1
Input-output structure of US economy, detailed interindustry transactions for 541 industries, and components of final demand, 1982 benchmark data, 2708–17
Manufacturing annual survey, 1990: establishments, employment, finances, inventories, and energy use, by SIC 2- to 4-digit industry, 2506–14.2
Manufacturing annual survey, 1990: finances and operations, by SIC 2- and 3-digit industry and State, 2506–14.3
Manufacturing energy use and prices, 1988 survey, series, 3166–13
Minerals offshore lease sales environmental and economic impacts in coastal areas, final statement series, 5736–7
Natl Energy Strategy plans for conservation, R&D, security, and pollution reduction, technical rpt series, 3006–13
Natl Energy Strategy Strategic Petroleum Reserve and energy efficiency issues, 1991 hearings, 21368–142
Natural and supplemental gas production, prices, trade, use, reserves, and pipeline company finances, by firm and State, monthly rpt with articles, 3162–4
Natural gas interstate pipeline company detailed financial and operating data, by firm, 1990, annual rpt, 3164–38
Natural gas supply, demand, prices, and distribution, by State, 1986-90 annual rpt, 3164–4
Natural gas use, by end-use sector and PAD district, seasonal weekly rpt, 3162–45
New England States electric power sales, Fed Reserve 1st District, monthly rpt, 9373–2
Oil and gas primary use prohibited for power and industrial plants, exemptions, and gas use by State, 1980-91, annual rpt, 3334–1
Oil products prices, sales, and purchases of refiners, processors, and distributors, by product, end-use sector, PAD district, and State, 1991, annual rpt, 3164–85
Oil products sales and purchases of refiners, processors, and distributors, by product, end-use sector, PAD district, and State, monthly rpt, 3162–11
Oil refinery capacity, openings, closings, and acquisitions by plant, and fuel used by PAD district, 1991, annual rpt, 3164–2.1
Pacific basin countries energy supply and demand, and implications for US trade, country rpt series, 3406–6
Pacific Northwest electric power capacity and use, by energy source, forecast under alternative load and demand cases, 1991-2012, annual rpt, 3224–3
Prices and spending for fuel, by type, end-use sector, and State, 1990, annual rpt, 3164–64
Prices of fuel, by type, end-use sector, and region, projected 1991-2030, 3166–6.60
Productivity of labor, capital, and other inputs in manufacturing, changes by selected industry, various periods 1949-88, article, 6722–1.345
Recycling of municipal and industrial waste, costs, revenues, and secondary products trade and related energy use and pollution reductions, 1991 hearings, 21368–139
Solar collector and photovoltaic cell shipments by end-use sector and State, and trade, 1990, annual rpt, 3164–62
Statistical Abstract of US, 1992 annual data compilation, 2324–1.19
TVA electric power purchases and resales, with electricity use, average bills, and rates by customer class, by distributor, 1991, annual tables, 9804–14
TVA electric power purchases of municipal and cooperative distributors, and prices and use by distributor and consumer sector, monthly rpt, 9802–1

TVA energy use by fuel type, and conservation costs and savings, FY91, annual rpt, 9804–26
Warehouse services finances, and inventory, by SIC 3- to 4-digit industry, 1990 survey, annual rpt, 2413–14
Wood, waste, and alcohol fuel use, by end-use sector and region, 1990, annual rpt, 3164–97
see also Agricultural energy use
see also Electric power and heat cogeneration
see also Transportation energy use

Industrial arts
Enrollment in vocational education, and academic and other credits earned, by subject and student characteristics, high school classes of 1982 and 1987, 4838–50
Enrollment in vocational education, student and teacher characteristics, and outcomes, for secondary and postsecondary instns, 1970s-90, 4828–42
Teachers of vocational education, by subject area and selected characteristics, for public high schools, 1987/88, 4836–3.9

Industrial capacity and utilization
Business activity indicators, 1990, annual rpt, 9364–5.9
Business cycle duration and strength indicators, late 1940s-91, article, 9373–1.301
Capacity use rates for manufacturers from 1948, and for mining and utilities, 1967-91, annual rpt, 204–1.3
Economic indicators and components, and Fed Reserve 4th District business and financial conditions, monthly chartbook, 9377–10
Economic indicators and components, current data and annual trends, monthly rpt, 23842–1.3
Economic indicators, monthly rpt, 9362–1.2
Electric power capacity and use in Pacific Northwest, by energy source, forecast under alternative load and demand cases, 1991-2012, annual rpt, 3224–3
Electric power plants production and capital costs, operations, and fuel use, by fuel type, plant, utility, and location, 1990, annual rpt, 3164–9
Electric power plants production, capacity, sales, and fuel stocks, use, and costs, by State, 1986-90, annual rpt, 3164–11
Electric utilities privately owned, finances and operations, detailed data, 1990, annual rpt, 3164–23
Energy supply, demand, and prices, by fuel type and end-use sector, projections and underlying assumptions, 1995-2010, annual rpt, 3164–90
Energy supply, demand, and prices, by fuel type and end-use sector, with foreign comparisons, 1981-90, annual fact book, 3164–76
Energy supply, demand, and prices, by fuel type and end-use sector, with foreign comparisons, 1991 and trends from 1949, annual rpt, 3164–74
Exports, imports, balances, US consumption, and operations of industries affected, by industry, 1989-91, annual rpt, 9884–25
Fuel oxygenate supply, blending in gasoline, and plant capacity and use, by PAD district, monthly rpt, 3162–6.4
Gasoline (oxygenated) supply and demand in carbon monoxide nonattainment areas, forecast winter 1992/93, article, 3162–24.301
Hydroelectric power generation and capacity, for TVA projects, 1990, annual rpt, 9804–7
Imports and tariff provisions effect on US industries and products, investigations with background financial and operating data, series, 9886–4
Imports injury to US industries from foreign subsidized products and sales at less than fair value, investigations with background financial and operating data, series, 9886–19
Imports injury to US industries from foreign subsidized products, investigations with background financial and operating data, series, 9886–15
Imports injury to US industries from sales at less than fair value, investigations with background financial and operating data, series, 9886–14
Imports under Generalized System of Preferences, status, and US tariffs, with trade by country and US economic impacts, for selected commodities, 1987-91, annual rpt, 9884–23
Manufacturing capacity use, by SIC 2- to 4-digit industry, 1990, annual Current Industrial Rpt, 2506–3.7
Militarily strategic manufacturing industries finances, operations, and intl competitiveness, series, 2026–1
Natural gas interstate pipeline capacity, use, contract deliveries, and prices, by region, State, and firm, 1990, 3168–125
Nuclear power plant capacity, generation, and capacity use, monthly rpt, 3162–24.8
Nuclear power plant capacity, generation, and capacity use, monthly 1973-88, 3168–123.8
Nuclear power plant safety standards and research, design, licensing, construction, operation, and finances, with data by reactor, quarterly journal, 3352–4
Oil refinery capacity and use, weekly rpt, 3162–32
Oil refinery capacity, openings, closings, and acquisitions by plant, and fuel used by PAD district, 1991, annual rpt, 3164–2.1
Oil refinery capacity use, 1989-90, annual rpt, 3164–44.3
Oil refinery operating and idle capacity, inputs by type, and oil quality, by PAD district, monthly rpt, 3162–6.2
OPEC oil production and capacity, by member, monthly rpt, 9112–2
Pacific basin countries energy supply and demand, and implications for US trade, country rpt series, 3406–6
Southwestern Fed Power System financial statements, sales by customer, and operations and costs by project, FY91, annual rpt, 3244–1
Statistical Abstract of US, 1992 annual data compilation, 2324–1.27
Steel imports of US under voluntary restraint agreement, by product, customs district, and country, with US industry operating data, quarterly rpt, 9882–13
Steel trade, by product, country, and customs district, with US industry operating data, 1989-June 1992, semiannual rpt, 9882–15
Uranium mill capacity by plant, and production, by operating status, 1987-91, annual rpt, 3164–65.1
Uranium mining and milling industries finances and operations, with selected foreign comparisons, 1970s-90 and projected to 2005, annual rpt, 3164–82

Industrial location
see Industrial siting

Industrial management
see Business management
see Consultants
see Executives and managers
see Industrial siting
see Labor-management relations, general

Industrial plants and equipment
Arson incidents by whether structure occupied, property value, and arrest rate, by property type, 1991, annual rpt, 6224–2.1
Assets and debts of private sector, balance sheets by segment, 1960-91, semiannual rpt, 9365–4.1
Business statistics, detailed data for major industries and economic indicators, *Survey of Current Business*, monthly rpt, 2702–1.16
Business statistics, detailed data for major industries and economic indicators, 1960-91, *Survey of Current Business* biennial supplement, 2704–1
Capital (fixed), govt and private nonresidential structures and equipment, residential capital, and consumer-owned durable goods, 1925-90, annual article, 2702–1.305; 2702–1.306; 2702–1.327; 2702–1.338
Coastal areas construction authorized by permit, by building type, 1970-89, 2176–8.3
Construction (industrial and commercial) contracts, *Survey of Current Business*, cyclical indicators, monthly rpt, 2702–1.1
Construction put in place, permits, housing sales, costs, material prices, and employment, quarterly rpt with articles, 2042–1
Construction put in place, value of new public and private structures, by type, monthly rpt, 2382–4
County Business Patterns, 1989: employment, establishments, and payroll, by SIC 2- to 4-digit industry and county, annual State rpt series, 2326–8
County Business Patterns, 1990: employment, establishments, and payroll, by SIC 2- to 4-digit industry and county, annual State rpt series, 2326–6
Economic indicators and components, and Fed Reserve 4th District business and financial conditions, monthly chartbook, 9377–10
Employment, earnings, and hours, by SIC 1- to 4-digit industry, monthly 1989-Feb 1992, annual rpt, 6744–4
Employment of minorities and women, by occupation, SIC 1- to 3-digit industry, State, and MSA, 1991, annual rpt, 9244–1
Energy producers finances and operations, by energy type for US firms domestic and foreign operations, 1990, annual rpt, 3164–44
Energy use and prices for manufacturing industries, 1988 survey, series, 3166–13

Expenditures for plant and equipment, by major industry group, quarterly rpt, 2502–2
Exports and imports between US and outlying areas, by detailed commodity and mode of transport, 1991, annual rpt, 2424–11
Exports and imports of US, by country and detailed commodity, monthly rpt, 2422–12
Exports and imports of US, by Harmonized System 6-digit commodity and country, 1991, annual rpt, 2424–13
Exports and imports of US, by selected country, country group, and commodity group, 1991, annual rpt, 2044–37
Exports and imports of US, by transport mode, country, and SITC 1- to 3-digit commodity, 1991, annual rpt, 2424–12
Exports, imports, and balances of US for manufactured goods, by SITC 2-digit commodity and country, quarterly rpt, 2042–35
Exports of US, detailed Schedule B commodities with countries of destination, 1991, annual rpt, 2424–10
Fishery employment, vessels, plants, and cooperatives, by State, 1990, annual rpt, 2164–1.10
Foreign direct investment in US, major transactions by type, industry, country, and US location, 1990, annual rpt, 2044–20
Input-output structure of US economy, detailed interindustry transactions for 84 industries, and components of final demand, 1987, annual article, 2702–1.316
Input-output structure of US economy, detailed interindustry transactions for 541 industries, and components of final demand, 1982 benchmark data, 2708–17
Labor productivity, indexes of output, hours, and employment by SIC 2- to 4-digit industry, 1967-90, annual rpt, 6824–1.3
Lumber (pulpwood) production and mill receipts in North Central States, by species, mill, State, and county, 1990, annual rpt, 1204–19
Manufacturing annual survey, 1990: finances and operations, by SIC 2- to 4-digit industry, series, 2506–14
Manufacturing census, 1987: concentration of largest firms measured by value added, and for shipments by SIC 2- and 4-digit industry, subject rpt, 2497–6
Manufacturing census, 1987: shipments of manufacturers products, by customer class and SIC 2- and 4-digit industry, subject rpt, 2497–4
Manufacturing finances and operations, by SIC 2- to 4-digit industry, forecast 1992, annual rpt, 2044–28
Meat plants inspected and certified for exporting to US, by country, 1991, annual listing, 1374–2
Meat production, livestock slaughter, and slaughter plants, by species and State, 1991, annual rpt, 1623–10
Militarily strategic manufacturing industries finances, operations, and intl competitiveness, series, 2026–1
Military prime contract awards, by category, contractor type, and State, FY89-91, annual rpt, 3544–11
Military prime contract awards, by detailed procurement category, FY88-91, annual rpt, 3544–18
Mineral Industry Surveys, commodity reviews of production, trade, use, and industry operations, advance annual rpt series, 5614–5
Minerals Yearbook, Vol 1, 1989: commodity reviews of production, use, trade, prices, and mining operations, annual rpt, 5604–33
Mines occupational deaths, by circumstances and selected victim characteristics, semiannual rpt series, 6662–3
Multinatl firms US affiliates, finances, and operations, by industry, world area of parent firm, and State, 1989-90, annual rpt, 2704–4
Natl income and product accounts, comprehensive accounts and components, benchmark revisions, 1929-88, 2708–5
Natl income and product accounts, comprehensive accounts and components, *Survey of Current Business*, monthly rpt, 2702–1.28
Natural gas interstate pipeline company detailed financial and operating data, by firm, 1990, annual rpt, 3164–38
Occupational deaths, by equipment type, circumstances, and OSHA standards violated, series, 6606–2
Occupational injury and illness rates, by SIC 2- to 4-digit industry, 1989-90, annual rpt, 6844–7
Occupational injury and illness rates, by SIC 2- to 4-digit industry, 1990, annual rpt, 6844–1
OECD trade, total and for 4 major countries, and US trade by country, by commodity, 1980-90, world area rpt series, 9116–1
Oil and gas primary use prohibited for power and industrial plants, exemptions, and gas use by State, 1980-91, annual rpt, 3334–1
Oil refinery capacity, openings, closings, and acquisitions by plant, and fuel used by PAD district, 1991, annual rpt, 3164–2.1
Petrochemicals industries contract labor accidents, injuries, safety programs operations, and employee characteristics, 1986-91, 6608–6
Price indexes (producer), by stage of processing and detailed commodity, monthly rpt, 6762–6
Price indexes (producer), by stage of processing and detailed commodity, monthly 1991, annual rpt, 6764–2
Production, shipments, trade, stocks, orders, use, and firms, by product, periodic Current Industrial Rpt series, 2506–12
Savings instns failures, inventory of real estate assets available from Resolution Trust Corp, 1991, semiannual listing, 9722–2.1
Savings instns failures, inventory of real estate assets available from Resolution Trust Corp, 1992, semiannual listing, 9722–2.8
Science, engineering, and technical employment in manufacturing, by field and industry, 1989, triennial rpt, 9627–23
Shipbuilding and repair facilities, capacity, and employment, by shipyard, 1991, annual rpt, 7704–9
Solar collector and photovoltaic cell shipments by end-use sector and State, and trade, 1990, annual rpt, 3164–62
Tax (income) returns of corporations, income and tax items by asset size and detailed industry, 1989, annual rpt, 8304–4; 8304–21
Technology-intensive industries intl competitiveness, with background data by industry and foreign comparisons, 1960s-91, GAO rpt, 26123–406
Telephone and telegraph firms detailed finances and operations, 1990, annual rpt, 9284–6
Uranium tailings at inactive mills, remedial action proposals, costs, site characteristics, and environmental, socioeconomic, and health impacts, series, 3356–4
Water use by end use, well withdrawals, and public supply deliveries, by county, State rpt series, 5666–24
see also Business firms and establishments, number
see also Business machines and equipment
see also Capital investments, general
see also Capital investments, specific industry
see also Depreciation
see also Electric power plants and equipment
see also Foundries
see also Grain storage and facilities
see also Industrial capacity and utilization
see also Industrial robots
see also Industrial siting
see also Railroad equipment and vehicles
see also Warehouses
see also under By Commodity in the "Index by Categories"

Industrial pollution
see Air pollution
see Environmental pollution and control
see Hazardous waste and disposal
see Lead poisoning and pollution
see Marine pollution
see Noise
see Water pollution

Industrial production
Bank deposits, reserves, and loans, relation to industrial production, 1920s-70s, article, 9377–1.302
Business cycle recession and expansion duration indicators, 1850s-1990, working paper, 9375–13.83
China economic performance and trade, 1980-91, annual rpt, 9114–5
Competitiveness (intl) of US industries, with selected foreign and US operating data by major firm and product, series, 2046–12
Economic indicators and components, and Fed Reserve 4th District business and financial conditions, monthly chartbook, 9377–10
Economic indicators and components, current data and annual trends, monthly rpt, 23842–1.3
Economic indicators, monthly rpt, 9362–1.2
Electric power demand, and industrial and employment impacts of capacity shortfalls and new power plants, by selected State, 1960s-80s and projected to 2000, hearing, 21248–163
Forecasts of economic conditions and employment, alternative BLS projections to 2005 and trends 1975-90, biennial rpt, 6744–19

Forecasts of industrial production and unemployment, performance of consumer sentiment surveys, 1991 working paper, 9371–10.69
Forecasts of industrial production, performance of Natl Assn of Purchasing Managers manufacturing activity index and production-worker hours, 1980s-91, article, 9371–1.301
Foreign and US economic conditions, and trade devs and balances, with data by selected country and country group, monthly rpt, 9882–14
Foreign countries *Background Notes*, summary social, political, and economic data, series, 7006–2
Foreign countries economic conditions and implications for US, periodic country rpt series, 2046–4
Foreign countries economic indicators, and trade and investment flows, for selected countries and country groups, selected years 1946-91, annual rpt, 204–1.9
GDP forecasts for current quarter, performance of monthly advance indicators, 1981-91, article, 9393–8.305
Imports and tariff provisions effect on US industries and products, investigations with background financial and operating data, series, 9886–4
Imports injury to US industries from foreign subsidized products, investigations with background financial and operating data, series, 9886–15
Imports injury to US industries from sales at less than fair value, investigations with background financial and operating data, series, 9886–14
Industry finances and operations, by SIC 2- to 4-digit industry, forecast 1992, annual rpt, 2044–28
Input-output structure of US economy, detailed interindustry transactions for 84 industries, and components of final demand, 1987, annual article, 2702–1.316
Input-output structure of US economy, detailed interindustry transactions for 541 industries, and components of final demand, 1982 benchmark data, 2708–17
Israel economic conditions, US investment and export opportunities, and trade practices, 1992 rpt, 2008–32
Manufacturing annual survey, 1990: value of shipments, by SIC 4- to 5-digit product class, 2506–14.1
Manufacturing census, 1987: concentration of largest firms measured by value added, and for shipments by SIC 2- and 4-digit industry, subject rpt, 2497–6
Manufacturing census, 1987: exporting establishments, shipments, and employment, by SIC 2-digit industry and State, 2506–16.2
Manufacturing census, 1987: shipments of manufacturers products, by customer class and SIC 2- and 4-digit industry, subject rpt, 2497–4
Manufacturing industries operations and performance, analytical rpt series, 2506–16
Manufacturing production over business cycles, relation to market structure and other factor inputs, for durable and nondurable goods, 1991 working paper, 9375–13.70
Manufacturing shipments and new and unfilled orders, 1950-91, annual rpt, 204–1.3
Manufacturing shipments, inventories, and orders, by SIC 2- to 3-digit industry, monthly Current Industrial Rpt, 2506–3.1
Middle Atlantic States manufacturing business outlook, monthly survey rpt, 9387–11
Militarily strategic manufacturing industries finances, operations, and intl competitiveness, series, 2026–1
Military spending reductions, economic impacts of Bush Admin plans by industry and State, FY92-97, 26306–6.167
Money supply relation to industrial production and consumer spending, 1960s-91, working paper, 9377–9.131
OECD intl trade position for US and 4 countries, and factors affecting US competition, quarterly pamphlet, 2042–25
Overseas Business Reports: economic conditions, investment and export opportunities, and trade practices, country market research rpt series, 2046–6
Population size and demographic changes impacts on economic conditions, with background data, 1950s-80s and projected to 2010, 23848–226
Southeastern US manufacturing conditions, survey methodology and selected results, Dec 1991-July 1992, article, 9371–1.307
Soviet Union and US economic and sociodemographic indicators, selected years 1970-90, handbook, 2328–80
Statistical Abstract of US, 1992 annual data compilation, 2324–1.27
Survey of Current Business, detailed data for major industries and economic indicators, monthly rpt, 2702–1
Survey of Current Business, detailed data for major industries and economic indicators, 1960-91, biennial supplement, 2704–1
Tennessee Valley economic conditions, and compared to US, alternative projections 1992-2010 and trends from 1929, annual rpt, 9804–27
see also Business inventories
see also Business orders
see also Gross Domestic Product
see also Industrial capacity and utilization
see also Industrial production indexes
see also Industrial purchasing
see also Labor productivity
see also Production costs
see also Productivity
see also Value added tax
see also under names of specific industries or industry groups

Industrial production indexes
Business activity indicators, 1990, annual rpt, 9364–5.9
Business cycle recovery industrial production, relation to depth of decline, alternative indexes, model results, 1880s-1991, technical paper, 9379–12.82
Economic indicators and components, current data and annual trends, monthly rpt, 23842–1.3
Economic indicators compounded annual rates of change, monthly rpt, 9391–3
Economic indicators, monthly rpt, 9362–1.2
Forecasts of production, performance of regional indexes by SIC 2-digit manufacturing industry, 1992 working paper, 9375–13.85
Foreign and US economic conditions, for major industrial countries, monthly rpt, 9112–1
Foreign and US industrial production indexes and CPI, for US and 6 OECD countries, current data and annual trends, monthly rpt, 23842–1.7
Foreign and US industrial production indexes, for 7 OECD countries, *Survey of Current Business*, monthly rpt, 2702–1.1
Foreign countries economic conditions and implications for US, periodic country rpt series, 2046–4
Metals industries economic performance indicators and indexes, by commodity, monthly rpt, 5602–5
Middle Atlantic States manufacturing output index, monthly rpt, 9387–12
Production and capacity use indexes, by SIC 2- to 4-digit industry, monthly rpt, 9365–2.24
Production indexes for selected manufacturing groups, 1947-91, annual rpt, 204–1.3
Southeastern States, Fed Reserve 5th District, economic indicators by State, quarterly rpt, 9389–16
Statistical Abstract of US, 1992 annual data compilation, 2324–1.27
Survey of Current Business, detailed data for major industries and economic indicators, monthly rpt, 2702–1.3
Survey of Current Business, detailed data for major industries and economic indicators, 1960-91, biennial supplement, 2704–1

Industrial purchasing
Contracts (long-term sales) escalation clauses, use of Producer Price Index, methodology, 1991 rpt, 6888–23
Manufacturing census, 1987: shipments of manufacturers products, by customer class and SIC 2- and 4-digit industry, subject rpt, 2497–4
Natl income and product accounts, comprehensive accounts and components, benchmark revisions, 1929-88, 2708–5
Natl income and product accounts, comprehensive accounts and components, *Survey of Current Business*, monthly rpt, 2702–1.28
see also Business orders

Industrial relations
see Labor-management relations, general
see Work stoppages

Industrial robots
Competitiveness (intl) of US high technology industries, with background data by industry and foreign comparisons, 1960s-91, GAO rpt, 26123–406
Exports and imports between US and outlying areas, by detailed commodity and mode of transport, 1991, annual rpt, 2424–11
Exports of US, detailed Schedule B commodities with countries of destination, 1991, annual rpt, 2424–10
Manufacturing finances and operations, by SIC 2- to 4-digit industry, forecast 1992, annual rpt, 2044–28
Manufacturing industries important to military, finances, operations, and intl competitiveness, 1991 rpt, 2026–1.1

NSF R&D grant awards, by div and program, FY90, periodic rpt, 9626–7.3
Shipments, trade, use, and firms, annual Current Industrial Rpt, discontinued, 2506–12.32
Soviet Union and US economic and sociodemographic indicators, selected years 1970-90, handbook, 2328–80
Statistical Abstract of US, 1992 annual data compilation, 2324–1.27

Industrial siting
Farmland value, rent, taxes, foreign ownership, and transfers by probable use and lender type, with data by region and State, 1981-92, article, 1561–16.302
Food processing industry location factors, rankings, 1988 survey, 9088–37
Historic and natural natl landmarks damaged and threatened, with owner, location, damage type, and recommended remedial action, 1990, annual listing, 5544–16
Kidney dialysis facilities distribution related to area characteristics and facility ownership, 1982, article, 4652–1.306
Neighborhood quality, indicators and attitudes of renter households, by whether receiving and eligible for HUD assistance, householder characteristics, and location, 1989, biennial rpt, 5184–11
Nuclear power plant safety standards and research, design, licensing, construction, operation, and finances, with data by reactor, quarterly journal, 3352–4
Nuclear radiation exposure of population near commercial reactors, by body site, age group, and selected plant, 1988, annual rpt, 9634–7
Office location factors, rankings of importance, and ratings for Chicago, 1992 working paper, 9375–13.78
Radioactive waste and spent fuel generation, inventory, and disposal, 1960s-90 and projected to 2020, annual rpt, 3364–2
Unemployed displaced workers, layoffs and recalls by layoff reason, industry, firm size, and State, 2nd half 1988, 6406–6.36
Unemployed displaced workers, layoffs and unemployment insurance claims by reason, industry, selected characteristics, and State, quarterly press release, 6742–23
Unemployed displaced workers, layoffs and unemployment insurance claims by reason, industry, selected characteristics, MSA, and State, 1990, annual rpt, 6744–18
Water quality, chemistry, hydrology, and other characteristics, local area studies, series, 5666–27

Industrial standards
Auto and light truck fuel economy performance by make, standards, and enforcement, 1978-94 model years, annual rpt, 7764–9
Calibration of measurement systems, standard reference materials specifications and availability, 1992 biennial listing, 2214–2
Computer systems purchase and use, and data recording, processing, and transfer, Fed Govt standards, series, 2216–2
Export and import product standards under GATT, Natl Inst of Standards and Technology info activities, and proposed standards by agency and country, 1991, annual rpt, 2214–6
Exports of goods, services, and investment, trade barriers, impacts, and US actions, by country, 1991, annual rpt, 444–2
Intl and domestic standards dev for production, controls, and processes in US and EC, 1980s-91, 26358–257
Natl Inst of Standards and Technology rpts, 1991, annual listing, 2214–1
Nuclear power plant safety standards and research, design, licensing, construction, operation, and finances, with data by reactor, quarterly journal, 3352–4
Performance, weights, and measures standards dev, proposals, and policies, 1992 annual conf, 2214–7
Rope (wire) used for mine hoists, characteristics by type, 1991 rpt, 5608–172
Textile products trade regulations of foreign countries, and US exports, by commodity and country, 1989-91, biennial rpt, 2044–18
see also Quality control and testing
see also Weights and measures

Industry
see Business and industry
see under By Industry in the "Index by Categories"

Industry wage surveys
BLS data collection, analysis, and presentation methods, by program, 1992 rpt, 6888–1
Hospital employees and wages by occupation, and benefits, by region and selected MSA, 1991 survey, 6787–6.254
Metalworking machinery and die and tool manufacturing, wages and production workers by occupation, and benefits, by selected MSA, 1990 survey, 6787–6.253
Wages, hours, and employment by occupation, and benefits, for selected locations, industry survey rpt series, 6787–6
see also Area wage surveys

INF treaty
see Intermediate-Range Nuclear Forces Treaty

Infant formula
see Dairy industry and products

Infant health
see Breast-feeding
see Infant mortality
see Obstetrics and gynecology
see Pediatrics
see Prenatal care

Infant mortality
Costa Rica and Guatemala life expectancy, and death rate by cause and age, by sex, 1984 and trends from 1900, working paper, 2326–18.64
Costa Rica economic indicators and reform issues, mid 1970s-90, working paper, 9916–13.5
Czechoslovakia health care system, spending, and population health condition indicators, 1988-89, article, 4042–3.363
Deaths and rates, by cause, age, sex, marital status, race, and State, 1989, US Vital Statistics advance annual rpt, 4146–5.124
Deaths and rates, by cause, age, sex, race, and State, preliminary 1989-91 and trends from 1960, US Vital Statistics annual rpt, 4144–7
Deaths and rates, by detailed location, cause, and demographic characteristics, 1989, US Vital Statistics annual rpt, 4144–3
Deaths of infants, risk factors, and health and prevention issues, for US and selected countries, 1990 conf, 4148–28
Deaths recorded in 121 cities, by age group and for infants, weekly rpt, 4202–1
Developing countries economic and social conditions from 1960s, and Intl Dev Cooperation Agency and AID activities and funding, FY91-93, annual rpt, 9904–4
Developing countries population size, life expectancy, and fertility, trends and forecasts, country rpt series, 2326–24
Foreign and US infant mortality rate, and births of low birthweight and to teen and older mothers, 1980s, article, 4652–1.324
Foreign countries and cities population density, and distribution, life expectancy, and infant mortality by world region, 1991, fact sheet, 2326–17.50
Foreign countries *Background Notes*, summary social, political, and economic data, series, 7006–2
Foreign countries economic, social, political, and geographic summary data, by country, 1992, annual factbook, 9114–2
Foreign countries population size, growth rates, and components of change, by country, projected 1990-2020 and trends from 1950, biennial rpt, 2324–9
Health condition and care indicators, 1950s-90 with health improvement and disease prevention goals for 1990, annual data compilation, 4144–11
Indian Health Service and tribal facilities and use, and Indians health and other characteristics, by IHS region, 1980s-90, annual chartbook, 4084–7
Indian Health Service facilities, funding, operations, and Indian health and other characteristics, 1950s-91, annual chartbook, 4084–1
Latin America economic and social conditions, resources, trade, and aid, 1992, annual factbook, 9914–14
OECD members health care costs, hospital use, resources, and economic and health indicators, by country, 1960s-90, article, 4652–1.322
Ohio poverty, hunger, and public welfare program operations and indicators of need, by county, 1991 hearing, 21968–58
Palau admin, and social, economic, and govtl data, FY91, annual rpt, 7004–6
Soviet Union and US economic and sociodemographic indicators, selected years 1970-90, handbook, 2328–80
Statistical Abstract of US, 1992 annual data compilation, 2324–1.2
Sudden infant death syndrome incidence correlation to kindergarten absence rate, local area study, 1992 article, 4042–3.331
Vietnam population size, components of change, and selected characteristics, 1979, 1989, and projected to 2050, 2326–18.65
Vital statistics provisional data, monthly rpt, 4142–1
see also Fetal deaths

Infective and parasitic diseases
Blood banks safety violations, FDA enforcement, disease transmittal, and Houston regional center activities and finances, 1970s-91, hearings, 21368–134

Cancer (leukemia) virus infection among Japan island village residents, relation to selected characteristics, 1984-86 study, article, 4472–1.319
Cases of acute and chronic conditions, disability, absenteeism, and health services use, by selected characteristics, 1990, annual rpt, 4147–10.182; 4147–10.183
Child infectious disease cases, and related disability and health care, by disease, health insurance status, and other characteristics, 1988, 4147–10.181
Cytomegalovirus (congenital) disease cases, by infant, mother, and birth characteristics, type of impairment, State, and Canada Province, 1990-91, 4202–7.314
Deaths and rates, by cause, age, sex, marital status, race, and State, 1989, US Vital Statistics advance annual rpt, 4146–5.124
Deaths and rates, by cause and age, preliminary 1990-91, US Vital Statistics annual rpt, 4144–7
Deaths and rates, by cause and selected social, demographic, and employment characteristics, 1979-85, natl longitudinal study, 4478–186
Deaths and rates, by cause, provisional data, monthly rpt, 4142–1.2
Deaths and rates, by detailed location, cause, and demographic characteristics, 1989, US Vital Statistics annual rpt, 4144–3
Dracunculiasis cases, and surveillance and eradication programs, for India, Pakistan, and Africa, 1980s-91, article, 4202–7.307
Drug abuse indicators for selected metro areas, research results, data collection, and policy issues, 1992 semiannual conf, 4492–5
Drug abusers bacterial infections, by pre-injection skin cleaning habits, 1988-89 local area study, article, 4042–3.361
Foreign travel vaccination needs by country, and disease prevention recommendations, 1992 annual rpt, 4204–11
Health condition and care indicators, 1950s-90 with health improvement and disease prevention goals for 1990, annual data compilation, 4144–11
Hepatitis cases by infection source, age, sex, race, and State, and deaths, by strain, 1989 and trends from 1966, 4205–2
HHS financial aid, by program, recipient, State, and city, FY91, annual regional listings, 4004–3
Hospital discharges and length of stay, by diagnosis, patient and instn characteristics, procedure performed, and payment source, 1990, annual rpt, 4147–13.112
Hospital discharges and length of stay by region and diagnosis, and procedures performed, by age and sex, 1990, annual rpt, 4146–8.211
Hospital discharges and length of stay under old and new survey designs, by diagnosis, patient and instn characteristics, and procedure, Jan-Mar 1988, 4147–13.110
Hospital discharges by detailed diagnostic and procedure category, primary diagnosis, and length of stay, by age, sex, and region, 1990, annual rpt, 4147–13.111
Human papillomavirus infection and c-myc gene overexpression related to cervical cancer relapse and metastasis risk, 1984-88 study, article, 4472–1.348
Immigrant and nonimmigrant visa applicants refused, and refusals overcome, by reason, FY90, annual rpt, 7184–1.3
Indian Health Service, tribal, and contract facilities hospitalization, by diagnosis, age, sex, and service area, FY91, annual rpt, 4084–5
Intestinal parasites lab isolations, by State and organism, 1987, article, 4202–7.306
Kuwait oil fires set by Iraq, pollution levels, disease cases, and US remediation and monitoring spending, 1991 rpt, 9188–117
Lyme disease surveillance activities of State health depts, 1992 article, 4042–3.364
Malaria cases in US, for military personnel and US and foreign natls, and by country of infection, 1966-90, annual rpt, 4205–4
Measles cases in Arkansas, with risk factors and vaccination rates, 1986, article, 4042–3.301
Morbidity and Mortality Weekly Report, infectious notifiable disease cases and deaths, and other public health issues, periodic journal, 4202–7
Morbidity and Mortality Weekly Report, infectious notifiable disease cases by age, race, and State, and deaths, 1940s-91, annual rpt, 4204–1
Morbidity and Mortality Weekly Report, infectious notifiable disease cases by State, and public health issues, 4202–1
Morbidity and Mortality Weekly Report, special supplements, series, 4206–2
Natl Inst of Allergy and Infectious Diseases activities, grants by recipient and location, and disease cases, FY84-91, annual rpt, 4474–30
Neurological Disorders and Stroke Natl Inst activities, and disorder cases, FY91, annual rpt, 4474–25
New Zealand measles cases, by age and district, 1991, article, 4202–7.321
OECD members health care costs, hospital use, resources, and economic and health indicators, by country, 1960s-90, article, 4652–1.322
Philippines Mount Pinatubo volcanic eruptions, evacuation camps infective disease cases and deaths, 1991, article, 4202–7.320
Physicians visits, by patient and practice characteristics, diagnosis, and services provided, 1989, annual rpt, 4147–13.109
Polio cases in Latin America, by country, 1990-91, article, 4202–7.309
Refugees, displaced persons, and population affected by famine, CDC recommendations for disease surveillance, control, and prevention, with background data, 1978-91, 4206–2.63
Spain, Catalonia infectious disease surveillance, interval between onset and public health agency notification, 1982-86, article, 4042–3.349
see also Acquired immune deficiency syndrome
see also Animal diseases and zoonoses
see also Food and waterborne diseases
see also Pneumonia and influenza
see also Rabies
see also Septicemia
see also Sexually transmitted diseases
see also Tuberculosis
see also Vaccination and vaccines
see also under By Disease in the "Index by Categories"

Inflammable materials
Injuries from use of consumer products, by severity, victim age, and detailed product, 1991, annual rpt, 9164–6
Textile products trade regulations of foreign countries, and US exports, by commodity and country, 1989-91, biennial rpt, 2044–18
Transport of hazardous material, accidents, casualties, and damage, by mode of transport, with DOT control activities, 1990, annual rpt, 7304–4

Inflation
Budget of US, CBO analysis of revenue and spending alternatives and projections of economic indicators, FY93-97, annual rpt, 26304–3
CPI and Personal Consumption Expenditure Index inflation measures under alternative weighting systems, monthly rpt, periodic article, 6762–2
Developing countries economic and social conditions from 1960s, and Intl Dev Cooperation Agency and AID activities and funding, FY91-93, annual rpt, 9904–4
Dollar exchange rate relation to interest rates and inflation, model description and results, 1974-90, technical paper, 9366–7.279
Economic indicators and relation to govt finances by level of govt, selected years 1929-91, annual rpt, 10044–1
Economic indicators compounded annual rates of change, monthly rpt, 9391–3
Economic indicators performance, and Fed Reserve monetary policy objectives, as of July 1992, semiannual rpt, 9362–4
Forecasts of economic indicators, 1992-93 and trends from 1948, annual article, 9383–6.301
Forecasts of economic indicators, 1993-94 and trends from 1948, annual article, 9383–6.303
Forecasts of inflation, performance of expected long run inflation rate and commodity price indexes, 1960s-90, article, 9377–1.303
Foreign and US currencies shares of intl transactions, with background data, for 5 countries, 1960s-80s, 9381–10.129
Foreign and US economic indicators, trade balances, and exchange rates, for selected OECD and Asian countries, 1992 semiannual rpt, 8002–14
Foreign countries economic and monetary trends, compounded annual rates of change and quarterly indicators for US and 7 major industrialized countries, quarterly rpt, 9391–7
GNP implicit price deflators, monthly rpt, quarterly data, 23842–1.1
Gold standard relation to inflation, with background data for UK, US, France, and Italy, 1730s-1930s, working paper, 9377–9.136
Haiti economic conditions, 1985-91, working paper, 9916–13.3
Health care costs, use, and structure of private and public delivery systems, indicators, issues, and foreign comparisons, 1960s-80s, technical paper, 8006–6.1

Health care spending and factors in increase, with background data and foreign comparisons, various periods 1929-90, technical paper, 9366–6.296
Hyperinflationary periods relative price changes and money demand behavior, for Germany, 1920-23, and for PRC, 1946-49, working paper, 9371–10.86
Interest rates relation to inflation, 1959-91, article, 9379–1.306
Latin America economic and social conditions, resources, trade, and aid, 1992, annual factbook, 9914–14
Mail order catalog price changes, and relation to inflation, by item, 1953-87, working paper, 9375–13.76
Metals industries economic performance indicators and indexes, by commodity, monthly rpt, 5602–5
Natl income and product accounts and components, *Survey of Current Business*, monthly rpt, 2702–1.23
Natl income and product accounts, comprehensive accounts and components, benchmark revisions, 1929-88, 2708–5
Natl income and product accounts, comprehensive accounts and components, *Survey of Current Business*, monthly rpt, 2702–1.30
OECD countries current account balance and net assets, relation to inflation, unemployment rate, and govt lending, 1970s-89, technical paper, 9366–7.274
OECD pension plan finances, participation, and benefits, for 9 countries, with data by firm and worker characteristics, 1990 conf, 6688–2
Poverty population impact of inflation, alternative models assessment, 1992 article, 9377–1.306
Purchasing power of dollar, monthly 1963-91, *Survey of Current Business* biennial supplement, 2704–1
Seignorage sources, use, and impacts of inflation, 1950s-90, article, 9391–1.307
South America inflation relation to money supply, for 5 countries, 1970s-90, technical paper, 9379–12.91
Statistical Abstract of US, 1992 annual data compilation, 2324–1.15
Survey of Current Business, detailed data for major industries and economic indicators, monthly rpt, 2702–1.4
Survey of Current Business, detailed financial and business data, and economic indicators, monthly rpt, 2702–1.3
see also Consumer Price Index
see also Cost of living
see also Food prices
see also Interest rates
see also Monetary policy
see also Money supply
see also Price regulation
see also Prices
see also Producer Price Index

Influenza
see Pneumonia and influenza

Information access
see Freedom of information
see Government information
see Information sciences
see Information services
see Information storage and retrieval systems

Information sciences
Access, policy, technology, and other info services issues, recommendations, 1991 conf, 15638–16
Degrees awarded in higher education, by level, field, race, and sex, 1989/90 and trends from 1980/81, annual rpt, 4844–17
Natl Commission on Libraries and Info Science activities, FY91, annual rpt, 15634–1
NSF R&D grant awards, by div and program, periodic rpt series, 9626–7
Research and demonstration projects for libraries, and funding, FY67-86, listing, 4878–5
Training in library science, grants for disadvantaged students, by instn and State, FY91, annual listing, 4874–1
see also CD-ROM technology and use
see also Computer sciences

Information services
Access, policy, technology, and other info services issues, recommendations, 1991 conf, 15638–16
County Business Patterns, 1989: employment, establishments, and payroll, by SIC 2- to 4-digit industry and county, annual State rpt series, 2326–8
County Business Patterns, 1990: employment, establishments, and payroll, by SIC 2- to 4-digit industry and county, annual State rpt series, 2326–6
Family planning and population activities of AID, grants by project and recipient, and contraceptive shipments, by country, FY91, annual rpt series, 9914–13
Finances and operations, by SIC 2- to 4-digit industry, forecast 1992, annual rpt, 2044–28
Weather services activities and funding, by Federal agency, planned FY92-93, annual rpt, 2144–2
see also Government information
see also Information storage and retrieval systems
see also Libraries
see also Mass media
see also Research

Information storage and retrieval systems
Air Force fiscal mgmt system operations and techniques, quarterly rpt, 3602–1
Census Bur geographic levels of data coverage, maps, and reference products, 1992 rpt, 2308–67
Criminal justice systems of States, activities, employment, funding, and data collection, by State, 1970s-91, annual rpt, 6064–40
Education discrimination natl survey participation and data coverage, school district administrators views, 1991 survey, 4826–1.33
Educational Resources Info Center (ERIC) data base, foreign and US providers, 1992 biennial listing, 4814–4
Fed Govt data processing use and dev, Natl Archives special collection, 1988 rpt, 9516–1.8
Fed Govt info storage and transmission on electronic formats, costs and revenues for 4 agencies, FY85-91, GAO rpt, 26125–47
Fed Govt standards for data recording, processing, and transfer, and for purchase and use of computer systems, series, 2216–2
Fingerprint identification automated system participation of State, city, county, and special district police agencies, 1990, annual rpt, 6064–39
Fingerprint identification system of FBI, automation costs, staff, and workload, FY90 and projected to FY2000, 26358–253
Glaciology intl research summaries, methodology, and bibls, series, 2156–18
Health and vital statistics data collection, and use for planning and evaluation, 1989 biennial conf papers, 4164–2
Library of Congress activities, acquisitions, services, and financial statements, FY91, annual rpt, 26404–1
Police employment, spending, and operations, for State, city, county, and special district agencies, 1990, annual rpt, 6064–39
Pollution (water) discharge permits, and EPA info system coverage and costs, 1991-92, GAO rpt, 26125–46
R&D facilities of higher education instns, space and equipment adequacy, needs, and funding by source, by instn type and control, 1992, biennial rpt, 9624–25
Survey of Income and Program Participation, data collection, methodology, and availability, 1991 users guide, 2628–24
Survey of Income and Program Participation, data collection, methodology, and comparisons to other data bases, working paper series, 2626–10
Voter registration and verification data storage and retrieval systems use and characteristics, for selected counties, 1992 rpt, 9278–8
see also CD-ROM catalogs and guides
see also CD-ROM releases
see also CD-ROM technology and use
see also Computer data file guides
see also Computer industry and products
see also Computer networks
see also Microforms
see also Statistical programs and activities

Information Ventures, Inc.
"Review of Literature on Herbicides, Including Phenoxy Herbicides and Associated Dioxins: Volume XIX Analysis of Recent Literature on Health Effects; and Volume XX Annotated Bibliography of Recent Literature on Health Effects", 8706–1.5

Infrastructure
see Public works

Ing, Donna
"Laboratory-Based Surveillance for Rotavirus, U.S., Jan. 1989-May 1991", 4202–7.317

Ingels, Steven J.
"First Follow-Up: Dropout Component Data File User's Manual. National Education Longitudinal Study of 1988", 4826–9.17
"First Follow-Up: Student Component Data File User's Manual. National Education Longitudinal Study of 1988", 4826–9.14
"First Follow-Up: Teacher Component Data File User's Manual. National Education Longitudinal Study of 1988", 4826–9.18

Inhalation therapy
see Respiratory therapy
Inheritance tax
see Estate tax
Injuries
see Accidental deaths
see Accidents and accident prevention
see Agricultural accidents and safety
see Aviation accidents and safety
see Drowning
see Marine accidents and safety
see Mine accidents and safety
see Occupational health and safety
see Railroad accidents and safety
see Spinal cord injuries
see Traffic accidents and safety
see Transportation accidents and safety
Inland water transportation
Army Corps of Engineers activities and projects, FY88 and trends from 1800s, annual rpt, 3754–1.1
Army Corps of Engineers activities and projects, FY89 and trends from 1800s, annual rpt, 3754–1.2
Army Corps of Engineers activities and projects, FY90 and trends from 1800s, annual rpt, 3754–1.3
Army Corps of Engineers water resources dev projects, characteristics, and costs, 1950s-89, biennial State rpt series, 3756–1
Army Corps of Engineers water resources dev projects, characteristics, and costs, 1950s-91, biennial State rpt series, 3756–2
Coal and coke production, shipments, and trade, by State of origin and destination, end-use sector, and mode of transport, quarterly rpt, 3162–37.1
Coal mining restrictions on public land, impacts on production, costs, and demand, by region, 1985-88 and projected to 2075, 5668–125
Coal production, stocks, and shipments, by State of origin and destination, end-use sector, and mode of transport, quarterly rpt, 3162–8
County Business Patterns, 1989: employment, establishments, and payroll, by SIC 2- to 4-digit industry and county, annual State rpt series, 2326–8
County Business Patterns, 1990: employment, establishments, and payroll, by SIC 2- to 4-digit industry and county, annual State rpt series, 2326–6
Employment, earnings, and hours, by SIC 1- to 4-digit industry, monthly 1989-Feb 1992, annual rpt, 6744–4
Energy use by mode of transport, fuel supply, and demographic and economic factors of vehicle use, 1970s-90, annual rpt, 3304–5
Exports and imports (waterborne) of US, by type of service, customs district, port, and world area, monthly rpt, 2422–7
Fed Govt Inland Waterways Trust Fund financial condition, monthly rpt, 8102–9.8
Foreign countries economic, social, political, and geographic summary data, by country, 1992, annual factbook, 9114–2
Freight (shipborne domestic), by major commodity group, vessel type, and port, 1987-89, annual rpt, 7704–7
Freight (waterborne domestic and foreign) by commodity, traffic, and passengers, by port and waterway, 1989, annual rpt, 3754–3
Govt employment and payroll, by function, level of govt, and jurisdiction, annual rpt series, 2466–1
Govt finances, by level of govt, State, and for large cities and counties, annual rpt series, 2466–2
Grain shipments and rates for barge and rail loadings, periodic situation rpt with articles, 1561–4
Military and personal property shipments, passenger traffic, and costs, by service branch and mode of transport, FY91, annual rpt, 3704–15
Occupational injury and illness rates, by SIC 2- to 4-digit industry, 1989-90, annual rpt, 6844–7
Occupational injury and illness rates, by SIC 2- to 4-digit industry, 1990, annual rpt, 6844–1
Ohio River basin waterway facilities, freight by commodity and port, and recreation, by waterway, 1988-89, annual rpt, 3754–6
Price indexes (producer), by stage of processing and detailed commodity, monthly rpt, 6762–6
Price indexes (producer), by stage of processing and detailed commodity, monthly 1991, annual rpt, 6764–2
Soviet Union and US economic and sociodemographic indicators, selected years 1970-90, handbook, 2328–80
St Lawrence Seaway Dev Corp finances and activities, with Seaway cargo tonnage, and shipping costs compared to other US ports, 1990, annual rpt, 7744–1
St Lawrence Seaway ship, cargo, and passenger traffic, and toll revenue, 1991 and trends from 1959, annual rpt, 7744–2
Statistical Abstract of US, 1992 annual data compilation, 2324–1.22
TVA finances and operations by program and facility, FY91, annual rpt, 9804–32
User fees financing of transportation infrastructure, with data on hwys, airports, and waterways, 1985-91, 26306–6.170
see also Barges
see also Dredging
Inner cities
see Central cities
Inoculation
see Vaccination and vaccines
Input-output analysis
Agricultural productivity indicators for Brazil, 1968-87, 1528–331
Employment and economic conditions, alternative BLS projections to 2005 and trends 1975-90, biennial rpt, 6744–19
Input-output structure of US economy, detailed interindustry transactions for 84 industries, and components of final demand, 1987, annual article, 2702–1.316
Input-output structure of US economy, detailed interindustry transactions for 541 industries, and components of final demand, 1982 benchmark data, 2708–17
Regional multipliers for BEA input-output model by industry and State, and methodology, 1992 guide, 2708–47
Insecticides
see Pesticides
Inspection of industrial products
see Quality control and testing
Inspectors General reports
see Federal Inspectors General reports
Installment credit
see Consumer credit
Institute of American Indian and Alaska Native Culture and Arts Development
Education funding by Federal agency, program, and recipient type, and instn spending, 1960s-91, annual rpt, 4824–8
Institute of Peace
see U.S. Institute of Peace
Instructional materials
see Educational materials
Instruments and measuring devices
Calibration of measurement systems, standard reference materials specifications and availability, 1992 biennial listing, 2214–2
Collective bargaining agreements expiring during year, and workers covered, by firm, union, industry group, and State, 1992, annual rpt, 6784–9
County Business Patterns, 1989: employment, establishments, and payroll, by SIC 2- to 4-digit industry and county, annual State rpt series, 2326–8
County Business Patterns, 1990: employment, establishments, and payroll, by SIC 2- to 4-digit industry and county, annual State rpt series, 2326–6
Electronic communications systems and related products shipments, trade, use, and firms, 1991, annual Current Industrial Rpt, 2506–12.35
Employment, earnings, and hours, by SIC 1- to 4-digit industry, monthly 1989-Feb 1992, annual rpt, 6744–4
Employment of minorities and women, by occupation, SIC 1- to 3-digit industry, State, and MSA, 1991, annual rpt, 9244–1
Employment, unemployment, and labor force characteristics, by region and census div, 1991, annual rpt, 6744–7.1
Energy use and prices, by fuel type and manufacturing industry, 1974-88, 3166–15.3
Energy use and prices for manufacturing industries, 1988 survey, series, 3166–13
Exports and imports between US and outlying areas, by detailed commodity and mode of transport, 1991, annual rpt, 2424–11
Exports and imports of US, by country and detailed commodity, monthly rpt, 2422–12
Exports and imports of US, by Harmonized System 6-digit commodity and country, 1991, annual rpt, 2424–13
Exports and imports of US, by selected country, country group, and commodity group, 1991, annual rpt, 2044–37
Exports and imports of US, by transport mode, country, and SITC 1- to 3-digit commodity, 1991, annual rpt, 2424–12
Exports, imports, and balances of US for manufactured goods, by SITC 2-digit commodity and country, quarterly rpt, 2042–35
Exports of US, detailed commodities by country, monthly CD-ROM, 2422–13

Exports of US, detailed Schedule B commodities with countries of destination, 1991, annual rpt, 2424–10
Freight (waterborne domestic and foreign) by commodity, traffic, and passengers, by port and waterway, 1989, annual rpt, 3754–3
Glassware shipments, trade, use, and firms, by product, 1991, annual Current Industrial Rpt, 2506–9.3
Hazardous substances industrial releases and reduction methods under EPA regulation, by chemical, source, industry, and location, 1989, annual rpt, 9234–6
Hazardous substances industrial releases and reduction methods under EPA regulation, with chemical stocks and use, facility directory, 1987-89, annual CD-ROM, 9234–7
Imports, exports, and employment impacts, by SIC 2- to 4-digit industry and commodity, quarterly rpt, 2322–2
Imports of US, detailed commodities by country, monthly CD-ROM, 2422–14
Imports of US given duty-free treatment for value of US material sent abroad, by commodity and country, 1987-90, annual rpt, 9884–14
Industrial control equipment shipments, trade, use, and firms, by product, 1991, annual Current Industrial Rpt, 2506–12.11
Injuries from use of consumer products, by severity, victim age, and detailed product, 1991, annual rpt, 9164–6
Input-output structure of US economy, detailed interindustry transactions for 84 industries, and components of final demand, 1987, annual article, 2702–1.316
Input-output structure of US economy, detailed interindustry transactions for 541 industries, and components of final demand, 1982 benchmark data, 2708–17
Labor productivity, indexes of output, hours, and employment by SIC 2- to 4-digit industry, 1967-90, annual rpt, 6824–1.3
Manufacturing annual survey, 1990: finances and operations, by SIC 2- to 4-digit industry, series, 2506–14
Manufacturing census, 1987: concentration of largest firms measured by value added, and for shipments by SIC 2- and 4-digit industry, subject rpt, 2497–6
Manufacturing census, 1987: shipments of manufacturers products, by customer class and SIC 2- and 4-digit industry, subject rpt, 2497–4
Manufacturing corporations financial statements, by selected SIC 2- to 3-digit industry, quarterly rpt, 2502–1
Manufacturing finances and operations, by SIC 2- to 4-digit industry, forecast 1992, annual rpt, 2044–28
Manufacturing industries operations and performance, analytical rpt series, 2506–16
Manufacturing production, shipments, inventories, orders, and pollution control costs, periodic Current Industrial Rpt series, 2506–3
Military prime contract awards, by detailed procurement category, FY88-91, annual rpt, 3544–18
Multinatl firms US affiliates finances and operations, by industry, country of parent firm, and State, 1987, 2708–48
Multinatl US firms and foreign affiliates finances and operations, by industry and country, 1989 benchmark survey, annual rpt, 2704–5
Natural gas interstate pipeline company detailed financial and operating data, by firm, 1990, annual rpt, 3164–38
Occupational injury and illness rates, by SIC 2- to 4-digit industry, 1989-90, annual rpt, 6844–7
Occupational injury and illness rates, by SIC 2- to 4-digit industry, 1990, annual rpt, 6844–1
OECD trade, total and for 4 major countries, and US trade by country, by commodity, 1980-90, world area rpt series, 9116–1
Pacific territories population and housing detailed characteristics, by location, 1990 Census of Population and Housing, series, 2551–8
Pipelines inspections using internal electronic devices, costs and effectiveness, 1985-91, GAO rpt, 26113–594
Pollution abatement capital and operating costs, by SIC 2- to 4-digit industry and State, 1990, annual Current Industrial Rpt, 2506–3.6
Price indexes (producer), by stage of processing and detailed commodity, monthly rpt, 6762–6
Price indexes (producer), by stage of processing and detailed commodity, monthly 1991, annual rpt, 6764–2
Puerto Rico and other US possessions corporations income tax returns, income and tax items, and employment, by selected industry, 1989, article, 8302–2.326
Science, engineering, and technical employment in manufacturing, by field and industry, 1989, triennial rpt, 9627–23
Shipments, trade, use, and firms, for instruments and related products by detailed type, 1991, annual Current Industrial Rpt, 2506–12.26
Standards dev, proposals, and policies, for weights, measures, and performance, 1992 annual conf, 2214–7
Tariff Schedule of US, classifications and rates of duty by detailed imported commodity, 1993 base edition, 9886–13
Tax (income) returns of corporations, income and tax items by asset size and detailed industry, 1989, annual rpt, 8304–4; 8304–21
Tax (income) returns of corporations with foreign tax credit, income and tax items by industry group, 1988, biennial article, 8302–2.316
see also Aeronautical navigation
see also Medical supplies and equipment
see also Radar
see also Scientific equipment and apparatus
see also Watches and clocks
see also under By Commodity in the "Index by Categories"
see also under By Industry in the "Index by Categories"

Instruments, musical
see Musical instruments

Insulation
Buildings (commercial and residential) energy conservation technologies use, costs, efficiency, and residential tax credits, 1970s-90 and projected to 2010, 26358–259
Commercial buildings energy use, costs, and conservation, by building characteristics, survey rpt series, 3166–8
Exports and imports between US and outlying areas, by detailed commodity and mode of transport, 1991, annual rpt, 2424–11
Exports and imports of US, by country and detailed commodity, monthly rpt, 2422–12
Exports and imports of US, by Harmonized System 6-digit commodity and country, 1991, annual rpt, 2424–13
Exports of US, detailed Schedule B commodities with countries of destination, 1991, annual rpt, 2424–10
Housing (rental) units, total, with HUD assistance by program, and eligible for aid, by unit, household, and neighborhood characteristics, and location, 1989, biennial rpt, 5184–11
Housing and households detailed characteristics, and unit and neighborhood quality, MSA surveys, series, 2485–6
Housing energy use, costs, and conservation, and household and housing characteristics, survey rpt series, 3166–7
Injuries from use of consumer products, by severity, victim age, and detailed product, 1991, annual rpt, 9164–6
Manufacturing annual survey, 1990: finances and operations, by SIC 2- to 4-digit industry, series, 2506–14
Price indexes (producer), by stage of processing and detailed commodity, monthly rpt, 6762–6
Price indexes (producer) for building materials, by type, quarterly rpt, 2042–1.5
Stockpiling of strategic material by Fed Govt, activity, and inventory by commodity, as of Sept 1991, semiannual rpt, 3542–22

Insurance and insurance industry
Asset risk assessment for insurance companies, with financial ratios by firm type and financial status, 1990 and trends from 1900s, article, 9373–1.314; 9373–27.3
Bombings with insurance fraud motive, 1987-91, annual rpt, 8484–4.1
Bond (municipal) insurer finances and capital adequacy indicators, by firm and sector, 1986-90, hearing, 21248–173
Budget of US, obligations and authority by function, agency, and program, with summaries and analyses, FY93, annual rpt, 104–2
Collective bargaining agreements expiring during year, and workers covered, by firm, union, industry group, and State, 1992, annual rpt, 6784–9
Consumer Expenditure Survey, spending by category, and income, by selected household characteristics, 1991, annual press release, 6726–1.53

County Business Patterns, 1989: employment, establishments, and payroll, by SIC 2- to 4-digit industry and county, annual State rpt series, 2326–8
County Business Patterns, 1990: employment, establishments, and payroll, by SIC 2- to 4-digit industry and county, annual State rpt series, 2326–6
Court civil and criminal caseloads for Federal district, appeals, and bankruptcy courts, by type of suit and offense, circuit, and district, 1991, annual rpt, 18204–11
Court civil and criminal caseloads for Federal district, appeals, and special courts, 1991, annual rpt, 18204–8
Electric utilities privately owned, finances and operations, detailed data, 1990, annual rpt, 3164–23
Employment Cost Index and alternative measure of compensation costs, by component, occupation, industry group, union status, and location, 1975-92, annual rpt, 6744–20
Employment, earnings, and hours, by SIC 1- to 4-digit industry, monthly 1989-Feb 1992, annual rpt, 6744–4
Employment of minorities and women, by occupation, SIC 1- to 3-digit industry, State, and MSA, 1991, annual rpt, 9244–1
Export credit activity of Eximbank and 6 OECD countries, 1990, annual rpt, 9254–3
Exports and imports of services, direct and among multinatl firms affiliates, by industry and world area, 1986-91, article, 2702–1.336
Exports, imports, tariffs, and industry operating data for insurance, 1991 rpt, 9885–12.2
Farm finances, assets, liabilities, and debt by lender type, by State, 1960-89, 1548–384
Farm finances, debts, assets, and receipts, and lenders financial condition, quarterly rpt with articles, 1541–1
Farm loans by purpose and source, quarterly rpt, 9365–3.10
Farmland value, rent, taxes, foreign ownership, and transfers by probable use and lender type, with data by region and State, 1981-92, article, 1561–16.302
Fed Govt spending in States, by type, program, agency, and State, FY91, annual rpt, 2464–2
Finances and operations, by SIC 2- to 4-digit industry, forecast 1992, annual rpt, 2044–28
Finances of insurance companies, by insurance type and firm, with some intl comparisons, 1991 conf, 9373–3.35
Finances of insurance industry, and failures, with data by firm and State, 1990 hearing, 25528–119
Financial condition of insurance industry, operations, assets, junk bond holdings, and State regulation, with intl comparisons, 1991 hearings, 25268–79
Flow-of-funds accounts, savings, investments, and credit statements, quarterly rpt, 9365–3.3
Foreign direct investment in US, by industry group and world area, 1989-91, annual article, 2702–1.331
Foreign insurance excise tax collections of IRS, quarterly rpt, 8302–2.1
Input-output structure of US economy, detailed interindustry transactions for 541 industries, and components of final demand, 1982 benchmark data, 2708–17
Mail volume to and from households, use, and views, by class, source, content, and household characteristics, FY87-90, annual rpt, 9864–10
Mortgage applications, dispositions, and secondary loan market sales, by purpose, lender type, and applicant and neighborhood characteristics, 1991, article, 9362–1.307
Mortgage loan activity, by type of lender, loan, and mortgaged property, monthly press release, 5142–18
Mortgage loan activity, by type of lender, loan, and mortgaged property, quarterly press release, 5142–30
Mortgages FHA-insured, activities, audits, and financial statements, FY90-91, annual rpt, 5144–26
Mortgages FHA-insured by State, financing costs, and loans in force and claims by loan-to-value ratio, 1970s-80s, hearings, 21248–162
Mortgages FHA-insured, financial, property, and borrower characteristics, by metro area, 1991, annual rpt, 5144–24
Mortgages FHA-insured, financial, property, and borrower characteristics, by State, 1991, annual rpt, 5144–1; 5144–25
Mortgages FHA-insured, financial, property, and borrower characteristics, 1991, annual rpt, 5144–17; 5144–23
Mortgages FHA-insured, insurance fund financial condition with background housing and mortgage data, 1970s-90s, hearing, 25248–128
Multinatl firms US affiliates finances and operations, by industry, country of parent firm, and State, 1987, 2708–48
Multinatl firms US affiliates, finances, and operations, by industry, world area of parent firm, and State, 1989-90, annual rpt, 2704–4
Multinatl US firms and foreign affiliates finances and operations, by industry and country, 1989 benchmark survey, annual rpt, 2704–5
Natural gas interstate pipeline company detailed financial and operating data, by firm, 1990, annual rpt, 3164–38
Occupational injury and illness rates, by SIC 2- to 4-digit industry, 1989-90, annual rpt, 6844–7
Occupational injury and illness rates, by SIC 2- to 4-digit industry, 1990, annual rpt, 6844–1
Occupational Outlook Handbook, 1992-93, biennial rpt, 6744–1
Pension Benefit Guaranty Corp activities and finances, FY91, annual rpt, 9674–1
Pension Benefit Guaranty Corp single- and multi-employer funds balances, FY91, article, 9391–16.309
Postal Service special services revenue and volume, quarterly rpt, 9862–1
Public opinion on taxes, spending, and govt efficiency, by respondent characteristics, 1992 survey, annual rpt, 10044–2
SEC registration, firms required to file annual rpts, as of Sept 1991, annual listing, 9734–5
Small business finances, operations, owner characteristics, and Federal contracts, 1980s-90, annual rpt, 9764–6
Southeastern US employment by industry div, earnings, and hours, for 8 States, quarterly press release, 6942–7
Statistical Abstract of US, 1992 annual data compilation, 2324–1.16
Student guaranteed loans, defaults, and collections, by type of loan, lender, and guarantee agency, with data by State and top lender, FY91, annual rpt, 4804–38
Tax (excise) collections of IRS, by source, quarterly rpt, 8302–1
Tax (income) returns filed, by type of filer, selected income items, quarterly rpt, 8302–2.1
Tax (income) returns of corporations, income and tax items by asset size and detailed industry, 1989, annual rpt, 8304–4; 8304–21
Tax (income) returns of corporations with foreign tax credit, income and tax items by industry group, 1988, biennial article, 8302–2.316
Tax (income) returns of partnerships, income statement and balance sheet items, by industry group, 1990, annual article, 8302–2.314
Tax (income) returns of sole proprietorships, income statement items, by industry group, 1990, annual article, 8302–2.317; 8302–2.320
Tax collections of State govts by detailed type of tax, and tax rates, by State, FY91, annual rpt, 2466–2.7
Tax exempt organizations and employee plans listed on IRS masterfile, determinations, applications, and rulings, FY91, annual rpt, 8304–3.2
Tax rates and revenue of State and local govts, by source and State, 1992 and historical trends, annual rpt, 10044–1
see also Agricultural insurance
see also Automobile insurance
see also Census of Financial, Insurance, and Real Estate Industries
see also Deposit insurance
see also Disability benefits and insurance
see also Employee benefits
see also Federal Deposit Insurance Corp.
see also Federal Savings and Loan Insurance Corp.
see also Health insurance
see also Life insurance
see also Medicare
see also Old-Age, Survivors, Disability, and Health Insurance
see also Property and casualty insurance
see also Servicepersons life insurance programs
see also Surety bonds
see also Unemployment insurance
see also Workers compensation
see also under By Industry in the "Index by Categories"

Integrated circuits
see Semiconductors

Integrated Postsecondary Education Data System
Finances of higher education instns, revenue by source and spending by function, by State and instn control, FY82-90, annual rpt, 4844–6

Glossary for IPEDS, 1992 rpt, 4848–47
Higher education enrollment, faculty, finances, and degrees, by instn level and control, and State, FY88, annual rpt, 4844–13

Intellectual property
see Copyright
see Patents
see Trademarks

Intelligence levels
Army personnel with low aptitude test scores, by sex and race, FY89-90, GAO rpt, 26123–373
Military reserve forces personnel strengths and characteristics, by component, quarterly rpt, 3542–4
see also Educational tests
see also Literacy and illiteracy
see also Mental health and illness
see also Mental retardation

Intelligence services
see also Bureau of Intelligence and Research, State Department
see also Central Intelligence Agency
see also Defense Intelligence Agency
see also Defense Security Assistance Agency
see also Detective and protective services
see also Espionage
see also Military intelligence

INTELSAT
see International Telecommunications Satellite Organization

Inter-American Development Bank
Loan activity by purpose and country, and funds by source, FY90, annual rpt, 15344–1.7
Loans and grants for economic and military aid from US and intl agencies, by program and country, FY46-91, annual rpt, 9914–5

Inter-American Foundation
Activities, grants by recipient, and fellowships of IAF, by country, FY91, annual rpt, 14424–1
Budget of US, authoritative financial statements with appropriations, outlays, and receipts, by category and agency, FY91, annual rpt, 8104–2.2
Budget of US, obligations and authority by function, agency, and program, with summaries and analyses, FY93, annual rpt, 104–2
Grants by program area, and fellowships by field and instn, by country, with IAF finances and staff, FY72-91, annual rpt, 14424–2
Grants of IAF, project characteristics, area benefits, and investment returns, for 8 projects, 1970s-88, 14428–1
Latin America economic and social conditions, resources, trade, and aid, 1992, annual factbook, 9914–14

Interagency Council on the Homeless
Assistance for homeless of Fed Govt by program and agency, and indicators of need, 1990, annual rpt, 14364–1

Interagency Forum on Aging-Related Statistics
Activities of Forum, and contacts, 1989-90, annual rpt, 14324–1

Interagency Scientific Committee To Address the Conservation of the Northern Spotted Owl
Conservation methods, timber industry impacts, and Federal and State spending, 1980s-95, 1208–388
Findings and recommendations, 1990 rpt, 1208–385

Interagency Task Force on Acid Precipitation
Emissions of acid rain constituents, and environmental, economic, and health effects, 1985-89 and alternative projections to 2030, 14358–4
Research on acid rain, activities, and funding by Federal agency, FY91-92, 14358–3

Interdepartment Radio Advisory Committee
Radio frequency assignments for Federal use, by agency, 1st half 1992, semiannual rpt, 2802–1

Interest groups
see Lobbying and lobbying groups
see Nonprofit organizations and foundations
see Political action committees

Interest payments
Agricultural Stabilization and Conservation Service producer payments, by program and State, 1991, annual table, 1804–12
AID loans repayment status and terms by program and country, and status of predecessor agency loans, quarterly rpt, 9912–3
Bank deposits availability policies, with background data, 1980s-90, last issue of annual report, 9364–13
Banks (insured commercial and savings) finances, for foreign and domestic offices, by asset size, 1990, annual rpt, 9294–4.2
Banks (insured commercial and savings) financial condition and performance, by asset size and region, quarterly rpt, 9292–1
Banks and thrifts finances and operations by deposit size, Fed Reserve functional cost analysis, 1991, annual rpt, 9364–6
Budget of US, authoritative financial statements with appropriations, outlays, and receipts, by category and agency, FY91, annual rpt, 8104–2.2
Budget of US, Bush Admin proposals, with detail for defense budgets, and historical data from FY34, FY93, 108–46
Budget of US, CBO analysis and review of FY93 budget by function, annual rpt, 26304–2
Budget of US, CBO analysis of revenue and spending alternatives and projections of economic indicators, FY93-97, annual rpt, 26304–3
Budget of US, House concurrent resolution, with spending and revenue targets, FY93 and projected to FY97, annual rpt, 21264–2
Budget of US, midsession review of FY93 budget, by function, annual rpt, 104–7
Budget of US, obligations and authority by function, agency, and program, with summaries and analyses, FY93, annual rpt, 104–2
Budget of US, receipts by source, outlays by agency and program, and balances, monthly rpt, 8102–3
Business statistics, detailed data for major industries and economic indicators, 1960-91, *Survey of Current Business* biennial supplement, 2704–1
Consumer interest paid to business, and interest received as personal income, 1959-91, annual rpt, 204–1.1
Credit card issuers, and banks credit operations, costs and revenue, mid 1970s-91, article, 9362–1.306
Credit unions federally insured, finances by instn characteristics and State, as of June 1992, semiannual rpt, 9532–6
Credit unions federally insured, finances, 1990-91, annual rpt, 9534–1
Developing countries debt to foreign lenders, and IMF credit outstanding, by country, 1985-91, annual rpt, 9114–7
Electric power distribution loans from REA, and borrower operating and financial data, by firm and State, 1991, annual rpt, 1244–1
Electric power plants production and capital costs, operations, and fuel use, by fuel type, plant, utility, and location, 1990, annual rpt, 3164–9
Electric utilities finances and operations, detailed data for publicly and privately owned firms, 1990, annual rpt, 3164–11.4
Electric utilities finances and operations, detailed data for publicly owned firms, 1990, annual rpt, 3164–24
Electric utilities privately owned, finances and operations, detailed data, 1990, annual rpt, 3164–23
Energy producers finances and operations, by energy type for US firms domestic and foreign operations, 1990, annual rpt, 3164–44.1
Farm production itemized costs, by farm sales size and region, 1991, annual rpt, 1614–3
Farm production itemized costs, receipts, and returns, by commodity and region, 1975-90, annual rpt, 1544–20
Farm production itemized costs, receipts, and returns, by crop and State, 1987-89, annual rpt, 1544–24
Farm sector balance sheet, and receipts by detailed commodity, by State, 1986-90, annual rpt, 1544–18
Fed Govt finances, cash and debt transactions, daily tables, 8102–4
Fed Govt programs under Ways and Means Committee jurisdiction, finances, operations, and participant characteristics, FY70s-91, annual rpt, 21784–11
Fed Govt trust funds financial condition, by fund, periodic rpt series, 8102–9
Fed Natl Mortgage Assn activities and finances, 1991, annual rpt, 9474–1
Finance companies assets, operating ratios, and growth indicators, for top 20 firms, 1980s-90, article, 9385–1.309
Financial operations of Fed Govt, detailed data, *Treasury Bulletin*, quarterly rpt, 8002–4
FmHA activities, and loans and grants by program and State, FY91 and trends from FY70, annual rpt, 1184–17
Foreign-controlled US firms transactions with related foreign persons, by type, industry div, and country, 1988, article, 8302–2.318
Foreign govts and private obligors debt to US, by country and program, periodic rpt, 8002–6
Govt direct spending and employment, by function and level of govt, selected years 1962-87, 10048–53
Govt finances, by level of govt, State, and for large cities and counties, annual rpt series, 2466–2

Govt finances, tax systems and revenue, and fiscal structure, by level of govt and State, 1992 with historical trends, annual rpt, 10044–1
Govt revenues and spending by level of govt, natl income and product accounts, 1959-91, annual rpt, 204–1.6
Income (household, family, and personal), by source, detailed characteristics, and region, 1991, annual Current Population Rpt, 2546–6.76
Income from US sources and tax withheld for foreign natls not residing in US, by country and tax treaty status, 1989, annual article, 8302–2.308
Income tax returns of foreign corporations and individuals, and US entities abroad, detailed data compilation, 1970s-89, quinquennial rpt, 8308–31
Mortgages FHA-insured, financial, property, and borrower characteristics, by metro area, 1991, annual rpt, 5144–24
Mortgages FHA-insured, financial, property, and borrower characteristics, by State, 1991, annual rpt, 5144–1
Mortgages FHA-insured, financial, property, and borrower characteristics, 1991, annual rpt, 5144–23
Multinatl firms US affiliates, finances, and operations, by industry, world area of parent firm, and State, 1989-90, annual rpt, 2704–4
Multinatl firms US affiliates gross product, by component, industry, and country of parent firm, 1987-90, article, 2702–1.342
Natl income and product accounts and components, *Survey of Current Business*, monthly rpt, 2702–1.23
Natl income and product accounts benchmark revisions of GDP and natl income, various periods 1959-80, tables, 2702–1.307
Natl income and product accounts, comprehensive accounts and components, benchmark revisions, 1929-88, 2708–5
Natl income and product accounts, comprehensive accounts and components, *Survey of Current Business*, monthly rpt, 2702–1.29; 2702–1.31
Natural gas interstate pipeline company detailed financial and operating data, by firm, 1990, annual rpt, 3164–38
Nonprofit charitable and other tax exempt organizations finances, by category and size of assets and contributions, 1988, annual article, 8302–2.315
OASDHI, Medicaid, SSI, and related programs benefits, beneficiary characteristics, and trust funds, selected years 1937-90, annual rpt, 4744–3
Older persons income and sources, by whether OASDI beneficiary, poverty status, and other characteristics, 1990, biennial rpt, 4744–26
Postal Service activities, finances, and mail volume and subsidies, FY91, annual rpt, 9864–5.3
Public debt, net interest paid by Fed Govt, monthly rpt, quarterly and annual data, 23842–1.6
Rice production, practices, costs, and land tenure, by production area, 1988, 1568–309
Rural Electrification Admin activities and finances, and loans by State, FY91 and trends from FY36, annual rpt, 1244–3
Rural Telephone Program loan activity, by State, FY91, annual tables, 1244–8
Savings and loan assns, FHLB 6th District insured members financial condition and operations by State, quarterly rpt, 9302–23
Savings instns financial statements, for instns insured by Savings Assn Insurance Fund by FHLB district and State, and for FDIC-insured savings banks, 1989, annual rpt, 8434–1
Savings instns insured by Savings Assn Insurance Fund, assets, liabilities, and deposit and loan activity, by conservatorship status, monthly rpt, 8432–1
Southeastern States, Fed Reserve 5th District insured commercial banks financial statements, by State, quarterly rpt, 9389–18
Survey of Current Business, detailed financial and business data, and economic indicators, monthly rpt, 2702–1.3
Tax (income) returns filed, by type of filer, selected income items, quarterly rpt, 8302–2.1
Tax (income) returns for foreign corporate activity in US, selected income and tax items, by industry div and selected country, 1988, article, 8302–2.309
Tax (income) returns of corporations, income and tax items by asset size and detailed industry, 1989, annual rpt, 8304–4; 8304–21
Tax (income) returns of corporations, summary data by asset size and industry div, 1989, annual article, 8302–2.321
Tax (income) returns of corporations with foreign tax credit, income and tax items by industry group, 1988, biennial article, 8302–2.316
Tax (income) returns of individuals, by filing status, tax item, and income level, 1991, annual article, 8302–2.319
Tax (income) returns of individuals, detailed data, 1988, annual rpt, 8304–2
Tax (income) returns of individuals, selected income and tax items by income level, preliminary 1990, annual article, 8302–2.307
Tax (income) returns of individuals with foreign earned income, income and tax items by income level and occupation, 1987, article, 8302–2.301
Tax (income) returns of partnerships, income statement and balance sheet items, by industry group, 1990, annual article, 8302–2.314
Tax (income) returns of sole proprietorships, income statement items, by industry group, 1990, annual article, 8302–2.317; 8302–2.320
Tax (income) withholding and related documents filed, by type and IRS service center, 1991 and projected 1992-99, annual rpt, 8304–22
Tax exempt organizations finances, with data by type, size, State, and for largest organizations, late 1940s-80s, compilation of papers, 8308–35
Tax exempt organizations with unrelated business income, finances by organization type, 1987, article, 8302–2.306
Telephone and telegraph firms detailed finances and operations, 1990, annual rpt, 9284–6
Telephone firms borrowing under Rural Telephone Program, and financial and operating data, by State, 1991, annual rpt, 1244–2
Truck rates for fruit and vegetables paid by shippers and receivers, by commodity and city, and fleet itemized costs per mile, weekly rpt, 1311–22
Unemployment insurance programs of States, benefits, coverage, exhaustions, and finances, 1990, annual tables, 6404–10

Interest rates

Bank deposits interest rates deregulation impacts on bank asset risk, alternative model descriptions and results, 1970s-80s, working paper, 9379–14.15
Bank deposits interest rates relation to market concentration, regulation, migration, and other factors, 1980s, technical paper, 9366–6.297
Banking and financial conditions, 1990, annual rpt, 9364–5
Banks (insured commercial and FDIC-insured savings) assets, income, and financial ratios, by asset size and State, quarterly rpt, 13002–3
Banks interest rates on deposits, relation to measures of bank financial strength and other indicators, 1984-91, technical paper, 9366–6.300
Banks loan interest rates and default risk relation to GDP and money supply, model description and results, 1992 working paper, 9387–8.283
Banks profitability, balance sheet and income statement items, and financial ratios, by asset size, 1985-91, annual article, 9362–1.305
Bond (junk) holdings of Resolution Trust Corp, quarterly press release, 9722–4
Bond yields and interest rates on public and private securities, 1929-91, annual rpt, 204–1.5
Budget of US, CBO analysis of revenue and spending alternatives and projections of economic indicators, FY93-97, annual rpt, 26304–3
Business cycle duration and strength indicators, late 1940s-91, article, 9373–1.301
Business statistics, detailed data for major industries and economic indicators, *Survey of Current Business*, monthly rpt, 2702–1.8
Business statistics, detailed data for major industries and economic indicators, 1960-91, *Survey of Current Business* biennial supplement, 2704–1
Credit (installment) outstanding and terms, by lender and credit type, monthly rpt, 9365–2.6
Credit card issuers disclosure of terms and conditions to consumers, with finances and operations, 1991 hearing, 21248–175
Credit unions federally insured, finances by instn characteristics and State, as of June 1992, semiannual rpt, 9532–6
Credit unions with low income membership, financial, operating, and membership data, 1982-91, 9536–1.8
Discount rate relation to Fed funds rate, model description and results, 1955-90, technical paper, 9379–12.90

Economic indicators and components, and Fed Reserve 4th District business and financial conditions, monthly chartbook, 9377–10
Economic indicators and components, current data and annual trends, monthly rpt, 23842–1.5
Economic indicators forecasting performance of interest rate spreads, 1950s-90, working paper, 9375–13.67
Economic indicators performance, and Fed Reserve monetary policy objectives, as of July 1992, semiannual rpt, 9362–4
Eurodollar deposit rates, interest arbitrage, and other short-term rates, current and 4-year trends, weekly chartbook, 9365–1.5
Exchange rate relation to interest rates and inflation, model description and results, 1974-90, technical paper, 9366–7.279
Exchange rates relation to domestic interest rates, productivity, and other factors, for US and 3 OECD countries, 1970s-90, working paper, 9393–10.21
Export credit activity of Eximbank and 6 OECD countries, 1990, annual rpt, 9254–3
Farm credit, terms, delinquency, agricultural bank failures, and credit conditions by Fed Reserve District, quarterly rpt, 9365–3.10
Farm loan rates relation to Treasury bill interest rates, 1991 article, 1541–1.306
Farm loan short-term interest rate setting factors of large and small banks, 1991 article, 1541-1.307
Farm mortgage and other loans interest rates, by lender type, quarterly rpt with articles, 1541–1
Farm prices received and paid, by commodity and State, monthly rpt, 1629–1
Fed Financing Bank holdings and transactions, by borrower, monthly press release, 12802–1
Fed funds rate impact on stock prices, 1974-79, technical paper, 4746–26.19
Fed Govt debt issued, redeemed, and outstanding, by series and source, and gifts to reduce debt, monthly rpt, 8242–2
Fed Govt financial operations, detailed data, *Treasury Bulletin*, quarterly rpt, 8002–4
Fed Reserve banks interest rates, Dec 1991, annual rpt, 9364–1.1
Fed Reserve Bd discount rate changes relation to Treasury bill rates, alternative estimates, 1970s-80s, article, 9391–1.314
Fed Reserve discount rates relation to monetary and fiscal policy, model description and results, 1970s-91, working paper, 9379–14.20
Financial and business detailed statistics, *Fed Reserve Bulletin*, monthly rpt with articles, 9362–1
Financial and economic analysis of banking and nonbanking sectors, working paper series, 9381–10
Financial and monetary conditions, selected US summary data, weekly rpt, 9391–4
Financial instruments and home mortgages interest rates, monthly rpt, 9365–2.14
FmHA guaranteed loan program, characteristics of borrowers, lenders, and loans, FY88, 1548–386
Food marketing cost indexes, by expense category, monthly rpt with articles, 1502–4
Forecasts of interest rates, performance of short- and long-term rate spreads, for US and 6 EC countries, 1950s-91, technical paper, 9385–8.136
Foreign and US economic conditions, and trade devs and balances, with data by selected country and country group, monthly rpt, 9882–14
Foreign and US long-term interest rates relation to rates of return to capital, economic policies, and other factors, by country, 1960s-90, article, 9385–1.301
Foreign central banks discount and short-term interest rates, monthly rpt, 9362–1.3
Foreign countries economic conditions and implications for US, periodic country rpt series, 2046–4
Foreign countries economic conditions, policy, and trade practices, by country, 1989-91, annual rpt, 21384–5
Futures trading in selected commodities and financial instruments and indexes, for NYC, Chicago, and other markets activity, biweekly rpt, 11922–5
GDP forecasting performance of selected economic indicators over selected forecast periods and business cycles, 1960s-91, article, 9375–1.307
GNP and employment impact of interest rate spreads, various periods 1959-91, technical paper, 9385–8.131
GNP and employment related to oil prices and interest rates, late 1940s-91, article, 9389–1.304
Housing and households detailed characteristics, and unit and neighborhood quality, MSA surveys, series, 2485–6
Inflation relation to interest rates, 1959-91, article, 9379–1.306
Loans (consumer) of banks, relation to bank-auto finance company interest rate spread, tax reform, and other factors, 1970s-91, working paper, 9379–12.88
Monetary aggregate (M2) growth relation to Resolution Trust Corp failed thrift resolution activity and other factors, 1990-91, article, 9379–1.303
Monetary policy impacts on interest rates, 1992 working paper, 9375–13.80
Monetary policy impacts on money supply and interest rates, and regression results for alternative indexes, 1950s-88, working paper, 9387–8.259
Monetary trends, Fed Reserve Bank of St Louis monthly rpt, 9391–2
Money demand relation to income growth and interest rates, model description and results, 1992 working paper, 9387–8.279
Money supply impact on interest rate, alternative model results, 1950s-90, technical paper, 9371–10.75
Mortgage applications to FHA for new and existing units, refinancings, and housing starts, monthly rpt, 5142–44
Mortgage, bond, and other interest rates, quarterly rpt, 2042–1.5
Mortgage interest fixed and adjustable rates and fees offered, by region, weekly rpt, 9412–3
Mortgage interest rate differential among cities, and relation to bank market conditions, 1987-88, technical paper, 9366–1.162
Mortgages (conventional) terms at closing, by lender type, with periodic data by district, State, and for 32 MSAs, monthly rpt, 9442–2
Mortgages (conventional) terms at closing, for fixed- and adjustable-rate loans by purpose, FHLB district, State, and selected MSA, 1960s-91, annual rpt, 9444–2
Mortgages (fixed rate) profitability of thrifts, relation to interest rate spread and other operating ratios, model results, 1991 technical paper, 9366–6.289
Mortgages FHA-insured, financial, property, and borrower characteristics, 1991, annual rpt, 5144–17
Mortgages FHA-insured for 1-family units, by loan type and mortgage characteristics, quarterly rpt, 5142–45
Mortgages FHA-insured, secondary market prices and yields, and interest rates on construction and conventional mortgage loans, by region, monthly press release, 5142–20
North Central States farm credit conditions and economic devs, Fed Reserve 7th District, monthly rpt, 9375–10
North Central States farm credit conditions, earnings, and expenses, Fed Reserve 9th District, quarterly rpt, 9383–11
North Central States, FHLB 6th District and natl cost of funds indexes for savings instns, and mortgage and Treasury bill rates, monthly rpt, 9302–38
North Central States, FHLB 7th District and natl cost of funds indexes for savings instns, and mortgage rates, monthly rpt, 9302–30
Rural Electrification Admin activities and finances, and loans by State, FY91 and trends from FY36, annual rpt, 1244–3
Savings and loan assns, FHLB 6th District insured members financial condition and operations by State, quarterly rpt, 9302–23
Savings instns failure resolution activity of Resolution Trust Corp, brokered deposits, fees, and interest rates by instn and region, as of July 1991, hearing, 21248–171
Savings instns holdings of low-grade (junk) bonds and relation to stock volatility and deposit interest rates, late 1980s, working paper, 9375–13.69
Savings instns insured by Savings Assn Insurance Fund, assets, liabilities, and deposit and loan activity, by conservatorship status, monthly rpt, 8432–1
Securities (intl) returns, relation to interest rates and other factors, model description, 1992 technical paper, 9385–8.137
Small Business Admin dev company loan program and debenture sale activity, with data by firm, industry div, State, and region, quarterly rpt, 9762–6
Small Business Admin direct and guaranteed loans, principal outstanding, and losses, by program, borrower race and sex, and State, 1950s-90, GAO rpt, 26113–554
Small Business Admin guaranteed loans issued under regular, certified, and preferred lender programs, selected characteristics, FY83-90, GAO rpt, 26113–581

Small business financing sources, and business financial data by size, type, and industry, 1980s-90, annual rpt, 9764–6.2
Southwestern US farm credit conditions and real estate values, Fed Reserve 11th District, quarterly rpt, 9379–11
Statistical Abstract of US, 1992 annual data compilation, 2324–1.16
Student guaranteed loans, defaults, and collections, by type of loan, lender, and guarantee agency, with data by State and top lender, FY91, annual rpt, 4804–38
Student Loan Marketing Assn activities and finances, 1991, annual rpt, 9784–1
Student loan Perkins program income, losses, and Federal and school contributions, late 1950s-89, GAO rpt, 26121–440
Survey of Current Business, detailed financial and business data, and economic indicators, monthly rpt, 2702–1.1
Taiwan monetary and foreign exchange policies, with money supply, interest rates, and other economic indicators, 1980s, article, 9393–8.303
Treasury bill interest rates, factors affecting before- and after-tax real rates, model description and results, 1960s-89, working paper, 9373–27.6
Treasury bill offerings, auction results by Fed Reserve District, and terms, periodic press release series, 8002–7
Treasury bills, notes, and bonds market bid yields at constant maturities, *Treasury Bulletin*, quarterly rpt, 8002–4.9
Western States, FHLB 11th District and natl cost of funds indexes for savings instns, and mortgage and Treasury bill rates, monthly rpt, 9302–38

Intergovernmental relations
Assistance (financial and nonfinancial) of Fed Govt, 1992 base edition, annual listing, 104–5
Intergovernmental Perspective, quarterly journal, 10042–1
Investigations of Federal agency and program operations, summaries of findings, as of 1991, annual GAO rpt, 26104–5.3
Public opinion on taxes, spending, and govt efficiency, by respondent characteristics, 1992 survey, annual rpt, 10044–2
see also Federal-local relations
see also Federal-State relations
see also Foreign relations
see also International cooperation in law enforcement
see also Interstate compacts
see also Interstate relations
see also Regional planning
see also State-local relations

Interindustry transactions
see Input-output analysis

Interior Department
see Department of Interior

Intermediate-Range Nuclear Forces Treaty
Status of arms control treaties and agreements, and Arms Control and Disarmament Agency activities, 1991, annual rpt, 9824–2

Internal Revenue Service
Activities of IRS, collection, enforcement, and litigation, with data by type of tax, region, and State, FY91, annual rpt, 8304–3
Admin and compliance issues, and taxpayer views, 1991 conf, 8304–25
Budget of US, obligations and authority by function, agency, and program, with summaries and analyses, FY93, annual rpt, 104–2
Corporations income tax compliance, and IRS enforcement activities, 1970s-92, hearing, 25408–118
Corporations income tax compliance issues for large firms, with income, taxes paid, and tax credits, 1988, GAO rpt, 26119–405
Corporations income tax returns, income and tax items by asset size and detailed industry, 1989, annual rpt, 8304–4; 8304–21
Criminal undercover investigations of IRS and costs by criminal activity, and success rates, by region, mid 1980s-90, GAO rpt, 26119–394
Earned income tax credit advance payment option, participation, taxpayer awareness, employer burden, and IRS administration, 1989-90, GAO rpt, 26119–378
Employee benefit plan applications to IRS, and coverage, by disposition and plan type, FY91, annual rpt, 8304–23
Enforcement of tax payment activities of IRS, and related collections, FY88-92, hearing, 21788–217
Ethical climate at IRS, misconduct, reporting and retaliation, and staff and mgmt integrity, employees views, 1991 GAO rpt, 26119–366
Excise tax collections of IRS, by source, quarterly rpt, 8302–1
Foreign corporations and individuals, and US entities abroad, detailed data compilation for income tax returns, 1970s-89, quinquennial rpt, 8308–31
Individual income tax returns, detailed data, 1988, annual rpt, 8304–2
Intangible assets from acquired businesses, tax deductions for amortization, IRS unresolved audits, and claims allowed, 1991 GAO rpt, 26119–365
Luxury tax revenue, and related IRS administrative costs, FY91 and projected to FY95, GAO rpt, 26119–385
Money laundering investigation activities of States and Fed Govt, and use of IRS large cash transaction rpts, by State, 1985-91, GAO rpt, 26119–430
Returns and supplemental documents filed, by type, FY91 and projected to FY2000, semiannual rpt, 8302–4
Returns filed, by type, IRS service center, and whether full-paid, refund, and electronically filed, 1990 and projected to 1998, semiannual rpt, 8302–7
Returns filed, by type of filer, detailed preliminary and supplementary data, quarterly rpt with articles, 8302–2
Returns filed, by type of tax and IRS district, 1990 and projected 1991-98, annual rpt, 8304–24
Returns filed, by type of tax, region, and IRS service center, projected 1991-98 and trends from 1978, annual rpt, 8304–9
Returns filed using alternative methods, with fraud, and conventional form preparation time and processing costs, 1986-92, GAO rpt, 26119–400
Returns processing and taxpayer info activity, electronic and experimental filings, and refunds, for individual income tax, periodic press release, 8302–6
Tax exempt organizations finances, with data by type, size, State, and for largest organizations, late 1940s-80s, compilation of papers, 8308–35
Telephone system of IRS for income tax questions, improvements in accuracy, 1989-91, GAO rpt, 26119–418
Wage reporting by employers, SSA and IRS reconciliation of records, late 1970s-80s, GAO rpt, 26121–477
Withholding and related documents filed, by type and IRS service center, 1991 and projected 1992-99, annual rpt, 8304–22
Withholding tax delinquent accounts of Federal agencies, and compared to other taxpayers, 1990, hearing, 21788–206

Internal security
Court civil and criminal caseloads for Federal district, appeals, and special courts, 1991, annual rpt, 18204–8
DOE contractor computer system security and controls at Strategic Petroleum Reserve offices, 1991, 3006–5.27
Fed Govt employees and hirees background checks by OPM, efficiency, and agency managers views on timeliness and quality, FY90, GAO rpt, 26119–373
Info Security Oversight Office monitoring of Federal security measures and classification actions, FY91, annual rpt, 9454–21
IRS internal audits, and employee and nonemployee violations, FY91, annual rpt, 8304–3.1
Labor laws enacted, by State, 1991, annual article, 6722–1.309
Labor productivity of Federal employees, indexes of output and labor costs by function, FY67-90, annual rpt, 6824–1.6
Natl Archives and Records Admin activities, finances, holdings, and staff, FY91, annual rpt, 9514–2
Nuclear weapons facilities of DOE, security deficiencies by type and facility, 1989-90, GAO rpt, 26113–557
Persian Gulf War classification actions monitored by Info Security Oversight Office, FY91, annual rpt, 9454–21
US attorneys civil and criminal cases by type and disposition, and collections, by Federal district, FY91, annual rpt, 6004–2.7

International agreements
see Executive agreements
see Trade agreements
see Treaties and conventions

International assistance
Africa (sub-Saharan) economic, social, and political conditions, with US aid by program and country, 1991 rpt, 7008–58
African Dev Foundation dev grants and fellowships, by country, FY84-91, annual rpt, 9034–1
AID activities, finances, and staff, by program and country, FY90, GAO rpt, 26123–382
AID and Intl Dev Cooperation Agency activities and funding, FY91-93, with developing countries economic and social conditions from 1960s, annual rpt, 9904–4

AID contracts and grants for technical and support services, by instn, country, and State, FY91, annual listing, 9914–7
AID contracts, grants, and cooperative agreements with higher education instns, by project, instn, and country, FY91, annual listing, 9914–6
AID dev projects and socioeconomic impacts, evaluation rpt series, 9916–1
AID economic aid to developing countries, obligations and disbursements by country, quarterly rpt, 9912–4
AID loans repayment status and terms by program and country, and status of predecessor agency loans, quarterly rpt, 9912–3
Background Notes, foreign countries summary social, political, and economic data, series, 7006–2
Budget of US, balances of budget authority obligated and unobligated, by function and agency, FY90-93, annual rpt, 104–8
Budget of US, House concurrent resolution, with spending and revenue targets, FY93 and projected to FY97, annual rpt, 21264–2
Budget of US, obligations and authority by function, agency, and program, with summaries and analyses, FY93, annual rpt, 104–2
Budget of US, receipts by source, outlays by agency and program, and balances, monthly rpt, 8102–3
Currency (foreign) accounts owned by US under AID admin and by foreign govts with joint AID control, status by program and country, quarterly rpt, 9912–1
Currency (foreign) holdings of US, transactions and balances by program and country, 1st half FY92, semiannual rpt, 8102–7
Debt to US of foreign govts and private obligors, by country and program, periodic rpt, 8002–6
Developing countries economic, population, and agricultural data, US and other aid sources, and AID activity, country rpt series, 9916–12
Disasters, casualties, damage, and aid by US and others, by country, FY91 and trends from FY64, annual rpt, 9914–12
Eastern Europe economic aid by donor country, and Poland and Hungary exports by world area, 1988-91, GAO rpt, 26123–386
Eastern Europe export industries dev potential, with trade and industry finances and operations, for 5 countries, 1985-90, 9886–4.179
Economic conditions in foreign countries and implications for US, periodic country rpt series, 2046–4
Economic conditions, policy, and trade practices, by country, 1989-91, annual rpt, 21384–5
Economic, social, political, and geographic summary data, by country, 1992, annual factbook, 9114–2
Energy use and aid for developing countries, 1991 hearings, 25318–83
Exports and imports between US and outlying areas, by detailed commodity and mode of transport, 1991, annual rpt, 2424–11
Exports and imports of US, by Harmonized System 6-digit commodity and country, 1991, annual rpt, 2424–13
Exports of US, detailed Schedule B commodities with countries of destination, 1991, annual rpt, 2424–10
Family planning and population activities of AID, grants by project and recipient, and contraceptive shipments, by country, FY91, annual rpt series, 9914–13
Fed Govt contingent liabilities and claims paid on insured and guaranteed contracts with foreign obligors, by country and program, periodic rpt, 8002–12
Fed Govt economic and military aid, by program and country, selected years 1940-89, annual rpt, 15344–1.1
Financial instns (intl) funds by source and disbursements by purpose, by country, with US policy review, FY90, annual rpt, 15344–1
Food supply, needs, and aid for developing countries, status and alternative forecasts, world area rpt series, 1526–8
Housing and urban dev program of AID, FY91, annual rpt, 9914–4
Human rights conditions in 170 countries, and US economic and military aid, 1991, annual rpt, 21384–3
Inter-American Foundation activities, grants by recipient, and fellowships, by country, FY91, annual rpt, 14424–1
Latin America dev grants of Inter-American Foundation by program area, and fellowships by field and instn, by country, FY72-91, annual rpt, 14424–2
Latin America dev grants of Inter-American Foundation, project characteristics, area benefits, and investment returns, for 8 projects, 1970s-88, 14428–1
Latin America economic and social conditions, resources, trade, and aid, 1992, annual factbook, 9914–14
Latin America economic conditions, trade, and foreign aid, working paper series, 9916–13
Loans and grants for economic and military aid from US and intl agencies, by program and country, FY46-91, annual rpt, 9914–5
Loans and loan guarantees of Fed Govt, outstanding amounts by agency and program, *Treasury Bulletin*, quarterly rpt, 8002–4.11
Natl income and product accounts, comprehensive accounts and components, benchmark revisions, 1929-88, 2708–5
Natl income and product accounts, comprehensive accounts and components, *Survey of Current Business*, monthly rpt, 2702–1.26
NATO members, Japan, and South Korea economic aid to developing countries and Eastern Europe, 1980-90, annual rpt, 3544–28
Nicaragua economic and dev aid of US by type, and foreign debt by creditor, FY90-91, GAO rpt, 26123–398
Peace Corps activities, funding by program, and volunteers, by country, FY93, annual rpt, 9654–1
R&D funding by Fed Govt, by detailed function, program, and agency, FY91-93, annual rpt, 9627–9
Rice exports under Federal programs, periodic situation rpt, 1561–8
Statistical Abstract of US, 1992 annual data compilation, 2324–1.29; 2324–1.31
Voluntary agencies foreign aid programs, funding, and outlays, by agency, 1990, annual rpt, 9914–9
see also Export-Import Bank
see also Military assistance
see also Public Law 480
see also Refugees
see also War relief

International Atomic Energy Agency
Safety inspection activities and emergency response procedures of IAEA since 1986 Chernobyl accident, 1991, GAO rpt, 26123–367

International Bank for Reconstruction and Development
Loan activity by purpose and country, and funds by source, FY90, annual rpt, 15344–1.4
Loans and grants for economic and military aid from US and intl agencies, by program and country, FY46-91, annual rpt, 9914–5
UN participation of US, and member and nonmember shares of UN budget by country, FY89-91, annual rpt, 7004–5
see also International Development Association
see also International Finance Corp.

International Boundary and Water Commission, U.S. and Mexico
Budget of US, obligations and authority by function, agency, and program, with summaries and analyses, FY93, annual rpt, 104–2
Hydroelectric power plants capacity and other characteristics, for western US, FY91, annual rpt, 3254–1
Labor unions recognized in Fed Govt, agreements and membership by agency and facility, as of Jan 1991, biennial listing, 9844–14

International cooperation in conservation
Debt burden indicators, conversion agreement terms, and swaps for conservation funds, by selected developing country, 1987-90, hearing, 25368–181
Developing countries economic and social conditions from 1960s, and Intl Dev Cooperation Agency and AID activities and funding, FY91-93, annual rpt, 9904–4
Eastern Europe environmental remediation costs, and aid by donor, by country, 1991 hearing, 25368–181
EPA pollution control grant program activities, monthly rpt, 9182–8
Forests (tropical) condition, conservation methods, and biological diversity issues, 1992 rpt, 26358–262
Kuwait oil fires set by Iraq, pollution levels, disease cases, and US remediation and monitoring spending, 1991 rpt, 9188–117
Marine Mammal Protection Act admin, and populations, strandings, and catch permits by species and location, 1988-89, annual rpt, 2164–11
Marine mammals protection, Federal and intl regulatory and research activities, 1991, annual rpt, 14734–1
Treaties and other bilateral and multilateral agreements of US in force, by country, as of Jan 1992, annual listing, 7004–1

see also International cooperation in environmental sciences

International cooperation in cultural activities
Arts Natl Endowment activities and grants, FY91, annual rpt, 9564–3
Smithsonian Instn activities and finances, FY91, annual rpt, 29574–1
Treaties and other bilateral and multilateral agreements of US in force, by country, as of Jan 1992, annual listing, 7004–1
see also Educational exchanges
see also Exchange of persons programs

International cooperation in environmental sciences
Developing countries economic and social conditions from 1960s, and Intl Dev Cooperation Agency and AID activities and funding, FY91-93, annual rpt, 9904–4
Geological Survey activities and funding, FY91, annual rpt, 5664–8
Glaciology intl research summaries, methodology, and bibls, series, 2156–18
Global climate change contributing pollutants, atmospheric concentrations by location, and monitoring activities, 1990, annual rpt, 2144–28
Global climate change contributing pollutants, emissions by monitoring site and country, and temperature change by world area and US region, 1860s-1990, annual rpt, 3004–33
Industrial pollutant concentrations and costs by process and waste prevention or treatment method, biennial conf, suspended, 9184–22
Kuwait oil fires set by Iraq, pollution levels, disease cases, and US remediation and monitoring spending, 1991 rpt, 9188–117
Kuwait oil fires set by Iraqi forces, air pollution levels by substance and site, as of Mar 1991, 9188–116
Kuwait oil fires set by Iraqi forces, air pollution levels, health effects, intl monitoring activities, and wells affected, 1991, GAO rpt, 26113–566
Oceanographic research and distribution activities of World Data Center A by country, and cruises by ship, 1990, annual rpt, 2144–15
Treaties and other bilateral and multilateral agreements of US in force, by country, as of Jan 1992, annual listing, 7004–1
Weather services activities and funding, by Federal agency, planned FY92-93, annual rpt, 2144–2
see also International cooperation in conservation

International cooperation in law enforcement
Developing countries economic and social conditions from 1960s, and Intl Dev Cooperation Agency and AID activities and funding, FY91-93, annual rpt, 9904–4
Drug (illegal) production, eradication, and seizures, by substance, with US aid, by country, 1988-92, annual rpt, 7004–17
Drug abuse indicators for selected metro areas, research results, data collection, and policy issues, 1992 semiannual conf, 4492–5
Drug enforcement aid of US, by country, FY90, annual rpt, 21384–3
Marshals Service activities, FY91, annual rpt, 6294–1
Terrorism incidents in US, related activity, and casualties, by attack type, target, group, and location, 1991, annual rpt, 6224–6
Treaties and other bilateral and multilateral agreements of US in force, by country, as of Jan 1992, annual listing, 7004–1

International cooperation in science and technology
Agricultural research grants of USDA, by program, subagency, and country, FY92, annual listing, 1954–3
Allergy and Infectious Diseases Natl Inst activities, grants by recipient and location, and disease cases, FY84-91, annual rpt, 4474–30
Assistance (financial and nonfinancial) of Fed Govt, 1992 base edition, annual listing, 104–5
Cancer Natl Inst activities, grants by recipient, and cancer deaths and cases, FY91 and trends, annual rpt, 4474–13
Dental Research Natl Inst research and training grants, by recipient, FY90, annual listing, 4474–19
Hazardous material transport accidents, casualties, and damage, by mode of transport, with DOT control activities, 1990, annual rpt, 7304–4
Heart, Lung, and Blood Natl Inst activities, and grants by recipient and location, FY91 and disease trends from 1940, annual rpt, 4474–15
Industry (US) intl competitiveness, with selected foreign and US operating data by major firm and product, series, 2046–12
NASA R&D funding to higher education instns, by field, instn, and State, FY91, annual listing, 9504–7
NSF grants and contracts, by field, recipient, and State, FY90, annual rpt, 9624–26
NSF R&D grant awards, by div and program, periodic rpt series, 9626–7
Nuclear power plant safety inspection activities and emergency response procedures of Intl Atomic Energy Agency since 1986 Chernobyl accident, 1991, GAO rpt, 26123–367
Spacecraft launches and other activities of NASA and USSR, with flight data, 1957-91, annual rpt, 9504–6.1
Standards for production, controls, and processes, domestic and intl dev in US and EC, 1980s-91, 26358–257
Treaties and other bilateral and multilateral agreements of US in force, by country, as of Jan 1992, annual listing, 7004–1
see also European Space Agency
see also International cooperation in environmental sciences
see also Technology transfer

International corporations
see Foreign corporations
see Multinational corporations

International crime
Bank of Credit and Commerce Intl financial statements, audits, and selected loan data, 1984-90, hearing, 25388–60
see also Air piracy
see also International cooperation in law enforcement
see also Smuggling
see also Terrorism

International debts
see Foreign debts

International Development Association
Loan activity by purpose and country, and funds by source, FY90, annual rpt, 15344–1.5
Loans and grants for economic and military aid from US and intl agencies, by program and country, FY46-91, annual rpt, 9914–5
UN participation of US, and member and nonmember shares of UN budget by country, FY89-91, annual rpt, 7004–5

International Development Cooperation Agency
see U.S. International Development Cooperation Agency

International economic relations
see Balance of payments
see Foreign competition
see Foreign debts
see Foreign economic relations
see Foreign investments
see Foreign trade
see International finance
see Multinational corporations

International employees
Admissions to US of aliens, by country, FY81-91, annual rpt, 6264–2.3
Immigrants and nonimmigrants admitted to US, alien workers, visitors, deportations, and naturalizations, FY91, annual summary rpt, 6264–7
UN employment, and US natls share of staff, by agency, as of Dec 1991, annual rpt, 7004–5
UNESCO fiscal mgmt, spending, staff, and funding sources, mid 1970s-92, GAO rpt, 26123–84

International finance
Banks (foreign) loans to US business by location of issuer, with impact of change in Fed Reserve Bd reserve requirements, 1980s-91, article, 9385–1.307
Banks (US) foreign lending at all US and foreign offices, by country group and country, quarterly rpt, 13002–1
Banks balance sheets, by Fed Reserve District, for major banks in NYC, and for US branches and agencies of foreign banks, weekly rpt, 9365–1.3
Capital movements between US and foreign countries, *Treasury Bulletin*, quarterly rpt, 8002–4.13
Finance (intl) and financial policy, and external factors affecting US economy, technical paper series, 9366–7
Financial and economic analysis, technical paper series, 9385–8
Financial instns (intl) funds by source and disbursements by purpose, by country, with US policy review, FY90, annual rpt, 15344–1
Financial markets (intl) performance of foreign and US bank and securities firms, finances and competitiveness issues, 1980s, compilation of papers, 9385–10
Foreign and US intl transactions, debt, security holdings, interest and exchange rates, and US reserve assets, monthly rpt, 9362–1.3
see also African Development Bank
see also African Development Fund
see also Asian Development Bank

see also Balance of payments
see also Eurocurrency
see also Export-Import Bank
see also Foreign debts
see also Foreign economic relations
see also Foreign exchange
see also Foreign investments
see also Inter-American Development Bank
see also International Bank for Reconstruction and Development
see also International Development Association
see also International Monetary Fund
see also International reserves
see also Multinational corporations
see also Organization for Economic Cooperation and Development
see also Overseas Private Investment Corp.
see also Special Drawing Rights

International Finance Corp.
Financial statements of IFC, 1991 hearing, 21248–169
Loan activity by purpose and country, FY90, annual rpt, 15344–1.6
Loans and grants for economic and military aid from US and intl agencies, by program and country, FY46-91, annual rpt, 9914–5

International Joint Commission, U.S. and Canada
Activities of Commission, biennial rpt, discontinued, 14644–3
Great Lakes flood prevention activities of Army Corps of Engineers and Intl Joint Commission, monthly rpt and supplements, 3752–1
Great Lakes industrial water pollution emissions, comparison of State, EPA, Intl Joint Commission, and Ontario standards, 1991 rpt, 14648–29
Great Lakes Science Advisory Board research activities and water quality goals, FY91, biennial rpt, 14644–6
Great Lakes water quality, and pollution control policy and activities, 1991 biennial rpt, 14644–1
Mink and otter population, breeding, trapping, pollutant levels, and research status, for Great Lakes area, 1991 conf, 14648–27
Pollution (air) levels in Detroit area, by pollutant and site, 1970s-90, 14648–28

International labor
see Alien workers
see Foreign labor conditions
see International employees

International law
see also Citizenship
see also Diplomatic and consular service
see also Executive agreements
see also International cooperation in law enforcement
see also International military forces
see also International sanctions
see also Maritime law
see also Passports and visas
see also Territorial waters
see also Treaties and conventions

International military forces
UN peacekeeping operations costs by mission, and assessment rates by country, 1948-92, GAO rpt, 26123–404
US military aid, arms sales, and training programs costs and budget requests, by program, world region, and country, FY91-93, annual rpt, 7144–13

International Monetary Fund
Budget of US, authoritative financial statements with appropriations, outlays, and receipts, by category and agency, FY91, annual rpt, 8104–2.2
Developing countries debt to foreign lenders, and IMF credit outstanding, by country, 1985-91, annual rpt, 9114–7
Fed Govt receipts by source and outlays by agency, *Treasury Bulletin*, quarterly rpt, 8002–4.1
Financial statements of IMF, and proposed funding quotas by member country, 1991 hearing, 21248–169
Investment (intl) position of US, by component, industry, world region, and country, 1990-91, annual article, 2702–1.323
Loan activity and voting power, by member country, FY90, annual rpt, 15344–1.3
Reserve assets of US by type, *Treasury Bulletin*, quarterly rpt, 8002–4.12

International organizations
AID economic aid to developing countries, obligations and disbursements by country, quarterly rpt, 9912–4
AID loans repayment status and terms by program and country, and status of predecessor agency loans, quarterly rpt, 9912–3
Budget of US, obligations and authority by function, agency, and program, with summaries and analyses, FY93, annual rpt, 104–2
Financial instns (intl) funds by source and disbursements by purpose, by country, with US policy review, FY90, annual rpt, 15344–1
Loans and grants for economic and military aid from US and intl agencies, by program and country, FY46-91, annual rpt, 9914–5
Loans of US banks to foreigners at all US and foreign offices, by country group and country, quarterly rpt, 13002–1
Membership, date established, and purpose of intl organizations, 1992 listing, annual rpt, 9114–2
Military aid of US, arms sales, and training, by country, FY50-91, annual rpt, 3904–3
Refugee migration, and intl aid programs, by world area and country of origin and asylum, 1991, annual rpt, 7004–15
Standards for production, controls, and processes, domestic and intl dev in US and EC, 1980s-91, 26358–257
Treaties and other bilateral and multilateral agreements of US in force, by country, as of Jan 1992, annual listing, 7004–1
Voluntary agencies foreign aid programs, funding, and outlays, by agency, 1990, annual rpt, 9914–9
see also African Development Bank
see also African Development Fund
see also Asian Development Bank
see also Association of Southeast Asian Nations
see also Central Treaty Organization
see also Common markets and free trade areas
see also European Space Agency
see also Inter-American Development Bank
see also International Atomic Energy Agency
see also International Bank for Reconstruction and Development
see also International Development Association
see also International employees
see also International Finance Corp.
see also International military forces
see also International Monetary Fund
see also International Telecommunications Satellite Organization
see also North Atlantic Treaty Organization
see also Organization for Economic Cooperation and Development
see also Red Cross
see also United Nations
see also Warsaw Pact

International relations
see Diplomatic and consular service
see Foreign economic relations
see Foreign relations
see International military forces
see International sanctions
see Military intervention
see Military invasion and occupation
see Treaties and conventions
see United Nations

International reserves
Currency (foreign) holdings of US, transactions and balances by program and country, 1st half FY92, semiannual rpt, 8102–7
Eastern Europe transition to market economies, economic conditions, trade, and foreign investment, by country, 1990-91, 9118–13
Economic conditions in foreign countries and implications for US, periodic country rpt series, 2046–4
Economic indicators and components, current data and annual trends, monthly rpt, 23842–1.7
Flow-of-funds accounts, savings, investments, and credit statements, quarterly rpt, 9365–3.3
Foreign and US intl transactions, debt, security holdings, interest and exchange rates, and US reserve assets, monthly rpt, 9362–1.3
Reserve assets of US by type, *Treasury Bulletin*, quarterly rpt, 8002–4.12
Statistical Abstract of US, 1992 annual data compilation, 2324–1.29; 2324–1.31
see also Special Drawing Rights

International sanctions
Tuna production, consumption, trade, and impacts of US dolphin protection embargo, 1989-92, article, 9882–16.303
see also Boycotts

International Telecommunications Satellite Organization
Launchings of satellites and other space objects since 1957, quarterly listing, 9502–2

International trade
see Balance of payments
see Foreign competition
see Foreign exchange
see Foreign investments
see Foreign trade
see Foreign trade promotion
see Maritime law
see Multinational corporations
see Ships and shipping
see Tariffs and foreign trade controls

see Trade agreements
International Trade Administration
Andean Trade Preference Act duty-free exports from 4 countries to US, and business opportunities, 1989-91, 2048–161
Budget of US, obligations and authority by function, agency, and program, with summaries and analyses, FY93, annual rpt, 104–2
Business America, foreign and domestic commerce, and US investment and trade opportunities, biweekly journal, 2042–24
Caribbean Basin Initiative export and investment incentives, contact listing, bibl, and US imports country, 1983-91, annual rpt, 2044–36
Competitiveness (intl) of US industries, with selected foreign and US operating data by major firm and product, series, 2046–12
Construction put in place, permits, housing sales, costs, material prices, and employment, quarterly rpt with articles, 2042–1
Eastern Europe imports from US, and trade and dev opportunities, monthly rpt, 2042–33
Eastern Europe trade with US, by commodity and country, 1987-91 and outlook for 1992, 2048–158
Exports and imports of US, by selected country, country group, and commodity group, 1991, annual rpt, 2044–37
Exports, imports, and balances of US, by selected country, country group, and commodity group, preliminary data, monthly rpt, 2042–34
Exports, imports, and balances of US for manufactured goods, by SITC 2-digit commodity and country, quarterly rpt, 2042–35
Exports of manufactured goods for US and major competitors, market share rpts, annual listing, discontinued, 2044–6
Exports of manufactured goods, total and for US and major competitors, by country of destination, annual commodity market share rpt series, discontinued, 2046–13
Exports of manufactured goods, total and for US and major competitors, by SITC 1- to 5-digit commodity, annual country market share rpt series, discontinued, 2046–2
Foreign countries economic conditions and implications for US, periodic country rpt series, 2046–4
Foreign countries economic indicators, and trade and trade flows by commodity, by country, data compilation, monthly CD-ROM, 2002–6
Industry finances and operations, by SIC 2- to 4-digit industry, forecast 1992, annual rpt, 2044–28
Investment (foreign direct) in US, major transactions by type, industry, country, and US location, 1990, annual rpt, 2044–20
Japan economic conditions, US investment and export opportunities, and trade practices, forecast 1991-93 and trends from 1988, 2048–159
Latin America and Caribbean country imports from US, by State of origin and country, 1987 and 1990, 2048–160
Latin America trade, and balance of trade with US, by country, annual rpt, suspended, 2044–34
Mexico imports from US, by industry and State, 1987-91, 2048–154
OECD intl trade position for US and 4 countries, and factors affecting US competition, quarterly pamphlet, 2042–25
Overseas Business Reports: economic conditions, investment and export opportunities, and trade practices, country market research rpt series, 2046–6
Plumbing fixtures production, and imports from US and other sources, for 15 countries, 1991 rpt, 2048–156
Soviet Union trade and investment opportunities for US firms, contact listing, bibl, and background economic data, 1991 rpt, 2048–157
Textile Agreement Category System import classification codes, correlation with TSUSA, 1993 annual rpt, 2044–31
Textile and apparel exports of US, by product group and country, quarterly rpt, 2042–36
Textile and apparel foreign market conditions for US exports, with domestic industry operations, country rpt series, 2046–15
Textile imports, by country of origin, monthly rpt, 2042–27
Textile imports, by product and country of origin, monthly rpt series, 2046–8; 2046–9
Textile products trade regulations of foreign countries, and US exports, by commodity and country, 1989-91, biennial rpt, 2044–18
see also Foreign Trade Zones Board
International Trade Commission
see U.S. International Trade Commission
International transactions
see Balance of payments
Interstate agreements
see Interstate compacts
Interstate commerce
Communications services revenue and expenses, itemized by SIC 2- to 4-digit kind of business, 1990, annual rpt, 2413–15
Criminal case processing in Federal district courts, and dispositions, by offense, district, and offender characteristics, 1989, annual data compilation, 6064–29
Criminal cases by type and disposition, and collections, for US attorneys, by Federal district, FY91, annual rpt, 6004–2.1
Criminal sentences for Federal offenses, guidelines by offense and circumstances, series, 17668–1
Mail order sales from out of State, tax revenue losses by State, 1990-92, 10048–84
Telecommunications domestic and intl rates, by type of service and area served, 1990, annual rpt, 9284–6.6
Telephone service subscribership, charges, and local and long distance firm finances and operations, late 1970s-92, semiannual rpt, 9282–7
see also Antitrust law
see also Buses
see also Freight
see also Inland water transportation
see also Pipelines
see also Railroads
see also Ships and shipping
see also Transportation and transportation equipment
see also Trucks and trucking industry
Interstate Commerce Commission
Activities of ICC, and employment and finances of regulated carriers, as of FY91, annual rpt, 9484–1
Budget of US, authoritative financial statements with appropriations, outlays, and receipts, by category and agency, FY91, annual rpt, 8104–2.2
Budget of US, obligations and authority by function, agency, and program, with summaries and analyses, FY93, annual rpt, 104–2
Bus (Class I) passengers and selected revenue data, for individual large carriers, quarterly rpt, 9482–13
Labor unions recognized in Fed Govt, agreements and membership by agency and facility, as of Jan 1991, biennial listing, 9844–14
Railroad employment by occupational group, for Class I line-haul railroads, monthly rpt, 9482–3
Railroad employment, earnings, and hours, by occupation for Class I railroads, 1991, annual table, 9484–5
Railroad revenue, income, freight, and rate of return, by Class I freight railroad and district, quarterly rpt, 9482–2
Truck, bus, and rail carriers finances and operations, detailed data, 1990, annual rpt series, 9486–5
Truck, bus, and rail carriers finances and operations, detailed data, 1991, annual rpt series, 9486–6
Truck transport of household goods, financial and operating data by firm, quarterly rpt, 9482–14
Truck transport of household goods, performance and disposition of damage claims, for selected carriers, 1991, annual rpt, 9484–11
Truck transport of property, financial and operating data by region and firm, quarterly rpt, 9482–5
Interstate Commission on the Potomac River Basin
Budget of US, authoritative financial statements with appropriations, outlays, and receipts, by category and agency, FY91, annual rpt, 8104–2.2
Interstate compacts
Radioactive low-level waste disposal activities of States and interstate compacts, with data by disposal facility and reactor, 1990, annual rpt, 3004–36
Interstate relations
Child support overdue payments deducted from wages, interstate enforcement effectiveness, 1991, GAO rpt, 26121–445
see also Interstate compacts
see also Regional planning
Inventions
Energy-related inventions recommended by Natl Inst of Standards and Technology for DOE support, awards, and evaluation status, 1991, annual listing, 2214–5
Fed Govt employee incentive awards, costs, and benefits, by award type and agency, FY90, annual rpt, 9844–20

see also Patents
see also Technological innovations
see also Technology transfer
Inventories
see Agricultural stocks
see Agricultural surpluses
see Business inventories
see Energy stocks and inventories
see Stockpiling
Inventory of Mental Health Organizations and General Hospital Mental Health Services
Facilities, patients, services, and staff characteristics, *Statistical Notes* series, 4506–3
Investigations
see Congressional investigations
see Criminal investigations
see Government investigations
Investment Advisory Council
Small Business Investment Company program financial performance, findings and recommendations, 1992 rpt, 9768–24
Investments
Airline finances, by carrier, carrier group, and for total certificated system, quarterly rpt, 7302–7
Assets and debts of private sector, balance sheets by segment, 1960-91, semiannual rpt, 9365–4.1
Banking and financial conditions, 1990, annual rpt, 9364–5
Banks (commercial) loans and investments, 1972-91, annual rpt, 204–1.5
Banks (natl) charters, mergers, liquidations, enforcement cases, and financial performance, with data by instn and State, quarterly rpt, 8402–3
Banks reserve requirements of Fed Reserve Bd relation to GNP and investment, 1991 working paper, 9375–13.72
Business statistics, detailed data for major industries and economic indicators, 1960-91, *Survey of Current Business* biennial supplement, 2704–1
Capital gains and other tax changes, impacts on stock prices and returns, model description and results, 1992 technical paper, 9379–12.97
Capital gains counted as income, and other income definitions effects on household income and poverty status, by recipient characteristics, 1991, annual Current Population Rpt, 2546–6.78
Capital gains tax rates impacts on taxpayer gains and long-term revenues, 1990 technical paper, 8006–6.4
Capital gains tax rates relation to tax revenues, mid 1950s-80s, technical paper, 8006–6.3
County Business Patterns, 1989: employment, establishments, and payroll, by SIC 2- to 4-digit industry and county, annual State rpt series, 2326–8
County Business Patterns, 1990: employment, establishments, and payroll, by SIC 2- to 4-digit industry and county, annual State rpt series, 2326–6
Credit Union Natl Admin Central Liquidity Facility financial statements, FY91, annual rpt, 9534–5
Credit unions federally insured, finances by instn characteristics and State, as of June 1992, semiannual rpt, 9532–6
Credit unions federally insured, finances, 1990-91, annual rpt, 9534–1
Credit unions financial performance and regulation, with background data, 1960s-90, GAO rpt, 26119–364
Economic indicators and components, and Fed Reserve 4th District business and financial conditions, monthly chartbook, 9377–10
Economic indicators and components, current data and annual trends, monthly rpt, 23842–1.5
Economic Report of the President for 1992, with economic trends from 1959, annual rpt, 204–1.1
Electric power distribution loans from REA, and borrower operating and financial data, by firm and State, 1991, annual rpt, 1244–1
Electric utilities finances and operations, detailed data for publicly and privately owned firms, 1990, annual rpt, 3164–11.4
Electric utilities finances and operations, detailed data for publicly owned firms, 1990, annual rpt, 3164–24
Electric utilities privately owned, finances and operations, detailed data, 1990, annual rpt, 3164–23
Energy producers finances and operations, by energy type for US firms domestic and foreign operations, 1990, annual rpt, 3164–44
Flow-of-funds accounts, savings, investments, and credit statements, quarterly rpt, 9365–3.3
Forecasts of economic conditions and employment, alternative BLS projections to 2005 and trends 1975-90, biennial rpt, 6744–19
Households financial services use, by account type and instn type and location, 1989 survey, article, 9362–1.303
Housing (rental) units, total, with HUD assistance by program, and eligible for aid, by unit, household, and neighborhood characteristics, and location, 1989, biennial rpt, 5184–11
Housing units owned for recreation and investment, by selected unit characteristics, 1989, biennial rpt supplement, 2485–13
Income (household, family, and personal), by source, detailed characteristics, and region, 1991, annual Current Population Rpt, 2546–6.76
Income (personal) per capita and by source, and employment, by industry div, State, MSA, and county, 1969-90, annual CD-ROM, 2704–7
Income tax returns of foreign corporations and individuals, and US entities abroad, detailed data compilation, 1970s-89, quinquennial rpt, 8308–31
Input-output structure of US economy, detailed interindustry transactions for 84 industries, and components of final demand, 1987, annual article, 2702–1.316
Insurance company asset risk assessment, with financial ratios by firm type and financial status, 1990 and trends from 1900s, article, 9373–1.314; 9373–27.3
Insurance company finances, by insurance type and firm, with some intl comparisons, 1991 conf, 9373–3.35
Loan commitments impact on business investment, 1980-84, working paper, 9381–10.128
Monetary trends, Fed Reserve Bank of St Louis monthly rpt, 9391–2
Multinatl firms US affiliates, finances, and operations, by industry, world area of parent firm, and State, 1989-90, annual rpt, 2704–4
Multinatl US firms and foreign affiliates finances and operations, by industry and country, 1989 benchmark survey, annual rpt, 2704–5
Natl income and product accounts and components, *Survey of Current Business*, monthly rpt, 2702–1.23
Natl income and product accounts benchmark revisions, methodological changes and revised summary tables, 1959-91, article, 2702–1.302
Natl income and product accounts benchmark revisions of GDP and natl income, various periods 1959-80, tables, 2702–1.307
Natl income and product accounts, comprehensive accounts and components, benchmark revisions, 1929-88, 2708–5
Natl income and product accounts, comprehensive accounts and components, *Survey of Current Business*, monthly rpt, 2702–1.28
Natural gas interstate pipeline company detailed financial and operating data, by firm, 1990, annual rpt, 3164–38
Nonprofit charitable and other tax exempt organizations finances, by category and size of assets and contributions, 1988, annual article, 8302–2.315
Nonprofit charitable organizations finances, with data by State and for top 10 instns, 1988, article, 8302–2.302
North Central States business and economic conditions, Fed Reserve 9th District, quarterly journal, 9383–19
North Central States, FHLB 6th District insured S&Ls financial condition and operations by State, quarterly rpt, 9302–23
Older persons and younger adults household income, by source, household composition, and age group, 1984 and 1989, article, 4742–1.304
Older persons and younger adults household income, by source, household composition, race, and age group, 1984-89, 4746–26.20
Older persons income and sources, by OASDI beneficiary and poverty status, and other characteristics, 1990, biennial chartbook, 4744–25
Older persons income and sources, by whether OASDI beneficiary, poverty status, and other characteristics, 1990, biennial rpt, 4744–26
Older persons socioeconomic characteristics, 1900s-90 and projected to 2050, biennial chartbook, 12904–1
Pacific territories population and housing detailed characteristics, by location, 1990 Census of Population and Housing, series, 2551–8
Pension systems of State and local govts, finances, coverage, and benefits, by system, FY90, annual rpt, 2466–2.4

Poverty status of population and families, by detailed characteristics, 1991, annual Current Population Rpt, 2546–6.77
Railroad (Class I) finances and operations, detailed data by firm, class of service, and district, 1990, annual rpt, 9486–5.1
Railroad (Class I) finances and operations, detailed data by firm, class of service, and district, 1991, annual rpt, 9486–6.1
Savings instns financial statements, for instns insured by Savings Assn Insurance Fund by FHLB district and State, and for FDIC-insured savings banks, 1989, annual rpt, 8434–1
Small business R&D grants of Fed Govt, project sales by type and dev funding by source, by agency and selected firm, 1984-91, GAO rpt, 26113–393
Southeastern States, Fed Reserve 5th District insured commercial banks financial statements, by State, quarterly rpt, 9389–18
Statistical Abstract of US, 1992 annual data compilation, 2324–1.14
Survey of Current Business, detailed financial and business data, and economic indicators, monthly rpt, 2702–1.3
Tax (estate) returns property and tax data, by size of gross estate and State, 1989-90, article, 8302–2.305
Tax (income) returns filed, by type of filer, selected income items, quarterly rpt, 8302–2.1
Tax (income) returns for foreign corporate activity in US, selected income and tax items, by industry div and selected country, 1988, article, 8302–2.309
Tax (income) returns of corporations, income and tax items by asset size and detailed industry, 1989, annual rpt, 8304–4; 8304–21
Tax (income) returns of individuals, by filing status, tax item, and income level, 1991, annual article, 8302–2.319
Tax (income) returns of individuals, detailed data, 1988, annual rpt, 8304–2
Tax (income) returns of individuals, selected income and tax items by income level, preliminary 1990, annual article, 8302–2.307
Tax (income) returns of partnerships, income statement and balance sheet items, by industry group, 1990, annual article, 8302–2.314
Tax (income) withholding and related documents filed, by type and IRS service center, 1991 and projected 1992-99, annual rpt, 8304–22
Tax exempt organizations finances, with data by type, size, State, and for largest organizations, late 1940s-80s, compilation of papers, 8308–35
Tax exempt organizations with unrelated business income, finances by organization type, 1987, article, 8302–2.306
Telephone and telegraph firms detailed finances and operations, 1990, annual rpt, 9284–6
Telephone firms borrowing under Rural Telephone Program, and financial and operating data, by State, 1991, annual rpt, 1244–2
Trust assets of banks, trust companies, and S&Ls, by type of asset and fund, selected firm, and State, 1991, annual rpt, 13004–1
West Central States economic indicators, Fed Reserve 10th District, quarterly rpt, 9381–16.2
Western States, FHLB 11th District shareholder instns, offices, and financial condition, 1992 annual listing, 9304–23
see also Capital investments, general
see also Capital investments, specific industry
see also Divestiture
see also Foreign investments
see also Futures trading
see also Government securities
see also Individual retirement arrangements
see also Joint ventures
see also Loans
see also Mortgages
see also Mutual funds
see also New York Stock Exchange
see also Options trading
see also Securities
see also Stock exchanges
see also Venture capital

Inyo County, Calif.
Water (groundwater) supply, quality, chemistry, and use, 1920s-89 and projected to 2015, local area rpt, 5666–28.15

Iohp, Kidsen
"Hepatitis B Immunization Campaign for Children in the Federated States of Micronesia", 4042–3.357

Iowa
Banks (insured commercial and savings) deposits by instn, State, MSA, and county, as of June 1991, annual regional rpt, 9295–3.5
Birds (dabbling duck) nesting activity in north-central Iowa, by habitat characteristics and species, 1984-85, technical rpt, 5506–12.5
Coal production and mines by county, prices, productivity, miners, and reserves, by mining method and State, 1990-91, annual rpt, 3164–25
County Business Patterns, 1990: employment, establishments, and payroll, by SIC 2- to 4-digit industry and county, annual State rpt, 2326–6.17
Deaths and rates, by detailed location, cause, and demographic characteristics, 1989, US Vital Statistics annual rpt, 4144–3.1
Employment, earnings, and hours, by selected SIC 1- to 4-digit industry, State, and for 275 MSAs, 1987-92, 6748–81
Fed Govt spending in States and local areas, by type, State, county, and city, FY91, annual rpt, 2464–3
Fed Govt spending in States, by type, program, agency, and State, FY91, annual rpt, 2464–2
HHS financial aid, by program, recipient, State, and city, FY91, annual regional listing, 4004–3.7
Hospital deaths of Medicare patients, actual and expected rates by diagnosis, and hospital characteristics, by instn, FY90 annual State rpt, 4654–14.16
Housing census, 1990: inventory, occupancy, and costs, State fact sheet, 2326–21.17
Housing census, 1990: summary unit characteristics, by householder race and age, county, place, and urban-rural location, State rpt, 2471–1.17
Military prime contract awards, by contractor, service branch, State, and city, FY91, annual rpt, 3544–22
Mineral Industry Surveys, State reviews of production, 1991, preliminary annual rpt, 5614–6
Minerals (strategic) deposits in North Central States, characteristics, 1992 compilation of papers, 5668–127
Multinatl firms US affiliates finances and operations, by industry, country of parent firm, and State, 1987, 2708–48
Physicians, by specialty, age, sex, and location of training and practice, 1990, State rpt, 4116–6.16
Population and housing census, 1990: detailed geographic coverage, State CD-ROM, 2551–9.4
Population and housing census, 1990: summary characteristics, by county, subdiv, and place, State rpt, 2551–7.17
Population census, 1990: population characteristics and living arrangements, by county, place, and urban-rural location, State rpt, 2531–1.17
Statistical Abstract of US, 1992 annual data compilation, 2324–1
Timber harvest and industrial roundwood production, by species and product, 1988 State rpt, 1206–10.13
Timber in Iowa, resources and removals by species, forest and tree characteristics, ownership, and county, 1988-90 and trends from 1973-74, 1208–75
Water quality, chemistry, hydrology, and other characteristics, 1991 local area study, 5666–27.34
Water resources data collection and analysis activities of USGS Water Resources Div District, with project descriptions, 1990 rpt, 5666–26.17
see also Davenport, Iowa
see also under By State in the "Index by Categories"

Iran
Agricultural trade of US, by detailed commodity and country, 1991, annual rpt, 1524–8
Agricultural trade of US, by detailed commodity and country, 1991, semiannual rpt, 1522–4
AID loans repayment status and terms by program and country, and status of predecessor agency loans, quarterly rpt, 9912–3
Boycotts (intl) by OPEC and other countries, US firms and individuals cooperation and tax benefits denied, 1990, article, 8302–2.323
Economic and military aid and loans from US and intl agencies, by program and country, FY46-91, annual rpt, 9914–5
Economic and social conditions of developing countries from 1960s, and Intl Dev Cooperation Agency and AID activities and funding, FY91-93, annual rpt, 9904–4
Economic conditions, policy, and trade practices, by country, 1989-91, annual rpt, 21384–5
Economic, social, political, and geographic summary data, by country, 1992, annual factbook, 9114–2
Exports and imports of US, by commodity and country, 1980-90, world area rpt, 9116–1.6

Exports and imports of US, by transport mode, country, and SITC 1- to 3-digit commodity, 1991, annual rpt, 2424–12
Exports of US, detailed Schedule B commodities with countries of destination, 1991, annual rpt, 2424–10
Human rights conditions in 170 countries, and US economic and military aid, 1991, annual rpt, 21384–3
Military spending, arms trade, and force strengths, with govt spending and population, by country, 1979-89, annual rpt, 9824–1
Minerals Yearbook, Vol 3, 1989: foreign country review of production, trade, and policy, by commodity, annual rpt, 5604–35.3
Oil production, and exports and prices for US, by major exporting country, detailed data, monthly rpt with articles, 3162–24
Oil production, and exports and prices for US, by major exporting country, detailed data, monthly 1973-88, 3168–123
Oil production, stocks, use, and trade, by selected country and country group, monthly rpt, 3162–42
Population size, growth rates, and components of change, by country, projected 1990-2020 and trends from 1950, biennial rpt, 2324–9
Refugee migration, and intl aid programs, by world area and country of origin and asylum, 1991, annual rpt, 7004–15
UN voting record and share of votes in agreement with US, by issue, country, and world area, 1991, annual rpt, 7004–18

Iraq
Agricultural trade of US, by detailed commodity and country, 1991, annual rpt, 1524–8
Agricultural trade of US, by detailed commodity and country, 1991, semiannual rpt, 1522–4
Banca Nazionale del Lavoro Atlanta office loans to Iraq, with purpose and exporting country and company involved, 1991 hearing, 21248–165
Boycotts (intl) by OPEC and other countries, US firms and individuals cooperation and tax benefits denied, 1990, article, 8302–2.323
Economic and military aid and loans from US and intl agencies, by program and country, FY46-91, annual rpt, 9914–5
Economic and social conditions of developing countries from 1960s, and Intl Dev Cooperation Agency and AID activities and funding, FY91-93, annual rpt, 9904–4
Economic conditions, policy, and trade practices, by country, 1989-91, annual rpt, 21384–5
Economic, social, political, and geographic summary data, by country, 1992, annual factbook, 9114–2
Exports and imports of US, by commodity and country, 1980-90, world area rpt, 9116–1.6
Exports and imports of US, by transport mode, country, and SITC 1- to 3-digit commodity, 1991, annual rpt, 2424–12
Exports, imports, and balances of US for manufactured goods, by SITC 2-digit commodity and country, quarterly rpt, 2042–35
Human rights conditions in 170 countries, and US economic and military aid, 1991, annual rpt, 21384–3
Military spending, arms trade, and force strengths, with govt spending and population, by country, 1979-89, annual rpt, 9824–1
Minerals Yearbook, Vol 3, 1989: foreign country review of production, trade, and policy, by commodity, annual rpt, 5604–35.3
Oil production and exports to US, by major exporting country, detailed data, monthly rpt with articles, 3162–24
Oil production and exports to US, by major exporting country, detailed data, monthly 1973-88, 3168–123
Oil production, stocks, use, and trade, by selected country and country group, monthly rpt, 3162–42
Population size, growth rates, and components of change, by country, projected 1990-2020 and trends from 1950, biennial rpt, 2324–9
Refugee migration, and intl aid programs, by world area and country of origin and asylum, 1991, annual rpt, 7004–15
UN voting record and share of votes in agreement with US, by issue, country, and world area, 1991, annual rpt, 7004–18

Ireland
Agricultural trade of US, by detailed commodity and country, 1991, annual rpt, 1524–8
Agricultural trade of US, by detailed commodity and country, 1991, semiannual rpt, 1522–4
AID loans repayment status and terms by program and country, and status of predecessor agency loans, quarterly rpt, 9912–3
Background Notes, summary social, political, and economic data, 1991 rpt, 7006–2.3
Cuba trade, by commodity and country, mid 1980s-91, 9118–8
Economic and military aid and loans from US and intl agencies, by program and country, FY46-91, annual rpt, 9914–5
Economic and social conditions of developing countries from 1960s, and Intl Dev Cooperation Agency and AID activities and funding, FY91-93, annual rpt, 9904–4
Economic conditions, income, production, prices, employment, and trade, 1992 periodic country rpt, 2046–4.21
Economic conditions, policy, and trade practices, by country, 1989-91, annual rpt, 21384–5
Economic, social, political, and geographic summary data, by country, 1992, annual factbook, 9114–2
Exports and imports of US, by Harmonized System 6-digit commodity and country, 1991, annual rpt, 2424–13
Exports and imports of US, by selected country, country group, and commodity group, 1991, annual rpt, 2044–37
Exports and imports of US, by transport mode, country, and SITC 1- to 3-digit commodity, 1991, annual rpt, 2424–12
Exports, imports, and balances of US for manufactured goods, by SITC 2-digit commodity and country, quarterly rpt, 2042–35
Exports of US, detailed Schedule B commodities with countries of destination, 1991, annual rpt, 2424–10
Health care costs and components, services use, resources, and economic indicators, by OECD country, 1960s-90, article, 4652–1.322
Human rights conditions in 170 countries, and US economic and military aid, 1991, annual rpt, 21384–3
Labor conditions, union coverage, and work accidents, 1992 annual country rpt, 6366–4.31
Military spending, arms trade, and force strengths, with govt spending and population, by country, 1979-89, annual rpt, 9824–1
Multinatl US firms and foreign affiliates finances and operations, by industry and country, 1989 benchmark survey, annual rpt, 2704–5
Multinatl US firms foreign affiliates, income statement items by asset size, industry, and country, 1988, biennial article, 8302–2.322
Oil production, stocks, use, and trade, by selected country and country group, monthly rpt, 3162–42
Population size, growth rates, and components of change, by country, projected 1990-2020 and trends from 1950, biennial rpt, 2324–9
Refugee migration, and intl aid programs, by world area and country of origin and asylum, 1991, annual rpt, 7004–15
Tax revenue, by level of govt and type of tax, for OECD countries, mid 1960s-90, annual rpt, 10044–1.2
UN voting record and share of votes in agreement with US, by issue, country, and world area, 1991, annual rpt, 7004–18
see also under By Foreign Country in the "Index by Categories"

Ireland, Peter N.
"Endogenous Financial Innovation and the Demand for Money", 9389–19.34
"Financial Evolution and the Long-Run Behavior of Velocity: New Evidence from U.S. Regional Data", 9389–1.301

Irick, Christine
"Retirement-Age Couples by Type of Wife's Social Security Benefit", 4746–26.12

Iron and steel industry
Building materials shipments and PPI, by type, quarterly rpt, 2042–1.5; 2042–1.6
Business statistics, detailed data for major industries and economic indicators, *Survey of Current Business*, monthly rpt, 2702–1.16
Business statistics, detailed data for major industries and economic indicators, 1960-91, *Survey of Current Business* biennial supplement, 2704–1
Carbon and alloy steel products from Brazil at less than fair value, injury to US industry, investigation with background financial and operating data, 1992 rpt, 9886–14.356
Carbon steel (flat-rolled) products from 21 countries, injury to US industry from foreign subsidized and less than fair value imports, investigation with background financial and operating data, 1992 rpt, 9886–19.85

China minerals production and trade, by commodity, 1989-90, annual rpt, 5604–38
Coal coke use and costs in steel industry, effects of Clean Air Act, 1985-91 and projected to 2003, 5606–5.10
County Business Patterns, 1989: employment, establishments, and payroll, by SIC 2- to 4-digit industry and county, annual State rpt series, 2326–8
County Business Patterns, 1990: employment, establishments, and payroll, by SIC 2- to 4-digit industry and county, annual State rpt series, 2326–6
Drums and pails (steel shipping) shipments, trade, use, and firms, quarterly Current Industrial Rpt, 2506–11.5
Eastern Europe export industries dev potential, with trade and industry finances and operations, for 5 countries, 1985-90, 9886–4.179
Employment, earnings, and hours, by SIC 1- to 4-digit industry, monthly 1989-Feb 1992, annual rpt, 6744–4
Employment of minorities and women, by occupation, SIC 1- to 3-digit industry, State, and MSA, 1991, annual rpt, 9244–1
Energy use and prices for manufacturing industries, 1988 survey, series, 3166–13
Exports and imports between US and outlying areas, by detailed commodity and mode of transport, 1991, annual rpt, 2424–11
Exports and imports of steel, by product, country, and customs district, with US industry operating data, 1989-June 1992, semiannual rpt, 9882–15
Exports and imports of US, by country and detailed commodity, monthly rpt, 2422–12
Exports and imports of US, by Harmonized System 6-digit commodity and country, 1991, annual rpt, 2424–13
Exports and imports of US, by selected country, country group, and commodity group, 1991, annual rpt, 2044–37
Exports and imports of US, by transport mode, country, and SITC 1- to 3-digit commodity, 1991, annual rpt, 2424–12
Exports, imports, and balances of US for manufactured goods, by SITC 2-digit commodity and country, quarterly rpt, 2042–35
Exports, imports, and intl competitiveness of US industries, trends and outlook, quarterly rpt with articles, 9882–16
Exports of US, detailed commodities by country, monthly CD-ROM, 2422–13
Exports of US, detailed Schedule B commodities with countries of destination, 1991, annual rpt, 2424–10
Ferrosilicon from 6 countries, injury to US industry from foreign subsidized and less than fair value imports, investigation with background financial and operating data, 1992 rpt, 9886–19.84
Financial and economic performance indicators and indexes for metals industries, by commodity, monthly rpt, 5602–5
Foreign and US hourly compensation costs, for iron and steel industry by country, 1975-90, 6826–3.8
Foreign countries economic, social, political, and geographic summary data, by country, 1992, annual factbook, 9114–2
Foreign countries mineral production, reserves, and industry role in domestic economy and world supply, world area and country rpt series, 5606–1
Freight (waterborne domestic and foreign) by commodity, traffic, and passengers, by port and waterway, 1989, annual rpt, 3754–3
Hwy construction material prices and indexes for Federal-aid system, by type of material and urban-rural location, quarterly rpt, 7552–7
Hwy construction material prices and indexes for Federal-aid system, by type of material, quarterly press release, 7552–16
Hwy construction material use by type, and spending, by State, 1940s-91, annual rpt, 7554–29
Imports injury to US industries from foreign subsidized products and sales at less than fair value, investigations with background financial and operating data, series, 9886–19
Imports injury to US industries from foreign subsidized products, investigations with background financial and operating data, series, 9886–15
Imports of steel under voluntary restraint agreement, by product, customs district, and country, with US industry operating data, quarterly rpt, 9882–13
Imports of US, detailed commodities by country, monthly CD-ROM, 2422–14
Imports of US given duty-free treatment for value of US material sent abroad, by commodity and country, 1987-90, annual rpt, 9884–14
Input-output structure of US economy, detailed interindustry transactions for 84 industries, and components of final demand, 1987, annual article, 2702–1.316
Input-output structure of US economy, detailed interindustry transactions for 541 industries, and components of final demand, 1982 benchmark data, 2708–17
Manufacturing annual survey, 1990: finances and operations, by SIC 2- to 4-digit industry, series, 2506–14
Manufacturing census, 1987: concentration of largest firms measured by value added, and for shipments by SIC 2- and 4-digit industry, subject rpt, 2497–6
Manufacturing census, 1987: shipments of manufacturers products, by customer class and SIC 2- and 4-digit industry, subject rpt, 2497–4
Manufacturing corporations financial statements, by selected SIC 2- to 3-digit industry, quarterly rpt, 2502–1
Manufacturing finances and operations, by SIC 2- to 4-digit industry, forecast 1992, annual rpt, 2044–28
Military and personal property shipments, passenger traffic, and costs, by service branch and mode of transport, FY91, annual rpt, 3704–15
Mineral Industry Surveys, commodity review of production, trade, stocks, and use, monthly rpt, 5612–1.11; 5612–1.12
Minerals Yearbook, Vol 1, 1989: commodity reviews of production, use, trade, prices, and mining operations, annual rpt, 5604–33
Minerals Yearbook, Vol 1, 1990: commodity reviews of production, reserves, supply, use, and trade, annual rpt series, 5604–20
Minerals Yearbook, Vol 1, 1991: commodity reviews of production, reserves, supply, use, and trade, annual rpt series, 5604–15
Minerals Yearbook, Vol 2, 1989: State reviews of production and sales by commodity, and business activity, annual rpt series, 5604–16
Minerals Yearbook, Vol 2, 1990: State reviews of production and sales by commodity, and business activity, annual rpt series, 5604–22
Minerals Yearbook, Vol 3, 1989: foreign country reviews of production, trade, and policy, by commodity, annual rpt, 5604–35
Mines (metal) and related operations occupational injuries and incidence, employment, and hours, 1990, annual rpt, 6664–3
Multinatl US firms and foreign affiliates finances and operations, by industry and country, 1989 benchmark survey, annual rpt, 2704–5
North Central States business and economic conditions, Fed Reserve 9th District, quarterly journal, 9383–19
Occupational injury and illness rates, by SIC 2- to 4-digit industry, 1989-90, annual rpt, 6844–7
Occupational injury and illness rates, by SIC 2- to 4-digit industry, 1990, annual rpt, 6844–1
OECD trade, total and for 4 major countries, and US trade by country, by commodity, 1980-90, world area rpt series, 9116–1
Ohio River basin waterway facilities, freight by commodity and port, and recreation, by waterway, 1988-89, annual rpt, 3754–6
Plumbing fixtures production, and imports from US and other sources, for 15 countries, 1991 rpt, 2048–156
Pollution (air) abatement equipment shipments by industry, and new and backlog orders, by product, 1991, annual Current Industrial Rpt, 2506–12.5
Price indexes (producer), by stage of processing and detailed commodity, monthly rpt, 6762–6
Price indexes (producer), by stage of processing and detailed commodity, monthly 1991, annual rpt, 6764–2
Production, prices, trade, and foreign and US industry devs, by commodity, bimonthly rpt, 5602–4
Production, prices, trade, use, employment, tariffs, and stockpiles, by mineral, with foreign comparisons, 1987-91, annual rpt, 5604–18
Production, shipments, trade, stocks, and material used, for primary metals by product, periodic Current Industrial Rpt series, 2506–10
Production, trade, use, and foreign investment in US industry, for minerals, 1985-90 and projected to 2000, annual rpt, 5304–5
Productivity of labor and capital, and indexes of output, hours, and employment, 1967-90, annual rpt, 6824–1.2; 6824–1.3; 6824–1.5

Rope (steel wire) from South Korea and Mexico at less than fair value, injury to US industry, investigation with background financial and operating data, 1992 rpt, 9886–14.346
Rope (wire) used for mine hoists, characteristics by type, 1991 rpt, 5608–172
Science, engineering, and technical employment in manufacturing, by field and industry, 1989, triennial rpt, 9627–23
Soviet Union and US economic and sociodemographic indicators, selected years 1970-90, handbook, 2328–80
Soviet Union minerals production and exports, by commodity and Republic, 1975-90, annual rpt, 5604–39
Statistical Abstract of US, 1992 annual data compilation, 2324–1.27
Tax (income) returns of corporations, income and tax items by asset size and detailed industry, 1989, annual rpt, 8304–4; 8304–21
Waterworks compact ductile iron fittings from PRC at less than fair value, injury to US industry, investigation with background financial and operating data, 1992 rpt, 9886–14.358
see also under By Commodity in the "Index by Categories"

Irrigation
Acreage of irrigated farmland, farm characteristics, and water and fuel sources, by State and leading county, 1950s-88, 1588–122
Agricultural Conservation Program participation and payments, by practice and State, FY91, annual rpt, 1804–7
Army Corps of Engineers activities and projects, FY88 and trends from 1800s, annual rpt, 3754–1.1
Army Corps of Engineers activities and projects, FY89 and trends from 1800s, annual rpt, 3754–1.2
Army Corps of Engineers activities and projects, FY90 and trends from 1800s, annual rpt, 3754–1.3
Army Corps of Engineers water resources dev projects, characteristics, and costs, 1950s-89, biennial State rpt series, 3756–1
Army Corps of Engineers water resources dev projects, characteristics, and costs, 1950s-91, biennial State rpt series, 3756–2
Colorado River Storage Project finances and activities in western States, FY91, annual rpt, 5824–3
Columbia River Power System projects, plant investment allocation schedule, FY91, annual rpt, 3224–1
Conservation program of USDA, acreage, projects, participation, and funding, by State, 1936-90, quinquennial rpt, 1808–1
Costs of production (itemized), receipts, and returns, by crop and State, 1987-89, annual rpt, 1544–24
Costs of production, itemized by farm sales size and region, 1991, annual rpt, 1614–3
County Business Patterns, 1989: employment, establishments, and payroll, by SIC 2- to 4-digit industry and county, annual State rpt series, 2326–8
County Business Patterns, 1990: employment, establishments, and payroll, by SIC 2- to 4-digit industry and county, annual State rpt series, 2326–6
Environmental Quality, status of problems, protection programs, research, and intl issues, 1991 annual rpt, 484–1
Farm production inputs, finances, mgmt, and land value and transfers, periodic situation rpt with articles, 1561–16
Farm production itemized costs, receipts, and returns, by commodity and region, 1975-90, annual rpt, 1544–20
FmHA activities, and loans and grants by program and State, FY91 and trends from FY70, annual rpt, 1184–17
Groundwater supply, quality, chemistry, and use, State and local area rpt series, 5666–28
Groundwater supply, quality, chemistry, other characteristics, and use, regional rpt series, 5666–25
Groundwater use by purpose and State, and depletion, 1980s, 10048–82
Indian and govt lands under Bur of Indian Affairs mgmt, acreage, leases, and use, 1989, annual rpt, 5704–12
Livestock grazing forage demand, and meat supply and demand, indicators, 1960s-90 and projected to 2030, 1208–404
Occupational injury and illness rates, by SIC 2- to 4-digit industry, 1989-90, annual rpt, 6844–7
Occupational injury and illness rates, by SIC 2- to 4-digit industry, 1990, annual rpt, 6844–1
Rice production, practices, costs, and land tenure, by production area, 1988, 1568–309
Statistical Abstract of US, 1992 annual data compilation, 2324–1.23
Water quality, chemistry, hydrology, and other characteristics, local area studies, series, 5666–27
Water supply in US and southern Canada, streamflow, surface and groundwater conditions, and reservoir levels, by location, monthly rpt, 5662–3
Water use by end use, well withdrawals, and public supply deliveries, by county, State rpt series, 5666–24
Western Area Power Admin activities by plant, financial statements, and sales by customer, FY91, annual rpt, 3254–1
Western US irrigation projects of Reclamation Bur, crop production and acreage by commodity, State, and project, 1990, annual rpt, 5824–12
Western US water supply, storage by reservoir and State, and streamflow conditions, as of Oct 1992, annual rpt, 1264–4
see also Watershed projects

IRS
see Internal Revenue Service

Irvine, Audrey
"Impact of Medicare Payment Policy on Home Health Resources Utilization", 4652–1.302

Islands
see Coral reefs and islands

Isola, Jorma
"Association of Overexpression of Tumor Suppressor Protein p53 with Rapid Cell Proliferation and Poor Prognosis in Node-Negative Breast Cancer Patients", 4472–1.329

Israel
Agricultural trade by commodity and country, prices, and world market devs, monthly rpt, 1922–12
Agricultural trade of US, by detailed commodity and country, 1991, annual rpt, 1524–8
Agricultural trade of US, by detailed commodity and country, 1991, semiannual rpt, 1522–4
AID economic aid to developing countries, obligations and disbursements by country, quarterly rpt, 9912–4
AID loans repayment status and terms by program and country, and status of predecessor agency loans, quarterly rpt, 9912–3
Economic and military aid and loans from US and intl agencies, by program and country, FY46-91, annual rpt, 9914–5
Economic and social conditions of developing countries from 1960s, and Intl Dev Cooperation Agency and AID activities and funding, FY91-93, annual rpt, 9904–4
Economic conditions, policy, and trade practices, by country, 1989-91, annual rpt, 21384–5
Economic conditions, US investment and export opportunities, and trade practices, for Israel, 1992 rpt, 2008–32
Economic, social, political, and geographic summary data, by country, 1992, annual factbook, 9114–2
Exports and imports of US, by Harmonized System 6-digit commodity and country, 1991, annual rpt, 2424–13
Exports and imports of US, by selected country, country group, and commodity group, 1991, annual rpt, 2044–37
Exports and imports of US, by transport mode, country, and SITC 1- to 3-digit commodity, 1991, annual rpt, 2424–12
Exports, imports, and balances of US for manufactured goods, by SITC 2-digit commodity and country, quarterly rpt, 2042–35
Exports, imports, and balances of US with major trading partners, by product category, 1987-91, annual chartbook, 9884–21
Exports of US, detailed Schedule B commodities with countries of destination, 1991, annual rpt, 2424–10
Human rights conditions in 170 countries, and US economic and military aid, 1991, annual rpt, 21384–3
Imports of goods, services, and investment from US, trade barriers, impacts, and US actions, by country, 1991, annual rpt, 444–2
Labor conditions, union coverage, and work accidents, 1991 annual country rpt, 6366–4.6
Labor conditions, union coverage, and work accidents, 1992 annual country rpt, 6366–4.42
Military aid of US, arms sales, and training programs costs and budget requests, by program, world region, and country, FY91-93, annual rpt, 7144–13
Military spending, arms trade, and force strengths, with govt spending and population, by country, 1979-89, annual rpt, 9824–1

Minerals Yearbook, Vol 3, 1989: foreign country review of production, trade, and policy, by commodity, annual rpt, 5604–35.3
Multinatl US firms and foreign affiliates finances and operations, by industry and country, 1989 benchmark survey, annual rpt, 2704–5
Multinatl US firms foreign affiliates, income statement items by asset size, industry, and country, 1988, biennial article, 8302–2.322
Population size, growth rates, and components of change, by country, projected 1990-2020 and trends from 1950, biennial rpt, 2324–9
Refugee migration, and intl aid programs, by world area and country of origin and asylum, 1991, annual rpt, 7004–15
Spacecraft and satellite launches since 1957, quarterly listing, 9502–2
Steel trade, by product, country, and customs district, with US industry operating data, 1989-June 1992, semiannual rpt, 9882–15
UN voting record and share of votes in agreement with US, by issue, country, and world area, 1991, annual rpt, 7004–18
see also under By Foreign Country in the "Index by Categories"

Israilevich, Philip R.
"Estimating Monthly Regional Value Added by Combining Regional Input with National Production Data", 9375–13.85

Italy
Agricultural trade of US, by detailed commodity and country, 1991, annual rpt, 1524–8
Agricultural trade of US, by detailed commodity and country, 1991, semiannual rpt, 1522–4
AID economic aid to developing countries, obligations and disbursements by country, quarterly rpt, 9912–4
AID loans repayment status and terms by program and country, and status of predecessor agency loans, quarterly rpt, 9912–3
Cuba trade, by commodity and country, mid 1980s-91, 9118–8
Debt (public) burden on future generations, for Italy, alternative forecasts, 1992 working paper, 9377–9.139
Dollar exchange rates of selected currencies, weekly chartbook, 9365–1.5
Drug abuse indicators, by world region and selected country, 1992 semiannual conf, 4492–5.2
Economic and military aid and loans from US and intl agencies, by program and country, FY46-91, annual rpt, 9914–5
Economic and monetary trends, compounded annual rates of change and quarterly indicators for US and 7 major industrialized countries, quarterly rpt, 9391–7
Economic conditions, and oil supply and demand, for major industrial countries, monthly rpt, 9112–1
Economic conditions, consumer and stock prices and production indexes, for 7 OECD countries, *Survey of Current Business*, monthly rpt, 2702–1.1
Economic conditions, income, production, prices, employment, and trade, 1992 periodic country rpt, 2046–4.29
Economic conditions, policy, and trade practices, by country, 1989-91, annual rpt, 21384–5
Economic indicators, and dollar exchange rates, for selected OECD countries, 1992 semiannual rpt, 8002–14
Economic, social, political, and geographic summary data, by country, 1992, annual factbook, 9114–2
Energy production by type, and oil trade, and use, by country group and selected country, monthly rpt, 9112–2
European Monetary Union impacts on France, Germany, and Italy monetary policies, 1992 technical paper, 9385–8.145
Export credit activity of Eximbank and 6 OECD countries, 1990, annual rpt, 9254–3
Exports and imports of US by country, and trade shifts by commodity, 1991, annual rpt, 9884–25
Exports and imports of US, by Harmonized System 6-digit commodity and country, 1991, annual rpt, 2424–13
Exports and imports of US, by selected country, country group, and commodity group, 1991, annual rpt, 2044–37
Exports and imports of US, by transport mode, country, and SITC 1- to 3-digit commodity, 1991, annual rpt, 2424–12
Exports, imports, and balances of US for manufactured goods, by SITC 2-digit commodity and country, quarterly rpt, 2042–35
Exports, imports, and balances of US with major trading partners, by product category, 1987-91, annual chartbook, 9884–21
Exports of US, detailed Schedule B commodities with countries of destination, 1991, annual rpt, 2424–10
Gold standard relation to inflation, with background data for UK, US, France, and Italy, 1730s-1930s, working paper, 9377–9.136
Hazelnut production, supply, trade, and use, for 3 countries and US, 1990-93, annual article, 1925–34.338
Health care costs and components, services use, resources, and economic indicators, by OECD country, 1960s-90, article, 4652–1.322
Human rights conditions in 170 countries, and US economic and military aid, 1991, annual rpt, 21384–3
Imports of goods, services, and investment from US, trade barriers, impacts, and US actions, by country, 1991, annual rpt, 444–2
Intl transactions of US with 9 countries, 1989-91, *Survey of Current Business*, monthly rpt, annual table, 2702–1.33
Labor conditions, union coverage, and work accidents, 1992 annual country rpt, 6366–4.23
Military spending, arms trade, and force strengths, with govt spending and population, by country, 1979-89, annual rpt, 9824–1
Multinatl US firms and foreign affiliates finances and operations, by industry and country, 1989 benchmark survey, annual rpt, 2704–5
Multinatl US firms foreign affiliates, income statement items by asset size, industry, and country, 1988, biennial article, 8302–2.322
Musical instrument (woodwind) key pads from Italy at less than fair value, injury to US industry, investigation with background financial and operating data, 1992 rpt, 9886–14.364
Non-Hodgkin's lymphoma incidence in Italy, by sex and geographic area, aggregate 1983-87, article, 4472–1.336
Nuclear power generation in US and 20 countries, monthly rpt, 3162–24.10
Nuclear power generation in US and 20 countries, monthly 1973-88, 3168–123.10
Oil production, stocks, use, and trade, by selected country and country group, monthly rpt, 3162–42
Oil production, use, stocks, and exports to US, by country, detailed data, monthly rpt with articles, 3162–24
Oil production, use, stocks, and exports to US, by country, detailed data, monthly 1973-88, 3168–123
Pollution (air) contributing to global warming, emissions by monitoring site and country, and temperature change by world area and US region, 1860s-1990, annual rpt, 3004–33
Population size, growth rates, and components of change, by country, projected 1990-2020 and trends from 1950, biennial rpt, 2324–9
Potassium hydroxide from 3 countries at less than fair value, injury to US industry, investigation with background financial and operating data, 1992 rpt, 9886–14.339
Refugee migration, and intl aid programs, by world area and country of origin and asylum, 1991, annual rpt, 7004–15
Science and Engineering Indicators, employment, education, R&D funding, and industry impacts, with foreign comparisons, 1960s-91, biennial rpt, 9624–10
Sexually transmitted disease cases in Italy by disease and sex, and surveillance activities, Sept 1990-June 1991, article, 4202–7.311
Ships in world merchant fleet, tonnage, and new ship construction and deliveries, by vessel type and country, as of Jan 1992, annual rpt, 7704–3
Spacecraft and satellite launches since 1957, quarterly listing, 9502–2
Steel (carbon flat-rolled) products from 21 countries, injury to US industry from foreign subsidized and less than fair value imports, investigation with background financial and operating data, 1992 rpt, 9886–19.85
Steel trade, by product, country, and customs district, with US industry operating data, 1989-June 1992, semiannual rpt, 9882–15
Tax (estate) returns for nonresident aliens, property and tax data, by estate size and decedent country of residence, 1986, article, 8302–2.310
Tax (income) returns for foreign corporate activity in US, selected income and tax items, by industry div and selected country, 1988, article, 8302–2.309

Tax revenue, by level of govt and type of tax, for OECD countries, mid 1960s-90, annual rpt, 10044–1.2
Telecommunications industry intl competitiveness, structure, and devs, with background data and foreign comparisons, 1991 rpt, 2808–30
Transportation energy use, fuel prices, vehicle registrations, and mileage, by selected country, 1950-89, annual rpt, 3304–5.1
UN voting record and share of votes in agreement with US, by issue, country, and world area, 1991, annual rpt, 7004–18
see also San Marino
see also Vatican City
see also under By Foreign Country in the "Index by Categories"

Ivory Coast
Agricultural trade of US, by detailed commodity and country, 1991, annual rpt, 1524–8
Agricultural trade of US, by detailed commodity and country, 1991, semiannual rpt, 1522–4
AID economic aid to developing countries, obligations and disbursements by country, quarterly rpt, 9912–4
AID loans repayment status and terms by program and country, and status of predecessor agency loans, quarterly rpt, 9912–3
Economic and military aid and loans from US and intl agencies, by program and country, FY46-91, annual rpt, 9914–5
Economic and social conditions of developing countries from 1960s, and Intl Dev Cooperation Agency and AID activities and funding, FY91-93, annual rpt, 9904–4
Economic conditions, income, production, prices, employment, and trade, 1992 periodic country rpt, 2046–4.23
Economic, social, political, and geographic summary data, by country, 1992, annual factbook, 9114–2
Exports and imports of US, by commodity and country, 1980-90, world area rpt, 9116–1.2
Exports and imports of US, by transport mode, country, and SITC 1- to 3-digit commodity, 1991, annual rpt, 2424–12
Exports of US, detailed Schedule B commodities with countries of destination, 1991, annual rpt, 2424–10
Food supply, needs, and aid for developing countries, status and alternative forecasts, 1992 world area rpt, 1526–8.2
Human rights conditions in 170 countries, and US economic and military aid, 1991, annual rpt, 21384–3
Military aid of US, arms sales, and training programs costs and budget requests, by program, world region, and country, FY91-93, annual rpt, 7144–13
Military spending, arms trade, and force strengths, with govt spending and population, by country, 1979-89, annual rpt, 9824–1
Minerals Yearbook, Vol 3, 1989: foreign country review of production, trade, and policy, by commodity, annual rpt, 5604–35.1
Population size, growth rates, and components of change, by country, projected 1990-2020 and trends from 1950, biennial rpt, 2324–9
Refugee migration, and intl aid programs, by world area and country of origin and asylum, 1991, annual rpt, 7004–15
UN voting record and share of votes in agreement with US, by issue, country, and world area, 1991, annual rpt, 7004–18

Jabine, Thomas B.
"Survey of Income and Program Participation (SIPP): Quality Profile", 2628–34

Jackson County, Mo.
Housing and households characteristics, and unit and neighborhood quality, by MSA location for 11 MSAs, 1986 survey, supplement, 2485–8

Jackson, Georgia P.
"Electric Household Appliances and Certain Heating Equipment, Industry and Trade Summary", 9885–9.4

Jackson, Miss.
Wages by occupation, and benefits, for office and plant workers, 1992 survey, periodic MSA rpt, 6785–17.1
see also under By City and By SMSA or MSA in the "Index by Categories"

Jacksonville, Fla.
Freight (waterborne domestic and foreign) by commodity, traffic, and passengers, by port and waterway, 1989, annual rpt, 3754–3.1; 3754–3.2
Housing starts and completions authorized by building permits in 40 MSAs, quarterly rpt, 2382–9
see also under By City and By SMSA or MSA in the "Index by Categories"

Jaditz, Ted
"Testing for Nonlinear Dynamics", 6886–6.85

Jagger, Craig
"Outlook for U.S. Wheat in 1992 or 'A Dry Year in Kansas Is Followed by ...?'", 1504–9.1

Jails
see Correctional institutions

Jamaica
Agricultural trade of US, by detailed commodity and country, 1991, annual rpt, 1524–8
Agricultural trade of US, by detailed commodity and country, 1991, semiannual rpt, 1522–4
AID economic aid to developing countries, obligations and disbursements by country, quarterly rpt, 9912–4
AID loans repayment status and terms by program and country, and status of predecessor agency loans, quarterly rpt, 9912–3
Economic and military aid and loans from US and intl agencies, by program and country, FY46-91, annual rpt, 9914–5
Economic and social conditions of developing countries from 1960s, and Intl Dev Cooperation Agency and AID activities and funding, FY91-93, annual rpt, 9904–4
Economic and social conditions, resources, and trade, and aid, 1992, annual factbook, 9914–14
Economic conditions, policy, and trade practices, by country, 1989-91, annual rpt, 21384–5
Economic, population, and agricultural data, US and other aid sources, and AID activity, 1992 country rpt, 9916–12.69
Economic, social, political, and geographic summary data, by country, 1992, annual factbook, 9114–2
Exports and imports of US, by commodity and country, 1980-90, world area rpt, 9116–1.4
Exports and imports of US, by Harmonized System 6-digit commodity and country, 1991, annual rpt, 2424–13
Exports and imports of US, by transport mode, country, and SITC 1- to 3-digit commodity, 1991, annual rpt, 2424–12
Exports, imports, and balances of US for manufactured goods, by SITC 2-digit commodity and country, quarterly rpt, 2042–35
Exports of US, detailed Schedule B commodities with countries of destination, 1991, annual rpt, 2424–10
Human rights conditions in 170 countries, and US economic and military aid, 1991, annual rpt, 21384–3
Labor conditions, union coverage, and work accidents, 1991 annual country rpt, 6366–4.4
Military aid of US, arms sales, and training programs costs and budget requests, by program, world region, and country, FY91-93, annual rpt, 7144–13
Military spending, arms trade, and force strengths, with govt spending and population, by country, 1979-89, annual rpt, 9824–1
Multinatl US firms and foreign affiliates finances and operations, by industry and country, 1989 benchmark survey, annual rpt, 2704–5
Multinatl US firms foreign affiliates, income statement items by asset size, industry, and country, 1988, biennial article, 8302–2.322
Population size, growth rates, and components of change, by country, projected 1990-2020 and trends from 1950, biennial rpt, 2324–9
Refugee migration, and intl aid programs, by world area and country of origin and asylum, 1991, annual rpt, 7004–15
Steel trade, by product, country, and customs district, with US industry operating data, 1989-June 1992, semiannual rpt, 9882–15
Tax (income) returns of Foreign Sales Corps, assets, and income and tax items, by industry, country of incorporation, and transaction pricing method, 1987, article, 8302–2.311
UN voting record and share of votes in agreement with US, by issue, country, and world area, 1991, annual rpt, 7004–18
see also under By Foreign Country in the "Index by Categories"

James River
Freight (waterborne domestic and foreign) by commodity, traffic, and passengers, by port and waterway, 1989, annual rpt, 3754–3.1
Ships in Natl Defense Reserve Fleet at James River, as of July 1991, semiannual listing, 7702–2

Jamison, Ellen
"World Population Profile: 1991", 2324–9
Janitorial and maintenance services
County Business Patterns, 1989: employment, establishments, and payroll, by SIC 2- to 4-digit industry and county, annual State rpt series, 2326–8
County Business Patterns, 1990: employment, establishments, and payroll, by SIC 2- to 4-digit industry and county, annual State rpt series, 2326–6
Employment and economic conditions, alternative BLS projections to 2005 and trends 1975-90, biennial rpt, 6744–19
Employment, earnings, and hours, by SIC 1- to 4-digit industry, monthly 1989-Feb 1992, annual rpt, 6744–4
Labor demand, turnover, and training completions, by detailed occupation, 1990 and projected to 2005, biennial rpt, 6744–3
Occupational injury and illness rates, by SIC 2- to 4-digit industry, 1989-90, annual rpt, 6844–7
Occupational injury and illness rates, by SIC 2- to 4-digit industry, 1990, annual rpt, 6844–1
Occupational Outlook Handbook, 1992-93, biennial rpt, 6744–1
Pacific territories population and housing detailed characteristics, by location, 1990 Census of Population and Housing, series, 2551–8
Postal Service operating costs, itemized by class of mail, FY91, annual rpt, 9864–4
Schools asbestos contamination, inspection and abatement effectiveness, staff and parental notification, and inspector and janitorial training, as of 1990, 9238–71
see also Domestic workers and services
Jankowski, John E., Jr.
"Federal R&D Funding by Budget Function, FY91-93", 9627–9
Jankowski, Louis W.
"Jail Inmates, 1991", 6066–25.48
"Probation and Parole, 1990", 6066–25.43
Japan
Agricultural exports of US, for grains, oilseed products, hides, skins, and cotton, by country, weekly rpt, 1922–3
Agricultural imports of Japan, total and from US, by commodity, 1989-91, article, 1925–34.313
Agricultural production, prices, and trade, by country, 1980s and forecast 1992, annual world region rpt, 1524–4.3
Agricultural trade by commodity and country, prices, and world market devs, monthly rpt, 1922–12
Agricultural trade of US, by detailed commodity and country, 1991, annual rpt, 1524–8
Agricultural trade of US, by detailed commodity and country, 1991, semiannual rpt, 1522–4
AID loans repayment status and terms by program and country, and status of predecessor agency loans, quarterly rpt, 9912–3
Auto and auto parts trade, production, and labor conditions, for US and compared to Canada and Mexico, 1950s-90, 6366–3.28
Auto fuel economy improvements from new technologies, 1987-90 and alternative projections to 2010, 26358–251
Auto industry finances and operations, trade by country, and prices of selected US and foreign models, monthly rpt, 9882–8
Auto parts trade with Japan and other countries, 1985-90 and forecast to 1994, annual rpt, 2004–10
Auto sales and production of US industry and Japanese assembly plants in US, and imports, 1979-90, article, 6722–1.313
Autos (minivans) from Japan at less than fair value, injury to US industry, investigation with background financial and operating data, 1992 rpt, 9886–14.351
Banks reserve and overdraft requirements of Fed Reserve and 3 foreign central banks, with balance sheets and deposit balances, 1989-90, article, 9377–1.307
Beef imports from US and Australia, by type and quota status, 1988-92, semiannual rpt, 1925–33.2
Cancer (leukemia) virus infection among Japan island village residents, relation to selected characteristics, 1984-86 study, article, 4472–1.319
Cherry production, imports from US, and prices, for Japan, 1988-92, article, 1925–34.339
Construction activity in Japan, by type and region, selected years 1985-91, article, 2042–1.307
Corporations (*keiretsu*) equity and debt financing by shareholding banks, with model results, 1960s-70, article, 9393–8.302
Corporations (*keiretsu* and independent) ownership and concentration indicators, for Japan, 1984, technical paper, 9366–6.288
Cuba trade, by commodity and country, mid 1980s-91, 9118–8
Currency (foreign and US) shares of intl transactions, with background data, for 5 countries, 1960s-80s, 9381–10.129
Dollar exchange rate trade-weighted index of Fed Reserve Bank of Dallas, by world area, monthly rpt, 9379–13
Dollar exchange rates of mark and yen, impact of central bank policy interventions, 1985-89, article, 9391–1.310
Dollar exchange rates of mark and yen, spot and forward market bid-ask spreads impacts of central bank intervention, mid 1980s-91, article, 9377–1.305
Dollar exchange rates of yen and mark, impact of central bank policy interventions and other factors, various periods 1983-90, working paper, 9377–9.138
Dollar exchange rates of yen and mark, impact of central bank policy interventions, 1987-90, working paper, 9377–9.134
Economic and military aid and loans from US and intl agencies, by program and country, FY46-91, annual rpt, 9914–5
Economic and monetary trends, compounded annual rates of change and quarterly indicators for US and 7 major industrialized countries, quarterly rpt, 9391–7
Economic conditions, and oil supply and demand, for major industrial countries, monthly rpt, 9112–1
Economic conditions, consumer and stock prices and production indexes, for 7 OECD countries, *Survey of Current Business*, monthly rpt, 2702–1.1
Economic conditions, policy, and trade practices, by country, 1989-91, annual rpt, 21384–5
Economic conditions, US investment and export opportunities, and trade practices, for Japan, forecast 1991-93 and trends from 1988, 2048–159
Economic indicators, and dollar exchange rates, for selected OECD countries, 1992 semiannual rpt, 8002–14
Economic, social, political, and geographic summary data, by country, 1992, annual factbook, 9114–2
Energy production by type, and oil trade, and use, by country group and selected country, monthly rpt, 9112–2
Energy supply and demand, by fuel and end-use sector, 1950s-87 and forecast to 1995, 3166–6.58
Energy use and imports by fuel type, and gasoline prices, for Japan, 1970s-80s, hearing, 21448–45
Energy use and production, by fuel type, country, and country group, projected 1995-2010 and trends from 1970, annual rpt, 3164–84
Exchange rate variability and other factors, relation to inter- and intra-industry foreign trade for US, Germany, and Japan, 1960s-88, working paper, 9371–10.81
Export credit activity of Eximbank and 6 OECD countries, 1990, annual rpt, 9254–3
Exports and imports among US, Canada, and Japan related to domestic and foreign prices and income, 1965-87, technical paper, 9366–7.276
Exports and imports, intl position of US and 4 OECD countries, and factors affecting US competition, quarterly pamphlet, 2042–25
Exports and imports of OECD, total and for 4 major countries, and US trade by country, by commodity, 1980-90, world area rpt series, 9116–1
Exports and imports of US by country, and trade shifts by commodity, 1991, annual rpt, 9884–25
Exports and imports of US, by Harmonized System 6-digit commodity and country, 1991, annual rpt, 2424–13
Exports and imports of US, by selected country, country group, and commodity group, 1991, annual rpt, 2044–37
Exports and imports of US, by transport mode, country, and SITC 1- to 3-digit commodity, 1991, annual rpt, 2424–12
Exports and imports, trade agreements and relations, and USITC investigations, 1991, annual rpt, 9884–5
Exports, imports, and balances of US, by selected country, country group, and commodity group, preliminary data, monthly rpt, 2042–34
Exports, imports, and balances of US for manufactured goods, by SITC 2-digit commodity and country, quarterly rpt, 2042–35
Exports, imports, and balances of US with major trading partners, by product category, 1987-91, annual chartbook, 9884–21

Exports of US, detailed Schedule B commodities with countries of destination, 1991, annual rpt, 2424–10
Farmland and agricultural industries in US, Japan investment, with data by State and county, late 1960s-90, 1528–332
Financial markets (intl) performance of foreign and US bank and securities firms, finances and competitiveness issues, 1980s, compilation of papers, 9385–10
Fish (billfish) tagged and recovered by location, and Japan catch in US waters, 1950-90, annual rpt, 2164–7
Fish (tuna) catch in Japan, trade, tariffs, prices, holdings, and consumption, by species, 1977-90, 2166–19.11
Fish and shellfish aquaculture in US and Japan, mgmt, methods, and biological data for selected species, 1990 conf, annual rpt, 2164–15
Germany unification economic impacts for Germany, US, Japan, and worldwide, alternative projections 1991-99, technical paper, 9366–7.275
Health care costs and components, services use, resources, and economic indicators, by OECD country, 1960s-90, article, 4652–1.322
Human rights conditions in 170 countries, and US economic and military aid, 1991, annual rpt, 21384–3
Imports of goods, services, and investment from US, trade barriers, impacts, and US actions, by country, 1991, annual rpt, 444–2
Imports of US given duty-free treatment for value of US material sent abroad, by commodity and country, 1987-90, annual rpt, 9884–14
Insurance company finances, by insurance type and firm, with some intl comparisons, 1991 conf, 9373–3.35
Interest and exchange rates, security yields, and stock indexes, for selected foreign countries, weekly chartbook, 9365–1.5
Interest rates (long term) relation to rates of return to capital, economic policies, and other factors, US and 4 countries, 1960s-90, article, 9385–1.301
Investment (foreign direct) in US, by industry group and world area, 1989-91, annual article, 2702–1.331
Investment (foreign direct) in US, major transactions by type, industry, country, and US location, 1990, annual rpt, 2044–20
Labor conditions, union coverage, and work accidents, 1992 annual country rpt, 6366–4.29
Labor costs (manufacturing) and productivity, by selected country, 1950s-91, press release, 6726–1.55
Labor costs and indexes, by selected country, 1991, semiannual rpt, 6822–3
Lenses (aspherical ophthalmoscopy) from Japan at less than fair value, injury to US industry, investigation with background financial and operating data, 1992 rpt, 9886–14.343
Manufacturing industry (US) intl competitiveness, trade and economic policies with background data and foreign comparisons, 1991 rpt, 26358–252
Mexico trade with US and other countries, foreign investment, and maquiladoras operations, 1980s-91, GAO rpt, 26119–417
Military spending and indicators of ability to support common defense, for NATO members, Japan, and South Korea, 1970s-90, annual rpt, 3544–28
Military spending, arms trade, and force strengths, with govt spending and population, by country, 1979-89, annual rpt, 9824–1
Minerals production, trade, use, and foreign investment in US industry, 1985-90 and projected to 2000, annual rpt, 5304–5
Minerals Yearbook, Vol 3, 1989: foreign country review of production, trade, and policy, by commodity, annual rpt, 5604–35.2
Monetary policies and central bank regulation in US and 5 countries, 1980-91, article, 9385–1.308
Motor vehicle industry finances, and average fleet fuel economy, by selected firm, 1991 hearings, 21368–138
Multinatl firms US affiliates finances and operations, by industry, country of parent firm, and State, 1987, 2708–48
Multinatl firms US affiliates, finances, and operations, by industry, world area of parent firm, and State, 1989-90, annual rpt, 2704–4
Multinatl US firms and foreign affiliates finances and operations, by industry and country, 1989 benchmark survey, annual rpt, 2704–5
Multinatl US firms foreign affiliates, income statement items by asset size, industry, and country, 1988, biennial article, 8302–2.322
Natural gas and liquefied gas trade of US with 5 countries, by US firm, 1955-91, annual article, 3162–4.301
Nuclear power generation in US and 20 countries, monthly rpt, 3162–24.10
Nuclear power generation in US and 20 countries, monthly 1973-88, 3168–123.10
Occupational injuries and illnesses in Japan and US, and lost workday and death rates, late 1950s-88, article, 6722–1.318
Oil production, stocks, use, and trade, by selected country and country group, monthly rpt, 3162–42
Oil supply, demand, and stock forecasts, by world area, quarterly rpt, 3162–34
Oil use and stocks for selected OECD countries, monthly rpt, 3162–24.10
Oil use and stocks for selected OECD countries, 1973-88, 3168–123.10
Pension plan finances, participation, and benefits, for 9 OECD countries, with data by firm and worker characteristics, 1990 conf, 6688–2
Persian Gulf War allied and other countries cash and in-kind contributions, by type and country, 1990-91, GAO rpt, 26123–371
Persian Gulf War allied countries cash and in-kind contributions, by type and country, and status of DOD accounts, as of Sept 1991, annual GAO rpt, 26104–24
Pollution (air) contributing to global warming, emissions by monitoring site and country, and temperature change by world area and US region, 1860s-1990, annual rpt, 3004–33
Population size, growth rates, and components of change, by country, projected 1990-2020 and trends from 1950, biennial rpt, 2324–9
Poultry imports of Japan, by country, 1990-91, semiannual rpt, 1925–33.1
Public interest and expectations for science and technology, 1990 survey, biennial rpt, 9624–10.7
R&D activities of US firms in Japan, employee characteristics, and mgmt views on benefits and drawbacks, 1991 rpt, 9628–88
Rails (steel) from 3 countries at less than fair value, injury to US industry, investigation with background financial and operating data, 1992 rpt, 9886–14.349
Raisin imports of 3 countries, and Chile exports, by country of origin and destination, 1988-91, semiannual article, 1925–34.321
Refugee migration, and intl aid programs, by world area and country of origin and asylum, 1991, annual rpt, 7004–15
Savings rates, and ratio of aged to working age population, for US, Japan, and West Germany, 1980s-90, article, 9387–1.302
Science and Engineering Indicators, employment, education, R&D funding, and industry impacts, with foreign comparisons, 1960s-91, biennial rpt, 9624–10
Semiconductor and related equipment sales, by US and Japanese firm, 1970s-88, annual rpt, 15034–1.1
Semiconductor fabrication and packing materials market share of Japan, 1970s-90, annual rpt, 15034–1.4
Semiconductor industry (US) intl competitiveness, indicators and comparisons to Japan and Europe, 1980s and projected to 1994, working paper, 15036–1.1
Ships in world merchant fleet, tonnage, and new ship construction and deliveries, by vessel type and country, as of Jan 1992, annual rpt, 7704–3
Soybean meal and oil demand for Japan, model description and results, 1992 article, 1561–3.305
Spacecraft and satellite launches since 1957, quarterly listing, 9502–2
Steel (carbon flat-rolled) products from 21 countries, injury to US industry from foreign subsidized and less than fair value imports, investigation with background financial and operating data, 1992 rpt, 9886–19.85
Steel imports of US under voluntary restraint agreement, by product, customs district, and country, with US industry operating data, quarterly rpt, 9882–13
Steel trade, by product, country, and customs district, with US industry operating data, 1989-June 1992, semiannual rpt, 9882–15
Tax (income) final withholding systems use in 4 countries, and feasibility of US adoption, with background data, 1986-92, GAO rpt, 26119–400
Tax (income) returns for foreign corporate activity in US, selected income and tax items, by industry div and selected country, 1988, article, 8302–2.309
Tax (income) returns, income, and tax withheld for foreign partners of US partnerships, by country, 1990, article, 8302–2.324

Tax (income and capital) policies, with background data, for EC, Japan, and US, mid 1960s-91, article, 9373–1.316
Tax revenue, by level of govt and type of tax, for OECD countries, mid 1960s-90, annual rpt, 10044–1.2
Technological info transfer between US and Japan, activities and researcher and student exchanges, 1988-89, GAO rpt, 26123–379
Technology-intensive industries intl competitiveness, with background data by industry and foreign comparisons, 1960s-91, GAO rpt, 26123–406
Telecommunications industry intl competitiveness, structure, and devs, with background data and foreign comparisons, 1991 rpt, 2808–30
Tidal currents, daily time and velocity by station for North America and Asia coasts, forecast 1993, annual rpt, 2174–1.2
Timber in northwestern US and British Columbia, production, prices, trade, and employment, quarterly rpt, 1202–3
Tools (electric cutting and sanding) from Japan at less than fair value, injury to US industry, investigation with background financial and operating data, 1992 rpt, 9886–14.355
Transportation energy use, fuel prices, vehicle registrations, and mileage, by selected country, 1950-89, annual rpt, 3304–5.1
Travel to US and Canada, market analysis with trip and traveler characteristics, and traveler views on selected destination cities and package tours, 1989, country rpt, 2906–2.19; 2906–2.22; 2906–2.23
Travel to US and Canada, market analysis with trip and traveler characteristics, 1989, country rpt, 2906–2.15
Travel to US, spending by world area of residence, and economic impact, by spending category and State, 1989, 2908–28
UN voting record and share of votes in agreement with US, by issue, country, and world area, 1991, annual rpt, 7004–18
see also under By Foreign Country in the "Index by Categories"

Japan-U.S. Friendship Commission
Budget of US, authoritative financial statements with appropriations, outlays, and receipts, by category and agency, FY91, annual rpt, 8104–2.2
Budget of US, obligations and authority by function, agency, and program, with summaries and analyses, FY93, annual rpt, 104–2
Education funding by Federal agency, program, and recipient type, and instn spending, 1960s-91, annual rpt, 4824–8

Jarrow, Robert A.
"Option Pricing with Random Volatilities in Complete Markets", 9371–10.74

Jasinski, Stephen M.
"Bismuth—Uses, Supply, and Technology", 5608–175

Jaussaud, Renee
"Records of the Department of the Interior, Record Group 48", 9516–2.1

Jefferson County, Colo.
Housing and households characteristics, and unit and neighborhood quality, by MSA location for 11 MSAs, 1986 survey, supplement, 2485–8

Jefferson Parish, La.
Housing and households characteristics, and unit and neighborhood quality, by MSA location for 11 MSAs, 1986 survey, supplement, 2485–8

Jeffery, Robert W.
"Pilot Study of AIDS Risk in the General Population", 4042–3.311

Jencks, Stephen F.
"Containing U.S. Health Care Costs: What Bullet To Bite?", 4652–1.310

Jennings, Jerry T.
"Who's Helping Out? Support Networks Among American Families: 1988", 2546–20.21

Jereb, John A.
"Tuberculosis Morbidity in the U.S.: Final Data, 1990", 4202–7.302

Jervis, Lance
"1991 Promotion Activities Under Federal Milk Orders", 1317–4.304

Jet fuel
see Aviation fuels

Jewelry
Consumer holdings of durable goods, by type, in current and constant dollars, 1925-90, annual article, 2702–1.305
Consumer holdings of durable goods, by type, in current and constant dollars, 1988-91, annual article, 2702–1.327
Consumer spending, natl income and product account benchmark revisions, 1929-88, 2708–5
Consumer spending, natl income and product accounts, comprehensive accounts and components, *Survey of Current Business*, monthly rpt, 2702–1.25
County Business Patterns, 1989: employment, establishments, and payroll, by SIC 2- to 4-digit industry and county, annual State rpt series, 2326–8
County Business Patterns, 1990: employment, establishments, and payroll, by SIC 2- to 4-digit industry and county, annual State rpt series, 2326–6
CPI by component for US city average, and by selected metro area, region, and population size, monthly rpt, 6762–2
Employment, earnings, and hours, by SIC 1- to 4-digit industry, monthly 1989-Feb 1992, annual rpt, 6744–4
Exports and imports between US and outlying areas, by detailed commodity and mode of transport, 1991, annual rpt, 2424–11
Exports and imports of US, by Harmonized System 6-digit commodity and country, 1991, annual rpt, 2424–13
Exports and imports of US, by transport mode, country, and SITC 1- to 3-digit commodity, 1991, annual rpt, 2424–12
Exports of US, detailed Schedule B commodities with countries of destination, 1991, annual rpt, 2424–10
Imports of bicycles and costume jewelry from PRC and other countries, 1986-91, article, 9882–2.301
Imports of US given duty-free treatment for value of US material sent abroad, by commodity and country, 1987-90, annual rpt, 9884–14
Injuries from use of consumer products and related activities, by severity and victim age and sex, 1990, annual rpt, 9164–7
Injuries from use of consumer products, by severity, victim age, and detailed product, 1991, annual rpt, 9164–6
Input-output structure of US economy, detailed interindustry transactions for 541 industries, and components of final demand, 1982 benchmark data, 2708–17
Manufacturing annual survey, 1990: finances and operations, by SIC 2- to 4-digit industry, series, 2506–14
Manufacturing census, 1987: concentration of largest firms measured by value added, and for shipments by SIC 2- and 4-digit industry, subject rpt, 2497–6
Manufacturing census, 1987: shipments of manufacturers products, by customer class and SIC 2- and 4-digit industry, subject rpt, 2497–4
Manufacturing finances and operations, by SIC 2- to 4-digit industry, forecast 1992, annual rpt, 2044–28
Occupational injury and illness rates, by SIC 2- to 4-digit industry, 1989-90, annual rpt, 6844–7
Occupational injury and illness rates, by SIC 2- to 4-digit industry, 1990, annual rpt, 6844–1
Occupational Outlook Handbook, 1992-93, biennial rpt, 6744–1
OECD trade, total and for 4 major countries, and US trade by country, by commodity, 1980-90, world area rpt series, 9116–1
Price indexes (producer), by stage of processing and detailed commodity, monthly rpt, 6762–6
Price indexes (producer), by stage of processing and detailed commodity, monthly 1991, annual rpt, 6764–2
Price indexes for department store inventories, by class of item, monthly table, 6762–7
Retail trade sales and inventories, by kind of business, region, and selected State, MSA, and city, monthly rpt, 2413–3
Retail trade sales, inventories, purchases, gross margin, and accounts receivable, by SIC 2- to 4-digit kind of business and form of ownership, 1990, annual rpt, 2413–5
Science, engineering, and technical employment in manufacturing, by field and industry, 1989, triennial rpt, 9627–23
Tax (luxury) revenue, and related IRS administrative costs, FY91 and projected to FY95, GAO rpt, 26119–385
Thefts, and value of property stolen and recovered, by property type, 1991, annual rpt, 6224–2.1
see also Gemstones

JHK and Associates
"INFORM Evaluation", 7558–119

Jinkins, John E.
"Financial Characteristics of Vegetable Farms in 1990", 1561–11.304
"Measuring Farm and Ranch Business Diversity", 1541–1.314

Job Corps
Forest Service employment and human resource program participation, FY91, annual rpt, 1204–1.4

Participants characteristics, activities, and funding, for Employment and Training Admin programs, FY86-88, annual rpt, 6404–17

Job creation

Budget of US, Bush Admin proposals, with detail for defense budgets, and historical data from FY34, FY93, 108–46

Disabled persons workshops finances, operations, and Federal procurement, FY82-91, annual rpt, 11714–1

Economic Dev Admin activities, and funding by program, recipient, State, and county, FY91 and cumulative from FY66, annual rpt, 2064–2

Electric power demand, and industrial and employment impacts of capacity shortfalls and new power plants, by selected State, 1960s-80s and projected to 2000, hearing, 21248–163

Enterprise zone programs in rural areas, jobs created and saved, and firms participating, by industry, 1986, article, 1502–7.303

Enterprise zone programs of States, business investment and jobs created, and incentive programs, by State, 1992 annual rpt, 5124–9

Small business finances, operations, owner characteristics, and Federal contracts, 1980s-90, annual rpt, 9764–6

Statistical Abstract of US, 1992 annual data compilation, 2324–1.17

Tax (income) returns filed, by type of filer, selected income items, quarterly rpt, 8302–2.1

Tax (income) returns of individuals, by filing status, tax item, and income level, 1991, annual article, 8302–2.319

Tennessee Valley economic conditions, and compared to US, alternative projections 1992-2010 and trends from 1929, annual rpt, 9804–27

Job discrimination

see Discrimination in employment

Job placement

see Employment services

Job tenure

Black Americans social and economic characteristics, for South and total US, 1991 and trends from 1950, annual Current Population Rpt, 2546–1.463

Deaths during 1986, decedents health condition, services use, habits, and social, employment, and other characteristics, 4147–20.19

Disabled persons work experience following OASDI benefit award, by selected characteristics, 1980s, article, 4742–1.312

Disabled persons work history before and after SSI application, by age, diagnosis, industry div, and sex, aggregate 1937-87, article, 4742–1.308

Education (elementary and secondary) schools, teachers, staff, and enrollment, by selected characteristics, 1987/88-1988/89, 4836–3.10

Education data compilation, 1992 annual rpt, 4824–2

Fed Bur of Prisons correctional staff by selected characteristics, and inmates, by facility, data compilation, 1992 annual rpt, 6064–6.1

Fed Govt civilian employees demographic and employment characteristics, as of Sept 1991, annual article, 9842–1.301

Fed Govt employment of minorities, disabled, and veterans, and years of service, by occupation, age, sex, and agency, as of Sept 1990, biennial rpt, 9844–27

Fed Govt Senior Executive Service members characteristics, entries, exits, and awards, FY79-91, annual rpt, 9844–36

Law enforcement officer assaults and deaths by circumstances, agency, victim and offender characteristics, and location, 1990, annual rpt, 6224–3

Leave benefits in small business compared to larger firms and govts, by occupational group, 1989-90, article, 6722–1.315

Military health care personnel, and accessions by training source, by occupation, specialty, and service branch, FY90, annual rpt, 3544–24

Military homosexual personnel discharges by pay grade, tenure, race, sex, and occupation, and investigations, by service branch, 1980s-90, GAO rpt, 26123–392

Mines occupational deaths, by circumstances and selected victim characteristics, semiannual rpt series, 6662–3

NASA Apollo era science and engineering staff background and characteristics, 1958-70, 9508–39

NASA staff characteristics and personnel actions, FY91, annual rpt, 9504–1

Occupational changes within firm, by worker characteristics, 1986-87, article, 6742–1.301

OECD pension plan finances, participation, and benefits, for 9 countries, with data by firm and worker characteristics, 1990 conf, 6688–2

Petrochemicals industries contract labor accidents, injuries, safety programs operations, and employee characteristics, 1986-91, 6608–6

Population economic well-being indicators, by selected characteristics and household income and income-to-poverty ratio, 1984, 2546–20.22

Railroad employment and compensation, by age, sex, occupation, and years of service, 1985, annual rpt, 9704–2.4

Science and engineering employment characteristics of minorities, women, and disabled, by field, 1970s-91, biennial rpt, 9624–20.1

Teachers and administrators in private schools, pay, work conditions, and selected characteristics, by school type and affiliation, 1987/88, 4836–3.8

Teachers of vocational education, by subject area and selected characteristics, for public high schools, 1987/88, 4836–3.9

Tenure with current employer compared to 1983, and employment in same occupation in 1990, by sex, age, and race, 1991, press release, 6726–1.47

Unemployed displaced workers job search and placement aid effectiveness, relation to previous employment and other characteristics, 1979-87 studies, 15496–1.14

Vocational education enrollment, student and teacher characteristics, and outcomes, for secondary and postsecondary instns, 1970s-90, 4828–42

Younger workers jobs held and weeks worked since age 18, by age, sex, and race, 1978-90, 6726–2.3

see also Labor mobility

see also Labor turnover

Job training

see Apprenticeship

see Employee development

see Manpower training programs

see Vocational education and training

see Vocational rehabilitation

Job Training Partnership Act

Displaced worker employment and training services, and layoff alternatives, indicators of effectiveness, 1980s, 15498–28

Expenditures of Fed Govt in States, by type, program, agency, and State, FY91, annual rpt, 2464–2

Fraud and abuse in DOL programs, audits and investigations, 2nd half FY92, semiannual rpt, 6302–2

Labor Dept activities and funding, by program and State, FY91, annual rpt, 6304–1

Participants characteristics, activities, and funding, for Employment and Training Admin programs, FY86-88, annual rpt, 6404–17

Rural areas employment and population characteristics, and role of education and training in economic dev, 1960s-80s, compilation of papers, 1598–277

Rural areas JTPA programs costs and outcomes, FY87, article, 1502–7.305

State and local govt JTPA admin, funding, effectiveness, and participants, GAO rpt series, 26106–8

Unemployed displaced workers and other hard-to-serve groups, factors contributing to unemployment, and training programs operations, series, 15496–1

Unemployment, employment, and labor force of States and local areas eligible for JTPA funding, monthly rpt, special supplement, 6742–22

Job vacancy

Data on labor turnover, job openings, and new hires and wages, pilot survey results, costs, and methodology, 1990-91, 6728–40

Education (elementary and secondary) schools, teachers, staff, and enrollment, by selected characteristics, 1987/88-1988/89, 4836–3.10

Help-wanted ads index and ratio to unemployment, *Survey of Current Business*, cyclical indicators, monthly rpt, 2702–1.1

Hospital employment and job vacancy rate, by occupation, and instn size and control, 1981-88, annual rpt, 4114–12

Indian Health Service employment of Indians and non-Indians, training, hires, and quits, by occupation, FY90, annual rpt, 4084–6

Labor force, wages, hours, and payroll costs, by major industry group and demographic characteristics, *Survey of Current Business*, monthly rpt, 2702–1.7

New England States economic indicators, Fed Reserve 1st District, monthly rpt, 9373–2

North Central States business and economic conditions, Fed Reserve 9th District, quarterly journal, 9383–19

Occupational separations, replacement rates, and related job openings, estimation procedures with data by occupation, age, and sex, late 1980s and projected to 2005, 6748–84

OECD pension plan finances, participation, and benefits, for 9 countries, with data by firm and worker characteristics, 1990 conf, 6688–2
Prison employment requirements for new and expanded Federal facilities, by occupation, FY87-95, GAO rpt, 26119–397
Statistical Abstract of US, 1992 annual data compilation, 2324–1.13
VA health care staff and turnover, by occupation, physician specialty, and location, 1991, annual rpt, 8604–8
see also Labor turnover

Jobs
see Employee performance and appraisal
see Employment and unemployment, general
see Employment and unemployment, local and regional
see Employment and unemployment, specific industry
see Job creation
see Job tenure
see Job vacancy
see Labor turnover
see Minority employment
see Occupations
see Part-time employment
see Temporary and seasonal employment
see Veterans employment
see Women's employment
see Youth employment
see under By Occupation in the "Index by Categories"

Johnson, Cheryl
"Value-Added for the U.S. Agricultural Sector", 1541–1.321
"Why U.S. Farm Income Is Record High", 1541–1.302

Johnson, Clifford L.
"Overweight Adults in the U.S.", 4147–16.6

Johnson, Craig E.
"Wetlands: Status and Trends in the Conterminous U.S. Mid-1970's to Mid-1980's", 5508–89

Johnson, David
"Team Behavior in the Family: An Analysis of the Rotten Kid Theorem", 6886–6.86

Johnson, Doyle C.
"Net Cash Income and Selected Characteristics of U.S. Farms Producing Fruits, Tree Nuts, and Berries", 1561–6.301
"1992 Floriculture and Environmental Horticulture Outlook", 1504–9.1

Johnson, Eugene G.
"NAEP 1990 Technical Report", 4896–8.5

Johnson, Jesse L.
"Paints, Inks, and Related Items, Industry and Trade Summary", 9885–11.3

Johnson, Mae D.
"U.S. Textile Imports and Exports", 1561–1.301

Johnson, Ronald
"Bank Capital Ratios, Asset Growth, and the Stock Market", 9385–1.311
"Price-Adjustment Delays in the Secondary Market for Developing Country Debt and the Estimation of Asset Pricing Models", 9385–8.132

Johnson, Tony G.
"Forest Statistics for the Northern Mountains of Virginia, 1992", 1206–6.16
"Forest Statistics for the Southern Piedmont of Virginia, 1991", 1206–6.14
"Forest Statistics for Virginia, 1992", 1206–6.18

Johnson, Walter R.
"Numerical Modeling of Storm Surges in Norton Sound", 2176–1.40

Johnston Atoll
Minerals offshore lease sales environmental and economic impacts in coastal areas, 1990 final statement, 5736–7.1

Johnston, Lloyd D.
"Smoking, Drinking, and Illicit Drug Use Among American Secondary School Students, College Students and Young Adults, 1975-91", 4494–4

Johnston, Paul V.
"Trade Dependency Index Tables for Total, Merchandise, and Agricultural Trade, 1960-88", 1528–328

Joines, Douglas H.
"IRAs and Saving: Evidence from a Panel of Taxpayers", 9381–10.126

Joint committees
see Congressional joint committees

Joint Economic Committee
Eastern Europe transition to market economies, economic conditions, trade, and foreign investment, by country, 1990-91, 9118–13
Economic indicators and components, current data and annual trends, monthly rpt, 23842–1
Economic Report of the President for 1991, economic effects of budget proposals, and trends and projections, 1940s-95, annual hearings, 23844–4
Economic Report of the President for 1992, Joint Economic Committee critique and policy recommendations, annual rpt, 23844–2
Economic review and outlook for US, analysis of Bush Admin and private projections, with small business views, 1991 hearings, 23848–230
Employment situation, earnings, hours, and other BLS economic indicators, transcripts of BLS Commissioner's monthly testimony, periodic rpt, 23846–4
Married-couple families income, and spouses labor force participation and hours worked, by income class, 1979 and 1989, 23848–225
Military spending reductions, economic impacts by defense contractor, industry, State, and congressional district, 1989-90 hearings, 23848–224
Population size and demographic changes impacts on economic conditions, with background data, 1950s-80s and projected to 2010, 23848–226
Statistical programs of Fed Govt, funding by agency, and BLS programs improvement spending, 1991 hearing, 23848–227

Joint Taxation Committee
Economic performance and income distribution impacts of tax policy, issues and background data, with foreign comparisons, 1991 and trends, 21788–211

Joint Typhoon Warning Center
"Western North Pacific Typhoons—1991", 2152–8.303

Joint ventures
AID dev projects and socioeconomic impacts, evaluation rpt series, 9916–1
Eastern Europe export industries dev potential, with trade and industry finances and operations, for 5 countries, 1985-90, 9886–4.179
Energy resources of US, foreign direct investment by energy type and firm, and US affiliates operations, as of 1990, annual rpt, 3164–80
Food marketing cooperatives exports under intl business arrangements, 1985-88, 1128–69
Foreign direct investment in US, major transactions by type, industry, country, and US location, 1990, annual rpt, 2044–20
Japan investment in US farmland and agricultural industries, with data by State and county, late 1960s-90, 1528–332
Japan R&D activities of US firms, employee characteristics, and mgmt views on benefits and drawbacks, 1991 rpt, 9628–88
Militarily strategic manufacturing industries finances, operations, and intl competitiveness, series, 2026–1
Uranium reserves and industry operations, by region and State, various periods 1966-91, annual rpt, 3164–65.1

Joliet, Ill.
Housing vacancy rates for single and multifamily units and mobile homes, by city and ZIP code, 1992, annual MSA rpt, 9304–18.5

Jolly, James H.
"Materials Flow of Zinc in the U.S., 1850-1990", 5608–176

Jones, Lee R.
"1990 Science Report Card: NAEP's Assessment of Fourth, Eighth, and Twelfth Graders. National Assessment of Educational Progress", 4896–8.3

Jordan
Agricultural trade of US, by detailed commodity and country, 1991, annual rpt, 1524–8
Agricultural trade of US, by detailed commodity and country, 1991, semiannual rpt, 1522–4
AID economic aid to developing countries, obligations and disbursements by country, quarterly rpt, 9912–4
AID loans repayment status and terms by program and country, and status of predecessor agency loans, quarterly rpt, 9912–3
Boycotts (intl) by OPEC and other countries, US firms and individuals cooperation and tax benefits denied, 1990, article, 8302–2.323
Economic and military aid and loans from US and intl agencies, by program and country, FY46-91, annual rpt, 9914–5
Economic and social conditions of developing countries from 1960s, and Intl Dev Cooperation Agency and AID activities and funding, FY91-93, annual rpt, 9904–4
Economic conditions, policy, and trade practices, by country, 1989-91, annual rpt, 21384–5
Economic, social, political, and geographic summary data, by country, 1992, annual factbook, 9114–2

Electric power plants (oil shale-fired) feasibility assessment with background data, for Jordan, 1990 rpt, 3008–127
Exports and imports of US, by commodity and country, 1980-90, world area rpt, 9116–1.6
Exports and imports of US, by transport mode, country, and SITC 1- to 3-digit commodity, 1991, annual rpt, 2424–12
Exports of US, detailed Schedule B commodities with countries of destination, 1991, annual rpt, 2424–10
Human rights conditions in 170 countries, and US economic and military aid, 1991, annual rpt, 21384–3
Labor conditions, union coverage, and work accidents, 1992 annual country rpt, 6366–4.38
Military aid of US, arms sales, and training programs costs and budget requests, by program, world region, and country, FY91-93, annual rpt, 7144–13
Military spending, arms trade, and force strengths, with govt spending and population, by country, 1979-89, annual rpt, 9824–1
Minerals Yearbook, Vol 3, 1989: foreign country review of production, trade, and policy, by commodity, annual rpt, 5604–35.3
Population size, growth rates, and components of change, by country, projected 1990-2020 and trends from 1950, biennial rpt, 2324–9
Refugee migration, and intl aid programs, by world area and country of origin and asylum, 1991, annual rpt, 7004–15
UN voting record and share of votes in agreement with US, by issue, country, and world area, 1991, annual rpt, 7004–18

Journalism
County Business Patterns, 1989: employment, establishments, and payroll, by SIC 2- to 4-digit industry and county, annual State rpt series, 2326–8
County Business Patterns, 1990: employment, establishments, and payroll, by SIC 2- to 4-digit industry and county, annual State rpt series, 2326–6
Foreign countries media representatives admitted to US, by country, FY81-91, annual rpt, 6264–2.3
Labor demand, turnover, and training completions, by detailed occupation, 1990 and projected to 2005, biennial rpt, 6744–3
Occupational Outlook Handbook, 1992-93, biennial rpt, 6744–1
Public confidence in people running selected social instns, 1972-88 surveys, biennial rpt, 9624–10.7
see also Freedom of the press
see also Newspapers
see also Periodicals

Joyce, Philip
"Budgeting for Administrative Costs Under Credit Reform", 26306–6.166

Judges
Administrative law judges views toward establishment of separate ALJ agency, 1992, GAO report, 26119–428
Criminal caseload, positions authorized, misconduct, terms, salaries, and selected other characteristics of judges, data compilation, 1992 annual rpt, 6064–6.5
Criminal justice systems activities, spending, and employment, by level of govt, data compilation, 1992 annual rpt, 6064–6.1
Federal district and appeals court judgeships and visiting judge services, 1960s-91, annual rpt, 18204–8.11; 18204–8.15; 18204–8.30
Federal district court personnel, by court, 1991, annual report, 17664–1
Judicial Conf proceedings and findings, spring 1992, semiannual rpt, 18202–2
Labor demand, turnover, and training completions, by detailed occupation, 1990 and projected to 2005, biennial rpt, 6744–3
Occupational Outlook Handbook, 1992-93, biennial rpt, 6744–1
Pension systems of State and local govts, finances, coverage, and benefits, by system, FY90, annual rpt, 2466–2.4
Sentences under Federal mandatory minimum provisions, by defendant characteristics, and views on justice system impacts, FY90, 17668–2
States criminal justice systems activities, employment, funding, and data collection, by State, 1970s-91, annual rpt, 6064–40
Wiretaps authorized, costs, arrests, trials, and convictions, by offense and jurisdiction, 1991, annual rpt, 18204–7
Workers compensation contested claims, caseload, and commissioners and hearing officers, by State, 1987-90, annual rpt, 6504–9
see also Judicial ethics
see also Judicial powers
see also Judicial reform

Judgments, civil procedure
Claims Court caseload by type of suit, and judgments, FY92, annual rpt, 18224–1
Discrimination in employment, Civil Rights Act issues, EEOC cases by issue, damage awards, and sexual harassment complaints and company policies, late 1970s-91, hearing, 21348–120
Fed Govt accounts receivable, delinquent debt cases and collections of Justice Dept and private law firms, pilot project results, FY91, annual rpt, 6004–20
Fed Govt benefit programs overpayment recovery and judgment enforcement cases filed in Federal district courts, 1991, annual rpt, 18204–8.14
Federal district, appeals, and bankruptcy courts, civil cases terminated by circuit and district, 1991, annual rpt, 18204–11
Nuclear Regulatory Commission activities, finances, and staff, with data for individual power plants, FY91, annual rpt, 9634–2
Tax collection, enforcement, and litigation activity of IRS, with data by type of tax, region, and State, FY91, annual rpt, 8304–3
Tax Court of US caseloads and recoveries, FY92, annual tables, 18224–5
Tax Court of US caseloads and tax due, by disposition, FY91, annual tables, 18224–3
US attorneys case processing and collections, by case type and Federal district, FY91, annual rpt, 6004–2
see also Child support and alimony
see also Fines and settlements

Judicial Branch
see Administrative Office of the U.S. Courts
see Court of International Trade
see Court of Military Appeals
see Federal bankruptcy courts
see Federal courts of appeals
see Federal district courts
see Federal Judicial Center
see Supreme Court
see U.S. Court of Appeals for the Federal Circuit

Judicial Conference of the U.S.
Proceedings and findings of conf, spring 1992, semiannual rpt, 18202–2
Proceedings and findings of semiannual confs, 1991, annual rpt, 18204–8

Judicial ethics
Judges misconduct cases by disposition, and judicial conduct commissions staff and budgets, by State, data compilation, 1992 annual rpt, 6064–6.1; 6064–6.5
Judicial Conf proceedings and findings, spring 1992, semiannual rpt, 18202–2
Justice Dept employee misconduct investigations, by type of allegation and penalty, 1988-90, GAO rpt, 26119–380
Public opinion on crime and crime-related issues, by respondent characteristics, data compilation, 1992 annual rpt, 6064–6.2

Judicial powers
Judicial Conf proceedings and findings, spring 1992, semiannual rpt, 18202–2

Judicial reform
Judicial Conf proceedings and findings, spring 1992, semiannual rpt, 18202–2
Sentences for Federal crimes, guidelines use and results by offense and district, and Sentencing Commission activities, 1991, annual rpt, 17664–1
Sentences for Federal crimes, guidelines use and results by offense, 1984-1990, 6066–19.68
Sentences for Federal offenses, guidelines by offense and circumstances, series, 17668–1
Sentences for Federal offenses, guidelines impacts on sentence disparity by offender race and other characteristics, 1985-90, GAO rpt, 26119–415
Sentences under Federal mandatory minimum provisions, by defendant characteristics, and views on justice system impacts, FY90, 17668–2
Tort and other civil litigation reform recommendations, with background data, 1960-90, 048–3

Junior colleges
Black higher education instns enrollment, finances, staff, and degrees, by instn and selected student characteristics, 1970s-90, 4848–46
Condition of Education, detail for elementary, secondary, and higher education, 1920s-91 and projected to 2002, annual rpt, 4824–1
Degrees awarded in higher education, by level, field, race, and sex, 1989/90 and trends from 1980/81, annual rpt, 4844–17
Digest of Education Statistics, 1992 annual data compilation, 4824–2
Enrollment and degrees awarded in higher education, by sex, full- and part-time status, and instn level and control, fall 1991, annual rpt, 4844–16

Enrollment, by grade, instn type and control, and student characteristics, 1989 and trends from 1947, annual Current Population Rpt, 2546–1.459
Enrollment, degrees, teachers, and spending, 1977/78-1990/91 and alternative projections to 2002/2003, annual rpt, 4824–4
Enrollment, faculty, finances, and degrees in higher education, by instn level and control, and State, FY88, annual rpt, 4844–13
Enrollment in higher education, by level, race, and sex, fall 1980-90, biennial rpt, 4844–15
Enrollment, tuition, control, location, and other characteristics of higher education instns, 1991/92, biennial listing, 4844–3
Faculty and staff of higher education instns, by occupation, full- and part-time status, sex, and instn type and control, fall 1989, biennial rpt, 4844–18
High school class of 1972: community college attendance, by selected characteristics, natl longitudinal study, 1970s-86, 4888–7
Noncollegiate instns enrollment and program completion, by sex and instn level and control, fall 1990, annual rpt, 4844–19
Occupational qualification and skill improvement training, workers participating by training source, occupation, age, sex, and race, 1991, 6728–32
Pell grants and applicants, by tuition, family and student income, instn type and control, and State, 1990/91, annual rpt, 4804–1
R&D and related funding of Fed Govt to higher education and nonprofit instns, by field, instn, agency, and State, FY90, annual rpt, 9627–17
Statistical Abstract of US, 1992 annual data compilation, 2324–1.4
Student aid and other sources of support, with student expenses and characteristics, by instn type and control, 1987 study, series, 4846–3; 4846–5
Teachers in higher education, and salaries, by faculty rank, sex, instn type and control, and State, 1990/91, annual rpt, 4844–8
Tuition and other student charges, by public and private 2- and 4-year higher education instn, and State, 1991/92, annual listing, 4844–10
Vocational education enrollment, student and teacher characteristics, and outcomes, for secondary and postsecondary instns, 1970s-90, 4828–42

Juries
Employee paid leave days for jury duty, for State and local govt employees, 1990, biennial rpt, 6784–21
Federal district court grand and petit juror use and costs, trials, and trial days, by court, annual rpt, discontinued, 18204–4
Federal district court grand and petit juror use, by circuit and district, 1991, annual rpt, 18204–11
Federal district court grand and petit juror use, June 1987-91, annual rpt, 18204–8
Fees paid, and jury use and service, by State and for Federal system, data compilation, 1992 annual rpt, 6064–6.1
Public opinion on crime and crime-related issues, by respondent characteristics, data compilation, 1992 annual rpt, 6064–6.2
State court chief prosecutors employment characteristics, and felony case prosecution procedures, 1990 survey, 6066–25.46
US attorneys case processing and collections, by case type and Federal district, FY91, annual rpt, 6004–2

Jurisdiction
see Administration of justice
see Administrative law and procedure
see Courts
see Law

Justice Department
see Department of Justice

Juvenile courts and cases
Case processing, and juveniles detained, by age, sex, race, and offense, data compilation, 1992 annual rpt, 6064–6.5
Caseloads of Federal district courts, 1991, annual rpt, 18204–8.18
Data on juvenile justice issues, young offenders, and victims, series, 6066–27
Federal district court caseloads, 1991, annual rpt, 18204–11
Statistical Abstract of US, 1992 annual data compilation, 2324–1.5
US attorneys civil and criminal cases by type and disposition, and collections, by Federal district, FY91, annual rpt, 6004–2.1
Youth health condition, risk factors, and preventive and treatment services use and availability, 1970s-80s, 26358–234.2

Juvenile delinquency
Arrests, by offense, offender characteristics, and location, 1991, annual rpt, 6224–2.2
Data on crime, criminal justice admin and enforcement, and public opinion, data compilation, 1992 annual rpt, 6064–6
Data on juvenile justice issues, young offenders, and victims, series, 6066–27
Indian and Alaska Native youth health condition and behavioral patterns, by sex and grade, 1988-90, 4088–3
Sentences for Federal offenses, guidelines by offense and circumstances, series, 17668–1
Women in jail, by criminal background and sociodemographic characteristics, with comparisons to men, 1989, 6066–19.66
Youth health condition, risk factors, and preventive and treatment services use and availability, 1970s-80s, 26358–234.2
see also Juvenile courts and cases
see also Juvenile detention and correctional institutions
see also Missing persons and runaways

Juvenile detention and correctional institutions
Data on juvenile justice issues, young offenders, and victims, series, 6066–27
Education (compensatory) programs in juvenile facilities, activities, participant and staff characteristics, and outcomes, 1991 rpts, 4808–40
Facilities, population, and juveniles held with adults, by State, FY90, annual rpt, 6064–34
Facilities, population, employment, spending, and other characteristics of correctional instns, by State and for Fed Govt, 1990, annual rpt, 6064–26.3; 6068–218
Federal correctional instns prisoners and staff, by selected characteristics, region, and instn, FY89, annual rpt, 6244–1.1
Jail juvenile population, by sex, 1978-90, annual rpt, 6064–26.1
Jail population by sex, race, and for 25 jurisdictions, and instn conditions, 1990-91, annual rpt, 6066–25.48
Population census, 1990: institutionalized population and persons in group quarters, by sex, race, county, place, and urban-rural location, State rpt series, 2531–1
Population in juvenile facilities, by resident characteristics and facility type, late 1970s-89, 6068–250
Population in juvenile facilities, by resident characteristics and facility type, 1977-89, annual rpt, 6064–35
Prisoners and movements, by offense, location, and selected other characteristics, data compilation, 1992 annual rpt, 6064–6.6
States criminal justice systems activities, employment, funding, and data collection, by State, 1970s-91, annual rpt, 6064–40
Statistical Abstract of US, 1992 annual data compilation, 2324–1.5
Youth health condition, risk factors, and preventive and treatment services use and availability, 1970s-80s, 26358–234.2

Kahl, Anne
"Geriatric Education Centers Address Medication Issues Affecting Older Adults", 4042–3.303

Kahler, Lucinda R.
"Factors Associated with Rates of Participation in WIC by Eligible Pregnant Women", 4042–3.305

Kahn, Arthur L.
"SSI Recipients by State and County", 4744–27

Kalamazoo, Mich.
see also under By City and By SMSA or MSA in the "Index by Categories"

Kalcevic, Deborah
"Experience of the Stafford Loan Program and Options for Change", 26306–3.120

Kampuchea
see Cambodia

Kane, Edward J.
"Incentive Conflict in Deposit-Institution Regulation: Evidence from Australia", 9375–13.82

Kane, Michael D.
"Top 100 Cooperatives, 1990 Financial Profile", 1124–3

Kane, Sally
"Climate Change: Economic Implications for World Agriculture", 1528–326

Kannan, Rajagopalan
"Paying for Highways, Airways, and Waterways: How Can Users Be Charged?", 26306–6.170

Kansas
Banks (insured commercial and savings) deposits by instn, State, MSA, and county, as of June 1991, annual regional rpt, 9295–3.5
Coal production and mines by county, prices, productivity, miners, and reserves, by mining method and State, 1990-91, annual rpt, 3164–25

County Business Patterns, 1990: employment, establishments, and payroll, by SIC 2- to 4-digit industry and county, annual State rpt, 2326–6.18
Deaths and rates, by detailed location, cause, and demographic characteristics, 1989, US Vital Statistics annual rpt, 4144–3.1
Employment, earnings, and hours, by selected SIC 1- to 4-digit industry, State, and for 275 MSAs, 1987-92, 6748–81
Fed Govt spending in States and local areas, by type, State, county, and city, FY91, annual rpt, 2464–3
Fed Govt spending in States, by type, program, agency, and State, FY91, annual rpt, 2464–2
Financial and economic devs, Fed Reserve 10th District, quarterly rpt, 9381–16
HHS financial aid, by program, recipient, State, and city, FY91, annual regional listing, 4004–3.7
Hospital deaths of Medicare patients, actual and expected rates by diagnosis, and hospital characteristics, by instn, FY90 annual State rpt, 4654–14.17
Housing census, 1990: inventory, occupancy, and costs, State fact sheet, 2326–21.18
Housing census, 1990: summary unit characteristics, by householder race and age, county, place, and urban-rural location, State rpt, 2471–1.18
Land Mgmt Bur activities in southwestern US, FY91, annual rpt, 5724–15
Military prime contract awards, by contractor, service branch, State, and city, FY91, annual rpt, 3544–22
Mineral Industry Surveys, State reviews of production, 1991, preliminary annual rpt, 5614–6
Minerals (strategic) deposits in North Central States, characteristics, 1992 compilation of papers, 5668–127
Multinatl firms US affiliates finances and operations, by industry, country of parent firm, and State, 1987, 2708–48
Physicians, by specialty, age, sex, and location of training and practice, 1990, State rpt, 4116–6.17
Population and housing census, 1990: detailed geographic coverage, State CD-ROM, 2551–9.4
Population and housing census, 1990: summary characteristics, by county, subdiv, and place, State rpt, 2551–7.18
Population census, 1990: population characteristics and living arrangements, by county, place, and urban-rural location, State rpt, 2531–1.18
Statistical Abstract of US, 1992 annual data compilation, 2324–1
Water (groundwater) supply, quality, chemistry, and use, 1987, State rpt, 5666–28.21
Water quality, chemistry, hydrology, and other characteristics, 1990 local area study, 5666–27.26
Water use by end use, well withdrawals, and public supply deliveries, by county, 1987, State rpt, 5666–24.17
see also Kansas City, Kans.
see also Topeka, Kans.
see also Wichita, Kans.
see also under By State in the "Index by Categories"

Kansas City, Kans.
CPI by component for US city average, and by selected metro area, region, and population size, monthly rpt, 6762–2
Drug test results at arrest, by drug type, offense, and sex, for selected urban areas, quarterly rpt, 6062–3
Housing and households characteristics, and unit and neighborhood quality, by MSA location for 11 MSAs, 1986 survey, supplement, 2485–8
Housing starts and completions authorized by building permits in 40 MSAs, quarterly rpt, 2382–9
Housing vacancy rates for single and multifamily units and mobile homes, by city and ZIP code, 1992, annual MSA rpt, 9304–22.3
see also under By City and By SMSA or MSA in the "Index by Categories"

Kansas City, Mo.
CPI by component for US city average, and by selected metro area, region, and population size, monthly rpt, 6762–2
Drug test results at arrest, by drug type, offense, and sex, for selected urban areas, quarterly rpt, 6062–3
Housing and households characteristics, and unit and neighborhood quality, by MSA location for 11 MSAs, 1986 survey, supplement, 2485–8
Housing starts and completions authorized by building permits in 40 MSAs, quarterly rpt, 2382–9
Housing vacancy rates for single and multifamily units and mobile homes, by city and ZIP code, 1992, annual MSA rpt, 9304–22.3
see also under By City and By SMSA or MSA in the "Index by Categories"

Kappus, Karl K.
"Results of Testing for Intestinal Parasites by State Diagnostic Laboratories, U.S., 1987", 4202–7.306

Karsten, Richard A.
"Summary of Water Resources Activities of the USGS in Iowa, FY90", 5666–26.17

Karvounis, Paula
"Corporation Income Tax Returns, 1989", 8302–2.321

Kash, Kathryn M.
"Psychological Distress and Surveillance Behaviors of Women with a Family History of Breast Cancer", 4472–1.301

Kashyap, Anil K.
"Internal Net Worth and the Investment Process: An Application to U.S. Agriculture", 9375–13.77
"Production and Inventory Control at the General Motors Corporation During the 1920s and 1930s", 9375–13.87
"Sticky Prices: New Evidence from Retail Catalogs", 9375–13.76

Kask, Christopher
"Manufacturing Productivity and Labor Costs in 14 Economies", 6722–1.304

Kasman, Bruce
"Comparison of Monetary Policy Operating Procedures in Six Industrial Countries", 9385–1.308

Kato, Ikuko
"Vitamin Supplement Use and Its Correlates Among Elderly Japanese Men Residing on Oahu, HI", 4042–3.373

Kaufman, George G.
"Incentive Conflict in Deposit-Institution Regulation: Evidence from Australia", 9375–13.82

Kaufman, Phillip
"Characteristics of At-Risk Students in NELS:88. National Education Longitudinal Study of 1988", 4826–9.16
"Comparison of Vocational and Non-Vocational Public School Teachers of Grades 9 to 12. Schools and Staffing Survey", 4836–3.9
"Dropout Rates in the U.S.: 1991", 4834–23

Kautz, J. Edward
"Effects of Harvest on Feral Rock Dove Survival, Nest Success, and Population Size", 5506–12.4

Kavanagh, Barbara
"Asset-Backed Commercial Paper Programs", 9362–1.302

Kazakhstan
Agricultural production, prices, and trade, for former USSR republics, 1960s-91 and forecast 1992, annual rpt, 1524–4.1
Economic, social, political, and geographic summary data, by country, 1992, annual factbook, 9114–2
Embassies of US in former Soviet republics and Baltic States, positions planned by function, and filled, 1992, GAO rpt, 26123–403
Energy supply and use, and social, economic, and political indicators for former Soviet Republics and Baltic States, 1989-90, 3168–126
Energy use and production of former USSR Republics, by fuel type, 1990, annual rpt, 3164–84.2
Exports and imports of US with Communist and transitional economy countries, by detailed commodity and country, quarterly rpt with articles, 9882–2
Ferrosilicon from 6 countries, injury to US industry from foreign subsidized and less than fair value imports, investigation with background financial and operating data, 1992 rpt, 9886–19.84
Livestock and meat inventories, use, and imports, by former USSR republic, 1986-93, semiannual rpt, 1925–33.2
Population size and characteristics of former Soviet Republics and Baltic States, 1989-92, 9118–19
Uranium resources and production of CIS, by state, 1992 article, 3164–65

Keating, John W.
"Structural Approaches to Vector Autoregressions", 9391–1.316

Keck, Merle E.
"Relationship of Fixed and Vehicular Lighting to Accidents", 7558–118

Keeton, William R.
"Reconstruction Finance Corporation: Would It Work Today?", 9381–1.304

Kelsay, Laura E.
"Cartographic Records in the National Archives of the U.S. Relating to American Indians", 9516–1.4

Kemper, Brenda
"Significant Features of Fiscal Federalism, Volume 2, Revenues and Expenditures", 10044–1.2
"Significant Features of Fiscal Federalism, 1992 Edition. Volume 1. Budget Processes and Tax Systems", 10044–1.1

Kennedy, Eric
"Destination Japan: A Business Guide for the 90s", 2048–159

Kennedy, Lenna
"Children Receiving SSI Payments, December 1991", 4742–1.316

Kennewick, Wash.
Radiation exposure of population near Hanford, Wash, nuclear plant, with methodology, 1944-91, series, 3356–5

Kenney, Justin
"Monitor National Marine Sanctuary", 2152–8.304

Kennickell, Arthur B.
"Changes in Family Finances from 1983 to 1989: Evidence from the Survey of Consumer Finances", 9362–1.301
"Estimation of Household Net Worth Using Model-Based and Design-Based Weights: Evidence from the 1989 Survey of Consumer Finances", 9368–91

Kenny, Joan F.
"Reported Water Use in Kansas, 1987", 5666–24.17

Kenosha, Wis.
Housing vacancy rates for single and multifamily units and mobile homes, by city and ZIP code, 1991, annual MSA rpt, 9304–18.3

Kent County, Del.
Water use by end use, well withdrawals, and public supply deliveries, by county, 1983-86, State rpt, 5666–24.10

Kent, Joseph H.
"Influenza Surveillance—U.S., 1991-92", 4202–7.325

Kenton County, Ky.
Housing and households characteristics, and unit and neighborhood quality, by MSA location for 11 MSAs, 1986 survey, supplement, 2485–8

Kentucky
Appalachian Regional Commission funding, by project and State, planned FY92, annual rpt, 9084–3
Banks (insured commercial and savings) deposits by instn, State, MSA, and county, as of June 1991, annual regional rpt, 9295–3.3
Births of low birthweight to Medicaid patients, by prenatal care source and adequacy, and other risk factors, for 2 States, late 1980s, article, 4042–3.304
Coal production and mines by county, prices, productivity, miners, and reserves, by mining method and State, 1990-91, annual rpt, 3164–25
County Business Patterns, 1990: employment, establishments, and payroll, by SIC 2- to 4-digit industry and county, annual State rpt, 2326–6.19
Deaths and rates, by detailed location, cause, and demographic characteristics, 1989, US Vital Statistics annual rpt, 4144–3.1
Economic and banking conditions, for Fed Reserve 8th District, quarterly rpt with articles, 9391–16
Economic indicators and components, and Fed Reserve 4th District business and financial conditions, monthly chartbook, 9377–10
Employment by industry div, earnings, and hours, for 8 southeastern States, quarterly press release, 6942–7
Employment, earnings, and hours, by selected SIC 1- to 4-digit industry, State, and for 275 MSAs, 1987-92, 6748–81
Fed Govt spending in States and local areas, by type, State, county, and city, FY91, annual rpt, 2464–3
Fed Govt spending in States, by type, program, agency, and State, FY91, annual rpt, 2464–2
HHS financial aid, by program, recipient, State, and city, FY91, annual regional listing, 4004–3.4
Hospital deaths of Medicare patients, actual and expected rates by diagnosis, and hospital characteristics, by instn, FY90 annual State rpt, 4654–14.18
Housing census, 1990: summary unit characteristics, by householder race and age, county, place, and urban-rural location, State rpt, 2471–1.19
Medicaid impacts on State budgets, and program financing, cost control measures, enrollment, and services coverage, by selected State, 1960s-80s and projected to 1997, 10176–3.6
Military prime contract awards, by contractor, service branch, State, and city, FY91, annual rpt, 3544–22
Mineral Industry Surveys, State reviews of production, 1991, preliminary annual rpt, 5614–6
Multinatl firms US affiliates finances and operations, by industry, country of parent firm, and State, 1987, 2708–48
Physicians, by specialty, age, sex, and location of training and practice, 1990, State rpt, 4116–6.18
Population and housing census, 1990: detailed geographic coverage, State CD-ROM, 2551–9.6
Population and housing census, 1990: population and housing characteristics, detailed geographic coverage, State CD-ROM, 2551–10.24
Population and housing census, 1990: summary characteristics, by county, subdiv, and place, State rpt, 2551–7.19
Population census, 1990: population characteristics and living arrangements, by county, place, and urban-rural location, State rpt, 2531–1.19
Statistical Abstract of US, 1992 annual data compilation, 2324–1
Textile mill employment, earnings, and hours, for 8 Southeastern States, quarterly press release, 6942–1
Timber and pulpwood production, by product, 1986, State rpt, 1206–15.12
see also Hopkinsville, Ky.
see also Kenton County, Ky.
see also Louisville, Ky.
see also Paducah, Ky.
see also under By State in the "Index by Categories"

Kenya
Agricultural trade of US, by detailed commodity and country, 1991, annual rpt, 1524–8
Agricultural trade of US, by detailed commodity and country, 1991, semiannual rpt, 1522–4
AID economic aid to developing countries, obligations and disbursements by country, quarterly rpt, 9912–4
AID loans repayment status and terms by program and country, and status of predecessor agency loans, quarterly rpt, 9912–3
Economic and military aid and loans from US and intl agencies, by program and country, FY46-91, annual rpt, 9914–5
Economic and social conditions of developing countries from 1960s, and Intl Dev Cooperation Agency and AID activities and funding, FY91-93, annual rpt, 9904–4
Economic conditions, income, production, prices, employment, and trade, 1991 periodic country rpt, 2046–4.10
Economic conditions, investment and export opportunities, and trade practices, 1992 country market research rpt, 2046–6.7
Economic conditions, policy, and trade practices, by country, 1989-91, annual rpt, 21384–5
Economic, social, political, and geographic summary data, by country, 1992, annual factbook, 9114–2
Exports and imports of US, by commodity and country, 1980-90, world area rpt, 9116–1.2
Exports and imports of US, by transport mode, country, and SITC 1- to 3-digit commodity, 1991, annual rpt, 2424–12
Exports of US, detailed Schedule B commodities with countries of destination, 1991, annual rpt, 2424–10
Food supply, needs, and aid for developing countries, status and alternative forecasts, 1992 world area rpt, 1526–8.2
Human rights conditions in 170 countries, and US economic and military aid, 1991, annual rpt, 21384–3
Military aid of US, arms sales, and training programs costs and budget requests, by program, world region, and country, FY91-93, annual rpt, 7144–13
Military spending, arms trade, and force strengths, with govt spending and population, by country, 1979-89, annual rpt, 9824–1
Minerals Yearbook, Vol 3, 1989: foreign country review of production, trade, and policy, by commodity, annual rpt, 5604–35.1
Population size, growth rates, and components of change, by country, projected 1990-2020 and trends from 1950, biennial rpt, 2324–9
Population size, life expectancy, and fertility, trends and projections, 1992 country rpt, 2326–24.1
Refugee migration, and intl aid programs, by world area and country of origin and asylum, 1991, annual rpt, 7004–15
Steel trade, by product, country, and customs district, with US industry operating data, 1989-June 1992, semiannual rpt, 9882–15
UN voting record and share of votes in agreement with US, by issue, country, and world area, 1991, annual rpt, 7004–18

Keough, Kristin
"Current Funds Revenues and Expenditures of Institutions of Higher Education: FY82-90", 4844–6

Kern County, Calif.
Water (groundwater) supply, quality, chemistry, and use, 1920s-89 and projected to 2015, local area rpt, 5666–28.15
Kerns, Wilmer L.
"Private Social Welfare Expenditures, 1972-90", 4742–1.323
Kerosene
Business statistics, detailed data for major industries and economic indicators, 1960-91, *Survey of Current Business* biennial supplement, 2704–1
Consumption of energy, by detailed fuel type, end-use sector, and State, 1960-90, State Energy Data System annual rpt, 3164–39
Exports and imports of US, by country and detailed commodity, monthly rpt, 2422–12
Foreign and US energy production, trade, use, and reserves, and oil and refined products supply and prices, by country, 1981-90, annual rpt, 3164–50
Freight (waterborne domestic and foreign) by commodity, traffic, and passengers, by port and waterway, 1989, annual rpt, 3754–3
Housing (low income) energy aid, funding sources, costs, and participation, by State, FY90, annual rpt, 4584–1
Housing (rental) units, total, with HUD assistance by program, and eligible for aid, by unit, household, and neighborhood characteristics, and location, 1989, biennial rpt, 5184–11
Housing and households detailed characteristics, and unit and neighborhood quality, MSA surveys, series, 2485–6
Housing energy prices, by fuel type and State, 1990 and forecast 1991-92, 3166–6.61
Housing energy use, costs, and conservation, and household and housing characteristics, survey rpt series, 3166–7
Injuries from use of consumer products, by severity, victim age, and detailed product, 1991, annual rpt, 9164–6
Pacific basin countries energy supply and demand, and implications for US trade, country rpt series, 3406–6
Price indexes (producer), by stage of processing and detailed commodity, monthly rpt, 6762–6
Price indexes (producer), by stage of processing and detailed commodity, monthly 1991, annual rpt, 6764–2
Prices and spending for fuel, by type, end-use sector, and State, 1990, annual rpt, 3164–64
Prices and volume of oil products sold and purchased by refiners, processors, and distributors, by product, end-use sector, PAD district, and State, monthly rpt, 3162–11; 3164–85
Sales and deliveries of fuel oil and kerosene, by end-use, PAD district, and State, 1990, annual rpt, 3164–94
Supply, demand, and movement of crude oil, gas liquids, and refined products, by PAD district and State, 1991, annual rpt, 3164–2
Supply, demand, and prices, by fuel type and end-use sector, alternative projections by region, 1990-2010, annual rpt, 3164–96
Supply, demand, and prices, by fuel type and end-use sector, alternative projections 1990-2010, annual rpt, 3164–75
Supply, demand, and prices, by fuel type and end-use sector, with foreign comparisons, 1991 and trends from 1949, annual rpt, 3164–74.1
Supply, demand, trade, stocks, and refining of oil and gas liquids, by detailed product, State, and PAD district, monthly rpt with articles, 3162–6
Kidnapping
Aircraft hijackings, on-board explosions, and other crimes, US and foreign incidents, 1986-90, annual rpt, 7504–31
Child abductions, runaways, and missing and exploited children, and Office of Juvenile Justice and Delinquency Prevention activities, FY90, annual rpt, 6064–36
Court civil and criminal caseloads for Federal district, appeals, and bankruptcy courts, by type of suit and offense, circuit, and district, 1991, annual rpt, 18204–11
Court civil and criminal caseloads for Federal district, appeals, and special courts, 1991, annual rpt, 18204–8
Court criminal case processing in Federal courts by disposition, and prisoners, by offense and jurisdiction, data compilation, 1992 annual rpt, 6064–6.5; 6064–6.6
Court criminal case processing in Federal district courts, and dispositions, by offense, district, and offender characteristics, 1989, annual data compilation, 6064–29
Court criminal case processing in Federal district courts, and dispositions, by offense, 1980-91, annual rpt, 6064–31
Prison and parole admissions and releases, sentence length, and time served, by offense and offender characteristics, 1988, annual rpt, 6064–33
Prisoners in Federal and contract instns, by selected characteristics, region, and Federal instn, FY89, annual rpt, 6244–1.1
Sentences for Federal crimes, guidelines use and results by offense and district, and Sentencing Commission activities, 1991, annual rpt, 17664–1
Sentences for Federal offenses, guidelines by offense and circumstances, series, 17668–1
Terrorism (intl) incidents, casualties, and attacks on US targets, by attack type and country, 1991, annual rpt, 7004–22
Terrorism (intl) incidents, casualties, and attacks on US targets, by attack type and world area, 1991, annual rpt, 7004–13
US attorneys civil and criminal cases by type and disposition, and collections, by Federal district, FY91, annual rpt, 6004–2.1
Wiretaps authorized, costs, arrests, trials, and convictions, by offense and jurisdiction, 1991, annual rpt, 18204–7
Women in jail, by criminal background and sociodemographic characteristics, with comparisons to men, 1989, 6066–19.66
see also Hostages
Kidney diseases
see Urogenital diseases
Kieffer, Edith
"Area-Level Predictors of Use of Prenatal Care in Diverse Populations", 4042–3.366
Kilkenny, Maureen
"Nonfarm Prospects Under Agricultural Liberalization", 1502–3.301
Killeen, Tex.
see also under By City and By SMSA or MSA in the "Index by Categories"
Kim, C. S.
"Changing Structure of the U.S. Flour Milling Industry", 1502–3.301
Kim, Dongcheol
"Margin Requirements, Price Fluctuations, and Market Participation in Metal and Stock Index Futures", 9385–8.127
Kim, Sun B.
"Use of Equity Positions by Banks: The Japanese Evidence", 9393–8.302
Kindergarten
see Preschool education
King County, Wash.
Housing and households characteristics, and unit and neighborhood quality, by MSA location for 11 MSAs, 1987 survey, supplement, 2485–8
King, Mary C.
"Occupational Segregation by Race and Sex, 1940-88", 6722–1.321
Kingston, N.Y
Wages by occupation, for office and plant workers, 1992 survey, periodic MSA rpt, 6785–3.4
Kiribati
Economic, social, political, and geographic summary data, by country, 1992, annual factbook, 9114–2
Exports and imports of US, by transport mode, country, and SITC 1- to 3-digit commodity, 1991, annual rpt, 2424–12
Exports of US, detailed Schedule B commodities with countries of destination, 1991, annual rpt, 2424–10
Human rights conditions in 170 countries, and US economic and military aid, 1991, annual rpt, 21384–3
Population size, growth rates, and components of change, by country, projected 1990-2020 and trends from 1950, biennial rpt, 2324–9
Kisker, Ellen E.
"Profile of Child Care Settings: Early Education and Care in 1990", 4808–39
Kitchen utensils and appliances
see Household appliances and equipment
see Household supplies and utensils
Kitzmiller, John
"Television Receivers and Video Monitors, Industry and Trade Summary", 9885–12.1
Kiwifruit
see Fruit and fruit products
Klaas, Erwin E.
"Dabbling Duck Recruitment in Relation to Habitat and Predators at Union Slough National Wildlife Refuge, Iowa", 5506–12.5
Klatsky, Arthur L.
"Alcohol and Coronary Artery Disease", 4482–1.301
Klein, Michael W.
"Real Exchange Rate and Foreign Direct Investment in the U.S.: Relative Wealth vs. Relative Wage Effects", 9373–27.10

Klein, Terry M.
"Alcohol Involvement in Fatal Traffic Crashes, 1990", 7764–16

Klerman, Jacob A.
"Random-Effects Approach to Attrition Bias in the SIPP Health Insurance Data", 2626–10.147

Kliesen, Kevin L.
"Agriculture in 1991: The Decline Continues", 9391–16.308
"District Agricultural Banks Ride High in the Saddle", 9391–16.306
"Emerging Importance of Aquaculture", 9391–16.301
"Recent Credit Crunch: The Neglected Dimensions", 9391–1.315

Klitgaard, Thomas
"U.S. Imports in the 1980s: Some Insights from a Disaggregate Analysis", 9385–8.138

Kneller, Robert W.
"Cigarette Smoking and Other Risk Factors for Progression of Precancerous Stomach Lesions", 4472–1.334

Knight, Richard R.
"Yellowstone Grizzly Bear Investigations, Annual Report of the Interagency Study Team, 1991", 5544–4

Knoxville, Tenn.
Wages by occupation, and benefits for office and plant workers, 1992 survey, periodic MSA rpt, 6785–3.4
see also under By City and By SMSA or MSA in the "Index by Categories"

Knudson, Mary
"Intellectual Property Rights and the Private Seed Industry", 1548–388

Koch, Hugo
"Office Visits Involving X-rays, National Ambulatory Medical Care Survey: U.S., 1977", 4147–16.6
"1978 Summary: National Ambulatory Medical Care Survey", 4147–16.6

Kocher, Susie
"Inventory of Parks and Recreation Facilities on the Coast of Washington and Oregon", 5738–40.3

Kochhar, Satya
"Denial of SSI Applications Because of Excess Resources", 4742–1.317

Kodrzycki, Yolanda K.
"What Past Recoveries Say About the Outlook for New England", 9373–1.315

Koenig, Evan F.
"Do Interest Rates Help Predict Inflation?", 9379–1.306
"Forecasting Turning Points: Is a Two-State Characterization of the Business Cycle Appropriate?", 9379–12.95
"Nominal Feedback Rules for Monetary Policy: Some Comments", 9379–12.92

Koenig, Steven R.
"Farmer Mac: Can It Help Indebted Farm Operators?", 1541–1.304
"Profile of Participants in FmHA's Guaranteed Farm Loan Programs", 1548–386

Kokoski, Mary F.
"Price of Giving: Taxes, Education, and Econometric Issues", 6886–6.83

Kollias, Sotirios
"Structure and Regulation of Insurance Markets in Europe", 9373–3.35

Kominski, Robert
"Educational Attainment in the U.S.: March 1991 and 1990", 2546–1.460
"School Enrollment—Social and Economic Characteristics of Students: October 1990", 2546–1.459

Komisar, Harriet L.
"Rural Hospitals and Medicare's Prospective Payment System", 26306–6.164

Koonin, Lisa M.
"Abortion Surveillance—U.S., 1989", 4202–7.324

Kopcke, Richard W.
"Capitalization and Portfolio Risk of Insurance Companies", 9373–1.314; 9373–27.3
"Economic Rents, the Demand for Capital, and Financial Structure", 9373–27.8
"Insurance Companies as Financial Intermediaries: Risk and Return", 9373–3.35
"Profits and Stock Prices: The Importance of Being Earnest", 9373–1.306
"Tobin's q, Economic Rents, and the Optimal Stock of Capital", 9373–27.11

Kopka, Teresita L.
"Characteristics of Doctorate Recipients: 1979, 1984, and 1989", 4848–44

Korb, Roslyn
"Postsecondary Education Facilities Inventory and Classification Manual", 4848–48
"Postsecondary Student Outcomes: A Feasibility Study", 4848–45

Korda, Holly
"Medicaid Payment Methodologies for Inpatient Hospital Services", 17206–2.35

Korea, North
Agricultural trade of US, by detailed commodity and country, 1991, annual rpt, 1524–8
Agricultural trade of US, by detailed commodity and country, 1991, semiannual rpt, 1522–4
Economic and social conditions of developing countries from 1960s, and Intl Dev Cooperation Agency and AID activities and funding, FY91-93, annual rpt, 9904–4
Economic, social, political, and geographic summary data, by country, 1992, annual factbook, 9114–2
Export licensing, monitoring, and enforcement activities, FY91, annual rpt, 2024–1
Exports and imports of US, by transport mode, country, and SITC 1- to 3-digit commodity, 1991, annual rpt, 2424–12
Exports and imports of US with Communist and transitional economy countries, by detailed commodity and country, quarterly rpt with articles, 9882–2
Human rights conditions in 170 countries, and US economic and military aid, 1991, annual rpt, 21384–3
Military spending, arms trade, and force strengths, with govt spending and population, by country, 1979-89, annual rpt, 9824–1
Minerals Yearbook, Vol 3, 1989: foreign country review of production, trade, and policy, by commodity, annual rpt, 5604–35.2
Population size, growth rates, and components of change, by country, projected 1990-2020 and trends from 1950, biennial rpt, 2324–9

Korea, South
Agricultural production, prices, and trade, by country, 1980s and forecast 1992, annual world region rpt, 1524–4.3
Agricultural trade by commodity and country, prices, and world market devs, monthly rpt, 1922–12
Agricultural trade of US, by detailed commodity and country, 1991, annual rpt, 1524–8
Agricultural trade of US, by detailed commodity and country, 1991, semiannual rpt, 1522–4
AID loans repayment status and terms by program and country, and status of predecessor agency loans, quarterly rpt, 9912–3
Computer memory components from South Korea at less than fair value, injury to US industry, investigation with background financial and operating data, 1992 rpt, 9886–14.348
Debt burden indicators for 8 developing countries, alternative projections 1991-2000 and trends from 1974, technical paper, 9366–7.271
Economic and military aid and loans from US and intl agencies, by program and country, FY46-91, annual rpt, 9914–5
Economic and monetary trends, compounded annual rates of change and annual indicators for US and 15 trading partners, quarterly rpt, annual supplement, 9391–7
Economic and social conditions of developing countries from 1960s, and Intl Dev Cooperation Agency and AID activities and funding, FY91-93, annual rpt, 9904–4
Economic conditions, and oil supply and demand, for major industrial countries, monthly rpt, 9112–1
Economic conditions, policy, and trade practices, by country, 1989-91, annual rpt, 21384–5
Economic, social, political, and geographic summary data, by country, 1992, annual factbook, 9114–2
Export and import balances of US, and dollar exchange rates, with 5 Asian countries, 1992 semiannual rpt, 8002–14
Exports and imports of US, by commodity and country, 1980-90, world area rpt, 9116–1.3
Exports and imports of US by country, and trade shifts by commodity, 1991, annual rpt, 9884–25
Exports and imports of US, by Harmonized System 6-digit commodity and country, 1991, annual rpt, 2424–13
Exports and imports of US, by selected country, country group, and commodity group, 1991, annual rpt, 2044–37
Exports and imports of US, by transport mode, country, and SITC 1- to 3-digit commodity, 1991, annual rpt, 2424–12
Exports and imports, trade agreements and relations, and USITC investigations, 1991, annual rpt, 9884–5
Exports, imports, and balances of US for manufactured goods, by SITC 2-digit commodity and country, quarterly rpt, 2042–35
Exports, imports, and balances of US with major trading partners, by product category, 1987-91, annual chartbook, 9884–21

Exports of US, detailed Schedule B commodities with countries of destination, 1991, annual rpt, 2424–10
Human rights conditions in 170 countries, and US economic and military aid, 1991, annual rpt, 21384–3
Imports of goods, services, and investment from US, trade barriers, impacts, and US actions, by country, 1991, annual rpt, 444–2
Imports of US given duty-free treatment for value of US material sent abroad, by commodity and country, 1987-90, annual rpt, 9884–14
Manufacturing industry (US) intl competitiveness, trade and economic policies with background data and foreign comparisons, 1991 rpt, 26358–252
Military aid of US, arms sales, and training programs costs and budget requests, by program, world region, and country, FY91-93, annual rpt, 7144–13
Military spending and indicators of ability to support common defense, for NATO members, Japan, and South Korea, 1970s-90, annual rpt, 3544–28
Military spending, arms trade, and force strengths, with govt spending and population, by country, 1979-89, annual rpt, 9824–1
Minerals Yearbook, Vol 3, 1989: foreign country review of production, trade, and policy, by commodity, annual rpt, 5604–35.2
Multinatl US firms and foreign affiliates finances and operations, by industry and country, 1989 benchmark survey, annual rpt, 2704–5
Multinatl US firms foreign affiliates, income statement items by asset size, industry, and country, 1988, biennial article, 8302–2.322
Mushroom (canned) trade, supply, and demand, for selected countries, 1980s-92, article, 1925–34.333
Nuclear power generation in US and 20 countries, monthly rpt, 3162–24.10
Nuclear power generation in US and 20 countries, monthly 1973-88, 3168–123.10
Persian Gulf War allied countries cash and in-kind contributions, by type and country, and status of DOD accounts, as of Sept 1991, annual GAO rpt, 26104–24
Pipe fittings (stainless steel) from 2 countries at less than fair value, injury to US industry, investigation with background financial and operating data, 1992 rpt, 9886–14.354
Pipes (welded stainless steel) from South Korea and Taiwan at less than fair value, injury to US industry, investigation with background financial and operating data, 1992 rpt, 9886–14.338; 9886–14.365
Pipes and tubes (welded nonalloy steel) from 6 countries at less than fair value, injury to US industry, investigation with background financial and operating data, 1992 rpt, 9886–14.361
Pollution (air) contributing to global warming, emissions by monitoring site and country, and temperature change by world area and US region, 1860s-1990, annual rpt, 3004–33
Population size, growth rates, and components of change, by country, projected 1990-2020 and trends from 1950, biennial rpt, 2324–9
Refugee migration, and intl aid programs, by world area and country of origin and asylum, 1991, annual rpt, 7004–15
Ships in world merchant fleet, tonnage, and new ship construction and deliveries, by vessel type and country, as of Jan 1992, annual rpt, 7704–3
Spacecraft and satellite launches since 1957, quarterly listing, 9502–2
Steel (carbon flat-rolled) products from 21 countries, injury to US industry from foreign subsidized and less than fair value imports, investigation with background financial and operating data, 1992 rpt, 9886–19.85
Steel imports of US under voluntary restraint agreement, by product, customs district, and country, with US industry operating data, quarterly rpt, 9882–13
Steel trade, by product, country, and customs district, with US industry operating data, 1989-June 1992, semiannual rpt, 9882–15
Steel wire rope from South Korea and Mexico at less than fair value, injury to US industry, investigation with background financial and operating data, 1992 rpt, 9886–14.346
Sweaters from 3 countries at less than fair value, injury to US industry, investigation supplement, 1992 rpt, 9886–14.363
Tax (income) returns of Foreign Sales Corps, assets, and income and tax items, by industry, country of incorporation, and transaction pricing method, 1987, article, 8302–2.311
Timber in northwestern US and British Columbia, production, prices, trade, and employment, quarterly rpt, 1202–3
Travel to US and Canada, market analysis with detailed trip and traveler characteristics, 1990-91, country rpt, 2906–2.18
Travel to US and Canada, market analysis with trip and traveler characteristics, 1990-91, country rpt, 2906–2.16
see also under By Foreign Country in the "Index by Categories"

Korobow, Leon
"Financial Leverage Versus Return on Book Equity at Bank Holding Companies in 1988, 1986, 1980", 9385–8.134
"Using Cluster Analysis as a Tool for Economic and Financial Analysis", 9385–8.128

Kost, Kathryn
"Health Risks and Benefits of Contraceptive Use in the U.S.", 4164–2

Kotlikoff, Laurence J.
"Estimating a Firm's Age-Productivity Profile Using the Present Value of Workers' Earnings", 9377–9.128

Kottman, Stacy E.
"Regional Employment by Industry: Do Returns to Capital Matter?", 9371–1.306

Kovar, Mary G.
"Longitudinal Study of Aging: 1984-90. Vital and Health Statistics Series 1", 4147–1.28

Kowalczyk, George I.
"Physician Customary Charges and Medicare Payment Experience: Study Findings", 4652–1.307

Kowalik, Zygmunt
"Numerical Modeling of Storm Surges in Norton Sound", 2176–1.40
"Numerical Modeling of Storm Surges in the Beaufort and Chukchi Seas", 2176–1.40

Kozak, Lola J.
"Estimates from Two Survey Designs: National Hospital Discharge Survey. Vital and Health Statistics Series 13", 4147–13.110

Kozo, Thomas L.
"Superstructure Icing and Wave Hindcast Statistics in the Navarin and St. George Basin Areas", 2176–1.40
"Yukon Delta Oceanography and Meteorology", 2176–1.40

Kraenzle, Charles A.
"Co-ops' Share of Farm Marketings, Production Supplies at 27 Percent", 1122–1.302

Krasner, Melvin
"Trends in Health and Health Care Among Blacks and Hispanics in New York City During the 1980s", 4164–2

Kraus, Lewis E.
"Chartbook on Work Disability in the U.S.", 4948–11

Krause, Kenneth R.
"Beef Cow-Calf Industry, 1964-87; Location and Size", 1568–251
"Nation's Changing Beef Cow Herd", 1561–7.301

Kraushaar, Jonathan M.
"Fiber Deployment Update, End of Year 1991", 9284–18

Kretzmer, Peter E.
"How Important Are Monetary and Fiscal Policy in Explaining Postwar Aggregate U.S. Data? A Vector Autoregressive Approach", 9381–10.132

Krisberg, Barry
"Juveniles Taken into Custody: FY90 Report", 6064–35
"National Juvenile Custody Trends, 1978-89", 6068–250

Kroe, Elaine
"Basic Student Charges at Postsecondary Institutions: Academic Year 1991-92. Tuition and Required Fees and Room and Board Charges at 4-year, 2-Year, and Public Less-than-2-Year Institutions", 4844–10
"1991-92 Directory of Postsecondary Institutions", 4844–3

Kruger, Linda E.
"Assessment of Non-Economic Impacts to Coastal Recreation and Tourism Resultant from Oil and Gas Development: A Review of Selected Literature and Example Methodology", 5738–40.1

Ku, Leighton
"Patterns of HIV Risk and Preventive Behaviors Among Teenage Men", 4042–3.313

Kulwicki, Anahid
"Cigarette Use Among Arab Americans in the Detroit Metropolitan Area", 4042–3.360

Kumar, Vikram
"Exchange Rate Variability and International Trade", 9371–1.304
"Note on Forward Biases and Equilibrium Foreign Exchange Hedging in a Production Economy", 9371–10.85
"Real Effects of Exchange Risk on International Trade", 9371–10.81

Kunkel, Jeffrey L.
"Average Wages for 1985-90 for Indexing Under the Social Security Act", 4706–2.133

Kushi, Lawrence H.
"Dietary Fat and Postmenopausal Breast Cancer", 4472–1.328

Kutscher, Ronald E.
"New BLS Projections: Findings and Implications", 6744–19

Kuttner, Kenneth N.
"Estimating Monthly Regional Value Added by Combining Regional Input with National Production Data", 9375–13.85
"Why Does the Paper-Bill Spread Predict Real Economic Activity?", 9375–13.67

Kuwait
Agricultural trade of US, by detailed commodity and country, 1991, annual rpt, 1524–8
Agricultural trade of US, by detailed commodity and country, 1991, semiannual rpt, 1522–4
Apple imports of 5 Persian Gulf countries, by country of origin, 1981-90, article, 1925–34.322
Boycotts (intl) by OPEC and other countries, US firms and individuals cooperation and tax benefits denied, 1990, article, 8302–2.323
Economic and military aid and loans from US and intl agencies, by program and country, FY46-91, annual rpt, 9914–5
Economic and social conditions of developing countries from 1960s, and Intl Dev Cooperation Agency and AID activities and funding, FY91-93, annual rpt, 9904–4
Economic conditions, policy, and trade practices, by country, 1989-91, annual rpt, 21384–5
Economic, social, political, and geographic summary data, by country, 1992, annual factbook, 9114–2
Exports and imports of US, by commodity and country, 1980-90, world area rpt, 9116–1.6
Exports and imports of US, by Harmonized System 6-digit commodity and country, 1991, annual rpt, 2424–13
Exports and imports of US, by transport mode, country, and SITC 1- to 3-digit commodity, 1991, annual rpt, 2424–12
Exports, imports, and balances of US for manufactured goods, by SITC 2-digit commodity and country, quarterly rpt, 2042–35
Exports of US, detailed Schedule B commodities with countries of destination, 1991, annual rpt, 2424–10
Human rights conditions in 170 countries, and US economic and military aid, 1991, annual rpt, 21384–3
Iraq invasion of Kuwait, oil production disruption impacts on futures prices, family budgets, and oil firms, 1990 hearings, 25408–116
Labor conditions, union coverage, and work accidents, 1992 annual country rpt, 6366–4.37
Military spending, arms trade, and force strengths, with govt spending and population, by country, 1979-89, annual rpt, 9824–1
Minerals Yearbook, Vol 3, 1989: foreign country review of production, trade, and policy, by commodity, annual rpt, 5604–35.3
Oil fires set by Iraq, pollution levels, disease cases, and US remediation and monitoring spending, 1991 rpt, 9188–117
Oil fires set in Kuwait by Iraqi forces, air pollution levels by substance and site, as of Mar 1991, 9188–116
Oil fires set in Kuwait by Iraqi forces, air pollution levels, health effects, intl monitoring activities, and wells affected, 1991, GAO rpt, 26113–566
Oil production and exports to US, by major exporting country, detailed data, monthly rpt with articles, 3162–24
Oil production and exports to US, by major exporting country, detailed data, monthly 1973-88, 3168–123
Oil production, stocks, use, and trade, by selected country and country group, monthly rpt, 3162–42
Persian Gulf War allied countries cash and in-kind contributions, by type and country, and status of DOD accounts, as of Sept 1991, annual GAO rpt, 26104–24
Population size, growth rates, and components of change, by country, projected 1990-2020 and trends from 1950, biennial rpt, 2324–9
Refugee migration, and intl aid programs, by world area and country of origin and asylum, 1991, annual rpt, 7004–15
UN voting record and share of votes in agreement with US, by issue, country, and world area, 1991, annual rpt, 7004–18
see also under By Foreign Country in the "Index by Categories"

Kvitek, Rikk G.
"Shallow Subtidal Survey of the Washington Outer Coast and Olympic National Park To Determine the Distribution, Fate, and Effects of Spilled Bunker C Fuel Oil", 5738–38.3

Kydland, Finn E.
"Gold Standard as a Rule", 9377–9.136
"On the Econometrics of World Business Cycles", 9377–9.124

Kyrgyzstan
Agricultural production, prices, and trade, for former USSR republics, 1960s-91 and forecast 1992, annual rpt, 1524–4.1
Economic, social, political, and geographic summary data, by country, 1992, annual factbook, 9114–2
Embassies of US in former Soviet republics and Baltic States, positions planned by function, and filled, 1992, GAO rpt, 26123–403
Energy supply and use, and social, economic, and political indicators for former Soviet Republics and Baltic States, 1989-90, 3168–126
Energy use and production of former USSR Republics, by fuel type, 1990, annual rpt, 3164–84.2
Exports and imports of US with Communist and transitional economy countries, by detailed commodity and country, quarterly rpt with articles, 9882–2
Livestock and meat inventories, use, and imports, by former USSR republic, 1986-93, semiannual rpt, 1925–33.2
Population size and characteristics of former Soviet Republics and Baltic States, 1989-92, 9118–19

Labeling
Exports of goods, services, and investment, trade barriers, impacts, and US actions, by country, 1991, annual rpt,, 444–2
Hazardous substances occupational exposure, employer compliance with info and training regulations, inspections, and fines, by firm size and industry div, 1989-91, GAO rpt, 26121–439
Imports detained by FDA, by reason, product, shipper, brand, and country, monthly listing, 4062–2
Public opinion on taxes, spending, and govt efficiency, by respondent characteristics, 1992 survey, annual rpt, 10044–2
Textile products trade regulations of foreign countries, and US exports, by commodity and country, 1989-91, biennial rpt, 2044–18
see also Generic products
see also Trademarks

Labelle, Roberta
"Financial Incentives and Medical Practice: Evidence from Ontario on the Effect of Changes in Physician Fees on Medical Care Utilization", 17266–2.3

Labor
see terms listed under Employment and unemployment, general; Labor supply and demand; and Occupations

Labor Agreement Information Retrieval System
Collective bargaining agreements of Federal employees, coverage, unions, and location, by agency, for contracts expiring 1992, semiannual listing, 9847–1

Labor costs and cost indexes
BLS data collection, analysis, and presentation methods, by program, 1992 rpt, 6888–1
Business statistics, detailed data for major industries and economic indicators, *Survey of Current Business*, monthly rpt, 2702–1
Business statistics, detailed data for major industries and economic indicators, 1960-91, *Survey of Current Business* biennial supplement, 2704–1
Costs and productivity of labor for private, nonfarm business, and manufacturing sectors, revised data, quarterly rpt, 6822–2
Costs and productivity of labor, indexes, preliminary data, quarterly rpt, 6822–1
Economic indicators compounded annual rates of change, monthly rpt, 9391–3
Economic indicators, prices, labor costs, and productivity, BLS econometric analyses and methodology, working paper series, 6886–6
Employer Cost Index by region, quarterly press release, 6942–8
Employment and Earnings, detailed data, monthly rpt, 6742–2.7

Employment Cost Index and alternative measure of compensation costs, by component, occupation, industry group, union status, and location, 1975-92, annual rpt, 6744–20
Employment Cost Index and percent change by occupational group, industry div, region, and metro-nonmetro area, quarterly press release, 6782–5
Employment Cost Index changes for nonfarm workers, by occupation, industry div, region, and bargaining status, monthly rpt, 6782–1
Employment Cost Index, current data and annual trends, monthly rpt, 23842–1.2
Employment, earnings, and hours, by SIC 1- to 4-digit industry, monthly 1989-Feb 1992, annual rpt, 6744–4
Employment, earnings, and hours, monthly press release, 6742–5
Employment, earnings, hours, and productivity, by industry div, selected years 1946-91, annual rpt, 204–1.2
Fed Govt labor productivity, indexes of output and labor costs by function, FY67-90, annual rpt, 6824–4
Food marketing cost indexes, by expense category, monthly rpt with articles, 1502–4
Foreign and US industrial output, compensation, unit labor costs, and indexes, Monthly Labor Review, 6722–1.6
Foreign and US manufacturing hourly compensation costs, by industry and country, series, 6826–3
Foreign and US manufacturing labor costs and indexes, by selected country, 1991, semiannual rpt, 6822–3
Foreign and US manufacturing labor productivity and costs, by selected country, 1950s-91, press release, 6726–1.55
Foreign and US manufacturing labor productivity and unit costs, for 14 countries, 1960s-90, article, 6722–1.304
Foreign direct investment in US, relation to exchange rate and relative labor costs and wealth indicators, for 7 countries, 1980s, working paper, 9373–27.10
Health Care Financing Review, provider prices, price inputs and indexes, and labor, quarterly journal, 4652–1.1
Health condition and care indicators, 1950s-90 with health improvement and disease prevention goals for 1990, annual data compilation, 4144–11
Hospital financial performance under Medicare, 1977-89, article, 4652–1.315
Hospital reimbursement by Medicare under prospective payment system, analyses of alternative payment plans, series, 17206–1
Hospital reimbursement by Medicare under prospective payment system, and effect on services, finances, and beneficiary payments, 1980-91, annual rpt, 17204–2
Hospital wage index, effect of occupation mix adjustment, by California labor market area, 1988, 17206–2.31
Hourly costs, by component, industry and occupational group, worker class, and firm size, monthly rpt, annual tables, 6782–1.2
Hourly costs, by component, occupational group, industry div, union coverage, region, 1992, annual rpt, 6744–21
Metals industries economic performance indicators and indexes, by commodity, monthly rpt, 5602–5
Monthly Labor Review, output, compensation, unit labor costs, and indexes, 6722–1.1; 6722–1.3; 6722–1.5
Statistical Abstract of US, 1992 annual data compilation, 2324–1.13
Tennessee Valley economic conditions, and compared to US, alternative projections 1992-2010 and trends from 1929, annual rpt, 9804–27
see also Employee benefits
see also Payroll
see also Social security tax
see also Unemployment insurance tax
see also Workers compensation

Labor Department
see Department of Labor

Labor force
see Employment and unemployment, general
see Employment and unemployment, local and regional
see Employment and unemployment, specific industry
see Foreign labor conditions
see Labor supply and demand

Labor law
Alien workers discrimination and other employment-related problems in NYC, hotline calls, 1988, 6366–6.7
Alien workers legalization and employer sanctions reform provisions, wage impacts, model results, 1987-89, working paper, 6366–6.8
Alien workers legalization applications and other Immigration Reform and Control Act provisions impacts on Los Angeles wages and working conditions, 1980s-91, working paper, 6366–6.9
Black lung benefits and claims by State, trust fund receipts by source, and disbursements, 1991, annual rpt, 6504–3
Child labor certification and injury reporting procedures of States, relation to proposed Federal guidelines, 1991, GAO rpt, 26121–451
Collective bargaining devs, 1991, annual narrative article, 6722–1.307
Court civil and criminal caseloads for Federal district, appeals, and bankruptcy courts, by type of suit and offense, circuit, and district, 1991, annual rpt, 18204–11
Court civil and criminal caseloads for Federal district, appeals, and special courts, 1991, annual rpt, 18204–8
Court criminal case processing in Federal district courts, and dispositions, by offense, district, and offender characteristics, 1989, annual data compilation, 6064–29
Court criminal case processing in Federal district courts, and dispositions, by offense, 1980-91, annual rpt, 6064–31
Discrimination complaints of Federal employees, processing, and disposition, by complaint type and agency, FY90, annual rpt, 9244–11
Fed Govt employment discrimination complaint processing and counseling costs, by agency, FY91, GAO rpt, 26119–388
Fed Labor Relations Authority and Fed Service Impasses Panel activities, and cases by union, agency, and disposition, FY86-91, annual rpt, 13364–1
Immigration Reform and Control Act employer sanctions impacts on labor markets, with data for selected industries and metro areas, 1980s, working paper, 6366–6.10
Industrial relations devs and collective bargaining agreements expiring during month, Monthly Labor Review, 6722–1
Insurance (health) under multiple employer welfare arrangements, coverage, unpaid claims, and regulation, by State, 1988-91, GAO rpt, 26121–443
Leave for family reasons, State law provisions and employer compliance, for 4 States, 1987-91, hearing, 25548–105
Military prime contract awards, by size and type of contract, service branch, competitive status, category, and labor standard, FY91, annual rpt, 3544–19
Natl Labor Relations Board activities, cases, elections conducted, and litigation, FY90, annual rpt, 9584–1
State labor laws enacted, by State, 1991 annual article, 6722–1.309
Supreme Court docket labor-related cases, 1991-92, annual narrative article, 6722–1.308
Unemployment insurance laws of States, changes in coverage, benefits, tax rates, and penalties, by State, 1991, annual article, 6722–1.311
Unemployment insurance programs of States, benefits, coverage, and tax provisions, as of July 1992, semiannual listing, 6402–7
Unemployment insurance programs of States, comparison of law provisions, as of Jan 1992, semiannual revisions to base edition, 6402–2
US attorneys civil and criminal cases by type and disposition, and collections, by Federal district, FY91, annual rpt, 6004–2.1; 6004–2.7
Workers compensation laws of States and Fed Govt, 1992 annual rpt, 6504–11
Workers compensation laws of States, changes in coverage, benefits, and premium rates, by State, 1991, annual article, 6722–1.310
Workers compensation programs of States, admin, coverage, benefits, finances, processing, and staff, 1988-91, annual rpt, 6504–9
see also Minimum wage

Labor-management relations, general
Assistance (financial and nonfinancial) of Fed Govt, 1992 base edition, annual listing, 104–5
BLS data collection, analysis, and presentation methods, by program, 1992 rpt, 6888–1
Bombing incidents and casualties, by target, circumstances, and State, 1987-91, annual rpt, 8484–4.1
Collective bargaining agreements expiring during year, and workers covered, by firm, union, industry group, and State, 1992, annual rpt, 6784–9
Collective bargaining agreements expiring during year, and workers covered, by industry and level of govt, 1993, annual press release, 6726–1.54

Collective bargaining contract expirations, and industrial relations devs, current statistics and articles, Monthly Labor Review, 6722–1
Collective bargaining contract expirations, wage increases, and coverage, by major industry group, 1991, annual article, 6722–1.306
Collective bargaining devs, 1991, annual narrative article, 6722–1.307
Collective bargaining wage and benefit changes, quarterly press release, 6782–2
Collective bargaining wage changes and coverage, by industry and whether contract includes escalator clause and lump sum payment, 1982-91, annual article, 6722–1.325
Foreign countries labor conditions, union coverage, and work accidents, annual country rpt series, 6366–4
Labor laws enacted, by State, 1991, annual article, 6722–1.309
Mediation and arbitration activities of Fed Mediation and Conciliation Service, and cases by issue, region, and State, FY85-90, annual rpt, 9344–1
Mines drug abuse screening and employee aid programs activities and policies, by mineral and firm size, 1989, 6668–8
Natl Labor Relations Board activities, cases, elections conducted, and litigation, FY90, annual rpt, 9584–1
Occupational Outlook Handbook, 1992-93, biennial rpt, 6744–1
OECD pension plan finances, participation, and benefits, for 9 countries, with data by firm and worker characteristics, 1990 conf, 6688–2
Railroad and airline labor disputes, and Federal mediation activities and caseloads, with data by carrier and union, FY87-88, annual rpt, 9604–1
Representation elections conducted by NLRB, results, monthly rpt, 9582–2
Sexual harassment complaints and company policies, 1988 survey, hearing, 21348–120
Statistical Abstract of US, 1992 annual data compilation, 2324–1.13
Unemployed displaced workers, layoffs and unemployment insurance claims by reason, industry, selected characteristics, MSA, and State, 1990, annual rpt, 6744–18
Wage and benefit changes from collective bargaining and mgmt decisions, by industry div, monthly rpt, 6782–1
see also Absenteeism
see also Discrimination in employment
see also Employee benefits
see also Employee performance and appraisal
see also Escalator clauses
see also Labor-management relations in government
see also Labor unions
see also Pensions and pension funds
see also Personnel management
see also Work conditions
see also Work stoppages

Labor-management relations in government
Background checks of employees and hirees by OPM, efficiency, and Federal agency managers views on timeliness and quality, FY90, GAO rpt, 26119–373
Canada and US civil service merit systems operations, pay, appointments, and promotions, late 1980s-91, 9498–16
Collective bargaining agreements expiring during year, and workers covered, by firm, union, industry group, and State, 1992, annual rpt, 6784–9
Collective bargaining agreements expiring during year, and workers covered, by industry and level of govt, 1993, annual press release, 6726–1.54
Collective bargaining contract expirations, wage increases, and coverage, by major industry group, 1991, annual article, 6722–1.306
Discrimination complaints of Federal employees, processing and counseling costs, by agency, FY91, GAO rpt, 26119–388
Discrimination complaints of Federal employees, processing, and disposition, by complaint type and agency, FY90, annual rpt, 9244–11
Fed Govt civilian employees demographic and employment characteristics, as of Sept 1991, annual article, 9842–1.301
Fed Govt collective bargaining agreements, coverage, unions, and location, by agency, for contracts expiring 1992, semiannual listing, 9847–1
Fed Govt employees misconduct reporting, awareness of protection and other factors influencing reporting, 1992 survey, GAO rpt, 26119–413
Fed Govt labor-mgmt relations program operations and effectiveness, agency and union representatives views, 1990-91 surveys, GAO rpt, 26119–367
Fed Govt labor unions recognized, agreements and membership by agency and facility, as of Jan 1991, biennial listing, 9844–14
Fed Labor Relations Authority and Fed Service Impasses Panel activities, and cases by union, agency, and disposition, FY86-91, annual rpt, 13364–1
IRS ethical climate, misconduct, reporting and retaliation, and staff and mgmt integrity, employees views, 1991 GAO rpt, 26119–366
Mediation and arbitration activities of Fed Mediation and Conciliation Service, and cases by issue, region, and State, FY85-90, annual rpt, 9344–1
Merit system oversight and enforcement activities of OPM, series, 9496–2
Merit Systems Protection Board decisions on appeals of Fed Govt personnel actions, by agency and region, FY91, annual rpt, 9494–2
NASA staff characteristics and personnel actions, FY91, annual rpt, 9504–1
Police employment, spending, and operations, for State, city, county, and special district agencies, 1990, annual rpt, 6064–39
Quality mgmt practices of Fed Govt, employee views, 1992 survey, GAO rpt, 26119–425
State and local govt collective bargaining, wage and benefit changes and coverage, 1st half 1992, semiannual press release, 6782–6
Statistical Abstract of US, 1992 annual data compilation, 2324–1.9
Supervisors (first-line) in Fed Govt, performance ratings by self, superiors, and subordinates, 1991 survey, 9498–15
Wage and benefit changes from collective bargaining and mgmt decisions, by industry div, monthly rpt, 6782–1
see also Civil service system

Labor mobility
Adult education and literacy programs funding, enrollment, and student characteristics and benefits, 1987-90, fact sheet, 4806–4.1; 4806–4.4
Adult education and literacy programs funding, enrollment by State, and student characteristics and benefits, 1987-90, fact sheet, 4806–4.2
Displaced workers job search and placement aid effectiveness, relation to previous employment and other characteristics, 1979-87 studies, 15496–1.14
Fed Govt Senior Executive Service members characteristics, entries, exits, and awards, FY79-91, annual rpt, 9844–36
Housing (rental) total, HUD-assisted by program, and eligible for aid, recent movers by reason, selected characteristics, and location, 1989, biennial rpt, 5184–11
Housing characteristics of recent movers for new and previous unit, and household characteristics, MSA surveys, series, 2485–6
Housing unit and household characteristics of recent movers, and reason for move, by tenure, 1989, 2486–1.12
Labor force status transition rates, and relation to unemployment rate, by sex, 1980-89, working paper, 9377–9.129
Migration, immigration, and mover characteristics compared to nonmovers, 1987-90, annual Current Population Rpt, 2546–1.456
Migration since 1990, mover characteristics by same or different area, and compared to nonmovers, 1991, annual Current Population Rpt, 2546–1.464
NYC housing supply, occupancy, condition, and household characteristics, by tenure and borough, 1991 triennial survey, 2488–3
Occupational changes since 1990, and tenure with current employer compared to 1983, by sex, age, and race, 1991, press release, 6726–1.47
Occupational changes within firm, by worker characteristics, 1986-87, article, 6742–1.301
Occupational separations, replacement rates, and related job openings, estimation procedures with data by occupation, age, and sex, late 1980s and projected to 2005, 6748–84
OECD pension plan finances, participation, and benefits, for 9 countries, with data by firm and worker characteristics, 1990 conf, 6688–2
Regional employment mobility index, by industry, aggregate 1969-90, article, 9371–1.306
Unemployed persons finding work, by characteristics of worker and new job, aggregate 1986-89, 2546–20.20
Unemployed persons finding work by industry div, and earnings, by sector and sex, aggregate 1987-89, fact sheet, 2326–17.47

see also Job tenure
see also Labor turnover
see also Migrant workers
see also Migration

Labor productivity

Age of workers relation to wages and productivity, by sex and occupation, model description and results, 1991 working paper, 9377–9.128

Alcohol abuse direct and indirect costs, 1985, article, 4482–1.311

Auto and auto parts trade, production, and labor conditions, for US and compared to Canada and Mexico, 1950s-90, 6366–3.28

Auto assembly plant productivity and relation to labor reserves, model description and results, 1991 working paper, 6886–6.89

BLS data collection, analysis, and presentation methods, by program, 1992 rpt, 6888–1

Coal production and mines by county, prices, productivity, miners, and reserves, by mining method and State, 1990-91, annual rpt, 3164–25

Coal production per work hour, 1990 and trends from 1949, annual rpt, 3164–74.4

Coal production, reserves, use, and prices by State, exports by country, and employment, 1900s-90, biennial rpt, 3164–79

Competitiveness (intl) of US industries, with selected foreign and US operating data by major firm and product, series, 2046–12

Containers (wood) industry productivity trends and technological devs, 1977-89, article, 6722–1.344

Degree awards relation to productivity, effects of selection bias, model description and results, 1991 working paper, 6886–6.81

Economic indicators and components, current data and annual trends, monthly rpt, 23842–1.2

Economic Report of the President for 1992, Joint Economic Committee critique and policy recommendations, annual rpt, 23844–2

Employment and unemployment current statistics, Monthly Labor Review, 6722–1.1

Exchange rates relation to domestic interest rates, productivity, and other factors, for US and 3 OECD countries, 1970s-90, working paper, 9393–10.21

Export and import balances relation to productivity and capital investment, for selected countries, 1960s-90, working paper, 9393–10.22

Farm production inputs, output, and productivity, by commodity and region, 1947-90, annual rpt, 1544–17

Fish fresh and frozen products industry productivity trends and technological devs, 1972-90, article, 6722–1.342

Food marketing sector finances, operations, and merger activity, for processors and distributors, 1991, annual rpt, 1544–22

Food prices (farm-retail), marketing cost components, and industry finances and productivity, 1960s-91, annual rpt, 1544–9.3

Foreign and US industrial output, compensation, unit labor costs, and indexes, Monthly Labor Review, 6722–1.6

Foreign and US manufacturing labor productivity and costs, by selected country, 1950s-91, press release, 6726–1.55

Foreign and US manufacturing labor productivity and unit costs, for 14 countries, 1960s-90, article, 6722–1.304

Foreign countries labor conditions, union coverage, and work accidents, annual country rpt series, 6366–4

Hospital financial performance under Medicare, 1977-89, article, 4652–1.315

Hospital reimbursement by Medicare under prospective payment system, and effect on services, finances, and beneficiary payments, 1980-91, annual rpt, 17204–2

Hospital reimbursement by Medicare under prospective payment system, methodology, inputs, and data by diagnostic group, 1992 annual rpt, 17204–1

Hours worked relation to labor productivity over business cycle, model descriptions and results, 1940s-91, article, 9383–6.302

Imports injury to US industries from foreign subsidized products and sales at less than fair value, investigations with background financial and operating data, series, 9886–19

Mines (coal) and related operations occupational injuries and incidence, employment, and hours, 1990, annual rpt, 6664–4

Nuts and bolts industry productivity trends and technological devs, 1958-90, article, 6722–1.343

Oil and gas industry labor productivity, 1959-87, article, 6722–1.316

Output, compensation, labor and nonlabor unit costs, and indexes, Monthly Labor Review, 6722–1.5

Output per hour, and compensation and unit labor costs, percent change, monthly rpt, 6742–2.7

Output per hour, and compensation and unit labor costs, 1959-91, annual rpt, 204–1.1; 204–1.2

Pacific Northwest population, households, employment, income, fuel prices, and electricity demand, alternative forecasts 1991-2010, annual rpt, 3224–3.3

Productivity and costs of labor for private, nonfarm business, and manufacturing sectors, revised data, quarterly rpt, 6822–2

Productivity and costs of labor, indexes, preliminary data, quarterly rpt, 6822–1

Productivity of labor, capital, and other inputs in manufacturing, changes by selected industry, various periods 1949-88, article, 6722–1.345

Productivity of labor for US and foreign countries, and impacts of investment spending, 1950s-91, article, 9381–1.308

Productivity of labor, indexes of output, hours, and employment by SIC 2- to 4-digit industry, 1967-90, annual rpt, 6824–1

Railroad industry productivity measures, late 1950s-80s, article, 6722–1.337

Science and Engineering Indicators, employment, education, R&D funding, and industry impacts, with foreign comparisons, 1960s-91, biennial rpt, 9624–10.6

Small business finances, operations, owner characteristics, and Federal contracts, 1980s-90, annual rpt, 9764–6

Statistical Abstract of US, 1992 annual data compilation, 2324–1.13

Technological devs effect on labor force, composition, and productivity, 1970s-90 and projected to 2005, industry rpt series, 6826–2

Technology-intensive capital investment relation to productivity, by industry sector, 1940s-80s, technical paper, 9385–8.130

Technology-intensive capital investment relation to productivity growth, 1950s-89, article, 9385–1.310

Tennessee Valley economic conditions, and compared to US, alternative projections 1992-2010 and trends from 1929, annual rpt, 9804–27

Traffic accidents direct and indirect costs, by cost type, payment source, and severity, 1980s, 7558–114

Wages relation to labor productivity, model description and results, late 1940s-90, working paper, 9393–10.20

see also Employee performance and appraisal
see also Government efficiency
see also Industrial production indexes
see also Labor costs and cost indexes
see also Production costs

Labor supply and demand

Census of Population and Housing, 1990: summary characteristics, by county, subdiv, and place, State rpt series, 2551–7

Economic indicators and components, current data and annual trends, monthly rpt, 23842–1.2

Fiscal policy (supply side) of Reagan Admin, economic impacts, 1980s and trends from 1960s, technical paper, 9385–1.304

Forecasts of economic conditions and employment, alternative BLS projections to 2005 and trends 1975-90, biennial rpt, 6744–19

Forecasts of labor force status by age, sex, and race, accuracy of BLS forecasts made 1970s-80s, as of 1990, article, 6722–1.334

Immigrant visa applicants on waiting lists at consular office, by preference class, world region, and for top countries, as of Jan 1992, 7188–1

Labor demand, turnover, and training completions, by detailed occupation, 1990 and projected to 2005, biennial rpt, 6744–3

Labor force, wages, hours, and payroll costs, by major industry group and demographic characteristics, *Survey of Current Business*, monthly rpt, 2702–1.7

Lumber and paper products industries labor demand elasticities, 1992 rpt, 1208–416

Monthly Labor Review, current statistics and articles, 6722–1

New England States economic indicators, Fed Reserve 1st District, monthly rpt, 9373–2

Population size and demographic changes impacts on economic conditions, with background data, 1950s-80s and projected to 2010, 23848–226

Recruiting and job search costs for employers and job candidates, model description and results, 1992 working paper, 6886–6.95
Recruitment visits at colleges by Federal agencies and private companies, and school officials views, 1991, GAO rpt, 26119–377
Rural areas economic conditions and dev, quarterly journal, 1502–8
Rural areas job skill and educational requirements, impacts of industrial and occupational shifts, 1970s-80s and projected to 2000, article, 1502–7.302
Statistical Abstract of US, 1992 annual data compilation, 2324–1.13
see also Absenteeism
see also Agricultural labor
see also Alien workers
see also Blue collar workers
see also Child labor
see also Clerical workers
see also Employee benefits
see also Employee development
see also Employment and unemployment, general
see also Employment and unemployment, local and regional
see also Employment and unemployment, specific industry
see also Federal employees
see also Forced labor
see also Foreign labor conditions
see also Health occupations
see also Hours of labor
see also Job tenure
see also Job vacancy
see also Labor law
see also Labor-management relations, general
see also Labor mobility
see also Labor productivity
see also Labor turnover
see also Labor unions
see also Manpower training programs
see also Merchant seamen
see also Migrant workers
see also Military personnel
see also Minority employment
see also Occupational health and safety
see also Occupational testing and certification
see also Occupations
see also Old-Age, Survivors, Disability, and Health Insurance
see also Part-time employment
see also Pensions and pension funds
see also Production workers
see also Professional and technical workers
see also Retirement
see also Sales workers
see also State and local employees
see also Temporary and seasonal employment
see also Underemployment
see also Unemployment insurance
see also Unpaid family workers
see also Vacations and holidays
see also Veterans employment
see also Women's employment
see also Youth employment
see also under names of specific occupations

Labor turnover
AFDC applicants recently unemployed, characteristics of prior job and unemployment insurance eligibility, for Maryland, 1988-90, hearing, 21788–207
Air traffic control and airway facilities staff, by employment and other characteristics, FY90, annual rpt, 7504–41
Army line officer accessions, involuntary separations, and strengths under alternative force reduction plans, FY90-95, 26306–3.121
BLS data collection, analysis, and presentation methods, by program, 1992 rpt, 6888–1
Business statistics, detailed data for major industries and economic indicators, 1960-91, *Survey of Current Business* biennial supplement, 2704–1
Child day care and early childhood education programs availability, demand, use, costs, and provider and enrollee characteristics, 1990 survey, 4808–39
Criminal justice systems activities, spending, and employment, by level of govt, data compilation, 1992 annual rpt, 6064–6.1
Customs Service mgmt and trade law enforcement effectiveness, staff and broker survey results, 1992 GAO rpt, 26119–420
Data on labor turnover, job openings, and new hires and wages, pilot survey results, costs, and methodology, 1990-91, 6728–40
Deaths during 1986, decedents health condition, services use, habits, and social, employment, and other characteristics, 4147–20.19
Displaced worker employment and training services, and layoff alternatives, indicators of effectiveness, 1980s, 15498–28
Displaced worker training programs spending, participation, and placements by State, 1990, GAO rpt, 26121–481
Displaced workers and homemakers Pell grants recipients, by family income and grant level, 1990/91, annual rpt, 4804–1
Displaced workers and other hard-to-serve groups, factors contributing to unemployment, and training programs operations, series, 15496–1
Displaced workers in Southeast US, and layoff events, by State, industry div, and reason for separation, 1990-91, press release, 6946–3.25
Displaced workers, layoffs and recalls by layoff reason, industry, firm size, and State, 2nd half 1988, 6406–6.36
Displaced workers, layoffs and unemployment insurance claims by reason, industry, selected characteristics, and State, quarterly press release, 6742–23
Displaced workers, layoffs and unemployment insurance claims by reason, industry, selected characteristics, MSA, and State, 1990, annual rpt, 6744–18
Displaced workers losing job 1979-89, by industry, as of Jan 1990, article, 6722–1.340
Displaced workers losing job 1987-92, labor force status by employment and other characteristics, as of Jan 1992, biennial press release, 6726–1.48
DOT employment, by subagency, occupation, and selected personnel characteristics, FY91, annual rpt, 7304–18
Education (elementary and secondary) schools, teachers, staff, and enrollment, by selected characteristics, 1987/88-1988/89, 4836–3.10
Fed Govt bank regulatory agencies pay comparability and turnover, by occupation, 1991, GAO rpt, 26119–368
Fed Govt civilian employees accessions and separations, by citizenship status and agency for DC metro area and elsewhere, bimonthly rpt, 9842–1.3
Fed Govt employment of minorities, women, and disabled, by agency and occupation, FY90, annual rpt, 9244–10
Fed Govt personnel action appeals, decisions of Merit Systems Protection Board by agency and region, FY91, annual rpt, 9494–2
Fed Govt Senior Executive Service members characteristics, entries, exits, and awards, FY79-91, annual rpt, 9844–36
Forecasts of economic conditions and employment, alternative BLS projections to 2005 and trends 1975-90, biennial rpt, 6744–19
Fruit and vegetable processing industry in California, workers affected by plant closings, 1977-86, working paper, 6366–6.5
Health insurance coverage for State and local govt employees during layoff, 1990, biennial rpt, 6784–21
Households composition, income, benefits, and labor force status, Survey of Income and Program Participation methodology, working paper series, 2626–10
Imports, exports, and employment impacts, by SIC 2- to 4-digit industry and commodity, quarterly rpt, 2322–2
Indian Health Service employment of Indians and non-Indians, training, hires, and quits, by occupation, FY90, annual rpt, 4084–6
Labor demand, turnover, and training completions, by detailed occupation, 1990 and projected to 2005, biennial rpt, 6744–3
Labor force not at work, unemployed, and working less than 35 hours, by reason, sex, race, region, and State, 1991, annual rpt, 6744–7.1; 6744–7.2
Labor laws enacted, by State, 1991, annual article, 6722–1.309
Military enlistments and reenlistment rates, by service branch, FY79-91, annual rpt, 3544–1.2
Military personnel reductions planned by service branch, and women and minorities affected by Army and Air Force plans, FY90-91, GAO rpt, 26123–373
Military recruits and reenlistment rates, by service branch, quarterly rpt, 3542–14.4
Military recruits by race, and reenlistments, by sex and service branch, quarterly press release, 3542–7
Military reserves attrition rates, by component, FY91, annual rpt, 3544–31.1
NASA Apollo era science and engineering staff background and characteristics, 1958-70, 9508–39

NASA staff characteristics and personnel actions, FY91, annual rpt, 9504–1
Nuclear power plant occupational radiation exposure, by site, 1968-89, annual rpt, 9634–3
Occupational changes within firm, by worker characteristics, 1986-87, article, 6742–1.301
Occupational separations, replacement rates, and related job openings, estimation procedures with data by occupation, age, and sex, late 1980s and projected to 2005, 6748–84
OECD pension plan finances, participation, and benefits, for 9 countries, with data by firm and worker characteristics, 1990 conf, 6688–2
Older persons socioeconomic characteristics, 1900s-90 and projected to 2050, biennial chartbook, 12904–1
Small business finances, operations, owner characteristics, and Federal contracts, 1980s-90, annual rpt, 9764–6
State and local govt employment of minorities and women, by occupation, function, pay level, and State, 1991, annual rpt, 9244–6
Teachers leaving profession and subsequent employment, by school level and control, 1987-89, annual rpt, 4824–1
Unemployed persons finding work, by characteristics of worker and new job, aggregate 1986-89, 2546–20.20
Unemployment by reason, detailed data, monthly rpt, 6742–2
Unemployment by reason, monthly press release, 6742–5
Unemployment by reason, transcripts of BLS Commissioner's monthly testimony, periodic rpt, 23846–4
Unemployment, by reason, 1947-91, annual rpt, 204–1.2
VA health care staff and turnover, by occupation, physician specialty, and location, 1991, annual rpt, 8604–8
see also Job tenure
see also Job vacancy

Labor unions

Auto and auto parts trade, production, and labor conditions, for US and compared to Canada and Mexico, 1950s-90, 6366–3.28
BLS data collection, analysis, and presentation methods, by program, 1992 rpt, 6888–1
Coal industry retirees pension and health trust funds financial condition, employer contributions, and beneficiaries, late 1970s-92, GAO rpt, 26121–469; 26121–471
Collective bargaining agreements expiring during year, and workers covered, by firm, union, industry group, and State, 1992, annual rpt, 6784–9
County Business Patterns, 1989: employment, establishments, and payroll, by SIC 2- to 4-digit industry and county, annual State rpt series, 2326–8
County Business Patterns, 1990: employment, establishments, and payroll, by SIC 2- to 4-digit industry and county, annual State rpt series, 2326–6
Coverage by unions of workers and earnings, by age, sex, race, occupational group, and industry div, monthly rpt, annual article, 6782–1.2
Coverage by unions of workers and earnings, by age, sex, race, occupational group, and industry div, 1990-91, annual press release, 6726–1.44
Criminal sentences for Federal offenses, guidelines by offense and circumstances, series, 17668–1
Election campaign-related internal communications of firms and assns, spending by organization, location, and candidate, 1991-92, biennial rpt, 9274–3
Elections for representation conducted by NLRB, results, monthly rpt, 9582–2
Employment and earnings by union affiliation, monthly rpt, periodic data, 6742–2
Employment Cost Index and alternative measure of compensation costs, by component, occupation, industry group, union status, and location, 1975-92, annual rpt, 6744–20
Employment Cost Index and percent change by occupational group, industry div, region, and metro-nonmetro area, quarterly press release, 6782–5
Employment Cost Index, by industry sector and union status, monthly rpt, 6782–1.1
Employment, earnings, and hours, by SIC 1- to 4-digit industry, monthly 1989-Feb 1992, annual rpt, 6744–4
Fed Govt collective bargaining agreements, coverage, unions, and location, by agency, for contracts expiring 1992, semiannual listing, 9847–1
Fed Govt labor unions recognized, agreements and membership by agency and facility, as of Jan 1991, biennial listing, 9844–14
Fed Labor Relations Authority and Fed Service Impasses Panel activities, and cases by union, agency, and disposition, FY86-91, annual rpt, 13364–1
Foreign and US labor union membership, for 12 countries, 1955-90, article, 6722–1.305
Foreign countries economic, social, political, and geographic summary data, by country, 1992, annual factbook, 9114–2
Foreign countries labor conditions, union coverage, and work accidents, annual country rpt series, 6366–4
Input-output structure of US economy, detailed interindustry transactions for 541 industries, and components of final demand, 1982 benchmark data, 2708–17
Labor hourly costs, by component, occupational group, industry div, union coverage, and region, 1992, annual rpt, 6744–21
Multinatl firms US affiliates, finances, and operations, by industry, world area of parent firm, and State, 1989-90, annual rpt, 2704–4
Natl Labor Relations Board activities, cases, elections conducted, and litigation, FY90, annual rpt, 9584–1
Petrochemicals industries contract labor accidents, injuries, safety programs operations, and employee characteristics, 1986-91, 6608–6
Police employment, spending, and operations, for State, city, county, and special district agencies, 1990, annual rpt, 6064–39
Political action committees, by type, 1974-91, semiannual press release, 9276–1.96
Political action committees, by type, 1974-92, semiannual press release, 9276–1.107
Political action committees contributions by party, and finances, by PAC type, 1991-92, press release, 9276–1.106; 9276–1.110
Political campaign finances reported to Fed Election Commission, by type of filer, 1990 natl elections, biennial rpt series, 9276–2
Railroad and airline labor disputes, and Federal mediation activities and caseloads, with data by carrier and union, FY87-88, annual rpt, 9604–1
Statistical Abstract of US, 1992 annual data compilation, 2324–1.13
Trade adjustment aid for workers, petitions by disposition, selected industry, union, and State, monthly rpt, 6402–13
Wage and benefit changes from collective bargaining and mgmt decisions, by industry div, monthly rpt, 6782–1
Work stoppages, workers involved, and days idle, 1991 and trends from 1947, annual press release, 6784–12
see also Industry wage surveys
see also Labor-management relations, general
see also Labor-management relations in government

Laboratories

AIDS patients costs and service use under Medicaid, for California, 1984-86, article, 4652–1.301
Clinical labs test performance standards and proficiency testing, HHS regulations, 1992 rpt, 4206–2.52
County Business Patterns, 1989: employment, establishments, and payroll, by SIC 2- to 4-digit industry and county, annual State rpt series, 2326–8
County Business Patterns, 1990: employment, establishments, and payroll, by SIC 2- to 4-digit industry and county, annual State rpt series, 2326–6
DOE R&D projects and funding at natl labs, universities, and other instns, periodic summary rpt series, 3004–18
Drug (illegal) production, eradication, and seizures, by substance, with US aid, by country, 1988-92, annual rpt, 7004–17
Employment, earnings, and hours, by SIC 1- to 4-digit industry, monthly 1989-Feb 1992, annual rpt, 6744–4
Energy use in commercial buildings, costs, and conservation, by building characteristics, survey rpt series, 3166–8
Health care facilities excluded from Medicare prospective payment system, quality standards and review, certification, accreditation, and licensing, 1991 survey, 17206–2.41
Indian Health Service facilities, funding, operations, and Indian health and other characteristics, 1950s-91, annual chartbook, 4084–1
Medicare admin and research, and HCFA affirmative action and accreditation programs, FY87, annual rpt, 4654–5
Medicare and Medicaid beneficiaries and program operations, 1992, annual fact book, 4654–18

Medicare facilities, by type and State, 1990, and by type, 1967-90, annual rpt, 4744–3.5
Medicare reimbursement of hospitals under prospective payment system, and effect on services, finances, and beneficiary payments, 1980-91, annual rpt, 17204–2
Tax (income) returns of corporations, income and tax items by asset size and detailed industry, 1989, annual rpt, 8304–4; 8304–21
Tax (income) returns of sole proprietorships, income statement items, by industry group, 1990, annual article, 8302–2.317; 8302–2.320
Veterinary Services Natl Labs activities, biologic drug products evaluation and disease testing, FY91, annual rpt, 1394–17
see also Clinical laboratory technicians
see also Department of Energy National Laboratories

Laczniak, Randall J.
"Ground-Water Use and Levels in the Southern Coastal Plain of Virginia", 5666–28.20

Lafayette, Mo.
see also under By City and By SMSA or MSA in the "Index by Categories"

LaFayette, Russell A.
"Southwestern Riparian-Stream Ecosystems: Research Design, Complexity, and Opportunity", 1208–390

LAIRS
see Labor Agreement Information Retrieval System

Lake County, Ill.
CPI by component for US city average, and by region, population size, and for 15 metro areas, monthly rpt, 6762–1
CPI by component for US city average, and by selected metro area, region, and population size, monthly rpt, 6762–2
Housing starts and completions authorized by building permits in 40 MSAs, quarterly rpt, 2382–9

Lake County, Ind.
CPI by component for US city average, and by region, population size, and for 15 metro areas, monthly rpt, 6762–1
CPI by component for US city average, and by selected metro area, region, and population size, monthly rpt, 6762–2

Lakeland, Fla.
see also under By City and By SMSA or MSA in the "Index by Categories"

Lakes and lakeshores
Acid rain environmental, economic, and health effects, and pollutant emissions, 1985-89 and alternative projections to 2030, 14358–4
Army Corps of Engineers activities and projects, FY88 and trends from 1800s, annual rpt, 3754–1.1
Army Corps of Engineers activities and projects, FY89 and trends from 1800s, annual rpt, 3754–1.2
Army Corps of Engineers activities and projects, FY90 and trends from 1800s, annual rpt, 3754–1.3
Army Corps of Engineers water resources dev projects, characteristics, and costs, 1950s-89, biennial State rpt series, 3756–1
Army Corps of Engineers water resources dev projects, characteristics, and costs, 1950s-91, biennial State rpt series, 3756–2
Bridges over navigable waters, with type of bridge and use, owner, dimensions, and location, 1991 regional listing series, 7406–5
Disease (waterborne) outbreaks and cases, by type, source, and location, 1989-90, article, 4202–7.301
Environmental conditions, fish, wildlife, use, and mgmt, for individual coastal and riparian ecosystems, series, 5506–9
Environmental Quality, status of problems, protection programs, research, and intl issues, 1991 annual rpt, 484–1
Fish Hatchery Natl System activities and deliveries, by species, hatchery, and jurisdiction of waters stocked, FY91, annual rpt, 5504–10
Freight (waterborne domestic and foreign) by commodity, traffic, and passengers, by port and waterway, 1989, annual rpt, 3754–3
Natl park system sites acreage and descriptions, 1991, biennial listing, 5544–5
Natl park system visits and overnight stays, by park and State, monthly rpt, 5542–4
Natl parks and other land under Natl Park Service mgmt, acreage by site, ownership, and region, FY92, semiannual rpt, 5542–1
Public lands acreage, grants, use, revenues, and allocations, by State, FY91, annual rpt, 5724–1.2
Water quality, chemistry, hydrology, and other characteristics, local area studies, series, 5666–27
Water supply and quality in streams and lakes, and groundwater levels in wells, by drainage basin, 1990, annual State rpt series, 5666–10
Water supply and quality in streams and lakes, and groundwater levels in wells, by drainage basin, 1990-91, annual CD-ROM, 5664–18
Water supply and quality in streams and lakes, and groundwater levels in wells, by drainage basin, 1991, annual State rpt series, 5666–12
Western US activities of Reclamation Bur, land and population served, and recreation areas, by location, 1990, annual rpt, 5824–12
see also Dredging
see also Great Lakes
see also Reservoirs
see also Wetlands

Laliberte, Lucie
"Reconciliation of the U.S.-Canadian Current Account", 2702–1.341

Lamison-White, Leatha
"Income, Poverty, and Wealth in the U.S.: A Chart Book", 2546–6.75

Lammers, Norma P.
"Jail Construction in California", 6066–30.1

Lamson, Neil I.
"Stand Development and Yields of Appalachian Hardwood Stands Managed with Single-Tree Selection for at Least 30 Years", 1208–394

Lancaster, Pa.
see also under By City and By SMSA or MSA in the "Index by Categories"

Land
see Arid zones
see Farms and farmland
see Forests and forestry
see Geography
see Homesteads
see Land area
see Land ownership and rights
see Land reform
see Land use
see Pasture and rangeland
see Property condemnation
see Property tax
see Property value
see Public lands
see Real estate business
see Reclamation of land
see Soil pollution
see Soils and soil conservation
see Topography

Land area
Alabama timber acreage and value, by species, forest type, ownership, and county, 1990, series, 1206–30
Alaska timber acreage and resources, by species, ownership class, and inventory unit, series, 1206–9
Census of Population and Housing, 1990: summary characteristics, households, and land area, by county, subdiv, and place, State rpt series, 2551–1
Coal mining restrictions on public land, impacts on production, costs, and demand, by region, 1985-88 and projected to 2075, 5668–125
Desert areas public grazing acreage, use, fees, and endangered species, 1988-90, GAO rpt, 26113–552
DOE real property owned and leased, by type, subagency, contractor, and site, FY91, annual rpt, 3004–28
Fires (wild) and acreage burned, by type of land, ownership, cause, region, and State, 1984-90, annual rpt, 1204–4
Fish and Wildlife Service restoration programs funding, land purchases, and project listing, by State, FY90, annual rpt, 5504–1
Foreign countries economic, social, political, and geographic summary data, by country, 1992, annual factbook, 9114–2
Foreign countries *Geographic Notes*, boundaries, claims, nomenclature, and other devs, quarterly rpt, 7142–3
Foreign countries population size, growth rate, and area, for 94 largest cities, 1991 biennial rpt, 2324–9
Forest Service activities and finances, by region and State, FY91, annual rpt, 1204–1.1
Forests (natl) and other lands under Forest Service mgmt, acreage by forest and location, 1991 and historic trends, annual rpt, 1204–2
Forests (natl) revenue share paid to States, and acreage, by forest, county, and congressional district, FY92, annual rpt, 1204–33
Forests (tropical) condition, conservation methods, and biological diversity issues, 1992 rpt, 26358–262

Indian and govt lands under Bur of Indian Affairs mgmt, acreage, leases, and use, 1989, annual rpt, 5704–12
Military base support costs by function, and personnel and acreage by installation, by service branch, FY93, annual rpt, 3504–11
Montana timber outside natl forests, acreage, resources, and mortality, by species and ownership class, 1988-89, 1206–25
New Mexico Caballo Resource Area public land mgmt, and grazing, environmental, and leasing activities, FY90-91, annual rpt, 5724–17
Northeastern US timber resources and removals, by species, ownership, and county, State rpt series, 1206–12
Park natl system and other land under Natl Park Service mgmt, acreage by site, ownership, and region, FY92, semiannual rpt, 5542–1
Park natl system sites acreage and descriptions, 1991, biennial listing, 5544–5
Public lands acreage, grants, use, revenues, and allocations, by State, FY91 and trends, annual rpt, 5724–1
Public lands minerals resources and availability, State rpt series, 5606–7
Real estate assets of failed thrifts, inventory of properties available from Resolution Trust Corp, semiannual listing series, 9722–2
Southern US timber resources and removals, by species, ownership, State, and county, series, 1206–8
Statistical Abstract of US, 1992 annual data compilation, 2324–1; 2324–1.6
Tennessee timber acreage and resources, by species, ownership class, and county, 1989, series, 1206–27
Timber and orchard damage from natural disaster, USDA restoration aid and program participation by practice and State, FY91, annual rpt, 1804–24
Timber insect and disease incidence and damage, and control activities, State rpt series, 1206–49
Timber insect and disease incidence and damage, annual regional rpt series, 1206–11
Timber planting and stand improvement, by ownership and State, FY91, annual rpt, 1204–7
Washington State timber acreage and resources, by species, ownership class, and county, 1988-89 with harvest trends from 1955, series, 1206–28
Water resources data collection and analysis activities of USGS Water Resources Div Districts, with project descriptions, series, 5666–26
Western US activities of Reclamation Bur, land and population served, and recreation areas, by location, 1990, annual rpt, 5824–12
Wetlands acreage acquired by Fed Govt, and costs, by site and State, FY92, annual rpt, 14784–1
Wetlands acreage, and agreements and payments to farmers under Water Bank Program, by State, 1972-91, annual rpt, 1804–21
Wetlands acreage and losses, by wetland type, 1970s-80s, 5508–89
Wetlands acreage in Florida, by wetland type, 1970s-80s, 5508–119
Wetlands preservation under Water Bank Program, acreage, agreements, and payments, by State, monthly rpt, 1802–5
Wildlife refuges and other land under Fish and Wildlife Service mgmt, acreage by site and State, as of Sept 1992, annual rpt, 5504–8
Wisconsin timber resources and removals, by species, forest type, ownership, and county, series, 1206–34
see also Farms and farmland
see also Land use

Land, Eric
"Soaps, Detergents, and Surface-Active Agents, Industry and Trade Summary", 9885–11.1

Land ownership and rights
Alabama timber acreage and value, by species, forest type, ownership, and county, 1990, series, 1206–30
Alabama timber acreage converted from nonforest use, reforested, and harvested, for pine, 1950s-90, 1208–409
Alaska oil, gas, and coal reserve acreage, by ownership, 1991 rpt, 5608–174
Alaska timber acreage and resources, by species, ownership class, and inventory unit, series, 1206–9
Assets and debts of private sector, balance sheets by segment, 1960-91, semiannual rpt, 9365–4.1
Farm acreage owned and rented by region, and method of acquisition of owned acreage, for young farm operators, 1992 article, 1541–1.319
Farm production inputs, finances, mgmt, and land value and transfers, periodic situation rpt with articles, 1561–16
Farmland in US owned by foreigners, holdings, acquisitions, and disposals by land use, owner type and country, and State, 1991, annual rpt, 1584–2
Farmland in US owned by foreigners, holdings, acreage, and value by land use, owner country, State, and county, 1991, annual rpt, 1584–3
Foreign direct investment in US by country, and finances, employment, and acreage owned, by industry group of business acquired or established, 1985-91, annual article, 2702–1.320
Foreign direct investment in US, major transactions by type, industry, country, and US location, 1990, annual rpt, 2044–20
Historic and natural natl landmarks damaged and threatened, with owner, location, damage type, and recommended remedial action, 1990, annual listing, 5544–16
Indian and govt lands under Bur of Indian Affairs mgmt, acreage, leases, and use, 1989, annual rpt, 5704–12
Indian land ownership, multiple ownership, and Bur of Indian Affairs records maintenance, for 12 reservations, 1991, GAO rpt, 26113–559
Indian tribes in Pacific Northwest, OCS oil and gas lease and dev environmental, economic, and cultural impacts, with background data, 1970s-92, 5738–35
Iowa timber resources and removals, by species, forest and tree characteristics, ownership, and county, 1988-90 and trends from 1973-74, 1208–75
Loan activity for mortgages, by type of lender, loan, and mortgaged property, quarterly press release, 5142–30
Louisiana timber resources, by ownership, forest and tree characteristics, and parish, 1991, series, 1206–35
Michigan fuelwood production, by species, land ownership, survey region, county, and location, 1986, 1208–412
Minerals foreign and US supply under alternative market conditions, reserves, and background industry data, series, 5606–4
Minnesota fuelwood production, by species, land ownership, and location, 1988, 1208–398
Minnesota timber acreage, resources, and removals, by ownership, forest and tree characteristics, and county, 1990, series, 1206–24
Missouri fuelwood production, by species, land ownership, and location, 1987, 1208–399
Missouri timber resources and removals, by species, forest and tree characteristics, ownership, and county, 1987-89 and trends from 1959, 1208–76
Missouri timber resources and removals by species, land ownership, and county, 1988-89, series, 1206–3
Montana timber outside natl forests, acreage, resources, and mortality, by species and ownership class, 1988-89, 1206–25
Multinatl firms US affiliates, finances, and operations, by industry, world area of parent firm, and State, 1989-90, annual rpt, 2704–4
New Mexico Caballo Resource Area public land mgmt, and grazing, environmental, and leasing activities, FY90-91, annual rpt, 5724–17
Northeastern US timber resources and removals, by species, ownership, and county, State rpt series, 1206–12
Oregon lumber production, and industry operations, by county, 1988, 1208–280
Pacific Northwest northern spotted owl conservation methods, findings and recommendations, 1990 rpt, 1208–385
Park natl system and other land under Natl Park Service mgmt, acreage by site, ownership, and region, FY92, semiannual rpt, 5542–1
Rice production, practices, costs, and land tenure, by production area, 1988, 1568–309
Rocky Mountain States timber and mill residue production, by species, ownership, and county, series, 1206–17
Southern US timber resources and removals, by species, ownership, State, and county, series, 1206–8
Soybean tillage systems impacts on yield and inputs use and costs, 1990, article, 1561–3.304
Tax (income) returns filed, by type of filer, selected income items, quarterly rpt, 8302–2.1
Tennessee timber acreage and resources, by species, ownership class, and county, 1989, series, 1206–27

Timber insect and disease incidence and damage, and control activities, State rpt series, 1206–49
Timber insect and disease incidence and damage, annual regional rpt series, 1206–11
Timber insect and disease incidence and damage, by State, 1990, annual rpt, 1204–8
Timber planting and stand improvement, by ownership and State, FY91, annual rpt, 1204–7
Tobacco (flue-cured) farms and farm operators, by region and selected characteristics, 1970s-87, 1568–307
Uranium reserves and industry operations, by region and State, various periods 1966-91, annual rpt, 3164–65.1
Virginia timber resources, growth, and removals, by species, ownership, treatment, and county, 1990-92, series, 1206–6
Washington State timber acreage and resources, by species, ownership class, and county, 1988-89 with harvest trends from 1955, series, 1206–28
Wisconsin timber resources and removals, by species, forest type, ownership, and county, series, 1206–34
see also Government supplies and property
see also Homesteads
see also Housing tenure
see also Land reform
see also Public lands
see also Real estate business
see also Vacant and abandoned property

Land reform
Forests (tropical) condition, conservation methods, and biological diversity issues, 1992 rpt, 26358–262
Russia land transfers to private activity, by land use, 1991-92, 1524–4.1

Land use
Coastal areas environmental conditions and mgmt, for individual areas, conf series, 2146–8
Coastal areas environmental impacts of economic dev and population growth, 1960-80s and projected to 2010, series, 2176–8
Developing countries economic, population, and agricultural data, US and other aid sources, and AID activity, country rpt series, 9916–12
Environmental Quality, status of problems, protection programs, research, and intl issues, 1991 annual rpt, 484–1
Foreign countries economic, social, political, and geographic summary data, by country, 1992, annual factbook, 9114–2
Foreign ownership of US farmland, holdings, acquisitions, and disposals by land use, owner type and country, and State, 1991, annual rpt, 1584–2
Foreign ownership of US farmland, holdings, acreage, and value by land use, owner country, State, and county, 1991, annual rpt, 1584–3
Indian and govt lands under Bur of Indian Affairs mgmt, acreage, leases, and use, 1989, annual rpt, 5704–12
Latin America economic and social conditions, resources, trade, and aid, 1992, annual factbook, 9914–14
Research (agricultural) funding and staffing for USDA, State agencies, and other instns, by topic, FY91, annual rpt, 1744–2
Statistical Abstract of US, 1992 annual data compilation, 2324–1.6
Uranium tailings at inactive mills, remedial action proposals, costs, site characteristics, and environmental, socioeconomic, and health impacts, series, 3356–4
Water (groundwater) supply, quality, chemistry, and use, State and local area rpt series, 5666–28
Water quality, chemistry, hydrology, and other characteristics, local area studies, series, 5666–27
see also City and town planning
see also Farms and farmland
see also Forests and forestry
see also Industrial siting
see also Land ownership and rights
see also Land reform
see also Mines and mineral resources
see also Pasture and rangeland
see also Property condemnation
see also Public lands
see also Reclamation of land
see also Regional planning
see also Zoning and zoning laws

Lande, James L.
"Telephone Rates Update", 9282–8

Landefeld, J. Steven
"Rates of Return on Direct Investment", 2702–1.330

Landfills
Hazardous substances industrial releases and reduction methods under EPA regulation, with chemical stocks and use, facility directory, 1987-89, annual CD-ROM, 9234–7
Industrial waste generation, disposal, and regulation, by industry and State, mid 1980s-90, 26358–256
Methane recovered from landfills, use by region, 1990, annual rpt, 3164–97

Landscape protection
see Environmental pollution and control
see Land use

Lang, William W.
""Flight to Quality" in Bank Lending and Economic Activity", 9387–8.283

Langan, Patrick A.
"Recidivism of Felons on Probation, 1986-89", 6066–19.65

Lange, Mark D.
"Cotton Mill Use in the 1990s", 1504–9.1

Lange, W. Robert
"Deaths Among Members of the Public Health Service Commissioned Corps, 1965-89", 4042–3.316

Language arts
Copyrights Register activities, registrations by material type, and fees, FY91 and trends from 1790, annual rpt, 26404–2
Degrees awarded in higher education, by level, field, race, and sex, 1989/90 and trends from 1980/81, annual rpt, 4844–17
DOD Dependents Schools basic skills and college entrance test scores, 1991-92, annual rpt, 3504–16
Education data compilation, 1992 annual rpt, 4824–2
Elementary and secondary students educational performance in math, science, reading, and writing, 1969-90, 4898–32
Fed Govt aid to higher education and nonprofit instns for R&D and related activities, by field, instn, agency, and State, FY90, annual rpt, 9627–17
Higher education grad programs enrollment in science and engineering, by field, source of funds, and characteristics of student and instn, 1990, annual rpt, 9627–7
Natl Education Goals progress indicators, by State, 1992, annual rpt, 15914–1
Natl Endowment for Arts activities and grants, FY91, annual rpt, 9564–3
Vocational education enrollment, and academic and other credits earned, by subject and student characteristics, high school classes of 1982 and 1987, 4838–50
see also Area studies
see also Writers and writing

Language use and ability
Asian and Hispanic students proficiency in English and language at home, by selected characteristics, 1988 eighth grade class, natl longitudinal survey, 1992 rpt, 4826–9.12
Census of Population and Housing, 1990: population and housing characteristics, detailed geographic coverage, State CD-ROM series, 2551–10
Census of Population and Housing, 1990: summary characteristics, by county, subdiv, and place, State rpt series, 2551–7
Condition of Education, detail for elementary, secondary, and higher education, 1920s-91 and projected to 2002, annual rpt, 4824–1
Digest of Education Statistics, 1992 annual data compilation, 4824–2
Eighth grade class of 1988: educational performance and conditions, characteristics, attitudes, activities, and plans, natl longitudinal survey, series, 4826–9
Elementary and secondary students educational performance in math, science, reading, and writing, 1969-90, 4898–32
Elementary and secondary students writing ability and scores, 1990 natl assessments, 4896–8.4
Immigrant and nonimmigrant visa applicants refused, and refusals overcome, by reason, FY90, annual rpt, 7184–1.3
Pacific territories population and housing detailed characteristics, by location, 1990 Census of Population and Housing, series, 2551–8
Population and labor force characteristics, 1940s-90 and projected to 2000, 15496–1.16
Vocational education enrollment, student and teacher characteristics, and outcomes, for secondary and postsecondary instns, 1970s-90, 4828–42
see also Bilingual education
see also Compensatory education
see also Foreign languages
see also Language arts
see also Learning disabilities
see also Literacy and illiteracy
see also Reading ability and habits
see also Speech pathology and audiology
see also Writers and writing

Lansing, Mich.
see also under By City and By SMSA or MSA in the "Index by Categories"

Laos
Agricultural trade of US, by detailed commodity and country, 1991, annual rpt, 1524–8
Agricultural trade of US, by detailed commodity and country, 1991, semiannual rpt, 1522–4
AID loans repayment status and terms by program and country, and status of predecessor agency loans, quarterly rpt, 9912–3
Economic and military aid and loans from US and intl agencies, by program and country, FY46-91, annual rpt, 9914–5
Economic, social, political, and geographic summary data, by country, 1992, annual factbook, 9114–2
Export licensing, monitoring, and enforcement activities, FY91, annual rpt, 2024–1
Exports and imports of US, by transport mode, country, and SITC 1- to 3-digit commodity, 1991, annual rpt, 2424–12
Exports and imports of US with Communist and transitional economy countries, by detailed commodity and country, quarterly rpt with articles, 9882–2
Human rights conditions in 170 countries, and US economic and military aid, 1991, annual rpt, 21384–3
Military aid of US, arms sales, and training programs costs and budget requests, by program, world region, and country, FY91-93, annual rpt, 7144–13
Military spending, arms trade, and force strengths, with govt spending and population, by country, 1979-89, annual rpt, 9824–1
Minerals Yearbook, Vol 3, 1989: foreign country review of production, trade, and policy, by commodity, annual rpt, 5604–35.2
Population size, growth rates, and components of change, by country, projected 1990-2020 and trends from 1950, biennial rpt, 2324–9
Refugee migration, and intl aid programs, by world area and country of origin and asylum, 1991, annual rpt, 7004–15
Refugees from Indochina, arrivals, and departures, by country of origin and resettlement, camp, and ethnicity, monthly rpt, 7002–4
UN voting record and share of votes in agreement with US, by issue, country, and world area, 1991, annual rpt, 7004–18

LaPlante, Mitchell P.
"Assistive Technology Devices and Home Accessibility Features: Prevalence, Payment, Need, and Trends", 4146–8.219
"Disability in Basic Life Activities Across the Life Span", 4946–1.1
"Disability Risks of Chronic Illnesses and Impairments", 4946–1.2

Larceny
see Robbery and theft

Larsen, Max
"Residential Fuelwood Consumption in the Southeastern U.S.", 9806–9.12

Larson, Frederic R.
"Timberland Resources of the Kenai Peninsula, Alaska, 1987", 1206–9.23

Larson, James A.
"Texas Upland Cotton Acreage Abandonment and Harvested Yield: A Historical Perspective", 1561–1.303

Larson, Jerry D.
"Ground-Water Use and Levels in the Southern Coastal Plain of Virginia", 5666–28.20

Las Vegas, Nev.
Housing starts and completions authorized by building permits in 40 MSAs, quarterly rpt, 2382–9
see also under By City and By SMSA or MSA in the "Index by Categories"

Lasers
Exports and imports of US, by Harmonized System 6-digit commodity and country, 1991, annual rpt, 2424–13
Price indexes (producer), by stage of processing and detailed commodity, monthly rpt, 6762–6
Price indexes (producer), by stage of processing and detailed commodity, monthly 1991, annual rpt, 6764–2
Shipments, trade, use, and firms, for electronic communications systems and related products, 1991, annual Current Industrial Rpt, 2506–12.35

Lasker, Roz D.
"Survey of Visits and Consultations", 17266–2.5
"Variation in Medicare Global Service Policies: Relationship to Current Payment and Implications for a Fee Schedule", 17266–2.2

Latin America
Agricultural trade by commodity and country, prices, and world market devs, monthly rpt, 1922–12
Cholera surveillance in Latin America, activities and CDC recommendations, 1992 narrative article, 4202–7.310
Construction contract awards and billings, by country of contractor and world area of award, 1990, annual article, 2042–1.304
Drug abuse indicators, by world region and selected country, 1992 semiannual conf, 4492–5.2
Economic and social conditions of developing countries from 1960s, and Intl Dev Cooperation Agency and AID activities and funding, FY91-93, annual rpt, 9904–4
Economic and social conditions, resources, and trade, and aid, 1992, annual factbook, 9914–14
Economic conditions, trade, and foreign aid, for Latin America, working paper series, 9916–13
Energy production by type, and oil trade, and use, by country group and selected country, monthly rpt, 9112–2
Energy use and production, by fuel type, country, and country group, projected 1995-2010 and trends from 1970, annual rpt, 3164–84
Exports and imports (waterborne) of US, by type of service, customs district, port, and world area, monthly rpt, 2422–7
Exports and imports of Latin America, and balance of trade with US, by country, annual rpt, suspended, 2044–34
Exports and imports of US, by Harmonized System 6-digit commodity and country, 1991, annual rpt, 2424–13
Exports and imports of US, by selected country, country group, and commodity group, 1991, annual rpt, 2044–37
Exports and imports of US, by transport mode, country, and SITC 1- to 3-digit commodity, 1991, annual rpt, 2424–12
Exports, imports, and balances of US with major trading partners, by product category, 1987-91, annual chartbook, 9884–21
Exports, investment, debt, and tariffs of 7 Latin America countries, and trade and investment policy liberalization issues, mid 1960s-91, 9886–4.184
Family planning and population activities of AID, grants by project and recipient, and contraceptive shipments, by country, FY91, annual rpt series, 9914–13
Food supply, needs, and aid for developing countries, status and alternative forecasts, 1992 world area rpt, 1526–8.2
Immigrant and nonimmigrant visas of US issued and refused, by class, issuing office, and nationality, FY90, annual rpt, 7184–1
Immigrants admitted to US, by class of admission, country of birth, and MSA of destination, FY91, advance annual rpt, 6264–4
Immigrants and legalized aliens, by occupational group and country of birth, preliminary FY91, annual tables, 6264–1
Immigrants and nonimmigrants admitted to US, alien workers, visitors, deportations, and naturalizations, FY91, annual summary rpt, 6264–7
Immigration to US, alien workers, visitors, deportations, and naturalizations, by country, FY91 and trends from 1820, annual rpt, 6264–2
Income tax returns of foreign corporations and individuals, and US entities abroad, detailed data compilation, 1970s-89, quinquennial rpt, 8308–31
Inter-American Foundation activities, grants by recipient, and fellowships, by country, FY91, annual rpt, 14424–1
Inter-American Foundation dev grants by program area, and fellowships by field and instn, by country, FY72-91, annual rpt, 14424–2
Inter-American Foundation dev grants, project characteristics, area benefits, and investment returns, for 8 projects, 1970s-88, 14428–1
Investment (foreign direct) in US, by industry group and world area, 1989-91, annual article, 2702–1.331
Investment (foreign direct) of US, by industry group and world area, 1989-91, annual article, 2702–1.332
Loans of US banks to foreigners at all US and foreign offices, by country group and country, quarterly rpt, 13002–1
Military aid of US, arms sales, and training programs costs and budget requests, by program, world region, and country, FY91-93, annual rpt, 7144–13
Military spending, arms trade, and force strengths, with govt spending and population, by country, 1979-89, annual rpt, 9824–1

Multinatl firms US affiliates finances and operations, by industry, country of parent firm, and State, 1987, 2708–48
Multinatl firms US affiliates, finances, and operations, by industry, world area of parent firm, and State, 1989-90, annual rpt, 2704–4
Multinatl US firms and foreign affiliates finances and operations, by industry and country, 1989 benchmark survey, annual rpt, 2704–5
Peace Corps activities, funding by program, and volunteers, by country, FY93, annual rpt, 9654–1
Polio cases in Latin America, by country, 1990-91, article, 4202–7.309
Productivity of labor for US and foreign countries, and impacts of investment spending, 1950s-91, article, 9381–1.308
Refugee arrivals in US by world area and country of origin, and quotas, monthly rpt, 7002–4
Refugee arrivals in US by world area of origin and State of settlement, and Federal aid, FY91-92 and proposed FY93 allocations, annual rpt, 7004–16
Refugee migration, and intl aid programs, by world area and country of origin and asylum, 1991, annual rpt, 7004–15
Sexual activity among young unmarried adults, contraceptives use, and AIDS risk knowledge, by sex and Latin American country, 1984-91, article, 4202–7.323
Steel trade, by product, country, and customs district, with US industry operating data, 1989-June 1992, semiannual rpt, 9882–15
Tax (income) returns for foreign corporate activity in US, selected income and tax items, by industry div and selected country, 1988, article, 8302–2.309
Terrorism (intl) incidents, casualties, and attacks on US targets, by attack type and world area, 1991, annual rpt, 7004–13
Tide height and time daily at coastal points, forecast 1993, annual rpt, 2174–2.2; 2174–2.3
Tobacco production and use in Latin America, Canada, and US, and related economic, health, and social issues, 1950s-92, annual rpt, 4204–18
Travel to and from US, and travel receipts and payments, by world area, with data by country, 1985-90, annual rpt, 2904–10
Travel to and from US on US and foreign flag air carriers, by country, world area, and US port, monthly rpt, 7302–2
Travel to US, spending by world area of residence, and economic impact, by spending category and State, 1989, 2908–28
UN voting record and share of votes in agreement with US, by issue, country, and world area, 1991, annual rpt, 7004–18
US military and civilian personnel and dependents, by service branch, world area, and country, quarterly rpt, 3542–20
Weather conditions and effect on agriculture, by US region, State, and city, and world area, weekly rpt, 2182–7
Weather events and anomalies, precipitation and temperature for US and foreign locations, weekly rpt, 2182–6
see also Andean Group
see also Anguilla
see also Antigua and Barbuda
see also Argentina
see also Aruba
see also Bahamas
see also Belize
see also Bermuda
see also Bolivia
see also Brazil
see also British Virgin Islands
see also Caribbean area
see also Caribbean Community
see also Cayman Islands
see also Central America
see also Central American Common Market
see also Chile
see also Colombia
see also Costa Rica
see also Cuba
see also Dominica
see also Dominican Republic
see also Ecuador
see also El Salvador
see also French Guiana
see also Grenada
see also Guatemala
see also Guyana
see also Haiti
see also Honduras
see also Inter-American Development Bank
see also Jamaica
see also Latin American Integration Association
see also Mexico
see also Netherlands Antilles
see also Nicaragua
see also Panama
see also Paraguay
see also Peru
see also Puerto Rico
see also South America
see also St. Christopher and Nevis
see also St. Lucia
see also St. Vincent and The Grenadines
see also Suriname
see also Trinidad and Tobago
see also Uruguay
see also U.S. Virgin Islands
see also Venezuela
see also under By Foreign Country in the "Index by Categories"

Latin American Free Trade Association
see Latin American Integration Association

Latin American Integration Association
Exports, imports, membership, and trade impacts of regional preferential trading arrangements, by group, late 1940s-91, article, 9373–1.308
Steel trade, by product, country, and customs district, with US industry operating data, 1989-June 1992, semiannual rpt, 9882–15

Latinos
see Hispanic Americans
see Mexicans in the U.S.

Latvia
Agricultural production, prices, and trade, for former USSR republics, 1960s-91 and forecast 1992, annual rpt, 1524–4.1
Agricultural trade of US with Eastern Europe, by commodity group and country, 1988-91, 1928–11
Economic conditions, policy, and trade practices, by country, 1989-91, annual rpt, 21384–5
Economic, social, political, and geographic summary data, by country, 1992, annual factbook, 9114–2
Embassies of US in former Soviet republics and Baltic States, positions planned by function, and filled, 1992, GAO rpt, 26123–403
Energy supply and use, and social, economic, and political indicators for former Soviet Republics and Baltic States, 1989-90, 3168–126
Energy use and production of former USSR Republics, by fuel type, 1990, annual rpt, 3164–84.2
Human rights conditions in 170 countries, and US economic and military aid, 1991, annual rpt, 21384–3
Livestock and meat inventories, use, and imports, by former USSR republic, 1986-93, semiannual rpt, 1925–33.2
Military aid of US, arms sales, and training programs costs and budget requests, by program, world region, and country, FY91-93, annual rpt, 7144–13
Older population and selected characteristics, 1980s and projected to 2020, country rpt, 2326–19.8
Population size and characteristics of former Soviet Republics and Baltic States, 1989-92, 9118–19
Refugee migration, and intl aid programs, by world area and country of origin and asylum, 1991, annual rpt, 7004–15

Latzy, John
"Controlled Foreign Corporations, 1988", 8302–2.322
"Transactions Between Foreign Controlled Corporations and Related Foreign Persons, 1988: Data Release", 8302–2.318

Laundry and cleaning services
County Business Patterns, 1989: employment, establishments, and payroll, by SIC 2- to 4-digit industry and county, annual State rpt series, 2326–8
County Business Patterns, 1990: employment, establishments, and payroll, by SIC 2- to 4-digit industry and county, annual State rpt series, 2326–6
CPI by component for US city average, and by selected metro area, region, and population size, monthly rpt, 6762–2
Employment, earnings, and hours, by SIC 1- to 4-digit industry, monthly 1989-Feb 1992, annual rpt, 6744–4
Employment of minorities and women, by occupation, SIC 1- to 3-digit industry, State, and MSA, 1991, annual rpt, 9244–1
Input-output structure of US economy, detailed interindustry transactions for 541 industries, and components of final demand, 1982 benchmark data, 2708–17
Labor productivity, indexes of output, hours, and employment by SIC 2- to 4-digit industry, 1967-90, annual rpt, 6824–1.4
Occupational injury and illness rates, by SIC 2- to 4-digit industry, 1989-90, annual rpt, 6844–7
Occupational injury and illness rates, by SIC 2- to 4-digit industry, 1990, annual rpt, 6844–1
Tax (income) returns of partnerships, income statement and balance sheet items, by industry group, 1990, annual article, 8302–2.314

Tax (income) returns of sole proprietorships, income statement items, by industry group, 1990, annual article, 8302–2.317; 8302–2.320
VA health care facilities energy use and conservation, by facility, quarterly rpt, 8602–9
see also Janitorial and maintenance services

Law
Foreign countries economic, social, political, and geographic summary data, by country, 1992, annual factbook, 9114–2
Smoking, tobacco, and health impacts research rpts, 1991 annual report, 4204–19
Tobacco use by minors, effectiveness of local ordinance enforcing penalties on retailers, 1989-90 local area study, article, 4042–3.336
see also Administration of justice
see also Administrative law and procedure
see also Alcoholic beverages control laws
see also Antitrust law
see also Building codes
see also Civil procedure
see also Commercial law
see also Constitutional law
see also Courts
see also Criminal procedure
see also Due process of law
see also Environmental regulation
see also Financial institutions regulation
see also Government-citizen lawsuits
see also International cooperation in law enforcement
see also Labor law
see also Law enforcement
see also Lawyers and legal services
see also Legal aid
see also Legal education
see also Maritime law
see also Medical regulation
see also Military law
see also State laws
see also Tax laws and courts
see also Traffic laws and courts
see also U.S. statutes
see also Zoning and zoning laws

Law enforcement
Data on crime, criminal justice admin and enforcement, and public opinion, data compilation, 1992 annual rpt, 6064–6
Education data compilation, 1992 annual rpt, 4824–2
Expenditures, employment, and payroll, by activity, level of govt, and State, FY90, annual rpt, 6066–25.50
Palau admin, and social, economic, and govtl data, FY91, annual rpt, 7004–6
States criminal justice systems activities, employment, funding, and data collection, by State, 1970s-91, annual rpt, 6064–40
Statistical Abstract of US, 1992 annual data compilation, 2324–1.5
see also Administration of justice
see also Administrative law and procedure
see also Arrest
see also Campus security
see also Correctional institutions
see also Courts
see also Crime and criminals
see also Criminal investigations
see also Criminal procedure
see also Electronic surveillance
see also Federal aid to law enforcement
see also Forensic sciences
see also International cooperation in law enforcement
see also Juvenile detention and correctional institutions
see also Organized crime
see also Police
see also Pretrial detention and release
see also Searches and seizures
see also State funding for public safety
see also Traffic laws and courts

Law of the sea
see Maritime law

Law schools
see Legal education

Lawler, John V.
"U.S. Textile Imports and Exports", 1561–1.301

Lawn and garden equipment
County Business Patterns, 1989: employment, establishments, and payroll, by SIC 2- to 4-digit industry and county, annual State rpt series, 2326–8
County Business Patterns, 1990: employment, establishments, and payroll, by SIC 2- to 4-digit industry and county, annual State rpt series, 2326–6
CPI by component for US city average, and by selected metro area, region, and population size, monthly rpt, 6762–2
Exports and imports between US and outlying areas, by detailed commodity and mode of transport, 1991, annual rpt, 2424–11
Exports and imports of US, by Harmonized System 6-digit commodity and country, 1991, annual rpt, 2424–13
Exports, imports, tariffs, and industry operating data for farm machinery and lawn equipment, 1992 rpt, 9885–9.3
Exports of US, detailed Schedule B commodities with countries of destination, 1991, annual rpt, 2424–10
Injuries from use of consumer products and related activities, by severity and victim age and sex, 1990, annual rpt, 9164–7
Injuries from use of consumer products, by severity, victim age, and detailed product, 1991, annual rpt, 9164–6
Injuries from use of consumer products, related deaths and costs, and recalls by brand, by product type, FY90, annual rpt, 9164–2
Labor productivity, indexes of output, hours, and employment by SIC 2- to 4-digit industry, 1967-90, annual rpt, 6824–1.3
Manufacturing annual survey, 1990: finances and operations, by SIC 2- to 4-digit industry, series, 2506–14
Manufacturing census, 1987: concentration of largest firms measured by value added, and for shipments by SIC 2- and 4-digit industry, subject rpt, 2497–6
Manufacturing census, 1987: shipments of manufacturers products, by customer class and SIC 2- and 4-digit industry, subject rpt, 2497–4
Manufacturing finances and operations, by SIC 2- to 4-digit industry, forecast 1992, annual rpt, 2044–28
Occupational injury and illness rates, by SIC 2- to 4-digit industry, 1989-90, annual rpt, 6844–7
Occupational injury and illness rates, by SIC 2- to 4-digit industry, 1990, annual rpt, 6844–1
Price indexes (producer), by stage of processing and detailed commodity, monthly rpt, 6762–6
Price indexes (producer), by stage of processing and detailed commodity, monthly 1991, annual rpt, 6764–2
Productivity of labor and capital, and indexes of output, hours, and employment, 1967-90, annual rpt, 6824–1.5

Lawrence Berkeley Laboratory
"Prediction of Release Rates for a Potential Waste Repository at Yucca Mountain", 3368–4
see also Department of Energy National Laboratories

Lawrence Livermore National Laboratory
see also Department of Energy National Laboratories

Lawrence, Mass.
CPI by component for US city average, and by region, population size, and for 15 metro areas, monthly rpt, 6762–1
CPI by component for US city average, and by selected metro area, region, and population size, monthly rpt, 6762–2
Wages by occupation, and benefits, for office and plant workers, 1991 survey, periodic MSA rpt, 6785–16.3

Lawyers and legal services
AFDC hearings dispositions, by type of claimant representation, FY90, annual rpt, 4584–3.4
County Business Patterns, 1989: employment, establishments, and payroll, by SIC 2- to 4-digit industry and county, annual State rpt series, 2326–8
County Business Patterns, 1990: employment, establishments, and payroll, by SIC 2- to 4-digit industry and county, annual State rpt series, 2326–6
CPI by component for US city average, and by selected metro area, region, and population size, monthly rpt, 6762–2
Employment and economic conditions, alternative BLS projections to 2005 and trends 1975-90, biennial rpt, 6744–19
Employment and spending for law enforcement, by activity and level of govt, data compilation, 1992 annual rpt, 6064–6.1
Employment, earnings, and hours, by SIC 1- to 4-digit industry, monthly 1989-Feb 1992, annual rpt, 6744–4
Exports and imports of services, direct and among multinatl firms affiliates, by industry and world area, 1986-91, article, 2702–1.336
Fed Govt accounts receivable, delinquent debt cases and collections of Justice Dept and private law firms, pilot project results, FY91, annual rpt, 6004–20
Federal judicial personnel, by position, June 1990-91, annual rpt, 18204–8.11
Finances and operations, by SIC 2- to 4-digit industry, forecast 1992, annual rpt, 2044–28
Foreign countries interests represented by former US govt officials, activities and individuals, FY86-91, GAO rpt, 26123–134

Govt spending, employment and payroll, by activity, level of govt, and State, FY90, annual rpt, 6066–25.50
House of Representatives salaries, expenses, and contingent fund disbursement, detailed listings, quarterly rpt, 21942–1
Input-output structure of US economy, detailed interindustry transactions for 541 industries, and components of final demand, 1982 benchmark data, 2708–17
Labor demand, turnover, and training completions, by detailed occupation, 1990 and projected to 2005, biennial rpt, 6744–3
Merit Systems Protection Board activities, staff, and finances, FY91, annual rpt, 9494–5
Multinatl firms US affiliates finances and operations, by industry, country of parent firm, and State, 1987, 2708–48
Multinatl US firms and foreign affiliates finances and operations, by industry and country, 1989 benchmark survey, annual rpt, 2704–5
Natl income and product accounts, comprehensive accounts and components, benchmark revisions, 1929-88, 2708–5
Natl income and product accounts, comprehensive accounts and components, *Survey of Current Business*, monthly rpt, 2702–1.25
Occupational injury and illness rates, by SIC 2- to 4-digit industry, 1989-90, annual rpt, 6844–7
Occupational injury and illness rates, by SIC 2- to 4-digit industry, 1990, annual rpt, 6844–1
Occupational Outlook Handbook, 1992-93, biennial rpt, 6744–1
Pacific territories population and housing detailed characteristics, by location, 1990 Census of Population and Housing, series, 2551–8
Senate receipts, itemized expenses by payee, and balances, 1st half FY92, semiannual listing, 25922–1
Sentences under Federal mandatory minimum provisions, by defendant characteristics, and views on justice system impacts, FY90, 17668–2
States criminal justice systems activities, employment, funding, and data collection, by State, 1970s-91, annual rpt, 6064–40
Statistical Abstract of US, 1992 annual data compilation, 2324–1.5
Tax (income) returns of corporations, income and tax items by asset size and detailed industry, 1989, annual rpt, 8304–4; 8304–21
Tax (income) returns of partnerships, income statement and balance sheet items, by industry group, 1990, annual article, 8302–2.314
Tax (income) returns of sole proprietorships, income statement items, by industry group, 1990, annual article, 8302–2.317; 8302–2.320
Tax exempt organizations and employee plans listed on IRS masterfile, determinations, applications, and rulings, FY91, annual rpt, 8304–3.2
Traffic accidents direct and indirect costs, by cost type, payment source, and severity, 1980s, 7558–114
Workers compensation contested claims cases represented by attorneys, by State, 1987-90, annual rpt, 6504–9
Workers compensation laws of States and Fed Govt, 1992 annual rpt, 6504–11
see also Judges
see also Legal aid
see also Legal arbitration and mediation
see also Legal education
see also Legal ethics
see also U.S. attorneys

Layoffs
see Labor turnover

Lazenby, Helen C.
"National Health Accounts: Lessons from the U.S. Experience", 4652–1.323

Lead and lead industry
Business statistics, detailed data for major industries and economic indicators, *Survey of Current Business*, monthly rpt, 2702–1.16
Business statistics, detailed data for major industries and economic indicators, 1960-91, *Survey of Current Business* biennial supplement, 2704–1
Byproducts of primary metals mining, production and prices by commodity, 1965-90, 5608–170
Castings (nonferrous) shipments, by metal type, 1991, annual Current Industrial Rpt, 2506–10.5
Exports and imports between US and outlying areas, by detailed commodity and mode of transport, 1991, annual rpt, 2424–11
Exports and imports of US, by country and detailed commodity, monthly rpt, 2422–12
Exports and imports of US, by Harmonized System 6-digit commodity and country, 1991, annual rpt, 2424–13
Exports and imports of US, by transport mode, country, and SITC 1- to 3-digit commodity, 1991, annual rpt, 2424–12
Exports of US, detailed Schedule B commodities with countries of destination, 1991, annual rpt, 2424–10
Input-output structure of US economy, detailed interindustry transactions for 541 industries, and components of final demand, 1982 benchmark data, 2708–17
Manufacturing annual survey, 1990: finances and operations, by SIC 2- to 4-digit industry, series, 2506–14
Manufacturing finances and operations, by SIC 2- to 4-digit industry, forecast 1992, annual rpt, 2044–28
Mineral Industry Surveys, commodity review of production, trade, stocks, and use, monthly rpt, 5612–1.13
Mineral Industry Surveys, State reviews of production, 1991, preliminary annual rpt, 5614–6
Minerals Yearbook, Vol 1, 1989: commodity reviews of production, use, trade, prices, and mining operations, annual rpt, 5604–33
Minerals Yearbook, Vol 1, 1990: commodity review of production, reserves, supply, use, and trade, annual rpt, 5604–20.35
Minerals Yearbook, Vol 2, 1989: State reviews of production and sales by commodity, and business activity, annual rpt series, 5604–16
Minerals Yearbook, Vol 2, 1990: State reviews of production and sales by commodity, and business activity, annual rpt series, 5604–22
Minerals Yearbook, Vol 3, 1989: foreign country reviews of production, trade, and policy, by commodity, annual rpt, 5604–35
Mines (metal) and related operations occupational injuries and incidence, employment, and hours, 1990, annual rpt, 6664–3
Price indexes (producer), by stage of processing and detailed commodity, monthly rpt, 6762–6
Price indexes (producer), by stage of processing and detailed commodity, monthly 1991, annual rpt, 6764–2
Production in 5 western States, and prices, for 5 nonferrous metals, 1848-1990, 5608–178
Production, prices, trade, and foreign and US industry devs, by commodity, bimonthly rpt, 5602–4
Production, prices, trade, use, employment, tariffs, and stockpiles, by mineral, with foreign comparisons, 1987-91, annual rpt, 5604–18
Production, trade, use, and foreign investment in US industry, for minerals, 1985-90 and projected to 2000, annual rpt, 5304–5
Steel (hot-rolled) products containing lead or bismuth from 4 countries, injury to US industry from foreign subsidized and less than fair value imports, investigation with background financial and operating data, 1992 rpt, 9886–19.82
Stockpiling of strategic material by Fed Govt, activity, and inventory by commodity, as of Sept 1991, semiannual rpt, 3542–22
Stockpiling of strategic material, inventories and needs, by commodity, 1992, annual rpt, 3544–37
see also Lead poisoning and pollution

Lead poisoning and pollution
Air pollution levels for 6 pollutants, and measurements exceeding natl standards, by site, 1990-91, annual rpt, 9194–5
Air pollution levels for 6 pollutants, by source and selected MSA, 1982-91, annual rpt, 9194–1
California OCS oil and gas dev impacts on water quality, marine life, and sediments, by site, 1986-90, annual rpt, 5734–11
Carcinogens chemistry, sources, environment and health risks, and regulation, by substance and brand, 1991 annual rpt, 4044–15
Coastal and estuarine pollutant concentrations in fish, shellfish, and environment, series, 2176–3
Environmental Quality, status of problems, protection programs, research, and intl issues, 1991 annual rpt, 484–1
Great Lakes industrial water pollution emissions, comparison of State, EPA, Intl Joint Commission, and Ontario standards, 1991 rpt, 14648–29
Health condition and care indicators, 1950s-90 with health improvement and disease prevention goals for 1990, annual data compilation, 4144–11

Imports detained by FDA, by reason, product, shipper, brand, and country, monthly listing, 4062–2
Industrial hazardous substances releases and reduction methods under EPA regulation, by chemical, source, industry, and location, 1989, annual rpt, 9234–6
Industrial hazardous substances releases and reduction methods under EPA regulation, with chemical stocks and use, facility directory, 1987-89, annual CD-ROM, 9234–7
Paint (lead-based) abatement costs and results, demonstration project design and findings, 1991 rpt, 5188–131
Paint (lead-based) abatement programs for low- and moderate-income housing, HUD grants to public agencies, 1992 press release, 5006–3.102
Tax (excise) on hazardous waste generation and disposal, rates, and firms filing returns, by substance type, 1989, annual article, 8302–2.303
Water quality, chemistry, hydrology, and other characteristics, local area studies, series, 5666–27
Water supply and quality in streams and lakes, and groundwater levels in wells, by drainage basin, 1990, annual State rpt series, 5666–10
Water supply and quality in streams and lakes, and groundwater levels in wells, by drainage basin, 1990-91, annual CD-ROM, 5664–18
Water supply and quality in streams and lakes, and groundwater levels in wells, by drainage basin, 1991, annual State rpt series, 5666–12

Leading indicators
see Economic indicators

Leak, William B.
"Ecology and Management of Northern Hardwood Forests in New England", 1208–405

Learning disabilities
Digest of Education Statistics, 1992 annual data compilation, 4824–2
Special education programs, enrollment by age, staff, funding, and needs, by type of handicap and State, 1990/91, annual rpt, 4944–4

Leasing
see Mineral leases
see Motor vehicle rental
see Oil and gas leases
see Rental industries

Leather industry and products
Business statistics, detailed data for major industries and economic indicators, *Survey of Current Business*, monthly rpt, 2702–1.14
Business statistics, detailed data for major industries and economic indicators, 1960-91, *Survey of Current Business* biennial supplement, 2704–1
Collective bargaining agreements expiring during year, and workers covered, by firm, union, industry group, and State, 1992, annual rpt, 6784–9
County Business Patterns, 1989: employment, establishments, and payroll, by SIC 2- to 4-digit industry and county, annual State rpt series, 2326–8
County Business Patterns, 1990: employment, establishments, and payroll, by SIC 2- to 4-digit industry and county, annual State rpt series, 2326–6
Employment, earnings, and hours, by SIC 1- to 4-digit industry, monthly 1989-Feb 1992, annual rpt, 6744–4
Energy use and prices, by fuel type and manufacturing industry, 1974-88, 3166–15.3
Energy use and prices for manufacturing industries, 1988 survey, series, 3166–13
Exports and imports between US and outlying areas, by detailed commodity and mode of transport, 1991, annual rpt, 2424–11
Exports and imports of dairy, livestock, and poultry products, by commodity and country, FAS monthly circular, 1925–32
Exports and imports of US, by country and detailed commodity, monthly rpt, 2422–12
Exports and imports of US, by Harmonized System 6-digit commodity and country, 1991, annual rpt, 2424–13
Exports and imports of US, by selected country, country group, and commodity group, 1991, annual rpt, 2044–37
Exports and imports of US, by transport mode, country, and SITC 1- to 3-digit commodity, 1991, annual rpt, 2424–12
Exports, imports, and balances of US for manufactured goods, by SITC 2-digit commodity and country, quarterly rpt, 2042–35
Exports of US, detailed commodities by country, monthly CD-ROM, 2422–13
Exports of US, detailed Schedule B commodities with countries of destination, 1991, annual rpt, 2424–10
Freight (waterborne domestic and foreign) by commodity, traffic, and passengers, by port and waterway, 1989, annual rpt, 3754–3
Hazardous substances industrial releases and reduction methods under EPA regulation, by chemical, source, industry, and location, 1989, annual rpt, 9234–6
Hazardous substances industrial releases and reduction methods under EPA regulation, with chemical stocks and use, facility directory, 1987-89, annual CD-ROM, 9234–7
Imports, exports, and employment impacts, by SIC 2- to 4-digit industry and commodity, quarterly rpt, 2322–2
Imports of US, detailed commodities by country, monthly CD-ROM, 2422–14
Imports of US given duty-free treatment for value of US material sent abroad, by commodity and country, 1987-90, annual rpt, 9884–14
Input-output structure of US economy, detailed interindustry transactions for 84 industries, and components of final demand, 1987, annual article, 2702–1.316
Input-output structure of US economy, detailed interindustry transactions for 541 industries, and components of final demand, 1982 benchmark data, 2708–17
Luggage, storage, and carrying cases production, shipments, and trade, annual Current Industrial Rpt, discontinued, 2506–6.13
Manufacturing annual survey, 1990: finances and operations, by SIC 2- to 4-digit industry, series, 2506–14
Manufacturing census, 1987: concentration of largest firms measured by value added, and for shipments by SIC 2- and 4-digit industry, subject rpt, 2497–6
Manufacturing census, 1987: shipments of manufacturers products, by customer class and SIC 2- and 4-digit industry, subject rpt, 2497–4
Manufacturing finances and operations, by SIC 2- to 4-digit industry, forecast 1992, annual rpt, 2044–28
Manufacturing industries operations and performance, analytical rpt series, 2506–16
Manufacturing production, shipments, inventories, orders, and pollution control costs, periodic Current Industrial Rpt series, 2506–3
Mexico imports from US, by industry and State, 1987-91, 2048–154
Multinatl firms US affiliates finances and operations, by industry, country of parent firm, and State, 1987, 2708–48
Multinatl US firms and foreign affiliates finances and operations, by industry and country, 1989 benchmark survey, annual rpt, 2704–5
Occupational injury and illness rates, by SIC 2- to 4-digit industry, 1989-90, annual rpt, 6844–7
Occupational injury and illness rates, by SIC 2- to 4-digit industry, 1990, annual rpt, 6844–1
OECD trade, total and for 4 major countries, and US trade by country, by commodity, 1980-90, world area rpt series, 9116–1
Pacific territories population and housing detailed characteristics, by location, 1990 Census of Population and Housing, series, 2551–8
Pollution abatement capital and operating costs, by SIC 2- to 4-digit industry and State, 1990, annual Current Industrial Rpt, 2506–3.6
Price indexes (producer), by stage of processing and detailed commodity, monthly rpt, 6762–6
Price indexes (producer), by stage of processing and detailed commodity, monthly 1991, annual rpt, 6764–2
Puerto Rico and other US possessions corporations income tax returns, income and tax items, and employment, by selected industry, 1989, article, 8302–2.326
Science, engineering, and technical employment in manufacturing, by field and industry, 1989, triennial rpt, 9627–23
Tariff Schedule of US, classifications and rates of duty by detailed imported commodity, 1993 base edition, 9886–13
Tax (income) returns of corporations, income and tax items by asset size and detailed industry, 1989, annual rpt, 8304–4; 8304–21
Tax (income) returns of sole proprietorships, income statement items, by industry group, 1990, annual article, 8302–2.317; 8302–2.320
see also Hides and skins
see also Shoes and shoe industry
see also under By Commodity in the "Index by Categories"

see also under By Industry in the "Index by Categories"

Leatherberry, Earl C.
"Forest Statistics for Minnesota's Central Hardwood Unit, 1990", 1206–24.11
"Timber Resource of Missouri's Eastern Ozarks, 1989", 1206–3.6
"Wisconsin's Timberland Plantations, 1983", 1206–34.9

Lebanon
Agricultural trade of US, by detailed commodity and country, 1991, annual rpt, 1524–8
Agricultural trade of US, by detailed commodity and country, 1991, semiannual rpt, 1522–4
AID economic aid to developing countries, obligations and disbursements by country, quarterly rpt, 9912–4
AID loans repayment status and terms by program and country, and status of predecessor agency loans, quarterly rpt, 9912–3
Boycotts (intl) by OPEC and other countries, US firms and individuals cooperation and tax benefits denied, 1990, article, 8302–2.323
Economic and military aid and loans from US and intl agencies, by program and country, FY46-91, annual rpt, 9914–5
Economic and social conditions of developing countries from 1960s, and Intl Dev Cooperation Agency and AID activities and funding, FY91-93, annual rpt, 9904–4
Economic, social, political, and geographic summary data, by country, 1992, annual factbook, 9114–2
Exports and imports of US, by transport mode, country, and SITC 1- to 3-digit commodity, 1991, annual rpt, 2424–12
Exports of US, detailed Schedule B commodities with countries of destination, 1991, annual rpt, 2424–10
Hostages held in Lebanon, and releases, listing as of 1991, annual rpt, 7004–13; 7004–22
Human rights conditions in 170 countries, and US economic and military aid, 1991, annual rpt, 21384–3
Military aid of US, arms sales, and training programs costs and budget requests, by program, world region, and country, FY91-93, annual rpt, 7144–13
Military spending, arms trade, and force strengths, with govt spending and population, by country, 1979-89, annual rpt, 9824–1
Minerals Yearbook, Vol 3, 1989: foreign country review of production, trade, and policy, by commodity, annual rpt, 5604–35.3
Population size, growth rates, and components of change, by country, projected 1990-2020 and trends from 1950, biennial rpt, 2324–9
Refugee migration, and intl aid programs, by world area and country of origin and asylum, 1991, annual rpt, 7004–15
UN voting record and share of votes in agreement with US, by issue, country, and world area, 1991, annual rpt, 7004–18

Lebanon, Pa.
Wages by occupation, and benefits for office and plant workers, 1992 survey, periodic MSA rpt, 6785–3.4

LeBlanc, Linda A.
"Unlocking Learning: Chapter 1 in Correctional Facilities. National Study of the Chapter 1 Neglected or Delinquent Program: Final Report", 4808–40.1; 4808–40.2

LeClere , Felicia B.
"Prevalence of Major Digestive Disorders and Bowel Symptoms, 1989", 4146–8.213

Lee, Elizabeth N.
"Poultry, Industry and Trade Summary", 9885–8.6

Lee, I-Min
"Quetelet's Index and Risk of Colon Cancer in College Alumni", 4472–1.339

Lee, Mei L.
"Output and Inflation Components of Medical Care and Other Spending Changes", 4652–1.308

Leeper, Eric M.
"Consumer Attitudes and Business Cycles", 9371–10.69
"Dynamic Impacts of Monetary Policy: An Exercise in Tentative Identification", 9371–10.89
"In Search of the Liquidity Effect", 9371–10.75

Lefkowitz, Doris C.
"Health Insurance, Use of Health Services, and Health Care Expenditures", 4186–8.24

Legal aid
Aliens (illegal) held in Immigration and Naturalization Service detention facilities pending hearings, and legal aid requests, 1980s-91, GAO rpt, 26119–409
Assistance (financial and nonfinancial) of Fed Govt, 1992 base edition, annual listing, 104–5
Drug abuse by mothers, treatment and other services use, referrals, needs, and barriers, for 13 NIDA-funded programs, 1990/91 survey, 4498–76
Employment and spending for law enforcement, by activity and level of govt, data compilation, 1992 annual rpt, 6064–6.1
Employment in Federal district courts, by court, 1991, annual report, 17664–1
Expenditures, employment, and payroll, by activity, level of govt, and State, FY90, annual rpt, 6066–25.50
Expenditures of Fed Govt in States, by type, program, agency, and State, FY91, annual rpt, 2464–2
Judicial Conf proceedings and findings, spring 1992, semiannual rpt, 18202–2
Public defender workloads in Federal district courts, and Equal Access to Justice Act petitions and decisions, 1991, annual rpt, 18204–8.3; 18204–8.9; 18204–8.25
States criminal justice systems activities, employment, funding, and data collection, by State, 1970s-91, annual rpt, 6064–40

Legal arbitration and mediation
Community Relations Service investigation and mediation of minority discrimination disputes, activities and funding, FY91, annual rpt, 6004–9
FmHA activities, and loans and grants by program and State, FY91 and trends from FY70, annual rpt, 1184–17
Labor disputes of airlines and railroads, Natl Mediation Board activities and caseloads, with data by carrier, union, and occupation, FY87-88, annual rpt, 9604–1
Labor-mgmt mediation and arbitration activities of Fed Mediation and Conciliation Service, and cases by issue, region, and State, FY85-90, annual rpt, 9344–1
Securities dispute arbitration between brokers and investors, outcomes related to forum type and other factors, 1992 GAO rpt, 26119–401

Legal education
Degrees awarded in higher education, by level, field, race, and sex, 1989/90 and trends from 1980/81, annual rpt, 4844–17
Digest of Education Statistics, 1992 annual data compilation, 4824–2

Legal ethics
Public opinion on crime and crime-related issues, by respondent characteristics, data compilation, 1992 annual rpt, 6064–6.2
see also Judicial ethics

Legal services
see Lawyers and legal services
see Legal aid

Legal Services Corp.
Budget of US, authoritative financial statements with appropriations, outlays, and receipts, by category and agency, FY91, annual rpt, 8104–2.2
Budget of US, obligations and authority by function, agency, and program, with summaries and analyses, FY93, annual rpt, 104–2
Expenditures of Fed Govt in States, by type, program, agency, and State, FY91, annual rpt, 2464–2

Legislative bodies
see Congress
see House of Representatives
see Senate
see State legislatures

Leibowitz, Arnold H.
"Role of Foreign Medical Graduates in the Delivery of Health Care in the U.S.: The Immigration Ramifications", 6366–6.2

Leigh, Barbara C.
"Alcohol Consumption and Sexual Risk-Taking in Adolescents", 4482–1.304

Leimer, Dean R.
"Mathematical Demonstration of the Pareto Optimality of Pay-As-You-Go Social Security Programs in a Closed Economy", 4746–26.18
"On the Existence of Pareto-Superior Reversals of Dynamically Inefficient Social Security Programs", 4746–26.17
"Pareto Optimality of Existing Pay-As-You-Go Social Security Programs", 4746–26.16
"Social Security, Uncertainty Adjustments, and the Consumption Decision", 4746–26.9

Leisure
see Recreation

Lemieux, Jeffrey
"Projections of National Health Expenditures", 26306–6.175

Leonard, Barbara
"Financial and Time Costs to Parents of Severely Disabled Children", 4042–3.329
Leonard, Mary L.
"Pollution Abatement and Control Expenditures, 1972-90", 2702–1.321
Leonesio, Michael V.
"Economic Retirement Studies: An Annotated Bibliography", 4746–26.14
"Social Security and Older Workers", 4746–26.22
Lesotho
Agricultural trade of US, by detailed commodity and country, 1991, annual rpt, 1524–8
Agricultural trade of US, by detailed commodity and country, 1991, semiannual rpt, 1522–4
AID economic aid to developing countries, obligations and disbursements by country, quarterly rpt, 9912–4
Economic and military aid and loans from US and intl agencies, by program and country, FY46-91, annual rpt, 9914–5
Economic and social conditions of developing countries from 1960s, and Intl Dev Cooperation Agency and AID activities and funding, FY91-93, annual rpt, 9904–4
Economic, population, and agricultural data, US and other aid sources, and AID activity, 1991 country rpt, 9916–12.58
Economic, social, political, and geographic summary data, by country, 1992, annual factbook, 9114–2
Exports and imports of US, by transport mode, country, and SITC 1- to 3-digit commodity, 1991, annual rpt, 2424–12
Exports of US, detailed Schedule B commodities with countries of destination, 1991, annual rpt, 2424–10
Human rights conditions in 170 countries, and US economic and military aid, 1991, annual rpt, 21384–3
Military aid of US, arms sales, and training programs costs and budget requests, by program, world region, and country, FY91-93, annual rpt, 7144–13
Military spending, arms trade, and force strengths, with govt spending and population, by country, 1979-89, annual rpt, 9824–1
Minerals Yearbook, Vol 3, 1989: foreign country review of production, trade, and policy, by commodity, annual rpt, 5604–35.1
Population size, growth rates, and components of change, by country, projected 1990-2020 and trends from 1950, biennial rpt, 2324–9
Refugee migration, and intl aid programs, by world area and country of origin and asylum, 1991, annual rpt, 7004–15
UN voting record and share of votes in agreement with US, by issue, country, and world area, 1991, annual rpt, 7004–18
Letter carriers
see Postal employees
Leveille, Gilbert A.
"Future Foods and Fads", 1504–9.1
Levine, Richard M.
"Mineral Industries of the USSR, 1990", 5604–39
Levit, Katharine R.
"Business, Households, and Governments: Health Care Costs, 1990", 4652–1.309
Lewerenz, George
"Inventory and Analysis of Federal Population Research, FY90", 4474–9
Lewin/ICF
"Evaluation of Winners and Losers Under Medicare's Prospective Payment System", 17206–2.38
"Examination of Winners and Losers Under Medicare's Prospective Payment System: A Synthesis of the Evidence", 17206–2.36
Lewis, Frank R.
"Acute Care Treatment", 4208–35
Lexington, Ky.
see also under By City and By SMSA or MSA in the "Index by Categories"
LGL Ltd.
"Acoustic Effects of Oil Production Activities on Bowhead and White Whales Visible During Spring Migration Near Point Barrow, Alaska—1990 Phase: Sound Propagation and Whale Responses to Playbacks of Continuous Drilling Noise from an Ice Platform, as Studied in Pack Ice Conditions", 5738–27
Li, Anlong
"Binomial Approximation in Financial Models: Computational Simplicity and Convergence", 9377–9.132
Libel and slander
Court caseloads for Federal district courts, 1991, annual rpt, 18204–8.18
Court civil and criminal caseloads for Federal district, appeals, and bankruptcy courts, by type of suit and offense, circuit, and district, 1991, annual rpt, 18204–11
Liberia
Agricultural trade of US, by detailed commodity and country, 1991, annual rpt, 1524–8
Agricultural trade of US, by detailed commodity and country, 1991, semiannual rpt, 1522–4
AID economic aid to developing countries, obligations and disbursements by country, quarterly rpt, 9912–4
AID loans repayment status and terms by program and country, and status of predecessor agency loans, quarterly rpt, 9912–3
Economic and military aid and loans from US and intl agencies, by program and country, FY46-91, annual rpt, 9914–5
Economic and social conditions of developing countries from 1960s, and Intl Dev Cooperation Agency and AID activities and funding, FY91-93, annual rpt, 9904–4
Economic, social, political, and geographic summary data, by country, 1992, annual factbook, 9114–2
Exports and imports of US, by transport mode, country, and SITC 1- to 3-digit commodity, 1991, annual rpt, 2424–12
Exports of US, detailed Schedule B commodities with countries of destination, 1991, annual rpt, 2424–10
Food supply, needs, and aid for developing countries, status and alternative forecasts, 1992 world area rpt, 1526–8.2
Human rights conditions in 170 countries, and US economic and military aid, 1991, annual rpt, 21384–3
Military spending, arms trade, and force strengths, with govt spending and population, by country, 1979-89, annual rpt, 9824–1
Minerals Yearbook, Vol 3, 1989: foreign country review of production, trade, and policy, by commodity, annual rpt, 5604–35.1
Multinatl US firms foreign affiliates, income statement items by asset size, industry, and country, 1988, biennial article, 8302–2.322
Population size, growth rates, and components of change, by country, projected 1990-2020 and trends from 1950, biennial rpt, 2324–9
Refugee migration, and intl aid programs, by world area and country of origin and asylum, 1991, annual rpt, 7004–15
Ships in world merchant fleet, tonnage, and new ship construction and deliveries, by vessel type and country, as of Jan 1992, annual rpt, 7704–3
UN voting record and share of votes in agreement with US, by issue, country, and world area, 1991, annual rpt, 7004–18
Librarians
Blind and disabled persons library services, readership, circulation, staff, funding, and holdings, FY91, annual listing, 26404–3
Digest of Education Statistics, 1992 annual data compilation, 4824–2
Elementary and secondary public school systems enrollment, finances, staff, and high school grads, by State, FY89-90, annual rpt, 4834–6
Employment and payroll, by function and level of govt, annual rpt series, 2466–1
Fed Govt labor productivity, indexes of output and labor costs by function, FY67-90, annual rpt, 6824–1.6
Indian and Hawaii Native public libraries services, project listing and funding by tribe and State, FY90, annual rpt, 4874–5
Labor demand, turnover, and training completions, by detailed occupation, 1990 and projected to 2005, biennial rpt, 6744–3
Occupational Outlook Handbook, 1992-93, biennial rpt, 6744–1
Public libraries finances, staff, and operations, by State and population size, 1990, annual rpt, 4824–6
Training in library science, grants for disadvantaged students, by instn and State, FY91, annual listing, 4874–1
VA health care facilities trainees, by detailed program and city, FY91, annual rpt, 8704–4
Libraries
Access, policy, technology, and other info services issues, recommendations, 1991 conf, 15638–16
Audiovisual activities and spending of Fed Govt, by whether performed in-house and agency, FY91, annual rpt, 9514–1
Banks in Fed Reserve System, expenses and operations itemized by service, office, and district, 1991, annual rpt, 9364–11
Blind and disabled persons library services, readership, circulation, staff, funding, and holdings, FY91, annual listing, 26404–3
County Business Patterns, 1989: employment, establishments, and payroll, by SIC 2- to 4-digit industry and county, annual State rpt series, 2326–8

County Business Patterns, 1990: employment, establishments, and payroll, by SIC 2- to 4-digit industry and county, annual State rpt series, 2326–6
Depository libraries for Federal publications, 1992 annual listing, 2214–1; 2304–2
Digest of Education Statistics, 1992 annual data compilation, 4824–2
Elementary and secondary students reading performance and factors affecting proficiency, 1988 and 1990 natl assessments, 4898–33
Govt direct spending and employment, by function and level of govt, selected years 1962-87, 10048–53
Govt finances, by level of govt, State, and for large cities and counties, annual rpt series, 2466–2
Higher education enrollment, faculty, finances, and degrees, by instn level and control, and State, FY88, annual rpt, 4844–13
Higher education instn revenue by source and spending by function, by State and instn control, FY82-90, annual rpt, 4844–6
Library of Congress activities, acquisitions, services, and financial statements, FY91, annual rpt, 26404–1
Natl Archives and Records Admin activities, finances, holdings, and staff, FY91, annual rpt, 9514–2
Natl income and product accounts, comprehensive accounts and components, benchmark revisions, 1929-88, 2708–5
Natl income and product accounts, comprehensive accounts and components, *Survey of Current Business*, monthly rpt, 2702–1.26
Occupational injury and illness rates, by SIC 2- to 4-digit industry, 1989-90, annual rpt, 6844–7
Peace Inst activities and finances, FY90-91, biennial rpt, 29594–1
Presidential libraries holdings, use, and costs, by instn, FY91, annual rpt, 9514–2
Public libraries finances, staff, and operations, by State and population size, 1990, annual rpt, 4824–6
School and public libraries, selected data, 1991 edition, annual rpt, 4824–2.30
Statistical Abstract of US, 1992 annual data compilation, 2324–1.4
see also Federal aid to libraries
see also Librarians
see also Medical libraries

Library of Congress
Activities, acquisitions, services, and financial statements of LC, FY91, annual rpt, 26404–1
Blind and disabled persons library services, readership, circulation, staff, funding, and holdings, FY91, annual listing, 26404–3
Budget of US, authoritative financial statements with appropriations, outlays, and receipts, by category and agency, FY91, annual rpt, 8104–2.2
Budget of US, obligations and authority by function, agency, and program, with summaries and analyses, FY93, annual rpt, 104–2
Buildings and grounds under Capitol Architect supervision, itemized outlays by payee and function, 2nd half FY91, semiannual rpt, 25922–2
Copyrights Register activities, registrations by material type, and fees, FY91 and trends from 1790, annual rpt, 26404–2
Education funding by Federal agency, program, and recipient type, and instn spending, 1960s-91, annual rpt, 4824–8
Labor unions recognized in Fed Govt, agreements and membership by agency and facility, as of Jan 1991, biennial listing, 9844–14
Publications and products of LC, 1992-93, biennial listing, 26404–6
see also Congressional Research Service
see also Copyright Royalty Tribunal

Library sciences
see Information sciences

Libya
Agricultural trade of US, by detailed commodity and country, 1991, annual rpt, 1524–8
Agricultural trade of US, by detailed commodity and country, 1991, semiannual rpt, 1522–4
AID loans repayment status and terms by program and country, and status of predecessor agency loans, quarterly rpt, 9912–3
Boycotts (intl) by OPEC and other countries, US firms and individuals cooperation and tax benefits denied, 1990, article, 8302–2.323
Economic and military aid and loans from US and intl agencies, by program and country, FY46-91, annual rpt, 9914–5
Economic and social conditions of developing countries from 1960s, and Intl Dev Cooperation Agency and AID activities and funding, FY91-93, annual rpt, 9904–4
Economic, social, political, and geographic summary data, by country, 1992, annual factbook, 9114–2
Exports and imports of US, by commodity and country, 1980-90, world area rpt, 9116–1.6
Exports and imports of US, by transport mode, country, and SITC 1- to 3-digit commodity, 1991, annual rpt, 2424–12
Human rights conditions in 170 countries, and US economic and military aid, 1991, annual rpt, 21384–3
Military spending, arms trade, and force strengths, with govt spending and population, by country, 1979-89, annual rpt, 9824–1
Minerals Yearbook, Vol 3, 1989: foreign country review of production, trade, and policy, by commodity, annual rpt, 5604–35.1
Oil production and exports to US, by major exporting country, detailed data, monthly rpt with articles, 3162–24
Oil production and exports to US, by major exporting country, detailed data, monthly 1973-88, 3168–123
Oil production, stocks, use, and trade, by selected country and country group, monthly rpt, 3162–42
Pan Am Flight 103 bombing in 1988 and other terrorist incidents, role of Libya, 1991, annual rpt, 7004–13
Population size, growth rates, and components of change, by country, projected 1990-2020 and trends from 1950, biennial rpt, 2324–9
UN voting record and share of votes in agreement with US, by issue, country, and world area, 1991, annual rpt, 7004–18

Licenses and permits
Aircraft registered with FAA, by type and characteristics of aircraft, make, carrier, State, and county, 1991, annual rpt, 7504–3
Alcohol sale permits revoked and suspended, fines, and inspections, for Bur of Alcohol, Tobacco, and Firearms, FY78-90, hearing, 21788–217
Animal protection, licensing, and inspection activities of USDA, and animals used in research, by State, FY90, annual rpt, 1394–10
Auto, van, and light truck ownership and operating costs, by vehicle size and year of operation, 1991 model year, biennial rpt, 7554–21
Boat registrations, by class, propulsion type, hull material, and State, 1991, annual rpt, 7404–1.1
Budget of US, authoritative financial statements with appropriations, outlays, and receipts, by category and agency, FY91, annual rpt, 8104–2.2
Child day care and early childhood education programs availability, demand, use, costs, and provider and enrollee characteristics, 1990 survey, 4808–39
Coal Surface Mining Reclamation and Enforcement Office activities and funding, by State and Indian tribe, FY91, annual rpt, 5644–1
Communications services revenue and expenses, itemized by SIC 2- to 4-digit kind of business, 1990, annual rpt, 2413–15
Credit unions federally insured, finances, 1990-91, annual rpt, 9534–1
Drug and medical device applications submitted to FDA, by disposition, quarterly rpt, annual data, 4062–3
Drug marketing application processing of FDA, by drug, purpose, and producer, 1991, annual rpt, 4064–14
Electric power and industrial plants exempt from oil and gas primary use prohibition, 1991, annual rpt, 3334–1
Electric power plants certification applications filed with FERC, for small production and cogeneration facilities, FY80-91, annual listing, 3084–13
Endangered species listing and mgmt activities of Fish and Wildlife Service and Natl Marine Fisheries Service, FY74-91, GAO rpt, 26113–578
Energy suppliers rate regulation, and hydroelectric project licensing, for FERC, FY91, annual rpt, 3084–9
Export licensing, monitoring, and enforcement activities, FY91, annual rpt, 2024–1
Exports and imports of services, direct and among multinatl firms affiliates, by industry and world area, 1986-91, article, 2702–1.336
Exports of goods, services, and investment, trade barriers, impacts, and US actions, by country, 1991, annual rpt, 444–2
Farm production itemized costs, by farm sales size and region, 1991, annual rpt, 1614–3

FCC licensing activities, by class of operation, FY91, annual rpt, 9284–4
Firearms dealers licensed by Bur of Alcohol, Tobacco and Firearms, views on regulatory inspections, 1992 survey, GAO rpt, 26119–429
Food marketing cooperatives exports under intl business arrangements, 1985-88, 1128–69
Forest Service activities and finances, by region and State, FY91, annual rpt, 1204–1
Govt finances, by level of govt, State, and for large cities and counties, annual rpt series, 2466–2
Govt finances, tax systems and revenue, and fiscal structure, by level of govt and State, 1992 with historical trends, annual rpt, 10044–1
Grazing of livestock on public desert areas, acreage, use, fees, and endangered species, 1988-90, GAO rpt, 26113–552
Grazing of livestock on public rangeland, allotments, permits, acreage, and stocking rates, by BLM State office, as of Sept 1991, GAO rpt, 26113–582
Hazardous material transport license applications by disposition, and certified test facilities by State and country, 1990, annual rpt, 7304–4
Health care facilities excluded from Medicare prospective payment system, quality standards and review, certification, accreditation, and licensing, 1991 survey, 17206–2.41
Home drug infusion therapy use, equipment, industry finances, and Medicare coverage options, 1992 rpt, 26358–258
Hospital closings relation to hospital and community characteristics, by metro-nonmetro location, 1980-87, article, 4042–3.341
Hydroelectric power plants licensing by FERC, impacts of environmental laws, with staffing and plant safety incidents, 1980s-90s, GAO rpt, 26113–599
Indian and govt lands under Bur of Indian Affairs mgmt, acreage, leases, and use, 1989, annual rpt, 5704–12
Kidney end-stage disease treatment facilities approved by Medicare, dialysis and transplant services and ownership, 1991 annual listing, 4654–17
Marine Mammal Protection Act admin, and populations, strandings, and catch permits by species and location, 1988-89, annual rpt, 2164–11
Meat plants inspected and certified for exporting to US, by country, 1991, annual listing, 1374–2
Medicare admin and research, and HCFA affirmative action and accreditation programs, FY87, annual rpt, 4654–5
Nuclear power plant operating licenses, and construction permits granted and pending, monthly rpt, 3162–24.8
Nuclear power plant operating licenses, and construction permits granted and pending, monthly 1973-88, 3168–123.8
Nuclear power plant safety standards and research, design, licensing, construction, operation, and finances, with data by reactor, quarterly journal, 3352–4
Nuclear power plant spent fuel storage capacity and inventories, by reactor, as of 1987, 3166–6.59
Nuclear Regulatory Commission activities, finances, and staff, with data for individual power plants, FY91, annual rpt, 9634–2
Nursing homes certification requirements, beds, and staff and training needs, by State, 1990, 17206–2.37
Pollution (water) discharge permits, and EPA info system coverage and costs, 1991-92, GAO rpt, 26125–46
Public lands acreage and use, and Land Mgmt Bur activities and finances, annual State rpt series, 5724–11
Public lands acreage, grants, use, revenues, and allocations, by State, FY91, annual rpt, 5724–1.2; 5724–1.3
R&D licenses for university activities supported by NSF and NIH, transfer to private firms, related income, and scientists associated with licensees, FY89-90, GAO rpt, 26113–575
Radio frequency assignments for mobile communications, effects of auctioning frequencies, 1990, 26306–6.169
Rail line abandonment, construction, and acquisition certificate applications, by disposition, FY89-91, annual rpt, 9484–1.1
SEC activities, securities industry finances, and exchange activity, selected years 1938-FY91, annual rpt, 9734–2
Small Business Admin dev company loan program and debenture sale activity, with data by firm, industry div, State, and region, quarterly rpt, 9762–6
Small Business Admin loan and contract activity by program and firm, and financial condition, FY91, annual rpt, 9764–1
Small Business Investment Companies capital holdings, SBA obligation, and ownership, as of July 1992, semiannual listing, 9762–4
Truck itemized costs per mile, finances, and operations, for agricultural carriers, 1991, annual rpt, 1311–15
Truck rates for fruit and vegetables paid by shippers and receivers, by commodity and city, and fleet itemized costs per mile, weekly rpt, 1311–22
TV channel allocation and license status, for commercial and noncommercial UHF and VHF stations by market, as of June 1992, semiannual rpt, 9282–6
USDA revenue, by source and subagency, FY88-92, GAO rpt, 26113–602
Waste (industrial) generation, disposal, and regulation, by industry and State, mid 1980s-90, 26358–256
West Central States drilling permits, by State, quarterly rpt, 9381–16.2
see also Building permits
see also Drivers licenses
see also Hunting and fishing licenses
see also Mineral leases
see also Motor vehicle registrations
see also Occupational testing and certification
see also Oil and gas leases
see also Royalties
see also Water permits

Licking County, Ohio
Housing and households characteristics, and unit and neighborhood quality, by MSA location for 11 MSAs, 1987 survey, supplement, 2485–8

Lidderdale, Tancred
"Demand, Supply, and Price Outlook for Oxygenated Gasoline, Winter 1992-93", 3162–24.301

Liebman, Jeffrey B.
"Capital Costs, Industrial Mix, and the Composition of Business Investment", 9373–1.304

Liebrand, Carolyn B.
"Southern Dairy Farmers' Evaluation of Milk Handlers", 1128–67
"Value of Cooperative Benefits to Southern Dairy Farmers", 1128–68

Liechtenstein
Agricultural trade of US, by detailed commodity and country, 1991, semiannual rpt, 1522–4
Economic, social, political, and geographic summary data, by country, 1992, annual factbook, 9114–2
Exports and imports of US, by transport mode, country, and SITC 1- to 3-digit commodity, 1991, annual rpt, 2424–12
Human rights conditions in 170 countries, and US economic and military aid, 1991, annual rpt, 21384–3
Multinatl US firms foreign affiliates, income statement items by asset size, industry, and country, 1988, biennial article, 8302–2.322
Population size, growth rates, and components of change, by country, projected 1990-2020 and trends from 1950, biennial rpt, 2324–9
UN voting record and share of votes in agreement with US, by issue, country, and world area, 1991, annual rpt, 7004–18

Life expectancy
Alcohol abuse direct and indirect costs, 1985, article, 4482–1.311
Cancer (breast) cases, survival, and death rates, by age, and change by birth cohort, 1970s-90s, article, 4472–1.341
Cancer (breast) disease-free survival probability relation to tumor size, histology, and other characteristics, study, 1992 article, 4472–1.335
Costa Rica and Guatemala life expectancy, and death rate by cause and age, by sex, 1984 and trends from 1900, working paper, 2326–18.64
Costa Rica economic indicators and reform issues, mid 1970s-90, working paper, 9916–13.5
Czechoslovakia health care system, spending, and population health condition indicators, 1988-89, article, 4042–3.363
Developing countries aged population and selected characteristics, 1980s and projected to 2020, country rpt series, 2326–19
Developing countries economic and social conditions from 1960s, and Intl Dev Cooperation Agency and AID activities and funding, FY91-93, annual rpt, 9904–4
Developing countries population size, life expectancy, and fertility, trends and forecasts, country rpt series, 2326–24
Foreign and US aged population and characteristics, by country, 1991 and projected to 2020, wallchart, 2328–82
Foreign countries and cities population density, and distribution, life expectancy, and infant mortality by world region, 1991, fact sheet, 2326–17.50

Foreign countries *Background Notes*, summary social, political, and economic data, series, 7006–2
Foreign countries economic, social, political, and geographic summary data, by country, 1992, annual factbook, 9114–2
Foreign countries population size, growth rates, and components of change, by country, projected 1990-2020 and trends from 1950, biennial rpt, 2324–9
Health condition and care indicators, 1950s-90 with health improvement and disease prevention goals for 1990, annual data compilation, 4144–11
Indian cancer cases, and incidence and survival rates, with comparisons to whites, for 2 States, 1982-87, article, 4472–1.347
Indian deaths, years of productive life lost, and life expectancy at birth, by IHS region, 1986-88, annual chartbook, 4084–7
Indian Health Service facilities, funding, operations, and Indian health and other characteristics, 1950s-91, annual chartbook, 4084–1
Latin America economic and social conditions, resources, trade, and aid, 1992, annual factbook, 9914–14
Life expectancy, and death rates by cause, by sex and age, 1900s-89 and projected to 2080, actuarial rpt, 4706–1.107
Life expectancy, by sex, income, education, and labor force status, for whites, 1979-85, article, 4042–3.347
Life tables, abridged, 1989, US Vital Statistics advance annual rpt, 4146–5.124
Life tables, 1991, and life expectancy by race and sex, from 1950, US Vital Statistics annual rpt, 4144–7
OECD members health care costs, hospital use, resources, and economic and health indicators, by country, 1960s-90, article, 4652–1.322
Older persons socioeconomic characteristics, 1900s-90 and projected to 2050, biennial chartbook, 12904–1
Older population, and health, economic, and other characteristics, with foreign comparisons, 1980s-91 with trends and projections, Current Population Rpt, 2546–2.165
Population size and components of change, alternative projections 1990-2080 and trends from 1900, annual actuarial rpt, 4706–1.106
Soviet Union and US economic and sociodemographic indicators, selected years 1970-90, handbook, 2328–80
Statistical Abstract of US, 1992 annual data compilation, 2324–1.2
Traffic accidents direct and indirect costs, by cost type, payment source, and severity, 1980s, 7558–114
Transplants of organs, failures, deaths, and survival rates, by hospital, 1987-89, annual rpt series, 4104–17
Vietnam population size, components of change, and selected characteristics, 1979, 1989, and projected to 2050, 2326–18.65

Life insurance

Asset risk assessment for insurance companies, with financial ratios by firm type and financial status, 1990 and trends from 1900s, article, 9373–1.314; 9373–27.3
Assets and debts of private sector, balance sheets by segment, 1960-91, semiannual rpt, 9365–4.1
Assets and liabilities of financial instns, by instn type, 1990, annual rpt, 9364–5.4
Assets and liabilities of life insurance companies, monthly rpt, 9362–1.4
Assets of life insurance industry by type, and South Central States guaranty fund limits, 1992 article, 9391–16.310
Consumer spending, natl income and product account benchmark revisions, 1929-88, 2708–5
Consumer spending, natl income and product accounts, comprehensive accounts and components, *Survey of Current Business*, monthly rpt, 2702–1.25
Economies of scale and other efficiency measures for life insurance industry, by asset size, 1989, technical paper, 9385–8.144
Employer-provided life insurance benefits, by plan type, age, occupation, and annual salary, 1990, article, 6722–1.346
Employment, earnings, and hours, by SIC 1- to 4-digit industry, monthly 1989-Feb 1992, annual rpt, 6744–4
Expenditures, coverage, and benefits for social welfare programs, late 1930s-90, annual rpt, 4744–3.1
Failures of life and health insurance companies, and State guaranty fund assessments, by State, 1975-90, GAO rpt, 26119–392
Farm loans at risk of default, lender losses, and selected farm financial indicators, by type of farm and lender, 1984-89, 1548–383
Fed Govt civilian employees demographic and employment characteristics, as of Sept 1991, annual article, 9842–1.301
Fed Govt civilian employees health and life insurance program coverage and finances, annual rpt, discontinued, 9844–35
Fed Govt civilian employees retirement, health, and life insurance benefits, coverage and finances of 4 programs, FY86-90, annual rpt, 9844–37
Fed Govt civilian employees work-years, pay rates, and benefits use and costs, by agency, FY90, annual rpt, 9844–31
Finances and operations, by SIC 2- to 4-digit industry, forecast 1992, annual rpt, 2044–28
Finances of insurance companies, by insurance type and firm, with some intl comparisons, 1991 conf, 9373–3.35
Financial condition of insurance industry, operations, assets, junk bond holdings, and State regulation, with intl comparisons, 1991 hearings, 25268–79
Health care (long-term) financing reform issues, 1991 rpt, 10176–3.7
Households net worth distribution under alternative sample weighting systems to account for inconsistency in survey design and response rates, 1992 rpt, 9368–91
Multinatl US firms and foreign affiliates finances and operations, by industry and country, 1989 benchmark survey, annual rpt, 2704–5
Occupational injury and illness rates, by SIC 2- to 4-digit industry, 1989-90, annual rpt, 6844–7
Occupational injury and illness rates, by SIC 2- to 4-digit industry, 1990, annual rpt, 6844–1
Population economic well-being indicators, by selected characteristics and household income and income-to-poverty ratio, 1984, 2546–20.22
State and local govt employees benefit plan coverage and provisions, by plan type, 1990, biennial rpt, 6784–21
Statistical Abstract of US, 1992 annual data compilation, 2324–1.16
Tax (estate) returns property and tax data, by size of gross estate and State, 1989-90, article, 8302–2.305
Tax exclusion for employee benefits, Federal revenue forgone and coverage indicators, by benefit type, 1950s-80s and projected to 1995, GAO rpt, 26119–389
Tax exempt organizations and employee plans listed on IRS masterfile, determinations, applications, and rulings, FY91, annual rpt, 8304–3.2
Transit systems finances and operations, by mode, size of fleet and urban area, region, and for 518 systems, 1990, annual rpt, 7884–4
Veterans and servicepersons life insurance, actuarial analyses of VA programs, 1991, annual rpt, 8604–1
Veterans and servicepersons life insurance of VA, finances and coverage by program and State, 1991, annual rpt, 8604–4
see also Area wage surveys
see also Old-Age, Survivors, Disability, and Health Insurance
see also Servicepersons life insurance programs

Light

see also Fiber optics
see also Lasers
see also Lighting equipment

Lighthouses and lightships

Mariners Weather Log, quarterly journal, 2152–8

Lighting equipment

Auto parts trade with Japan and other countries, 1985-90 and forecast to 1994, annual rpt, 2004–10
Bulb production, shipments, stocks, trade, and firms, by type, monthly and quarterly Current Industrial Rpts, 2506–12.13; 2506–12.33
Commercial buildings energy use, costs, and conservation, by building characteristics, survey rpt series, 3166–8
Commercial buildings lighting energy use and conservation, by building characteristics, 1986, 3166–15.1
County Business Patterns, 1989: employment, establishments, and payroll, by SIC 2- to 4-digit industry and county, annual State rpt series, 2326–8
County Business Patterns, 1990: employment, establishments, and payroll, by SIC 2- to 4-digit industry and county, annual State rpt series, 2326–6
Energy conservation programs of States, Federal aid and savings, by State, 1990, annual rpt, 3304–1
Energy conservation technologies for housing and commercial buildings, use, costs, efficiency, and residential tax credits, 1970s-90 and projected to 2010, 26358–259

Energy natl strategy Strategic Petroleum Reserve and energy efficiency issues, 1991 hearings, 21368–142
Exports and imports between US and outlying areas, by detailed commodity and mode of transport, 1991, annual rpt, 2424–11
Exports and imports of US, by Harmonized System 6-digit commodity and country, 1991, annual rpt, 2424–13
Exports and imports of US, by transport mode, country, and SITC 1- to 3-digit commodity, 1991, annual rpt, 2424–12
Exports, imports, tariffs, and industry operating data for lamps and lighting fittings, 1992 rpt, 9885–10.2
Exports of US, detailed Schedule B commodities with countries of destination, 1991, annual rpt, 2424–10
Fluorescent light ballast shipments, trade, and firms, by ballast type, quarterly Current Industrial Rpt, 2506–12.14
Glassware shipments, trade, use, and firms, by product, 1991, annual Current Industrial Rpt, 2506–9.3
Housing (rental) units, total, with HUD assistance by program, and eligible for aid, by unit, household, and neighborhood characteristics, and location, 1989, biennial rpt, 5184–11
Injuries from use of consumer products and related activities, by severity and victim age and sex, 1990, annual rpt, 9164–7
Injuries from use of consumer products, by severity, victim age, and detailed product, 1991, annual rpt, 9164–6
Input-output structure of US economy, detailed interindustry transactions for 84 industries, and components of final demand, 1987, annual article, 2702–1.316
Input-output structure of US economy, detailed interindustry transactions for 541 industries, and components of final demand, 1982 benchmark data, 2708–17
Labor productivity, indexes of output, hours, and employment by SIC 2- to 4-digit industry, 1967-90, annual rpt, 6824–1.3
Manufacturing annual survey, 1990: finances and operations, by SIC 2- to 4-digit industry, series, 2506–14
Manufacturing census, 1987: concentration of largest firms measured by value added, and for shipments by SIC 2- and 4-digit industry, subject rpt, 2497–6
Manufacturing finances and operations, by SIC 2- to 4-digit industry, forecast 1992, annual rpt, 2044–28
Occupational injury and illness rates, by SIC 2- to 4-digit industry, 1989-90, annual rpt, 6844–7
Occupational injury and illness rates, by SIC 2- to 4-digit industry, 1990, annual rpt, 6844–1
Office furniture shipments and exports, by product, 1991, annual Current Industrial Rpt, 2506–7.8
Price indexes (producer), by stage of processing and detailed commodity, monthly rpt, 6762–6
Price indexes (producer), by stage of processing and detailed commodity, monthly 1991, annual rpt, 6764–2
Shipments, trade, firms, and use, for lighting fixtures by product, 1991, annual Current Industrial Rpt, 2506–12.19
Traffic accidents impacts of roadway lighting, by circumstances, 1991 rpt, 7558–118
Wiring devices and supplies shipments, trade, use, and firms, by product, 1991, annual Current Industrial Rpt, 2506–12.18

Lilja, Janice G.
"Research on WIC Participation Effects on Medicaid Costs", 1504–9.1

Lime
see Nonmetallic minerals and mines

Lindgren, Sue A.
"Anti-Drug Abuse Formula Grants: Justice Variable Passthrough Data, 1990", 6066–23.7
"Justice Expenditure and Employment, 1990", 6066–25.50

Linens
see Household supplies and utensils

Ling, K. Charles
"Value of Cooperative Benefits to Southern Dairy Farmers", 1128–68

Lino, Mark
"Overview of Home-Based Work: Results from a Regional Research Project", 1702–1.307
"Payments of Child Support and Alimony", 1702–1.305
"Young Husband-Wife Households with Children", 1702–1.302

Liquefied natural gas
see Natural gas liquids

Liquefied petroleum gas
Business statistics, detailed data for major industries and economic indicators, *Survey of Current Business*, monthly rpt, 2702–1.17
Business statistics, detailed data for major industries and economic indicators, 1960-91, *Survey of Current Business* biennial supplement, 2704–1
Consumption of energy, by detailed fuel type, end-use sector, and State, 1960-90, State Energy Data System annual rpt, 3164–39
Exports and imports between US and outlying areas, by detailed commodity and mode of transport, 1991, annual rpt, 2424–11
Exports and imports of US, by country and detailed commodity, monthly rpt, 2422–12
Exports and imports of US, by Harmonized System 6-digit commodity and country, 1991, annual rpt, 2424–13
Exports and imports of US, by transport mode, country, and SITC 1- to 3-digit commodity, 1991, annual rpt, 2424–12
Exports of US, detailed Schedule B commodities with countries of destination, 1991, annual rpt, 2424–10
Farm prices received and paid, by commodity and State, monthly rpt, 1629–1
Farm prices received and paid, by commodity and State, 1991, annual rpt, 1629–5
Farm production inputs supply, demand, and prices, 1970s-91 and projected to 1996, article, 1561–16.301
Farm production inputs supply, demand, and prices, 1980s-92, article, 1561–16.304
Farm production itemized costs, by farm sales size and region, 1991, annual rpt, 1614–3
Foreign and US energy production, trade, use, and reserves, and oil and refined products supply and prices, by country, 1981-90, annual rpt, 3164–50
Freight (waterborne domestic and foreign) by commodity, traffic, and passengers, by port and waterway, 1989, annual rpt, 3754–3
Futures trading in selected commodities and financial instruments and indexes, for NYC, Chicago, and other markets activity, biweekly rpt, 11922–5
Heating fuels production, imports, stocks, and prices, by selected PAD district and State, seasonal weekly rpt, 3162–45
Housing (low income) energy aid, funding sources, costs, and participation, by State, FY90, annual rpt, 4584–1
Housing (rental) units, total, with HUD assistance by program, and eligible for aid, by unit, household, and neighborhood characteristics, and location, 1989, biennial rpt, 5184–11
Housing and households detailed characteristics, and unit and neighborhood quality, MSA surveys, series, 2485–6
Housing energy prices, by fuel type and State, 1990 and forecast 1991-92, 3166–6.61
Housing energy use, costs, and conservation, and household and housing characteristics, survey rpt series, 3166–7
Manufacturing energy use and prices, by fuel type and industry, 1974-88, 3166–15.3
Manufacturing energy use and prices, 1988 survey, series, 3166–13
Naval Petroleum and Oil Shale Reserves production and revenue by fuel type, sales by purchaser, and wells, by reserve, FY91, annual rpt, 3334–3
Pacific basin countries energy supply and demand, and implications for US trade, country rpt series, 3406–6
Price indexes (producer), by stage of processing and detailed commodity, monthly rpt, 6762–6
Prices and spending for fuel, by type, end-use sector, and State, 1990, annual rpt, 3164–64
Prices of fuel, by type, end-use sector, and region, projected 1991-2030, 3166–6.60
Statistical Abstract of US, 1992 annual data compilation, 2324–1.25
Supply, demand, and movement of crude oil, gas liquids, and refined products, by PAD district and State, 1991, annual rpt, 3164–2
Supply, demand, and prices, by fuel type and end-use sector, alternative projections by region, 1990-2010, annual rpt, 3164–96
Supply, demand, and prices, by fuel type and end-use sector, alternative projections 1990-2010, annual rpt, 3164–75
Supply, demand, and prices, by fuel type and end-use sector, projections and underlying assumptions, 1995-2010, annual rpt, 3164–90
Supply, demand, and prices, by fuel type and end-use sector, with foreign comparisons, 1991 and trends from 1949, annual rpt, 3164–74.1; 3164–74.2
Supply, demand, and prices, by fuel type, end-use sector, and country, detailed data, monthly rpt with articles, 3162–24

Supply, demand, and prices, by fuel type, end-use sector, and country, detailed data, monthly 1973-88, 3168–123
Supply, demand, trade, stocks, and refining of oil and gas liquids, by detailed product, State, and PAD district, monthly rpt with articles, 3162–6
Tax rates for gasoline and other motor fuel, by city and State, monthly rpt, 7552–1
Transportation energy use by mode, fuel supply, and demographic and economic factors of vehicle use, 1970s-90, annual rpt, 3304–5

Liquor and liquor industry
Appalachia food processing firms, employment, and shipments, and farm production, by commodity and State, 1960s-90, 9088–37
Business statistics, detailed data for major industries and economic indicators, *Survey of Current Business*, monthly rpt, 2702–1.13
Business statistics, detailed data for major industries and economic indicators, 1960-91, *Survey of Current Business* biennial supplement, 2704–1
Corn and barley feed and industrial use, revised estimates 1980s-91, article, 1561–4.301
County Business Patterns, 1989: employment, establishments, and payroll, by SIC 2- to 4-digit industry and county, annual State rpt series, 2326–8
County Business Patterns, 1990: employment, establishments, and payroll, by SIC 2- to 4-digit industry and county, annual State rpt series, 2326–6
CPI by component for US city average, and by selected metro area, region, and population size, monthly rpt, 6762–2
Employment, earnings, and hours, by SIC 1- to 4-digit industry, monthly 1989-Feb 1992, annual rpt, 6744–4
Exports and imports (agricultural) of US, by detailed commodity and country, 1991, semiannual rpt, 1522–4
Exports and imports between US and outlying areas, by detailed commodity and mode of transport, 1991, annual rpt, 2424–11
Exports and imports of US, by Harmonized System 6-digit commodity and country, 1991, annual rpt, 2424–13
Exports and imports of US, by transport mode, country, and SITC 1- to 3-digit commodity, 1991, annual rpt, 2424–12
Exports of US, detailed Schedule B commodities with countries of destination, 1991, annual rpt, 2424–10
Food marketing sector finances, operations, and merger activity, for processors and distributors, 1991, annual rpt, 1544–22
Freight (waterborne domestic and foreign) by commodity, traffic, and passengers, by port and waterway, 1989, annual rpt, 3754–3
Govt direct spending and employment, by function and level of govt, selected years 1962-87, 10048–53
Govt finances, by level of govt, State, and for large cities and counties, annual rpt series, 2466–2
Grain (feed) consumption, by end use, periodic situation rpt with articles, 1561–4
Grain production, prices, trade, and export inspections by US port and country of destination, by grain type, weekly rpt, 1313–2
Input-output structure of US economy, detailed interindustry transactions for 541 industries, and components of final demand, 1982 benchmark data, 2708–17
Manufacturing annual survey, 1990: finances and operations, by SIC 2- to 4-digit industry, series, 2506–14
Manufacturing census, 1987: concentration of largest firms measured by value added, and for shipments by SIC 2- and 4-digit industry, subject rpt, 2497–6
Manufacturing census, 1987: shipments of manufacturers products, by customer class and SIC 2- and 4-digit industry, subject rpt, 2497–4
Manufacturing finances and operations, by SIC 2- to 4-digit industry, forecast 1992, annual rpt, 2044–28
Molasses supply, use, wholesale prices by market, and imports by country, 1986-91, annual rpt, 1311–19
Natl income and product accounts, comprehensive accounts and components, benchmark revisions, 1929-88, 2708–5
Natl income and product accounts, comprehensive accounts and components, *Survey of Current Business*, monthly rpt, 2702–1.26
Occupational injury and illness rates, by SIC 2- to 4-digit industry, 1989-90, annual rpt, 6844–7
Occupational injury and illness rates, by SIC 2- to 4-digit industry, 1990, annual rpt, 6844–1
Price indexes (producer), by stage of processing and detailed commodity, monthly rpt, 6762–6
Price indexes (producer), by stage of processing and detailed commodity, monthly 1991, annual rpt, 6764–2
Production of distilled spirits, stocks, materials used, and taxable and tax-free removals, by State, monthly rpt, 8486–1.3
Retail trade sales and inventories, by kind of business, region, and selected State, MSA, and city, monthly rpt, 2413–3
Retail trade sales, by kind of business, advance monthly rpt, 2413–2
Retail trade sales, inventories, purchases, gross margin, and accounts receivable, by SIC 2- to 4-digit kind of business and form of ownership, 1990, annual rpt, 2413–5
Soviet Union and US economic and sociodemographic indicators, selected years 1970-90, handbook, 2328–80
State govt liquor store employment and payroll, by State, 1991, annual rpt series, 2466–1.1
State govt liquor store labor productivity and indexes of output, FY67-90, annual rpt, 6824–1.6
Statistical Abstract of US, 1992 annual data compilation, 2324–1.27
Tax (excise) collections of IRS, by source, quarterly rpt, 8302–2.1
Tax (income) returns of corporations, income and tax items by asset size and detailed industry, 1989, annual rpt, 8304–4; 8304–21
Tax (income) returns of sole proprietorships, income statement items, by industry group, 1990, annual article, 8302–2.320
Tax collections of State govts by detailed type of tax, and tax rates, by State, FY91, annual rpt, 2466–2.7
Tax enforcement activities and collections of Bur of Alcohol, Tobacco, and Firearms and IRS, 1991 hearing, 21788–217
Tax rates and revenue of State and local govts, by source and State, 1992 and historical trends, annual rpt, 10044–1
Tax revenue, by level of govt, type of tax, State, and selected large county, quarterly rpt, 2462–3
Wholesale trade sales and inventories, by SIC 2- to 3-digit kind of business, monthly rpt, 2413–7
see also Alcohol abuse and treatment
see also Alcohol use
see also Alcoholic beverages control laws
see also Beer and breweries
see also Wine and winemaking

Liquor laws
see Alcoholic beverages control laws

Literacy and illiteracy
Adult education and literacy programs funding, enrollment, and activities, fact sheet series, 4806–4
Adult literacy and English as a second language programs, Education Dept and State programs, enrollment, and funding, by State, 1988-91, 4808–41
Aliens excluded and deported from US by cause and country, 1892-1991, annual rpt, 6264–2.5
Costa Rica economic indicators and reform issues, mid 1970s-90, working paper, 9916–13.5
Developing countries aged population and selected characteristics, 1980s and projected to 2020, country rpt series, 2326–19
Developing countries economic and social conditions from 1960s, and Intl Dev Cooperation Agency and AID activities and funding, FY91-93, annual rpt, 9904–4
Foreign and US aged population and characteristics, by country, 1991 and projected to 2020, wallchart, 2328–82
Foreign countries economic, social, political, and geographic summary data, by country, 1992, annual factbook, 9114–2
Latin America economic and social conditions, resources, trade, and aid, 1992, annual factbook, 9914–14
Natl Education Goals progress indicators, by State, 1992, annual rpt, 15914–1
Pacific territories population and housing detailed characteristics, by location, 1990 Census of Population and Housing, series, 2551–8
Preschool child and parent literacy activities under Even Start program, and grants by recipient, FY90, annual listing, 4804–41
Workplace literacy program of Education Dept, project descriptions and funding, FY91, annual listing, 4804–40
Workplace literacy programs, demonstration projects funding and participants, FY88-90, 4808–43
Young adults literacy and reading scores, by race and education, 1985, annual rpt, 4824–2.28

see also Reading ability and habits
Literature
see Language arts
Lithuania
Agricultural production, prices, and trade, for former USSR republics, 1960s-91 and forecast 1992, annual rpt, 1524–4.1
Agricultural trade of US with Eastern Europe, by commodity group and country, 1988-91, 1928–11
Economic conditions, policy, and trade practices, by country, 1989-91, annual rpt, 21384–5
Economic, social, political, and geographic summary data, by country, 1992, annual factbook, 9114–2
Embassies of US in former Soviet republics and Baltic States, positions planned by function, and filled, 1992, GAO rpt, 26123–403
Energy supply and use, and social, economic, and political indicators for former Soviet Republics and Baltic States, 1989-90, 3168–126
Energy use and production of former USSR Republics, by fuel type, 1990, annual rpt, 3164–84.2
Human rights conditions in 170 countries, and US economic and military aid, 1991, annual rpt, 21384–3
Livestock and meat inventories, use, and imports, by former USSR republic, 1986-93, semiannual rpt, 1925–33.2
Military aid of US, arms sales, and training programs costs and budget requests, by program, world region, and country, FY91-93, annual rpt, 7144–13
Older population and selected characteristics, 1980s and projected to 2020, country rpt, 2326–19.8
Population size and characteristics of former Soviet Republics and Baltic States, 1989-92, 9118–19
Refugee migration, and intl aid programs, by world area and country of origin and asylum, 1991, annual rpt, 7004–15
UN voting record and share of votes in agreement with US, by issue, country, and world area, 1991, annual rpt, 7004–18
Litow, Leon
"Estimates of Median Four-Person Family Income, by State: 1974-89", 2626–2.60
Little, Arthur D., Inc.
"Final Report on Monitoring Hydrocarbons and Trace Metals in Beaufort Sea Sediments and Organisms", 5738–33
Little, Jane S.
"Lessons from Variations in State Medicaid Expenditures", 9373–1.303
"Public-Private Cost Shifts in Nursing Home Care", 9373–1.311
"Why State Medicaid Costs Vary: A First Look", 9373–27.1
Little, Marilyn
"Credit Union Industry Performance, 1991", 9381–14
Little Rock, Ark.
Economic and banking conditions, for Fed Reserve 8th District, quarterly rpt with articles, 9391–16
Freight (waterborne domestic and foreign) by commodity, traffic, and passengers, by port and waterway, 1989, annual rpt, 3754–3.2
see also under By City and By SMSA or MSA in the "Index by Categories"
Little White Salmon National Fish Hatchery
Activities of hatchery, late 1890s-1980s, 5508–114
Liu, Korbin
"International Infant Mortality Rankings: A Look Behind the Numbers", 4652–1.324
Livestock and livestock industry
Agricultural Conservation Program acreage and projects, by State, 1936-90, quinquennial rpt, 1808–1
Agricultural Stabilization and Conservation Service producer payments, by program and State, 1991, annual table, 1804–12
Agricultural Statistics, 1991, annual rpt, 1004–1
Business statistics, detailed data for major industries and economic indicators, *Survey of Current Business*, monthly rpt, 2702–1.13
Business statistics, detailed data for major industries and economic indicators, 1960-91, *Survey of Current Business* biennial supplement, 2704–1
Cattle (dairy) slaughtered under Federal inspection, 1991, annual rpt, 1317–1.6
Cattle and calves for beef and milk, by State, as of July 1992, semiannual press release, 1623–1
Cattle and calves for beef, ranches, inventory, producers, and returns, by herd size and region, mid 1940s-91, 1568–251
Cattle and calves loss to predators, disease, and other causes, by region and State, 1991, 1618–22
Cattle and calves on feed, inventory and marketings by State, monthly release, 1623–2
Cattle in beef herds, by region, 1964, 1978, and 1987, article, 1561–7.301
Coastal and riparian areas environmental conditions, fish, wildlife, use, and mgmt, for individual ecosystems, series, 5506–9
Desert areas public grazing acreage, use, fees, and endangered species, 1988-90, GAO rpt, 26113–552
Economic Indicators of the Farm Sector, balance sheets, and receipts by detailed commodity, by State, 1986-90, annual rpt, 1544–18
Exports and imports (agricultural) commodity and country, prices, and world market devs, monthly rpt, 1922–12
Exports and imports (agricultural) of US, by commodity and country, bimonthly rpt, 1522–1
Exports and imports (agricultural) of US, by detailed commodity and country, 1991, annual rpt, 1524–8
Exports and imports (agricultural) of US, by detailed commodity and country, 1991, semiannual rpt, 1522–4
Exports and imports between US and outlying areas, by detailed commodity and mode of transport, 1991, annual rpt, 2424–11
Exports and imports of dairy, livestock, and poultry products, by commodity and country, FAS monthly circular, 1925–32
Exports and imports of US, by country and detailed commodity, monthly rpt, 2422–12
Exports and imports of US, by Harmonized System 6-digit commodity and country, 1991, annual rpt, 2424–13
Exports and imports of US, by transport mode, country, and SITC 1- to 3-digit commodity, 1991, annual rpt, 2424–12
Exports of US, detailed commodities by country, monthly CD-ROM, 2422–13
Exports of US, detailed Schedule B commodities with countries of destination, 1991, annual rpt, 2424–10
Farm credit, terms, delinquency, agricultural bank failures, and credit conditions by Fed Reserve District, quarterly rpt, 9365–3.10
Farm finances, assets, liabilities, and debt by lender type, by State, 1960-89, 1548–384
Farm financial and marketing conditions, forecast 1992, annual chartbook, 1504–8
Farm financial and marketing conditions, forecast 1992, annual conf, 1504–9
Farm income, cash marketing receipts ranked by commodity and State, 1990, 1548–385
Farm livestock inventory, and prices and ratios to feed price, by selected animal, 1975-90, article, 1541–1.302
Farm sector assets by type, and real and nonreal estate debt, including and excluding operator households, by sales size, 1960-89, 1548–387
Foreign and US livestock, poultry, and dairy production, trade, and use, by selected country, FAS semiannual circular series, 1925–33
Foreign countries agricultural production, prices, and trade, by country, 1980-91 and forecast 1992, annual world area rpt series, 1524–4
Freight (waterborne domestic and foreign) by commodity, traffic, and passengers, by port and waterway, 1989, annual rpt, 3754–3
Futures and options trading volume, by commodity and exchange, FY91, annual rpt, 11924–2
Futures trading in selected commodities and financial instruments and indexes, for NYC, Chicago, and other markets activity, biweekly rpt, 11922–5
Imports of US, detailed commodities by country, monthly CD-ROM, 2422–14
Indian and govt lands under Bur of Indian Affairs mgmt, acreage, leases, and use, 1989, annual rpt, 5704–12
Input-output structure of US economy, detailed interindustry transactions for 84 industries, and components of final demand, 1987, annual article, 2702–1.316
Input-output structure of US economy, detailed interindustry transactions for 541 industries, and components of final demand, 1982 benchmark data, 2708–17
Marketing data for livestock, meat, and wool, by species and market, weekly rpt, 1315–1
Natl forests timber sales, expenses, and operations, by region, State, and forest, FY91, annual rpts, 1204–36
Natl rangeland livestock grazing, BLM mgmt, officials views, 1980s-90, GAO rpt, 26113–567
New Mexico Caballo Resource Area public land mgmt, and grazing, environmental, and leasing activities, FY90-91, annual rpt, 5724–17

Packers purchases and feeding, and livestock markets, dealers, and sales, by State, 1990, annual rpt, 1384–1
Price indexes (producer), by stage of processing and detailed commodity, monthly rpt, 6762–6
Prices received and paid by farmers, by commodity and State, monthly rpt, 1629–1
Prices received and paid by farmers, by commodity and State, 1991, annual rpt, 1629–5
Production inputs, output, and productivity for farms, by commodity and region, 1947-90, annual rpt, 1544–17
Production, inventory, and prices of meat, USDA forecasts accuracy, 1980s, GAO rpt, 26131–93
Production itemized costs, by farm sales size and region, 1991, annual rpt, 1614–3
Production itemized costs, receipts, and returns, by commodity and region, 1988-90, annual rpt, 1544–20
Production, prices, receipts, and disposition for meat animals, by species and State, 1990-91, annual rpt, 1623–8
Production, prices, trade, and marketing, by commodity, current situation and forecast, monthly rpt with articles, 1502–4
Production, prices, trade, and stocks, monthly rpt, 1561–17
Production, prices, trade, stocks, and use, periodic situation rpt with articles, 1561–7
Public lands acreage and use, and Land Mgmt Bur activities and finances, annual State rpt series, 5724–11
Public lands acreage, grants, use, revenues, and allocations, by State, FY91, annual rpt, 5724–1.2
Public rangeland livestock grazing allotments, permits, acreage, and stocking rates, by BLM State office, as of Sept 1991, GAO rpt, 26113–582
Radionuclide concentrations in air, water, humans, animals, and milk near Nevada and other nuclear test sites, 1990, annual rpt, 9194–17
Sheep and lamb trade, tariffs, and industry operating data, 1991 rpt, 9885–8.1
Sheep and wool production, use, and prices, and operations costs and returns, for western US, 1920s-90, 1548–382
Sheep slaughter, stock, and feeder lamb and ewe prices, weekly and biweekly rpt, 1315–2
Slaughter and meat production, by livestock type and State, monthly rpt, 1623–9
Slaughter of livestock, meat production, and slaughter plants, by species and State, 1991, annual rpt, 1623–10
Soviet Union and US economic and sociodemographic indicators, selected years 1970-90, handbook, 2328–80
Statistical Abstract of US, 1992 annual data compilation, 2324–1.23
Swine and pork trade, tariffs, and industry operating data, 1992 rpt, 9885–8.5
Swine inventory, value, farrowings, and farms, by State, quarterly release, 1623–3
Tax (income) returns of partnerships, income statement and balance sheet items, by industry group, 1990, annual article, 8302–2.314
Thefts, and value of property stolen and recovered, by property type, 1991, annual rpt, 6224–2.1
Water use by end use, well withdrawals, and public supply deliveries, by county, State rpt series, 5666–24
Wolf (gray) kills of livestock, and farmer compensation claims and payments, for Minnesota, late 1970s-80s, 5508–115
see also Animal diseases and zoonoses
see also Dairy industry and products
see also Hides and skins
see also Meat and meat products
see also Pasture and rangeland
see also Poultry industry and products
see also Veterinary medicine
see also under By Commodity in the "Index by Categories"

Living arrangements
AFDC beneficiaries demographic and financial characteristics, by State, FY90, annual rpt, 4584–7
Census of Population and Housing, 1990: detailed geographic coverage, State CD-ROM series, 2551–9
Census of Population and Housing, 1990: population and housing characteristics, detailed geographic coverage, State CD-ROM series, 2551–10
Census of Population and Housing, 1990: summary characteristics, households, and land area, by county, subdiv, and place, State rpt series, 2551–1
Census of Population, 1990: population characteristics and living arrangements, by county, place, and urban-rural location, State rpt series, 2531–1
Census of Population, 1990: population characteristics and living arrangements, for Native American, urban, and metro areas, series, 2531–2
Child living arrangements, and women's marriage and divorce experience, by race, 1970s-90, Current Population Rpt, 2546–2.166
Children (handicapped) enrollment by age, and special education programs staff, funding, and needs, by type of handicap and State, 1990/91, annual rpt, 4944–4
Consumer Income, socioeconomic characteristics of persons, families, and households, detailed cross-tabulations, Current Population Rpt series, 2546–6
Deaths during 1986, decedents health condition, services use, habits, and social, employment, and other characteristics, 4147–20.19
Developing countries aged population and selected characteristics, 1980s and projected to 2020, country rpt series, 2326–19
Drug abuse by mothers, treatment and other services use, referrals, needs, and barriers, for 13 NIDA-funded programs, 1990/91 survey, 4498–76
Family members supporting others outside household, by relationship, recipient living arrangements, and provider characteristics, 1988, Current Population Rpt, 2546–20.21
Foreign and US aged population and characteristics, by country, 1991 and projected to 2020, wallchart, 2328–82
Households composition, income, benefits, and labor force status, Survey of Income and Program Participation methodology, working paper series, 2626–10
Income (household) and poverty status under alternative income definitions, by recipient characteristics, 1979-91, annual Current Population Rpt, 2546–6.78
Income (personal) relative to median, by race and selected other characteristics, mid 1960s-89, Current Population Rpt, 2546–6.73
Indian and Alaska Native youth health condition and behavioral patterns, by sex and grade, 1988-90, 4088–3
Living arrangements, family relationships, and marital status, by selected characteristics, 1991, annual Current Population Rpt, 2546–1.461
Older persons living arrangements, by poverty status, 1991, annual rpt, 4744–3.1
Older persons socioeconomic characteristics, 1900s-90 and projected to 2050, biennial chartbook, 12904–1
Older population, and health, economic, and other characteristics, with foreign comparisons, 1980s-91 with trends and projections, Current Population Rpt, 2546–2.165
Pacific territories population and housing detailed characteristics, by location, 1990 Census of Population and Housing, series, 2551–8
Population economic well-being indicators, by selected characteristics and household income and income-to-poverty ratio, 1984, 2546–20.22
Poverty status of families, by detailed characteristics, 1980 and 1988, GAO rpt, 26131–102
Single parent families in own and others homes, by financial, housing, and other characteristics, 1989, 2486–1.14
Single person and nonfamily households social, economic and housing characteristics, by tenure, 1989, 2486–1.15
Statistical Abstract of US, 1992 annual data compilation, 2324–1.1
Supplemental Security Income and Medicaid eligibility and payment provisions, and beneficiaries living arrangements, by State, 1992, annual rpt, 4704–13
Supplemental Security Income recipients, by eligibility type and living arrangement, 1990, annual rpt, 4744–3.8
Supplemental Security Income recipients, by race, sex, living arrangements, age, eligibility, and State, quarterly rpt, 4742–1.2
VA health care services, needs, availability, structure, and funding, 1991 compilation of papers, 8608–9
Veterans post-traumatic stress cases by period of service, and VA treatment and rehabilitation program operations and staff, by site, FY91, annual rpt, 8704–6
Women (older) living alone, income by source, and expenses by type, by marital status, 1988-89, article, 1702–1.301
see also Caregivers and caregiving
see also Families and households
see also Foster home care
see also Group homes for the handicapped
see also Group quarters
see also Homeless population
see also Housing condition and occupancy

see also Rooming and boarding houses
see also Transient housing
Living standard
see Cost of living
see Family budgets
see Personal and household income
see Quality of life
Lloyd, Karen
"Outpatient Payment Policy Reform", 17206–1.15
Lo, Andrew W.
"Sources and Nature of Long-Term Memory in the Business Cycle", 9377–9.125
Loan delinquency and default
AID loans repayment status and terms by program and country, and status of predecessor agency loans, quarterly rpt, 9912–3
Banks (insured commercial and FDIC-insured savings) assets, income, and financial ratios, by asset size and State, quarterly rpt, 13002–3
Banks (insured commercial and savings) finances, for foreign and domestic offices, by asset size, 1990, annual rpt, 9294–4.2
Banks (insured commercial and savings) financial condition and performance, by asset size and region, quarterly rpt, 9292–1
Banks (natl) charters, mergers, liquidations, enforcement cases, and financial performance, with data by instn and State, quarterly rpt, 8402–3
Banks and thrifts finances and operations by deposit size, Fed Reserve functional cost analysis, 1991, annual rpt, 9364–6
Banks in Fed Reserve 8th District, financial performance indicators by asset size, 1988-91, annual article, 9391–16.307
Banks in Fed Reserve 9th District, finances and performance ratios, by State, quarterly journal, 9383–19
Banks in Texas, loan losses relation to loan volume growth and other factors, mid 1970s-90, article, 9379–1.305
Banks loan interest rates and default risk relation to GDP and money supply, model description and results, 1992 working paper, 9387–8.283
Banks profitability, balance sheet and income statement items, and financial ratios, by asset size, 1985-91, annual article, 9362–1.305
Bond (junk) issues by rating, and defaults by bond type, late 1970s-80s, working paper, 9373–27.14
Budget of US, obligations and authority by function, agency, and program, with summaries and analyses, FY93, annual rpt, 104–2
Credit card issuers disclosure of terms and conditions to consumers, with finances and operations, 1991 hearing, 21248–175
Credit unions (federally-insured) financial performance, by charter type and region, 1st half 1992, semiannual rpt, 9532–7
Credit unions federally insured, finances by instn characteristics and State, as of June 1992, semiannual rpt, 9532–6
Credit unions federally insured, finances, 1990-91, annual rpt, 9534–1
Credit unions financial performance and regulation, with background data, 1960s-90, GAO rpt, 26119–364
Credit unions with low income membership, financial, operating, and membership data, 1982-91, 9536–1.8
DOD programs fraud and abuse, audits and investigations, 2nd half FY92, semiannual rpt, 3542–18
Electric power distribution loans from REA, and borrower operating and financial data, by firm and State, 1991, annual rpt, 1244–1
Farm Credit System financial condition, quarterly rpt, 9262–2
Farm Credit System financial statements and loan activity by lender type, and borrower characteristics, 1991, annual rpt, 9264–2
Farm credit, terms, delinquency, agricultural bank failures, and credit conditions by Fed Reserve District, quarterly rpt, 9365–3.10
Farm finances, debts, assets, and receipts, and lenders financial condition, quarterly rpt with articles, 1541–1
Farm loan guarantees of FmHA, characteristics of borrowers, lenders, and loans, FY88, 1548–386
Farm loans at risk of default, lender losses, and selected farm financial indicators, by type of farm and lender, 1984-89, 1548–383
Fed Govt accounts receivable, delinquent debt cases and collections of Justice Dept and private law firms, pilot project results, FY91, annual rpt, 6004–20
Fed Govt foreign loan and credit arrearages, by program and country, as of Dec 1989, annual rpt, 15344–1.1
Fed Home Loan Mortgage Corp activities and financial statements, 1991, annual rpt, 9414–1
Financial instns loan loss computations for tax returns under alternative methods, 1991 rpt, 8008–157
FmHA activities, and loans and grants by program and State, FY91 and trends from FY70, annual rpt, 1184–17
FmHA loan guarantees to business and industry in rural areas, by State and industry, and closures and defaults, FY74-91, GAO rpt, 26113–591
FmHA loans and borrower supervision activities in farm and housing programs, by type and State, monthly rpt, 1182–1
FmHA loans, delinquencies, and lending practices, by loan program, FY88-91, GAO rpt, 26113–569
FmHA property acquired through foreclosure, acreage, value, and sales, for farm and nonfarm property by State, monthly rpt, 1182–6
FmHA property acquired through foreclosure, 1-family homes, value, sales, and leases, by State, monthly rpt, 1182–7
Foreign govts and private obligors debt to US, by country and program, periodic rpt, 8002–6
GSA programs fraud and abuse, audits and investigations, 1st half FY92, semiannual rpt, 9452–8
Interior Dept programs fraud and abuse, audits and investigations, 2nd half FY92, semiannual rpt, 5302–2
Labor Dept programs fraud and abuse, audits and investigations, 2nd half FY92, semiannual rpt, 6302–2
Military contractor debts owed to Fed Govt and deferred, status by service branch and firm, 1980-91, GAO rpt, 26123–400
Mortgage applications of minorities, for Boston by disposition and financial characteristics, with problems in analyzing lender disclosure statements, 1990, working paper, 9373–27.15
Mortgage foreclosure court caseloads for Federal district courts, 1991, annual rpt, 18204–8.14; 18204–8.18; 18204–11
Mortgage purchases, sales, and other activity of Fed Home Loan Mortgage Corp, 1990, annual rpt, 5184–8
Mortgage purchases, sales, and other activity of Fed Natl Mortgage Assn, 1991, annual rpt, 5184–9; 9474–1
Mortgages FHA-insured, and foreclosures, by State and county, 1991 and cumulative from 1934, annual rpt, 5144–15
Natural gas interstate pipeline company detailed financial and operating data, by firm, 1990, annual rpt, 3164–38
North Central States, FHLB 6th District insured S&Ls financial condition and operations by State, quarterly rpt, 9302–23
Rural Electrification Admin activities and finances, and loans by State, FY91 and trends from FY36, annual rpt, 1244–3
Rural Telephone Program loan activity, by State, FY91, annual tables, 1244–8
Savings instns failures, financial performance of instns under Resolution Trust Corp conservatorship, quarterly rpt, 9722–5
Savings instns insured by Savings Assn Insurance Fund, assets, liabilities, and deposit and loan activity, by conservatorship status, monthly rpt, 8432–1
Small Business Admin direct and guaranteed loans, principal outstanding, and losses, by program, borrower race and sex, and State, 1950s-90, GAO rpt, 26113–554
Small Business Admin guaranteed loans issued under regular, certified, and preferred lender programs, selected characteristics, FY83-90, GAO rpt, 26113–581
Small Business Admin loan guarantee program participants finances, operations, characteristics, and views, 1991 survey, 9768–25
Small Business Investment Company finances, losses, and program operations, 1980s-91, 25728–44
Small business loan collateral adequacy for failed firms, with loan liquidation recoveries and losses, FY89, GAO rpt, 26113–553
South Central States agricultural banks financial ratios, and farm finances and production growth, by State, 1980s-92, annual article, 9391–16.308
Southeastern States, Fed Reserve 5th District insured commercial banks financial statements, by State, quarterly rpt, 9389–18
Southeastern States, Fed Reserve 8th District banking and economic conditions, quarterly rpt with articles, 9391–16
Southeastern States, FHLB 4th District, employment and housing indicators by State, quarterly rpt, 9302–36

Statistical Abstract of US, 1992 annual data compilation, 2324–1.16
Student guaranteed loan participation and default rates, for correspondence schools, FY87-89, GAO rpt, 26121–448
Student guaranteed loan Stafford program, borrowers and likelihood of default by selected characteristics, 1989-90, 26306–3.120
Student guaranteed loans, defaults, and collections, by type of loan, lender, and guarantee agency, with data by State and top lender, FY91, annual rpt, 4804–38
Student Loan Marketing Assn activities and finances, 1991, annual rpt, 9784–1
Student loan Perkins program income, losses, and Federal and school contributions, late 1950s-89, GAO rpt, 26121–440
Student loans of Fed Govt in default, losses, and rates, by instn and State, as of June 1991, annual rpt, 4804–18
Student supplemental and parent loans and defaults, for freshmen and other students, by whether proprietary instn, FY89-91, GAO rpt, 26121–473
Tax (income) returns filed, by type of filer, selected income items, quarterly rpt, 8302–2.1
Tax (income) returns of corporations, income and tax items by asset size and detailed industry, 1989, annual rpt, 8304–4; 8304–21
Tax (income) returns of partnerships, income statement and balance sheet items, by industry group, 1990, annual article, 8302–2.314
Tax (income) returns of sole proprietorships, income statement items, by industry group, 1990, annual article, 8302–2.317
Tax exempt organizations with unrelated business income, finances by organization type, 1987, article, 8302–2.306
US attorneys case processing and collections, by case type and Federal district, FY91, annual rpt, 6004–2
USDA programs fraud and abuse, audits and investigations, FY92, semiannual rpt, 1002–4
VA benefit overpayment and home loan debt repayment waiver cases and dispositions, FY88-91, hearing, 21768–67
VA mortgage loan activity, defaults, and property acquired, FY67-91, annual rpt, 8604–5.3

Loans
Bank of Credit and Commerce Intl financial statements, audits, and selected loan data, 1984-90, hearing, 25388–60
Banking activity, consumer credit, and interest rates, monthly rpt series, 9365–2
Banking and financial conditions, 1990, annual rpt, 9364–5
Banks (commercial) loans and investments, 1972-91, annual rpt, 204–1.5
Banks (insured commercial and savings) finances, for foreign and domestic offices, by asset size, 1990, annual rpt, 9294–4.2
Banks (insured commercial and savings) financial condition and performance, by asset size and region, quarterly rpt, 9292–1
Banks (natl) charters, mergers, liquidations, enforcement cases, and financial performance, with data by instn and State, quarterly rpt, 8402–3
Banks and thrifts finances and operations by deposit size, Fed Reserve functional cost analysis, 1991, annual rpt, 9364–6
Banks and thrifts in New England, deposits by type and loans, relation to capital/asset ratios, by instn size, 1990-91, working paper, 9373–27.4
Banks capital availability impacts on lending, 1992 working paper, 9379–14.19
Banks in Fed Reserve System, expenses and operations itemized by service, office, and district, 1991, annual rpt, 9364–11
Banks loan amounts outstanding, for commercial and Fed Reserve banks, monthly rpt, 9362–1.1
Banks loan terms, monthly rpt, quarterly data, 9362–1.4
Banks mergers antitrust issues, with background financial data by State and selected instn, 1991 hearing, 21248–176
Banks profitability, balance sheet and income statement items, and financial ratios, by asset size, 1985-91, annual article, 9362–1.305
Business statistics, detailed data for major industries and economic indicators, 1960-91, *Survey of Current Business* biennial supplement, 2704–1
Election campaign finances to FEC, by type of filer, 1990 natl elections, biennial rpt series, 9276–2
Fed Financing Bank holdings and transactions, by borrower, monthly press release, 12802–1
Fed Govt financial operations, detailed data, *Treasury Bulletin*, quarterly rpt, 8002–4
Fed Reserve banks finances and staff, 1991, annual rpt, 9364–1.1
Financial, banking, and mortgage market activity, weekly rpt series, 9365–1
Intl financial markets performance of foreign and US bank and securities firms, finances and competitiveness issues, 1980s, compilation of papers, 9385–10
Monetary trends, Fed Reserve Bank of St Louis monthly rpt, 9391–2
New England States economic indicators, Fed Reserve 1st District, monthly rpt, 9373–2
New England States, FHLB 1st District thrift instns, financial condition, and locations, 1992, annual listing, 9304–26
Nonprofit charitable and other tax exempt organizations finances, by category and size of assets and contributions, 1988, annual article, 8302–2.315
North Central States, FHLB 6th District insured S&Ls financial condition and operations by State, quarterly rpt, 9302–23
Savings instns financial statements, for instns insured by Savings Assn Insurance Fund by FHLB district and State, and for FDIC-insured savings banks, 1989, annual rpt, 8434–1
Savings instns insured by Savings Assn Insurance Fund, assets, liabilities, and deposit and loan activity, by conservatorship status, monthly rpt, 8432–1
Securities credit issues of stockbrokers and other nonbank lenders, and brokers balance sheet, as of June 1991, annual rpt, 9365–5.1
Southeastern States, Fed Reserve 5th District, economic indicators by State, quarterly rpt, 9389–16
Southeastern States, Fed Reserve 5th District insured commercial banks financial statements, by State, quarterly rpt, 9389–18
Southeastern States, Fed Reserve 8th District banking and economic conditions, quarterly rpt with articles, 9391–16
Survey of Current Business, detailed financial and business data, and economic indicators, monthly rpt, 2702–1.1
Tax (income) returns of corporations, income and tax items by asset size and detailed industry, 1989, annual rpt, 8304–4
Tax exempt organizations finances, with data by type, size, State, and for largest organizations, late 1940s-80s, compilation of papers, 8308–35
West Central States economic indicators, Fed Reserve 10th District, quarterly rpt, 9381–16.2
Western States, FHLB 11th District shareholder instns, offices, and financial condition, 1992 annual listing, 9304–23
see also Agricultural credit
see also Commercial credit
see also Consumer credit
see also Credit
see also Credit unions
see also Discrimination in credit
see also Export-Import Bank
see also Farm Credit System
see also Federal aid programs
see also Federal aid to arts and humanities
see also Federal aid to education
see also Federal aid to higher education
see also Federal aid to highways
see also Federal aid to housing
see also Federal aid to law enforcement
see also Federal aid to libraries
see also Federal aid to local areas
see also Federal aid to medical education
see also Federal aid to medicine
see also Federal aid to railroads
see also Federal aid to rural areas
see also Federal aid to States
see also Federal aid to transportation
see also Federal aid to vocational education
see also Federal funding for energy programs
see also Federal funding for research and development
see also Finance companies
see also Foreign debts
see also Government and business
see also Government assets and liabilities
see also Interest payments
see also Interest rates
see also International assistance
see also Loan delinquency and default
see also Military assistance
see also Mortgages
see also Public debt
see also Student aid
see also Veterans benefits and pensions
see also Veterans housing

Lobbying and lobbying groups
Foreign countries interests represented by former US govt officials, activities and individuals, FY86-91, GAO rpt, 26123–134
see also Political action committees

Local-Federal relations
see Federal-local relations
Local government
Alaska rural areas population characteristics, and energy resources dev effects, series, 5736–5
Arts funding, by level of govt, State, and selected city, FY86-92, GAO rpt, 26119–371
Construction put in place, value of new public and private structures, by type, monthly rpt, 2382–4
Criminal justice spending of State and local govts, by State, 1988-90, 6066–23.7
Criminal justice systems activities, spending, and employment, by level of govt, data compilation, 1992 annual rpt, 6064–6.1
Expenditures (direct) and employment, by function and level of govt, selected years 1962-87, 10048–53
Finances of govts, by level of govt, State, and for large cities and counties, annual rpt series, 2466–2
Finances of govts, tax systems and revenue, and fiscal structure, by level of govt and State, 1992 and historical trends, annual rpt, 10044–1
Finances of State and local govts, revenue by source and outlays by type, 1987-91, annual article, 2702–1.311
Finances of State and local govts, spending and Federal grants by function, 1960s-91 and proposed to 1997, article, 9362–1.309
Finances, structure, and service delivery of local govts in metro areas, local area rpt series, 10046–9
Fiscal condition of State and local govts, with data by State and selected city, 1991 hearing, 21268–44
Flow-of-funds accounts, savings, investments, and credit statements, quarterly rpt, 9365–3.3
Hwy Statistics, detailed data by State, 1991, annual rpt, 7554–1
Job Training Partnership Act State and local admin, funding, effectiveness, and participants, GAO rpt series, 26106–8
Natl income and product accounts, comprehensive accounts and components, benchmark revisions, 1929-88, 2708–5
Natl income and product accounts, comprehensive accounts and components, *Survey of Current Business*, monthly rpt, 2702–1.26
Public opinion on taxes, spending, and govt efficiency, by respondent characteristics, 1992 survey, annual rpt, 10044–2
Retirement systems of State and local govts, cash and security holdings and finances, quarterly rpt, 2462–2
Science and Engineering Indicators, employment, education, R&D funding, and industry impacts, with foreign comparisons, 1960s-91, biennial rpt, 9624–10
Statistical Abstract of US, 1992 annual data compilation, 2324–1.9
see also Census of Governments
see also City and town planning
see also Federal aid to local areas
see also Federal-local relations
see also Fire departments
see also Municipal bonds
see also Police
see also School districts
see also Special districts
see also State and local employees
see also State and local employees pay
see also State and local taxes
see also State funding for local areas
see also State-local relations
see also Zoning and zoning laws
Location of industries
see Industrial siting
Lodging
see Hotels and motels
see Rooming and boarding houses
Loewenstein, Mark A.
"Bidding for Workers", 6886–6.95
Logistics
Fed Govt labor productivity, indexes of output and labor costs by function, FY67-90, annual rpt, 6824–1.6
Merchant ship crew supply, wartime needs, training, and sources, 1970s-90 and alternative projections to 2000, 7708–5
Military and personal property shipments by commercial cariers, and cost savings from bill audits and rate negotiations, FY99-91, GAO rpt, 26123–369
Military and personal property shipments, passenger traffic, and costs, by service branch and mode of transport, FY91, annual rpt, 3704–15
Military budget, manpower needs, costs, and force readiness by service branch, FY93, annual rpt, 3504–1
Military budget, R&D appropriations by item, service branch, and defense agency, FY91-93, annual rpt, 3544–33
Persian Gulf War aircraft, tank, and personnel carrier deployment and operating capability, and spare parts availability, 1990-91, GAO rpt, 26123–375
Persian Gulf War allied and other countries cash and in-kind contributions, by type and country, 1990-91, GAO rpt, 26123–371
Persian Gulf War chemical protective suits and masks contractor deliveries and field inspections, 1990-91, GAO rpt, 26123–387
Persian Gulf War costs to US by category and service branch, and offsetting contributions by allied country, monthly rpt, 102–3
Reserve forces personnel and equipment strengths, and readiness, by reserve component, FY91, annual rpt, 3544–31
see also Military supplies and property
Long Beach, Calif.
Housing and households characteristics, unit and neighborhood quality, and journey to work by MSA location, for 11 MSAs, 1985 survey, supplement, 2485–8
Housing and households characteristics, 1989 survey, MSA fact sheet, 2485–11.13
Housing and households detailed characteristics, and unit and neighborhood quality, by location, 1989 survey, MSA rpt, 2485–6.3
Housing starts and completions authorized by building permits in 40 MSAs, quarterly rpt, 2382–9
Wages by occupation, and benefits, for office and plant workers, 1991 survey, periodic MSA rpt, 6785–16.6
Long, DeWitt
"Nonresident Alien Estates, 1986", 8302–2.310
Long, Edward R.
"Status and Trends in Toxicants and the Potential for Their Biological Effects in Tampa Bay, Fla.", 2176–3.15
Long Island, N.Y.
CPI by component for US city average, and by region, population size, and for 15 metro areas, monthly rpt, 6762–1
CPI by component for US city average, and by selected metro area, region, and population size, monthly rpt, 6762–2
Housing starts and completions authorized by building permits in 40 MSAs, quarterly rpt, 2382–9
Hwy traffic mgmt and info electronic system, demonstration program results, late 1980s, 7558–119
Long, Michael
"Ohio Timber Products Output, 1989", 1206–15.11
Long, Wayne S.
"State and Local Government Workers Covered Under Social Security, 1987", 4742–1.315
Longitudinal Study of Aging
Design of survey, and data collection and estimation procedures, 1984-90, 4147–1.28
Longmont, Colo.
Housing vacancy rates for single and multifamily units and mobile homes, by city and ZIP code, 1992, annual MSA rpt, 9304–22.1
Longnecker, Matthew P.
"Serum a-Tocopherol Concentration in Relation to Subsequent Colorectal Cancer: Pooled Data from Five Cohorts", 4472–1.308
Longshoremen
Deaths involving cargo handling by circumstances, and OSHA standards violated, 1975-84, 6606–2.18
Employment shipboard, shipyard, and longshore, FY90-91, annual rpt, 7704–14.3
Labor supply in 4 coastal regions, monthly rpt, 7702–1
Workers compensation laws of States and Fed Govt, 1992 annual rpt, 6504–11
Workers compensation programs under Federal admin, finances and operations, FY91, annual rpt, 6504–10
Lorain, Ohio
CPI by component for US city average, and by region, population size, and for 15 metro areas, monthly rpt, 6762–1
CPI by component for US city average, and by selected metro area, region, and population size, monthly rpt, 6762–2
Lord, Ron
"Restructuring in Centrally-Planned Economies and the Outlook for Sugar", 1504–9.1
Los Alamos Scientific Laboratory
see also Department of Energy National Laboratories
Los Angeles, Calif.
Auto alternative fuels use in Federal fleet, energy economy performance at 4 sites, FY91, annual rpt, 3304–28
Banks loan activity in low income and minority communities, 1991 hearing, 21248–176

Commuters, by county of residence and work, for top 10 metro areas, 1990 Census of Population, press release, 2328–84
CPI by component for US city average, and by region, population size, and for 15 metro areas, monthly rpt, 6762–1
CPI by component for US city average, and by selected metro area, region, and population size, monthly rpt, 6762–2
Drug abuse indicators for selected metro areas, research results, data collection, and policy issues, 1992 semiannual conf, 4492–5
Drug test results at arrest, by drug type, offense, and sex, for selected urban areas, quarterly rpt, 6062–3
Freight (waterborne domestic and foreign) by commodity, traffic, and passengers, by port and waterway, 1989, annual rpt, 3754–3.4
Fruit and vegetable shipments, and arrivals by city, by mode of transport and State and country of origin, 1990, annual rpt, 1311–4.2
Heroin prices and purity in 19 metro areas and Puerto Rico, by world area of origin, quarterly rpt, 6282–2
Housing and households characteristics, unit and neighborhood quality, and journey to work by MSA location, for 11 MSAs, 1985 survey, supplement, 2485–8
Housing and households characteristics, 1989 survey, MSA fact sheet, 2485–11.13
Housing and households detailed characteristics, and unit and neighborhood quality, by location, 1989 survey, MSA rpt, 2485–6.3
Housing rental and sales, discrimination against blacks and Hispanics in selected metro areas, 1989 study, 5186–16.2
Housing starts and completions authorized by building permits in 40 MSAs, quarterly rpt, 2382–9
Immigration Reform and Control Act employer sanctions impacts on labor markets, with data for selected industries and metro areas, 1980s, working paper, 6366–6.10
Oil prices by product, for 4 cities, seasonal weekly rpt, 3162–45
Wages by occupation, and benefits, for office and plant workers, 1991 survey, periodic MSA rpt, 6785–16.6
see also under By City and By SMSA or MSA in the "Index by Categories"

Los Angeles County, Calif.
Alien workers legalization applications and other Immigration Reform and Control Act provisions impacts on Los Angeles wages and working conditions, 1980s-91, working paper, 6366–6.9
Housing and households characteristics, unit and neighborhood quality, and journey to work by MSA location, for 11 MSAs, 1985 survey, supplement, 2485–8
Housing and households detailed characteristics, and unit and neighborhood quality, by location, 1989 survey, MSA rpt, 2485–6.3

Losey, Art
"Pesticide Re-registration Dilemma and Its Impact", 1504–9.1

Lotteries
Govt finances, tax systems and revenue, and fiscal structure, by level of govt and State, 1992 with historical trends, annual rpt, 10044–1
State govt revenue by source, spending and debt by function, and holdings, FY91, annual rpt, 2466–2.6
State govt tax collections by detailed type of tax, and tax rates, by State, FY91, annual rpt, 2466–2.7
Statistical Abstract of US, 1992 annual data compilation, 2324–1.9

Loudoun County, Va.
Fed Govt land acquisition and dev projects in DC metro area, characteristics and funding by agency and project, FY92-96, annual rpt, 15454–1

Loughlin, Thomas R.
"Incidental Catch of Marine Mammals by Foreign and Joint Venture Trawl Vessels in the U.S. EEZ of the North Pacific, 1973-88", 2168–129

Louisiana
Banks (insured commercial and savings) deposits by instn, State, MSA, and county, as of June 1991, annual regional rpt, 9295–3.4
Coal production and mines by county, prices, productivity, miners, and reserves, by mining method and State, 1990-91, annual rpt, 3164–25
Deaths and rates, by detailed location, cause, and demographic characteristics, 1989, US Vital Statistics annual rpt, 4144–3.1
Economic indicators by State and MSA, Fed Reserve 6th District, quarterly rpt, 9371–14
Employment by industry div, earnings, and hours, by southwestern State, monthly rpt, 6962–2
Employment, earnings, and hours, by selected SIC 1- to 4-digit industry, State, and for 275 MSAs, 1987-92, 6748–81
Estuary environmental and fishery conditions, research results and methodology, 1992 rpt, 2176–7.28
Fed Govt spending in States and local areas, by type, State, county, and city, FY91, annual rpt, 2464–3
Fed Govt spending in States, by type, program, agency, and State, FY91, annual rpt, 2464–2
Fish (catfish) raised on farms, inventory, stocks, and production, by major producer State, quarterly rpt, 1631–18
Floods in Mississippi River and Gulf of Mexico basins, precipitation and water levels by site, damage, and deaths, 1982-83, 5666–27.33
HHS financial aid, by program, recipient, State, and city, FY91, annual regional listing, 4004–3.6
Hospital deaths of Medicare patients, actual and expected rates by diagnosis, and hospital characteristics, by instn, FY90 annual State rpt, 4654–14.19
Housing census, 1990: inventory, occupancy, and costs, State fact sheet, 2326–21.20
Housing census, 1990: summary unit characteristics, by householder race and age, county, place, and urban-rural location, State rpt, 2471–1.20
Military prime contract awards, by contractor, service branch, State, and city, FY91, annual rpt, 3544–22
Mineral Industry Surveys, State reviews of production, 1991, preliminary annual rpt, 5614–6
Multinatl firms US affiliates finances and operations, by industry, country of parent firm, and State, 1987, 2708–48
Physicians, by specialty, age, sex, and location of training and practice, 1990, State rpt, 4116–6.19
Population and housing census, 1990: detailed geographic coverage, State CD-ROM, 2551–9.7
Population and housing census, 1990: population and housing characteristics, detailed geographic coverage, State CD-ROM, 2551–10.25
Population and housing census, 1990: summary characteristics, by county, subdiv, and place, State rpt, 2551–7.20
Population census, 1990: population characteristics and living arrangements, by county, place, and urban-rural location, State rpt, 2531–1.20
Rice market activities, prices, inspections, sales, trade, supply, and use, for US and selected foreign markets, weekly rpt, 1313–8
Rice production, practices, costs, and land tenure, by production area, 1988, 1568–309
Rice stocks on and off farms and total in all positions, periodic rpt, 1621–7
Shrimp harvesters impacts of Gulf Coast fishery closure, and nonfishing job skills, 1987, article, 2162–1.301
Statistical Abstract of US, 1992 annual data compilation, 2324–1
Timber in Louisiana, resources by ownership, forest and tree characteristics, and parish, 1991, series, 1206–35
Water quality, chemistry, hydrology, and other characteristics, 1991 local area study, 5666–27.34
see also Baton Rouge, La.
see also Jefferson Parish, La.
see also New Orleans, La.
see also St. Tammany Parish, La.
see also under By State in the "Index by Categories"

Louisville, Ky.
Economic and banking conditions, for Fed Reserve 8th District, quarterly rpt with articles, 9391–16
Freight (waterborne domestic and foreign) by commodity, traffic, and passengers, by port and waterway, 1989, annual rpt, 3754–3.2
Wages by occupation, and benefits, for office and plant workers, 1991 survey, periodic MSA rpt, 6785–16.3
see also under By City and By SMSA or MSA in the "Index by Categories"

Loungani, Prakash
"Effect of Changes in Reserve Requirements on Investment and GNP", 9375–13.72

Love, John M.
"Forecasting Fresh Apple Prices for Selected Months in the Marketing Season", 1561–6.303
"Produce Industry's Challenge To Double Demand for Fresh Vegetables", 1561–11.301

"Transitions to Kindergarten: Final Report of the National Transition Study", 4808–44
"U.S. Processing Snap Bean Industry: A Commodity Highlight", 1561–11.305

Love, Milton
"Maturity and Fecundity in the Rockfishes, *Sebastes* spp., a Review", 2162–1.302

Love, Timothy G.
"Effects of the Gates Park Fire on Recreation Choices", 1208–422

Low-income energy assistance
Assistance for low income households, coverage and impacts on energy use and costs, selected years FY79-89, 4588–2
Assistance for low income households energy use, by type of aid, from FY82, and by State, FY90, annual rpt, 4744–3.9
Assistance for low income households, funding sources, costs, and participation, by State, FY90, annual rpt, 4584–1
Expenditures of Fed Govt in States, by type, program, agency, and State, FY91, annual rpt, 2464–2
HHS financial aid, by program, recipient, State, and city, FY91, annual regional listings, 4004–3
Income (median) for 4-person family, by State, 1969 and 1974-89, technical paper, 2626–2.60
Natl income and product accounts, comprehensive accounts and components, benchmark revisions, 1929-88, 2708–5
Natl income and product accounts, comprehensive accounts and components, *Survey of Current Business*, monthly rpt, 2702–1.26
Ohio poverty, hunger, and public welfare program operations and indicators of need, by county, 1991 hearing, 21968–58
Oil company overcharge settlements funds received, and conservation and energy aid spending, by outlying area, 1990, GAO rpt, 26113–564
States low income housing energy aid, program characteristics by State, FY91, annual rpt, 4584–2

Low-income housing
American Housing Survey: unit and households detailed characteristics, and unit and neighborhood quality, MSA rpt series, 2485–6
Community Dev Block Grant activities and funding, by program, FY75-91, annual rpt, 5124–8
Disabled persons low income housing capital advances and rental aid of HUD, by recipient, FY92, press release, 5006–3.98
Fed Govt financial and nonfinancial domestic aid, 1992 base edition, annual listing, 104–5
Fed Govt spending in States, by type, program, agency, and State, FY91, annual rpt, 2464–2
Fed Home Loan Banks affordable housing program operations, 1990, hearing, 21248–170
FmHA activities, and loans and grants by program and State, FY91 and trends from FY70, annual rpt, 1184–17
FmHA loans and borrower supervision activities in farm and housing programs, by type and State, monthly rpt, 1182–1
HUD funding for community housing groups planning dev, by training organization, 1992, press release, 5006–3.93
HUD grants for low income rental housing and homeownership assistance, by recipient, FY92, press release, 5006–3.86
HUD grants to aid housing purchase in depressed areas, by recipient, 1991, press release, 5006–3.84
HUD grants to aid purchase of low income housing units, by recipient, 1992, press release, 5006–3.101
HUD grants to aid purchase of multifamily housing units, by recipient, 1992, press release, 5006–3.91
HUD grants to housing organizations to assist first time low income buyers, by recipient, 1992, press release, 5006–3.94
Income (household) and poverty status under alternative income definitions, by recipient characteristics, 1979-91, annual Current Population Rpt, 2546–6.78
Mortgage activity impact of lending program for low- and moderate-income neighborhoods in Philadelphia, with background data, 1980s, working paper, 9387–8.266
Mortgages FHA-insured for 1-family units, by loan type and mortgage characteristics, quarterly rpt, 5142–45
NYC housing supply, occupancy, condition, and household characteristics, by tenure and borough, 1991 triennial survey, 2488–3
Older persons low income housing capital advances and rental aid of HUD, by recipient, FY91, press release, 5006–3.88
Older persons low income housing capital advances and rental aid of HUD, by recipient, FY92, press release, 5006–3.97
Paint (lead-based) abatement programs for low- and moderate-income housing, HUD grants to public agencies, 1992 press release, 5006–3.102
Pension funds (public) investment in housing, and public and private funds holdings of mortgages, mortgage-backed securities, and govt securities, 1986-90, 5188–134
Poverty status of population and families, by detailed characteristics, 1991, annual Current Population Rpt, 2546–6.77
Public opinion on taxes, spending, and govt efficiency, by respondent characteristics, 1992 survey, annual rpt, 10044–2
Regulation on land use and rent control, impacts on housing affordability and availability, and low income housing condition, 1991 hearing, 21248–174
Supply of low income rental housing in rural areas, FmHA loans and impacts of programs to maintain supply and to deter mortgage prepayment, 1988-91, GAO rpt, 26113–586
Tax credits for low income housing developers, with subsidies, project and tenant characteristics, and investor returns, 1987-88, 5188–133
Urban areas fiscal, economic, and social conditions, as of FY92, biennial rpt, 5184–7
see also Low-income energy assistance
see also Public housing
see also Rent supplements

Low, Walton H.
"Reconnaissance Investigation of Water Quality, Bottom Sediment, and Biota Associated with Irrigation Drainage in the American Falls Reservoir Area, Idaho, 1988-89", 5666–27.24

Lowell, B. Lindsay
"Circular Mobility, Migrant Communities, and Policy Restrictions: Unauthorized Flows from Mexico", 6366–6.11

Lowenstein, Ronnie
"Impact of the Current Defense Build-Down", 9385–1.313

LPG
see Liquefied petroleum gas

LSD
see Drug abuse and treatment

Lucier, Gary
"Financial Characteristics of Vegetable Farms in 1990", 1561–11.304

Luckett, Charles A.
"Developments in the Pricing of Credit Card Services", 9362–1.306

Ludwick, David E.
"Live Swine and Fresh, Chilled, or Frozen Pork, Industry and Trade Summary", 9885–8.5

Luebeck, E. Georg
"Multistage Carcinogenesis: Population-Based Model for Colon Cancer", 4472–1.311

Lukasiewicz, John
"Occupational Employment Projections", 6744–19

Lukes, James J.
"Ceramic Floor and Wall Tiles, Industry and Trade Summary", 9885–13.2

Lumber industry and products
Alaska timber acreage and resources, by species, ownership class, and inventory unit, series, 1206–9
Business statistics, detailed data for major industries and economic indicators, *Survey of Current Business*, monthly rpt, 2702–1.15
Business statistics, detailed data for major industries and economic indicators, 1960-91, *Survey of Current Business* biennial supplement, 2704–1
California lumber mills, operations, timber use by species and origin, and residue use, by product and county, 1988, 1208–108
Canada softwood lumber, costs and production compared to US, 1970s-91, hearing, 21728–78
Collective bargaining agreements expiring during year, and workers covered, by firm, union, industry group, and State, 1992, annual rpt, 6784–9
Containers (wood) industry productivity trends and technological devs, 1977-89, article, 6722–1.344
County Business Patterns, 1989: employment, establishments, and payroll, by SIC 2- to 4-digit industry and county, annual State rpt series, 2326–8
County Business Patterns, 1990: employment, establishments, and payroll, by SIC 2- to 4-digit industry and county, annual State rpt series, 2326–6
Disaster damage to timber and orchards, USDA restoration aid and program participation by practice and State, FY91, annual rpt, 1804–24
Douglas fir (young growth) lumber and veneer recovery and quality, effects of timber stand and log characteristics, model description and results, 1991 rpt, 1208–413
Employment, earnings, and hours, by SIC 1- to 4-digit industry, monthly 1989-Feb 1992, annual rpt, 6744–4

Employment of minorities and women, by occupation, SIC 1- to 3-digit industry, State, and MSA, 1991, annual rpt, 9244–1
Employment, unemployment, and labor force characteristics, by region and census div, 1991, annual rpt, 6744–7.1
Energy use and prices, by fuel type and manufacturing industry, 1974-88, 3166–15.3
Energy use and prices for manufacturing industries, 1988 survey, series, 3166–13
Environmental Quality, status of problems, protection programs, research, and intl issues, 1991 annual rpt, 484–1
Export licensing, monitoring, and enforcement activities, FY91, annual rpt, 2024–1
Exports and imports (agricultural) commodity and country, prices, and world market devs, monthly rpt, 1922–12
Exports and imports between US and outlying areas, by detailed commodity and mode of transport, 1991, annual rpt, 2424–11
Exports and imports of US, by country and detailed commodity, monthly rpt, 2422–12
Exports and imports of US by country, and trade shifts by commodity, 1991, annual rpt, 9884–25
Exports and imports of US, by Harmonized System 6-digit commodity and country, 1991, annual rpt, 2424–13
Exports and imports of US, by selected country, country group, and commodity group, 1991, annual rpt, 2044–37
Exports and imports of US, by transport mode, country, and SITC 1- to 3-digit commodity, 1991, annual rpt, 2424–12
Exports, imports, and balances of US for manufactured goods, by SITC 2-digit commodity and country, quarterly rpt, 2042–35
Exports, imports, and export promotion of US lumber and wood products by country, and trade balance, by commodity, FAS periodic circular, 1925–36
Exports, imports, tariffs, and industry operating data for agricultural, fishery, and forest products, commodity rpt series, 9885–8
Exports of US, detailed commodities by country, monthly CD-ROM, 2422–13
Exports of US, detailed Schedule B commodities with countries of destination, 1991, annual rpt, 2424–10
Exports of US hardwood lumber to Europe and Asia, by species and country, 1981-90, 1208–373
Farm financial and marketing conditions, forecast 1992, annual conf, 1504–9
Florida industrial roundwood lumber production, by product and county, 1967-89, 1208–352
Freight (waterborne domestic and foreign) by commodity, traffic, and passengers, by port and waterway, 1989, annual rpt, 3754–3
Futures and options trading volume, by commodity and exchange, FY91, annual rpt, 11924–2
Futures trading in selected commodities and financial instruments and indexes, for NYC, Chicago, and other markets activity, biweekly rpt, 11922–5
Georgia industrial roundwood lumber production, by product, 1986 and 1989, 1208–393
Hazardous substances industrial releases and reduction methods under EPA regulation, by chemical, source, industry, and location, 1989, annual rpt, 9234–6
Hazardous substances industrial releases and reduction methods under EPA regulation, with chemical stocks and use, facility directory, 1987-89, annual CD-ROM, 9234–7
Hwy construction material use by type, and spending, by State, 1940s-91, annual rpt, 7554–29
Imports, exports, and employment impacts, by SIC 2- to 4-digit industry and commodity, quarterly rpt, 2322–2
Imports of softwood lumber from Canada, injury to US industry from foreign subsidized products, investigation with background financial and operating data, 1992 rpt, 9886–15.80
Imports of US, detailed commodities by country, monthly CD-ROM, 2422–14
Imports of US given duty-free treatment for value of US material sent abroad, by commodity and country, 1987-90, annual rpt, 9884–14
Injuries from use of consumer products, by severity, victim age, and detailed product, 1991, annual rpt, 9164–6
Input-output structure of US economy, detailed interindustry transactions for 84 industries, and components of final demand, 1987, annual article, 2702–1.316
Input-output structure of US economy, detailed interindustry transactions for 541 industries, and components of final demand, 1982 benchmark data, 2708–17
Iowa timber resources and removals, by species, forest and tree characteristics, ownership, and county, 1988-90 and trends from 1973-74, 1208–75
Labor demand elasticities for lumber and paper products industries, 1992 rpt, 1208–416
Labor productivity, indexes of output, hours, and employment by SIC 2- to 4-digit industry, 1967-90, annual rpt, 6824–1.3
Latin America economic and social conditions, resources, trade, and aid, 1992, annual factbook, 9914–14
Louisiana timber resources, by ownership, forest and tree characteristics, and parish, 1991, series, 1206–35
Manufacturing annual survey, 1990: finances and operations, by SIC 2- to 4-digit industry, series, 2506–14
Manufacturing census, 1987: concentration of largest firms measured by value added, and for shipments by SIC 2- and 4-digit industry, subject rpt, 2497–6
Manufacturing census, 1987: shipments of manufacturers products, by customer class and SIC 2- and 4-digit industry, subject rpt, 2497–4
Manufacturing finances and operations, by SIC 2- to 4-digit industry, forecast 1992, annual rpt, 2044–28
Manufacturing industries operations and performance, analytical rpt series, 2506–16
Manufacturing production, shipments, inventories, orders, and pollution control costs, periodic Current Industrial Rpt series, 2506–3
Mexico imports from US, by industry and State, 1987-91, 2048–154
Military prime contract awards, by detailed procurement category, FY88-91, annual rpt, 3544–18
Minnesota timber acreage, resources, and removals, by ownership, forest and tree characteristics, and county, 1990, series, 1206–24
Missouri timber resources and removals, by species, forest and tree characteristics, ownership, and county, 1987-89 and trends from 1959, 1208–76
Multinatl firms US affiliates finances and operations, by industry, country of parent firm, and State, 1987, 2708–48
Multinatl US firms and foreign affiliates finances and operations, by industry and country, 1989 benchmark survey, annual rpt, 2704–5
Natl forests revenue, by source, forest, and State, FY91, annual rpt, 1204–34
Natl forests timber sales and harvests, by State, FY91, annual rpt, 1204–1
Natl forests timber sales, expenses, and operations, by region, State, and forest, FY91, annual rpts, 1204–36
North Central States pulpwood production and mill receipts, by species, mill, State, and county, 1990, annual rpt, 1204–19
North Central States pulpwood production in 3 States, by species and county, 1990, 1208–397
North Central States timber harvest and industrial roundwood production, by product and county, State rpt series, 1206–10
North Central States timber harvest, estimation methodology, 1991 rpt, 1208–419
Northeastern US hardwood forests ecology and mgmt, 1992, 1208–405
Northeastern US industrial roundwood production by product, State rpt series, 1206–15
Northeastern US pulpwood production by species and county, and shipments, by State, 1990, annual rpt, 1204–18
Northeastern US timber resources and removals, by species, ownership, and county, State rpt series, 1206–12
Northwestern US and British Columbia forest industry production, prices, trade, and employment, quarterly rpt, 1202–3
Occupational injury and illness rates and lost workdays, for selected industries, 1978-89, compilation of papers, 6728–41
Occupational injury and illness rates, by SIC 2- to 4-digit industry, 1989-90, annual rpt, 6844–7
Occupational injury and illness rates, by SIC 2- to 4-digit industry, 1990, annual rpt, 6844–1
Occupational Outlook Handbook, 1992-93, biennial rpt, 6744–1
OECD trade, total and for 4 major countries, and US trade by country, by commodity, 1980-90, world area rpt series, 9116–1
Oregon lumber production, and industry operations, by county, 1988, 1208–280

Owl (northern spotted) conservation methods in Pacific Northwest, timber industry impacts, and Federal and State spending, 1980s-95, 1208–388
Pacific Northwest Indian tribes environmental, economic, and cultural impacts of OCS oil and gas lease and dev, with background data, 1970s-92, 5738–35
Pacific Northwest population, households, employment, income, fuel prices, and electricity demand, alternative forecasts 1991-2010, annual rpt, 3224–3.3
Pacific territories population and housing detailed characteristics, by location, 1990 Census of Population and Housing, series, 2551–8
Pine (ponderosa) fenceposts service life and costs, by preservative treatment method and site, 1992 rpt, 1208–406
Pollution abatement capital and operating costs, by SIC 2- to 4-digit industry and State, 1990, annual Current Industrial Rpt, 2506–3.6
Preservatives for lumber products, performance test results by preservative type, late 1930s-80s, 1208–391
Price indexes (producer), by stage of processing and detailed commodity, monthly rpt, 6762–6
Price indexes (producer), by stage of processing and detailed commodity, monthly 1991, annual rpt, 6764–2
Prices (stumpage) for sawtimber sold from natl forests in Pacific Northwest, monthly 1975-89, 1208–387
Prices of lumber, by grade and Pacific Northwest species, 1971-90 and projected to 2040, 1208–424
Production, prices, employment, and trade, for hardwood lumber and products, quarterly rpt, 1202–4
Production, shipments, PPI, stocks, and trade of lumber products, by type, quarterly rpt, 2042–1.5; 2042–1.6
Production, shipments, trade, stocks, and use of wood, paper, and related products, periodic Current Industrial Rpt series, 2506–7
Public lands acreage and use, and Land Mgmt Bur activities and finances, annual State rpt series, 5724–11
Public lands acreage, grants, use, revenues, and allocations, by State, FY91, annual rpt, 5724–1.2
Rocky Mountain States timber and mill residue production, by species, ownership, and county, series, 1206–17
Science, engineering, and technical employment in manufacturing, by field and industry, 1989, triennial rpt, 9627–23
Southeastern US pulpwood and residue prices, spending, and transport shares by mode, 1989-90, annual rpt, 1204–22
Southern US timber resources and removals, by species, ownership, State, and county, series, 1206–8
Southern US veneer log receipts, production, and shipments, by species and State, with residue use, 1988, 1208–407
Soviet Union and US economic and sociodemographic indicators, selected years 1970-90, handbook, 2328–80
Soviet Union timber exports to US, related insect and disease infestation in Western US, economic and environmental impacts, 1991 and projected to 2040, 1208–389
Statistical Abstract of US, 1992 annual data compilation, 2324–1.24
Tariff Schedule of US, classifications and rates of duty by detailed imported commodity, 1993 base edition, 9886–13
Tax (income) returns of corporations, income and tax items by asset size and detailed industry, 1989, annual rpt, 8304–4; 8304–21
Tax (income) returns of partnerships, income statement and balance sheet items, by industry group, 1990, annual article, 8302–2.314
Tax (income) returns of sole proprietorships, income statement items, by industry group, 1990, annual article, 8302–2.317; 8302–2.320
Tropical woods kiln drying time relation to moisture content and other properties, for 650 species, 1991 rpt, 1208–392
Veneer recovered from Douglas-fir logs and blocks at Oregon and Washington mills, by grade and type, 1981-83 study, 1208–396
Virginia industrial roundwood production, shipments, and residue volume, by species, product, and location, 1987-89, 1208–138
Virginia timber resources, growth, and removals, by species, ownership, treatment, and county, 1990-92, series, 1206–6
Wholesale trade sales and inventories, by SIC 2- to 3-digit kind of business, monthly rpt, 2413–7
Wisconsin timber resources and removals, by species, forest type, ownership, and county, series, 1206–34
Wood, waste, and alcohol fuel use, by end-use sector and region, 1990, annual rpt, 3164–97
see also Forests and forestry
see also Furniture and furnishings
see also Gum and wood chemicals
see also Paper and paper products
see also Wood fuel
see also under By Commodity in the "Index by Categories"
see also under By Industry in the "Index by Categories"

Lung diseases
see Black lung disease
see Pneumonia and influenza
see Respiratory diseases
see Tuberculosis

Luppold, William G.
"New Estimates of Hardwood-Log Exports to Europe and Asia", 1208–373

Luther, Dennis
"Toys and Models, Industry and Trade Summary", 9885–10.1

Luxembourg
Agricultural trade of US, by detailed commodity and country, 1991, annual rpt, 1524–8
Agricultural trade of US, by detailed commodity and country, 1991, semiannual rpt, 1522–4
AID loans repayment status and terms by program and country, and status of predecessor agency loans, quarterly rpt, 9912–3
Cuba trade, by commodity and country, mid 1980s-91, 9118–8
Economic and military aid and loans from US and intl agencies, by program and country, FY46-91, annual rpt, 9914–5
Economic, social, political, and geographic summary data, by country, 1992, annual factbook, 9114–2
Exports and imports of US, by selected country, country group, and commodity group, 1991, annual rpt, 2044–37
Exports and imports of US, by transport mode, country, and SITC 1- to 3-digit commodity, 1991, annual rpt, 2424–12
Exports, imports, and balances of US for manufactured goods, by SITC 2-digit commodity and country, quarterly rpt, 2042–35
Exports of US, detailed Schedule B commodities with countries of destination, 1991, annual rpt, 2424–10
Health care costs and components, services use, resources, and economic indicators, by OECD country, 1960s-90, article, 4652–1.322
Human rights conditions in 170 countries, and US economic and military aid, 1991, annual rpt, 21384–3
Intl transactions of US with 9 countries, 1989-91, *Survey of Current Business*, monthly rpt, annual table, 2702–1.33
Military spending, arms trade, and force strengths, with govt spending and population, by country, 1979-89, annual rpt, 9824–1
Multinatl US firms and foreign affiliates finances and operations, by industry and country, 1989 benchmark survey, annual rpt, 2704–5
Multinatl US firms foreign affiliates, income statement items by asset size, industry, and country, 1988, biennial article, 8302–2.322
Oil production, stocks, use, and trade, by selected country and country group, monthly rpt, 3162–42
Population size, growth rates, and components of change, by country, projected 1990-2020 and trends from 1950, biennial rpt, 2324–9
Rails (steel) from 3 countries at less than fair value, injury to US industry, investigation with background financial and operating data, 1992 rpt, 9886–14.349
Refugee migration, and intl aid programs, by world area and country of origin and asylum, 1991, annual rpt, 7004–15
Spacecraft and satellite launches since 1957, quarterly listing, 9502–2
Steel trade, by product, country, and customs district, with US industry operating data, 1989-June 1992, semiannual rpt, 9882–15
Tax revenue, by level of govt and type of tax, for OECD countries, mid 1960s-90, annual rpt, 10044–1.2
UN voting record and share of votes in agreement with US, by issue, country, and world area, 1991, annual rpt, 7004–18
see also under By Foreign Country in the "Index by Categories"

Lyle, Faye
"Worker Rights in U.S. Policy, 1991", 6366–4.11

Lyme disease
see Infective and parasitic diseases

Ma, L.
"Case-Control Study of Factors Associated with Failure To Detect Breast Cancer by Mammography", 4472–1.316

Maas, Kenneth M.
"Land Ownership and the Regulatory Framework for Oil, Gas, and Coal Leasing in Alaska", 5608–174

Macao
Agricultural trade of US, by detailed commodity and country, 1991, annual rpt, 1524–8
Agricultural trade of US, by detailed commodity and country, 1991, semiannual rpt, 1522–4
Economic, social, political, and geographic summary data, by country, 1992, annual factbook, 9114–2
Exports and imports of US, by transport mode, country, and SITC 1- to 3-digit commodity, 1991, annual rpt, 2424–12
Exports, imports, and balances of US for manufactured goods, by SITC 2-digit commodity and country, quarterly rpt, 2042–35
Exports of US, detailed Schedule B commodities with countries of destination, 1991, annual rpt, 2424–10
Human rights conditions in 170 countries, and US economic and military aid, 1991, annual rpt, 21384–3
Minerals Yearbook, Vol 3, 1989: foreign country review of production, trade, and policy, by commodity, annual rpt, 5604–35.2
Population size, growth rates, and components of change, by country, projected 1990-2020 and trends from 1950, biennial rpt, 2324–9
Refugee migration, and intl aid programs, by world area and country of origin and asylum, 1991, annual rpt, 7004–15

MacDorman, Marian F.
"Advance Report of Final Mortality Statistics, 1989", 4146–5.124

Mace, Douglas J.
"Effect of the 65 MPH Speed Limit on Travel Speeds and Related Crashes", 7768–121

Macedonia
Economic, social, political, and geographic summary data, by country, 1992, annual factbook, 9114–2

Machine-readable data file guides
see CD-ROM catalogs and guides
see Computer data file guides

Machine tools
see Machines and machinery industry

Machines and machinery industry
Business statistics, detailed data for major industries and economic indicators, *Survey of Current Business*, monthly rpt, 2702–1.16
Business statistics, detailed data for major industries and economic indicators, 1960-91, *Survey of Current Business* biennial supplement, 2704–1
Capital expenditures for plant and equipment, by major industry group, quarterly rpt, 2502–2
Collective bargaining agreements expiring during year, and workers covered, by firm, union, industry group, and State, 1992, annual rpt, 6784–9
Communist and transitional economy countries trade with US, by detailed commodity and country, quarterly rpt with articles, 9882–2
Construction machinery PPI, quarterly rpt, 2042–1.5
County Business Patterns, 1989: employment, establishments, and payroll, by SIC 2- to 4-digit industry and county, annual State rpt series, 2326–8
County Business Patterns, 1990: employment, establishments, and payroll, by SIC 2- to 4-digit industry and county, annual State rpt series, 2326–6
Cuba trade, by commodity and country, mid 1980s-91, 9118–8
Eastern Europe export industries dev potential, with trade and industry finances and operations, for 5 countries, 1985-90, 9886–4.179
Employment, earnings, and hours, by SIC 1- to 4-digit industry, monthly 1989-Feb 1992, annual rpt, 6744–4
Employment of minorities and women, by occupation, SIC 1- to 3-digit industry, State, and MSA, 1991, annual rpt, 9244–1
Employment, unemployment, and labor force characteristics, by region and census div, 1991, annual rpt, 6744–7.1
Energy use and prices, by fuel type and manufacturing industry, 1974-88, 3166–15.3
Energy use and prices for manufacturing industries, 1988 survey, series, 3166–13
Exports and imports between US and outlying areas, by detailed commodity and mode of transport, 1991, annual rpt, 2424–11
Exports and imports of US, by country and detailed commodity, monthly rpt, 2422–12
Exports and imports of US by country, and trade shifts by commodity, 1991, annual rpt, 9884–25
Exports and imports of US, by Harmonized System 6-digit commodity and country, 1991, annual rpt, 2424–13
Exports and imports of US, by transport mode, country, and SITC 1- to 3-digit commodity, 1991, annual rpt, 2424–12
Exports, imports, tariffs, and industry operating data for machinery and equipment, commodity rpt series, 9885–9
Exports of agricultural products and nonelectrical machinery, *Survey of Current Business*, monthly rpt, 2702–1.1
Exports of US, detailed commodities by country, monthly CD-ROM, 2422–13
Exports of US, detailed Schedule B commodities with countries of destination, 1991, annual rpt, 2424–10
Foreign direct investment in US, by industry group and world area, 1989-91, annual article, 2702–1.331
Foreign direct investment of US, by industry group and world area, 1989-91, annual article, 2702–1.332
Freight (waterborne domestic and foreign) by commodity, traffic, and passengers, by port and waterway, 1989, annual rpt, 3754–3
Hazardous substances industrial releases and reduction methods under EPA regulation, by chemical, source, industry, and location, 1989, annual rpt, 9234–6
Hazardous substances industrial releases and reduction methods under EPA regulation, with chemical stocks and use, facility directory, 1987-89, annual CD-ROM, 9234–7
Imports, exports, and employment impacts, by SIC 2- to 4-digit industry and commodity, quarterly rpt, 2322–2
Imports of US, detailed commodities by country, monthly CD-ROM, 2422–14
Imports of US given duty-free treatment for value of US material sent abroad, by commodity and country, 1987-90, annual rpt, 9884–14
Injuries from use of consumer products, by severity, victim age, and detailed product, 1991, annual rpt, 9164–6
Input-output structure of US economy, detailed interindustry transactions for 84 industries, and components of final demand, 1987, annual article, 2702–1.316
Input-output structure of US economy, detailed interindustry transactions for 541 industries, and components of final demand, 1982 benchmark data, 2708–17
Labor productivity, indexes of output, hours, and employment by SIC 2- to 4-digit industry, 1967-90, annual rpt, 6824–1.3
Manufacturing annual survey, 1990: finances and operations, by SIC 2- to 4-digit industry, series, 2506–14
Manufacturing census, 1987: concentration of largest firms measured by value added, and for shipments by SIC 2- and 4-digit industry, subject rpt, 2497–6
Manufacturing census, 1987: shipments of manufacturers products, by customer class and SIC 2- and 4-digit industry, subject rpt, 2497–4
Manufacturing corporations financial statements, by selected SIC 2- to 3-digit industry, quarterly rpt, 2502–1
Manufacturing finances and operations, by SIC 2- to 4-digit industry, forecast 1992, annual rpt, 2044–28
Manufacturing industries operations and performance, analytical rpt series, 2506–16
Manufacturing production, shipments, inventories, orders, and pollution control costs, periodic Current Industrial Rpt series, 2506–3
Mexico imports from US, by industry and State, 1987-91, 2048–154
Military and personal property shipments, passenger traffic, and costs, by service branch and mode of transport, FY91, annual rpt, 3704–15
Military prime contract awards, by detailed procurement category, FY88-91, annual rpt, 3544–18
Multinatl firms US affiliates finances and operations, by industry, country of parent firm, and State, 1987, 2708–48
Multinatl firms US affiliates, finances, and operations, by industry, world area of parent firm, and State, 1989-90, annual rpt, 2704–4

Multinatl US firms and foreign affiliates finances and operations, by industry and country, 1989 benchmark survey, annual rpt, 2704–5
Multinatl US firms foreign affiliates, income statement items by asset size, industry, and country, 1988, biennial article, 8302–2.322
Natl income and product accounts, comprehensive accounts and components, benchmark revisions, 1929-88, 2708–5
Natl income and product accounts, comprehensive accounts and components, *Survey of Current Business*, monthly rpt, 2702–1.28
Occupational deaths, by equipment type, circumstances, and OSHA standards violated, series, 6606–2
Occupational injury and illness rates, by SIC 2- to 4-digit industry, 1989-90, annual rpt, 6844–7
Occupational injury and illness rates, by SIC 2- to 4-digit industry, 1990, annual rpt, 6844–1
OECD trade, total and for 4 major countries, and US trade by country, by commodity, 1980-90, world area rpt series, 9116–1
Pacific territories population and housing detailed characteristics, by location, 1990 Census of Population and Housing, series, 2551–8
Pollution abatement capital and operating costs, by SIC 2- to 4-digit industry and State, 1990, annual Current Industrial Rpt, 2506–3.6
Price indexes (producer), by stage of processing and detailed commodity, monthly rpt, 6762–6
Price indexes (producer), by stage of processing and detailed commodity, monthly 1991, annual rpt, 6764–2
Production, shipments, trade, stocks, orders, use, and firms, by product, periodic Current Industrial Rpt series, 2506–12
Puerto Rico and other US possessions corporations income tax returns, income and tax items, and employment, by selected industry, 1989, article, 8302–2.326
Rubber mechanical goods shipments, by product, 1991, annual Current Industrial Rpt, 2506–8.17
Science, engineering, and technical employment in manufacturing, by field and industry, 1989, triennial rpt, 9627–23
Soviet Union and US economic and sociodemographic indicators, selected years 1970-90, handbook, 2328–80
Tariff Schedule of US, classifications and rates of duty by detailed imported commodity, 1993 base edition, 9886–13
Tax (income) returns of corporations, income and tax items by asset size and detailed industry, 1989, annual rpt, 8304–4; 8304–21
Tax (income) returns of corporations with foreign tax credit, income and tax items by industry group, 1988, biennial article, 8302–2.316
Tax (income) returns of partnerships, income statement and balance sheet items, by industry group, 1990, annual article, 8302–2.314
Tax (income) returns of sole proprietorships, income statement items, by industry group, 1990, annual article, 8302–2.317; 8302–2.320
Technological devs effect on labor force, composition, and productivity, 1970s-90 and projected to 2005, industry rpt, 6826–2.9
Textile and apparel foreign market conditions for US exports, with domestic industry operations, country rpt series, 2046–15
Wages and production workers by occupation, and benefits, for metalworking machinery and die and tool manufacturing, by selected MSA, 1990 survey, 6787–6.253
Wholesale trade sales and inventories, by SIC 2- to 3-digit kind of business, monthly rpt, 2413–7
see also Agricultural machinery and equipment
see also Electric power plants and equipment
see also Electrical machinery and equipment
see also Engines and motors
see also Hardware
see also Industrial plants and equipment
see also Industrial robots
see also Lawn and garden equipment
see also Tools
see also Transportation and transportation equipment
see also Vending machines and stands
see also under By Commodity in the "Index by Categories"
see also under By Industry in the "Index by Categories"

MacLean, Colin D.
"Preliminary Timber Resource Statistics for Southwest Washington", 1206–28.4
"Preliminary Timber Resource Statistics for the Olympic Peninsula, Washington", 1206–28.5
"Preliminary Timber Resource Statistics for the Puget Sound Area, Washington", 1206–28.6

MacLennan, R.
"Increasing Incidence of Cutaneous Melanoma in Queensland, Australia", 4472–1.344

Macon, Ga.
see also under By City and By SMSA or MSA in the "Index by Categories"

Macro International, Inc.
"Medically Based Programs Serving Maternal Substance Abusers and Their Children: A Survey of NIDA Grantees", 4498–76

Madagascar
Agricultural trade of US, by detailed commodity and country, 1991, annual rpt, 1524–8
Agricultural trade of US, by detailed commodity and country, 1991, semiannual rpt, 1522–4
AID economic aid to developing countries, obligations and disbursements by country, quarterly rpt, 9912–4
AID loans repayment status and terms by program and country, and status of predecessor agency loans, quarterly rpt, 9912–3
Economic and military aid and loans from US and intl agencies, by program and country, FY46-91, annual rpt, 9914–5
Economic and social conditions of developing countries from 1960s, and Intl Dev Cooperation Agency and AID activities and funding, FY91-93, annual rpt, 9904–4
Economic, population, and agricultural data, US and other aid sources, and AID activity, 1992 country rpt, 9916–12.72
Economic, social, political, and geographic summary data, by country, 1992, annual factbook, 9114–2
Exports and imports of US, by transport mode, country, and SITC 1- to 3-digit commodity, 1991, annual rpt, 2424–12
Exports of US, detailed Schedule B commodities with countries of destination, 1991, annual rpt, 2424–10
Human rights conditions in 170 countries, and US economic and military aid, 1991, annual rpt, 21384–3
Military aid of US, arms sales, and training programs costs and budget requests, by program, world region, and country, FY91-93, annual rpt, 7144–13
Military spending, arms trade, and force strengths, with govt spending and population, by country, 1979-89, annual rpt, 9824–1
Minerals Yearbook, Vol 3, 1989: foreign country review of production, trade, and policy, by commodity, annual rpt, 5604–35.1
Population size, growth rates, and components of change, by country, projected 1990-2020 and trends from 1950, biennial rpt, 2324–9
Refugee migration, and intl aid programs, by world area and country of origin and asylum, 1991, annual rpt, 7004–15
UN voting record and share of votes in agreement with US, by issue, country, and world area, 1991, annual rpt, 7004–18

Madigan, Edward R.
"New Opportunities for Agriculture", 1504–9.1
"Opportunities To Teach Better Nutrition", 1504–9.1

Madison, James, Memorial Fellowship Foundation
Education funding by Federal agency, program, and recipient type, and instn spending, 1960s-91, annual rpt, 4824–8

Madison, Wis.
see also under By City and By SMSA or MSA in the "Index by Categories"

Madrigal, Vicente
"Form Invariance in Biased Sampling Problems", 9371–10.87
"Risk Neutral Valuation, Asymmetric Information, and the Efficient Markets Hypothesis", 9371–10.77

Magazines
see Periodicals

Magistrates
see Judges

Magnesium
see Metals and metal industries

Maharaj, Vishwanie
"By-catch from the Artisanal Shrimp Trawl Fishery, Gulf of Paria, Trinidad", 2162–1.302

Mahler, Susan J.
"Environmental Excise Taxes, 1989", 8302–2.303

Mail
see Postal service
Mail order
see Direct marketing
Mailath, George J.
"When Do Regulators Close Banks? When Should They?", 9387-8.263
Maine
Banks (insured commercial and savings) deposits by instn, State, MSA, and county, as of June 1991, annual regional rpt, 9295-3.1
Coastal areas environmental conditions and mgmt, 1989 conf, 2146-8.1
County Business Patterns, 1990: employment, establishments, and payroll, by SIC 2- to 4-digit industry and county, annual State rpt, 2326-6.21
Deaths and rates, by detailed location, cause, and demographic characteristics, 1989, US Vital Statistics annual rpt, 4144-3.1
Economic indicators for New England States, Fed Reserve 1st District, monthly rpt, 9373-2
Employment, earnings, and hours, by selected SIC 1- to 4-digit industry, State, and for 275 MSAs, 1987-92, 6748-81
Fed Govt spending in States and local areas, by type, State, county, and city, FY91, annual rpt, 2464-3
Fed Govt spending in States, by type, program, agency, and State, FY91, annual rpt, 2464-2
HHS financial aid, by program, recipient, State, and city, FY91, annual regional listing, 4004-3.1
Hospital deaths of Medicare patients, actual and expected rates by diagnosis, and hospital characteristics, by instn, FY90 annual State rpt, 4654-14.20
Housing census, 1990: inventory, occupancy, and costs, State fact sheet, 2326-21.21
Housing census, 1990: summary unit characteristics, by householder race and age, county, place, and urban-rural location, State rpt, 2471-1.21
Military prime contract awards, by contractor, service branch, State, and city, FY91, annual rpt, 3544-22
Mineral Industry Surveys, State reviews of production, 1991, preliminary annual rpt, 5614-6
Multinatl firms US affiliates finances and operations, by industry, country of parent firm, and State, 1987, 2708-48
Physicians, by specialty, age, sex, and location of training and practice, 1990, State rpt, 4116-6.20
Pollutant concentrations in coastal and estuarine fish, shellfish, and environment, late 1970s-89, local area rpt, 2176-3.17
Population and housing census, 1990: detailed geographic coverage, State CD-ROM, 2551-9.1
Population and housing census, 1990: population and housing characteristics, detailed geographic coverage, State CD-ROM, 2551-10.10
Population and housing census, 1990: summary characteristics, by county, subdiv, and place, State rpt, 2551-7.21
Population census, 1990: population characteristics and living arrangements, by county, place, and urban-rural location, State rpt, 2531-1.21
Potato production, acreage, shipments, and arrivals, for Maine by variety, and compared to other States and Canada, 1991-92, annual rpt, 1311-26
Statistical Abstract of US, 1992 annual data compilation, 2324-1
Water resources dev projects of Army Corps of Engineers, characteristics, and costs, 1950s-91, biennial State rpt, 3756-2.20
Water supply in northeastern US, precipitation and stream runoff by station, monthly rpt, 2182-3
see also under By State in the "Index by Categories"
Maintenance services
see Janitorial and maintenance services
Makuc, Diane M.
"Health Service Areas for the U.S. Vital and Health Statistics Series 2", 4147-2.113
Malagasy Republic
see Madagascar
Malaria
see Infective and parasitic diseases
Malawi
Agricultural trade of US, by detailed commodity and country, 1991, annual rpt, 1524-8
Agricultural trade of US, by detailed commodity and country, 1991, semiannual rpt, 1522-4
AID economic aid to developing countries, obligations and disbursements by country, quarterly rpt, 9912-4
AID loans repayment status and terms by program and country, and status of predecessor agency loans, quarterly rpt, 9912-3
Economic and military aid and loans from US and intl agencies, by program and country, FY46-91, annual rpt, 9914-5
Economic and social conditions of developing countries from 1960s, and Intl Dev Cooperation Agency and AID activities and funding, FY91-93, annual rpt, 9904-4
Economic conditions, income, production, prices, employment, and trade, 1992 periodic country rpt, 2046-4.17
Economic, social, political, and geographic summary data, by country, 1992, annual factbook, 9114-2
Exports and imports of US, by transport mode, country, and SITC 1- to 3-digit commodity, 1991, annual rpt, 2424-12
Exports of US, detailed Schedule B commodities with countries of destination, 1991, annual rpt, 2424-10
Food supply, needs, and aid for developing countries, status and alternative forecasts, 1992 world area rpt, 1526-8.2
Human rights conditions in 170 countries, and US economic and military aid, 1991, annual rpt, 21384-3
Military aid of US, arms sales, and training programs costs and budget requests, by program, world region, and country, FY91-93, annual rpt, 7144-13
Military spending, arms trade, and force strengths, with govt spending and population, by country, 1979-89, annual rpt, 9824-1
Minerals Yearbook, Vol 3, 1989: foreign country review of production, trade, and policy, by commodity, annual rpt, 5604-35.1
Population size, growth rates, and components of change, by country, projected 1990-2020 and trends from 1950, biennial rpt, 2324-9
Refugee migration, and intl aid programs, by world area and country of origin and asylum, 1991, annual rpt, 7004-15
UN voting record and share of votes in agreement with US, by issue, country, and world area, 1991, annual rpt, 7004-18
Malaysia
Agricultural trade of US, by detailed commodity and country, 1991, annual rpt, 1524-8
Agricultural trade of US, by detailed commodity and country, 1991, semiannual rpt, 1522-4
AID loans repayment status and terms by program and country, and status of predecessor agency loans, quarterly rpt, 9912-3
Background Notes, summary social, political, and economic data, 1991 rpt, 7006-2.6
Cuba trade, by commodity and country, mid 1980s-91, 9118-8
Economic and military aid and loans from US and intl agencies, by program and country, FY46-91, annual rpt, 9914-5
Economic and social conditions of developing countries from 1960s, and Intl Dev Cooperation Agency and AID activities and funding, FY91-93, annual rpt, 9904-4
Economic conditions, policy, and trade practices, by country, 1989-91, annual rpt, 21384-5
Economic, social, political, and geographic summary data, by country, 1992, annual factbook, 9114-2
Exports and imports of US, by commodity and country, 1980-90, world area rpt, 9116-1.3
Exports and imports of US, by Harmonized System 6-digit commodity and country, 1991, annual rpt, 2424-13
Exports and imports of US, by selected country, country group, and commodity group, 1991, annual rpt, 2044-37
Exports and imports of US, by transport mode, country, and SITC 1- to 3-digit commodity, 1991, annual rpt, 2424-12
Exports, imports, and balances of US for manufactured goods, by SITC 2-digit commodity and country, quarterly rpt, 2042-35
Exports of US, detailed Schedule B commodities with countries of destination, 1991, annual rpt, 2424-10
Human rights conditions in 170 countries, and US economic and military aid, 1991, annual rpt, 21384-3
Imports of goods, services, and investment from US, trade barriers, impacts, and US actions, by country, 1991, annual rpt, 444-2
Imports of US given duty-free treatment for value of US material sent abroad, by commodity and country, 1987-90, annual rpt, 9884-14
Military aid of US, arms sales, and training programs costs and budget requests, by program, world region, and country, FY91-93, annual rpt, 7144-13
Military spending, arms trade, and force strengths, with govt spending and population, by country, 1979-89, annual rpt, 9824-1

Minerals Yearbook, Vol 3, 1989: foreign country review of production, trade, and policy, by commodity, annual rpt, 5604–35.2
Multinatl US firms and foreign affiliates finances and operations, by industry and country, 1989 benchmark survey, annual rpt, 2704–5
Multinatl US firms foreign affiliates, income statement items by asset size, industry, and country, 1988, biennial article, 8302–2.322
Oil exports to US by OPEC and non-OPEC countries, monthly rpt, 3162–24.3
Oil exports to US by OPEC and non-OPEC countries, monthly 1973-88, 3168–123.3
Population size, growth rates, and components of change, by country, projected 1990-2020 and trends from 1950, biennial rpt, 2324–9
Refugee migration, and intl aid programs, by world area and country of origin and asylum, 1991, annual rpt, 7004–15
Rubber thread from Malaysia at less than fair value, injury to US industry, investigation with background financial and operating data, 1992 rpt, 9886–14.360
Steel trade, by product, country, and customs district, with US industry operating data, 1989-June 1992, semiannual rpt, 9882–15
UN voting record and share of votes in agreement with US, by issue, country, and world area, 1991, annual rpt, 7004–18
see also under By Foreign Country in the "Index by Categories"

Maldives
Economic and military aid and loans from US and intl agencies, by program and country, FY46-91, annual rpt, 9914–5
Economic, social, political, and geographic summary data, by country, 1992, annual factbook, 9114–2
Exports and imports of US, by transport mode, country, and SITC 1- to 3-digit commodity, 1991, annual rpt, 2424–12
Exports of US, detailed Schedule B commodities with countries of destination, 1991, annual rpt, 2424–10
Human rights conditions in 170 countries, and US economic and military aid, 1991, annual rpt, 21384–3
Military aid of US, arms sales, and training programs costs and budget requests, by program, world region, and country, FY91-93, annual rpt, 7144–13
Population size, growth rates, and components of change, by country, projected 1990-2020 and trends from 1950, biennial rpt, 2324–9
Refugee migration, and intl aid programs, by world area and country of origin and asylum, 1991, annual rpt, 7004–15
UN voting record and share of votes in agreement with US, by issue, country, and world area, 1991, annual rpt, 7004–18

Malecki, Richard A.
"Effects of Harvest on Feral Rock Dove Survival, Nest Success, and Population Size", 5506–12.4

Mali
Agricultural trade of US, by detailed commodity and country, 1991, annual rpt, 1524–8
Agricultural trade of US, by detailed commodity and country, 1991, semiannual rpt, 1522–4
AID economic aid to developing countries, obligations and disbursements by country, quarterly rpt, 9912–4
AID loans repayment status and terms by program and country, and status of predecessor agency loans, quarterly rpt, 9912–3
Economic and military aid and loans from US and intl agencies, by program and country, FY46-91, annual rpt, 9914–5
Economic and social conditions of developing countries from 1960s, and Intl Dev Cooperation Agency and AID activities and funding, FY91-93, annual rpt, 9904–4
Economic conditions, income, production, prices, employment, and trade, 1992 periodic country rpt, 2046–4.22
Economic, social, political, and geographic summary data, by country, 1992, annual factbook, 9114–2
Exports and imports of US, by transport mode, country, and SITC 1- to 3-digit commodity, 1991, annual rpt, 2424–12
Exports of US, detailed Schedule B commodities with countries of destination, 1991, annual rpt, 2424–10
Human rights conditions in 170 countries, and US economic and military aid, 1991, annual rpt, 21384–3
Military aid of US, arms sales, and training programs costs and budget requests, by program, world region, and country, FY91-93, annual rpt, 7144–13
Military spending, arms trade, and force strengths, with govt spending and population, by country, 1979-89, annual rpt, 9824–1
Minerals Yearbook, Vol 3, 1989: foreign country review of production, trade, and policy, by commodity, annual rpt, 5604–35.1
Population size, growth rates, and components of change, by country, projected 1990-2020 and trends from 1950, biennial rpt, 2324–9
Refugee migration, and intl aid programs, by world area and country of origin and asylum, 1991, annual rpt, 7004–15
UN voting record and share of votes in agreement with US, by issue, country, and world area, 1991, annual rpt, 7004–18

Malkki, Rita M.
"Famine-Affected, Refugee, and Displaced Populations: Recommendations for Public Health Issues", 4206–2.63

Malnutrition
see Nutrition and malnutrition

Malpractice
see Medical malpractice

Malta
Agricultural trade of US, by detailed commodity and country, 1991, annual rpt, 1524–8
Agricultural trade of US, by detailed commodity and country, 1991, semiannual rpt, 1522–4
AID loans repayment status and terms by program and country, and status of predecessor agency loans, quarterly rpt, 9912–3
Economic and military aid and loans from US and intl agencies, by program and country, FY46-91, annual rpt, 9914–5
Economic, social, political, and geographic summary data, by country, 1992, annual factbook, 9114–2
Exports and imports of US, by transport mode, country, and SITC 1- to 3-digit commodity, 1991, annual rpt, 2424–12
Exports of US, detailed Schedule B commodities with countries of destination, 1991, annual rpt, 2424–10
Human rights conditions in 170 countries, and US economic and military aid, 1991, annual rpt, 21384–3
Military aid of US, arms sales, and training programs costs and budget requests, by program, world region, and country, FY91-93, annual rpt, 7144–13
Military spending, arms trade, and force strengths, with govt spending and population, by country, 1979-89, annual rpt, 9824–1
Population size, growth rates, and components of change, by country, projected 1990-2020 and trends from 1950, biennial rpt, 2324–9
Refugee migration, and intl aid programs, by world area and country of origin and asylum, 1991, annual rpt, 7004–15
Ships in world merchant fleet, tonnage, and new ship construction and deliveries, by vessel type and country, as of Jan 1992, annual rpt, 7704–3
UN voting record and share of votes in agreement with US, by issue, country, and world area, 1991, annual rpt, 7004–18

Malvinas
see Falkland Islands (Malvinas)

Mammography
Cancer (breast) cases undetected by mammography, by tumor and reproductive characteristics, 1976-86 local area study, article, 4472–1.316
Older women's mammography use relation to views and participation in promotional workshop, local area study, 1992 article, 4042–3.337
Poor black women's cervical and breast cancer screening, effects of in-home promotion program, 1989-92, article, 4042–3.338
Use of mammography and promotion costs, by recruitment method, 1988-90 study, article, 4472–1.318
Use of mammography, and reasons for nonuse, by age, race, income, and State, 1987-89, article, 4202–7.313
Views of women on mammography and cancer, 1990 local area survey, article, 4042–3.370

Management
see Business management
see Consultants
see Executives and managers
see Government efficiency
see Health facilities administration
see Labor-management relations, general
see Labor-management relations in government
see School administration and staff

Manatees
see Marine mammals

Manchester, Joyce
"Economic Effects of the Savings and Loan Crisis", 26306–6.165
Manea, Sally Jo
"Hepatitis B Immunization Campaign for Children in the Federated States of Micronesia", 4042–3.357
Manegold, James G.
"IRAs and Saving: Evidence from a Panel of Taxpayers", 9381–10.126
Mangeno, J. J.
"Environmental Monitoring and Disposal of Radioactive Wastes from U.S. Naval Nuclear-Powered Ships and Their Support Facilities, 1991", 3804–11
"Occupational Radiation Exposure from U.S. Naval Nuclear Propulsion Plants and Their Support Facilities, 1991", 3804–10
Mangold, Robert D.
"Tree Planting in the U.S., 1991", 1204–7
Mann, Catherine L.
"Fiscal Implications of the Transition from Planned to Market Economy", 9366–7.278
Manned space flight
see Astronauts
Manning, Carol A.
"Evaluation of an Alternative Method for Hiring Air Traffic Control Specialists with Prior Military Experience", 7506–10.101
"Identifying Ability Requirements for Operators of Future Automated Air Traffic Control Systems", 7506–10.122
Manning, Carolyn A.
"Summary of Reported Water Use for Arkansas Counties", 5666–24.12
Manpower
see Labor supply and demand
see under names of specific occupations
Manpower training programs
Assistance (block and categorical grants) programs for State and local govts, FY91, biennial listing, 10044–8
Assistance (financial and nonfinancial) of Fed Govt, 1992 base edition, annual listing, 104–5
Assistance programs of Fed Govt for public welfare, employment, and training, coordination issues with background data, 1991 rpt, 15498–29
Budget of US, CBO analysis and review of FY93 budget by function, annual rpt, 26304–2
Budget of US, obligations and authority by function, agency, and program, with summaries and analyses, FY93, annual rpt, 104–2
Displaced worker employment and training services, and layoff alternatives, indicators of effectiveness, 1980s, 15498–28
Displaced worker training programs spending, participation, and placements by State, 1990, GAO rpt, 26121–481
Drug abuse by mothers, treatment and other services use, referrals, needs, and barriers, for 13 NIDA-funded programs, 1990/91 survey, 4498–76
Employment and Training Admin activities, funding, and participant characteristics, by program, FY86-88, annual rpt, 6404–17
Employment, earnings, and hours, by SIC 1- to 4-digit industry, monthly 1989-Feb 1992, annual rpt, 6744–4
Expenditures of Fed Govt in States, by type, program, agency, and State, FY91, annual rpt, 2464–2
HHS financial aid, by program, recipient, State, and city, FY91, annual regional listings, 4004–3
Homeless persons aid by program and Federal agency, and indicators of need, 1990, annual rpt, 14364–1
Input-output structure of US economy, detailed interindustry transactions for 541 industries, and components of final demand, 1982 benchmark data, 2708–17
Job Training Partnership Act programs in rural areas, costs and outcomes, FY87, article, 1502–7.305
Job Training Partnership Act State and local admin, funding, effectiveness, and participants, GAO rpt series, 26106–8
Job Training Partnership Act, unemployment, employment, and labor force of States and local areas eligible for funding, monthly rpt, special supplement, 6742–22
Labor Dept activities and funding, by program and State, FY91, annual rpt, 6304–1
Labor laws enacted, by State, 1991, annual article, 6722–1.309
Natl Commission for Employment Policy activities and rpts, 1991 annual rpt, 15494–1
Natl income and product accounts, comprehensive accounts and components, benchmark revisions, 1929-88, 2708–5
Natl income and product accounts, comprehensive accounts and components, *Survey of Current Business*, monthly rpt, 2702–1.26
Occupational qualification and skill improvement training, workers participating by training source, occupation, age, sex, and race, 1991, 6728–32
Ohio poverty, hunger, and public welfare program operations and indicators of need, by county, 1991 hearing, 21968–58
Unemployed displaced workers and other hard-to-serve groups, factors contributing to unemployment, and training programs operations, series, 15496–1
see also Apprenticeship
see also Employee development
see also Military training
see also Vocational education and training
see also Vocational rehabilitation
see also Work incentive programs
see also Youth Conservation Corps
Mansfield, Ohio
Wages by occupation, and benefits for office and plant workers, 1992 survey, periodic MSA rpt, 6785–3.4
Mansfield, Wendy
"Office for Civil Rights Survey Redesign: A Feasibility Survey", 4826–1.33
"Public School Principal Survey on Safe, Disciplined, and Drug-Free Schools", 4826–1.32
Manufactured housing
see Mobile homes
Manufacturing
Business statistics, detailed data for major industries and economic indicators, *Survey of Current Business*, monthly rpt, 2702–1
Business statistics, detailed data for major industries and economic indicators, 1960-91, *Survey of Current Business* biennial supplement, 2704–1
Capital expenditures for plant and equipment, by industry div, monthly rpt, quarterly data, 23842–1.1
Capital expenditures for plant and equipment, by major industry group, quarterly rpt, 2502–2
Capital investment in manufacturing, relation to cash flow and other factors, 1992 working paper, 9375–13.81
Capital investment relation to cash flow and other factors, model description and results, 1950s-80s, technical paper, 9385–8.129
Capital investment relation to debt/collateral ratios, model description and results, 1950s-80, working paper, 9377–9.141
Census Bur data files and rpts, coverage and availability, 1992 annual listing, 2304–2
Coal receipts and prices at manufacturing plants, by SIC 2-digit industry, quarterly rpt, 3162–37.2
Collective bargaining agreements expiring during year, and workers covered, by firm, union, industry group, and State, 1992, annual rpt, 6784–9
Collective bargaining wage and benefit changes, quarterly press release, 6782–2
Collective bargaining wage changes and coverage, by industry and whether contract includes escalator clause and lump sum payment, 1982-91, annual article, 6722–1.325
Communist and transitional economy countries trade with US, by detailed commodity and country, quarterly rpt with articles, 9882–2
Competitiveness (intl) of US manufacturing industry, trade and economic policies with background data and foreign comparisons, 1991 rpt, 26358–252
County Business Patterns, 1989: employment, establishments, and payroll, by SIC 2- to 4-digit industry and county, annual State rpt series, 2326–8
County Business Patterns, 1990: employment, establishments, and payroll, by SIC 2- to 4-digit industry and county, annual State rpt series, 2326–6
Cuba trade, by commodity and country, mid 1980s-91, 9118–8
Deaths and rates, by cause and selected social, demographic, and employment characteristics, 1979-85, natl longitudinal study, 4478–186
Debt/asset ratios in manufacturing, impact on employment changes over the business cycle, 1960s-84, technical paper, 9366–6.286
Earnings and hours of work, weekly averages, monthly rpt, 23842–1.2
Economies of scale in output, technology, and trade, model description and results, 1992 technical paper, 9383–20.22
Employment and Earnings, detailed data, monthly rpt, 6742–2.5; 6742–2.6
Employment Cost Index and alternative measure of compensation costs, by component, occupation, industry group, union status, and location, 1975-92, annual rpt, 6744–20
Employment Cost Index and percent change by occupational group, industry div, region, and metro-nonmetro area, quarterly press release, 6782–5

Employment, earnings, and hours, by industry div and major manufacturing group, Monthly Labor Review, 6722–1.2
Employment, earnings, and hours, by selected SIC 1- to 4-digit industry, State, and for 275 MSAs, 1987-92, 6748–81
Employment, earnings, and hours, by SIC 1- to 4-digit industry, monthly 1989-Feb 1992, annual rpt, 6744–4
Employment, earnings, and hours, monthly press release, 6742–5
Employment in manufacturing and nonagricultural industries, by MSA, 1990-91, annual press release, 6946–3.24
Employment of minorities and women, by occupation, SIC 1- to 3-digit industry, State, and MSA, 1991, annual rpt, 9244–1
Employment situation, earnings, hours, and other BLS economic indicators, transcripts of BLS Commissioner's monthly testimony, periodic rpt, 23846–4
Employment, unemployment, and labor force characteristics, by region, State, and selected metro area, 1991, annual rpt, 6744–7
Energy use and prices, by fuel type and manufacturing industry, 1974-88, 3166–15.3
Energy use and prices for manufacturing industries, 1988 survey, series, 3166–13
Energy use in commercial buildings, costs, and conservation, by building characteristics, survey rpt series, 3166–8
Export and import price indexes, by selected end-use category, monthly press release, 6762–15
Export and import price indexes for goods and services, and dollar exchange rate indexes, quarterly press release, 6762–13
Exports and imports between US and outlying areas, by detailed commodity and mode of transport, 1991, annual rpt, 2424–11
Exports and imports of US, by country and detailed commodity, monthly rpt, 2422–12
Exports and imports of US by country, and trade shifts by commodity, 1991, annual rpt, 9884–25
Exports and imports of US, by Harmonized System 6-digit commodity and country, 1991, annual rpt, 2424–13
Exports and imports of US, by transport mode, country, and SITC 1- to 3-digit commodity, 1991, annual rpt, 2424–12
Exports, imports, and balances of US, by selected country, country group, and commodity group, preliminary data, monthly rpt, 2042–34
Exports, imports, and balances of US for manufactured goods, by SITC 2-digit commodity and country, quarterly rpt, 2042–35
Exports, imports, and balances of US with major trading partners, by product category, 1987-91, annual chartbook, 9884–21
Exports, imports, and trade flows, by country and commodity, with background economic indicators, data compilation, monthly CD-ROM, 2002–6
Exports, imports, tariffs, and industry operating data for miscellaneous manufactured products, commodity rpt series, 9885–10
Exports of manufactured goods, total and for US and major competitors, by country of destination, annual commodity market share rpt series, discontinued, 2046–13
Exports of manufactured goods, total and for US and major competitors, by SITC 1- to 5-digit commodity, annual country market share rpt series, discontinued, 2046–2
Exports of US, detailed commodities by country, monthly CD-ROM, 2422–13
Fed Govt labor productivity, indexes of output and labor costs by function, FY67-90, annual rpt, 6824–1.6
Finances and operations, by SIC 2- to 4-digit industry, forecast 1992, annual rpt, 2044–28
Financial statements for manufacturing, mining, and trade corporations, by selected SIC 2- to 3-digit industry, quarterly rpt, 2502–1
Foreign and US manufacturing labor costs and indexes, by selected country, 1991, semiannual rpt, 6822–3
Foreign and US manufacturing labor productivity and costs, by selected country, 1950s-91, press release, 6726–1.55
Foreign and US manufacturing labor productivity and unit costs, for 14 countries, 1960s-90, article, 6722–1.304
Foreign-controlled US firms transactions with related foreign persons, by type, industry div, and country, 1988, article, 8302–2.318
Foreign countries economic conditions, policy, and trade practices, by country, 1989-91, annual rpt, 21384–5
Foreign countries economic, social, political, and geographic summary data, by country, 1992, annual factbook, 9114–2
Foreign direct investment in US, by industry group and world area, 1989-91, annual article, 2702–1.331
Foreign direct investment in US, major transactions by type, industry, country, and US location, 1990, annual rpt, 2044–20
Foreign direct investment of US, by industry group and world area, 1989-91, annual article, 2702–1.332
Gross State Product by component, industry div, and State, 1977-89, article, 2702–1.303
Hazardous substances industrial releases and reduction methods under EPA regulation, by chemical, source, industry, and location, 1989, annual rpt, 9234–6
Hazardous substances industrial releases and reduction methods under EPA regulation, with chemical stocks and use, facility directory, 1987-89, annual CD-ROM, 9234–7
Hazardous substances industrial releases and reduction methods under EPA regulation, with chemical stocks and use, facility directory, 1991 CD-ROM user guide, 9238–70
Import price indexes for manufactured and nonmanufactured goods, changes by world area, 1991-92, article, 6722–1.327
Imports, exports, and employment impacts, by SIC 2- to 4-digit industry and commodity, quarterly rpt, 2322–2
Imports of US, detailed commodities by country, monthly CD-ROM, 2422–14
Income tax returns of foreign corporations and individuals, and US entities abroad, detailed data compilation, 1970s-89, quinquennial rpt, 8308–31
Input-output structure of US economy, detailed interindustry transactions for 84 industries, and components of final demand, 1987, annual article, 2702–1.316
Input-output structure of US economy, detailed interindustry transactions for 541 industries, and components of final demand, 1982 benchmark data, 2708–17
Inventories related to sales, by industry sector, model description and results, late 1960s-91, article, 9389–1.302
Labor hourly costs, by component, occupational group, industry div, union coverage, and region, 1992, annual rpt, 6744–21
Latin America economic and social conditions, resources, trade, and aid, 1992, annual factbook, 9914–14
Mexico imports from US, by industry and State, 1987-91, 2048–154
Middle Atlantic States manufacturing business outlook, monthly survey rpt, 9387–11
Middle Atlantic States manufacturing output index, monthly rpt, 9387–12
Minority- and woman-owned businesses and owner characteristics, by industry, employment and sales size, and form of ownership, 1987 survey, 2328–59
Multinatl firms US affiliates finances and operations, by industry, country of parent firm, and State, 1987, 2708–48
Multinatl firms US affiliates, finances, and operations, by industry, world area of parent firm, and State, 1989-90, annual rpt, 2704–4
Multinatl US firms and foreign affiliates finances and operations, by industry and country, 1989 benchmark survey, annual rpt, 2704–5
Multinatl US firms foreign affiliates, income statement items by asset size, industry, and country, 1988, biennial article, 8302–2.322
Natl income and product accounts, comprehensive accounts and components, benchmark revisions, 1929-88, 2708–5
Natl income and product accounts, comprehensive accounts and components, *Survey of Current Business*, monthly rpt, 2702–1.29
Occupational injuries, illnesses, and lost workdays, by SIC 2-digit industry, 1990-91, annual press release, 6844–3
Occupational injury and illness rates by circumstances and establishment size, and methodology for computing rates, 1988, industry rpt, 6886–4.1
Occupational injury and illness rates, by SIC 2- to 4-digit industry, 1989-90, annual rpt, 6844–7
Occupational injury and illness rates, by SIC 2- to 4-digit industry, 1990, annual rpt, 6844–1
Occupational Outlook Handbook, 1992-93, biennial rpt, 6744–1
Operations and performance of manufacturing industries, analytical rpt series, 2506–16

Pacific Northwest population, households, employment, income, fuel prices, and electricity demand, alternative forecasts 1991-2010, annual rpt, 3224–3.3
Pacific territories population and housing detailed characteristics, by location, 1990 Census of Population and Housing, series, 2551–8
Price indexes (producer), by stage of processing and detailed commodity, monthly rpt, 6762–6
Price indexes (producer), by stage of processing and detailed commodity, monthly 1991, annual rpt, 6764–2
Producer Price Index, by major commodity group and subgroup, and processing stage, monthly press release, 6762–5
Production and capacity use indexes, by SIC 2- to 4-digit industry, monthly rpt, 9365–2.24
Production forecasts, performance of regional indexes by SIC 2-digit manufacturing industry, 1992 working paper, 9375–13.85
Production, shipments, inventories, and new orders, monthly rpt, 23842–1.3
Productivity and costs of labor for private, nonfarm business, and manufacturing sectors, revised data, quarterly rpt, 6822–2
Productivity and costs of labor, indexes, preliminary data, quarterly rpt, 6822–1
Productivity of labor, capital, and other inputs in manufacturing, changes by selected industry, various periods 1949-88, article, 6722–1.345
Productivity relation to high technology capital investment, by industry sector, 1940s-80s, technical paper, 9385–8.130
Profits in manufacturing relation to real exchange rate, model description and results, 1992 technical paper, 9385–8.142
Puerto Rico and other US possessions corporations income tax returns, income and tax items, and employment, by selected industry, 1989, article, 8302–2.326
Recycling in manufacturing industries, fuel savings, and CO2 emissions reductions, 1988 and projected to 1995, hearing, 21368–140
Science, engineering, and technical employment in manufacturing, by field and industry, 1989, triennial rpt, 9627–23
SEC registration, firms required to file annual rpts, as of Sept 1991, annual listing, 9734–5
Shipments, inventories, orders, capacity use, and pollution control costs of manufacturers, periodic Current Industrial Rpt series, 2506–3
Small Business Admin loan guarantee program participants finances, operations, characteristics, and views, 1991 survey, 9768–25
Small business finances, operations, owner characteristics, and Federal contracts, 1980s-90, annual rpt, 9764–6
Southeastern States, Fed Reserve 5th District, economic indicators by State, quarterly rpt, 9389–16
Southeastern US employment by industry div, earnings, and hours, for 8 States, quarterly press release, 6942–7
Southeastern US manufacturing conditions, survey methodology and selected results, Dec 1991-July 1992, article, 9371–1.307
Statistical Abstract of US, 1992 annual data compilation, 2324–1.17; 2324–1.27
Tariff Schedule of US, classifications and rates of duty by detailed imported commodity, 1993 base edition, 9886–13
Tax (income) returns filed, by type of filer, selected income items, quarterly rpt, 8302–2.1
Tax (income) returns for foreign corporate activity in US, selected income and tax items, by industry div and selected country, 1988, article, 8302–2.309
Tax (income) returns of corporations, income and tax items by asset size and detailed industry, 1989, annual rpt, 8304–4; 8304–21
Tax (income) returns of corporations with foreign tax credit, income and tax items by industry group, 1988, biennial article, 8302–2.316
Tax (income) returns of Foreign Sales Corps, assets, and income and tax items, by industry, country of incorporation, and transaction pricing method, 1987, article, 8302–2.311
Tax (income) returns of Interest Charge-Domestic Intl Sales Corps, assets and selected income and tax items, by detailed industry, 1987, article, 8302–2.312
Tax (income) returns of partnerships, income statement and balance sheet items, by industry group, 1990, annual article, 8302–2.314
Tax (income) returns of sole proprietorships, income statement items, by industry group, 1990, annual article, 8302–2.317; 8302–2.320
Technology-intensive capital investment relation to productivity growth, 1950s-89, article, 9385–1.310
Technology-intensive industries intl competitiveness, with background data by industry and foreign comparisons, 1960s-91, GAO rpt, 26123–406
Technology transfer by Federal R&D labs to small manufacturers, promotional programs activities and grants to States, late 1980s-91, GAO rpt, 26113–551
Tennessee Valley economic conditions, and compared to US, alternative projections 1992-2010 and trends from 1929, annual rpt, 9804–27
Trade zones (US) operations and movement of goods, by zone and commodity, FY90, annual rpt, 2044–30
Unemployed displaced workers job search and placement aid effectiveness, relation to previous employment and other characteristics, 1979-87 studies, 15496–1.14
Unemployed displaced workers, layoffs and unemployment insurance claims by reason, industry, selected characteristics, and State, quarterly press release, 6742–23
Unemployed displaced workers, layoffs and unemployment insurance claims by reason, industry, selected characteristics, MSA, and State, 1990, annual rpt, 6744–18
Wage and benefit changes from collective bargaining and mgmt decisions, by industry div, monthly rpt, 6782–1
Wages by occupation, and benefits for office and plant workers, periodic MSA survey rpt series, 6785–12; 6785–16; 6785–17
Waste (industrial) generation, disposal, and regulation, by industry and State, mid 1980s-90, 26358–256
see also Aerospace industry
see also Aircraft
see also Aluminum and aluminum industry
see also Annual Survey of Manufactures
see also Business machines and equipment
see also Cement and concrete
see also Census of Manufactures
see also Chemicals and chemical industry
see also Clay industry and products
see also Clothing and clothing industry
see also Copper and copper industry
see also Dyeing and coloring materials
see also Electrical machinery and equipment
see also Electronics industry and products
see also Food and food industry
see also Furniture and furnishings
see also Furs and fur industry
see also Glass and glass industry
see also Gum and wood chemicals
see also Household appliances and equipment
see also Ice, manufactured
see also Industrial capacity and utilization
see also Industrial plants and equipment
see also Industrial production
see also Industrial production indexes
see also Instruments and measuring devices
see also Iron and steel industry
see also Leather industry and products
see also Lumber industry and products
see also Machines and machinery industry
see also Metals and metal industries
see also Motor vehicle industry
see also Musical instruments
see also Paints and varnishes
see also Paper and paper products
see also Petroleum and petroleum industry
see also Pharmaceutical industry
see also Plastics and plastics industry
see also Printing and publishing industry
see also Production workers
see also Rubber and rubber industry
see also Shipbuilding and repairing
see also Sporting goods
see also Stone products and quarries
see also Textile industry and fabrics
see also Tires and tire industry
see also Tobacco industry and products
see also Toys and games
see also Transportation and transportation equipment
see also Zinc and zinc industry
see also under By Commodity in the "Index by Categories"
see also under By Industry in the "Index by Categories"

Manufacturing Energy Consumption Survey
Consumption and prices of energy, by fuel type and manufacturing industry, 1974-88, 3166–15.3
Design and questionnaire dev for 1991 survey, 3166–15.2

Manzella, Sharon A.
"Distribution of Kemp's Ridley Sea Turtles (Lepidochelys kempi) Along the Texas Coast: An Atlas", 2168–132

Maps
Alaska minerals resources and geologic characteristics, compilation of papers, 1990, annual rpt, 5664–15
Alaska minerals resources, production, oil and gas leases, reserves, and exploratory wells, with maps and bibl, 1990, annual rpt, 5664–11
Alaska OCS environmental conditions and oil dev impacts, compilation of papers, series, 2176–1
Birds (mourning dove) population, by hunting and nonhunting State, 1966-92, annual rpt, 5504–15
Birds (northern spotted owl) conservation methods in Pacific Northwest, findings and recommendations, 1990 rpt, 1208–385
Birds (northern spotted owl) conservation methods in Pacific Northwest, timber industry impacts, and Federal and State spending, 1980s-95, 1208–388
Birds (waterfowl) population, habitat conditions, and migratory flight forecasts, for Canada and US by region, 1992 and trends from 1955, annual rpt, 5504–27
Birds (waterfowl) refuge and breeding area acreage acquired by Fed Govt, and costs, by site and State, FY92, annual rpt, 14784–1
Census Bur data files and rpts, coverage and availability, 1992 annual listing, 2304–2
Census Bur geographic levels of data coverage, maps, and reference products, 1992 rpt, 2308–67
Census Bur rpts and data files, coverage, availability, and use, series, 2326–7
Census of Population and Housing, 1990: maps and cartographic products availability, listing, 2308–66
Census of Population and Housing, 1990: summary characteristics, households, and land area, by county, subdiv, and place, State rpt series, 2551–1
Coastal and riparian areas environmental conditions, fish, wildlife, use, and mgmt, for individual ecosystems, series, 5506–9
Coastal areas environmental conditions and mgmt, for individual areas, conf series, 2146–8
DC metro area land acquisition and dev projects of Fed Govt, characteristics and funding by agency and project, FY92-96, annual rpt, 15454–1
Developing countries economic, population, and agricultural data, US and other aid sources, and AID activity, country rpt series, 9916–12
Disasters and natl security incidents and mgmt, with data by major event and State, 1992 annual rpt, 9434–6
Energy use, costs, and conservation, and household and housing characteristics, survey rpt series, 3166–7
Estuaries approved and restricted for shellfish harvest, and pollution sources, by estuary, State, and coastal region, with maps, 1990, quinquennial rpt, 2178–33
Fed Govt publications and other holdings of Natl Archives, special collections, series, 9516–1
Foreign countries economic, social, political, and geographic summary data, by country, 1992, annual factbook, 9114–2
Foreign countries *Geographic Notes*, boundaries, claims, nomenclature, and other devs, quarterly rpt, 7142–3
Geological Survey rpts and research journal articles, monthly listing, 5662–1
Geological Survey rpts, 1991, annual listing, 5664–4
Glaciology intl research summaries, methodology, and bibls, series, 2156–18
Great Lakes Science Advisory Board research activities and water quality goals, FY91, biennial rpt, 14644–6
Housing rental and sales, discrimination against blacks and Hispanics in selected metro areas, 1989 study, 5186–16.2
Hurricanes and tropical storms in Pacific and Indian Oceans, paths and surveillance, 1991, annual rpt, 3804–8
Marine Fisheries Review, US and foreign fisheries resources, dev, mgmt, and research, quarterly journal, 2162–1
Mariners Weather Log, quarterly journal, 2152–8
Military contracts, payroll, and personnel, by service branch and location, with top 5 contractors and maps, by State and country, FY91, annual rpt, 3544–29
Minerals (strategic) supply and characteristics of individual deposits, by country, commodity rpt series, 5666–21
Minerals production, reserves, and industry role in domestic economy and world supply, world area and country rpt, series, 5606–1
Natural gas pipelines and owners, and fields, as of Sept 1990, map, 3088–21
Ocean pollution, estuary, and coastal waters monitoring and assessment, NOAA activities and funding, FY90, annual rpt, 2174–9
Ohio River basin waterway facilities, freight by commodity and port, and recreation, by waterway, 1988-89, annual rpt, 3754–6
Pollution (air) levels for 6 pollutants, by source and selected MSA, 1982-91, annual rpt, 9194–1
Public lands minerals resources and availability, State rpt series, 5606–7
Radon and other radionuclide levels in air, water, soil, and uranium mill tailings, by site and region, 1950s-80s, compilation of papers, 5668–126
Soil surveys and maps for counties, 1899-1991, annual listing, 1264–11
Soviet Union former Republics and Baltic States energy supply and use, and social, economic, and political indicators, 1989-90, 3168–126
Soviet Union former Republics and Baltic States population size and characteristics, 1989-92, 9118–19
Timber in Pacific Northwest, old-growth forests plant and wildlife population and species diversity, 1991 compilation of papers, 1208–386
Timber insect and disease incidence and damage, and control activities, State rpt series, 1206–49
Timber insect and disease incidence and damage, by State, 1990, annual rpt, 1204–8
Turtles (sea) sightings, strandings, and incidental catch, for Kemp's ridley turtles on Texas coast, late 1940s-90, 2168–132
Uranium tailings at inactive mills, remedial action proposals, costs, site characteristics, and environmental, socioeconomic, and health impacts, series, 3356–4
Water (groundwater) supply, quality, chemistry, and use, State and local area rpt series, 5666–28
Water (groundwater) supply, quality, chemistry, other characteristics, and use, regional rpt series, 5666–25
Water quality, chemistry, hydrology, and other characteristics, local area studies, series, 5666–27
Water resources dev projects of Army Corps of Engineers, characteristics, and costs, 1950s-89, biennial State rpt series, 3756–1
Water resources dev projects of Army Corps of Engineers, characteristics, and costs, 1950s-91, biennial State rpt series, 3756–2
Water supply in US and southern Canada, streamflow, surface and groundwater conditions, and reservoir levels, by location, monthly rpt, 5662–3
Water supply in western US, and snow survey results, annual State rpt series, 1264–14
Water use by end use, well withdrawals, and public supply deliveries, by county, State rpt series, 5666–24
Weather conditions and effect on agriculture, by US region, State, and city, and world area, weekly rpt, 2182–7
Weather events and anomalies, precipitation and temperature for US and foreign locations, weekly rpt, 2182–6
Weather forecasts for US and Northern Hemisphere, precipitation and temperature by location, semimonthly rpt, 2182–1
see also Cartography

Marella, Richard L.
"Public-Supply Water Use in Florida, 1987", 5666–24.13

Mariana Islands
see Guam
see Northern Mariana Islands

Maricopa County, Ariz.
Housing and households characteristics, unit and neighborhood quality, and journey to work by MSA location, for 11 MSAs, 1985 survey, supplement, 2485–8
Housing and households detailed characteristics, and unit and neighborhood quality, by location, 1989 survey, MSA rpt, 2485–6.9

Marijuana
Abuse of drugs and alcohol, by selected characteristics, 1991 survey, annual rpt series, 4494–5
Abuse of drugs, indicators for selected metro areas, research results, data collection, and policy issues, 1992 semiannual conf, 4492–5
Abuse of drugs, treatment, biological and behavioral factors, and addiction potential of new drugs, research results, 1991 annual conf, 4494–11
Airline and aviation safety employees drug testing and results, by drug type and occupational group, 1991, semiannual rpt, 7502–17
Arrests, by offense, offender characteristics, and location, 1991, annual rpt, 6224–2.2

Arrests for drug- and nondrug-related offenses, urine test results by drug type, offense, and sex, for selected urban areas, quarterly rpt, 6062–3
Coast Guard enforcement activities, 1st half FY92, semiannual rpt, 7402–4
Court civil and criminal caseloads for Federal district, appeals, and bankruptcy courts, by type of suit and offense, circuit, and district, 1991, annual rpt, 18204–11
Court civil and criminal caseloads for Federal district, appeals, and special courts, 1991, annual rpt, 18204–8
Crime relationship to drug abuse and trafficking, and enforcement data, series, 6066–29
Cultivation of marijuana, DEA and local agencies eradication activities by State, and drug potency and prices, 1982-91, annual rpt, 6284–4
DC metro area drug, alcohol, and tobacco use, user characteristics, and consequences, series, 4496–12
Fed Govt drug abuse and trafficking reduction programs activities, funding, staff, and Bush Admin budget request, by Federal agency, FY91-93, annual rpt, 234–2
Foreign countries drug production, eradication, and seizures, by illegal substance, with US aid, by country, 1988-92, annual rpt, 7004–17
Health condition and care indicators, 1950s-90 with health improvement and disease prevention goals for 1990, annual data compilation, 4144–11
Immigration and Naturalization Service illegal alien and narcotics activities, FY84-91, annual rpt, 6264–2.5
Immigration and Naturalization Service illegal alien and narcotics activities, FY91, annual summary rpt, 6264–7
Police and sheriff depts drug enforcement activities, and employee drug testing policies, 1990, 6066–19.67
Prices of illegal drugs by type and selected metro area, and cocaine and heroin purity, quarterly rpt, 6282–1
Prices of illegal drugs by type, stage of processing, and country of origin, 1991, annual rpt, 6284–7
Public opinion on crime and crime-related issues, by respondent characteristics, data compilation, 1992 annual rpt, 6064–6.2
Research on drug abuse and treatment, summaries of findings, resource materials, and grant listings, bimonthly rpt, 4492–4
Sentences for Federal offenses, guidelines by offense and circumstances, series, 17668–1
Sentences under Federal mandatory minimum provisions, by defendant characteristics, and views on justice system impacts, FY90, 17668–2
Supply of drugs in US by country of origin, abuse, prices, and seizures, by substance, 1991, annual rpt, 6284–2
Testing for drugs, urinalysis methods accuracy by drug type, 1991, 6068–247
Women arrestees drug abuse history and selected other characteristics, for 4 cities, 1988-89, 6068–246
Youth drug, alcohol, and cigarette use and attitudes, by substance type and selected characteristics, 1975-91 surveys, press release, 4008–116; 4494–4

Marine accidents and safety
Accidents involving ships and marine facilities, casualties, circumstances, Coast Guard investigation results, periodic rpt, suspended, 9612–4
Alaska coast shipwrecks, characteristics, deaths, cargo, and whale catch, by vessel and location, 1763-1937, 5738–34
Boat registrations, and accidents, casualties, and damage by cause, by vessel characteristics and State, 1991, annual rpt, 7404–1
Coast Guard search and rescue missions, and lives and property lost and saved, by district and assisting unit, FY91, annual rpt, 7404–2
Diving (underwater) accidents, illnesses, and deaths, by circumstances, diver characteristics, and location, 1970-90, annual rpt, 2144–29
Diving (underwater sport and occupational) deaths, by circumstances, diver characteristics, and location, annual rpt, discontinued, 2144–5
DOT planning and safety grants, by program, State, and for 40 SMSAs, FY89, annual rpt, 7304–7
Fed Govt spending in States, by type, program, agency, and State, FY91, annual rpt, 2464–2
Hazardous material transport accidents, casualties, and damage, by mode of transport, with DOT control activities, 1990, annual rpt, 7304–4
Injury and illness rates and causes, by SIC 2- to 4-digit industry, 1990, annual rpt, 6844–1
Occupational injury and illness rates, by SIC 2- to 4-digit industry, 1989-90, annual rpt, 6844–7
Oil and gas OCS leasing and exploration activity, production, revenue, and environmental studies, by location, quarterly rpt, 5732–1
Recreational boats and engines recalls for safety-related defects, by make, periodic listing, 7402–5
Statistical Abstract of US, 1992 annual data compilation, 2324–1.22
Weather services activities and funding, by Federal agency, planned FY92-93, annual rpt, 2144–2
see also Drowning
see also Oil spills

Marine Corps
Accidents during training activities, and deaths by cause, by service branch, FY88-91, GAO rpt, 26123–397
Base support costs by function, and personnel and acreage by installation, by service branch, FY93, annual rpt, 3504–11
Black military and civilian DOD personnel, by sex, grade, and period of service, and lists of award recipients, officers, and service academy grads, 1770s-90, 3548–22
Budget of DOD, organization, personnel, weapons, and property, by service branch, State, and country, 1992 annual summary rpt, 3504–13
Budget of DOD, procurement appropriations by item, service branch, and defense agency, FY91-93, annual rpt, 3544–32
Budget of DOD, weapons acquisition costs by system and service branch, FY91-93, annual rpt, 3504–2
Commercial activities of DOD performed in-house, and work-years, by service branch, installation, and State, FY91, annual rpt, 3544–25
Criminal case processing in military courts, and prisoners by facility, by service branch, data compilation, 1992 annual rpt, 6064–6.6
Deaths by cause, age, race, and rank, and personnel captured and missing, by service branch, FY91, annual rpt, 3544–40
Health care facilities of DOD in US and abroad, beds, admissions, outpatient visits, and births, by service branch, quarterly rpt, 3542–15
Homosexual military personnel discharges by pay grade, tenure, race, sex, and occupation, and investigations, by service branch, 1980s-90, GAO rpt, 26123–392
Persian Gulf War Operation Desert Storm deployment, by sex, race, rank, and service branch, 1990-91, GAO rpt, 26123–394
Personnel active duty enlisted accessions by race, and goals, by sex and service branch, quarterly press release, 3542–7
Personnel needs, costs, and force readiness, by service branch, FY93, annual rpt, 3504–1
Personnel occupational distribution, by race, sex, and service branch, FY90, GAO rpt, 26123–381
Personnel reductions planned by service branch, and women and minorities affected by Army and Air Force plans, FY90-91, GAO rpt, 26123–373
Personnel reserve and active duty force mix and costs under alternative reduction cases, by service branch, 1990 and projected to 1997, 26306–6.172
Personnel strengths, for active duty, civilians, and dependents, by service branch and US and foreign location, quarterly rpt, 3542–20
Personnel strengths, for active duty, civilians, and reserves, by service branch, FY91 and trends, annual rpt, 3544–1
Personnel strengths, for active duty, civilians, and reserves, by service branch, quarterly rpt, 3542–14
Personnel strengths in US and abroad, by service branch, world area, and country, quarterly press release, 3542–9
Personnel strengths, summary by service branch, monthly press release, 3542–2
Shipments by DOD of military and personal property, passenger traffic, and costs, by service branch and mode of transport, FY91, annual rpt, 3704–15
Training and education programs of DOD, funding, staff, students, and facilities, by service branch, FY93, annual rpt, 3504–5
see also Marine Reserve

Marine Mammal Commission
Budget of US, authoritative financial statements with appropriations, outlays, and receipts, by category and agency, FY91, annual rpt, 8104–2.2
Budget of US, obligations and authority by function, agency, and program, with summaries and analyses, FY93, annual rpt, 104–2

Fishing (net) operations off California, marine mammals and birds incidental catch, 1984-85, 14738–13
Hawaii humpback whale habitat impacts of human activities, with data on shipping, whale watching, coastal construction, and aircraft, 1980s-90, 14738–14
Protection of marine mammals, Federal and intl regulatory and research activities, with bibl, 1991, annual rpt, 14734–1
Research on marine mammals, Federal funding by topic, recipient, and agency, FY91, annual rpt, 14734–2

Marine Mammal Protection Act
Admin of Act, and marine mammal population, strandings, and catch permits by species and location, 1988-89, annual rpt, 2164–11

Marine mammals
Alaska OCS environmental conditions and oil dev impacts, compilation of papers, series, 2176–1
Alaska rural areas population characteristics, and energy resources dev effects, series, 5736–5
Coastal and riparian areas environmental conditions, fish, wildlife, use, and mgmt, for individual ecosystems, series, 5506–9
Dolphin protection embargo impacts on US tuna imports, by country, 1989-92, article, 9882–16.303
Dolphin protection issues, and US tuna fishery competitiveness, investigation with background financial and operating data and foreign comparisons, 1992 rpt, 9886–4.187
Environmental Quality, status of problems, protection programs, research, and intl issues, 1991 annual rpt, 484–1
Fishing (net) operations off California, marine mammals and birds incidental catch, 1984-85, 14738–13
Fishing trawl vessels incidental catch of marine mammals, by species, vessel flag and type, and North Pacific region, 1965-88, 2168–129
Manatees killed in Florida and other US waters, by cause, 1978-91, annual rpt, 14734–1
Minerals offshore lease sales environmental and economic impacts in coastal areas, final statement series, 5736–7
Otters (sea) population, and relocation project results, for California, 1982-90, annual rpt, 5504–12
Otters (sea) population off California coast, 1982-91, annual rpt, 14734–1
Pollutant concentrations in tissue of marine mammals, by species and pollutant type, for Alaska, 1987-91, 2218–87
Population and mgmt of marine mammals, by species and region, 1988-90, annual rpt, 2164–22
Population of marine mammals, strandings, and catch permits by species and location, 1988-89, annual rpt, 2164–11
Porpoise kills by tuna fishery, and Federal and intl marine mammal protection activity, with bibl, 1991, annual rpt, 14734–1
Protection of marine mammals, activities, funding, populations, and harvests, by species, 1990, annual rpt, 5504–12
Protection of marine mammals, Federal and intl regulatory and research activities, with bibl, 1991, annual rpt, 14734–1
Research on marine mammals, Federal funding by topic, recipient, and agency, FY91, annual rpt, 14734–2
Whale catch off Alaska, for total fleet and for vessels later wrecked, 1750s-1937, 5738–34
Whales (bowhead) catch and quota for Eskimos, and other marine mammals harvest, 1970s-91, annual rpt, 14734–1
Whales (bowhead and white) migration through Beaufort Sea, behavior impacts of oil drilling and aircraft noise, spring 1990, 5738–27
Whales (humpback) habitat impacts of human activities in Hawaii, with data on shipping, whale watching, coastal construction, and aircraft, 1980s-90, 14738–14
Whales population and behavior in Chukchi and Beaufort Seas, by endangered species, 1982-91, 5738–32
Whales population and behavior in Chukchi and Beaufort Seas, by endangered species, 1990, 5738–36

Marine pollution
Alaska Beaufort Sea pollutant concentrations in sediment and marine life, by contaminant and site, 1985-89, 5738–33
Alaska OCS environmental conditions and oil dev impacts, compilation of papers, series, 2176–1
California OCS oil and gas dev impacts on water quality, marine life, and sediments, by site, 1986-90, annual rpt, 5734–11
Coastal and estuarine pollutant concentrations in fish, shellfish, and environment, series, 2176–3
Coastal and riparian areas environmental conditions, fish, wildlife, use, and mgmt, for individual ecosystems, series, 5506–9
Coastal areas and watersheds pollution indicators, by location, 1980s-90, 2178–35
Coastal areas environmental conditions and mgmt, for individual areas, conf series, 2146–8
Environmental quality indicators, NOAA monitoring results, 1991 annual summary rpt, 2144–27
Estuary environmental conditions, research results and methodology, series, 2176–7
Health effects of selected pollutants on animals by species and on humans, and environmental levels, series, 5506–14
Justice Dept enforcement of environmental laws, activities, FY83-92, annual press release, 6004–22
Marine mammals protection, Federal and intl regulatory and research activities, 1991, annual rpt, 14734–1
Marine mammals tissue pollutant concentrations, by species and pollutant type, for Alaska, 1987-91, 2218–87
Minerals offshore lease sales environmental and economic impacts in coastal areas, final statement series, 5736–7
NOAA activities and funding for ocean pollution, estuary, and coastal waters monitoring and assessment, FY90, annual rpt, 2174–9
Oil and gas OCS production water discharges, for Pacific lands under Federal lease by drilling platform, 1960s-90, annual rpt, 5734–9
Oil and gas OCS production water discharges, treatment costs by method, 1992 rpt, 3166–6.66
Radioactive waste from Navy nuclear-powered vessels and support facilities, releases in harbors, and public exposure, 1970s-91, annual rpt, 3804–11
Research and distribution of oceanographic data, World Data Center A activities by country, and cruises by ship, 1990, annual rpt, 2144–15
Research on ocean pollution, monitoring, and resources dev activities of Fed Govt, funding and project descriptions, FY89, annual listing, 2144–23
Research on ocean pollution, monitoring, and resources dev activities of Fed Govt, 5-year plan and funding by agency, FY87-92, triennial rpt, 2148–56
Research on ocean pollution, project rpts and data files, FY84-87, listing, 2158–51
Shellfish harvest in estuaries, approved and restricted areas, and pollution sources, by estuary, State, and coastal region, 1990, quinquennial rpt, 2178–33
see also Oil spills

Marine Reserve
Personnel and equipment strengths, and readiness, by reserve component, FY91, annual rpt, 3544–31
Personnel strengths and characteristics, by reserve component, quarterly rpt, 3542–4
Personnel strengths for reserve components, by selected characteristics, FY91, annual rpt, 3544–1.5

Marine resources
Fish and shellfish resources and catch, marine mammal and sea turtle population, and mgmt, by species and region, 1988-90, annual rpt, 2164–22
Pacific Marine Environmental Lab research activities and bibl, FY91, annual rpt, 2144–21
see also Coastal areas
see also Continental shelf
see also Coral reefs and islands
see also Fish and fishing industry
see also Marine mammals
see also Marine pollution
see also Marine resources conservation
see also Offshore mineral resources
see also Offshore oil and gas
see also Oil spills
see also Shellfish
see also Water resources development

Marine resources conservation
Coastal and riparian areas environmental conditions, fish, wildlife, use, and mgmt, for individual ecosystems, series, 5506–9
Coastal areas environmental conditions and mgmt, for individual areas, conf series, 2146–8
Coastal areas environmental mgmt programs of States, activities and Federal funding, FY90-91, biennial rpt, 2174–8
Environmental Quality, status of problems, protection programs, research, and intl issues, 1991 annual rpt, 484–1
Estuary environmental conditions, research results and methodology, series, 2176–7
Marine Fisheries Review, US and foreign fisheries resources, dev, mgmt, and research, quarterly journal, 2162–1
NOAA oceanographic and other research activities, FY87-88, biennial rpt, 2144–6

Research on ocean pollution, monitoring, and resources dev activities of Fed Govt, funding and project descriptions, FY89, annual listing, 2144–23
Research on ocean pollution, monitoring, and resources dev activities of Fed Govt, 5-year plan and funding by agency, FY87-92, triennial rpt, 2148–56
see also Marine mammals
see also Marine pollution

Marine safety
see Marine accidents and safety

Marital status
see Marriage and divorce
see Widows and widowers
see under By Marital Status in the "Index by Categories"

Maritime academies
see Service academies

Maritime Administration
Activities, finances, and subsidies of MarAd, and world merchant fleet operations, FY91, annual rpt, 7704–14
Budget of US, obligations and authority by function, agency, and program, with summaries and analyses, FY93, annual rpt, 104–2
Containers (intermodal) and equipment owned by shipping and leasing companies, inventory by type and size, 1991, annual rpt, 7704–10
Employment of DOT, by subagency, occupation, and selected personnel characteristics, FY91, annual rpt, 7304–18
Foreign and US merchant ships, tonnage, and new ship construction and deliveries, by vessel type and country, as of Jan 1992, annual rpt, 7704–3
Foreign-flag ships owned by US firms and foreign affiliates, by type, owner, and country of registry and construction, as of July 1991, semiannual rpt, 7702–3
Freight (shipborne domestic), by major commodity group, vessel type, and port, 1987-89, annual rpt, 7704–7
Merchant ship crew supply, wartime needs, training, and sources, 1970s-90 and alternative projections to 2000, 7708–5
Merchant ships in US fleet and Natl Defense Reserve Fleet, vessels, tonnage, and owner, as of July 1991, semiannual listing, 7702–2
Port improvement capital expenditures and financing methods, by region and selected port, 1946-89, 7708–6
Shipbuilding and repair facilities, capacity, and employment, by shipyard, 1991, annual rpt, 7704–9
Shipbuilding and repair subsidy elimination proposals of US and OECD, impacts on industry and trade, with data on US-flag vessels, 1980s-91, 9886–4.183
Ships in US merchant fleet, operating subsidies, construction, and ship-related employment, monthly rpt, 7702–1

Maritime industry
see Inland water transportation
see Longshoremen
see Marine accidents and safety
see Merchant seamen
see Shipbuilding and operating subsidies
see Shipbuilding and repairing
see Ships and shipping

Maritime law
Court civil and criminal caseloads for Federal district, appeals, and bankruptcy courts, by type of suit and offense, circuit, and district, 1991, annual rpt, 18204–11
Court civil and criminal caseloads for Federal district, appeals, and special courts, 1991, annual rpt, 18204–8
Marine Mammal Protection Act admin, and populations, strandings, and catch permits by species and location, 1988-89, annual rpt, 2164–11
Maritime Commission activities, case filings by type and disposition, and civil penalties by shipper, FY91, annual rpt, 9334–1
Treaties and other bilateral and multilateral agreements of US in force, by country, as of Jan 1992, annual listing, 7004–1
US attorneys civil and criminal cases by type and disposition, and collections, by Federal district, FY91, annual rpt, 6004–2.5

Market Facts of Canada Ltd.
"Pleasure Travel Markets to North America", 2906–2

Market research
Agricultural, fishery, and forest products trade, tariffs, and industry operating data, commodity rpt series, 9885–8
Agricultural production, consumption, and policies for selected countries, and US export dev and promotion, monthly journal, 1922–2
Agricultural trade by commodity and country, prices, and world market devs, monthly rpt, 1922–12
Agricultural trade, outlook and current situation, quarterly rpt, 1542–4
Business America, foreign and domestic commerce, and US investment and trade opportunities, biweekly journal, 2042–24
Energy supply and demand for Pacific basin, and implications for US trade, country rpt series, 3406–6
Energy technologies export markets, competitiveness, and promotion, for US industries, 1992 technical rpt, 3006–13.5
Exports, imports, and trade flows, by country and commodity, with background economic indicators, data compilation, monthly CD-ROM, 2002–6
Exports of manufactured goods for US and major competitors, market share rpts, annual listing, discontinued, 2044–6
Exports of manufactured goods, total and for US and major competitors, by country of destination, annual commodity market share rpt series, discontinued, 2046–13
Exports of manufactured goods, total and for US and major competitors, by SITC 1- to 5-digit commodity, annual country market share rpt series, discontinued, 2046–2
Fish and shellfish foreign market conditions for US products, country rpt series, 2166–19
Israel economic conditions, US investment and export opportunities, and trade practices, 1992 rpt, 2008–32
Japan economic conditions, US investment and export opportunities, and trade practices, forecast 1991-93 and trends from 1988, 2048–159
Occupational Outlook Handbook, 1992-93, biennial rpt, 6744–1
Overseas Business Reports: economic conditions, investment and export opportunities, and trade practices, country market research rpt series, 2046–6
Plumbing fixtures production, and imports from US and other sources, for 15 countries, 1991 rpt, 2048–156
Soviet Union trade and investment opportunities for US firms, contact listing, bibl, and background economic data, 1991 rpt, 2048–157
Textile and apparel foreign market conditions for US exports, with domestic industry operations, country rpt series, 2046–15
Travel to US and Canada, market analysis with detailed trip and traveler characteristics, country rpt series, 2906–2
Travel to US, market research data available from US Travel and Tourism Admin, 1992, annual rpt, 2904–15
see also Consumer surveys

Market shares
see Economic concentration and diversification

Marketing
Drug (prescription) prices in US and other countries, industry profits, and R&D and marketing spending, 1980s-91 and projected to 2000, 25148–44
Minority Business Dev Centers mgmt and financial aid, and characteristics of businesses, by region and State, FY91, annual rpt, 2104–6
Occupational Outlook Handbook, 1992-93, biennial rpt, 6744–1
Savings instns financial statements, for instns insured by Savings Assn Insurance Fund by FHLB district and State, and for FDIC-insured savings banks, 1989, annual rpt, 8434–1
see also Advertising
see also Agricultural marketing
see also Competition
see also Consumer credit
see also Consumer protection
see also Consumer surveys
see also Credit
see also Direct marketing
see also Economic concentration and diversification
see also Foreign trade promotion
see also Generic products
see also Labeling
see also Market research
see also Packaging and containers
see also Price regulation
see also Prices
see also Retail trade
see also Sales promotion
see also Sales workers
see also Shopping centers
see also Wholesale trade
see also under names of specific commodities or commodity groups

Marketing quotas
see Agricultural production quotas and price supports

Marks, Gary
"HIV-Infected Men's Practices in Notifying Past Sexual Partners of Infection Risk", 4042–3.310

Markstrom, Donald C.
"Service Life of Treated and Untreated Black Hills Ponderosa Pine Fenceposts", 1208–406
Marlor, Felice S.
"Federal Nonfarm Business Credit Assistance: An Analysis of Disbursements to Rural Areas", 1548–389
Marquez, Jaime
"Autonomy of Trade Elasticities: Choice and Consequences", 9366–7.276
Marriage and divorce
AFDC beneficiaries demographic and financial characteristics, by State, FY90, annual rpt, 4584–7
Asian and Pacific Islands Americans social and economic characteristics, for West and total US, 1990-91, Current Population Report, 2546–1.462
Black Americans social and economic characteristics, for South and total US, 1991 and trends from 1950, annual Current Population Rpt, 2546–1.463
Business owner and business characteristics, for minority- and women-owned firms, by industry, employment and sales size, and form of ownership, 1987 survey, 2328–59
Census of Population and Housing, 1990: detailed geographic coverage, State CD-ROM series, 2551–9
Census of Population and Housing, 1990: population and housing characteristics, detailed geographic coverage, State CD-ROM series, 2551–10
Census of Population, 1990: population characteristics and living arrangements, by county, place, and urban-rural location, State rpt series, 2531–1
Census of Population, 1990: population characteristics and living arrangements, for Native American, urban, and metro areas, series, 2531–2
Consumer Income, socioeconomic characteristics of persons, families, and households, detailed cross-tabulations, Current Population Rpt series, 2546–6
Deaths and rates, by cause and selected social, demographic, and employment characteristics, 1979-85, natl longitudinal study, 4478–186
Deaths during 1986, decedents health condition, services use, habits, and social, employment, and other characteristics, 4147–20.19
Educational attainment, by social and demographic characteristics and location, 1991 and trends from 1940, biennial Current Population Rpt, 2546–1.460
Farm population, by employment, social, and economic characteristics, and region, 1990, annual Current Population Rpt, 2546–1.458
Households and family characteristics, by location, 1991, annual Current Population Rpt, 2546–1.457
Households composition, income, benefits, and labor force status, Survey of Income and Program Participation methodology, working paper series, 2626–10
Housing (rental) total, HUD-assisted by program, and eligible for aid, recent movers by reason, selected characteristics, and location, 1989, biennial rpt, 5184–11
Immigrant and nonimmigrant visas of US issued and refused, by class, issuing office, and nationality, FY90, annual rpt, 7184–1
Immigration to US, alien workers, visitors, deportations, and naturalizations, by country, FY91 and trends from 1820, annual rpt, 6264–2
Income (household) and poverty status under alternative income definitions, by recipient characteristics, 1979-91, annual Current Population Rpt, 2546–6.78
Interracial and interethnic married couples, 1970, 1980, and 1991, annual Current Population Rpt, 2546–1.461
Living arrangements, family relationships, and marital status, by selected characteristics, 1991, annual Current Population Rpt, 2546–1.461
Marriages, divorces, and rates, by State, preliminary 1990-91, US Vital Statistics annual rpt, 4144–7
Migration, immigration, and mover characteristics compared to nonmovers, 1987-90, annual Current Population Rpt, 2546–1.456
Migration since 1990, mover characteristics by same or different area, and compared to nonmovers, 1991, annual Current Population Rpt, 2546–1.464
Never-married share of population, by sex and age, 1970 and 1991, Current Population Rpt, fact sheet, 2546–2.163
OASDI beneficiary data collection system design compared to earlier surveys, with summary results, 1992 article, 4742–1.313
OASDI benefits and beneficiaries, by category, age, and sex, quarterly rpt, 4742–1.1
Older persons socioeconomic characteristics, 1900s-90 and projected to 2050, biennial chartbook, 12904–1
Pacific territories population and housing detailed characteristics, by location, 1990 Census of Population and Housing, series, 2551–8
Population economic well-being indicators, by selected characteristics and household income and income-to-poverty ratio, 1984, 2546–20.22
Population size and components of change, alternative projections 1990-2080 and trends from 1900, annual actuarial rpt, 4706–1.106
Railroad employee benefits and beneficiaries, by type, FY90, annual rpt, 9704–2.2
Railroad retirement benefits for divorced spouses, monthly rpt, 9702–2
Research on population and reproduction, Federal funding by project, FY90, annual listing, 4474–9
Single mothers family income, and impacts of child care, govt and child support payments, taxes, and marriage, with data by State, 1970s-91, 21788–212
Single parent families in own and others homes, by financial, housing, and other characteristics, 1989, 2486–1.14
Soviet Union and US economic and sociodemographic indicators, selected years 1970-90, handbook, 2328–80
Statistical Abstract of US, 1992 annual data compilation, 2324–1.1; 2324–1.2
Tax (income) returns of individuals, by filing status, tax item, and income level, 1991, annual article, 8302–2.319
Vital statistics provisional data, monthly rpt, 4142–1
Women's marriage, divorce, and remarriage by age, and child living arrangements, by race, 1970s-90, Current Population Rpt, 2546–2.166
see also Births out of wedlock
see also Child support and alimony
see also Domestic relations courts and cases
see also Families and households
see also Widows and widowers
see also under By Marital Status in the "Index by Categories"
Marsden, Mary E.
"Prevalence of Drug Use in the D.C. Metropolitan Area Household Population: 1990", 4496–12.1
Marshall Islands
Agricultural trade of US, by detailed commodity and country, 1991, annual rpt, 1524–8
Agricultural trade of US, by detailed commodity and country, 1991, semiannual rpt, 1522–4
Banks (insured commercial and savings) deposits by instn, State, MSA, and county, as of June 1991, annual regional rpt, 9295–3.6
Economic, social, political, and geographic summary data, by country, 1992, annual factbook, 9114–2
Exports and imports of US, by transport mode, country, and SITC 1- to 3-digit commodity, 1991, annual rpt, 2424–12
Exports of US, detailed Schedule B commodities with countries of destination, 1991, annual rpt, 2424–10
Human rights conditions in 170 countries, and US economic and military aid, 1991, annual rpt, 21384–3
Nuclear Claims Trust Fund for Marshall Islands, financial condition, with health care benefits and enrollment, 1987-92, GAO rpt, 26123–405
Physicians, by specialty, age, sex, and location of training and practice, 1990, State rpt, 4116–6.53
Population size, growth rates, and components of change, by country, projected 1990-2020 and trends from 1950, biennial rpt, 2324–9
UN voting record and share of votes in agreement with US, by issue, country, and world area, 1991, annual rpt, 7004–18
Marshall, Mary P.
"Water Resources Activities in New York, FY89", 5666–26.22
Marshals Service
see U.S. Marshals Service
Marshes
see Wetlands
Martin, Cathy R.
"Water Resources Activities, North Dakota District, FY90", 5666–26.20
Martin, Elwood M.
"Preliminary Estimates of Waterfowl Harvest and Hunter Activity in the U.S. During the 1991 Hunting Season", 5504–28
"Sandhill Crane Harvest and Hunter Activity in the Central Flyway During the 1991-92 Hunting Season", 5504–31

Martin, Peter
"Ground-Water Flow System in Indian Wells Valley, Kern, Inyo, and San Bernardino Counties, California", 5666–28.15
Martinez, Steve W.
"Domestic Food Assistance Programs: Measuring Benefits to Producers", 1548–390
Martini, Alberto
"Impact of Survey and Questionnaire Design on Longitudinal Labor Force Measures", 2626–10.145
Martinique
Economic and social conditions, resources, and trade, and aid, 1992, annual factbook, 9914–14
Exports and imports of US, by transport mode, country, and SITC 1- to 3-digit commodity, 1991, annual rpt, 2424–12
Exports of US, detailed Schedule B commodities with countries of destination, 1991, annual rpt, 2424–10
Martino, Orlando
"Mineral Economy of Mexico. Mineral Perspectives", 5606–1.18
Maryland
AFDC applicants recently unemployed, characteristics of prior job and unemployment insurance eligibility, for Maryland, 1988-90, hearing, 21788–207
Appalachian Regional Commission funding, by project and State, planned FY92, annual rpt, 9084–3
Apple production, marketing, and prices, for Appalachia and compared to other States, 1989-92, annual rpt, 1311–13
Banks (insured commercial), Fed Reserve 5th District members financial statements, by State, quarterly rpt, 9389–18
Banks (insured commercial and savings) deposits by instn, State, MSA, and county, as of June 1991, annual regional rpt, 9295–3.2
Coal production and mines by county, prices, productivity, miners, and reserves, by mining method and State, 1990-91, annual rpt, 3164–25
Deaths and rates, by detailed location, cause, and demographic characteristics, 1989, US Vital Statistics annual rpt, 4144–3.1
Economic indicators by State, Fed Reserve 5th District, quarterly rpt, 9389–16
Employment and housing indicators by State, FHLB 4th District, quarterly rpt, 9302–36
Employment, earnings, and hours, by selected SIC 1- to 4-digit industry, State, and for 275 MSAs, 1987-92, 6748–81
Fed Govt spending in States and local areas, by type, State, county, and city, FY91, annual rpt, 2464–3
Fed Govt spending in States, by type, program, agency, and State, FY91, annual rpt, 2464–2
HHS financial aid, by program, recipient, State, and city, FY91, annual regional listing, 4004–3.3
Hospital deaths of Medicare patients, actual and expected rates by diagnosis, and hospital characteristics, by instn, FY90 annual State rpt, 4654–14.21
Housing census, 1990: summary unit characteristics, by householder race and age, county, place, and urban-rural location, State rpt, 2471–1.22
Military prime contract awards, by contractor, service branch, State, and city, FY91, annual rpt, 3544–22
Mineral Industry Surveys, State reviews of production, 1991, preliminary annual rpt, 5614–6
Multinatl firms US affiliates finances and operations, by industry, country of parent firm, and State, 1987, 2708–48
Physicians, by specialty, age, sex, and location of training and practice, 1990, State rpt, 4116–6.21
Population and housing census, 1990: detailed geographic coverage, State CD-ROM, 2551–9.5
Population and housing census, 1990: population and housing characteristics, detailed geographic coverage, State CD-ROM, 2551–10.11
Population and housing census, 1990: summary characteristics, by county, subdiv, and place, State rpt, 2551–7.22
Population census, 1990: population characteristics and living arrangements, by county, place, and urban-rural location, State rpt, 2531–1.22
Statistical Abstract of US, 1992 annual data compilation, 2324–1
Timber resources and removals, by species, ownership class, and county, 1976 and 1986, State rpt, 1206–12.16
Water use by end use, well withdrawals, and public supply deliveries, by county, 1987, State rpt, 5666–24.15
see also Anne Arundel County, Md.
see also Baltimore, Md.
see also Montgomery County, Md.
see also Prince George's County, Md.
see also Washington County, Md.
see also under By State in the "Index by Categories"
Mass media
AIDS public knowledge, attitudes, info sources, and testing, 1991 survey, 4146–8.218
Alcohol use, knowledge, attitudes, and info sources of youth, series, 4006–10
Fed Govt audiovisual activities and spending, by whether performed in-house and agency, FY91, annual rpt, 9514–1
Statistical Abstract of US, 1992 annual data compilation, 2324–1.18
see also Advertising
see Journalism
see also Motion pictures
see also Newspapers
see also Periodicals
see also Public broadcasting
see also Radio
see also Television
Mass transit
see Airlines
see Buses
see National Railroad Passenger Corp.
see Railroads
see Subways
see Urban transportation
Massachusetts
Banks (insured commercial and savings) deposits by instn, State, MSA, and county, as of June 1991, annual regional rpt, 9295–3.1
County Business Patterns, 1990: employment, establishments, and payroll, by SIC 2- to 4-digit industry and county, annual State rpt, 2326–6.23
Cranberry production, prices, use, and acreage, for selected States, 1990-91 and forecast 1992, annual rpt, 1621–18.5
Deaths and rates, by detailed location, cause, and demographic characteristics, 1989, US Vital Statistics annual rpt, 4144–3.1
Economic indicators for New England States, Fed Reserve 1st District, monthly rpt, 9373–2
Employment, earnings, and hours, by selected SIC 1- to 4-digit industry, State, and for 275 MSAs, 1987-92, 6748–81
Fed Govt spending in States and local areas, by type, State, county, and city, FY91, annual rpt, 2464–3
Fed Govt spending in States, by type, program, agency, and State, FY91, annual rpt, 2464–2
HHS financial aid, by program, recipient, State, and city, FY91, annual regional listing, 4004–3.1
Hospital deaths of Medicare patients, actual and expected rates by diagnosis, and hospital characteristics, by instn, FY90 annual State rpt, 4654–14.22
Housing census, 1990: inventory, occupancy, and costs, State fact sheet, 2326–21.23
Housing census, 1990: summary unit characteristics, by householder race and age, county, place, and urban-rural location, State rpt, 2471–1.23
Military prime contract awards, by contractor, service branch, State, and city, FY91, annual rpt, 3544–22
Mineral Industry Surveys, State reviews of production, 1991, preliminary annual rpt, 5614–6
Multinatl firms US affiliates finances and operations, by industry, country of parent firm, and State, 1987, 2708–48
Physicians, by specialty, age, sex, and location of training and practice, 1990, State rpt, 4116–6.22
Population and housing census, 1990: detailed geographic coverage, State CD-ROM, 2551–9.1
Population and housing census, 1990: population and housing characteristics, detailed geographic coverage, State CD-ROM, 2551–10.26
Population and housing census, 1990: summary characteristics, by county, subdiv, and place, State rpt, 2551–7.23
Population census, 1990: population characteristics and living arrangements, by county, place, and urban-rural location, State rpt, 2531–1.23
Statistical Abstract of US, 1992 annual data compilation, 2324–1
Wages by occupation, and benefits for office and plant workers, 1992 survey, periodic MSA rpt, 6785–3.4
Water resources dev projects of Army Corps of Engineers, characteristics, and costs, 1950s-91, biennial State rpt, 3756–2.22
Water supply in northeastern US, precipitation and stream runoff by station, monthly rpt, 2182–3
Water use by end use, well withdrawals, and public supply deliveries, by county, 1986, State rpt, 5666–24.16
see also Boston, Mass.
see also Brockton, Mass.

see also Cambridge, Mass.
see also Chelsea, Mass.
see also Haverhill, Mass.
see also Lawrence, Mass.
see also Salem, Mass.
see also Worcester, Mass.
see also under By State in the "Index by Categories"

Mataloni, Raymond J., Jr.
"U.S. Multinational Companies: Operations in 1990", 2702–1.329

Maternal deaths
Abortion (induced and spontaneous), related maternal deaths, 1972-87, annual article, 4202–7.324
Deaths and rates, by cause and age, preliminary 1990-91, US Vital Statistics annual rpt, 4144–7
Deaths and rates, by cause, provisional data, monthly rpt, 4142–1.2
Deaths and rates, by detailed location, cause, and demographic characteristics, 1989, US Vital Statistics annual rpt, 4144–3
Deaths related to pregnancy, 1989, US Vital Statistics advance annual rpt, 4146–5.124
Health condition and care indicators, 1950s-90 with health improvement and disease prevention goals for 1990, annual data compilation, 4144–11
Indian Health Service and tribal facilities and use, and Indians health and other characteristics, by IHS region, 1980s-90, annual chartbook, 4084–7

Maternity
Alcohol-related diagnoses hospital discharges and length of stay, by age, sex, race, and region, 1979-85, 4488–10.5
Cancer (liver) risk for women relation to parity and oral contraceptives use, 1985-86, article, 4472–1.331
Disability related to pregnancy, absenteeism, and health services use, by selected characteristics, 1990, annual rpt, 4147–10.182
Disability related to pregnancy, absenteeism, and health services use, by selected characteristics, 1991, annual rpt, 4147–10.183
Drug abuse and treatment, research on biological and behavioral factors and addiction potential of new drugs, 1991 annual conf, 4494–11
Health condition and care indicators, 1950s-90 with health improvement and disease prevention goals for 1990, annual data compilation, 4144–11
Health condition of children and mothers, and services use, indicators by age, race, and poverty status 1988, 4478–197
Health survey of mothers with and without children with birth defects, reasons for participation, 1990, article, 4042–3.377
Homeless mothers and children nutrient intake, body measurements, and blood chemistry, 1989-90 local area study, article, 4042–3.330
Hospital discharges and length of stay, by diagnosis, patient and instn characteristics, procedure performed, and payment source, 1990, annual rpt, 4147–13.112
Hospital discharges and length of stay by region and diagnosis, and procedures performed, by age and sex, 1990, annual rpt, 4146–8.211
Hospital discharges and length of stay under old and new survey designs, by diagnosis, patient and instn characteristics, and procedure, Jan-Mar 1988, 4147–13.110
Hospital discharges by detailed diagnostic and procedure category, primary diagnosis, and length of stay, by age, sex, and region, 1990, annual rpt, 4147–13.111
Indian Health Service and tribal facilities and use, and Indians health and other characteristics, by IHS region, 1980s-90, annual chartbook, 4084–7
Indian Health Service facilities, funding, operations, and Indian health and other characteristics, 1950s-91, annual chartbook, 4084–1
OECD members health care costs, hospital use, resources, and economic and health indicators, by country, 1960s-90, article, 4652–1.322
Outcomes of pregnancy, probabilities by gestation week, 1980, article, 4042–3.324
Prisoners in Federal and State instns known to be pregnant, 1990, quinquennial rpt, 6068–218
Smoking among pregnant women, by age and marital status, for Indians in Washington State, mid 1980s, article, 4042–3.306
Smoking, tobacco, and health impacts research rpts, 1991 annual report, 4204–19
Statistical Abstract of US, 1992 annual data compilation, 2324–1.2
see also Birth defects
see also Births
see also Births out of wedlock
see also Birthweight
see also Breast-feeding
see also Family planning
see also Fertility
see also Fetal deaths
see also Infant mortality
see also Maternal deaths
see also Maternity benefits
see also Maternity homes
see also Midwives
see also Obstetrics and gynecology
see also Prenatal care
see also Teenage pregnancy

Maternity benefits
Assistance (financial and nonfinancial) of Fed Govt, 1992 base edition, annual listing, 104–5
Assistance of Fed Govt for maternal and child health services, block grant beneficiary and taxpayer equity among States, issues, alternative allocation formulas, and background data, 1992 GAO rpt, 26121–454
Employee maternity leave policies, for US and selected countries, 1990 conf, 4148–28
Food aid program of USDA for women, infants, and children, participant referrals to social service programs, by type and reason, 1990 local area study, article, 4042–3.318
Food aid program of USDA for women, infants, and children, participants and costs by State and Indian agency, FY90, annual tables, 1364–12
Food aid program of USDA for women, infants, and children, participants by race, State, and Indian agency, 1991, annual rpt, 1364–16
Food aid program of USDA for women, infants, and children, participants, clinics, and costs, by State and Indian agency, monthly tables, 1362–16
Food aid program of USDA for women, infants, and children, prenatal enrollment, by selected maternal and prenatal care characteristics, 1988-89 local area study, article, 4042–3.305
Food aid program of USDA for women, infants, and children, prenatal participation effects on birthweight and health and social welfare costs, 1960s-90, GAO rpt, 26121–458
Food stamp recipient household size, composition, income, and income and deductions allowed, summer 1989, annual rpt, 1364–8
Foreign countries social security programs coverage, funding, eligibility, and benefits, by country, 1991, biennial rpt, 4746–4.62
HHS financial aid, by program, recipient, State, and city, FY91, annual regional listings, 4004–3
Labor laws enacted, by State, 1991, annual article, 6722–1.309
Medicaid prenatal care program costs and benefits, for Missouri, 1988, article, 4042–3.365
State and local govt employees benefit plan coverage and provisions, by plan type, 1990, biennial rpt, 6784–21

Maternity homes
Population census, 1990: institutionalized population and persons in group quarters, by sex, race, county, place, and urban-rural location, State rpt series, 2531–1

Mathematic models and modeling
Alaska rural areas population characteristics, and energy resources dev effects, series, 5736–5
Electric utilities conservation programs, impacts on prices and revenue requirements, alternative projections 1990-2010, 3308–105
Energy Info Admin forecasting and data analysis models, 1992, annual listing, 3164–87
Energy supply, demand, distribution, and regulatory impacts, series, 3166–6
Lumber (tropical wood) kiln drying time relation to moisture content and other properties, for 650 species, 1991 rpt, 1208–392
Lumber and veneer recovery and quality from young growth Douglas fir, effects of timber stand and log characteristics, model description and results, 1991 rpt, 1208–413
Nuclear radiation exposure of population near commercial reactors, by body site, age group, and selected plant, 1988, annual rpt, 9634–7
Radiation exposure of population near Hanford, Wash, nuclear plant, with methodology, 1944-91, series, 3356–5
Recreational use of natl forests, factors affecting regional growth, shift-share analysis, 1992 rpt, 1208–423
Unemployment insurance programs of States and Fed Govt, benefits adequacy, and work disincentives, series, 6406–6
Weather forecasts accuracy evaluations, for US, UK, and European systems, quarterly rpt, 2182–8

see also Economic and econometric models
Mathematica Policy Research, Inc.
"Assignment and the Participating Physician Program: An Analysis of Beneficiary Awareness, Understanding, and Experience", 17266–2.1
"Profile of Child Care Settings: Early Education and Care in 1990", 4808–39
Mathematics
Condition of Education, detail for elementary, secondary, and higher education, 1920s-91 and projected to 2002, annual rpt, 4824–1
Degrees awarded in higher education, by level, field, race, and sex, 1989/90 and trends from 1980/81, annual rpt, 4844–17
DOD Dependents Schools basic skills and college entrance test scores, 1991-92, annual rpt, 3504–16
Education data compilation, 1992 annual rpt, 4824–2
Eighth grade class of 1988: educational performance and conditions, characteristics, attitudes, activities, and plans, natl longitudinal survey, series, 4826–9
Elementary and secondary students computer and calculator use and availability, by grade level, 1990 natl assessment, fact sheet, 4896–9.1
Elementary and secondary students educational performance in math, science, reading, and writing, 1969-90, 4898–32
Elementary and secondary students reading and math proficiency, and dropouts, by race, 1970s-90, 4838–52
Employment of scientists and engineers, and related topics, advance rpt series, 9626–8
Employment of scientists, engineers, and technicians in manufacturing, by field and industry, 1989, triennial rpt, 9627–23
Employment, unemployment, and labor force characteristics, by region and census div, 1991, annual rpt, 6744–7.1
Fed Govt aid to higher education and nonprofit instns for R&D and related activities, by field, instn, agency, and State, FY90, annual rpt, 9627–17
Foreign and US students science and math proficiency, intl assessment results and other indicators by selected country, 1960s-80s, 4838–51
Goldwater, Barry, Scholarship Foundation awards and finances, FY87-91, annual rpt, 10404–1
Higher education grad programs enrollment in science and engineering, by field, source of funds, and characteristics of student and instn, 1990, annual rpt, 9627–7
Indians and Alaska Natives education condition, indicators and comparisons to other groups, 1980s-90, 4808–42.1
Labor demand, turnover, and training completions, by detailed occupation, 1990 and projected to 2005, biennial rpt, 6744–3
Minority group, women, and disabled persons employment and education in science and engineering, by field, mid 1970s-91, biennial rpt, 9624–20
NASA R&D funding to higher education instns, by field, instn, and State, FY91, annual listing, 9504–7
Natl assessment of elementary and high school students, science and math education, 1985/86, series, 4896–6
Natl Education Goals progress indicators, by State, 1992, annual rpt, 15914–1
NSF activities, finances, and funding by program, FY91, annual rpt, 9624–6
Occupational Outlook Handbook, 1992-93, biennial rpt, 6744–1
R&D facilities of higher education instns, space and equipment adequacy, needs, and funding by source, by instn type and control, 1992, biennial rpt, 9624–25
R&D funding by higher education instns and federally funded centers, by field, instn, and State, FY90, annual rpt, 9627–13
Science and Engineering Indicators, employment, education, R&D funding, and industry impacts, with foreign comparisons, 1960s-91, biennial rpt, 9624–10
Teachers of science and math, professional dev project of Education Dept, school district participation by State, 1989/90, GAO rpt, 26121–488
Vocational education enrollment, and academic and other credits earned, by subject and student characteristics, high school classes of 1982 and 1987, 4838–50
see also Computer sciences
see also Mathematic models and modeling
see also Statisticians
Mattoon, Richard H.
"Can the States Solve the Health Care Crisis?", 9375–1.308
"State and Local Governments' Reaction to Recession", 9375–1.303
Mauritania
Agricultural trade of US, by detailed commodity and country, 1991, annual rpt, 1524–8
Agricultural trade of US, by detailed commodity and country, 1991, semiannual rpt, 1522–4
AID economic aid to developing countries, obligations and disbursements by country, quarterly rpt, 9912–4
Background Notes, summary social, political, and economic data, 1992 rpt, 7006–2.25
Economic and military aid and loans from US and intl agencies, by program and country, FY46-91, annual rpt, 9914–5
Economic and social conditions of developing countries from 1960s, and Intl Dev Cooperation Agency and AID activities and funding, FY91-93, annual rpt, 9904–4
Economic conditions, income, production, prices, employment, and trade, 1991 periodic country rpt, 2046–4.6
Economic conditions, income, production, prices, employment, and trade, 1992 periodic country rpt, 2046–4.51
Economic, social, political, and geographic summary data, by country, 1992, annual factbook, 9114–2
Exports and imports of US, by transport mode, country, and SITC 1- to 3-digit commodity, 1991, annual rpt, 2424–12
Exports of US, detailed Schedule B commodities with countries of destination, 1991, annual rpt, 2424–10
Human rights conditions in 170 countries, and US economic and military aid, 1991, annual rpt, 21384–3
Military spending, arms trade, and force strengths, with govt spending and population, by country, 1979-89, annual rpt, 9824–1
Minerals Yearbook, Vol 3, 1989: foreign country review of production, trade, and policy, by commodity, annual rpt, 5604–35.1
Population size, growth rates, and components of change, by country, projected 1990-2020 and trends from 1950, biennial rpt, 2324–9
Refugee migration, and intl aid programs, by world area and country of origin and asylum, 1991, annual rpt, 7004–15
UN voting record and share of votes in agreement with US, by issue, country, and world area, 1991, annual rpt, 7004–18
Mauritius
Agricultural trade of US, by detailed commodity and country, 1991, annual rpt, 1524–8
Agricultural trade of US, by detailed commodity and country, 1991, semiannual rpt, 1522–4
AID economic aid to developing countries, obligations and disbursements by country, quarterly rpt, 9912–4
AID loans repayment status and terms by program and country, and status of predecessor agency loans, quarterly rpt, 9912–3
Economic and military aid and loans from US and intl agencies, by program and country, FY46-91, annual rpt, 9914–5
Economic and social conditions of developing countries from 1960s, and Intl Dev Cooperation Agency and AID activities and funding, FY91-93, annual rpt, 9904–4
Economic, social, political, and geographic summary data, by country, 1992, annual factbook, 9114–2
Exports and imports of US, by transport mode, country, and SITC 1- to 3-digit commodity, 1991, annual rpt, 2424–12
Exports of US, detailed Schedule B commodities with countries of destination, 1991, annual rpt, 2424–10
Human rights conditions in 170 countries, and US economic and military aid, 1991, annual rpt, 21384–3
Military aid of US, arms sales, and training programs costs and budget requests, by program, world region, and country, FY91-93, annual rpt, 7144–13
Military spending, arms trade, and force strengths, with govt spending and population, by country, 1979-89, annual rpt, 9824–1
Minerals Yearbook, Vol 3, 1989: foreign country review of production, trade, and policy, by commodity, annual rpt, 5604–35.1
Population size, growth rates, and components of change, by country, projected 1990-2020 and trends from 1950, biennial rpt, 2324–9
Refugee migration, and intl aid programs, by world area and country of origin and asylum, 1991, annual rpt, 7004–15

UN voting record and share of votes in agreement with US, by issue, country, and world area, 1991, annual rpt, 7004–18

May, Dennis M.
"Forest Resources of Tennessee", 1206–27.11
"Production and Receipts of Veneer Logs in the Southeastern and Midsouth States, 1988", 1208–407

May, Noal D.
"Exposures from Headset Interference Tones", 7506–10.100

May, Philip A.
"Fetal Alcohol Effects Among North American Indians", 4482–1.310

Mayfield, Max
"Eastern North Pacific Hurricane Season—1991", 2152–8.302

Mayor, Adrienne
"Derelict Ships", 2152–8.304

McAllen, Tex.
see also under By City and By SMSA or MSA in the "Index by Categories"

McAllister, Patrick H.
"Floating Ceilings on Deposit Interest Rates", 9366–6.300

McAndrews, James J.
"Results of a Survey of ATM Network Pricing", 9387–8.270

McAuley, James B.
"Trichinosis Surveillance, U.S., 1987-90", 4202–7.304

McBride, William D.
"Conventional and Conservation Tillage Systems in Soybean Production, 1990", 1561–3.304

McCarty, Timothy P.
"Agricultural and Horticultural Machinery, Industry and Trade Summary", 9885–9.3

McCauley, Robert N.
"Foreign Bank Credit to U.S. Corporations: The Implications of Offshore Loans", 9385–1.307

McClelland, Robert
"Price of Giving: Taxes, Education, and Econometric Issues", 6886–6.83

McClure, J. D.
"Analysis of Transporting Highway Route-Controlled Quantities: An Overview of 1985-90", 3008–129

McCoy, H. Virginia
"Effects of Migration on Cancer Incidence and Resources for Prevention and Treatment in Florida", 4042–3.339

McCoy, John L.
"Health of Retired Workers: Survival Status and Medicare Service Use", 4652–1.319

McDonald, Bradley J.
"Intra-Industry Trade Indexes for Canada, Mexico, and the U.S., 1962-87", 1528–327

McDonald, Donald A.
"Status and Trends in Concentrations of Selected Contaminants in Boston Harbor Sediments and Biota", 2176–3.14

McDonald, Douglas C.
"Federal Sentencing in Transition, 1986-90", 6066–19.68

McDowell, John M.
"Labor Market Consequences of U.S. Immigration: A Survey", 6366–6.1

McDowell, Lena
"Public Elementary and Secondary Schools and Agencies in the U.S. and Outlying Areas: School Year 1990-91", 4834–17

McElravey, John
"Capital Adequacy and the Growth of U.S. Banks", 9375–13.88

McElroy, Robert G.
"Farm Income Outlook: Following 1990's Records", 1504–9.1

McEwen, J. Thomas
"Assessing Criminal Justice Needs", 6066–20.22

McFadden, Michael C.
"Measurement of Streamflow Gains and Losses on Mission Creek at Santa Barbara, Calif., July and September 1987", 5666–27.29

McGath, Chris
"Calculating State-Level Estimates of USDA's Farm Income Accounts", 1541–1.313

McGlone, James M.
"Federal Nonfarm Business Credit Assistance: An Analysis of Disbursements to Rural Areas", 1548–389

McGovern, Nancy Y.
"Records in the National Archives Relating to the Early Involvement of the U.S. Government in Data Processing, 1880's to 1950's", 9516–1.8

McGranahan, David
"Can the Rural Economy Be Competitive? Lessons from the Data", 1504–9.1

McGuire, Michael R.
"Encapsulation of Pesticides in Starch", 1504–9.1

MCI Communications
Fiber optics and copper wire mileage and access lines, and fiber systems investment, by telecommunications firm, 1985-91, annual rpt, 9284–18
Finances and operations of local and long distance firms, subscribership, and charges, late 1970s-92, semiannual rpt, 9282–7
Intl telecommunications operations of US carriers, finances, rates, and traffic by service type, firm, and country, 1975-90, annual rpt, 9284–17

McIntire, Robert J.
"New Seasonal Adjustment Factors for Household Data Series", 6742–2.307
"Revision of Seasonally Adjusted Labor Force Series", 6742–2.302

McKewan, W. M.
"Wire Ropes Used for Hoisting in U.S. Mines", 5608–172

McKinney Homeless Assistance Act
Assistance for homeless of Fed Govt by program and agency, and indicators of need, 1990, annual rpt, 14364–1
Assistance for homeless of Fed Govt, program descriptions and funding, by agency and State, FY91, annual GAO rpt, 26104–21
Housing and support services projects for homeless, funding, and clients, by organization, FY87 and FY90, GAO rpt, 26113–593
Housing for homeless persons in rehabilitated single occupancy units, funding and characteristics, by city, FY87-91, GAO rpt, 26113–596
HUD support services grants for homeless families in transitional housing, by recipient, 1991, press release, 5006–3.87

McLain, William H.
"Montana's Timber Production and Mill Residue, 1988", 1206–17.12

McLanahan, Leona O.
"Water Resources Investigations in Pennsylvania: Programs and Activities of the USGS, 1990-91", 5666–26.25

McLaughlin, Josetta S.
"U.S. and Japanese Work Injury and Illness Experience", 6722–1.318

McLean, Garnet A.
"Effects of Seating Configuration and Number of Type III Exits on Emergency Aircraft Evacuation", 7506–10.124

McLemore, Thomas
"1978 Summary: National Ambulatory Medical Care Survey", 4147–16.6

McMaster University
"Financial Incentives and Medical Practice: Evidence from Ontario on the Effect of Changes in Physician Fees on Medical Care Utilization", 17266–2.3

McMillen, Marilyn M.
"Detailed Characteristics of Private Schools and Staff: 1987-88", 4836–3.8

McNees, Stephen K.
"How Large Are Economic Forecast Errors?", 9373–1.313
"1990-91 Recession in Historical Perspective", 9373–1.301

McNeil, John
"Measuring the Effect of Benefits and Taxes on Income and Poverty: 1979-91", 2546–6.78
"Trends in Relative Income: 1964-89", 2546–6.73
"Workers with Low Earnings: 1964-90", 2546–6.74

McWilliams, William H.
"Forest Statistics for West-Central Alabama Counties, 1990", 1206–30.11
"Recent Trends in Afforestation and Reforestation of Nonindustrial Private Pine Forests in Alabama", 1208–409

MDS Associates
"Status of Appalachian Regional Commission Primary Care Projects", 9088–38

Mearns, Alan J.
"Contaminant Trends in the Southern California Bight: Inventory and Assessment", 2176–3.16

Measles
see Infective and parasitic diseases

Measures
see Industrial standards
see Instruments and measuring devices
see Weights and measures

Meat and meat products
Agricultural Statistics, 1991, annual rpt, 1004–1
Appalachia food processing firms, employment, and shipments, and farm production, by commodity and State, 1960s-90, 9088–37
Beef consumption and retail prices, and size of cattle herds by region, 1960s-91, article, 1561–7.301
Business statistics, detailed data for major industries and economic indicators, *Survey of Current Business*, monthly rpt, 2702–1.13
Business statistics, detailed data for major industries and economic indicators, 1960-91, *Survey of Current Business* biennial supplement, 2704–1

Canada-US trade agreement issues, with data on Canada fertilizer and agricultural production and trade, 1960s-90s, hearing, 25368–179
Cancer (colorectal) risk relation to diet, for men, 1986-88, article, 4472–1.302
Cold storage food stocks by commodity and census div, and warehouse space use, by State, monthly rpt, 1631–5
Cold storage food stocks by commodity, and warehouse space use, by census div, 1991, annual rpt, 1631–11
Consumption and trade of meat products, and other indicators of grazing forage demand, 1960s-90 and projected to 2030, 1208–404
Consumption of food, dietary composition, and nutrient intake, natl survey methodology changes and sample results, 1990 rpt, 1358–6
Consumption, supply, trade, prices, spending, and indexes, by food commodity, 1990, annual rpt, 1544–4
County Business Patterns, 1989: employment, establishments, and payroll, by SIC 2- to 4-digit industry and county, annual State rpt series, 2326–8
County Business Patterns, 1990: employment, establishments, and payroll, by SIC 2- to 4-digit industry and county, annual State rpt series, 2326–6
CPI by component for US city average, and by selected metro area, region, and population size, monthly rpt, 6762–2
Deaths during 1986, decedents health condition, services use, habits, and social, employment, and other characteristics, 4147–20.19
Eastern Europe export industries dev potential, with trade and industry finances and operations, for 5 countries, 1985-90, 9886–4.179
Employment, earnings, and hours, by SIC 1- to 4-digit industry, monthly 1989-Feb 1992, annual rpt, 6744–4
Employment of minorities and women, by occupation, SIC 1- to 3-digit industry, State, and MSA, 1991, annual rpt, 9244–1
Exports and imports (agricultural) commodity and country, prices, and world market devs, monthly rpt, 1922–12
Exports and imports (agricultural) of US, by commodity and country, bimonthly rpt, 1522–1
Exports and imports (agricultural) of US, by detailed commodity and country, 1991, annual rpt, 1524–8
Exports and imports (agricultural) of US, by detailed commodity and country, 1991, semiannual rpt, 1522–4
Exports and imports between US and outlying areas, by detailed commodity and mode of transport, 1991, annual rpt, 2424–11
Exports and imports of dairy, livestock, and poultry products, by commodity and country, FAS monthly circular, 1925–32
Exports and imports of US, by country and detailed commodity, monthly rpt, 2422–12
Exports and imports of US, by Harmonized System 6-digit commodity and country, 1991, annual rpt, 2424–13
Exports and imports of US, by selected country, country group, and commodity group, 1991, annual rpt, 2044–37
Exports and imports of US, by transport mode, country, and SITC 1- to 3-digit commodity, 1991, annual rpt, 2424–12
Exports of US, detailed Schedule B commodities with countries of destination, 1991, annual rpt, 2424–10
Farm financial and marketing conditions, forecast 1992, annual chartbook, 1504–8
Foreign and US livestock, poultry, and dairy production, trade, and use, by selected country, FAS semiannual circular series, 1925–33
Foreign countries agricultural production, prices, and trade, by country, 1980-91 and forecast 1992, annual world area rpt series, 1524–4
Freight (waterborne domestic and foreign) by commodity, traffic, and passengers, by port and waterway, 1989, annual rpt, 3754–3
Futures and options trading volume, by commodity and exchange, FY91, annual rpt, 11924–2
Futures trading in selected commodities and financial instruments and indexes, for NYC, Chicago, and other markets activity, biweekly rpt, 11922–5
Input-output structure of US economy, detailed interindustry transactions for 541 industries, and components of final demand, 1982 benchmark data, 2708–17
Inspections and certification of meat plants for export to US, listing by country, 1991, annual rpt, 1374–2
Inspections and rejection of meat from Canada, by US port of entry, 1989-91, hearing, 21368–141
Inspections of meat and poultry for domestic use and export, and rejections by cause, by type of animal and product, FY90, annual rpt, 1374–3
Inspections of meat imports between US and Canada, 1989-91, GAO rpt, 26113–595
Labor productivity, indexes of output, hours, and employment by SIC 2- to 4-digit industry, 1967-90, annual rpt, 6824–1.3
Lamb and mutton production, stocks, trade, and consumption, 1950s-90, 1548–382
Lamb and sheep exports, imports, tariffs, and industry operating data, 1991 rpt, 9885–8.1
Manufacturing annual survey, 1990: finances and operations, by SIC 2- to 4-digit industry, series, 2506–14
Manufacturing census, 1987: concentration of largest firms measured by value added, and for shipments by SIC 2- and 4-digit industry, subject rpt, 2497–6
Manufacturing census, 1987: shipments of manufacturers products, by customer class and SIC 2- and 4-digit industry, subject rpt, 2497–4
Manufacturing finances and operations, by SIC 2- to 4-digit industry, forecast 1992, annual rpt, 2044–28
Marketing data for livestock, meat, and wool, by species and market, weekly rpt, 1315–1
Multinatl US firms and foreign affiliates finances and operations, by industry and country, 1989 benchmark survey, annual rpt, 2704–5
Nutrient, caloric, and waste composition, detailed data for raw, processed, and prepared foods, 1992 rpt, 1356–3.17
Occupational injury and illness rates and lost workdays, for selected industries, 1978-89, compilation of papers, 6728–41
Occupational injury and illness rates, by SIC 2- to 4-digit industry, 1989-90, annual rpt, 6844–7
Occupational injury and illness rates, by SIC 2- to 4-digit industry, 1990, annual rpt, 6844–1
OECD trade, total and for 4 major countries, and US trade by country, by commodity, 1980-90, world area rpt series, 9116–1
Pork and live swine trade, tariffs, and industry operating data, 1992 rpt, 9885–8.5
Price indexes (producer), by stage of processing and detailed commodity, monthly rpt, 6762–6
Price indexes (producer), by stage of processing and detailed commodity, monthly 1991, annual rpt, 6764–2
Prices (farm-retail) for food, marketing cost components, and industry finances and productivity, 1920s-91, annual rpt, 1544–9
Prices (producer and retail) of meat and fish, 1987-92, semiannual situation rpt, 1561–15.3
Production, inventory, and prices of meat, USDA forecasts accuracy, 1980s, GAO rpt, 26131–93
Production of meat and livestock slaughter, by livestock type and State, monthly rpt, 1623–9
Production of meat, by species and State, 1991, annual rpt, 1623–10
Production, prices, receipts, and disposition for meat animals, by species and State, 1990-91, annual rpt, 1623–8
Production, prices, trade, and marketing, by commodity, current situation and forecast, monthly rpt with articles, 1502–4
Production, prices, trade, and stocks, monthly rpt, 1561–17
Production, prices, trade, stocks, and use, periodic situation rpt with articles, 1561–7
Retail trade sales and inventories, by kind of business, region, and selected State, MSA, and city, monthly rpt, 2413–3
Retail trade sales, inventories, purchases, gross margin, and accounts receivable, by SIC 2- to 4-digit kind of business and form of ownership, 1990, annual rpt, 2413–5
Science, engineering, and technical employment in manufacturing, by field and industry, 1989, triennial rpt, 9627–23
Soviet Union and US economic and sociodemographic indicators, selected years 1970-90, handbook, 2328–80
Statistical Abstract of US, 1992 annual data compilation, 2324–1.23
Supply and demand indicators for livestock and dairy products, and for selected foreign and US crops, monthly rpt, 1522–5
Tax (income) returns of corporations, income and tax items by asset size and detailed industry, 1989, annual rpt, 8304–4; 8304–21

Trichinosis cases in US, by type of meat and State, 1987-90, article, 4202–7.304
Weight and volume conversion factors for agricultural commodities and products, 1992 rpt, 1508–3
see also Oils, oilseeds, and fats
see also Poultry industry and products
see also under By Commodity in the "Index by Categories"

Meckstroth, Alicia
"Private Foundation and Charitable Trust Statistics, 1989: Data Release", 8302–2.325
"Private Foundations, 1988", 8302–2.302

Medals
see Awards, medals, and prizes
see Military awards, decorations, and medals

Media
see Mass media

Mediation
see Legal arbitration and mediation

Medicaid
AIDS cases among children, hospital use and charges by instn and patient characteristics, and payment source, 1986-87, 4186–6.16
AIDS patients costs and service use under Medicaid, and service needs, for New Jersey waiver program, 1987-89, article, 4652–1.317
AIDS patients costs and service use under Medicaid, for California, 1984-86, article, 4652–1.301
AIDS virus-related Medicaid claims and payments, by sex, age, risk group, eligibility, and source of care, for Michigan, mid 1980s, article, 4042–3.348
Auto safety, child restraints use among Medicaid recipients by selected characteristics, local area study, 1992 article, 4042–3.312
Beneficiaries and program operations, for Medicare and Medicaid, 1992, annual fact book, 4654–18
Benefits, beneficiaries, and spells of participation, by aid program and recipient characteristics, 1987-88, Current Population Rpt, 2546–20.25
Benefits, beneficiary characteristics, and trust funds of OASDHI, Medicaid, SSI, and related programs, selected years 1937-90, annual rpt, 4744–3
Births of low birthweight to Medicaid patients, by prenatal care source and adequacy, and other risk factors, for 2 States, late 1980s, article, 4042–3.304
Budget deficit forecasting accuracy, contributing factors, and analysis of major programs, FY91, annual GAO rpt, 26104–23
Budget of US, CBO analysis of revenue and spending alternatives and projections of economic indicators, FY93-97, annual rpt, 26304–3
Census of Population and intercensal data use in Federal formula grant allocation, with data by program and State, FY91, 25408–120
Child and maternal health condition and services use, indicators by age, race, and poverty status, 1988, 4478–197
Child health screenings for Medicaid eligible population, rural physicians participation effects of promotional mailing, for North Carolina, 1990, article, 4042–3.358
Children (handicapped) formal and informal care, outlays and time spent relation to diagnosis and other characteristics, 1988, article, 4042–3.329
Children (handicapped) with special needs, insurance coverage, and health care services use, by selected characteristics, 1988, 4146–8.216
Costs, use, and structure of private and public health care delivery, indicators, issues, and foreign comparisons, 1960s-80s, technical paper, 8006–6.1
Coverage, eligibility, and payment provisions of States for Medicaid, as of March 1992, annual rpt, 4654–19
Coverage, funding, and costs, with reform recommendations, for Medicaid, mid 1960s-92, 10048–83
Coverage under health insurance and govt aid, with background data 1960s-91 and govt fiscal impacts projected to 2002, 26306–6.174
Coverage under health insurance, by insurance type and selected characteristics, 1985-90, 2546–20.23
Diabetes patients physician office visits, by characteristics of patient, physician, and visit, 1989, 4146–8.212
Economic Report of the President for 1991, economic effects of budget proposals, and trends and projections, 1940s-95, annual hearings, 23844–4
Eligibility and payment provisions for SSI and Medicaid, by State, 1992, annual rpt, 4704–13
Expenditures for health care by businesses, households, and govts, 1965-90, annual article, 4652–1.309
Expenditures for Medicaid by States, outlay differentials, with data by service type and eligibility category, FY89, article, 9373–1.303
Expenditures for Medicaid of States, impacts of cost containment and other factors, with data by eligibility type, mid 1970s-90, working paper, 9373–27.1
Expenditures of Fed Govt in States, by type, program, agency, and State, FY91, annual rpt, 2464–2
Finances of govts, tax systems and revenue, and fiscal structure, by level of govt and State, 1992 and historical trends, annual rpt, 10044–1
Food aid program of USDA for women, infants, and children, prenatal participation effects on birthweight and health and social welfare costs, 1960s-90, GAO rpt, 26121–458
Fraud in State programs, funding for remediation by State, FY91, annual regional listings, 4004–3
Health condition and care indicators, 1950s-90 with health improvement and disease prevention goals for 1990, annual data compilation, 4144–11
HHS financial aid, by program, recipient, State, and city, FY91, annual regional listings, 4004–3
Hispanic Americans health insurance coverage, by source, employment and poverty status, and origin, 1987-90, GAO rpt, 26131–97
Hospital closures in 1990, operating characteristics, current use, and location, annual rpt, 4004–35
Hospital discharges and length of stay, by diagnosis, patient and instn characteristics, procedure performed, and payment source, 1990, annual rpt, 4147–13.112
Hospital discharges, by payment source, diagnosis, patient characteristics, and region, and procedures performed, 1990, 4146–8.221
Households composition, income, benefits, and labor force status, Survey of Income and Program Participation methodology, working paper series, 2626–10
Income (household) and poverty status under alternative income definitions, by recipient characteristics, 1979-91, annual Current Population Rpt, 2546–6.78
Internist office visits, by characteristics of patient, physician, and visit, 1989, 4146–8.214
Long term health care financing reform issues, 1991 rpt, 10176–3.7
Medicare premiums and out-of-pocket costs paid by Medicaid, eligibility and participation, by State, 1991, hearing, 21148–67
Mental health care facilities, staff, patients, and finances, 1970s-91, biennial rpt, 4094–1
Mental health care of affective disorder patients, by patient and facility characteristics, 1986, 4506–3.49
Nursing home compliance with Medicare and Medicaid regulations, and patient characteristics, by facility, suspended annual State rpt series, 4654–15
Nursing home reimbursement rates of Medicaid, and ratio to private resident payments, by State, FY89, article, 9373–1.311
Nursing homes certification requirements, beds, and staff and training needs, by State, 1990, 17206–2.37
Older persons ability to pay out of pocket health care costs, indicators by selected characteristics, 1984, article, 4742–1.307
Oregon Medicaid waiver proposal for managed care, services priorities dev procedures and issues, with background data, 1992 rpt, 26358–254
Physicians payment and participation in Medicaid by service type, and cost compared to Medicare, by State, FY89, 17266–1.4
Physicians payment by Medicare under fee schedule, methodology with data by procedure and specialty, 1992, annual rpt, 17264–1
Physicians payment by Medicare, vulnerable beneficiaries services use prior to fee schedule implementation, 1986-90, annual rpt, 17266–1.8
Physicians visits, by patient and practice characteristics, diagnosis, and services provided, 1989, annual rpt, 4147–13.109
Population economic well-being indicators, by selected characteristics and household income and income-to-poverty ratio, 1984, 2546–20.22
Poverty status of population and families, by detailed characteristics, 1991, annual Current Population Rpt, 2546–6.77
Prenatal care program of Medicaid, costs and benefits, for Missouri, 1988, article, 4042–3.365

Prenatal care under Medicaid eligibility expansion, coverage, use, and costs, by State, 1990-91, 4008–120
Public opinion on OASDHI and health care system operations and reform issues, 1991 surveys, 10176–2.2
Research activities and grants of HCFA, by program, FY91, annual listing, 4654–10
State and local govt fiscal condition, with data by State and selected city, 1991 hearing, 21268–44
State govt budget balances, balances as share of outlays, and costs of Medicaid coverage expansion, FY89-92, hearing, 21408–129
States budget impacts of Medicaid, and other Advisory Commission on Social Security findings and recommendations, 1991 quadrennial rpt, 10178–1
States budget impacts of Medicaid, and program financing, cost control measures, enrollment, and services coverage, by selected State, 1960s-80s and projected to 1997, 10176–3.6
Statistical Abstract of US, 1992 annual data compilation, 2324–1.3
Supplemental Security Income work incentive programs, participant characteristics, by program, 1982-91, article, 4742–1.305
Traffic accident injury hospitalization, costs, and discharges, by payment source and State, mid 1980s-90, 7768–122
VA health care services, needs, availability, structure, and funding, 1991 compilation of papers, 8608–9
Veterans health care, patients, visits, costs, and operating beds, by VA and contract facility, and region, quarterly rpt, 8602–4
Youth health condition, risk factors, and preventive and treatment services use and availability, 1970s-80s, 26358–234.3

Medical assistance

Assistance (financial and nonfinancial) of Fed Govt, 1992 base edition, annual listing, 104–5
Budget of US, Bush Admin proposals, with detail for defense budgets, and historical data from FY34, FY93, 108–46
Chronology of income maintenance and health care financing, major private and public actions, 1636-1991, quadrennial rpt, 10178–1
Coverage under health insurance and govt aid, with background data 1960s-91 and govt fiscal impacts projected to 2002, 26306–6.174
Crime victim compensation and support service programs funding, by offense and State, FY88-90, biennial rpt, 6064–37
Developing countries economic and social conditions from 1960s, and Intl Dev Cooperation Agency and AID activities and funding, FY91-93, annual rpt, 9904–4
Drug abuse by mothers, treatment and other services use, referrals, needs, and barriers, for 13 NIDA-funded programs, 1990/91 survey, 4498–76
Expenditures, coverage, and benefits for social welfare programs, late 1930s-90, annual rpt, 4744–3.1
Expenditures for health care and factors in costs, with data by payment source and service type, 1960s-90 and projected to 2000, 26306–6.175
Expenditures for health care and factors in increase, with background data and foreign comparisons, various periods 1929-90, technical paper, 9366–6.296
Expenditures for health care by businesses, households, and govts, 1965-90, annual article, 4652–1.309
Expenditures for health care by funding source, 1990, with trends and indexes by service type from 1960, article, 4652–1.323
Expenditures for public welfare by program, FY50s-89, annual article, 4742–1.319
Expenditures for public welfare programs, by program type and level of govt, FY65-89, annual article, 4742–1.302
Health care services use and total and out-of-pocket spending, by type of insurance coverage and selected characteristics, 1987, 4186–8.24
Health condition and care indicators, 1950s-90 with health improvement and disease prevention goals for 1990, annual data compilation, 4144–11
Hispanic Americans health insurance coverage, by source, employment and poverty status, and origin, 1987-90, GAO rpt, 26131–97
Homeless persons aid by program and Federal agency, and indicators of need, 1990, annual rpt, 14364–1
Homeless persons aid programs of Fed Govt, program descriptions and funding, by agency and State, FY87-91, annual GAO rpt, 26104–21
Hospital discharges and length of stay, by diagnosis, patient and instn characteristics, procedure performed, and payment source, 1990, annual rpt, 4147–13.112
Hospital trauma center cases and deaths by injury type, costs, and payment sources, with data for selected areas, 1991 hearing, 21348–123
Marshall Islands Nuclear Claims Trust Fund financial condition, and health care benefits and enrollment, 1987-92, GAO rpt, 26123–405
Older persons socioeconomic characteristics, 1900s-90 and projected to 2050, biennial chartbook, 12904–1
Population economic well-being indicators, by selected characteristics and household income and income-to-poverty ratio, 1984, 2546–20.22
Private health insurance denial because of poor health, coverage under public insurance, 1987, 4186–8.23
Public opinion on OASDHI and health care system operations and reform issues, 1991 surveys, 10176–2.2
Reform of health care system, issues with data on insurance administrative and employer costs, coverage, public views, and Canada and UK systems, 1950s-91, hearings, 25368–180
Research activities and grants of HCFA, by program, FY91, annual listing, 4654–10
Traffic accident injury hospitalization, costs, and discharges, by payment source and State, mid 1980s-90, 7768–122
Women, infants, and children food aid program of USDA, participant referrals to social service programs, by type and reason, 1990 local area study, article, 4042–3.318
see also Maternity benefits
see also Medicaid
see also Medicare
see also State funding for health and hospitals

Medical centers

see Hospitals
see Military health facilities and services
see Veterans health facilities and services

Medical costs

Accident deaths and injuries prevention, and treatment, 1991 conf papers, 4208–35
AIDS virus-related Medicaid claims and payments, by sex, age, risk group, eligibility, and source of care, for Michigan, mid 1980s, article, 4042–3.348
Alcohol abuse direct and indirect costs, 1985, article, 4482–1.311
Bone marrow donors, minority recruitment, Federal aid, transplants, costs, payment sources, 1987-92, GAO rpt, 26121–487
Business statistics, detailed data for major industries and economic indicators, 1960-91, *Survey of Current Business* biennial supplement, 2704–1
Cancer patients hospitalized by purpose and body site, case classification effect on charges and length of stay, FY85, article, 4652–1.304
Children (handicapped) formal and informal care, outlays and time spent relation to diagnosis and other characteristics, 1988, article, 4042–3.329
Consumer Expenditure Survey, spending by category, and income, by selected household characteristics, 1991, annual press release, 6726–1.53
Consumer Expenditure Survey, spending by category, selected household characteristics, and region, quarterly rpt, 6762–14
Consumer Product Safety Commission activities, recalls by brand, and casualties and medical costs, by product type, FY90, annual rpt, 9164–2
Costs, use, and structure of private and public health care delivery, indicators, issues, and foreign comparisons, 1960s-80s, technical paper, 8006–6.1
CPI by component for US city average, and by selected metro area, region, and population size, monthly rpt, 6762–2
Crime victimization rates, by victim and offender characteristics, circumstances, and offense, 1990 survey, annual rpt, 6066–3.47
Czechoslovakia health care system, spending, and population health condition indicators, 1988-89, article, 4042–3.363
Deaths during 1986, decedents health condition, services use, habits, and social, employment, and other characteristics, 4147–20.19
Disabled persons assistive technology equipment and home accessibility features, use, payment sources, and unmet needs, by age, 1990, 4146–8.219
Disease direct and indirect costs, by diagnosis, 1989, annual rpt, 4474–15
Drug (prescription) prices charged to VA and Fed Govt, by manufacturer and drug, 1990-91, hearing, 21768–68
Drug (prescription) prices charged to wholesalers, retailers, VA, and Fed Govt, for 29 drugs, 1985-91, GAO rpt, 26121–472

Drug (prescription) prices in Canada and US, by brand and vendor, 1991, GAO rpt, 26121–482
Drug (prescription) prices in US and other countries, industry profits, and R&D and marketing spending, 1980s-91 and projected to 2000, 25148–44
Drug abuse services availability, need, use, outcome, costs, funding sources, and cost-effectiveness, series, 4496–11
Drug abuse treatment services costs, effectiveness, and financing issues, 1991 conf papers, 4498–80
Economic indicators and components, current data and annual trends, monthly rpt, 23842–1.4
Expenditures (private) for social welfare, by category, 1970s-90, annual article, 4742–1.323
Expenditures, coverage, and benefits for social welfare programs, late 1930s-90, annual rpt, 4744–3.1
Expenditures for health care, and CPI for selected services, 1980s-91, and nursing home population by sex, projected to 2040, article, 1702–1.309
Expenditures for health care and factors in costs, with data by payment source and service type, 1960s-90 and projected to 2000, 26306–6.175
Expenditures for health care and factors in increase, with background data and foreign comparisons, various periods 1929-90, technical paper, 9366–6.296
Expenditures for health care by businesses, households, and govts, 1965-90, annual article, 4652–1.309
Expenditures for health care by funding source, 1990, with trends and indexes by service type from 1960, article, 4652–1.323
Expenditures for health care, growth rates by component, 1970s-90, article, 4652–1.310
Expenditures for public welfare by program, FY50s-89, annual article, 4742–1.319
Expenditures, output, and price growth rates for health care compared to selected other personal consumption expenditures, 1965-90, article, 4652–1.308
Expenditures per capita for health care by State, 1990, and relation to income, services availability, rate control, and other factors, 1982, GAO rpt, 26121–444
Expenditures, use, payment sources, and admin of health care services, with foreign comparisons, 1970s-90, chartbook, 21788–213
Fed Govt employees compensation costs, and vocational rehabilitation costs and workload, FY82-90, GAO rpt, 26119–381
Fire-related injuries by severity, and deaths, by ignition source, victim age, and treatment location, 1984-85 local area study, article, 4042–3.340
Food aid program of USDA for women, infants, and children, prenatal participation effects on birthweight and health and social welfare costs, 1960s-90, GAO rpt, 26121–458
Food stamp recipient household size, composition, income, and income and deductions allowed, summer 1989, annual rpt, 1364–8
Ford Motor Co and foreign subsidiaries employee health care costs, with data on foreign and US health care systems, 1987-90, article, 9882–16.302
Foreign and US aged population and characteristics, by country, 1991 and projected to 2020, wallchart, 2328–82
Foreign and US health care administrative costs for all and public programs, by selected OECD country, mid 1970s-90, article, 4652–1.325
Govt direct spending and employment, by function and level of govt, selected years 1962-87, 10048–53
Health Care Financing Review, quarterly journal, 4652–1
Health care provider prices, price inputs and indexes, and labor, quarterly journal, 4652–1.1
Health care services use and total and out-of-pocket spending, by type of insurance coverage and selected characteristics, 1987, 4186–8.24
Health condition and care indicators, 1950s-90 with health improvement and disease prevention goals for 1990, annual data compilation, 4144–11
Home drug infusion therapy use, equipment, industry finances, and Medicare coverage options, 1992 rpt, 26358–258
Hospital capital, operating, and total costs, model estimates of factors affecting variation, 1985-89, article, 4652–1.313
Hospital costs and use, data compilation project analyses, series, 4186–6
Hospital costs per capita in ratesetting States, and HMO enrollment, 1980s-90, article, 4652–1.311
Hospital financial performance under Medicare, 1977-89, article, 4652–1.315
Hospital reimbursement by Medicaid, provisions by State, 1991, 17206–2.35
Hospital reimbursement by Medicare under prospective payment system, and effect on services, finances, and beneficiary payments, 1980-91, annual rpt, 17204–2
Hospital reimbursement by Medicare under prospective payment system, case mix index and payments impacts of cost and charge weights, FY85-87, article, 4652–1.318
Hospital reimbursement by Medicare under prospective payment system, impacts on costs, industry structure and operations, and quality of care, series, 17206–2
Hospital reimbursement by Medicare under prospective payment system, methodology, inputs, and data by diagnostic group, 1992 annual rpt, 17204–1
Hospital trauma center cases and deaths by injury type, costs, and payment sources, with data for selected areas, 1991 hearing, 21348–123
Infant (newborn) intensive care, assessment of alternative case mix groupings intended to improve cost homogeneity, 1985, article, 4652–1.303
Mental health care facilities, staff, patients, and finances, 1970s-91, biennial rpt, 4094–1
Military health care benefits and costs under Civilian Health and Medical Program of Uniformed Services, FY85-90, annual chartbook, 3504–23
Natl income and product accounts and components, *Survey of Current Business*, monthly rpt, 2702–1.23
Natl income and product accounts, comprehensive accounts and components, benchmark revisions, 1929-88, 2708–5
Natl income and product accounts, comprehensive accounts and components, *Survey of Current Business*, monthly rpt, 2702–1.25
Neurological Disorders and Stroke Natl Inst activities, and disorder cases, FY91, annual rpt, 4474–25
Neurosciences research and public policy issues, series, 26356–9
OECD members health care costs, hospital use, resources, and economic and health indicators, by country, 1960s-90, article, 4652–1.322
Older persons ability to pay out of pocket health care costs, indicators by selected characteristics, 1984, article, 4742–1.307
Older persons socioeconomic characteristics, 1900s-90 and projected to 2050, biennial chartbook, 12904–1
Older population, and health, economic, and other characteristics, with foreign comparisons, 1980s-91 with trends and projections, Current Population Rpt, 2546–2.165
Pacemaker lead implants, failures, and costs, by model, 1992 GAO rpt, 26131–103
Physicians payment by Medicare under fee schedule, analyses of costs and other issues, series, 17266–1
Physicians payment by Medicare under fee schedule, impacts on beneficiaries, practice, and program finances, series, 17266–2
Public health innovation contest winners, project descriptions and costs, 1991, article, 4042–3.322
Public opinion on OASDHI and health care system operations and reform issues, 1991 surveys, 10176–2.2
Research activities and grants of HCFA, by program, FY91, annual listing, 4654–10
Statistical Abstract of US, 1992 annual data compilation, 2324–1.3
Tax (income) returns filed, by type of filer, selected income items, quarterly rpt, 8302–2.1
Tax (income) returns of individuals, detailed data, 1988, annual rpt, 8304–2
Tax (income) returns of individuals, selected income and tax items by income level, preliminary 1990, annual article, 8302–2.307
Tobacco production and use in Latin America, Canada, and US, and related economic, health, and social issues, 1950s-92, annual rpt, 4204–18
Traffic accident injury hospitalization, costs, and discharges, by payment source and State, mid 1980s-90, 7768–122
Traffic accidents direct and indirect costs, by cost type, payment source, and severity, 1980s, 7558–114
VA and non-VA facilities health services sharing contracts, by service type and region, FY91, annual rpt, 8704–5
VA health care benefits and program operations spending, FY67-91, annual rpt, 8604–5.1

VA health care services income eligibility and copayment enforcement, and revenue forgone from unreported income, 1987-91, GAO rpt, 26121–479
VA health care services, needs, availability, structure, and funding, 1991 compilation of papers, 8608–9
VA hospitals admissions and discharges by diagnosis, facilities operating costs, and other VA activities, FY91, annual rpt, 8604–3.2
Vital and Health Statistics series: health condition, medical costs, and use of facilities and services, 4147–10
see also Health care reform
see also Health insurance
see also Medicaid
see also Medical assistance
see also Medical regulation
see also Medicare

Medical education
Board and care home violations of State drug handling and dispensing regulations, for 3 metro areas, 1990-91, GAO rpt, 26121–447
Degree (PhD) recipients in higher education, by field and selected characteristics, 1979, 1984, and 1989, 4848–44
Degrees awarded in higher education, by level, field, race, and sex, 1989/90 and trends from 1980/81, annual rpt, 4844–17
Digest of Education Statistics, 1992 annual data compilation, 4824–2
Enrollment and applicants for medical schools, 1950s-88, series, 4006–8
Enrollment in science and engineering grad programs, by field, source of funds, and characteristics of student and instn, 1990, annual rpt, 9627–7
Foreign students and applicants for US medical schools, 1978-87, working paper, 6366–6.2
Health care professionals supply and education, by professional and other characteristics, and location, 1960s-92 and projected to 2020, biennial rpt, 4114–8
Health condition and care indicators, 1950s-90 with health improvement and disease prevention goals for 1990, annual data compilation, 4144–11
High school enrollment in vocational education, and academic and other credits earned, by subject and student characteristics, classes of 1982 and 1987, 4838–50
Higher education enrollment, faculty, finances, and degrees, by instn level and control, and State, FY88, annual rpt, 4844–13
Hospital multiple admissions of Medicare beneficiaries, by reason and characteristics of instn and patient, 1985, 4008–117
Hospital operations of higher education instns, revenue and spending by State and instn control, FY82-90, annual rpt, 4844–6
Hospital reimbursement by Medicare under prospective payment system, analyses of alternative payment plans, series, 17206–1
Hospital reimbursement by Medicare under prospective payment system, and effect on services, finances, and beneficiary payments, 1980-91, annual rpt, 17204–2
Hospital reimbursement by Medicare under prospective payment system, diagnosis related group code assignment and effects on care and instn finances, series, 4006–7
Hospital reimbursement by Medicare under prospective payment system, impacts on costs, industry structure and operations, and quality of care, series, 17206–2
Hospital reimbursement by Medicare under prospective payment system, methodology, inputs, and data by location, 1992 annual rpt, 17204–1
Hospital reimbursement by Medicare under prospective payment system, rural area instns financial performance and impacts of PPS policy changes, 1991 rpt, 26306–6.164
Mental health care facilities, staff, patients, and finances, 1970s-91, biennial rpt, 4094–1
Military health care personnel, and accessions by training source, by occupation, specialty, and service branch, FY90, annual rpt, 3544–24
Military training and education programs funding, staff, students, and facilities, by service branch, FY93, annual rpt, 3504–5
Nursing homes certification requirements, beds, and staff and training needs, by State, 1990, 17206–2.37
Physicians, by specialty, age, sex, and location of training and practice, 1990, State rpt series, 4116–6
Physicians recently graduating, specialties, school debt, and practice settings, and medical school funding sources, 1970s-91, hearing, 21368–135
R&D facilities of higher education instns, space and equipment adequacy, needs, and funding by source, by instn type and control, 1992, biennial rpt, 9624–25
Radiation protection and health physics enrollment and degrees granted by instn and State, and grad placement, by student characteristics, 1991, annual rpt, 3004–7
Radiation protection and health physics enrollment and degrees granted by instn and State, and women grads plans and employment, 1991, annual rpt, 3006–8.19
VA Geriatric Research, Education and Clinical Centers activities and finances, FY88, annual rpt, 8704–8
VA health care facilities trainees, by detailed program and city, FY91, annual rpt, 8704–4
VA health care services, needs, availability, structure, and funding, 1991 compilation of papers, 8608–9
Vocational education enrollment, student and teacher characteristics, and outcomes, for secondary and postsecondary instns, 1970s-90, 4828–42
Youth health condition, risk factors, and preventive and treatment services use and availability, 1970s-80s, 26358–234.3
see also Federal aid to medical education
see also Foreign medical graduates
see also Medical research

Medical equipment
see Medical supplies and equipment

Medical ethics
Blood banks safety violations, FDA enforcement, disease transmittal, and Houston regional center activities and finances, 1970s-91, hearings, 21368–134
see also Human experimentation
see also Medical malpractice
see also Scientific ethics

Medical examinations and tests
AIDS and tuberculosis cases in prisons, test results, and control and treatment policies, by location, 1990 survey, annual rpt, 6064–22
AIDS public knowledge, attitudes, info sources, and testing, 1991 survey, 4146–8.218
AIDS virus patient lab testing for T-lymphocytes, specimen handling, and worker safety, CDC guidelines, 1992 rpt, 4206–2.58
AIDS virus type 2 antibody testing, CDC recommendations, 1992 rpt, 4206–2.62
Aviation medicine research and test results, technical rpt series, 7506–10
Births and rates, by characteristics of birth, infant, and mother, and presence of maternal risk factors and birth defects, 1989, 4146–5.125
Cancer (breast) screening use relation to cancer anxiety, for high-risk women, 1992 article, 4472–1.301
Cancer (breast and cervical) screening use and reasons for nonuse, by age, race, income, and State, 1987-89, article, 4202–7.313
Cancer (cervical and breast) screening among poor black women, effects of in-home promotion program, 1989-92, article, 4042–3.338
Cancer (colorectal) deaths relation to cancer screening use, 1979-88 local area study, article, 4472–1.349
Cancer (colorectal) early detection screening program effectiveness, 1984-88 study, article, 4042–3.333
Cancer patients hospitalized by purpose and body site, case classification effect on charges and length of stay, FY85, article, 4652–1.304
Child day care and early childhood education programs availability, demand, use, costs, and provider and enrollee characteristics, 1990 survey, 4808–39
Child health screenings for Medicaid eligible population, rural physicians participation effects of promotional mailing, for North Carolina, 1990, article, 4042–3.358
Cholesterol serum testing, public awareness and use, 1987-88 local area study, article, 4042–3.335
Diabetes patients physician office visits, by characteristics of patient, physician, and visit, 1989, 4146–8.212
Digestive diseases (chronic) prevalence, and procedures performed, by disease and patient characteristics, 1989, 4146–8.213
Health condition and care indicators, 1950s-90 with health improvement and disease prevention goals for 1990, annual data compilation, 4144–11
Hospital discharges and length of stay, by diagnosis, patient and instn characteristics, procedure performed, and payment source, 1990, annual rpt, 4147–13.112

Hospital discharges and length of stay by region and diagnosis, and procedures performed, by age and sex, 1990, annual rpt, 4146–8.211
Hospital discharges and length of stay under old and new survey designs, by diagnosis, patient and instn characteristics, and procedure, Jan-Mar 1988, 4147–13.110
Hospital discharges by detailed diagnostic and procedure category, primary diagnosis, and length of stay, by age, sex, and region, 1990, annual rpt, 4147–13.111
Hypertension cases, stroke and heart disease risk, and drug dosages, with diagnosis and treatment methods, 1992 quadrennial rpt, 4478–198
Indian and Alaska Native youth health condition and behavioral patterns, by sex and grade, 1988-90, 4088–3
Indian Health Service facilities, funding, operations, and Indian health and other characteristics, 1950s-91, annual chartbook, 4084–1
Indian Health Service outpatient services provided, by reason for visit and age, FY90, annual rpt, 4084–2
Indian Health Service, tribal, and contract facilities hospitalization, by diagnosis, age, sex, and service area, FY91, annual rpt, 4084–5
Insurance (health) coverage and provisions of employee benefit plans, by plan type, for State and local govt employees, 1990, biennial rpt, 6784–21
Internist office visits, by characteristics of patient, physician, and visit, 1989, 4146–8.214
Intestinal parasites lab isolations, by State and organism, 1987, article, 4202–7.306
Maternal and child health indicators and services use, by age, race, and poverty status, 1988, 4478–197
Medicaid payment and participation by service type, and cost compared to Medicare, by State, FY89, 17266–1.4
Medicare enrollees magnetic resonance imaging, endoscopic, and CAT scan procedures use rate, by State, 1986-90, annual rpt, 17266–1.7
Medicare payment of physicians, reforms impacts on services, and monitoring methods, 1992 annual rpt, 4004–34
Medicare payment of physicians, vulnerable beneficiaries services use prior to fee schedule implementation, 1986-90, annual rpt, 17266–1.8
Payment sources expected for hospital discharges, by diagnosis, patient characteristics, and region, and procedures performed, 1990, 4146–8.221
Pediatrician office visits, by characteristics of patient and visit, 1989, 4146–8.210
Physicians visits, by patient and practice characteristics, diagnosis, and services provided, 1989, annual rpt, 4147–13.109
Physicians visits, by patient and practice characteristics, diagnosis, and services provided, 1990, advance rpt, 4146–8.215
Tuberculosis screening, treatment, and control among migrant farmworkers, CDC guidelines, 1992 rpt, 4206–2.60
VA health care services, needs, availability, structure, and funding, 1991 compilation of papers, 8608–9
Veterans health care, patients, visits, costs, and operating beds, by VA and contract facility, and region, quarterly rpt, 8602–4
Youth health condition, risk factors, and preventive and treatment services use and availability, 1970s-80s, 26358–234.3
see also Autopsies
see also Drug and alcohol testing
see also Mammography
see also X-rays

Medical facilities and services
see Health facilities and services

Medical instruments
see Medical supplies and equipment

Medical insurance
see Blue Cross-Blue Shield
see Health insurance
see Health maintenance organizations
see Medicaid
see Medicare

Medical libraries
Assistance (financial and nonfinancial) of Fed Govt, 1992 base edition, annual listing, 104–5
HHS financial aid, by program, recipient, State, and city, FY91, annual regional listings, 4004–3
NIH grants and contracts, quarterly listing, 4432–1
VA health care facilities trainees, by detailed program and city, FY91, annual rpt, 8704–4

Medical malpractice
Costs, use, and structure of private and public health care delivery, indicators, issues, and foreign comparisons, 1960s-80s, technical paper, 8006–6.1
Court caseloads for Federal district courts, 1991, annual rpt, 18204–8.14; 18204–8.18
Court civil and criminal caseloads for Federal district, appeals, and bankruptcy courts, by type of suit and offense, circuit, and district, 1991, annual rpt, 18204–11
Obstetrics rural practitioners malpractice insurance subsidy program funding and participation, for North Carolina, 1989-92, article, 4042–3.355
Physicians income, practice revenue, hours worked, and malpractice insurance premiums paid, late 1970s-90, technical paper, 9366–6.296
States medical boards licensing and discipline of health professionals, 1950s-88, series, 4006–8

Medical personnel
see Health occupations

Medical regulation
Board and care home violations of State drug handling and dispensing regulations, for 3 metro areas, 1990-91, GAO rpt, 26121–447
Drug (prescription) advertising in medical journals, accuracy, info completeness, and violations of FDA regulations, 1990, 4008–119
Drug marketing application processing of FDA, by drug, purpose, and producer, 1991, annual rpt, 4064–14
FDA investigations and regulatory activities, quarterly rpt, 4062–3
FDA regulations dev timeliness, with status and processing time for selected regulations, 1991, GAO rpt, 26121–453
Health Care Financing Admin research activities and grants, by program, FY91, annual listing, 4654–10
Health Care Financing Review, quarterly journal, 4652–1
HHS financial aid, by program, recipient, State, and city, FY91, annual regional listings, 4004–3
HHS programs fraud and abuse, audits and investigations, 1st half FY92, semiannual rpt, 4002–6
Hospital closings relation to hospital and community characteristics, by metro-nonmetro location, 1980-87, article, 4042–3.341
Hospital costs per capita in ratesetting States, and HMO enrollment, 1980s-90, article, 4652–1.311
Hospital reimbursement by Medicare under prospective payment system, analyses of alternative payment plans, series, 17206–1
Hospital reimbursement by Medicare under prospective payment system, and effect on services, finances, and beneficiary payments, 1980-91, annual rpt, 17204–2
Hospital reimbursement by Medicare under prospective payment system, diagnosis related group code assignment and effects on care and instn finances, series, 4006–7
Hospital reimbursement by Medicare under prospective payment system, impacts on costs, industry structure and operations, and quality of care, series, 17206–2
Hospital reimbursement by Medicare under prospective payment system, methodology, inputs, and data by location, 1992 annual rpt, 17204–1
Insurance (health) coverage of selected services, State mandates, 1990, 10176–3.2
Insurance (health) under multiple employer welfare arrangements, coverage, unpaid claims, and regulation, by State, 1988-91, GAO rpt, 26121–443
Kidney end-stage disease treatment facilities approved by Medicare, dialysis and transplant services and ownership, 1991 annual listing, 4654–17
Labs (clinical) test performance standards and proficiency testing, HHS regulations, 1992 rpt, 4206–2.52
Medicaid coverage, eligibility, and payment provisions of States, as of March 1992, annual rpt, 4654–19
Medicare admin and research, and HCFA affirmative action and accreditation programs, FY87, annual rpt, 4654–5
Medicare financial and admin issues, Inspector General rpts, series, 4006–11
Medicare payment of physicians under fee schedule, methodology with data by procedure and specialty, 1992, annual rpt, 17264–1
New health care technologies, coverage under Medicare, risks and benefit evaluations, series, 4186–10
Nursing home reimbursement by Medicare under prospective payment system, service availability, use, patient characteristics, and quality of care indicators, late 1980s-90, 17206–1.14
OASDI and Medicare trust fund finances, economic assumptions, outlook, and health care system reform issues, series, 10176–1

Physicians payment by Medicare, impacts of reforms on services, and monitoring methods, 1992 annual rpt, 4004–34
Physicians payment by Medicare under fee schedule, adjustment factor recommendations, 1993, annual rpt, 4004–33
Physicians payment by Medicare under fee schedule, analyses of costs and other issues, series, 17266–1
Physicians payment by Medicare under fee schedule, impacts on beneficiaries, practice, and program finances, series, 17266–2
Physicians payment by Medicare under fee schedule, impacts on charges by specialty and State, 1992 and 1996, hearing, 25368–178
Physicians payment by Medicare, volume performance standard recommendations, FY93, annual rpt, 4004–32
States medical boards licensing and discipline of health professionals, 1950s-88, series, 4006–8
States rate controls and other factors relation to per capita spending for health care, 1982, GAO rpt, 26121–444
Utilization review organizations assessment of health services for insurance firms, with URO finances, operations, and staff, 1990, GAO rpt, 26121–490
VA hospitals compliance with accreditation commission quality assurance standards, by facility and region, 1989-90, GAO rpt, 26121–441
Workers compensation regulation of physician fees and hospital rates, provisions by State, 1992 annual rpt, 6504–11
see also Health care reform

Medical research

Agent Orange exposure health effects, literature review, 1990, annual rpt series, 8706–1
Alcohol abuse research, treatment programs, and patient characteristics and health effects, quarterly journal, 4482–1
Allergy and Infectious Diseases Natl Inst activities, grants by recipient and location, and disease cases, FY84-91, annual rpt, 4474–30
Assistance (financial and nonfinancial) of Fed Govt, 1992 base edition, annual listing, 104–5
Aviation medicine research and test results, technical rpt series, 7506–10
Biological warfare agent vaccine dev and production of Salk Inst, and Army contract costs by component, late 1970s-91, GAO rpt, 26123–374
Budget of US, obligations and authority by function, agency, and program, with summaries and analyses, FY93, annual rpt, 104–2
Cancer (breast) research funding, cases, and deaths, 1970s-90, GAO rpt, 26131–92
Cancer epidemiology and biochemistry research, semimonthly journal, 4472–1
Cancer Natl Inst activities, grants by recipient, and cancer deaths and cases, FY91 and trends, annual rpt, 4474–13
Cancer Natl Inst epidemiology and biometry activities, FY91, annual rpt, 4474–29
Dental Research Natl Inst research and training grants, by recipient, FY90, annual listing, 4474–19
Developing countries family planning and population activities of AID, grants by project and recipient, and contraceptive shipments, by country, FY91, annual rpt series, 9914–13
Drug (prescription) prices in US and other countries, industry profits, and R&D and marketing spending, 1980s-91 and projected to 2000, 25148–44
Drug abuse and treatment, research on biological and behavioral factors and addiction potential of new drugs, 1991 annual conf, 4494–11
Drug abuse and treatment research summaries, and resource materials and grant listings, bimonthly rpt, 4492–4
Drug abuse prevention services evaluation, methodological issues, 1991 conf, 4498–78
Drug abuse services availability, need, use, outcome, costs, funding sources, and cost-effectiveness, series, 4496–11
Expenditures (private) for social welfare, by category, 1970s-90, annual article, 4742–1.323
Expenditures for public welfare by program, FY50s-89, annual article, 4742–1.319
Expenditures for R&D and related activities of higher education and nonprofit instns by Fed Govt, by field, instn, agency, and State, FY90, annual rpt, 9627–17
Expenditures for R&D by Fed Govt, by detailed function, program, and agency, FY91-93, annual rpt, 9627–9
Expenditures for R&D by higher education instns and federally funded centers, by field, instn, and State, FY90, annual rpt, 9627–13
General Medical Sciences Natl Inst activities, budget, and research and training funding by program, FY91, annual rpt, 4474–38
Health condition and care indicators, 1950s-90 with health improvement and disease prevention goals for 1990, annual data compilation, 4144–11
Health condition and quality of life measurement, rpts and other info sources, quarterly listing, 4122–1
Heart, Lung, and Blood Natl Inst activities and Advisory Council recommendations, 1991 narrative rpt, 4474–22
Heart, Lung, and Blood Natl Inst activities, and grants by recipient and location, FY91 and disease trends from 1940, annual rpt, 4474–15
HHS financial aid, by program, recipient, State, and city, FY91, annual regional listings, 4004–3
Higher education instn R&D facilities space and equipment adequacy, needs, and funding by source, by instn type and control, 1992, biennial rpt, 9624–25
Kidney end-stage disease research of CDC and HCFA, project listing, 1991, annual rpt, 4654–16
Labor supply and education of health professionals, by professional and other characteristics, and location, 1960s-92 and projected to 2020, biennial rpt, 4114–8
Medicare coverage of new health care technologies, risks and benefit evaluations, series, 4186–10
Military health care personnel, and accessions by training source, by occupation, specialty, and service branch, FY90, annual rpt, 3544–24
Neurological Disorders and Stroke Natl Inst activities, and disorder cases, FY91, annual rpt, 4474–25
Neurosciences research and public policy issues, series, 26356–9
NIH activities, staff, funding, and facilities, historical data, 1991 annual rpt, 4434–1
NIH grants and contracts, by inst and type of recipient, FY82-91, annual rpt, 4434–9
NIH grants and contracts, quarterly listing, 4432–1
NIH rpts, 1992 annual listing, 4434–2
Nutrition biomedical and behavioral research and training, NIH activities and funding by inst, FY90, annual rpt, 4434–15
Physicians, by specialty, age, sex, and location of training and practice, 1990, State rpt series, 4116–6
Pollutants health effects, concentrations in food and environment, sources, human intake, and regulation, series, 9186–8
Pollutants health effects for animals by species and for humans, and environmental levels, for selected substances, series, 5506–14
Public health innovation contest winners, project descriptions and costs, 1991, article, 4042–3.322
Reproduction and population research, Fed Govt funding by project, FY90, annual listing, 4474–9
Reproduction and population research, Natl Inst of Child Health and Human Dev funding and activities, 1991, annual rpt, 4474–33
Science and Engineering Indicators, employment, education, R&D funding, and industry impacts, with foreign comparisons, 1960s-91, biennial rpt, 9624–10
Smoking and health effects, with trends in smoking, related disease and death, and public attitudes, literature review, 1992 annual rpt, 4204–18
Smoking prevalence, health effects, and control strategies effectiveness, research results, series, 4476–7
Smoking, tobacco, and health impacts research rpts, 1991 annual report, 4204–19
Toxicology Natl Program research and testing activities, FY90 and planned FY91, annual rpt, 4044–16
VA Geriatric Research, Education and Clinical Centers activities and finances, FY88, annual rpt, 8704–8
VA health care facilities physicians, dentists, and nurses, by selected employment characteristics and VA district, quarterly rpt, 8602–6
VA health care facilities trainees, by detailed program and city, FY91, annual rpt, 8704–4
VA health care services, needs, availability, structure, and funding, 1991 compilation of papers, 8608–9
VA health care staff and turnover, by occupation, physician specialty, and location, 1991, annual rpt, 8604–8
Vaccination research rpts, 1991 annual listing, 4204–16
Women awarded NIH research and training grants, by recipient characteristics, inst, and host instn, FY90, annual rpt, 4434–18

see also Animal experimentation
see also Epidemiology and epidemiologists
see also Human experimentation

Medical supplies and equipment
Consumer holdings of durable goods, by type, in current and constant dollars, 1925-90, annual article, 2702–1.305
Consumer holdings of durable goods, by type, in current and constant dollars, 1988-91, annual article, 2702–1.327
Consumer spending, natl income and product account benchmark revisions, 1929-88, 2708–5
Consumer spending, natl income and product accounts, comprehensive accounts and components, *Survey of Current Business*, monthly rpt, 2702–1.25
County Business Patterns, 1989: employment, establishments, and payroll, by SIC 2- to 4-digit industry and county, annual State rpt series, 2326–8
County Business Patterns, 1990: employment, establishments, and payroll, by SIC 2- to 4-digit industry and county, annual State rpt series, 2326–6
CPI by component for US city average, and by selected metro area, region, and population size, monthly rpt, 6762–2
Cuba trade, by commodity and country, mid 1980s-91, 9118–8
Disability (functional) prevalence and severity, by type of activity needing assistance, age, and sex, 1979-80, 4946–1.1
Disabled persons assistive technology equipment and home accessibility features, use, payment sources, and unmet needs, by age, 1990, 4146–8.219
Eastern Europe export industries dev potential, with trade and industry finances and operations, for 5 countries, 1985-90, 9886–4.179
Employment, earnings, and hours, by SIC 1- to 4-digit industry, monthly 1989-Feb 1992, annual rpt, 6744–4
Employment of minorities and women, by occupation, SIC 1- to 3-digit industry, State, and MSA, 1991, annual rpt, 9244–1
Expenditures for health care by funding source, 1990, with trends and indexes by service type from 1960, article, 4652–1.323
Exports and imports between US and outlying areas, by detailed commodity and mode of transport, 1991, annual rpt, 2424–11
Exports and imports of US, by country and detailed commodity, monthly rpt, 2422–12
Exports and imports of US, by Harmonized System 6-digit commodity and country, 1991, annual rpt, 2424–13
Exports and imports of US, by transport mode, country, and SITC 1- to 3-digit commodity, 1991, annual rpt, 2424–12
Exports of US, detailed Schedule B commodities with countries of destination, 1991, annual rpt, 2424–10
FDA investigations and regulatory activities, quarterly rpt, 4062–3
Health Care Financing Review, provider prices, price inputs and indexes, and labor, quarterly journal, 4652–1.1
Hearing aid performance test results, by make and model, 1992 annual rpt, 8704–3
Home drug infusion therapy use, equipment, industry finances, and Medicare coverage options, 1992 rpt, 26358–258
Imports detained by FDA, by reason, product, shipper, brand, and country, monthly listing, 4062–2
Imports of US given duty-free treatment for value of US material sent abroad, by commodity and country, 1987-90, annual rpt, 9884–14
Injuries from use of consumer products, by severity, victim age, and detailed product, 1991, annual rpt, 9164–6
Input-output structure of US economy, detailed interindustry transactions for 541 industries, and components of final demand, 1982 benchmark data, 2708–17
Intravenous needle use and other drug abuse, by selected characteristics, 1991 survey, annual rpt series, 4494–5
Lenses (aspherical ophthalmoscopy) from Japan at less than fair value, injury to US industry, investigation with background financial and operating data, 1992 rpt, 9886–14.343
Manufacturing annual survey, 1990: finances and operations, by SIC 2- to 4-digit industry, series, 2506–14
Manufacturing census, 1987: concentration of largest firms measured by value added, and for shipments by SIC 2- and 4-digit industry, subject rpt, 2497–6
Manufacturing census, 1987: shipments of manufacturers products, by customer class and SIC 2- and 4-digit industry, subject rpt, 2497–4
Manufacturing finances and operations, by SIC 2- to 4-digit industry, forecast 1992, annual rpt, 2044–28
Military prime contract awards, by category, contractor type, and State, FY89-91, annual rpt, 3544–11
Military prime contract awards, by detailed procurement category, FY88-91, annual rpt, 3544–18
Multinatl US firms and foreign affiliates finances and operations, by industry and country, 1989 benchmark survey, annual rpt, 2704–5
Occupational injury and illness rates, by SIC 2- to 4-digit industry, 1989-90, annual rpt, 6844–7
Occupational injury and illness rates, by SIC 2- to 4-digit industry, 1990, annual rpt, 6844–1
OECD trade, total and for 4 major countries, and US trade by country, by commodity, 1980-90, world area rpt series, 9116–1
Pacemaker lead implants, failures, and costs, by model, 1992 GAO rpt, 26131–103
Price indexes (producer), by stage of processing and detailed commodity, monthly rpt, 6762–6
Price indexes (producer), by stage of processing and detailed commodity, monthly 1991, annual rpt, 6764–2
Radiation from electronic devices, incidents by type of device, and FDA control activities, 1991, annual rpt, 4064–13
Science, engineering, and technical employment in manufacturing, by field and industry, 1989, triennial rpt, 9627–23
Shipments, trade, use, and firms, for electronic medical equipment, by product, 1991, annual Current Industrial Rpt, 2506–12.34
Shipments, trade, use, and firms, for instruments and related products by detailed type, 1991, annual Current Industrial Rpt, 2506–12.26
Tax (income) returns of corporations, income and tax items by asset size and detailed industry, 1989, annual rpt, 8304–4; 8304–21
VA health care services, needs, availability, structure, and funding, 1991 compilation of papers, 8608–9
see also Biologic drug products
see also Drugs
see also Prosthetics and orthotics
see also Vaccination and vaccines
see also X-rays

Medical technicians
see Allied health personnel
see Clinical laboratory technicians
see Health occupations

Medical transplants
Bone marrow donors, minority recruitment, Federal aid, transplants, costs, payment sources, 1987-92, GAO rpt, 26121–487
Data on health condition and care, indicators, 1988 natl survey, CD-ROM, 4147–10.184
Heart transplants and other cardiac surgical procedures, rehabilitation risks and benefit evaluation for Medicare coverage, 1991 rpt, 4186–10.8
Hospital deaths of Medicare patients, actual and expected rates by diagnosis, with hospital characteristics, by instn, FY90, annual State rpt series, 4654–14
Insurance (health) coverage and provisions of employee benefit plans, by plan type, for State and local govt employees, 1990, biennial rpt, 6784–21
Kidney end-stage disease treatment facilities approved by Medicare, dialysis and transplant services and ownership, 1991 annual listing, 4654–17
Kidney end-stage disease treatment facilities, Medicare enrollment and reimbursement, survival, and patient characteristics, 1984-90, annual rpt, 4654–16
Organ transplants, failures, deaths, and survival rates, by hospital, 1987-89, annual rpt series, 4104–17
Pacemaker lead implants, failures, and costs, by model, 1992 GAO rpt, 26131–103
Statistical Abstract of US, 1992 annual data compilation, 2324–1.3
VA health care services, needs, availability, structure, and funding, 1991 compilation of papers, 8608–9

Medicare
Actuarial studies, Medicare and OASDI future cost estimates and past experience analyses, series, 4706–1
Admin and research of Medicare, and HCFA affirmative action and accreditation programs, FY87, annual rpt, 4654–5
Advisory Commission on Social Security findings and recommendations on OASDHI and health care system status and reform, series, 10176–3
Advisory Commission on Social Security findings and recommendations on

OASDHI and health care system status and reform, 1991 quadrennial rpt, 10178–1
Assistance (financial and nonfinancial) of Fed Govt, 1992 base edition, annual listing, 104–5
Assistance of Fed Govt, by type, program, agency, and State, FY91, annual rpt, 2464–2
Beneficiaries and program operations, for Medicare and Medicaid, 1992, annual fact book, 4654–18
Benefits, beneficiary characteristics, and trust funds of OASDHI, Medicaid, SSI, and related programs, selected years 1937-90, annual rpt, 4744–3
Benefits overpayment recovery and judgment enforcement cases filed in Federal district courts, 1991, annual rpt, 18204–8.14
Budget of US, Bush Admin proposals, with detail for defense budgets, and historical data from FY34, FY93, 108–46
Budget of US, CBO analysis and review of FY93 budget by function, annual rpt, 26304–2
Budget of US, CBO analysis of revenue and spending alternatives and projections of economic indicators, FY93-97, annual rpt, 26304–3
Budget of US, House concurrent resolution, with spending and revenue targets, FY93 and projected to FY97, annual rpt, 21264–2
Budget of US, midsession review of FY93 budget, by function, annual rpt, 104–7
Budget of US, obligations and authority by function, agency, and program, with summaries and analyses, FY93, annual rpt, 104–2
Budget of US, receipts by source, outlays by agency and program, and balances, monthly rpt, 8102–3
Cancer patients hospitalized by purpose and body site, case classification effect on charges and length of stay, FY85, article, 4652–1.304
Costs, use, and structure of private and public health care delivery, indicators, issues, and foreign comparisons, 1960s-80s, technical paper, 8006–6.1
Coverage (universal) for health care, costs of alternative funding proposals, with background data, 1991 rpt, 26306–6.163
Coverage of new health care technologies under Medicare, risks and benefit evaluations, series, 4186–10
Coverage under health insurance and govt aid, with background data 1960s-91 and govt fiscal impacts projected to 2002, 26306–6.174
Coverage under health insurance, by insurance type and selected characteristics, 1985-90, 2546–20.23
Diabetes patients physician office visits, by characteristics of patient, physician, and visit, 1989, 4146–8.212
Expenditures for health care by businesses, households, and govts, 1965-90, annual article, 4652–1.309
Fed Govt civilian employees retirement, health, and life insurance benefits, coverage and finances of 4 programs, FY86-90, annual rpt, 9844–37.4
Finances and operations of programs under Ways and Means Committee jurisdiction, FY70s-91, annual rpt, 21784–11
Finances of Fed Govt, cash and debt transactions, daily tables, 8102–4
Financial and admin issues for Medicare, Inspector General rpts, series, 4006–11
Health Care Financing Review, quarterly journal, 4652–1
Health care services use and total and out-of-pocket spending, by type of insurance coverage and selected characteristics, 1987, 4186–8.24
Health condition and care indicators, 1950s-90 with health improvement and disease prevention goals for 1990, annual data compilation, 4144–11
Health maintenance organizations reimbursement by Medicare under prospective payment system, alternative methods for determining local payment, 1991, article, 4652–1.321
HHS financial aid, by program, recipient, State, and city, FY91, annual regional listings, 4004–3
Hispanic Americans health insurance coverage, by source, employment and poverty status, and origin, 1987-90, GAO rpt, 26131–97
Home drug infusion therapy use, equipment, industry finances, and Medicare coverage options, 1992 rpt, 26358–258
Home health care for Medicare and non-Medicare patients, services use and nursing visits, for Virginia, 1983-85, article, 4652–1.302
Hospital closures in 1990, operating characteristics, current use, and location, annual rpt, 4004–35
Hospital deaths of Medicare patients, actual and expected rates by diagnosis, with hospital characteristics, by instn, FY90, annual State rpt series, 4654–14
Hospital discharges and length of stay, by diagnosis, patient and instn characteristics, procedure performed, and payment source, 1990, annual rpt, 4147–13.112
Hospital discharges, by payment source, diagnosis, patient characteristics, and region, and procedures performed, 1990, 4146–8.221
Hospital financial performance under Medicare, 1977-89, article, 4652–1.315
Hospital Insurance trust fund finances, mid 1960s-91 and alternative projections to 2066, annual rpt, 4654–11
Hospital multiple admissions of Medicare beneficiaries, by reason and characteristics of instn and patient, 1985, 4008–117
Hospital reimbursement by Medicare under prospective payment system, analyses of alternative payment plans, series, 17206–1
Hospital reimbursement by Medicare under prospective payment system, and effect on services, finances, and beneficiary payments, 1980-91, annual rpt, 17204–2
Hospital reimbursement by Medicare under prospective payment system, case mix index and payments impacts of cost and charge weights, FY85-87, article, 4652–1.318
Hospital reimbursement by Medicare under prospective payment system, diagnosis related group code assignment and effects on care and instn finances, series, 4006–7
Hospital reimbursement by Medicare under prospective payment system, impacts on costs, industry structure and operations, and quality of care, series, 17206–2
Hospital reimbursement by Medicare under prospective payment system, impacts on operating costs and margins, 1980s, article, 4652–1.312
Hospital reimbursement by Medicare under prospective payment system, methodology, inputs, and data by diagnostic group, 1992 annual rpt, 17204–1
Hospital reimbursement by Medicare under prospective payment system, omitted services impacts on hospital revenue, FY85, article, 4652–1.316
Hospital reimbursement by Medicare under prospective payment system, rural area instns financial performance and impacts of PPS policy changes, 1991 rpt, 26306–6.164
Income (household) and poverty status under alternative income definitions, by recipient characteristics, 1979-91, annual Current Population Rpt, 2546–6.78
Internist office visits, by characteristics of patient, physician, and visit, 1989, 4146–8.214
Kidney end-stage disease treatment facilities approved by Medicare, dialysis and transplant services and ownership, 1991 annual listing, 4654–17
Kidney end-stage disease treatment facilities, Medicare enrollment and reimbursement, survival, and patient characteristics, 1984-90, annual rpt, 4654–16
Medicaid coverage of Medicare premiums and out-of-pocket costs, eligibility and participation, by State, 1991, hearing, 21148–67
Mental health care facilities, staff, patients, and finances, 1970s-91, biennial rpt, 4094–1
Mental health care of affective disorder patients, by patient and facility characteristics, 1986, 4506–3.49
Natl income and product accounts, comprehensive accounts and components, benchmark revisions, 1929-88, 2708–5
Natl income and product accounts, comprehensive accounts and components, *Survey of Current Business*, monthly rpt, 2702–1.26
Nursing home compliance with Medicare and Medicaid regulations, and patient characteristics, by facility, suspended annual State rpt series, 4654–15
OASDHI trust funds finances, FY91 with projections, annual article, 4742–1.314
Older persons ability to pay out of pocket health care costs, indicators by selected characteristics, 1984, article, 4742–1.307
Physicians payment by Medicare, impacts of reforms on services, and monitoring methods, 1992 annual rpt, 4004–34
Physicians payment by Medicare under fee schedule, adjustment factor recommendations, 1993, annual rpt, 4004–33
Physicians payment by Medicare under fee schedule, analyses of costs and other issues, series, 17266–1
Physicians payment by Medicare under fee schedule, impacts on beneficiaries, practice, and program finances, series, 17266–2

Physicians payment by Medicare under fee schedule, impacts on charges by specialty and State, 1992 and 1996, hearing, 25368–178
Physicians payment by Medicare under fee schedule, methodology with data by procedure and specialty, 1992, annual rpt, 17264–1
Physicians payment by Medicare under reasonable charge method, effect of customary charges in selected States, 1987-89, article, 4652–1.307
Physicians payment by Medicare, volume performance standard recommendations, FY93, annual rpt, 4004–32
Physicians visits, by patient and practice characteristics, diagnosis, and services provided, 1989, annual rpt, 4147–13.109
Population economic well-being indicators, by selected characteristics and household income and income-to-poverty ratio, 1984, 2546–20.22
Poverty status of population and families, by detailed characteristics, 1991, annual Current Population Rpt, 2546–6.77
Private health insurance denial because of poor health, coverage under public insurance, 1987, 4186–8.23
Public debt burden on future generations forecast under alternative tax, OASDI, and Medicare policies, 1992 working paper, 9377–9.137
Public opinion on OASDHI and health care system operations and reform issues, 1991 surveys, 10176–2.2
Research activities and grants of HCFA, by program, FY91, annual listing, 4654–10
Retirees health and other characteristics related to Medicare use and charges 2 years later, 1984, article, 4652–1.319
Statistical Abstract of US, 1992 annual data compilation, 2324–1.3
Supplemental private insurance for Medicare, loss ratio performance, by firm, 1988-89, GAO rpt, 26121–452
Supplementary Medical Insurance trust fund finances, mid 1960s-91 and projected to 2065, annual rpt, 4654–12
Tax collections under OASDHI, for Hospital Insurance, quarterly rpt, 4742–1.4
Traffic accident injury hospitalization, costs, and discharges, by payment source and State, mid 1980s-90, 7768–122
Trust funds finances of OASDHI, FY91 and projected to 2066, annual rpt, 4654–8
Trust funds financial condition, for Hospital Insurance, monthly rpt, 8102–9.15
Trust funds financial condition, for Medicare, monthly rpt, 8102–9.3
Trust funds of OASDI and Medicare, finances, economic assumptions, and outlook, with health care system reform issues, series, 10176–1
VA health care services, needs, availability, structure, and funding, 1991 compilation of papers, 8608–9
see also Old-Age, Survivors, Disability, and Health Insurance

Medicine
see also Anesthesiology
see also Aviation medicine
see also Biologic drug products
see also Chemotherapy
see also Chiropractic and naturopathy
see also Dentists and dentistry
see also Diseases and disorders
see also Drugs
see also Epidemiology and epidemiologists
see also Federal aid to medical education
see also Federal aid to medicine
see also Geriatrics
see also Health care reform
see also Health condition
see also Health education
see also Health facilities administration
see also Health facilities and services
see also Health insurance
see also Health maintenance organizations
see also Health occupations
see also Hospitals
see also Mammography
see also Medicaid
see also Medical assistance
see also Medical costs
see also Medical education
see also Medical ethics
see also Medical examinations and tests
see also Medical libraries
see also Medical malpractice
see also Medical regulation
see also Medical research
see also Medical supplies and equipment
see also Medical transplants
see also Medicare
see also Nurses and nursing
see also Nursing homes
see also Obstetrics and gynecology
see also Optometry
see also Orthopedics
see also Osteopathy
see also Pathology
see also Pediatrics
see also Pharmaceutical industry
see also Pharmacists and pharmacy
see also Physicians
see also Physiology
see also Podiatry
see also Prenatal care
see also Preventive medicine
see also Psychiatry
see also Public health
see also Regional medical programs
see also State funding for health and hospitals
see also Surgeons and surgery
see also Vaccination and vaccines
see also Veterinary medicine

Medin, Dean E.
"Birds of a Great Basin Sagebrush Habitat in East-Central Nevada", 1208–402

Mediterranean Sea
Tide height and time daily at coastal points, forecast 1993, annual rpt, 2174–2.4
Weather (marine) forecast areas, and broadcast schedules and stations worldwide, as of Sept 1992, annual rpt, 2184–3
Weather (marine) forecast broadcast schedules worldwide, periodic rpt, 2182–9

Medrich, Elliott A.
"International Mathematics and Science Assessments: What Have We Learned?", 4838–51
"Overview and Inventory of State Requirements for School Coursework and Attendance", 4838–52

Meeks, Ronald L.
"Indian Health Service and Tribal Hospital Inpatient Workload Summary for FY91 and Comparison with Previous Year", 4084–4
"Utilization of IHS and Tribal Direct and Contract General Hospitals, FY90 and U.S. Non-Federal Short-Stay Hospitals, CY89", 4084–5

Meers, Christine
"Crewing the Merchant Marine for Mobilization", 7708–5

Mehl, Georg M.
"U.S. Exports to Latin America and the Caribbean: A State by State Overview 1987-90", 2048–160
"U.S. Exports to Mexico: A State-by-State Overview, 1987-91", 2048–154

Mehra, Yash P.
"Deficits and Long-Term Interest Rates: An Empirical Note", 9389–19.33
"In Search of a Stable, Short-Run M1 Demand Function", 9389–1.303

Meisenheimer, Joseph R., II
"Job Market Slid in Early 1991, Then Struggled To Find Footing", 6722–1.312

Melancon, J. Michael
"Estimated Oil and Gas Reserves, Gulf of Mexico, Dec. 31, 1990", 5734–6

Melbourne, Fla.
see also under By City and By SMSA or MSA in the "Index by Categories"

Melick, William R.
"Purchasing Power Parity and Uncovered Interest Rate Parity: The U.S. 1974-90", 9366–7.279

Melons
see Fruit and fruit products

Membership organizations
American Historical Assn financial statements, and membership by State, 1990, annual rpt, 29574–2
Consumer spending, natl income and product account benchmark revisions, 1929-88, 2708–5
Consumer spending, natl income and product accounts, comprehensive accounts and components, *Survey of Current Business*, monthly rpt, 2702–1.25
County Business Patterns, 1989: employment, establishments, and payroll, by SIC 2- to 4-digit industry and county, annual State rpt series, 2326–8
County Business Patterns, 1990: employment, establishments, and payroll, by SIC 2- to 4-digit industry and county, annual State rpt series, 2326–6
CPI by component for US city average, and by selected metro area, region, and population size, monthly rpt, 6762–2
Election campaign-related internal communications of firms and assns, spending by organization, location, and candidate, 1991-92, biennial rpt, 9274–3
Employment, earnings, and hours, by SIC 1- to 4-digit industry, monthly 1989-Feb 1992, annual rpt, 6744–4
Mail volume to and from households, use, and views, by class, source, content, and household characteristics, FY87-90, annual rpt, 9864–10
Physical fitness clubs memberships for Federal employees, agency costs, and personnel directors views on OPM guidelines and admin leave use, 1991-92, GAO rpt, 26119–393

Police employment, spending, and operations, for State, city, county, and special district agencies, 1990, annual rpt, 6064–39
Railroad (Amtrak) finances, executive office travel expenses and staff years, and membership dues by assn, FY88-92, GAO rpt, 26113–573
Tax exempt organizations and employee plans listed on IRS masterfile, determinations, applications, and rulings, FY91, annual rpt, 8304–3.2
see also Associations
see also Cooperatives
see also Credit unions
see also Labor unions
see also Rural cooperatives

Memorials
see Monuments and memorials

Memphis, Tenn.
Economic and banking conditions, for Fed Reserve 8th District, quarterly rpt with articles, 9391–16
Freight (waterborne domestic and foreign) by commodity, traffic, and passengers, by port and waterway, 1989, annual rpt, 3754–3.2
Wages by occupation, for office and plant workers, 1991 survey, periodic MSA rpt, 6785–12.4
see also under By City and By SMSA or MSA in the "Index by Categories"

Men
AIDS cases by risk group, race, sex, age, State, and MSA, and deaths, quarterly rpt, 4202–9
AIDS virus-infected men notification of sexual partners, relation to risk behavior and other characteristics, 1988-89 local area study, article, 4042–3.310
Alcohol abuse impacts on sexual function, for men with cirrhosis of liver, 1992 article, 4482–1.307
Asian and Pacific Islands Americans social and economic characteristics, for West and total US, 1990-91, Current Population Report, 2546–1.462
Black Americans social and economic characteristics, for South and total US, 1991 and trends from 1950, annual Current Population Rpt, 2546–1.463
Cancer (breast) risk for women relation to incidence among male relatives, 1978-79, article, 4472–1.330
Cancer (colon) risk for men relation to weight-height index at college entrance and in middle age, and level of physical exercise, 1962-88 study, article, 4472–1.339
Cancer (prostate) risk relation to presence of genetic mutations, 1992 article, 4472–1.322
Census of Population and Housing, 1990: detailed geographic coverage, State CD-ROM series, 2551–9
Census of Population and Housing, 1990: population and housing characteristics, detailed geographic coverage, State CD-ROM series, 2551–10
Census of Population, 1990: population characteristics and living arrangements, by county, place, and urban-rural location, State rpt series, 2531–1
Census of Population, 1990: population characteristics and living arrangements, for Native American, urban, and metro areas, series, 2531–2
Crimes, arrests, and rates, by offense, offender characteristics, population size, and jurisdiction, 1991, annual rpt, 6224–2.1; 6224–2.2
Deaths and rates, by cause and selected social, demographic, and employment characteristics, 1979-85, natl longitudinal study, 4478–186
Deaths and rates, by detailed location, cause, and demographic characteristics, 1989, US Vital Statistics annual rpt, 4144–3
Drug, alcohol, and cigarette use, by selected characteristics, 1991 survey, annual rpt series, 4494–5
Health condition and care indicators, 1950s-90 with health improvement and disease prevention goals for 1990, annual data compilation, 4144–11
Homicide and suicide among young black men, by day of week, with comparisons to whites and women, 1979-85, article, 4042–3.323
Households composition, income, benefits, and labor force status, Survey of Income and Program Participation methodology, working paper series, 2626–10
Military draft registrants by State, FY91, annual rpt, 9744–1
Nurses employed by VA, men RNs, licensed practical nurses, and nursing assistants, by grade, quarterly rpt, 8602–6
OASDHI, Medicaid, SSI, and related programs benefits, beneficiary characteristics, and trust funds, selected years 1937-90, annual rpt, 4744–3
Pacific territories population and housing detailed characteristics, by location, 1990 Census of Population and Housing, series, 2551–8
Population economic well-being indicators, by selected characteristics and household income and income-to-poverty ratio, 1984, 2546–20.22
Prison and community-based facilities, population, employment, spending, and other characteristics, by State and for Fed Govt, 1990, quinquennial rpt, 6068–218
Prisoners, characteristics, and movements, by State, 1990, annual rpt, 6064–26
Prisoners in Federal and contract instns, by selected characteristics, region, and Federal instn, FY89, annual rpt, 6244–1.1
Science and Engineering Indicators, employment, education, R&D funding, and industry impacts, with foreign comparisons, 1960s-91, biennial rpt, 9624–10
Statistical Abstract of US, 1992 annual data compilation, 2324–1
Teenage boys AIDS risk behavior, sexual activity, and drug and condom use, 1988, article, 4042–3.313
Veterans (Vietnam) labor force status and earnings, by whether served in Southeast Asia, presence and severity of disability, and selected other characteristics, 1989, article, 6722–1.326
see also Families and households
see also under By Sex in the "Index by Categories"

Menke, Terri
"Universal Health Insurance Coverage Using Medicare's Payment Rates", 26306–6.163

Mental health and illness
Affective disorder patients mental health care services, by patient and facility characteristics, 1986, 4506–3.49
Alcohol-related disorder hospital discharges and length of stay, by diagnosis, sex, age, and race, 1979-89, 4486–1.16
Assistance (financial and nonfinancial) of Fed Govt, 1992 base edition, annual listing, 104–5
Biological factors in major mental disorders, with cases, research funding, and treatment methods, 1980s-91, 26356–9.4
Chronic fatigue syndrome physical and mental symptoms prevalence, by sex, 1981-84, article, 4042–3.354
Court insanity caseloads for Federal district courts, 1991, annual rpt, 18204–8.14; 18204–8.18; 18204–11
Deaths during 1986, decedents health condition, services use, habits, and social, employment, and other characteristics, 4147–20.19
Education (special) enrollment by age, staff, funding, and needs, by type of handicap and State, 1990/91, annual rpt, 4944–4
Family life and relationships quality and other issues, views of parents and children, 1990 survey, 15528–2
Head Start handicapped enrollment, by handicap, State, and for Indian and migrant programs, 1988/89, annual rpt, 4584–4
Health condition and care indicators, 1950s-90 with health improvement and disease prevention goals for 1990, annual data compilation, 4144–11
Homeless persons transitional housing and support services program, outcome relation to client characteristics and services, FY87-90, GAO rpt, 26113–549
Hospital discharges and length of stay, by diagnosis, patient and instn characteristics, procedure performed, and payment source, 1990, annual rpt, 4147–13.112
Hospital discharges and length of stay by region and diagnosis, and procedures performed, by age and sex, 1990, annual rpt, 4146–8.211
Hospital discharges and length of stay under old and new survey designs, by diagnosis, patient and instn characteristics, and procedure, Jan-Mar 1988, 4147–13.110
Hospital discharges by detailed diagnostic and procedure category, primary diagnosis, and length of stay, by age, sex, and region, 1990, annual rpt, 4147–13.111
Housing (public) for aged, placement of younger mentally disabled tenants, behavioral problems, and services, 1990 survey, GAO rpt, 26113–590
Immigrant and nonimmigrant visa applicants refused, and refusals overcome, by reason, FY90, annual rpt, 7184–1.3
Indian and Alaska Native youth health condition and behavioral patterns, by sex and grade, 1988-90, 4088–3
Indian Health Service, tribal, and contract facilities hospitalization, by diagnosis, age, sex, and service area, FY91, annual rpt, 4084–5

Indians and Alaska Natives education condition, indicators and comparisons to other groups, 1980s-90, 4808–42.1
Law enforcement officer assaults and deaths by circumstances, agency, victim and offender characteristics, and location, 1990, annual rpt, 6224–3
OECD members health care costs, hospital use, resources, and economic and health indicators, by country, 1960s-90, article, 4652–1.322
Physicians visits, by patient and practice characteristics, diagnosis, and services provided, 1989, annual rpt, 4147–13.109
Post-traumatic stress disorder cases among Persian Gulf veterans, and VA program use, by site, 1991, annual rpt, 8704–7
Post-traumatic stress disorder cases among veterans by period of service, and VA treatment and rehabilitation program operations and staff, by site, FY91, annual rpt, 8704–6
Prevalence of mental illness among adults by diagnosis, and health services use, 1980-83, article, 4042–3.368
Serious mental illness among adults, functional limitations, govt aid, drugs used, visits to professionals, and other characteristics, 1989, 4146–8.220
Veterans disability and death compensation cases of VA, by entitlement type, period of service, and sex, as of Mar 1992, annual rpt, 8604–13
Working age persons with disability, labor force status, type and cause of disability, and other characteristics, 1970s-89, chartbook, 4948–11
Youth health condition, risk factors, and preventive and treatment services use and availability, 1970s-80s, 26358–234.2; 26358–234.3
see also Alzheimer's disease
see also Commitment
see also Intelligence levels
see also Mental health facilities and services
see also Mental retardation
see also Neurological disorders
see also Psychiatry
see also Psychology
see also Stress
see also Suicide

Mental health facilities and services
Assistance (financial and nonfinancial) of Fed Govt, 1992 base edition, annual listing, 104–5
Child and maternal health condition and services use, indicators by age, race, and poverty status, 1988, 4478–197
Crime victim compensation and support service programs funding, by offense and State, FY88-90, biennial rpt, 6064–37
Criminal sentences for Federal offenses, guidelines by offense and circumstances, series, 17668–1
Deaths during 1986, decedents health condition, services use, habits, and social, employment, and other characteristics, 4147–20.19
Employment, earnings, and hours, by SIC 1- to 4-digit industry, monthly 1989-Feb 1992, annual rpt, 6744–4
Facilities for mental health care, staff, patients, and finances, 1970s-91, biennial rpt, 4094–1
Facilities, patients, services, and staff characteristics, *Statistical Notes* series, 4506–3
Health condition and care indicators, 1950s-90 with health improvement and disease prevention goals for 1990, annual data compilation, 4144–11
HHS financial aid, by program, recipient, State, and city, FY91, annual regional listings, 4004–3
Homeless persons aid programs of Fed Govt, program descriptions and funding, by agency and State, FY87-91, annual GAO rpt, 26104–21
Homeless persons transitional housing and support services, HUD grants by community, 1991, press release, 5006–3.80
Homeless persons with mental illness, HUD rent assistance and support services grants, by recipient, 1992, press release, 5006–3.89
Hospital deaths of Medicare patients, actual and expected rates by diagnosis, with hospital characteristics, by instn, FY90, annual State rpt series, 4654–14
Institutionalized population and persons in group quarters, by sex, race, county, place, and urban-rural location, 1990 Census of Population, State rpt series, 2531–1
Insurance (health) coverage and provisions of employee benefit plans, by plan type, for State and local govt employees, 1990, biennial rpt, 6784–21
Medicaid beneficiaries and payments, and Medicare facilities, mid 1960s-90, annual rpt, 4744–3.5; 4744–3.6
Medicaid coverage, eligibility, and payment provisions of States, as of March 1992, annual rpt, 4654–19
Medicare admin and research, and HCFA affirmative action and accreditation programs, FY87, annual rpt, 4654–5
Medicare and Medicaid beneficiaries and program operations, 1992, annual fact book, 4654–18
Medicare reimbursement of hospitals under prospective payment system, and effect on services, finances, and beneficiary payments, 1980-91, annual rpt, 17204–2
Medicare reimbursement of hospitals under prospective payment system, methodology, inputs, and data by diagnostic group, 1992 annual rpt, 17204–1
Military health care benefits and costs under Civilian Health and Medical Program of Uniformed Services, FY85-90, annual chartbook, 3504–23
Prison and community-based facilities, population, employment, spending, and other characteristics, by State and for Fed Govt, 1990, annual rpt, 6064–26.3
Quality standards and review for health care facilities excluded from Medicare prospective payment system, certification, accreditation, and licensing, 1991 survey, 17206–2.41
Serious mental illness among adults, functional limitations, govt aid, drugs used, visits to professionals, and other characteristics, 1989, 4146–8.220
Statistical Abstract of US, 1992 annual data compilation, 2324–1.3
VA health care facilities inpatient deaths, results of quality of care reviews, 1986 and 1989, 8708–1
VA health care services, needs, availability, structure, and funding, 1991 compilation of papers, 8608–9
VA hospitals admissions and discharges by diagnosis, facilities operating costs, and other VA activities, FY91, annual rpt, 8604–3.2
Veterans (Persian Gulf) post-traumatic stress disorder cases, and VA program use, by site, 1991, annual rpt, 8704–7
Veterans health care, patients, visits, costs, and operating beds, by VA and contract facility, and region, quarterly rpt, 8602–4
Veterans post-traumatic stress cases by period of service, and VA treatment and rehabilitation program operations and staff, by site, FY91, annual rpt, 8704–6
Youth health condition, risk factors, and preventive and treatment services use and availability, 1970s-80s, 26358–234.2
see also Psychiatry

Mental retardation
Birth defect records use to forecast school-age mental retardation cases, accuracy, 1992 article, 4042–3.327
Disability and work limitations of persons with chronic health conditions, by condition, age, and sex, 1983-86, 4946–1.2
Education (special) enrollment by age, staff, funding, and needs, by type of handicap and State, 1990/91, annual rpt, 4944–4
Facilities for mental health, partial care services and patient characteristics, by instn type and State, 1970s-88, 4506–3.51
Head Start handicapped enrollment, by handicap, State, and for Indian and migrant programs, 1988/89, annual rpt, 4584–4
Health care providers communication skills with mentally retarded patients, training materials effectiveness, 1992 article, 4042–3.328
HHS financial aid, by program, recipient, State, and city, FY91, annual regional listings, 4004–3
Immigrant and nonimmigrant visa applicants refused, and refusals overcome, by reason, FY90, annual rpt, 7184–1.3
Institutionalized population and persons in group quarters, by sex, race, county, place, and urban-rural location, 1990 Census of Population, State rpt series, 2531–1
Job training demonstration project for mentally retarded SSI beneficiaries, participant characteristics, 1985-87, article, 4742–1.301
Medicaid coverage, eligibility, and payment provisions of States, as of March 1992, annual rpt, 4654–19
Medicaid coverage, funding, and costs, with reform recommendations, mid 1960s-92, 10048–83
Medicaid outlay differentials among States, with data by service type and eligibility category, FY89, article, 9373–1.303
Statistical Abstract of US, 1992 annual data compilation, 2324–1.3

Merchant marine
see Merchant seamen
see Ships and shipping
Merchant seamen
Employment, by type and ownership of vessel and license status of sailor, monthly rpt, 7702–1
Employment shipboard, shipyard, and longshore, FY90-91, annual rpt, 7704–14.3
Fed Govt civilian employees work-years, pay rates, and benefits use and costs, by agency, FY90, annual rpt, 9844–31
Group quarters for ship crews, population by race and sex, 1990 Census of Population, State rpt series, 2531–1
Immigration and Naturalization Service illegal alien and narcotics activities, FY84-91, annual rpt, 6264–2.5
Labor supply, wartime needs, training, and sources, for merchant ship crews, 1970s-90 and alternative projections to 2000, 7708–5
Statistical Abstract of US, 1992 annual data compilation, 2324–1.22
Mercury pollution
California OCS oil and gas dev impacts on water quality, marine life, and sediments, by site, 1986-90, annual rpt, 5734–11
Coastal and estuarine pollutant concentrations in fish, shellfish, and environment, series, 2176–3
Great Lakes industrial water pollution emissions, comparison of State, EPA, Intl Joint Commission, and Ontario standards, 1991 rpt, 14648–29
Industrial hazardous substances releases and reduction methods under EPA regulation, by chemical, source, industry, and location, 1989, annual rpt, 9234–6
Industrial hazardous substances releases and reduction methods under EPA regulation, with chemical stocks and use, facility directory, 1987-89, annual CD-ROM, 9234–7
Marine mammals tissue pollutant concentrations, by species and pollutant type, for Alaska, 1987-91, 2218–87
Tax (excise) on hazardous waste generation and disposal, rates, and firms filing returns, by substance type, 1989, annual article, 8302–2.303
Water quality, chemistry, hydrology, and other characteristics, local area studies, series, 5666–27
Water supply and quality in streams and lakes, and groundwater levels in wells, by drainage basin, 1990, annual State rpt series, 5666–10
Water supply and quality in streams and lakes, and groundwater levels in wells, by drainage basin, 1990-91, annual CD-ROM, 5664–18
Water supply and quality in streams and lakes, and groundwater levels in wells, by drainage basin, 1991, annual State rpt series, 5666–12
Mergers
see Business acquisitions and mergers
Meridian Corp.
"Southeastern Regional Biomass Energy Program. Six Year Report: 1983-89", 9806–9.11
Merit Systems Protection Board
Appeals decisions on Fed Govt personnel actions, by agency and region, FY91, annual rpt, 9494–2
Budget of US, authoritative financial statements with appropriations, outlays, and receipts, by category and agency, FY91, annual rpt, 8104–2.2
Budget of US, obligations and authority by function, agency, and program, with summaries and analyses, FY93, annual rpt, 104–2
Canada and US civil service merit systems operations, pay, appointments, and promotions, late 1980s-91, 9498–16
Labor unions recognized in Fed Govt, agreements and membership by agency and facility, as of Jan 1991, biennial listing, 9844–14
Personnel Mgmt Office merit system oversight and enforcement activities, series, 9496–2
Procurement operations of Fed Govt, employees job performance, and views on policies and practices, 1991 survey, 9498–17
Staffing, finances, and activities of the Merit Systems Protection Board, FY91, annual rpt, 9494–5
Supervisors (first-line) in Fed Govt, performance ratings by self, superiors, and subordinates, 1991 survey, 9498–15
Merriner, J. V.
"Assessment and Management of Atlantic and Gulf Menhaden Stocks", 2162–1.303
Mertens, Henry W.
"Effects of Color Vision Deficiency on Detection of Color-Highlighted Targets in a Simulated Air Traffic Control Display", 7506–10.102
"Performance of Color-Dependent Tasks of Air Traffic Control Specialists as a Function of Type and Degree of Color Vision Deficiency", 7506–10.123
"Validity of Clinical Color Vision Tests for Air Traffic Control Specialists", 7506–10.125
Merzel, Cheryl
"New Jersey's Medicaid Waiver for Acquired Immunodeficiency Syndrome", 4652–1.317
Mesa, Ariz.
Housing and households characteristics, unit and neighborhood quality, and journey to work by MSA location, for 11 MSAs, 1985 survey, supplement, 2485–8
Housing and households detailed characteristics, and unit and neighborhood quality, by location, 1989 survey, MSA rpt, 2485–6.9
Mester, Loretta J.
"Debt Covenants and Renegotiation", 9387–8.272
"Efficiency in the Savings and Loan Industry", 9387–8.277
"Further Evidence Concerning Expense Preference and the Fed", 9387–8.267
"Perpetual Signaling with Imperfectly Correlated Costs", 9387–8.271
"Quality and Risk-Adjusted Cost Function for Banks: Evidence on the 'Too-Big-To-Fail' Doctrine", 9387–8.260
"When Do Regulators Close Banks? When Should They?", 9387–8.263
Metabolic and endocrine diseases
Cases of acute and chronic conditions, disability, absenteeism, and health services use, by selected characteristics, 1990, annual rpt, 4147–10.182; 4147–10.183
HHS financial aid, by program, recipient, State, and city, FY91, annual regional listings, 4004–3
Hospital discharges and length of stay, by diagnosis, patient and instn characteristics, procedure performed, and payment source, 1990, annual rpt, 4147–13.112
Hospital discharges and length of stay by region and diagnosis, and procedures performed, by age and sex, 1990, annual rpt, 4146–8.211
Hospital discharges and length of stay under old and new survey designs, by diagnosis, patient and instn characteristics, and procedure, Jan-Mar 1988, 4147–13.110
Hospital discharges by detailed diagnostic and procedure category, primary diagnosis, and length of stay, by age, sex, and region, 1990, annual rpt, 4147–13.111
Indian Health Service, tribal, and contract facilities hospitalization, by diagnosis, age, sex, and service area, FY91, annual rpt, 4084–5
OECD members health care costs, hospital use, resources, and economic and health indicators, by country, 1960s-90, article, 4652–1.322
Physicians visits, by patient and practice characteristics, diagnosis, and services provided, 1989, annual rpt, 4147–13.109
Pollutants health effects, concentrations in food and environment, sources, human intake, and regulation, series, 9186–8
see also Allergies
see also Diabetes
see also Immunity disorders
see also Nutrition and malnutrition
see also under By Disease in the "Index by Categories"
Metals and metal industries
Alaska minerals resources, production, oil and gas leases, reserves, and exploratory wells, with maps and bibl, 1990, annual rpt, 5664–11
Bismuth reserves, production, and US trade, by country, and US consumption by end use, 1980s-90, 5608–175
Building materials production and PPI, by type, quarterly rpt, 2042–1.5; 2042–1.6
Business statistics, detailed data for major industries and economic indicators, *Survey of Current Business*, monthly rpt, 2702–1.16
Business statistics, detailed data for major industries and economic indicators, 1960-91, *Survey of Current Business* biennial supplement, 2704–1
Capital expenditures for plant and equipment, by major industry group, quarterly rpt, 2502–2
Coin and medal production by denomination, capacity, and facility improvement funding, by mint, with monetary metals purchases, projected FY92-96, hearing, 21248–164
Coin production and monetary metals use and holdings of US Mint, by metal type, FY91, annual rpt, 8204–1

Collective bargaining agreements expiring during year, and workers covered, by firm, union, industry group, and State, 1992, annual rpt, 6784–9
County Business Patterns, 1989: employment, establishments, and payroll, by SIC 2- to 4-digit industry and county, annual State rpt series, 2326–8
County Business Patterns, 1990: employment, establishments, and payroll, by SIC 2- to 4-digit industry and county, annual State rpt series, 2326–6
Cuba trade, by commodity and country, mid 1980s-91, 9118–8
DOE R&D projects and funding at natl labs, universities, and other instns, FY91, annual summary rpt, 3004–18.3
Drug abuse screening and employee aid programs activities and policies in mining, by mineral and firm size, 1989, 6668–8
Employment, earnings, and hours, by SIC 1- to 4-digit industry, monthly 1989-Feb 1992, annual rpt, 6744–4
Employment of minorities and women, by occupation, SIC 1- to 3-digit industry, State, and MSA, 1991, annual rpt, 9244–1
Employment, unemployment, and labor force characteristics, by region and census div, 1991, annual rpt, 6744–7.1
Energy use and prices, by fuel type and manufacturing industry, 1974-88, 3166–15.3
Energy use and prices for manufacturing industries, 1988 survey, series, 3166–13
Explosives and blasting agents use, by type, industry, and State, 1991, Mineral Industry Surveys, annual rpt, 5614–22
Exports and imports between US and outlying areas, by detailed commodity and mode of transport, 1991, annual rpt, 2424–11
Exports and imports of US, by country and detailed commodity, monthly rpt, 2422–12
Exports and imports of US by country, and trade shifts by commodity, 1991, annual rpt, 9884–25
Exports and imports of US, by Harmonized System 6-digit commodity and country, 1991, annual rpt, 2424–13
Exports and imports of US, by selected country, country group, and commodity group, 1991, annual rpt, 2044–37
Exports and imports of US, by transport mode, country, and SITC 1- to 3-digit commodity, 1991, annual rpt, 2424–12
Exports, imports, and balances of US for manufactured goods, by SITC 2-digit commodity and country, quarterly rpt, 2042–35
Exports, imports, tariffs, and industry operating data for minerals and metals industries, commodity rpt series, 9885–13
Exports of US, detailed commodities by country, monthly CD-ROM, 2422–13
Exports of US, detailed Schedule B commodities with countries of destination, 1991, annual rpt, 2424–10
Financial and economic performance indicators and indexes for metals industries, by commodity, monthly rpt, 5602–5
Foreign and US minerals industries operations, trends, and projections for selected countries, series, 5606–5
Foreign and US minerals supply under alternative market conditions, reserves, and background industry data, series, 5606–4
Foreign countries mineral production, reserves, and industry role in domestic economy and world supply, world area and country rpt series, 5606–1
Foreign direct investment in US, by industry group and world area, 1989-91, annual article, 2702–1.331
Foreign direct investment of US, by industry group and world area, 1989-91, annual article, 2702–1.332
Freight (waterborne domestic and foreign) by commodity, traffic, and passengers, by port and waterway, 1989, annual rpt, 3754–3
Futures and options trading volume, by commodity and exchange, FY91, annual rpt, 11924–2
Futures contracts margin requirements for metals and stock index futures, impact on prices, volatility, and trading activity, 1970s-90, technical paper, 9385–8.127
Futures trading in selected commodities and financial instruments and indexes, for NYC, Chicago, and other markets activity, biweekly rpt, 11922–5
Hazardous substances industrial releases and reduction methods under EPA regulation, by chemical, source, industry, and location, 1989, annual rpt, 9234–6
Hazardous substances industrial releases and reduction methods under EPA regulation, with chemical stocks and use, facility directory, 1987-89, annual CD-ROM, 9234–7
Imports, exports, and employment impacts, by SIC 2- to 4-digit industry and commodity, quarterly rpt, 2322–2
Imports of US, detailed commodities by country, monthly CD-ROM, 2422–14
Imports of US given duty-free treatment for value of US material sent abroad, by commodity and country, 1987-90, annual rpt, 9884–14
Input-output structure of US economy, detailed interindustry transactions for 84 industries, and components of final demand, 1987, annual article, 2702–1.316
Input-output structure of US economy, detailed interindustry transactions for 541 industries, and components of final demand, 1982 benchmark data, 2708–17
Labor productivity, indexes of output, hours, and employment by SIC 2- to 4-digit industry, 1967-90, annual rpt, 6824–1.3
Machinery for metalworking, shipments, unfilled orders, trade, and use, quarterly Current Industrial Rpt, 2506–12.12
Magnesium from Canada, injury to US industry from foreign subsidized and less than fair value imports, investigation with background financial and operating data, 1992 rpt, 9886–19.86
Manufacturing annual survey, 1990: finances and operations, by SIC 2- to 4-digit industry, series, 2506–14
Manufacturing census, 1987: concentration of largest firms measured by value added, and for shipments by SIC 2- and 4-digit industry, subject rpt, 2497–6
Manufacturing census, 1987: shipments of manufacturers products, by customer class and SIC 2- and 4-digit industry, subject rpt, 2497–4
Manufacturing corporations financial statements, by selected SIC 2- to 3-digit industry, quarterly rpt, 2502–1
Manufacturing finances and operations, by SIC 2- to 4-digit industry, forecast 1992, annual rpt, 2044–28
Manufacturing industries operations and performance, analytical rpt series, 2506–16
Manufacturing production, shipments, inventories, orders, and pollution control costs, periodic Current Industrial Rpt series, 2506–3
Mexico imports from US, by industry and State, 1987-91, 2048–154
Military prime contract awards, by detailed procurement category, FY88-91, annual rpt, 3544–18
Mineral Industry Surveys, commodity reviews of production, trade, stocks, and use, monthly rpt series, 5612–1
Mineral Industry Surveys, commodity reviews of production, trade, stocks, and use, quarterly rpt series, 5612–2
Mineral Industry Surveys, commodity reviews of production, trade, use, and industry operations, advance annual rpt series, 5614–5
Mineral Industry Surveys, State reviews of production, 1991, preliminary annual rpt, 5614–6
Minerals Yearbook, Vol 1, 1989: commodity reviews of production, use, trade, prices, and mining operations, annual rpt, 5604–33
Minerals Yearbook, Vol 1, 1990: commodity reviews of production, reserves, supply, use, and trade, annual rpt series, 5604–20
Minerals Yearbook, Vol 1, 1991: commodity reviews of production, reserves, supply, use, and trade, annual rpt series, 5604–15
Minerals Yearbook, Vol 2, 1989: State reviews of production and sales by commodity, and business activity, annual rpt series, 5604–16
Minerals Yearbook, Vol 2, 1990: State reviews of production and sales by commodity, and business activity, annual rpt series, 5604–22
Minerals Yearbook, Vol 3, 1989: foreign country reviews of production, trade, and policy, by commodity, annual rpt, 5604–35
Multinatl firms US affiliates finances and operations, by industry, country of parent firm, and State, 1987, 2708–48
Multinatl firms US affiliates, finances, and operations, by industry, world area of parent firm, and State, 1989-90, annual rpt, 2704–4
Multinatl US firms and foreign affiliates finances and operations, by industry and country, 1989 benchmark survey, annual rpt, 2704–5
Multinatl US firms foreign affiliates, income statement items by asset size, industry, and country, 1988, biennial article, 8302–2.322

Natl income and product accounts, comprehensive accounts and components, benchmark revisions, 1929-88, 2708–5
Natl income and product accounts, comprehensive accounts and components, *Survey of Current Business*, monthly rpt, 2702–1.29
Occupational deaths in mining accidents, by circumstances and selected victim characteristics, semiannual rpt series, 6662–3
Occupational injuries and incidence, employment, and hours in metal mines and related operations, 1990, annual rpt, 6664–3
Occupational injuries by circumstances, employment, and hours, for mining industries by type of operation and State, quarterly rpt, 6662–1
Occupational injury and illness rates and lost workdays, by State, for structural metal fabrication industry, 1989, article, 6722–1.301
Occupational injury and illness rates and lost workdays, for selected industries, 1978-89, compilation of papers, 6728–41
Occupational injury and illness rates, by SIC 2- to 4-digit industry, 1989-90, annual rpt, 6844–7
Occupational injury and illness rates, by SIC 2- to 4-digit industry, 1990, annual rpt, 6844–1
OECD trade, total and for 4 major countries, and US trade by country, by commodity, 1980-90, world area rpt series, 9116–1
Pacific territories population and housing detailed characteristics, by location, 1990 Census of Population and Housing, series, 2551–8
Price indexes (producer), by stage of processing and detailed commodity, monthly rpt, 6762–6
Price indexes (producer), by stage of processing and detailed commodity, monthly 1991, annual rpt, 6764–2
Production and prices of primary metals mining byproducts, by commodity, 1965-90, 5608–170
Production, prices, trade, use, employment, tariffs, and stockpiles, by mineral, with foreign comparisons, 1987-91, annual rpt, 5604–18
Production, shipments, trade, stocks, and material used, for primary metals by product, periodic Current Industrial Rpt series, 2506–10
Production, trade, use, and foreign investment in US industry, for minerals, 1985-90 and projected to 2000, annual rpt, 5304–5
Public lands minerals resources and availability, State rpt series, 5606–7
Puerto Rico and other US possessions corporations income tax returns, income and tax items, and employment, by selected industry, 1989, article, 8302–2.326
Science, engineering, and technical employment in manufacturing, by field and industry, 1989, triennial rpt, 9627–23
Shipments, trade, and inventories of intermediate metal products, periodic Current Industrial Rpt series, 2506–11
Soviet Union minerals production and exports, by commodity and Republic, 1975-90, annual rpt, 5604–39
Statistical Abstract of US, 1992 annual data compilation, 2324–1.25; 2324–1.27
Stockpiling of strategic material, inventories and needs, by commodity, 1992, annual rpt, 3544–37
Tariff Schedule of US, classifications and rates of duty by detailed imported commodity, 1993 base edition, 9886–13
Tax (income) returns of corporations, income and tax items by asset size and detailed industry, 1989, annual rpt, 8304–4; 8304–21
Tax (income) returns of corporations with foreign tax credit, income and tax items by industry group, 1988, biennial article, 8302–2.316
Tax (income) returns of sole proprietorships, income statement items, by industry group, 1990, annual article, 8302–2.317; 8302–2.320
see also Abrasive materials
see also Aluminum and aluminum industry
see also Copper and copper industry
see also Foundries
see also Gold
see also Hardware
see also Iron and steel industry
see also Lead and lead industry
see also Lead poisoning and pollution
see also Mercury pollution
see also Offshore mineral resources
see also Scrap metals
see also Silver
see also Stockpiling
see also Strategic materials
see also Tin and tin industry
see also Trace metals
see also Uranium
see also Zinc and zinc industry
see also under By Commodity in the "Index by Categories"
see also under By Industry in the "Index by Categories"

Meteorological satellites
Fed Govt weather services activities and funding, by agency, planned FY92-93, annual rpt, 2144–2
Glaciology intl research summaries, methodology, and bibls, series, 2156–18
Hurricanes and tropical storms in Pacific and Indian Oceans, paths and surveillance, 1991, annual rpt, 3804–8
Launchings and other activities of NASA and Soviet Union, with flight data, 1957-91, annual rpt, 9504–6.1
Microwave radiometry applications for satellites, research summaries and bibl, 1992 rpt, 2156–18.24
Ocean weather forecast areas, and broadcast schedules and stations worldwide, as of Sept 1992, annual rpt, 2184–3
Ocean weather forecast broadcast schedules worldwide, periodic rpt, 2182–9

Meteorology
Agricultural research funding and staffing for USDA, State agencies, and other instns, by topic, FY91, annual rpt, 1744–2
Atlantic Oceanographic and Meteorological Lab research activities and bibl, FY91, annual rpt, 2144–19
Carbon dioxide in atmosphere, DOE R&D programs and funding at natl labs, universities, and other instns, FY92, annual summary rpt, 3004–18.10
Data collection and analysis issues for weather conditions and forecasts, 1991 annual conf, 2184–10
Fed Govt weather services activities and funding, by agency, planned FY92-93, annual rpt, 2144–2
Forecasts accuracy, evaluations for US, UK, and European systems, quarterly rpt, 2182–8
Glaciology intl research summaries, methodology, and bibls, series, 2156–18
Great Lakes Environmental Research Lab activities, FY91 annual rpt, 2144–26
Labor demand, turnover, and training completions, by detailed occupation, 1990 and projected to 2005, biennial rpt, 6744–3
Occupational Outlook Handbook, 1992-93, biennial rpt, 6744–1
Oceanographic research and distribution activities of World Data Center A by country, and cruises by ship, 1990, annual rpt, 2144–15
Pacific Marine Environmental Lab research activities and bibl, FY91, annual rpt, 2144–21
Pacific Ocean temperature, current, and wind, by equatorial eastern site and depth, 1983-87, 2148–62
see also Global climate change
see also Meteorological satellites
see also Stratosphere
see also Weather
see also Weather control

Methane
see Natural gas and gas industry

Methanol
see Alcohol fuels

Methodology
Agricultural Economics Research, quarterly journal, 1502–3
Agricultural research funding and staffing for USDA, State agencies, and other instns, by topic, FY91, annual rpt, 1744–2
AIDS virus infection among drug abusers, disease progression longitudinal studies, 1987 conf papers, 4498–79
Air traffic and other aviation activity forecasts of FAA, 1992 annual conf, 7504–28
Alaska OCS environmental conditions and oil dev impacts, compilation of papers, series, 2176–1
Astronomical tables, time conversion factors, and listing of observatories worldwide, 1993, annual rpt, 3804–7
Aviation medicine research and test results, technical rpt series, 7506–10
Budget deficit forecasting accuracy, contributing factors, and analysis of major programs, FY91, annual GAO rpt, 26104–23
Canada and US current accounts balance reconciliation adjustment methodology, with background data, 1990-91, article, 2702–1.341
Disease and injury prevention activities effectiveness, evaluation methodologies, 1992 rpt, 4206–2.53

Drug abuse prevention services evaluation, methodological issues, 1991 conf, 4498-78
Electric utilities conservation programs, energy savings measurement methodology, 1991, compilation of papers, 3308-102
Employment, earnings, and hours benchmarks by SIC 2- to 4-digit industry, 1984-91, and revised seasonal adjustment factors by major industry group, 1992, semiannual article, 6742-2.306
Employment, earnings, and hours, seasonal adjustment factors by major industry group, Nov 1991-Apr 1992, semiannual article, 6742-2.301
Energy natl strategy plans for conservation, R&D, security, and pollution reduction, technical rpt series, 3006-13
Energy use and conservation, survey results and methodology, series, 3166-15
Energy use, costs, and conservation, and household and housing characteristics, survey rpt series, 3166-7
Estuary environmental conditions, research results and methodology, series, 2176-7
Farm production value-added calculation methodology, with background data, 1988-91, article, 1541-1.321
Finance (intl) and financial policy, and external factors affecting US economy, technical paper series, 9366-7
Financial and economic analysis and forecasting methodology, technical paper series, 9366-6; 9377-9
Financial and economic analysis of banking and nonbanking sectors, working paper series, 9381-10
Financial instns loan loss computations for tax returns under alternative methods, 1991 rpt, 8008-157
Fires on public lands, prevention activities evaluation methods and effectiveness, 1989 survey, 1208-417
Fires on wildlands, ecology, mgmt, cultural impacts, and historic patterns, 1990 conf, 1208-415
Foreign countries economic and social conditions, working paper series, 2326-18
GDP use to measure real output, and effect of alternative price weights, 1959-90, article, 2702-1.314
Glaciology intl research summaries, methodology, and bibls, series, 2156-18
Global climate change contributing pollutants, emissions by monitoring site and country, and temperature change by world area and US region, 1860s-1990, annual rpt, 3004-33
Global climate change impacts on mountain grassland vegetation, monitoring study results, 1969 and 1988, 1208-425
Great Lakes industrial water pollution emissions, comparison of State, EPA, Intl Joint Commission, and Ontario standards, 1991 rpt, 14648-29
Health care spending by funding source, 1990, with trends and indexes by service type from 1960, article, 4652-1.323
Health condition and quality of life measurement, rpts and other info sources, quarterly listing, 4122-1
High school dropout rates, and subsequent completion, by student and school characteristics, alternative estimates, 1991, annual rpt, 4834-23
Hospital deaths of Medicare patients, actual and expected rates by diagnosis, with hospital characteristics, by instn, FY90, annual State rpt series, 4654-14
Households net worth distribution under alternative sample weighting systems to account for inconsistency in survey design and response rates, 1992 rpt, 9368-91
Inflation measured by CPI and Personal Consumption Expenditure Index, under alternative weighting systems, monthly rpt, periodic article, 6762-2
Input-output model of BEA, regional multipliers by industry and State, and methodology, 1992 guide, 2708-47
Juvenile facilities compensatory education programs activities, participant and staff characteristics, and outcomes, 1991 rpts, 4808-40
Labor force and economic data series of BLS, collection, analysis, and presentation methods, by program, 1992 rpt, 6888-1
Labor Intl Affairs Bur research contracts, FY83-91, annual listing, 6364-1
Labor separations, replacement rates, and related job openings, estimation procedures with data by occupation, age, and sex, late 1980s and projected to 2005, 6748-84
Meat production, inventory, and price forecasts of USDA, accuracy, 1980s, GAO rpt, 26131-93
Medicare payment of physicians under fee schedule, analyses of costs and other issues, series, 17266-1
Medicare payment of physicians under fee schedule, impacts on beneficiaries, practice, and program finances, series, 17266-2
Medicare payment of physicians under fee schedule, methodology with data by procedure and specialty, 1992, annual rpt, 17264-1
Medicare reimbursement of hospitals under prospective payment system, analyses of alternative payment plans, series, 17206-1
Medicare reimbursement of hospitals under prospective payment system, impacts on costs, industry structure and operations, and quality of care, series, 17206-2
Medicare reimbursement of hospitals under prospective payment system, methodology, inputs, and data by diagnostic group, 1992 annual rpt, 17204-1
Natl income and product accounts benchmark revisions, methodological changes and revised summary tables, 1959-91, article, 2702-1.302
Natl income and product accounts benchmark revisions of personal income, and reconciliation with adjusted gross income, 1959-90, article, 2702-1.318
Natl income and product accounts revisions, methodology, and data sources, various periods 1989-92, annual article, 2702-1.324
OASDI and Medicare trust fund finances, economic assumptions, outlook, and health care system reform issues, series, 10176-1
Occupational injury and illness rates by circumstances and establishment size, and methodology for computing rates, industry rpt series, 6886-4
Producer Price Index use in sales contract escalation clauses, methodology, 1991 rpt, 6888-23
Production, price, and supply forecasts used for USDA commodity program outlays, accuracy, 1975-88, GAO rpt, 26131-94
Property inventory and classification methods for higher education instns, 1992 guidelines, 4848-48
Small business use of Census Bur economic data in planning decisions, case studies, 1991 rpt, 2628-33
Social security programs and related issues, technical paper series, 4746-26
Statistical Abstract of US, 1992 annual data compilation, 2324-1
Timber in North Central States, harvest estimation methodology, 1991 rpt, 1208-419
Timber in Rocky Mountains and southwest US, old growth forests ecology, mgmt, and research methods, 1992 conf, 1208-421
Unemployment insurance programs of States and Fed Govt, benefits adequacy, and work disincentives, series, 6406-6
Uranium tailings at inactive mills, remedial action proposals, costs, site characteristics, and environmental, socioeconomic, and health impacts, series, 3356-4
Weather forecasts accuracy evaluations, for US, UK, and European systems, quarterly rpt, 2182-8
Wildlife habitats assessment use of forest inventories, with data for northern coastal California, as of 1985, 1208-414
see also Classifications
see also Demonstration and pilot projects
see also Economic and econometric models
see also Mathematic models and modeling
see also Seasonal adjustment factors
see also Statistical programs and activities
see also under names of individual surveys (listed under Surveys)

Metropolitan areas
see Central cities
see Metropolitan Statistical Areas
see Suburbs
see Urban areas
see under By City, By SMSA or MSA, and By Urban-Rural and Metro-Nonmetro in the "Index by Categories"

Metropolitan Statistical Areas
American Housing Survey, data coverage, products, and metro areas surveyed 1974-94, 2328-89
Census Bur geographic levels of data coverage, maps, and reference products, 1992 rpt, 2308-67
Census of Housing, 1990: summary unit characteristics, by householder race and age, county, place, and urban-rural location, State rpt series, 2471-1
Census of Population and Housing, 1990: population and housing characteristics, detailed geographic coverage, State CD-ROM series, 2551-10
Census of Population and Housing, 1990: summary characteristics, households, and land area, by region, State, MSA, and city, US rpt, 2551-1.1
Census of Population, 1990: population characteristics and living arrangements, by county, place, and urban-rural location, State rpt series, 2531-1

Consumer Income, socioeconomic characteristics of persons, families, and households, detailed cross-tabulations, Current Population Rpt series, 2546–6
Crimes, arrests by offender characteristics, and rates, by offense, and law enforcement employees, by population size and jurisdiction, 1991, annual rpt, 6224–2
Definitions of MSAs and central cities, and revisions, 1992, annual listing, 104–32
Govt finances, structure, and service delivery in large metro areas, local area rpt series, 10046–9
Housing starts and completions authorized by building permits in 40 MSAs, quarterly rpt, 2382–9
Income (personal) per capita and by source, and employment, by industry div, State, MSA, and county, 1969-90, annual CD-ROM, 2704–7
Migration, immigration, and mover characteristics compared to nonmovers, 1987-90, annual Current Population Rpt, 2546–1.456
Migration, population change, and areas losing population, by region, State, and metro-nonmetro location, 1980s and trends from 1940, Current Population Rpt, 2546–2.164
Migration since 1990, mover characteristics by same or different area, and compared to nonmovers, 1991, annual Current Population Rpt, 2546–1.464
Statistical Abstract of US, 1992 annual data compilation, 2324–1
see also Area wage surveys
see also Central business districts
see also Central cities
see also under By SMSA or MSA in the "Index by Categories"

Mexican Americans
see Hispanic Americans
see Mexicans in the U.S.

Mexicans in the U.S.
Admissions to US of immigrants, alien workers, and visitors, deportations, and naturalizations, by country, FY91 and trends from 1820, annual rpt, 6264–2
Admissions to US of immigrants and nonimmigrants, alien workers, deportations, and naturalizations, FY91, annual summary rpt, 6264–7
Alcohol use among Mexican American women, by whether immigrant and occupational group, 1992 article, 4482–1.309
Clothing and other industries employment of aliens, and impacts on local economies, with background data, 1990 working paper, 6366–6.6
Educational enrollment, by grade, instn type and control, and student characteristics, 1990 and trends from 1947, annual Current Population Rpt, 2546–1.459
Illegal immigration from Mexico, and cyclic migration between US and Mexico, 1960s-80s, working paper, 6366–6.11
Immigrants admitted to US, by class of admission, country of birth, and MSA of destination, FY91, advance annual rpt, 6264–4

Mexico
Agricultural trade by commodity and country, prices, and world market devs, monthly rpt, 1922–12
Agricultural trade of Mexico with US and Canada, and impacts of North American Free Trade Agreement, 1980s-90, 1528–330
Agricultural trade of Mexico with US, and impacts of North American Free Trade Agreement, 1980s-2000, article, 9381–1.307
Agricultural trade of US, by detailed commodity and country, 1991, annual rpt, 1524–8
Agricultural trade of US, by detailed commodity and country, 1991, semiannual rpt, 1522–4
Agricultural trade tariffs affected by North American Free Trade Agreement, and NAFTA quotas, by commodity, 1992 article, 1925–34.332
AID economic aid to developing countries, obligations and disbursements by country, quarterly rpt, 9912–4
AID loans repayment status and terms by program and country, and status of predecessor agency loans, quarterly rpt, 9912–3
Air pollution levels for 6 pollutants, and measurements exceeding natl standards, by site, 1990-91, annual rpt, 9194–5
Auto and auto parts trade, production, and labor conditions, for US and compared to Canada and Mexico, 1950s-90, 6366–3.28
Auto parts trade with Japan and other countries, 1985-90 and forecast to 1994, annual rpt, 2004–10
Capital investment spending by industry, and impacts of relative price changes and intl debt crisis, for Mexico, 1980s, technical paper, 9366–7.270
Clothing exports to US, and domestic and US-owned industry production costs and operations, for Caribbean area and Mexico, impacts of North American Free Trade Agreement, 1992 rpt, 9886–4.186
Cuba trade, by commodity and country, mid 1980s-91, 9118–8
Debt burden indicators for 8 developing countries, alternative projections 1991-2000 and trends from 1974, technical paper, 9366–7.271
Dollar exchange rate trade-weighted index of Fed Reserve Bank of Dallas, by world area, monthly rpt, 9379–13
Drug abuse indicators, by world region and selected country, 1991 semiannual conf, 4492–5.1
Drug abuse indicators, by world region and selected country, 1992 semiannual conf, 4492–5.2
Economic and military aid and loans from US and intl agencies, by program and country, FY46-91, annual rpt, 9914–5
Economic and monetary trends, compounded annual rates of change and annual indicators for US and 15 trading partners, quarterly rpt, annual supplement, 9391–7
Economic and social conditions of developing countries from 1960s, and Intl Dev Cooperation Agency and AID activities and funding, FY91-93, annual rpt, 9904–4
Economic and social conditions, resources, and trade, and aid, 1992, annual factbook, 9914–14
Economic conditions, policy, and trade practices, by country, 1989-91, annual rpt, 21384–5
Economic, population, and agricultural data, US and other aid sources, and AID activity, 1992 country rpt, 9916–12.63
Economic, social, political, and geographic summary data, by country, 1992, annual factbook, 9114–2
Electric power supply, demand, and trade of Mexico and US, with data by fuel source, utility, and region, 1970s-89 and projected to 2000, 3408–2
Exports (duty-free) of Caribbean area to US, by commodity and country, with consumer and industry impacts, 1984-91, annual rpt, 9884–20
Exports and imports among US, Canada, and Mexico, intraindustry trade indexes by commodity, 1962-87, 1528–327
Exports and imports of Mexico with US and other countries, foreign investment, and maquiladoras operations, 1980s-91, GAO rpt, 26119–417
Exports and imports of US, by commodity and country, 1980-90, world area rpt, 9116–1.5
Exports and imports of US by country, and trade shifts by commodity, 1991, annual rpt, 9884–25
Exports and imports of US, by Harmonized System 6-digit commodity and country, 1991, annual rpt, 2424–13
Exports and imports of US, by selected country, country group, and commodity group, 1991, annual rpt, 2044–37
Exports and imports of US, by transport mode, country, and SITC 1- to 3-digit commodity, 1991, annual rpt, 2424–12
Exports and imports of US, Canada, and Mexico, economic impacts of North American Free Trade Agreement, alternative model descriptions, 1992 conf, 9886–4.182
Exports and imports, trade agreements and relations, and USITC investigations, 1991, annual rpt, 9884–5
Exports, imports, and balances of US, by selected country, country group, and commodity group, preliminary data, monthly rpt, 2042–34
Exports, imports, and balances of US for manufactured goods, by SITC 2-digit commodity and country, quarterly rpt, 2042–35
Exports, imports, and balances of US with major trading partners, by product category, 1987-91, annual chartbook, 9884–21
Exports, imports, and tariffs between Mexico and US, by commodity, impacts of North American Free Trade Agreement and compared to EC expansion to Mediterranean, 1970s-80s, 6366–3.29
Exports of US, detailed Schedule B commodities with countries of destination, 1991, annual rpt, 2424–10
Farm financial and marketing conditions, forecast 1992, annual chartbook, 1504–8
Fruit trade between Mexico and US, 1989-91, and US tariffs under proposed North American Free Trade Agreement, 1992, by commodity, article, 1561–6.304

Heroin prices and purity in 19 metro areas and Puerto Rico, by world area of origin, quarterly rpt, 6282–2
Human rights conditions in 170 countries, and US economic and military aid, 1991, annual rpt, 21384–3
Imports of goods, services, and investment from US, trade barriers, impacts, and US actions, by country, 1991, annual rpt, 444–2
Imports of Latin America and Caribbean countries from US, by State of origin, 1987 and 1990, 2048–160
Imports of Mexico from US, by industry and State, 1987-91, 2048–154
Imports of US given duty-free treatment for value of US material sent abroad, by commodity and country, 1987-90, annual rpt, 9884–14
Inflation relation to money supply, for 5 South America countries, 1970s-90, technical paper, 9379–12.91
Intl transactions of US with 9 countries, 1989-91, *Survey of Current Business*, monthly rpt, annual table, 2702–1.33
Labor conditions, union coverage, and work accidents, 1992 annual country rpt, 6366–4.51
Limestone (crushed) from Mexico at less than fair value, injury to US industry, investigation with background financial and operating data, 1992 rpt, 9886–14.353
Maquiladora plants environmental regulation enforcement activities, staff, and funding, 1989-92, GAO rpt, 26119–416
Military aid of US, arms sales, and training programs costs and budget requests, by program, world region, and country, FY91-93, annual rpt, 7144–13
Military spending, arms trade, and force strengths, with govt spending and population, by country, 1979-89, annual rpt, 9824–1
Minerals production, reserves, and industry role in domestic economy and world supply, 1992 country rpt, 5606–1.18
Multinatl US firms and foreign affiliates finances and operations, by industry and country, 1989 benchmark survey, annual rpt, 2704–5
Multinatl US firms foreign affiliates, income statement items by asset size, industry, and country, 1988, biennial article, 8302–2.322
Natural gas and liquefied gas trade of US with 5 countries, by US firm, 1955-91, annual article, 3162–4.301
Natural gas imports and contracted supply from Canada and Mexico, by US pipeline firm, 1989-90, annual rpt, 3164–33.6
North American Free Trade Agreement proposal economic and trade impacts on Mexico and US, with data on maquiladora plants, 1980s-90, hearings, 21788–210
Nuclear power generation in US and 20 countries, monthly rpt, 3162–24.10
Nuclear power generation in US and 20 countries, monthly 1973-88, 3168–123.10
Oil production, and exports and prices for US, by major exporting country, detailed data, monthly rpt with articles, 3162–24
Oil production, and exports and prices for US, by major exporting country, detailed data, monthly 1973-88, 3168–123
Oil production, stocks, use, and trade, by selected country and country group, monthly rpt, 3162–42
Oil supply, demand, and stock forecasts, by world area, quarterly rpt, 3162–34
Oranges acreage, yield, and production, by Mexico State, 1990/91-1991/92, article, 1925–34.309
Pesticide residue on Mexico fruit and vegetable exports to US, US and Mexico standards and violations, FY79-91, GAO rpt, 26113–585
Pineapple (canned fruit and juice) production and exports, by country, and Mexico export prices, selected years 1987-92, annual article, 1925–34.327
Pipes and tubes (welded nonalloy steel) from 6 countries at less than fair value, injury to US industry, investigation with background financial and operating data, 1992 rpt, 9886–14.361
Pollution (air) contributing to global warming, emissions by monitoring site and country, and temperature change by world area and US region, 1860s-1990, annual rpt, 3004–33
Population size, growth rates, and components of change, by country, projected 1990-2020 and trends from 1950, biennial rpt, 2324–9
Poultry imports of Mexico from US, 1990-91, semiannual rpt, 1925–33.1
Refugee migration, and intl aid programs, by world area and country of origin and asylum, 1991, annual rpt, 7004–15
Spacecraft and satellite launches since 1957, quarterly listing, 9502–2
Steel (carbon flat-rolled) products from 21 countries, injury to US industry from foreign subsidized and less than fair value imports, investigation with background financial and operating data, 1992 rpt, 9886–19.85
Steel imports of US under voluntary restraint agreement, by product, customs district, and country, with US industry operating data, quarterly rpt, 9882–13
Steel trade, by product, country, and customs district, with US industry operating data, 1989-June 1992, semiannual rpt, 9882–15
Steel wire rope from South Korea and Mexico at less than fair value, injury to US industry, investigation with background financial and operating data, 1992 rpt, 9886–14.346
Strawberry trade of US and Mexico, and Mexico and Chile supply and use, 1987-92, annual article, 1925–34.315
Tax (estate) returns for nonresident aliens, property and tax data, by estate size and decedent country of residence, 1986, article, 8302–2.310
Tax (income) returns, income, and tax withheld for foreign partners of US partnerships, by country, 1990, article, 8302–2.324
Telecommunications domestic and intl rates, by type of service and area served, 1990, annual rpt, 9284–6.6
Textile and apparel foreign market conditions for US exports, with domestic industry operations, 1992 country rpt, 2046–15.3; 2046–15.4
Tobacco production and use in Latin America, Canada, and US, and related economic, health, and social issues, 1950s-92, annual rpt, 4204–18
Trade agreement with US, impacts on truck traffic at border crossings, Customs Service staff needs, and hwy improvement costs, projected to 2000 with trends from 1986, GAO rpt, 26123–368
Travel to and from US, and travel receipts and payments, by world area, with data by country, 1985-90, annual rpt, 2904–10
Travel to and from US, by world area, forecast 1992-93, annual rpt, 2904–9
Travel to US, spending by world area of residence, and economic impact, by spending category and State, 1989, 2908–28
UN voting record and share of votes in agreement with US, by issue, country, and world area, 1991, annual rpt, 7004–18
Water supplied by US from Colorado River Basin, for Mexico, 1981-85, annual rpt, 5824–6
Wetlands conservation projects, acreage, and costs, for Canada and Mexico, FY92, 14784–1
see also Gulf of Mexico
see also Mexicans in the U.S.
see also under By Foreign Country in the "Index by Categories"

Meyer, E.
"Heavy-Duty Trucks in Crashes, NASS, 1979-86", 7768–124

Meyer, Leslie A.
"Assessment of USDA's Cotton Supply and Demand Estimates", 1561–1.302
"Texas Upland Cotton Acreage Abandonment and Harvested Yield: A Historical Perspective", 1561–1.303

Meyer, Stephen A.
"Saving and Demographics: Some International Comparisons", 9387–1.302

Miami, Fla.
CPI by component for US city average, and by region, population size, and for 15 metro areas, monthly rpt, 6762–1
CPI by component for US city average, and by selected metro area, region, and population size, monthly rpt, 6762–2
Drug abuse indicators for selected metro areas, research results, data collection, and policy issues, 1992 semiannual conf, 4492–5
Drug test results at arrest, by drug type, offense, and sex, for selected urban areas, quarterly rpt, 6062–3
Fruit and vegetable shipments, and arrivals by city, by mode of transport and State and country of origin, 1991, annual rpt, 1311–4.1
Heroin prices and purity in 19 metro areas and Puerto Rico, by world area of origin, quarterly rpt, 6282–2
Housing and households characteristics, and unit and neighborhood quality, by MSA location for 11 MSAs, 1986 survey, supplement, 2485–8
Housing starts and completions authorized by building permits in 40 MSAs, quarterly rpt, 2382–9
Wages by occupation, for office and plant workers, 1991 survey, periodic MSA rpt, 6785–16.3

see also under By City and By SMSA or MSA in the "Index by Categories"
Micarelli, William F.
"History of the 1987 Economic Censuses", 2628–16
Michigan
Banks (insured commercial and savings) deposits by instn, State, MSA, and county, as of June 1991, annual regional rpt, 9295–3.3
Business and economic conditions, Fed Reserve 9th District, quarterly journal, 9383–19
Celery acreage planted and growing, by growing area, monthly rpt, 1621–14
Deaths and rates, by detailed location, cause, and demographic characteristics, 1989, US Vital Statistics annual rpt, 4144–3.1
Employment, earnings, and hours, by selected SIC 1- to 4-digit industry, State, and for 275 MSAs, 1987-92, 6748–81
Fed Govt spending in States and local areas, by type, State, county, and city, FY91, annual rpt, 2464–3
Fed Govt spending in States, by type, program, agency, and State, FY91, annual rpt, 2464–2
HHS financial aid, by program, recipient, State, and city, FY91, annual regional listing, 4004–3.5
Hospital deaths of Medicare patients, actual and expected rates by diagnosis, and hospital characteristics, by instn, FY90 annual State rpt, 4654–14.23
Housing census, 1990: inventory, occupancy, and costs, State fact sheet, 2326–21.24
Housing census, 1990: summary unit characteristics, by householder race and age, county, place, and urban-rural location, State rpt, 2471–1.24
Local areas economic conditions and public services impacts of reductions in Federal aid, for Michigan, with background data, 1970s-91, GAO rpt, 26121–483
Lumber (pulpwood) production in 3 North Central States, by species and county, 1990, 1208–397
Medicaid claims and payments for HIV patients, by sex, age, risk group, eligibility, and source of care, for Michigan, mid 1980s, article, 4042–3.348
Military prime contract awards, by contractor, service branch, State, and city, FY91, annual rpt, 3544–22
Mineral Industry Surveys, State reviews of production, 1991, preliminary annual rpt, 5614–6
Multinatl firms US affiliates finances and operations, by industry, country of parent firm, and State, 1987, 2708–48
Physicians, by specialty, age, sex, and location of training and practice, 1990, State rpt, 4116–6.23
Pollution (air) levels in Detroit area, by pollutant and site, 1970s-90, 14648–28
Population and housing census, 1990: detailed geographic coverage, State CD-ROM, 2551–9.3
Population and housing census, 1990: summary characteristics, by county, subdiv, and place, State rpt, 2551–7.24
Population census, 1990: population characteristics and living arrangements, by county, place, and urban-rural location, State rpt, 2531–1.24
Savings and loan assns, FHLB 6th District insured members financial condition and operations by State, quarterly rpt, 9302–23
Statistical Abstract of US, 1992 annual data compilation, 2324–1
Wood fuel production in Michigan, by species, land ownership, survey region, county, and location, 1986, 1208–412
see also Ann Arbor, Mich.
see also Detroit, Mich.
see also Oakland County, Mich.
see also Wayne County, Mich.
see also under By State in the "Index by Categories"
Microforms
Census Bur activities, rpts, and user services, monthly rpt, 2302–3
Census Bur data coverage and availability for economic censuses and related statistics, 1992 preliminary guide, 2308–5
Census Bur data files and rpts, coverage and availability, 1992 annual listing, 2304–2
Census Bur geographic levels of data coverage, maps, and reference products, 1992 rpt, 2308–67
Census Bur rpts and data files, coverage, availability, and use, series, 2326–7
Census Bur rpts and data files, monthly listing, 2302–6
Census of Population and Housing, 1990: data coverage, collection procedures, products and services availability, and uses, guide, 2555–1
Education Dept rpts, 1992 semiannual listing, 4812–1
Educational Resources Info Center (ERIC) data base, foreign and US providers, 1992 biennial listing, 4814–4
Fed Govt agencies administrative records and other holdings of Natl Archives, final inventories, series, 9516–2
Fed Govt standards for data recording, processing, and transfer, and for purchase and use of computer systems, series, 2216–2
Geological Survey rpts and research journal articles, monthly listing, 5662–1
Library of Congress activities, acquisitions, services, and financial statements, FY91, annual rpt, 26404–1
Library of Congress rpts and products, 1992-93, biennial listing, 26404–6
Natl Archives and Records Admin activities, finances, holdings, and staff, FY91, annual rpt, 9514–2
Natl Inst of Standards and Technology rpts, 1991, annual listing, 2214–1
Price indexes (producer), by stage of processing and detailed commodity, monthly rpt, 6762–6
Micronesia Federated States
Agricultural trade of US, by detailed commodity and country, 1991, annual rpt, 1524–8
Agricultural trade of US, by detailed commodity and country, 1991, semiannual rpt, 1522–4
Banks (insured commercial and savings) deposits by instn, State, MSA, and county, as of June 1991, annual regional rpt, 9295–3.6
Economic, social, political, and geographic summary data, by country, 1992, annual factbook, 9114–2
Exports and imports of US, by transport mode, country, and SITC 1- to 3-digit commodity, 1991, annual rpt, 2424–12
Exports of US, detailed Schedule B commodities with countries of destination, 1991, annual rpt, 2424–10
Hepatitis B vaccination coverage of children, by island, for Micronesia, 1988-90, article, 4042–3.357
Human rights conditions in 170 countries, and US economic and military aid, 1991, annual rpt, 21384–3
Physicians, by specialty, age, sex, and location of training and practice, 1990, State rpt, 4116–6.53
Population size, growth rates, and components of change, by country, projected 1990-2020 and trends from 1950, biennial rpt, 2324–9
UN voting record and share of votes in agreement with US, by issue, country, and world area, 1991, annual rpt, 7004–18
Middle Atlantic States
Bridges over navigable waters, with type of bridge and use, owner, dimensions, and location, 1991 regional listing, 7406–5.3
Deaths and rates, by cause and selected social, demographic, and employment characteristics, 1979-85, natl longitudinal study, 4478–186
Economic conditions, Fed Reserve 3rd District, quarterly rpt, 9387–10
Economic indicator forecasts for Middle Atlantic States, performance of vector autoregression models, 1992 working paper, 9387–8.282
Economic indicators and cyclical devs and outlook, by Fed Reserve Bank District, periodic rpt, 9362–8
Economic indicators forecasts and errors, for Fed Reserve 3rd District by State, 1980s-93, article, 9387–1.303
Energy supply, demand, and prices, by fuel type and end-use sector, alternative projections by region, 1990-2010, annual rpt, 3164–96
Financial and economic devs, Fed Reserve Bank of Philadelphia bimonthly journal, 9387–1
Financial and economic devs, Fed Reserve Bank of Richmond bimonthly journal, 9389–1
Fishing (ocean sport) activities, and catch by species, by angler characteristics and State, 1990-91, annual coastal area rpt, 2166–17.1
Freight (waterborne domestic and foreign) by commodity, traffic, and passengers, by port and waterway, 1989, annual rpt, 3754–3.1
HHS financial aid, by program, recipient, State, and city, FY91, annual regional listing, 4004–3.2; 4004–3.3
Lumber (pulpwood) production by species and county, and shipments, by northeastern State, 1990, annual rpt, 1204–18
Manufacturing business outlook, for Fed Reserve 3rd District, monthly survey rpt, 9387–11
Manufacturing output index for Middle Atlantic States, monthly rpt, 9387–12
Peanut production, prices, stocks, exports, use, inspection, and quality, by region and State, 1982-91, annual rpt, 1311–5

Statistical Abstract of US, 1992 annual data compilation, 2324–1
Tide height and tidal current velocity daily at Middle Atlantic coastal stations, forecast 1993, annual rpt, 2174–11
Tide height and time daily at coastal points, forecast 1993, annual rpt, 2174–2.3
see also Appalachia
see also under By Census Division in the "Index by Categories"
see also under names of individual States

Middle East
Agricultural trade by commodity and country, prices, and world market devs, monthly rpt, 1922–12
Agricultural trade of US, by commodity and country, bimonthly rpt, 1522–1
Agricultural trade of US, by detailed commodity and country, 1991, annual rpt, 1524–8
Agricultural trade of US, by detailed commodity and country, 1991, semiannual rpt, 1522–4
AID contracts and grants for technical and support services, by instn, country, and State, FY91, annual listing, 9914–7
AID economic aid to developing countries, obligations and disbursements by country, quarterly rpt, 9912–4
AID loans repayment status and terms by program and country, and status of predecessor agency loans, quarterly rpt, 9912–3
Boycotts (intl) by OPEC and other countries, US firms and individuals cooperation and tax benefits denied, 1990, article, 8302–2.323
Construction contract awards and billings, by country of contractor and world area of award, 1990, annual article, 2042–1.304
Economic and military aid and loans from US and intl agencies, by program and country, FY46-91, annual rpt, 9914–5
Economic and social conditions of developing countries from 1960s, and Intl Dev Cooperation Agency and AID activities and funding, FY91-93, annual rpt, 9904–4
Energy producers finances and operations, by energy type for US firms domestic and foreign operations, 1990, annual rpt, 3164–44.2
Energy production by type, and oil trade, and use, by country group and selected country, monthly rpt, 9112–2
Energy use and production, by fuel type, country, and country group, projected 1995-2010 and trends from 1970, annual rpt, 3164–84
Exports and imports of OECD, total and for 4 major countries, and US trade by country, by commodity, 1980-90, world area rpt, 9116–1.6
Exports and imports of US, by Harmonized System 6-digit commodity and country, 1991, annual rpt, 2424–13
Exports and imports of US, by selected country, country group, and commodity group, 1991, annual rpt, 2044–37
Exports and imports of US, by transport mode, country, and SITC 1- to 3-digit commodity, 1991, annual rpt, 2424–12
Family planning and population activities of AID, grants by project and recipient, and contraceptive shipments, by country, FY91, annual rpt series, 9914–13
Immigrants and nonimmigrants admitted to US, alien workers, visitors, deportations, and naturalizations, FY91, annual summary rpt, 6264–7
Immigration to US, alien workers, visitors, deportations, and naturalizations, by country, FY91 and trends from 1820, annual rpt, 6264–2
Imports of goods, services, and investment from US, trade barriers, impacts, and US actions, by country, 1991, annual rpt, 444–2
Investment (foreign direct) in US, by industry group and world area, 1989-91, annual article, 2702–1.331
Investment (foreign direct) of US, by industry group and world area, 1989-91, annual article, 2702–1.332
Military aid of US, arms sales, and training, by country, FY50-91, annual rpt, 3904–3
Military aid of US, arms sales, and training programs costs and budget requests, by program, world region, and country, FY91-93, annual rpt, 7144–13
Military arms trade and force strengths of Middle Eastern countries, and impacts of voluntary arms trade reductions, mid 1960s-91 and projected to 2002, 26306–6.173
Military spending, arms trade, and force strengths, with govt spending and population, by country, 1979-89, annual rpt, 9824–1
Minerals Yearbook, Vol 3, 1989: foreign country review of production, trade, and policy, by commodity, annual rpt, 5604–35.3
Multinatl firms US affiliates finances and operations, by industry, country of parent firm, and State, 1987, 2708–48
Multinatl firms US affiliates, finances, and operations, by industry, world area of parent firm, and State, 1989-90, annual rpt, 2704–4
Multinatl US firms and foreign affiliates finances and operations, by industry and country, 1989 benchmark survey, annual rpt, 2704–5
Multinatl US firms foreign affiliates, income statement items by asset size, industry, and country, 1988, biennial article, 8302–2.322
Oil imports from Persian Gulf, US and OECD dependence indicators, and US military supply, late 1970s-80s and supply disruptions from 1951, 3166–6.65
Persian Gulf War allied and other countries cash and in-kind contributions, by type and country, 1990-91, GAO rpt, 26123–371
Persian Gulf War costs to US by category and service branch, and offsetting contributions by allied country, monthly rpt, 102–3
Population size, growth rates, and components of change, by country, projected 1990-2020 and trends from 1950, biennial rpt, 2324–9
Refugee arrivals in US by world area and country of origin, and quotas, monthly rpt, 7002–4
Refugee arrivals in US by world area of origin and State of settlement, and Federal aid, FY91-92 and proposed FY93 allocations, annual rpt, 7004–16
Refugee migration, and intl aid programs, by world area and country of origin and asylum, 1991, annual rpt, 7004–15
Terrorism (intl) incidents, casualties, and attacks on US targets, by attack type and country, 1991, annual rpt, 7004–22
Terrorism (intl) incidents, casualties, and attacks on US targets, by attack type and world area, 1991, annual rpt, 7004–13
Tide height and time daily at coastal points, forecast 1993, annual rpt, 2174–2.5
Travel to and from US, and travel receipts and payments, by world area, with data by country, 1985-90, annual rpt, 2904–10
Travel to US, by characteristics of visit and traveler, country, port city, and State of destination, quarterly rpt, 2902–1
Travel to US, spending by world area of residence, and economic impact, by spending category and State, 1989, 2908–28
UN voting record and share of votes in agreement with US, by issue, country, and world area, 1991, annual rpt, 7004–18
US military and civilian personnel and dependents, by service branch, world area, and country, quarterly rpt, 3542–20
Weather forecasts for US and Northern Hemisphere, precipitation and temperature by location, semimonthly rpt, 2182–1
see also Bahrain
see also Central Treaty Organization
see also Cyprus
see also Egypt
see also Iran
see also Iraq
see also Israel
see also Jordan
see also Kuwait
see also Lebanon
see also Mediterranean Sea
see also Oman
see also Organization of Petroleum Exporting Countries
see also Qatar
see also Saudi Arabia
see also Syria
see also Turkey
see also United Arab Emirates
see also Yemen
see also Yemen, North
see also Yemen, South
see also under By Foreign Country in the "Index by Categories"

Middlesex County, N.J.
Housing and households characteristics, and unit and neighborhood quality, by MSA location for 11 MSAs, 1987 survey, supplement, 2485–8
Wages by occupation, for office and plant workers, 1991 survey, periodic MSA rpt, 6785–12.3

Midtlyng, Karen S.
"Water Resources Activities of the USGS in Montana, Oct. 1989-Sept. 1991", 5666–26.21

Midway Islands
Economic, social, political, and geographic summary data, by country, 1992, annual factbook, 9114–2

Midwestern States
see North Central States
see under By Region in the "Index by Categories"

Midwives
Indian Health Service and tribal facility outpatient visits, by type of provider, selected hospital, and service area, FY91, annual rpt, 4084–3
Infant health, deaths and risk factors, and prevention issues, for US and selected countries, 1990 conf, 4148–28
Malpractice insurance subsidy program for rural obstetrics practitioners, funding and participation, for North Carolina, 1989-92, article, 4042–3.355
Military health care personnel, and accessions by training source, by occupation, specialty, and service branch, FY90, annual rpt, 3544–24

Migrant workers
Assistance (financial and nonfinancial) of Fed Govt, 1992 base edition, annual listing, 104–5
Education (special) enrollment by age, staff, funding, and needs, by type of handicap and State, 1990/91, annual rpt, 4944–4
Education in Head Start programs, enrollment, funding, and staff, FY91, annual rpt, 4584–5
Food stamp recipient household size, composition, income, and income and deductions allowed, summer 1989, annual rpt, 1364–8
Group quarters for agricultural workers, population by race and sex, 1990 Census of Population, State rpt series, 2531–1
Head Start handicapped enrollment, by handicap, State, and for Indian and migrant programs, 1988/89, annual rpt, 4584–4
HHS financial aid, by program, recipient, State, and city, FY91, annual regional listings, 4004–3
Housing census, 1990: summary unit characteristics, by householder race and age, county, place, and urban-rural location, State rpt series, 2471–1
Pacific territories population and housing detailed characteristics, by location, 1990 Census of Population and Housing, series, 2551–8
Tuberculosis screening, treatment, and control among migrant farmworkers, CDC guidelines, 1992 rpt, 4206–2.60

Migration
Bank deposits interest rates relation to market concentration, regulation, migration, and other factors, 1980s, technical paper, 9366–6.297
Cancer incidence impacts of migration, and treatment resources availability, for Florida by county, 1980, article, 4042–3.339
Census of Population and Housing, 1990: population and housing characteristics, detailed geographic coverage, State CD-ROM series, 2551–10
Census of Population and Housing, 1990: summary characteristics, by county, subdiv, and place, State rpt series, 2551–7
Consumer Income, socioeconomic characteristics of persons, families, and households, detailed cross-tabulations, Current Population Rpt series, 2546–6
Education spending in local areas, impacts of high school grads in- and out-migration, model description and results, 1980s, technical paper, 9379–12.81
Foreign countries *Geographic Notes*, boundaries, claims, nomenclature, and other devs, quarterly rpt, 7142–3
Higher education enrollment of State and out-of-State residents, by State, fall 1988, annual rpt, 4824–2.17
Households and housing detailed characteristics, and unit and neighborhood quality, by location, 1989, biennial rpt supplement, 2485–13
Households and housing unit summary characteristics, 1989 and trends, chartbook, 2486–2.1
Households composition, income, benefits, and labor force status, Survey of Income and Program Participation methodology, working paper series, 2626–10
Households moving rates by tenure and age, and housing value by mobility status and region, 1989, fact sheet, 2326–17.38
Housing (rental) total, HUD-assisted by program, and eligible for aid, recent movers by reason, selected characteristics, and location, 1989, biennial rpt, 5184–11
Housing and households characteristics, and unit and neighborhood quality, by MSA location for 11 MSAs, 1987 survey, supplement, 2485–8
Housing and households characteristics, MSA surveys, fact sheet series, 2485–11
Housing and households detailed characteristics, and unit and neighborhood quality, 1989, wallchart, 2485–12
Housing characteristics of recent movers for new and previous unit, and household characteristics, MSA surveys, series, 2485–6
Housing unit and household characteristics of recent movers, and reason for move, by tenure, 1989, 2486–1.12
NYC housing supply, occupancy, condition, and household characteristics, by tenure and borough, 1991 triennial survey, 2488–3
Older population, and health, economic, and other characteristics, with foreign comparisons, 1980s-91 with trends and projections, Current Population Rpt, 2546–2.165
Pacific territories population and housing detailed characteristics, by location, 1990 Census of Population and Housing, series, 2551–8
Population and housing summary data and trends, 1970s-91, Current Population Rpt, fact sheet, 2546–2.163
Population migration during the 1980s, by census region, division, State, and metro-nonmetro area, with trends from 1940, 2546–2.164
Population migration, immigration, and mover characteristics compared to nonmovers, 1987-90, annual Current Population Rpt, 2546–1.456
Population migration since 1990, mover characteristics by same or different area, and compared to nonmovers, 1991, annual Current Population Rpt, 2546–1.464
Population size and demographic changes impacts on economic conditions, with background data, 1950s-80s and projected to 2010, 23848–226
Population size, July 1981-89 and compared to 1980 and 1990, annual press release, 2324–10
Research on population and reproduction, Federal funding by project, FY90, annual listing, 4474–9
Research on population and reproduction, Natl Inst of Child Health and Human Dev funding and activities, 1991, annual rpt, 4474–33
Soviet Union former Republics and Baltic States population size and characteristics, 1989-92, 9118–19
Statistical Abstract of US, 1992 annual data compilation, 2324–1.1
see also Alien workers
see also Immigration and emigration
see also Labor mobility
see also Mexicans in the U.S.
see also Migrant workers
see also Refugees
see also Relocation

Migratory Bird Conservation Commission
Refuges and breeding areas for migratory waterfowl, acreage acquired by Fed Govt, and costs, by site and State, FY92, annual rpt, 14784–1
Wetlands wildlife and migratory bird habitat acquisition, funding by State, 1992, press release, 5306–4.13; 5306–4.16

Mikelsons, Maris
"Housing Discrimination Study: Mapping Patterns of Steering for Five Metropolitan Areas", 5186–16.2
"Housing Discrimination Study: Replication of 1977 Study Measures with Current Data", 5186–16.6

Milburn, Nelda J.
"Performance of Color-Dependent Tasks of Air Traffic Control Specialists as a Function of Type and Degree of Color Vision Deficiency", 7506–10.123
"Validity of Clinical Color Vision Tests for Air Traffic Control Specialists", 7506–10.125

Miles, Patrick D.
"Timber Resource of Missouri's Southwest Ozarks, 1989", 1206–3.7

Military academies
see Service academies

Military aircraft
Budget of DOD, organization, personnel, weapons, and property, by service branch, State, and country, 1992 annual summary rpt, 3504–13
Budget of DOD, procurement appropriations by item, service branch, and defense agency, FY91-93, annual rpt, 3544–32
Budget of DOD, programs, policies, and operations, FY91, annual rpt, 3544–2
Budget of DOD, weapons acquisition costs by system and service branch, FY91-93, annual rpt, 3504–2
Coast Guard enforcement activities, 1st half FY92, semiannual rpt, 7402–4
Coast Guard search and rescue missions, and lives and property lost and saved, by district and assisting unit, FY91, annual rpt, 7404–2
Expenditures and obligations of DOD, by function and service branch, quarterly rpt, 3542–3
Exports and imports of US, by Harmonized System 6-digit commodity and country, 1991, annual rpt, 2424–13
Exports of US, detailed Schedule B commodities with countries of destination, 1991, annual rpt, 2424–10

Foreign countries military aid and arms sales of US, by weapon type, as of Sept 1991, annual rpt, 3904–3
Foreign countries military spending, arms trade, and force strengths, with govt spending and population, by country, 1979-89, annual rpt, 9824–1
Helicopter (Apache) use and performance during Persian Gulf War, 1991, GAO rpt, 26123–378
Manufacturing annual survey, 1990: value of shipments, by SIC 4- to 5-digit product class, 2506–14.1
Natl Guard activities, personnel, and facilities, FY91, annual rpt, 3504–22
Natl income and product accounts, comprehensive accounts and components, benchmark revisions, 1929-88, 2708–5
Natl income and product accounts, comprehensive accounts and components, *Survey of Current Business*, monthly rpt, 2702–1.26
NATO and Warsaw Pact military forces reductions and ceilings under CFE treaty, inspections, and US compliance costs and savings, 1991 hearings, 25388–59
NATO, Japan, and South Korea military spending and indicators of ability to support common defense, by country, 1970s-90, annual rpt, 3544–28
Officials (Federal) and Congress members use of military aircraft, and aircraft inventory characteristics, 1989-91, GAO rpt, 26123–384
Officials (Federal) use of military aircraft, trips of 11 officials by reason, with costs and reimbursements, 1989-91, GAO rpt, 26111–78
Persian Gulf War aircraft, tank, and personnel carrier deployment and operating capability, and spare parts availability, 1990-91, GAO rpt, 26123–375
Price indexes (producer), by stage of processing and detailed commodity, monthly rpt, 6762–6
Price indexes (producer), by stage of processing and detailed commodity, monthly 1991, annual rpt, 6764–2
Procurement, DOD prime contract awards by category, contract and contractor type, and service branch, FY82-1st half FY92, semiannual rpt, 3542–1
Procurement, DOD prime contract awards by category, contractor type, and State, FY89-91, annual rpt, 3544–11
Procurement, DOD prime contract awards by detailed procurement category, FY88-91, annual rpt, 3544–18
Procurement, DOD prime contract awards by size and type of contract, service branch, competitive status, category, and labor standard, FY91, annual rpt, 3544–19
Reserve forces personnel and equipment strengths, and readiness, by reserve component, FY91, annual rpt, 3544–31
Sales, orders, backlog, and firms, by product for govt, military, and other customers, 1991, annual Current Industrial Rpt, 2506–12.22
Shipments by DOD of military and personal property, passenger traffic, and costs, by service branch and mode of transport, FY91, annual rpt, 3704–15

Military airlift
Budget of DOD, programs, policies, and operations, FY91, annual rpt, 3544–2
Persian Gulf War costs to US by category and service branch, and offsetting contributions by allied country, monthly rpt, 102–3
Shipments by DOD of military and personal property, passenger traffic, and costs, by service branch and mode of transport, FY91, annual rpt, 3704–15

Military appropriations
see Defense budgets and appropriations

Military assistance
Assistance (military) of US, arms sales, and training programs costs and budget requests, by program, world region, and country, FY91-93, annual rpt, 7144–13
Budget of DOD, organization, personnel, weapons, and property, by service branch, State, and country, 1992 annual summary rpt, 3504–13
Budget of DOD, programs, policies, and operations, FY91, annual rpt, 3544–2
Budget of DOD, R&D appropriations by item, service branch, and defense agency, FY91-93, annual rpt, 3544–33
Currency (foreign) holdings of US, transactions and balances by program and country, 1st half FY92, semiannual rpt, 8102–7
Debt to US of foreign govts and private obligors, by country and program, periodic rpt, 8002–6
Developing countries economic and social conditions from 1960s, and Intl Dev Cooperation Agency and AID activities and funding, FY91-93, annual rpt, 9904–4
Economic and military aid and loans from US and intl agencies, by program and country, FY46-91, annual rpt, 9914–5
Economic conditions in foreign countries and implications for US, periodic country rpt series, 2046–4
Economic indicators and components, current data and annual trends, monthly rpt, 23842–1.7
Expenditures for DOD base support by function, and personnel and acreage by installation, by service branch, FY93, annual rpt, 3504–11
Foreign countries military and economic aid of US, by program and country, selected years 1940-89, annual rpt, 15344–1.1
Human rights conditions in 170 countries, and US economic and military aid, 1991, annual rpt, 21384–3
Latin America economic and social conditions, resources, trade, and aid, 1992, annual factbook, 9914–14
Loans and loan guarantees of Fed Govt, outstanding amounts by agency and program, *Treasury Bulletin*, quarterly rpt, 8002–4.11
Natl income and product accounts, comprehensive accounts and components, benchmark revisions, 1929-88, 2708–5
Natl income and product accounts, comprehensive accounts and components, *Survey of Current Business*, monthly rpt, 2702–1.26
Persian Gulf War allied and other countries cash and in-kind contributions, by type and country, 1990-91, GAO rpt, 26123–371
Persian Gulf War allied countries cash and in-kind contributions, by type and country, and status of DOD accounts, as of Sept 1991, annual GAO rpt, 26104–24
Persian Gulf War costs to US by category and service branch, and offsetting contributions by allied country, monthly rpt, 102–3
Statistical Abstract of US, 1992 annual data compilation, 2324–1.11; 2324–1.29
Treaties and agreements on arms control, status and Arms Control and Disarmament Agency activities, 1991, annual rpt, 9824–2
Treaties and other bilateral and multilateral agreements of US in force, by country, as of Jan 1992, annual listing, 7004–1
see also Arms trade

Military aviation
Air traffic control and airway facilities improvement activities under Aviation System Capital Investment Plan, 1981-91 and projected to 2006, annual rpt, 7504–12
Air traffic controller academy grads and military hires, training performance, facility assignments, and selected characteristics, 1988, 7506–10.101
Atlantic Ocean intl air traffic and passengers, by aviation type and route, alternative forecasts 1992-2010 and trends from 1982, annual rpt, 7504–44
Black military and civilian DOD personnel, by sex, grade, and period of service, and lists of award recipients, officers, and service academy grads, 1770s-90, 3548–22
Budget of DOD, personnel needs, costs, and force readiness by service branch, FY93, annual rpt, 3504–1
Civil aircraft joint use of military airfields, passenger enplanements by State, 1990, annual rpt, 7504–48.2
Instrument flight rule aircraft handled, by user type, FAA traffic control center, and region, FY85-91 and projected to FY2005, annual rpt, 7504–15
Natl Guard activities, personnel, and facilities, FY91, annual rpt, 3504–22
Navy personnel strengths, accessions, and attrition, detailed statistics, quarterly rpt, 3802–4
Reserve forces personnel and equipment strengths, and readiness, by reserve component, FY91, annual rpt, 3544–31
Traffic, aircraft, carriers, airports, and FAA activities, detailed data, 1981-90, annual rpt, 7504–1
Traffic, aircraft, pilots, airports, and fuel use, forecast FY92-2003 and trends from FY82, annual rpt, 7504–6
Traffic and other aviation activity forecasts of FAA, 1992 annual conf, 7504–28
Traffic and passenger and freight enplanements, by airport, 1960s-91 and projected to 2010, hub area rpt series, 7506–7
Traffic and passenger enplanements, by airport, region, and State, projected FY92-2005 and trends from FY83, annual rpt, 7504–7
Traffic, capacity, and performance, by carrier and type of operation, monthly rpt, 7302–6

Traffic levels at FAA air traffic control facilities, by airport and State, FY91, annual rpt, 7504–27
Training and education programs of DOD, funding, staff, students, and facilities, by service branch, FY93, annual rpt, 3504–5
see also Military aircraft
see also Military airlift

Military awards, decorations, and medals
Black military and civilian DOD personnel, by sex, grade, and period of service, and lists of award recipients, officers, and service academy grads, 1770s-90, 3548–22

Military bases, posts, and reservations
Army strategic capability, force strengths, budget, and mgmt, FY79-93, annual rpt, 3704–13
Bombing incidents and casualties, by target, circumstances, and State, 1987-91, annual rpt, 8484–4.1
Budget of DOD, base construction and family housing appropriations by facility, service branch, and location, FY91-93, annual rpt, 3544–39
Budget of DOD, organization, personnel, weapons, and property, by service branch, State, and country, 1992 annual summary rpt, 3504–13
Budget of DOD, programs, policies, and operations, FY91, annual rpt, 3544–2
Budget of US, Bush Admin proposals, with detail for defense budgets, and historical data from FY34, FY93, 108–46.2
Business statistics, detailed data for major industries and economic indicators, 1960-91, *Survey of Current Business* biennial supplement, 2704–1
Closings and realignment of bases, DOD appropriations by facility, service branch, and location, FY91-93, annual rpt, 3544–39
Closings of bases in Germany, US liability for local natl employee severance pay, projected FY91-95, GAO rpt, 26123–383
Commercial activities of DOD performed in-house, and work-years, by service branch, installation, and State, FY91, annual rpt, 3544–25
Construction put in place, by type of construction, quarterly rpt, 2042–1.1
Construction put in place, value of new public and private structures, by type, monthly rpt, 2382–4
Construction, renovation, and closure of bases, DOD budget requests by project, service branch, State, and country, FY93, annual rpt, 3544–15
Construction spending by Fed Govt, by type of structure, FY85-92, annual article, 2042–1.303
Expenditures for contracts and payroll, and personnel, by service branch and location, with top 5 contractors and maps, by State and country, FY91, annual rpt, 3544–29
Fish Hatchery Natl System activities and deliveries, by species, hatchery, and jurisdiction of waters stocked, FY91, annual rpt, 5504–10
Hazardous substances underground storage tanks on military bases, DOD compliance with EPA regulations, 1988-91, GAO rpt, 26123–395
Hazardous waste site remedial action at military installations, activities and funding by site and State, FY91, annual rpt, 3544–36
Idaho Snake River area birds of prey, rodent, and vegetation distribution and characteristics, research results, 1991, annual rpt, 5724–14
Input-output structure of US economy, detailed interindustry transactions for 541 industries, and components of final demand, 1982 benchmark data, 2708–17
Minerals resources and availability on public lands, State rpt series, 5606–7
Natl Guard activities, personnel, and facilities, FY91, annual rpt, 3504–22
Natl income and product accounts, comprehensive accounts and components, benchmark revisions, 1929-88, 2708–5
Natl income and product accounts, comprehensive accounts and components, *Survey of Current Business*, monthly rpt, 2702–1.26
NATO military base construction projects, and US funding, by project status, 1985-93, GAO rpt, 26123–388
Pentagon personnel, FY45-91, annual rpt, 3544–1.1
Personnel (civilian and military) of DOD, by service branch, major installation, and State, as of Sept 1991, annual rpt, 3544–7
Reserve forces personnel and equipment strengths, and readiness, by reserve component, FY91, annual rpt, 3544–31
Support of bases, DOD outlays by function, and personnel and acreage by installation, by service branch, FY93, annual rpt, 3504–11
Terrorism (intl) incidents, casualties, and attacks on US targets, by attack type and country, 1991, annual rpt, 7004–22
Terrorism (intl) incidents, casualties, and attacks on US targets, by attack type and world area, 1991, annual rpt, 7004–13
Training and education programs of DOD, funding, staff, students, and facilities, by service branch, FY93, annual rpt, 3504–5
see also Military housing
see also Military post exchanges and commissaries
see also Military prisons

Military benefits and pensions
Benefits and beneficiaries of govt pension plans, by type of plan and eligibility, and level of govt, 1960s-80s, annual article, 4742–1.318
Budget of DOD, programs, policies, and operations, FY91, annual rpt, 3544–2
Disability retirement cases of DOD, by disposition, tenure, and whether receiving VA benefits, 1980s-90, GAO rpt, 26121–470
Expenditures and obligations of DOD, by function and service branch, quarterly rpt, 3542–3
Expenditures, coverage, and benefits for social welfare programs, late 1930s-90, annual rpt, 4744–3.1; 4744–3.3
Expenditures for contracts and payroll, and personnel, by service branch and location, with top 5 contractors and maps, by State and country, FY91, annual rpt, 3544–29
Expenditures of Fed Govt in States, by type, program, agency, and State, FY91, annual rpt, 2464–2
Income (household, family, and personal), by source, detailed characteristics, and region, 1991, annual Current Population Rpt, 2546–6.76
Income and sources of aged, by whether OASDI beneficiary, poverty status, and other characteristics, 1990, biennial rpt, 4744–26
Pacific territories population and housing detailed characteristics, by location, 1990 Census of Population and Housing, series, 2551–8
Pension annuitants, DOD retired military personnel, FY50-91, annual rpt, 3544–1.4
see also Civilian Health and Medical Program of the Uniformed Services
see also Servicepersons life insurance programs
see also Veterans benefits and pensions

Military cemeteries and funerals
Acreage and descriptions of natl park system sites, 1991, biennial listing, 5544–5
Acreage of land under Natl Park Service mgmt, by site, ownership, and region, FY92, semiannual rpt, 5542–1
Air traffic and costs for transport of military personnel and human remains, FY91, annual rpt, 3704–15
American Battle Monuments Commission activities, expenses, and visitors by site, FY87, annual rpt, 9064–1
Assistance (block and categorical grants) programs for State and local govts, FY91, biennial listing, 10044–8
Burials in natl cemeteries, and disposition of gravesites, by location, FY91, annual rpt, 8604–3.3
Burials in natl cemeteries by period of service, markers furnished, and VA grants to State cemeteries, FY73-91, annual rpt, 8604–5.3

Military contracts and procurement
see Defense contracts and procurement

Military courts
see Court of Military Appeals
see Courts-martial and courts of inquiry

Military dependents
Dependents of DOD military and civilian personnel, by service branch and location, FY91, annual rpt, 3544–1.4
Dependents of DOD military and civilian personnel, by service branch and US and foreign location, quarterly rpt, 3542–20
Health care facilities of DOD in US and abroad, beds, admissions, outpatient visits, and births, by service branch, quarterly rpt, 3542–15
Pacific territories population and housing detailed characteristics, by location, 1990 Census of Population and Housing, series, 2551–8
Schools for DOD dependents, student basic skills and college entrance test scores, 1991-92, annual rpt, 3504–16
see also Civilian Health and Medical Program of the Uniformed Services

Military education
Commercial activities of DOD performed in-house, and work-years, by service branch, installation, and State, FY91, annual rpt, 3544–25
Degrees awarded in higher education, by level, field, race, and sex, 1989/90 and trends from 1980/81, annual rpt, 4844–17
Expenditures, staff, students, and facilities for DOD training and education programs, by service branch, FY93, annual rpt, 3504–5

Health care personnel, and accessions by training source, by occupation, specialty, and service branch, FY90, annual rpt, 3544–24
Navy personnel strengths, accessions, and attrition, detailed statistics, quarterly rpt, 3802–4
see also Military training
see also Reserve Officers Training Corps
see also Service academies

Military expenditures
see Defense budgets and appropriations
see Defense contracts and procurement
see Defense expenditures
see Military assistance

Military funerals
see Military cemeteries and funerals

Military health facilities and services
Admissions, beds, outpatient visits, and births in DOD health facilities in US and abroad, by service branch, quarterly rpt, 3542–15
Commercial activities of DOD performed in-house, and work-years, by service branch, installation, and State, FY91, annual rpt, 3544–25
Employment, and accessions by training source, by occupation, specialty, and service branch, FY90, annual rpt, 3544–24
Procurement, DOD prime contract awards by detailed procurement category, FY88-91, annual rpt, 3544–18
VA and non-VA facilities health services sharing contracts, by service type, FY80-90, compilation of papers, 8608–9
see also Civilian Health and Medical Program of the Uniformed Services
see also Veterans health facilities and services

Military housing
Army strategic capability, force strengths, budget, and mgmt, FY79-93, annual rpt, 3704–13
Budget of DOD, base construction and family housing appropriations by facility, service branch, and location, FY91-93, annual rpt, 3544–39
Budget of US, Bush Admin proposals, with detail for defense budgets, and historical data from FY34, FY93, 108–46.2
Construction, renovation, and closure for bases, DOD budget requests by project, service branch, State, and country, FY93, annual rpt, 3544–15
Expenditures and obligations of DOD, by function and service branch, quarterly rpt, 3542–3
Mortgages FHA-insured for 1-family units, by loan type and mortgage characteristics, quarterly rpt, 5142–45
Pacific territories population and housing detailed characteristics, by location, 1990 Census of Population and Housing, series, 2551–8
Population census, 1990: institutionalized population and persons in group quarters, by sex, race, county, place, and urban-rural location, State rpt series, 2531–1
Population census, 1990: institutionalized population and persons in group quarters, for Native American, urban, and metro areas, series, 2531–2

Military intelligence
Budget of DOD, personnel needs, costs, and force readiness by service branch, FY93, annual rpt, 3504–1
Budget of DOD, programs, policies, and operations, FY91, annual rpt, 3544–2
Budget of DOD, R&D appropriations by item, service branch, and defense agency, FY91-93, annual rpt, 3544–33
Espionage against Federal and military agencies, US natls convicted by selected personal, employment, and espionage characteristics, 1945-89, hearings, 25428–2
see also Defense Intelligence Agency
see also Defense Security Assistance Agency

Military intervention
Black military and civilian DOD personnel, by sex, grade, and period of service, and lists of award recipients, officers, and service academy grads, 1770s-90, 3548–22
Deaths by cause, age, race, and rank, and personnel captured and missing, by service branch, FY91, annual rpt, 3544–40
Participants, deaths, veterans living, and compensation and pension recipients, for each US war, 1775-1991, annual rpt, 8604–2
Persian Gulf War aircraft, tank, and personnel carrier deployment and operating capability, and spare parts availability, 1990-91, GAO rpt, 26123–375
Persian Gulf War allied and other countries cash and in-kind contributions, by type and country, 1990-91, GAO rpt, 26123–371
Persian Gulf War allied contributions to Operation Desert Storm offsetting US costs, by country, as of Mar-Apr 1992, annual rpt, 3544–28
Persian Gulf War allied countries cash and in-kind contributions, by type and country, and status of DOD accounts, as of Sept 1991, annual GAO rpt, 26104–24
Persian Gulf War allied countries funding contributions, impact on budget deficit, FY91-97, annual rpt, 21264–2
Persian Gulf War Apache helicopter use and performance, 1991, GAO rpt, 26123–378
Persian Gulf War Army and Air Natl Guard units and personnel mobilized, FY91, annual rpt, 3504–22
Persian Gulf War budget impact, CBO analysis, FY93-97, annual rpt, 26304–3
Persian Gulf War budget impact, OMB analysis, FY93, annual rpt, 104–2.2
Persian Gulf War chemical protective suits and masks contractor deliveries and field inspections, 1990-91, GAO rpt, 26123–387
Persian Gulf War classification actions monitored by Info Security Oversight Office, FY91, annual rpt, 9454–21
Persian Gulf War costs to US by category and service branch, and offsetting contributions by allied country, monthly rpt, 102–3
Persian Gulf War costs to US, offsetting contributions by allied country, as of Jan 1982, annual rpt, 3544–2
Persian Gulf War crude oil drawdowns from Strategic Petroleum Reserve, contract deliveries by purchasing firm, 1st quarter 1991, quarterly rpt, supplement, 3002–13
Persian Gulf War impacts on US budget deficit, FY91, annual GAO rpt, 26104–23
Persian Gulf War merchant ships under US flag activated, crew size, and time needed to activate, Sept 1990, 7708–5
Persian Gulf War Natl Defense Reserve Fleet deployment and availability, 1990-91, GAO rpt, 26123–376
Persian Gulf War Operation Desert Storm deployment, by sex, race, rank, and service branch, 1990-91, GAO rpt, 26123–394
Persian Gulf War Operation Desert Storm impacts on weekly draft registrations, Jan-Mar 1991, annual rpt, 9744–1
Persian Gulf War shipping operations of Military Sealift Command, FY91, annual rpt, 3804–14
Persian Gulf War shipping operations of Military Sealift Command, 1991, annual rpt, 7704–14
Persian Gulf War US military retirees called to active duty, FY91, annual rpt, 3544–31.1
Persian Gulf War US reserve forces mobilization, by component, 1990-91, annual rpt, 3544–31.2
Persian Gulf War veterans post-traumatic stress disorder cases, and VA program use, by site, 1991, annual rpt, 8704–7

Military invasion and occupation
Iraq invasion of Kuwait, oil production disruption impacts on futures prices, family budgets, and oil firms, 1990 hearings, 25408–116
Kuwait oil fires set by Iraq, pollution levels, disease cases, and US remediation and monitoring spending, 1991 rpt, 9188–117
Kuwait oil fires set by Iraqi forces, air pollution levels by substance and site, as of Mar 1991, 9188–116
Kuwait oil fires set by Iraqi forces, air pollution levels, health effects, intl monitoring activities, and wells affected, 1991, GAO rpt, 26113–566

Military law
Navy personnel strengths, accessions, and attrition, detailed statistics, quarterly rpt, 3802–4
US attorneys civil and criminal cases by type and disposition, and collections, by Federal district, FY91, annual rpt, 6004–2.1
see also Court of Military Appeals
see also Courts-martial and courts of inquiry

Military occupation
see Military invasion and occupation

Military pay
Budget of DOD, organization, personnel, weapons, and property, by service branch, State, and country, 1992 annual summary rpt, 3504–13
Budget of DOD, programs, policies, and operations, FY91, annual rpt, 3544–2
Budget of US, Bush Admin proposals, with detail for defense budgets, and historical data from FY34, FY93, 108–46.2
Claims Court caseload by type of suit, and judgments, FY92, annual rpt, 18224–1

Drug enforcement activities of DOD, funding by purpose, FY89-91, GAO rpt, 26123–390
Expenditures and obligations of DOD, by function and service branch, quarterly rpt, 3542–3
Germany natls working at US military bases scheduled for closing, US liability for severance pay, projected FY91-95, GAO rpt, 26123–383
Homosexual military personnel discharges by pay grade, tenure, race, sex, and occupation, and investigations, by service branch, 1980s-90, GAO rpt, 26123–392
Income (household, family, and personal), by source, detailed characteristics, and region, 1991, annual Current Population Rpt, 2546–6.76
Income (personal) per capita and by source, and employment, by industry div, State, MSA, and county, 1969-90, annual CD-ROM, 2704–7
Natl Guard activities, personnel, and facilities, FY91, annual rpt, 3504–22
Natl income and product accounts and components, *Survey of Current Business*, monthly rpt, 2702–1.23
Natl income and product accounts, comprehensive accounts and components, benchmark revisions, 1929-88, 2708–5
Natl income and product accounts, comprehensive accounts and components, *Survey of Current Business*, monthly rpt, 2702–1.26
OASDHI coverage of employment and earnings, and social security contributions, by age, sex, race, State, and county, 1988, annual rpt, 4744–29
Occupational Outlook Handbook, 1992-93, biennial rpt, 6744–1
Payroll and employment, by function, level of govt, and State, 1991, annual rpt, 2466–1.1
Payroll of Fed Govt, by State and county, FY91, annual rpt, 2464–3.1
Payroll of Fed Govt, spending for civilian, military, and postal workers by State, FY91, annual rpt, 2464–2
Payroll, personnel, and contracts spending, by service branch and location, with top 5 contractors and maps, by State and country, FY91, annual rpt, 3544–29
Persian Gulf War costs to US by category and service branch, and offsetting contributions by allied country, monthly rpt, 102–3
Reserve forces personnel strengths and characteristics, by component, quarterly rpt, 3542–4
Sealift Military Command shipping operations, finances, and personnel, FY91, annual rpt, 3804–14
Statistical Abstract of US, 1992 annual data compilation, 2324–1.11
see also Military benefits and pensions

Military personnel

Agent Orange exposure health effects, literature review, 1990, annual rpt series, 8706–1
Aliens serving in US armed forces, citizenship petitions granted by country, FY07-91, annual rpt, 6264–2.4
Army line officer accessions, involuntary separations, and strengths under alternative force reduction plans, FY90-95, 26306–3.121
Army strategic capability, force strengths, budget, and mgmt, FY79-93, annual rpt, 3704–13
Auto rental age restrictions impacts on military personnel, with personnel by age, and rental receipts by company, 1991, GAO rpt, 26123–391
Base support costs by function, and personnel and acreage by installation, by service branch, FY93, annual rpt, 3504–11
Black military and civilian DOD personnel, by sex, grade, and period of service, and lists of award recipients, officers, and service academy grads, 1770s-90, 3548–22
Budget of DOD, organization, personnel, weapons, and property, by service branch, State, and country, 1992 annual summary rpt, 3504–13
Budget of DOD, personnel needs, costs, and force readiness by service branch, FY93, annual rpt, 3504–1
Budget of DOD, programs, policies, and operations, FY91, annual rpt, 3544–2
Budget of US, Bush Admin proposals, with detail for defense budgets, and historical data from FY34, FY93, 108–46.2
Business statistics, detailed data for major industries and economic indicators, 1960-91, *Survey of Current Business* biennial supplement, 2704–1
Coast Guard military and civilian employment, by grade, sex, race, and location, FY91, annual rpt, 7304–18
Coast Guard search and rescue missions, and lives and property lost and saved, by district and assisting unit, FY91, annual rpt, 7404–2
Criminal case processing in military courts, and prisoners by facility, by service branch, data compilation, 1992 annual rpt, 6064–6.5; 6064–6.6
Deaths by cause, age, race, and rank, and personnel captured and missing, by service branch, FY91, annual rpt, 3544–40
Discrimination issues in Army, personnel, promotion, and training by race and sex, annual rpt, discontinued, 3704–10
Economic indicators and components, current data and annual trends, monthly rpt, 23842–1.2
Employee leave benefits in small business compared to larger firms and govts, by occupational group, 1989-90, article, 6722–1.315
Employee paid leave days for military duty, for State and local govt employees, 1990, biennial rpt, 6784–21
Employment and Earnings, detailed data, monthly rpt, 6742–2.4
Employment and payroll, by function, level of govt, and State, 1991, annual rpt, 2466–1.1
Employment situation, earnings, hours, and other BLS economic indicators, transcripts of BLS Commissioner's monthly testimony, periodic rpt, 23846–4
Espionage against Federal and military agencies, US natls convicted by selected personal, employment, and espionage characteristics, 1945-89, hearings, 25428–2
Food stamp recipient household size, composition, income, and income and deductions allowed, summer 1989, annual rpt, 1364–8
Foreign countries economic, social, political, and geographic summary data, by country, 1992, annual factbook, 9114–2
Foreign countries military aid of US, arms sales, and training programs costs and budget requests, by program, world region, and country, FY91-93, annual rpt, 7144–13
Foreign countries military spending, arms trade, and force strengths, with govt spending and population, by country, 1979-89, annual rpt, 9824–1
Health care facilities of DOD in US and abroad, beds, admissions, outpatient visits, and births, by service branch, quarterly rpt, 3542–15
Health care personnel, and accessions by training source, by occupation, specialty, and service branch, FY90, annual rpt, 3544–24
Health care professionals supply and education, by professional and other characteristics, and location, 1960s-92 and projected to 2020, biennial rpt, 4114–8
Homosexual military personnel discharges by pay grade, tenure, race, sex, and occupation, and investigations, by service branch, 1980s-90, GAO rpt, 26123–392
Income (household, family, and personal), by source, detailed characteristics, and region, 1991, annual Current Population Rpt, 2546–6.76
Labor force, wages, hours, and payroll costs, by major industry group and demographic characteristics, *Survey of Current Business*, monthly rpt, 2702–1.7
Malaria cases in US, for military personnel and US and foreign natls, and by country of infection, 1966-90, annual rpt, 4205–4
Migration, immigration, and mover characteristics compared to nonmovers, 1987-90, annual Current Population Rpt, 2546–1.456
Migration since 1990, mover characteristics by same or different area, and compared to nonmovers, 1991, annual Current Population Rpt, 2546–1.464
Natl Guard activities, personnel, and facilities, FY91, annual rpt, 3504–22
NATO, Japan, and South Korea military spending and indicators of ability to support common defense, by country, 1970s-90, annual rpt, 3544–28
Navy personnel radiation exposure on nuclear-powered vessels and at support facilities, and injury claims, 1950s-91, annual rpt, 3804–10
Navy personnel strengths, accessions, and attrition, detailed statistics, quarterly rpt, 3802–4
OASDHI coverage of employment and earnings, and social security contributions, by age, sex, race, State, and county, 1988, annual rpt, 4744–29
Occupational Outlook Handbook, 1992-93, biennial rpt, 6744–1
Pacific territories population and housing detailed characteristics, by location, 1990 Census of Population and Housing, series, 2551–8

Persian Gulf War allied and other countries cash and in-kind contributions, by type and country, 1990-91, GAO rpt, 26123–371
Persian Gulf War Operation Desert Storm deployment, by sex, race, rank, and service branch, 1990-91, GAO rpt, 26123–394
Personnel (civilian) of DOD, by service branch and defense agency, with summary military employment data, quarterly rpt, 3542–16
Personnel (civilian and military) of DOD, by service branch, major installation, and State, as of Sept 1991, annual rpt, 3544–7
Personnel (civilian and military) of DOD, FY85-93, GAO rpt, 26123–399
Personnel active duty enlisted accessions by race, and goals, by sex and service branch, quarterly press release, 3542–7
Personnel, contracts, and payroll spending, by service branch and location, with top 5 contractors and maps, by State and country, FY91, annual rpt, 3544–29
Personnel occupational distribution, by race, sex, and service branch, FY90, GAO rpt, 26123–381
Personnel reserve and active duty force mix and costs under alternative reduction cases, by service branch, 1990 and projected to 1997, 26306–6.172
Personnel strengths, for active duty, civilians, and dependents, by service branch and US and foreign location, quarterly rpt, 3542–20
Personnel strengths, for active duty, civilians, and reserves, by service branch, FY91 and trends, annual rpt, 3544–1
Personnel strengths, for active duty, civilians, and reserves, by service branch, quarterly rpt, 3542–14
Personnel strengths in US and abroad, by service branch, world area, and country, quarterly press release, 3542–9
Personnel strengths, summary by service branch, monthly press release, 3542–2
Physicians, by specialty, age, sex, and location of training and practice, 1990, State rpt series, 4116–6
Reductions in active duty force planned by service branch, and women and minorities affected by Army and Air Force plans, FY90-91, GAO rpt, 26123–373
Reserve forces personnel and equipment strengths, and readiness, by reserve component, FY91, annual rpt, 3544–31
Reserve forces personnel strengths and characteristics, by component, quarterly rpt, 3542–4
Sealift Military Command shipping operations, finances, and personnel, FY91, annual rpt, 3804–14
Statistical Abstract of US, 1992 annual data compilation, 2324–1.11
Terrorism (intl) incidents, casualties, and attacks on US targets, by attack type and country, 1991, annual rpt, 7004–22
Terrorism (intl) incidents, casualties, and attacks on US targets, by attack type and world area, 1991, annual rpt, 7004–13
Terrorism incidents in US, related activity, and casualties, by attack type, target, group, and location, 1991, annual rpt, 6224–6
Transport of personnel by DOD, and costs, by service branch and mode of transport, FY91, annual rpt, 3704–15
War participants, deaths, veterans living, and compensation and pension recipients, for each US war, 1775-1991, annual rpt, 8604–2
World War II soldier survey results, questionnaire forms, and related rpts, Natl Archives special collection, 1991 rpt, 9516–1.10
see also Courts-martial and courts of inquiry
see also Military benefits and pensions
see also Military dependents
see also Military education
see also Military pay
see also Military training
see also Retired military personnel
see also Selective service
see also Veterans
see also Voluntary military service

Military policy
see Arms trade
see Defense budgets and appropriations
see Military assistance
see Military strategy
see National defense

Military post exchanges and commissaries
Financial statements of Army and Air Force Exchange Service, 1990, annual rpt, 3504–21
Labor productivity of Federal employees, indexes of output and labor costs by function, FY67-90, annual rpt, 6824–1.6
Labor unions recognized in Fed Govt, agreements and membership by agency and facility, as of Jan 1991, biennial listing, 9844–14
Operations, listing by post exchange and location worldwide, 1991-92, annual rpt, 3504–10
Poultry and egg production, prices, receipts, trade, and disposition, by species, 1960-90, annual rpt, 1564–13

Military prisons
Prisoners in Federal instns, admissions, releases, and recidivism, by region, monthly rpt series, 6242–1
Prisoners in military prisons, and capacity, by service branch and facility, data compilation, 1992 annual rpt, 6064–6.6

Military reserves
see Armed services reserves

Military science
Budget of DOD, R&D appropriations by item, service branch, and defense agency, FY91-93, annual rpt, 3544–33
see also Arms control and disarmament
see also Civil defense
see also Defense research
see also Logistics
see also Military strategy

Military service
see Selective service
see Voluntary military service

Military service academies
see Service academies

Military services
see Armed services

Military strategy
Army strategic capability, force strengths, budget, and mgmt, FY79-93, annual rpt, 3704–13
Base support costs by function, and personnel and acreage by installation, by service branch, FY93, annual rpt, 3504–11
Budget of DOD, personnel needs, costs, and force readiness by service branch, FY93, annual rpt, 3504–1
Budget of DOD, programs, policies, and operations, FY91, annual rpt, 3544–2
Budget of DOD, R&D appropriations by item, service branch, and defense agency, FY91-93, annual rpt, 3544–33
Foreign countries military aid of US, arms sales, and training programs costs and budget requests, by program, world region, and country, FY91-93, annual rpt, 7144–13
Personnel reserve and active duty force mix and costs under alternative reduction cases, by service branch, 1990 and projected to 1997, 26306–6.172
Reserve forces personnel and equipment strengths, and readiness, by reserve component, FY91, annual rpt, 3544–31
Stockpiling of strategic material, inventories and needs, by commodity, 1992, annual rpt, 3544–37

Military supplies and property
Bombing incidents and casualties by target and circumstances, and explosives theft and recovery, by State, 1987-91, annual rpt, 8484–4
Budget of DOD, programs, policies, and operations, FY91, annual rpt, 3544–2
Budget of DOD, R&D appropriations by item, service branch, and defense agency, FY91-93, annual rpt, 3544–33
Budget of DOD, weapons acquisition costs by system and service branch, FY91-93, annual rpt, 3504–2
Budget of US, Bush Admin proposals, with detail for defense budgets, and historical data from FY34, FY93, 108–46.2
Capital (fixed), govt and private nonresidential structures and equipment, residential capital, and consumer-owned durable goods, 1925-90, annual article, 2702–1.305; 2702–1.327
Chemical protective suits and masks contractor deliveries and field inspections during Persian Gulf War, 1990-91, GAO rpt, 26123–387
Commercial activities of DOD performed in-house, and work-years, by service branch, installation, and State, FY91, annual rpt, 3544–25
Electric power plants of Fed Govt, conversion to alternative fuels, 1992, annual rpt, 3334–2
Expenditures and obligations of DOD, by function and service branch, quarterly rpt, 3542–3
Expenditures for DOD base support by function, and personnel and acreage by installation, by service branch, FY93, annual rpt, 3504–11
Exports and imports of US, by country and detailed commodity, monthly rpt, 2422–12
Foreign countries military aid and arms sales of US, by weapon type, as of Sept 1991, annual rpt, 3904–3
Foreign countries military aid of US, arms sales, and training programs costs and budget requests, by program, world region, and country, FY91-93, annual rpt, 7144–13
Freight (waterborne domestic and foreign) by commodity, traffic, and passengers, by port and waterway, 1989, annual rpt, 3754–3

Instruments and related products shipments, trade, use, and firms, by detailed type, 1991, annual Current Industrial Rpt, 2506–12.26
Inventory of DOD property, supplies, and equipment, by service branch, annual rpt, discontinued, 3544–6
Mexico imports from US, by industry and State, 1987-91, 2048–154
Oil imports from Persian Gulf, US and OECD dependence indicators, and US military supply, late 1970s-80s and supply disruptions from 1951, 3166–6.65
Persian Gulf War aircraft, tank, and personnel carrier deployment and operating capability, and spare parts availability, 1990-91, GAO rpt, 26123–375
Persian Gulf War allied and other countries cash and in-kind contributions, by type and country, 1990-91, GAO rpt, 26123–371
Persian Gulf War allied countries cash and in-kind contributions, by type and country, and status of DOD accounts, as of Sept 1991, annual GAO rpt, 26104–24
Persian Gulf War costs to US by category and service branch, and offsetting contributions by allied country, monthly rpt, 102–3
Reserve forces personnel and equipment strengths, and readiness, by reserve component, FY91, annual rpt, 3544–31
Sealift Military Command shipping operations, finances, and personnel, FY91, annual rpt, 3804–14
Shipments by DOD of military and personal property, passenger traffic, and costs, by service branch and mode of transport, FY91, annual rpt, 3704–15
Shipments of military and personal property by commercial cariers, and cost savings from bill audits and rate negotiations, FY99-91, GAO rpt, 26123–369
Theft and fraud losses of military supplies, and inventory control measures adequacy, 1988-91, GAO rpt, 26123–377
see also Ammunition
see also Arms trade
see also Defense contracts and procurement
see also Logistics
see also Military assistance
see also Military bases, posts, and reservations
see also Military vehicles
see also Military weapons

Military training
Accidents during training activities, and deaths by cause, by service branch, FY88-91, GAO rpt, 26123–397
Budget of DOD, organization, personnel, weapons, and property, by service branch, State, and country, 1992 annual summary rpt, 3504–13
Budget of DOD, personnel needs, costs, and force readiness by service branch, FY93, annual rpt, 3504–1
Budget of DOD, programs, policies, and operations, FY91, annual rpt, 3544–2
Budget of DOD, R&D appropriations by item, service branch, and defense agency, FY91-93, annual rpt, 3544–33
Commercial activities of DOD performed in-house, and work-years, by service branch, installation, and State, FY91, annual rpt, 3544–25
Expenditures for DOD base support by function, and personnel and acreage by installation, by service branch, FY93, annual rpt, 3504–11
Expenditures, staff, students, and facilities for DOD training and education programs, by service branch, FY93, annual rpt, 3504–5
Foreign countries economic and military aid loans and grants from US and intl agencies, by program and country, FY46-91, annual rpt, 9914–5
Foreign countries human rights conditions in 170 countries, and US economic and military aid, 1991, annual rpt, 21384–3
Foreign countries military aid of US, arms sales, and training, by country, FY50-91, annual rpt, 3904–3
Foreign countries military aid of US, arms sales, and training programs costs and budget requests, by program, world region, and country, FY91-93, annual rpt, 7144–13
Health care personnel, and accessions by training source, by occupation, specialty, and service branch, FY90, annual rpt, 3544–24
Natl Guard activities, personnel, and facilities, FY91, annual rpt, 3504–22
Navy personnel strengths, accessions, and attrition, detailed statistics, quarterly rpt, 3802–4
Occupational qualification and skill improvement training, workers participating by training source, occupation, age, sex, and race, 1991, 6728–32
Procurement, DOD prime contract awards by detailed procurement category, FY88-91, annual rpt, 3544–18
Reserve forces personnel and equipment strengths, and readiness, by reserve component, FY91, annual rpt, 3544–31
see also Military education
see also Reserve Officers Training Corps
see also Service academies

Military tribunals
see Courts-martial and courts of inquiry

Military vehicles
Budget of DOD, procurement appropriations by item, service branch, and defense agency, FY91-93, annual rpt, 3544–32
Budget of DOD, programs, policies, and operations, FY91, annual rpt, 3544–2
Budget of DOD, weapons acquisition costs by system and service branch, FY91-93, annual rpt, 3504–2
Coast Guard search and rescue missions, and lives and property lost and saved, by district and assisting unit, FY91, annual rpt, 7404–2
Energy use by mode of transport, fuel supply, and demographic and economic factors of vehicle use, 1970s-90, annual rpt, 3304–5
Exports and imports of US, by country and detailed commodity, monthly rpt, 2422–12
Exports and imports of US, by Harmonized System 6-digit commodity and country, 1991, annual rpt, 2424–13
Exports of US, detailed Schedule B commodities with countries of destination, 1991, annual rpt, 2424–10
Foreign countries military aid and arms sales of US, by weapon type, as of Sept 1991, annual rpt, 3904–3
Foreign countries military spending, arms trade, and force strengths, with govt spending and population, by country, 1979-89, annual rpt, 9824–1
Input-output structure of US economy, detailed interindustry transactions for 541 industries, and components of final demand, 1982 benchmark data, 2708–17
Manufacturing annual survey, 1990: finances and operations, by SIC 2- to 4-digit industry, series, 2506–14
Manufacturing census, 1987: concentration of largest firms measured by value added, and for shipments by SIC 2- and 4-digit industry, subject rpt, 2497–6
Manufacturing census, 1987: shipments of manufacturers products, by customer class and SIC 2- and 4-digit industry, subject rpt, 2497–4
NATO and Warsaw Pact military forces reductions and ceilings under CFE treaty, inspections, and US compliance costs and savings, 1991 hearings, 25388–59
Persian Gulf War aircraft, tank, and personnel carrier deployment and operating capability, and spare parts availability, 1990-91, GAO rpt, 26123–375
Persian Gulf War allied and other countries cash and in-kind contributions, by type and country, 1990-91, GAO rpt, 26123–371
Persian Gulf War allied countries cash and in-kind contributions, by type and country, and status of DOD accounts, as of Sept 1991, annual GAO rpt, 26104–24
Procurement, DOD prime contract awards by category, contract and contractor type, and service branch, FY82-1st half FY92, semiannual rpt, 3542–1
Procurement, DOD prime contract awards by category, contractor type, and State, FY89-91, annual rpt, 3544–11
Procurement, DOD prime contract awards by detailed procurement category, FY88-91, annual rpt, 3544–18
Shipments by DOD of military and personal property, passenger traffic, and costs, by service branch and mode of transport, FY91, annual rpt, 3704–15

Military weapons
Army strategic capability, force strengths, budget, and mgmt, FY79-93, annual rpt, 3704–13
Budget of DOD, organization, personnel, weapons, and property, by service branch, State, and country, 1992 annual summary rpt, 3504–13
Budget of DOD, programs, policies, and operations, FY91, annual rpt, 3544–2
Budget of DOD, R&D appropriations by item, service branch, and defense agency, FY91-93, annual rpt, 3544–33
Czechoslovakia military weapons production in Czech and Slovak regions, and domestic and export arms sales, 1987-90, hearing, 25408–115
Foreign countries military aid of US, arms sales, and training programs costs and budget requests, by program, world region, and country, FY91-93, annual rpt, 7144–13

Foreign countries military spending, arms trade, and force strengths, with govt spending and population, by country, 1979-89, annual rpt, 9824–1
NATO and Warsaw Pact military forces reductions and ceilings under CFE treaty, as of Nov 1990, 9828–1
NATO and Warsaw Pact military forces reductions and ceilings under CFE treaty, inspections, and US compliance costs and savings, 1991 hearings, 25388–59
Price indexes (producer), by stage of processing and detailed commodity, monthly 1991, annual rpt, 6764–2
Sealift Military Command shipping operations, finances, and personnel, FY91, annual rpt, 3804–14
Shipments by DOD of military and personal property, passenger traffic, and costs, by service branch and mode of transport, FY91, annual rpt, 3704–15
see also Ammunition
see also Arms trade
see also Chemical and biological warfare agents
see also Defense contracts and procurement
see also Defense expenditures
see also Military aircraft
see also Military assistance
see also Military vehicles
see also Missiles and rockets
see also Naval vessels
see also Nuclear weapons
see also Torpedoes

Militia
see National Guard

Milk and milk products
see Dairy industry and products

Miller, Glenn H., Jr.
"Changing Economy of the Tenth District", 9381–1.306
"Tenth District: Matching a Nation in Recovery", 9381–1.302

Miller, Louisa F.
"Marriage, Divorce, and Remarriage in the 1990's", 2546–2.166

Miller, Michael A.
"Time-Off Benefits in Small Establishments", 6722–1.315

Miller, Preston J.
"Real Effects of Monetary Policy in a World Economy", 9383–20.24

Miller, Randy
"Controlled Foreign Corporations, 1988", 8302–2.322
"Foreign Recipients of U.S. Income, 1989", 8302–2.308

Miller, T.
"Costs of Highway Crashes", 7558–114

Miller, William L.
"Exploratory Study of the Relationship Between Hypertension and Diet Diversity Among Saba Islanders", 4042–3.343

Mills, Leonard O.
"Effects of Countercyclical Monetary Policy on Money and Interest Rates: An Evaluation of Evidence from FOMC Documents", 9387–8.259
"Have Regional Per-Capita Incomes Converged?", 9387–8.257

Miltenberger, R. P.
"Brookhaven National Laboratory, Site Environmental Report for 1990", 3324–2.9

Milwaukee, Wis.
CPI by component for US city average, and by selected metro area, region, and population size, monthly rpt, 6762–2
see also under By City and By SMSA or MSA in the "Index by Categories"

Mine accidents and safety
Alaska occupational injury deaths, by cause, occupation, and industry, early 1980s, article, 4042–3.307
Coal miners working under unsupported mine roof, reasons, supervisor reactions, and preventive measures, 1989-90 survey, 5608–173
Coal mining and related operations occupational injuries and incidence, employment, and hours, 1990, annual rpt, 6664–4
Coal mining disabling injuries and deaths, 1937-90, biennial rpt, 3164–79
Deaths in mining accidents, by circumstances and selected victim characteristics, semiannual rpt series, 6662–3
Diesel engines exhaust in underground mines, emissions measurement and control, 1992 conf, 5608–177
Drug abuse screening and employee aid programs activities and policies in mining, by mineral and firm size, 1989, 6668–8
Fed Govt spending in States, by type, program, agency, and State, FY91, annual rpt, 2464–2
Injuries by circumstances, employment, and hours, for mining industries by type of operation and State, quarterly rpt, 6662–1
Injuries, illnesses, and lost workdays, by SIC 2-digit industry, 1990-91, annual press release, 6844–3
Injury and illness rates by SIC 2- to 4-digit industry, and deaths by cause and industry div, 1990, annual rpt, 6844–1
Injury and illness rates, by SIC 2- to 4-digit industry, 1989-90, annual rpt, 6844–7
Metal mines and related operations occupational injuries and incidence, employment, and hours, 1990, annual rpt, 6664–3
Nonmetallic minerals mines and related operations occupational injuries and incidence, employment, and hours, 1990, annual rpt, 6664–1
Sand and gravel mines and related operations occupational injuries and incidence, employment, and hours, 1990, annual rpt, 6664–2
Statistical Abstract of US, 1992 annual data compilation, 2324–1.25
Stone mines and related operations occupational injuries and incidence, employment, and hours, 1990, annual rpt, 6664–5
see also Black lung disease

Mine Safety and Health Administration
Budget of US, obligations and authority by function, agency, and program, with summaries and analyses, FY93, annual rpt, 104–2
Coal mining and related operations occupational injuries and incidence, employment, and hours, 1990, annual rpt, 6664–4
Deaths in mining accidents, by circumstances and selected victim characteristics, semiannual rpt series, 6662–3
Drug abuse screening and employee aid programs activities and policies in mining, by mineral and firm size, 1989, 6668–8
Expenditures of Fed Govt in States, by type, program, agency, and State, FY91, annual rpt, 2464–2
Injuries by circumstances, employment, and hours, for mining industries by type of operation and State, quarterly rpt, 6662–1
Inspections, closure orders, and violations contested and upheld, for Federal and State occupational safety agencies, FY91, GAO rpt, 26121–461
Metal mines and related operations occupational injuries and incidence, employment, and hours, 1990, annual rpt, 6664–3
Nonmetallic minerals mines and related operations occupational injuries and incidence, employment, and hours, 1990, annual rpt, 6664–1
Sand and gravel mines and related operations occupational injuries and incidence, employment, and hours, 1990, annual rpt, 6664–2
Stone mines and related operations occupational injuries and incidence, employment, and hours, 1990, annual rpt, 6664–5

Mineral Industry Surveys
Explosives and blasting agents use, by type, industry, and State, 1991, annual rpt, 5614–22
Lime producing firms and plants, with operating data, 1991, annual listing, 5614–31
Peat producing firms, with operating data, 1991, annual listing, 5614–32
Phosphate rock production, prices, sales, trade, and use, 1992, annual rpt, 5614–20
Potash production, prices, trade, use, and sales, 1991 and 1992 crop years, annual rpt, 5614–19
Production of minerals, 1991, annual preliminary rpt, 5614–6
Production, trade, stocks, and use of minerals, monthly commodity rpt series, 5612–1
Production, trade, stocks, and use of minerals, quarterly commodity rpt series, 5612–2
Production, trade, use, and industry operations, advance annual commodity rpt series, 5614–5

Mineral leases
Coal and other fossil fuel production on Federal land, 1991 and trends from 1949, annual rpt, 3164–74.1
Coal leasing activity on Federal and Indian lands, acreage, production, and revenues, by State, 1981-90, biennial rpt, 3164–79
Expenditures of Fed Govt in States, by type, program, agency, and State, FY91, annual rpt, 2464–2
Fed Govt receipts by source and outlays by agency, *Treasury Bulletin*, quarterly rpt, 8002–4.1
Flow-of-funds accounts, savings, investments, and credit statements, quarterly rpt, 9365–3.3
Forest Service activities and finances, by region and State, FY91, annual rpt, 1204–1

Forests (natl) revenue, by source, forest, and State, FY91, annual rpt, 1204–34
Geothermal resources, power plant capacity and operating status, leases, and wells, by location, 1960s-95, 3308–87
Indian and govt lands under Bur of Indian Affairs mgmt, acreage, leases, and use, 1989, annual rpt, 5704–12
Land Mgmt Bur activities and funding by State, FY90, annual rpt, 5724–13
Land Mgmt Bur activities in southwestern US, FY91, annual rpt, 5724–15
Multinatl firms US affiliates, finances, and operations, by industry, world area of parent firm, and State, 1989-90, annual rpt, 2704–4
New Mexico Caballo Resource Area public land mgmt, and grazing, environmental, and leasing activities, FY90-91, annual rpt, 5724–17
Offshore minerals lease sales environmental and economic impacts in coastal areas, final statement series, 5736–7
Production and revenue from oil, gas, and minerals on Federal and Indian lands, by State, 1991 and trends from 1920, annual rpt, 5734–2
Public lands acreage and use, and Land Mgmt Bur activities and finances, annual State rpt series, 5724–11
Public lands acreage, grants, use, revenues, and allocations, by State, FY91 and trends, annual rpt, 5724–1
Public lands minerals resources and availability, State rpt series, 5606–7
USDA revenue, by source and subagency, FY88-92, GAO rpt, 26113–602
see also Oil and gas leases

Minerals Management Service
Alaska Beaufort Sea pollutant concentrations in sediment and marine life, by contaminant and site, 1985-89, 5738–33
Alaska rural areas population characteristics, and energy resources dev effects, series, 5736–5
Budget of US, obligations and authority by function, agency, and program, with summaries and analyses, FY93, annual rpt, 104–2
California OCS oil and gas dev impacts on water quality, marine life, and sediments, by site, 1986-90, annual rpt, 5734–11
Expenditures of Fed Govt in States, by type, program, agency, and State, FY91, annual rpt, 2464–2
Fish (anadromous species) population, migration, and habitat conditions, for coastal Beaufort Sea, summer 1990, 5738–37
Gulf of Mexico oil and gas leases, by company and tract, 1990, annual rpt, 5734–8
Gulf of Mexico oil and gas reserves, production, and leasing status, by location, 1990, annual rpt, 5734–6
Offshore minerals lease sales environmental and economic impacts in coastal areas, final statement series, 5736–7
Oil and gas OCS leasing and exploration activity, production, revenue, and environmental studies, by location, quarterly rpt, 5732–1
Oil and gas OCS reserves, geophysical data collection activities and costs, by region, 1976-90, 5738–41
Oil and gas OCS reserves of Fed Govt, leasing and exploration activity, production, revenue, and costs, by ocean area, FY91, annual rpt, 5734–4
Oil, gas, and minerals production and revenue on Federal and Indian land, by State, 1991 and trends from 1920, annual rpt, 5734–2
Oil spill off Washington coast in 1988, pollutant levels and impacts on marine biota, by site, as of 1990, 5738–38
Oregon OCS rocky banks fish and invertebrate population and habitats, 1988-90, 5738–39
Pacific Northwest Indian tribes environmental, economic, and cultural impacts of OCS oil and gas lease and dev, with background data, 1970s-92, 5738–35
Pacific Ocean OCS oil and gas production, and wells, by drilling platform under Federal lease, 1960s-90, annual rpt, 5734–9
Pacific Ocean OCS oil and gas production, reserves, and wells drilled by location, 1990, annual rpt, 5734–7
Ships wrecked off Alaska, characteristics, deaths, cargo, and whale catch, by vessel and location, 1763-1937, 5738–34
Washington and Oregon coastal areas recreation resources, and impacts of OCS oil and gas dev, 1983-88, 5738–40
Whales (bowhead and white) migration through Beaufort Sea, behavior impacts of oil drilling and aircraft noise, spring 1990, 5738–27
Whales population and behavior in Chukchi and Beaufort Seas, by endangered species, 1982-91, 5738–32
Whales population and behavior in Chukchi and Beaufort Seas, by endangered species, 1990, 5738–36

Mines and mineral resources
Alaska minerals resources and geologic characteristics, compilation of papers, 1990, annual rpt, 5664–15
Alaska minerals resources, production, oil and gas leases, reserves, and exploratory wells, with maps and bibl, 1990, annual rpt, 5664–11
Capital expenditures for plant and equipment, by industry div, monthly rpt, quarterly data, 23842–1.1
Capital expenditures for plant and equipment, by major industry group, quarterly rpt, 2502–2
Census Bur data files and rpts, coverage and availability, 1992 annual listing, 2304–2
China minerals production and trade, by commodity, 1989-90, annual rpt, 5604–38
Communist and transitional economy countries trade with US, by detailed commodity and country, quarterly rpt with articles, 9882–2
County Business Patterns, 1989: employment, establishments, and payroll, by SIC 2- to 4-digit industry and county, annual State rpt series, 2326–8
County Business Patterns, 1990: employment, establishments, and payroll, by SIC 2- to 4-digit industry and county, annual State rpt series, 2326–6
Deaths and rates, by cause and selected social, demographic, and employment characteristics, 1979-85, natl longitudinal study, 4478–186
Employment and Earnings, detailed data, monthly rpt, 6742–2.5
Employment, earnings, and hours, by selected SIC 1- to 4-digit industry, State, and for 275 MSAs, 1987-92, 6748–81
Employment, earnings, and hours, by SIC 1- to 4-digit industry, monthly 1989-Feb 1992, annual rpt, 6744–4
Employment, earnings, and hours, monthly press release, 6742–5
Employment of minorities and women, by occupation, SIC 1- to 3-digit industry, State, and MSA, 1991, annual rpt, 9244–1
Employment situation, earnings, hours, and other BLS economic indicators, transcripts of BLS Commissioner's monthly testimony, periodic rpt, 23846–4
Employment, unemployment, and labor force characteristics, by region and census div, 1991, annual rpt, 6744–7.1
Energy use by mode of transport, fuel supply, and demographic and economic factors of vehicle use, 1970s-90, annual rpt, 3304–5
Equipment for mining and construction, trade, tariffs, and industry operating data, 1992 rpt, 9885–9.2
Explosives and blasting agents use, by type, industry, and State, 1991, Mineral Industry Surveys, annual rpt, 5614–22
Exports and imports between US and outlying areas, by detailed commodity and mode of transport, 1991, annual rpt, 2424–11
Exports and imports of US, by country and detailed commodity, monthly rpt, 2422–12
Exports and imports of US by country, and trade shifts by commodity, 1991, annual rpt, 9884–25
Exports and imports of US, by Harmonized System 6-digit commodity and country, 1991, annual rpt, 2424–13
Exports and imports of US, by transport mode, country, and SITC 1- to 3-digit commodity, 1991, annual rpt, 2424–12
Exports, imports, tariffs, and industry operating data for minerals and metals industries, commodity rpt series, 9885–13
Exports of US, detailed Schedule B commodities with countries of destination, 1991, annual rpt, 2424–10
Fed Govt financial and nonfinancial domestic aid, 1992 base edition, annual listing, 104–5
Finances and operations, by SIC 2- to 4-digit industry, forecast 1992, annual rpt, 2044–28
Financial statements for manufacturing, mining, and trade corporations, by selected SIC 2- to 3-digit industry, quarterly rpt, 2502–1
Foreign and US minerals industries operations, trends, and projections for selected countries, series, 5606–5
Foreign and US minerals supply under alternative market conditions, reserves, and background industry data, series, 5606–4
Foreign countries mineral production, reserves, and industry role in domestic economy and world supply, world area and country rpt series, 5606–1

Foreign direct investment in US, by industry group and world area, 1989-91, annual article, 2702–1.331
Foreign direct investment in US, major transactions by type, industry, country, and US location, 1990, annual rpt, 2044–20
Foreign direct investment of US, by industry group and world area, 1989-91, annual article, 2702–1.332
Geological Survey activities and funding, FY91, annual rpt, 5664–8
Gross State Product by component, industry div, and State, 1977-89, article, 2702–1.303
Imports, exports, and employment impacts, by SIC 2- to 4-digit industry and commodity, quarterly rpt, 2322–2
Imports of US given duty-free treatment for value of US material sent abroad, by commodity and country, 1987-90, annual rpt, 9884–14
Income tax returns of foreign corporations and individuals, and US entities abroad, detailed data compilation, 1970s-89, quinquennial rpt, 8308–31
Input-output structure of US economy, detailed interindustry transactions for 541 industries, and components of final demand, 1982 benchmark data, 2708–17
Machinery and equipment for mining, shipments, firms, and exports by product, 1991, annual Current Industrial Rpt, 2506–12.4
Manufacturing census, 1987: concentration of largest firms measured by value added, and for shipments by SIC 2- and 4-digit industry, subject rpt, 2497–6
Mexico imports from US, by industry and State, 1987-91, 2048–154
Mineral Industry Surveys, commodity reviews of production, trade, stocks, and use, monthly rpt series, 5612–1
Mineral Industry Surveys, commodity reviews of production, trade, stocks, and use, quarterly rpt series, 5612–2
Mineral Industry Surveys, commodity reviews of production, trade, use, and industry operations, advance annual rpt series, 5614–5
Mineral Industry Surveys, State reviews of production, 1991, preliminary annual rpt, 5614–6
Minerals Yearbook, Vol 1, 1989: commodity reviews of production, use, trade, prices, and mining operations, annual rpt, 5604–33
Minerals Yearbook, Vol 1, 1990: commodity reviews of production, reserves, supply, use, and trade, annual rpt series, 5604–20
Minerals Yearbook, Vol 1, 1991: commodity reviews of production, reserves, supply, use, and trade, annual rpt series, 5604–15
Minerals Yearbook, Vol 2, 1989: State reviews of production and sales by commodity, and business activity, annual rpt series, 5604–16
Minerals Yearbook, Vol 2, 1990: State reviews of production and sales by commodity, and business activity, annual rpt series, 5604–22
Minerals Yearbook, Vol 3: foreign country reviews of production, trade, and policy, by commodity, annual rpt series, suspended, 5604–17
Minerals Yearbook, Vol 3, 1989: foreign country reviews of production, trade, and policy, by commodity, annual rpt, 5604–35
Multinatl firms US affiliates finances and operations, by industry, country of parent firm, and State, 1987, 2708–48
Multinatl firms US affiliates, finances, and operations, by industry, world area of parent firm, and State, 1989-90, annual rpt, 2704–4
Multinatl US firms and foreign affiliates finances and operations, by industry and country, 1989 benchmark survey, annual rpt, 2704–5
Multinatl US firms foreign affiliates, income statement items by asset size, industry, and country, 1988, biennial article, 8302–2.322
Natl income and product accounts, comprehensive accounts and components, benchmark revisions, 1929-88, 2708–5
Natl income and product accounts, comprehensive accounts and components, *Survey of Current Business*, monthly rpt, 2702–1.29
OECD trade, total and for 4 major countries, and US trade by country, by commodity, 1980-90, world area rpt series, 9116–1
Ohio River basin waterway facilities, freight by commodity and port, and recreation, by waterway, 1988-89, annual rpt, 3754–6
Pacific territories population and housing detailed characteristics, by location, 1990 Census of Population and Housing, series, 2551–8
Pollution abatement capital spending, for mining, petroleum refining, and electric utilities, 1990, annual Current Industrial Rpt, 2506–3.6
Price indexes (producer), by stage of processing and detailed commodity, monthly rpt, 6762–6
Price indexes (producer), by stage of processing and detailed commodity, monthly 1991, annual rpt, 6764–2
Producer Price Index, by major commodity group and subgroup, and processing stage, monthly press release, 6762–5
Production and capacity use indexes, by SIC 2- to 4-digit industry, monthly rpt, 9365–2.24
Production, prices, trade, and foreign and US industry devs, by commodity, bimonthly rpt, 5602–4
Production, prices, trade, use, employment, tariffs, and stockpiles, by mineral, with foreign comparisons, 1987-91, annual rpt, 5604–18
Production, trade, use, and foreign investment in US industry, for minerals, 1985-90 and projected to 2000, annual rpt, 5304–5
Public lands acreage and use, and Land Mgmt Bur activities and finances, annual State rpt series, 5724–11
Public lands minerals resources and availability, State rpt series, 5606–7
Publications and patents of Mines Bur, monthly listing, 5602–2
Real estate assets of failed thrifts, inventory of properties available from Resolution Trust Corp, 1991, semiannual listing, 9722–2.7
Real estate assets of failed thrifts, inventory of properties available from Resolution Trust Corp, 1992, semiannual listing, 9722–2.14
Rope (wire) used for mine hoists, characteristics by type, 1991 rpt, 5608–172
SEC registration, firms required to file annual rpts, as of Sept 1991, annual listing, 9734–5
Small business finances, operations, owner characteristics, and Federal contracts, 1980s-90, annual rpt, 9764–6
Southeastern US employment by industry div, earnings, and hours, for 8 States, quarterly press release, 6942–7
Soviet Union minerals production and exports, by commodity and Republic, 1975-90, annual rpt, 5604–39
Statistical Abstract of US, 1992 annual data compilation, 2324–1.15; 2324–1.25
Tariff Schedule of US, classifications and rates of duty by detailed imported commodity, 1993 base edition, 9886–13
Tax (income) returns filed, by type of filer, selected income items, quarterly rpt, 8302–2.1
Tax (income) returns for foreign corporate activity in US, selected income and tax items, by industry div and selected country, 1988, article, 8302–2.309
Tax (income) returns of corporations, income and tax items by asset size and detailed industry, 1989, annual rpt, 8304–4; 8304–21
Tax (income) returns of corporations with foreign tax credit, income and tax items by industry group, 1988, biennial article, 8302–2.316
Tax (income) returns of partnerships, income statement and balance sheet items, by industry group, 1990, annual article, 8302–2.314
Tax (income) returns of sole proprietorships, income statement items, by industry group, 1990, annual article, 8302–2.317; 8302–2.320
Wage and benefit changes from collective bargaining and mgmt decisions, by industry div, monthly rpt, 6782–1
Wages by occupation, and benefits, for office and plant workers, periodic MSA survey rpt series, 6785–16; 6785–17
Waste (industrial) generation, disposal, and regulation, by industry and State, mid 1980s-90, 26358–256
Water (groundwater) supply, quality, chemistry, other characteristics, and use, regional rpt series, 5666–25
Water use by end use, well withdrawals, and public supply deliveries, by county, State rpt series, 5666–24
Wetlands acid neutralizing capability for mining runoff, with pollutant levels and site characteristics, for Pennsylvania, 1987-90, 5608–171
Wholesale trade sales and inventories, by SIC 2- to 3-digit kind of business, monthly rpt, 2413–7
see also Abrasive materials
see also Advanced materials
see also Aluminum and aluminum industry
see also Cement and concrete
see also Census of Mineral Industries

see also Clay industry and products
see also Coal and coal mining
see also Copper and copper industry
see also Gases
see also Gemstones
see also Gold
see also Iron and steel industry
see also Lead and lead industry
see also Metals and metal industries
see also Mine accidents and safety
see also Mineral leases
see also Natural gas and gas industry
see also Nonmetallic minerals and mines
see also Offshore oil and gas
see also Oil shale
see also Petroleum and petroleum industry
see also Phosphate
see also Potash
see also Radioactive materials
see also Sand and gravel
see also Severance taxes
see also Silver
see also Stockpiling
see also Stone products and quarries
see also Strategic materials
see also Tin and tin industry
see also Uranium
see also Zinc and zinc industry
see also under By Industry in the "Index by Categories"

Minimum income
see Income maintenance

Minimum wage
Fair Labor Standards Act minimum wage rates, 1938-91, annual rpt, 4744–3.1
Foreign countries labor conditions, union coverage, and work accidents, annual country rpt series, 6366–4
Labor laws enacted, by State, 1991, annual article, 6722–1.309
Statistical Abstract of US, 1992 annual data compilation, 2324–1.13

Mining
see Mine accidents and safety
see Mines and mineral resources

Mink
see Wildlife and wildlife conservation

Minneapolis, Minn.
CPI by component for US city average, and by selected metro area, region, and population size, monthly rpt, 6762–2
Drug abuse indicators for selected metro areas, research results, data collection, and policy issues, 1992 semiannual conf, 4492–5
Housing and households characteristics, unit and neighborhood quality, and journey to work by MSA location, for 11 MSAs, 1985 survey, supplement, 2485–8
Housing and households characteristics, 1989 survey, MSA fact sheet, 2485–11.11
Housing and households detailed characteristics, and unit and neighborhood quality, by location, 1989 survey, MSA rpt, 2485–6.7
Housing starts and completions authorized by building permits in 40 MSAs, quarterly rpt, 2382–9
see also under By City and By SMSA or MSA in the "Index by Categories"

Minnesota
Banks (insured commercial and savings) deposits by instn, State, MSA, and county, as of June 1991, annual regional rpt, 9295–3.5
Business and economic conditions, Fed Reserve 9th District, quarterly journal, 9383–19
County Business Patterns, 1990: employment, establishments, and payroll, by SIC 2- to 4-digit industry and county, annual State rpt, 2326–6.25
Dairy prices, by product and selected area, with related marketing data, 1991, annual rpt, 1317–1
Deaths and rates, by detailed location, cause, and demographic characteristics, 1989, US Vital Statistics annual rpt, 4144–3.1
Employment, earnings, and hours, by selected SIC 1- to 4-digit industry, State, and for 275 MSAs, 1987-92, 6748–81
Fed Govt spending in States and local areas, by type, State, county, and city, FY91, annual rpt, 2464–3
Fed Govt spending in States, by type, program, agency, and State, FY91, annual rpt, 2464–2
HHS financial aid, by program, recipient, State, and city, FY91, annual regional listing, 4004–3.5
Hospital deaths of Medicare patients, actual and expected rates by diagnosis, and hospital characteristics, by instn, FY90 annual State rpt, 4654–14.24
Housing census, 1990: inventory, occupancy, and costs, State fact sheet, 2326 21.25
Housing census, 1990: summary unit characteristics, by householder race and age, county, place, and urban-rural location, State rpt, 2471–1.25
Lumber (pulpwood) production in 3 North Central States, by species and county, 1990, 1208–397
Military prime contract awards, by contractor, service branch, State, and city, FY91, annual rpt, 3544–22
Mineral Industry Surveys, State reviews of production, 1991, preliminary annual rpt, 5614–6
Multinatl firms US affiliates finances and operations, by industry, country of parent firm, and State, 1987, 2708–48
Physicians, by specialty, age, sex, and location of training and practice, 1990, State rpt, 4116–6.24
Population and housing census, 1990: detailed geographic coverage, State CD-ROM, 2551–9.4
Population and housing census, 1990: summary characteristics, by county, subdiv, and place, State rpt, 2551–7.25
Population census, 1990: population characteristics and living arrangements, by county, place, and urban-rural location, State rpt, 2531–1.25
Potato production, acreage, prices, and shipments, for 7 major producer States, and compared to other States, 1970s-92, annual rpt, 1311–29
Statistical Abstract of US, 1992 annual data compilation, 2324–1
Timber in Minnesota, acreage, resources, and removals, by ownership, forest and tree characteristics, and county, 1990, series, 1206–24
Water supply and quality in streams and lakes, and groundwater levels in wells, by drainage basin, 1990, annual State rpt, 5666–10.22
Wolf (gray) kills of livestock, and farmer compensation claims and payments, for Minnesota, late 1970s-80s, 5508–115
Wood fuel production in Minnesota, by species, land ownership, and location, 1988, 1208–398
see also Hennepin County, Minn.
see also Minneapolis, Minn.
see also St. Cloud, Minn.
see also St. Paul, Minn.
see also under By State in the "Index by Categories"

Minority Business Development Agency
Budget of US, obligations and authority by function, agency, and program, with summaries and analyses, FY93, annual rpt, 104–2
Fed Govt minority businesses funding, by program and agency, FY91, annual rpt, 2104–5
Mgmt and financial aid from Minority Business Dev Centers, and characteristics of businesses, by region and State, FY91, annual rpt, 2104–6

Minority businesses
Airway facilities and services contract awards of FAA to minority- and woman-owned businesses, FY87-90, annual rpt, 7504–37
Banks minority-owned, selected assets and liabilities, 1990, annual rpt, 9364–5.11
Community Dev Block Grant activities and funding, by program, FY75-91, annual rpt, 5124–8
DOE contracts and grants, by category, State, and for top contractors, FY91, annual rpt, 3004–21
DOE procurement contract awards to small businesses, by business type and subagency, FY90, annual rpt, 3004–35
Fed Govt accounts receivable, delinquent debt cases and collections of Justice Dept and private law firms, pilot project results, FY91, annual rpt, 6004–20
Fed Govt financial and nonfinancial domestic aid, 1992 base edition, annual listing, 104–5
Fed Govt minority businesses funding, by program and agency, FY91, annual rpt, 2104–5
Fed Govt procurement set-aside contract awards to minority business, by State, FY90, GAO rpt, 26113–563
Fed Govt procurement set-aside contracts for minority businesses, by participant race and sex, industry, firm, and State, FY90, annual rpt, 9764–8
Hwy construction minority contractor training, funding by region, FY92, annual release, 7554–40
Indian population and Indian-owned firms, by State for North Central States, selected years 1987-90, article, 9383–19.304
Mgmt and financial aid from Minority Business Dev Centers, and characteristics of businesses, by region and State, FY91, annual rpt, 2104–6
Military contractor subcontract awards to small and disadvantaged business, by firm and service branch, quarterly rpt, 3542–17
Military prime contract awards in labor surplus areas, by service branch, State, and area, 1st half FY92, semiannual rpt, 3542–19

NASA procurement contract awards, by type, contractor, State, and country, FY92 with trends from 1961, semiannual rpt, 9502–6
Owner and business characteristics, for minority- and woman-owned firms, by industry, employment and sales size, and form of ownership, 1987 survey, 2328–59
R&D funding by Fed Govt to small business, by program area, agency, MSA, and State, FY90, annual rpt, 9764–7
Small Business Admin dev company loan program and debenture sale activity, with data by firm, industry div, State, and region, quarterly rpt, 9762–6
Small Business Admin loan and contract activity by program and firm, and financial condition, FY91, annual rpt, 9764–1
Small Business Admin loan guarantee program participants finances, operations, characteristics, and views, 1991 survey, 9768–25
Small business finances, operations, owner characteristics, and Federal contracts, 1980s-90, annual rpt, 9764–6
Small Business Investment Companies capital holdings, SBA obligation, and ownership, as of July 1992, semiannual listing, 9762–4
Small Business Investment Company program financial performance, findings and recommendations, 1992 rpt, 9768–24
Statistical Abstract of US, 1992 annual data compilation, 2324–1.17
Tax (income) admin and compliance issues, and taxpayer views, 1991 conf, 8304–25
see also Survey of Minority-Owned Business Enterprises
see also Women-owned businesses

Minority employment

Apprenticeship programs regulation, participation of minorities and women, and earnings, by occupation, 1990, GAO rpt, 26121–446
Asian and Pacific Islands Americans social and economic characteristics, for West and total US, 1990-91, Current Population Report, 2546–1.462
Black Americans social and economic characteristics, for South and total US, 1991 and trends from 1950, annual Current Population Rpt, 2546–1.463
Black and white women's occupational differences, and compared to men, selected years 1940-88, article, 6722–1.321
Black women's labor force status, earnings, and other economic status indicators, and compared to whites, various periods 1939-88, 11048–191
Census of Population and Housing, 1990: population and housing characteristics, detailed geographic coverage, State CD-ROM series, 2551–10
Central America immigrants in DC, by selected employment and other characteristics, and reasons for migration, 1985-88, working paper, 6366–6.3
Colombia immigrants employment in New England textile industry, by selected characteristics, 1960s-80s, working paper, 6366–6.4
Dallas-Fort Worth metro area employment, earnings, hours, and CPI changes, late 1970s-91, annual rpt, 6964–2
DOT activities by subagency, budget, and summary accident data, FY89, annual rpt, 7304–1
DOT employment, by subagency, occupation, and selected personnel characteristics, FY91, annual rpt, 7304–18
Education data, detail for elementary, secondary, and higher education, 1920s-91 and projected to 2002, annual rpt, 4824–1
Educational attainment, by social and demographic characteristics and location, 1991 and trends from 1940, biennial Current Population Rpt, 2546–1.460
Educational enrollment, by grade, instn type and control, and student characteristics, 1990 and trends from 1947, annual Current Population Rpt, 2546–1.459
Employment and economic conditions, alternative BLS projections to 2005 and trends 1975-90, biennial rpt, 6744–19
Employment, earnings, and hours, monthly press release, 6742–5
Employment of minorities and women by industry sector, and govt salaries, by occupation, mid 1960s-90, chartbook, 9248–20
Employment of minorities and women, by occupation, SIC 1- to 3-digit industry, State, and MSA, 1991, annual rpt, 9244–1
Employment, unemployment, and labor force characteristics, by region, State, and selected metro area, 1991, annual rpt, 6744–7
Epidemic Intelligence Service of CDC, minority grads by race and current employer, 1950s-80s, article, 4042–3.374
Fed Equal Opportunity Recruitment Program activity, and employment by sex, race, pay grade, and occupational group, FY91, annual rpt, 9844–33
Fed Govt civilian employees demographic and employment characteristics, as of Sept 1991, annual article, 9842–1.301
Fed Govt civilian employees demographic characteristics, by agency, 1990, GAO rpt, 26119–383
Fed Govt employment of minorities, women, and disabled, by agency and occupation, FY90, annual rpt, 9244–10
Health Care Financing Admin affirmative action employment, by category, FY87, annual rpt, 4654–5
Health care professionals supply and education, by professional and other characteristics, and location, 1960s-92 and projected to 2020, biennial rpt, 4114–8
Hispanic Americans health insurance coverage, by source, employment and poverty status, and origin, 1987-90, GAO rpt, 26131–97
Income (household, family, and personal), by source, detailed characteristics, and region, 1991, annual Current Population Rpt, 2546–6.76
Indian Health Service and tribal facilities and use, and Indians health and other characteristics, by IHS region, 1980s-90, annual chartbook, 4084–7
Indian tribes in Pacific Northwest, OCS oil and gas lease and dev environmental, economic, and cultural impacts, with background data, 1970s-92, 5738–35
IRS employment of minorities and women, compared to Fed Govt and total civilian labor force, FY91, annual rpt, 8304–3.3
Job Training Partnership Act education and worker training program participants, by selected characteristics, 1986-88, 15496–1.15
Labor demand, turnover, and training completions, by detailed occupation, 1990 and projected to 2005, biennial rpt, 6744–3
Labor force status, by race, detailed Hispanic origin, and sex, quarterly rpt, 6742–18
Labor force status, by worker characteristics and industry group, 1990-91, annual article, 6722–1.312
Labor force status, experience, and unemployment duration, by race and sex, 1990-91, annual press release, 6726–1.51
Labor force, wages, hours, and payroll costs, by major industry group and demographic characteristics, *Survey of Current Business*, monthly rpt, 2702–1.7
Merit Systems Protection Board activities, staff, and finances, FY91, annual rpt, 9494–5
Military personnel deployment in Operation Desert Storm, by sex, race, rank, and service branch, 1990-91, GAO rpt, 26123–394
Military personnel occupational distribution, by race, sex, and service branch, FY90, GAO rpt, 26123–381
Military personnel reductions planned by service branch, and women and minorities affected by Army and Air Force plans, FY90-91, GAO rpt, 26123–373
Military recruits by race, and goals, by sex and service branch, quarterly press release, 3542–7
NASA minority and women employment, by installation, FY82-91, FY91, annual rpt, 9504–6.2
NASA staff characteristics and personnel actions, FY91, annual rpt, 9504–1
NIH research and training grants awarded to women, by recipient characteristics, inst, and host instn, FY90, annual rpt, 4434–18
OASDHI coverage of employment and earnings, and social security contributions, by age, sex, race, State, and county, 1988, annual rpt, 4744–29
Population economic well-being indicators, by selected characteristics and household income and income-to-poverty ratio, 1984, 2546–20.22
Poverty relation to low earnings, by work experience during year, household relationship, sex, race, age, and education, 1960s-90, Current Population Rpt, 2546–6.74
Poverty status of population and families, by detailed characteristics, 1991, annual Current Population Rpt, 2546–6.77
Science and engineering employment and education of minorities, women, and disabled, by field, mid 1970s-91, biennial rpt, 9624–20
Small Business Admin minority and women employment, and hiring goals, FY91, annual rpt, 9764–9
Southeastern US layoff events and separations, by State, industry div, and reason for separation, 1990-91, press release, 6946–3.25

SSA minority, handicapped, and women employees, by pay grade, FY91, annual rpt, 4704–6
State and local govt employment of minorities and women, by occupation, function, pay level, and State, 1991, annual rpt, 9244–6
Statistical Abstract of US, 1992 annual data compilation, 2324–1.13
Unemployed displaced workers job search and placement aid effectiveness, relation to previous employment and other characteristics, 1979-87 studies, 15496–1.14
Unemployed persons finding work, by characteristics of worker and new job, aggregate 1986-89, 2546–20.20
see also Discrimination in employment
see also Minority businesses
see also Racial discrimination
see also under By Race and Ethnic Group in the "Index by Categories"

Minority groups
AFDC beneficiaries demographic and financial characteristics, by State, FY90, annual rpt, 4584–7
AIDS prevention program for minority youth, interactive videodisc presentation effectiveness, 1992 article, 4042–3.332
Arab Americans smoking status, duration, and cigarettes smoked daily, by age, sex, ethnicity, education, and income, local area study, 1992 article, 4042–3.360
Arts Natl Endowment activities and grants, FY91, annual rpt, 9564–3
Bone marrow donors, minority recruitment, Federal aid, transplants, costs, payment sources, 1987-92, GAO rpt, 26121–487
Census of Population and Housing, 1990: data summary, use, and availability, fact sheet, 2326–23.2
Census of Population and Housing, 1990: detailed geographic coverage, State CD-ROM series, 2551–9
Census of Population and Housing, 1990: population and housing characteristics, detailed geographic coverage, State CD-ROM series, 2551–10
Census of Population and Housing, 1990: summary characteristics, households, and land area, by county, subdiv, and place, State rpt series, 2551–1
Census of Population, 1990: minority group participation in census, effectiveness and quality of outreach and promotional programs, hearing, 21628–103
Census of Population, 1990: population characteristics and living arrangements, by county, place, and urban-rural location, State rpt series, 2531–1
Census of Population, 1990: population characteristics and living arrangements, for Native American, urban, and metro areas, series, 2531–2
Child day care and early childhood education programs availability, demand, use, costs, and provider and enrollee characteristics, 1990 survey, 4808–39
Education (elementary and secondary) enrollment, staff, finances, operations, programs, and policies, 1987/88 biennial survey, series, 4836–3
Education data compilation, 1992 annual rpt, 4824–2
Education data, detail for elementary, secondary, and higher education, 1920s-91 and projected to 2002, annual rpt, 4824–1
Educational performance and conditions, characteristics, attitudes, activities, and plans, 1988 8th grade class, natl longitudinal survey, series, 4826–9
Fed Govt employment of minorities, disabled, and veterans, and years of service, by occupation, age, sex, and agency, as of Sept 1990, biennial rpt, 9844–27
Food aid program of USDA for women, infants, and children, participants by race, State, and Indian agency, 1991, annual rpt, 1364–16
Foreign countries *Background Notes*, summary social, political, and economic data, series, 7006–2
Foreign countries economic, social, political, and geographic summary data, by country, 1992, annual factbook, 9114–2
Health sciences research and training grants and contracts of Natl Inst of General Medical Sciences, by program, FY91, annual rpt, 4474–38
Heart, Lung, and Blood Natl Inst activities, and grants by recipient and location, FY91 and disease trends from 1940, annual rpt, 4474–15
HHS financial aid, by program, recipient, State, and city, FY91, annual regional listings, 4004–3
High school dropouts and rates, and data collection and reporting methods evaluation, 1992 rpt, 4838–49
Higher education degrees awarded, by level, field, race, and sex, 1989/90 and trends from 1980/81, annual rpt, 4844–17
Higher education enrollment, by level, race, and sex, fall 1980-90, biennial rpt, 4844–15
Higher education enrollment, completion, and degrees, for minorities by race, sex, and type of instn, 1970s-90, 26306–3.122
Households composition, income, benefits, and labor force status, Survey of Income and Program Participation methodology, working paper series, 2626–10
Housing census, 1990: summary unit characteristics, by householder race and age, county, place, and urban-rural location, State rpt series, 2471–1
Military service academies prep schools costs and student performance indicators, 1988-90, GAO rpt, 26123–380
Pacific territories population and housing detailed characteristics, by location, 1990 Census of Population and Housing, series, 2551–8
Prenatal care adequacy relation to mothers ethnic group and other characteristics, for Hawaii, 1992 article, 4042–3.366
Science and engineering grad enrollment, by field, source of funds, and characteristics of student and instn, 1990, annual rpt, 9627–7
Science and Engineering Indicators, employment, education, R&D funding, and industry impacts, with foreign comparisons, 1960s-91, biennial rpt, 9624–10
Soviet Union and US economic and sociodemographic indicators, selected years 1970-90, handbook, 2328–80
Soviet Union former Republics and Baltic States energy supply and use, and social, economic, and political indicators, 1989-90, 3168–126
Statistical Abstract of US, 1992 annual data compilation, 2324–1
Student aid targeted to minority groups, higher education instns with awards and funding sources, by instn level and control, 1989/90, hearings, 21408–130
Tuberculosis prevention and control among at-risk minority and homeless populations, CDC recommendations, 1992 rpt, 4206–2.55
Vietnam population size, components of change, and selected characteristics, 1979, 1989, and projected to 2050, 2326–18.65
see also Alaska Natives
see also Ancestry
see also Asian Americans
see also Black Americans
see also Black students
see also Civil rights
see also Hispanic Americans
see also Indians
see also Minority businesses
see also Minority employment
see also Pacific Islands Americans
see also Racial discrimination
see also Survey of Minority-Owned Business Enterprises
see also under By Race and Ethnic Group in the "Index by Categories"

Minority-Owned Business Enterprise Survey
see Survey of Minority-Owned Business Enterprises

Mint Bureau
see U.S. Mint

Mint oil
see Spices and herbs

Mintz, M. M.
"Forecast of Transportation Energy Demand Through the Year 2010", 3008–124

Miscarriage
see Fetal deaths

Mishel, Lawrence
"Upgrading Workers' Skills Not Sufficient To Jump-Start Rural Economy", 1502–7.302

Missiaen, Edmond
"Outlook for Horticultural Products", 1504–9.1

Missiles and rockets
County Business Patterns, 1989: employment, establishments, and payroll, by SIC 2- to 4-digit industry and county, annual State rpt series, 2326–8
County Business Patterns, 1990: employment, establishments, and payroll, by SIC 2- to 4-digit industry and county, annual State rpt series, 2326–6
Employment, earnings, and hours, by SIC 1- to 4-digit industry, monthly 1989-Feb 1992, annual rpt, 6744–4
Exports of US, detailed Schedule B commodities with countries of destination, 1991, annual rpt, 2424–10
Foreign countries military aid and arms sales of US, by weapon type, as of Sept 1991, annual rpt, 3904–3
Foreign countries military spending, arms trade, and force strengths, with govt spending and population, by country, 1979-89, annual rpt, 9824–1

Input-output structure of US economy, detailed interindustry transactions for 541 industries, and components of final demand, 1982 benchmark data, 2708–17
Manufacturing annual survey, 1990: value of shipments, by SIC 4- to 5-digit product class, 2506–14.1
Manufacturing census, 1987: concentration of largest firms measured by value added, and for shipments by SIC 2- and 4-digit industry, subject rpt, 2497–6
Manufacturing census, 1987: shipments of manufacturers products, by customer class and SIC 2- and 4-digit industry, subject rpt, 2497–4
Manufacturing finances and operations, by SIC 2- to 4-digit industry, forecast 1992, annual rpt, 2044–28
Military budget, organization, personnel, weapons, and property, by service branch, State, and country, 1992 annual summary rpt, 3504–13
Military budget, procurement appropriations by item, service branch, and defense agency, FY91-93, annual rpt, 3544–32
Military budget, programs, and policies, FY91, annual rpt, 3544–2
Military outlays and obligations, by function and service branch, quarterly rpt, 3542–3
Military prime contract awards, by category, contract and contractor type, and service branch, FY82-1st half FY92, semiannual rpt, 3542–1
Military prime contract awards, by category, contractor type, and State, FY89-91, annual rpt, 3544–11
Military prime contract awards, by detailed procurement category, FY88-91, annual rpt, 3544–18
Military prime contract awards, by size and type of contract, service branch, competitive status, category, and labor standard, FY91, annual rpt, 3544–19
Military weapons acquisition costs by system and service branch, DOD budget, FY91-93, annual rpt, 3504–2
Natl income and product accounts, comprehensive accounts and components, benchmark revisions, 1929-88, 2708–5
Natl income and product accounts, comprehensive accounts and components, *Survey of Current Business*, monthly rpt, 2702–1.26
NATO, Japan, and South Korea military spending and indicators of ability to support common defense, by country, 1970s-90, annual rpt, 3544–28
Navy weapons systems parts purchases from foreign suppliers and US contractors, by State and country, 1988, 2026–1.3
Statistical Abstract of US, 1992 annual data compilation, 2324–1.11

Missing persons and runaways
Arrests, by offense, offender characteristics, and location, data compilation, 1992 annual rpt, 6064–6.4
Arrests, by offense, offender characteristics, and location, 1991, annual rpt, 6224–2.2
Child abductions, runaways, and missing and exploited children, and Office of Juvenile Justice and Delinquency Prevention activities, FY90, annual rpt, 6064–36
Children missing, by suspected cause, 1988, annual rpt, 6064–34
HHS financial aid, by program, recipient, State, and city, FY91, annual regional listings, 4004–3
Juvenile arrests, by sex, race, disposition, and offense, 1990, 6066–27.8
Military deaths by cause, age, race, and rank, and personnel captured and missing, by service branch, FY91, annual rpt, 3544–40
Youths entering runaway and homeless centers, by selected characteristics, data compilation, 1992 annual rpt, 6064–6.6

Missions and missionaries
Malaria cases in US, for military personnel and US and foreign natls, and by country of infection, 1966-90, annual rpt, 4205–4

Mississippi
Appalachian Regional Commission funding, by project and State, planned FY92, annual rpt, 9084–3
Banks (insured commercial and savings) deposits by instn, State, MSA, and county, as of June 1991, annual regional rpt, 9295–3.4
County Business Patterns, 1990: employment, establishments, and payroll, by SIC 2- to 4-digit industry and county, annual State rpt, 2326–6.26
Deaths and rates, by detailed location, cause, and demographic characteristics, 1989, US Vital Statistics annual rpt, 4144–3.1
Economic indicators by State and MSA, Fed Reserve 6th District, quarterly rpt, 9371–14
Employment by industry div, earnings, and hours, for 8 southeastern States, quarterly press release, 6942–7
Employment, earnings, and hours, by selected SIC 1- to 4-digit industry, State, and for 275 MSAs, 1987-92, 6748–81
Estuary environmental and fishery conditions, research results and methodology, 1992 rpt, 2176–7.28
Fed Govt spending in States and local areas, by type, State, county, and city, FY91, annual rpt, 2464–3
Fed Govt spending in States, by type, program, agency, and State, FY91, annual rpt, 2464–2
Fish (catfish) raised on farms, inventory, stocks, and production, by major producer State, quarterly rpt, 1631–18
Floods in Mississippi River and Gulf of Mexico basins, precipitation and water levels by site, damage, and deaths, 1982-83, 5666–27.33
HHS financial aid, by program, recipient, State, and city, FY91, annual regional listing, 4004–3.4
Hospital deaths of Medicare patients, actual and expected rates by diagnosis, and hospital characteristics, by instn, FY90 annual State rpt, 4654–14.25
Housing census, 1990: inventory, occupancy, and costs, State fact sheet, 2326–21.26
Housing census, 1990: summary unit characteristics, by householder race and age, county, place, and urban-rural location, State rpt, 2471–1.26
Military prime contract awards, by contractor, service branch, State, and city, FY91, annual rpt, 3544–22
Mineral Industry Surveys, State reviews of production, 1991, preliminary annual rpt, 5614–6
Multinatl firms US affiliates finances and operations, by industry, country of parent firm, and State, 1987, 2708–48
Physicians, by specialty, age, sex, and location of training and practice, 1990, State rpt, 4116–6.25
Population and housing census, 1990: detailed geographic coverage, State CD-ROM, 2551–9.6
Population and housing census, 1990: summary characteristics, by county, subdiv, and place, State rpt, 2551–7.26
Population census, 1990: population characteristics and living arrangements, by county, place, and urban-rural location, State rpt, 2531–1.26
Poverty, hunger, and public welfare program operations and indicators of need, for Mississippi, 1991 hearing, 21968–57
Radionuclide concentrations in air, water, humans, animals, and milk near Nevada and other nuclear test sites, 1990, annual rpt, 9194–17
Rice stocks on and off farms and total in all positions, periodic rpt, 1621–7
Statistical Abstract of US, 1992 annual data compilation, 2324–1
Textile mill employment, earnings, and hours, for 8 Southeastern States, quarterly press release, 6942–1
Water resources data collection and analysis activities of USGS Water Resources Div District, with project descriptions, 1991 rpt, 5666–26.27
see also Columbus, Miss.
see also Jackson, Miss.
see also Vicksburg, Miss.
see also under By State in the "Index by Categories"

Mississippi River
Army Corps of Engineers water resources dev projects, characteristics, and costs, 1950s-89, biennial State rpt series, 3756–1
Army Corps of Engineers water resources dev projects, characteristics, and costs, 1950s-91, biennial State rpt series, 3756–2
Freight (shipborne domestic), by major commodity group, vessel type, and port, 1987-89, annual rpt, 7704–7
Freight (waterborne domestic and foreign) by commodity, traffic, and passengers, by port and waterway, 1989, annual rpt, 3754–3.2
Water quality, chemistry, hydrology, and other characteristics, 1991 local area study, 5666–27.34
Water supply and quality in streams and lakes, and groundwater levels in wells, by drainage basin, 1990, annual State rpt series, 5666–10
Water supply and quality in streams and lakes, and groundwater levels in wells, by drainage basin, 1991, annual State rpt series, 5666–12
Water supply in US and southern Canada, streamflow, surface and groundwater conditions, and reservoir levels, by location, monthly rpt, 5662–3

Missouri
Banks (insured commercial and savings) deposits by instn, State, MSA, and county, as of June 1991, annual regional rpt, 9295–3.5

Coal production and mines by county, prices, productivity, miners, and reserves, by mining method and State, 1990-91, annual rpt, 3164–25
County Business Patterns, 1990: employment, establishments, and payroll, by SIC 2- to 4-digit industry and county, annual State rpt, 2326–6.27
Deaths and rates, by detailed location, cause, and demographic characteristics, 1989, US Vital Statistics annual rpt, 4144–3.1
Economic and banking conditions, for Fed Reserve 8th District, quarterly rpt with articles, 9391–16
Employment, earnings, and hours, by selected SIC 1- to 4-digit industry, State, and for 275 MSAs, 1987-92, 6748–81
Fed Govt spending in States and local areas, by type, State, county, and city, FY91, annual rpt, 2464–3
Fed Govt spending in States, by type, program, agency, and State, FY91, annual rpt, 2464–2
Financial and economic devs, Fed Reserve 10th District, quarterly rpt, 9381–16
Floods in Mississippi River and Gulf of Mexico basins, precipitation and water levels by site, damage, and deaths, 1982-83, 5666–27.33
Heart disease risk factors prevalence in Missouri, 1989-90, article, 4042–3.302
HHS financial aid, by program, recipient, State, and city, FY91, annual regional listing, 4004–3.7
Hospital deaths of Medicare patients, actual and expected rates by diagnosis, and hospital characteristics, by instn, FY90 annual State rpt, 4654–14.26
Housing census, 1990: inventory, occupancy, and costs, State fact sheet, 2326–21.27
Housing census, 1990: summary unit characteristics, by householder race and age, county, place, and urban-rural location, State rpt, 2471–1.27
Military prime contract awards, by contractor, service branch, State, and city, FY91, annual rpt, 3544–22
Mineral Industry Surveys, State reviews of production, 1991, preliminary annual rpt, 5614–6
Minerals (strategic) deposits in North Central States, characteristics, 1992 compilation of papers, 5668–127
Minerals Yearbook, Vol 2, 1990: State review of production and sales by commodity, and business activity, annual rpt, 5604–22.26
Multinatl firms US affiliates finances and operations, by industry, country of parent firm, and State, 1987, 2708–48
Physicians, by specialty, age, sex, and location of training and practice, 1990, State rpt, 4116–6.26
Population and housing census, 1990: detailed geographic coverage, State CD-ROM, 2551–9.4
Population and housing census, 1990: summary characteristics, by county, subdiv, and place, State rpt, 2551–7.27
Population census, 1990: population characteristics and living arrangements, by county, place, and urban-rural location, State rpt, 2531–1.27
Prenatal care program of Medicaid, costs and benefits, for Missouri, 1988, article, 4042–3.365
Rice stocks on and off farms and total in all positions, periodic rpt, 1621–7
Statistical Abstract of US, 1992 annual data compilation, 2324–1
Timber in Missouri, resources and removals by species, forest and tree characteristics, ownership, and county, 1987-89 and trends from 1959, 1208–76
Timber in Missouri, resources and removals by species, land ownership, and county, 1988-89, series, 1206–3
Unemployed displaced workers job search and placement aid effectiveness, relation to previous employment and other characteristics, 1979-87 studies, 15496–1.14
Water quality, chemistry, hydrology, and other characteristics, 1991 local area study, 5666–27.34
Wood fuel production in Missouri, by species, land ownership, and location, 1987, 1208–399
see also Jackson County, Mo.
see also Kansas City, Mo.
see also St. Louis, Mo.
see also under By State in the "Index by Categories"

Missouri River
Army Corps of Engineers water resources dev projects, characteristics, and costs, 1950s-89, biennial State rpt series, 3756–1
Army Corps of Engineers water resources dev projects, characteristics, and costs, 1950s-91, biennial State rpt series, 3756–2
Birds (least tern and piping plover) and habitat levels of selenium and other pollutants, for Missouri River in South Dakota, 1988-90, 5508–118
Freight (waterborne domestic and foreign) by commodity, traffic, and passengers, by port and waterway, 1989, annual rpt, 3754–3.2
Water quality, chemistry, hydrology, and other characteristics, 1991 local area study, 5666–27.34
Water supply and quality in streams and lakes, and groundwater levels in wells, by drainage basin, 1990, annual State rpt series, 5666–10
Water supply and quality in streams and lakes, and groundwater levels in wells, by drainage basin, 1991, annual State rpt series, 5666–12
Water supply in US and southern Canada, streamflow, surface and groundwater conditions, and reservoir levels, by location, monthly rpt, 5662–3

Misurelli, Denby
"Plastics Recycling Portends New Wave of Future Exports", 9882–16.301

Miwa, Hiroshi
"RNA Expression of the WT1 Gene in Wilms' Tumors in Relation to Histology", 4472–1.304

Mobile, Ala.
Freight (waterborne domestic and foreign) by commodity, traffic, and passengers, by port and waterway, 1989, annual rpt, 3754–3.2
Wages by occupation, and benefits for office and plant workers, 1992 survey, periodic MSA rpt, 6785–3.6
see also under By City and By SMSA or MSA in the "Index by Categories"

Mobile homes
Alteration and repair of owner-occupied homes, costs and structural, household, financial, and project characteristics, 1987, 2486–1.13
American Housing Survey: unit and household characteristics of recent movers, and reason for move, by tenure, 1989, 2486–1.12
American Housing Survey: unit and households characteristics, and unit and neighborhood quality, by MSA location for 11 MSAs, 1987 survey, supplement, 2485–8
American Housing Survey: unit and households detailed characteristics, and unit and neighborhood quality, MSA rpt series, 2485–6
American Housing Survey: unit and households detailed characteristics, and unit and neighborhood quality, 1989, biennial rpt supplement, 2485–13
Census of Housing, 1990: summary unit characteristics, by householder race and age, county, place, and urban-rural location, State rpt series, 2471–1
County Business Patterns, 1989: employment, establishments, and payroll, by SIC 2- to 4-digit industry and county, annual State rpt series, 2326–8
County Business Patterns, 1990: employment, establishments, and payroll, by SIC 2- to 4-digit industry and county, annual State rpt series, 2326–6
Employment, earnings, and hours, by SIC 1- to 4-digit industry, monthly 1989-Feb 1992, annual rpt, 6744–4
Energy use, costs, and conservation, and household and housing characteristics, survey rpt series, 3166–7
Finance companies credit outstanding and leasing activities, by credit type, monthly rpt, 9365–2.7
Housing (rental) units, total, with HUD assistance by program, and eligible for aid, by unit, household, and neighborhood characteristics, and location, 1989, biennial rpt, 5184–11
Housing and households summary characteristics, 1989 and trends, chartbook, 2486–2.1
Injuries from use of consumer products, by severity, victim age, and detailed product, 1991, annual rpt, 9164–6
Input-output structure of US economy, detailed interindustry transactions for 541 industries, and components of final demand, 1982 benchmark data, 2708–17
Loan activity of savings instns insured by Savings Assn Insurance Fund by FHLB district and State, and for FDIC-insured savings banks, 1989, annual rpt, 8434–1
Loans FHA-insured, financial, property, and borrower characteristics, by State, 1991, annual rpt, 5144–1; 5144–25
Loans FHA-insured, financial, property, and borrower characteristics, 1991, annual rpt, 5144–23
Loans for mobile homes, monthly rpt, 23842–1.5

Loans for mobile homes outstanding, *Survey of Current Business*, monthly rpt, 2702–1.8
Manufacturing annual survey, 1990: finances and operations, by SIC 2- to 4-digit industry, series, 2506–14
Manufacturing census, 1987: concentration of largest firms measured by value added, and for shipments by SIC 2- and 4-digit industry, subject rpt, 2497–6
Manufacturing census, 1987: shipments of manufacturers products, by customer class and SIC 2- and 4-digit industry, subject rpt, 2497–4
Military and personal property shipments, passenger traffic, and costs, by service branch and mode of transport, FY91, annual rpt, 3704–15
Natl income and product accounts, comprehensive accounts and components, benchmark revisions, 1929-88, 2708–5
Natl income and product accounts, comprehensive accounts and components, *Survey of Current Business*, monthly rpt, 2702–1.28
New single and multifamily units, by structural and financial characteristics, inside-outside MSAs, and region, 1987-91, annual rpt, 2384–1
North Central States, FHLB 7th District housing vacancy rates for single and multifamily units and mobile homes, by ZIP code, annual MSA rpt series, 9304–18
Occupational injury and illness rates and lost workdays, for selected industries, 1978-89, compilation of papers, 6728–41
Occupational injury and illness rates, by SIC 2- to 4-digit industry, 1989-90, annual rpt, 6844–7
Occupational injury and illness rates, by SIC 2- to 4-digit industry, 1990, annual rpt, 6844–1
Pacific Northwest population, households, employment, income, fuel prices, and electricity demand, alternative forecasts 1991-2010, annual rpt, 3224–3.3
Pacific territories population and housing detailed characteristics, by location, 1990 Census of Population and Housing, series, 2551–8
Price indexes (producer), by stage of processing and detailed commodity, monthly rpt, 6762–6
Price indexes (producer), by stage of processing and detailed commodity, monthly 1991, annual rpt, 6764–2
Savings instns failures, inventory of real estate assets available from Resolution Trust Corp, 1991, semiannual listing, 9722–2.5
Savings instns failures, inventory of real estate assets available from Resolution Trust Corp, 1992, semiannual listing, 9722–2.12
Shipments and PPI for mobile homes, quarterly rpt, 2042–1.2; 2042–1.5
Shipments of mobile homes, and credit, selected years 1963-91, *Survey of Current Business* biennial supplement, 2704–1
Shipments of mobile homes, by State, monthly rpt, quarterly table, 2382–5
Shipments of mobile homes, by State, 1989-91, annual rpt, 2384–2
Shipments of mobile homes, dealer inventories, and home characteristics, by region, and placements and prices by State, monthly rpt, 2382–1
Shipments of mobile homes, *Survey of Current Business*, monthly rpt, 2702–1.5
Single parent families in own and others homes, by financial, housing, and other characteristics, 1989, 2486–1.14
Single person and nonfamily households social, economic and housing characteristics, by tenure, 1989, 2486–1.15
Statistical Abstract of US, 1992 annual data compilation, 2324–1.26
Vacant housing characteristics, and occupancy and vacancy rates, by tenure and location, 1960s-91, annual rpt, 2484–1
West Central States, FHLB 10th District housing vacancy rates for single and multifamily units and mobile homes, by ZIP code, annual MSA rpt series, 9304–22
Western States, FHLB 12th District housing vacancy rates for single and multifamily units and mobile homes, by ZIP code, annual MSA rpt series, 9304–21
see also Recreational vehicles

Mobile radio
Finances of communications services, itemized revenue and expenses by SIC 2- to 4-digit kind of business, 1990, annual rpt, 2413–15
Licensing activities of FCC, by class of operation, FY91, annual rpt, 9284–4
Licensing of frequencies for mobile communications, effects of auctioning frequencies, 1990, 26306–6.169
Manufacturing finances and operations, by SIC 2- to 4-digit industry, forecast 1992, annual rpt, 2044–28
Price indexes (producer), by stage of processing and detailed commodity, monthly rpt, 6762–6
Price indexes (producer), by stage of processing and detailed commodity, monthly 1991, annual rpt, 6764–2
Shipments, trade, use, and firms, for electronic communications systems and related products, 1991, annual Current Industrial Rpt, 2506–12.35
Telephone firms borrowing under Rural Telephone Program, and financial and operating data, by State, 1991, annual rpt, 1244–2
Telephone firms mobile operations and revenue, 1990, annual rpt, 9284–6.2
Telephone service subscribership, charges, and local and long distance firm finances and operations, late 1970s-92, semiannual rpt, 9282–7
TV (UHF) channels reassigned for land mobile use, by market, as of June 1992, semiannual rpt, 9282–6

Mobile telephones
see Mobile radio

Mobility
see Labor mobility
see Migration
see Mobility limitations
see Transportation assistance

Mobility limitations
Cases of acute and chronic conditions, disability, absenteeism, and health services use, by selected characteristics, 1990, annual rpt, 4147–10.182; 4147–10.183
Census of Population and Housing, 1990: population and housing characteristics, detailed geographic coverage, State CD-ROM series, 2551–10
Census of Population and Housing, 1990: summary characteristics, by county, subdiv, and place, State rpt series, 2551–7
Child infectious disease cases, and related disability and health care, by disease, health insurance status, and other characteristics, 1988, 4147–10.181
Children (handicapped) enrollment by age, and special education programs staff, funding, and needs, by type of handicap and State, 1990/91, annual rpt, 4944–4
Chronic health conditions causing disability, prevalence and services use and needs, series, 4946–1
Deaths during 1986, decedents health condition, services use, habits, and social, employment, and other characteristics, 4147–20.19
Educational attainment relation to health condition and care, indicators by selected characteristics, 1989, 4147–10.180
Equipment (assistive technology) and home accessibility features, use, payment sources, and unmet needs, by age, 1990, 4146–8.219
Fire-related injuries by severity, and deaths, by ignition source, victim age, and treatment location, 1984-85 local area study, article, 4042–3.340
Health condition and care indicators, 1950s-90 with health improvement and disease prevention goals for 1990, annual data compilation, 4144–11
Insurance (health) coverage of persons, by insurance type and selected characteristics, 1985-90, 2546–20.23
Insurance (health) denial by private carriers because of poor health, by selected characteristics, 1987, 4186–8.23
Mental health care facilities, staff, patients, and finances, 1970s-91, biennial rpt, 4094–1
Mental illness (serious) among adults, functional limitations, govt aid, drugs used, visits to professionals, and other characteristics, 1989, 4146–8.220
Older persons care by family members and others, caregiver quit probability related to selected characteristics, 1982, article, 4652–1.305
Older persons socioeconomic characteristics, 1900s-90 and projected to 2050, biennial chartbook, 12904–1
Older population, and health, economic, and other characteristics, with foreign comparisons, 1980s-91 with trends and projections, Current Population Rpt, 2546–2.165
Pacific territories population and housing detailed characteristics, by location, 1990 Census of Population and Housing, series, 2551–8
Population economic well-being indicators, by selected characteristics and household income and income-to-poverty ratio, 1984, 2546–20.22

Traffic accidents direct and indirect costs, by cost type, payment source, and severity, 1980s, 7558–114
Transit systems grants of Federal Transit Admin, by city and State, FY91, annual rpt, 7884–10
Transplants of organs, failure and death risk by selected transplant and patient characteristics, 1987-89, annual rpt, 4104–17.1
Working age persons with disability, labor force status, type and cause of disability, and other characteristics, 1970s-89, chartbook, 4948–11
Youth health condition, risk factors, and preventive and treatment services use and availability, 1970s-80s, 26358–234.2; 26358–234.3
see also Architectural barriers to the handicapped

Mobs
see Riots and disorders

Models
see Demonstration and pilot projects
see Economic and econometric models
see Mathematic models and modeling

Modems
see Telecommunication

Modesto, Calif.
see also under By City and By SMSA or MSA in the "Index by Categories"

Moffatt, Ronald E.
"Oceanographic Data Exchange, 1990", 2144–15

Mohamedshah, Yusuf M.
"Investigation of Passing Accidents Using the HSIS Data Base", 7552–3.301

Molasses
see Sugar industry and products

Moldova
Agricultural production, prices, and trade, for former USSR republics, 1960s-91 and forecast 1992, annual rpt, 1524–4.1
Economic, social, political, and geographic summary data, by country, 1992, annual factbook, 9114–2
Embassies of US in former Soviet republics and Baltic States, positions planned by function, and filled, 1992, GAO rpt, 26123–403
Energy supply and use, and social, economic, and political indicators for former Soviet Republics and Baltic States, 1989-90, 3168–126
Energy use and production of former USSR Republics, by fuel type, 1990, annual rpt, 3164–84.2
Exports and imports of US with Communist and transitional economy countries, by detailed commodity and country, quarterly rpt with articles, 9882–2
Livestock and meat inventories, use, and imports, by former USSR republic, 1986-93, semiannual rpt, 1925–33.2
Population size and characteristics of former Soviet Republics and Baltic States, 1989-92, 9118–19

Moline, Ill.
Wages by occupation, and benefits, for office and plant workers, 1992 survey, periodic MSA rpt, 6785–17.1

Monaco
Economic, social, political, and geographic summary data, by country, 1992, annual factbook, 9114–2
Exports and imports of US, by transport mode, country, and SITC 1- to 3-digit commodity, 1991, annual rpt, 2424–12
Population size, growth rates, and components of change, by country, projected 1990-2020 and trends from 1950, biennial rpt, 2324–9

Mondschean, Thomas H.
"Empirical Test of the Incentive Effects of Deposit Insurance: The Case of Junk Bonds at Savings and Loan Associations", 9375–13.69
"Ex Ante Risk and Ex Post Collapse of S&Ls in the 1980s", 9375–1.306
"Market Value Accounting for Commercial Banks", 9375–1.301

Monetary policy
Banks in Fed Reserve System, expenses and operations itemized by service, office, and district, 1991, annual rpt, 9364–11
Economic indicators impacts of monetary policy, alternative model results, mid 1970s-91, technical paper, 9385–1.306; 9385–8.135
Economic indicators relation to monetary policy shocks, model description and results, 1970s-92, working paper, 9371–10.89
Economic policy and banking practices, technical paper series, 9366–1
Economic Report of the President for 1991, economic effects of budget proposals, and trends and projections, 1940s-95, annual hearings, 23844–4
Economic Report of the President for 1992, Joint Economic Committee critique and policy recommendations, annual rpt, 23844–2
Economic Report of the President for 1992, with economic trends from 1929, annual rpt, 204–1
European Monetary Union impacts on France, Germany, and Italy monetary policies, 1992 technical paper, 9385–8.145
Fed Reserve Bd and Reserve banks finances, staff, and review of monetary policy and economic devs, 1991, annual rpt, 9364–1
Fed Reserve Bd discount rate changes relation to Treasury bill rates, alternative estimates, 1970s-80s, article, 9391–1.314
Fed Reserve Bd reserve requirements and other policy actions impacts on M1 and M2 growth, 1959-92, article, 9391–1.313
Fed Reserve discount rates relation to monetary and fiscal policy, model description and results, 1970s-91, working paper, 9379–14.20
Fed Reserve monetary policy objectives, analysis and economic performance, 1950s-90 and projected to FY95, hearings, 21248–160
Fed Reserve monetary policy objectives, and performance of major economic indicators, as of July 1992, semiannual rpt, 9362–4
Fed Reserve System, Bd of Governors, and district banks financial statements, performance, and fiscal services, 1991-92, annual rpt, 9364–10
Financial and economic analysis of banking and nonbanking sectors, working paper series, 9381–10
Financial and economic analysis, technical paper series, 8006–6; 9379–12; 9383–20; 9389–19; 9393–10
Financial and economic devs, Fed Reserve Bank of Dallas quarterly journal, 9379–1
Financial and economic devs, Fed Reserve Bank of Minneapolis quarterly journal, 9383–6
Financial and economic devs, Fed Reserve Bank of New York quarterly journal, 9385–1
Financial and economic devs, Fed Reserve Bank of Philadelphia bimonthly journal, 9387–1
Financial and economic devs, Fed Reserve Bank of St Louis bimonthly journal, 9391–1
Foreign and US monetary policy and central bank regulation, for 6 countries, 1980-90, article, 9385–1.308
Free trade and currency zones devs, and impacts on monetary policy, 1991 conf, 9381–13.1
GNP seasonal growth relation to monetary, fiscal, and demand indicators, 1991 working paper, 9375–13.74
GNP variability relation to monetary and fiscal policies, 1950s-91, working paper, 9381–10.132
Gold standard relation to inflation, with background data for UK, US, France, and Italy, 1730s-1930s, working paper, 9377–9.136
Great Depression monetary policy conduct of Fed Reserve, with discount rate and other policy indicators, selected qtrs 1923-31, article, 9391–1.306
Interest rate impacts of monetary policy, 1992 working paper, 9375–13.80
Military spending reductions, economic impacts by defense contractor, industry, State, and congressional district, 1989-90 hearings, 23848–224
Money supply and interest rate impacts of monetary policy, and regression results for alternative indexes, 1950s-88, working paper, 9387–8.259
Productivity shocks impacts on business cycles, and relation to monetary, fiscal, and demand indicators, 1991 working paper, 9375–13.73
Singapore economic conditions and monetary policy, with exchange rate and money supply related to foreign prices and other factors, 1960s-90, article, 9379–1.304
Taiwan monetary and foreign exchange policies, with money supply, interest rates, and other economic indicators, 1980s, article, 9393–8.303
see also Credit
see also Fiscal policy
see also Foreign exchange
see also Inflation
see also Money supply

Money laundering
Drug-related money laundering operations, US and foreign govts enforcement activities, 1991, annual rpt, 7004–17
IRS undercover criminal investigations and costs by criminal activity, and success rates, by region, mid 1980s-90, GAO rpt, 26119–394
States and Fed Govt money laundering investigation activities, and use of IRS large cash transaction rpts, by State, 1985-91, GAO rpt, 26119–430

Treasury Dept money laundering investigations, civil penalty cases workload, processing, and disposition, 1985-91, GAO rpt, 26119–390

Money market funds
see Mutual funds

Money supply
Banks loan interest rates and default risk relation to GDP and money supply, model description and results, 1992 working paper, 9387–8.283
Business statistics, detailed data for major industries and economic indicators, *Survey of Current Business*, monthly rpt, 2702–1.8
Business statistics, detailed data for major industries and economic indicators, 1960-91, *Survey of Current Business* biennial supplement, 2704–1
Currency and coin outstanding and in circulation, by type and denomination, and per capita, *Treasury Bulletin*, quarterly rpt, 8002–4.10
Currency in circulation and removed, and Fed Reserve costs of new currency, 1990-92, annual rpt, 9364–10.2
Demand deposit velocity changes, by region, 1940s-80s, article, 9389–1.301
Economic indicators and components, and Fed Reserve 4th District business and financial conditions, monthly chartbook, 9377–10
Economic indicators and components, current data and annual trends, monthly rpt, 23842–1.5
Fed Reserve Bd reserve requirements and other policy actions impacts on M1 and M2 growth, 1959-92, article, 9391–1.313
Fed Reserve monetary policy objectives, analysis and economic performance, 1950s-90 and projected to FY95, hearings, 21248–160
Fed Reserve monetary policy objectives, and performance of major economic indicators, as of July 1992, semiannual rpt, 9362–4
Financial and economic analysis and forecasting methodology, technical paper series, 9366–6
Financial and economic analysis, technical paper series, 9383–20; 9385–8; 9393–10
Financial and economic devs, Fed Reserve Bank of St Louis bimonthly journal, 9391–1
Financial and monetary conditions, selected US summary data, weekly rpt, 9391–4
Foreign and US economic conditions, for major industrial countries, monthly rpt, 9112–1
Foreign countries economic and monetary trends, compounded annual rates of change and quarterly indicators for US and 7 major industrialized countries, quarterly rpt, 9391–7
Foreign countries economic conditions and implications for US, periodic country rpt series, 2046–4
GDP forecasting performance of selected economic indicators over selected forecast periods and business cycles, 1960s-91, article, 9375–1.307
GNP, inflation, and interest rates relation to M1, alternative model results and forecast errors, 1950s-91, article, 9389–1.303
Interest rates relation to money supply, alternative model results, 1950s-90, technical paper, 9371–10.75
Monetary aggregate (M2) growth relation to Resolution Trust Corp failed thrift resolution activity and other factors, 1990-91, article, 9379–1.303
Monetary aggregate (M2) growth relation to Resolution Trust Corp failed thrift resolution activity, 1990-91, technical paper, 9379–12.83
Monetary aggregates and money stock, 1987-90, annual rpt, 9364–5.1
Monetary aggregates, money stock measures and components, monthly rpt, 9362–1.1
Monetary aggregates relation to GDP, for M2 including and excluding small time deposits and other components, 1960s-91, article, 9385–1.305
Monetary base alternative measures, assessment, 1991 article, 9391–1.302
Monetary policy impacts on money supply and interest rates, and regression results for alternative indexes, 1950s-88, working paper, 9387–8.259
Monetary policy shocks impact on economic indicators, model description and results, 1970s-92, working paper, 9371–10.89
Monetary trends, Fed Reserve Bank of St Louis monthly rpt, 9391–2
Money demand, alternative model description and results, 1970s-85, article, 9391–1.303
Money demand relation to income growth and interest rates, model description and results, 1992 working paper, 9387–8.279
Money stock components, 1959-91, annual rpt, 204–1.5
Production and consumer spending relation to money supply, 1960s-91, working paper, 9377–9.131
Seignorage sources, use, and impacts of inflation, 1950s-90, article, 9391–1.307
Singapore economic conditions and monetary policy, with exchange rate and money supply related to foreign prices and other factors, 1960s-90, article, 9379–1.304
South America inflation relation to money supply, for 5 countries, 1970s-90, technical paper, 9379–12.91
Statistical Abstract of US, 1992 annual data compilation, 2324–1.16
Survey of Current Business, detailed financial and business data, and economic indicators, monthly rpt, 2702–1.1
Taiwan monetary and foreign exchange policies, with money supply, interest rates, and other economic indicators, 1980s, article, 9393–8.303
see also Coins and coinage
see also Counterfeiting and forgery
see also Credit
see also Eurocurrency
see also Flow-of-funds accounts
see also Foreign exchange
see also International reserves
see also Monetary policy
see also Money laundering
see also Special foreign currency programs

Mongolia
Agricultural trade of US, by detailed commodity and country, 1991, annual rpt, 1524–8
Agricultural trade of US, by detailed commodity and country, 1991, semiannual rpt, 1522–4
Economic and military aid and loans from US and intl agencies, by program and country, FY46-91, annual rpt, 9914–5
Economic and social conditions of developing countries from 1960s, and Intl Dev Cooperation Agency and AID activities and funding, FY91-93, annual rpt, 9904–4
Economic, social, political, and geographic summary data, by country, 1992, annual factbook, 9114–2
Exports and imports of US, by transport mode, country, and SITC 1- to 3-digit commodity, 1991, annual rpt, 2424–12
Exports and imports of US with Communist and transitional economy countries, by detailed commodity and country, quarterly rpt with articles, 9882–2
Exports of US, detailed Schedule B commodities with countries of destination, 1991, annual rpt, 2424–10
Human rights conditions in 170 countries, and US economic and military aid, 1991, annual rpt, 21384–3
Military aid of US, arms sales, and training programs costs and budget requests, by program, world region, and country, FY91-93, annual rpt, 7144–13
Military spending, arms trade, and force strengths, with govt spending and population, by country, 1979-89, annual rpt, 9824–1
Minerals Yearbook, Vol 3, 1989: foreign country review of production, trade, and policy, by commodity, annual rpt, 5604–35.2
Population size, growth rates, and components of change, by country, projected 1990-2020 and trends from 1950, biennial rpt, 2324–9
Refugee migration, and intl aid programs, by world area and country of origin and asylum, 1991, annual rpt, 7004–15
UN voting record and share of votes in agreement with US, by issue, country, and world area, 1991, annual rpt, 7004–18

Monheit, Alan C.
"Health Insurance, Use of Health Services, and Health Care Expenditures", 4186–8.24

Monopolies and cartels
Gasoline service stations price competition and divorcement from oil companies, issues with data by firm, city, and State, 1991 hearing, 25528–120
OPEC and other countries intl boycotts, US firms and individuals cooperation and tax benefits denied, 1990, article, 8302–2.323
Shipping industry structure, rates, and effects of Shipping Act, by route, 1980s, 9408–54
see also Antitrust law
see also Organization of Petroleum Exporting Countries

Monroe County, N.Y.
Housing and households characteristics, and unit and neighborhood quality, by MSA location for 11 MSAs, 1986 survey, supplement, 2485–8

Montana
- Banks (insured commercial and savings) deposits by instn, State, MSA, and county, as of June 1991, annual regional rpt, 9295–3.6
- Bears (grizzly) in Yellowstone Natl Park area, monitoring results, 1991, annual rpt, 5544–4
- Business and economic conditions, Fed Reserve 9th District, quarterly journal, 9383–19
- Camping in wilderness areas, impacts on plants and soils, 1979-90 studies, 1208–395
- Coal production and mines by county, prices, productivity, miners, and reserves, by mining method and State, 1990-91, annual rpt, 3164–25
- County Business Patterns, 1990: employment, establishments, and payroll, by SIC 2- to 4-digit industry and county, annual State rpt, 2326–6.28
- Deaths and rates, by detailed location, cause, and demographic characteristics, 1989, US Vital Statistics annual rpt, 4144–3.1
- Employment, earnings, and hours, by selected SIC 1- to 4-digit industry, State, and for 275 MSAs, 1987-92, 6748–81
- Fed Govt spending in States and local areas, by type, State, county, and city, FY91, annual rpt, 2464–3
- Fed Govt spending in States, by type, program, agency, and State, FY91, annual rpt, 2464–2
- HHS financial aid, by program, recipient, State, and city, FY91, annual regional listing, 4004–3.8
- Hospital deaths of Medicare patients, actual and expected rates by diagnosis, and hospital characteristics, by instn, FY90 annual State rpt, 4654–14.27
- Hospitals in rural areas, Medicare admission rates and charges, by instn, patient, and care characteristics, mid 1980s, 17206–2.33
- Housing census, 1990: inventory, occupancy, and costs, State fact sheet, 2326–21.28
- Housing census, 1990: summary unit characteristics, by householder race and age, county, place, and urban-rural location, State rpt, 2471–1.28
- Indian health risk behavior, by region and for Montana, mid 1980s, article, 4042–3.346
- Metals (nonferrous) production in 5 western States, and prices, for 5 metals, 1848-1990, 5608–178
- Military prime contract awards, by contractor, service branch, State, and city, FY91, annual rpt, 3544–22
- Mineral Industry Surveys, State reviews of production, 1991, preliminary annual rpt, 5614–6
- Multinatl firms US affiliates finances and operations, by industry, country of parent firm, and State, 1987, 2708–48
- Physicians, by specialty, age, sex, and location of training and practice, 1990, State rpt, 4116–6.27
- Population and housing census, 1990: detailed geographic coverage, State CD-ROM, 2551–9.8
- Population and housing census, 1990: population and housing characteristics, detailed geographic coverage, State CD-ROM, 2551–10.15
- Population and housing census, 1990: summary characteristics, by county, subdiv, and place, State rpt, 2551–7.28
- Population census, 1990: population characteristics and living arrangements, by county, place, and urban-rural location, State rpt, 2531–1.28
- Population, households, employment, income, fuel prices, and electricity demand for Pacific Northwest, alternative forecasts 1991-2010 with trends from 1980, annual rpt, 3224–3.3
- *Statistical Abstract of US*, 1992 annual data compilation, 2324–1
- Timber in Montana outside natl forests, acreage, resources, and mortality by species and ownership class, 1988-89, series, 1206–25
- Timber in Montana, production and mill residue, by species, ownership, and county, 1988, 1206–17.12
- Timber in northwestern US and British Columbia, production, prices, trade, and employment, quarterly rpt, 1202–3
- Timber insect and disease incidence and damage, and control activities, 1990, State rpt, 1206–49.2
- Timber insect and disease incidence and damage, and control activities, 1991, State rpt, 1206–49.3
- Water resources data collection and analysis activities of USGS Water Resources Div District, with project descriptions, 1991 rpt, 5666–26.21
- Water resources dev projects of Army Corps of Engineers, characteristics, and costs, 1950s-91, biennial State rpt, 3756–2.27
- Water supply, and snow survey results, 1990, annual State rpt, 1264–14.2
- *see also* Billings, Mont.
- *see also* under By State in the "Index by Categories"

Montenegro
- Economic, social, political, and geographic summary data, by country, 1992, annual factbook, 9114–2

Monterey, Calif.
- Wages by occupation, and benefits, for office and plant workers, 1992 survey, periodic MSA rpt, 6785–3.3

Montgomery, Ala.
- Wages by occupation, and benefits for office and plant workers, 1992 survey, periodic MSA rpt, 6785–3.5
- *see also* under By City and By SMSA or MSA in the "Index by Categories"

Montgomery County, Md.
- Fed Govt land acquisition and dev projects in DC metro area, characteristics and funding by agency and project, FY92-96, annual rpt, 15454–1

Montgomery County, Pa.
- Housing and households characteristics, unit and neighborhood quality, and journey to work by MSA location, for 11 MSAs, 1985 survey, supplement, 2485–8
- Housing and households detailed characteristics, and unit and neighborhood quality, by location, 1989 survey, MSA rpt, 2485–6.4

Montserrat
- Economic and social conditions, resources, and trade, and aid, 1992, annual factbook, 9914–14
- Exports and imports of US, by transport mode, country, and SITC 1- to 3-digit commodity, 1991, annual rpt, 2424–12
- Exports of US, detailed Schedule B commodities with countries of destination, 1991, annual rpt, 2424–10

Monuments and memorials
- Acreage and descriptions of natl park system sites, 1991, biennial listing, 5544–5
- Acreage of land under Forest Service mgmt, by forest and location, 1991, annual rpt, 1204–2
- Acreage of land under Natl Park Service mgmt, by site, ownership, and region, FY92, semiannual rpt, 5542–1
- American Battle Monuments Commission activities, expenses, and visitors by site, FY87, annual rpt, 9064–1
- Damaged and threatened natl historic and natural landmarks, with owner, location, damage type, and recommended remedial action, 1990, annual listing, 5544–16
- DC metro area land acquisition and dev projects of Fed Govt, characteristics and funding by agency and project, FY92-96, annual rpt, 15454–1
- Visits and overnight stays in natl park system, by park and State, monthly rpt, 5542–4
- Visits and overnight stays in natl park system, by park and State, 1991, annual rpt, 5544–12

Moolgavkar, Suresh H.
- "Multistage Carcinogenesis: Population-Based Model for Colon Cancer", 4472–1.311

Mooney, Michael J.
- "Overdue", 2152–8.304
- "Titanic Memorial", 2152–8.301

Moonlighting
- Fed Govt employees moonlighting, selected characteristics of 2nd job and Federal position, FY88-90, GAO rpt, 26119–386
- Home-based workers and hours, by worker characteristics, occupational group and industry div, 1991, press release, 6726–1.32
- *Statistical Abstract of US*, 1992 annual data compilation, 2324–1.13
- Teachers and administrators in private schools, pay, work conditions, and selected characteristics, by school type and affiliation, 1987/88, 4836–3.8

Moore, David
- "Auctioning Radio Spectrum Licenses", 26306–6.169

Moore, Robert R.
- "Brokered Deposits and Thrift Institutions", 9379–14.17
- "Brokered Deposits: Determinants and Implications for Thrift Institutions", 9379–15.301
- "Role of Bank Capital in Bank Loan Growth: Market and Accounting Measures", 9379–14.19

Moore, Sue E.
- "Aerial Surveys of Endangered Whales in the Alaskan Chukchi and Western Beaufort Seas, 1990", 5738–36
- "Distribution, Abundance and Behavior of Endangered Whales in the Alaskan Chukchi and Western Beaufort Seas, 1991: with a Review, 1982-91", 5738–32

Morality
see Ethics and morality

Moran, Larry R.
"Motor Vehicles, Model Year 1992", 2702–1.339

Moran, Peter J.
"Increasing Flower Consumption Through Marketing", 1504–9.1

Morbidity
see Diseases and disorders

Morehart, Mitchell J.
"Debt Repayment Capacity of Commercial Farm Operators: How Much Debt Can Farmers Afford?", 1541–1.312
"Financial Condition of Dairy Farms, 1987-90", 1561–2.301
"Financial Conditions for the 1990's", 1504–9.1
"Major Statistical Series of the U.S. Department of Agriculture, Volume 12: Costs of Production", 1506–1.1

Moreno, Ramon
"Exchange Rate Policy and Shocks to Asset Markets: The Case of Taiwan in the 1980s", 9393–8.303

Morgan, Donald P.
"Imperfect Information and Financial Constraints: New Evidence Using Bank Loan Commitments", 9381–10.128

Morgan, Frank B.
"Race/Ethnicity Trends in Degrees Conferred by Institutions of Higher Education: 1980-81 Through 1989-90", 4844–17

Morgan, George A.
"Mineral Economy of Guinea. Mineral Perspectives", 5606–1.20

Morgan, Nancy
"Joint Products: The Case of Japanese Demand for Soybean Meal and Oil", 1561–3.305

Morgan, Paul B.
"Primer on the Japanese Banking System", 9366–7.273

Morisse, Kathryn A.
"U.S. International Transactions in 1991", 9362–1.304

Morocco
Agricultural subsidies to producers and consumers in Morocco, by selected commodity, 1970s-90, 1528–329
Agricultural trade of US, by detailed commodity and country, 1991, annual rpt, 1524–8
Agricultural trade of US, by detailed commodity and country, 1991, semiannual rpt, 1522–4
AID economic aid to developing countries, obligations and disbursements by country, quarterly rpt, 9912–4
AID loans repayment status and terms by program and country, and status of predecessor agency loans, quarterly rpt, 9912–3
Almond production, trade, use, and stocks, for 6 countries and US, 1990-93, annual article, 1925–34.337
Economic and military aid and loans from US and intl agencies, by program and country, FY46-91, annual rpt, 9914–5
Economic and social conditions of developing countries from 1960s, and Intl Dev Cooperation Agency and AID activities and funding, FY91-93, annual rpt, 9904–4
Economic conditions, policy, and trade practices, by country, 1989-91, annual rpt, 21384–5
Economic, social, political, and geographic summary data, by country, 1992, annual factbook, 9114–2
Exports and imports of US, by commodity and country, 1980-90, world area rpt, 9116–1.6
Exports and imports of US, by transport mode, country, and SITC 1- to 3-digit commodity, 1991, annual rpt, 2424–12
Exports of US, detailed Schedule B commodities with countries of destination, 1991, annual rpt, 2424–10
Food supply, needs, and aid for developing countries, status and alternative forecasts, 1992 world area rpt, 1526–8.2
Human rights conditions in 170 countries, and US economic and military aid, 1991, annual rpt, 21384–3
Labor conditions, union coverage, and work accidents, 1992 annual country rpt, 6366–4.20
Military aid of US, arms sales, and training programs costs and budget requests, by program, world region, and country, FY91-93, annual rpt, 7144–13
Military spending, arms trade, and force strengths, with govt spending and population, by country, 1979-89, annual rpt, 9824–1
Minerals Yearbook, Vol 3, 1989: foreign country review of production, trade, and policy, by commodity, annual rpt, 5604–35.1
Multinatl US firms foreign affiliates, income statement items by asset size, industry, and country, 1988, biennial article, 8302–2.322
Phosphate rock exports of Morocco by country of destination, Mineral Industry Surveys, monthly rpt, periodic table, 5612–1.30
Population size, growth rates, and components of change, by country, projected 1990-2020 and trends from 1950, biennial rpt, 2324–9
Refugee migration, and intl aid programs, by world area and country of origin and asylum, 1991, annual rpt, 7004–15
UN voting record and share of votes in agreement with US, by issue, country, and world area, 1991, annual rpt, 7004–18

Morris, Leo
"Sexual Experience and Use of Contraception Among Young Adults in Latin America", 4202–7.323

Morris, Mark O.
"Jail Construction in California", 6066–30.1

Morris, Melissa D.
"Transportation Energy Data Book: Edition 12", 3304–5

Morris, Victor
"What About (Hurricane) Bob?", 2152–8.301

Morrison, Diane M.
"Alcohol Consumption and Sexual Risk-Taking in Adolescents", 4482–1.304

Morrison, Howard I.
"Herbicides and Cancer", 4472–1.356

Mortality
see Accidental deaths
see Child mortality
see Deaths
see Fetal deaths
see Homicide
see Infant mortality
see Life expectancy
see Maternal deaths
see Suicide
see Traffic accident fatalities
see Vital statistics

Mortgages
Alteration and repair of owner-occupied homes, costs and structural, household, financial, and project characteristics, 1987, 2486–1.13
American Housing Survey: unit and household characteristics of recent movers, and reason for move, by tenure, 1989, 2486–1.12
American Housing Survey: unit and households detailed characteristics, and unit and neighborhood quality, MSA rpt series, 2485–6
American Housing Survey: unit and households detailed characteristics, and unit and neighborhood quality, 1989, wallchart, 2485–12
Applications for mortgages, dispositions, and secondary loan market sales, by purpose, lender type, and applicant and neighborhood characteristics, 1991, article, 9362–1.307
Assets and debts of private sector, balance sheets by segment, 1960-91, semiannual rpt, 9365–4.1
Banks (insured commercial and savings) finances, for foreign and domestic offices, by asset size, 1990, annual rpt, 9294–4.2
Banks and thrifts finances and operations by deposit size, Fed Reserve functional cost analysis, 1991, annual rpt, 9364–6
Banks credit operations costs and revenue, by credit type, mid 1970s-91, article, 9362–1.306
Business statistics, detailed data for major industries and economic indicators, *Survey of Current Business*, monthly rpt, 2702–1.5; 2702–1.8
Business statistics, detailed data for major industries and economic indicators, 1960-91, *Survey of Current Business* biennial supplement, 2704–1
Census of Population and Housing, 1990: population and housing characteristics, detailed geographic coverage, State CD-ROM series, 2551–10
Census of Population and Housing, 1990: summary characteristics, by county, subdiv, and place, State rpt series, 2551–7
Costs of housing exceeding 28% of gross income, families income by source and expenses by type, by tenure and other characteristics, 1989, article, 1702–1.304
County Business Patterns, 1989: employment, establishments, and payroll, by SIC 2- to 4-digit industry and county, annual State rpt series, 2326–8
County Business Patterns, 1990: employment, establishments, and payroll, by SIC 2- to 4-digit industry and county, annual State rpt series, 2326–6

Credit unions financial performance and regulation, with background data, 1960s-90, GAO rpt, 26119-364
Credit unions with low income membership, financial, operating, and membership data, 1982-91, 9536-1.8
Debt outstanding, by type of property and holder, 1940-91, annual rpt, 204-1.5
Families financial status, income, net worth, and assets and debt by type, by income and selected characteristics, 1983 and 1989, article, 9362-1.301
Farm sector assets by type, and real and nonreal estate debt, including and excluding operator households, by sales size, 1960-89, 1548-387
Fed Govt spending in States, by type, program, agency, and State, FY91, annual rpt, 2464-2
Fed Home Loan Mortgage Corp activities and financial statements, 1991, annual rpt, 9414-1
Fed Home Loan Mortgage Corp financial condition and capital adequacy, 1990, annual rpt, 5184-8
Fed Housing Financing Bd new home mortgage yields, monthly rpt, 23842-1.5
Fed Natl Mortgage Assn activities and finances, 1991, annual rpt, 5184-9; 9474-1
Fed Natl Mortgage Assn, Fed Home Loan Mortgage Corp, and FHLBs finances, 1991 hearings, 21248-170
FHA-insured mortgage activities, audits, and financial statements, FY90-91, annual rpt, 5144-26
FHA-insured mortgages, and foreclosures, by State and county, 1991 and cumulative from 1934, annual rpt, 5144-15
FHA-insured mortgages by State, financing costs, and loans in force and claims by loan-to-value ratio, 1970s-80s, hearings, 21248-162
FHA-insured mortgages, financial, property, and borrower characteristics, by metro area, 1991, annual rpt, 5144-24
FHA-insured mortgages, financial, property, and borrower characteristics, by State, 1991, annual rpt, 5144-1; 5144-25
FHA-insured mortgages, financial, property, and borrower characteristics, 1991, annual rpt, 5144-17; 5144-23
FHA-insured mortgages for 1-family units, by loan type and mortgage characteristics, quarterly rpt, 5142-45
FHA-insured mortgages secondary market prices and yields, and interest rates on construction and conventional mortgage loans, by region, monthly press release, 5142-20
FHA mortgage applications for new and existing units, refinancings, and housing starts, monthly rpt, 5142-44
FHA mortgage insurance fund financial condition, with background housing and mortgage data, 1970s-90s, hearing, 25248-128
Finance companies credit outstanding and leasing activities, by credit type, monthly rpt, 9365-2.7
Flow-of-funds accounts, savings, investments, and credit statements, quarterly rpt, 9365-3.3
FmHA property acquired through foreclosure, 1-family homes, value, sales, and leases, by State, monthly rpt, 1182-7
Foreclosure of mortgages, caseloads for Federal district courts, 1991, annual rpt, 18204-8.14; 18204-8.18; 18204-11
Futures and options trading volume, by commodity and exchange, FY91, annual rpt, 11924-2
Govt Natl Mortgage Assn finances, and mortgage-backed securities program, FY91, annual rpt, 5144-6
Home mortgage market activity and debt outstanding, 1987-90, annual rpt, 9364-5.7
Households financial services use, by account type and instn type and location, 1989 survey, article, 9362-1.303
Households net worth distribution under alternative sample weighting systems to account for inconsistency in survey design and response rates, 1992 rpt, 9368-91
Housing and households summary characteristics, 1989 and trends, chartbook, 2486-2.1
Housing units completed, single and multifamily units by structural and financial characteristics, and location, 1987-91, annual rpt, 2384-1
Illinois S&Ls, mortgage interest fixed and adjustable rates and fees offered, monthly rpt, discontinued, 9302-6
Interest fixed and adjustable rates and fees on mortgages offered, by region, weekly rpt, 9412-3
Interest rates for commercial paper, govt securities, other financial instruments, and home mortgages, monthly rpt, 9365-2.14
Interest rates on mortgages, differential among cities, and relation to bank market conditions, 1987-88, technical paper, 9366-1.162
Interest rates on new mortgages for previously occupied homes, monthly rpt, 9302-30; 9302-38
Intl financial markets performance of foreign and US bank and securities firms, finances and competitiveness issues, 1980s, compilation of papers, 9385-10
Loan activity for mortgages, by type of lender, loan, and mortgaged property, monthly press release, 5142-18
Loan activity for mortgages, by type of lender, loan, and mortgaged property, quarterly press release, 5142-30
Low- and moderate-income neighborhood lending program in Philadelphia, impacts on mortgage activity, with background data, 1980s, working paper, 9387-8.266
Low income rental housing in rural areas, FmHA loans and impacts of programs to maintain supply and to deter mortgage prepayment, 1988-91, GAO rpt, 26113-586
Minority- and woman-owned businesses and owner characteristics, by industry, employment and sales size, and form of ownership, 1987 survey, 2328-59
Minority groups mortgage applications, for Boston by disposition and financial characteristics, with problems in analyzing lender disclosure statements, 1990, working paper, 9373-27.15
New England States banks and thrifts real estate lending impacts of capital losses, with financial ratios, 1980s-91, article, 9373-27.12
New England States economic indicators, Fed Reserve 1st District, monthly rpt, 9373-2
New England States, FHLB 1st District thrift instns, financial condition, and locations, 1992, annual listing, 9304-26
Nonprofit charitable organizations finances, with data by State and for top 10 instns, 1988, article, 8302-2.302
North Central States business and economic conditions, Fed Reserve 9th District, quarterly journal, 9383-19
North Central States, FHLB 6th District insured S&Ls financial condition and operations by State, quarterly rpt, 9302-23
NYC housing supply, occupancy, condition, and household characteristics, by tenure and borough, 1991 triennial survey, 2488-3
Originations of mortgages, by State, 1982-90, annual press release, 5144-21
Pacific territories population and housing detailed characteristics, by location, 1990 Census of Population and Housing, series, 2551-8
Pension funds (public) investment in housing, and public and private funds holdings of mortgages, mortgage-backed securities, and govt securities, 1986-90, 5188-134
Real estate agent fees for mortgage banker referrals, and other issues, consumer views, 1989 survey, hearings, 21248-161
Recreation and investment housing units owned, by selected characteristics, 1989, biennial rpt supplement, 2485-13
Savings instns failure resolution activity and finances of Resolution Trust Corp, with data by asset type, State, region, and instn, monthly rpt, 9722-3
Savings instns failures, financial performance of instns under Resolution Trust Corp conservatorship, quarterly rpt, 9722-5
Savings instns finances and operations by district and State, mortgage loan activity, and FHLB finances, annual rpt, discontinued, 8434-3
Savings instns financial statements, for instns insured by Savings Assn Insurance Fund by FHLB district and State, and for FDIC-insured savings banks, 1989, annual rpt, 8434-1
Savings instns insured by Savings Assn Insurance Fund, assets, liabilities, and deposit and loan activity, by conservatorship status, monthly rpt, 8432-1
Savings instns profitability on fixed-rate mortgages, relation to interest rate spread and other operating ratios, model results, 1991 technical paper, 9366-6.289
Securities backed by mortgages, impacts of mortgage prepayment on present value, and returns compared to other investments, 1992, article, 9371-1.308
Single parent families in own and others homes, by financial, housing, and other characteristics, 1989, 2486-1.14
Single person and nonfamily households social, economic and housing characteristics, by tenure, 1989, 2486-1.15
Small business financing sources, and business financial data by size, type, and industry, 1980s-90, annual rpt, 9764-6.2

Southeastern States, Fed Reserve 5th District, economic indicators by State, quarterly rpt, 9389–16
Southeastern States, Fed Reserve 5th District insured commercial banks financial statements, by State, quarterly rpt, 9389–18
Southeastern States, Fed Reserve 8th District banking and economic conditions, quarterly rpt with articles, 9391–16
Southeastern States, FHLB 4th District, employment and housing indicators by State, quarterly rpt, 9302–36
State and local govt employees pension system cash and security holdings and finances, quarterly rpt, 2462–2
Statistical Abstract of US, 1992 annual data compilation, 2324–1.16
Survey of Current Business, detailed financial and business data, and economic indicators, monthly rpt, 2702–1.1
Tax (income) returns filed, by type of filer, selected income items, quarterly rpt, 8302–2.1
Tax (income) returns of corporations, income and tax items by asset size and detailed industry, 1989, annual rpt, 8304–4; 8304–21
Tax (income) returns of individuals, by filing status, tax item, and income level, 1991, annual article, 8302–2.319
Tax (income) returns of individuals, detailed data, 1988, annual rpt, 8304–2
Tax (income) withholding and related documents filed, by type and IRS service center, 1991 and projected 1992-99, annual rpt, 8304–22
Tax exempt organizations finances, with data by type, size, State, and for largest organizations, late 1940s-80s, compilation of papers, 8308–35
Terms on conventional mortgages at closing, by lender type, with periodic data by district, State, and for 32 MSAs, monthly rpt, 9442–2
Terms on conventional mortgages at closing, for fixed- and adjustable-rate loans by purpose, FHLB district, State, and selected MSA, 1960s-91, annual rpt, 9444–2
Terms, yields, secondary market activity, and debt outstanding, monthly rpt, 9362–1.1
Trust assets of banks, trust companies, and S&Ls, by type of asset and fund, selected firm, and State, 1991, annual rpt, 13004–1
Western States, FHLB 11th District shareholder instns, offices, and financial condition, 1992 annual listing, 9304–23
Wisconsin S&Ls, mortgage interest fixed and adjustable rates and fees offered, monthly rpt, discontinued, 9302–7
see also Agricultural credit
see also Farm Credit System
see also Veterans housing

Morton, Danielle C.
"Prisoners in 1991", 6066–25.47

Moseley, James R.
"Matching USDA Programs with Environmental Needs", 1504–9.1

Moser, James T.
"Determining Margin for Futures Contracts: The Role of Private Interests and the Relevance of Excess Volatility", 9375–1.302

Mosher, William D.
"Reproductive Impairments Among Currently Married Couples: U.S, 1976", 4147–16.6

Moss, Abigail J.
"Changes in Cigarette Smoking and Current Smoking Practices Among Adults: U.S., 1978", 4147–16.6

Moss, Carol P.
"Water Resources Activities of the Mississippi District, 1990-91", 5666–26.27

Mosser, Patricia C.
"Changes in Monetary Policy Effectiveness: Evidence from Large Macroeconometric Models", 9385–1.306
"Large Model Comparisons of Monetary Policy Sensitivity", 9385–8.135

Motels
see Hotels and motels

Mothers
see Births
see Breast-feeding
see Families and households
see Fertility
see Maternal deaths
see Maternity
see Maternity benefits
see Maternity homes
see Parents
see Teenage pregnancy
see Women

Motion pictures
Copyrights Register activities, registrations by material type, and fees, FY91 and trends from 1790, annual rpt, 26404–2
County Business Patterns, 1989: employment, establishments, and payroll, by SIC 2- to 4-digit industry and county, annual State rpt series, 2326–8
County Business Patterns, 1990: employment, establishments, and payroll, by SIC 2- to 4-digit industry and county, annual State rpt series, 2326–6
Employment, earnings, and hours, by SIC 1- to 4-digit industry, monthly 1989-Feb 1992, annual rpt, 6744–4
Exports and imports between US and outlying areas, by detailed commodity and mode of transport, 1991, annual rpt, 2424–11
Exports and imports of US, by country and detailed commodity, monthly rpt, 2422–12
Exports and imports of US, by Harmonized System 6-digit commodity and country, 1991, annual rpt, 2424–13
Exports and imports of US, by transport mode, country, and SITC 1- to 3-digit commodity, 1991, annual rpt, 2424–12
Exports of US, detailed Schedule B commodities with countries of destination, 1991, annual rpt, 2424–10
Fed Govt audiovisual activities and spending, by whether performed in-house and agency, FY91, annual rpt, 9514–1
Fed Govt publications and other holdings of Natl Archives, special collections, series, 9516–1
Finances and operations, by SIC 2- to 4-digit industry, forecast 1992, annual rpt, 2044–28
Households entertainment spending, recreation participation by activity, and video product and pet ownership, 1970s-90, article, 1702–1.303
Input-output structure of US economy, detailed interindustry transactions for 541 industries, and components of final demand, 1982 benchmark data, 2708–17
Libraries (public) finances, staff, and operations, by State and population size, 1990, annual rpt, 4824–6
Library of Congress activities, acquisitions, services, and financial statements, FY91, annual rpt, 26404–1
Multinatl firms US affiliates finances and operations, by industry, country of parent firm, and State, 1987, 2708–48
Multinatl US firms and foreign affiliates finances and operations, by industry and country, 1989 benchmark survey, annual rpt, 2704–5
Natl Archives and Records Admin activities, finances, holdings, and staff, FY91, annual rpt, 9514–2
Natl Endowment for Arts activities and grants, FY91, annual rpt, 9564–3
Natl income and product accounts, comprehensive accounts and components, benchmark revisions, 1929-88, 2708–5
Natl income and product accounts, comprehensive accounts and components, *Survey of Current Business*, monthly rpt, 2702–1.29
Occupational injury and illness rates, by SIC 2- to 4-digit industry, 1989-90, annual rpt, 6844–7
Price indexes (producer), by stage of processing and detailed commodity, monthly rpt, 6762–6
Soviet Union and US economic and sociodemographic indicators, selected years 1970-90, handbook, 2328–80
Tax (income) returns of corporations, income and tax items by asset size and detailed industry, 1989, annual rpt, 8304–4; 8304–21
Tax (income) returns of sole proprietorships, income statement items, by industry group, 1990, annual article, 8302–2.317; 8302–2.320
see also Video recordings and equipment

Motor Freight Transportation and Warehousing Survey
Finances and inventory of truck and warehouse services, by SIC 2- to 4-digit industry, 1990 survey, annual rpt, 2413–14

Motor fuels
Alternative fuels pollutant emissions by fuel type, and alcohol fuel production and inputs, 1991 hearing, 25318–82
Alternative fuels use in Federal fleet, energy economy performance at 4 sites, FY91, annual rpt, 3304–28
Bus exhaust emissions reduction programs, funding, and alternative fuel bus dev, periodic rpt, 7882–3
Fuel oil and kerosene sales and deliveries, by end-use, PAD district, and State, 1990, annual rpt, 3164–94
Injuries from use of consumer products and related activities, by severity and victim age and sex, 1990, annual rpt, 9164–7
Oxygenate supply and blending in gasoline, by PAD district, monthly data, weekly rpt, 3162–32.3
Oxygenate supply, blending in gasoline, and plant capacity and use, by PAD district, monthly rpt, 3162–6.4

Price indexes (producer), by stage of processing and detailed commodity, monthly rpt, 6762–6
Prices and spending for fuel, by type, end-use sector, and State, 1990, annual rpt, 3164–64
Prices of fuel, by type, end-use sector, and region, projected 1991-2030, 3166–6.60
see also Aviation fuels
see also Diesel fuel
see also Fuel tax
see also Gasohol
see also Gasoline
see also Transportation energy use

Motor transportation
see Automobiles
see Buses
see Motor vehicle industry
see Motorcycles
see Taxicabs
see Traffic accidents and safety
see Trucks and trucking industry

Motor vehicle exhaust
Abatement spending by govts, business, and consumers, 1972-90, annual article, 2702–1.321
Bus exhaust emissions reduction programs, funding, and alternative fuel bus dev, periodic rpt, 7882–3
Emissions levels for 6 pollutants, by source and selected MSA, 1982-91, annual rpt, 9194–1
Energy natl strategy auto fuel economy standards and alternative fuels issues, 1991 hearings, 21368–138
Energy use by mode of transport, fuel supply, and demographic and economic factors of vehicle use, 1970s-90, annual rpt, 3304–5
Older autos retirement programs proposals costs, savings, and emissions and energy use reductions, 1992 rpt, 26358–263
Oxygenate supply and blending in gasoline, by PAD district, monthly data, weekly rpt, 3162–32.3
Oxygenate supply, blending in gasoline, and plant capacity and use, by PAD district, monthly rpt, 3162–6.4
Philadelphia metro area transit service operations, costs and benefits, and local economic and air pollution impacts, 1970s-90 and projected to 2020, 7308–205

Motor vehicle exports and imports
Business statistics, detailed data for major industries and economic indicators, 1960-91, *Survey of Current Business* biennial supplement, 2704–1
Energy economy improvements from new technologies, 1987-90 and alternative projections to 2010, 26358–251
Energy economy performance of autos and light trucks by make, standards, and enforcement, 1978-94 model years, annual rpt, 7764–9
Energy economy test results for US and foreign makes, 1993 model year, annual rpt, 3304–11
Energy use by mode of transport, fuel supply, and demographic and economic factors of vehicle use, 1970s-90, annual rpt, 3304–5
Exports and imports between US and outlying areas, by detailed commodity and mode of transport, 1991, annual rpt, 2424–11
Exports and imports by country, US industry finances and operations, and prices of selected US and foreign models, monthly rpt, 9882–8
Exports and imports of US, by country and detailed commodity, monthly rpt, 2422–12
Exports and imports of US, by Harmonized System 6-digit commodity and country, 1991, annual rpt, 2424–13
Exports and imports of US, by selected country, country group, and commodity group, 1991, annual rpt, 2044–37
Exports and imports of US, by transport mode, country, and SITC 1- to 3-digit commodity, 1991, annual rpt, 2424–12
Exports, imports, and balances of US for manufactured goods, by SITC 2-digit commodity and country, quarterly rpt, 2042–35
Exports, imports, and intl competitiveness of US industries, trends and outlook, quarterly rpt with articles, 9882–16
Exports, imports, production, and labor conditions in autos and auto part industries, for US and compared to Canada and Mexico, 1950s-90, 6366–3.28
Exports of US, detailed Schedule B commodities with countries of destination, 1991, annual rpt, 2424–10
Imports, exports, and employment impacts, by SIC 2- to 4-digit industry and commodity, quarterly rpt, 2322–2
Imports of autos and parts, *Survey of Current Business*, monthly rpt, 2702–1.1
Imports of US given duty-free treatment for value of US material sent abroad, by commodity and country, 1987-90, annual rpt, 9884–14
Input-output structure of US economy, detailed interindustry transactions for 541 industries, and components of final demand, 1982 benchmark data, 2708–17
Japan and other auto imports of US, 1979-90, article, 6722–1.313
Minivans from Japan at less than fair value, injury to US industry, investigation with background financial and operating data, 1992 rpt, 9886–14.351
Natl income and product accounts, comprehensive accounts and components, benchmark revisions, 1929-88, 2708–5
Natl income and product accounts, comprehensive accounts and components, *Survey of Current Business*, monthly rpt, 2702–1.27
OECD intl trade position for US and 4 countries, and factors affecting US competition, quarterly pamphlet, 2042–25
OECD trade, total and for 4 major countries, and US trade by country, by commodity, 1980-90, world area rpt series, 9116–1
Parts (auto) trade with Japan and other countries, 1985-90 and forecast to 1994, annual rpt, 2004–10
Price indexes for exports and imports, by selected end-use category, monthly press release, 6762–15
Safety of domestic and foreign autos, crash test results by model, model years 1987-91, 7768–111
Safety of domestic and foreign autos, crash test results by model, press release series, 7766–7
Sales and prices for domestic and import autos and trucks, and auto production and inventories, 1992 model year, annual article, 2702–1.339
Sales of domestic and imported cars, monthly rpt, quarterly data, 23842–1.1
Statistical Abstract of US, 1992 annual data compilation, 2324–1.21
Theft rates of new autos, by make and model, 1990 model year, annual rpt, 7764–21
Waterborne commerce (domestic and foreign) of US, freight by commodity, traffic, and passengers, by port and waterway, 1989, annual rpt, 3754–3

Motor vehicle fleets
DOE fleet, and fuel efficiency, by vehicle type, FY91, annual rpt, 3004–27
Energy use by fuel type, and miles traveled, by transport mode, projected 1990-2010 and trends from 1960s, 3008–124
Energy use, size, and trip characteristics, for motor vehicle fleets by type, 1970s-90, annual rpt, 3304–5.3
Fed Govt auto fleet alternative fuels use, energy economy performance at 4 sites, FY91, annual rpt, 3304–28
Police agencies employment, spending, and operations, FY90, 6066–25.44
Police employment, spending, and operations, for State, city, county, and special district agencies, 1990, annual rpt, 6064–39
Postal Service operating costs, itemized by class of mail, FY91, annual rpt, 9864–4
Registrations, by public and private ownership, vehicle type, and State, 1991, annual rpt, 7554–1.2
Sheriffs' agencies employment, spending, and operations, FY90, 6066–25.45
Truck and warehouse services finances and inventory, by SIC 2- to 4-digit industry, 1990 survey, annual rpt, 2413–14
Truck rates for fruit and vegetables paid by shippers and receivers, by commodity and city, and fleet itemized costs per mile, weekly rpt, 1311–22
TVA energy use by fuel type, and conservation costs and savings, FY91, annual rpt, 9804–26

Motor vehicle industry
Business statistics, detailed data for major industries and economic indicators, *Survey of Current Business*, monthly rpt, 2702–1.22
Capital expenditures for plant and equipment, by major industry group, quarterly rpt, 2502–2
Competitiveness (intl) of US industries, and trade, trends and outlook, quarterly rpt with articles, 9882–16
County Business Patterns, 1989: employment, establishments, and payroll, by SIC 2- to 4-digit industry and county, annual State rpt series, 2326–8
County Business Patterns, 1990: employment, establishments, and payroll, by SIC 2- to 4-digit industry and county, annual State rpt series, 2326–6
Economic indicators and components, and Fed Reserve 4th District business and financial conditions, monthly chartbook, 9377–10

Electric-powered autos, R&D activity and DOE funding shares, FY91, annual rpt, 3304–2
Employment, earnings, and hours, by SIC 1- to 4-digit industry, monthly 1989-Feb 1992, annual rpt, 6744–4
Employment of minorities and women, by occupation, SIC 1- to 3-digit industry, State, and MSA, 1991, annual rpt, 9244–1
Employment, unemployment, and labor force characteristics, by region and census div, 1991, annual rpt, 6744–7.1
Finances and operations of US auto industry, trade by country, and prices of selected US and foreign models, monthly rpt, 9882–8
Finances of auto industry, and average fleet fuel economy, by selected firm, 1991 hearings, 21368–138
Foreign and US hourly compensation costs, for motor vehicle industry by country, 1975-90, 6826–3.8
Input-output structure of US economy, detailed interindustry transactions for 84 industries, and components of final demand, 1987, annual article, 2702–1.316
Input-output structure of US economy, detailed interindustry transactions for 541 industries, and components of final demand, 1982 benchmark data, 2708–17
Mail volume to and from households, use, and views, by class, source, content, and household characteristics, FY87-90, annual rpt, 9864–10
Manufacturing annual survey, 1990: finances and operations, by SIC 2- to 4-digit industry, series, 2506–14
Manufacturing census, 1987: concentration of largest firms measured by value added, and for shipments by SIC 2- and 4-digit industry, subject rpt, 2497–6
Manufacturing census, 1987: shipments of manufacturers products, by customer class and SIC 2- and 4-digit industry, subject rpt, 2497–4
Manufacturing corporations financial statements, by selected SIC 2- to 3-digit industry, quarterly rpt, 2502–1
Manufacturing finances and operations, by SIC 2- to 4-digit industry, forecast 1992, annual rpt, 2044–28
Mexico and US economic and trade impacts of proposed North American Free Trade Agreement, with data on maquiladora plants, 1980s-90, hearings, 21788–210
Multinatl firms US affiliates finances and operations, by industry, country of parent firm, and State, 1987, 2708–48
Multinatl US firms and foreign affiliates finances and operations, by industry and country, 1989 benchmark survey, annual rpt, 2704–5
Multinatl US firms foreign affiliates, income statement items by asset size, industry, and country, 1988, biennial article, 8302–2.322
Natl income and product accounts, comprehensive accounts and components, benchmark revisions, 1929-88, 2708–5
Natl income and product accounts, comprehensive accounts and components, *Survey of Current Business*, monthly rpt, 2702–1.24; 2702–1.31
Occupational injury and illness rates, by SIC 2- to 4-digit industry, 1989-90, annual rpt, 6844–7
Occupational injury and illness rates, by SIC 2- to 4-digit industry, 1990, annual rpt, 6844–1
Price indexes (producer), by stage of processing and detailed commodity, monthly rpt, 6762–6
Price indexes (producer), by stage of processing and detailed commodity, monthly 1991, annual rpt, 6764–2
Production and capacity use indexes, by SIC 2- to 4-digit industry, monthly rpt, 9365–2.24
Production, labor conditions, and trade of autos and auto parts, for US and compared to Canada and Mexico, 1950s-90, 6366–3.28
Productivity in auto assembly plants and relation to labor reserves, model description and results, 1991 working paper, 6886–6.89
Productivity of labor and capital, and indexes of output, hours, and employment, 1967-90, annual rpt, 6824–1.3; 6824–1.5
Recalls of motor vehicles and equipment with safety-related defects, by make, monthly listing, 7762–12
Recalls of motor vehicles and equipment with safety-related defects, by make, quarterly listing, 7762–2
Science, engineering, and technical employment in manufacturing, by field and industry, 1989, triennial rpt, 9627–23
Soviet Union and US economic and sociodemographic indicators, selected years 1970-90, handbook, 2328–80
Statistical Abstract of US, 1992 annual data compilation, 2324–1.21
Tax (income) returns of corporations, income and tax items by asset size and detailed industry, 1989, annual rpt, 8304–4; 8304–21
Tax (income) returns of corporations with foreign tax credit, income and tax items by industry group, 1988, biennial article, 8302–2.316
see also Automobile repair and maintenance
see also Automobiles
see also Buses
see also Chrysler Corp.
see also Ford Motor Co.
see also General Motors Corp.
see also Motor vehicle exhaust
see also Motor vehicle exports and imports
see also Motor vehicle fleets
see also Motor vehicle parts and supplies
see also Motor vehicle registrations
see also Motor vehicle rental
see also Motor vehicle safety devices
see also Motorcycles
see also Recreational vehicles
see also Tires and tire industry
see also Trucks and trucking industry

Motor vehicle parts and supplies
Consumer spending, natl income and product account benchmark revisions, 1929-88, 2708–5
Consumer spending, natl income and product accounts, comprehensive accounts and components, *Survey of Current Business*, monthly rpt, 2702–1.25
County Business Patterns, 1989: employment, establishments, and payroll, by SIC 2- to 4-digit industry and county, annual State rpt series, 2326–8
County Business Patterns, 1990: employment, establishments, and payroll, by SIC 2- to 4-digit industry and county, annual State rpt series, 2326–6
CPI by component for US city average, and by selected metro area, region, and population size, monthly rpt, 6762–2
Eastern Europe export industries dev potential, with trade and industry finances and operations, for 5 countries, 1985-90, 9886–4.179
Exports and imports between US and outlying areas, by detailed commodity and mode of transport, 1991, annual rpt, 2424–11
Exports and imports of auto parts with Japan and other countries, 1985-90 and forecast to 1994, annual rpt, 2004–10
Exports of US, detailed Schedule B commodities with countries of destination, 1991, annual rpt, 2424–10
Input-output structure of US economy, detailed interindustry transactions for 541 industries, and components of final demand, 1982 benchmark data, 2708–17
Instruments and related products shipments, trade, use, and firms, by detailed type, 1991, annual Current Industrial Rpt, 2506–12.26
Labor productivity, indexes of output, hours, and employment by SIC 2- to 4-digit industry, 1967-90, annual rpt, 6824–1.3
Manufacturing annual survey, 1990: finances and operations, by SIC 2- to 4-digit industry, series, 2506–14
Manufacturing census, 1987: concentration of largest firms measured by value added, and for shipments by SIC 2- and 4-digit industry, subject rpt, 2497–6
Manufacturing census, 1987: shipments of manufacturers products, by customer class and SIC 2- and 4-digit industry, subject rpt, 2497–4
Occupational injury and illness rates, by SIC 2- to 4-digit industry, 1989-90, annual rpt, 6844–7
Price indexes (producer), by stage of processing and detailed commodity, monthly rpt, 6762–6
Price indexes (producer), by stage of processing and detailed commodity, monthly 1991, annual rpt, 6764–2
Production, labor conditions, and trade of autos and auto parts, for US and compared to Canada and Mexico, 1950s-90, 6366–3.28
Quality changes in autos since last model year, factory and retail value, 1993 model year, annual press release, 6764–3
Recalls of motor vehicles and equipment with safety-related defects, by make, monthly listing, 7762–12
Recalls of motor vehicles and equipment with safety-related defects, by make, quarterly listing, 7762–2
Tax (excise) on auto equipment of Fed Govt and States, 1991, annual rpt, 7554–1
see also Batteries
see also Engines and motors
see also Mobile radio

see also Motor vehicle safety devices
see also Tires and tire industry

Motor vehicle registrations

Business statistics, detailed data for major industries and economic indicators, *Survey of Current Business*, monthly rpt, 2702–1.22

Colorado off-road vehicle use, owner expenses, and views on proposed registration fee, 1986-88, hearing, 25318–85

Costs of owning and operating autos, vans, and light trucks, by vehicle size and year of operation, 1991 model year, biennial rpt, 7554–21

CPI by component for US city average, and by selected metro area, region, and population size, monthly rpt, 6762–2

Energy use by mode of transport, fuel supply, and demographic and economic factors of vehicle use, 1970s-90, annual rpt, 3304–5

Foreign countries transportation energy use, fuel prices, vehicle registrations, and mileage, by selected country, 1950-89, annual rpt, 3304–5.1

Govt finances, tax systems and revenue, and fiscal structure, by level of govt and State, 1992 with historical trends, annual rpt, 10044–1

Hwy receipts by source, and spending by function, by level of govt and State, 1991, annual rpt, 7554–1.3

Hwy Statistics, registrations, by public and private ownership, vehicle type, and State, 1991, annual rpt, 7554–1.2

Hwy Statistics, summary data by State, 1990-91, annual rpt, 7554–24

Hwy Statistics, summary data with trends and projections, 1992 chartbook, 7554–41

Natl income and product accounts, comprehensive accounts and components, benchmark revisions, 1929-88, 2708–5

Natl income and product accounts, comprehensive accounts and components, *Survey of Current Business*, monthly rpt, 2702–1.26

Registrations and fuel use, by vehicle type, 1960-91, annual rpt, 3164–74.1

Revenue, by level of govt, type of tax, State, and selected large county, quarterly rpt, 2462–3

Revenue of State govts by detailed source, and tax rates, by State, FY91, annual rpt, 2466–2.7

State govt revenue by source, spending and debt by function, and holdings, FY91, annual rpt, 2466–2.6

Statistical Abstract of US, 1992 annual data compilation, 2324–1.21

Motor vehicle rental

Age restrictions for auto rental impacts on military personnel, with personnel by age, and rental receipts by company, 1991, GAO rpt, 26123–391

Communications services revenue and expenses, itemized by SIC 2- to 4-digit kind of business, 1990, annual rpt, 2413–15

County Business Patterns, 1989: employment, establishments, and payroll, by SIC 2- to 4-digit industry and county, annual State rpt series, 2326–8

County Business Patterns, 1990: employment, establishments, and payroll, by SIC 2- to 4-digit industry and county, annual State rpt series, 2326–6

Employment, earnings, and hours, by SIC 1- to 4-digit industry, monthly 1989-Feb 1992, annual rpt, 6744–4

Energy use, size, and trip characteristics, for motor vehicle fleets by type, 1970s-90, annual rpt, 3304–5.3

Finance companies credit outstanding and leasing activities, by credit type, monthly rpt, 9365–2.7

Multinatl US firms and foreign affiliates finances and operations, by industry and country, 1989 benchmark survey, annual rpt, 2704–5

Price indexes (producer), by stage of processing and detailed commodity, monthly rpt, 6762–6

Price indexes (producer), by stage of processing and detailed commodity, monthly 1991, annual rpt, 6764–2

Travel to US, by characteristics of visit and traveler, world area of origin, and US destination, 1991 survey, annual rpt, 2904–12

Truck and warehouse services finances and inventory, by SIC 2- to 4-digit industry, 1990 survey, annual rpt, 2413–14

Motor vehicle safety

see Motor vehicle safety devices
see Traffic accident fatalities
see Traffic accidents and safety

Motor vehicle safety devices

Accident deaths and injuries prevention, and treatment, 1991 conf papers, 4208–35

Child restraints use among Medicaid recipients by selected characteristics, local area study, 1992 article, 4042–3.312

Child restraints use, related injuries by severity, 1991, annual rpt, 9164–6

Child safety seats recalls, by make, monthly listing, 7762–12

Crash test results by domestic and foreign model, model years 1987-91, 7768–111

Crash test results by domestic and foreign model, press release series, 7766–7

Exports and imports of US, by Harmonized System 6-digit commodity and country, 1991, annual rpt, 2424–13

Indian health risk behavior, by region and for Montana, mid 1980s, article, 4042–3.346

Natl Hwy Traffic Safety Admin activities and grants, and fatal traffic accident data, 1990, annual rpt, 7764–1

Quality changes in autos since last model year, factory and retail value, 1993 model year, annual press release, 6764–3

Recalls of motor vehicles and equipment with safety-related defects, by make, monthly listing, 7762–12

Recalls of motor vehicles and equipment with safety-related defects, by make, quarterly listing, 7762–2

Seat belt and motorcycle helmet use, and other circumstances of fatal accidents, 1991, semiannual rpt, 7762–11

Seat belt and motorcycle helmet use, and other detailed circumstances of fatal accidents, 1990, annual rpt, 7764–10

Seat belt nonuse and other health risk behavior, prevalence by age, State, and other characteristics, 1986-90, article, 4202–7.305

Seat belt use and alcohol involvement, for drivers killed and surviving fatal accidents, 1990, annual rpt, 7764–16

Seat belt use, and other circumstances of accidents, 1990, annual rpt, 7764–18

Seat belts (automatic) and air bags, availability and impact on traffic accident deaths, 1980s-91, 7768–123

Shoulder belt use, for manual and automatic restraints, by auto make and model, 1986-90 model years, study results, article, 4042–3.320

Truck accidents, casualties, and damage, by circumstances and characteristics of persons and vehicles involved, 1989, annual rpt, 7554–9

Motor vehicle theft

Court civil and criminal caseloads for Federal district, appeals, and bankruptcy courts, by type of suit and offense, circuit, and district, 1991, annual rpt, 18204–11

Court civil and criminal caseloads for Federal district, appeals, and special courts, 1991, annual rpt, 18204–8

Court criminal case processing in Federal district courts, and dispositions, by offense, district, and offender characteristics, 1989, annual data compilation, 6064–29

Court criminal case processing in Federal district courts, and dispositions, by offense, 1980-91, annual rpt, 6064–31

Crime, criminal justice admin and enforcement, and public opinion, data compilation, 1992 annual rpt, 6064–6

Crime Index by population size and region, and offenses by large city, 1st half 1992, semiannual rpt, 6222–1

Crimes, arrests by offender characteristics, and rates, by offense, and law enforcement employees, by population size and jurisdiction, 1991, annual rpt, 6224–2

Juvenile arrests, by sex, race, disposition, and offense, 1990, 6066–27.8

Prison and parole admissions and releases, sentence length, and time served, by offense and offender characteristics, 1988, annual rpt, 6064–33

Prisoners in Federal and contract instns, by selected characteristics, region, and Federal instn, FY89, annual rpt, 6244–1.1

Sentences for Federal crimes, guidelines use and results by offense and district, and Sentencing Commission activities, 1991, annual rpt, 17664–1

Sentences for Federal offenses, guidelines by offense and circumstances, series, 17668–1

States criminal justice systems activities, employment, funding, and data collection, by State, 1970s-91, annual rpt, 6064–40

Theft rates of new autos, by make and model, 1990 model year, annual rpt, 7764–21

US attorneys civil and criminal cases by type and disposition, and collections, by Federal district, FY91, annual rpt, 6004–2.1; 6004–2.7

Victimization rates, by victim and offender characteristics, circumstances, and offense, survey rpt series, 6066–3

Victimizations, by offense and whether reported to police, 1990-91, press release, 6068–249

Victimizations of households, by offense, household characteristics, and location, 1975-91, annual rpt, 6066–25.49
Women in jail, by criminal background and sociodemographic characteristics, with comparisons to men, 1989, 6066–19.66

Motorcycle gangs
see Organized crime

Motorcycles
Accidents (fatal), circumstances, and characteristics of persons and vehicles involved, 1991, semiannual rpt, 7762–11
Accidents (fatal), deaths, and rates, by circumstances, characteristics of persons and vehicles involved, and location, 1990, annual rpt, 7764–10
Accidents at hwy-railroad grade-crossings, detailed data by State and railroad, 1991, annual rpt, 7604–2
Accidents, casualties, circumstances, and characteristics of persons and vehicles involved, 1990, annual rpt, 7764–18
Commuting to work, by mode, trip duration, and work location, 1980 and 1990, 7558–120
CPI by component for US city average, and by selected metro area, region, and population size, monthly rpt, 6762–2
Drivers licenses issued and in force by age and sex, fees, and renewal, by license class and State, 1990, annual rpt, 7554–16
Energy use and vehicle registrations, by vehicle type, 1960-91, annual rpt, 3164–74.1
Energy use by mode of transport, fuel supply, and demographic and economic factors of vehicle use, 1970s-90, annual rpt, 3304–5
Exports and imports between US and outlying areas, by detailed commodity and mode of transport, 1991, annual rpt, 2424–11
Exports and imports of US, by country and detailed commodity, monthly rpt, 2422–12
Exports and imports of US, by Harmonized System 6-digit commodity and country, 1991, annual rpt, 2424–13
Exports and imports of US, by transport mode, country, and SITC 1- to 3-digit commodity, 1991, annual rpt, 2424–12
Exports of US, detailed Schedule B commodities with countries of destination, 1991, annual rpt, 2424–10
Housing and households characteristics, unit and neighborhood quality, and journey to work by MSA location, for 11 MSAs, 1985 survey, supplement, 2485–8
Housing and households detailed characteristics, and unit and neighborhood quality, by location, 1989, biennial rpt supplement, 2485–13
Hwy Statistics, detailed data by State, 1991, annual rpt, 7554–1
Hwy Statistics, summary data by State, 1990-91, annual rpt, 7554–24
Input-output structure of US economy, detailed interindustry transactions for 541 industries, and components of final demand, 1982 benchmark data, 2708–17
Manufacturing annual survey, 1990: finances and operations, by SIC 2- to 4-digit industry, series, 2506–14
Manufacturing finances and operations, by SIC 2- to 4-digit industry, forecast 1992, annual rpt, 2044–28
Occupational injury and illness rates, by SIC 2- to 4-digit industry, 1989-90, annual rpt, 6844–7
OECD trade, total and for 4 major countries, and US trade by country, by commodity, 1980-90, world area rpt series, 9116–1
Pacific territories population and housing detailed characteristics, by location, 1990 Census of Population and Housing, series, 2551–8
Price indexes (producer), by stage of processing and detailed commodity, monthly rpt, 6762–6
Price indexes (producer), by stage of processing and detailed commodity, monthly 1991, annual rpt, 6764–2
Recalls of motor vehicles and equipment with safety-related defects, by make, monthly listing, 7762–12
Recalls of motor vehicles and equipment with safety-related defects, by make, quarterly listing, 7762–2
Statistical Abstract of US, 1992 annual data compilation, 2324–1.21
Travel patterns, personal and household characteristics, and auto and public transport use, 1990 survey, series, 7556–6

Motors
see Engines and motors

Mott, Frank L.
"Maternal-Child Health Data from the NLSY: 1988 Tabulations and Summary Discussion", 4478–197

Mountain, David G.
"Oceanographic Observations in the Inner New York Bight in Support of the 12-Mile Dumpsite Study, 1987-89", 2168–130

Mountain-Plains States
see Western States
see under By Region in the "Index by Categories"

Movie industry
see Motion pictures
see Video recordings and equipment

Mozambique
Agricultural trade of US, by detailed commodity and country, 1991, annual rpt, 1524–8
Agricultural trade of US, by detailed commodity and country, 1991, semiannual rpt, 1522–4
AID economic aid to developing countries, obligations and disbursements by country, quarterly rpt, 9912–4
Economic and military aid and loans from US and intl agencies, by program and country, FY46-91, annual rpt, 9914–5
Economic and social conditions of developing countries from 1960s, and Intl Dev Cooperation Agency and AID activities and funding, FY91-93, annual rpt, 9904–4
Economic conditions, income, production, prices, employment, and trade, 1992 periodic country rpt, 2046–4.61
Economic, social, political, and geographic summary data, by country, 1992, annual factbook, 9114–2
Exports and imports of US, by transport mode, country, and SITC 1- to 3-digit commodity, 1991, annual rpt, 2424–12
Exports of US, detailed Schedule B commodities with countries of destination, 1991, annual rpt, 2424–10
Food supply, needs, and aid for developing countries, status and alternative forecasts, 1992 world area rpt, 1526–8.2
Human rights conditions in 170 countries, and US economic and military aid, 1991, annual rpt, 21384–3
Military aid of US, arms sales, and training programs costs and budget requests, by program, world region, and country, FY91-93, annual rpt, 7144–13
Military spending, arms trade, and force strengths, with govt spending and population, by country, 1979-89, annual rpt, 9824–1
Minerals Yearbook, Vol 3, 1989: foreign country review of production, trade, and policy, by commodity, annual rpt, 5604–35.1
Population size, growth rates, and components of change, by country, projected 1990-2020 and trends from 1950, biennial rpt, 2324–9
Refugee migration, and intl aid programs, by world area and country of origin and asylum, 1991, annual rpt, 7004–15
UN voting record and share of votes in agreement with US, by issue, country, and world area, 1991, annual rpt, 7004–18

MPR Associates, Inc.
"Characteristics of At-Risk Students in NELS:88. National Education Longitudinal Study of 1988", 4826–9.16
"Comparison of Vocational and Non-Vocational Public School Teachers of Grades 9 to 12. Schools and Staffing Survey", 4836–3.9
"Language Characteristics and Academic Achievement: A Look at Asian and Hispanic Eighth Graders in National Education Longitudinal Study of 1988", 4826–9.12
"Parental Financial Support for Undergraduate Education: 1987 National Postsecondary Student Aid Study", 4846–3.11
"Profile of American Eighth-Grade Mathematics and Science Instruction. National Education Longitudinal Study of 1988", 4826–9.13

MSA
see Metropolitan Statistical Areas
see under By SMSA or MSA in the "Index by Categories"

Mueggler, Walter F.
"Cliff Lake Bench Research Natural Area: Problems Encountered in Monitoring Vegetation Change on Mountain Grasslands", 1208–425

Muller, Charlotte F.
"Why Do Some Caregivers of Disabled and Frail Elderly Quit?", 4652–1.305

Muller, L. Scott
"Disability Beneficiaries Who Work and Their Experience Under Program Incentives", 4742–1.312

Mullins, William H.
"Reconnaissance Investigation of Water Quality, Bottom Sediment, and Biota Associated with Irrigation Drainage in the American Falls Reservoir Area, Idaho, 1988-89", 5666–27.24

Multifiber Arrangement
see Trade agreements
Multilateral development banks
see African Development Bank
see Asian Development Bank
see Inter-American Development Bank
see International Bank for Reconstruction and Development
Multinational corporations
Banks (insured commercial and savings) deposits by instn, State, MSA, and county, as of June 1991, annual regional rpt series, 9295–3
Banks (insured commercial and savings) finances, for foreign and domestic offices, by asset size, 1990, annual rpt, 9294–4.2
Banks (natl) charters, mergers, liquidations, enforcement cases, and financial performance, with data by instn and State, quarterly rpt, 8402–3
Banks (US) foreign branches assets and liabilities, by world region and country, quarterly rpt, 9365–3.7
Banks (US) foreign lending at all US and foreign offices, by country group and country, quarterly rpt, 13002–1
Banks balance sheets, by Fed Reserve District, for major banks in NYC, and for US branches and agencies of foreign banks, weekly rpt, 9365–1.3
Capital expenditures of multinatl US firms foreign affiliates, by major industry group, world area, and country, 1987-92, semiannual article, 2702–1.312; 2702–1.335
Currency (foreign) positions of US firms and foreign branches or affiliates, *Treasury Bulletin*, quarterly rpt, 8002–4.14
Employees of intl corporations transferred to US, by country, FY81-91, annual rpt, 6264–2.3
Employment and trade of foreign-controlled US firms compared to US multinatl firms, 1988, article, 9391–1.309
Energy producers finances and operations, by energy type for US firms domestic and foreign operations, 1990, annual rpt, 3164–44
Energy resources of US, foreign direct investment by energy type and firm, and US affiliates operations, as of 1990, annual rpt, 3164–80
Finances and operations of foreign firms US affiliates, by industry, country of parent firm, and State, 1987, 2708–48
Finances and operations of foreign firms US affiliates, by industry, country of parent firm, and State, 1987, article, 2702–1.340
Finances and operations of foreign firms US affiliates, by industry div, country of parent firm, and State, 1989-90, annual article, 2702–1.319; 2702–1.337
Finances and operations of foreign firms US affiliates, by industry, world area of parent firm, and State, 1989-90, annual rpt, 2704–4
Finances and operations of multinatl US firms and foreign affiliates, by industry and country, 1989 benchmark survey, annual rpt, 2704–5
Finances and operations of multinatl US firms and foreign affiliates, by industry and world area, 1989-90, annual article, 2702–1.329
Finances and tax burdens of corporations under domestic and foreign control, 1983-87, GAO rpt, 26119–411
Foreign-controlled US firms transactions with related foreign persons, by type, industry div, and country, 1988, article, 8302–2.318
Foreign direct investment in US, by industry group and world area, 1989-91, annual article, 2702–1.331
Foreign direct investment in US by top 10 countries, factors affecting rate of return, and compared to returns for US firms, 1980s-91, article, 2702–1.330
Foreign direct investment in US, major transactions by type, industry, country, and US location, 1990, annual rpt, 2044–20
Foreign direct investment of US, by industry group and world area, 1989-91, annual article, 2702–1.332
GDP contribution of multinatl firms US affiliates, by component, industry, and country of parent firm, 1987-90, article, 2702–1.342
Imports of US given duty-free treatment for value of US material sent abroad, by commodity and country, 1987-90, annual rpt, 9884–14
Income tax compliance issues, for multinatl firms US affiliates with income and tax data by industry group, 1987-89, press release, 8008–155
Income tax returns of foreign corporations and individuals, and US entities abroad, detailed data compilation, 1970s-89, quinquennial rpt, 8308–31
Insurance industry financial condition, operations, assets, junk bond holdings, and State regulation, with intl comparisons, 1991 hearings, 25268–79
Latin America economic and social conditions, resources, trade, and aid, 1992, annual factbook, 9914–14
Militarily strategic manufacturing industries finances, operations, and intl competitiveness, series, 2026–1
Oil company effective income tax rates, with background income and tax data for domestic and foreign operations, 1977-89, 3168–124
Royalties and fees received and paid by multinatl firms US affiliates, and nonbank and manufacturing employment in Fed Reserve 8th District, 1970s-90, article, 9391–16.302
Services trade of US, direct and among multinatl firms affiliates, by industry and world area, 1986-91, article, 2702–1.336
Ships under foreign flag owned by US firms and foreign affiliates, by type, owner, and country of registry and construction, as of July 1991, semiannual rpt, 7702–3
Statistical Abstract of US, 1992 annual data compilation, 2324–1.16; 2324–1.17
Tax (income) and effective rates on US, foreign, and worldwide income, by company and industry, 1980s, GAO rpt, 26119–289
Tax (income) returns for foreign corporate activity in US, selected income and tax items, by industry div and selected country, 1988, article, 8302–2.309
Tax (income) returns of corporations with foreign tax credit, income and tax items by industry group, 1988, biennial article, 8302–2.316
Tax (income) returns of multinatl US firms foreign affiliates, income statement items by asset size, industry, and country, 1988, biennial article, 8302–2.322
Multnomah County, Oreg.
Housing and households characteristics, and unit and neighborhood quality, by MSA location for 11 MSAs, 1986 survey, supplement, 2485–8
Municipal bonds
Business statistics, detailed data for major industries and economic indicators, 1960-91, *Survey of Current Business* biennial supplement, 2704–1
Finances of govts, by level of govt, State, and for large cities and counties, annual rpt series, 2466–2
Finances of govts, tax systems and revenue, and fiscal structure, by level of govt and State, 1992 and historical trends, annual rpt, 10044–1
Futures and options trading volume, by commodity and exchange, FY91, annual rpt, 11924–2
Futures trading in selected commodities and financial instruments and indexes, for NYC, Chicago, and other markets activity, biweekly rpt, 11922–5
Hwy receipts by source, and spending by function, by level of govt and State, 1991, annual rpt, 7554–1.3
Insurers of municipal bonds, finances and capital adequacy indicators, by firm and sector, 1986-90, hearing, 21248–173
Interest rates for commercial paper, govt securities, other financial instruments, and home mortgages, monthly rpt, 9365–2.14
Issues by local govts, 1990, annual rpt, 9364–5.5
State and local govt employees pension system cash and security holdings and finances, quarterly rpt, 2462–2
Tax (estate) returns property and tax data, by size of gross estate and State, 1989-90, article, 8302–2.305
Tax exemption for municipal bond interest, economic impacts, 1980s-90, article, 9373–1.310
Trust assets of banks, trust companies, and S&Ls, by type of asset and fund, selected firm, and State, 1991, annual rpt, 13004–1
Yields on corporate, Treasury, and municipal long-term bonds, *Treasury Bulletin*, quarterly rpt, 8002–4.9
Yields on govt and private issues, weekly rpt, 9391–4
Yields, *Survey of Current Business*, cyclical indicators, monthly rpt, 2702–1.1
Municipal government
see Census of Governments
see Local government
see State and local employees
see State and local taxes
Municipal transportation
see Urban transportation
Munnell, Alicia H.
"Are Pensions Worth the Cost?", 9373–27.2
"Current Taxation of Qualified Pension Plans: Has the Time Come?", 9373–1.305
"Mortgage Lending in Boston: Interpreting HMDA Data", 9373–27.15

"Taxation of Capital Income in a Global Economy: An Overview", 9373–1.316
"What Is the Impact of Pensions on Saving?", 9373–27.5

Murder
see Homicide

Murphy, R. Dennis
"Analysis of Department Store Reference Pricing in Metropolitan Washington", 9408–57

Murphy, William T.
"Audiovisual Records in the National Archives of the U.S. Relating to World War II", 9516–1.3

Murray, J. J.
"Ice Patrol—A Titanic Legacy", 2152–8.301

Musculoskeletal diseases
Cases of acute and chronic conditions, disability, absenteeism, and health services use, by selected characteristics, 1990, annual rpt, 4147–10.182; 4147–10.183
Children (handicapped) enrollment by age, and special education programs staff, funding, and needs, by type of handicap and State, 1990/91, annual rpt, 4944–4
Chronic fatigue syndrome physical and mental symptoms prevalence, by sex, 1981-84, article, 4042–3.354
Computer video display terminal use relation to musculoskeletal disorders, among telephone industry workers, 1990, 4248–93
Deaths and rates, by cause, age, sex, marital status, race, and State, 1989, US Vital Statistics advance annual rpt, 4146–5.124
Dental Research Natl Inst research and training grants, by recipient, FY90, annual listing, 4474–19
Disability and work limitations of persons with chronic health conditions, by condition, age, and sex, 1983-86, 4946–1.2
Head Start handicapped enrollment, by handicap, State, and for Indian and migrant programs, 1988/89, annual rpt, 4584–4
HHS financial aid, by program, recipient, State, and city, FY91, annual regional listings, 4004–3
Hip fractures and repair procedures, actual and expected death rates for Medicare hospital providers, by instn, 1990, annual State rpt series, 4654–14
Hospital discharges and length of stay, by diagnosis, patient and instn characteristics, procedure performed, and payment source, 1990, annual rpt, 4147–13.112
Hospital discharges and length of stay by region and diagnosis, and procedures performed, by age and sex, 1990, annual rpt, 4146–8.211
Hospital discharges and length of stay under old and new survey designs, by diagnosis, patient and instn characteristics, and procedure, Jan-Mar 1988, 4147–13.110
Hospital discharges by detailed diagnostic and procedure category, primary diagnosis, and length of stay, by age, sex, and region, 1990, annual rpt, 4147–13.111
Insurance (health) denial by private carriers because of poor health, by selected characteristics, 1987, 4186–8.23
Neurological Disorders and Stroke Natl Inst activities, and disorder cases, FY91, annual rpt, 4474–25
OECD members health care costs, hospital use, resources, and economic and health indicators, by country, 1960s-90, article, 4652–1.322
Physicians visits, by patient and practice characteristics, diagnosis, and services provided, 1989, annual rpt, 4147–13.109
see also under By Disease in the "Index by Categories"

Museums
County Business Patterns, 1989: employment, establishments, and payroll, by SIC 2- to 4-digit industry and county, annual State rpt series, 2326–8
County Business Patterns, 1990: employment, establishments, and payroll, by SIC 2- to 4-digit industry and county, annual State rpt series, 2326–6
DC metro area land acquisition and dev projects of Fed Govt, characteristics and funding by agency and project, FY92-96, annual rpt, 15454–1
Education Dept research libraries funding, by project, instn, and State, FY90, annual listing, 4874–2
Employment, earnings, and hours, by SIC 1- to 4-digit industry, monthly 1989-Feb 1992, annual rpt, 6744–4
Fed Govt spending in States, by type, program, agency, and State, FY91, annual rpt, 2464–2
Inst of Museum Services activities and finances, and grants by recipient, FY91, annual rpt, 9564–7
Inst of Museum Services grants, by recipient, annual press release series, discontinued, 9564–6
Mail volume to and from households, use, and views, by class, source, content, and household characteristics, FY87-90, annual rpt, 9864–10
Military museums, listing, 1992 annual summary rpt, 3504–13
Natl Archives and Records Admin activities, finances, holdings, and staff, FY91, annual rpt, 9514–2
Natl Endowment for Arts activities and grants, FY91, annual rpt, 9564–3
Natl Endowment for Humanities activities and grants, FY91, annual rpt, 9564–2
Occupational injury and illness rates, by SIC 2- to 4-digit industry, 1989-90, annual rpt, 6844–7
Occupational injury and illness rates, by SIC 2- to 4-digit industry, 1990, annual rpt, 6844–1
Occupational Outlook Handbook, 1992-93, biennial rpt, 6744–1
Smithsonian Instn activities and finances, FY91, annual rpt, 29574–1
see also Zoological parks

Musgrave, John C.
"Fixed Reproducible Tangible Wealth in the U.S., Revised Estimates", 2702–1.305
"Fixed Reproducible Tangible Wealth in the U.S., 1988-91", 2702–1.327

Mushrooms
see Vegetables and vegetable products

Music
Communications services revenue and expenses, itemized by SIC 2- to 4-digit kind of business, 1990, annual rpt, 2413–15
Copyrights Register activities, registrations by material type, and fees, FY91 and trends from 1790, annual rpt, 26404–2
Exports and imports of sheet music, by country, 1991, annual rpt, 2424–13
Exports of sheet music, by country of destination, 1991, annual rpt, 2424–10
Industry finances and operations, by SIC 2- to 4-digit industry, forecast 1992, annual rpt, 2044–28
Labor demand, turnover, and training completions, by detailed occupation, 1990 and projected to 2005, biennial rpt, 6744–3
Library of Congress activities, acquisitions, services, and financial statements, FY91, annual rpt, 26404–1
Natl Endowment for Arts activities and grants, FY91, annual rpt, 9564–3
Occupational Outlook Handbook, 1992-93, biennial rpt, 6744–1

Musical instruments
County Business Patterns, 1989: employment, establishments, and payroll, by SIC 2- to 4-digit industry and county, annual State rpt series, 2326–8
County Business Patterns, 1990: employment, establishments, and payroll, by SIC 2- to 4-digit industry and county, annual State rpt series, 2326–6
Employment, earnings, and hours, by SIC 1- to 4-digit industry, monthly 1989-Feb 1992, annual rpt, 6744–4
Exports and imports between US and outlying areas, by detailed commodity and mode of transport, 1991, annual rpt, 2424–11
Exports and imports of US, by country and detailed commodity, monthly rpt, 2422–12
Exports and imports of US, by Harmonized System 6-digit commodity and country, 1991, annual rpt, 2424–13
Exports of US, detailed Schedule B commodities with countries of destination, 1991, annual rpt, 2424–10
Injuries from use of consumer products, by severity, victim age, and detailed product, 1991, annual rpt, 9164–6
Input-output structure of US economy, detailed interindustry transactions for 541 industries, and components of final demand, 1982 benchmark data, 2708–17
Manufacturing annual survey, 1990: finances and operations, by SIC 2- to 4-digit industry, series, 2506–14
Manufacturing census, 1987: concentration of largest firms measured by value added, and for shipments by SIC 2- and 4-digit industry, subject rpt, 2497–6
Manufacturing census, 1987: shipments of manufacturers products, by customer class and SIC 2- and 4-digit industry, subject rpt, 2497–4
Manufacturing finances and operations, by SIC 2- to 4-digit industry, forecast 1992, annual rpt, 2044–28
Occupational injury and illness rates, by SIC 2- to 4-digit industry, 1989-90, annual rpt, 6844–7
Occupational injury and illness rates, by SIC 2- to 4-digit industry, 1990, annual rpt, 6844–1
OECD trade, total and for 4 major countries, and US trade by country, by commodity, 1980-90, world area rpt series, 9116–1

Price indexes (producer), by stage of processing and detailed commodity, monthly rpt, 6762–6
Price indexes (producer), by stage of processing and detailed commodity, monthly 1991, annual rpt, 6764–2
Science, engineering, and technical employment in manufacturing, by field and industry, 1989, triennial rpt, 9627–23
Woodwind key pads from Italy at less than fair value, injury to US industry, investigation with background financial and operating data, 1992 rpt, 9886–14.364

Mutual funds
Assets and debts of private sector, balance sheets by segment, 1960-91, semiannual rpt, 9365–4.1
Assets of trusts under mgmt of banks, trust companies, and S&Ls, by type of asset and fund, selected firm, and State, 1990, annual rpt, 13004–1
Credit unions federally insured, finances by instn characteristics and State, as of June 1992, semiannual rpt, 9532–6
Credit unions federally insured, finances, 1990-91, annual rpt, 9534–1
Finances and operations, by SIC 2- to 4-digit industry, forecast 1992, annual rpt, 2044–28
Finances of open-end investment companies, monthly 1990, annual rpt, 9364–5.6
Financial and monetary conditions, selected US summary data, weekly rpt, 9391–4
Flow-of-funds accounts, savings, investments, and credit statements, quarterly rpt, 9365–3.3
Foreign and US economic conditions, for major industrial countries, monthly rpt, 9112–1
Mail volume to and from households, use, and views, by class, source, content, and household characteristics, FY87-90, annual rpt, 9864–10
Statistical Abstract of US, 1992 annual data compilation, 2324–1.16

Myanmar
Economic and social conditions of developing countries from 1960s, and Intl Dev Cooperation Agency and AID activities and funding, FY91-93, annual rpt, 9904–4
UN voting record and share of votes in agreement with US, by issue, country, and world area, 1991, annual rpt, 7004–18
see also Burma

Myers, Forest
"Deposit Growth, Nonperforming Assets, and Return on Assets, by County", 9381–14

Myers, Jennifer G.
"Longitudinal Examination of Applicants to the Air Traffic Control Supervisory Identification and Development Program", 7506–10.116
"Survey of Aviation Medical Examiners: Information and Attitudes About the Pre-Employment and Pre-Appointment Drug Testing Program", 7506–10.115

NAFTA
see North American Free Trade Agreement

Nakagawara, Van B.
"Prevalence of Artificial Lens Implants in the Civil Airman Population", 7506–10.114

Nakamura, Leonard I.
"Bank Branching", 9387–8.281
"Commercial Bank Information: Implications for the Structure of Banking", 9387–8.264
""Flight to Quality" in Bank Lending and Economic Activity", 9387–8.283

Nam, Jun-mo
"Cigarette Smoking, Alcohol, and Nasopharyngeal Carcinoma: A Case-Control Study Among U.S. Whites", 4472–1.312

Namibia
Agricultural trade of US, by detailed commodity and country, 1991, annual rpt, 1524–8
Agricultural trade of US, by detailed commodity and country, 1991, semiannual rpt, 1522–4
Economic and social conditions of developing countries from 1960s, and Intl Dev Cooperation Agency and AID activities and funding, FY91-93, annual rpt, 9904–4
Economic conditions, income, production, prices, employment, and trade, 1992 periodic country rpt, 2046–4.37
Economic, social, political, and geographic summary data, by country, 1992, annual factbook, 9114–2
Exports and imports of US, by transport mode, country, and SITC 1- to 3-digit commodity, 1991, annual rpt, 2424–12
Exports of US, detailed Schedule B commodities with countries of destination, 1991, annual rpt, 2424–10
Human rights conditions in 170 countries, and US economic and military aid, 1991, annual rpt, 21384–3
Military aid of US, arms sales, and training programs costs and budget requests, by program, world region, and country, FY91-93, annual rpt, 7144–13
Minerals Yearbook, Vol 3, 1989: foreign country review of production, trade, and policy, by commodity, annual rpt, 5604–35.1
Population size, growth rates, and components of change, by country, projected 1990-2020 and trends from 1950, biennial rpt, 2324–9
Refugee migration, and intl aid programs, by world area and country of origin and asylum, 1991, annual rpt, 7004–15
UN voting record and share of votes in agreement with US, by issue, country, and world area, 1991, annual rpt, 7004–18

Nance, James M.
"Demographic Profile of Participants in Two Gulf of Mexico Inshore Shrimp Fisheries and Their Response to the Texas Closure", 2162–1.301

Nandi, Chandana
"Maternal Pregravid Weight, Age, and Smoking Status as Risk Factors for Low Birth Weight Births", 4042–3.367

Napa, Calif.
Wages by occupation, and benefits, for office and plant workers, 1992 survey, periodic MSA rpt, 6785–3.3

Narcotics
see Drug abuse and treatment
see Drug and narcotics offenses
see Drugs

NASA
see National Aeronautics and Space Administration

Nashville, Tenn.
Freight (waterborne domestic and foreign) by commodity, traffic, and passengers, by port and waterway, 1989, annual rpt, 3754–3.2
Wages by occupation, for office and plant workers, 1992 survey, periodic MSA rpt, 6785–17.3
see also under By City and By SMSA or MSA in the "Index by Categories"

Nassau County, N.Y.
Housing and households characteristics, and unit and neighborhood quality, by MSA location for 11 MSAs, 1987 survey, supplement, 2485–8
Wages by occupation, and benefits, for office and plant workers, 1991 survey, periodic MSA rpt, 6785–16.4

Nassif, Joseph
"Trends in Per Capita Consumption in Central America, 1969-89", 9916–13.4

National accounts
see National income and product accounts

National Adolescent Student Health Survey
Alcohol use and abuse by 8th and 10th graders, by sex, race, Hispanic origin, and grade, 1987, article, 4482–1.302

National Advisory Committee on Semiconductors
Competitiveness (intl) of US semiconductor industry, status, and outlook, working paper series, 15036–1
Competitiveness (intl) of US semiconductor industry, status, outlook, and Federal policy, 1980s, annual rpt, 15034–1

National Advisory Council on Educational Research and Improvement
Office of Educational Research and Improvement activities, FY91, annual narrative rpt, 4814–1

National Advisory Council on Indian Education
Activities of NACIE, with Indian education funding of Fed Govt, enrollment, program grants, and fellowships by State, 1980s-FY91, annual rpt, 14874–1

National Advisory Council on International Monetary and Financial Policies
Intl financial instns funds by source and disbursements by purpose, by country, with US policy review, FY90, annual rpt, 15344–1

National Aeronautics and Space Administration
Accidents, casualties, damage, and safety activities of NASA, FY91, annual rpt, 9504–4
Activities and budgets for aeronautics and space by Federal agency, and foreign programs, 1957-FY91, annual rpt, 9504–9
Activities and finances of NASA, and data on US and USSR space launches, 1957-91, annual rpt, 9504–6

Apollo era science and engineering staff background and characteristics, 1958-70, 9508–39
Budget of US, authoritative financial statements with appropriations, outlays, and receipts, by category and agency, FY91, annual rpt, 8104–2.2
Budget of US, obligations and authority by function, agency, and program, with summaries and analyses, FY93, annual rpt, 104–2
Education (cooperative) programs of NASA and contractors, activities, 1991, 9508–41
Education funding by Federal agency, program, and recipient type, and instn spending, 1960s-91, annual rpt, 4824–8
Employee characteristics and personnel actions, FY91, annual rpt, 9504–1
Expenditures of Fed Govt in States, by type, program, agency, and State, FY91, annual rpt, 2464–2
Fraud and abuse in NASA programs, audits and investigations, 2nd half FY92, semiannual rpt, 9502–9
Labor unions recognized in Fed Govt, agreements and membership by agency and facility, as of Jan 1991, biennial listing, 9844–14
Launch schedules and technical descriptions of NASA projects, press release series, 9506–2
Launchings of satellites and other space objects since 1957, quarterly listing, 9502–2
Procurement contract awards of NASA, by type, contractor, State, and country, FY92 with trends from 1961, semiannual rpt, 9502–6
R&D and related funding of Fed Govt to higher education and nonprofit instns, by field, instn, agency, and State, FY90, annual rpt, 9627–17
R&D funding by NASA to higher education instns, by field, instn, and State, FY91, annual listing, 9504–7
Space station *Freedom* technical characteristics, funding, and contracts by State, 1985-92 and projected 1997-2002, 9508–40

National Agricultural Statistics Service
Budget of US, obligations and authority by function, agency, and program, with summaries and analyses, FY93, annual rpt, 104–2
Meat production, inventory, and price forecasts of USDA, accuracy, 1980s, GAO rpt, 26131–93
see also Agricultural Statistics Board

National Ambulatory Medical Care Survey
Diabetes patients physician office visits, by characteristics of patient, physician, and visit, 1989, 4146–8.212
Internist office visits, by characteristics of patient, physician, and visit, 1989, 4146–8.214
Otitis media patients physician office visits, by specialty and characteristics of patient and visit, 1975-90, 4146–8.217
Pediatrician office visits, by characteristics of patient and visit, 1989, 4146–8.210
Physicians visits, by patient and practice characteristics, diagnosis, and services provided, 1989, annual rpt, 4147–13.109
Physicians visits, by patient and practice characteristics, diagnosis, and services provided, 1990, advance rpt, 4146–8.215

National Archives and Records Administration
Activities, finances, holdings, and staff of NARA, FY91, annual rpt, 9514–2
Audiovisual activities and spending of Fed Govt, by whether performed in-house and agency, FY91, annual rpt, 9514–1
Budget of US, authoritative financial statements with appropriations, outlays, and receipts, by category and agency, FY91, annual rpt, 8104–2.2
Budget of US, obligations and authority by function, agency, and program, with summaries and analyses, FY93, annual rpt, 104–2
Education funding by Federal agency, program, and recipient type, and instn spending, 1960s-91, annual rpt, 4824–8
Fed Govt agencies administrative records and other holdings of Natl Archives, final inventories, series, 9516–2
Fed Govt publications and other holdings of Natl Archives, special collections, series, 9516–1
Labor unions recognized in Fed Govt, agreements and membership by agency and facility, as of Jan 1991, biennial listing, 9844–14

National Assessment of Educational Progress
Educational performance by subject and selected student characteristics, standard test results and credits, 1992 edition, annual rpt, 4824–2.12
Elementary and secondary students educational performance, and factors affecting proficiency, by selected characteristics, 1990 natl assessments, subject rpt series, 4896–8
Elementary and secondary students educational performance in math, science, reading, and writing, 1969-90, 4898–32
Elementary and secondary students educational performance, issues and special topics, natl assessments, fact sheet series, 4896–9
Reading performance and factors affecting proficiency, for elementary and secondary students, 1988 and 1990 natl assessments, 4898–33
Science and engineering enrollment, performance, curricula, student aid sources, and career plans, by sex and race, 1970s-91, biennial rpt, 9624–20.2
Science and math education, natl assessment of elementary and high school students, 1985/86, series, 4896–6

National Association of Blue Shield Plans
see Blue Cross-Blue Shield

National Association of State Public Health Veterinarians, Inc.
"Compendium of Animal Rabies Control, 1992", 4206–2.57

National Bureau of Standards
see National Institute of Standards and Technology

National Cancer Institute
Activities of NCI epidemiology and biometry programs, FY91, annual rpt, 4474–29
Activities of NCI, grants by recipient, and cancer deaths and cases, FY91 and trends, annual rpt, 4474–13
Contracts and grants of NCI, by recipient and location, annual listing, discontinued, 4474–28
Research on cancer epidemiology and biochemistry, semimonthly journal, 4472–1
Smoking prevalence, health effects, and control strategies effectiveness, research results, series, 4476–7
Telephone helpline of NCI, calls by caller type, 1983-90, article, 4042–3.325

National Capital Planning Commission
Budget of US, authoritative financial statements with appropriations, outlays, and receipts, by category and agency, FY91, annual rpt, 8104–2.2
Budget of US, obligations and authority by function, agency, and program, with summaries and analyses, FY93, annual rpt, 104–2
Land acquisition and dev projects of Fed Govt in DC metro area, characteristics and funding by agency and project, FY92-96, annual rpt, 15454–1

National Center for Appropriate Technology
"State Catalog of FY91 Low Income Home Energy Assistance Program Characteristics", 4584–2

National Center for Education Statistics
see Office of Educational Research and Improvement

National Center for Health Services Research and Health Care Technology Assessment
see Agency for Health Care Policy and Research

National Center for Health Statistics
Cancer death rates and annual change, by body site, sex, and race, comparability of local registry and natl data, 1975-88, article, 4472–1.320
Data collection for health and vital statistics, and use for planning and evaluation, 1991 biennial conf, 4164–2
Deaths and rates, by detailed location, cause, and demographic characteristics, 1989, US Vital Statistics annual rpt, 4144–3
Foreign and US health data collection and availability, by country, 1991, biennial listing, 4124–8
Health condition and care indicators, 1950s-90 with health improvement and disease prevention goals for 1990, annual data compilation, 4144–11
Health condition and quality of life measurement, rpts and other info sources, quarterly listing, 4122–1
Infant health, deaths and risk factors, and prevention issues, for US and selected countries, 1990 conf, 4148–28
Publications of NCHS, quarterly listing, 4122–2
Publications of NCHS, 1990-91, annual listing, 4124–1
Vital and Health Statistics Natl Committee activities, FY91, annual narrative rpt, 4164–1
Vital and Health Statistics series: advance data rpts, 4146–8
Vital and Health Statistics series: death rates for selected causes and population groups, 4147–20
Vital and Health Statistics series: health care facilities use and labor force, 4147–13

Vital and Health Statistics series: health condition, medical costs, and use of facilities and services, 4147–10
Vital and Health Statistics series: methodology, survey design, and data evaluation, 4147–2
Vital and Health Statistics series: natality, marriage, and divorce trends, 4147–21
Vital and Health Statistics series: program and data collection procedures, 4147–1
Vital and Health Statistics series: reprints of advance data rpts, 4147–16
Vital statistics, preliminary 1990-91 and trends from 1960, annual rpt, 4144–7
Vital statistics provisional data, monthly rpt, 4142–1
Vital statistics provisional data, supplements to monthly rpts, series, 4146–5

National Center on Child Abuse and Neglect
Assistance for child abuse and neglect prevention and treatment, and disabled infant protection, by State, annual listing, issuing agency transfer, 4604–14
Assistance for child abuse and neglect prevention and treatment, and disabled infant protection, by State, FY91, annual listing, 4584–6
Assistance for child abuse and neglect prevention and treatment, discretionary grants, FY91, annual listing, 4584–9

National Clearinghouse for Smoking and Health
see Office on Smoking and Health

National Commission for Employment Policy
Activities and rpts of NCEP, 1991 annual rpt, 15494–1
Assistance programs of Fed Govt for public welfare, employment, and training, coordination issues with background data, 1991 rpt, 15498–29
Displaced worker employment and training services, and layoff alternatives, indicators of effectiveness, 1980s, 15498–28
Unemployed displaced workers and other hard-to-serve groups, factors contributing to unemployment, and training programs operations, series, 15496–1

National Commission on Children
Family life and relationships quality and other issues, views of parents and children, 1990 survey, 15528–2

National Commission on Libraries and Information Science
Access, policy, technology, and other info services issues, recommendations, 1991 conf, 15638–16
Activities of NCLIS, FY91, annual rpt, 15634–1
Budget of US, authoritative financial statements with appropriations, outlays, and receipts, by category and agency, FY91, annual rpt, 8104–2.2
Budget of US, obligations and authority by function, agency, and program, with summaries and analyses, FY93, annual rpt, 104–2
Expenditures for education by Federal agency, program, and recipient type, and instn spending, 1960s-91, annual rpt, 4824–8

National commissions
see Federal boards, committees, and commissions
see Federal independent agencies

National Credit Union Administration
Assets, members, and location of credit unions, 1992 annual listing, 9534–6
Budget of US, authoritative financial statements with appropriations, outlays, and receipts, by category and agency, FY91, annual rpt, 8104–2.2
Budget of US, obligations and authority by function, agency, and program, with summaries and analyses, FY93, annual rpt, 104–2
Finances of federally insured credit unions, by instn characteristics and State, as of June 1992, semiannual rpt, 9532–6
Finances, operations, and regulation of credit unions, series, 9536–1
Financial performance of federally-insured credit unions, by charter type and region, 1st half 1992, semiannual rpt, 9532–7
Financial statements of Central Liquidity Facility, FY91, annual rpt, 9534–5
Financial statements of NCUA and credit unions, 1990-91, annual rpt, 9534–1
Insurance fund of NCUA, losses and financial statements, with federally insured credit union finances, mergers, and closings, FY91, annual rpt, 9534–7
Regulation and financial performance of credit unions, with background data, 1960s-90, GAO rpt, 26119–364

National Crime Survey
see also National Crime Victimization Survey

National Crime Victimization Survey
Data collection, methodology, and use, technical rpt series, 6066–23
Victimization rates, by victim and offender characteristics, circumstances, and offense, survey rpt series, 6066–3
Victimizations, by offense and whether reported to police, 1990-91, press release, 6068–249

National debt
see Foreign debts
see Government assets and liabilities
see Public debt

National defense
Foreign countries economic, social, political, and geographic summary data, by country, 1992, annual factbook, 9114–2
Investigations of GAO, 1991, listing, 26106–10.6
Middle East arms trade and force strengths, and impacts of voluntary arms trade reductions, by country, mid 1960s-91 and projected to 2002, 26306–6.173
Public confidence in people running selected social instns, 1972-88 surveys, biennial rpt, 9624–10.7
see also Armed services
see also Armed services reserves
see also Arms control and disarmament
see also Arms trade
see also Chemical and biological warfare agents
see also Civil defense
see also Defense agencies
see also Defense budgets and appropriations
see also Defense contracts and procurement
see also Defense expenditures
see also Defense industries
see also Defense research
see also Department of Defense
see also Espionage
see also Internal security
see also Logistics
see also Military aircraft
see also Military airlift
see also Military assistance
see also Military aviation
see also Military awards, decorations, and medals
see also Military bases, posts, and reservations
see also Military benefits and pensions
see also Military education
see also Military health facilities and services
see also Military housing
see also Military intelligence
see also Military intervention
see also Military invasion and occupation
see also Military law
see also Military pay
see also Military personnel
see also Military post exchanges and commissaries
see also Military prisons
see also Military science
see also Military strategy
see also Military supplies and property
see also Military training
see also Military vehicles
see also Military weapons
see also National Guard
see also Naval vessels
see also Nuclear weapons
see also Service academies
see also Strategic materials
see also War

National Dropout Statistics Field Test
Data collection and reporting methods evaluation, and results, for high school dropout surveys, 1992 rpt, 4838–49

National Education Goals Panel
Natl Education Goals progress indicators, by State, 1992, annual rpt, 15914–1

National Education Longitudinal Survey
Eighth grade class of 1988: educational performance and conditions, characteristics, attitudes, activities, and plans, natl longitudinal survey, series, 4826–9
High school dropout rates, by selected characteristics, 1988 survey, 4826–10.3
High school dropouts and transfers between public and private schools, by instn control, income level, and race, 1990 survey, 4826–10.4

National Endowment for the Arts
see National Foundation on the Arts and the Humanities

National Endowment for the Humanities
see National Foundation on the Arts and the Humanities

National Environmental Policy Act
Environmental Quality, status of problems, protection programs, research, and intl issues, 1991 annual rpt, 484–1

National Environmental Satellite, Data, and Information Service
Glaciology intl research summaries, methodology, and bibls, series, 2156–18
Heating and cooling degree days weighted by population, by census div and State, with area-weighted temperature and precipitation, monthly rpt, 2152–13
Mariners Weather Log, quarterly journal, 2152–8

Ocean pollution research projects, rpts and data files, FY84-87, listing, 2158–51
Pacific Ocean subsurface temperature data collection activities, annual rpt, discontinued, 2154–12
Storms and unusual weather phenomena characteristics, casualties, and property damage, by State, monthly listing, 2152–3
Weather data for surface and upper air, averages by foreign and US station, monthly rpt, 2152–4

National Fire Protection Association
"Analysis Report on Fire Fighter Fatalities", 9434–8

National forests
Acreage, grants, use, revenues, and allocations, for public lands by State, FY91 and trends, annual rpt, 5724–1
Acreage of land under Forest Service mgmt, by forest and location, 1991 and historic trends, annual rpt, 1204–2
Alabama timber acreage and value, by species, forest type, ownership, and county, 1990, series, 1206–30
Alaska timber acreage and resources, by species, ownership class, and inventory unit, series, 1206–9
Black Hills Natl Forest mountain pine beetle infestation and ponderosa pine mortality, 1989-91, 1208–408
California lumber mills, operations, timber use by species and origin, and residue use, by product and county, 1988, 1208–108
Expenditures of Fed Govt in States, by type, program, agency, and State, FY91, annual rpt, 2464–2
Fires (wild) and acreage burned, by type of land, ownership, cause, region, and State, 1984-90, annual rpt, 1204–4
Forest Service activities and finances, by region and State, FY91, annual rpt, 1204–1
Forest Service recreation uses fund outlays by purpose, and wilderness mgmt funds reprogrammed to other activities, FY88-90, GAO rpt, 26113–550
Insect and disease incidence and damage in forests, and control activities, State rpt series, 1206–49
Insect and disease incidence and damage in forests, annual regional rpt series, 1206–11
Insect and disease incidence and damage in forests, by State, 1990, annual rpt, 1204–8
Land Mgmt Bur activities and funding by State, FY90, annual rpt, 5724–13
Minerals resources and availability on public lands, State rpt series, 5606–7
Minnesota timber acreage, resources, and removals, by ownership, forest and tree characteristics, and county, 1990, series, 1206–24
Missouri timber resources and removals, by species, forest and tree characteristics, ownership, and county, 1987-89 and trends from 1959, 1208–76
Missouri timber resources and removals by species, land ownership, and county, 1988-89, series, 1206–3
Northeastern US timber resources and removals, by species, ownership, and county, State rpt series, 1206–12
Northwestern US and British Columbia forest industry production, prices, trade, and employment, quarterly rpt, 1202–3
Oregon lumber production, and industry operations, by county, 1988, 1208–280
Owl (northern spotted) conservation methods in Pacific Northwest, findings and recommendations, 1990 rpt, 1208–385
Owl (northern spotted) conservation methods in Pacific Northwest, timber industry impacts, and Federal and State spending, 1980s-95, 1208–388
Planting and stand improvement, by ownership and State, FY91, annual rpt, 1204–7
Recreational use of natl forests, by type of activity and State, 1991, annual rpt, 1204–17
Recreational use of natl forests, factors affecting regional growth, shift-share analysis, 1992 rpt, 1208–423
Revenue of natl forest land, by source, forest, and State, FY91, annual rpt, 1204–34
Revenue of natl forest land, share paid to States, and acreage, by forest, county, and congressional district, FY92, annual rpt, 1204–33
Rocky Mountain States timber and mill residue production, by species, ownership, and county, series, 1206–17
Statistical Abstract of US, 1992 annual data compilation, 2324–1.7; 2324–1.24
Timber sales of Forest Service, expenses, and operations, by region, State, and natl forest, FY91, annual rpts, 1204–36
Timber stumpage prices, for sawtimber sold from natl forests in Pacific Northwest, monthly 1975-89, 1208–387
Virginia timber resources, growth, and removals, by species, ownership, treatment, and county, 1990-92, series, 1206–6
Washington State timber acreage and resources, by species, ownership class, and county, 1988-89 with harvest trends from 1955, series, 1206–28
Water quality and fish population in southwestern US streams, impacts of land mgmt and forest fires, 1980s-91, 1208–390
Wisconsin timber resources and removals, by species, forest type, ownership, and county, series, 1206–34
see also Wilderness areas

National Foundation on the Arts and the Humanities
Arts Natl Endowment activities and grants, FY91, annual rpt, 9564–3
Budget of US, authoritative financial statements with appropriations, outlays, and receipts, by category and agency, FY91, annual rpt, 8104–2.2
Budget of US, obligations and authority by function, agency, and program, with summaries and analyses, FY93, annual rpt, 104–2
Education funding by Federal agency, program, and recipient type, and instn spending, 1960s-91, annual rpt, 4824–8
Expenditures of Fed Govt in States, by type, program, agency, and State, FY91, annual rpt, 2464–2
Humanities Natl Endowment activities and grants, FY91, annual rpt, 9564–2
Museum Services Inst activities and finances, and grants by recipient, FY91, annual rpt, 9564–7
Museum Services Inst grants, by recipient, annual press release series, discontinued, 9564–6

National Governors Association
"1991 Catalogue of State Medicaid Program Changes", 4654–19.1

National grasslands
Acreage and use of public lands, and Land Mgmt Bur activities and finances, annual State rpt series, 5724–11
Acreage, grants, use, revenues, and allocations, for public lands by State, FY91 and trends, annual rpt, 5724–1
Acreage of land under Forest Service mgmt, by forest and location, 1991, annual rpt, 1204–2
Expenditures of Fed Govt in States, by type, program, agency, and State, FY91, annual rpt, 2464–2
Forest Service activities and finances, by region and State, FY91, annual rpt, 1204–1.1
Grazing of livestock on natl rangeland, BLM mgmt, officials views, 1980s-90, GAO rpt, 26113–567
Grazing of livestock on public rangeland, allotments, permits, acreage, and stocking rates, by BLM State office, as of Sept 1991, GAO rpt, 26113–582
Land Mgmt Bur activities and funding by State, FY90, annual rpt, 5724–13
Land Mgmt Bur activities in southwestern US, FY91, annual rpt, 5724–15

National Guard
Activities, personnel, and facilities of Army and Air Natl Guard, FY91, annual rpt, 3504–22
Expenditures of Fed Govt in States, by type, program, agency, and State, FY91, annual rpt, 2464–2
Labor unions recognized in Fed Govt, agreements and membership by agency and facility, as of Jan 1991, biennial listing, 9844–14
Personnel and equipment strengths, and readiness, by reserve component, FY91, annual rpt, 3544–31
Personnel strengths and characteristics, by reserve component, quarterly rpt, 3542–4
Personnel strengths for reserve components, by selected characteristics, FY91, annual rpt, 3544–1.5
Statistical Abstract of US, 1992 annual data compilation, 2324–1.11
Training and education programs of DOD, funding, staff, students, and facilities, by service branch, FY93, annual rpt, 3504–5

National Health and Nutrition Examination Survey
Design of survey sample, and estimation procedures, 1992 rpt, 4147–2.115
Epidemiologic Followup Study to NHANES I, design and procedures, 1992 rpt, 4147–1.29

National Health Examination Survey
see National Health and Nutrition Examination Survey

National Health Interview Survey
Design of survey sample and linkage with Natl Hospital Discharge Survey, 1992 rpt, 4147–2.114
Disability (functional) prevalence and severity, by type of activity needing assistance, age, and sex, 1979-80, 4946–1.1
Disability and work limitations of persons with chronic health conditions, by condition, age, and sex, 1983-86, 4946–1.2
Health condition, medical costs, and use of health facilities and services, Vital and Health Statistics series, 4147–10
Vital and Health Statistics series: advance data rpts, 4146–8
Vital and Health Statistics series: reprints of advance data rpts, 4147–16

National Health Interview Survey on Child Health
Children (handicapped) with special needs, insurance coverage, and health care services use, by selected characteristics, 1988, 4146–8.216

National Health Service Corps
Assistance (financial) of HHS, by program, recipient, State, and city, FY91, annual regional listings, 4004–3

National Health Survey
see National Ambulatory Medical Care Survey
see National Health and Nutrition Examination Survey
see National Health Interview Survey
see National Health Interview Survey on Child Health
see National Hospital Discharge Survey
see National Medical Expenditure Survey
see National Natality Survey

National Heart, Lung, and Blood Institute
Activities and grants of NHLBI, and Advisory Council recommendations, annual narrative rpt, data coverage transfer, 4474–11
Activities of NHLBI, and Advisory Council recommendations, 1991 narrative rpt, 4474–22
Activities of NHLBI, and grants by recipient and location, FY91 and disease trends from 1940, annual rpt, 4474–15
Deaths and rates, by cause and selected social, demographic, and employment characteristics, 1979-85, natl longitudinal study, 4478–186
Hypertension cases, stroke and heart disease risk, and drug dosages, with diagnosis and treatment methods, 1992 quadrennial rpt, 4478–198

National Highway Traffic Safety Administration
Accidents (fatal), circumstances, and characteristics of persons and vehicles involved, 1991, semiannual rpt, 7762–11
Accidents (fatal), deaths, and rates, by circumstances, characteristics of persons and vehicles involved, and location, 1990, annual rpt, 7764–10
Accidents and casualties, by driver age and sex, 1990, 7768–105
Accidents, casualties, circumstances, and characteristics of persons and vehicles involved, 1990, annual rpt, 7764–18
Activities of NHTSA, grants awarded, and fatal traffic accident data, 1990, annual rpt, 7764–1
Auto safety, crash test results by domestic and foreign model, model years 1987-91, 7768–111
Auto safety crash test results, by domestic and foreign model, press release series, 7766–7
Auto theft rates of new cars, by make and model, 1990 model year, annual rpt, 7764–21
Budget of US, obligations and authority by function, agency, and program, with summaries and analyses, FY93, annual rpt, 104–2
Deaths in traffic accidents by region, and death rates for miles traveled, monthly rpt, 7762–7
Driving while intoxicated enforcement incentive grants of NHTSA, by State, 1992 press release, 7306–10.4
Drunk drivers and others involved in fatal accidents, alcohol levels by circumstances and characteristics of persons and vehicles, 1990, annual rpt, 7764–16
Employment of DOT, by subagency, occupation, and selected personnel characteristics, FY91, annual rpt, 7304–18
Energy economy performance of autos and light trucks by make, standards, and enforcement, 1978-94 model years, annual rpt, 7764–9
Expenditures of Fed Govt in States, by type, program, agency, and State, FY91, annual rpt, 2464–2
Hospitalization for traffic accident injuries, costs, and discharges, by payment source and State, mid 1980s-90, 7768–122
Recalls of motor vehicles and equipment with safety-related defects, by make, monthly listing, 7762–12
Recalls of motor vehicles and equipment with safety-related defects, by make, quarterly listing, 7762–2
Seat belts (automatic) and air bags, availability and impact on traffic accident deaths, 1980s-91, 7768–123
Speed limit impacts on traffic deaths and speeds, for States with 55 and 65 mph limit, 1986-90, 7764–15
Speed limit impacts on traffic speeds and accidents, for States with 55 and 65 mph limit, 1983-89, 7768–121
Tire quality ratings, by type and brand, as of Feb 1992, annual rpt, 7764–17
Truck accidents, circumstances, and characteristics of vehicles and persons involved, 1979-86, 7768–124

National Hospital Discharge Survey
Design of survey sample and linkage with Natl Health Interview Survey, 1992 rpt, 4147–2.114
Discharges and length of stay, by diagnosis, patient and instn characteristics, procedure performed, and payment source, 1990, annual rpt, 4147–13.112
Discharges and length of stay by region and diagnosis, and procedures performed, by age and sex, 1990, annual rpt, 4146–8.211
Discharges and length of stay under old and new survey designs, by diagnosis, patient and instn characteristics, and procedure, Jan-Mar 1988, 4147–13.110
Discharges by detailed diagnostic and procedure category, primary diagnosis, and length of stay, by age, sex, and region, 1990, annual rpt, 4147–13.111
Payment sources expected for hospital discharges, by diagnosis, patient characteristics, and region, and procedures performed, 1990, 4146–8.221

National Household Education Survey
Adult education participation, by selected characteristics, 1991 survey, 4826–10.5
Child care arrangements prior to 1st grade, by setting and parents' educational level, 1991 survey, 4826–10.2
Reading and TV viewing activities of children at home, by grade level, 1991 survey, 4826–10.1

National Household Survey on Drug Abuse
Abuse of drugs and alcohol, by selected characteristics, 1991 survey, annual rpt series, 4494–5
DC metro area drug, alcohol, and tobacco use, user characteristics, and consequences, series, 4496–12

National income and product accounts
Budget of US, CBO analysis of revenue and spending alternatives and projections of economic indicators, FY93-97, annual rpt, 26304–3
Budget of US, historical data, selected years FY34-91 and projected to FY97, 108–46.5
Budget of US, obligations and authority by function, agency, and program, with summaries and analyses, FY93, annual rpt, 104–2
Budget of US, receipts and outlays on natl income and product basis, FY93, annual article, 2702–1.310
Business statistics, detailed data for major industries and economic indicators, *Survey of Current Business*, monthly rpt, 2702–1
Business statistics, detailed data for major industries and economic indicators, 1960-91, *Survey of Current Business* biennial supplement, 2704–1
Economic indicators and components, current data and annual trends, monthly rpt, 23842–1.6
Economic Report of the President for 1992, with economic trends from 1929, annual rpt, 204–1.1
Exports, imports, and trade flows, by country and commodity, with background economic indicators, data compilation, monthly CD-ROM, 2002–6
Flow-of-funds accounts, savings, investments, and credit statements, quarterly rpt, 9365–3.3
Govt revenue by source and outlays by type, for State and local govts, 1987-91, annual article, 2702–1.311
Govt revenue by source and spending by function, natl income and product accounts, *Survey of Current Business*, monthly rpt, 2702–1.26
Govt revenues and spending by level of govt, natl income and product accounts, 1959-91, annual rpt, 204–1.6
Health care spending by funding source, 1990, with trends and indexes by service type from 1960, article, 4652–1.323
Income (personal) natl income and product accounts benchmark revisions, and reconciliation with adjusted gross income, 1959-90, article, 2702–1.318
Intl transactions in natl income and product accounts, *Survey of Current Business*, monthly rpt, 2702–1.27

Natl income and product accounts and components, summary data 1959-91, tables, 2702–1.334
Natl income and product accounts and components, *Survey of Current Business*, monthly rpt, 2702–1.23
Natl income and product accounts benchmark revisions, methodological changes and revised summary tables, 1959-91, article, 2702–1.302
Natl income and product accounts benchmark revisions of GDP and natl income, various periods 1959-80, tables, 2702–1.307
Natl income and product accounts benchmark revisions of personal income and outlays, monthly 1987-91, tables, 2702–1.301
Natl income and product accounts, comprehensive accounts and components, benchmark revisions, 1929-88, 2708–5
Natl income and product accounts, comprehensive accounts and components, *Survey of Current Business*, monthly rpt, 2702–1.24
Natl income and product accounts, index to annual and monthly tables, 1992 article, 2702–1.304; 2702–1.325
Natl income and product accounts revisions, methodology, and data sources, various periods 1989-92, annual article, 2702–1.324
Natl income and product accounts revisions to GDP, personal income, and selected foreign transactions, various periods 1959-90, tables, 2702–1.313
Statistical Abstract of US, 1992 annual data compilation, 2324–1.14
Tax (income) returns filed, by type of filer, selected income items, quarterly rpt, 8302–2.1
see also Gross Domestic Product
see also Gross National Product

National Institute for Occupational Safety and Health
Toxicology Natl Program research and testing activities, FY90 and planned FY91, annual rpt, 4044–16

National Institute of Allergy and Infectious Diseases
Activities of NIAID, grants by recipient and location, and disease cases, FY84-91, annual rpt, 4474–30

National Institute of Child Health and Human Development
Maternal and child health indicators and services use, by age, race, and poverty status, 1988, 4478–197
Research on population and reproduction, Federal funding by project, FY90, annual listing, 4474–9
Research on population and reproduction, NICHD funding and activities, 1991, annual rpt, 4474–33

National Institute of Dental Research
Grants for research and training awarded by Inst, by recipient instn, FY90, annual listing, 4474–19

National Institute of Education
see also Office of Educational Research and Improvement

National Institute of Environmental Health Sciences
Toxicology Natl Program research and testing activities, FY90 and planned FY91, annual rpt, 4044–16

National Institute of General Medical Sciences
Activities of NIGMS, budget, and research and training funding by program, FY91, annual rpt, 4474–38

National Institute of Justice
AIDS and tuberculosis cases in prisons, test results, and control and treatment policies, by location, 1990 survey, annual rpt, 6064–22
Correctional facilities construction issues and projects, series, 6066–30
Crime and criminal justice research results, series, 6066–20
Drug control street-level task forces enforcement activities, impacts on crime, and residents views, local area studies, 1992 rpt, 6068–251
Drug enforcement programs of State and local govts, FY91, annual rpt, 6064–32
Drug test results at arrest, by drug type, offense, and sex, for selected urban areas, quarterly rpt, 6062–3
Drug testing, urinalysis methods accuracy by drug type, 1991, 6068–247

National Institute of Mental Health
Facilities for mental health care, staff, patients, and finances, 1970s-91, biennial rpt, 4094–1
Facilities, patients, services, and staff characteristics, *Statistical Notes* series, 4506–3
Mental health care facilities, staff, patients, and finances, biennial rpt, issuing agency change, 4504–9

National Institute of Neurological Disorders and Stroke
Activities of NINDS, and disorder cases, FY91, annual rpt, 4474–25

National Institute of Standards and Technology
Budget of US, obligations and authority by function, agency, and program, with summaries and analyses, FY93, annual rpt, 104–2
Computer systems purchase and use, and data recording, processing, and transfer, Fed Govt standards, series, 2216–2
Energy-related inventions recommended by NIST for DOE support, awards, and evaluation status, 1991, annual listing, 2214–5
GATT Standards Code info activities of NIST, and proposed standards by agency and country, 1991, annual rpt, 2214–6
Marine mammals tissue pollutant concentrations, by species and pollutant type, for Alaska, 1987-91, 2218–87
Market potential of industrial and Federal labs technological innovations, results of annual *R&D 100* awards competition, 1960s-90, 2218–86
Measurement systems calibration, standard reference materials specifications and availability, 1992 biennial listing, 2214–2
Publications of NIST, 1991, annual listing, 2214–1
Weights, measures, and performance standards dev, proposals, and policies, 1992 annual conf, 2214–7

National Institute on Aging
Population size and characteristics of aged, series, 2326–25

National Institute on Alcohol Abuse and Alcoholism
Abuse of alcohol, and related injury and illness, series, 4486–1
Health effects of alcohol abuse, 1979-85, series, 4488–10
Research on alcoholism, treatment programs, and patient characteristics, quarterly journal, 4482–1

National Institute on Drug Abuse
Abuse of drugs and alcohol, by selected characteristics, 1991 survey, annual rpt series, 4494–5
Abuse of drugs, indicators for selected metro areas, research results, data collection, and policy issues, 1992 semiannual conf, 4492–5
AIDS prevention programs for drug abusers and their sexual partners, client characteristics, and outcomes, for selected metro areas, 1989 annual conf, 4494–12
AIDS virus infection among drug abusers, disease progression longitudinal studies, 1987 conf papers, 4498–79
DC metro area drug, alcohol, and tobacco use, user characteristics, and consequences, series, 4496–12
Drug abuse prevention services evaluation, methodological issues, 1991 conf, 4498–78
Drug abuse treatment services costs, effectiveness, and financing issues, 1991 conf papers, 4498–80
Mothers abusing drugs, treatment and other services use, referrals, needs, and barriers, for 13 NIDA-funded programs, 1990/91 survey, 4498–76
Prisoners and parolees drug abuse treatment and education programs, activities, costs, and outcomes, 1990 conf, 4498–77
Research on drug abuse and trafficking reduction, NIDA and Office of Justice Programs funding, 1970s-91, GAO rpt, 26131–99
Research on drug abuse and treatment, biological and behavioral factors, and addiction potential of new drugs, 1991 annual conf, 4494–11
Research on drug abuse and treatment, summaries of findings, resource materials, and grant listings, bimonthly rpt, 4492–4
Research on drug abuse services availability, need, use, outcome, costs, funding sources, and cost-effectiveness, series, 4496–11
Youth drug, alcohol, and cigarette use and attitudes, by substance type and selected characteristics, 1975-91 surveys, annual rpt, 4494–4

National Institutes of Health
Activities, staff, funding, and facilities of NIH, historical data, 1991 annual rpt, 4434–1
Assistance (financial) of HHS, by program, recipient, State, and city, FY91, annual regional listings, 4004–3
Budget of US, obligations and authority by function, agency, and program, with summaries and analyses, FY93, annual rpt, 104–2
Cancer (breast) research funding, cases, and deaths, 1970s-90, GAO rpt, 26131–92
Grants and awards of NIH, quarterly listing, 4432–1

Grants and contracts of NIH, by inst and type of recipient, FY82-91, annual rpt, 4434–9
Nutrition biomedical and behavioral research and training, NIH activities and funding by inst, FY90, annual rpt, 4434–15
Publications of NIH, 1992 annual listing, 4434–2
R&D licenses for university activities supported by NSF and NIH, transfer to private firms, related income, and scientists associated with licensees, FY89-90, GAO rpt, 26113–575
Toxicology Natl Program research and testing activities, FY90 and planned FY91, annual rpt, 4044–16
Women awarded NIH research and training grants, by recipient characteristics, inst, and host instn, FY90, annual rpt, 4434–18
see also Division of Research Grants, NIH
see also National Cancer Institute
see also National Heart, Lung, and Blood Institute
see also National Institute of Allergy and Infectious Diseases
see also National Institute of Child Health and Human Development
see also National Institute of Dental Research
see also National Institute of Environmental Health Sciences
see also National Institute of General Medical Sciences
see also National Institute of Mental Health
see also National Institute of Neurological Disorders and Stroke
see also National Institute on Aging
see also National Institute on Alcohol Abuse and Alcoholism
see also National Institute on Drug Abuse
see also National Library of Medicine

National Labor Relations Board
Activities, cases, elections conducted, and litigation, FY90, annual rpt, 9584–1
Budget of US, authoritative financial statements with appropriations, outlays, and receipts, by category and agency, FY91, annual rpt, 8104–2.2
Budget of US, obligations and authority by function, agency, and program, with summaries and analyses, FY93, annual rpt, 104–2
Labor unions recognized in Fed Govt, agreements and membership by agency and facility, as of Jan 1991, biennial listing, 9844–14
Representation elections conducted by NLRB, results, monthly rpt, 9582–2

National Library of Medicine
Electronic info storage and transmission costs and revenues for 4 Federal agencies, FY85-91, GAO rpt, 26125–47

National Longitudinal Mortality Study
Deaths and rates, by cause and selected social, demographic, and employment characteristics, 1979-85, natl longitudinal study, 4478–186

National Longitudinal Study of High School Seniors
Community college attendance, by selected characteristics, 1972 high school class, natl longitudinal study, 1970s-86, 4888–7

National Longitudinal Survey of Mature Women
Older women's employment patterns, with background data, 1992 rpt, 6726–2.4

National Longitudinal Survey of Young Men
Youth unemployment research based on natl longitudinal surveys, review of studies conducted 1977-88, 6728–42

National Longitudinal Survey of Young Women
Employment part-time of women, transitions by marital status and whether young children present, 1988 and trends from 1978, 6726–2.2
Youth unemployment research based on natl longitudinal surveys, review of studies conducted 1977-88, 6728–42

National Longitudinal Survey of Youth
Child care arrangements of younger working mothers, and costs, by selected characteristics, 1988, 6726–2.1
Employment history of younger workers, jobs held and weeks worked since age 18, by age, sex, and race, 1978-90, 6726–2.3
Maternal and child health indicators and services use, by age, race, and poverty status, 1988, 4478–197
Youth unemployment research based on natl longitudinal surveys, review of studies conducted 1977-88, 6728–42

National Longitudinal Surveys of Labor Market Experience
Family members labor force status, impacts on household, series, 6726–2
see also National Longitudinal Survey of Mature Women
see also National Longitudinal Survey of Young Men
see also National Longitudinal Survey of Young Women
see also National Longitudinal Survey of Youth

National Marine Fisheries Service
Aquaculture in US and Japan, mgmt, methods, and biological data for selected species, 1990 conf, annual rpt, 2164–15
Atlantic Ocean fish and shellfish distribution, bottom trawl survey results by species and location, periodic rpt series, 2164–18
Bass (striped) stocks status on Atlantic coast, and sport and commercial catch by State, 1979-90, annual rpt, 5504–29
Billfish catch in Gulf of Mexico, by species and location, 1990, annual rpt, 2164–23
Billfish tagged and recovered by location, and Japan catch in US waters, 1950-90, annual rpt, 2164–7
Cold storage holdings of fish and shellfish, by product and species, preliminary data, monthly press release, 2162–2
Endangered species listing and mgmt activities of Fish and Wildlife Service and NMFS, FY74-91, GAO rpt, 26113–578
Fish and shellfish catch and stocks in northwest Atlantic, by species and location, 1887-1991 and forecast to 1993, semiannual conf, 2162–9
Fish and shellfish resources and catch, marine mammal and sea turtle population, and mgmt, by species and region, 1988-90, annual rpt, 2164–22
Fish catch, trade, use, and fishery operations, with selected foreign data, by species, 1980s-91, annual rpt, 2164–1
Fish meal and oil production and trade, quarterly tables, 2162–3
Fishing (ocean sport) activities, and catch by species, by angler characteristics and State, annual coastal area rpt series, 2166–17
Foreign countries market conditions for US fish and shellfish products, country rpt series, 2166–19
Game fish tagging and research activities, by species, 1990, annual rpt, 2164–24
Marine Fisheries Review, US and foreign fisheries resources, dev, mgmt, and research, quarterly journal, 2162–1
Marine Mammal Protection Act admin, and populations, strandings, and catch permits by species and location, 1988-89, annual rpt, 2164–11
Marine mammals incidental catch by fishing trawl vessels, by species, vessel flag and type, and North Pacific location, 1965-88, 2168–129
New York Bight ocean floor shellfish and other species abundance, and impacts of sewage sludge disposal site phaseout, by site, 1980s, 2168–128
New York Bight water temperature, salinity, and density, by site and depth, 1987-89, 2168–130
Pacific Ocean (northern) fish catch, driftnet fishing impacts, and fish feeding, habitat, and other characteristics, 1988 conf, 2168–131
Production of processed fish by location, and trade, by species and product, 1988-91, annual rpts, 2166–6
Sharks and other fish tagged and recovered, by species, 1991, annual rpt, 2164–21
Turtles (sea) sightings, strandings, and incidental catch, for Kemp's ridley turtles on Texas coast, late 1940s-90, 2168–132

National Mediation Board
Activities and caseloads of NMB, and railroad and airline labor disputes, with data by carrier and union, FY87-88, annual rpt, 9604–1
Budget of US, authoritative financial statements with appropriations, outlays, and receipts, by category and agency, FY91, annual rpt, 8104–2.2
Budget of US, obligations and authority by function, agency, and program, with summaries and analyses, FY93, annual rpt, 104–2
see also National Railroad Adjustment Board

National Medical Care Expenditure Survey
see also National Medical Expenditure Survey

National Medical Expenditure Survey
Data on health care use and costs, methodology and findings of natl survey, series, 4186–8

National monuments
see Monuments and memorials

National Mortality Followback Survey
Deaths during 1986, decedents health condition, services use, habits, and social, employment, and other characteristics, 4147–20.19

National Narcotics Intelligence Consumers Committee
Supply of drugs in US by country of origin, abuse, prices, and seizures, by substance, 1991, annual rpt, 6284–2

National Natality Survey
Birth, marriage, and divorce trends, series, 4147–21
National Ocean Service
Alaska OCS environmental conditions and oil dev impacts, compilation of papers, series, 2176–1
Coastal areas environmental impacts of economic dev and population growth, 1960-80s and projected to 2010, series, 2176–8
Coastal areas environmental mgmt programs of States, activities and Federal funding, FY90-91, biennial rpt, 2174–8
Estuary environmental conditions, research results and methodology, series, 2176–7
Great Lakes water level benchmarks, for Intl Datum 1985, pamphlet, 2178–34
Great Lakes water levels, daily and monthly averages by site, 1991 and cumulative from 1900, annual rpt, 2174–3
Great Lakes water levels, monthly and annual averages by station, 1860-1990, quinquennial rpt, 2178–1
Marine mammals tissue pollutant concentrations, by species and pollutant type, for Alaska, 1987-91, 2218–87
Middle Atlantic States tide height and tidal current velocity daily at selected coastal stations, forecast 1993, annual rpt, 2174–11
Pollutant concentrations in coastal and estuarine fish, shellfish, and environment, series, 2176–3
Pollution of oceans, estuaries, and coastal waters monitoring and assessment, NOAA activities and funding, FY90, annual rpt, 2174–9
Shellfish harvest in estuaries, approved and restricted areas, and pollution sources, by estuary, State, and coastal region, 1990, quinquennial rpt, 2178–33
Tidal currents, daily time and velocity by station for North America and Asia coasts, forecast 1993, annual rpts, 2174–1
Tide height and time daily at coastal points worldwide, forecast 1993, annual rpt series, 2174–2
National Oceanic and Atmospheric Administration
Atlantic Oceanographic and Meteorological Lab research activities and bibl, FY91, annual rpt, 2144–19
Budget of US, obligations and authority by function, agency, and program, with summaries and analyses, FY93, annual rpt, 104–2
Climate Monitoring and Diagnostics Lab activities, and atmospheric concentrations of global climate change contributing pollutants, by location, 1990, annual rpt, 2144–28
Coastal areas and watersheds pollution indicators, by location, 1980s-90, 2178–35
Coastal areas environmental conditions and mgmt, for individual areas, conf series, 2146–8
Diving (underwater) accidents, illnesses, and deaths, by circumstances, diver characteristics, and location, 1970-90, annual rpt, 2144–29
Diving (underwater sport and occupational) deaths, by circumstances, diver characteristics, and location, annual rpt, discontinued, 2144–5
Environmental quality indicators, NOAA monitoring results, 1991 annual summary rpt, 2144–27
Environmental Research Labs of NOAA, staff rpts, FY91, annual listing, 2144–25
Estuary environmental conditions and mgmt, for individual areas, conf series, discontinued, 2146–6
Expenditures of Fed Govt in States, by type, program, agency, and State, FY91, annual rpt, 2464–2
Fish (anadromous species) population, migration, and habitat conditions, for coastal Beaufort Sea, summer 1990, 5738–37
Great Lakes Environmental Research Lab activities, FY91 annual rpt, 2144–26
Hurricanes in northwest Atlantic Ocean, correlation with Sahel Africa rainfall, 1947-90, 2148–61
Ocean pollution research, monitoring, and resources dev activities of Fed Govt, funding and project descriptions, FY89, annual rpt, 2144–23
Oceanographic research and distribution activities of World Data Center A by country, and cruises by ship, 1990, annual rpt, 2144–15
Pacific Marine Environmental Lab research activities and bibl, FY91, annual rpt, 2144–21
Pacific Ocean temperature, current, and wind, by equatorial eastern site and depth, 1983-87, 2148–62
Research activities of NOAA, FY87-88, biennial rpt, 2144–6
Research on ocean pollution, monitoring, and resources dev activities of Fed Govt, 5-year plan and funding by agency, FY87-92, triennial rpt, 2148–56
Shellfish harvest in estuaries, approved and restricted areas by State and coastal region, triennial rpt, issuing agency change, 2148–50
Weather services activities and funding, by Federal agency, planned FY92-93, annual rpt, 2144–2
see also National Environmental Satellite, Data, and Information Service
see also National Marine Fisheries Service
see also National Ocean Service
see also National Weather Service
National Park Service
Acreage and descriptions of natl park system sites, 1991, biennial listing, 5544–5
Acreage of land under NPS mgmt, by site, ownership, and region, FY92, semiannual rpt, 5542–1
Bears (grizzly) in Yellowstone Natl Park area, monitoring results, 1991, annual rpt, 5544–4
Budget of US, obligations and authority by function, agency, and program, with summaries and analyses, FY93, annual rpt, 104–2
Expenditures of Fed Govt in States, by type, program, agency, and State, FY91, annual rpt, 2464–2
Historic and natural natl landmarks damaged and threatened, with owner, location, damage type, and recommended remedial action, 1990, annual listing, 5544–16
Historic Preservation Fund grants, by State, FY93, annual press release, 5544–9
Land and Water Conservation Fund allocations for outdoor recreation area dev, by State, FY93, annual table, 5544–15
Owl (northern spotted) conservation methods in Pacific Northwest, findings and recommendations, 1990 rpt, 1208–385
Visits and overnight stays in natl park system, by park and State, monthly rpt, 5542–4
Visits and overnight stays in natl park system, by park and State, 1991, annual rpt, 5544–12
National parks
Acreage and descriptions of natl park system sites, 1991, biennial listing, 5544–5
Acreage of land under Natl Park Service mgmt, by site, ownership, and region, FY92, semiannual rpt, 5542–1
Bears (grizzly) in Yellowstone Natl Park area, monitoring results, 1991, annual rpt, 5544–4
Blue Ridge Parkway impacts on local economic conditions and employment, by expense type, 1987, 7556–8.4
Blue Ridge Parkway traffic accidents, deaths, and circumstances, 1984-87, 7556–8.2
Business statistics, detailed data for major industries and economic indicators, 1960-91, *Survey of Current Business* biennial supplement, 2704–1
Crimes committed in natl parks, by offense, data compilation, 1992 annual rpt, 6064–6.3
Environmental Quality, status of problems, protection programs, research, and intl issues, 1991 annual rpt, 484–1
Minerals resources and availability on public lands, State rpt series, 5606–7
Statistical Abstract of US, 1992 annual data compilation, 2324–1.7
Visits and overnight stays in natl park system, by park and State, monthly rpt, 5542–4
Visits and overnight stays in natl park system, by park and State, 1991, annual rpt, 5544–12
Visits in natl park system, *Survey of Current Business*, monthly rpt, 2702–1.10
Washington and Oregon coastal areas tourism and recreation facilities and economic impacts, by county, 1983-88, 5738–40.3
see also National forests
see also National trails
see also Wilderness areas
see also Wildlife refuges
National planning
see Economic policy
see Fiscal policy
see Monetary policy
National Postsecondary Student Aid Study
Assistance and other sources of support, with student expenses and characteristics, by instn type and control, 1990 triennial study, series, 4846–5
National Prosecutor Survey
State court chief prosecutors employment characteristics, and felony case prosecution procedures, 1990 survey, 6066–25.46

National Railroad Adjustment Board
Activities and caseloads of NRAB, and railroad and airline labor disputes, with data by carrier and union, FY87-88, annual rpt, 9604–1
National Railroad Passenger Corp.
Energy use by mode of transport, fuel supply, and demographic and economic factors of vehicle use, 1970s-90, annual rpt, 3304–5
Finances and ridership of Amtrak, FY79-89, annual rpt, 7304–1
Finances, executive office travel expenses and staff years, and membership dues by assn, for Amtrak, FY88-92, GAO rpt, 26113–573
Operations and finances of Amtrak, FY91, annual rpt, 29524–1
Passenger cost and travel time, for buses, air travel, and Amtrak, by selected route, 1980s-1992, GAO rpt, 26113–583
National Renewable Energy Laboratory
"Photovoltaic Energy Program Summary", 3304–20
National school lunch and breakfast programs
see School lunch and breakfast programs
National Science Foundation
Activities of NSF, finances, and funding by program, FY91, annual rpt, 9624–6
Activities of Science Resources Studies Div, rpts and project descriptions, annual listing, suspended, 9624–21
Budget of US, authoritative financial statements with appropriations, outlays, and receipts, by category and agency, FY91, annual rpt, 8104–2.2
Budget of US, obligations and authority by function, agency, and program, with summaries and analyses, FY93, annual rpt, 104–2
Education funding by Federal agency, program, and recipient type, and instn spending, 1960s-91, annual rpt, 4824–8
Education in science and engineering, grad programs enrollment by field, source of funds, and characteristics of student and instn, 1990, annual rpt, 9627–7
Employment of scientists and engineers, and related topics, advance rpt series, 9626–8
Engineering research and education grants of NSF, FY91, annual listing, 9624–24
Expenditures of Fed Govt in States, by type, program, agency, and State, FY91, annual rpt, 2464–2
Fraud and abuse in NSF programs, audits and investigations, 2nd half FY92, semiannual rpt, 9622–1
Grants and contracts of NSF, by field, recipient, and State, FY90, annual rpt, 9624–26
Higher education and nonprofit instns R&D and related activities funding by Fed Govt, by field, instn, agency, and State, FY90, annual rpt, 9627–17
Higher education instn and federally funded center R&D funding, by field, instn, and State, FY90, annual rpt, 9627–13
Higher education instn R&D facilities space and equipment adequacy, needs, and funding by source, by instn type and control, 1992, biennial rpt, 9624–25
Higher education instn science and engineering curricula improvement grants of NSF, recipient characteristics and views, 1985-87, 9628–87
Japan R&D activities of US firms, employee characteristics, and mgmt views on benefits and drawbacks, 1991 rpt, 9628–88
Labor force, Federal and university research funding, and educational data, for science and engineering, series, 9626–6
Labor unions recognized in Fed Govt, agreements and membership by agency and facility, as of Jan 1991, biennial listing, 9844–14
Manufacturing employment of scientists, engineers, and technicians, by field and industry, 1989, triennial rpt, 9627–23
Minority group, women, and disabled persons employment and education in science and engineering, by field, mid 1970s-91, biennial rpt, 9624–20
Publications of NSF, 1992 annual listing, 9624–16
R&D funding by Fed Govt, by detailed function, program, and agency, FY91-93, annual rpt, 9627–9
R&D grant awards of NSF, by div and program, periodic rpt series, 9626–7
R&D licenses for university activities supported by NSF and NIH, transfer to private firms, related income, and scientists associated with licensees, FY89-90, GAO rpt, 26113–575
Science and Engineering Indicators, employment, education, R&D funding, and industry impacts, with foreign comparisons, 1960s-91, biennial rpt, 9624–10
Undergrad research grants of NSF, administrator and recipient characteristics and views, 1987-89, 9628–86
National security
see Internal security
see National defense
National Security Council
Budget of US, authoritative financial statements with appropriations, outlays, and receipts, by category and agency, FY91, annual rpt, 8104–2.2
Budget of US, obligations and authority by function, agency, and program, with summaries and analyses, FY93, annual rpt, 104–2
National stockpiles
see Stockpiling
National Survey of Professional, Administrative, Technical, and Clerical Pay
BLS data collection, analysis, and presentation methods, by program, 1992 rpt, 6888–1
National Technical Information Service
Computer software and documentation available from NTIS, 1992 annual listing, 2224–2
Electronic info storage and transmission costs and revenues for 4 Federal agencies, FY85-91, GAO rpt, 26125–47
EPA rpts in NTIS collection, quarterly listing, 9182–5
National Telecommunications and Information Administration
Budget of US, obligations and authority by function, agency, and program, with summaries and analyses, FY93, annual rpt, 104–2
Expenditures of Fed Govt in States, by type, program, agency, and State, FY91, annual rpt, 2464–2
Publications of NTIA, FY91, annual listing, 2804–3
Radio frequency assignments for Federal use, by agency, 1st half 1992, semiannual rpt, 2802–1
Telecommunications industry intl competitiveness, structure, and devs, with background data and foreign comparisons, 1991 rpt, 2808–30
National Toxicology Program
Carcinogens chemistry, sources, environment and health risks, and regulation, by substance and brand, 1991 annual rpt, 4044–15
Research and testing activities under program, FY90 and planned FY91, annual rpt, 4044–16
National trails
Acreage and descriptions of natl park system sites, 1991, biennial listing, 5544–5
Acreage of land under Natl Park Service mgmt, by site, ownership, and region, FY92, semiannual rpt, 5542–1
Forest Service activities and finances, by region and State, FY91, annual rpt, 1204–1.1
Visits and overnight stays in natl park system, by park and State, 1991, annual rpt, 5544–12
National Transportation Safety Board
Activities of NTSB, with investigations and recommendations, and accidents and casualties by mode, 1990, annual rpt, 9614–1
Aircraft accidents and circumstances, for US operations of domestic and foreign airlines and general aviation, periodic rpt, 9612–1
Aircraft accidents, casualties, and damage, for commercial operations by detailed circumstances, 1988, annual rpt, 9614–2
Aircraft accidents, deaths, and circumstances, by carrier and carrier type, preliminary 1991, annual press release, 9614–9
Budget of US, authoritative financial statements with appropriations, outlays, and receipts, by category and agency, FY91, annual rpt, 8104–2.2
Budget of US, obligations and authority by function, agency, and program, with summaries and analyses, FY93, annual rpt, 104–2
Deaths in transportation accidents, by mode, 1990-91, annual press release, 9614–6
Rail rapid transit systems safety, operating, and funding characteristics, 1988-89, 9618–19
Railroad accidents, casualties, circumstances, and railroad involved, 1988, annual rpt, 9614–8
Railroad accidents, circumstances, severity, and railroad involved, periodic rpt, periodicity change, 9612–3
Railroad accidents involving hazardous materials, casualties, and circumstances, 1984-89, 9618–18
Ships and marine facilities accidents, casualties, circumstances, Coast Guard investigation results, periodic rpt, suspended, 9612–4

National Trust for Historic Preservation
Grants to Natl Trust and to States, FY93, annual press release, 5544–9

National Veterinary Services Laboratories
Activities of NVSL, biologic drug product evaluation and disease testing, FY91, annual rpt, 1394–17

National Weather Service
Data collection and analysis issues for weather conditions and forecasts, 1991 annual conf, 2184–10
Forecasts accuracy, evaluations for US, UK, and European systems, quarterly rpt, 2182–8
Forecasts of precipitation and temperature for US and Northern Hemisphere, by location, semimonthly rpt, 2182–1
Northeastern US water supply, precipitation and stream runoff by station, monthly rpt, 2182–3
Ocean surface temperature by ocean and for US coastal areas, and Bering Sea ice conditions, monthly rpt, 2182–5
Ocean weather forecast areas, and broadcast schedules and stations worldwide, as of Sept 1992, annual rpt, 2184–3
Ocean weather forecast broadcast schedules worldwide, periodic rpt, 2182–9
Precipitation and temperature for US and foreign locations, major events and anomalies, weekly rpt, 2182–6
Weather conditions and effect on agriculture, by US region, State, and city, and world area, weekly rpt, 2182–7
Weather trends and deviations, by world region, 1880s-1990, annual chartbook, 2184–9
Western US water supply, streamflow and reservoir storage forecasts by stream and station, Jan-May monthly rpt, 1262–1

National Wildlife Refuge System
see Wildlife refuges

Nationality
see Citizenship

Nationalization
see Government ownership

Nationwide Food Consumption Survey
Food consumption, dietary composition, and nutrient intake, natl survey methodology changes and sample results, 1990 rpt, 1358–6

Nationwide Personal Transportation Study
Households and personal travel patterns, characteristics, and auto and public transport use, 1990 survey, series, 7556–6
Travel patterns, personal and household characteristics, and auto use, 1990 survey, annual rpt, 7554–1.6

Native Americans
see Alaska Natives
see Indians

Nativity
see Birthplace

NATO
see North Atlantic Treaty Organization

Natural disasters
see Avalanches
see Disasters
see Drought
see Earthquakes
see Floods
see Forest fires
see Storms
see Volcanoes

Natural fibers
Business statistics, detailed data for major industries and economic indicators, 1960-91, *Survey of Current Business* biennial supplement, 2704–1
County Business Patterns, 1989: employment, establishments, and payroll, by SIC 2- to 4-digit industry and county, annual State rpt series, 2326–8
County Business Patterns, 1990: employment, establishments, and payroll, by SIC 2- to 4-digit industry and county, annual State rpt series, 2326–6
Employment, earnings, and hours, by SIC 1- to 4-digit industry, monthly 1989-Feb 1992, annual rpt, 6744–4
Exports and imports (agricultural) of US, by commodity and country, bimonthly rpt, 1522–1
Exports and imports (agricultural) of US, by detailed commodity and country, 1991, annual rpt, 1524–8
Exports and imports (agricultural) of US, by detailed commodity and country, 1991, semiannual rpt, 1522–4
Exports and imports between US and outlying areas, by detailed commodity and mode of transport, 1991, annual rpt, 2424–11
Exports and imports of textiles, raw fiber equivalents by product, country, and world region, 1989-90, article, 1561–1.301
Exports and imports of US, by country and detailed commodity, monthly rpt, 2422–12
Exports and imports of US, by Harmonized System 6-digit commodity and country, 1991, annual rpt, 2424–13
Exports and imports of US, by transport mode, country, and SITC 1- to 3-digit commodity, 1991, annual rpt, 2424–12
Exports of US, detailed Schedule B commodities with countries of destination, 1991, annual rpt, 2424–10
Exports of US textiles and apparel, by product group and country, quarterly rpt, 2042–36
Foreign countries agricultural production, prices, and trade, by country, 1980-91 and forecast 1992, annual world area rpt series, 1524–4
Foreign countries market conditions for US textile and apparel exports, with domestic industry operations, country rpt series, 2046–15
Imports of textiles, by country of origin, monthly rpt, 2042–27
Imports of textiles, by product and country of origin, monthly rpt series, 2046–8; 2046–9
Imports of textiles under Multifiber Arrangement by product and country, and status of bilateral agreements, 1988-91, annual rpt, 9884–18
Manufacturing annual survey, 1990: finances and operations, by SIC 2- to 4-digit industry, series, 2506–14
OECD trade, total and for 4 major countries, and US trade by country, by commodity, 1980-90, world area rpt series, 9116–1
Price indexes (producer), by stage of processing and detailed commodity, monthly rpt, 6762–6
Price indexes (producer), by stage of processing and detailed commodity, monthly 1991, annual rpt, 6764–2
Production, prices, trade, and use of natural fibers, periodic situation rpt with articles, 1561–1
Production, trade, sales, stocks, and material used, by product, region, and State, periodic Current Industrial Rpt series, 2506–5
Statistical Abstract of US, 1992 annual data compilation, 2324–1.27
Stockpiling of strategic material by Fed Govt, activity, and inventory by commodity, as of Sept 1991, semiannual rpt, 3542–22
Stockpiling of strategic material, inventories and needs, by commodity, 1992, annual rpt, 3544–37
see also Cotton
see also Silk
see also Wool and wool trade

Natural gas and gas industry
Auto alternative fuels pollutant emissions by fuel type, and alcohol fuel production and inputs, 1991 hearing, 25318–82
Business statistics, detailed data for major industries and economic indicators, *Survey of Current Business*, monthly rpt, 2702–1.12
Business statistics, detailed data for major industries and economic indicators, 1960-91, *Survey of Current Business* biennial supplement, 2704–1
Census of Population and Housing, 1990: summary characteristics, by county, subdiv, and place, State rpt series, 2551–7
Commercial buildings energy use, costs, and conservation, by building characteristics, survey rpt series, 3166–8
Construction put in place (public and private), by type, quarterly rpt, 2042–1.1
Construction put in place, value of new public and private structures, by type, monthly rpt, 2382–4
Consumer spending, natl income and product account benchmark revisions, 1929-88, 2708–5
Consumer spending, natl income and product accounts, comprehensive accounts and components, *Survey of Current Business*, monthly rpt, 2702–1.25
Consumption of energy, by detailed fuel type, end-use sector, and State, 1960-90, State Energy Data System annual rpt, 3164–39
County Business Patterns, 1989: employment, establishments, and payroll, by SIC 2- to 4-digit industry and county, annual State rpt series, 2326–8
County Business Patterns, 1990: employment, establishments, and payroll, by SIC 2- to 4-digit industry and county, annual State rpt series, 2326–6
Developing countries energy efficiency improvement issues and devs, with data by end use and country, 1980s-90, 26358–260
Electric power and industrial plants prohibited from oil and gas primary use, exemptions, and gas use by State, 1980-91, annual rpt, 3334–1
Electric power plants (steam) fuel receipts, costs, and quality, by fuel, plant, utility, and State, 1991, annual rpt, 3164–42

Electric power plants and capacity, by fuel used, owner, location, and operating status, 1991 and for units planned 1992-2001, annual listing, 3164-36
Electric power plants production and capital costs, operations, and fuel use, by fuel type, plant, utility, and location, 1990, annual rpt, 3164-9
Electric power plants production, capacity, sales, and fuel stocks, use, and costs, by State, 1986-90, annual rpt, 3164-11
Electric power plants production, fuel use, stocks, and costs by fuel type, and sales, by State, monthly rpt, with articles, 3162-35
Electric power supply, demand, and trade of Mexico and US, with data by fuel source, utility, and region, 1970s-89 and projected to 2000, 3408-2
Employment, earnings, and hours, by SIC 1- to 4-digit industry, monthly 1989-Feb 1992, annual rpt, 6744-4
Employment of minorities and women, by occupation, SIC 1- to 3-digit industry, State, and MSA, 1991, annual rpt, 9244-1
Environmental Quality, status of problems, protection programs, research, and intl issues, 1991 annual rpt, 484-1
Farm production itemized costs, by farm sales size and region, 1991, annual rpt, 1614-3
Finances and operations, by SIC 2- to 4-digit industry, forecast 1992, annual rpt, 2044-28
Finances and operations of energy producers, by energy type for US firms domestic and foreign operations, 1990, annual rpt, 3164-44
Foreign and US energy production, trade, use, and reserves, and oil and refined products supply and prices, by country, 1981-90, annual rpt, 3164-50
Foreign and US energy supply and demand, by major fuel and end-use sector, 1950s-87 and forecast to 1995, 3166-6.58
Foreign and US energy use and production, by fuel type, country, and country group, projected 1995-2010 and trends from 1970, annual rpt, 3164-84
Foreign and US natural gas production, by market economy country, monthly rpt, 9112-2
Foreign and US oil dependency, energy demand, and efficiency measures, for 6 OECD countries, 1970s-80s, working paper, 9375-13.79
Foreign countries mineral production, reserves, and industry role in domestic economy and world supply, world area and country rpt series, 5606-1
Foreign direct investment in US energy sources by type and firm, and US affiliates operations, as of 1990, annual rpt, 3164-80
Futures and options trading volume, by commodity and exchange, FY91, annual rpt, 11924-2
Futures market for natural gas, prices and contract activity, 1990-92, article, 3162-4.302
Futures trading in selected commodities and financial instruments and indexes, for NYC, Chicago, and other markets activity, biweekly rpt, 11922-5
Govt employment and payroll, by function, level of govt, and jurisdiction, annual rpt series, 2466-1
Heating fuels production, imports, stocks, and prices, by selected PAD district and State, seasonal weekly rpt, 3162-45
Helium and other components of natural gas, analyses of individual wells and pipelines, 1985-91, annual rpt, 5604-2
Helium and other components of natural gas, analyses of individual wells and pipelines, 1986-90, 5608-132
Housing (low income) energy aid, funding sources, costs, and participation, by State, FY90, annual rpt, 4584-1
Housing (rental) market absorption rates, by whether utilities included in rent, 1990, annual Current Housing Rpt, 2484-2
Housing (rental) units, total, with HUD assistance by program, and eligible for aid, by unit, household, and neighborhood characteristics, and location, 1989, biennial rpt, 5184-11
Housing and households detailed characteristics, and unit and neighborhood quality, MSA surveys, series, 2485-6
Housing energy use, costs, and conservation, and household and housing characteristics, survey rpt series, 3166-7
Housing heating and air conditioning equipment shipments by type of fuel used, quarterly rpt, 2042-1.6
Housing units completed, single and multifamily units by structural and financial characteristics, and location, 1987-91, annual rpt, 2384-1
Input-output structure of US economy, detailed interindustry transactions for 541 industries, and components of final demand, 1982 benchmark data, 2708-17
Japan energy use and imports by fuel type, and gasoline prices, 1970s-80s, hearing, 21448-45
Labor productivity in oil and gas industry, 1959-87, article, 6722-1.316
Labor productivity, indexes of output, hours, and employment by SIC 2- to 4-digit industry, 1967-90, annual rpt, 6824-1.4
Manufacturing energy use and prices, by fuel type and industry, 1974-88, 3166-15.3
Manufacturing energy use and prices, 1988 survey, series, 3166-13
Methane production in coal fields, and proved reserves, by State, 1989-91, 3164-46.3
Methane recovered from landfills, use by region, 1990, annual rpt, 3164-97
Minerals Yearbook, Vol 3, 1989: foreign country reviews of production, trade, and policy, by commodity, annual rpt, 5604-35
Multinatl firms US affiliates finances and operations, by industry, country of parent firm, and State, 1987, 2708-48
Natl Energy Strategy fossil fuel, electric power, conservation, and pollution reduction issues, 1991 hearings, 21368-136
Natl Energy Strategy plans for conservation, R&D, security, and pollution reduction, technical rpt series, 3006-13
Naval Petroleum and Oil Shale Reserves production and revenue by fuel type, sales by purchaser, and wells, by reserve, FY91, annual rpt, 3334-3
Occupational injury and illness rates, by SIC 2- to 4-digit industry, 1989-90, annual rpt, 6844-7
Occupational injury and illness rates, by SIC 2- to 4-digit industry, 1990, annual rpt, 6844-1
Pacific basin countries energy supply and demand, and implications for US trade, country rpt series, 3406-6
Pacific territories population and housing detailed characteristics, by location, 1990 Census of Population and Housing, series, 2551-8
Pipeline (interstate) capacity, use, contract deliveries, and prices, by State, region, and firm, 1990, 3168-125
Pollution (air) contributing to global warming, emissions by monitoring site and country, and temperature change by world area and US region, 1860s-1990, annual rpt, 3004-33
Production and reserves of oil, gas, and gas liquids, by State and substate area, 1991, annual rpt, 3164-46
Production, dev, and distribution firms revenues and income, quarterly rpt, 3162-38
Production, prices, trade, use, reserves, pipeline finances, and wells classified, for natural and supplemental gas, by firm and State, monthly rpt with articles, 3162-4
Romania energy production and trade, 1970s-91, with capital investment projected to 2000, GAO rpt, 26123-402
Soviet Union and US economic and sociodemographic indicators, selected years 1970-90, handbook, 2328-80
Soviet Union gas production, by selected region and former Republic, 1980s-88, annual rpt, 23844-2
Statistical Abstract of US, 1992 annual data compilation, 2324-1.19; 2324-1.25
Supply, demand, and distribution of energy, and regulatory impacts, series, 3166-6
Supply, demand, and prices, by fuel type and end-use sector, alternative projections by region, 1990-2010, annual rpt, 3164-96
Supply, demand, and prices, by fuel type and end-use sector, alternative projections 1990-2010, annual rpt, 3164-75
Supply, demand, and prices, by fuel type and end-use sector, projections and underlying assumptions, 1995-2010, annual rpt, 3164-90
Supply, demand, and prices, by fuel type and end-use sector, with foreign comparisons, 1981-90, annual fact book, 3164-76
Supply, demand, and prices, by fuel type and end-use sector, with foreign comparisons, 1991 and trends from 1949, annual rpt, 3164-74
Supply, demand, and prices, by fuel type, end-use sector, and country, detailed data, monthly rpt with articles, 3162-24
Supply, demand, and prices, by fuel type, end-use sector, and country, detailed data, monthly 1973-88, 3168-123
Supply, demand, and prices of energy, forecasts by resource type, quarterly rpt, 3162-34
Supply, demand, and prices of oil and gas, alternative projections, annual rpt, discontinued, 3164-89

Supply, demand, prices, and distribution of natural gas, by State, 1986-90, annual rpt, 3164–4
Tax (income) returns of corporations, income and tax items by asset size and detailed industry, 1989, annual rpt, 8304–4; 8304–21
Transit systems finances and operations, by mode, size of fleet and urban area, region, and for 518 systems, 1990, annual rpt, 7884–4
Transportation energy use by fuel type, and miles traveled, by mode, projected 1990-2010 and trends from 1960s, 3008–124
Transportation energy use by mode, fuel supply, and demographic and economic factors of vehicle use, 1970s-90, annual rpt, 3304–5
Utilities privately owned, detailed finances and operations by firm, 1990, annual rpt, 3164–23
VA health care facilities energy use and conservation, by facility, quarterly rpt, 8602–9
see also Energy exploration and drilling
see also Liquefied petroleum gas
see also Natural gas exports and imports
see also Natural gas liquids
see also Natural gas prices
see also Natural gas reserves
see also Offshore oil and gas
see also Oil and gas leases
see also Pipelines
see also under By Commodity in the "Index by Categories"

Natural gas exports and imports
Eastern Europe and USSR natural gas trade, by country, monthly rpt, 9112–2
Exports and imports between US and outlying areas, by detailed commodity and mode of transport, 1991, annual rpt, 2424–11
Exports and imports of gas, by country of origin and destination, 1989, annual rpt, 3164–50.3
Exports and imports of US, by country and detailed commodity, monthly rpt, 2422–12
Exports and imports of US, by Harmonized System 6-digit commodity and country, 1991, annual rpt, 2424–13
Exports and imports of US, by selected country, country group, and commodity group, 1991, annual rpt, 2044–37
Exports and imports of US, by transport mode, country, and SITC 1- to 3-digit commodity, 1991, annual rpt, 2424–12
Exports, imports, production, prices, use, reserves, and pipeline finances, for natural gas, by firm and State, monthly rpt with articles, 3162–4
Exports of US, detailed Schedule B commodities with countries of destination, 1991, annual rpt, 2424–10
Foreign countries mineral production, reserves, and industry role in domestic economy and world supply, world area and country rpt series, 5606–1
Heating fuels production, imports, stocks, and prices, by selected PAD district and State, seasonal weekly rpt, 3162–45
Imports and contracted supply of gas from Canada and Mexico, by US pipeline firm, 1990-91, annual rpt, 3164–33.6
Input-output structure of US economy, detailed interindustry transactions for 541 industries, and components of final demand, 1982 benchmark data, 2708–17
Liquids (gas) supply, demand, and movement, by PAD district and State, 1991, annual rpt, 3164–2
Liquids (gas) supply, demand, trade, stocks, and refining, by detailed product and PAD district, monthly rpt with articles, 3162–6
Pacific basin countries energy supply and demand, and implications for US trade, country rpt series, 3406–6
Pipeline interstate company gas reserves and production, by firm, 1963-91 and deliverability projected to 2011, annual rpt, 3164–33
Supply, demand, and prices, by fuel type and end-use sector, alternative projections by region, 1990-2010, annual rpt, 3164–96
Supply, demand, and prices, by fuel type and end-use sector, alternative projections 1990-2010, annual rpt, 3164–75
Supply, demand, and prices, by fuel type and end-use sector, projections and underlying assumptions, 1995-2010, annual rpt, 3164–90
Supply, demand, and prices, by fuel type and end-use sector, with foreign comparisons, 1991 and trends from 1949, annual rpt, 3164–74
Supply, demand, and prices, by fuel type, end-use sector, and country, detailed data, monthly rpt with articles, 3162–24
Supply, demand, and prices, by fuel type, end-use sector, and country, detailed data, monthly 1973-88, 3168–123
Supply, demand, and prices of energy, forecasts by resource type, quarterly rpt, 3162–34

Natural gas liquids
Exports and imports between US and outlying areas, by detailed commodity and mode of transport, 1991, annual rpt, 2424–11
Exports and imports of natural gas and liquefied gas with 5 countries, and average price, by US firm, 1955-91, annual article, 3162–4.301
Exports and imports of US, by Harmonized System 6-digit commodity and country, 1991, annual rpt, 2424–13
Exports of US, detailed Schedule B commodities with countries of destination, 1991, annual rpt, 2424–10
Foreign and US natural gas plant liquids production, by country group and selected country, monthly rpt, 3162–42
Minerals Yearbook, Vol 3, 1989: foreign country reviews of production, trade, and policy, by commodity, annual rpt, 5604–35
Occupational injury and illness rates, by SIC 2- to 4-digit industry, 1989-90, annual rpt, 6844–7
Occupational injury and illness rates, by SIC 2- to 4-digit industry, 1990, annual rpt, 6844–1
Pacific basin countries energy supply and demand, and implications for US trade, country rpt series, 3406–6
Price indexes (producer), by stage of processing and detailed commodity, monthly rpt, 6762–6
Price indexes (producer), by stage of processing and detailed commodity, monthly 1991, annual rpt, 6764–2
Production and reserves of oil, gas, and gas liquids, by State and substate area, 1991, annual rpt, 3164–46
Statistical Abstract of US, 1992 annual data compilation, 2324–1.25
Supply, demand, and movement of crude oil, gas liquids, and refined products, by PAD district and State, 1991, annual rpt, 3164–2
Supply, demand, and prices, by fuel type and end-use sector, with foreign comparisons, 1991 and trends from 1949, annual rpt, 3164–74
Supply, demand, and prices, by fuel type, end-use sector, and country, detailed data, monthly 1973-88, 3168–123
Supply, demand, trade, stocks, and refining of oil and gas liquids, by detailed product, State, and PAD district, monthly rpt with articles, 3162–6

Natural gas prices
CPI by component for US city average, and by selected metro area, region, and population size, monthly rpt, 6762–2
Electric power plants (steam) fuel receipts, costs, and quality, by fuel, plant, utility, and State, 1991, annual rpt, 3164–42
Electric power plants prices paid for fossil fuels, FY90-91, annual rpt, 3084–9
Electric power plants production, capacity, sales, and fuel stocks, use, and costs, by State, 1986-90, annual rpt, 3164–11
Electric power plants production, fuel use, stocks, and costs by fuel type, and sales, by State, monthly rpt, with articles, 3162–35
Exports and imports of natural gas and liquefied gas with 5 countries, and average price, by US firm, 1955-91, annual article, 3162–4.301
Food marketing cost indexes, by expense category, monthly rpt with articles, 1502–4
Heating fuels production, imports, stocks, and prices, by selected PAD district and State, seasonal weekly rpt, 3162–45
Housing energy prices, by fuel type and State, 1990 and forecast 1991-92, 3166–6.61
Manufacturing energy use and prices, by fuel type and industry, 1974-88, 3166–15.3
Naval Petroleum and Oil Shale Reserves sales and contract prices, by purchaser and reserve, FY91, annual rpt, 3334–3
Pacific basin countries energy supply and demand, and implications for US trade, country rpt series, 3406–6
Pacific Northwest population, households, employment, income, fuel prices, and electricity demand, alternative forecasts 1991-2010, annual rpt, 3224–3.3
Pipeline (interstate) capacity, use, contract deliveries, and prices, by State, region, and firm, 1990, 3168–125
Prices and spending for fuel, by type, end-use sector, and State, 1990, annual rpt, 3164–64
Prices of fuel, by type, end-use sector, and region, projected 1991-2030, 3166–6.60
Prices, production, trade, use, reserves, and pipeline company finances, for natural gas, by firm and State, monthly rpt with articles, 3162–4

Prices, supply, and demand, by fuel type and end-use sector, alternative projections by region, 1990-2010, annual rpt, 3164–96
Prices, supply, and demand, by fuel type and end-use sector, alternative projections 1990-2010, annual rpt, 3164–75
Prices, supply, and demand, by fuel type and end-use sector, projections and underlying assumptions, 1995-2010, annual rpt, 3164–90
Prices, supply, and demand, by fuel type and end-use sector, with foreign comparisons, 1981-90, annual fact book, 3164–76
Prices, supply, and demand, by fuel type and end-use sector, with foreign comparisons, 1991 and trends from 1949, annual rpt, 3164–74
Prices, supply, and demand for natural gas, by consuming sector and State, 1930-90, annual rpt, 3164–4
Prices, supply, and demand of energy, forecasts by resource type, quarterly rpt, 3162–34
Producer price indexes, by stage of processing and detailed commodity, monthly rpt, 6762–6
Producer price indexes, by stage of processing and detailed commodity, monthly 1991, annual rpt, 6764–2
VA health care facilities energy use and conservation, by facility, quarterly rpt, 8602–9
Wholesale and wellhead prices to electric plants, and prices to residential customers, monthly rpt, 3162–24.9
Wholesale and wellhead prices to electric plants, and prices to residential customers, monthly 1973-88, 3168–123.9

Natural gas reserves
Alaska minerals resources, production, oil and gas leases, reserves, and exploratory wells, with maps and bibl, 1990, annual rpt, 5664–11
Alaska oil, gas, and coal reserve acreage, by ownership, 1991 rpt, 5608–174
Field codes and locations, for oil and gas, 1991, annual listing, 3164–70
Field locations, for natural gas, as of Sept 1990, map, 3088–21
Foreign and US energy reserves, by type of fuel and country, as of Jan 1991, annual rpt, 3164–50.6
Foreign countries mineral production, reserves, and industry role in domestic economy and world supply, world area and country rpt series, 5606–1
Foreign countries oil and gas reserves and discoveries, by country and country group, quarterly rpt, suspended, 3162–43
Gulf of Mexico oil and gas reserves, production, and leasing status, by location, 1990, annual rpt, 5734–6
Offshore oil and gas reserves of Fed Govt, production, leasing and exploration activity, revenue, and costs, by ocean area, FY91, annual rpt, 5734–4
Pacific basin countries energy supply and demand, and implications for US trade, country rpt series, 3406–6
Pacific Ocean OCS oil and gas production, reserves, and wells drilled by location, 1990, annual rpt, 5734–7
Pipeline interstate company gas reserves and production, by firm, 1963-91 and deliverability projected to 2011, annual rpt, 3164–33
Producers finances and operations, by energy type for US firms domestic and foreign operations, 1990, annual rpt, 3164–44.2
Public lands minerals resources and availability, State rpt series, 5606–7
Reserves and production of oil, gas, and gas liquids, by State and substate area, 1991, annual rpt, 3164–46
Reserves and storage of natural gas, by consuming sector, census div, and State, 1930-90, annual rpt, 3164–4
Reserves, production, and ultimate recovery of oil and gas, by location, with field technical characteristics, series, 3166–14
Reserves, production, prices, trade, use, reserves, and pipeline finances, for natural and supplemental gas, by firm and State, monthly rpt with articles, 3162–4
Supply, demand, and prices, by fuel type and end-use sector, projections and underlying assumptions, 1995-2010, annual rpt, 3164–90
Supply, demand, and prices, by fuel type and end-use sector, with foreign comparisons, 1991 and trends from 1949, annual rpt, 3164–74

Natural resources
Developing countries economic, population, and agricultural data, US and other aid sources, and AID activity, country rpt series, 9916–12
Foreign countries economic, social, political, and geographic summary data, by country, 1992, annual factbook, 9114–2
Overseas Business Reports: economic conditions, investment and export opportunities, and trade practices, country market research rpt series, 2046–6
see also Conservation of natural resources
see also Energy resources and consumption
see also Fish and fishing industry
see also Forests and forestry
see also Geothermal resources
see also Marine resources
see also Mines and mineral resources
see also Plants and vegetation
see also Reclamation of land
see also Severance taxes
see also State funding for natural resources and conservation
see also Strategic materials
see also Water area
see also Water power
see also Water resources development
see also Water supply and use

Naturalization
see Citizenship

Naturopathy
see Chiropractic and naturopathy

Nauru
Economic, social, political, and geographic summary data, by country, 1992, annual factbook, 9114–2
Exports and imports of US, by transport mode, country, and SITC 1- to 3-digit commodity, 1991, annual rpt, 2424–12
Human rights conditions in 170 countries, and US economic and military aid, 1991, annual rpt, 21384–3
Minerals Yearbook, Vol 3, 1989: foreign country review of production, trade, and policy, by commodity, annual rpt, 5604–35.2
Population size, growth rates, and components of change, by country, projected 1990-2020 and trends from 1950, biennial rpt, 2324–9

Navajo and Hopi Indian Relocation Commission
Budget of US, obligations and authority by function, agency, and program, with summaries and analyses, FY93, annual rpt, 104–2
see also Office of Navajo and Hopi Indian Relocation

Naval Observatory
see U.S. Naval Observatory

Naval Oceanography Command
Hurricanes and tropical storms in Pacific and Indian Oceans, paths and surveillance, 1991, annual rpt, 3804–8
Research cruise ships characteristics, by higher education instn and Federal agency, 1992, annual listing, 3804–6

Naval Petroleum Reserves
Production and revenue by fuel type, sales by purchaser, and wells, by reserve, FY91, annual rpt, 3334–3
Property (real) of DOE owned and leased, by type, subagency, contractor, and site, FY91, annual rpt, 3004–28
Radiation and other pollutant releases from DOE contractor research lab and nuclear weapons facilities, monitoring results, 1992 annual site rpt, 3324–2.10

Naval vessels
Budget of DOD, organization, personnel, weapons, and property, by service branch, State, and country, 1992 annual summary rpt, 3504–13
Budget of DOD, personnel needs, costs, and force readiness by service branch, FY93, annual rpt, 3504–1
Budget of DOD, procurement appropriations by item, service branch, and defense agency, FY91-93, annual rpt, 3544–32
Budget of DOD, programs, policies, and operations, FY91, annual rpt, 3544–2
Budget of DOD, weapons acquisition costs by system and service branch, FY91-93, annual rpt, 3504–2
Coast Guard enforcement activities, 1st half FY92, semiannual rpt, 7402–4
Coast Guard search and rescue missions, and lives and property lost and saved, by district and assisting unit, FY91, annual rpt, 7404–2
Expenditures and obligations of DOD, by function and service branch, quarterly rpt, 3542–3
Foreign countries military aid and arms sales of US, by weapon type, as of Sept 1991, annual rpt, 3904–3
Foreign countries military spending, arms trade, and force strengths, with govt spending and population, by country, 1979-89, annual rpt, 9824–1
Foreign-flag ships subject to US control, by type and country of registry and construction, as of July 1991, semiannual rpt, 7702–3
Manufacturing annual survey, 1990: finances and operations, by SIC 2- to 4-digit industry, series, 2506–14

Military Sealift Command shipping operations, finances, and personnel, FY91, annual rpt, 3804–14
Natl Defense Reserve Fleet inventory, by location, as of July 1991, semiannual listing, 7702–2
Natl Defense Reserve Fleet inventory from FY45, and ships and tonnage by vessel type, with location, FY91, annual rpt, 7704–14.2; 7704–14.4
Natl Defense Reserve Fleet inventory, use in Persian Gulf War, and revenue from scrap sales, 1987-91, GAO rpt, 26123–376
Natl income and product accounts, comprehensive accounts and components, benchmark revisions, 1929-88, 2708–5
Natl income and product accounts, comprehensive accounts and components, *Survey of Current Business*, monthly rpt, 2702–1.26
NATO, Japan, and South Korea military spending and indicators of ability to support common defense, by country, 1970s-90, annual rpt, 3544–28
Persian Gulf War allied and other countries cash and in-kind contributions, by type and country, 1990-91, GAO rpt, 26123–371
Persian Gulf War allied countries cash and in-kind contributions, by type and country, and status of DOD accounts, as of Sept 1991, annual GAO rpt, 26104–24
Persian Gulf War costs to US by category and service branch, and offsetting contributions by allied country, monthly rpt, 102–3
Price indexes (producer), by stage of processing and detailed commodity, monthly 1991, annual rpt, 6764–2
Procurement, DOD prime contract awards by category, contract and contractor type, and service branch, FY82-1st half FY92, semiannual rpt, 3542–1
Procurement, DOD prime contract awards by category, contractor type, and State, FY89-91, annual rpt, 3544–11
Procurement, DOD prime contract awards by detailed procurement category, FY88-91, annual rpt, 3544–18
Procurement, DOD prime contract awards by size and type of contract, service branch, competitive status, category, and labor standard, FY91, annual rpt, 3544–19
Shipbuilding and repair subsidy elimination proposals of US and OECD, impacts on industry and trade, with data on US-flag vessels, 1980s-91, 9886–4.183
Shipbuilding contract costs and funding of Navy, FY83-91, GAO rpt, 26123–401
see also Nuclear-powered ships
see also Submarines

Navigation
Army Corps of Engineers water resources dev projects, characteristics, and costs, 1950s-89, biennial State rpt series, 3756–1
Army Corps of Engineers water resources dev projects, characteristics, and costs, 1950s-91, biennial State rpt series, 3756–2
Exports and imports between US and outlying areas, by detailed commodity and mode of transport, 1991, annual rpt, 2424–11
Exports and imports of US, by Harmonized System 6-digit commodity and country, 1991, annual rpt, 2424–13
Exports of US, detailed Schedule B commodities with countries of destination, 1991, annual rpt, 2424–10
Fed Govt financial and nonfinancial domestic aid, 1992 base edition, annual listing, 104–5
Instruments and related products shipments, trade, use, and firms, by detailed type, 1991, annual Current Industrial Rpt, 2506–12.26
Mariners Weather Log, quarterly journal, 2152–8
see also Aeronautical navigation
see also Lighthouses and lightships
see also Marine accidents and safety
see also Radar

Navy
Accidents during training activities, and deaths by cause, by service branch, FY88-91, GAO rpt, 26123–397
Black military and civilian DOD personnel, by sex, grade, and period of service, and lists of award recipients, officers, and service academy grads, 1770s-90, 3548–22
Budget of DOD, organization, personnel, weapons, and property, by service branch, State, and country, 1992 annual summary rpt, 3504–13
Criminal case processing in military courts, and prisoners by facility, by service branch, data compilation, 1992 annual rpt, 6064–6.6
Deaths by cause, age, race, and rank, and personnel captured and missing, by service branch, FY91, annual rpt, 3544–40
Health care facilities of DOD in US and abroad, beds, admissions, outpatient visits, and births, by service branch, quarterly rpt, 3542–15
Historic audiovisual records of naval activity, Natl Archives special collection, 1975 rpt, 9516–1.6
Homosexual military personnel discharges by pay grade, tenure, race, sex, and occupation, and investigations, by service branch, 1980s-90, GAO rpt, 26123–392
Military Sealift Command shipping operations, finances, and personnel, FY91, annual rpt, 3804–14
Officers newly commissioned, share from service academies, and academy attrition, 1970s-91 and projected to FY97, GAO rpt, 26123–389
Persian Gulf War costs to US by category and service branch, and offsetting contributions by allied country, monthly rpt, 102–3
Persian Gulf War Operation Desert Storm deployment, by sex, race, rank, and service branch, 1990-91, GAO rpt, 26123–394
Personnel (civilian and military) of DOD, by service branch, major installation, and State, as of Sept 1991, annual rpt, 3544–7
Personnel active duty enlisted accessions by race, and goals, by sex and service branch, quarterly press release, 3542–7
Personnel, contracts, and payroll, by service branch and location, with top 5 contractors and maps, by State and country, FY91, annual rpt, 3544–29
Personnel needs, costs, and force readiness, by service branch, FY93, annual rpt, 3504–1
Personnel occupational distribution, by race, sex, and service branch, FY90, GAO rpt, 26123–381
Personnel reductions planned by service branch, and women and minorities affected by Army and Air Force plans, FY90-91, GAO rpt, 26123–373
Personnel reserve and active duty force mix and costs under alternative reduction cases, by service branch, 1990 and projected to 1997, 26306–6.172
Personnel strengths, accessions, and attrition, detailed statistics for Navy and Naval Reserve, quarterly rpt, 3802–4
Personnel strengths, for active duty, civilians, and dependents, by service branch and US and foreign location, quarterly rpt, 3542–20
Personnel strengths, for active duty, civilians, and reserves, by service branch, FY91 and trends, annual rpt, 3544–1
Personnel strengths, for active duty, civilians, and reserves, by service branch, quarterly rpt, 3542–14
Personnel strengths in US and abroad, by service branch, world area, and country, quarterly press release, 3542–9
Personnel strengths, summary by service branch, monthly press release, 3542–2
Reserve forces personnel and equipment strengths, and readiness, by reserve component, FY91, annual rpt, 3544–31
Reserve forces personnel strengths and characteristics, by component, quarterly rpt, 3542–4
Training and education programs of DOD, funding, staff, students, and facilities, by service branch, FY93, annual rpt, 3504–5
see also Department of Navy
see also Marine Corps
see also Naval Petroleum Reserves
see also Naval vessels

Near East
see Middle East

Nebraska
Banks (insured commercial and savings) deposits by instn, State, MSA, and county, as of June 1991, annual regional rpt, 9295–3.5
County Business Patterns, 1990: employment, establishments, and payroll, by SIC 2- to 4-digit industry and county, annual State rpt, 2326–6.29
Deaths and rates, by detailed location, cause, and demographic characteristics, 1989, US Vital Statistics annual rpt, 4144–3.1
Employment, earnings, and hours, by selected SIC 1- to 4-digit industry, State, and for 275 MSAs, 1987-92, 6748–81
Fed Govt spending in States and local areas, by type, State, county, and city, FY91, annual rpt, 2464–3
Fed Govt spending in States, by type, program, agency, and State, FY91, annual rpt, 2464–2
Financial and economic devs, Fed Reserve 10th District, quarterly rpt, 9381–16
HHS financial aid, by program, recipient, State, and city, FY91, annual regional listing, 4004–3.7

Hospital deaths of Medicare patients, actual and expected rates by diagnosis, and hospital characteristics, by instn, FY90 annual State rpt, 4654–14.28
Housing census, 1990: inventory, occupancy, and costs, State fact sheet, 2326–21.29
Housing census, 1990: summary unit characteristics, by householder race and age, county, place, and urban-rural location, State rpt, 2471–1.29
Military prime contract awards, by contractor, service branch, State, and city, FY91, annual rpt, 3544–22
Mineral Industry Surveys, State reviews of production, 1991, preliminary annual rpt, 5614–6
Minerals (strategic) deposits in North Central States, characteristics, 1992 compilation of papers, 5668–127
Multinatl firms US affiliates finances and operations, by industry, country of parent firm, and State, 1987, 2708–48
Physicians, by specialty, age, sex, and location of training and practice, 1990, State rpt, 4116–6.28
Population and housing census, 1990: detailed geographic coverage, State CD-ROM, 2551–9.4
Population and housing census, 1990: summary characteristics, by county, subdiv, and place, State rpt, 2551–7.29
Population census, 1990: population characteristics and living arrangements, by county, place, and urban-rural location, State rpt, 2531–1.29
Statistical Abstract of US, 1992 annual data compilation, 2324–1
Water quality, chemistry, hydrology, and other characteristics, 1990 local area study, 5666–27.26
Water quality, chemistry, hydrology, and other characteristics, 1991 local area study, 5666–27.34
Water resources dev projects of Army Corps of Engineers, characteristics, and costs, 1950s-91, biennial State rpt, 3756–2.28
see also Omaha, Nebr.
see also under By State in the "Index by Categories"

Neef, Arthur
"Manufacturing Productivity and Labor Costs in 14 Economies", 6722–1.304

Negotiable orders of withdrawal accounts
Banks (insured commercial) domestic and foreign office consolidated financial statements, monthly rpt, quarterly data, 9362–1.4
Banks (insured commercial and savings) finances, for foreign and domestic offices, by asset size, 1990, annual rpt, 9294–4.2
Debits, deposits, and deposit turnover, for commercial banks by type of account, monthly rpt, 9365–2.5
Savings instns insured by Savings Assn Insurance Fund, assets, liabilities, and deposit and loan activity, by conservatorship status, monthly rpt, 8432–1
Service fees, minimum balances, and services offered by banks and thrifts, by service type, 1991, annual rpt, 9364–12
Southeastern States, Fed Reserve 5th District insured commercial banks financial statements, by State, quarterly rpt, 9389–18

Negotiations
see Labor-management relations, general
see Labor-management relations in government
see Legal arbitration and mediation
see Strategic Arms Reduction Talks
see Treaties and conventions

Negroes
see Black Americans

Neighborhood Reinvestment Corp.
Budget of US, authoritative financial statements with appropriations, outlays, and receipts, by category and agency, FY91, annual rpt, 8104–2.2
Budget of US, obligations and authority by function, agency, and program, with summaries and analyses, FY93, annual rpt, 104–2
Contracting practices of NRC, and oversight of local grantees, with grantee listing, FY88-91, GAO rpt, 26113–587

Neighborhoods
Census Bur data coverage and availability for statistics on counties, cities, and small areas, 1991 rpt, 2326–7.82
Census Bur data coverage and availability for statistics on small areas, religious and other groups use, 1991 rpt, 2326–7.85
Crime and crime-related issues, public opinion by respondent characteristics, data compilation, 1992 annual rpt, 6064–6.2
Drug control street-level task forces enforcement activities, impacts on crime, and residents views, local area studies, 1992 rpt, 6068–251
Financial services use by households, by account type and instn type and location, 1989, article, 9362–1.303
Housing affordability and availability, impacts of govt land use regulations and rent control, and low income housing condition, 1991 hearing, 21248–174
Housing unit and household characteristics of recent movers, and reason for move, by tenure, 1989, 2486–1.12
Mortgage activity impact of lending program for low- and moderate-income neighborhoods in Philadelphia, with background data, 1980s, working paper, 9387–8.266
Quality of housing and neighborhoods, attitudes of homeowners by whether home improvements made, 1987, 2486–1.13
Quality of housing and neighborhoods, indicators and attitudes, by householder type and location, for 11 MSAs, 1987 survey, supplement, 2485–8
Quality of housing and neighborhoods, indicators and attitudes, by householder type and location, 1989, biennial rpt supplement, 2485–13
Quality of housing and neighborhoods, indicators and attitudes, MSA surveys, series, 2485–6
Quality of housing and neighborhoods, indicators and attitudes, 1989, wallchart, 2485–12
Racial discrimination in housing rental and sales, for blacks and Hispanics in selected metro areas, 1989 study, series, 5186–16
Rental housing units, total, with HUD assistance by program, and eligible for aid, by unit, household, and neighborhood characteristics, and location, 1989, biennial rpt, 5184–11
see also Blocks, city
see also Census tracts
see also Community development
see also Wards, city
see also ZIP codes

Nelson, Charles
"Estimates of Median Four-Person Family Income, by State: 1974-89", 2626–2.60

Nelson, Lyle
"Assignment and the Participating Physician Program: An Analysis of Beneficiary Awareness, Understanding, and Experience", 17266–2.1

Nelson, Merwyn R.
"Maternal Pregravid Weight, Age, and Smoking Status as Risk Factors for Low Birth Weight Births", 4042–3.367

Nelson, Richard R.
"State Labor Legislation Enacted in 1991", 6722–1.309

Nelson, William J., Jr.
"Workers' Compensation: Coverage, Benefits, and Costs, 1989", 4742–1.311
"Workers' Compensation: 1984-88 Benchmark Revisions", 4742–1.322

Nelson, William R.
"Ninety Years of Salmon Culture at Little White Salmon National Fish Hatchery", 5508–114

Neoplasms
Agent Orange exposure health effects, literature review, 1990, annual rpt series, 8706–1
Breast and cervical cancer deaths and rates by State, and in situ case rates by age, by race, 1970s-86, article, 4202–7.312
Breast and cervical cancer screening use and reasons for nonuse, by age, race, income, and State, 1987-89, article, 4202–7.313
Breast cancer research funding, cases, and deaths, 1970s-90, GAO rpt, 26131–92
Breast cancer risk of hormone replacement therapy for menopause, 1992 rpt, 26358–261
Cancer (mesothelioma) patient deaths, by cause of death reported on death certificates, for Massachusetts, 1982-89, article, 4042–3.351
Cervical and breast cancer screening among poor black women, effects of in-home promotion program, 1989-92, article, 4042–3.338
Colorectal cancer early detection screening program effectiveness, 1984-88 study, article, 4042–3.333
Contraceptives failures and health risks to women, with pregnancy, abortion, and cancer death rates, 1980s, conf paper, 4164–2
Deaths and rates, by cause, age, sex, marital status, race, and State, 1989, US Vital Statistics advance annual rpt, 4146–5.124
Deaths and rates, by cause and age, preliminary 1990-91, US Vital Statistics annual rpt, 4144–7
Deaths and rates, by cause and selected social, demographic, and employment characteristics, 1979-85, natl longitudinal study, 4478–186
Deaths and rates, by detailed location, cause, and demographic characteristics, 1989, US Vital Statistics annual rpt, 4144–3
Deaths and rates for cancer, by body site, provisional data, monthly rpt, 4142–1.2

Deaths during 1986, decedents health condition, services use, habits, and social, employment, and other characteristics, 4147–20.19
Disability and work limitations of persons with chronic health conditions, by condition, age, and sex, 1983-86, 4946–1.2
Health condition and care indicators, 1950s-90 with health improvement and disease prevention goals for 1990, annual data compilation, 4144–11
HHS financial aid, by program, recipient, State, and city, FY91, annual regional listings, 4004–3
Hospital deaths of Medicare patients, actual and expected rates by diagnosis, with hospital characteristics, by instn, FY90, annual State rpt series, 4654–14
Hospital discharges and length of stay, by diagnosis, patient and instn characteristics, procedure performed, and payment source, 1990, annual rpt, 4147–13.112
Hospital discharges and length of stay by region and diagnosis, and procedures performed, by age and sex, 1990, annual rpt, 4146–8.211
Hospital discharges and length of stay under old and new survey designs, by diagnosis, patient and instn characteristics, and procedure, Jan-Mar 1988, 4147–13.110
Hospital discharges by detailed diagnostic and procedure category, primary diagnosis, and length of stay, by age, sex, and region, 1990, annual rpt, 4147–13.111
Hospitalization of cancer patients by purpose and body site, case classification effect on charges and length of stay, FY85, article, 4652–1.304
Hyperthermia therapy used with cancer chemotherapy, risks and benefit evaluation for Medicare coverage, 1991 rpt, 4186–10.7
Indian Health Service and tribal facilities and use, and Indians health and other characteristics, by IHS region, 1980s-90, annual chartbook, 4084–7
Indian Health Service facilities, funding, operations, and Indian health and other characteristics, 1950s-91, annual chartbook, 4084–1
Indian Health Service, tribal, and contract facilities hospitalization, by diagnosis, age, sex, and service area, FY91, annual rpt, 4084–5
Mammography and cancer views of women, 1990 local area survey, article, 4042–3.370
Migration impacts on cancer incidence, and treatment resources availability, for Florida by county, 1980, article, 4042–3.339
Natl Cancer Inst activities, grants by recipient, and cancer deaths and cases, FY91 and trends, annual rpt, 4474–13
Natl Cancer Inst epidemiology and biometry activities, FY91, annual rpt, 4474–29
Navy personnel radiation exposure on nuclear-powered vessels and at support facilities, and injury claims, 1950s-91, annual rpt, 3804–10
OECD members health care costs, hospital use, resources, and economic and health indicators, by country, 1960s-90, article, 4652–1.322
Older population, and health, economic, and other characteristics, with foreign comparisons, 1980s-91 with trends and projections, Current Population Rpt, 2546–2.165
PHS Commissioned Corps members deaths, by cause, 1965-89, article, 4042–3.316
Physicians visits, by patient and practice characteristics, diagnosis, and services provided, 1989, annual rpt, 4147–13.109
Pollutants health effects, concentrations in food and environment, sources, human intake, and regulation, series, 9186–8
Research on cancer epidemiology and biochemistry, semimonthly journal, 4472–1
Smoking and health effects, with trends in smoking, related disease and death, and public attitudes, literature review, 1992 annual rpt, 4204–18
Smoking control strategies effectiveness, with data on research funding, smoking prevalence, cancer deaths, and taxation, 1900s-91, 4476–7.1
Smoking, tobacco, and health impacts research rpts, 1991 annual report, 4204–19
Statistical Abstract of US, 1992 annual data compilation, 2324–1.2
see also Carcinogens
see also Mammography
see also under By Disease in the "Index by Categories"

Nepal
Agricultural trade of US, by detailed commodity and country, 1991, annual rpt, 1524–8
Agricultural trade of US, by detailed commodity and country, 1991, semiannual rpt, 1522–4
AID economic aid to developing countries, obligations and disbursements by country, quarterly rpt, 9912–4
AID loans repayment status and terms by program and country, and status of predecessor agency loans, quarterly rpt, 9912–3
Economic and military aid and loans from US and intl agencies, by program and country, FY46-91, annual rpt, 9914–5
Economic and social conditions of developing countries from 1960s, and Intl Dev Cooperation Agency and AID activities and funding, FY91-93, annual rpt, 9904–4
Economic, social, political, and geographic summary data, by country, 1992, annual factbook, 9114–2
Exports and imports of US, by transport mode, country, and SITC 1- to 3-digit commodity, 1991, annual rpt, 2424–12
Exports of US, detailed Schedule B commodities with countries of destination, 1991, annual rpt, 2424–10
Human rights conditions in 170 countries, and US economic and military aid, 1991, annual rpt, 21384–3
Military aid of US, arms sales, and training programs costs and budget requests, by program, world region, and country, FY91-93, annual rpt, 7144–13
Military spending, arms trade, and force strengths, with govt spending and population, by country, 1979-89, annual rpt, 9824–1
Minerals Yearbook, Vol 3, 1989: foreign country review of production, trade, and policy, by commodity, annual rpt, 5604–35.2
Population size, growth rates, and components of change, by country, projected 1990-2020 and trends from 1950, biennial rpt, 2324–9
Refugee migration, and intl aid programs, by world area and country of origin and asylum, 1991, annual rpt, 7004–15
UN voting record and share of votes in agreement with US, by issue, country, and world area, 1991, annual rpt, 7004–18

Nepheline syenite
see Chemicals and chemical industry

Nervous system disorders
see Neurological disorders

Netherlands
Agricultural trade of US, by detailed commodity and country, 1991, annual rpt, 1524–8
Agricultural trade of US, by detailed commodity and country, 1991, semiannual rpt, 1522–4
AID loans repayment status and terms by program and country, and status of predecessor agency loans, quarterly rpt, 9912–3
Cuba trade, by commodity and country, mid 1980s-91, 9118–8
Drug abusers needle sharing, by selected characteristics, for Amsterdam, Netherlands, 1989-90 survey, article, 4042–3.369
Economic and military aid and loans from US and intl agencies, by program and country, FY46-91, annual rpt, 9914–5
Economic and monetary trends, compounded annual rates of change and annual indicators for US and 15 trading partners, quarterly rpt, annual supplement, 9391–7
Economic conditions, income, production, prices, employment, and trade, 1992 periodic country rpt, 2046–4.60
Economic conditions, investment and export opportunities, and trade practices, 1992 country market research rpt, 2046–6.3
Economic conditions, policy, and trade practices, by country, 1989-91, annual rpt, 21384–5
Economic, social, political, and geographic summary data, by country, 1992, annual factbook, 9114–2
Exports and imports of US, by Harmonized System 6-digit commodity and country, 1991, annual rpt, 2424–13
Exports and imports of US, by selected country, country group, and commodity group, 1991, annual rpt, 2044–37
Exports and imports of US, by transport mode, country, and SITC 1- to 3-digit commodity, 1991, annual rpt, 2424–12
Exports, imports, and balances of US for manufactured goods, by SITC 2-digit commodity and country, quarterly rpt, 2042–35
Exports of US, detailed Schedule B commodities with countries of destination, 1991, annual rpt, 2424–10
Health care costs and components, services use, resources, and economic indicators, by OECD country, 1960s-90, article, 4652–1.322

Human rights conditions in 170 countries, and US economic and military aid, 1991, annual rpt, 21384–3
Interest and exchange rates, security yields, and stock indexes, for selected foreign countries, weekly chartbook, 9365–1.5
Intl transactions of US with 9 countries, 1989-91, *Survey of Current Business*, monthly rpt, annual table, 2702–1.33
Investment (foreign direct) in US, major transactions by type, industry, country, and US location, 1990, annual rpt, 2044–20
Labor conditions, union coverage, and work accidents, 1991 annual country rpt, 6366–4.9
Labor conditions, union coverage, and work accidents, 1992 annual country rpt, 6366–4.45
Military spending, arms trade, and force strengths, with govt spending and population, by country, 1979-89, annual rpt, 9824–1
Multinatl firms US affiliates finances and operations, by industry, country of parent firm, and State, 1987, 2708–48
Multinatl firms US affiliates, finances, and operations, by industry, world area of parent firm, and State, 1989-90, annual rpt, 2704–4
Multinatl US firms and foreign affiliates finances and operations, by industry and country, 1989 benchmark survey, annual rpt, 2704–5
Multinatl US firms foreign affiliates, income statement items by asset size, industry, and country, 1988, biennial article, 8302–2.322
Nuclear power generation in US and 20 countries, monthly rpt, 3162–24.10
Nuclear power generation in US and 20 countries, monthly 1973-88, 3168–123.10
Oil exports to US by OPEC and non-OPEC countries, monthly rpt, 3162–24.3
Oil exports to US by OPEC and non-OPEC countries, monthly 1973-88, 3168–123.3
Oil production, stocks, use, and trade, by selected country and country group, monthly rpt, 3162–42
Pension plan finances, participation, and benefits, for 9 OECD countries, with data by firm and worker characteristics, 1990 conf, 6688–2
Population size, growth rates, and components of change, by country, projected 1990-2020 and trends from 1950, biennial rpt, 2324–9
Poverty definitions in US and Netherlands, comparison of minimum income measures, 1991 working paper, 6886–6.84
Refugee migration, and intl aid programs, by world area and country of origin and asylum, 1991, annual rpt, 7004–15
Spacecraft and satellite launches since 1957, quarterly listing, 9502–2
Steel (carbon flat-rolled) products from 21 countries, injury to US industry from foreign subsidized and less than fair value imports, investigation with background financial and operating data, 1992 rpt, 9886–19.85
Steel trade, by product, country, and customs district, with US industry operating data, 1989-June 1992, semiannual rpt, 9882–15
Tax (income) returns for foreign corporate activity in US, selected income and tax items, by industry div and selected country, 1988, article, 8302–2.309
Tax (income) returns, income, and tax withheld for foreign partners of US partnerships, by country, 1990, article, 8302–2.324
Tax (income) returns of Foreign Sales Corps, assets, and income and tax items, by industry, country of incorporation, and transaction pricing method, 1987, article, 8302–2.311
Tax revenue, by level of govt and type of tax, for OECD countries, mid 1960s-90, annual rpt, 10044–1.2
UN voting record and share of votes in agreement with US, by issue, country, and world area, 1991, annual rpt, 7004–18
see also Netherlands Antilles
see also under By Foreign Country in the "Index by Categories"

Netherlands Antilles
Agricultural trade of US, by detailed commodity and country, 1991, annual rpt, 1524–8
Agricultural trade of US, by detailed commodity and country, 1991, semiannual rpt, 1522–4
Economic and social conditions, resources, and trade, and aid, 1992, annual factbook, 9914–14
Economic, social, political, and geographic summary data, by country, 1992, annual factbook, 9114–2
Exports and imports of US, by Harmonized System 6-digit commodity and country, 1991, annual rpt, 2424–13
Exports and imports of US, by selected country, country group, and commodity group, 1991, annual rpt, 2044–37
Exports and imports of US, by transport mode, country, and SITC 1- to 3-digit commodity, 1991, annual rpt, 2424–12
Exports of US, detailed Schedule B commodities with countries of destination, 1991, annual rpt, 2424–10
Hypertension relation to diet diversity among Saba Islands residents, 1983-86 study, article, 4042–3.343
Multinatl US firms and foreign affiliates finances and operations, by industry and country, 1989 benchmark survey, annual rpt, 2704–5
Multinatl US firms foreign affiliates, income statement items by asset size, industry, and country, 1988, biennial article, 8302–2.322
Oil exports to US by OPEC and non-OPEC countries, monthly rpt, 3162–24.3
Oil exports to US by OPEC and non-OPEC countries, monthly 1973-88, 3168–123.3
Population size, growth rates, and components of change, by country, projected 1990-2020 and trends from 1950, biennial rpt, 2324–9
Steel trade, by product, country, and customs district, with US industry operating data, 1989-June 1992, semiannual rpt, 9882–15
Tax (income) returns for foreign corporate activity in US, selected income and tax items, by industry div and selected country, 1988, article, 8302–2.309
see also under By Foreign Country in the "Index by Categories"

Networks
see Computer networks
see Information storage and retrieval systems
see Public broadcasting
see Radio
see Television

Neuberger, Jonathan A.
"Risk and Return in Banking: Evidence from Bank Stock Returns", 9393–8.301

Neumann, Manfred J.
"Seigniorage in the U.S.: How Much Does the U.S. Government Make from Money Production?", 9391–1.307

Neunlist, Lindsay L.
"Limited Income Credit Unions", 9536–1.8

Neurological disorders
Aircraft pilot neuropsychological screening tests accuracy, 1992 technical rpt, 7506–10.107
Cancer (brain) diagnostic accuracy without use of computerized tomography scans and magnetic resonance imaging, 1985-89, article, 4472–1.309
Cancer (brain) risk relation to menopausal status and ovary removal, Germany study, 1992 article, 4472–1.340
Cancer deaths and rates, by body site and selected social, demographic, and employment characteristics, 1979-85, natl longitudinal study, 4478–186
Cancer deaths and rates, by body site, provisional data, monthly rpt, 4142–1.2
Cases of acute and chronic conditions, disability, absenteeism, and health services use, by selected characteristics, 1990, annual rpt, 4147–10.182; 4147–10.183
Chronic fatigue syndrome physical and mental symptoms prevalence, by sex, 1981-84, article, 4042–3.354
Disability and work limitations of persons with chronic health conditions, by condition, age, and sex, 1983-86, 4946–1.2
HHS financial aid, by program, recipient, State, and city, FY91, annual regional listings, 4004–3
Hospital discharges and length of stay, by diagnosis, patient and instn characteristics, procedure performed, and payment source, 1990, annual rpt, 4147–13.112
Hospital discharges and length of stay by region and diagnosis, and procedures performed, by age and sex, 1990, annual rpt, 4146–8.211
Hospital discharges and length of stay under old and new survey designs, by diagnosis, patient and instn characteristics, and procedure, Jan-Mar 1988, 4147–13.110
Hospital discharges by detailed diagnostic and procedure category, primary diagnosis, and length of stay, by age, sex, and region, 1990, annual rpt, 4147–13.111
Indian Health Service, tribal, and contract facilities hospitalization, by diagnosis, age, sex, and service area, FY91, annual rpt, 4084–5
Infectious notifiable disease cases, by age, race, and State, and deaths, 1940s-91, annual rpt, 4204–1
Morbidity and Mortality Weekly Report, infectious notifiable disease cases by State, and public health issues, 4202–1

Natl Inst of Neurological Disorders and Stroke activities, and disorder cases, FY91, annual rpt, 4474–25
Occupational repetitive motion injury rates by selected industry, with data for California, 1980s, hearing, 21408–128
OECD members health care costs, hospital use, resources, and economic and health indicators, by country, 1960s-90, article, 4652–1.322
Physicians visits, by patient and practice characteristics, diagnosis, and services provided, 1989, annual rpt, 4147–13.109
Pollutants health effects, concentrations in food and environment, sources, human intake, and regulation, series, 9186–8
Research in neurosciences and public policy issues, series, 26356–9
Sleep disorder diagnosis and treatment, risks and benefit evaluation for Medicare coverage, 1992 rpt, 4186–10.9
Spina bifida and other neural tube birth defects prevention through prenatal use of folic acid supplements, findings and CDC recommendations, 1992 rpt, 4206–2.64
Veterans disability and death compensation cases of VA, by entitlement type, period of service, sex, age, and State, FY90, annual rpt, 8604–7
Veterans health care, patients, visits, costs, and operating beds, by VA and contract facility, and region, quarterly rpt, 8602–4
see also Alzheimer's disease
see also Learning disabilities
see also Mental health and illness
see also Rabies
see also Spinal cord injuries
see also under By Disease in the "Index by Categories"

Nevada
Banks (insured commercial and savings) deposits by instn, State, MSA, and county, as of June 1991, annual regional rpt, 9295–3.6
Birds in western US Great Basin sagebrush habitat, population density by species, 1978-83 studies, 1208–402
County Business Patterns, 1990: employment, establishments, and payroll, by SIC 2- to 4-digit industry and county, annual State rpt, 2326–6.30
Deaths and rates, by detailed location, cause, and demographic characteristics, 1989, US Vital Statistics annual rpt, 4144–3.1
DOE mgmt and operating contract admin at Nevada Field Office, funding, property value, and staff, FY88-90, 3006–5.31
Employment, earnings, and hours, by selected SIC 1- to 4-digit industry, State, and for 275 MSAs, 1987-92, 6748–81
Fed Govt spending in States and local areas, by type, State, county, and city, FY91, annual rpt, 2464–3
Fed Govt spending in States, by type, program, agency, and State, FY91, annual rpt, 2464–2
HHS financial aid, by program, recipient, State, and city, FY91, annual regional listing, 4004–3.9
Hospital deaths of Medicare patients, actual and expected rates by diagnosis, and hospital characteristics, by instn, FY90 annual State rpt, 4654–14.29
Housing census, 1990: inventory, occupancy, and costs, State fact sheet, 2326–21.30
Housing census, 1990: summary unit characteristics, by householder race and age, county, place, and urban-rural location, State rpt, 2471–1.30
Land Mgmt Bur activities and finances, and public land acreage and use, FY90, annual State rpt, 5724–11.1
Land Mgmt Bur activities and finances, and public land acreage and use, FY91, annual State rpt, 5724–11.3
Metals (nonferrous) production in 5 western States, and prices, for 5 metals, 1848-1990, 5608–178
Military prime contract awards, by contractor, service branch, State, and city, FY91, annual rpt, 3544–22
Mineral Industry Surveys, State reviews of production, 1991, preliminary annual rpt, 5614–6
Multinatl firms US affiliates finances and operations, by industry, country of parent firm, and State, 1987, 2708–48
Physicians, by specialty, age, sex, and location of training and practice, 1990, State rpt, 4116–6.29
Population and housing census, 1990: detailed geographic coverage, State CD-ROM, 2551–9.8
Population and housing census, 1990: population and housing characteristics, detailed geographic coverage, State CD-ROM, 2551–10.15
Population and housing census, 1990: summary characteristics, by county, subdiv, and place, State rpt, 2551–7.30
Population census, 1990: population characteristics and living arrangements, by county, place, and urban-rural location, State rpt, 2531–1.30
Radioactive low-level waste disposal activities of States and interstate compacts, with data by disposal facility and reactor, 1990, annual rpt, 3004–36
Radioactive waste repository sites, storage containers radionuclide releases at proposed Nevada site, 1990 rpt, 3368–4
Radionuclide concentrations in air, water, humans, animals, and milk near Nevada and other nuclear test sites, 1990, annual rpt, 9194–17
Statistical Abstract of US, 1992 annual data compilation, 2324–1
Water (groundwater) supply, quality, chemistry, and use, FY87, local area rpt, 5666–28.22
Water quality, chemistry, hydrology, and other characteristics, 1991 local area study, 5666–27.32
Water supply and quality in streams and lakes, and groundwater levels in wells, by drainage basin, 1990, annual State rpt, 5666–10.27
Water supply and quality in streams and lakes, and groundwater levels in wells, by drainage basin, 1991, annual State rpt, 5666–12.27
Water supply, and snow survey results, monthly State rpt, 1266–2.6
see also Clark County, Nev.
see also Las Vegas, Nev.
see also Reno, Nev.
see also under By State in the "Index by Categories"

New Britain, Conn.
Housing and households characteristics, and unit and neighborhood quality, by MSA location for 11 MSAs, 1987 survey, supplement, 2485–8
Wages by occupation, for office and plant workers, 1992 survey, periodic MSA rpt, 6785–17.2

New Caledonia
Economic, social, political, and geographic summary data, by country, 1992, annual factbook, 9114–2
Exports and imports of US, by transport mode, country, and SITC 1- to 3-digit commodity, 1991, annual rpt, 2424–12
Exports of US, detailed Schedule B commodities with countries of destination, 1991, annual rpt, 2424–10
Minerals Yearbook, Vol 3, 1989: foreign country review of production, trade, and policy, by commodity, annual rpt, 5604–35.2
Population size, growth rates, and components of change, by country, projected 1990-2020 and trends from 1950, biennial rpt, 2324–9

New England
see Northeast States
see under By Census Division in the "Index by Categories"

New Guinea
see Papua New Guinea

New Hampshire
Banks (insured commercial and savings) deposits by instn, State, MSA, and county, as of June 1991, annual regional rpt, 9295–3.1
County Business Patterns, 1990: employment, establishments, and payroll, by SIC 2- to 4-digit industry and county, annual State rpt, 2326–6.31
Deaths and rates, by detailed location, cause, and demographic characteristics, 1989, US Vital Statistics annual rpt, 4144–3.1
Economic indicators for New England States, Fed Reserve 1st District, monthly rpt, 9373–2
Employment, earnings, and hours, by selected SIC 1- to 4-digit industry, State, and for 275 MSAs, 1987-92, 6748–81
Fed Govt spending in States and local areas, by type, State, county, and city, FY91, annual rpt, 2464–3
Fed Govt spending in States, by type, program, agency, and State, FY91, annual rpt, 2464–2
HHS financial aid, by program, recipient, State, and city, FY91, annual regional listing, 4004–3.1
Hospital deaths of Medicare patients, actual and expected rates by diagnosis, and hospital characteristics, by instn, FY90 annual State rpt, 4654–14.30
Housing census, 1990: inventory, occupancy, and costs, State fact sheet, 2326–21.31
Housing census, 1990: summary unit characteristics, by householder race and age, county, place, and urban-rural location, State rpt, 2471–1.31
Hubbard Brook Experimental Forest hydrology and climate data, 1956-89, 1208–410
Military prime contract awards, by contractor, service branch, State, and city, FY91, annual rpt, 3544–22

Mineral Industry Surveys, State reviews of production, 1991, preliminary annual rpt, 5614–6
Multinatl firms US affiliates finances and operations, by industry, country of parent firm, and State, 1987, 2708–48
Physicians, by specialty, age, sex, and location of training and practice, 1990, State rpt, 4116–6.30
Population and housing census, 1990: detailed geographic coverage, State CD-ROM, 2551–9.1
Population and housing census, 1990: population and housing characteristics, detailed geographic coverage, State CD-ROM, 2551–10.26
Population and housing census, 1990: summary characteristics, by county, subdiv, and place, State rpt, 2551–7.31
Population census, 1990: population characteristics and living arrangements, by county, place, and urban-rural location, State rpt, 2531–1.31
Statistical Abstract of US, 1992 annual data compilation, 2324–1
Water supply in northeastern US, precipitation and stream runoff by station, monthly rpt, 2182–3
see also under By State in the "Index by Categories"

New Haven, Conn.
see also under By City and By SMSA or MSA in the "Index by Categories"

New Hebrides
see Vanuatu

New Jersey
AIDS patients costs and service use under Medicaid, and service needs, for New Jersey waiver program, 1987-89, article, 4652–1.317
Banks (insured commercial and savings) deposits by instn, State, MSA, and county, as of June 1991, annual regional rpt, 9295–3.1
Cranberry production, prices, use, and acreage, for selected States, 1990-91 and forecast 1992, annual rpt, 1621–18.5
Deaths and rates, by detailed location, cause, and demographic characteristics, 1989, US Vital Statistics annual rpt, 4144–3.1
Employment, earnings, and hours, by selected SIC 1- to 4-digit industry, State, and for 275 MSAs, 1987-92, 6748–81
Employment growth and unemployment rates, Fed Reserve 3rd District, quarterly rpt, 9387–10
Fed Govt spending in States and local areas, by type, State, county, and city, FY91, annual rpt, 2464–3
Fed Govt spending in States, by type, program, agency, and State, FY91, annual rpt, 2464–2
HHS financial aid, by program, recipient, State, and city, FY91, annual regional listing, 4004–3.2
Hospital deaths of Medicare patients, actual and expected rates by diagnosis, and hospital characteristics, by instn, FY90 annual State rpt, 4654–14.31
Housing census, 1990: summary unit characteristics, by householder race and age, county, place, and urban-rural location, State rpt, 2471–1.32
Military prime contract awards, by contractor, service branch, State, and city, FY91, annual rpt, 3544–22
Mineral Industry Surveys, State reviews of production, 1991, preliminary annual rpt, 5614–6
Multinatl firms US affiliates finances and operations, by industry, country of parent firm, and State, 1987, 2708–48
Physicians, by specialty, age, sex, and location of training and practice, 1990, State rpt, 4116–6.31
Population and housing census, 1990: detailed geographic coverage, State CD-ROM, 2551–9.2
Population and housing census, 1990: population and housing characteristics, detailed geographic coverage, State CD-ROM, 2551–10.36; 2551–10.37
Population and housing census, 1990: summary characteristics, by county, subdiv, and place, State rpt, 2551–7.32
Population census, 1990: population characteristics and living arrangements, by county, place, and urban-rural location, State rpt, 2531–1.32
Statistical Abstract of US, 1992 annual data compilation, 2324–1
Water quality, chemistry, hydrology, and other characteristics, 1990 local area study, 5666–27.27
see also Atlantic City, N.J.
see also Bergen County, N.J.
see also Hunterdon County, N.J.
see also Middlesex County, N.J.
see also Newark, N.J.
see also Somerset County, N.J.
see also Trenton, N.J.
see also under By State in the "Index by Categories"

New London, Conn.
see also under By City and By SMSA or MSA in the "Index by Categories"

New Mexico
Banks (insured commercial and savings) deposits by instn, State, MSA, and county, as of June 1991, annual regional rpt, 9295–3.6
Caballo Resource Area public land mgmt, and grazing, environmental, and leasing activities, FY90-91, annual rpt, 5724–17
Coal production and mines by county, prices, productivity, miners, and reserves, by mining method and State, 1990-91, annual rpt, 3164–25
County Business Patterns, 1990: employment, establishments, and payroll, by SIC 2- to 4-digit industry and county, annual State rpt, 2326–6.33
Deaths and rates, by detailed location, cause, and demographic characteristics, 1989, US Vital Statistics annual rpt, 4144–3.1
Employment by industry div, earnings, and hours, by southwestern State, monthly rpt, 6962–2
Employment, earnings, and hours, by selected SIC 1- to 4-digit industry, State, and for 275 MSAs, 1987-92, 6748–81
Fed Govt spending in States and local areas, by type, State, county, and city, FY91, annual rpt, 2464–3
Fed Govt spending in States, by type, program, agency, and State, FY91, annual rpt, 2464–2
Financial and economic devs, Fed Reserve 10th District, quarterly rpt, 9381–16
HHS financial aid, by program, recipient, State, and city, FY91, annual regional listing, 4004–3.6
Hospital deaths of Medicare patients, actual and expected rates by diagnosis, and hospital characteristics, by instn, FY90 annual State rpt, 4654–14.32
Housing census, 1990: inventory, occupancy, and costs, State fact sheet, 2326–21.33
Housing census, 1990: summary unit characteristics, by householder race and age, county, place, and urban-rural location, State rpt, 2471–1.33
Land Mgmt Bur activities in southwestern US, FY91, annual rpt, 5724–15
Military prime contract awards, by contractor, service branch, State, and city, FY91, annual rpt, 3544–22
Mineral Industry Surveys, State reviews of production, 1991, preliminary annual rpt, 5614–6
Multinatl firms US affiliates finances and operations, by industry, country of parent firm, and State, 1987, 2708–48
Peppers (dried chili and paprika) acreage and production in California and New Mexico, 1971-91, FAS annual circular, 1925–15.1
Physicians, by specialty, age, sex, and location of training and practice, 1990, State rpt, 4116–6.32
Population and housing census, 1990: detailed geographic coverage, State CD-ROM, 2551–9.8
Population and housing census, 1990: population and housing characteristics, detailed geographic coverage, State CD-ROM, 2551–10.9
Population and housing census, 1990: summary characteristics, by county, subdiv, and place, State rpt, 2551–7.33
Population census, 1990: population characteristics and living arrangements, by county, place, and urban-rural location, State rpt, 2531–1.33
Potash production, prices, trade, use, and sales, 1991-92 crop years, Mineral Industry Surveys, annual rpt, 5614–19
Radiation and other pollutant releases from DOE contractor research lab and nuclear weapons facilities, monitoring results, 1991 annual site rpt, 3324–2.4
Statistical Abstract of US, 1992 annual data compilation, 2324–1
Water quality and fish population in southwestern US streams, impacts of land mgmt and forest fires, 1980s-91, 1208–390
Water supply, and snow survey results, monthly State rpt, 1266–2.11
see also Albuquerque, N.Mex.
see also under By State in the "Index by Categories"

New Orleans, La.
CPI by component for US city average, and by selected metro area, region, and population size, monthly rpt, 6762–2
Drug abuse indicators for selected metro areas, research results, data collection, and policy issues, 1992 semiannual conf, 4492–5
Drug test results at arrest, by drug type, offense, and sex, for selected urban areas, quarterly rpt, 6062–3

Freight (waterborne domestic and foreign) by commodity, traffic, and passengers, by port and waterway, 1989, annual rpt, 3754–3.2
Fruit and vegetable shipments, and arrivals by city, by mode of transport and State and country of origin, 1990, annual rpt, 1311–4.2
Heroin prices and purity in 19 metro areas and Puerto Rico, by world area of origin, quarterly rpt, 6282–2
Housing and households characteristics, and unit and neighborhood quality, by MSA location for 11 MSAs, 1986 survey, supplement, 2485–8
Housing starts and completions authorized by building permits in 40 MSAs, quarterly rpt, 2382–9
Wages by occupation, and benefits, for office and plant workers, 1991 survey, periodic MSA rpt, 6785–16.1
see also under By City and By SMSA or MSA in the "Index by Categories"

New York Bight
Freight (waterborne domestic and foreign) by commodity, traffic, and passengers, by port and waterway, 1989, annual rpt, 3754–3.1
Shellfish and other species abundance on New York Bight floor, and impacts of sewage sludge disposal site phaseout, by site, 1980s, 2168–128
Water temperature, salinity, and density, by New York Bight site and depth, 1987-89, 2168–130

New York City
Alien workers discrimination and other employment-related problems in NYC, hotline calls, 1988, 6366–6.7
Banks (commercial) debits to demand deposits, and demand deposits and turnover, monthly rpt, 9365–2.5
Banks balance sheets, by Fed Reserve District, for major banks in NYC, and for US branches and agencies of foreign banks, weekly rpt, 9365–1.3
Commuters, by county of residence and work, for top 10 metro areas, 1990 Census of Population, press release, 2328–84
CPI by component for US city average, and by region, population size, and for 15 metro areas, monthly rpt, 6762–1
CPI by component for US city average, and by selected metro area, region, and population size, monthly rpt, 6762–2
Drug (heroin) seizures by Federal agencies, with NYC street prices and purity, FY82-91, GAO rpt, 26119–404
Drug abuse indicators for selected metro areas, research results, data collection, and policy issues, 1992 semiannual conf, 4492–5
Drug test results at arrest, by drug type, offense, and sex, for selected urban areas, quarterly rpt, 6062–3
Freight (waterborne domestic and foreign) by commodity, traffic, and passengers, by port and waterway, 1989, annual rpt, 3754–3.1
Fruit and vegetable shipments, and arrivals by city, by mode of transport and State and country of origin, 1991, annual rpt, 1311–4.1
Fruit and vegetable wholesale prices in NYC by State, and shipments and arrivals by mode of transport, by commodity, weekly rpt, 1311–20
Fruit and vegetable wholesale prices in NYC, Chicago, and selected shipping points, by crop, 1991, annual rpt, 1311–8
Fruit and vegetable wholesale prices in NYC-Newark, and arrivals by mode of transport, by commodity and State, 1990, annual rpt, 1311–21
Health condition and care indicators, for blacks and Hispanics in NYC, 1980s, conf paper, 4164–2
Heroin prices and purity in 19 metro areas and Puerto Rico, by world area of origin, quarterly rpt, 6282–2
Housing affordability and availability, impacts of govt land use regulations and rent control, and low income housing condition, 1991 hearing, 21248–174
Housing and households characteristics, and unit and neighborhood quality, by MSA location for 11 MSAs, 1987 survey, supplement, 2485–8
Housing rental and sales, discrimination against blacks and Hispanics in selected metro areas, 1989 study, 5186–16.2
Housing starts and completions authorized by building permits in 40 MSAs, quarterly rpt, 2382–9
Housing supply, occupancy, condition, and household characteristics, for NYC by tenure and borough, 1991 triennial survey, 2488–3
Immigration Reform and Control Act employer sanctions impacts on labor markets, with data for selected industries and metro areas, 1980s, working paper, 6366–6.10
Infectious notifiable disease cases and current outbreaks, by region and State, weekly rpt, 4202–1
Infectious notifiable disease cases, by age and State, and deaths, 1940s-91, annual rpt, 4204–1
Oil prices by product, for 4 cities, seasonal weekly rpt, 3162–45
Strikes, replacement workers hired, and impacts on firm operating capacity, with data for NYC, 1984-88, hearing, 21348–121
see also under By City and By SMSA or MSA in the "Index by Categories"

New York State
Appalachian Regional Commission funding, by project and State, planned FY92, annual rpt, 9084–3
Banks (insured commercial and savings) deposits by instn, State, MSA, and county, as of June 1991, annual regional rpt, 9295–3.1
Banks (multinatl) US branches assets and liabilities, total and for 3 States, monthly rpt, quarterly data, 9362–1.4
Birds (pigeon) population and survival rates in central New York, by harvest level, 1981-83, technical rpt, 5506–12.4
Celery acreage planted and growing, by growing area, monthly rpt, 1621–14
Dairy prices, by product and selected area, with related marketing data, 1991, annual rpt, 1317–1
Deaths and rates, by detailed location, cause, and demographic characteristics, 1989, US Vital Statistics annual rpt, 4144–3.1
Employment, earnings, and hours, by selected SIC 1- to 4-digit industry, State, and for 275 MSAs, 1987-92, 6748–81
Fed Govt spending in States and local areas, by type, State, county, and city, FY91, annual rpt, 2464–3
Fed Govt spending in States, by type, program, agency, and State, FY91, annual rpt, 2464–2
HHS financial aid, by program, recipient, State, and city, FY91, annual regional listing, 4004–3.2
Hospital deaths of Medicare patients, actual and expected rates by diagnosis, and hospital characteristics, by instn, FY90 annual State rpt, 4654–14.33
Housing census, 1990: summary unit characteristics, by householder race and age, county, place, and urban-rural location, State rpt, 2471–1.34
Indian low birthweight births, compared to whites and blacks, for New York, 1980s, article, 4042–3.359
Military prime contract awards, by contractor, service branch, State, and city, FY91, annual rpt, 3544–22
Mineral Industry Surveys, State reviews of production, 1991, preliminary annual rpt, 5614–6
Multinatl firms US affiliates finances and operations, by industry, country of parent firm, and State, 1987, 2708–48
Physicians, by specialty, age, sex, and location of training and practice, 1990, State rpt, 4116–6.33
Population and housing census, 1990: detailed geographic coverage, State CD-ROM, 2551–9.2
Population and housing census, 1990: population and housing characteristics, detailed geographic coverage, State CD-ROM, 2551–10.38; 2551–10.39; 2551–10.40
Population and housing census, 1990: summary characteristics, by county, subdiv, and place, State rpt, 2551–7.34
Population census, 1990: population characteristics and living arrangements, by county, place, and urban-rural location, State rpt, 2531–1.34
Radiation and other pollutant releases from DOE contractor research lab and nuclear weapons facilities, monitoring results, 1992 annual site rpt, 3324–2.5; 3324–2.9
Statistical Abstract of US, 1992 annual data compilation, 2324–1
Water resources data collection and analysis activities of USGS Water Resources Div District, with project descriptions, 1991 rpt, 5666–26.22
Water supply and quality in streams and lakes, and groundwater levels in wells, by drainage basin, 1991, annual State rpt, 5666–12.31
Water supply in northeastern US, precipitation and stream runoff by station, monthly rpt, 2182–3
see also Albany, N.Y.
see also Buffalo, N.Y.
see also Kingston, N.Y.
see also Long Island, N.Y.
see also Monroe County, N.Y.
see also Nassau County, N.Y.

see also New York Bight
see also New York City
see also Niagara Falls, N.Y.
see also Ontario County, N.Y.
see also Orange County, N.Y.
see also Poughkeepsie, N.Y.
see also Rochester, N.Y.
see also Schenectady, N.Y.
see also Suffolk County, N.Y.
see also Troy, N.Y.
see also under By State in the "Index by Categories"

New York Stock Exchange
Business statistics, detailed data for major industries and economic indicators, 1960-91, *Survey of Current Business* biennial supplement, 2704–1
Price indexes of NYSE for common stock, by type, 1966-91 with trends from 1952, annual rpt, 204–1.7
Stockbrokers with NYSE membership, securities credit issues, as of June 1991, annual rpt, 9365–5.1
Trading related to option and futures expirations, impacts on market decline of Nov 1991, 9738–22
Trading volume on NYSE, monthly rpt, 9362–1.1
Trading volume, securities listed by type, and finances, by exchange, selected years 1938-90, annual rpt, 9734–2.1; 9734–2.2

New Zealand
Agricultural production, prices, and trade, by country, 1980s and forecast 1992, annual world region rpt, 1524–4.3
Agricultural trade of US, by detailed commodity and country, 1991, annual rpt, 1524–8
Agricultural trade of US, by detailed commodity and country, 1991, semiannual rpt, 1522–4
Cuba trade, by commodity and country, mid 1980s-91, 9118–8
Economic and military aid and loans from US and intl agencies, by program and country, FY46-91, annual rpt, 9914–5
Economic and monetary trends, compounded annual rates of change and annual indicators for US and 15 trading partners, quarterly rpt, annual supplement, 9391–7
Economic conditions, policy, and trade practices, by country, 1989-91, annual rpt, 21384–5
Economic, social, political, and geographic summary data, by country, 1992, annual factbook, 9114–2
Exports and imports of US, by Harmonized System 6-digit commodity and country, 1991, annual rpt, 2424–13
Exports and imports of US, by selected country, country group, and commodity group, 1991, annual rpt, 2044–37
Exports and imports of US, by transport mode, country, and SITC 1- to 3-digit commodity, 1991, annual rpt, 2424–12
Exports, imports, and balances of US for manufactured goods, by SITC 2-digit commodity and country, quarterly rpt, 2042–35
Exports of US, detailed Schedule B commodities with countries of destination, 1991, annual rpt, 2424–10
Health care costs and components, services use, resources, and economic indicators, by OECD country, 1960s-90, article, 4652–1.322
Human rights conditions in 170 countries, and US economic and military aid, 1991, annual rpt, 21384–3
Imports of goods, services, and investment from US, trade barriers, impacts, and US actions, by country, 1991, annual rpt, 444–2
Kiwifruit from New Zealand at less than fair value, injury to US industry, investigation with background financial and operating data, 1992 rpt, 9886–14.345
Measles cases in New Zealand, by age and district, 1991, article, 4202–7.321
Military spending, arms trade, and force strengths, with govt spending and population, by country, 1979-89, annual rpt, 9824–1
Minerals Yearbook, Vol 3, 1989: foreign country review of production, trade, and policy, by commodity, annual rpt, 5604–35.2
Multinatl US firms and foreign affiliates finances and operations, by industry and country, 1989 benchmark survey, annual rpt, 2704–5
Multinatl US firms foreign affiliates, income statement items by asset size, industry, and country, 1988, biennial article, 8302–2.322
Oil production, stocks, use, and trade, by selected country and country group, monthly rpt, 3162–42
Oil supply, demand, and stock forecasts, by world area, quarterly rpt, 3162–34
Population size, growth rates, and components of change, by country, projected 1990-2020 and trends from 1950, biennial rpt, 2324–9
Refugee migration, and intl aid programs, by world area and country of origin and asylum, 1991, annual rpt, 7004–15
Steel (carbon flat-rolled) products from 21 countries, injury to US industry from foreign subsidized and less than fair value imports, investigation with background financial and operating data, 1992 rpt, 9886–19.85
Tax revenue, by level of govt and type of tax, for OECD countries, mid 1960s-90, annual rpt, 10044–1.2
UN voting record and share of votes in agreement with US, by issue, country, and world area, 1991, annual rpt, 7004–18
see also under By Foreign Country in the "Index by Categories"

Newark, N.J.
Drug abuse indicators for selected metro areas, research results, data collection, and policy issues, 1992 semiannual conf, 4492–5
Fruit and vegetable shipments, and arrivals by city, by mode of transport and State and country of origin, 1991, annual rpt, 1311–4.1
Fruit and vegetable wholesale prices in NYC-Newark, and arrivals by mode of transport, by commodity and State, 1990, annual rpt, 1311–21
Heroin prices and purity in 19 metro areas and Puerto Rico, by world area of origin, quarterly rpt, 6282–2
Housing and households characteristics, and unit and neighborhood quality, by MSA location for 11 MSAs, 1987 survey, supplement, 2485–8
Wages by occupation, and benefits, for office and plant workers, 1992 survey, periodic MSA rpt, 6785–17.1

Newcomb, Polly A.
"Screening Sigmoidoscopy and Colorectal Cancer Mortality", 4472–1.349

Newman, Douglas
"Effects of Environmental Actions on Tuna Trade", 9882–16.303
"Poultry, Industry and Trade Summary", 9885–8.6

Newman, Judy L.
"Presidential Popularity, Presidential Policies", 9393–10.17

Newport News, Va.
Housing starts and completions authorized by building permits in 40 MSAs, quarterly rpt, 2382–9

News reporting
see Freedom of the press
see Journalism

Newspapers
Advertising in newspapers, spending by ad type, *Survey of Current Business*, monthly rpt, 2702–1.6
Advertising in newspapers, spending by ad type, 1960-91, *Survey of Current Business* biennial supplement, 2704–1
Cigarette ad and promotion costs by media, and market shares, by cigarette type, with sales and use, 1963-89, annual rpt, 9404–4
County Business Patterns, 1989: employment, establishments, and payroll, by SIC 2- to 4-digit industry and county, annual State rpt series, 2326–8
County Business Patterns, 1990: employment, establishments, and payroll, by SIC 2- to 4-digit industry and county, annual State rpt series, 2326–6
CPI by component for US city average, and by selected metro area, region, and population size, monthly rpt, 6762–2
Employment, earnings, and hours, by SIC 1- to 4-digit industry, monthly 1989-Feb 1992, annual rpt, 6744–4
Employment of minorities and women, by occupation, SIC 1- to 3-digit industry, State, and MSA, 1991, annual rpt, 9244–1
Exports and imports between US and outlying areas, by detailed commodity and mode of transport, 1991, annual rpt, 2424–11
Exports and imports of US, by Harmonized System 6-digit commodity and country, 1991, annual rpt, 2424–13
Exports of US, detailed Schedule B commodities with countries of destination, 1991, annual rpt, 2424–10
Foreign travel to US and Canada, market analyses with detailed trip and traveler characteristics, country rpt series, 2906–2
Input-output structure of US economy, detailed interindustry transactions for 541 industries, and components of final demand, 1982 benchmark data, 2708–17
Mail volume to and from households, use, and views, by class, source, content, and household characteristics, FY87-90, annual rpt, 9864–10
Manufacturing annual survey, 1990: finances and operations, by SIC 2- to 4-digit industry, series, 2506–14

Manufacturing census, 1987: concentration of largest firms measured by value added, and for shipments by SIC 2- and 4-digit industry, subject rpt, 2497–6
Manufacturing census, 1987: shipments of manufacturers products, by customer class and SIC 2- and 4-digit industry, subject rpt, 2497–4
Manufacturing finances and operations, by SIC 2- to 4-digit industry, forecast 1992, annual rpt, 2044–28
Multinatl US firms and foreign affiliates finances and operations, by industry and country, 1989 benchmark survey, annual rpt, 2704–5
Occupational injury and illness rates, by SIC 2- to 4-digit industry, 1989-90, annual rpt, 6844–7
Occupational injury and illness rates, by SIC 2- to 4-digit industry, 1990, annual rpt, 6844–1
Price indexes (producer), by stage of processing and detailed commodity, monthly rpt, 6762–6
Price indexes (producer), by stage of processing and detailed commodity, monthly 1991, annual rpt, 6764–2
Recycling of paper by grade, with newsprint collection, recycling capacity by company, and curbside pickup operations, by State, 1970s-80s and projected to 1995, hearing, 25318–84
Science, engineering, and technical employment in manufacturing, by field and industry, 1989, triennial rpt, 9627–23
Soviet Union and US economic and sociodemographic indicators, selected years 1970-90, handbook, 2328–80
Statistical Abstract of US, 1992 annual data compilation, 2324–1.18
Tax (income) returns of corporations, income and tax items by asset size and detailed industry, 1989, annual rpt, 8304–4; 8304–21
see also Journalism

Newsprint
see Paper and paper products

Niagara Falls, N.Y.
CPI by component for US city average, and by selected metro area, region, and population size, monthly rpt, 6762–2

Niagara River
Water levels in Great Lakes, monthly and annual averages by station, 1860-1990, quinquennial rpt, 2178–1

Nicaragua
Agricultural trade of US, by detailed commodity and country, 1991, annual rpt, 1524–8
Agricultural trade of US, by detailed commodity and country, 1991, semiannual rpt, 1522–4
AID economic aid to developing countries, obligations and disbursements by country, quarterly rpt, 9912–4
AID loans repayment status and terms by program and country, and status of predecessor agency loans, quarterly rpt, 9912–3
Economic and dev aid of US by type, and foreign debt by creditor, for Nicaragua, FY90-91, GAO rpt, 26123–398
Economic and military aid and loans from US and intl agencies, by program and country, FY46-91, annual rpt, 9914–5
Economic and social conditions of developing countries from 1960s, and Intl Dev Cooperation Agency and AID activities and funding, FY91-93, annual rpt, 9904–4
Economic and social conditions, resources, and trade, and aid, 1992, annual factbook, 9914–14
Economic conditions, policy, and trade practices, by country, 1989-91, annual rpt, 21384–5
Economic indicators for Central America by country, 1969-89, working paper, 9916–13.4
Economic, population, and agricultural data, US and other aid sources, and AID activity, 1991 country rpt, 9916–12.56
Economic, social, political, and geographic summary data, by country, 1992, annual factbook, 9114–2
Exports and imports of US, by commodity and country, 1980-90, world area rpt, 9116–1.5
Exports and imports of US, by transport mode, country, and SITC 1- to 3-digit commodity, 1991, annual rpt, 2424–12
Exports of US, detailed Schedule B commodities with countries of destination, 1991, annual rpt, 2424–10
Food supply, needs, and aid for developing countries, status and alternative forecasts, 1992 world area rpt, 1526–8.2
Human rights conditions in 170 countries, and US economic and military aid, 1991, annual rpt, 21384–3
Military aid of US, arms sales, and training programs costs and budget requests, by program, world region, and country, FY91-93, annual rpt, 7144–13
Military spending, arms trade, and force strengths, with govt spending and population, by country, 1979-89, annual rpt, 9824–1
Population size, growth rates, and components of change, by country, projected 1990-2020 and trends from 1950, biennial rpt, 2324–9
Refugee migration, and intl aid programs, by world area and country of origin and asylum, 1991, annual rpt, 7004–15
UN voting record and share of votes in agreement with US, by issue, country, and world area, 1991, annual rpt, 7004–18

Nicotine
see Smoking

Nielsen, Rosemarie
"Effects of Adopting a Value-Added Tax", 26306–6.168

Niger
Agricultural trade of US, by detailed commodity and country, 1991, annual rpt, 1524–8
Agricultural trade of US, by detailed commodity and country, 1991, semiannual rpt, 1522–4
AID economic aid to developing countries, obligations and disbursements by country, quarterly rpt, 9912–4
AID loans repayment status and terms by program and country, and status of predecessor agency loans, quarterly rpt, 9912–3
Economic and military aid and loans from US and intl agencies, by program and country, FY46-91, annual rpt, 9914–5
Economic and social conditions of developing countries from 1960s, and Intl Dev Cooperation Agency and AID activities and funding, FY91-93, annual rpt, 9904–4
Economic conditions, income, production, prices, employment, and trade, 1991 periodic country rpt, 2046–4.4
Economic, social, political, and geographic summary data, by country, 1992, annual factbook, 9114–2
Exports and imports of US, by transport mode, country, and SITC 1- to 3-digit commodity, 1991, annual rpt, 2424–12
Exports of US, detailed Schedule B commodities with countries of destination, 1991, annual rpt, 2424–10
Human rights conditions in 170 countries, and US economic and military aid, 1991, annual rpt, 21384–3
Military aid of US, arms sales, and training programs costs and budget requests, by program, world region, and country, FY91-93, annual rpt, 7144–13
Military spending, arms trade, and force strengths, with govt spending and population, by country, 1979-89, annual rpt, 9824–1
Minerals Yearbook, Vol 3, 1989: foreign country review of production, trade, and policy, by commodity, annual rpt, 5604–35.1
Population size, growth rates, and components of change, by country, projected 1990-2020 and trends from 1950, biennial rpt, 2324–9
Refugee migration, and intl aid programs, by world area and country of origin and asylum, 1991, annual rpt, 7004–15
UN voting record and share of votes in agreement with US, by issue, country, and world area, 1991, annual rpt, 7004–18

Nigeria
Agricultural trade of US, by detailed commodity and country, 1991, annual rpt, 1524–8
Agricultural trade of US, by detailed commodity and country, 1991, semiannual rpt, 1522–4
AID economic aid to developing countries, obligations and disbursements by country, quarterly rpt, 9912–4
AID loans repayment status and terms by program and country, and status of predecessor agency loans, quarterly rpt, 9912–3
Drug abuse indicators, by world region and selected country, 1992 semiannual conf, 4492–5.2
Economic and military aid and loans from US and intl agencies, by program and country, FY46-91, annual rpt, 9914–5
Economic and social conditions of developing countries from 1960s, and Intl Dev Cooperation Agency and AID activities and funding, FY91-93, annual rpt, 9904–4
Economic conditions, income, production, prices, employment, and trade, 1992 periodic country rpt, 2046–4.39
Economic conditions, policy, and trade practices, by country, 1989-91, annual rpt, 21384–5
Economic, social, political, and geographic summary data, by country, 1992, annual factbook, 9114–2

Exports and imports of US, by commodity and country, 1980-90, world area rpt, 9116–1.2
Exports and imports of US, by Harmonized System 6-digit commodity and country, 1991, annual rpt, 2424–13
Exports and imports of US, by selected country, country group, and commodity group, 1991, annual rpt, 2044–37
Exports and imports of US, by transport mode, country, and SITC 1- to 3-digit commodity, 1991, annual rpt, 2424–12
Exports, imports, and balances of US for manufactured goods, by SITC 2-digit commodity and country, quarterly rpt, 2042–35
Exports of US, detailed Schedule B commodities with countries of destination, 1991, annual rpt, 2424–10
Food supply, needs, and aid for developing countries, status and alternative forecasts, 1992 world area rpt, 1526–8.2
Human rights conditions in 170 countries, and US economic and military aid, 1991, annual rpt, 21384–3
Imports of goods, services, and investment from US, trade barriers, impacts, and US actions, by country, 1991, annual rpt, 444–2
Military aid of US, arms sales, and training programs costs and budget requests, by program, world region, and country, FY91-93, annual rpt, 7144–13
Military spending, arms trade, and force strengths, with govt spending and population, by country, 1979-89, annual rpt, 9824–1
Minerals Yearbook, Vol 3, 1989: foreign country review of production, trade, and policy, by commodity, annual rpt, 5604–35.1
Multinatl US firms and foreign affiliates finances and operations, by industry and country, 1989 benchmark survey, annual rpt, 2704–5
Multinatl US firms foreign affiliates, income statement items by asset size, industry, and country, 1988, biennial article, 8302–2.322
Oil production, and exports and prices for US, by major exporting country, detailed data, monthly rpt with articles, 3162–24
Oil production, and exports and prices for US, by major exporting country, detailed data, monthly 1973-88, 3168–123
Oil production, stocks, use, and trade, by selected country and country group, monthly rpt, 3162–42
Population size, growth rates, and components of change, by country, projected 1990-2020 and trends from 1950, biennial rpt, 2324–9
Refugee migration, and intl aid programs, by world area and country of origin and asylum, 1991, annual rpt, 7004–15
Steel trade, by product, country, and customs district, with US industry operating data, 1989-June 1992, semiannual rpt, 9882–15
UN voting record and share of votes in agreement with US, by issue, country, and world area, 1991, annual rpt, 7004–18
see also under By Foreign Country in the "Index by Categories"

NIH
see National Institutes of Health

Nikishka, Alaska
Tide height and time daily at coastal points, forecast 1993, annual rpt, 2174–2.1

NIMH
see National Institute of Mental Health

NOAA
see National Oceanic and Atmospheric Administration

Nobel Prize
see Awards, medals, and prizes

Noell, Jay
"Undergraduate Enrollment and Completion Among Minorities", 26306–3.122

Noise
Air traffic controller and pilot hearing impacts of headset interference tones, 1992 technical rpt, 7506–10.100
Electric utilities privately owned, pollution abatement outlays by type of pollutant and equipment, and firm, 1990, annual rpt, 3164–23
Fed Govt financial and nonfinancial domestic aid, 1991 base edition with supplements, annual listing, 104–5
Health condition and care indicators, 1950s-90 with health improvement and disease prevention goals for 1990, annual data compilation, 4144–11
Neighborhood and housing quality, indicators and attitudes, by householder type and location, for 11 MSAs, 1987 survey, supplement, 2485–8
Neighborhood and housing quality, indicators and attitudes, by householder type and location, 1989, biennial rpt supplement, 2485–13
Neighborhood and housing quality, indicators and attitudes, MSA surveys, series, 2485–6
Neighborhood quality, indicators and attitudes of renter households, by whether receiving and eligible for HUD assistance, householder characteristics, and location, 1989, biennial rpt, 5184–11
Uranium tailings at inactive mills, remedial action proposals, costs, site characteristics, and environmental, socioeconomic, and health impacts, series, 3356–4
Whales (bowhead and white) migration through Beaufort Sea, behavior impacts of oil drilling and aircraft noise, spring 1990, 5738–27
see also Aircraft noise

Nolan, K. Michael
"Suspended-Sediment Budgets for Four Drainage Basins Tributary to Lake Tahoe, California and Nevada, 1984-87", 5666–27.32

Nolley, Jean W.
"Bulletin of Hardwood Market Statistics", 1202–4

Non-ferrous metals industry
see Aluminum and aluminum industry
see Copper and copper industry
see Lead and lead industry
see Metals and metal industries
see Tin and tin industry
see Zinc and zinc industry

Nonappropriated funds
Budget of US, CBO analysis of revenue and spending alternatives and projections of economic indicators, FY93-97, annual rpt, 26304–3
Budget of US, obligations and authority by function, agency, and program, with summaries and analyses, FY93, annual rpt, 104–2

Nonmarket economies
see Centrally planned economies

Nonmetallic minerals and mines
Alaska minerals resources, production, oil and gas leases, reserves, and exploratory wells, with maps and bibl, 1990, annual rpt, 5664–11
Business statistics, detailed data for major industries and economic indicators, 1960-91, *Survey of Current Business* biennial supplement, 2704–1
Cancer risk relation to occupational fluoride dust exposure, 1992 article, 4472–1.359
County Business Patterns, 1989: employment, establishments, and payroll, by SIC 2- to 4-digit industry and county, annual State rpt series, 2326–8
County Business Patterns, 1990: employment, establishments, and payroll, by SIC 2- to 4-digit industry and county, annual State rpt series, 2326–6
DOE R&D projects and funding at natl labs, universities, and other instns, FY91, annual summary rpt, 3004–18.3
Drug abuse screening and employee aid programs activities and policies in mining, by mineral and firm size, 1989, 6668–8
Employment, earnings, and hours, by SIC 1- to 4-digit industry, monthly 1989-Feb 1992, annual rpt, 6744–4
Employment of minorities and women, by occupation, SIC 1- to 3-digit industry, State, and MSA, 1991, annual rpt, 9244–1
Exports and imports between US and outlying areas, by detailed commodity and mode of transport, 1991, annual rpt, 2424–11
Exports and imports of US, by country and detailed commodity, monthly rpt, 2422–12
Exports and imports of US, by Harmonized System 6-digit commodity and country, 1991, annual rpt, 2424–13
Exports and imports of US, by selected country, country group, and commodity group, 1991, annual rpt, 2044–37
Exports and imports of US, by transport mode, country, and SITC 1- to 3-digit commodity, 1991, annual rpt, 2424–12
Exports, imports, and balances of US for manufactured goods, by SITC 2-digit commodity and country, quarterly rpt, 2042–35
Exports of US, detailed commodities by country, monthly CD-ROM, 2422–13
Exports of US, detailed Schedule B commodities with countries of destination, 1991, annual rpt, 2424–10
Fluorspar and other minerals trade, tariffs, and industry operating data, 1992 rpt, 9885–13.1
Foreign and US minerals industries operations, trends, and projections for selected countries, series, 5606–5
Foreign and US minerals supply under alternative market conditions, reserves, and background industry data, series, 5606–4
Freight (waterborne domestic and foreign) by commodity, traffic, and passengers, by port and waterway, 1989, annual rpt, 3754–3

Imports, exports, and employment impacts, by SIC 2- to 4-digit industry and commodity, quarterly rpt, 2322–2
Imports of US, detailed commodities by country, monthly CD-ROM, 2422–14
Input-output structure of US economy, detailed interindustry transactions for 84 industries, and components of final demand, 1987, annual article, 2702–1.316
Input-output structure of US economy, detailed interindustry transactions for 541 industries, and components of final demand, 1982 benchmark data, 2708–17
Labor productivity, indexes of output, hours, and employment by SIC 2- to 4-digit industry, 1967-90, annual rpt, 6824–1.2
Lime producing firms and plants, with operating data, 1991, Mineral Industry Surveys, annual listing, 5614–31
Limestone (crushed) from Mexico at less than fair value, injury to US industry, investigation with background financial and operating data, 1992 rpt, 9886–14.353
Manufacturing annual survey, 1990: finances and operations, by SIC 2- to 4-digit industry, series, 2506–14
Manufacturing census, 1987: concentration of largest firms measured by value added, and for shipments by SIC 2- and 4-digit industry, subject rpt, 2497–6
Manufacturing census, 1987: shipments of manufacturers products, by customer class and SIC 2- and 4-digit industry, subject rpt, 2497–4
Mineral Industry Surveys, commodity reviews of production, trade, stocks, and use, monthly rpt series, 5612–1
Mineral Industry Surveys, commodity reviews of production, trade, stocks, and use, quarterly rpt series, 5612–2
Mineral Industry Surveys, commodity reviews of production, trade, use, and industry operations, advance annual rpt series, 5614–5
Mineral Industry Surveys, State reviews of production, 1991, preliminary annual rpt, 5614–6
Minerals Yearbook, Vol 1, 1989: commodity reviews of production, use, trade, prices, and mining operations, annual rpt, 5604–33
Minerals Yearbook, Vol 1, 1990: commodity reviews of production, reserves, supply, use, and trade, annual rpt series, 5604–20
Minerals Yearbook, Vol 1, 1991: commodity reviews of production, reserves, supply, use, and trade, annual rpt series, 5604–15
Minerals Yearbook, Vol 2, 1989: State reviews of production and sales by commodity, and business activity, annual rpt series, 5604–16
Minerals Yearbook, Vol 2, 1990: State reviews of production and sales by commodity, and business activity, annual rpt series, 5604–22
Minerals Yearbook, Vol 3, 1989: foreign country reviews of production, trade, and policy, by commodity, annual rpt, 5604–35
Multinatl firms US affiliates finances and operations, by industry, country of parent firm, and State, 1987, 2708–48
Multinatl US firms and foreign affiliates finances and operations, by industry and country, 1989 benchmark survey, annual rpt, 2704–5
Occupational deaths in mining accidents, by circumstances and selected victim characteristics, semiannual rpt series, 6662–3
Occupational injuries and incidence, employment, and hours in nonmetallic minerals mines and related operations, 1990, annual rpt, 6664–1
Occupational injury and illness rates, by SIC 2- to 4-digit industry, 1989-90, annual rpt, 6844–7
Occupational injury and illness rates, by SIC 2- to 4-digit industry, 1990, annual rpt, 6844–1
Peat producing firms, with operating data, 1991, Mineral Industry Surveys, annual listing, 5614–32
Price indexes (producer), by stage of processing and detailed commodity, monthly rpt, 6762–6
Price indexes (producer), by stage of processing and detailed commodity, monthly 1991, annual rpt, 6764–2
Production, prices, trade, use, employment, tariffs, and stockpiles, by mineral, with foreign comparisons, 1987-91, annual rpt, 5604–18
Production, trade, use, and foreign investment in US industry, for minerals, 1985-90 and projected to 2000, annual rpt, 5304–5
Public lands minerals resources and availability, State rpt series, 5606–7
Publications and patents of Mines Bur, monthly listing, 5602–2
Salt production capacity, by firm and facility, 1991, annual listing, 5614–30
Soviet Union minerals production and exports, by commodity and Republic, 1975-90, annual rpt, 5604–39
Statistical Abstract of US, 1992 annual data compilation, 2324–1.25
Talc health effects, concentrations in food and environment, sources, human intake, and regulation, 1992 rpt, 9186–8.38
Tax (income) returns of corporations, income and tax items by asset size and detailed industry, 1989, annual rpt, 8304–4; 8304–21
Tax (income) returns of corporations with foreign tax credit, income and tax items by industry group, 1988, biennial article, 8302–2.316
Tax (income) returns of sole proprietorships, income statement items, by industry group, 1990, annual article, 8302–2.317; 8302–2.320
see also Asbestos contamination
see also Cement and concrete
see also Clay industry and products
see also Coal and coal mining
see also Fertilizers
see also Gases
see also Gemstones
see also Glass and glass industry
see also Natural gas and gas industry
see also Offshore mineral resources
see also Offshore oil and gas
see also Oil shale
see also Petroleum and petroleum industry
see also Phosphate
see also Potash
see also Pottery and porcelain products
see also Sand and gravel
see also Stockpiling
see also Stone products and quarries
see also Strategic materials
see also under By Commodity in the "Index by Categories"

Nonmetropolitan areas
see Rural areas
see under By Urban-Rural and Metro-Nonmetro in the "Index by Categories"

Nonprofit organizations and foundations
AID contracts and grants for technical and support services, by instn, country, and State, FY91, annual listing, 9914–7
AID loans repayment status and terms by program and country, and status of predecessor agency loans, quarterly rpt, 9912–3
Allergy and Infectious Diseases Natl Inst activities, grants by recipient and location, and disease cases, FY84-91, annual rpt, 4474–30
Arts Natl Endowment activities and grants, FY91, annual rpt, 9564–3
Assets and debts of private sector, balance sheets by segment, 1960-91, semiannual rpt, 9365–4.1
Blind and disabled persons reading materials from nonprofit agencies, FY91, annual listing, 26404–3
Child day care and early childhood education programs availability, demand, use, costs, and provider and enrollee characteristics, 1990 survey, 4808–39
County Business Patterns, 1989: employment, establishments, and payroll, by SIC 2- to 4-digit industry and county, annual State rpt series, 2326–8
County Business Patterns, 1990: employment, establishments, and payroll, by SIC 2- to 4-digit industry and county, annual State rpt series, 2326–6
Dental Research Natl Inst research and training grants, by recipient, FY90, annual listing, 4474–19
Disabled persons low income housing capital advances and rental aid of HUD, by recipient, FY92, press release, 5006–3.98
Disabled persons workshops finances, operations, and Federal procurement, FY82-91, annual rpt, 11714–1
DOE contracts and grants, by category, State, and for top contractors, FY91, annual rpt, 3004–21
Energy conservation aid of Fed Govt to public and nonprofit private instns, by building type and State, 1991, annual rpt, 3304–15
Fed Govt financial and nonfinancial domestic aid, 1992 base edition, annual listing, 104–5
Finances of nonprofit charitable and other exempt organizations, by asset and contributions size and category, 1988, annual article, 8302–2.315
Finances of nonprofit charitable organizations, summary data by asset size, 1989, article, 8302–2.325
Finances of nonprofit charitable organizations, with data by State and for top 10 instns, 1988, article, 8302–2.302

Finances of tax exempt organizations, with data by type, size, State, and for largest organizations, late 1940s-80s, compilation of papers, 8308–35
Foreign countries aid programs of private voluntary agencies, funding, and outlays, by agency, 1990, annual rpt, 9914–9
Foreign countries disasters, casualties, damage, and aid by US and others, FY91 and trends from FY64, annual rpt, 9914–12
Health care facilities for kidney end-stage disease treatment, by ownership, 1986-90, annual rpt, 4654–16.5
Health condition and care indicators, 1950s-90 with health improvement and disease prevention goals for 1990, annual data compilation, 4144–11
HHS financial aid, by program, recipient, State, and city, FY91, annual regional listings, 4004–3
Higher education enrollment, tuition, control, location, and other instn characteristics, 1991/92, biennial listing, 4844–3
Hospital deaths of Medicare patients, actual and expected rates by diagnosis, with hospital characteristics, by instn, FY90, annual State rpt series, 4654–14
Housing (low income rental) in rural areas, FmHA loans and impacts of programs to maintain supply and to deter mortgage prepayment, 1988-91, GAO rpt, 26113–586
Humanities Natl Endowment activities and grants, FY91, annual rpt, 9564–2
Investment funds (collective) assets, instns involved, and accounts, by type of fund and holding, 1991, annual rpt, 13004–1.3
Kidney end-stage disease treatment facilities approved by Medicare, dialysis and transplant services and ownership, 1991 annual listing, 4654–17
Mail operating costs of USPS, itemized by class of mail, FY91, annual rpt, 9864–4
Mail revenue and subsidy for revenue forgone, by class of mail, FY91, and volume from FY87, annual rpt, 9864–1
Mail revenue, costs, and volume, by class of mail, FY91, annual rpt, 9864–2
Mail volume, revenues, and subsidies for revenue forgone, by class of mail, FY91, annual rpt, 9864–5
Mail volume to and from households, use, and views, by class, source, content, and household characteristics, FY87-90, annual rpt, 9864–10
Mental health care facilities, staff, and patient characteristics, *Statistical Notes* series, 4506–3
Military prime contract awards, by category, contract and contractor type, and service branch, FY82-1st half FY92, semiannual rpt, 3542–1
Military prime contract awards, by category, contractor type, and State, FY89-91, annual rpt, 3544–11
Military prime contract awards for R&D, for top 500 contractors, FY91, annual listing, 3544–4
Military prime contract awards for R&D to US and foreign nonprofit instns and govt agencies, by instn and location, FY91, annual listing, 3544–17
NASA funding by program and type of performer, and contract awards by State, FY91, annual rpt, 9504–6.2
NASA procurement contract awards, by type, contractor, State, and country, FY92 with trends from 1961, semiannual rpt, 9502–6
Natl income and product accounts and components, *Survey of Current Business*, monthly rpt, 2702–1.23
Natl income and product accounts, comprehensive accounts and components, benchmark revisions, 1929-88, 2708–5
Natl income and product accounts, comprehensive accounts and components, *Survey of Current Business*, monthly rpt, 2702–1.29
Neighborhood Dev Demonstration program evaluation, grantee organization characteristics, activities, finances, and private sector support, 1984-89, 5188–119
NIH grants and contracts, by inst and type of recipient, FY82-91, annual rpt, 4434–9
NSF grants and contracts, by field, recipient, and State, FY90, annual rpt, 9624–26
NSF R&D grant awards, by div and program, periodic rpt series, 9626–7
Older persons low income housing capital advances and rental aid of HUD, by recipient, FY91, press release, 5006–3.88
Older persons low income housing capital advances and rental aid of HUD, by recipient, FY92, press release, 5006–3.97
Pacific territories population and housing detailed characteristics, by location, 1990 Census of Population and Housing, series, 2551–8
R&D and related funding of Fed Govt to higher education and nonprofit instns, by field, instn, agency, and State, FY89, advance annual rpt, 9626–8.2; 9627–17.1
Refugee arrivals and resettlement in US, by age, sex, sponsoring agency, State, and country, monthly rpt, 4592–1
Science and Engineering Indicators, employment, education, R&D funding, and industry impacts, with foreign comparisons, 1960s-91, biennial rpt, 9624–10
Science and engineering labor force, Federal and university research funding, and educational data, series, 9626–6
Statistical Abstract of US, 1992 annual data compilation, 2324–1.12; 2324–1.28
see also Membership organizations
see also Political action committees
see also Religious organizations

Norfolk, Va.
Freight (waterborne domestic and foreign) by commodity, traffic, and passengers, by port and waterway, 1989, annual rpt, 3754–3.1
Housing starts and completions authorized by building permits in 40 MSAs, quarterly rpt, 2382–9
see also under By City and By SMSA or MSA in the "Index by Categories"

Norry, Leonard J.
"Homeowners and Home Improvements: 1987", 2486–1.13

North America
Agricultural exports of US, for grains, oilseed products, hides, skins, and cotton, by country, weekly rpt, 1922–3
Agricultural trade of US, by commodity and country, bimonthly rpt, 1522–1
Agricultural trade of US, by detailed commodity and country, 1991, semiannual rpt, 1522–4
Air traffic and passengers, for intl routes over north Atlantic, by aviation type and route, alternative forecasts 1992-2010 and trends from 1982, annual rpt, 7504–44
Air traffic and passengers, for intl routes over Pacific, by route, alternative forecasts 1992-2010 and trends from 1980, annual rpt, 7504–51
Exports and imports (waterborne) of US, by type of service, customs district, port, and world area, monthly rpt, 2422–7
Exports, imports, and balances of US with major trading partners, by product category, 1987-91, annual chartbook, 9884–21
Immigrant and nonimmigrant visas of US issued and refused, by class, issuing office, and nationality, FY90, annual rpt, 7184–1
Immigrants admitted to US, by class of admission, country of birth, and MSA of destination, FY91, advance annual rpt, 6264–4
Immigrants and legalized aliens, by occupational group and country of birth, preliminary FY91, annual tables, 6264–1
Military spending, arms trade, and force strengths, with govt spending and population, by country, 1979-89, annual rpt, 9824–1
Terrorism (intl) incidents, casualties, and attacks on US targets, by attack type and world area, 1991, annual rpt, 7004–13
Tidal currents, daily time and velocity by station for North America and Asia coasts, forecast 1993, annual rpts, 2174–1
Tide height and time daily at coastal points, forecast 1993, annual rpt, 2174–2.2; 2174–2.3
Travel to and from US on US and foreign flag air carriers, by country, world area, and US port, monthly rpt, 7302–2
US military and civilian personnel and dependents, by service branch, world area, and country, quarterly rpt, 3542–20
Weather events and anomalies, precipitation and temperature for US and foreign locations, weekly rpt, 2182–6
Weather forecasts for US and Northern Hemisphere, precipitation and temperature by location, semimonthly rpt, 2182–1
see also Canada
see also Caribbean area
see also Greenland
see also Gulf of Mexico
see also Mexico
see also St. Pierre and Miquelon
see also under By Foreign Country in the "Index by Categories"

North American Free Trade Agreement
Agricultural trade tariffs affected by NAFTA, and NAFTA quotas, by commodity, 1992 article, 1925–34.332
Clothing exports to US, and domestic and US-owned industry production costs and

operations, for Caribbean area and Mexico, impacts of NAFTA, 1992 rpt, 9886–4.186
Employment impacts of NAFTA, issues and alternative estimates, 1992 rpt, 6366–3.30
Exports and imports of US, Canada, and Mexico, economic impacts of NAFTA, alternative model descriptions, 1992 conf, 9886–4.182
Exports and imports, trade agreements and relations, and USITC investigations, 1991, annual rpt, 9884–5
Mexico agricultural trade with US and Canada, and impacts of NAFTA, 1980s-90, 1528–330
Mexico agricultural trade with US, and impacts of NAFTA, 1980s-2000, article, 9381–1.307
Mexico and US economic and trade impacts of NAFTA proposal, with data on maquiladora plants, 1980s-90, hearings, 21788–210
Mexico fruit trade with US, 1989-91, and US tariffs under NAFTA proposal, 1992, by commodity, article, 1561–6.304
Mexico trade with US, and tariffs, by commodity, impacts of NAFTA compared to EC expansion to Mediterranean, 1970s-80s, 6366–3.29
Mexico-US trade agreement impacts on truck traffic at border crossings, Customs Service staff needs, and hwy improvement costs, projected to 2000 with trends from 1986, GAO rpt, 26123–368

North Atlantic Treaty Organization
Base construction and family housing, DOD appropriations by facility, service branch, and location, FY91-93, annual rpt, 3544–39
Base construction projects of NATO, and US funding, by project status, 1985-93, GAO rpt, 26123–388
Base construction, renovation, and closure, DOD budget requests by project, service branch, State, and country, FY93, annual rpt, 3544–15
DOD civilian and military personnel and dependents, by service branch and US and foreign location, quarterly rpt, 3542–20
Exports and imports of NATO members with Council for Mutual Economic Assistance Europe members, by country, annual rpt, discontinued, 7144–5
Exports and imports of NATO members with PRC, by country, annual rpt, discontinued, 7144–14
Military budget, procurement appropriations by item, service branch, and defense agency, FY91-93, annual rpt, 3544–32
Military forces reductions and ceilings for NATO and Warsaw Pact under CFE treaty, as of Nov 1990, 9828–1
Military forces reductions and ceilings for NATO and Warsaw Pact under CFE treaty, inspections, and US compliance costs and savings, 1991 hearings, 25388–59
Military personnel active duty and reserve end strengths of NATO, by country, 1988 and 1991, 26306–6.172
Military personnel of DOD abroad, by service branch, world area, and country, quarterly press release, 3542–9
Military personnel of US abroad, by country, FY91, annual rpt, 3544–1.2
Military personnel of US abroad, by service branch, outlying area, and country, quarterly rpt, 3542–14.5
Military spending and indicators of ability to support common defense, for NATO members, Japan, and South Korea, 1970s-90, annual rpt, 3544–28
Military spending, arms trade, and force strengths, with govt spending and population, by country, 1979-89, annual rpt, 9824–1
Officials of NATO, admissions to US, by country, FY81-91, annual rpt, 6264–2.3
Spacecraft and satellite launches since 1957, quarterly listing, 9502–2
UN voting record and share of votes in agreement with US, by issue, country, and world area, 1991, annual rpt, 7004–18

North Carolina
Appalachian Regional Commission funding, by project and State, planned FY92, annual rpt, 9084–3
Banks (insured commercial), Fed Reserve 5th District members financial statements, by State, quarterly rpt, 9389–18
Banks (insured commercial and savings) deposits by instn, State, MSA, and county, as of June 1991, annual regional rpt, 9295–3.2
Births of low birthweight to Medicaid patients, by prenatal care source and adequacy, and other risk factors, for 2 States, late 1980s, article, 4042–3.304
Blue Ridge Parkway impacts on local economic conditions and employment, by expense type, 1987, 7556–8.4
Blue Ridge Parkway traffic accidents, deaths, and circumstances, 1984-87, 7556–8.2
Child health screenings for Medicaid eligible population, rural physicians participation effects of promotional mailing, for North Carolina, 1990, article, 4042–3.358
County Business Patterns, 1990: employment, establishments, and payroll, by SIC 2- to 4-digit industry and county, annual State rpt, 2326–6.35
Deaths and rates, by detailed location, cause, and demographic characteristics, 1989, US Vital Statistics annual rpt, 4144–3.1
Economic indicators by State, Fed Reserve 5th District, quarterly rpt, 9389–16
Employment and housing indicators by State, FHLB 4th District, quarterly rpt, 9302–36
Employment by industry div, earnings, and hours, for 8 southeastern States, quarterly press release, 6942–7
Employment, earnings, and hours, by selected SIC 1- to 4-digit industry, State, and for 275 MSAs, 1987-92, 6748–81
Fed Govt spending in States and local areas, by type, State, county, and city, FY91, annual rpt, 2464–3
Fed Govt spending in States, by type, program, agency, and State, FY91, annual rpt, 2464–2
HHS financial aid, by program, recipient, State, and city, FY91, annual regional listing, 4004–3.4
Hospital deaths of Medicare patients, actual and expected rates by diagnosis, and hospital characteristics, by instn, FY90 annual State rpt, 4654–14.34
Housing census, 1990: inventory, occupancy, and costs, State fact sheet, 2326–21.35
Housing census, 1990: summary unit characteristics, by householder race and age, county, place, and urban-rural location, State rpt, 2471–1.35
Military prime contract awards, by contractor, service branch, State, and city, FY91, annual rpt, 3544–22
Mineral Industry Surveys, State reviews of production, 1991, preliminary annual rpt, 5614–6
Multinatl firms US affiliates finances and operations, by industry, country of parent firm, and State, 1987, 2708–48
Obstetrics rural practitioners malpractice insurance subsidy program funding and participation, for North Carolina, 1989-92, article, 4042–3.355
Physicians, by specialty, age, sex, and location of training and practice, 1990, State rpt, 4116–6.34
Population and housing census, 1990: detailed geographic coverage, State CD-ROM, 2551–9.5
Population and housing census, 1990: summary characteristics, by county, subdiv, and place, State rpt, 2551–7.35
Population census, 1990: population characteristics and living arrangements, by county, place, and urban-rural location, State rpt, 2531–1.35
Statistical Abstract of US, 1992 annual data compilation, 2324–1
Textile mill employment, earnings, and hours, for 8 Southeastern States, quarterly press release, 6942–1
see also Charlotte, N.C.
see also Gastonia, N.C.
see also Greensboro, N.C.
see also High Point, N.C.
see also Wilmington, N.C.
see also Winston-Salem, N.C.
see also under By State in the "Index by Categories"

North Central States
Banking industry structure, performance, and financial devs, for Fed Reserve 10th District, 1991, annual rpt, 9381–14
Birds (duck) breeding population, by species, State, and Canada Province, 1991-92 and trends from 1955, annual rpt, 5504–30
Bridges over navigable waters, with type of bridge and use, owner, dimensions, and location, 1991 regional listing, 7406–5.3
Business and economic conditions, Fed Reserve 9th District, quarterly journal, 9383–19
CPI by component for US city average, and by selected metro area, region, and population size, monthly rpt, 6762–2
Dairy prices, by product and selected area, with related marketing data, 1991, annual rpt, 1317–1
Deaths and rates, by cause and selected social, demographic, and employment characteristics, 1979-85, natl longitudinal study, 4478–186
Economic indicators and cyclical devs and outlook, by Fed Reserve Bank District, periodic rpt, 9362–8
Energy supply, demand, and prices, by fuel type and end-use sector, alternative projections by region, 1990-2010, annual rpt, 3164–96

Farm credit conditions and economic devs, Fed Reserve 7th District, monthly rpt, 9375–10
Farm credit conditions, earnings, and expenses, Fed Reserve 9th District, quarterly rpt, 9383–11
Financial and economic analysis, and economic issues affecting North Central States, working paper series, 9375–13
Financial and economic devs, Fed Reserve Bank of Chicago bimonthly journal, 9375–1
Financial and economic devs, Fed Reserve Bank of Cleveland quarterly journal, 9377–1
Financial and economic devs, Fed Reserve Bank of Kansas City quarterly journal, 9381–1
Financial and economic devs, Fed Reserve Bank of Minneapolis quarterly journal, 9383–6
Financial and economic devs, Fed Reserve Bank of St Louis bimonthly journal, 9391–1
Freight (waterborne domestic and foreign) by commodity, traffic, and passengers, by port and waterway, 1989, annual rpt, 3754–3.2; 3754–3.3
HHS financial aid, by program, recipient, State, and city, FY91, annual regional listing, 4004–3.5; 4004–3.7
Housing vacancy rates for single and multifamily units and mobile homes in FHLB 10th District, by ZIP code, annual MSA rpt series, 9304–22
Indian population and Indian-owned firms, by State for North Central States, selected years 1987-90, article, 9383–19.304
Lumber (industrial roundwood) production and timber harvest for North Central States, by product and county, State rpt series, 1206–10
Lumber (pulpwood) production and mill receipts in North Central States, by species, mill, State, and county, 1990, annual rpt, 1204–19
Lumber (pulpwood) production in 3 North Central States, by species and county, 1990, 1208–397
Pollution (air) regulation under Clean Air Act 1990 amendments, economic impacts with background data for Midwest and US, 1992 article, 9375–1.304
Savings and loan assns, FHLB 6th District insured members financial condition and operations by State, quarterly rpt, 9302–23
Savings and loan assns, FHLB 8th District members, locations, assets, and savings, 1992, annual listing, 9304–9
Savings instns, FHLB 6th and 11th District and natl cost of funds indexes, and mortgage and Treasury bill rates, monthly rpt, 9302–38
Savings instns, FHLB 7th District and natl cost of funds indexes, and mortgage rates, monthly rpt, 9302–30
Savings instns, FHLB 7th District members assets and deposits by instn and market area, 1987, annual rpt, discontinued, 9304–28
Services (producer) industries in Midwest, employment concentration by industry group, MSA, and urban-rural location, 1970s-89, article, 9375–1.305
Statistical Abstract of US, 1992 annual data compilation, 2324–1
Swine inventory, value, farrowings, and farms, by State, quarterly release, 1623–3
Temperature annual and seasonal averages by US region, and departures from normal by world area, 1860s-1990, annual rpt, 3004–33
Timber in Great Lakes area, aspen forest vegetation, climate, and other environmental characteristics, 1991 rpt, 1208–418
Timber in North Central States, harvest estimation methodology, 1991 rpt, 1208–419
Water storage and carriage facilities of Reclamation Bur, capacity, and operating status, as of Sept 1990, biennial listing, 5824–7
see also under By Region in the "Index by Categories"
see also under names of individual States

North Dakota

Banks (insured commercial and savings) deposits by instn, State, MSA, and county, as of June 1991, annual regional rpt, 9295–3.5
Birds (duck) population and nesting success in south-central North Dakota, by species, with habitat conditions, 1960s-81, 5508–120
Business and economic conditions, Fed Reserve 9th District, quarterly journal, 9383–19
Coal production and mines by county, prices, productivity, miners, and reserves, by mining method and State, 1990-91, annual rpt, 3164–25
County Business Patterns, 1990: employment, establishments, and payroll, by SIC 2- to 4-digit industry and county, annual State rpt, 2326–6.36
Deaths and rates, by detailed location, cause, and demographic characteristics, 1989, US Vital Statistics annual rpt, 4144–3.1
Employment, earnings, and hours, by selected SIC 1- to 4-digit industry, State, and for 275 MSAs, 1987-92, 6748–81
Fed Govt spending in States and local areas, by type, State, county, and city, FY91, annual rpt, 2464–3
Fed Govt spending in States, by type, program, agency, and State, FY91, annual rpt, 2464–2
HHS financial aid, by program, recipient, State, and city, FY91, annual regional listing, 4004–3.8
Hospital deaths of Medicare patients, actual and expected rates by diagnosis, and hospital characteristics, by instn, FY90 annual State rpt, 4654–14.35
Housing census, 1990: inventory, occupancy, and costs, State fact sheet, 2326–21.36
Housing census, 1990: summary unit characteristics, by householder race and age, county, place, and urban-rural location, State rpt, 2471–1.36
Military prime contract awards, by contractor, service branch, State, and city, FY91, annual rpt, 3544–22
Mineral Industry Surveys, State reviews of production, 1991, preliminary annual rpt, 5614–6
Multinatl firms US affiliates finances and operations, by industry, country of parent firm, and State, 1987, 2708–48
Physicians, by specialty, age, sex, and location of training and practice, 1990, State rpt, 4116–6.35
Population and housing census, 1990: detailed geographic coverage, State CD-ROM, 2551–9.4
Population and housing census, 1990: population and housing characteristics, detailed geographic coverage, State CD-ROM, 2551–10.43
Population and housing census, 1990: summary characteristics, by county, subdiv, and place, State rpt, 2551–7.36
Population census, 1990: population characteristics and living arrangements, by county, place, and urban-rural location, State rpt, 2531–1.36
Potato production, acreage, prices, and shipments, for 7 major producer States, and compared to other States, 1970s-92, annual rpt, 1311–29
Statistical Abstract of US, 1992 annual data compilation, 2324–1
Water resources data collection and analysis activities of USGS Water Resources Div Districts, with project descriptions, 1991 rpt, 5666–26.20
Water supply and quality in streams and lakes, and groundwater levels in wells, by drainage basin, 1990, annual State rpt, 5666–10.33
see also under By State in the "Index by Categories"

North, David S.

"IRCA Did Not Do Much to the Labor Market: A Los Angeles County Case Study", 6366–6.9

North Sea

Oil supply, demand, and stock forecasts, by world area, quarterly rpt, 3162–34

Northeast States

Construction, real estate, and other economic performance indicators, for New England compared to Texas and other areas, 1970s-91, article, 9373–1.302
CPI by component for US city average, and by selected metro area, region, and population size, monthly rpt, 6762–2
Dairy prices, by product and selected area, with related marketing data, 1991, annual rpt, 1317–1
Deaths and rates, by cause and selected social, demographic, and employment characteristics, 1979-85, natl longitudinal study, 4478–186
Economic and financial devs, Fed Reserve Bank of Boston quarterly journal, 9373–25
Economic indicators and cyclical devs and outlook, by Fed Reserve Bank District, periodic rpt, 9362–8
Economic indicators for New England States, Fed Reserve 1st District, monthly rpt, 9373–2
Electric power demand, and industrial and employment impacts of capacity shortfalls and new power plants, by selected State, 1960s-80s and projected to 2000, hearing, 21248–163
Energy supply, demand, and prices, by fuel type and end-use sector, alternative projections by region, 1990-2010, annual rpt, 3164–96

Financial and economic analysis, and economic issues affecting Northeast States, working paper series, 9373–27
Financial and economic devs, Fed Reserve Bank of Boston bimonthly journal, 9373–1
Fishing (ocean sport) activities, and catch by species, by angler characteristics and State, 1990-91, annual coastal area rpt, 2166–17.1
Freight (waterborne domestic and foreign) by commodity, traffic, and passengers, by port and waterway, 1989, annual rpt, 3754–3.1
Govt retirement systems investment policy assessment, with system assets and liabilities, by New England State, 1992 article, 9373–25.301
HHS financial aid, by program, recipient, State, and city, FY91, annual regional listing, 4004–3.1
Hurricane Bob atmospheric pressure and wind speeds, by location, Aug 1991, article, 2152–8.301
Immigrants from Colombia employed in New England textile industry, by selected characteristics, 1960s-80s, working paper, 6366–6.4
Lumber (industrial roundwood) production in northeastern US, by product, State rpt series, 1206–15
Lumber (pulpwood) production by species and county, and shipments, by northeastern State, 1990, annual rpt, 1204–18
Pollutant concentrations in coastal and estuarine fish, shellfish, and environment, late 1970s-89, local area rpt, 2176–3.14
Savings banks insured by Bank Insurance Fund, financial condition and performance, by asset size and region, quarterly rpt, 9292–1.2
Savings instns, FHLB 1st District members, financial condition, and locations, 1992, annual listing, 9304–26
Savings instns, FHLB 1st District members financial operations compared to banks, and related economic and housing indicators, bimonthly rpt with articles, suspended, 9302–4
Shipborne commerce (domestic) of US, freight by major commodity group, vessel type, and port, 1987-89, annual rpt, 7704–7
Statistical Abstract of US, 1992 annual data compilation, 2324–1
Temperature annual and seasonal averages by US region, and departures from normal by world area, 1860s-1990, annual rpt, 3004–33
Tide height and time daily at coastal points, forecast 1993, annual rpt, 2174–2.3
Timber in northeastern US, hardwood forests ecology and mgmt, 1992, 1208–405
Timber in northeastern US, resources and removals by species, ownership class, and county, State rpt series, 1206–12
Water supply in northeastern US, precipitation and stream runoff by station, monthly rpt, 2182–3
see also Appalachia
see also under By Region in the "Index by Categories"
see also under names of individual States

Northern Mariana Islands
Banks (insured commercial and savings) deposits by instn, State, MSA, and county, as of June 1991, annual regional rpt, 9295–3.6
Economic, social, political, and geographic summary data, by country, 1992, annual factbook, 9114–2
Exports and imports between US and outlying areas, by detailed commodity and mode of transport, 1991, annual rpt, 2424–11
Fed Govt spending in States and local areas, by type, State, county, and city, FY91, annual rpt, 2464–3
Fed Govt spending in States, by type, program, agency, and State, FY91, annual rpt, 2464–2
HHS financial aid, by program, recipient, State, and city, FY91, annual regional listing, 4004–3.9
Oil company overcharge settlements funds received, and conservation and energy aid spending, by outlying area, 1990, GAO rpt, 26113–564
Physicians, by specialty, age, sex, and location of training and practice, 1990, State rpt, 4116–6.53
Population and housing census, 1990: detailed characteristics, by location, outlying area rpt, 2551–8.2
Population size, growth rates, and components of change, by country, projected 1990-2020 and trends from 1950, biennial rpt, 2324–9
Statistical Abstract of US, 1992 annual data compilation, 2324–1.30
Supplemental Security Income recipients, by race, sex, living arrangements, age, eligibility, and State, quarterly rpt, 4742–1.2
see also Saipan, Northern Mariana Islands
see also under By Outlying Area in the "Index by Categories"

Northern spotted owl
see Endangered species

Norton, Arthur J.
"Marriage, Divorce, and Remarriage in the 1990's", 2546–2.166

Norway
Agricultural trade of US, by detailed commodity and country, 1991, annual rpt, 1524–8
Agricultural trade of US, by detailed commodity and country, 1991, semiannual rpt, 1522–4
AID loans repayment status and terms by program and country, and status of predecessor agency loans, quarterly rpt, 9912–3
Background Notes, summary social, political, and economic data, 1992 rpt, 7006–2.26
Cuba trade, by commodity and country, mid 1980s-91, 9118–8
Economic and military aid and loans from US and intl agencies, by program and country, FY46-91, annual rpt, 9914–5
Economic conditions, income, production, prices, employment, and trade, 1992 periodic country rpt, 2046–4.42
Economic conditions, investment and export opportunities, and trade practices, 1992 country market research rpt, 2046–6.1
Economic conditions, policy, and trade practices, by country, 1989-91, annual rpt, 21384–5
Economic, social, political, and geographic summary data, by country, 1992, annual factbook, 9114–2
Exports and imports of US, by Harmonized System 6-digit commodity and country, 1991, annual rpt, 2424–13
Exports and imports of US, by selected country, country group, and commodity group, 1991, annual rpt, 2044–37
Exports and imports of US, by transport mode, country, and SITC 1- to 3-digit commodity, 1991, annual rpt, 2424–12
Exports, imports, and balances of US for manufactured goods, by SITC 2-digit commodity and country, quarterly rpt, 2042–35
Exports of US, detailed Schedule B commodities with countries of destination, 1991, annual rpt, 2424–10
Health care costs and components, services use, resources, and economic indicators, by OECD country, 1960s-90, article, 4652–1.322
Human rights conditions in 170 countries, and US economic and military aid, 1991, annual rpt, 21384–3
Imports of goods, services, and investment from US, trade barriers, impacts, and US actions, by country, 1991, annual rpt, 444–2
Labor conditions, union coverage, and work accidents, 1991 annual country rpt, 6366–4.15
Military spending, arms trade, and force strengths, with govt spending and population, by country, 1979-89, annual rpt, 9824–1
Multinatl US firms and foreign affiliates finances and operations, by industry and country, 1989 benchmark survey, annual rpt, 2704–5
Multinatl US firms foreign affiliates, income statement items by asset size, industry, and country, 1988, biennial article, 8302–2.322
Oil exports to US by OPEC and non-OPEC countries, monthly rpt, 3162–24.3
Oil exports to US by OPEC and non-OPEC countries, monthly 1973-88, 3168–123.3
Oil production, stocks, use, and trade, by selected country and country group, monthly rpt, 3162–42
Population size, growth rates, and components of change, by country, projected 1990-2020 and trends from 1950, biennial rpt, 2324–9
Refugee migration, and intl aid programs, by world area and country of origin and asylum, 1991, annual rpt, 7004–15
Ships in world merchant fleet, tonnage, and new ship construction and deliveries, by vessel type and country, as of Jan 1992, annual rpt, 7704–3
Steel trade, by product, country, and customs district, with US industry operating data, 1989-June 1992, semiannual rpt, 9882–15
Tax revenue, by level of govt and type of tax, for OECD countries, mid 1960s-90, annual rpt, 10044–1.2
UN voting record and share of votes in agreement with US, by issue, country, and world area, 1991, annual rpt, 7004–18

see also under By Foreign Country in the "Index by Categories"
Nose and throat disorders
Cancer (esophageal) risk for relatives of cases in Yaocun Commune, Linxian, PRC, 1989, article, 4472–1.315
Cancer (nasopharyngeal) death risk by level of smoking and alcohol use, 1986, article, 4472–1.312
Cancer deaths and rates, by body site and selected social, demographic, and employment characteristics, 1979-85, natl longitudinal study, 4478–186
Cases of acute and chronic conditions, disability, absenteeism, and health services use, by selected characteristics, 1990, annual rpt, 4147–10.182; 4147–10.183
Disability and work limitations of persons with chronic health conditions, by condition, age, and sex, 1983-86, 4946–1.2
Tonsillitis and other infectious disease cases among children, and related disability and health care, by health insurance status and other characteristics, 1988, 4147–10.181
Notifiable diseases
see Infective and parasitic diseases
NOW accounts
see Negotiable orders of withdrawal accounts
NSF
see National Science Foundation
Nuclear accidents and safety
DOE contractor nuclear weapons facilities, contract fees, environmental and safety enforcement activity, and salaries, by contractor and facility, 1987-88, hearing, 21408–127
Hanford, Wash, nuclear plant, nearby population radiation exposure, with methodology, 1944-91, series, 3356–5
Incidents and mgmt of disasters and natl security threats, with data by major event and State, 1992 annual rpt, 9434–6
Inspections, regulatory, and licensing activities of NRC, budget and staff, by program, FY91-93, annual rpt, 9634–9
Inspections, regulatory, and licensing activities of NRC, with data for individual power plants, FY91, annual rpt, 9634–2
Intl Atomic Energy Agency Nuclear power plant safety inspection activities and emergency response procedures since 1986 Chernobyl accident, 1991, GAO rpt, 26123–367
Radiation exposure of population near commercial reactors, by body site, age group, and selected plant, 1988, annual rpt, 9634–7
Radiation exposure of workers at nuclear power plants and related facilities, by site, 1968-89, annual rpt, 9634–3
Radiation protection and health physics enrollment and degrees granted by instn and State, and grad placement, by student characteristics, 1991, annual rpt, 3004–7
Radiation protection and health physics enrollment and degrees granted by instn and State, and women grads plans and employment, 1991, annual rpt, 3006–8.19
Safety standards and research, design, licensing, construction, operation, and finances, for nuclear power plants with data by reactor, quarterly journal, 3352–4
Nuclear explosives and explosions
Marshall Islands Nuclear Claims Trust Fund financial condition, and health care benefits and enrollment, 1987-92, GAO rpt, 26123–405
Radionuclide concentrations in air, water, humans, animals, and milk near Nevada and other nuclear test sites, 1990, annual rpt, 9194–17
see also Nuclear weapons
Nuclear fallout
see Nuclear explosives and explosions
Nuclear industries
see Nuclear power
Nuclear medicine and radiology
Blue Cross-Blue Shield plans changes in physician costs per enrollee and for selected procedures, mid 1980s, article, 4652–1.320
Cancer (brain) diagnostic accuracy without use of computerized tomography scans and magnetic resonance imaging, 1985-89, article, 4472–1.309
Cancer (breast) risk relation to radiotherapy treatment for primary breast cancer, study, 1992 article, 4472–1.333
Cancer (secondary) risk for chronic lymphocytic leukemia, by treatment method, 1992 article, 4472–1.343
Cancer risk relation to radiologic Thorotrast exposure, Denmark study, 1992 article, 4472–1.338
Equipment shipments, trade, use, and firms, for electronic medical equipment by product, 1991, annual Current Industrial Rpt, 2506–12.34
FDA investigations and regulatory activities, quarterly rpt, 4062–3
Hospital discharges and length of stay, by diagnosis, patient and instn characteristics, procedure performed, and payment source, 1990, annual rpt, 4147–13.112
Hospital discharges and length of stay under old and new survey designs, by diagnosis, patient and instn characteristics, and procedure, Jan-Mar 1988, 4147–13.110
Hospital discharges by detailed diagnostic and procedure category, primary diagnosis, and length of stay, by age, sex, and region, 1990, annual rpt, 4147–13.111
Hospital employment and job vacancy rate, by occupation, and instn size and control, 1981-88, annual rpt, 4114–12
Labor demand, turnover, and training completions, by detailed occupation, 1990 and projected to 2005, biennial rpt, 6744–3
Labor supply and education of health professionals, by professional and other characteristics, and location, 1960s-92 and projected to 2020, biennial rpt, 4114–8
Labor supply of physicians, by specialty, age, sex, and location of training and practice, 1990, State rpt series, 4116–6
Manufacturing finances and operations, by SIC 2- to 4-digit industry, forecast 1992, annual rpt, 2044–28
Medicare admin and research, and HCFA affirmative action and accreditation programs, FY87, annual rpt, 4654–5
Medicare enrollees magnetic resonance imaging, endoscopic, and CAT scan procedures use rate, by State, 1986-90, annual rpt, 17266–1.7
Medicare payment of physicians, reforms impacts on services, and monitoring methods, 1992 annual rpt, 4004–34
Medicare payment of physicians under fee schedule, impacts on charges by specialty and State, 1992 and 1996, hearing, 25368–178
Medicare payment of physicians under fee schedule, methodology with data by procedure and specialty, 1992, annual rpt, 17264–1
Medicare reimbursement of hospitals under prospective payment system, ambulatory surgery and radiology proposed reform, 1992 rpt, 17206–1.15
Military health care personnel, and accessions by training source, by occupation, specialty, and service branch, FY90, annual rpt, 3544–24
Occupational Outlook Handbook, 1992-93, biennial rpt, 6744–1
Physicians visits, by patient and practice characteristics, diagnosis, and services provided, 1989, annual rpt, 4147–13.109
Physicians visits, by patient and practice characteristics, diagnosis, and services provided, 1990, advance rpt, 4146–8.215
Quality standards and review for health care facilities excluded from Medicare prospective payment system, certification, accreditation, and licensing, 1991 survey, 17206–2.41
Radiation exposure of workers at nuclear power plants and related facilities, by site, 1968-89, annual rpt, 9634–3
Radiation from electronic devices, incidents by type of device, and FDA control activities, 1991, annual rpt, 4064–13
Radiation protection and health physics enrollment and degrees granted by instn and State, and grad placement, by student characteristics, 1991, annual rpt, 3004–7
Radiation protection and health physics enrollment and degrees granted by instn and State, and women grads plans and employment, 1991, annual rpt, 3006–8.19
VA health care facilities physicians, dentists, and nurses, by selected employment characteristics and VA district, quarterly rpt, 8602–6
VA health care facilities trainees, by detailed program and city, FY91, annual rpt, 8704–4
VA health care services, needs, availability, structure, and funding, 1991 compilation of papers, 8608–9
VA health care staff and turnover, by occupation, physician specialty, and location, 1991, annual rpt, 8604–8
Waste (radioactive) generation, inventory, and disposal, 1960s-90 and projected to 2020, annual rpt, 3364–2
see also Mammography
see also X-rays
Nuclear power
Construction costs and status for nuclear power plants, and capacity, by plant, annual rpt, discontinued, 3164–69
Consumption of energy, by detailed fuel type, end-use sector, and State, 1960-90, State Energy Data System annual rpt, 3164–39
Criminal cases by type and disposition, and collections, for US attorneys, by Federal district, FY91, annual rpt, 6004–2.1

DOE R&D projects and funding at natl labs, universities, and other instns, FY88-90, triennial summary rpt, 3004–18.5
DOE real property owned and leased, by type, subagency, contractor, and site, FY91, annual rpt, 3004–28
Engineering (nuclear) enrollment and degrees by instn and State, and women grads plans and employment, 1974-90, annual rpt, 3006–8.18
Engineering (nuclear) enrollment and degrees granted by instn and State, and grad placement, by student characteristics, 1991, annual rpt, 3004–5
Environmental Quality, status of problems, protection programs, research, and intl issues, 1991 annual rpt, 484–1
Exports and imports of US, by Harmonized System 6-digit commodity and country, 1991, annual rpt, 2424–13
Exports of US, detailed Schedule B commodities with countries of destination, 1991, annual rpt, 2424–10
Finances and operations of energy producers, by energy type for US firms domestic and foreign operations, 1990, annual rpt, 3164–44
Foreign and US energy production and use, by energy type and country, 1981-90, annual rpt, 3164–50.1; 3164–50.5; 3164–50.7
Foreign and US energy supply and demand, by major fuel and end-use sector, 1950s-87 and forecast to 1995, 3166–6.58
Foreign and US energy use and production, by fuel type, country, and country group, projected 1995-2010 and trends from 1970, annual rpt, 3164–84
Foreign and US nuclear power generation, by market economy country, monthly rpt, 9112–2
Foreign and US oil dependency, energy demand, and efficiency measures, for 6 OECD countries, 1970s-80s, working paper, 9375–13.79
Govt direct spending and employment, by function and level of govt, selected years 1962-87, 10048–53
Great Lakes Science Advisory Board research activities and water quality goals, FY91, biennial rpt, 14644–6
Japan energy use and imports by fuel type, and gasoline prices, 1970s-80s, hearing, 21448–45
Mexico and US electric power supply, demand, and trade, with data by fuel source, utility, and region, 1970s-89 and projected to 2000, 3408–2
Natl Energy Strategy nuclear power, waste mgmt, and uranium enrichment issues, 1991 hearings, 21368–137
Natl Energy Strategy plans for conservation, R&D, security, and pollution reduction, technical rpt series, 3006–13
Pacific basin countries energy supply and demand, and implications for US trade, country rpt series, 3406–6
Power plants (nuclear) capacity and uranium needs, projected 1990-2005, annual rpt, 3164–82
Power plants and capacity, by fuel used, owner, location, and operating status, 1991, and for units planned 1992-2001, annual listing, 3164–36
Power plants capacity and investment by fuel type, and industrial and employment impacts of new power plants, by selected State, 1960s-80s and projected to 2000, hearing, 21248–163
Power plants capital and production costs, operations, and fuel use, by fuel type, plant, utility, and location, 1990, annual rpt, 3164–9
Power plants decommissioning and nuclear waste site remedial actions, bibl, 1991 annual listing, 3354–12
Power plants production, capacity, and fuel use, by fuel type, census div, and State, 1986-90, annual rpt, 3164–11.1
Power plants production, fuel use, stocks, and costs by fuel type, and sales, by State, monthly rpt, 3162–35
Prices and spending for fuel, by type, end-use sector, and State, 1990, annual rpt, 3164–64
Public knowledge, interest, and expectations for science and technology, 1990 survey, biennial rpt, 9624–10.7
Reactors for domestic use and export by function and operating status, with owner, operating characteristics, and location, 1991, annual listing, 3354–15
Regulatory, inspection, and licensing activities of NRC, budget and staff, by program, FY91-93, annual rpt, 9634–9
Regulatory, inspection, and licensing activities of NRC, with data for individual power plants, FY91, annual rpt, 9634–2
Rural Electrification Admin financed electric power plants, with location, capacity, and owner, as of Jan 1992, annual listing, 1244–6
Scientists and engineers employed in nuclear-related industries, by industry sector and occupation, 1983-91, 3006–8.20
Statistical Abstract of US, 1992 annual data compilation, 2324–1.19
Supply, demand, and prices, by fuel type and end-use sector, alternative projections by region, 1990-2010, annual rpt, 3164–96
Supply, demand, and prices, by fuel type and end-use sector, alternative projections 1990-2010, annual rpt, 3164–75
Supply, demand, and prices, by fuel type and end-use sector, projections and underlying assumptions, 1995-2010, annual rpt, 3164–90
Supply, demand, and prices, by fuel type and end-use sector, with foreign comparisons, 1981-90, annual fact book, 3164–76
Supply, demand, and prices, by fuel type and end-use sector, with foreign comparisons, 1991 and trends from 1949, annual rpt, 3164–74
Supply, demand, and prices, by fuel type, end-use sector, and country, detailed data, monthly rpt with articles, 3162–24
Supply, demand, and prices, by fuel type, end-use sector, and country, detailed data, monthly 1973-88, 3168–123
Supply, demand, and prices of energy, forecasts by resource type, quarterly rpt, 3162–34
TVA finances and operations by program and facility, FY91, annual rpt, 9804–32
Utilities finances and operations, detailed data for privately owned firms, 1990, annual rpt, 3164–23
Utilities finances and operations, detailed data for publicly owned firms, 1990, annual rpt, 3164–24
see also Nuclear accidents and safety
see also Nuclear explosives and explosions
see also Nuclear-powered ships
see also Nuclear weapons
see also Radiation
see also Radioactive waste and disposal
see also Uranium

Nuclear-powered ships
Budget of DOD, programs, policies, and operations, FY91, annual rpt, 3544–2
Radiation exposure of Navy personnel on nuclear-powered vessels and at support facilities, and injury claims, 1950s-91, annual rpt, 3804–10
Radioactive waste from Navy nuclear-powered vessels and support facilities, releases in harbors, and public exposure, 1970s-91, annual rpt, 3804–11
Reactors for domestic use and export by function and operating status, with owner, operating characteristics, and location, 1991, annual listing, 3354–15

Nuclear radiation
see Radiation

Nuclear Regulatory Commission
Activities, finances, and staff of NRC, with data for individual power plants, FY91, annual rpt, 9634–2
Activities of NRC, budget, staff, and activities by program, FY91-93, annual rpt, 9634–9
Budget of US, authoritative financial statements with appropriations, outlays, and receipts, by category and agency, FY91, annual rpt, 8104–2.2
Budget of US, obligations and authority by function, agency, and program, with summaries and analyses, FY93, annual rpt, 104–2
Education funding by Federal agency, program, and recipient type, and instn spending, 1960s-91, annual rpt, 4824–8
Labor unions recognized in Fed Govt, agreements and membership by agency and facility, as of Jan 1991, biennial listing, 9844–14
Nuclear engineering enrollment and degrees granted by instn and State, and grad placement, by student characteristics, 1991, annual rpt, 3004–5
Occupational radiation exposure at nuclear power plants and related facilities, by site, 1968-89, annual rpt, 9634–3
R&D and related funding of Fed Govt to higher education and nonprofit instns, by field, instn, agency, and State, FY90, annual rpt, 9627–17
Radiation exposure of population near commercial reactors, by body site, age group, and selected plant, 1988, annual rpt, 9634–7
Radiation protection and health physics enrollment and degrees granted by instn and State, and grad placement, by student characteristics, 1991, annual rpt, 3004–7
Radioactive materials shipments on US hwys, by material type, carrier, and shipper, 1985-90, 3008–129

Nuclear Waste Fund
see Government trust funds
Nuclear weapons
Budget of US, Bush Admin proposals, with detail for defense budgets, and historical data from FY34, FY93, 108–46.2
Budget of US, obligations and authority by function, agency, and program, with summaries and analyses, FY93, annual rpt, 104–2
DOE contractor nuclear weapons facilities, contract fees, environmental and safety enforcement activity, and salaries, by contractor and facility, 1987-88, hearing, 21408–127
DOE contractor research lab and nuclear weapons facilities radiation and other pollutant releases, monitoring results, annual site rpt series, 3324–2
Military budget, programs, and policies, FY91, annual rpt, 3544–2
Military prime contract awards, by detailed procurement category, FY88-91, annual rpt, 3544–18
NATO, Japan, and South Korea military spending and indicators of ability to support common defense, by country, 1970s-90, annual rpt, 3544–28
Reactors for domestic use and export by function and operating status, with owner, operating characteristics, and location, 1991, annual listing, 3354–15
Scientists and engineers employed in nuclear-related industries, by industry sector and occupation, 1983-91, 3006–8.20
Security at DOE nuclear weapons facilities, deficiencies by type and facility, 1989-90, GAO rpt, 26113–557
Treaties and agreements on arms control, status and Arms Control and Disarmament Agency activities, 1991, annual rpt, 9824–2
UN voting record and share of votes in agreement with US, by issue, country, and world area, 1991, annual rpt, 7004–18
Waste (low-level radioactive) from DOE military activities, disposal methods and costs, 1991, 3006–5.30
Waste (radioactive) from DOE military activities, repository research, transport, and disposal costs under alternative systems, 1983-89 and projected to 2094, 3368–5
Waste (radioactive) generation, inventory, and disposal, 1960s-90 and projected to 2020, annual rpt, 3364–2
see also Intermediate-Range Nuclear Forces Treaty
see also Nuclear explosives and explosions
see also Strategic Arms Reduction Talks
Numismatics
see Coins and coinage
Nurseries and nursery products
see Flowers and nursery products
Nursery schools
see Preschool education
Nurses and nursing
AIDS patients costs and service use under Medicaid, and service needs, for New Jersey waiver program, 1987-89, article, 4652–1.317
Earnings, annual average percent changes for selected occupational groups, selected MSAs, monthly rpt, 6782–1.1
Education in science and engineering, grad programs enrollment by field, source of funds, and characteristics of student and instn, 1990, annual rpt, 9627–7
Health condition and care indicators, 1950s-90 with health improvement and disease prevention goals for 1990, annual data compilation, 4144–11
HHS financial aid, by program, recipient, State, and city, FY91, annual regional listings, 4004–3
Home drug infusion therapy use, equipment, industry finances, and Medicare coverage options, 1992 rpt, 26358–258
Home health care for Medicare and non-Medicare patients, services use and nursing visits, for Virginia, 1983-85, article, 4652–1.302
Hospital deaths of Medicare patients, actual and expected rates by diagnosis, with hospital characteristics, by instn, FY90, annual State rpt series, 4654–14
Hospital employees and wages by occupation, and benefits, by region and selected MSA, 1991 survey, 6787–6.254
Hospital employment and job vacancy rate, by occupation, and instn size and control, 1981-88, annual rpt, 4114–12
Indian Health Service and tribal facility outpatient visits, by type of provider, selected hospital, and service area, FY91, annual rpt, 4084–3
Indian Health Service facilities, funding, operations, and Indian health and other characteristics, 1950s-91, annual chartbook, 4084–1
Insurance (health) coverage and provisions of employee benefit plans, by plan type, for State and local govt employees, 1990, biennial rpt, 6784–21
Labor demand, turnover, and training completions, by detailed occupation, 1990 and projected to 2005, biennial rpt, 6744–3
Labor supply and education of health professionals, by professional and other characteristics, and location, 1960s-92 and projected to 2020, biennial rpt, 4114–8
Medicare reimbursement of hospitals under prospective payment system, and effect on services, finances, and beneficiary payments, 1980-91, annual rpt, 17204–2
Mental health care facilities, staff, and patient characteristics, *Statistical Notes* series, 4506–3
Mental health care facilities, staff, patients, and finances, 1970s-91, biennial rpt, 4094–1
Military health care personnel, and accessions by training source, by occupation, specialty, and service branch, FY90, annual rpt, 3544–24
Military reserve medical personnel, by specialty and reserve component, FY91, annual rpt, 3544–31.1
Navy personnel strengths, accessions, and attrition, detailed statistics, quarterly rpt, 3802–4
Nursing homes certification requirements, beds, and staff and training needs, by State, 1990, 17206–2.37
Occupational Outlook Handbook, 1992-93, biennial rpt, 6744–1
OECD members health care costs, hospital use, resources, and economic and health indicators, by country, 1960s-90, article, 4652–1.322
Rural areas health care access for counties without hospitals and in which the only hospital closed, 1987-89, 17206–2.30
Soviet Union and US economic and sociodemographic indicators, selected years 1970-90, handbook, 2328–80
Statistical Abstract of US, 1992 annual data compilation, 2324–1.3
Tax (income) returns of sole proprietorships, income statement items, by industry group, 1990, annual article, 8302–2.317; 8302–2.320
VA health care facilities employment, FY67-91, annual rpt, 8604–5.1
VA health care facilities physicians, dentists, and nurses, by selected employment characteristics and VA district, quarterly rpt, 8602–6
VA health care facilities trainees, by detailed program and city, FY91, annual rpt, 8704–4
VA health care professionals employment, by district and facility, quarterly rpt, 8602–4
VA health care services, needs, availability, structure, and funding, 1991 compilation of papers, 8608–9
VA health care staff and turnover, by occupation, physician specialty, and location, 1991, annual rpt, 8604–8
see also Midwives
Nursing homes
AIDS patients costs and service use under Medicaid, for California, 1984-86, article, 4652–1.301
Certification requirements for nursing homes, beds, and staff and training needs, by State, 1990, 17206–2.37
Construction put in place, private and public, by type and region, monthly rpt, annual tables, 2382–4
Consumer spending, natl income and product account benchmark revisions, 1929-88, 2708–5
Consumer spending, natl income and product accounts, comprehensive accounts and components, *Survey of Current Business*, monthly rpt, 2702–1.25
Costs, use, and structure of private and public health care delivery, indicators, issues, and foreign comparisons, 1960s-80s, technical paper, 8006–6.1
County Business Patterns, 1989: employment, establishments, and payroll, by SIC 2- to 4-digit industry and county, annual State rpt series, 2326–8
County Business Patterns, 1990: employment, establishments, and payroll, by SIC 2- to 4-digit industry and county, annual State rpt series, 2326–6
Deaths during 1986, decedents health condition, services use, habits, and social, employment, and other characteristics, 4147–20.19
Employer-provided HMO and fee-for-service plan coverage of hospital care alternatives, 1989, article, 6722–1.302
Employment, earnings, and hours, by SIC 1- to 4-digit industry, monthly 1989-Feb 1992, annual rpt, 6744–4
Employment in nursing homes, 1981-88, annual rpt, 4114–12
Employment of minorities and women, by occupation, SIC 1- to 3-digit industry, State, and MSA, 1991, annual rpt, 9244–1

Energy use in commercial buildings, costs, and conservation, by building characteristics, survey rpt series, 3166–8
Expenditures and price indexes for nursing home services, and instn revenues, 1980s and projected to 1993, 10176–3.2; 10176–3.7
Expenditures for health care and factors in costs, with data by payment source and service type, 1960s-90 and projected to 2000, 26306–6.175
Expenditures for health care by funding source, 1990, with trends and indexes by service type from 1960, article, 4652–1.323
Expenditures, use, payment sources, and admin of health care services, with foreign comparisons, 1970s-90, chartbook, 21788–213
Family members supporting others outside household, by relationship, recipient living arrangements, and provider characteristics, 1988, Current Population Rpt, 2546–20.21
Govt finances, by level of govt, State, and for large cities and counties, annual rpt series, 2466–2
Health Care Financing Admin research activities and grants, by program, FY91, annual listing, 4654–10
Health Care Financing Review, provider prices, price inputs and indexes, and labor, quarterly journal, 4652–1.1
Health condition and care indicators, 1950s-90 with health improvement and disease prevention goals for 1990, annual data compilation, 4144–11
Input-output structure of US economy, detailed interindustry transactions for 541 industries, and components of final demand, 1982 benchmark data, 2708–17
Institutionalized population and persons in group quarters, by sex, race, county, place, and urban-rural location, 1990 Census of Population, State rpt series, 2531–1
Medicaid coverage, eligibility, and payment provisions of States, as of March 1992, annual rpt, 4654–19
Medicaid coverage, funding, and costs, with reform recommendations, mid 1960s-92, 10048–83
Medicaid outlay differentials among States, with data by service type and eligibility category, FY89, article, 9373–1.303
Medicaid reimbursement rates for nursing homes, and ratio to private resident payments, by State, FY89, article, 9373–1.311
Medicare admin and research, and HCFA affirmative action and accreditation programs, FY87, annual rpt, 4654–5
Medicare and Medicaid beneficiaries and program operations, 1992, annual fact book, 4654–18
Medicare and Medicaid enrollees, benefits, reimbursements, and services use, mid 1960s-90, annual rpt, 4744–3.5; 4744–3.6
Medicare and Medicaid regulations, nursing home compliance and patient characteristics, by facility, suspended annual State rpt series, 4654–15
Medicare reimbursement of hospitals under prospective payment system, and effect on services, finances, and beneficiary payments, 1980-91, annual rpt, 17204–2
Medicare reimbursement of hospitals under prospective payment system, methodology, inputs, and data by diagnostic group, 1992 annual rpt, 17204–1
Medicare reimbursement of nursing homes under prospective payment system, service availability, use, patient characteristics, and quality of care indicators, late 1980s-90, 17206–1.14
Occupational injury and illness rates and lost workdays, for selected industries, 1978-89, compilation of papers, 6728–41
Occupational injury and illness rates, by SIC 2- to 4-digit industry, 1989-90, annual rpt, 6844–7
Occupational injury and illness rates, by SIC 2- to 4-digit industry, 1990, annual rpt, 6844–1
Older persons health and long-term care needs, financial issues with background data, 1991 rpt, 10176–1.3
Older persons socioeconomic characteristics, 1900s-90 and projected to 2050, biennial chartbook, 12904–1
Older population, and health, economic, and other characteristics, with foreign comparisons, 1980s-91 with trends and projections, Current Population Rpt, 2546–2.165
Pacific territories population and housing detailed characteristics, by location, 1990 Census of Population and Housing, series, 2551–8
Population at risk of nursing home use, and admissions, by sex, projected 1990-2040, article, 1702–1.309
Quality of care in nursing homes, assessment methods using residents health condition, 1991 conf paper, 4164–2
Quality standards and review for health care facilities excluded from Medicare prospective payment system, certification, accreditation, and licensing, 1991 survey, 17206–2.41
Rural areas health care access for counties without hospitals and in which the only hospital closed, 1987-89, 17206–2.30
Statistical Abstract of US, 1992 annual data compilation, 2324–1.3
Supplemental Security Income and Medicaid eligibility and payment provisions, and beneficiaries living arrangements, by State, 1992, annual rpt, 4704–13
Tax (income) returns of corporations, income and tax items by asset size and detailed industry, 1989, annual rpt, 8304–4; 8304–21
Tax (income) returns of sole proprietorships, income statement items, by industry group, 1990, annual article, 8302–2.317; 8302–2.320
VA health care services, needs, availability, structure, and funding, 1991 compilation of papers, 8608–9
Veterans characteristics, and VA activities and programs, FY91, annual rpt, 8604–3
Veterans health care, patients, visits, costs, and operating beds, by VA and contract facility, and region, quarterly rpt, 8602–4
Vital and Health Statistics series: health care facilities use and labor force, 4147–13

Nutrition and malnutrition
Deaths and rates, by cause, age, sex, marital status, race, and State, 1989, US Vital Statistics advance annual rpt, 4146–5.124
Deaths and rates, by cause, provisional data, monthly rpt, 4142–1.2
Deaths and rates, by detailed location, cause, and demographic characteristics, 1989, US Vital Statistics annual rpt, 4144–3
Developing countries economic and social conditions from 1960s, and Intl Dev Cooperation Agency and AID activities and funding, FY91-93, annual rpt, 9904–4
Developing countries food supply, needs, and aid, status and alternative forecasts, world area rpt series, 1526–8
Education natl goals progress indicators, by State, 1992, annual rpt, 15914–1
Farm financial and marketing conditions, forecast 1992, annual conf, 1504–9
Fed Govt financial and nonfinancial domestic aid, 1992 base edition, annual listing, 104–5
Foreign countries agricultural research grants of USDA, by program, subagency, and country, FY92, annual listing, 1954–3
Foreign countries disasters, casualties, damage, and aid by US and others, FY91 and trends from FY64, annual rpt, 9914–12
Health condition and care indicators, 1950s-90 with health improvement and disease prevention goals for 1990, annual data compilation, 4144–11
HHS financial aid, by program, recipient, State, and city, FY91, annual regional listings, 4004–3
Homeless mothers and children nutrient intake, body measurements, and blood chemistry, 1989-90 local area study, article, 4042–3.330
Hypertension relation to diet diversity among Saba Islands residents, 1983-86 study, article, 4042–3.343
Latin America economic and social conditions, resources, trade, and aid, 1992, annual factbook, 9914–14
Mexican American obese women participation in weight loss and nutrition education programs, effectiveness, local area study, 1992 article, 4042–3.356
Mississippi poverty, hunger, and public welfare program operations and indicators of need, 1991 hearing, 21968–57
NIH nutrition biomedical and behavioral research and training activities and funding, by inst, FY90, annual rpt, 4434–15
Older persons in poverty, by health, nutrition, assistance, and other characteristics, 1990, GAO rpt, 26131–100
Public service announcements on nutrition displayed in supermarkets, effectiveness, local area study, 1992 article, 4042–3.371
Refugees, displaced persons, and population affected by famine, CDC recommendations for disease surveillance, control, and prevention, with background data, 1978-91, 4206–2.63

Research and education grants, USDA competitive awards by program and recipient, FY91, annual listing, 1764–1
Statistical Abstract of US, 1992 annual data compilation, 2324–1.3
Youth health condition, risk factors, and preventive and treatment services use and availability, 1970s-80s, 26358–234.2
see also Breast-feeding
see also Dietitians and nutritionists
see also Food assistance
see also Food consumption
see also Food ingredients and additives
see also Food supply
see also Obesity
see also School lunch and breakfast programs
see also Vitamins and nutrients
see also under By Disease in the "Index by Categories"

Nuts
Agricultural Statistics, 1991, annual rpt, 1004–1
Almond production, trade, use, and stocks, for 6 countries and US, 1990-93, annual article, 1925–34.337
Almond production, 1990-92, annual rpt, 1621–18.4
Cold storage food stocks by commodity and census div, and warehouse space use, by State, monthly rpt, 1631–5
Cold storage food stocks by commodity, and warehouse space use, by census div, 1991, annual rpt, 1631–11
Confectionery shipments, trade, use, and ingredients used, by product, 1991, annual Current Industrial Rpt, 2506–4.5
Consumption, supply, trade, prices, spending, and indexes, by food commodity, 1990, annual rpt, 1544–4
Exports and imports (agricultural) of US, by commodity and country, bimonthly rpt, 1522–1
Exports and imports (agricultural) of US, by detailed commodity and country, 1991, annual rpt, 1524–8
Exports and imports (agricultural) of US, by detailed commodity and country, 1991, semiannual rpt, 1522–4
Exports and imports between US and outlying areas, by detailed commodity and mode of transport, 1991, annual rpt, 2424–11
Exports and imports of US, by country and detailed commodity, monthly rpt, 2422–12
Exports and imports of US, by Harmonized System 6-digit commodity and country, 1991, annual rpt, 2424–13
Exports of US, detailed Schedule B commodities with countries of destination, 1991, annual rpt, 2424–10
Farm income, acreage, prices received, and production costs, for fruit, nut, and berry operations by commodity and region, 1987, article, 1561–6.301
Farm sector balance sheet, and receipts by detailed commodity, by State, 1986-90, annual rpt, 1544–18
Fertilizer and pesticide use and application rates, by type, crop, and State, 1991, 1616–1.3
Foreign and US fresh and processed fruit, vegetable, and nut production and trade, FAS monthly circular with articles, 1925–34
Hazelnut production, supply, trade, and use, for 3 countries and US, 1990-93, annual article, 1925–34.338
Hazelnut production, 1990-92, annual rpt, 1621–18.6
Input-output structure of US economy, detailed interindustry transactions for 541 industries, and components of final demand, 1982 benchmark data, 2708–17
Irrigation projects of Reclamation Bur in western US, crop production and acreage by commodity, State, and project, 1990, annual rpt, 5824–12
Macadamia nut industry competitiveness, investigation with background financial and operating data and foreign comparisons, 1992 rpt, 9886–4.189
Manufacturing annual survey, 1990: finances and operations, by SIC 2- to 4-digit industry, series, 2506–14
Manufacturing census, 1987: concentration of largest firms measured by value added, and for shipments by SIC 2- and 4-digit industry, subject rpt, 2497–6
Manufacturing census, 1987: shipments of manufacturers products, by customer class and SIC 2- and 4-digit industry, subject rpt, 2497–4
Pecan production and prices by State, and US trade by country, late 1980s-91, annual rpt, 1311–28
Pecan wholesale prices at selected shipping points, 1991, annual rpt, 1311–8
Pistachio production, trade, stocks, and use, for 5 countries, and US exports by country, 1987/88-1992/93, annual article, 1925–34.345
Pistachio production, 1990-92, annual rpt, 1621–18.7
Price indexes (producer), by stage of processing and detailed commodity, monthly rpt, 6762–6
Price indexes (producer), by stage of processing and detailed commodity, monthly 1991, annual rpt, 6764–2
Prices (wholesale) of fruit and vegetables in NYC by State, and shipments and arrivals by mode of transport, by commodity, weekly rpt, 1311–20
Prices (wholesale) of fruit and vegetables in NYC-Newark, and arrivals by mode of transport, by commodity and State, 1990, annual rpt, 1311–21
Prices received and paid by farmers, by commodity and State, monthly rpt, 1629–1
Prices received and paid by farmers, by commodity and State, 1991, annual rpt, 1629–5
Production, farms, acreage, and related data, by selected crop and State, monthly rpt, 1621–1
Production, prices, and use of fruit and nuts, annual rpt series, 1621–18
Production, prices, trade, stocks, and use, by selected crop, periodic situation rpt with articles, 1561–6
Statistical Abstract of US, 1992 annual data compilation, 2324–1.23
Walnut production, trade, stocks, and use, for 6 countries, 1990/91-1992/93, annual article, 1925–34.344
Weight and volume conversion factors for agricultural commodities and products, 1992 rpt, 1508–3
see also Oils, oilseeds, and fats
see also Peanuts

Nye, Lendell G.
"Confirmatory Factor Analysis of Burnout Dimensions: Correlations with Job Stressors and Aspects of Social Support and Job Satisfaction", 7506–10.103
"Dimensionality and Construct Validity of the Perceptions of Organizational Politics Scale (POPS)", 7506–10.106
"Gender, Equity, and Job Satisfaction", 7506–10.105
"Organizational Goal Congruence and Job Attitudes Revisited", 7506–10.104

Oak Ridge National Laboratory
"Assessment of Using Oil Shale for Power Production in the Hashemite Kingdom of Jordan", 3008–127
"Biomass Energy Development in Yunnan Province, China, Preliminary Evaluation", 3308–103
"Comparison of Methods To Integrate DSM and Supply Resources in Electric-Utility Planning", 3308–100
"Effects of Utility DSM Programs on Risk", 3308–105
"Electric-Utility DSM Programs: Terminology and Reporting Formats", 3308–101
"Electric-Utility DSM Programs: 1990 Data and Forecasts to 2000", 3308–106
"Handbook of Evaluation of Utility DSM Programs", 3308–102
"Integrated Data Base for 1991: U.S. Spent Fuel and Radioactive Waste Inventories, Projections, and Characteristics", 3364–2
"Nuclear Facility Decommissioning and Site Remedial Actions: A Selected Bibliography, Volume 12", 3354–12
"Public Involvement in Integrated Resource Planning: A Study of Demand-Side Management Collaboratives", 3308–104
"Transportation Energy Data Book: Edition 12", 3304–5
"Trends '91: A Compendium of Data on Global Change", 3004–33
see also Department of Energy National Laboratories

Oak, Steven W.
"Incidence and Impact of Oak Decline in Western Virginia, 1986", 1208–384

Oakerson, Ronald J.
"Metropolitan Organization: The Allegheny County Case", 10046–9.2

Oakland, Calif.
CPI by component for US city average, and by region, population size, and for 15 metro areas, monthly rpt, 6762–1
CPI by component for US city average, and by selected metro area, region, and population size, monthly rpt, 6762–2
Drug control street-level task forces enforcement activities, impacts on crime, and residents views, local area studies, 1992 rpt, 6068–251
Fruit and vegetable shipments, and arrivals by city, by mode of transport and State and country of origin, 1990, annual rpt, 1311–4.2
Housing and households characteristics, unit and neighborhood quality, and journey to work by MSA location, for 11 MSAs, 1985 survey, supplement, 2485–8

Housing and households characteristics, 1989 survey, MSA fact sheet, 2485–11.8
Housing and households detailed characteristics, and unit and neighborhood quality, by location, 1989 survey, MSA rpt, 2485–6.8
see also under By City and By SMSA or MSA in the "Index by Categories"

Oakland County, Mich.
Housing and households characteristics, unit and neighborhood quality, and journey to work by MSA location, for 11 MSAs, 1985 survey, supplement, 2485–8
Housing and households detailed characteristics, and unit and neighborhood quality, by location, 1989 survey, MSA rpt, 2485–6.2

OASDHI
see Old-Age, Survivors, Disability, and Health Insurance

Obesity
Cancer (colon) risk for men relation to weight-height index at college entrance and in middle age, and level of physical exercise, 1962-88 study, article, 4472–1.339
Diabetes patients physician office visits, by characteristics of patient, physician, and visit, 1989, 4146–8.212
Health condition and care indicators, 1950s-90 with health improvement and disease prevention goals for 1990, annual data compilation, 4144–11
Health risk behavior, prevalence of 7 habits, by age, State, and other characteristics, 1986-90, article, 4202–7.305
Heart disease risk factors prevalence in Missouri, 1989-90, article, 4042–3.302
Indian health risk behavior, by region and for Montana, mid 1980s, article, 4042–3.346
Mexican American obese women participation in weight loss and nutrition education programs, effectiveness, local area study, 1992 article, 4042–3.356

Obscenity and pornography
Child abductions, runaways, and missing and exploited children, and Office of Juvenile Justice and Delinquency Prevention activities, FY90, annual rpt, 6064–36
Court criminal case processing in Federal district courts, and dispositions, by offense, district, and offender characteristics, 1989, annual data compilation, 6064–29
Court criminal case processing in Federal district courts, and dispositions, by offense, 1980-91, annual rpt, 6064–31
Postal Service inspection activities, 2nd half FY92, semiannual rpt, 9862–2
Public opinion on crime and crime-related issues, by respondent characteristics, data compilation, 1992 annual rpt, 6064–6.2
Sentences for Federal offenses, guidelines by offense and circumstances, series, 17668–1
US attorneys civil and criminal cases by type and disposition, and collections, by Federal district, FY91, annual rpt, 6004–2.1

Obstetrics and gynecology
Health condition and care indicators, 1950s-90 with health improvement and disease prevention goals for 1990, annual data compilation, 4144–11
Hospital discharges and length of stay, by diagnosis, patient and instn characteristics, procedure performed, and payment source, 1990, annual rpt, 4147–13.112
Hospital discharges and length of stay by region and diagnosis, and procedures performed, by age and sex, 1990, annual rpt, 4146–8.211
Hospital discharges by detailed diagnostic and procedure category, primary diagnosis, and length of stay, by age, sex, and region, 1990, annual rpt, 4147–13.111
Indian Health Service and tribal facility outpatient visits, by type of provider, selected hospital, and service area, FY91, annual rpt, 4084–3
Indian Health Service outpatient services provided, by reason for visit and age, FY90, annual rpt, 4084–2
Indian Health Service, tribal, and contract facilities hospitalization, by diagnosis, age, sex, and service area, FY91, annual rpt, 4084–5
Infant health, deaths and risk factors, and prevention issues, for US and selected countries, 1990 conf, 4148–28
Labor supply and education of health professionals, by professional and other characteristics, and location, 1960s-92 and projected to 2020, biennial rpt, 4114–8
Labor supply of physicians, by specialty, age, sex, and location of training and practice, 1990, State rpt series, 4116–6
Malpractice insurance subsidy program for rural obstetrics practitioners, funding and participation, for North Carolina, 1989-92, article, 4042–3.355
Medicaid payment and participation by service type, and cost compared to Medicare, by State, FY89, 17266–1.4
Menopause treatment with hormone replacement therapy, use, health risks, and research funding, 1992 rpt, 26358–261
Military health care benefits and costs under Civilian Health and Medical Program of Uniformed Services, FY85-90, annual chartbook, 3504–23
Military health care personnel, and accessions by training source, by occupation, specialty, and service branch, FY90, annual rpt, 3544–24
Payment sources expected for hospital discharges, by diagnosis, patient characteristics, and region, and procedures performed, 1990, 4146–8.221
VA health care facilities physicians, dentists, and nurses, by selected employment characteristics and VA district, quarterly rpt, 8602–6
VA health care staff and turnover, by occupation, physician specialty, and location, 1991, annual rpt, 8604–8
Visits to physicians, by patient and practice characteristics, diagnosis, and services provided, 1989, annual rpt, 4147–13.109
Visits to physicians, by patient and practice characteristics, diagnosis, and services provided, 1990, advance rpt, 4146–8.215
see also Maternity
see also Midwives
see also Prenatal care

Occupational health and safety
Aircraft accidents and circumstances, for US operations of domestic and foreign airlines and general aviation, periodic rpt, 9612–1
Aircraft flight attendant work hour limitation proposals, with emergency evacuations and related casualties by incident, 1975-89, hearing, 21648–68
Aircraft pilot and flight attendant occupational injuries, illnesses, and lost workdays, for commercial carriers, mid 1970s-88, article, 6722–1.320
Alaska occupational injury deaths, by cause, occupation, and industry, early 1980s, article, 4042–3.307
Assistance (financial and nonfinancial) of Fed Govt, 1992 base edition, annual listing, 104–5
Auto and auto parts trade, production, and labor conditions, for US and compared to Canada and Mexico, 1950s-90, 6366–3.28
Aviation medicine research and test results, technical rpt series, 7506–10
BLS data collection, analysis, and presentation methods, by program, 1992 rpt, 6888–1
Cancer (leukemia) patients ras oncogene activation risk from occupational dust and chemical exposure, 1992 article, 4472–1.352
Cancer (pancreatic) death risk relation to occupational DDT exposure and other characteristics, 1982 article, 4472–1.314
Cancer risk relation to occupational fluoride dust exposure, 1992 article, 4472–1.359
Cancer risk relation to occupational herbicide exposure, 1992 article, 4472–1.356
Carcinogens chemistry, sources, environment and health risks, and regulation, by substance and brand, 1991 annual rpt, 4044–15
Child labor certification and injury reporting procedures of States, relation to proposed Federal guidelines, 1991, GAO rpt, 26121–451
Computer video display terminal use relation to musculoskeletal disorders, among telephone industry workers, 1990, 4248–93
Criminal cases by type and disposition, and collections, for US attorneys, by Federal district, FY91, annual rpt, 6004–2.1
Data on health condition and care, indicators, 1988 natl survey, CD-ROM, 4147–10.184
Deaths related to work injuries, by equipment type, circumstances, and OSHA standards violated, series, 6606–2
Deaths related to work injuries, data collection program of BLS and States, with results by selected worker characteristics, 1991, article, 6722–1.338
Disability, acute and chronic health conditions, absenteeism, and health services use, by selected characteristics, 1990, annual rpt, 4147–10.182; 4147–10.183
Diving (underwater) accidents, illnesses, and deaths, by circumstances, diver characteristics, and location, 1970-90, annual rpt, 2144–29

Electronic monitoring of employees, effects on mental and physical health and job satisfaction, for local telephone company workers, 1989, hearings, 21348–122
Fed Govt block and categorical grant programs for State and local govts, FY91, biennial listing, 10044–8
Fed Govt spending in States, by type, program, agency, and State, FY91, annual rpt, 2464–2
Fire fighter and civilian injuries and deaths in arson cases, 1986-89, 9438–14
Fire fighter deaths, by cause, circumstances, and location, 1990, annual rpt, 9434–8
Foreign countries labor conditions, union coverage, and work accidents, annual country rpt series, 6366–4
Grocery stores occupational injury and illness rates, and lost workdays by State, 1990, article, 6722–1.339
Hazardous substances industrial releases and reduction methods under EPA regulation, with chemical stocks and use, facility directory, 1987-89, annual CD-ROM, 9234–7
Hazardous substances occupational exposure, employer compliance with info and training regulations, employer views by firm size and industry div, 1989-91, GAO rpt, 26121–456
Hazardous substances occupational exposure, employer compliance with info and training regulations, inspections, and fines, by firm size and industry div, 1989-91, GAO rpt, 26121–439
Health care professionals supply and education, by professional and other characteristics, and location, 1960s-92 and projected to 2020, biennial rpt, 4114–8
Health condition and care indicators, 1950s-90 with health improvement and disease prevention goals for 1990, annual data compilation, 4144–11
HHS financial aid, by program, recipient, State, and city, FY91, annual regional listings, 4004–3
Injuries, illnesses, and lost workdays, by industry div and major manufacturing group, Monthly Labor Review, 6722–1.7
Injuries, illnesses, and lost workdays, by SIC 2-digit industry, 1990-91, annual press release, 6844–3
Injury and illness rates and lost workdays, for selected industries, 1978-89, compilation of papers, 6728–41
Injury and illness rates by circumstances and establishment size, and methodology for computing rates, industry rpt series, 6886–4
Injury and illness rates by SIC 2- to 4-digit industry, and deaths by cause and industry div, 1990, annual rpt, 6844–1
Injury and illness rates, by SIC 2- to 4-digit industry, 1989-90, annual rpt, 6844–7
Inspections, closure orders, and violations contested and upheld, for Federal and State occupational safety agencies, FY91, GAO rpt, 26121–461
Japan and US occupational injuries and illnesses, and lost workday and death rates, late 1950s-88, article, 6722–1.318
Labor laws enacted, by State, 1991, annual article, 6722–1.309
Law enforcement officer deaths by circumstances, agency, victim characteristics, and location, 1990, annual rpt, 6224–3
Metal structural fabrication industry occupational injury and illness rates and lost workdays, by State, 1989, 6722–1.301
NASA accidents, casualties, damage, and safety activities, FY91, annual rpt, 9504–4
Navy personnel radiation exposure on nuclear-powered vessels and at support facilities, and injury claims, 1950s-91, annual rpt, 3804–10
Nuclear power plant occupational radiation exposure, by site, 1968-89, annual rpt, 9634–3
Nuclear weapons facilities of DOE, contractor fees, environmental and safety enforcement activity, and salaries, by contractor and facility, 1987-88, hearing, 21408–127
Occupational Outlook Handbook, 1992-93, biennial rpt, 6744–1
Occupational Safety and Health Admin activities and grants, press release series, 6606–3
Occupational Safety and Health Admin penalties assessed compared to maximum allowable, by firm size and region, FY89, GAO rpt, 26121–455
Petrochemicals industries contract labor accidents, injuries, safety programs operations, and employee characteristics, 1986-91, 6608–6
Physicians, by specialty, age, sex, and location of training and practice, 1990, State rpt series, 4116–6
Pollutants health effects, concentrations in food and environment, sources, human intake, and regulation, series, 9186–8
Postal Service employment and related expenses, FY91, annual rpt, 9864–5.1
Prevention of accidental injury and death, and treatment, 1991 conf papers, 4208–35
Radiation protection and health physics enrollment and degrees granted by instn and State, and grad placement, by student characteristics, 1991, annual rpt, 3004–7
Radiation protection and health physics enrollment and degrees granted by instn and State, and women grads plans and employment, 1991, annual rpt, 3006–8.19
Railroad accidents, casualties, and damage, by cause, railroad, and State, 1991, annual rpt, 7604–1
Railroad accidents, casualties, and damage, Fed Railroad Admin activities, and safety inspectors by State, 1990, annual rpt, 7604–12
Railroad accidents, casualties, circumstances, and railroad involved, 1988, annual rpt, 9614–8
Railroad accidents caused by human factors, and safety impacts of engineer work scheduling, 1989-90, GAO rpt, 26113–579
Railroad accidents involving hazardous materials, casualties, and circumstances, 1984-89, 9618–18
Railroad-hwy grade-crossing accidents, detailed data by State and railroad, 1991, annual rpt, 7604–2
Railroad safety violation claims settled, by carrier, FY91, annual rpt, 7604–10
Repetitive motion injury rates by selected industry, with data for California, 1980s, hearing, 21408–128
Soft drink industry occupational injury and illness rate and lost workdays, for 7 States, mid 1970s-90, article, 6722–1.319
Statistical Abstract of US, 1992 annual data compilation, 2324–1.13
Truck accidents, casualties, and damage, by circumstances and characteristics of persons and vehicles involved, 1989, annual rpt, 7554–9
Truck accidents, circumstances, and characteristics of vehicles and persons involved, 1979-86, 7768–124
Vermont smoking laws compliance of employers, 1989, article, 4042–3.375
see also Agricultural accidents and safety
see also Assaults on police
see also Black lung disease
see also Mine accidents and safety
see also Workers compensation

Occupational Safety and Health Administration
Activities and grants of OSHA, press release series, 6606–3
Budget of US, obligations and authority by function, agency, and program, with summaries and analyses, FY93, annual rpt, 104–2
Deaths related to work injuries, by equipment type, circumstances, and OSHA standards violated, series, 6606–2
Expenditures of Fed Govt in States, by type, program, agency, and State, FY91, annual rpt, 2464–2
Hazardous substances occupational exposure, employer compliance with info and training regulations, employer views by firm size and industry div, 1989-91, GAO rpt, 26121–456
Hazardous substances occupational exposure, employer compliance with info and training regulations, inspections, and fines, by firm size and industry div, 1989-91, GAO rpt, 26121–439
Inspections, closure orders, and violations contested and upheld, for Federal and State occupational safety agencies, FY91, GAO rpt, 26121–461
Penalties assessed by OSHA compared to maximum allowable, by firm size and region, FY89, GAO rpt, 26121–455
Petrochemicals industries contract labor accidents, injuries, safety programs operations, and employee characteristics, 1986-91, 6608–6

Occupational Safety and Health Review Commission
Budget of US, obligations and authority by function, agency, and program, with summaries and analyses, FY93, annual rpt, 104–2
Labor unions recognized in Fed Govt, agreements and membership by agency and facility, as of Jan 1991, biennial listing, 9844–14

Occupational testing and certification
Air traffic control supervisor selection, relation to screening test and technical training performance, 1980s, technical rpt, 7506–10.116
Air traffic controller academy grads and military hires, training performance, facility assignments, and selected characteristics, 1988, 7506–10.101

Air traffic controller screening results relation to intelligence test scores, 1992 technical rpt, 7506–10.126
Air traffic controller visual skills test, evaluation, 1992 technical rpt, 7506–10.108
Aircraft pilot and nonpilot certificates held and issued, by type of certificate, region, State, and for women, 1990, annual rpt, 7504–1.7
Aircraft pilot and nonpilot certificates held, by type of certificate, age, sex, region, and State, 1991, annual rpt, 7504–2
Aircraft pilot neuropsychological screening tests accuracy, 1992 technical rpt, 7506–10.107
Diving (underwater) accidents, illnesses, and deaths, by circumstances, diver characteristics, and location, 1970-90, annual rpt, 2144–29
Education (elementary and secondary) schools, teachers, staff, and enrollment, by selected characteristics, 1987/88-1988/89, 4836–3.10
Health care professionals licensing and disciplinary actions of State medical boards, 1950s-88, series, 4006–8
Merchant ship crew supply, wartime needs, training, and sources, 1970s-90 and alternative projections to 2000, 7708–5
Nursing homes certification requirements, beds, and staff and training needs, by State, 1990, 17206–2.37
Physicians and dentists with board certification, VA employment by specialty, quarterly rpt, 8602–6
Physicians, by specialty, age, sex, and location of training and practice, 1990, State rpt series, 4116–6
Physicians with board certification, and other characteristics of Medicare hospital providers, by instn, 1990, annual State rpt series, 4654–14
Police employment, spending, and operations, for State, city, county, and special district agencies, 1990, annual rpt, 6064–39
Teacher testing for State certification, listing of laws, 1992 annual data compilation, 4824–2.14
Teachers and other special education staff, training, degrees, and certification, by field and State, FY89, annual rpt, 4944–4
Training for job qualification and skill improvement, workers participating by training source, occupation, age, sex, and race, 1991, 6728–32
Vocational education enrollment, student and teacher characteristics, and outcomes, for secondary and postsecondary instns, 1970s-90, 4828–42

Occupational therapy
Hospital employment and job vacancy rate, by occupation, and instn size and control, 1981-88, annual rpt, 4114–12
Labor demand, turnover, and training completions, by detailed occupation, 1990 and projected to 2005, biennial rpt, 6744–3
Labor supply and education of health professionals, by professional and other characteristics, and location, 1960s-92 and projected to 2020, biennial rpt, 4114–8
Mental health care of affective disorder patients, by patient and facility characteristics, 1986, 4506–3.49
Military health care personnel, and accessions by training source, by occupation, specialty, and service branch, FY90, annual rpt, 3544–24
Occupational Outlook Handbook, 1992-93, biennial rpt, 6744–1
Special education programs, enrollment by age, staff, funding, and needs, by type of handicap and State, 1990/91, annual rpt, 4944–4
VA health care staff and turnover, by occupation, physician specialty, and location, 1991, annual rpt, 8604–8
see also Vocational rehabilitation

Occupational training
see Employee development
see Vocational education and training

Occupational wage surveys
see Area wage surveys
see Industry wage surveys

Occupations
Census of Population and Housing, 1990: industry and occupation classification codes, alphabetical index, 2628–1
Census of Population and Housing, 1990: industry and occupation classification codes, classified index, 2628–2
Census of Population and Housing, 1990: population and housing characteristics, detailed geographic coverage, State CD-ROM series, 2551–10
Credit unions finances, by occupational membership category, as of June 1992, semiannual rpt, 9532–6
Criminal sentences for Federal offenses, guidelines by offense and circumstances, series, 17668–1
Earnings distribution among and within selected groups, by demographic and employment characteristics, late 1960s-80s, article, 6722–1.328
Forecasts of employment by occupation, accuracy of BLS forecasts for 1990 made 1980, article, 6722–1.336
Forecasts of employment by occupation, accuracy of BLS forecasts for 1990 made 1982, article, 6742–1.302
Labor demand, turnover, and training completions, by detailed occupation, 1990 and projected to 2005, biennial rpt, 6744–3
Occupational Outlook Handbook, 1992-93, biennial rpt, 6744–1
Occupational Outlook Quarterly, journal, 6742–1
Pacific territories population and housing detailed characteristics, by location, 1990 Census of Population and Housing, series, 2551–8
Separations, replacement rates, and related job openings, estimation procedures with data by occupation, age, and sex, late 1980s and projected to 2005, 6748–84
Statistical Abstract of US, 1992 annual data compilation, 2324–1.13
Technological devs effect on labor force, composition, and productivity, 1970s-90 and projected to 2005, industry rpt series, 6826–2
Wage differentials relation to worker occupation and employer, model description and results, 1991 working paper, 9377–9.130
Women's labor force status, earnings, and other characteristics, with comparisons to men, fact sheet series, 6564–1
see also Agricultural labor
see also Blue collar workers
see also Business management
see also Clergy
see also Clerical workers
see also Consultants
see also Domestic workers and services
see also Employee development
see also Engineers and engineering
see also Executives and managers
see also Health occupations
see also Job tenure
see also Judges
see also Lawyers and legal services
see also Librarians
see also Military personnel
see also Occupational testing and certification
see also Pilots
see also Postal employees
see also Production workers
see also Professional and technical workers
see also Sales workers
see also Scientists and technicians
see also Service workers
see also Teachers
see also Vocational education and training
see also Vocational guidance
see also Writers and writing
see also under By Occupation in the "Index by Categories"

Ocean liners
see Passenger ships

Ocean pollution
see Marine pollution

Ocean resources
see Marine resources

Oceania
Agricultural exports of US, for grains, oilseed products, hides, skins, and cotton, by country, weekly rpt, 1922–3
Agricultural trade by commodity and country, prices, and world market devs, monthly rpt, 1922–12
Agricultural trade of US, by commodity and country, bimonthly rpt, 1522–1
Agricultural trade of US, by detailed commodity and country, 1991, annual rpt, 1524–8
Agricultural trade of US, by detailed commodity and country, 1991, semiannual rpt, 1522–4
Cancer death rates, by body site, sex, and world area, 1969 and annual percent change 1969-86, article, 4472–1.306
Economic and military aid and loans from US and intl agencies, by program and country, FY46-91, annual rpt, 9914–5
Energy supply and demand for Pacific basin, and implications for US trade, country rpt series, 3406–6
Exports and imports (waterborne) of US, by type of service, customs district, port, and world area, monthly rpt, 2422–7
Immigrant and nonimmigrant visas of US issued and refused, by class, issuing office, and nationality, FY90, annual rpt, 7184–1
Immigrants admitted to US, by class of admission, country of birth, and MSA of destination, FY91, advance annual rpt, 6264–4
Immigrants and legalized aliens, by occupational group and country of birth, preliminary FY91, annual tables, 6264–1

Immigrants and nonimmigrants admitted to US, alien workers, visitors, deportations, and naturalizations, FY91, annual summary rpt, 6264–7
Immigration to US, alien workers, visitors, deportations, and naturalizations, by country, FY91 and trends from 1820, annual rpt, 6264–2
Income tax returns of foreign corporations and individuals, and US entities abroad, detailed data compilation, 1970s-89, quinquennial rpt, 8308–31
Military spending, arms trade, and force strengths, with govt spending and population, by country, 1979-89, annual rpt, 9824–1
Minerals Yearbook, Vol 3, 1989: foreign country review of production, trade, and policy, by commodity, annual rpt, 5604–35.2
Multinatl US firms foreign affiliates, income statement items by asset size, industry, and country, 1988, biennial article, 8302–2.322
Peace Corps activities, funding by program, and volunteers, by country, FY93, annual rpt, 9654–1
Pollution (air) contributing to global warming, emissions by monitoring site and country, and temperature change by world area and US region, 1860s-1990, annual rpt, 3004–33
Population size, growth rates, and components of change, by country, projected 1990-2020 and trends from 1950, biennial rpt, 2324–9
Tax (income) returns for foreign corporate activity in US, selected income and tax items, by industry div and selected country, 1988, article, 8302–2.309
Tide height and time daily at coastal points, forecast 1993, annual rpt, 2174–2.5
Travel to and from US on US and foreign flag air carriers, by country, world area, and US port, monthly rpt, 7302–2
Travel to US, by characteristics of visit and traveler, country, port city, and State of destination, quarterly rpt, 2902–1
Travel to US, spending by world area of residence, and economic impact, by spending category and State, 1989, 2908–28
US military and civilian personnel and dependents, by service branch, world area, and country, quarterly rpt, 3542–20
see also American Samoa
see also Australia
see also Cook Islands
see also Fiji
see also French Polynesia
see also Guam
see also Johnston Atoll
see also Kiribati
see also Marshall Islands
see also Micronesia Federated States
see also Nauru
see also New Caledonia
see also New Zealand
see also Northern Mariana Islands
see also Palau
see also Papua New Guinea
see also Solomon Islands
see also Tonga
see also Tuvalu
see also Vanuatu
see also Western Samoa
see also under By Foreign Country in the "Index by Categories"

Oceanography
Alaska minerals resources and geologic characteristics, compilation of papers, 1990, annual rpt, 5664–15
Alaska OCS environmental conditions and oil dev impacts, compilation of papers, series, 2176–1
Atlantic Oceanographic and Meteorological Lab research activities and bibl, FY91, annual rpt, 2144–19
Coastal areas environmental conditions and mgmt, for individual areas, conf series, 2146–8
Environmental quality indicators, NOAA monitoring results, 1991 annual summary rpt, 2144–27
Fed Govt aid to higher education and nonprofit instns for R&D and related activities, by field, instn, agency, and State, FY90, annual rpt, 9627–17
Higher education grad programs enrollment in science and engineering, by field, source of funds, and characteristics of student and instn, 1990, annual rpt, 9627–7
Minerals offshore lease sales environmental and economic impacts in coastal areas, final statement series, 5736–7
NASA R&D funding to higher education instns, by field, instn, and State, FY91, annual listing, 9504–7
New York Bight water temperature, salinity, and density, by site and depth, 1987-89, 2168–130
NOAA oceanographic and other research activities, FY87-88, biennial rpt, 2144–6
Pacific Marine Environmental Lab research activities and bibl, FY91, annual rpt, 2144–21
Pacific Ocean subsurface temperature data collection activities, annual rpt, discontinued, 2154–12
Pacific Ocean temperature, current, and wind, by equatorial eastern site and depth, 1983-87, 2148–62
R&D funding by higher education instns and federally funded centers, by field, instn, and State, FY90, annual rpt, 9627–13
Science and Engineering Indicators, employment, education, R&D funding, and industry impacts, with foreign comparisons, 1960s-91, biennial rpt, 9624–10
Ships for oceanographic research, vessel characteristics by higher education instn and Federal agency, 1992, annual listing, 3804–6
Temperature of sea surface by ocean and for US coastal areas, and Bering Sea ice conditions, monthly rpt, 2182–5
Weather conditions and forecasts, data collection and analysis issues, 1991 annual conf, 2184–10
Weather trends and deviations, by world region, 1880s-1990, annual chartbook, 2184–9
World Data Center A oceanographic research and data distribution activities by country, and cruises by ship, 1990, annual rpt, 2144–15
see also Ice conditions
see also Marine pollution
see also Marine resources
see also Marine resources conservation
see also Navigation
see also Tides and currents

Oceans and seas
see Arctic Ocean
see Atlantic Ocean
see Bering Sea
see Chukchi Sea
see Coastal areas
see Continental shelf
see Coral reefs and islands
see Gulf of Alaska
see Gulf of Mexico
see Indian Ocean
see Marine accidents and safety
see Marine pollution
see Marine resources
see Marine resources conservation
see Mediterranean Sea
see North Sea
see Oceanography
see Offshore mineral resources
see Offshore oil and gas
see Pacific Ocean
see Tides and currents
see Tsunamis

O'Connell, Martin
"Who's Minding the Kids? Child Care Arrangements: Fall 1988", 2546–20.24

O'Donnell, Robert D.
"Candidate Automated Test Battery for Neuropsychological Screening of Airmen: Design and Preliminary Validation", 7506–10.107

OECD
see Organization for Economic Cooperation and Development

Office buildings
see Commercial buildings
see Public buildings

Office equipment
see Business machines and equipment
see Computer industry and products
see Office supplies

Office for Victims of Crime
Victims of crime, compensation and support service programs funding, by offense and State, FY88-90, biennial rpt, 6064–37
Victims of crime, compensation and support service programs operations, series, 6066–31

Office of Education
see Department of Education

Office of Educational Research and Improvement
Activities of OERI, FY91, annual narrative rpt, 4814–1
Budget of US, obligations and authority by function, agency, and program, with summaries and analyses, FY93, annual rpt, 104–2
Condition of Education, detail for elementary, secondary, and higher education, 1920s-91 and projected to 2002, annual rpt, 4824–1
Condition of Education, summary trends, 1970s-91, annual pamphlet, 4824–10
Degree (PhD) recipients in higher education, by field and selected characteristics, 1979, 1984, and 1989, 4848–44

Digest of Education Statistics, 1992 annual data compilation, 4824–2
Drug abuse prevention programs in schools, Education Dept recognition program, 1989/90-1990/91, annual listing, 4814–2
Education data collection, processing, and reporting standards, 1991 narrative rpt, 4828–41
Education data, enrollment, degrees, teachers, and spending, 1977/78-1990/91 and alternative projections to 2002/2003, annual rpt, 4824–4
Education data, enrollment, finances, teachers, and other characteristics, by State, 1969-89, 4828–33
Education data, selected trends and projections 1979-2002, annual pamphlet, 4824–9
Education data, 1940s-95, pamphlet, 4828–35
Education data, 1960s-91, annual pamphlet, 4824–3
Education issues, special topics, series, 4826–10
Educational Resources Info Center (ERIC) data base, foreign and US providers, 1992 biennial listing, 4814–4
Eighth grade class of 1988: educational performance and conditions, characteristics, attitudes, activities, and plans, natl longitudinal survey, series, 4826–9
Elementary and secondary education enrollment, staff, finances, operations, programs, and policies, 1987/88 biennial survey, series, 4836–3
Elementary and secondary education enrollment, teachers, high school grads, and spending, by instn control and State, 1992/93, annual rpt, 4834–19
Elementary and secondary public school agencies, by enrollment size and location, fall 1990, annual listing, 4834–1
Elementary and secondary public school systems enrollment, finances, staff, and high school grads, by State, FY89-90, annual rpt, 4834–6
Elementary and secondary public schools and enrollment, by State, 1990/91, annual rpt, 4834–17
Fast Response Survey System, estimates for education data, series, 4826–1
Fed Govt education funding by agency, program, and recipient type, and instn spending, 1960s-91, annual rpt, 4824–8
Foreign and US students science and math proficiency, intl assessment results and other indicators by selected country, 1960s-80s, 4838–51
High school class of 1972: community college attendance, by selected characteristics, natl longitudinal study, 1970s-86, 4888–7
High school classes of 1980 and 1982: education, employment, and family characteristics, activities, and attitudes, natl longitudinal study, series, 4826–2
High school dropout rates, and subsequent completion, by student and school characteristics, alternative estimates, 1991, annual rpt, 4834–23
High school dropouts and rates, and data collection and reporting methods evaluation, 1992 rpt, 4838–49
Higher education data collection system, glossary, 1992 rpt, 4848–47
Higher education degrees awarded, by level, field, race, and sex, 1989/90 and trends from 1980/81, annual rpt, 4844–17
Higher education enrollment and degrees awarded, by sex, full- and part-time status, and instn level and control, fall 1991, annual rpt, 4844–16
Higher education enrollment, by level, race, and sex, fall 1980-90, biennial rpt, 4844–15
Higher education enrollment, faculty, finances, and degrees, by instn level and control, and State, FY88, annual rpt, 4844–13
Higher education enrollment, tuition, control, location, and other instn characteristics, 1991/92, biennial listing, 4844–3
Higher education faculty and staff, by occupation, full- and part-time status, sex, and instn type and control, fall 1989, biennial rpt, 4844–18
Higher education instn physical plant inventory and classification methods, 1992 guidelines, 4848–48
Higher education instn revenue by source and spending by function, by State and instn control, FY82-90, annual rpt, 4844–6
Higher education instn student aid and other sources of support, with student expenses and characteristics, by instn type and control, 1987 triennial study, series, 4846–3; 4846–5
Higher education instn tuition and other charges, by public and private 2- and 4-year instn, and State, 1991/92, annual listing, 4844–10
Higher education noncollegiate instns enrollment and program completions, by sex and instn level and control, fall 1990, annual rpt, 4844–19
Higher education student performance, instns data collection activities, by instn level and control, 1991, 4848–45
Libraries (public) finances, staff, and operations, by State and population size, 1990, annual rpt, 4824–6
Libraries (public) services for Indians and Hawaii Natives, project listing and funding by tribe and State, FY90, annual rpt, 4874–5
Libraries (research) funding of Education Dept, by project, instn, and State, FY90, annual listing, 4874–2
Library research and demonstration projects and funding, FY67-86, listing, 4878–5
Library science training grants for disadvantaged students, by instn and State, FY91, annual listing, 4874–1
Publications of Education Dept, semiannual listing, 4812–1
Publications of Natl Center for Education Statistics, periodic listing, 4822–1
Research on education, field projects funding and descriptions, FY90-91, annual listing, 4884–1
Teachers in higher education, and salaries, by faculty rank, sex, instn type and control, and State, 1990/91, annual rpt, 4844–8
Vocational education enrollment, student and teacher characteristics, and outcomes, for secondary and postsecondary instns, 1970s-90, 4828–42

Office of Federal Statistical Policy and Standards
see Office of Management and Budget

Office of Government Ethics
Budget of US, obligations and authority by function, agency, and program, with summaries and analyses, FY93, annual rpt, 104–2
Fed Govt agencies ethics regulation, activities, and staff, 1991, biennial rpt, 9834–1

Office of Grants and Program Systems, USDA
Research and education grants, USDA competitive awards by program and recipient, FY91, annual listing, 1764–1

Office of Human Development Services
see also Administration for Children, Youth, and Families
see also Administration on Aging
see also National Center on Child Abuse and Neglect

Office of International Cooperation and Development, USDA
Budget of US, obligations and authority by function, agency, and program, with summaries and analyses, FY93, annual rpt, 104–2
Research grants of USDA, by program, subagency, and country, FY92, annual listing, 1954–3

Office of International Policy, SSA
Social security programs, research rpt series, 4746–4

Office of Justice Programs
Activities and funding of OJP, FY91, annual rpt, 6064–18
Budget of US, obligations and authority by function, agency, and program, with summaries and analyses, FY93, annual rpt, 104–2
Drug abuse and trafficking reduction research funding by Natl Inst on Drug Abuse and OJP, 1970s-91, GAO rpt, 26131–99
Drug abuse treatment, prevention, and enforcement grants by State, and State allocations by program, FY87-90, 6068–252
Drug control street-level task forces enforcement activities, impacts on crime, and residents views, local area studies, 1992 rpt, 6068–251
Expenditures of Fed Govt in States, by type, program, agency, and State, FY91, annual rpt, 2464–2
see also Bureau of Justice Assistance
see also Bureau of Justice Statistics
see also National Institute of Justice
see also Office for Victims of Crime
see also Office of Juvenile Justice and Delinquency Prevention

Office of Juvenile Justice and Delinquency Prevention
Activities of OJJDP, with background data, FY90, annual rpt, 6064–34
Data on juvenile justice issues, young offenders, and victims, series, 6066–27
Facilities for juveniles, population by resident characteristics and facility type, late 1970s-89, 6068–250
Facilities for juveniles, population by resident characteristics and facility type, 1977-89, annual rpt, 6064–35

Missing, abducted, runaway, and exploited children, and OJJDP activities, FY90, annual rpt, 6064–36

Office of Management and Budget

Assistance (financial and nonfinancial) of Fed Govt, 1992 base edition, annual listing, 104–5

Budget deficit forecasting accuracy, contributing factors, and analysis of major programs, FY91, annual GAO rpt, 26104–23

Budget deficit reduction under Gramm-Rudman Act, OMB sequestration estimates, by category, FY92, annual rpt, 104–27

Budget of US, authoritative financial statements with appropriations, outlays, and receipts, by category and agency, FY91, annual rpt, 8104–2.2

Budget of US, authority rescissions and deferrals, monthly rpt, 102–2

Budget of US, balances of budget authority obligated and unobligated, by function and agency, FY90-93, annual rpt, 104–8

Budget of US, Bush Admin proposals, with detail for defense budgets, and historical data from FY34, FY93, 108–46

Budget of US, midsession review of FY93 budget, by function, annual rpt, 104–7

Budget of US, obligations and authority by function, agency, and program, with summaries and analyses, FY93, annual rpt, 104–2

Fraud and abuse in Fed Govt, audits and investigations by agency, FY91, annual rpt, 104–29

Info collection of Fed Govt under Paperwork Reduction Act, respondent burden, OMB reviews, violations, and major info systems proposals, 1981-92, annual rpt, 104–26

MSA and central city definitions and revisions, 1992, annual listing, 104–32

Persian Gulf War costs to US by category and service branch, and offsetting contributions by allied country, monthly rpt, 102–3

Office of Minority Business Enterprise

see Minority Business Development Agency

Office of National Drug Control Policy

Abuse, treatment, and enforcement issues, series, 236–1

Budget of US, obligations and authority by function, agency, and program, with summaries and analyses, FY93, annual rpt, 104–2

Drug abuse and trafficking reduction programs activities, funding, staff, and Bush Admin budget request, by Federal agency, FY91-93, annual rpt, 234–2

Drug abuse and trafficking reduction programs funding, and Bush Admin budget request, by Federal agency, FY91-93, annual rpt, 234–1

Enforcement, abuse, and treatment issues, series, 236–3

Office of Navajo and Hopi Indian Relocation

Activities and caseloads of relocation program, monthly rpt, 16002–1

see also Navajo and Hopi Indian Relocation Commission

Office of Personnel Management

Background checks of employees and hirees by OPM, efficiency, and Federal agency managers views on timeliness and quality, FY90, GAO rpt, 26119–373

Budget of US, authoritative financial statements with appropriations, outlays, and receipts, by category and agency, FY91, annual rpt, 8104–2.2

Budget of US, obligations and authority by function, agency, and program, with summaries and analyses, FY93, annual rpt, 104–2

Civil service retirement system actuarial valuation, FY79-91 and projected to FY2065, annual rpt, 9844–34

Collective bargaining agreements of Federal employees, coverage, unions, and location, by agency, for contracts expiring 1992, semiannual listing, 9847–1

Employment (civilian) of Fed Govt, work-years, pay rates, and benefits use and costs, by agency, FY90, annual rpt, 9844–31

Employment and payroll (civilian) of Fed Govt, by agency in DC metro area, total US, and abroad, bimonthly rpt, 9842–1

Employment and payroll (civilian) of Fed Govt, by pay system, agency, and location, 1991, annual rpt, 9844–6

Equal Opportunity Recruitment Program activity, and Fed Govt employment by sex, race, pay grade, and occupational group, FY91, annual rpt, 9844–33

Fed Govt civilian employees retirement, health, and life insurance benefits, coverage and finances of 4 programs, FY86-90, annual rpt, 9844–37

Incentive awards to Federal employees, costs, and benefits, by award type and agency, FY90, annual rpt, 9844–20

Insurance (health and life) programs of Fed Govt, coverage and finances, annual rpt, discontinued, 9844–35

Labor unions recognized in Fed Govt, agreements and membership by agency and facility, as of Jan 1991, biennial listing, 9844–14

Merit system oversight and enforcement activities of OPM, series, 9496–2

Minority group, disabled, and veteran employment in Fed Govt, and years of service, by occupation, age, sex, and agency, as of Sept 1990, biennial rpt, 9844–27

Physical fitness clubs memberships for Federal employees, agency costs, and personnel directors views on OPM guidelines and admin leave use, 1991-92, GAO rpt, 26119–393

Recruitment for Federal entry-level professional positions, reasons for accepting or declining offer, 1990 surveys, GAO rpt, 26119–387

Recruitment visits at colleges by Federal agencies and private companies, and school officials views, 1991, GAO rpt, 26119–377

Senior Executive Service members characteristics, entries, exits, and awards, FY79-91, annual rpt, 9844–36

White collar employees of Fed Govt, views on work conditions and schedules, 1992 survey, 9848–41

Office of Policy Development

Budget of US, obligations and authority by function, agency, and program, with summaries and analyses, FY93, annual rpt, 104–2

Office of Policy, SSA

Employment and earnings covered under OASDHI, and social security contributions, by age, sex, race, State, and county, 1988, annual rpt, 4744–29

Social security programs, research rpt series, 4746–4

see also Office of International Policy, SSA

see also Office of Research and Statistics, SSA

Office of Research and Statistics, SSA

Income, tax, and transfer payments distribution and equity, analyses and alternative estimates, series, 4746–14

OASDHI, Medicaid, SSI, and related programs benefits, beneficiary characteristics, and trust funds, selected years 1937-90, annual rpt, 4744–3

Older persons income and sources, by OASDI beneficiary and poverty status, and other characteristics, 1990, biennial chartbook, 4744–25

Older persons income and sources, by whether OASDI beneficiary, poverty status, and other characteristics, 1990, biennial rpt, 4744–26

Social Security Bulletin, OASDHI and other program operations and beneficiary characteristics, from 1940, quarterly journal, 4742–1

Social security programs and related issues, technical paper series, 4746–26

Social security programs, research rpt series, 4746–4

Supplemental Security Income payments and beneficiaries, by type of eligibility, State, and county, Dec 1990, annual rpt, 4744–27

Office of Science and Technology Policy

Budget of US, authoritative financial statements with appropriations, outlays, and receipts, by category and agency, FY91, annual rpt, 8104–2.2

Budget of US, obligations and authority by function, agency, and program, with summaries and analyses, FY93, annual rpt, 104–2

Office of Special Counsel

see U.S. Office of Special Counsel

Office of Special Education and Rehabilitative Services

Blind-operated vending facilities on Federal and non-Federal property, finances and operations by agency and State, FY91, annual rpt, 4944–2

Budget of US, obligations and authority by function, agency, and program, with summaries and analyses, FY93, annual rpt, 104–2

Disabled persons rehabilitation, Federal and State activities and funding, FY90, annual rpt, 4944–1

Disabled persons with chronic health conditions, prevalence and services use and needs, series, 4946–1

Disabled workers labor force status, type and cause of disability, and other characteristics, 1970s-89, chartbook, 4948–11

Enrollment by age, staff, funding, and needs of special education programs, by type of handicap and State, 1990/91, annual rpt, 4944–4

Vocational rehabilitation cases of State agencies, by disposition and State, FY91 and trends from FY21, annual rpt, 4944–5

Office of Surface Mining Reclamation and Enforcement
Activities and funding of OSM, by State and Indian tribe, FY91, annual rpt, 5644–1
Budget of US, obligations and authority by function, agency, and program, with summaries and analyses, FY93, annual rpt, 104–2
Expenditures of Fed Govt in States, by type, program, agency, and State, FY91, annual rpt, 2464–2
Office of Technology Assessment
Activities of OTA, and rpts, FY91, annual rpt, 26354–3
AIDS prevalence, prevention, and treatment issues, series, 26356–6
Auto fuel economy improvements from new technologies, 1987-90 and alternative projections to 2010, 26358–251
Autos (older) retirement programs proposals costs, savings, and emissions and energy use reductions, 1992 rpt, 26358–263
Budget of US, obligations and authority by function, agency, and program, with summaries and analyses, FY93, annual rpt, 104–2
Developing countries energy efficiency improvement issues and devs, with data by end use and country, 1980s-90, 26358–260
Drug infusion therapy in home, use, equipment, industry finances, and Medicare coverage options, 1992 rpt, 26358–258
Educational testing costs, achievement scores by selected State, and attendance and testing policies, with foreign comparisons, 1970s-91, 26358–255
Energy conservation technologies for housing and commercial buildings, use, costs, efficiency, and residential tax credits, 1970s-90 and projected to 2010, 26358–259
FBI fingerprint identification system automation costs, staff, and workload, FY90 and projected to FY2000, 26358–253
Forests (tropical) condition, conservation methods, and biological diversity issues, 1992 rpt, 26358–262
Manufacturing industry (US) intl competitiveness, trade and economic policies with background data and foreign comparisons, 1991 rpt, 26358–252
Medicaid waiver proposal of Oregon for managed care, services priorities dev procedures and issues, with background data, 1992 rpt, 26358–254
Menopause treatment with hormone replacement therapy, use, health risks, and research funding, 1992 rpt, 26358–261
Neurosciences research and public policy issues, series, 26356–9
Standards for production, controls, and processes, domestic and intl dev in US and EC, 1980s-91, 26358–257
Waste (industrial) generation, disposal, and regulation, by industry and State, mid 1980s-90, 26358–256
Youth health condition, risk factors, and preventive and treatment services use and availability, 1970s-80s, 26358–234
Office of Territorial and International Affairs
American Samoa govt finances, with data on health and farm spending and employment, mid 1980s-91, GAO rpt, 26123–385
Budget of US, obligations and authority by function, agency, and program, with summaries and analyses, FY93, annual rpt, 104–2
Expenditures of Fed Govt in States, by type, program, agency, and State, FY91, annual rpt, 2464–2
Office of the Comptroller of Currency
Activities of Comptroller, and natl banks charters, mergers, liquidations, and financial performance, with data by instn and State, quarterly rpt, 8402–3
Budget of US, obligations and authority by function, agency, and program, with summaries and analyses, FY93, annual rpt, 104–2
Employee pay comparability among Federal bank regulatory agencies, and turnover, by occupation, 1991, GAO rpt, 26119–368
Office of the Secretary of Defense
Base construction, renovation, and closure, DOD budget requests by project, service branch, State, and country, FY93, annual rpt, 3544–15
Budget of DOD, base construction and family housing appropriations by facility, service branch, and location, FY91-93, annual rpt, 3544–39
Budget of DOD, procurement appropriations by item, service branch, and defense agency, FY91-93, annual rpt, 3544–32
Budget of DOD, programs, policies, and operations, FY91, annual rpt, 3544–2
Budget of DOD, R&D appropriations by item, service branch, and defense agency, FY91-93, annual rpt, 3544–33
Commercial activities of DOD performed in-house, and work-years, by service branch, installation, and State, FY91, annual rpt, 3544–25
Deaths by cause, age, race, and rank, and personnel captured and missing, by service branch, FY91, annual rpt, 3544–40
Expenditures and obligations of DOD, by function and service branch, quarterly rpt, 3542–3
Expenditures for contracts and payroll, and personnel, by service branch and location, with top 5 contractors and maps, by State and country, FY91, annual rpt, 3544–29
Fraud and abuse in DOD programs, audits and investigations, 2nd half FY92, semiannual rpt, 3542–18
Hazardous waste site remedial action at military installations, activities and funding by site and State, FY91, annual rpt, 3544–36
Health care facilities of DOD in US and abroad, beds, admissions, outpatient visits, and births, by service branch, quarterly rpt, 3542–15
Health care personnel, and accessions by training source, by occupation, specialty, and service branch, FY90, annual rpt, 3544–24
NATO, Japan, and South Korea military spending and indicators of ability to support common defense, by country, 1970s-90, annual rpt, 3544–28
Personnel (civilian) of DOD, by service branch and defense agency, with summary military employment data, quarterly rpt, 3542–16
Personnel (civilian and military) of DOD, by service branch, major installation, and State, as of Sept 1991, annual rpt, 3544–7
Personnel active duty enlisted accessions by race, and goals, by sex and service branch, quarterly press release, 3542–7
Personnel strengths, for active duty, civilians, and dependents, by service branch and US and foreign location, quarterly rpt, 3542–20
Personnel strengths, for active duty, civilians, and reserves, by service branch, FY91 and trends, annual rpt, 3544–1
Personnel strengths, for active duty, civilians, and reserves, by service branch, quarterly rpt, 3542–14
Personnel strengths in US and abroad, by service branch, world area, and country, quarterly press release, 3542–9
Personnel strengths, summary by service branch, monthly press release, 3542–2
Procurement, DOD prime contract awards by category, contract and contractor type, and service branch, FY82-1st half FY92, semiannual rpt, 3542–1
Procurement, DOD prime contract awards by category, contractor type, and State, FY89-91, annual rpt, 3544–11
Procurement, DOD prime contract awards by contractor, service branch, State, and city, FY91, annual rpt, 3544–22
Procurement, DOD prime contract awards by detailed procurement category, FY88-91, annual rpt, 3544–18
Procurement, DOD prime contract awards by service branch and State, 1st half FY92, semiannual rpt, 3542–5
Procurement, DOD prime contract awards by size and type of contract, service branch, competitive status, category, and labor standard, FY91, annual rpt, 3544–19
Procurement, DOD prime contract awards for top 100 contractors, FY91, annual listing, 3544–5
Procurement, DOD prime contract awards in labor surplus areas, by service branch, State, and area, 1st half FY92, semiannual rpt, 3542–19
Procurement, subcontract awards by DOD contractors to small and disadvantaged business, by firm and service branch, quarterly rpt, 3542–17
Property, supply, and equipment inventory of DOD, by service branch, annual rpt, discontinued, 3544–6
Publications of DOD Directorate for Info Operations and Rpts, 1991 listing, 3548–21
R&D prime contract awards of DOD, for top 500 contractors, FY91, annual listing, 3544–4
R&D prime contract awards of DOD to US and foreign nonprofit instns and govt agencies, by instn and location, FY91, annual listing, 3544–17
Reserve forces personnel and equipment strengths, and readiness, by reserve component, FY91, annual rpt, 3544–31

Reserve forces personnel strengths and characteristics, by component, quarterly rpt, 3542–4
Strategic material stockpile inventories and needs, by commodity, 1992, annual rpt, 3544–37
Strategic material stockpiling by Fed Govt, activity, and inventory by commodity, as of Sept 1991, semiannual rpt, 3542–22

Office of the Secretary of Energy
Activities and finances of DOE, summary energy supply and demand data, and bibl, 1990, annual rpt, 3024–2
Budget of DOE, authority by program and subagency, FY92, annual rpt, 3024–5

Office of the Special Representative for Trade Negotiations
see Office of the U.S. Trade Representative

Office of the U.S. Trade Representative
Budget of US, authoritative financial statements with appropriations, outlays, and receipts, by category and agency, FY91, annual rpt, 8104–2.2
Budget of US, obligations and authority by function, agency, and program, with summaries and analyses, FY93, annual rpt, 104–2
Export and import agreements, negotiations, and related legislation, 1991, annual rpt, 444–1
Exports of goods, services, and investment, trade barriers, impacts, and US actions, by country, 1991, annual rpt, 444–2

Office of the Vice President
Budget of US, authoritative financial statements with appropriations, outlays, and receipts, by category and agency, FY91, annual rpt, 8104–2.2
Budget of US, obligations and authority by function, agency, and program, with summaries and analyses, FY93, annual rpt, 104–2

Office of Thrift Supervision
Budget of US, obligations and authority by function, agency, and program, with summaries and analyses, FY93, annual rpt, 104–2
Employee pay comparability among Federal bank regulatory agencies, and turnover, by occupation, 1991, GAO rpt, 26119–368
Housing finance studies, technical paper series, 8436–1
Savings instns finances and operations by district and State, mortgage loan activity, and FHLB finances, annual rpt, discontinued, 8434–3
Savings instns financial statements, for instns insured by Savings Assn Insurance Fund by FHLB district and State, and for FDIC-insured savings banks, 1989, annual rpt, 8434–1
Savings instns insured by Savings Assn Insurance Fund, assets, liabilities, and deposit and loan activity, by conservatorship status, monthly rpt, 8432–1
Savings instns insured by Savings Assn Insurance Fund, finances by profitability group, district, and State, quarterly rpt, 8432–4
Savings instns insured by Savings Assn Insurance Fund, offices, and deposits, by OTS district, State, MSA, and county, 1991, annual rpt, 8434–5
see also Federal Home Loan Bank Board

Office of Transportation, USDA
Hwys and bridges in rural areas, conditions and funding, discontinued series, 1276–1
Truck transport of fruit and vegetables, itemized costs per mile by item for fleets and owner-operator trucks, monthly table, discontinued, 1272–1

Office of Vocational and Adult Education
Adult education and literacy programs funding, enrollment, and activities, fact sheet series, 4806–4

Office on Smoking and Health
Research on smoking and health, publications, 1991 annual report, 4204–19
Research on smoking and health, with trends in smoking, related disease and death, and public attitudes, literature review, 1992 annual rpt, 4204–18

Office supplies
Banks in Fed Reserve System, expenses and operations itemized by service, office, and district, 1991, annual rpt, 9364–11
County Business Patterns, 1989: employment, establishments, and payroll, by SIC 2- to 4-digit industry and county, annual State rpt series, 2326–8
County Business Patterns, 1990: employment, establishments, and payroll, by SIC 2- to 4-digit industry and county, annual State rpt series, 2326–6
Employment, earnings, and hours, by SIC 1- to 4-digit industry, monthly 1989-Feb 1992, annual rpt, 6744–4
Exports and imports between US and outlying areas, by detailed commodity and mode of transport, 1991, annual rpt, 2424–11
Exports and imports of US, by country and detailed commodity, monthly rpt, 2422–12
Exports and imports of US, by Harmonized System 6-digit commodity and country, 1991, annual rpt, 2424–13
Exports and imports of US, by transport mode, country, and SITC 1- to 3-digit commodity, 1991, annual rpt, 2424–12
Exports of US, detailed Schedule B commodities with countries of destination, 1991, annual rpt, 2424–10
House of Representatives salaries, expenses, and contingent fund disbursement, detailed listings, quarterly rpt, 21942–1
Injuries from use of consumer products and related activities, by severity and victim age and sex, 1990, annual rpt, 9164–7
Injuries from use of consumer products, by severity, victim age, and detailed product, 1991, annual rpt, 9164–6
Manufacturing annual survey, 1990: finances and operations, by SIC 2- to 4-digit industry, series, 2506–14
Manufacturing census, 1987: concentration of largest firms measured by value added, and for shipments by SIC 2- and 4-digit industry, subject rpt, 2497–6
Manufacturing census, 1987: shipments of manufacturers products, by customer class and SIC 2- and 4-digit industry, subject rpt, 2497–4
Military prime contract awards, by detailed procurement category, FY88-91, annual rpt, 3544–18
Occupational injury and illness rates, by SIC 2- to 4-digit industry, 1989-90, annual rpt, 6844–7
Occupational injury and illness rates, by SIC 2- to 4-digit industry, 1990, annual rpt, 6844–1
Price indexes (producer), by stage of processing and detailed commodity, monthly rpt, 6762–6
Price indexes (producer), by stage of processing and detailed commodity, monthly 1991, annual rpt, 6764–2
Science, engineering, and technical employment in manufacturing, by field and industry, 1989, triennial rpt, 9627–23
Senate receipts, itemized expenses by payee, and balances, 1st half FY92, semiannual listing, 25922–1

Office workers
see Clerical workers

Official publications
see Government documents

Officials
Air travel by Federal officials aboard military aircraft, trips of 11 officials by reason, with costs and reimbursements, 1989-91, GAO rpt, 26111–78
Air travel by Federal officials and Congress aboard military aircraft, and aircraft inventory characteristics, 1989-91, GAO rpt, 26123–384
Corrupt govt officials prosecuted and convicted, by judicial district and level of govt, 1970-90, annual rpt, 6004–13
Criminal case processing in Federal courts, by offense, disposition, and jurisdiction, data compilation, 1992 annual rpt, 6064–6.5
Foreign and NATO officials admitted to US, by country, FY81-91, annual rpt, 6264–2.3
Foreign countries economic, social, political, and geographic summary data, by country, 1992, annual factbook, 9114–2
Foreign countries interests represented by former US govt officials, activities and individuals, FY86-91, GAO rpt, 26123–134
Foreign govts Chiefs of State and Cabinet members, by country, bimonthly listing, 9112–4
Pension systems of State and local govts, finances, coverage, and benefits, by system, FY90, annual rpt, 2466–2.4
Workers compensation programs of States, top officials, salaries, and hours, by State, as of 1990, annual rpt, 6504–9
see also Congressional employees
see also Executives and managers
see also Federal employees
see also Government employees
see also International employees
see also Presidential appointments
see also State and local employees

Offshore mineral resources
Environmental and economic impacts in coastal areas of offshore minerals lease sales, final statement series, 5736–7
Production and revenue from oil, gas, and minerals on Federal and Indian lands, by State, 1991 and trends from 1920, annual rpt, 5734–2
see also Offshore oil and gas

Offshore oil and gas
Alaska Beaufort Sea pollutant concentrations in sediment and marine life, by contaminant and site, 1985-89, 5738–33
Alaska minerals resources, production, oil and gas leases, reserves, and exploratory wells, with maps and bibl, 1990, annual rpt, 5664–11
Alaska OCS environmental conditions and oil dev impacts, compilation of papers, series, 2176–1
California OCS oil and gas dev impacts on water quality, marine life, and sediments, by site, 1986-90, annual rpt, 5734–11
Coastal and riparian areas environmental conditions, fish, wildlife, use, and mgmt, for individual ecosystems, series, 5506–9
Drilling rigs construction financing guarantees of MarAd, FY91, annual rpt, 7704–14.1
Field codes and locations, for oil and gas, 1991, annual listing, 3164–70
Gulf of Mexico oil and gas leases, by company and tract, 1990, annual rpt, 5734–8
Gulf of Mexico oil and gas reserves, production, and leasing status, by location, 1990, annual rpt, 5734–6
Latin America economic and social conditions, resources, trade, and aid, 1992, annual factbook, 9914–14
Lease revenue sharing payments for OCS oil and gas by State, 1992 annual press release, 5306–4.14
Leasing and exploration activity, production, revenue, and environmental studies, for Federal OCS lands by location, quarterly rpt, 5732–1
Natural and supplemental gas production, prices, trade, use, reserves, and pipeline company finances, by firm and State, monthly rpt with articles, 3162–4
Natural gas supply, demand, prices, and distribution, by State, 1986-90 annual rpt, 3164–4
Pacific basin countries energy supply and demand, and implications for US trade, country rpt series, 3406–6
Pacific Northwest Indian tribes environmental, economic, and cultural impacts of OCS oil and gas lease and dev, with background data, 1970s-92, 5738–35
Pacific Ocean OCS oil and gas production, and wells, by drilling platform under Federal lease, 1960s-90, annual rpt, 5734–9
Pacific Ocean OCS oil and gas production, reserves, and wells drilled by location, 1990, annual rpt, 5734–7
Price indexes (producer), by stage of processing and detailed commodity, monthly 1991, annual rpt, 6764–2
Producers finances and operations, by energy type for US firms domestic and foreign operations, 1990, annual rpt, 3164–44.2
Production and reserves of oil, gas, and gas liquids, by State and substate area, 1991, annual rpt, 3164–46
Production and revenue from oil, gas, and minerals on Federal and Indian lands, by State, 1991 and trends from 1920, annual rpt, 5734–2
Production, leasing and exploration activity, revenue, and costs, for Fed Govt OCS oil and gas reserves, by ocean area, FY91, annual rpt, 5734–4
Reserves of OCS oil and gas, geophysical data collection activities and costs, by region, 1976-90, 5738–41
Reserves, production, and ultimate recovery of oil and gas, by location, with field technical characteristics, series, 3166–14
Seismic exploration crews and activity, monthly rpt, 3162–24.5
Seismic exploration crews and activity, monthly 1973-88, 3168–123.5
Statistical Abstract of US, 1992 annual data compilation, 2324–1.25
Supply, demand, and prices, by fuel type and end-use sector, alternative projections by region, 1990-2010, annual rpt, 3164–96
Supply, demand, and prices, by fuel type and end-use sector, with foreign comparisons, 1991 and trends from 1949, annual rpt, 3164–74.1; 3164–74.2
Washington and Oregon coastal areas recreation resources, and impacts of OCS oil and gas dev, 1983-88, 5738–40
Water discharges from oil and gas OCS production, for Pacific lands under Federal lease by drilling platform, 1960s-90, annual rpt, 5734–9
Water discharges from oil and gas OCS production, treatment costs by method, 1992 rpt, 3166–6.66
Whales population and behavior in Chukchi and Beaufort Seas, by endangered species, 1982-91, 5738–32

Ogden, Utah
Housing starts and completions authorized by building permits in 40 MSAs, quarterly rpt, 2382–9
Housing vacancy rates for single and multifamily units and mobile homes, by city and ZIP code, 1992, annual MSA rpt, 9304–21.2
Wages by occupation, for office and plant workers, 1991 survey, periodic MSA rpt, 6785–12.2
Wages by occupation, for office and plant workers, 1992 survey, periodic MSA rpt, 6785–17.3

O'Hanlon, Michael
"Limiting Conventional Arms Exports to the Middle East", 26306–6.173

Ohio
Appalachian Regional Commission funding, by project and State, planned FY92, annual rpt, 9084–3
Banks (insured commercial and savings) deposits by instn, State, MSA, and county, as of June 1991, annual regional rpt, 9295–3.3
Coal production and mines by county, prices, productivity, miners, and reserves, by mining method and State, 1990-91, annual rpt, 3164–25
County Business Patterns, 1990: employment, establishments, and payroll, by SIC 2- to 4-digit industry and county, annual State rpt, 2326–6.37
Deaths and rates, by detailed location, cause, and demographic characteristics, 1989, US Vital Statistics annual rpt, 4144–3.1
Economic indicators and components, and Fed Reserve 4th District business and financial conditions, monthly chartbook, 9377–10
Electric power demand, and industrial and employment impacts of capacity shortfalls and new power plants, by selected State, 1960s-80s and projected to 2000, hearing, 21248–163
Employment, earnings, and hours, by selected SIC 1- to 4-digit industry, State, and for 275 MSAs, 1987-92, 6748–81
Fed Govt spending in States and local areas, by type, State, county, and city, FY91, annual rpt, 2464–3
Fed Govt spending in States, by type, program, agency, and State, FY91, annual rpt, 2464–2
HHS financial aid, by program, recipient, State, and city, FY91, annual regional listing, 4004–3.5
Hospital deaths of Medicare patients, actual and expected rates by diagnosis, and hospital characteristics, by instn, FY90 annual State rpt, 4654–14.36
Housing census, 1990: inventory, occupancy, and costs, State fact sheet, 2326–21.37
Housing census, 1990: summary unit characteristics, by householder race and age, county, place, and urban-rural location, State rpt, 2471–1.37
Military prime contract awards, by contractor, service branch, State, and city, FY91, annual rpt, 3544–22
Mineral Industry Surveys, State reviews of production, 1991, preliminary annual rpt, 5614–6
Multinatl firms US affiliates finances and operations, by industry, country of parent firm, and State, 1987, 2708–48
Physicians, by specialty, age, sex, and location of training and practice, 1990, State rpt, 4116–6.36
Population and housing census, 1990: detailed geographic coverage, State CD-ROM, 2551–9.3
Population and housing census, 1990: summary characteristics, by county, subdiv, and place, State rpt, 2551–7.37
Population census, 1990: population characteristics and living arrangements, by county, place, and urban-rural location, State rpt, 2531–1.37
Poverty, hunger, and public welfare program operations and indicators of need, for Ohio by county, 1991 hearing, 21968–58
Statistical Abstract of US, 1992 annual data compilation, 2324–1
Timber and pulpwood production, by product, 1989, State rpt, 1206–15.11
Water resources data collection and analysis activities of USGS Water Resources Div District, with project descriptions, 1991 rpt, 5666–26.23
Water resources dev projects of Army Corps of Engineers, characteristics, and costs, 1950s-91, biennial State rpt, 3756–2.36
see also Akron, Ohio
see also Cincinnati, Ohio
see also Cleveland, Ohio
see also Columbus, Ohio
see also Franklin County, Ohio
see also Hamilton, Ohio
see also Licking County, Ohio

see also Lorain, Ohio
see also Mansfield, Ohio
see also Toledo, Ohio
see also under By State in the "Index by Categories"

Ohio River
Army Corps of Engineers water resources dev projects, characteristics, and costs, 1950s-89, biennial State rpt series, 3756–1
Army Corps of Engineers water resources dev projects, characteristics, and costs, 1950s-91, biennial State rpt series, 3756–2
Freight (shipborne domestic), by major commodity group, vessel type, and port, 1987-89, annual rpt, 7704–7
Freight (waterborne) by commodity and port, waterway facilities, and recreation, for Ohio River basin by waterway, 1988-89, annual rpt, 3754–6
Freight (waterborne domestic and foreign) by commodity, traffic, and passengers, by port and waterway, 1989, annual rpt, 3754–3.2
Water quality, chemistry, hydrology, and other characteristics, 1991 local area study, 5666–27.34
Water supply and quality in streams and lakes, and groundwater levels in wells, by drainage basin, 1990, annual State rpt series, 5666–10
Water supply and quality in streams and lakes, and groundwater levels in wells, by drainage basin, 1991, annual State rpt series, 5666–12
Water supply in US and southern Canada, streamflow, surface and groundwater conditions, and reservoir levels, by location, monthly rpt, 5662–3

Ohmann, Janet L.
"Wildlife Habitats of the North Coast of California: New Techniques for Extensive Forest Inventory", 1208–414

Oil
see Aviation fuels
see Diesel fuel
see Fuel oil
see Gasoline
see Kerosene
see Offshore oil and gas
see Oil and gas leases
see Oil depletion allowances
see Oil shale
see Oil spills
see Oils, oilseeds, and fats
see Petroleum and petroleum industry
see Petroleum exports and imports
see Petroleum prices
see Petroleum reserves

Oil and gas leases
Alaska minerals resources, production, oil and gas leases, reserves, and exploratory wells, with maps and bibl, 1990, annual rpt, 5664–11
Alaska OCS environmental conditions and oil dev impacts, compilation of papers, series, 2176–1
Coastal and riparian areas environmental conditions, fish, wildlife, use, and mgmt, for individual ecosystems, series, 5506–9
Forest Service activities and finances, by region and State, FY91, annual rpt, 1204–1.1
Gulf of Mexico oil and gas leases, by company and tract, 1990, annual rpt, 5734–8
Gulf of Mexico oil and gas reserves, production, and leasing status, by location, 1990, annual rpt, 5734–6
Land Mgmt Bur activities in southwestern US, FY91, annual rpt, 5724–15
Naval Petroleum and Oil Shale Reserves production and revenue by fuel type, sales by purchaser, and wells, by reserve, FY91, annual rpt, 3334–3
New Mexico Caballo Resource Area public land mgmt, and grazing, environmental, and leasing activities, FY90-91, annual rpt, 5724–17
Offshore oil and gas leases, revenue sharing payments by State, 1992 annual press release, 5306–4.14
Offshore oil and gas leasing and exploration activity, production, revenue, and environmental studies, by location, quarterly rpt, 5732–1
Offshore oil and gas reserves of Fed Govt, production, leasing and exploration activity, revenue, and costs, by ocean area, FY91, annual rpt, 5734–4
Pacific Northwest Indian tribes environmental, economic, and cultural impacts of OCS oil and gas lease and dev, with background data, 1970s-92, 5738–35
Pacific Ocean OCS oil and gas production, and wells, by drilling platform under Federal lease, 1960s-90, annual rpt, 5734–9
Production and revenue from oil, gas, and minerals on Federal and Indian lands, by State, 1991 and trends from 1920, annual rpt, 5734–2
Public lands acreage and use, and Land Mgmt Bur activities and finances, annual State rpt series, 5724–11
Public lands acreage, grants, use, revenues, and allocations, by State, FY91, annual rpt, 5724–1.2
Statistical Abstract of US, 1992 annual data compilation, 2324–1.25
Washington and Oregon coastal areas recreation resources, and impacts of OCS oil and gas dev, 1983-88, 5738–40

Oil depletion allowances
Producers finances and operations, by energy type for US firms domestic and foreign operations, 1990, annual rpt, 3164–44.1

Oil shale
Jordan oil shale-fired electric power plants, feasibility assessment with background data, 1990 rpt, 3008–127
Naval Petroleum and Oil Shale Reserves production and revenue by fuel type, sales by purchaser, and wells, by reserve, FY91, annual rpt, 3334–3
Occupational injuries and incidence, employment, and hours in nonmetallic minerals mines and related operations, 1990, annual rpt, 6664–1
Reserves and ultimate recovery of oil and gas, by reservoir characteristics, geologic province, region, and field, 1989, 3166–14.2

Oil spills
Alaska OCS environmental conditions and oil dev impacts, compilation of papers, series, 2176–1
Alaska oil spill from Exxon Valdez, analysis of proposals for clean-up of Exxon Valdez oil spill, Budget of US, FY93, annual rpt, 104–2.2
Alaska oil spill from tanker Exxon Valdez, impacts on marine mammals, and resulting legislation, 1991 annual rpt, 14734–1
Claims Court caseload by type of suit, and judgments, FY92, annual rpt, 18224–1
Coastal and riparian areas environmental conditions, fish, wildlife, use, and mgmt, for individual ecosystems, series, 5506–9
Coastal areas environmental conditions and mgmt, for individual areas, conf series, 2146–8
Economic impacts of oil spills on coastal communities, model description and results, 1991 rpt, 5738–40.2
Environmental Quality, status of problems, protection programs, research, and intl issues, 1991 annual rpt, 484–1
Justice Dept enforcement of environmental laws, activities, FY83-92, annual press release, 6004–22
NOAA activities and funding for ocean pollution, estuary, and coastal waters monitoring and assessment, FY90, annual rpt, 2174–9
Statistical Abstract of US, 1992 annual data compilation, 2324–1.6
Washington State oil spill off northern coast in 1988, pollutant levels and impacts on marine biota, by site, as of 1990, 5738–38

Oil wells
see Energy exploration and drilling

Oils, oilseeds, and fats
Acreage planted and harvested, by crop and State, 1990-91 and planned as of June 1992, annual rpt, 1621–23
Acreage planted, by selected crop and State, 1983-91 and planned 1992, annual rpt, 1621–22
Agricultural Stabilization and Conservation Service soybean and oilseed programs, 1955-91, annual fact sheet, 1806–4.5
Agricultural Statistics, 1991, annual rpt, 1004–1
Cancer (colorectal) risk relation to diet, for men, 1986-88, article, 4472–1.302
Communist and transitional economy countries trade with US, by detailed commodity and country, quarterly rpt with articles, 9882–2
Confectionery shipments, trade, use, and ingredients used, by product, 1991, annual Current Industrial Rpt, 2506–4.5
Consumption of food, dietary composition, and nutrient intake, natl survey methodology changes and sample results, 1990 rpt, 1358–6
Consumption, supply, trade, prices, spending, and indexes, by food commodity, 1990, annual rpt, 1544–4
Cotton linters production, stocks, use, and prices, monthly rpt, 1309–10
Cottonseed prices and quality, by State, seasonal weekly rpt, 1309–14
Cottonseed quality factors, by State, 1991 crop, annual rpt, 1309–5

County Business Patterns, 1989: employment, establishments, and payroll, by SIC 2- to 4-digit industry and county, annual State rpt series, 2326–8
County Business Patterns, 1990: employment, establishments, and payroll, by SIC 2- to 4-digit industry and county, annual State rpt series, 2326–6
CPI by component for US city average, and by selected metro area, region, and population size, monthly rpt, 6762–2
Employment, earnings, and hours, by SIC 1- to 4-digit industry, monthly 1989-Feb 1992, annual rpt, 6744–4
Exports and imports (agricultural) commodity and country, prices, and world market devs, monthly rpt, 1922–12
Exports and imports (agricultural) of US, by commodity and country, bimonthly rpt, 1522–1
Exports and imports (agricultural) of US, by detailed commodity and country, 1991, annual rpt, 1524–8
Exports and imports (agricultural) of US, by detailed commodity and country, 1991, semiannual rpt, 1522–4
Exports and imports between US and outlying areas, by detailed commodity and mode of transport, 1991, annual rpt, 2424–11
Exports and imports of dairy, livestock, and poultry products, by commodity and country, FAS monthly circular, 1925–32
Exports and imports of US, by country and detailed commodity, monthly rpt, 2422–12
Exports and imports of US, by Harmonized System 6-digit commodity and country, 1991, annual rpt, 2424–13
Exports and imports of US, by selected country, country group, and commodity group, 1991, annual rpt, 2044–37
Exports and imports of US, by transport mode, country, and SITC 1- to 3-digit commodity, 1991, annual rpt, 2424–12
Exports, imports, tariffs, and industry operating data for oilseeds, 1992 rpt, 9885–8.4
Exports of grains, oilseed products, hides, skins, and cotton, by country, weekly rpt, dropped data, 1922–3
Exports of US, detailed Schedule B commodities with countries of destination, 1991, annual rpt, 2424–10
Farm financial and marketing conditions, forecast 1992, annual chartbook, 1504–8
Farm financial and marketing conditions, forecast 1992, annual conf, 1504–9
Farm sector balance sheet, and receipts by detailed commodity, by State, 1986-90, annual rpt, 1544–18
Fish (processed) production by location, and trade, by species and product, 1988-91, annual rpts, 2166–6
Fish catch, trade, use, and fishery operations, with selected foreign data, by species, 1980s-91, annual rpt, 2164–1
Fish meal and oil production and trade, quarterly tables, 2162–3
Foreign and US agricultural production, acreage, and yield for selected crops, forecasts by selected world region and country, FAS monthly circular, 1925–28
Foreign and US oils, oilseeds, and fats production and trade, FAS periodic circular series, 1925–1
Foreign countries agricultural production, prices, and trade, by country, 1980-91 and forecast 1992, annual world area rpt series, 1524–4
Freight (waterborne domestic and foreign) by commodity, traffic, and passengers, by port and waterway, 1989, annual rpt, 3754–3
Futures and options trading volume, by commodity and exchange, FY91, annual rpt, 11924–2
Input-output structure of US economy, detailed interindustry transactions for 541 industries, and components of final demand, 1982 benchmark data, 2708–17
Inspections of meat and poultry for domestic use and export, and rejections by cause, by type of animal and product, FY90, annual rpt, 1374–3
Manufacturing annual survey, 1990: finances and operations, by SIC 2- to 4-digit industry, series, 2506–14
Manufacturing census, 1987: concentration of largest firms measured by value added, and for shipments by SIC 2- and 4-digit industry, subject rpt, 2497–6
Manufacturing census, 1987: shipments of manufacturers products, by customer class and SIC 2- and 4-digit industry, subject rpt, 2497–4
Nutrient, caloric, and waste composition, detailed data for raw, processed, and prepared foods, 1992 rpt, 1356–3.17
Occupational injury and illness rates, by SIC 2- to 4-digit industry, 1989-90, annual rpt, 6844–7
Occupational injury and illness rates, by SIC 2- to 4-digit industry, 1990, annual rpt, 6844–1
OECD trade, total and for 4 major countries, and US trade by country, by commodity, 1980-90, world area rpt series, 9116–1
Price indexes (producer), by stage of processing and detailed commodity, monthly rpt, 6762–6
Price indexes (producer), by stage of processing and detailed commodity, monthly 1991, annual rpt, 6764–2
Prices (farm-retail) for food, marketing cost components, and industry finances and productivity, 1920s-91, annual rpt, 1544–9
Prices received and paid by farmers, by commodity and State, monthly rpt, 1629–1
Prices received and paid by farmers, by commodity and State, 1991, annual rpt, 1629–5
Prices received by farmers and production value, by detailed crop and State, 1989-91, annual rpt, 1621–2
Production, farms, acreage, and related data, by selected crop and State, monthly rpt, 1621–1
Production inputs, output, and productivity for farms, by commodity and region, 1947-90, annual rpt, 1544–17
Production of oil and fat, consumption by end use, and stocks, by type, monthly Current Industrial Rpt, 2506–4.4
Production of oil, crushings, and stocks, by oilseed type and State, monthly Current Industrial Rpt, 2506–4.3
Production, prices, trade, and export inspections by US port and country of destination, by grain type, weekly rpt, 1313–2
Production, prices, trade, and marketing, by commodity, current situation and forecast, monthly rpt with articles, 1502–4
Production, prices, trade, and use of oils and fats, periodic situation rpt with articles, 1561–3
Science, engineering, and technical employment in manufacturing, by field and industry, 1989, triennial rpt, 9627–23
Soviet Union and US economic and sociodemographic indicators, selected years 1970-90, handbook, 2328–80
Sunflower seed stocks by region and market city, and seed inspected for export, weekly rpt, 1313–4
Tallow and grease foreign and US production, trade, and use, by selected country, FAS semiannual circular series, 1925–33
Weight and volume conversion factors for agricultural commodities and products, 1992 rpt, 1508–3
see also Animal feed
see also Corn
see also Peanuts
see also Soybeans
see also under By Commodity in the "Index by Categories"

O'Keefe, John
"Bank Failure Resolutions: Implications for Banking Industry Structure, Conduct and Performance", 9292–4.304

Oklahoma
Banks (insured commercial and savings) deposits by instn, State, MSA, and county, as of June 1991, annual regional rpt, 9295–3.4
Coal production and mines by county, prices, productivity, miners, and reserves, by mining method and State, 1990-91, annual rpt, 3164–25
Deaths and rates, by detailed location, cause, and demographic characteristics, 1989, US Vital Statistics annual rpt, 4144–3.1
Employment by industry div, earnings, and hours, by southwestern State, monthly rpt, 6962–2
Employment, earnings, and hours, by selected SIC 1- to 4-digit industry, State, and for 275 MSAs, 1987-92, 6748–81
Fed Govt spending in States and local areas, by type, State, county, and city, FY91, annual rpt, 2464–3
Fed Govt spending in States, by type, program, agency, and State, FY91, annual rpt, 2464–2
Financial and economic devs, Fed Reserve 10th District, quarterly rpt, 9381–16
HHS financial aid, by program, recipient, State, and city, FY91, annual regional listing, 4004–3.6
Hospital deaths of Medicare patients, actual and expected rates by diagnosis, and hospital characteristics, by instn, FY90 annual State rpt, 4654–14.37
Housing census, 1990: inventory, occupancy, and costs, State fact sheet, 2326–21.38
Housing census, 1990: summary unit characteristics, by householder race and age, county, place, and urban-rural location, State rpt, 2471–1.38

Land Mgmt Bur activities in southwestern US, FY91, annual rpt, 5724–15
Medicare payment of physicians, reforms impacts on services, and monitoring methods, 1992 annual rpt, 4004–34
Military prime contract awards, by contractor, service branch, State, and city, FY91, annual rpt, 3544–22
Mineral Industry Surveys, State reviews of production, 1991, preliminary annual rpt, 5614–6
Minerals (strategic) deposits in North Central States, characteristics, 1992 compilation of papers, 5668–127
Multinatl firms US affiliates finances and operations, by industry, country of parent firm, and State, 1987, 2708–48
Physicians, by specialty, age, sex, and location of training and practice, 1990, State rpt, 4116–6.37
Population and housing census, 1990: detailed geographic coverage, State CD-ROM, 2551–9.7
Population and housing census, 1990: summary characteristics, by county, subdiv, and place, State rpt, 2551–7.38
Population census, 1990: population characteristics and living arrangements, by county, place, and urban-rural location, State rpt, 2531–1.38
Statistical Abstract of US, 1992 annual data compilation, 2324–1
Water supply and quality in streams and lakes, and groundwater levels in wells, by drainage basin, 1990, annual State rpt, 5666–10.35
see also Oklahoma City, Okla.
see also under By State in the "Index by Categories"

Oklahoma City, Okla.
Housing and households characteristics, 1988 survey, MSA fact sheet, 2485–11.2
see also under By City and By SMSA or MSA in the "Index by Categories"

Old age
see Aged and aging

Old age assistance
Assistance (financial and nonfinancial) of Fed Govt, 1992 base edition, annual listing, 104–5
Benefits, beneficiaries, and spells of participation, by aid program and recipient characteristics, 1987-88, Current Population Rpt, 2546–20.25
Energy aid for low income households, funding sources, costs, and participation, by State, FY90, annual rpt, 4584–1
Energy aid for low income households, program characteristics by State, FY91, annual rpt, 4584–2
Fed Govt programs under Ways and Means Committee jurisdiction, finances, operations, and participant characteristics, FY70s-91, annual rpt, 21784–11
Food stamp eligibility and payment errors, by type, recipient characteristics, and State, FY90, annual rpt, 1364–15
Food stamp recipient household size, composition, income, and income and deductions allowed, summer 1989, annual rpt, 1364–8
Foreign countries social security programs coverage, funding, eligibility, and benefits, by country, 1991, biennial rpt, 4746–4.62
HHS financial aid, by program, recipient, State, and city, FY91, annual regional listings, 4004–3
Housing (low income) for aged, HUD capital advances and rental aid by recipient, FY91, press release, 5006–3.88
Housing (low income) for aged, HUD capital advances and rental aid by recipient, FY92, press release, 5006–3.97
Housing (public) for aged, placement of younger mentally disabled tenants, behavioral problems, and services, 1990 survey, GAO rpt, 26113–590
Medicaid and SSI recipients, by eligibility type, from 1970s, and by State, 1990, annual rpt, 4744–3.8
Medicaid coverage, funding, and costs, with reform recommendations, mid 1960s-92, 10048–83
Older persons socioeconomic characteristics, 1900s-90 and projected to 2050, biennial chartbook, 12904–1
Outlying areas income maintenance beneficiaries and payments, by program and area, quarterly FY90, annual rpt, 4584–3.1; 4584–3.2
Outlying areas programs and provisions, FY89-90, annual rpt, 4584–8
Poor aged persons, by health, nutrition, assistance, and other characteristics, 1990, GAO rpt, 26131–100
Senior Community Service Employment program participant characteristics, FY87, annual rpt, 6404–17
see also Medicare
see also Old-Age, Survivors, Disability, and Health Insurance
see also Pensions and pension funds
see also Supplemental Security Income

Old-Age, Survivors, Disability, and Health Insurance
Actuarial studies, Medicare and OASDI future cost estimates and past experience analyses, series, 4706–1
Actuarial studies of OASDHI programs, series, 4706–2
Admin of OASDHI and SSI, case processing, staff, and client problems with contacting SSA offices, 1980s-90, hearing, 25148–45
Advisory Commission on Social Security findings and recommendations on OASDHI and health care system status and reform, series, 10176–3
Advisory Commission on Social Security findings and recommendations on OASDHI and health care system status and reform, 1991 quadrennial rpt, 10178–1
Assistance (financial and nonfinancial) of Fed Govt, 1992 base edition, annual listing, 104–5
Assistance of Fed Govt, by type, program, agency, and State, FY91, annual rpt, 2464–2
Benefits, beneficiary characteristics, and trust funds of OASDHI, Medicaid, SSI, and related programs, selected years 1937-90, annual rpt, 4744–3
Benefits by county, FY91, annual regional listings, 4004–3
Benefits overpayment, and overpaid beneficiaries characteristics, for OASDI and SSI, late 1970s-90, GAO rpt, 26121–484
Budget of US, balances of budget authority obligated and unobligated, by function and agency, FY90-93, annual rpt, 104–8
Budget of US, CBO analysis and review of FY93 budget by function, annual rpt, 26304–2
Budget of US, CBO analysis of revenue and spending alternatives and projections of economic indicators, FY93-97, annual rpt, 26304–3
Budget of US, House concurrent resolution, with spending and revenue targets, FY93 and projected to FY97, annual rpt, 21264–2
Budget of US, midsession review of FY93 budget, by function, annual rpt, 104–7
Budget of US, obligations and authority by function, agency, and program, with summaries and analyses, FY93, annual rpt, 104–2
Budget of US, receipts by source, outlays by agency and program, and balances, monthly rpt, 8102–3
Court civil and criminal caseloads for Federal district, appeals, and bankruptcy courts, by type of suit and offense, circuit, and district, 1991, annual rpt, 18204–11
Court civil and criminal caseloads for Federal district, appeals, and special courts, 1991, annual rpt, 18204–8
Data on OASDHI beneficiaries, collection system design and compared to earlier surveys, with summary results, 1992 article, 4742–1.313
Disability benefit applications under OASDI and SSI, dispositions, awards, and administrative law judge hearing outcomes, by race, 1988, GAO rpt, 26121–459
Disability Insurance beneficiaries deaths and survival, by selected characteristics, for persons entitled 1972 and 1985, article, 4742–1.321
Disability Insurance eligibility determinations by States, caseloads, Federal funding, and State directors views, 1980s-91, hearing, 21148–63
Expenditures (direct) and employment, by function and level of govt, selected years 1962-87, 10048–53
Expenditures of Fed Govt by type, and other finances, selected years 1952-90, annual rpt, 10044–1
Fed Govt civilian employees demographic and employment characteristics, as of Sept 1991, annual article, 9842–1.301
Finances and operations of programs under Ways and Means Committee jurisdiction, FY70s-91, annual rpt, 21784–11
Finances of govts, revenue by source, spending by function, debt, and assets, by level of govt, FY90, annual rpt, 2466–2.2
Finances of SSA programs, and litigation, FY91, annual rpt, 4704–6
Food stamp recipient household size, composition, income, and income and deductions allowed, summer 1989, annual rpt, 1364–8
Households composition, income, benefits, and labor force status, Survey of Income and Program Participation methodology, working paper series, 2626–10
Income (household) and poverty status under alternative income definitions, by recipient characteristics, 1979-91, annual Current Population Rpt, 2546–6.78

Income tax returns of individuals, detailed data, 1988, annual rpt, 8304–2
Mental health care facilities, staff, patients, and finances, 1970s-91, biennial rpt, 4094–1
Natl income and product accounts, comprehensive accounts and components, benchmark revisions, 1929-88, 2708–5
Natl income and product accounts, comprehensive accounts and components, *Survey of Current Business*, monthly rpt, 2702–1.25
Older persons and younger adults household income, by source, household composition, and age group, 1984 and 1989, article, 4742–1.304
Older persons and younger adults household income, by source, household composition, race, and age group, 1984-89, 4746–26.20
Older persons income and sources, by OASDI beneficiary and poverty status, and other characteristics, 1990, biennial chartbook, 4744–25
Older persons income and sources, by whether OASDI beneficiary, poverty status, and other characteristics, 1990, biennial rpt, 4744–26
Pacific territories population and housing detailed characteristics, by location, 1990 Census of Population and Housing, series, 2551–8
Population economic well-being indicators, by selected characteristics and household income and income-to-poverty ratio, 1984, 2546–20.22
Poverty status of population and families, by detailed characteristics, 1991, annual Current Population Rpt, 2546–6.77
Public debt burden on future generations forecast under alternative tax, OASDI, and Medicare policies, 1992 working paper, 9377–9.137
Public opinion on OASDHI and health care system operations and reform issues, series, 10176–2
Railroad retirement and unemployment insurance accounts status, and interchange with OASDHI fund, FY90, annual rpt, 9704–2.1
Research on social security programs and related issues, technical paper series, 4746–26
Retirees health and other characteristics related to Medicare use and charges 2 years later, 1984, article, 4652–1.319
Retirement earnings test of OASI, liberalization effect on beneficiaries and Federal revenue, 1991 hearing, 21788–215
Social Security Bulletin, OASDHI and other program operations and beneficiary characteristics, from 1940, quarterly journal, 4742–1
State and local govt employees OASDHI coverage, by system, FY90, annual rpt, 2466–2.4
State and local govt employees OASDI coverage under voluntary Federal-State agreements, 1987, article, 4742–1.315
Statistical Abstract of US, 1992 annual data compilation, 2324–1.12
Student aid Pell grants and applicants, by tuition, income level, instn type and control, and State, 1990/91, annual rpt, 4804–1
Tax (income) returns of individuals, by filing status, tax item, and income level, 1991, annual article, 8302–2.319
Tax (income) returns of individuals, selected income and tax items by income level, preliminary 1990, annual article, 8302–2.307
Trust funds finances, FY91 with projections, annual article, 4742–1.314
Trust funds finances of OASDHI, FY91 and projected to 2066, annual rpt, 4654–8
Trust funds finances of OASDHI, impacts of Federal debt, with background data, 1990-2065, technical paper, 8006–6.6
Trust funds finances of OASDI, 1937-FY91 and alternative projections to 2070, annual rpt, 4704–4
Trust funds financial condition, for Disability Insurance, monthly rpt, 8102–9.14
Trust funds financial condition, for OASI, monthly rpt, 8102–9.2
Trust funds of OASDI and Medicare, finances, economic assumptions, and outlook, with health care system reform issues, series, 10176–1
US attorneys civil cases, by type and disposition, FY91, annual rpt, 6004–2.5
see also Medicare
see also Social security tax

Olive, Kenneth E.
"Attitudes of Patients Toward Smoking by Health Professionals", 4042–3.334

Oliveira, Victor J.
"Concentrations of Hired and Contract Labor Expenses", 1541–1.305
"Profile of Hired Farmworkers, 1990 Annual Averages", 1598–278

Omaha, Nebr.
Drug test results at arrest, by drug type, offense, and sex, for selected urban areas, quarterly rpt, 6062–3
see also under By City and By SMSA or MSA in the "Index by Categories"

Oman
Agricultural trade of US, by detailed commodity and country, 1991, annual rpt, 1524–8
Agricultural trade of US, by detailed commodity and country, 1991, semiannual rpt, 1522–4
AID economic aid to developing countries, obligations and disbursements by country, quarterly rpt, 9912–4
AID loans repayment status and terms by program and country, and status of predecessor agency loans, quarterly rpt, 9912–3
Apple imports of 5 Persian Gulf countries, by country of origin, 1981-90, article, 1925–34.322
Borders (maritime) of Oman, geographic coordinates, as of 1982, 7006–8.8
Boycotts (intl) by OPEC and other countries, US firms and individuals cooperation and tax benefits denied, 1990, article, 8302–2.323
Economic and military aid and loans from US and intl agencies, by program and country, FY46-91, annual rpt, 9914–5
Economic and social conditions of developing countries from 1960s, and Intl Dev Cooperation Agency and AID activities and funding, FY91-93, annual rpt, 9904–4
Economic conditions, policy, and trade practices, by country, 1989-91, annual rpt, 21384–5
Economic, social, political, and geographic summary data, by country, 1992, annual factbook, 9114–2
Exports and imports of US, by commodity and country, 1980-90, world area rpt, 9116–1.6
Exports and imports of US, by transport mode, country, and SITC 1- to 3-digit commodity, 1991, annual rpt, 2424–12
Exports of US, detailed Schedule B commodities with countries of destination, 1991, annual rpt, 2424–10
Human rights conditions in 170 countries, and US economic and military aid, 1991, annual rpt, 21384–3
Military aid of US, arms sales, and training programs costs and budget requests, by program, world region, and country, FY91-93, annual rpt, 7144–13
Military spending, arms trade, and force strengths, with govt spending and population, by country, 1979-89, annual rpt, 9824–1
Minerals Yearbook, Vol 3, 1989: foreign country review of production, trade, and policy, by commodity, annual rpt, 5604–35.3
Population size, growth rates, and components of change, by country, projected 1990-2020 and trends from 1950, biennial rpt, 2324–9
Refugee migration, and intl aid programs, by world area and country of origin and asylum, 1991, annual rpt, 7004–15
Steel trade, by product, country, and customs district, with US industry operating data, 1989-June 1992, semiannual rpt, 9882–15
UN voting record and share of votes in agreement with US, by issue, country, and world area, 1991, annual rpt, 7004–18

Omnibus Budget Reconciliation Act
Budget of US, CBO analysis of revenue and spending alternatives and projections of economic indicators, FY93-97, annual rpt, 26304–3

On-line information systems
see Computer networks
see Information storage and retrieval systems

O'Neill, K. L.
"Can Thymidine Kinase Levels in Breast Tumors Predict Disease Recurrence?", 4472–1.355

Onions
see Vegetables and vegetable products

Ontario County, N.Y.
Housing and households characteristics, and unit and neighborhood quality, by MSA location for 11 MSAs, 1986 survey, supplement, 2485–8

Ontario Province, Canada
Great Lakes industrial water pollution emissions, comparison of State, EPA, Intl Joint Commission, and Ontario standards, 1991 rpt, 14648–29
Health service use related to change in physician fee and other variables, regression results for 28 common services, for Ontario, Canada, 1975-87, 17266–2.3
Pollution (air) levels in Detroit area, by pollutant and site, 1970s-90, 14648–28

OPEC
see Organization of Petroleum Exporting Countries
Open housing
see Discrimination in housing
Operating costs
see Business income and expenses, general
see Business income and expenses, specific industry
see Operating ratios
see Production costs
Operating ratios
Agricultural cooperatives finances, aggregate for top 100 assns by commodity group, 1990, annual rpt, 1124–3
Agricultural, fishery, and forest products trade, tariffs, and industry operating data, commodity rpt series, 9885–8
Agricultural Outlook, production, prices, marketing, and trade, by commodity, forecast and current situation, monthly rpt with articles, 1502–4
Air traffic, capacity, and performance, by carrier and type of operation, monthly rpt, 7302–6
Air traffic, capacity, and performance for medium regionals, by carrier, quarterly rpt, 7302–8
Airline finances and operations, summary data, quarterly rpt, 7502–16
Airline finances, by carrier, carrier group, and for total certificated system, quarterly rpt, 7302–7
Airline operations and passenger, cargo, and mail traffic, by type of service, air carrier, State, and country, 1981-90, annual rpt, 7504–1.6
Bank holding companies capital requirements impacts on asset growth, 1989-91, working paper, 9375–13.88
Bank holding companies, financial ratios, banks held, and equity financing relation to regulatory capital standards, 1970s-90, technical paper, 9366–6.291
Bank holding companies return on equity relation to leverage-related and other financial ratios, 1980s, technical paper, 9385–8.134
Bank holding companies stock prices relation to capital and assets, 1990-92, article, 9385–1.311
Banking and economic conditions, for Fed Reserve 8th District, quarterly rpt with articles, 9391–16
Banking industry structure, performance, and financial devs, for Fed Reserve 10th District, 1991, annual rpt, 9381–14
Banking system reform impacts on consumers, with background data, 1991 hearing, 21248–167
Banks (agricultural) financial ratios, for South Central States, 1990-91, annual article, 9391–16.308
Banks (FDIC-insured) return on assets, by region and State, 1991, annual rpt, 9294–1
Banks (insured commercial) financial ratios, by State, 1987-90, annual rpt, 9294–4
Banks (insured commercial and FDIC-insured savings) assets, income, and financial ratios, by asset size and State, quarterly rpt, 13002–3
Banks (insured commercial and savings) financial condition and performance, by asset size and region, quarterly rpt, 9292–1
Banks (natl) charters, mergers, liquidations, enforcement cases, and financial performance, with data by instn and State, quarterly rpt, 8402–3
Banks acquisitions purchase price relation to target and acquiring banks financial ratios variability and asset size, 1980s, working paper, 9371–10.80
Banks agricultural loans share of all loans, with market shares and returns on assets, by bank size, 1970s-80s, working paper, 9381–10.122
Banks and thrifts finances and operations by deposit size, Fed Reserve functional cost analysis, 1991, annual rpt, 9364–6
Banks and thrifts financial performance relation to market concentration, 1992 working paper, 9371–10.88
Banks and thrifts in New England, assets and liabilities by type, and deposits relation to capital/asset ratios, by instn type and size, 1980s-91, article, 9373–1.309
Banks and thrifts in New England, deposits by type and loans, relation to capital/asset ratios, by instn size, 1990-91, working paper, 9373–27.4
Banks and thrifts in New England, real estate lending impacts of capital losses, with financial ratios, 1980s-91, article, 9373–27.12
Banks assets composition and securitization, relation to risk and liquidity indicators, model description and results, 1980s-91, technical paper, 9366–6.295
Banks capital aid by Reconstruction Finance Corp, impact on solvency status and financial ratios, 1920s-40, article, 9381–1.304
Banks dividends on common stock, relation to earnings, capital, and other factors, 1989-90, article, 9292–4.302
Banks finances, examination ratings, and failure resolution costs and methods, 1980s-91, article, 9292–4.301
Banks financial performance in Fed Reserve 10th District, by State, quarterly rpt, 9381–16
Banks financial performance indicators, by bank, 1991-92, hearings, 25248–127
Banks financial performance relation to growth in State personal income, 1980s-90, working paper, 9377–9.135
Banks financial ratios, for agricultural and small banks in South Central States, by State, as of 1991 and trends from 1985, article, 9391–16.306
Banks in Fed Reserve 3rd District, assets, income, and rates of return, by major instn, quarterly rpt, annual table, 9387–10
Banks in Fed Reserve 6th District, financial ratios by asset size and State, 1986-90, annual article, 9371–1.305
Banks in Fed Reserve 8th District, financial performance indicators by asset size, 1988-91, annual article, 9391–16.307
Banks in Fed Reserve 9th District, finances and performance ratios, by State, quarterly journal, 9383–19
Banks in Texas, loan losses relation to loan volume growth and other factors, mid 1970s-90, article, 9379–1.305
Banks in Texas, loans and financial ratios relation to economic indicators, 1970s-90, working paper, 9379–14.16
Banks interest rates on deposits, relation to measures of bank financial strength and other indicators, 1984-91, technical paper, 9366–6.300
Banks mergers impacts on noninterest expense ratios, with background data for total and southeastern US, 1980s-90, article, 9371–1.303
Banks mergers impacts on operating costs, 1982-86, working paper, 9371–10.78
Banks profitability, balance sheet and income statement items, and financial ratios, by asset size, 1985-91, annual article, 9362–1.305
Banks profitability relation to market concentration, efficiency indicators, and regulation, model description and results, 1980s, technical paper, 9366–6.290
Banks seasonal borrowing from Fed Reserve, participants financial and other characteristics, Fed Reserve 8th District, 1984-90, article, 9391–1.311
Banks securities new issues by type of instrument, relation to primary capital ratio and other factors, 1983-86, working paper, 9371–10.79
Banks uninsured deposits by type and bank size, and relation to bank size and selected operating ratios, 1980s-91, technical paper, 9385–8.126
Building materials industry finances and operations, by SIC 4-digit industry, selected years 1977-89, article, 2042–1.302
Bus (Class I) passengers and selected revenue data, for individual large carriers, quarterly rpt, 9482–13
Business statistics, detailed data for major industries and economic indicators, *Survey of Current Business*, monthly rpt, 2702–1.3
Capital costs over business cycles relation to firm size and financial distress indicators, 1960s-91, article, 9385–1.312
Chemical and energy products trade, tariffs, and industry operating data, commodity rpt series, 9885–11
Corporate profits by industry div, stockholders equity, and costs per unit of output, 1947-91, annual rpt, 204–1.1; 204–1.7
Corporations financial statements for manufacturing, mining, and trade, by selected SIC 2- to 3-digit industry, quarterly rpt, 2502–1
Corporations profits by industry div, profit tax liability, and dividends, monthly rpt, quarterly data, 23842–1.1
Corporations profits, natl compounded annual rates of change, monthly rpt, 9391–3
Corporations under domestic and foreign control, finances and tax burdens, 1983-87, GAO rpt, 26119–411
Credit card issuers, and banks credit operations, costs and revenue, mid 1970s-91, article, 9362–1.306
Credit Union Natl Admin Central Liquidity Facility financial statements, FY91, annual rpt, 9534–5
Credit unions (federally-insured) financial performance, by charter type and region, 1st half 1992, semiannual rpt, 9532–7
Credit unions federally insured, finances by instn characteristics and State, as of June 1992, semiannual rpt, 9532–6

Credit unions federally insured, finances, mergers, closings, and insurance fund losses and financial statements, FY91, annual rpt, 9534–7

Credit unions federally insured, finances, 1990-91, annual rpt, 9534–1

Credit unions financial performance and regulation, with background data, 1960s-90, GAO rpt, 26119–364

Credit unions with low income membership, financial, operating, and membership data, 1982-91, 9536–1.8

Electric power distribution loans from REA, and borrower operating and financial data, by firm and State, 1991, annual rpt, 1244–1

Electric utilities privately owned, finances and operations, detailed data, 1990, annual rpt, 3164–23

Electronics and services trade, tariffs, and industry operating data, commodity rpt series, 9885–12

Energy producers finances and operations, by energy type for US firms domestic and foreign operations, 1990, annual rpt, 3164–44

Energy resources of US, foreign direct investment by energy type and firm, and US affiliates operations, as of 1990, annual rpt, 3164–80

Farm credit, terms, delinquency, agricultural bank failures, and credit conditions by Fed Reserve District, quarterly rpt, 9365–3.10

Farm finances, assets, liabilities, and debt by lender type, by State, 1960-89, 1548–384

Farm finances, debts, assets, and receipts, and lenders financial condition, quarterly rpt with articles, 1541–1

Farm loan guarantees of FmHA, characteristics of borrowers, lenders, and loans, FY88, 1548–386

Farm loans at risk of default, lender losses, and selected farm financial indicators, by type of farm and lender, 1984-89, 1548–383

Farm production itemized costs, receipts, and returns, by crop and State, 1987-89, annual rpt, 1544–24

Farm sector balance sheet, and marketing receipts by detailed commodity, by State, 1986-90, annual rpt, 1544–18

Fed Natl Mortgage Assn, Fed Home Loan Mortgage Corp, and FHLBs finances, 1991 hearings, 21248–170

Finance companies assets, operating ratios, and growth indicators, for top 20 firms, 1980s-90, article, 9385–1.309

Financial instns reform issues, with finances, impacts of deposit insurance changes, and views of depositors and bankers, 1991 hearings, 25248–129

Financial markets (intl) performance of foreign and US bank and securities firms, finances and competitiveness issues, 1980s, compilation of papers, 9385–10

Food prices (farm-retail), marketing cost components, and industry finances and productivity, 1960s-91, annual rpt, 1544–9.3

Fruit and nut production, prices, trade, stocks, and use, by selected crop, periodic situation rpt with articles, 1561–6

Grocery store profits and prices relation to market concentration, literature review, 1990 rpt, 9408–56

Hospital closings, financial and operating characteristics related to instn and area characteristics, 1985-88, 17206–2.28

Hospital financial performance under Medicare, 1977-89, article, 4652–1.315

Hospital reimbursement by Medicare under prospective payment system, analyses of alternative payment plans, series, 17206–1

Hospital reimbursement by Medicare under prospective payment system, and effect on services, finances, and beneficiary payments, 1980-91, annual rpt, 17204–2

Hospital reimbursement by Medicare under prospective payment system, impacts on costs, industry structure and operations, and quality of care, series, 17206–2

Hospital reimbursement by Medicare under prospective payment system, methodology, inputs, and data by diagnostic group, 1992 annual rpt, 17204–1

Hospital reimbursement by Medicare under prospective payment system, rural area instns financial performance and impacts of PPS policy changes, 1991 rpt, 26306–6.164

Imports and tariff provisions effect on US industries and products, investigations with background financial and operating data, series, 9886–4

Imports injury to US industries from foreign subsidized products and sales at less than fair value, investigations with background financial and operating data, series, 9886–19

Imports injury to US industries from foreign subsidized products, investigations with background financial and operating data, series, 9886–15

Imports injury to US industries from sales at less than fair value, investigations with background financial and operating data, series, 9886–14

Income tax returns of foreign corporations and individuals, and US entities abroad, detailed data compilation, 1970s-89, quinquennial rpt, 8308–31

Industry (US) intl competitiveness, with selected foreign and US operating data by major firm and product, series, 2046–12

Insurance company asset risk assessment, with financial ratios by firm type and financial status, 1990 and trends from 1900s, article, 9373–1.314; 9373–27.3

Insurance company finances, by insurance type and firm, with some intl comparisons, 1991 conf, 9373–3.35

Insurance industry finances, failures, and regulation, with data by firm and State, 1990 hearing, 25528–119

Insurance industry financial condition, operations, assets, junk bond holdings, and State regulation, with intl comparisons, 1991 hearings, 25268–79

Machinery and equipment trade, tariffs, and industry operating data, commodity rpt series, 9885–9

Manufacturing capital investment relation to debt/collateral ratios, model description and results, 1950s-80, working paper, 9377–9.141

Manufacturing debt/asset ratios impact on employment changes over the business cycle, 1960s-84, technical paper, 9366–6.286

Manufacturing investment spending relation to cash flow and other factors, model description and results, 1950s-80s, technical paper, 9385–8.129

Manufacturing trade, tariffs, and industry operating data, commodity rpt series, 9885–10

Militarily strategic manufacturing industries finances, operations, and intl competitiveness, series, 2026–1

Minerals and metals trade, tariffs, and industry operating data, commodity rpt series, 9885–13

Minerals foreign and US supply under alternative market conditions, reserves, and background industry data, series, 5606–4

Multinatl firms US affiliates income tax compliance issues, with income and tax data by industry group, 1987-89, press release, 8008–155

Natural gas interstate pipeline company detailed financial and operating data, by firm, 1990, annual rpt, 3164–38

Nonprofit charitable organizations finances, with data by State and for top 10 instns, 1988, article, 8302–2.302

Oil company production and imports by type, and financial data, 1975-90, annual rpt, 3164–74.1

Railroad employment and finances, for ICC-regulated carriers, as of FY91, annual rpt, 9484–1

Railroad freight, by commodity and region of origin and destination, 1989, annual rpt, 7604–6

Railroad revenue, income, freight, and rate of return, by Class I freight railroad and district, quarterly rpt, 9482–2

Retail trade inventory/sales ratios, by selected kind of business, monthly rpt, 2413–3.2

Retail trade sales, inventories, purchases, gross margin, and accounts receivable, by SIC 2- to 4-digit kind of business and form of ownership, 1990, annual rpt, 2413–5

Savings and loan assns, FHLB 6th District insured members financial condition and operations by State, quarterly rpt, 9302–23

Savings instns brokered deposits relation to size and selected financial ratios, late 1980s-91, article, 9379–15.301

Savings instns brokered deposits relation to size and selected financial ratios, 1st qtr 1991, working paper, 9379–14.17

Savings instns conversion from mutual to stock ownership, financial performance for Fed Reserve 1st District instns, 1980s-90, article, 9373–1.307

Savings instns economies of scale and other efficiency indicators for mutual and stock instns, model description and results, 1991, working paper, 9387–8.277

Savings instns failure resolution costs, impacts of capital standards relaxation, 1979-92, working paper, 9377–9.140

Savings instns financial ratios, for high and low risk S&Ls, 1987, article, 9375–1.306

Savings instns financial statements, for instns insured by Savings Assn Insurance Fund by FHLB district and State, and for FDIC-insured savings banks, 1989, annual rpt, 8434–1

Savings instns insured by Savings Assn Insurance Fund, assets, liabilities, and deposit and loan activity, by conservatorship status, monthly rpt, 8432–1
Savings instns insured by Savings Assn Insurance Fund, finances by profitability group, district, and State, quarterly rpt, 8432–4
Savings instns profitability on fixed-rate mortgages, relation to interest rate spread and other operating ratios, model results, 1991 technical paper, 9366–6.289
Securities industry finances, for broker-dealers and individual stock exchanges and clearing agencies, 1986-90, annual rpt, 9734–2.1
Semiconductor industry capital investment and R&D spending under alternative tax proposals, and asset/equity ratios by selected firm, 1980s-91, working paper, 15036–1.2
Small business financing sources, and business financial data by size, type, and industry, 1980s-90, annual rpt, 9764–6.2
Small Business Investment Company program financial performance, findings and recommendations, 1992 rpt, 9768–24
Steel imports of US under voluntary restraint agreement, by product, customs district, and country, with US industry operating data, quarterly rpt, 9882–13
Steel trade, by product, country, and customs district, with US industry operating data, 1989-June 1992, semiannual rpt, 9882–15
Stock (common) prices and earnings ratios, current data and annual trends, monthly rpt, 23842–1.5
Stock prices relation to corporate earnings, model results with data for Ford Motor Co, 1950s-90, article, 9373–1.306
Telecommunications finances, rates, and traffic for US carriers intl operations, by service type, firm, and country, 1975-90, annual rpt, 9284–17
Telephone and telegraph firms detailed finances and operations, 1990, annual rpt, 9284–6
Telephone firms borrowing under Rural Telephone Program, and financial and operating data, by State, 1991, annual rpt, 1244–2
Transit systems finances and operations, by mode, size of fleet and urban area, region, and for 518 systems, 1990, annual rpt, 7884–4
Truck, bus, and rail carriers regulated by ICC, employment and finances, as of FY91, annual rpt, 9484–1
Truck itemized costs per mile, finances, and operations, for agricultural carriers, 1991, annual rpt, 1311–15
Truck transport of household goods, financial and operating data by firm, quarterly rpt, 9482–14
Truck transport of property, financial and operating data by region and firm, quarterly rpt, 9482–5
Unemployment insurance programs of States, benefits, coverage, exhaustions, and finances, 1990, annual tables, 6404–10
Uranium mining and milling industries finances and operations, with selected foreign comparisons, 1970s-90 and projected to 2005, annual rpt, 3164–82
Workers compensation coverage, benefits, costs, and insurers performance, 1939-88, article, 4742–1.322
see also Agricultural productivity
see also Industrial capacity and utilization
see also Labor productivity
see also Productivity

OPIC
see Overseas Private Investment Corp.

Opinion and attitude surveys
AIDS public knowledge, attitudes, info sources, and testing, 1991 survey, 4146–8.218
Banking system reform issues, with top instn finances, fiscal impacts, and views of depositors, bankers, and regulators on deposit insurance, 1991 hearings, 21248–168
Confidence in people running selected social instns, 1973-90 surveys, biennial rpt, 9624–10.7
Crime and crime-related issues, public opinion by respondent characteristics, data compilation, 1992 annual rpt, 6064–6.2
Crime victimization rates, by offense, reasons for reporting and not reporting crime to police, and police response, 1990 survey, annual rpt, 6066–3.47
Criminal justice systems problems, assessments of State and local officials, 1990, 6066–20.22
Criminal sentences under Federal mandatory minimum provisions by defendant characteristics, and views on justice system impacts, FY90, 17668–2
Drug, alcohol, and cigarette use and attitudes of youth, by substance type and selected characteristics, 1975-91 surveys, annual rpt, 4494–4
Education (elementary and secondary) schools, teachers, staff, and enrollment, by selected characteristics, 1987/88-1988/89, 4836–3.10
Education data compilation, 1992 annual rpt, 4824–2.6; 4824–2.12
Education data, detail for elementary, secondary, and higher education, 1920s-91 and projected to 2002, annual rpt, 4824–1
Educational performance and conditions, characteristics, attitudes, activities, and plans, 1988 8th grade class, natl longitudinal survey, series, 4826–9
Educational performance of elementary and secondary students, and factors affecting proficiency, by selected characteristics, 1990 natl assessments, subject rpt series, 4896–8
Educational performance of elementary and secondary students in math, science, reading, and writing, 1969-90, 4898–32
Educational performance of elementary and secondary students, issues and special topics, natl assessments, fact sheet series, 4896–9
Educational performance of elementary and secondary students, reading proficiency and related factors, 1988 and 1990 natl assessments, 4898–33
Family life and relationships quality and other issues, views of parents and children, 1990 survey, 15528–2
Fed Govt employees views on work condition, 1991 survey, GAO rpt, 26119–406
Fed Govt labor-mgmt relations program operations and effectiveness, agency and union representatives views, 1990-91 surveys, GAO rpt, 26119–367
Fed Govt procurement operations employees job performance, and views on policies and practices, 1991 survey, 9498–17
Fed Govt recruitment for Federal entry-level professional positions, reasons for accepting or declining offer, 1990 surveys, GAO rpt, 26119–387
Fed Govt Senior Executive Service members views on work environment, 1989 and 1991 surveys, GAO rpt, 26119–402
Fed Govt white collar employees views on work conditions and schedules, 1992 survey, 9848–41
Financial instns reform issues, with finances, impacts of deposit insurance changes, and views of depositors and bankers, 1991 hearings, 25248–129
Health care system reform issues, with data on insurance administrative and employer costs, coverage, public views, and Canada and UK systems, 1950s-91, hearings, 25368–180
High school classes of 1980 and 1982: education, employment, and family characteristics, activities, and attitudes, natl longitudinal study, series, 4826–2
Homeownership values, reasons, and barriers, views by race and tenure, 1992 survey, 9478–1
Homosexuals holding selected jobs, public opinion, 1977-91 surveys, GAO rpt, 26123–392.1
Housing (rental) units, total, with HUD assistance by program, and eligible for aid, by unit, household, and neighborhood characteristics, and location, 1989, biennial rpt, 5184–11
Housing alteration and repair for owner-occupied units, with opinion of structure and neighborhood, 1987, 2486–1.13
Housing and neighborhood quality, indicators and attitudes, by householder type and location, for 11 MSAs, 1987 survey, supplement, 2485–8
Housing and neighborhood quality, indicators and attitudes, by householder type and location, 1989, biennial rpt supplement, 2485–13
Housing and neighborhood quality, indicators and attitudes, MSA surveys, series, 2485–6
Indian and Alaska Native youth health condition and behavioral patterns, by sex and grade, 1988-90, 4088–3
Mammography and cancer views of women, 1990 local area survey, article, 4042–3.370
OASDHI and health care system operations and reform issues, public opinion, series, 10176–2
Pregnancy health survey, reasons for participation for mothers with and without children with birth defects, 1990, article, 4042–3.377
Presidential approval rating and political party affiliation impact on defense spending and transfer payments, model description and results, 1950s-88, working paper, 9393–10.17

Schools crime victimization, drug availability, and preventive measures, with student views, 1989 survey, 6066–3.46
Schools safety, discipline, and student drug use, elementary and secondary school principals views, 1991 survey, 4826–1.32
Science and technology public knowledge, interest, and expectations, 1990 survey, biennial rpt, 9624–10.7
Smoking cessation clinics success rates, and participants smoking history, views on program, and other characteristics, 1987-88 local area study, article, 4042–3.314
Tax (income) admin and compliance issues, and taxpayer views, 1991 conf, 8304–25
Taxes, spending, and govt efficiency, public opinion by respondent characteristics, 1992 survey, annual rpt, 10044–2
Teachers and administrators in private schools, pay, work conditions, and selected characteristics, by school type and affiliation, 1987/88, 4836–3.8
Teachers of vocational education, by subject area and selected characteristics, for public high schools, 1987/88, 4836–3.9
World War II soldier survey results, questionnaire forms, and related rpts, Natl Archives special collection, 1991 rpt, 9516–1.10
Youth alcohol use, knowledge, attitudes, and info sources, series, 4006–10
Youth drug, alcohol, and cigarette use and attitudes, by substance type and selected characteristics, 1975-91 surveys, press release, 4008–116
see also Business outlook and attitude surveys
see also Consumer surveys
see also Foreign opinion of U.S.
see also Market research

Options
see Futures trading
see Options trading

Options trading
Arbitration of securities disputes between brokers and investors, outcomes related to forum type and other factors, 1992 GAO rpt, 26119–401
Banks (insured commercial and savings) finances, for foreign and domestic offices, by asset size, 1990, annual rpt, 9294–4.2
Intl financial markets performance of foreign and US bank and securities firms, finances and competitiveness issues, 1980s, compilation of papers, 9385–10
Market decline of Nov 1991, impacts of trading related to option and futures expirations, 9738–22
Trading activity by commodity and exchange, and Commodity Futures Trading Commission oversight, FY91, annual rpt, 11924–2
see also Futures trading

Optoelectronics
see Fiber optics

Optometry
County Business Patterns, 1989: employment, establishments, and payroll, by SIC 2- to 4-digit industry and county, annual State rpt series, 2326–8
County Business Patterns, 1990: employment, establishments, and payroll, by SIC 2- to 4-digit industry and county, annual State rpt series, 2326–6
CPI by component for US city average, and by selected metro area, region, and population size, monthly rpt, 6762–2
Degrees awarded in higher education, by level, field, race, and sex, 1989/90 and trends from 1980/81, annual rpt, 4844–17
Health condition and care indicators, 1950s-90 with health improvement and disease prevention goals for 1990, annual data compilation, 4144–11
Indian Health Service and tribal facility outpatient visits, by type of provider, selected hospital, and service area, FY91, annual rpt, 4084–3
Insurance (health) coverage and provisions of employee benefit plans, by plan type, for State and local govt employees, 1990, biennial rpt, 6784–21
Labor demand, turnover, and training completions, by detailed occupation, 1990 and projected to 2005, biennial rpt, 6744–3
Labor supply and education of health professionals, by professional and other characteristics, and location, 1960s-92 and projected to 2020, biennial rpt, 4114–8
Labor supply of physicians, by specialty, age, sex, and location of training and practice, 1990, State rpt series, 4116–6
Lenses (aspherical ophthalmoscopy) from Japan at less than fair value, injury to US industry, investigation with background financial and operating data, 1992 rpt, 9886–14.343
Medicare payment of physicians under fee schedule, methodology with data by procedure and specialty, 1992, annual rpt, 17264–1
Military health care personnel, and accessions by training source, by occupation, specialty, and service branch, FY90, annual rpt, 3544–24
Occupational Outlook Handbook, 1992-93, biennial rpt, 6744–1
Tax (income) returns of sole proprietorships, income statement items, by industry group, 1990, annual article, 8302–2.317; 8302–2.320
VA health care facilities trainees, by detailed program and city, FY91, annual rpt, 8704–4
VA health care services, needs, availability, structure, and funding, 1991 compilation of papers, 8608–9
see also Vision

Orange County, N.Y.
Wages by occupation, for office and plant workers, 1992 survey, periodic MSA rpt, 6785–3.4

Oranges
see Citrus fruits

Orders
see Business orders

Ordnance
see Ammunition
see Military supplies and property
see Military weapons

Oregon
Banks (insured commercial and savings) deposits by instn, State, MSA, and county, as of June 1991, annual regional rpt, 9295–3.6
Birds (northern spotted owl) conservation methods in Pacific Northwest, findings and recommendations, 1990 rpt, 1208–385
Birds (northern spotted owl) conservation methods in Pacific Northwest, timber industry impacts, and Federal and State spending, 1980s-95, 1208–388
Camping in wilderness areas, impacts on plants and soils, 1979-90 studies, 1208–395
Coastal areas recreation resources, and impacts of OCS oil and gas dev, for Washington and Oregon, 1983-88, 5738–40
Cranberry production, prices, use, and acreage, for selected States, 1990-91 and forecast 1992, annual rpt, 1621–18.5
Deaths and rates, by detailed location, cause, and demographic characteristics, 1989, US Vital Statistics annual rpt, 4144–3.1
Employment, earnings, and hours, by selected SIC 1- to 4-digit industry, State, and for 275 MSAs, 1987-92, 6748–81
Fed Govt spending in States and local areas, by type, State, county, and city, FY91, annual rpt, 2464–3
Fed Govt spending in States, by type, program, agency, and State, FY91, annual rpt, 2464–2
Fish and invertebrate population and habitats, for Oregon OCS rocky banks, 1988-90, 5738–39
Fishing (ocean sport) activities, and catch by species, by angler characteristics and State, 1987-89, annual coastal area rpt, 2166–17.2
Hazelnut production, 1990-92, annual rpt, 1621–18.6
HHS financial aid, by program, recipient, State, and city, FY91, annual regional listing, 4004–3.10
Hospital deaths of Medicare patients, actual and expected rates by diagnosis, and hospital characteristics, by instn, FY90 annual State rpt, 4654–14.38
Housing census, 1990: inventory, occupancy, and costs, State fact sheet, 2326–21.39
Housing census, 1990: summary unit characteristics, by householder race and age, county, place, and urban-rural location, State rpt, 2471–1.39
Indian tribes in Pacific Northwest, OCS oil and gas lease and dev environmental, economic, and cultural impacts, with background data, 1970s-92, 5738–35
Land Mgmt Bur activities and finances, and public land acreage and use, FY91, annual State rpt, 5724–11.2
Land Mgmt Bur activities and funding by State, FY90, annual rpt, 5724–13
Lumber (veneer) recovered from Douglas-fir logs and blocks at Oregon and Washington mills, by grade and type, 1981-83 study, 1208–396
Lumber production, and industry operations, for Oregon by county, 1988, 1208–280
Medicaid impacts on State budgets, and program financing, cost control measures, enrollment, and services coverage, by selected State, 1960s-80s and projected to 1997, 10176–3.6
Medicaid waiver proposal of Oregon for managed care, services priorities dev procedures and issues, with background data, 1992 rpt, 26358–254
Medicare payment of physicians, reforms impacts on services, and monitoring methods, 1992 annual rpt, 4004–34

Metals (nonferrous) production in 5 western States, and prices, for 5 metals, 1848-1990, 5608–178
Military prime contract awards, by contractor, service branch, State, and city, FY91, annual rpt, 3544–22
Mineral Industry Surveys, State reviews of production, 1991, preliminary annual rpt, 5614–6
Multinatl firms US affiliates finances and operations, by industry, country of parent firm, and State, 1987, 2708–48
Physicians, by specialty, age, sex, and location of training and practice, 1990, State rpt, 4116–6.38
Population and housing census, 1990: detailed geographic coverage, State CD-ROM, 2551–9.9
Population and housing census, 1990: population and housing characteristics, detailed geographic coverage, State CD-ROM, 2551–10.2
Population and housing census, 1990: summary characteristics, by county, subdiv, and place, State rpt, 2551–7.39
Population census, 1990: population characteristics and living arrangements, by county, place, and urban-rural location, State rpt, 2531–1.39
Population, households, employment, income, fuel prices, and electricity demand for Pacific Northwest, alternative forecasts 1991-2010 with trends from 1980, annual rpt, 3224–3.3
Potato production, acreage, prices, and shipments, for 7 major producer States, and compared to other States, 1970s-92, annual rpt, 1311–29
Radiation exposure of population near Hanford, Wash, nuclear plant, with methodology, 1944-91, series, 3356–5
Statistical Abstract of US, 1992 annual data compilation, 2324–1
Timber in northwestern US and British Columbia, production, prices, trade, and employment, quarterly rpt, 1202–3
Timber in Oregon, acreage on railroad grant lands returned to Federal ownership, by county, FY91, annual rpt, 5724–1.1
Timber in Pacific Northwest, old-growth forests plant and wildlife population and species diversity, 1991 compilation of papers, 1208–386
Water resources dev projects of Army Corps of Engineers, characteristics, and costs, 1950s-91, biennial State rpt, 3756–2.38
Water supply, and snow survey results, monthly State rpt, 1266–2.7
Water supply in Oregon, streamflow by station and reservoir storage, 1992, annual rpt, 1264–9
see also Multnomah County, Oreg.
see also Portland, Oreg.
see also Washington County, Oreg.
see also under By State in the "Index by Categories"

Oregon State University
"Fish Assemblages of Rocky Banks of the Pacific Northwest, Final Report", 5738–39

Organ transplants
see Medical transplants

Organization for Economic Cooperation and Development
Current account balance and net assets, relation to inflation, unemployment rate, and govt lending, for OECD countries, 1970s-89, technical paper, 9366–7.274
Economic conditions, and oil supply and demand, for major industrial countries, monthly rpt, 9112–1
Economic indicators, and dollar exchange rates, for selected OECD countries, 1992 semiannual rpt, 8002–14
Energy production by type, and oil trade, and use, by country group and selected country, monthly rpt, 9112–2
Energy supply and demand, by fuel and end-use sector, 1950s-87 and forecast to 1995, 3166–6.58
Energy use and production, by fuel type, country, and country group, projected 1995-2010 and trends from 1970, annual rpt, 3164–84
Exchange rate variability indicators, by selected OECD country, various periods 1959-90, article, 9371–1.304
Exports and imports, intl position of US and 4 OECD countries, and factors affecting US competition, quarterly pamphlet, 2042–25
Exports and imports of OECD members, by country, annual rpt, discontinued, 7144–10
Exports and imports of OECD, total and for 4 major countries, and US trade by country, by commodity, 1980-90, world area rpt series, 9116–1
GNP and GNP growth for OECD members, by country, annual rpt, discontinued, 7144–8
Govt budget surplus and deficit, and govt debt privately held, turnover, and selling procedures, for OECD members, FY91, 8008–154
Health care costs and components, services use, resources, and economic indicators, by OECD country, 1960s-90, article, 4652–1.322
Health care spending per capita and as share of GDP, for 10 OECD countries, 1988-89, 10176–3.2
Industrial production, consumer price, and stock price indexes for 6 OECD countries and US, *Survey of Current Business*, monthly rpt, 2702–1.1
Industrial production indexes and CPI, for US and 6 OECD countries, current data and annual trends, monthly rpt, 23842–1.7
Labor costs and indexes, by selected country, 1991, semiannual rpt, 6822–3
Latin America economic and social conditions, resources, trade, and aid, 1992, annual factbook, 9914–14
Military spending, arms trade, and force strengths, with govt spending and population, by country, 1979-89, annual rpt, 9824–1
Oil and refined products stocks of OECD, quarterly 1987-90, annual rpt, 3164–50.2
Oil imports from Persian Gulf, US and OECD dependence indicators, and US military supply, late 1970s-80s and supply disruptions from 1951, 3166–6.65
Oil production, stocks, use, and trade, by selected country and country group, monthly rpt, 3162–42
Oil stocks and use by OECD countries, selected years 1960-91, annual rpt, 3164–74.8
Oil supply, demand, and stock forecasts, by world area, quarterly rpt, 3162–34
Oil use and stocks for selected OECD countries, monthly rpt, 3162–24.10
Oil use and stocks for selected OECD countries, 1973-88, 3168–123.10
Pension plan finances, participation, and benefits, for 9 OECD countries, with data by firm and worker characteristics, 1990 conf, 6688–2
Productivity of labor for US and foreign countries, and impacts of investment spending, 1950s-91, article, 9381–1.308
Shipbuilding and repair subsidy elimination proposals of US and OECD, impacts on industry and trade, with data on US-flag vessels, 1980s-91, 9886–4.183
Statistical Abstract of US, 1992 annual data compilation, 2324–1.31
Tax revenue, by level of govt and type of tax, for OECD countries, mid 1960s-90, annual rpt, 10044–1.2
Telecommunications industry intl competitiveness, structure, and devs, with background data and foreign comparisons, 1991 rpt, 2808–30

Organization of Petroleum Exporting Countries
Boycotts (intl) by OPEC and other countries, US firms and individuals cooperation and tax benefits denied, 1990, article, 8302–2.323
Energy supply and demand, by fuel and end-use sector, 1950s-87 and forecast to 1995, 3166–6.58
Energy use and production, by fuel type, country, and country group, projected 1995-2010 and trends from 1970, annual rpt, 3164–84
Exports and imports of US by country, and trade shifts by commodity, 1991, annual rpt, 9884–25
Exports and imports of US, by world area, quarterly pamphlet, 2042–25
Income tax returns of foreign corporations and individuals, and US entities abroad, detailed data compilation, 1970s-89, quinquennial rpt, 8308–31
Investment (direct) in US oil and other industries, by OPEC members, as of 1990, annual rpt, 3164–80
Investment (foreign direct) of US, by industry group and world area, 1989-91, annual article, 2702–1.332
Loans of US banks to foreigners at all US and foreign offices, by country group and country, quarterly rpt, 13002–1
Military spending, arms trade, and force strengths, with govt spending and population, by country, 1979-89, annual rpt, 9824–1
Multinatl firms US affiliates, finances, and operations, by industry, world area of parent firm, and State, 1989-90, annual rpt, 2704–4
Multinatl US firms and foreign affiliates finances and operations, by industry and country, 1989 benchmark survey, annual rpt, 2704–5
Multinatl US firms foreign affiliates capital expenditures, by major industry group, world area, and country, 1987-92, semiannual article, 2702–1.312

Multinatl US firms foreign affiliates capital expenditures, by major industry group, world area, and country, 1988-92, semiannual article, 2702–1.335
Oil crude, gas liquids, and refined products supply, demand, and movement, by PAD district and State, 1991, annual rpt, 3164–2
Oil import costs, by crude type and country or group of origin, monthly rpt, 3162–11
Oil import costs, by crude type and country or group of origin, 1991, annual rpt, 3164–85
Oil prices of OPEC and non-OPEC countries, weekly rpt, 3162–32
Oil prices of OPEC, monthly rpt, 9112–1
Oil production, and exports and prices for US, by major exporting country, detailed data, monthly rpt with articles, 3162–24
Oil production, and exports and prices for US, by major exporting country, detailed data, monthly 1973-88, 3168–123
Oil production and exports to US, by OPEC member, 1960-91, annual rpt, 3164–74.2; 3164–74.8
Oil production, capacity, use, and exports by country, by OPEC member, monthly rpt, 9112–2
Oil production, stocks, use, and trade, by selected country and country group, monthly rpt, 3162–42
Oil, refined products, and gas liquids supply, demand, trade, stocks, and refining, by detailed product, State, and PAD district, monthly rpt with articles, 3162–6
Tariffs and excise taxes on oil imports from OPEC, economic impacts, model description and results, 1992 technical paper, 9379–12.96

Organized crime
Court civil and criminal caseloads for Federal district, appeals, and bankruptcy courts, by type of suit and offense, circuit, and district, 1991, annual rpt, 18204–11
Court civil and criminal caseloads for Federal district, appeals, and special courts, 1991, annual rpt, 18204–8
Court criminal case processing in Federal district courts, and dispositions, by offense, district, and offender characteristics, 1989, annual data compilation, 6064–29
Court criminal case processing in Federal district courts, and dispositions, by offense, 1980-91, annual rpt, 6064–31
Homicides and rate, by weapon, circumstances, and victim characteristics, and years of potential life lost, 1980s, article, 4202–7.315
IRS undercover criminal investigations and costs by criminal activity, and success rates, by region, mid 1980s-90, GAO rpt, 26119–394
Labor Dept programs fraud and abuse, audits and investigations, 2nd half FY92, semiannual rpt, 6302–2
Motorcycle gangs bombings, casualties, and stolen explosive recoveries, 1987-91, annual rpt, 8484–4.1
Prison and parole admissions and releases, sentence length, and time served, by offense and offender characteristics, 1988, annual rpt, 6064–33
Prisoners in Federal and contract instns, by selected characteristics, region, and Federal instn, FY89, annual rpt, 6244–1.1
Sentences for Federal crimes, guidelines use and results by offense and district, and Sentencing Commission activities, 1991, annual rpt, 17664–1
Sentences for Federal offenses, guidelines by offense and circumstances, series, 17668–1
US attorneys civil and criminal cases by type and disposition, and collections, by Federal district, FY91, annual rpt, 6004–2.1; 6004–2.7
Wiretaps authorized, costs, arrests, trials, and convictions, by offense and jurisdiction, 1991, annual rpt, 18204–7
see also Money laundering

Organized labor
see Labor unions

Oriental Americans
see Asian Americans

Orlando, Fla.
Housing starts and completions authorized by building permits in 40 MSAs, quarterly rpt, 2382–9
Wages by occupation, and benefits for office and plant workers, 1992 survey, periodic MSA rpt, 6785–3.6
Water (groundwater) supply, quality, chemistry, and use, 1987-89, local area rpt, 5666–28.19
see also under By City and By SMSA or MSA in the "Index by Categories"

Orlando, S. Paul, Jr.
"Analysis of Salinity Structure and Stability for Texas Estuaries", 2176–7.26

Orphan drugs
see Drugs

Orr, James
"Evolution of U.S. Trade with China", 9385–1.303

Orthopedics
Labor supply and education of health professionals, by professional and other characteristics, and location, 1960s-92 and projected to 2020, biennial rpt, 4114–8
Labor supply of physicians, by specialty, age, sex, and location of training and practice, 1990, State rpt series, 4116–6
Medicare payment of physicians, reforms impacts on services, and monitoring methods, 1992 annual rpt, 4004–34
Military health care personnel, and accessions by training source, by occupation, specialty, and service branch, FY90, annual rpt, 3544–24
VA health care facilities physicians, dentists, and nurses, by selected employment characteristics and VA district, quarterly rpt, 8602–6
VA health care staff and turnover, by occupation, physician specialty, and location, 1991, annual rpt, 8604–8
Visits to physicians, by patient and practice characteristics, diagnosis, and services provided, 1989, annual rpt, 4147–13.109
Visits to physicians, by patient and practice characteristics, diagnosis, and services provided, 1990, advance rpt, 4146–8.215
see also Podiatry
see also Prosthetics and orthotics

Orthotics
see Prosthetics and orthotics

O'Shea, Robert
"Large-Scale Study of Freedom from Smoking Clinics—Factors in Quitting", 4042–3.314

Osteopathy
County Business Patterns, 1989: employment, establishments, and payroll, by SIC 2- to 4-digit industry and county, annual State rpt series, 2326–8
County Business Patterns, 1990: employment, establishments, and payroll, by SIC 2- to 4-digit industry and county, annual State rpt series, 2326–6
Degrees awarded in higher education, by level, field, race, and sex, 1989/90 and trends from 1980/81, annual rpt, 4844–17
Health condition and care indicators, 1950s-90 with health improvement and disease prevention goals for 1990, annual data compilation, 4144–11
Labor supply and education of health professionals, by professional and other characteristics, and location, 1960s-92 and projected to 2020, biennial rpt, 4114–8
Medicare reimbursement of hospitals under prospective payment system, and effect on services, finances, and beneficiary payments, 1980-91, annual rpt, 17204–2
Tax (income) returns of sole proprietorships, income statement items, by industry group, 1990, annual article, 8302–2.317; 8302–2.320
Visits to physicians, by patient and practice characteristics, diagnosis, and services provided, 1990, advance rpt, 4146–8.215

Osterberg, William P.
"Debt, Collateral, and U.S. Manufacturing Investment: 1954-80", 9377–9.141
"Intervention and the Bid-Ask Spread in G-3 Foreign Exchange Rates", 9377–1.305
"New Results on the Impact of Central-Bank Intervention on Deviations from Uncovered Interest Parity", 9377–9.138

Otis, Joanne
"Predicting and Reinforcing Children's Intentions To Wear Protective Helmets While Bicycling", 4042–3.326

Otitis media
see Ear diseases and infections

Otters
see Marine mammals
see Wildlife and wildlife conservation

Outdoor recreation
see Recreation

Outer continental shelf
see Continental shelf

Outlying areas
see American Samoa
see Census of Outlying Areas
see Guam
see Midway Islands
see Northern Mariana Islands
see Puerto Rico
see Territories of the U.S.
see U.S. Virgin Islands
see Wake Island
see under By Outlying Area in the "Index by Categories"

Output of labor
see Labor productivity

Overman, JoAnne R.
"GATT Standards Code Activities of the National Institute of Standards and Technology, 1991", 2214–6

Overseas Private Investment Corp.
Budget of US, authoritative financial statements with appropriations, outlays, and receipts, by category and agency, FY91, annual rpt, 8104–2.2
Budget of US, obligations and authority by function, agency, and program, with summaries and analyses, FY93, annual rpt, 104–2
Debt to US of foreign govts and private obligors, by country and program, periodic rpt, 8002–6
Labor unions recognized in Fed Govt, agreements and membership by agency and facility, as of Jan 1991, biennial listing, 9844–14
Liabilities (contingent) and claims paid by Fed Govt on federally insured and guaranteed contracts with foreign obligors, by country and program, periodic rpt, 8002–12
Loans and grants for economic and military aid from US and intl agencies, by program and country, FY46-91, annual rpt, 9914–5
Loans, loan guarantees, and grants of Fed Govt, administrative costs budget accounting, by program and agency, 1992 rpt, 26306–6.166

Overtime
Customs inspectors overtime pay issues, 1991 hearing, 21788–214
Employment and Earnings, detailed data, monthly rpt, 6742–2.6
Employment, earnings, and hours, by SIC 1- to 4-digit industry, monthly 1989-Feb 1992, annual rpt, 6744–4
Fed Govt civilian employees work-years by schedule, overtime, holidays, and personnel cost components, FY90-91, annual article, 9842–1.303
Fed Govt civilian employees work-years, pay rates, and benefits use and costs, by agency, FY90, annual rpt, 9844–31
Labor force, wages, hours, and payroll costs, by major industry group and demographic characteristics, *Survey of Current Business*, monthly rpt, 2702–1.7
Police employment, spending, and operations, for State, city, county, and special district agencies, 1990, annual rpt, 6064–39
Railroad employment, earnings, and hours, by occupation for Class I railroads, 1991, annual table, 9484–5
Survey of Current Business, detailed financial and business data, and economic indicators, monthly rpt, 2702–1.1
see also Area wage surveys

Overweight
see Obesity

Owen, Park T.
"Nuclear Facility Decommissioning and Site Remedial Actions: A Selected Bibliography, Volume 12", 3354–12

Owens, Raymond E.
"Identifying Credit Crunches", 9389–19.32

Owls
see Birds and bird conservation

Ownership of enterprise
Aluminum plant ownership, capacity, energy and aluminum sources, and startup and closing dates, by US and foreign plant and location, 1990, annual listing, 5604–49
Capital (fixed), govt and private nonresidential structures and equipment, residential capital, and consumer-owned durable goods, 1925-90, annual article, 2702–1.305; 2702–1.306; 2702–1.327; 2702–1.338
Child day care and early childhood education programs availability, demand, use, costs, and provider and enrollee characteristics, 1990 survey, 4808–39
Farm crop subsidies of USDA, deficiency payments by payment size and producer form of organization, 1990, GAO rpt, 26113–574
Farm loan guarantees of FmHA, characteristics of borrowers, lenders, and loans, FY88, 1548–386
Health Care Financing Review, provider prices, price inputs and indexes, and labor, quarterly journal, 4652–1.1
Home drug infusion therapy use, equipment, industry finances, and Medicare coverage options, 1992 rpt, 26358–258
Hospital deaths of Medicare patients, actual and expected rates by diagnosis, with hospital characteristics, by instn, FY90, annual State rpt series, 4654–14
Hospital discharges and length of stay under old and new survey designs, by diagnosis, patient and instn characteristics, and procedure, Jan-Mar 1988, 4147–13.110
Hospital multiple admissions of Medicare beneficiaries, by reason and characteristics of instn and patient, 1985, 4008–117
Hospital reimbursement by Medicare under prospective payment system, analyses of alternative payment plans, series, 17206–1
Hospital reimbursement by Medicare under prospective payment system, and effect on services, finances, and beneficiary payments, 1980-91, annual rpt, 17204–2
Hospital reimbursement by Medicare under prospective payment system, diagnosis related group code assignment and effects on care and instn finances, series, 4006–7
Hospital reimbursement by Medicare under prospective payment system, impacts on costs, industry structure and operations, and quality of care, series, 17206–2
Hospital reimbursement by Medicare under prospective payment system, rural area instns financial performance and impacts of PPS policy changes, 1991 rpt, 26306–6.164
Income tax returns of foreign corporations and individuals, and US entities abroad, detailed data compilation, 1970s-89, quinquennial rpt, 8308–31
Kidney dialysis facilities distribution related to area characteristics and facility ownership, 1982, article, 4652–1.306
Lumber mills, operations, log use by species and origin, and residue use, for California by product and county, 1988, 1208–108
Mental health care facilities, staff, and patient characteristics, *Statistical Notes* series, 4506–3
Minerals production, reserves, and industry role in domestic economy and world supply, world area and country rpt, series, 5606–1
Natl income and product accounts, comprehensive accounts and components, benchmark revisions, 1929-88, 2708–5
Natl income and product accounts, comprehensive accounts and components, *Survey of Current Business*, monthly rpt, 2702–1.24
Savings instns conversion from mutual to stock ownership, financial performance for Fed Reserve 1st District instns, 1980s-90, article, 9373–1.307
Savings instns economies of scale and scope, for mutual and stock instns by asset size, model description and results, 1989 technical paper, 8436–1.7
Savings instns financial statements, for instns insured by Savings Assn Insurance Fund by FHLB district and State, and for FDIC-insured savings banks, 1989, annual rpt, 8434–1
Securities purchases, sales, and holdings, by issuer and type and ownership of security, monthly listing, 9732–2
Ships under foreign flag owned by US firms and foreign affiliates, by type, owner, and country of registry and construction, as of July 1991, semiannual rpt, 7702–3
Small Business Admin guaranteed loans issued under regular, certified, and preferred lender programs, selected characteristics, FY83-90, GAO rpt, 26113–581
Small Business Admin loan guarantee program participants finances, operations, characteristics, and views, 1991 survey, 9768–25
Small business finances, operations, owner characteristics, and Federal contracts, 1980s-90, annual rpt, 9764–6
Small Business Investment Companies capital holdings, SBA obligation, and ownership, as of July 1992, semiannual listing, 9762–4
Tax (income) returns filed, by type of return and IRS district, 1990 and projected 1991-98, annual rpt, 8304–24
Tax (income) returns filed, by type of tax and IRS region and service center, projected 1991-98 and trends from 1978, annual rpt, 8304–9
see also Bank holding companies
see also Business acquisitions and mergers
see also Cooperatives
see also Corporations
see also Divestiture
see also Employee ownership
see also Foreign corporations
see also Franchises
see also Government corporations and enterprises
see also Government ownership
see also Holding companies
see also Joint ventures
see also Minority businesses
see also Monopolies and cartels
see also Multinational corporations
see also Partnerships
see also Proprietorships
see also Rural cooperatives
see also Securities
see also Self-employment
see also Women-owned businesses

Ozone
see Air pollution
see Stratosphere

Pacemakers
see Medical supplies and equipment
Pacific Islands Americans
Census of Population and Housing, 1990: Pacific territories detailed characteristics, by location, series, 2551–8
Census of Population, 1990: population characteristics and living arrangements, by county, place, and urban-rural location, State rpt series, 2531–1
Census of Population, 1990: population characteristics and living arrangements, for Native American, urban, and metro areas, series, 2531–2
Education data compilation, 1992 annual rpt, 4824–2
Eighth grade class of 1988: Asian and Hispanic students proficiency in English and language at home, by selected characteristics, natl longitudinal survey, 1992 rpt, 4826–9.12
Housing census, 1990: summary unit characteristics, by householder race and age, county, place, and urban-rural location, State rpt series, 2471–1
Population social and economic characteristics, for Asian and Pacific Islands Americans, for West and total US, 1990-91, Current Population Rpt, 2546–1.462
Statistical Abstract of US, 1992 annual data compilation, 2324–1
Pacific Marine Environmental Laboratory
see National Oceanic and Atmospheric Administration
Pacific Northwest
see Western States
Pacific Northwest Laboratory
"Population Dose Commitments Due to Radioactive Releases from Nuclear Power Plant Sites in 1988", 9634–7
see also Department of Energy National Laboratories
Pacific Ocean
Air traffic and passengers, for intl routes over Pacific, by route, alternative forecasts 1992-2010 and trends from 1980, annual rpt, 7504–51
Coastal areas environmental conditions and mgmt, for individual areas, conf series, 2146–8
Environmental summary data, and intl claims and disputes, 1992 annual factbook, 9114–2
Fish and shellfish resources and catch, marine mammal and sea turtle population, and mgmt, by species and region, 1988-90, annual rpt, 2164–22
Fish catch, driftnet fishing impacts, and fish feeding, habitat, and other characteristics, for north Pacific Ocean, 1988 conf, 2168–131
Fish catch, trade, use, and fishery operations, with selected foreign data, by species, 1980s-91, annual rpt, 2164–1
Fishing (ocean sport) activities, and catch by species, by angler characteristics and State, 1987-89, annual coastal area rpt, 2166–17.2
Freight (waterborne domestic and foreign) by commodity, traffic, and passengers, by port and waterway, 1989, annual rpt, 3754–3.4
Hurricanes and tropical storms in north Pacific Ocean, characteristics, 1991, annual article, 2152–8.302; 2152–8.303
Hurricanes and tropical storms in Pacific and Indian Oceans, paths and surveillance, 1991, annual rpt, 3804–8
Indian tribes in Pacific Northwest, OCS oil and gas lease and dev environmental, economic, and cultural impacts, with background data, 1970s-92, 5738–35
Marine Fisheries Review, US and foreign fisheries resources, dev, mgmt, and research, quarterly journal, 2162–1
Marine Mammal Protection Act admin, and populations, strandings, and catch permits by species and location, 1988-89, annual rpt, 2164–11
Marine mammals incidental catch by fishing trawl vessels, by species, vessel flag and type, and North Pacific location, 1965-88, 2168–129
Mariners Weather Log, quarterly journal, 2152–8
Minerals offshore lease sales environmental and economic impacts in coastal areas, 1990 final statement, 5736–7.1
Oil and gas dev impacts on California OCS water quality, marine life, and sediments, by site, 1986-90, annual rpt, 5734–11
Oil and gas OCS production, and wells, for Pacific lands under Federal lease, by drilling platform, 1960s-90, annual rpt, 5734–9
Oil and gas OCS production, reserves, and wells drilled, for Pacific Ocean by location, 1990, annual rpt, 5734–7
Oil and gas OCS reserves of Fed Govt, leasing and exploration activity, production, revenue, and costs, by ocean area, FY91, annual rpt, 5734–4
Port improvement capital expenditures and financing methods, by region and selected port, 1946-89, 7708–6
Research activities of Pacific Marine Environmental Lab, and bibl, FY91, annual rpt, 2144–21
Shellfish harvest in estuaries, approved and restricted areas, and pollution sources, by estuary, State, and coastal region, 1990, quinquennial rpt, 2178–33
Temperature (subsurface) of Pacific Ocean, data collection activities, annual rpt, discontinued, 2154–12
Temperature, current, and wind, by equatorial eastern Pacific site and depth, 1983-87, 2148–62
Temperature of sea surface by ocean and for US coastal areas, and Bering Sea ice conditions, monthly rpt, 2182–5
Tidal currents, daily time and velocity by station for North America and Asia coasts, forecast 1993, annual rpt, 2174–1.2
Tide height and time daily at coastal points, forecast 1993, annual rpt, 2174–2.2; 2174–2.5
Weather (marine) forecast areas, and broadcast schedules and stations worldwide, as of Sept 1992, annual rpt, 2184–3
Weather (marine) forecast broadcast schedules worldwide, periodic rpt, 2182–9
see also Bering Sea
see also Gulf of Alaska
see also Oceania
Pacific States
see Western States
see under By Census Division in the "Index by Categories"
Pacifism
Inst of Peace activities and finances, FY90-91, biennial rpt, 29594–1
Packaging and containers
Bottles (plastic) production, shipments, and firms, by end use, annual rpt, discontinued, 2506–8.10
Business statistics, detailed data for major industries and economic indicators, *Survey of Current Business*, monthly rpt, 2702–1.18; 2702–1.20
Business statistics, detailed data for major industries and economic indicators, 1960-91, *Survey of Current Business* biennial supplement, 2704–1
Closures for containers, shipments, trade, use, and firms, quarterly Current Industrial Rpt, 2506–11.4
County Business Patterns, 1989: employment, establishments, and payroll, by SIC 2- to 4-digit industry and county, annual State rpt series, 2326–8
County Business Patterns, 1990: employment, establishments, and payroll, by SIC 2- to 4-digit industry and county, annual State rpt series, 2326–6
Drums and pails (steel shipping) shipments, trade, use, and firms, quarterly Current Industrial Rpt, 2506–11.5
Employment, earnings, and hours, by SIC 1- to 4-digit industry, monthly 1989-Feb 1992, annual rpt, 6744–4
Employment of minorities and women, by occupation, SIC 1- to 3-digit industry, State, and MSA, 1991, annual rpt, 9244–1
Exports and imports between US and outlying areas, by detailed commodity and mode of transport, 1991, annual rpt, 2424–11
Exports and imports of US, by country and detailed commodity, monthly rpt, 2422–12
Exports and imports of US, by Harmonized System 6-digit commodity and country, 1991, annual rpt, 2424–13
Exports and imports of US, by transport mode, country, and SITC 1- to 3-digit commodity, 1991, annual rpt, 2424–12
Exports of US, detailed Schedule B commodities with countries of destination, 1991, annual rpt, 2424–10
Farm prices received and paid, by commodity and State, monthly rpt, 1629–1
Farm production itemized costs, by farm sales size and region, 1991, annual rpt, 1614–3
Food marketing cost indexes, by expense category, monthly rpt with articles, 1502–4
Food prices (farm-retail), marketing cost components, and industry finances and productivity, 1920s-91, annual rpt, 1544–9
Food products and commodities, weight and volume conversion factors, 1992 rpt, 1508–3
Freight (waterborne domestic and foreign) by commodity, traffic, and passengers, by port and waterway, 1989, annual rpt, 3754–3

Fruit and vegetable wholesale prices in NYC by State, and shipments and arrivals by mode of transport, by commodity, weekly rpt, 1311-20
Fruit and vegetable wholesale prices in NYC, Chicago, and selected shipping points, by crop, 1991, annual rpt, 1311-8
Fruit and vegetable wholesale prices in NYC-Newark, and arrivals by mode of transport, by commodity and State, 1990, annual rpt, 1311-21
Glass container production, shipments, stocks, trade, and use, by type, monthly Current Industrial Report, 2506-9.4
Hazardous material transport cylinder test facilities, certifications by State and country, 1990, annual rpt, 7304-4
Hazardous waste mgmt and environmental protection standards compliance activities of Bonneville Power Admin, 1991, annual rpt, 3224-6
Injuries from use of consumer products and related activities, by severity and victim age and sex, 1990, annual rpt, 9164-7
Injuries from use of consumer products, by severity, victim age, and detailed product, 1991, annual rpt, 9164-6
Injuries from use of consumer products, related deaths and costs, and recalls by brand, by product type, FY90, annual rpt, 9164-2
Input-output structure of US economy, detailed interindustry transactions for 84 industries, and components of final demand, 1987, annual article, 2702-1.316
Input-output structure of US economy, detailed interindustry transactions for 541 industries, and components of final demand, 1982 benchmark data, 2708-17
Labor productivity, indexes of output, hours, and employment by SIC 2- to 4-digit industry, 1967-90, annual rpt, 6824-1.3
Manufacturing annual survey, 1990: finances and operations, by SIC 2- to 4-digit industry, series, 2506-14
Manufacturing census, 1987: concentration of largest firms measured by value added, and for shipments by SIC 2- and 4-digit industry, subject rpt, 2497-6
Manufacturing census, 1987: shipments of manufacturers products, by customer class and SIC 2- and 4-digit industry, subject rpt, 2497-4
Manufacturing finances and operations, by SIC 2- to 4-digit industry, forecast 1992, annual rpt, 2044-28
Military prime contract awards, by detailed procurement category, FY88-91, annual rpt, 3544-18
Occupational injury and illness rates, by SIC 2- to 4-digit industry, 1989-90, annual rpt, 6844-7
Occupational injury and illness rates, by SIC 2- to 4-digit industry, 1990, annual rpt, 6844-1
Plastic packaging by resin type, and municipal solid waste composition by weight, 1990-91, article, 9882-16.301
Price indexes (producer), by stage of processing and detailed commodity, monthly rpt, 6762-6
Price indexes (producer), by stage of processing and detailed commodity, monthly 1991, annual rpt, 6764-2
Radioactive waste repository sites, storage containers radionuclide releases at proposed Nevada site, 1990 rpt, 3368-4
Rice shipments, by end use, package size, and State of origin and destination, 1960s-89, biennial rpt, 1564-11
Science, engineering, and technical employment in manufacturing, by field and industry, 1989, triennial rpt, 9627-23
Tax (income) returns of corporations, income and tax items by asset size and detailed industry, 1989, annual rpt, 8304-4; 8304-21
Waste (low-level radioactive) from DOE military activities, disposal methods and costs, 1991, 3006-5.30
Wood containers industry productivity trends and technological devs, 1977-89, article, 6722-1.344
see also Containerization
see also Labeling
see also under By Commodity in the "Index by Categories"

Packard, Michael
"Effects of Removing 70- and 71-Year-Olds from Coverage Under the Social Security Earnings Test", 4746-26.13

Packers and Stockyards Administration
Budget of US, obligations and authority by function, agency, and program, with summaries and analyses, FY93, annual rpt, 104-2
Livestock packers purchases and feeding, and livestock markets, dealers, and sales, by State, 1990, annual rpt, 1384-1

Padding, Paul I.
"Preliminary 1991, Final 1987-90. Estimates of Age and Sex Compositions of Harvested Ducks and Geese", 5504-32

Paducah, Ky.
Water quality, chemistry, hydrology, and other characteristics, 1991 local area study, 5666-27.30

Paffenbarger, Ralph S., Jr.
"Quetelet's Index and Risk of Colon Cancer in College Alumni", 4472-1.339

Pain
see Diseases and disorders

Paints and varnishes
Business statistics, detailed data for major industries and economic indicators, *Survey of Current Business*, monthly rpt, 2702-1.11
Business statistics, detailed data for major industries and economic indicators, 1960-91, *Survey of Current Business* biennial supplement, 2704-1
County Business Patterns, 1989: employment, establishments, and payroll, by SIC 2- to 4-digit industry and county, annual State rpt series, 2326-8
County Business Patterns, 1990: employment, establishments, and payroll, by SIC 2- to 4-digit industry and county, annual State rpt series, 2326-6
Employment, earnings, and hours, by SIC 1- to 4-digit industry, monthly 1989-Feb 1992, annual rpt, 6744-4
Exports and imports between US and outlying areas, by detailed commodity and mode of transport, 1991, annual rpt, 2424-11
Exports and imports of US, by country and detailed commodity, monthly rpt, 2422-12
Exports and imports of US, by Harmonized System 6-digit commodity and country, 1991, annual rpt, 2424-13
Exports and imports of US, by transport mode, country, and SITC 1- to 3-digit commodity, 1991, annual rpt, 2424-12
Exports, imports, tariffs, and industry operating data for paints and inks, 1992 rpt, 9885-11.3
Exports of US, detailed Schedule B commodities with countries of destination, 1991, annual rpt, 2424-10
Freight (waterborne domestic and foreign) by commodity, traffic, and passengers, by port and waterway, 1989, annual rpt, 3754-3
Housing alteration and repair spending, by property and job characteristics, and region, quarterly rpt, annual tables, 2382-7.2
Injuries from use of consumer products and related activities, by severity and victim age and sex, 1990, annual rpt, 9164-7
Injuries from use of consumer products, by severity, victim age, and detailed product, 1991, annual rpt, 9164-6
Input-output structure of US economy, detailed interindustry transactions for 84 industries, and components of final demand, 1987, annual article, 2702-1.316
Input-output structure of US economy, detailed interindustry transactions for 541 industries, and components of final demand, 1982 benchmark data, 2708-17
Labor productivity, indexes of output, hours, and employment by SIC 2- to 4-digit industry, 1967-90, annual rpt, 6824-1.3
Lead paint abatement costs and results, demonstration project design and findings, 1991 rpt, 5188-131
Lead paint abatement for low and moderate income housing, HUD grants to public agencies, 1992 press release, 5006-3.102
Manufacturing annual survey, 1990: finances and operations, by SIC 2- to 4-digit industry, series, 2506-14
Manufacturing census, 1987: concentration of largest firms measured by value added, and for shipments by SIC 2- and 4-digit industry, subject rpt, 2497-6
Manufacturing census, 1987: shipments of manufacturers products, by customer class and SIC 2- and 4-digit industry, subject rpt, 2497-4
Manufacturing finances and operations, by SIC 2- to 4-digit industry, forecast 1992, annual rpt, 2044-28
Occupational injury and illness rates, by SIC 2- to 4-digit industry, 1989-90, annual rpt, 6844-7
Occupational injury and illness rates, by SIC 2- to 4-digit industry, 1990, annual rpt, 6844-1
OECD trade, total and for 4 major countries, and US trade by country, by commodity, 1980-90, world area rpt series, 9116-1
Oil and fat production, consumption by end use, and stocks, by type, monthly Current Industrial Rpt, 2506-4.4
Oils, oilseeds, and fats production, prices, trade, and use, periodic situation rpt with articles, 1561-3

Price indexes (producer), by stage of processing and detailed commodity, monthly rpt, 6762–6
Price indexes (producer), by stage of processing and detailed commodity, monthly 1991, annual rpt, 6764–2
Production and sales of synthetic organic chemicals, and manufacturer listing, by product, 1990, annual rpt, 9884–3
Production by State, shipments, trade, and use, by product for inorganic chemicals, 1991, annual Current Industrial Rpt, 2506–8.14
Production of synthetic organic chemicals, by detailed product, quarterly rpt, 9882–1
Science, engineering, and technical employment in manufacturing, by field and industry, 1989, triennial rpt, 9627–23
Shipments and PPI for building materials, by type, quarterly rpt, 2042–1.5; 2042–1.6
Shipments, trade, and use of paint and related products, quarterly Current Industrial Rpt, 2506–8.4
Shipments, trade, and use of paint and related products, 1991, annual Current Industrial Rpt, 2506–8.16
Tax (income) returns of corporations, income and tax items by asset size and detailed industry, 1989, annual rpt, 8304–4; 8304–21
see also Dyeing and coloring materials
see also under By Commodity in the "Index by Categories"

Paisner, Alan M.
"BLS Regional Offices: Contribution to Wage Programs", 6722–1.333

Pakistan
Agricultural trade by commodity and country, prices, and world market devs, monthly rpt, 1922–12
Agricultural trade of US, by detailed commodity and country, 1991, annual rpt, 1524–8
Agricultural trade of US, by detailed commodity and country, 1991, semiannual rpt, 1522–4
AID economic aid to developing countries, obligations and disbursements by country, quarterly rpt, 9912–4
AID loans repayment status and terms by program and country, and status of predecessor agency loans, quarterly rpt, 9912–3
Background Notes, summary social, political, and economic data, 1992 rpt, 7006–2.23
Boycotts (intl) by OPEC and other countries, US firms and individuals cooperation and tax benefits denied, 1990, article, 8302–2.323
Cotton production, trade, and use, for selected countries, FAS monthly circular, 1925–4.2
Dracunculiasis cases, and surveillance and eradication programs, for India, Pakistan, and Africa, 1980s-91, article, 4202–7.307
Economic and military aid and loans from US and intl agencies, by program and country, FY46-91, annual rpt, 9914–5
Economic and social conditions of developing countries from 1960s, and Intl Dev Cooperation Agency and AID activities and funding, FY91-93, annual rpt, 9904–4
Economic conditions, income, production, prices, employment, and trade, 1992 periodic country rpt, 2046–4.19
Economic conditions, investment and export opportunities, and trade practices, 1992 country market research rpt, 2046–6.5
Economic conditions, policy, and trade practices, by country, 1989-91, annual rpt, 21384–5
Economic, social, political, and geographic summary data, by country, 1992, annual factbook, 9114–2
Energy supply and demand, and implications for US trade, 1992 country rpt, 3406–6.11
Exports and imports of US, by commodity and country, 1980-90, world area rpt, 9116–1.3
Exports and imports of US, by Harmonized System 6-digit commodity and country, 1991, annual rpt, 2424–13
Exports and imports of US, by transport mode, country, and SITC 1- to 3-digit commodity, 1991, annual rpt, 2424–12
Exports, imports, and balances of US for manufactured goods, by SITC 2-digit commodity and country, quarterly rpt, 2042–35
Exports of US, detailed Schedule B commodities with countries of destination, 1991, annual rpt, 2424–10
Food supply, needs, and aid for developing countries, status and alternative forecasts, 1992 world area rpt, 1526–8.2
Human rights conditions in 170 countries, and US economic and military aid, 1991, annual rpt, 21384–3
Imports of goods, services, and investment from US, trade barriers, impacts, and US actions, by country, 1991, annual rpt, 444–2
Military spending, arms trade, and force strengths, with govt spending and population, by country, 1979-89, annual rpt, 9824–1
Minerals Yearbook, Vol 3, 1989: foreign country review of production, trade, and policy, by commodity, annual rpt, 5604–35.2
Nuclear power generation in US and 20 countries, monthly rpt, 3162–24.10
Nuclear power generation in US and 20 countries, monthly 1973-88, 3168–123.10
Population size, growth rates, and components of change, by country, projected 1990-2020 and trends from 1950, biennial rpt, 2324–9
Refugee migration, and intl aid programs, by world area and country of origin and asylum, 1991, annual rpt, 7004–15
Spacecraft and satellite launches since 1957, quarterly listing, 9502–2
UN voting record and share of votes in agreement with US, by issue, country, and world area, 1991, annual rpt, 7004–18
see also under By Foreign Country in the "Index by Categories"

Palau
Agricultural trade of US, by detailed commodity and country, 1991, semiannual rpt, 1522–4
Banks (insured commercial and savings) deposits by instn, State, MSA, and county, as of June 1991, annual regional rpt, 9295–3.6
Economic, social, political, and geographic summary data, by country, 1992, annual factbook, 9114–2
Exports and imports of US, by transport mode, country, and SITC 1- to 3-digit commodity, 1991, annual rpt, 2424–12
Exports of US, detailed Schedule B commodities with countries of destination, 1991, annual rpt, 2424–10
Population and housing census, 1990: detailed characteristics, by location, outlying area rpt, 2551–8.4
Population social, economic, health, and govtl data, for Palau, FY91, annual rpt, 7004–6

Pan American World Airways
Bombing of Pan Am Flight 103 in 1988 and other terrorist incidents, role of Libya, 1991, annual rpt, 7004–13

Panama
Agricultural trade of US, by detailed commodity and country, 1991, annual rpt, 1524–8
Agricultural trade of US, by detailed commodity and country, 1991, semiannual rpt, 1522–4
AID economic aid to developing countries, obligations and disbursements by country, quarterly rpt, 9912–4
AID loans repayment status and terms by program and country, and status of predecessor agency loans, quarterly rpt, 9912–3
Background Notes, summary social, political, and economic data, 1992 rpt, 7006–2.11
Cuba trade, by commodity and country, mid 1980s-91, 9118–8
Economic and military aid and loans from US and intl agencies, by program and country, FY46-91, annual rpt, 9914–5
Economic and social conditions of developing countries from 1960s, and Intl Dev Cooperation Agency and AID activities and funding, FY91-93, annual rpt, 9904–4
Economic and social conditions, resources, and trade, and aid, 1992, annual factbook, 9914–14
Economic conditions, policy, and trade practices, by country, 1989-91, annual rpt, 21384–5
Economic, population, and agricultural data, US and other aid sources, and AID activity, 1991 country rpt, 9916–12.55
Economic, social, political, and geographic summary data, by country, 1992, annual factbook, 9114–2
Exports and imports of US, by commodity and country, 1980-90, world area rpt, 9116–1.5
Exports and imports of US, by Harmonized System 6-digit commodity and country, 1991, annual rpt, 2424–13
Exports and imports of US, by transport mode, country, and SITC 1- to 3-digit commodity, 1991, annual rpt, 2424–12
Exports, imports, and balances of US for manufactured goods, by SITC 2-digit commodity and country, quarterly rpt, 2042–35
Exports of US, detailed Schedule B commodities with countries of destination, 1991, annual rpt, 2424–10
Human rights conditions in 170 countries, and US economic and military aid, 1991, annual rpt, 21384–3

Labor conditions, union coverage, and work accidents, 1991 annual country rpt, 6366–4.7
Labor conditions, union coverage, and work accidents, 1992 annual country rpt, 6366–4.27
Military aid of US, arms sales, and training programs costs and budget requests, by program, world region, and country, FY91-93, annual rpt, 7144–13
Military spending, arms trade, and force strengths, with govt spending and population, by country, 1979-89, annual rpt, 9824–1
Multinatl US firms and foreign affiliates finances and operations, by industry and country, 1989 benchmark survey, annual rpt, 2704–5
Multinatl US firms foreign affiliates, income statement items by asset size, industry, and country, 1988, biennial article, 8302–2.322
Population size, growth rates, and components of change, by country, projected 1990-2020 and trends from 1950, biennial rpt, 2324–9
Refugee migration, and intl aid programs, by world area and country of origin and asylum, 1991, annual rpt, 7004–15
Ships in world merchant fleet, tonnage, and new ship construction and deliveries, by vessel type and country, as of Jan 1992, annual rpt, 7704–3
Steel trade, by product, country, and customs district, with US industry operating data, 1989-June 1992, semiannual rpt, 9882–15
UN voting record and share of votes in agreement with US, by issue, country, and world area, 1991, annual rpt, 7004–18
see also Panama Canal
see also under By Foreign Country in the "Index by Categories"

Panama Canal
Immigrants admitted to US, by class and country, FY85-91, annual rpt, 6264–2.1
Traffic and tolls of Canal by commodity, and local public utilities and services, FY91, annual rpt, 9664–3

Panama Canal Commission
Activities and finances of Commission, with Canal traffic and local govt operations, FY91, annual rpt, 9664–3
Budget of US, authoritative financial statements with appropriations, outlays, and receipts, by category and agency, FY91, annual rpt, 8104–2.2
Budget of US, obligations and authority by function, agency, and program, with summaries and analyses, FY93, annual rpt, 104–2

Paper and paper products
Business statistics, detailed data for major industries and economic indicators, *Survey of Current Business*, monthly rpt, 2702–1.18
Business statistics, detailed data for major industries and economic indicators, 1960-91, *Survey of Current Business* biennial supplement, 2704–1
California lumber mills, operations, timber use by species and origin, and residue use, by product and county, 1988, 1208–108
Capital expenditures for plant and equipment, by major industry group, quarterly rpt, 2502–2
Collective bargaining agreements expiring during year, and workers covered, by firm, union, industry group, and State, 1992, annual rpt, 6784–9
County Business Patterns, 1989: employment, establishments, and payroll, by SIC 2- to 4-digit industry and county, annual State rpt series, 2326–8
County Business Patterns, 1990: employment, establishments, and payroll, by SIC 2- to 4-digit industry and county, annual State rpt series, 2326–6
CPI by component for US city average, and by selected metro area, region, and population size, monthly rpt, 6762–2
Employment, earnings, and hours, by SIC 1- to 4-digit industry, monthly 1989-Feb 1992, annual rpt, 6744–4
Employment of minorities and women, by occupation, SIC 1- to 3-digit industry, State, and MSA, 1991, annual rpt, 9244–1
Employment, unemployment, and labor force characteristics, by region and census div, 1991, annual rpt, 6744–7.1
Energy use and prices, by fuel type and manufacturing industry, 1974-88, 3166–15.3
Energy use and prices for manufacturing industries, 1988 survey, series, 3166–13
Exports and imports between US and outlying areas, by detailed commodity and mode of transport, 1991, annual rpt, 2424–11
Exports and imports of US, by country and detailed commodity, monthly rpt, 2422–12
Exports and imports of US, by Harmonized System 6-digit commodity and country, 1991, annual rpt, 2424–13
Exports and imports of US, by selected country, country group, and commodity group, 1991, annual rpt, 2044–37
Exports and imports of US, by transport mode, country, and SITC 1- to 3-digit commodity, 1991, annual rpt, 2424–12
Exports, imports, and balances of US for manufactured goods, by SITC 2-digit commodity and country, quarterly rpt, 2042–35
Exports of US, detailed commodities by country, monthly CD-ROM, 2422–13
Exports of US, detailed Schedule B commodities with countries of destination, 1991, annual rpt, 2424–10
Freight (waterborne domestic and foreign) by commodity, traffic, and passengers, by port and waterway, 1989, annual rpt, 3754–3
Hazardous substances industrial releases and reduction methods under EPA regulation, by chemical, source, industry, and location, 1989, annual rpt, 9234–6
Hazardous substances industrial releases and reduction methods under EPA regulation, with chemical stocks and use, facility directory, 1987-89, annual CD-ROM, 9234–7
Imports, exports, and employment impacts, by SIC 2- to 4-digit industry and commodity, quarterly rpt, 2322–2
Imports of US, detailed commodities by country, monthly CD-ROM, 2422–14
Imports of US given duty-free treatment for value of US material sent abroad, by commodity and country, 1987-90, annual rpt, 9884–14
Injuries from use of consumer products, by severity, victim age, and detailed product, 1991, annual rpt, 9164–6
Input-output structure of US economy, detailed interindustry transactions for 84 industries, and components of final demand, 1987, annual article, 2702–1.316
Input-output structure of US economy, detailed interindustry transactions for 541 industries, and components of final demand, 1982 benchmark data, 2708–17
Labor demand elasticities for lumber and paper products industries, 1992 rpt, 1208–416
Labor productivity, indexes of output, hours, and employment by SIC 2- to 4-digit industry, 1967-90, annual rpt, 6824–1.3
Manufacturing annual survey, 1990: finances and operations, by SIC 2- to 4-digit industry, series, 2506–14
Manufacturing census, 1987: concentration of largest firms measured by value added, and for shipments by SIC 2- and 4-digit industry, subject rpt, 2497–6
Manufacturing census, 1987: shipments of manufacturers products, by customer class and SIC 2- and 4-digit industry, subject rpt, 2497–4
Manufacturing corporations financial statements, by selected SIC 2- to 3-digit industry, quarterly rpt, 2502–1
Manufacturing finances and operations, by SIC 2- to 4-digit industry, forecast 1992, annual rpt, 2044–28
Manufacturing industries operations and performance, analytical rpt series, 2506–16
Manufacturing production, shipments, inventories, orders, and pollution control costs, periodic Current Industrial Rpt series, 2506–3
Mexico imports from US, by industry and State, 1987-91, 2048–154
Multinatl firms US affiliates finances and operations, by industry, country of parent firm, and State, 1987, 2708–48
Multinatl US firms and foreign affiliates finances and operations, by industry and country, 1989 benchmark survey, annual rpt, 2704–5
Newsprint trade, tariffs, and industry operating data, 1992 rpt, 9885–8.8
North Central States pulpwood production and mill receipts, by species, mill, State, and county, 1990, annual rpt, 1204–19
Northeastern US pulpwood production by species and county, and shipments, by State, 1990, annual rpt, 1204–18
Occupational injury and illness rates, by SIC 2- to 4-digit industry, 1989-90, annual rpt, 6844–7
Occupational injury and illness rates, by SIC 2- to 4-digit industry, 1990, annual rpt, 6844–1
OECD trade, total and for 4 major countries, and US trade by country, by commodity, 1980-90, world area rpt series, 9116–1
Pacific Northwest population, households, employment, income, fuel prices, and electricity demand, alternative forecasts 1991-2010, annual rpt, 3224–3.3
Pollution (air) abatement equipment shipments by industry, and new and backlog orders, by product, 1991, annual Current Industrial Rpt, 2506–12.5

Pollution (water) industrial emissions in Great Lakes, comparison of State, EPA, Intl Joint Commission, and Ontario standards, 1991 rpt, 14648–29
Pollution abatement capital and operating costs, by SIC 2- to 4-digit industry and State, 1990, annual Current Industrial Rpt, 2506–3.6
Price indexes (producer), by stage of processing and detailed commodity, monthly rpt, 6762–6
Price indexes (producer), by stage of processing and detailed commodity, monthly 1991, annual rpt, 6764–2
Production, shipments, trade, stocks, and use, by paper and pulp product and State, , annual Current Industrial Rpt, discontinued, 2506–7.10
Puerto Rico and other US possessions corporations income tax returns, income and tax items, and employment, by selected industry, 1989, article, 8302–2.326
Recycling in manufacturing industries, fuel savings, and CO2 emissions reductions, 1988 and projected to 1995, hearing, 21368–140
Recycling of municipal and industrial waste, costs, revenues, and secondary products trade and related energy use and pollution reductions, 1991 hearings, 21368–139
Recycling of paper by grade, with newsprint collection, recycling capacity by company, and curbside pickup operations, by State, 1970s-80s and projected to 1995, hearing, 25318–84
Science, engineering, and technical employment in manufacturing, by field and industry, 1989, triennial rpt, 9627–23
Southeastern US pulpwood and residue prices, spending, and transport shares by mode, 1989-90, annual rpt, 1204–22
Soviet Union and US economic and sociodemographic indicators, selected years 1970-90, handbook, 2328–80
Statistical Abstract of US, 1992 annual data compilation, 2324–1.24
Tariff Schedule of US, classifications and rates of duty by detailed imported commodity, 1993 base edition, 9886–13
Tax (income) returns of corporations, income and tax items by asset size and detailed industry, 1989, annual rpt, 8304–4; 8304–21
Tax (income) returns of sole proprietorships, income statement items, by industry group, 1990, annual article, 8302–2.317; 8302–2.320
Wholesale trade sales and inventories, by SIC 2- to 3-digit kind of business, monthly rpt, 2413–7
Wood, waste, and alcohol fuel use, by end-use sector and region, 1990, annual rpt, 3164–97
see also under By Commodity in the "Index by Categories"
see also under By Industry in the "Index by Categories"

Paper gold
see Special Drawing Rights

Paperwork
see Government forms and paperwork

Paperwork Reduction Act
Info collection of Fed Govt under Act, respondent burden, OMB reviews, violations, and major info systems proposals, 1981-92, annual rpt, 104–26

Papua New Guinea
Agricultural trade of US, by detailed commodity and country, 1991, annual rpt, 1524–8
Agricultural trade of US, by detailed commodity and country, 1991, semiannual rpt, 1522–4
Economic and military aid and loans from US and intl agencies, by program and country, FY46-91, annual rpt, 9914–5
Economic, social, political, and geographic summary data, by country, 1992, annual factbook, 9114–2
Exports and imports of US, by transport mode, country, and SITC 1- to 3-digit commodity, 1991, annual rpt, 2424–12
Exports of US, detailed Schedule B commodities with countries of destination, 1991, annual rpt, 2424–10
Human rights conditions in 170 countries, and US economic and military aid, 1991, annual rpt, 21384–3
Military aid of US, arms sales, and training programs costs and budget requests, by program, world region, and country, FY91-93, annual rpt, 7144–13
Military spending, arms trade, and force strengths, with govt spending and population, by country, 1979-89, annual rpt, 9824–1
Minerals Yearbook, Vol 3, 1989: foreign country review of production, trade, and policy, by commodity, annual rpt, 5604–35.2
Population size, growth rates, and components of change, by country, projected 1990-2020 and trends from 1950, biennial rpt, 2324–9
Refugee migration, and intl aid programs, by world area and country of origin and asylum, 1991, annual rpt, 7004–15
UN voting record and share of votes in agreement with US, by issue, country, and world area, 1991, annual rpt, 7004–18

Paraguay
Agricultural trade of US, by detailed commodity and country, 1991, annual rpt, 1524–8
Agricultural trade of US, by detailed commodity and country, 1991, semiannual rpt, 1522–4
AID economic aid to developing countries, obligations and disbursements by country, quarterly rpt, 9912–4
AID loans repayment status and terms by program and country, and status of predecessor agency loans, quarterly rpt, 9912–3
Economic and military aid and loans from US and intl agencies, by program and country, FY46-91, annual rpt, 9914–5
Economic and social conditions of developing countries from 1960s, and Intl Dev Cooperation Agency and AID activities and funding, FY91-93, annual rpt, 9904–4
Economic and social conditions, resources, and trade, and aid, 1992, annual factbook, 9914–14
Economic conditions, policy, and trade practices, by country, 1989-91, annual rpt, 21384–5
Economic, social, political, and geographic summary data, by country, 1992, annual factbook, 9114–2
Exports and imports of US, by transport mode, country, and SITC 1- to 3-digit commodity, 1991, annual rpt, 2424–12
Exports of US, detailed Schedule B commodities with countries of destination, 1991, annual rpt, 2424–10
Human rights conditions in 170 countries, and US economic and military aid, 1991, annual rpt, 21384–3
Imports of goods, services, and investment from US, trade barriers, impacts, and US actions, by country, 1991, annual rpt, 444–2
Military aid of US, arms sales, and training programs costs and budget requests, by program, world region, and country, FY91-93, annual rpt, 7144–13
Military spending, arms trade, and force strengths, with govt spending and population, by country, 1979-89, annual rpt, 9824–1
Population size, growth rates, and components of change, by country, projected 1990-2020 and trends from 1950, biennial rpt, 2324–9
UN voting record and share of votes in agreement with US, by issue, country, and world area, 1991, annual rpt, 7004–18

Paraplegia
see Spinal cord injuries

Paraprofessionals
Child day care and early childhood education programs availability, demand, use, costs, and provider and enrollee characteristics, 1990 survey, 4808–39
Education (special) enrollment by age, staff, funding, and needs, by type of handicap and State, 1990/91, annual rpt, 4944–4
Labor demand, turnover, and training completions, by detailed occupation, 1990 and projected to 2005, biennial rpt, 6744–3
Occupational Outlook Handbook, 1992-93, biennial rpt, 6744–1
State and local govt employment of minorities and women, by occupation, function, pay level, and State, 1991, annual rpt, 9244–6
see also Allied health personnel

Parcel services
see Postal service

Pardons
Criminal case processing in Federal courts, by offense, disposition, and jurisdiction, data compilation, 1992 annual rpt, 6064–6.5

Parents
Asian and Pacific Islands Americans social and economic characteristics, for West and total US, 1990-91, Current Population Report, 2546–1.462
Black Americans social and economic characteristics, for South and total US, 1991 and trends from 1950, annual Current Population Rpt, 2546–1.463
Census of Population and Housing, 1990: summary characteristics, by county, subdiv, and place, State rpt series, 2551–7

Census of Population, 1990: population characteristics and living arrangements, by county, place, and urban-rural location, State rpt series, 2531–1
Census of Population, 1990: population characteristics and living arrangements, for Native American, urban, and metro areas, series, 2531–2
Consumer Income, socioeconomic characteristics of persons, families, and households, detailed cross-tabulations, Current Population Rpt series, 2546–6
Divorced and absent fathers child support payment and visitation practices, and mothers with custody, by employment and other characteristics, 1988, article, 6722–1.329
Divorced parents poverty rates, effects of child support enforcement provisions, model results, 1976-83, working paper, 6886–6.87
Drug abuse by mothers, treatment and other services use, referrals, needs, and barriers, for 13 NIDA-funded programs, 1990/91 survey, 4498–76
Education data compilation, 1992 annual rpt, 4824–2
Education data, detail for elementary, secondary, and higher education, 1920s-91 and projected to 2002, annual rpt, 4824–1
Education in science and math, achievement relation to parental involvement, natl assessment of elementary and high school students, 1985/86, 4896–6.7
Education programs for preschool students transition to kindergarten, and factors affecting activities, 1989-90 study, 4808–44
Educational performance and conditions, characteristics, attitudes, activities, and plans, 1988 8th grade class, natl longitudinal survey, series, 4826–9
Educational performance of elementary and secondary students, and factors affecting proficiency, by selected characteristics, 1990 natl assessments, subject rpt series, 4896–8
Educational performance of elementary and secondary students in math, science, reading, and writing, 1969-90, 4898–32
Educational performance of elementary and secondary students, reading proficiency and related factors, 1988 and 1990 natl assessments, 4898–33
Employee benefit plan coverage and provisions, by plan type, for State and local govt employees, 1990, biennial rpt, 6784–21
Employee leave for family reasons, State law provisions and employer compliance, for 4 States, 1987-91, hearing, 25548–105
Employment part-time of women, transitions by marital status and whether young children present, 1988 and trends from 1978, 6726–2.2
Family life and relationships quality and other issues, views of parents and children, 1990 survey, 15528–2
Family members supporting others outside household, by relationship, recipient living arrangements, and provider characteristics, 1988, Current Population Rpt, 2546–20.21
Foreign countries social security programs coverage, funding, eligibility, and benefits, by country, 1991, biennial rpt, 4746–4.62
Grandchildren in households, and families with grandchildren present, by presence of parents and race, 1991, annual Current Population Rpt, 2546–1.461
Handicapped children's formal and informal care, outlays and time spent relation to diagnosis and other characteristics, 1988, article, 4042–3.329
Higher education instn student financial support by parents, by type and funding sources, and student, parent, and instn characteristics, fall 1986, 4846–3.11
Higher education PhD degree recipients, by field and selected characteristics, 1979, 1984, and 1989, 4848–44
Households composition, income, benefits, and labor force status, Survey of Income and Program Participation methodology, working paper series, 2626–10
Immigrant and nonimmigrant visas of US issued and refused, by class, issuing office, and nationality, FY90, annual rpt, 7184–1
Jail population of women, by criminal background and sociodemographic characteristics, 1989, 6066–19.66
Labor force status of family members and earnings, by family composition and race, quarterly press release, 6742–21
Literacy program for preschoolers and parents, Even Start program activities and grants by recipient, FY90, annual listing, 4804–41
Living arrangements, family relationships, and marital status, by selected characteristics, 1991, annual Current Population Rpt, 2546–1.461
OASDI benefits and beneficiaries, by category, age, and sex, quarterly rpt, 4742–1.1
Pacific territories population and housing detailed characteristics, by location, 1990 Census of Population and Housing, series, 2551–8
Population economic well-being indicators, by selected characteristics and household income and income-to-poverty ratio, 1984, 2546–20.22
Poverty relation to low earnings, by work experience during year, household relationship, sex, race, age, and education, 1960s-90, Current Population Rpt, 2546–6.74
Prisoners (women) in State instns, by whether abused, and other characteristics, data compilation, 1992 annual rpt, 6064–6.6
Reading to children, frequency by child's grade level, 1991 survey, 4826–10.1
Student supplemental and parent loans and defaults, for freshmen and other students, by whether proprietary instn, FY89-91, GAO rpt, 26121–473
Supplemental Security Income child beneficiaries and benefits, by selected characteristics, family income status, and State, 1991, article, 4742–1.316
Tax (income) returns of individuals, detailed data, 1988, annual rpt, 8304–2
Veterans compensation and pension recipients, for each US war, 1775-1991, annual rpt, 8604–2
Veterans disability and death compensation and pension cases, by type of entitlement and period of service, monthly rpt, 8602–5
Veterans disability and death compensation cases of VA, by entitlement type, period of service, and sex, as of Mar 1992, annual rpt, 8604–13
Veterans disability and death compensation cases of VA, by entitlement type, period of service, sex, age, and State, FY90, annual rpt, 8604–7
Women's labor force status and characteristics, 1960s-90, chartbook, 6748–85
see also Adoption
see also Child day care
see also Child support and alimony
see also Children
see also Families and households
see also Maternity
see also Maternity benefits
see also Single parents
see also Teenage pregnancy

Pari-mutuel wagering
Consumer spending, natl income and product account benchmark revisions, 1929-88, 2708–5
Consumer spending, natl income and product accounts, comprehensive accounts and components, *Survey of Current Business*, monthly rpt, 2702–1.25
State govt revenue by source, spending and debt by function, and holdings, FY91, annual rpt, 2466–2.6
State govt tax collections by detailed type of tax, and tax rates, by State, FY91, annual rpt, 2466–2.7
Statistical Abstract of US, 1992 annual data compilation, 2324–1.9
Tax rates and revenue of State and local govts, by source and State, 1992 and historical trends, annual rpt, 10044–1
see also Horse racing

Parigi, Bruno M.
"Bank Branching", 9387–8.281

Park, Sangkyun
"Behavior of Uninsured Deposits: Market Discipline or 'Too Big To Fail?' ", 9385–8.126
"Loan Contraction Within a Framework of Moral Hazard", 9385–8.133

Park, Thae S.
"Federal Personal Income Tax Liabilities and Payments: Revised and Updated Estimates, 1959-91", 2702–1.326
"Relationship Between Personal Income and Adjusted Gross Income: New Estimates for 1989-90 and Revisions for 1959-88", 2702–1.318

Parker, Martin R., Jr.
"Synthesis of Safety Research: Adverse Environmental Conditions", 7558–98.1

Parking facilities
Apartment completions by region and metro-nonmetro location, and absorption rate, by size and rent class, preliminary 1991, annual Current Housing Rpt, 2484–3
Apartment market absorption rates and characteristics for nonsubsidized furnished and unfurnished units, 1990, annual Current Housing Rpt, 2484–2
Auto, van, and light truck ownership and operating costs, by vehicle size and year of operation, 1991 model year, biennial rpt, 7554–21

Costs for monthly parking, for 8 cities, 1992 GAO rpt, 26113–597
County Business Patterns, 1989: employment, establishments, and payroll, by SIC 2- to 4-digit industry and county, annual State rpt series, 2326–8
County Business Patterns, 1990: employment, establishments, and payroll, by SIC 2- to 4-digit industry and county, annual State rpt series, 2326–6
Crime victimization rates, by victim and offender characteristics, circumstances, and offense, 1990 survey, annual rpt, 6066–3.47
DC metro area land acquisition and dev projects of Fed Govt, characteristics and funding by agency and project, FY92-96, annual rpt, 15454–1
Energy use in commercial buildings, costs, and conservation, by building characteristics, survey rpt series, 3166–8
Govt direct spending and employment, by function and level of govt, selected years 1962-87, 10048–53
Govt revenue by source, spending by function, debt, and assets, by level of govt, FY90, annual rpt, 2466–2.2
Home mortgages FHA-insured, financial, property, and borrower characteristics, by metro area, 1991, annual rpt, 5144–24
Home mortgages FHA-insured, financial, property, and borrower characteristics, by State, 1991, annual rpt, 5144–1; 5144–25
Home mortgages FHA-insured, financial, property, and borrower characteristics, 1991, annual rpt, 5144–17; 5144–23
Housing (rental) units, total, with HUD assistance by program, and eligible for aid, by unit, household, and neighborhood characteristics, and location, 1989, biennial rpt, 5184–11
Housing and households characteristics, and unit and neighborhood quality, by MSA location for 11 MSAs, 1987 survey, supplement, 2485–8
Housing and households detailed characteristics, and unit and neighborhood quality, by location, 1989, biennial rpt supplement, 2485–13
Housing and households detailed characteristics, and unit and neighborhood quality, MSA surveys, series, 2485–6
Housing units completed, single and multifamily units by structural and financial characteristics, and location, 1987-91, annual rpt, 2384–1
Housing units completed, single and multifamily units by structural characteristics, monthly rpt, quarterly tables, 2382–2.2
Occupational injury and illness rates, by SIC 2- to 4-digit industry, 1989-90, annual rpt, 6844–7
Occupational injury and illness rates, by SIC 2- to 4-digit industry, 1990, annual rpt, 6844–1
Single parent families in own and others homes, by financial, housing, and other characteristics, 1989, 2486–1.14
Tax (income) returns of partnerships, income statement and balance sheet items, by industry group, 1990, annual article, 8302–2.314
Tax (income) returns of sole proprietorships, income statement items, by industry group, 1990, annual article, 8302–2.317; 8302–2.320

Parkinson, Patrick
"Clearance and Settlement in U.S. Securities Markets", 9366–1.163

Parks
Acreage of land under Natl Park Service mgmt, by site, ownership, and region, FY92, semiannual rpt, 5542–1
Govt employment and payroll, by function, level of govt, and jurisdiction, annual rpt series, 2466–1
Statistical Abstract of US, 1992 annual data compilation, 2324–1.7
see also National parks
see also State parks
see also Zoological parks

Parks, Roger B.
"Metropolitan Organization: The Allegheny County Case", 10046–9.2

Parks, Wesley W.
"Review of Indian Ocean Fisheries for Skipjack Tuna, *Katsuwonus pelamis*, and Yellowfin Tuna, *Thunnus albacares*", 2162–1.301

Parlett, Ralph L.
"1992 Food Price Outlook", 1504–9.1

Parochial schools
see Private schools

Parole and probation
Admissions and releases from prison and parole, sentence length, and time served, by offense and offender characteristics, 1988, annual rpt, 6064–33
Caseloads, decisions, and activities of US Parole Commission, FY88-91, annual rpt, 6004–3
Crime, criminal justice admin and enforcement, and public opinion, data compilation, 1992 annual rpt, 6064–6
Drug abuse and trafficking offenders losing Federal benefits under new sentencing guidelines, by selected characteristics, 1990-91, GAO rpt, 26119–398
Drug abuse treatment and education programs for prisoners and parolees, activities, costs, and outcomes, 1990 conf, 4498–77
Fed Probation System admissions, discharges, and caseloads, by type of supervision, 1991, annual rpt, 18204–8.6; 18204–8.19
Fed Probation System caseload, by circuit and district, 1991, annual rpt, 18204–11
Federal correctional instn inmates, admissions, releases, and recidivism, by region, monthly rpt series, 6242–1
Federal criminal sentencing, guidelines use and results by offense and district, and Sentencing Commission activities, 1991, annual rpt, 17664–1
Federal criminal sentencing, guidelines use and results by offense, 1984-1990, 6066–19.68
Federal district court criminal case processing and dispositions, by offense, district, and offender characteristics, 1989, annual data compilation, 6064–29
Judicial Conf proceedings and findings, spring 1992, semiannual rpt, 18202–2
Parole and probation population, entries, and exits, by State, 1990, annual rpt, 6066–25.43
Prisoners, characteristics, and movements, by State, 1990, annual rpt, 6064–26
Prisoners in Federal and State instns by selected characteristics, releases, staff, and instn size, with data by region and State, late 1970s-91, 6068–248
Probation population, by offender characteristics, sentence conditions, whether rearrested, and offense, 1986-89, 6066–19.65
Sentences for Federal offenses, guidelines by offense and circumstances, series, 17668–1
Sentences under Federal mandatory minimum provisions, by defendant characteristics, and views on justice system impacts, FY90, 17668–2
States criminal justice systems activities, employment, funding, and data collection, by State, 1970s-91, annual rpt, 6064–40
US attorneys civil and criminal cases by type and disposition, and collections, by Federal district, FY91, annual rpt, 6004–2.1
Women in jail, by criminal background and sociodemographic characteristics, with comparisons to men, 1989, 6066–19.66

Parsons, Carol A.
"Immigration and Regional Labor Market Performance in the U.S. Apparel Industry", 6366–6.6

Part-time employment
AFDC beneficiaries demographic and financial characteristics, by State, FY90, annual rpt, 4584–7
Black women's labor force status, earnings, and other economic status indicators, and compared to whites, various periods 1939-88, 11048–191
Child care arrangements of mothers employed and in school, and costs, by age of child and characteristics of mother, 1988, Current Population Rpt, 2546–20.24
Consumer Income, socioeconomic characteristics of persons, families, and households, detailed cross-tabulations, Current Population Rpt series, 2546–6
Credit unions federally insured, finances by instn characteristics and State, as of June 1992, semiannual rpt, 9532–6
Displaced workers losing job 1987-92, labor force status by employment and other characteristics, as of Jan 1992, biennial press release, 6726–1.48
DOT employment, by subagency, occupation, and selected personnel characteristics, FY91, annual rpt, 7304–18
Drug, alcohol, and cigarette use, by selected characteristics, 1991 survey, annual rpt series, 4494–5
Economic indicators and components, current data and annual trends, monthly rpt, 23842–1.2
Education data compilation, 1992 annual rpt, 4824–2
Educational enrollment, by grade, instn type and control, and student characteristics, 1990 and trends from 1947, annual Current Population Rpt, 2546–1.459
Employment and Earnings, detailed data, monthly rpt, 6742–2
Employment, earnings, and hours, monthly press release, 6742–5

Employment situation, earnings, hours, and other BLS economic indicators, transcripts of BLS Commissioner's monthly testimony, periodic rpt, 23846–4
Employment, unemployment, and labor force characteristics, by region and State, 1991, annual rpt, 6744–7.1; 6744–7.2
Farm operators working part-time, selected characteristics of operation, 1987, young readers pamphlet, 2346–1.6
Fed Govt civilian employees demographic and employment characteristics, as of Sept 1991, annual article, 9842–1.301
Fed Govt civilian employees work-years, pay rates, and benefits use and costs, by agency, FY90, annual rpt, 9844–31
Fed Govt civilian employment and payroll, by agency in DC metro area, total US, and abroad, bimonthly rpt, 9842–1
Federal district court magistrate full- and part-time positions, 1991, annual rpt, 18204–8.11
Food stamp recipient household size, composition, income, and income and deductions allowed, summer 1989, annual rpt, 1364–8
Govt employment and payroll, by function, level of govt, and jurisdiction, annual rpt series, 2466–1
High school class of 1991: college enrollment, and labor force participation of grads and dropouts, by race and sex, annual press release, 6726–1.46
Higher education faculty and staff, by occupation, full- and part-time status, sex, and instn type and control, fall 1989, biennial rpt, 4844–18
Hospital employees and wages by occupation, and benefits, by region and selected MSA, 1991 survey, 6787–6.254
Hospital employment and job vacancy rate, by occupation, and instn size and control, 1981-88, annual rpt, 4114–12
Hospital reimbursement by Medicare under prospective payment system, and effect on services, finances, and beneficiary payments, 1980-91, annual rpt, 17204–2
Households composition, income, benefits, and labor force status, Survey of Income and Program Participation methodology, working paper series, 2626–10
Income (household) and poverty status under alternative income definitions, by recipient characteristics, 1979-91, annual Current Population Rpt, 2546–6.78
Insurance (health) coverage of persons, by insurance type and selected characteristics, 1985-90, 2546–20.23
Labor demand, turnover, and training completions, by detailed occupation, 1990 and projected to 2005, biennial rpt, 6744–3
Labor force status, experience, and unemployment duration, by race and sex, 1990-91, annual press release, 6726–1.51
Labor force status transition rates, and relation to unemployment rate, by sex, 1980-89, working paper, 9377–9.129
Mental health care facilities, staff, patients, and finances, 1970s-91, biennial rpt, 4094–1
Military health care personnel, by full- and part-time status, occupation, and service branch, FY90, annual rpt, 3544–24.7
Military service branches civilian employment, with summary military employment data, quarterly rpt, 3542–16
Monthly Labor Review, current statistics and articles, 6722–1
NASA staff characteristics and personnel actions, FY91, annual rpt, 9504–1
Occupational Outlook Handbook, 1992-93, biennial rpt, 6744–1
Older persons income by source, for married OASI beneficiaries by work and eligibility pattern of wife, 1982, article, 4746–26.12
Older persons labor force status, income sources, and reasons for not working, with data by occupation, sex, and race, 1989-90 and projected to 2050, 21148–65
Older persons socioeconomic characteristics, 1900s-90 and projected to 2050, biennial chartbook, 12904–1
Pacific territories population and housing detailed characteristics, by location, 1990 Census of Population and Housing, series, 2551–8
Police agencies employment, spending, and operations, FY90, 6066–25.44
Police employment, spending, and operations, for State, city, county, and special district agencies, 1990, annual rpt, 6064–39
Poverty status of families, by detailed characteristics, 1980 and 1988, GAO rpt, 26131–102
Public assistance benefits, beneficiaries, and spells of participation, by aid program and recipient characteristics, 1987-88, Current Population Rpt, 2546–20.25
Sheriffs' agencies employment, spending, and operations, FY90, 6066–25.45
Small Business Admin loan guarantee program participants finances, operations, characteristics, and views, 1991 survey, 9768–25
Small business finances, operations, owner characteristics, and Federal contracts, 1980s-90, annual rpt, 9764–6
State and local govt employees benefit plan coverage and provisions, by plan type, 1990, biennial rpt, 6784–21
State and local govt employment of minorities and women, by occupation, function, pay level, and State, 1991, annual rpt, 9244–6
State court chief prosecutors employment characteristics, and felony case prosecution procedures, 1990 survey, 6066–25.46
Statistical Abstract of US, 1992 annual data compilation, 2324–1.13
Union coverage of workers and earnings, by age, sex, race, occupational group, and industry div, 1990-91, annual press release, 6726–1.44
VA employment characteristics and activities, FY91, annual rpt, 8604–3.4
VA health care facilities physicians, dentists, and nurses, by selected employment characteristics and VA district, quarterly rpt, 8602–6
VA health care professionals employment, by district and facility, quarterly rpt, 8602–4
VA physicians and dentists full- and part-time staff and vacancies, by specialty, 1991, annual rpt, 8604–8
Wages of full- and part-time workers, by selected characteristics, quarterly press release, 6742–20
Women (married) working part time, by whether voluntarily and income class, 1979 and 1989, 23848–225
Women's labor force status and characteristics, 1960s-90, chartbook, 6748–85
Women's part-time employment transitions, by marital status and whether young children present, 1988 and trends from 1978, 6726–2.2
see also Moonlighting
see also Temporary and seasonal employment
see also Underemployment
see also Worksharing

Partlan, John
"Small Time Deposits and the Recent Weakness in M2", 9385–1.305

Partnerships
Farmland in US owned by foreigners, holdings, acquisitions, and disposals by land use, owner type and country, and State, 1991, annual rpt, 1584–2
Foreign partners of US partnerships, detailed data compilation for income tax returns, 1970s-89, quinquennial rpt, 8308–31
Foreign partners of US partnerships, income and tax withheld, by country, 1990, article, 8302–2.324
Income and losses of partnerships, impact of 1986 Tax Reform Act, by profit status and selected industry, 1980s, article, 8302–2.313
Minority- and woman-owned businesses and owner characteristics, by industry, employment and sales size, and form of ownership, 1987 survey, 2328–59
Retail trade sales, inventories, purchases, gross margin, and accounts receivable, by SIC 2- to 4-digit kind of business and form of ownership, 1990, annual rpt, 2413–5
Small Business Admin loan guarantee program participants finances, operations, characteristics, and views, 1991 survey, 9768–25
Small business finances, operations, owner characteristics, and Federal contracts, 1980s-90, annual rpt, 9764–6
Small Business Investment Companies capital holdings, SBA obligation, and ownership, as of July 1992, semiannual listing, 9762–4
Statistical Abstract of US, 1992 annual data compilation, 2324–1.17
Tax (income) collection, enforcement, and litigation activity of IRS, with data by type of tax, region, and State, FY91, annual rpt, 8304–3
Tax (income) returns and supplemental documents filed, by type, FY91 and projected to FY2000, semiannual rpt, 8302–4
Tax (income) returns filed, by type of filer, selected income items, quarterly rpt, 8302–2.1
Tax (income) returns filed, by type of return and IRS district, 1990 and projected 1991-98, annual rpt, 8304–24
Tax (income) returns filed, by type of tax and IRS region and service center, projected 1991-98 and trends from 1978, annual rpt, 8304–9

Tax (income) returns of individuals, detailed data, 1988, annual rpt, 8304–2
Tax (income) returns of partnerships, income statement and balance sheet items, by industry group, 1990, annual article, 8302–2.314
Tax (income) withholding and related documents filed, by type and IRS service center, 1991 and projected 1992-99, annual rpt, 8304–22
Tax returns and supplemental documents filed, by type, 1990 and projected to 1999, annual article, 8302–2.304
see also Joint ventures

Pasch, Richard J.
"North Atlantic Hurricanes—1991", 2152–8.302

Pasek, Judith E.
"Status and Trends of Mountain Pine Beetle Populations in the Bear Mountain and White House Gulch Areas on the Harney Ranger District, Black Hills National Forest, South Dakota", 1208–408

Passenger ships
Construction and operating subsidies of MarAd by firm, and ship deliveries and fleet by country, by vessel type, FY91, annual rpt, 7704–14.1; 7704–14.2
Foreign-flag ships owned by US firms and foreign affiliates, by type, owner, and country of registry and construction, as of July 1991, semiannual rpt, 7702–3
Foreign travel to US, by characteristics of visit and traveler, country, port city, and State of destination, monthly rpt, 2902–1
Sanitation inspection scores for passenger cruise ships, biweekly rpt, 4202–10
St Lawrence Seaway ship, cargo, and passenger traffic, and toll revenue, 1991 and trends from 1959, annual rpt, 7744–2
Tax (excise) collections of IRS, by source, quarterly rpt, 8302–1
Traffic, freight by commodity, and passengers, domestic and foreign waterborne commerce by port and waterway, 1989, annual rpt, 3754–3

Passmore, Wayne
"Can Retail Depositories Fund Mortgages Profitably?", 9366–6.289

Passport Office
see Bureau of Consular Affairs, State Department

Passports and visas
Applicants for immigrant visas on waiting lists at consular office, by preference class, world region, and for top countries, as of Jan 1992, 7188–1
Applications for passports handled by Federal district courts, by circuit and district, 1991, annual rpt, 18204–8.27
Business statistics, detailed data for major industries and economic indicators, 1960-91, *Survey of Current Business* biennial supplement, 2704–1
Criminal cases by type and disposition, and collections, for US attorneys, by Federal district, FY91, annual rpt, 6004–2.1
Criminal sentences for Federal offenses, guidelines by offense and circumstances, series, 17668–1
Foreign travel to US, by characteristics of visit and traveler, country, port city, and State of destination, monthly rpt, 2902–1
Passports issued, *Survey of Current Business*, monthly rpt, 2702–1.10
Residency (temporary) applications of aliens, by occupation, age, sex, marital status, and country, 1988-91, 4808–41
Visas of US issued and refused to immigrants and nonimmigrants, by class, issuing office, and nationality, FY90, annual rpt, 7184–1

Pasture and rangeland
Agricultural Statistics, 1991, annual rpt, 1004–1
Cattle and calves for beef, ranches, inventory, producers, and returns, by herd size and region, mid 1940s-91, 1568–251
Conservation program of USDA, acreage, projects, participation, and funding, by State, 1936-90, quinquennial rpt, 1808–1
Conservation program of USDA, participation and payments by practice and State, FY91, annual rpt, 1804–7
Desert areas public grazing acreage, use, fees, and endangered species, 1988-90, GAO rpt, 26113–552
Economic Indicators of the Farm Sector, itemized production costs, receipts, and returns, by commodity and region, 1975-90, annual rpt, 1544–20
Environmental Quality, status of problems, protection programs, research, and intl issues, 1991 annual rpt, 484–1
Farm prices received and paid, by commodity and State, monthly rpt, 1629–1
Farm production itemized costs, by farm sales size and region, 1991, annual rpt, 1614–3
FmHA activities, and loans and grants by program and State, FY91 and trends from FY70, annual rpt, 1184–17
Foreign ownership of US farmland, holdings, acquisitions, and disposals by land use, owner type and country, and State, 1991, annual rpt, 1584–2
Foreign ownership of US farmland, holdings, acreage, and value by land use, owner country, State, and county, 1991, annual rpt, 1584–3
Indian and govt lands under Bur of Indian Affairs mgmt, acreage, leases, and use, 1989, annual rpt, 5704–12
Irrigation projects of Reclamation Bur in western US, crop production and acreage by commodity, State, and project, 1990, annual rpt, 5824–12
Livestock grazing forage demand, and meat supply and demand, indicators, 1960s-90 and projected to 2030, 1208–404
Natl forests revenue, by source, forest, and State, FY91, annual rpt, 1204–34
New Mexico Caballo Resource Area public land mgmt, and grazing, environmental, and leasing activities, FY90-91, annual rpt, 5724–17
Public lands acreage, grants, use, revenues, and allocations, by State, FY91, annual rpt, 5724–1.2
Public lands grazing and receipts, by animal type and State, FY91, annual rpt, 1204–1.1
Rental of pasture, and cattle grazing rates, by region and State, 1986-92, article, 1561–16.302
Research and education grants, USDA competitive awards by program and recipient, FY91, annual listing, 1764–1
Sheep and wool production, use, and prices, and operations costs and returns, for western US, 1920s-90, 1548–382
Southwestern US farm credit conditions and real estate values, Fed Reserve 11th District, quarterly rpt, 9379–11
see also National grasslands

Patent and Trademark Office
Activities of PTO, applications, grants, fees, and litigation, FY71-90, annual rpt, 2244–1
Budget of US, obligations and authority by function, agency, and program, with summaries and analyses, FY93, annual rpt, 104–2
Grants of patents to US and foreign applicants, by State and country, FY90-91, annual press release, 2244–2
Patents (US) granted to US and foreign applicants, by applicant and country, 1960s-91, annual rpt, 2244–3

Patents
Applications, grants, fees, and litigation, for patents and trademarks, FY71-90, annual rpt, 2244–1
Claims Court caseload by type of suit, and judgments, FY92, annual rpt, 18224–1
County Business Patterns, 1989: employment, establishments, and payroll, by SIC 2- to 4-digit industry and county, annual State rpt series, 2326–8
County Business Patterns, 1990: employment, establishments, and payroll, by SIC 2- to 4-digit industry and county, annual State rpt series, 2326–6
Court civil and criminal caseloads for Federal district, appeals, and bankruptcy courts, by type of suit and offense, circuit, and district, 1991, annual rpt, 18204–11
Court civil and criminal caseloads for Federal district, appeals, and special courts, 1991, annual rpt, 18204–8
Exports of goods, services, and investment, trade barriers, impacts, and US actions, by country, 1991, annual rpt, 444–2
Fed Govt employee incentive awards, costs, and benefits, by award type and agency, FY90, annual rpt, 9844–20
Foreign countries economic conditions, policy, and trade practices, by country, 1989-91, annual rpt, 21384–5
Grants of patents to US and foreign applicants, by applicant and country, 1960s-91, annual rpt, 2244–3
Grants of patents to US and foreign applicants, by State and country, FY90-91, annual press release, 2244–2
Higher education instn R&D supported by NSF and NIH, license transfer to private firms, related income, and scientists associated with licensees, FY89-90, GAO rpt, 26113–575
Intl competitiveness of US high technology industries, with background data by industry and foreign comparisons, 1960s-91, GAO rpt, 26123–406
Land Mgmt Bur activities and finances, and public land acreage and use, annual State rpt series, 5724–11
Lands (public) acreage, grants, use, revenues, and allocations, by State, FY91, annual rpt, 5724–1.2
Market potential of industrial and Federal labs technological innovations, results of annual *R&D 100* awards competition, 1960s-90, 2218–86

Mines Bur rpts and patents, monthly listing, 5602–2
NSF grantees retaining patent rights and number transferred to NSF, FY91, annual rpt, 9624–6
Overseas Business Reports: economic conditions, investment and export opportunities, and trade practices, country market research rpt series, 2046–6
Science and Engineering Indicators, employment, education, R&D funding, and industry impacts, with foreign comparisons, 1960s-91, biennial rpt, 9624–10.5; 9624–10.6
Seed varieties patent protection, and wheat farmer profitability of using purchased seed, 1986-89, 1548–388
Statistical Abstract of US, 1992 annual data compilation, 2324–1.17
see also Trademarks

Pathology

Aviation medicine research and test results, technical rpt series, 7506–10
Education in science and engineering, grad programs enrollment by field, source of funds, and characteristics of student and instn, 1990, annual rpt, 9627–7
Labor supply and education of health professionals, by professional and other characteristics, and location, 1960s-92 and projected to 2020, biennial rpt, 4114–8
Labor supply of physicians, by specialty, age, sex, and location of training and practice, 1990, State rpt series, 4116–6
Medicare payment of physicians under fee schedule, methodology with data by procedure and specialty, 1992, annual rpt, 17264–1
Military health care personnel, and accessions by training source, by occupation, specialty, and service branch, FY90, annual rpt, 3544–24
VA health care facilities physicians, dentists, and nurses, by selected employment characteristics and VA district, quarterly rpt, 8602–6
VA health care services, needs, availability, structure, and funding, 1991 compilation of papers, 8608–9
VA health care staff and turnover, by occupation, physician specialty, and location, 1991, annual rpt, 8604–8
see also Diseases and disorders
see also Medical examinations and tests

Pattison, David

"Review of the Net Revenue Estimates in Robbins and Robbins, 'Paying People Not To Work' ", 4746–26.10
"Simulating Aggregate and Distributional Effects of Various Plans for Modifying the Retirement Earnings Test", 4746–26.15

Paulozzi, Leonard J.

"Evaluation of the Vermont Worksite Smoking Law", 4042–3.375

Payment-in-kind program, USDA

see Agricultural production quotas and price supports

Payroll

Appalachia food processing firms, employment, and shipments, and farm production, by commodity and State, 1960s-90, 9088–37
Banks (Fed Reserve) and branch officers, staff, and salary, 1991, annual rpt, 9364–1.1
Banks and thrifts finances and operations by deposit size, Fed Reserve functional cost analysis, 1991, annual rpt, 9364–6
Banks in Fed Reserve System, expenses and operations itemized by service, office, and district, 1991, annual rpt, 9364–11
Building materials industry finances and operations, by SIC 4-digit industry, selected years 1977-89, article, 2042–1.302
Communications services revenue and expenses, itemized by SIC 2- to 4-digit kind of business, 1990, annual rpt, 2413–15
Costs (hourly) of labor, by component, industry and occupational group, worker class, and firm size, monthly rpt, annual tables, 6782–1.2
Costs (hourly) of labor, by component, occupational group, industry div, union coverage, and region, 1992, annual rpt, 6744–21
County Business Patterns, 1989: employment, establishments, and payroll, by SIC 2- to 4-digit industry and county, annual State rpt series, 2326–8
County Business Patterns, 1990: employment, establishments, and payroll, by SIC 2- to 4-digit industry and county, annual State rpt series, 2326–6
Credit unions federally insured, finances by instn characteristics and State, as of June 1992, semiannual rpt, 9532–6
Disabled persons workshops finances, operations, and Federal procurement, FY82-91, annual rpt, 11714–1
Electric utilities privately owned, finances and operations, detailed data, 1990, annual rpt, 3164–23
Fed Reserve System, Bd of Governors, and district banks financial statements, performance, and fiscal services, 1991-92, annual rpt, 9364–10
Foreign and US manufacturing hourly compensation costs, by industry and country, series, 6826–3
Foreign travelers to US, spending by world area of residence, and economic impacts, by spending category and State, 1989, 2908–28
Gross State Product by component, industry div, and State, 1977-89, article, 2702–1.303
Health Care Financing Review, provider prices, price inputs and indexes, and labor, quarterly journal, 4652–1.1
Manufacturing annual survey, 1990: establishments, employment, finances, inventories, and energy use, by SIC 2- to 4-digit industry, 2506–14.2
Manufacturing annual survey, 1990: finances and operations, by SIC 2- and 3-digit industry and State, 2506–14.3
Manufacturing census, 1987: concentration of largest firms measured by value added, and for shipments by SIC 2- and 4-digit industry, subject rpt, 2497–6
Militarily strategic manufacturing industries finances, operations, and intl competitiveness, series, 2026–1
Multinatl firms US affiliates finances and operations, by industry, country of parent firm, and State, 1987, 2702–1.340; 2708–48
Multinatl firms US affiliates finances and operations, by industry div, country of parent firm, and State, 1989-90, annual article, 2702–1.319
Multinatl firms US affiliates, finances, and operations, by industry, world area of parent firm, and State, 1989-90, annual rpt, 2704–4
Multinatl firms US affiliates gross product, by component, industry, and country of parent firm, 1987-90, article, 2702–1.342
Multinatl US firms and foreign affiliates finances and operations, by industry and country, 1989 benchmark survey, annual rpt, 2704–5
Multinatl US firms and foreign affiliates finances and operations, by industry and world area, 1988, annual article, 2702–1.329
Natl income and product accounts, comprehensive accounts and components, benchmark revisions, 1929-88, 2708–5
Natl income and product accounts, comprehensive accounts and components, *Survey of Current Business*, monthly rpt, 2702–1.29
Natural gas interstate pipeline company detailed financial and operating data, by firm, 1990, annual rpt, 3164–38
Nonprofit charitable and other tax exempt organizations finances, by category and size of assets and contributions, 1988, annual article, 8302–2.315
Nonprofit charitable organizations finances, with data by State and for top 10 instns, 1988, article, 8302–2.302
Nuclear weapons facilities of DOE, contractor fees, environmental and safety enforcement activity, and salaries, by contractor and facility, 1987-88, hearing, 21408–127
Railroad (Class I) finances and operations, detailed data by firm, class of service, and district, 1990, annual rpt, 9486–5.1
Railroad (Class I) finances and operations, detailed data by firm, class of service, and district, 1991, annual rpt, 9486–6.1
Savings instns financial statements, for instns insured by Savings Assn Insurance Fund by FHLB district and State, and for FDIC-insured savings banks, 1989, annual rpt, 8434–1
Small Business Admin loan guarantee program participants finances, operations, characteristics, and views, 1991 survey, 9768–25
Southeastern States, Fed Reserve 5th District insured commercial banks financial statements, by State, quarterly rpt, 9389–18
Statistical Abstract of US, 1992 annual data compilation, 2324–1.17
Steel imports of US under voluntary restraint agreement, by product, customs district, and country, with US industry operating data, quarterly rpt, 9882–13
Steel trade, by product, country, and customs district, with US industry operating data, 1989-June 1992, semiannual rpt, 9882–15
Tax (income) returns filed, by type of filer, selected income items, quarterly rpt, 8302–2.1
Tax (income) returns of partnerships, income statement and balance sheet items, by industry group, 1990, annual article, 8302–2.314

Tax (income) returns of sole proprietorships, income statement items, by industry group, 1990, annual article, 8302–2.317; 8302–2.320
Tax exempt organizations finances, with data by type, size, State, and for largest organizations, late 1940s-80s, compilation of papers, 8308–35
Tax exempt organizations with unrelated business income, finances by organization type, 1987, article, 8302–2.306
Telephone and telegraph firms detailed finances and operations, 1990, annual rpt, 9284–6
Truck and bus interstate carriers finances and operations, by district, 1990, annual rpt, 9486–5.3
Truck and warehouse services finances and inventory, by SIC 2- to 4-digit industry, 1990 survey, annual rpt, 2413–14
Truck, bus, and rail carriers regulated by ICC, employment and finances, as of FY91, annual rpt, 9484–1
Truck interstate carriers finances and operations, by district, 1990, annual rpt, 9486–5.2
see also Agricultural wages
see also Earnings, general
see also Earnings, specific industry
see also Educational employees pay
see also Federal pay
see also Government pay
see also Military pay
see also Social security tax
see also State and local employees pay
see also Unemployment insurance tax
see also Wage deductions

Payroll tax
see Social security tax
see Unemployment insurance tax

Peace Corps
Activities of PC, funding by program, and volunteers, by country, FY93, annual rpt, 9654–1
Budget of US, authoritative financial statements with appropriations, outlays, and receipts, by category and agency, FY91, annual rpt, 8104–2.2
Budget of US, obligations and authority by function, agency, and program, with summaries and analyses, FY93, annual rpt, 104–2
Developing countries economic and social conditions from 1960s, and Intl Dev Cooperation Agency and AID activities and funding, FY91-93, annual rpt, 9904–4
Expenditures for economic and military aid, by program and country, FY46-91, annual rpt, 9914–5
Human rights conditions in 170 countries, and US economic and military aid, 1991, annual rpt, 21384–3
Labor unions recognized in Fed Govt, agreements and membership by agency and facility, as of Jan 1991, biennial listing, 9844–14
Latin America economic and social conditions, resources, trade, and aid, 1992, annual factbook, 9914–14
Palau admin, and social, economic, and govtl data, FY91, annual rpt, 7004–6

Peace Institute
see U.S. Institute of Peace

Peacekeeping forces
see International military forces

Peach, Richard
"Impact of the Current Defense Build-Down", 9385–1.313

Peaches
see Fruit and fruit products

Peanuts
Acreage planted and harvested, by crop and State, 1990-91 and planned as of June 1992, annual rpt, 1621–23
Acreage planted, by selected crop and State, 1983-91 and planned 1992, annual rpt, 1621–22
Agricultural Stabilization and Conservation Service peanut programs, 1978-91, annual fact sheet, 1806–4.3
Agricultural Statistics, 1991, annual rpt, 1004–1
CCC financial condition and major commodity program operations, FY63-88, annual chartbook, 1824–2
Cold storage food stocks by commodity, and warehouse space use, by census div, 1991, annual rpt, 1631–11
Confectionery shipments, trade, use, and ingredients used, by product, 1991, annual Current Industrial Rpt, 2506–4.5
Consumption, supply, trade, prices, spending, and indexes, by food commodity, 1990, annual rpt, 1544–4
Exports and imports (agricultural) of US, by detailed commodity and country, 1991, annual rpt, 1524–8
Exports and imports (agricultural) of US, by detailed commodity and country, 1991, semiannual rpt, 1522–4
Exports and imports between US and outlying areas, by detailed commodity and mode of transport, 1991, annual rpt, 2424–11
Exports and imports of US, by country and detailed commodity, monthly rpt, 2422–12
Exports and imports of US, by Harmonized System 6-digit commodity and country, 1991, annual rpt, 2424–13
Exports of US, detailed Schedule B commodities with countries of destination, 1991, annual rpt, 2424–10
Fertilizer and pesticide use and application rates, by type, crop, and State, 1991, 1616–1.1
Foreign and US oils, oilseeds, and fats production and trade, FAS periodic circular series, 1925–1
Price indexes (producer), by stage of processing and detailed commodity, monthly 1991, annual rpt, 6764–2
Prices received and paid by farmers, by commodity and State, 1991, annual rpt, 1629–5
Prices received by farmers and production value, by detailed crop and State, 1989-91, annual rpt, 1621–2
Production and US exports by country, prices, and stocks, for peanuts, weekly rpt, 1311–1
Production, farms, acreage, and related data, by selected crop and State, monthly rpt, 1621–1
Production itemized costs, receipts, and returns, by commodity and region, 1975-90, annual rpt, 1544–20
Production itemized costs, receipts, and returns, by crop and State, 1987-89, annual rpt, 1544–24
Production, prices, stocks, exports, use, inspection, and quality, for peanuts, by region and State, 1980-90, annual rpt, 1311–5
Production, prices, trade, and use of oils and fats, periodic situation rpt with articles, 1561–3
Stocks, millings, and use, by peanut grade and type, monthly rpt, 1621–6
Truck rates for fruit and vegetables paid by shippers and receivers, by commodity and city, and fleet itemized costs per mile, weekly rpt, 1311–22

Pearrow, Joan
"U.S. Imports of Fruits and Vegetables Under Plant Quarantine Regulations, FY89", 1524–7

Peat
see Nonmetallic minerals and mines

Pebsworth, Vicky
"Role of Specialty Societies and Physicians in the Commission's Evaluation of Relative Work Values", 17266–2.8

Pecans
see Nuts

Peden, Edgar A.
"Output and Inflation Components of Medical Care and Other Spending Changes", 4652–1.308

Pedestrians
Accident deaths involving alcohol, by driver and victim blood alcohol levels, and other characteristics, 1977-88, annual rpt, 4486–1.12
Accident deaths involving alcohol, by driver and victim blood alcohol levels, and other characteristics, 1977-89, annual rpt, 4486–1.14
Accidents (fatal), circumstances, and characteristics of persons and vehicles involved, 1991, semiannual rpt, 7762–11
Accidents (fatal), deaths, and rates, by circumstances, characteristics of persons and vehicles involved, and location, 1990, annual rpt, 7764–10
Accidents at hwy-railroad grade-crossings, detailed data by State and railroad, 1991, annual rpt, 7604–2
Accidents, casualties, circumstances, and characteristics of persons and vehicles involved, 1990, annual rpt, 7764–18
Commuting to work, by mode, trip duration, and work location, 1980 and 1990, 7558–120
Pacific territories population and housing detailed characteristics, by location, 1990 Census of Population and Housing, series, 2551–8
Safety research on traffic issues, literature review, with data on accidents and impact of safety measures, 1961-90, 7558–98
Travel patterns, personal and household characteristics, and auto and public transport use, 1990 survey, series, 7556–6

Pediatrics
Adolescent health specialists, views on training, and Federal aid for training, 1991 rpt, 26358–234.3
Health condition and care indicators, 1950s-90 with health improvement and disease prevention goals for 1990, annual data compilation, 4144–11

HHS financial aid, by program, recipient, State, and city, FY91, annual regional listings, 4004–3
Indian Health Service outpatient services provided, by reason for visit and age, FY90, annual rpt, 4084–2
Indian Health Service, tribal, and contract facilities hospitalization, by diagnosis, age, sex, and service area, FY91, annual rpt, 4084–5
Infant (newborn) intensive care, assessment of alternative case mix groupings intended to improve cost homogeneity, 1985, article, 4652–1.303
Labor supply and education of health professionals, by professional and other characteristics, and location, 1960s-92 and projected to 2020, biennial rpt, 4114–8
Labor supply of physicians, by specialty, age, sex, and location of training and practice, 1990, State rpt series, 4116–6
Medicaid payment and participation by service type, and cost compared to Medicare, by State, FY89, 17266–1.4
Military health care personnel, and accessions by training source, by occupation, specialty, and service branch, FY90, annual rpt, 3544–24
Office visits to pediatricians, by characteristics of patient and visit, 1989, 4146–8.210
Otitis media patients physician office visits, by specialty and characteristics of patient and visit, 1975-90, 4146–8.217
VA health care facilities physicians, dentists, and nurses, by selected employment characteristics and VA district, quarterly rpt, 8602–6
Visits to physicians, by patient and practice characteristics, diagnosis, and services provided, 1989, annual rpt, 4147–13.109
Visits to physicians, by patient and practice characteristics, diagnosis, and services provided, 1990, advance rpt, 4146–8.215

Peek, Joe
"Capital Crunch in New England", 9373–1.309
"Capital Crunch: Neither a Borrower Nor a Lender Be", 9373–27.4
"Measurement and Determinants of Single-Family House Prices", 9373–27.7
"Role of Real Estate in the New England Credit Crunch", 9373–27.12
"Treasury Bill Rates in the 1970s and 1980s", 9373–27.6

Pell grants
see Student aid

Penalties
see Fines and settlements
see Judgments, civil procedure
see Sentences, criminal procedure

Pennsylvania
Appalachian Regional Commission funding, by project and State, planned FY92, annual rpt, 9084–3
Apple production, marketing, and prices, for Appalachia and compared to other States, 1989-92, annual rpt, 1311–13
Banks (insured commercial and savings) deposits by instn, State, MSA, and county, as of June 1991, annual regional rpt, 9295–3.1
Coal (Pennsylvania anthracite) production, weekly rpt, 3162–1
Coal production and mines by county, prices, productivity, miners, and reserves, by mining method and State, 1990-91, annual rpt, 3164–25
Dairy prices, by product and selected area, with related marketing data, 1991, annual rpt, 1317–1
Deaths and rates, by detailed location, cause, and demographic characteristics, 1989, US Vital Statistics annual rpt, 4144–3.1
Economic indicators and components, and Fed Reserve 4th District business and financial conditions, monthly chartbook, 9377–10
Employment, earnings, and hours, by selected SIC 1- to 4-digit industry, State, and for 275 MSAs, 1987-92, 6748–81
Employment growth and unemployment rates, Fed Reserve 3rd District, quarterly rpt, 9387–10
Fed Govt spending in States and local areas, by type, State, county, and city, FY91, annual rpt, 2464–3
Fed Govt spending in States, by type, program, agency, and State, FY91, annual rpt, 2464–2
HHS financial aid, by program, recipient, State, and city, FY91, annual regional listing, 4004–3.3
Hospital deaths of Medicare patients, actual and expected rates by diagnosis, and hospital characteristics, by instn, FY90 annual State rpt, 4654–14.39
Housing census, 1990: summary unit characteristics, by householder race and age, county, place, and urban-rural location, State rpt, 2471–1.40
Medicaid impacts on State budgets, and program financing, cost control measures, enrollment, and services coverage, by selected State, 1960s-80s and projected to 1997, 10176–3.6
Military prime contract awards, by contractor, service branch, State, and city, FY91, annual rpt, 3544–22
Mineral Industry Surveys, State reviews of production, 1991, preliminary annual rpt, 5614–6
Multinatl firms US affiliates finances and operations, by industry, country of parent firm, and State, 1987, 2708–48
Physicians, by specialty, age, sex, and location of training and practice, 1990, State rpt, 4116–6.39
Population and housing census, 1990: detailed geographic coverage, State CD-ROM, 2551–9.2
Population and housing census, 1990: summary characteristics, by county, subdiv, and place, State rpt, 2551–7.40
Population census, 1990: population characteristics and living arrangements, by county, place, and urban-rural location, State rpt, 2531–1.40
Radiation and other pollutant releases from DOE contractor research lab and nuclear weapons facilities, monitoring results, 1992 annual site rpt, 3324–2.6
Statistical Abstract of US, 1992 annual data compilation, 2324–1
Uranium tailings at inactive mills, remedial action activities by site, and funding, FY91, annual rpt, 3354–9
Water resources data collection and analysis activities of USGS Water Resources Div District, with project descriptions, 1991 rpt, 5666–26.25
Water supply and quality in streams and lakes, and groundwater levels in wells, by drainage basin, 1990, annual State rpt, 5666–10.37
Wetlands acid neutralizing capability for mining runoff, with pollutant levels and site characteristics, for Pennsylvania, 1987-90, 5608–171
see also Allegheny County, Pa.
see also Delaware County, Pa.
see also Harrisburg, Pa.
see also Lebanon, Pa.
see also Montgomery County, Pa.
see also Philadelphia, Pa.
see also Pittsburgh, Pa.
see also Westmoreland County, Pa.
see also York, Pa.
see also under By State in the "Index by Categories"

Pennsylvania Avenue Development Corp.
Budget of US, authoritative financial statements with appropriations, outlays, and receipts, by category and agency, FY91, annual rpt, 8104–2.2
Budget of US, obligations and authority by function, agency, and program, with summaries and analyses, FY93, annual rpt, 104–2

Pensacola, Fla.
see also under By City and By SMSA or MSA in the "Index by Categories"

Pension and Welfare Benefits Administration
Budget of US, obligations and authority by function, agency, and program, with summaries and analyses, FY93, annual rpt, 104–2
OECD pension plan finances, participation, and benefits, for 9 countries, with data by firm and worker characteristics, 1990 conf, 6688–2

Pension Benefit Guaranty Corp.
Activities and finances of PBGC, FY91, annual rpt, 9674–1
Assets and liabilities of top 50 underfunded plans guaranteed by PBGC, 1991, annual press release, 9674–2
Budget of US, conversion of deposit insurance and PBGC budget authority and outlays from cash to accrual accounting basis, FY93, 108–46.1
Budget of US, obligations and authority by function, agency, and program, with summaries and analyses, FY93, annual rpt, 104–2
Finances and operations of programs under Ways and Means Committee jurisdiction, FY70s-91, annual rpt, 21784–11
Insurance funds of PBGC for single- and multi-employer plans, balances, FY91, article, 9391–16.309
Labor unions recognized in Fed Govt, agreements and membership by agency and facility, as of Jan 1991, biennial listing, 9844–14
Terminations of pension plans, liabilities, assets, and PBGC recoveries and losses, with top 50 underfunded plans, mid 1970s-91, article, 9371–1.302

Pensions and pension funds
Assets and debts of private sector, balance sheets by segment, 1960-91, semiannual rpt, 9365–4.1
Assets and liabilities of top 50 underfunded plans guaranteed by Pension Benefit Guaranty Corp, 1991, annual press release, 9674–2
Assets of private and public pension funds, 1981-90, annual rpt, 9364–5.12
Chile social security system replacement with private pension system, economic impacts, 1970s-90, technical paper, 9385–8.123
Coal industry retirees pension and health trust funds financial condition, employer contributions, and beneficiaries, late 1970s-92, GAO rpt, 26121–469; 26121–471
Consumer Expenditure Survey, spending by category, and income, by selected household characteristics, 1991, annual press release, 6726–1.53
Costs of employee compensation, by component, occupation, industry group, union status, and location, 1975-92, annual rpt, 6744–20.2
Eastern Europe pension systems finances and provisions, 1950s-90 and alternative projections to 2025, technical paper, 8006–6.7
Expenditures (private) for social welfare, by category, 1970s-90, annual article, 4742–1.323
Expenditures, coverage, and benefits for social welfare programs, late 1930s-90, annual rpt, 4744–3.1; 4744–3.3
Flow-of-funds accounts, savings, investments, and credit statements, quarterly rpt, 9365–3.3
Health insurance benefits of pension plans, accounting standards changes, and impacts on firm finances, with background data, 1986-89, technical paper, 9366–6.298
Households composition, income, benefits, and labor force status, Survey of Income and Program Participation methodology, working paper series, 2626–10
Housing (rental) units, total, with HUD assistance by program, and eligible for aid, by unit, household, and neighborhood characteristics, and location, 1989, biennial rpt, 5184–11
Income (household) of aged and younger adults, by source, household composition, and age group, 1984 and 1989, article, 4742–1.304
Income (household, family, and personal), by source, detailed characteristics, and region, 1991, annual Current Population Rpt, 2546–6.76
Income and sources of aged, by OASDI beneficiary and poverty status, and other characteristics, 1990, biennial rpt, 4744–25
Income and sources of aged, by whether OASDI beneficiary, poverty status, and other characteristics, 1990, biennial rpt, 4744–26
Insurance funds of Pension Benefit Guaranty Corp for single- and multi-employer plans, balances, FY91, article, 9391–16.309
Labor hourly costs, by component, industry and occupational group, worker class, and firm size, monthly rpt, annual tables, 6782–1.2
Labor hourly costs, by component, occupational group, industry div, union coverage, and region, 1992, annual rpt, 6744–21
Mortgage loan activity, by type of lender, loan, and mortgaged property, monthly press release, 5142–18
Mortgage loan activity, by type of lender, loan, and mortgaged property, quarterly press release, 5142–30
Mortgage, mortgage-backed security, and govt security holdings of public and private pension funds, and public funds investment in housing, 1986-90, 5188–134
Natl income and product accounts, comprehensive accounts and components, benchmark revisions, 1929-88, 2708–5
Natl income and product accounts, comprehensive accounts and components, *Survey of Current Business*, monthly rpt, 2702–1.28
OASDI beneficiary data collection system design compared to earlier surveys, with summary results, 1992 article, 4742–1.313
Occupational injury and illness rates, by SIC 2- to 4-digit industry, 1989-90, annual rpt, 6844–7
OECD pension plan finances, participation, and benefits, for 9 countries, with data by firm and worker characteristics, 1990 conf, 6688–2
Older persons income by source, for married OASI beneficiaries by work and eligibility pattern of wife, 1982, article, 4746–26.12
Older persons income sources, assets, and health care financing issues, 1991 rpt, 10176–3.3; 10176–3.4
Older persons socioeconomic characteristics, 1900s-90 and projected to 2050, biennial chartbook, 12904–1
Pacific territories population and housing detailed characteristics, by location, 1990 Census of Population and Housing, series, 2551–8
Pension Benefit Guaranty Corp activities and finances, FY91, annual rpt, 9674–1
Population economic well-being indicators, by selected characteristics and household income and income-to-poverty ratio, 1984, 2546–20.22
Poverty status of population and families, by detailed characteristics, 1991, annual Current Population Rpt, 2546–6.77
Railroad (Amtrak) finances and operations, FY91, annual rpt, 29524–1
Railroad employee benefits and beneficiaries by type, and railroad employment and payroll, FY90, annual rpt, 9704–2
Railroad employee benefits program finances and beneficiaries, FY91, annual rpt, 9704–1
Railroad retirement, survivors, unemployment, and health insurance programs, monthly rpt, 9702–2
Securities holdings by shareholder type, and mgmt and executive pay issues, with data by company, 1991 hearing, 25248–130
Small business finances, operations, owner characteristics, and Federal contracts, 1980s-90, annual rpt, 9764–6
State and local govt employees benefit plan coverage and provisions, by plan type, 1990, biennial rpt, 6784–21
Statistical Abstract of US, 1992 annual data compilation, 2324–1.12
Survivor benefits and coverage for spouses under pension plans, by income level, age, and sex, 1989, GAO rpt, 26121–450
Tax (excise) collections of IRS, by source, quarterly rpt, 8302–1
Tax (income) exclusion for employer contributions to pension plans and plan earnings, tax revenue losses by plan type, FY90-92, working paper, 9373–27.2
Tax (income) returns filed, by type of filer, selected income items, quarterly rpt, 8302–2.1
Tax (income) returns of individuals, detailed data, 1988, annual rpt, 8304–2
Tax (income) returns of individuals, selected income and tax items by income level, preliminary 1990, annual article, 8302–2.307
Tax (income) withholding and related documents filed, by type and IRS service center, 1991 and projected 1992-99, annual rpt, 8304–22
Tax and other assistance programs under Ways and Means Committee jurisdiction, finances, operations, and participant characteristics, FY70s-91, annual rpt, 21784–11
Tax exclusion for employee benefits, Federal revenue forgone and coverage indicators, by benefit type, 1950s-80s and projected to 1995, GAO rpt, 26119–389
Tax exclusion of pension plan earnings and contributions, cost and benefit issues with background data, 1970s-FY92, article, 9373–1.305
Tax exempt organizations and employee plans listed on IRS masterfile, determinations, applications, and rulings, FY91, annual rpt, 8304–3.2
Telephone and telegraph firms detailed finances and operations, 1990, annual rpt, 9284–6.2; 9284–6.3
Terminations of pension plans, liabilities, assets, and Pension Benefit Guarantee Corp recoveries and losses, with top 50 underfunded plans, mid 1970s-91, article, 9371–1.302
see also Area wage surveys
see also Civil service pensions
see also Individual retirement arrangements
see also Military benefits and pensions
see also Old-Age, Survivors, Disability, and Health Insurance
see also Social security
see also Veterans benefits and pensions

People's Democratic Republic of Yemen
see Yemen, South

People's Republic of China
see China, Peoples Republic

Peoria, Ill.
see also under By City and By SMSA or MSA in the "Index by Categories"

Per capita income
see Personal and household income

Perez, Agnes M.
"Introducing a Broiler Retail Weight Consumption Series", 1561–7.302
"U.S. Egg and Poultry Statistical Series, 1960-90", 1564–13

Perez, Jacob
"Forgery and Fraud-Related Offenses in 6 States, 1983-88", 6066–19.64
Perez-Lopez, Jorge F.
"U.S. Employment Effects of a North American Free Trade Agreement: A Survey of Issues and Estimated Employment Effects", 6366–3.30
Perez, Michael A.
"Incidental Catch of Marine Mammals by Foreign and Joint Venture Trawl Vessels in the U.S. EEZ of the North Pacific, 1973-88", 2168–129
Performing arts
Copyrights Register activities, registrations by material type, and fees, FY91 and trends from 1790, annual rpt, 26404–2
County Business Patterns, 1989: employment, establishments, and payroll, by SIC 2- to 4-digit industry and county, annual State rpt series, 2326–8
County Business Patterns, 1990: employment, establishments, and payroll, by SIC 2- to 4-digit industry and county, annual State rpt series, 2326–6
Households entertainment spending, recreation participation by activity, and video product and pet ownership, 1970s-90, article, 1702–1.303
Labor demand, turnover, and training completions, by detailed occupation, 1990 and projected to 2005, biennial rpt, 6744–3
Natl Endowment for Arts activities and grants, FY91, annual rpt, 9564–3
Natl park system sites acreage and descriptions, 1991, biennial listing, 5544–5
Occupational Outlook Handbook, 1992-93, biennial rpt, 6744–1
Statistical Abstract of US, 1992 annual data compilation, 2324–1.7
Tax (income) returns of sole proprietorships, income statement items, by industry group, 1990, annual article, 8302–2.317; 8302–2.320
see also Dance
see also Motion pictures
see also Theater
Periodicals
Cigarette ad and promotion costs by media, and market shares, by cigarette type, with sales and use, 1963-89, annual rpt, 9404–4
Copyrights Register activities, registrations by material type, and fees, FY91 and trends from 1790, annual rpt, 26404–2
County Business Patterns, 1989: employment, establishments, and payroll, by SIC 2- to 4-digit industry and county, annual State rpt series, 2326–8
County Business Patterns, 1990: employment, establishments, and payroll, by SIC 2- to 4-digit industry and county, annual State rpt series, 2326–6
Employment, earnings, and hours, by SIC 1- to 4-digit industry, monthly 1989-Feb 1992, annual rpt, 6744–4
Exports and imports between US and outlying areas, by detailed commodity and mode of transport, 1991, annual rpt, 2424–11
Exports and imports of US, by country and detailed commodity, monthly rpt, 2422–12
Exports and imports of US, by Harmonized System 6-digit commodity and country, 1991, annual rpt, 2424–13
Exports of US, detailed Schedule B commodities with countries of destination, 1991, annual rpt, 2424–10
Foreign travel to US and Canada, market analyses with detailed trip and traveler characteristics, country rpt series, 2906–2
House of Representatives salaries, expenses, and contingent fund disbursement, detailed listings, quarterly rpt, 21942–1
Input-output structure of US economy, detailed interindustry transactions for 541 industries, and components of final demand, 1982 benchmark data, 2708–17
Libraries (public) finances, staff, and operations, by State and population size, 1990, annual rpt, 4824–6
Libraries for blind and handicapped, readership, circulation, staff, funding, and holdings, FY91, annual listing, 26404–3
Library of Congress activities, acquisitions, services, and financial statements, FY91, annual rpt, 26404–1
Mail revenue and subsidy for revenue forgone, by class of mail, FY91, and volume from FY87, annual rpt, 9864–1
Mail volume to and from households, use, and views, by class, source, content, and household characteristics, FY87-90, annual rpt, 9864–10
Manufacturing annual survey, 1990: finances and operations, by SIC 2- to 4-digit industry, series, 2506–14
Manufacturing census, 1987: concentration of largest firms measured by value added, and for shipments by SIC 2- and 4-digit industry, subject rpt, 2497–6
Manufacturing census, 1987: shipments of manufacturers products, by customer class and SIC 2- and 4-digit industry, subject rpt, 2497–4
Manufacturing finances and operations, by SIC 2- to 4-digit industry, forecast 1992, annual rpt, 2044–28
Occupational injury and illness rates, by SIC 2- to 4-digit industry, 1989-90, annual rpt, 6844–7
Occupational injury and illness rates, by SIC 2- to 4-digit industry, 1990, annual rpt, 6844–1
Price indexes (producer), by stage of processing and detailed commodity, monthly rpt, 6762–6
Price indexes (producer), by stage of processing and detailed commodity, monthly 1991, annual rpt, 6764–2
Science, engineering, and technical employment in manufacturing, by field and industry, 1989, triennial rpt, 9627–23
Senate receipts, itemized expenses by payee, and balances, 1st half FY92, semiannual listing, 25922–1
Soviet Union and US economic and sociodemographic indicators, selected years 1970-90, handbook, 2328–80
Soviet Union trade and investment opportunities for US firms, contact listing, bibl, and background economic data, 1991 rpt, 2048–157
Statistical Abstract of US, 1992 annual data compilation, 2324–1.18
Tax (income) returns of corporations, income and tax items by asset size and detailed industry, 1989, annual rpt, 8304–4; 8304–21
see also Journalism
see also Newspapers
see also Research journals
Perkins, Craig
"National Corrections Reporting Program, 1988", 6064–33
Perlack, R. D.
"Biomass Energy Development in Yunnan Province, China, Preliminary Evaluation", 3308–103
Perloff, Betty P.
"Effects of Procedural Differences Between 1977 and 1987 in the Nationwide Food Consumption Survey on Estimates of Food and Nutrient Intakes: Results of the USDA 1988 Bridging Study", 1358–6
Permits
see Building permits
see Drivers licenses
see Hunting and fishing licenses
see Licenses and permits
see Occupational testing and certification
see Water permits
Perquisites
see Employee benefits
see Employee bonuses and work incentives
see Employee ownership
Perry, Charles A.
"Statistical Comparison of Selected Chemical Constituents in Water from Chemigation and Conventional Irrigation Wells in Kansas, 1987", 5666–28.21
Perry, Janet
"Economic Well-Being of Farm Operator Households, 1990", 1541–1.315
Persian Gulf
see Middle East
Persian Gulf War
see Military intervention
Personal and household income
AFDC application denials and hearings decisions, by reason and State, FY90, annual rpt, 4584–3.3; 4584–3.4
AFDC beneficiaries demographic and financial characteristics, by State, FY90, annual rpt, 4584–7
Alien nonresidents income from US sources and tax withheld by country and US tax treaty status, 1989, annual article, 8302–2.308
Asian and Pacific Islands Americans social and economic characteristics, for West and total US, 1990-91, Current Population Report, 2546–1.462
Banks financial performance relation to growth in State personal income, 1980s-90, working paper, 9377–9.135
Black Americans social and economic characteristics, for South and total US, 1991 and trends from 1950, annual Current Population Rpt, 2546–1.463
Black women's labor force status, earnings, and other economic status indicators, and compared to whites, various periods 1939-88, 11048–191
BLS data collection, analysis, and presentation methods, by program, 1992 rpt, 6888–1
Business statistics, detailed data for major industries and economic indicators, *Survey of Current Business*, monthly rpt, 2702–1

Business statistics, detailed data for major industries and economic indicators, 1960-91, *Survey of Current Business* biennial supplement, 2704–1
Census of Population and Housing, 1990: population and housing characteristics, detailed geographic coverage, State CD-ROM series, 2551–10
Census of Population and Housing, 1990: summary characteristics, by county, subdiv, and place, State rpt series, 2551–7
City (central) and suburbs per capita income, by city, 1991 hearings, 21308–28
Consumer Income, socioeconomic characteristics of persons, families, and households, detailed cross-tabulations, Current Population Rpt series, 2546–6
Costa Rica economic indicators and reform issues, mid 1970s-90, working paper, 9916–13.5
Deaths and rates, by cause and selected social, demographic, and employment characteristics, 1979-85, natl longitudinal study, 4478–186
Developing countries aged population and selected characteristics, 1980s and projected to 2020, country rpt series, 2326–19
Developing countries aided by Peace Corps, quality of life indicators, FY93, annual rpt, 9654–1
Disabled persons work experience following OASDI benefit award, by selected characteristics, 1980s, article, 4742–1.312
Distribution and equity of income, tax, and transfer payments, analyses and alternative estimates, series, 4746–14
Economic indicators and components, and Fed Reserve 4th District business and financial conditions, monthly chartbook, 9377–10
Economic indicators and relation to govt finances by level of govt, selected years 1929-91, annual rpt, 10044–1
Economic indicators compounded annual rates of change, monthly rpt, 9391–3
Economic indicators, monthly rpt, 9362–1.2
Economic Report of the President for 1991, economic effects of budget proposals, and trends and projections, 1940s-95, annual hearings, 23844–4
Economic Report of the President for 1992, Joint Economic Committee critique and policy recommendations, annual rpt, 23844–2
Economic Report of the President for 1992, with economic trends from 1929, annual rpt, 204–1
Educational attainment, by social and demographic characteristics and location, 1991 and trends from 1940, biennial Current Population Rpt, 2546–1.460
Energy use by mode of transport, fuel supply, and demographic and economic factors of vehicle use, 1970s-90, annual rpt, 3304–5
Families financial status, income, net worth, and assets and debt by type, by income and selected characteristics, 1983 and 1989, article, 9362–1.301
Family income and Federal tax rates, by income level, late 1970s-94, 21788–212
Family median income for 4 persons, by State, 1969 and 1974-89, technical paper, 2626–2.60
Family members supporting others outside household, by relationship and provider characteristics, 1988, fact sheet, 2326–17.48
Family members supporting others outside household, by relationship, recipient living arrangements, and provider characteristics, 1988, Current Population Rpt, 2546–20.21
Food stamp recipient household size, composition, income, and income and deductions allowed, summer 1989, annual rpt, 1364–8
Health care spending per capita by State, 1990, and relation to income, services availability, rate control, and other factors, 1982, GAO rpt, 26121–444
Home mortgages FHA-insured, financial, property, and borrower characteristics, by metro area, 1991, annual rpt, 5144–24
Home mortgages FHA-insured, financial, property, and borrower characteristics, by State, 1991, annual rpt, 5144–1; 5144–25
Home mortgages FHA-insured, financial, property, and borrower characteristics, 1991, annual rpt, 5144–23
Hospital closings relation to hospital and community characteristics, by metro-nonmetro location, 1980-87, article, 4042–3.341
Households (single person and nonfamily) social, economic and housing characteristics, by tenure, 1989, 2486–1.15
Households and family characteristics, by location, 1991, annual Current Population Rpt, 2546–1.457
Households and housing characteristics, and unit and neighborhood quality, by MSA location for 11 MSAs, 1987 survey, supplement, 2485–8
Households and housing characteristics, MSA surveys, fact sheet series, 2485–11
Households and housing detailed characteristics, and unit and neighborhood quality, by location, 1989, biennial rpt supplement, 2485–13
Households and housing detailed characteristics, and unit and neighborhood quality, MSA surveys, series, 2485–6
Households and housing detailed characteristics, and unit and neighborhood quality, 1989, wallchart, 2485–12
Households and housing unit characteristics of recent movers, and reason for move, by tenure, 1989, 2486–1.12
Households and housing unit summary characteristics, 1989 and trends, chartbook, 2486–2.1
Households, family, and personal income, by source, detailed characteristics, and region, 1991, annual Current Population Rpt, 2546–6.76
Households, family, and personal income, wealth, and poverty measures, 1960s-90, Current Population Rpt, chartbook, 2546–6.75
Households income and poverty status under alternative income definitions, by recipient characteristics, 1991, annual Current Population Rpt, 2546–6.78
Households income and wealth distribution by selected characteristics, with foreign comparisons, 1992 compilation of papers, Current Population Rpt, 2546–6.79
Households income distribution, by household composition, 1970 and 1990, fact sheet, 2326–17.40
Households income transition between higher and lower income levels, 1979-88, 8008–156
Households net worth distribution under alternative sample weighting systems to account for inconsistency in survey design and response rates, 1992 rpt, 9368–91
Housing (low income) eligibility, tenants reported income agreement with tax records, 1989-90, GAO rpt, 26121–468
Housing (rental) units, total, with HUD assistance by program, and eligible for aid, by unit, household, and neighborhood characteristics, and location, 1989, biennial rpt, 5184–11
Housing costs exceeding 28% of gross income, families income by source and expenses by type, by tenure and other characteristics, 1989, article, 1702–1.304
Imports demand relation to prices and household income, model description and results, 1992 technical paper, 9385–8.141
Income tax returns of foreign corporations and individuals, and US entities abroad, detailed data compilation, 1970s-89, quinquennial rpt, 8308–31
Married-couple families income, and spouses labor force participation and hours worked, by income class, 1979 and 1989, 23848–225
Married couples aged 18-25, income and expenses by wife's employment status and family size, 1988-89, article, 1702–1.302
Migration, immigration, and mover characteristics compared to nonmovers, 1987-90, annual Current Population Rpt, 2546–1.456
Migration since 1990, mover characteristics by same or different area, and compared to nonmovers, 1991, annual Current Population Rpt, 2546–1.464
Money demand relation to income growth and interest rates, model description and results, 1992 working paper, 9387–8.279
Mortgage applications, dispositions, and secondary loan market sales, by purpose, lender type, and applicant and neighborhood characteristics, 1991, article, 9362–1.307
Mortgage applications of minorities, for Boston by disposition and financial characteristics, with problems in analyzing lender disclosure statements, 1990, working paper, 9373–27.15
Natl income and product accounts and components, summary data 1959-91, tables, 2702–1.334
Natl income and product accounts and components, *Survey of Current Business*, monthly rpt, 2702–1.23
Natl income and product accounts benchmark revisions, methodological changes and revised summary tables, 1959-91, article, 2702–1.302
Natl income and product accounts benchmark revisions of GDP and natl income, various periods 1959-80, tables, 2702–1.307

Natl income and product accounts benchmark revisions of personal income and outlays, monthly 1987-91, tables, 2702–1.301

Natl income and product accounts benchmark revisions of personal income, and reconciliation with adjusted gross income, 1959-90, article, 2702–1.318

Natl income and product accounts, comprehensive accounts and components, benchmark revisions, 1929-88, 2708–5

Natl income and product accounts, comprehensive accounts and components, *Survey of Current Business*, monthly rpt, 2702–1.28

Natl income and product accounts revisions to GDP, personal income, and selected foreign transactions, various periods 1959-90, tables, 2702–1.313

New England States economic indicators, Fed Reserve 1st District, monthly rpt, 9373–2

North Central States business and economic conditions, Fed Reserve 9th District, quarterly journal, 9383–19

NYC housing supply, occupancy, condition, and household characteristics, by tenure and borough, 1991 triennial survey, 2488–3

OASDI beneficiary data collection system design compared to earlier surveys, with summary results, 1992 article, 4742–1.313

OASDI benefits share of personal income, by selected characteristics, 1986-90, annual rpt, 4744–3.1; 4744–3.3

Older persons ability to pay out of pocket health care costs, indicators by selected characteristics, 1984, article, 4742–1.307

Older persons and younger adults household income, by source, household composition, and age group, 1984 and 1989, article, 4742–1.304

Older persons and younger adults household income, by source, household composition, race, and age group, 1984-89, 4746–26.20

Older persons economic status compared to other age groups, 1990 and trends from 1947, 4746–26.24

Older persons income and sources, by OASDI beneficiary and poverty status, and other characteristics, 1990, biennial chartbook, 4744–25

Older persons income and sources, by whether OASDI beneficiary, poverty status, and other characteristics, 1990, biennial rpt, 4744–26

Older persons income by source, for married OASI beneficiaries by work and eligibility pattern of wife, 1982, article, 4746–26.12

Older persons income, net worth, and poverty status, compared to other age groups, 1988-90, article, 4742–1.320

Older persons income sources, assets, and health care financing issues, 1991 rpt, 10176–3.3; 10176–3.4

Older persons labor force status, income sources, and reasons for not working, with data by occupation, sex, and race, 1989-90 and projected to 2050, 21148–65

Older persons socioeconomic characteristics, 1900s-90 and projected to 2050, biennial chartbook, 12904–1

Pacific Northwest population, households, employment, income, fuel prices, and electricity demand, alternative forecasts 1991-2010, annual rpt, 3224–3.3

Pacific territories population and housing detailed characteristics, by location, 1990 Census of Population and Housing, series, 2551–8

Partnership losses and total income of high-income individuals, by average tax rate, 1985-89, article, 8302–2.313

Personal and per capita income, and earnings by industry group, by region and State, 1989-91, annual article, 2702–1.328

Personal income (per capita and total), by State, MSA, county, and metro-nonmetro location, 1988-90, annual article, 2702–1.317

Personal income (taxable and total), and income tax liability and payments, quarterly 1959-91, article, 2702–1.326

Personal income by source, disposition, and disposable income, 1959-91, annual rpt, 204–1.1

Personal income, by source, monthly rpt, 23842–1.1

Personal income per capita and by source, and employment, by industry div, State, MSA, and county, 1969-90, annual CD-ROM, 2704–7

Personal income per capita, by region compared to total US, alternative model results, 1929-87, working paper, 9387–8.257

Personal income relative to median, by race and selected other characteristics, mid 1960s-89, Current Population Rpt, 2546–6.73

Personal income totals, by region, census div, and State, quarterly article, 2702–1.34

Philadelphia metro area transit service operations, costs and benefits, and local economic and air pollution impacts, 1970s-90 and projected to 2020, 7308–205

Population and housing summary data and trends, 1970s-91, Current Population Rpt, fact sheet, 2546–2.163

Population economic well-being indicators, by selected characteristics and household income and income-to-poverty ratio, 1984, 2546–20.22

Poverty status of families, by detailed characteristics, 1980 and 1988, GAO rpt, 26131–102

Rural areas economic conditions and dev, quarterly journal, 1502–8

Single mothers family income, and impacts of child care, govt and child support payments, taxes, and marriage, with data by State, 1970s-91, 21788–212

Single parent families in own and others homes, by financial, housing, and other characteristics, 1989, 2486–1.14

Southeastern States, Fed Reserve 5th District, economic indicators by State, quarterly rpt, 9389–16

Southeastern States, Fed Reserve 6th District, economic indicators by State and MSA, quarterly rpt, 9371–14

Southeastern States, Fed Reserve 8th District banking and economic conditions, quarterly rpt with articles, 9391–16

Statistical Abstract of US, 1992 annual data compilation, 2324–1.14

Student aid Pell grants and applicants, by tuition, income level, instn type and control, and State, 1990/91, annual rpt, 4804–1

Supplemental Security Income child beneficiaries and benefits, by selected characteristics, family income status, and State, 1991, article, 4742–1.316

Survey of Income and Program Participation, data collection, methodology, and availability, 1991 users guide, 2628–24

Survey of Income and Program Participation, household composition, income, benefits, and labor force status, methodology, working paper series, 2626–10

Survey of Income and Program Participation, household income and socioeconomic characteristics, special study series, 2546–20

Tax (income) returns filed, by type of filer, selected income items, quarterly rpt, 8302–2.1

Tax (income) returns of individuals, detailed data, 1988, annual rpt, 8304–2

Tax (income) returns of individuals, selected income and tax items by income level, preliminary 1990, annual article, 8302–2.307

Tax policy impacts on economic performance and income distribution, issues and background data, with foreign comparisons, 1991 and trends, 21788–211

Tennessee Valley economic conditions, and compared to US, alternative projections 1992-2010 and trends from 1929, annual rpt, 9804–27

Travel to US, by characteristics of visit and traveler, world area of origin, and US destination, 1991 survey, annual rpt, 2904–12

VA health care services income eligibility and copayment enforcement, and revenue forgone from unreported income, 1987-91, GAO rpt, 26121–479

Wealth (personal) under alternative measures, by age group, 1984, technical paper, 4746–26.11

West Central States economic indicators, Fed Reserve 10th District, quarterly rpt, 9381–16.2

Women (older) living alone, income by source, and expenses by type, by marital status, 1988-89, article, 1702–1.301

Women in jail, by criminal background and sociodemographic characteristics, with comparisons to men, 1989, 6066–19.66

Women's labor force status, earnings, and other characteristics, with comparisons to men, fact sheet series, 6564–1

see also Child support and alimony
see also Earnings, general
see also Earnings, local and regional
see also Earnings, specific industry
see also Family budgets
see also Tips and tipping
see also under By Income in the "Index by Categories"

Personal assets
see Wealth
Personal care products
Carcinogens chemistry, sources, environment and health risks, and regulation, by substance and brand, 1991 annual rpt, 4044–15
Consumer spending, natl income and product account benchmark revisions, 1929-88, 2708–5
Consumer spending, natl income and product accounts, comprehensive accounts and components, *Survey of Current Business*, monthly rpt, 2702–1.25
CPI by component for US city average, and by selected metro area, region, and population size, monthly rpt, 6762–2
Dental fluoride products use by children, by frequency of dental visits and selected characteristics, 1983-89, 4146–8.222
Electric housewares and fans shipments, trade, use, and firms, by product, 1991, annual Current Industrial Rpt, 2506–12.15
Exports and imports between US and outlying areas, by detailed commodity and mode of transport, 1991, annual rpt, 2424–11
Exports and imports of US, by Harmonized System 6-digit commodity and country, 1991, annual rpt, 2424–13
Exports and imports of US, by selected country, country group, and commodity group, 1991, annual rpt, 2044–37
Exports, imports, and balances of US for manufactured goods, by SITC 2-digit commodity and country, quarterly rpt, 2042–35
Exports of US, detailed Schedule B commodities with countries of destination, 1991, annual rpt, 2424–10
Injuries from use of consumer products and related activities, by severity and victim age and sex, 1990, annual rpt, 9164–7
Injuries from use of consumer products, by severity, victim age, and detailed product, 1991, annual rpt, 9164–6
Injuries from use of consumer products, related deaths and costs, and recalls by brand, by product type, FY90, annual rpt, 9164–2
Manufacturing annual survey, 1990: finances and operations, by SIC 2- to 4-digit industry, series, 2506–14
Manufacturing census, 1987: concentration of largest firms measured by value added, and for shipments by SIC 2- and 4-digit industry, subject rpt, 2497–6
Manufacturing census, 1987: shipments of manufacturers products, by customer class and SIC 2- and 4-digit industry, subject rpt, 2497–4
Manufacturing finances and operations, by SIC 2- to 4-digit industry, forecast 1992, annual rpt, 2044–28
Price indexes (producer), by stage of processing and detailed commodity, monthly rpt, 6762–6
Price indexes (producer), by stage of processing and detailed commodity, monthly 1991, annual rpt, 6764–2
Price indexes for department store inventories, by class of item, monthly table, 6762–7
Toxicology Natl Program research and testing activities, FY90 and planned FY91, annual rpt, 4044–16
see also Contraceptives
see also Cosmetics and toiletries
see also Drugs
see also Vitamins and nutrients
see also under By Commodity in the "Index by Categories"
Personal consumption
BLS data collection, analysis, and presentation methods, by program, 1992 rpt, 6888–1
Business statistics, detailed data for major industries and economic indicators, 1960-91, *Survey of Current Business* biennial supplement, 2704–1
Central America economic indicators, by country, 1969-89, working paper, 9916–13.4
Economic indicators and components, and Fed Reserve 4th District business and financial conditions, monthly chartbook, 9377–10
Economic indicators and components, current data and annual trends, monthly rpt, 23842–1.1
Economic indicators compounded annual rates of change, monthly rpt, 9391–3
Expenditures by category, and income, by selected household characteristics, 1991 survey, annual press release, 6726–1.53
Expenditures by category, selected household characteristics, and region, Consumer Expenditure Survey, quarterly rpt, 6762–14
Expenditures by category, various periods 1917-90, fact sheet, 2326–17.42
Expenditures by category, 1959-91, annual rpt, 204–1.1
Expenditures on selected durable goods and services, 1980-90, article, 6722–1.324
Family Economics Review, consumer goods prices and supply, and home economics, quarterly journal, 1702–1
Forecasts of durable goods spending, performance of consumer sentiment index and other economic indicators, 1950s-90, article, 9393–8.304
Forecasts of economic conditions and employment, alternative BLS projections to 2005 and trends 1975-90, biennial rpt, 6744–19
GNP seasonal growth relation to monetary, fiscal, and demand indicators, 1991 working paper, 9375–13.74
Inflation measured by CPI and Personal Consumption Expenditure Index, under alternative weighting systems, monthly rpt, periodic article, 6762–2
Input-output structure of US economy, detailed interindustry transactions for 84 industries, and components of final demand, 1987, annual article, 2702–1.316
Input-output structure of US economy, detailed interindustry transactions for 541 industries, and components of final demand, 1982 benchmark data, 2708–17
Money supply relation to industrial production and consumer spending, 1960s-91, working paper, 9377–9.131
Natl income and product accounts and components, *Survey of Current Business*, monthly rpt, 2702–1.23
Natl income and product accounts benchmark revisions, methodological changes and revised summary tables, 1959-91, article, 2702–1.302
Natl income and product accounts benchmark revisions of GDP and natl income, various periods 1959-80, tables, 2702–1.307
Natl income and product accounts benchmark revisions of personal income and outlays, monthly 1987-91, tables, 2702–1.301
Natl income and product accounts, comprehensive accounts and components, benchmark revisions, 1929-88, 2708–5
Natl income and product accounts, comprehensive accounts and components, *Survey of Current Business*, monthly rpt, 2702–1.25
Older persons socioeconomic characteristics, 1900s-90 and projected to 2050, biennial chartbook, 12904–1
Pollution abatement spending by govts, business, and consumers, 1972-90, annual article, 2702–1.321
Productivity shocks impacts on business cycles, and relation to monetary, fiscal, and demand indicators, 1991 working paper, 9375–13.73
Retail trade sales per capita, 1990, annual rpt, 2413–5
Statistical Abstract of US, 1992 annual data compilation, 2324–1.14
Survey of Current Business, detailed financial and business data, and economic indicators, monthly rpt, 2702–1.3
Travel to US, by characteristics of visit and traveler, world area of origin, and US destination, 1991 survey, annual rpt, 2904–12
see also Cost of living
see also Family budgets
see also Food consumption
see also Housing energy use
see also Wealth
Personal debt
Black women's labor force status, earnings, and other economic status indicators, and compared to whites, various periods 1939-88, 11048–191
Credit card issuers disclosure of terms and conditions to consumers, with finances and operations, 1991 hearing, 21248–175
Credit cards held by household income, age, and card type, and debt outstanding, with issuer costs and revenue, 1970s-80, article, 9362–1.306
Debt and assets of private sector, balance sheets by segment, 1960-91, semiannual rpt, 9365–4.1
Debt outstanding, by sector and type of debt and holder, monthly rpt, 9362–1.1
Economic indicators and components, and Fed Reserve 4th District business and financial conditions, monthly chartbook, 9377–10
Families financial status, income, net worth, and assets and debt by type, by income and selected characteristics, 1983 and 1989, article, 9362–1.301
Flow-of-funds accounts, savings, investments, and credit statements, quarterly rpt, 9365–3.3
Higher education PhD degree recipients, by field and selected characteristics, 1979, 1984, and 1989, 4848–44

Households composition, income, benefits, and labor force status, Survey of Income and Program Participation methodology, working paper series, 2626–10
Households financial services use, by account type and instn type and location, 1989 survey, article, 9362–1.303
Households net worth distribution under alternative sample weighting systems to account for inconsistency in survey design and response rates, 1992 rpt, 9368–91
Physicians recently graduating, specialties, school debt, and practice settings, and medical school funding sources, 1970s-91, hearing, 21368–135
Population economic well-being indicators, by selected characteristics and household income and income-to-poverty ratio, 1984, 2546–20.22
Tax (estate) returns property and tax data, by size of gross estate and State, 1989-90, article, 8302–2.305
see also Consumer credit
see also Credit bureaus and agencies
see also Loans
see also Mortgages

Personal income
see Personal and household income

Personal property
see Housing tenure
see Land ownership and rights
see Ownership of enterprise
see Personal debt
see Property
see Savings
see Wealth

Personick, Martin E.
"Job Hazards Underscored in Woodworking Study", 6728–41
"Nursing Home Aides Experience Increase in Serious Injuries", 6728–41
"Profiles in Safety and Health: Eating and Drinking Places", 6728–41
"Profiles in Safety and Health: Fabricated Structural Metal", 6722–1.301; 6728–41
"Profiles in Safety and Health: Occupational Hazards of Meatpacking", 6728–41
"Profiles in Safety and Health: Retail Grocery Stores", 6722–1.339
"Profiles in Safety and Health: Roofing and Sheet Metal Work", 6728–41
"Profiles in Safety and Health: The Soft Drink Industry", 6722–1.319; 6728–41
"Profiles in Safety and Health: Work Hazards of Mobile Homes", 6728–41

Personnel management
Airline and aviation safety employees drug testing and results, by drug type and occupational group, 1991, semiannual rpt, 7502–17
Criminal justice systems activities, spending, and employment, by level of govt, data compilation, 1992 annual rpt, 6064–6.1
Fed Govt merit system oversight and enforcement activities of OPM, series, 9496–2
Labor demand, turnover, and training completions, by detailed occupation, 1990 and projected to 2005, biennial rpt, 6744–3
Minority Business Dev Centers mgmt and financial aid, and characteristics of businesses, by region and State, FY91, annual rpt, 2104–6
Police and sheriff depts drug enforcement activities, and employee drug testing policies, 1990, 6066–19.67
see also Employee development
see also Employee performance and appraisal

Peru
Agricultural trade of US, by detailed commodity and country, 1991, annual rpt, 1524–8
Agricultural trade of US, by detailed commodity and country, 1991, semiannual rpt, 1522–4
AID economic aid to developing countries, obligations and disbursements by country, quarterly rpt, 9912–4
AID loans repayment status and terms by program and country, and status of predecessor agency loans, quarterly rpt, 9912–3
Cuba trade, by commodity and country, mid 1980s-91, 9118–8
Debt burden indicators for 8 developing countries, alternative projections 1991-2000 and trends from 1974, technical paper, 9366–7.271
Economic and military aid and loans from US and intl agencies, by program and country, FY46-91, annual rpt, 9914–5
Economic and social conditions of developing countries from 1960s, and Intl Dev Cooperation Agency and AID activities and funding, FY91-93, annual rpt, 9904–4
Economic and social conditions, resources, and trade, and aid, 1992, annual factbook, 9914–14
Economic conditions, policy, and trade practices, by country, 1989-91, annual rpt, 21384–5
Economic, population, and agricultural data, US and other aid sources, and AID activity, 1991 country rpt, 9916–12.53
Economic, social, political, and geographic summary data, by country, 1992, annual factbook, 9114–2
Exports (duty free) under Andean Trade Preference Act from 4 countries to US, and business opportunities, 1989-91, 2048–161
Exports and imports of US, by commodity and country, 1980-90, world area rpt, 9116–1.7
Exports and imports of US, by Harmonized System 6-digit commodity and country, 1991, annual rpt, 2424–13
Exports and imports of US, by selected country, country group, and commodity group, 1991, annual rpt, 2044–37
Exports and imports of US, by transport mode, country, and SITC 1- to 3-digit commodity, 1991, annual rpt, 2424–12
Exports, imports, and balances of US for manufactured goods, by SITC 2-digit commodity and country, quarterly rpt, 2042–35
Exports of US, detailed Schedule B commodities with countries of destination, 1991, annual rpt, 2424–10
Food supply, needs, and aid for developing countries, status and alternative forecasts, 1992 world area rpt, 1526–8.2
Fruit, vegetable, nut, and cut flower imports of US from Andean countries, 1989 and 1991, article, 1925–34.317
Human rights conditions in 170 countries, and US economic and military aid, 1991, annual rpt, 21384–3
Inflation relation to money supply, for 5 South America countries, 1970s-90, technical paper, 9379–12.91
Military aid of US, arms sales, and training programs costs and budget requests, by program, world region, and country, FY91-93, annual rpt, 7144–13
Military spending, arms trade, and force strengths, with govt spending and population, by country, 1979-89, annual rpt, 9824–1
Multinatl US firms and foreign affiliates finances and operations, by industry and country, 1989 benchmark survey, annual rpt, 2704–5
Multinatl US firms foreign affiliates, income statement items by asset size, industry, and country, 1988, biennial article, 8302–2.322
Oil production, investment needs, and exports, for 8 South America countries, 1980s-90 and projected to 2010, GAO rpt, 26123–396
Population size, growth rates, and components of change, by country, projected 1990-2020 and trends from 1950, biennial rpt, 2324–9
Refugee migration, and intl aid programs, by world area and country of origin and asylum, 1991, annual rpt, 7004–15
Steel trade, by product, country, and customs district, with US industry operating data, 1989-June 1992, semiannual rpt, 9882–15
UN voting record and share of votes in agreement with US, by issue, country, and world area, 1991, annual rpt, 7004–18
see also under By Foreign Country in the "Index by Categories"

Pesticides
Agricultural Outlook, production, prices, marketing, and trade, by commodity, forecast and current situation, monthly rpt with articles, 1502–4
Apple (processed) demand and impacts of selected market factors, 1980s-91, 1548–392
Assistance (financial and nonfinancial) of Fed Govt, 1992 base edition, annual listing, 104–5
Birds (least tern and piping plover) and habitat levels of selenium and other pollutants, for Missouri River in South Dakota, 1988-90, 5508–118
Bonneville Power Admin hazardous waste mgmt and environmental protection standards compliance activities, 1991, annual rpt, 3224–6
Cancer (pancreatic) death risk relation to occupational DDT exposure and other characteristics, 1982 article, 4472–1.314
Cancer risk relation to occupational herbicide exposure, 1992 article, 4472–1.356
Carcinogens chemistry, sources, environment and health risks, and regulation, by substance and brand, 1991 annual rpt, 4044–15
Coastal and estuarine pollutant concentrations in fish, shellfish, and environment, series, 2176–3

Coastal areas and watersheds pollution indicators, by location, 1980s-90, 2178–35
Criminal cases by type and disposition, and collections, for US attorneys, by Federal district, FY91, annual rpt, 6004–2.1
Environmental Quality, status of problems, protection programs, research, and intl issues, 1991 annual rpt, 484–1
EPA pollution control grant program activities, monthly rpt, 9182–8
EPA R&D programs and funding, planned FY92, annual listing, 9184–17
Exports and imports (agricultural) of US, by commodity and country, bimonthly rpt, 1522–1
Exports and imports (agricultural) of US, by detailed commodity and country, 1991, annual rpt, 1524–8
Exports and imports (agricultural) of US, by detailed commodity and country, 1991, semiannual rpt, 1522–4
Exports and imports between US and outlying areas, by detailed commodity and mode of transport, 1991, annual rpt, 2424–11
Exports and imports of US, by country and detailed commodity, monthly rpt, 2422–12
Exports and imports of US, by Harmonized System 6-digit commodity and country, 1991, annual rpt, 2424–13
Exports and imports of US, by transport mode, country, and SITC 1- to 3-digit commodity, 1991, annual rpt, 2424–12
Exports of US, detailed Schedule B commodities with countries of destination, 1991, annual rpt, 2424–10
Farm fertilizer and pesticide use, and application rates, by type, crop, and State, series, 1616–1
Farm prices received and paid, by commodity and State, monthly rpt, 1629–1
Farm production inputs, finances, mgmt, and land value and transfers, periodic situation rpt with articles, 1561–16
Farm production itemized costs, by farm sales size and region, 1991, annual rpt, 1614–3
Farm production itemized costs, receipts, and returns, by commodity and region, 1975-90, annual rpt, 1544–20
Farm production itemized costs, receipts, and returns, by crop and State, 1987-89, annual rpt, 1544–24
Food imports with pesticide residue, FDA enforcement, with contaminated shipments distributed, damages assessed and paid, and repeat offenders, FY88-90, GAO rpt, 26113–598
Forest Service activities and finances, by region and State, FY91, annual rpt, 1204–1
Freight (waterborne domestic and foreign) by commodity, traffic, and passengers, by port and waterway, 1989, annual rpt, 3754–3
Great Lakes industrial water pollution emissions, comparison of State, EPA, Intl Joint Commission, and Ontario standards, 1991 rpt, 14648–29
Health effects of selected pollutants, concentrations in food and environment, sources, human intake, and regulation, series, 9186–8
Health effects of selected pollutants on animals by species and on humans, and environmental levels, series, 5506–14
Imports detained by FDA, by reason, product, shipper, brand, and country, monthly listing, 4062–2
Industrial hazardous substances releases and reduction methods under EPA regulation, by chemical, source, industry, and location, 1989, annual rpt, 9234–6
Industrial hazardous substances releases and reduction methods under EPA regulation, with chemical stocks and use, facility directory, 1987-89, annual CD-ROM, 9234–7
Injuries from use of consumer products, by severity, victim age, and detailed product, 1991, annual rpt, 9164–6
Lumber preservatives performance test results, by type, late 1930s-80s, 1208–391
Manufacturing annual survey, 1990: finances and operations, by SIC 2- to 4-digit industry, series, 2506–14
Manufacturing finances and operations, by SIC 2- to 4-digit industry, forecast 1992, annual rpt, 2044–28
Marine mammals tissue pollutant concentrations, by species and pollutant type, for Alaska, 1987-91, 2218–87
Mexico fruit and vegetable exports to US, US and Mexico standards for pesticide residue and violations, FY79-91, GAO rpt, 26113–585
OECD trade, total and for 4 major countries, and US trade by country, by commodity, 1980-90, world area rpt series, 9116–1
Price indexes (producer), by stage of processing and detailed commodity, monthly rpt, 6762–6
Price indexes (producer), by stage of processing and detailed commodity, monthly 1991, annual rpt, 6764–2
Prices received and paid by farmers, by commodity and State, 1991, annual rpt, 1629–5
Production and sales of synthetic organic chemicals, and manufacturer listing, by product, 1990, annual rpt, 9884–3
Production, trade, and additives, by pesticide type, with manufacturers listing, annual rpt, discontinued, 1804–5
Public opinion on taxes, spending, and govt efficiency, by respondent characteristics, 1992 survey, annual rpt, 10044–2
Rice production, practices, costs, and land tenure, by production area, 1988, 1568–309
Soybean tillage systems impacts on yield and inputs use and costs, 1990, article, 1561–3.304
Statistical Abstract of US, 1992 annual data compilation, 2324–1.6
Timber insect and disease incidence and damage, and control activities, State rpt series, 1206–49
Timber insect and disease incidence and damage, annual regional rpt series, 1206–11
Toxicology Natl Program research and testing activities, FY90 and planned FY91, annual rpt, 4044–16
Water (groundwater) pesticide contamination, vulnerability indicators by State and county, 1987-89, GAO rpt, 26131–91
Water (groundwater) supply, quality, chemistry, and use, State and local area rpt series, 5666–28
Water quality, chemistry, hydrology, and other characteristics, local area studies, series, 5666–27
Water supply and quality in streams and lakes, and groundwater levels in wells, by drainage basin, 1990, annual State rpt series, 5666–10
Water supply and quality in streams and lakes, and groundwater levels in wells, by drainage basin, 1990-91, annual CD-ROM, 5664–18
Water supply and quality in streams and lakes, and groundwater levels in wells, by drainage basin, 1991, annual State rpt series, 5666–12
Wetlands in natl wildlife refuges in South Dakota, pesticide levels and water toxicity indicators, 1990, 5508–117
see also Dioxins

Pests and pest control
Agricultural Conservation Program acreage and projects, by State, 1936-90, quinquennial rpt, 1808–1
Agricultural research and education grants, USDA competitive awards by program and recipient, FY91, annual listing, 1764–1
Agricultural research funding and staffing for USDA, State agencies, and other instns, by topic, FY91, annual rpt, 1744–2
Agricultural research grants of USDA, by program, subagency, and country, FY92, annual listing, 1954–3
County Business Patterns, 1989: employment, establishments, and payroll, by SIC 2- to 4-digit industry and county, annual State rpt series, 2326–8
County Business Patterns, 1990: employment, establishments, and payroll, by SIC 2- to 4-digit industry and county, annual State rpt series, 2326–6
Foreign countries disasters, casualties, damage, and aid by US and others, FY91 and trends from FY64, annual rpt, 9914–12
Forest Service activities and finances, by region and State, FY91, annual rpt, 1204–1.2
Housing and neighborhood quality, indicators and attitudes, by householder type and location, for 11 MSAs, 1987 survey, supplement, 2485–8
Housing and neighborhood quality, indicators and attitudes, by householder type and location, 1989, biennial rpt supplement, 2485–13
Housing and neighborhood quality, indicators and attitudes, MSA surveys, series, 2485–6
Imports detained by FDA, by reason, product, shipper, brand, and country, monthly listing, 4062–2
Labor demand, turnover, and training completions, by detailed occupation, 1990 and projected to 2005, biennial rpt, 6744–3
Mountain pine beetle infestation in Black Hills Natl Forest, and ponderosa pine mortality, 1989-91, 1208–408
Neighborhood quality, indicators and attitudes of renter households, by whether

receiving and eligible for HUD assistance, householder characteristics, and location, 1989, biennial rpt, 5184–11
Sugarcane clones yields, stability, and fungi resistance, 1991/92, annual rpt, 1704–2
Timber in Great Lakes area, aspen forest vegetation, climate, and other environmental characteristics, 1991 rpt, 1208–418
Timber in northeastern US, hardwood forests ecology and mgmt, 1992, 1208–405
Timber in Rocky Mountains and southwest US, old growth forests ecology, mgmt, and research methods, 1992 conf, 1208–421
Timber in southeastern US, resources mgmt and research, 1990 biennial conf papers, 1204–35
Timber in Virginia, oak decline disease incidence and losses, 1986, 1208–384
Timber in western US, insect and disease infestation from lumber imports from USSR, economic and environmental impacts, 1991 and projected to 2040, 1208–389
Timber insect and disease incidence and damage, and control activities, State rpt series, 1206–49
Timber insect and disease incidence and damage, annual regional rpt series, 1206–11
Timber insect and disease incidence and damage, by State, 1990, annual rpt, 1204–8
see also Pesticides

Pet food and supplies
County Business Patterns, 1989: employment, establishments, and payroll, by SIC 2- to 4-digit industry and county, annual State rpt series, 2326–8
County Business Patterns, 1990: employment, establishments, and payroll, by SIC 2- to 4-digit industry and county, annual State rpt series, 2326–6
CPI by component for US city average, and by selected metro area, region, and population size, monthly rpt, 6762–2
Exports and imports (agricultural) of US, by detailed commodity and country, 1991, semiannual rpt, 1522–4
Exports and imports between US and outlying areas, by detailed commodity and mode of transport, 1991, annual rpt, 2424–11
Exports and imports of US, by Harmonized System 6-digit commodity and country, 1991, annual rpt, 2424–13
Exports of US, detailed Schedule B commodities with countries of destination, 1991, annual rpt, 2424–10
Injuries from use of consumer products and related activities, by severity and victim age and sex, 1990, annual rpt, 9164–7
Injuries from use of consumer products, by severity, victim age, and detailed product, 1991, annual rpt, 9164–6
Input-output structure of US economy, detailed interindustry transactions for 541 industries, and components of final demand, 1982 benchmark data, 2708–17
Manufacturing annual survey, 1990: finances and operations, by SIC 2- to 4-digit industry, series, 2506–14
Manufacturing census, 1987: concentration of largest firms measured by value added, and for shipments by SIC 2- and 4-digit industry, subject rpt, 2497–6
Manufacturing census, 1987: shipments of manufacturers products, by customer class and SIC 2- and 4-digit industry, subject rpt, 2497–4
Occupational injury and illness rates, by SIC 2- to 4-digit industry, 1989-90, annual rpt, 6844–7
Occupational injury and illness rates, by SIC 2- to 4-digit industry, 1990, annual rpt, 6844–1
Price indexes (producer), by stage of processing and detailed commodity, monthly rpt, 6762–6
Price indexes (producer), by stage of processing and detailed commodity, monthly 1991, annual rpt, 6764–2
Rice shipments, by end use, package size, and State of origin and destination, 1960s-89, biennial rpt, 1564–11

Peters, A. T.
"Effects of the Clean Air Act, Amendment of 1990 on the U.S. Coke and Steel Industry and Foreign Trade Balance", 5606–5.10

Peters, Robert H.
"Miners' Views About Why People Go Under Unsupported Roof and How To Stop Them", 5608–173

Petersen, Bruce C.
"Market Structure, Technology, and the Cyclicality of Output", 9375–13.70
"R&D and Internal Finance: A Panel Study of Small Firms in High-Tech Industries", 9375–13.75

Petersen, Donna J.
"Seasonal Variation in Adolescent Conceptions, Induced Abortions, and Late Initiation of Prenatal Care", 4042–3.372

Peterson, Gary R.
"Availability of Primary Copper in Market-Economy Countries. A Minerals Availability Appraisal", 5606–4.30

Peterson, Pamela P.
"Choice of Capital Instruments by Banking Organizations", 9371–10.79

Petrochemicals
Consumption of fossil fuel by end use, and trade, by type, 1991 and trends from 1949, annual rpt, 3164–74.1; 3164–74.2
County Business Patterns, 1989: employment, establishments, and payroll, by SIC 2- to 4-digit industry and county, annual State rpt series, 2326–8
County Business Patterns, 1990: employment, establishments, and payroll, by SIC 2- to 4-digit industry and county, annual State rpt series, 2326–6
Employment, earnings, and hours, by SIC 1- to 4-digit industry, monthly 1989-Feb 1992, annual rpt, 6744–4
Exports and imports between US and outlying areas, by detailed commodity and mode of transport, 1991, annual rpt, 2424–11
Exports and imports of US, by country and detailed commodity, monthly rpt, 2422–12
Exports and imports of US, by Harmonized System 6-digit commodity and country, 1991, annual rpt, 2424–13
Exports and imports of US, by transport mode, country, and SITC 1- to 3-digit commodity, 1991, annual rpt, 2424–12
Exports of US, detailed Schedule B commodities with countries of destination, 1991, annual rpt, 2424–10
Freight (waterborne domestic and foreign) by commodity, traffic, and passengers, by port and waterway, 1989, annual rpt, 3754–3
Industrial hazardous substances releases and reduction methods under EPA regulation, with chemical stocks and use, facility directory, 1987-89, annual CD-ROM, 9234–7
Manufacturing annual survey, 1990: finances and operations, by SIC 2- to 4-digit industry, series, 2506–14
Manufacturing finances and operations, by SIC 2- to 4-digit industry, forecast 1992, annual rpt, 2044–28
Occupational injury and illness rates, by SIC 2- to 4-digit industry, 1989-90, annual rpt, 6844–7
Occupational injury and illness rates, by SIC 2- to 4-digit industry, 1990, annual rpt, 6844–1
Occupational safety programs for contract labor in petrochemicals industries, accidents, injuries, and employee characteristics, 1986-91, 6608–6
Pacific basin countries energy supply and demand, and implications for US trade, country rpt series, 3406–6
Price indexes (producer), by stage of processing and detailed commodity, monthly rpt, 6762–6
Price indexes (producer), by stage of processing and detailed commodity, monthly 1991, annual rpt, 6764–2
Prices and spending for fuel, by type, end-use sector, and State, 1990, annual rpt, 3164–64
Production and sales of synthetic organic chemicals, and manufacturer listing, by product, 1990, annual rpt, 9884–3
Production, dev, and distribution firms revenues and income, quarterly rpt, 3162–38
Production of synthetic organic chemicals, by detailed product, quarterly rpt, 9882–1
Supply, demand, and movement of crude oil, gas liquids, and refined products, by PAD district and State, 1991, annual rpt, 3164–2
Supply, demand, and prices, by fuel type and end-use sector, alternative projections by region, 1990-2010, annual rpt, 3164–96
Supply, demand, and prices, by fuel type and end-use sector, alternative projections 1990-2010, annual rpt, 3164–75
Supply, demand, trade, stocks, and refining of oil and gas liquids, by detailed product, State, and PAD district, monthly rpt with articles, 3162–6
Tax (excise) on hazardous waste generation and disposal, rates, and firms filing returns, by substance type, 1989, annual article, 8302–2.303

Petroleum and petroleum industry
Business statistics, detailed data for major industries and economic indicators, *Survey of Current Business*, monthly rpt, 2702–1.17

Business statistics, detailed data for major industries and economic indicators, 1960-91, *Survey of Current Business* biennial supplement, 2704–1
Capital expenditures for plant and equipment, by major industry group, quarterly rpt, 2502–2
Census of Population and Housing, 1990: summary characteristics, by county, subdiv, and place, State rpt series, 2551–7
Collective bargaining agreements expiring during year, and workers covered, by firm, union, industry group, and State, 1992, annual rpt, 6784–9
Consumption of energy, by detailed fuel type, end-use sector, and State, 1960-90, State Energy Data System annual rpt, 3164–39
County Business Patterns, 1989: employment, establishments, and payroll, by SIC 2- to 4-digit industry and county, annual State rpt series, 2326–8
County Business Patterns, 1990: employment, establishments, and payroll, by SIC 2- to 4-digit industry and county, annual State rpt series, 2326–6
Crude oil trade, tariffs, and industry operating data, 1992 rpt, 9885–11.4
Developing countries energy efficiency improvement issues and devs, with data by end use and country, 1980s-90, 26358–260
Electric power and industrial plants prohibited from oil and gas primary use, exemptions, and gas use by State, 1980-91, annual rpt, 3334–1
Electric power plants (steam) fuel receipts, costs, and quality, by fuel, plant, utility, and State, 1991, annual rpt, 3164–42
Electric power plants and capacity, by fuel used, owner, location, and operating status, 1991 and for units planned 1992-2001, annual listing, 3164–36
Electric power plants production and capital costs, operations, and fuel use, by fuel type, plant, utility, and location, 1990, annual rpt, 3164–9
Electric power plants production, capacity, sales, and fuel stocks, use, and costs, by State, 1986-90, annual rpt, 3164–11
Electric power plants production, fuel use, stocks, and costs by fuel type, and sales, by State, monthly rpt, with articles, 3162–35
Electric power supply, demand, and trade of Mexico and US, with data by fuel source, utility, and region, 1970s-89 and projected to 2000, 3408–2
Employment, earnings, and hours, by SIC 1- to 4-digit industry, monthly 1989-Feb 1992, annual rpt, 6744–4
Employment of minorities and women, by occupation, SIC 1- to 3-digit industry, State, and MSA, 1991, annual rpt, 9244–1
Energy use and prices, by fuel type and manufacturing industry, 1974-88, 3166–15.3
Environmental Quality, status of problems, protection programs, research, and intl issues, 1991 annual rpt, 484–1
Environmental regulation impacts on oil resources recovery, under alternative oil price, technology, and regulatory assumptions, projected 1990-2015, 3338–2
Farm production itemized costs, by farm sales size and region, 1991, annual rpt, 1614–3
Finances and operations, by SIC 2- to 4-digit industry, forecast 1992, annual rpt, 2044–28
Finances and operations of energy producers, by energy type for US firms domestic and foreign operations, 1990, annual rpt, 3164–44
Foreign and US economic conditions, for major industrial countries, monthly rpt, 9112–1
Foreign and US energy production, trade, use, and reserves, and oil and refined products supply and prices, by country, 1981-90, annual rpt, 3164–50
Foreign and US energy supply and demand, by major fuel and end-use sector, 1950s-87 and forecast to 1995, 3166–6.58
Foreign and US energy use and production, by fuel type, country, and country group, projected 1995-2010 and trends from 1970, annual rpt, 3164–84
Foreign and US oil dependency, energy demand, and efficiency measures, for 6 OECD countries, 1970s-80s, working paper, 9375–13.79
Foreign and US oil production, stocks, use, and trade, by country group and selected country, monthly rpt, 3162–42
Foreign and US oil production, trade, and use, by country group and selected country, monthly rpt, 9112–2
Foreign countries economic conditions, policy, and trade practices, by country, 1989-91, annual rpt, 21384–5
Foreign direct investment in US, by industry group and world area, 1989-91, annual article, 2702–1.331
Foreign direct investment in US energy sources by type and firm, and US affiliates operations, as of 1990, annual rpt, 3164–80
Foreign direct investment of US, by industry group and world area, 1989-91, annual article, 2702–1.332
Freight (waterborne domestic and foreign) by commodity, traffic, and passengers, by port and waterway, 1989, annual rpt, 3754–3
Futures trading in selected commodities and financial instruments and indexes, for NYC, Chicago, and other markets activity, biweekly rpt, 11922–5
Hazardous substances industrial releases and reduction methods under EPA regulation, by chemical, source, industry, and location, 1989, annual rpt, 9234–6
Hazardous substances industrial releases and reduction methods under EPA regulation, with chemical stocks and use, facility directory, 1987-89, annual CD-ROM, 9234–7
Heating fuels production, imports, stocks, and prices, by selected PAD district and State, seasonal weekly rpt, 3162–45
Hwy construction material use by type, and spending, by State, 1940s-91, annual rpt, 7554–29
Input-output structure of US economy, detailed interindustry transactions for 84 industries, and components of final demand, 1987, annual article, 2702–1.316
Input-output structure of US economy, detailed interindustry transactions for 541 industries, and components of final demand, 1982 benchmark data, 2708–17
Iraq invasion of Kuwait, oil production disruption impacts on futures prices, family budgets, and oil firms, 1990 hearings, 25408–116
Kuwait oil fires set by Iraqi forces, air pollution levels by substance and site, as of Mar 1991, 9188–116
Kuwait oil fires set by Iraqi forces, air pollution levels, health effects, intl monitoring activities, and wells affected, 1991, GAO rpt, 26113–566
Labor productivity in oil and gas industry, 1959-87, article, 6722–1.316
Labor productivity, indexes of output, hours, and employment by SIC 2- to 4-digit industry, 1967-90, annual rpt, 6824–1.2; 6824–1.3
Lumber preservatives performance test results, by type, late 1930s-80s, 1208–391
Manufacturing annual survey, 1990: finances and operations, by SIC 2- to 4-digit industry, series, 2506–14
Manufacturing census, 1987: concentration of largest firms measured by value added, and for shipments by SIC 2- and 4-digit industry, subject rpt, 2497–6
Manufacturing census, 1987: shipments of manufacturers products, by customer class and SIC 2- and 4-digit industry, subject rpt, 2497–4
Manufacturing corporations financial statements, by selected SIC 2- to 3-digit industry, quarterly rpt, 2502–1
Manufacturing energy use and prices, 1988 survey, series, 3166–13
Manufacturing production, shipments, inventories, orders, and pollution control costs, periodic Current Industrial Rpt series, 2506–3
Military and personal property shipments, passenger traffic, and costs, by service branch and mode of transport, FY91, annual rpt, 3704–15
Military prime contract awards, by category, contractor type, and State, FY89-91, annual rpt, 3544–11
Military prime contract awards, by size and type of contract, service branch, competitive status, category, and labor standard, FY91, annual rpt, 3544–19
Military Sealift Command shipping operations, finances, and personnel, FY91, annual rpt, 3804–14
Minerals Yearbook, Vol 3, 1989: foreign country reviews of production, trade, and policy, by commodity, annual rpt, 5604–35
Multinatl firms US affiliates finances and operations, by industry, country of parent firm, and State, 1987, 2708–48
Multinatl firms US affiliates, finances, and operations, by industry, world area of parent firm, and State, 1989-90, annual rpt, 2704–4
Multinatl US firms and foreign affiliates finances and operations, by industry and country, 1989 benchmark survey, annual rpt, 2704–5
Multinatl US firms foreign affiliates, income statement items by asset size, industry, and country, 1988, biennial article, 8302–2.322

Natl Energy Strategy fossil fuel, electric power, conservation, and pollution reduction issues, 1991 hearings, 21368–136
Natl Energy Strategy plans for conservation, R&D, security, and pollution reduction, technical rpt series, 3006–13
Natl income and product accounts, comprehensive accounts and components, benchmark revisions, 1929-88, 2708–5
Natl income and product accounts, comprehensive accounts and components, *Survey of Current Business*, monthly rpt, 2702–1.25
Occupational injury and illness rates, by SIC 2- to 4-digit industry, 1989-90, annual rpt, 6844–7
Occupational injury and illness rates, by SIC 2- to 4-digit industry, 1990, annual rpt, 6844–1
Ohio River basin waterway facilities, freight by commodity and port, and recreation, by waterway, 1988-89, annual rpt, 3754–6
Pacific basin countries energy supply and demand, and implications for US trade, country rpt series, 3406–6
Pollution (air) abatement equipment shipments by industry, and new and backlog orders, by product, 1991, annual Current Industrial Rpt, 2506–12.5
Pollution (air) contributing to global warming, emissions by monitoring site and country, and temperature change by world area and US region, 1860s-1990, annual rpt, 3004–33
Pollution abatement capital and operating costs, by SIC 2- to 4-digit industry and State, 1990, annual Current Industrial Rpt, 2506–3.6
Production and reserves of oil, gas, and gas liquids, by State and substate area, 1991, annual rpt, 3164–46
Production, dev, and distribution firms revenues and income, quarterly rpt, 3162–38
Puerto Rico and other US possessions corporations income tax returns, income and tax items, and employment, by selected industry, 1989, article, 8302–2.326
Purchases and sales of oil products by refiners, processors, and distributors, by product, end-use sector, PAD district, and State, monthly rpt, 3162–11; 3164–85
Romania energy production and trade, 1970s-91, with capital investment projected to 2000, GAO rpt, 26123–402
Science, engineering, and technical employment in manufacturing, by field and industry, 1989, triennial rpt, 9627–23
South America oil production, investment needs, and exports, for 8 countries, 1980s-90 and projected to 2010, GAO rpt, 26123–396
Soviet Union and US economic and sociodemographic indicators, selected years 1970-90, handbook, 2328–80
Soviet Union former Republics and Baltic States energy supply and use, and social, economic, and political indicators, 1989-90, 3168–126
Soviet Union oil production, and exports by country or world region of destination, 1980s-89, annual rpt, 23844–2
Statistical Abstract of US, 1992 annual data compilation, 2324–1.19; 2324–1.25
Supply and demand of oil and refined products, refinery capacity and use, and prices, weekly rpt, 3162–32
Supply, demand, and distribution of energy, and regulatory impacts, series, 3166–6
Supply, demand, and movement of crude oil, gas liquids, and refined products, by PAD district and State, 1991, annual rpt, 3164–2
Supply, demand, and prices, by fuel type and end-use sector, alternative projections by region, 1990-2010, annual rpt, 3164–96
Supply, demand, and prices, by fuel type and end-use sector, alternative projections 1990-2010, annual rpt, 3164–75
Supply, demand, and prices, by fuel type and end-use sector, projections and underlying assumptions, 1995-2010, annual rpt, 3164–90
Supply, demand, and prices, by fuel type and end-use sector, with foreign comparisons, 1981-90, annual fact book, 3164–76
Supply, demand, and prices, by fuel type and end-use sector, with foreign comparisons, 1991 and trends from 1949, annual rpt, 3164–74
Supply, demand, and prices, by fuel type, end-use sector, and country, detailed data, monthly rpt with articles, 3162–24
Supply, demand, and prices, by fuel type, end-use sector, and country, detailed data, monthly 1973-88, 3168–123
Supply, demand, and prices of energy, forecasts by resource type, quarterly rpt, 3162–34
Supply, demand, and prices of oil and gas, alternative projections, annual rpt, discontinued, 3164–89
Supply, demand, trade, stocks, and refining of oil and gas liquids, by detailed product, State, and PAD district, monthly rpt with articles, 3162–6
Supply of oil products, EIA and alternative estimates, 1981-90, annual article, 3162–6.302
Tax (excise) on hazardous waste generation and disposal, rates, and firms filing returns, by substance type, 1989, annual article, 8302–2.303
Tax (income) effective rates for oil companies, with background income and tax data for domestic and foreign operations, 1977-89, 3168–124
Tax (income) returns of corporations, income and tax items by asset size and detailed industry, 1989, annual rpt, 8304–4; 8304–21
Tax (income) returns of corporations with foreign tax credit, income and tax items by industry group, 1988, biennial article, 8302–2.316
Transportation energy use by fuel type, and miles traveled, by mode, projected 1990-2010 and trends from 1960s, 3008–124
Underground storage of oil, Federal trust fund for leaking tanks, financial condition, monthly rpt, 8102–9.11
Used oil sources, disposal methods, and toxic substance content, 1991 hearings, 21368–139
Water (groundwater) supply, quality, chemistry, other characteristics, and use, regional rpt series, 5666–25
Wholesale trade sales and inventories, by SIC 2- to 3-digit kind of business, monthly rpt, 2413–7
see also Asphalt and tar
see also Aviation fuels
see also Diesel fuel
see also Energy exploration and drilling
see also Fuel oil
see also Gasoline
see also Gasoline service stations
see also Kerosene
see also Liquefied petroleum gas
see also Motor fuels
see also Natural gas and gas industry
see also Naval Petroleum Reserves
see also Offshore oil and gas
see also Oil and gas leases
see also Oil depletion allowances
see also Oil shale
see also Oil spills
see also Organization of Petroleum Exporting Countries
see also Petrochemicals
see also Petroleum exports and imports
see also Petroleum prices
see also Petroleum reserves
see also Petroleum stocks
see also Pipelines
see also Strategic Petroleum Reserve
see also Synthetic fuels
see also Trans-Alaska Pipeline System
see also Windfall profit tax
see also under By Commodity in the "Index by Categories"
see also under By Industry in the "Index by Categories"

Petroleum exports and imports
Business statistics, detailed data for major industries and economic indicators, *Survey of Current Business*, monthly rpt, 2702–1.17
Business statistics, detailed data for major industries and economic indicators, 1960-91, *Survey of Current Business* biennial supplement, 2704–1
Crude oil trade, tariffs, and industry operating data, 1992 rpt, 9885–11.4
Cuba trade, by commodity and country, mid 1980s-91, 9118–8
Export licensing, monitoring, and enforcement activities, FY91, annual rpt, 2024–1
Exports and imports between US and outlying areas, by detailed commodity and mode of transport, 1991, annual rpt, 2424–11
Exports and imports of US, by country and detailed commodity, monthly rpt, 2422–12
Exports and imports of US, by Harmonized System 6-digit commodity and country, 1991, annual rpt, 2424–13
Exports and imports of US, by selected country, country group, and commodity group, 1991, annual rpt, 2044–37
Exports and imports of US, by transport mode, country, and SITC 1- to 3-digit commodity, 1991, annual rpt, 2424–12
Exports, imports, production, and use, by country group and selected country, monthly rpt, 9112–2

Exports, imports, production, use, and stocks of oil, by country group and selected country, monthly rpt, 3162–42
Exports of US, detailed Schedule B commodities with countries of destination, 1991, annual rpt, 2424–10
Foreign and US energy supply and demand, by major fuel and end-use sector, 1950s-87 and forecast to 1995, 3166–6.58
Foreign and US oil production, trade, and stocks, by product and country, 1987-90, annual rpt, 3164–50.2
Heating fuels production, imports, stocks, and prices, by selected PAD district and State, seasonal weekly rpt, 3162–45
Imports, exports, and employment impacts, by SIC 2- to 4-digit industry and commodity, quarterly rpt, 2322–2
Imports of oil and refined products, *Survey of Current Business*, monthly rpt, 2702–1.1
Input-output structure of US economy, detailed interindustry transactions for 541 industries, and components of final demand, 1982 benchmark data, 2708–17
Intl transactions summary, 1980s-91, annual article, 9362–1.304
Japan energy use and imports by fuel type, and gasoline prices, 1970s-80s, hearing, 21448–45
Latin America economic and social conditions, resources, trade, and aid, 1992, annual factbook, 9914–14
Mexico imports from US, by industry and State, 1987-91, 2048–154
Natl Energy Strategy Strategic Petroleum Reserve and energy efficiency issues, 1991 hearings, 21368–142
Natl income and product accounts, comprehensive accounts and components, benchmark revisions, 1929-88, 2708–5
Natl income and product accounts, comprehensive accounts and components, *Survey of Current Business*, monthly rpt, 2702–1.27
OECD intl trade position for US and 4 countries, and factors affecting US competition, quarterly pamphlet, 2042–25
OECD trade, total and for 4 major countries, and US trade by country, by commodity, 1980-90, world area rpt series, 9116–1
Pacific basin countries energy supply and demand, and implications for US trade, country rpt series, 3406–6
Persian Gulf oil exports, US and OECD dependence indicators, and US military supply, late 1970s-80s and supply disruptions from 1951, 3166–6.65
Price indexes for exports and imports, by selected end-use category, monthly press release, 6762–15
Prices and volume of oil products sold and purchased by refiners, processors, and distributors, by product, end-use sector, PAD district, and State, 1991, annual rpt, 3164–85
South America oil production, investment needs, and exports, for 8 countries, 1980s-90 and projected to 2010, GAO rpt, 26123–396
Statistical Abstract of US, 1992 annual data compilation, 2324–1.19
Strategic Petroleum Reserve oil deliveries, by country and State of origin, quarterly rpt, annual data, 3002–13
Supply and demand of oil and refined products, refinery capacity and use, and prices, weekly rpt, 3162–32
Supply, demand, and movement of crude oil, gas liquids, and refined products, by PAD district and State, 1991, annual rpt, 3164–2
Supply, demand, and prices, by fuel type and end-use sector, alternative projections by region, 1990-2010, annual rpt, 3164–96
Supply, demand, and prices, by fuel type and end-use sector, alternative projections 1990-2010, annual rpt, 3164–75
Supply, demand, and prices, by fuel type and end-use sector, with foreign comparisons, 1981-90, annual fact book, 3164–76
Supply, demand, and prices, by fuel type and end-use sector, with foreign comparisons, 1991 and trends from 1949, annual rpt, 3164–74
Supply, demand, and prices, by fuel type, end-use sector, and country, detailed data, monthly rpt with articles, 3162–24
Supply, demand, and prices, by fuel type, end-use sector, and country, detailed data, monthly 1973-88, 3168–123
Supply, demand, and prices of energy, forecasts by resource type, quarterly rpt, 3162–34
Supply, demand, trade, stocks, and refining of oil and gas liquids, by detailed product, State, and PAD district, monthly rpt with articles, 3162–6
Supply of oil products, EIA and alternative estimates, 1981-90, annual article, 3162–6.302
Tariffs and excise taxes on oil imports from OPEC, economic impacts, model description and results, 1992 technical paper, 9379–12.96
Waterborne commerce (domestic and foreign) of US, freight by commodity, traffic, and passengers, by port and waterway, 1989, annual rpt, 3754–3

Petroleum prices

Airline fuel prices for domestic and intl operations, quarterly rpt, 7502–16
Alaska minerals resources, production, oil and gas leases, reserves, and exploratory wells, with maps and bibl, 1990, annual rpt, 5664–11
Auto fuel economy improvements from new technologies, 1987-90 and alternative projections to 2010, 26358–251
Business statistics, detailed data for major industries and economic indicators, *Survey of Current Business*, monthly rpt, 2702–1.17
Business statistics, detailed data for major industries and economic indicators, 1960-91, *Survey of Current Business* biennial supplement, 2704–1
CPI by component for US city average, and by selected metro area, region, and population size, monthly rpt, 6762–2
Economic indicators impact of oil price increases, 1970s-91, article, 9391–1.301
Electric power plants (steam) fuel receipts, costs, and quality, by fuel, plant, utility, and State, 1991, annual rpt, 3164–42
Electric power plants prices paid for fossil fuels, FY90-91, annual rpt, 3084–9
Electric power plants production, capacity, sales, and fuel stocks, use, and costs, by State, 1986-90, annual rpt, 3164–11
Electric power plants production, fuel use, stocks, and costs by fuel type, and sales, by State, monthly rpt, with articles, 3162–35
Environmental regulation impacts on oil resources recovery, under alternative oil price, technology, and regulatory assumptions, projected 1990-2015, 3338–2
Farm prices received and paid, by commodity and State, monthly rpt, 1629–1
Farm prices received and paid, by commodity and State, 1991, annual rpt, 1629–5
Farm production inputs supply, demand, and prices, 1970s-91 and projected to 1996, article, 1561–16.301
Farm production inputs supply, demand, and prices, 1980s-92, article, 1561–16.304
Food marketing cost indexes, by expense category, monthly rpt with articles, 1502–4
Foreign and US energy production, trade, use, and reserves, and oil and refined products supply and prices, by country, 1981-90, annual rpt, 3164–50
Foreign and US energy use and production, by fuel type, country, and country group, projected 1995-2010 and trends from 1970, annual rpt, 3164–84
Foreign countries transportation energy use, fuel prices, vehicle registrations, and mileage, by selected country, 1950-89, annual rpt, 3304–5.1
Gasoline service stations price competition and divorcement from oil companies, issues with data by firm, city, and State, 1991 hearing, 25528–120
GNP and employment related to oil prices and interest rates, late 1940s-91, article, 9389–1.304
Heating fuels production, imports, stocks, and prices, by selected PAD district and State, seasonal weekly rpt, 3162–45
Housing energy prices, by fuel type and State, 1990 and forecast 1991-92, 3166–6.61
Import and export price indexes, by selected end-use category, monthly press release, 6762–15
Iraq invasion of Kuwait, oil production disruption impacts on futures prices, family budgets, and oil firms, 1990 hearings, 25408–116
Japan energy use and imports by fuel type, and gasoline prices, 1970s-80s, hearing, 21448–45
Manufacturing energy use and prices, by fuel type and industry, 1974-88, 3166–15.3
Naval Petroleum and Oil Shale Reserves sales and contract prices, by purchaser and reserve, FY91, annual rpt, 3334–3
OPEC oil sales price, monthly rpt, 9112–1
Overcharge settlements of oil companies, funds received, and conservation and energy aid spending, by outlying area, 1990, GAO rpt, 26113–564

Overcharge settlements, use in low income energy assistance, by State, FY90, annual rpt, 4584–1
Pacific basin countries energy supply and demand, and implications for US trade, country rpt series, 3406–6
Pacific Northwest population, households, employment, income, fuel prices, and electricity demand, alternative forecasts 1991-2010, annual rpt, 3224–3.3
Prices and spending for fuel, by type, end-use sector, and State, 1990, annual rpt, 3164–64
Prices of fuel, by type, end-use sector, and region, projected 1991-2030, 3166–6.60
Prices of imported and domestic oil and wholesale and retail fuels, and dealer margins, monthly rpt, 3162–24.9
Prices of imported and domestic oil and wholesale and retail fuels, and dealer margins, monthly 1975-88, 3168–123.9
Prices of oil and refined products, spot market, OPEC, non-OPEC, and refiners costs, weekly rpt, 3162–32
Prices, supply, and demand, by fuel type and end-use sector, alternative projections by region, 1990-2010, annual rpt, 3164–96
Prices, supply, and demand, by fuel type and end-use sector, alternative projections 1990-2010, annual rpt, 3164–75
Prices, supply, and demand, by fuel type and end-use sector, projections and underlying assumptions, 1995-2010, annual rpt, 3164–90
Prices, supply, and demand, by fuel type and end-use sector, with foreign comparisons, 1981-90, annual fact book, 3164–76
Prices, supply, and demand, by fuel type and end-use sector, with foreign comparisons, 1991 and trends from 1949, annual rpt, 3164–74
Prices, supply, and demand of energy, forecasts by resource type, quarterly rpt, 3162–34
Producer price indexes, by stage of processing and detailed commodity, monthly rpt, 6762–6
Producer price indexes, by stage of processing and detailed commodity, monthly 1991, annual rpt, 6764–2
Refined product prices and sales volume, 1989-90, annual rpt, 3164–44.3
Refiners, processors, and distributors sales and purchases, by product, end-use sector, PAD district, and State, monthly rpt, 3162–11
Refiners, processors, and distributors sales and purchases, by product, end-use sector, PAD district, and State, 1991, annual rpt, 3164–85
Statistical Abstract of US, 1992 annual data compilation, 2324–1.15
Texas (west) crude oil prices, quarterly rpt, 9381–16.2
Transportation energy use by mode, fuel supply, and demographic and economic factors of vehicle use, 1970s-90, annual rpt, 3304–5.2
VA health care facilities energy use and conservation, by facility, quarterly rpt, 8602–9

Petroleum reserves
Alaska Arctic Natl Wildlife Refuge oil reserves and production, alternative forecasts 1985-2015, 3166–6.64
Alaska minerals resources, production, oil and gas leases, reserves, and exploratory wells, with maps and bibl, 1990, annual rpt, 5664–11
Alaska oil, gas, and coal reserve acreage, by ownership, 1991 rpt, 5608–174
Environmental regulation impacts on oil resources recovery, under alternative oil price, technology, and regulatory assumptions, projected 1990-2015, 3338–2
Field codes and locations, for oil and gas, 1991, annual listing, 3164–70
Foreign and US energy reserves, by type of fuel and country, as of Jan 1991, annual rpt, 3164–50.6
Foreign and US energy use and production, by fuel type, country, and country group, projected 1995-2010 and trends from 1970, annual rpt, 3164–84
Foreign countries oil and gas reserves and discoveries, by country and country group, quarterly rpt, suspended, 3162–43
Foreign countries oil reserves, production, and resource lifespan under alternative production rates, trends and projections, discontinued series, 3166–9
Gulf of Mexico oil and gas reserves, production, and leasing status, by location, 1990, annual rpt, 5734–6
Offshore oil and gas reserves of Fed Govt, production, leasing and exploration activity, revenue, and costs, by ocean area, FY91, annual rpt, 5734–4
Pacific basin countries energy supply and demand, and implications for US trade, country rpt series, 3406–6
Pacific Ocean OCS oil and gas production, reserves, and wells drilled by location, 1990, annual rpt, 5734–7
Producers finances and operations, by energy type for US firms domestic and foreign operations, 1990, annual rpt, 3164–44.2
Public lands minerals resources and availability, State rpt series, 5606–7
Research on enhanced oil recovery under DOE contract, project summaries, funding, and bibl, quarterly rpt, 3002–14
Reserves and production of oil, gas, and gas liquids, by State and substate area, 1991, annual rpt, 3164–46
Reserves, production, and ultimate recovery of oil and gas, by location, with field technical characteristics, series, 3166–14
Supply, demand, and prices, by fuel type and end-use sector, projections and underlying assumptions, 1995-2010, annual rpt, 3164–90
Supply, demand, and prices, by fuel type and end-use sector, with foreign comparisons, 1991 and trends from 1949, annual rpt, 3164–74
see also Natural gas reserves
see also Naval Petroleum Reserves
see also Strategic Petroleum Reserve

Petroleum stocks
Business statistics, detailed data for major industries and economic indicators, *Survey of Current Business*, monthly rpt, 2702–1.17
Electric power plants production, capacity, sales, and fuel stocks, use, and costs, by State, 1986-90, annual rpt, 3164–11
Electric power plants production, fuel use, stocks, and costs by fuel type, and sales, by State, monthly rpt, with articles, 3162–35
Heating fuels production, imports, stocks, and prices, by selected PAD district and State, seasonal weekly rpt, 3162–45
OECD oil crude and refined products stocks, quarterly 1987-90, annual rpt, 3164–50.2
OECD oil stocks, for US and 16 countries, monthly rpt, 9112–2
OECD oil stocks, monthly rpt, 3162–42
Pacific basin countries energy supply and demand, and implications for US trade, country rpt series, 3406–6
Supply and demand of oil and refined products, refinery capacity and use, and prices, weekly rpt, 3162–32
Supply, demand, and movement of crude oil, gas liquids, and refined products, by PAD district and State, 1991, annual rpt, 3164–2
Supply, demand, and prices, by fuel type and end-use sector, alternative projections 1990-2010, annual rpt, 3164–75
Supply, demand, and prices, by fuel type and end-use sector, with foreign comparisons, 1991 and trends from 1949, annual rpt, 3164–74.2
Supply, demand, and prices, by fuel type, end-use sector, and country, detailed data, monthly rpt with articles, 3162–24
Supply, demand, and prices, by fuel type, end-use sector, and country, detailed data, monthly 1973-88, 3168–123
Supply, demand, and prices of energy, forecasts by resource type, quarterly rpt, 3162–34
Supply, demand, trade, stocks, and refining of oil and gas liquids, by detailed product, State, and PAD district, monthly rpt with articles, 3162–6
see also Naval Petroleum Reserves
see also Strategic Petroleum Reserve

Pets
Households entertainment spending, recreation participation by activity, and video product and pet ownership, 1970s-90, article, 1702–1.303
Rabies vaccination schedules and dosages for pets and livestock by species, and disease outbreak control, CDC recommendations, 1992 rpt, 4206–2.57
Statistical Abstract of US, 1992 annual data compilation, 2324–1.7
see also Pet food and supplies

Petska, Tom
"Partnerships, Partners, and Tax Shelters After Tax Reform, 1987-89", 8302–2.313

Pfannenstiel, Judy C.
"Unlocking Learning: Chapter 1 in Correctional Facilities. National Study of the Chapter 1 Neglected or Delinquent Program: Effective Practices Study Findings", 4808–40.3

Pharmaceutical industry
Competitiveness (intl) of US high technology industries, with background data by industry and foreign comparisons, 1960s-91, GAO rpt, 26123–406

County Business Patterns, 1989: employment, establishments, and payroll, by SIC 2- to 4-digit industry and county, annual State rpt series, 2326–8
County Business Patterns, 1990: employment, establishments, and payroll, by SIC 2- to 4-digit industry and county, annual State rpt series, 2326–6
Employment, earnings, and hours, by SIC 1- to 4-digit industry, monthly 1989-Feb 1992, annual rpt, 6744–4
Employment of minorities and women, by occupation, SIC 1- to 3-digit industry, State, and MSA, 1991, annual rpt, 9244–1
Input-output structure of US economy, detailed interindustry transactions for 84 industries, and components of final demand, 1987, annual article, 2702–1.316
Input-output structure of US economy, detailed interindustry transactions for 541 industries, and components of final demand, 1982 benchmark data, 2708–17
Labor productivity, indexes of output, hours, and employment by SIC 2- to 4-digit industry, 1967-90, annual rpt, 6824–1.3
Manufacturing annual survey, 1990: finances and operations, by SIC 2- to 4-digit industry, series, 2506–14
Manufacturing census, 1987: concentration of largest firms measured by value added, and for shipments by SIC 2- and 4-digit industry, subject rpt, 2497–6
Manufacturing census, 1987: shipments of manufacturers products, by customer class and SIC 2- and 4-digit industry, subject rpt, 2497–4
Manufacturing corporations financial statements, by selected SIC 2- to 3-digit industry, quarterly rpt, 2502–1
Manufacturing finances and operations, by SIC 2- to 4-digit industry, forecast 1992, annual rpt, 2044–28
Marketing applications for drugs, FDA processing by drug, purpose, and producer, 1991, annual rpt, 4064–14
Multinatl US firms and foreign affiliates finances and operations, by industry and country, 1989 benchmark survey, annual rpt, 2704–5
Occupational injury and illness rates, by SIC 2- to 4-digit industry, 1989-90, annual rpt, 6844–7
Occupational injury and illness rates, by SIC 2- to 4-digit industry, 1990, annual rpt, 6844–1
Price indexes (producer), by stage of processing and detailed commodity, monthly rpt, 6762–6
Price indexes (producer), by stage of processing and detailed commodity, monthly 1991, annual rpt, 6764–2
Production and sales of synthetic organic chemicals, and manufacturer listing, by product, 1990, annual rpt, 9884–3
Profitability of prescription drug industry, R&D and marketing spending, and FDA drug approvals by firm, 1980s-91 and projected to 2000, 25148–44
Puerto Rico and other US possessions corporations income tax returns, income and tax items, and employment, by selected industry, 1989, article, 8302–2.326
Puerto Rico statehood referendum proposal, with background data on Federal outlays, economic conditions, and finances of corporations with tax-favored status, 1940s-88, hearing, 21448–46
Science, engineering, and technical employment in manufacturing, by field and industry, 1989, triennial rpt, 9627–23
Tax (income) returns of corporations, income and tax items by asset size and detailed industry, 1989, annual rpt, 8304–4; 8304–21
Technological devs effect on labor force, composition, and productivity, 1970s-90 and projected to 2005, industry rpt, 6826–2.9
Wholesale trade sales and inventories, by SIC 2- to 3-digit kind of business, monthly rpt, 2413–7
Women's representation in clinical drug trials, and FDA policy guidance, 1988-91, GAO rpt, 26121–486
see also Biologic drug products
see also Drugs
see also Drugstores
see also Pharmacists and pharmacy

Pharmacists and pharmacy
AIDS virus-related Medicaid claims and payments, by sex, age, risk group, eligibility, and source of care, for Michigan, mid 1980s, article, 4042–3.348
Degrees awarded in higher education, by level, field, race, and sex, 1989/90 and trends from 1980/81, annual rpt, 4844–17
Drug (prescription) advertising in medical journals, accuracy, info completeness, and violations of FDA regulations, 1990, 4008–119
Education in science and engineering, grad programs enrollment by field, source of funds, and characteristics of student and instn, 1990, annual rpt, 9627–7
General Medical Sciences Natl Inst activities, budget, and research and training funding by program, FY91, annual rpt, 4474–38
Health condition and care indicators, 1950s-90 with health improvement and disease prevention goals for 1990, annual data compilation, 4144–11
Hospital employment and job vacancy rate, by occupation, and instn size and control, 1981-88, annual rpt, 4114–12
Indian Health Service and tribal facility outpatient visits, by type of provider, selected hospital, and service area, FY91, annual rpt, 4084–3
Labor demand, turnover, and training completions, by detailed occupation, 1990 and projected to 2005, biennial rpt, 6744–3
Labor supply and education of health professionals, by professional and other characteristics, and location, 1960s-92 and projected to 2020, biennial rpt, 4114–8
Licensing and discipline of pharmacists by State medical boards, with medical school enrollment and applications, 1950s-88, 4006–8.5
Military health care personnel, and accessions by training source, by occupation, specialty, and service branch, FY90, annual rpt, 3544–24
Occupational Outlook Handbook, 1992-93, biennial rpt, 6744–1
VA health care facilities trainees, by detailed program and city, FY91, annual rpt, 8704–4
VA health care staff and turnover, by occupation, physician specialty, and location, 1991, annual rpt, 8604–8
VA pharmacy medications dispensed by type, patient-oriented hours, and fee-basis prescriptions filled by VA and non-VA pharmacies, FY89-91, annual rpt, 8604–3.2
see also Drugs
see also Drugstores

Phelan, Daniel J.
"Water Use in the St. Jones River Basin, Kent County, Delaware, 1983-86", 5666–24.10

Phelps, Robert B.
"Outlook for Timber Products", 1504–9.1

Philadelphia, Pa.
Commuters, by county of residence and work, for top 10 metro areas, 1990 Census of Population, press release, 2328–84
Commuting accessibility of central business district, impact on housing prices, for Philadelphia, 1970-88, working paper, 9387–8.258
CPI by component for US city average, and by region, population size, and for 15 metro areas, monthly rpt, 6762–1
CPI by component for US city average, and by selected metro area, region, and population size, monthly rpt, 6762–2
Drug abuse indicators for selected metro areas, research results, data collection, and policy issues, 1992 semiannual conf, 4492–5
Drug test results at arrest, by drug type, offense, and sex, for selected urban areas, quarterly rpt, 6062–3
Employment growth and unemployment rates, Fed Reserve 3rd District, quarterly rpt, 9387–10
Freight (waterborne domestic and foreign) by commodity, traffic, and passengers, by port and waterway, 1989, annual rpt, 3754–3.1
Fruit and vegetable shipments, and arrivals by city, by mode of transport and State and country of origin, 1991, annual rpt, 1311–4.1
Heroin prices and purity in 19 metro areas and Puerto Rico, by world area of origin, quarterly rpt, 6282–2
Housing and households characteristics, unit and neighborhood quality, and journey to work by MSA location, for 11 MSAs, 1985 survey, supplement, 2485–8
Housing and households characteristics, 1989 survey, MSA fact sheet, 2485–11.5
Housing and households detailed characteristics, and unit and neighborhood quality, by location, 1989 survey, MSA rpt, 2485–6.4
Mortgage activity impact of lending program for low- and moderate-income neighborhoods in Philadelphia, with background data, 1980s, working paper, 9387–8.266
Transit system in Philadelphia metro area, operations, costs and benefits, and local economic and air pollution impacts, 1970s-90 and projected to 2020, 7308–205

Unemployed displaced workers job search and placement aid effectiveness, relation to previous employment and other characteristics, 1979-87 studies, 15496–1.14
Wages by occupation, and benefits, for office and plant workers, 1991 survey, periodic MSA rpt, 6785–16.5
see also under By City and By SMSA or MSA in the "Index by Categories"

Philanthropy
see Gifts and private contributions
see Nonprofit organizations and foundations

Philippines
Agricultural trade by commodity and country, prices, and world market devs, monthly rpt, 1922–12
Agricultural trade of US, by detailed commodity and country, 1991, annual rpt, 1524–8
Agricultural trade of US, by detailed commodity and country, 1991, semiannual rpt, 1522–4
AID economic aid to developing countries, obligations and disbursements by country, quarterly rpt, 9912–4
AID loans repayment status and terms by program and country, and status of predecessor agency loans, quarterly rpt, 9912–3
Debt burden indicators for 8 developing countries, alternative projections 1991-2000 and trends from 1974, technical paper, 9366–7.271
Economic and military aid and loans from US and intl agencies, by program and country, FY46-91, annual rpt, 9914–5
Economic and social conditions of developing countries from 1960s, and Intl Dev Cooperation Agency and AID activities and funding, FY91-93, annual rpt, 9904–4
Economic conditions, income, production, prices, employment, and trade, 1991 periodic country rpt, 2046–4.8
Economic conditions, investment and export opportunities, and trade practices, 1992 country market research rpt, 2046–6.2
Economic conditions, policy, and trade practices, by country, 1989-91, annual rpt, 21384–5
Economic, population, and agricultural data, US and other aid sources, and AID activity, 1990 country rpt, 9916–12.50
Economic, social, political, and geographic summary data, by country, 1992, annual factbook, 9114–2
Exports and imports of US, by commodity and country, 1980-90, world area rpt, 9116–1.3
Exports and imports of US, by Harmonized System 6-digit commodity and country, 1991, annual rpt, 2424–13
Exports and imports of US, by selected country, country group, and commodity group, 1991, annual rpt, 2044–37
Exports and imports of US, by transport mode, country, and SITC 1- to 3-digit commodity, 1991, annual rpt, 2424–12
Exports, imports, and balances of US for manufactured goods, by SITC 2-digit commodity and country, quarterly rpt, 2042–35
Exports of US, detailed Schedule B commodities with countries of destination, 1991, annual rpt, 2424–10
Food supply, needs, and aid for developing countries, status and alternative forecasts, 1992 world area rpt, 1526–8.2
Fruit (fresh) imports of Philippines by country, and vegetable exports, by commodity, 1987-90, article, 1925–34.303
Hostages kidnapped in Philippines, listing as of 1991, 7004–22
Human rights conditions in 170 countries, and US economic and military aid, 1991, annual rpt, 21384–3
Imports of goods, services, and investment from US, trade barriers, impacts, and US actions, by country, 1991, annual rpt, 444–2
Labor conditions, union coverage, and work accidents, 1992 annual country rpt, 6366–4.22
Military aid of US, arms sales, and training programs costs and budget requests, by program, world region, and country, FY91-93, annual rpt, 7144–13
Military spending, arms trade, and force strengths, with govt spending and population, by country, 1979-89, annual rpt, 9824–1
Minerals Yearbook, Vol 3, 1989: foreign country review of production, trade, and policy, by commodity, annual rpt, 5604–35.2
Mount Pinatubo, Philippines, volcanic eruptions, evacuation camps infective disease cases and deaths, 1991, article, 4202–7.320
Multinatl US firms and foreign affiliates finances and operations, by industry and country, 1989 benchmark survey, annual rpt, 2704–5
Multinatl US firms foreign affiliates, income statement items by asset size, industry, and country, 1988, biennial article, 8302–2.322
Pineapple (canned fruit and juice) production and exports, by country, and Mexico export prices, selected years 1987-92, annual article, 1925–34.327
Pineapple (canned fruit and juice) production and exports, for 2 countries, forecast 1992, semiannual article, 1925–34.346
Population size, growth rates, and components of change, by country, projected 1990-2020 and trends from 1950, biennial rpt, 2324–9
Refugee migration, and intl aid programs, by world area and country of origin and asylum, 1991, annual rpt, 7004–15
Ships in world merchant fleet, tonnage, and new ship construction and deliveries, by vessel type and country, as of Jan 1992, annual rpt, 7704–3
Steel trade, by product, country, and customs district, with US industry operating data, 1989-June 1992, semiannual rpt, 9882–15
Tidal currents, daily time and velocity by station for North America and Asia coasts, forecast 1993, annual rpt, 2174–1.2
UN voting record and share of votes in agreement with US, by issue, country, and world area, 1991, annual rpt, 7004–18
US veterans living abroad, disability and death compensation cases by entitlement type, period of service, sex, and age, FY90, annual rpt, 8604–7
US veterans living abroad, VA expenses by type and location, FY91, annual rpt, 8604–3.4
US veterans programs spending, by US and foreign location, FY91, annual rpt, 8604–6
see also under By Foreign Country in the "Index by Categories"

Philips, Peter
"Effect of Immigration Reform on Collective Bargaining in the California Fruit and Vegetable Processing Industry", 6366–6.5

Phillips, Keith R.
"Regional Wage Divergence and National Wage Inequality", 9379–1.307

Philosophy
see Arts and the humanities

Phoenix, Ariz.
Drug abuse indicators for selected metro areas, research results, data collection, and policy issues, 1992 semiannual conf, 4492–5
Drug test results at arrest, by drug type, offense, and sex, for selected urban areas, quarterly rpt, 6062–3
Heroin prices and purity in 19 metro areas and Puerto Rico, by world area of origin, quarterly rpt, 6282–2
Housing and households characteristics, unit and neighborhood quality, and journey to work by MSA location, for 11 MSAs, 1985 survey, supplement, 2485–8
Housing and households characteristics, 1989 survey, MSA fact sheet, 2485–11.4
Housing and households detailed characteristics, and unit and neighborhood quality, by location, 1989 survey, MSA rpt, 2485–6.9
Housing starts and completions authorized by building permits in 40 MSAs, quarterly rpt, 2382–9
see also under By City and By SMSA or MSA in the "Index by Categories"

Phonographic equipment and recordings
see Home video and audio equipment
see Recording industry

Phosphate
County Business Patterns, 1989: employment, establishments, and payroll, by SIC 2- to 4-digit industry and county, annual State rpt series, 2326–8
County Business Patterns, 1990: employment, establishments, and payroll, by SIC 2- to 4-digit industry and county, annual State rpt series, 2326–6
Exports and imports (agricultural) of US, by detailed commodity and country, 1991, semiannual rpt, 1522–4
Fertilizer (inorganic) shipments, trade, use, and firms, by product and State, with stocks, 1991, annual Current Industrial Rpt, 2506–8.13
Fertilizer consumption, by type and region, 1947-90, annual rpt, 1544–17.2
Freight (waterborne domestic and foreign) by commodity, traffic, and passengers, by port and waterway, 1989, annual rpt, 3754–3
Futures trading in selected commodities and financial instruments and indexes, for NYC, Chicago, and other markets activity, biweekly rpt, 11922–5
Manufacturing annual survey, 1990: finances and operations, by SIC 2- to 4-digit industry, series, 2506–14

Mineral Industry Surveys, commodity review of production, trade, and use, advance data, 1991, annual rpt, 5614–5.4
Mineral Industry Surveys, commodity review of production, trade, stocks, and use, monthly rpt, 5612–1.30
Minerals Yearbook, Vol 3, 1989: foreign country reviews of production, trade, and policy, by commodity, annual rpt, 5604–35
Mines (nonmetallic minerals) and related operations occupational injuries and incidence, employment, and hours, 1990, annual rpt, 6664–1
Price indexes (producer), by stage of processing and detailed commodity, monthly 1991, annual rpt, 6764–2
Production of phosphate rock, prices, sales, trade, and use, 1992, Mineral Industry Surveys, annual rpt, 5614–20
Production, prices, trade, and foreign and US industry devs, by commodity, bimonthly rpt, 5602–4
Production, prices, trade, use, employment, tariffs, and stockpiles, by mineral, with foreign comparisons, 1987-91, annual rpt, 5604–18

Photography and photographic equipment
County Business Patterns, 1989: employment, establishments, and payroll, by SIC 2- to 4-digit industry and county, annual State rpt series, 2326–8
County Business Patterns, 1990: employment, establishments, and payroll, by SIC 2- to 4-digit industry and county, annual State rpt series, 2326–6
CPI by component for US city average, and by selected metro area, region, and population size, monthly rpt, 6762–2
Employment, earnings, and hours, by SIC 1- to 4-digit industry, monthly 1989-Feb 1992, annual rpt, 6744–4
Exports and imports between US and outlying areas, by detailed commodity and mode of transport, 1991, annual rpt, 2424–11
Exports and imports of US, by country and detailed commodity, monthly rpt, 2422–12
Exports and imports of US, by Harmonized System 6-digit commodity and country, 1991, annual rpt, 2424–13
Exports and imports of US, by transport mode, country, and SITC 1- to 3-digit commodity, 1991, annual rpt, 2424–12
Exports of US, detailed Schedule B commodities with countries of destination, 1991, annual rpt, 2424–10
Fed Govt publications and other holdings of Natl Archives, special collections, series, 9516–1
Film (dry, photoresist) from Japan at less than fair value, injury to US industry, investigation with background financial and operating data, 1992 rpt, 9886–14.359
Film and paper (photographic) trade, tariffs, and industry operating data, 1992 rpt, 9885–10.4
Imports of US given duty-free treatment for value of US material sent abroad, by commodity and country, 1987-90, annual rpt, 9884–14
Injuries from use of consumer products, by severity, victim age, and detailed product, 1991, annual rpt, 9164–6
Input-output structure of US economy, detailed interindustry transactions for 541 industries, and components of final demand, 1982 benchmark data, 2708–17
Labor demand, turnover, and training completions, by detailed occupation, 1990 and projected to 2005, biennial rpt, 6744–3
Labor productivity, indexes of output, hours, and employment by SIC 2- to 4-digit industry, 1967-90, annual rpt, 6824–1.3
Library of Congress activities, acquisitions, services, and financial statements, FY91, annual rpt, 26404–1
Manufacturing annual survey, 1990: finances and operations, by SIC 2- to 4-digit industry, series, 2506–14
Manufacturing census, 1987: concentration of largest firms measured by value added, and for shipments by SIC 2- and 4-digit industry, subject rpt, 2497–6
Manufacturing census, 1987: shipments of manufacturers products, by customer class and SIC 2- and 4-digit industry, subject rpt, 2497–4
Manufacturing finances and operations, by SIC 2- to 4-digit industry, forecast 1992, annual rpt, 2044–28
Military prime contract awards, by category, contractor type, and State, FY89-91, annual rpt, 3544–11
Military prime contract awards, by detailed procurement category, FY88-91, annual rpt, 3544–18
Multinatl US firms and foreign affiliates finances and operations, by industry and country, 1989 benchmark survey, annual rpt, 2704–5
Natl Archives and Records Admin activities, finances, holdings, and staff, FY91, annual rpt, 9514–2
Occupational injury and illness rates, by SIC 2- to 4-digit industry, 1989-90, annual rpt, 6844–7
Occupational injury and illness rates, by SIC 2- to 4-digit industry, 1990, annual rpt, 6844–1
Occupational Outlook Handbook, 1992-93, biennial rpt, 6744–1
OECD trade, total and for 4 major countries, and US trade by country, by commodity, 1980-90, world area rpt series, 9116–1
Price indexes (producer), by stage of processing and detailed commodity, monthly rpt, 6762–6
Price indexes (producer), by stage of processing and detailed commodity, monthly 1991, annual rpt, 6764–2
Science, engineering, and technical employment in manufacturing, by field and industry, 1989, triennial rpt, 9627–23
Senate receipts, itemized expenses by payee, and balances, 1st half FY92, semiannual listing, 25922–1
Statistical Abstract of US, 1992 annual data compilation, 2324–1.7
Tax (income) returns of corporations, income and tax items by asset size and detailed industry, 1989, annual rpt, 8304–4; 8304–21
Tax (income) returns of sole proprietorships, income statement items, by industry group, 1990, annual article, 8302–2.317; 8302–2.320

PHS
see Public Health Service

Physical characteristics
see also Birthweight
see also Body measurements
see also Disabled and handicapped persons
see also Health condition
see also Obesity

Physical education and training
Special education programs, enrollment by age, staff, funding, and needs, by type of handicap and State, 1990/91, annual rpt, 4944–4

Physical exercise
Cancer (colon) risk for men relation to weight-height index at college entrance and in middle age, and level of physical exercise, 1962-88 study, article, 4472–1.339
Cancer (colon) risk relation to diet, aspirin use, exercise, and other factors, 1982-88, article, 4472–1.346
Deaths during 1986, decedents health condition, services use, habits, and social, employment, and other characteristics, 4147–20.19
Fed Govt employees physical fitness clubs memberships, agency costs, and personnel directors views on OPM guidelines and admin leave use, 1991-92, GAO rpt, 26119–393
Fed Govt financial and nonfinancial domestic aid, 1992 base edition, annual listing, 104–5
Health condition and care indicators, 1950s-90 with health improvement and disease prevention goals for 1990, annual data compilation, 4144–11
Health risk behavior, prevalence of 7 habits, by age, State, and other characteristics, 1986-90, article, 4202–7.305
Heart disease risk factors prevalence in Missouri, 1989-90, article, 4042–3.302
Households entertainment spending, recreation participation by activity, and video product and pet ownership, 1970s-90, article, 1702–1.303
Indian health risk behavior, by region and for Montana, mid 1980s, article, 4042–3.346
Injuries from use of consumer products and related activities, by severity and victim age and sex, 1990, annual rpt, 9164–7
Injuries from use of consumer products, by severity, victim age, and detailed product, 1991, annual rpt, 9164–6
Pulse rate relation to blood pressure and other physical, demographic, and behavioral characteristics, 1971-74, article, 4042–3.321
see also Physical education and training
see also Sports and athletics

Physical sciences
Degree (PhD) recipients in higher education, by field and selected characteristics, 1979, 1984, and 1989, 4848–44
Degrees awarded in higher education, by level, field, race, and sex, 1989/90 and trends from 1980/81, annual rpt, 4844–17
DOE R&D projects and funding at natl labs, universities, and other instns, periodic summary rpt series, 3004–18

Employment of scientists and engineers, and related topics, advance rpt series, 9626–8
Employment of scientists, engineers, and technicians in manufacturing, by field and industry, 1989, triennial rpt, 9627–23
Fed Govt aid to higher education and nonprofit instns for R&D and related activities, by field, instn, agency, and State, FY90, annual rpt, 9627–17
Higher education grad programs enrollment in science and engineering, by field, source of funds, and characteristics of student and instn, 1990, annual rpt, 9627–7
Labor demand, turnover, and training completions, by detailed occupation, 1990 and projected to 2005, biennial rpt, 6744–3
Minority group, women, and disabled persons employment and education in science and engineering, by field, mid 1970s-91, biennial rpt, 9624–20
NASA R&D funding to higher education instns, by field, instn, and State, FY91, annual listing, 9504–7
NSF activities, finances, and funding by program, FY91, annual rpt, 9624–6
Occupational Outlook Handbook, 1992-93, biennial rpt, 6744–1
R&D facilities of higher education instns, space and equipment adequacy, needs, and funding by source, by instn type and control, 1992, biennial rpt, 9624–25
R&D funding by higher education instns and federally funded centers, by field, instn, and State, FY90, annual rpt, 9627–13
Science and Engineering Indicators, employment, education, R&D funding, and industry impacts, with foreign comparisons, 1960s-91, biennial rpt, 9624–10
see also Astronomy
see also Chemistry
see also Earth sciences
see also Environmental sciences
see also Geography
see also Mathematics
see also Oceanography
see also Physics

Physical therapy
Hospital employment and job vacancy rate, by occupation, and instn size and control, 1981-88, annual rpt, 4114–12
Labor demand, turnover, and training completions, by detailed occupation, 1990 and projected to 2005, biennial rpt, 6744–3
Labor supply and education of health professionals, by professional and other characteristics, and location, 1960s-92 and projected to 2020, biennial rpt, 4114–8
Medicare admin and research, and HCFA affirmative action and accreditation programs, FY87, annual rpt, 4654–5
Medicare and Medicaid beneficiaries and program operations, 1992, annual fact book, 4654–18
Military health care personnel, and accessions by training source, by occupation, specialty, and service branch, FY90, annual rpt, 3544–24
Occupational Outlook Handbook, 1992-93, biennial rpt, 6744–1
Special education programs, enrollment by age, staff, funding, and needs, by type of handicap and State, 1990/91, annual rpt, 4944–4
VA health care staff and turnover, by occupation, physician specialty, and location, 1991, annual rpt, 8604–8

Physically handicapped
see Blind
see Deaf
see Disabled and handicapped persons

Physician Payment Review Commission
Medicare payment of physicians under fee schedule, methodology with data by procedure and specialty, 1992, annual rpt, 17264–1
Physicians payment by Medicare under fee schedule, analyses of costs and other issues, series, 17266–1
Physicians payment by Medicare under fee schedule, impacts on beneficiaries, practice, and program finances, series, 17266–2

Physicians
Acute and chronic health conditions, disability, absenteeism, and health services use, by selected characteristics, 1990, annual rpt, 4147–10.182; 4147–10.183
AIDS patients costs and service use under Medicaid, and service needs, for New Jersey waiver program, 1987-89, article, 4652–1.317
AIDS patients costs and service use under Medicaid, for California, 1984-86, article, 4652–1.301
AIDS virus-related Medicaid claims and payments, by sex, age, risk group, eligibility, and source of care, for Michigan, mid 1980s, article, 4042–3.348
Allergy and Infectious Diseases Natl Inst activities, grants by recipient and location, and disease cases, FY84-91, annual rpt, 4474–30
Blue Cross-Blue Shield plans changes in physician costs per enrollee and for selected procedures, mid 1980s, article, 4652–1.320
Child infectious disease cases, and related disability and health care, by disease, health insurance status, and other characteristics, 1988, 4147–10.181
Children (handicapped) with special needs, insurance coverage, and health care services use, by selected characteristics, 1988, 4146–8.216
Cholesterol treatment practices and views of primary care physicians, 1986 local area study, article, 4042–3.345
Community and migrant health center physicians hospital admitting privileges, status and issues, 1991, GAO rpt, 26121–465
Costs, use, and structure of private and public health care delivery, indicators, issues, and foreign comparisons, 1960s-80s, technical paper, 8006–6.1
County Business Patterns, 1989: employment, establishments, and payroll, by SIC 2- to 4-digit industry and county, annual State rpt series, 2326–8
County Business Patterns, 1990: employment, establishments, and payroll, by SIC 2- to 4-digit industry and county, annual State rpt series, 2326–6
CPI by component for US city average, and by selected metro area, region, and population size, monthly rpt, 6762–2
Czechoslovakia health care system, spending, and population health condition indicators, 1988-89, article, 4042–3.363
Data on health condition and care, indicators, 1988 natl survey, CD-ROM, 4147–10.184
Deaths during 1986, decedents health condition, services use, habits, and social, employment, and other characteristics, 4147–20.19
Developing countries population/physician ratios, by country, 1960s-92, annual rpt, 9904–4
Diabetes patients physician office visits, by characteristics of patient, physician, and visit, 1989, 4146–8.212
Drug (prescription) advertising in medical journals, accuracy, info completeness, and violations of FDA regulations, 1990, 4008–119
Education debt, specialties, and preferred practice setting for recent physician grads, and medical school funding sources, 1970s-91, hearing, 21368–135
Educational attainment relation to health condition and care, indicators by selected characteristics, 1989, 4147–10.180
Employment, earnings, and hours, by SIC 1- to 4-digit industry, monthly 1989-Feb 1992, annual rpt, 6744–4
Expenditures for health care and factors in costs, with data by payment source and service type, 1960s-90 and projected to 2000, 26306–6.175
Expenditures for health care by funding source, 1990, with trends and indexes by service type from 1960, article, 4652–1.323
Health Care Financing Review, provider prices, price inputs and indexes, and labor, quarterly journal, 4652–1.1
Health condition and care indicators, 1950s-90 with health improvement and disease prevention goals for 1990, annual data compilation, 4144–11
Hospital deaths of Medicare patients, actual and expected rates by diagnosis, with hospital characteristics, by instn, FY90, annual State rpt series, 4654–14
Hospital employment and job vacancy rate, by occupation, and instn size and control, 1981-88, annual rpt, 4114–12
Hospital outpatient and inpatient leading diagnoses and procedures, and costs by setting, 1987, article, 4652–1.314
Income, practice revenue, hours worked, and malpractice insurance premiums paid, for physicians, late 1970s-90, technical paper, 9366–6.296
Indian Health Service and tribal facility outpatient visits, by type of provider, selected hospital, and service area, FY91, annual rpt, 4084–3
Input-output structure of US economy, detailed interindustry transactions for 541 industries, and components of final demand, 1982 benchmark data, 2708–17
Insurance (health) coverage and provisions of employee benefit plans, by plan type, for State and local govt employees, 1990, biennial rpt, 6784–21

Internist office visits, by characteristics of patient, physician, and visit, 1989, 4146–8.214
Labor demand, turnover, and training completions, by detailed occupation, 1990 and projected to 2005, biennial rpt, 6744–3
Labor supply and education of health professionals, by professional and other characteristics, and location, 1960s-92 and projected to 2020, biennial rpt, 4114–8
Labor supply of physicians, by specialty, age, sex, and location of training and practice, 1990, State rpt series, 4116–6
Medicaid coverage, funding, and costs, with reform recommendations, mid 1960s-92, 10048–83
Medicaid outlay differentials among States, with data by service type and eligibility category, FY89, article, 9373–1.303
Medicaid payment and participation by service type, and cost compared to Medicare, by State, FY89, 17266–1.4
Medicare and Medicaid beneficiaries and program operations, 1992, annual fact book, 4654–18
Medicare and Medicaid enrollees, benefits, reimbursements, and services use, mid 1960s-90, annual rpt, 4744–3.5; 4744–3.6
Medicare payment of physicians, reforms impacts on services, and monitoring methods, 1992 annual rpt, 4004–34
Medicare payment of physicians under fee schedule, adjustment factor recommendations, 1993, annual rpt, 4004–33
Medicare payment of physicians under fee schedule, analyses of costs and other issues, series, 17266–1
Medicare payment of physicians under fee schedule, impacts on beneficiaries, practice, and program finances, series, 17266–2
Medicare payment of physicians under fee schedule, impacts on charges by specialty and State, 1992 and 1996, hearing, 25368–178
Medicare payment of physicians under fee schedule, methodology with data by procedure and specialty, 1992, annual rpt, 17264–1
Medicare payment of physicians under reasonable charge method, effect of customary charges in selected States, 1987-89, article, 4652–1.307
Medicare payment of physicians, volume performance standard recommendations, FY93, annual rpt, 4004–32
Medicare providers identification number assignment by carriers, operations, 1989-90, 4006–11.1
Medicare reimbursement of hospitals under prospective payment system, and effect on services, finances, and beneficiary payments, 1980-91, annual rpt, 17204–2
Medicare reimbursement of hospitals under prospective payment system, methodology, inputs, and data by diagnostic group, 1992 annual rpt, 17204–1
Mental health care facilities, staff, patients, and finances, 1970s-91, biennial rpt, 4094–1
Military health care benefits and costs under Civilian Health and Medical Program of Uniformed Services, FY85-90, annual chartbook, 3504–23
Military health care personnel, and accessions by training source, by occupation, specialty, and service branch, FY90, annual rpt, 3544–24
Military reserve medical personnel, by specialty and reserve component, FY91, annual rpt, 3544–31.1
Navy personnel strengths, accessions, and attrition, detailed statistics, quarterly rpt, 3802–4
Occupational Outlook Handbook, 1992-93, biennial rpt, 6744–1
OECD members health care costs, hospital use, resources, and economic and health indicators, by country, 1960s-90, article, 4652–1.322
Older persons health and long-term care needs, financial issues with background data, 1991 rpt, 10176–1.3
Older persons visits to physicians, by age group, and compared to nonaged, 1989, 12904–1
Oregon Medicaid waiver proposal for managed care, services priorities dev procedures and issues, with background data, 1992 rpt, 26358–254
Otitis media patients physician office visits, by specialty and characteristics of patient and visit, 1975-90, 4146–8.217
Population economic well-being indicators, by selected characteristics and household income and income-to-poverty ratio, 1984, 2546–20.22
Retirees health and other characteristics related to Medicare use and charges 2 years later, 1984, article, 4652–1.319
Rural areas health care access for counties without hospitals and in which the only hospital closed, 1987-89, 17206–2.30
Rural areas physician supply, by practice type, 1980s, article, 1502–7.304
Soviet Union and US economic and sociodemographic indicators, selected years 1970-90, handbook, 2328–80
Statistical Abstract of US, 1992 annual data compilation, 2324–1.3
Tax (income) returns of corporations, income and tax items by asset size and detailed industry, 1989, annual rpt, 8304–4; 8304–21
Tax (income) returns of partnerships, income statement and balance sheet items, by industry group, 1990, annual article, 8302–2.314
Tax (income) returns of sole proprietorships, income statement items, by industry group, 1990, annual article, 8302–2.317; 8302–2.320
Time and effort in patient visits, office personnel services, and coding manual use in billing, by selected specialty, 1989 survey, 17266–2.5
VA health care facilities employment, FY67-91, annual rpt, 8604–5.1
VA health care facilities physicians, dentists, and nurses, by selected employment characteristics and VA district, quarterly rpt, 8602–6
VA health care facilities trainees, by detailed program and city, FY91, annual rpt, 8704–4
VA health care professionals employment, by district and facility, quarterly rpt, 8602–4
VA health care services, needs, availability, structure, and funding, 1991 compilation of papers, 8608–9
VA health care staff and turnover, by occupation, physician specialty, and location, 1991, annual rpt, 8604–8
Veterans post-traumatic stress cases by period of service, and VA treatment and rehabilitation program operations and staff, by site, FY91, annual rpt, 8704–6
Visits to physicians, by patient and practice characteristics, diagnosis, and services provided, 1989, annual rpt, 4147–13.109
Visits to physicians, by patient and practice characteristics, diagnosis, and services provided, 1990, advance rpt, 4146–8.215
Workers compensation laws of States and Fed Govt, 1992 annual rpt, 6504–11
Youth health condition, risk factors, and preventive and treatment services use and availability, 1970s-80s, 26358–234.2; 26358–234.3
see also Anesthesiology
see also Foreign medical graduates
see also Geriatrics
see also Medical education
see also Medical ethics
see also Medical malpractice
see also Nuclear medicine and radiology
see also Obstetrics and gynecology
see also Orthopedics
see also Osteopathy
see also Pathology
see also Pediatrics
see also Podiatry
see also Psychiatry
see also Surgeons and surgery

Physics

Budget of US, obligations and authority by function, agency, and program, with summaries and analyses, FY93, annual rpt, 104–2
DOE R&D projects and funding at natl labs, universities, and other instns, FY91, annual summary rpt, 3004–18.3; 3004–18.4
Fed Govt aid to higher education and nonprofit instns for R&D and related activities, by field, instn, agency, and State, FY90, annual rpt, 9627–17
Higher education grad programs enrollment in science and engineering, by field, source of funds, and characteristics of student and instn, 1990, annual rpt, 9627–7
NASA R&D funding to higher education instns, by field, instn, and State, FY91, annual listing, 9504–7
Occupational Outlook Handbook, 1992-93, biennial rpt, 6744–1
R&D funding by higher education instns and federally funded centers, by field, instn, and State, FY90, annual rpt, 9627–13
Science and Engineering Indicators, employment, education, R&D funding, and industry impacts, with foreign comparisons, 1960s-91, biennial rpt, 9624–10
Superconducting super collider and other large-scale R&D projects of Fed Govt, issues and impacts on other research, 1991 hearings, 21268–43

Superconducting super collider construction costs, and funding by source, FY88-91 and projected to FY99, 3006–5.28
Superconducting Super Collider particle accelerator program of DOE, conventional facility construction funding and estimated and actual costs, 1988-99, 3006–5.32

Physiology
Aviation medicine research and test results, technical rpt series, 7506–10
Education in science and engineering, grad programs enrollment by field, source of funds, and characteristics of student and instn, 1990, annual rpt, 9627–7

Pierce County, Wash.
Housing and households characteristics, and unit and neighborhood quality, by MSA location for 11 MSAs, 1987 survey, supplement, 2485–8

Pierce, John P.
"Promoting Smoking Cessation in the U.S.: Effect of Public Service Announcements on the Cancer Information Service Telephone Line", 4472–1.313

Pierrot, Lane
"Structuring U.S. Forces After the Cold War: Costs and Effects of Increased Reliance on the Reserves", 26306–6.172

Pigments
see Dyeing and coloring materials
see Paints and varnishes

Pigott, Charles
"Determinants of Long-Term Interest Rates: An Empirical Study of Several Industrial Countries", 9385–1.301

Pilot projects
see Demonstration and pilot projects

Pilots
Accidents and circumstances, for US operations of domestic and foreign airlines and general aviation, periodic rpt, 9612–1
Accidents, casualties, and damage for air carriers, by detailed circumstances, 1988, annual rpt, 9614–2
Air traffic control and pilot errors, runway incursions, and near collisions, monthly rpt, 7502–15
Air traffic, pilots, airports, and fuel use, forecast FY92-2003 and trends from FY82, annual rpt, 7504–6
Certificates for pilots and nonpilots held and issued, by type of certificate, region, State, and for women, 1990, annual rpt, 7504–1.7
Certificates for pilots and nonpilots held, by type of certificate, age, sex, region, and State, 1991, annual rpt, 7504–2
Drug testing and results for airline and aviation safety employees, by drug type and occupational group, 1991, semiannual rpt, 7502–17
Eye defect (aphakia) and artificial lens implants among pilots, by sex and class of medical certificate, 1982-85, technical rpt, 7506–10.114
Flight service station workload of FAA, pilot briefs, contacts, and flight plans by facility, projected FY92-2002 and trends from FY83, annual rpt, 7504–39
General aviation pilots and aircraft, by FAA region and State, 1991, annual rpt, 7504–3.3
Instrument-rated and total pilots in Natl Airspace System, 1991-2005, annual rpt, 7504–12
Labor demand, turnover, and training completions, by detailed occupation, 1990 and projected to 2005, biennial rpt, 6744–3
Medical research and test results for aviation, technical rpt series, 7506–10
Occupational injuries, illnesses, and lost workdays, for commercial airline pilots and flight attendants, mid 1970s-88, article, 6722–1.320
Occupational Outlook Handbook, 1992-93, biennial rpt, 6744–1

Pine Bluff, Ark.
Wages by occupation, and benefits for office and plant workers, 1992 survey, periodic MSA rpt, 6785–3.4

Pineapples
see Fruit and fruit products

Pinellas County, Fla.
Housing and households characteristics, unit and neighborhood quality, and journey to work by MSA location, for 11 MSAs, 1985 survey, supplement, 2485–8

Pinkston, Elizabeth
"Paying for Highways, Airways, and Waterways: How Can Users Be Charged?", 26306–6.170

Pipelines
Bridges over navigable waters, with type of bridge and use, owner, dimensions, and location, 1991 regional listing series, 7406–5
Coal and coke production, shipments, and trade, by State of origin and destination, end-use sector, and mode of transport, quarterly rpt, 3162–37.1
Coal production, stocks, and shipments, by State of origin and destination, end-use sector, and mode of transport, quarterly rpt, 3162–8
Construction put in place and cost indexes, by type of construction, quarterly rpt, 2042–1.1; 2042–1.5
Construction put in place, value of new public and private structures, by type, monthly rpt, 2382–4
County Business Patterns, 1989: employment, establishments, and payroll, by SIC 2- to 4-digit industry and county, annual State rpt series, 2326–8
County Business Patterns, 1990: employment, establishments, and payroll, by SIC 2- to 4-digit industry and county, annual State rpt series, 2326–6
DOT activities by subagency, budget, and summary accident data, FY89, annual rpt, 7304–1
DOT planning and safety grants, by program, State, and for 40 SMSAs, FY89, annual rpt, 7304–7
Employment, earnings, and hours, by SIC 1- to 4-digit industry, monthly 1989-Feb 1992, annual rpt, 6744–4
Energy producers finances and operations, by energy type for US firms domestic and foreign operations, 1990, annual rpt, 3164–44.1
Energy use by fuel type, and miles traveled, by transport mode, projected 1990-2010 and trends from 1960s, 3008–124
Energy use by mode of transport, fuel supply, and demographic and economic factors of vehicle use, 1970s-90, annual rpt, 3304–5
Exports and imports between US and outlying areas, by detailed commodity and mode of transport, 1991, annual rpt, 2424–11
Exports and imports of US, by Harmonized System 6-digit commodity and country, 1991, annual rpt, 2424–13
Exports of US, detailed Schedule B commodities with countries of destination, 1991, annual rpt, 2424–10
Foreign countries economic, social, political, and geographic summary data, by country, 1992, annual factbook, 9114–2
Input-output structure of US economy, detailed interindustry transactions for 541 industries, and components of final demand, 1982 benchmark data, 2708–17
Inspections of pipelines using internal electronic devices, costs and effectiveness, 1985-91, GAO rpt, 26113–594
Labor productivity, indexes of output, hours, and employment by SIC 2- to 4-digit industry, 1967-90, annual rpt, 6824–1.4
Military and personal property shipments, passenger traffic, and costs, by service branch and mode of transport, FY91, annual rpt, 3704–15
Multinatl firms US affiliates finances and operations, by industry, country of parent firm, and State, 1987, 2708–48
Natural and supplemental gas production, prices, trade, use, reserves, and pipeline company finances, by firm and State, monthly rpt with articles, 3162–4
Natural gas composition and helium levels, analyses of individual wells and pipelines, by selected State and county, 1986-90, 5608–132
Natural gas composition and helium levels, analyses of individual wells and pipelines, 1985-91, annual rpt, 5604–2
Natural gas interstate pipeline capacity, use, contract deliveries, and prices, by region, State, and firm, 1990, 3168–125
Natural gas interstate pipeline company detailed financial and operating data, by firm, 1990, annual rpt, 3164–38
Natural gas interstate pipeline company reserves and production, by firm, 1963-91 and deliverability projected to 2011, last issue of annual rpt, 3164–33
Natural gas interstate pipeline company sales and price trends, monthly rpt, 3162–24.4; 3162–24.9
Natural gas interstate pipeline company sales and price trends, monthly 1973-88, 3168–123.4; 3168–123.9
Natural gas pipelines and owners, and fields, as of Sept 1990, map, 3088–21
Natural gas supply, demand, prices, and distribution, by State, 1986-90 annual rpt, 3164–4
Natural gas trade over pipelines, alternative projections, 1990-2010, annual rpt, 3164–96
Occupational injury and illness rates, by SIC 2- to 4-digit industry, 1989-90, annual rpt, 6844–7
Occupational injury and illness rates, by SIC 2- to 4-digit industry, 1990, annual rpt, 6844–1
Offshore oil and gas reserves of Fed Govt, production, leasing and exploration activity, revenue, and costs, by ocean area, FY91, annual rpt, 5734–4

Oil and refined products stocks, and interdistrict shipments by mode of transport, monthly rpt, 3162–6.3
Oil company effective income tax rates, with background income and tax data for domestic and foreign operations, 1977-89, 3168–124
Oil crude, gas liquids, and refined products supply, demand, and movement, by PAD district and State, 1991, annual rpt, 3164–2
Pacific basin countries energy supply and demand, and implications for US trade, country rpt series, 3406–6
Price indexes (producer), by stage of processing and detailed commodity, monthly rpt, 6762–6
Price indexes (producer), by stage of processing and detailed commodity, monthly 1991, annual rpt, 6764–2
Reclamation Bur irrigation activities, finances, and project impacts in western US, 1990, annual rpt, 5824–12
Soviet Union and US economic and sociodemographic indicators, selected years 1970-90, handbook, 2328–80
Soviet Union former Republics and Baltic States energy supply and use, and social, economic, and political indicators, 1989-90, 3168–126
Statistical Abstract of US, 1992 annual data compilation, 2324–1.21
Tax (income) returns of corporations, income and tax items by asset size and detailed industry, 1989, annual rpt, 8304–4; 8304–21
Water storage and carriage facilities of Reclamation Bur, capacity, and operating status, as of Sept 1990, biennial listing, 5824–7
see also Trans-Alaska Pipeline System

Pisano, Paul A.
"Investigation of Passing Accidents on Two-Lane, Two-Way Roads", 7552–3.301

Pisarski, Alan E.
"New Perspectives in Commuting, Based on Early Data from the 1990 Decennial Census and the 1990 Nationwide Personal Transportation Study", 7558–120
"Travel Behavior Issues in the 1990's: 1990 Nationwide Personal Transportation Survey", 7556–6.3

Pistachios
see Nuts

Pitcher, C. B.
"Construction Material Trends: Data from the Census and Survey of Manufactures", 2042–1.302

Pittsburgh, Pa.
CPI by component for US city average, and by region, population size, and for 15 metro areas, monthly rpt, 6762–1
CPI by component for US city average, and by selected metro area, region, and population size, monthly rpt, 6762–2
Freight (waterborne domestic and foreign) by commodity, traffic, and passengers, by port and waterway, 1989, annual rpt, 3754–3.2
Fruit and vegetable shipments, and arrivals by city, by mode of transport and State and country of origin, 1991, annual rpt, 1311–4.1
Govt finances, structure, and service delivery, 1992 local area rpt, 10046–9.2
Housing and households characteristics, and unit and neighborhood quality, by MSA location for 11 MSAs, 1986 survey, supplement, 2485–8
Unemployed displaced workers job search and placement aid effectiveness, relation to previous employment and other characteristics, 1979-87 studies, 15496–1.14
Wages by occupation, and benefits, for office and plant workers, 1992 survey, periodic MSA rpt, 6785–17.1
see also under By City and By SMSA or MSA in the "Index by Categories"

Place of birth
see Birthplace

Planned parenthood
see Contraceptives
see Family planning

Planning
see City and town planning
see Economic policy
see Health planning and evaluation
see Logistics
see Military strategy
see Regional planning

Plants and equipment
see Business firms and establishments, number
see Capital investments, general
see Capital investments, specific industry
see Electric power plants and equipment
see Industrial plants and equipment
see Industrial robots

Plants and vegetation
Alaska Copper River Delta wetland environmental conditions, 1987, 1208–401
Camping in wilderness areas, impacts on plants and soils, 1979-90 studies, 1208–395
Coastal and riparian areas environmental conditions, fish, wildlife, use, and mgmt, for individual ecosystems, series, 5506–9
Exports and imports of US, by country and detailed commodity, monthly rpt, 2422–12
Exports and imports of US, by transport mode, country, and SITC 1- to 3-digit commodity, 1991, annual rpt, 2424–12
Fires on wildlands, ecology, mgmt, cultural impacts, and historic patterns, 1990 conf, 1208–415
Global climate change impacts on mountain grassland vegetation, monitoring study results, 1969 and 1988, 1208–425
Idaho Snake River area birds of prey, rodent, and vegetation distribution and characteristics, research results, 1991, annual rpt, 5724–14
Natl historic and natural landmarks damaged and threatened, with owner, location, damage type, and recommended remedial action, 1990, annual listing, 5544–16
Pacific Northwest old-growth forests plant and wildlife population and species diversity, 1991 compilation of papers, 1208–386
Radiation and other pollutant releases from DOE contractor research lab and nuclear weapons facilities, monitoring results, annual site rpt series, 3324–2
Research on fish and wildlife population, habitat, and mgmt, technical rpt series, 5506–12
Water quality, chemistry, hydrology, and other characteristics, local area studies, series, 5666–27
Wetlands acid neutralizing capability for mining runoff, with pollutant levels and site characteristics, for Pennsylvania, 1987-90, 5608–171
Wetlands and riparian soil and plant characteristics, series, 5506–10
see also Botany
see also Farms and farmland
see also Flowers and nursery products
see also Forests and forestry
see also Horticulture
see also Pasture and rangeland

Plastics and plastics industry
Bottles (plastic) production, shipments, and firms, by end use, annual rpt, discontinued, 2506–8.10
Building materials production and PPI, by type, quarterly rpt, 2042–1.5; 2042–1.6
Business statistics, detailed data for major industries and economic indicators, *Survey of Current Business*, monthly rpt, 2702–1.11
Business statistics, detailed data for major industries and economic indicators, 1960-91, *Survey of Current Business* biennial supplement, 2704–1
County Business Patterns, 1989: employment, establishments, and payroll, by SIC 2- to 4-digit industry and county, annual State rpt series, 2326–8
County Business Patterns, 1990: employment, establishments, and payroll, by SIC 2- to 4-digit industry and county, annual State rpt series, 2326–6
Employment, earnings, and hours, by SIC 1- to 4-digit industry, monthly 1989-Feb 1992, annual rpt, 6744–4
Employment of minorities and women, by occupation, SIC 1- to 3-digit industry, State, and MSA, 1991, annual rpt, 9244–1
Energy use and prices for manufacturing industries, 1988 survey, series, 3166–13
Exports and imports between US and outlying areas, by detailed commodity and mode of transport, 1991, annual rpt, 2424–11
Exports and imports of US, by country and detailed commodity, monthly rpt, 2422–12
Exports and imports of US, by Harmonized System 6-digit commodity and country, 1991, annual rpt, 2424–13
Exports and imports of US, by selected country, country group, and commodity group, 1991, annual rpt, 2044–37
Exports and imports of US, by transport mode, country, and SITC 1- to 3-digit commodity, 1991, annual rpt, 2424–12
Exports, imports, and balances of US for manufactured goods, by SITC 2-digit commodity and country, quarterly rpt, 2042–35
Exports of US, detailed commodities by country, monthly CD-ROM, 2422–13
Exports of US, detailed Schedule B commodities with countries of destination, 1991, annual rpt, 2424–10

Freight (waterborne domestic and foreign) by commodity, traffic, and passengers, by port and waterway, 1989, annual rpt, 3754–3
Hose and belting shipments, trade, use, and firms, by product, annual Current Industrial Rpt, discontinued, 2506–8.12
Imports, exports, and employment impacts, by SIC 2- to 4-digit industry and commodity, quarterly rpt, 2322–2
Imports of US, detailed commodities by country, monthly CD-ROM, 2422–14
Injuries from use of consumer products, by severity, victim age, and detailed product, 1991, annual rpt, 9164–6
Input-output structure of US economy, detailed interindustry transactions for 84 industries, and components of final demand, 1987, annual article, 2702–1.316
Input-output structure of US economy, detailed interindustry transactions for 541 industries, and components of final demand, 1982 benchmark data, 2708–17
Labor productivity, indexes of output, hours, and employment by SIC 2- to 4-digit industry, 1967-90, annual rpt, 6824–1.3
Manufacturing annual survey, 1990: finances and operations, by SIC 2- to 4-digit industry, series, 2506–14
Manufacturing census, 1987: concentration of largest firms measured by value added, and for shipments by SIC 2- and 4-digit industry, subject rpt, 2497–6
Manufacturing census, 1987: shipments of manufacturers products, by customer class and SIC 2- and 4-digit industry, subject rpt, 2497–4
Manufacturing corporations financial statements, by selected SIC 2- to 3-digit industry, quarterly rpt, 2502–1
Manufacturing finances and operations, by SIC 2- to 4-digit industry, forecast 1992, annual rpt, 2044–28
Multinatl firms US affiliates finances and operations, by industry, country of parent firm, and State, 1987, 2708–48
Multinatl US firms and foreign affiliates finances and operations, by industry and country, 1989 benchmark survey, annual rpt, 2704–5
Occupational injury and illness rates, by SIC 2- to 4-digit industry, 1989-90, annual rpt, 6844–7
Occupational injury and illness rates, by SIC 2- to 4-digit industry, 1990, annual rpt, 6844–1
OECD trade, total and for 4 major countries, and US trade by country, by commodity, 1980-90, world area rpt series, 9116–1
Oil and fat production, consumption by end use, and stocks, by type, monthly Current Industrial Rpt, 2506–4.4
Packaging materials by resin type, and municipal solid waste composition by weight, 1990-91, article, 9882–16.301
Plumbing fixtures shipments, stocks, trade, use, and firms, by product, quarterly Current Industrial Rpt, 2506–11.2
Price indexes (producer), by stage of processing and detailed commodity, monthly rpt, 6762–6
Price indexes (producer), by stage of processing and detailed commodity, monthly 1991, annual rpt, 6764–2
Production and sales of synthetic organic chemicals, and manufacturer listing, by product, 1990, annual rpt, 9884–3
Production of synthetic organic chemicals, by detailed product, quarterly rpt, 9882–1
Recycling of municipal and industrial waste, costs, revenues, and secondary products trade and related energy use and pollution reductions, 1991 hearings, 21368–139
Science, engineering, and technical employment in manufacturing, by field and industry, 1989, triennial rpt, 9627–23
Shoe production, shipments, trade, and use, by product, 1991, annual Current Industrial Rpt, 2506–6.8
Tariff Schedule of US, classifications and rates of duty by detailed imported commodity, 1993 base edition, 9886–13
Tax (income) returns of corporations, income and tax items by asset size and detailed industry, 1989, annual rpt, 8304–4; 8304–21
see also Petrochemicals
see also Polymers
see also under By Commodity in the "Index by Categories"
see also under By Industry in the "Index by Categories"

Plato, Gerald
"Managing Price Risk with Diammonium Phosphate and Anhydrous Ammonia Futures Contracts", 1561–16.301

Plumbing and heating
Business statistics, detailed data for major industries and economic indicators, *Survey of Current Business*, monthly rpt, 2702–1.16
Business statistics, detailed data for major industries and economic indicators, 1960-91, *Survey of Current Business* biennial supplement, 2704–1
Census of Population and Housing, 1990: summary characteristics, by county, subdiv, and place, State rpt series, 2551–7
Commercial buildings energy use, costs, and conservation, by building characteristics, survey rpt series, 3166–8
County Business Patterns, 1989: employment, establishments, and payroll, by SIC 2- to 4-digit industry and county, annual State rpt series, 2326–8
County Business Patterns, 1990: employment, establishments, and payroll, by SIC 2- to 4-digit industry and county, annual State rpt series, 2326–6
Employment, earnings, and hours, by SIC 1- to 4-digit industry, monthly 1989-Feb 1992, annual rpt, 6744–4
Energy aid for low income households, coverage and impacts on energy use and costs, selected years FY79-89, 4588–2
Energy aid for low income households, funding sources, costs, and participation, by State, FY90, annual rpt, 4584–1
Energy conservation programs of States, Federal aid and savings, by State, 1990, annual rpt, 3304–1
Energy conservation technologies for housing and commercial buildings, use, costs, efficiency, and residential tax credits, 1970s-90 and projected to 2010, 26358–259
Energy natl strategy Strategic Petroleum Reserve and energy efficiency issues, 1991 hearings, 21368–142
Energy supply, demand, and prices, by fuel type and end-use sector, projections and underlying assumptions, 1995-2010, annual rpt, 3164–90
Energy supply, demand, and prices, by fuel type and end-use sector, with foreign comparisons, 1991 and trends from 1949, annual rpt, 3164–74
Energy use, costs, and conservation, and household and housing characteristics, survey rpt series, 3166–7
Exports and imports between US and outlying areas, by detailed commodity and mode of transport, 1991, annual rpt, 2424–11
Exports and imports of US, by Harmonized System 6-digit commodity and country, 1991, annual rpt, 2424–13
Exports, imports, tariffs, and industry operating data for household appliances and heating equipment, 1992 rpt, 9885–9.4
Exports of US, detailed Schedule B commodities with countries of destination, 1991, annual rpt, 2424–10
Furnace shipments, trade, use, and firms, 1991, annual Current Industrial Rpt, 2506–12.7
Heating equipment shipments, inventories, exports, and firms, by product, annual Current Industrial Rpt, discontinued, 2506–11.6
Home mortgages FHA-insured, financial, property, and borrower characteristics, by metro area, 1991, annual rpt, 5144–24
Home mortgages FHA-insured, financial, property, and borrower characteristics, by State, 1991, annual rpt, 5144–1; 5144–25
Home mortgages FHA-insured, financial, property, and borrower characteristics, 1991, annual rpt, 5144–17; 5144–23
Households (single person and nonfamily) social, economic and housing characteristics, by tenure, 1989, 2486–1.15
Housing (low income) energy aid, program characteristics by assistance type and State, FY91, annual rpt, 4584–2
Housing (rental) units, total, with HUD assistance by program, and eligible for aid, by unit, household, and neighborhood characteristics, and location, 1989, biennial rpt, 5184–11
Housing alteration and repair for owner-occupied units, costs and structural, household, financial, and project characteristics, 1987, 2486–1.13
Housing alteration and repair spending, by property and job characteristics, and region, quarterly rpt, annual tables, 2382–7.2
Housing and households characteristics, and unit and neighborhood quality, by MSA location for 11 MSAs, 1987 survey, supplement, 2485–8
Housing and households characteristics, MSA surveys, fact sheet series, 2485–11
Housing and households detailed characteristics, and unit and neighborhood quality, by location, 1989, biennial rpt supplement, 2485–13

Housing and households detailed characteristics, and unit and neighborhood quality, MSA surveys, series, 2485–6
Housing and population census, 1990: population and housing characteristics, detailed geographic coverage, State CD-ROM series, 2551–10
Housing unit and household characteristics of recent movers, and reason for move, by tenure, 1989, 2486–1.12
Housing units completed, single and multifamily units by structural and financial characteristics, and location, 1987-91, annual rpt, 2384–1
Housing units completed, single and multifamily units by structural characteristics, monthly rpt, quarterly tables, 2382–2.2
Indian Health Service funding for housing sanitary facilities, and needs, FY60-91, annual rpt, 4084–1
Injuries from use of consumer products and related activities, by severity and victim age and sex, 1990, annual rpt, 9164–7
Injuries from use of consumer products, by severity, victim age, and detailed product, 1991, annual rpt, 9164–6
Injuries from use of consumer products, related deaths and costs, and recalls by brand, by product type, FY90, annual rpt, 9164–2
Input-output structure of US economy, detailed interindustry transactions for 541 industries, and components of final demand, 1982 benchmark data, 2708–17
Labor productivity, indexes of output, hours, and employment by SIC 2- to 4-digit industry, 1967-90, annual rpt, 6824–1.3
Manufacturing annual survey, 1990: finances and operations, by SIC 2- to 4-digit industry, series, 2506–14
Manufacturing census, 1987: concentration of largest firms measured by value added, and for shipments by SIC 2- and 4-digit industry, subject rpt, 2497–6
Manufacturing census, 1987: shipments of manufacturers products, by customer class and SIC 2- and 4-digit industry, subject rpt, 2497–4
Manufacturing finances and operations, by SIC 2- to 4-digit industry, forecast 1992, annual rpt, 2044–28
Military prime contract awards, by detailed procurement category, FY88-91, annual rpt, 3544–18
NYC housing supply, occupancy, condition, and household characteristics, by tenure and borough, 1991 triennial survey, 2488–3
Occupational injury and illness rates, by SIC 2- to 4-digit industry, 1989-90, annual rpt, 6844–7
Occupational injury and illness rates, by SIC 2- to 4-digit industry, 1990, annual rpt, 6844–1
Pacific territories population and housing detailed characteristics, by location, 1990 Census of Population and Housing, series, 2551–8
Pipe fittings (carbon steel) from 2 countries at less than fair value, injury to US industry, investigation with background financial and operating data, 1992 rpt, 9886–14.352
Pipe fittings (stainless steel) from 2 countries at less than fair value, injury to US industry, investigation with background financial and operating data, 1992 rpt, 9886–14.354
Pipes (welded stainless steel) from South Korea and Taiwan at less than fair value, injury to US industry, investigation with background financial and operating data, 1992 rpt, 9886–14.338; 9886–14.365
Pipes and tubes (welded nonalloy steel) from 6 countries at less than fair value, injury to US industry, investigation with background financial and operating data, 1992 rpt, 9886–14.361
Price indexes (producer), by stage of processing and detailed commodity, monthly rpt, 6762–6
Producer price indexes, by stage of processing and detailed commodity, monthly 1991, annual rpt, 6764–2
Production of plumbing fixtures, and imports from US and other sources, for 15 countries, 1991 rpt, 2048–156
Production, shipments, and PPI for building materials, by type, quarterly rpt, 2042–1.5; 2042–1.6
R&D facilities of higher education instns, space and equipment adequacy, needs, and funding by source, by instn type and control, 1992, biennial rpt, 9624–25
Shipments, trade, use, and firms, for appliances by product, 1991, annual Current Industrial Rpt, 2506–12.16
Single parent families in own and others homes, by financial, housing, and other characteristics, 1989, 2486–1.14
Solar collector and photovoltaic cell shipments by end-use sector and State, and trade, 1990, annual rpt, 3164–62
Statistical Abstract of US, 1992 annual data compilation, 2324–1.26
Tax (income) returns of corporations, income and tax items by asset size and detailed industry, 1989, annual rpt, 8304–4; 8304–21
TVA electric power purchases of municipal and cooperative distributors, and prices and use by distributor and consumer sector, monthly rpt, 9802–1
Waterworks compact ductile iron fittings from PRC at less than fair value, injury to US industry, investigation with background financial and operating data, 1992 rpt, 9886–14.358
see also Air conditioning
see also Electric power and heat cogeneration
see also Household appliances and equipment

Plummer, Charles
"U.S. Tomato Statistics, 1960-90", 1568–310

Pluta, Mark J.
"Early Estimates. National Postsecondary Statistics, Collegiate and Noncollegiate: Fall 1991", 4844–16

Pneumonia and influenza
AIDS patient vaccination schedules for prevention of *Pneumocystis carinii*, dosages, and precautions, CDC recommendations, 1992 rpt, 4206–2.54
Cases of acute and chronic conditions, disability, absenteeism, and health services use, by selected characteristics, 1990, annual rpt, 4147–10.182; 4147–10.183
Child infectious disease cases, and related disability and health care, by disease, health insurance status, and other characteristics, 1988, 4147–10.181
Deaths and rates, by cause, age, sex, marital status, race, and State, 1989, US Vital Statistics advance annual rpt, 4146–5.124
Deaths and rates, by cause and age, preliminary 1990-91, US Vital Statistics annual rpt, 4144–7
Deaths and rates, by cause and selected social, demographic, and employment characteristics, 1979-85, natl longitudinal study, 4478–186
Deaths and rates, by cause, provisional data, monthly rpt, 4142–1.2
Deaths and rates, by detailed location, cause, and demographic characteristics, 1989, US Vital Statistics annual rpt, 4144–3
Deaths recorded in 121 cities, weekly rpt, 4202–1
Health condition and care indicators, 1950s-90 with health improvement and disease prevention goals for 1990, annual data compilation, 4144–11
Hospital deaths of Medicare patients, actual and expected rates by diagnosis, with hospital characteristics, by instn, FY90, annual State rpt series, 4654–14
Influenza cases, by strain, 1983-91, article, 4202–7.316
Influenza cases, by strain, 1986-92, article, 4202–7.325
Morbidity and Mortality Weekly Report, infectious notifiable disease cases by State, and public health issues, 4202–1
OECD members health care costs, hospital use, resources, and economic and health indicators, by country, 1960s-90, article, 4652–1.322
Vaccination for influenza, schedules, dosages, and precautions, CDC guidelines, 1992 rpt, 4206–2.59

Podgursky, Michael
"Industrial Structure of Job Displacement, 1979-89", 6722–1.340

Podiatry
County Business Patterns, 1989: employment, establishments, and payroll, by SIC 2- to 4-digit industry and county, annual State rpt series, 2326–8
County Business Patterns, 1990: employment, establishments, and payroll, by SIC 2- to 4-digit industry and county, annual State rpt series, 2326–6
Degrees awarded in higher education, by level, field, race, and sex, 1989/90 and trends from 1980/81, annual rpt, 4844–17
Health condition and care indicators, 1950s-90 with health improvement and disease prevention goals for 1990, annual data compilation, 4144–11
HHS financial aid, by program, recipient, State, and city, FY91, annual regional listings, 4004–3
Indian Health Service and tribal facility outpatient visits, by type of provider, selected hospital, and service area, FY91, annual rpt, 4084–3
Labor demand, turnover, and training completions, by detailed occupation, 1990 and projected to 2005, biennial rpt, 6744–3

Labor supply and education of health professionals, by professional and other characteristics, and location, 1960s-92 and projected to 2020, biennial rpt, 4114–8
Medicare payment of physicians under fee schedule, methodology with data by procedure and specialty, 1992, annual rpt, 17264–1
Military health care personnel, and accessions by training source, by occupation, specialty, and service branch, FY90, annual rpt, 3544–24
Occupational Outlook Handbook, 1992-93, biennial rpt, 6744–1
VA health care facilities trainees, by detailed program and city, FY91, annual rpt, 8704–4
VA health care services, needs, availability, structure, and funding, 1991 compilation of papers, 8608–9

Poisoning and drug reaction
AIDS patient vaccination schedules for prevention of *Pneumocystis carinii*, dosages, and precautions, CDC recommendations, 1992 rpt, 4206–2.54
Alcohol-related deaths, by cause, State, and county, annual averages 1979-80 and 1983-85, 4488–10.4
Drug abuse indicators for selected metro areas, research results, data collection, and policy issues, 1992 semiannual conf, 4492–5
Health condition and care indicators, 1950s-90 with health improvement and disease prevention goals for 1990, annual data compilation, 4144–11
Hepatitis B eradication through universal childhood vaccination, with schedules, dosages, and precautions, CDC recommendations, 1991 rpt, 4206–2.49
HHS financial aid, by program, recipient, State, and city, FY91, annual regional listings, 4004–3
Homicides, by circumstance, victim and offender relationship, and type of weapon, 1991, annual rpt, 6224–2.1
Influenza vaccination schedules, dosages, and precautions, CDC recommendations, 1992 rpt, 4206–2.59
Injuries from use of consumer products, by severity, victim age, and detailed product, 1991, annual rpt, 9164–6
Occupational illness rates, by cause and SIC 2- to 3-digit industry, 1990, annual rpt, 6844–1
Pollutants health effects, concentrations in food and environment, sources, human intake, and regulation, series, 9186–8
Pollutants health effects for animals by species and for humans, and environmental levels, for selected substances, series, 5506–14
Prevention of accidental injury and death, and treatment, 1991 conf papers, 4208–35
Research and testing activities under Natl Toxicology Program, FY90 and planned FY91, annual rpt, 4044–16
Vaccination for pertussis, schedules, dosages, and precautions, CDC guidelines, 1992 rpt, 4206–2.51
Vaccination for smallpox, schedules, dosages, and precautions, CDC guidelines, 1991 rpt, 4206–2.50
Vaccination of adults for selected diseases, by age and target group, schedules, dosages, and precautions, CDC guidelines, 1991 rpt, 4206–2.48
Vaccine (acellular) for pertussis, CDC guidelines for schedules, dosages, and precautions, 1992 rpt, 4206–2.65
Vaccine adverse reactions, Morbidity and Mortality Weekly Report, 4202–1
see also Food and waterborne diseases
see also Lead poisoning and pollution

Poland
Agricultural trade of US, by detailed commodity and country, 1991, annual rpt, 1524–8
Agricultural trade of US, by detailed commodity and country, 1991, semiannual rpt, 1522–4
Agricultural trade of US with Eastern Europe, by commodity group and country, 1988-91, 1928–11
AID economic aid to developing countries, obligations and disbursements by country, quarterly rpt, 9912–4
AID loans repayment status and terms by program and country, and status of predecessor agency loans, quarterly rpt, 9912–3
Economic and military aid and loans from US and intl agencies, by program and country, FY46-91, annual rpt, 9914–5
Economic and social conditions of developing countries from 1960s, and Intl Dev Cooperation Agency and AID activities and funding, FY91-93, annual rpt, 9904–4
Economic conditions, policy, and trade practices, by country, 1989-91, annual rpt, 21384–5
Economic, social, political, and geographic summary data, by country, 1992, annual factbook, 9114–2
Export industries dev potential, with trade and industry finances and operations, for 5 Eastern Europe countries, 1985-90, 9886–4.179
Export licensing, monitoring, and enforcement activities, FY91, annual rpt, 2024–1
Exports and imports of US, by commodity and country, 1980-90, world area rpt, 9116–1.1
Exports and imports of US, by transport mode, country, and SITC 1- to 3-digit commodity, 1991, annual rpt, 2424–12
Exports and imports of US with Communist and transitional economy countries, by detailed commodity and country, quarterly rpt with articles, 9882–2
Exports and imports of US with Eastern Europe, by commodity and country, 1987-91 and outlook for 1992, 2048–158
Exports, imports, and balances of US for manufactured goods, by SITC 2-digit commodity and country, quarterly rpt, 2042–35
Exports of Poland and Hungary, by world area, 1988-91, GAO rpt, 26123–386
Exports of US, detailed Schedule B commodities with countries of destination, 1991, annual rpt, 2424–10
Human rights conditions in 170 countries, and US economic and military aid, 1991, annual rpt, 21384–3
Imports of goods, services, and investment from US, trade barriers, impacts, and US actions, by country, 1991, annual rpt, 444–2
Market economy transition of Eastern Europe countries, trade, and foreign investment, by country, 1990-91, 9118–13
Military aid of US, arms sales, and training programs costs and budget requests, by program, world region, and country, FY91-93, annual rpt, 7144–13
Military spending, arms trade, and force strengths, with govt spending and population, by country, 1979-89, annual rpt, 9824–1
Minerals production of Poland, by commodity, 1988-90, annual rpt, 5604–39
Pension systems finances and provisions in Eastern Europe, 1950s-90 and alternative projections to 2025, technical paper, 8006–6.7
Pollution (air) contributing to global warming, emissions by monitoring site and country, and temperature change by world area and US region, 1860s-1990, annual rpt, 3004–33
Population size, growth rates, and components of change, by country, projected 1990-2020 and trends from 1950, biennial rpt, 2324–9
Refugee migration, and intl aid programs, by world area and country of origin and asylum, 1991, annual rpt, 7004–15
Steel (carbon flat-rolled) products from 21 countries, injury to US industry from foreign subsidized and less than fair value imports, investigation with background financial and operating data, 1992 rpt, 9886–19.85
Steel imports of US under voluntary restraint agreement, by product, customs district, and country, with US industry operating data, quarterly rpt, 9882–13
Steel trade, by product, country, and customs district, with US industry operating data, 1989-June 1992, semiannual rpt, 9882–15
Tax reform issues in transition to market economy, with tax rates, revenue, and govt spending compared to EC, by selected country, late 1960s-91, technical paper, 9366–7.278
UN voting record and share of votes in agreement with US, by issue, country, and world area, 1991, annual rpt, 7004–18

Polar bears
see Marine mammals

Polednak, Anthony P.
"Awareness and Use of Blood Cholesterol Tests in 40—74-Year-Olds by Educational Level", 4042–3.335

Police
Auto fleet size, trip characteristics, and energy use, by fleet type, 1970s-90, annual rpt, 3304–5.3
Bombing incidents and casualties, by target, circumstances, and State, 1987-91, annual rpt, 8484–4.1
Bombing incidents, casualties, and damage, by target, circumstances, and State, 1991, annual rpt, 6224–5
Crime, criminal justice admin and enforcement, and public opinion, data compilation, 1992 annual rpt, 6064–6

Crime victimization, by offense and whether reported to police, 1990-91, press release, 6068–249
Crime victimization rates, by offense, reasons for reporting and not reporting crime to police, and police response, 1990 survey, annual rpt, 6066–3.47
Drug control street-level task forces enforcement activities, impacts on crime, and residents views, local area studies, 1992 rpt, 6068–251
Drug enforcement activities of police and sheriff depts, and employee drug testing policies, 1990, 6066–19.67
Employee benefit plan coverage and provisions, by plan type, for State and local govt employees, 1990, biennial rpt, 6784–21
Employment and payroll, by activity, level of govt, and State, FY90, annual rpt, 6066–25.50
Employment and payroll, by function and level of govt, annual rpt series, 2466–1
Employment, funding, data collection, and other activities of State criminal justice systems, by State, 1970s-91, annual rpt, 6064–40
Employment of State and local law enforcement personnel and officers, by sex, population size, census div, and jurisdiction, as of Oct 1991, annual rpt, 6224–2.3
Employment, spending, and operations, for State, city, county, and special district police agencies, 1990, annual rpt, 6064–39
Employment, spending, and operations of law enforcement agencies, FY90, 6066–25.44
Expenditures (direct) and employment, by function and level of govt, selected years 1962-87, 10048–53
Expenditures by function, and revenues by source, natl income and product account benchmark revisions, 1929-88, 2708–5
Expenditures by function, and revenues by source, natl income and product accounts, *Survey of Current Business*, monthly rpt, 2702–1.26
Finances of govts, by level of govt, State, and for large cities and counties, annual rpt series, 2466–2
Govt finances, tax systems and revenue, and fiscal structure, by level of govt and State, 1992 with historical trends, annual rpt, 10044–1
Labor demand, turnover, and training completions, by detailed occupation, 1990 and projected to 2005, biennial rpt, 6744–3
Local govts in metro areas, finances, structure, and service delivery, local area rpt series, 10046–9
Minority group and women employment in State and local govt, by occupation, function, and pay level, 1991, annual rpt, 9244–6.4
Neighborhood and housing quality, indicators and attitudes, by householder type and location, for 11 MSAs, 1987 survey, supplement, 2485–8
Occupational Outlook Handbook, 1992-93, biennial rpt, 6744–1
Pension plans for police and firefighters, participation requirements, and earnings replacement, 1990, article, 6722–1.350
Sheriffs' agencies employment, spending, and operations, FY90, 6066–25.45
Statistical Abstract of US, 1992 annual data compilation, 2324–1.5
Traffic fatal accidents, deaths, and rates, by circumstances, characteristics of persons and vehicles involved, and location, 1990, annual rpt, 7764–10
see also Assaults on police
see also Detective and protective services
see also Federal aid to law enforcement
see also Law enforcement
see also State police

Policy Development and Research, HUD
American Housing Survey: unit and households characteristics, MSA fact sheet series, 2485–11
Budget of US, obligations and authority by function, agency, and program, with summaries and analyses, FY93, annual rpt, 104–2
Fed Home Loan Mortgage Corp financial condition and capital adequacy, 1990, annual rpt, 5184–8
Fed Natl Mortgage Assn activities and finances, 1991, annual rpt, 5184–9
Lead paint abatement costs and results, demonstration project design and findings, 1991 rpt, 5188–131
Low income housing developers tax credits, subsidies, project and tenant characteristics, and investor returns, 1987-88, 5188–133
Neighborhood Dev Demonstration program evaluation, grantee organization characteristics, activities, finances, and private sector support, 1984-89, 5188–119
Pension funds (public) investment in housing, and public and private funds holdings of mortgages, mortgage-backed securities, and govt securities, 1986-90, 5188–134
Public housing residents educational attainment, by selected characteristics, 1980s, 5188–132
Racial discrimination in housing rental and sales, for blacks and Hispanics in selected metro areas, 1989 study, series, 5186–16
Rental housing units, total, with HUD assistance by program, and eligible for aid, by unit, household, and neighborhood characteristics, and location, 1989, biennial rpt, 5184–11
Urban areas fiscal, economic, and social conditions, as of FY92, biennial rpt, 5184–7

Policy Studies Associates, Inc.
"Unlocking Learning: Chapter 1 in Correctional Facilities. National Study of the Chapter 1 Neglected or Delinquent Program", 4808–40

Polio
see Infective and parasitic diseases

Political action committees
Committees, by type, 1974-91, semiannual press release, 9276–1.96
Committees, by type, 1974-92, semiannual press release, 9276–1.107
Congressional election campaign receipts and spending, by candidate and State, late 1980s-92, press release, 9276–1.102; 9276–1.103; 9276–1.112
Congressional election campaign receipts and spending, by candidate and State, 1980s-92, press release, 9276–1.108
Finances of PACs and contributions by party, by PAC type, 1991-92, press release, 9276–1.106; 9276–1.110
Financing of campaigns and Fed Election Commission activities, various periods 1975-91, annual rpt, 9274–1
Funding of campaigns by PACs and other sources, 1990 natl elections, biennial rpt series, 9276–2
Statistical Abstract of US, 1992 annual data compilation, 2324–1.8

Political broadcasting
see also Radio Free Europe
see also Radio Liberty

Political campaign funds
see Campaign funds
see Political action committees

Political conventions
Finances reported to Fed Election Commission, by type of filer, 1990 natl elections, biennial rpt series, 9276–2
Tax (income) return checkoff for contribution to presidential campaign fund, receipts and outlays, mid 1970s-91 and alternative projections to 1993, hearing, 21428–10

Political ethics
Fed Govt agencies ethics regulation, activities, and staff, 1991, biennial rpt, 9834–1
Fed Govt employees misconduct reporting, awareness of protection and other factors influencing reporting, 1992 survey, GAO rpt, 26119–413
Govt employees political activities prohibited under Hatch Act, cases initiated, FY91, annual rpt, 9894–1
IRS ethical climate, misconduct, reporting and retaliation, and staff and mgmt integrity, employees views, 1991 GAO rpt, 26119–366
Justice Dept employee misconduct investigations, by type of allegation and penalty, 1988-90, GAO rpt, 26119–380
Public opinion on crime and crime-related issues, by respondent characteristics, data compilation, 1992 annual rpt, 6064–6.2
see also Conflict of interests
see also Corruption and bribery
see also Lobbying and lobbying groups

Political parties
Campaign finances and Fed Election Commission activities, various periods 1975-91, annual rpt, 9274–1
Campaign finances, elections, procedures, and Fed Election Commission activities, press release series, 9276–1
Campaign finances reported to Fed Election Commission, by type of filer, 1990 natl elections, biennial rpt series, 9276–2
County Business Patterns, 1989: employment, establishments, and payroll, by SIC 2- to 4-digit industry and county, annual State rpt series, 2326–8
County Business Patterns, 1990: employment, establishments, and payroll, by SIC 2- to 4-digit industry and county, annual State rpt series, 2326–6
Foreign countries *Background Notes*, summary social, political, and economic data, series, 7006–2
Foreign countries economic, social, political, and geographic summary data, by country, 1992, annual factbook, 9114–2

Foreign countries human rights conditions in 170 countries, 1991, annual rpt, 21384–3
Presidential approval rating and political party affiliation impact on defense spending and transfer payments, model description and results, 1950s-88, working paper, 9393–10.17
Statistical Abstract of US, 1992 annual data compilation, 2324–1.8
Votes cast by party, candidate, and State, 1990 natl elections, biennial rpt, 21944–3
see also Communist parties
see also Democratic Party
see also Political conventions
see also Republican Party

Political rights
see Civil rights

Political science
Degrees awarded in higher education, by level, field, race, and sex, 1989/90 and trends from 1980/81, annual rpt, 4844–17
Fed Govt aid to higher education and nonprofit instns for R&D and related activities, by field, instn, agency, and State, FY90, annual rpt, 9627–17
Higher education grad programs enrollment in science and engineering, by field, source of funds, and characteristics of student and instn, 1990, annual rpt, 9627–7
R&D funding by higher education instns and federally funded centers, by field, instn, and State, FY90, annual rpt, 9627–13

Polls
see Elections
see Opinion and attitude surveys

Pollution
see Acid rain
see Air pollution
see Asbestos contamination
see Dioxins
see Environmental pollution and control
see Environmental regulation
see Global climate change
see Marine pollution
see Mercury pollution
see Motor vehicle exhaust
see Noise
see Radiation
see Radon
see Soil pollution
see Water pollution

Polymers
Exports and imports of US, by country and detailed commodity, monthly rpt, 2422–12
Farm financial and marketing conditions, forecast 1992, annual conf, 1504–9
Production, trade, use, and foreign investment in US industry, for minerals, 1985-90 and projected to 2000, annual rpt, 5304–5

Pompano Beach, Fla.
Housing starts and completions authorized by building permits in 40 MSAs, quarterly rpt, 2382–9
Wages by occupation, and benefits for office and plant workers, 1991 survey, periodic MSA rpt, 6785–3.1

Poor
see Homeless population
see Poverty

Population census
see Census of Population
see Census of Population and Housing

Population characteristics
Agricultural research funding and staffing for USDA, State agencies, and other instns, by topic, FY91, annual rpt, 1744–2
Alaska rural areas population characteristics, and energy resources dev effects, series, 5736–5
Census Bur data files and rpts, coverage and availability, 1992 annual listing, 2304–2
Census of Housing, 1990: summary unit characteristics, by householder race and age, county, place, and urban-rural location, State rpt series, 2471–1
Census of Population and Housing, 1990: data summary, use, and availability, for selected long form questions, fact sheet series, 2326–23
Census of Population and Housing, 1990: detailed geographic coverage, State CD-ROM series, 2551–9
Census of Population and Housing, 1990: population and housing characteristics, detailed geographic coverage, State CD-ROM series, 2551–10
Census of Population and Housing, 1990: summary characteristics, by county, subdiv, and place, State rpt series, 2551–7
Census of Population and Housing, 1990: summary characteristics, households, and land area, by county, subdiv, and place, State rpt series, 2551–1
Census of Population, 1990: population characteristics and living arrangements, by county, place, and urban-rural location, State rpt series, 2531–1
Census of Population, 1990: population characteristics and living arrangements, for Native American, urban, and metro areas, series, 2531–2
Coastal areas environmental and economic impacts of offshore minerals lease sales, final statement series, 5736–7
Current Population Reports, demographic, social, and economic characteristics, series, 2546–1
Current Population Reports, demographic subjects, special study series, 2546–2
Current Population Reports, income and socioeconomic characteristics of persons, families, and households, detailed cross-tabulations, series, 2546–6
Data on population and housing, and policy issues, fact sheet series, 2326–17
Developing countries economic and social conditions from 1960s, and Intl Dev Cooperation Agency and AID activities and funding, FY91-93, annual rpt, 9904–4
Developing countries economic, population, and agricultural data, US and other aid sources, and AID activity, country rpt series, 9916–12
Economic well-being indicators, by selected population characteristics and household income and income-to-poverty ratio, 1984, 2546–20.22
Employment and economic conditions, alternative BLS projections to 2005 and trends 1975-90, biennial rpt, 6744–19
Foreign countries *Background Notes*, summary social, political, and economic data, series, 7006–2
Foreign countries economic and social conditions, working paper series, 2326–18
Foreign countries economic, social, political, and geographic summary data, by country, 1992, annual factbook, 9114–2
Foreign countries population size, growth rates, and components of change, by country, projected 1990-2020 and trends from 1950, biennial rpt, 2324–9
Housing prices and adjustments for quality changes, analysis of factors, 1950s-80s, working paper, 9373–27.7
Latin America economic and social conditions, resources, trade, and aid, 1992, annual factbook, 9914–14
Mississippi poverty, hunger, and public welfare program operations and indicators of need, 1991 hearing, 21968–57
Overseas Business Reports: economic conditions, investment and export opportunities, and trade practices, country market research rpt series, 2046–6
Pacific territories population and housing detailed characteristics, by location, 1990 Census of Population and Housing, series, 2551–8
Palau admin, and social, economic, and govtl data, FY91, annual rpt, 7004–6
Population and labor force characteristics, 1940s-90 and projected to 2000, 15496–1.16
Research on population and reproduction, Federal funding by project, FY90, annual listing, 4474–9
Research on population and reproduction, Natl Inst of Child Health and Human Dev funding and activities, 1991, annual rpt, 4474–33
Rural areas employment and population characteristics, and role of education and training in economic dev, 1960s-80s, compilation of papers, 1598–277
Soviet Union and US economic and sociodemographic indicators, selected years 1970-90, handbook, 2328–80
Soviet Union former Republics and Baltic States population size and characteristics, 1989-92, 9118–19
Statistical Abstract of US, 1992 annual data compilation, 2324–1.1
Survey of Income and Program Participation, household composition, income, benefits, and labor force status, methodology, working paper series, 2626–10
Uranium tailings at inactive mills, remedial action proposals, costs, site characteristics, and environmental, socioeconomic, and health impacts, series, 3356–4
see also Aged and aging
see also Ancestry
see also Birthplace
see also Body measurements
see also Children
see also Disabled and handicapped persons
see also Earnings, general
see also Educational attainment
see also Educational enrollment
see also Employment and unemployment, general

see also Families and households
see also Farm population
see also Fertility
see also Health condition
see also Homeless population
see also Housing condition and occupancy
see also Intelligence levels
see also Labor supply and demand
see also Life expectancy
see also Living arrangements
see also Marriage and divorce
see also Men
see also Migration
see also Minority groups
see also Nutrition and malnutrition
see also Occupations
see also Personal and household income
see also Personal consumption
see also Population projections
see also Population size
see also Poverty
see also Quality of life
see also Vital statistics
see also Wealth
see also Women
see also Youth

Population projections

Coastal areas environmental impacts of economic dev and population growth, 1960-80s and projected to 2010, series, 2176–8

Current Population Reports, population estimates and projections, by region and State, series, 2546–3

Developing countries aged population and selected characteristics, 1980s and projected to 2020, country rpt series, 2326–19

Developing countries population size, life expectancy, and fertility, trends and forecasts, country rpt series, 2326–24

Economic conditions impacts of population size and demographic changes, with background data, 1950s-80s and projected to 2010, 23848–226

Employment and economic conditions, alternative BLS projections to 2005 and trends 1975-90, biennial rpt, 6744–19

Employment by occupation, accuracy of BLS forecasts for 1990 made 1980, article, 6722–1.336

Employment by occupation, accuracy of BLS forecasts for 1990 made 1982, article, 6742–1.302

Foreign and US aged population and characteristics, by country, 1991 and projected to 2020, wallchart, 2328–82

Foreign countries and cities population density, and distribution, life expectancy, and infant mortality by world region, 1991, fact sheet, 2326–17.50

Foreign countries economic and social conditions, working paper series, 2326–18

Foreign countries economic indicators, and trade and trade flows by commodity, by country, data compilation, monthly CD-ROM, 2002–6

Foreign countries population size, growth rates, and components of change, by country, projected 1990-2020 and trends from 1950, biennial rpt, 2324–9

Health condition and care indicators, 1950s-90 with health improvement and disease prevention goals for 1990, annual data compilation, 4144–11

Households, share by composition and householder age, projected to 2000, chartbook, 2486–2.1

Labor force status by age, sex, and race, accuracy of BLS forecasts made 1970s-80s, as of 1990, article, 6722–1.334

Mentally retarded school-age cases, forecasts using birth defect records, accuracy, 1992 article, 4042–3.327

Nursing home use risk, and admissions, by sex, projected 1990-2040, article, 1702–1.309

OASDHI future cost estimates, actuarial study series, 4706–1

Older persons labor force status, income sources, and reasons for not working, with data by occupation, sex, and race, 1989-90 and projected to 2050, 21148–65

Older persons population size and characteristics, series, 2326–25

Older persons socioeconomic characteristics, 1900s-90 and projected to 2050, biennial chartbook, 12904–1

Older population, and health, economic, and other characteristics, with foreign comparisons, 1980s-91 with trends and projections, Current Population Rpt, 2546–2.165

Pacific Northwest population, households, employment, income, fuel prices, and electricity demand, alternative forecasts 1991-2010, annual rpt, 3224–3.3

Population size and components of change, alternative projections 1990-2080 and trends from 1900, annual actuarial rpt, 4706–1.106

Population size, by race and Hispanic origin, 1992 and projected 2000-2050, press release, 2328–85

Voting age population, by sex, age, race, and State, forecast 1992 general elections, with votes cast from 1930, Current Population Rpt, 2546–3.170

Population size

Appalachia population, by State and county, 1980 and 1990, annual rpt, 9084–1

Census of Housing, 1990: summary unit characteristics, by householder race and age, county, place, and urban-rural location, State rpt series, 2471–1

Census of Population and Housing, 1990: detailed geographic coverage, State CD-ROM series, 2551–9

Census of Population and Housing, 1990: Indian tribes population size, with data by State, press release, 2328–86

Census of Population and Housing, 1990: population and housing characteristics, detailed geographic coverage, State CD-ROM series, 2551–10

Census of Population and Housing, 1990: summary characteristics, by county, subdiv, and place, State rpt series, 2551–7

Census of Population and Housing, 1990: summary characteristics, households, and land area, by county, subdiv, and place, State rpt series, 2551–1

Census of Population, 1990: data adjustment in intercensal data for census undercounts, final decision with data by region and State, 2328–90

Census of Population, 1990: data adjustment in intercensal data for census undercounts, recommendations with alternative undercount estimates, 2628–36

Census of Population, 1990: population characteristics and living arrangements, by county, place, and urban-rural location, State rpt series, 2531–1

Census of Population, 1990: population characteristics and living arrangements, for Native American, urban, and metro areas, series, 2531–2

Central America economic indicators, by country, 1969-89, working paper, 9916–13.4

Coastal areas environmental impacts of economic dev and population growth, 1960-80s and projected to 2010, series, 2176–8

Costa Rica economic indicators and reform issues, mid 1970s-90, working paper, 9916–13.5

Crimes, arrests by offender characteristics, and rates, by offense, and law enforcement employees, by population size and jurisdiction, 1991, annual rpt, 6224–2

Current Population Reports, demographic, social, and economic characteristics, series, 2546–1

Current Population Reports, demographic subjects, special study series, 2546–2

Current Population Reports, population estimates and projections, by region and State, series, 2546–3

Current Population Reports, population estimates for civilian, resident, and total population, monthly rpt, 2542–1

Data on population and housing, and policy issues, fact sheet series, 2326–17

Developing countries aged population and selected characteristics, 1980s and projected to 2020, country rpt series, 2326–19

Developing countries aided by Peace Corps, quality of life indicators, FY93, annual rpt, 9654–1

Developing countries economic and social conditions from 1960s, and Intl Dev Cooperation Agency and AID activities and funding, FY91-93, annual rpt, 9904–4

Developing countries economic, population, and agricultural data, US and other aid sources, and AID activity, country rpt series, 9916–12

Developing countries population size, life expectancy, and fertility, trends and forecasts, country rpt series, 2326–24

Economic conditions impacts of population size and demographic changes, with background data, 1950s-80s and projected to 2010, 23848–226

Economic indicators and relation to govt finances by level of govt, selected years 1929-91, annual rpt, 10044–1

Energy use by mode of transport, fuel supply, and demographic and economic factors of vehicle use, 1970s-90, annual rpt, 3304–5

Environmental Quality, status of problems, protection programs, research, and intl issues, 1991 annual rpt, 484–1

Foreign countries and cities population density, and distribution, life expectancy, and infant mortality by world region, 1991, fact sheet, 2326–17.50

Foreign countries *Background Notes*, summary social, political, and economic data, series, 7006–2
Foreign countries economic and social conditions, working paper series, 2326–18
Foreign countries economic conditions and implications for US, periodic country rpt series, 2046–4
Foreign countries economic indicators, and trade and trade flows by commodity, by country, data compilation, monthly CD-ROM, 2002–6
Foreign countries economic, social, political, and geographic summary data, by country, 1992, annual factbook, 9114–2
Foreign countries *Geographic Notes*, boundaries, claims, nomenclature, and other devs, quarterly rpt, 7142–3
Foreign countries military spending, arms trade, and force strengths, with govt spending and population, by country, 1979-89, annual rpt, 9824–1
Foreign countries population size, growth rates, and components of change, by country, projected 1990-2020 and trends from 1950, biennial rpt, 2324–9
Health care spending and factors in increase, with background data and foreign comparisons, various periods 1929-90, technical paper, 9366–6.296
Health condition and care indicators, 1950s-90 with health improvement and disease prevention goals for 1990, annual data compilation, 4144–11
Israel economic conditions, US investment and export opportunities, and trade practices, 1992 rpt, 2008–32
Latin America economic and social conditions, resources, trade, and aid, 1992, annual factbook, 9914–14
NATO, Japan, and South Korea military spending and indicators of ability to support common defense, by country, 1970s-90, annual rpt, 3544–28
OECD members health care costs, hospital use, resources, and economic and health indicators, by country, 1960s-90, article, 4652–1.322
Older persons population size and characteristics, series, 2326–25
Older persons socioeconomic characteristics, 1900s-90 and projected to 2050, biennial chartbook, 12904–1
Older population, and health, economic, and other characteristics, with foreign comparisons, 1980s-91 with trends and projections, Current Population Rpt, 2546–2.165
Pacific Northwest Indian tribes environmental, economic, and cultural impacts of OCS oil and gas lease and dev, with background data, 1970s-92, 5738–35
Pacific Northwest population, households, employment, income, fuel prices, and electricity demand, alternative forecasts 1991-2010, annual rpt, 3224–3.3
Pacific territories population and housing detailed characteristics, by location, 1990 Census of Population and Housing, series, 2551–8
Palau admin, and social, economic, and govtl data, FY91, annual rpt, 7004–6
Population of US, monthly 1961-88, *Survey of Current Business* biennial supplement, 2704–1
Population size, by age, selected years 1929-91, annual rpt, 204–1.2
Population size, July 1991-92, by region, census div, and State, annual press release, 2324–10
Research on population and reproduction, Federal funding by project, FY90, annual listing, 4474–9
Research on population and reproduction, Natl Inst of Child Health and Human Dev funding and activities, 1991, annual rpt, 4474–33
Rural areas economic conditions and dev, quarterly journal, 1502–8
Soviet Union and US economic and sociodemographic indicators, selected years 1970-90, handbook, 2328–80
Soviet Union former Republics and Baltic States energy supply and use, and social, economic, and political indicators, 1989-90, 3168–126
Soviet Union former Republics and Baltic States population size and characteristics, 1989-92, 9118–19
Statistical Abstract of US, 1992 annual data compilation, 2324–1.1
Tennessee Valley economic conditions, and compared to US, alternative projections 1992-2010 and trends from 1929, annual rpt, 9804–27
Vietnam population size, components of change, and selected characteristics, 1979, 1989, and projected to 2050, 2326–18.65
Vital statistics provisional data, monthly rpt, 4142–1
Voting age population, by State, 1992 general elections, press release, 9276–1.100
Voting age population, by State, 1992 primary elections, press release, 9276–1.97
see also Births
see also Deaths
see also Family planning
see also Farm population
see also Fertility
see also Immigration and emigration
see also Migration
see also Population projections
see also Vital statistics

Porcelain products
see Pottery and porcelain products

Porcella, Ronald L.
"Catalogue of U.S. Geological Survey Strong-Motion Records, 1990", 5664–14

Pork
see Meat and meat products

Pornography
see Obscenity and pornography

Porpoises
see Marine mammals

Porter, Kenneth E.
"Availability of Primary Copper in Market-Economy Countries. A Minerals Availability Appraisal", 5606–4.30

Porterville, Calif.
Wages by occupation, and benefits for office and plant workers, 1991 survey, periodic MSA rpt, 6785–12.1

Portland, Oreg.
CPI by component for US city average, and by selected metro area, region, and population size, monthly rpt, 6762–2
Drug test results at arrest, by drug type, offense, and sex, for selected urban areas, quarterly rpt, 6062–3
Freight (waterborne domestic and foreign) by commodity, traffic, and passengers, by port and waterway, 1989, annual rpt, 3754–3.4
Housing and households characteristics, and unit and neighborhood quality, by MSA location for 11 MSAs, 1986 survey, supplement, 2485–8
Wages by occupation, for office and plant workers, 1991 survey, periodic MSA rpt, 6785–12.1
see also under By City and By SMSA or MSA in the "Index by Categories"

Ports
see Harbors and ports

Portugal
Agricultural trade of US, by detailed commodity and country, 1991, annual rpt, 1524–8
Agricultural trade of US, by detailed commodity and country, 1991, semiannual rpt, 1522–4
AID economic aid to developing countries, obligations and disbursements by country, quarterly rpt, 9912–4
AID loans repayment status and terms by program and country, and status of predecessor agency loans, quarterly rpt, 9912–3
Cuba trade, by commodity and country, mid 1980s-91, 9118–8
Economic and military aid and loans from US and intl agencies, by program and country, FY46-91, annual rpt, 9914–5
Economic and social conditions of developing countries from 1960s, and Intl Dev Cooperation Agency and AID activities and funding, FY91-93, annual rpt, 9904–4
Economic conditions, income, production, prices, employment, and trade, 1992 periodic country rpt, 2046–4.45
Economic conditions, policy, and trade practices, by country, 1989-91, annual rpt, 21384–5
Economic, social, political, and geographic summary data, by country, 1992, annual factbook, 9114–2
Exports and imports of US, by transport mode, country, and SITC 1- to 3-digit commodity, 1991, annual rpt, 2424–12
Exports, imports, and balances of US for manufactured goods, by SITC 2-digit commodity and country, quarterly rpt, 2042–35
Exports of US, detailed Schedule B commodities with countries of destination, 1991, annual rpt, 2424–10
Health care costs and components, services use, resources, and economic indicators, by OECD country, 1960s-90, article, 4652–1.322
Human rights conditions in 170 countries, and US economic and military aid, 1991, annual rpt, 21384–3
Imports of goods, services, and investment from US, trade barriers, impacts, and US actions, by country, 1991, annual rpt, 444–2

Labor conditions, union coverage, and work accidents, 1992 annual country rpt, 6366–4.21
Military aid of US, arms sales, and training programs costs and budget requests, by program, world region, and country, FY91-93, annual rpt, 7144–13
Military spending, arms trade, and force strengths, with govt spending and population, by country, 1979-89, annual rpt, 9824–1
Multinatl US firms and foreign affiliates finances and operations, by industry and country, 1989 benchmark survey, annual rpt, 2704–5
Multinatl US firms foreign affiliates, income statement items by asset size, industry, and country, 1988, biennial article, 8302–2.322
Oil production, stocks, use, and trade, by selected country and country group, monthly rpt, 3162–42
Population size, growth rates, and components of change, by country, projected 1990-2020 and trends from 1950, biennial rpt, 2324–9
Refugee migration, and intl aid programs, by world area and country of origin and asylum, 1991, annual rpt, 7004–15
Steel trade, by product, country, and customs district, with US industry operating data, 1989-June 1992, semiannual rpt, 9882–15
Tax revenue, by level of govt and type of tax, for OECD countries, mid 1960s-90, annual rpt, 10044–1.2
UN voting record and share of votes in agreement with US, by issue, country, and world area, 1991, annual rpt, 7004–18
see also Macao
see also under By Foreign Country in the "Index by Categories"

Post exchanges
see Military post exchanges and commissaries

Post, Mitchell A.
"Effect of a Rating Change on Commercial Paper Outstandings", 9366–6.299
"Evolution of the U.S. Commercial Paper Market Since 1980", 9362–1.308

Post-traumatic stress disorder
see Mental health and illness

Postal employees
Assaults and deaths of law enforcement officers, by circumstances, agency, victim and offender characteristics, and location, 1991, annual rpt, 6224–3
Automation impacts on USPS labor hours, by task, 1990-91 with projected use of selected equipment to 1995, GAO rpt, 26119–395
Competition and rate increases impacts on USPS mail volume and employment, with evaluation of alternative forecast models, 1970s-80s and forecast to 1995, GAO rpt, 26119–384
Costs to USPS of personnel, by segment and occupation, FY91, annual rpt, 9864–2
Employment (civilian) of Fed Govt, work-years, pay rates, and benefits use and costs, by agency, FY90, annual rpt, 9844–31
Employment and economic conditions, alternative BLS projections to 2005 and trends 1975-90, biennial rpt, 6744–19
Employment and payroll, by function, level of govt, and State, 1991, annual rpt, 2466–1.1
Employment and related expenses of USPS, FY91, annual rpt, 9864–5
Employment, earnings, and hours, by SIC 1- to 4-digit industry, monthly 1989-Feb 1992, annual rpt, 6744–4
Health insurance programs for Federal civilian employees, enrollment, profits, and administrative costs, by plan, 1984-90, GAO rpt, 26119–376
Hours of work, allocations in post offices with high and low workloads, effectiveness, FY89-90, GAO rpt, 26119–379
Inspection activities of USPS, FY91, annual rpt, 9864–9
Labor demand, turnover, and training completions, by detailed occupation, 1990 and projected to 2005, biennial rpt, 6744–3
Labor unions recognized in Fed Govt, agreements and membership by agency and facility, as of Jan 1991, biennial listing, 9844–14
Occupational Outlook Handbook, 1992-93, biennial rpt, 6744–1
Pay and benefit costs, by type, for USPS, FY90-91, annual article, 9842–1.303
Payroll and other operating costs of USPS, itemized by class of mail, FY91, annual rpt, 9864–4
Payroll of Fed Govt, spending for civilian, military, and postal workers by State, FY91, annual rpt, 2464–2
Postal Service activities, financial statements, and employment, FY87-91, annual rpt, 9864–1
Productivity of Federal employees, indexes of output and labor costs by function, FY67-90, annual rpt, 6824–1.6

Postal Rate Commission
Ratesetting and mail volume forecasts, evaluation of alternative models, 1992 GAO rpt, 26119–384

Postal service
Air mail (foreign and US) carried by US scheduled service carriers, by carrier, monthly rpt, 7302–6
Air mail carried by US certificated carriers, by airport and carrier, 1991, annual rpt, 7504–35
Air mail, passenger, and cargo traffic, and airline operations, by type of service, air carrier, State, and country, 1981-90, annual rpt, 7504–1.6
Air traffic, and passenger and freight enplanements, by airport, 1960s-91 and projected to 2010, hub area rpt series, 7506–7
Airline finances, by carrier, carrier group, and for total certificated system, quarterly rpt, 7302–7
Airline operations and passenger, cargo, and mail traffic, by type of service, air carrier, State, and country, 1981-90, annual rpt, 7504–1.4
Automation impacts on USPS labor hours, by task, 1990-91 with projected use of selected equipment to 1995, GAO rpt, 26119–395
Banks in Fed Reserve System, expenses and operations itemized by service, office, and district, 1991, annual rpt, 9364–11
Bombing incidents and casualties, by target, circumstances, and State, 1987-91, annual rpt, 8484–4.1
Bombing incidents, casualties, and damage, by target, circumstances, and State, 1991, annual rpt, 6224–5
Budget of US, obligations and authority by function, agency, and program, with summaries and analyses, FY93, annual rpt, 104–2
Competition and rate increases impacts on USPS mail volume and employment, with evaluation of alternative forecast models, 1970s-80s and forecast to 1995, GAO rpt, 26119–384
Court civil and criminal caseloads for Federal district, appeals, and bankruptcy courts, by type of suit and offense, circuit, and district, 1991, annual rpt, 18204–11
Court civil and criminal caseloads for Federal district, appeals, and special courts, 1991, annual rpt, 18204–8
CPI by component for US city average, and by selected metro area, region, and population size, monthly rpt, 6762–2
Criminal case processing in Federal courts by disposition, and prisoners, by offense and jurisdiction, data compilation, 1992 annual rpt, 6064–6.5
Criminal cases by type and disposition, and collections, for US attorneys, by Federal district, FY91, annual rpt, 6004–2.1; 6004–2.7
Criminal sentences for Federal offenses, guidelines by offense and circumstances, series, 17668–1
Delivery on-time of 1st class mail, impacts of USPS standards revisions, 1990-91, GAO rpt, 26119–431
Expenditures (direct) and employment, by function and level of govt, selected years 1962-87, 10048–53
Expenditures by function, and revenues by source, natl income and product account benchmark revisions, 1929-88, 2708–5
Expenditures by function, and revenues by source, natl income and product accounts, *Survey of Current Business*, monthly rpt, 2702–1.26
Expenditures of Fed Govt, by function, FY90, annual rpt, 2466–2.2
Exports and imports of philatelic material, by country, 1991, annual rpt, 2424–13
Exports of philatelic material, by country of destination, 1991, annual rpt, 2424–10
Finances of Fed Govt, cash and debt transactions, daily tables, 8102–4
Foreign and US domestic postal rates, for 14 countries, 1991, annual rpt, 9864–5.1
Foreign govts and private obligors debt to US, by country and program, periodic rpt, 8002–6
Govt finances, tax systems and revenue, and fiscal structure, by level of govt and State, 1992 with historical trends, annual rpt, 10044–1
House of Representatives salaries, expenses, and contingent fund disbursement, detailed listings, quarterly rpt, 21942–1
Households incoming and outgoing mail volume, use, and views, by class, source, content, and household characteristics, FY87-90, annual rpt, 9864–10
Inspection activities of USPS, FY91, annual rpt, 9864–9

Inspection activities of USPS, 2nd half FY92, semiannual rpt, 9862–2
Parcel deliveries to and from households, carrier preferences, and content, for USPS and competitors, FY87-90, annual rpt, 9864–10
Post offices, siting, and routes historical records, Natl Archives special collection, 1975 rpt, 9516–1.5
Price indexes (producer), by stage of processing and detailed commodity, monthly rpt, 6762–6
Price indexes (producer), by stage of processing and detailed commodity, monthly 1991, annual rpt, 6764–2
Revenue and subsidy for revenue forgone, by class of mail, FY91, annual rpt, 9864–5
Revenue and volume by class of mail, and special service transactions, quarterly rpt, 9862–1
Revenue and volume, by class of mail and type of service, FY87-91, annual rpt, 9864–1
Revenue, costs, and volume, by class of mail, FY91, annual rpt, 9864–2
Senate receipts, itemized expenses by payee, and balances, 1st half FY92, semiannual listing, 25922–1
Soviet Union and US economic and sociodemographic indicators, selected years 1970-90, handbook, 2328–80
Statistical Abstract of US, 1992 annual data compilation, 2324–1.18
Theft of mail, Federal prisoners by selected characteristics, FY89, annual rpt, 6244–1.1
see also Postal employees
see also ZIP codes

Potash

Fertilizer consumption, by type and region, 1947-90, annual rpt, 1544–17.2
Minerals Yearbook, Vol 1, 1990: commodity review of production, reserves, supply, use, and trade, annual rpt, 5604–20.47
Minerals Yearbook, Vol 3, 1989: foreign country reviews of production, trade, and policy, by commodity, annual rpt, 5604–35
Mines (nonmetallic minerals) and related operations occupational injuries and incidence, employment, and hours, 1990, annual rpt, 6664–1
Price indexes (producer), by stage of processing and detailed commodity, monthly 1991, annual rpt, 6764–2
Production of potash, prices, trade, use, and sales, 1991 and 1992 crop years, Mineral Industry Surveys, annual rpt, 5614–19
Production, prices, trade, use, employment, tariffs, and stockpiles, by mineral, with foreign comparisons, 1987-91, annual rpt, 5604–18
Production, trade, use, and foreign investment in US industry, for minerals, 1985-90 and projected to 2000, annual rpt, 5304–5

Potassium hydroxide

see Chemicals and chemical industry

Potatoes

see Vegetables and vegetable products

Potomac River

Army Corps of Engineers water resources dev projects, characteristics, and costs, 1950s-89, biennial State rpt series, 3756–1
Army Corps of Engineers water resources dev projects, characteristics, and costs, 1950s-91, biennial State rpt series, 3756–2
Fish (striped bass) stocks status on Atlantic coast, and sport and commercial catch by State, 1979-90, annual rpt, 5504–29
Freight (waterborne domestic and foreign) by commodity, traffic, and passengers, by port and waterway, 1989, annual rpt, 3754–3.1
Water supply and quality in streams and lakes, and groundwater levels in wells, by drainage basin, 1990, annual State rpt series, 5666–10
Water supply and quality in streams and lakes, and groundwater levels in wells, by drainage basin, 1991, annual State rpt series, 5666–12
Water supply in US and southern Canada, streamflow, surface and groundwater conditions, and reservoir levels, by location, monthly rpt, 5662–3

Pottery and porcelain products

County Business Patterns, 1989: employment, establishments, and payroll, by SIC 2- to 4-digit industry and county, annual State rpt series, 2326–8
County Business Patterns, 1990: employment, establishments, and payroll, by SIC 2- to 4-digit industry and county, annual State rpt series, 2326–6
Employment, earnings, and hours, by SIC 1- to 4-digit industry, monthly 1989-Feb 1992, annual rpt, 6744–4
Exports and imports between US and outlying areas, by detailed commodity and mode of transport, 1991, annual rpt, 2424–11
Exports and imports of US, by country and detailed commodity, monthly rpt, 2422–12
Exports and imports of US, by Harmonized System 6-digit commodity and country, 1991, annual rpt, 2424–13
Exports and imports of US, by transport mode, country, and SITC 1- to 3-digit commodity, 1991, annual rpt, 2424–12
Exports of US, detailed Schedule B commodities with countries of destination, 1991, annual rpt, 2424–10
Injuries from use of consumer products, by severity, victim age, and detailed product, 1991, annual rpt, 9164–6
Input-output structure of US economy, detailed interindustry transactions for 541 industries, and components of final demand, 1982 benchmark data, 2708–17
Manufacturing annual survey, 1990: finances and operations, by SIC 2- to 4-digit industry, series, 2506–14
Manufacturing census, 1987: concentration of largest firms measured by value added, and for shipments by SIC 2- and 4-digit industry, subject rpt, 2497–6
Manufacturing census, 1987: shipments of manufacturers products, by customer class and SIC 2- and 4-digit industry, subject rpt, 2497–4
Occupational injury and illness rates, by SIC 2- to 4-digit industry, 1989-90, annual rpt, 6844–7
Occupational injury and illness rates, by SIC 2- to 4-digit industry, 1990, annual rpt, 6844–1
Plumbing fixtures production, and imports from US and other sources, for 15 countries, 1991 rpt, 2048–156
Plumbing fixtures shipments, stocks, trade, use, and firms, by product, quarterly Current Industrial Rpt, 2506–11.2
Price indexes (producer), by stage of processing and detailed commodity, monthly rpt, 6762–6
Price indexes (producer), by stage of processing and detailed commodity, monthly 1991, annual rpt, 6764–2
Science, engineering, and technical employment in manufacturing, by field and industry, 1989, triennial rpt, 9627–23

Poughkeepsie, N.Y.

Wages by occupation, for office and plant workers, 1991 survey, periodic MSA rpt, 6785–16.4
Wages by occupation, for office and plant workers, 1992 survey, periodic MSA rpt, 6785–3.4

Poullier, Jean-Pierre

"Administrative Costs in Selected Industrialized Countries", 4652–1.325

Poultry industry and products

Agricultural Statistics, 1991, annual rpt, 1004–1
Appalachia food processing firms, employment, and shipments, and farm production, by commodity and State, 1960s-90, 9088–37
Broiler retail weight consumption revised conversion factors, 1960s-91, article, 1561–7.302
Business statistics, detailed data for major industries and economic indicators, *Survey of Current Business*, monthly rpt, 2702–1.13
Business statistics, detailed data for major industries and economic indicators, 1960-91, *Survey of Current Business* biennial supplement, 2704–1
Cold storage food stocks by commodity and census div, and warehouse space use, by State, monthly rpt, 1631–5
Cold storage food stocks by commodity, and warehouse space use, by census div, 1991, annual rpt, 1631–11
Consumption of chicken broilers and other poultry, 1970-89, 1208–404
Consumption, supply, trade, prices, spending, and indexes, by food commodity, 1990, annual rpt, 1544–4
County Business Patterns, 1989: employment, establishments, and payroll, by SIC 2- to 4-digit industry and county, annual State rpt series, 2326–8
County Business Patterns, 1990: employment, establishments, and payroll, by SIC 2- to 4-digit industry and county, annual State rpt series, 2326–6
CPI by component for US city average, and by selected metro area, region, and population size, monthly rpt, 6762–2
Eastern Europe export industries dev potential, with trade and industry finances and operations, for 5 countries, 1985-90, 9886–4.179
Egg production and layer inventory, by State, 1990-91, annual rpt, 1625–7
Egg production by type of product, and eggs broken under Federal inspection by region, monthly rpt, 1625–2

Eggs set and chicks placed in broiler hatcheries, by State, weekly rpt, 1625–11
Employment, earnings, and hours, by SIC 1- to 4-digit industry, monthly 1989-Feb 1992, annual rpt, 6744–4
Exports and imports (agricultural) commodity and country, prices, and world market devs, monthly rpt, 1922–12
Exports and imports (agricultural) of US, by commodity and country, bimonthly rpt, 1522–1
Exports and imports (agricultural) of US, by detailed commodity and country, 1991, annual rpt, 1524–8
Exports and imports (agricultural) of US, by detailed commodity and country, 1991, semiannual rpt, 1522–4
Exports and imports between US and outlying areas, by detailed commodity and mode of transport, 1991, annual rpt, 2424–11
Exports and imports of dairy, livestock, and poultry products, by commodity and country, FAS monthly circular, 1925–32
Exports and imports of US, by country and detailed commodity, monthly rpt, 2422–12
Exports and imports of US, by Harmonized System 6-digit commodity and country, 1991, annual rpt, 2424–13
Exports and imports of US, by transport mode, country, and SITC 1- to 3-digit commodity, 1991, annual rpt, 2424–12
Exports, imports, tariffs, and industry operating data for poultry products, 1992 rpt, 9885–8.6
Exports of US, detailed Schedule B commodities with countries of destination, 1991, annual rpt, 2424–10
Farm financial and marketing conditions, forecast 1992, annual chartbook, 1504–8
Farm financial and marketing conditions, forecast 1992, annual conf, 1504–9
Farm income, cash marketing receipts ranked by commodity and State, 1990, 1548–385
Farm sector assets by type, and real and nonreal estate debt, including and excluding operator households, by sales size, 1960-89, 1548–387
Farm sector balance sheet, and receipts by detailed commodity, by State, 1986-90, annual rpt, 1544–18
Foreign and US livestock, poultry, and dairy production, trade, and use, by selected country, FAS semiannual circular series, 1925–33
Foreign countries agricultural production, prices, and trade, by country, 1980-91 and forecast 1992, annual world area rpt series, 1524–4
Futures and options trading volume, by commodity and exchange, FY91, annual rpt, 11924–2
Input-output structure of US economy, detailed interindustry transactions for 541 industries, and components of final demand, 1982 benchmark data, 2708–17
Inspections of meat and poultry for domestic use and export, and rejections by cause, by type of animal and product, FY90, annual rpt, 1374–3
Inspections of poultry slaughter by Fed Govt, pounds certified, and condemnations by cause, by State, monthly rpt, 1625–3
Labor productivity, indexes of output, hours, and employment by SIC 2- to 4-digit industry, 1967-90, annual rpt, 6824–1.3
Manufacturing annual survey, 1990: finances and operations, by SIC 2- to 4-digit industry, series, 2506–14
Manufacturing census, 1987: concentration of largest firms measured by value added, and for shipments by SIC 2- and 4-digit industry, subject rpt, 2497–6
Manufacturing census, 1987: shipments of manufacturers products, by customer class and SIC 2- and 4-digit industry, subject rpt, 2497–4
Manufacturing finances and operations, by SIC 2- to 4-digit industry, forecast 1992, annual rpt, 2044–28
Natl Poultry Improvement Plan participating hatcheries and birds, by species and disease program, 1992, annual listing, 1394–15
Nutrient, caloric, and waste composition, detailed data for raw, processed, and prepared foods, 1992 rpt, 1356–3.17
Occupational injury and illness rates, by SIC 2- to 4-digit industry, 1989-90, annual rpt, 6844–7
Occupational injury and illness rates, by SIC 2- to 4-digit industry, 1990, annual rpt, 6844–1
Price indexes (producer), by stage of processing and detailed commodity, monthly rpt, 6762–6
Price indexes (producer), by stage of processing and detailed commodity, monthly 1991, annual rpt, 6764–2
Prices (farm-retail) for food, marketing cost components, and industry finances and productivity, 1920s-91, annual rpt, 1544–9
Prices (producer and retail) of meat and fish, 1987-92, semiannual situation rpt, 1561–15.3
Prices and marketing of poultry and eggs, by selected region, State, and city, monthly and weekly 1991, annual rpt, 1317–2
Prices received and paid by farmers, by commodity and State, monthly rpt, 1629–1
Prices received and paid by farmers, by commodity and State, 1991, annual rpt, 1629–5
Production and inventories for chickens, eggs, and turkeys, monthly rpt, 1625–1
Production and prices for chickens, eggs, and turkeys, by State, 1990-91, annual rpt, 1625–5
Production inputs, output, and productivity for farms, by commodity and region, 1947-90, annual rpt, 1544–17
Production, inventory, and prices of meat, USDA forecasts accuracy, 1980s, GAO rpt, 26131–93
Production itemized costs, by farm sales size and region, 1991, annual rpt, 1614–3
Production of chicken and turkey hatcheries, by State, 1990-91, annual rpt, 1625–8
Production, prices, receipts, trade, and disposition, for poultry species and eggs, 1960-90, annual rpt, 1564–13
Production, prices, trade, and marketing, by commodity, current situation and forecast, monthly rpt with articles, 1502–4
Production, prices, trade, and stocks, monthly rpt, 1561–17
Production, prices, trade, stocks, and use, periodic situation rpt with articles, 1561–7
Statistical Abstract of US, 1992 annual data compilation, 2324–1.23
Supply and demand indicators for livestock and dairy products, and for selected foreign and US crops, monthly rpt, 1522–5
Tax (income) returns of partnerships, income statement and balance sheet items, by industry group, 1990, annual article, 8302–2.314
Turkey hatcheries egg inventory and poult placements, by region, monthly rpt, 1625–10
Turkeys raised by State, and losses by region, 1990-91, and hatchery plans, 1992, annual rpt, 1625–6
Weight and volume conversion factors for agricultural commodities and products, 1992 rpt, 1508–3

Poverty

Agricultural Conservation Program participation by low-income farmers, by State, FY91, annual rpt, 1804–7
Asian and Pacific Islands Americans social and economic characteristics, for West and total US, 1990-91, Current Population Report, 2546–1.462
Banks loan activity in low income and minority communities, 1991 hearing, 21248–176
Black Americans social and economic characteristics, for South and total US, 1991 and trends from 1950, annual Current Population Rpt, 2546–1.463
Black women's labor force status, earnings, and other economic status indicators, and compared to whites, various periods 1939-88, 11048–191
Budget of US, House Budget Committee analysis of Bush Admin proposals and economic assumptions, FY93, 21268–42
Cancer (cervical and breast) screening among poor black women, effects of in-home promotion program, 1989-92, article, 4042–3.338
CCC dairy price support program foreign donations and domestic donations to poor, schools, Prisons Bur, and VA, monthly rpt, 1802–2
Census of Population and Housing, 1990: population and housing characteristics, detailed geographic coverage, State CD-ROM series, 2551–10
Census of Population and Housing, 1990: summary characteristics, by county, subdiv, and place, State rpt series, 2551–7
Child care arrangements of mothers employed and in school, and costs, by age of child and characteristics of mother, 1988, Current Population Rpt, 2546–20.24
Child day care and early childhood education programs availability, demand, use, costs, and provider and enrollee characteristics, 1990 survey, 4808–39
Child support enforcement provisions effects on divorced parents poverty rate, model results, 1976-83, working paper, 6886–6.87
Condition of Education, detail for elementary, secondary, and higher education, 1920s-91 and projected to 2002, annual rpt, 4824–1

Consumer Income, socioeconomic characteristics of persons, families, and households, detailed cross-tabulations, Current Population Rpt series, 2546–6
Costa Rica economic indicators and reform issues, mid 1970s-90, working paper, 9916–13.5
Credit unions with low income membership, financial, operating, and membership data, 1982-91, 9536–1.8
DC metro area drug, alcohol, and tobacco use, user characteristics, and consequences, series, 4496–12
Dental fluoride products use by children, by frequency of dental visits and selected characteristics, 1983-89, 4146–8.222
Developing countries economic and social conditions from 1960s, and Intl Dev Cooperation Agency and AID activities and funding, FY91-93, annual rpt, 9904–4
Digestive diseases (chronic) prevalence, and procedures performed, by disease and patient characteristics, 1989, 4146–8.213
Disabled workers labor force status, type and cause of disability, and other characteristics, 1970s-89, chartbook, 4948–11
Drug abuse by mothers, treatment and other services use, referrals, needs, and barriers, for 13 NIDA-funded programs, 1990/91 survey, 4498–76
Earnings (low) relation to poverty, by work experience during year, household relationship, sex, race, age, and education, 1960s-90, Current Population Rpt, 2546–6.74
Economic Report of the President for 1992, Joint Economic Committee critique and policy recommendations, annual rpt, 23844–2
Education programs for preschool students transition to kindergarten, and factors affecting activities, 1989-90 study, 4808–44
Employment and unemployment in metro and nonmetro poverty and nonpoverty areas, monthly rpt, quarterly data, 6742–2.9
Families in poverty, by detailed characteristics, 1980 and 1988, GAO rpt, 26131–102
Family and population poverty status, by race, 1971-90, annual rpt, 204–1.1
Farm population, by employment, social, and economic characteristics, and region, 1990, annual Current Population Rpt, 2546–1.458
Food spending of women-headed households, by item and selected characteristics, and compared to other households, 1970s-88, 1548–391
Foreign countries labor conditions, union coverage, and work accidents, annual country rpt series, 6366–4
Health care services use and total and out-of-pocket spending, by type of insurance coverage and selected characteristics, 1987, 4186–8.24
Health condition and care relation to education, indicators by selected characteristics, 1989, 4147–10.180
Health risk behavior, prevalence of 7 habits, by age, State, and other characteristics, 1986-90, article, 4202–7.305
High school dropouts and transfers between public and private schools, by instn control, income level, and race, 1990 survey, 4826–10.4
Hispanic Americans health insurance coverage, by source, employment and poverty status, and origin, 1987-90, GAO rpt, 26131–97
Households (single person and nonfamily) social, economic and housing characteristics, by tenure, 1989, 2486–1.15
Households and housing unit summary characteristics, 1989 and trends, chartbook, 2486–2.1
Households composition, income, benefits, and labor force status, Survey of Income and Program Participation methodology, working paper series, 2626–10
Households, family, and personal income, wealth, and poverty measures, 1960s-90, Current Population Rpt, chartbook, 2546–6.75
Households income transition between higher and lower income levels, 1979-88, 8008–156
Housing (rental) units, total, with HUD assistance by program, and eligible for aid, by unit, household, and neighborhood characteristics, and location, 1989, biennial rpt, 5184–11
Housing and households characteristics, and unit and neighborhood quality, by MSA location for 11 MSAs, 1987 survey, supplement, 2485–8
Housing and households detailed characteristics, and unit and neighborhood quality, by location, 1989, biennial rpt supplement, 2485–13
Housing and households detailed characteristics, and unit and neighborhood quality, MSA surveys, series, 2485–6
Housing unit and household characteristics of recent movers, and reason for move, by tenure, 1989, 2486–1.12
Immigrant and nonimmigrant visa applicants refused, and refusals overcome, by reason, FY90, annual rpt, 7184–1.3
Income (household) and poverty status under alternative income definitions, by recipient characteristics, 1979-91, annual Current Population Rpt, 2546–6.78
Income (household) and wealth distribution by selected characteristics, with foreign comparisons, 1992 compilation of papers, Current Population Rpt, 2546–6.79
Income (minimum) measures for poverty definitions, comparison of US and Netherlands measures, 1991 working paper, 6886–6.84
Income (personal) relative to median, by race and selected other characteristics, mid 1960s-89, Current Population Rpt, 2546–6.73
Income (poverty) guidelines and derivation, by family size, 1992 with trends from 1965, article, 4742–1.310
Indian Health Service and tribal facilities and use, and Indians health and other characteristics, by IHS region, 1980s-90, annual chartbook, 4084–7
Inflation impact on poverty population, alternative models assessment, 1992 article, 9377–1.306
Insurance (health) denial by private carriers because of poor health, by selected characteristics, 1987, 4186–8.23
Latin America economic and social conditions, resources, trade, and aid, 1992, annual factbook, 9914–14
Maternal and child health indicators and services use, by age, race, and poverty status, 1988, 4478–197
Medicaid coverage, funding, and costs, with reform recommendations, mid 1960s-92, 10048–83
Medicare payment of physicians, vulnerable beneficiaries services use prior to fee schedule implementation, 1986-90, annual rpt, 17266–1.8
Medicare premiums and out-of-pocket costs paid by Medicaid, eligibility and participation, by State, 1991, hearing, 21148–67
Mental health care facilities, staff, patients, and finances, 1970s-91, biennial rpt, 4094–1
Mental illness (serious) among adults, functional limitations, govt aid, drugs used, visits to professionals, and other characteristics, 1989, 4146–8.220
Migration, immigration, and mover characteristics compared to nonmovers, 1987-90, annual Current Population Rpt, 2546–1.456
Migration since 1990, mover characteristics by same or different area, and compared to nonmovers, 1991, annual Current Population Rpt, 2546–1.464
Mississippi poverty, hunger, and public welfare program operations and indicators of need, 1991 hearing, 21968–57
NYC housing supply, occupancy, condition, and household characteristics, by tenure and borough, 1991 triennial survey, 2488–3
OASDI beneficiary data collection system design compared to earlier surveys, with summary results, 1992 article, 4742–1.313
OASI retirement earnings test, liberalization effect on beneficiaries and Federal revenue, 1991 hearing, 21788–215
Ohio poverty, hunger, and public welfare program operations and indicators of need, by county, 1991 hearing, 21968–58
Older persons and younger adults household income, by source, household composition, and age group, 1984 and 1989, article, 4742–1.304
Older persons and younger adults household income, by source, household composition, race, and age group, 1984-89, 4746–26.20
Older persons economic status compared to other age groups, 1990 and trends from 1947, 4746–26.24
Older persons in poverty, by health, nutrition, assistance, and other characteristics, 1990, GAO rpt, 26131–100
Older persons income and sources, by OASDI beneficiary and poverty status, and other characteristics, 1990, biennial chartbook, 4744–25
Older persons income and sources, by whether OASDI beneficiary, poverty status, and other characteristics, 1990, biennial rpt, 4744–26

Older persons socioeconomic characteristics, 1900s-90 and projected to 2050, biennial chartbook, 12904–1
Older population, and health, economic, and other characteristics, with foreign comparisons, 1980s-91 with trends and projections, Current Population Rpt, 2546–2.165
Pacific territories population and housing detailed characteristics, by location, 1990 Census of Population and Housing, series, 2551–8
Population and families in poverty, by detailed socioeconomic characteristics, 1991, annual Current Population Rpt, 2546–6.77
Population and labor force characteristics, 1940s-90 and projected to 2000, 15496–1.16
Population economic well-being indicators, by selected characteristics and household income and income-to-poverty ratio, 1984, 2546–20.22
Population in poverty, and impacts of selected cash and noncash benefits and benefit changes, 1980s, 21788–212
Population poverty status by age group and living arrangements, and family poverty threshold, late 1930s-91, annual rpt, 4744–3.1
Rural areas economic conditions and dev, quarterly journal, 1502–8
Single parent families in own and others homes, by financial, housing, and other characteristics, 1989, 2486–1.14
Statistical Abstract of US, 1992 annual data compilation, 2324–1.14
Tax policy impacts on economic performance and income distribution, issues and background data, with foreign comparisons, 1991 and trends, 21788–211
Telephone local service charges and low-income subsidies, by region, company, and city, 1980s-91, semiannual rpt, 9282–8
Women's labor force status, earnings, and other characteristics, with comparisons to men, fact sheet series, 6564–1
see also Aid to Families with Dependent Children
see also Food assistance
see also Food stamp programs
see also Homeless population
see also Income maintenance
see also Low-income energy assistance
see also Low-income housing
see also Public welfare programs
see also State funding for social welfare
see also under By Income in the "Index by Categories"

Power plants
see Electric power plants and equipment

Power resources
see terms listed under Energy resources and consumption

Powers, Susan
"Statistical Needs in Eastern Europe", 6722–1.317

Prawiraatmadja, Widhyawan
"Indonesia: Asia Pacific Energy Series Country Report", 3406–6.9

PRC
see China, Peoples Republic

Precious metals
see Gold
see Silver

Precious stones
see Gemstones

Precipitation
see Weather

Predictions
see Projections and forecasts

Prefabricated buildings
County Business Patterns, 1989: employment, establishments, and payroll, by SIC 2- to 4-digit industry and county, annual State rpt series, 2326–8
County Business Patterns, 1990: employment, establishments, and payroll, by SIC 2- to 4-digit industry and county, annual State rpt series, 2326–6
Employment, earnings, and hours, by SIC 1- to 4-digit industry, monthly 1989-Feb 1992, annual rpt, 6744–4
Exports and imports between US and outlying areas, by detailed commodity and mode of transport, 1991, annual rpt, 2424–11
Exports and imports of US, by country and detailed commodity, monthly rpt, 2422–12
Exports and imports of US, by Harmonized System 6-digit commodity and country, 1991, annual rpt, 2424–13
Exports and imports of US, by transport mode, country, and SITC 1- to 3-digit commodity, 1991, annual rpt, 2424–12
Exports, imports, tariffs, and industry operating data for prefabricated buildings, 1992 rpt, 9885–10.3
Exports of US, detailed Schedule B commodities with countries of destination, 1991, annual rpt, 2424–10
Input-output structure of US economy, detailed interindustry transactions for 541 industries, and components of final demand, 1982 benchmark data, 2708–17
Manufacturing annual survey, 1990: finances and operations, by SIC 2- to 4-digit industry, series, 2506–14
Manufacturing census, 1987: concentration of largest firms measured by value added, and for shipments by SIC 2- and 4-digit industry, subject rpt, 2497–6
Manufacturing census, 1987: shipments of manufacturers products, by customer class and SIC 2- and 4-digit industry, subject rpt, 2497–4
Manufacturing finances and operations, by SIC 2- to 4-digit industry, forecast 1992, annual rpt, 2044–28
Mortgages FHA-insured, financial, property, and borrower characteristics, by State, 1991, annual rpt, 5144–1
Occupational injury and illness rates, by SIC 2- to 4-digit industry, 1989-90, annual rpt, 6844–7
Occupational injury and illness rates, by SIC 2- to 4-digit industry, 1990, annual rpt, 6844–1
Price indexes (producer), by stage of processing and detailed commodity, monthly rpt, 6762–6
Price indexes (producer), by stage of processing and detailed commodity, monthly 1991, annual rpt, 6764–2
Price indexes (producer) for building materials, by type, quarterly rpt, 2042–1.5
Science, engineering, and technical employment in manufacturing, by field and industry, 1989, triennial rpt, 9627–23
see also Mobile homes

Pregnancy
see Abortion
see Births out of wedlock
see Fetal deaths
see Maternal deaths
see Maternity
see Obstetrics and gynecology
see Prenatal care
see Teenage pregnancy

Prenatal care
Births and rates, by characteristics of birth, infant, and mother, and presence of maternal risk factors and birth defects, 1989, 4146–5.125
Births of low birthweight to Medicaid patients, by prenatal care source and adequacy, and other risk factors, for 2 States, late 1980s, article, 4042–3.304
Drug abuse by mothers, treatment and other services use, referrals, needs, and barriers, for 13 NIDA-funded programs, 1990/91 survey, 4498–76
Education natl goals progress indicators, by State, 1992, annual rpt, 15914–1
Food aid program of USDA for women, infants, and children, prenatal participation effects on birthweight and health and social welfare costs, 1960s-90, GAO rpt, 26121–458
Hawaii prenatal care adequacy relation to mothers ethnic group and other characteristics, 1992 article, 4042–3.366
Health condition and care indicators, 1950s-90 with health improvement and disease prevention goals for 1990, annual data compilation, 4144–11
Health condition of children and mothers, and services use, indicators by age, race, and poverty status 1988, 4478–197
HHS financial aid, by program, recipient, State, and city, FY91, annual regional listings, 4004–3
Indian low birthweight births, compared to whites and blacks, for New York, 1980s, article, 4042–3.359
Indians prenatal care and adverse birth outcomes, relation to local services availability, 1980-85, conf paper, 4164–2
Infant health, deaths and risk factors, and prevention issues, for US and selected countries, 1990 conf, 4148–28
Medicaid eligibility expansion for prenatal care, coverage, use, and costs, by State, 1990-91, 4008–120
Medicaid prenatal care program costs and benefits, for Missouri, 1988, article, 4042–3.365
Mississippi poverty, hunger, and public welfare program operations and indicators of need, 1991 hearing, 21968–57
Smoking among pregnant women, by age and marital status, for Indians in Washington State, mid 1980s, article, 4042–3.306
Spina bifida and other neural tube birth defects prevention through prenatal use of folic acid supplements, findings and CDC recommendations, 1992 rpt, 4206–2.64

Statistical Abstract of US, 1992 annual data compilation, 2324–1.2
Teenage abortion and late prenatal care initiation, risk relation to season of conception, 1979-86, article, 4042–3.372
Women, infants, and children food aid program of USDA, prenatal enrollment, by selected maternal and prenatal care characteristics, 1988-89 local area study, article, 4042–3.305

Prero, Aaron J.
"Transitional Employment Training for SSI Recipients with Mental Retardation", 4742–1.301

Preschool education
Availability, demand, use, and costs of child day care and early childhood education programs and provider and enrollee characteristics, 1990 survey, 4808–39
Census of Population and Housing, 1990: summary characteristics, by county, subdiv, and place, State rpt series, 2551–7
Child care arrangements of mothers employed and in school, and costs, by age of child and characteristics of mother, 1988, Current Population Rpt, 2546–20.24
Child care arrangements prior to 1st grade, by setting and parents' educational level, 1991 survey, 4826–10.2
Condition of Education, detail for elementary, secondary, and higher education, 1920s-91 and projected to 2002, annual rpt, 4824–1
Digest of Education Statistics, 1992 annual data compilation, 4824–2
Drug abuse by mothers, treatment and other services use, referrals, needs, and barriers, for 13 NIDA-funded programs, 1990/91 survey, 4498–76
Enrollment, by grade, instn type and control, and student characteristics, 1989 and trends from 1947, annual Current Population Rpt, 2546–1.459
Enrollment, finances, staff, and high school grads, for elementary and secondary public school systems by State, FY89-90, annual rpt, 4834–6
Handicapped children early education project descriptions, 1991/92, annual listing, 4944–10
HHS financial aid, by program, recipient, State, and city, FY91, annual regional listings, 4004–3
Kindergarten students transition from preschool, programs and factors affecting activities, 1989-90 study, 4808–44
Literacy program for preschoolers and parents, Even Start program activities and grants by recipient, FY90, annual listing, 4804–41
Natl Education Goals progress indicators, by State, 1992, annual rpt, 15914–1
Pacific territories population and housing detailed characteristics, by location, 1990 Census of Population and Housing, series, 2551–8
Special education programs, enrollment by age, staff, funding, and needs, by type of handicap and State, 1990/91, annual rpt, 4944–4
Statistical Abstract of US, 1992 annual data compilation, 2324–1.4
see also Head Start Project

Prescott, Edward C.
"Liquidity Constraints in Economies with Aggregate Fluctuations: A Quantitative Exploration", 9383–20.19

Prescription drugs
see Drugs

Presidency of the U.S.
Approval rating and political party of president, impact on defense spending and transfer payments, model description and results, 1950s-88, working paper, 9393–10.17
Election (presidential) campaign Federal matching funds receipts, by candidate, 1992 primary elections, press release, 9276–1.98
Election (presidential) campaign Federal matching funds requested, by candidate, 1992 primary elections, press release, 9276–1.104
Election (presidential) campaign receipts and expenditures, by type, and by candidate and party, 1992 primary elections, press release, 9276–1.99
Election (presidential) campaign spending limits for candidates, and voting age population, by State, 1992 primary elections, press release, 9276–1.97
Election campaign finances and FEC activities, various periods 1975-91, annual rpt, 9274–1
Election campaign finances to FEC, by type of filer, 1990 natl elections, biennial rpt series, 9276–2
Election campaign-related internal communications of firms and assns, spending by organization, location, and candidate, 1991-92, biennial rpt, 9274–3
Election participation since 1930, and voting age population, by sex, age, race, and State, forecast 1992 general elections, Current Population Rpt, 2546–3.170
Election voter turnout by age and sex, 1990 congressional elections, with trends from 1964, fact sheet, 2326–17.39
Libraries (presidential) holdings, use, and costs, by instn, FY91, annual rpt, 9514–2
Presidential election campaign fund contributions from income tax return checkoff, receipts and outlays, mid 1970s-91 and alternative projections to 1993, hearing, 21428–10
Statistical Abstract of US, 1992 annual data compilation, 2324–1.8
Threats against President, criminal case processing and dispositions in Federal district court, 1980-91, annual rpt, 6064–31
Threats against President, criminal case processing and dispositions in Federal district court, 1989, annual data compilation, 6064–29
Threats against President, prisoners in Federal instns by race and sex, FY89, annual rpt, 6244–1.1
see also Executive Office of the President
see also Presidential appointments

Presidential advisory bodies
see Federal boards, committees, and commissions
see under names of individual Presidential commissions (starting with Presidential or President's)

Presidential appointments
Employment (noncareer) of Fed Govt, conversions to career appointments, by pay grade and agency, 1988-89, GAO rpt, 26119–382
Former US govt officials representing foreign interests, activities and individuals, FY86-91, GAO rpt, 26123–134
Judges appointed to district and appeals courts, by previous experience and other characteristics, data compilation, 1992 annual rpt, 6064–6.1
Senior Executive Service members characteristics, entries, exits, and awards, FY79-91, annual rpt, 9844–36
Senior Executive Service noncareer and Schedule C appointments, by agency, 1990-91, GAO rpt, 26119–412

Presidential commissions
see Federal boards, committees, and commissions
see under names of individual Presidential commissions (starting with Presidential or President's)

Presidential-congressional relations
see Congressional-executive relations

Presidential powers
see also Congressional-executive relations
see also Executive agreements
see also Executive impoundment of appropriated funds
see also Presidential appointments

President's Council on Competitiveness
Tort and other civil litigation reform recommendations, with background data, 1960-90, 048–3

Press
see Freedom of the press
see Journalism
see Newspapers

Pressure groups
see Lobbying and lobbying groups
see Political action committees

Prete, Lawrence
"Electric Utility Demand-Side Management", 3162–35.302
"Nonutility Power Producers", 3162–35.301

Pretrial detention and release
Aliens (illegal) held in Immigration and Naturalization Service detention facilities pending hearings, and legal aid requests, 1980s-91, GAO rpt, 26119–409
Criminal activity while on release, Federal sentencing guidelines by offense and circumstances, series, 17668–1
Criminal case processing in Federal courts, by offense, disposition, and jurisdiction, data compilation, 1992 annual rpt, 6064–6.5
Drug test results at arrest, by drug type, offense, and sex, for selected urban areas, quarterly rpt, 6062–3
Federal district court criminal case processing and dispositions, by offense, district, and offender characteristics, 1989, annual data compilation, 6064–29
Federal district court pretrial reports, detention, supervision, and bail violations, 1991, annual rpt, 18204–8.23
Federal district court pretrial service cases, by type of bail rpt, circuit, and district, 1991, annual rpt, 18204–11
Marshals Service activities, FY91, annual rpt, 6294–1

Prisoners in Federal and contract instns, by selected characteristics, region, and Federal instn, FY89, annual rpt, 6244–1.1
US attorneys civil and criminal cases by type and disposition, and collections, by Federal district, FY91, annual rpt, 6004–2.1
see also Habeas corpus

Preventive medicine
AIDS prevention programs for drug abusers and their sexual partners, client characteristics, and outcomes, for selected metro areas, 1989 annual conf, 4494–12
AIDS public knowledge, attitudes, info sources, and testing, 1991 survey, 4146–8.218
Cancer (breast) symptoms duration prior to seeking care, for black and white women, by selected characteristics, 1985-86 local area study, article, 4472–1.323
Child and maternal health condition and services use, indicators by age, race, and poverty status, 1988, 4478–197
Diabetes patients physician office visits, by characteristics of patient, physician, and visit, 1989, 4146–8.212
Disease and injury prevention activities effectiveness, evaluation methodologies, 1992 rpt, 4206–2.53
Health condition and care indicators, 1950s-90 with health improvement and disease prevention goals for 1990, annual data compilation, 4144–11
HHS financial aid, by program, recipient, State, and city, FY91, annual regional listings, 4004–3
HHS public health innovation contest winners, project descriptions and costs, 1991, article, 4042–3.322
House of Representatives salaries, expenses, and contingent fund disbursement, detailed listings, quarterly rpt, 21942–1
Indian and Alaska Native youth health condition and behavioral patterns, by sex and grade, 1988-90, 4088–3
Indian Health Service outpatient services provided, by reason for visit and age, FY90, annual rpt, 4084–2
Labor supply and education of health professionals, by professional and other characteristics, and location, 1960s-92 and projected to 2020, biennial rpt, 4114–8
Medicare coverage of new health care technologies, risks and benefit evaluations, series, 4186–10
Medicare payment of physicians, vulnerable beneficiaries services use prior to fee schedule implementation, 1986-90, annual rpt, 17266–1.8
Menopause treatment with hormone replacement therapy, use, health risks, and research funding, 1992 rpt, 26358–261
Military health care personnel, and accessions by training source, by occupation, specialty, and service branch, FY90, annual rpt, 3544–24
Morbidity and Mortality Weekly Report, infectious notifiable disease cases by State, and public health issues, 4202–1
Older persons health education centers medication mgmt and other preventive health activities, and Federal funding, FY83-91, article, 4042–3.303
Older persons health promotion program, costs and effectiveness of case mgmt and health education, 1980-83 local area study, article, 4042–3.342
Pediatrician office visits, by characteristics of patient and visit, 1989, 4146–8.210
Physicians, by specialty, age, sex, and location of training and practice, 1990, State rpt series, 4116–6
Public Health Reports, bimonthly journal, 4042–3
Research activities and grants of HCFA, by program, FY91, annual listing, 4654–10
Senate receipts, itemized expenses by payee, and balances, 1st half FY92, semiannual listing, 25922–1
Smoking cessation TV promotion campaign, hotline calls by sex, race, age, and education, aggregate 1983-87, article, 4472–1.313
Smoking prevalence, health effects, and control strategies effectiveness, research results, series, 4476–7
Smoking, tobacco, and health impacts research rpts, 1991 annual report, 4204–19
Youth health condition, risk factors, and preventive and treatment services use and availability, 1970s-80s, 26358–234
see also Health maintenance organizations
see also Medical examinations and tests
see also Prenatal care
see also Vaccination and vaccines

Price indexes
see Consumer Price Index
see Producer Price Index

Price regulation
Energy suppliers rate regulation, and hydroelectric project licensing, for FERC, FY91, annual rpt, 3084–9
Health care spending per capita by State, 1990, and relation to income, services availability, rate control, and other factors, 1982, GAO rpt, 26121–444
Hospital costs per capita in ratesetting States, and HMO enrollment, 1980s-90, article, 4652–1.311
Hospital reimbursement by Medicaid and States rate-setting, adjustments for volume fluctuation, 1991, 17206–2.34
Hospital reimbursement by Medicaid, provisions by State, 1991, 17206–2.35
Insurance (health) reforms of States to improve small business access, provisions with background data by State, 1991, GAO rpt, 26121–462
Medicare payment of physicians under fee schedule, impacts on charges by specialty and State, 1992 and 1996, hearing, 25368–178
Physicians payment by Medicare, impacts of reforms on services, and monitoring methods, 1992 annual rpt, 4004–34
Physicians payment by Medicare under fee schedule, adjustment factor recommendations, 1993, annual rpt, 4004–33
Stock market decline of Nov 1991, impacts of trading related to option and futures expirations, 9738–22
Telephone service subscribership, charges, and local and long distance firm finances and operations, late 1970s-92, semiannual rpt, 9282–7
Transport tariff schedules submitted to ICC, by disposition and mode of transport, FY91, annual rpt, 9484–1.1
see also Agricultural production quotas and price supports
see also Rent control

Price, Rumi K.
"Estimating the Prevalence of Chronic Fatigue Syndrome and Associated Symptoms in the Community", 4042–3.354

Prices
Airline consumer complaints to DOT about service by US and foreign carrier, and for travel and cargo service, by reason, monthly rpt, 7302–11
Business activity indicators, 1990, annual rpt, 9364–5.9
Business cycle recession and expansion duration indicators, 1850s-1990, working paper, 9375–13.83
Business statistics, detailed data for major industries and economic indicators, *Survey of Current Business*, monthly rpt, 2702–1
Business statistics, detailed data for major industries and economic indicators, 1960-91, *Survey of Current Business* biennial supplement, 2704–1
Department store advertised sale prices and references to competitors prices, and actual consumer savings, 1990-91 local area study, 9408–57
Department store inventory price indexes, by class of item, monthly table, 6762–7
Economic indicators, monthly rpt, 9362–1.2
Exchange rates relation to domestic and foreign relative prices, for US and 7 other countries, model description and results 1970s-90, working paper, 9381–10.123
Export and import price indexes, by selected end-use category, monthly press release, 6762–15
Export and import price indexes for goods and services, and dollar exchange rate indexes, quarterly press release, 6762–13
Exports, imports, and trade flows, by country and commodity, with background economic indicators, data compilation, monthly CD-ROM, 2002–6
Fiscal policy (supply side) of Reagan Admin, economic impacts, 1980s and trends from 1960s, technical paper, 9385–1.304; 9385–8.125
Foreign and US economic conditions, and trade devs and balances, with data by selected country and country group, monthly rpt, 9882–14
Foreign and US economic conditions, for major industrial countries, monthly rpt, 9112–1
Foreign countries economic indicators, and trade and investment flows, for selected countries and country groups, selected years 1946-91, annual rpt, 204–1.9
Haiti economic conditions, 1985-91, working paper, 9916–13.3
Import price indexes for manufactured and nonmanufactured goods, changes by world area, 1991-92, article, 6722–1.327
Imports and tariff provisions effect on US industries and products, investigations with background financial and operating data, series, 9886–4

Imports injury to US industries from foreign subsidized products and sales at less than fair value, investigations with background financial and operating data, series, 9886–19
Imports injury to US industries from foreign subsidized products, investigations with background financial and operating data, series, 9886–15
Imports injury to US industries from sales at less than fair value, investigations with background financial and operating data, series, 9886–14
Intl investment position of US, by component, industry, world region, and country, 1990-91, annual article, 2702–1.323
Mail order catalog price changes, and relation to inflation, by item, 1953-87, working paper, 9375–13.76
Middle Atlantic States manufacturing business outlook, monthly survey rpt, 9387–11
Natl income and product accounts and components, *Survey of Current Business*, monthly rpt, 2702–1.23
Statistical Abstract of US, 1992 annual data compilation, 2324–1.15
Telecommunications domestic and intl rates, by type of service and area served, 1990, annual rpt, 9284–6.6
Telecommunications finances, rates, and traffic for US carriers intl operations, by service type, firm, and country, 1975-90, annual rpt, 9284–17
Telephone local service charges and low-income subsidies, by region, company, and city, 1980s-91, semiannual rpt, 9282–8
Telephone service subscribership, charges, and local and long distance firm finances and operations, late 1970s-92, semiannual rpt, 9282–7
Tennessee Valley economic conditions, and compared to US, alternative projections 1992-2010 and trends from 1929, annual rpt, 9804–27
see also Agricultural prices
see also Agricultural production quotas and price supports
see also Coal prices
see also Consumer Price Index
see also Electric power prices
see also Energy prices
see also Family budgets
see also Food prices
see also Housing costs and financing
see also Inflation
see also Medical costs
see also Natural gas prices
see also Petroleum prices
see also Price regulation
see also Producer Price Index
see also Professionals' fees
see also under names of specific commodities or commodity groups

Priester, Jeanne M.
"Extension System's Commitment to Independent Living for Older Americans", 1504–9.1

Primary Metropolitan Statistical Areas
see Metropolitan Statistical Areas

Prince George's County, Md.
Fed Govt land acquisition and dev projects in DC metro area, characteristics and funding by agency and project, FY92-96, annual rpt, 15454–1
Housing and households characteristics, unit and neighborhood quality, and journey to work by MSA location, for 11 MSAs, 1985 survey, supplement, 2485–8
Housing and households detailed characteristics, and unit and neighborhood quality, by location, 1989 survey, MSA rpt, 2485–6.1

Prince William County, Va.
Fed Govt land acquisition and dev projects in DC metro area, characteristics and funding by agency and project, FY92-96, annual rpt, 15454–1

Prince William Sound, Alaska
Oil spill from tanker Exxon Valdez, impacts on marine mammals, and resulting legislation, 1991 annual rpt, 14734–1
Tide height and time daily at coastal points, forecast 1993, annual rpt, 2174–2.1

Printing and publishing industry
Banks in Fed Reserve System, expenses and operations itemized by service, office, and district, 1991, annual rpt, 9364–11
Collective bargaining agreements expiring during year, and workers covered, by firm, union, industry group, and State, 1992, annual rpt, 6784–9
County Business Patterns, 1989: employment, establishments, and payroll, by SIC 2- to 4-digit industry and county, annual State rpt series, 2326–8
County Business Patterns, 1990: employment, establishments, and payroll, by SIC 2- to 4-digit industry and county, annual State rpt series, 2326–6
CPI by component for US city average, and by selected metro area, region, and population size, monthly rpt, 6762–2
Employment, earnings, and hours, by SIC 1- to 4-digit industry, monthly 1989-Feb 1992, annual rpt, 6744–4
Employment of minorities and women, by occupation, SIC 1- to 3-digit industry, State, and MSA, 1991, annual rpt, 9244–1
Employment, unemployment, and labor force characteristics, by region and census div, 1991, annual rpt, 6744–7.1
Energy use and prices, by fuel type and manufacturing industry, 1974-88, 3166–15.3
Energy use and prices for manufacturing industries, 1988 survey, series, 3166–13
Exports and imports between US and outlying areas, by detailed commodity and mode of transport, 1991, annual rpt, 2424–11
Exports and imports of US, by country and detailed commodity, monthly rpt, 2422–12
Exports and imports of US, by Harmonized System 6-digit commodity and country, 1991, annual rpt, 2424–13
Exports and imports of US, by transport mode, country, and SITC 1- to 3-digit commodity, 1991, annual rpt, 2424–12
Exports of US, detailed commodities by country, monthly CD-ROM, 2422–13
Exports of US, detailed Schedule B commodities with countries of destination, 1991, annual rpt, 2424–10
Fed Govt labor productivity, indexes of output and labor costs by function, FY67-90, annual rpt, 6824–1.6
Freight (waterborne domestic and foreign) by commodity, traffic, and passengers, by port and waterway, 1989, annual rpt, 3754–3
GPO activities, finances, and production, FY91, annual rpt, 26204–1
GPO activities, staff, and productivity, 1970s-90 and projected to 2000, 26208–4
Hazardous substances industrial releases and reduction methods under EPA regulation, by chemical, source, industry, and location, 1989, annual rpt, 9234–6
Hazardous substances industrial releases and reduction methods under EPA regulation, with chemical stocks and use, facility directory, 1987-89, annual CD-ROM, 9234–7
Imports, exports, and employment impacts, by SIC 2- to 4-digit industry and commodity, quarterly rpt, 2322–2
Imports of US, detailed commodities by country, monthly CD-ROM, 2422–14
Input-output structure of US economy, detailed interindustry transactions for 84 industries, and components of final demand, 1987, annual article, 2702–1.316
Input-output structure of US economy, detailed interindustry transactions for 541 industries, and components of final demand, 1982 benchmark data, 2708–17
Mail volume to and from households, use, and views, by class, source, content, and household characteristics, FY87-90, annual rpt, 9864–10
Manufacturing annual survey, 1990: finances and operations, by SIC 2- to 4-digit industry, series, 2506–14
Manufacturing census, 1987: concentration of largest firms measured by value added, and for shipments by SIC 2- and 4-digit industry, subject rpt, 2497–6
Manufacturing census, 1987: shipments of manufacturers products, by customer class and SIC 2- and 4-digit industry, subject rpt, 2497–4
Manufacturing corporations financial statements, by selected SIC 2- to 3-digit industry, quarterly rpt, 2502–1
Manufacturing finances and operations, by SIC 2- to 4-digit industry, forecast 1992, annual rpt, 2044–28
Manufacturing industries operations and performance, analytical rpt series, 2506–16
Manufacturing production, shipments, inventories, orders, and pollution control costs, periodic Current Industrial Rpt series, 2506–3
Mexico imports from US, by industry and State, 1987-91, 2048–154
Military and personal property shipments, passenger traffic, and costs, by service branch and mode of transport, FY91, annual rpt, 3704–15
Military prime contract awards, by detailed procurement category, FY88-91, annual rpt, 3544–18
Multinatl firms US affiliates finances and operations, by industry, country of parent firm, and State, 1987, 2708–48

Multinatl US firms and foreign affiliates finances and operations, by industry and country, 1989 benchmark survey, annual rpt, 2704–5
Occupational injury and illness rates, by SIC 2- to 4-digit industry, 1989-90, annual rpt, 6844–7
Occupational injury and illness rates, by SIC 2- to 4-digit industry, 1990, annual rpt, 6844–1
Pacific territories population and housing detailed characteristics, by location, 1990 Census of Population and Housing, series, 2551–8
Pollution abatement capital and operating costs, by SIC 2- to 4-digit industry and State, 1990, annual Current Industrial Rpt, 2506–3.6
Price indexes (producer), by stage of processing and detailed commodity, monthly rpt, 6762–6
Price indexes (producer), by stage of processing and detailed commodity, monthly 1991, annual rpt, 6764–2
Puerto Rico and other US possessions corporations income tax returns, income and tax items, and employment, by selected industry, 1989, article, 8302–2.326
Science, engineering, and technical employment in manufacturing, by field and industry, 1989, triennial rpt, 9627–23
Statistical Abstract of US, 1992 annual data compilation, 2324–1.18
Tax (income) returns of corporations, income and tax items by asset size and detailed industry, 1989, annual rpt, 8304–4; 8304–21
Tax (income) returns of partnerships, income statement and balance sheet items, by industry group, 1990, annual article, 8302–2.314
Tax (income) returns of sole proprietorships, income statement items, by industry group, 1990, annual article, 8302–2.317; 8302–2.320
see also Books and bookselling
see also Copyright
see also Microforms
see also Newspapers
see also Periodicals
see also Writers and writing
see also under By Industry in the "Index by Categories"

Prison sentences
see Sentences, criminal procedure

Prison work programs
Facilities, population, employment, spending, and other characteristics of correctional instns, by State and for Fed Govt, 1990, quinquennial rpt, 6068–218
Fed Bur of Prisons admin offices and correctional instns, facility characteristics, 1992, annual listing, 6244–4
Fed Prison Industries finances and operations, FY91, annual rpt, 6244–3
Fed Prison Industries sales, by commodity and Federal agency, FY91, annual rpt, 6244–5
Participants of work release programs, and provisions for using inmate labor for prison construction, by State, data compilation, 1992 annual rpt, 6064–6.1; 6064–6.6

Prisoners
Admissions and releases from prison and parole, sentence length, and time served, by offense and offender characteristics, 1988, annual rpt, 6064–33
AIDS and tuberculosis cases in prisons, test results, and control and treatment policies, by location, 1990 survey, annual rpt, 6064–22
Court criminal case processing in Federal district courts, and dispositions, by offense, 1980-91, annual rpt, 6064–31
Criminal activity in prison, Federal sentencing guidelines by offense and circumstances, series, 17668–1
Drug abuse indicators for selected metro areas, research results, data collection, and policy issues, 1992 semiannual conf, 4492–5
Drug abuse treatment and education programs for prisoners and parolees, activities, costs, and outcomes, 1990 conf, 4498–77
Drug smuggling interdiction, inmate and staff testing, and treatment programs, by prison characteristics, 1989-90, 6066–19.70
Drunk driving arrests, sentencing, and prisoner drinking patterns and other characteristics, 1989, 6066–19.69
Fed Bur of Prisons activities, and inmate and staff characteristics, 1991, annual rpt, 6244–2
Federal correctional instn inmates, admissions, releases, and recidivism, by region, monthly rpt series, 6242–1
Federal correctional instns prisoners and staff, by selected characteristics, region, and instn, FY89, annual rpt, 6244–1.1
Foreign countries human rights conditions in 170 countries, 1991, annual rpt, 21384–3
HHS financial aid, by program, recipient, State, and city, FY91, annual regional listings, 4004–3
Jail population by sex, race, and for 25 jurisdictions, and instn conditions, 1990-91, annual rpt, 6066–25.48
Marshals Service activities, FY91, annual rpt, 6294–1
Mental health care facilities, staff, patients, and finances, 1970s-91, biennial rpt, 4094–1
Pacific territories population and housing detailed characteristics, by location, 1990 Census of Population and Housing, series, 2551–8
Petitions of prisoners, and dispositions in Federal district and appeals courts, by type, 1991, annual rpt, 18204–8; 18204–11
Population and movements of prisoners, by offense, location, and selected other characteristics, data compilation, 1992 annual rpt, 6064–6.6
Population census, 1990: institutionalized population and persons in group quarters, by sex, race, county, place, and urban-rural location, State rpt series, 2531–1
Population census, 1990: institutionalized population and persons in group quarters, for Native American, urban, and metro areas, series, 2531–2
Population, facilities, employment, spending, and other characteristics of correctional instns, by State and for Fed Govt, 1990, quinquennial rpt, 6068–218
Population of Federal and State instns by selected characteristics, releases, staff, and instn size, with data by region and State, late 1970s-91, 6068–248
Population of Federal and State instns by sex, admissions, and instn capacity and overcrowding, by State, 1980s-91, annual rpt, 6066–25.47
Population of prisoners, characteristics, and movements, by State, 1990, annual rpt, 6064–26
States criminal justice systems activities, employment, funding, and data collection, by State, 1970s-91, annual rpt, 6064–40
Statistical Abstract of US, 1992 annual data compilation, 2324–1.5
US attorneys civil and criminal cases by type and disposition, and collections, by Federal district, FY91, annual rpt, 6004–2.1
Veterans post-traumatic stress cases by period of service, and VA treatment and rehabilitation program operations and staff, by site, FY91, annual rpt, 8704–6
Women in jail, by criminal background and sociodemographic characteristics, with comparisons to men, 1989, 6066–19.66
see also Community-based correctional programs
see also Parole and probation
see also Prison work programs
see also Prisoners of war

Prisoners of war
Mental illness (post-traumatic stress) among veterans by period of service, and VA treatment and rehabilitation program operations and staff, FY91, annual rpt, 8704–6
Military deaths by cause, age, race, and rank, and personnel captured and missing, by service branch, FY91, annual rpt, 3544–40
Veterans health care, patients, visits, costs, and operating beds, by VA and contract facility, and region, quarterly rpt, 8602–4
Vietnam Orderly Departure Program, former re-education camp prisoners arrivals in US and refugee camps, monthly rpt, 7002–4

Prisons
see Correctional institutions
see Juvenile detention and correctional institutions
see Military prisons
see Prison work programs
see Prisoners
see Sentences, criminal procedure

Pristas, Paul J.
"Big Game Fishing in Northern Gulf of Mexico During 1990", 2164–23

Privacy
see Right of privacy

Private schools
Bilingual education enrollment, and eligible students not enrolled, by State, 1990-91, annual rpt, 4804–14
Black higher education instns enrollment, finances, staff, and degrees, by instn and selected student characteristics, 1970s-90, 4848–46
Census of Population and Housing, 1990: summary characteristics, by county, subdiv, and place, State rpt series, 2551–7
Child day care and early childhood education programs availability, demand, use, costs, and provider and enrollee characteristics, 1990 survey, 4808–39

Condition of Education, detail for elementary, secondary, and higher education, 1920s-91 and projected to 2002, annual rpt, 4824–1
Data on education, enrollment, degrees, teachers, and spending, 1977/78-1990/91 and alternative projections to 2002/2003, annual rpt, 4824–4
Digest of Education Statistics, 1992 annual data compilation, 4824–2
Education data, selected trends and projections 1979-2002, annual pamphlet, 4824–9
Eighth grade class of 1988: educational performance and conditions, characteristics, attitudes, activities, and plans, natl longitudinal survey, series, 4826–9
Elementary and secondary education enrollment, staff, finances, operations, programs, and policies, 1987/88 biennial survey, series, 4836–3
Elementary and secondary education enrollment, teachers, high school grads, and spending, by instn control and State, 1992/93, annual rpt, 4834–19
Elementary and secondary students educational performance, and factors affecting proficiency, by selected characteristics, 1990 natl assessments, subject rpt series, 4896–8
Elementary and secondary students educational performance in math, science, reading, and writing, 1969-90, 4898–32
Enrollment, by grade, instn type and control, and student characteristics, 1989 and trends from 1947, annual Current Population Rpt, 2546–1.459
Enrollment, staff, and spending, by instn level and control, and teacher salaries, 1980s-93, annual press release, 4804–19
High school classes of 1980 and 1982: education, employment, and family characteristics, activities, and attitudes, natl longitudinal study, series, 4826–2
High school dropout rates, and subsequent completion, by student and school characteristics, alternative estimates, 1991, annual rpt, 4834–23
High school dropouts and transfers between public and private schools, by instn control, income level, and race, 1990 survey, 4826–10.4
Higher education enrollment and degrees awarded, by sex, full- and part-time status, and instn level and control, fall 1991, annual rpt, 4844–16
Higher education enrollment, by level, race, and sex, fall 1980-90, biennial rpt, 4844–15
Higher education enrollment, faculty, finances, and degrees, by instn level and control, and State, FY88, annual rpt, 4844–13
Higher education enrollment, tuition, control, location, and other instn characteristics, 1991/92, biennial listing, 4844–3
Higher education faculty and staff, by occupation, full- and part-time status, sex, and instn type and control, fall 1989, biennial rpt, 4844–18
Higher education instn revenue by source and spending by function, by State and instn control, FY82-90, annual rpt, 4844–6
Higher education instn student aid and other sources of support, with student expenses and characteristics, by instn type and control, 1987 triennial study, series, 4846–3; 4846–5
Higher education instn tuition and other charges, by public and private 2- and 4-year instn, and State, 1991/92, annual listing, 4844–10
Higher education noncollegiate instns enrollment and program completions, by sex and instn level and control, fall 1990, annual rpt, 4844–19
Higher education student performance, instns data collection activities, by instn level and control, 1991, 4848–45
Housing and households characteristics, and unit and neighborhood quality, by MSA location for 11 MSAs, 1987 survey, supplement, 2485–8
Housing and households detailed characteristics, and unit and neighborhood quality, by location, 1989, biennial rpt supplement, 2485–13
Indian education funding of Fed Govt, with enrollment, program grants, and fellowships by State, 1980s-FY91, annual rpt, 14874–1
Minority group targeted student aid, higher education instns with awards and funding sources, by instn level and control, 1989/90, hearings, 21408–130
Pacific territories population and housing detailed characteristics, by location, 1990 Census of Population and Housing, series, 2551–8
Pell grants and applicants, by tuition, family and student income, instn type and control, and State, 1990/91, annual rpt, 4804–1
R&D facilities of higher education instns, space and equipment adequacy, needs, and funding by source, by instn type and control, 1992, biennial rpt, 9624–25
R&D funding by Fed Govt for higher education instns, indirect costs and effects of alternative reimbursement policies, FY89, GAO rpt, 26113–592
R&D funding by higher education instns and federally funded centers, by field, instn, and State, FY90, annual rpt, 9627–13
Science and engineering grad enrollment, by field, source of funds, and characteristics of student and instn, 1990, annual rpt, 9627–7
Science and math education, natl assessment of elementary and high school students, 1985/86, series, 4896–6
Statistical Abstract of US, 1992 annual data compilation, 2324–1.4
Student loan Perkins program income, losses, and Federal and school contributions, late 1950s-89, GAO rpt, 26121–440
Teachers in higher education, and salaries, by faculty rank, sex, instn type and control, and State, 1990/91, annual rpt, 4844–8
Vocational education enrollment, student and teacher characteristics, and outcomes, for secondary and postsecondary instns, 1970s-90, 4828–42

Privileges and immunities
Witnesses immunity requests by Federal prosecutors to US Attorney General, and witnesses involved, data compilation, 1992 annual rpt, 6064–6.5
Prizes
see Awards, medals, and prizes
Prizzi, Laura Y.
"Individual Income Tax Returns, 1991: Taxpayer Usage Study", 8302–2.319
Probation
see Parole and probation
Processed foods
see Food and food industry
see Food ingredients and additives
Procurement
see Business orders
see Defense contracts and procurement
see Government contracts and procurement
see Industrial purchasing
Producer Price Index
Agricultural Outlook, production, prices, marketing, and trade, by commodity, forecast and current situation, monthly rpt with articles, 1502–4
BLS data collection, analysis, and presentation methods, by program, 1992 rpt, 6888–1
Building materials PPI, by type, quarterly rpt, 2042–1.5
Business statistics, detailed data for major industries and economic indicators, *Survey of Current Business*, monthly rpt, 2702–1
Business statistics, detailed data for major industries and economic indicators, 1960-91, *Survey of Current Business* biennial supplement, 2704–1
Dairy products PPI, monthly rpt, 1317–4.2
Economic indicators and components, and Fed Reserve 4th District business and financial conditions, monthly chartbook, 9377–10
Economic indicators and components, current data and annual trends, monthly rpt, 23842–1.4
Economic indicators compounded annual rates of change, monthly rpt, 9391–3
Economic indicators, monthly rpt, 9362–1.2
Food consumption, supply, trade, prices, spending, and indexes, by commodity, 1990, annual rpt, 1544–4
Footwear production, employment, use, prices, and US trade by country, quarterly rpt, 9882–6
Lumber (hardwood) production, prices, employment, and trade, quarterly rpt, 1202–4
Meat and fish retail and producer prices, 1987-92, semiannual situation rpt, 1561–15.3
Metals industries economic performance indicators and indexes, by commodity, monthly rpt, 5602–5
Monthly Labor Review, CPI and PPI current statistics, 6722–1.4
North Central States farm credit conditions and economic devs, Fed Reserve 7th District, monthly rpt, 9375–10
OECD intl trade position for US and 4 countries, and factors affecting US competition, quarterly pamphlet, 2042–25
Price indexes (consumer and producer), by commodity group, selected years 1929-91, annual rpt, 204–1.4

Price indexes (producer), by major commodity group and subgroup, and processing stage, monthly press release, 6762–5
Price indexes (producer), by stage of processing and detailed commodity, monthly rpt, 6762–6
Price indexes (producer), by stage of processing and detailed commodity, monthly 1991, annual rpt, 6764–2
Price indexes (producer), changes for selected items by stage of processing, 1987-91, article, 6722–1.323
Sales contract escalation clauses, use of Producer Price Index, methodology, 1991 rpt, 6888–23
Statistical Abstract of US, 1992 annual data compilation, 2324–1.15
Telephone local service charges and low-income subsidies, by region, company, and city, 1980s-91, semiannual rpt, 9282–8

Product safety

Bovine somatotropin (bST) dairy industry use, effectiveness of FDA testing for human and animal safety, 1991, GAO rpt, 26131–101
Consumer Product Safety Commission activities, recalls by brand, and casualties and medical costs, by product type, FY90, annual rpt, 9164–2
FDA investigations and regulatory activities, quarterly rpt, 4062–3
Imports detained by FDA, by reason, product, shipper, brand, and country, monthly listing, 4062–2
Injuries from use of consumer products and related activities, by severity and victim age and sex, 1990, annual rpt, 9164–7
Injuries from use of consumer products, by severity, victim age, and detailed product, 1991, annual rpt, 9164–6
Pacemaker lead implants, failures, and costs, by model, 1992 GAO rpt, 26131–103
Radiation from electronic devices, incidents by type of device, and FDA control activities, 1991, annual rpt, 4064–13
Statistical Abstract of US, 1992 annual data compilation, 2324–1.3
Torts for product liability, caseloads for Federal district courts, 1991, annual rpt, 18204–8.14; 18204–11
see also Defective products
see also Food ingredients and additives
see also Food inspection
see also Hazardous substances
see also Inflammable materials
see also Motor vehicle safety devices
see also Poisoning and drug reaction
see also Quality control and testing

Production

see Agricultural production
see Industrial production
see Industrial production indexes
see Producer Price Index
see Production costs
see Productivity
see Value added tax

Production capacity and utilization

see Industrial capacity and utilization

Production costs

Auto quality changes since last model year, factory and retail value, 1993 model year, annual press release, 6764–3
Competitiveness (intl) of US industries, with selected foreign and US operating data by major firm and product, series, 2046–12
Food prices (farm-retail), marketing cost components, and industry finances and productivity, 1920s-91, annual rpt, 1544–9
Manufacturing annual survey, 1990: finances and operations, by SIC 2- and 3-digit industry and State, 2506–14.3
Minerals foreign and US supply under alternative market conditions, reserves, and background industry data, series, 5606–4
Tax (income) returns of corporations, income and tax items by asset size and detailed industry, 1989, annual rpt, 8304–4; 8304–21
see also Agricultural production costs
see also Business income and expenses, general
see also Business income and expenses, specific industry
see also Capital investments, general
see also Capital investments, specific industry
see also Energy production costs
see also Labor costs and cost indexes
see also Payroll
see also Producer Price Index

Production Credit Associations

see Farm Credit System

Production workers

Black Americans social and economic characteristics, for South and total US, 1991 and trends from 1950, annual Current Population Rpt, 2546–1.463
Building materials industry finances and operations, by SIC 4-digit industry, selected years 1977-89, article, 2042–1.302
Business statistics, detailed data for major industries and economic indicators, 1960-91, *Survey of Current Business* biennial supplement, 2704–1
Dallas-Fort Worth metro area employment, earnings, hours, and CPI changes, late 1970s-91, annual rpt, 6964–2
Earnings and hours, by industry div and major manufacturing group, Monthly Labor Review, 6722–1.2
Earnings, annual average percent changes for selected occupational groups, selected MSAs, monthly rpt, 6782–1.1
Employment and Earnings, detailed data, monthly rpt, 6742–2.6
Employment and economic conditions, alternative BLS projections to 2005 and trends 1975-90, biennial rpt, 6744–19
Employment Cost Index and alternative measure of compensation costs, by component, occupation, industry group, union status, and location, 1975-92, annual rpt, 6744–20
Employment, earnings, and hours, by SIC 1- to 4-digit industry, monthly 1989-Feb 1992, annual rpt, 6744–4
Employment, earnings, and hours, monthly press release, 6742–5
Employment situation, earnings, hours, and other BLS economic indicators, transcripts of BLS Commissioner's monthly testimony, periodic rpt, 23846–4
Foreign and US manufacturing hourly compensation costs, by industry and country, series, 6826–3
Houston metro area employment, earnings, hours, and CPI changes, 1970s-91, annual rpt, 6964–1
Imports injury to US industries from foreign subsidized products, investigations with background financial and operating data, series, 9886–15
Imports injury to US industries from sales at less than fair value, investigations with background financial and operating data, series, 9886–14
Industry finances and operations, by SIC 2- to 4-digit industry, forecast 1992, annual rpt, 2044–28
Labor demand, turnover, and training completions, by detailed occupation, 1990 and projected to 2005, biennial rpt, 6744–3
Manufacturing annual survey, 1990: establishments, employment, finances, inventories, and energy use, by SIC 2- to 4-digit industry, 2506–14.2
Manufacturing annual survey, 1990: finances and operations, by SIC 2- and 3-digit industry and State, 2506–14.3
Manufacturing census, 1987: concentration of largest firms measured by value added, and for shipments by SIC 2- and 4-digit industry, subject rpt, 2497–6
Multinatl US firms and foreign affiliates finances and operations, by industry and country, 1989 benchmark survey, annual rpt, 2704–5
Natl income and product accounts, comprehensive accounts and components, benchmark revisions, 1929-88, 2708–5
Natl income and product accounts, comprehensive accounts and components, *Survey of Current Business*, monthly rpt, 2702–1.29
Occupational Outlook Handbook, 1992-93, biennial rpt, 6744–1
Pacific territories population and housing detailed characteristics, by location, 1990 Census of Population and Housing, series, 2551–8
Southeastern US manufacturing hours and earnings, for 8 States, quarterly press release, 6942–7
Southwestern US employment by industry div, earnings, and hours, by State, monthly rpt, 6962–2
Statistical Abstract of US, 1992 annual data compilation, 2324–1.13
Training for job qualification and skill improvement, workers participating by training source, occupation, age, sex, and race, 1991, 6728–32
see also under By Occupation in the "Index by Categories"

Productivity

Banks productivity, inefficiencies, and economies of scale, alternative model descriptions and results, 1991 working paper, 9377–9.126
Business cycle impacts of productivity shocks, and relation to monetary, fiscal, and demand indicators, 1991 working paper, 9375–13.73
Economic indicators compounded annual rates of change, monthly rpt, 9391–3
Economic indicators, prices, labor costs, and productivity, BLS econometric analyses and methodology, working paper series, 6886–6

Fiscal policy (supply side) of Reagan Admin, economic impacts, 1980s and trends from 1960s, technical paper, 9385–1.304; 9385–8.125
Foreign and US industrial output, compensation, unit labor costs, and indexes, Monthly Labor Review, 6722–1.6
Health care spending and factors in increase, with background data and foreign comparisons, various periods 1929-90, technical paper, 9366–6.296
Monthly Labor Review, output, compensation, labor and nonlabor unit costs, and indexes, 6722–1.5
OECD intl trade position for US and 4 countries, and factors affecting US competition, quarterly pamphlet, 2042–25
Productivity of labor, capital, and other inputs in manufacturing, changes by selected industry, various periods 1949-88, article, 6722–1.345
Railroad industry productivity measures, late 1950s-80s, article, 6722–1.337
Technology-intensive capital investment relation to productivity, by industry sector, 1940s-80s, technical paper, 9385–8.130
Technology-intensive capital investment relation to productivity growth, 1950s-89, article, 9385–1.310
see also Agricultural productivity
see also Government efficiency
see also Industrial capacity and utilization
see also Industrial production indexes
see also Labor productivity

Professional and technical workers
Air traffic control and airway facilities staff, by employment and other characteristics, FY90, annual rpt, 7504–41
Aircraft mechanics certified by FAA, by age, sex, region, and State, 1991, annual rpt, 7504–2
Black Americans social and economic characteristics, for South and total US, 1991 and trends from 1950, annual Current Population Rpt, 2546–1.463
Deaths and rates, by cause and selected social, demographic, and employment characteristics, 1979-85, natl longitudinal study, 4478–186
Educational attainment, by social and demographic characteristics and location, 1991 and trends from 1940, biennial Current Population Rpt, 2546–1.460
Employment and economic conditions, alternative BLS projections to 2005 and trends 1975-90, biennial rpt, 6744–19
Employment and unemployment during recessions, 1948-91, annual article, 6722–1.312
Employment Cost Index and alternative measure of compensation costs, by component, occupation, industry group, union status, and location, 1975-92, annual rpt, 6744–20
Employment, earnings, and hours, monthly press release, 6742–5
Employment situation, earnings, hours, and other BLS economic indicators, transcripts of BLS Commissioner's monthly testimony, periodic rpt, 23846–4
Employment, unemployment, and labor force characteristics, by region, State, and selected metro area, 1991, annual rpt, 6744–7
Fed Govt employment of minorities, women, and disabled, by agency and occupation, FY90, annual rpt, 9244–10
Fed Govt white collar employees views on work conditions and schedules, 1992 survey, 9848–41
Higher education faculty and staff, by occupation, full- and part-time status, sex, and instn type and control, fall 1989, biennial rpt, 4844–18
Immigrant and nonimmigrant visas of US issued and refused, by class, issuing office, and nationality, FY90, annual rpt, 7184–1
Immigrants and legalized aliens, by occupational group and country of birth, preliminary FY91, annual tables, 6264–1
Immigration to US, alien workers, visitors, deportations, and naturalizations, by country, FY91 and trends from 1820, annual rpt, 6264–2
Income (household, family, and personal), by source, detailed characteristics, and region, 1991, annual Current Population Rpt, 2546–6.76
Labor demand, turnover, and training completions, by detailed occupation, 1990 and projected to 2005, biennial rpt, 6744–3
Labor hourly costs, by component, occupational group, industry div, union coverage, and region, 1992, annual rpt, 6744–21
Labor unions recognized in Fed Govt, agreements and membership by agency and facility, as of Jan 1991, biennial listing, 9844–14
Minority group and women employment, by occupation, SIC 1- to 3- digit industry, State, and MSA, 1991, annual rpt, 9244–1
Occupational Outlook Handbook, 1992-93, biennial rpt, 6744–1
Pacific territories population and housing detailed characteristics, by location, 1990 Census of Population and Housing, series, 2551–8
Prison employment requirements for new and expanded Federal facilities, by occupation, FY87-95, GAO rpt, 26119–397
State and local govt employment of minorities and women, by occupation, function, pay level, and State, 1991, annual rpt, 9244–6
Training for job qualification and skill improvement, workers participating by training source, occupation, age, sex, and race, 1991, 6728–32
Transit systems finances and operations, by mode, size of fleet and urban area, region, and for 518 systems, 1990, annual rpt, 7884–4
Wages by occupation, and benefits, for office and plant workers, periodic MSA survey rpt series, 6785–16; 6785–17
see also Area wage surveys
see also Consultants
see also Engineers and engineering
see also Executives and managers
see also Health occupations
see also Industry wage surveys
see also Paraprofessionals
see also Scientists and technicians
see also under By Occupation in the "Index by Categories"
see also under names of specific professions

Professional associations
see Associations

Professionals' fees
Health Care Financing Review, provider prices, price inputs and indexes, and labor, quarterly journal, 4652–1.1
Medicaid coverage, funding, and costs, with reform recommendations, mid 1960s-92, 10048–83
Physicians costs per enrollee and for selected procedures, changes under Blue Cross-Blue Shield plans, mid 1980s, article, 4652–1.320
Physicians income and liability costs, 1980s-90, 26306–6.175
Physicians payment by Medicare, impacts of reforms on services, and monitoring methods, 1992 annual rpt, 4004–34
Physicians payment by Medicare under fee schedule, adjustment factor recommendations, 1993, annual rpt, 4004–33
Physicians payment by Medicare under fee schedule, analyses of costs and other issues, series, 17266–1
Physicians payment by Medicare under fee schedule, impacts on beneficiaries, practice, and program finances, series, 17266–2
Physicians payment by Medicare under fee schedule, impacts on charges by specialty and State, 1992 and 1996, hearing, 25368–178
Physicians payment by Medicare under fee schedule, methodology with data by procedure and specialty, 1992, annual rpt, 17264–1
Physicians payment by Medicare under reasonable charge method, effect of customary charges in selected States, 1987-89, article, 4652–1.307
Physicians payment issues, HCFA research activities and grants, FY91, annual listing, 4654–10

Profits
see Business income and expenses, general
see Business income and expenses, specific industry
see Farm income
see Operating ratios

Project HOPE
"Classifications Systems for PPS-Excluded and Non-PPS Providers", 17206–2.29

Project listings
see Demonstration and pilot projects
see Directories

Projections and forecasts
Acid rain environmental, economic, and health effects, and pollutant emissions, 1985-89 and alternative projections to 2030, 14358–4
AIDS prevention and control plans, cases, and Federal funding, 1980s-94, 4048–22
Air traffic (passenger), and aircraft operations by type, by airport and State, projected FY92-2005 and trends from FY83, annual rpt, 7504–7
Air traffic and other aviation activity forecasts of FAA, 1992 annual conf, 7504–28
Air traffic, and passenger and freight enplanements, by airport, 1960s-91 and projected to 2010, hub area rpt series, 7506–7

Air traffic and passengers, for intl routes over north Atlantic, by aviation type and route, alternative forecasts 1992-2010 and trends from 1982, annual rpt, 7504–44
Air traffic and passengers, for intl routes over Pacific, by route, alternative forecasts 1992-2010 and trends from 1980, annual rpt, 7504–51
Air traffic control and airway facilities improvement activities under Aviation System Capital Investment Plan, 1981-91 and projected to 2006, annual rpt, 7504–12
Air traffic, pilots, airports, and fuel use, forecast FY92-2003 and trends from FY82, annual rpt, 7504–6
Aircraft flight service station workload of FAA, pilot briefs, contacts, and flight plans by facility, projected FY92-2002 and trends from FY83, annual rpt, 7504–39
Aircraft handled by instrument flight rule, by user type, FAA traffic control center, and region, FY85-91 and projected to FY2005, annual rpt, 7504–15
Airport capacity improvement projects and funding, traffic, and delays, by major airport, 1988-90 and forecast to 2000, annual rpt, 7504–43
Autos (older) retirement programs proposals costs, savings, and emissions and energy use reductions, 1992 rpt, 26358–263
Bank Insurance Fund finances projected under alternative assumptions about bank failures and assets involved, 1991-93, hearing, 21248–166
Banking system reform issues, with top instn finances, fiscal impacts, and views of depositors, bankers, and regulators on deposit insurance, 1991 hearings, 21248–168
Banks failures forecasting performance of asset risk indicators and other factors, 1980s-91, article, 9379–15.302
Budget deficit forecasting accuracy, contributing factors, and analysis of major programs, FY91, annual GAO rpt, 26104–23
Budget deficits impacts on GNP and public and foreign debt, projected under alternative reduction policies, 1990-2020 with intl comparisons from 1981, GAO rpt, 26109–5
Budget of US, Bush Admin proposals, with detail for defense budgets, and historical data from FY34, FY93, 108–46
Budget of US, CBO analysis and review of FY93 budget by function, annual rpt, 26304–2
Budget of US, CBO analysis of revenue and spending alternatives and projections of economic indicators, FY93-97, annual rpt, 26304–3
Budget of US, House concurrent resolution, with spending and revenue targets, FY93 and projected to FY97, annual rpt, 21264–2
Budget of US, midsession review of FY93 budget, by function, annual rpt, 104–7
Budget of US, obligations and authority by function, agency, and program, with summaries and analyses, FY93, annual rpt, 104–2
Business cycle forecasting performance of BEA economic indicators, 1948-91, technical paper, 9379–12.95
Business cycle recession forecasting performance of economic indicators and experimental indexes, 1992 working paper, 9375–13.84
Coastal areas environmental impacts of economic dev and population growth, 1960-80s and projected to 2010, series, 2176–8
Coin and medal production by denomination, capacity, and facility improvement funding, by mint, with monetary metals purchases, projected FY92-96, hearing, 21248–164
Construction put in place, housing starts, and Fed Govt investment outlays, projected 1992-96 and trends from 1980, annual article, 2042–1.304
Consumer spending forecast performance of consumer sentiment index and other economic indicators, 1950s-90, article, 9393–8.304
Developing countries debt burden indicators, for 8 countries, alternative projections 1991-2000 and trends from 1974, technical paper, 9366–7.271
Developing countries economic, population, and agricultural data, US and other aid sources, and AID activity, country rpt series, 9916–12
Dollar exchange rate forecasting performance of forward rates, 1991 working paper, 9371–10.68
Eastern Europe pension systems finances and provisions, 1950s-90 and alternative projections to 2025, technical paper, 8006–6.7
Economic and social conditions of foreign countries, working paper series, 2326–18
Economic conditions and employment, alternative BLS projections to 2005 and trends 1975-90, biennial rpt, 6744–19
Economic indicators forecasting performance of alternative models, 1992 article, 9391–1.316
Economic indicators forecasting performance of interest rate spreads, 1950s-90, working paper, 9375–13.67
Economic indicators forecasting performance of selected forecasters by indicator, 1950s-92, article, 9373–1.313
Economic indicators forecasts and errors, for Fed Reserve 3rd District by State, 1980s-93, article, 9387–1.303
Economic indicators forecasts, 1991-92 and trends from 1948, annual article, 9383–6.301
Economic indicators forecasts, 1993-94 and trends from 1948, annual article, 9383–6.303
Economic Report of the President for 1991, economic effects of budget proposals, and trends and projections, 1940s-95, annual hearings, 23844–4
Economic Report of the President for 1992, with economic trends from 1929, annual rpt, 204–1
Economic review and outlook for US, analysis of Bush Admin and private projections, with small business views, 1991 hearings, 23848–230
Education data, enrollment, degrees, teachers, and spending, 1977/78-1990/91 and alternative projections to 2002/2003, annual rpt, 4824–4
Employment and GNP, accuracy of BLS forecasts made late 1970s-85, as of 1990, article, 6722–1.335
Exchange rate forecasting performance of alternative models, 1970s-91, working paper, 9381–10.125
Fed Govt agencies budget requests and program costs and characteristics, series, 26306–3
Fed Govt civil service retirement system actuarial valuation, FY79-91 and projected to FY2065, annual rpt, 9844–34
Fed Govt programs of congressional interest, objectives, feasibility, benefits, and costs, series, 26306–6
Financial and economic analysis and forecasting methodology, technical paper series, 9366–6
Financial instns reform issues, with finances, impacts of deposit insurance changes, and views of depositors and bankers, 1991 hearings, 25248–129
GDP forecasting performance of selected economic indicators over selected forecast periods and business cycles, 1960s-91, article, 9375–1.307
GDP forecasts for current quarter, performance of monthly advance indicators, 1981-91, article, 9393–8.305
Germany unification economic impacts for Germany, US, Japan, and worldwide, alternative projections 1991-99, technical paper, 9366–7.275
Global climate change and contributing pollutants emissions, literature review, 1980s and projected to 2075, 3338–3
GPO activities, staff, and productivity, 1970s-90 and projected to 2000, 26208–4
Great Lakes and connecting channels water levels, and forecasts, semimonthly rpt, 3752–2
Health care professionals supply and education, by professional and other characteristics, and location, 1960s-92 and projected to 2020, biennial rpt, 4114–8
Higher education grads labor force status, job degree requirements, and outlook, 1980s-90 and projected to 2005, article, 6722–1.331
Housing real prices projected under alternative population assumptions, 1991-2000, article, 9381–1.305
Industrial production and unemployment forecasting performance of consumer sentiment surveys, 1991 working paper, 9371–10.69
Industrial production forecasting performance of Natl Assn of Purchasing Managers manufacturing activity index and production-worker hours, 1980s-91, article, 9371–1.301
Industry (US) intl competitiveness, with selected foreign and US operating data by major firm and product, series, 2046–12
Industry finances and operations, by SIC 2- to 4-digit industry, forecast 1992, annual rpt, 2044–28
Inflation forecasting performance of expected long run inflation rate and commodity price indexes, 1960s-90, article, 9377–1.303
Interest rate forecasting performance of short- and long-term rate spreads, for US and 6 EC countries, 1950s-91, technical paper, 9385–8.136

Italy public debt burden on future generations, alternative forecasts, 1992 working paper, 9377–9.139
Labor demand in rural areas, job skill and educational requirements impacts of industrial and occupational shifts, 1970s-80s and projected to 2000, article, 1502–7.302
Labor demand, turnover, and training completions, by detailed occupation, 1990 and projected to 2005, biennial rpt, 6744–3
Labor separations, replacement rates, and related job openings, estimation procedures with data by occupation, age, and sex, late 1980s and projected to 2005, 6748–84
Mail order sales from out of State, tax revenue losses by State, 1990-92, 10048–84
Mail volume and employment of USPS, impacts of competition and rate increases, with evaluation of alternative forecast models, 1970s-80s and forecast to 1995, GAO rpt, 26119–384
Manufacturing output forecasts, performance of regional indexes by SIC 2-digit industry, 1992 working paper, 9375–13.85
Medicare Hospital Insurance trust fund finances, mid 1960s-91 and alternative projections to 2066, annual rpt, 4654–11
Merchant ship crew supply, wartime needs, training, and sources, 1970s-90 and alternative projections to 2000, 7708–5
Mexico-US trade agreement impacts on truck traffic at border crossings, Customs Service staff needs, and hwy improvement costs, projected to 2000 with trends from 1986, GAO rpt, 26123–368
Middle Atlantic States economic indicators, forecasting performance of vector autoregression models, 1992 working paper, 9387–8.282
Military officers newly commissioned, share from service academies, and academy attrition, 1970s-91 and projected to FY97, GAO rpt, 26123–389
Military spending reductions, economic impacts by defense contractor, industry, State, and congressional district, 1989-90 hearings, 23848–224
Military spending reductions, economic impacts of alternative plans, with data by industry and State, various periods 1949-87, article, 9385–1.313
Minerals foreign and US supply under alternative market conditions, reserves, and background industry data, series, 5606–4
Minerals industry operations, trends, and projections for selected countries, series, 5606–5
Minerals offshore lease sales environmental and economic impacts in coastal areas, final statement series, 5736–7
Monetary policy objectives of Fed Reserve, analysis and economic performance, 1950s-90 and projected to FY95, hearings, 21248–160
North American Free Trade Agreement proposal for Canada, US, and Mexico, economic impacts, alternative model descriptions, 1992 conf, 9886–4.182
North Central States business and economic conditions, Fed Reserve 9th District, quarterly journal, 9383–19
OASDHI future cost estimates, actuarial study series, 4706–1
OASDHI trust funds finances, FY91 and projected to 2066, annual rpt, 4654–8
OASDHI trust funds finances, FY91 with projections, annual article, 4742–1.314
OASDI and Medicare trust fund finances, economic assumptions, outlook, and health care system reform issues, series, 10176–1
OASDI trust funds finances, 1937-FY91 and alternative projections to 2070, annual rpt, 4704–4
Occupational Outlook Handbook, 1992-93, biennial rpt, 6744–1
Pacific Northwest population, households, employment, income, and fuel prices, alternative projections, annual rpt, suspended, 3224–5
Pacific Northwest population, households, employment, income, fuel prices, and electricity demand, alternative forecasts 1991-2010, annual rpt, 3224–3.3
Philadelphia metro area transit service operations, costs and benefits, and local economic and air pollution impacts, 1970s-90 and projected to 2020, 7308–205
Prison employment requirements for new and expanded Federal facilities, by occupation, FY87-95, GAO rpt, 26119–397
Public debt burden on future generations forecast under alternative tax, OASDI, and Medicare policies, 1992 working paper, 9377–9.137
Public works financing, use, and condition, 1990 hearing, 21648–67
R&D funding of Fed Govt for large-scale projects, issues and impacts on other research, with data for space station and super collider, 1991 hearings, 21268–43
R&D spending of major firms, by industry group, planned 1990-91, 9626–6.38
Radioactive waste and spent fuel generation, inventory, and disposal, 1960s-90 and projected to 2020, annual rpt, 3364–2
Railroad retirement system actuarial evaluation, 1991 and projected to 2016, annual rpt, 9704–1
Recycling in manufacturing industries, fuel savings, and CO2 emissions reductions, 1988 and projected to 1995, hearing, 21368–140
Recycling of paper by grade, with newsprint collection, recycling capacity by company, and curbside pickup operations, by State, 1970s-80s and projected to 1995, hearing, 25318–84
Retirement age, and older persons labor force status, by sex, 1950s-90 and projected to 2005, article, 6722–1.332
Savings instns failures, costs and budget deficit and economic impacts, 1980s and projected to 2010, 26306–6.165
Semiconductor materials supply and demand, and semiconductor firms by State, late 1980s and projected to 1993, hearing, 21708–130
Statistical Abstract of US, 1992 annual data compilation, 2324–1
Stock returns forecasting performance of alternative models, descriptions and results, 1992 technical paper, 9385–8.146
Stockpiling of strategic material, inventories and needs, by commodity, 1992, annual rpt, 3544–37
Tax (income) returns and supplemental documents filed, by type, FY91 and projected to FY2000, semiannual rpt, 8302–4
Tax (income) returns filed, by type, IRS service center, and whether full-paid, refund, and electronically filed, 1990 and projected to 1998, semiannual rpt, 8302–7
Tax (income) withholding and related documents filed, by type and IRS service center, 1991 and projected 1992-99, annual rpt, 8304–22
Tax returns and supplemental documents filed, by type, 1990 and projected to 1999, annual article, 8302–2.304
Tax returns filed, by type of tax and IRS district, 1990 and projected 1991-98, annual rpt, 8304–24
Tax returns filed, by type of tax and IRS region and service center, projected 1991-98 and trends from 1978, annual rpt, 8304–9
Tennessee Valley economic conditions, and compared to US, alternative projections 1992-2010 and trends from 1929, annual rpt, 9804–27
Tidal currents, daily time and velocity by station for North America and Asia coasts, forecast 1993, annual rpts, 2174–1
Tide height and tidal current velocity daily at Middle Atlantic coastal stations, forecast 1993, annual rpt, 2174–11
Tide height and time daily at coastal points worldwide, forecast 1993, annual rpt series, 2174–2
Unemployment by selected characteristics, health insurance coverage, and unemployment insurance benefits exhaustion, 1988-91 and projected to 1996, hearing, 21788–209
VA health care services, needs, availability, structure, and funding, findings and recommendations, 1991 rpt, 8608–8
VA health care services, needs, availability, structure, and funding, 1991 compilation of papers, 8608–9
Wastewater treatment and collection facility construction funding needs and Fed Govt grants, by State, 1990 and projected to 2010, biennial rpt, 9204–7
Wastewater treatment plants construction loan funds for local govts, costs and State officials views by State, projected 1991-2000, GAO rpt, 26113–561
Water (groundwater) supply, quality, chemistry, other characteristics, and use, regional rpt series, 5666–25
Water quality, chemistry, hydrology, and other characteristics, local area studies, series, 5666–27
Water supply in western US, streamflow and reservoir storage forecasts by stream and station, Jan-May monthly rpt, 1262–1
Weather (marine) forecast areas, and broadcast schedules and stations worldwide, as of Sept 1992, annual rpt, 2184–3

Weather (marine) forecast broadcast schedules worldwide, periodic rpt, 2182–9
Weather conditions and forecasts, data collection and analysis issues, 1991 annual conf, 2184–10
Weather forecasts accuracy evaluations, for US, UK, and European systems, quarterly rpt, 2182–8
Weather forecasts for US and Northern Hemisphere, precipitation and temperature by location, semimonthly rpt, 2182–1
Women's labor force status, and employment by industry group and occupation, 1990 and projected to 2005, fact sheet, 6564–1.1
see also Agricultural forecasts
see also Energy projections
see also Population projections

Property
Older persons income by source, for married OASI beneficiaries by work and eligibility pattern of wife, 1982, article, 4746–26.12
see also Business assets and liabilities, general
see also Business assets and liabilities, specific industry
see also Capital investments, general
see also Capital investments, specific industry
see also Educational facilities
see also Farms and farmland
see also Government supplies and property
see also Housing condition and occupancy
see also Housing tenure
see also Land ownership and rights
see also Land use
see also Military bases, posts, and reservations
see also Military supplies and property
see also Mortgages
see also Property and casualty insurance
see also Property condemnation
see also Property damage and loss
see also Property tax
see also Property value
see also Public buildings
see also Public lands
see also Real estate business
see also Rent
see also Surplus government property
see also Vacant and abandoned property
see also Wealth

Property and casualty insurance
Asset risk assessment for insurance companies, with financial ratios by firm type and financial status, 1990 and trends from 1900s, article, 9373–1.314; 9373–27.3
Budget of US, obligations and authority by function, agency, and program, with summaries and analyses, FY93, annual rpt, 104–2
Business statistics, detailed data for major industries and economic indicators, 1960-91, *Survey of Current Business* biennial supplement, 2704–1
Communications services revenue and expenses, itemized by SIC 2- to 4-digit kind of business, 1990, annual rpt, 2413–15
County Business Patterns, 1989: employment, establishments, and payroll, by SIC 2- to 4-digit industry and county, annual State rpt series, 2326–8
County Business Patterns, 1990: employment, establishments, and payroll, by SIC 2- to 4-digit industry and county, annual State rpt series, 2326–6
Crime insurance policies under Federal program by State, and claims paid, data compilation, 1992 annual rpt, 6064–6.3
Finances and operations, by SIC 2- to 4-digit industry, forecast 1992, annual rpt, 2044–28
Finances of insurance companies, by insurance type and firm, with some intl comparisons, 1991 conf, 9373–3.35
Financial condition of insurance industry, operations, assets, junk bond holdings, and State regulation, with intl comparisons, 1991 hearings, 25268–79
Health Care Financing Review, provider prices, price inputs and indexes, and labor, quarterly journal, 4652–1.1
Home mortgages FHA-insured, financial, property, and borrower characteristics, by metro area, 1991, annual rpt, 5144–24
Home mortgages FHA-insured, financial, property, and borrower characteristics, by State, 1991, annual rpt, 5144–1
Home mortgages FHA-insured, financial, property, and borrower characteristics, 1991, annual rpt, 5144–17; 5144–23
Housing (rental) units, total, with HUD assistance by program, and eligible for aid, by unit, household, and neighborhood characteristics, and location, 1989, biennial rpt, 5184–11
Housing and households detailed characteristics, and unit and neighborhood quality, MSA surveys, series, 2485–6
Marine and war-risk insurance approved for US and foreign vessels, FY91, annual rpt, 7704–14.4
NYC housing supply, occupancy, condition, and household characteristics, by tenure and borough, 1991 triennial survey, 2488–3
Obstetrics rural practitioners malpractice insurance subsidy program funding and participation, for North Carolina, 1989-92, article, 4042–3.355
Occupational injury and illness rates, by SIC 2- to 4-digit industry, 1989-90, annual rpt, 6844–7
Occupational injury and illness rates, by SIC 2- to 4-digit industry, 1990, annual rpt, 6844–1
Physicians income and liability costs, 1980s-90, 26306–6.175
Physicians income, practice revenue, hours worked, and malpractice insurance premiums paid, late 1970s-90, technical paper, 9366–6.296
Statistical Abstract of US, 1992 annual data compilation, 2324–1.16
Transit systems finances and operations, by mode, size of fleet and urban area, region, and for 518 systems, 1990, annual rpt, 7884–4
Truck and warehouse services finances and inventory, by SIC 2- to 4-digit industry, 1990 survey, annual rpt, 2413–14
Truck itemized costs per mile, finances, and operations, for agricultural carriers, 1991, annual rpt, 1311–15
Truck rates for fruit and vegetables paid by shippers and receivers, by commodity and city, and fleet itemized costs per mile, weekly rpt, 1311–22
see also Automobile insurance

Property condemnation
Claims Court caseload by type of suit, and judgments, FY92, annual rpt, 18224–1
Court civil and criminal caseloads for Federal district, appeals, and bankruptcy courts, by type of suit and offense, circuit, and district, 1991, annual rpt, 18204–11
Court civil and criminal caseloads for Federal district, appeals, and special courts, 1991, annual rpt, 18204–8
Housing (rental) total, HUD-assisted by program, and eligible for aid, recent movers by reason, selected characteristics, and location, 1989, biennial rpt, 5184–11
US attorneys land condemnation cases, by disposition and district, FY91, annual rpt, 6004–2.6

Property damage and loss
Aircraft accidents and circumstances, for US operations of domestic and foreign airlines and general aviation, periodic rpt, 9612–1
Aircraft accidents, casualties, and damage, for commercial operations by detailed circumstances, 1988, annual rpt, 9614–2
Arson cases, civilian and fire fighter casualties, and property damage, 1986-89, 9438–14
Arson incidents by whether structure occupied, property value, and arrest rate, by property type, 1991, annual rpt, 6224–2.1
Boat accidents, casualties, and damage, by cause, vessel characteristics, and State, 1991, annual rpt, 7404–1.1
Bombing incidents and casualties, by target, circumstances, and State, 1987-91, annual rpt, 8484–4.1
Bombing incidents, casualties, and damage, by target, circumstances, and State, 1991, annual rpt, 6224–5
Coast Guard search and rescue missions, and lives and property lost and saved, by district and assisting unit, FY91, annual rpt, 7404–2
Court civil and criminal caseloads for Federal district, appeals, and special courts, 1991, annual rpt, 18204–8
Crime victimization rates, by victim and offender characteristics, circumstances, and offense, 1990 survey, annual rpt, 6066–3.47
Crimes, by characteristics of victim and offender, circumstances, and location, data compilation, 1992 annual rpt, 6064–6.3
Disasters and natl security incidents and mgmt, with data by major event and State, 1992 annual rpt, 9434–6
Earthquake risk for Federal buildings and employees, by agency and region, 1989, with location and size of major events from 1600s, GAO rpt, 26119–399
Farmland damaged by natural disaster, Emergency Conservation Program funding by region and State, monthly rpt, 1802–13
Fires, casualties, losses, and US Fire Admin activities, funding, and training programs, FY91, annual rpt, 9434–7
Fish (trout) raised on farms, production, sales, prices, and losses, 1991-92, annual rpt, 1631–16
Floods in Mississippi River and Gulf of Mexico basins, precipitation and water levels by site, damage, and deaths, 1982-83, 5666–27.33

Foreign countries disasters, casualties, damage, and aid by US and others, FY91 and trends from FY64, annual rpt, 9914–12
Hazardous material transport accidents, casualties, and damage, by mode of transport, with DOT control activities, 1990, annual rpt, 7304–4
Housing (rental) total, HUD-assisted by program, and eligible for aid, recent movers by reason, selected characteristics, and location, 1989, biennial rpt, 5184–11
Housing unit and household characteristics of recent movers, and reason for move, by tenure, 1989, 2486–1.12
Hurricane Andrew atmospheric pressure, wind speeds, deaths, and damage, by location, Aug 1992, article, 2152–8.304
Military personnel personal property shipped worldwide, and loss and damage claims, FY91, annual rpt, 3704–15
NASA accidents, casualties, damage, and safety activities, FY91, annual rpt, 9504–4
Panama Canal fires, and related property loss, FY90-91, annual rpt, 9664–3.2
Railroad accidents, casualties, and damage, by cause, railroad, and State, 1991, annual rpt, 7604–1
Railroad accidents, casualties, and damage, Fed Railroad Admin activities, and safety inspectors by State, 1990, annual rpt, 7604–12
Railroad accidents, casualties, circumstances, and railroad involved, 1988, annual rpt, 9614–8
Railroad accidents, casualties, damage, and circumstances, by incident, 1988, annual rpt, 7604–3
Railroad accidents involving hazardous materials, casualties, and circumstances, 1984-89, 9618–18
Ships in world merchant fleet, tonnage, and new ship construction and deliveries, by vessel type and country, as of Jan 1992, annual rpt, 7704–3
Ships wrecked off Alaska, characteristics, deaths, cargo, and whale catch, by vessel and location, 1763-1937, 5738–34
Statistical Abstract of US, 1992 annual data compilation, 2324–1.5
Storms and unusual weather phenomena characteristics, casualties, and property damage, by State, monthly listing, 2152–3
Tax (income) returns of individuals, by filing status, tax item, and income level, 1991, annual article, 8302–2.319
Tax (income) returns of individuals, detailed data, 1988, annual rpt, 8304–2
Tax (income) returns of individuals, selected income and tax items by income level, preliminary 1990, annual article, 8302–2.307
Thefts, and value of property stolen and recovered, by property type, 1991, annual rpt, 6224–2.1
Timber in western US, insect and disease infestation from lumber imports from USSR, economic and environmental impacts, 1991 and projected to 2040, 1208–389
Timber insect and disease incidence and damage, and control activities, State rpt series, 1206–49
Timber insect and disease incidence and damage, annual regional rpt series, 1206–11
Timber insect and disease incidence and damage, by State, 1990, annual rpt, 1204–8
Traffic accidents, casualties, circumstances, and characteristics of persons and vehicles involved, 1990, annual rpt, 7764–18
Traffic accidents direct and indirect costs, by cost type, payment source, and severity, 1980s, 7558–114
Transit systems accidents and casualties by circumstances, damage, and ridership, by mode, 1990, annual rpt, 7884–13
Truck accidents, casualties, and damage, by circumstances and characteristics of persons and vehicles involved, 1989, annual rpt, 7554–9
Truck transport of household goods, performance and disposition of damage claims, for selected carriers, 1991, annual rpt, 9484–11
see also Robbery and theft

Property loss
see Property damage and loss

Property tax
Banks in Fed Reserve System, expenses and operations itemized by service, office, and district, 1991, annual rpt, 9364–11
Collections of taxes, by level of govt, type of tax, State, and selected counties, quarterly rpt, 2462–3
Farm prices received and paid, by commodity and State, monthly rpt, 1629–1
Farm production itemized costs, by farm sales size and region, 1991, annual rpt, 1614–3
Farmland value, rent, taxes, foreign ownership, and transfers by probable use and lender type, with data by region and State, 1981-92, article, 1561–16.302
Finances of govts, by level of govt, State, and for large cities and counties, annual rpt series, 2466–2
Finances of govts, tax systems and revenue, and fiscal structure, by level of govt and State, 1992 and historical trends, annual rpt, 10044–1
Home mortgages FHA-insured, financial, property, and borrower characteristics, by metro area, 1991, annual rpt, 5144–24
Home mortgages FHA-insured, financial, property, and borrower characteristics, by State, 1991, annual rpt, 5144–1
Home mortgages FHA-insured, financial, property, and borrower characteristics, 1991, annual rpt, 5144–17; 5144–23
Housing alteration and repair for owner-occupied units, costs and structural, household, financial, and project characteristics, 1987, 2486–1.13
Housing and households detailed characteristics, and unit and neighborhood quality, MSA surveys, series, 2485–6
Housing and households summary characteristics, 1989 and trends, chartbook, 2486–2.1
Hwy receipts by source, and spending by function, by level of govt and State, 1991, annual rpt, 7554–1.3
Income tax returns of individuals, detailed data, 1988, annual rpt, 8304–2
Natl income and product accounts and components, *Survey of Current Business*, monthly rpt, 2702–1.23
Natl income and product accounts, comprehensive accounts and components, benchmark revisions, 1929-88, 2708–5
Natl income and product accounts, comprehensive accounts and components, *Survey of Current Business*, monthly rpt, 2702–1.26
NYC housing supply, occupancy, condition, and household characteristics, by tenure and borough, 1991 triennial survey, 2488–3
Public lands, Fed Govt payments to local govts in lieu of property taxes, by State, FY92, annual press release, 5306–4.15
Public opinion on taxes, spending, and govt efficiency, by respondent characteristics, 1992 survey, annual rpt, 10044–2
State govt tax collections by detailed type of tax, and tax rates, by State, FY91, annual rpt, 2466–2.7
Statistical Abstract of US, 1992 annual data compilation, 2324–1.9
Telephone and telegraph firms detailed finances and operations, 1990, annual rpt, 9284–6.2; 9284–6.3
Transit systems finances and operations, by mode, size of fleet and urban area, region, and for 518 systems, 1990, annual rpt, 7884–4

Property value
AFDC beneficiaries demographic and financial characteristics, by State, FY90, annual rpt, 4584–7
Assets and debts of private sector, balance sheets by segment, 1960-91, semiannual rpt, 9365–4.1
Banks (insured commercial and savings) finances, for foreign and domestic offices, by asset size, 1990, annual rpt, 9294–4.2
Capital (fixed), govt and private nonresidential structures and equipment, residential capital, and consumer-owned durable goods, 1925-90, annual article, 2702–1.305; 2702–1.306; 2702–1.327; 2702–1.338
Census of Population and Housing, 1990: data summary, use, and availability, fact sheet, 2326–23.1
Commuting accessibility of central business district, impact on housing prices, for Philadelphia, 1970-88, working paper, 9387–8.258
Construction put in place, value of new public and private structures, by type, monthly rpt, 2382–4
DOE mgmt and operating contract admin at Nevada Field Office, funding, property value, and staff, FY88-90, 3006–5.31
DOE real property owned and leased, by type, subagency, contractor, and site, FY91, annual rpt, 3004–28
Economic Report of the President for 1992, with economic trends from 1929, annual rpt, 204–1.10
Electric utilities privately owned, finances and operations, detailed data, 1990, annual rpt, 3164–23
Families financial status, income, net worth, and assets and debt by type, by income and selected characteristics, 1983 and 1989, article, 9362–1.301

Farm credit, terms, delinquency, agricultural bank failures, and credit conditions by Fed Reserve District, quarterly rpt, 9365–3.10
Farm finances, assets, liabilities, and debt by lender type, by State, 1960-89, 1548–384
Farm loan guarantees of FmHA, characteristics of borrowers, lenders, and loans, FY88, 1548–386
Farm production inputs, finances, mgmt, and land value and transfers, periodic situation rpt with articles, 1561–16
Farm sector assets by type, and real and nonreal estate debt, including and excluding operator households, by sales size, 1960-89, 1548–387
Farmland in US owned by foreigners, holdings, acquisitions, and disposals by land use, owner type and country, and State, 1991, annual rpt, 1584–2
Farmland in US owned by foreigners, holdings, acreage, and value by land use, owner country, State, and county, 1991, annual rpt, 1584–3
Farmland irrigated, farm characteristics, and water and fuel sources, by State and leading county, 1950s-88, 1588–122
Fish and Wildlife Service restoration programs funding, land purchases, and project listing, by State, FY90, annual rpt, 5504–1
FmHA property acquired through foreclosure, acreage, value, and sales, for farm and nonfarm property by State, monthly rpt, 1182–6
FmHA property acquired through foreclosure, 1-family homes, value, sales, and leases, by State, monthly rpt, 1182–7
Foreign direct investment in US, major transactions by type, industry, country, and US location, 1990, annual rpt, 2044–20
Home mortgages FHA-insured, financial, property, and borrower characteristics, by metro area, 1991, annual rpt, 5144–24
Home mortgages FHA-insured, financial, property, and borrower characteristics, by State, 1991, annual rpt, 5144–1; 5144–25
Home mortgages FHA-insured, financial, property, and borrower characteristics, 1991, annual rpt, 5144–17; 5144–23
Homeownership values, reasons, and barriers, views by race and tenure, 1992 survey, 9478–1
Households (single person and nonfamily) social, economic and housing characteristics, by tenure, 1989, 2486–1.15
Households moving rates by tenure and age, and housing value by mobility status and region, 1989, fact sheet, 2326–17.38
Households net worth distribution under alternative sample weighting systems to account for inconsistency in survey design and response rates, 1992 rpt, 9368–91
Housing alteration and repair for owner-occupied units, costs and structural, household, financial, and project characteristics, 1987, 2486–1.13
Housing and households characteristics, and unit and neighborhood quality, by MSA location for 11 MSAs, 1987 survey, supplement, 2485–8
Housing and households detailed characteristics, and unit and neighborhood quality, by location, 1989, biennial rpt supplement, 2485–13
Housing and households detailed characteristics, and unit and neighborhood quality, MSA surveys, series, 2485–6
Housing and households detailed characteristics, and unit and neighborhood quality, 1989, wallchart, 2485–12
Housing and households summary characteristics, 1989 and trends, chartbook, 2486–2.1
Housing and population census, 1990: population and housing characteristics, detailed geographic coverage, State CD-ROM series, 2551–10
Housing and population census, 1990: summary characteristics, households, and land area, by county, subdiv, and place, State rpt series, 2551–1
Housing census, 1990: median value and rent, by State and region, and compared to 1970 and 1980, fact sheet, 2328–83
Housing census, 1990: summary unit characteristics, by householder race and age, county, place, and urban-rural location, State rpt series, 2471–1
Housing unit and household characteristics of recent movers, and reason for move, by tenure, 1989, 2486–1.12
Housing units (1-family) sold and for sale by price, stage of construction, months on market, and region, monthly rpt, 2382–3
Housing units completed, single and multifamily units by structural and financial characteristics, and location, 1987-91, annual rpt, 2384–1
Housing vacancy and occupancy rates, and vacant unit characteristics, by tenure and location, 1960s-91, annual rpt, 2484–1
Natural gas interstate pipeline company detailed financial and operating data, by firm, 1990, annual rpt, 3164–38
North Central States farm credit conditions and farmland market values, Fed Reserve 9th District, quarterly rpt, 9383–11
NYC housing supply, occupancy, condition, and household characteristics, by tenure and borough, 1991 triennial survey, 2488–3
Pacific territories population and housing detailed characteristics, by location, 1990 Census of Population and Housing, series, 2551–8
Population economic well-being indicators, by selected characteristics and household income and income-to-poverty ratio, 1984, 2546–20.22
Public lands acreage, grants, use, revenues, and allocations, by State, FY91 and trends, annual rpt, 5724–1
Real estate assets of failed thrifts, sales by Resolution Trust Corp, and disposition of other assets, 1990-91, GAO rpt, 26119–372
Savings instns financial statements, for instns insured by Savings Assn Insurance Fund by FHLB district and State, and for FDIC-insured savings banks, 1989, annual rpt, 8434–1
School districts in Dallas, educational quality relation to property values, model description and results, 1985-87, technical paper, 9379–12.94
Single parent families in own and others homes, by financial, housing, and other characteristics, 1989, 2486–1.14
Southeastern States, Fed Reserve 5th District, economic indicators by State, quarterly rpt, 9389–16
Southeastern States, Fed Reserve 6th District, economic indicators by State and MSA, quarterly rpt, 9371–14
Southwestern US farm credit conditions and real estate values, Fed Reserve 11th District, quarterly rpt, 9379–11
Statistical Abstract of US, 1992 annual data compilation, 2324–1.23; 2324–1.26
Tax (estate) returns for nonresident aliens, property and tax data, by estate size and decedent country of residence, 1986, article, 8302–2.310
Tax (estate) returns property and tax data, by size of gross estate and State, 1989-90, article, 8302–2.305
Tax (income) returns of corporations, income and tax items by asset size and detailed industry, 1989, annual rpt, 8304–4; 8304–21
Trust assets of banks, trust companies, and S&Ls, by type of asset and fund, selected firm, and State, 1991, annual rpt, 13004–1
Vacant housing characteristics and costs, and occupancy and vacancy rates, by region and metro-nonmetro location, quarterly rpt, 2482–1
West Central States farm real estate values, farm loan trends, and regional farm price index, Fed Reserve 10th District, quarterly rpt, 9381–16.1
Wetlands acreage acquired by Fed Govt, and costs, by site and State, FY92, annual rpt, 14784–1
Wildlife refuges and other land under Fish and Wildlife Service mgmt, acreage by site and State, as of Sept 1992, annual rpt, 5504–8

Proprietorships

Minority- and woman-owned businesses and owner characteristics, by industry, employment and sales size, and form of ownership, 1987 survey, 2328–59
Natl income and product accounts, comprehensive accounts and components, benchmark revisions, 1929-88, 2708–5
Natl income and product accounts, comprehensive accounts and components, *Survey of Current Business*, monthly rpt, 2702–1.24
Retail trade sales, inventories, purchases, gross margin, and accounts receivable, by SIC 2- to 4-digit kind of business and form of ownership, 1990, annual rpt, 2413–5
Small Business Admin loan guarantee program participants finances, operations, characteristics, and views, 1991 survey, 9768–25
Small business finances, operations, owner characteristics, and Federal contracts, 1980s-90, annual rpt, 9764–6
Statistical Abstract of US, 1992 annual data compilation, 2324–1.17
Tax (income) returns filed, by type of filer, selected income items, quarterly rpt, 8302–2.1
Tax (income) returns of sole proprietorships, income statement items, by industry group, 1990, annual article, 8302–2.317; 8302–2.320

Prospective Payment Assessment Commission
Hospital reimbursement by Medicare under prospective payment system, analyses of alternative payment plans, series, 17206–1
Hospital reimbursement by Medicare under prospective payment system, and effect on services, finances, and beneficiary payments, 1980-91, annual rpt, 17204–2
Hospital reimbursement by Medicare under prospective payment system, impacts on costs, industry structure and operations, and quality of care, series, 17206–2
Hospital reimbursement by Medicare under prospective payment system, methodology, inputs, and data by diagnostic group, 1992 annual rpt, 17204–1

Prosthetics and orthotics
Exports and imports between US and outlying areas, by detailed commodity and mode of transport, 1991, annual rpt, 2424–11
Exports and imports of US, by country and detailed commodity, monthly rpt, 2422–12
Exports and imports of US, by Harmonized System 6-digit commodity and country, 1991, annual rpt, 2424–13
Exports of US, detailed Schedule B commodities with countries of destination, 1991, annual rpt, 2424–10
Injuries from use of consumer products, by severity, victim age, and detailed product, 1991, annual rpt, 9164–6
Price indexes (producer), by stage of processing and detailed commodity, monthly rpt, 6762–6
Price indexes (producer), by stage of processing and detailed commodity, monthly 1991, annual rpt, 6764–2
Statistical Abstract of US, 1992 annual data compilation, 2324–1.3
Use, payment sources, and unmet needs for assistive technology equipment and home accessibility features, by age, 1990, 4146–8.219
VA health care facilities trainees, by detailed program and city, FY91, annual rpt, 8704–4
VA health care services, needs, availability, structure, and funding, 1991 compilation of papers, 8608–9

Prostitution
Arrests and prisoners, by offense, offender characteristics, and location, data compilation, 1992 annual rpt, 6064–6.6
Arrests, by offense, offender characteristics, and location, data compilation, 1992 annual rpt, 6064–6.4
Arrests, by offense, offender characteristics, and location, 1991, annual rpt, 6224–2.2
Immigrant and nonimmigrant visa applicants refused, and refusals overcome, by reason, FY90, annual rpt, 7184–1.3
Juvenile arrests, by sex, race, disposition, and offense, 1990, 6066–27.8
Public opinion on crime and crime-related issues, by respondent characteristics, data compilation, 1992 annual rpt, 6064–6.2
Sentences for Federal offenses, guidelines by offense and circumstances, series, 17668–1
US attorneys civil and criminal cases by type and disposition, and collections, by Federal district, FY91, annual rpt, 6004–2.1

Protective services
see Campus security
see Detective and protective services
see Security devices

Providence, R.I.
Wages by occupation, for office and plant workers, 1992 survey, periodic MSA rpt, 6785–3.5
see also under By City and By SMSA or MSA in the "Index by Categories"

Provo, Utah
see also under By City and By SMSA or MSA in the "Index by Categories"

Prowse, Stephen D.
"Structure of Corporate Ownership in Japan", 9366–6.288

Psychiatry
Affective disorder patients mental health care services, by patient and facility characteristics, 1986, 4506–3.49
Health condition and care indicators, 1950s-90 with health improvement and disease prevention goals for 1990, annual data compilation, 4144–11
Labor supply and education of health professionals, by professional and other characteristics, and location, 1960s-92 and projected to 2020, biennial rpt, 4114–8
Labor supply of physicians, by specialty, age, sex, and location of training and practice, 1990, State rpt series, 4116–6
Medicaid payment and participation by service type, and cost compared to Medicare, by State, FY89, 17266–1.4
Medicare payment of physicians under fee schedule, methodology with data by procedure and specialty, 1992, annual rpt, 17264–1
Mental health care facilities, staff, and patient characteristics, *Statistical Notes* series, 4506–3
Mental health care facilities, staff, patients, and finances, 1970s-91, biennial rpt, 4094–1
Military health care personnel, and accessions by training source, by occupation, specialty, and service branch, FY90, annual rpt, 3544–24
VA health care facilities physicians, dentists, and nurses, by selected employment characteristics and VA district, quarterly rpt, 8602–6
VA health care facilities trainees, by detailed program and city, FY91, annual rpt, 8704–4
VA health care staff and turnover, by occupation, physician specialty, and location, 1991, annual rpt, 8604–8
Visits to physicians, by patient and practice characteristics, diagnosis, and services provided, 1989, annual rpt, 4147–13.109
Visits to physicians, by patient and practice characteristics, diagnosis, and services provided, 1990, advance rpt, 4146–8.215

Psychological disorders
see Mental health and illness

Psychology
Aviation medicine research and test results, technical rpt series, 7506–10
Degrees awarded in higher education, by level, field, race, and sex, 1989/90 and trends from 1980/81, annual rpt, 4844–17
Drug abuse and treatment, research on biological and behavioral factors and addiction potential of new drugs, 1991 annual conf, 4494–11
Education (special) enrollment by age, staff, funding, and needs, by type of handicap and State, 1990/91, annual rpt, 4944–4
Fed Govt aid to higher education and nonprofit instns for R&D and related activities, by field, instn, agency, and State, FY90, annual rpt, 9627–17
Higher education grad programs enrollment in science and engineering, by field, source of funds, and characteristics of student and instn, 1990, annual rpt, 9627–7
Labor demand, turnover, and training completions, by detailed occupation, 1990 and projected to 2005, biennial rpt, 6744–3
Minority group, women, and disabled persons employment and education in science and engineering, by field, mid 1970s-91, biennial rpt, 9624–20
NASA R&D funding to higher education instns, by field, instn, and State, FY91, annual listing, 9504–7
Occupational Outlook Handbook, 1992-93, biennial rpt, 6744–1
R&D facilities of higher education instns, space and equipment adequacy, needs, and funding by source, by instn type and control, 1992, biennial rpt, 9624–25
R&D funding by higher education instns and federally funded centers, by field, instn, and State, FY90, annual rpt, 9627–13
Science and Engineering Indicators, employment, education, R&D funding, and industry impacts, with foreign comparisons, 1960s-91, biennial rpt, 9624–10

Public administration
Budget of US, CBO analysis and review of FY93 budget by function, annual rpt, 26304–2
Budget of US, House concurrent resolution, with spending and revenue targets, FY93 and projected to FY97, annual rpt, 21264–2
Budget of US, midsession review of FY93 budget, by function, annual rpt, 104–7
Budget of US, obligations and authority by function, agency, and program, with summaries and analyses, FY93, annual rpt, 104–2
Budget of US, receipts by source, outlays by agency and program, and balances, monthly rpt, 8102–3
Census Bur data files and rpts, coverage and availability, 1992 annual listing, 2304–2
Deaths and rates, by cause and selected social, demographic, and employment characteristics, 1979-85, natl longitudinal study, 4478–186
Employment and payroll, by function and level of govt, annual rpt series, 2466–1
Expenditures (direct) and employment, by function and level of govt, selected years 1962-87, 10048–53
Fed Govt agencies and program operations investigations, summaries of findings, as of 1991, annual GAO rpt, 26104–5.4
Finances of govts, by level of govt, State, and for large cities and counties, annual rpt series, 2466–2
Labor demand, turnover, and training completions, by detailed occupation, 1990 and projected to 2005, biennial rpt, 6744–3

Minority group and women employment in State and local govt, by occupation, function, pay level, and State, 1991, annual rpt, 9244–6
Natl income and product accounts, comprehensive accounts and components, benchmark revisions, 1929-88, 2708–5
Natl income and product accounts, comprehensive accounts and components, *Survey of Current Business*, monthly rpt, 2702–1.26
Pacific territories population and housing detailed characteristics, by location, 1990 Census of Population and Housing, series, 2551–8
Public confidence in people running selected social instns, 1972-88 surveys, biennial rpt, 9624–10.7
Truman, Harry S, Scholarship Foundation finances, and awards by student characteristics, FY91, annual rpt, 14314–1
see also Administrative law and procedure
see also Civil service system
see also Federal boards, committees, and commissions
see also Federal employees
see also Federal executive departments
see also Federal independent agencies
see also Government and business
see also Government assets and liabilities
see also Government efficiency
see also Government employees
see also Government revenues
see also Government spending
see also Government supplies and property
see also Labor-management relations in government
see also Local government
see also Officials
see also Political science
see also Public services
see also School administration and staff
see also School boards
see also State and local employees
see also State government
see also under By Industry in the "Index by Categories"

Public assistance
see Public welfare programs

Public broadcasting
Fed Govt spending in States, by type, program, agency, and State, FY91, annual rpt, 2464–2
Licensing activities of FCC, by class of operation, FY91, annual rpt, 9284–4
Natl Endowment for Arts activities and grants, FY91, annual rpt, 9564–3
Statistical Abstract of US, 1992 annual data compilation, 2324–1.18
TV channel allocation and license status, for commercial and noncommercial UHF and VHF stations by market, as of June 1992, semiannual rpt, 9282–6
see also Educational broadcasting

Public buildings
Alteration and repair spending for commercial and public buildings, by type, size, age, and region, 1989, 2388–4
Alteration and repair spending for commercial and public buildings, by type, 1989, article, 2042–1.305
Arson incidents by whether structure occupied, property value, and arrest rate, by property type, 1991, annual rpt, 6224–2.1
Audiovisual activities and spending of Fed Govt, by whether performed in-house and agency, FY91, annual rpt, 9514–1
Budget of US, authoritative financial statements with appropriations, outlays, and receipts, by category and agency, FY91, annual rpt, 8104–2.2
Capital (fixed), govt and private nonresidential structures and equipment, residential capital, and consumer-owned durable goods, 1925-90, annual article, 2702–1.305; 2702–1.327
Capitol Architect activities, funding, costs, and contracts, FY89, annual rpt, 25944–1
Capitol Architect outlays for salaries, supplies, and services, itemized by payee and function, 2nd half FY91, semiannual rpt, 25922–2
Construction put in place, permits, housing sales, costs, material prices, and employment, quarterly rpt with articles, 2042–1
Construction put in place, value of new public and private structures, by type, monthly rpt, 2382–4
Criminal cases by type and disposition, and collections, for US attorneys, by Federal district, FY91, annual rpt, 6004–2.1
DC metro area land acquisition and dev projects of Fed Govt, characteristics and funding by agency and project, FY92-96, annual rpt, 15454–1
Disabled and aged persons access and services availability at election polling places, by State, 1990 natl elections, hearing, 21428–11
Disabled persons access to Federal and federally funded facilities, complaints by disposition and State, FY91, annual rpt, 17614–1
DOE energy use, costs, and conservation, by end use, fuel type, and field office, FY91, annual rpt, 3004–27
DOE real property owned and leased, by type, subagency, contractor, and site, FY91, annual rpt, 3004–28
Earthquake risk for Federal buildings and employees, by agency and region, 1989, with location and size of major events from 1600s, GAO rpt, 26119–399
Energy conservation aid of Fed Govt to public and nonprofit private instns, by building type and State, 1991, annual rpt, 3304–15
Energy use in commercial buildings, costs, and conservation, by building characteristics, survey rpt series, 3166–8
Expenditures (direct) and employment, by function and level of govt, selected years 1962-87, 10048–53
Fed Govt labor productivity, indexes of output and labor costs by function, FY67-90, annual rpt, 6824–1.6
Fed Reserve banks finances and staff, 1991, annual rpt, 9364–1.1
Govt finances, by level of govt, State, and for large cities and counties, annual rpt series, 2466–2
GSA activities and finances, FY91, annual rpt, 9454–1
Historic and natural natl landmarks damaged and threatened, with owner, location, damage type, and recommended remedial action, 1990, annual listing, 5544–16
Input-output structure of US economy, detailed interindustry transactions for 541 industries, and components of final demand, 1982 benchmark data, 2708–17
Mint (US) building improvement and new equipment funding, by facility, projected FY92-96, hearing, 21248–164
NIH activities, staff, funding, and facilities, historical data, 1991 annual rpt, 4434–1
Postal Service activities, finances, and mail volume and subsidies, FY91, annual rpt, 9864–5.3
Postal Service operating costs, itemized by class of mail, FY91, annual rpt, 9864–4
Postal Service revenue, costs, and volume, by service type and class of mail, FY91, annual rpt, 9864–2
Statistical Abstract of US, 1992 annual data compilation, 2324–1.10
TVA energy use by fuel type, and conservation costs and savings, FY91, annual rpt, 9804–26
see also Educational facilities

Public contracts
see Defense contracts and procurement
see Government contracts and procurement

Public debt
Borrowing and debt issues, by level of govt, selected years 1929-91, annual rpt, 204–1.5; 204–1.6
Budget deficit reduction under Gramm-Rudman Act, CBO sequestration estimates, FY93, annual rpt, 26304–6
Budget deficit reduction under Gramm-Rudman Act, OMB sequestration estimates, by category, FY92, annual rpt, 104–27
Budget deficits impacts on GNP and public and foreign debt, projected under alternative reduction policies, 1990-2020 with intl comparisons from 1981, GAO rpt, 26109–5
Budget of US, authoritative financial statements with appropriations, outlays, and receipts, by agency, FY91, annual rpt, 8104–2
Budget of US, Bush Admin proposals, with detail for defense budgets, and historical data from FY34, FY93, 108–46
Budget of US, CBO analysis and review of FY93 budget by function, annual rpt, 26304–2
Budget of US, CBO analysis of revenue and spending alternatives and projections of economic indicators, FY93-97, annual rpt, 26304–3
Budget of US, House Budget Committee analysis of Bush Admin proposals and economic assumptions, FY93, 21268–42
Budget of US, House concurrent resolution, with spending and revenue targets, FY93 and projected to FY97, annual rpt, 21264–2
Budget of US, midsession review of FY93 budget, by function, annual rpt, 104–7
Budget of US, obligations and authority by function, agency, and program, with summaries and analyses, FY93, annual rpt, 104–2
Budget of US, receipts by source, outlays by agency and program, and balances, monthly rpt, 8102–3
Business statistics, detailed data for major industries and economic indicators, *Survey of Current Business*, monthly rpt, 2702–1.8

Business statistics, detailed data for major industries and economic indicators, 1960-91, *Survey of Current Business* biennial supplement, 2704–1
Debt outstanding by type of holder, and total and per capita Federal debt, 1929-89, hearing, 25368–177
Economic indicators and components, and Fed Reserve 4th District business and financial conditions, monthly chartbook, 9377–10
Expenditures (direct) and employment, by function and level of govt, selected years 1962-87, 10048–53
Fed Govt debt, by type and holder, monthly rpt, 9362–1.1
Fed Govt debt, by type and holder, 1990, annual rpt, 9364–5.5
Fed Govt debt interest payments, monthly rpt, quarterly and annual data, 23842–1.6
Fed Govt debt issued, redeemed, and outstanding, by series and source, and gifts to reduce debt, monthly rpt, 8242–2
Fed Govt finances, cash and debt transactions, daily tables, 8102–4
Fed Govt financial operations, detailed data, *Treasury Bulletin*, quarterly rpt, 8002–4
Fed Govt financial transactions, *Survey of Current Business*, monthly rpt, 2702–1.8
Fed Govt receipts, expenditures, and debt, Fed Reserve Bank of St Louis monthly rpt, 9391–3
Finances of govts, by level of govt, State, and for large cities and counties, annual rpt series, 2466–2
Fiscal policy (supply side) of Reagan Admin, economic impacts, 1980s and trends from 1960s, technical paper, 9385–1.304; 9385–8.125
Forecasts of public debt burden on future generations under alternative tax, OASDI, and Medicare policies, 1992 working paper, 9377–9.137
Foreign countries economic conditions and implications for US, periodic country rpt series, 2046–4
Foreign countries economic conditions, policy, and trade practices, by country, 1989-91, annual rpt, 21384–5
Govt finances, tax systems and revenue, and fiscal structure, by level of govt and State, 1992 with historical trends, annual rpt, 10044–1
Health insurance and govt aid coverage, with background data 1960s-91 and govt fiscal impacts projected to 2002, 26306–6.174
Italy public debt burden on future generations, alternative forecasts, 1992 working paper, 9377–9.139
Latin America economic and social conditions, resources, trade, and aid, 1992, annual factbook, 9914–14
Natl income and product accounts, comprehensive accounts and components, benchmark revisions, 1929-88, 2708–5
Natl income and product accounts, comprehensive accounts and components, *Survey of Current Business*, monthly rpt, 2702–1.26
NATO, Japan, and South Korea military spending and indicators of ability to support common defense, by country, 1970s-90, annual rpt, 3544–28
OASDHI trust funds finances impacts of Federal debt, with background data, 1990-2065, technical paper, 8006–6.6
Port improvement capital expenditures and financing methods, by region and selected port, 1946-89, 7708–6
Postal Service activities, finances, and mail volume and subsidies, FY91, annual rpt, 9864–5.3
Savings rate relation to Federal debt and deficits, 1980s, technical paper, 8006–6.5
State govt budget balances, balances as share of outlays, and costs of Medicaid coverage expansion, FY89-92, hearing, 21408–129
Statistical Abstract of US, 1992 annual data compilation, 2324–1.9
Tax returns filed with contributions to retire public debt, FY91 and cumulative from 1982, annual rpt, 8304–3.1
see also Foreign debts
see also Government securities
see also Municipal bonds
see also U.S. savings bonds

Public defenders
see Legal aid

Public demonstrations
see also Right of assembly
see also Riots and disorders

Public documents
see Government documents

Public finance
see Budget of the U.S.
see Fiscal policy
see Government assets and liabilities
see Government revenues
see Government securities
see Government spending
see Monetary policy
see Public debt
see Taxation

Public health
Appalachian Regional Commission health care services projects by State, and project listing, 1960s-80s, 9088–38
Assistance (financial and nonfinancial) of Fed Govt, 1992 base edition, annual listing, 104–5
Budget of US, House concurrent resolution, with spending and revenue targets, FY93 and projected to FY97, annual rpt, 21264–2
Criminal cases by type and disposition, and collections, for US attorneys, by Federal district, FY91, annual rpt, 6004–2.1
Employment and payroll, by function and level of govt, annual rpt series, 2466–1
Expenditures by function, and revenues by source, natl income and product account benchmark revisions, 1929-88, 2708–5
Expenditures by function, and revenues by source, natl income and product accounts, *Survey of Current Business*, monthly rpt, 2702–1.26
Expenditures for public welfare by program, FY50s-89, annual article, 4742–1.319
Expenditures for public welfare programs, by program type and level of govt, FY65-89, annual article, 4742–1.302
Expenditures of Fed Govt in States, by type, program, agency, and State, FY91, annual rpt, 2464–2
Foreign and US health care administrative costs for all and public programs, by selected OECD country, mid 1970s-90, article, 4652–1.325
Govt finances, by level of govt, State, and for large cities and counties, annual rpt series, 2466–2
Health condition and care indicators, 1950s-90 with health improvement and disease prevention goals for 1990, annual data compilation, 4144–11
HHS financial aid, by program, recipient, State, and city, FY91, annual regional listings, 4004–3
HHS public health innovation contest winners, project descriptions and costs, 1991, article, 4042–3.322
Labor supply and education of health professionals, by professional and other characteristics, and location, 1960s-92 and projected to 2020, biennial rpt, 4114–8
Morbidity and Mortality Weekly Report, infectious notifiable disease cases and deaths, and other public health issues, periodic journal, 4202–7
Morbidity and Mortality Weekly Report, special supplements, series, 4206–2
NIH rpts, 1992 annual listing, 4434–2
OECD members health care costs, hospital use, resources, and economic and health indicators, by country, 1960s-90, article, 4652–1.322
Physicians, by specialty, age, sex, and location of training and practice, 1990, State rpt series, 4116–6
Public Health Reports, bimonthly journal, 4042–3
San Antonio, Tex, govt funding for public housing and health, with background data, 1989-91, hearing, 21248–172
State and local govt employment of minorities and women, by occupation, function, and pay level, 1991, annual rpt, 9244–6.4
see also Accidents and accident prevention
see also Air pollution
see also Asbestos contamination
see also Birth defects
see also Carcinogens
see also Child abuse and neglect
see also Child welfare
see also Community health services
see also Diseases and disorders
see also Domestic violence
see also Environmental pollution and control
see also Epidemiology and epidemiologists
see also Food inspection
see also Hazardous substances
see also Health condition
see also Health education
see also Health facilities administration
see also Health facilities and services
see also Health insurance
see also Health maintenance organizations
see also Health occupations
see also Infant mortality
see also Lead poisoning and pollution
see also Medicaid
see also Medical assistance
see also Medical costs
see also Medical education
see also Medical research
see also Medical supplies and equipment
see also Medical transplants
see also Mental health facilities and services
see also Mercury pollution
see also Noise
see also Occupational health and safety

see also Pesticides
see also Pests and pest control
see also Poisoning and drug reaction
see also Preventive medicine
see also Radiation
see also Refuse and refuse disposal
see also Regional medical programs
see also Sewage and wastewater systems
see also Smoking
see also Soil pollution
see also State funding for health and hospitals
see also State funding for public safety
see also Vaccination and vaccines
see also Water supply and use

Public Health Service

AIDS prevention and control plans, cases, and Federal funding, 1980s-94, 4048–22
Budget of US, obligations and authority by function, agency, and program, with summaries and analyses, FY93, annual rpt, 104–2
Carcinogens chemistry, sources, environment and health risks, and regulation, by substance and brand, 1991 annual rpt, 4044–15
Commissioned Corps of PHS, deaths of members by cause, 1965-89, article, 4042–3.316
Physicians, by specialty, age, sex, and location of training and practice, 1990, State rpt series, 4116–6
Public Health Reports, bimonthly journal, 4042–3
Toxicology Natl Program research and testing activities, FY90 and planned FY91, annual rpt, 4044–16
see also Agency for Health Care Policy and Research
see also Alcohol, Drug Abuse and Mental Health Administration
see also Bureau of Health Professions
see also Center for Mental Health Services
see also Centers for Disease Control
see also Food and Drug Administration
see also Health Resources and Services Administration
see also Indian Health Service
see also National Center for Health Statistics
see also National Institute for Occupational Safety and Health
see also National Institute of Mental Health
see also National Institute on Alcohol Abuse and Alcoholism
see also National Institute on Drug Abuse
see also National Institutes of Health
see also National Library of Medicine
see also Office on Smoking and Health

Public housing

AFDC beneficiaries demographic and financial characteristics, by State, FY90, annual rpt, 4584–7
American Housing Survey: unit and households detailed characteristics, and unit and neighborhood quality, MSA rpt series, 2485–6
Benefits, beneficiaries, and spells of participation, by aid program and recipient characteristics, 1987-88, Current Population Rpt, 2546–20.25
Construction put in place, permits, housing sales, costs, material prices, and employment, quarterly rpt with articles, 2042–1
Construction put in place, value of new public and private structures, by type, monthly rpt, 2382–4
Drug treatment and anticrime programs for public housing, HUD grants by recipient, FY91, press release, 5006–3.81
Drug treatment and anticrime programs for public housing, HUD grants by recipient, FY92, press release, 5006–3.99
Educational attainment of public housing residents, by selected characteristics, 1980s, 5188–132
Eligibility for low income housing, tenants reported income agreement with tax records, 1989-90, GAO rpt, 26121–468
Employment and payroll, by function and level of govt, annual rpt series, 2466–1
Expenditures for public welfare by program, FY50s-89, annual article, 4742–1.319
Expenditures of Fed Govt in States, by type, program, agency, and State, FY91, annual rpt, 2464–2
Govt finances, by level of govt, State, and for large cities and counties, annual rpt series, 2466–2
Housing (rental) units, total, with HUD assistance by program, and eligible for aid, by unit, household, and neighborhood characteristics, and location, 1989, biennial rpt, 5184–11
HUD activities, and housing programs operations and funding, 1990, annual rpt, 5004–10
Living arrangements, family relationships, and marital status, by selected characteristics, 1991, annual Current Population Rpt, 2546–1.461
NYC housing supply, occupancy, condition, and household characteristics, by tenure and borough, 1991 triennial survey, 2488–3
Older persons public housing, placement of younger mentally disabled tenants, behavioral problems, and services, 1990 survey, GAO rpt, 26113–590
Population economic well-being indicators, by selected characteristics and household income and income-to-poverty ratio, 1984, 2546–20.22
San Antonio, Tex, govt funding for public housing and health, with background data, 1989-91, hearing, 21248–172
Single person and nonfamily households social, economic and housing characteristics, by tenure, 1989, 2486–1.15
Statistical Abstract of US, 1992 annual data compilation, 2324–1.26
Tenant assns in public and Indian housing, HUD project mgmt and operation training grants by recipient, FY91, press release, 5006–3.77
Tenant assns in public and Indian housing, HUD project mgmt and operation training grants by recipient, FY92, press release, 5006–3.100
see also Low-income housing

Public lands

Acreage and use of public lands, and Land Mgmt Bur activities and finances, annual State rpt series, 5724–11
Acreage, grants, use, revenues, and allocations, for public lands by State, FY91 and trends, annual rpt, 5724–1
Acreage of land under Natl Park Service mgmt, by site, ownership, and region, FY92, semiannual rpt, 5542–1
Alaska oil, gas, and coal reserve acreage, by ownership, 1991 rpt, 5608–174
Army Corps of Engineers recreation facilities mgmt, acreage, visits, and non-Federal public and private dev alternatives, 1980s-90, 3758–8
Bur of Indian Affairs mgmt of tribal and govt lands, acreage, leases, and use, 1989, annual rpt, 5704–12
Coal mining restrictions on public land, impacts on production, costs, and demand, by region, 1985-88 and projected to 2075, 5668–125
Coal Surface Mining Reclamation and Enforcement Office activities and funding, by State and Indian tribe, FY91, annual rpt, 5644–1
Criminal cases by type and disposition, and collections, for US attorneys, by Federal district, FY91, annual rpt, 6004–2.1
DC metro area land acquisition and dev projects of Fed Govt, characteristics and funding by agency and project, FY92-96, annual rpt, 15454–1
Desert areas public grazing acreage, use, fees, and endangered species, 1988-90, GAO rpt, 26113–552
Environmental Quality, status of problems, protection programs, research, and intl issues, 1991 annual rpt, 484–1
Fires on public lands, prevention activities evaluation methods and effectiveness, 1989 survey, 1208–417
Fires on wildlands, ecology, mgmt, cultural impacts, and historic patterns, 1990 conf, 1208–415
Fish and Wildlife Service restoration programs funding, land purchases, and project listing, by State, FY90, annual rpt, 5504–1
Land Mgmt Bur activities and funding by State, FY90, annual rpt, 5724–13
Landmarks (natl historic and natural) damaged and threatened, with owner, location, damage type, and recommended remedial action, 1990, annual listing, 5544–16
Local govt receipts from Fed Govt in lieu of property taxes on public lands, by State, FY92, annual press release, 5306–4.15
Minerals resources and availability on public lands, State rpt series, 5606–7
Missouri timber resources and removals, by species, forest and tree characteristics, ownership, and county, 1987-89 and trends from 1959, 1208–76
New Mexico Caballo Resource Area public land mgmt, and grazing, environmental, and leasing activities, FY90-91, annual rpt, 5724–17
NIH activities, staff, funding, and facilities, historical data, 1991 annual rpt, 4434–1
Northeastern US timber resources and removals, by species, ownership, and county, State rpt series, 1206–12
Northwestern US and British Columbia forest industry production, prices, trade, and employment, quarterly rpt, 1202–3
Pacific Northwest northern spotted owl conservation methods, findings and recommendations, 1990 rpt, 1208–385

Private landowners restriction of access to public lands, reasons and impacts on recreation and land mgmt activities, 1991-92 surveys, GAO rpt, 26113–571
Rocky Mountain States timber and mill residue production, by species, ownership, and county, series, 1206–17
Southern US timber resources and removals, by species, ownership, State, and county, series, 1206–8
Southwestern US activities of Land Mgmt Bur, FY91, annual rpt, 5724–15
Statistical Abstract of US, 1992 annual data compilation, 2324–1.6; 2324–1.7; 2324–1.10
Tennessee timber acreage and resources, by species, ownership class, and county, 1989, series, 1206–27
Uranium reserves and industry operations, by region and State, various periods 1966-91, annual rpt, 3164–65.1
Western US activities of Reclamation Bur, land and population served, and recreation areas, by location, 1990, annual rpt, 5824–12
Wisconsin timber resources and removals, by species, forest type, ownership, and county, series, 1206–34
see also Homesteads
see also Military bases, posts, and reservations
see also Mineral leases
see also National forests
see also National grasslands
see also National parks
see also National trails
see also Oil and gas leases
see also Parks
see also Public buildings
see also State forests
see also State parks
see also Wilderness areas
see also Wildlife refuges

Public Law 480
Agricultural Statistics, 1991, annual rpt, 1004–1
CCC dairy price support program foreign donations and domestic donations to poor, schools, Prisons Bur, and VA, monthly rpt, 1802–2
Concessional sales agreements, market value, and shipping costs, by country, annual rpt, discontinued, 1924–6
Credit sales (long-term) allocations under PL 480, periodic press release, discontinued, 1922–7
Credit sales agreement terms, by commodity and country, FY90, annual rpt, 15344–1.11
Currency (foreign) accounts owned by US under AID admin and by foreign govts with joint AID control, status by program and country, quarterly rpt, 9912–1
Currency (foreign) holdings of US, transactions and balances by program and country, 1st half FY92, semiannual rpt, 8102–7
Developing countries economic and social conditions from 1960s, and Intl Dev Cooperation Agency and AID activities and funding, FY91-93, annual rpt, 9904–4
Disasters, casualties, damage, and aid by US and others, by country, FY91 and trends from FY64, annual rpt, 9914–12
Human rights conditions in 170 countries, and US economic and military aid, 1991, annual rpt, 21384–3
Latin America economic and social conditions, resources, trade, and aid, 1992, annual factbook, 9914–14
Loan repayment status and terms by program and country, AID and predecessor agencies, quarterly rpt, 9912–3
Oils, oilseeds, and fats foreign and US production and trade, FAS periodic circular series, 1925–1
Rice exports under Federal programs, periodic situation rpt, 1561–8
Title I and II aid, by country, FY46-91, annual rpt, 9914–5
Voluntary agencies foreign aid programs, funding, and outlays, by agency, 1990, annual rpt, 9914–9

Public opinion
see Consumer surveys
see Opinion and attitude surveys

Public ownership
see Government ownership

Public relations
County Business Patterns, 1989: employment, establishments, and payroll, by SIC 2- to 4-digit industry and county, annual State rpt series, 2326–8
County Business Patterns, 1990: employment, establishments, and payroll, by SIC 2- to 4-digit industry and county, annual State rpt series, 2326–6
Finances and operations, by SIC 2- to 4-digit industry, forecast 1992, annual rpt, 2044–28
Labor demand, turnover, and training completions, by detailed occupation, 1990 and projected to 2005, biennial rpt, 6744–3
Occupational Outlook Handbook, 1992-93, biennial rpt, 6744–1
see also Advertising
see also Lobbying and lobbying groups

Public schools
see Elementary and secondary education
see Higher education
see terms listed under Education and beginning with School

Public service employment
Forest Service employment and human resource program participation, FY91, annual rpt, 1204–1.4
Probation population, by offender characteristics, sentence conditions, whether rearrested, and offense, 1986-89, 6066–19.65
Senior Community Service Employment program participant characteristics, FY87, annual rpt, 6404–17
Student Community Service Learning work-study program, earnings and operations, 1986-90, GAO rpt, 26121–449
see also Job Corps

Public services
Budget of US, authoritative financial statements with appropriations, outlays, and receipts, by category and agency, FY91, annual rpt, 8104–2.2
Community Dev Block Grant activities and funding, by program, FY75-91, annual rpt, 5124–8
Educational facilities community services spending by elementary and secondary public school systems, by State, FY90, annual rpt, 4834–6
Expenditures (direct) and employment, by function and level of govt, selected years 1962-87, 10048–53
Fed Govt labor productivity, indexes of output and labor costs by function, FY67-90, annual rpt, 6824–1.6
Labor productivity of govt employees, indexes of output and labor costs by function, FY67-90, annual rpt, 6824–1.6
Local govts in metro areas, finances, structure, and service delivery, local area rpt series, 10046–9
Michigan local areas economic conditions and public services impacts of reductions in Federal aid, with background data, 1970s-91, GAO rpt, 26121–483
Neighborhood quality, indicators and attitudes of renter households, by whether receiving and eligible for HUD assistance, householder characteristics, and location, 1989, biennial rpt, 5184–11
Public opinion on taxes, spending, and govt efficiency, by respondent characteristics, 1992 survey, annual rpt, 10044–2
see also Community health services
see also Fire departments
see also Police
see also Public health
see also Public service employment
see also Public utilities
see also Public welfare programs
see also Public works
see also Sewage and wastewater systems
see also Social security
see also Social services
see also Special districts
see also User fees
see also Water supply and use

Public transportation
see Subways
see Urban transportation

Public utilities
Bombing incidents and casualties, by target, circumstances, and State, 1987-91, annual rpt, 8484–4.1
Bombing incidents, casualties, and damage, by target, circumstances, and State, 1991, annual rpt, 6224–5
Business statistics, detailed data for major industries and economic indicators, 1960-91, *Survey of Current Business* biennial supplement, 2704–1
Capital expenditures for plant and equipment, by industry div, monthly rpt, quarterly data, 23842–1.1
Capital expenditures for plant and equipment, by major industry group, quarterly rpt, 2502–2
Capital investment changes relation to changes in costs, by asset type and industry div, late 1950s-80s, article, 9373–1.304
Collective bargaining agreements expiring during year, and workers covered, by firm, union, industry group, and State, 1992, annual rpt, 6784–9
Communications services revenue and expenses, itemized by SIC 2- to 4-digit kind of business, 1990, annual rpt, 2413–15

Construction put in place and cost indexes, by type of construction, quarterly rpt, 2042–1.1; 2042–1.5
Construction put in place, value of new public and private structures, by type, monthly rpt, 2382–4
Consumer Expenditure Survey, spending by category, selected household characteristics, and region, quarterly rpt, 6762–14
Costa Rica economic indicators and reform issues, mid 1970s-90, working paper, 9916–13.5
County Business Patterns, 1989: employment, establishments, and payroll, by SIC 2- to 4-digit industry and county, annual State rpt series, 2326–8
County Business Patterns, 1990: employment, establishments, and payroll, by SIC 2- to 4-digit industry and county, annual State rpt series, 2326–6
CPI by component for US city average, and by selected metro area, region, and population size, monthly rpt, 6762–2
Deaths and rates, by cause and selected social, demographic, and employment characteristics, 1979-85, natl longitudinal study, 4478–186
Employment and Earnings, detailed data, monthly rpt, 6742–2.5
Employment Cost Index and alternative measure of compensation costs, by component, occupation, industry group, union status, and location, 1975-92, annual rpt, 6744–20
Employment, earnings, and hours, by SIC 1- to 4-digit industry, monthly 1989-Feb 1992, annual rpt, 6744–4
Employment, earnings, and hours, monthly press release, 6742–5
Employment of minorities and women, by occupation, SIC 1- to 3-digit industry, State, and MSA, 1991, annual rpt, 9244–1
Employment situation, earnings, hours, and other BLS economic indicators, transcripts of BLS Commissioner's monthly testimony, periodic rpt, 23846–4
Employment, unemployment, and labor force characteristics, by region, State, and selected metro area, 1991, annual rpt, 6744–7
Energy conservation programs of States, Federal aid and savings, by State, 1990, annual rpt, 3304–1
Expenditures (direct) and employment, by function and level of govt, selected years 1962-87, 10048–53
Foreign direct investment in US, major transactions by type, industry, country, and US location, 1990, annual rpt, 2044–20
Govt employment and payroll, by function, level of govt, and jurisdiction, annual rpt series, 2466–1
Govt finances, by level of govt, State, and for large cities and counties, annual rpt series, 2466–2
Home mortgages FHA-insured, financial, property, and borrower characteristics, 1991, annual rpt, 5144–17
Input-output structure of US economy, detailed interindustry transactions for 84 industries, and components of final demand, 1987, annual article, 2702–1.316
Input-output structure of US economy, detailed interindustry transactions for 541 industries, and components of final demand, 1982 benchmark data, 2708–17
Labor productivity, indexes of output, hours, and employment by SIC 2- to 4-digit industry, 1967-90, annual rpt, 6824–1.4
Mail volume to and from households, use, and views, by class, source, content, and household characteristics, FY87-90, annual rpt, 9864–10
Minority- and woman-owned businesses and owner characteristics, by industry, employment and sales size, and form of ownership, 1987 survey, 2328–59
Multinatl firms US affiliates finances and operations, by industry, country of parent firm, and State, 1987, 2708–48
Multinatl US firms foreign affiliates, income statement items by asset size, industry, and country, 1988, biennial article, 8302–2.322
Natl income and product accounts, comprehensive accounts and components, benchmark revisions, 1929-88, 2708–5
Natl income and product accounts, comprehensive accounts and components, *Survey of Current Business*, monthly rpt, 2702–1.26; 2702–1.29
Occupational injuries, illnesses, and lost workdays, by SIC 2-digit industry, 1990-91, annual press release, 6844–3
Occupational injury and illness rates by circumstances and establishment size, and methodology for computing rates, 1988, industry rpt, 6886–4.2
Occupational injury and illness rates, by SIC 2- to 4-digit industry, 1989-90, annual rpt, 6844–7
Occupational injury and illness rates, by SIC 2- to 4-digit industry, 1990, annual rpt, 6844–1
Pacific territories population and housing detailed characteristics, by location, 1990 Census of Population and Housing, series, 2551–8
Production and capacity use indexes, by SIC 2- to 4-digit industry, monthly rpt, 9365–2.24
SEC registration, firms required to file annual rpts, as of Sept 1991, annual listing, 9734–5
Small business finances, operations, owner characteristics, and Federal contracts, 1980s-90, annual rpt, 9764–6
Southeastern US employment by industry div, earnings, and hours, for 8 States, quarterly press release, 6942–7
State and local govt employment of minorities and women, by occupation, function, and pay level, 1991, annual rpt, 9244–6.4
Stock (common) price indexes, current data and annual trends, monthly rpt, 23842–1.5
Tax (income) returns filed, by type of filer, selected income items, quarterly rpt, 8302–2.1
Tax (income) returns for foreign corporate activity in US, selected income and tax items, by industry div and selected country, 1988, article, 8302–2.309
Tax (income) returns of corporations, income and tax items by asset size and detailed industry, 1989, annual rpt, 8304–4; 8304–21
Tax (income) returns of corporations with foreign tax credit, income and tax items by industry group, 1988, biennial article, 8302–2.316
Tax (income) returns of partnerships, income statement and balance sheet items, by industry group, 1990, annual article, 8302–2.314
Tax (income) returns of sole proprietorships, income statement items, by industry group, 1990, annual article, 8302–2.317; 8302–2.320
Tax collections of State govts by detailed type of tax, and tax rates, by State, FY91, annual rpt, 2466–2.7
Tax rates and revenue of State and local govts, by source and State, 1992 and historical trends, annual rpt, 10044–1
Tax revenue, by level of govt, type of tax, State, and selected large county, quarterly rpt, 2462–3
Uranium marketing, contracts, prices, utility shipments, and trade, 1982-91 and projected to 2001, annual rpt, 3164–65.2
Wage and benefit changes from collective bargaining and mgmt decisions, by industry div, monthly rpt, 6782–1
Wages by occupation, and benefits for office and plant workers, periodic MSA survey rpt series, 6785–12; 6785–16; 6785–17
see also Buses
see also Cable television
see also Census of Transportation, Communications, and Utilities Industries
see also Communications industries
see also Electric power
see also Electric power plants and equipment
see also Electric power prices
see also Mobile radio
see also Radio
see also Railroads
see also Refuse and refuse disposal
see also Rural electrification
see also Sewage and wastewater systems
see also Subways
see also Telecommunication
see also Telegraph
see also Telephones and telephone industry
see also Television
see also Water supply and use
see also under By Industry in the "Index by Categories"

Public Utility Holding Company Act
Electric utilities operation under PUHCA, with capacity and construction costs, late 1960s-80s, 3006–13.1

Public welfare programs
Assistance (financial and nonfinancial) of Fed Govt, 1992 base edition, annual listing, 104–5
Assistance programs of Fed Govt for public welfare, employment, and training, coordination issues with background data, 1991 rpt, 15498–29
Assistance programs under Ways and Means Committee jurisdiction, finances, operations, and participant characteristics, FY70s-91, annual rpt, 21784–11
Benefits, beneficiary characteristics, and trust funds of OASDHI, Medicaid, SSI, and related programs, selected years 1937-90, annual rpt, 4744–3
Black women's labor force status, earnings, and other economic status indicators, and compared to whites, various periods 1939-88, 11048–191

Budget of US, Bush Admin proposals, with detail for defense budgets, and historical data from FY34, FY93, 108–46
Budget of US, CBO analysis and review of FY93 budget by function, annual rpt, 26304–2
Budget of US, CBO analysis of revenue and spending alternatives and projections of economic indicators, FY93-97, annual rpt, 26304–3
Budget of US, House concurrent resolution, with spending and revenue targets, FY93 and projected to FY97, annual rpt, 21264–2
Budget of US, obligations and authority by function, agency, and program, with summaries and analyses, FY93, annual rpt, 104–2
Budget of US, receipts by source, outlays by agency and program, and balances, monthly rpt, 8102–3
Drug abuse by mothers, treatment and other services use, referrals, needs, and barriers, for 13 NIDA-funded programs, 1990/91 survey, 4498–76
Employment and payroll, by function and level of govt, annual rpt series, 2466–1
Expenditures (direct) and employment, by function and level of govt, selected years 1962-87, 10048–53
Expenditures for public welfare by program, FY50s-89, annual article, 4742–1.319
Expenditures for public welfare programs, by program type and level of govt, FY65-89, annual article, 4742–1.302
Finances of govts, by level of govt, State, and for large cities and counties, annual rpt series, 2466–2
Finances of govts, tax systems and revenue, and fiscal structure, by level of govt and State, 1992 and historical trends, annual rpt, 10044–1
Fraud and abuse in HHS programs, audits and investigations, 1st half FY92, semiannual rpt, 4002–6
HHS financial aid, by program, recipient, State, and city, FY91, annual regional listings, 4004–3
Housing (rental) units, total, with HUD assistance by program, and eligible for aid, by unit, household, and neighborhood characteristics, and location, 1989, biennial rpt, 5184–11
Income (household) and poverty status under alternative income definitions, by recipient characteristics, 1979-91, annual Current Population Rpt, 2546–6.78
Income (household, family, and personal), by source, detailed characteristics, and region, 1991, annual Current Population Rpt, 2546–6.76
Insurance (health) coverage of persons, by insurance type and selected characteristics, 1985-90, 2546–20.23
Investigations of Federal agency and program operations, summaries of findings, as of 1991, annual GAO rpt, 26104–5.3
Labor productivity of Federal employees, indexes of output and labor costs by function, FY67-90, annual rpt, 6824–1.6
Mississippi poverty, hunger, and public welfare program operations and indicators of need, 1991 hearing, 21968–57
Natl income and product accounts, comprehensive accounts and components, benchmark revisions, 1929-88, 2708–5
Natl income and product accounts, comprehensive accounts and components, *Survey of Current Business*, monthly rpt, 2702–1.26
NYC housing supply, occupancy, condition, and household characteristics, by tenure and borough, 1991 triennial survey, 2488–3
Older persons income and sources, by OASDI beneficiary and poverty status, and other characteristics, 1990, biennial chartbook, 4744–25
Older persons income and sources, by whether OASDI beneficiary, poverty status, and other characteristics, 1990, biennial rpt, 4744–26
Population economic well-being indicators, by selected characteristics and household income and income-to-poverty ratio, 1984, 2546–20.22
Poverty population, and impacts of selected cash and noncash benefits and benefit changes, 1980s, 21788–212
Poverty status of families, by detailed characteristics, 1980 and 1988, GAO rpt, 26131–102
Poverty status of population and families, by detailed characteristics, 1991, annual Current Population Rpt, 2546–6.77
R&D funding by Fed Govt, by detailed function, program, and agency, FY91-93, annual rpt, 9627–9
Refugee arrivals in US by world area of origin and State of settlement, and Federal aid, FY91-92 and proposed FY93 allocations, annual rpt, 7004–16
State and local govt employment of minorities and women, by occupation, function, and pay level, 1991, annual rpt, 9244–6.4
Statistical Abstract of US, 1992 annual data compilation, 2324–1.12
Survey of Income and Program Participation, data collection, methodology, and availability, 1991 users guide, 2628–24
Survey of Income and Program Participation, household composition, income, benefits, and labor force status, methodology, working paper series, 2626–10
see also Aid to blind
see also Aid to disabled and handicapped persons
see also Aid to Families with Dependent Children
see also Child day care
see also Child welfare
see also Disability benefits and insurance
see also Disaster relief
see also Food assistance
see also Food stamp programs
see also Foster home care
see also Homemaker services
see also Income maintenance
see also Legal aid
see also Low-income energy assistance
see also Maternity benefits
see also Medicaid
see also Medical assistance
see also Medicare
see also Old age assistance
see also Public service employment
see also Rent supplements
see also School lunch and breakfast programs
see also Social security
see also Social services
see also Social work
see also State funding for social welfare
see also Supplemental Security Income
see also Transportation assistance
see also Vocational rehabilitation
see also Work incentive programs

Public works
Appalachian Regional Commission funding, by project and State, planned FY92, annual rpt, 9084–3
Army Corps of Engineers activities, FY90, annual rpt, 3754–1
Assistance (financial and nonfinancial) of Fed Govt, 1992 base edition, annual listing, 104–5
Budget of US, authoritative financial statements with appropriations, outlays, and receipts, by category and agency, FY91, annual rpt, 8104–2.2
Budget of US, House concurrent resolution, with spending and revenue targets, FY93 and projected to FY97, annual rpt, 21264–2
Budget of US, obligations and authority by function, agency, and program, with summaries and analyses, FY93, annual rpt, 104–2
Community Dev Block Grant activities and funding, by program, FY75-91, annual rpt, 5124–8
Construction put in place, permits, housing sales, costs, material prices, and employment, quarterly rpt with articles, 2042–1
Economic Dev Admin activities, and funding by program, recipient, State, and county, FY91 and cumulative from FY66, annual rpt, 2064–2
Expenditures, financing, use, and condition of public works, 1990 hearing, 21648–67
Fed Govt spending in States, by type, program, agency, and State, FY91, annual rpt, 2464–2
Fiscal policy (supply side) of Reagan Admin, economic impacts, 1980s and trends from 1960s, technical paper, 9385–1.304; 9385–8.125
Investigations of GAO, 1991-92, listing, 26106–10.7
Lands (public) acreage, grants, use, revenues, and allocations, by State, FY91, annual rpt, 5724–1.2
Neighborhood and housing quality, indicators and attitudes, by householder type and location, 1989, biennial rpt supplement, 2485–13
Port improvement capital expenditures and financing methods, by region and selected port, 1946-89, 7708–6
Reclamation Bur irrigation activities, finances, and project impacts in western US, 1990, annual rpt, 5824–12
Statistical Abstract of US, 1992 annual data compilation, 2324–1.9
Wastewater treatment and collection facility construction funding needs and Fed Govt grants, by State, 1990 and projected to 2010, biennial rpt, 9204–7

see also Public buildings
see also Public service employment
see also Sewage and wastewater systems
see also Water resources development

Publications catalogs
see Bibliographies
see Government publications lists

Publishing industry
see Printing and publishing industry

Puerto Rico
Banks (insured commercial and savings) deposits by instn, State, MSA, and county, as of June 1991, annual regional rpt, 9295–3.1
Cement (portland) shipments to Puerto Rico, quarterly rpt, 2042–1.6
Coffee production for Puerto Rico and Hawaii, 1950s-91, FAS periodic circular, 1925–5
Corporations operating in Puerto Rico and other US possessions, income tax return items, and employment, by selected industry, 1989, article, 8302–2.326
Deaths and rates, by detailed location, cause, and demographic characteristics, 1989, US Vital Statistics annual rpt, 4144–3.2
Drug abuse indicators, by world region and selected country, 1991 semiannual conf, 4492–5.1
Drug industry employee salaries and tax benefits, for Puerto Rico, 1991 rpt, 25148–44
Economic, social, political, and geographic summary data, by country, 1992, annual factbook, 9114–2
Employment, earnings, and hours, by selected SIC 1- to 4-digit industry, State, and for 275 MSAs, 1987-92, 6748–81
Exports and imports between US and outlying areas, by detailed commodity and mode of transport, 1991, annual rpt, 2424–11
Fed Govt spending in States and local areas, by type, State, county, and city, FY91, annual rpt, 2464–3
Fed Govt spending in States, by type, program, agency, and State, FY91, annual rpt, 2464–2
Fires (wild) and acreage burned, by type of land, ownership, cause, region, and State, 1984-90, annual rpt, 1204–4
Food assistance program in Puerto Rico, funding and restrictions, FY90-91, GAO rpt, 26113–580
Freight (waterborne domestic and foreign) by commodity, traffic, and passengers, by port and waterway, 1989, annual rpt, 3754–3.2
Heroin prices and purity in 19 metro areas and Puerto Rico, by world area of origin, quarterly rpt, 6282–2
HHS financial aid, by program, recipient, State, and city, FY91, annual regional listing, 4004–3.2
Higher education enrollment, faculty, finances, and degrees, by instn level and control, and State, FY88, annual rpt, 4844–13
Hospital deaths of Medicare patients, actual and expected rates by diagnosis, and hospital characteristics, by instn, FY90 annual State rpt, 4654–14.40
Housing census, 1990: inventory, occupancy, and costs, State fact sheet, 2326–21.53
Hurricane Hugo disaster loan offices of SBA, staff and salary and support costs, for Puerto Rico and Virgin Islands, 1989-91, GAO rpt, 26113–576
Mineral Industry Surveys, State reviews of production, 1991, preliminary annual rpt, 5614–6
Multinatl US firms foreign affiliates, income statement items by asset size, industry, and country, 1988, biennial article, 8302–2.322
OASDHI coverage of employment and earnings, and social security contributions, by age, sex, race, State, and county, 1988, annual rpt, 4744–29
Oil company overcharge settlements funds received, and conservation and energy aid spending, by outlying area, 1990, GAO rpt, 26113–564
Oil exports to US by OPEC and non-OPEC countries, monthly rpt, 3162–24.3
Oil exports to US by OPEC and non-OPEC countries, monthly 1973-88, 3168–123.3
Physicians, by specialty, age, sex, and location of training and practice, 1990, State rpt, 4116–6.40
Population and housing census, 1990: summary characteristics, households, and land area, by county, subdiv, and place, State rpt, 2551–1.53
Population census, 1990: population characteristics and living arrangements, by county, place, and urban-rural location, State rpt, 2531–1.53
Population size, growth rates, and components of change, by country, projected 1990-2020 and trends from 1950, biennial rpt, 2324–9
Poultry and egg production, prices, receipts, trade, and disposition, by species, 1960-90, annual rpt, 1564–13
Statehood for Puerto Rico, referendum proposal with background data on Federal outlays, economic conditions, and finances of corporations with tax-favored status, 1940s-88, hearing, 21448–46
Statistical Abstract of US, 1992 annual data compilation, 2324–1; 2324–1.30
Sugarcane growers, acreage, yield, and cane sugar production, quarterly situation rpt with articles, 1561–14
Tax (estate) returns for nonresident aliens, property and tax data, by estate size and decedent country of residence, 1986, article, 8302–2.310
Tax (excise) collections of IRS, by source, region, and State, quarterly rpt, annual table, 8302–1
Terrorism incidents in US, related activity, and casualties, by attack type, target, group, and location, 1991, annual rpt, 6224–6
Tobacco production, prices, stocks, taxes by State, and trade and production by country, 1991, annual rpt, 1319–1
VA programs spending, by US and foreign location, FY91, annual rpt, 8604–6
Wages by occupation, and benefits for office and plant workers, 1991 survey, periodic labor market area rpt, 6785–3.2
Water resources data collection and analysis activities of USGS Water Resources Div District, with project descriptions, 1990 rpt, 5666–26.19
Weather conditions and effect on agriculture, by US region, State, and city, and world area, weekly rpt, 2182–7
see also under By Outlying Area in the "Index by Categories"

Puffer, Cynthia A.
"Reregistration of Minor Use Pesticides: Some Observations and Implications", 1561–16.301

Puget Sound
Indian tribes in Pacific Northwest, OCS oil and gas lease and dev environmental, economic, and cultural impacts, with background data, 1970s-92, 5738–35

Puidak, Peter
"Social Security Implications of a Reunified Germany", 4742–1.306

Punishment
see Capital punishment
see Fines and settlements
see Judgments, civil procedure
see Sentences, criminal procedure
see Student discipline

Purchasing
see Industrial purchasing

Purchasing power
see Personal and household income

Putnam, Judith J.
"Food Consumption, Prices, and Expenditures, 1970-90", 1544–4

Qatar
Agricultural trade of US, by detailed commodity and country, 1991, annual rpt, 1524–8
Agricultural trade of US, by detailed commodity and country, 1991, semiannual rpt, 1522–4
Apple imports of 5 Persian Gulf countries, by country of origin, 1981-90, article, 1925–34.322
Background Notes, summary social, political, and economic data, 1992 rpt, 7006–2.19
Boycotts (intl) by OPEC and other countries, US firms and individuals cooperation and tax benefits denied, 1990, article, 8302–2.323
Economic and social conditions of developing countries from 1960s, and Intl Dev Cooperation Agency and AID activities and funding, FY91-93, annual rpt, 9904–4
Economic, social, political, and geographic summary data, by country, 1992, annual factbook, 9114–2
Exports and imports of US, by commodity and country, 1980-90, world area rpt, 9116–1.6
Exports and imports of US, by transport mode, country, and SITC 1- to 3-digit commodity, 1991, annual rpt, 2424–12
Exports of US, detailed Schedule B commodities with countries of destination, 1991, annual rpt, 2424–10
Human rights conditions in 170 countries, and US economic and military aid, 1991, annual rpt, 21384–3
Military spending, arms trade, and force strengths, with govt spending and population, by country, 1979-89, annual rpt, 9824–1
Minerals Yearbook, Vol 3, 1989: foreign country review of production, trade, and policy, by commodity, annual rpt, 5604–35.3

Oil production and exports to US, by major exporting country, detailed data, monthly rpt with articles, 3162–24
Oil production and exports to US, by major exporting country, detailed data, monthly 1973-88, 3168–123
Oil production, stocks, use, and trade, by selected country and country group, monthly rpt, 3162–42
Population size, growth rates, and components of change, by country, projected 1990-2020 and trends from 1950, biennial rpt, 2324–9
Refugee migration, and intl aid programs, by world area and country of origin and asylum, 1991, annual rpt, 7004–15
UN voting record and share of votes in agreement with US, by issue, country, and world area, 1991, annual rpt, 7004–18

Quality control and testing
Cotton acreage planted by State and county, and fiber quality, by variety, 1992, annual rpt, 1309–6
Cotton fiber and processing test results, by variety, region, State, and production area, 1991, annual rpt, 1309–16
Cotton fiber grade, staple, and mike, for upland and American pima cotton by State, monthly rpt, 1309–11
Cotton fiber grade, staple, mike, and other quality indicators, for upland cotton by classing office, weekly rpt, 1309–15
Cotton quality, by State, 1991, annual rpt, 1309–7
Cotton quality, supply, and carryover, 1991-92, annual rpt, 1309–8
Cottonseed prices and quality, by State, seasonal weekly rpt, 1309–14
Cottonseed quality factors, by State, 1991 crop, annual rpt, 1309–5
Equipment for industrial control, shipments, trade, use, and firms, 1991, annual Current Industrial Rpt, 2506–12.11
Fed Govt agencies programs and services performance evaluation measures use, dev, and effectiveness, 1991 survey, GAO rpt, 26119–396
Fed Govt quality mgmt practices, employee views, 1992 survey, GAO rpt, 26119–425
General Motors production and inventory control system efficiency, model description and results, 1992 working paper, 9375–13.87
Hearing aid performance test results, by make and model, 1992 annual rpt, 8704–3
Labor demand, turnover, and training completions, by detailed occupation, 1990 and projected to 2005, biennial rpt, 6744–3
Labs (clinical) test performance standards and proficiency testing, HHS regulations, 1992 rpt, 4206–2.52
Measurement systems calibration, standard reference materials specifications and availability, 1992 biennial listing, 2214–2
Nuclear reactors for domestic use and export by function and operating status, with owner, operating characteristics, and location, 1991 annual listing, 3354–15
Occupational Outlook Handbook, 1992-93, biennial rpt, 6744–1
Strategic Petroleum Reserve crude oil specifications and physical and chemical analyses results, 1991, 3338–5
Textile products trade regulations of foreign countries, and US exports, by commodity and country, 1989-91, biennial rpt, 2044–18
Tire quality ratings, by type and brand, as of Feb 1992, annual rpt, 7764–17
see also Food inspection
see also Government inspections

Quality of life
Cancer clinical trials quality-of-life data collection, patient compliance rate, 1988-91 local area studies, article, 4472–1.326
Data on health condition and quality of life measures, rpts and other info sources, quarterly listing, 4122–1
Family life and relationships quality and other issues, views of parents and children, 1990 survey, 15528–2
Households composition, income, benefits, and labor force status, Survey of Income and Program Participation methodology, working paper series, 2626–10
Housing and neighborhood quality, indicators and attitudes, MSA surveys, series, 2485–6
Latin America economic and social conditions, resources, trade, and aid, 1992, annual factbook, 9914–14
Neighborhood and housing quality, indicators and attitudes, by householder type and location, for 11 MSAs, 1987 survey, supplement, 2485–8
Neighborhood and housing quality, indicators and attitudes, by householder type and location, 1989, biennial rpt supplement, 2485–13
Population economic well-being indicators, by selected characteristics and household income and income-to-poverty ratio, 1984, 2546–20.22
Rental housing units, total, with HUD assistance by program, and eligible for aid, by unit, household, and neighborhood characteristics, and location, 1989, biennial rpt, 5184–11
see also Health condition
see also Housing condition and occupancy
see also Living arrangements
see also Poverty
see also Work conditions

Qualters, Judith R.
"Breast and Cervical Cancer Surveillance, U.S., 1973-87", 4202–7.312

Quarries and quarrying
see Sand and gravel
see Stone products and quarries

Quasi-official agencies
see American National Red Cross
see Government corporations and enterprises
see Legal Services Corp.
see National Railroad Passenger Corp.
see Smithsonian Institution
see U.S. Institute of Peace

Quebec Province, Canada
Exports and imports, trade agreements and relations, and USITC investigations, 1991, annual rpt, 9884–5

Questionnaires
see Consumer surveys
see Opinion and attitude surveys
see Statistical programs and activities
see under names of individual surveys (listed under Surveys)

Quinlin, Stephen V.
"Maternal-Child Health Data from the NLSY: 1988 Tabulations and Summary Discussion", 4478–197

Quits
see Labor turnover

Raab, Jonathan
"Public Involvement in Integrated Resource Planning: A Study of Demand-Side Management Collaboratives", 3308–104

Rabies
Cases of rabies in animals and humans by State, and deaths, 1940s-91, annual rpt, 4204–1
Foreign countries rabies-free, and disease prevention recommendations, 1992 annual rpt, 4204–11
Morbidity and Mortality Weekly Report, infectious notifiable disease cases by State, and public health issues, 4202–1
Vaccination of pets and livestock for rabies, schedules and dosages by species, and disease outbreak control, CDC recommendations, 1992, 4206–2.57

Race/ethnic groups
see Alaska Natives
see Ancestry
see Asian Americans
see Black Americans
see Hispanic Americans
see Indians
see Minority employment
see Minority groups
see Pacific Islands Americans
see Racial discrimination
see under By Race and Ethnic Group in the "Index by Categories"

Racial discrimination
Banks loan activity in low income and minority communities, 1991 hearing, 21248–176
Community Relations Service investigation and mediation of minority discrimination disputes, activities and funding, FY91, annual rpt, 6004–9
Criminal sentences for Federal offenses, guidelines impacts on sentence disparity by offender race and other characteristics, 1985-90, GAO rpt, 26119–415
Disability benefit applications under OASDI and SSI, dispositions, awards, and administrative law judge hearing outcomes, by race, 1988, GAO rpt, 26121–459
Fed Equal Opportunity Recruitment Program activity, and employment by sex, race, pay grade, and occupational group, FY91, annual rpt, 9844–33
Foreign countries human rights conditions in 170 countries, 1991, annual rpt, 21384–3
Housing rental and sales, discrimination against blacks and Hispanics in selected metro areas, 1989 study, series, 5186–16
Labor laws enacted, by State, 1991, annual article, 6722–1.309
Mortgage applications of minorities, for Boston by disposition and financial characteristics, with problems in analyzing lender disclosure statements, 1990, working paper, 9373–27.15

Racketeering
see Organized crime
Radar
Air traffic control operations of FAA, by service and aviation type, and facility, 1981-90, annual rpt, 7504–1.2
Air traffic levels at FAA-operated control facilities, including instrument operations, by airport and State, FY91, annual rpt, 7504–27
Exports and imports between US and outlying areas, by detailed commodity and mode of transport, 1991, annual rpt, 2424–11
Exports and imports of US, by Harmonized System 6-digit commodity and country, 1991, annual rpt, 2424–13
Exports of US, detailed Schedule B commodities with countries of destination, 1991, annual rpt, 2424–10
Hurricanes and tropical storms in Pacific and Indian Oceans, paths and surveillance, 1991, annual rpt, 3804–8
Instruments and related products shipments, trade, use, and firms, by detailed type, 1991, annual Current Industrial Rpt, 2506–12.26
Military weapons acquisition costs by system and service branch, DOD budget, FY91-93, annual rpt, 3504–2
Price indexes (producer), by stage of processing and detailed commodity, monthly 1991, annual rpt, 6764–2
Radiation from electronic devices, incidents by type of device, and FDA control activities, 1991, annual rpt, 4064–13
Shipments, trade, use, and firms, for electronic communications systems and related products, 1991, annual Current Industrial Rpt, 2506–12.35
Radbill, Larry M.
"Extended Measures of Well-Being", 2546–20.22
Raddatz, C. T.
"Occupational Radiation Exposure at Commercial Nuclear Power Reactors and Other Facilities, 1989", 9634–3
Radiation
Aircraft crew radiation exposure and health risks, 1992 technical rpt, 7506–10.98
Assistance (financial and nonfinancial) of Fed Govt, 1992 base edition, annual listing, 104–5
Atmosphere (surface) radiation levels, by selected site, 1990, annual rpt, 2144–28
DOE contractor research lab and nuclear weapons facilities radiation and other pollutant releases, monitoring results, annual site rpt series, 3324–2
DOE R&D projects and funding at natl labs, universities, and other instns, FY88-90, triennial summary rpt, 3004–18.5
Electronic devices radiation incidents by type of device, and FDA control activities, 1991, annual rpt, 4064–13
Environmental levels of radon and other radionuclides in air, water, soil, and uranium mill tailings, by site and region, 1950s-80s, compilation of papers, 5668–126
Environmental radiation and radionuclide concentrations in air, water, and milk, monitoring results by site, quarterly rpt, 9192–5
EPA R&D programs and funding, planned FY92, annual listing, 9184–17
FDA investigations and regulatory activities, quarterly rpt, 4062–3
Hanford, Wash, nuclear plant, nearby population radiation exposure, with methodology, 1944-91, series, 3356–5
Health condition and care indicators, 1950s-90 with health improvement and disease prevention goals for 1990, annual data compilation, 4144–11
Health physics and radiation protection enrollment and degrees granted by instn and State, and grad placement, by student characteristics, 1991, annual rpt, 3004–7
Health physics and radiation protection enrollment and degrees granted by instn and State, and women grads plans and employment, 1973-91, annual rpt, 3006–8.19
Instruments and related products shipments, trade, use, and firms, by detailed type, 1991, annual Current Industrial Rpt, 2506–12.26
Navy nuclear-powered vessels and support facilities radioactive waste, releases in harbors, and public exposure, 1970s-91, annual rpt, 3804–11
Navy personnel radiation exposure on nuclear-powered vessels and at support facilities, and injury claims, 1950s-91, annual rpt, 3804–10
Nuclear weapons test areas in Nevada and other sites, radionuclide concentrations in air, water, humans, animals, and milk, 1990, annual rpt, 9194–17
Radiation exposure of population near commercial reactors, by body site, age group, and selected plant, 1988, annual rpt, 9634–7
Research and testing activities under Natl Toxicology Program, FY90 and planned FY91, annual rpt, 4044–16
Uranium tailings at inactive mills, remedial action proposals, costs, site characteristics, and environmental, socioeconomic, and health impacts, series, 3356–4
Water supply and quality in streams and lakes, and groundwater levels in wells, by drainage basin, 1990, annual State rpt series, 5666–10
Water supply and quality in streams and lakes, and groundwater levels in wells, by drainage basin, 1990-91, annual CD-ROM, 5664–18
Water supply and quality in streams and lakes, and groundwater levels in wells, by drainage basin, 1991, annual State rpt series, 5666–12
see also Nuclear accidents and safety
see also Nuclear explosives and explosions
see also Nuclear medicine and radiology
see also Nuclear power
see also Nuclear weapons
see also Radioactive materials
see also Radioactive waste and disposal
see also Radon
see also Uranium
see also X-rays
Radiation Control for Health and Safety Act
FDA admin of Act, and radiation incidents involving electronic devices, 1991, annual rpt, 4064–13
Radin, Beryl A.
"Managing Rural Policy Initiatives in the Intergovernmental System", 1504–9.1
Radio
Employment, earnings, and hours, by SIC 1- to 4-digit industry, monthly 1989-Feb 1992, annual rpt, 6744–4
Equipment shipments, trade, use, and firms, for electronic communications systems and related products, 1991, annual Current Industrial Rpt, 2506–12.35
Fed Govt radio frequency assignments, by agency, 1st half 1992, semiannual rpt, 2802–1
Finances and operations, by SIC 2- to 4-digit industry, forecast 1992, annual rpt, 2044–28
Finances of communications services, itemized revenue and expenses by SIC 2- to 4-digit kind of business, 1990, annual rpt, 2413–15
Foreign countries economic, social, political, and geographic summary data, by country, 1992, annual factbook, 9114–2
Input-output structure of US economy, detailed interindustry transactions for 541 industries, and components of final demand, 1982 benchmark data, 2708–17
Licensing activities of FCC, by class of operation, FY91, annual rpt, 9284–4
Occupational injury and illness rates, by SIC 2- to 4-digit industry, 1989-90, annual rpt, 6844–7
Occupational Outlook Handbook, 1992-93, biennial rpt, 6744–1
Price indexes (producer), by stage of processing and detailed commodity, monthly rpt, 6762–6
Price indexes (producer), by stage of processing and detailed commodity, monthly 1991, annual rpt, 6764–2
Stations on the air, by class of operation, monthly press release, 9282–4
Statistical Abstract of US, 1992 annual data compilation, 2324–1.18
Weather (marine) forecast areas, and broadcast schedules and stations worldwide, as of Sept 1992, annual rpt, 2184–3
Weather (marine) forecast broadcast schedules worldwide, periodic rpt, 2182–9
see also Home video and audio equipment
see also Mobile radio
Radio Free Europe
Broadcasting and financial data for Radio Free Europe and Radio Liberty, FY91, annual rpt, 10314–1
Radio Liberty
Broadcasting and financial data for Radio Free Europe and Radio Liberty, FY91, annual rpt, 10314–1
Radioactive materials
Criminal sentences for Federal offenses, guidelines by offense and circumstances, series, 17668–1
Environmental Quality, status of problems, protection programs, research, and intl issues, 1991 annual rpt, 484–1
Exports and imports of US, by country and detailed commodity, monthly rpt, 2422–12
Exports and imports of US, by transport mode, country, and SITC 1- to 3-digit commodity, 1991, annual rpt, 2424–12

FDA investigations and regulatory activities, quarterly rpt, 4062–3
Freight (waterborne domestic and foreign) by commodity, traffic, and passengers, by port and waterway, 1989, annual rpt, 3754–3
Inventory discrepancies for nuclear materials at DOE and contractor facilities, 1990/91, annual rpt, 3344–2
Minerals Yearbook, Vol 1, 1989: commodity reviews of production, use, trade, prices, and mining operations, annual rpt, 5604–33
Minerals Yearbook, Vol 3, 1989: foreign country reviews of production, trade, and policy, by commodity, annual rpt, 5604–35
Nuclear Regulatory Commission activities, finances, and staff, with data for individual power plants, FY91, annual rpt, 9634–2
OECD trade, total and for 4 major countries, and US trade by country, by commodity, 1980-90, world area rpt series, 9116–1
Safety standards and research, design, licensing, construction, operation, and finances, for nuclear power plants with data by reactor, quarterly journal, 3352–4
Shipments of radioactive materials on US hwys, by material type, carrier, and shipper, 1985-90, 3008–129
see also Radiation
see also Radioactive waste and disposal
see also Radon
see also Uranium

Radioactive waste and disposal
DOE activities and finances, summary energy supply and demand data, and bibl, 1990, annual rpt, 3024–2
DOE contractor research lab and nuclear weapons facilities radiation and other pollutant releases, monitoring results, annual site rpt series, 3324–2
Military activities of DOE, low-level radioactive waste disposal methods and costs, 1991, 3006–5.30
Natl Energy Strategy nuclear power, waste mgmt, and uranium enrichment issues, 1991 hearings, 21368–137
Navy nuclear-powered vessels and support facilities radioactive waste, releases in harbors, and public exposure, 1970s-91, annual rpt, 3804–11
Nuclear power plant occupational radiation exposure, by site, 1968-89, annual rpt, 9634–3
Nuclear Regulatory Commission activities, finances, and staff, with data for individual power plants, FY91, annual rpt, 9634–2
Nuclear Waste Fund finances, and DOE Civilian Radioactive Waste Mgmt Office R&D costs, FY90-91, annual rpt, 3364–1
Nuclear Waste Fund finances, and DOE Civilian Radioactive Waste Mgmt Program costs, quarterly rpt, 3362–1
Regulatory, inspection, and licensing activities of NRC, budget and staff, by program, FY91-93, annual rpt, 9634–9
Repository sites for nuclear waste, remedial actions, and uranium mill tailings mgmt, bibl, 1991 annual listing, 3354–12
Repository sites for radioactive waste, storage containers radionuclide releases at proposed Nevada site, 1990 rpt, 3368–4
Repository sites research, and waste transport and disposal systems, alternative cost estimates, 1983-89 and projected to 2094, 3368–5
Safety standards and research, design, licensing, construction, operation, and finances, for nuclear power plants with data by reactor, quarterly journal, 3352–4
Scientists and engineers employed in nuclear-related industries, by industry sector and occupation, 1983-91, 3006–8.20
Shipments of radioactive materials on US hwys, by material type, carrier, and shipper, 1985-90, 3008–129
Spent fuel and radioactive waste generation, inventory, and disposal, 1960s-90 and projected to 2020, annual rpt, 3364–2
Spent fuel deliveries to DOE for disposal, by utility and reactor, projected 1998-2007, annual rpt, 3364–5
Spent fuel from nuclear power plants and additional storage capacity needed, by reactor, projected 1991-2040, annual rpt, 3354–2
Spent fuel from nuclear power plants, discharges, storage capacity, and inventories, by reactor, 1968-90, 3166–6.62
Spent fuel from nuclear power plants, storage capacity and inventories, by reactor, as of 1987, 3166–6.59
State and interstate compact low-level radioactive disposal activities, with data by disposal facility and reactor, 1990, annual rpt, 3004–36
Uranium tailings at inactive mills, remedial action activities by site, and funding, FY91, annual rpt, 3354–9
Uranium tailings at inactive mills, remedial action proposals, costs, site characteristics, and environmental, socioeconomic, and health impacts, series, 3356–4
Weapons (nuclear) facilities of DOE, contractor fees, environmental and safety enforcement activity, and salaries, by contractor and facility, 1987-88, hearing, 21408–127

Radiology
see Nuclear medicine and radiology
see X-rays

Radner, Daniel B.
"Alternative Estimates of Economic Well-Being by Age Using Data on Wealth and Income", 4746–26.11
"Assessment of the Economic Status of the Aged", 4746–26.24
"Changes in the Incomes of Age Groups, 1984-89", 4742–1.304; 4746–26.20
"Economic Status of the Aged", 4742–1.320

Radon
Environmental levels of radon and other radionuclides in air, water, soil, and uranium mill tailings, by site and region, 1950s-80s, compilation of papers, 5668–126
EPA pollution control grant program activities, monthly rpt, 9182–8
Indoor air radon levels, by county and State, annual rpt, discontinued, 9194–19

Raffel, Marshall W.
"Czechoslovakia's Changing Health Care System", 4042–3.363

Raffel, Norma K.
"Czechoslovakia's Changing Health Care System", 4042–3.363

Rago, Paul J.
"Emergency Striped Bass Research Study, Report for 1990", 5504–29

Railroad accidents and safety
Accidents and casualties on transit systems by circumstances, damage, and ridership, by mode, 1990, annual rpt, 7884–13
Accidents, and mgmt of disasters and natl security threats, with data by major event and State, 1992 annual rpt, 9434–6
Accidents, casualties, and damage, by cause, railroad, and State, 1991, annual rpt, 7604–1
Accidents, casualties, and damage involving railroads, Fed Railroad Admin activities, and safety inspectors by State, 1990, annual rpt, 7604–12
Accidents, casualties, circumstances, and railroad involved, 1988, annual rpt, 9614–8
Accidents, casualties, damage, and circumstances, by incident, 1988, annual rpt, 7604–3
DOT activities by subagency, budget, and summary accident data, FY89, annual rpt, 7304–1
Engineers work schedules impacts on safety, and rail accidents caused by human factors, 1989-90, GAO rpt, 26113–579
Hazardous material transport accidents, casualties, and damage, by mode of transport, with DOT control activities, 1990, annual rpt, 7304–4
Hazardous materials transport by rail, accidents, casualties, and circumstances, 1984-89, 9618–18
Hwy-railroad grade-crossing accidents, detailed data by State and railroad, 1991, annual rpt, 7604–2
Hwy safety program funding by State, and accident and death reductions, FY91, annual rpt, 7554–26
Injury and illness rates, by SIC 2- to 4-digit industry, 1990, annual rpt, 6844–1
Occupational injury and illness rates, by SIC 2- to 4-digit industry, 1989-90, annual rpt, 6844–7
Rapid rail transit systems safety, operating, and funding characteristics, 1988-89, 9618–19
Safety violation claims settled, by rail carrier, FY91, annual rpt, 7604–10

Railroad equipment and vehicles
Amtrak finances and operations, FY91, annual rpt, 29524–1
Business statistics, detailed data for major industries and economic indicators, *Survey of Current Business*, monthly rpt, 2702–1.22
Business statistics, detailed data for major industries and economic indicators, 1960-91, *Survey of Current Business* biennial supplement, 2704–1
Cars, ownership, and supply, by type, selected years FY76-91, annual rpt, 9484–1
Construction put in place (public and private), by type, quarterly rpt, 2042–1.1

Construction put in place, value of new public and private structures, by type, monthly rpt, 2382–4
County Business Patterns, 1989: employment, establishments, and payroll, by SIC 2- to 4-digit industry and county, annual State rpt series, 2326–8
County Business Patterns, 1990: employment, establishments, and payroll, by SIC 2- to 4-digit industry and county, annual State rpt series, 2326–6
Employment, earnings, and hours, by SIC 1- to 4-digit industry, monthly 1989-Feb 1992, annual rpt, 6744–4
Exports and imports between US and outlying areas, by detailed commodity and mode of transport, 1991, annual rpt, 2424–11
Exports and imports of US, by country and detailed commodity, monthly rpt, 2422–12
Exports and imports of US, by Harmonized System 6-digit commodity and country, 1991, annual rpt, 2424–13
Exports and imports of US, by transport mode, country, and SITC 1- to 3-digit commodity, 1991, annual rpt, 2424–12
Exports of US, detailed Schedule B commodities with countries of destination, 1991, annual rpt, 2424–10
Finances and operations of Class I railroads, detailed data by firm, class of service, and district, 1990, annual rpt, 9486–5.1
Finances and operations of Class I railroads, detailed data by firm, class of service, and district, 1991, annual rpt, 9486–6.1
Fuel oil and kerosene sales and deliveries, by end-use, PAD district, and State, 1990, annual rpt, 3164–94
Imports of US given duty-free treatment for value of US material sent abroad, by commodity and country, 1987-90, annual rpt, 9884–14
Input-output structure of US economy, detailed interindustry transactions for 541 industries, and components of final demand, 1982 benchmark data, 2708–17
Manufacturing annual survey, 1990: finances and operations, by SIC 2- to 4-digit industry, series, 2506–14
Manufacturing census, 1987: concentration of largest firms measured by value added, and for shipments by SIC 2- and 4-digit industry, subject rpt, 2497–6
Manufacturing census, 1987: shipments of manufacturers products, by customer class and SIC 2- and 4-digit industry, subject rpt, 2497–4
Military prime contract awards, by detailed procurement category, FY88-91, annual rpt, 3544–18
Occupational injury and illness rates, by SIC 2- to 4-digit industry, 1989-90, annual rpt, 6844–7
Occupational injury and illness rates, by SIC 2- to 4-digit industry, 1990, annual rpt, 6844–1
OECD trade, total and for 4 major countries, and US trade by country, by commodity, 1980-90, world area rpt series, 9116–1
Price indexes (producer), by stage of processing and detailed commodity, monthly rpt, 6762–6
Price indexes (producer), by stage of processing and detailed commodity, monthly 1991, annual rpt, 6764–2
Productivity of labor and capital, and indexes of output, hours, and employment, 1967-90, annual rpt, 6824–1.5
Rails (steel) from 3 countries at less than fair value, injury to US industry, investigation with background financial and operating data, 1992 rpt, 9886–14.349
Rapid rail transit systems safety, operating, and funding characteristics, 1988-89, 9618–19
Science, engineering, and technical employment in manufacturing, by field and industry, 1989, triennial rpt, 9627–23
Soviet Union and US economic and sociodemographic indicators, selected years 1970-90, handbook, 2328–80
Transit systems finances, equipment, and ridership characteristics, 1985-90, biennial rpt, 7884–8
Urban areas transit systems grants of Federal Transit Admin, by city and State, FY91, annual rpt, 7884–10
see also Railroad accidents and safety

Railroad Retirement Board
Budget of US, authoritative financial statements with appropriations, outlays, and receipts, by category and agency, FY91, annual rpt, 8104–2.2
Budget of US, obligations and authority by function, agency, and program, with summaries and analyses, FY93, annual rpt, 104–2
Labor unions recognized in Fed Govt, agreements and membership by agency and facility, as of Jan 1991, biennial listing, 9844–14
Railroad employee benefits and beneficiaries by type, and railroad employment and payroll, FY90, annual rpt, 9704–2
Railroad employee benefits program finances and beneficiaries, FY91, annual rpt, 9704–1
Railroad retirement, survivors, unemployment, and health insurance programs, monthly rpt, 9702–2

Railroads
Bridges over navigable waters, with type of bridge and use, owner, dimensions, and location, 1991 regional listing series, 7406–5
Business statistics, detailed data for major industries and economic indicators, *Survey of Current Business*, monthly rpt, 2702–1.10
Business statistics, detailed data for major industries and economic indicators, 1960-91, *Survey of Current Business* biennial supplement, 2704–1
Capital expenditures for plant and equipment, by major industry group, quarterly rpt, 2502–2
Coal mining restrictions on public land, impacts on production, costs, and demand, by region, 1985-88 and projected to 2075, 5668–125
Commuting to work, by mode, trip duration, and work location, 1980 and 1990, 7558–120
Container (intermodal) traffic by mode, use of containers over legal weight for hwy use, and California enforcement activity, 1960s-88, hearing, 21648–65
Electric utilities privately owned, finances and operations, detailed data, 1990, annual rpt, 3164–23
Employee benefit program finances and beneficiaries, FY91, annual rpt, 9704–1
Employee benefits and beneficiaries by type, and railroad employment and payroll, FY90, annual rpt, 9704–2
Employee retirement, disability, and unemployment insurance programs, beneficiaries, payments, and collections, quarterly rpt, 4742–1.1; 4742–1.4
Employee retirement, survivors, unemployment, and health insurance programs, monthly rpt, 9702–2
Employee retirement, unemployment, and disability benefits, and program finances, late 1930s-89, annual rpt, 4744–3
Employment by functional group, for Class I line-haul railroads, monthly rpt, 9482–3
Employment, earnings, and hours, by occupation for Class I railroads, 1991, annual table, 9484–5
Employment, earnings, and hours, by SIC 1- to 4-digit industry, monthly 1989-Feb 1992, annual rpt, 6744–4
Energy use by fuel type, and miles traveled, by transport mode, projected 1990-2010 and trends from 1960s, 3008–124
Energy use by mode of transport, fuel supply, and demographic and economic factors of vehicle use, 1970s-90, annual rpt, 3304–5
Finances and employment of ICC-regulated carriers, as of FY91, annual rpt, 9484–1
Finances and operations, by SIC 2- to 4-digit industry, forecast 1992, annual rpt, 2044–28
Finances and operations of Class I railroads, detailed data by firm, class of service, and district, 1990, annual rpt, 9486–5.1
Finances and operations of Class I railroads, detailed data by firm, class of service, and district, 1991, annual rpt, 9486–6.1
Finances and operations of transit systems, by mode, size of fleet and urban area, region, and for 518 systems, 1990, annual rpt, 7884–4
Finances, equipment, and ridership characteristics of transit systems, 1985-90, biennial rpt, 7884–8
Fires (wild) and acreage burned, by type of land, ownership, cause, region, and State, 1984-90, annual rpt, 1204–4
Foreign countries economic, social, political, and geographic summary data, by country, 1992, annual factbook, 9114–2
Freight shipped by rail, by commodity and region of origin and destination, 1989, annual rpt, 7604–6
Grain shipments and rates for barge and rail loadings, periodic situation rpt with articles, 1561–4
Input-output structure of US economy, detailed interindustry transactions for 541 industries, and components of final demand, 1982 benchmark data, 2708–17
Labor disputes of railroads, and Federal mediation activities and caseloads, with data by carrier and union, FY87-88, annual rpt, 9604–1

Labor productivity, indexes of output, hours, and employment by SIC 2- to 4-digit industry, 1967-90, annual rpt, 6824–1.4
Military and personal property shipments, passenger traffic, and costs, by service branch and mode of transport, FY91, annual rpt, 3704–15
Occupational Outlook Handbook, 1992-93, biennial rpt, 6744–1
Pensions and other income sources of aged, by whether OASDI beneficiary, poverty status, and other characteristics, 1990, biennial rpt, 4744–26
Price indexes (producer), by stage of processing and detailed commodity, monthly rpt, 6762–6
Price indexes (producer), by stage of processing and detailed commodity, monthly 1991, annual rpt, 6764–2
Productivity measures for railroad industry, late 1950s-80s, article, 6722–1.337
Revenue, income, freight, and rate of return, by Class I freight railroad and district, quarterly rpt, 9482–2
Soviet Union and US economic and sociodemographic indicators, selected years 1970-90, handbook, 2328–80
Statistical Abstract of US, 1992 annual data compilation, 2324–1.21
Tax (income) returns of corporations, income and tax items by asset size and detailed industry, 1989, annual rpt, 8304–4; 8304–21
Travel to US, by characteristics of visit and traveler, world area of origin, and US destination, 1991 survey, annual rpt, 2904–12
Unemployment insurance claims and covered unemployment by program, and extended benefit triggers, by State, weekly rpt, 6402–15
Unemployment insurance claims, by program, weekly press release, 6402–14
see also Consolidated Rail Corp.
see also Federal aid to railroads
see also Freight
see also High-speed ground transportation
see also National Railroad Passenger Corp.
see also Railroad accidents and safety
see also Railroad equipment and vehicles
see also Subways
see also Urban transportation

Rainfall
see Weather

Rainy River
see Souris-Red-Rainy Rivers

Raisins
see Fruit and fruit products

Raleigh, N.C.
see also under By City and By SMSA or MSA in the "Index by Categories"

Randall, Richard E.
"Insurance Companies as Financial Intermediaries: Risk and Return", 9373–3.35
"Procyclical Application of Bank Capital Requirements", 9373–26

Randolph, Robert F.
"Miners' Views About Why People Go Under Unsupported Roof and How To Stop Them", 5608–173

Rantoul, Ill.
Wages by occupation, for office and plant workers, 1991 survey, periodic MSA rpt, 6785–12.2

Rape
Arrests and criminal case processing through sentencing, cases and duration by disposition and offense, for selected cities, 1988, annual rpt, 6064–27
Court criminal case processing in Federal district courts, and dispositions, by offense, district, and offender characteristics, 1989, annual data compilation, 6064–29
Court criminal case processing in Federal district courts, and dispositions, by offense, 1980-91, annual rpt, 6064–31
Crime, criminal justice admin and enforcement, and public opinion, data compilation, 1992 annual rpt, 6064–6
Crime Index by population size and region, and offenses by large city, 1st half 1992, semiannual rpt, 6222–1
Crimes, arrests by offender characteristics, and rates, by offense, and law enforcement employees, by population size and jurisdiction, 1991, annual rpt, 6224–2
Executions of prisoners, by offense and race, 1930-90, annual rpt, 6064–26.6
Juvenile arrests, by sex, race, disposition, and offense, 1990, 6066–27.8
Prison and parole admissions and releases, sentence length, and time served, by offense and offender characteristics, 1988, annual rpt, 6064–33
Prisoners in Federal and contract instns, by selected characteristics, region, and Federal instn, FY89, annual rpt, 6244–1.1
Probation population, by offender characteristics, sentence conditions, whether rearrested, and offense, 1986-89, 6066–19.65
Sentences for Federal offenses, guidelines by offense and circumstances, series, 17668–1
States criminal justice systems activities, employment, funding, and data collection, by State, 1970s-91, annual rpt, 6064–40
Statistical Abstract of US, 1992 annual data compilation, 2324–1.5
Victimization rates, by victim and offender characteristics, circumstances, and offense, survey rpt series, 6066–3
Victimizations, by offense and whether reported to police, 1990-91, press release, 6068–249
Victimizations of households, by offense, household characteristics, and location, 1975-91, annual rpt, 6066–25.49
Women in jail, by criminal background and sociodemographic characteristics, with comparisons to men, 1989, 6066–19.66

Rapid transit
see High-speed ground transportation
see Subways
see Urban transportation

Rappaport, Edward N.
"Eastern North Pacific Hurricane Season—1991", 2152–8.302
"Hurricane Andrew—A Preliminary Look", 2152–8.304

Ras al-Khaimah
see United Arab Emirates

Rasinski, Kenneth
"High School and Beyond Fourth Follow-Up Contractor Report", 4826–2.54

Rasmussen, P. G.
"New Test of Scanning and Monitoring Ability: Methods and Initial Results", 7506–10.108

Ratnofsky, Alexander
"Unlocking Learning: Chapter 1 in Correctional Facilities. National Study of the Chapter 1 Neglected or Delinquent Program: Longitudinal Study Findings", 4808–40.2

Ravikumar, B.
"Neoclassical Model of Seasonal Fluctuations", 9387–8.262

Raw materials
see Stockpiling
see Strategic materials
see terms listed under Agricultural commodities
see terms listed under Commodities
see terms listed under Natural resources

Rawlings, Steve W.
"Household and Family Characteristics: March 1991", 2546–1.457

Rawlins, Scott D.
"Impact of Trade and Environmental Regulations on U.S. Nursery and Greenhouse Producers", 1504–9.1

Ray, Geraldine
"Young Husband-Wife Households with Children", 1702–1.302

Rayon
see Synthetic fibers and fabrics

RCA Global Communications
Finances and operations, detail for telegraph firms, 1990, annual rpt, 9284–6.3

REA
see Rural Electrification Administration

Reactors
see Electric power plants and equipment
see Nuclear power

Reading ability and habits
Child reading and TV viewing activities at home, by grade level, 1991 survey, 4826–10.1
Condition of Education, detail for elementary, secondary, and higher education, 1920s-91 and projected to 2002, annual rpt, 4824–1
Digest of Education Statistics, 1992 annual data compilation, 4824–2
DOD Dependents Schools basic skills and college entrance test scores, 1991-92, annual rpt, 3504–16
Eighth grade class of 1988: educational performance and conditions, characteristics, attitudes, activities, and plans, natl longitudinal survey, series, 4826–9
Elementary and secondary students educational performance in math, science, reading, and writing, 1969-90, 4898–32
Elementary and secondary students reading and math proficiency, and dropouts, by race, 1970s-90, 4838–52
Elementary and secondary students reading performance and factors affecting proficiency, 1988 and 1990 natl assessments, 4898–33
Foreign travel to US and Canada, market analyses with detailed trip and traveler characteristics, country rpt series, 2906–2
Natl Education Goals progress indicators, by State, 1992, annual rpt, 15914–1
Statistical Abstract of US, 1992 annual data compilation, 2324–1.7

see also Literacy and illiteracy
Reading, Pa.
see also under By City and By SMSA or MSA in the "Index by Categories"
Real estate
see Apartment houses
see Commercial buildings
see Condominiums and cooperatives
see Farms and farmland
see Government supplies and property
see Homesteads
see Housing condition and occupancy
see Housing construction
see Housing costs and financing
see Housing supply and requirements
see Housing tenure
see Industrial plants and equipment
see Land area
see Land ownership and rights
see Land reform
see Land use
see Military bases, posts, and reservations
see Mortgages
see Property
see Property value
see Public buildings
see Public lands
see Real estate business
see Reclamation of land
Real estate business
Business statistics, detailed data for major industries and economic indicators, 1960-91, *Survey of Current Business* biennial supplement, 2704–1
Collective bargaining agreements expiring during year, and workers covered, by firm, union, industry group, and State, 1992, annual rpt, 6784–9
County Business Patterns, 1989: employment, establishments, and payroll, by SIC 2- to 4-digit industry and county, annual State rpt series, 2326–8
County Business Patterns, 1990: employment, establishments, and payroll, by SIC 2- to 4-digit industry and county, annual State rpt series, 2326–6
Discrimination in housing rental and sales, for blacks and Hispanics in selected metro areas, 1989 study, series, 5186–16
Employment, earnings, and hours, by SIC 1- to 4-digit industry, monthly 1989-Feb 1992, annual rpt, 6744–4
Employment, unemployment, and labor force characteristics, by region and census div, 1991, annual rpt, 6744–7.1
Flow-of-funds accounts, savings, investments, and credit statements, quarterly rpt, 9365–3.3
Foreign direct investment in US, by industry group and world area, 1989-91, annual article, 2702–1.331
Foreign direct investment in US, major transactions by type, industry, country, and US location, 1990, annual rpt, 2044–20
Foreign direct investment in US, relation to exchange rate and relative labor costs and wealth indicators, for 7 countries, 1980s, working paper, 9373–27.10
Input-output structure of US economy, detailed interindustry transactions for 541 industries, and components of final demand, 1982 benchmark data, 2708–17
Mail volume to and from households, use, and views, by class, source, content, and household characteristics, FY87-90, annual rpt, 9864–10
Mortgage banker referral fees paid to real estate agents, and other issues, consumer views, 1989 survey, hearings, 21248–161
Multinatl firms US affiliates finances and operations, by industry, country of parent firm, and State, 1987, 2708–48
Multinatl firms US affiliates, finances, and operations, by industry, world area of parent firm, and State, 1989-90, annual rpt, 2704–4
Multinatl US firms and foreign affiliates finances and operations, by industry and country, 1989 benchmark survey, annual rpt, 2704–5
Multinatl US firms foreign affiliates, income statement items by asset size, industry, and country, 1988, biennial article, 8302–2.322
Natl income and product accounts, comprehensive accounts and components, benchmark revisions, 1929-88, 2708–5
Natl income and product accounts, comprehensive accounts and components, *Survey of Current Business*, monthly rpt, 2702–1.29
North Central States farm credit conditions, earnings, and expenses, Fed Reserve 9th District, quarterly rpt, 9383–11
Occupational injury and illness rates, by SIC 2- to 4-digit industry, 1989-90, annual rpt, 6844–7
Occupational injury and illness rates, by SIC 2- to 4-digit industry, 1990, annual rpt, 6844–1
Occupational Outlook Handbook, 1992-93, biennial rpt, 6744–1
Partnership income and losses impact of 1986 Tax Reform Act, by profit status and selected industry, 1980s, article, 8302–2.313
Resolution Trust Corp real estate assets marketing activities, real estate industry views, 1991 survey, GAO rpt, 26119–422
Savings instns failure resolution activity of Resolution Trust Corp, assets, deposits, and assets availability and sales, periodic press release, 9722–1
Savings instns failures, inventory of real estate assets available from Resolution Trust Corp, semiannual listing series, 9722–2
Savings instns failures, Resolution Trust Corp sales of real estate and other assets, 1990-91, GAO rpt, 26119–372
SEC registration, firms required to file annual rpts, as of Sept 1991, annual listing, 9734–5
Small business finances, operations, owner characteristics, and Federal contracts, 1980s-90, annual rpt, 9764–6
Southeastern US employment by industry div, earnings, and hours, for 8 States, quarterly press release, 6942–7
Statistical Abstract of US, 1992 annual data compilation, 2324–1.16
Supply and demand for housing and commercial real estate, market activity indicators by region, quarterly rpt, 9292–6
Tax (income) returns of corporations, income and tax items by asset size and detailed industry, 1989, annual rpt, 8304–4; 8304–21
Tax (income) returns of partnerships, income statement and balance sheet items, by industry group, 1990, annual article, 8302–2.314
Tax (income) returns of sole proprietorships, income statement items, by industry group, 1990, annual article, 8302–2.317; 8302–2.320
Wage and benefit changes from collective bargaining and mgmt decisions, by industry div, monthly rpt, 6782–1
see also Census of Financial, Insurance, and Real Estate Industries
see also Housing costs and financing
see also Housing sales
see also Property value
see also Rent
see also under By Industry in the "Index by Categories"
Reardon, Jack
"Safety and Health Experience of Pilots and Flight Attendants", 6722–1.320
Reardon, Leo B.
"Study of Health Care Access in Counties Where the Only Hospital Closed", 17206–2.30
Reaves, Brian A.
"Drug Enforcement by Police and Sheriffs' Departments, 1990", 6066–19.67
"Law Enforcement Management and Administrative Statistics, 1990: Data for Individual State and Local Agencies with 100 or More Officers", 6064–39
"Sheriffs' Departments, 1990", 6066–25.45
"State and Local Police Departments, 1990", 6066–25.44
Recession
see Business cycles
Rechnitzer, James R.
"Black Lung Benefits Act: Annual Report on Administration of the Act During 1991", 6504–3
Recidivism
Drug abuse and trafficking offenders losing Federal benefits under new sentencing guidelines, by selected characteristics, 1990-91, GAO rpt, 26119–398
Drug abuse treatment and education programs for prisoners and parolees, activities, costs, and outcomes, 1990 conf, 4498–77
Drug abuse treatment services costs, effectiveness, and financing issues, 1991 conf papers, 4498–80
Electronic monitoring of criminal releases by State, completions, violations, and new offenses, 1989, 6066–20.23
Federal district court criminal case processing and dispositions, by offense, district, and offender characteristics, 1989, annual data compilation, 6064–29
Parole discharges, by whether parole revoked, sentence length, time served, offense, and offender characteristics, 1988, annual rpt, 6064–33
Prisoners and movements, by offense, location, and selected other characteristics, data compilation, 1992 annual rpt, 6064–6.6
Prisoners in Federal instns, admissions, releases, and recidivism, by region, monthly rpt series, 6242–1
Probation population, by offender characteristics, sentence conditions, whether rearrested, and offense, 1986-89, 6066–19.65

Sentences for Federal offenses, guidelines by offense and circumstances, series, 17668–1
Women in jail, by criminal background and sociodemographic characteristics, with comparisons to men, 1989, 6066–19.66

Recksiek, Conrad
"By-catch from the Artisanal Shrimp Trawl Fishery, Gulf of Paria, Trinidad", 2162–1.302

Reclamation of land
Agricultural Conservation Program acreage and projects, by State, 1936-90, quinquennial rpt, 1808–1
Coal Surface Mining Reclamation and Enforcement Office activities and funding, by State and Indian tribe, FY91, annual rpt, 5644–1
Fed Govt spending in States, by type, program, agency, and State, FY91, annual rpt, 2464–2
Public lands acreage, grants, use, revenues, and allocations, by State, FY91 and trends, annual rpt, 5724–1
see also Irrigation

Reconstruction Finance Corp.
Capital aid to banks by Reconstruction Finance Corp, impact on solvency status and financial ratios, 1920s-40, article, 9381–1.304

Recording industry
Copyrights Register activities, registrations by material type, and fees, FY91 and trends from 1790, annual rpt, 26404–2
County Business Patterns, 1989: employment, establishments, and payroll, by SIC 2- to 4-digit industry and county, annual State rpt series, 2326–8
County Business Patterns, 1990: employment, establishments, and payroll, by SIC 2- to 4-digit industry and county, annual State rpt series, 2326–6
Exports and imports between US and outlying areas, by detailed commodity and mode of transport, 1991, annual rpt, 2424–11
Exports and imports of US, by country and detailed commodity, monthly rpt, 2422–12
Exports and imports of US, by Harmonized System 6-digit commodity and country, 1991, annual rpt, 2424–13
Exports of US, detailed Schedule B commodities with countries of destination, 1991, annual rpt, 2424–10
Fed Govt audiovisual activities and spending, by whether performed in-house and agency, FY91, annual rpt, 9514–1
Fed Govt publications and other holdings of Natl Archives, special collections, series, 9516–1
House of Representatives salaries, expenses, and contingent fund disbursement, detailed listings, quarterly rpt, 21942–1
Input-output structure of US economy, detailed interindustry transactions for 541 industries, and components of final demand, 1982 benchmark data, 2708–17
Libraries (public) finances, staff, and operations, by State and population size, 1990, annual rpt, 4824–6
Libraries for blind and handicapped, readership, circulation, staff, funding, and holdings, FY91, annual listing, 26404–3
Library of Congress activities, acquisitions, services, and financial statements, FY91, annual rpt, 26404–1
Manufacturing annual survey, 1990: finances and operations, by SIC 2- to 4-digit industry, series, 2506–14
Manufacturing census, 1987: concentration of largest firms measured by value added, and for shipments by SIC 2- and 4-digit industry, subject rpt, 2497–6
Manufacturing census, 1987: shipments of manufacturers products, by customer class and SIC 2- and 4-digit industry, subject rpt, 2497–4
Natl Archives and Records Admin activities, finances, holdings, and staff, FY91, annual rpt, 9514–2
Occupational injury and illness rates, by SIC 2- to 4-digit industry, 1989-90, annual rpt, 6844–7
Occupational injury and illness rates, by SIC 2- to 4-digit industry, 1990, annual rpt, 6844–1
OECD trade, total and for 4 major countries, and US trade by country, by commodity, 1980-90, world area rpt series, 9116–1
Price indexes (producer), by stage of processing and detailed commodity, monthly rpt, 6762–6
Price indexes (producer), by stage of processing and detailed commodity, monthly 1991, annual rpt, 6764–2
Senate receipts, itemized expenses by payee, and balances, 1st half FY92, semiannual listing, 25922–1
Statistical Abstract of US, 1992 annual data compilation, 2324–1.7
see also Video recordings and equipment

Recreation
Accident deaths and injuries prevention, and treatment, 1991 conf papers, 4208–35
Aircraft accidents and circumstances, for US operations of domestic and foreign airlines and general aviation, periodic rpt, 9612–1
Aircraft pilot and nonpilot certificates held, by type of certificate, age, sex, region, and State, 1991, annual rpt, 7504–2
Army Corps of Engineers recreation facilities mgmt, acreage, visits, and non-Federal public and private dev alternatives, 1980s-90, 3758–8
Army Corps of Engineers water resources dev projects, characteristics, and costs, 1950s-89, biennial State rpt series, 3756–1
Army Corps of Engineers water resources dev projects, characteristics, and costs, 1950s-91, biennial State rpt series, 3756–2
Assistance (block and categorical grants) programs for State and local govts, FY91, biennial listing, 10044–8
Bombing incidents, casualties, and damage, by target, circumstances, and State, 1991, annual rpt, 6224–5
Budget of US, obligations and authority by function, agency, and program, with summaries and analyses, FY93, annual rpt, 104–2
Coastal areas construction authorized by permit, by building type, 1970-89, 2176–8.3
Coastal areas environmental conditions and mgmt, for individual areas, conf series, 2146–8
Colorado River Storage Project finances and activities in western States, FY91, annual rpt, 5824–3
Construction authorized by building permits, by type of construction, region, State, and MSA, quarterly rpt, 2042–1.3
Construction put in place, private and public, by type and region, monthly rpt, annual tables, 2382–4
Consumer Expenditure Survey, spending by category, and income, by selected household characteristics, 1991, annual press release, 6726–1.53
Consumer Expenditure Survey, spending by category, selected household characteristics, and region, quarterly rpt, 6762–14
County Business Patterns, 1989: employment, establishments, and payroll, by SIC 2- to 4-digit industry and county, annual State rpt series, 2326–8
County Business Patterns, 1990: employment, establishments, and payroll, by SIC 2- to 4-digit industry and county, annual State rpt series, 2326–6
CPI by component for US city average, and by selected metro area, region, and population size, monthly rpt, 6762–2
Deaths and rates, by cause and selected social, demographic, and employment characteristics, 1979-85, natl longitudinal study, 4478–186
Employment, earnings, and hours, by SIC 1- to 4-digit industry, monthly 1989-Feb 1992, annual rpt, 6744–4
Environmental Quality, status of problems, protection programs, research, and intl issues, 1991 annual rpt, 484–1
Farmland value, rent, taxes, foreign ownership, and transfers by probable use and lender type, with data by region and State, 1981-92, article, 1561–16.302
Fed Govt financial and nonfinancial domestic aid, 1992 base edition, annual listing, 104–5
Fed Govt spending in States, by type, program, agency, and State, FY91, annual rpt, 2464–2
FmHA activities, and loans and grants by program and State, FY91 and trends from FY70, annual rpt, 1184–17
FmHA loans, by type, borrower race, and State, quarterly rpt, 1182–5
Food and alcoholic beverage spending, by place of purchase, 1970-91, annual rpt, 1544–4.5
Forests (natl) revenue, by source, forest, and State, FY91, annual rpt, 1204–34
Govt direct spending and employment, by function and level of govt, selected years 1962-87, 10048–53
Govt employment and payroll, by function, level of govt, and jurisdiction, annual rpt series, 2466–1
Govt finances, by level of govt, State, and for large cities and counties, annual rpt series, 2466–2
Households entertainment spending, recreation participation by activity, and video product and pet ownership, 1970s-90, article, 1702–1.303

Housing (rental) total, HUD-assisted by program, and eligible for aid, recent movers by reason, selected characteristics, and location, 1989, biennial rpt, 5184–11
Housing units owned for recreation and investment, by selected unit characteristics, 1989, biennial rpt supplement, 2485–13
Injuries from use of consumer products and related activities, by severity and victim age and sex, 1990, annual rpt, 9164–7
Injuries from use of consumer products, by severity, victim age, and detailed product, 1991, annual rpt, 9164–6
Input-output structure of US economy, detailed interindustry transactions for 84 industries, and components of final demand, 1987, annual article, 2702–1.316
Input-output structure of US economy, detailed interindustry transactions for 541 industries, and components of final demand, 1982 benchmark data, 2708–17
Labor demand, turnover, and training completions, by detailed occupation, 1990 and projected to 2005, biennial rpt, 6744–3
Land and Water Conservation Fund allocations for outdoor recreation area dev, by State, FY93, annual table, 5544–15
Land Mgmt Bur activities and funding by State, FY90, annual rpt, 5724–13
Mail volume to and from households, use, and views, by class, source, content, and household characteristics, FY87-90, annual rpt, 9864–10
Multinatl US firms and foreign affiliates finances and operations, by industry and country, 1989 benchmark survey, annual rpt, 2704–5
Natl income and product accounts, comprehensive accounts and components, benchmark revisions, 1929-88, 2708–5
Natl income and product accounts, comprehensive accounts and components, *Survey of Current Business*, monthly rpt, 2702–1.25
New Mexico Caballo Resource Area public land mgmt, and grazing, environmental, and leasing activities, FY90-91, annual rpt, 5724–17
Occupational injury and illness rates, by SIC 2- to 4-digit industry, 1989-90, annual rpt, 6844–7
Occupational injury and illness rates, by SIC 2- to 4-digit industry, 1990, annual rpt, 6844–1
Occupational Outlook Handbook, 1992-93, biennial rpt, 6744–1
Ohio River basin waterway facilities, freight by commodity and port, and recreation, by waterway, 1988-89, annual rpt, 3754–6
Pacific territories population and housing detailed characteristics, by location, 1990 Census of Population and Housing, series, 2551–8
Public lands acreage and use, and Land Mgmt Bur activities and finances, annual State rpt series, 5724–11
Public lands acreage, grants, use, revenues, and allocations, by State, FY91, annual rpt, 5724–1.2
Real estate assets of failed thrifts, inventory of properties available from Resolution Trust Corp, 1991, semiannual listing, 9722–2.1
Real estate assets of failed thrifts, inventory of properties available from Resolution Trust Corp, 1992, semiannual listing, 9722–2.8
Statistical Abstract of US, 1992 annual data compilation, 2324–1.7
Tax (income) returns of corporations, income and tax items by asset size and detailed industry, 1989, annual rpt, 8304–4; 8304–21
Tax (income) returns of partnerships, income statement and balance sheet items, by industry group, 1990, annual article, 8302–2.314
Tax (income) returns of sole proprietorships, income statement items, by industry group, 1990, annual article, 8302–2.317; 8302–2.320
Tax collections of State govts by detailed type of tax, and tax rates, by State, FY91, annual rpt, 2466–2.7
Travel patterns, personal and household characteristics, and auto and public transport use, 1990 survey, series, 7556–6
TVA finances and operations by program and facility, FY91, annual rpt, 9804–32
VA health care facilities trainees, by detailed program and city, FY91, annual rpt, 8704–4
Washington and Oregon coastal areas recreation resources, and impacts of OCS oil and gas dev, 1983-88, 5738–40
Western US activities of Reclamation Bur, land and population served, and recreation areas, by location, 1990, annual rpt, 5824–12
Youth health condition, risk factors, and preventive and treatment services use and availability, 1970s-80s, 26358–234.2
see also Boats and boating
see also Camping
see also Fishing, sport
see also Horse racing
see also Hunting and trapping
see also Motion pictures
see also National forests
see also National parks
see also National trails
see also Parks
see also Recreational vehicles
see also Sporting goods
see also Sports and athletics
see also State forests
see also Swimming
see also Swimming pools
see also Travel and tourism
see also Wilderness areas
see also Winter sports

Recreational vehicles
Accidents (fatal), deaths, and rates, by circumstances, characteristics of persons and vehicles involved, and location, 1990, annual rpt, 7764–10
Accidents involving consumer products and related activities, injuries by severity and victim age and sex, 1990, annual rpt, 9164–7
Accidents involving consumer products, injuries by severity, victim age, and detailed product, 1991, annual rpt, 9164–6
Colorado off-road vehicle use, owner expenses, and views on proposed registration fee, 1986-88, hearing, 25318–85
County Business Patterns, 1989: employment, establishments, and payroll, by SIC 2- to 4-digit industry and county, annual State rpt series, 2326–8
County Business Patterns, 1990: employment, establishments, and payroll, by SIC 2- to 4-digit industry and county, annual State rpt series, 2326–6
Employment, earnings, and hours, by SIC 1- to 4-digit industry, monthly 1989-Feb 1992, annual rpt, 6744–4
Energy use by mode of transport, fuel supply, and demographic and economic factors of vehicle use, 1970s-90, annual rpt, 3304–5
Exports and imports of US, by Harmonized System 6-digit commodity and country, 1991, annual rpt, 2424–13
Exports of US, detailed Schedule B commodities with countries of destination, 1991, annual rpt, 2424–10
Input-output structure of US economy, detailed interindustry transactions for 541 industries, and components of final demand, 1982 benchmark data, 2708–17
Manufacturing annual survey, 1990: finances and operations, by SIC 2- to 4-digit industry, series, 2506–14
Manufacturing census, 1987: concentration of largest firms measured by value added, and for shipments by SIC 2- and 4-digit industry, subject rpt, 2497–6
Manufacturing census, 1987: shipments of manufacturers products, by customer class and SIC 2- and 4-digit industry, subject rpt, 2497–4
Natl park system visits and overnight stays, by park and State, monthly rpt, 5542–4
Natl park system visits and overnight stays, by park and State, 1991, annual rpt, 5544–12
Occupational injury and illness rates, by SIC 2- to 4-digit industry, 1989-90, annual rpt, 6844–7
Occupational injury and illness rates, by SIC 2- to 4-digit industry, 1990, annual rpt, 6844–1
OECD trade, total and for 4 major countries, and US trade by country, by commodity, 1980-90, world area rpt series, 9116–1
Price indexes (producer), by stage of processing and detailed commodity, monthly rpt, 6762–6
Price indexes (producer), by stage of processing and detailed commodity, monthly 1991, annual rpt, 6764–2
Statistical Abstract of US, 1992 annual data compilation, 2324–1.21

Recruiting
see Voluntary military service

Recycling of waste materials
Business statistics, detailed data for major industries and economic indicators, 1960-91, *Survey of Current Business* biennial supplement, 2704–1
County Business Patterns, 1989: employment, establishments, and payroll, by SIC 2- to 4-digit industry and county, annual State rpt series, 2326–8

County Business Patterns, 1990: employment, establishments, and payroll, by SIC 2- to 4-digit industry and county, annual State rpt series, 2326–6
Electric power plants and capacity, by fuel used, owner, location, and operating status, 1991 and for units planned 1992-2001, annual listing, 3164–36
Electric power plants certification applications filed with FERC, for small production and cogeneration facilities, FY80-91, annual listing, 3084–13
Employment, earnings, and hours, by SIC 1- to 4-digit industry, monthly 1989-Feb 1992, annual rpt, 6744–4
Energy from municipal waste combustion, and waste generation, 1990 and projected 1995-2010, annual rpt, 3164–90
Energy from waste materials, alternative projections 1990-2010, annual rpt, 3164–75
Energy from waste materials, ethanol feedstocks availability by source, and potential production, 1991 hearing, 25318–82
Energy from waste materials, use by source and region, 1990, annual rpt, 3164–97
Environmental Quality, status of problems, protection programs, research, and intl issues, 1991 annual rpt, 484–1
Exports and imports between US and outlying areas, by detailed commodity and mode of transport, 1991, annual rpt, 2424–11
Exports and imports of US, by country and detailed commodity, monthly rpt, 2422–12
Exports and imports of US, by Harmonized System 6-digit commodity and country, 1991, annual rpt, 2424–13
Exports and imports of US, by transport mode, country, and SITC 1- to 3-digit commodity, 1991, annual rpt, 2424–12
Exports of US, detailed Schedule B commodities with countries of destination, 1991, annual rpt, 2424–10
Hazardous substances industrial releases and reduction methods under EPA regulation, with chemical stocks and use, facility directory, 1987-89, annual CD-ROM, 9234–7
Industrial hazardous substances releases and reduction methods under EPA regulation, by chemical, source, industry, and location, 1989, annual rpt, 9234–6
Input-output structure of US economy, detailed interindustry transactions for 84 industries, and components of final demand, 1987, annual article, 2702–1.316
Input-output structure of US economy, detailed interindustry transactions for 541 industries, and components of final demand, 1982 benchmark data, 2708–17
Lumber (industrial roundwood) production and timber harvest for North Central States, by product and county, State rpt series, 1206–10
Lumber (industrial roundwood) production, by product, for Georgia, 1986 and 1989, 1208–393
Lumber (industrial roundwood) production for Florida, by product and county, 1987 and 1989, 1208–352
Lumber (industrial roundwood) production in Iowa, plant residue by use and type, 1988, 1208–75
Lumber (industrial roundwood) production in Missouri, plant residue by use and type, 1987, 1208–76
Lumber (industrial roundwood) production in northeastern US, by product, State rpt series, 1206–15
Lumber (industrial roundwood) production in Virginia, shipments, and residue volume, by species, product, and location, 1987-89, 1208–138
Lumber (pulpwood) production and mill receipts in North Central States, by species, mill, State, and county, 1990, annual rpt, 1204–19
Lumber (pulpwood and residue) prices, spending, and transport shares by mode, for southeast US, 1989-90, annual rpt, 1204–22
Lumber (veneer) receipts, production, and shipments, by species and southern State, with residue use, 1988, 1208–407
Lumber mills, operations, log use by species and origin, and residue use, for California by product and county, 1988, 1208–108
Lumber production, and industry operations, for Oregon by county, 1988, 1208–280
Lumber production and mill residue for Rocky Mountain States, by species, ownership, and county, series, 1206–17
Manufacturing industries recycling, fuel savings, and CO2 emissions reductions, 1988 and projected to 1995, hearing, 21368–140
Mexico imports from US, by industry and State, 1987-91, 2048–154
Minerals and metal recycling, by commodity, 1987-91, annual rpt, 5604–18
Minerals Yearbook, Vol 1, 1989: commodity reviews of production, use, trade, prices, and mining operations, annual rpt, 5604–33
Municipal and industrial waste recycling, costs, revenues, and secondary products trade and related energy use and pollution reductions, 1991 hearings, 21368–139
Paper (waste) use and inventories, *Survey of Current Business*, monthly rpt, 2702–1.18
Paper recycling by grade, with newsprint collection, recycling capacity by company, and curbside pickup operations, by State, 1970s-80s and projected to 1995, hearing, 25318–84
Plastic packaging by resin type, and municipal solid waste composition by weight, 1990-91, article, 9882–16.301
Price indexes (producer), by stage of processing and detailed commodity, monthly rpt, 6762–6
Price indexes (producer), by stage of processing and detailed commodity, monthly 1991, annual rpt, 6764–2
Statistical Abstract of US, 1992 annual data compilation, 2324–1.6; 2324–1.24
see also Biomass energy
see also Scrap metals

Red Cross
Refugee migration, and intl aid programs, by world area and country of origin and asylum, 1991, annual rpt, 7004–15
see also American National Red Cross

Red River
Freight (waterborne domestic and foreign) by commodity, traffic, and passengers, by port and waterway, 1989, annual rpt, 3754–3.2
Water supply and quality in streams and lakes, and groundwater levels in wells, by drainage basin, 1990, annual State rpt series, 5666–10
Water supply and quality in streams and lakes, and groundwater levels in wells, by drainage basin, 1991, annual State rpt series, 5666–12
Water supply in US and southern Canada, streamflow, surface and groundwater conditions, and reservoir levels, by location, monthly rpt, 5662–3

Red River of the North
see Souris-Red-Rainy Rivers

Redick, Richard W.
"Availability and Distribution of Psychiatric Beds, U.S. and Each State, 1988", 4506–3.48
"Patient Care Episodes in Mental Health Organizations, U.S.: Selected Years from 1955 to 1988", 4506–3.50

Redman, John
"Federal Job Training for the Poor May Be More Cost Effective in Rural Areas", 1502–7.305

Redmiles, Lissa
"Individual Foreign Earned Income and Tax Credit, 1987", 8302–2.301
"International Boycott Participation, 1990: Data Release", 8302–2.323

Reed, A. J.
"Expectations, Demand Shifts, and Milk Supply Response", 1502–3.303

Reed, Fred W.
"Sequelae of Traveling Substantial Distances for Prenatal Care and Birthing: The Use of Birth and Linked Birth/Infant Death Records To Assess Racial Differentials in Health Care", 4164–2

Reeder, John G.
"Oilseeds, Industry and Trade Summary", 9885–8.4

Reeder, Richard J.
"State Enterprise Zones in Nonmetro Areas: Are They Working?", 1502–7.303

Reform
see Educational reform
see Health care reform
see Judicial reform
see Land reform
see Rehabilitation of criminals
see Tax reform

Refrigeration
see Air conditioning
see Cold storage and refrigeration
see Household appliances and equipment

Refugees
Admissions to US of immigrants, alien workers, and visitors, deportations, and naturalizations, by country, FY91 and trends from 1820, annual rpt, 6264–2
Admissions to US of immigrants and nonimmigrants, alien workers, deportations, and naturalizations, FY91, annual summary rpt, 6264–7
Admissions to US of immigrants, by class of admission, country of birth, and MSA of destination, FY91, advance annual rpt, 6264–4

AID economic aid to developing countries, obligations and disbursements by country, quarterly rpt, 9912–4
Amerasian refugees arrivals in US, by State, monthly rpt, 4592–1
Amerasian refugees immigrant visas issued, by preference class and country of birth, FY88-90, annual rpt, 7184–1
Arrivals and resettlement in US, by age, sex, sponsoring agency, State, and country, monthly rpt, 4592–1
Arrivals in US by world area of origin and State of settlement, and Federal aid, FY91-92 and proposed FY93 allocations, annual rpt, 7004–16
Arrivals in US, by world area of origin, processing, and nationality, monthly rpt, 7002–4
Assistance (financial and nonfinancial) of Fed Govt, 1992 base edition, annual listing, 104–5
Cuba and Haiti refugees resettlement activities of Community Relations Service, FY91, annual rpt, 6004–9
Disease surveillance, control, and prevention among refugees, displaced persons, and population affected by famine, CDC recommendations with background data, 1978-91, 4206–2.63
Education (bilingual) enrollment, and eligible students not enrolled, by State, 1990-91, annual rpt, 4804–14
Fed Govt spending in States, by type, program, agency, and State, FY91, annual rpt, 2464–2
Foreign countries disasters, casualties, damage, and aid by US and others, FY91 and trends from FY64, annual rpt, 9914–12
Foreign countries *Geographic Notes*, boundaries, claims, nomenclature, and other devs, quarterly rpt, 7142–3
HHS financial aid, by program, recipient, State, and city, FY91, annual regional listings, 4004–3
Indochina refugees, arrivals, and departures, by country of origin and resettlement, camp, and ethnicity, monthly rpt, 7002–4
Indochina refugees arrivals and resettlement in US, by State, monthly rpt, 4592–1
Indochina refugees suffering stressful events during migration, by event type and ethnic group, 1990 local area study, 15496–1.16
Migration of refugees, and intl aid programs, by world area and country of origin and asylum, 1991, annual rpt, 7004–15
Persian Gulf War allied and other countries cash and in-kind contributions, by type and country, 1990-91, GAO rpt, 26123–371
Statistical Abstract of US, 1992 annual data compilation, 2324–1.1
UN voting record and share of votes in agreement with US, by issue, country, and world area, 1991, annual rpt, 7004–18
Vietnam population size, components of change, and selected characteristics, 1979, 1989, and projected to 2050, 2326–18.65

Refuse and refuse disposal
Agricultural Conservation Program acreage and projects, by State, 1936-90, quinquennial rpt, 1808–1
Air pollution levels for 6 pollutants, by source and selected MSA, 1982-91, annual rpt, 9194–1
Army Corps of Engineers activities and projects, FY88 and trends from 1800s, annual rpt, 3754–1.1
Army Corps of Engineers activities and projects, FY89 and trends from 1800s, annual rpt, 3754–1.2
Army Corps of Engineers activities and projects, FY90 and trends from 1800s, annual rpt, 3754–1.3
Assistance (financial and nonfinancial) of Fed Govt, 1992 base edition, annual listing, 104–5
County Business Patterns, 1989: employment, establishments, and payroll, by SIC 2- to 4-digit industry and county, annual State rpt series, 2326–8
County Business Patterns, 1990: employment, establishments, and payroll, by SIC 2- to 4-digit industry and county, annual State rpt series, 2326–6
CPI by component for US city average, and by selected metro area, region, and population size, monthly rpt, 6762–2
Electric utilities privately owned, pollution abatement outlays by type of pollutant and equipment, and firm, 1990, annual rpt, 3164–23
Employment, earnings, and hours, by SIC 1- to 4-digit industry, monthly 1989-Feb 1992, annual rpt, 6744–4
Environmental Quality, status of problems, protection programs, research, and intl issues, 1991 annual rpt, 484–1
Expenditures for pollution abatement by govts, business, and consumers, 1972-90, annual article, 2702–1.321
Fires (wild) and acreage burned, by type of land, ownership, cause, region, and State, 1984-90, annual rpt, 1204–4
Govt direct spending and employment, by function and level of govt, selected years 1962-87, 10048–53
Govt employment and payroll, by function, level of govt, and jurisdiction, annual rpt series, 2466–1
Govt finances, by level of govt, State, and for large cities and counties, annual rpt series, 2466–2
Housing (rental) units, total, with HUD assistance by program, and eligible for aid, by unit, household, and neighborhood characteristics, and location, 1989, biennial rpt, 5184–11
Housing and households detailed characteristics, and unit and neighborhood quality, MSA surveys, series, 2485–6
Incinerators air pollution abatement equipment shipments, by product, 1991, annual Current Industrial Rpt, 2506–12.5
Industrial waste generation, disposal, and regulation, by industry and State, mid 1980s-90, 26358–256
Manufacturing pollution abatement capital and operating costs, by SIC 2- to 4-digit industry and State, 1990, annual Current Industrial Rpt, 2506–3.6
Military prime contract awards, by detailed procurement category, FY88-91, annual rpt, 3544–18
Neighborhood and housing quality, indicators and attitudes, by householder type and location, for 11 MSAs, 1987 survey, supplement, 2485–8
Neighborhood and housing quality, indicators and attitudes, by householder type and location, 1989, biennial rpt supplement, 2485–13
Neighborhood and housing quality, indicators and attitudes, MSA surveys, series, 2485–6
Neighborhood quality, indicators and attitudes of renter households, by whether receiving and eligible for HUD assistance, householder characteristics, and location, 1989, biennial rpt, 5184–11
Occupational injury and illness rates, by SIC 2- to 4-digit industry, 1989-90, annual rpt, 6844–7
Occupational injury and illness rates, by SIC 2- to 4-digit industry, 1990, annual rpt, 6844–1
Plastic packaging by resin type, and municipal solid waste composition by weight, 1990-91, article, 9882–16.301
Public opinion on taxes, spending, and govt efficiency, by respondent characteristics, 1992 survey, annual rpt, 10044–2
State and local govt employment of minorities and women, by occupation, function, and pay level, 1991, annual rpt, 9244–6.4
Statistical Abstract of US, 1992 annual data compilation, 2324–1.6
see also Hazardous waste and disposal
see also Landfills
see also Radioactive waste and disposal
see also Recycling of waste materials
see also Sewage and wastewater systems

Regional medical programs
Appalachian Regional Commission health care services projects by State, and project listing, 1960s-80s, 9088–38
HHS financial aid, by program, recipient, State, and city, FY91, annual regional listings, 4004–3
Hospital closings relation to hospital and community characteristics, by metro-nonmetro location, 1980-87, article, 4042–3.341
Kidney end-stage disease treatment facilities, Medicare enrollment and reimbursement, survival, and patient characteristics, 1984-90, annual rpt, 4654–16
VA and non-VA facilities health services sharing contracts, by service type and region, FY91, annual rpt, 8704–5
VA and non-VA facilities health services sharing contracts, by service type, FY80-90, compilation of papers, 8608–9

Regional planning
Appalachia local dev projects, and funding by source, by program and State, FY91, annual rpt, 9084–1
Appalachian Regional Commission funding, by project and State, planned FY92, annual rpt, 9084–3
Assistance (financial and nonfinancial) of Fed Govt, 1992 base edition, annual listing, 104–5
Coastal areas environmental conditions and mgmt, for individual areas, conf series, 2146–8
DC metro area land acquisition and dev projects of Fed Govt, characteristics and funding by agency and project, FY92-96, annual rpt, 15454–1
Fed Govt spending in States, by type, program, agency, and State, FY91, annual rpt, 2464–2
Occupational Outlook Handbook, 1992-93, biennial rpt, 6744–1

Wetlands (coastal) mapping projects status, costs, and methods, 1990 conf, 5508–116
see also Regional medical programs

Regions of the U.S.
see Appalachia
see Middle Atlantic States
see North Central States
see Northeast States
see Southeastern States
see Southwestern States
see Western States
see under By Region, By Census Division, and By State in the "Index by Categories"
see under names of individual States

Regions of the world
see Africa
see Antarctica
see Arctic
see Arctic Ocean
see Asia
see Atlantic Ocean
see Caribbean area
see Central America
see Eastern Europe
see Europe
see Gulf of Alaska
see Gulf of Mexico
see Indian Ocean
see Latin America
see Mediterranean Sea
see Middle East
see North America
see North Sea
see Oceania
see Pacific Ocean
see South America
see Southeast Asia

Regulation
see Administrative law and procedure
see Antitrust law
see Environmental regulation
see Financial institutions regulation
see Government and business
see Government forms and paperwork
see Government inspections
see Interstate commerce
see Licenses and permits
see Medical regulation
see Price regulation
see under names of individual agencies (listed under Federal independent agencies)

Rehabilitation
see Drug abuse and treatment
see Housing maintenance and repair
see Rehabilitation of criminals
see Rehabilitation of the disabled
see Veterans rehabilitation
see Vocational rehabilitation

Rehabilitation of criminals
Boot camp correctional facilities and population, by selected characteristics, 1990, quinquennial rpt, 6068–218
Education funding by Federal agency, program, and recipient type, and instn spending, 1960s-91, annual rpt, 4824–8
Job Training Partnership Act education and worker training program participants, by selected characteristics, 1986-88, 15496–1.15
Sex offenders treatment programs for adults and juveniles, by program type and State, data compilation, 1992 annual rpt, 6064–6.1; 6064–6.6
Shock incarceration programs participation and operations, 1991, annual rpt, 6064–32
Shock incarceration programs provisions and participation, by State, data compilation, 1992 annual rpt, 6064–6.6
see also Community-based correctional programs
see also Pardons
see also Parole and probation
see also Prison work programs
see also Recidivism

Rehabilitation of the disabled
Accident deaths and injuries prevention, and treatment, 1991 conf papers, 4208–35
Facilities excluded from Medicare prospective payment system, quality standards and review, certification, accreditation, and licensing, 1991 survey, 17206–2.41
Fed Govt and State rehabilitation activities and funding, FY91, annual rpt, 4944–1
Fed Govt spending in States, by type, program, agency, and State, FY91, annual rpt, 2464–2
Heart transplants and other cardiac surgical procedures, rehabilitation risks and benefit evaluation for Medicare coverage, 1991 rpt, 4186–10.8
Hospital deaths of Medicare patients, actual and expected rates by diagnosis, with hospital characteristics, by instn, FY90, annual State rpt series, 4654–14
Hospital discharges by detailed diagnostic and procedure category, primary diagnosis, and length of stay, by age, sex, and region, 1990, annual rpt, 4147–13.111
Medicare admin and research, and HCFA affirmative action and accreditation programs, FY87, annual rpt, 4654–5
Medicare and Medicaid beneficiaries and program operations, 1992, annual fact book, 4654–18
Medicare reimbursement of hospitals under prospective payment system, and effect on services, finances, and beneficiary payments, 1980-91, annual rpt, 17204–2
Medicare reimbursement of hospitals under prospective payment system, methodology, inputs, and data by diagnostic group, 1992 annual rpt, 17204–1
OASDI benefits and beneficiaries, by category, age, and sex, quarterly rpt, 4742–1.1
Physicians, by specialty, age, sex, and location of training and practice, 1990, State rpt series, 4116–6
Workers compensation laws of States and Fed Govt, 1992 annual rpt, 6504–11
see also Group homes for the handicapped
see also Occupational therapy
see also Physical therapy
see also Respiratory therapy
see also Sheltered workshops
see also Special education
see also Speech pathology and audiology
see also Veterans rehabilitation
see also Vocational rehabilitation

Reid, Angus, Group, Inc.
"Canadian Pleasure Travel Market Study: Final Report", 2906–2.24

Reid, J. Norman
"Building National Strategies for Rural Economic Development", 1504–9.1

Reid, Max
"Oil Shocks, Monetary Policy, and Economic Activity", 9389–1.304

Reid, Robert N.
"Benthic Macrofauna of the New York Bight, 1979-89", 2168–128

Reimund, Donn A.
"Structural Change in the U.S. Farm Sector, 1974-87: Thirteenth Annual Family Farm Report to Congress", 1504–4

Reinsdorf, Marshall B.
"Effect of Price Dispersion on Cost of Living Indexes", 6886–6.82

Reisinger, Anne L.
"Monitoring Access: Report to Congress", 17266–1.5

Reitzes, James D.
"Analysis of the Maritime Industry and the Effects of 1984 Shipping Act", 9408–54

Rekitar, Jakov A.
"USSR Construction Sector", 2042–1.301

Relief
see Disaster relief
see Food assistance
see Income maintenance
see International assistance
see Low-income energy assistance
see Public welfare programs
see Refugees
see State funding for social welfare
see Transportation assistance
see War relief

Religion
Cancer (pancreatic) death risk relation to occupational DDT exposure and other characteristics, 1982 article, 4472–1.314
Degrees awarded in higher education, by level, field, race, and sex, 1989/90 and trends from 1980/81, annual rpt, 4844–17
Education data compilation, 1992 annual rpt, 4824–2
Foreign countries *Background Notes,* summary social, political, and economic data, series, 7006–2
Foreign countries economic, social, political, and geographic summary data, by country, 1992, annual factbook, 9114–2
Infant health, deaths and risk factors, and prevention issues, for US and selected countries, 1990 conf, 4148–28
Statistical Abstract of US, 1992 annual data compilation, 2324–1.1
see also Clergy
see also Missions and missionaries
see also Religious liberty
see also Religious organizations

Religious liberty
Foreign countries human rights conditions in 170 countries, 1991, annual rpt, 21384–3

Religious organizations
Books (religious) exports of US by country, 1991, annual rpt, 2424–10; 2424–11
Buildings (commercial and public) alteration and repair spending, by type, size, age, and region, 1989, 2388–4
Census Bur data coverage and availability for statistics on small areas, religious and other groups use, 1991 rpt, 2326–7.85
Child day care and early childhood education programs availability, demand, use, costs, and provider and enrollee characteristics, 1990 survey, 4808–39

Construction put in place, and authorized by selected MSA, by type and region, quarterly rpt, 2042–1.1; 2042–1.3
Construction put in place, value of new public and private structures, by type, monthly rpt, 2382–4
Consumer spending, natl income and product account benchmark revisions, 1929-88, 2708–5
Consumer spending, natl income and product accounts, comprehensive accounts and components, *Survey of Current Business*, monthly rpt, 2702–1.25
County Business Patterns, 1989: employment, establishments, and payroll, by SIC 2- to 4-digit industry and county, annual State rpt series, 2326–8
County Business Patterns, 1990: employment, establishments, and payroll, by SIC 2- to 4-digit industry and county, annual State rpt series, 2326–6
Education (elementary and secondary) schools, teachers, staff, and enrollment, by selected characteristics, 1987/88-1988/89, 4836–3.10
Finances of tax exempt organizations, with data by type, size, State, and for largest organizations, late 1940s-80s, compilation of papers, 8308–35
Finances of tax exempt organizations with unrelated business income, by organization type, 1987, article, 8302–2.306
Group housing in religious instns, population by race and sex, 1990 Census of Population, State rpt series, 2531–1
Hospital deaths of Medicare patients, actual and expected rates by diagnosis, with hospital characteristics, by instn, FY90, annual State rpt series, 4654–14
Input-output structure of US economy, detailed interindustry transactions for 541 industries, and components of final demand, 1982 benchmark data, 2708–17
Mail volume to and from households, use, and views, by class, source, content, and household characteristics, FY87-90, annual rpt, 9864–10
Public confidence in people running selected social instns, 1972-88 surveys, biennial rpt, 9624–10.7
Schools (Catholic) dropouts, and transfers to public and other private schools, by income level and race, 1990 survey, 4826–10.4
Schools (elementary and secondary), enrollment, teachers, high school grads, and spending, by instn control and State, 1992/93, annual rpt, 4834–19
Schools (higher education) enrollment, tuition, control, location, and other characteristics, 1991/92, biennial listing, 4844–3
Schools (private elementary and secondary), students, and staff characteristics, by school type and affiliation, 1987/88, 4836–3.8
Schools conditions, educational performance, and student characteristics, attitudes, activities, and plans, 1988 8th grade class, natl longitudinal survey, series, 4826–9
Schools, students, staff, finances, and facilities, data compilation, 1992 annual rpt, 4824–2
Statistical Abstract of US, 1992 annual data compilation, 2324–1.1
Tax exempt organizations and employee plans listed on IRS masterfile, determinations, applications, and rulings, FY91, annual rpt, 8304–3.2
Terrorism (intl) incidents, casualties, and attacks on US targets, by attack type and country, 1991, annual rpt, 7004–22
Terrorism incidents in US, related activity, and casualties, by attack type, target, group, and location, 1991, annual rpt, 6224–6
see also Clergy
see also Missions and missionaries

Relocation
Housing (rental) total, HUD-assisted by program, and eligible for aid, recent movers by reason, selected characteristics, and location, 1989, biennial rpt, 5184–11
Housing characteristics of recent movers for new and previous unit, and household characteristics, MSA surveys, series, 2485–6
Housing unit and household characteristics of recent movers, and reason for move, by tenure, 1989, 2486–1.12
Indian (Navajo and Hopi) relocation program activities and caseloads, monthly rpt, 16002–1
NYC housing supply, occupancy, condition, and household characteristics, by tenure and borough, 1991 triennial survey, 2488–3
Railroad accidents involving hazardous materials, casualties, and circumstances, 1984-89, 9618–18
Railroad accidents involving hazardous materials, damage, and persons evacuated, by cause, railroad, and State, 1991, annual rpt, 7604–1
Railroad accidents involving hazardous materials, damage, and persons evacuated, by incident, 1988, annual rpt, 7604–3
Small business use of Census Bur economic data in planning decisions, case studies, 1991 rpt, 2628–33
Unemployed displaced workers, layoffs and recalls by layoff reason, industry, firm size, and State, 2nd half 1988, 6406–6.36
Unemployed displaced workers, layoffs and unemployment insurance claims by reason, industry, selected characteristics, and State, quarterly press release, 6742–23
Unemployed displaced workers, layoffs and unemployment insurance claims by reason, industry, selected characteristics, MSA, and State, 1990, annual rpt, 6744–18
see also Migration

Remedial education
Eighth grade class of 1988: educational performance and conditions, characteristics, attitudes, activities, and plans, natl longitudinal survey, series, 4826–9
Elementary and secondary education enrollment, staff, finances, operations, programs, and policies, 1987/88 biennial survey, series, 4836–3
Higher education remedial instruction and tutoring offerings, by instn type and control, 1980-92, annual rpt, 4824–2.21
Occupational qualification and skill improvement training, workers participating by training source, occupation, age, sex, and race, 1991, 6728–32
Statistical Abstract of US, 1992 annual data compilation, 2324–1.4
see also Compensatory education
see also Special education

Remolona, Eli M.
"Finance Companies, Bank Competition, and Niche Markets", 9385–1.309

Rendleman, C. Matthew
"Agrichemical Reduction Policy: Its Effect on Income and Income Distribution", 1502–3.302

Renewable energy resources
see Alcohol fuels
see Biomass energy
see Geothermal resources
see Hydroelectric power
see Solar energy
see Water power
see Wind energy
see Wood fuel

Reno, Nev.
Wages by occupation, and benefits for office and plant workers, 1992 survey, periodic MSA rpt, 6785–3.4
see also under By City and By SMSA or MSA in the "Index by Categories"

Rent
American Housing Survey: unit and household characteristics of recent movers, and reason for move, by tenure, 1989, 2486–1.12
American Housing Survey: unit and households detailed characteristics, and unit and neighborhood quality, MSA rpt series, 2485–6
Apartment and condominium completions by rent class and sales price, and market absorption rates, quarterly rpt, 2482–2
Apartment completions by region and metro-nonmetro location, and absorption rate, by size and rent class, preliminary 1991, annual Current Housing Rpt, 2484–3
Apartment market absorption rates and characteristics for nonsubsidized furnished and unfurnished units, 1990, annual Current Housing Rpt, 2484–2
Banks and thrifts finances and operations by deposit size, Fed Reserve functional cost analysis, 1991, annual rpt, 9364–6
Banks in Fed Reserve System, expenses and operations itemized by service, office, and district, 1991, annual rpt, 9364–11
Budget of US, authoritative financial statements with appropriations, outlays, and receipts, by category and agency, FY91, annual rpt, 8104–2.2
Business statistics, detailed data for major industries and economic indicators, 1960-91, *Survey of Current Business* biennial supplement, 2704–1
Census of Housing, 1990: inventory, occupancy, and costs, State fact sheet series, 2326–21
Census of Housing, 1990: median value and rent, by State and region, and compared to 1970 and 1980, fact sheet, 2328–83
Census of Housing, 1990: summary unit characteristics, by householder race and age, county, place, and urban-rural location, State rpt series, 2471–1

Census of Population and Housing, 1990: data summary, use, and availability, fact sheet, 2326–23.1
Census of Population and Housing, 1990: detailed geographic coverage, State CD-ROM series, 2551–9
Census of Population and Housing, 1990: population and housing characteristics, detailed geographic coverage, State CD-ROM series, 2551–10
Census of Population and Housing, 1990: summary characteristics, by county, subdiv, and place, State rpt series, 2551–7
Census of Population and Housing, 1990: summary characteristics, households, and land area, by county, subdiv, and place, State rpt series, 2551–1
Commercial real estate supply and demand, market activity indicators by region, quarterly rpt, 9292–6
Communications services revenue and expenses, itemized by SIC 2- to 4-digit kind of business, 1990, annual rpt, 2413–15
Costs of housing exceeding 28% of gross income, families income by source and expenses by type, by tenure and other characteristics, 1989, article, 1702–1.304
CPI by component for US city average, and by selected metro area, region, and population size, monthly rpt, 6762–2
Discrimination in housing rental and sales, for blacks and Hispanics in selected metro areas, 1989 study, series, 5186–16
DOE real property owned and leased, by type, subagency, contractor, and site, FY91, annual rpt, 3004–28
Electric utilities privately owned, finances and operations, detailed data, 1990, annual rpt, 3164–23
Farm production itemized costs, by farm sales size and region, 1991, annual rpt, 1614–3
Farm production itemized costs, receipts, and returns, by commodity and region, 1975-90, annual rpt, 1544–20
Farm sector balance sheet, and marketing receipts by detailed commodity, by State, 1986-90, annual rpt, 1544–18
Farmland irrigated, farm characteristics, and water and fuel sources, by State and leading county, 1950s-88, 1588–122
Farmland value, rent, taxes, foreign ownership, and transfers by probable use and lender type, with data by region and State, 1981-92, article, 1561–16.302
FmHA property acquired through foreclosure, 1-family homes, value, sales, and leases, by State, monthly rpt, 1182–7
House of Representatives salaries, expenses, and contingent fund disbursement, detailed listings, quarterly rpt, 21942–1
Housing (rental) units, total, with HUD assistance by program, and eligible for aid, by unit, household, and neighborhood characteristics, and location, 1989, biennial rpt, 5184–11
Housing and households summary characteristics, 1989 and trends, chartbook, 2486–2.1
Housing energy use, costs, and conservation, and household and housing characteristics, survey rpt series, 3166–7
Income (personal) per capita and by source, and employment, by industry div, State, MSA, and county, 1969-90, annual CD-ROM, 2704–7
Income tax returns of foreign corporations and individuals, and US entities abroad, detailed data compilation, 1970s-89, quinquennial rpt, 8308–31
Natl income and product accounts and components, *Survey of Current Business*, monthly rpt, 2702–1.23
Natl income and product accounts, comprehensive accounts and components, benchmark revisions, 1929-88, 2708–5
Natl income and product accounts, comprehensive accounts and components, *Survey of Current Business*, monthly rpt, 2702–1.28
Natural gas interstate pipeline company detailed financial and operating data, by firm, 1990, annual rpt, 3164–38
Nonprofit charitable and other tax exempt organizations finances, by category and size of assets and contributions, 1988, annual article, 8302–2.315
Nonprofit charitable organizations finances, with data by State and for top 10 instns, 1988, article, 8302–2.302
NYC housing supply, occupancy, condition, and household characteristics, by tenure and borough, 1991 triennial survey, 2488–3
Pacific territories population and housing detailed characteristics, by location, 1990 Census of Population and Housing, series, 2551–8
Railroad (Class I) finances and operations, detailed data by firm, class of service, and district, 1990, annual rpt, 9486–5.1
Railroad (Class I) finances and operations, detailed data by firm, class of service, and district, 1991, annual rpt, 9486–6.1
Rice production, practices, costs, and land tenure, by production area, 1988, 1568–309
Senate receipts, itemized expenses by payee, and balances, 1st half FY92, semiannual listing, 25922–1
Statistical Abstract of US, 1992 annual data compilation, 2324–1.26
Survey of Current Business, detailed financial and business data, and economic indicators, monthly rpt, 2702–1.3
Tax (income) returns filed, by type of filer, selected income items, quarterly rpt, 8302–2.1
Tax (income) returns of corporations, income and tax items by asset size and detailed industry, 1989, annual rpt, 8304–4; 8304–21
Tax (income) returns of individuals, detailed data, 1988, annual rpt, 8304–2
Tax (income) returns of partnerships, income statement and balance sheet items, by industry group, 1990, annual article, 8302–2.314
Tax (income) returns of sole proprietorships, income statement items, by industry group, 1990, annual article, 8302–2.317; 8302–2.320
Tax exempt organizations finances, with data by type, size, State, and for largest organizations, late 1940s-80s, compilation of papers, 8308–35
Tax exempt organizations with unrelated business income, finances by organization type, 1987, article, 8302–2.306
Telephone and telegraph firms detailed finances and operations, 1990, annual rpt, 9284–6.2; 9284–6.3
Truck and warehouse services finances and inventory, by SIC 2- to 4-digit industry, 1990 survey, annual rpt, 2413–14
Vacant housing characteristics and costs, and occupancy and vacancy rates, by region and metro-nonmetro location, quarterly rpt, 2482–1
Vacant housing characteristics, and occupancy and vacancy rates, by tenure and location, 1960s-91, annual rpt, 2484–1
see also Housing tenure
see also Motor vehicle rental
see also Rent control
see also Rent supplements
see also Rental industries

Rent control
American Housing Survey: unit and household characteristics of recent movers, and reason for move, by tenure, 1989, 2486–1.12
American Housing Survey: unit and households detailed characteristics, and unit and neighborhood quality, MSA rpt series, 2485–6
Construction of multifamily housing, and impacts of rent control, by selected city, 1991 hearing, 21248–174
Housing (rental) units, total, with HUD assistance by program, and eligible for aid, by unit, household, and neighborhood characteristics, and location, 1989, biennial rpt, 5184–11
NYC housing supply, occupancy, condition, and household characteristics, by tenure and borough, 1991 triennial survey, 2488–3
Single parent families in own and others homes, by financial, housing, and other characteristics, 1989, 2486–1.14
Single person and nonfamily households social, economic and housing characteristics, by tenure, 1989, 2486–1.15

Rent supplements
American Housing Survey: unit and household characteristics of recent movers, and reason for move, by tenure, 1989, 2486–1.12
American Housing Survey: unit and households detailed characteristics, and unit and neighborhood quality, MSA rpt series, 2485–6
Disabled persons low income housing capital advances and rental aid of HUD, by recipient, FY92, press release, 5006–3.98
Eligibility for low income housing, tenants reported income agreement with tax records, 1989-90, GAO rpt, 26121–468
Expenditures of Fed Govt in States, by type, program, agency, and State, FY91, annual rpt, 2464–2
Homeless persons housing in rehabilitated single occupancy units, funding and characteristics, by city, FY87-91, GAO rpt, 26113–596
Homeless persons housing in rehabilitated single occupancy units, HUD grants by community, 1991, press release, 5006–3.82

Homeless persons housing in rehabilitated single occupancy units, HUD grants by community, 1992, press release, 5006–3.90
Homeless persons with mental illness, HUD rent assistance and support services grants, by recipient, 1992, press release, 5006–3.89
Housing (rental) units, total, with HUD assistance by program, and eligible for aid, by unit, household, and neighborhood characteristics, and location, 1989, biennial rpt, 5184–11
HUD activities, and housing programs operations and funding, 1990, annual rpt, 5004–10
Low income housing developers tax credits, subsidies, project and tenant characteristics, and investor returns, 1987-88, 5188–133
NYC housing supply, occupancy, condition, and household characteristics, by tenure and borough, 1991 triennial survey, 2488–3
Older persons low income housing capital advances and rental aid of HUD, by recipient, FY91, press release, 5006–3.88
Older persons low income housing capital advances and rental aid of HUD, by recipient, FY92, press release, 5006–3.97
Population economic well-being indicators, by selected characteristics and household income and income-to-poverty ratio, 1984, 2546–20.22
Rehabilitation of rental housing, HUD funding and activities by program and region, FY91, annual rpt, 5124–7
Single parent families in own and others homes, by financial, housing, and other characteristics, 1989, 2486–1.14
Supply of low income rental housing in rural areas, FmHA loans and impacts of programs to maintain supply and to deter mortgage prepayment, 1988-91, GAO rpt, 26113–586

Rental industries

Banks (insured commercial and savings) finances, for foreign and domestic offices, by asset size, 1990, annual rpt, 9294–4.2
Containers (intermodal) and equipment owned by shipping and leasing companies, inventory by type and size, 1991, annual rpt, 7704–10
County Business Patterns, 1989: employment, establishments, and payroll, by SIC 2- to 4-digit industry and county, annual State rpt series, 2326–8
County Business Patterns, 1990: employment, establishments, and payroll, by SIC 2- to 4-digit industry and county, annual State rpt series, 2326–6
Employment, earnings, and hours, by SIC 1- to 4-digit industry, monthly 1989-Feb 1992, annual rpt, 6744–4
Finance companies credit outstanding and leasing activities, by credit type, monthly rpt, 9365–2.7
Finances and operations, by SIC 2- to 4-digit industry, forecast 1992, annual rpt, 2044–28
Hospital financial performance under Medicare, 1977-89, article, 4652–1.315
Input-output structure of US economy, detailed interindustry transactions for 541 industries, and components of final demand, 1982 benchmark data, 2708–17
Military prime contract awards, by detailed procurement category, FY88-91, annual rpt, 3544–18
Multinatl US firms and foreign affiliates finances and operations, by industry and country, 1989 benchmark survey, annual rpt, 2704–5
Occupational injury and illness rates, by SIC 2- to 4-digit industry, 1989-90, annual rpt, 6844–7
Southeastern States, Fed Reserve 5th District insured commercial banks financial statements, by State, quarterly rpt, 9389–18
Tax (income) returns of corporations, income and tax items by asset size and detailed industry, 1989, annual rpt, 8304–4; 8304–21
Tax (income) returns of partnerships, income statement and balance sheet items, by industry group, 1990, annual article, 8302–2.314
Tax (income) returns of sole proprietorships, income statement items, by industry group, 1990, annual article, 8302–2.317; 8302–2.320
Truck and warehouse services finances and inventory, by SIC 2- to 4-digit industry, 1990 survey, annual rpt, 2413–14
see also Motor vehicle rental

Renter households

see Housing tenure

Renzema, Marc

"Use of Electronic Monitoring in the U.S.: 1989 Update", 6066–20.23

Reorganization of government

see Government reorganization

Repair industries

Airline and aviation safety employees drug testing and results, by drug type and occupational group, 1991, semiannual rpt, 7502–17
Buildings (commercial and public) alteration and repair spending, by type, size, age, and region, 1989, 2388–4
Buildings (commercial and public) alteration and repair spending, by type, 1989, article, 2042–1.305
Communications services revenue and expenses, itemized by SIC 2- to 4-digit kind of business, 1990, annual rpt, 2413–15
County Business Patterns, 1989: employment, establishments, and payroll, by SIC 2- to 4-digit industry and county, annual State rpt series, 2326–8
County Business Patterns, 1990: employment, establishments, and payroll, by SIC 2- to 4-digit industry and county, annual State rpt series, 2326–6
CPI by component for US city average, and by selected metro area, region, and population size, monthly rpt, 6762–2
Employment, earnings, and hours, by SIC 1- to 4-digit industry, monthly 1989-Feb 1992, annual rpt, 6744–4
Employment, unemployment, and labor force characteristics, by region and census div, 1991, annual rpt, 6744–7.1
Farm production itemized costs, receipts, and returns, by commodity and region, 1975-90, annual rpt, 1544–20
Farm production itemized costs, receipts, and returns, by crop and State, 1987-89, annual rpt, 1544–24
Fed Govt labor productivity, indexes of output and labor costs by function, FY67-90, annual rpt, 6824–1.6
Input-output structure of US economy, detailed interindustry transactions for 541 industries, and components of final demand, 1982 benchmark data, 2708–17
Military prime contract awards, by detailed procurement category, FY88-91, annual rpt, 3544–18
Multinatl firms US affiliates finances and operations, by industry, country of parent firm, and State, 1987, 2708–48
Multinatl US firms and foreign affiliates finances and operations, by industry and country, 1989 benchmark survey, annual rpt, 2704–5
Natl income and product accounts, comprehensive accounts and components, benchmark revisions, 1929-88, 2708–5
Natl income and product accounts, comprehensive accounts and components, *Survey of Current Business*, monthly rpt, 2702–1.29
Occupational injury and illness rates, by SIC 2- to 4-digit industry, 1989-90, annual rpt, 6844–7
Occupational injury and illness rates, by SIC 2- to 4-digit industry, 1990, annual rpt, 6844–1
Occupational Outlook Handbook, 1992-93, biennial rpt, 6744–1
Rice production, practices, costs, and land tenure, by production area, 1988, 1568–309
Tax (income) returns filed, by type of filer, selected income items, quarterly rpt, 8302–2.1
Tax (income) returns of corporations, income and tax items by asset size and detailed industry, 1989, annual rpt, 8304–4; 8304–21
Tax (income) returns of partnerships, income statement and balance sheet items, by industry group, 1990, annual article, 8302–2.314
Tax (income) returns of sole proprietorships, income statement items, by industry group, 1990, annual article, 8302–2.317; 8302–2.320
Transit systems finances and operations, by mode, size of fleet and urban area, region, and for 518 systems, 1990, annual rpt, 7884–4
see also Automobile repair and maintenance
see also Housing maintenance and repair
see also Shipbuilding and repairing

Repak, Terry A.

" 'They Come on Behalf of Their Children': Central American Families in Washington, D.C.", 6366–6.3

Republic of China

see Taiwan

Republic of Korea

see Korea, South

Republic of Yemen

see Yemen

Republican Party

Campaign finances, elections, procedures, and Fed Election Commission activities, press release series, 9276–1
Campaign finances reported to Fed Election Commission, by type of filer, 1990 natl elections, biennial rpt series, 9276–2

Campaign-related internal communications of firms and assns, spending by organization, location, and candidate, 1991-92, biennial rpt, 9274–3
Statistical Abstract of US, 1992 annual data compilation, 2324–1.8
Votes cast by party, candidate, and State, 1990 natl elections, biennial rpt, 21944–3

Research
County Business Patterns, 1989: employment, establishments, and payroll, by SIC 2- to 4-digit industry and county, annual State rpt series, 2326–8
County Business Patterns, 1990: employment, establishments, and payroll, by SIC 2- to 4-digit industry and county, annual State rpt series, 2326–6
Crime and criminal justice research results, series, 6066–20
Employment, earnings, and hours, by SIC 1- to 4-digit industry, monthly 1989-Feb 1992, annual rpt, 6744–4
Environmental Quality, status of problems, protection programs, research, and intl issues, 1991 annual rpt, 484–1
Fulbright-Hays academic exchanges, grants by purpose, and foreign govt share of costs, by country, FY91, annual rpt, 10324–1
Great Lakes Science Advisory Board research activities and water quality goals, FY91, biennial rpt, 14644–6
Higher education enrollment, faculty, finances, and degrees, by instn level and control, and State, FY88, annual rpt, 4844–13
Higher education instn revenue by source and spending by function, by State and instn control, FY82-90, annual rpt, 4844–6
Juvenile justice issues, data on young offenders and victims, series, 6066–27
Occupational injury and illness rates, by SIC 2- to 4-digit industry, 1989-90, annual rpt, 6844–7
Occupational injury and illness rates, by SIC 2- to 4-digit industry, 1990, annual rpt, 6844–1
Tax (income) returns filed, by type of filer, selected income items, quarterly rpt, 8302–2.1
Tax (income) returns of corporations, income and tax items by asset size and detailed industry, 1989, annual rpt, 8304–21
see also Agricultural sciences and research
see also Animal experimentation
see also Business outlook and attitude surveys
see also Consumer surveys
see also Defense research
see also Demonstration and pilot projects
see also Educational research
see also Energy research and development
see also Federal funding for research and development
see also Human experimentation
see also Market research
see also Medical research
see also Opinion and attitude surveys
see also Research and development
see also Research journals
see also Statistical programs and activities
see also under specific academic and scientific disciplines

Research & Training Associates, Inc.
"Unlocking Learning: Chapter 1 in Correctional Facilities. National Study of the Chapter 1 Neglected or Delinquent Program", 4808–40

Research and development
Arkansas govt science agency research grants and industry sponsors matching funds, and Federal R&D aid to higher education instns, mid 1980s-90, hearing, 21708–131
County Business Patterns, 1989: employment, establishments, and payroll, by SIC 2- to 4-digit industry and county, annual State rpt series, 2326–8
County Business Patterns, 1990: employment, establishments, and payroll, by SIC 2- to 4-digit industry and county, annual State rpt series, 2326–6
Employment of scientists and engineers, by sex, race, and primary work activity, 1986, biennial rpt, 9624–20.1
Environmental Quality, status of problems, protection programs, research, and intl issues, 1991 annual rpt, 484–1
Food marketing sector R&D spending, 1984-90, annual rpt, 1544–22.3
Foreign direct investment by method and industry div, and affiliated firms R&D spending, pay, employment, and trade compared to US-owned firms, 1980-90, article, 9391–1.309
Higher education instn and federally funded center R&D funding, by field, instn, and State, FY90, annual rpt, 9627–13
Higher education instn R&D facilities space and equipment adequacy, needs, and funding by source, by instn type and control, 1992, biennial rpt, 9624–25
Higher education PhD degree recipients employment plans, by employer type, work activity, and field, 1979, 1984, and 1989, 4848–44
Hwy construction and design R&D, quarterly journal, 7552–3
Industry (US) intl competitiveness, with selected foreign and US operating data by major firm and product, series, 2046–12
Input-output structure of US economy, detailed interindustry transactions for 541 industries, and components of final demand, 1982 benchmark data, 2708–17
Intl competitiveness of US high technology industries, with background data by industry and foreign comparisons, 1960s-91, GAO rpt, 26123–406
Japan R&D activities of US firms, employee characteristics, and mgmt views on benefits and drawbacks, 1991 rpt, 9628–88
Machinery and equipment trade, tariffs, and industry operating data, commodity rpt series, 9885–9
Manufacturing employment of scientists, engineers, and technicians, by field and industry, 1989, triennial rpt, 9627–23
Manufacturing industry (US) intl competitiveness, trade and economic policies with background data and foreign comparisons, 1991 rpt, 26358–252
Militarily strategic manufacturing industries finances, operations, and intl competitiveness, series, 2026–1
Multinatl firms US affiliates, finances, and operations, by industry, world area of parent firm, and State, 1989-90, annual rpt, 2704–4
Multinatl US firms and foreign affiliates finances and operations, by industry and country, 1989 benchmark survey, annual rpt, 2704–5
Multinatl US firms and foreign affiliates finances and operations, by industry and world area, 1988, annual article, 2702–1.329
Pollution abatement spending by govts, business, and consumers, 1972-90, annual article, 2702–1.321
Science and Engineering Indicators, employment, education, R&D funding, and industry impacts, with foreign comparisons, 1960s-91, biennial rpt, 9624–10
Science and engineering labor force, Federal and university research funding, and educational data, series, 9626–6
Semiconductor industry (US) intl competitiveness, status, and outlook, working paper series, 15036–1
Small businesses in high technology, R&D funding relation to finances, 1991 working paper, 9375–13.75
Statistical Abstract of US, 1992 annual data compilation, 2324–1.20
Tax (income) returns of corporations, income and tax items by asset size and detailed industry, 1989, annual rpt, 8304–4
Transit systems research rpts, 1991, annual listing, 7884–11
see also Defense research
see also Demonstration and pilot projects
see also Energy research and development
see also Federal funding for research and development
see also Federally Funded R&D Centers
see also Inventions
see also Technological innovations

Research journals
Alcohol abuse research, treatment programs, and patient characteristics and health effects, quarterly journal, 4482–1
Cancer epidemiology and biochemistry research, semimonthly journal, 4472–1
Ceramics (advanced) research publication releases in 6 countries, by subfield, selected years 1965-90, hearing, 21708–130
Drug (prescription) advertising in medical journals, accuracy, info completeness, and violations of FDA regulations, 1990, 4008–119
Drug abuse and treatment research summaries, and resource materials and grant listings, bimonthly rpt, 4492–4
Forest Service Rocky Mountain Forest and Range Experiment Station rpts, 1980-89, listing, 1208–403
Geological Survey rpts and research journal articles, monthly listing, 5662–1
Geological Survey rpts, 1991, annual listing, 5664–4
Health Care Financing Review, quarterly journal, 4652–1
Health condition and quality of life measurement, rpts and other info sources, quarterly listing, 4122–1
Intl competitiveness of US high technology industries, with background data by industry and foreign comparisons, 1960s-91, GAO rpt, 26123–406

Morbidity and Mortality Weekly Report, infectious notifiable disease cases and deaths, and other public health issues, periodic journal, 4202–7
Morbidity and Mortality Weekly Report, infectious notifiable disease cases by State, and public health issues, 4202–1
NOAA Environmental Research Labs rpts, FY91, annual listing, 2144–25
NSF rpts, 1992 annual listing, 9624–16
Nuclear power plant decommissioning and radioactive waste site remedial actions, bibl, 1991 annual listing, 3354–12
Public Health Reports, bimonthly journal, 4042–3
Scientific journal articles, by field for foreign and US sources, 1973-87, biennial rpt, 9624–10.5
Social Security Bulletin, OASDHI and other program operations and beneficiary characteristics, from 1940, quarterly journal, 4742–1
Transit systems research rpts, 1991, annual listing, 7884–11
VA Geriatric Research, Education and Clinical Centers activities and finances, FY88, annual rpt, 8704–8
Vaccination research rpts, 1991 annual listing, 4204–16

Research Triangle Institute
"Prevalence of Drug Use in the D.C. Metropolitan Area Household Population: 1990", 4496–12.1

Reserve components
see Armed services reserves
see Coast Guard Reserve
see Marine Reserve
see National Guard

Reserve Officers Training Corps
Black military and civilian DOD personnel, by sex, grade, and period of service, and lists of award recipients, officers, and service academy grads, 1770s-90, 3548–22
Budget of DOD, organization, personnel, weapons, and property, by service branch, State, and country, 1992 annual summary rpt, 3504–13
Expenditures for education by Federal agency, program, and recipient type, and instn spending, 1960s-91, annual rpt, 4824–8
Expenditures, staff, students, and facilities for DOD training and education programs, by service branch, FY93, annual rpt, 3504–5
Health care personnel, and accessions by training source, by occupation, specialty, and service branch, FY90, annual rpt, 3544–24

Reservoirs
Agricultural Conservation Program acreage and projects, by State, 1936-90, quinquennial rpt, 1808–1
Agricultural Conservation Program participation and payments, by practice and State, FY91, annual rpt, 1804–7
Army Corps of Engineers activities and projects, FY88 and trends from 1800s, annual rpt, 3754–1.1
Army Corps of Engineers activities and projects, FY89 and trends from 1800s, annual rpt, 3754–1.2
Army Corps of Engineers activities and projects, FY90 and trends from 1800s, annual rpt, 3754–1.3
Army Corps of Engineers water resources dev projects, characteristics, and costs, 1950s-89, biennial State rpt series, 3756–1
Army Corps of Engineers water resources dev projects, characteristics, and costs, 1950s-91, biennial State rpt series, 3756–2
Colorado River Basin Federal reservoir and power operations and revenues, 1991-92, annual rpt, 5824–6
Colorado water supply, streamflow, precipitation, and reservoir storage, 1992 water year, annual rpt, 1264–13
Fish Hatchery Natl System activities and deliveries, by species, hatchery, and jurisdiction of waters stocked, FY91, annual rpt, 5504–10
Oregon water supply, streamflow by station and reservoir storage, 1992, annual rpt, 1264–9
Public lands acreage, grants, use, revenues, and allocations, by State, FY91, annual rpt, 5724–1.2
Reclamation Bur irrigation activities, finances, and project impacts in western US, 1990, annual rpt, 5824–12
Reclamation Bur water storage and carriage facilities, capacity, and operating status, as of Sept 1990, biennial listing, 5824–7
Tennessee Valley river control activities, and hydroelectric power generation and capacity, 1990, annual rpt, 9804–7
TVA finances and operations by program and facility, FY91, annual rpt, 9804–32
Water quality, chemistry, hydrology, and other characteristics, local area studies, series, 5666–27
Water supply and quality in streams and lakes, and groundwater levels in wells, by drainage basin, 1990, annual State rpt series, 5666–10
Water supply and quality in streams and lakes, and groundwater levels in wells, by drainage basin, 1990-91, annual CD-ROM, 5664–18
Water supply and quality in streams and lakes, and groundwater levels in wells, by drainage basin, 1991, annual State rpt series, 5666–12
Water supply in US and southern Canada, streamflow, surface and groundwater conditions, and reservoir levels, by location, monthly rpt, 5662–3
Western US water supply, and snow survey results, monthly State rpt series, 1266–2
Western US water supply, storage by reservoir and State, and streamflow conditions, as of Oct 1992, annual rpt, 1264–4
Western US water supply, streamflow and reservoir storage forecasts by stream and station, Jan-May monthly rpt, 1262–1

Residential energy use
see Housing energy use

Resins
see Gum and wood chemicals
see Plastics and plastics industry
see Polymers

Resolution Trust Corp.
Activities and finances of RTC, with data on savings instn conservatorships by instn and State, 1990, annual rpt, 9724–1
Assets disposition by RTC, use of private contractors, fees paid, and location of assets, 1990-91, GAO rpt, 26119–424
Bond (junk) holdings of RTC, quarterly press release, 9722–4
Budget deficit forecasting accuracy, contributing factors, and analysis of major programs, FY91, annual GAO rpt, 26104–23
Budget of US, authoritative financial statements with appropriations, outlays, and receipts, by category and agency, FY91, annual rpt, 8104–2.2
Budget of US, CBO analysis of revenue and spending alternatives and projections of economic indicators, FY93-97, annual rpt, 26304–3
Budget of US, obligations and authority by function, agency, and program, with summaries and analyses, FY93, annual rpt, 104–2
Fed Govt finances, cash and debt transactions, daily tables, 8102–4
Fraud and abuse in RTC programs, audits and investigations, 2nd half FY92, semiannual rpt, 9722–6
Monetary aggregate (M2) growth relation to RTC failed thrift resolution activity and other factors, 1990-91, article, 9379–1.303
Monetary aggregate (M2) growth relation to RTC failed thrift resolution activity, 1990-91, technical paper, 9379–12.83
Obligation limits compliance by RTC, with balance sheet, quarterly GAO rpt, 26102–6
Real estate assets marketing activities of RTC, real estate industry views, 1991 survey, GAO rpt, 26119–422
Real estate assets of failed thrifts, inventory of properties available from RTC, semiannual listing series, 9722–2
Real estate assets of failed thrifts, sales by RTC, and disposition of other assets, 1990-91, GAO rpt, 26119–372
Savings instns failure resolution activity and finances of RTC, with data by asset type, State, region, and instn, monthly rpt, 9722–3
Savings instns failure resolution activity of RTC, assets, deposits, and assets availability and sales, periodic press release, 9722–1
Savings instns failure resolution activity of RTC, brokered deposits, fees, and interest rates by instn and region, as of July 1991, hearing, 21248–171
Savings instns failures, financial performance of instns under RTC conservatorship, quarterly rpt, 9722–5

Resorts
see Hotels and motels

Respiratory diseases
Acid rain environmental, economic, and health effects, and pollutant emissions, 1985-89 and alternative projections to 2030, 14358–4
Cancer (lung) risk relation to environmental smoke exposure, for nonsmoking women, local area study, 1992 article, 4472–1.342
Cancer (mesothelioma) patient deaths, by cause of death reported on death certificates, for Massachusetts, 1982-89, article, 4042–3.351
Cancer (ovarian and lung) MDR1 gene levels, by type of treatment, 1992 article, 4472–1.345

Cancer deaths and rates, by body site and selected social, demographic, and employment characteristics, 1979-85, natl longitudinal study, 4478–186
Cancer deaths and rates, by body site, provisional data, monthly rpt, 4142–1.2
Cases of acute and chronic conditions, disability, absenteeism, and health services use, by selected characteristics, 1990, annual rpt, 4147–10.182; 4147–10.183
Deaths and rates, by cause, age, sex, marital status, race, and State, 1989, US Vital Statistics advance annual rpt, 4146–5.124
Deaths and rates, by cause and age, preliminary 1990-91, US Vital Statistics annual rpt, 4144–7
Deaths and rates, by cause and selected social, demographic, and employment characteristics, 1979-85, natl longitudinal study, 4478–186
Deaths and rates, by cause, provisional data, monthly rpt, 4142–1.2
Deaths and rates, by detailed location, cause, and demographic characteristics, 1989, US Vital Statistics annual rpt, 4144–3
Deaths during 1986, decedents health condition, services use, habits, and social, employment, and other characteristics, 4147–20.19
Disability and work limitations of persons with chronic health conditions, by condition, age, and sex, 1983-86, 4946–1.2
Health condition and care indicators, 1950s-90 with health improvement and disease prevention goals for 1990, annual data compilation, 4144–11
HHS financial aid, by program, recipient, State, and city, FY91, annual regional listings, 4004–3
Hospital deaths of Medicare patients, actual and expected rates by diagnosis, with hospital characteristics, by instn, FY90, annual State rpt series, 4654–14
Hospital discharges and length of stay, by diagnosis, patient and instn characteristics, procedure performed, and payment source, 1990, annual rpt, 4147–13.112
Hospital discharges and length of stay by region and diagnosis, and procedures performed, by age and sex, 1990, annual rpt, 4146–8.211
Hospital discharges and length of stay under old and new survey designs, by diagnosis, patient and instn characteristics, and procedure, Jan-Mar 1988, 4147–13.110
Hospital discharges by detailed diagnostic and procedure category, primary diagnosis, and length of stay, by age, sex, and region, 1990, annual rpt, 4147–13.111
Hospitalization for pulmonary edema and respiratory failure, diagnostic coding errors, substandard care, and Medicare costs, 1980s, 4006–7.6
Hungary child respiratory disease cases, by type, age, and air pollution levels, for Sopron, 1990, article, 4202–7.319
Indian Health Service, tribal, and contract facilities hospitalization, by diagnosis, age, sex, and service area, FY91, annual rpt, 4084–5
Medicare payment of physicians, reforms impacts on services, and monitoring methods, 1992 annual rpt, 4004–34
Natl Heart, Lung, and Blood Inst activities, and Advisory Council recommendations, 1991 narrative rpt, 4474–22
Natl Heart, Lung, and Blood Inst activities, and grants by recipient and location, FY91 and disease trends from 1940, annual rpt, 4474–15
Natl Inst of Allergy and Infectious Diseases activities, grants by recipient and location, and disease cases, FY84-91, annual rpt, 4474–30
Occupational illness rates, by cause and SIC 2- to 3-digit industry, 1990, annual rpt, 6844–1
OECD members health care costs, hospital use, resources, and economic and health indicators, by country, 1960s-90, article, 4652–1.322
Physicians visits, by patient and practice characteristics, diagnosis, and services provided, 1989, annual rpt, 4147–13.109
Pollutants health effects, concentrations in food and environment, sources, human intake, and regulation, series, 9186–8
Smoking and health effects, with trends in smoking, related disease and death, and public attitudes, literature review, 1992 annual rpt, 4204–18
Smoking control strategies effectiveness, with data on research funding, smoking prevalence, cancer deaths, and taxation, 1900s-91, 4476–7.1
Smoking, tobacco, and health impacts research rpts, 1991 annual report, 4204–19
Transplants of hearts and lungs, failures, deaths, and survival rates, by hospital, 1987-89, annual rpt, 4104–17.5
Veterans disability and death compensation cases of VA, by entitlement type, period of service, and sex, as of Mar 1992, annual rpt, 8604–13
Veterans disability and death compensation cases of VA, by entitlement type, period of service, sex, age, and State, FY90, annual rpt, 8604–7
see also Black lung disease
see also Nose and throat disorders
see also Pneumonia and influenza
see also Respiratory therapy
see also Tuberculosis
see also under By Disease in the "Index by Categories"

Respiratory therapy
Hospital employment and job vacancy rate, by occupation, and instn size and control, 1981-88, annual rpt, 4114–12
Intermittent positive pressure breathing therapy risks and benefit evaluation for Medicare coverage, 1991 rpt, 4186–10.6
Labor demand, turnover, and training completions, by detailed occupation, 1990 and projected to 2005, biennial rpt, 6744–3
Labor supply and education of health professionals, by professional and other characteristics, and location, 1960s-92 and projected to 2020, biennial rpt, 4114–8
Occupational Outlook Handbook, 1992-93, biennial rpt, 6744–1
VA health care staff and turnover, by occupation, physician specialty, and location, 1991, annual rpt, 8604–8

Response Analysis Corp.
"Low Income Home Energy Trends, 1979-89", 4588–2

Rest homes
see Nursing homes

Restaurants and drinking places
Agricultural Statistics, 1991, annual rpt, 1004–1
Blind-operated vending facilities on Federal and non-Federal property, finances and operations by agency and State, FY91, annual rpt, 4944–2
Business statistics, detailed data for major industries and economic indicators, *Survey of Current Business*, monthly rpt, 2702–1.10
Business statistics, detailed data for major industries and economic indicators, 1960-91, *Survey of Current Business* biennial supplement, 2704–1
Collective bargaining agreements expiring during year, and workers covered, by firm, union, industry group, and State, 1992, annual rpt, 6784–9
Consumer Expenditure Survey, spending by category, and income, by selected household characteristics, 1991, annual press release, 6726–1.53
Consumer Expenditure Survey, spending by category, selected household characteristics, and region, quarterly rpt, 6762–14
Consumer research, food marketing, legislation, and regulation devs, and consumption and price trends, quarterly journal, 1541–7
Consumer spending, natl income and product account benchmark revisions, 1929-88, 2708–5
Consumer spending, natl income and product accounts, comprehensive accounts and components, *Survey of Current Business*, monthly rpt, 2702–1.25
County Business Patterns, 1989: employment, establishments, and payroll, by SIC 2- to 4-digit industry and county, annual State rpt series, 2326–8
County Business Patterns, 1990: employment, establishments, and payroll, by SIC 2- to 4-digit industry and county, annual State rpt series, 2326–6
CPI by component for US city average, and by selected metro area, region, and population size, monthly rpt, 6762–2
Crime victimization rates, by victim and offender characteristics, circumstances, and offense, 1990 survey, annual rpt, 6066–3.47
Employment and receipts of travel-related industries, 1988, 7556–8.3
Employment, earnings, and hours, by SIC 1- to 4-digit industry, monthly 1989-Feb 1992, annual rpt, 6744–4
Energy use in commercial buildings, costs, and conservation, by building characteristics, survey rpt series, 3166–8
Expenditures for food and alcoholic beverages by place of purchase, and CPI, 1970-91, annual rpt, 1544–4.5
Expenditures for food at and away from home, by selected characteristics, 1989, article, 1702–1.308
Fast food nutrient, caloric, and waste composition, 1992 rpt, 1356–3.17

Finances, operations, and merger activity, for food processors and distributors, 1991, annual rpt, 1544–22
Food product manufacturers shipments to eating and drinking outlets in own and other firms, by SIC 4-digit industry, 1987 Census of Manufactures, subject rpt, 2497–4
Foreign travelers to US, spending by world area of residence, and economic impacts, by spending category and State, 1989, 2908–28
Higher education instn room and board charges, and meals covered, by public and private 2- and 4-year instn, and State, 1991/92, annual listing, 4844–10
Immigration Reform and Control Act employer sanctions impacts on labor markets, with data for selected industries and metro areas, 1980s, working paper, 6366–6.10
Input-output structure of US economy, detailed interindustry transactions for 84 industries, and components of final demand, 1987, annual article, 2702–1.316
Input-output structure of US economy, detailed interindustry transactions for 541 industries, and components of final demand, 1982 benchmark data, 2708–17
Insurance (health) coverage of food service employees, 1988-89, hearings, 25368–180
Labor productivity, indexes of output, hours, and employment by SIC 2- to 4-digit industry, 1967-90, annual rpt, 6824–1.4
Mail volume to and from households, use, and views, by class, source, content, and household characteristics, FY87-90, annual rpt, 9864–10
Multinatl firms US affiliates finances and operations, by industry, country of parent firm, and State, 1987, 2708–48
Occupational injury and illness rates and lost workdays, for selected industries, 1978-89, compilation of papers, 6728–41
Occupational injury and illness rates, by SIC 2- to 4-digit industry, 1989-90, annual rpt, 6844–7
Occupational injury and illness rates, by SIC 2- to 4-digit industry, 1990, annual rpt, 6844–1
Occupational Outlook Handbook, 1992-93, biennial rpt, 6744–1
Pacific territories population and housing detailed characteristics, by location, 1990 Census of Population and Housing, series, 2551–8
Prices (farm-retail) for food, marketing cost components, and industry finances and productivity, 1920s-91, annual rpt, 1544–9
Sales and inventories, by kind of retail business, region, and selected State, MSA, and city, monthly rpt, 2413–3
Sales, inventories, purchases, gross margin, and accounts receivable, by SIC 2- to 4-digit kind of business and form of ownership, 1990, annual rpt, 2413–5
Sales of retailers, by kind of business, advance monthly rpt, 2413–2
Savings instns failures, inventory of real estate assets available from Resolution Trust Corp, 1991, semiannual listing, 9722–2.1
Savings instns failures, inventory of real estate assets available from Resolution Trust Corp, 1992, semiannual listing, 9722–2.8
Statistical Abstract of US, 1992 annual data compilation, 2324–1.28
Tax (income) returns of corporations, income and tax items by asset size and detailed industry, 1989, annual rpt, 8304–4; 8304–21
Tax (income) returns of partnerships, income statement and balance sheet items, by industry group, 1990, annual article, 8302–2.314
Tax (income) returns of sole proprietorships, income statement items, by industry group, 1990, annual article, 8302–2.317; 8302–2.320
Technological devs effect on labor force, composition, and productivity, 1970s-90 and projected to 2005, industry rpt, 6826–2.9
Women-headed households food spending, by item and selected characteristics, and compared to other households, 1970s-88, 1548–391

Restitution
see Crime victim compensation
see Fines and settlements

Retail centers
see Shopping centers

Retail trade
Buildings (commercial and public) alteration and repair spending, by type, size, age, and region, 1989, 2388–4
Business activity indicators, 1990, annual rpt, 9364–5.9
Business statistics, detailed data for major industries and economic indicators, *Survey of Current Business*, monthly rpt, 2702–1.6
Business statistics, detailed data for major industries and economic indicators, 1960-91, *Survey of Current Business* biennial supplement, 2704–1
Census Bur data files and rpts, coverage and availability, 1992 annual listing, 2304–2
Coastal areas construction authorized by permit, by building type, 1970-89, 2176–8.3
Collective bargaining agreements expiring during year, and workers covered, by firm, union, industry group, and State, 1992, annual rpt, 6784–9
County Business Patterns, 1989: employment, establishments, and payroll, by SIC 2- to 4-digit industry and county, annual State rpt series, 2326–8
County Business Patterns, 1990: employment, establishments, and payroll, by SIC 2- to 4-digit industry and county, annual State rpt series, 2326–6
Credit (installment) outstanding and terms, by lender and credit type, monthly rpt, 9365–2.6
Credit (installment) outstanding, by type of holder, *Survey of Current Business*, monthly rpt, 2702–1.8
Deaths and rates, by cause and selected social, demographic, and employment characteristics, 1979-85, natl longitudinal study, 4478–186
Earnings, weekly averages, monthly rpt, 23842–1.2
Economic indicators and components, and Fed Reserve 4th District business and financial conditions, monthly chartbook, 9377–10
Economic indicators compounded annual rates of change, monthly rpt, 9391–3
Economic indicators, monthly rpt, 9362–1.2
Employment and Earnings, detailed data, monthly rpt, 6742–2.5
Employment Cost Index and alternative measure of compensation costs, by component, occupation, industry group, union status, and location, 1975-92, annual rpt, 6744–20
Employment, earnings, and hours, by selected SIC 1- to 4-digit industry, State, and for 275 MSAs, 1987-92, 6748–81
Employment, earnings, and hours, by SIC 1- to 4-digit industry, monthly 1989-Feb 1992, annual rpt, 6744–4
Employment, earnings, and hours, monthly press release, 6742–5
Employment of minorities and women, by occupation, SIC 1- to 3-digit industry, State, and MSA, 1991, annual rpt, 9244–1
Employment situation, earnings, hours, and other BLS economic indicators, transcripts of BLS Commissioner's monthly testimony, periodic rpt, 23846–4
Employment, unemployment, and labor force characteristics, by region and census div, 1991, annual rpt, 6744–7.1
Finance companies credit outstanding and leasing activities, by credit type, monthly rpt, 9365–2.7
Finances and operations, by SIC 2- to 4-digit industry, forecast 1992, annual rpt, 2044–28
Financial statements for manufacturing, mining, and trade corporations, by selected SIC 2- to 3-digit industry, quarterly rpt, 2502–1
Foreign-controlled US firms transactions with related foreign persons, by type, industry div, and country, 1988, article, 8302–2.318
Foreign direct investment in US, by industry group and world area, 1989-91, annual article, 2702–1.331
Foreign direct investment in US, major transactions by type, industry, country, and US location, 1990, annual rpt, 2044–20
Foreign direct investment of US, by industry group and world area, 1989-91, annual article, 2702–1.332
Foreign travelers to US, spending by world area of residence, and economic impacts, by spending category and State, 1989, 2908–28
GDP forecasts for current quarter, performance of monthly advance indicators, 1981-91, article, 9393–8.305
Gross State Product by component, industry div, and State, 1977-89, article, 2702–1.303
Income tax returns of foreign corporations and individuals, and US entities abroad, detailed data compilation, 1970s-89, quinquennial rpt, 8308–31
Input-output structure of US economy, detailed interindustry transactions for 541 industries, and components of final demand, 1982 benchmark data, 2708–17

Inventories related to sales, by industry sector, model description and results, late 1960s-91, article, 9389–1.302
Labor productivity, indexes of output, hours, and employment by SIC 2- to 4-digit industry, 1967-90, annual rpt, 6824–1.4
Manufacturing census, 1987: shipments of manufacturers products, by customer class and SIC 2- and 4-digit industry, subject rpt, 2497–4
Minority- and woman-owned businesses and owner characteristics, by industry, employment and sales size, and form of ownership, 1987 survey, 2328–59
Multinatl firms US affiliates finances and operations, by industry, country of parent firm, and State, 1987, 2708–48
Multinatl firms US affiliates, finances, and operations, by industry, world area of parent firm, and State, 1989-90, annual rpt, 2704–4
Multinatl US firms and foreign affiliates finances and operations, by industry and country, 1989 benchmark survey, annual rpt, 2704–5
Multinatl US firms foreign affiliates, income statement items by asset size, industry, and country, 1988, biennial article, 8302–2.322
Natl income and product accounts, comprehensive accounts and components, benchmark revisions, 1929-88, 2708–5
Natl income and product accounts, comprehensive accounts and components, *Survey of Current Business*, monthly rpt, 2702–1.29
New England States economic indicators, Fed Reserve 1st District, monthly rpt, 9373–2
North Central States business and economic conditions, Fed Reserve 9th District, quarterly journal, 9383–19
Occupational injuries, illnesses, and lost workdays, by SIC 2-digit industry, 1990-91, annual press release, 6844–3
Occupational injury and illness rates by circumstances and establishment size, and methodology for computing rates, 1988, industry rpt, 6886–4.4
Occupational injury and illness rates, by SIC 2- to 4-digit industry, 1989-90, annual rpt, 6844–7
Occupational injury and illness rates, by SIC 2- to 4-digit industry, 1990, annual rpt, 6844–1
Pacific territories population and housing detailed characteristics, by location, 1990 Census of Population and Housing, series, 2551–8
Puerto Rico and other US possessions corporations income tax returns, income and tax items, and employment, by selected industry, 1989, article, 8302–2.326
Sales and inventories, by kind of retail business, region, and selected State, MSA, and city, monthly rpt, 2413–3
Sales and inventories, monthly rpt, 23842–1.3
Sales, inventories, purchases, gross margin, and accounts receivable, by SIC 2- to 4-digit kind of business and form of ownership, 1990, annual rpt, 2413–5
Sales of retailers, by kind of business, advance monthly rpt, 2413–2
SEC registration, firms required to file annual rpts, as of Sept 1991, annual listing, 9734–5
Small Business Admin loan guarantee program participants finances, operations, characteristics, and views, 1991 survey, 9768–25
Small business finances, operations, owner characteristics, and Federal contracts, 1980s-90, annual rpt, 9764–6
Southeastern US employment by industry div, earnings, and hours, for 8 States, quarterly press release, 6942–7
Soviet Union and US economic and sociodemographic indicators, selected years 1970-90, handbook, 2328–80
Statistical Abstract of US, 1992 annual data compilation, 2324–1.28
Tax (income) returns filed, by type of filer, selected income items, quarterly rpt, 8302–2.1
Tax (income) returns of corporations, income and tax items by asset size and detailed industry, 1989, annual rpt, 8304–4; 8304–21
Tax (income) returns of corporations with foreign tax credit, income and tax items by industry group, 1988, biennial article, 8302–2.316
Tax (income) returns of partnerships, income statement and balance sheet items, by industry group, 1990, annual article, 8302–2.314
Tax (income) returns of sole proprietorships, income statement items, by industry group, 1990, annual article, 8302–2.317; 8302–2.320
Wage and benefit changes from collective bargaining and mgmt decisions, by industry div, monthly rpt, 6782–1
Wages by occupation, and benefits for office and plant workers, periodic MSA survey rpt series, 6785–12; 6785–16; 6785–17
see also Advertising
see also Census of Retail Trade
see also Consumer credit
see also Consumer protection
see also Credit cards
see also Department stores
see also Direct marketing
see also Drugstores
see also Food stores
see also Gasoline service stations
see also Labeling
see also Military post exchanges and commissaries
see also Packaging and containers
see also Restaurants and drinking places
see also Sales promotion
see also Sales workers
see also Shopping centers
see also Vending machines and stands
see also Warehouses
see also Wholesale trade
see also under By Industry in the "Index by Categories"
see also under names of specific commodities or commodity groups

Retired military personnel
Annuitants, DOD retired military personnel, FY50-91, annual rpt, 3544–1.4
Black military and civilian DOD personnel, by sex, grade, and period of service, and lists of award recipients, officers, and service academy grads, 1770s-90, 3548–22
Budget of DOD, organization, personnel, weapons, and property, by service branch, State, and country, 1992 annual summary rpt, 3504–13
Fed Govt civilian employees demographic and employment characteristics, as of Sept 1991, annual article, 9842–1.301
Health care facilities of DOD in US and abroad, beds, admissions, outpatient visits, and births, by service branch, quarterly rpt, 3542–15
Health care retired personnel, by specialty, FY90, annual rpt, 3544–24.8
Navy personnel strengths, accessions, and attrition, detailed statistics, quarterly rpt, 3802–4
Pacific territories population and housing detailed characteristics, by location, 1990 Census of Population and Housing, series, 2551–8
Persian Gulf War US military retirees called to active duty, FY91, annual rpt, 3544–31.1
Reserve forces personnel and equipment strengths, and readiness, by reserve component, FY91, annual rpt, 3544–31
Reserve forces personnel strengths and characteristics, by component, quarterly rpt, 3542–4
see also Civilian Health and Medical Program of the Uniformed Services
see also Military benefits and pensions
see also Veterans

Retired Senior Volunteer Program
Activities and funding of ACTION, by program, FY91, annual rpt, 9024–2

Retirement
Age at retirement, and older persons labor force status, by sex, 1950s-90 and projected to 2005, article, 6722–1.332
Air traffic control and airway facilities staff, by employment and other characteristics, FY90, annual rpt, 7504–41
Deaths during 1986, decedents health condition, services use, habits, and social, employment, and other characteristics, 4147–20.19
DOT employment, by subagency, occupation, and selected personnel characteristics, FY91, annual rpt, 7304–18
Fed Govt civilian employees demographic characteristics, by agency, 1990, GAO rpt, 26119–383
Fed Govt personnel action appeals, decisions of Merit Systems Protection Board by agency and region, FY91, annual rpt, 9494–2
Financial status of families, income, net worth, and assets and debt by type, by income and selected characteristics, 1983 and 1989, article, 9362–1.301
Health insurance coverage for State and local govt employees after retirement, 1990, biennial rpt, 6784–21
Insurance (health) provided by employer, costs and cost factors by industry div and firm size, 1987-91, GAO rpt, 26121–485
Medicare service use and charges of retirees related to prior health and other characteristics, 1984, article, 4652–1.319
NASA staff characteristics and personnel actions, FY91, annual rpt, 9504–1
OASI benefits, earnings, and tax revenues under alternative eligibility criteria, 1990, technical paper, 4746–26.15

OECD pension plan finances, participation, and benefits, for 9 countries, with data by firm and worker characteristics, 1990 conf, 6688–2
Older persons socioeconomic characteristics, 1900s-90 and projected to 2050, biennial chartbook, 12904–1
Population size and components of change, alternative projections 1990-2080 and trends from 1900, annual actuarial rpt, 4706–1.106
Poverty status of population and families, by detailed characteristics, 1991, annual Current Population Rpt, 2546–6.77
Public opinion on OASDHI and health care system operations and reform issues, 1991 surveys, 10176–2.2
Research on employment and retirement, bibl, 1990 listing, 4746–26.14
see also Civil service pensions
see also Employee benefits
see also Individual retirement arrangements
see also Old age assistance
see also Old-Age, Survivors, Disability, and Health Insurance
see also Pensions and pension funds
see also Retired military personnel
see also Retired Senior Volunteer Program

Reunion
Economic and social conditions of developing countries from 1960s, and Intl Dev Cooperation Agency and AID activities and funding, FY91-93, annual rpt, 9904–4
Economic, social, political, and geographic summary data, by country, 1992, annual factbook, 9114–2
Exports and imports of US, by transport mode, country, and SITC 1- to 3-digit commodity, 1991, annual rpt, 2424–12
Minerals Yearbook, Vol 3, 1989: foreign country review of production, trade, and policy, by commodity, annual rpt, 5604–35.1
Population size, growth rates, and components of change, by country, projected 1990-2020 and trends from 1950, biennial rpt, 2324–9

Revenue sharing
Education funding by Federal agency, program, and recipient type, and instn spending, 1960s-91, annual rpt, 4824–8
Forests (natl) revenue share paid to States, and acreage, by forest, county, and congressional district, FY92, annual rpt, 1204–33
Govt finances, by level of govt, State, and for large cities and counties, annual rpt series, 2466–2
Govt finances, tax systems and revenue, and fiscal structure, by level of govt and State, 1992 with historical trends, annual rpt, 10044–1
Hwy Trust Fund receipts by source, and apportionments, by State, 1991, annual rpt, 7554–1.3
Oil and gas OCS leases, revenue sharing payments by State, 1992 annual press release, 5306–4.14

Revzin, A. M.
"New Test of Scanning and Monitoring Ability: Methods and Initial Results", 7506–10.108

Reynolds, Bruce J.
"International Business Arrangements Used by Cooperatives", 1128–69

Rhind, Constance
"Experience of the Stafford Loan Program and Options for Change", 26306–3.120

Rhoades, Stephen A.
"Evidence on the Size of Banking Markets from Mortgage Loan Rates in Twenty Cities", 9366–1.162

Rhode Island
Banks (insured commercial and savings) deposits by instn, State, MSA, and county, as of June 1991, annual regional rpt, 9295–3.1
County Business Patterns, 1990: employment, establishments, and payroll, by SIC 2- to 4-digit industry and county, annual State rpt, 2326–6.41
Deaths and rates, by detailed location, cause, and demographic characteristics, 1989, US Vital Statistics annual rpt, 4144–3.1
Economic indicators for New England States, Fed Reserve 1st District, monthly rpt, 9373–2
Employment, earnings, and hours, by selected SIC 1- to 4-digit industry, State, and for 275 MSAs, 1987-92, 6748–81
Fed Govt spending in States and local areas, by type, State, county, and city, FY91, annual rpt, 2464–3
Fed Govt spending in States, by type, program, agency, and State, FY91, annual rpt, 2464–2
HHS financial aid, by program, recipient, State, and city, FY91, annual regional listing, 4004–3.1
Hospital deaths of Medicare patients, actual and expected rates by diagnosis, and hospital characteristics, by instn, FY90 annual State rpt, 4654–14.41
Housing census, 1990: inventory, occupancy, and costs, State fact sheet, 2326–21.41
Housing census, 1990: summary unit characteristics, by householder race and age, county, place, and urban-rural location, State rpt, 2471–1.41
Military prime contract awards, by contractor, service branch, State, and city, FY91, annual rpt, 3544–22
Mineral Industry Surveys, State reviews of production, 1991, preliminary annual rpt, 5614–6
Multinatl firms US affiliates finances and operations, by industry, country of parent firm, and State, 1987, 2708–48
Physicians, by specialty, age, sex, and location of training and practice, 1990, State rpt, 4116–6.41
Population and housing census, 1990: detailed geographic coverage, State CD-ROM, 2551–9.1
Population and housing census, 1990: population and housing characteristics, detailed geographic coverage, State CD-ROM, 2551–10.10
Population and housing census, 1990: summary characteristics, by county, subdiv, and place, State rpt, 2551–7.41
Population census, 1990: population characteristics and living arrangements, by county, place, and urban-rural location, State rpt, 2531–1.41
State govt pension funds use to balance budgets, with data for 2 States, 1991 hearing, 21148–66
Statistical Abstract of US, 1992 annual data compilation, 2324–1
Water (groundwater) supply, quality, chemistry, and use, 1989, State rpt, 5666–28.18
Water supply in northeastern US, precipitation and stream runoff by station, monthly rpt, 2182–3
see also Providence, R.I.
see also under By State in the "Index by Categories"

Rhodesia
see Zimbabwe

Rice
Acreage planted and harvested, by crop and State, 1990-91 and planned as of June 1992, annual rpt, 1621–23
Acreage planted, by selected crop and State, 1983-91 and planned 1992, annual rpt, 1621–22
Acreage reduction and conservation programs participation of rice farmers, by State, 1986-91, article, 1561–8.303
Acreage reduction program compliance, enrollment, and yield on planted acreage, by commodity and State, annual press release series, 1004–20
Agricultural Stabilization and Conservation Service producer payments, by program and State, 1991, annual table, 1804–12
Agricultural Stabilization and Conservation Service rice programs, 1980-92, annual fact sheet, 1806–4.1
Agricultural Statistics, 1991, annual rpt, 1004–1
Beer production, stocks, material used, tax-free removals, and taxable removals by State, monthly rpt, 8486–1.1
Business statistics, detailed data for major industries and economic indicators, *Survey of Current Business*, monthly rpt, 2702–1.13
Business statistics, detailed data for major industries and economic indicators, 1960-91, *Survey of Current Business* biennial supplement, 2704–1
CCC certificate exchange activity, by commodity, biweekly press release, 1802–16
Consumption, supply, trade, prices, spending, and indexes, by food commodity, 1990, annual rpt, 1544–4
County Business Patterns, 1989: employment, establishments, and payroll, by SIC 2- to 4-digit industry and county, annual State rpt series, 2326–8
County Business Patterns, 1990: employment, establishments, and payroll, by SIC 2- to 4-digit industry and county, annual State rpt series, 2326–6
Export licensing, monitoring, and enforcement activities, FY91, annual rpt, 2024–1
Exports and imports (agricultural) commodity and country, prices, and world market devs, monthly rpt, 1922–12
Exports and imports (agricultural) of US, by commodity and country, bimonthly rpt, 1522–1
Exports and imports (agricultural) of US, by detailed commodity and country, 1991, annual rpt, 1524–8

Exports and imports (agricultural) of US, by detailed commodity and country, 1991, semiannual rpt, 1522–4
Exports and imports between US and outlying areas, by detailed commodity and mode of transport, 1991, annual rpt, 2424–11
Exports and imports of US, by country and detailed commodity, monthly rpt, 2422–12
Exports and imports of US, by Harmonized System 6-digit commodity and country, 1991, annual rpt, 2424–13
Exports and imports of US, by transport mode, country, and SITC 1- to 3-digit commodity, 1991, annual rpt, 2424–12
Exports of grains, oilseed products, hides, skins, and cotton, by country, weekly rpt, dropped data, 1922–3
Exports of US, detailed Schedule B commodities with countries of destination, 1991, annual rpt, 2424–10
Farm income, cash marketing receipts ranked by commodity and State, 1990, 1548–385
Farm sector balance sheet, and receipts by detailed commodity, by State, 1986-90, annual rpt, 1544–18
Fertilizer and pesticide use and application rates, by type, crop, and State, 1991, 1616–1.1
Foreign and US agricultural production, acreage, and yield for selected crops, forecasts by selected world region and country, FAS monthly circular, 1925–28
Foreign and US agricultural supply and demand indicators, by selected crop, monthly rpt, 1522–5
Foreign and US grain production, prices, trade, stocks, and use, FAS periodic circular series, 1925–2
Foreign and US rice production, prices, trade, stocks, and use, periodic situation rpt, 1561–8
Foreign countries agricultural production, prices, and trade, by country, 1980-91 and forecast 1992, annual world area rpt series, 1524–4
Freight (waterborne domestic and foreign) by commodity, traffic, and passengers, by port and waterway, 1989, annual rpt, 3754–3
Futures and options trading volume, by commodity and exchange, FY91, annual rpt, 11924–2
Futures trading in selected commodities and financial instruments and indexes, for NYC, Chicago, and other markets activity, biweekly rpt, 11922–5
Input-output structure of US economy, detailed interindustry transactions for 541 industries, and components of final demand, 1982 benchmark data, 2708–17
Irrigation projects of Reclamation Bur in western US, crop production and acreage by commodity, State, and project, 1990, annual rpt, 5824–12
Labor productivity, indexes of output, hours, and employment by SIC 2- to 4-digit industry, 1967-90, annual rpt, 6824–1.3
Loan support programs of USDA for grains, activity and status by grain and State, monthly rpt, 1802–3
Manufacturing annual survey, 1990: finances and operations, by SIC 2- to 4-digit industry, series, 2506–14
Manufacturing census, 1987: concentration of largest firms measured by value added, and for shipments by SIC 2- and 4-digit industry, subject rpt, 2497–6
Manufacturing census, 1987: shipments of manufacturers products, by customer class and SIC 2- and 4-digit industry, subject rpt, 2497–4
OECD trade, total and for 4 major countries, and US trade by country, by commodity, 1980-90, world area rpt series, 9116–1
Price (season average) forecasts for rice using futures settlement prices, 1990-92, article, 1561–8.301
Price indexes (producer), by stage of processing and detailed commodity, monthly rpt, 6762–6
Price indexes (producer), by stage of processing and detailed commodity, monthly 1991, annual rpt, 6764–2
Price support and other CCC program outlays, with production and marketing outlook, by commodity, projected 1991-97, annual rpt, 26306–6.171
Prices, market activities, inspections, sales, trade, supply, and use of rice, for US and selected foreign markets, weekly rpt, 1313–8
Prices received and paid by farmers, by commodity and State, monthly rpt, 1629–1
Prices received and paid by farmers, by commodity and State, 1991, annual rpt, 1629–5
Prices received by farmers and production value, by detailed crop and State, 1989-91, annual rpt, 1621–2
Production, farms, acreage, and related data, by selected crop and State, monthly rpt, 1621–1
Production itemized costs, receipts, and returns, by commodity and region, 1975-90, annual rpt, 1544–20
Production itemized costs, receipts, and returns, by crop and State, 1987-89, annual rpt, 1544–24
Production, practices, costs, and land tenure, for rice, by production area, 1988, 1568–309
Production, prices, trade, and marketing, by commodity, current situation and forecast, monthly rpt with articles, 1502–4
Shipments of rice, by end use, package size, and State of origin and destination, 1960s-89, biennial rpt, 1564–11
Soviet Union and US economic and sociodemographic indicators, selected years 1970-90, handbook, 2328–80
Spain rice acreage and yield, by region, mid 1930s-91, article, 1561–8.304
Stocks of grain on and off farms, by crop, quarterly rpt, 1621–4
Stocks of rice on and off farms and total, periodic rpt, 1621–7

Rice, Dorothy P.
"Burden of Caring for Alzheimer's Disease Patients", 4164–2
"Economic Cost of Alcohol Abuse", 4482–1.311

Rice, Kenneth
"Sole Proprietorship Return Preliminary Statistics, 1990: Data Release", 8302–2.317

Rice, Virginia H.
"Cigarette Use Among Arab Americans in the Detroit Metropolitan Area", 4042–3.360

Richardson, David H.
"Social Security, Uncertainty Adjustments, and the Consumption Decision", 4746–26.9

Richardson, Ralph M.
"Co-ops' Net Income Up, Sales Down Slightly in 1991", 1122–1.307
"Farmer Cooperative Statistics, 1990", 1124–1

Richardson, W. John
"Acoustic Effects of Oil Production Activities on Bowhead and White Whales Visible During Spring Migration Near Point Barrow, Alaska—1990 Phase: Sound Propagation and Whale Responses to Playbacks of Continuous Drilling Noise from an Ice Platform, as Studied in Pack Ice Conditions", 5738–27

Richland, Wash.
Radiation exposure of population near Hanford, Wash, nuclear plant, with methodology, 1944-91, series, 3356–5

Richmond, Va.
see also under By City and By SMSA or MSA in the "Index by Categories"

Richter, Albert J.
"Changing Public Sector: Shifts in Governmental Spending and Employment", 10048–53

Ries, Peter W.
"Educational Differences in Health Status and Health Care. Vital and Health Statistics Series 10", 4147–10.180

Rigby, Donald E.
"SSI Work Incentive Participants, September 1991", 4742–1.305

Right of assembly
Foreign countries human rights conditions in 170 countries, 1991, annual rpt, 21384–3

Right of privacy
Criminal sentences for Federal offenses, guidelines by offense and circumstances, series, 17668–1
Employee electronic monitoring effects on mental and physical health and job satisfaction, for local telephone company workers, 1989, hearings, 21348–122
Foreign countries human rights conditions in 170 countries, 1991, annual rpt, 21384–3
Labor laws enacted, by State, 1991, annual article, 6722–1.309
see also Electronic surveillance

Right to counsel
see also Legal aid

Riley, Margaret
"Private Foundations, 1988", 8302–2.302

Rimer, Barbara K.
"Multistrategy Health Education Program To Increase Mammography Use Among Women Ages 65 and Older", 4042–3.337

Rinne, John N.
"Southwestern Riparian-Stream Ecosystems: Research Design, Complexity, and Opportunity", 1208–390

Rio Grande River
Water supply and quality in streams and lakes, and groundwater levels in wells, by drainage basin, 1990, annual State rpt series, 5666–10
Water supply and quality in streams and lakes, and groundwater levels in wells, by drainage basin, 1991, annual State rpt series, 5666–12

Water supply in US and southern Canada, streamflow, surface and groundwater conditions, and reservoir levels, by location, monthly rpt, 5662–3

Riots and disorders

Foreign countries disasters, casualties, damage, and aid by US and others, FY91 and trends from FY64, annual rpt, 9914–12

Mgmt of disasters and natl security threats, with data by major event and State, 1992 annual rpt, 9434–6

Minority group discrimination disputes investigation and mediation activities and funding of Community Relations Service, FY91, annual rpt, 6004–9

Police response to disturbances, officers assaulted and killed, by circumstances, 1990, annual rpt, 6224–3

Prisoners in State and Federal instns, violations by type, 1990, quinquennial rpt, 6068–218

Terrorism (intl) incidents, casualties, and attacks on US targets, by attack type and country, 1991, annual rpt, 7004–22

US attorneys civil and criminal cases by type and disposition, and collections, by Federal district, FY91, annual rpt, 6004–2.1

Riou, Guy

"Human Papillomavirus-Negative Status and c-myc Gene Overexpression: Independent Prognostic Indicators of Distant Metastasis for Early-Stage Invasive Cervical Cancers", 4472–1.348

Ritchken, Peter

"On Markovian Representations of the Term Structure", 9377–9.145

Ritchko, Sue Ann

"Second Century of Food Composition Research", 1504–9.1

Rivers and waterways

Acid rain environmental, economic, and health effects, and pollutant emissions, 1985-89 and alternative projections to 2030, 14358–4

Army Corps of Engineers activities and projects, FY88 and trends from 1800s, annual rpt, 3754–1.1

Army Corps of Engineers activities and projects, FY89 and trends from 1800s, annual rpt, 3754–1.2

Army Corps of Engineers activities and projects, FY90 and trends from 1800s, annual rpt, 3754–1.3

Army Corps of Engineers water resources dev projects, characteristics, and costs, 1950s-89, biennial State rpt series, 3756–1

Army Corps of Engineers water resources dev projects, characteristics, and costs, 1950s-91, biennial State rpt series, 3756–2

Canada-US boundary waters, Intl Joint Commission activities, biennial rpt, discontinued, 14644–3

Coast Guard search and rescue missions, and lives and property lost and saved, by district and assisting unit, FY91, annual rpt, 7404–2

Colorado water supply, streamflow, precipitation, and reservoir storage, 1992 water year, annual rpt, 1264–13

Disease (waterborne) outbreaks and cases, by type, source, and location, 1989-90, article, 4202–7.301

Environmental conditions, fish, wildlife, use, and mgmt, for individual coastal and riparian ecosystems, series, 5506–9

Environmental Quality, status of problems, protection programs, research, and intl issues, 1991 annual rpt, 484–1

Fish catch, trade, use, and fishery operations, with selected foreign data, by species, 1980s-91, annual rpt, 2164–1

Fish Hatchery Natl System activities and deliveries, by species, hatchery, and jurisdiction of waters stocked, FY91, annual rpt, 5504–10

Foreign countries *Geographic Notes*, boundaries, claims, nomenclature, and other devs, quarterly rpt, 7142–3

Forest Service activities and finances, by region and State, FY91, annual rpt, 1204–1.1

Freight (shipborne domestic), by major commodity group, vessel type, and port, 1987-89, annual rpt, 7704–7

Freight (waterborne domestic and foreign) by commodity, traffic, and passengers, by port and waterway, 1989, annual rpt, 3754–3

Hazardous substances industrial releases and reduction methods under EPA regulation, by chemical, source, industry, and location, 1989, annual rpt, 9234–6

Hydroelectric power plants retired, characteristics and location, as of 1992, annual listing, 3084–12

Natl forests and other land under Forest Service mgmt, acreage by forest and location, 1991, annual rpt, 1204–2

Natl park system sites acreage and descriptions, 1991, biennial listing, 5544–5

Natl park system visits and overnight stays, by park and State, monthly rpt, 5542–4

Natl park system visits and overnight stays, by park and State, 1991, annual rpt, 5544–12

Natl parks and other land under Natl Park Service mgmt, acreage by site, ownership, and region, FY92, semiannual rpt, 5542–1

Northeastern US water supply, precipitation and stream runoff by station, monthly rpt, 2182–3

Oregon water supply, streamflow by station and reservoir storage, 1992, annual rpt, 1264–9

Public lands acreage, grants, use, revenues, and allocations, by State, FY91, annual rpt, 5724–1.2

Soil and plant characteristics in wetlands and riparian areas, series, 5506–10

Southwestern US streams water quality and fish population impacts of land mgmt and forest fires, 1980s-91, 1208–390

Statistical Abstract of US, 1992 annual data compilation, 2324–1.6

Vermont White River basin stream recreation use by activity, time, and location, 1987, 1208–400

Wastewater treatment and collection facility construction funding needs and Fed Govt grants, by State, 1990 and projected to 2010, biennial rpt, 9204–7

Water quality, chemistry, hydrology, and other characteristics, local area studies, series, 5666–27

Water supply and quality in streams and lakes, and groundwater levels in wells, by drainage basin, 1990, annual State rpt series, 5666–10

Water supply and quality in streams and lakes, and groundwater levels in wells, by drainage basin, 1990-91, annual CD-ROM, 5664–18

Water supply and quality in streams and lakes, and groundwater levels in wells, by drainage basin, 1991, annual State rpt series, 5666–12

Water supply in US and southern Canada, streamflow, surface and groundwater conditions, and reservoir levels, by location, monthly rpt, 5662–3

Western US water supply, and snow survey results, monthly State rpt series, 1266–2

Western US water supply, storage by reservoir and State, and streamflow conditions, as of Oct 1992, annual rpt, 1264–4

Western US water supply, streamflow and reservoir storage forecasts by stream and station, Jan-May monthly rpt, 1262–1

see also Arkansas River
see also Bridges and tunnels
see also Canals
see also Chesapeake Bay
see also Colorado River
see also Columbia River
see also Dams
see also Delaware River
see also Dredging
see also Estuaries
see also Floods
see also Great Lakes
see also Harbors and ports
see also Hudson River
see also Illinois River
see also James River
see also Lakes and lakeshores
see also Mississippi River
see also Missouri River
see also New York Bight
see also Niagara River
see also Ohio River
see also Potomac River
see also Puget Sound
see also Red River
see also Rio Grande River
see also San Francisco Bay
see also Snake River
see also Souris-Red-Rainy Rivers
see also St. Lawrence River
see also Susquehanna River
see also Tennessee River
see also Water resources development
see also Willamette River

Riverside, Calif.

CPI by component for US city average, and by region, population size, and for 15 metro areas, monthly rpt, 6762–1

CPI by component for US city average, and by selected metro area, region, and population size, monthly rpt, 6762–2

Housing and households characteristics, and unit and neighborhood quality, by MSA location for 11 MSAs, 1986 survey, supplement, 2485–8

Housing starts and completions authorized by building permits in 40 MSAs, quarterly rpt, 2382–9

see also under By City and By SMSA or MSA in the "Index by Categories"

RMC Research Corp.
"Transitions to Kindergarten: Final Report of the National Transition Study", 4808–44

Roads
see Highways, streets, and roads

Robbery and theft
Arrests and criminal case processing through sentencing, cases and duration by disposition and offense, for selected cities, 1988, annual rpt, 6064–27
Assaults and deaths of law enforcement officers, by circumstances, agency, victim and offender characteristics, and location, 1991, annual rpt, 6224–3
Cattle and calves loss to predators, disease, and other causes, by region and State, 1991, 1618–22
Court civil and criminal caseloads for Federal district, appeals, and bankruptcy courts, by type of suit and offense, circuit, and district, 1991, annual rpt, 18204–11
Court civil and criminal caseloads for Federal district, appeals, and special courts, 1991, annual rpt, 18204–8
Court criminal case processing in Federal district courts, and dispositions, by offense, district, and offender characteristics, 1989, annual data compilation, 6064–29
Court criminal case processing in Federal district courts, and dispositions, by offense, 1980-91, annual rpt, 6064–31
Crime, criminal justice admin and enforcement, and public opinion, data compilation, 1992 annual rpt, 6064–6
Crime Index by population size and region, and offenses by large city, 1st half 1992, semiannual rpt, 6222–1
Crimes, arrests by offender characteristics, and rates, by offense, and law enforcement employees, by population size and jurisdiction, 1991, annual rpt, 6224–2
Drug control street-level task forces enforcement activities, impacts on crime, and residents views, local area studies, 1992 rpt, 6068–251
Drug test results at arrest, by drug type, offense, and sex, for selected urban areas, quarterly rpt, 6062–3
Explosives theft and recovery, by type and State, 1987-91, annual rpt, 8484–4
Homicides, by circumstance, victim and offender relationship, and type of weapon, 1991, annual rpt, 6224–2.1
IRS internal audits, and employee and nonemployee violations, FY91, annual rpt, 8304–3.1
Juvenile arrests, by sex, race, disposition, and offense, 1990, 6066–27.8
Military supplies theft and fraud losses, and inventory control measures adequacy, 1988-91, GAO rpt, 26123–377
Postal Service inspection activities, 2nd half FY92, semiannual rpt, 9862–2
Prison and parole admissions and releases, sentence length, and time served, by offense and offender characteristics, 1988, annual rpt, 6064–33
Prisoners in Federal and contract instns, by selected characteristics, region, and Federal instn, FY89, annual rpt, 6244–1.1
Probation population, by offender characteristics, sentence conditions, whether rearrested, and offense, 1986-89, 6066–19.65
Sentences for Federal crimes, guidelines use and results by offense and district, and Sentencing Commission activities, 1991, annual rpt, 17664–1
Sentences for Federal crimes, guidelines use and results by offense, 1984-1990, 6066–19.68
Sentences for Federal offenses, guidelines by offense and circumstances, series, 17668–1
Sentences for Federal offenses, guidelines impacts on sentence disparity by offender race and other characteristics, 1985-90, GAO rpt, 26119–415
States criminal justice systems activities, employment, funding, and data collection, by State, 1970s-91, annual rpt, 6064–40
Statistical Abstract of US, 1992 annual data compilation, 2324–1.5
US attorneys civil and criminal cases by type and disposition, and collections, by Federal district, FY91, annual rpt, 6004–2.1
Victimization rates, by victim and offender characteristics, circumstances, and offense, survey rpt series, 6066–3
Victimizations, by offense and whether reported to police, 1990-91, press release, 6068–249
Victimizations of households, by offense, household characteristics, and location, 1975-91, annual rpt, 6066–25.49
Wiretaps authorized, costs, arrests, trials, and convictions, by offense and jurisdiction, 1991, annual rpt, 18204–7
Women in jail, by criminal background and sociodemographic characteristics, with comparisons to men, 1989, 6066–19.66
see also Federal Inspectors General reports
see also Motor vehicle theft
see also Security devices

Roberds, William
"Budget Constraints and Time-Series Evidence on Consumption: Comment", 9371–10.90
"Legal Restrictions and Welfare in a Simple Model of Money", 9371–10.72

Robertson, Leon
"Home and Leisure Injury Prevention", 4208–35

Robertson, Susan E.
"Million Dollar Measles Outbreak: Epidemiology, Risk Factors, and a Selective Revaccination Strategy", 4042–3.301

Robinson, Donald B.
"Tuberculosis in a Small Semi-Rural County", 4042–3.319

Robinson, Kenneth L.
"State Enterprise Zones in Nonmetro Areas: Are They Working?", 1502–7.303

Robles, Annette
"State of Native American Youth Health", 4088–3

Robotics
see Automation
see Industrial robots

Rochester, N.Y.
Housing and households characteristics, and unit and neighborhood quality, by MSA location for 11 MSAs, 1986 survey, supplement, 2485–8
Wages by occupation, and benefits, for office and plant workers, 1991 survey, periodic MSA rpt, 6785–16.4
see also under By City and By SMSA or MSA in the "Index by Categories"

Rock Hill, S.C.
Housing starts and completions authorized by building permits in 40 MSAs, quarterly rpt, 2382–9

Rock Island, Ill.
Freight (waterborne domestic and foreign) by commodity, traffic, and passengers, by port and waterway, 1989, annual rpt, 3754–3.2; 3754–3.3
Wages by occupation, and benefits, for office and plant workers, 1992 survey, periodic MSA rpt, 6785–17.1

Rockefeller, Winthrop
"Managing Rural Policy in a Federal System of Government", 1504–9.1

Rockets
see Missiles and rockets

Rockford, Ill.
see also under By City and By SMSA or MSA in the "Index by Categories"

Rodano, Edith M.
"Technical Assistance and Safety Programs: FY91 Project Directory", 7884–1

Rodrigues, Anthony P.
"Tests of Mean-Variance Efficiency of International Equity Markets", 9385–8.137

Rodriguez-Archila, Laura
"Advertising, Industry and Trade Summary", 9885–12.3
"Lamps and Lighting Fittings, Industry and Trade Summary", 9885–10.2

Rogers, Carolyn C.
"Health and Social Characteristics of the Nonmetro Elderly", 1504–9.1

Rogers, Denise M.
"Characteristics of Farmland Owners and Their Participation in the Farmland Market, 1970-88", 1561–16.302

Rogers, George
"Timber Resource Statistics for the Chatham Area of the Tongass National Forest, Alaska, 1982", 1206–9.26
"Timber Resource Statistics for the Ketchikan Area of the Tongass National Forest, Alaska, 1985", 1206–9.24
"Timber Resource Statistics for the Stikine Area of the Tongass National Forest, Alaska, 1984", 1206–9.25

Rogers, John
"Participant Evaluation and Cost of a Community-Based Health Promotion Program for Elders", 4042–3.342

Rogers, R. Mark
"Forecasting Industrial Production: Purchasing Managers' Versus Production-Worker Hours Data", 9371–1.301
"Tracking Manufacturing: The Survey of Southeastern Manufacturing Conditions", 9371–1.307

Rogoff, Kenneth
"Global Versus Country-Specific Productivity Shocks and the Current Account", 9393–10.22

Rogot, Eugene
"Life Expectancy by Employment Status, Income, and Education in the National Longitudinal Mortality Study", 4042–3.347

"Second Data Book. A Mortality Study of 1.3 Million Persons by Demographic, Social, and Economic Factors: 1979-85 Follow-Up. U.S. National Longitudinal Mortality Study", 4478–186

Romain, Robert F.
"Canada's Broiler Supply Management Program: A Shield from U.S. Price Volatility?", 1502–3.302

Romania
Agricultural trade of US, by detailed commodity and country, 1991, annual rpt, 1524–8
Agricultural trade of US, by detailed commodity and country, 1991, semiannual rpt, 1522–4
Agricultural trade of US with Eastern Europe, by commodity group and country, 1988-91, 1928–11
Economic and military aid and loans from US and intl agencies, by program and country, FY46-91, annual rpt, 9914–5
Economic and social conditions of developing countries from 1960s, and Intl Dev Cooperation Agency and AID activities and funding, FY91-93, annual rpt, 9904–4
Economic conditions, policy, and trade practices, by country, 1989-91, annual rpt, 21384–5
Economic, social, political, and geographic summary data, by country, 1992, annual factbook, 9114–2
Energy production and trade for Romania, 1970s-91, with capital investment projected to 2000, GAO rpt, 26123–402
Export industries dev potential, with trade and industry finances and operations, for 5 Eastern Europe countries, 1985-90, 9886–4.179
Export licensing, monitoring, and enforcement activities, FY91, annual rpt, 2024–1
Exports and imports of US, by commodity and country, 1980-90, world area rpt, 9116–1.1
Exports and imports of US, by transport mode, country, and SITC 1- to 3-digit commodity, 1991, annual rpt, 2424–12
Exports and imports of US with Communist and transitional economy countries, by detailed commodity and country, quarterly rpt with articles, 9882–2
Exports and imports of US with Eastern Europe, by commodity and country, 1987-91 and outlook for 1992, 2048–158
Exports and imports of US with Romania, and US import tariff rates, by commodity, 1985-91, GAO rpt, 26119–414
Exports, imports, and balances of US for manufactured goods, by SITC 2-digit commodity and country, quarterly rpt, 2042–35
Exports of US, detailed Schedule B commodities with countries of destination, 1991, annual rpt, 2424–10
Human rights conditions in 170 countries, and US economic and military aid, 1991, annual rpt, 21384–3
Market economy transition of Eastern Europe countries, trade, and foreign investment, by country, 1990-91, 9118–13
Military aid of US, arms sales, and training programs costs and budget requests, by program, world region, and country, FY91-93, annual rpt, 7144–13
Military spending, arms trade, and force strengths, with govt spending and population, by country, 1979-89, annual rpt, 9824–1
Pipes and tubes (welded nonalloy steel) from 6 countries at less than fair value, injury to US industry, investigation with background financial and operating data, 1992 rpt, 9886–14.361
Pollution (air) contributing to global warming, emissions by monitoring site and country, and temperature change by world area and US region, 1860s-1990, annual rpt, 3004–33
Population size, growth rates, and components of change, by country, projected 1990-2020 and trends from 1950, biennial rpt, 2324–9
Refugee migration, and intl aid programs, by world area and country of origin and asylum, 1991, annual rpt, 7004–15
Steel (carbon flat-rolled) products from 21 countries, injury to US industry from foreign subsidized and less than fair value imports, investigation with background financial and operating data, 1992 rpt, 9886–19.85
Steel imports of US under voluntary restraint agreement, by product, customs district, and country, with US industry operating data, quarterly rpt, 9882–13
Steel trade, by product, country, and customs district, with US industry operating data, 1989-June 1992, semiannual rpt, 9882–15
Tobacco and cigarette production, prices, use, and trade, for Romania, 1980-91, article, 1925–16.301
UN voting record and share of votes in agreement with US, by issue, country, and world area, 1991, annual rpt, 7004–18

Romero, Carol J.
"Assisting Dislocated Workers: Alternatives to Layoffs, and the Role of the Employment Service Under the Economic Dislocation and Worker Adjustment Assistance Act (EDWAA)", 15498–28
"Changing Nation—Its Changing Labor Force", 15496–1.16
"Potential Effectiveness of the Employment Service in Serving Dislocated Workers Under EDWAA: Evidence from the 1980s", 15496–1.14

Rooming and boarding houses
Board and care home violations of State drug handling and dispensing regulations, for 3 metro areas, 1990-91, GAO rpt, 26121–447
Census of Population and Housing, 1990: population and housing characteristics, detailed geographic coverage, State CD-ROM series, 2551–10
Census of Population, 1990: population characteristics and living arrangements, by county, place, and urban-rural location, State rpt series, 2531–1
County Business Patterns, 1989: employment, establishments, and payroll, by SIC 2- to 4-digit industry and county, annual State rpt series, 2326–8
County Business Patterns, 1990: employment, establishments, and payroll, by SIC 2- to 4-digit industry and county, annual State rpt series, 2326–6
Homeless persons housing in rehabilitated single occupancy units, funding and characteristics, by city, FY87-91, GAO rpt, 26113–596
Rental housing units, total, with HUD assistance by program, and eligible for aid, by unit, household, and neighborhood characteristics, and location, 1989, biennial rpt, 5184–11
Supplemental Security Income and Medicaid eligibility and payment provisions, and beneficiaries living arrangements, by State, 1992, annual rpt, 4704–13
Tax (income) returns of sole proprietorships, income statement items, by industry group, 1990, annual article, 8302–2.317; 8302–2.320

Rosenbaum, Paula
"Large-Scale Study of Freedom from Smoking Clinics—Factors in Quitting", 4042–3.314

Rosengren, Eric S.
"Capital Crunch in New England", 9373–1.309
"Capital Crunch: Neither a Borrower Nor a Lender Be", 9373–27.4
"Defaults of Original Issue High-Yield Convertible Bonds", 9373–27.14
"Failed Bank Resolution and the Collateral Crunch: The Advantages of Adopting Transferable Puts", 9373–27.13
"Real Exchange Rate and Foreign Direct Investment in the U.S.: Relative Wealth vs. Relative Wage Effects", 9373–27.10
"Role of Real Estate in the New England Credit Crunch", 9373–27.12

Rosenheck, Robert
"Age and Cohort Effects in PTSD", 8704–6
"Causal Model of the Etiology of PTSD", 8704–6
"Long-Term Sequelae of Combat in World War II, Korea and Vietnam: A Comparative Study", 8704–6

Rosenthal, Neal H.
"Evaluating the 1990 Projections of Occupational Employment", 6722–1.336
"How Accurate Are the Employment Projections in the *Occupational Outlook Handbook*?", 6742–1.302

Rosenthal, Stanley L.
"Note on Relationships Between Western Sahel Rainfall and U.S. Hurricane Activity", 2148–61

Rossi, Clifford V.
"Thrift Industry Cost Structure and Competitive Viability", 8436–1.7

Rosson, James F., Jr.
"Forest Statistics for Northwest Louisiana Parishes, 1991", 1206–35.11
"Forest Statistics for South Delta Louisiana Parishes, 1991", 1206–35.9
"Forest Statistics for Southeast Louisiana Parishes, 1991", 1206–35.10
"Forest Statistics for Southwest Louisiana Parishes, 1991", 1206–35.8

ROTC
see Reserve Officers Training Corps

Roth, Lisa
"Relationship Between Family Homelessness, Insurance Coverage, Health Status, and Health Care-Seeking Behavior", 4164–2

Rourke, John P.
"Producer Milk Marketed Under Federal Milk Orders by State of Origin", 1317–4.301
"Producer Structure in Federal Milk Order Markets", 1317–4.303
Roussopoulos, Sue M.
"Forest Statistics for Minnesota's Prairie Unit, 1990", 1206–24.12
"Wisconsin's Timberland Plantations, 1983", 1206–34.9
Rowe, Brenda J.
"Unlocking Learning: Chapter 1 in Correctional Facilities. National Study of the Chapter 1 Neglected or Delinquent Program: Effective Practices Study Findings", 4808–40.3
Royalties
Budget of US, authoritative financial statements with appropriations, outlays, and receipts, by category and agency, FY91, annual rpt, 8104–2.2
Copyright royalty fees for cable and satellite TV and funds available for distribution, 1990-91, annual rpt, 26404–2
Exports and imports of services, direct and among multinatl firms affiliates, by industry and world area, 1986-91, article, 2702–1.336
Foreign-controlled US firms royalties and license fees paid to and received from foreign parents, 1982-90, article, 9391–1.309
Forest Service activities and finances, by region and State, FY91, annual rpt, 1204–1.1
Multinatl firms US affiliates, royalties and fees received and paid, and nonbank and manufacturing employment in Fed Reserve 8th District, 1970s-90, article, 9391–16.302
Multinatl US firms and foreign affiliates finances and operations, by industry and country, 1989 benchmark survey, annual rpt, 2704–5
Natl income and product accounts, comprehensive accounts and components, benchmark revisions, 1929-88, 2708–5
Natl income and product accounts, comprehensive accounts and components, *Survey of Current Business*, monthly rpt, 2702–1.26
Natural gas interstate pipeline company detailed financial and operating data, by firm, 1990, annual rpt, 3164–38
Naval Petroleum and Oil Shale Reserves production and revenue by fuel type, sales by purchaser, and wells, by reserve, FY91, annual rpt, 3334–3
Oil and gas OCS leasing and exploration activity, production, revenue, and environmental studies, by location, quarterly rpt, 5732–1
Oil, gas, and minerals production and revenue on Federal and Indian land, by State, 1991 and trends from 1920, annual rpt, 5734–2
Public lands acreage and use, and Land Mgmt Bur activities and finances, annual State rpt series, 5724–11
Tax (income) returns filed, by type of filer, selected income items, quarterly rpt, 8302–2.1
Tax (income) returns of corporations, income and tax items by asset size and detailed industry, 1989, annual rpt, 8304–4; 8304–21
Tax (income) returns of individuals, detailed data, 1988, annual rpt, 8304–2
Tax (income) returns of partnerships, income statement and balance sheet items, by industry group, 1990, annual article, 8302–2.314
USDA revenue, by source and subagency, FY88-92, GAO rpt, 26113–602
Rubber and rubber industry
Business statistics, detailed data for major industries and economic indicators, *Survey of Current Business*, monthly rpt, 2702–1.19
Business statistics, detailed data for major industries and economic indicators, 1960-91, *Survey of Current Business* biennial supplement, 2704–1
Capital expenditures for plant and equipment, by major industry group, quarterly rpt, 2502–2
Collective bargaining agreements expiring during year, and workers covered, by firm, union, industry group, and State, 1992, annual rpt, 6784–9
County Business Patterns, 1989: employment, establishments, and payroll, by SIC 2- to 4-digit industry and county, annual State rpt series, 2326–8
County Business Patterns, 1990: employment, establishments, and payroll, by SIC 2- to 4-digit industry and county, annual State rpt series, 2326–6
Employment, earnings, and hours, by SIC 1- to 4-digit industry, monthly 1989-Feb 1992, annual rpt, 6744–4
Employment, unemployment, and labor force characteristics, by region and census div, 1991, annual rpt, 6744–7.1
Exports and imports (agricultural) of US, by commodity and country, bimonthly rpt, 1522–1
Exports and imports (agricultural) of US, by detailed commodity and country, 1991, annual rpt, 1524–8
Exports and imports (agricultural) of US, by detailed commodity and country, 1991, semiannual rpt, 1522–4
Exports and imports between US and outlying areas, by detailed commodity and mode of transport, 1991, annual rpt, 2424–11
Exports and imports of US, by country and detailed commodity, monthly rpt, 2422–12
Exports and imports of US, by Harmonized System 6-digit commodity and country, 1991, annual rpt, 2424–13
Exports and imports of US, by selected country, country group, and commodity group, 1991, annual rpt, 2044–37
Exports and imports of US, by transport mode, country, and SITC 1- to 3-digit commodity, 1991, annual rpt, 2424–12
Exports, imports, and balances of US for manufactured goods, by SITC 2-digit commodity and country, quarterly rpt, 2042–35
Exports of US, detailed commodities by country, monthly CD-ROM, 2422–13
Exports of US, detailed Schedule B commodities with countries of destination, 1991, annual rpt, 2424–10
Footwear production, employment, use, prices, and US trade by country, quarterly rpt, 9882–6
Foreign countries agricultural production, prices, and trade, by country, 1980-91 and forecast 1992, annual world area rpt series, 1524–4
Freight (waterborne domestic and foreign) by commodity, traffic, and passengers, by port and waterway, 1989, annual rpt, 3754–3
Hose and belting shipments, trade, use, and firms, by product, annual Current Industrial Rpt, discontinued, 2506–8.12
Imports, exports, and employment impacts, by SIC 2- to 4-digit industry and commodity, quarterly rpt, 2322–2
Imports of US, detailed commodities by country, monthly CD-ROM, 2422–14
Input-output structure of US economy, detailed interindustry transactions for 84 industries, and components of final demand, 1987, annual article, 2702–1.316
Input-output structure of US economy, detailed interindustry transactions for 541 industries, and components of final demand, 1982 benchmark data, 2708–17
Labor productivity, indexes of output, hours, and employment by SIC 2- to 4-digit industry, 1967-90, annual rpt, 6824–1.3
Manufacturing annual survey, 1990: finances and operations, by SIC 2- to 4-digit industry, series, 2506–14
Manufacturing census, 1987: concentration of largest firms measured by value added, and for shipments by SIC 2- and 4-digit industry, subject rpt, 2497–6
Manufacturing census, 1987: shipments of manufacturers products, by customer class and SIC 2- and 4-digit industry, subject rpt, 2497–4
Manufacturing corporations financial statements, by selected SIC 2- to 3-digit industry, quarterly rpt, 2502–1
Manufacturing finances and operations, by SIC 2- to 4-digit industry, forecast 1992, annual rpt, 2044–28
Manufacturing production, shipments, inventories, orders, and pollution control costs, periodic Current Industrial Rpt series, 2506–3
Multinatl firms US affiliates finances and operations, by industry, country of parent firm, and State, 1987, 2708–48
Multinatl US firms and foreign affiliates finances and operations, by industry and country, 1989 benchmark survey, annual rpt, 2704–5
Occupational injury and illness rates, by SIC 2- to 4-digit industry, 1989-90, annual rpt, 6844–7
Occupational injury and illness rates, by SIC 2- to 4-digit industry, 1990, annual rpt, 6844–1
OECD trade, total and for 4 major countries, and US trade by country, by commodity, 1980-90, world area rpt series, 9116–1
Pacific territories population and housing detailed characteristics, by location, 1990 Census of Population and Housing, series, 2551–8
Pollution abatement capital and operating costs, by SIC 2- to 4-digit industry and State, 1990, annual Current Industrial Rpt, 2506–3.6

Price indexes (producer), by stage of processing and detailed commodity, monthly rpt, 6762–6
Price indexes (producer), by stage of processing and detailed commodity, monthly 1991, annual rpt, 6764–2
Production and sales of synthetic organic chemicals, and manufacturer listing, by product, 1990, annual rpt, 9884–3
Production, shipments, trade, stocks, and firms, by rubber product, annual Current Industrial Rpt, discontinued, 2506–8.7
Puerto Rico and other US possessions corporations income tax returns, income and tax items, and employment, by selected industry, 1989, article, 8302–2.326
Science, engineering, and technical employment in manufacturing, by field and industry, 1989, triennial rpt, 9627–23
Shipments of rubber mechanical goods, by product, 1991, annual Current Industrial Rpt, 2506–8.17
Shoe production, shipments, trade, and use, by product, 1991, annual Current Industrial Rpt, 2506–6.8
Stockpiling of strategic material by Fed Govt, activity, and inventory by commodity, as of Sept 1991, semiannual rpt, 3542–22
Stockpiling of strategic material, inventories and needs, by commodity, 1992, annual rpt, 3544–37
Tariff Schedule of US, classifications and rates of duty by detailed imported commodity, 1993 base edition, 9886–13
Tax (income) returns of corporations, income and tax items by asset size and detailed industry, 1989, annual rpt, 8304–4; 8304–21
Thread (rubber) from Malaysia at less than fair value, injury to US industry, investigation with background financial and operating data, 1992 rpt, 9886–14.360
see also Tires and tire industry
see also under By Commodity in the "Index by Categories"
see also under By Industry in the "Index by Categories"

Rubin, Laura S.
"State and Local Government Sector: Long-Term Trends and Recent Fiscal Pressures", 9362–1.309

Rubinger, Bruce
"Survey of Direct U.S. Private Capital Investment in Research and Development Facilities in Japan", 9628–88

Rudich, Robert
"Safety Management Information Statistics (SAMIS) 1990 Annual Report", 7884–13

Ruelle, Richard
"Contaminant Evaluation of Interior Least Tern and Piping Plover Eggs and Chicks on the Missouri River, South Dakota", 5508–118
"Pesticide and Toxicity Evaluation of Wetland Waters and Sediments on National Wildlife Refuges in South Dakota", 5508–117

Rugs
see Carpets and rugs

Ruiz-Tiben, Ernesto
"Surveillance of Dracunculiasis, 1981-91", 4202–7.307

Runaways
see Missing persons and runaways

Runkle, David E.
"Bleak Outlook for the U.S. Economy", 9383–6.301
"No Relief in Sight for the U.S. Economy", 9383–6.303

Runner, Diana
"Changes in Unemployment Insurance Legislation in 1991", 6722–1.311

Rural areas
Alaska rural areas population characteristics, and energy resources dev effects, series, 5736–5
Asian and Pacific Islands Americans social and economic characteristics, for West and total US, 1990-91, Current Population Report, 2546–1.462
Businesses in rural areas, Fed Govt credit assistance by program and county characteristics, 1983-89, 1548–389
Census of Housing, 1990: summary unit characteristics, by householder race and age, county, place, and urban-rural location, State rpt series, 2471–1
Census of Population and Housing, 1990: population and housing characteristics, detailed geographic coverage, State CD-ROM series, 2551–10
Census of Population, 1990: population characteristics and living arrangements, by county, place, and urban-rural location, State rpt series, 2531–1
Crime Index by population size and region, and offenses by large city, 1st half 1992, semiannual rpt, 6222–1
Crime victimization in cities, suburbs, and rural areas, by offense, circumstances, and victim and offender characteristics, 1987-89, 6066–3.48
Crime victimization of households, by offense, household characteristics, and location, 1975-91, annual rpt, 6066–25.49
Crimes, arrests by offender characteristics, and rates, by offense, and law enforcement employees, by population size and jurisdiction, 1991, annual rpt, 6224–2
Deaths and rates, by cause and selected social, demographic, and employment characteristics, 1979-85, natl longitudinal study, 4478–186
Economic and social conditions, dev, and problems in rural areas, periodic journal, 1502–7
Economic conditions and dev in rural areas, quarterly journal, 1502–8
Educational enrollment, by grade, instn type and control, and student characteristics, 1990 and trends from 1947, annual Current Population Rpt, 2546–1.459
Employment and population characteristics in rural areas, and role of education and training in economic dev, 1960s-80s, compilation of papers, 1598–277
Enterprise zone programs in rural areas, jobs created and saved, and firms participating, by industry, 1986, article, 1502–7.303
Health care access in rural areas by service type, for selected counties with closed or no hospital, 1991 rpt, 17206–2.30
Health condition and care indicators, 1950s-90 with health improvement and disease prevention goals for 1990, annual data compilation, 4144–11
Home mortgages FHA-insured, financial, property, and borrower characteristics, by metro area, 1991, annual rpt, 5144–24
Home mortgages FHA-insured, financial, property, and borrower characteristics, by State, 1991, annual rpt, 5144–1; 5144–25
Home mortgages FHA-insured, financial, property, and borrower characteristics, 1991, annual rpt, 5144–23
Hospital closings, financial and operating characteristics compared to instns remaining open, 1985-88, 17206–2.27
Hospital reimbursement by Medicare under prospective payment system, rural area instns financial performance and impacts of PPS policy changes, 1991 rpt, 26306–6.164
Hospitals in rural areas, Medicare admission rates and charges, by instn, patient, and care characteristics, mid 1980s, 17206–2.33
Hospitals in rural areas, Medicare-dependent instns financial performance under cost-based adjustment, FY89, 17206–2.42
Households and family characteristics, by location, 1991, annual Current Population Rpt, 2546–1.457
Housing (low income rental) in rural areas, FmHA loans and impacts of programs to maintain supply and to deter mortgage prepayment, 1988-91, GAO rpt, 26113–586
Housing (rental) units, total, with HUD assistance by program, and eligible for aid, by unit, household, and neighborhood characteristics, and location, 1989, biennial rpt, 5184–11
Housing and households detailed characteristics, and unit and neighborhood quality, by location, 1989, biennial rpt supplement, 2485–13
Housing vacancy and occupancy rates, and vacant unit characteristics and costs, by region and metro-nonmetro location, quarterly rpt, 2482–1
Hwy Statistics, detailed data by State, 1991, annual rpt, 7554–1
Hwy traffic volume on rural roads and city streets, monthly rpt, 7552–8
Income (household) and poverty status under alternative income definitions, by recipient characteristics, 1979-91, annual Current Population Rpt, 2546–6.78
Income (personal) relative to median, by race and selected other characteristics, mid 1960s-89, Current Population Rpt, 2546–6.73
Job Training Partnership Act programs in rural areas, costs and outcomes, FY87, article, 1502–7.305
Labor demand in rural areas, job skill and educational requirements impacts of industrial and occupational shifts, 1970s-80s and projected to 2000, article, 1502–7.302
Loan guarantees of FmHA to business and industry in rural areas, by State and industry, and closures and defaults, FY74-91, GAO rpt, 26113–591

Medicare payment of physicians, vulnerable beneficiaries services use prior to fee schedule implementation, 1986-90, annual rpt, 17266–1.8
Obstetrics rural practitioners malpractice insurance subsidy program funding and participation, for North Carolina, 1989-92, article, 4042–3.355
Pacific territories population and housing detailed characteristics, by location, 1990 Census of Population and Housing, series, 2551–8
Physicians payment by Medicare under fee schedule, methodology with data by procedure and specialty, 1992, annual rpt, 17264–1
Physicians supply in rural areas, by practice type, 1980s, article, 1502–7.304
Poverty status of population and families, by detailed characteristics, 1991, annual Current Population Rpt, 2546–6.77
Research (agricultural) funding and staffing for USDA, State agencies, and other instns, by topic, FY91, annual rpt, 1744–2
Statistical Abstract of US, 1992 annual data compilation, 2324–1
Telephone firms borrowing under Rural Telephone Program, and financial and operating data, by State, 1991, annual rpt, 1244–2
Traffic accidents on rural 2-lane roads related to passing, by circumstances and severity, 1992 article, 7552–3.301
VA health care services, needs, availability, structure, and funding, 1991 compilation of papers, 8608–9
Vietnam population size, components of change, and selected characteristics, 1979, 1989, and projected to 2050, 2326–18.65
see also Farm income
see also Farm population
see also Farms and farmland
see also Federal aid to rural areas
see also Migrant workers
see also Rural electrification
see also under Agriculture and terms beginning with Agricultural
see also under By Urban-Rural and Metro-Nonmetro in the "Index by Categories"

Rural cooperatives
Agricultural cooperatives finances, aggregate for top 100 assns by commodity group, 1990, annual rpt, 1124–3
Agricultural cooperatives, finances, and membership, by type of service, commodity, and State, 1990, annual rpt, 1124–1
Agricultural cooperatives finances, operations, activities, and current issues, monthly journal, 1122–1
Agricultural cooperatives, finances, operations, activities, and membership, commodity rpt series, 1126–1
Agricultural research funding and staffing for USDA, State agencies, and other instns, by topic, FY91, annual rpt, 1744–2
Agricultural Statistics, 1991, annual rpt, 1004–1
Electric cooperatives financed by REA, finances and operations, 1988-90, annual rpt, 3164–24.3
Electric power distribution loans from REA, and borrower operating and financial data, by firm and State, 1991, annual rpt, 1244–1
Electric power plants and capacity, by fuel used, owner, location, and operating status, 1991 and for units planned 1992-2001, annual listing, 3164–36
Electric power plants financed by REA, with location, capacity, and owner, as of Jan 1992, annual listing, 1244–6
Electric power purchases from TVA and resales, with use, average bills, and rates by customer class, by distributor, 1991, annual tables, 9804–14
Electric power purchases of municipal and cooperative distributors, and prices and use by distributor and consumer sector, for TVA, monthly rpt, 9802–1
Electric power sales and revenue, by end-use sector, consumption level, and utility, 1990, annual rpt, 3164–91
Electric power sales by customer, activities by plant, and financial statements of Western Area Power Admin, FY91, annual rpt, 3254–1
Electric power sales by customer, for Southwestern Fed Power System, FY91, annual rpt, 3244–1
Electric power sales by customer, plants, and capacity of Southeastern Power Admin, FY91, annual rpt, 3234–1
Electric power sales of Bonneville Power Admin, by customer, FY91, annual rpt, 3224–1
Electric power sales, revenue, and rates of Bonneville Power Admin, by customer and customer type, 1991, semiannual rpt, 3222–1
Farm finances, assets, liabilities, and debt by lender type, by State, 1960-89, 1548–384
Farm sector assets by type, and real and nonreal estate debt, including and excluding operator households, by sales size, 1960-89, 1548–387
Farm sector balance sheet, and receipts by detailed commodity, by State, 1986-90, annual rpt, 1544–18
Food marketing cooperatives exports under intl business arrangements, 1985-88, 1128–69
Milk handlers (cooperative and proprietary) performance, views of dairy farmers in southern States, 1989 survey, 1128–67
Milk order and cooperative prices, by selected area, 1991, annual rpt, 1317–1.5
Milk producer prices received from cooperatives and proprietary handlers, by characteristics of cooperative membership and operation, 1989 survey, 1128–68
Statistical Abstract of US, 1992 annual data compilation, 2324–1.23
Tax exempt organizations and employee plans listed on IRS masterfile, determinations, applications, and rulings, FY91, annual rpt, 8304–3.2
Tax returns filed, by type of tax and IRS district, 1990 and projected 1991-98, annual rpt, 8304–24
Tax returns filed, by type of tax and IRS region and service center, projected 1991-98 and trends from 1978, annual rpt, 8304–9
Telephone firms borrowing under Rural Telephone Program, and financial and operating data, by State, 1991, annual rpt, 1244–2
Telephone firms borrowing under Rural Telephone Program, loan activity by State, FY91, annual tables, 1244–8
Telephone rural cooperative bank financial statements, FY91, annual rpt, 1244–4
Tobacco stocks held by grower cooperatives, by type, quarterly rpt, 1319–3

Rural electrification
Agricultural Statistics, 1991, annual rpt, 1004–1
Bonneville Power Admin mgmt of Fed Columbia River Power System, finances, operations, and sales by customer, FY91, annual rpt, 3224–1
Bonneville Power Admin sales, revenues, and rates, by customer and customer type, 1991, semiannual rpt, 3222–1
Capacity and plants, by fuel used, owner, location, and operating status, 1991, and for units planned 1992-2001, annual listing, 3164–36
Cooperatives financed by REA, finances and operations, 1988-90, annual rpt, 3164–24.3
Cooperatives, membership, and revenue for Rural Electric Cooperatives, by State, 1990, annual rpt, 1124–1
Loans by State, and REA activities and finances, FY91 and trends from FY36, annual rpt, 1244–3
Loans of REA, and borrower operating and financial data, by distribution firm and State, 1991, annual rpt, 1244–1
Plants financed by REA, with location, capacity, and owner, as of Jan 1992, annual listing, 1244–6
Purchases (wholesale) of REA borrowers, by borrower, supplier, and State, annual rpt, discontinued, 1244–5
Sales and revenue, by end-use sector, consumption level, and utility, 1990, annual rpt, 3164–91
Southeastern Power Admin sales by customer, plants, capacity, and Southeastern Fed Power Program financial statements, FY91, annual rpt, 3234–1
Southwestern Fed Power System financial statements, sales by customer, and operations and costs by project, FY91, annual rpt, 3244–1
TVA electric power purchases and resales, with electricity use, average bills, and rates by customer class, by distributor, 1991, annual tables, 9804–14
Western Area Power Admin activities by plant, financial statements, and sales by customer, FY91, annual rpt, 3254–1

Rural Electrification Administration
Activities and finances of REA, and loans by State, FY91 and trends from FY36, annual rpt, 1244–3
Budget of US, obligations and authority by function, agency, and program, with summaries and analyses, FY93, annual rpt, 104–2
Cooperatives financed by REA, finances and operations, 1988-90, annual rpt, 3164–24.3
Loans of REA, and borrower operating and financial data, by distribution firm and State, 1991, annual rpt, 1244–1
Plants financed by REA, with location, capacity, and owner, as of Jan 1992, annual listing, 1244–6

Purchases (wholesale) of REA borrowers, by borrower, supplier, and State, annual rpt, discontinued, 1244–5
see also Rural Telephone Bank

Rural Telephone Bank
Financial statements of Bank, FY91, annual rpt, 1244–4
Loans by State, and REA activities and finances, FY91 and trends from FY36, annual rpt, 1244–3
Loans to telephone firms under Rural Telephone Program, activity by State, FY91, annual tables, 1244–8
Loans under Rural Telephone Program, and borrower operations and finances, by State, 1991, annual rpt, 1244–2

Rush, Mark
"Effect of Changes in Reserve Requirements on Investment and GNP", 9375–13.72

Russia
Agricultural production, prices, and trade, for former USSR republics, 1960s-91 and forecast 1992, annual rpt, 1524–4.1
Economic, social, political, and geographic summary data, by country, 1992, annual factbook, 9114–2
Energy supply and use, and social, economic, and political indicators for former Soviet Republics and Baltic States, 1989-90, 3168–126
Energy use and production of former USSR Republics, by fuel type, 1990, annual rpt, 3164–84.2
Exports and imports of US with Communist and transitional economy countries, by detailed commodity and country, quarterly rpt with articles, 9882–2
Ferrosilicon from 6 countries, injury to US industry from foreign subsidized and less than fair value imports, investigation with background financial and operating data, 1992 rpt, 9886–19.84
Livestock and meat inventories, use, and imports, by former USSR republic, 1986-93, semiannual rpt, 1925–33.2
Population size and characteristics of former Soviet Republics and Baltic States, 1989-92, 9118–19
Uranium resources and production of CIS, by state, 1992 article, 3164–65
see also Soviet Union

Rutledge, Gary L.
"Pollution Abatement and Control Expenditures, 1972-90", 2702–1.321

Rwanda
Agricultural trade of US, by detailed commodity and country, 1991, annual rpt, 1524–8
Agricultural trade of US, by detailed commodity and country, 1991, semiannual rpt, 1522–4
AID economic aid to developing countries, obligations and disbursements by country, quarterly rpt, 9912–4
Economic and military aid and loans from US and intl agencies, by program and country, FY46-91, annual rpt, 9914–5
Economic and social conditions of developing countries from 1960s, and Intl Dev Cooperation Agency and AID activities and funding, FY91-93, annual rpt, 9904–4
Economic conditions, income, production, prices, employment, and trade, 1991 periodic country rpt, 2046–4.9
Economic, population, and agricultural data, US and other aid sources, and AID activity, 1992 country rpt, 9916–12.68
Economic, social, political, and geographic summary data, by country, 1992, annual factbook, 9114–2
Exports and imports of US, by transport mode, country, and SITC 1- to 3-digit commodity, 1991, annual rpt, 2424–12
Human rights conditions in 170 countries, and US economic and military aid, 1991, annual rpt, 21384–3
Military aid of US, arms sales, and training programs costs and budget requests, by program, world region, and country, FY91-93, annual rpt, 7144–13
Military spending, arms trade, and force strengths, with govt spending and population, by country, 1979-89, annual rpt, 9824–1
Minerals Yearbook, Vol 3, 1989: foreign country review of production, trade, and policy, by commodity, annual rpt, 5604–35.1
Population size, growth rates, and components of change, by country, projected 1990-2020 and trends from 1950, biennial rpt, 2324–9
Refugee migration, and intl aid programs, by world area and country of origin and asylum, 1991, annual rpt, 7004–15
UN voting record and share of votes in agreement with US, by issue, country, and world area, 1991, annual rpt, 7004–18

Ryan, James T.
"Balance Sheet Outlook for the Farm Sector in 1992", 1504–9.1
"Debt Repayment Capacity of Commercial Farm Operators: How Much Debt Can Farmers Afford?", 1541–1.312
"Farmer Mac: Can It Help Indebted Farm Operators?", 1541–1.304

Ryan White Comprehensive AIDS Resources Emergency Act
AIDS patients health care and support services funding under Ryan White CARE Act, and Federal grants by metro area, 1991, article, 4042–3.352

Rye
see Grains and grain products

Ryscavage, Paul
"Impact of Demographic, Social, and Economic Change on the Distribution of Income", 2546–6.79
"Impact of Survey and Questionnaire Design on Longitudinal Labor Force Measures", 2626–10.145
"Job Creation During the Late 1980's: Dynamic Aspects of Employment Growth", 2546–20.20
"Trends in Income and Wealth of the Elderly in the 1980s", 2546–6.79; 2626–10.144

Sabo, Carol
"Electric-Utility DSM Programs: Terminology and Reporting Formats", 3308–101

Sabotage
Aircraft hijackings, on-board explosions, and other crimes, US and foreign incidents, 1986-90, annual rpt, 7504–31
Kuwait oil fires set by Iraqi forces, air pollution levels by substance and site, as of Mar 1991, 9188–116
Kuwait oil fires set by Iraqi forces, air pollution levels, health effects, intl monitoring activities, and wells affected, 1991, GAO rpt, 26113–566
Sentences for Federal offenses, guidelines by offense and circumstances, series, 17668–1
Terrorism (intl) incidents, casualties, and attacks on US targets, by attack type and country, 1991, annual rpt, 7004–22
Terrorism (intl) incidents, casualties, and attacks on US targets, by attack type and world area, 1991, annual rpt, 7004–13
Terrorism incidents in US, related activity, and casualties, by attack type, target, group, and location, 1991, annual rpt, 6224–6
US attorneys civil and criminal cases by type and disposition, and collections, by Federal district, FY91, annual rpt, 6004–2.1

Sacramento, Calif.
Freight (waterborne domestic and foreign) by commodity, traffic, and passengers, by port and waterway, 1989, annual rpt, 3754–3.4
Housing starts and completions authorized by building permits in 40 MSAs, quarterly rpt, 2382–9
see also under By City and By SMSA or MSA in the "Index by Categories"

Sadeghi, M. M.
"Prediction of Release Rates for a Potential Waste Repository at Yucca Mountain", 3368–4

Sadura, Anna
"Quality-of-Life Assessment: Patient Compliance with Questionnaire Completion", 4472–1.326

Safety
see Accidents and accident prevention
see Aviation accidents and safety
see Marine accidents and safety
see Mine accidents and safety
see Motor vehicle safety devices
see Occupational health and safety
see Product safety
see Railroad accidents and safety
see State funding for public safety
see Traffic accident fatalities
see Traffic accidents and safety
see Transportation accidents and safety

Saginaw, Mich.
see also under By City and By SMSA or MSA in the "Index by Categories"

Sagoe, John A.
"Relative Drying Times of 650 Tropical Woods: Estimation by Green Moisture Content, Specific Gravity, and Green Weight Density", 1208–392

Saiger, Aaron J.
"State Strategic Planning Under the Drug Formula Grant Program", 6068–252

Sailors
see Merchant seamen
see Military personnel

Saint
see under terms beginning St.

Saipan, Northern Mariana Islands
Occupational health and safety violations and penalties assessed by OSHA, for Saipan garment factories, Mar 1992, press release, 6606–3.10

Salant, Priscilla
"Europeans Strive To Untangle Rural from Agricultural Policy", 1502–7.301
Salaries
see Agricultural wages
see Earnings, general
see Earnings, local and regional
see Earnings, specific industry
see Educational employees pay
see Federal pay
see Government pay
see Minimum wage
see Payroll
see Professionals' fees
see State and local employees pay
Salassi, Michael E.
"U.S. Rice Production Practices and Costs, 1988", 1568–309
Salem, Mass.
CPI by component for US city average, and by region, population size, and for 15 metro areas, monthly rpt, 6762–1
CPI by component for US city average, and by selected metro area, region, and population size, monthly rpt, 6762–2
Salem, Oreg.
see also under By City and By SMSA or MSA in the "Index by Categories"
Sales, business
see Business income and expenses, general
see Business income and expenses, specific industry
see Farm income
Sales promotion
Cigarette ad and promotion costs by media, and market shares, by cigarette type, with sales and use, 1963-89, annual rpt, 9404–4
Electric utilities finances and operations, detailed data for publicly and privately owned firms, 1990, annual rpt, 3164–11.4
Electric utilities finances and operations, detailed data for publicly owned firms, 1990, annual rpt, 3164–24
Electric utilities privately owned, finances and operations, detailed data, 1990, annual rpt, 3164–23
Milk order advertising and promotion finances, and producer participation, by region, 1991, annual article, 1317–4.304
Natural gas interstate pipeline company detailed financial and operating data, by firm, 1990, annual rpt, 3164–38
see also Advertising
see also Direct marketing
see also Foreign trade promotion
see also Market research
see also Sales workers
Sales tax
Auto, van, and light truck ownership and operating costs, by vehicle size and year of operation, 1991 model year, biennial rpt, 7554–21
Collections of taxes, by level of govt, type of tax, State, and selected counties, quarterly rpt, 2462–3
Finances of govts, by level of govt, State, and for large cities and counties, annual rpt series, 2466–2
Finances of govts, tax systems and revenue, and fiscal structure, by level of govt and State, 1992 and historical trends, annual rpt, 10044–1
Income tax returns of individuals, detailed data, 1988, annual rpt, 8304–2
Mail order sales from out of State, tax revenue losses by State, 1990-92, 10048–84
Natl income and product accounts and components, *Survey of Current Business*, monthly rpt, 2702–1.23
Natl income and product accounts, comprehensive accounts and components, benchmark revisions, 1929-88, 2708–5
Natl income and product accounts, comprehensive accounts and components, *Survey of Current Business*, monthly rpt, 2702–1.26
North Central States business and economic conditions, Fed Reserve 9th District, quarterly journal, 9383–19
Public opinion on taxes, spending, and govt efficiency, by respondent characteristics, 1992 survey, annual rpt, 10044–2
Retail trade sales tax as share of sales, by SIC 2- to 4-digit kind of business, 1990, annual rpt, 2413–5
Transit systems finances and operations, by mode, size of fleet and urban area, region, and for 518 systems, 1990, annual rpt, 7884–4
West Central States economic indicators, Fed Reserve 10th District, quarterly rpt, 9381–16.2
see also Excise tax
see also Fuel tax
see also Value added tax
Sales workers
Deaths and rates, by cause and selected social, demographic, and employment characteristics, 1979-85, natl longitudinal study, 4478–186
Educational attainment, by social and demographic characteristics and location, 1991 and trends from 1940, biennial Current Population Rpt, 2546–1.460
Employment and economic conditions, alternative BLS projections to 2005 and trends 1975-90, biennial rpt, 6744–19
Employment Cost Index and alternative measure of compensation costs, by component, occupation, industry group, union status, and location, 1975-92, annual rpt, 6744–20
Employment, earnings, and hours, monthly press release, 6742–5
Employment, unemployment, and labor force characteristics, by region, State, and selected metro area, 1991, annual rpt, 6744–7
Immigrants and legalized aliens, by occupational group and country of birth, preliminary FY91, annual tables, 6264–1
Immigration to US, alien workers, visitors, deportations, and naturalizations, by country, FY91 and trends from 1820, annual rpt, 6264–2
Income (household, family, and personal), by source, detailed characteristics, and region, 1991, annual Current Population Rpt, 2546–6.76
Labor demand, turnover, and training completions, by detailed occupation, 1990 and projected to 2005, biennial rpt, 6744–3
Minority group and women employment, by occupation, SIC 1- to 3- digit industry, State, and MSA, 1991, annual rpt, 9244–1
Occupational Outlook Handbook, 1992-93, biennial rpt, 6744–1
Older persons labor force status, income sources, and reasons for not working, with data by occupation, sex, and race, 1989-90 and projected to 2050, 21148–65
Pacific territories population and housing detailed characteristics, by location, 1990 Census of Population and Housing, series, 2551–8
Training for job qualification and skill improvement, workers participating by training source, occupation, age, sex, and race, 1991, 6728–32
see also under By Occupation in the "Index by Categories"
Salin, Victoria
"Cigarettes, Industry and Trade Summary", 9885–8.2
Salinas, Calif.
Wages by occupation, and benefits, for office and plant workers, 1992 survey, periodic MSA rpt, 6785–3.3
see also under By City and By SMSA or MSA in the "Index by Categories"
Salinity control
see Water pollution
Salk Institute
Biological warfare agent vaccine dev and production of Salk Inst, and Army contract costs by component, late 1970s-91, GAO rpt, 26123–374
Sallie Mae
see Student Loan Marketing Association
Salmon
see Aquaculture
Salt
see Nonmetallic minerals and mines
Salt Lake City, Utah
Housing starts and completions authorized by building permits in 40 MSAs, quarterly rpt, 2382–9
Housing vacancy rates for single and multifamily units and mobile homes, by city and ZIP code, 1992, annual MSA rpt, 9304–21.2
Wages by occupation, for office and plant workers, 1991 survey, periodic MSA rpt, 6785–12.2
Wages by occupation, for office and plant workers, 1992 survey, periodic MSA rpt, 6785–17.3
see also under By City and By SMSA or MSA in the "Index by Categories"
Saluter, Arlene F.
"Marital Status and Living Arrangements: March 1991", 2546–1.461
Salvage
see also Recycling of waste materials
see also Scrap metals
Samoa
see American Samoa
see Western Samoa
Samolyk, Katherine A.
"Bank Performance and Regional Economic Growth: Evidence of a Regional Credit Channel", 9377–9.135
San Antonio, Tex.
Drug test results at arrest, by drug type, offense, and sex, for selected urban areas, quarterly rpt, 6062–3
Govt funding for public housing and health, for San Antonio, with background data, 1989-91, hearing, 21248–172

Housing and households characteristics, and unit and neighborhood quality, by MSA location for 11 MSAs, 1986 survey, supplement, 2485–8
Housing rental and sales, discrimination against blacks and Hispanics in selected metro areas, 1989 study, 5186–16.2
Housing starts and completions authorized by building permits in 40 MSAs, quarterly rpt, 2382–9
Wages by occupation, for office and plant workers, 1991 survey, periodic MSA rpt, 6785–12.1
see also under By City and By SMSA or MSA in the "Index by Categories"

San Bernardino, Calif.
Housing and households characteristics, and unit and neighborhood quality, by MSA location for 11 MSAs, 1986 survey, supplement, 2485–8
Housing starts and completions authorized by building permits in 40 MSAs, quarterly rpt, 2382–9

San Bernardino County, Calif.
Water (groundwater) supply, quality, chemistry, and use, 1920s-89 and projected to 2015, local area rpt, 5666–28.15

San Diego, Calif.
Auto alternative fuels use in Federal fleet, energy economy performance at 4 sites, FY91, annual rpt, 3304–28
Commuters, by county of residence and work, for top 10 metro areas, 1990 Census of Population, press release, 2328–84
CPI by component for US city average, and by selected metro area, region, and population size, monthly rpt, 6762–2
Drug abuse indicators for selected metro areas, research results, data collection, and policy issues, 1992 semiannual conf, 4492–5
Drug test results at arrest, by drug type, offense, and sex, for selected urban areas, quarterly rpt, 6062–3
Heroin prices and purity in 19 metro areas and Puerto Rico, by world area of origin, quarterly rpt, 6282–2
Housing and households characteristics, and unit and neighborhood quality, by MSA location for 11 MSAs, 1987 survey, supplement, 2485–8
Housing starts and completions authorized by building permits in 40 MSAs, quarterly rpt, 2382–9
Wages by occupation, for office and plant workers, 1991 survey, periodic MSA rpt, 6785–16.3
see also under By City and By SMSA or MSA in the "Index by Categories"

San Francisco Bay
Ships in Natl Defense Reserve Fleet at Suisun Bay, as of July 1991, semiannual listing, 7702–2

San Francisco, Calif.
Commuters, by county of residence and work, for top 10 metro areas, 1990 Census of Population, press release, 2328–84
CPI by component for US city average, and by region, population size, and for 15 metro areas, monthly rpt, 6762–1
CPI by component for US city average, and by selected metro area, region, and population size, monthly rpt, 6762–2
Drug abuse indicators for selected metro areas, research results, data collection, and policy issues, 1992 semiannual conf, 4492–5
Freight (waterborne domestic and foreign) by commodity, traffic, and passengers, by port and waterway, 1989, annual rpt, 3754–3.4
Fruit and vegetable shipments, and arrivals by city, by mode of transport and State and country of origin, 1990, annual rpt, 1311–4.2
Heroin prices and purity in 19 metro areas and Puerto Rico, by world area of origin, quarterly rpt, 6282–2
Housing and households characteristics, unit and neighborhood quality, and journey to work by MSA location, for 11 MSAs, 1985 survey, supplement, 2485–8
Housing and households characteristics, 1989 survey, MSA fact sheet, 2485–11.8
Housing and households detailed characteristics, and unit and neighborhood quality, by location, 1989 survey, MSA rpt, 2485–6.8
Wages by occupation, for office and plant workers, 1992 survey, periodic MSA rpt, 6785–17.3
Water (groundwater) supply, quality, chemistry, and use, 1976-88, local area rpt, 5666–28.16
see also under By City and By SMSA or MSA in the "Index by Categories"

San Jose, Calif.
Commuters, by county of residence and work, for top 10 metro areas, 1990 Census of Population, press release, 2328–84
CPI by component for US city average, and by region, population size, and for 15 metro areas, monthly rpt, 6762–1
CPI by component for US city average, and by selected metro area, region, and population size, monthly rpt, 6762–2
Drug test results at arrest, by drug type, offense, and sex, for selected urban areas, quarterly rpt, 6062–3
Housing and households characteristics, 1988 survey, MSA fact sheet, 2485–11.1
see also under By City and By SMSA or MSA in the "Index by Categories"

San Marino
Economic, social, political, and geographic summary data, by country, 1992, annual factbook, 9114–2
Exports and imports of US, by transport mode, country, and SITC 1- to 3-digit commodity, 1991, annual rpt, 2424–12
Population size, growth rates, and components of change, by country, projected 1990-2020 and trends from 1950, biennial rpt, 2324–9

Sana
see Yemen, North

Sanctions
see International sanctions

Sand and gravel
County Business Patterns, 1989: employment, establishments, and payroll, by SIC 2- to 4-digit industry and county, annual State rpt series, 2326–8
County Business Patterns, 1990: employment, establishments, and payroll, by SIC 2- to 4-digit industry and county, annual State rpt series, 2326–6
Drug abuse screening and employee aid programs activities and policies in mining, by mineral and firm size, 1989, 6668–8
Exports and imports between US and outlying areas, by detailed commodity and mode of transport, 1991, annual rpt, 2424–11
Exports of US, detailed Schedule B commodities with countries of destination, 1991, annual rpt, 2424–10
Input-output structure of US economy, detailed interindustry transactions for 541 industries, and components of final demand, 1982 benchmark data, 2708–17
Mineral Industry Surveys, commodity review of production, trade, stocks, and use, quarterly rpt, 5612–2.20
Minerals Yearbook, Vol 1, 1989: commodity reviews of production, use, trade, prices, and mining operations, annual rpt, 5604–33
Minerals Yearbook, Vol 1, 1990: commodity review of production, reserves, supply, use, and trade, annual rpt, 5604–20.51
Minerals Yearbook, Vol 3, 1989: foreign country reviews of production, trade, and policy, by commodity, annual rpt, 5604–35
Occupational injuries and incidence, employment, and hours in sand and gravel mines and related operations, 1990, annual rpt, 6664–2
Occupational injuries by circumstances, employment, and hours, for mining industries by type of operation and State, quarterly rpt, 6662–1
Price indexes (producer) and sales of building materials, by type, quarterly rpt, 2042–1.6
Price indexes (producer), by stage of processing and detailed commodity, monthly rpt, 6762–6
Price indexes (producer), by stage of processing and detailed commodity, monthly 1991, annual rpt, 6764–2
Producers of sand and gravel, listing, 1990, Mineral Industry Surveys, advance annual rpt, 5614–5.1; 5614–5.6
Producers of sand and gravel, listing, 1991, Mineral Industry Surveys, advance annual rpt, 5614–5.18
Production, trade, use, and foreign investment in US industry, for minerals, 1985-90 and projected to 2000, annual rpt, 5304–5

Sandia National Laboratories
see also Department of Energy National Laboratories

Sanitary engineering
see Plumbing and heating
see Refuse and refuse disposal
see Sewage and wastewater systems

Sankarasubramanian, L.
"On Markovian Representations of the Term Structure", 9377–9.145

Santa Ana, Calif.
Housing and households characteristics, and unit and neighborhood quality, by MSA location for 11 MSAs, 1986 survey, supplement, 2485–8
Housing starts and completions authorized by building permits in 40 MSAs, quarterly rpt, 2382–9
Wages by occupation, for office and plant workers, 1991 survey, periodic MSA rpt, 6785–16.3

Santa Barbara, Calif.
Water quality, chemistry, hydrology, and other characteristics, 1991 local area study, 5666–27.29
see also under By City and By SMSA or MSA in the "Index by Categories"
Santa Barbara County, Calif.
Water (groundwater) supply, quality, chemistry, and use, 1987-88, local area rpt, 5666–28.17
Santa Rosa, Calif.
see also under By City and By SMSA or MSA in the "Index by Categories"
Santamaria, Marco
"Privatizing Social Security: The Chilean Case", 9385–8.123
Sao Tome and Principe
Agricultural trade of US, by detailed commodity and country, 1991, semiannual rpt, 1522–4
AID economic aid to developing countries, obligations and disbursements by country, quarterly rpt, 9912–4
Economic and military aid and loans from US and intl agencies, by program and country, FY46-91, annual rpt, 9914–5
Economic and social conditions of developing countries from 1960s, and Intl Dev Cooperation Agency and AID activities and funding, FY91-93, annual rpt, 9904–4
Economic, social, political, and geographic summary data, by country, 1992, annual factbook, 9114–2
Exports and imports of US, by transport mode, country, and SITC 1- to 3-digit commodity, 1991, annual rpt, 2424–12
Human rights conditions in 170 countries, and US economic and military aid, 1991, annual rpt, 21384–3
Military aid of US, arms sales, and training programs costs and budget requests, by program, world region, and country, FY91-93, annual rpt, 7144–13
Military spending, arms trade, and force strengths, with govt spending and population, by country, 1979-89, annual rpt, 9824–1
Minerals Yearbook, Vol 3, 1989: foreign country review of production, trade, and policy, by commodity, annual rpt, 5604–35.1
Population size, growth rates, and components of change, by country, projected 1990-2020 and trends from 1950, biennial rpt, 2324–9
UN voting record and share of votes in agreement with US, by issue, country, and world area, 1991, annual rpt, 7004–18
Sarasota, Fla.
see also under By City and By SMSA or MSA in the "Index by Categories"
Sargent, James D.
"Referrals of Participants in an Urban WIC Program to Health and Welfare Services", 4042–3.318
Sass, Steven
"Public Pension Dos and Don'ts", 9373–25.301
Satellites
Foreign and US space launchings and characteristics of craft and flight, 1957-91, annual rpt, 9504–9.1
Launchings and other activities of NASA and Soviet Union, with flight data, 1957-91, annual rpt, 9504–6.1
Launchings of satellites and other space objects since 1957, quarterly listing, 9502–2
Military weapons acquisition costs by system and service branch, DOD budget, FY91-93, annual rpt, 3504–2
NASA project launch schedules and technical descriptions, press release series, 9506–2
see also Communications satellites
see also Meteorological satellites
Saudi Arabia
Agricultural trade by commodity and country, prices, and world market devs, monthly rpt, 1922–12
Agricultural trade of US, by detailed commodity and country, 1991, annual rpt, 1524–8
Agricultural trade of US, by detailed commodity and country, 1991, semiannual rpt, 1522–4
Boycotts (intl) by OPEC and other countries, US firms and individuals cooperation and tax benefits denied, 1990, article, 8302–2.323
Economic and military aid and loans from US and intl agencies, by program and country, FY46-91, annual rpt, 9914–5
Economic and social conditions of developing countries from 1960s, and Intl Dev Cooperation Agency and AID activities and funding, FY91-93, annual rpt, 9904–4
Economic conditions, policy, and trade practices, by country, 1989-91, annual rpt, 21384–5
Economic, social, political, and geographic summary data, by country, 1992, annual factbook, 9114–2
Exports and imports of US, by commodity and country, 1980-90, world area rpt, 9116–1.6
Exports and imports of US, by Harmonized System 6-digit commodity and country, 1991, annual rpt, 2424–13
Exports and imports of US, by selected country, country group, and commodity group, 1991, annual rpt, 2044–37
Exports and imports of US, by transport mode, country, and SITC 1- to 3-digit commodity, 1991, annual rpt, 2424–12
Exports, imports, and balances of US for manufactured goods, by SITC 2-digit commodity and country, quarterly rpt, 2042–35
Exports, imports, and balances of US with major trading partners, by product category, 1987-91, annual chartbook, 9884–21
Exports of US, detailed Schedule B commodities with countries of destination, 1991, annual rpt, 2424–10
Human rights conditions in 170 countries, and US economic and military aid, 1991, annual rpt, 21384–3
Military spending, arms trade, and force strengths, with govt spending and population, by country, 1979-89, annual rpt, 9824–1
Minerals Yearbook, Vol 3, 1989: foreign country review of production, trade, and policy, by commodity, annual rpt, 5604–35.3
Multinatl US firms and foreign affiliates finances and operations, by industry and country, 1989 benchmark survey, annual rpt, 2704–5
Multinatl US firms foreign affiliates, income statement items by asset size, industry, and country, 1988, biennial article, 8302–2.322
Oil production, and exports and prices for US, by major exporting country, detailed data, monthly rpt with articles, 3162–24
Oil production, and exports and prices to US, by major exporting country, detailed data, monthly 1973-88, 3168–123
Oil production, stocks, use, and trade, by selected country and country group, monthly rpt, 3162–42
Persian Gulf War allied countries cash and in-kind contributions, by type and country, and status of DOD accounts, as of Sept 1991, annual GAO rpt, 26104–24
Population size, growth rates, and components of change, by country, projected 1990-2020 and trends from 1950, biennial rpt, 2324–9
Refugee migration, and intl aid programs, by world area and country of origin and asylum, 1991, annual rpt, 7004–15
Spacecraft and satellite launches since 1957, quarterly listing, 9502–2
Steel trade, by product, country, and customs district, with US industry operating data, 1989-June 1992, semiannual rpt, 9882–15
UN voting record and share of votes in agreement with US, by issue, country, and world area, 1991, annual rpt, 7004–18
see also under By Foreign Country in the "Index by Categories"
Saunders, Norman C.
"BLS Employment Projections for 1990: An Evaluation", 6722–1.335
"U.S. Economy into the 21st Century", 6744–19
Sauter, Steven
"Health Hazard Evaluation Report: U.S. West Communications, Phoenix, Ariz.; Minneapolis, Minn.; Denver, Colo.", 4248–93
Savannah, Ga.
Freight (waterborne domestic and foreign) by commodity, traffic, and passengers, by port and waterway, 1989, annual rpt, 3754–3.1
Wages by occupation, for office and plant workers, 1992 survey, periodic MSA rpt, 6785–3.5
see also under By City and By SMSA or MSA in the "Index by Categories"
Savannah River Plant, S.C.
Radiation and other pollutant releases from DOE contractor research lab and nuclear weapons facilities, monitoring results, 1991 annual site rpt, 3324–2.2; 3324–2.15
Westinghouse Co procurement from govt supply sources, for Savannah River nuclear weapons plant operations, 1990-91, 3006–5.33
Savings
Banks and thrifts finances and operations by deposit size, Fed Reserve functional cost analysis, 1991, annual rpt, 9364–6
Budget deficits and Fedeal debts impacts on savings rate, 1980s, technical paper, 8006–6.5
Business statistics, detailed data for major industries and economic indicators, 1960-91, *Survey of Current Business* biennial supplement, 2704–1

Deposits, debits, and deposit turnover at financial instns, 1990, annual rpt, 9364–5.1
Economic indicators and components, and Fed Reserve 4th District business and financial conditions, monthly chartbook, 9377–10
Economic indicators compounded annual rates of change, monthly rpt, 9391–3
Economic indicators, monthly rpt, 9362–1.2
Employee compensation costs, by component, occupation, industry group, union status, and location, 1975-92, annual rpt, 6744–20.2
Families financial status, income, net worth, and assets and debt by type, by income and selected characteristics, 1983 and 1989, article, 9362–1.301
Financial and monetary conditions, selected US summary data, weekly rpt, 9391–4
Fiscal policy (supply side) of Reagan Admin, economic impacts, 1980s and trends from 1960s, technical paper, 9385–1.304; 9385–8.125
Flow-of-funds accounts, savings, investments, and credit statements, quarterly rpt, 9365–3.3
Foreign and US savings rates, and ratio of aged to working age population, for US, Japan, and West Germany, 1980s-90, article, 9387–1.302
Foreign countries economic conditions and implications for US, periodic country rpt series, 2046–4
Foreign countries economic conditions, policy, and trade practices, by country, 1989-91, annual rpt, 21384–5
Higher education instn student financial support by parents, by type and funding sources, and student, parent, and instn characteristics, fall 1986, 4846–3.11
Households financial services use, by account type and instn type and location, 1989 survey, article, 9362–1.303
IRA contributions impact on savings, 1979-84, working paper, 9381–10.126
Latin America economic and social conditions, resources, trade, and aid, 1992, annual factbook, 9914–14
Monetary trends, Fed Reserve Bank of St Louis monthly rpt, 9391–2
Natl income and product accounts and components, *Survey of Current Business*, monthly rpt, 2702–1.23
Natl income and product accounts benchmark revisions, methodological changes and revised summary tables, 1959-91, article, 2702–1.302
Natl income and product accounts benchmark revisions of GDP and natl income, various periods 1959-80, tables, 2702–1.307
Natl income and product accounts benchmark revisions of personal income and outlays, monthly 1987-91, tables, 2702–1.301
Natl income and product accounts, comprehensive accounts and components, benchmark revisions, 1929-88, 2708–5
Natl income and product accounts, comprehensive accounts and components, *Survey of Current Business*, monthly rpt, 2702–1.28
Older persons income and sources, by whether OASDI beneficiary, poverty status, and other characteristics, 1990, biennial rpt, 4744–26
Older persons income by source, for married OASI beneficiaries by work and eligibility pattern of wife, 1982, article, 4746–26.12
Personal, business, and govt gross saving and investment from 1959, and personal savings by type, 1946-91, annual rpt, 204–1.1
Personal, business, and govt savings, *Survey of Current Business*, monthly rpt, 2702–1.1
Southeastern States, Fed Reserve 5th District insured commercial banks financial statements, by State, quarterly rpt, 9389–18
Statistical Abstract of US, 1992 annual data compilation, 2324–1.14
Supplemental Security Income applicants denied benefits because assets exceeded limits by asset type, and later eligibility, 1989, article, 4742–1.317
Survey of Current Business, detailed financial and business data, and economic indicators, monthly rpt, 2702–1.3
see also Bank deposits
see also Certificates of deposit
see also Credit unions
see also Individual retirement arrangements
see also Investments
see also Negotiable orders of withdrawal accounts
see also Savings institutions

Savings Association Insurance Fund
Deposits in SAIF-insured thrifts, and offices, by region, State, MSA, and county, 1991, annual rpt, 8434–5
Finances and operations of FDIC, insured deposits, and finances of banks needing FDIC aid, 1991 and trends from 1934, annual rpt, 9294–1
Finances of thrifts insured by SAIF, by profitability group, district, and State, quarterly rpt, 8432–4
Financial statements of SAIF-insured thrifts by FHLB district and State, and for FDIC-insured savings banks, 1989, annual rpt, 8434–1

Savings bonds
see U.S. savings bonds

Savings institutions
Assets and liabilities of depository instns, monthly rpt, 9362–1.1
Assets and liabilities of financial instns, by instn type, 1990, annual rpt, 9364–5.4
Assets, liabilities, and deposit and loan activity, for thrifts insured by Savings Assn Insurance Fund, by conservatorship status, monthly rpt, 8432–1
Banks (insured commercial and FDIC-insured savings) assets, income, and financial ratios, by asset size and State, quarterly rpt, 13002–3
Banks financial performance, risk assessment, and regulation, 1991 annual conf papers, 9375–7
Bond (junk) holdings of Resolution Trust Corp, quarterly press release, 9722–4
Bond (junk) holdings of S&Ls and relation to stock volatility and deposit interest rates, late 1980s, working paper, 9375–13.69
Business statistics, detailed data for major industries and economic indicators, 1960-91, *Survey of Current Business* biennial supplement, 2704–1
County Business Patterns, 1989: employment, establishments, and payroll, by SIC 2- to 4-digit industry and county, annual State rpt series, 2326–8
County Business Patterns, 1990: employment, establishments, and payroll, by SIC 2- to 4-digit industry and county, annual State rpt series, 2326–6
Credit (installment) outstanding and terms, by lender and credit type, monthly rpt, 9365–2.6
Deposits (brokered) relation to thrift size and selected financial ratios, late 1980s-91, article, 9379–15.301
Deposits (brokered) relation to thrift size and selected financial ratios, 1st qtr 1991, working paper, 9379–14.17
Deposits in insured commercial and savings banks, by instn, State, MSA, and county, as of June 1991, annual regional rpt series, 9295–3
Deposits in thrifts insured by Savings Assn Insurance Fund, and offices, by region, State, MSA, and county, 1991, annual rpt, 8434–5
Economic indicators and components, and Fed Reserve 4th District business and financial conditions, monthly chartbook, 9377–10
Economies of scale and other efficiency indicators for mutual and stock thrifts, model description and results, 1991, working paper, 9387–8.277
Economies of scale and scope, for mutual and stock thrifts by asset size, model description and results, 1989 technical paper, 8436–1.7
Employment, earnings, and hours, by SIC 1- to 4-digit industry, monthly 1989-Feb 1992, annual rpt, 6744–4
Failures of thrifts, costs and budget deficit and economic impacts, 1980s and projected to 2010, 26306–6.165
Failures of thrifts, financial performance of instns under Resolution Trust Corp conservatorship, quarterly rpt, 9722–5
Failures of thrifts, resolution activity and finances of Resolution Trust Corp, with data by asset type, State, region, and instn, monthly rpt, 9722–3
Failures of thrifts, resolution activity of Resolution Trust Corp, assets, deposits, and assets availability and sales, periodic press release, 9722–1
Failures of thrifts, resolution activity of Resolution Trust Corp, brokered deposits, fees, and interest rates by instn and region, as of July 1991, hearing, 21248–171
Failures of thrifts, resolution activity of Resolution Trust Corp impact on M2 growth, 1990-91, article, 9379–1.303
Failures of thrifts, resolution activity of Resolution Trust Corp impact on M2 growth, 1990-91, technical paper, 9379–12.83
Failures of thrifts, resolution costs impacts of capital standards relaxation, 1979-92, working paper, 9377–9.140
Farm loan guarantees of FmHA, characteristics of borrowers, lenders, and loans, FY88, 1548–386

Fed Home Loan Bank System members and assets, annual listing, discontinued, 9314–5
Finances and operations, by SIC 2- to 4-digit industry, forecast 1992, annual rpt, 2044–28
Finances and operations of savings instns by district and State, mortgage loan activity, and FHLB finances, annual rpt, discontinued, 8434–3
Finances of banks and thrifts, by instn type, 1991, annual rpt, 13004–2
Finances of insured commercial and savings banks, by State, 1990, annual rpt, 9294–4
Finances of thrifts insured by Savings Assn Insurance Fund, by profitability group, district, and State, quarterly rpt, 8432–4
Financial condition and performance of insured commercial and savings banks, by asset size and region, quarterly rpt, 9292–1
Financial condition of savings instns, and devs, working paper series, 9379–14
Financial performance of thrifts converting from mutual to stock ownership, Fed Reserve 1st District, 1980s-90, article, 9373–1.307
Financial ratios of high and low risk S&Ls, 1987, article, 9375–1.306
Financial statements of thrifts insured by Savings Assn Insurance Fund by FHLB district and State, and for FDIC-insured savings banks, 1989, annual rpt, 8434–1
Flow-of-funds accounts, savings, investments, and credit statements, quarterly rpt, 9365–3.3
Fraud and abuse in financial instns, Justice Dept enforcement activity, staff, and case dispositions by instn type, 1988-92, 6008–35
Fraud and abuse in thrifts, Federal indictments and case dispositions, periodic press release, 6002–3; 6008–33
Households financial services use, by account type and instn type and location, 1989 survey, article, 9362–1.303
Mortgage applications, dispositions, and secondary loan market sales, by purpose, lender type, and applicant and neighborhood characteristics, 1991, article, 9362–1.307
Mortgages (fixed rate) profitability of thrifts, relation to interest rate spread and other operating ratios, model results, 1991 technical paper, 9366–6.289
New England States banks and thrifts, assets and liabilities by type, and deposits relation to capital/asset ratios, by instn type and size, 1980s-91, article, 9373–1.309
New England States banks and thrifts, deposits by type and loans relation to capital/asset ratios, by instn size, 1990-91, working paper, 9373–27.4
New England States banks and thrifts real estate lending impacts of capital losses, with financial ratios, 1980s-91, article, 9373–27.12
New England States, FHLB 1st District thrift instns, financial condition, and locations, 1992, annual listing, 9304–26
New England States, FHLB 1st District thrifts financial operations compared to banks, and housing industry indicators, bimonthly rpt with articles, suspended, 9302–4
North Central States, FHLB 6th District and natl cost of funds indexes for savings instns, and mortgage rates, monthly rpt, 9302–38
North Central States, FHLB 6th District insured S&Ls financial condition and operations by State, quarterly rpt, 9302–23
North Central States, FHLB 7th District and natl cost of funds indexes for savings instns, and mortgage rates, monthly rpt, 9302–30
North Central States, FHLB 7th District savings instns, assets and deposits by instn and market area, annual rpt, discontinued, 9304–28
North Central States, FHLB 8th District S&Ls, locations, assets, and savings, 1992, annual listing, 9304–9
Occupational injury and illness rates, by SIC 2- to 4-digit industry, 1989-90, annual rpt, 6844–7
Occupational injury and illness rates, by SIC 2- to 4-digit industry, 1990, annual rpt, 6844–1
Real estate assets of failed thrifts, inventory of properties available from Resolution Trust Corp, semiannual listing series, 9722–2
Real estate assets of failed thrifts, sales by Resolution Trust Corp, and disposition of other assets, 1990-91, GAO rpt, 26119–372
Regulatory issues for savings instns, 1989 annual conf, 9304–24
Resolution Trust Corp programs fraud and abuse, audits and investigations, 2nd half FY92, semiannual rpt, 9722–6
Service fees, minimum balances, and services offered by banks and thrifts, by service type, 1991, annual rpt, 9364–12
Southeastern States, Fed Reserve 5th District, economic indicators by State, quarterly rpt, 9389–16
Southeastern States, FHLB 4th District thrifts finances, by State, discontinued annual rpt series, 9304–29
Statistical Abstract of US, 1992 annual data compilation, 2324–1.16
Tax (income) returns of corporations, income and tax items by asset size and detailed industry, 1989, annual rpt, 8304–4; 8304–21
Trust assets of banks, trust companies, and S&Ls, by type of asset and fund, selected firm, and State, 1991, annual rpt, 13004–1
West Central States economic indicators, Fed Reserve 10th District, quarterly rpt, 9381–16.2
West Central States, FHLB 10th District thrifts, locations, assets, and deposits, 1992, annual listing, 9304–17
Western States, FHLB 11th District and natl cost of funds indexes for savings instns, and mortgage rates, monthly rpt, 9302–38
Western States, FHLB 11th District shareholder instns, offices, and financial condition, 1992 annual listing, 9304–23
see also Mortgages

SBA
see Small Business Administration

Schaffer, Donna
"Mothers' Motivations To Participate in a Pregnancy Health Survey", 4042–3.377

Schappert, Susan M.
"National Ambulatory Medical Care Survey: 1989 Summary. Vital and Health Statistics Series 13", 4147–13.109
"National Ambulatory Medical Care Survey: 1990 Summary", 4146–8.215
"Office Visits for Diabetes Mellitus: U.S., 1989", 4146–8.212
"Office Visits for Otitis Media: U.S., 1975-90", 4146–8.217

Schaub, James D.
"Outlook Story for Oilseeds", 1504–9.1

Schaub, John
"Outlook for Production Inputs", 1504–9.1

Schaupp, Willis C., Jr.
"Status and Trends of Mountain Pine Beetle Populations in the Bear Mountain and White House Gulch Areas on the Harney Ranger District, Black Hills National Forest, South Dakota", 1208–408

Schenectady, N.Y.
Wages by occupation, for office and plant workers, 1991 survey, periodic MSA rpt, 6785–3.1

Schieber, George J.
"Containing U.S. Health Care Costs: What Bullet To Bite?", 4652–1.310
"U.S. Health Expenditure Performance: An International Comparison and Data Update", 4652–1.322

Schilling, Robert F.
"15-Month Followup of Women Methadone Patients Taught Skills To Reduce Heterosexual HIV Transmission", 4042–3.353

Schinke, Steven P.
"Feasibility of Interactive Videodisc Technology To Teach Minority Youth About Preventing HIV Infection", 4042–3.332

Schlehofer, Brigitte
"Association Between Brain Tumors and Menopausal Status", 4472–1.340

Schmitt, Carl M.
"Students at Less-Than-4-Year Institutions: 1987 National Postsecondary Student Aid Study", 4846–3.12

Schneider, Dona
"Blue Thursday? Homicide and Suicide Among Urban 15—24-Year-Old Black Male Americans", 4042–3.323

Schnick, Rosalie A.
"Therapeutic Compounds", 1504–9.1

Schnitzer, Patricia G.
"Surveillance of Traumatic Occupational Fatalities in Alaska—Implications for Prevention", 4042–3.307

Schoenman, Julie A.
"Classifications Systems for PPS-Excluded and Non-PPS Providers", 17206–2.29

Schoepfle, Gregory K.
"U.S. Employment Effects of a North American Free Trade Agreement: A Survey of Issues and Estimated Employment Effects", 6366–3.30

Scholarships
see Student aid

Scholl, Russell B.
"International Investment Position of the U.S. in 1991", 2702–1.323

School administration and staff
Athletic depts at NCAA Div I schools, staff by race, and income, by sex and position, 1990/91, GAO rpt, 26121–476
Black higher education instns enrollment, finances, staff, and degrees, by instn and selected student characteristics, 1970s-90, 4848–46
Condition of Education, detail for elementary, secondary, and higher education, 1920s-91 and projected to 2002, annual rpt, 4824–1
County Business Patterns, 1989: employment, establishments, and payroll, by SIC 2- to 4-digit industry and county, annual State rpt series, 2326–8
County Business Patterns, 1990: employment, establishments, and payroll, by SIC 2- to 4-digit industry and county, annual State rpt series, 2326–6
Data on education, enrollment, finances, teachers, and other characteristics, by State, 1969-89, 4828–33
Data on education, 1940s-95, pamphlet, 4828–35
Digest of Education Statistics, 1992 annual data compilation, 4824–2
DOD Dependents Schools and Uniformed Services University of Health Sciences civilian and military personnel, quarterly rpt, 3542–14.1
Elementary and secondary education enrollment, staff, finances, operations, programs, and policies, 1987/88 biennial survey, series, 4836–3
Elementary and secondary public school systems enrollment, finances, staff, and high school grads, by State, FY89-90, annual rpt, 4834–6
Elementary and secondary school system mgmt by higher education instn, Chelsea, Mass and Boston University demonstration program operations and results, 1988-90, 4808–38
Employment and direct spending, by function and level of govt, selected years 1967-87, 10048–53
Employment and economic conditions, alternative BLS projections to 2005 and trends 1975-90, biennial rpt, 6744–19
Employment and payroll, by function and level of govt, annual rpt series, 2466–1
Employment and payroll of State and local govts, monthly rpt, 6742–4
Employment, earnings, and hours, by selected SIC 1- to 4-digit industry, State, and for 275 MSAs, 1987-92, 6748–81
Employment, earnings, and hours, by SIC 1- to 4-digit industry, monthly 1989-Feb 1992, annual rpt, 6744–4
Employment, enrollment, and spending, by instn level and control, and teachers salaries, 1980s-93, annual press release, 4804–19
Employment, unemployment, and labor force characteristics, by region and census div, 1991, annual rpt, 6744–7.1
Head Start enrollment, funding, and staff, FY91, annual rpt, 4584–5
Higher education faculty and staff, by occupation, full- and part-time status, sex, and instn type and control, fall 1989, biennial rpt, 4844–18
Higher education PhD degree recipients employment plans, by employer type, work activity, and field, 1979, 1984, and 1989, 4848–44
Juvenile facilities compensatory education programs activities, participant and staff characteristics, and outcomes, 1991 rpts, 4808–40
Labor demand, turnover, and training completions, by detailed occupation, 1990 and projected to 2005, biennial rpt, 6744–3
Minority group and women employment by industry sector, and govt salaries, by occupation, mid 1960s-90, chartbook, 9248–20
Occupational injury and illness rates, by SIC 2- to 4-digit industry, 1989-90, annual rpt, 6844–7
Occupational injury and illness rates, by SIC 2- to 4-digit industry, 1990, annual rpt, 6844–1
Occupational Outlook Handbook, 1992-93, biennial rpt, 6744–1
Pacific territories population and housing detailed characteristics, by location, 1990 Census of Population and Housing, series, 2551–8
Principals views on safety, discipline, and student drug use, for elementary and secondary schools, 1991 survey, 4826–1.32
Private elementary and secondary schools, students, and staff characteristics, by school type and affiliation, 1987/88, 4836–3.8
Public confidence in people running selected social instns, 1972-88 surveys, biennial rpt, 9624–10.7
School districts efficient use of staff, model description and results for Texas, 1987-89, technical paper, 9379–12.80
Science and engineering grad enrollment, by field, source of funds, and characteristics of student and instn, 1990, annual rpt, 9627–7
Science and Engineering Indicators, employment, education, R&D funding, and industry impacts, with foreign comparisons, 1960s-91, biennial rpt, 9624–10
Science and engineering labor force, Federal and university research funding, and educational data, series, 9626–6
Science and math achievement relation to selected school characteristics, natl assessment of elementary and high school students, 1985/86, 4896–6.7
Special education programs, enrollment by age, staff, funding, and needs, by type of handicap and State, 1990/91, annual rpt, 4944–4
Statistical Abstract of US, 1992 annual data compilation, 2324–1.4
see also Campus security
see also Educational employees pay
see also Educational finance
see also School boards
see also School districts
see also Teachers

School boards
Elementary and secondary public school agencies, by enrollment size and location, fall 1990, annual listing, 4834–1

School buildings
see Educational facilities

School busing
Accidents (fatal), deaths, and rates, by circumstances, characteristics of persons and vehicles involved, and location, 1990, annual rpt, 7764–10
Accidents at hwy-railroad grade-crossings, detailed data by State and railroad, 1991, annual rpt, 7604–2
County Business Patterns, 1989: employment, establishments, and payroll, by SIC 2- to 4-digit industry and county, annual State rpt series, 2326–8
County Business Patterns, 1990: employment, establishments, and payroll, by SIC 2- to 4-digit industry and county, annual State rpt series, 2326–6
Digest of Education Statistics, 1992 annual data compilation, 4824–2
Drivers licenses issued and in force by age and sex, fees, and renewal, by license class and State, 1990, annual rpt, 7554–16
Employment, earnings, and hours, by SIC 1- to 4-digit industry, monthly 1989-Feb 1992, annual rpt, 6744–4
Energy use by mode of transport, fuel supply, and demographic and economic factors of vehicle use, 1970s-90, annual rpt, 3304–5
Occupational injury and illness rates, by SIC 2- to 4-digit industry, 1989-90, annual rpt, 6844–7
Occupational injury and illness rates, by SIC 2- to 4-digit industry, 1990, annual rpt, 6844–1
Travel patterns, personal and household characteristics, and auto and public transport use, 1990 survey, series, 7556–6

School desegregation
see Discrimination in education

School districts
Budget efficiency measures for school districts, model description and results, 1992 technical paper, 9379–12.87
Compensatory education grants, and allocation by function, for 8 school districts, 1990/91, GAO rpt, 26121–478
Districts, schools, and enrollment, by State and for selected systems, 1991 annual data compilation, 4824–2.10
Elementary and secondary public school agencies, by enrollment size and location, fall 1990, annual listing, 4834–1
Elementary and secondary public schools and enrollment, by State, 1990/91, annual rpt, 4834–17
Elementary and secondary schools, teachers, staff, and enrollment, by selected characteristics, 1987/88-88/89, 4836–3.10
Employment and payroll, by function, level of govt, and State, 1991, annual rpt, 2466–1.1
Expenditures (direct) and employment, by function and level of govt, selected years 1962-87, 10048–53
Finances of govts, by level of govt, State, and for large cities and counties, annual rpt series, 2466–2
Finances, structure, and service delivery of local govts in metro areas, local area rpt series, 10046–9
Finances, tax systems and revenue, and fiscal structure, by level of govt and State, 1992 and historical trends, annual rpt, 10044–1

Property values relation to school district educational quality, for Dallas, model description and results, 1985-87, technical paper, 9379–12.94
R&D and related funding of Fed Govt to higher education and nonprofit instns, by field, instn, agency, and State, FY90, annual rpt, 9627–17
Science and math teacher dev project of Education Dept, school district participation by State, 1989/90, GAO rpt, 26121–488
Staff use and efficiency of school districts, model description and results for Texas, 1987-89, technical paper, 9379–12.80
see also School boards

School dropouts
Appalachia local dev projects, and funding by source, by program and State, FY91, annual rpt, 9084–1
Asian and Pacific Islands Americans social and economic characteristics, for West and total US, 1990-91, Current Population Report, 2546–1.462
Census of Population and Housing, 1990: summary characteristics, by county, subdiv, and place, State rpt series, 2551–7
Condition of Education, detail for elementary, secondary, and higher education, 1920s-91 and projected to 2002, annual rpt, 4824–1
Credit availability relation to college attainment, model description and results, 1991 working paper, 6886–6.92
Digest of Education Statistics, 1992 annual data compilation, 4824–2
Eighth grade class of 1988: educational performance and conditions, characteristics, attitudes, activities, and plans, natl longitudinal survey, series, 4826–9
Elementary and secondary students reading and math proficiency, and dropouts, by race, 1970s-90, 4838–52
High school class of 1991: college enrollment, and labor force participation of grads and dropouts, by race and sex, annual press release, 6726–1.46
High school dropout rates, and subsequent completion, by student and school characteristics, alternative estimates, 1991, annual rpt, 4834–23
High school dropout rates, by selected characteristics, 1988 survey, 4826–10.3
High school dropouts and rates, and data collection and reporting methods evaluation, 1992 rpt, 4838–49
High school dropouts and transfers between public and private schools, by instn control, income level, and race, 1990 survey, 4826–10.4
High school dropouts in Chelsea, Mass, by sex, race, and grade, impacts of Boston University mgmt of local school system, 1988-90, 4808–38
Income (household) and poverty status under alternative income definitions, by recipient characteristics, 1979-91, annual Current Population Rpt, 2546–6.78
Income (household, family, and personal), by source, detailed characteristics, and region, 1991, annual Current Population Rpt, 2546–6.76
Income (personal) relative to median, by race and selected other characteristics, mid 1960s-89, Current Population Rpt, 2546–6.73
Indians and Alaska Natives education condition, indicators and comparisons to other groups, 1980s-90, 4808–42.1
Juvenile facilities compensatory education programs activities, participant and staff characteristics, and outcomes, 1991 rpts, 4808–40
Military officers newly commissioned, share from service academies, and academy attrition, 1970s-91 and projected to FY97, GAO rpt, 26123–389
Natl Education Goals progress indicators, by State, 1992, annual rpt, 15914–1
Pacific territories population and housing detailed characteristics, by location, 1990 Census of Population and Housing, series, 2551–8
Population educational enrollment status and attainment, by selected characteristics, 1990 and trends from 1947, annual Current Population Rpt, 2546–1.459
Poverty relation to low earnings, by work experience during year, household relationship, sex, race, age, and education, 1960s-90, Current Population Rpt, 2546–6.74
Single parent families in own and others homes, by financial, housing, and other characteristics, 1989, 2486–1.14
Special education programs, enrollment by age, staff, funding, and needs, by type of handicap and State, 1990/91, annual rpt, 4944–4
Statistical Abstract of US, 1992 annual data compilation, 2324–1.4
see also Educational retention rates

School enrollment
see Educational enrollment

School finance
see Educational finance
see Tuition and fees

School lunch and breakfast programs
CCC dairy price support program foreign donations and domestic donations to poor, schools, Prisons Bur, and VA, monthly rpt, 1802–2
Consumer research, food marketing, legislation, and regulation devs, and consumption and price trends, quarterly journal, 1541–7
Criminal cases by type and disposition, and collections, for US attorneys, by Federal district, FY91, annual rpt, 6004–2.1
Eighth grade class of 1988: educational performance and conditions, characteristics, attitudes, activities, and plans, natl longitudinal survey, series, 4826–9
Elementary and secondary education enrollment, staff, finances, operations, programs, and policies, 1987/88 biennial survey, series, 4836–3
Eligibility for free lunch, share of enrollment by State, 1990/91, annual rpt, 4834–17
Expenditures for education by Federal agency, program, and recipient type, and instn spending, 1960s-91, annual rpt, 4824–8
Fed Govt financial and nonfinancial domestic aid, 1992 base edition, annual listing, 104–5
Income (household) and poverty status under alternative income definitions, by recipient characteristics, 1979-91, annual Current Population Rpt, 2546–6.78
Poverty status of population and families, by detailed characteristics, 1991, annual Current Population Rpt, 2546–6.77
Processing of food donations for school lunch programs, contracts, and processors problems with State reporting requirements, with data by State, 1989-91, GAO rpt, 26113–555
Statistical Abstract of US, 1992 annual data compilation, 2324–1.12
USDA child nutrition programs funding, by program and State, FY90-91, annual rpt, 4824–2.27

Schools
see Educational facilities
see Private schools
see terms listed under Education and beginning with School

Schools and Staffing Survey
Elementary and secondary education enrollment, staff, finances, operations, programs, and policies, 1987/88 biennial survey, series, 4836–3

Schramm, Wayne F.
"Weighing Costs and Benefits of Adequate Prenatal Care for 12,023 Births in Missouri's Medicaid Program, 1988", 4042–3.365

Schreft, Stacey L.
"Identifying Credit Crunches", 9389–19.32

Schulte, Joann M.
"Chancroid in the U.S., 1981-90: Evidence for Underreporting of Cases", 4202–7.318

Schulz, Carl O.
"Review of Literature on Herbicides, Including Phenoxy Herbicides and Associated Dioxins: Volume XVII Analysis of Recent Literature on Health Effects; and Volume XVIII Annotated Bibliography of Recent Literature on Health Effects", 8706–1.4

Schumann, Laurence
"Effects of FTC Antitrust Challenges on Rival Firms 1981-87: An Analysis of the Use of Stock Returns To Determine the Competitive Effects of Horizontal Mergers", 9408–55

Schuster, Ervin G.
"Assessing Forest Service Recreation Trends with Shift-share Analysis", 1208–423

Schwartz, Anne
"Comments on the President's Budget for FY93", 17266–2.11

Schwartz, Rachel M.
"Explaining Resource Consumption Among Non-Normal Neonates", 4652–1.303

Schweitzer, Martin
"Public Involvement in Integrated Resource Planning: A Study of Demand-Side Management Collaboratives", 3308–104

Schwenk, F. N.
"Economic Status of Rural Older Americans", 1504–9.1
"Income and Expenditures of Older Widowed, Divorced, and Never-Married Women Who Live Alone", 1702–1.301

Schwenk, Nancy E.
"Health Care Trends", 1702–1.309
"Trends in Entertainment", 1702–1.303

Science and technology
Higher education instn R&D facilities space and equipment adequacy, needs, and funding by source, by instn type and control, 1992, biennial rpt, 9624–25
Natl Inst of Standards and Technology rpts, 1991, annual listing, 2214–1
NSF grants and contracts, by field, recipient, and State, FY90, annual rpt, 9624–26
NSF R&D grant awards, by div and program, periodic rpt series, 9626–7
NSF rpts, 1992 annual listing, 9624–16
Public knowledge, interest, and expectations for science and technology, 1990 survey, biennial rpt, 9624–10.7
Science and Engineering Indicators, employment, education, R&D funding, and industry impacts, with foreign comparisons, 1960s-91, biennial rpt, 9624–10
see also Agricultural sciences and research
see also Astronomy
see also Atmospheric sciences
see also Aviation sciences
see also Biological sciences
see also Biotechnology
see also Botany
see also CD-ROM technology and use
see also Chemistry
see also Computer sciences
see also Defense research
see also Department of Energy National Laboratories
see also Earth sciences
see also Educational research
see also Educational technology
see also Energy research and development
see also Engineers and engineering
see also Environmental sciences
see also Federal aid to medicine
see also Federal funding for energy programs
see also Federal funding for research and development
see also Federally Funded R&D Centers
see also Forensic sciences
see also Genetics
see also Information sciences
see also International cooperation in science and technology
see also Inventions
see also Mathematics
see also Medical research
see also Meteorology
see also Military science
see also Oceanography
see also Physical sciences
see also Physics
see also Physiology
see also Psychology
see also Research
see also Research and development
see also Scientific education
see also Scientific equipment and apparatus
see also Scientific ethics
see also Scientists and technicians
see also Social sciences
see also Space programs
see also Space sciences
see also Technological innovations
see also Technology transfer
see also Zoology

Science Applications International Corp.
"Aerial Surveys of Endangered Whales in the Alaskan Chukchi and Western Beaufort Seas, 1990", 5738–36
"Distribution, Abundance and Behavior of Endangered Whales in the Alaskan Chukchi and Western Beaufort Seas, 1991: with a Review, 1982-91", 5738–32

Scientex Corporation
"Accidents Reported by Motor Carriers of Property, 1989", 7554–9

Scientific education
Assistance (financial and nonfinancial) of Fed Govt, 1992 base edition, annual listing, 104–5
Condition of Education, detail for elementary, secondary, and higher education, 1920s-91 and projected to 2002, annual rpt, 4824–1
Degrees (PhD) in science and engineering, holders by field, instn, employment prospects, sex, race, and other characteristics, 1960s-90, advance annual rpt, 9626–8.1
Degrees awarded in higher education, by level, field, race, and sex, 1989/90 and trends from 1980/81, annual rpt, 4844–17
Degrees awarded in science and engineering, and ratio to population and job openings, 1970s-90 and projected to 2005, article, 6722–1.314
Digest of Education Statistics, 1992 annual data compilation, 4824–2
DOD Dependents Schools basic skills and college entrance test scores, 1991-92, annual rpt, 3504–16
Eighth grade class of 1988: science and math course participation, instruction, and performance, by selected characteristics, natl longitudinal survey, 1992 rpt, 4826–9.13
Elementary and secondary students educational performance in math, science, reading, and writing, 1969-90, 4898–32
Elementary and secondary students science performance, and student and teacher attitudes, by selected characteristics, 1990 natl assessments, 4896–8.3
Enrollment in science and engineering grad programs, by field, source of funds, and characteristics of student and instn, 1990, annual rpt, 9627–7
Fed Govt aid to higher education and nonprofit instns for R&D and related activities, by field, instn, agency, and State, FY90, annual rpt, 9627–17
Foreign and US students science and math proficiency, intl assessment results and other indicators by selected country, 1960s-80s, 4838–51
Goldwater, Barry, Scholarship Foundation awards and finances, FY87-91, annual rpt, 10404–1
Graduate level enrollment in science and engineering, by field, source of funds, and characteristics of student and instn, 1990, annual rpt, 9626–8.3
Higher education instn science and engineering curricula improvement grants of NSF, recipient characteristics and views, 1985-87, 9628–87
Labor force, Federal and university research funding, and educational data, for science and engineering, series, 9626–6
Minority group, women, and disabled persons employment and education in science and engineering, by field, mid 1970s-91, biennial rpt, 9624–20
NASA Apollo era science and engineering staff background and characteristics, 1958-70, 9508–39
Natl assessment of elementary and high school students, science and math education, 1985/86, series, 4896–6
Natl Education Goals progress indicators, by State, 1992, annual rpt, 15914–1
NSF activities, finances, and funding by program, FY91, annual rpt, 9624–6
NSF grants and contracts, by field, recipient, and State, FY90, annual rpt, 9624–26
NSF R&D grant awards, by div and program, periodic rpt series, 9626–7
Nuclear engineering enrollment and degrees granted by instn and State, and grad placement, by student characteristics, 1991, annual rpt, 3004–5
Radiation protection and health physics enrollment and degrees granted by instn and State, and grad placement, by student characteristics, 1991, annual rpt, 3004–7
Radiation protection and health physics enrollment and degrees granted by instn and State, and women grads plans and employment, 1991, annual rpt, 3006–8.19
Science and Engineering Indicators, employment, education, R&D funding, and industry impacts, with foreign comparisons, 1960s-91, biennial rpt, 9624–10
Teachers of science and math, professional dev project of Education Dept, school district participation by State, 1989/90, GAO rpt, 26121–488
Undergrad research grants of NSF, administrator and recipient characteristics and views, 1987-89, 9628–86
Vocational education enrollment, and academic and other credits earned, by subject and student characteristics, high school classes of 1982 and 1987, 4838–50
Vocational education enrollment, student and teacher characteristics, and outcomes, for secondary and postsecondary instns, 1970s-90, 4828–42

Scientific equipment and apparatus
Calibration of measurement systems, standard reference materials specifications and availability, 1992 biennial listing, 2214–2
DOE R&D projects and funding at natl labs, universities, and other instns, periodic summary rpt series, 3004–18
Eastern Europe export industries dev potential, with trade and industry finances and operations, for 5 countries, 1985-90, 9886–4.179
Employment, earnings, and hours, by SIC 1- to 4-digit industry, monthly 1989-Feb 1992, annual rpt, 6744–4
Exports and imports between US and outlying areas, by detailed commodity and mode of transport, 1991, annual rpt, 2424–11
Exports and imports of US, by country and detailed commodity, monthly rpt, 2422–12

Exports and imports of US, by transport mode, country, and SITC 1- to 3-digit commodity, 1991, annual rpt, 2424–12
Exports of US, detailed Schedule B commodities with countries of destination, 1991, annual rpt, 2424–10
Glassware shipments, trade, use, and firms, by product, 1991, annual Current Industrial Rpt, 2506–9.3
HHS financial aid, by program, recipient, State, and city, FY91, annual regional listings, 4004–3
Higher education instn science and engineering curricula improvement grants of NSF, recipient characteristics and views, 1985-87, 9628–87
Imports of US given duty-free treatment for value of US material sent abroad, by commodity and country, 1987-90, annual rpt, 9884–14
Input-output structure of US economy, detailed interindustry transactions for 541 industries, and components of final demand, 1982 benchmark data, 2708–17
Manufacturing census, 1987: concentration of largest firms measured by value added, and for shipments by SIC 2- and 4-digit industry, subject rpt, 2497–6
Manufacturing census, 1987: shipments of manufacturers products, by customer class and SIC 2- and 4-digit industry, subject rpt, 2497–4
Manufacturing finances and operations, by SIC 2- to 4-digit industry, forecast 1992, annual rpt, 2044–28
Mexico imports from US, by industry and State, 1987-91, 2048–154
NSF activities, finances, and funding by program, FY91, annual rpt, 9624–6
Occupational injury and illness rates, by SIC 2- to 4-digit industry, 1989-90, annual rpt, 6844–7
Occupational injury and illness rates, by SIC 2- to 4-digit industry, 1990, annual rpt, 6844–1
Oceanographic research cruise ships characteristics, by higher education instn and Federal agency, 1992, annual listing, 3804–6
OECD trade, total and for 4 major countries, and US trade by country, by commodity, 1980-90, world area rpt series, 9116–1
Price indexes (producer), by stage of processing and detailed commodity, monthly rpt, 6762–6
Price indexes (producer), by stage of processing and detailed commodity, monthly 1991, annual rpt, 6764–2
Science and Engineering Indicators, employment, education, R&D funding, and industry impacts, with foreign comparisons, 1960s-91, biennial rpt, 9624–10.5
Science, engineering, and technical employment in manufacturing, by field and industry, 1989, triennial rpt, 9627–23
Seismographs (portable) from Canada, injury to US industry from foreign subsidized imports, investigation with background financial and operating data, 1992 rpt, 9886–15.79
Shipments, trade, use, and firms, for instruments and related products by detailed type, 1991, annual Current Industrial Rpt, 2506–12.26
Standards dev, proposals, and policies, for weights, measures, and performance, 1992 annual conf, 2214–7
see also Medical supplies and equipment

Scientific ethics
Public knowledge, interest, and expectations for science and technology, 1990 survey, biennial rpt, 9624–10.7
see also Medical ethics

Scientific research
see Research

Scientists and technicians
Agricultural research funding and staffing for USDA, State agencies, and other instns, by topic, FY91, annual rpt, 1744–2
DOT employment, by subagency, occupation, and selected personnel characteristics, FY91, annual rpt, 7304–18
Electronics industry production and labor conditions, in 10 MSAs, EC, and top producer countries, late 1970s-80s, article, 9393–8.307
Employment and economic conditions, alternative BLS projections to 2005 and trends 1975-90, biennial rpt, 6744–19
Employment of scientists and engineers, and related topics, advance rpt series, 9626–8
Employment of scientists, engineers, and technicians by industry and occupation, and degrees awarded, 1970s-90 and projected to 2005, article, 6722–1.314
Environmental Quality, status of problems, protection programs, research, and intl issues, 1991 annual rpt, 484–1
Japan R&D activities of US firms, employee characteristics, and mgmt views on benefits and drawbacks, 1991 rpt, 9628–88
Labor demand, turnover, and training completions, by detailed occupation, 1990 and projected to 2005, biennial rpt, 6744–3
Labor force, Federal and university research funding, and educational data, for science and engineering, series, 9626–6
Manufacturing employment of scientists, engineers, and technicians, by field and industry, 1989, triennial rpt, 9627–23
Minority group, women, and disabled persons employment and education in science and engineering, by field, mid 1970s-91, biennial rpt, 9624–20
NASA Apollo era science and engineering staff background and characteristics, 1958-70, 9508–39
NASA staff characteristics and personnel actions, FY91, annual rpt, 9504–1
Nuclear engineering enrollment and degrees granted by instn and State, and grad placement, by student characteristics, 1991, annual rpt, 3004–5
Nuclear-related employment of scientists and engineers, by industry sector and occupation, 1983-91, 3006–8.20
Occupational Outlook Handbook, 1992-93, biennial rpt, 6744–1
Public confidence in people running selected social instns, 1972-88 surveys, biennial rpt, 9624–10.7
Radiation protection and health physics enrollment and degrees granted by instn and State, and grad placement, by student characteristics, 1991, annual rpt, 3004–7
Science and Engineering Indicators, employment, education, R&D funding, and industry impacts, with foreign comparisons, 1960s-91, biennial rpt, 9624–10
Statistical Abstract of US, 1992 annual data compilation, 2324–1.20
see also Scientific education
see also Scientific ethics
see also Statisticians
see also under specific scientific disciplines (listed under Science and technology)

Scotland
see United Kingdom

Scott, Charles G.
"Disabled SSI Recipients Who Work", 4742–1.308

Scott, Edwin L.
"Cooperative Game Fish Tagging Program Annual Newsletter, 1990", 2164–24

Scranton, Pa.
see also under By City and By SMSA or MSA in the "Index by Categories"

Scrap metals
Business statistics, detailed data for major industries and economic indicators, *Survey of Current Business*, monthly rpt, 2702–1.16
Business statistics, detailed data for major industries and economic indicators, 1960-91, *Survey of Current Business* biennial supplement, 2704–1
Exports and imports between US and outlying areas, by detailed commodity and mode of transport, 1991, annual rpt, 2424–11
Exports and imports of US, by country and detailed commodity, monthly rpt, 2422–12
Exports and imports of US, by Harmonized System 6-digit commodity and country, 1991, annual rpt, 2424–13
Exports and imports of US, by transport mode, country, and SITC 1- to 3-digit commodity, 1991, annual rpt, 2424–12
Exports of US, detailed Schedule B commodities with countries of destination, 1991, annual rpt, 2424–10
Financial and economic performance indicators and indexes for metals industries, by commodity, monthly rpt, 5602–5
Freight (waterborne domestic and foreign) by commodity, traffic, and passengers, by port and waterway, 1989, annual rpt, 3754–3
Input-output structure of US economy, detailed interindustry transactions for 541 industries, and components of final demand, 1982 benchmark data, 2708–17
Labor productivity, indexes of output, hours, and employment by SIC 2- to 4-digit industry, 1967-90, annual rpt, 6824–1.4
Mineral Industry Surveys, commodity review of production, trade, stocks, and use, monthly rpt, 5612–1.11
Minerals Yearbook, Vol 1, 1989: commodity reviews of production, use, trade, prices, and mining operations, annual rpt, 5604–33
Minerals Yearbook, Vol 1, 1990: commodity reviews of production, reserves, supply, use, and trade, annual rpt series, 5604–20

Minerals Yearbook, Vol 1, 1991: commodity reviews of production, reserves, supply, use, and trade, annual rpt series, 5604–15
Minerals Yearbook, Vol 3, 1989: foreign country reviews of production, trade, and policy, by commodity, annual rpt, 5604–35
Price indexes (producer), by stage of processing and detailed commodity, monthly rpt, 6762–6
Price indexes (producer), by stage of processing and detailed commodity, monthly 1991, annual rpt, 6764–2
Production, prices, trade, use, employment, tariffs, and stockpiles, by mineral, with foreign comparisons, 1987-91, annual rpt, 5604–18
Recycling of municipal and industrial waste, costs, revenues, and secondary products trade and related energy use and pollution reductions, 1991 hearings, 21368–139
Ships in Natl Defense Reserve Fleet, use in Persian Gulf War, and revenue from scrap sales, 1987-91, GAO rpt, 26123–376

Scroggins, Carol D.
"Consumer Attitudes Toward Labeling", 1504–9.1

Sea pollution
see Marine pollution

Sea turtles
see Endangered species

SEACO, Inc.
see Science Applications International Corp.

Seafood
see Fish and fishing industry
see Shellfish

Seamen
see Merchant seamen

Searches and seizures
Airport security operations to prevent hijacking, screening results, enforcement actions, and hijacking attempts, 1990, annual rpt, 7504–49
Bombing incidents and casualties by target and circumstances, and explosives theft and recovery, by State, 1987-91, annual rpt, 8484–4
Bombing incidents, casualties, and damage, by target, circumstances, and State, 1991, annual rpt, 6224–5
Coast Guard enforcement activities, 1st half FY92, semiannual rpt, 7402–4
Counterfeiting and other Secret Service investigations and arrests by type, and dispositions, FY91 and trends from FY82, annual rpt, 8464–1
Drug (heroin) seizures by Federal agencies, with NYC street prices and purity, FY82-91, GAO rpt, 26119–404
Drug (illegal) and related property seizures by Federal agencies, by type, data compilation, 1992 annual rpt, 6064–6.4
Drug (illegal) arrests and related property seizures assisted by Natl Guard, FY89-91, annual rpt, 3504–22
Drug (illegal) production, eradication, and seizures, by substance, with US aid, by country, 1988-92, annual rpt, 7004–17
Drug (illegal) supply in US by country of origin, abuse, prices, and seizures, by substance, 1991, annual rpt, 6284–2
Drug abuse and trafficking reduction programs activities, funding, staff, and Bush Admin budget request, by Federal agency, FY91-93, annual rpt, 234–2
Drug abuse indicators for selected metro areas, research results, data collection, and policy issues, 1992 semiannual conf, 4492–5
Drug enforcement activities of police and sheriff depts, and employee drug testing policies, 1990, 6066–19.67
FDA investigations and regulatory activities, quarterly rpt, 4062–3
Foreign countries human rights conditions in 170 countries, 1991, annual rpt, 21384–3
Immigration and Naturalization Service illegal alien and narcotics activities, FY84-91, annual rpt, 6264–2.5
Justice Dept Asset Forfeiture Program seizures, finances, and disbursements, FY85-91, annual rpt, 6004–21
LSD trafficking, abuse, and enforcement, and DEA field div activities, 1980s-91, 6288–9
Marijuana crop eradication activities of DEA and local agencies, and weapons and assets seized, by State, 1982-91, annual rpt, 6284–4
Marshals Service activities, FY91, annual rpt, 6294–1
Tax litigation and enforcement activity of IRS, FY91, annual rpt, 8304–3.1
Warrants issued for search and arrest, caseloads of Federal district courts, by circuit and district, 1991, annual rpt, 18204–8.26

Seashores
Army Corps of Engineers activities and projects, FY88 and trends from 1800s, annual rpt, 3754–1.1
Army Corps of Engineers activities and projects, FY89 and trends from 1800s, annual rpt, 3754–1.2
Army Corps of Engineers activities and projects, FY90 and trends from 1800s, annual rpt, 3754–1.3
Army Corps of Engineers water resources dev projects, characteristics, and costs, 1950s-89, biennial State rpt series, 3756–1
Army Corps of Engineers water resources dev projects, characteristics, and costs, 1950s-91, biennial State rpt series, 3756–2
Environmental conditions, fish, wildlife, use, and mgmt, for individual coastal and riparian ecosystems, series, 5506–9
Environmental mgmt of coastal areas, State activities and Federal funding, FY90-91, biennial rpt, 2174–8
Minerals offshore lease sales environmental and economic impacts in coastal areas, final statement series, 5736–7
Natl park system sites acreage and descriptions, 1991, biennial listing, 5544–5
Natl park system visits and overnight stays, by park and State, monthly rpt, 5542–4
Natl park system visits and overnight stays, by park and State, 1991, annual rpt, 5544–12
Natl parks and other land under Natl Park Service mgmt, acreage by site, ownership, and region, FY92, semiannual rpt, 5542–1
Washington and Oregon coastal areas recreation resources, and impacts of OCS oil and gas dev, 1983-88, 5738–40

Seaside, Calif.
Wages by occupation, and benefits, for office and plant workers, 1992 survey, periodic MSA rpt, 6785–3.3

Seasonal adjustment factors
Balance of payments, seasonal adjustment statistical discrepancy, monthly rpt, 23842–1.7
Construction put in place, value of new public and private structures, by type, monthly rpt, 2382–4
Employment, earnings, and hours benchmarks by SIC 2- to 4-digit industry, 1984-91, and revised seasonal adjustment factors by major industry group, 1992, semiannual article, 6742–2.306
Employment, earnings, and hours, by SIC 1- to 4-digit industry, monthly 1989-Feb 1992, annual rpt, 6744–4
Employment, earnings, and hours, seasonal adjustment factors by major industry group, Nov 1991-Apr 1992, semiannual article, 6742–2.301
Employment situation, earnings, hours, and other BLS economic indicators, transcripts of BLS Commissioner's monthly testimony, periodic rpt, 23846–4
Housing starts, by units per structure and metro-nonmetro location, and mobile home placements and prices, by region, monthly rpt, 2382–1
Housing units (1-family) sold and for sale by price, stage of construction, months on market, and region, monthly rpt, 2382–3
Housing units authorized, by region, State, selected MSA, and permit-issuing place, monthly rpt, 2382–5
Labor force and economic data series of BLS, collection, analysis, and presentation methods, by program, 1992 rpt, 6888–1
Labor force data series of BLS, seasonal adjustment factors, 1992, semiannual article, 6742–2.302; 6742–2.307
Labor force, revised estimates based on 1991 seasonal adjustment factors, monthly 1987-91, annual tables, 6742–2.304
Monetary aggregates and components weekly and monthly Fed Reserve seasonal adjustment factors, monthly rpt with articles, 9362–1
Retail trade sales and inventories, by kind of business, region, and selected State, MSA, and city, monthly rpt, 2413–3
Timber stumpage prices, for sawtimber sold from natl forests in Pacific Northwest, monthly 1975-89, 1208–387
Wholesale trade sales and inventories, by SIC 2- to 3-digit kind of business, monthly rpt, 2413–7

Seasonal and summer employment
see Temporary and seasonal employment

Seasonal variations
Bears (grizzly) in Yellowstone Natl Park area, monitoring results, 1991, annual rpt, 5544–4
Crimes committed, monthly 1985-89, annual rpt, 6224–2.1
Economic indicators impact of seasonal variations, model description and results, 1940s-80s, working paper, 9387–8.262
Energy supply, demand, and prices, forecasts by resource type, quarterly rpt, 3162–34
Teenage abortion and late prenatal care initiation, risk relation to season of conception, 1979-86, article, 4042–3.372

Temperature annual and seasonal averages by US region, and departures from normal by world area, 1860s-1990, annual rpt, 3004–33
Traffic fatal accidents, deaths, and rates, by circumstances, characteristics of persons and vehicles involved, and location, 1990, annual rpt, 7764–10
Truck accidents, circumstances, and characteristics of vehicles and persons involved, 1979-86, 7768–124
see also Business cycles
see also Seasonal adjustment factors

Seat belts
see Motor vehicle safety devices

Seattle, Wash.
Air traffic, and passenger and freight enplanements, by airport, 1960s-91 and projected to 2010, hub area rpt, 7506–7.44
CPI by component for US city average, and by selected metro area, region, and population size, monthly rpt, 6762–2
Drug abuse indicators for selected metro areas, research results, data collection, and policy issues, 1992 semiannual conf, 4492–5
Freight (waterborne domestic and foreign) by commodity, traffic, and passengers, by port and waterway, 1989, annual rpt, 3754–3.4
Fruit and vegetable shipments, and arrivals by city, by mode of transport and State and country of origin, 1990, annual rpt, 1311–4.2
Heroin prices and purity in 19 metro areas and Puerto Rico, by world area of origin, quarterly rpt, 6282–2
Housing and households characteristics, and unit and neighborhood quality, by MSA location for 11 MSAs, 1987 survey, supplement, 2485–8
Housing starts and completions authorized by building permits in 40 MSAs, quarterly rpt, 2382–9
see also under By City and By SMSA or MSA in the "Index by Categories"

Seburn, Patrick W.
"Evolution of Employer-Provided Defined Benefit Pensions", 6722–1.303

SEC
see Securities and Exchange Commission

Secondary education
see Elementary and secondary education

Secret Service
see U.S. Secret Service

Securities
Arbitration of securities disputes between brokers and investors, outcomes related to forum type and other factors, 1992 GAO rpt, 26119–401
Asset-backed commercial paper programs, with data on commercial paper outstanding, 1960s-91, article, 9362–1.302
Assets and debts of private sector, balance sheets by segment, 1960-91, semiannual rpt, 9365–4.1
Bank holding companies stock prices relation to capital and assets, 1990-92, article, 9385–1.311
Banking and financial conditions, 1990, annual rpt, 9364–5
Banks (insured commercial and savings) finances, for foreign and domestic offices, by asset size, 1990, annual rpt, 9294–4.2
Banks (natl) charters, mergers, liquidations, enforcement cases, and financial performance, with data by instn and State, quarterly rpt, 8402–3
Banks assets valuation impact of market value accounting for debt securities, by bank asset size, 1990, GAO rpt, 26111–77
Banks dividends on common stock, relation to earnings, capital, and other factors, 1989-90, article, 9292–4.302
Banks in Fed Reserve System, expenses and operations itemized by service, office, and district, 1991, annual rpt, 9364–11
Banks securities new issues by type of instrument, relation to primary capital ratio and other factors, 1983-86, working paper, 9371–10.79
Banks stock returns relation to returns on industrial stocks and long-term bonds, model description and results, 1970s-90, article, 9393–8.301
Business statistics, detailed data for major industries and economic indicators, *Survey of Current Business*, monthly rpt, 2702–1.8
Business statistics, detailed data for major industries and economic indicators, 1960-91, *Survey of Current Business* biennial supplement, 2704–1
Commercial paper outstanding, by issuer and holder type, and foreign firms paper issued by US subsidiaries and foreign offices, 1980s-91, article, 9362–1.308
Commercial paper ratings of bank holding companies relation to total commercial paper outstanding, 1980s-90, technical paper, 9366–6.299
Corporations securities holdings by shareholder type, and mgmt and executive pay issues, with data by company, 1991 hearing, 25248–130
Court civil and criminal caseloads for Federal district, appeals, and bankruptcy courts, by type of suit and offense, circuit, and district, 1991, annual rpt, 18204–11
Court civil and criminal caseloads for Federal district, appeals, and special courts, 1991, annual rpt, 18204–8
Credit (securities) issues of stockbrokers and other nonbank lenders, and brokers balance sheet, as of June 1991, annual rpt, 9365–5.1
Credit unions federally insured, finances by instn characteristics and State, as of June 1992, semiannual rpt, 9532–6
Developing countries debt securities prices on secondary market, relation to stock price indexes and other factors, model description and results, 1980s-90, technical paper, 9385–8.132
Economic and monetary trends, compounded annual rates of change and quarterly indicators for US and 7 major industrialized countries, quarterly rpt, 9391–7
Electric utilities privately owned, finances and operations, detailed data, 1990, annual rpt, 3164–23
Families financial status, income, net worth, and assets and debt by type, by income and selected characteristics, 1983 and 1989, article, 9362–1.301
Fed funds rate impact on stock prices, 1974-79, technical paper, 4746–26.19
Flow-of-funds accounts, savings, investments, and credit statements, quarterly rpt, 9365–3.3
Foreign and US industrial stock indexes and long-term govt bond yields, for selected countries, weekly chartbook, 9365–1.5
Foreign and US stock price indexes, for 7 OECD countries, *Survey of Current Business*, monthly rpt, 2702–1.1
Foreign direct investment in US, relation to exchange rate and relative labor costs and wealth indicators, for 7 countries, 1980s, working paper, 9373–27.10
Foreign govts assets and liabilities, and transactions in securities, monthly rpt, 9362–1.3
Fraud involving securities, US attorneys cases by disposition, FY91, annual rpt, 6004–2.1
Futures and options trading volume, by commodity and exchange, FY91, annual rpt, 11924–2
Households net worth distribution under alternative sample weighting systems to account for inconsistency in survey design and response rates, 1992 rpt, 9368–91
Insider trading, Federal sentencing guidelines by offense and circumstances, series, 17668–1
Insurance company asset risk assessment, with financial ratios by firm type and financial status, 1990 and trends from 1900s, article, 9373–1.314; 9373–27.3
Insurance company finances, by insurance type and firm, with some intl comparisons, 1991 conf, 9373–3.35
Insurance industry financial condition, operations, assets, junk bond holdings, and State regulation, with intl comparisons, 1991 hearings, 25268–79
Interest rates for commercial paper, govt securities, other financial instruments, and home mortgages, monthly rpt, 9365–2.14
Intl investment position of US, by component, industry, world region, and country, 1990-91, annual article, 2702–1.323
Intl transactions in long-term domestic and foreign securities, purchases and sales, by country, *Treasury Bulletin*, quarterly rpt, 8002–4.13
Intl transactions summary, 1980s-91, annual article, 9362–1.304
Intl transactions, *Survey of Current Business*, monthly rpt, quarterly tables, 2702–1.33
Issues outstanding, trading, and turnover, by type of instrument, 1990, technical paper, 9366–1.163
Low-grade junk bond holdings of RTC, quarterly press release, 9722–4
Low-grade junk bond issues by rating, and defaults by bond type, late 1970s-80s, working paper, 9373–27.14
Margin requirements set by Fed Reserve Board, 1934-74, annual rpt, 9364–1.2
Merger announcements and antitrust challenges impact on stock returns of rival firms, 1980s, 9408–55
Mortgage-backed securities present value impacts of mortgage prepayment, and returns compared to other investments, 1992, article, 9371–1.308
Mortgage-backed securities program of Govt Natl Mortgage Assn, private issues, FY91, annual rpt, 5144–6

Mortgage-backed security conduits lending activity, by type of loan and mortgaged property, monthly press release, 5142–18
Mortgage-backed security conduits lending activity, by type of loan and mortgaged property, quarterly press release, 5142–30
Mortgage, mortgage-backed security, and govt security holdings of public and private pension funds, and public funds investment in housing, 1986-90, 5188–134
Multinatl firms US affiliates, finances, and operations, by industry, world area of parent firm, and State, 1989-90, annual rpt, 2704–4
Natural gas interstate pipeline company detailed financial and operating data, by firm, 1990, annual rpt, 3164–38
Nonprofit charitable and other tax exempt organizations finances, by category and size of assets and contributions, 1988, annual article, 8302–2.315
Nonprofit charitable organizations finances, with data by State and for top 10 instns, 1988, article, 8302–2.302
Pools of finance company credit upon which securities have been issued, by credit type, monthly rpt, 9365–2.7
Pools of installment credit upon which securities have been issued, by credit type, monthly rpt, 9365–2.6
Price indexes of common stock, trading volume, margin credit, and new govt and corporate issues, monthly rpt, 9362–1.1
Prices and yields of common stock and bonds, current data and annual trends, monthly rpt, 23842–1.5
Prices of common stock relation to corporate earnings, model results with data for Ford Motor Co, 1950s-90, article, 9373–1.306
Purchases, sales, and holdings, by issuer and type and ownership of security, monthly listing, 9732–2
Returns on stock, forecasting performance of alternative models, descriptions and results, 1992 technical paper, 9385–8.146
Returns on stock, volatility relation to economic indicators, model description and results, 1920s-90, technical paper, 9385–8.124
Savings instns conversion from mutual to stock ownership, chief executive stock holdings and stock price changes, 1986-87, article, 9373–1.307
Savings instns failure resolution activity of Resolution Trust Corp, assets, deposits, and assets availability and sales, periodic press release, 9722–1
Savings instns financial statements, for instns insured by Savings Assn Insurance Fund by FHLB district and State, and for FDIC-insured savings banks, 1989, annual rpt, 8434–1
Savings instns holdings of low-grade (junk) bonds and relation to stock volatility and deposit interest rates, late 1980s, working paper, 9375–13.69
Savings instns insured by Savings Assn Insurance Fund, assets, liabilities, and deposit and loan activity, by conservatorship status, monthly rpt, 8432–1
SEC activities, securities industry finances, and exchange activity, selected years 1938-FY91, annual rpt, 9734–2
SEC registration, firms required to file annual rpts, as of Sept 1991, annual listing, 9734–5
Small business capital formation sources and issues, 1991 annual conf, 9734–4
Small business financing sources, and business financial data by size, type, and industry, 1980s-90, annual rpt, 9764–6.2
Southeastern States, Fed Reserve 5th District insured commercial banks financial statements, by State, quarterly rpt, 9389–18
Southeastern States, Fed Reserve 8th District banking and economic conditions, quarterly rpt with articles, 9391–16
State and local govt employees pension system cash and security holdings and finances, quarterly rpt, 2462–2
Statistical Abstract of US, 1992 annual data compilation, 2324–1.16
Taiwan monetary and foreign exchange policies, with money supply, interest rates, and other economic indicators, 1980s, article, 9393–8.303
Tax (estate) returns for nonresident aliens, property and tax data, by estate size and decedent country of residence, 1986, article, 8302–2.310
Tax (estate) returns property and tax data, by size of gross estate and State, 1989-90, article, 8302–2.305
Tax (income) returns of corporations, income and tax items by asset size and detailed industry, 1989, annual rpt, 8304–4; 8304–21
Tax exempt organizations finances, with data by type, size, State, and for largest organizations, late 1940s-80s, compilation of papers, 8308–35
Tax on capital gains and other changes, impacts on stock prices and returns, model description and results, 1992 technical paper, 9379–12.97
Telephone and telegraph firms detailed finances and operations, 1990, annual rpt, 9284–6
Treasury tax and loan account deposits, Fed Reserve Banks mgmt of securities held as collateral, 1991, GAO rpt, 26111–80
Trust assets of banks, trust companies, and S&Ls, by type of asset and fund, selected firm, and State, 1991, annual rpt, 13004–1
Yields, interest rates, prices, and offerings, by type of bond and issuing sector, selected years 1929-91, annual rpt, 204–1.5; 204–1.7
Yields on corporate, Treasury, and municipal long-term bonds, *Treasury Bulletin*, quarterly rpt, 8002–4.9
Yields on govt and private issues, weekly rpt, 9391–4
see also American Stock Exchange
see also Foreign investments
see also Government securities
see also Municipal bonds
see also Mutual funds
see also New York Stock Exchange
see also Options trading
see also Stockbrokers
see also Tax exempt securities
see also U.S. savings bonds

Securities and Exchange Commission
Activities of SEC, securities industry finances, and exchange activity, selected years 1938-FY91, annual rpt, 9734–2
Arbitration of securities disputes between brokers and investors, outcomes related to forum type and other factors, 1992 GAO rpt, 26119–401
Budget of US, authoritative financial statements with appropriations, outlays, and receipts, by category and agency, FY91, annual rpt, 8104–2.2
Budget of US, obligations and authority by function, agency, and program, with summaries and analyses, FY93, annual rpt, 104–2
Corporations required to file annual rpts with SEC, as of Sept 1991, annual listing, 9734–5
Govt securities market performance, regulation, and reform issues, with auction results, 1990-91, 8008–154
Labor unions recognized in Fed Govt, agreements and membership by agency and facility, as of Jan 1991, biennial listing, 9844–14
Market decline of Nov 1991, impacts of trading related to option and futures expirations, 9738–22
Securities purchases, sales, and holdings, by issuer and type and ownership of security, monthly listing, 9732–2
Small business capital formation sources and issues, 1991 annual conf, 9734–4

Securities exchange
see American Stock Exchange
see New York Stock Exchange
see Stock exchanges

Securities Investor Protection Corp.
Regulatory activity and finances of SIPC, 1970s-91, GAO rpt, 26119–419

Security clearance
see Internal security

Security devices
Exports and imports of US, by Harmonized System 6-digit commodity and country, 1991, annual rpt, 2424–13
Exports of US, detailed Schedule B commodities with countries of destination, 1991, annual rpt, 2424–10
Licensing activities of FCC, by class of operation, FY91, annual rpt, 9284–4
Price indexes (producer), by stage of processing and detailed commodity, monthly rpt, 6762–6
Price indexes (producer), by stage of processing and detailed commodity, monthly 1991, annual rpt, 6764–2
Shipments, trade, use, and firms, for electronic communications systems and related products, 1991, annual Current Industrial Rpt, 2506–12.35

Security services
see Campus security
see Detective and protective services
see Internal security
see Security devices

Sedition
see Subversive activities

Seeds
Agricultural Statistics, 1991, annual rpt, 1004–1
Exports and imports (agricultural) commodity and country, prices, and world market devs, monthly rpt, 1922–12

Exports and imports (agricultural) of US, by commodity and country, bimonthly rpt, 1522–1
Exports and imports (agricultural) of US, by detailed commodity and country, 1991, annual rpt, 1524–8
Exports and imports (agricultural) of US, by detailed commodity and country, 1991, semiannual rpt, 1522–4
Exports and imports between US and outlying areas, by detailed commodity and mode of transport, 1991, annual rpt, 2424–11
Exports and imports of US, by country and detailed commodity, monthly rpt, 2422–12
Exports and imports of US, by Harmonized System 6-digit commodity and country, 1991, annual rpt, 2424–13
Exports of seeds, by type, world region, and country, FAS quarterly rpt, 1925–13
Exports of US, detailed Schedule B commodities with countries of destination, 1991, annual rpt, 2424–10
Farm production inputs, finances, mgmt, and land value and transfers, periodic situation rpt with articles, 1561–16
Farm production itemized costs, by farm sales size and region, 1991, annual rpt, 1614–3
Farm production itemized costs, receipts, and returns, by commodity and region, 1975-90, annual rpt, 1544–20
Farm production itemized costs, receipts, and returns, by crop and State, 1987-89, annual rpt, 1544–24
Farm sector balance sheet, and marketing receipts by detailed commodity, by State, 1986-90, annual rpt, 1544–18
Feed production, acreage, stocks, use, trade, prices, and price supports, periodic situation rpt with articles, 1561–4
Input-output structure of US economy, detailed interindustry transactions for 541 industries, and components of final demand, 1982 benchmark data, 2708–17
Irrigation projects of Reclamation Bur in western US, crop production and acreage by commodity, State, and project, 1990, annual rpt, 5824–12
Patent protection for seed varieties, and wheat farmer profitability of using purchased seed, 1986-89, 1548–388
Potato production, prices, stocks, and use, by State, 1980s-91, annual rpt, 1621–11
Prices received and paid by farmers, by commodity and State, monthly rpt, 1629–1
Prices received and paid by farmers, by commodity and State, 1991, annual rpt, 1629–5
Production, farms, acreage, and related data, by selected crop and State, monthly rpt, 1621–1
Rice production, practices, costs, and land tenure, by production area, 1988, 1568–309
see also Oils, oilseeds, and fats

Seeman, Isadore
"National Mortality Followback Survey: 1986 Summary, U.S.", 4147–20.19

Segal, William
"Effect of Immigration Reform on Collective Bargaining in the California Fruit and Vegetable Processing Industry", 6366–6.5

Segelquist, Charles A.
"Synthesis of Soil-Plant Correspondence Data from Twelve Wetland Studies Throughout the U.S.", 5506–10.13

Segregation
see Discrimination in education
see Discrimination in housing
see School busing

Seifert, Mary L.
"New Seasonal Adjustment Factors for the Establishment Data Series", 6742–2.301

Seignorage
see Coins and coinage

Seismographs
see Scientific equipment and apparatus

Seizures
see Searches and seizures

Selby, Maija L.
"Increasing Participation by Private Physicians in the EPSDT Program in Rural North Carolina", 4042–3.358

Seldovia, Alaska
Tide height and time daily at coastal points, forecast 1993, annual rpt, 2174–2.1

Selective service
Registrants by State, FY91, annual rpt, 9744–1
see also Draft evasion and protest
see also Voluntary military service

Selective Service System
Activities of SSS, and registrants by State, FY91, annual rpt, 9744–1
Budget of US, authoritative financial statements with appropriations, outlays, and receipts, by category and agency, FY91, annual rpt, 8104–2.2
Budget of US, obligations and authority by function, agency, and program, with summaries and analyses, FY93, annual rpt, 104–2
Labor unions recognized in Fed Govt, agreements and membership by agency and facility, as of Jan 1991, biennial listing, 9844–14

Self-employment
AFDC beneficiaries demographic and financial characteristics, by State, FY90, annual rpt, 4584–7
Asian and Pacific Islands Americans social and economic characteristics, for West and total US, 1990-91, Current Population Report, 2546–1.462
Black Americans social and economic characteristics, for South and total US, 1991 and trends from 1950, annual Current Population Rpt, 2546–1.463
Employment and Earnings, detailed data, monthly rpt, 6742–2
Employment and economic conditions, alternative BLS projections to 2005 and trends 1975-90, biennial rpt, 6744–19
Employment, earnings, and hours, monthly press release, 6742–5
Employment situation, earnings, hours, and other BLS economic indicators, transcripts of BLS Commissioner's monthly testimony, periodic rpt, 23846–4
Farm and nonfarm business income of self employed, 1989, article, 1541–1.301
Farm labor, wages, hours, and perquisites, by State, monthly rpt, 1631–1
Farm operators nonfarm self-employment income by source and farm profit and loss, and tax burden, 1987, article, 1541–1.320
Farm population, by employment, social, and economic characteristics, and region, 1990, annual Current Population Rpt, 2546–1.458
Food stamp recipient household size, composition, income, and income and deductions allowed, summer 1989, annual rpt, 1364–8
Home-based workers and hours, by worker characteristics, occupational group and industry div, 1991, press release, 6726–1.52
Home-based workers by selected characteristics, and views, 1989, article, 1702–1.307
Income (household, family, and personal), by source, detailed characteristics, and region, 1991, annual Current Population Rpt, 2546–6.76
Labor demand, turnover, and training completions, by detailed occupation, 1990 and projected to 2005, biennial rpt, 6744–3
Minority- and woman-owned businesses and owner characteristics, by industry, employment and sales size, and form of ownership, 1987 survey, 2328–59
Natl income and product accounts, comprehensive accounts and components, benchmark revisions, 1929-88, 2708–5
Natl income and product accounts, comprehensive accounts and components, *Survey of Current Business*, monthly rpt, 2702–1.29
NYC housing supply, occupancy, condition, and household characteristics, by tenure and borough, 1991 triennial survey, 2488–3
OASDHI coverage of employment and earnings, late 1930s-90, annual rpt, 4744–3.1; 4744–3.2
Occupational Outlook Handbook, 1992-93, biennial rpt, 6744–1
Older persons income and sources, by whether OASDI beneficiary, poverty status, and other characteristics, 1990, biennial rpt, 4744–26
Pacific territories population and housing detailed characteristics, by location, 1990 Census of Population and Housing, series, 2551–8
Poverty status of population and families, by detailed characteristics, 1991, annual Current Population Rpt, 2546–6.77
Small business finances, operations, owner characteristics, and Federal contracts, 1980s-90, annual rpt, 9764–6
Statistical Abstract of US, 1992 annual data compilation, 2324–1.13
Tax (income) returns of individuals, by filing status, tax item, and income level, 1991, annual article, 8302–2.319
Tax (income) returns of individuals, detailed data, 1988, annual rpt, 8304–2
Tax rates and revenue of State and local govts, by source and State, 1992 and historical trends, annual rpt, 10044–1
Training for job qualification and skill improvement, workers participating by training source, occupation, age, sex, and race, 1991, 6728–32
Veterans (Vietnam) labor force status and earnings, by whether served in Southeast Asia, presence and severity of disability, and selected other characteristics, 1989, article, 6722–1.326

SEMATECH
Expenditures, funding sources, and effectiveness in improving US competitive position, for SEMATECH consortium, 1980s-92, GAO rpt, 26113–588
Semiconductors
Competitiveness (intl) of US high technology industries, with background data by industry and foreign comparisons, 1960s-91, GAO rpt, 26123–406
Competitiveness (intl) of US semiconductor industry, status, and outlook, working paper series, 15036–1
Competitiveness (intl) of US semiconductor industry, status, outlook, and Federal policy, 1980s, annual rpt, 15034–1
County Business Patterns, 1989: employment, establishments, and payroll, by SIC 2- to 4-digit industry and county, annual State rpt series, 2326–8
County Business Patterns, 1990: employment, establishments, and payroll, by SIC 2- to 4-digit industry and county, annual State rpt series, 2326–6
Exports and imports between US and outlying areas, by detailed commodity and mode of transport, 1991, annual rpt, 2424–11
Exports and imports of US, by Harmonized System 6-digit commodity and country, 1991, annual rpt, 2424–13
Exports of US, detailed Schedule B commodities with countries of destination, 1991, annual rpt, 2424–10
Film (dry, photoresist) from Japan at less than fair value, injury to US industry, investigation with background financial and operating data, 1992 rpt, 9886–14.359
Input-output structure of US economy, detailed interindustry transactions for 541 industries, and components of final demand, 1982 benchmark data, 2708–17
Labor productivity, indexes of output, hours, and employment by SIC 2- to 4-digit industry, 1967-90, annual rpt, 6824–1.3
Manufacturing annual survey, 1990: finances and operations, by SIC 2- to 4-digit industry, series, 2506–14
Manufacturing census, 1987: concentration of largest firms measured by value added, and for shipments by SIC 2- and 4-digit industry, subject rpt, 2497–6
Manufacturing finances and operations, by SIC 2- to 4-digit industry, forecast 1992, annual rpt, 2044–28
Manufacturing industries important to military, finances, operations, and intl competitiveness, 1991 rpt, 2026–1.2
Occupational injury and illness rates, by SIC 2- to 4-digit industry, 1989-90, annual rpt, 6844–7
Occupational injury and illness rates, by SIC 2- to 4-digit industry, 1990, annual rpt, 6844–1
Price indexes (producer), by stage of processing and detailed commodity, monthly rpt, 6762–6
Price indexes (producer), by stage of processing and detailed commodity, monthly 1991, annual rpt, 6764–2
R&D consortium of semiconductor manufacturers, funding, outlays, and effectiveness in improving US competitive position, 1980s-92, GAO rpt, 26113–588
Shipments, trade, use, and firms, for semiconductors, printed circuit boards, and other electronic components, 1991, annual Current Industrial Rpt, 2506–12.36
Statistical Abstract of US, 1992 annual data compilation, 2324–1.27
Supply and demand of semiconductor materials, and semiconductor firms by State, late 1980s and projected to 1993, hearing, 21708–130
Senate
Budget of US, authoritative financial statements with appropriations, outlays, and receipts, by category and agency, FY91, annual rpt, 8104–2.2
Budget of US, obligations and authority by function, agency, and program, with summaries and analyses, FY93, annual rpt, 104–2
Buildings and grounds under Capitol Architect supervision, itemized outlays by payee and function, 2nd half FY91, semiannual rpt, 25922–2
Election (general) Federal and non-Federal party transfers, by State, 1992 House and Senate elections, press release, 9276–1.111; 9276–1.113
Election (senate) campaign spending limits for candidates, and voting age population, by State, 1992 general elections, press release, 9276–1.100
Election campaign finances and FEC activities, various periods 1975-91, annual rpt, 9274–1
Election campaign finances to FEC, by type of filer, 1990 natl elections, biennial rpt series, 9276–2
Election campaign receipts and spending of congressional candidates, by candidate and State, late 1980s-92, press release, 9276–1.102; 9276–1.103; 9276–1.108; 9276–1.112
Election campaign-related internal communications of firms and assns, spending by organization, location, and candidate, 1991-92, biennial rpt, 9274–3
Finances of Senate, receipts, itemized expenses by payee, and balances, 1st half FY92, semiannual listing, 25922–1
Former US govt officials representing foreign interests, activities and individuals, FY86-91, GAO rpt, 26123–134
Statistical Abstract of US, 1992 annual data compilation, 2324–1.8
Votes cast by party, candidate, and State, 1990 natl elections, biennial rpt, 21944–3
see also Senate Documents
see also Senate Special Publications
see also under names of individual committees (starting with Senate or Joint)
see also under names of individual subcommittees (starting with Subcommittee)
Senate Aging Committee, Special
Drug (prescription) prices in US and other countries, industry profits, and R&D and marketing spending, 1980s-91 and projected to 2000, 25148–44
OASDHI and SSI admin, case processing, staff, and client problems with contacting SSA offices, 1980s-90, hearing, 25148–45
Older persons socioeconomic characteristics, 1900s-90 and projected to 2050, biennial chartbook, 12904–1
Senate Agriculture and Forestry Committee
see Senate Agriculture, Nutrition, and Forestry Committee
Senate Agriculture, Nutrition, and Forestry Committee
Bee colony rentals, and pollinated crop value, by crop, 1989, hearings, 25168–78
Infant formula bid prices and contracts awarded by States under USDA food aid program for women, infants, and children, late 1980s-91, hearing, 25528–118
Senate Banking, Housing, and Urban Affairs Committee
Banks financial performance indicators, by bank, 1991-92, hearings, 25248–127
Financial instns reform issues, with finances, impacts of deposit insurance changes, and views of depositors and bankers, 1991 hearings, 25248–129
Mortgages FHA-insured, insurance fund financial condition with background housing and mortgage data, 1970s-90s, hearing, 25248–128
Securities holdings by shareholder type, and mgmt and executive pay issues, with data by company, 1991 hearing, 25248–130
Senate Commerce, Science and Transportation Committee
Insurance industry financial condition, operations, assets, junk bond holdings, and State regulation, with intl comparisons, 1991 hearings, 25268–79
Senate Documents
Capitol Architect outlays for salaries, supplies, and services, itemized by payee and function, 2nd half FY91, semiannual rpt, 25922–2
Finances of Senate, receipts, itemized expenses by payee, and balances, 1st half FY92, semiannual listing, 25922–1
Senate Energy and Natural Resources Committee
Alternative fuels pollutant emissions by fuel type, and alcohol fuel production and inputs, 1991 hearing, 25318–82
Energy policy and program proposals, 1991 hearings, 25318–83
Recycling of paper by grade, with newsprint collection, recycling capacity by company, and curbside pickup operations, by State, 1970s-80s and projected to 1995, hearing, 25318–84
Wilderness areas acreage by State, and Colorado off-road vehicle use, owner expenses, and views on registration fee, 1986-88, hearing, 25318–85
Senate Finance Committee
Canada-US trade agreement issues, with data on Canada fertilizer and agricultural production and trade, 1960s-90s, hearing, 25368–179
Debt outstanding by type of holder, and total and per capita Federal debt, 1929-89, hearing, 25368–177
Developing countries debt burden indicators, conversion agreement terms, and swaps for conservation funds, by selected country, 1987-90, hearing, 25368–181
Foreign countries economic conditions, policy, and trade practices, by country, 1989-91, annual rpt, 21384–5
Health care system reform issues, with data on insurance administrative and employer costs, coverage, public views, and Canada and UK systems, 1950s-91, hearings, 25368–180

Medicare payment of physicians under fee schedule, impacts on charges by specialty and State, 1992 and 1996, hearing, 25368–178

Senate Foreign Relations Committee
Bank of Credit and Commerce Intl financial statements, audits, and selected loan data, 1984-90, hearing, 25388–60
Economic conditions, policy, and trade practices, by country, 1989-91, annual rpt, 21384–5
Human rights conditions in 170 countries, and US economic and military aid, 1991, annual rpt, 21384–3
NATO and Warsaw Pact military forces reductions and ceilings under CFE treaty, inspections, and US compliance costs and savings, 1991 hearings, 25388–59

Senate Governmental Affairs Committee
Assistance (formula grants) of Fed Govt, use of adjusted census and intercensal data for allocation, with data by program and State, FY91, 25408–120
Census of Population, 1990: data accuracy, evaluation, and adjustment issues, hearing, 21628–99
Census of Population, 1990: data adjustment for undercounts, issues, 1991, 25408–119
Iraq invasion of Kuwait, oil production disruption impacts on futures prices, family budgets, and oil firms, 1990 hearings, 25408–116
Military weapons trade of 32 countries, 1984-88, hearing, 25408–115
Tax (income) compliance of corporations, and IRS enforcement activities, 1970s-92, hearing, 25408–118

Senate Human Resources Committee
see Senate Labor and Human Resources Committee

Senate Intelligence Committee, Select
Espionage against Federal and military agencies, US natls convicted by selected personal, employment, and espionage characteristics, 1945-89, hearings, 25428–2

Senate Judiciary Committee
Food aid program of USDA for women, infants, and children, State contract awards and bid prices for infant formula, late 1980s-91, hearing, 25528–118
Gasoline service stations price competition and divorcement from oil companies, issues with data by firm, city, and State, 1991 hearing, 25528–120
Insurance industry finances, failures, and regulation, with data by firm and State, 1990 hearing, 25528–119

Senate Labor and Human Resources Committee
Employee leave for family reasons, State law provisions and employer compliance, for 4 States, 1987-91, hearing, 25548–105

Senate Labor and Public Welfare Committee
see Senate Labor and Human Resources Committee

Senate Small Business Committee
Small Business Investment Company finances, losses, and program operations, 1980s-91, 25728–44

Senate Special Publications
Capitol Architect activities, funding, costs, and contracts, FY89, annual rpt, 25944–1

Senegal
Agricultural trade of US, by detailed commodity and country, 1991, annual rpt, 1524–8
Agricultural trade of US, by detailed commodity and country, 1991, semiannual rpt, 1522–4
AID economic aid to developing countries, obligations and disbursements by country, quarterly rpt, 9912–4
AID loans repayment status and terms by program and country, and status of predecessor agency loans, quarterly rpt, 9912–3
Economic and military aid and loans from US and intl agencies, by program and country, FY46-91, annual rpt, 9914–5
Economic and social conditions of developing countries from 1960s, and Intl Dev Cooperation Agency and AID activities and funding, FY91-93, annual rpt, 9904–4
Economic conditions, income, production, prices, employment, and trade, 1991 periodic country rpt, 2046–4.5
Economic conditions, income, production, prices, employment, and trade, 1992 periodic country rpt, 2046–4.50
Economic, population, and agricultural data, US and other aid sources, and AID activity, 1991 country rpt, 9916–12.52
Economic, social, political, and geographic summary data, by country, 1992, annual factbook, 9114–2
Exports and imports of US, by transport mode, country, and SITC 1- to 3-digit commodity, 1991, annual rpt, 2424–12
Exports of US, detailed Schedule B commodities with countries of destination, 1991, annual rpt, 2424–10
Food supply, needs, and aid for developing countries, status and alternative forecasts, 1992 world area rpt, 1526–8.2
Human rights conditions in 170 countries, and US economic and military aid, 1991, annual rpt, 21384–3
Military aid of US, arms sales, and training programs costs and budget requests, by program, world region, and country, FY91-93, annual rpt, 7144–13
Military spending, arms trade, and force strengths, with govt spending and population, by country, 1979-89, annual rpt, 9824–1
Population size, growth rates, and components of change, by country, projected 1990-2020 and trends from 1950, biennial rpt, 2324–9
Refugee migration, and intl aid programs, by world area and country of origin and asylum, 1991, annual rpt, 7004–15
UN voting record and share of votes in agreement with US, by issue, country, and world area, 1991, annual rpt, 7004–18

Senior citizens
see Aged and aging

Senior Companion Program
Activities and funding of ACTION, by program, FY91, annual rpt, 9024–2

Sentences, criminal procedure
AFDC fraud cases, referrals, and disposition, by State, FY90, annual rpt, 4584–3.5
Antitrust criminal enforcement activities of Justice Dept by industry div and offense, sentencing, and labor costs, FY90, GAO rpt, 26119–375
Assaults and deaths of law enforcement officers, by circumstances, agency, victim and offender characteristics, and location, 1991, annual rpt, 6224–3
Banks and thrifts fraud cases, Justice Dept investigation and prosecution activities, 1989-92, GAO rpt, 26119–426
Corrupt govt officials prosecuted and convicted, by judicial district and level of govt, 1970-90, annual rpt, 6004–13
Counterfeiting and other Secret Service investigations and arrests by type, and dispositions, FY91 and trends from FY82, annual rpt, 8464–1
Crime, criminal justice admin and enforcement, and public opinion, data compilation, 1992 annual rpt, 6064–6
Drug abuse and trafficking offenders losing Federal benefits under new sentencing guidelines, by selected characteristics, 1990-91, GAO rpt, 26119–398
Drug abuse indicators for selected metro areas, research results, data collection, and policy issues, 1992 semiannual conf, 4492–5
Drunk driving arrests, sentencing, and prisoner drinking patterns and other characteristics, 1989, 6066–19.69
Environmental laws enforcement activities of EPA and State govts, FY91, annual rpt, 9184–21
Environmental laws enforcement activities of Justice Dept, FY83-91, press release, 6008–37
Environmental laws enforcement activities of Justice Dept, FY83-92, annual press release, 6004–22
Federal correctional instns prisoners, by selected characteristics, region, and instn, FY89, annual rpt, 6244–1.1
Federal criminal sentencing, guidelines by offense and circumstances, series, 17668–1
Federal criminal sentencing, guidelines impacts on sentence disparity by offender race and other characteristics, 1985-90, GAO rpt, 26119–415
Federal criminal sentencing, guidelines use and results by offense and district, and Sentencing Commission activities, 1991, annual rpt, 17664–1
Federal criminal sentencing, guidelines use and results by offense, 1984-1990, 6066–19.68
Federal criminal sentencing under mandatory minimum provisions by defendant characteristics, and views on justice system impacts, FY90, 17668–2
Federal district court criminal case processing and dispositions, by offense, district, and offender characteristics, 1989, annual data compilation, 6064–29
Federal district court criminal case processing and dispositions, by offense, 1980-91, annual rpt, 6064–31
Federal district court dispositions of criminal defendants, 1991, annual rpt, 18204–8.18
Felony case processing from arrest to sentencing, cases and duration by disposition and offense, for selected cities, 1988, annual rpt, 6064–27
Financial instns fraud and abuse, Justice Dept enforcement activity, staff, and case dispositions by instn type, 1988-92, 6008–35

Fraud and forgery arrests, case dispositions, and sentencing, by age, sex, race, and offense type, 1983-88, 6066–19.64
Immigration and nationality violations, prosecutions, fines, imprisonment, and convictions, and deportation and exclusion cases, FY85-91, annual rpt, 6264–2.5
Juvenile facilities population, by resident characteristics and facility type, late 1970s-89, 6068–250
Juvenile facilities population, by resident characteristics and facility type, 1977-89, annual rpt, 6064–35
Prison and parole admissions and releases, sentence length, and time served, by offense and offender characteristics, 1988, annual rpt, 6064–33
Prisoners in Federal and State instns, admissions and outcomes by sentence and inmate characteristics, by State, 1990, annual rpt, 6064–26.4
Prisoners in Federal and State instns by selected characteristics, releases, staff, and instn size, with data by region and State, late 1970s-91, 6068–248
Prisoners in Federal and State instns by sex, admissions, and instn capacity and overcrowding, by State, 1980s-91, annual rpt, 6066–25.47
Probation population, by offender characteristics, sentence conditions, whether rearrested, and offense, 1986-89, 6066–19.65
Savings instns fraud and abuse, Federal indictments and case dispositions, periodic press release, 6002–3; 6008–33
Statistical Abstract of US, 1992 annual data compilation, 2324–1.5
Tax litigation and enforcement activity of IRS, FY91, annual rpt, 8304–3.1
US attorneys civil and criminal cases by type and disposition, and collections, by Federal district, FY91, annual rpt, 6004–2.1; 6004–2.2
VA programs fraud and abuse, audits and investigations, 2nd half FY92, semiannual rpt, 8602–1
Women in jail, by criminal background and sociodemographic characteristics, with comparisons to men, 1989, 6066–19.66
see also Capital punishment
see also Commitment
see also Crime victim compensation
see also Fines and settlements
see also Pardons
see also Parole and probation

Separation of powers
see also Congressional-executive relations

Septicemia
Deaths and rates, by cause, age, sex, marital status, race, and State, 1989, US Vital Statistics advance annual rpt, 4146–5.124
Deaths and rates, by cause and age, preliminary 1990-91, US Vital Statistics annual rpt, 4144–7
Deaths and rates, by cause and selected social, demographic, and employment characteristics, 1979-85, natl longitudinal study, 4478–186
Deaths and rates, by cause, provisional data, monthly rpt, 4142–1.2
Deaths and rates, by detailed location, cause, and demographic characteristics, 1989, US Vital Statistics annual rpt, 4144–3
Health condition and care indicators, 1950s-90 with health improvement and disease prevention goals for 1990, annual data compilation, 4144–11
Hospital deaths of Medicare patients, actual and expected rates by diagnosis, with hospital characteristics, by instn, FY90, annual State rpt series, 4654–14
Hospitalization for septicemia, diagnostic coding errors, substandard care, and Medicare costs, 1980s, 4006–7.8

Serbia
Economic, social, political, and geographic summary data, by country, 1992, annual factbook, 9114–2
see also Montenegro

Servants
see Domestic workers and services

Service academies
Black military and civilian DOD personnel, by sex, grade, and period of service, and lists of award recipients, officers, and service academy grads, 1770s-90, 3548–22
Budget of DOD, organization, personnel, weapons, and property, by service branch, State, and country, 1992 annual summary rpt, 3504–13
Enrollment, staff, outlays, and facilities for DOD training and education programs, by service branch, FY93, annual rpt, 3504–5
Enrollment, tuition, control, location, and other characteristics of higher education instns, 1991/92, biennial listing, 4844–3
Expenditures for education by Federal agency, program, and recipient type, and instn spending, 1960s-91, annual rpt, 4824–8
Maritime academy students receiving Fed Govt aid, monthly rpt, 7702–1
Merchant ship crew supply, wartime needs, training, and sources, 1970s-90 and alternative projections to 2000, 7708–5
Officer candidates, by service branch, quarterly rpt, 3542–14
Officer candidates, FY46-91, annual rpt, 3544–1.2
Officers newly commissioned, share from service academies, and academy attrition, 1970s-91 and projected to FY97, GAO rpt, 26123–389
Prep schools for service academies, costs and student performance indicators, various periods 1988-90, GAO rpt, 26123–380
Ships on loan to maritime academies, vessels and tonnage, as of July 1991, semiannual listing, 7702–2
Tuition and other student charges, by public and private 2- and 4-year higher education instn, and State, 1991/92, annual listing, 4844–10

Service industries
Alien nonresidents income from US sources and tax withheld by country and US tax treaty status, 1989, annual article, 8302–2.308
Business statistics, detailed data for major industries and economic indicators, *Survey of Current Business*, monthly rpt, 2702–1
Business statistics, detailed data for major industries and economic indicators, 1960-91, *Survey of Current Business* biennial supplement, 2704–1
Canada and US current accounts balance reconciliation adjustment methodology, with background data, 1990-91, article, 2702–1.341
Capital expenditures for plant and equipment, by major industry group, quarterly rpt, 2502–2
Census Bur data files and rpts, coverage and availability, 1992 annual listing, 2304–2
Collective bargaining agreements expiring during year, and workers covered, by firm, union, industry group, and State, 1992, annual rpt, 6784–9
Collective bargaining wage and benefit changes, quarterly press release, 6782–2
Collective bargaining wage changes and coverage, by industry and whether contract includes escalator clause and lump sum payment, 1982-91, annual article, 6722–1.325
Consumer spending, monthly rpt, quarterly data, 23842–1.1
Consumer spending on selected durable goods and services, 1980-90, article, 6722–1.324
County Business Patterns, 1989: employment, establishments, and payroll, by SIC 2- to 4-digit industry and county, annual State rpt series, 2326–8
County Business Patterns, 1990: employment, establishments, and payroll, by SIC 2- to 4-digit industry and county, annual State rpt series, 2326–6
Deaths and rates, by cause and selected social, demographic, and employment characteristics, 1979-85, natl longitudinal study, 4478–186
Economic indicators and components, current data and annual trends, monthly rpt, 23842–1.7
Economic indicators compounded annual rates of change, monthly rpt, 9391–3
Employment and Earnings, detailed data, monthly rpt, 6742–2.5
Employment concentration in midwestern US producer services industries by industry group, MSA, and urban-rural location, 1970s-89, article, 9375–1.305
Employment Cost Index and alternative measure of compensation costs, by component, occupation, industry group, union status, and location, 1975-92, annual rpt, 6744–20
Employment Cost Index and percent change by occupational group, industry div, region, and metro-nonmetro area, quarterly press release, 6782–5
Employment, earnings, and hours, by selected SIC 1- to 4-digit industry, State, and for 275 MSAs, 1987-92, 6748–81
Employment, earnings, and hours, by SIC 1- to 4-digit industry, monthly 1989-Feb 1992, annual rpt, 6744–4
Employment, earnings, and hours, monthly press release, 6742–5
Employment of minorities and women, by occupation, SIC 1- to 3-digit industry, State, and MSA, 1991, annual rpt, 9244–1
Employment situation, earnings, hours, and other BLS economic indicators, transcripts of BLS Commissioner's monthly testimony, periodic rpt, 23846–4
Employment, unemployment, and labor force characteristics, by region, State, and selected metro area, 1991, annual rpt, 6744–7

Export and import price indexes for goods and services, and dollar exchange rate indexes, quarterly press release, 6762–13
Exports and imports of services, direct and among multinatl firms affiliates, by industry and world area, 1986-91, article, 2702–1.336
Exports, imports, tariffs, and industry operating data for electronics and service industries, commodity rpt series, 9885–12
Exports of goods, services, and investment, trade barriers, impacts, and US actions, by country, 1991, annual rpt, 444–2
Finances and operations, by SIC 2- to 4-digit industry, forecast 1992, annual rpt, 2044–28
Foreign direct investment in US, major transactions by type, industry, country, and US location, 1990, annual rpt, 2044–20
Foreign direct investment of US, by industry group and world area, 1989-91, annual article, 2702–1.332
Gross State Product by component, industry div, and State, 1977-89, article, 2702–1.303
Home-based workers and hours, by worker characteristics, occupational group and industry div, 1991, press release, 6726–1.52
House of Representatives salaries, expenses, and contingent fund disbursement, detailed listings, quarterly rpt, 21942–1
Income tax returns of foreign corporations and individuals, and US entities abroad, detailed data compilation, 1970s-89, quinquennial rpt, 8308–31
Input-output structure of US economy, detailed interindustry transactions for 84 industries, and components of final demand, 1987, annual article, 2702–1.316
Input-output structure of US economy, detailed interindustry transactions for 541 industries, and components of final demand, 1982 benchmark data, 2708–17
Intl transactions summary, 1980s-91, annual article, 9362–1.304
Labor hourly costs, by component, industry and occupational group, worker class, and firm size, monthly rpt, annual tables, 6782–1.2
Labor hourly costs, by component, occupational group, industry div, union coverage, and region, 1992, annual rpt, 6744–21
Mail volume to and from households, use, and views, by class, source, content, and household characteristics, FY87-90, annual rpt, 9864–10
Military contracts, payroll, and personnel, by service branch and location, with top 5 contractors and maps, by State and country, FY91, annual rpt, 3544–29
Military prime contract awards, by category, contract and contractor type, and service branch, FY82-1st half FY92, semiannual rpt, 3542–1
Military prime contract awards, by category, contractor type, and State, FY89-91, annual rpt, 3544–11
Military prime contract awards, by detailed procurement category, FY88-91, annual rpt, 3544–18
Military prime contract awards, by size and type of contract, service branch, competitive status, category, and labor standard, FY91, annual rpt, 3544–19
Minority- and woman-owned businesses and owner characteristics, by industry, employment and sales size, and form of ownership, 1987 survey, 2328–59
Multinatl firms US affiliates finances and operations, by industry, country of parent firm, and State, 1987, 2708–48
Multinatl firms US affiliates, finances, and operations, by industry, world area of parent firm, and State, 1989-90, annual rpt, 2704–4
Multinatl US firms and foreign affiliates finances and operations, by industry and country, 1989 benchmark survey, annual rpt, 2704–5
Multinatl US firms foreign affiliates, income statement items by asset size, industry, and country, 1988, biennial article, 8302–2.322
Natl income and product accounts, comprehensive accounts and components, benchmark revisions, 1929-88, 2708–5
Natl income and product accounts, comprehensive accounts and components, *Survey of Current Business*, monthly rpt, 2702–1.29
Occupational injuries, illnesses, and lost workdays, by SIC 2-digit industry, 1990-91, annual press release, 6844–3
Occupational injury and illness rates by circumstances and establishment size, and methodology for computing rates, 1988, industry rpt, 6886–4.5
Occupational injury and illness rates, by SIC 2- to 4-digit industry, 1989-90, annual rpt, 6844–7
Occupational injury and illness rates, by SIC 2- to 4-digit industry, 1990, annual rpt, 6844–1
Pacific territories population and housing detailed characteristics, by location, 1990 Census of Population and Housing, series, 2551–8
Price indexes (producer), by stage of processing and detailed commodity, monthly 1991, annual rpt, 6764–2
Puerto Rico and other US possessions corporations income tax returns, income and tax items, and employment, by selected industry, 1989, article, 8302–2.326
SEC registration, firms required to file annual rpts, as of Sept 1991, annual listing, 9734–5
Senate receipts, itemized expenses by payee, and balances, 1st half FY92, semiannual listing, 25922–1
Small Business Admin loan guarantee program participants finances, operations, characteristics, and views, 1991 survey, 9768–25
Small business finances, operations, owner characteristics, and Federal contracts, 1980s-90, annual rpt, 9764–6
Southeastern US employment by industry div, earnings, and hours, for 8 States, quarterly press release, 6942–7
Statistical Abstract of US, 1992 annual data compilation, 2324–1.28
Tax (income) returns filed, by type of filer, selected income items, quarterly rpt, 8302–2.1
Tax (income) returns for foreign corporate activity in US, selected income and tax items, by industry div and selected country, 1988, article, 8302–2.309
Tax (income) returns of corporations, income and tax items by asset size and detailed industry, 1989, annual rpt, 8304–4; 8304–21
Tax (income) returns of corporations with foreign tax credit, income and tax items by industry group, 1988, biennial article, 8302–2.316
Tax (income) returns of partnerships, income statement and balance sheet items, by industry group, 1990, annual article, 8302–2.314
Tax (income) returns of sole proprietorships, income statement items, by industry group, 1990, annual article, 8302–2.317; 8302–2.320
Wage and benefit changes from collective bargaining and mgmt decisions, by industry div, monthly rpt, 6782–1
Wages by occupation, and benefits for office and plant workers, periodic MSA survey rpt series, 6785–12; 6785–16; 6785–17
see also Accounting and auditing
see also Adult day care
see also Advertising
see also Agricultural services
see also Associations
see also Automobile repair and maintenance
see also Barber and beauty shops
see also Census of Service Industries
see also Child day care
see also Consultants
see also Courier services
see also Credit bureaus and agencies
see also Detective and protective services
see also Direct marketing
see also Domestic workers and services
see also Gasoline service stations
see also Health facilities and services
see also Hotels and motels
see also Information services
see also Janitorial and maintenance services
see also Labor unions
see also Laundry and cleaning services
see also Lawyers and legal services
see also Legal aid
see also Membership organizations
see also Motion pictures
see also Motor vehicle rental
see also Museums
see also Nonprofit organizations and foundations
see also Public relations
see also Public services
see also Rental industries
see also Repair industries
see also Service workers
see also Travel agencies
see also under By Industry in the "Index by Categories"

Service stations
see Gasoline service stations

Service workers
Black Americans social and economic characteristics, for South and total US, 1991 and trends from 1950, annual Current Population Rpt, 2546–1.463
Deaths and rates, by cause and selected social, demographic, and employment characteristics, 1979-85, natl longitudinal study, 4478–186

Educational attainment, by social and demographic characteristics and location, 1991 and trends from 1940, biennial Current Population Rpt, 2546–1.460
Employment and economic conditions, alternative BLS projections to 2005 and trends 1975-90, biennial rpt, 6744–19
Employment Cost Index and alternative measure of compensation costs, by component, occupation, industry group, union status, and location, 1975-92, annual rpt, 6744–20
Employment, earnings, and hours, monthly press release, 6742–5
Employment situation, earnings, hours, and other BLS economic indicators, transcripts of BLS Commissioner's monthly testimony, periodic rpt, 23846–4
Employment, unemployment, and labor force characteristics, by region, State, and selected metro area, 1991, annual rpt, 6744–7
Higher education faculty and staff, by occupation, full- and part-time status, sex, and instn type and control, fall 1989, biennial rpt, 4844–18
Immigrants and legalized aliens, by occupational group and country of birth, preliminary FY91, annual tables, 6264–1
Immigration to US, alien workers, visitors, deportations, and naturalizations, by country, FY91 and trends from 1820, annual rpt, 6264–2
Income (household, family, and personal), by source, detailed characteristics, and region, 1991, annual Current Population Rpt, 2546–6.76
Labor demand, turnover, and training completions, by detailed occupation, 1990 and projected to 2005, biennial rpt, 6744–3
Labor hourly costs, by component, occupational group, industry div, union coverage, and region, 1992, annual rpt, 6744–21
Minority group and women employment, by occupation, SIC 1- to 3- digit industry, State, and MSA, 1991, annual rpt, 9244–1
Occupational Outlook Handbook, 1992-93, biennial rpt, 6744–1
Pacific territories population and housing detailed characteristics, by location, 1990 Census of Population and Housing, series, 2551–8
State and local govt employment of minorities and women, by occupation, function, pay level, and State, 1991, annual rpt, 9244–6
Training for job qualification and skill improvement, workers participating by training source, occupation, age, sex, and race, 1991, 6728–32
see also Area wage surveys
see also Domestic workers and services
see also Health occupations
see also Industry wage surveys
see also Police
see also Service industries
see also under By Occupation in the "Index by Categories"

Servicepersons life insurance programs
Actuarial analyses of VA life insurance programs for veterans and servicepersons, 1991, annual rpt, 8604–1
Budget of US, obligations and authority by function, agency, and program, with summaries and analyses, FY93, annual rpt, 104–2
Expenditures for VA programs, by State, county, and congressional district, FY91, annual rpt, 8604–6
Finances and activities of VA life insurance programs, FY67-91, annual rpt, 8604–5.3
Finances and coverage of VA life insurance for veterans and servicepersons, by program and State, 1991, annual rpt, 8604–4
Finances and operations of VA insurance programs, FY91 and cumulative from 1965, annual rpt, 8604–3.3
see also Veterans benefits and pensions

Set-aside programs
see Agricultural production quotas and price supports
see Defense contracts and procurement
see Minority businesses
see Small business

Seth, Rama
"Foreign Bank Credit to U.S. Corporations: The Implications of Offshore Loans", 9385–1.307

Setia, Parveen P.
"Current Status of the Environmental Reserve and the Conservation Compliance Programs: Implications for U.S. Wheat Area", 1561–12.302
"Developments in the Spanish Rice Market Since Joining the European Community: Implications for the U.S. Rice Industry", 1561–8.304
"Risk Analysis of Planting Flexibility Choices on Rice Farms in the Mississippi River Delta", 1561–8.302
"Uncertainty and Planting Flexibility Choices on Spring Wheat Farms", 1561–12.303

Settlements
see Fines and settlements

Severance taxes
Energy producers finances and operations, by energy type for US firms domestic and foreign operations, 1990, annual rpt, 3164–44
Finances of govts, tax systems and revenue, and fiscal structure, by level of govt and State, 1992 and historical trends, annual rpt, 10044–1
Natl income and product accounts, comprehensive accounts and components, benchmark revisions, 1929-88, 2708–5
Natl income and product accounts, comprehensive accounts and components, *Survey of Current Business*, monthly rpt, 2702–1.26
Oil company effective income tax rates, with background income and tax data for domestic and foreign operations, 1977-89, 3168–124
State govt revenue by source, spending and debt by function, and holdings, FY91, annual rpt, 2466–2.6
State govt tax collections by detailed type of tax, and tax rates, by State, FY91, annual rpt, 2466–2.7
Statistical Abstract of US, 1992 annual data compilation, 2324–1.9

Severson, Richard
"German Housing/Construction Market", 2042–1.306

Sewage and wastewater systems
Army Corps of Engineers activities and projects, FY88 and trends from 1800s, annual rpt, 3754–1.1
Army Corps of Engineers activities and projects, FY89 and trends from 1800s, annual rpt, 3754–1.2
Army Corps of Engineers activities and projects, FY90 and trends from 1800s, annual rpt, 3754–1.3
Assistance (financial and nonfinancial) of Fed Govt, 1992 base edition, annual listing, 104–5
Building materials PPI, by construction industry, monthly rpt, 6762–6
Census of Population and Housing, 1990: summary characteristics, by county, subdiv, and place, State rpt series, 2551–7
Coastal areas and watersheds pollution indicators, by location, 1980s-90, 2178–35
Coastal areas environmental conditions and mgmt, for individual areas, conf series, 2146–8
Construction of wastewater treatment and collection facilities, funding needs and Federal grants, by State, 1990 and projected to 2010, biennial rpt, 9204–7
Construction of wastewater treatment plants, loan funds for local govts, costs and State officials views by State, projected 1991-2000, GAO rpt, 26113–561
Construction put in place (public and private), by type, quarterly rpt, 2042–1.1
Construction put in place, value of new public and private structures, by type, monthly rpt, 2382–4
Construction spending by Fed Govt, by type of structure, FY85-92, annual article, 2042–1.303
Environmental Quality, status of problems, protection programs, research, and intl issues, 1991 annual rpt, 484–1
EPA grants to State and local govts for wastewater treatment facility construction, by project, monthly listing, discontinued, 9202–3
EPA pollution control grant program activities, monthly rpt, 9182–8
EPA R&D programs and funding, planned FY92, annual listing, 9184–17
Expenditures for pollution abatement by govts, business, and consumers, 1972-90, annual article, 2702–1.321
Expenditures of Fed Govt in States, by type, program, agency, and State, FY91, annual rpt, 2464–2
FmHA activities, and loans and grants by program and State, FY91 and trends from FY70, annual rpt, 1184–17
Govt direct spending and employment, by function and level of govt, selected years 1962-87, 10048–53
Govt employment and payroll, by function, level of govt, and jurisdiction, annual rpt series, 2466–1
Govt finances, by level of govt, State, and for large cities and counties, annual rpt series, 2466–2
Govt finances, tax systems and revenue, and fiscal structure, by level of govt and State, 1992 with historical trends, annual rpt, 10044–1

Groundwater supply, quality, chemistry, and use, State and local area rpt series, 5666–28
Groundwater supply, quality, chemistry, other characteristics, and use, regional rpt series, 5666–25
Housing (rental) units, total, with HUD assistance by program, and eligible for aid, by unit, household, and neighborhood characteristics, and location, 1989, biennial rpt, 5184–11
Housing and households characteristics, and unit and neighborhood quality, by MSA location for 11 MSAs, 1987 survey, supplement, 2485–8
Housing and households detailed characteristics, and unit and neighborhood quality, by location, 1989, biennial rpt supplement, 2485–13
Housing and households detailed characteristics, and unit and neighborhood quality, MSA surveys, series, 2485–6
Housing and population census, 1990: population and housing characteristics, detailed geographic coverage, State CD-ROM series, 2551–10
Indian Health Service funding for housing sanitary facilities, and needs, FY60-91, annual rpt, 4084–1
Industrial hazardous substances releases and reduction methods under EPA regulation, by chemical, source, industry, and location, 1989, annual rpt, 9234–6
Industrial hazardous substances releases and reduction methods under EPA regulation, with chemical stocks and use, facility directory, 1987-89, annual CD-ROM, 9234–7
Input-output structure of US economy, detailed interindustry transactions for 541 industries, and components of final demand, 1982 benchmark data, 2708–17
Manufacturing pollution abatement capital and operating costs, by SIC 2- to 4-digit industry and State, 1990, annual Current Industrial Rpt, 2506–3.6
Military prime contract awards, by detailed procurement category, FY88-91, annual rpt, 3544–18
Natl income and product accounts, comprehensive accounts and components, benchmark revisions, 1929-88, 2708–5
Natl income and product accounts, comprehensive accounts and components, *Survey of Current Business*, monthly rpt, 2702–1.28
New York Bight ocean floor shellfish and other species abundance, and impacts of sewage sludge disposal site phaseout, by site, 1980s, 2168–128
Pacific territories population and housing detailed characteristics, by location, 1990 Census of Population and Housing, series, 2551–8
Pollutants health effects, concentrations in food and environment, sources, human intake, and regulation, series, 9186–8
Population size and demographic changes impacts on economic conditions, with background data, 1950s-80s and projected to 2010, 23848–226
Shellfish harvest in estuaries, approved and restricted areas, and pollution sources, by estuary, State, and coastal region, 1990, quinquennial rpt, 2178–33
Ship (passenger) sanitary inspection scores, biweekly rpt, 4202–10
Water quality, chemistry, hydrology, and other characteristics, local area studies, series, 5666–27
Water use by end use, well withdrawals, and public supply deliveries, by county, State rpt series, 5666–24

Sex
see Homosexuality
see Men
see Sex crimes
see Sex discrimination
see Sex education
see Sexual behavior
see Sexual sterilization
see Sexually transmitted diseases
see Women
see under By Sex in the "Index by Categories"

Sex crimes
Aliens excluded and deported from US by cause and country, 1892-1991, annual rpt, 6264–2.5
Arrests, by offense, offender characteristics, and location, 1991, annual rpt, 6224–2.2
Child abductions, runaways, and missing and exploited children, and Office of Juvenile Justice and Delinquency Prevention activities, FY90, annual rpt, 6064–36
Court civil and criminal caseloads for Federal district, appeals, and bankruptcy courts, by type of suit and offense, circuit, and district, 1991, annual rpt, 18204–11
Court civil and criminal caseloads for Federal district, appeals, and special courts, 1991, annual rpt, 18204–8
Court criminal case processing in Federal district courts, and dispositions, by offense, district, and offender characteristics, 1989, annual data compilation, 6064–29
Court criminal case processing in Federal district courts, and dispositions, by offense, 1980-91, annual rpt, 6064–31
Crime, criminal justice admin and enforcement, and public opinion, data compilation, 1992 annual rpt, 6064–6
Drug test results at arrest, by drug type, offense, and sex, for selected urban areas, quarterly rpt, 6062–3
Homicides, by circumstance, victim and offender relationship, and type of weapon, 1991, annual rpt, 6224–2.1
Immigrant and nonimmigrant visa applicants refused, and refusals overcome, by reason, FY90, annual rpt, 7184–1.3
Juvenile arrests, by sex, race, disposition, and offense, 1990, 6066–27.8
Labor laws enacted, by State, 1991, annual article, 6722–1.309
Prison and parole admissions and releases, sentence length, and time served, by offense and offender characteristics, 1988, annual rpt, 6064–33
Prisoners in Federal and contract instns, by selected characteristics, region, and Federal instn, FY89, annual rpt, 6244–1.1
Sentences for Federal crimes, guidelines use and results by offense and district, and Sentencing Commission activities, 1991, annual rpt, 17664–1
Sentences for Federal offenses, guidelines by offense and circumstances, series, 17668–1
Treatment programs for adult and juvenile sex offenders, by program type and State, data compilation, 1992 annual rpt, 6064–6.1; 6064–6.6
US attorneys civil and criminal cases by type and disposition, and collections, by Federal district, FY91, annual rpt, 6004–2.1
Victims of crime, compensation and support service programs funding, by offense and State, FY88-90, biennial rpt, 6064–37
Women in jail, by criminal background and sociodemographic characteristics, with comparisons to men, 1989, 6066–19.66
see also Prostitution
see also Rape

Sex discrimination
Educational equity program for women, grants and contracts by project, type, and State, 1988-92, annual rpt, 4804–2
FAA employees job satisfaction, impacts of promotion and pay equity by sex, 1992 technical rpt, 7506–10.105
Fed Equal Opportunity Recruitment Program activity, and employment by sex, race, pay grade, and occupational group, FY91, annual rpt, 9844–33
Foreign countries human rights conditions in 170 countries, 1991, annual rpt, 21384–3
Harassment (sexual) complaints and company policies, 1988 survey, hearing, 21348–120
Labor laws enacted, by State, 1991, annual article, 6722–1.309
Washington State govt employees comparable worth agreement, compliance costs and indicators of success, mid 1980s-93, GAO rpt, 26119–410

Sex education
Youth health condition, risk factors, and preventive and treatment services use and availability, 1970s-80s, 26358–234.2

Sexual behavior
AIDS cases at VA health care centers by sex, race, risk factor, and facility, and AIDS prevention and treatment issues, quarterly rpt, 8702–1
AIDS cases by risk group, race, sex, age, State, and MSA, and deaths, quarterly rpt, 4202–9
AIDS knowledge, attitudes, and risk behaviors of women in methadone maintenance programs, effects of life skills training, 1988-89 local area study, article, 4042–3.353
AIDS prevention programs for drug abusers and their sexual partners, client characteristics, and outcomes, for selected metro areas, 1989 annual conf, 4494–12
AIDS virus-infected men notification of sexual partners, relation to risk behavior and other characteristics, 1988-89 local area study, article, 4042–3.310
Alcohol abuse impacts on sexual function, for men with cirrhosis of liver, 1992 article, 4482–1.307
HHS financial aid, by program, recipient, State, and city, FY91, annual regional listings, 4004–3
Homeless youths health conditions and risk behaviors, 1990 local area study, article, 4042–3.344
Indian and Alaska Native youth health condition and behavioral patterns, by sex and grade, 1988-90, 4088–3

Latin America young unmarried adults sexual activity, contraceptives use, and AIDS risk knowledge, by sex and country, 1984-91, article, 4202-7.323
Population sexual partners in lifetime and past year, by selected characteristics, 1988 local area study, article, 4042-3.311
Research on population and reproduction, Federal funding by project, FY90, annual listing, 4474-9
Teenage boys AIDS risk behavior, sexual activity, and drug and condom use, 1988, article, 4042-3.313
see also Contraceptives
see also Family planning
see also Homosexuality
see also Obscenity and pornography
see also Sex crimes
see also Sexually transmitted diseases

Sexual harassment
see Sex discrimination

Sexual sterilization
Abortions by method, patient characteristics, and State, and related deaths, 1970-89, annual article, 4202-7.324
Cancer (brain) risk relation to menopausal status and ovary removal, Germany study, 1992 article, 4472-1.340
Deaths during 1986, decedents health condition, services use, habits, and social, employment, and other characteristics, 4147-20.19
Developing countries family planning and population activities of AID, grants by project and recipient, and contraceptive shipments, by country, FY91, annual rpt series, 9914-13
Developing countries population size, life expectancy, and fertility, trends and forecasts, country rpt series, 2326-24
Foreign countries contraception use by women, by age and country, 1991 biennial rpt, 2324-9
Health condition and care indicators, 1950s-90 with health improvement and disease prevention goals for 1990, annual data compilation, 4144-11
Hospital discharges and length of stay, by diagnosis, patient and instn characteristics, procedure performed, and payment source, 1990, annual rpt, 4147-13.112
Hysterectomies and prostatectomies performed by Medicare hospital providers, actual and expected death rates by instn, 1990, annual State rpt series, 4654-14
Hysterectomy rate, by age, diagnosis, and region, 1970s-80s, 26358-261
Research on population and reproduction, Federal funding by project, FY90, annual listing, 4474-9

Sexually transmitted diseases
Chancroid cases and surveillance, 1981-90, article, 4202-7.318
Condom use promotion effectiveness in prevention of sexually transmitted disease reinfection, 1988 local area study, article, 4042-3.376
Deaths and rates, by cause, age, sex, marital status, race, and State, 1989, US Vital Statistics advance annual rpt, 4146-5.124
Deaths and rates, by cause, provisional data, monthly rpt, 4142-1.2
Deaths and rates, by detailed location, cause, and demographic characteristics, 1989, US Vital Statistics annual rpt, 4144-3
Developing countries family planning and population activities of AID, grants by project and recipient, and contraceptive shipments, by country, FY91, annual rpt series, 9914-13
Health condition and care indicators, 1950s-90 with health improvement and disease prevention goals for 1990, annual data compilation, 4144-11
HHS financial aid, by program, recipient, State, and city, FY91, annual regional listings, 4004-3
Italy STD cases by disease and sex, and surveillance activities, Sept 1990-June 1991, article, 4202-7.311
Morbidity and Mortality Weekly Report, infectious notifiable disease cases by age, race, and State, and deaths, 1940s-91, annual rpt, 4204-1
Morbidity and Mortality Weekly Report, infectious notifiable disease cases by State, and public health issues, 4202-1
Natl Inst of Allergy and Infectious Diseases activities, grants by recipient and location, and disease cases, FY84-91, annual rpt, 4474-30
Syphilis case rate, by sex, race, and region, 1990, article, 4202-7.303
Youth health condition, risk factors, and preventive and treatment services use and availability, 1970s-80s, 26358-234.2
see also Acquired immune deficiency syndrome
see also under By Disease in the "Index by Categories"

Seychelles
Agricultural trade of US, by detailed commodity and country, 1991, annual rpt, 1524-8
Agricultural trade of US, by detailed commodity and country, 1991, semiannual rpt, 1522-4
AID economic aid to developing countries, obligations and disbursements by country, quarterly rpt, 9912-4
Economic and military aid and loans from US and intl agencies, by program and country, FY46-91, annual rpt, 9914-5
Economic and social conditions of developing countries from 1960s, and Intl Dev Cooperation Agency and AID activities and funding, FY91-93, annual rpt, 9904-4
Economic, social, political, and geographic summary data, by country, 1992, annual factbook, 9114-2
Exports and imports of US, by transport mode, country, and SITC 1- to 3-digit commodity, 1991, annual rpt, 2424-12
Exports of US, detailed Schedule B commodities with countries of destination, 1991, annual rpt, 2424-10
Human rights conditions in 170 countries, and US economic and military aid, 1991, annual rpt, 21384-3
Military aid of US, arms sales, and training programs costs and budget requests, by program, world region, and country, FY91-93, annual rpt, 7144-13
Minerals Yearbook, Vol 3, 1989: foreign country review of production, trade, and policy, by commodity, annual rpt, 5604-35.1
Population size, growth rates, and components of change, by country, projected 1990-2020 and trends from 1950, biennial rpt, 2324-9
UN voting record and share of votes in agreement with US, by issue, country, and world area, 1991, annual rpt, 7004-18

Shack-Marquez, Janice
"Changes in Family Finances from 1983 to 1989: Evidence from the Survey of Consumer Finances", 9362-1.301

Shaffer, Sherrill
"Optimal Linear Taxation of Polluting Firms", 9387-8.280
"Potential Merger Synergies Among Large Commercial Banks", 9387-8.256
"Revenue-Restricted Cost Study of 100 Large Banks", 9387-8.274
"Structure, Conduct, Performance, and Welfare", 9387-8.276

Shale oil
see Oil shale

Shank, Susan E.
"New Labor Force Data for Census Regions and Divisions", 6742-2.303

Shankar, A. S.
"Inhalation Toxicology Research Institute, Albuquerque, N.Mex., Site Environmental Report, 1990", 3324-2.4

Shapouri, Hosein
"Sheep Production in 11 Western States", 1548-382

Sharjah
see United Arab Emirates

Sharp, Gerald B.
"Use of Restraint Devices To Prevent Collision Injuries and Deaths Among Welfare-Supported Children", 4042-3.312

Sharpe, Steven A.
"Consumer Switching Costs, Market Structure and Prices: The Theory and Its Application in the Bank Deposit Market", 9366-6.297
"Debt and Employment Volatility over the Business Cycle", 9366-6.286

Shaw, Gary M.
"Mothers' Motivations To Participate in a Pregnancy Health Survey", 4042-3.377

Shea, Martina
"Characteristics of Recipients and the Dynamics of Program Participation: 1987-88", 2546-20.25
"Poverty in the U.S.: 1991", 2546-6.77

Sheboygan County, Wis.
Housing vacancy rates for single and multifamily units and mobile homes, by city and ZIP code, 1989, annual MSA rpt, 9304-18.2

Sheep
see Livestock and livestock industry

Sheffield, Raymond M.
"Hurricane Hugo: Effects on South Carolina's Forest Resource", 1208-411

Sheikh, Patricia R.
"Outlook for Cotton", 1504-9.1

Shekhter, Elaina
"Partnership Returns, 1990", 8302-2.314

Shelburne, Robert C.
"North American Free Trade Agreement: Comparisons with and Lessons from Southern EC Enlargement", 6366-3.29
"Trade and Employment Effects of the Caribbean Basin Economic Recovery Act", 6364-2

Shelley, Kristina J.
"Future of Jobs for College Graduates", 6722-1.331

Shellfish
Alaska Beaufort Sea pollutant concentrations in sediment and marine life, by contaminant and site, 1985-89, 5738–33
Alaska OCS environmental conditions and oil dev impacts, compilation of papers, series, 2176–1
Aquaculture in US and Japan, mgmt, methods, and biological data for selected species, 1990 conf, annual rpt, 2164–15
Atlantic Ocean fish and shellfish catch and stocks, by species and northwest location, 1887-1991 and forecast to 1993, semiannual conf, 2162–9
Atlantic Ocean fish and shellfish distribution, bottom trawl survey results by species and location, periodic rpt series, 2164–18
Coastal and riparian areas environmental conditions, fish, wildlife, use, and mgmt, for individual ecosystems, series, 5506–9
Coastal areas environmental conditions and mgmt, for individual areas, conf series, 2146–8
Cold storage holdings of fish and shellfish, by product and species, preliminary data, monthly press release, 2162–2
Consumption, supply, trade, prices, spending, and indexes, by food commodity, 1990, annual rpt, 1544–4
Disease cases and outbreaks related to fish and shellfish consumption, by species, cause, and State, 1969-87, hearing, 21568–51
Environmental Quality, status of problems, protection programs, research, and intl issues, 1991 annual rpt, 484–1
Estuaries approved and restricted for shellfish harvest, and pollution sources, by estuary, State, and coastal region, 1990, quinquennial rpt, 2178–33
Estuary environmental conditions, research results and methodology, series, 2176–7
Exports and imports (agricultural) of US, by detailed commodity and country, 1991, annual rpt, 1524–8
Exports and imports (agricultural) of US, by detailed commodity and country, 1991, semiannual rpt, 1522–4
Exports and imports between US and outlying areas, by detailed commodity and mode of transport, 1991, annual rpt, 2424–11
Exports and imports of US, by country and detailed commodity, monthly rpt, 2422–12
Exports and imports of US, by Harmonized System 6-digit commodity and country, 1991, annual rpt, 2424–13
Exports and imports of US, by transport mode, country, and SITC 1- to 3-digit commodity, 1991, annual rpt, 2424–12
Exports of US, detailed Schedule B commodities with countries of destination, 1991, annual rpt, 2424–10
Foreign countries market conditions for US fish and shellfish products, country rpt series, 2166–19
Freight (waterborne domestic and foreign) by commodity, traffic, and passengers, by port and waterway, 1989, annual rpt, 3754–3
Landings and trade of commercial fisheries, by species, 1980-91, semiannual rpt, 1561–15.1
Landings, resources, and mgmt, for fish and shellfish species and region, 1988-90, annual rpt, 2164–22
Landings, trade, use, and fishery operations, with selected foreign data, by species, 1980s-91, annual rpt, 2164–1
Manufacturing annual survey, 1990: finances and operations, by SIC 2- to 4-digit industry, series, 2506–14
Marine Fisheries Review, US and foreign fisheries resources, dev, mgmt, and research, quarterly journal, 2162–1
New York Bight ocean floor shellfish and other species abundance, and impacts of sewage sludge disposal site phaseout, by site, 1980s, 2168–128
Nutrient, caloric, and waste composition, detailed data for raw, processed, and prepared foods, 1992 rpt, 1356–3.17
Pacific Northwest Indian tribes environmental, economic, and cultural impacts of OCS oil and gas lease and dev, with background data, 1970s-92, 5738–35
Pollutant concentrations in coastal and estuarine fish, shellfish, and environment, series, 2176–3
Price indexes (producer), by stage of processing and detailed commodity, monthly rpt, 6762–6
Price indexes (producer), by stage of processing and detailed commodity, monthly 1991, annual rpt, 6764–2
Production of processed fish by location, and trade, by species and product, 1988-91, annual rpts, 2166–6
Shrimp catch by region, and US trade by country, 1980-90, article, 1561–15.301
Shrimp catch impacts of sea turtle excluder devices, by device type, for Texas fishery, 1983-87 and projected to 1997, article, 2162–1.302
Statistical Abstract of US, 1992 annual data compilation, 2324–1.24
Weight and volume conversion factors for agricultural commodities and products, 1992 rpt, 1508–3

Sheltered workshops
Finances, operations, and Federal procurement from sheltered workshops, FY82-91, annual rpt, 11714–1

Shepard, Lloyd S.
"Analysis of Acid Precipitation Samples Collected by State Agencies: January-December 1989", 9194–20

Sheriffs' departments
see Police

Sherman, Deborah J.
"Neglected Health Care Needs of Street Youth", 4042–3.344

Sherman, William F.
"Records of the Accounting Offices of the Department of the Treasury, Record Group 217", 9516–2.2

Sherwood-Call, Carolyn
"Changing Geographical Patterns of Electronic Components Activity", 9393–8.307

Shields, Dennis A.
"USDA's Method of Estimating Fruit and Tree Nut Production", 1561–6.302

Shipbuilding and operating subsidies
Assistance (financial and nonfinancial) of Fed Govt, 1992 base edition, annual listing, 104–5
DOT activities by subagency, budget, and summary accident data, FY89, annual rpt, 7304–1
DOT planning and safety grants, by program, State, and for 40 SMSAs, FY89, annual rpt, 7304–7
Elimination of shipbuilding and repair subsidies, US and OECD proposals impacts on industry and trade, with data on US-flag vessels, 1980s-91, 9886–4.183
Freight (waterborne) sponsored by Fed Govt, total and US-flag share by agency and program, 1990, annual rpt, 7704–14.3
MarAd activities, finances, subsidies, and world merchant fleet operations, FY91, annual rpt, 7704–14
Merchant ships in US fleet, operating subsidies, construction, and ship-related employment, monthly rpt, 7702–1

Shipbuilding and repairing
Costs of merchant ship construction and conversion by owner and builder, fleet size, and employment, monthly rpt, 7702–1
County Business Patterns, 1989: employment, establishments, and payroll, by SIC 2- to 4-digit industry and county, annual State rpt series, 2326–8
County Business Patterns, 1990: employment, establishments, and payroll, by SIC 2- to 4-digit industry and county, annual State rpt series, 2326–6
Employment, earnings, and hours, by SIC 1- to 4-digit industry, monthly 1989-Feb 1992, annual rpt, 6744–4
Employment of minorities and women, by occupation, SIC 1- to 3-digit industry, State, and MSA, 1991, annual rpt, 9244–1
Employment shipboard, shipyard, and longshore, FY90-91, annual rpt, 7704–14.3
Exports and imports between US and outlying areas, by detailed commodity and mode of transport, 1991, annual rpt, 2424–11
Exports and imports of US, by country and detailed commodity, monthly rpt, 2422–12
Exports and imports of US, by Harmonized System 6-digit commodity and country, 1991, annual rpt, 2424–13
Exports and imports of US, by transport mode, country, and SITC 1- to 3-digit commodity, 1991, annual rpt, 2424–12
Exports of US, detailed Schedule B commodities with countries of destination, 1991, annual rpt, 2424–10
Facilities for shipbuilding and repair, capacity, and employment, by shipyard, 1991, annual rpt, 7704–9
Foreign and US merchant ships, tonnage, and new ship construction and deliveries, by vessel type and country, as of Jan 1992, annual rpt, 7704–3
Foreign-flag ships owned by US firms and foreign affiliates, by type, owner, and country of registry and construction, as of July 1991, semiannual rpt, 7702–3
Freight (waterborne domestic and foreign) by commodity, traffic, and passengers, by port and waterway, 1989, annual rpt, 3754–3

Manufacturing annual survey, 1990: finances and operations, by SIC 2- to 4-digit industry, series, 2506–14
Manufacturing census, 1987: concentration of largest firms measured by value added, and for shipments by SIC 2- and 4-digit industry, subject rpt, 2497–6
Manufacturing census, 1987: shipments of manufacturers products, by customer class and SIC 2- and 4-digit industry, subject rpt, 2497–4
Manufacturing finances and operations, by SIC 2- to 4-digit industry, forecast 1992, annual rpt, 2044–28
Merchant ships in US fleet and Natl Defense Reserve Fleet, vessels, tonnage, and owner, as of July 1991, semiannual listing, 7702–2
Military budget, procurement appropriations by item, service branch, and defense agency, FY91-93, annual rpt, 3544–32
Navy nuclear-powered vessels and support facilities radioactive waste, releases in harbors, and public exposure, 1970s-91, annual rpt, 3804–11
Navy personnel radiation exposure on nuclear-powered vessels and at support facilities, and injury claims, 1950s-91, annual rpt, 3804–10
Navy ship construction contract costs and funding, FY83-91, GAO rpt, 26123–401
Occupational injury and illness rates, by SIC 2- to 4-digit industry, 1989-90, annual rpt, 6844–7
Occupational injury and illness rates, by SIC 2- to 4-digit industry, 1990, annual rpt, 6844–1
OECD trade, total and for 4 major countries, and US trade by country, by commodity, 1980-90, world area rpt series, 9116–1
Price indexes (producer), by stage of processing and detailed commodity, monthly rpt, 6762–6
Price indexes (producer), by stage of processing and detailed commodity, monthly 1991, annual rpt, 6764–2
Science, engineering, and technical employment in manufacturing, by field and industry, 1989, triennial rpt, 9627–23
Statistical Abstract of US, 1992 annual data compilation, 2324–1.22
Tax (income) returns of corporations, income and tax items by asset size and detailed industry, 1989, annual rpt, 8304–4; 8304–21
see also Shipbuilding and operating subsidies

Shipments
see Foreign trade
see Freight
see Industrial production

Shipping Act
Shipping industry structure, rates, and effects of Shipping Act, by route, 1980s, 9408–54

Ships and shipping
Coastal areas environmental conditions and mgmt, for individual areas, conf series, 2146–8
Container (intermodal) traffic by mode, use of containers over legal weight for hwy use, and California enforcement activity, 1960s-88, hearing, 21648–65
Containers (intermodal) and equipment owned by shipping and leasing companies, inventory by type and size, 1991, annual rpt, 7704–10
County Business Patterns, 1989: employment, establishments, and payroll, by SIC 2- to 4-digit industry and county, annual State rpt series, 2326–8
County Business Patterns, 1990: employment, establishments, and payroll, by SIC 2- to 4-digit industry and county, annual State rpt series, 2326–6
Employment, earnings, and hours, by SIC 1- to 4-digit industry, monthly 1989-Feb 1992, annual rpt, 6744–4
Energy use by fuel type, and miles traveled, by transport mode, projected 1990-2010 and trends from 1960s, 3008–124
Energy use by mode of transport, fuel supply, and demographic and economic factors of vehicle use, 1970s-90, annual rpt, 3304–5
Exports and imports (waterborne) of US, by type of service, customs district, port, and world area, monthly rpt, 2422–7
Exports and imports between US and outlying areas, by detailed commodity and mode of transport, 1991, annual rpt, 2424–11
Exports of US, detailed commodities by country, monthly CD-ROM, 2422–13
Finances and operations, by SIC 2- to 4-digit industry, forecast 1992, annual rpt, 2044–28
Fishery employment, vessels, plants, and cooperatives, by State, 1990, annual rpt, 2164–1.10
Fishing fleet characteristics, for Atlantic and Gulf menhaden fisheries, 1955-88, article, 2162–1.303
Foreign and US merchant ships, tonnage, and new ship construction and deliveries, by vessel type and country, as of Jan 1992, annual rpt, 7704–3
Foreign and US merchant ships, tonnage, shipments, crews, and other operations, as of 1991, annual rpt, 7704–14
Foreign-flag ships owned by US firms and foreign affiliates, by type, owner, and country of registry and construction, as of July 1991, semiannual rpt, 7702–3
Freight rates, industry structure, and impacts of Shipping Act, by route, 1980s, 9408–54
Fuel oil and kerosene sales and deliveries, by end-use, PAD district, and State, 1990, annual rpt, 3164–94
Hawaii humpback whale habitat impacts of human activities, with data on shipping, whale watching, coastal construction, and aircraft, 1980s-90, 14738–14
Imports of US, detailed commodities by country, monthly CD-ROM, 2422–14
Input-output structure of US economy, detailed interindustry transactions for 541 industries, and components of final demand, 1982 benchmark data, 2708–17
Iraq registration and govt control of merchant ships, listing of vessels, 1991, hearing, 21248–165
Latin America economic and social conditions, resources, trade, and aid, 1992, annual factbook, 9914–14
Maritime Commission activities, case filings by type and disposition, and civil penalties by shipper, FY91, annual rpt, 9334–1
Merchant ships in US fleet and Natl Defense Reserve Fleet, vessels, tonnage, and owner, as of July 1991, semiannual listing, 7702–2
Merchant vessel logbooks, Natl Archives special collection, 1992 rpt, 9516–1.9
Minerals offshore lease sales environmental and economic impacts in coastal areas, final statement series, 5736–7
Multinatl firms US affiliates finances and operations, by industry, country of parent firm, and State, 1987, 2708–48
Occupational Outlook Handbook, 1992-93, biennial rpt, 6744–1
Oceanographic research and distribution activities of World Data Center A by country, and cruises by ship, 1990, annual rpt, 2144–15
Oceanographic research cruise ships characteristics, by higher education instn and Federal agency, 1992, annual listing, 3804–6
Overseas Business Reports: economic conditions, investment and export opportunities, and trade practices, country market research rpt series, 2046–6
Panama Canal traffic and tolls, by commodity, flag of vessel, and trade route, FY91, annual rpt, 9664–3.1
Price indexes (producer), by stage of processing and detailed commodity, monthly rpt, 6762–6
Price indexes (producer), by stage of processing and detailed commodity, monthly 1991, annual rpt, 6764–2
Soviet Union and US economic and sociodemographic indicators, selected years 1970-90, handbook, 2328–80
St Lawrence Seaway Dev Corp finances and activities, with Seaway cargo tonnage, and shipping costs compared to other US ports, 1990, annual rpt, 7744–1
St Lawrence Seaway ship, cargo, and passenger traffic, and toll revenue, 1991 and trends from 1959, annual rpt, 7744–2
Statistical Abstract of US, 1992 annual data compilation, 2324–1.22
Tax (income) returns of corporations, income and tax items by asset size and detailed industry, 1989, annual rpt, 8304–4; 8304–21
Tax (income) returns of sole proprietorships, income statement items, by industry group, 1990, annual article, 8302–2.317; 8302–2.320
Traffic, freight by commodity, and passengers, domestic and foreign waterborne commerce by port and waterway, 1989, annual rpt, 3754–3
Traffic of waterborne domestic and foreign freight, by US port, 1990, annual rpt, 3754–7
Weather rpts and gale and wave observations received from ships, quarterly journal, 2152–8
see also Barges
see also Boats and boating
see also Freight
see also Harbors and ports
see also Inland water transportation
see also Longshoremen
see also Marine accidents and safety
see also Maritime law

see also Merchant seamen
see also Naval vessels
see also Navigation
see also Nuclear-powered ships
see also Oil spills
see also Passenger ships
see also Shipbuilding and operating subsidies
see also Shipbuilding and repairing
see also Tanker ships

Shock incarceration
see Rehabilitation of criminals

Shoes and shoe industry
Business statistics, detailed data for major industries and economic indicators, *Survey of Current Business*, monthly rpt, 2702–1.14
Business statistics, detailed data for major industries and economic indicators, 1960-91, *Survey of Current Business* biennial supplement, 2704–1
Consumer spending, natl income and product account benchmark revisions, 1929-88, 2708–5
Consumer spending, natl income and product accounts, comprehensive accounts and components, *Survey of Current Business*, monthly rpt, 2702–1.25
County Business Patterns, 1989: employment, establishments, and payroll, by SIC 2- to 4-digit industry and county, annual State rpt series, 2326–8
County Business Patterns, 1990: employment, establishments, and payroll, by SIC 2- to 4-digit industry and county, annual State rpt series, 2326–6
CPI by component for US city average, and by selected metro area, region, and population size, monthly rpt, 6762–2
Employment, earnings, and hours, by SIC 1- to 4-digit industry, monthly 1989-Feb 1992, annual rpt, 6744–4
Employment of minorities and women, by occupation, SIC 1- to 3-digit industry, State, and MSA, 1991, annual rpt, 9244–1
Exports and imports between US and outlying areas, by detailed commodity and mode of transport, 1991, annual rpt, 2424–11
Exports and imports of US, by country and detailed commodity, monthly rpt, 2422–12
Exports and imports of US, by Harmonized System 6-digit commodity and country, 1991, annual rpt, 2424–13
Exports and imports of US, by selected country, country group, and commodity group, 1991, annual rpt, 2044–37
Exports and imports of US, by transport mode, country, and SITC 1- to 3-digit commodity, 1991, annual rpt, 2424–12
Exports, imports, and balances of US for manufactured goods, by SITC 2-digit commodity and country, quarterly rpt, 2042–35
Exports, imports, and intl competitiveness of US industries, trends and outlook, quarterly rpt with articles, 9882–16
Exports of US, detailed Schedule B commodities with countries of destination, 1991, annual rpt, 2424–10
Imports of US given duty-free treatment for value of US material sent abroad, by commodity and country, 1987-90, annual rpt, 9884–14
Injuries from use of consumer products, by severity, victim age, and detailed product, 1991, annual rpt, 9164–6
Input-output structure of US economy, detailed interindustry transactions for 84 industries, and components of final demand, 1987, annual article, 2702–1.316
Input-output structure of US economy, detailed interindustry transactions for 541 industries, and components of final demand, 1982 benchmark data, 2708–17
Manufacturing annual survey, 1990: finances and operations, by SIC 2- to 4-digit industry, series, 2506–14
Manufacturing census, 1987: concentration of largest firms measured by value added, and for shipments by SIC 2- and 4-digit industry, subject rpt, 2497–6
Manufacturing census, 1987: shipments of manufacturers products, by customer class and SIC 2- and 4-digit industry, subject rpt, 2497–4
Manufacturing finances and operations, by SIC 2- to 4-digit industry, forecast 1992, annual rpt, 2044–28
Occupational injury and illness rates, by SIC 2- to 4-digit industry, 1989-90, annual rpt, 6844–7
Occupational injury and illness rates, by SIC 2- to 4-digit industry, 1990, annual rpt, 6844–1
OECD trade, total and for 4 major countries, and US trade by country, by commodity, 1980-90, world area rpt series, 9116–1
Price indexes (producer), by stage of processing and detailed commodity, monthly rpt, 6762–6
Price indexes (producer), by stage of processing and detailed commodity, monthly 1991, annual rpt, 6764–2
Price indexes for department store inventories, by class of item, monthly table, 6762–7
Production, employment, use, prices, and US trade by country, quarterly rpt, 9882–6
Production, shipments, trade, and use of shoes, by product, 1991, annual Current Industrial Rpt, 2506–6.8
Production, shipments, trade, and use of shoes, quarterly Current Industrial Rpt, 2506–6.7
Productivity of labor and capital, and indexes of output, hours, and employment, 1967-90, annual rpt, 6824–1.3; 6824–1.5
Retail trade sales and inventories, by kind of business, region, and selected State, MSA, and city, monthly rpt, 2413–3
Retail trade sales, by kind of business, advance monthly rpt, 2413–2
Retail trade sales, inventories, purchases, gross margin, and accounts receivable, by SIC 2- to 4-digit kind of business and form of ownership, 1990, annual rpt, 2413–5
Science, engineering, and technical employment in manufacturing, by field and industry, 1989, triennial rpt, 9627–23
Tax (income) returns of corporations, income and tax items by asset size and detailed industry, 1989, annual rpt, 8304–4; 8304–21
see also under By Commodity in the "Index by Categories"

Shopping centers
Mail volume to and from households, use, and views, by class, source, content, and household characteristics, FY87-90, annual rpt, 9864–10
Neighborhood and housing quality, indicators and attitudes, by householder type and location, for 11 MSAs, 1987 survey, supplement, 2485–8
Statistical Abstract of US, 1992 annual data compilation, 2324–1.28

Short, Kathleen S.
"Extended Measures of Well-Being", 2546–20.22
"Health Insurance Coverage, 1987-90", 2546–20.23

Short, Sara D.
"Financial Condition of Dairy Farms, 1987-90", 1561–2.301
"Outlook for Dairy", 1504–9.1

Shreveport, La.
see also under By City and By SMSA or MSA in the "Index by Categories"

Shrimp
see Shellfish

Shriner, Susan
"Victim Programs To Serve Native Americans", 6066–31.1

Shumofsky, Nina
"Corporation Income Tax Returns, 1989", 8302–2.321

Shumway, C. Richard
"State-Level Output Supply and Input Demand Elasticities for Agricultural Commodities", 1502–3.303

Sibert, Anne
"Can Unconventional Preferences Explain Risk Premia in the Foreign Exchange Markets?", 9381–10.131
"Public Finance and Coordination Problems in a Common Currency Area", 9381–10.127
"Strategic Capital Taxation in Large, Open Economies with Mobile Capital", 9381–10.130

Sickmund, Melissa
"Juvenile Court Drug and Alcohol Cases: 1985-88", 6066–27.7
"Offenders in Juvenile Court, 1988", 6066–27.9

Sickness
see Absenteeism
see Diseases and disorders
see Health condition
see Hospitalization

Siegel, Jacob S.
"Trends in Retirement Age by Sex, 1950-2005", 6722–1.332

Siegel, Paul Z.
"Behavioral Risk Factor Surveillance, 1986-90", 4202–7.305

Siegel, William C.
"Forestry Implications of Water Quality and Wetland Law", 1504–9.1

Sieling, Mark
"Productivity in the Nuts and Bolts Industry, 1958-90", 6722–1.343

Siems, Thomas F.
"Quantifying Management's Role in Bank Survival", 9379–1.302

Sienkiewicz, Joseph M.
"Observation", 2152–8.303
Sierra Leone
Agricultural trade of US, by detailed commodity and country, 1991, annual rpt, 1524–8
Agricultural trade of US, by detailed commodity and country, 1991, semiannual rpt, 1522–4
AID economic aid to developing countries, obligations and disbursements by country, quarterly rpt, 9912–4
Economic and military aid and loans from US and intl agencies, by program and country, FY46-91, annual rpt, 9914–5
Economic and social conditions of developing countries from 1960s, and Intl Dev Cooperation Agency and AID activities and funding, FY91-93, annual rpt, 9904–4
Economic, social, political, and geographic summary data, by country, 1992, annual factbook, 9114–2
Exports and imports of US, by transport mode, country, and SITC 1- to 3-digit commodity, 1991, annual rpt, 2424–12
Exports of US, detailed Schedule B commodities with countries of destination, 1991, annual rpt, 2424–10
Human rights conditions in 170 countries, and US economic and military aid, 1991, annual rpt, 21384–3
Military aid of US, arms sales, and training programs costs and budget requests, by program, world region, and country, FY91-93, annual rpt, 7144–13
Military spending, arms trade, and force strengths, with govt spending and population, by country, 1979-89, annual rpt, 9824–1
Minerals Yearbook, Vol 3, 1989: foreign country review of production, trade, and policy, by commodity, annual rpt, 5604–35.1
Population size, growth rates, and components of change, by country, projected 1990-2020 and trends from 1950, biennial rpt, 2324–9
Refugee migration, and intl aid programs, by world area and country of origin and asylum, 1991, annual rpt, 7004–15
UN voting record and share of votes in agreement with US, by issue, country, and world area, 1991, annual rpt, 7004–18
Sigler, Stella
"Analyses of Natural Gases, 1986-90", 5608–132
Silk
Broadwoven gray goods production, by fabric type, quarterly Current Industrial Rpt, 2506–5.11
Exports and imports (agricultural) of US, by detailed commodity and country, 1991, annual rpt, 1524–8
Exports and imports (agricultural) of US, by detailed commodity and country, 1991, semiannual rpt, 1522–4
Exports and imports between US and outlying areas, by detailed commodity and mode of transport, 1991, annual rpt, 2424–11
Exports and imports of textiles, raw fiber equivalents by product, country, and world region, 1989-90, article, 1561–1.301
Exports and imports of US, by country and detailed commodity, monthly rpt, 2422–12
Exports and imports of US, by Harmonized System 6-digit commodity and country, 1991, annual rpt, 2424–13
Exports and imports of US, by transport mode, country, and SITC 1- to 3-digit commodity, 1991, annual rpt, 2424–12
Exports of US, detailed Schedule B commodities with countries of destination, 1991, annual rpt, 2424–10
Exports of US textiles and apparel, by product group and country, quarterly rpt, 2042–36
Imports of silk-blend textiles, by product and country of origin, monthly rpt, 2046–8.6
Imports of textiles, by country of origin, monthly rpt, 2042–27
Imports of textiles, by product and country of origin, monthly rpt series, 2046–8; 2046–9
Manufacturing annual survey, 1990: finances and operations, by SIC 2- to 4-digit industry, series, 2506–14
Production, prices, trade, and use of natural fibers, periodic situation rpt with articles, 1561–1
Sill, Keith
"Empirical Investigation of Money Demand in the Cash-In-Advance Model Framework", 9387–8.279
Silver
Business statistics, detailed data for major industries and economic indicators, *Survey of Current Business*, monthly rpt, 2702–1.8
Business statistics, detailed data for major industries and economic indicators, 1960-91, *Survey of Current Business* biennial supplement, 2704–1
Coin production and monetary metals use and holdings of US Mint, by metal type, FY91, annual rpt, 8204–1
County Business Patterns, 1989: employment, establishments, and payroll, by SIC 2- to 4-digit industry and county, annual State rpt series, 2326–8
County Business Patterns, 1990: employment, establishments, and payroll, by SIC 2- to 4-digit industry and county, annual State rpt series, 2326–6
Exports and imports between US and outlying areas, by detailed commodity and mode of transport, 1991, annual rpt, 2424–11
Exports and imports of US, by country and detailed commodity, monthly rpt, 2422–12
Exports and imports of US, by Harmonized System 6-digit commodity and country, 1991, annual rpt, 2424–13
Exports and imports of US, by transport mode, country, and SITC 1- to 3-digit commodity, 1991, annual rpt, 2424–12
Exports of US, detailed Schedule B commodities with countries of destination, 1991, annual rpt, 2424–10
Foreign countries mineral production, reserves, and industry role in domestic economy and world supply, world area and country rpt series, 5606–1
Futures and options trading volume, by commodity and exchange, FY91, annual rpt, 11924–2
Futures trading in selected commodities and financial instruments and indexes, for NYC, Chicago, and other markets activity, biweekly rpt, 11922–5
Mineral Industry Surveys, commodity review of production, trade, stocks, and use, monthly rpt, 5612–1.10
Mineral Industry Surveys, State reviews of production, 1991, preliminary annual rpt, 5614–6
Minerals Yearbook, Vol 1, 1989: commodity reviews of production, use, trade, prices, and mining operations, annual rpt, 5604–33
Minerals Yearbook, Vol 1, 1990: commodity review of production, reserves, supply, use, and trade, annual rpt, 5604–20.53
Minerals Yearbook, Vol 2, 1989: State reviews of production and sales by commodity, and business activity, annual rpt series, 5604–16
Minerals Yearbook, Vol 2, 1990: State reviews of production and sales by commodity, and business activity, annual rpt series, 5604–22
Minerals Yearbook, Vol 3, 1989: foreign country reviews of production, trade, and policy, by commodity, annual rpt, 5604–35
Mines (metal) and related operations occupational injuries and incidence, employment, and hours, 1990, annual rpt, 6664–3
Price indexes (producer), by stage of processing and detailed commodity, monthly rpt, 6762–6
Production and prices of primary metals mining byproducts, by commodity, 1965-90, 5608–170
Production in 5 western States, and prices, for 5 nonferrous metals, 1848-1990, 5608–178
Production, prices, trade, use, employment, tariffs, and stockpiles, by mineral, with foreign comparisons, 1987-91, annual rpt, 5604–18
Production, trade, use, and foreign investment in US industry, for minerals, 1985-90 and projected to 2000, annual rpt, 5304–5
Stockpiling of strategic material by Fed Govt, activity, and inventory by commodity, as of Sept 1991, semiannual rpt, 3542–22
Stockpiling of strategic material, inventories and needs, by commodity, 1992, annual rpt, 3544–37
Silvestri, George
"Occupational Employment Projections", 6744–19
Simanis, Joseph G.
"Social Security Reform in Four East European Countries", 4742–1.303
Simons, Brad D.
"Relationship of Polyps to Cancer of the Large Intestine", 4472–1.325
Simons, Katerina
"Failed Bank Resolution and the Collateral Crunch: The Advantages of Adopting Transferable Puts", 9373–27.13
"Mutual-to-Stock Conversions by New England Savings Banks: Where Has All the Money Gone?", 9373–1.307

Simpson, William T.
"Relative Drying Times of 650 Tropical Woods: Estimation by Green Moisture Content, Specific Gravity, and Green Weight Density", 1208–392

Singapore
Agricultural production, prices, and trade, by country, 1980s and forecast 1992, annual world region rpt, 1524–4.3
Agricultural trade of US, by detailed commodity and country, 1991, annual rpt, 1524–8
Agricultural trade of US, by detailed commodity and country, 1991, semiannual rpt, 1522–4
AID economic aid to developing countries, obligations and disbursements by country, quarterly rpt, 9912–4
Cuba trade, by commodity and country, mid 1980s-91, 9118–8
Drug abuse indicators, by world region and selected country, 1992 semiannual conf, 4492–5.2
Economic and military aid and loans from US and intl agencies, by program and country, FY46-91, annual rpt, 9914–5
Economic and monetary trends, compounded annual rates of change and annual indicators for US and 15 trading partners, quarterly rpt, annual supplement, 9391–7
Economic and social conditions of developing countries from 1960s, and Intl Dev Cooperation Agency and AID activities and funding, FY91-93, annual rpt, 9904–4
Economic conditions and monetary policy in Singapore, with exchange rate and money supply related to foreign prices and other factors, for Singapore, 1960s-90, article, 9379–1.304
Economic conditions, income, production, prices, employment, and trade, 1992 periodic country rpt, 2046–4.65
Economic conditions, policy, and trade practices, by country, 1989-91, annual rpt, 21384–5
Economic, social, political, and geographic summary data, by country, 1992, annual factbook, 9114–2
Export and import balances of US, and dollar exchange rates, with 5 Asian countries, 1992 semiannual rpt, 8002–14
Exports and imports of US, by commodity and country, 1980-90, world area rpt, 9116–1.3
Exports and imports of US by country, and trade shifts by commodity, 1991, annual rpt, 9884–25
Exports and imports of US, by Harmonized System 6-digit commodity and country, 1991, annual rpt, 2424–13
Exports and imports of US, by selected country, country group, and commodity group, 1991, annual rpt, 2044–37
Exports and imports of US, by transport mode, country, and SITC 1- to 3-digit commodity, 1991, annual rpt, 2424–12
Exports, imports, and balances of US for manufactured goods, by SITC 2-digit commodity and country, quarterly rpt, 2042–35
Exports of US, detailed Schedule B commodities with countries of destination, 1991, annual rpt, 2424–10
Human rights conditions in 170 countries, and US economic and military aid, 1991, annual rpt, 21384–3
Imports of goods, services, and investment from US, trade barriers, impacts, and US actions, by country, 1991, annual rpt, 444–2
Imports of US given duty-free treatment for value of US material sent abroad, by commodity and country, 1987-90, annual rpt, 9884–14
Military aid of US, arms sales, and training programs costs and budget requests, by program, world region, and country, FY91-93, annual rpt, 7144–13
Military spending, arms trade, and force strengths, with govt spending and population, by country, 1979-89, annual rpt, 9824–1
Minerals Yearbook, Vol 3, 1989: foreign country review of production, trade, and policy, by commodity, annual rpt, 5604–35.2
Multinatl US firms and foreign affiliates finances and operations, by industry and country, 1989 benchmark survey, annual rpt, 2704–5
Multinatl US firms foreign affiliates, income statement items by asset size, industry, and country, 1988, biennial article, 8302–2.322
Population size, growth rates, and components of change, by country, projected 1990-2020 and trends from 1950, biennial rpt, 2324–9
Refugee migration, and intl aid programs, by world area and country of origin and asylum, 1991, annual rpt, 7004–15
Ships in world merchant fleet, tonnage, and new ship construction and deliveries, by vessel type and country, as of Jan 1992, annual rpt, 7704–3
Steel trade, by product, country, and customs district, with US industry operating data, 1989-June 1992, semiannual rpt, 9882–15
UN voting record and share of votes in agreement with US, by issue, country, and world area, 1991, annual rpt, 7004–18
Vegetable imports of Singapore, for fresh and processed types, 1986-90, article, 1925–34.305
see also under By Foreign Country in the "Index by Categories"

Singer, Florence
"Weather in U.S. Agriculture: Monthly Temperature and Precipitation by State and Farm Production Region, 1950-90", 1544–28

Single parents
AFDC Job Opportunities and Basic Skills Training program State admin, and Unemployed Parent program caseloads and payments by State, 1991 GAO rpt, 26131–96
AFDC unemployed parent cases and payments, by State, quarterly FY90, annual rpt, 4584–3.1
Asian and Pacific Islands Americans social and economic characteristics, for West and total US, 1990-91, Current Population Report, 2546–1.462
Benefits, beneficiaries, and spells of participation, by aid program and recipient characteristics, 1987-88, Current Population Rpt, 2546–20.25
Black Americans social and economic characteristics, for South and total US, 1991 and trends from 1950, annual Current Population Rpt, 2546–1.463
Census of Population and Housing, 1990: summary characteristics, by county, subdiv, and place, State rpt series, 2551–7
Census of Population, 1990: population characteristics and living arrangements, by county, place, and urban-rural location, State rpt series, 2531–1
Census of Population, 1990: population characteristics and living arrangements, for Native American, urban, and metro areas, series, 2531–2
Child care arrangements of mothers employed and in school, and costs, by age of child and characteristics of mother, 1988, Current Population Rpt, 2546–20.24
Child care arrangements of younger working mothers, and costs, by selected characteristics, 1988, 6726–2.1
Child living arrangements, and women's marriage and divorce experience, by race, 1970s-90, Current Population Rpt, 2546–2.166
Child support payment and visitation practices of absent fathers, and mothers with custody, by employment and other characteristics, 1988, article, 6722–1.329
Families headed by single parents in own and others homes, by financial, housing, and other characteristics, 1989, 2486–1.14
Food spending of women-headed households, by item and selected characteristics, and compared to other households, 1970s-88, 1548–391
Food stamp recipient household size, composition, income, and income and deductions allowed, summer 1989, annual rpt, 1364–8
Higher education instn student financial support by parents, by type and funding sources, and student, parent, and instn characteristics, fall 1986, 4846–3.11
Homeownership rate by marital status, and single parents share of family households, by race, 1989, fact sheet, 2326–17.44
Households and family characteristics, by location, 1991, annual Current Population Rpt, 2546–1.457
Housing (rental) units, total, with HUD assistance by program, and eligible for aid, by unit, household, and neighborhood characteristics, and location, 1989, biennial rpt, 5184–11
Income (family) of single mothers, and impacts of child care, govt and child support payments, taxes, and marriage, with data by State, 1970s-91, 21788–212
Income (household) and poverty status under alternative income definitions, by recipient characteristics, 1979-91, annual Current Population Rpt, 2546–6.78
Insurance (health) coverage of persons, by insurance type and selected characteristics, 1985-90, 2546–20.23
Job Training Partnership Act education and worker training program participants, by selected characteristics, 1986-88, 15496–1.15

Job Training Partnership Act support services and supplementary payments, and impact on single parent participation, 199091, 26106–8.15
Living arrangements, family relationships, and marital status, by selected characteristics, 1991, annual Current Population Rpt, 2546–1.461
Pacific territories population and housing detailed characteristics, by location, 1990 Census of Population and Housing, series, 2551–8
Population economic well-being indicators, by selected characteristics and household income and income-to-poverty ratio, 1984, 2546–20.22
Poverty relation to low earnings, by work experience during year, household relationship, sex, race, age, and education, 1960s-90, Current Population Rpt, 2546–6.74
Poverty status of families, by detailed characteristics, 1980 and 1988, GAO rpt, 26131–102
Statistical Abstract of US, 1992 annual data compilation, 2324–1.1
Supplemental Security Income child beneficiaries and benefits, by selected characteristics, family income status, and State, 1991, article, 4742–1.316

Singleton, Christopher J.
"Auto Industry Jobs in the 1980's: A Decade of Transition", 6722–1.313

Skelton, David T.
"Use of Electronic Monitoring in the U.S.: 1989 Update", 6066–20.23

Skin diseases
Cancer (invasive melanoma) cases in Queensland, Australia, by sex, 1979/80 and 1987, article, 4472–1.344
Cancer (melanoma) tumor characteristics agreement in physician records and tumor registry, 1992 article, 4472–1.354
Cancer deaths and rates, by body site and selected social, demographic, and employment characteristics, 1979-85, natl longitudinal study, 4478–186
Cancer deaths and rates, by body site, provisional data, monthly rpt, 4142–1.2
Cases of acute and chronic conditions, disability, absenteeism, and health services use, by selected characteristics, 1990, annual rpt, 4147–10.182; 4147–10.183
Disability and work limitations of persons with chronic health conditions, by condition, age, and sex, 1983-86, 4946–1.2
Hospital discharges and length of stay, by diagnosis, patient and instn characteristics, procedure performed, and payment source, 1990, annual rpt, 4147–13.112
Hospital discharges and length of stay by region and diagnosis, and procedures performed, by age and sex, 1990, annual rpt, 4146–8.211
Hospital discharges and length of stay under old and new survey designs, by diagnosis, patient and instn characteristics, and procedure, Jan-Mar 1988, 4147–13.110
Hospital discharges by detailed diagnostic and procedure category, primary diagnosis, and length of stay, by age, sex, and region, 1990, annual rpt, 4147–13.111
Indian Health Service, tribal, and contract facilities hospitalization, by diagnosis, age, sex, and service area, FY91, annual rpt, 4084–5
Occupational illness rates, by cause and SIC 2- to 3-digit industry, 1990, annual rpt, 6844–1
OECD members health care costs, hospital use, resources, and economic and health indicators, by country, 1960s-90, article, 4652–1.322
Physicians visits, by patient and practice characteristics, diagnosis, and services provided, 1989, annual rpt, 4147–13.109
Pollutants health effects, concentrations in food and environment, sources, human intake, and regulation, series, 9186–8
see also under By Disease in the "Index by Categories"

Skinner, Robert A.
"Assessment of USDA's Cotton Supply and Demand Estimates", 1561–1.302
"Outlook for Cotton", 1504–9.1

Skyjacking
see Air piracy

Slander
see Libel and slander

Slaten, Douglas D.
"Outbreak of Bacillus cereus Food Poisoning—Are Caterers Supervised Sufficiently?", 4042–3.350

Slave labor
see Forced labor

Sleemi, Fehmida
"Wage and Compensation Changes in Settlements, 1991", 6722–1.325

Sleep disorders
see Neurological disorders

Slovenia
Economic, social, political, and geographic summary data, by country, 1992, annual factbook, 9114–2

Slum clearance
see Urban renewal

Small business
Army Corps of Engineers dredging contracts to small businesses, costs and bidding activity, FY90-92, GAO rpt, 26113–589
Bank deposit insurance coverage of households and small businesses, and value of insurance to banks by instn, 1970s-90, hearing, 21408–126
Capital formation sources and issues for small business, 1991 annual conf, 9734–4
Census Bur economic data use by small business for planning decisions, case studies, 1991 rpt, 2628–33
Developing countries economic and social conditions from 1960s, and Intl Dev Cooperation Agency and AID activities and funding, FY91-93, annual rpt, 9904–4
DOE contracts and grants, by category, State, and for top contractors, FY91, annual rpt, 3004–21
DOE procurement contract awards to small businesses, by business type and subagency, FY90, annual rpt, 3004–35
DOE R&D projects and funding at natl labs, universities, and other instns, periodic summary rpt series, 3004–18
Economic review and outlook for US, analysis of Bush Admin and private projections, with small business views, 1991 hearings, 23848–230
Employee leave benefits in small business compared to larger firms and govts, by occupational group, 1989-90, article, 6722–1.315
Fed Govt financial and nonfinancial domestic aid, 1992 base edition, annual listing, 104–5
Fed Govt spending in States, by type, program, agency, and State, FY91, annual rpt, 2464–2
Finances, operations, owner characteristics, and Federal contracts, for small business, 1980s-90, annual rpt, 9764–6
Forests (natl) set-aside sales in Pacific Northwest region, quarterly rpt, 1202–3
Health sciences research and training grants and contracts of Natl Inst of General Medical Sciences, by program, FY91, annual rpt, 4474–38
HHS financial aid, by program, recipient, State, and city, FY91, annual regional listings, 4004–3
Insurance (health) provided by small businesses, cost and access issues, 1991 hearings, 21788–218
Insurance (health) reforms of States to improve small business access, provisions with background data by State, 1991, GAO rpt, 26121–462
Insurance (life) benefits of employer-sponsored plans by plan type, age, occupation, and salary, 1990, article, 6722–1.346
Loan and debenture sale activity under SBA dev company program, with data by firm, industry div, State, and region, quarterly rpt, 9762–6
Loan guarantee program of SBA, participants finances, operations, characteristics, and views, 1991 survey, 9768–25
Loans (direct and guaranteed) of SBA, principal outstanding, and losses, by program, borrower race and sex, and State, 1950s-90, GAO rpt, 26113–554
Loans (guaranteed) of SBA issued under regular, certified, and preferred lender programs, selected characteristics, FY83-90, GAO rpt, 26113–581
Loans and finances of SBA, and small business contracts, by firm and location, FY91, annual rpt, 9764–1
Loans for small business, collateral adequacy for failed firms, with loan liquidation recoveries and losses, FY89, GAO rpt, 26113–553
Military contractor subcontract awards to small and disadvantaged business, by firm and service branch, quarterly rpt, 3542–17
Military prime contract awards, by category, contract and contractor type, and service branch, FY82-1st half FY92, semiannual rpt, 3542–1
Military prime contract awards for R&D, for top 500 contractors, FY91, annual listing, 3544–4
Military prime contract awards in labor surplus areas, by service branch, State, and area, 1st half FY92, semiannual rpt, 3542–19
Minority- and woman-owned businesses and owner characteristics, by industry, employment and sales size, and form of ownership, 1987 survey, 2328–59

Minority business Federal procurement set-aside contracts, by participant race and sex, industry, firm, and State, FY90, annual rpt, 9764–8
Minority business Federal procurement set-aside contracts, by State, FY90, GAO rpt, 26113–563
Minority business funding, by program and Federal agency, FY91, annual rpt, 2104–5
NASA procurement contract awards, by type, contractor, State, and country, FY92 with trends from 1961, semiannual rpt, 9502–6
R&D funding by Fed Govt to small business, by program area, agency, MSA, and State, FY90, annual rpt, 9764–7
R&D funding by small high technology firms relation to firm finances, 1991 working paper, 9375–13.75
R&D grants of Fed Govt to small business, project commercial success indicators and other characteristics of firms involved, 1988-90 survey, chartbook, 9768–23
R&D grants of Fed Govt to small business, project sales by type and dev funding by source, by agency and selected firm, 1984-91, GAO rpt, 26113–393
Research and education grants, USDA competitive awards by program and recipient, FY91, annual listing, 1764–1
Rural areas businesses credit assistance of Fed Govt, by program and county characteristics, 1983-89, 1548–389
Rural areas tourism-related and other small businesses, SBA loans, FY86-1st half FY91, hearing, 21728–79
Statistical Abstract of US, 1992 annual data compilation, 2324–1.17
Tax (income) admin and compliance issues, and taxpayer views, 1991 conf, 8304–25
Tax (income) returns filed, by type of filer, selected income items, quarterly rpt, 8302–2.1
Tax (income) returns of corporations, income and tax items by asset size and detailed industry, 1989, annual rpt, 8304–4
Tax collection activity of IRS, by type of tax, FY91, annual rpt, 8304–3.1
Technology transfer by Federal R&D labs to small manufacturers, promotional programs activities and grants to States, late 1980s-91, GAO rpt, 26113–551
Tree planting on govt land contracted to small businesses, Federal grants, State funding, and projects, by State, FY91, annual rpt, 9764–10
Workers compensation laws of States and Fed Govt, 1992 annual rpt, 6504–11
see also Franchises
see also Small Business Investment Companies
see also Venture capital

Small Business Administration
Activities of SBA, financial condition, and loans and contracts by firm, FY91, annual rpt, 9764–1
Budget of US, authoritative financial statements with appropriations, outlays, and receipts, by category and agency, FY91, annual rpt, 8104–2.2
Budget of US, Bush Admin proposals, with detail for defense budgets, and historical data from FY34, FY93, 108–46.3
Budget of US, obligations and authority by function, agency, and program, with summaries and analyses, FY93, annual rpt, 104–2
Fraud and abuse in SBA programs, audits and investigations, 1st half FY92, semiannual rpt, 9762–5
Hurricane Hugo disaster loan offices of SBA, staff and salary and support costs, for Puerto Rico and Virgin Islands, 1989-91, GAO rpt, 26113–576
Labor unions recognized in Fed Govt, agreements and membership by agency and facility, as of Jan 1991, biennial listing, 9844–14
Loan and debenture sale activity under SBA dev company program, with data by firm, industry div, State, and region, quarterly rpt, 9762–6
Loan guarantee program of SBA, participants finances, operations, characteristics, and views, 1991 survey, 9768–25
Loans (direct and guaranteed) of SBA, principal outstanding, and losses, by program, borrower race and sex, and State, 1950s-90, GAO rpt, 26113–554
Loans (guaranteed) of SBA issued under regular, certified, and preferred lender programs, selected characteristics, FY83-90, GAO rpt, 26113–581
Loans for small business, collateral adequacy for failed firms, with loan liquidation recoveries and losses, FY89, GAO rpt, 26113–553
Mgmt and financial aid from Minority Business Dev Centers, and SBA financial assistance, by region, FY91, annual rpt, 2104–6
Minority business Federal procurement set-aside contracts, by participant race and sex, industry, firm, and State, FY90, annual rpt, 9764–8
Minority business Federal procurement set-aside contracts, by State, FY90, GAO rpt, 26113–563
Minority group and women employment in SBA, and hiring goals, FY91, annual rpt, 9764–9
R&D funding by Fed Govt to small business, by program area, agency, MSA, and State, FY90, annual rpt, 9764–7
R&D grants of Fed govt to small business, project commercial success indicators and other characteristics of firms involved, 1988-90 survey, chartbook, 9768–23
R&D grants of Fed Govt to small business, project sales by type and dev funding by source, by agency and selected firm, 1984-91, GAO rpt, 26113–393
Rural areas tourism-related and other small businesses, SBA loans, FY86-1st half FY91, hearing, 21728–79
Small business finances, operations, owner characteristics, and Federal contracts, 1980s-90, annual rpt, 9764–6
Small Business Investment Companies capital holdings, SBA obligation, and ownership, as of July 1992, semiannual listing, 9762–4
Small Business Investment Company finances, losses, and program operations, 1980s-91, 25728–44
Small Business Investment Company program financial performance, findings and recommendations, 1992 rpt, 9768–24
Tree planting on govt land contracted to small businesses, Federal grants, State funding, and projects, by State, FY91, annual rpt, 9764–10

Small Business Investment Companies
Capital holdings, SBA obligation, and ownership of SBICs, as of July 1992, semiannual listing, 9762–4
Finances and losses of SBICs, and program operations, FY80s-91, 25728–44
Financial performance of SBICs, findings and recommendations, 1992 rpt, 9768–24
Financing disbursements by SBICs, 1980-90, annual rpt, 9764–6.2
Fraud and abuse in SBA programs, audits and investigations, 1st half FY92, semiannual rpt, 9762–5
Rural areas businesses credit assistance of Fed Govt, by program and county characteristics, 1983-89, 1548–389
Tax (income) returns of corporations, income and tax items by asset size and detailed industry, 1989, annual rpt, 8304–4; 8304–21

Smetana, Richard D.
"Concerns of the Grain Industry", 1504–9.1

Smith, Allan H.
"Serum 2,3,7,8-Tetrachlorodibenzo-p-dioxin Levels of New Zealand Pesticide Applicators and Their Implication for Cancer Hypotheses", 4472–1.303

Smith, Dolores S.
"Expanded HMDA Data on Residential Lending: One Year Later", 9362–1.307

Smith, H. Clay
"Stand Development and Yields of Appalachian Hardwood Stands Managed with Single-Tree Selection for at Least 30 Years", 1208–394

Smith, Jo Ann
"Nutrition Labeling: We're on Our Way", 1504–9.1

Smith, Joseph W.
"Atlantic and Gulf Menhaden Purse Seine Fisheries: Origins, Harvesting Technologies, Biostatistical Monitoring, Recent Trends in Fisheries Statistics, and Forecasting", 2162–1.303
"Biological Analysis of Two Management Options for the Atlantic Menhaden Fishery", 2162–1.303

Smith, Marvin M.
"Reductions in the Army Officer Corps", 26306–3.121

Smith, Stephen D.
"Convexity Trap: Pitfalls in Financing Mortgage Portfolios and Related Securities", 9371–1.308
"Form Invariance in Biased Sampling Problems", 9371–10.87
"Note on Competition, Fixed Costs, and the Profitability of Depository Intermediaries", 9371–10.88
"Note on Forward Biases and Equilibrium Foreign Exchange Hedging in a Production Economy", 9371–10.85
"Risk Neutral Valuation, Asymmetric Information, and the Efficient Markets Hypothesis", 9371–10.77

Smith, Steven A.
"INFORM Evaluation", 7558–119

Smith, W. Brad
"Assessing Removals for North Central Forest Inventories", 1208–419
"Production and Sources of Residential Fuelwood from Roundwood in Michigan", 1208–412
"Timber Industry of Iowa: An Assessment of Timber Product Output and Use, 1988", 1206–10.13
"Timber Resource of Missouri's Northwest Ozarks, 1989", 1206–3.5

Smithsonian Institution
Activities and finances of Instn, FY91, annual rpt, 29574–1
American Historical Assn financial statements, and membership by State, 1990, annual rpt, 29574–2
Budget of US, authoritative financial statements with appropriations, outlays, and receipts, by category and agency, FY91, annual rpt, 8104–2.2
Budget of US, obligations and authority by function, agency, and program, with summaries and analyses, FY93, annual rpt, 104–2
Education funding by Federal agency, program, and recipient type, and instn spending, 1960s-91, annual rpt, 4824–8
Labor unions recognized in Fed Govt, agreements and membership by agency and facility, as of Jan 1991, biennial listing, 9844–14

Smog
see Air pollution

Smoking
Airline consumer complaints to DOT about service, by reason and US and foreign carrier, monthly rpt, 7302–11
Arab Americans smoking status, duration, and cigarettes smoked daily, by age, sex, ethnicity, education, and income, local area study, 1992 article, 4042–3.360
Births and rates, by characteristics of birth, infant, and mother, and presence of maternal risk factors and birth defects, 1989, 4146–5.125
Births of low birthweight, risk relation to mothers smoking, weight, and age, 1988, article, 4042–3.367
Cancer (breast) risk relation to estrogen replacement therapy use, body mass index, and other risk factors, 1987-89 NYC study, article, 4472–1.350
Cancer (lung) risk relation to carcinogen metabolizing activity of 2 enzymes, 1987, article, 4472–1.307
Cancer (lung) risk relation to environmental smoke exposure, for nonsmoking women, local area study, 1992 article, 4472–1.342
Cancer (nasopharyngeal) death risk by level of smoking and alcohol use, 1986, article, 4472–1.312
Cancer (pancreatic) death risk relation to occupational DDT exposure and other characteristics, 1982 article, 4472–1.314
Cancer (stomach) risk relation to smoking and alcohol use, 1989-90 local area study, article, 4472–1.334
Cessation of smoking, clinics success rates, and participants smoking history, views on program, and other characteristics, 1987-88 local area study, article, 4042–3.314
Cessation of smoking TV promotion campaign, hotline calls by sex, race, age, and education, aggregate 1983-87, article, 4472–1.313
Cessation programs ratings by consumers, 1992 article, 4042–3.308
Consumption of cigarettes and cigars, *Survey of Current Business*, monthly rpt, 2702–1.13
Consumption of cigarettes and other tobacco products per capita, and total spending, 1986-91, annual rpt, 1319–1.4
Consumption of cigarettes and smokeless tobacco, by selected characteristics, 1991 survey, annual rpt series, 4494–5
Consumption of tobacco products, quarterly situation rpt with articles, 1561–10
DC metro area drug, alcohol, and tobacco use, user characteristics, and consequences, series, 4496–12
Deaths during 1986, decedents health condition, services use, habits, and social, employment, and other characteristics, 4147–20.19
Diving (underwater) accidents, illnesses, and deaths, by circumstances, diver characteristics, and location, 1970-90, annual rpt, 2144–29
Fires (wild) and acreage burned, by type of land, ownership, cause, region, and State, 1984-90, annual rpt, 1204–4
Health condition and care indicators, 1950s-90 with health improvement and disease prevention goals for 1990, annual data compilation, 4144–11
Health risk behavior, prevalence of 7 habits, by age, State, and other characteristics, 1986-90, article, 4202–7.305
Heart disease risk factors prevalence in Missouri, 1989-90, article, 4042–3.302
Hospital employees smoking, patients views by smoking history, 1989 local area study, article, 4042–3.334
Indian and Alaska Native youth health condition and behavioral patterns, by sex and grade, 1988-90, 4088–3
Indian health risk behavior, by region and for Montana, mid 1980s, article, 4042–3.346
Injuries from use of consumer products and related activities, by severity and victim age and sex, 1990, annual rpt, 9164–7
Injuries from use of consumer products, by severity, victim age, and detailed product, 1991, annual rpt, 9164–6
Labor laws enacted, by State, 1991, annual article, 6722–1.309
Latin America, Canada, and US tobacco production and use, and related economic, health, and social issues, 1950s-92, annual rpt, 4204–18
Maternal and child health indicators and services use, by age, race, and poverty status, 1988, 4478–197
Nicotine, tar, and carbon monoxide content of cigarettes, by brand, 1990, 9408–53
Older population, and health, economic, and other characteristics, with foreign comparisons, 1980s-91 with trends and projections, Current Population Rpt, 2546–2.165
Pregnant women smoking, by age and marital status, for Indians in Washington State, mid 1980s, article, 4042–3.306
Prevention of drug abuse, evaluation of services, methodological issues, 1991 conf, 4498–78
Pulse rate relation to blood pressure and other physical, demographic, and behavioral characteristics, 1971-74, article, 4042–3.321
Research on smoking and health, with trends in smoking, related disease and death, and public attitudes, literature review, 1992 annual rpt, 4204–18
Research on smoking prevalence, health effects, and control strategies effectiveness, series, 4476–7
Research on smoking, tobacco, and health impacts, publications, 1991 annual report, 4204–19
Schools safety, discipline, and student drug use, elementary and secondary school principals views, 1991 survey, 4826–1.32
Statistical Abstract of US, 1992 annual data compilation, 2324–1.3
Switzerland tobacco and cigarette production, trade, and use, 1980s-92, article, 1925–16.315
Tuberculosis cases, by risk factor, in Washington County, Md, 1975-90, article, 4042–3.319
Turkey tobacco and cigarette production, trade, and use, 1980s-92, article, 1925–16.313
Vermont smoking laws compliance of employers, 1989, article, 4042–3.375
Youth drug, alcohol, and cigarette use and attitudes, by substance type and selected characteristics, 1975-91 surveys, press release, 4008–116; 4494–4
Youth health condition, risk factors, and preventive and treatment services use and availability, 1970s-80s, 26358–234.2
see also Tobacco industry and products

SMSA
see Metropolitan Statistical Areas
see under By SMSA or MSA in the "Index by Categories"

Smuggling
Aliens (illegal) smuggled into US, and smugglers located, FY84-90, annual rpt, 6264–2.5
Prisoners in Federal and contract instns, by selected characteristics, region, and Federal instn, FY89, annual rpt, 6244–1.1
Prisoners in State and Federal instns, violations by type, 1990, quinquennial rpt, 6068–218
Sentences for Federal offenses, guidelines by offense and circumstances, series, 17668–1

Snack foods
see Food and food industry

Snake River
Birds of prey, rodent, and vegetation distribution and characteristics, for Idaho Snake River area, research results, 1991, annual rpt, 5724–14
Fish (salmon) conservation spending by organization, and population, for Columbia River basin, 1970-91, GAO rpt, 26113–577
Freight (waterborne domestic and foreign) by commodity, traffic, and passengers, by port and waterway, 1989, annual rpt, 3754–3.4

Water supply and quality in streams and lakes, and groundwater levels in wells, by drainage basin, 1990, annual State rpt series, 5666–10
Water supply and quality in streams and lakes, and groundwater levels in wells, by drainage basin, 1991, annual State rpt series, 5666–12
Water supply in US and southern Canada, streamflow, surface and groundwater conditions, and reservoir levels, by location, monthly rpt, 5662–3

Snell, Tracy L.
"Prisoners in 1991", 6066–25.47
"Women in Jail, 1989", 6066–19.66

Snyder, Howard N.
"Arrests of Youth, 1990", 6066–27.8

Snyder, Thomas D.
"Digest of Education Statistics, 1992", 4824–2

Soap and detergent industry
County Business Patterns, 1989: employment, establishments, and payroll, by SIC 2- to 4-digit industry and county, annual State rpt series, 2326–8
County Business Patterns, 1990: employment, establishments, and payroll, by SIC 2- to 4-digit industry and county, annual State rpt series, 2326–6
CPI by component for US city average, and by selected metro area, region, and population size, monthly rpt, 6762–2
Employment, earnings, and hours, by SIC 1- to 4-digit industry, monthly 1989-Feb 1992, annual rpt, 6744–4
Employment of minorities and women, by occupation, SIC 1- to 3-digit industry, State, and MSA, 1991, annual rpt, 9244–1
Exports and imports between US and outlying areas, by detailed commodity and mode of transport, 1991, annual rpt, 2424–11
Exports and imports of US, by country and detailed commodity, monthly rpt, 2422–12
Exports and imports of US, by Harmonized System 6-digit commodity and country, 1991, annual rpt, 2424–13
Exports and imports of US, by transport mode, country, and SITC 1- to 3-digit commodity, 1991, annual rpt, 2424–12
Exports, imports, tariffs, and industry operating data for soap, detergent, and surface-active agent products, 1991 rpt, 9885–11.1
Exports of US, detailed Schedule B commodities with countries of destination, 1991, annual rpt, 2424–10
Freight (waterborne domestic and foreign) by commodity, traffic, and passengers, by port and waterway, 1989, annual rpt, 3754–3
Injuries from use of consumer products and related activities, by severity and victim age and sex, 1990, annual rpt, 9164–7
Injuries from use of consumer products, by severity, victim age, and detailed product, 1991, annual rpt, 9164–6
Input-output structure of US economy, detailed interindustry transactions for 541 industries, and components of final demand, 1982 benchmark data, 2708–17
Labor productivity, indexes of output, hours, and employment by SIC 2- to 4-digit industry, 1967-90, annual rpt, 6824–1.3
Manufacturing annual survey, 1990: finances and operations, by SIC 2- to 4-digit industry, series, 2506–14
Manufacturing census, 1987: concentration of largest firms measured by value added, and for shipments by SIC 2- and 4-digit industry, subject rpt, 2497–6
Manufacturing census, 1987: shipments of manufacturers products, by customer class and SIC 2- and 4-digit industry, subject rpt, 2497–4
Manufacturing finances and operations, by SIC 2- to 4-digit industry, forecast 1992, annual rpt, 2044–28
Multinatl US firms and foreign affiliates finances and operations, by industry and country, 1989 benchmark survey, annual rpt, 2704–5
Occupational injury and illness rates, by SIC 2- to 4-digit industry, 1989-90, annual rpt, 6844–7
Occupational injury and illness rates, by SIC 2- to 4-digit industry, 1990, annual rpt, 6844–1
Oil and fat production, consumption by end use, and stocks, by type, monthly Current Industrial Rpt, 2506–4.4
Oils, oilseeds, and fats production, prices, trade, and use, periodic situation rpt with articles, 1561–3
Price indexes (producer), by stage of processing and detailed commodity, monthly rpt, 6762–6
Price indexes (producer), by stage of processing and detailed commodity, monthly 1991, annual rpt, 6764–2
Production and sales of synthetic organic chemicals, and manufacturer listing, by product, 1990, annual rpt, 9884–3
Science, engineering, and technical employment in manufacturing, by field and industry, 1989, triennial rpt, 9627–23
Tax (income) returns of corporations, income and tax items by asset size and detailed industry, 1989, annual rpt, 8304–4; 8304–21
Toxicology Natl Program research and testing activities, FY90 and planned FY91, annual rpt, 4044–16

Social indicators
see Quality of life
see under names of specific indicators (listed under Population characteristics)

Social sciences
Degree (PhD) recipients in higher education, by field and selected characteristics, 1979, 1984, and 1989, 4848–44
Degrees awarded in higher education, by level, field, race, and sex, 1989/90 and trends from 1980/81, annual rpt, 4844–17
DOD Dependents Schools basic skills and college entrance test scores, 1991-92, annual rpt, 3504–16
Education data compilation, 1992 annual rpt, 4824–2
Employment of scientists and engineers, and related topics, advance rpt series, 9626–8
Fed Govt aid to higher education and nonprofit instns for R&D and related activities, by field, instn, agency, and State, FY90, annual rpt, 9627–17
Higher education grad programs enrollment in science and engineering, by field, source of funds, and characteristics of student and instn, 1990, annual rpt, 9627–7
Labor demand, turnover, and training completions, by detailed occupation, 1990 and projected to 2005, biennial rpt, 6744–3
Minority group, women, and disabled persons employment and education in science and engineering, by field, mid 1970s-91, biennial rpt, 9624–20
NASA R&D funding to higher education instns, by field, instn, and State, FY91, annual listing, 9504–7
NSF activities, finances, and funding by program, FY91, annual rpt, 9624–6
Occupational Outlook Handbook, 1992-93, biennial rpt, 6744–1
R&D facilities of higher education instns, space and equipment adequacy, needs, and funding by source, by instn type and control, 1992, biennial rpt, 9624–25
R&D funding by higher education instns and federally funded centers, by field, instn, and State, FY90, annual rpt, 9627–13
Research on population and reproduction, Federal funding by project, FY90, annual listing, 4474–9
Science and Engineering Indicators, employment, education, R&D funding, and industry impacts, with foreign comparisons, 1960s-91, biennial rpt, 9624–10
Vocational education enrollment, and academic and other credits earned, by subject and student characteristics, high school classes of 1982 and 1987, 4838–50
see also Anthropology
see also Economics
see also Geography
see also History
see also Political science
see also Psychology
see also Sociology

Social security
Admin of social insurance programs, direct govt spending and employment by level of govt, selected years 1962-87, 10048–53
Chile social security system replacement with private pension system, economic impacts, 1970s-90, technical paper, 9385–8.123
Expenditures for public welfare programs, by program type and level of govt, FY65-89, annual article, 4742–1.302
Foreign countries social security programs coverage, funding, eligibility, and benefits, by country, 1991, biennial rpt, 4746–4.62
Numbers for social security, new issues, 1937-90, annual rpt, 4744–3.2
Research on social security programs and related issues, technical paper series, 4746–26
Research on social security programs, series, 4746–4
Statistical Abstract of US, 1992 annual data compilation, 2324–1.12
see also Aid to Families with Dependent Children
see also Health insurance

see also Health maintenance organizations
see also Income maintenance
see also Medicaid
see also Medicare
see also Old age assistance
see also Old-Age, Survivors, Disability, and Health Insurance
see also Public welfare programs
see also Social security tax
see also Supplemental Security Income
see also Unemployment insurance
see also Workers compensation

Social Security Administration
Activities, litigation, finances, and staff of SSA, FY91, annual rpt, 4704–6
Actuarial studies, Medicare and OASDI future cost estimates and past experience analyses, series, 4706–1
Actuarial studies of OASDHI programs, series, 4706–2
Admin of OASDHI and SSI, case processing, staff, and client problems with contacting SSA offices, 1980s-90, hearing, 25148–45
Assistance (financial) of HHS, by program, recipient, State, and city, FY91, annual regional listings, 4004–3
Budget of US, obligations and authority by function, agency, and program, with summaries and analyses, FY93, annual rpt, 104–2
Disability Insurance eligibility determinations by States, caseloads, Federal funding, and State directors views, 1980s-91, hearing, 21148–63
OASDI and SSI benefit overpayments, and overpaid beneficiaries characteristics, late 1970s-90, GAO rpt, 26121–484
OASDI trust funds finances, 1937-FY91 and alternative projections to 2070, annual rpt, 4704–4
Public opinion on OASDHI and health care system operations and reform issues, 1991 surveys, 10176–2.2
Supplemental Security Income and Medicaid eligibility and payment provisions, and beneficiaries living arrangements, by State, 1992, annual rpt, 4704–13
Wage reporting by employers, SSA and IRS reconciliation of records, late 1970s-80s, GAO rpt, 26121–477
see also Office of International Policy, SSA
see also Office of Policy, SSA
see also Office of Research and Statistics, SSA

Social security tax
Budget of US, authoritative financial statements with appropriations, outlays, and receipts, by category and agency, FY91, annual rpt, 8104–2.2
Budget of US, CBO analysis and review of FY93 budget by function, annual rpt, 26304–2
Budget of US, CBO analysis of revenue and spending alternatives and projections of economic indicators, FY93-97, annual rpt, 26304–3
Budget of US, historical data, selected years FY34-91 and projected to FY97, 108–46.5
Budget of US, obligations and authority by function, agency, and program, with summaries and analyses, FY93, annual rpt, 104–2
Budget of US, receipts by source, outlays by agency and program, and balances, monthly rpt, 8102–3
Business statistics, detailed data for major industries and economic indicators, 1960-91, *Survey of Current Business* biennial supplement, 2704–1
Collections, enforcement, and litigation activity of IRS, with data by type of tax, region, and State, FY91, annual rpt, 8304–3
Collections of Fed Govt, by source, *Treasury Bulletin*, quarterly rpt, 8002–4.1
Collections of tax, beneficiaries, and benefit payments for social insurance programs, quarterly rpt, 4742–1.4
Communications services revenue and expenses, itemized by SIC 2- to 4-digit kind of business, 1990, annual rpt, 2413–15
Employee compensation costs, by component, occupation, industry group, union status, and location, 1975-92, annual rpt, 6744–20.2
Employment and earnings covered under OASDHI, and social security contributions, by age, sex, race, State, and county, 1988, annual rpt, 4744–29
Fed Govt civilian employees work-years, pay rates, and benefits use and costs, by agency, FY90, annual rpt, 9844–31
Fed Govt internal revenue and refunds, by type of tax, quarterly rpt, 8302–2.1
Finances and operations of programs under Ways and Means Committee jurisdiction, FY70s-91, annual rpt, 21784–11
Finances of SSA programs, and litigation, FY91, annual rpt, 4704–6
Foreign countries social security programs coverage, funding, eligibility, and benefits, by country, 1991, biennial rpt, 4746–4.62
Health care spending by businesses, households, and govts, 1965-90, annual article, 4652–1.309
Income (household) and poverty status under alternative income definitions, by recipient characteristics, 1979-91, annual Current Population Rpt, 2546–6.78
Income tax returns of individuals, detailed data, 1988, annual rpt, 8304–2
Labor hourly costs, by component, industry and occupational group, worker class, and firm size, monthly rpt, annual tables, 6782–1.2
Labor hourly costs, by component, occupational group, industry div, union coverage, and region, 1992, annual rpt, 6744–21
Medicare contributions and disbursements, by State, 1985, 4006–11.4
Medicare Hospital Insurance tax rates and recommendations under alternative economic and fiscal assumptions, 1991 rpt, 10176–1.2
Medicare Hospital Insurance trust fund finances, mid 1960s-91 and alternative projections to 2066, annual rpt, 4654–11
Natl income and product accounts and components, *Survey of Current Business*, monthly rpt, 2702–1.23
Natl income and product accounts, comprehensive accounts and components, benchmark revisions, 1929-88, 2708–5
Natl income and product accounts, comprehensive accounts and components, *Survey of Current Business*, monthly rpt, 2702–1.29
OASDHI, Medicaid, SSI, and related programs benefits, beneficiary characteristics, and trust funds, selected years 1937-90, annual rpt, 4744–3
OASDHI trust funds finances, FY91 and projected to 2066, annual rpt, 4654–8
OASDHI trust funds finances, FY91 with projections, annual article, 4742–1.314
OASDI trust funds finances, 1937-FY91 and alternative projections to 2070, annual rpt, 4704–4
OASI benefits, earnings, and tax revenues under alternative eligibility criteria, 1990, technical paper, 4746–26.15
Pension plan earnings and contributions tax exclusions, cost and benefit issues with background data, 1970s-FY92, article, 9373–1.305
Public opinion on taxes, spending, and govt efficiency, by respondent characteristics, 1992 survey, annual rpt, 10044–2
Self-employment social security tax forms returned, by income level, 1991, annual article, 8302–2.319
State and local govt tax rates and revenue, by source and State, 1992 and historical trends, annual rpt, 10044–1
Statistical Abstract of US, 1992 annual data compilation, 2324–1.12
Survey of Current Business, detailed financial and business data, and economic indicators, monthly rpt, 2702–1.3
Telephone and telegraph firms detailed finances and operations, 1990, annual rpt, 9284–6.2; 9284–6.3
Transit systems finances and operations, by mode, size of fleet and urban area, region, and for 518 systems, 1990, annual rpt, 7884–4

Social services
AIDS patients health care and support services funding under Ryan White CARE Act, and Federal grants by metro area, 1991, article, 4042–3.352
Assistance (block and categorical grants) programs for State and local govts, FY91, biennial listing, 10044–8
Assistance (financial and nonfinancial) of Fed Govt, 1992 base edition, annual listing, 104–5
Assistance (formula grants) of Fed Govt, use of adjusted census and intercensal data for allocation, with data by program and State, FY91, 25408–120
Budget of US, midsession review of FY93 budget, by function, annual rpt, 104–7
Budget of US, obligations and authority by function, agency, and program, with summaries and analyses, FY93, annual rpt, 104–2
Budget of US, receipts by source, outlays by agency and program, and balances, monthly rpt, 8102–3
County Business Patterns, 1989: employment, establishments, and payroll, by SIC 2- to 4-digit industry and county, annual State rpt series, 2326–8
County Business Patterns, 1990: employment, establishments, and payroll, by SIC 2- to 4-digit industry and county, annual State rpt series, 2326–6

Employment, earnings, and hours, by SIC 1- to 4-digit industry, monthly 1989-Feb 1992, annual rpt, 6744–4
Expenditures (direct) and employment, by function and level of govt, selected years 1962-87, 10048–53
Expenditures (private) for social welfare, by category, 1970s-90, annual article, 4742–1.323
Fed Govt programs under Ways and Means Committee jurisdiction, finances, operations, and participant characteristics, FY70s-91, annual rpt, 21784–11
Fed Govt spending in States, by type, program, agency, and State, FY91, annual rpt, 2464–2
Govt employment and payroll, by function, level of govt, and jurisdiction, annual rpt series, 2466–1
HHS financial aid, by program, recipient, State, and city, FY91, annual regional listings, 4004–3
Homeless families in transitional housing, HUD support services grants by recipient, 1991, press release, 5006–3.87
Homeless persons housing and support services projects, funding, and clients, by organization, FY87 and FY90, GAO rpt, 26113–593
Input-output structure of US economy, detailed interindustry transactions for 84 industries, and components of final demand, 1987, annual article, 2702–1.316
Input-output structure of US economy, detailed interindustry transactions for 541 industries, and components of final demand, 1982 benchmark data, 2708–17
Military in-house commercial activities work-years, by service branch, State, and installation, FY91, annual rpt, 3544–25
Military prime contract awards, by detailed procurement category, FY88-91, annual rpt, 3544–18
Multinatl firms US affiliates finances and operations, by industry, country of parent firm, and State, 1987, 2708–48
Occupational injury and illness rates, by SIC 2- to 4-digit industry, 1989-90, annual rpt, 6844–7
Occupational injury and illness rates, by SIC 2- to 4-digit industry, 1990, annual rpt, 6844–1
R&D funding by Fed Govt, by detailed function, program, and agency, FY91-93, annual rpt, 9627–9
Tax (income) returns of corporations, income and tax items by asset size and detailed industry, 1989, annual rpt, 8304–4; 8304–21
see also Adult day care
see also Caregivers and caregiving
see also Child day care
see also Child welfare
see also Community health services
see also Counselors and counseling
see also Disaster relief
see also Foster home care
see also Group homes for the handicapped
see also Home health services
see also Homemaker services
see also Legal aid
see also School lunch and breakfast programs
see also Social work
see also Vocational rehabilitation
see also Work incentive programs

Social work
Education (special) enrollment by age, staff, funding, and needs, by type of handicap and State, 1990/91, annual rpt, 4944–4
Hospital employment and job vacancy rate, by occupation, and instn size and control, 1981-88, annual rpt, 4114–12
Labor demand, turnover, and training completions, by detailed occupation, 1990 and projected to 2005, biennial rpt, 6744–3
Mental health care facilities, staff, and patient characteristics, *Statistical Notes* series, 4506–3
Mental health care facilities, staff, patients, and finances, 1970s-91, biennial rpt, 4094–1
Military health care personnel, and accessions by training source, by occupation, specialty, and service branch, FY90, annual rpt, 3544–24
Occupational Outlook Handbook, 1992-93, biennial rpt, 6744–1
VA health care facilities trainees, by detailed program and city, FY91, annual rpt, 8704–4
VA health care services, needs, availability, structure, and funding, 1991 compilation of papers, 8608–9
VA health care staff and turnover, by occupation, physician specialty, and location, 1991, annual rpt, 8604–8
see also Counselors and counseling
see also Social services

Sociology
Fed Govt aid to higher education and nonprofit instns for R&D and related activities, by field, instn, agency, and State, FY90, annual rpt, 9627–17
Higher education grad programs enrollment in science and engineering, by field, source of funds, and characteristics of student and instn, 1990, annual rpt, 9627–7
Occupational Outlook Handbook, 1992-93, biennial rpt, 6744–1
R&D funding by higher education instns and federally funded centers, by field, instn, and State, FY90, annual rpt, 9627–13

Soft drink industry and products
Appalachia food processing firms, employment, and shipments, and farm production, by commodity and State, 1960s-90, 9088–37
Consumption, supply, trade, prices, spending, and indexes, by food commodity, 1990, annual rpt, 1544–4
County Business Patterns, 1989: employment, establishments, and payroll, by SIC 2- to 4-digit industry and county, annual State rpt series, 2326–8
County Business Patterns, 1990: employment, establishments, and payroll, by SIC 2- to 4-digit industry and county, annual State rpt series, 2326–6
CPI by component for US city average, and by selected metro area, region, and population size, monthly rpt, 6762–2
Employment, earnings, and hours, by SIC 1- to 4-digit industry, monthly 1989-Feb 1992, annual rpt, 6744–4
Exports and imports (agricultural) of US, by detailed commodity and country, 1991, semiannual rpt, 1522–4
Exports and imports between US and outlying areas, by detailed commodity and mode of transport, 1991, annual rpt, 2424–11
Exports and imports of US, by Harmonized System 6-digit commodity and country, 1991, annual rpt, 2424–13
Exports of US, detailed Schedule B commodities with countries of destination, 1991, annual rpt, 2424–10
Input-output structure of US economy, detailed interindustry transactions for 541 industries, and components of final demand, 1982 benchmark data, 2708–17
Labor productivity, indexes of output, hours, and employment by SIC 2- to 4-digit industry, 1967-90, annual rpt, 6824–1.3
Manufacturing annual survey, 1990: finances and operations, by SIC 2- to 4-digit industry, series, 2506–14
Manufacturing census, 1987: concentration of largest firms measured by value added, and for shipments by SIC 2- and 4-digit industry, subject rpt, 2497–6
Manufacturing census, 1987: shipments of manufacturers products, by customer class and SIC 2- and 4-digit industry, subject rpt, 2497–4
Manufacturing finances and operations, by SIC 2- to 4-digit industry, forecast 1992, annual rpt, 2044–28
Occupational injury and illness rate and lost workdays, for soft drink industry in 7 States, mid 1970s-90, article, 6722–1.319
Occupational injury and illness rates and lost workdays, for selected industries, 1978-89, compilation of papers, 6728–41
Occupational injury and illness rates, by SIC 2- to 4-digit industry, 1989-90, annual rpt, 6844–7
Occupational injury and illness rates, by SIC 2- to 4-digit industry, 1990, annual rpt, 6844–1
Price indexes (producer), by stage of processing and detailed commodity, monthly rpt, 6762–6
Price indexes (producer), by stage of processing and detailed commodity, monthly 1991, annual rpt, 6764–2
Tax (income) returns of corporations, income and tax items by asset size and detailed industry, 1989, annual rpt, 8304–4; 8304–21
Vending machine shipments by product, trade, and use, 1991, Current Industrial Rpt, 2506–12.10

Software
see Computer industry and products

Soil Conservation Service
Budget of US, obligations and authority by function, agency, and program, with summaries and analyses, FY93, annual rpt, 104–2
Colorado water supply, streamflow, precipitation, and reservoir storage, 1992 water year, annual rpt, 1264–13
Conservation of soil and water, USDA funding by program and State, annual rpt, discontinued, 1264–12
Cost sharing payments and eligibility requirements for USDA agricultural and water conservation programs, FY88-92, GAO rpt, 26113–572

County soil surveys and maps, 1899-1991, annual listing, 1264–11
Expenditures of Fed Govt in States, by type, program, agency, and State, FY91, annual rpt, 2464–2
Oregon water supply, streamflow by station and reservoir storage, 1992, annual rpt, 1264–9
Revenue of USDA, by source and subagency, FY88-92, GAO rpt, 26113–602
Western US water supply, and snow survey results, annual State rpt series, 1264–14
Western US water supply, and snow survey results, monthly State rpt series, 1266–2
Western US water supply, storage by reservoir and State, and streamflow conditions, as of Oct 1992, annual rpt, 1264–4
Western US water supply, streamflow and reservoir storage forecasts by stream and station, Jan-May monthly rpt, 1262–1

Soil pollution
Agricultural Conservation Program acreage and projects, by State, 1936-90, quinquennial rpt, 1808–1
Coastal and riparian areas environmental conditions, fish, wildlife, use, and mgmt, for individual ecosystems, series, 5506–9
DOE contractor research lab and nuclear weapons facilities radiation and other pollutant releases, monitoring results, annual site rpt series, 3324–2
Hazardous waste site remedial action under Superfund, current and proposed sites descriptions and status, periodic listings, series, 9216–3
Health effects of selected pollutants, concentrations in food and environment, sources, human intake, and regulation, series, 9186–8
Health effects of selected pollutants on animals by species and on humans, and environmental levels, series, 5506–14
Industrial hazardous substances releases and reduction methods under EPA regulation, by chemical, source, industry, and location, 1989, annual rpt, 9234–6
Industrial hazardous substances releases and reduction methods under EPA regulation, with chemical stocks and use, facility directory, 1987-89, annual CD-ROM, 9234–7
Natl historic and natural landmarks damaged and threatened, with owner, location, damage type, and recommended remedial action, 1990, annual listing, 5544–16
Oil resources recovery impacts of environmental regulation, under alternative oil price, technology, and regulatory assumptions, projected 1990-2015, 3338–2
Radioactive waste and spent fuel generation, inventory, and disposal, 1960s-90 and projected to 2020, annual rpt, 3364–2
Radon and other radionuclide levels in air, water, soil, and uranium mill tailings, by site and region, 1950s-80s, compilation of papers, 5668–126
Uranium tailings at inactive mills, remedial action proposals, costs, site characteristics, and environmental, socioeconomic, and health impacts, series, 3356–4

Soils and soil conservation
Agricultural Conservation Program acreage and projects, by State, 1936-90, quinquennial rpt, 1808–1
Agricultural Statistics, 1991, annual rpt, 1004–1
Army Corps of Engineers activities and projects, FY88 and trends from 1800s, annual rpt, 3754–1.1
Army Corps of Engineers activities and projects, FY89 and trends from 1800s, annual rpt, 3754–1.2
Army Corps of Engineers activities and projects, FY90 and trends from 1800s, annual rpt, 3754–1.3
Camping in wilderness areas, impacts on plants and soils, 1979-90 studies, 1208–395
Coastal and riparian areas environmental conditions, fish, wildlife, use, and mgmt, for individual ecosystems, series, 5506–9
Coastal areas and watersheds pollution indicators, by location, 1980s-90, 2178–35
Conservation of soil and water, USDA funding by program and State, annual rpt, discontinued, 1264–12
Conservation program of USDA, participation and payments by practice and State, FY91, annual rpt, 1804–7
Conservation programs of USDA, cost sharing payments and eligibility requirements, FY88-92, GAO rpt, 26113–572
County Business Patterns, 1989: employment, establishments, and payroll, by SIC 2- to 4-digit industry and county, annual State rpt series, 2326–8
County Business Patterns, 1990: employment, establishments, and payroll, by SIC 2- to 4-digit industry and county, annual State rpt series, 2326–6
County soil surveys and maps, 1899-1991, annual listing, 1264–11
Emergency Conservation Program for farmland damaged by natural disaster, aid and participation by State, FY91, annual rpt, 1804–22
Emergency Conservation Program for farmland damaged by natural disaster, funding by region and State, monthly rpt, 1802–13
Environmental Quality, status of problems, protection programs, research, and intl issues, 1991 annual rpt, 484–1
Expenditures of Fed Govt in States, by type, program, agency, and State, FY91, annual rpt, 2464–2
Farm production inputs, finances, mgmt, and land value and transfers, periodic situation rpt with articles, 1561–16
Fed Govt financial and nonfinancial domestic aid, 1992 base edition, annual listing, 104–5
Fires on wildlands, ecology, mgmt, cultural impacts, and historic patterns, 1990 conf, 1208–415
Forests (aspen) vegetation, climate, and other environmental characteristics, for upper Great Lakes area, 1991 rpt, 1208–418
Historic and natural natl landmarks damaged and threatened, with owner, location, damage type, and recommended remedial action, 1990, annual listing, 5544–16
Indian and govt lands under Bur of Indian Affairs mgmt, acreage, leases, and use, 1989, annual rpt, 5704–12
Northeastern US hardwood forests ecology and mgmt, 1992, 1208–405
Public lands acreage, grants, use, revenues, and allocations, by State, FY91, annual rpt, 5724–1.2
Research and education grants, USDA competitive awards by program and recipient, FY91, annual listing, 1764–1
Soybean tillage systems impacts on yield and inputs use and costs, 1990, article, 1561–3.304
Timber in southeastern US, resources mgmt and research, 1990 biennial conf papers, 1204–35
Timber sales of Forest Service, expenses, and operations, by region, State, and natl forest, FY91, annual rpts, 1204–36
Water quality, chemistry, hydrology, and other characteristics, local area studies, series, 5666–27
Wetlands and riparian soil and plant characteristics, series, 5506–10
Wheat acreage enrolled in soils and wetlands conservation programs, and production impacts, by State, 1991, article, 1561–12.302
see also Flood control
see also Reclamation of land
see also Soil pollution

Solar energy
Building design using solar energy and passive solar, costs, savings, and characteristics, discontinued series, 3306–5
Collector (solar) and photovoltaic module shipments, by type and end use, 1974-90, annual rpt, 3164–74.7
Electric power plants and capacity, by fuel used, owner, location, and operating status, 1991 and for units planned 1992-2001, annual listing, 3164–36
Electric power plants certification applications filed with FERC, for small production and cogeneration facilities, FY80-91, annual listing, 3084–13
Equipment shipments by end-use sector and State, and trade, for collectors and photovoltaic cells, 1990, annual rpt, 3164–62
Exports of US, detailed Schedule B commodities with countries of destination, 1991, annual rpt, 2424–10
Housing (rental) units, total, with HUD assistance by program, and eligible for aid, by unit, household, and neighborhood characteristics, and location, 1989, biennial rpt, 5184–11
Housing and households detailed characteristics, and unit and neighborhood quality, MSA surveys, series, 2485–6
Housing energy use, costs, and conservation, and household and housing characteristics, survey rpt series, 3166–7
Pacific territories population and housing detailed characteristics, by location, 1990 Census of Population and Housing, series, 2551–8
Photovoltaic R&D sponsored by DOE, projects, funding, and rpts, FY91, annual listing, 3304–20
Statistical Abstract of US, 1992 annual data compilation, 2324–1.19

Supply, demand, and prices, by fuel type and end-use sector, alternative projections 1990-2010, annual rpt, 3164–75
Supply, demand, and prices, by fuel type and end-use sector, projections and underlying assumptions, 1995-2010, annual rpt, 3164–90
Supply, demand, and prices, by fuel type and end-use sector, with foreign comparisons, 1981-90, annual fact book, 3164–76

Solar Energy Research Institute
"Photovoltaic Energy Program Summary", 3304–20
see also Department of Energy National Laboratories

Soldiers
see Military personnel

Soldiers' and Airmen's Home
Budget of US, obligations and authority by function, agency, and program, with summaries and analyses, FY93, annual rpt, 104–2
Labor unions recognized in Fed Govt, agreements and membership by agency and facility, as of Jan 1991, biennial listing, 9844–14

Soldiers pay and allowances
see Military benefits and pensions
see Military pay

Sole proprietorships
see Proprietorships

Solid waste
see Landfills
see Recycling of waste materials
see Refuse and refuse disposal
see Sewage and wastewater systems

Solomon, David J.
"HIV Infection Treatment Costs Under Medicaid in Michigan", 4042–3.348

Solomon Islands
Economic, social, political, and geographic summary data, by country, 1992, annual factbook, 9114–2
Exports and imports of US, by transport mode, country, and SITC 1- to 3-digit commodity, 1991, annual rpt, 2424–12
Human rights conditions in 170 countries, and US economic and military aid, 1991, annual rpt, 21384–3
Military aid of US, arms sales, and training programs costs and budget requests, by program, world region, and country, FY91-93, annual rpt, 7144–13
Minerals Yearbook, Vol 3, 1989: foreign country review of production, trade, and policy, by commodity, annual rpt, 5604–35.2
Population size, growth rates, and components of change, by country, projected 1990-2020 and trends from 1950, biennial rpt, 2324–9
UN voting record and share of votes in agreement with US, by issue, country, and world area, 1991, annual rpt, 7004–18

Somalia
Agricultural trade of US, by detailed commodity and country, 1991, annual rpt, 1524–8
Agricultural trade of US, by detailed commodity and country, 1991, semiannual rpt, 1522–4
AID economic aid to developing countries, obligations and disbursements by country, quarterly rpt, 9912–4
AID loans repayment status and terms by program and country, and status of predecessor agency loans, quarterly rpt, 9912–3
Economic and military aid and loans from US and intl agencies, by program and country, FY46-91, annual rpt, 9914–5
Economic and social conditions of developing countries from 1960s, and Intl Dev Cooperation Agency and AID activities and funding, FY91-93, annual rpt, 9904–4
Economic, social, political, and geographic summary data, by country, 1992, annual factbook, 9114–2
Exports and imports of US, by commodity and country, 1980-90, world area rpt, 9116–1.2
Exports and imports of US, by transport mode, country, and SITC 1- to 3-digit commodity, 1991, annual rpt, 2424–12
Exports of US, detailed Schedule B commodities with countries of destination, 1991, annual rpt, 2424–10
Food supply, needs, and aid for developing countries, status and alternative forecasts, 1992 world area rpt, 1526–8.2
Human rights conditions in 170 countries, and US economic and military aid, 1991, annual rpt, 21384–3
Military spending, arms trade, and force strengths, with govt spending and population, by country, 1979-89, annual rpt, 9824–1
Minerals Yearbook, Vol 3, 1989: foreign country review of production, trade, and policy, by commodity, annual rpt, 5604–35.1
Population size, growth rates, and components of change, by country, projected 1990-2020 and trends from 1950, biennial rpt, 2324–9
Refugee migration, and intl aid programs, by world area and country of origin and asylum, 1991, annual rpt, 7004–15
UN voting record and share of votes in agreement with US, by issue, country, and world area, 1991, annual rpt, 7004–18

Somerset County, N.J.
Wages by occupation, for office and plant workers, 1991 survey, periodic MSA rpt, 6785–12.3

Sommer, Steve S.
"Pattern of p53 Gene Mutations in Breast Cancers of Women of the Midwestern U.S.", 4472–1.305

Sondheimer, John A.
"U.S. International Sales and Purchases of Private Services: U.S. Cross-Border Transactions, 1986-91; and Sales by Affiliates, 1989-90", 2702–1.336

Sonu, Sunee C.
"Japan's Tuna Market", 2166–19.11

Sorrentino, Constance
"Union Membership Statistics in 12 Countries", 6722–1.305

Souris-Red-Rainy Rivers
Water supply and quality in streams and lakes, and groundwater levels in wells, by drainage basin, 1990, annual State rpt series, 5666–10
Water supply and quality in streams and lakes, and groundwater levels in wells, by drainage basin, 1991, annual State rpt series, 5666–12
Water supply in US and southern Canada, streamflow, surface and groundwater conditions, and reservoir levels, by location, monthly rpt, 5662–3

South Africa
Agricultural trade of US, by detailed commodity and country, 1991, annual rpt, 1524–8
Agricultural trade of US, by detailed commodity and country, 1991, semiannual rpt, 1522–4
AID economic aid to developing countries, obligations and disbursements by country, quarterly rpt, 9912–4
Economic and military aid and loans from US and intl agencies, by program and country, FY46-91, annual rpt, 9914–5
Economic and social conditions of developing countries from 1960s, and Intl Dev Cooperation Agency and AID activities and funding, FY91-93, annual rpt, 9904–4
Economic conditions, income, production, prices, employment, and trade, 1991 periodic country rpt, 2046–4.1
Economic conditions, income, production, prices, employment, and trade, 1992 periodic country rpt, 2046–4.44
Economic conditions, investment and export opportunities, and trade practices, 1992 country market research rpt, 2046–6.8
Economic conditions, policy, and trade practices, by country, 1989-91, annual rpt, 21384–5
Economic, social, political, and geographic summary data, by country, 1992, annual factbook, 9114–2
Exports and imports of US, by commodity and country, 1980-90, world area rpt, 9116–1.2
Exports and imports of US, by Harmonized System 6-digit commodity and country, 1991, annual rpt, 2424–13
Exports and imports of US, by selected country, country group, and commodity group, 1991, annual rpt, 2044–37
Exports and imports of US, by transport mode, country, and SITC 1- to 3-digit commodity, 1991, annual rpt, 2424–12
Exports, imports, and balances of US for manufactured goods, by SITC 2-digit commodity and country, quarterly rpt, 2042–35
Exports of US, detailed Schedule B commodities with countries of destination, 1991, annual rpt, 2424–10
Human rights conditions in 170 countries, and US economic and military aid, 1991, annual rpt, 21384–3
Intl transactions of US with 9 countries, 1989-91, *Survey of Current Business*, monthly rpt, annual table, 2702–1.33
Labor conditions, union coverage, and work accidents, 1992 annual country rpt, 6366–4.34
Military spending, arms trade, and force strengths, with govt spending and population, by country, 1979-89, annual rpt, 9824–1
Minerals Yearbook, Vol 3, 1989: foreign country review of production, trade, and policy, by commodity, annual rpt, 5604–35.1
Multinatl US firms and foreign affiliates finances and operations, by industry and country, 1989 benchmark survey, annual rpt, 2704–5

Multinatl US firms foreign affiliates, income statement items by asset size, industry, and country, 1988, biennial article, 8302–2.322
Nuclear power generation in US and 20 countries, monthly rpt, 3162–24.10
Nuclear power generation in US and 20 countries, monthly 1973-88, 3168–123.10
Pollution (air) contributing to global warming, emissions by monitoring site and country, and temperature change by world area and US region, 1860s-1990, annual rpt, 3004–33
Population size, growth rates, and components of change, by country, projected 1990-2020 and trends from 1950, biennial rpt, 2324–9
Raisin and prune production, trade, use, and stocks, by country, and South Africa production by raisin type, 1988-92, semiannual article, 1925–34.321
Refugee migration, and intl aid programs, by world area and country of origin and asylum, 1991, annual rpt, 7004–15
Steel imports of US under voluntary restraint agreement, by product, customs district, and country, with US industry operating data, quarterly rpt, 9882–13
Steel trade, by product, country, and customs district, with US industry operating data, 1989-June 1992, semiannual rpt, 9882–15
UN voting record and share of votes in agreement with US, by issue, country, and world area, 1991, annual rpt, 7004–18
see also under By Foreign Country in the "Index by Categories"

South America

Agricultural exports of US, for grains, oilseed products, hides, skins, and cotton, by country, weekly rpt, 1922–3
Agricultural trade of US, by commodity and country, bimonthly rpt, 1522–1
Agricultural trade of US, by detailed commodity and country, 1991, annual rpt, 1524–8
Agricultural trade of US, by detailed commodity and country, 1991, semiannual rpt, 1522–4
AID contracts and grants for technical and support services, by instn, country, and State, FY91, annual listing, 9914–7
AID economic aid to developing countries, obligations and disbursements by country, quarterly rpt, 9912–4
AID loans repayment status and terms by program and country, and status of predecessor agency loans, quarterly rpt, 9912–3
Economic and military aid and loans from US and intl agencies, by program and country, FY46-91, annual rpt, 9914–5
Economic and social conditions of developing countries from 1960s, and Intl Dev Cooperation Agency and AID activities and funding, FY91-93, annual rpt, 9904–4
Economic and social conditions, resources, and trade, and aid, 1992, annual factbook, 9914–14
Economic conditions, trade, and foreign aid, for Latin America, working paper series, 9916–13
Exports (duty-free) of Caribbean area to US, by commodity and country, with consumer and industry impacts, 1984-91, annual rpt, 9884–20
Exports and imports of OECD, total and for 4 major countries, and US trade by country, by commodity, 1980-90, world area rpt, 9116–1.7
Immigrants admitted to US, by class of admission, country of birth, and MSA of destination, FY91, advance annual rpt, 6264–4
Immigrants and legalized aliens, by occupational group and country of birth, preliminary FY91, annual tables, 6264–1
Immigrants and nonimmigrants admitted to US, alien workers, visitors, deportations, and naturalizations, FY91, annual summary rpt, 6264–7
Immigration to US, alien workers, visitors, deportations, and naturalizations, by country, FY91 and trends from 1820, annual rpt, 6264–2
Imports of Latin America and Caribbean countries from US, by State of origin, 1987 and 1990, 2048–160
Inter-American Foundation activities, grants by recipient, and fellowships, by country, FY91, annual rpt, 14424–1
Inter-American Foundation dev grants by program area, and fellowships by field and instn, by country, FY72-91, annual rpt, 14424–2
Investment (foreign direct) of US, by industry group and world area, 1989-91, annual article, 2702–1.332
Loans of US banks to foreigners at all US and foreign offices, by country group and country, quarterly rpt, 13002–1
Military aid of US, arms sales, and training, by country, FY50-91, annual rpt, 3904–3
Military aid of US, arms sales, and training programs costs and budget requests, by program, world region, and country, FY91-93, annual rpt, 7144–13
Multinatl US firms and foreign affiliates finances and operations, by industry and country, 1989 benchmark survey, annual rpt, 2704–5
Multinatl US firms foreign affiliates, income statement items by asset size, industry, and country, 1988, biennial article, 8302–2.322
Oil production, investment needs, and exports, for 8 South America countries, 1980s-90 and projected to 2010, GAO rpt, 26123–396
Peace Corps activities, funding by program, and volunteers, by country, FY93, annual rpt, 9654–1
Population size, growth rates, and components of change, by country, projected 1990-2020 and trends from 1950, biennial rpt, 2324–9
Terrorism (intl) incidents, casualties, and attacks on US targets, by attack type and country, 1991, annual rpt, 7004–22
Tobacco production and use in Latin America, Canada, and US, and related economic, health, and social issues, 1950s-92, annual rpt, 4204–18
Travel to US, by characteristics of visit and traveler, country, port city, and State of destination, quarterly rpt, 2902–1
see also Andean Group
see also Argentina
see also Bolivia
see also Brazil
see also Chile
see also Colombia
see also Ecuador
see also Falkland Islands (Malvinas)
see also French Guiana
see also Guyana
see also Inter-American Development Bank
see also Latin American Integration Association
see also Paraguay
see also Peru
see also Suriname
see also Uruguay
see also Venezuela
see also under By Foreign Country in the "Index by Categories"

South Carolina

Appalachian Regional Commission funding, by project and State, planned FY92, annual rpt, 9084–3
Banks (insured commercial), Fed Reserve 5th District members financial statements, by State, quarterly rpt, 9389–18
Banks (insured commercial and savings) deposits by instn, State, MSA, and county, as of June 1991, annual regional rpt, 9295–3.2
County Business Patterns, 1990: employment, establishments, and payroll, by SIC 2- to 4-digit industry and county, annual State rpt, 2326–6.42
Deaths and rates, by detailed location, cause, and demographic characteristics, 1989, US Vital Statistics annual rpt, 4144–3.1
Economic indicators by State, Fed Reserve 5th District, quarterly rpt, 9389–16
Employment and housing indicators by State, FHLB 4th District, quarterly rpt, 9302–36
Employment by industry div, earnings, and hours, for 8 southeastern States, quarterly press release, 6942–7
Employment, earnings, and hours, by selected SIC 1- to 4-digit industry, State, and for 275 MSAs, 1987-92, 6748–81
Fed Govt spending in States and local areas, by type, State, county, and city, FY91, annual rpt, 2464–3
Fed Govt spending in States, by type, program, agency, and State, FY91, annual rpt, 2464–2
HHS financial aid, by program, recipient, State, and city, FY91, annual regional listing, 4004–3.4
Hospital deaths of Medicare patients, actual and expected rates by diagnosis, and hospital characteristics, by instn, FY90 annual State rpt, 4654–14.42
Housing census, 1990: inventory, occupancy, and costs, State fact sheet, 2326–21.42
Housing census, 1990: summary unit characteristics, by householder race and age, county, place, and urban-rural location, State rpt, 2471–1.42
Military prime contract awards, by contractor, service branch, State, and city, FY91, annual rpt, 3544–22
Mineral Industry Surveys, State reviews of production, 1991, preliminary annual rpt, 5614–6
Multinatl firms US affiliates finances and operations, by industry, country of parent firm, and State, 1987, 2708–48

Peaches production, marketing, and prices in 3 southeastern States and Appalachia, 1991, annual rpt, 1311–12
Physicians, by specialty, age, sex, and location of training and practice, 1990, State rpt, 4116–6.42
Population and housing census, 1990: detailed geographic coverage, State CD-ROM, 2551–9.5
Population and housing census, 1990: population and housing characteristics, detailed geographic coverage, State CD-ROM, 2551–10.51
Population and housing census, 1990: summary characteristics, by county, subdiv, and place, State rpt, 2551–7.42
Population census, 1990: population characteristics and living arrangements, by county, place, and urban-rural location, State rpt, 2531–1.42
Radiation and other pollutant releases from DOE contractor research lab and nuclear weapons facilities, monitoring results, 1991 annual site rpt, 3324–2.2; 3324–2.15
Radioactive low-level waste disposal activities of States and interstate compacts, with data by disposal facility and reactor, 1990, annual rpt, 3004–36
Statistical Abstract of US, 1992 annual data compilation, 2324–1
Textile mill employment, earnings, and hours, for 8 Southeastern States, quarterly press release, 6942–1
see also Charleston, S.C.
see also Columbia, S.C.
see also Florence, S.C.
see also Rock Hill, S.C.
see also Sumter, S.C.
see also under By State in the "Index by Categories"

South, D. W.
"Fossil Energy Perspective on Global Climate Change", 3338–3

South Dakota
Banks (insured commercial and savings) deposits by instn, State, MSA, and county, as of June 1991, annual regional rpt, 9295–3.5
Birds (least tern and piping plover) and habitat levels of selenium and other pollutants, for Missouri River in South Dakota, 1988-90, 5508–118
Business and economic conditions, Fed Reserve 9th District, quarterly journal, 9383–19
County Business Patterns, 1990: employment, establishments, and payroll, by SIC 2- to 4-digit industry and county, annual State rpt, 2326–6.43
Deaths and rates, by detailed location, cause, and demographic characteristics, 1989, US Vital Statistics annual rpt, 4144–3.1
Employment, earnings, and hours, by selected SIC 1- to 4-digit industry, State, and for 275 MSAs, 1987-92, 6748–81
Fed Govt spending in States and local areas, by type, State, county, and city, FY91, annual rpt, 2464–3
Fed Govt spending in States, by type, program, agency, and State, FY91, annual rpt, 2464–2
HHS financial aid, by program, recipient, State, and city, FY91, annual regional listing, 4004–3.8
Hospital deaths of Medicare patients, actual and expected rates by diagnosis, and hospital characteristics, by instn, FY90 annual State rpt, 4654–14.43
Housing census, 1990: inventory, occupancy, and costs, State fact sheet, 2326–21.43
Housing census, 1990: summary unit characteristics, by householder race and age, county, place, and urban-rural location, State rpt, 2471–1.43
Military prime contract awards, by contractor, service branch, State, and city, FY91, annual rpt, 3544–22
Mineral Industry Surveys, State reviews of production, 1991, preliminary annual rpt, 5614–6
Multinatl firms US affiliates finances and operations, by industry, country of parent firm, and State, 1987, 2708–48
Pesticide levels and water toxicity indicators, for natl wildlife refuge wetlands in South Dakota, 1990, 5508–117
Physicians, by specialty, age, sex, and location of training and practice, 1990, State rpt, 4116–6.43
Population and housing census, 1990: detailed geographic coverage, State CD-ROM, 2551–9.4
Population and housing census, 1990: population and housing characteristics, detailed geographic coverage, State CD-ROM, 2551–10.52
Population and housing census, 1990: summary characteristics, by county, subdiv, and place, State rpt, 2551–7.43
Population census, 1990: population characteristics and living arrangements, by county, place, and urban-rural location, State rpt, 2531–1.43
Statistical Abstract of US, 1992 annual data compilation, 2324–1
Timber in Black Hills Natl Forest, mountain pine beetle infestation and ponderosa pine mortality, 1989-91, 1208–408
Water resources data collection and analysis activities of USGS Water Resources Div District, with project descriptions, 1991 rpt, 5666–26.16
see also under By State in the "Index by Categories"

South West Africa
see Namibia

Southeast Asia
Agricultural trade of US, by detailed commodity and country, 1991, annual rpt, 1524–8
Agricultural trade of US, by detailed commodity and country, 1991, semiannual rpt, 1522–4
AID economic aid to developing countries, obligations and disbursements by country, quarterly rpt, 9912–4
Economic and military aid and loans from US and intl agencies, by program and country, FY46-91, annual rpt, 9914–5
Economic and social conditions of developing countries from 1960s, and Intl Dev Cooperation Agency and AID activities and funding, FY91-93, annual rpt, 9904–4
Exports and imports of US, by Harmonized System 6-digit commodity and country, 1991, annual rpt, 2424–13
Exports and imports of US, by selected country, country group, and commodity group, 1991, annual rpt, 2044–37
Exports and imports of US, by transport mode, country, and SITC 1- to 3-digit commodity, 1991, annual rpt, 2424–12
Exports, imports, and balances of US for manufactured goods, by SITC 2-digit commodity and country, quarterly rpt, 2042–35
Food supply, needs, and aid for developing countries, status and alternative forecasts, 1992 world area rpt, 1526–8.2
Heroin prices and purity in 19 metro areas and Puerto Rico, by world area of origin, quarterly rpt, 6282–2
Immigrants and nonimmigrants admitted to US, alien workers, visitors, deportations, and naturalizations, FY91, annual summary rpt, 6264–7
Immigration to US, alien workers, visitors, deportations, and naturalizations, by country, FY91 and trends from 1820, annual rpt, 6264–2
Military aid of US, arms sales, and training, by country, FY50-91, annual rpt, 3904–3
Military spending, arms trade, and force strengths, with govt spending and population, by country, 1979-89, annual rpt, 9824–1
Minerals Yearbook, Vol 3, 1989: foreign country review of production, trade, and policy, by commodity, annual rpt, 5604–35.2
Productivity of labor for US and foreign countries, and impacts of investment spending, 1950s-91, article, 9381–1.308
Refugee arrivals and resettlement in US, by age, sex, sponsoring agency, State, and country, monthly rpt, 4592–1
Refugee arrivals in US by world area of origin and State of settlement, and Federal aid, FY91-92 and proposed FY93 allocations, annual rpt, 7004–16
Refugee migration, and intl aid programs, by world area and country of origin and asylum, 1991, annual rpt, 7004–15
Refugees from Indochina, arrivals, and departures, by country of origin and resettlement, camp, and ethnicity, monthly rpt, 7002–4
Tide height and time daily at coastal points, forecast 1993, annual rpt, 2174–2.5
Weather conditions and effect on agriculture, by US region, State, and city, and world area, weekly rpt, 2182–7
see also Association of Southeast Asian Nations
see also Brunei
see also Burma
see also Cambodia
see also Christmas Island
see also Indonesia
see also Laos
see also Malaysia
see also Myanmar
see also Philippines
see also Singapore
see also Thailand
see also Vietnam
see also under By Foreign Country in the "Index by Categories"

Southeastern Pennsylvania Transit Authority
Operations of SEPTA, costs and benefits, and local economic and air pollution impacts, 1970s-90 and projected to 2020, 7308–205
Southeastern Power Administration
Finances and operations of Federal power admins and electric utilities, 1990, annual rpt, 3164–24.2
Sales by customer, plants, and capacity of SEPA, and Southeastern Fed Power Program financial statements, FY91, annual rpt, 3234–1
Southeastern Research Institute, Inc.
"Final Case Study for the National Scenic Byways Study: Case Study of the Economic Impact of the Blue Ridge Parkway", 7556–8.4
Southeastern States
Banks (insured commercial), Fed Reserve 5th District members financial statements, by State, quarterly rpt, 9389–18
Banks mergers impacts on noninterest expense ratios, with background data for total and southeastern US, 1980s-90, article, 9371–1.303
Black Americans social and economic characteristics, for South and total US, 1991 and trends from 1950, annual Current Population Rpt, 2546–1.463
Civil War era geographic records for southern US, Natl Archives special collection, 1973 rpt, 9516–1.2
CPI by component for US city average, and by selected metro area, region, and population size, monthly rpt, 6762–2
Dairy prices, by product and selected area, with related marketing data, 1991, annual rpt, 1317–1
Deaths and rates, by cause and selected social, demographic, and employment characteristics, 1979-85, natl longitudinal study, 4478–186
Economic and banking conditions, for Fed Reserve 8th District, quarterly rpt with articles, 9391–16
Economic indicators and cyclical devs and outlook, by Fed Reserve Bank District, periodic rpt, 9362–8
Economic indicators by State and MSA, Fed Reserve 6th District, quarterly rpt, 9371–14
Economic indicators by State, Fed Reserve 5th District, quarterly rpt, 9389–16
Electric power sales by customer, plants, and capacity of Southeastern Power Admin, FY91, annual rpt, 3234–1
Employment and housing indicators by State, FHLB 4th District, quarterly rpt, 9302–36
Employment by industry div, earnings, and hours, for 8 southeastern States, quarterly press release, 6942–7
Employment conditions in southeastern States, with comparisons to other regions, press release series, 6946–3
Energy supply, demand, and prices, by fuel type and end-use sector, alternative projections by region, 1990-2010, annual rpt, 3164–96
Financial and banking devs in southeastern States, working paper series, 9371–10
Financial and economic devs, Fed Reserve Bank of Atlanta bimonthly journal, 9371–1
Financial and economic devs, Fed Reserve Bank of Richmond bimonthly journal, 9389–1
Financial and economic devs, Fed Reserve Bank of St Louis bimonthly journal, 9391–1
Fishing (ocean sport) activities, and catch by species, by angler characteristics and State, 1990-91, annual coastal area rpt, 2166–17.1
Freight (waterborne domestic and foreign) by commodity, traffic, and passengers, by port and waterway, 1989, annual rpt, 3754–3.1; 3754–3.2
HHS financial aid, by program, recipient, State, and city, FY91, annual regional listing, 4004–3.3; 4004–3.4
Housing vacancy rates for single and multifamily units and mobile homes in FHLB 9th District, discontinued annual MSA rpt series, 9304–19
Hurricane Andrew atmospheric pressure, wind speeds, deaths, and damage, by location, Aug 1992, article, 2152–8.304
Lumber (pulpwood and residue) prices, spending, and transport shares by mode, for southeast US, 1989-90, annual rpt, 1204–22
Lumber (veneer) receipts, production, and shipments, by species and southern State, with residue use, 1988, 1208–407
Milk handlers (cooperative and proprietary) performance, views of dairy farmers in southern States, 1989 survey, 1128–67
Peaches production, marketing, and prices in 3 southeastern States and Appalachia, 1991, annual rpt, 1311–12
Peanut production, prices, stocks, exports, use, inspection, and quality, by region and State, 1982-91, annual rpt, 1311–5
Rice production, practices, costs, and land tenure, by production area, 1988, 1568–309
Savings instns, FHLB 4th District members finances, by State, 1985-89, discontinued annual rpt series, 9304–29
Shipborne commerce (domestic) of US, freight by major commodity group, vessel type, and port, 1987-89, annual rpt, 7704–7
Statistical Abstract of US, 1992 annual data compilation, 2324–1
Swine inventory, value, farrowings, and farms, by State, quarterly release, 1623–3
Temperature annual and seasonal averages by US region, and departures from normal by world area, 1860s-1990, annual rpt, 3004–33
Textile mill employment, earnings, and hours, for 8 Southeastern States, quarterly press release, 6942–1
Textile mill employment in southern US, 1951-91, annual rpt, 6944–1
Tide height and time daily at coastal points, forecast 1993, annual rpt, 2174–2.3
Timber in southeastern US, resources mgmt and research, 1990 biennial conf papers, 1204–35
Timber in southern US, resources and removals by species, ownership, State, and county, series, 1206–8
see also Appalachia
see also under By Region in the "Index by Categories"
see also under names of individual States
Southwestern Power Administration
Finances and operations of Federal power admins and electric utilities, 1990, annual rpt, 3164–24.2
Financial statements, sales by customer, and operations and costs by project, for Southwestern Fed Power System, FY91, annual rpt, 3244–1
Property (real) of DOE owned and leased, by type, subagency, contractor, and site, FY91, annual rpt, 3004–28
Southwestern States
Deaths and rates, by cause and selected social, demographic, and employment characteristics, 1979-85, natl longitudinal study, 4478–186
Dental caries and baby bottle tooth decay prevalence among Head Start children in southwest US, by characteristics of child and area, 1992 article, 4042–3.317
Desert areas public grazing acreage, use, fees, and endangered species, 1988-90, GAO rpt, 26113–552
Economic indicators and cyclical devs and outlook, by Fed Reserve Bank District, periodic rpt, 9362–8
Electric power sales by customer, activities by plant, and financial statements of Western Area Power Admin, FY91, annual rpt, 3254–1
Electric power sales by customer, financial statements, and operations and costs by project, for Southwestern Fed Power System, FY91, annual rpt, 3244–1
Employment by industry div, earnings, and hours, by southwestern State, monthly rpt, 6962–2
Energy supply, demand, and prices, by fuel type and end-use sector, alternative projections by region, 1990-2010, annual rpt, 3164–96
Farm credit conditions and real estate values, Fed Reserve 11th District, quarterly rpt, 9379–11
Financial and economic devs, Fed Reserve Bank of Dallas quarterly journal, 9379–1
HHS financial aid, by program, recipient, State, and city, FY91, annual regional listing, 4004–3.6
Land Mgmt Bur activities in southwestern US, FY91, annual rpt, 5724–15
Peanut production, prices, stocks, exports, use, inspection, and quality, by region and State, 1982-91, annual rpt, 1311–5
Statistical Abstract of US, 1992 annual data compilation, 2324–1
Temperature annual and seasonal averages by US region, and departures from normal by world area, 1860s-1990, annual rpt, 3004–33
Timber in Rocky Mountains and southwest US, old growth forests ecology, mgmt, and research methods, 1992 conf, 1208–421
Timber insect and disease incidence and damage, 1991, annual regional rpt, 1206–11.2
Water quality and fish population in southwestern US streams, impacts of land mgmt and forest fires, 1980s-91, 1208–390
Water storage and carriage facilities of Reclamation Bur, capacity, and operating status, as of Sept 1990, biennial listing, 5824–7

see also under By Region in the "Index by Categories"
see also under names of individual States

Soviet Union

Agricultural exports of US, for grains, oilseed products, hides, skins, and cotton, by country, weekly rpt, 1922–3
Agricultural, oil, and gas production indicators for former USSR, by region and selected Republic, 1980s-90, annual rpt, 23844–2
Agricultural production, prices, and trade, for former USSR republics, 1960s-91 and forecast 1992, annual rpt, 1524–4.1
Agricultural trade by commodity and country, prices, and world market devs, monthly rpt, 1922–12
Agricultural trade of US, by detailed commodity and country, 1991, annual rpt, 1524–8
Agricultural trade of US, by detailed commodity and country, 1991, semiannual rpt, 1522–4
Arms Control and Disarmament Agency activities, and treaties status, 1991, annual rpt, 9824–2
Cocoa bean imports of USSR, by country, 1986-90, semiannual rpt, 1925–9.1
Construction activity and building materials production, for USSR, 1985-92, article, 2042–1.301
Cotton production, trade, and use, for selected countries, FAS monthly circular, 1925–4.2
Cuba trade, by commodity and country, mid 1980s-91, 9118–8
Economic and military aid and loans from US and intl agencies, by program and country, FY46-91, annual rpt, 9914–5
Economic and social conditions of developing countries from 1960s, and Intl Dev Cooperation Agency and AID activities and funding, FY91-93, annual rpt, 9904–4
Economic and sociodemographic indicators of USSR and US, selected years 1970-90, handbook, 2328–80
Economic conditions, policy, and trade practices, by country, 1989-91, annual rpt, 21384–5
Economic, social, political, and geographic summary data, by country, 1992, annual factbook, 9114–2
Energy use and production, by fuel type, country, and country group, projected 1995-2010 and trends from 1970, annual rpt, 3164–84
Export, import, and investment opportunities for US firms in USSR, contact listing, bibl, and background economic data, 1991 rpt, 2048–157
Export licensing, monitoring, and enforcement activities, FY91, annual rpt, 2024–1
Exports and imports of US, by commodity and country, 1980-90, world area rpt, 9116–1.1
Exports and imports of US, by Harmonized System 6-digit commodity and country, 1991, annual rpt, 2424–13
Exports and imports of US, by selected country, country group, and commodity group, 1991, annual rpt, 2044–37
Exports and imports of US, by transport mode, country, and SITC 1- to 3-digit commodity, 1991, annual rpt, 2424–12
Exports and imports of US with Communist and transitional economy countries, by detailed commodity and country, quarterly rpt with articles, 9882–2
Exports, imports, and balances of US for manufactured goods, by SITC 2-digit commodity and country, quarterly rpt, 2042–35
Exports of US, detailed Schedule B commodities with countries of destination, 1991, annual rpt, 2424–10
Former Soviet Republics and Baltic States energy supply and use, and social, economic, and political indicators, 1989-90, 3168–126
Former Soviet Republics and Baltic States population size and characteristics, 1989-92, 9118–19
Former Soviet Republics and Baltic States, US embassy positions planned by function, and filled, 1992, GAO rpt, 26123–403
Grain production, supply, trade, and use, by country and world region, forecasts and trends, FAS monthly circular, 1925–2.1
Human rights conditions in 170 countries, and US economic and military aid, 1991, annual rpt, 21384–3
Military aid of US, arms sales, and training, by country, FY50-91, annual rpt, 3904–3
Military aid of US, arms sales, and training programs costs and budget requests, by program, world region, and country, FY91-93, annual rpt, 7144–13
Military forces reductions and ceilings for NATO and Warsaw Pact under CFE treaty, as of Nov 1990, 9828–1
Military spending, arms trade, and force strengths, with govt spending and population, by country, 1979-89, annual rpt, 9824–1
Minerals production and exports of USSR, by commodity, 1975-90, annual rpt, 5604–39
Officials appearances in and outside USSR, annual rpt, discontinued, 9114–1
Oil and gas production by region, use, and trade by country, monthly rpt, 9112–2
Oil production and exports to US, by major exporting country, detailed data, monthly rpt with articles, 3162–24
Oil production and exports to US, by major exporting country, detailed data, monthly 1973-88, 3168–123
Oil production, stocks, use, and trade, by selected country and country group, monthly rpt, 3162–42
Oil supply, demand, and stock forecasts, by world area, quarterly rpt, 3162–34
Pension systems finances and provisions in Eastern Europe, 1950s-90 and alternative projections to 2025, technical paper, 8006–6.7
Pollution (air) contributing to global warming, emissions by monitoring site and country, and temperature change by world area and US region, 1860s-1990, annual rpt, 3004–33
Population size, growth rates, and components of change, by country, projected 1990-2020 and trends from 1950, biennial rpt, 2324–9
Poultry and egg production, trade, and use in former USSR republics, 1986-92, semiannual rpt, 1925–33.1
Radio Free Europe and Radio Liberty broadcast and financial data, FY91, annual rpt, 10314–1
Refugee arrivals in US by world area and country of origin, and quotas, monthly rpt, 7002–4
Refugee arrivals in US by world area of origin and State of settlement, and Federal aid, FY91-92 and proposed FY93 allocations, annual rpt, 7004–16
Refugee migration, and intl aid programs, by world area and country of origin and asylum, 1991, annual rpt, 7004–15
Space launchings and characteristics of craft and flight, by country, 1957-91, annual rpt, 9504–9.1
Spacecraft and satellite launches since 1957, quarterly listing, 9502–2
Spacecraft launches and other activities of NASA and USSR, with flight data, 1957-91, annual rpt, 9504–6.1
Steel trade, by product, country, and customs district, with US industry operating data, 1989-June 1992, semiannual rpt, 9882–15
Strategic Arms Reduction Treaty between US and USSR, protocols, and nuclear systems inventory agreements, as of 1990, 9828–26
Timber in western US, insect and disease infestation from lumber imports from USSR, economic and environmental impacts, 1991 and projected to 2040, 1208–389
UN voting record and share of votes in agreement with US, by issue, country, and world area, 1991, annual rpt, 7004–18
Uranium from USSR at less than fair value, injury to US industry, investigation with background financial and operating data, 1991 rpt, 9886–14.337
Uranium imports impacts on US industry, with data on DOE enrichment program and stocks, 1980s-92, GAO rpt, 26113–584
Weather conditions and effect on agriculture, by US region, State, and city, and world area, weekly rpt, 2182–7
see also Armenia
see also Azerbaijan
see also Byelarus
see also Commonwealth of Independent States
see also Estonia
see also Georgia, Republic of
see also Kazakhstan
see also Kyrgyzstan
see also Latvia
see also Lithuania
see also Moldova
see also Russia
see also Tajikistan
see also Turkmenistan
see also Ukraine
see also Uzbekistan
see also under By Foreign Country in the "Index by Categories"

Soybeans

Acreage planted and harvested, by crop and State, 1990-91 and planned as of June 1992, annual rpt, 1621–23
Acreage planted, by selected crop and State, 1983-91 and planned 1992, annual rpt, 1621–22

Agricultural Stabilization and Conservation Service soybean and oilseed programs, 1955-91, annual fact sheet, 1806-4.5
Agricultural Statistics, 1991, annual rpt, 1004-1
Beer production, stocks, material used, tax-free removals, and taxable removals by State, monthly rpt, 8486-1.1
CCC certificate exchange activity, by commodity, biweekly press release, 1802-16
CCC financial condition and major commodity program operations, FY63-88, annual chartbook, 1824-2
County Business Patterns, 1989: employment, establishments, and payroll, by SIC 2- to 4-digit industry and county, annual State rpt series, 2326-8
County Business Patterns, 1990: employment, establishments, and payroll, by SIC 2- to 4-digit industry and county, annual State rpt series, 2326-6
Export licensing, monitoring, and enforcement activities, FY91, annual rpt, 2024-1
Exports and imports (agricultural) commodity and country, prices, and world market devs, monthly rpt, 1922-12
Exports and imports (agricultural) of US, by commodity and country, bimonthly rpt, 1522-1
Exports and imports (agricultural) of US, by detailed commodity and country, 1991, annual rpt, 1524-8
Exports and imports (agricultural) of US, by detailed commodity and country, 1991, semiannual rpt, 1522-4
Exports and imports between US and outlying areas, by detailed commodity and mode of transport, 1991, annual rpt, 2424-11
Exports and imports of US, by country and detailed commodity, monthly rpt, 2422-12
Exports and imports of US, by Harmonized System 6-digit commodity and country, 1991, annual rpt, 2424-13
Exports of grains, oilseed products, hides, skins, and cotton, by country, weekly rpt, dropped data, 1922-3
Exports of US, detailed Schedule B commodities with countries of destination, 1991, annual rpt, 2424-10
Farm sector balance sheet, and receipts by detailed commodity, by State, 1986-90, annual rpt, 1544-18
Fed Crop Insurance Corp financial performance, and effect of alternative price forecasts on program costs, 1983-89, GAO rpt, 26131-95
Fertilizer and pesticide use and application rates, by type, crop, and State, 1991, 1616-1.1
Foreign and US agricultural production, acreage, and yield for selected crops, forecasts by selected world region and country, FAS monthly circular, 1925-28
Foreign and US agricultural supply and demand indicators, by selected crop, monthly rpt, 1522-5
Foreign and US oils, oilseeds, and fats production and trade, FAS periodic circular series, 1925-1
Foreign countries agricultural production, prices, and trade, by country, 1980-91 and forecast 1992, annual world area rpt series, 1524-4
Freight (waterborne domestic and foreign) by commodity, traffic, and passengers, by port and waterway, 1989, annual rpt, 3754-3
Futures and options trading volume, by commodity and exchange, FY91, annual rpt, 11924-2
Futures contracts, stocks in deliverable position by type, weekly table, 11922-4.3
Futures trading in selected commodities and financial instruments and indexes, for NYC, Chicago, and other markets activity, biweekly rpt, 11922-5
Input-output structure of US economy, detailed interindustry transactions for 541 industries, and components of final demand, 1982 benchmark data, 2708-17
Inspections of grain for domestic use and export, and foreign buyers complaints, FY92, annual rpt, 1294-1
Irrigation projects of Reclamation Bur in western US, crop production and acreage by commodity, State, and project, 1990, annual rpt, 5824-12
Loan support programs of USDA for grains, activity and status by grain and State, monthly rpt, 1802-3
Manufacturing census, 1987: concentration of largest firms measured by value added, and for shipments by SIC 2- and 4-digit industry, subject rpt, 2497-6
Manufacturing census, 1987: shipments of manufacturers products, by customer class and SIC 2- and 4-digit industry, subject rpt, 2497-4
OECD trade, total and for 4 major countries, and US trade by country, by commodity, 1980-90, world area rpt series, 9116-1
Price (season average) forecasts for soybeans using futures settlement prices, 1986-92, article, 1561-3.303
Price indexes (producer), by stage of processing and detailed commodity, monthly rpt, 6762-6
Price indexes (producer), by stage of processing and detailed commodity, monthly 1991, annual rpt, 6764-2
Price support and other CCC program outlays, with production and marketing outlook, by commodity, projected 1991-97, annual rpt, 26306-6.171
Prices received and paid by farmers, by commodity and State, monthly rpt, 1629-1
Prices received and paid by farmers, by commodity and State, 1991, annual rpt, 1629-5
Prices received by farmers and production value, by detailed crop and State, 1989-91, annual rpt, 1621-2
Production, farms, acreage, and related data, by selected crop and State, monthly rpt, 1621-1
Production itemized costs, receipts, and returns, by commodity and region, 1975-90, annual rpt, 1544-20
Production itemized costs, receipts, and returns, by crop and State, 1987-89, annual rpt, 1544-24
Production of oil and fat, consumption by end use, and stocks, by type, monthly Current Industrial Rpt, 2506-4.4
Production of oil, crushings, and stocks, by oilseed type and State, monthly Current Industrial Rpt, 2506-4.3
Production, price, and supply forecasts used for USDA commodity program outlays, accuracy, 1975-88, GAO rpt, 26131-94
Production, prices, trade, and export inspections by US port and country of destination, by grain type, weekly rpt, 1313-2
Production, prices, trade, and marketing, by commodity, current situation and forecast, monthly rpt with articles, 1502-4
Production, prices, trade, and use of oils and fats, periodic situation rpt with articles, 1561-3
Rail loadings of grain and soybeans, periodic situation rpt with articles, 1561-4
Research and education grants, USDA competitive awards by program and recipient, FY91, annual listing, 1764-1
Soviet Union and US economic and sociodemographic indicators, selected years 1970-90, handbook, 2328-80
Stocks of grain by region and market city, and grain inspected for export, by type, weekly rpt, 1313-4
Stocks of grain on and off farms, by crop, quarterly rpt, 1621-4
Weight and volume conversion factors for agricultural commodities and products, 1992 rpt, 1508-3

Space program accidents and safety
Accidents, casualties, damage, and safety activities of NASA, FY91, annual rpt, 9504-4

Space programs
Budget of US, CBO analysis and review of FY93 budget by function, annual rpt, 26304-2
Budget of US, CBO analysis of revenue and spending alternatives and projections of economic indicators, FY93-97, annual rpt, 26304-3
Budget of US, obligations and authority by function, agency, and program, with summaries and analyses, FY93, annual rpt, 104-2
Employment and payroll, by function, level of govt, and State, 1991, annual rpt, 2466-1.1
Expenditures (direct) and employment, by function and level of govt, selected years 1962-87, 10048-53
Expenditures of Fed Govt, by function, FY90, annual rpt, 2466-2.2
Expenditures of Fed Govt by type, and other finances, selected years 1952-90, annual rpt, 10044-1
Expenditures of Fed Govt in States, by type, program, agency, and State, FY91, annual rpt, 2464-2
Fed Govt aeronautics and space activities and budgets, by agency, and foreign programs, 1957-FY91, annual rpt, 9504-9
Finances and operations, by SIC 2- to 4-digit industry, forecast 1992, annual rpt, 2044-28
Fraud and abuse in NASA programs, audits and investigations, 2nd half FY92, semiannual rpt, 9502-9
Military budget, programs, and policies, FY91, annual rpt, 3544-2
Military weapons acquisition costs by system and service branch, DOD budget, FY91-93, annual rpt, 3504-2

NASA activities and finances, and data on US and USSR space launches, 1957-91, annual rpt, 9504-6
NASA project launch schedules and technical descriptions, press release series, 9506-2
Natl income and product accounts, comprehensive accounts and components, benchmark revisions, 1929-88, 2708-5
Natl income and product accounts, comprehensive accounts and components, *Survey of Current Business*, monthly rpt, 2702-1.26
Nuclear reactors for domestic use and export by function and operating status, with owner, operating characteristics, and location, 1991 annual listing, 3354-15
Procurement contract awards of NASA, by type, contractor, State, and country, FY92 with trends from 1961, semiannual rpt, 9502-6
Public knowledge, interest, and expectations for science and technology, 1990 survey, biennial rpt, 9624-10.7
Space Station Freedom and other large-scale R&D projects of Fed Govt, issues and impacts on other research, 1991 hearings, 21268-43
Space station *Freedom* technical characteristics, funding, and contracts by State, 1985-92 and projected 1997-2002, 9508-40
Statistical Abstract of US, 1992 annual data compilation, 2324-1.20
see also Communications satellites
see also Meteorological satellites
see also Satellites
see also Space program accidents and safety
see also Space sciences
see also Spacecraft

Space sciences
Apollo era science and engineering staff background and characteristics, 1958-70, 9508-39
Expenditures for R&D by Fed Govt, by detailed function, program, and agency, FY91-93, annual rpt, 9627-9
NASA activities and finances, and data on US and USSR space launches, 1957-91, annual rpt, 9504-6
NASA project launch schedules and technical descriptions, press release series, 9506-2
NASA R&D funding to higher education instns, by field, instn, and State, FY91, annual listing, 9504-7
Procurement contract awards of NASA, by type, contractor, State, and country, FY92 with trends from 1961, semiannual rpt, 9502-6
R&D funding by higher education instns and federally funded centers, by field, instn, and State, FY90, annual rpt, 9627-13
Science and Engineering Indicators, employment, education, R&D funding, and industry impacts, with foreign comparisons, 1960s-91, biennial rpt, 9624-10

Spacecraft
County Business Patterns, 1989: employment, establishments, and payroll, by SIC 2- to 4-digit industry and county, annual State rpt series, 2326-8
County Business Patterns, 1990: employment, establishments, and payroll, by SIC 2- to 4-digit industry and county, annual State rpt series, 2326-6
Exports and imports of US, by country and detailed commodity, monthly rpt, 2422-12
Exports, imports, tariffs, and industry operating data for aircraft, spacecraft, and related equipment, 1991 rpt, 9885-9.1
Foreign and US space launchings and characteristics of craft and flight, 1957-91, annual rpt, 9504-9.1
Launch schedules and technical descriptions of NASA projects, press release series, 9506-2
Launchings by US and USSR, 1957-91, annual rpt, 9504-6
Launchings of satellites and other space objects since 1957, quarterly listing, 9502-2
Manufacturing annual survey, 1990: value of shipments, by SIC 4- to 5-digit product class, 2506-14.1
Manufacturing census, 1987: concentration of largest firms measured by value added, and for shipments by SIC 2- and 4-digit industry, subject rpt, 2497-6
Manufacturing finances and operations, by SIC 2- to 4-digit industry, forecast 1992, annual rpt, 2044-28
Military prime contract awards, by detailed procurement category, FY88-91, annual rpt, 3544-18
Military weapons acquisition costs by system and service branch, DOD budget, FY91-93, annual rpt, 3504-2
Occupational injury and illness rates, by SIC 2- to 4-digit industry, 1990, annual rpt, 6844-1
Space station *Freedom* technical characteristics, funding, and contracts by State, 1985-92 and projected 1997-2002, 9508-40
see also Communications satellites
see also Meteorological satellites
see also Satellites
see also Space program accidents and safety

Spain
Agricultural trade of US, by detailed commodity and country, 1991, annual rpt, 1524-8
Agricultural trade of US, by detailed commodity and country, 1991, semiannual rpt, 1522-4
AID loans repayment status and terms by program and country, and status of predecessor agency loans, quarterly rpt, 9912-3
Cuba trade, by commodity and country, mid 1980s-91, 9118-8
Disease (infectious) surveillance, interval between onset and public health agency notification, for Catalonia, 1982-86, article, 4042-3.349
Drug abuse indicators, by world region and selected country, 1992 semiannual conf, 4492-5.2
Economic and military aid and loans from US and intl agencies, by program and country, FY46-91, annual rpt, 9914-5
Economic and monetary trends, compounded annual rates of change and annual indicators for US and 15 trading partners, quarterly rpt, annual supplement, 9391-7
Economic and social conditions of developing countries from 1960s, and Intl Dev Cooperation Agency and AID activities and funding, FY91-93, annual rpt, 9904-4
Economic conditions, income, production, prices, employment, and trade, 1992 periodic country rpt, 2046-4.32
Economic conditions, policy, and trade practices, by country, 1989-91, annual rpt, 21384-5
Economic, social, political, and geographic summary data, by country, 1992, annual factbook, 9114-2
Exports and imports of US, by Harmonized System 6-digit commodity and country, 1991, annual rpt, 2424-13
Exports and imports of US, by selected country, country group, and commodity group, 1991, annual rpt, 2044-37
Exports and imports of US, by transport mode, country, and SITC 1- to 3-digit commodity, 1991, annual rpt, 2424-12
Exports, imports, and balances of US for manufactured goods, by SITC 2-digit commodity and country, quarterly rpt, 2042-35
Exports, imports, and tariffs between Mexico and US, by commodity, impacts of North American Free Trade Agreement and compared to EC expansion to Mediterranean, 1970s-80s, 6366-3.29
Exports of US, detailed Schedule B commodities with countries of destination, 1991, annual rpt, 2424-10
Hazelnut production, supply, trade, and use, for 3 countries and US, 1990-93, annual article, 1925-34.338
Health care costs and components, services use, resources, and economic indicators, by OECD country, 1960s-90, article, 4652-1.322
Human rights conditions in 170 countries, and US economic and military aid, 1991, annual rpt, 21384-3
Imports of goods, services, and investment from US, trade barriers, impacts, and US actions, by country, 1991, annual rpt, 444-2
Labor conditions, union coverage, and work accidents, 1991 annual country rpt, 6366-4.10
Military aid of US, arms sales, and training programs costs and budget requests, by program, world region, and country, FY91-93, annual rpt, 7144-13
Military spending, arms trade, and force strengths, with govt spending and population, by country, 1979-89, annual rpt, 9824-1
Multinatl US firms and foreign affiliates finances and operations, by industry and country, 1989 benchmark survey, annual rpt, 2704-5
Multinatl US firms foreign affiliates, income statement items by asset size, industry, and country, 1988, biennial article, 8302-2.322
Nuclear power generation in US and 20 countries, monthly rpt, 3162-24.10
Nuclear power generation in US and 20 countries, monthly 1973-88, 3168-123.10
Oil exports to US by OPEC and non-OPEC countries, monthly rpt, 3162-24.3

Oil exports to US by OPEC and non-OPEC countries, monthly 1973-88, 3168–123.3
Oil production, stocks, use, and trade, by selected country and country group, monthly rpt, 3162–42
Pollution (air) contributing to global warming, emissions by monitoring site and country, and temperature change by world area and US region, 1860s-1990, annual rpt, 3004–33
Population size, growth rates, and components of change, by country, projected 1990-2020 and trends from 1950, biennial rpt, 2324–9
Refugee migration, and intl aid programs, by world area and country of origin and asylum, 1991, annual rpt, 7004–15
Rice acreage and yield of Spain, by region, mid 1930s-91, article, 1561–8.304
Saffron acreage and production in Spain, 1960s-88, FAS annual circular, 1925–15.1
Spacecraft and satellite launches since 1957, quarterly listing, 9502–2
Steel (carbon flat-rolled) products from 21 countries, injury to US industry from foreign subsidized and less than fair value imports, investigation with background financial and operating data, 1992 rpt, 9886–19.85
Steel trade, by product, country, and customs district, with US industry operating data, 1989-June 1992, semiannual rpt, 9882–15
Tax revenue, by level of govt and type of tax, for OECD countries, mid 1960s-90, annual rpt, 10044–1.2
UN voting record and share of votes in agreement with US, by issue, country, and world area, 1991, annual rpt, 7004–18
see also under By Foreign Country in the "Index by Categories"

Spalding, Josephine
"Prefabricated Buildings, Industry and Trade Summary", 9885–10.3

Spanish heritage Americans
see Hispanic Americans

Spanish Sahara
see Western Sahara

Spatz, Karen J.
"International Business Arrangements Used by Cooperatives", 1128–69

Special districts
Census Bur data coverage and availability for statistics on counties, cities, and small areas, 1991 rpt, 2326–7.82
Employment and payroll, by function, level of govt, and State, 1991, annual rpt, 2466–1.1
Enterprise zone programs in rural areas, jobs created and saved, and firms participating, by industry, 1986, article, 1502–7.303
Enterprise zone programs of States, business investment and jobs created, and incentive programs, by State, 1992 annual rpt, 5124–9
Expenditures (direct) and employment, by function and level of govt, selected years 1962-87, 10048–53
Finances of govts, by level of govt, State, and for large cities and counties, annual rpt series, 2466–2
Finances, structure, and service delivery of local govts in metro areas, local area rpt series, 10046–9
Finances, tax systems and revenue, and fiscal structure, by level of govt and State, 1992 and historical trends, annual rpt, 10044–1
Guam detailed population and housing characteristics, by urban-rural area, election district, and place, 1990 census, Pacific outlying area rpt, 2551–8.3
Minority group and women employment in State and local govt, by occupation, function, pay grade, and level of govt, 1991, annual rpt, 9244–6.3
Police employment, spending, and operations, for State, city, county, and special district agencies, 1990, annual rpt, 6064–39
see also School districts

Special Drawing Rights
Assets and debts of private sector, balance sheets by segment, 1960-91, semiannual rpt, 9365–4.1
Budget of US, authoritative financial statements with appropriations, outlays, and receipts, by category and agency, FY91, annual rpt, 8104–2.2
Economic indicators and components, current data and annual trends, monthly rpt, 23842–1.7
Fed Govt receipts by source and outlays by agency, *Treasury Bulletin*, quarterly rpt, 8002–4.1
Fed Reserve banks finances and staff, 1991, annual rpt, 9364–1.1
Flow-of-funds accounts, savings, investments, and credit statements, quarterly rpt, 9365–3.3
Investment (intl) position of US, by component, industry, world region, and country, 1990-91, annual article, 2702–1.323
Reserve assets of US by type, *Treasury Bulletin*, quarterly rpt, 8002–4.12
Reserve assets of US, monthly rpt, 9362–1.3

Special education
Assistance (financial and nonfinancial) of Fed Govt, 1992 base edition, annual listing, 104–5
Bilingual education enrollment, and eligible students not enrolled, by State, 1990-91, annual rpt, 4804–14
Data on education, enrollment, finances, teachers, and other characteristics, by State, 1969-89, 4828–33
Digest of Education Statistics, 1992 annual data compilation, 4824–2
Discrimination in education, natl survey participation and data coverage, school district administrators views, 1991 survey, 4826–1.33
Early childhood education for handicapped children, project descriptions, 1991/92, annual listing, 4944–10
Elementary and secondary education enrollment, staff, finances, operations, programs, and policies, 1987/88 biennial survey, series, 4836–3
Elementary and secondary public school agencies, by enrollment size and location, fall 1990, annual listing, 4834–1
Enrollment by age, staff, funding, and needs of special education programs, by type of handicap and State, 1990/91, annual rpt, 4944–4
Enrollment in public elementary and secondary schools, and facilities, by State, 1990/91, annual rpt, 4834–17
Expenditures for education by Federal agency, program, and recipient type, and instn spending, 1960s-91, annual rpt, 4824–8
Expenditures of Fed Govt in States, by type, program, agency, and State, FY91, annual rpt, 2464–2
Food aid program of USDA for women, infants, and children, prenatal participation effects on birthweight and health and social welfare costs, 1960s-90, GAO rpt, 26121–458
Head Start enrollment, funding, and staff, FY91, annual rpt, 4584–5
Head Start handicapped enrollment, by handicap, State, and for Indian and migrant programs, 1988/89, annual rpt, 4584–4
Mental health care of affective disorder patients, by patient and facility characteristics, 1986, 4506–3.49
Statistical Abstract of US, 1992 annual data compilation, 2324–1.4
see also Compensatory education
see also Remedial education

Special foreign currency programs
AID and Intl Dev Cooperation Agency activities and funding, FY91-93, with developing countries economic and social conditions from 1960s, annual rpt, 9904–4
Budget of US, obligations and authority by function, agency, and program, with summaries and analyses, FY93, annual rpt, 104–2
Currency (foreign) accounts owned by US under AID admin and by foreign govts with joint AID control, status by program and country, quarterly rpt, 9912–1
Currency (foreign) holdings of US, transactions and balances by program and country, 1st half FY92, semiannual rpt, 8102–7
Military outlays and obligations, by function and service branch, quarterly rpt, 3542–3

Speech pathology and audiology
Cases of acute and chronic conditions, disability, absenteeism, and health services use, by selected characteristics, 1990, annual rpt, 4147–10.182; 4147–10.183
Disability and work limitations of persons with chronic health conditions, by condition, age, and sex, 1983-86, 4946–1.2
Education in science and engineering, grad programs enrollment by field, source of funds, and characteristics of student and instn, 1990, annual rpt, 9627–7
Fed Govt employment of minorities, disabled, and veterans, and years of service, by occupation, age, sex, and agency, as of Sept 1990, biennial rpt, 9844–27
Head Start handicapped enrollment, by handicap, State, and for Indian and migrant programs, 1988/89, annual rpt, 4584–4
Hospital employment and job vacancy rate, by occupation, and instn size and control, 1981-88, annual rpt, 4114–12
Labor demand, turnover, and training completions, by detailed occupation, 1990 and projected to 2005, biennial rpt, 6744–3

Labor supply and education of health professionals, by professional and other characteristics, and location, 1960s-92 and projected to 2020, biennial rpt, 4114–8
Military health care personnel, and accessions by training source, by occupation, specialty, and service branch, FY90, annual rpt, 3544–24
Occupational Outlook Handbook, 1992-93, biennial rpt, 6744–1
Special education programs, enrollment by age, staff, funding, and needs, by type of handicap and State, 1990/91, annual rpt, 4944–4
VA health care facilities trainees, by detailed program and city, FY91, annual rpt, 8704–4
VA health care staff and turnover, by occupation, physician specialty, and location, 1991, annual rpt, 8604–8
see also Ear diseases and infections

Spencer, John S., Jr.
"Timber Resource of Missouri, Statistical Report, 1989", 1208–76

Spendable earnings
see Earnings, general
see Personal and household income

Spices and herbs
Agricultural Statistics, 1991, annual rpt, 1004–1
Consumption, supply, trade, prices, spending, and indexes, by food commodity, 1990, annual rpt, 1544–4
CPI by component for US city average, and by selected metro area, region, and population size, monthly rpt, 6762–2
Exports and imports (agricultural) of US, by commodity and country, bimonthly rpt, 1522–1
Exports and imports (agricultural) of US, by detailed commodity and country, 1991, annual rpt, 1524–8
Exports and imports (agricultural) of US, by detailed commodity and country, 1991, semiannual rpt, 1522–4
Exports and imports between US and outlying areas, by detailed commodity and mode of transport, 1991, annual rpt, 2424–11
Exports and imports of US, by country and detailed commodity, monthly rpt, 2422–12
Exports and imports of US, by Harmonized System 6-digit commodity and country, 1991, annual rpt, 2424–13
Exports and imports of US, by transport mode, country, and SITC 1- to 3-digit commodity, 1991, annual rpt, 2424–12
Exports of essential oils, by type and country, FAS monthly circular with articles, 1925–34
Exports of US, detailed Schedule B commodities with countries of destination, 1991, annual rpt, 2424–10
Foreign and US tea and herbal production, prices, and trade, FAS annual circular series, 1925–15
Foreign countries agricultural production, prices, and trade, by country, 1980-91 and forecast 1992, annual world area rpt series, 1524–4
Imports of fruits and vegetables under quarantine, by crop, country, and port of entry, FY89, annual rpt, 1524–7
Irrigation projects of Reclamation Bur in western US, crop production and acreage by commodity, State, and project, 1990, annual rpt, 5824–12
Mint oil production, yield, and farm prices by State, and NYC spot prices, 1989-92, FAS annual circular, 1925–15.2
Nutrient, caloric, and waste composition, detailed data for raw, processed, and prepared foods, 1992 rpt, 1356–3.17
Price indexes (producer), by stage of processing and detailed commodity, monthly rpt, 6762–6
Price indexes (producer), by stage of processing and detailed commodity, monthly 1991, annual rpt, 6764–2
Prices (wholesale) of fruit and vegetables in NYC by State, and shipments and arrivals by mode of transport, by commodity, weekly rpt, 1311–20
Prices (wholesale) of fruit and vegetables in NYC-Newark, and arrivals by mode of transport, by commodity and State, 1990, annual rpt, 1311–21
Prices received by farmers and production value, by detailed crop and State, 1989-91, annual rpt, 1621–2
Statistical Abstract of US, 1992 annual data compilation, 2324–1.23

Spies
see Espionage

Spina bifida
see Birth defects

Spinal cord injuries
Disability and work limitations of persons with chronic health conditions, by condition, age, and sex, 1983-86, 4946–1.2
Natl Inst of Neurological Disorders and Stroke activities, and disorder cases, FY91, annual rpt, 4474–25
VA health care services, needs, availability, structure, and funding, 1991 compilation of papers, 8608–9
Veterans health care, patients, visits, costs, and operating beds, by VA and contract facility, and region, quarterly rpt, 8602–4

Spinelli, Felix
"Regulatory Reform in Australia and New Zealand", 1524–4.3

Spletzer, James R.
"Testing for the Presence of Liquidity Constraints in Post-Secondary Educational Attainment", 6886–6.92

Spokane, Wash.
see also under By City and By SMSA or MSA in the "Index by Categories"

Sporting goods
Consumer holdings of durable goods, by type, in current and constant dollars, 1925-90, annual article, 2702–1.305
Consumer holdings of durable goods, by type, in current and constant dollars, 1988-91, annual article, 2702–1.327
County Business Patterns, 1989: employment, establishments, and payroll, by SIC 2- to 4-digit industry and county, annual State rpt series, 2326–8
County Business Patterns, 1990: employment, establishments, and payroll, by SIC 2- to 4-digit industry and county, annual State rpt series, 2326–6
CPI by component for US city average, and by selected metro area, region, and population size, monthly rpt, 6762–2
Employment, earnings, and hours, by SIC 1- to 4-digit industry, monthly 1989-Feb 1992, annual rpt, 6744–4
Exports and imports between US and outlying areas, by detailed commodity and mode of transport, 1991, annual rpt, 2424–11
Exports and imports of US, by country and detailed commodity, monthly rpt, 2422–12
Exports and imports of US, by Harmonized System 6-digit commodity and country, 1991, annual rpt, 2424–13
Exports of US, detailed Schedule B commodities with countries of destination, 1991, annual rpt, 2424–10
Imports of US given duty-free treatment for value of US material sent abroad, by commodity and country, 1987-90, annual rpt, 9884–14
Injuries from use of consumer products and related activities, by severity and victim age and sex, 1990, annual rpt, 9164–7
Injuries from use of consumer products, by severity, victim age, and detailed product, 1991, annual rpt, 9164–6
Injuries from use of consumer products, related deaths and costs, and recalls by brand, by product type, FY90, annual rpt, 9164–2
Input-output structure of US economy, detailed interindustry transactions for 541 industries, and components of final demand, 1982 benchmark data, 2708–17
Manufacturing annual survey, 1990: finances and operations, by SIC 2- to 4-digit industry, series, 2506–14
Manufacturing census, 1987: concentration of largest firms measured by value added, and for shipments by SIC 2- and 4-digit industry, subject rpt, 2497–6
Manufacturing census, 1987: shipments of manufacturers products, by customer class and SIC 2- and 4-digit industry, subject rpt, 2497–4
Manufacturing finances and operations, by SIC 2- to 4-digit industry, forecast 1992, annual rpt, 2044–28
Military prime contract awards, by detailed procurement category, FY88-91, annual rpt, 3544–18
Occupational injury and illness rates, by SIC 2- to 4-digit industry, 1989-90, annual rpt, 6844–7
Occupational injury and illness rates, by SIC 2- to 4-digit industry, 1990, annual rpt, 6844–1
Price indexes (producer), by stage of processing and detailed commodity, monthly rpt, 6762–6
Price indexes (producer), by stage of processing and detailed commodity, monthly 1991, annual rpt, 6764–2
Retail trade sales and inventories, by kind of business, region, and selected State, MSA, and city, monthly rpt, 2413–3
Retail trade sales, inventories, purchases, gross margin, and accounts receivable, by SIC 2- to 4-digit kind of business and form of ownership, 1990, annual rpt, 2413–5
Statistical Abstract of US, 1992 annual data compilation, 2324–1.7
Tax (excise) collections of IRS, by source, quarterly rpt, 8302–1; 8302–2.1

Tax (income) returns of sole proprietorships, income statement items, by industry group, 1990, annual article, 8302–2.317; 8302–2.320
see also Bicycles
see also Boats and boating
see also Recreational vehicles

Sports and athletics
Bowling centers occupational injury and illness rates, 1990, annual rpt, 6844–1
Consumer spending, natl income and product account benchmark revisions, 1929-88, 2708–5
Consumer spending, natl income and product accounts, comprehensive accounts and components, *Survey of Current Business*, monthly rpt, 2702–1.25
County Business Patterns, 1989: employment, establishments, and payroll, by SIC 2- to 4-digit industry and county, annual State rpt series, 2326–8
County Business Patterns, 1990: employment, establishments, and payroll, by SIC 2- to 4-digit industry and county, annual State rpt series, 2326–6
CPI by component for US city average, and by selected metro area, region, and population size, monthly rpt, 6762–2
Diving (underwater) accidents, illnesses, and deaths, by circumstances, diver characteristics, and location, 1970-90, annual rpt, 2144–29
Households entertainment spending, recreation participation by activity, and video product and pet ownership, 1970s-90, article, 1702–1.303
Injuries from use of consumer products and related activities, by severity and victim age and sex, 1990, annual rpt, 9164–7
Injuries from use of consumer products, by severity, victim age, and detailed product, 1991, annual rpt, 9164–6
Input-output structure of US economy, detailed interindustry transactions for 541 industries, and components of final demand, 1982 benchmark data, 2708–17
Labor demand, turnover, and training completions, by detailed occupation, 1990 and projected to 2005, biennial rpt, 6744–3
Military service academies prep schools costs and student performance indicators, 1988-90, GAO rpt, 26123–380
NCAA Div I athletic depts staff by race, and income, by sex and position, 1990/91, GAO rpt, 26121–476
Statistical Abstract of US, 1992 annual data compilation, 2324–1.7
Tax (income) returns of sole proprietorships, income statement items, by industry group, 1990, annual article, 8302–2.317; 8302–2.320
see also Basketball
see also Bicycles
see also Boats and boating
see also Fishing, sport
see also Football
see also Golf
see also Horse racing
see also Physical exercise
see also Sporting goods
see also Swimming
see also Swimming pools
see also Winter sports

Spoth, Richard
"Simulating Smokers' Acceptance of Modifications in a Cessation Program", 4042–3.308

Springfield, Mass.
see also under By City and By SMSA or MSA in the "Index by Categories"

Springfield, Mo.
see also under By City and By SMSA or MSA in the "Index by Categories"

Spyratos, Frederique
"Multiparametric Prognostic Evaluation of Biological Factors in Primary Breast Cancer", 4472–1.335

Sri Lanka
Agricultural trade of US, by detailed commodity and country, 1991, annual rpt, 1524–8
Agricultural trade of US, by detailed commodity and country, 1991, semiannual rpt, 1522–4
AID economic aid to developing countries, obligations and disbursements by country, quarterly rpt, 9912–4
AID loans repayment status and terms by program and country, and status of predecessor agency loans, quarterly rpt, 9912–3
Economic and military aid and loans from US and intl agencies, by program and country, FY46-91, annual rpt, 9914–5
Economic and social conditions of developing countries from 1960s, and Intl Dev Cooperation Agency and AID activities and funding, FY91-93, annual rpt, 9904–4
Economic conditions, income, production, prices, employment, and trade, 1992 periodic country rpt, 2046–4.52
Economic, social, political, and geographic summary data, by country, 1992, annual factbook, 9114–2
Exports and imports of US, by transport mode, country, and SITC 1- to 3-digit commodity, 1991, annual rpt, 2424–12
Exports, imports, and balances of US for manufactured goods, by SITC 2-digit commodity and country, quarterly rpt, 2042–35
Exports of US, detailed Schedule B commodities with countries of destination, 1991, annual rpt, 2424–10
Food supply, needs, and aid for developing countries, status and alternative forecasts, 1992 world area rpt, 1526–8.2
Human rights conditions in 170 countries, and US economic and military aid, 1991, annual rpt, 21384–3
Labor conditions, union coverage, and work accidents, 1992 annual country rpt, 6366–4.43
Military aid of US, arms sales, and training programs costs and budget requests, by program, world region, and country, FY91-93, annual rpt, 7144–13
Military spending, arms trade, and force strengths, with govt spending and population, by country, 1979-89, annual rpt, 9824–1
Minerals Yearbook, Vol 3, 1989: foreign country review of production, trade, and policy, by commodity, annual rpt, 5604–35.2
Population size, growth rates, and components of change, by country, projected 1990-2020 and trends from 1950, biennial rpt, 2324–9
Refugee migration, and intl aid programs, by world area and country of origin and asylum, 1991, annual rpt, 7004–15
UN voting record and share of votes in agreement with US, by issue, country, and world area, 1991, annual rpt, 7004–18

Srinivasan, Aruna
"Are There Cost Savings from Bank Mergers?", 9371–1.303
"Cost Savings Associated with Bank Mergers", 9371–10.78

St. Christopher and Nevis
Agricultural trade of US, by detailed commodity and country, 1991, semiannual rpt, 1522–4
Economic and social conditions, resources, and trade, and aid, 1992, annual factbook, 9914–14
Economic, social, political, and geographic summary data, by country, 1992, annual factbook, 9114–2
Exports and imports of US, by transport mode, country, and SITC 1- to 3-digit commodity, 1991, annual rpt, 2424–12
Exports of US, detailed Schedule B commodities with countries of destination, 1991, annual rpt, 2424–10
Human rights conditions in 170 countries, and US economic and military aid, 1991, annual rpt, 21384–3
Military aid of US, arms sales, and training programs costs and budget requests, by program, world region, and country, FY91-93, annual rpt, 7144–13
Population size, growth rates, and components of change, by country, projected 1990-2020 and trends from 1950, biennial rpt, 2324–9
UN voting record and share of votes in agreement with US, by issue, country, and world area, 1991, annual rpt, 7004–18

St. Clair County, Ill.
Housing and households characteristics, and unit and neighborhood quality, by MSA location for 11 MSAs, 1987 survey, supplement, 2485–8

St. Cloud, Minn.
Wages by occupation, and benefits, for office and plant workers, 1992 survey, periodic MSA rpt, 6785–17.2

St. Croix County, Wis.
Housing vacancy rates for single and multifamily units and mobile homes, by city and ZIP code, 1991, annual MSA rpt, 9304–18.4

St. Kitts-Nevis
see St. Christopher and Nevis

St. Lawrence River
Traffic on Seaway for ships, cargo, and passengers, and toll revenue, 1991 and trends from 1959, annual rpt, 7744–2
Water levels in Great Lakes, monthly and annual averages by station, 1860-1990, quinquennial rpt, 2178–1
Water levels of Great Lakes and connecting channels, and forecasts, semimonthly rpt, 3752–2
Water supply and quality in streams and lakes, and groundwater levels in wells, by drainage basin, 1990, annual State rpt series, 5666–10
Water supply and quality in streams and lakes, and groundwater levels in wells, by drainage basin, 1991, annual State rpt series, 5666–12

Water supply in northeastern US, precipitation and stream runoff by station, monthly rpt, 2182–3
Water supply in US and southern Canada, streamflow, surface and groundwater conditions, and reservoir levels, by location, monthly rpt, 5662–3

St. Lawrence Seaway Development Corp.
Activities and finances of Corp, 1990, annual rpt, 7744–1
Budget of US, obligations and authority by function, agency, and program, with summaries and analyses, FY93, annual rpt, 104–2
Employment of DOT, by subagency, occupation, and selected personnel characteristics, FY91, annual rpt, 7304–18
Traffic on Seaway for ships, cargo, and passengers, and toll revenue, 1991 and trends from 1959, annual rpt, 7744–2

St. Louis, Mo.
CPI by component for US city average, and by region, population size, and for 15 metro areas, monthly rpt, 6762–1
CPI by component for US city average, and by selected metro area, region, and population size, monthly rpt, 6762–2
Drug abuse indicators for selected metro areas, research results, data collection, and policy issues, 1992 semiannual conf, 4492–5
Drug test results at arrest, by drug type, offense, and sex, for selected urban areas, quarterly rpt, 6062–3
Economic and banking conditions, for Fed Reserve 8th District, quarterly rpt with articles, 9391–16
Freight (waterborne domestic and foreign) by commodity, traffic, and passengers, by port and waterway, 1989, annual rpt, 3754–3.2
Fruit and vegetable shipments, and arrivals by city, by mode of transport and State and country of origin, 1990, annual rpt, 1311–4.2
Heroin prices and purity in 19 metro areas and Puerto Rico, by world area of origin, quarterly rpt, 6282–2
Housing and households characteristics, and unit and neighborhood quality, by MSA location for 11 MSAs, 1987 survey, supplement, 2485–8
Housing starts and completions authorized by building permits in 40 MSAs, quarterly rpt, 2382–9
State and local govt employees wages by occupation, and benefits, 1991 survey, periodic MSA rpt, 6785–15.2
Wages by occupation, and benefits, for office and plant workers, 1992 survey, periodic MSA rpt, 6785–17.2
see also under By City and By SMSA or MSA in the "Index by Categories"

St. Lucia
Agricultural trade of US, by detailed commodity and country, 1991, semiannual rpt, 1522–4
Economic and social conditions, resources, and trade, and aid, 1992, annual factbook, 9914–14
Economic, social, political, and geographic summary data, by country, 1992, annual factbook, 9114–2
Exports and imports of US, by transport mode, country, and SITC 1- to 3-digit commodity, 1991, annual rpt, 2424–12
Exports of US, detailed Schedule B commodities with countries of destination, 1991, annual rpt, 2424–10
Human rights conditions in 170 countries, and US economic and military aid, 1991, annual rpt, 21384–3
Military aid of US, arms sales, and training programs costs and budget requests, by program, world region, and country, FY91-93, annual rpt, 7144–13
Population size, growth rates, and components of change, by country, projected 1990-2020 and trends from 1950, biennial rpt, 2324–9
UN voting record and share of votes in agreement with US, by issue, country, and world area, 1991, annual rpt, 7004–18

St. Paul, Minn.
CPI by component for US city average, and by selected metro area, region, and population size, monthly rpt, 6762–2
Drug abuse indicators for selected metro areas, research results, data collection, and policy issues, 1992 semiannual conf, 4492–5
Freight (waterborne domestic and foreign) by commodity, traffic, and passengers, by port and waterway, 1989, annual rpt, 3754–3.2; 3754–3.3
Housing and households characteristics, unit and neighborhood quality, and journey to work by MSA location, for 11 MSAs, 1985 survey, supplement, 2485–8
Housing and households characteristics, 1989 survey, MSA fact sheet, 2485–11.11
Housing and households detailed characteristics, and unit and neighborhood quality, by location, 1989 survey, MSA rpt, 2485–6.7
Housing starts and completions authorized by building permits in 40 MSAs, quarterly rpt, 2382–9
see also under By City and By SMSA or MSA in the "Index by Categories"

St. Petersburg, Fla.
CPI by component for US city average, and by selected metro area, region, and population size, monthly rpt, 6762–2
Housing and households characteristics, unit and neighborhood quality, and journey to work by MSA location, for 11 MSAs, 1985 survey, supplement, 2485–8
Housing and households characteristics, 1989 survey, MSA fact sheet, 2485–11.12
Housing starts and completions authorized by building permits in 40 MSAs, quarterly rpt, 2382–9
Wages by occupation, and benefits, for office and plant workers, 1991 survey, periodic MSA rpt, 6785–16.3

St. Pierre and Miquelon
Exports and imports of US, by transport mode, country, and SITC 1- to 3-digit commodity, 1991, annual rpt, 2424–12

St. Tammany Parish, La.
Housing and households characteristics, and unit and neighborhood quality, by MSA location for 11 MSAs, 1986 survey, supplement, 2485–8

St. Vincent and The Grenadines
Agricultural trade of US, by detailed commodity and country, 1991, semiannual rpt, 1522–4
Economic and social conditions, resources, and trade, and aid, 1992, annual factbook, 9914–14
Economic, social, political, and geographic summary data, by country, 1992, annual factbook, 9114–2
Exports and imports of US, by transport mode, country, and SITC 1- to 3-digit commodity, 1991, annual rpt, 2424–12
Exports of US, detailed Schedule B commodities with countries of destination, 1991, annual rpt, 2424–10
Human rights conditions in 170 countries, and US economic and military aid, 1991, annual rpt, 21384–3
Military aid of US, arms sales, and training programs costs and budget requests, by program, world region, and country, FY91-93, annual rpt, 7144–13
Population size, growth rates, and components of change, by country, projected 1990-2020 and trends from 1950, biennial rpt, 2324–9
UN voting record and share of votes in agreement with US, by issue, country, and world area, 1991, annual rpt, 7004–18

Stahmer, C. B.
"Newsprint, Industry and Trade Summary", 9885–8.8

Staiert, Jim
"Higher Net Income Improves Growth of Largest Co-ops", 1122–1.306
"Largest Co-ops Rebound To Post $101 Million Increase in Income", 1122–1.305
"Nation's Cooperatives Rebuild Unallocated Equity", 1122–1.308

Stamford, Conn.
see also under By City and By SMSA or MSA in the "Index by Categories"

Stamps, James
"U.S. Market Access in Latin America: Recent Liberalization Measures and Remaining Barriers (With a Special Case Study on Chile). Report to the Committee on Finance of the U.S. Senate on Investigation No. 332-318 Under Section 332 of the Tariff Act of 1930", 9886–4.184

Standard Consolidated Areas
see Metropolitan Statistical Areas

Standard Industrial Classification
Census Bur data collection and statistical program plans, advisory committees findings and recommendations, 1992 conf, 2628–35
Census of Population and Housing, 1990: industry and occupation classification codes, alphabetical index, 2628–1
Census of Population and Housing, 1990: industry and occupation classification codes, classified index, 2628–2
Input-output structure of US economy, detailed interindustry transactions for 541 industries, and components of final demand, 1982 benchmark data, 2708–17

Standard Metropolitan Statistical Areas
see Metropolitan Statistical Areas
see under By SMSA or MSA in the "Index by Categories"
see under By Urban-Rural and Metro-Nonmetro in the "Index by Categories"

Standard of living
see Cost of living
see Family budgets
see Personal and household income
see Quality of life
Standards
see Industrial standards
see Quality control and testing
see Weights and measures
Stanford University
Radiation and other pollutant releases from DOE contractor research lab and nuclear weapons facilities, monitoring results, 1992 annual site rpt, 3324–2.11
Stanley, Stephen
"Evidence of Improved Inventory Control", 9389–1.302
Stark, Lloyd R.
"Study of Natural Wetlands Associated with Acid Mine Drainage", 5608–171
START
see Strategic Arms Reduction Talks
State aid programs
see Aid to Families with Dependent Children
see Medicaid
see Medical assistance
see State funding for economic development
see State funding for education
see State funding for health and hospitals
see State funding for higher education
see State funding for local areas
see State funding for public safety
see State funding for social welfare
see State government spending
see Supplemental Security Income
see Unemployment insurance
see Workers compensation
State and local employees
American Samoa govt finances, with data on health and farm spending and employment, mid 1980s-91, GAO rpt, 26123–385
Asian and Pacific Islands Americans social and economic characteristics, for West and total US, 1990-91, Current Population Report, 2546–1.462
Black Americans social and economic characteristics, for South and total US, 1991 and trends from 1950, annual Current Population Rpt, 2546–1.463
Business statistics, detailed data for major industries and economic indicators, 1960-91, *Survey of Current Business* biennial supplement, 2704–1
Corrupt govt officials prosecuted and convicted, by judicial district and level of govt, 1970-90, annual rpt, 6004–13
Criminal justice systems activities, spending, and employment, by level of govt, data compilation, 1992 annual rpt, 6064–6.1
Criminal justice systems of States, activities, employment, funding, and data collection, by State, 1970s-91, annual rpt, 6064–40
DC govt finances, revenue by source, financial statements, and employment, with income in central city and suburbs compared to other cities, 1991 hearings, 21308–28
DC govt workers compensation under Fed Govt admin, program finances and operations, FY91, annual rpt, 6504–10
Employee benefit plan coverage and provisions, by plan type, for State and local govt employees, 1990, biennial rpt, 6784–21
Employment and direct spending, by function and level of govt, selected years 1967-87, 10048–53
Employment and payroll, by function and level of govt, annual rpt series, 2466–1
Employment and payroll of State and local govts, monthly rpt, 6742–4
Employment Cost Index and percent change by occupational group, industry div, region, and metro-nonmetro area, quarterly press release, 6782–5
Employment, earnings, and hours, by selected SIC 1- to 4-digit industry, State, and for 275 MSAs, 1987-92, 6748–81
Employment, earnings, and hours, by SIC 1- to 4-digit industry, monthly 1989-Feb 1992, annual rpt, 6744–4
Employment situation, earnings, hours, and other BLS economic indicators, transcripts of BLS Commissioner's monthly testimony, periodic rpt, 23846–4
Health Care Financing Review, provider prices, price inputs and indexes, and labor, quarterly journal, 4652–1.1
Health care professionals supply and education, by professional and other characteristics, and location, 1960s-92 and projected to 2020, biennial rpt, 4114–8
Insurance (life) benefits of employer-sponsored plans by plan type, age, occupation, and salary, 1990, article, 6722–1.346
Law enforcement spending, employment, and payroll, by activity, level of govt, and State, FY90, annual rpt, 6066–25.50
Leave benefits in small business compared to larger firms and govts, by occupational group, 1989-90, article, 6722–1.315
Libraries (public) finances, staff, and operations, by State and population size, 1990, annual rpt, 4824–6
Local govts in metro areas, finances, structure, and service delivery, local area rpt series, 10046–9
Minority group and women employment by industry sector, and govt salaries, by occupation, mid 1960s-90, chartbook, 9248–20
Minority group and women employment in State and local govt, by occupation, function, pay level, and State, 1991, annual rpt, 9244–6
OASDI coverage of State and local govt employees under voluntary Federal-State agreements, 1987, article, 4742–1.315
Occupational Outlook Handbook, 1992-93, biennial rpt, 6744–1
Pacific territories population and housing detailed characteristics, by location, 1990 Census of Population and Housing, series, 2551–8
Prison and community-based facilities, population, employment, spending, and other characteristics, by State and for Fed Govt, 1990, annual rpt, 6064–26.3; 6068–218
Prison drug smuggling interdiction, inmate and staff testing, and treatment programs, by instn characteristics, 1989-90, 6066–19.70
Prisoners in Federal and State instns by selected characteristics, releases, staff, and instn size, with data by region and State, late 1970s-91, 6068–248
Productivity of State and local employees, indexes of output by function, FY64-90, annual rpt, 6824–1.6
Prosecutors (chief) in State courts, employment characteristics, and felony case prosecution procedures, 1990 survey, 6066–25.46
Railroad accidents, casualties, and damage, Fed Railroad Admin activities, and safety inspectors by State, 1990, annual rpt, 7604–12
Science and engineering labor force, Federal and university research funding, and educational data, series, 9626–6
Southwestern US employment by industry div, earnings, and hours, by State, monthly rpt, 6962–2
Statistical Abstract of US, 1992 annual data compilation, 2324–1.9
Training for job qualification and skill improvement, workers participating by training source, occupation, age, sex, and race, 1991, 6728–32
Transit systems finances and operations, by mode, size of fleet and urban area, region, and for 518 systems, 1990, annual rpt, 7884–4
Veterans (Vietnam) labor force status and earnings, by whether served in Southeast Asia, presence and severity of disability, and selected other characteristics, 1989, article, 6722–1.326
see also Civil service pensions
see also Civil service system
see also Fire departments
see also Labor-management relations in government
see also Officials
see also Police
see also State and local employees pay
see also State police
see also Teachers
State and local employees pay
Collective bargaining wage and benefit changes and coverage, monthly rpt, 6782–1
Collective bargaining wage and benefit changes and coverage, 1st half 1992, semiannual press release, 6782–6
Costs (hourly) of labor, by component, occupational group, industry div, union coverage, and region, 1992, annual rpt, 6744–21
Criminal justice systems activities, spending, and employment, by level of govt, data compilation, 1992 annual rpt, 6064–6.1
Employment and payroll, by function and level of govt, annual rpt series, 2466–1
Employment Cost Index and alternative measure of compensation costs, by component, occupation, industry group, union status, and location, 1975-92, annual rpt, 6744–20
Finances of govts, by level of govt, State, and for large cities and counties, annual rpt series, 2466–2
Income (household, family, and personal), by source, detailed characteristics, and region, 1991, annual Current Population Rpt, 2546–6.76
Income (personal) per capita and by source, and employment, by industry div, State, MSA, and county, 1969-90, annual CD-ROM, 2704–7

Law enforcement spending, employment, and payroll, by activity, level of govt, and State, FY90, annual rpt, 6066–25.50
Libraries (public) finances, staff, and operations, by State and population size, 1990, annual rpt, 4824–6
Minority group and women employment in State and local govt, by occupation, function, pay level, and State, 1991, annual rpt, 9244–6
Natl income and product accounts and components, *Survey of Current Business*, monthly rpt, 2702–1.23
Natl income and product accounts, comprehensive accounts and components, benchmark revisions, 1929-88, 2708–5
Natl income and product accounts, comprehensive accounts and components, *Survey of Current Business*, monthly rpt, 2702–1.26
Occupational Outlook Handbook, 1992-93, biennial rpt, 6744–1
Pacific territories population and housing detailed characteristics, by location, 1990 Census of Population and Housing, series, 2551–8
Payroll and employment of State and local govts, monthly rpt, 6742–4
Police agencies employment, spending, and operations, FY90, 6066–25.44
Police employment, spending, and operations, for State, city, county, and special district agencies, 1990, annual rpt, 6064–39
Prison construction and operating costs, capacity, and inmates, for Federal and State facilities, 1985-89, GAO rpt, 26119–407
Sheriffs' agencies employment, spending, and operations, FY90, 6066–25.45
Statistical Abstract of US, 1992 annual data compilation, 2324–1.9
Transit systems finances and operations, by mode, size of fleet and urban area, region, and for 518 systems, 1990, annual rpt, 7884–4
Wages by occupation, and benefits, for State and local govt workers, 1991 survey, periodic MSA rpt, 6785–15
Washington State govt employees comparable worth agreement, compliance costs and indicators of success, mid 1980s-93, GAO rpt, 26119–410
Workers compensation programs of States, top officials, salaries, and hours, by State, as of 1990, annual rpt, 6504–9
see also Civil service pensions
see also Educational employees pay

State and local taxes

Blue Ridge Parkway impacts on local economic conditions and employment, by expense type, 1987, 7556–8.4
Collections of taxes, by level of govt, type of tax, State, and selected counties, quarterly rpt, 2462–3
DC govt finances, revenue by source, financial statements, and employment, with income in central city and suburbs compared to other cities, 1991 hearings, 21308–28
Energy producers finances and operations, by energy type for US firms domestic and foreign operations, 1990, annual rpt, 3164–44
Estate taxes of States, credits filed in Fed Govt estate tax returns, by State, 1990, article, 8302–2.305
Finances of govts, by level of govt, State, and for large cities and counties, annual rpt series, 2466–2
Finances of govts, revenue and spending by level of govt, natl income and product accounts, 1959-91, annual rpt, 204–1.6
Finances of govts, tax systems and revenue, and fiscal structure, by level of govt and State, 1992 and historical trends, annual rpt, 10044–1
Finances of State and local govts, obligations and resources compared to Fed Govt, 1960s-90, GAO rpt, 26121–457
Fiscal condition of State and local govts, with data by State and selected city, 1991 hearing, 21268–44
Foreign travelers to US, spending by world area of residence, and economic impacts, by spending category and State, 1989, 2908–28
Hwy receipts by source, and spending by function, by level of govt and State, 1991, annual rpt, 7554–1.3
Hwy scenic routes impacts on local economic conditions, by State, county, and selected byway, late 1980s, 7556–8.1
Income (household) and poverty status under alternative income definitions, by recipient characteristics, 1979-91, annual Current Population Rpt, 2546–6.78
Income tax returns of individuals, detailed data, 1988, annual rpt, 8304–2
Income tax returns of individuals, selected income and tax items by income level, preliminary 1990, annual article, 8302–2.307
Local govts in metro areas, finances, structure, and service delivery, local area rpt series, 10046–9
Mail order sales from out of State, tax revenue losses by State, 1990-92, 10048–84
Maternal and child health services block grant beneficiary and taxpayer equity among States, issues, alternative allocation formulas, and background data, 1992 GAO rpt, 26121–454
Natl income and product accounts and components, *Survey of Current Business*, monthly rpt, 2702–1.23
Natl income and product accounts, comprehensive accounts and components, benchmark revisions, 1929-88, 2708–5
Natl income and product accounts, comprehensive accounts and components, *Survey of Current Business*, monthly rpt, 2702–1.26
New England States economic indicators, Fed Reserve 1st District, monthly rpt, 9373–2
Philadelphia metro area transit service operations, costs and benefits, and local economic and air pollution impacts, 1970s-90 and projected to 2020, 7308–205
Public opinion on taxes, spending, and govt efficiency, by respondent characteristics, 1992 survey, annual rpt, 10044–2
Statistical Abstract of US, 1992 annual data compilation, 2324–1.9
Telephone and telegraph firms detailed finances and operations, 1990, annual rpt, 9284–6.2
Transit systems finances and operations, by mode, size of fleet and urban area, region, and for 518 systems, 1990, annual rpt, 7884–4
Washington and Oregon coastal areas tourism and recreation facilities and economic impacts, by county, 1983-88, 5738–40.3
see also Excise tax
see also Fuel tax
see also Property tax
see also Revenue sharing
see also Sales tax
see also Severance taxes

State courts

Expenditures and employment for law enforcement, by activity and level of govt, data compilation, 1992 annual rpt, 6064–6.1
Expenditures, employment, and payroll, by activity, level of govt, and State, FY90, annual rpt, 6066–25.50
Felony court filings, dispositions, and sentence lengths, by sentence type, and offense and offender characteristics, data compilation, 1992 annual rpt, 6064–6.5
Prosecutors (chief) in State courts, employment characteristics, and felony case prosecution procedures, 1990 survey, 6066–25.46
US attorneys work hours, by type of court and Federal district, FY91, annual rpt, 6004–2.6
Wiretaps authorized, costs, arrests, trials, and convictions, by offense and jurisdiction, 1991, annual rpt, 18204–7
see also Domestic relations courts and cases

State Department

see Department of State

State forests

California lumber mills, operations, timber use by species and origin, and residue use, by product and county, 1988, 1208–108
Minnesota timber acreage, resources, and removals, by ownership, forest and tree characteristics, and county, 1990, series, 1206–24
Missouri timber resources and removals, by species, forest and tree characteristics, ownership, and county, 1987-89 and trends from 1959, 1208–76
Missouri timber resources and removals by species, land ownership, and county, 1988-89, series, 1206–3
Owl (northern spotted) conservation methods in Pacific Northwest, findings and recommendations, 1990 rpt, 1208–385
Planting and stand improvement, by ownership and State, FY91, annual rpt, 1204–7
Tennessee timber acreage and resources, by species, ownership class, and county, 1989, series, 1206–27
Virginia timber resources, growth, and removals, by species, ownership, treatment, and county, 1990-92, series, 1206–6
Wisconsin timber resources and removals, by species, forest type, ownership, and county, series, 1206–34

State funding for economic development
Appalachia local dev projects, and funding by source, by program and State, FY91, annual rpt, 9084–1
Arkansas govt science agency research grants and industry sponsors matching funds, and Federal R&D aid to higher education instns, mid 1980s-90, hearing, 21708–131
Community Dev Block Grant activities and funding, by program, FY75-91, annual rpt, 5124–8
Construction put in place, value of new public and private structures, by type, monthly rpt, 2382–4
Enterprise zone programs of States, business investment and jobs created, and incentive programs, by State, 1992 annual rpt, 5124–9
Expenditures (direct) and employment, by function and level of govt, selected years 1962-87, 10048–53
Finances of govts, by level of govt, State, and for large cities and counties, annual rpt series, 2466–2
Finances of govts, tax systems and revenue, and fiscal structure, by level of govt and State, 1992 and historical trends, annual rpt, 10044–1
Natl income and product accounts, comprehensive accounts and components, benchmark revisions, 1929-88, 2708–5
Natl income and product accounts, comprehensive accounts and components, *Survey of Current Business*, monthly rpt, 2702–1.26
New England States govt retirement systems investment policy assessment, with system assets and liabilities, by State, 1992 article, 9373–25.301

State funding for education
Adult education and literacy programs funding, enrollment, and activities, fact sheet series, 4806–4
Digest of Education Statistics, 1992 annual data compilation, 4824–2
Elementary and secondary public school systems enrollment, finances, staff, and high school grads, by State, FY89-90, annual rpt, 4834–6
Expenditures (direct) and employment, by function and level of govt, selected years 1962-87, 10048–53
Finances of govts, by level of govt, State, and for large cities and counties, annual rpt series, 2466–2
Finances of govts, tax systems and revenue, and fiscal structure, by level of govt and State, 1992 and historical trends, annual rpt, 10044–1
Input-output structure of US economy, detailed interindustry transactions for 541 industries, and components of final demand, 1982 benchmark data, 2708–17
Libraries (public) finances, staff, and operations, by State and population size, 1990, annual rpt, 4824–6
Natl income and product accounts, comprehensive accounts and components, benchmark revisions, 1929-88, 2708–5
Natl income and product accounts, comprehensive accounts and components, *Survey of Current Business*, monthly rpt, 2702–1.26
School lunch programs food donations processing, contracts, and processors problems with State reporting requirements, with data by State, 1989-91, GAO rpt, 26113–555
Special education programs, enrollment by age, staff, funding, and needs, by type of handicap and State, 1990/91, annual rpt, 4944–4
see also State funding for higher education

State funding for health and hospitals
American Samoa govt finances, with data on health and farm spending and employment, mid 1980s-91, GAO rpt, 26123–385
Board and care home violations of State drug handling and dispensing regulations, for 3 metro areas, 1990-91, GAO rpt, 26121–447
Drug abuse services availability, need, use, outcome, costs, funding sources, and cost-effectiveness, series, 4496–11
Drug abuse treatment, prevention, and enforcement grants by State, and State allocations by program, FY87-90, 6068–252
Employment and payroll, by function, level of govt, and State, 1991, annual rpt, 2466–1.1
Expenditures (direct) and employment, by function and level of govt, selected years 1962-87, 10048–53
Expenditures for health care and factors in costs, with data by payment source and service type, 1960s-90 and projected to 2000, 26306–6.175
Expenditures for health care by businesses, households, and govts, 1965-90, annual article, 4652–1.309
Expenditures for health care by funding source, 1990, with trends and indexes by service type from 1960, article, 4652–1.323
Finances of govts, by level of govt, State, and for large cities and counties, annual rpt series, 2466–2
Finances of govts, tax systems and revenue, and fiscal structure, by level of govt and State, 1992 and historical trends, annual rpt, 10044–1
Health condition and care indicators, 1950s-90 with health improvement and disease prevention goals for 1990, annual data compilation, 4144–11
Hospital cost of charity cases and patients bad debts, and relation to operating margin, by selected MSA and urban-rural location, 1980s, 17206–2.32
Input-output structure of US economy, detailed interindustry transactions for 541 industries, and components of final demand, 1982 benchmark data, 2708–17
Insurance (health) reforms of States to improve small business access, provisions with background data by State, 1991, GAO rpt, 26121–462
Mental health care facilities, staff, and patient characteristics, *Statistical Notes* series, 4506–3
Mental health care facilities, staff, patients, and finances, 1970s-91, biennial rpt, 4094–1
Natl income and product accounts, comprehensive accounts and components, benchmark revisions, 1929-88, 2708–5
Natl income and product accounts, comprehensive accounts and components, *Survey of Current Business*, monthly rpt, 2702–1.26
Obstetrics rural practitioners malpractice insurance subsidy program funding and participation, for North Carolina, 1989-92, article, 4042–3.355
Physicians recently graduating, specialties, school debt, and practice settings, and medical school funding sources, 1970s-91, hearing, 21368–135
Veterans health care, patients, visits, costs, and operating beds, by VA and contract facility, and region, quarterly rpt, 8602–4
see also Medicaid

State funding for higher education
Agricultural research funding and staffing for USDA, State agencies, and other instns, by topic, FY91, annual rpt, 1744–2
Black higher education instns enrollment, finances, staff, and degrees, by instn and selected student characteristics, 1970s-90, 4848–46
Finances, enrollment, faculty, and degrees in higher education, by instn level and control, and State, FY88, annual rpt, 4844–13
Finances of govts, by level of govt, State, and for large cities and counties, annual rpt series, 2466–2
Finances of govts, tax systems and revenue, and fiscal structure, by level of govt and State, 1992 and historical trends, annual rpt, 10044–1
Finances of higher education instns, revenue by source and spending by function, by State and instn control, FY82-90, annual rpt, 4844–6
Input-output structure of US economy, detailed interindustry transactions for 541 industries, and components of final demand, 1982 benchmark data, 2708–17
Natl income and product accounts, comprehensive accounts and components, benchmark revisions, 1929-88, 2708–5
Natl income and product accounts, comprehensive accounts and components, *Survey of Current Business*, monthly rpt, 2702–1.26
R&D facilities of higher education instns, space and equipment adequacy, needs, and funding by source, by instn type and control, 1992, biennial rpt, 9624–25
R&D funding by higher education instns and federally funded centers, by field, instn, and State, FY90, advance annual rpt, 9626–8.5
R&D funding by higher education instns and federally funded centers, by field, instn, and State, FY90, annual rpt, 9627–13
R&D funding by higher education instns and federally funded centers, by field, instn, and State, FY91, advance annual rpt, 9626–8.7
Student aid and other sources of support, with student expenses and characteristics, by instn type and control, 1987 study, series, 4846–3; 4846–5
Student guaranteed loans, defaults, and collections, by type of loan, lender, and guarantee agency, with data by State and top lender, FY91, annual rpt, 4804–38

State funding for local areas
Appalachia local dev projects, and funding by source, by program and State, FY91, annual rpt, 9084–1
Community Dev Block Grant activities and funding, by program, FY75-91, annual rpt, 5124–8
Drug enforcement grants of Fed Govt, and allocations to local govts, by State, FY91, annual rpt, 6064–38
Drug enforcement grants to States, and allocations to local areas, by State, FY87-91, 236–3.1
Enterprise zone programs of States, business investment and jobs created, and incentive programs, by State, 1992 annual rpt, 5124–9
Expenditures (direct) and employment, by function and level of govt, selected years 1962-87, 10048–53
Finances of govts, by level of govt, State, and for large cities and counties, annual rpt series, 2466–2
Finances of govts, tax systems and revenue, and fiscal structure, by level of govt and State, 1992 and historical trends, annual rpt, 10044–1
Hwy receipts by source, and spending by function, by level of govt and State, 1991, annual rpt, 7554–1.3
Hwy Statistics, summary data by State, 1990-91, annual rpt, 7554–24
Statistical Abstract of US, 1992 annual data compilation, 2324–1.9
Transit systems finances and operations, by mode, size of fleet and urban area, region, and for 518 systems, 1990, annual rpt, 7884–4
Wastewater treatment plants construction loan funds for local govts, costs and State officials views by State, projected 1991-2000, GAO rpt, 26113–561

State funding for natural resources and conservation
Coal Surface Mining Reclamation and Enforcement Office activities and funding, by State and Indian tribe, FY91, annual rpt, 5644–1
Coastal areas environmental mgmt programs of States, activities and Federal funding, FY90-91, biennial rpt, 2174–8
Employment and payroll, by function, level of govt, and State, 1991, annual rpt, 2466–1.1
Enforcement of environmental laws by EPA and State govts, activities, FY91, annual rpt, 9184–21
Expenditures (direct) and employment, by function and level of govt, selected years 1962-87, 10048–53
Finances of govts, by level of govt, State, and for large cities and counties, annual rpt series, 2466–2
Input-output structure of US economy, detailed interindustry transactions for 541 industries, and components of final demand, 1982 benchmark data, 2708–17
Natl income and product accounts, comprehensive accounts and components, benchmark revisions, 1929-88, 2708–5
Natl income and product accounts, comprehensive accounts and components, *Survey of Current Business*, monthly rpt, 2702–1.26
Radioactive low-level waste disposal activities of States and interstate compacts, with data by disposal facility and reactor, 1990, annual rpt, 3004–36
Tree planting on govt land contracted to small businesses, Federal grants, State funding, and projects, by State, FY91, annual rpt, 9764–10
Uranium tailings at inactive mills, remedial action activities by site, and funding, FY91, annual rpt, 3354–9
Wastewater treatment plants construction loan funds for local govts, costs and State officials views by State, projected 1991-2000, GAO rpt, 26113–561
Wetlands (coastal) conservation funding by project, 1992 press release, 5306–4.12

State funding for public safety
California jail population and overcrowding by county, and instn construction funding, 1980s, 6066–30.1
Crime victim compensation and support service programs funding, by offense and State, FY88-90, biennial rpt, 6064–37
Criminal justice spending of State and local govts, by State, 1988-90, 6066–23.7
Criminal justice systems activities, spending, and employment, by level of govt, data compilation, 1992 annual rpt, 6064–6.1
Criminal justice systems of States, activities, employment, funding, and data collection, by State, 1970s-91, annual rpt, 6064–40
Drug abuse treatment, prevention, and enforcement grants by State, and State allocations by program, FY87-90, 6068–252
Drug enforcement grants to States, and allocations to local areas, by State, FY87-91, 236–3.1
Employment and payroll, by function, level of govt, and State, 1991, annual rpt, 2466–1.1
Expenditures (direct) and employment, by function and level of govt, selected years 1962-87, 10048–53
Finances of govts, by level of govt, State, and for large cities and counties, annual rpt series, 2466–2
Finances of govts, tax systems and revenue, and fiscal structure, by level of govt and State, 1992 and historical trends, annual rpt, 10044–1
Input-output structure of US economy, detailed interindustry transactions for 541 industries, and components of final demand, 1982 benchmark data, 2708–17
Law enforcement spending, employment, and payroll, by activity, level of govt, and State, FY90, annual rpt, 6066–25.50
Natl income and product accounts, comprehensive accounts and components, benchmark revisions, 1929-88, 2708–5
Natl income and product accounts, comprehensive accounts and components, *Survey of Current Business*, monthly rpt, 2702–1.26
Occupational safety enforcement activities of Federal and State agencies, inspections, closure orders, and violations contested and upheld, FY91, GAO rpt, 26121–461
Police agencies employment, spending, and operations, FY90, 6066–25.44
Prison and community-based facilities, population, employment, spending, and other characteristics, by State and for Fed Govt, 1990, annual rpt, 6064–26.3; 6068–218
Prison construction and operating costs, capacity, and inmates, for Federal and State facilities, 1985-89, GAO rpt, 26119–407
Sheriffs' agencies employment, spending, and operations, FY90, 6066–25.45
Truck and bus safety inspections of States, and vehicles and drivers ordered out of service, FY85-89, annual rpt, 7304–1.2
see also State police

State funding for social welfare
Blind persons by age, older blind persons by State, and State rehabilitation services, 1989, 21148–64
Child abuse and neglect prevention and treatment, and disabled infant protection, grants by State, FY91, annual listing, 4584–6
Child abuse and neglect prevention and treatment, discretionary grants, FY91, annual listing, 4584–9
Child day care and early childhood education programs availability, demand, use, costs, and provider and enrollee characteristics, 1990 survey, 4808–39
Child Support Enforcement Program collections for non-AFDC clients, administrative costs, and user fees, by State, with Federal shares of costs, 1990, GAO rpt, 26121–463
Employment and payroll, by function, level of govt, and State, 1991, annual rpt, 2466–1.1
Expenditures (direct) and employment, by function and level of govt, selected years 1962-87, 10048–53
Finances of govts, by level of govt, State, and for large cities and counties, annual rpt series, 2466–2
Finances of govts, tax systems and revenue, and fiscal structure, by level of govt and State, 1992 and historical trends, annual rpt, 10044–1
Foster care programs of States, Federal funding and children served, by State, 1981-89, hearing, 21788–208
Infant formula bid prices and contracts awarded by States under USDA food aid program for women, infants, and children, late 1980s-91, hearing, 25528–118
Input-output structure of US economy, detailed interindustry transactions for 541 industries, and components of final demand, 1982 benchmark data, 2708–17
Job Training Partnership Act State and local admin, funding, effectiveness, and participants, GAO rpt series, 26106–8
Natl income and product accounts, comprehensive accounts and components, benchmark revisions, 1929-88, 2708–5
Natl income and product accounts, comprehensive accounts and components, *Survey of Current Business*, monthly rpt, 2702–1.26
Unemployed displaced worker training programs spending, participation, and placements by State, 1990, GAO rpt, 26121–481
Vocational rehabilitation cases of State agencies, by disposition and State, FY91 and trends from FY21, annual rpt, 4944–5
Vocational rehabilitation programs of Fed Govt and States, activities and funding, FY91, annual rpt, 4944–1

see also Aid to Families with Dependent Children
see also Medicaid
see also Supplemental Security Income
see also Unemployment insurance
see also Workers compensation

State funding for transportation
Bus (intercity) deregulation in 1982, impacts on service, ridership, and State and Federal funding, with background data, 1980s-92, GAO rpt, 26113–583
Employment and payroll, by function, level of govt, and State, 1991, annual rpt, 2466–1.1
Expenditures (direct) and employment, by function and level of govt, selected years 1962-87, 10048–53
Finances of govts, by level of govt, State, and for large cities and counties, annual rpt series, 2466–2
Finances of govts, tax systems and revenue, and fiscal structure, by level of govt and State, 1992 and historical trends, annual rpt, 10044–1
Hwy funding, costs for completion, and mileage of Federal-aid system, by State, 1989-91 and projected to FY93, 21648–66
Hwy scenic routes and mileage, by govt ownership, land use and usage restrictions, and other characteristics, 1990, 7558–112
Hwy Statistics, detailed data by State, 1991, annual rpt, 7554–1
Hwy Statistics, summary data by State, 1990-91, annual rpt, 7554–24
Input-output structure of US economy, detailed interindustry transactions for 541 industries, and components of final demand, 1982 benchmark data, 2708–17
Mexico-US trade agreement impacts on truck traffic at border crossings, Customs Service staff needs, and hwy improvement costs, projected to 2000 with trends from 1986, GAO rpt, 26123–368
Natl income and product accounts, comprehensive accounts and components, benchmark revisions, 1929-88, 2708–5
Natl income and product accounts, comprehensive accounts and components, *Survey of Current Business*, monthly rpt, 2702–1.26
Rail rapid transit systems safety, operating, and funding characteristics, 1988-89, 9618–19
Transit systems finances and operations, by mode, size of fleet and urban area, region, and for 518 systems, 1990, annual rpt, 7884–4
Transit systems finances, equipment, and ridership characteristics, 1985-90, biennial rpt, 7884–8
User fees financing of transportation infrastructure, with data on hwys, airports, and waterways, 1985-91, 26306–6.170

State government
Budget balancing by State govts using pension funds, with data for 2 States, 1991 hearing, 21148–66
Finances of govts, by level of govt, State, and for large cities and counties, annual rpt series, 2466–2
Finances of govts, tax systems and revenue, and fiscal structure, by level of govt and State, 1992 and historical trends, annual rpt, 10044–1
Finances of State and local govts, revenue by source and outlays by type, 1987-91, annual article, 2702–1.311
Fiscal condition of State and local govts, with data by State and selected city, 1991 hearing, 21268–44
Public opinion on taxes, spending, and govt efficiency, by respondent characteristics, 1992 survey, annual rpt, 10044–2
Science and Engineering Indicators, employment, education, R&D funding, and industry impacts, with foreign comparisons, 1960s-91, biennial rpt, 9624–10
Securities issued by State and local govts and corporations, 1990, annual rpt, 9364–5.5
Statistical Abstract of US, 1992 annual data compilation, 2324–1.8; 2324–1.9
see also Census of Governments
see also Federal aid to States
see also Federal-State relations
see also Interstate compacts
see also Interstate relations
see also State and local employees
see also State and local employees pay
see also State and local taxes
see also State courts
see also State forests
see also State funding for economic development
see also State funding for education
see also State funding for health and hospitals
see also State funding for higher education
see also State funding for local areas
see also State funding for natural resources and conservation
see also State funding for public safety
see also State funding for social welfare
see also State funding for transportation
see also State government spending
see also State laws
see also State legislatures
see also State-local relations
see also State parks
see also State police
see also under By State in the "Index by Categories"
see also under names of individual States

State government spending
American Samoa govt finances, with data on health and farm spending and employment, mid 1980s-91, GAO rpt, 26123–385
Arts funding, by level of govt, State, and selected city, FY86-92, GAO rpt, 26119–371
Budget balances of States as share of outlays, and cost of Medicaid coverage expansion, FY89-92, hearing, 21408–129
Expenditures (direct) and employment, by function and level of govt, selected years 1962-87, 10048–53
Finances of govts, by level of govt, State, and for large cities and counties, annual rpt series, 2466–2
Finances of govts, tax systems and revenue, and fiscal structure, by level of govt and State, 1992 and historical trends, annual rpt, 10044–1
Finances of State and local govts, revenue by source and outlays by type, 1987-91, annual article, 2702–1.311
Finances of State and local govts, spending and Federal grants by function, 1960s-91 and proposed to 1997, article, 9362–1.309
Fiscal condition of State and local govts, with data by State and selected city, 1991 hearing, 21268–44
Flow-of-funds accounts, savings, investments, and credit statements, quarterly rpt, 9365–3.3
Gross State product impacts on govt spending, with data by industry div and State, 1960s-86, working paper, 9377–9.133
Natl income and product accounts, comprehensive accounts and components, benchmark revisions, 1929-88, 2708–5
Natl income and product accounts, comprehensive accounts and components, *Survey of Current Business*, monthly rpt, 2702–1.26
Palau admin, and social, economic, and govtl data, FY91, annual rpt, 7004–6
Science and Engineering Indicators, employment, education, R&D funding, and industry impacts, with foreign comparisons, 1960s-91, biennial rpt, 9624–10.4
see also Aid to Families with Dependent Children
see also Medicaid
see also Medical assistance
see also State funding for economic development
see also State funding for education
see also State funding for health and hospitals
see also State funding for higher education
see also State funding for local areas
see also State funding for natural resources and conservation
see also State funding for public safety
see also State funding for social welfare
see also State funding for transportation
see also Supplemental Security Income
see also Unemployment insurance
see also Workers compensation

State Hospital Data Project
Costs and use of hospitals, data compilation project analyses, series, 4186–6

State laws
AFDC provisions, by State, FY89-90, annual rpt, 4584–8
Black lung benefits and claims by State, trust fund receipts by source, and disbursements, 1991, annual rpt, 6504–3
Board and care home violations of State drug handling and dispensing regulations, for 3 metro areas, 1990-91, GAO rpt, 26121–447
Capital punishment sentencing provisions of States, 1990, annual rpt, 6064–26.6
Child day care and early childhood education programs availability, demand, use, costs, and provider and enrollee characteristics, 1990 survey, 4808–39
Child labor certification and injury reporting procedures of States, relation to proposed Federal guidelines, 1991, GAO rpt, 26121–451
Criminal law statutes of States, and public opinion, data compilation, 1992 annual rpt, 6064–6.1; 6064–6.2
Education (elementary and secondary) curricula, competency, and attendance requirements of States, with background data, 1970s-90, 4838–52

Finances of govts, tax systems and revenue, and fiscal structure, by level of govt and State, 1992 and historical trends, annual rpt, 10044–1
Great Lakes industrial water pollution emissions, comparison of State, EPA, Intl Joint Commission, and Ontario standards, 1991 rpt, 14648–29
Insurance (health) coverage of selected services, State mandates, 1990, 10176–3.2
Insurance (health) reforms of States to improve small business access, provisions with background data by State, 1991, GAO rpt, 26121–462
Labor laws enacted, by State, 1991, annual article, 6722–1.309
Medicaid coverage, eligibility, and payment provisions of States, as of March 1992, annual rpt, 4654–19
Nursing homes certification requirements, beds, and staff and training needs, by State, 1990, 17206–2.37
Supplemental Security Income and Medicaid eligibility and payment provisions, and beneficiaries living arrangements, by State, 1992, annual rpt, 4704–13
Unemployment insurance laws of States, changes in coverage, benefits, tax rates, and penalties, by State, 1991, annual article, 6722–1.311
Unemployment insurance programs of States, benefits, coverage, and tax provisions, as of July 1992, semiannual listing, 6402–7
Unemployment insurance programs of States, comparison of law provisions, as of Jan 1992, semiannual revisions to base edition, 6402–2
Vermont smoking laws compliance of employers, 1989, article, 4042–3.375
Workers compensation laws of States and Fed Govt, 1992 annual rpt, 6504–11
Workers compensation laws of States, changes in coverage, benefits, and premium rates, by State, 1991, annual article, 6722–1.310
Workers compensation programs of States, admin, coverage, benefits, finances, processing, and staff, 1988-91, annual rpt, 6504–9
see also Alcoholic beverages control laws
see also Financial institutions regulation
see also Traffic laws and courts

State legislatures
Statistical Abstract of US, 1992 annual data compilation, 2324–1.8

State-local relations
Boundary review commission activities in 12 States, 1989, 10048–85
see also State funding for local areas

State parks
Statistical Abstract of US, 1992 annual data compilation, 2324–1.7
Washington and Oregon coastal areas tourism and recreation facilities and economic impacts, by county, 1983-88, 5738–40.3
see also State forests

State police
Assaults and deaths of law enforcement officers, by circumstances, agency, victim and offender characteristics, and location, 1991, annual rpt, 6224–3
Drug enforcement activities of police and sheriff depts, and employee drug testing policies, 1990, 6066–19.67
Employment and payroll, by activity, level of govt, and State, FY90, annual rpt, 6066–25.50
Employment and spending for law enforcement, by activity and level of govt, data compilation, 1992 annual rpt, 6064–6.1
Employment, funding, data collection, and other activities of State criminal justice systems, by State, 1970s-91, annual rpt, 6064–40
Employment of State and local law enforcement personnel and officers, by sex, population size, census div, and jurisdiction, as of Oct 1991, annual rpt, 6224–2.3
Employment, spending, and operations, for State, city, county, and special district police agencies, 1990, annual rpt, 6064–39
Employment, spending, and operations of law enforcement agencies, FY90, 6066–25.44

State taxation
see State and local taxes

States
see terms beginning with State
see under By State in the "Index by Categories"
see under names of individual States

States, Alan E.
"Canola and the Common Market, A Producer's Perspective", 1504–9.1

States' rights
see Federal-State relations

Statistical programs and activities
Agricultural data collection, Economic Research Service activities, funding, and staff, by branch, planned FY92, annual rpt, 1504–6
Agricultural data collection, methodology, and use, for major time series of USDA, series, 1506–1
BLS major economic indicators, methodology, and time series revisions, transcripts of BLS Commissioner's monthly testimony, periodic rpt, 23846–4
Cancer cases among Indians, and racial misclassification in Natl Cancer Inst registry, 1974-89, article, 4472–1.324
Cancer clinical trials quality-of-life data collection, patient compliance rate, 1988-91 local area studies, article, 4472–1.326
Cancer death rates and annual change, by body site, sex, and race, comparability of local registry and natl data, 1975-88, article, 4472–1.320
Cancer Natl Inst epidemiology and biometry activities, FY91, annual rpt, 4474–29
Census Bur activities, rpts, and user services, monthly rpt, 2302–3
Census Bur data collection and statistical program plans, advisory committees findings and recommendations, 1992 conf, 2628–35
Census Bur data collection methodology, programs, and measurement techniques, technical paper series, 2626–2
Census Bur data coverage and availability for economic censuses and related statistics, 1992 preliminary guide, 2308–5
Census Bur data files and rpts, coverage and availability, 1992 annual listing, 2304–2
Census Bur planning for 2000 decennial census and economic statistics program improvement, FY92 budget proposals, hearing, 21628–98
Census Bur rpts and data files, coverage, availability, and use, series, 2326–7
Computer systems purchase and use, and data recording, processing, and transfer, Fed Govt standards, series, 2216–2
Crime and criminal justice data collection, methodology, and use, technical rpt series, 6066–23
Crime and criminal justice research results, series, 6066–20
Crime, criminal justice admin and enforcement, and public opinion, data compilation, 1992 annual rpt, 6064–6
Criminal justice systems of States, activities, employment, funding, and data collection, by State, 1970s-91, annual rpt, 6064–40
Developing countries family planning and population activities of AID, grants by project and recipient, and contraceptive shipments, by country, FY91, annual rpt series, 9914–13
DOE data collection forms and related rpts, 1991, annual listing, 3164–86
Drug abuse indicators for selected metro areas, research results, data collection, and policy issues, 1992 semiannual conf, 4492–5
Education data collection, processing, and reporting standards, 1991 narrative rpt, 4828–41
Educational performance, higher education instns data collection activities, by instn level and control, 1991, 4848–45
Electric utilities conservation programs data reporting guidelines, with background data, 1991 rpt, 3308–101
Employment and economic conditions, alternative BLS projections to 2005 and trends 1975-90, biennial rpt, 6744–19
Employment Cost Index methodology, occupational definitions, and coverage, quarterly press release, 6782–5
Energy Info Admin activities, 1991, annual rpt, 3164–29
Farm income accounts of USDA, State-level expense data sources and adjustment factors, 1990, article, 1541–1.313
Fed Govt financial and nonfinancial domestic aid, 1992 base edition, annual listing, 104–5
Fed Govt info collection effects of Paperwork Reduction Act, with respondent burden, OMB reviews, violations, and major info systems proposals, 1981-92, annual rpt, 104–26
Fed Govt statistical programs funding by agency, and BLS programs improvement spending, 1991 hearing, 23848–227
Fed Reserve data concordance for *Federal Reserve Bulletin* and *Annual Statistical Digest*, 1990 annual rpt, 9364–8
Fed Reserve System statistical series additions and revisions, monthly rpt with articles, 9362–1
Glaciology intl research summaries, methodology, and bibls, series, 2156–18
Health and vital statistics data collection, and use for planning and evaluation, 1989 biennial conf papers, 4164–2

Health Care Financing Admin research activities and grants, by program, FY91, annual listing, 4654–10
Health data collection and availability, by country, 1991, biennial listing, 4124–8
HHS financial aid, by program, recipient, State, and city, FY91, annual regional listings, 4004–3
Juvenile facilities population, by resident characteristics and facility type, 1977-89, annual rpt, 6064–35
Labor force and economic data series of BLS, collection, analysis, and presentation methods, by program, 1992 rpt, 6888–1
Labor turnover, job openings, and new hires and wages, pilot survey results, costs, and methodology, 1990-91, 6728–40
Medicare payment of physicians, payment reforms impact on service availability, monitoring activity, 1991, annual rpt, 17266–1.5
Medicare payment of physicians, reforms impacts on services, and monitoring methods, 1992 annual rpt, 4004–34
Medicare payment of physicians, vulnerable beneficiaries services use prior to fee schedule implementation, 1986-90, annual rpt, 17266–1.8
Minerals Yearbook, data collection and availability, annual rpt, discontinued, 5604–48
Natl Hwy Traffic Safety Admin activities and grants, and fatal traffic accident data, 1990, annual rpt, 7764–1
OASDHI programs actuarial studies, series, 4706–2
OASDI beneficiary data collection system design compared to earlier surveys, with summary results, 1992 article, 4742–1.313
OASDI data file on 10% of beneficiaries, description and use, 1992 article, 4742–1.309
Oil and gas OCS reserves, geophysical data collection activities and costs, by region, 1976-90, 5738–41
Oil products supply, EIA and alternative estimates, 1981-90, annual article, 3162–6.302
Older population data sources of Fed Govt, interagency forum activities, and contacts, 1989-90, annual rpt, 14324–1
Pain and pain-related conditions, data available from NCHS, with bibl, 1992 rpt, 4147–1.27
Population and reproduction research, Fed Govt funding by project, FY90, annual listing, 4474–9
Poverty income guidelines and derivation, by family size, 1992 with trends from 1965, article, 4742–1.310
Vital and Health Statistics series and other NCHS rpts, 1990-91, annual listing, 4124–1
Vital and Health Statistics series: methodology, survey design, and data evaluation, 4147–2
Vital and Health Statistics series: program and data collection procedures, 4147–1
Wetlands (coastal) mapping projects status, costs, and methods, 1990 conf, 5508–116
see also Business outlook and attitude surveys
see also Classifications
see also Computer data file guides
see also Consumer surveys
see also Economic and econometric models
see also Mathematic models and modeling
see also Methodology
see also Opinion and attitude surveys
see also Seasonal adjustment factors
see also Statisticians
see also under names of individual surveys (listed under Surveys)

Statisticians
Labor demand, turnover, and training completions, by detailed occupation, 1990 and projected to 2005, biennial rpt, 6744–3
Occupational Outlook Handbook, 1992-93, biennial rpt, 6744–1

Steel industry
see Iron and steel industry

Steele, Christine E.
"Full-Time Federal Civilian Employment in White- and Blue-Collar Occupations as of Sept. 30, 1991", 9842–1.302
"Profile of the 'Typical' Federal Civilian Employee, Sept. 30, 1991", 9842–1.301

Stefanski, Robert J.
"Potential El Nino Impacts on U.S. Feed Grain Production", 1561–4.302

Steinberg, Doug
"Inventory of Parks and Recreation Facilities on the Coast of Washington and Oregon", 5738–40.3

Steindel, Charles
"Industry Productivity and High-Tech Investment", 9385–8.130
"Manufacturing Productivity and High-Tech Investment", 9385–1.310

Steller, Rose M.
"Live Sheep and Meat of Sheep, Industry and Trade Summary", 9885–8.1

Stephan, James J.
"Census of State and Federal Correctional Facilities, 1990", 6068–218

Steppleton, Carolyn D.
"Georgia's Timber Industry—An Assessment of Timber Product Output and Use, 1989", 1208–393

Sterilization
see Sexual sterilization

Steroids
see Hormones

Stevedores
see Longshoremen

Stevens, E. J.
"Comparing Central Banks' Rulebooks", 9377–1.307

Stewart, Jean E.
"Composition of Foods. Baked Products: Raw, Processed, Prepared", 1356–3.18

Stewart, Kenneth J.
"Energy, Food Prices Helped Slow Inflation in 1991", 6722–1.322

Stinson, Frederick S.
"U.S. Alcohol Epidemiologic Data Reference Manual. Volume 4: Hospital Discharges with Alcohol-Related Conditions, Hospital Discharge Survey, 1979-85", 4488–10.5

Stipe, Lawrence E.
"Montana Forest Pest Conditions and Program Highlights, 1991", 1206–49.3

Stock exchanges
Business statistics, detailed data for major industries and economic indicators, 1960-91, *Survey of Current Business* biennial supplement, 2704–1
County Business Patterns, 1989: employment, establishments, and payroll, by SIC 2- to 4-digit industry and county, annual State rpt series, 2326–8
County Business Patterns, 1990: employment, establishments, and payroll, by SIC 2- to 4-digit industry and county, annual State rpt series, 2326–6
Index futures exchange activity in NYC, Chicago, and other futures markets, biweekly rpt, 11922–5
Prices, trading, and customer financing, 1990, annual rpt, 9364–5.4
Statistical Abstract of US, 1992 annual data compilation, 2324–1.16
Tax (income) returns of corporations, income and tax items by asset size and detailed industry, 1989, annual rpt, 8304–4; 8304–21
Trading volume, securities listed by type, and finances, by exchange, selected years 1938-90, annual rpt, 9734–2.1; 9734–2.2
see also American Stock Exchange
see also New York Stock Exchange
see also Securities

Stock, James H.
"Procedure for Predicting Recessions with Leading Indicators: Econometric Issues and Recent Performance", 9375–13.84

Stock market
see American Stock Exchange
see New York Stock Exchange
see Securities
see Stock exchanges
see Stockbrokers

Stockbrokers
Arbitration of securities disputes between brokers and investors, outcomes related to forum type and other factors, 1992 GAO rpt, 26119–401
Assets and liabilities of stockbrokers, 1990, annual rpt, 9364–5.13
County Business Patterns, 1989: employment, establishments, and payroll, by SIC 2- to 4-digit industry and county, annual State rpt series, 2326–8
County Business Patterns, 1990: employment, establishments, and payroll, by SIC 2- to 4-digit industry and county, annual State rpt series, 2326–6
Credit (securities) issues of stockbrokers and other nonbank lenders, and brokers balance sheet, as of June 1991, annual rpt, 9365–5.1
Employment, earnings, and hours, by SIC 1- to 4-digit industry, monthly 1989-Feb 1992, annual rpt, 6744–4
Finances and operations, by SIC 2- to 4-digit industry, forecast 1992, annual rpt, 2044–28
Finances of stockbrokers, 1986-90, annual rpt, 9734–2.1
Flow-of-funds accounts, savings, investments, and credit statements, quarterly rpt, 9365–3.3
Households financial services use, by account type and instn type and location, 1989 survey, article, 9362–1.303
Input-output structure of US economy, detailed interindustry transactions for 541 industries, and components of final demand, 1982 benchmark data, 2708–17
Intl financial markets performance of foreign and US bank and securities firms, finances and competitiveness issues, 1980s, compilation of papers, 9385–10

Mail volume to and from households, use, and views, by class, source, content, and household characteristics, FY87-90, annual rpt, 9864–10
Multinatl firms US affiliates finances and operations, by industry, country of parent firm, and State, 1987, 2708–48
Occupational injury and illness rates, by SIC 2- to 4-digit industry, 1989-90, annual rpt, 6844–7
Occupational injury and illness rates, by SIC 2- to 4-digit industry, 1990, annual rpt, 6844–1
Occupational Outlook Handbook, 1992-93, biennial rpt, 6744–1
Regulatory activity and finances of Securities Investor Protection Corp, 1970s-91, GAO rpt, 26119–419
Savings instns failure resolution activity of Resolution Trust Corp, brokered deposits, fees, and interest rates by instn and region, as of July 1991, hearing, 21248–171
Securities purchases, sales, and holdings, by issuer and type and ownership of security, monthly listing, 9732–2
Tax (income) returns of corporations, income and tax items by asset size and detailed industry, 1989, annual rpt, 8304–4; 8304–21
Tax (income) returns of partnerships, income statement and balance sheet items, by industry group, 1990, annual article, 8302–2.314
Tax (income) returns of sole proprietorships, income statement items, by industry group, 1990, annual article, 8302–2.317; 8302–2.320
Tax (income) withholding and related documents filed, by type and IRS service center, 1991 and projected 1992-99, annual rpt, 8304–22

Stockpiling
Mineral Industry Surveys, commodity reviews of production, trade, stocks, and use, monthly rpt series, 5612–1
Mineral Industry Surveys, commodity reviews of production, trade, use, and industry operations, advance annual rpt series, 5614–5
Minerals production, prices, trade, use, employment, tariffs, and stockpiles, by mineral, with foreign comparisons, 1987-91, annual rpt, 5604–18
Strategic material stockpile inventories and needs, by commodity, 1992, annual rpt, 3544–37
Strategic material stockpiling by Fed Govt, activity, and inventory by commodity, as of Sept 1991, semiannual rpt, 3542–22
see also Naval Petroleum Reserves
see also Strategic Petroleum Reserve

Stocks
see Agricultural stocks
see Business inventories
see Coal stocks
see Energy stocks and inventories
see Options trading
see Petroleum stocks
see Securities
see Stock exchanges
see Stockbrokers
see Stockpiling

Stockton, Calif.
see also under By City and By SMSA or MSA in the "Index by Categories"

Stockwell, Heather G.
"Environmental Tobacco Smoke and Lung Cancer Risk in Nonsmoking Women", 4472–1.342

Stoddard, Susan
"Chartbook on Work Disability in the U.S.", 4948–11

Stone, Michael P.
"Strategic Force, Strategic Vision for the 1990s and Beyond. A Statement on the Posture of the U.S. Army, FY93", 3704–13

Stone products and quarries
Business statistics, detailed data for major industries and economic indicators, *Survey of Current Business*, monthly rpt, 2702–1.20
Business statistics, detailed data for major industries and economic indicators, 1960-91, *Survey of Current Business* biennial supplement, 2704–1
Capital expenditures for plant and equipment, by major industry group, quarterly rpt, 2502–2
Collective bargaining agreements expiring during year, and workers covered, by firm, union, industry group, and State, 1992, annual rpt, 6784–9
County Business Patterns, 1989: employment, establishments, and payroll, by SIC 2- to 4-digit industry and county, annual State rpt series, 2326–8
County Business Patterns, 1990: employment, establishments, and payroll, by SIC 2- to 4-digit industry and county, annual State rpt series, 2326–6
Drug abuse screening and employee aid programs activities and policies in mining, by mineral and firm size, 1989, 6668–8
Employment, earnings, and hours, by SIC 1- to 4-digit industry, monthly 1989-Feb 1992, annual rpt, 6744–4
Employment, unemployment, and labor force characteristics, by region and census div, 1991, annual rpt, 6744–7.1
Energy use and prices, by fuel type and manufacturing industry, 1974-88, 3166–15.3
Energy use and prices for manufacturing industries, 1988 survey, series, 3166–13
Exports and imports between US and outlying areas, by detailed commodity and mode of transport, 1991, annual rpt, 2424–11
Exports and imports of US, by country and detailed commodity, monthly rpt, 2422–12
Exports and imports of US, by Harmonized System 6-digit commodity and country, 1991, annual rpt, 2424–13
Exports and imports of US, by transport mode, country, and SITC 1- to 3-digit commodity, 1991, annual rpt, 2424–12
Exports of US, detailed commodities by country, monthly CD-ROM, 2422–13
Exports of US, detailed Schedule B commodities with countries of destination, 1991, annual rpt, 2424–10
Foreign countries mineral production, reserves, and industry role in domestic economy and world supply, world area and country rpt series, 5606–1
Freight (waterborne domestic and foreign) by commodity, traffic, and passengers, by port and waterway, 1989, annual rpt, 3754–3
Hazardous substances industrial releases and reduction methods under EPA regulation, by chemical, source, industry, and location, 1989, annual rpt, 9234–6
Hazardous substances industrial releases and reduction methods under EPA regulation, with chemical stocks and use, facility directory, 1987-89, annual CD-ROM, 9234–7
Hwy construction material use by type, and spending, by State, 1940s-91, annual rpt, 7554–29
Imports, exports, and employment impacts, by SIC 2- to 4-digit industry and commodity, quarterly rpt, 2322–2
Imports of US, detailed commodities by country, monthly CD-ROM, 2422–14
Input-output structure of US economy, detailed interindustry transactions for 84 industries, and components of final demand, 1987, annual article, 2702–1.316
Input-output structure of US economy, detailed interindustry transactions for 541 industries, and components of final demand, 1982 benchmark data, 2708–17
Labor productivity, indexes of output, hours, and employment by SIC 2- to 4-digit industry, 1967-90, annual rpt, 6824–1.2
Limestone (crushed) from Mexico at less than fair value, injury to US industry, investigation with background financial and operating data, 1992 rpt, 9886–14.353
Manufacturing annual survey, 1990: finances and operations, by SIC 2- to 4-digit industry, series, 2506–14
Manufacturing census, 1987: concentration of largest firms measured by value added, and for shipments by SIC 2- and 4-digit industry, subject rpt, 2497–6
Manufacturing industries operations and performance, analytical rpt series, 2506–16
Manufacturing production, shipments, inventories, orders, and pollution control costs, periodic Current Industrial Rpt series, 2506–3
Mexico imports from US, by industry and State, 1987-91, 2048–154
Mineral Industry Surveys, commodity review of production, trade, stocks, and use, quarterly rpt, 5612–2.20
Mineral Industry Surveys, commodity reviews of production, trade, use, and industry operations, advance annual rpt series, 5614–5
Mineral Industry Surveys, State reviews of production, 1991, preliminary annual rpt, 5614–6
Minerals Yearbook, Vol 1, 1989: commodity reviews of production, use, trade, prices, and mining operations, annual rpt, 5604–33
Minerals Yearbook, Vol 1, 1990: commodity review of production, reserves, supply, use, and trade, annual rpt, 5604–20.1; 5604–20.55
Minerals Yearbook, Vol 2, 1989: State reviews of production and sales by commodity, and business activity, annual rpt series, 5604–16

Minerals Yearbook, Vol 2, 1990: State reviews of production and sales by commodity, and business activity, annual rpt series, 5604–22
Minerals Yearbook, Vol 3, 1989: foreign country reviews of production, trade, and policy, by commodity, annual rpt, 5604–35
Multinatl firms US affiliates finances and operations, by industry, country of parent firm, and State, 1987, 2708–48
Multinatl US firms and foreign affiliates finances and operations, by industry and country, 1989 benchmark survey, annual rpt, 2704–5
Occupational injuries and incidence, employment, and hours in stone mines and related operations, 1990, annual rpt, 6664–5
Occupational injuries by circumstances, employment, and hours, for mining industries by type of operation and State, quarterly rpt, 6662–1
Occupational injury and illness rates, by SIC 2- to 4-digit industry, 1989-90, annual rpt, 6844–7
Occupational injury and illness rates, by SIC 2- to 4-digit industry, 1990, annual rpt, 6844–1
Ohio River basin waterway facilities, freight by commodity and port, and recreation, by waterway, 1988-89, annual rpt, 3754–6
Pacific territories population and housing detailed characteristics, by location, 1990 Census of Population and Housing, series, 2551–8
Pollution abatement capital and operating costs, by SIC 2- to 4-digit industry and State, 1990, annual Current Industrial Rpt, 2506–3.6
Price indexes (producer) and sales of building materials, by type, quarterly rpt, 2042–1.5; 2042–1.6
Price indexes (producer), by stage of processing and detailed commodity, monthly rpt, 6762–6
Price indexes (producer), by stage of processing and detailed commodity, monthly 1991, annual rpt, 6764–2
Production, prices, trade, use, employment, tariffs, and stockpiles, by mineral, with foreign comparisons, 1987-91, annual rpt, 5604–18
Production, trade, use, and foreign investment in US industry, for minerals, 1985-90 and projected to 2000, annual rpt, 5304–5
Science, engineering, and technical employment in manufacturing, by field and industry, 1989, triennial rpt, 9627–23
Tariff Schedule of US, classifications and rates of duty by detailed imported commodity, 1993 base edition, 9886–13
Tax (income) returns of corporations, income and tax items by asset size and detailed industry, 1989, annual rpt, 8304–4; 8304–21
Tax (income) returns of sole proprietorships, income statement items, by industry group, 1990, annual article, 8302–2.317; 8302–2.320
see also Abrasive materials
see also Cement and concrete
see also Oil shale
see also Phosphate
see also Potash
see also Sand and gravel
see also under By Industry in the "Index by Categories"

Stone, Roy B.
"Floods of December 1982 to May 1983 in the Central and Southern Mississippi River and the Gulf of Mexico Basins", 5666–27.33

Stonitsch, Laura A.
"Construction and Mining Equipment, Industry and Trade Summary", 9885–9.2

Storage
see Agricultural stocks
see Cold storage and refrigeration
see Grain storage and facilities
see Packaging and containers
see Stockpiling
see Warehouses

Storm, Hans H.
"Adjuvant Radiotherapy and Risk of Contralateral Breast Cancer", 4472–1.333
"Cancer Incidence Among Danish Thorotrast-Exposed Patients", 4472–1.338

Storms
Coastal areas environmental conditions and mgmt, for individual areas, conf series, 2146–8
Farm water supply, crop moisture, and drought indexes, weekly rpt, seasonal data, 2182–7
Farmland damaged by natural disaster, Emergency Conservation Program aid and participation by State, FY91, annual rpt, 1804–22
Foreign countries disasters, casualties, damage, and aid by US and others, FY91 and trends from FY64, annual rpt, 9914–12
Hurricane Andrew atmospheric pressure, wind speeds, deaths, and damage, by location, Aug 1992, article, 2152–8.304
Hurricane Bob atmospheric pressure and wind speeds, by location, Aug 1991, article, 2152–8.301
Hurricane Hugo damage to timber resources in South Carolina, inventory by county, species, and damage class, as of 1990, 1208–411
Hurricane Hugo disaster loan offices of SBA, staff and salary and support costs, for Puerto Rico and Virgin Islands, 1989-91, GAO rpt, 26113–576
Hurricanes and tropical storms in Pacific and Indian Oceans, paths and surveillance, 1991, annual rpt, 3804–8
Hurricanes in northwest Atlantic Ocean, correlation with Sahel Africa rainfall, 1947-90, 2148–61
Incidents and mgmt of disasters and natl security threats, with data by major event and State, 1992 annual rpt, 9434–6
Lightning and other causes of wildfires, and acreage burned, by type of land, ownership, region, and State, 1984-90, annual rpt, 1204–4
Mariners Weather Log, quarterly journal, 2152–8
Precipitation and temperature for US and foreign locations, major events and anomalies, weekly rpt, 2182–6
Statistical Abstract of US, 1992 annual data compilation, 2324–1.6
Weather phenomena and storm characteristics, casualties, and property damage, by State, monthly listing, 2152–3
Weather trends and deviations, by world region, 1880s-1990, annual chartbook, 2184–9
see also Floods

Straka, John W.
"Demand for Older Workers: The Neglected Side of a Labor Market", 4746–14.16; 4746–26.21

Strand, John A.
"Monitoring of Olympic National Park Beaches To Determine Fate and Effects of Spilled Bunker C Fuel Oil", 5738–38.1

Strategic Arms Reduction Talks
Soviet Union and US START treaty, protocols, and nuclear systems inventory agreements, as of 1990, 9828–26
Status of arms control treaties and agreements, and Arms Control and Disarmament Agency activities, 1991, annual rpt, 9824–2

Strategic materials
Bismuth reserves, production, and US trade, by country, and US consumption by end use, 1980s-90, 5608–175
Mineral Industry Surveys, commodity reviews of production, trade, stocks, and use, monthly rpt series, 5612–1
Mineral Industry Surveys, commodity reviews of production, trade, use, and industry operations, advance annual rpt series, 5614–5
Minerals (strategic) supply and characteristics of individual deposits, by country, commodity rpt series, 5666–21
Minerals production, reserves, and industry role in domestic economy and world supply, 1991 world area rpt, 5606–1.19
North Central States strategic minerals deposits, characteristics, 1992 compilation of papers, 5668–127
Nuclear material inventory discrepancies at DOE and contractor facilities, 1990/91, annual rpt, 3344–2
Prices of sensitive materials, and indexes, *Survey of Current Business*, cyclical indicators, monthly rpt, 2702–1.1
Statistical Abstract of US, 1992 annual data compilation, 2324–1.25
see also Naval Petroleum Reserves
see also Stockpiling
see also Strategic Petroleum Reserve
see also Uranium

Strategic Petroleum Reserve
Capacity, inventory, fill rate, and finances of SPR, quarterly rpt, 3002–13
Contractor computer system security and controls at SPR offices, 1991, 3006–5.27
Crude oil imports, domestic deliveries, and stocks, 1977-91, annual rpt, 3164–74.2
Crude oil specifications and physical and chemical analyses results, for SPR, 1991, 3338–5
Energy supply, demand, and prices, forecasts by resource type, quarterly rpt, 3162–34
Military Sealift Command shipping operations, finances, and personnel, FY91, annual rpt, 3804–14

Natl Energy Strategy SPR and energy efficiency issues, 1991 hearings, 21368–142
Oil imports and withdrawals from stocks, monthly rpt, 3162–24.3
Oil imports and withdrawals from stocks, monthly 1973-88, 3168–123.3
Persian Gulf War crude oil drawdowns from SPR, contract deliveries by purchasing firm, 1st quarter 1991, quarterly rpt, supplement, 3002–13
Property (real) of DOE owned and leased, by type, subagency, contractor, and site, FY91, annual rpt, 3004–28
Statistical Abstract of US, 1992 annual data compilation, 2324–1.19
Supply and demand of oil and refined products, refinery capacity and use, and prices, weekly rpt, 3162–32
Supply, demand, and movement of crude oil, gas liquids, and refined products, by PAD district and State, 1991, annual rpt, 3164–2
Supply, demand, and prices, by fuel type and end-use sector, alternative projections 1990-2010, annual rpt, 3164–75

Stratosphere
Global climate change contributing pollutants, atmospheric concentrations by location, and monitoring activities, 1990, annual rpt, 2144–28
Ozone depletion in stratosphere over Northern Hemisphere, by latitude band, 1969-86, GAO rpt, 26113–562
Ozone depletion in stratosphere, USDA competitive research grants by recipient, FY91, annual rpt, 1764–1
Weather conditions and forecasts, data collection and analysis issues, 1991 annual conf, 2184–10
Weather trends and deviations, by world region, 1880s-1990, annual chartbook, 2184–9

Straw, J. Ashley, Jr.
"American Woodcock Harvest and Breeding Population Status, 1992", 5504–11

Strawberries
see Fruit and fruit products

Streams
see Rivers and waterways

Streetcars
see Urban transportation

Streets
see Highways, streets, and roads

Stress
Cancer (breast) screening use relation to cancer anxiety, for high-risk women, 1992 article, 4472–1.301
Employee electronic monitoring effects on mental and physical health and job satisfaction, for local telephone company workers, 1989, hearings, 21348–122
Health condition and care indicators, 1950s-90 with health improvement and disease prevention goals for 1990, annual data compilation, 4144–11
Indian and Alaska Native youth health condition and behavioral patterns, by sex and grade, 1988-90, 4088–3

Strickland, Roger
"Calculating State-Level Estimates of USDA's Farm Income Accounts", 1541–1.313
"Ranking of States and Commodities by Cash Receipts, 1990", 1548–385
"Value-Added for the U.S. Agricultural Sector", 1541–1.321
"Why U.S. Farm Income Is Record High", 1541–1.302

Strikes and lockouts
see Work stoppages

Stroke
see Cerebrovascular diseases

Strongin, Steven
"Market Structure, Technology, and the Cyclicality of Output", 9375–13.70

Student aid
African Dev Foundation dev grants and fellowships, by country, FY84-91, annual rpt, 9034–1
Allergy and Infectious Diseases Natl Inst activities, grants by recipient and location, and disease cases, FY84-91, annual rpt, 4474–30
Arts Natl Endowment activities and grants, FY91, annual rpt, 9564–3
Assistance (financial and nonfinancial) of Fed Govt, 1992 base edition, annual listing, 104–5
Assistance and other sources of support, with student expenses and characteristics, by instn type and control, 1987 study, series, 4846–3; 4846–5
Assistance of Fed Govt, by type, program, agency, and State, FY91, annual rpt, 2464–2
Benefits overpayment recovery and judgment enforcement cases filed in Federal district courts, 1991, annual rpt, 18204–8.14
Black higher education instns enrollment, finances, staff, and degrees, by instn and selected student characteristics, 1970s-90, 4848–46
Condition of Education, detail for elementary, secondary, and higher education, 1920s-91 and projected to 2002, annual rpt, 4824–1
Correspondence schools guaranteed student loan participation and default rates, FY87-89, GAO rpt, 26121–448
Credit availability relation to college attainment, model description and results, 1991 working paper, 6886–6.92
Degree (PhD) recipients in higher education, by field and selected characteristics, 1979, 1984, and 1989, 4848–44
Dental Research Natl Inst research and training grants, by recipient, FY90, annual listing, 4474–19
Education Dept financial aid programs, 1992 annual listing, 4804–3
Expenditures and participation, by Federal student aid program, instn type and control, and State, annual rpt, discontinued, 4804–28
Expenditures for education by Federal agency, program, and recipient type, and instn spending, 1960s-91, annual rpt, 4824–8
Expenditures for student aid supplemental grants, loans, and work-study awards, Federal shares by instn and State, 1992/93, annual listing, 4804–17
Flow-of-funds accounts, savings, investments, and credit statements, quarterly rpt, 9365–3.3
Fraud and abuse in Education Dept programs, audits and investigations, 2nd half FY92, semiannual rpt, 4802–1
Fulbright-Hays academic exchanges, grants by purpose, and foreign govt share of costs, by country, FY91, annual rpt, 10324–1
Goldwater, Barry, Scholarship Foundation awards and finances, FY87-91, annual rpt, 10404–1
Guaranteed student loan activity, by program, guarantee agency, and State, quarterly rpt, 4802–2
Guaranteed student loan activity under Stafford program, Education Dept collection of lender origination fees, 1980s-91, GAO rpt, 26121–467
Guaranteed student loan Stafford program, borrowers and likelihood of default by selected characteristics, 1989-90, 26306–3.120
Guaranteed student loans, defaults, and collections, by type of loan, lender, and guarantee agency, with data by State and top lender, FY91, annual rpt, 4804–38
Health care professionals supply and education, by professional and other characteristics, and location, 1960s-92 and projected to 2020, biennial rpt, 4114–8
Health sciences research and training grants and contracts of Natl Inst of General Medical Sciences, by program, FY91, annual rpt, 4474–38
Heart, Lung, and Blood Natl Inst activities, and grants by recipient and location, FY91 and disease trends from 1940, annual rpt, 4474–15
HHS financial aid, by program, recipient, State, and city, FY91, annual regional listings, 4004–3
Higher education enrollment, faculty, finances, and degrees, by instn level and control, and State, FY88, annual rpt, 4844–13
Higher education instn revenue by source and spending by function, by State and instn control, FY82-90, annual rpt, 4844–6
Higher education instn tuition, fees, and student aid awards, by State, late 1950s-92, annual rpt, 4824–2.22
Higher education instn undergrad research grants of NSF, administrator and recipient characteristics and views, 1987-89, 9628–86
Humanities Natl Endowment activities and grants, FY91, annual rpt, 9564–2
Income (household, family, and personal), by source, detailed characteristics, and region, 1991, annual Current Population Rpt, 2546–6.76
Indian education funding of Fed Govt, with enrollment, program grants, and fellowships by State, 1980s-FY91, annual rpt, 14874–1
Indian Health Service employment of Indians and non-Indians, training, hires, and quits, by occupation, FY90, annual rpt, 4084–6
Inter-American Foundation activities, grants by recipient, and fellowships, by country, FY91, annual rpt, 14424–1
Latin America dev grants of Inter-American Foundation by program area, and fellowships by field and instn, by country, FY72-91, annual rpt, 14424–2
Library science training grants for disadvantaged students, by instn and State, FY91, annual listing, 4874–1

Loan activity of savings instns insured by Savings Assn Insurance Fund by FHLB district and State, and for FDIC-insured savings banks, 1989, annual rpt, 8434–1
Loans and loan guarantees of Fed Govt, outstanding amounts by agency and program, *Treasury Bulletin*, quarterly rpt, 8002–4.11
Loans of Fed Govt to students, defaults, losses, and rates, by instn and State, as of June 1991, annual rpt, 4804–18
Maritime academy students receiving Fed Govt aid, monthly rpt, 7702–1
Military health care personnel, and accessions by training source, by occupation, specialty, and service branch, FY90, annual rpt, 3544–24
Military training and education programs funding, staff, students, and facilities, by service branch, FY93, annual rpt, 3504–5
Minority group targeted student aid, higher education instns with awards and funding sources, by instn level and control, 1989/90, hearings, 21408–130
NIH grants and contracts, by inst and type of recipient, FY82-91, annual rpt, 4434–9
NIH grants and contracts, quarterly listing, 4432–1
NIH research and training grants awarded to women, by recipient characteristics, inst, and host instn, FY90, annual rpt, 4434–18
NSF grants and contracts, by field, recipient, and State, FY90, annual rpt, 9624–26
Peace Inst activities and finances, FY90-91, biennial rpt, 29594–1
Pell grants and applicants, by tuition, family and student income, instn type and control, and State, 1990/91, annual rpt, 4804–1
Perkins student loan program income, losses, and Federal and school contributions, late 1950s-89, GAO rpt, 26121–440
Reproduction and population research, Natl Inst of Child Health and Human Dev funding and activities, 1991, annual rpt, 4474–33
Science and engineering enrollment, performance, curricula, student aid sources, and career plans, by sex and race, 1970s-91, biennial rpt, 9624–20.2
Science and engineering grad enrollment, by field, source of funds, and characteristics of student and instn, 1990, annual rpt, 9627–7
Science and Engineering Indicators, employment, education, R&D funding, and industry impacts, with foreign comparisons, 1960s-91, biennial rpt, 9624–10
Science fellowship and traineeship funding of Fed Govt, by field, instn, agency, and State, FY90, annual rpt, 9627–17
Statistical Abstract of US, 1992 annual data compilation, 2324–1.4
Student Loan Marketing Assn activities and finances, 1991, annual rpt, 9784–1
Supplemental and parent loans and defaults, for freshmen and other students, by whether proprietary instn, FY89-91, GAO rpt, 26121–473
Truman, Harry S, Scholarship Foundation finances, and awards by student characteristics, FY91, annual rpt, 14314–1
Truman, Harry S, Scholarship Fund receipts by source, transfers, and investment holdings and transactions, monthly rpt, 14312–1
US attorneys civil and criminal cases by type and disposition, and collections, by Federal district, FY91, annual rpt, 6004–2.1; 6004–2.5
see also School lunch and breakfast programs
see also Veterans education
see also Work-study programs

Student Community Service Program
Activities and funding of ACTION, by program, FY91, annual rpt, 9024–2

Student discipline
Crime victimization in schools, drug availability, and preventive measures, with student views, 1989 survey, 6066–3.46
Digest of Education Statistics, 1992 annual data compilation, 4824–2
Discrimination in education, natl survey participation and data coverage, school district administrators views, 1991 survey, 4826–1.33
Eighth grade class of 1988: educational performance and conditions, characteristics, attitudes, activities, and plans, natl longitudinal survey, series, 4826–9
Elementary and secondary schools, teachers, staff, and enrollment, by selected characteristics, 1987/88-88/89, 4836–3.10
High school dropout rates, and subsequent completion, by student and school characteristics, alternative estimates, 1991, annual rpt, 4834–23
Natl Education Goals progress indicators, by State, 1992, annual rpt, 15914–1
Principals views on safety, discipline, and student drug use, for elementary and secondary schools, 1991 survey, 4826–1.32
Private elementary and secondary schools, students, and staff characteristics, by school type and affiliation, 1987/88, 4836–3.8

Student employment
see Work-study programs
see Youth employment

Student Loan Marketing Association
Activities and finances of Sallie Mae, 1991, annual rpt, 9784–1
Budget of US, financial statements of federally sponsored enterprises, FY93, annual rpt, 104–2.6
Guaranteed student loans, defaults, and collections, by type of loan, lender, and guarantee agency, with data by State and top lender, FY91, annual rpt, 4804–38

Student loans
see Student aid

Students
Aircraft pilot and nonpilot certificates held, by type of certificate, age, sex, region, and State, 1991, annual rpt, 7504–2
Child care arrangements of mothers employed and in school, and costs, by age of child and characteristics of mother, 1988, Current Population Rpt, 2546–20.24
Condition of Education, detail for elementary, secondary, and higher education, 1920s-91 and projected to 2002, annual rpt, 4824–1
Crime victimization in schools, drug availability, and preventive measures, with student views, 1989 survey, 6066–3.46
Data on education, enrollment, finances, teachers, and other characteristics, by State, 1969-89, 4828–33
Data on education, special topics, series, 4826–10
Deaths and rates, by cause and selected social, demographic, and employment characteristics, 1979-85, natl longitudinal study, 4478–186
Digest of Education Statistics, 1992 annual data compilation, 4824–2
Disability, acute and chronic health conditions, absenteeism, and health services use, by selected characteristics, 1990, annual rpt, 4147–10.182; 4147–10.183
Drug, alcohol, and cigarette use and attitudes of youth, by substance type and selected characteristics, 1975-91 surveys, annual rpt, 4494–4
Drug, alcohol, and cigarette use and attitudes of youth, by substance type, 1975-91 surveys, press release, 4008–116
Eighth grade class of 1988: educational performance and conditions, characteristics, attitudes, activities, and plans, natl longitudinal survey, series, 4826–9
Elementary and secondary education enrollment, staff, finances, operations, programs, and policies, 1987/88 biennial survey, series, 4836–3
Food stamp recipient household size, composition, income, and income and deductions allowed, summer 1989, annual rpt, 1364–8
Health condition and care relation to education, indicators by selected characteristics, 1989, 4147–10.180
High school classes of 1980 and 1982: education, employment, and family characteristics, activities, and attitudes, natl longitudinal study, series, 4826–2
Higher education instn student aid and other sources of support, with student expenses and characteristics, by instn type and control, 1987 triennial study, series, 4846–3; 4846–5
Indian and Alaska Native youth health condition and behavioral patterns, by sex and grade, 1988-90, 4088–3
Juvenile facilities compensatory education programs activities, participant and staff characteristics, and outcomes, 1991 rpts, 4808–40
Natl Education Goals progress indicators, by State, 1992, annual rpt, 15914–1
OASDI beneficiaries and benefits, selected characteristics with data by State, late 1930s-90, annual rpt, 4744–3.3; 4744–3.4
OASDI benefits and beneficiaries, by category, age, and sex, quarterly rpt, 4742–1.1
Pacific territories population and housing detailed characteristics, by location, 1990 Census of Population and Housing, series, 2551–8
Population census, 1990: institutionalized population and persons in group quarters, by sex, race, county, place, and urban-rural location, State rpt series, 2531–1

Population census, 1990: institutionalized population and persons in group quarters, for Native American, urban, and metro areas, series, 2531–2
Poverty status of population and families, by detailed characteristics, 1991, annual Current Population Rpt, 2546–6.77
Private elementary and secondary schools, students, and staff characteristics, by school type and affiliation, 1987/88, 4836–3.8
see also Black students
see also Educational attainment
see also Educational enrollment
see also Educational performance
see also Educational retention rates
see also Educational tests
see also Foreign students
see also Learning disabilities
see also National Assessment of Educational Progress
see also School dropouts
see also Student aid
see also Student Community Service Program
see also Student discipline
see also Tuition and fees

Stuhr, David P.
"Financial Leverage Versus Return on Book Equity at Bank Holding Companies in 1988, 1986, 1980", 9385–8.134
"Using Cluster Analysis as a Tool for Economic and Financial Analysis", 9385–8.128

Stuver, Sherri O.
"Case-Control Study of Factors Associated with Human T-Cell Leukemia Virus Type I Infection in Southern Miyazaki, Japan", 4472–1.319

Subcommittee on Agricultural Production and Stabilization of Prices. Senate
Bee colony rentals, and pollinated crop value, by crop, 1989, hearings, 25168–78

Subcommittee on Antitrust, Monopolies and Business Rights. Senate
Gasoline service stations price competition and divorcement from oil companies, issues with data by firm, city, and State, 1991 hearing, 25528–120
Infant formula bid prices and contracts awarded by States under USDA food aid program for women, infants, and children, late 1980s-91, hearing, 25528–118
Insurance industry finances, failures, and regulation, with data by firm and State, 1990 hearing, 25528–119

Subcommittee on Aviation. House
Flight attendant work hour limitation proposals, with emergency evacuations and related casualties by incident, 1975-89, hearing, 21648–68

Subcommittee on Census and Population. House
Census Bur planning for 2000 decennial census and economic statistics program improvement, FY92 budget proposals, hearing, 21628–98
Census of Population, local govts participation in 1990 census and plans for 2000 census, hearing, 21628–100
Census of Population, 1990: data accuracy and enumeration methodology issues, hearing, 21628–97
Census of Population, 1990: data accuracy, evaluation, and adjustment issues, hearing, 21628–99
Census of Population, 1990: data adjustment for undercounts, Commerce Dept decision against adjustment, hearing, 21628–101
Census of Population, 1990: data adjustment for undercounts, evaluation of advisability, with error rates by race and selected city, hearing, 21628–102
Census of Population, 1990: minority group participation in census, effectiveness and quality of outreach and promotional programs, hearing, 21628–103
Census of Population, 2000: planning activities, and review of 1990 census operations, hearing, 21628–104

Subcommittee on Children, Family, Drugs and Alcoholism. Senate
Employee leave for family reasons, State law provisions and employer compliance, for 4 States, 1987-91, hearing, 25548–105

Subcommittee on Commerce, Consumer, and Monetary Affairs. House
Bank deposit insurance coverage of households and small businesses, and value of insurance to banks by instn, 1970s-90, hearing, 21408–126

Subcommittee on Commerce, Consumer Protection, and Competitiveness. House
Meat from Canada inspected and rejected, by US port of entry, 1989-91, hearing, 21368–141
Recycling in manufacturing industries, fuel savings, and CO2 emissions reductions, 1988 and projected to 1995, hearing, 21368–140

Subcommittee on Consumer Affairs and Coinage. House
Banking system reform impacts on consumers, with background data, 1991 hearing, 21248–167
Coin and medal production by denomination, capacity, and facility improvement funding, by mint, with monetary metals purchases, projected FY92-96, hearing, 21248–164
Credit card issuers disclosure of terms and conditions to consumers, with finances and operations, 1991 hearing, 21248–175

Subcommittee on Deficits, Debt Management and International Debt. Senate
Developing countries debt burden indicators, conversion agreement terms, and swaps for conservation funds, by selected country, 1987-90, hearing, 25368–181

Subcommittee on Domestic Monetary Policy. House
Monetary policy objectives of Fed Reserve, analysis and economic performance, 1950s-90 and projected to FY95, hearings, 21248–160

Subcommittee on Economic Stabilization. House
Electric power demand, and industrial and employment impacts of capacity shortfalls and new power plants, by selected State, 1960s-80s and projected to 2000, hearing, 21248–163

Subcommittee on Elections. House
Polling places access and services availability for aged and disabled, by State, 1990 natl elections, hearing, 21428–11
Tax (income) return checkoff for contribution to presidential campaign fund, receipts and outlays, mid 1970s-91 and alternative projections to 1993, hearing, 21428–10

Subcommittee on Employment and Housing. House
Occupational repetitive motion injury rates by selected industry, with data for California, 1980s, hearing, 21408–128

Subcommittee on Energy and Power. House
Natl Energy Strategy auto fuel economy standards and alternative fuels issues, 1991 hearings, 21368–138
Natl Energy Strategy fossil fuel, electric power, conservation, and pollution reduction issues, 1991 hearings, 21368–136
Natl Energy Strategy nuclear power, waste mgmt, and uranium enrichment issues, 1991 hearings, 21368–137
Natl Energy Strategy Strategic Petroleum Reserve and energy efficiency issues, 1991 hearings, 21368–142

Subcommittee on Energy Regulation and Conservation. Senate
Alternative fuels pollutant emissions by fuel type, and alcohol fuel production and inputs, 1991 hearing, 25318–82
Recycling of paper by grade, with newsprint collection, recycling capacity by company, and curbside pickup operations, by State, 1970s-80s and projected to 1995, hearing, 25318–84

Subcommittee on Environment, Energy, and Natural Resources. House
Hazardous waste generated, and treated by process, by State, 1987-89 and projected to 2009, hearing, 21408–132
Indian trust fund overpayments and shortages, by account, 1970s-91, hearing, 21408–131
Nuclear weapons facilities of DOE, contractor fees, environmental and safety enforcement activity, and salaries, by contractor and facility, 1987-88, hearing, 21408–127

Subcommittee on European Affairs. Senate
NATO and Warsaw Pact military forces reductions and ceilings under CFE treaty, inspections, and US compliance costs and savings, 1991 hearings, 25388–59

Subcommittee on Financial Institutions Supervision, Regulation, and Insurance. House
Banking system reform issues, with top instn finances, fiscal impacts, and views of depositors, bankers, and regulators on deposit insurance, 1991 hearings, 21248–168
Savings instns failure resolution activity of Resolution Trust Corp, brokered deposits, fees, and interest rates by instn and region, as of July 1991, hearing, 21248–171

Subcommittee on Fisheries and Wildlife Conservation and the Environment. House
Disease cases and outbreaks related to fish and shellfish consumption, by species, cause, and State, 1969-87, hearing, 21568–51

Subcommittee on Government Information and Regulation. Senate
Assistance (formula grants) of Fed Govt, use of adjusted census and intercensal data for allocation, with data by program and State, FY91, 25408–120
Census of Population, 1990: data accuracy, evaluation, and adjustment issues, hearing, 21628–99

Census of Population, 1990: data adjustment for undercounts, issues, 1991, 25408–119

Subcommittee on Health and Environment. House
Physicians recently graduating, specialties, school debt, and practice settings, and medical school funding sources, 1970s-91, hearing, 21368–135

Subcommittee on Health. House
Insurance (health) provided by small businesses, cost and access issues, 1991 hearings, 21788–218
Unemployment by selected characteristics, health insurance coverage, and unemployment insurance benefits exhaustion, 1988-91 and projected to 1996, hearing, 21788–209

Subcommittee on Hospitals and Health Care. House
Drug (prescription) prices charged to VA and Fed Govt, by manufacturer and drug, 1990-91, hearing, 21768–68

Subcommittee on Housing and Community Development. House
Fed Natl Mortgage Assn, Fed Home Loan Mortgage Corp, and FHLBs finances, 1991 hearings, 21248–170
Housing affordability and availability, impacts of govt land use regulations and rent control, and low income housing condition, 1991 hearing, 21248–174
Mortgages FHA-insured by State, financing costs, and loans in force and claims by loan-to-value ratio, 1970s-80s, hearings, 21248–162
Real estate agent fees for mortgage banker referrals, and other issues, consumer views, 1989 survey, hearings, 21248–161
San Antonio, Tex, govt funding for public housing and health, with background data, 1989-91, hearing, 21248–172

Subcommittee on Housing and Memorial Affairs. House
VA benefit overpayment and home loan debt repayment waiver cases and dispositions, FY88-91, hearing, 21768–67

Subcommittee on Housing and Urban Affairs. Senate
Mortgages FHA-insured, insurance fund financial condition with background housing and mortgage data, 1970s-90s, hearing, 25248–128

Subcommittee on Human Resources and Intergovernmental Relations. House
Minority group targeted student aid, higher education instns with awards and funding sources, by instn level and control, 1989/90, hearings, 21408–130
State govt budget balances, balances as share of outlays, and costs of Medicaid coverage expansion, FY89-92, hearing, 21408–129

Subcommittee on Human Resources. House
AFDC applicants recently unemployed, characteristics of prior job and unemployment insurance eligibility, for Maryland, 1988-90, hearing, 21788–207
Foster care programs of States, Federal funding and children served, by State, 1981-89, hearing, 21788–208
Single mothers family income, and impacts of child care, govt and child support payments, taxes, and marriage, with data by State, 1970s-91, 21788–212

Subcommittee on Insular and International Affairs. House
Puerto Rico statehood referendum proposal, with background data on Federal outlays, economic conditions, and finances of corporations with tax-favored status, 1940s-88, hearing, 21448–46

Subcommittee on International Development, Finance, Trade and Monetary Policy. House
Intl Monetary Fund financial statements, and proposed funding quotas by member country, 1991 hearing, 21248–169

Subcommittee on International Trade. Senate
Canada-US trade agreement issues, with data on Canada fertilizer and agricultural production and trade, 1960s-90s, hearing, 25368–179

Subcommittee on Investigations and Oversight, Public Works and Transportation. House
Container (intermodal) traffic by mode, use of containers over legal weight for hwy use, and California enforcement activity, 1960s-88, hearing, 21648–65

Subcommittee on Investigations, Permanent. Senate
Military weapons trade of 32 countries, 1984-88, hearing, 25408–115
Tax (income) compliance of corporations, and IRS enforcement activities, 1970s-92, hearing, 25408–118

Subcommittee on Investment, Jobs, and Prices. House
State govt pension funds use to balance budgets, with data for 2 States, 1991 hearing, 21148–66

Subcommittee on Labor-Management Relations. House
Electronic monitoring of employees, effects on mental and physical health and job satisfaction, for local telephone company workers, 1989, hearings, 21348–122
Hospital trauma center cases and deaths by injury type, costs, and payment sources, with data for selected areas, 1991 hearing, 21348–123
Strikes, replacement workers hired, and impacts on firm operating capacity, with data for NYC, 1984-88, hearing, 21348–121

Subcommittee on Medicare and Long-Term Care. Senate
Physicians payment by Medicare under fee schedule, impacts on charges by specialty and State, 1992 and 1996, hearing, 25368–178

Subcommittee on National Parks and Public Lands. House
Colorado River Storage Project power sales, and Glen Canyon Dam operations, 1960s-80s, hearing, 21448–47

Subcommittee on Oversight and Investigations, Energy and Commerce. House
Blood banks safety violations, FDA enforcement, disease transmittal, and Houston regional center activities and finances, 1970s-91, hearings, 21368–134

Subcommittee on Oversight. House
Customs inspectors overtime pay issues, 1991 hearing, 21788–214
Tax (withholding) delinquent accounts of Federal agencies, and compared to other taxpayers, 1990, hearing, 21788–206
Tax enforcement activities and collections of Bur of Alcohol, Tobacco, and Firearms and IRS, 1991 hearing, 21788–217

Subcommittee on Policy Research and Insurance. House
Bond (municipal) insurer finances and capital adequacy indicators, by firm and sector, 1986-90, hearing, 21248–173
Housing affordability and availability, impacts of govt land use regulations and rent control, and low income housing condition, 1991 hearing, 21248–174

Subcommittee on Procurement, Tourism, and Rural Development. House
Small Business Admin loans to tourism-related and other small businesses in rural areas, FY86-1st half FY91, hearing, 21728–79

Subcommittee on Public Lands, National Parks and Forests. Senate
Wilderness areas acreage by State, and Colorado off-road vehicle use, owner expenses, and views on registration fee, 1986-88, hearing, 25318–85

Subcommittee on Regulation, Business Opportunities, and Energy. House
Lumber (softwood) from Canada, costs and production compared to US, 1970s-91, hearing, 21728–78

Subcommittee on Retirement Income and Employment. House
OASDI Disability Insurance eligibility determinations by States, caseloads, Federal funding, and State directors views, 1980s-91, hearing, 21148–63

Subcommittee on Science. House
Arkansas govt science agency research grants and industry sponsors matching funds, and Federal R&D aid to higher education instns, mid 1980s-90, hearing, 21708–131

Subcommittee on Securities. Senate
Corporations securities holdings by shareholder type, and mgmt and executive pay issues, with data by company, 1991 hearing, 25248–130

Subcommittee on Social Security. House
OASI retirement earnings test, liberalization effect on beneficiaries and Federal revenue, 1991 hearing, 21788–215

Subcommittee on Taxation and Debt Management. Senate
Debt outstanding by type of holder, and total and per capita Federal debt, 1929-89, hearing, 25368–177

Subcommittee on Technology and Competitiveness. House
EC govt subsidies, by industry sector and for Airbus Industrie, by country, 1980s-91, hearing, 21708–132
Materials (critical) industry status and intl competitiveness, with data on semiconductors and advanced ceramics, 1991 hearing, 21708–130

Subcommittee on Technology and National Security. Joint
Eastern Europe transition to market economies, economic conditions, trade, and foreign investment, by country, 1990-91, 9118–13
Population size and demographic changes impacts on economic conditions, with background data, 1950s-80s and projected to 2010, 23848–226

Subcommittee on Terrorism, Narcotics, and International Operations. Senate
Bank of Credit and Commerce Intl financial statements, audits, and selected loan data, 1984-90, hearing, 25388–60
Subcommittee on Trade. House
Mexico and US economic and trade impacts of proposed North American Free Trade Agreement, with data on maquiladora plants, 1980s-90, hearings, 21788–210
Subcommittee on Transportation and Hazardous Materials. House
Recycling of municipal and industrial waste, costs, revenues, and secondary products trade and related energy use and pollution reductions, 1991 hearings, 21368–139
Subcommittee on Water, Power and Offshore Energy Resources. House
Colorado River Storage Project power sales, and Glen Canyon Dam operations, 1960s-80s, hearing, 21448–47
Japan energy use and imports by fuel type, and gasoline prices, 1970s-80s, hearing, 21448–45
Submarines
Foreign countries military spending, arms trade, and force strengths, with govt spending and population, by country, 1979-89, annual rpt, 9824–1
Military weapons acquisition costs by system and service branch, DOD budget, FY91-93, annual rpt, 3504–2
Navy weapons systems parts purchases from foreign suppliers and US contractors, by State and country, 1988, 2026–1.3
NOAA oceanographic and other research activities, FY87-88, biennial rpt, 2144–6
Nuclear reactors for domestic use and export by function and operating status, with owner, operating characteristics, and location, 1991 annual listing, 3354–15
Radiation exposure of Navy personnel on nuclear-powered vessels and at support facilities, and injury claims, 1950s-91, annual rpt, 3804–10
Radioactive waste from Navy nuclear-powered vessels and support facilities, releases in harbors, and public exposure, 1970s-91, annual rpt, 3804–11
Submerged lands
see also Continental shelf
see also Offshore oil and gas
Subsidies
Budget of US, obligations and authority by function, agency, and program, with summaries and analyses, FY93, annual rpt, 104–2
EC govt subsidies, by industry sector and for Airbus Industrie, by country, 1980s-91, hearing, 21708–132
Loans, loan guarantees, and grants of Fed Govt, administrative costs budget accounting, by program and agency, 1992 rpt, 26306–6.166
Manufacturing industry (US) intl competitiveness, trade and economic policies with background data and foreign comparisons, 1991 rpt, 26358–252
Minerals depletion allowance of foreign countries and US, by nonfuel mineral, 1987-91, annual rpt, 5604–18
Minority- and woman-owned businesses and owner characteristics, by industry, employment and sales size, and form of ownership, 1987 survey, 2328–59
Minority business funding, by program and Federal agency, FY91, annual rpt, 2104–5
Natl income and product accounts and components, *Survey of Current Business*, monthly rpt, 2702–1.23
Natl income and product accounts, comprehensive accounts and components, benchmark revisions, 1929-88, 2708–5
Natl income and product accounts, comprehensive accounts and components, *Survey of Current Business*, monthly rpt, 2702–1.26
Postal Service activities, finances, and mail volume and subsidies, FY91, annual rpt, 9864–5.3
Postal Service operating costs, itemized by class of mail, FY91, annual rpt, 9864–4
Postal Service subsidy for revenue forgone, by class of mail, FY91, annual rpt, 9864–1
Telephone local service charges and low-income subsidies, by region, company, and city, 1980s-91, semiannual rpt, 9282–8
see also Agricultural production quotas and price supports
see also Agricultural subsidies
see also Federal aid programs
see also Federal aid to arts and humanities
see also Federal aid to education
see also Federal aid to higher education
see also Federal aid to highways
see also Federal aid to housing
see also Federal aid to law enforcement
see also Federal aid to libraries
see also Federal aid to local areas
see also Federal aid to medical education
see also Federal aid to medicine
see also Federal aid to railroads
see also Federal aid to rural areas
see also Federal aid to States
see also Federal aid to transportation
see also Federal aid to vocational education
see also Federal funding for energy programs
see also Federal funding for research and development
see also Rent supplements
see also Shipbuilding and operating subsidies
see also State funding for economic development
see also State funding for education
see also State funding for health and hospitals
see also State funding for higher education
see also State funding for local areas
see also State funding for natural resources and conservation
see also State funding for public safety
see also State funding for social welfare
see also State funding for transportation
see also State government spending
see also Tax expenditures
see also Tax incentives and shelters
see also Trade adjustment assistance
Substance abuse
see Alcohol abuse and treatment
see Cocaine
see Drug abuse and treatment
see Drug and alcohol testing
see Marijuana
see Smoking
Substance Abuse and Mental Health Services Administration
see also Alcohol, Drug Abuse and Mental Health Administration
see also Center for Mental Health Services
Suburbs
Census of Housing, 1990: summary unit characteristics, by householder race and age, county, place, and urban-rural location, State rpt series, 2471–1
Census of Population and Housing, 1990: summary characteristics, households, and land area, by region, State, MSA, and city, US rpt, 2551–1.1
Census of Population, 1990: population characteristics and living arrangements, by county, place, and urban-rural location, State rpt series, 2531–1
Crime Index by population size and region, and offenses by large city, 1st half 1992, semiannual rpt, 6222–1
Crime victimization in cities, suburbs, and rural areas, by offense, circumstances, and victim and offender characteristics, 1987-89, 6066–3.48
Crime victimization of households, by offense, household characteristics, and location, 1975-91, annual rpt, 6066–25.49
Crimes, arrests by offender characteristics, and rates, by offense, and law enforcement employees, by population size and jurisdiction, 1991, annual rpt, 6224–2
Educational enrollment, by grade, instn type and control, and student characteristics, 1990 and trends from 1947, annual Current Population Rpt, 2546–1.459
Employment and unemployment in metro and nonmetro areas, monthly rpt, quarterly data, 6742–2.9
Home mortgages FHA-insured, financial, property, and borrower characteristics, by metro area, 1991, annual rpt, 5144–24
Home mortgages FHA-insured, financial, property, and borrower characteristics, by State, 1991, annual rpt, 5144–1; 5144–25
Home mortgages FHA-insured, financial, property, and borrower characteristics, 1991, annual rpt, 5144–23
Households and family characteristics, by location, 1991, annual Current Population Rpt, 2546–1.457
Housing (rental) units, total, with HUD assistance by program, and eligible for aid, by unit, household, and neighborhood characteristics, and location, 1989, biennial rpt, 5184–11
Housing and households characteristics, MSA surveys, fact sheet series, 2485–11
Housing and households detailed characteristics, and unit and neighborhood quality, by location, 1989, biennial rpt supplement, 2485–13
Housing and households detailed characteristics, and unit and neighborhood quality, MSA surveys, series, 2485–6
Housing unit and household characteristics of recent movers, and reason for move, by tenure, 1989, 2486–1.12
Housing vacancy and occupancy rates, and vacant unit characteristics and costs, by region and metro-nonmetro location, quarterly rpt, 2482–1

Income (household) and poverty status under alternative income definitions, by recipient characteristics, 1979-91, annual Current Population Rpt, 2546–6.78
Income (personal) relative to median, by race and selected other characteristics, mid 1960s-89, Current Population Rpt, 2546–6.73
Income per capita for central cities and suburbs, by city, 1991 hearings, 21308–28
Migration, immigration, and mover characteristics compared to nonmovers, 1987-90, annual Current Population Rpt, 2546–1.456
Migration, population change, and areas losing population, by region, State, and metro-nonmetro location, 1980s and trends from 1940, Current Population Rpt, 2546–2.164
Migration since 1990, mover characteristics by same or different area, and compared to nonmovers, 1991, annual Current Population Rpt, 2546–1.464
see also Neighborhoods
see also Urban renewal
see also under By Urban-Rural and Metro-Nonmetro in the "Index by Categories"

Subversive activities
Aliens excluded and deported from US by cause and country, 1892-1991, annual rpt, 6264–2.5
Bombing incidents and casualties, by target, circumstances, and State, 1987-91, annual rpt, 8484–4.1
Court criminal case processing in Federal district courts, and dispositions, by offense, district, and offender characteristics, 1989, annual data compilation, 6064–29
Foreign countries human rights conditions in 170 countries, 1991, annual rpt, 21384–3
Immigrant and nonimmigrant visa applicants refused, and refusals overcome, by reason, FY90, annual rpt, 7184–1.3
Prisoners in Federal and contract instns, by selected characteristics, region, and Federal instn, FY89, annual rpt, 6244–1.1
Sentences for Federal offenses, guidelines by offense and circumstances, series, 17668–1
US attorneys civil and criminal cases by type and disposition, and collections, by Federal district, FY91, annual rpt, 6004–2.1; 6004–2.7
see also Espionage
see also Internal security
see also Sabotage
see also Terrorism

Subways
Accidents and casualties on transit systems by circumstances, damage, and ridership, by mode, 1990, annual rpt, 7884–13
Accidents, casualties, and damage, by circumstances and system, annual rpt, discontinued, 7884–5
Energy use by mode of transport, fuel supply, and demographic and economic factors of vehicle use, 1970s-90, annual rpt, 3304–5
Finances and operations of transit systems, by mode, size of fleet and urban area, region, and for 518 systems, 1990, annual rpt, 7884–4
Finances, equipment, and ridership characteristics of transit systems, 1985-90, biennial rpt, 7884–8
Manufacturing annual survey, 1990: finances and operations, by SIC 2- to 4-digit industry, series, 2506–14
Safety, operating, and funding characteristics of rail rapid transit systems, 1988-89, 9618–19
Urban areas transit systems grants of Federal Transit Admin, by city and State, FY91, annual rpt, 7884–10

Sudan
Agricultural trade of US, by detailed commodity and country, 1991, annual rpt, 1524–8
Agricultural trade of US, by detailed commodity and country, 1991, semiannual rpt, 1522–4
AID economic aid to developing countries, obligations and disbursements by country, quarterly rpt, 9912–4
AID loans repayment status and terms by program and country, and status of predecessor agency loans, quarterly rpt, 9912–3
Economic and military aid and loans from US and intl agencies, by program and country, FY46-91, annual rpt, 9914–5
Economic and social conditions of developing countries from 1960s, and Intl Dev Cooperation Agency and AID activities and funding, FY91-93, annual rpt, 9904–4
Economic conditions, income, production, prices, employment, and trade, 1992 periodic country rpt, 2046–4.46
Economic, social, political, and geographic summary data, by country, 1992, annual factbook, 9114–2
Exports and imports of US, by transport mode, country, and SITC 1- to 3-digit commodity, 1991, annual rpt, 2424–12
Exports of US, detailed Schedule B commodities with countries of destination, 1991, annual rpt, 2424–10
Food supply, needs, and aid for developing countries, status and alternative forecasts, 1992 world area rpt, 1526–8.2
Human rights conditions in 170 countries, and US economic and military aid, 1991, annual rpt, 21384–3
Military spending, arms trade, and force strengths, with govt spending and population, by country, 1979-89, annual rpt, 9824–1
Minerals Yearbook, Vol 3, 1989: foreign country review of production, trade, and policy, by commodity, annual rpt, 5604–35.1
Population size, growth rates, and components of change, by country, projected 1990-2020 and trends from 1950, biennial rpt, 2324–9
Refugee migration, and intl aid programs, by world area and country of origin and asylum, 1991, annual rpt, 7004–15
UN voting record and share of votes in agreement with US, by issue, country, and world area, 1991, annual rpt, 7004–18

Suffolk County, N.Y.
Housing and households characteristics, and unit and neighborhood quality, by MSA location for 11 MSAs, 1987 survey, supplement, 2485–8
Wages by occupation, and benefits, for office and plant workers, 1991 survey, periodic MSA rpt, 6785–16.4

Sugar industry and products
Acreage planted and harvested, by crop and State, 1990-91 and planned as of June 1992, annual rpt, 1621–23
Acreage planted, by selected crop and State, 1983-91 and planned 1992, annual rpt, 1621–22
Agricultural Stabilization and Conservation Service sugar programs, 1991-92, annual fact sheet, 1806–4.13
Agricultural Statistics, 1991, annual rpt, 1004–1
Alcoholic beverages production, stocks, materials used, and taxable and tax-free removals, for beer and distilled spirits by State, monthly rpt, 8486–1.1; 8486–1.3
Business statistics, detailed data for major industries and economic indicators, *Survey of Current Business*, monthly rpt, 2702–1.13
Business statistics, detailed data for major industries and economic indicators, 1960-91, *Survey of Current Business* biennial supplement, 2704–1
Cloned sugarcane yields, stability, and fungi resistance, 1991/92, annual rpt, 1704–2
Consumption, supply, trade, prices, spending, and indexes, by food commodity, 1990, annual rpt, 1544–4
County Business Patterns, 1989: employment, establishments, and payroll, by SIC 2- to 4-digit industry and county, annual State rpt series, 2326–8
County Business Patterns, 1990: employment, establishments, and payroll, by SIC 2- to 4-digit industry and county, annual State rpt series, 2326–6
CPI by component for US city average, and by selected metro area, region, and population size, monthly rpt, 6762–2
Cuba trade, by commodity and country, mid 1980s-91, 9118–8
Employment, earnings, and hours, by SIC 1- to 4-digit industry, monthly 1989-Feb 1992, annual rpt, 6744–4
Exports and imports (agricultural) commodity and country, prices, and world market devs, monthly rpt, 1922–12
Exports and imports (agricultural) of US, by commodity and country, bimonthly rpt, 1522–1
Exports and imports (agricultural) of US, by detailed commodity and country, 1991, annual rpt, 1524–8
Exports and imports (agricultural) of US, by detailed commodity and country, 1991, semiannual rpt, 1522–4
Exports and imports between US and outlying areas, by detailed commodity and mode of transport, 1991, annual rpt, 2424–11
Exports and imports of US, by country and detailed commodity, monthly rpt, 2422–12
Exports and imports of US, by Harmonized System 6-digit commodity and country, 1991, annual rpt, 2424–13
Exports and imports of US, by selected country, country group, and commodity group, 1991, annual rpt, 2044–37
Exports and imports of US, by transport mode, country, and SITC 1- to 3-digit commodity, 1991, annual rpt, 2424–12

Exports, imports, tariffs, and industry operating data for natural sweeteners, 1992 rpt, 9885–8.9
Exports of US, detailed Schedule B commodities with countries of destination, 1991, annual rpt, 2424–10
Farm financial and marketing conditions, forecast 1992, annual chartbook, 1504–8
Farm financial and marketing conditions, forecast 1992, annual conf, 1504–9
Farm income, cash marketing receipts ranked by commodity and State, 1990, 1548–385
Farm sector balance sheet, and receipts by detailed commodity, by State, 1986-90, annual rpt, 1544–18
Foreign and US production, prices, trade, and use, FAS periodic circular series, 1925–14
Foreign countries agricultural production, prices, and trade, by country, 1980-91 and forecast 1992, annual world area rpt series, 1524–4
Freight (waterborne domestic and foreign) by commodity, traffic, and passengers, by port and waterway, 1989, annual rpt, 3754–3
Futures and options trading volume, by commodity and exchange, FY91, annual rpt, 11924–2
Futures trading in selected commodities and financial instruments and indexes, for NYC, Chicago, and other markets activity, biweekly rpt, 11922–5
Imports of sugar and sugar-containing products under quota, by country, weekly rpt, periodicity change, 1922–9
Input-output structure of US economy, detailed interindustry transactions for 541 industries, and components of final demand, 1982 benchmark data, 2708–17
Irrigation projects of Reclamation Bur in western US, crop production and acreage by commodity, State, and project, 1990, annual rpt, 5824–12
Labor productivity, indexes of output, hours, and employment by SIC 2- to 4-digit industry, 1967-90, annual rpt, 6824–1.3
Latin America economic and social conditions, resources, trade, and aid, 1992, annual factbook, 9914–14
Manufacturing annual survey, 1990: finances and operations, by SIC 2- to 4-digit industry, series, 2506–14
Manufacturing census, 1987: concentration of largest firms measured by value added, and for shipments by SIC 2- and 4-digit industry, subject rpt, 2497–6
Manufacturing census, 1987: shipments of manufacturers products, by customer class and SIC 2- and 4-digit industry, subject rpt, 2497–4
Molasses (feed) wholesale prices by market area, and trade, weekly rpt, 1311–16
Molasses supply, use, wholesale prices by market, and imports by country, 1986-91, annual rpt, 1311–19
Occupational injury and illness rates, by SIC 2- to 4-digit industry, 1989-90, annual rpt, 6844–7
Occupational injury and illness rates, by SIC 2- to 4-digit industry, 1990, annual rpt, 6844–1
OECD trade, total and for 4 major countries, and US trade by country, by commodity, 1980-90, world area rpt series, 9116–1
Price indexes (producer), by stage of processing and detailed commodity, monthly rpt, 6762–6
Price indexes (producer), by stage of processing and detailed commodity, monthly 1991, annual rpt, 6764–2
Prices (farm-retail) for food, marketing cost components, and industry finances and productivity, 1920s-91, annual rpt, 1544–9
Prices received and paid by farmers, by commodity and State, 1991, annual rpt, 1629–5
Prices received by farmers and production value, by detailed crop and State, 1989-91, annual rpt, 1621–2
Production, farms, acreage, and related data, by selected crop and State, monthly rpt, 1621–1
Production inputs, output, and productivity for farms, by commodity and region, 1947-90, annual rpt, 1544–17
Production, prices, trade, and marketing, by commodity, current situation and forecast, monthly rpt with articles, 1502–4
Production, prices, trade, supply, and use, quarterly situation rpt with articles, 1561–14
Science, engineering, and technical employment in manufacturing, by field and industry, 1989, triennial rpt, 9627–23
Soviet Union and US economic and sociodemographic indicators, selected years 1970-90, handbook, 2328–80
Statistical Abstract of US, 1992 annual data compilation, 2324–1.23
Tax (income) returns of corporations, income and tax items by asset size and detailed industry, 1989, annual rpt, 8304–4; 8304–21
Weight and volume conversion factors for agricultural commodities and products, 1992 rpt, 1508–3
see also Candy and confectionery products
see also Syrups and sweeteners
see also under By Commodity in the "Index by Categories"

Sugarman, Jonathan R.
"Serum Cholesterol Concentrations Among Navajo Indians", 4042–3.309
"Using the Behavioral Risk Factor Surveillance System To Monitor Year 2000 Objectives Among American Indians", 4042–3.346

Suicide
Alcohol-related deaths, by cause, State, and county, annual averages 1979-80 and 1983-85, 4488–10.4
Black young men homicide and suicide victims, by day of week, and compared to whites and women, 1979-85, article, 4042–3.323
Deaths and rates, by cause, age, sex, marital status, race, and State, 1989, US Vital Statistics advance annual rpt, 4146–5.124
Deaths and rates, by cause and age, preliminary 1990-91, US Vital Statistics annual rpt, 4144–7
Deaths and rates, by cause and selected social, demographic, and employment characteristics, 1979-85, natl longitudinal study, 4478–186
Deaths and rates, by cause, provisional data, monthly rpt, 4142–1.2
Deaths and rates, by detailed location, cause, and demographic characteristics, 1989, US Vital Statistics annual rpt, 4144–3
Deaths by cause, age, race, and sex, with health improvement and disease prevention goals for 1990, 1950s-90, annual data compilation, 4144–11
Drug abuse treatment services costs, effectiveness, and financing issues, 1991 conf papers, 4498–80
Indian and Alaska Native youth health condition and behavioral patterns, by sex and grade, 1988-90, 4088–3
Indian Health Service and tribal facilities and use, and Indians health and other characteristics, by IHS region, 1980s-90, annual chartbook, 4084–7
Indian Health Service facilities, funding, operations, and Indian health and other characteristics, 1950s-91, annual chartbook, 4084–1
Military deaths by cause, age, race, and rank, and personnel captured and missing, by service branch, FY91, annual rpt, 3544–40
PHS Commissioned Corps members deaths, by cause, 1965-89, article, 4042–3.316
Prison deaths in State and Fed Govt facilities, by cause, 1990, quinquennial rpt, 6068–218
Prisoners and movements, by offense, location, and selected other characteristics, data compilation, 1992 annual rpt, 6064–6.6
Prisoners in Federal and State instns, deaths by cause, sex, and State, 1990, annual rpt, 6064–26.3; 6064–26.4
Prisoners in jails, deaths by cause, 1990-91, annual rpt, 6066–25.48
Statistical Abstract of US, 1992 annual data compilation, 2324–1.2
Youth health condition, risk factors, and preventive and treatment services use and availability, 1970s-80s, 26358–234.2

Sulfanilic acid
see Chemicals and chemical industry

Suligoi, Barbara
"National Surveillance System for Sexually Transmitted Diseases in Italy", 4202–7.311

Sullivan, David F.
"State and Local Government Fiscal Position in 1991", 2702–1.311

Sullivan, Gordon R.
"Strategic Force, Strategic Vision for the 1990s and Beyond. A Statement on the Posture of the U.S. Army, FY93", 3704–13

Sullivan, Patrick J.
"Profile of Participants in FmHA's Guaranteed Farm Loan Programs", 1548–386

Sulvetta, Margaret B.
"Achieving Cost Control in the Hospital Outpatient Department", 4652–1.314

Summers, Lawrence H.
"Macroeconomic Policy and Long-Run Growth", 9381–1.308

Sumter, S.C.
Wages by occupation, and benefits for office and plant workers, 1992 survey, periodic MSA rpt, 6785–3.6

Sundell, Paul A.
"Determinants of Short-term Agricultural Loan Rates at Commercial Banks", 1541–1.307
Sunflower seeds
see Oils, oilseeds, and fats
Sung, John F.
"Cancer Screening Intervention Among Black Women in Inner-City Atlanta—Design of a Study", 4042–3.338
Sunshine, Jonathan H.
"Medicare's Share in U.S. Physicians' Revenues", 17266–2.4
"Partial Care in Mental Health Organizations, U.S. and Each State, 1988", 4506–3.51
Superconducting super collider
see Physics
Superfund
see Hazardous waste and disposal
Supermarkets
see Food stores
Supervisors
see Business management
see Executives and managers
Supplemental Security Income
Admin of OASDHI and SSI, case processing, staff, and client problems with contacting SSA offices, 1980s-90, hearing, 25148–45
AFDC beneficiaries demographic and financial characteristics, by State, FY90, annual rpt, 4584–7
Benefit applicants denied SSI because assets exceeded limits by asset type, and later eligibility, 1989, article, 4742–1.317
Benefit applications under OASDI and SSI, dispositions, awards, and administrative law judge hearing outcomes, by race, 1988, GAO rpt, 26121–459
Benefits and beneficiaries of SSI, by type of eligibility, State, and county, Dec 1989, annual rpt, 4744–27
Benefits, beneficiaries, and recipient characteristics, with data by State, 1970s-90, annual rpt, 4744–3.8
Benefits, beneficiaries, and spells of participation, by aid program and recipient characteristics, 1987-88, Current Population Rpt, 2546–20.25
Benefits by county, FY91, annual regional listings, 4004–3
Benefits overpayment, and overpaid beneficiaries characteristics, for OASDI and SSI, late 1970s-90, GAO rpt, 26121–484
Budget of US, obligations and authority by function, agency, and program, with summaries and analyses, FY93, annual rpt, 104–2
Child beneficiaries of SSI, and benefits, by selected characteristics, family income status, and State, 1991, article, 4742–1.316
Court caseloads for SSI claims in Federal district courts, 1991, annual rpt, 18204–8.14; 18204–11
Disabled persons work history before and after SSI application, by age, diagnosis, industry div, and sex, aggregate 1937-87, article, 4742–1.308
Eligibility and payment provisions for SSI and Medicaid, and beneficiaries living arrangements, by State, 1992, annual rpt, 4704–13
Expenditures, coverage, and benefits for social welfare programs, late 1930s-90, annual rpt, 4744–3.1
Expenditures of Fed Govt in States, by type, program, agency, and State, FY91, annual rpt, 2464–2
Finances and operations of programs under Ways and Means Committee jurisdiction, FY70s-91, annual rpt, 21784–11
Finances of Fed Govt, cash and debt transactions, daily tables, 8102–4
Finances of SSA programs, and litigation, FY91, annual rpt, 4704–6
Food aid program of USDA for women, infants, and children, prenatal participation effects on birthweight and health and social welfare costs, 1960s-90, GAO rpt, 26121–458
Food stamp recipient household size, composition, income, and income and deductions allowed, summer 1989, annual rpt, 1364–8
Households composition, income, benefits, and labor force status, Survey of Income and Program Participation methodology, working paper series, 2626–10
Households, family, and personal income, by source, detailed characteristics, and region, 1991, annual Current Population Rpt, 2546–6.76
Mental health care facilities, staff, patients, and finances, 1970s-91, biennial rpt, 4094–1
Mentally retarded SSI beneficiaries transitional job training demonstration project participant characteristics, 1985-87, article, 4742–1.301
Natl income and product accounts, comprehensive accounts and components, benchmark revisions, 1929-88, 2708–5
Natl income and product accounts, comprehensive accounts and components, *Survey of Current Business*, monthly rpt, 2702–1.26
Older persons income and sources, by whether OASDI beneficiary, poverty status, and other characteristics, 1990, biennial rpt, 4744–26
Population economic well-being indicators, by selected characteristics and household income and income-to-poverty ratio, 1984, 2546–20.22
Public opinion on OASDHI and health care system operations and reform issues, 1991 surveys, 10176–2.2
Social Security Bulletin, OASDHI and other program operations and beneficiary characteristics, from 1940, quarterly journal, 4742–1
Statistical Abstract of US, 1992 annual data compilation, 2324–1.12
Vocational rehabilitation cases of State agencies, by social, employment, and disability characteristics, FY91, annual rpt, 4944–1
Work incentive programs for SSI beneficiaries, participant characteristics, by program, 1982-91, article, 4742–1.305
Supplementary wage benefits
see Employee benefits
Supreme Court
Budget of US, authoritative financial statements with appropriations, outlays, and receipts, by category and agency, FY91, annual rpt, 8104–2.2
Budget of US, obligations and authority by function, agency, and program, with summaries and analyses, FY93, annual rpt, 104–2
Buildings and grounds under Capitol Architect supervision, itemized outlays by payee and function, 2nd half FY91, semiannual rpt, 25922–2
Caseloads, dispositions, and backlog, for Supreme Court, Oct 1986-90, annual rpt, 18204–8.16
Crime, criminal justice admin and enforcement, and public opinion, data compilation, 1992 annual rpt, 6064–6
Criminal case processing in Federal courts, by offense, disposition, and jurisdiction, data compilation, 1992 annual rpt, 6064–6.5
Labor-related cases on Supreme Court docket, 1991-92, annual narrative article, 6722–1.308
Public confidence in people running selected social instns, 1972-88 surveys, biennial rpt, 9624–10.7
Public opinion on crime and crime-related issues, by respondent characteristics, data compilation, 1992 annual rpt, 6064–6.2
Statistical Abstract of US, 1992 annual data compilation, 2324–1.5
Writs of certiorari for review by Supreme Court on writs filed in Federal courts of appeals, petitions and disposition, 1991, annual rpt, 18204–8.17
Surety bonds
Food imports with pesticide residue, FDA enforcement, with contaminated shipments distributed, damages assessed and paid, and repeat offenders, FY88-90, GAO rpt, 26113–598
Livestock packers purchases and feeding, and livestock markets, dealers, and sales, by State, 1990, annual rpt, 1384–1
Minority business funding, by program and Federal agency, FY91, annual rpt, 2104–5
Rural areas businesses credit assistance of Fed Govt, by program and county characteristics, 1983-89, 1548–389
Small Business Admin loans, contract awards, and surety bonds, by firm, State, and city, FY91, annual rpt, 9764–1
Surgeons and surgery
Births and rates, by characteristics of birth, infant, and mother, and presence of maternal risk factors and birth defects, 1989, 4146–5.125
Blue Cross-Blue Shield plans changes in physician costs per enrollee and for selected procedures, mid 1980s, article, 4652–1.320
Cancer patients hospitalized by purpose and body site, case classification effect on charges and length of stay, FY85, article, 4652–1.304
Cataract surgery reimbursement by Medicare, savings from denial of claims for unnecessary and poor service, 1988, 4006–11.2; 4006–11.3
Deaths of Medicare patients, actual and expected rates by diagnosis, with hospital characteristics, by instn, FY90, annual State rpt series, 4654–14
Diabetes patients physician office visits, by characteristics of patient, physician, and visit, 1989, 4146–8.212

Fees (global) inclusion of preoperative and postoperative visits, duration, and setting, for 160 surgical procedures, 1990 survey, 17266–2.6
Fees for surgical procedures, and services included, for 4 common procedures, 1988, 17266–2.2
Health Care Financing Review, provider prices, price inputs and indexes, and labor, quarterly journal, 4652–1.1
Health condition and care indicators, 1950s-90 with health improvement and disease prevention goals for 1990, annual data compilation, 4144–11
Hepatitis cases by infection source, age, sex, race, and State, and deaths, by strain, 1989 and trends from 1966, 4205–2
Hospital discharges and length of stay, by diagnosis, patient and instn characteristics, procedure performed, and payment source, 1990, annual rpt, 4147–13.112
Hospital discharges and length of stay by region and diagnosis, and procedures performed, by age and sex, 1990, annual rpt, 4146–8.211
Hospital discharges and length of stay under old and new survey designs, by diagnosis, patient and instn characteristics, and procedure, Jan-Mar 1988, 4147–13.110
Hospital discharges by detailed diagnostic and procedure category, primary diagnosis, and length of stay, by age, sex, and region, 1990, annual rpt, 4147–13.111
Hospital discharges for surgery not related to diagnosis at admission, diagnostic coding errors, substandard care, and Medicare costs, 1980s, 4006–7.7
Hospital outpatient and inpatient leading diagnoses and procedures, and costs by setting, 1987, article, 4652–1.314
Insurance (health) coverage and provisions of employee benefit plans, by plan type, for State and local govt employees, 1990, biennial rpt, 6784–21
Insurance (health) provided by employer for inpatient and outpatient surgery, 1989-90, article, 6722–1.349
Labor supply and education of health professionals, by professional and other characteristics, and location, 1960s-92 and projected to 2020, biennial rpt, 4114–8
Labor supply of physicians, by specialty, age, sex, and location of training and practice, 1990, State rpt series, 4116–6
Medicaid payment and participation by service type, and cost compared to Medicare, by State, FY89, 17266–1.4
Medicare and Medicaid beneficiaries and program operations, 1992, annual fact book, 4654–18
Medicare coverage of new health care technologies, risks and benefit evaluations, series, 4186–10
Medicare payment of physicians, reforms impacts on services, and monitoring methods, 1992 annual rpt, 4004–34
Medicare payment of physicians under fee schedule, analyses of costs and other issues, series, 17266–1
Medicare payment of physicians under fee schedule, impacts on beneficiaries, practice, and program finances, series, 17266–2
Medicare payment of physicians under fee schedule, methodology with data by procedure and specialty, 1992, annual rpt, 17264–1
Medicare payment of physicians under reasonable charge method, effect of customary charges in selected States, 1987-89, article, 4652–1.307
Medicare payment of physicians, volume performance standard recommendations, FY93, annual rpt, 4004–32
Medicare reimbursement of hospitals under prospective payment system, ambulatory surgery and radiology proposed reform, 1992 rpt, 17206–1.15
Military health care benefits and costs under Civilian Health and Medical Program of Uniformed Services, FY85-90, annual chartbook, 3504–23
Military health care personnel, and accessions by training source, by occupation, specialty, and service branch, FY90, annual rpt, 3544–24
Occupational Outlook Handbook, 1992-93, biennial rpt, 6744–1
Payment sources expected for hospital discharges, by diagnosis, patient characteristics, and region, and procedures performed, 1990, 4146–8.221
Quality standards and review for health care facilities excluded from Medicare prospective payment system, certification, accreditation, and licensing, 1991 survey, 17206–2.41
Statistical Abstract of US, 1992 annual data compilation, 2324–1.3
VA health care facilities physicians, dentists, and nurses, by selected employment characteristics and VA district, quarterly rpt, 8602–6
VA health care facilities trainees, by detailed program and city, FY91, annual rpt, 8704–4
VA health care services, needs, availability, structure, and funding, 1991 compilation of papers, 8608–9
VA health care staff and turnover, by occupation, physician specialty, and location, 1991, annual rpt, 8604–8
Veterans health care, patients, visits, costs, and operating beds, by VA and contract facility, and region, quarterly rpt, 8602–4
Visits to physicians, by patient and practice characteristics, diagnosis, and services provided, 1989, annual rpt, 4147–13.109
Visits to physicians, by patient and practice characteristics, diagnosis, and services provided, 1990, advance rpt, 4146–8.215
see also Medical transplants

Suriname
Agricultural trade of US, by detailed commodity and country, 1991, annual rpt, 1524–8
Agricultural trade of US, by detailed commodity and country, 1991, semiannual rpt, 1522–4
AID economic aid to developing countries, obligations and disbursements by country, quarterly rpt, 9912–4
AID loans repayment status and terms by program and country, and status of predecessor agency loans, quarterly rpt, 9912–3
Economic and military aid and loans from US and intl agencies, by program and country, FY46-91, annual rpt, 9914–5
Economic and social conditions of developing countries from 1960s, and Intl Dev Cooperation Agency and AID activities and funding, FY91-93, annual rpt, 9904–4
Economic and social conditions, resources, and trade, and aid, 1992, annual factbook, 9914–14
Economic, social, political, and geographic summary data, by country, 1992, annual factbook, 9114–2
Exports and imports of US, by transport mode, country, and SITC 1- to 3-digit commodity, 1991, annual rpt, 2424–12
Exports of US, detailed Schedule B commodities with countries of destination, 1991, annual rpt, 2424–10
Human rights conditions in 170 countries, and US economic and military aid, 1991, annual rpt, 21384–3
Military aid of US, arms sales, and training programs costs and budget requests, by program, world region, and country, FY91-93, annual rpt, 7144–13
Military spending, arms trade, and force strengths, with govt spending and population, by country, 1979-89, annual rpt, 9824–1
Population size, growth rates, and components of change, by country, projected 1990-2020 and trends from 1950, biennial rpt, 2324–9
Refugee migration, and intl aid programs, by world area and country of origin and asylum, 1991, annual rpt, 7004–15
UN voting record and share of votes in agreement with US, by issue, country, and world area, 1991, annual rpt, 7004–18

Surmieda, Maria R.
"Surveillance in Evacuation Camps After the Eruption of Mt. Pinatubo, Philippines", 4202–7.320

Surplus government property
Assistance (financial and nonfinancial) of Fed Govt, 1992 base edition, annual listing, 104–5
Budget of US, authoritative financial statements with appropriations, outlays, and receipts, by category and agency, FY91, annual rpt, 8104–2.2
Developing countries economic and social conditions from 1960s, and Intl Dev Cooperation Agency and AID activities and funding, FY91-93, annual rpt, 9904–4
Foreign countries aid programs of private voluntary agencies, funding, and outlays, by agency, 1990, annual rpt, 9914–9
Foreign countries military aid of US, arms sales, and training, by country, FY50-91, annual rpt, 3904–3
Homeless persons aid organizations receipt of surplus Federal property donations, value by State, 1990, annual rpt, 14364–1
Inventory of Fed Govt assets targeted for disposition by type, and related employment and contracts, by agency, FY90, GAO rpt, 26119–369
Jails providing housing to Marshals Service prisoners, funding and surplus property awards, FY91, annual rpt, 6294–1
Ships in Natl Defense Reserve Fleet, use in Persian Gulf War, and revenue from scrap sales, 1987-91, GAO rpt, 26123–376

Surveillance
see Electronic surveillance
see Espionage
Survey of Characteristics of Business Owners
Data collection, coverage, availability, and procedural history, 1987 economic censuses, 2628–16
Survey of Consumer Finances
Families financial status, income, net worth, and assets and debt by type, by income and selected characteristics, 1983 and 1989, article, 9362–1.301
Households financial services use, by account type and instn type and location, 1989 survey, article, 9362–1.303
Households net worth distribution under alternative sample weighting systems to account for inconsistency in survey design and response rates, 1992 rpt, 9368–91
Survey of Income and Program Participation
Data collection and processing, evaluation of errors, and bibl on methodology, for SIPP, 1990 rpt, 2628–34
Data collection and statistical program plans of Census Bur, advisory committees findings and recommendations, 1992 conf, 2628–35
Data collection, methodology, and availability, 1991 users guide, 2628–24
Data collection, methodology, and comparisons to other data bases, working paper series, 2626–10
Household Economic Studies, series, 2546–20
Population and housing data, and policy issues, fact sheet series, 2326–17
Survey of Minority-Owned Business Enterprises
Data collection, coverage, availability, and procedural history, 1987 economic censuses, 2628–16
Data coverage and availability for economic censuses and related statistics, 1992 preliminary guide, 2308–5
Data from economic censuses of 1987 and related programs, CD-ROM series, 2326–22
Data from economic censuses of 1987 and related programs, CD-ROM series, user guides, 2306–8
see also Characteristics of Business Owners Survey
Survey of Real Estate Trends
Supply and demand for housing and commercial real estate, market activity indicators by region, quarterly rpt, 9292–6
Survey of Southeastern Manufacturing Conditions
Southeastern US manufacturing conditions, survey methodology and selected results, Dec 1991-July 1992, article, 9371–1.307
Survey of Women-Owned Businesses
Data collection, coverage, availability, and procedural history, 1987 economic censuses, 2628–16
Data coverage and availability for economic censuses and related statistics, 1992 preliminary guide, 2308–5
Data from economic censuses of 1987 and related programs, CD-ROM series, 2326–22
Data from economic censuses of 1987 and related programs, CD-ROM series, user guides, 2306–8
see also Characteristics of Business Owners Survey
Surveys
see Aerial surveys
see American Housing Survey
see Annual Survey of Manufactures
see Area wage surveys
see Business outlook and attitude surveys
see Census of Agriculture
see Census of Construction Industries
see Census of Financial, Insurance, and Real Estate Industries
see Census of Governments
see Census of Housing
see Census of Manufactures
see Census of Mineral Industries
see Census of Outlying Areas
see Census of Population
see Census of Population and Housing
see Census of Retail Trade
see Census of Service Industries
see Census of Transportation
see Census of Transportation, Communications, and Utilities Industries
see Census of Wholesale Trade
see Characteristics of Business Owners Survey
see Client/Patient Sample Survey of Inpatient, Outpatient, and Partial Care Programs
see Commercial Buildings Energy Consumption Survey
see Consumer Expenditure Survey
see Consumer surveys
see Current Employment Survey
see Current Population Survey
see Economic censuses
see Enterprise Statistics Program
see Farm Costs and Returns Survey
see Fast Response Survey System
see High School and Beyond Survey
see High School Transcript Study
see Hospital Cost and Clinical Research Project
see Hospital Cost and Utilization Project
see Housing Discrimination Study
see Industry wage surveys
see Integrated Postsecondary Education Data System
see Inventory of Mental Health Organizations and General Hospital Mental Health Services
see Manufacturing Energy Consumption Survey
see Methodology
see Mineral Industry Surveys
see Motor Freight Transportation and Warehousing Survey
see National Adolescent Student Health Survey
see National Ambulatory Medical Care Survey
see National Assessment of Educational Progress
see National Crime Victimization Survey
see National Dropout Statistics Field Test
see National Education Longitudinal Survey
see National Health and Nutrition Examination Survey
see National Health Interview Survey
see National Health Interview Survey on Child Health
see National Hospital Discharge Survey
see National Household Education Survey
see National Household Survey on Drug Abuse
see National Longitudinal Mortality Study
see National Longitudinal Study of High School Seniors
see National Longitudinal Survey of Mature Women
see National Longitudinal Survey of Young Men
see National Longitudinal Survey of Young Women
see National Longitudinal Survey of Youth
see National Longitudinal Surveys of Labor Market Experience
see National Medical Expenditure Survey
see National Mortality Followback Survey
see National Natality Survey
see National Postsecondary Student Aid Study
see National Prosecutor Survey
see Nationwide Food Consumption Survey
see Nationwide Personal Transportation Study
see Opinion and attitude surveys
see Schools and Staffing Survey
see State Hospital Data Project
see Statistical programs and activities
see Survey of Characteristics of Business Owners
see Survey of Consumer Finances
see Survey of Income and Program Participation
see Survey of Minority-Owned Business Enterprises
see Survey of Real Estate Trends
see Survey of Southeastern Manufacturing Conditions
see Survey of Women-Owned Businesses
Survivors
see Old-Age, Survivors, Disability, and Health Insurance
see Widows and widowers
Susquehanna River
Freight (waterborne domestic and foreign) by commodity, traffic, and passengers, by port and waterway, 1989, annual rpt, 3754–3.1
Water supply and quality in streams and lakes, and groundwater levels in wells, by drainage basin, 1990, annual State rpt series, 5666–10
Water supply and quality in streams and lakes, and groundwater levels in wells, by drainage basin, 1991, annual State rpt series, 5666–12
Water supply in US and southern Canada, streamflow, surface and groundwater conditions, and reservoir levels, by location, monthly rpt, 5662–3
Susquehanna River Basin Commission
Budget of US, authoritative financial statements with appropriations, outlays, and receipts, by category and agency, FY91, annual rpt, 8104–2.2
Budget of US, obligations and authority by function, agency, and program, with summaries and analyses, FY93, annual rpt, 104–2
Swamps
see Wetlands
Swartzman, Julie
"Medicare's Share in U.S. Physicians' Revenues", 17266–2.4

Swaziland
Agricultural trade of US, by detailed commodity and country, 1991, annual rpt, 1524–8
Agricultural trade of US, by detailed commodity and country, 1991, semiannual rpt, 1522–4
AID economic aid to developing countries, obligations and disbursements by country, quarterly rpt, 9912–4
AID loans repayment status and terms by program and country, and status of predecessor agency loans, quarterly rpt, 9912–3
Economic and military aid and loans from US and intl agencies, by program and country, FY46-91, annual rpt, 9914–5
Economic and social conditions of developing countries from 1960s, and Intl Dev Cooperation Agency and AID activities and funding, FY91-93, annual rpt, 9904–4
Economic conditions, income, production, prices, employment, and trade, 1992 periodic country rpt, 2046–4.26
Economic, social, political, and geographic summary data, by country, 1992, annual factbook, 9114–2
Exports and imports of US, by transport mode, country, and SITC 1- to 3-digit commodity, 1991, annual rpt, 2424–12
Exports of US, detailed Schedule B commodities with countries of destination, 1991, annual rpt, 2424–10
Human rights conditions in 170 countries, and US economic and military aid, 1991, annual rpt, 21384–3
Military aid of US, arms sales, and training programs costs and budget requests, by program, world region, and country, FY91-93, annual rpt, 7144–13
Military spending, arms trade, and force strengths, with govt spending and population, by country, 1979-89, annual rpt, 9824–1
Minerals Yearbook, Vol 3, 1989: foreign country review of production, trade, and policy, by commodity, annual rpt, 5604–35.1
Population size, growth rates, and components of change, by country, projected 1990-2020 and trends from 1950, biennial rpt, 2324–9
Refugee migration, and intl aid programs, by world area and country of origin and asylum, 1991, annual rpt, 7004–15
UN voting record and share of votes in agreement with US, by issue, country, and world area, 1991, annual rpt, 7004–18

Sweaters
see Clothing and clothing industry

Sweden
Agricultural trade of US, by detailed commodity and country, 1991, annual rpt, 1524–8
Agricultural trade of US, by detailed commodity and country, 1991, semiannual rpt, 1522–4
AID loans repayment status and terms by program and country, and status of predecessor agency loans, quarterly rpt, 9912–3
Cuba trade, by commodity and country, mid 1980s-91, 9118–8
Economic and military aid and loans from US and intl agencies, by program and country, FY46-91, annual rpt, 9914–5
Economic conditions, income, production, prices, employment, and trade, 1992 periodic country rpt, 2046–4.33
Economic conditions, policy, and trade practices, by country, 1989-91, annual rpt, 21384–5
Economic, social, political, and geographic summary data, by country, 1992, annual factbook, 9114–2
Exports and imports of US, by Harmonized System 6-digit commodity and country, 1991, annual rpt, 2424–13
Exports and imports of US, by selected country, country group, and commodity group, 1991, annual rpt, 2044–37
Exports and imports of US, by transport mode, country, and SITC 1- to 3-digit commodity, 1991, annual rpt, 2424–12
Exports, imports, and balances of US for manufactured goods, by SITC 2-digit commodity and country, quarterly rpt, 2042–35
Exports of US, detailed Schedule B commodities with countries of destination, 1991, annual rpt, 2424–10
Health care costs and components, services use, resources, and economic indicators, by OECD country, 1960s-90, article, 4652–1.322
Human rights conditions in 170 countries, and US economic and military aid, 1991, annual rpt, 21384–3
Imports of goods, services, and investment from US, trade barriers, impacts, and US actions, by country, 1991, annual rpt, 444–2
Imports of US given duty-free treatment for value of US material sent abroad, by commodity and country, 1987-90, annual rpt, 9884–14
Income (household) and wealth distribution by selected characteristics, with foreign comparisons, 1992 compilation of papers, Current Population Rpt, 2546–6.79
Labor conditions, union coverage, and work accidents, 1992 annual country rpt, 6366–4.36
Military spending, arms trade, and force strengths, with govt spending and population, by country, 1979-89, annual rpt, 9824–1
Multinatl US firms and foreign affiliates finances and operations, by industry and country, 1989 benchmark survey, annual rpt, 2704–5
Multinatl US firms foreign affiliates, income statement items by asset size, industry, and country, 1988, biennial article, 8302–2.322
Nuclear power generation in US and 20 countries, monthly rpt, 3162–24.10
Nuclear power generation in US and 20 countries, monthly 1973-88, 3168–123.10
Oil production, stocks, use, and trade, by selected country and country group, monthly rpt, 3162–42
Population size, growth rates, and components of change, by country, projected 1990-2020 and trends from 1950, biennial rpt, 2324–9
Refugee migration, and intl aid programs, by world area and country of origin and asylum, 1991, annual rpt, 7004–15
Science and Engineering Indicators, employment, education, R&D funding, and industry impacts, with foreign comparisons, 1960s-91, biennial rpt, 9624–10
Spacecraft and satellite launches since 1957, quarterly listing, 9502–2
Steel (carbon flat-rolled) products from 21 countries, injury to US industry from foreign subsidized and less than fair value imports, investigation with background financial and operating data, 1992 rpt, 9886–19.85
Steel trade, by product, country, and customs district, with US industry operating data, 1989-June 1992, semiannual rpt, 9882–15
Tax revenue, by level of govt and type of tax, for OECD countries, mid 1960s-90, annual rpt, 10044–1.2
Transportation energy use, fuel prices, vehicle registrations, and mileage, by selected country, 1950-89, annual rpt, 3304–5.1
UN voting record and share of votes in agreement with US, by issue, country, and world area, 1991, annual rpt, 7004–18
see also under By Foreign Country in the "Index by Categories"

Sweeteners
see Honey and beekeeping
see Sugar industry and products
see Syrups and sweeteners

Swimming
Disease (waterborne) outbreaks and cases, by type, source, and location, 1989-90, article, 4202–7.301
Diving (underwater) research activities of NOAA, FY87-88, biennial rpt, 2144–6
Injuries from use of consumer products and related activities, by severity and victim age and sex, 1990, annual rpt, 9164–7
Injuries from use of consumer products, by severity, victim age, and detailed product, 1991, annual rpt, 9164–6
Vermont White River basin stream recreation use by activity, time, and location, 1987, 1208–400
see also Drowning
see also Swimming pools

Swimming pools
Apartment completions by region and metro-nonmetro location, and absorption rate, by size and rent class, preliminary 1991, annual Current Housing Rpt, 2484–3
Apartment market absorption rates and characteristics for nonsubsidized furnished and unfurnished units, 1990, annual Current Housing Rpt, 2484–2
Injuries from use of consumer products, by severity, victim age, and detailed product, 1991, annual rpt, 9164–6
Solar collector and photovoltaic cell shipments by end-use sector and State, and trade, 1990, annual rpt, 3164–62

Swine
see Livestock and livestock industry

Switzer, Josephine C.
"Catalogue of U.S. Geological Survey Strong-Motion Records, 1990", 5664–14

Switzerland
Agricultural trade of US, by detailed commodity and country, 1991, annual rpt, 1524–8

Agricultural trade of US, by detailed commodity and country, 1991, semiannual rpt, 1522–4
Background Notes, summary social, political, and economic data, 1991 rpt, 7006–2.5
Cuba trade, by commodity and country, mid 1980s-91, 9118–8
Economic and military aid and loans from US and intl agencies, by program and country, FY46-91, annual rpt, 9914–5
Economic and monetary trends, compounded annual rates of change and quarterly indicators for US and 7 major industrialized countries, quarterly rpt, 9391–7
Economic conditions, income, production, prices, employment, and trade, 1992 periodic country rpt, 2046–4.20; 2046–4.48
Economic conditions, policy, and trade practices, by country, 1989-91, annual rpt, 21384–5
Economic, social, political, and geographic summary data, by country, 1992, annual factbook, 9114–2
Exports and imports of US, by Harmonized System 6-digit commodity and country, 1991, annual rpt, 2424–13
Exports and imports of US, by selected country, country group, and commodity group, 1991, annual rpt, 2044–37
Exports and imports of US, by transport mode, country, and SITC 1- to 3-digit commodity, 1991, annual rpt, 2424–12
Exports, imports, and balances of US for manufactured goods, by SITC 2-digit commodity and country, quarterly rpt, 2042–35
Exports, imports, and balances of US with major trading partners, by product category, 1987-91, annual chartbook, 9884–21
Exports of US, detailed Schedule B commodities with countries of destination, 1991, annual rpt, 2424–10
Farmland in US owned by foreigners, holdings, acreage, and value by land use, owner country, State, and county, 1991, annual rpt, 1584–3
Financial markets (intl) performance of foreign and US bank and securities firms, finances and competitiveness issues, 1980s, compilation of papers, 9385–10
Health care costs and components, services use, resources, and economic indicators, by OECD country, 1960s-90, article, 4652–1.322
Human rights conditions in 170 countries, and US economic and military aid, 1991, annual rpt, 21384–3
Imports of goods, services, and investment from US, trade barriers, impacts, and US actions, by country, 1991, annual rpt, 444–2
Interest and exchange rates, security yields, and stock indexes, for selected foreign countries, weekly chartbook, 9365–1.5
Investment (foreign direct) in US, major transactions by type, industry, country, and US location, 1990, annual rpt, 2044–20
Labor conditions, union coverage, and work accidents, 1991 annual country rpt, 6366–4.2
Military spending, arms trade, and force strengths, with govt spending and population, by country, 1979-89, annual rpt, 9824–1
Monetary policies and central bank regulation in US and 5 countries, 1980-91, article, 9385–1.308
Multinatl firms US affiliates finances and operations, by industry, country of parent firm, and State, 1987, 2708–48
Multinatl firms US affiliates, finances, and operations, by industry, world area of parent firm, and State, 1989-90, annual rpt, 2704–4
Multinatl US firms and foreign affiliates finances and operations, by industry and country, 1989 benchmark survey, annual rpt, 2704–5
Multinatl US firms foreign affiliates, income statement items by asset size, industry, and country, 1988, biennial article, 8302–2.322
Nuclear power generation in US and 20 countries, monthly rpt, 3162–24.10
Nuclear power generation in US and 20 countries, monthly 1973-88, 3168–123.10
Oil production, stocks, use, and trade, by selected country and country group, monthly rpt, 3162–42
Population size, growth rates, and components of change, by country, projected 1990-2020 and trends from 1950, biennial rpt, 2324–9
Refugee migration, and intl aid programs, by world area and country of origin and asylum, 1991, annual rpt, 7004–15
Steel trade, by product, country, and customs district, with US industry operating data, 1989-June 1992, semiannual rpt, 9882–15
Tax (estate) returns for nonresident aliens, property and tax data, by estate size and decedent country of residence, 1986, article, 8302–2.310
Tax (income) returns for foreign corporate activity in US, selected income and tax items, by industry div and selected country, 1988, article, 8302–2.309
Tax (income) returns, income, and tax withheld for foreign partners of US partnerships, by country, 1990, article, 8302–2.324
Tax revenue, by level of govt and type of tax, for OECD countries, mid 1960s-90, annual rpt, 10044–1.2
Tobacco and cigarette production, use, and trade, for Switzerland, 1980s-92, article, 1925–16.315
see also under By Foreign Country in the "Index by Categories"

Symposiums
see Conferences

Synthetic fibers and fabrics
Business statistics, detailed data for major industries and economic indicators, *Survey of Current Business*, monthly rpt, 2702–1.21
Business statistics, detailed data for major industries and economic indicators, 1960-91, *Survey of Current Business* biennial supplement, 2704–1
Clothing and shoe production, shipments, trade, and use, by product, periodic Current Industrial Rpt series, 2506–6
County Business Patterns, 1989: employment, establishments, and payroll, by SIC 2- to 4-digit industry and county, annual State rpt series, 2326–8
County Business Patterns, 1990: employment, establishments, and payroll, by SIC 2- to 4-digit industry and county, annual State rpt series, 2326–6
Employment, earnings, and hours, by SIC 1- to 4-digit industry, monthly 1989-Feb 1992, annual rpt, 6744–4
Exports and imports between US and outlying areas, by detailed commodity and mode of transport, 1991, annual rpt, 2424–11
Exports and imports of textiles, raw fiber equivalents by product, country, and world region, 1989-90, article, 1561–1.301
Exports and imports of US, by country and detailed commodity, monthly rpt, 2422–12
Exports and imports of US, by Harmonized System 6-digit commodity and country, 1991, annual rpt, 2424–13
Exports and imports of US, by transport mode, country, and SITC 1- to 3-digit commodity, 1991, annual rpt, 2424–12
Exports of US, detailed Schedule B commodities with countries of destination, 1991, annual rpt, 2424–10
Exports of US textiles and apparel, by product group and country, quarterly rpt, 2042–36
Foreign countries market conditions for US textile and apparel exports, with domestic industry operations, country rpt series, 2046–15
Freight (waterborne domestic and foreign) by commodity, traffic, and passengers, by port and waterway, 1989, annual rpt, 3754–3
Glass (fibrous) production, shipments, and firms, by product, annual Current Industrial Rpt, discontinued, 2506–9.5
Imports of textiles, by country of origin, monthly rpt, 2042–27
Imports of textiles, by product and country of origin, monthly rpt series, 2046–8; 2046–9
Imports of textiles under Multifiber Arrangement by product and country, and status of bilateral agreements, 1988-91, annual rpt, 9884–18
Input-output structure of US economy, detailed interindustry transactions for 541 industries, and components of final demand, 1982 benchmark data, 2708–17
Labor productivity, indexes of output, hours, and employment by SIC 2- to 4-digit industry, 1967-90, annual rpt, 6824–1.3
Manufacturing annual survey, 1990: finances and operations, by SIC 2- to 4-digit industry, series, 2506–14
Manufacturing census, 1987: concentration of largest firms measured by value added, and for shipments by SIC 2- and 4-digit industry, subject rpt, 2497–6
Manufacturing census, 1987: shipments of manufacturers products, by customer class and SIC 2- and 4-digit industry, subject rpt, 2497–4
Manufacturing finances and operations, by SIC 2- to 4-digit industry, forecast 1992, annual rpt, 2044–28

Occupational injury and illness rates, by SIC 2- to 4-digit industry, 1989-90, annual rpt, 6844–7
Occupational injury and illness rates, by SIC 2- to 4-digit industry, 1990, annual rpt, 6844–1
Price indexes (producer), by stage of processing and detailed commodity, monthly rpt, 6762–6
Price indexes (producer), by stage of processing and detailed commodity, monthly 1991, annual rpt, 6764–2
Production, prices, trade, and use of cotton, wool, and synthetic fibers, periodic situation rpt with articles, 1561–1
Production, trade, sales, stocks, and material used, by product, region, and State, periodic Current Industrial Rpt series, 2506–5
Rayon yarn (high-tenacity filament) from Germany at less than fair value, injury to US industry, investigation with background financial and operating data, 1992 rpt, 9886–14.350
Science, engineering, and technical employment in manufacturing, by field and industry, 1989, triennial rpt, 9627–23
Statistical Abstract of US, 1992 annual data compilation, 2324–1.27
Sweaters from 3 countries at less than fair value, injury to US industry, investigation supplement, 1992 rpt, 9886–14.363

Synthetic food products
Nutrient, caloric, and waste composition of food, detailed data for raw, processed, and prepared foods, series, 1356–3

Synthetic fuels
Coal mining restrictions on public land, impacts on production, costs, and demand, by region, 1985-88 and projected to 2075, 5668–125
Electric power plants and capacity, by fuel used, owner, location, and operating status, 1991 and for units planned 1992-2001, annual listing, 3164–36

Synthetic products
see Advanced materials
see Chemicals and chemical industry
see Plastics and plastics industry
see Polymers
see Synthetic fibers and fabrics
see Synthetic food products
see Synthetic fuels

Syphilis
see Sexually transmitted diseases

Syracuse, N.Y.
see also under By City and By SMSA or MSA in the "Index by Categories"

Syria
Agricultural trade of US, by detailed commodity and country, 1991, annual rpt, 1524–8
Agricultural trade of US, by detailed commodity and country, 1991, semiannual rpt, 1522–4
AID economic aid to developing countries, obligations and disbursements by country, quarterly rpt, 9912–4
AID loans repayment status and terms by program and country, and status of predecessor agency loans, quarterly rpt, 9912–3
Boycotts (intl) by OPEC and other countries, US firms and individuals cooperation and tax benefits denied, 1990, article, 8302–2.323
Economic and military aid and loans from US and intl agencies, by program and country, FY46-91, annual rpt, 9914–5
Economic and social conditions of developing countries from 1960s, and Intl Dev Cooperation Agency and AID activities and funding, FY91-93, annual rpt, 9904–4
Economic conditions, income, production, prices, employment, and trade, 1992 periodic country rpt, 2046–4.27
Economic conditions, policy, and trade practices, by country, 1989-91, annual rpt, 21384–5
Economic, social, political, and geographic summary data, by country, 1992, annual factbook, 9114–2
Exports and imports of US, by commodity and country, 1980-90, world area rpt, 9116–1.6
Exports and imports of US, by transport mode, country, and SITC 1- to 3-digit commodity, 1991, annual rpt, 2424–12
Exports of US, detailed Schedule B commodities with countries of destination, 1991, annual rpt, 2424–10
Human rights conditions in 170 countries, and US economic and military aid, 1991, annual rpt, 21384–3
Military spending, arms trade, and force strengths, with govt spending and population, by country, 1979-89, annual rpt, 9824–1
Minerals Yearbook, Vol 3, 1989: foreign country review of production, trade, and policy, by commodity, annual rpt, 5604–35.3
Population size, growth rates, and components of change, by country, projected 1990-2020 and trends from 1950, biennial rpt, 2324–9
Refugee migration, and intl aid programs, by world area and country of origin and asylum, 1991, annual rpt, 7004–15
UN voting record and share of votes in agreement with US, by issue, country, and world area, 1991, annual rpt, 7004–18

Syron, Richard F.
"Procyclical Application of Bank Capital Requirements", 9373–26

Syrups and sweeteners
Agricultural Statistics, 1991, annual rpt, 1004–1
Carcinogens chemistry, sources, environment and health risks, and regulation, by substance and brand, 1991 annual rpt, 4044–15
Confectionery shipments, trade, use, and ingredients used, by product, 1991, annual Current Industrial Rpt, 2506–4.5
Consumption and trade by commodity, quarterly situation rpt with articles, 1561–14
Consumption, supply, trade, prices, spending, and indexes, by food commodity, 1990, annual rpt, 1544–4
Corn and barley feed and industrial use, revised estimates 1980s-91, article, 1561–4.301
County Business Patterns, 1989: employment, establishments, and payroll, by SIC 2- to 4-digit industry and county, annual State rpt series, 2326–8
County Business Patterns, 1990: employment, establishments, and payroll, by SIC 2- to 4-digit industry and county, annual State rpt series, 2326–6
Exports and imports (agricultural) of US, by commodity and country, bimonthly rpt, 1522–1
Exports and imports (agricultural) of US, by detailed commodity and country, 1991, annual rpt, 1524–8
Exports and imports (agricultural) of US, by detailed commodity and country, 1991, semiannual rpt, 1522–4
Exports and imports between US and outlying areas, by detailed commodity and mode of transport, 1991, annual rpt, 2424–11
Exports and imports of US, by country and detailed commodity, monthly rpt, 2422–12
Exports and imports of US, by Harmonized System 6-digit commodity and country, 1991, annual rpt, 2424–13
Exports, imports, tariffs, and industry operating data for natural sweeteners, 1992 rpt, 9885–8.9
Exports of US, detailed Schedule B commodities with countries of destination, 1991, annual rpt, 2424–10
Farm financial and marketing conditions, forecast 1992, annual conf, 1504–9
Futures and options trading volume, by commodity and exchange, FY91, annual rpt, 11924–2
Input-output structure of US economy, detailed interindustry transactions for 541 industries, and components of final demand, 1982 benchmark data, 2708–17
Manufacturing annual survey, 1990: finances and operations, by SIC 2- to 4-digit industry, series, 2506–14
Manufacturing census, 1987: concentration of largest firms measured by value added, and for shipments by SIC 2- and 4-digit industry, subject rpt, 2497–6
Manufacturing census, 1987: shipments of manufacturers products, by customer class and SIC 2- and 4-digit industry, subject rpt, 2497–4
Occupational injury and illness rates, by SIC 2- to 4-digit industry, 1989-90, annual rpt, 6844–7
Occupational injury and illness rates, by SIC 2- to 4-digit industry, 1990, annual rpt, 6844–1
Price indexes (producer), by stage of processing and detailed commodity, monthly rpt, 6762–6
Price indexes (producer), by stage of processing and detailed commodity, monthly 1991, annual rpt, 6764–2
Weight and volume conversion factors for agricultural commodities and products, 1992 rpt, 1508–3
see also Honey and beekeeping
see also Sugar industry and products

SysteMetrics Inc.
"Within DRG Case Complexity Change in FY90", 17206–2.39

Szymanski, William N.
"Uranium Industry of the Commonwealth of Independent States", 3164–65

Tacoma, Wash.
Air traffic, and passenger and freight enplanements, by airport, 1960s-91 and projected to 2010, hub area rpt, 7506–7.44

CPI by component for US city average, and by selected metro area, region, and population size, monthly rpt, 6762–2
Fruit and vegetable shipments, and arrivals by city, by mode of transport and State and country of origin, 1990, annual rpt, 1311–4.2
Housing starts and completions authorized by building permits in 40 MSAs, quarterly rpt, 2382–9
Housing vacancy rates for single and multifamily units and mobile homes, by city and ZIP code, 1992, annual MSA rpt, 9304–21.1
see also under By City and By SMSA or MSA in the "Index by Categories"

Taeuber, Cynthia M.
"Sixty-Five Plus in America", 2546–2.165

Taffel, Selma M.
"Health and Demographic Characteristics of Twin Births: U.S., 1988. Vital and Health Statistics Series 21", 4147–21.50

Taha, Fawzi A.
"Environmental Constraints in East and Southeast Asia: Potential for Changing Patterns of Agricultural Production and Trade", 1524–4.3
"World Wool Trade During the 1980's", 1561–1.304

Taiwan
Agricultural production, prices, and trade, by country, 1980s and forecast 1992, annual world region rpt, 1524–4.3
Agricultural trade by commodity and country, prices, and world market devs, monthly rpt, 1922–12
Agricultural trade of US, by detailed commodity and country, 1991, annual rpt, 1524–8
Agricultural trade of US, by detailed commodity and country, 1991, semiannual rpt, 1522–4
AID loans repayment status and terms by program and country, and status of predecessor agency loans, quarterly rpt, 9912–3
Economic and military aid and loans from US and intl agencies, by program and country, FY46-91, annual rpt, 9914–5
Economic conditions, and oil supply and demand, for major industrial countries, monthly rpt, 9112–1
Economic conditions, income, production, prices, employment, and trade, 1992 periodic country rpt, 2046–4.63
Economic conditions, policy, and trade practices, by country, 1989-91, annual rpt, 21384–5
Economic, social, political, and geographic summary data, by country, 1992, annual factbook, 9114–2
Export and import balances of US, and dollar exchange rates, with 5 Asian countries, 1992 semiannual rpt, 8002–14
Exports and imports of US, by commodity and country, 1980-90, world area rpt, 9116–1.3
Exports and imports of US by country, and trade shifts by commodity, 1991, annual rpt, 9884–25
Exports and imports of US, by Harmonized System 6-digit commodity and country, 1991, annual rpt, 2424–13
Exports and imports of US, by selected country, country group, and commodity group, 1991, annual rpt, 2044–37
Exports and imports of US, by transport mode, country, and SITC 1- to 3-digit commodity, 1991, annual rpt, 2424–12
Exports and imports, trade agreements and relations, and USITC investigations, 1991, annual rpt, 9884–5
Exports, imports, and balances of US for manufactured goods, by SITC 2-digit commodity and country, quarterly rpt, 2042–35
Exports, imports, and balances of US with major trading partners, by product category, 1987-91, annual chartbook, 9884–21
Exports of US, detailed Schedule B commodities with countries of destination, 1991, annual rpt, 2424–10
Human rights conditions in 170 countries, and US economic and military aid, 1991, annual rpt, 21384–3
Imports of goods, services, and investment from US, trade barriers, impacts, and US actions, by country, 1991, annual rpt, 444–2
Imports of US given duty-free treatment for value of US material sent abroad, by commodity and country, 1987-90, annual rpt, 9884–14
Labor conditions, union coverage, and work accidents, 1991 annual country rpt, 6366–4.8
Labor conditions, union coverage, and work accidents, 1992 annual country rpt, 6366–4.52
Lockwashers (helical spring) from PRC and Taiwan at less than fair value, injury to US industry, investigation with background financial and operating data, 1992 rpt, 9886–14.362
Manufacturing industry (US) intl competitiveness, trade and economic policies with background data and foreign comparisons, 1991 rpt, 26358–252
Military spending, arms trade, and force strengths, with govt spending and population, by country, 1979-89, annual rpt, 9824–1
Minerals Yearbook, Vol 3, 1989: foreign country review of production, trade, and policy, by commodity, annual rpt, 5604–35.2
Monetary and foreign exchange policies in Taiwan, with money supply, interest rates, and other economic indicators, 1980s, article, 9393–8.303
Multinatl US firms and foreign affiliates finances and operations, by industry and country, 1989 benchmark survey, annual rpt, 2704–5
Multinatl US firms foreign affiliates, income statement items by asset size, industry, and country, 1988, biennial article, 8302–2.322
Mushroom (canned) trade, supply, and demand, for selected countries, 1980s-92, article, 1925–34.333
Nuclear power generation in US and 20 countries, monthly rpt, 3162–24.10
Nuclear power generation in US and 20 countries, monthly 1973-88, 3168–123.10
Pipe fittings (stainless steel) from 2 countries at less than fair value, injury to US industry, investigation with background financial and operating data, 1992 rpt, 9886–14.354
Pipes (welded stainless steel) from South Korea and Taiwan at less than fair value, injury to US industry, investigation with background financial and operating data, 1992 rpt, 9886–14.338; 9886–14.365
Pipes and tubes (welded nonalloy steel) from 6 countries at less than fair value, injury to US industry, investigation with background financial and operating data, 1992 rpt, 9886–14.361
Population size, growth rates, and components of change, by country, projected 1990-2020 and trends from 1950, biennial rpt, 2324–9
Refugee migration, and intl aid programs, by world area and country of origin and asylum, 1991, annual rpt, 7004–15
Steel (carbon flat-rolled) products from 21 countries, injury to US industry from foreign subsidized and less than fair value imports, investigation with background financial and operating data, 1992 rpt, 9886–19.85
Steel trade, by product, country, and customs district, with US industry operating data, 1989-June 1992, semiannual rpt, 9882–15
Sweaters from 3 countries at less than fair value, injury to US industry, investigation supplement, 1992 rpt, 9886–14.363
Timber in northwestern US and British Columbia, production, prices, trade, and employment, quarterly rpt, 1202–3
see also under By Foreign Country in the "Index by Categories"

Tajikistan
Agricultural production, prices, and trade, for former USSR republics, 1960s-91 and forecast 1992, annual rpt, 1524–4.1
Economic, social, political, and geographic summary data, by country, 1992, annual factbook, 9114–2
Embassies of US in former Soviet republics and Baltic States, positions planned by function, and filled, 1992, GAO rpt, 26123–403
Energy supply and use, and social, economic, and political indicators for former Soviet Republics and Baltic States, 1989-90, 3168–126
Energy use and production of former USSR Republics, by fuel type, 1990, annual rpt, 3164–84.2
Exports and imports of US with Communist and transitional economy countries, by detailed commodity and country, quarterly rpt with articles, 9882–2
Livestock and meat inventories, use, and imports, by former USSR republic, 1986-93, semiannual rpt, 1925–33.2
Population size and characteristics of former Soviet Republics and Baltic States, 1989-92, 9118–19

Talc
see Nonmetallic minerals and mines

Tallman, Ellis W.
"Money Demand and Relative Prices in Hyperinflations: Evidence from Germany and China", 9371–10.86

Tallow and grease
see Oils, oilseeds, and fats

Tamaki, Junko A.
"Composition of Foods. Baked Products: Raw, Processed, Prepared", 1356–3.18

Tampa, Fla.
Coastal areas environmental conditions, fish, wildlife, use, and mgmt, 1990 rpt, 5506–9.43
CPI by component for US city average, and by selected metro area, region, and population size, monthly rpt, 6762–2
Housing and households characteristics, unit and neighborhood quality, and journey to work by MSA location, for 11 MSAs, 1985 survey, supplement, 2485–8
Housing and households characteristics, 1989 survey, MSA fact sheet, 2485–11.12
Housing starts and completions authorized by building permits in 40 MSAs, quarterly rpt, 2382–9
Pollutant concentrations in coastal and estuarine fish, shellfish, and environment, late 1970s-89, local area rpt, 2176–3.15
Wages by occupation, and benefits, for office and plant workers, 1991 survey, periodic MSA rpt, 6785–16.3
see also under By City and By SMSA or MSA in the "Index by Categories"

Tanker ships
Construction and operating subsidies of MarAd by firm, and ship deliveries and fleet by country, by vessel type, FY91, annual rpt, 7704–14.1; 7704–14.2
Construction and repair facilities, capacity, and employment, by shipyard, 1991, annual rpt, 7704–9
Exports and imports (waterborne) of US, by type of service, customs district, port, and world area, monthly rpt, 2422–7
Foreign and US merchant ships, tonnage, and new ship construction and deliveries, by vessel type and country, as of Jan 1992, annual rpt, 7704–3
Foreign-flag ships owned by US firms and foreign affiliates, by type, owner, and country of registry and construction, as of July 1991, semiannual rpt, 7702–3
Freight (shipborne domestic), by major commodity group, vessel type, and port, 1987-89, annual rpt, 7704–7
Freight (waterborne domestic and foreign) by commodity, traffic, and passengers, by port and waterway, 1989, annual rpt, 3754–3
Merchant ships in US fleet and Natl Defense Reserve Fleet, vessels, tonnage, and owner, as of July 1991, semiannual listing, 7702–2
Merchant ships in US fleet, operating subsidies, construction, and ship-related employment, monthly rpt, 7702–1
Military Sealift Command shipping operations, finances, and personnel, FY91, annual rpt, 3804–14
Oil and refined products stocks, and interdistrict shipments by mode of transport, monthly rpt, 3162–6.3
Oil company effective income tax rates, with background income and tax data for domestic and foreign operations, 1977-89, 3168–124
Oil crude, gas liquids, and refined products supply, demand, and movement, by PAD district and State, 1991, annual rpt, 3164–2
Oil tanker inbound freight price indexes, quarterly press release, 6762–13
St Lawrence Seaway ship, cargo, and passenger traffic, and toll revenue, 1991 and trends from 1959, annual rpt, 7744–2
Statistical Abstract of US, 1992 annual data compilation, 2324–1.22

Tanks
see Military vehicles

Tanner, D. Q.
"Surface Water-Quality Assessment of the Lower Kansas River Basin, Kansas and Nebraska: Concentrations of Major Metals and Trace Elements in Streambed Sediments, 1987", 5666–27.26

Tansey, John B.
"Georgia's Timber Industry—An Assessment of Timber Product Output and Use, 1989", 1208–393
"Production and Receipts of Veneer Logs in the Southeastern and Midsouth States, 1988", 1208–407

Tanzania
Agricultural trade of US, by detailed commodity and country, 1991, annual rpt, 1524–8
Agricultural trade of US, by detailed commodity and country, 1991, semiannual rpt, 1522–4
AID economic aid to developing countries, obligations and disbursements by country, quarterly rpt, 9912–4
AID loans repayment status and terms by program and country, and status of predecessor agency loans, quarterly rpt, 9912–3
Background Notes, summary social, political, and economic data, 1992 rpt, 7006–2.17
Economic and military aid and loans from US and intl agencies, by program and country, FY46-91, annual rpt, 9914–5
Economic and social conditions of developing countries from 1960s, and Intl Dev Cooperation Agency and AID activities and funding, FY91-93, annual rpt, 9904–4
Economic, population, and agricultural data, US and other aid sources, and AID activity, 1992 country rpt, 9916–12.71
Economic, social, political, and geographic summary data, by country, 1992, annual factbook, 9114–2
Exports and imports of US, by commodity and country, 1980-90, world area rpt, 9116–1.2
Exports and imports of US, by transport mode, country, and SITC 1- to 3-digit commodity, 1991, annual rpt, 2424–12
Exports of US, detailed Schedule B commodities with countries of destination, 1991, annual rpt, 2424–10
Food supply, needs, and aid for developing countries, status and alternative forecasts, 1992 world area rpt, 1526–8.2
Human rights conditions in 170 countries, and US economic and military aid, 1991, annual rpt, 21384–3
Military aid of US, arms sales, and training programs costs and budget requests, by program, world region, and country, FY91-93, annual rpt, 7144–13
Military spending, arms trade, and force strengths, with govt spending and population, by country, 1979-89, annual rpt, 9824–1
Minerals Yearbook, Vol 3, 1989: foreign country review of production, trade, and policy, by commodity, annual rpt, 5604–35.1
Population size, growth rates, and components of change, by country, projected 1990-2020 and trends from 1950, biennial rpt, 2324–9
Refugee migration, and intl aid programs, by world area and country of origin and asylum, 1991, annual rpt, 7004–15
UN voting record and share of votes in agreement with US, by issue, country, and world area, 1991, annual rpt, 7004–18

Tar
see Asphalt and tar
see Gum and wood chemicals

Tarhan, Vefa
"Does the Federal Reserve Affect Asset Prices?", 9375–13.80

Tariff Commission
see U.S. International Trade Commission

Tariffs and foreign trade controls
Agricultural, fishery, and forest products trade, tariffs, and industry operating data, commodity rpt series, 9885–8
Agricultural trade tariffs affected by North American Free Trade Agreement, and NAFTA quotas, by commodity, 1992 article, 1925–34.332
Bean (dried) prices by State, market activity, and foreign and US production, use, stocks, and trade, weekly rpt, 1311–17
Budget of US, authoritative financial statements with appropriations, outlays, and receipts, by category and agency, FY91, annual rpt, 8104–2.2
Budget of US, CBO analysis of revenue and spending alternatives and projections of economic indicators, FY93-97, annual rpt, 26304–3
Budget of US, historical data, selected years FY34-91 and projected to FY97, 108–46.5
Budget of US, obligations and authority by function, agency, and program, with summaries and analyses, FY93, annual rpt, 104–2
Budget of US, receipts by source, outlays by agency and program, and balances, monthly rpt, 8102–3
Business America, foreign and domestic commerce, and US investment and trade opportunities, biweekly journal, 2042–24
Caribbean area agricultural trade with US, by whether duty levied, commodity, and country, 1983 and 1987-91, annual article, 1925–34.329
Caribbean area duty-free exports to US, and imports from US, by country, and impact on US employment, by commodity, 1991, annual rpt, 6364–2
Caribbean area duty-free exports to US, by commodity and country, with consumer and industry impacts, 1984-91, annual rpt, 9884–20
Caribbean Basin Initiative export and investment incentives, contact listing, bibl, and US imports country, 1983-91, annual rpt, 2044–36
Chemical and energy products trade, tariffs, and industry operating data, commodity rpt series, 9885–11
Chile trade and investment policies, foreign direct investment, and US agricultural trade and tariffs, 1985-91, GAO rpt, 26119–408

Clothing exports to US, and domestic and US-owned industry production costs and operations, for Caribbean area and Mexico, impacts of North American Free Trade Agreement, 1992 rpt, 9886–4.186
Cotton, wool, and synthetic fiber production, prices, trade, and use, periodic situation rpt with articles, 1561–1
Criminal sentences for Federal offenses, guidelines by offense and circumstances, series, 17668–1
Customs Service activities and collections, bimonthly journal, 8142–2
Customs Service mgmt and trade law enforcement effectiveness, staff and broker survey results, 1992 GAO rpt, 26119–420
Dairy imports under quota by commodity, by country of origin, FAS monthly rpt, 1925–31
Electronics and services trade, tariffs, and industry operating data, commodity rpt series, 9885–12
Employment and industry impacts of trade, series, 6366–3
Energy producers finances and operations, by energy type for US firms domestic and foreign operations, 1990, annual rpt, 3164–44.1
Export and import agreements, negotiations, and related legislation, 1991, annual rpt, 444–1
Export licensing, monitoring, and enforcement activities, FY91, annual rpt, 2024–1
Exports and imports, trade agreements and relations, and USITC investigations, 1991, annual rpt, 9884–5
Exports, imports, and trade flows, by country and commodity, with background economic indicators, data compilation, monthly CD-ROM, 2002–6
Exports of goods, services, and investment, trade barriers, impacts, and US actions, by country, 1991, annual rpt, 444–2
Fed Govt receipts by source and outlays by agency, *Treasury Bulletin*, quarterly rpt, 8002–4.1
Fed Govt tax revenues, by type of tax, quarterly rpt, 2462–3
Fish and shellfish foreign market conditions for US products, country rpt series, 2166–19
Fish import duties collected, 1980s-91, annual rpt, 2164–1.6
Foreign countries agricultural production, prices, and trade, by country, 1980-91 and forecast 1992, annual world area rpt series, 1524–4
Foreign countries economic conditions, policy, and trade practices, by country, 1989-91, annual rpt, 21384–5
Generalized System of Preferences status, and US tariffs, with trade by country and US economic impacts, for selected commodities, 1987-91, annual rpt, 9884–23
Import restrictions and trade protectionism measures of US, Australia, Canada, and EC, cases initiated, 1980-85, article, 9379–1.301
Imports and tariff provisions effect on US industries and products, investigations with background financial and operating data, series, 9886–4
Imports injury to US industries from foreign subsidized products and sales at less than fair value, investigations with background financial and operating data, series, 9886–19
Imports injury to US industries from foreign subsidized products, investigations with background financial and operating data, series, 9886–15
Imports injury to US industries from sales at less than fair value, investigations with background financial and operating data, series, 9886–14
Imports injury to US industries, USITC rpts, 1984-91, annual listing, 9884–12
Imports of US given duty-free treatment for value of US material sent abroad, by commodity and country, 1987-90, annual rpt, 9884–14
Japan economic conditions, US investment and export opportunities, and trade practices, forecast 1991-93 and trends from 1988, 2048–159
Latin America, Canada, and US tobacco production and use, and related economic, health, and social issues, 1950s-92, annual rpt, 4204–18
Latin America exports, investment, debt, and tariffs for 7 countries, and trade and investment policy liberalization issues, mid 1960s-91, 9886–4.184
Lumber and wood products trade and export promotion of US by country, and trade balance, by commodity, FAS periodic circular, 1925–36
Machinery and equipment trade, tariffs, and industry operating data, commodity rpt series, 9885–9
Manufacturing industry (US) intl competitiveness, trade and economic policies with background data and foreign comparisons, 1991 rpt, 26358–252
Manufacturing trade, tariffs, and industry operating data, commodity rpt series, 9885–10
Maritime Commission activities, case filings by type and disposition, and civil penalties by shipper, FY91, annual rpt, 9334–1
Meat plants inspected and certified for exporting to US, by country, 1991, annual listing, 1374–2
Mexico and US economic and trade impacts of proposed North American Free Trade Agreement, with data on maquiladora plants, 1980s-90, hearings, 21788–210
Mexico fruit trade with US, 1989-91, and US tariffs under proposed North American Free Trade Agreement, 1992, by commodity, article, 1561–6.304
Mexico trade with US and other countries, foreign investment, and maquiladoras operations, 1980s-91, GAO rpt, 26119–417
Mineral Industry Surveys, commodity reviews of production, trade, use, and industry operations, advance annual rpt series, 5614–5
Minerals and metals trade, tariffs, and industry operating data, commodity rpt series, 9885–13
Minerals production, prices, trade, use, employment, tariffs, and stockpiles, by mineral, with foreign comparisons, 1987-91, annual rpt, 5604–18
Natl income and product accounts and components, *Survey of Current Business*, monthly rpt, 2702–1.23
Natl income and product accounts, comprehensive accounts and components, benchmark revisions, 1929-88, 2708–5
Natl income and product accounts, comprehensive accounts and components, *Survey of Current Business*, monthly rpt, 2702–1.26
Oil imports from OPEC, economic impacts of tariffs and excise taxes, model description and results, 1992 technical paper, 9379–12.96
Overseas Business Reports: economic conditions, investment and export opportunities, and trade practices, country market research rpt series, 2046–6
Romania trade with US, and US import tariff rates, by commodity, 1985-91, GAO rpt, 26119–414
Shipbuilding and repair subsidy elimination proposals of US and OECD, impacts on industry and trade, with data on US-flag vessels, 1980s-91, 9886–4.183
Sugar and honey foreign and US production, prices, trade, and use, FAS periodic circular series, 1925–14
Sugar and sugar product imports of US under quota, by country, weekly rpt, 1922–9
Tariff Schedule of US, classifications and rates of duty for detailed imported commodities, and codes for ports and foreign countries, 1992 base edition supplement, 9886–13
Textile and apparel foreign market conditions for US exports, with domestic industry operations, country rpt series, 2046–15
Textile products trade regulations of foreign countries, and US exports, by commodity and country, 1989-91, biennial rpt, 2044–18
US attorneys civil and criminal cases by type and disposition, and collections, by Federal district, FY91, annual rpt, 6004–2.1
USITC activities, investigations, and rpts, FY91, annual rpt, 9884–1
see also Common markets and free trade areas
see also Dumping
see also General Agreement on Tariffs and Trade
see also International sanctions
see also North American Free Trade Agreement

Tarone, Robert E.
"Implications of Birth Cohort Patterns in Interpreting Trends in Breast Cancer Rates", 4472–1.341

Tarrant County, Tex.
Housing and households characteristics, unit and neighborhood quality, and journey to work by MSA location, for 11 MSAs, 1985 survey, supplement, 2485–8
Housing and households detailed characteristics, and unit and neighborhood quality, by location, 1989 survey, MSA rpt, 2485–6.6

Tashjian, Michael D.
"Unlocking Learning: Chapter 1 in Correctional Facilities. National Study of the Chapter 1 Neglected or Delinquent Program: Descriptive Study Findings", 4808–40.4

Task Force on Defense, Foreign Policy and Space. House
R&D funding of Fed Govt for large-scale projects, issues and impacts on other research, with data for space station and super collider, 1991 hearings, 21268–43
Tatom, John A.
"Recent Credit Crunch: The Neglected Dimensions", 9391–1.315
"1990 Oil Price Hike in Perspective", 9391–1.301
Tax appeals
see Tax protests and appeals
Tax Court of the U.S.
Budget of US, authoritative financial statements with appropriations, outlays, and receipts, by category and agency, FY91, annual rpt, 8104–2.2
Budget of US, obligations and authority by function, agency, and program, with summaries and analyses, FY93, annual rpt, 104–2
Caseloads of Court and recoveries, FY92, annual tables, 18224–5
Caseloads of US Tax Court, and tax due, by disposition, FY91, annual tables, 18224–3
IRS enforcement and litigation activity, with data by type of tax, FY91, annual rpt, 8304–3.3
Tax courts
see Tax Court of the U.S.
see Tax laws and courts
Tax credits
see Tax expenditures
see Tax incentives and shelters
Tax delinquency and evasion
Corporations income tax compliance, and IRS enforcement activities, 1970s-92, hearing, 25408–118
Corporations income tax compliance issues for large firms, with income, taxes paid, and tax credits, 1988, GAO rpt, 26119–405
Court criminal case processing in Federal district courts, and dispositions, by offense, district, and offender characteristics, 1989, annual data compilation, 6064–29
Court criminal case processing in Federal district courts, and dispositions, by offense, 1980-91, annual rpt, 6064–31
Debt delinquent on Federal accounts, cases and collections of Justice Dept and private law firms, pilot project results, FY91, annual rpt, 6004–20
Fed Govt agencies delinquent withholding tax accounts, and compared to other taxpayers, 1990, hearing, 21788–206
Income tax admin and compliance issues, and taxpayer views, 1991 conf, 8304–25
IRS collections, enforcement, and litigation activity, with data by type of tax, region, and State, FY91, annual rpt, 8304–3
IRS undercover criminal investigations and costs by criminal activity, and success rates, by region, mid 1980s-90, GAO rpt, 26119–394
Sentences for Federal crimes, guidelines use and results by offense and district, and Sentencing Commission activities, 1991, annual rpt, 17664–1
Sentences for Federal offenses, guidelines by offense and circumstances, series, 17668–1
Tax enforcement activities and collections of Bur of Alcohol, Tobacco, and Firearms and IRS, 1991 hearing, 21788–217
Tax exempt organizations
Finances of nonprofit charitable and other exempt organizations, by asset and contributions size and category, 1988, annual article, 8302–2.315
Finances of tax exempt organizations, with data by type, size, State, and for largest organizations, late 1940s-80s, compilation of papers, 8308–35
Finances of tax exempt organizations with unrelated business income, by organization type, 1987, article, 8302–2.306
IRS collections, by excise tax source, quarterly rpt, 8302–1
IRS collections, enforcement, and litigation activity, with data by type of tax, region, and State, FY91, annual rpt, 8304–3
IRS tax returns and supplemental documents filed, by type, FY91 and projected to FY2000, semiannual rpt, 8302–4
IRS tax returns and supplemental documents filed, by type, 1990 and projected to 1999, annual article, 8302–2.304
IRS tax returns filed, by type of filer, quarterly rpt, 8302–2.1
IRS tax returns filed, by type of tax and IRS district, 1990 and projected 1991-98, annual rpt, 8304–24
IRS tax returns filed, by type of tax and IRS region and service center, projected 1991-98 and trends from 1978, annual rpt, 8304–9
Tax exempt securities
Assets and debts of private sector, balance sheets by segment, 1960-91, semiannual rpt, 9365–4.1
Families financial status, income, net worth, and assets and debt by type, by income and selected characteristics, 1983 and 1989, article, 9362–1.301
Finances of govts, tax systems and revenue, and fiscal structure, by level of govt and State, 1992 and historical trends, annual rpt, 10044–1
Flow-of-funds accounts, savings, investments, and credit statements, quarterly rpt, 9365–3.3
Higher education instn R&D facilities space and equipment adequacy, needs, and funding by source, by instn type and control, 1992, biennial rpt, 9624–25
Ownership of govt securities, dealer transactions and financing sources, and new State and local issues, monthly rpt, 9362–1.1
see also Municipal bonds
Tax expenditures
Budget of US, CBO analysis of revenue and spending alternatives and projections of economic indicators, FY93-97, annual rpt, 26304–3
Budget of US, House concurrent resolution, with spending and revenue targets, FY93 and projected to FY97, annual rpt, 21264–2
Budget of US, obligations and authority by function, agency, and program, with summaries and analyses, FY93, annual rpt, 104–2
Education funding by Federal agency, program, and recipient type, and instn spending, 1960s-91, annual rpt, 4824–8
Employee benefits tax exclusion, Federal revenue forgone and coverage indicators, by benefit type, 1950s-80s and projected to 1995, GAO rpt, 26119–389
Fed Govt programs under Ways and Means Committee jurisdiction, finances, operations, and participant characteristics, FY70s-91, annual rpt, 21784–11
Health care spending and factors in costs, with data by payment source and service type, 1960s-90 and projected to 2000, 26306–6.175
Mail order sales from out of State, tax revenue losses by State, 1990-92, 10048–84
Municipal bond interest tax exemption economic impacts, 1980s-90, article, 9373–1.310
Pension plan earnings and contributions tax exclusions, cost and benefit issues with background data, 1970s-FY92, article, 9373–1.305
Pension plans employer contributions and plan earnings income tax exclusions, tax revenue losses by plan type, FY90-92, working paper, 9373–27.2
Puerto Rico and other US possessions corporations income tax returns, income and tax items, and employment, by selected industry, 1989, article, 8302–2.326
Statistical Abstract of US, 1992 annual data compilation, 2324–1.10
Tax incentives and shelters
Boycotts (intl) by OPEC and other countries, US firms and individuals cooperation and tax benefits denied, 1990, article, 8302–2.323
Budget of US, CBO analysis and review of FY93 budget by function, annual rpt, 26304–2
Budget of US, CBO analysis of revenue and spending alternatives and projections of economic indicators, FY93-97, annual rpt, 26304–3
Budget of US, obligations and authority by function, agency, and program, with summaries and analyses, FY93, annual rpt, 104–2
Caribbean area duty-free exports to US, by commodity and country, with consumer and industry impacts, 1984-91, annual rpt, 9884–20
Caribbean Basin Initiative export and investment incentives, contact listing, bibl, and US imports country, 1983-91, annual rpt, 2044–36
Charitable contributions impacts of income tax policy, model description and results, 1991 working paper, 6886–6.83
Corporations income tax compliance issues for large firms, with income, taxes paid, and tax credits, 1988, GAO rpt, 26119–405
Corporations income tax returns, income and tax items by asset size and detailed industry, 1989, annual rpt, 8304–4; 8304–21
Corporations income tax returns, summary data by asset size and industry div, 1989, annual article, 8302–2.321
Corporations income taxes and effective rates on US, foreign, and worldwide income, by company and industry, 1980s, GAO rpt, 26119–289

Dependent care tax credit impacts of Family Support Act, Federal revenue losses and gains, FY88-93, 21788–212
Domestic Intl Sales Corps (Interest Charge) income tax returns, assets, and income and tax items, by detailed industry, 1987, article, 8302–2.312
Earned income tax credit advance payment option, participation, taxpayer awareness, employer burden, and IRS administration, 1989-90, GAO rpt, 26119–378
Electric utilities privately owned, finances and operations, detailed data, 1990, annual rpt, 3164–23
Energy conservation technologies for housing and commercial buildings, use, costs, efficiency, and residential tax credits, 1970s-90 and projected to 2010, 26358–259
Energy natl strategy fossil fuel, electric power, conservation, and pollution reduction issues, 1991 hearings, 21368–136
Energy producers finances and operations, by energy type for US firms domestic and foreign operations, 1990, annual rpt, 3164–44.1
Enterprise zone programs of States, business investment and jobs created, and incentive programs, by State, 1992 annual rpt, 5124–9
Estate tax returns for nonresident aliens, property and tax data, by estate size and decedent country of residence, 1986, article, 8302–2.310
Fed Govt programs under Ways and Means Committee jurisdiction, finances, operations, and participant characteristics, FY70s-91, annual rpt, 21784–11
Financial instns loan loss computations for tax returns under alternative methods, 1991 rpt, 8008–157
Foreign corporations and individuals, and US entities abroad, detailed data compilation for income tax returns, 1970s-89, quinquennial rpt, 8308–31
Foreign countries tax credits on corporate income tax returns, with income and tax items by industry group, 1988, biennial article, 8302–2.316
Foreign-earned income on US individual returns, income and tax items by income level and occupation, 1987, article, 8302–2.301
Foreign-owned corporate activity in US, income tax returns and selected income and tax items, by industry div and selected country, 1988, article, 8302–2.309
Foreign partners of US partnerships, income and tax withheld, by country, 1990, article, 8302–2.324
Foreign Sales Corps income tax returns, assets, and income and tax items, by industry, country of incorporation, and transaction pricing method, 1987, article, 8302–2.311
Gasohol and ethanol tax incentives, by State, as of 1991, annual rpt, 3164–97
Health care (long-term) financing reform issues, 1991 rpt, 10176–3.7
Health care system and OASDHI operations and reform issues, public opinion, 1991 surveys, 10176–2.2
Households income and poverty status under alternative income definitions, by recipient characteristics, 1991, annual Current Population Rpt, 2546–6.78
Housing (low income) developers tax credits, subsidies, project and tenant characteristics, and investor returns, 1987-88, 5188–133
Income tax admin and compliance issues, and taxpayer views, 1991 conf, 8304–25
Individual income tax returns, detailed data, 1988, annual rpt, 8304–2
Individual income tax returns, selected income and tax items by income level, preliminary 1990, annual article, 8302–2.307
Intangible assets from acquired businesses, tax deductions for amortization, IRS unresolved audits, and claims allowed, 1991 GAO rpt, 26119–365
Israel economic conditions, US investment and export opportunities, and trade practices, 1992 rpt, 2008–32
Litigation, enforcement, and collection activity of IRS, with data by type of tax, region, and State, FY91, annual rpt, 8304–3
Multinatl firms US affiliates income tax compliance issues, with income and tax data by industry group, 1987-89, press release, 8008–155
Multinatl US firms foreign affiliates, income statement items by asset size, industry, and country, 1988, biennial article, 8302–2.322
Natural gas interstate pipeline company detailed financial and operating data, by firm, 1990, annual rpt, 3164–38
Nonprofit charitable organizations finances, summary data by asset size, 1989, article, 8302–2.325
Partnership income and losses impact of 1986 Tax Reform Act, by profit status and selected industry, 1980s, article, 8302–2.313
Puerto Rico and other US possessions corporations income tax returns, income and tax items, and employment, by selected industry, 1989, article, 8302–2.326
Puerto Rico statehood referendum proposal, with background data on Federal outlays, economic conditions, and finances of corporations with tax-favored status, 1940s-88, hearing, 21448–46
Returns filed, by type of filer, detailed preliminary and supplementary data, quarterly rpt with articles, 8302–2
Small business capital formation sources and issues, 1991 annual conf, 9734–4
State and local govt tax rates and revenue, by source and State, 1992 and historical trends, annual rpt, 10044–1
Statistical Abstract of US, 1992 annual data compilation, 2324–1.17
Tax exempt organizations with unrelated business income, finances by organization type, 1987, article, 8302–2.306
Value added tax alternative proposals revenue impacts, with background data and intl comparisons, 1992 rpt, 26306–6.168
see also Individual retirement arrangements
see also Oil depletion allowances
see also Tax exempt organizations
see also Tax exempt securities
see also Tax expenditures

Tax laws and courts
Corporations income tax compliance, and IRS enforcement activities, 1970s-92, hearing, 25408–118
Court caseloads and recoveries, for US Tax Court, FY92, annual tables, 18224–5
Court caseloads for US Tax Court, and tax due, by disposition, FY91, annual tables, 18224–3
Court civil and criminal caseloads for Federal district, appeals, and bankruptcy courts, by type of suit and offense, circuit, and district, 1991, annual rpt, 18204–11
Court civil and criminal caseloads for Federal district, appeals, and special courts, 1991, annual rpt, 18204–8
Court criminal case processing in Federal courts by disposition, and prisoners, by offense and jurisdiction, data compilation, 1992 annual rpt, 6064–6.5; 6064–6.6
IRS collections, enforcement, and litigation activity, with data by type of tax, region, and State, FY91, annual rpt, 8304–3
Prison and parole admissions and releases, sentence length, and time served, by offense and offender characteristics, 1988, annual rpt, 6064–33
Prisoners in Federal and contract instns, by selected characteristics, region, and Federal instn, FY89, annual rpt, 6244–1.1
Sentences for Federal offenses, guidelines by offense and circumstances, series, 17668–1
Unemployment insurance programs of States, benefits, coverage, and tax provisions, as of July 1992, semiannual listing, 6402–7
US attorneys civil and criminal cases by type and disposition, and collections, by Federal district, FY91, annual rpt, 6004–2.1; 6004–2.5
see also Tax delinquency and evasion
see also Tax protests and appeals
see also Tax reform

Tax loopholes
see Tax incentives and shelters

Tax protests and appeals
Claims Court caseload by type of suit, and judgments, FY92, annual rpt, 18224–1
Court civil and criminal caseloads for Federal district, appeals, and bankruptcy courts, by type of suit and offense, circuit, and district, 1991, annual rpt, 18204–11
Court civil and criminal caseloads for Federal district, appeals, and special courts, 1991, annual rpt, 18204–8
IRS collections, enforcement, and litigation activity, with data by type of tax, region, and State, FY91, annual rpt, 8304–3

Tax reform
Brackets (income) simplification under tax reform in US and other countries, fiscal effects, late 1970s-92, working paper, 9377–9.143
Budget of US, CBO analysis of revenue and spending alternatives and projections of economic indicators, FY93-97, annual rpt, 26304–3
Budget of US, House Budget Committee analysis of Bush Admin proposals and economic assumptions, FY93, 21268–42

Capital gains and other tax changes, impacts on stock prices and returns, model description and results, 1992 technical paper, 9379–12.97
Eastern Europe transition to market economies, tax reform issues, with tax rates, revenue, and govt spending compared to EC, by selected country, late 1960s-91, technical paper, 9366–7.278
Income tax admin and compliance issues, and taxpayer views, 1991 conf, 8304–25
Income tax returns filed using alternative methods, with fraud, and conventional form preparation time and processing costs, 1986-92, GAO rpt, 26119–400
Loans (consumer) of banks, relation to bank-auto finance company interest rate spread, tax reform, and other factors, 1970s-91, working paper, 9379–12.88
Partnership income and losses impact of 1986 Tax Reform Act, by profit status and selected industry, 1980s, article, 8302–2.313
Returns and supplemental documents filed, by type, 1990 and projected to 1999, annual article, 8302–2.304
Semiconductor industry capital investment and R&D spending under alternative tax proposals, and asset/equity ratios by selected firm, 1980s-91, working paper, 15036–1.2

Tax sharing
see Revenue sharing

Taxation
Agricultural Statistics, 1991, annual rpt, 1004–1
Banks in Fed Reserve System, expenses and operations itemized by service, office, and district, 1991, annual rpt, 9364–11
Budget deficit forecasting accuracy, contributing factors, and analysis of major programs, FY91, annual GAO rpt, 26104–23
Budget of US, authoritative financial statements with appropriations, outlays, and receipts, by agency, FY91, annual rpt, 8104–2
Budget of US, CBO analysis and review of FY93 budget by function, annual rpt, 26304–2
Budget of US, CBO analysis of revenue and spending alternatives and projections of economic indicators, FY93-97, annual rpt, 26304–3
Budget of US, House concurrent resolution, with spending and revenue targets, FY93 and projected to FY97, annual rpt, 21264–2
Budget of US, obligations and authority by function, agency, and program, with summaries and analyses, FY93, annual rpt, 104–2
Budget of US, receipts by source, outlays by agency and program, and balances, monthly rpt, 8102–3
Business statistics, detailed data for major industries and economic indicators, 1960-91, *Survey of Current Business* biennial supplement, 2704–1
Communications services revenue and expenses, itemized by SIC 2- to 4-digit kind of business, 1990, annual rpt, 2413–15
Corporations income tax returns, income and tax items by asset size and detailed industry, 1989, annual rpt, 8304–4; 8304–21
Eastern Europe transition to market economies, tax reform issues, with tax rates, revenue, and govt spending compared to EC, by selected country, late 1960s-91, technical paper, 9366–7.278
Economic performance and income distribution impacts of tax policy, issues and background data, with foreign comparisons, 1991 and trends, 21788–211
Electric power demand, and industrial and employment impacts of capacity shortfalls and new power plants, by selected State, 1960s-80s and projected to 2000, hearing, 21248–163
Electric power plants production and capital costs, operations, and fuel use, by fuel type, plant, utility, and location, 1990, annual rpt, 3164–9
Fed Govt finances, cash and debt transactions, daily tables, 8102–4
Fed Govt internal revenue and refunds, by type of tax, quarterly rpt, 8302–2.1
Fed Govt receipts by source and outlays by agency, *Treasury Bulletin*, quarterly rpt, 8002–4.1
Fed Govt tax receipts, monthly rpt, quarterly and annual data, 23842–1.6
Finances of govts, tax systems and revenue, and fiscal structure, by level of govt and State, 1992 and historical trends, annual rpt, 10044–1
Financial and economic analysis, technical paper series, 8006–6
Flow-of-funds accounts, savings, investments, and credit statements, quarterly rpt, 9365–3.3
Foreign and US income and capital tax policies, with background data for EC, Japan, and US, mid 1960s-91, article, 9373–1.316
Foreign travelers to US, spending by world area of residence, and economic impacts, by spending category and State, 1989, 2908–28
Gross State Product by component, industry div, and State, 1977-89, article, 2702–1.303
Health care financing reform issues, 1991 rpt, 10176–3.2
Households composition, income, benefits, and labor force status, Survey of Income and Program Participation methodology, working paper series, 2626–10
Input-output structure of US economy, detailed interindustry transactions for 541 industries, and components of final demand, 1982 benchmark data, 2708–17
IRS collections, enforcement, and litigation activity, with data by type of tax, region, and State, FY91, annual rpt, 8304–3
Military spending reductions, economic impacts by defense contractor, industry, State, and congressional district, 1989-90 hearings, 23848–224
Multinatl firms US affiliates, finances, and operations, by industry, world area of parent firm, and State, 1989-90, annual rpt, 2704–4
Multinatl US firms and foreign affiliates finances and operations, by industry and country, 1989 benchmark survey, annual rpt, 2704–5
Natl income and product accounts and components, *Survey of Current Business*, monthly rpt, 2702–1.23
Natl income and product accounts, comprehensive accounts and components, benchmark revisions, 1929-88, 2708–5
Natl income and product accounts, comprehensive accounts and components, *Survey of Current Business*, monthly rpt, 2702–1.26
Natural gas interstate pipeline company detailed financial and operating data, by firm, 1990, annual rpt, 3164–38
Nonprofit charitable organizations finances, summary data by asset size, 1989, article, 8302–2.325
Nonprofit charitable organizations finances, with data by State and for top 10 instns, 1988, article, 8302–2.302
Oil resources recovery impacts of environmental regulation, under alternative oil price, technology, and regulatory assumptions, projected 1990-2015, 3338–2
Public debt burden on future generations forecast under alternative tax, OASDI, and Medicare policies, 1992 working paper, 9377–9.137
Public opinion on taxes, spending, and govt efficiency, by respondent characteristics, 1992 survey, annual rpt, 10044–2
Small Business Admin loan guarantee program participants finances, operations, characteristics, and views, 1991 survey, 9768–25
Statistical Abstract of US, 1992 annual data compilation, 2324–1.10
Tax exempt organizations with unrelated business income, finances by organization type, 1987, article, 8302–2.306
Telephone and telegraph firms detailed finances and operations, 1990, annual rpt, 9284–6
Telephone firms borrowing under Rural Telephone Program, and financial and operating data, by State, 1991, annual rpt, 1244–2
Treasury tax and loan account deposits, Fed Reserve Banks mgmt of securities held as collateral, 1991, GAO rpt, 26111–80
Truck and warehouse services finances and inventory, by SIC 2- to 4-digit industry, 1990 survey, annual rpt, 2413–14
Truck interstate carriers finances and operations, by district, 1990, annual rpt, 9486–5.2
see also Estate tax
see also Excise tax
see also Fuel tax
see also Gift tax
see also Income taxes
see also Licenses and permits
see also Oil depletion allowances
see also Property tax
see also Revenue sharing
see also Sales tax
see also Severance taxes
see also Social security tax
see also State and local taxes
see also Tariffs and foreign trade controls
see also Tax delinquency and evasion
see also Tax exempt organizations
see also Tax exempt securities
see also Tax expenditures
see also Tax incentives and shelters
see also Tax laws and courts
see also Tax protests and appeals

see also Tax reform
see also Unemployment insurance tax
see also Value added tax
see also Windfall profit tax
see also Withholding tax

Taxicabs
Auto fleet size, trip characteristics, and energy use, by fleet type, 1970s-90, annual rpt, 3304–5.3
Commuting to work, by mode, trip duration, and work location, 1980 and 1990, 7558–120
Consumer spending, natl income and product account benchmark revisions, 1929-88, 2708–5
Consumer spending, natl income and product accounts, comprehensive accounts and components, *Survey of Current Business*, monthly rpt, 2702–1.25
County Business Patterns, 1989: employment, establishments, and payroll, by SIC 2- to 4-digit industry and county, annual State rpt series, 2326–8
County Business Patterns, 1990: employment, establishments, and payroll, by SIC 2- to 4-digit industry and county, annual State rpt series, 2326–6
Drivers licenses issued and in force by age and sex, fees, and renewal, by license class and State, 1990, annual rpt, 7554–16
Employment, earnings, and hours, by SIC 1- to 4-digit industry, monthly 1989-Feb 1992, annual rpt, 6744–4
Housing and households characteristics, unit and neighborhood quality, and journey to work by MSA location, for 11 MSAs, 1985 survey, supplement, 2485–8
Housing and households detailed characteristics, and unit and neighborhood quality, by location, 1989, biennial rpt supplement, 2485–13
Occupational injury and illness rates, by SIC 2- to 4-digit industry, 1989-90, annual rpt, 6844–7
Occupational injury and illness rates, by SIC 2- to 4-digit industry, 1990, annual rpt, 6844–1
Pacific territories population and housing detailed characteristics, by location, 1990 Census of Population and Housing, series, 2551–8
Tax (income) returns of sole proprietorships, income statement items, by industry group, 1990, annual article, 8302–2.317; 8302–2.320
Travel to US, by characteristics of visit and traveler, world area of origin, and US destination, 1991 survey, annual rpt, 2904–12

Taylor, Bruce M.
"School Crime: A National Crime Victimization Survey Report", 6066–3.46

Taylor, Donald H., Jr.
"One State's Response to the Malpractice Insurance Crisis: North Carolina's Rural Obstetrical Care Incentive Program", 4042–3.355

Taylor, G. F.
"Quantity and Quality of Stormwater Runoff from Western Daytona Beach, Fla., and Adjacent Areas", 5666–27.28

Taylor, Jack A.
"ras Oncogene Activation and Occupational Exposures in Acute Myeloid Leukemia", 4472–1.352

Taylor, Jane E.
"Montana Forest Pest Conditions and Program Highlights, 1990", 1206–49.2

Taylor, Lori L.
"Measuring the Value of School Quality", 9379–12.94
"Student Emigration and the Willingness To Pay for Public Schools: A Test of the Publicness of Public High Schools in the U.S.", 9379–12.81

Taylor, Maureen H.
"Oceanographic Observations in the Inner New York Bight in Support of the 12-Mile Dumpsite Study, 1987-89", 2168–130

Taylor-Shirley, Katherine
"Profiles in Safety and Health: Occupational Hazards of Meatpacking", 6728–41

Tea
Agricultural Statistics, 1991, annual rpt, 1004–1
Business statistics, detailed data for major industries and economic indicators, *Survey of Current Business*, monthly rpt, 2702–1.13
Business statistics, detailed data for major industries and economic indicators, 1960-91, *Survey of Current Business* biennial supplement, 2704–1
Consumption, supply, trade, prices, spending, and indexes, by food commodity, 1990, annual rpt, 1544–4
Cuba trade, by commodity and country, mid 1980s-91, 9118–8
Exports and imports (agricultural) of US, by commodity and country, bimonthly rpt, 1522–1
Exports and imports (agricultural) of US, by detailed commodity and country, 1991, annual rpt, 1524–8
Exports and imports (agricultural) of US, by detailed commodity and country, 1991, semiannual rpt, 1522–4
Exports and imports between US and outlying areas, by detailed commodity and mode of transport, 1991, annual rpt, 2424–11
Exports and imports of US, by country and detailed commodity, monthly rpt, 2422–12
Exports and imports of US, by Harmonized System 6-digit commodity and country, 1991, annual rpt, 2424–13
Exports and imports of US, by transport mode, country, and SITC 1- to 3-digit commodity, 1991, annual rpt, 2424–12
Exports of US, detailed Schedule B commodities with countries of destination, 1991, annual rpt, 2424–10
Foreign and US tea and herbal production, prices, and trade, FAS annual circular series, 1925–15
Foreign countries agricultural production, prices, and trade, by country, 1980-91 and forecast 1992, annual world area rpt series, 1524–4
Manufacturing annual survey, 1990: finances and operations, by SIC 2- to 4-digit industry, series, 2506–14
Price indexes (producer), by stage of processing and detailed commodity, monthly rpt, 6762–6
Price indexes (producer), by stage of processing and detailed commodity, monthly 1991, annual rpt, 6764–2
Weight and volume conversion factors for agricultural commodities and products, 1992 rpt, 1508–3

Teacher education
Assistance (financial and nonfinancial) of Fed Govt, 1992 base edition, annual listing, 104–5
Child day care and early childhood education programs availability, demand, use, costs, and provider and enrollee characteristics, 1990 survey, 4808–39
Degree (PhD) recipients in higher education, by field and selected characteristics, 1979, 1984, and 1989, 4848–44
Degrees awarded in higher education, by level, field, race, and sex, 1989/90 and trends from 1980/81, annual rpt, 4844–17
Digest of Education Statistics, 1992 annual data compilation, 4824–2
Eighth grade class of 1988: educational performance and conditions, characteristics, attitudes, activities, and plans, natl longitudinal survey, series, 4826–9
Elementary and secondary students educational performance, and factors affecting proficiency, by selected characteristics, 1990 natl assessments, subject rpt series, 4896–8
Fulbright-Hays academic exchanges, grants by purpose, and foreign govt share of costs, by country, FY91, annual rpt, 10324–1
Science and Engineering Indicators, employment, education, R&D funding, and industry impacts, with foreign comparisons, 1960s-91, biennial rpt, 9624–10.1
Science and math teacher dev project of Education Dept, school district participation by State, 1989/90, GAO rpt, 26121–488
Special education staff, training, degrees, and certification, by field and State, FY89, annual rpt, 4944–4
Vocational education enrollment, student and teacher characteristics, and outcomes, for secondary and postsecondary instns, 1970s-90, 4828–42

Teachers
Black higher education instns enrollment, finances, staff, and degrees, by instn and selected student characteristics, 1970s-90, 4848–46
Child day care and early childhood education programs availability, demand, use, costs, and provider and enrollee characteristics, 1990 survey, 4808–39
Condition of Education, detail for elementary, secondary, and higher education, 1920s-91 and projected to 2002, annual rpt, 4824–1
Crime victimization in schools, drug availability, and preventive measures, with student views, 1989 survey, 6066–3.46
Data on education, enrollment, degrees, teachers, and spending, 1977/78-1990/91 and alternative projections to 2002/2003, annual rpt, 4824–4

Data on education, enrollment, finances, teachers, and other characteristics, by State, 1969-89, 4828–33
Data on education, selected trends and projections 1979-2002, annual pamphlet, 4824–9
Data on education, 1940s-95, pamphlet, 4828–35
Data on education, 1960s-91, annual pamphlet, 4824–3
Digest of Education Statistics, 1992 annual data compilation, 4824–2
Eighth grade class of 1988: educational performance and conditions, characteristics, attitudes, activities, and plans, natl longitudinal survey, series, 4826–9
Elementary and secondary education enrollment, staff, finances, operations, programs, and policies, 1987/88 biennial survey, series, 4836–3
Elementary and secondary education enrollment, teachers, high school grads, and spending, by instn control and State, 1992/93, annual rpt, 4834–19
Elementary and secondary public school agencies, by enrollment size and location, fall 1990, annual listing, 4834–1
Elementary and secondary public school systems enrollment, finances, staff, and high school grads, by State, FY89-90, annual rpt, 4834–6
Elementary and secondary students educational performance, and factors affecting proficiency, by selected characteristics, 1990 natl assessments, subject rpt series, 4896–8
Elementary and secondary students educational performance in math, science, reading, and writing, 1969-90, 4898–32
Elementary and secondary students educational performance, issues and special topics, natl assessments, fact sheet series, 4896–9
Employment and payroll, by function and level of govt, annual rpt series, 2466–1
Employment, enrollment, and spending, by instn level and control, and teachers salaries, 1980s-93, annual press release, 4804–19
Employment, unemployment, and labor force characteristics, by region and census div, 1991, annual rpt, 6744–7.1
Flight and ground instructors certificates held and issued, by region, State, and for women, 1990, annual rpt, 7504–1.7
Flight and ground instructors certified by FAA, by age, sex, region, and State, 1991, annual rpt, 7504–2
Fulbright-Hays academic exchanges, grants by purpose, and foreign govt share of costs, by country, FY91, annual rpt, 10324–1
Health care professionals supply and education, by professional and other characteristics, and location, 1960s-92 and projected to 2020, biennial rpt, 4114–8
Higher education enrollment, faculty, finances, and degrees, by instn level and control, and State, FY88, annual rpt, 4844–13
Higher education faculty and salaries, by rank, sex, instn type and control, and State, 1990/91, annual rpt, 4844–8
Higher education faculty and staff, by occupation, full- and part-time status, sex, and instn type and control, fall 1989, biennial rpt, 4844–18
Higher education PhD degree recipients employment plans, by employer type, work activity, and field, 1979, 1984, and 1989, 4848–44
Juvenile facilities compensatory education programs activities, participant and staff characteristics, and outcomes, 1991 rpts, 4808–40
Labor demand, turnover, and training completions, by detailed occupation, 1990 and projected to 2005, biennial rpt, 6744–3
Military service academies prep schools costs and student performance indicators, 1988-90, GAO rpt, 26123–380
Military training and education programs funding, staff, students, and facilities, by service branch, FY93, annual rpt, 3504–5
Natl Education Goals progress indicators, by State, 1992, annual rpt, 15914–1
Occupational Outlook Handbook, 1992-93, biennial rpt, 6744–1
Physicians, by specialty, age, sex, and location of training and practice, 1990, State rpt series, 4116–6
Private elementary and secondary schools, students, and staff characteristics, by school type and affiliation, 1987/88, 4836–3.8
Reading performance and factors affecting proficiency, for elementary and secondary students, 1988 and 1990 natl assessments, 4898–33
Science and engineering employment characteristics of minorities, women, and disabled, by field, 1970s-91, biennial rpt, 9624–20.1
Science and Engineering Indicators, employment, education, R&D funding, and industry impacts, with foreign comparisons, 1960s-91, biennial rpt, 9624–10
Science and engineering labor force, Federal and university research funding, and educational data, series, 9626–6
Science and math achievement relation to selected school characteristics, natl assessment of elementary and high school students, 1985/86, 4896–6.7
Special education programs, enrollment by age, staff, funding, and needs, by type of handicap and State, 1990/91, annual rpt, 4944–4
States elementary and secondary curricula, competency, and attendance requirements, with background data, 1970s-90, 4838–52
Statistical Abstract of US, 1992 annual data compilation, 2324–1.4
Vocational education enrollment, student and teacher characteristics, and outcomes, for secondary and postsecondary instns, 1970s-90, 4828–42
Vocational education teachers, by subject area and selected characteristics, for public high schools, 1987/88, 4836–3.9
see also Educational employees pay
see also Teacher education

Teaching aids and devices
see Educational materials
see Educational technology

Teague, Susan M.
"Tolerance of Beta Blocked Hypertensives During Orthostatic and Altitude Stresses", 7506–10.119

Technical assistance
see International assistance
see Military assistance

Technical Assistance and Training Corp.
"Survey of Substance Abuse Programs in the Mining Industry", 6668–8

Technical education
see Vocational education and training

Technicians
see Clinical laboratory technicians
see Scientists and technicians

Technological innovations
Auto (electric-powered) R&D activity and DOE funding shares, FY91, annual rpt, 3304–2
Auto fuel economy improvements from new technologies, 1987-90 and alternative projections to 2010, 26358–251
Capital investment in high technology equipment, relation to productivity growth, 1950s-89, article, 9385–1.310
Competitiveness (intl) of US high technology industries, with background data by industry and foreign comparisons, 1960s-91, GAO rpt, 26123–406
Containers (wood) industry productivity trends and technological devs, 1977-89, article, 6722–1.344
Economic indicators, prices, labor costs, and productivity, BLS econometric analyses and methodology, working paper series, 6886–6
Economies of scale in output, technology, and trade, model description and results, 1992 technical paper, 9383–20.22
Energy natl strategy fossil fuel, electric power, conservation, and pollution reduction issues, 1991 hearings, 21368–136
Engineering research and education grants of NSF, FY91, annual listing, 9624–24
Fish fresh and frozen products industry productivity trends and technological devs, 1972-90, article, 6722–1.342
Labor force, composition, and productivity effects of technological devs, 1970s-90 and projected to 2005, industry rpt series, 6826–2
Manufacturing industry (US) intl competitiveness, trade and economic policies with background data and foreign comparisons, 1991 rpt, 26358–252
Market potential of industrial and Federal labs technological innovations, results of annual ***R&D 100*** awards competition, 1960s-90, 2218–86
Medicare enrollees magnetic resonance imaging, endoscopic, and CAT scan procedures use rate, by State, 1986-90, annual rpt, 17266–1.7
NSF R&D grant awards, by div and program, periodic rpt series, 9626–7
Nuts and bolts industry productivity trends and technological devs, 1958-90, article, 6722–1.343
Productivity relation to high technology capital investment, by industry sector, 1940s-80s, technical paper, 9385–8.130

Science and Engineering Indicators, employment, education, R&D funding, and industry impacts, with foreign comparisons, 1960s-91, biennial rpt, 9624–10
Small business product and service R&D grants of Fed Govt, indicators of commercial success, FY88-90, chartbook, 9768–23
Small business R&D grants of Fed Govt, by program area, agency, MSA, and State, FY90, annual rpt, 9764–7
Small business R&D grants of Fed Govt, project sales by type and dev funding by source, by agency and selected firm, 1984-91, GAO rpt, 26113–393
Southeastern US high technology employment and pay, by industry and State, 1990, press release, 6946–3.23
Statistical Abstract of US, 1992 annual data compilation, 2324–1.27
Transit systems research rpts, 1991, annual listing, 7884–11
see also Advanced materials
see also Automation
see also Energy research and development
see also Fiber optics
see also Industrial robots
see also Inventions
see also Lasers
see also Patents
see also Polymers
see also Research
see also Research and development
see also Technology transfer

Technology
see Inventions
see Research
see Research and development
see Science and technology
see Technological innovations
see Technology transfer

Technology International, Inc.
"Survey of Direct U.S. Private Capital Investment in Research and Development Facilities in Japan", 9628–88

Technology transfer
AID contracts and grants for technical and support services, by instn, country, and State, FY91, annual listing, 9914–7
AID contracts, grants, and cooperative agreements with higher education instns, by project, instn, and country, FY91, annual listing, 9914–6
AID economic aid to developing countries, obligations and disbursements by country, quarterly rpt, 9912–4
Developing countries economic and social conditions from 1960s, and Intl Dev Cooperation Agency and AID activities and funding, FY91-93, annual rpt, 9904–4
Energy natl strategy plans for conservation and pollution reduction, funding for R&D and basic science activities, FY91-93, 3008–128
Energy technologies export markets, competitiveness, and promotion, for US industries, 1992 technical rpt, 3006–13.5
Export licensing, monitoring, and enforcement activities, FY91, annual rpt, 2024–1
Fed Govt R&D labs technology transfer to small manufacturers, promotional programs activities and grants to States, late 1980s-91, GAO rpt, 26113–551
HHS financial aid, by program, recipient, State, and city, FY91, annual regional listings, 4004–3
Higher education instn R&D supported by NSF and NIH, license transfer to private firms, related income, and scientists associated with licensees, FY89-90, GAO rpt, 26113–575
Japan and US technological info transfer activities, and researcher and student exchanges, 1988-89, GAO rpt, 26123–379
Market potential of industrial and Federal labs technological innovations, results of annual *R&D 100* awards competition, 1960s-90, 2218–86
Science and Engineering Indicators, employment, education, R&D funding, and industry impacts, with foreign comparisons, 1960s-91, biennial rpt, 9624–10.6
Treaties and other bilateral and multilateral agreements of US in force, by country, as of Jan 1992, annual listing, 7004–1

Teenage pregnancy
Abortions by method, patient characteristics, and State, and related deaths, 1970-89, annual article, 4202–7.324
Births and rates, by characteristics of birth, infant, and mother, and presence of maternal risk factors and birth defects, 1989, 4146–5.125
Births of low birthweight, risk relation to mothers smoking, weight, and age, 1988, article, 4042–3.367
Foreign and US infant mortality rate, and births of low birthweight and to teen and older mothers, 1980s, article, 4652–1.324
Health condition and care indicators, 1950s-90 with health improvement and disease prevention goals for 1990, annual data compilation, 4144–11
Health condition of children and mothers, and services use, indicators by age, race, and poverty status 1988, 4478–197
Indian and Alaska Native youth health condition and behavioral patterns, by sex and grade, 1988-90, 4088–3
Poverty status of families, by detailed characteristics, 1980 and 1988, GAO rpt, 26131–102
Research on population and reproduction, Federal funding by project, FY90, annual listing, 4474–9
Season of conception relation to risk of teenage abortion and late prenatal care initiation, 1979-86, article, 4042–3.372
Statistical Abstract of US, 1992 annual data compilation, 2324–1.2
Youth health condition, risk factors, and preventive and treatment services use and availability, 1970s-80s, 26358–234.2

Teenagers
see Elementary and secondary education
see Juvenile delinquency
see School dropouts
see Teenage pregnancy
see Youth
see Youth employment

Teigen, Lloyd D.
"Weather in U.S. Agriculture: Monthly Temperature and Precipitation by State and Farm Production Region, 1950-90", 1544–28

Teixeira, Ruy A.
"Upgrading Workers' Skills Not Sufficient To Jump-Start Rural Economy", 1502–7.302

Telecommunication
Air traffic control and airway facilities improvement activities under Aviation System Capital Investment Plan, 1981-91 and projected to 2006, annual rpt, 7504–12
Competitiveness (intl) of US high technology industries, with background data by industry and foreign comparisons, 1960s-91, GAO rpt, 26123–406
Competitiveness (intl) of US telecommunications industry, structure, and devs, with background data and foreign comparisons, 1991 rpt, 2808–30
Construction put in place, value of new public and private structures, by type, monthly rpt, 2382–4
County Business Patterns, 1989: employment, establishments, and payroll, by SIC 2- to 4-digit industry and county, annual State rpt series, 2326–8
County Business Patterns, 1990: employment, establishments, and payroll, by SIC 2- to 4-digit industry and county, annual State rpt series, 2326–6
Drug enforcement communications network for Federal agencies, funding for equipment and DOD support, FY88-91 and projected to FY87, GAO rpt, 26123–372
Equipment shipments, trade, use, and firms, for electronic communications systems and related products, 1991, annual Current Industrial Rpt, 2506–12.35
Exports and imports between US and outlying areas, by detailed commodity and mode of transport, 1991, annual rpt, 2424–11
Exports and imports of services, direct and among multinatl firms affiliates, by industry and world area, 1986-91, article, 2702–1.336
Exports and imports of US, by country and detailed commodity, monthly rpt, 2422–12
Exports and imports of US, by Harmonized System 6-digit commodity and country, 1991, annual rpt, 2424–13
Exports and imports of US, by transport mode, country, and SITC 1- to 3-digit commodity, 1991, annual rpt, 2424–12
Exports of US, detailed Schedule B commodities with countries of destination, 1991, annual rpt, 2424–10
Fed Govt labor productivity, indexes of output and labor costs by function, FY67-90, annual rpt, 6824–1.6
Fed Govt standards for data recording, processing, and transfer, and for purchase and use of computer systems, series, 2216–2
Fiber optics and copper wire mileage and access lines, and fiber systems investment, by telecommunications firm, 1985-91, annual rpt, 9284–18
Finances and operations, by SIC 2- to 4-digit industry, forecast 1992, annual rpt, 2044–28
Foreign countries economic, social, political, and geographic summary data, by country, 1992, annual factbook, 9114–2

GSA activities and finances, FY91, annual rpt, 9454–1
Input-output structure of US economy, detailed interindustry transactions for 84 industries, and components of final demand, 1987, annual article, 2702–1.316
Intl telecommunications operations of US carriers, finances, rates, and traffic by service type, firm, and country, 1975-90, annual rpt, 9284–17
Military budget, programs, and policies, FY91, annual rpt, 3544–2
Military budget, R&D appropriations by item, service branch, and defense agency, FY91-93, annual rpt, 3544–33
Modem shipments, trade, use, and firms, 1991, annual Current Industrial Rpt, 2506–12.35
Natl Telecommunications and Info Admin rpts, FY91, annual listing, 2804–3
Occupational Outlook Handbook, 1992-93, biennial rpt, 6744–1
Occupational repetitive motion injury rates by selected industry, with data for California, 1980s, hearing, 21408–128
OECD trade, total and for 4 major countries, and US trade by country, by commodity, 1980-90, world area rpt series, 9116–1
Price indexes (producer), by stage of processing and detailed commodity, monthly rpt, 6762–6
Price indexes (producer), by stage of processing and detailed commodity, monthly 1991, annual rpt, 6764–2
Rates for domestic and intl service, by type of service and area served, various dates 1990, annual rpt, 9284–6.6
Tax rates and revenue of State and local govts, by source and State, 1992 and historical trends, annual rpt, 10044–1
Wire and cable (insulated) shipments, trade, use, and firms, by product, 1991, annual Current Industrial Rpt, 2506–10.8
see also Communications satellites
see also Educational broadcasting
see also Mobile radio
see also Public broadcasting
see also Radio
see also Telegraph
see also Telephones and telephone industry
see also Television
see also under By Commodity in the "Index by Categories"

Telegraph
County Business Patterns, 1989: employment, establishments, and payroll, by SIC 2- to 4-digit industry and county, annual State rpt series, 2326–8
County Business Patterns, 1990: employment, establishments, and payroll, by SIC 2- to 4-digit industry and county, annual State rpt series, 2326–6
Exports and imports between US and outlying areas, by detailed commodity and mode of transport, 1991, annual rpt, 2424–11
Exports and imports of US, by Harmonized System 6-digit commodity and country, 1991, annual rpt, 2424–13
Exports of US, detailed Schedule B commodities with countries of destination, 1991, annual rpt, 2424–10
Finances and operations, detail for telegraph firms, 1990, annual rpt, 9284–6
Intl telecommunications operations of US carriers, finances, rates, and traffic by service type, firm, and country, 1975-90, annual rpt, 9284–17
Manufacturing annual survey, 1990: finances and operations, by SIC 2- to 4-digit industry, series, 2506–14
Occupational injury and illness rates, by SIC 2- to 4-digit industry, 1989-90, annual rpt, 6844–7
Postal Service Mailgram revenue, costs, and volume, FY91, annual rpt, 9864–2
Rates for domestic and intl service, by type of service and area served, various dates 1990, annual rpt, 9284–6.6
Shipments, trade, use, and firms, for electronic communications systems and related products, 1991, annual Current Industrial Rpt, 2506–12.35
Statistical Abstract of US, 1992 annual data compilation, 2324–1.18

Telephones and telephone industry
Agricultural Statistics, 1991, annual rpt, 1004–1
Banks in Fed Reserve System, expenses and operations itemized by service, office, and district, 1991, annual rpt, 9364–11
Bill payment transactions of households, by method, FY87-90, annual rpt, 9864–10
Cancer info telephone helpline of Natl Cancer Inst, calls by caller type, 1983-90, article, 4042–3.325
Census of Population and Housing, 1990: summary characteristics, by county, subdiv, and place, State rpt series, 2551–7
Construction put in place and cost indexes, by type of construction, quarterly rpt, 2042–1.1
Consumer spending, natl income and product account benchmark revisions, 1929-88, 2708–5
Consumer spending, natl income and product accounts, comprehensive accounts and components, *Survey of Current Business*, monthly rpt, 2702–1.25
County Business Patterns, 1989: employment, establishments, and payroll, by SIC 2- to 4-digit industry and county, annual State rpt series, 2326–8
County Business Patterns, 1990: employment, establishments, and payroll, by SIC 2- to 4-digit industry and county, annual State rpt series, 2326–6
CPI by component for US city average, and by selected metro area, region, and population size, monthly rpt, 6762–2
Criminal cases by type and disposition, and collections, for US attorneys, by Federal district, FY91, annual rpt, 6004–2.1
Electronics industry production and labor conditions, in 10 MSAs, EC, and top producer countries, late 1970s-80s, article, 9393–8.307
Emergency 911 telephone systems participation of sheriff's agencies, by area population size, 1987 and 1990, 6066–25.45
Emergency 911 telephone systems participation of State and local police, FY90, 6066–25.44
Emergency 911 telephone systems participation of State, city, county, and special district police agencies, 1990, annual rpt, 6064–39
Employee electronic monitoring effects on mental and physical health and job satisfaction, for local telephone company workers, 1989, hearings, 21348–122
Employment, earnings, and hours, by SIC 1- to 4-digit industry, monthly 1989-Feb 1992, annual rpt, 6744–4
Employment of minorities and women, by occupation, SIC 1- to 3-digit industry, State, and MSA, 1991, annual rpt, 9244–1
Exports and imports between US and outlying areas, by detailed commodity and mode of transport, 1991, annual rpt, 2424–11
Exports and imports of US, by country and detailed commodity, monthly rpt, 2422–12
Exports and imports of US, by Harmonized System 6-digit commodity and country, 1991, annual rpt, 2424–13
Exports of US, detailed Schedule B commodities with countries of destination, 1991, annual rpt, 2424–10
Farm prices received and paid, by commodity and State, monthly rpt, 1629–1
Fiber optics and copper wire mileage and access lines, and fiber systems investment, by telecommunications firm, 1985-91, annual rpt, 9284–18
Finances and operations, by SIC 2- to 4-digit industry, forecast 1992, annual rpt, 2044–28
Finances and operations, detail for telephone firms, 1990, annual rpt, 9284–6
Finances and operations of local and long distance firms, subscribership, and charges, late 1970s-92, semiannual rpt, 9282–7
Finances of communications services, itemized revenue and expenses by SIC 2- to 4-digit kind of business, 1990, annual rpt, 2413–15
Foreign countries economic, social, political, and geographic summary data, by country, 1992, annual factbook, 9114–2
House of Representatives salaries, expenses, and contingent fund disbursement, detailed listings, quarterly rpt, 21942–1
Households (single person and nonfamily) social, economic and housing characteristics, by tenure, 1989, 2486–1.15
Households and housing detailed characteristics, and unit and neighborhood quality, by location, 1989, biennial rpt supplement, 2485–13
Households with telephone available, for rental units and units receiving and eligible for HUD assistance, by location, 1989, biennial rpt, 5184–11
Households with telephones, MSA surveys, series, 2485–6
Housing and households characteristics, and unit and neighborhood quality, by MSA location for 11 MSAs, 1987 survey, supplement, 2485–8
Housing and population census, 1990: population and housing characteristics, detailed geographic coverage, State CD-ROM series, 2551–10
Housing unit and household characteristics of recent movers, and reason for move, by tenure, 1989, 2486–1.12

Indian Health Service and tribal facilities and use, and Indians health and other characteristics, by IHS region, 1980s-90, annual chartbook, 4084–7
Injuries from use of consumer products, by severity, victim age, and detailed product, 1991, annual rpt, 9164–6
Input-output structure of US economy, detailed interindustry transactions for 541 industries, and components of final demand, 1982 benchmark data, 2708–17
Intl telecommunications operations of US carriers, finances, rates, and traffic by service type, firm, and country, 1975-90, annual rpt, 9284–17
Labor productivity, indexes of output, hours, and employment by SIC 2- to 4-digit industry, 1967-90, annual rpt, 6824–1.4
Local telephone rates and low-income subsidies, by region, company, and city, 1980s-91, semiannual rpt, 9282–8
Long-distance telephone service rates, by company, city, and time of day, 1950s-90, annual rpt, 9284–6.7
Mail volume to and from households, use, and views, by class, source, content, and household characteristics, FY87-90, annual rpt, 9864–10
Manufacturing annual survey, 1990: finances and operations, by SIC 2- to 4-digit industry, series, 2506–14
Occupational injury and illness rates, by SIC 2- to 4-digit industry, 1989-90, annual rpt, 6844–7
Occupational injury and illness rates, by SIC 2- to 4-digit industry, 1990, annual rpt, 6844–1
Occupational musculoskeletal disorders from computer video display terminal use, among telephone industry workers, 1990, 4248–93
Pacific territories population and housing detailed characteristics, by location, 1990 Census of Population and Housing, series, 2551–8
Palau admin, and social, economic, and govtl data, FY91, annual rpt, 7004–6
Price indexes (producer), by stage of processing and detailed commodity, monthly rpt, 6762–6
Price indexes (producer), by stage of processing and detailed commodity, monthly 1991, annual rpt, 6764–2
Rates for domestic and intl service, by type of service and area served, various dates 1990, annual rpt, 9284–6.6
Rural Electrification Admin activities and finances, and loans by State, FY91 and trends from FY36, annual rpt, 1244–3
Rural Telephone Bank financial statements, FY91, annual rpt, 1244–4
Rural Telephone Cooperatives, membership, and revenue, by State, 1990, annual rpt, 1124–1
Rural Telephone Program loan activity, by State, FY91, annual tables, 1244–8
Rural Telephone Program loans, and borrower operations and finances, by State, 1991, annual rpt, 1244–2
Shipments, trade, use, and firms, for electronic communications systems and related products, 1991, annual Current Industrial Rpt, 2506–12.35
Single parent families in own and others homes, by financial, housing, and other characteristics, 1989, 2486–1.14
Soviet Union and US economic and sociodemographic indicators, selected years 1970-90, handbook, 2328–80
Statistical Abstract of US, 1992 annual data compilation, 2324–1.18
Tax (excise) collections of IRS, by source, quarterly rpt, 8302–1; 8302–2.1
Tax (income) aid telephone service activity of IRS, FY91, annual rpt, 8304–3
Tax (income) aid telephone system of IRS, improvements in accuracy, 1989-91, GAO rpt, 26119–418
Tax (income) returns filed using alternative methods, with fraud, and conventional form preparation time and processing costs, 1986-92, GAO rpt, 26119–400
Tax (income) returns of individuals, IRS processing and taxpayer info activity, electronic and experimental filings, and refunds, periodic press release, 8302–6
Telecommunications industry intl competitiveness, structure, and devs, with background data and foreign comparisons, 1991 rpt, 2808–30
see also Mobile radio

Television
Child reading and TV viewing activities at home, by grade level, 1991 survey, 4826–10.1
Education data compilation, 1992 annual rpt, 4824–2
Educational performance and conditions, characteristics, attitudes, activities, and plans, 1988 8th grade class, natl longitudinal survey, series, 4826–9
Educational performance of elementary and secondary students, and factors affecting proficiency, by selected characteristics, 1990 natl assessments, subject rpt series, 4896–8
Educational performance of elementary and secondary students in math, science, reading, and writing, 1969-90, 4898–32
Educational performance of elementary and secondary students, reading proficiency and related factors, 1988 and 1990 natl assessments, 4898–33
Employment, earnings, and hours, by SIC 1- to 4-digit industry, monthly 1989-Feb 1992, annual rpt, 6744–4
Equipment shipments, trade, use, and firms, for electronic communications systems and related products, 1991, annual Current Industrial Rpt, 2506–12.35
Finances of communications services, itemized revenue and expenses by SIC 2- to 4-digit kind of business, 1990, annual rpt, 2413–15
Foreign countries economic, social, political, and geographic summary data, by country, 1992, annual factbook, 9114–2
Input-output structure of US economy, detailed interindustry transactions for 541 industries, and components of final demand, 1982 benchmark data, 2708–17
Licensing activities of FCC, by class of operation, FY91, annual rpt, 9284–4
Licensing status and allocation of commercial and noncommercial UHF and VHF TV channels, by market, as of June 1992, semiannual rpt, 9282–6
Occupational injury and illness rates, by SIC 2- to 4-digit industry, 1989-90, annual rpt, 6844–7
Occupational Outlook Handbook, 1992-93, biennial rpt, 6744–1
Palau admin, and social, economic, and govtl data, FY91, annual rpt, 7004–6
Stations on the air, by class of operation, monthly press release, 9282–4
Statistical Abstract of US, 1992 annual data compilation, 2324–1.18
see also Cable television
see also Home video and audio equipment
see also Video recordings and equipment

Temperature
see Global climate change
see Weather

Temporary and seasonal employment
Air traffic control and airway facilities staff, by employment and other characteristics, FY90, annual rpt, 7504–41
Capitol Architect outlays for salaries, supplies, and services, itemized by payee and function, 2nd half FY91, semiannual rpt, 25922–2
DOT employment, by subagency, occupation, and selected personnel characteristics, FY91, annual rpt, 7304–18
Farm hired and contract labor costs, by farm type and sales size, and for top States and counties, 1987, article, 1541–1.305
Farm labor, wages, hours, and perquisites, by State, monthly rpt, 1631–1
Fed Govt civilian employees work-years, pay rates, and benefits use and costs, by agency, FY90, annual rpt, 9844–31
Fed Govt civilian employment and payroll, by agency in DC metro area, total US, and abroad, bimonthly rpt, 9842–1
Immigrants and nonimmigrants admitted to US, alien workers, visitors, deportations, and naturalizations, FY91, annual summary rpt, 6264–7
Immigration to US, alien workers, visitors, deportations, and naturalizations, by country, FY91 and trends from 1820, annual rpt, 6264–2
Income (household, family, and personal), by source, detailed characteristics, and region, 1991, annual Current Population Rpt, 2546–6.76
Military service branches civilian employment, with summary military employment data, quarterly rpt, 3542–16
NASA staff characteristics and personnel actions, FY91, annual rpt, 9504–1
Pacific territories population and housing detailed characteristics, by location, 1990 Census of Population and Housing, series, 2551–8
Petrochemicals industries contract labor accidents, injuries, safety programs operations, and employee characteristics, 1986-91, 6608–6
Postal Service activities, financial statements, and employment, FY87-91, annual rpt, 9864–1
Prison staff in Federal instns, by selected characteristics, region, and instn, FY89, annual rpt, 6244–1.2
Radiation exposure of workers at nuclear power plants and related facilities, by site, 1968-89, annual rpt, 9634–3
Small business finances, operations, owner characteristics, and Federal contracts, 1980s-90, annual rpt, 9764–6

Strikes, replacement workers hired, and impacts on firm operating capacity, with data for NYC, 1984-88, hearing, 21348–121
Unemployed displaced workers, layoffs and recalls by layoff reason, industry, firm size, and State, 2nd half 1988, 6406–6.36
Unemployed displaced workers, layoffs and unemployment insurance claims by reason, industry, selected characteristics, and State, quarterly press release, 6742–23
Unemployed displaced workers, layoffs and unemployment insurance claims by reason, industry, selected characteristics, MSA, and State, 1990, annual rpt, 6744–18
VA health care staff and turnover, by occupation, physician specialty, and location, 1991, annual rpt, 8604–8
Wages, hours, and employment by occupation, and benefits, for selected locations, industry survey rpt series, 6787–6
Youth labor force status by age, Apr and July 1992 and change from 1991, annual press release, 6744–13
Youth labor force status, by sex, race, and industry div, summer 1988-92, annual press release, 6744–14
see also Migrant workers
see also Part-time employment

Tennessee
Appalachian Regional Commission funding, by project and State, planned FY92, annual rpt, 9084–3
Banks (insured commercial and savings) deposits by instn, State, MSA, and county, as of June 1991, annual regional rpt, 9295–3.4
Coal production and mines by county, prices, productivity, miners, and reserves, by mining method and State, 1990-91, annual rpt, 3164–25
County Business Patterns, 1990: employment, establishments, and payroll, by SIC 2- to 4-digit industry and county, annual State rpt, 2326–6.44
Deaths and rates, by detailed location, cause, and demographic characteristics, 1989, US Vital Statistics annual rpt, 4144–3.1
Economic and banking conditions, for Fed Reserve 8th District, quarterly rpt with articles, 9391–16
Economic indicators by State and MSA, Fed Reserve 6th District, quarterly rpt, 9371–14
Employment by industry div, earnings, and hours, for 8 southeastern States, quarterly press release, 6942–7
Employment, earnings, and hours, by selected SIC 1- to 4-digit industry, State, and for 275 MSAs, 1987-92, 6748–81
Fed Govt spending in States and local areas, by type, State, county, and city, FY91, annual rpt, 2464–3
Fed Govt spending in States, by type, program, agency, and State, FY91, annual rpt, 2464–2
Floods in Mississippi River and Gulf of Mexico basins, precipitation and water levels by site, damage, and deaths, 1982-83, 5666–27.33
HHS financial aid, by program, recipient, State, and city, FY91, annual regional listing, 4004–3.4
Hospital deaths of Medicare patients, actual and expected rates by diagnosis, and hospital characteristics, by instn, FY90 annual State rpt, 4654–14.44
Housing census, 1990: inventory, occupancy, and costs, State fact sheet, 2326–21.44
Housing census, 1990: summary unit characteristics, by householder race and age, county, place, and urban-rural location, State rpt, 2471–1.44
Military prime contract awards, by contractor, service branch, State, and city, FY91, annual rpt, 3544–22
Mineral Industry Surveys, State reviews of production, 1991, preliminary annual rpt, 5614–6
Multinatl firms US affiliates finances and operations, by industry, country of parent firm, and State, 1987, 2708–48
Physicians, by specialty, age, sex, and location of training and practice, 1990, State rpt, 4116–6.44
Population and housing census, 1990: detailed geographic coverage, State CD-ROM, 2551–9.6
Population and housing census, 1990: summary characteristics, by county, subdiv, and place, State rpt, 2551–7.44
Population census, 1990: population characteristics and living arrangements, by county, place, and urban-rural location, State rpt, 2531–1.44
Radiation and other pollutant releases from DOE contractor research lab and nuclear weapons facilities, monitoring results, 1991 annual site rpt, 3324–2.7
Statistical Abstract of US, 1992 annual data compilation, 2324–1
Textile mill employment, earnings, and hours, for 8 Southeastern States, quarterly press release, 6942–1
Timber in Tennessee, acreage and resources by species, ownership class, and county, 1989, series, 1206–27
Water resources dev projects of Army Corps of Engineers, characteristics, and costs, 1950s-89, biennial State rpt, 3756–1.43
Water use by end use, well withdrawals, and public supply deliveries, by county, 1988, State rpt, 5666–24.14
see also Clarksville, Tenn.
see also Knoxville, Tenn.
see also Memphis, Tenn.
see also Nashville, Tenn.
see also Tennessee River
see also Tennessee Valley
see also under By State in the "Index by Categories"

Tennessee River
Army Corps of Engineers water resources dev projects, characteristics, and costs, 1950s-89, biennial State rpt series, 3756–1
Army Corps of Engineers water resources dev projects, characteristics, and costs, 1950s-91, biennial State rpt series, 3756–2
Freight (waterborne) by commodity and port, waterway facilities, and recreation, for Ohio River basin by waterway, 1988-89, annual rpt, 3754–6
Freight (waterborne domestic and foreign) by commodity, traffic, and passengers, by port and waterway, 1989, annual rpt, 3754–3.2
TVA river control activities, and hydroelectric power generation and capacity, 1990, annual rpt, 9804–7
Water supply and quality in streams and lakes, and groundwater levels in wells, by drainage basin, 1990, annual State rpt series, 5666–10
Water supply and quality in streams and lakes, and groundwater levels in wells, by drainage basin, 1991, annual State rpt series, 5666–12
see also Tennessee Valley

Tennessee Valley
Biomass energy program of TVA, operations, finances, and technological characteristics, series, 9806–9
Economic conditions in Tennessee Valley, and compared to US, alternative projections 1991-2010 and trends from 1920s, annual rpt, 9804–27
River control activities of TVA, and hydroelectric power generation and capacity, 1990, annual rpt, 9804–7
TVA finances and operations by program and facility, FY91, annual rpt, 9804–32

Tennessee Valley Authority
Biomass energy program of TVA, operations, finances, and technological characteristics, series, 9806–9
Budget of US, authoritative financial statements with appropriations, outlays, and receipts, by category and agency, FY91, annual rpt, 8104–2.2
Budget of US, obligations and authority by function, agency, and program, with summaries and analyses, FY93, annual rpt, 104–2
Economic conditions in Tennessee Valley, and compared to US, alternative projections 1991-2010 and trends from 1920s, annual rpt, 9804–27
Electric power purchases from TVA and resales, with use, average bills, and rates by customer class, by distributor, 1991, annual tables, 9804–14
Electric power purchases of municipal and cooperative distributors, and prices and use by distributor and consumer sector, for TVA, monthly rpt, 9802–1
Employment (civilian) of Fed Govt, work-years, pay rates, and benefits use and costs, by agency, FY90, annual rpt, 9844–31
Energy use of TVA by fuel type, and conservation costs and savings, FY91, annual rpt, 9804–26
Expenditures of Fed Govt in States, by type, program, agency, and State, FY91, annual rpt, 2464–2
Fed Govt finances, cash and debt transactions, daily tables, 8102–4
Fertilizer use, by type and State, 1991-92, annual rpt, 9804–30
Finances and operations by program and facility, FY91, annual rpt, 9804–32
Finances and operations of Federal power admins and electric utilities, 1990, annual rpt, 3164–24.2
Finances and power sales, FY91, annual rpt, 9804–1

Labor unions recognized in Fed Govt, agreements and membership by agency and facility, as of Jan 1991, biennial listing, 9844–14
Natl income and product accounts, comprehensive accounts and components, benchmark revisions, 1929-88, 2708–5
Natl income and product accounts, comprehensive accounts and components, *Survey of Current Business*, monthly rpt, 2702–1.26
Publications of TVA on fertilizer and agriculture, 1989-90 annual listing, 9804–28
River control activities of TVA, and hydroelectric power generation and capacity, 1990, annual rpt, 9804–7

Tenure
see Housing tenure
see Job tenure
see Land ownership and rights

Terhaar, Allen
"Changing Outlook for Feed Grain Trade", 1504–9.1

Territorial waters
Foreign countries economic, social, political, and geographic summary data, by country, 1992, annual factbook, 9114–2
Foreign countries *Geographic Notes*, boundaries, claims, nomenclature, and other devs, quarterly rpt, 7142–3
Foreign countries maritime claims and boundary agreements, series, 7006–8
Latin America economic and social conditions, resources, trade, and aid, 1992, annual factbook, 9914–14
Tuna industry competitiveness and dolphin protection issues, investigation with background financial and operating data and foreign comparisons, 1992 rpt, 9886–4.187
see also Continental shelf

Territories of the U.S.
Assistance (financial and nonfinancial) of Fed Govt, 1992 base edition, annual listing, 104–5
Census of Population and Housing, 1990: immigrants, by period of entry, citizenship, State, birthplace, and for top cities and counties, press release, 2328–88
Community Dev Block Grant activities and funding, by program, FY75-91, annual rpt, 5124–8
Corporations operating in Puerto Rico and other US possessions, income tax return items, and employment, by selected industry, 1989, article, 8302–2.326
Economic and military aid and loans from US and intl agencies, by program and country, FY46-91, annual rpt, 9914–5
Exports of US, detailed Schedule B commodities with countries of destination, 1991, annual rpt, 2424–10
Fed Govt civilian employees accessions and separations, by agency for DC metro area and elsewhere, bimonthly rpt, 9842–1.3
Fed Govt civilian employment and payroll, by pay system and location, 1991, annual rpt, 9844–6.1
Fed Govt spending in States and local areas, by type, State, county, and city, FY91, annual rpt, 2464–3
Food stamp recipient household size, composition, income, and income and deductions allowed, summer 1989, annual rpt, 1364–8
HHS financial aid, by program, recipient, State, and city, FY91, annual regional listing, 4004–3.2; 4004–3.9
Income maintenance beneficiaries and payments, by program and outlying area, quarterly FY90, annual rpt, 4584–3.1; 4584–3.2
Income tax returns of foreign corporations and individuals, and US entities abroad, detailed data compilation, 1970s-89, quinquennial rpt, 8308–31
Interior Dept programs fraud and abuse, audits and investigations, 2nd half FY92, semiannual rpt, 5302–2
Medicare enrollees living overseas, by eligibility and coverage type, FY87, annual rpt, 4654–5
Military and DOD civilian personnel and dependents, by service branch and US and foreign location, quarterly rpt, 3542–20
Military base support costs by function, and personnel and acreage by installation, by service branch, FY93, annual rpt, 3504–11
Military budget, organization, personnel, weapons, and property, by service branch, State, and country, 1992 annual summary rpt, 3504–13
Multinatl US firms foreign affiliates, income statement items by asset size, industry, and country, 1988, biennial article, 8302–2.322
Oil company overcharge settlements funds received, and conservation and energy aid spending, by outlying area, 1990, GAO rpt, 26113–564
Pacific territories admin, and Palau social, economic, and govtl data, FY91, annual rpt, 7004–6
Pollution (air) contributing to global warming, emissions by monitoring site and country, and temperature change by world area and US region, 1860s-1990, annual rpt, 3004–33
Population size, growth rates, and components of change, by country, projected 1990-2020 and trends from 1950, biennial rpt, 2324–9
R&D funding by higher education instns and federally funded centers, by field, instn, and State, FY90, annual rpt, 9627–13
Science and engineering grad enrollment, by field, source of funds, and characteristics of student and instn, 1990, annual rpt, 9627–7
Shipborne commerce (domestic) of US, freight by major commodity group, vessel type, and port, 1987-89, annual rpt, 7704–7
Statistical Abstract of US, 1992 annual data compilation, 2324–1.30
Tax (income) returns for foreign corporate activity in US, selected income and tax items, by industry div and selected country, 1988, article, 8302–2.309
Tax (income) returns of Foreign Sales Corps, assets, and income and tax items, by industry, country of incorporation, and transaction pricing method, 1987, article, 8302–2.311
TV channel allocation and license status, for commercial and noncommercial UHF and VHF stations by market, as of June 1992, semiannual rpt, 9282–6
VA expenses, by type and location, FY91, annual rpt, 8604–3.4
see also American Samoa
see also Guam
see also Midway Islands
see also Northern Mariana Islands
see also Puerto Rico
see also U.S. Virgin Islands
see also Wake Island
see also under By Outlying Area in the "Index by Categories"

Terrorism
Incidents of terrorism in US, related activity, and casualties, by attack type, target, group, and location, 1991, annual rpt, 6224–6
Intl terrorism incidents, casualties, and attacks on US targets, by attack type and country, 1991, annual rpt, 7004–22
Intl terrorism incidents, casualties, and attacks on US targets, by attack type and world area, 1968-91, annual rpt, 7004–13
Intl terrorism incidents involving US targets, by type of attack, and casualties, data compilation, 1992 annual rpt, 6064–6.3
Mgmt of disasters and natl security threats, with data by major event and State, 1992 annual rpt, 9434–6
see also Air piracy
see also Assassination
see also Hostages
see also Sabotage

Testa, William A.
"Job Flight and the Airline Industry: The Economic Impact of Airports on Chicago and Other Metro Areas", 9375–13.78
"Producer Services: Trends and Prospects for the Seventh District", 9375–1.305
"State and Local Governments' Reaction to Recession", 9375–1.303

Tests
see Drug and alcohol testing
see Educational tests
see Mammography
see Medical examinations and tests
see Occupational testing and certification
see Quality control and testing

Teutsch, Steven M.
"Framework for Assessing the Effectiveness of Disease and Injury Prevention", 4206–2.53

Texas
Banks (insured commercial and savings) deposits by instn, State, MSA, and county, as of June 1991, annual regional rpt, 9295–3.4
Banks in Texas, loan losses relation to loan volume growth and other factors, mid 1970s-90, article, 9379–1.305
Banks in Texas, loans and financial ratios relation to economic indicators, 1970s-90, working paper, 9379–14.16
Coal production and mines by county, prices, productivity, miners, and reserves, by mining method and State, 1990-91, annual rpt, 3164–25
Construction, real estate, and other economic performance indicators, for New England compared to Texas and other areas, 1970s-91, article, 9373–1.302
Cotton (upland) abandoned acreage relation to harvested yield and rainfall, for Texas, 1972-91, article, 1561–1.303
Dairy prices, by product and selected area, with related marketing data, 1991, annual rpt, 1317–1

Deaths and rates, by detailed location, cause, and demographic characteristics, 1989, US Vital Statistics annual rpt, 4144–3.1
Drug abuse indicators for selected metro areas, research results, data collection, and policy issues, 1992 semiannual conf, 4492–5
Employment by industry div, earnings, and hours, by southwestern State, with CPI by major component for 2 Texas MSAs, monthly rpt, 6962–2
Employment, earnings, and hours, by selected SIC 1- to 4-digit industry, State, and for 275 MSAs, 1987-92, 6748–81
Estuary environmental and fishery conditions, research results and methodology, 1992 rpt, 2176–7.28
Estuary environmental conditions, research results and methodology, 1991 local area rpt, 2176–7.26
Estuary environmental conditions, research results and methodology, 1992 local area rpt, 2176–7.27
Fed Govt spending in States and local areas, by type, State, county, and city, FY91, annual rpt, 2464–3
Fed Govt spending in States, by type, program, agency, and State, FY91, annual rpt, 2464–2
Financial instns in Texas and Federal Reserve 11th District, financial condition and devs, periodic journal, 9379–15
HHS financial aid, by program, recipient, State, and city, FY91, annual regional listing, 4004–3.6
Hospital deaths of Medicare patients, actual and expected rates by diagnosis, and hospital characteristics, by instn, FY90 annual State rpt, 4654–14.45
Hospitals in rural areas, Medicare admission rates and charges, by instn, patient, and care characteristics, mid 1980s, 17206–2.33
Housing census, 1990: summary unit characteristics, by householder race and age, county, place, and urban-rural location, State rpt, 2471–1.45
Land Mgmt Bur activities in southwestern US, FY91, annual rpt, 5724–15
Medicaid impacts on State budgets, and program financing, cost control measures, enrollment, and services coverage, by selected State, 1960s-80s and projected to 1997, 10176–3.6
Military prime contract awards, by contractor, service branch, State, and city, FY91, annual rpt, 3544–22
Mineral Industry Surveys, State reviews of production, 1991, preliminary annual rpt, 5614–6
Multinatl firms US affiliates finances and operations, by industry, country of parent firm, and State, 1987, 2708–48
Physicians, by specialty, age, sex, and location of training and practice, 1990, State rpt, 4116–6.45
Population and housing census, 1990: detailed geographic coverage, State CD-ROM, 2551–9.7
Population and housing census, 1990: summary characteristics, by county, subdiv, and place, State rpt, 2551–7.45
Population census, 1990: population characteristics and living arrangements, by county, place, and urban-rural location, State rpt, 2531–1.45
Radiation and other pollutant releases from DOE contractor research lab and nuclear weapons facilities, monitoring results, 1991 annual site rpt, 3324–2.1
Rice market activities, prices, inspections, sales, trade, supply, and use, for US and selected foreign markets, weekly rpt, 1313–8
Rice production, practices, costs, and land tenure, by production area, 1988, 1568–309
Rice stocks on and off farms and total in all positions, periodic rpt, 1621–7
Savings instns failures, inventory of real estate assets available from Resolution Trust Corp, 1991, semiannual listing, 9722–2.3
Savings instns failures, inventory of real estate assets available from Resolution Trust Corp, 1992, semiannual listing, 9722–2.10
Savings instns financial condition and devs, working paper series, 9379–14
School districts efficient use of staff, model description and results for Texas, 1987-89, technical paper, 9379–12.80
Shrimp catch impacts of sea turtle excluder devices, by device type, for Texas fishery, 1983-87 and projected to 1997, article, 2162–1.302
Shrimp harvesters impacts of Gulf Coast fishery closure, and nonfishing job skills, 1987, article, 2162–1.301
Statistical Abstract of US, 1992 annual data compilation, 2324–1
Turtles (sea) sightings, strandings, and incidental catch, for Kemp's ridley turtles on Texas coast, late 1940s-90, 2168–132
Uranium tailings at inactive Falls City mill, remedial action proposals, costs, site characteristics, and environmental, socioeconomic, and health impacts, 1991 rpt, 3356–4.10
Wages by occupation, and benefits for office and plant workers, 1992 survey, periodic labor market rpt, 6785–3.5
Water supply and quality in streams and lakes, and groundwater levels in wells, by drainage basin, 1990, annual State rpt, 5666–10.41
see also Abilene, Tex.
see also Arlington, Tex.
see also Austin, Tex.
see also Beaumont, Tex.
see also Bexar County, Tex.
see also Brazoria, Tex.
see also Collin County, Tex.
see also Corpus Christi, Tex.
see also Dallas County, Tex.
see also Dallas, Tex.
see also Fort Worth, Tex.
see also Galveston, Tex.
see also Guadalupe County, Tex.
see also Harris County, Tex.
see also Houston, Tex.
see also San Antonio, Tex.
see also Tarrant County, Tex.
see also under By State in the "Index by Categories"

Textile Agreement Category System
see Trade agreements

Textile industry and fabrics
Business statistics, detailed data for major industries and economic indicators, *Survey of Current Business*, monthly rpt, 2702–1.21
Business statistics, detailed data for major industries and economic indicators, 1960-91, *Survey of Current Business* biennial supplement, 2704–1
Capital expenditures for plant and equipment, by major industry group, quarterly rpt, 2502–2
Caribbean Basin Initiative export and investment incentives, contact listing, bibl, and US imports country, 1983-91, annual rpt, 2044–36
Collective bargaining agreements expiring during year, and workers covered, by firm, union, industry group, and State, 1992, annual rpt, 6784–9
County Business Patterns, 1989: employment, establishments, and payroll, by SIC 2- to 4-digit industry and county, annual State rpt series, 2326–8
County Business Patterns, 1990: employment, establishments, and payroll, by SIC 2- to 4-digit industry and county, annual State rpt series, 2326–6
Cuba trade, by commodity and country, mid 1980s-91, 9118–8
Eastern Europe export industries dev potential, with trade and industry finances and operations, for 5 countries, 1985-90, 9886–4.179
Employment, earnings, and hours, by selected SIC 1- to 4-digit industry, State, and for 275 MSAs, 1987-92, 6748–81
Employment, earnings, and hours, by SIC 1- to 4-digit industry, monthly 1989-Feb 1992, annual rpt, 6744–4
Employment of minorities and women, by occupation, SIC 1- to 3-digit industry, State, and MSA, 1991, annual rpt, 9244–1
Employment, unemployment, and labor force characteristics, by region and census div, 1991, annual rpt, 6744–7.1
Energy use and prices, by fuel type and manufacturing industry, 1974-88, 3166–15.3
Energy use and prices for manufacturing industries, 1988 survey, series, 3166–13
Exports and imports between US and outlying areas, by detailed commodity and mode of transport, 1991, annual rpt, 2424–11
Exports and imports of textiles, raw fiber equivalents by product, country, and world region, 1989-90, article, 1561–1.301
Exports and imports of US, by country and detailed commodity, monthly rpt, 2422–12
Exports and imports of US by country, and trade shifts by commodity, 1991, annual rpt, 9884–25
Exports and imports of US, by Harmonized System 6-digit commodity and country, 1991, annual rpt, 2424–13
Exports and imports of US, by selected country, country group, and commodity group, 1991, annual rpt, 2044–37
Exports and imports of US, by transport mode, country, and SITC 1- to 3-digit commodity, 1991, annual rpt, 2424–12
Exports, imports, and balances of US for manufactured goods, by SITC 2-digit commodity and country, quarterly rpt, 2042–35

Exports of US, detailed commodities by country, monthly CD-ROM, 2422–13
Exports of US, detailed Schedule B commodities with countries of destination, 1991, annual rpt, 2424–10
Exports of US textile products, and trade regulations of foreign countries, by commodity and country, 1989-91, biennial rpt, 2044–18
Exports of US textiles and apparel, by product group and country, quarterly rpt, 2042–36
Foreign countries market conditions for US textile and apparel exports, with domestic industry operations, country rpt series, 2046–15
Freight (waterborne domestic and foreign) by commodity, traffic, and passengers, by port and waterway, 1989, annual rpt, 3754–3
Hazardous substances industrial releases and reduction methods under EPA regulation, by chemical, source, industry, and location, 1989, annual rpt, 9234–6
Hazardous substances industrial releases and reduction methods under EPA regulation, with chemical stocks and use, facility directory, 1987-89, annual CD-ROM, 9234–7
Import classification codes under Textile Agreement Category System, correlation with TSUSA, 1993 annual rpt, 2044–31
Imports, exports, and employment impacts, by SIC 2- to 4-digit industry and commodity, quarterly rpt, 2322–2
Imports of textiles, by country of origin, monthly rpt, 2042–27
Imports of textiles, by product and country of origin, monthly rpt series, 2046–8; 2046–9
Imports of textiles under Multifiber Arrangement by product and country, and status of bilateral agreements, 1988-91, annual rpt, 9884–18
Imports of US, detailed commodities by country, monthly CD-ROM, 2422–14
Imports of US given duty-free treatment for value of US material sent abroad, by commodity and country, 1987-90, annual rpt, 9884–14
Input-output structure of US economy, detailed interindustry transactions for 84 industries, and components of final demand, 1987, annual article, 2702–1.316
Input-output structure of US economy, detailed interindustry transactions for 541 industries, and components of final demand, 1982 benchmark data, 2708–17
Labor productivity, indexes of output, hours, and employment by SIC 2- to 4-digit industry, 1967-90, annual rpt, 6824–1.3
Manufacturing annual survey, 1990: finances and operations, by SIC 2- to 4-digit industry, series, 2506–14
Manufacturing census, 1987: concentration of largest firms measured by value added, and for shipments by SIC 2- and 4-digit industry, subject rpt, 2497–6
Manufacturing census, 1987: shipments of manufacturers products, by customer class and SIC 2- and 4-digit industry, subject rpt, 2497–4
Manufacturing corporations financial statements, by selected SIC 2- to 3-digit industry, quarterly rpt, 2502–1
Manufacturing finances and operations, by SIC 2- to 4-digit industry, forecast 1992, annual rpt, 2044–28
Manufacturing industries operations and performance, analytical rpt series, 2506–16
Manufacturing production, shipments, inventories, orders, and pollution control costs, periodic Current Industrial Rpt series, 2506–3
Mexico imports from US, by industry and State, 1987-91, 2048–154
Military prime contract awards, by category, contract and contractor type, and service branch, FY82-1st half FY92, semiannual rpt, 3542–1
Multinatl firms US affiliates finances and operations, by industry, country of parent firm, and State, 1987, 2708–48
Multinatl US firms and foreign affiliates finances and operations, by industry and country, 1989 benchmark survey, annual rpt, 2704–5
New England textile industry employment of Colombian immigrants, by selected characteristics, 1960s-80s, working paper, 6366–6.4
Occupational injury and illness rates, by SIC 2- to 4-digit industry, 1989-90, annual rpt, 6844–7
Occupational injury and illness rates, by SIC 2- to 4-digit industry, 1990, annual rpt, 6844–1
Occupational repetitive motion injury rates by selected industry, with data for California, 1980s, hearing, 21408–128
OECD trade, total and for 4 major countries, and US trade by country, by commodity, 1980-90, world area rpt series, 9116–1
Pacific territories population and housing detailed characteristics, by location, 1990 Census of Population and Housing, series, 2551–8
Pollution abatement capital and operating costs, by SIC 2- to 4-digit industry and State, 1990, annual Current Industrial Rpt, 2506–3.6
Price indexes (producer), by stage of processing and detailed commodity, monthly rpt, 6762–6
Price indexes (producer), by stage of processing and detailed commodity, monthly 1991, annual rpt, 6764–2
Price indexes for department store inventories, by class of item, monthly table, 6762–7
Production, prices, trade, and use of cotton, wool, and synthetic fibers, periodic situation rpt with articles, 1561–1
Production, trade, sales, stocks, and material used, by product, region, and State, periodic Current Industrial Rpt series, 2506–5
Puerto Rico and other US possessions corporations income tax returns, income and tax items, and employment, by selected industry, 1989, article, 8302–2.326
Research (agricultural) funding and staffing for USDA, State agencies, and other instns, by topic, FY91, annual rpt, 1744–2
Science, engineering, and technical employment in manufacturing, by field and industry, 1989, triennial rpt, 9627–23
Southeastern US textile mill employment, earnings, and hours, for 8 States, quarterly press release, 6942–1
Southern US textile mill employment, 1951-91, annual rpt, 6944–1
Statistical Abstract of US, 1992 annual data compilation, 2324–1.27
Tariff Schedule of US, classifications and rates of duty by detailed imported commodity, 1993 base edition, 9886–13
Tax (income) returns of corporations, income and tax items by asset size and detailed industry, 1989, annual rpt, 8304–4; 8304–21
Tax (income) returns of sole proprietorships, income statement items, by industry group, 1990, annual article, 8302–2.317; 8302–2.320
Towels (shop) from Bangladesh at less than fair value, injury to US industry, investigation with background financial and operating data, 1992 rpt, 9886–14.340
see also Carpets and rugs
see also Clothing and clothing industry
see also Cotton
see also Natural fibers
see also Silk
see also Synthetic fibers and fabrics
see also Wool and wool trade
see also under By Commodity in the "Index by Categories"
see also under By Industry in the "Index by Categories"

Thacker, Stephen B.
"Survey of Graduates of the Epidemic Intelligence Service as an Approach To Enhancing Ethnic Diversity Among the Nation's Epidemiologists", 4042–3.374

Thackray, Richard I.
"Human Factors Evaluation of the Work Environment of Operators Engaged in the Inspection and Repair of Aging Aircraft", 7506–10.99

Thailand
Agricultural trade of US, by detailed commodity and country, 1991, annual rpt, 1524–8
Agricultural trade of US, by detailed commodity and country, 1991, semiannual rpt, 1522–4
AID economic aid to developing countries, obligations and disbursements by country, quarterly rpt, 9912–4
AID loans repayment status and terms by program and country, and status of predecessor agency loans, quarterly rpt, 9912–3
Background Notes, summary social, political, and economic data, 1991 rpt, 7006–2.4
Cuba trade, by commodity and country, mid 1980s-91, 9118–8
Drug abuse indicators, by world region and selected country, 1992 semiannual conf, 4492–5.2
Economic and military aid and loans from US and intl agencies, by program and country, FY46-91, annual rpt, 9914–5
Economic and social conditions of developing countries from 1960s, and Intl Dev Cooperation Agency and AID activities and funding, FY91-93, annual rpt, 9904–4
Economic conditions, income, production, prices, employment, and trade, 1992 periodic country rpt, 2046–4.16; 2046–4.58

Economic conditions, investment and export opportunities, and trade practices, 1992 country market research rpt, 2046–6.9
Economic conditions, policy, and trade practices, by country, 1989-91, annual rpt, 21384–5
Economic, population, and agricultural data, US and other aid sources, and AID activity, 1990 country rpt, 9916–12.49
Economic, social, political, and geographic summary data, by country, 1992, annual factbook, 9114–2
Exports and imports of US, by commodity and country, 1980-90, world area rpt, 9116–1.3
Exports and imports of US, by Harmonized System 6-digit commodity and country, 1991, annual rpt, 2424–13
Exports and imports of US, by selected country, country group, and commodity group, 1991, annual rpt, 2044–37
Exports and imports of US, by transport mode, country, and SITC 1- to 3-digit commodity, 1991, annual rpt, 2424–12
Exports, imports, and balances of US for manufactured goods, by SITC 2-digit commodity and country, quarterly rpt, 2042–35
Exports of US, detailed Schedule B commodities with countries of destination, 1991, annual rpt, 2424–10
Human rights conditions in 170 countries, and US economic and military aid, 1991, annual rpt, 21384–3
Imports of goods, services, and investment from US, trade barriers, impacts, and US actions, by country, 1991, annual rpt, 444–2
Military aid of US, arms sales, and training programs costs and budget requests, by program, world region, and country, FY91-93, annual rpt, 7144–13
Military spending, arms trade, and force strengths, with govt spending and population, by country, 1979-89, annual rpt, 9824–1
Minerals Yearbook, Vol 3, 1989: foreign country review of production, trade, and policy, by commodity, annual rpt, 5604–35.2
Multinatl US firms and foreign affiliates finances and operations, by industry and country, 1989 benchmark survey, annual rpt, 2704–5
Multinatl US firms foreign affiliates, income statement items by asset size, industry, and country, 1988, biennial article, 8302–2.322
Pineapple (canned fruit and juice) production and exports, for 2 countries, forecast 1992, semiannual article, 1925–34.346
Pipe fittings (carbon steel) from 2 countries at less than fair value, injury to US industry, investigation with background financial and operating data, 1992 rpt, 9886–14.352
Population size, growth rates, and components of change, by country, projected 1990-2020 and trends from 1950, biennial rpt, 2324–9
Refugee migration, and intl aid programs, by world area and country of origin and asylum, 1991, annual rpt, 7004–15
Rice market activities, prices, inspections, sales, trade, supply, and use, for US and selected foreign markets, weekly rpt, 1313–8
Shrimp artisanal fishery catch of shellfish and finfish, and disposition of by-catch, 1986-87, article, 2162–1.302
Steel trade, by product, country, and customs district, with US industry operating data, 1989-June 1992, semiannual rpt, 9882–15
UN voting record and share of votes in agreement with US, by issue, country, and world area, 1991, annual rpt, 7004–18
see also under By Foreign Country in the "Index by Categories"

Thaul, Susan
"Pediatric AIDS-Related Discharges in a Sample of U.S. Hospitals: Demographics, Diagnoses, and Resource Use", 4186–6.16

Theater
County Business Patterns, 1989: employment, establishments, and payroll, by SIC 2- to 4-digit industry and county, annual State rpt series, 2326–8
County Business Patterns, 1990: employment, establishments, and payroll, by SIC 2- to 4-digit industry and county, annual State rpt series, 2326–6
Input-output structure of US economy, detailed interindustry transactions for 541 industries, and components of final demand, 1982 benchmark data, 2708–17
Natl Endowment for Arts activities and grants, FY91, annual rpt, 9564–3

Theft
see Motor vehicle theft
see Robbery and theft

Therapy
see Chemotherapy
see Occupational therapy
see Physical therapy
see Rehabilitation of the disabled
see Respiratory therapy
see Speech pathology and audiology

Thermal power
see Electric power and heat cogeneration
see Geothermal resources

Third World countries
see Developing countries

Thodal, Carl E.
"Data on Ground-Water Quality, Carson Valley and Topaz Lake Areas, Douglas County, Nevada, for Year Ending September 1987", 5666–28.22

Thomas, R. Edward
"New Estimates of Hardwood-Log Exports to Europe and Asia", 1208–373

Thompson, J. Edward
"Modernization of the Food Label: An Initial Industry Impression", 1504–9.1

Thompson, James J.
"Inhalation Toxicology Research Institute, Albuquerque, N.Mex., Site Environmental Report, 1990", 3324–2.4

Thompson, Michael T.
"Forest Statistics for the Northern Piedmont of Virginia, 1992", 1206–6.15
"Forest Statistics for the Southern Mountains of Virginia, 1992", 1206–6.17
"Hurricane Hugo: Effects on South Carolina's Forest Resource", 1208–411

Thomson, James B.
"Capital Forbearance and Thrifts: An Ex Post Examination of Regulatory Gambling", 9377–9.140

Thor, Ann D.
"Accumulation of p53 Tumor Suppressor Gene Protein: An Independent Marker of Prognosis in Breast Cancers", 4472–1.317

Thorbecke, Willem
"Would Monetary Policy Be Effective if the OASDI Trust Funds Held Most Treasury Debt?", 4746–26.19

Thorne, P. D.
"Hanford Environmental Dose Reconstruction Project, Ground-Water Contribution to Dose from Past Hanford Operations", 3356–5.7

Thornton, Craig
"Transitional Employment Training for SSI Recipients with Mental Retardation", 4742–1.301

Thornton, Daniel L.
"Alternative Measures of the Monetary Base: What Are the Differences and Are They Important?", 9391–1.302
"Targeting M2: The Issue of Monetary Control", 9391–1.313

Thorsteinson, Lyman K.
"Arctic Fish Habitat Use Investigations: Nearshore Studies in the Alaskan Beaufort Sea, Summer 1990", 5738–37

Thrift institutions
see Credit unions
see Savings institutions

Throat disorders
see Nose and throat disorders

Throop, Adrian W.
"Consumer Sentiment: Its Causes and Effects", 9393–8.304
"Generalized Uncovered Interest Parity Model of Real Exchange Rates", 9393–10.21

Thun, Michael J.
"Risk Factors for Fatal Colon Cancer in a Large Prospective Study", 4472–1.346

Tibben, John
"Timber Industry of Iowa: An Assessment of Timber Product Output and Use, 1988", 1206–10.13

Tice, Thomas F.
"Prospects for the U.S. Feed Grain Sector", 1504–9.1

Tidal waves
see Tsunamis

Tides and currents
Alaska OCS environmental conditions and oil dev impacts, compilation of papers, series, 2176–1
California OCS oil and gas dev impacts on water quality, marine life, and sediments, by site, 1986-90, annual rpt, 5734–11
Coastal areas environmental conditions and mgmt, for individual areas, conf series, 2146–8
Coastal currents, for US by ocean region, monthly rpt, 2182–5
Coastal tidal currents, daily time and velocity by station for North America and Asia, forecast 1993, annual rpts, 2174–1
Coastal tide height and time daily at points worldwide, forecast 1993, annual rpt series, 2174–2
Estuary environmental conditions, research results and methodology, series, 2176–7

Great Lakes water levels, daily and monthly averages by site, 1991 and cumulative from 1900, annual rpt, 2174–3
Great Lakes water levels, monthly and annual averages by station, 1860-1990, quinquennial rpt, 2178–1
Mariners Weather Log, quarterly journal, 2152–8
Middle Atlantic States tide height and tidal current velocity daily at selected coastal stations, forecast 1993, annual rpt, 2174–11
Pacific Ocean temperature, current, and wind, by equatorial eastern site and depth, 1983-87, 2148–62
Weather conditions and forecasts, data collection and analysis issues, 1991 annual conf, 2184–10

Timber
see Forests and forestry
see Lumber industry and products
see Wood fuel

Time
see Chronologies
see Seasonal adjustment factors
see Seasonal variations
see Time of day

Time deposits
see Bank deposits
see Certificates of deposit

Time of day
Air traffic, and passenger and freight enplanements, by airport, 1960s-91 and projected to 2010, hub area rpt series, 7506–7
Aircraft accidents and circumstances, for US operations of domestic and foreign airlines and general aviation, periodic rpt, 9612–1
Aircraft accidents, casualties, and damage, for commercial operations by detailed circumstances, 1988, annual rpt, 9614–2
Airline consumer complaints by reason, passengers denied boarding, and late flights, by reporting carrier and airport, monthly rpt, 7302–11
Assaults and deaths of law enforcement officers, by circumstances, agency, victim and offender characteristics, and location, 1991, annual rpt, 6224–3
Boat accidents, casualties, and damage, by cause, vessel and operator characteristics, and State, 1991, annual rpt, 7404–1.2
Bombing incidents, casualties, and damage, by target, circumstances, and State, 1991, annual rpt, 6224–5
Commuting to work, by mode, trip duration, and work location, 1980 and 1990, 7558–120
Crime victimization rates, by victim and offender characteristics, circumstances, and offense, 1990 survey, annual rpt, 6066–3.47
Crimes, by characteristics of victim and offender, circumstances, and location, data compilation, 1992 annual rpt, 6064–6.3
Fire fighter deaths, by cause, circumstances, and location, 1990, annual rpt, 9434–8
Mines occupational deaths, by circumstances and selected victim characteristics, semiannual rpt series, 6662–3
Railroad accidents, casualties, circumstances, and railroad involved, 1988, annual rpt, 9614–8
Railroad accidents, casualties, damage, and circumstances, by incident, 1988, annual rpt, 7604–3
Railroad accidents involving hazardous materials, casualties, and circumstances, 1984-89, 9618–18
Railroad-hwy grade-crossing accidents, detailed data by State and railroad, 1991, annual rpt, 7604–2
Star position tables, planet coordinates, time conversion factors, and listing of observatories worldwide, 1993, annual rpt, 3804–7
Sunrise and sunset mean time every 5th day, by degree of latitude worldwide, forecast 1993, annual rpt series, 2174–2
Telephone rates for intl calls, and domestic long-distance rates by company, by time and area served, 1950s-90, annual rpt, 9284–6.6; 9284–6.7
Tidal currents, daily time and velocity by station for North America and Asia coasts, forecast 1993, annual rpts, 2174–1
Tide height and tidal current velocity daily at Middle Atlantic coastal stations, forecast 1993, annual rpt, 2174–11
Tide height and time daily at coastal points worldwide, forecast 1993, annual rpt series, 2174–2
Traffic accidents, casualties, circumstances, and characteristics of persons and vehicles involved, 1990, annual rpt, 7764–18
Traffic fatal accidents, alcohol levels of drivers and others, by circumstances and characteristics of persons and vehicles, 1990, annual rpt, 7764–16
Traffic fatal accidents, circumstances, and characteristics of persons and vehicles involved, 1991, semiannual rpt, 7762–11
Traffic fatal accidents, deaths, and rates, by circumstances, characteristics of persons and vehicles involved, and location, 1990, annual rpt, 7764–10
Traffic safety research, literature review, with data on accidents and impact of safety measures, 1961-90, 7558–98
Truck accidents, casualties, and damage, by circumstances and characteristics of persons and vehicles involved, 1989, annual rpt, 7554–9
Truck accidents, circumstances, and characteristics of vehicles and persons involved, 1979-86, 7768–124
Weather (marine) forecast areas, and broadcast schedules and stations worldwide, as of Sept 1992, annual rpt, 2184–3
Weather (marine) forecast broadcast schedules worldwide, periodic rpt, 2182–9

Tin and tin industry
Business statistics, detailed data for major industries and economic indicators, *Survey of Current Business*, monthly rpt, 2702–1.16
Business statistics, detailed data for major industries and economic indicators, 1960-91, *Survey of Current Business* biennial supplement, 2704–1
Exports and imports between US and outlying areas, by detailed commodity and mode of transport, 1991, annual rpt, 2424–11
Exports and imports of US, by country and detailed commodity, monthly rpt, 2422–12
Exports and imports of US, by Harmonized System 6-digit commodity and country, 1991, annual rpt, 2424–13
Exports and imports of US, by transport mode, country, and SITC 1- to 3-digit commodity, 1991, annual rpt, 2424–12
Exports of US, detailed Schedule B commodities with countries of destination, 1991, annual rpt, 2424–10
Foreign countries mineral production, reserves, and industry role in domestic economy and world supply, world area and country rpt series, 5606–1
Mineral Industry Surveys, commodity review of production, trade, stocks, and use, monthly rpt, 5612–1.24
Minerals Yearbook, Vol 1, 1989: commodity reviews of production, use, trade, prices, and mining operations, annual rpt, 5604–33
Minerals Yearbook, Vol 1, 1990: commodity review of production, reserves, supply, use, and trade, annual rpt, 5604–20.58
Minerals Yearbook, Vol 2, 1989: State reviews of production and sales by commodity, and business activity, annual rpt series, 5604–16
Minerals Yearbook, Vol 2, 1990: State reviews of production and sales by commodity, and business activity, annual rpt series, 5604–22
Minerals Yearbook, Vol 3, 1989: foreign country reviews of production, trade, and policy, by commodity, annual rpt, 5604–35
Mines (metal) and related operations occupational injuries and incidence, employment, and hours, 1990, annual rpt, 6664–3
OECD trade, total and for 4 major countries, and US trade by country, by commodity, 1980-90, world area rpt series, 9116–1
Price indexes (producer), by stage of processing and detailed commodity, monthly 1991, annual rpt, 6764–2
Production, prices, trade, use, employment, tariffs, and stockpiles, by mineral, with foreign comparisons, 1987-91, annual rpt, 5604–18
Statistical Abstract of US, 1992 annual data compilation, 2324–1.25
Stockpiling of strategic material by Fed Govt, activity, and inventory by commodity, as of Sept 1991, semiannual rpt, 3542–22
Stockpiling of strategic material, inventories and needs, by commodity, 1992, annual rpt, 3544–37

Tips and tipping
Tax (income) returns of individuals, by filing status, tax item, and income level, 1991, annual article, 8302–2.319
Tax (income) returns of individuals, detailed data, 1988, annual rpt, 8304–2

Tires and tire industry
Auto, van, and light truck ownership and operating costs, by vehicle size and year of operation, 1991 model year, biennial rpt, 7554–21
Business statistics, detailed data for major industries and economic indicators, *Survey of Current Business*, monthly rpt, 2702–1.19

Business statistics, detailed data for major industries and economic indicators, 1960-91, *Survey of Current Business* biennial supplement, 2704–1
County Business Patterns, 1989: employment, establishments, and payroll, by SIC 2- to 4-digit industry and county, annual State rpt series, 2326–8
County Business Patterns, 1990: employment, establishments, and payroll, by SIC 2- to 4-digit industry and county, annual State rpt series, 2326–6
CPI by component for US city average, and by selected metro area, region, and population size, monthly rpt, 6762–2
Employment, earnings, and hours, by SIC 1- to 4-digit industry, monthly 1989-Feb 1992, annual rpt, 6744–4
Employment of minorities and women, by occupation, SIC 1- to 3-digit industry, State, and MSA, 1991, annual rpt, 9244–1
Exports and imports between US and outlying areas, by detailed commodity and mode of transport, 1991, annual rpt, 2424–11
Exports and imports of US, by country and detailed commodity, monthly rpt, 2422–12
Exports and imports of US, by Harmonized System 6-digit commodity and country, 1991, annual rpt, 2424–13
Exports and imports of US, by transport mode, country, and SITC 1- to 3-digit commodity, 1991, annual rpt, 2424–12
Exports of US, detailed Schedule B commodities with countries of destination, 1991, annual rpt, 2424–10
Farm prices received and paid, by commodity and State, 1991, annual rpt, 1629–5
Input-output structure of US economy, detailed interindustry transactions for 541 industries, and components of final demand, 1982 benchmark data, 2708–17
Manufacturing annual survey, 1990: finances and operations, by SIC 2- to 4-digit industry, series, 2506–14
Manufacturing census, 1987: concentration of largest firms measured by value added, and for shipments by SIC 2- and 4-digit industry, subject rpt, 2497–6
Manufacturing census, 1987: shipments of manufacturers products, by customer class and SIC 2- and 4-digit industry, subject rpt, 2497–4
Manufacturing finances and operations, by SIC 2- to 4-digit industry, forecast 1992, annual rpt, 2044–28
Military prime contract awards, by detailed procurement category, FY88-91, annual rpt, 3544–18
Occupational injury and illness rates, by SIC 2- to 4-digit industry, 1989-90, annual rpt, 6844–7
Occupational injury and illness rates, by SIC 2- to 4-digit industry, 1990, annual rpt, 6844–1
Price indexes (producer), by stage of processing and detailed commodity, monthly rpt, 6762–6
Price indexes (producer), by stage of processing and detailed commodity, monthly 1991, annual rpt, 6764–2
Productivity of labor and capital, and indexes of output, hours, and employment, 1967-90, annual rpt, 6824–1.3; 6824–1.5
Quality ratings for tires, by type and brand, as of Feb 1992, annual rpt, 7764–17
Recalls of motor vehicles and equipment with safety-related defects, by make, monthly listing, 7762–12
Recalls of motor vehicles and equipment with safety-related defects, by make, quarterly listing, 7762–2
Science, engineering, and technical employment in manufacturing, by field and industry, 1989, triennial rpt, 9627–23
Soviet Union and US economic and sociodemographic indicators, selected years 1970-90, handbook, 2328–80
Tax (excise) collections of IRS, by source, quarterly rpt, 8302–1; 8302–2.1
Tire cord fabrics production, quarterly Current Industrial Rpt, 2506–5.11
Truck itemized costs per mile, finances, and operations, for agricultural carriers, 1991, annual rpt, 1311–15
Truck rates for fruit and vegetables paid by shippers and receivers, by commodity and city, and fleet itemized costs per mile, weekly rpt, 1311–22

Tobacco industry and products
Acreage planted and harvested, by crop and State, 1990-91 and planned as of June 1992, annual rpt, 1621–23
Acreage planted, by selected crop and State, 1983-91 and planned 1992, annual rpt, 1621–22
Advertising and promotion costs by media, and market shares, by cigarette type, with sales and use, 1963-89, annual rpt, 9404–4
Agricultural Stabilization and Conservation Service tobacco programs, 1960-92, annual fact sheet, 1806–4.4; 1806–4.6
Agricultural Stabilization and Conservation Service tobacco programs, 1988-92, annual fact sheet, 1806–4.7
Agricultural Statistics, 1991, annual rpt, 1004–1
Business statistics, detailed data for major industries and economic indicators, *Survey of Current Business*, monthly rpt, 2702–1.13
Business statistics, detailed data for major industries and economic indicators, 1960-91, *Survey of Current Business* biennial supplement, 2704–1
CCC financial condition and major commodity program operations, FY63-88, annual chartbook, 1824–2
Collective bargaining agreements expiring during year, and workers covered, by firm, union, industry group, and State, 1992, annual rpt, 6784–9
County Business Patterns, 1989: employment, establishments, and payroll, by SIC 2- to 4-digit industry and county, annual State rpt series, 2326–8
County Business Patterns, 1990: employment, establishments, and payroll, by SIC 2- to 4-digit industry and county, annual State rpt series, 2326–6
CPI by component for US city average, and by selected metro area, region, and population size, monthly rpt, 6762–2
Cuba trade, by commodity and country, mid 1980s-91, 9118–8
DC metro area drug, alcohol, and tobacco use, user characteristics, and consequences, series, 4496–12
Deaths during 1986, decedents health condition, services use, habits, and social, employment, and other characteristics, 4147–20.19
Eastern Europe tobacco and cigarette production, consumption, and trade, by country, 1985-91, article, 1561–10.303
Employment, earnings, and hours, by SIC 1- to 4-digit industry, monthly 1989-Feb 1992, annual rpt, 6744–4
Energy use and prices, by fuel type and manufacturing industry, 1974-88, 3166–15.3
Energy use and prices for manufacturing industries, 1988 survey, series, 3166–13
Exports and imports (agricultural) commodity and country, prices, and world market devs, monthly rpt, 1922–12
Exports and imports (agricultural) of US, by commodity and country, bimonthly rpt, 1522–1
Exports and imports (agricultural) of US, by detailed commodity and country, 1991, annual rpt, 1524–8
Exports and imports (agricultural) of US, by detailed commodity and country, 1991, semiannual rpt, 1522–4
Exports and imports between US and outlying areas, by detailed commodity and mode of transport, 1991, annual rpt, 2424–11
Exports and imports of US, by country and detailed commodity, monthly rpt, 2422–12
Exports and imports of US, by Harmonized System 6-digit commodity and country, 1991, annual rpt, 2424–13
Exports and imports of US, by selected country, country group, and commodity group, 1991, annual rpt, 2044–37
Exports and imports of US, by transport mode, country, and SITC 1- to 3-digit commodity, 1991, annual rpt, 2424–12
Exports, imports, tariffs, and industry operating data for cigarettes, 1991 rpt, 9885–8.2
Exports of US, detailed commodities by country, monthly CD-ROM, 2422–13
Exports of US, detailed Schedule B commodities with countries of destination, 1991, annual rpt, 2424–10
Farm financial and marketing conditions, forecast 1992, annual chartbook, 1504–8
Farm financial and marketing conditions, forecast 1992, annual conf, 1504–9
Farm income, cash marketing receipts ranked by commodity and State, 1990, 1548–385
Farm sector balance sheet, and receipts by detailed commodity, by State, 1986-90, annual rpt, 1544–18
Flue-cured tobacco farms and farm operators, by region and selected characteristics, 1970s-87, 1568–307
Foreign and US tobacco production, prices, and trade, FAS monthly circular with articles, 1925–16
Foreign countries agricultural production, prices, and trade, by country, 1980-91 and forecast 1992, annual world area rpt series, 1524–4

Freight (waterborne domestic and foreign) by commodity, traffic, and passengers, by port and waterway, 1989, annual rpt, 3754–3
Hazardous substances industrial releases and reduction methods under EPA regulation, by chemical, source, industry, and location, 1989, annual rpt, 9234–6
Hazardous substances industrial releases and reduction methods under EPA regulation, with chemical stocks and use, facility directory, 1987-89, annual CD-ROM, 9234–7
Illegal commerce in cigarettes, Federal sentencing guidelines by offense and circumstances, series, 17668–1
Illegal commerce in cigarettes, US attorneys cases by disposition, FY91, annual rpt, 6004–2.1
Imports, exports, and employment impacts, by SIC 2- to 4-digit industry and commodity, quarterly rpt, 2322–2
Imports of US, detailed commodities by country, monthly CD-ROM, 2422–14
Indian health risk behavior, by region and for Montana, mid 1980s, article, 4042–3.346
Input-output structure of US economy, detailed interindustry transactions for 84 industries, and components of final demand, 1987, annual article, 2702–1.316
Input-output structure of US economy, detailed interindustry transactions for 541 industries, and components of final demand, 1982 benchmark data, 2708–17
Labor productivity, indexes of output, hours, and employment by SIC 2- to 4-digit industry, 1967-90, annual rpt, 6824–1.3
Latin America, Canada, and US tobacco production and use, and related economic, health, and social issues, 1950s-92, annual rpt, 4204–18
Manufacturing annual survey, 1990: finances and operations, by SIC 2- to 4-digit industry, series, 2506–14
Manufacturing census, 1987: concentration of largest firms measured by value added, and for shipments by SIC 2- and 4-digit industry, subject rpt, 2497–6
Manufacturing census, 1987: shipments of manufacturers products, by customer class and SIC 2- and 4-digit industry, subject rpt, 2497–4
Manufacturing corporations financial statements, by selected SIC 2- to 3-digit industry, quarterly rpt, 2502–1
Manufacturing production, shipments, inventories, orders, and pollution control costs, periodic Current Industrial Rpt series, 2506–3
Marketing activity, prices, and sales, by grade and type of tobacco, market, and State, 1991, annual rpt series, 1319–5
Marketing of tobacco by cooperatives, 1989-91, article, 1122–1.304
Mexico imports from US, by industry and State, 1987-91, 2048–154
Multinatl firms US affiliates finances and operations, by industry, country of parent firm, and State, 1987, 2708–48
Multinatl US firms and foreign affiliates finances and operations, by industry and country, 1989 benchmark survey, annual rpt, 2704–5
Natl income and product accounts, comprehensive accounts and components, benchmark revisions, 1929-88, 2708–5
Natl income and product accounts, comprehensive accounts and components, *Survey of Current Business*, monthly rpt, 2702–1.25
Nicotine, tar, and carbon monoxide content of cigarettes, by brand, 1990, 9408–53
Occupational injury and illness rates, by SIC 2- to 4-digit industry, 1989-90, annual rpt, 6844–7
Occupational injury and illness rates, by SIC 2- to 4-digit industry, 1990, annual rpt, 6844–1
OECD trade, total and for 4 major countries, and US trade by country, by commodity, 1980-90, world area rpt series, 9116–1
Pollution abatement capital and operating costs, by SIC 2- to 4-digit industry and State, 1990, annual Current Industrial Rpt, 2506–3.6
Price indexes (producer), by stage of processing and detailed commodity, monthly rpt, 6762–6
Price indexes (producer), by stage of processing and detailed commodity, monthly 1991, annual rpt, 6764–2
Prices received and paid by farmers, by commodity and State, monthly rpt, 1629–1
Prices received and paid by farmers, by commodity and State, 1991, annual rpt, 1629–5
Prices received by farmers and production value, by detailed crop and State, 1989-91, annual rpt, 1621–2
Production, farms, acreage, and related data, by selected crop and State, monthly rpt, 1621–1
Production inputs, output, and productivity for farms, by commodity and region, 1947-90, annual rpt, 1544–17
Production, marketing, use, price supports, and trade, for tobacco, quarterly situation rpt with articles, 1561–10
Production, prices, stocks, and taxes by State, and trade and production by country, 1991, annual rpt, 1319–1
Production, prices, trade, and marketing, by commodity, current situation and forecast, monthly rpt with articles, 1502–4
Production, trade, and removals of tobacco products, by type, monthly rpt, 8486–1.4
Research on smoking, tobacco, and health impacts, publications, 1991 annual report, 4204–19
Science, engineering, and technical employment in manufacturing, by field and industry, 1989, triennial rpt, 9627–23
Smokeless tobacco use, by selected characteristics, 1991 survey, annual rpt series, 4494–5
Soviet Union and US economic and sociodemographic indicators, selected years 1970-90, handbook, 2328–80
Statistical Abstract of US, 1992 annual data compilation, 2324–1.27
Stocks, production, sales, and import inspections by country, for tobacco leaf by product, quarterly rpt, 1319–3
Tax (excise) collections of IRS, by source, quarterly rpt, 8302–2.1
Tax (income) returns of corporations, income and tax items by asset size and detailed industry, 1989, annual rpt, 8304–4; 8304–21
Tax collections of State govts by detailed type of tax, and tax rates, by State, FY91, annual rpt, 2466–2.7
Tax enforcement activities and collections of Bur of Alcohol, Tobacco, and Firearms and IRS, 1991 hearing, 21788–217
Tax rates and revenue of State and local govts, by source and State, 1992 and historical trends, annual rpt, 10044–1
Tax revenue, by level of govt, type of tax, State, and selected large county, quarterly rpt, 2462–3
Toxicology Natl Program research and testing activities, FY90 and planned FY91, annual rpt, 4044–16
Weight and volume conversion factors for agricultural commodities and products, 1992 rpt, 1508–3
Youth tobacco use, effectiveness of local ordinance enforcing penalties on retailers selling to minors, 1989-90 local area study, article, 4042–3.336
see also Smoking
see also under By Commodity in the "Index by Categories"
see also under By Industry in the "Index by Categories"

Todd, Richard M.
"Real Effects of Monetary Policy in a World Economy", 9383–20.24

Togo
Agricultural trade of US, by detailed commodity and country, 1991, annual rpt, 1524–8
Agricultural trade of US, by detailed commodity and country, 1991, semiannual rpt, 1522–4
AID economic aid to developing countries, obligations and disbursements by country, quarterly rpt, 9912–4
Economic and military aid and loans from US and intl agencies, by program and country, FY46-91, annual rpt, 9914–5
Economic and social conditions of developing countries from 1960s, and Intl Dev Cooperation Agency and AID activities and funding, FY91-93, annual rpt, 9904–4
Economic conditions, income, production, prices, employment, and trade, 1992 periodic country rpt, 2046–4.13
Economic, social, political, and geographic summary data, by country, 1992, annual factbook, 9114–2
Exports and imports of US, by transport mode, country, and SITC 1- to 3-digit commodity, 1991, annual rpt, 2424–12
Exports of US, detailed Schedule B commodities with countries of destination, 1991, annual rpt, 2424–10
Health surveillance system dev in Togo, 1986-91, article, 4202–7.322
Human rights conditions in 170 countries, and US economic and military aid, 1991, annual rpt, 21384–3
Military aid of US, arms sales, and training programs costs and budget requests, by program, world region, and country, FY91-93, annual rpt, 7144–13
Military spending, arms trade, and force strengths, with govt spending and population, by country, 1979-89, annual rpt, 9824–1

Minerals Yearbook, Vol 3, 1989: foreign country review of production, trade, and policy, by commodity, annual rpt, 5604–35.1
Population size, growth rates, and components of change, by country, projected 1990-2020 and trends from 1950, biennial rpt, 2324–9
Refugee migration, and intl aid programs, by world area and country of origin and asylum, 1991, annual rpt, 7004–15
UN voting record and share of votes in agreement with US, by issue, country, and world area, 1991, annual rpt, 7004–18

Toiletries
see Cosmetics and toiletries

Toledo, Ohio
Wages by occupation, and benefits for office and plant workers, 1992 survey, periodic MSA rpt, 6785–3.5
see also under By City and By SMSA or MSA in the "Index by Categories"

Tolls
Auto, van, and light truck ownership and operating costs, by vehicle size and year of operation, 1991 model year, biennial rpt, 7554–21
Hwy receipts by source, and spending by function, by level of govt and State, 1991, annual rpt, 7554–1.3
Natl income and product accounts, comprehensive accounts and components, benchmark revisions, 1929-88, 2708–5
Natl income and product accounts, comprehensive accounts and components, *Survey of Current Business*, monthly rpt, 2702–1.25
Panama Canal Commission finances and activities, with Canal traffic and local govt operations, FY91, annual rpt, 9664–3
St Lawrence Seaway ship, cargo, and passenger traffic, and toll revenue, 1991 and trends from 1959, annual rpt, 7744–2
State govt revenue by source, spending and debt by function, and holdings, FY91, annual rpt, 2466–2.6

Tomatoes
see Vegetables and vegetable products

Tonga
Economic, social, political, and geographic summary data, by country, 1992, annual factbook, 9114–2
Exports and imports of US, by transport mode, country, and SITC 1- to 3-digit commodity, 1991, annual rpt, 2424–12
Exports of US, detailed Schedule B commodities with countries of destination, 1991, annual rpt, 2424–10
Human rights conditions in 170 countries, and US economic and military aid, 1991, annual rpt, 21384–3
Military aid of US, arms sales, and training programs costs and budget requests, by program, world region, and country, FY91-93, annual rpt, 7144–13
Population size, growth rates, and components of change, by country, projected 1990-2020 and trends from 1950, biennial rpt, 2324–9

Tonsillitis
see Nose and throat disorders

Tool and die industry
see Machines and machinery industry

Toole, Michael J.
"Development of Health Surveillance in Togo, West Africa", 4202–7.322
"Famine-Affected, Refugee, and Displaced Populations: Recommendations for Public Health Issues", 4206–2.63

Tools
Business statistics, detailed data for major industries and economic indicators, 1960-91, *Survey of Current Business* biennial supplement, 2704–1
County Business Patterns, 1989: employment, establishments, and payroll, by SIC 2- to 4-digit industry and county, annual State rpt series, 2326–8
County Business Patterns, 1990: employment, establishments, and payroll, by SIC 2- to 4-digit industry and county, annual State rpt series, 2326–6
Electric cutting and sanding tools from Japan at less than fair value, injury to US industry, investigation with background financial and operating data, 1992 rpt, 9886–14.355
Employment, earnings, and hours, by SIC 1- to 4-digit industry, monthly 1989-Feb 1992, annual rpt, 6744–4
Employment of minorities and women, by occupation, SIC 1- to 3-digit industry, State, and MSA, 1991, annual rpt, 9244–1
Exports and imports between US and outlying areas, by detailed commodity and mode of transport, 1991, annual rpt, 2424–11
Exports and imports of US, by country and detailed commodity, monthly rpt, 2422–12
Exports and imports of US, by Harmonized System 6-digit commodity and country, 1991, annual rpt, 2424–13
Exports and imports of US, by transport mode, country, and SITC 1- to 3-digit commodity, 1991, annual rpt, 2424–12
Exports of US, detailed Schedule B commodities with countries of destination, 1991, annual rpt, 2424–10
Hand tools (power driven) US industry intl competitiveness, with selected foreign and US operating data, 1947-92, 2046–12.46
Imports of US given duty-free treatment for value of US material sent abroad, by commodity and country, 1987-90, annual rpt, 9884–14
Injuries from use of consumer products and related activities, by severity and victim age and sex, 1990, annual rpt, 9164–7
Injuries from use of consumer products, by severity, victim age, and detailed product, 1991, annual rpt, 9164–6
Injuries from use of consumer products, related deaths and costs, and recalls by brand, by product type, FY90, annual rpt, 9164–2
Input-output structure of US economy, detailed interindustry transactions for 541 industries, and components of final demand, 1982 benchmark data, 2708–17
Labor productivity, indexes of output, hours, and employment by SIC 2- to 4-digit industry, 1967-90, annual rpt, 6824–1.3
Manufacturing annual survey, 1990: finances and operations, by SIC 2- to 4-digit industry, series, 2506–14
Manufacturing census, 1987: concentration of largest firms measured by value added, and for shipments by SIC 2- and 4-digit industry, subject rpt, 2497–6
Manufacturing census, 1987: shipments of manufacturers products, by customer class and SIC 2- and 4-digit industry, subject rpt, 2497–4
Manufacturing finances and operations, by SIC 2- to 4-digit industry, forecast 1992, annual rpt, 2044–28
Military prime contract awards, by detailed procurement category, FY88-91, annual rpt, 3544–18
Multinatl US firms and foreign affiliates finances and operations, by industry and country, 1989 benchmark survey, annual rpt, 2704–5
Occupational injury and illness rates, by SIC 2- to 4-digit industry, 1989-90, annual rpt, 6844–7
Occupational injury and illness rates, by SIC 2- to 4-digit industry, 1990, annual rpt, 6844–1
OECD trade, total and for 4 major countries, and US trade by country, by commodity, 1980-90, world area rpt series, 9116–1
Price indexes (producer), by stage of processing and detailed commodity, monthly rpt, 6762–6
Price indexes (producer), by stage of processing and detailed commodity, monthly 1991, annual rpt, 6764–2
Science, engineering, and technical employment in manufacturing, by field and industry, 1989, triennial rpt, 9627–23
Statistical Abstract of US, 1992 annual data compilation, 2324–1.27
Wages and production workers by occupation, and benefits, for metalworking machinery and die and tool manufacturing, by selected MSA, 1990 survey, 6787–6.253
see also Agricultural machinery and equipment
see also Hardware
see also Household supplies and utensils
see also Lawn and garden equipment
see also Machines and machinery industry

Tootell, Geoffrey M.
"Back to the Future: Monetary Policy and the Twin Deficits", 9373–27.9
"Purchasing Power Parity Within the U.S.", 9373–1.312

Topeka, Kans.
Wages by occupation, for office and plant workers, 1992 survey, periodic MSA rpt, 6785–3.5

Topography
Foreign countries *Background Notes*, summary social, political, and economic data, series, 7006–2
Foreign countries economic, social, political, and geographic summary data, by country, 1992, annual factbook, 9114–2
Statistical Abstract of US, 1992 annual data compilation, 2324–1.6
Water quality, chemistry, hydrology, and other characteristics, local area studies, series, 5666–27
see also Arid zones
see also Cartography

see also Coastal areas
see also Lakes and lakeshores
see also Land area
see also Rivers and waterways
see also Seashores
see also Water area

Tornfelt, Evert E.
"Shipwrecks of the Alaskan Shelf and Shore", 5738–34

Toronto, Canada
Drug abuse indicators, by world region and selected country, 1992 semiannual conf, 4492–5.2

Torpedoes
Military weapons acquisition costs by system and service branch, DOD budget, FY91-93, annual rpt, 3504–2
Navy weapons systems parts purchases from foreign suppliers and US contractors, by State and country, 1988, 2026–1.3

Torts
Court civil and criminal caseloads for Federal district, appeals, and bankruptcy courts, by type of suit and offense, circuit, and district, 1991, annual rpt, 18204–11
Court civil and criminal caseloads for Federal district, appeals, and special courts, 1991, annual rpt, 18204–8
Reform recommendations for civil litigation, with background data, 1960-90, 048–3
US attorneys civil cases, by type and disposition, FY91, annual rpt, 6004–2.5

Toscano, Guy
"Fatal Work Injuries: Census for 31 States", 6722–1.338

Tourist travel
see Travel and tourism

Town planning
see City and town planning

Towner, Roy R.
"International Strategic Minerals Inventory Summary Report: Zirconium", 5666–21.12

Towns
see Central cities
see Cities
see Rural areas
see Suburbs
see Urban areas

Townsend, Richard T.
"Conservation and Protection of Humpback Whales in Hawaii—An Update", 14738–14

Toxic substances
see Dioxins
see Hazardous substances
see Hazardous waste and disposal
see Pesticides
see Poisoning and drug reaction

Toys and games
County Business Patterns, 1989: employment, establishments, and payroll, by SIC 2- to 4-digit industry and county, annual State rpt series, 2326–8
County Business Patterns, 1990: employment, establishments, and payroll, by SIC 2- to 4-digit industry and county, annual State rpt series, 2326–6
CPI by component for US city average, and by selected metro area, region, and population size, monthly rpt, 6762–2
Electronic communications systems and related products shipments, trade, use, and firms, 1991, annual Current Industrial Rpt, 2506–12.35
Employment, earnings, and hours, by SIC 1- to 4-digit industry, monthly 1989-Feb 1992, annual rpt, 6744–4
Employment of minorities and women, by occupation, SIC 1- to 3-digit industry, State, and MSA, 1991, annual rpt, 9244–1
Exports and imports between US and outlying areas, by detailed commodity and mode of transport, 1991, annual rpt, 2424–11
Exports and imports of US, by country and detailed commodity, monthly rpt, 2422–12
Exports and imports of US, by Harmonized System 6-digit commodity and country, 1991, annual rpt, 2424–13
Exports, imports, tariffs, and industry operating data for toys and models, 1991 rpt, 9885–10.1
Exports of US, detailed Schedule B commodities with countries of destination, 1991, annual rpt, 2424–10
Imports of US given duty-free treatment for value of US material sent abroad, by commodity and country, 1987-90, annual rpt, 9884–14
Injuries from use of consumer products and related activities, by severity and victim age and sex, 1990, annual rpt, 9164–7
Injuries from use of consumer products, by severity, victim age, and detailed product, 1991, annual rpt, 9164–6
Injuries from use of consumer products, related deaths and costs, and recalls by brand, by product type, FY90, annual rpt, 9164–2
Input-output structure of US economy, detailed interindustry transactions for 541 industries, and components of final demand, 1982 benchmark data, 2708–17
Manufacturing annual survey, 1990: finances and operations, by SIC 2- to 4-digit industry, series, 2506–14
Manufacturing census, 1987: concentration of largest firms measured by value added, and for shipments by SIC 2- and 4-digit industry, subject rpt, 2497–6
Manufacturing census, 1987: shipments of manufacturers products, by customer class and SIC 2- and 4-digit industry, subject rpt, 2497–4
Manufacturing finances and operations, by SIC 2- to 4-digit industry, forecast 1992, annual rpt, 2044–28
Occupational injury and illness rates, by SIC 2- to 4-digit industry, 1989-90, annual rpt, 6844–7
Occupational injury and illness rates, by SIC 2- to 4-digit industry, 1990, annual rpt, 6844–1
OECD trade, total and for 4 major countries, and US trade by country, by commodity, 1980-90, world area rpt series, 9116–1
Price indexes (producer), by stage of processing and detailed commodity, monthly rpt, 6762–6
Price indexes (producer), by stage of processing and detailed commodity, monthly 1991, annual rpt, 6764–2
Science, engineering, and technical employment in manufacturing, by field and industry, 1989, triennial rpt, 9627–23
see also Sporting goods

Trace metals
Acid rain distribution, pH levels, and composition, monitoring results by site, 1989, annual rpt, 9194–20
Acid rain environmental, economic, and health effects, and pollutant emissions, 1985-89 and alternative projections to 2030, 14358–4
Alaska Beaufort Sea pollutant concentrations in sediment and marine life, by contaminant and site, 1985-89, 5738–33
Alaska OCS environmental conditions and oil dev impacts, compilation of papers, series, 2176–1
Birds (least tern and piping plover) and habitat levels of selenium and other pollutants, for Missouri River in South Dakota, 1988-90, 5508–118
California OCS oil and gas dev impacts on water quality, marine life, and sediments, by site, 1986-90, annual rpt, 5734–11
Carcinogens chemistry, sources, environment and health risks, and regulation, by substance and brand, 1991 annual rpt, 4044–15
Coastal and estuarine pollutant concentrations in fish, shellfish, and environment, series, 2176–3
Coastal areas environmental conditions and mgmt, for individual areas, conf series, 2146–8
Environmental Quality, status of problems, protection programs, research, and intl issues, 1991 annual rpt, 484–1
Great Lakes industrial water pollution emissions, comparison of State, EPA, Intl Joint Commission, and Ontario standards, 1991 rpt, 14648–29
Health effects of selected pollutants, concentrations in food and environment, sources, human intake, and regulation, series, 9186–8
Health effects of selected pollutants on animals by species and on humans, and environmental levels, series, 5506–14
Industrial hazardous substances releases and reduction methods under EPA regulation, by chemical, source, industry, and location, 1989, annual rpt, 9234–6
Industrial hazardous substances releases and reduction methods under EPA regulation, with chemical stocks and use, facility directory, 1987-89, annual CD-ROM, 9234–7
Marine mammals tissue pollutant concentrations, by species and pollutant type, for Alaska, 1987-91, 2218–87
Toxicology Natl Program research and testing activities, FY90 and planned FY91, annual rpt, 4044–16
Water (groundwater) supply, quality, chemistry, and use, State and local area rpt series, 5666–28
Water quality, chemistry, hydrology, and other characteristics, local area studies, series, 5666–27
Water supply and quality in streams and lakes, and groundwater levels in wells, by drainage basin, 1990, annual State rpt series, 5666–10
Water supply and quality in streams and lakes, and groundwater levels in wells, by drainage basin, 1990-91, annual CD-ROM, 5664–18

Water supply and quality in streams and lakes, and groundwater levels in wells, by drainage basin, 1991, annual State rpt series, 5666–12
Wetlands acid neutralizing capability for mining runoff, with pollutant levels and site characteristics, for Pennsylvania, 1987-90, 5608–171
see also Lead poisoning and pollution
see also Mercury pollution

Tractors
see Agricultural machinery and equipment

Trade
see Agricultural exports and imports
see Arms trade
see Balance of payments
see Coal exports and imports
see Common markets and free trade areas
see Customs administration
see East-West trade
see Energy exports and imports
see Foreign competition
see Foreign trade
see Foreign trade promotion
see International assistance
see Interstate commerce
see Marketing
see Military assistance
see Motor vehicle exports and imports
see Natural gas exports and imports
see Petroleum exports and imports
see Retail trade
see Smuggling
see Tariffs and foreign trade controls
see Trade adjustment assistance
see Trade agreements
see Wholesale trade

Trade adjustment assistance
Assistance programs under Ways and Means Committee jurisdiction, finances, operations, and participant characteristics, FY70s-91, annual rpt, 21784–11
Displaced worker training programs spending, participation, and placements by State, 1990, GAO rpt, 26121–481
Economic Dev Admin activities, and funding by program, recipient, State, and county, FY91 and cumulative from FY66, annual rpt, 2064–2
Eligibility of workers, petitions by disposition, selected industry, union, and State, monthly rpt, 6402–13
Employment and Training Admin activities, funding, and participant characteristics, by program, FY86-88, annual rpt, 6404–17
Fed Govt financial and nonfinancial domestic aid, 1992 base edition, annual listing, 104–5

Trade agreements
Andean Trade Preference Act duty-free exports from 4 countries to US, and business opportunities, 1989-91, 2048–161
Bilateral and multilateral treaties and other agreements in force, by country, as of Jan 1992, annual listing, 7004–1
Canada-US trade agreement issues, with data on Canada fertilizer and agricultural production and trade, 1960s-90s, hearing, 25368–179
Caribbean Basin Initiative export and investment incentives, contact listing, bibl, and US imports country, 1983-91, annual rpt, 2044–36
EC economic integration impacts on domestic and intl agricultural conditions, 1990 conf, 1528–325
EC economic integration impacts on domestic economic conditions and US trade, with background data, 1986-91, 9886–4.181
Economic conditions, and trade devs and balances, with data by selected country and country group, monthly rpt, 9882–14
Employment and industry impacts of trade, series, 6366–3
Export and import agreements, negotiations, and related legislation, 1991, annual rpt, 444–1
Exports and imports, trade agreements and relations, and USITC investigations, 1991, annual rpt, 9884–5
Overseas Business Reports: economic conditions, investment and export opportunities, and trade practices, country market research rpt series, 2046–6
Shipbuilding and repair subsidy elimination proposals of US and OECD, impacts on industry and trade, with data on US-flag vessels, 1980s-91, 9886–4.183
Steel imports of US under voluntary restraint agreement, by product, customs district, and country, with US industry operating data, quarterly rpt, 9882–13
Textile Agreement Category System import classification codes, correlation with TSUSA, 1993 annual rpt, 2044–31
Textile imports under Multifiber Arrangement by product and country, and status of bilateral agreements, 1988-91, annual rpt, 9884–18
USITC activities, investigations, and rpts, FY91, annual rpt, 9884–1
see also Common markets and free trade areas
see also General Agreement on Tariffs and Trade
see also North American Free Trade Agreement
see also Tariffs and foreign trade controls

Trade balances
see Balance of payments
see Foreign trade

Trade fairs
see Exhibitions and trade fairs

Trade investigations
see Government investigations

Trade promotion
see Foreign trade promotion

Trade regulation
see Antitrust law
see Consumer protection
see Copyright
see Government and business
see Licenses and permits
see Patents
see Price regulation
see Tariffs and foreign trade controls
see Trade adjustment assistance
see Trademarks

Trade unions
see Labor unions

Trademarks
Applications, grants, fees, and litigation, for patents and trademarks, FY71-90, annual rpt, 2244–1
Court civil and criminal caseloads for Federal district, appeals, and bankruptcy courts, by type of suit and offense, circuit, and district, 1991, annual rpt, 18204–11
Court civil and criminal caseloads for Federal district, appeals, and special courts, 1991, annual rpt, 18204–8
Criminal sentences for Federal offenses, guidelines by offense and circumstances, series, 17668–1
Statistical Abstract of US, 1992 annual data compilation, 2324–1.17

Traffic accident fatalities
Accidents (fatal), circumstances, and characteristics of persons and vehicles involved, 1991, semiannual rpt, 7762–11
Accidents (fatal), deaths, and rates, by circumstances, characteristics of persons and vehicles involved, and location, 1990, annual rpt, 7764–10
Accidents and casualties, by driver age and sex, 1990, 7768–105
Accidents, casualties, and rates, by hwy type and State, 1989, annual rpt, 7554–2
Accidents, casualties, circumstances, and characteristics of persons and vehicles involved, 1990, annual rpt, 7764–18
Alaska occupational injury deaths, by cause, occupation, and industry, early 1980s, article, 4042–3.307
Alcohol-related deaths, by cause, State, and county, annual averages 1979-80 and 1983-85, 4488–10.4
Auto fuel economy from vehicle size reduction and other technological devs, and impacts on traffic deaths, 1991 hearings, 25318–83
Blue Ridge Parkway traffic accidents, deaths, and circumstances, 1984-87, 7556–8.2
Costs (direct and indirect) of traffic accidents, by cost type, payment source, and severity, 1980s, 7558–114
Deaths and rates, by cause, age, sex, marital status, race, and State, 1989, US Vital Statistics advance annual rpt, 4146–5.124
Deaths and rates, by cause and age, preliminary 1990-91, US Vital Statistics annual rpt, 4144–7
Deaths and rates, by cause and selected social, demographic, and employment characteristics, 1979-85, natl longitudinal study, 4478–186
Deaths and rates, by cause, provisional data, monthly rpt, 4142–1.2
Deaths and rates, by detailed location, cause, and demographic characteristics, 1989, US Vital Statistics annual rpt, 4144–3
Deaths by cause, age, race, and sex, 1950s-90, with health improvement and disease prevention goals for 1990, annual data compilation, 4144–11
Deaths in accidents, by vehicle type, 1980 and 1990, article, 1702–1.306
Deaths in traffic accidents by region, and death rates for miles traveled, monthly rpt, 7762–7
Deaths in traffic accidents by type of vehicle involved, and Natl Hwy Traffic Safety Admin activities, 1979-90, annual rpt, 7764–1
Drunk drivers and others involved in fatal accidents, alcohol levels by circumstances and characteristics of persons and vehicles, 1990, annual rpt, 7764–16
Drunk driving accidents and casualties, by alcohol level, data compilation, 1992 annual rpt, 6064–6.3

Drunk driving and other accidents involving alcohol, deaths by driver and victim blood alcohol levels, and other characteristics, 1977-88, annual rpt, 4486–1.12; 4486–1.14
Fire fighter deaths, by cause, circumstances, and location, 1990, annual rpt, 9434–8
Hospitalization for traffic accident injuries, costs, and discharges, by payment source and State, mid 1980s-90, 7768–122
Hwy Statistics, summary data with trends and projections, 1992 chartbook, 7554–41
Indian Health Service and tribal facilities and use, and Indians health and other characteristics, by IHS region, 1980s-90, annual chartbook, 4084–7
Indian Health Service facilities, funding, operations, and Indian health and other characteristics, 1950s-91, annual chartbook, 4084–1
Law enforcement officer assaults and deaths by circumstances, agency, victim and offender characteristics, and location, 1990, annual rpt, 6224–3
Occupational deaths, by cause and industry div, 1990, annual rpt, 6844–1
PHS Commissioned Corps members deaths, by cause, 1965-89, article, 4042–3.316
Prevention of accidental injury and death, and treatment, 1991 conf papers, 4208–35
Railroad-hwy grade-crossing accidents, detailed data by State and railroad, 1991, annual rpt, 7604–2
Safety program funding by State, and accident and death reductions, FY91, annual rpt, 7554–26
Seat belts (automatic) and air bags, availability and impact on traffic accident deaths, 1980s-91, 7768–123
Speed limit impacts on traffic deaths and speeds, for States with 55 and 65 mph limit, 1986-90, 7764–15
Statistical Abstract of US, 1992 annual data compilation, 2324–1.21
Truck accidents, casualties, and damage, by circumstances and characteristics of persons and vehicles involved, 1989, annual rpt, 7554–9

Traffic accidents and safety
Accidents and casualties, by driver age and sex, 1990, 7768–105
Accidents, casualties, and rates, by hwy type and State, 1989, annual rpt, 7554–2
Accidents, casualties, circumstances, and characteristics of persons and vehicles involved, 1990, annual rpt, 7764–18
Blue Ridge Parkway traffic accidents, deaths, and circumstances, 1984-87, 7556–8.2
Bridge replacement and repair program funding by bridge, and bridge status, by State, 1990, biennial rpt, 7554–27
Costs (direct and indirect) of traffic accidents, by cost type, payment source, and severity, 1980s, 7558–114
Disability, acute and chronic health conditions, absenteeism, and health services use, by selected characteristics, 1990, annual rpt, 4147–10.182; 4147–10.183
DOT activities by subagency, budget, and summary accident data, FY89, annual rpt, 7304–1
DOT planning and safety grants, by program, State, and for 40 SMSAs, FY89, annual rpt, 7304–7
Energy natl strategy auto fuel economy standards and alternative fuels issues, 1991 hearings, 21368–138
Fed Govt spending in States, by type, program, agency, and State, FY91, annual rpt, 2464–2
Hazardous material transport accidents, casualties, and damage, by mode of transport, with DOT control activities, 1990, annual rpt, 7304–4
Hospital trauma center cases and deaths by injury type, costs, and payment sources, with data for selected areas, 1991 hearing, 21348–123
Hospitalization for traffic accident injuries, costs, and discharges, by payment source and State, mid 1980s-90, 7768–122
Hwy Statistics, detailed data by State, 1991, annual rpt, 7554–1
Indian and Alaska Native youth health condition and behavioral patterns, by sex and grade, 1988-90, 4088–3
Lighting of roadways, impacts on traffic accidents by circumstances, 1991 rpt, 7558–118
NASA accidents, casualties, damage, and safety activities, FY91, annual rpt, 9504–4
Prevention of accidental injury and death, and treatment, 1991 conf papers, 4208–35
Railroad-hwy grade-crossing accidents and casualties, and Fed Railroad Admin activities, 1990, annual rpt, 7604–12
Railroad-hwy grade-crossing accidents, casualties, and damage, by cause, railroad, and State, 1991, annual rpt, 7604–1
Railroad-hwy grade-crossing accidents, casualties, circumstances, and railroad involved, 1988, annual rpt, 9614–8
Railroad-hwy grade-crossing accidents, casualties, damage, and circumstances, by incident, 1988, annual rpt, 7604–3
Railroad-hwy grade-crossing accidents, detailed data by State and railroad, 1991, annual rpt, 7604–2
Research on traffic safety, literature review, with data on accidents and impact of safety measures, 1961-90, 7558–98
Rural areas 2-lane roads, accidents related to passing by circumstances and severity, 1992 article, 7552–3.301
Safety of domestic and foreign autos, crash test results by model, model years 1987-91, 7768–111
Safety of domestic and foreign autos, crash test results by model, press release series, 7766–7
Safety program funding by State, and accident and death reductions, FY91, annual rpt, 7554–26
Scenic byways accidents and traffic, for selected routes, 1966-90, 7556–8.5
Speed limit impacts on traffic deaths and speeds, for States with 55 and 65 mph limit, 1986-90, 7764–15
Speed limit impacts on traffic speeds and accidents, for States with 55 and 65 mph limit, 1983-89, 7768–121
Statistical Abstract of US, 1992 annual data compilation, 2324–1.21
Truck accidents, casualties, and damage, by circumstances and characteristics of persons and vehicles involved, 1989, annual rpt, 7554–9
Truck accidents, circumstances, and characteristics of vehicles and persons involved, 1979-86, 7768–124
Trucks (long combination) hwy use and size restrictions, and accidents, by State, 1980s-90, GAO rpt, 26113–568
Trucks (wide) on narrow hwys, lane location characteristics and effects on other traffic, 1991 rpt, 7558–113
see also Driving while intoxicated
see also Motor vehicle safety devices
see also Pedestrians
see also Traffic accident fatalities
see also Traffic engineering
see also Traffic laws and courts

Traffic engineering
Accident deaths and injuries prevention, and treatment, 1991 conf papers, 4208–35
Appalachia hwy system and access roads funding and completion status, by State, quarterly tables, 9082–1
Carpool high occupancy vehicle lanes design, enforcement, and use in selected cities, 1991 conf, 7308–204
Construction zones temporary pavement markings impacts on driver performance, 1992 rpt, 7558–116
Construction zones traffic control and safety procedures and equipment, 1991 conf, 7558–115
Electronic traffic mgmt and info system, demonstration program results, late 1980s, 7558–119
Hwy construction and design R&D, quarterly journal, 7552–3
Hwy safety program funding by State, and accident and death reductions, FY91, annual rpt, 7554–26
Intersection traffic controls involvement in accidents, 1990, annual rpt, 7764–18
Intersection traffic controls involvement in fatal accidents, 1990, annual rpt, 7764–10
Lighting of roadways, impacts on traffic accidents by circumstances, 1991 rpt, 7558–118
Railroad-hwy grade-crossing accidents, detailed data by State and railroad, 1991, annual rpt, 7604–2
Research on traffic safety, literature review, with data on accidents and impact of safety measures, 1961-90, 7558–98
Research on transit systems, rpts, 1991, annual listing, 7884–11
Safety research and funding of DOT, project listing, FY90, annual rpt, 7764–1
Trucks (wide) on narrow hwys, lane location characteristics and effects on other traffic, 1991 rpt, 7558–113

Traffic laws and courts
Container (intermodal) traffic by mode, use of containers over legal weight for hwy use, and California enforcement activity, 1960s-88, hearing, 21648–65
Court civil and criminal caseloads for Federal district, appeals, and bankruptcy courts, by type of suit and offense, circuit, and district, 1991, annual rpt, 18204–11
Court civil and criminal caseloads for Federal district, appeals, and special courts, 1991, annual rpt, 18204–8

Court criminal case processing in Federal district courts, and dispositions, by offense, district, and offender characteristics, 1989, annual data compilation, 6064–29
Court criminal case processing in Federal district courts, and dispositions, by offense, 1980-91, annual rpt, 6064–31
Crime, criminal justice admin and enforcement, and public opinion, data compilation, 1992 annual rpt, 6064–6
Hwy Statistics, detailed data by State, 1991, annual rpt, 7554–1
Natl Hwy Traffic Safety Admin activities and grants, and fatal traffic accident data, 1990, annual rpt, 7764–1
Speed averages and vehicles exceeding 55 mph, by State, FY91, annual rpt, 7554–1.4
Speed averages and vehicles exceeding 55 mph, by State, quarterly rpt, 7552–14
Speed limit impacts on traffic deaths and speeds, for States with 55 and 65 mph limit, 1986-90, 7764–15
Speed limit impacts on traffic speeds and accidents, for States with 55 and 65 mph limit, 1983-89, 7768–121
Speed limit posted and alcohol involvement, for fatal accidents, 1990, annual rpt, 7764–16
Speed limit posted and other circumstances of accidents, 1990, annual rpt, 7764–18
Speed limit posted and other circumstances of fatal accidents, 1991, semiannual rpt, 7762–11
Speed limit posted, previous violations and license revocation of drivers involved, and other detailed circumstances of fatal accidents, 1990, annual rpt, 7764–10
Trucks (long combination) hwy use and size restrictions, and accidents, by State, 1980s-90, GAO rpt, 26113–568
Women in jail, by criminal background and sociodemographic characteristics, with comparisons to men, 1989, 6066–19.66
see also Driving while intoxicated

Traffic violations
see Traffic accidents and safety
see Traffic laws and courts

Trailer homes
see Mobile homes

Trails
see National trails

Training
see Apprenticeship
see Employee development
see Manpower training programs
see Military training
see Sheltered workshops
see Vocational education and training

Trainor, Cynthia
"Inorganic Acids, Industry and Trade Summary", 9885–11.2

Trans-Alaska Pipeline System
Oil shipments and capacity of TAPS, projected 1987-2015, 3166–6.64

Transfer payments
see terms listed under Income maintenance

Transient housing
County Business Patterns, 1989: employment, establishments, and payroll, by SIC 2- to 4-digit industry and county, annual State rpt series, 2326–8
County Business Patterns, 1990: employment, establishments, and payroll, by SIC 2- to 4-digit industry and county, annual State rpt series, 2326–6
HHS financial aid, by program, recipient, State, and city, FY91, annual regional listings, 4004–3
Homeless persons aid programs of Fed Govt, program descriptions and funding, by agency and State, FY87-91, annual GAO rpt, 26104–21
Homeless persons transitional housing and support services, HUD grants by community, 1991, press release, 5006–3.80
Homeless persons transitional housing and support services, HUD grants by community, 1992, press release, 5006–3.95
Homeless persons transitional housing and support services program, outcome relation to client characteristics and services, FY87-90, GAO rpt, 26113–549
Juvenile facilities population, by resident characteristics and facility type, late 1970s-89, 6068–250
Juvenile facilities population, by resident characteristics and facility type, 1977-89, annual rpt, 6064–35
Philippines Mount Pinatubo volcanic eruptions, evacuation camps infective disease cases and deaths, 1991, article, 4202–7.320
Population census, 1990: institutionalized population and persons in group quarters, by sex, race, county, place, and urban-rural location, State rpt series, 2531–1
Refugees, displaced persons, and population affected by famine, CDC recommendations for disease surveillance, control, and prevention, with background data, 1978-91, 4206–2.63
see also Group homes for the handicapped
see also Hotels and motels

Transportation accidents and safety
Accidents, and mgmt of disasters and natl security threats, with data by major event and State, 1992 annual rpt, 9434–6
Deaths in transportation accidents, by mode, 1990-91, annual press release, 9614–6
DOT activities by subagency, budget, and summary accident data, FY89, annual rpt, 7304–1
DOT safety monitoring activities, press release series, 7306–10
Fed Govt financial and nonfinancial domestic aid, 1992 base edition, annual listing, 104–5
Injuries from use of consumer products, by severity, victim age, and detailed product, 1991, annual rpt, 9164–6
Injury and illness rates by SIC 2- to 4-digit industry, and deaths by cause and industry div, 1990, annual rpt, 6844–1
Investigations and recommendations of Natl Transportation Safety Board, and accidents and casualties by mode, 1990, annual rpt, 9614–1
Investigations of GAO, 1991-92, listing, 26106–10.7
Occupational injuries, illnesses, and lost workdays, by SIC 2-digit industry, 1990-91, annual press release, 6844–3
Occupational injury and illness rates, by SIC 2- to 4-digit industry, 1989-90, annual rpt, 6844–7
Pipelines inspections using internal electronic devices, costs and effectiveness, 1985-91, GAO rpt, 26113–594
Statistical Abstract of US, 1992 annual data compilation, 2324–1.21
Subway accidents, casualties, and damage, by circumstances and system, annual rpt, discontinued, 7884–5
Transit systems accidents and casualties by circumstances, damage, and ridership, by mode, 1990, annual rpt, 7884–13
Transit systems finances and operations, by mode, size of fleet and urban area, region, and for 518 systems, 1990, annual rpt, 7884–4
Transit systems R&D projects and funding of Federal Transit Admin, FY91, annual listing, 7884–1
see also Aviation accidents and safety
see also Hazardous substances transport
see also Marine accidents and safety
see also Motor vehicle safety devices
see also Railroad accidents and safety
see also Traffic accident fatalities
see also Traffic accidents and safety
see also Traffic engineering

Transportation and transportation equipment
Business statistics, detailed data for major industries and economic indicators, *Survey of Current Business*, monthly rpt, 2702–1.22
Business statistics, detailed data for major industries and economic indicators, 1960-91, *Survey of Current Business* biennial supplement, 2704–1
Capital expenditures for plant and equipment, by industry div, monthly rpt, quarterly data, 23842–1.1
Capital expenditures for plant and equipment, by major industry group, quarterly rpt, 2502–2
Capital investment changes relation to changes in costs, by asset type and industry div, late 1950s-80s, article, 9373–1.304
Census Bur data files and rpts, coverage and availability, 1992 annual listing, 2304–2
Collective bargaining agreements expiring during year, and workers covered, by firm, union, industry group, and State, 1992, annual rpt, 6784–9
Consumer Expenditure Survey, spending by category, and income, by selected household characteristics, 1991, annual press release, 6726–1.53
Consumer Expenditure Survey, spending by category, selected household characteristics, and region, quarterly rpt, 6762–14
County Business Patterns, 1989: employment, establishments, and payroll, by SIC 2- to 4-digit industry and county, annual State rpt series, 2326–8
County Business Patterns, 1990: employment, establishments, and payroll, by SIC 2- to 4-digit industry and county, annual State rpt series, 2326–6
Cuba trade, by commodity and country, mid 1980s-91, 9118–8
Deaths and rates, by cause and selected social, demographic, and employment characteristics, 1979-85, natl longitudinal study, 4478–186
Developing countries economic, population, and agricultural data, US and other aid sources, and AID activity, country rpt series, 9916–12

Employment Cost Index and alternative measure of compensation costs, by component, occupation, industry group, union status, and location, 1975-92, annual rpt, 6744–20
Employment, earnings, and hours, by selected SIC 1- to 4-digit industry, State, and for 275 MSAs, 1987-92, 6748–81
Employment, earnings, and hours, by SIC 1- to 4-digit industry, monthly 1989-Feb 1992, annual rpt, 6744–4
Employment of minorities and women, by occupation, SIC 1- to 3-digit industry, State, and MSA, 1991, annual rpt, 9244–1
Employment, unemployment, and labor force characteristics, by region and census div, 1991, annual rpt, 6744–7.1
Energy use and prices, by fuel type and manufacturing industry, 1974-88, 3166–15.3
Energy use and prices for manufacturing industries, 1988 survey, series, 3166–13
Environmental Quality, status of problems, protection programs, research, and intl issues, 1991 annual rpt, 484–1
Exports and imports between US and outlying areas, by detailed commodity and mode of transport, 1991, annual rpt, 2424–11
Exports and imports of US, by Harmonized System 6-digit commodity and country, 1991, annual rpt, 2424–13
Exports and imports of US, by selected country, country group, and commodity group, 1991, annual rpt, 2044–37
Exports, imports, and balances of US for manufactured goods, by SITC 2-digit commodity and country, quarterly rpt, 2042–35
Exports of US, detailed commodities by country, monthly CD-ROM, 2422–13
Exports of US, detailed Schedule B commodities with countries of destination, 1991, annual rpt, 2424–10
Finances and operations of Class I rail and motor carriers, detailed data, 1990, annual rpt series, 9486–5
Finances and operations of Class I rail and motor carriers, detailed data, 1991, annual rpt series, 9486–6
Finances and operations of transit systems, by mode, size of fleet and urban area, region, and for 518 systems, 1990, annual rpt, 7884–4
Foreign countries economic, social, political, and geographic summary data, by country, 1992, annual factbook, 9114–2
Foreign direct investment in US, major transactions by type, industry, country, and US location, 1990, annual rpt, 2044–20
Foreign direct investment of US, by industry group and world area, 1989-91, annual article, 2702–1.332
Freight (waterborne domestic and foreign) by commodity, traffic, and passengers, by port and waterway, 1989, annual rpt, 3754–3
Govt direct spending and employment, by function and level of govt, selected years 1962-87, 10048–53
Hazardous substances industrial releases and reduction methods under EPA regulation, with chemical stocks and use, facility directory, 1987-89, annual CD-ROM, 9234–7
Imports, exports, and employment impacts, by SIC 2- to 4-digit industry and commodity, quarterly rpt, 2322–2
Imports of US, detailed commodities by country, monthly CD-ROM, 2422–14
Imports of US given duty-free treatment for value of US material sent abroad, by commodity and country, 1987-90, annual rpt, 9884–14
Industry finances and operations, by SIC 2- to 4-digit industry, forecast 1992, annual rpt, 2044–28
Input-output structure of US economy, detailed interindustry transactions for 84 industries, and components of final demand, 1987, annual article, 2702–1.316
Input-output structure of US economy, detailed interindustry transactions for 541 industries, and components of final demand, 1982 benchmark data, 2708–17
Investigations of GAO, 1991-92, listing, 26106–10.7
Manufacturing annual survey, 1990: finances and operations, by SIC 2- to 4-digit industry, series, 2506–14
Manufacturing census, 1987: concentration of largest firms measured by value added, and for shipments by SIC 2- and 4-digit industry, subject rpt, 2497–6
Manufacturing census, 1987: shipments of manufacturers products, by customer class and SIC 2- and 4-digit industry, subject rpt, 2497–4
Manufacturing corporations financial statements, by selected SIC 2- to 3-digit industry, quarterly rpt, 2502–1
Manufacturing industries operations and performance, analytical rpt series, 2506–16
Manufacturing production, shipments, inventories, orders, and pollution control costs, periodic Current Industrial Rpt series, 2506–3
Mexico imports from US, by industry and State, 1987-91, 2048–154
Military prime contract awards, by detailed procurement category, FY88-91, annual rpt, 3544–18
Multinatl firms US affiliates finances and operations, by industry, country of parent firm, and State, 1987, 2708–48
Multinatl US firms and foreign affiliates finances and operations, by industry and country, 1989 benchmark survey, annual rpt, 2704–5
Multinatl US firms foreign affiliates, income statement items by asset size, industry, and country, 1988, biennial article, 8302–2.322
Natl income and product accounts and components, *Survey of Current Business*, monthly rpt, 2702–1.23
Natl income and product accounts, comprehensive accounts and components, benchmark revisions, 1929-88, 2708–5
Natl income and product accounts, comprehensive accounts and components, *Survey of Current Business*, monthly rpt, 2702–1.29
Occupational injury and illness rates by circumstances and establishment size, and methodology for computing rates, 1988, industry rpt, 6886–4.2
Occupational injury and illness rates, by SIC 2- to 4-digit industry, 1989-90, annual rpt, 6844–7
Occupational injury and illness rates, by SIC 2- to 4-digit industry, 1990, annual rpt, 6844–1
Occupational Outlook Handbook, 1992-93, biennial rpt, 6744–1
OECD trade, total and for 4 major countries, and US trade by country, by commodity, 1980-90, world area rpt series, 9116–1
Pacific territories population and housing detailed characteristics, by location, 1990 Census of Population and Housing, series, 2551–8
Pollution abatement capital and operating costs, by SIC 2- to 4-digit industry and State, 1990, annual Current Industrial Rpt, 2506–3.6
Price indexes (producer), by stage of processing and detailed commodity, monthly rpt, 6762–6
Price indexes (producer), by stage of processing and detailed commodity, monthly 1991, annual rpt, 6764–2
Puerto Rico and other US possessions corporations income tax returns, income and tax items, and employment, by selected industry, 1989, article, 8302–2.326
Science, engineering, and technical employment in manufacturing, by field and industry, 1989, triennial rpt, 9627–23
SEC registration, firms required to file annual rpts, as of Sept 1991, annual listing, 9734–5
Small business finances, operations, owner characteristics, and Federal contracts, 1980s-90, annual rpt, 9764–6
Southeastern US employment by industry div, earnings, and hours, for 8 States, quarterly press release, 6942–7
Soviet Union and US economic and sociodemographic indicators, selected years 1970-90, handbook, 2328–80
Statistical Abstract of US, 1992 annual data compilation, 2324–1.21; 2324–1.22
Stock (common) price indexes, current data and annual trends, monthly rpt, 23842–1.5
Tariff Schedule of US, classifications and rates of duty by detailed imported commodity, 1993 base edition, 9886–13
Tax (income) returns filed, by type of filer, selected income items, quarterly rpt, 8302–2.1
Tax (income) returns of corporations, income and tax items by asset size and detailed industry, 1989, annual rpt, 8304–4; 8304–21
Tax (income) returns of corporations with foreign tax credit, income and tax items by industry group, 1988, biennial article, 8302–2.316
Tax (income) returns of partnerships, income statement and balance sheet items, by industry group, 1990, annual article, 8302–2.314
Tax (income) returns of sole proprietorships, income statement items, by industry group, 1990, annual article, 8302–2.317; 8302–2.320

Wage and benefit changes from collective bargaining and mgmt decisions, by industry div, monthly rpt, 6782–1
see also Air travel
see also Aircraft
see also Airlines
see also Automobile repair and maintenance
see also Automobiles
see also Aviation accidents and safety
see also Bicycles
see also Boats and boating
see also Bridges and tunnels
see also Buses
see also Canals
see also Census of Transportation
see also Census of Transportation, Communications, and Utilities Industries
see also Civil aviation
see also Commuting
see also Courier services
see also Drivers licenses
see also Federal aid to transportation
see also Ferries
see also Freight
see also Gasoline
see also General aviation
see also Harbors and ports
see also Hazardous substances transport
see also Helicopters
see also High-speed ground transportation
see also Highways, streets, and roads
see also Inland water transportation
see also Marine accidents and safety
see also Military vehicles
see also Motor fuels
see also Motor vehicle exhaust
see also Motor vehicle exports and imports
see also Motor vehicle fleets
see also Motor vehicle industry
see also Motor vehicle parts and supplies
see also Motor vehicle registrations
see also Motor vehicle rental
see also Motor vehicle safety devices
see also Motor vehicle theft
see also Motorcycles
see also Parking facilities
see also Passenger ships
see also Pipelines
see also Railroad accidents and safety
see also Railroad equipment and vehicles
see also Railroads
see also Recreational vehicles
see also Rivers and waterways
see also School busing
see also Shipbuilding and repairing
see also Ships and shipping
see also State funding for transportation
see also Subways
see also Tanker ships
see also Taxicabs
see also Traffic accident fatalities
see also Traffic accidents and safety
see also Transportation accidents and safety
see also Transportation assistance
see also Transportation energy use
see also Travel agencies
see also Travel and tourism
see also Trucks and trucking industry
see also Urban transportation
see also under By Commodity in the "Index by Categories"
see also under By Industry in the "Index by Categories"

Transportation assistance
Drug abuse by mothers, treatment and other services use, referrals, needs, and barriers, for 13 NIDA-funded programs, 1990/91 survey, 4498–76
Employer-provided transit fare subsidies, participation, and parking costs, by selected city, 1985-92, GAO rpt, 26113–597
Fed Govt employees transit subsidies, costs and participation by agency, 1992, GAO rpt, 26113–601

Transportation Department
see Department of Transportation

Transportation energy use
Auto and light truck fuel economy performance by make, standards, and enforcement, 1978-94 model years, annual rpt, 7764–9
Auto fuel economy from vehicle size reduction and other technological devs, and impacts on traffic deaths, 1991 hearings, 25318–83
Auto fuel economy improvements from new technologies, 1987-90 and alternative projections to 2010, 26358–251
Auto fuel economy test results for US and foreign makes, 1993 model year, annual rpt, 3304–11
Auto, van, and light truck ownership and operating costs, by vehicle size and year of operation, 1991 model year, biennial rpt, 7554–21
Business statistics, detailed data for major industries and economic indicators, *Survey of Current Business*, monthly rpt, 2702–1.12
Coal mining restrictions on public land, impacts on production, costs, and demand, by region, 1985-88 and projected to 2075, 5668–125
Conservation of energy, State programs aid from Fed Govt, and energy savings, by State, 1990, annual rpt, 3304–1
Consumer Expenditure Survey, spending by category, selected household characteristics, and region, quarterly rpt, 6762–14
Consumer spending, natl income and product account benchmark revisions, 1929-88, 2708–5
Consumer spending, natl income and product accounts, comprehensive accounts and components, *Survey of Current Business*, monthly rpt, 2702–1.25
Consumption of fuel by transport mode, fuel supply, and demographic and economic factors of vehicle use, 1970s-90, annual rpt, 3304–5
Consumption of motor fuel, by consuming sector and State, 1991, annual rpt, 7554–1.1
Costs of owning and operating autos, 1980, 1985, and 1991, article, 1702–1.306
CPI by component for US city average, and by selected metro area, region, and population size, monthly rpt, 6762–2
Developing countries energy efficiency improvement issues and devs, with data by end use and country, 1980s-90, 26358–260
DOE energy use, costs, and conservation, by end use, fuel type, and field office, FY91, annual rpt, 3004–27
Electric utilities privately owned, finances and operations, detailed data, 1990, annual rpt, 3164–23
Energy supply, demand, and prices, by fuel type and end-use sector, alternative projections by region, 1990-2010, annual rpt, 3164–96
Energy supply, demand, and prices, by fuel type and end-use sector, alternative projections 1990-2010, annual rpt, 3164–75
Energy supply, demand, and prices, by fuel type and end-use sector, projections and underlying assumptions, 1995-2010, annual rpt, 3164–90
Energy supply, demand, and prices, by fuel type and end-use sector, with foreign comparisons, 1981-90, annual fact book, 3164–76
Energy supply, demand, and prices, by fuel type and end-use sector, with foreign comparisons, 1991 and trends from 1949, annual rpt, 3164–74
Energy supply, demand, and prices, by fuel type, end-use sector, and country, detailed data, monthly rpt with articles, 3162–24
Energy supply, demand, and prices, by fuel type, end-use sector, and country, detailed data, monthly 1973-88, 3168–123
Energy use, by detailed fuel type, end-use sector, and State, 1960-90, State Energy Data System annual rpt, 3164–39
Energy use by fuel type, and miles traveled, by transport mode, projected 1990-2010 and trends from 1960s, 3008–124
Energy use by mode of transport, fuel supply, and demographic and economic factors of vehicle use, 1970s-90, annual rpt, 3304–5
Environmental Quality, status of problems, protection programs, research, and intl issues, 1991 annual rpt, 484–1
Foreign and US energy supply and demand, by major fuel and end-use sector, 1950s-87 and forecast to 1995, 3166–6.58
Foreign and US oil dependency, energy demand, and efficiency measures, for 6 OECD countries, 1970s-80s, working paper, 9375–13.79
Foreign countries transportation energy use, fuel prices, vehicle registrations, and mileage, by selected country, 1950-89, annual rpt, 3304–5.1
Gasohol use, by region, 1990, annual rpt, 3164–97
Gasoline and other motor fuel use, by consuming sector and State, 1991, annual rpt, 7554–1.1
Hwy Statistics, summary data by State, 1990-91, annual rpt, 7554–24
Hwy Statistics, summary data with trends and projections, 1992 chartbook, 7554–41
Input-output structure of US economy, detailed interindustry transactions for 541 industries, and components of final demand, 1982 benchmark data, 2708–17
Natl Energy Strategy auto fuel economy standards and alternative fuels issues, 1991 hearings, 21368–138
Natl Energy Strategy fossil fuel, electric power, conservation, and pollution reduction issues, 1991 hearings, 21368–136

Natl Energy Strategy plans for conservation, R&D, security, and pollution reduction, technical rpt series, 3006–13
Older autos retirement programs proposals costs, savings, and emissions and energy use reductions, 1992 rpt, 26358–263
Pacific basin countries energy supply and demand, and implications for US trade, country rpt series, 3406–6
Philadelphia metro area transit service operations, costs and benefits, and local economic and air pollution impacts, 1970s-90 and projected to 2020, 7308–205
Prices and spending for fuel, by type, end-use sector, and State, 1990, annual rpt, 3164–64
Prices of fuel, by type, end-use sector, and region, projected 1991-2030, 3166–6.60
R&D projects on automotive engines and powertrains, DOE contracts and funding by recipient, FY91, annual rpt, 3304–17
Rail rapid transit systems safety, operating, and funding characteristics, 1988-89, 9618–19
Statistical Abstract of US, 1992 annual data compilation, 2324–1.21
Transit systems finances and operations, by mode, size of fleet and urban area, region, and for 518 systems, 1990, annual rpt, 7884–4
Truck and warehouse services finances and inventory, by SIC 2- to 4-digit industry, 1990 survey, annual rpt, 2413–14
Truck itemized costs per mile, finances, and operations, for agricultural carriers, 1991, annual rpt, 1311–15
Truck rates for fruit and vegetables paid by shippers and receivers, by commodity and city, and fleet itemized costs per mile, weekly rpt, 1311–22
TVA energy use by fuel type, and conservation costs and savings, FY91, annual rpt, 9804–26
see also Aviation fuels
see also Motor vehicle exhaust

Trapping
see Hunting and trapping

Travel agencies
County Business Patterns, 1989: employment, establishments, and payroll, by SIC 2- to 4-digit industry and county, annual State rpt series, 2326–8
County Business Patterns, 1990: employment, establishments, and payroll, by SIC 2- to 4-digit industry and county, annual State rpt series, 2326–6
Foreign travel to US and Canada, market analyses with detailed trip and traveler characteristics, country rpt series, 2906–2
Foreign travel to US, by characteristics of visit and traveler, world area of origin, and US destination, 1991 survey, annual rpt, 2904–12
Occupational Outlook Handbook, 1992-93, biennial rpt, 6744–1
Price indexes (producer), by stage of processing and detailed commodity, monthly rpt, 6762–6
Price indexes (producer), by stage of processing and detailed commodity, monthly 1991, annual rpt, 6764–2
Statistical Abstract of US, 1992 annual data compilation, 2324–1.21

Travel and tourism
Amtrak finances, executive office travel expenses and staff years, and membership dues by assn, FY88-92, GAO rpt, 26113–573
Arrivals and departures of US and foreign natls, *Survey of Current Business*, monthly rpt, 2702–1.10
Auto and light truck fuel use, economy, and miles traveled, projected 1990-2010 and trends from 1960s, 3008–124
Auto use, travel patterns, and personal and household characteristics, 1950-90, annual rpt, 3304–5.4
Auto use, travel patterns, and personal and household characteristics, 1990 survey, annual rpt, 7554–1.6
Banks in Fed Reserve System, expenses and operations itemized by service, office, and district, 1991, annual rpt, 9364–11
Bus (Class I) passengers and selected revenue data, for individual large carriers, quarterly rpt, 9482–13
Business statistics, detailed data for major industries and economic indicators, 1960-91, *Survey of Current Business* biennial supplement, 2704–1
Canada and US current accounts balance reconciliation adjustment methodology, with background data, 1990-91, article, 2702–1.341
Consumer spending, natl income and product account benchmark revisions, 1929-88, 2708–5
Consumer spending, natl income and product accounts, comprehensive accounts and components, *Survey of Current Business*, monthly rpt, 2702–1.25
Eastern Europe export industries dev potential, with trade and industry finances and operations, for 5 countries, 1985-90, 9886–4.179
Employment and receipts of travel-related industries, 1988, 7556–8.3
Environmental Quality, status of problems, protection programs, research, and intl issues, 1991 annual rpt, 484–1
Exports and imports of services, direct and among multinatl firms affiliates, by industry and world area, 1986-91, article, 2702–1.336
Fed Govt labor productivity, indexes of output and labor costs by function, FY67-90, annual rpt, 6824–1.6
Finances and operations, by SIC 2- to 4-digit industry, forecast 1992, annual rpt, 2044–28
Foreign countries *Background Notes*, summary social, political, and economic data, travel notes, series, 7006–2
Foreign countries economic conditions and implications for US, periodic country rpt series, 2046–4
Foreign countries human rights conditions in 170 countries, 1991, annual rpt, 21384–3
Foreign travel balance of US, current and annual trends, monthly rpt, 23842–1.7
Foreign travel to and from US, and travel receipts and payments, by world area, with data by country, 1985-90, annual rpt, 2904–10
Foreign travel to and from US, by world area, forecast 1992-93, annual rpt, 2904–9
Foreign travel to US, admissions by country, FY81-91, annual rpt, 6264–2.3
Foreign travel to US, admissions by country, FY90-91, annual summary rpt, 6264–7
Foreign travel to US and Canada, market analyses with detailed trip and traveler characteristics, country rpt series, 2906–2
Foreign travel to US, by characteristics of visit and traveler, country, port city, and State of destination, monthly rpt, 2902–1
Foreign travel to US, by characteristics of visit and traveler, world area of origin, and US destination, 1991 survey, annual rpt, 2904–12
Foreign travel to US, market research data available from US Travel and Tourism Admin, 1992, annual rpt, 2904–15
Foreign travelers to US, spending by world area of residence, and economic impacts, by spending category and State, 1989, 2908–28
Forests (natl) recreational use, by type of activity and State, 1991, annual rpt, 1204–17
Hepatitis cases by infection source, age, sex, race, and State, and deaths, by strain, 1989 and trends from 1966, 4205–2
House of Representatives salaries, expenses, and contingent fund disbursement, detailed listings, quarterly rpt, 21942–1
Households and personal travel patterns, characteristics, and auto and public transport use, 1990 survey, series, 7556–6
Hwy scenic routes and mileage, by govt ownership, land use and usage restrictions, and other characteristics, 1990, 7558–112
Hwy scenic routes economic, safety, and other issues, series, 7556–8
Hwy Statistics, summary data by State, 1990-91, annual rpt, 7554–24
Hwy traffic volume on rural roads and city streets, monthly rpt, 7552–8
Input-output structure of US economy, detailed interindustry transactions for 541 industries, and components of final demand, 1982 benchmark data, 2708–17
Malaria cases in US, for military personnel and US and foreign natls, and by country of infection, 1966-90, annual rpt, 4205–4
Overseas Business Reports: economic conditions, investment and export opportunities, and trade practices, country market research rpt series, 2046–6
Palau admin, and social, economic, and govtl data, FY91, annual rpt, 7004–6
Philadelphia metro area transit service operations, costs and benefits, and local economic and air pollution impacts, 1970s-90 and projected to 2020, 7308–205
Price indexes (producer), by stage of processing and detailed commodity, monthly rpt, 6762–6
Railroad (Amtrak) finances and operations, FY91, annual rpt, 29524–1
Senate receipts, itemized expenses by payee, and balances, 1st half FY92, semiannual listing, 25922–1
Small Business Admin loans to tourism-related and other small businesses in rural areas, FY86-1st half FY91, hearing, 21728–79

Soviet Union and US economic and sociodemographic indicators, selected years 1970-90, handbook, 2328–80
Statistical Abstract of US, 1992 annual data compilation, 2324–1.7; 2324–1.21
Tax (income) returns of sole proprietorships, income statement items, by industry group, 1990, annual article, 8302–2.317; 8302–2.320
Travel patterns by mode, licensed drivers, auto operating costs, and traffic accident deaths, 1980s-91, article, 1702–1.306
Vaccination needs for intl travel by country, and disease prevention recommendations, 1992 annual rpt, 4204–11
Washington and Oregon coastal areas tourism and recreation facilities and economic impacts, by county, 1983-88, 5738–40.3
see also Air travel
see also Commuting
see also Passenger ships
see also Passports and visas
see also Transportation accidents and safety
see also Travel agencies

Travel and Tourism Administration
see U.S. Travel and Tourism Administration

Travis, Lois B.
"Second Cancers in Patients with Chronic Lymphocytic Leukemia", 4472–1.343

Treason
see Subversive activities

Treasury Department
see Department of Treasury

Treaties and conventions
Arms Control and Disarmament Agency activities, and treaties status, 1991, annual rpt, 9824–2
Bilateral and multilateral treaties and other agreements in force, by country, as of Jan 1992, annual listing, 7004–1
Copyright intl relations of US, by country, 1991, annual listing, 26404–2
Foreign countries economic, social, political, and geographic summary data, by country, 1992, annual factbook, 9114–2
Geographic Notes, foreign countries boundaries, claims, nomenclature, and other devs, quarterly rpt, 7142–3
Human rights conditions in 170 countries, and US economic and military aid, 1991, annual rpt, 21384–3
Maritime claims and boundary agreements of coastal countries, series, 7006–8
OASDI beneficiaries abroad, benefits, and eligibility based on intl agreement, by program type and country, 1990, annual rpt, 4744–3.3
Tax withheld and income from US sources for alien nonresidents, by country and tax treaty status, detailed data compilation for income tax returns, 1984-88, quinquennial rpt, 8308–31
Tax withheld and income from US sources for foreign natls not residing in US, by country and tax treaty status, 1989, annual article, 8302–2.308
Tuna industry competitiveness and dolphin protection issues, investigation with background financial and operating data and foreign comparisons, 1992 rpt, 9886–4.187
see also Executive agreements
see also Intermediate-Range Nuclear Forces Treaty
see also Strategic Arms Reduction Talks
see also Trade agreements
see also Treaty on Conventional Armed Forces in Europe

Treaty on Conventional Armed Forces in Europe
NATO and Warsaw Pact military forces reductions and ceilings under CFE treaty, as of Nov 1990, 9828–1
NATO and Warsaw Pact military forces reductions and ceilings under CFE treaty, inspections, and US compliance costs and savings, 1991 hearings, 25388–59
Status of arms control treaties and agreements, and Arms Control and Disarmament Agency activities, 1991, annual rpt, 9824–2

Trees
see Forests and forestry

Trehan, Bharat
"Modelling the Time Series Behavior of the Aggregate Wage Rate", 9393–10.20
"Predicting Contemporaneous Output", 9393–8.305

Trembley, Nancy
"FAA Air Traffic Activity, FY91", 7504–27

Trench, Elaine C.
"Ground-Water Resources of Rhode Island", 5666–28.18

Trenton, N.J.
CPI by component for US city average, and by region, population size, and for 15 metro areas, monthly rpt, 6762–1
CPI by component for US city average, and by selected metro area, region, and population size, monthly rpt, 6762–2
Wages by occupation, for office and plant workers, 1991 survey, periodic MSA rpt, 6785–12.3
see also under By City and By SMSA or MSA in the "Index by Categories"

Trials
Criminal case processing in Federal courts, by offense, disposition, and jurisdiction, data compilation, 1992 annual rpt, 6064–6.5
Federal district court civil and criminal trials, and time to trial and case disposition, 1991, annual rpt, 18204–8.14; 18204–8.18; 18204–8.29
Felony case processing from arrest to sentencing, cases and duration by disposition and offense, for selected cities, 1988, annual rpt, 6064–27
Tax litigation cases by type, function, and region, FY91, annual rpt, 8304–3.3
US attorneys case processing and collections, by case type and Federal district, FY91, annual rpt, 6004–2
Wiretaps authorized, costs, arrests, trials, and convictions, by offense and jurisdiction, 1991, annual rpt, 18204–7
see also Courts-martial and courts of inquiry
see also Domestic relations courts and cases
see also Juries

Trichinosis
see Food and waterborne diseases

Trinidad and Tobago
Agricultural trade of US, by detailed commodity and country, 1991, annual rpt, 1524–8
Agricultural trade of US, by detailed commodity and country, 1991, semiannual rpt, 1522–4
AID economic aid to developing countries, obligations and disbursements by country, quarterly rpt, 9912–4
Economic and military aid and loans from US and intl agencies, by program and country, FY46-91, annual rpt, 9914–5
Economic and social conditions, resources, and trade, and aid, 1992, annual factbook, 9914–14
Economic conditions, policy, and trade practices, by country, 1989-91, annual rpt, 21384–5
Economic, social, political, and geographic summary data, by country, 1992, annual factbook, 9114–2
Exports and imports of US, by commodity and country, 1980-90, world area rpt, 9116–1.4
Exports and imports of US, by Harmonized System 6-digit commodity and country, 1991, annual rpt, 2424–13
Exports and imports of US, by transport mode, country, and SITC 1- to 3-digit commodity, 1991, annual rpt, 2424–12
Exports, imports, and balances of US for manufactured goods, by SITC 2-digit commodity and country, quarterly rpt, 2042–35
Exports of US, detailed Schedule B commodities with countries of destination, 1991, annual rpt, 2424–10
Human rights conditions in 170 countries, and US economic and military aid, 1991, annual rpt, 21384–3
Military aid of US, arms sales, and training programs costs and budget requests, by program, world region, and country, FY91-93, annual rpt, 7144–13
Military spending, arms trade, and force strengths, with govt spending and population, by country, 1979-89, annual rpt, 9824–1
Multinatl US firms and foreign affiliates finances and operations, by industry and country, 1989 benchmark survey, annual rpt, 2704–5
Oil exports to US by OPEC and non-OPEC countries, monthly rpt, 3162–24.3
Oil exports to US by OPEC and non-OPEC countries, monthly 1973-88, 3168–123.3
Oil production, investment needs, and exports, for 8 South America countries, 1980s-90 and projected to 2010, GAO rpt, 26123–396
Population size, growth rates, and components of change, by country, projected 1990-2020 and trends from 1950, biennial rpt, 2324–9
Refugee migration, and intl aid programs, by world area and country of origin and asylum, 1991, annual rpt, 7004–15
Steel imports of US under voluntary restraint agreement, by product, customs district, and country, with US industry operating data, quarterly rpt, 9882–13
Steel trade, by product, country, and customs district, with US industry operating data, 1989-June 1992, semiannual rpt, 9882–15
UN voting record and share of votes in agreement with US, by issue, country, and world area, 1991, annual rpt, 7004–18
see also under By Foreign Country in the "Index by Categories"

Triplett, Jack E.
"Economic Theory and BEA's Alternative Quantity and Price Indexes", 2702–1.315
Trott, Edward A., Jr.
"Gross State Product by Industry, 1977-89", 2702–1.303
Trout
see Aquaculture
Troy, N.Y.
Wages by occupation, for office and plant workers, 1991 survey, periodic MSA rpt, 6785–3.1
TRT Telecommunications Corp.
Finances and operations, detail for telegraph firms, 1990, annual rpt, 9284–6.3
Finances, rates, and traffic for US telecommunications carriers intl operations, by service type, firm, and country, 1975-90, annual rpt, 9284–17
Trucks and trucking industry
Accidents (fatal), circumstances, and characteristics of persons and vehicles involved, 1991, semiannual rpt, 7762–11
Accidents (fatal), deaths, and rates, by circumstances, characteristics of persons and vehicles involved, and location, 1990, annual rpt, 7764–10
Accidents and persons involved, by circumstances, truck configuration, and injury severity, 1979-86, 7768–124
Accidents at hwy-railroad grade-crossings, detailed data by State and railroad, 1991, annual rpt, 7604–2
Accidents, casualties, and damage, by circumstances and characteristics of persons and trucks involved, 1989, annual rpt, 7554–9
Accidents, casualties, circumstances, and characteristics of persons and vehicles involved, 1990, annual rpt, 7764–18
Business statistics, detailed data for major industries and economic indicators, *Survey of Current Business*, monthly rpt, 2702–1.10; 2702–1.22
Business statistics, detailed data for major industries and economic indicators, 1960-91, *Survey of Current Business* biennial supplement, 2704–1
Collective bargaining agreements expiring during year, and workers covered, by firm, union, industry group, and State, 1992, annual rpt, 6784–9
Container (intermodal) traffic by mode, use of containers over legal weight for hwy use, and California enforcement activity, 1960s-88, hearing, 21648–65
Costs itemized per mile, finances, and operations, for agricultural carriers, 1991, annual rpt, 1311–15
County Business Patterns, 1989: employment, establishments, and payroll, by SIC 2- to 4-digit industry and county, annual State rpt series, 2326–8
County Business Patterns, 1990: employment, establishments, and payroll, by SIC 2- to 4-digit industry and county, annual State rpt series, 2326–6
CPI by component for US city average, and by selected metro area, region, and population size, monthly rpt, 6762–2
Drivers licenses issued and in force by age and sex, fees, and renewal, by license class and State, 1990, annual rpt, 7554–16
Employment, earnings, and hours, by SIC 1- to 4-digit industry, monthly 1989-Feb 1992, annual rpt, 6744–4
Employment of minorities and women, by occupation, SIC 1- to 3-digit industry, State, and MSA, 1991, annual rpt, 9244–1
Energy economy performance of autos and light trucks by make, standards, and enforcement, 1978-94 model years, annual rpt, 7764–9
Energy use and vehicle registrations, by vehicle type, 1960-91, annual rpt, 3164–74.1
Energy use by fuel type, and miles traveled, by transport mode, projected 1990-2010 and trends from 1960s, 3008–124
Energy use by mode of transport, fuel supply, and demographic and economic factors of vehicle use, 1970s-90, annual rpt, 3304–5
Engine and powertrain R&D projects, DOE contracts and funding by recipient, FY91, annual rpt, 3304–17
Exports and imports between US and outlying areas, by detailed commodity and mode of transport, 1991, annual rpt, 2424–11
Exports and imports by country, US industry finances and operations, and prices of selected US and foreign models, monthly rpt, 9882–8
Exports and imports of US, by country and detailed commodity, monthly rpt, 2422–12
Exports and imports of US, by Harmonized System 6-digit commodity and country, 1991, annual rpt, 2424–13
Exports and imports of US, by transport mode, country, and SITC 1- to 3-digit commodity, 1991, annual rpt, 2424–12
Exports of US, detailed Schedule B commodities with countries of destination, 1991, annual rpt, 2424–10
Farm production itemized costs, by farm sales size and region, 1991, annual rpt, 1614–3
Finances and employment of ICC-regulated carriers, as of FY91, annual rpt, 9484–1
Finances and inventory of truck and warehouse services, by SIC 2- to 4-digit industry, 1990 survey, annual rpt, 2413–14
Finances and operations, by SIC 2- to 4-digit industry, forecast 1992, annual rpt, 2044–28
Finances and operations of carriers of property, by region and firm, quarterly rpt, 9482–5
Finances and operations of interstate carriers, by district, 1990, annual rpt, 9486–5.2; 9486–5.3
Food prices (farm-retail), marketing cost components, and industry finances and productivity, 1960s-91, annual rpt, 1544–9.3
Fruit and vegetable truck delivery rates paid by shippers and receivers, by commodity and city, and fleet itemized costs per mile, weekly rpt, 1311–22
Household goods carriers financial and operating data by firm, quarterly rpt, 9482–14
Household goods carriers performance and disposition of damage claims, for selected carriers, 1991, annual rpt, 9484–11
Households with autos and trucks available, MSA surveys, series, 2485–6
Hwy Statistics, detailed data by State, 1991, annual rpt, 7554–1
Hwy Statistics, summary data by State, 1990-91, annual rpt, 7554–24
Input-output structure of US economy, detailed interindustry transactions for 541 industries, and components of final demand, 1982 benchmark data, 2708–17
Labor productivity, indexes of output, hours, and employment by SIC 2- to 4-digit industry, 1967-90, annual rpt, 6824–1.4
Long combination trucks hwy use and size restrictions, and accidents, by State, 1980s-90, GAO rpt, 26113–568
Manufacturing annual survey, 1990: finances and operations, by SIC 2- to 4-digit industry, series, 2506–14
Manufacturing census, 1987: shipments of manufacturers products, by customer class and SIC 2- and 4-digit industry, subject rpt, 2497–4
Mexico-US trade agreement impacts on truck traffic at border crossings, Customs Service staff needs, and hwy improvement costs, projected to 2000 with trends from 1986, GAO rpt, 26123–368
Multinatl firms US affiliates finances and operations, by industry, country of parent firm, and State, 1987, 2708–48
Natl income and product accounts and components, *Survey of Current Business*, monthly rpt, 2702–1.23
Natl income and product accounts, comprehensive accounts and components, benchmark revisions, 1929-88, 2708–5
Natl income and product accounts, comprehensive accounts and components, *Survey of Current Business*, monthly rpt, 2702–1.24; 2702–1.31
Occupational injury and illness rates, by SIC 2- to 4-digit industry, 1989-90, annual rpt, 6844–7
Occupational injury and illness rates, by SIC 2- to 4-digit industry, 1990, annual rpt, 6844–1
Occupational Outlook Handbook, 1992-93, biennial rpt, 6744–1
OECD trade, total and for 4 major countries, and US trade by country, by commodity, 1980-90, world area rpt series, 9116–1
Philadelphia metro area transit service operations, costs and benefits, and local economic and air pollution impacts, 1970s-90 and projected to 2020, 7308–205
Price indexes (producer), by stage of processing and detailed commodity, monthly rpt, 6762–6
Price indexes (producer), by stage of processing and detailed commodity, monthly 1991, annual rpt, 6764–2
Prices received and paid by farmers, by commodity and State, 1991, annual rpt, 1629–5
Production, labor conditions, and trade of autos and auto parts, for US and compared to Canada and Mexico, 1950s-90, 6366–3.28
Radioactive materials shipments on US hwys, by material type, carrier, and shipper, 1985-90, 3008–129

Recalls of motor vehicles and equipment with safety-related defects, by make, monthly listing, 7762–12
Safety of domestic and foreign autos, crash test results by model, model years 1987-91, 7768–111
Safety of domestic and foreign autos, crash test results by model, press release series, 7766–7
Safety research on traffic issues, literature review, with data on accidents and impact of safety measures, 1961-90, 7558–98
Sales and prices for domestic and import autos and trucks, and auto production and inventories, 1992 model year, annual article, 2702–1.339
Soviet Union and US economic and sociodemographic indicators, selected years 1970-90, handbook, 2328–80
Speed limit impacts on traffic speeds and accidents, for States with 55 and 65 mph limit, 1983-89, 7768–121
Statistical Abstract of US, 1992 annual data compilation, 2324–1.21
Tax (excise) collections of IRS, by source, quarterly rpt, 8302–1
Tax (excise) returns filed, by type of return and IRS district, 1990 and projected 1991-98, annual rpt, 8304 24
Tax (excise) returns filed, by type of tax and IRS region and service center, projected 1991-98 and trends from 1978, annual rpt, 8304–9
Tax (income) returns of corporations, income and tax items by asset size and detailed industry, 1989, annual rpt, 8304–4; 8304–21
Tax (income) returns of partnerships, income statement and balance sheet items, by industry group, 1990, annual article, 8302–2.314
Tax (income) returns of sole proprietorships, income statement items, by industry group, 1990, annual article, 8302–2.317; 8302–2.320
Trailer shipments, exports, and firms, by trailer type, monthly Current Industrial Rpt, 2506–12.25
Travel patterns, personal and household characteristics, and auto and public transport use, 1990 survey, series, 7556–6
Wide trucks on narrow hwys, lane location characteristics and effects on other traffic, 1991 rpt, 7558–113
see also Freight

Truman, Harry S., Scholarship Foundation
Awards by student characteristics, and Foundation finances, FY91, annual rpt, 14314–1
Budget of US, authoritative financial statements with appropriations, outlays, and receipts, by category and agency, FY91, annual rpt, 8104–2.2
Budget of US, obligations and authority by function, agency, and program, with summaries and analyses, FY93, annual rpt, 104–2
Expenditures for education by Federal agency, program, and recipient type, and instn spending, 1960s-91, annual rpt, 4824–8
Trust fund receipts by source, transfers, and investment holdings and transactions, monthly rpt, 14312–1

Trust funds
American Historical Assn financial statements, and membership by State, 1990, annual rpt, 29574–2
Assets and debts of private sector, balance sheets by segment, 1960-91, semiannual rpt, 9365–4.1
Assets of collective investment funds, instns involved, and accounts, by type of fund and holding, 1991, annual rpt, 13004–1.3
Assets of trusts under mgmt of banks, trust companies, and S&Ls, by type of asset and fund, selected firm, and State, 1991, annual rpt, 13004–1
County Business Patterns, 1989: employment, establishments, and payroll, by SIC 2- to 4-digit industry and county, annual State rpt series, 2326–8
County Business Patterns, 1990: employment, establishments, and payroll, by SIC 2- to 4-digit industry and county, annual State rpt series, 2326–6
Families financial status, income, net worth, and assets and debt by type, by income and selected characteristics, 1983 and 1989, article, 9362–1.301
Farmland in US owned by foreigners, holdings, acquisitions, and disposals by land use, owner type and country, and State, 1991, annual rpt, 1584–2
Higher education instn endowment funds, for top 100 instns, FY89, annual rpt, 4824–2.25
Higher education instn revenue by source and spending by function, by State and instn control, FY82-90, annual rpt, 4844–6
Households financial services use, by account type and instn type and location, 1989 survey, article, 9362–1.303
Households net worth distribution under alternative sample weighting systems to account for inconsistency in survey design and response rates, 1992 rpt, 9368–91
Income tax returns of foreign corporations and individuals, and US entities abroad, detailed data compilation, 1970s-89, quinquennial rpt, 8308–31
Mortgage loan activity, by type of lender, loan, and mortgaged property, monthly press release, 5142–18
Mortgage loan activity, by type of lender, loan, and mortgaged property, quarterly press release, 5142–30
Tax (income) returns of individuals, detailed data, 1988, annual rpt, 8304–2
Tax exempt organizations with unrelated business income, finances by organization type, 1987, article, 8302–2.306
Tax returns filed, by type of tax and IRS district, 1990 and projected 1991-98, annual rpt, 8304–24
Tax returns filed, by type of tax and IRS region and service center, projected 1991-98 and trends from 1978, annual rpt, 8304–9
see also Government trust funds
see also Pensions and pension funds
see also Unemployment trust funds

Trust Territory of the Pacific Islands
see Marshall Islands
see Micronesia Federated States
see Northern Mariana Islands
see Palau
see Territories of the U.S.

Tse, Pui-Kwan
"Mineral Industries of China, 1990", 5604–38

Tsunamis
Incidents and mgmt of disasters and natl security threats, with data by major event and State, 1992 annual rpt, 9434–6

Tuan, Francis
"China's Trade with Neighboring Countries Since the Early 1980's", 1524–4.2

Tuberculosis
Cases of TB, and rates, by patient characteristics, 1985 and 1990, article, 4202–7.302
Cattle TB cases and cooperative Federal-State eradication activities, by State, FY90-91, annual rpt, 1394–13
Deaths and rates, by cause, age, sex, marital status, race, and State, 1989, US Vital Statistics advance annual rpt, 4146–5.124
Deaths and rates, by cause, provisional data, monthly rpt, 4142–1.2
Deaths and rates, by detailed location, cause, and demographic characteristics, 1989, US Vital Statistics annual rpt, 4144–3
Drug-resistant TB cases, and AIDS-related cases, 1990-92, article, 4042–3.362
Health condition and care indicators, 1950s-90 with health improvement and disease prevention goals for 1990, annual data compilation, 4144–11
HHS financial aid, by program, recipient, State, and city, FY91, annual regional listings, 4004–3
Homeless population TB prevention, screening, and mgmt, CDC recommendations, 1992 rpt, 4206–2.55
Indian Health Service and tribal facilities and use, and Indians health and other characteristics, by IHS region, 1980s-90, annual chartbook, 4084–7
Indian Health Service facilities, funding, operations, and Indian health and other characteristics, 1950s-91, annual chartbook, 4084–1
Maryland, Washington County TB cases, by risk factor, 1975-90, article, 4042–3.319
Meat and poultry inspection for domestic use and export, and rejections by cause, by type of animal and product, FY90, annual rpt, 1374–3
Migrant farmworkers TB screening, treatment, and control, CDC guidelines, 1992 rpt, 4206–2.60
Minority group TB prevention, screening, and mgmt, CDC recommendations, 1992 rpt, 4206–2.55
Morbidity and Mortality Weekly Report, infectious notifiable disease cases by age, race, and State, and deaths, 1940s-91, annual rpt, 4204–1
Morbidity and Mortality Weekly Report, infectious notifiable disease cases by State, and public health issues, 4202–1
OECD members health care costs, hospital use, resources, and economic and health indicators, by country, 1960s-90, article, 4652–1.322
Prevention, screening, and outbreak mgmt for multidrug resistant TB, CDC guidelines, 1992 rpt, 4206–2.61
Prisoners AIDS and TB cases, test results, and control and treatment policies, by location, 1990 survey, annual rpt, 6064–22

see also under By Disease in the "Index by Categories"

Tucson, Ariz.
Housing starts and completions authorized by building permits in 40 MSAs, quarterly rpt, 2382–9
Wages by occupation, and benefits, for office and plant workers, 1992 survey, periodic MSA rpt, 6785–3.3
see also under By City and By SMSA or MSA in the "Index by Categories"

Tuition and fees
Black higher education instns enrollment, finances, staff, and degrees, by instn and selected student characteristics, 1970s-90, 4848–46
Child day care and early childhood education programs availability, demand, use, costs, and provider and enrollee characteristics, 1990 survey, 4808–39
Condition of Education, detail for elementary, secondary, and higher education, 1920s-91 and projected to 2002, annual rpt, 4824–1
Consumer spending, natl income and product account benchmark revisions, 1929-88, 2708–5
Consumer spending, natl income and product accounts, comprehensive accounts and components, *Survey of Current Business*, monthly rpt, 2702–1.25
CPI by component for US city average, and by selected metro area, region, and population size, monthly rpt, 6762–2
Digest of Education Statistics, 1992 annual data compilation, 4824–2
Health care professionals supply and education, by professional and other characteristics, and location, 1960s-92 and projected to 2020, biennial rpt, 4114–8
Higher education enrollment, faculty, finances, and degrees, by instn level and control, and State, FY88, annual rpt, 4844–13
Higher education enrollment, tuition, control, location, and other instn characteristics, 1991/92, biennial listing, 4844–3
Higher education instn revenue by source and spending by function, by State and instn control, FY82-90, annual rpt, 4844–6
Higher education instn student aid and other sources of support, with student expenses and characteristics, by instn type and control, 1987 triennial study, series, 4846–3; 4846–5
Higher education instn tuition and other charges, by public and private 2- and 4-year instn, and State, 1991/92, annual listing, 4844–10
Private elementary and secondary schools, students, and staff characteristics, by school type and affiliation, 1987/88, 4836–3.8
Statistical Abstract of US, 1992 annual data compilation, 2324–1.4
see also Student aid

Tulare County, Calif.
Wages by occupation, and benefits for office and plant workers, 1991 survey, periodic MSA rpt, 6785–12.1

Tulsa, Marilyn
"Outpatient Visits by Primary Health Provider, Indian Health Service and Tribally Operated Facilities, FY91", 4084–3
"Summary of Leading Causes for Outpatient Visits, Indian Health Service Direct and Contract Facilities, FY90", 4084–2

Tulsa, Okla.
see also under By City and By SMSA or MSA in the "Index by Categories"

Tuna
see Fish and fishing industry

Tunisia
Agricultural trade of US, by detailed commodity and country, 1991, annual rpt, 1524–8
Agricultural trade of US, by detailed commodity and country, 1991, semiannual rpt, 1522–4
AID economic aid to developing countries, obligations and disbursements by country, quarterly rpt, 9912–4
AID loans repayment status and terms by program and country, and status of predecessor agency loans, quarterly rpt, 9912–3
Cuba trade, by commodity and country, mid 1980s-91, 9118–8
Economic and military aid and loans from US and intl agencies, by program and country, FY46-91, annual rpt, 9914–5
Economic and social conditions of developing countries from 1960s, and Intl Dev Cooperation Agency and AID activities and funding, FY91-93, annual rpt, 9904–4
Economic conditions, policy, and trade practices, by country, 1989-91, annual rpt, 21384–5
Economic, social, political, and geographic summary data, by country, 1992, annual factbook, 9114–2
Exports and imports of US, by commodity and country, 1980-90, world area rpt, 9116–1.6
Exports and imports of US, by transport mode, country, and SITC 1- to 3-digit commodity, 1991, annual rpt, 2424–12
Exports of US, detailed Schedule B commodities with countries of destination, 1991, annual rpt, 2424–10
Food supply, needs, and aid for developing countries, status and alternative forecasts, 1992 world area rpt, 1526–8.2
Human rights conditions in 170 countries, and US economic and military aid, 1991, annual rpt, 21384–3
Labor conditions, union coverage, and work accidents, 1991 annual country rpt, 6366–4.13
Military aid of US, arms sales, and training programs costs and budget requests, by program, world region, and country, FY91-93, annual rpt, 7144–13
Military spending, arms trade, and force strengths, with govt spending and population, by country, 1979-89, annual rpt, 9824–1
Minerals Yearbook, Vol 3, 1989: foreign country review of production, trade, and policy, by commodity, annual rpt, 5604–35.1
Population size, growth rates, and components of change, by country, projected 1990-2020 and trends from 1950, biennial rpt, 2324–9
Refugee migration, and intl aid programs, by world area and country of origin and asylum, 1991, annual rpt, 7004–15
UN voting record and share of votes in agreement with US, by issue, country, and world area, 1991, annual rpt, 7004–18

Tunnels
see Bridges and tunnels

Turczyn, Kathleen M.
"Inventory of Pain Data from the National Center for Health Statistics. Vital and Health Statistics Series 1", 4147–1.27

Turgeon, Donna D.
"Toxic Contaminants in the Gulf of Maine", 2176–3.17

Turkey
Agricultural trade of US, by detailed commodity and country, 1991, annual rpt, 1524–8
Agricultural trade of US, by detailed commodity and country, 1991, semiannual rpt, 1522–4
AID economic aid to developing countries, obligations and disbursements by country, quarterly rpt, 9912–4
AID loans repayment status and terms by program and country, and status of predecessor agency loans, quarterly rpt, 9912–3
Almond production, trade, use, and stocks, for 6 countries and US, 1990-93, annual article, 1925–34.337
Cuba trade, by commodity and country, mid 1980s-91, 9118–8
Economic and military aid and loans from US and intl agencies, by program and country, FY46-91, annual rpt, 9914–5
Economic and social conditions of developing countries from 1960s, and Intl Dev Cooperation Agency and AID activities and funding, FY91-93, annual rpt, 9904–4
Economic conditions, income, production, prices, employment, and trade, 1992 periodic country rpt, 2046–4.57
Economic conditions, policy, and trade practices, by country, 1989-91, annual rpt, 21384–5
Economic, social, political, and geographic summary data, by country, 1992, annual factbook, 9114–2
Exports and imports of US, by Harmonized System 6-digit commodity and country, 1991, annual rpt, 2424–13
Exports and imports of US, by selected country, country group, and commodity group, 1991, annual rpt, 2044–37
Exports and imports of US, by transport mode, country, and SITC 1- to 3-digit commodity, 1991, annual rpt, 2424–12
Exports, imports, and balances of US for manufactured goods, by SITC 2-digit commodity and country, quarterly rpt, 2042–35
Exports of US, detailed Schedule B commodities with countries of destination, 1991, annual rpt, 2424–10
Hazelnut production, supply, trade, and use, for 3 countries and US, 1990-93, annual article, 1925–34.338
Health care costs and components, services use, resources, and economic indicators, by OECD country, 1960s-90, article, 4652–1.322

Hostages kidnapped in Turkey, listing as of 1991, 7004–22
Human rights conditions in 170 countries, and US economic and military aid, 1991, annual rpt, 21384–3
Imports of goods, services, and investment from US, trade barriers, impacts, and US actions, by country, 1991, annual rpt, 444–2
Military aid of US, arms sales, and training programs costs and budget requests, by program, world region, and country, FY91-93, annual rpt, 7144–13
Military spending, arms trade, and force strengths, with govt spending and population, by country, 1979-89, annual rpt, 9824–1
Minerals Yearbook, Vol 3, 1989: foreign country review of production, trade, and policy, by commodity, annual rpt, 5604–35.3
Multinatl US firms and foreign affiliates finances and operations, by industry and country, 1989 benchmark survey, annual rpt, 2704–5
Multinatl US firms foreign affiliates, income statement items by asset size, industry, and country, 1988, biennial article, 8302–2.322
Oil production, stocks, use, and trade, by selected country and country group, monthly rpt, 3162–42
Population size, growth rates, and components of change, by country, projected 1990-2020 and trends from 1950, biennial rpt, 2324–9
Raisin imports of EC member countries and Canada, and Turkey exports, by country, 1989-93, semiannual article, 1925–34.348
Refugee migration, and intl aid programs, by world area and country of origin and asylum, 1991, annual rpt, 7004–15
Steel trade, by product, country, and customs district, with US industry operating data, 1989-June 1992, semiannual rpt, 9882–15
Tax revenue, by level of govt and type of tax, for OECD countries, mid 1960s-90, annual rpt, 10044–1.2
Tobacco and cigarette production, use, and trade, for Turkey, 1980s-92, article, 1925–16.313
UN voting record and share of votes in agreement with US, by issue, country, and world area, 1991, annual rpt, 7004–18
see also under By Foreign Country in the "Index by Categories"

Turkeys
see Poultry industry and products

Turkmenistan
Agricultural production, prices, and trade, for former USSR republics, 1960s-91 and forecast 1992, annual rpt, 1524–4.1
Economic, social, political, and geographic summary data, by country, 1992, annual factbook, 9114–2
Embassies of US in former Soviet republics and Baltic States, positions planned by function, and filled, 1992, GAO rpt, 26123–403
Energy supply and use, and social, economic, and political indicators for former Soviet Republics and Baltic States, 1989-90, 3168–126
Energy use and production of former USSR Republics, by fuel type, 1990, annual rpt, 3164–84.2
Exports and imports of US with Communist and transitional economy countries, by detailed commodity and country, quarterly rpt with articles, 9882–2
Livestock and meat inventories, use, and imports, by former USSR republic, 1986-93, semiannual rpt, 1925–33.2
Population size and characteristics of former Soviet Republics and Baltic States, 1989-92, 9118–19

Turks and Caicos Islands
Economic and social conditions, resources, and trade, and aid, 1992, annual factbook, 9914–14
Exports and imports of US, by transport mode, country, and SITC 1- to 3-digit commodity, 1991, annual rpt, 2424–12

Turner, Margery A.
"Housing Discrimination Study: Analyzing Racial and Ethnic Steering", 5186–16.3
"Housing Discrimination Study: Mapping Patterns of Steering for Five Metropolitan Areas", 5186–16.2
"Housing Discrimination Study: Synthesis", 5186–16.1

Turnover of labor
see Job tenure
see Labor turnover

Turpentine
see Gum and wood chemicals

Tuvalu
Economic, social, political, and geographic summary data, by country, 1992, annual factbook, 9114–2
Exports and imports of US, by transport mode, country, and SITC 1- to 3-digit commodity, 1991, annual rpt, 2424–12
Population size, growth rates, and components of change, by country, projected 1990-2020 and trends from 1950, biennial rpt, 2324–9

TVA
see Tennessee Valley Authority

Uchida, Craig D.
"Modern Policing and the Control of Illegal Drugs: Testing New Strategies in Two American Cities", 6068–251

Uctum, Merih
"Financial Integration and the Transmission of Monetary Policy: The Case of France, Germany and Italy", 9385–8.145
"Money Markets and Common Monetary Policy in France, Germany and Italy", 9385–8.140

Udell, Gregory F.
"Securitization, Risk, and the Liquidity Problem in Banking", 9366–6.295

Uganda
Agricultural trade of US, by detailed commodity and country, 1991, annual rpt, 1524–8
Agricultural trade of US, by detailed commodity and country, 1991, semiannual rpt, 1522–4
AID cash transfers linked to nontraditional crop export programs, for Uganda, 1988-90, 9916–1.77
AID economic aid to developing countries, obligations and disbursements by country, quarterly rpt, 9912–4
AID loans repayment status and terms by program and country, and status of predecessor agency loans, quarterly rpt, 9912–3
Economic and military aid and loans from US and intl agencies, by program and country, FY46-91, annual rpt, 9914–5
Economic and social conditions of developing countries from 1960s, and Intl Dev Cooperation Agency and AID activities and funding, FY91-93, annual rpt, 9904–4
Economic conditions, income, production, prices, employment, and trade, 1992 periodic country rpt, 2046–4.34
Economic, social, political, and geographic summary data, by country, 1992, annual factbook, 9114–2
Exports and imports of US, by transport mode, country, and SITC 1- to 3-digit commodity, 1991, annual rpt, 2424–12
Exports of US, detailed Schedule B commodities with countries of destination, 1991, annual rpt, 2424–10
Human rights conditions in 170 countries, and US economic and military aid, 1991, annual rpt, 21384–3
Military aid of US, arms sales, and training programs costs and budget requests, by program, world region, and country, FY91-93, annual rpt, 7144–13
Military spending, arms trade, and force strengths, with govt spending and population, by country, 1979-89, annual rpt, 9824–1
Minerals Yearbook, Vol 3, 1989: foreign country review of production, trade, and policy, by commodity, annual rpt, 5604–35.1
Population size, growth rates, and components of change, by country, projected 1990-2020 and trends from 1950, biennial rpt, 2324–9
Refugee migration, and intl aid programs, by world area and country of origin and asylum, 1991, annual rpt, 7004–15
UN voting record and share of votes in agreement with US, by issue, country, and world area, 1991, annual rpt, 7004–18

Ukraine
Agricultural production, prices, and trade, for former USSR republics, 1960s-91 and forecast 1992, annual rpt, 1524–4.1
Economic, social, political, and geographic summary data, by country, 1992, annual factbook, 9114–2
Embassies of US in former Soviet republics and Baltic States, positions planned by function, and filled, 1992, GAO rpt, 26123–403
Energy supply and use, and social, economic, and political indicators for former Soviet Republics and Baltic States, 1989-90, 3168–126
Energy use and production of former USSR Republics, by fuel type, 1990, annual rpt, 3164–84.2
Exports and imports of US with Communist and transitional economy countries, by detailed commodity and country, quarterly rpt with articles, 9882–2
Ferrosilicon from 6 countries, injury to US industry from foreign subsidized and less than fair value imports, investigation with background financial and operating data, 1992 rpt, 9886–19.84

Livestock and meat inventories, use, and imports, by former USSR republic, 1986-93, semiannual rpt, 1925–33.2
Population size and characteristics of former Soviet Republics and Baltic States, 1989-92, 9118–19
UN voting record and share of votes in agreement with US, by issue, country, and world area, 1991, annual rpt, 7004–18
Uranium resources and production of CIS, by state, 1992 article, 3164–65

Ulbrich, Holley H.
"State Taxation of Interstate Mail Order Sales, Estimates of Revenue Potential 1990-92", 10048–84

Umm al-Qaiwain
see United Arab Emirates

Unconventional warfare
see Chemical and biological warfare agents

Underdeveloped countries
see Developing countries

Underemployment
Employment, earnings, and hours, monthly press release, 6742–5
Foreign countries labor conditions, union coverage, and work accidents, annual country rpt series, 6366–4
Older persons labor force status, income sources, and reasons for not working, with data by occupation, sex, and race, 1989-90 and projected to 2050, 21148–65
Women (married) working part time, by whether voluntarily and income class, 1979 and 1989, 23848–225
Youth labor force status, by sex, race, and industry div, summer 1988-92, annual press release, 6744–14

Underground economy
Drug (illegal) prices by type and selected metro area, and cocaine and heroin purity, quarterly rpt, 6282–1
Drug (illegal) prices by type, stage of processing, and country of origin, 1991, annual rpt, 6284–7
Heroin prices and purity in 19 metro areas and Puerto Rico, by world area of origin, quarterly rpt, 6282–2
see also Money laundering

Underground movements
see also Terrorism

Unemployment
see Employment and unemployment, general
see Employment and unemployment, local and regional
see Employment and unemployment, specific industry
see Labor turnover
see Public welfare programs
see Underemployment
see Unemployment insurance
see Unemployment insurance tax
see Work incentive programs

Unemployment insurance
AFDC applicants recently unemployed, characteristics of prior job and UI eligibility, for Maryland, 1988-90, hearing, 21788–207
AFDC beneficiaries demographic and financial characteristics, by State, FY90, annual rpt, 4584–7
Beneficiaries and taxes collected for social insurance programs since 1940, quarterly rpt, 4742–1.4
Beneficiaries exhausting UI benefits, by selected characteristics, 1991 hearing, 21788–209
Beneficiaries, taxes collected, and payments under Federal and State programs, since 1940, quarterly rpt, 4742–1.4
Benefits adequacy, State and Federal programs, and work disincentives, series, 6406–6
Benefits, claims, coverage, and exhaustions for UI, 1960-91, annual rpt, 204–1.2
Benefits, coverage, and tax provisions under State UI programs, as of Jan 1992, semiannual revisions to base edition, 6402–2
Benefits, coverage, and tax provisions under State UI programs, as of July 1992, semiannual listing, 6402–7
Benefits, coverage, exhaustions, and finances of State UI programs, 1990, annual tables, 6404–10
Benefits, coverage, tax rates, and penalties, changes under State UI programs, 1991, annual article, 6722–1.311
Budget of US, Bush Admin proposals, with detail for defense budgets, and historical data from FY34, FY93, 108–46
Budget of US, obligations and authority by function, agency, and program, with summaries and analyses, FY93, annual rpt, 104–2
Business statistics, detailed data for major industries and economic indicators, 1960-91, *Survey of Current Business* biennial supplement, 2704–1
Claims (initial) under State programs, *Survey of Current Business*, cyclical indicators, monthly rpt, 2702–1.1
Claims for UI and covered unemployment by program, and extended benefit triggers, by State, weekly rpt, 6402–15
Claims for UI, by program, weekly press release, 6402–14
Coverage of wages under UI, by industry div, State, and MSA, 1990-91, annual press releases, 6784–17
Displaced worker employment and training services, and layoff alternatives, indicators of effectiveness, 1980s, 15498–28
Displaced workers job search and placement aid effectiveness, relation to previous employment and other characteristics, 1979-87 studies, 15496–1.14
Displaced workers, layoffs and recalls by layoff reason, industry, firm size, and State, 2nd half 1988, 6406–6.36
Displaced workers, layoffs and UI claims by reason, industry, selected characteristics, and State, quarterly press release, 6742–23
Displaced workers, layoffs and UI claims by reason, industry, selected characteristics, MSA, and State, 1990, annual rpt, 6744–18
Economic indicators and components, current data and annual trends, monthly rpt, 23842–1.2
Economic Report of the President for 1991, economic effects of budget proposals, and trends and projections, 1940s-95, annual hearings, 23844–4
Expenditures (private) for social welfare, by category, 1970s-90, annual article, 4742–1.323
Expenditures, coverage, and benefits for social welfare programs, late 1930s-90, annual rpt, 4744–3.1; 4744–3.7
Expenditures for public welfare by program, FY50s-89, annual article, 4742–1.319
Expenditures of Fed Govt in States, by type, program, agency, and State, FY91, annual rpt, 2464–2
Finances and operations of programs under Ways and Means Committee jurisdiction, FY70s-91, annual rpt, 21784–11
Finances of Fed Govt, cash and debt transactions, daily tables, 8102–4
Finances of govts, revenue by source, spending by function, debt, and assets, by level of govt, FY90, annual rpt, 2466–2.2
Food stamp recipient household size, composition, income, and income and deductions allowed, summer 1989, annual rpt, 1364–8
Foreign countries social security programs coverage, funding, eligibility, and benefits, by country, 1991, biennial rpt, 4746–4.62
Households composition, income, benefits, and labor force status, Survey of Income and Program Participation methodology, working paper series, 2626–10
Income (household, family, and personal), by source, detailed characteristics, and region, 1991, annual Current Population Rpt, 2546–6.76
Income tax returns of individuals, by filing status, tax item, and income level, 1991, annual article, 8302–2.319
Income tax returns of individuals, detailed data, 1988, annual rpt, 8304–2
Income tax returns of individuals, selected income and tax items by income level, preliminary 1990, annual article, 8302–2.307
Labor Dept activities and funding, by program and State, FY91, annual rpt, 6304–1
Labor force, wages, hours, and payroll costs, by major industry group and demographic characteristics, *Survey of Current Business*, monthly rpt, 2702–1.7
Natl income and product accounts, comprehensive accounts and components, benchmark revisions, 1929-88, 2708–5
Natl income and product accounts, comprehensive accounts and components, *Survey of Current Business*, monthly rpt, 2702–1.25
North Central States business and economic conditions, Fed Reserve 9th District, quarterly journal, 9383–19
Older persons income and sources, by whether OASDI beneficiary, poverty status, and other characteristics, 1990, biennial rpt, 4744–26
Participants characteristics, activities, and funding, for Employment and Training Admin programs, FY86-88, annual rpt, 6404–17
Railroad employee benefits and beneficiaries by type, and railroad employment and payroll, FY90, annual rpt, 9704–2
Railroad employee benefits program finances and beneficiaries, FY91, annual rpt, 9704–1
Railroad retirement, survivors, unemployment, and health insurance programs, monthly rpt, 9702–2

Southeastern States, Fed Reserve 6th District, economic indicators by State and MSA, quarterly rpt, 9371–14
Southeastern US layoff events and separations, by State, industry div, and reason for separation, 1990-91, press release, 6946–3.25
State govt labor productivity, indexes of output by function, FY64-90, annual rpt, 6824–1.6
State govt revenue by source, spending and debt by function, and holdings, FY91, annual rpt, 2466–2.6
States UI programs quality appraisal results, FY91, annual rpt, 6404–16
Statistical Abstract of US, 1992 annual data compilation, 2324–1.12; 2324–1.13
see also Unemployment insurance tax
see also Unemployment trust funds

Unemployment insurance tax
Budget of US, authoritative financial statements with appropriations, outlays, and receipts, by category and agency, FY91, annual rpt, 8104–2.2
Budget of US, historical data, selected years FY34-91 and projected to FY97, 108–46.5
Budget of US, obligations and authority by function, agency, and program, with summaries and analyses, FY93, annual rpt, 104–2
Budget of US, receipts by source, outlays by agency and program, and balances, monthly rpt, 8102–3
Collections, enforcement, and litigation activity of IRS, with data by type of tax, region, and State, FY91, annual rpt, 8304–3
Collections of tax, beneficiaries, and benefit payments for social insurance programs, quarterly rpt, 4742–1.4
Costs (hourly) of labor, by component, industry and occupational group, worker class, and firm size, monthly rpt, annual tables, 6782–1.2
Costs (hourly) of labor, by component, occupational group, industry div, union coverage, and region, 1992, annual rpt, 6744–21
Employee compensation costs, by component, occupation, industry group, union status, and location, 1975-92, annual rpt, 6744–20.2
Fed Govt receipts by source and outlays by agency, *Treasury Bulletin*, quarterly rpt, 8002–4.1
Finances and operations of programs under Ways and Means Committee jurisdiction, FY70s-91, annual rpt, 21784–11
Finances of Fed Govt, cash and debt transactions, daily tables, 8102–4
Foreign countries social security programs coverage, funding, eligibility, and benefits, by country, 1991, biennial rpt, 4746–4.62
Railroad retirement, survivors, unemployment, and health insurance programs, monthly rpt, 9702–2
Returns and supplemental documents filed, by type, FY91 and projected to FY2000, semiannual rpt, 8302–4
State govt revenue by source, spending and debt by function, and holdings, FY91, annual rpt, 2466–2.6
States UI benefits, coverage, and tax provisions, as of July 1992, semiannual listing, 6402–7
States UI laws, changes in coverage, benefits, tax rates, and penalties, by State, 1991, annual article, 6722–1.311
States UI laws, comparison of provisions, as of Jan 1992, semiannual revisions to base edition, 6402–2
States UI programs benefits, coverage, exhaustions, and finances, 1990, annual tables, 6404–10
Transit systems finances and operations, by mode, size of fleet and urban area, region, and for 518 systems, 1990, annual rpt, 7884–4

Unemployment trust funds
Finances and operations of programs under Ways and Means Committee jurisdiction, FY70s-91, annual rpt, 21784–11
Financial condition of Federal UI trust funds, by State, monthly rpt, 8102–9.16
Financial condition of Federal UI trust funds, quarterly rpt, 8102–9.1
State govt revenue by source, spending and debt by function, and holdings, FY91, annual rpt, 2466–2.6
States UI programs benefits, coverage, exhaustions, and finances, 1990, annual tables, 6404–10

UNICOR
see Federal Prison Industries

Unions
see Labor unions

United Arab Emirates
Agricultural trade of US, by detailed commodity and country, 1991, annual rpt, 1524–8
Agricultural trade of US, by detailed commodity and country, 1991, semiannual rpt, 1522–4
Apple imports of 5 Persian Gulf countries, by country of origin, 1981-90, article, 1925–34.322
Boycotts (intl) by OPEC and other countries, US firms and individuals cooperation and tax benefits denied, 1990, article, 8302–2.323
Economic conditions, income, production, prices, employment, and trade, 1992 periodic country rpt, 2046–4.41
Economic conditions, policy, and trade practices, by country, 1989-91, annual rpt, 21384–5
Economic, social, political, and geographic summary data, by country, 1992, annual factbook, 9114–2
Exports and imports of US, by commodity and country, 1980-90, world area rpt, 9116–1.6
Exports and imports of US, by Harmonized System 6-digit commodity and country, 1991, annual rpt, 2424–13
Exports and imports of US, by selected country, country group, and commodity group, 1991, annual rpt, 2044–37
Exports and imports of US, by transport mode, country, and SITC 1- to 3-digit commodity, 1991, annual rpt, 2424–12
Exports, imports, and balances of US for manufactured goods, by SITC 2-digit commodity and country, quarterly rpt, 2042–35
Exports of US, detailed Schedule B commodities with countries of destination, 1991, annual rpt, 2424–10
Human rights conditions in 170 countries, and US economic and military aid, 1991, annual rpt, 21384–3
Military spending, arms trade, and force strengths, with govt spending and population, by country, 1979-89, annual rpt, 9824–1
Minerals Yearbook, Vol 3, 1989: foreign country review of production, trade, and policy, by commodity, annual rpt, 5604–35.3
Multinatl US firms and foreign affiliates finances and operations, by industry and country, 1989 benchmark survey, annual rpt, 2704–5
Oil production and exports to US, by major exporting country, detailed data, monthly rpt with articles, 3162–24
Oil production and exports to US, by major exporting country, detailed data, monthly 1973-88, 3168–123
Oil production, stocks, use, and trade, by selected country and country group, monthly rpt, 3162–42
Persian Gulf War allied countries cash and in-kind contributions, by type and country, and status of DOD accounts, as of Sept 1991, annual GAO rpt, 26104–24
Population size, growth rates, and components of change, by country, projected 1990-2020 and trends from 1950, biennial rpt, 2324–9
Refugee migration, and intl aid programs, by world area and country of origin and asylum, 1991, annual rpt, 7004–15
Steel trade, by product, country, and customs district, with US industry operating data, 1989-June 1992, semiannual rpt, 9882–15
UN voting record and share of votes in agreement with US, by issue, country, and world area, 1991, annual rpt, 7004–18
see also under By Foreign Country in the "Index by Categories"

United Arab Republic
see Egypt

United Kingdom
Agricultural trade of US, by detailed commodity and country, 1991, annual rpt, 1524–8
Agricultural trade of US, by detailed commodity and country, 1991, semiannual rpt, 1522–4
AID loans repayment status and terms by program and country, and status of predecessor agency loans, quarterly rpt, 9912–3
Banks reserve and overdraft requirements of Fed Reserve and 3 foreign central banks, with balance sheets and deposit balances, 1989-90, article, 9377–1.307
Corporations in US under foreign control, transactions of large corporations with related foreign persons, by type, industry div, and country, 1988, 8302–2.318
Cuba trade, by commodity and country, mid 1980s-91, 9118–8
Currency (foreign and US) shares of intl transactions, with background data, for 5 countries, 1960s-80s, 9381–10.129
Drug abuse indicators, by world region and selected country, 1991 semiannual conf, 4492–5.1
Drug abuse indicators, by world region and selected country, 1992 semiannual conf, 4492–5.2

Dyes (sulfur) from 3 countries at less than fair value, injury to US industry, investigation with background financial and operating data, 1992 rpt, 9886–14.347
Economic and military aid and loans from US and intl agencies, by program and country, FY46-91, annual rpt, 9914–5
Economic and monetary trends, compounded annual rates of change and quarterly indicators for US and 7 major industrialized countries, quarterly rpt, 9391–7
Economic conditions, and oil supply and demand, for major industrial countries, monthly rpt, 9112–1
Economic conditions, consumer and stock prices and production indexes, for 7 OECD countries, *Survey of Current Business*, monthly rpt, 2702–1.1
Economic conditions, income, production, prices, employment, and trade, 1992 periodic country rpt, 2046–4.53
Economic conditions, policy, and trade practices, by country, 1989-91, annual rpt, 21384–5
Economic indicators, and dollar exchange rates, for selected OECD countries, 1992 semiannual rpt, 8002–14
Economic, social, political, and geographic summary data, by country, 1992, annual factbook, 9114–2
Energy production by type, and oil trade, and use, by country group and selected country, monthly rpt, 9112–2
Export credit activity of Eximbank and 6 OECD countries, 1990, annual rpt, 9254–3
Exports and imports, intl position of US and 4 OECD countries, and factors affecting US competition, quarterly pamphlet, 2042–25
Exports and imports of OECD, total and for 4 major countries, and US trade by country, by commodity, 1980-90, world area rpt series, 9116–1
Exports and imports of US by country, and trade shifts by commodity, 1991, annual rpt, 9884–25
Exports and imports of US, by Harmonized System 6-digit commodity and country, 1991, annual rpt, 2424–13
Exports and imports of US, by selected country, country group, and commodity group, 1991, annual rpt, 2044–37
Exports and imports of US, by transport mode, country, and SITC 1- to 3-digit commodity, 1991, annual rpt, 2424–12
Exports, imports, and balances of US for manufactured goods, by SITC 2-digit commodity and country, quarterly rpt, 2042–35
Exports, imports, and balances of US with major trading partners, by product category, 1987-91, annual chartbook, 9884–21
Exports of US, detailed Schedule B commodities with countries of destination, 1991, annual rpt, 2424–10
Farmland in US owned by foreigners, holdings, acreage, and value by land use, owner country, State, and county, 1991, annual rpt, 1584–3
Financial markets (intl) performance of foreign and US bank and securities firms, finances and competitiveness issues, 1980s, compilation of papers, 9385–10
Gold standard relation to inflation, with background data for UK, US, France, and Italy, 1730s-1930s, working paper, 9377–9.136
Health care costs and components, services use, resources, and economic indicators, by OECD country, 1960s-90, article, 4652–1.322
Health care system reform issues, with data on insurance administrative and employer costs, coverage, public views, and Canada and UK systems, 1950s-91, hearings, 25368–180
Human rights conditions in 170 countries, and US economic and military aid, 1991, annual rpt, 21384–3
Imports of goods, services, and investment from US, trade barriers, impacts, and US actions, by country, 1991, annual rpt, 444–2
Imports of US given duty-free treatment for value of US material sent abroad, by commodity and country, 1987-90, annual rpt, 9884–14
Interest and exchange rates, security yields, and stock indexes, for selected foreign countries, weekly chartbook, 9365–1.5
Interest rates (long term) relation to rates of return to capital, economic policies, and other factors, US and 4 countries, 1960s-90, article, 9385–1.301
Investment (foreign direct) in US, major transactions by type, industry, country, and US location, 1990, annual rpt, 2044–20
Labor conditions, union coverage, and work accidents, 1992 annual country rpt, 6366–4.17; 6366–4.46
Military spending, arms trade, and force strengths, with govt spending and population, by country, 1979-89, annual rpt, 9824–1
Monetary policies and central bank regulation in US and 5 countries, 1980-91, article, 9385–1.308
Multinatl firms US affiliates finances and operations, by industry, country of parent firm, and State, 1987, 2708–48
Multinatl firms US affiliates, finances, and operations, by industry, world area of parent firm, and State, 1989-90, annual rpt, 2704–4
Multinatl US firms and foreign affiliates finances and operations, by industry and country, 1989 benchmark survey, annual rpt, 2704–5
Multinatl US firms foreign affiliates, income statement items by asset size, industry, and country, 1988, biennial article, 8302–2.322
Nuclear power generation in US and 20 countries, monthly rpt, 3162–24.10
Nuclear power generation in US and 20 countries, monthly 1973-88, 3168–123.10
Oil production, stocks, use, and trade, by selected country and country group, monthly rpt, 3162–42
Oil production, use, stocks, and exports and prices for US, by country, detailed data, monthly rpt with articles, 3162–24
Oil production, use, stocks, and exports and prices for US, by country, detailed data, monthly 1973-88, 3168–123
Pension plan finances, participation, and benefits, for 9 OECD countries, with data by firm and worker characteristics, 1990 conf, 6688–2
Pollution (air) contributing to global warming, emissions by monitoring site and country, and temperature change by world area and US region, 1860s-1990, annual rpt, 3004–33
Population size, growth rates, and components of change, by country, projected 1990-2020 and trends from 1950, biennial rpt, 2324–9
Potassium hydroxide from 3 countries at less than fair value, injury to US industry, investigation with background financial and operating data, 1992 rpt, 9886–14.339
Rails (steel) from 3 countries at less than fair value, injury to US industry, investigation with background financial and operating data, 1992 rpt, 9886–14.349
Refugee migration, and intl aid programs, by world area and country of origin and asylum, 1991, annual rpt, 7004–15
Science and Engineering Indicators, employment, education, R&D funding, and industry impacts, with foreign comparisons, 1960s-91, biennial rpt, 9624–10
Ships in world merchant fleet, tonnage, and new ship construction and deliveries, by vessel type and country, as of Jan 1992, annual rpt, 7704–3
Spacecraft and satellite launches since 1957, quarterly listing, 9502–2
Steel (carbon flat-rolled) products from 21 countries, injury to US industry from foreign subsidized and less than fair value imports, investigation with background financial and operating data, 1992 rpt, 9886–19.85
Steel (hot-rolled) products containing lead or bismuth from 4 countries, injury to US industry from foreign subsidized and less than fair value imports, investigation with background financial and operating data, 1992 rpt, 9886–19.82
Steel trade, by product, country, and customs district, with US industry operating data, 1989-June 1992, semiannual rpt, 9882–15
Tax (estate) returns for nonresident aliens, property and tax data, by estate size and decedent country of residence, 1986, article, 8302–2.310
Tax (income) final withholding systems use in 4 countries, and feasibility of US adoption, with background data, 1986-92, GAO rpt, 26119–400
Tax (income) returns for foreign corporate activity in US, selected income and tax items, by industry div and selected country, 1988, article, 8302–2.309
Tax (income) returns, income, and tax withheld for foreign partners of US partnerships, by country, 1990, article, 8302–2.324
Tax (value added) alternative proposals revenue impacts, with background data and intl comparisons, 1992 rpt, 26306–6.168
Tax revenue, by level of govt and type of tax, for OECD countries, mid 1960s-90, annual rpt, 10044–1.2
Tea imports of UK, and London auction prices, 1975-92, FAS annual circular, 1925–15.3

Telecommunications industry intl competitiveness, structure, and devs, with background data and foreign comparisons, 1991 rpt, 2808–30
Transportation energy use, fuel prices, vehicle registrations, and mileage, by selected country, 1950-89, annual rpt, 3304–5.1
Travel to US and Canada, market analysis with trip and traveler characteristics, and traveler views on selected destination cities and package tours, 1989, country rpt, 2906–2.19; 2906–2.20; 2906–2.21
Travel to US and Canada, market analysis with trip and traveler characteristics, 1989, country rpt, 2906–2.15
UN voting record and share of votes in agreement with US, by issue, country, and world area, 1991, annual rpt, 7004–18
Weather forecasts accuracy evaluations, for US, UK, and European systems, quarterly rpt, 2182–8
see also Gibraltar
see also under By Foreign Country in the "Index by Categories"

United Mine Workers of America
Retired coal industry workers pension and health trust funds financial condition, employer contributions, and beneficiaries, late 1970s-92, GAO rpt, 26121–469; 26121–471

United Nations
Background Notes, UN history, structure, and programs, 1991 rpt, 7006–2.2
Geographic Notes, foreign countries boundaries, claims, nomenclature, and other devs, quarterly rpt, 7142–3
Loans and grants for economic and military aid from US and intl agencies, by program and country, FY46-91, annual rpt, 9914–5
Peace Corps activities, funding by program, and volunteers, by country, FY93, annual rpt, 9654–1
Peacekeeping operations of UN, costs by mission, and assessment rates by country, 1948-92, GAO rpt, 26123–404
Refugee migration, and intl aid programs, by world area and country of origin and asylum, 1991, annual rpt, 7004–15
UNESCO fiscal mgmt, spending, staff, and funding sources, mid 1970s-92, GAO rpt, 26123–84
US participation in UN, and member and nonmember shares of UN budget by country, FY89-91, annual rpt, 7004–5
Voting record in UN and share of votes in agreement with US, by issue, country, and world area, 1991, annual rpt, 7004–18
see also International Atomic Energy Agency
see also International Bank for Reconstruction and Development
see also International Development Association
see also International Finance Corp.
see also International Monetary Fund

Universities
see Higher education

University of California at Davis
Radiation and other pollutant releases from DOE contractor research lab and nuclear weapons facilities, monitoring results, 1991 annual site rpt, 3324–2.3

University of Washington
"Effects of an Oil Spill and Freeze Event on Intertidal Community Structure in Washington", 5738–38.2

Unmanned space programs
see Communications satellites
see Meteorological satellites
see Satellites
see Space programs

Unpaid family workers
Asian and Pacific Islands Americans social and economic characteristics, for West and total US, 1990-91, Current Population Report, 2546–1.462
Black Americans social and economic characteristics, for South and total US, 1991 and trends from 1950, annual Current Population Rpt, 2546–1.463
Employment and Earnings, detailed data, monthly rpt, 6742–2
Employment, earnings, and hours, monthly press release, 6742–5
Employment situation, earnings, hours, and other BLS economic indicators, transcripts of BLS Commissioner's monthly testimony, periodic rpt, 23846–4
Farm labor, wages, hours, and perquisites, by State, monthly rpt, 1631–1
Farm population, by employment, social, and economic characteristics, and region, 1990, annual Current Population Rpt, 2546–1.458
Farm production itemized costs, receipts, and returns, by commodity and region, 1975-90, annual rpt, 1544–20
Health condition and care relation to education, indicators by selected characteristics, 1989, 4147–10.180
Home-based workers and hours, by worker characteristics, occupational group and industry div, 1991, press release, 6726–1.52
Housing alteration and repair for owner-occupied units, costs and structural, household, financial, and project characteristics, 1987, 2486–1.13
NYC housing supply, occupancy, condition, and household characteristics, by tenure and borough, 1991 triennial survey, 2488–3
Pacific territories population and housing detailed characteristics, by location, 1990 Census of Population and Housing, series, 2551–8

Unreported income
see Money laundering
see Tax delinquency and evasion
see Underground economy

Upper Volta
see Burkina Faso

Uranium
CIS uranium resources and production, by state, 1992 article, 3164–65
County Business Patterns, 1989: employment, establishments, and payroll, by SIC 2- to 4-digit industry and county, annual State rpt series, 2326–8
County Business Patterns, 1990: employment, establishments, and payroll, by SIC 2- to 4-digit industry and county, annual State rpt series, 2326–6
Enrichment facilities of DOE, financial statements, FY90-91, annual rpt, 3354–7
Exports and imports of US, by country and detailed commodity, monthly rpt, 2422–12
Exports and imports of US, by Harmonized System 6-digit commodity and country, 1991, annual rpt, 2424–13
Exports and imports of US, by transport mode, country, and SITC 1- to 3-digit commodity, 1991, annual rpt, 2424–12
Exports of US, detailed Schedule B commodities with countries of destination, 1991, annual rpt, 2424–10
Foreign countries mineral production, reserves, and industry role in domestic economy and world supply, world area and country rpt series, 5606–1
Foreign direct investment in US energy sources by type and firm, and US affiliates operations, as of 1990, annual rpt, 3164–80
Imports of uranium, impacts on US industry, with data on DOE enrichment program and stocks, 1980s-92, GAO rpt, 26113–584
Inventory discrepancies for nuclear materials at DOE and contractor facilities, 1990/91, annual rpt, 3344–2
Mill tailings mgmt, bibl, 1991 annual listing, 3354–12
Mills (inactive) uranium tailings, remedial action activities by site, and funding, FY91, annual rpt, 3354–9
Mills (inactive) uranium tailings, remedial action proposals, costs, site characteristics, and environmental, socioeconomic, and health impacts, series, 3356–4
Minerals Yearbook, Vol 2, 1989: State reviews of production and sales by commodity, and business activity, annual rpt series, 5604–16
Minerals Yearbook, Vol 2, 1990: State reviews of production and sales by commodity, and business activity, annual rpt series, 5604–22
Minerals Yearbook, Vol 3, 1989: foreign country reviews of production, trade, and policy, by commodity, annual rpt, 5604–35
Mines (metal) and related operations occupational injuries and incidence, employment, and hours, 1990, annual rpt, 6664–3
Mining and milling industries finances and operations, with selected foreign comparisons, 1970s-90 and projected to 2005, annual rpt, 3164–82
OECD trade, total and for 4 major countries, and US trade by country, by commodity, 1980-90, world area rpt series, 9116–1
Pacific basin countries energy supply and demand, and implications for US trade, country rpt series, 3406–6
Power plants capital and production costs, operations, and fuel use, by fuel type, plant, utility, and location, 1990, annual rpt, 3164–9
Production and prices of primary metals mining byproducts, by commodity, 1965-90, 5608–170
Public lands acreage, grants, use, revenues, and allocations, by State, FY91, annual rpt, 5724–1.2
Radioactive waste and spent fuel generation, inventory, and disposal, 1960s-90 and projected to 2020, annual rpt, 3364–2
Radon and other radionuclide levels in air, water, soil, and uranium mill tailings, by site and region, 1950s-80s, compilation of papers, 5668–126

Reserves, by recovery cost category, as of Dec 1990, annual rpt, 3164–74.1
Soviet Union exports of uranium at less than fair value, injury to US industry, investigation with background financial and operating data, 1991 rpt, 9886–14.337
Statistical Abstract of US, 1992 annual data compilation, 2324–1.19; 2324–1.25
Supply and industry operations for uranium, various periods 1947-91 and projected to 2001, annual rpt, 3164–65
Supply, demand, and prices, by fuel type and end-use sector, with foreign comparisons, 1981-90, annual fact book, 3164–76
Supply, demand, and prices, by fuel type and end-use sector, with foreign comparisons, 1991 and trends from 1949, annual rpt, 3164–74

Urban areas
AID housing and urban dev program, FY91, annual rpt, 9914–4
Asian and Pacific Islands Americans social and economic characteristics, for West and total US, 1990-91, Current Population Report, 2546–1.462
Census Bur geographic levels of data coverage, maps, and reference products, 1992 rpt, 2308–67
Census of Housing, 1990: summary unit characteristics, by householder race and age, county, place, and urban-rural location, State rpt series, 2471–1
Census of Population and Housing, 1990: population and housing characteristics, detailed geographic coverage, State CD-ROM series, 2551–10
Census of Population and Housing, 1990: summary characteristics, households, and land area, by region, State, MSA, and city, US rpt, 2551–1.1
Census of Population, 1990: population characteristics and living arrangements, by county, place, and urban-rural location, State rpt series, 2531–1
CPI by component for US city average, and by region, population size, and for 15 metro areas, monthly rpt, 6762–1
CPI by component for US city average, and by selected metro area, region, and population size, monthly rpt, 6762–2
Crime Index by population size and region, and offenses by large city, 1st half 1992, semiannual rpt, 6222–1
Crime victimization of households, by offense, household characteristics, and location, 1975-91, annual rpt, 6066–25.49
Crimes, arrests by offender characteristics, and rates, by offense, and law enforcement employees, by population size and jurisdiction, 1991, annual rpt, 6224–2
Deaths and rates, by cause and selected social, demographic, and employment characteristics, 1979-85, natl longitudinal study, 4478–186
Economic and social conditions in urban areas, as of FY92, biennial rpt, 5184–7
Educational enrollment, by grade, instn type and control, and student characteristics, 1990 and trends from 1947, annual Current Population Rpt, 2546–1.459
Environmental Quality, status of problems, protection programs, research, and intl issues, 1991 annual rpt, 484–1
Home mortgages FHA-insured, financial, property, and borrower characteristics, by metro area, 1991, annual rpt, 5144–24
Home mortgages FHA-insured, financial, property, and borrower characteristics, by State, 1991, annual rpt, 5144–1; 5144–25
Home mortgages FHA-insured, financial, property, and borrower characteristics, 1991, annual rpt, 5144–23
Households and family characteristics, by location, 1991, annual Current Population Rpt, 2546–1.457
Housing (rental) units, total, with HUD assistance by program, and eligible for aid, by unit, household, and neighborhood characteristics, and location, 1989, biennial rpt, 5184–11
Housing and households characteristics, and unit and neighborhood quality, by MSA location for 11 MSAs, 1987 survey, supplement, 2485–8
Housing and households detailed characteristics, and unit and neighborhood quality, by location, 1989, biennial rpt supplement, 2485–13
Housing unit and household characteristics of recent movers, and reason for move, by tenure, 1989, 2486–1.12
Housing vacancy and occupancy rates, and vacant unit characteristics and costs, by region and metro-nonmetro location, quarterly rpt, 2482–1
Hwy Statistics, detailed data by State, 1991, annual rpt, 7554–1
Maps and other cartographic records on urban areas, Natl Archives special collection, 1973 rpt, 9516–1.1
Medicare payment of physicians, vulnerable beneficiaries services use prior to fee schedule implementation, 1986-90, annual rpt, 17266–1.8
Pacific territories population and housing detailed characteristics, by location, 1990 Census of Population and Housing, series, 2551–8
Poverty status of population and families, by detailed characteristics, 1991, annual Current Population Rpt, 2546–6.77
Statistical Abstract of US, 1992 annual data compilation, 2324–1
Unemployment, by State and metro area, monthly press release, 6742–12
Vietnam population size, components of change, and selected characteristics, 1979, 1989, and projected to 2050, 2326–18.65
Water quality, chemistry, hydrology, and other characteristics, local area studies, series, 5666–27
see also Central business districts
see also Central cities
see also Cities
see also City and town planning
see also Community development
see also Local government
see also Metropolitan Statistical Areas
see also Neighborhoods
see also Relocation
see also Suburbs
see also Urban renewal
see also Urban transportation
see also Zoning and zoning laws
see also under By City, By SMSA or MSA, and By Urban-Rural and Metro-Nonmetro in the "Index by Categories"

Urban Development Action Grants
Expenditures of Fed Govt in States, by type, program, agency, and State, FY91, annual rpt, 2464–2

Urban Institute
"Costs of Highway Crashes", 7558–114
"Final Case Study for the National Scenic Byways Study: Economic Impacts of Scenic Byways", 7556–8.3

Urban Mass Transportation Administration
Employment of DOT, by subagency, occupation, and selected personnel characteristics, FY91, annual rpt, 7304–18
Expenditures of Fed Govt in States, by type, program, agency, and State, FY91, annual rpt, 2464–2
Subway accidents, casualties, and damage, by circumstances and system, annual rpt, discontinued, 7884–5
see also Federal Transit Administration

Urban planning
see City and town planning

Urban renewal
Govt finances, by level of govt, State, and for large cities and counties, annual rpt series, 2466–2
see also Community Development Block Grants
see also Relocation
see also Urban Development Action Grants

Urban transportation
Accidents and casualties on transit systems by circumstances, damage, and ridership, by mode, 1990, annual rpt, 7884–13
Budget of US, obligations and authority by function, agency, and program, with summaries and analyses, FY93, annual rpt, 104–2
Business statistics, detailed data for major industries and economic indicators, *Survey of Current Business*, monthly rpt, 2702–1.10
Business statistics, detailed data for major industries and economic indicators, 1960-91, *Survey of Current Business* biennial supplement, 2704–1
Carpool high occupancy vehicle lanes design, enforcement, and use in selected cities, 1991 conf, 7308–204
Census of Population and Housing, 1990: population and housing characteristics, detailed geographic coverage, State CD-ROM series, 2551–10
Census of Population and Housing, 1990: summary characteristics, by county, subdiv, and place, State rpt series, 2551–7
Child day care and early childhood education programs availability, demand, use, costs, and provider and enrollee characteristics, 1990 survey, 4808–39
Commuting to work, by mode, trip duration, and work location, 1980 and 1990, 7558–120
County Business Patterns, 1989: employment, establishments, and payroll, by SIC 2- to 4-digit industry and county, annual State rpt series, 2326–8
County Business Patterns, 1990: employment, establishments, and payroll, by SIC 2- to 4-digit industry and county, annual State rpt series, 2326–6

CPI by component for US city average, and by selected metro area, region, and population size, monthly rpt, 6762–2
Crime victimization rates, by victim and offender characteristics, circumstances, and offense, 1990 survey, annual rpt, 6066–3.47
DOT planning and safety grants, by program, State, and for 40 SMSAs, FY89, annual rpt, 7304–7
Employment, earnings, and hours, by SIC 1- to 4-digit industry, monthly 1989-Feb 1992, annual rpt, 6744–4
Energy use by mode of transport, fuel supply, and demographic and economic factors of vehicle use, 1970s-90, annual rpt, 3304–5
Fed Govt financial and nonfinancial domestic aid, 1992 base edition, annual listing, 104–5
Fed Govt spending in States, by type, program, agency, and State, FY91, annual rpt, 2464–2
Fed Transit Admin grants by State, and oversight, 1988-92, GAO rpt, 26113–600
Finances and operations of interstate carriers, 1990, annual rpt, 9486–5.3
Finances and operations of transit systems, by mode, size of fleet and urban area, region, and for 518 systems, 1990, annual rpt, 7884–4
Finances, equipment, and ridership characteristics of transit systems, 1985-90, biennial rpt, 7884–8
Foreign travelers to US, spending by world area of residence, and economic impacts, by spending category and State, 1989, 2908–28
Govt direct spending and employment, by function and level of govt, selected years 1962-87, 10048–53
Govt employment and payroll, by function, level of govt, and jurisdiction, annual rpt series, 2466–1
Housing (rental) total, HUD-assisted by program, and eligible for aid, recent movers by reason, selected characteristics, and location, 1989, biennial rpt, 5184–11
Housing and households characteristics, and unit and neighborhood quality, by MSA location for 11 MSAs, 1987 survey, supplement, 2485–8
Housing and households detailed characteristics, and unit and neighborhood quality, by location, 1989, biennial rpt supplement, 2485–13
Hwy receipts by source, and spending by function, by level of govt and State, 1991, annual rpt, 7554–1.3
Input-output structure of US economy, detailed interindustry transactions for 541 industries, and components of final demand, 1982 benchmark data, 2708–17
Multinatl firms US affiliates finances and operations, by industry, country of parent firm, and State, 1987, 2708–48
Natl income and product accounts, comprehensive accounts and components, benchmark revisions, 1929-88, 2708–5
Natl income and product accounts, comprehensive accounts and components, *Survey of Current Business*, monthly rpt, 2702–1.25
Occupational injury and illness rates, by SIC 2- to 4-digit industry, 1989-90, annual rpt, 6844–7
Occupational injury and illness rates, by SIC 2- to 4-digit industry, 1990, annual rpt, 6844–1
Pacific territories population and housing detailed characteristics, by location, 1990 Census of Population and Housing, series, 2551–8
Philadelphia metro area transit service operations, costs and benefits, and local economic and air pollution impacts, 1970s-90 and projected to 2020, 7308–205
Population size and demographic changes impacts on economic conditions, with background data, 1950s-80s and projected to 2010, 23848–226
R&D projects and funding of Federal Transit Admin, FY91, annual listing, 7884–1
Railroad (commuter) and other transit systems grants of Fed Transit Admin, FY93, annual rpt, 7884–12
Research and training grants of Federal Transit Admin to higher education instns, by project, FY92, annual listing, 7884–7
Research on transit systems, rpts, 1991, annual listing, 7884–11
Tax (income) returns of corporations, income and tax items by asset size and detailed industry, 1989, annual rpt, 8304–4; 8304–21
Tax (income) returns of sole proprietorships, income statement items, by industry group, 1990, annual article, 8302–2.317; 8302–2.320
Traffic volume on rural roads and city streets, monthly rpt, 7552–8
Transit systems and hwy programs funding, proposed FY92-97, 7558–117
Transit systems and hwys in urban areas, Federal aid by selected State, aggregate FY76-91, GAO rpt, 26113–570
Travel patterns, personal and household characteristics, and auto and public transport use, 1990 survey, series, 7556–6
Urban areas transit systems grants of Federal Transit Admin, by city and State, FY91, annual rpt, 7884–10
see also Buses
see also Commuting
see also Subways
see also Taxicabs
see also Traffic engineering
see also Transportation assistance

Urbana, Ill.
Wages by occupation, for office and plant workers, 1991 survey, periodic MSA rpt, 6785–12.2

Uri, Noel D.
"Energy Efficiency, Technological Change, and the Dieselization of U.S. Agriculture", 1561–16.301
"Forecasting the Prices Paid for Farm Inputs", 1561–16.301

Urogenital diseases
Alcohol abuse impacts on sexual function, for men with cirrhosis of liver, 1992 article, 4482–1.307
Cancer (breast) cases, survival, and death rates, by age, and change by birth cohort, 1970s-90s, article, 4472–1.341
Cancer (breast) death risk by presence of genetic mutations, and family breast cancer history, 1977-82, article, 4472–1.317
Cancer (breast) disease-free survival probability relation to tumor size, histology, and other characteristics, study, 1992 article, 4472–1.335
Cancer (breast) progression relation to loss of chromosomal heterozygosity, 1984-91 local area study, article, 4472–1.310
Cancer (breast) recurrence risk by thymidine kinase levels and estrogen receptor status, 1992 article, 4472–1.355
Cancer (breast) research funding, cases, and deaths, 1970s-90, GAO rpt, 26131–92
Cancer (breast) risk for women relation to incidence among male relatives, 1978-79, article, 4472–1.330
Cancer (breast) risk of postmenopausal women relation to dietary fat and other nutrient intake, 1986-89, article, 4472–1.328
Cancer (breast) risk relation to breast density, for Canada, 1992 article, 4472–1.332
Cancer (breast) risk relation to estrogen replacement therapy use, body mass index, and other risk factors, 1987-89 NYC study, article, 4472–1.350
Cancer (breast) risk relation to radiotherapy treatment for primary breast cancer, study, 1992 article, 4472–1.333
Cancer (breast) screening use relation to cancer anxiety, for high-risk women, 1992 article, 4472–1.301
Cancer (breast) severity relation to HER-2/neu gene amplification and overexpression, 1992 study, 4472–1.337
Cancer (breast) symptoms duration prior to seeking care, for black and white women, by selected characteristics, 1985-86 local area study, article, 4472–1.323
Cancer (breast) tumor genetic mutations, and presence relation to patient survival, 1992 article, 4472–1.329
Cancer (breast) tumor microvessel density and node status relation to patient survival and relapse, local area study, 1992 article, 4472–1.357
Cancer (breast) tumors with genetic mutations, 1992 article, 4472–1.305
Cancer (breast and cervical) deaths and rates by State, and in situ case rates by age, by race, 1970s-86, article, 4202–7.312
Cancer (breast and cervical) screening use and reasons for nonuse, by age, race, income, and State, 1987-89, article, 4202–7.313
Cancer (cervical) and dysplasia rates in Appalachian States, compared to total US, 1986-87, article, 4472–1.327
Cancer (cervical) relapse and metastasis risk related to c-myc gene overexpression and human papillomavirus infection, 1984-88 study, article, 4472–1.348
Cancer (cervical and breast) screening among poor black women, effects of in-home promotion program, 1989-92, article, 4042–3.338
Cancer (ovarian and lung) MDR1 gene levels, by type of treatment, 1992 article, 4472–1.345
Cancer (prostate) risk relation to presence of genetic mutations, 1992 article, 4472–1.322
Cancer (Wilms' tumor) patients with WT1 gene in kidney tissue, 1992 article, 4472–1.304

Cancer deaths and rates, by body site and selected social, demographic, and employment characteristics, 1979-85, natl longitudinal study, 4478–186
Cancer deaths and rates, by body site, provisional data, monthly rpt, 4142–1.2
Cases of acute and chronic conditions, disability, absenteeism, and health services use, by selected characteristics, 1990, annual rpt, 4147–10.182; 4147–10.183
Contraceptives failures and health risks to women, with pregnancy, abortion, and cancer death rates, 1980s, conf paper, 4164–2
Deaths and rates, by cause, age, sex, marital status, race, and State, 1989, US Vital Statistics advance annual rpt, 4146–5.124
Deaths and rates, by cause and age, preliminary 1990-91, US Vital Statistics annual rpt, 4144–7
Deaths and rates, by cause and selected social, demographic, and employment characteristics, 1979-85, natl longitudinal study, 4478–186
Deaths and rates, by cause, provisional data, monthly rpt, 4142–1.2
Deaths and rates, by detailed location, cause, and demographic characteristics, 1989, US Vital Statistics annual rpt, 4144–3
Disability and work limitations of persons with chronic health conditions, by condition, age, and sex, 1983-86, 4946–1.2
Health condition and care indicators, 1950s-90 with health improvement and disease prevention goals for 1990, annual data compilation, 4144–11
HHS financial aid, by program, recipient, State, and city, FY91, annual regional listings, 4004–3
Hospital deaths of Medicare patients, actual and expected rates by diagnosis, with hospital characteristics, by instn, FY90, annual State rpt series, 4654–14
Hospital discharges and length of stay, by diagnosis, patient and instn characteristics, procedure performed, and payment source, 1990, annual rpt, 4147–13.112
Hospital discharges and length of stay by region and diagnosis, and procedures performed, by age and sex, 1990, annual rpt, 4146–8.211
Hospital discharges and length of stay under old and new survey designs, by diagnosis, patient and instn characteristics, and procedure, Jan-Mar 1988, 4147–13.110
Hospital discharges by detailed diagnostic and procedure category, primary diagnosis, and length of stay, by age, sex, and region, 1990, annual rpt, 4147–13.111
Indian Health Service, tribal, and contract facilities hospitalization, by diagnosis, age, sex, and service area, FY91, annual rpt, 4084–5
Kidney dialysis facilities distribution related to area characteristics and facility ownership, 1982, article, 4652–1.306
Kidney dialysis services reimbursement by Medicare under prospective payment system, with costs, hospitalization, and patient characteristics, 1980s-93, 17206–1.17
Kidney end-stage disease program of Medicare, enrollment and program operations, 1992, annual fact book, 4654–18
Kidney end-stage disease program of Medicare, enrollment by age, sex, race, and region, and facilities, 1975-90, annual rpt, 4744–3.5
Kidney end-stage disease treatment facilities approved by Medicare, dialysis and transplant services and ownership, 1991 annual listing, 4654–17
Kidney end-stage disease treatment facilities, Medicare enrollment and reimbursement, survival, and patient characteristics, 1984-90, annual rpt, 4654–16
Kidney transplants, failures, deaths, and survival rates, by hospital, 1987-89, annual rpt, 4104–17.2
OECD members health care costs, hospital use, resources, and economic and health indicators, by country, 1960s-90, article, 4652–1.322
Physicians visits, by patient and practice characteristics, diagnosis, and services provided, 1989, annual rpt, 4147–13.109
Pollutants health effects, concentrations in food and environment, sources, human intake, and regulation, series, 9186–8
Research on population and reproduction, Federal funding by project, FY90, annual listing, 4474–9
see also Mammography
see also Sexually transmitted diseases
see also under By Disease in the "Index by Categories"

Uruguay
Agricultural trade of US, by detailed commodity and country, 1991, annual rpt, 1524–8
Agricultural trade of US, by detailed commodity and country, 1991, semiannual rpt, 1522–4
AID economic aid to developing countries, obligations and disbursements by country, quarterly rpt, 9912–4
AID loans repayment status and terms by program and country, and status of predecessor agency loans, quarterly rpt, 9912–3
Cuba trade, by commodity and country, mid 1980s-91, 9118–8
Economic and military aid and loans from US and intl agencies, by program and country, FY46-91, annual rpt, 9914–5
Economic and social conditions of developing countries from 1960s, and Intl Dev Cooperation Agency and AID activities and funding, FY91-93, annual rpt, 9904–4
Economic and social conditions, resources, and trade, and aid, 1992, annual factbook, 9914–14
Economic conditions, policy, and trade practices, by country, 1989-91, annual rpt, 21384–5
Economic, population, and agricultural data, US and other aid sources, and AID activity, 1992 country rpt, 9916–12.65
Economic, social, political, and geographic summary data, by country, 1992, annual factbook, 9114–2
Exports and imports of US, by commodity and country, 1980-90, world area rpt, 9116–1.7
Exports and imports of US, by transport mode, country, and SITC 1- to 3-digit commodity, 1991, annual rpt, 2424–12
Exports of US, detailed Schedule B commodities with countries of destination, 1991, annual rpt, 2424–10
Human rights conditions in 170 countries, and US economic and military aid, 1991, annual rpt, 21384–3
Labor conditions, union coverage, and work accidents, 1992 annual country rpt, 6366–4.44
Military aid of US, arms sales, and training programs costs and budget requests, by program, world region, and country, FY91-93, annual rpt, 7144–13
Military spending, arms trade, and force strengths, with govt spending and population, by country, 1979-89, annual rpt, 9824–1
Multinatl US firms foreign affiliates, income statement items by asset size, industry, and country, 1988, biennial article, 8302–2.322
Population size, growth rates, and components of change, by country, projected 1990-2020 and trends from 1950, biennial rpt, 2324–9
Refugee migration, and intl aid programs, by world area and country of origin and asylum, 1991, annual rpt, 7004–15
UN voting record and share of votes in agreement with US, by issue, country, and world area, 1991, annual rpt, 7004–18

U.S. Architectural and Transportation Barriers Compliance Board
Budget of US, authoritative financial statements with appropriations, outlays, and receipts, by category and agency, FY91, annual rpt, 8104–2.2
Budget of US, obligations and authority by function, agency, and program, with summaries and analyses, FY93, annual rpt, 104–2
Building access for disabled to Federal and federally funded facilities, complaints by disposition and State, FY91, annual rpt, 17614–1

U.S. Arms Control and Disarmament Agency
Activities of ACDA, and status of arms control treaties, 1991, annual rpt, 9824–2
Budget of US, authoritative financial statements with appropriations, outlays, and receipts, by category and agency, FY91, annual rpt, 8104–2.2
Budget of US, obligations and authority by function, agency, and program, with summaries and analyses, FY93, annual rpt, 104–2
Education funding by Federal agency, program, and recipient type, and instn spending, 1960s-91, annual rpt, 4824–8
Foreign countries military spending, arms trade, and force strengths, with govt spending and population, by country, 1979-89, annual rpt, 9824–1
NATO and Warsaw Pact military forces reductions and ceilings under CFE treaty, as of Nov 1990, 9828–1
Soviet Union and US Strategic Arms Reduction Treaty, protocols, and nuclear systems inventory agreements, as of 1990, 9828–26

U.S. Army Corps of Engineers
see Army Corps of Engineers
U.S. attorneys
Case processing and collections of US attorneys, by case type and Federal district, FY91, annual rpt, 6004–2
Court criminal case processing in Federal district courts, and dispositions, by offense, district, and offender characteristics, 1989, annual data compilation, 6064–29
Court criminal case processing in Federal district courts, and dispositions, by offense, 1980-91, annual rpt, 6064–31
Criminal case processing in Federal courts, by offense, disposition, and jurisdiction, data compilation, 1992 annual rpt, 6064–6.5
Debt delinquent on Federal accounts, cases and collections of Justice Dept and private law firms, pilot project results, FY91, annual rpt, 6004–20
Discrimination complaints of Federal employees, processing and counseling costs, by agency, FY91, GAO rpt, 26119–388
Federal district court personnel, by court, 1991, annual report, 17664–1
Sentences under Federal mandatory minimum provisions, by defendant characteristics, and views on justice system impacts, FY90, 17668–2
Victims of crime, compensation and support service programs funding, by offense and State, FY88-90, biennial rpt, 6064–37
U.S. Budget
see Budget of the U.S.
U.S. Claims Court
Caseloads of Court by type of suit, and judgments, FY92, annual rpt, 18224–1
Cases, judgments, and appeals, 1991, annual rpt, 18204–8.22
U.S. Coast Guard
see Coast Guard
U.S. Commission on Civil Rights
see Commission on Civil Rights
U.S. Court of Appeals for the Federal Circuit
Budget of US, obligations and authority by function, agency, and program, with summaries and analyses, FY93, annual rpt, 104–2
Cases filed and terminated, by source of appeal, 1991, annual rpt, 18204–8.17
Court of Intl Trade caseloads, decisions, and appeals, FY91-92, annual rpt, 18224–2
U.S. Court of International Trade
see Court of International Trade
U.S. Customs Service
Activities and collections of Customs Service, bimonthly journal, 8142–2
Activities, mgmt, and trade law enforcement effectiveness of Customs Service, staff and broker survey results, 1992 GAO rpt, 26119–420
Budget of US, obligations and authority by function, agency, and program, with summaries and analyses, FY93, annual rpt, 104–2
Drug (heroin) seizures by Federal agencies, with NYC street prices and purity, FY82-91, GAO rpt, 26119–404
Drug enforcement training of US for foreign govts, enrollment in US and host countries by program, FY91, annual rpt, 7004–17
Overtime pay for customs inspectors, issues, 1991 hearing, 21788–214

U.S. Fire Administration
Activities, funding, and training programs of USFA, with fires, casualties, and losses, FY91, annual rpt, 9434–7

U.S. Fish and Wildlife Service
see Fish and Wildlife Service

U.S. Geological Survey
see Geological Survey

U.S. Holocaust Memorial Council
Budget of US, authoritative financial statements with appropriations, outlays, and receipts, by category and agency, FY91, annual rpt, 8104–2.2
Budget of US, obligations and authority by function, agency, and program, with summaries and analyses, FY93, annual rpt, 104–2

U.S. Information Agency
Budget of US, authoritative financial statements with appropriations, outlays, and receipts, by category and agency, FY91, annual rpt, 8104–2.2
Budget of US, obligations and authority by function, agency, and program, with summaries and analyses, FY93, annual rpt, 104–2
Education funding by Federal agency, program, and recipient type, and instn spending, 1960s-91, annual rpt, 4824–8
Fulbright-Hays academic exchanges, grants by purpose, and foreign govt share of costs, by country, FY91, annual rpt, 10324–1
Labor unions recognized in Fed Govt, agreements and membership by agency and facility, as of Jan 1991, biennial listing, 9844–14
USIA programs fraud and abuse, audits and investigations, 1st half FY92, semiannual rpt, 9852–2

U.S. Institute of Peace
Activities and finances of Inst, FY90-91, biennial rpt, 29594–1
Education funding by Federal agency, program, and recipient type, and instn spending, 1960s-91, annual rpt, 4824–8

U.S. Interagency Air Assessment Team
Kuwait oil fires set by Iraqi forces, air pollution levels by substance and site, as of Mar 1991, 9188–116
Kuwait oil fires set by Iraqi forces, air pollution levels, health effects, intl monitoring activities, and wells affected, 1991, GAO rpt, 26113–566

U.S. International Development Cooperation Agency
Activities and funding of IDCA and AID, FY91-93, and developing countries economic and social conditions from 1960s, annual rpt, 9904–4
see also Agency for International Development
see also Overseas Private Investment Corp.

U.S. International Trade Commission
Activities, investigations, and rpts of USITC, FY91, annual rpt, 9884–1
Agricultural, fishery, and forest products trade, tariffs, and industry operating data, commodity rpt series, 9885–8
Auto industry finances and operations, trade by country, and prices of selected US and foreign models, monthly rpt, 9882–8
Budget of US, authoritative financial statements with appropriations, outlays, and receipts, by category and agency, FY91, annual rpt, 8104–2.2
Budget of US, obligations and authority by function, agency, and program, with summaries and analyses, FY93, annual rpt, 104–2
Caribbean area duty-free exports to US, by commodity and country, with consumer and industry impacts, 1984-91, annual rpt, 9884–20
Chemical and energy products trade, tariffs, and industry operating data, commodity rpt series, 9885–11
Chemicals (synthetic organic) production, by detailed product, quarterly rpt, 9882–1
Chemicals (synthetic organic) production, sales, and manufacturer listing, by product, 1990, annual rpt, 9884–3
Communist and transitional economy countries trade with US, by detailed commodity and country, quarterly rpt with articles, 9882–2
Electronics and services trade, tariffs, and industry operating data, commodity rpt series, 9885–12
Exports and imports of US by country, and trade shifts by commodity, semiannual rpt, periodicity change, 9882–9
Exports and imports of US by country, and trade shifts by commodity, 1991, annual rpt, 9884–25
Exports and imports, trade agreements and relations, and USITC investigations, 1991, annual rpt, 9884–5
Exports, imports, and balances of US with major trading partners, by product category, 1987-91, annual chartbook, 9884–21
Exports, imports, and intl competitiveness of US industries, trends and outlook, quarterly rpt with articles, 9882–16
Footwear production, employment, use, prices, and US trade by country, quarterly rpt, 9882–6
Foreign and US economic conditions, and trade devs and balances, with data by selected country and country group, monthly rpt, 9882–14
Generalized System of Preferences status, and US tariffs, with trade by country and US economic impacts, for selected commodities, 1987-91, annual rpt, 9884–23
Imports and tariff provisions effect on US industries and products, investigations with background financial and operating data, series, 9886–4
Imports injury to US industries from foreign subsidized products and sales at less than fair value, investigations with background financial and operating data, series, 9886–19
Imports injury to US industries from foreign subsidized products, investigations with background financial and operating data, series, 9886–15
Imports injury to US industries from sales at less than fair value, investigations with background financial and operating data, series, 9886–14
Imports of US given duty-free treatment for value of US material sent abroad, by commodity and country, 1987-90, annual rpt, 9884–14

Labor unions recognized in Fed Govt, agreements and membership by agency and facility, as of Jan 1991, biennial listing, 9844–14
Machinery and equipment trade, tariffs, and industry operating data, commodity rpt series, 9885–9
Manufacturing trade, tariffs, and industry operating data, commodity rpt series, 9885–10
Minerals and metals trade, tariffs, and industry operating data, commodity rpt series, 9885–13
Publications of USITC, 1984-91, annual listing, 9884–12
Steel imports of US under voluntary restraint agreement, by product, customs district, and country, with US industry operating data, quarterly rpt, 9882–13
Steel trade, by product, country, and customs district, with US industry operating data, 1989-June 1992, semiannual rpt, 9882–15
Tariff Schedule of US, classifications and rates of duty by detailed imported commodity, 1993 base edition, 9886–13
Textile imports under Multifiber Arrangement by product and country, and status of bilateral agreements, 1988-91, annual rpt, 9884–18

U.S.-Liberia Radio Corp.
Finances and operations, detail for telegraph firms, 1990, annual rpt, 9284–6.3
Finances, rates, and traffic for US telecommunications carriers intl operations, by service type, firm, and country, 1975-90, annual rpt, 9284–17

U.S. Marshals Service
Activities of USMS, FY91, annual rpt, 6294–1

U.S. Mint
Activities, finances, coin and medals production and holdings, and gold and silver transactions, by facility, FY91, annual rpt, 8204–1
Budget of US, obligations and authority by function, agency, and program, with summaries and analyses, FY93, annual rpt, 104–2
Coin and medal production by denomination, capacity, and facility improvement funding, by mint, with monetary metals purchases, projected FY92-96, hearing, 21248–164
Coin production of US Mint, for US by denomination and mint, monthly table, 8202–1

U.S. Naval Observatory
Star position tables, planet coordinates, time conversion factors, and listing of observatories worldwide, 1993, annual rpt, 3804–7

U.S. Nuclear Regulatory Commission
see Nuclear Regulatory Commission

U.S. Office of Special Counsel
Violations and prohibited political activity reported by Federal employees, cases by type, FY91, annual rpt, 9894–1

U.S. Parole Commission
Activities of Commission, and parole decisions and caseloads, FY88-91, annual rpt, 6004–3
Budget of US, obligations and authority by function, agency, and program, with summaries and analyses, FY93, annual rpt, 104–2
Parole granted, and hearing examiner caseload by disposition, by region, data compilation, 1992 annual rpt, 6064–6.1; 6064–6.6

U.S. Postal Rate Commission
see Postal Rate Commission

U.S. Postal Service
Activities of USPS, finances, and employment, FY87-91, annual rpt, 9864–1
Activities of USPS, finances, and mail volume and subsidies, FY91, annual rpt, 9864–5
Automation impacts on USPS labor hours, by task, 1990-91 with projected use of selected equipment to 1995, GAO rpt, 26119–395
Budget of US, authoritative financial statements with appropriations, outlays, and receipts, by category and agency, FY91, annual rpt, 8104–2.2
Budget of US, CBO analysis of revenue and spending alternatives and projections of economic indicators, FY93-97, annual rpt, 26304–3
Budget of US, obligations and authority by function, agency, and program, with summaries and analyses, FY93, annual rpt, 104–2
Competition and rate increases impacts on USPS mail volume and employment, with evaluation of alternative forecast models, 1970s-80s and forecast to 1995, GAO rpt, 26119–384
Costs of operations itemized by class of mail, FY91, annual rpt, 9864–4
Delivery on-time of 1st class mail, impacts of USPS standards revisions, 1990-91, GAO rpt, 26119–431
Employees work hour allocations in post offices with high and low workloads, effectiveness, FY89-90, GAO rpt, 26119–379
Expenditures of Fed Govt in States, by type, program, agency, and State, FY91, annual rpt, 2464–2
Households incoming and outgoing mail volume, use, and views, by class, source, content, and household characteristics, FY87-90, annual rpt, 9864–10
Input-output structure of US economy, detailed interindustry transactions for 541 industries, and components of final demand, 1982 benchmark data, 2708–17
Inspection activities of USPS, FY91, annual rpt, 9864–9
Inspection activities of USPS, 2nd half FY92, semiannual rpt, 9862–2
Post offices, siting, and routes historical records, Natl Archives special collection, 1975 rpt, 9516–1.5
Revenue and volume by class of mail, and special service transactions, quarterly rpt, 9862–1
Revenue, costs, and volume, by class of mail, FY91, annual rpt, 9864–2
Statistical Abstract of US, 1992 annual data compilation, 2324–1.18
see also Postal employees
see also Postal service

U.S. savings bonds
Assets and debts of private sector, balance sheets by segment, 1960-91, semiannual rpt, 9365–4.1
Banks in Fed Reserve System, expenses and operations itemized by service, office, and district, 1991, annual rpt, 9364–11
Farm sector balance sheet, and marketing receipts by detailed commodity, by State, 1986-90, annual rpt, 1544–18
Issues, redemptions, and bonds outstanding, by series, monthly table, 8242–1
Issues, redemptions, and bonds outstanding, monthly rpt, 8242–2
Sales and redemptions, *Treasury Bulletin*, quarterly rpt, 8002–4.7
Sales, redemptions, exchanges, and bonds outstanding, for series EE and HH, monthly rpt, 8442–1
Statistical Abstract of US, 1992 annual data compilation, 2324–1.10
Tax (estate) returns property and tax data, by size of gross estate and State, 1989-90, article, 8302–2.305

U.S. Savings Bonds Division
Savings bonds sold, redeemed, exchanged, and outstanding, for series EE and HH, monthly rpt, 8442–1

U.S. Secret Service
Budget of US, obligations and authority by function, agency, and program, with summaries and analyses, FY93, annual rpt, 104–2
Counterfeiting and other Secret Service investigations and arrests by type, and dispositions, FY91 and trends from FY82, annual rpt, 8464–1

U.S. Sentencing Commission
Activities of USSC, and sentencing guidelines use and results for Federal offenses by offense type and district, 1991, annual rpt, 17664–1
Budget of US, obligations and authority by function, agency, and program, with summaries and analyses, FY93, annual rpt, 104–2
Criminal sentences under Federal mandatory minimum provisions by defendant characteristics, and views on justice system impacts, FY90, 17668–2
Guidelines for sentencing, by Federal offense and circumstances, series, 17668–1

U.S. Soldiers Home
see Soldier's and Airmen's Home

US Sprint
Fiber optics and copper wire mileage and access lines, and fiber systems investment, by telecommunications firm, 1985-91, annual rpt, 9284–18
Finances and operations of local and long distance firms, subscribership, and charges, late 1970s-92, semiannual rpt, 9282–7
Intl telecommunications operations of US carriers, finances, rates, and traffic by service type, firm, and country, 1975-90, annual rpt, 9284–17

U.S. statutes
Assistance (block and categorical grants) programs for State and local govts, authorizing legislation, FY91, biennial listing, 10044–8
Assistance (financial and nonfinancial) of Fed Govt, authorizing legislation, 1992 base edition, annual listing, 104–5
Budget of US, debt subject to statutory limits, and legislative history, FY40-91 and projected to FY97, 108–46.5

Budget of US, debt subject to statutory limits, daily tables, 8102–4
Budget of US, statutory debt limit and debt subject to limit, monthly rpt, 8242–2
Child abductions, runaways, and missing and exploited children, and Office of Juvenile Justice and Delinquency Prevention activities, FY90, annual rpt, 6064–36
Court civil and criminal caseloads for Federal district, appeals, and bankruptcy courts, by type of suit and offense, circuit, and district, 1991, annual rpt, 18204–11
Court civil and criminal caseloads for Federal district, appeals, and special courts, 1991, annual rpt, 18204–8
Criminal case processing in Federal courts, by offense, disposition, and jurisdiction, data compilation, 1992 annual rpt, 6064–6.5
Fed Govt civilian pay legislation, 1945-90, annual rpt, 9844–6.5
Hwy funding and allocation methods, for Federal-aid system, FY92-97, 7558–107
Immigrants and nonimmigrants admitted to US, alien workers, visitors, deportations, and naturalizations, FY91, annual summary rpt, 6264–7
Immigration and nationality bills introduced and laws enacted, 77th-102nd Congresses, annual rpt, 6264–2.5
Imports injury to US industries, USITC activities, investigations, and rpts, FY91, annual rpt, 9884–1
Public lands minerals resources and availability, State rpt series, 5606–7
Sentences for Federal offenses, guidelines by offense and circumstances, series, 17668–1
Sentences under Federal mandatory minimum provisions, by defendant characteristics, and views on justice system impacts, FY90, 17668–2
Tariff Schedule of US, classifications and rates of duty by detailed imported commodity, 1993 base edition, 9886–13

U.S. Tax Court
see Tax Court of the U.S.

U.S. territories
see American Samoa
see Guam
see Puerto Rico
see Territories of the U.S.
see U.S. Virgin Islands
see under By Outlying Area in the "Index by Categories"

U.S. Travel and Tourism Administration
Budget of US, obligations and authority by function, agency, and program, with summaries and analyses, FY93, annual rpt, 104–2
Foreign travel to and from US, and travel receipts and payments, by world area, with data by country, 1985-90, annual rpt, 2904–10
Foreign travel to and from US, by world area, forecast 1992-93, annual rpt, 2904–9
Foreign travel to US and Canada, market analyses with detailed trip and traveler characteristics, country rpt series, 2906–2
Foreign travel to US, by characteristics of visit and traveler, country, port city, and State of destination, monthly rpt, 2902–1
Foreign travel to US, by characteristics of visit and traveler, world area of origin, and US destination, 1991 survey, annual rpt, 2904–12
Foreign travelers to US, spending by world area of residence, and economic impacts, by spending category and State, 1989, 2908–28
Market research data available from US Travel and Tourism Admin, 1992, annual rpt, 2904–15

U.S. Travel Data Center
"Final Case Study for the National Scenic Byways Study: Economic Impact of Travel on Scenic Byways", 7556–8.1
"Impact of International Visitor Spending on State Economies, 1989", 2908–28

U.S. Travel Service
see U.S. Travel and Tourism Administration

U.S. Virgin Islands
Banks (insured commercial and savings) deposits by instn, State, MSA, and county, as of June 1991, annual regional rpt, 9295–3.1
Deaths and rates, by detailed location, cause, and demographic characteristics, 1989, US Vital Statistics annual rpt, 4144–3.2
Drug abuse indicators, by world region and selected country, 1991 semiannual conf, 4492–5.1
Economic, social, political, and geographic summary data, by country, 1992, annual factbook, 9114–2
Employment, earnings, and hours, by selected SIC 1- to 4-digit industry, State, and for 275 MSAs, 1987-92, 6748–81
Exports and imports between US and outlying areas, by detailed commodity and mode of transport, 1991, annual rpt, 2424–11
Fed Govt spending in States and local areas, by type, State, county, and city, FY91, annual rpt, 2464–3
Fed Govt spending in States, by type, program, agency, and State, FY91, annual rpt, 2464–2
Freight (waterborne domestic and foreign) by commodity, traffic, and passengers, by port and waterway, 1989, annual rpt, 3754–3.2
HHS financial aid, by program, recipient, State, and city, FY91, annual regional listing, 4004–3.2
Hospital deaths of Medicare patients, actual and expected rates by diagnosis, and hospital characteristics, by instn, FY90 annual State rpt, 4654–14.40
Housing census, 1990: inventory, occupancy, and costs, State fact sheet, 2326–21.55
Hurricane Hugo disaster loan offices of SBA, staff and salary and support costs, for Puerto Rico and Virgin Islands, 1989-91, GAO rpt, 26113–576
Multinatl US firms foreign affiliates, income statement items by asset size, industry, and country, 1988, biennial article, 8302–2.322
OASDHI coverage of employment and earnings, and social security contributions, by age, sex, race, State, and county, 1988, annual rpt, 4744–29
Oil company overcharge settlements funds received, and conservation and energy aid spending, by outlying area, 1990, GAO rpt, 26113–564
Oil exports to US by OPEC and non-OPEC countries, monthly rpt, 3162–24.3
Oil exports to US by OPEC and non-OPEC countries, monthly 1973-88, 3168–123.3
Physicians, by specialty, age, sex, and location of training and practice, 1990, State rpt, 4116–6.54
Pollution (air) contributing to global warming, emissions by monitoring site and country, and temperature change by world area and US region, 1860s-1990, annual rpt, 3004–33
Population census, 1990: population characteristics and living arrangements, by county, place, and urban-rural location, State rpt, 2531–1.54
Population size, growth rates, and components of change, by country, projected 1990-2020 and trends from 1950, biennial rpt, 2324–9
Poultry and egg production, prices, receipts, trade, and disposition, by species, 1960-90, annual rpt, 1564–13
Statistical Abstract of US, 1992 annual data compilation, 2324–1.30
Tax (income) returns of Foreign Sales Corps, assets, and income and tax items, by industry, country of incorporation, and transaction pricing method, 1987, article, 8302–2.311
Water resources data collection and analysis activities of USGS Water Resources Div District, with project descriptions, 1990 rpt, 5666–26.19
see also under By Outlying Area in the "Index by Categories"

USDA
see Department of Agriculture

User fees
Army Corps of Engineers recreation facilities mgmt, acreage, visits, and non-Federal public and private dev alternatives, 1980s-90, 3758–8
Budget of US, authoritative financial statements with appropriations, outlays, and receipts, by category and agency, FY91, annual rpt, 8104–2.2
Budget of US, CBO analysis of revenue and spending alternatives and projections of economic indicators, FY93-97, annual rpt, 26304–3
Budget of US, House Budget Committee analysis of Bush Admin proposals and economic assumptions, FY93, 21268–42
Budget of US, obligations and authority by function, agency, and program, with summaries and analyses, FY93, annual rpt, 104–2
Child Support Enforcement Program collections for non-AFDC clients, administrative costs, and user fees, by State, with Federal shares of costs, 1990, GAO rpt, 26121–463
Copyrights Register activities, registrations by material type, and fees, FY91 and trends from 1790, annual rpt, 26404–2
Fed Reserve System, Bd of Governors, and district banks financial statements, performance, and fiscal services, 1991-92, annual rpt, 9364–10
Forest Service activities and finances, by region and State, FY91, annual rpt, 1204–1.1
Forests (natl) revenue, by source, forest, and State, FY91, annual rpt, 1204–34
Govt finances, by level of govt, State, and for large cities and counties, annual rpt series, 2466–2

Govt finances, tax systems and revenue, and fiscal structure, by level of govt and State, 1992 with historical trends, annual rpt, 10044–1
Grain inspected for domestic use and export, foreign buyers complaints, and handling facilities explosions, FY92, annual rpt, 1294–1
Grazing of livestock on public desert areas, acreage, use, fees, and endangered species, 1988-90, GAO rpt, 26113–552
HHS Freedom of Info Act requests, disposition, costs, and fees, 1991, annual rpt, 4004–21
Hwy funding and allocation methods, for Federal-aid system, FY92-97, 7558–107
Land Mgmt Bur activities and finances, and public land acreage and use, annual State rpt series, 5724–11
Lands (public) acreage, grants, use, revenues, and allocations, by State, FY91, annual rpt, 5724–1.2; 5724–1.3
Minority Business Dev Centers mgmt and financial aid, and characteristics of businesses, by region and State, FY91, annual rpt, 2104–6
Nuclear Waste Fund finances, and DOE Civilian Radioactive Waste Mgmt Office R&D costs, FY90-91, annual rpt, 3364–1
Nuclear Waste Fund finances, and DOE Civilian Radioactive Waste Mgmt Program costs, quarterly rpt, 3362–1
Patent and Trademark Office fee income, by source, FY88-91, annual rpt, 2244–1.1
Postal Service activities, finances, and mail volume and subsidies, FY91, annual rpt, 9864–5.3
Public opinion on taxes, spending, and govt efficiency, by respondent characteristics, 1992 survey, annual rpt, 10044–2
Transit systems finances and operations, by mode, size of fleet and urban area, region, and for 518 systems, 1990, annual rpt, 7884–4
Transportation infrastructure financing through user fees, with data on hwys, airports, and waterways, 1985-91, 26306–6.170
USDA revenue, by source and subagency, FY88-92, GAO rpt, 26113–602
see also Royalties
see also Tolls

USIA
see U.S. Information Agency

USMC
see Marine Corps

USSR
see Soviet Union

Utah
Banks (insured commercial and savings) deposits by instn, State, MSA, and county, as of June 1991, annual regional rpt, 9295–3.6
Coal production and mines by county, prices, productivity, miners, and reserves, by mining method and State, 1990-91, annual rpt, 3164–25
County Business Patterns, 1990: employment, establishments, and payroll, by SIC 2- to 4-digit industry and county, annual State rpt, 2326–6.46
Deaths and rates, by detailed location, cause, and demographic characteristics, 1989, US Vital Statistics annual rpt, 4144–3.1
Employment, earnings, and hours, by selected SIC 1- to 4-digit industry, State, and for 275 MSAs, 1987-92, 6748–81
Fed Govt spending in States and local areas, by type, State, county, and city, FY91, annual rpt, 2464–3
Fed Govt spending in States, by type, program, agency, and State, FY91, annual rpt, 2464–2
Forest fires effects on selected habitats, for Utah, 1992 rpt, 1208–420
HHS financial aid, by program, recipient, State, and city, FY91, annual regional listing, 4004–3.8
Hospital deaths of Medicare patients, actual and expected rates by diagnosis, and hospital characteristics, by instn, FY90 annual State rpt, 4654–14.46
Housing census, 1990: inventory, occupancy, and costs, State fact sheet, 2326–21.46
Housing census, 1990: summary unit characteristics, by householder race and age, county, place, and urban-rural location, State rpt, 2471–1.46
Land Mgmt Bur activities and finances, and public land acreage and use, FY91, annual State rpt, 5724–11.4
Medicaid impacts on State budgets, and program financing, cost control measures, enrollment, and services coverage, by selected State, 1960s-80s and projected to 1997, 10176–3.6
Military prime contract awards, by contractor, service branch, State, and city, FY91, annual rpt, 3544–22
Mineral Industry Surveys, State reviews of production, 1991, preliminary annual rpt, 5614–6
Multinatl firms US affiliates finances and operations, by industry, country of parent firm, and State, 1987, 2708–48
Physicians, by specialty, age, sex, and location of training and practice, 1990, State rpt, 4116–6.46
Population and housing census, 1990: detailed geographic coverage, State CD-ROM, 2551–9.8
Population and housing census, 1990: summary characteristics, by county, subdiv, and place, State rpt, 2551–7.46
Population census, 1990: population characteristics and living arrangements, by county, place, and urban-rural location, State rpt, 2531–1.46
Statistical Abstract of US, 1992 annual data compilation, 2324–1
Water salinity control program for Colorado River, participation and payments, FY87-91, annual rpt, 1804–23
Water supply and quality in streams and lakes, and groundwater levels in wells, by drainage basin, 1991, annual State rpt, 5666–12.42
Water supply, and snow survey results, monthly State rpt, 1266–2.8
Water supply, and snow survey results, 1991, annual State rpt, 1264–14.7
see also Ogden, Utah
see also Salt Lake City, Utah
see also under By State in the "Index by Categories"

Utica, N.Y.
see also under By City and By SMSA or MSA in the "Index by Categories"

Utilities
see Public utilities

Uzbekistan
Agricultural production, prices, and trade, for former USSR republics, 1960s-91 and forecast 1992, annual rpt, 1524–4.1
Economic, social, political, and geographic summary data, by country, 1992, annual factbook, 9114–2
Embassies of US in former Soviet republics and Baltic States, positions planned by function, and filled, 1992, GAO rpt, 26123–403
Energy supply and use, and social, economic, and political indicators for former Soviet Republics and Baltic States, 1989-90, 3168–126
Energy use and production of former USSR Republics, by fuel type, 1990, annual rpt, 3164–84.2
Exports and imports of US with Communist and transitional economy countries, by detailed commodity and country, quarterly rpt with articles, 9882–2
Livestock and meat inventories, use, and imports, by former USSR republic, 1986-93, semiannual rpt, 1925–33.2
Population size and characteristics of former Soviet Republics and Baltic States, 1989-92, 9118–19
Uranium resources and production of CIS, by state, 1992 article, 3164–65

VA
see Department of Veterans Affairs
see Veterans Administration

Vacant and abandoned property
Airport abandonments, by State, 1990, annual rpt, 7504–1.3
Alteration and repair spending for commercial and public buildings, by type, size, age, and region, 1989, 2388–4
Arson incidents by whether structure occupied, property value, and arrest rate, by property type, 1991, annual rpt, 6224–2.1
Coal Surface Mining Reclamation and Enforcement Office activities and funding, by State and Indian tribe, FY91, annual rpt, 5644–1
Commercial buildings energy use, costs, and conservation, by building characteristics, survey rpt series, 3166–8
Commercial real estate supply and demand, market activity indicators by region, quarterly rpt, 9292–6
Hospital closures in 1990, operating characteristics, current use, and location, annual rpt, 4004–35
Neighborhood and housing quality, indicators and attitudes, MSA surveys, series, 2485–6
Neighborhood quality, indicators and attitudes of renter households, by whether receiving and eligible for HUD assistance, householder characteristics, and location, 1989, biennial rpt, 5184–11
New England construction, real estate, and other economic performance indicators, compared to Texas and other areas, 1970s-91, article, 9373–1.302
Oil resources recovery impacts of environmental regulation, under alternative oil price, technology, and regulatory assumptions, projected 1990-2015, 3338–2

Rail line abandonment, construction, and acquisition certificate applications, by disposition, FY89-91, annual rpt, 9484–1.1
Uranium tailings at inactive mills, remedial action activities by site, and funding, FY91, annual rpt, 3354–9
Uranium tailings at inactive mills, remedial action proposals, costs, site characteristics, and environmental, socioeconomic, and health impacts, series, 3356–4
see also Housing condition and occupancy

Vacations and holidays
Employee benefit plan coverage and provisions, by plan type, for State and local govt employees, 1990, biennial rpt, 6784–21
Employee compensation costs, by component, occupation, industry group, union status, and location, 1975-92, annual rpt, 6744–20.2
Employee leave benefits in small business compared to larger firms and govts, by occupational group, 1989-90, article, 6722–1.315
Fed Govt civilian employees work-years by schedule, overtime, holidays, and personnel cost components, FY90-91, annual article, 9842–1.303
Fed Govt civilian employees work-years, pay rates, and benefits use and costs, by agency, FY90, annual rpt, 9844–31
Foreign countries economic, social, political, and geographic summary data, by country, 1992, annual factbook, 9114–2
Foreign countries holidays observed by businesses, by country, biweekly rpt, annual listing, 2042–24
GNP seasonal variations relation to labor hoarding and returns to scale, 1991 working paper, 9375–13.71
Labor force not at work, unemployed, and working less than 35 hours, by reason, sex, race, region, and State, 1991, annual rpt, 6744–7.1; 6744–7.2
Labor hourly costs, by component, industry and occupational group, worker class, and firm size, monthly rpt, annual tables, 6782–1.2
Labor hourly costs, by component, occupational group, industry div, union coverage, and region, 1992, annual rpt, 6744–21
Mail volume to and from households, use, and views, by class, source, content, and household characteristics, FY87-90, annual rpt, 9864–10
Overseas Business Reports: economic conditions, investment and export opportunities, and trade practices, country market research rpt series, 2046–6
Transit systems finances and operations, by mode, size of fleet and urban area, region, and for 518 systems, 1990, annual rpt, 7884–4
Travel patterns, personal and household characteristics, and auto and public transport use, 1990 survey, series, 7556–6
Travel to US, by characteristics of visit and traveler, world area of origin, and US destination, 1991 survey, annual rpt, 2904–12
Unemployed displaced workers, layoffs and recalls by layoff reason, industry, firm size, and State, 2nd half 1988, 6406–6.36
Unemployed displaced workers, layoffs and unemployment insurance claims by reason, industry, selected characteristics, and State, quarterly press release, 6742–23
Unemployed displaced workers, layoffs and unemployment insurance claims by reason, industry, selected characteristics, MSA, and State, 1990, annual rpt, 6744–18
see also Area wage surveys
see also Industry wage surveys

Vaccination and vaccines
Adult vaccination schedules, dosages, and precautions, by age, risk group, and disease, CDC recommendations, 1991 rpt, 4206–2.48
Biological warfare agent vaccine dev and production of Salk Inst, and Army contract costs by component, late 1970s-91, GAO rpt, 26123–374
Claims Court caseload by type of suit, and judgments, FY92, annual rpt, 18224–1
Developing countries economic and social conditions from 1960s, and Intl Dev Cooperation Agency and AID activities and funding, FY91-93, annual rpt, 9904–4.1
Exports and imports between US and outlying areas, by detailed commodity and mode of transport, 1991, annual rpt, 2424–11
Exports and imports of US, by Harmonized System 6-digit commodity and country, 1991, annual rpt, 2424–13
Exports of US, detailed Schedule B commodities with countries of destination, 1991, annual rpt, 2424–10
Foreign travel vaccination needs by country, and disease prevention recommendations, 1992 annual rpt, 4204–11
Health condition and care indicators, 1950s-90 with health improvement and disease prevention goals for 1990, annual data compilation, 4144–11
Hepatitis B eradication through universal childhood vaccination, with schedules, dosages, and precautions, CDC recommendations, 1991 rpt, 4206–2.49
Hepatitis B vaccination coverage of children, by island, for Micronesia, 1988-90, article, 4042–3.357
HHS financial aid, by program, recipient, State, and city, FY91, annual regional listings, 4004–3
Influenza vaccination schedules, dosages, and precautions, CDC recommendations, 1992 rpt, 4206–2.59
Insurance (health) coverage and provisions of employee benefit plans, by plan type, for State and local govt employees, 1990, biennial rpt, 6784–21
Kuwait child vaccinations, by disease, 1977-89, 9188–117
Latin America economic and social conditions, resources, trade, and aid, 1992, annual factbook, 9914–14
Manufacturing annual survey, 1990: value of shipments, by SIC 4- to 5-digit product class, 2506–14.1
Measles cases in Arkansas, with risk factors and vaccination rates, 1986, article, 4042–3.301
Morbidity and Mortality Weekly Report, infectious notifiable disease cases by State, and public health issues, 4202–1
Natl Inst of Allergy and Infectious Diseases activities, grants by recipient and location, and disease cases, FY84-91, annual rpt, 4474–30
Pertussis vaccination schedules, dosages, and precautions, CDC recommendations, 1992 rpt, 4206–2.51
Pertussis vaccination schedules, dosages, and precautions, for acellular vaccine, CDC recommendations, 1992 rpt, 4206–2.65
Pneumonia (*Pneumocystis carinii*) prevention in AIDS patients, vaccination schedules, dosages, and precautions, CDC recommendations, 1992 rpt, 4206–2.54
Price indexes (producer), by stage of processing and detailed commodity, monthly rpt, 6762–6
Price indexes (producer), by stage of processing and detailed commodity, monthly 1991, annual rpt, 6764–2
Rabies vaccination schedules and dosages for pets and livestock by species, and disease outbreak control, CDC recommendations, 1992 rpt, 4206–2.57
Research on immunization, 1991 annual listing, 4204–16
Shipments of vaccines and toxoids, by product type, 1987-90, 4205–22
Smallpox vaccination schedules, dosages, and precautions, CDC recommendations, 1991 rpt, 4206–2.50
Statistical Abstract of US, 1992 annual data compilation, 2324–1.3
Tax (excise) collections of IRS, by source, quarterly rpt, 8302–1

Vachris, Michelle A.
"New International Price Series Published by Nation and Region", 6722–1.327

Valdez, Alaska
Tide height and time daily at coastal points, forecast 1993, annual rpt, 2174–2.1

Vallejo, Calif.
Wages by occupation, and benefits, for office and plant workers, 1992 survey, periodic MSA rpt, 6785–3.3
see also under By City and By SMSA or MSA in the "Index by Categories"

Value added tax
Budget of US, CBO analysis of revenue and spending alternatives and projections of economic indicators, FY93-97, annual rpt, 26304–3
Fed Govt VAT revenue impacts of alternative proposals, with background data and intl comparisons, 1992 rpt, 26306–6.168

van Hees, Willem W.
"Timber Resource Statistics for the Chatham Area of the Tongass National Forest, Alaska, 1982", 1206–9.26
"Timber Resource Statistics for the Ketchikan Area of the Tongass National Forest, Alaska, 1985", 1206–9.24
"Timber Resource Statistics for the Stikine Area of the Tongass National Forest, Alaska, 1984", 1206–9.25
"Timberland Resources of the Kenai Peninsula, Alaska, 1987", 1206–9.23

Van Meir, Larry
"Revisions in Estimates of Food and Industrial Use for Feed Grains", 1561–4.301

Van Walleghem, Joe
"Update on Bank Branching and Interstate Banking Rules", 9381–14
Vancouver, Wash.
CPI by component for US city average, and by selected metro area, region, and population size, monthly rpt, 6762–2
Vandalism
Arrests, by offense, offender characteristics, and location, data compilation, 1992 annual rpt, 6064–6.4
Arrests, by offense, offender characteristics, and location, 1991, annual rpt, 6224–2.2
Bombing incidents and casualties, by target, circumstances, and State, 1987-91, annual rpt, 8484–4.1
Historic and natural natl landmarks damaged and threatened, with owner, location, damage type, and recommended remedial action, 1990, annual listing, 5544–16
Juvenile arrests, by sex, race, disposition, and offense, 1990, 6066–27.8
Neighborhood quality, indicators and attitudes of renter households, by whether receiving and eligible for HUD assistance, householder characteristics, and location, 1989, biennial rpt, 5184–11
Railroad accidents, casualties, and damage, by cause, railroad, and State, 1991, annual rpt, 7604–1
Railroad accidents, casualties, and damage, Fed Railroad Admin activities, and safety inspectors by State, 1990, annual rpt, 7604–12
Sentences for Federal offenses, guidelines by offense and circumstances, series, 17668–1
Vanderhorst, Paulette R.
"Integrated Postsecondary Education Data System Glossary", 4848–47
Vanuatu
Economic, social, political, and geographic summary data, by country, 1992, annual factbook, 9114–2
Exports and imports of US, by transport mode, country, and SITC 1- to 3-digit commodity, 1991, annual rpt, 2424–12
Human rights conditions in 170 countries, and US economic and military aid, 1991, annual rpt, 21384–3
Military aid of US, arms sales, and training programs costs and budget requests, by program, world region, and country, FY91-93, annual rpt, 7144–13
Population size, growth rates, and components of change, by country, projected 1990-2020 and trends from 1950, biennial rpt, 2324–9
UN voting record and share of votes in agreement with US, by issue, country, and world area, 1991, annual rpt, 7004–18
Varnishes
see Paints and varnishes
VAT
see Value added tax
Vatican City
Economic, social, political, and geographic summary data, by country, 1992, annual factbook, 9114–2
Exports and imports of US, by transport mode, country, and SITC 1- to 3-digit commodity, 1991, annual rpt, 2424–12
Vaughan, Denton R.
"Implementing an SSI Model Using the Survey of Income and Program Participation", 4746–26.23
"Income, Assets, and Health Insurance: Economic Resources for Meeting Acute Health Care Needs of the Aged", 4742–1.307
"Rationale for a SIPP-Based Microsimulation Model of SSI and OASDI", 4746–26.23
Vaughan, Douglas S.
"Assessment and Management of Atlantic and Gulf Menhaden Stocks", 2162–1.303
"Biological Analysis of Two Management Options for the Atlantic Menhaden Fishery", 2162–1.303
Vegetable oils
see Oils, oilseeds, and fats
Vegetables and vegetable products
Acreage planted and harvested, by crop and State, 1990-91 and planned as of June 1992, annual rpt, 1621–23
Acreage planted, by selected crop and State, 1983-91 and planned 1992, annual rpt, 1621–22
Agricultural Statistics, 1991, annual rpt, 1004–1
Appalachia food processing firms, employment, and shipments, and farm production, by commodity and State, 1960s-90, 9088–37
Bean (dried) prices by State, market activity, and foreign and US production, use, stocks, and trade, weekly rpt, 1311–17
Bean (dried) production and prices by State, exports and foreign production by country, and USDA food aid purchases, by bean type, 1986-91, annual rpt, 1311–18
Beans (snap) production, acreage, use, and price, by processing method, 1950s-91, article, 1561–11.305
Celery acreage planted and growing, by growing area, monthly rpt, 1621–14
Cold storage food stocks by commodity and census div, and warehouse space use, by State, monthly rpt, 1631–5
Cold storage food stocks by commodity, and warehouse space use, by census div, 1991, annual rpt, 1631–11
Consumption of fresh vegetables, and relation to prices and per capita income, 1950s-90, article, 1561–11.301
Consumption, supply, trade, prices, spending, and indexes, by food commodity, 1990, annual rpt, 1544–4
CPI by component for US city average, and by selected metro area, region, and population size, monthly rpt, 6762–2
Employment, earnings, and hours, by SIC 1- to 4-digit industry, monthly 1989-Feb 1992, annual rpt, 6744–4
Exports and imports (agricultural) of US, by commodity and country, bimonthly rpt, 1522–1
Exports and imports (agricultural) of US, by detailed commodity and country, 1991, annual rpt, 1524–8
Exports and imports (agricultural) of US, by detailed commodity and country, 1991, semiannual rpt, 1522–4
Exports and imports between US and outlying areas, by detailed commodity and mode of transport, 1991, annual rpt, 2424–11
Exports and imports of US, by country and detailed commodity, monthly rpt, 2422–12
Exports and imports of US, by Harmonized System 6-digit commodity and country, 1991, annual rpt, 2424–13
Exports and imports of US, by transport mode, country, and SITC 1- to 3-digit commodity, 1991, annual rpt, 2424–12
Exports of US, detailed Schedule B commodities with countries of destination, 1991, annual rpt, 2424–10
Farm financial and marketing conditions, forecast 1992, annual chartbook, 1504–8
Farm financial and marketing conditions, forecast 1992, annual conf, 1504–9
Farm financial condition, for vegetable operations, 1990, article, 1561–11.304
Farm income, cash marketing receipts ranked by commodity and State, 1990, 1548–385
Farm sector balance sheet, and receipts by detailed commodity, by State, 1986-90, annual rpt, 1544–18
Fertilizer and pesticide use and application rates, by type, crop, and State, series, 1616–1
Foreign and US fresh and processed fruit, vegetable, and nut production and trade, FAS monthly circular with articles, 1925–34
Foreign countries agricultural production, prices, and trade, by country, 1980-91 and forecast 1992, annual world area rpt series, 1524–4
Freight (waterborne domestic and foreign) by commodity, traffic, and passengers, by port and waterway, 1989, annual rpt, 3754–3
Imports of fruits and vegetables under quarantine, by crop, country, and port of entry, FY89, annual rpt, 1524–7
Imports of US given duty-free treatment for value of US material sent abroad, by commodity and country, 1987-90, annual rpt, 9884–14
Input-output structure of US economy, detailed interindustry transactions for 541 industries, and components of final demand, 1982 benchmark data, 2708–17
Irrigation projects of Reclamation Bur in western US, crop production and acreage by commodity, State, and project, 1990, annual rpt, 5824–12
Labor productivity, indexes of output, hours, and employment by SIC 2- to 4-digit industry, 1967-90, annual rpt, 6824–1.3
Latin America economic and social conditions, resources, trade, and aid, 1992, annual factbook, 9914–14
Manufacturing annual survey, 1990: finances and operations, by SIC 2- to 4-digit industry, series, 2506–14
Manufacturing finances and operations, by SIC 2- to 4-digit industry, forecast 1992, annual rpt, 2044–28
Mushroom (canned) trade, supply, and demand, for selected countries, 1980s-92, article, 1925–34.333
Mushroom production, sales, and prices, by State, 1966/67-1991/92 and planned 1992/93, annual rpt, 1631–9
Mushroom production, supply, use, and price, by variety, 1970-91, article, 1561–11.303

Nutrient, caloric, and waste composition, detailed data for raw, processed, and prepared foods, 1992 rpt, 1356–3.17
Occupational injury and illness rates, by SIC 2- to 4-digit industry, 1989-90, annual rpt, 6844–7
Occupational injury and illness rates, by SIC 2- to 4-digit industry, 1990, annual rpt, 6844–1
OECD trade, total and for 4 major countries, and US trade by country, by commodity, 1980-90, world area rpt series, 9116–1
Onions in summer storage, shrinkage and loss, 1989-91, annual rpts, 1621–25
Potato production, acreage, prices, and shipments, for 7 major producer States, and compared to other States, 1970s-92, annual rpt, 1311–29
Potato production, acreage, shipments, and arrivals, for Maine by variety, and compared to other States and Canada, 1991-92, annual rpt, 1311–26
Potato production, prices, stocks, and use, by State, 1980s-91, annual rpt, 1621–11
Potato production, stocks, processing, yields, and harvest losses, by State, periodic rpt, 1621–10
Price indexes (producer), by stage of processing and detailed commodity, monthly rpt, 6762–6
Price indexes (producer), by stage of processing and detailed commodity, monthly 1991, annual rpt, 6764–2
Prices (farm-retail) for food, marketing cost components, and industry finances and productivity, 1920s-91, annual rpt, 1544–9
Prices (wholesale) for fresh fruit and vegetables in NYC, Chicago, and selected shipping points, by crop, 1991, annual rpt, 1311–8
Prices (wholesale) of fruit and vegetables in NYC by State, and shipments and arrivals by mode of transport, by commodity, weekly rpt, 1311–20
Prices (wholesale) of fruit and vegetables in NYC-Newark, and arrivals by mode of transport, by commodity and State, 1990, annual rpt, 1311–21
Prices (wholesale) of tropical vegetables, by market for Florida and Central American produce, 1990/91, annual rpt, 1311–23
Prices of selected fresh and dried vegetables, relation to production, 1970s-91, article, 1561–11.302
Prices received and paid by farmers, by commodity and State, monthly rpt, 1629–1
Prices received and paid by farmers, by commodity and State, 1991, annual rpt, 1629–5
Prices received by farmers and production value, by detailed crop and State, 1989-91, annual rpt, 1621–2
Production, acreage, and yield, current and forecast for selected fresh and processing vegetables by State, periodic rpt, 1621–12
Production, farms, acreage, and related data, by selected crop and State, monthly rpt, 1621–1
Production inputs, output, and productivity for farms, by commodity and region, 1947-90, annual rpt, 1544–17
Production, prices, trade, and marketing, by commodity, current situation and forecast, monthly rpt with articles, 1502–4
Production, prices, trade, stocks, and use, for selected fresh and processing crops, periodic situation rpt with articles, 1561–11
Production, value, and acreage, for selected fresh and processing vegetables by State, 1989-91, annual rpts, 1621–25
Seed exports, by type, world region, and country, FAS quarterly rpt, 1925–13
Shipments by mode of transport, arrivals, and imports, for fruit and vegetables by commodity and State and country of origin, weekly rpt, 1311–3
Shipments of fruit and vegetables, and arrivals by city, by mode of transport and State and country of origin, 1991, annual rpt series, 1311–4
Soviet Union and US economic and sociodemographic indicators, selected years 1970-90, handbook, 2328–80
Statistical Abstract of US, 1992 annual data compilation, 2324–1.23
Tax (income) returns of corporations, income and tax items by asset size and detailed industry, 1989, annual rpt, 8304–21
Tax (income) returns of partnerships, income statement and balance sheet items, by industry group, 1990, annual article, 8302–2.314
Tomato (paste and canned) minimum grower price and processor subsidy, by EC country, 1985/86-1992/93, article, 1925–34.336
Tomato (processing) production, and paste and canned tomato supply, trade, and use, by selected country, 1988-92, article, 1925–34.304
Tomato (processing) production, processed imports of US by type, and canned and paste supply and use, by country, 1989-93, article, 1925–34.326
Tomato production, acreage, and yield by State, trade and production by country, stocks, shipments, and prices, 1960s-91, 1568–310
Truck rates for fruit and vegetables paid by shippers and receivers, by commodity and city, and fleet itemized costs per mile, weekly rpt, 1311–22
Truck rates for fruit and vegetables weekly by growing area and market, and shipments monthly by State and country of origin, 1991, annual rpt, 1311–15
Weight and volume conversion factors for agricultural commodities and products, 1992 rpt, 1508–3
see also Fruit and fruit products
see also under By Commodity in the "Index by Categories"

Vegetation
see Plants and vegetation

Veletto, Kimberly A.
"Corporate Foreign Tax Credit, 1988: An Industry Focus", 8302–2.316
"Foreign Recipients of U.S. Partnership Income, 1990: Data Release", 8302–2.324

Vending machines and stands
Blind-operated vending facilities on Federal and non-Federal property, finances and operations by agency and State, FY91, annual rpt, 4944–2
County Business Patterns, 1989: employment, establishments, and payroll, by SIC 2- to 4-digit industry and county, annual State rpt series, 2326–8
County Business Patterns, 1990: employment, establishments, and payroll, by SIC 2- to 4-digit industry and county, annual State rpt series, 2326–6
Electronic communications systems and related products shipments, trade, use, and firms, 1991, annual Current Industrial Rpt, 2506–12.35
Employment, earnings, and hours, by SIC 1- to 4-digit industry, monthly 1989-Feb 1992, annual rpt, 6744–4
Exports and imports between US and outlying areas, by detailed commodity and mode of transport, 1991, annual rpt, 2424–11
Exports and imports of US, by Harmonized System 6-digit commodity and country, 1991, annual rpt, 2424–13
Exports of US, detailed Schedule B commodities with countries of destination, 1991, annual rpt, 2424–10
Injuries from use of consumer products, by severity, victim age, and detailed product, 1991, annual rpt, 9164–6
Input-output structure of US economy, detailed interindustry transactions for 541 industries, and components of final demand, 1982 benchmark data, 2708–17
Manufacturing annual survey, 1990: finances and operations, by SIC 2- to 4-digit industry, series, 2506–14
Manufacturing census, 1987: concentration of largest firms measured by value added, and for shipments by SIC 2- and 4-digit industry, subject rpt, 2497–6
Manufacturing census, 1987: shipments of manufacturers products, by customer class and SIC 2- and 4-digit industry, subject rpt, 2497–4
Occupational injury and illness rates, by SIC 2- to 4-digit industry, 1989-90, annual rpt, 6844–7
Occupational injury and illness rates, by SIC 2- to 4-digit industry, 1990, annual rpt, 6844–1
Price indexes (producer), by stage of processing and detailed commodity, monthly rpt, 6762–6
Price indexes (producer), by stage of processing and detailed commodity, monthly 1991, annual rpt, 6764–2
Shipments of vending machines by product, trade, and use, 1991, Current Industrial Rpt, 2506–12.10
Tax (income) returns of sole proprietorships, income statement items, by industry group, 1990, annual article, 8302–2.317
Thefts, and value of property stolen and recovered, by property type, 1991, annual rpt, 6224–2.1

Veneman, Ann M.
"Turning Environmental Needs into Farm Opportunities", 1504–9.1

Venereal diseases
see Sexually transmitted diseases

Venezuela
Agricultural trade by commodity and country, prices, and world market devs, monthly rpt, 1922–12
Agricultural trade of US, by detailed commodity and country, 1991, annual rpt, 1524–8

Agricultural trade of US, by detailed commodity and country, 1991, semiannual rpt, 1522–4
AID economic aid to developing countries, obligations and disbursements by country, quarterly rpt, 9912–4
AID loans repayment status and terms by program and country, and status of predecessor agency loans, quarterly rpt, 9912–3
Cuba trade, by commodity and country, mid 1980s-91, 9118–8
Debt burden indicators for 8 developing countries, alternative projections 1991-2000 and trends from 1974, technical paper, 9366–7.271
Economic and military aid and loans from US and intl agencies, by program and country, FY46-91, annual rpt, 9914–5
Economic and monetary trends, compounded annual rates of change and annual indicators for US and 15 trading partners, quarterly rpt, annual supplement, 9391–7
Economic and social conditions of developing countries from 1960s, and Intl Dev Cooperation Agency and AID activities and funding, FY91-93, annual rpt, 9904–4
Economic and social conditions, resources, and trade, and aid, 1992, annual factbook, 9914–14
Economic conditions, policy, and trade practices, by country, 1989-91, annual rpt, 21384–5
Economic, social, political, and geographic summary data, by country, 1992, annual factbook, 9114–2
Exports and imports of US, by commodity and country, 1980-90, world area rpt, 9116–1.7
Exports and imports of US, by Harmonized System 6-digit commodity and country, 1991, annual rpt, 2424–13
Exports and imports of US, by selected country, country group, and commodity group, 1991, annual rpt, 2044–37
Exports and imports of US, by transport mode, country, and SITC 1- to 3-digit commodity, 1991, annual rpt, 2424–12
Exports, imports, and balances of US for manufactured goods, by SITC 2-digit commodity and country, quarterly rpt, 2042–35
Exports, imports, and balances of US with major trading partners, by product category, 1987-91, annual chartbook, 9884–21
Exports, investment, debt, and tariffs of 7 Latin America countries, and trade and investment policy liberalization issues, mid 1960s-91, 9886–4.184
Exports of US, detailed Schedule B commodities with countries of destination, 1991, annual rpt, 2424–10
Ferrosilicon from 6 countries, injury to US industry from foreign subsidized and less than fair value imports, investigation with background financial and operating data, 1992 rpt, 9886–19.84
Human rights conditions in 170 countries, and US economic and military aid, 1991, annual rpt, 21384–3
Imports of goods, services, and investment from US, trade barriers, impacts, and US actions, by country, 1991, annual rpt, 444–2
Intl transactions of US with 9 countries, 1989-91, *Survey of Current Business*, monthly rpt, annual table, 2702–1.33
Military aid of US, arms sales, and training programs costs and budget requests, by program, world region, and country, FY91-93, annual rpt, 7144–13
Military spending, arms trade, and force strengths, with govt spending and population, by country, 1979-89, annual rpt, 9824–1
Multinatl US firms and foreign affiliates finances and operations, by industry and country, 1989 benchmark survey, annual rpt, 2704–5
Multinatl US firms foreign affiliates, income statement items by asset size, industry, and country, 1988, biennial article, 8302–2.322
Oil production, and exports and prices for US, by major exporting country, detailed data, monthly rpt with articles, 3162–24
Oil production, and exports and prices for US, by major exporting country, detailed data, monthly 1973-88, 3168–123
Oil production, stocks, use, and trade, by selected country and country group, monthly rpt, 3162–42
Pipes and tubes (welded nonalloy steel) from 6 countries at less than fair value, injury to US industry, investigation with background financial and operating data, 1992 rpt, 9886–14.361
Population size, growth rates, and components of change, by country, projected 1990-2020 and trends from 1950, biennial rpt, 2324–9
Refugee migration, and intl aid programs, by world area and country of origin and asylum, 1991, annual rpt, 7004–15
Steel imports of US under voluntary restraint agreement, by product, customs district, and country, with US industry operating data, quarterly rpt, 9882–13
Steel trade, by product, country, and customs district, with US industry operating data, 1989-June 1992, semiannual rpt, 9882–15
Tax (estate) returns for nonresident aliens, property and tax data, by estate size and decedent country of residence, 1986, article, 8302–2.310
Travel to US and Canada, market analysis with detailed trip and traveler characteristics, 1990-91, country rpt, 2906–2.17
Travel to US and Canada, market analysis with trip and traveler characteristics, 1990-91, country rpt, 2906–2.16
UN voting record and share of votes in agreement with US, by issue, country, and world area, 1991, annual rpt, 7004–18
see also under By Foreign Country in the "Index by Categories"

Ventura, Calif.
see also under By City and By SMSA or MSA in the "Index by Categories"

Ventura, Stephanie J.
"Advance Report of New Data from the 1989 Birth Certificate", 4146–5.125

Venture capital
Minority- and woman-owned businesses and owner characteristics, by industry, employment and sales size, and form of ownership, 1987 survey, 2328–59
Small Business Admin dev company loan program and debenture sale activity, with data by firm, industry div, State, and region, quarterly rpt, 9762–6
Small business financing sources, and business financial data by size, type, and industry, 1980s-90, annual rpt, 9764–6.2
see also Small Business Investment Companies

Vermont
Banks (insured commercial and savings) deposits by instn, State, MSA, and county, as of June 1991, annual regional rpt, 9295–3.1
County Business Patterns, 1990: employment, establishments, and payroll, by SIC 2- to 4-digit industry and county, annual State rpt, 2326–6.47
Deaths and rates, by detailed location, cause, and demographic characteristics, 1989, US Vital Statistics annual rpt, 4144–3.1
Economic indicators for New England States, Fed Reserve 1st District, monthly rpt, 9373–2
Employment, earnings, and hours, by selected SIC 1- to 4-digit industry, State, and for 275 MSAs, 1987-92, 6748–81
Fed Govt spending in States and local areas, by type, State, county, and city, FY91, annual rpt, 2464–3
Fed Govt spending in States, by type, program, agency, and State, FY91, annual rpt, 2464–2
HHS financial aid, by program, recipient, State, and city, FY91, annual regional listing, 4004–3.1
Hospital deaths of Medicare patients, actual and expected rates by diagnosis, and hospital characteristics, by instn, FY90 annual State rpt, 4654–14.47
Housing census, 1990: summary unit characteristics, by householder race and age, county, place, and urban-rural location, State rpt, 2471–1.47
Military prime contract awards, by contractor, service branch, State, and city, FY91, annual rpt, 3544–22
Mineral Industry Surveys, State reviews of production, 1991, preliminary annual rpt, 5614–6
Multinatl firms US affiliates finances and operations, by industry, country of parent firm, and State, 1987, 2708–48
Physicians, by specialty, age, sex, and location of training and practice, 1990, State rpt, 4116–6.47
Population and housing census, 1990: detailed geographic coverage, State CD-ROM, 2551–9.1
Population and housing census, 1990: population and housing characteristics, detailed geographic coverage, State CD-ROM, 2551–10.10
Population and housing census, 1990: summary characteristics, by county, subdiv, and place, State rpt, 2551–7.47
Population census, 1990: population characteristics and living arrangements, by county, place, and urban-rural location, State rpt, 2531–1.47
Smoking laws in Vermont, employers compliance, 1989, article, 4042–3.375
Statistical Abstract of US, 1992 annual data compilation, 2324–1

Water supply in northeastern US, precipitation and stream runoff by station, monthly rpt, 2182–3
White River basin stream recreation use by activity, time, and location, 1987, 1208–400
see also under By State in the "Index by Categories"

Veterans
Agent Orange exposure health effects, literature review, 1990, annual rpt series, 8706–1
Census of Population and Housing, 1990: population and housing characteristics, detailed geographic coverage, State CD-ROM series, 2551–10
Census of Population and Housing, 1990: summary characteristics, by county, subdiv, and place, State rpt series, 2551–7
Deaths during 1986, decedents health condition, services use, habits, and social, employment, and other characteristics, 4147–20.19
Pacific territories population and housing detailed characteristics, by location, 1990 Census of Population and Housing, series, 2551–8
Population and characteristics of veterans, and VA activities and programs, FY91, annual rpt, 8604–3
Population of veterans, by period of service, FY67-91, annual rpt, 8604–5.1
Prisoners and movements, by offense, location, and selected other characteristics, data compilation, 1992 annual rpt, 6064–6.6
Statistical Abstract of US, 1992 annual data compilation, 2324–1.11
Tax exempt organizations and employee plans listed on IRS masterfile, determinations, applications, and rulings, FY91, annual rpt, 8304–3.2
War participants, deaths, veterans living, and compensation and pension recipients, for each US war, 1775-1991, annual rpt, 8604–2
see also Retired military personnel
see also Servicepersons life insurance programs
see also Veterans benefits and pensions
see also Veterans education
see also Veterans employment
see also Veterans health facilities and services
see also Veterans housing
see also Veterans rehabilitation

Veterans Administration
Mortgage applications, dispositions, and secondary loan market sales, by purpose, lender type, and applicant and neighborhood characteristics, 1991, article, 9362–1.307
Private health care providers payments from VA, by VA clinic, FY90, GAO rpt, 26121–474
see also Department of Veterans Affairs

Veterans Benefits Administration
Budget of US, obligations and authority by function, agency, and program, with summaries and analyses, FY93, annual rpt, 104–2

Veterans benefits and pensions
Assistance (financial and nonfinancial) of Fed Govt, 1992 base edition, annual listing, 104–5
Beneficiaries and taxes collected for social insurance programs since 1940, quarterly rpt, 4742–1.4
Benefits overpayment and home loan debts, VA repayment waiver cases and dispositions, FY88-91, hearing, 21768–67
Benefits overpayment recovery and judgment enforcement cases filed in Federal district courts, 1991, annual rpt, 18204–8.14
Budget of US, Bush Admin proposals, with detail for defense budgets, and historical data from FY34, FY93, 108–46
Budget of US, CBO analysis and review of FY93 budget by function, annual rpt, 26304–2
Budget of US, CBO analysis of revenue and spending alternatives and projections of economic indicators, FY93-97, annual rpt, 26304–3
Budget of US, House concurrent resolution, with spending and revenue targets, FY93 and projected to FY97, annual rpt, 21264–2
Budget of US, midsession review of FY93 budget, by function, annual rpt, 104–7
Budget of US, obligations and authority by function, agency, and program, with summaries and analyses, FY93, annual rpt, 104–2
Budget of US, receipts by source, outlays by agency and program, and balances, monthly rpt, 8102–3
Businesses in rural areas, Fed Govt credit assistance by program and county characteristics, 1983-89, 1548–389
Compensation and pension cases of VA, by type of entitlement and period of service, monthly rpt, 8602–5
Disability and death compensation cases of VA, by entitlement type, period of service, and sex, as of Mar 1992, annual rpt, 8604–13
Disability and death compensation cases of VA, by entitlement type, period of service, sex, age, and State, FY90, annual rpt, 8604–7
Expenditures (direct) and employment, by function and level of govt, selected years 1962-87, 10048–53
Expenditures and beneficiaries of VA compensation, health, and rehabilitation programs, FY67-91, annual rpt, 8604–5
Expenditures, coverage, and benefits for social welfare programs, late 1930s-90, annual rpt, 4744–3.3; 4744–3.7
Expenditures for public welfare by program, FY50s-89, annual article, 4742–1.319
Expenditures for public welfare programs, by program type and level of govt, FY65-89, annual article, 4742–1.302
Expenditures for VA programs, by State, county, and congressional district, FY91, annual rpt, 8604–6
Expenditures of Fed Govt in States, by type, program, agency, and State, FY91, annual rpt, 2464–2
Fraud and abuse in VA programs, audits and investigations, 2nd half FY92, semiannual rpt, 8602–1
Govt revenue by source, spending by function, debt, and assets, by level of govt, FY90, annual rpt, 2466–2.2
Homeless persons aid by program and Federal agency, and indicators of need, 1990, annual rpt, 14364–1
Homeless persons aid programs of Fed Govt, program descriptions and funding, by agency and State, FY87-91, annual GAO rpt, 26104–21
Households composition, income, benefits, and labor force status, Survey of Income and Program Participation methodology, working paper series, 2626–10
Income (household, family, and personal), by source, detailed characteristics, and region, 1991, annual Current Population Rpt, 2546–6.76
Insurance (life) for veterans and servicepersons, actuarial analyses of VA programs, 1991, annual rpt, 8604–1
Insurance (life) for veterans and servicepersons, finances and coverage by program and State, 1991, annual rpt, 8604–4
Lands (public) acreage and grants, by State, FY91 and trends, annual rpt, 5724–1.1
Loans and loan guarantees of Fed Govt, outstanding amounts by agency and program, *Treasury Bulletin*, quarterly rpt, 8002–4.11
Military disability retirement cases, by disposition, tenure, and whether receiving VA benefits, 1980s-90, GAO rpt, 26121–470
Natl income and product accounts, comprehensive accounts and components, benchmark revisions, 1929-88, 2708–5
Natl income and product accounts, comprehensive accounts and components, *Survey of Current Business*, monthly rpt, 2702–1.25
Older persons income and sources, by whether OASDI beneficiary, poverty status, and other characteristics, 1990, biennial rpt, 4744–26
Population economic well-being indicators, by selected characteristics and household income and income-to-poverty ratio, 1984, 2546–20.22
R&D funding by Fed Govt, by detailed function, program, and agency, FY91-93, annual rpt, 9627–9
Statistical Abstract of US, 1992 annual data compilation, 2324–1.11
US attorneys civil and criminal cases by type and disposition, and collections, by Federal district, FY91, annual rpt, 6004–2.1; 6004–2.5
VA activities and programs, and veterans characteristics, FY91, annual rpt, 8604–3
Vietnam veterans employment status, by whether served in Southeast Asia, presence and severity of disability, VA programs use, age, race, and occupation, 1991, biennial press release, 6726–1.49
War participants, deaths, veterans living, and compensation and pension recipients, for each US war, 1775-1991, annual rpt, 8604–2
see also Military benefits and pensions
see also Servicepersons life insurance programs
see also Veterans education

see also Veterans health facilities and services
see also Veterans housing

Veterans education

Assistance and other sources of support, with student expenses and characteristics, by instn type and control, 1987 study, series, 4846–3; 4846–5
Assistance under GI Bill and other programs, and participation by period of service and State, annual rpt, discontinued, 8604–9
Benefits overpayment and home loan debts, VA repayment waiver cases and dispositions, FY88-91, hearing, 21768–67
Budget of US, obligations and authority by function, agency, and program, with summaries and analyses, FY93, annual rpt, 104–2
Expenditures and beneficiaries of VA compensation, health, and rehabilitation programs, FY67-91, annual rpt, 8604–5
Expenditures for education by Federal agency, program, and recipient type, and instn spending, 1960s-91, annual rpt, 4824–8
High school class of 1972: community college attendance, by selected characteristics, natl longitudinal study, 1970s-86, 4888–7
Natl income and product accounts, comprehensive accounts and components, benchmark revisions, 1929-88, 2708–5
Natl income and product accounts, comprehensive accounts and components, *Survey of Current Business*, monthly rpt, 2702–1.25
Pell grants and applicants, by tuition, family and student income, instn type and control, and State, 1990/91, annual rpt, 4804–1
Reserves education benefits under GI Bill, eligible personnel and applications by component, 1991, annual rpt, 3544–31.1
Statistical Abstract of US, 1992 annual data compilation, 2324–1.11
Training benefits and participation, and other VA activities, FY91, annual rpt, 8604–3.3
Vietnam veterans labor force status and earnings, by whether served in Southeast Asia, presence and severity of disability, and sociodemographic characteristics 1989, article, 6722–1.326

Veterans employment

Business owner and business characteristics, for minority- and women-owned firms, by industry, employment and sales size, and form of ownership, 1987 survey, 2328–59
Business statistics, detailed data for major industries and economic indicators, 1960-91, *Survey of Current Business* biennial supplement, 2704–1
Disability and death compensation cases of VA, by entitlement type, period of service, and sex, as of Mar 1992, annual rpt, 8604–13
DOT employment, by subagency, occupation, and selected personnel characteristics, FY91, annual rpt, 7304–18
Employment and Training Admin activities, funding, and participant characteristics, by program, FY86-88, annual rpt, 6404–17
Fed Govt civilian employees demographic and employment characteristics, as of Sept 1991, annual article, 9842–1.301
Fed Govt employment of minorities, disabled, and veterans, and years of service, by occupation, age, sex, and agency, as of Sept 1990, biennial rpt, 9844–27
Fed Govt veteran employment by agency, and hiring practices, 1988-91, GAO rpt, 26119–391
Health care services of VA, needs, availability, structure, and funding, 1991 compilation of papers, 8608–9
Mental illness (post-traumatic stress) among veterans by period of service, and VA treatment and rehabilitation program operations and staff, FY91, annual rpt, 8704–6
Small Business Admin loan guarantee program participants finances, operations, characteristics, and views, 1991 survey, 9768–25
Unemployed displaced workers job search and placement aid effectiveness, relation to previous employment and other characteristics, 1979-87 studies, 15496–1.14
Unemployment insurance claims and covered unemployment by program, and extended benefit triggers, by State, weekly rpt, 6402–15
Unemployment insurance claims, by program, weekly press release, 6402–14
VA employment characteristics and activities, FY91, annual rpt, 8604–3.4
Vietnam veterans employment status, by age and race, monthly rpt, 6742–2
Vietnam veterans employment status, by age, monthly press release, 6742–5
Vietnam veterans employment status, by whether served in Southeast Asia, presence and severity of disability, VA programs use, age, race, and occupation, 1991, biennial press release, 6726–1.49
Vietnam veterans employment status, transcripts of BLS Commissioner's monthly testimony, periodic rpt, 23846–4
Vietnam veterans labor force status and earnings, by whether served in Southeast Asia, presence and severity of disability, and sociodemographic characteristics, 1989, article, 6722–1.326

Veterans Health Administration

Agent Orange exposure health effects, literature review, 1990, annual rpt series, 8706–1
Budget of US, obligations and authority by function, agency, and program, with summaries and analyses, FY93, annual rpt, 104–2
Deaths in VA health care facilities, results of quality of care reviews, 1986 and 1989, 8708–1
Geriatric Research, Education and Clinical Centers of VA, activities and finances, FY88, annual rpt, 8704–8
Mental illness (post-traumatic stress) among Persian Gulf veterans and VA program use, by site, 1991, annual rpt, 8704–7
Mental illness (post-traumatic stress) among veterans by period of service, and VA treatment and rehabilitation program operations and staff, FY91, annual rpt, 8704–6
Trainees of VA health care facilities, trainees by detailed program and city, FY91, annual rpt, 8704–4
see also Veterans Health Services and Research Administration

Veterans health facilities and services

Agent Orange exposure cases at VA health centers, and exemptions from copayment requirements, 1989, GAO rpt, 26121–464
AIDS cases at VA health care centers by sex, race, risk factor, and facility, and AIDS prevention and treatment issues, quarterly rpt, 8702–1
Assistance (block and categorical grants) programs for State and local govts, FY91, biennial listing, 10044–8
Assistance (financial and nonfinancial) of Fed Govt, 1992 base edition, annual listing, 104–5
Budget of US, CBO analysis of revenue and spending alternatives and projections of economic indicators, FY93-97, annual rpt, 26304–3
Budget of US, obligations and authority by function, agency, and program, with summaries and analyses, FY93, annual rpt, 104–2
Contracts for sharing health services among VA and non-VA facilities, by service type and region, FY91, annual rpt, 8704–5
Copayment and income eligibility for VA health care services, enforcement and revenue forgone from unreported income, 1987-91, GAO rpt, 26121–479
Deaths in VA health care facilities, results of quality of care reviews, 1986 and 1989, 8708–1
Drug (prescription) prices charged to VA and Fed Govt, by manufacturer and drug, 1990-91, hearing, 21768–68
Drug (prescription) prices charged to wholesalers, retailers, VA, and Fed Govt, for 29 drugs, 1985-91, GAO rpt, 26121–472
Employment of VA health facilities, and turnover, by occupation and location, 1991, annual rpt, 8604–8
Energy use and conservation of VA medical centers, by facility, quarterly rpt, 8602–9
Expenditures and beneficiaries of VA compensation, health, and rehabilitation programs, FY67-91, annual rpt, 8604–5
Expenditures for public welfare by program, FY50s-89, annual article, 4742–1.319
Expenditures for VA programs, by State, county, and congressional district, FY91, annual rpt, 8604–6
Fraud and abuse in VA programs, audits and investigations, 2nd half FY92, semiannual rpt, 8602–1
Geriatric Research, Education and Clinical Centers of VA, activities and finances, FY88, annual rpt, 8704–8
Health care services of VA, needs, availability, structure, and funding, 1991 compilation of papers, 8608–9
Health condition and care indicators, 1950s-90 with health improvement and disease prevention goals for 1990, annual data compilation, 4144–11
Kidney dialysis patients of VA, by treatment location and type, 1986-90, annual rpt, 4654–16.2

Mental health care facilities, staff, and patient characteristics, *Statistical Notes* series, 4506–3
Mental health care facilities, staff, patients, and finances, 1970s-91, biennial rpt, 4094–1
Mental illness (post-traumatic stress) among Persian Gulf veterans and VA program use, by site, 1991, annual rpt, 8704–7
Mental illness (post-traumatic stress) among veterans by period of service, and VA treatment and rehabilitation program operations and staff, FY91, annual rpt, 8704–6
Natl income and product accounts, comprehensive accounts and components, benchmark revisions, 1929-88, 2708–5
Natl income and product accounts, comprehensive accounts and components, *Survey of Current Business*, monthly rpt, 2702–1.25
Patients, visits, costs, and operating beds, by VA and contract facility, and region, quarterly rpt, 8602–4
Private health care providers payments from VA, by VA clinic, FY90, GAO rpt, 26121–474
Quality assurance standards of accreditation commission, VA hospitals compliance, by facility and region, 1989-90, GAO rpt, 26121–441
Statistical Abstract of US, 1992 annual data compilation, 2324–1.11
Trainees of VA health care facilities, trainees by detailed program and city, FY91, annual rpt, 8704–4
VA activities and programs, and veterans characteristics, FY91, annual rpt, 8604–3
VA health care services, needs, availability, structure, and funding, findings and recommendations, 1991 rpt, 8608–8
see also Military health facilities and services
see also Veterans benefits and pensions
see also Veterans rehabilitation

Veterans Health Services and Research Administration
AIDS cases at VA health care centers by sex, race, risk factor, and facility, and AIDS prevention and treatment issues, quarterly rpt, 8702–1
Contracts for sharing health services among VA and non-VA facilities, by service type and region, FY91, annual rpt, 8704–5
Health care staff and salary of VHSRA, by pay system and occupational group, 1991, annual rpt, 9844–6.3
Hearing aid performance test results, by make and model, 1992 annual rpt, 8704–3
see also Veterans Health Administration

Veterans hospitals
see Veterans health facilities and services

Veterans housing
American Housing Survey: unit and households detailed characteristics, and unit and neighborhood quality, MSA rpt series, 2485–6
Budget of US, obligations and authority by function, agency, and program, with summaries and analyses, FY93, annual rpt, 104–2
Business statistics, detailed data for major industries and economic indicators, 1960-91, *Survey of Current Business* biennial supplement, 2704–1
Expenditures for VA programs, by State, county, and congressional district, FY91, annual rpt, 8604–6
Expenditures of Fed Govt in States, by type, program, agency, and State, FY91, annual rpt, 2464–2
Mortgage loan activity, by type of lender, loan, and mortgaged property, quarterly press release, 5142–30
Mortgage loan activity of VA, defaults, and property acquired, FY67-91, annual rpt, 8604–5.3
Mortgage loans guaranteed by VA, and other activities, FY91, annual rpt, 8604–3.3
Mortgages FHA-insured for 1-family units, by loan type and mortgage characteristics, quarterly rpt, 5142–45
New single and multifamily units, by structural and financial characteristics, inside-outside MSAs, and region, 1987-91, annual rpt, 2384–1
New single-family houses sold and sales price by type of financing, monthly rpt, quarterly tables, 2382–3.2
Statistical Abstract of US, 1992 annual data compilation, 2324–1.11
VA benefit overpayment and home loan debt repayment waiver cases and dispositions, FY88-91, hearing, 21768–67

Veterans loans
see Veterans benefits and pensions
see Veterans housing

Veterans pensions
see Veterans benefits and pensions

Veterans rehabilitation
Expenditures and beneficiaries of VA compensation, health, and rehabilitation programs, FY67-91, annual rpt, 8604–5
Expenditures for VA programs, by State, county, and congressional district, FY91, annual rpt, 8604–6
Health care facilities of VA, trainees by detailed program and city, FY91, annual rpt, 8704–4
Mental illness (post-traumatic stress) among Persian Gulf veterans and VA program use, by site, 1991, annual rpt, 8704–7
Mental illness (post-traumatic stress) among veterans by period of service, and VA treatment and rehabilitation program operations and staff, FY91, annual rpt, 8704–6
Patients, visits, costs, and operating beds, by VA and contract facility, and region, quarterly rpt, 8602–4
VA activities and programs, and veterans characteristics, FY91, annual rpt, 8604–3
VA health care facilities physicians, dentists, and nurses, by selected employment characteristics and VA district, quarterly rpt, 8602–6
VA health care services, needs, availability, structure, and funding, 1991 compilation of papers, 8608–9

Veterinary medicine
Bovine somatotropin (bST) dairy industry use, effectiveness of FDA testing for human and animal safety, 1991, GAO rpt, 26131–101
Cattle tuberculosis cases and cooperative Federal-State eradication activities, by State, FY90-91, annual rpt, 1394–13
Cooperatives, finances, operations, activities, and membership, 1950s-89, commodity rpt, 1126–1.7
County Business Patterns, 1989: employment, establishments, and payroll, by SIC 2- to 4-digit industry and county, annual State rpt series, 2326–8
County Business Patterns, 1990: employment, establishments, and payroll, by SIC 2- to 4-digit industry and county, annual State rpt series, 2326–6
Dairy Herd Improvement Program cooperatives and cows tested, by State, 1990, annual rpt, 1124–1
Degrees awarded in higher education, by level, field, race, and sex, 1989/90 and trends from 1980/81, annual rpt, 4844–17
Drug (veterinary) PPI, monthly rpt, 6762–6
Drug (veterinary) PPI, monthly 1991, annual rpt, 6764–2
Drug shipments, trade, and use, by product, 1991, annual Current Industrial Rpt, 2506–8.5
Education in science and engineering, grad programs enrollment by field, source of funds, and characteristics of student and instn, 1990, annual rpt, 9627–7
Farm production itemized costs, by farm sales size and region, 1991, annual rpt, 1614–3
Farm production itemized costs, receipts, and returns, by commodity and region, 1988-90, annual rpt, 1544–20
FDA investigations and regulatory activities, quarterly rpt, 4062–3
Foreign countries agricultural research grants of USDA, by program, subagency, and country, FY92, annual listing, 1954–3
Health condition and care indicators, 1950s-90 with health improvement and disease prevention goals for 1990, annual data compilation, 4144–11
Injuries from use of consumer products, by severity, victim age, and detailed product, 1991, annual rpt, 9164–6
Lab animals protection, licensing, and inspection activities of USDA, by State, FY90, annual rpt, 1394–10
Labor demand, turnover, and training completions, by detailed occupation, 1990 and projected to 2005, biennial rpt, 6744–3
Labor supply and education of health professionals, by professional and other characteristics, and location, 1960s-92 and projected to 2020, biennial rpt, 4114–8
Military health care personnel, and accessions by training source, by occupation, specialty, and service branch, FY90, annual rpt, 3544–24
Natl Veterinary Services Labs activities, biologic drug products evaluation and disease testing, FY91, annual rpt, 1394–17
Occupational Outlook Handbook, 1992-93, biennial rpt, 6744–1
Rabies vaccination schedules and dosages for pets and livestock by species, and disease outbreak control, CDC recommendations, 1992 rpt, 4206–2.57
Research (agricultural) funding and staffing for USDA, State agencies, and other instns, by topic, FY91, annual rpt, 1744–2
Research and education grants, USDA competitive awards by program and recipient, FY91, annual listing, 1764–1

Tax (income) returns of corporations, income and tax items by asset size and detailed industry, 1989, annual rpt, 8304–4; 8304–21
Tax (income) returns of sole proprietorships, income statement items, by industry group, 1990, annual article, 8302–2.317; 8302–2.320
see also Animal diseases and zoonoses

Veum, Jonathan R.
"Interrelation of Child Support, Visitation, and Hours of Work", 6722–1.329
"Potential Effects of Mandatory Child Support Programs on Poverty", 6886–6.87

Vice Presidency of the U.S.
see Office of the Vice President

Vickery, Connie E.
"Development and Supermarket Field Testing of Videotaped Nutrition Messages for Cancer Risk Reduction", 4042–3.371

Vicksburg, Miss.
Freight (waterborne domestic and foreign) by commodity, traffic, and passengers, by port and waterway, 1989, annual rpt, 3754–3.2

Video recordings and equipment
AIDS prevention program for minority youth, interactive videodisc presentation effectiveness, 1992 article, 4042–3.332
Exports, imports, tariffs, and industry operating data for TV receivers and video monitors, 1992 rpt, 9885–12.1
Fed Govt audiovisual activities and spending, by whether performed in-house and agency, FY91, annual rpt, 9514–1
Libraries (public) finances, staff, and operations, by State and population size, 1990, annual rpt, 4824–6
Natl Archives and Records Admin activities, finances, holdings, and staff, FY91, annual rpt, 9514–2
Price indexes (producer), by stage of processing and detailed commodity, monthly rpt, 6762–6
Price indexes (producer), by stage of processing and detailed commodity, monthly 1991, annual rpt, 6764–2
Shipments, trade, use, and firms, for consumer electronics by product, 1991, annual Current Industrial Rpt, 2506–12.20
Shipments, trade, use, and firms, for electronic communications systems and related products, 1991, annual Current Industrial Rpt, 2506–12.35
Statistical Abstract of US, 1992 annual data compilation, 2324–1.7

Vietnam
Agricultural trade of US, by detailed commodity and country, 1991, annual rpt, 1524–8
Agricultural trade of US, by detailed commodity and country, 1991, semiannual rpt, 1522–4
AID loans repayment status and terms by program and country, and status of predecessor agency loans, quarterly rpt, 9912–3
Economic and military aid and loans from US and intl agencies, by program and country, FY46-91, annual rpt, 9914–5
Economic and social conditions of developing countries from 1960s, and Intl Dev Cooperation Agency and AID activities and funding, FY91-93, annual rpt, 9904–4
Economic, social, political, and geographic summary data, by country, 1992, annual factbook, 9114–2
Export licensing, monitoring, and enforcement activities, FY91, annual rpt, 2024–1
Exports and imports of US, by transport mode, country, and SITC 1- to 3-digit commodity, 1991, annual rpt, 2424–12
Exports and imports of US with Communist and transitional economy countries, by detailed commodity and country, quarterly rpt with articles, 9882–2
Food supply, needs, and aid for developing countries, status and alternative forecasts, 1992 world area rpt, 1526–8.2
Human rights conditions in 170 countries, and US economic and military aid, 1991, annual rpt, 21384–3
Military spending, arms trade, and force strengths, with govt spending and population, by country, 1979-89, annual rpt, 9824–1
Minerals Yearbook, Vol 3, 1989: foreign country review of production, trade, and policy, by commodity, annual rpt, 5604–35.2
Population size, components of change, and selected characteristics, for Vietnam, 1979, 1989, and projected to 2050, 2326–18.65
Population size, growth rates, and components of change, by country, projected 1990-2020 and trends from 1950, biennial rpt, 2324–9
Refugee arrivals in US by world area of origin and State of settlement, and Federal aid, FY91-92 and proposed FY93 allocations, annual rpt, 7004–16
Refugee migration, and intl aid programs, by world area and country of origin and asylum, 1991, annual rpt, 7004–15
Refugees from Indochina, arrivals, and departures, by country of origin and resettlement, camp, and ethnicity, monthly rpt, 7002–4
UN voting record and share of votes in agreement with US, by issue, country, and world area, 1991, annual rpt, 7004–18

Villarino, Margarita E.
"Multidrug-Resistant Tuberculosis Challenge to Public Health Efforts To Control Tuberculosis", 4042–3.362

Villezca-Becerra, Pedro A.
"State-Level Output Supply and Input Demand Elasticities for Agricultural Commodities", 1502–3.303

Vincennes, Ind.
Wages by occupation, and benefits for office and plant workers, 1992 survey, periodic MSA rpt, 6785–3.4

Vincent, Jeffrey R.
"Labor Demand by Forest Products Industries: A Review", 1208–416

Violence
Crimes, by characteristics of victim and offender, circumstances, and location, data compilation, 1992 annual rpt, 6064–6.3
Health condition and care indicators, 1950s-90 with health improvement and disease prevention goals for 1990, annual data compilation, 4144–11
Indian and Alaska Native youth health condition and behavioral patterns, by sex and grade, 1988-90, 4088–3
Prevention of accidental injury and death, and treatment, 1991 conf papers, 4208–35
see also Assassination
see also Assault
see also Assaults on police
see also Child abuse and neglect
see also Crime and criminals
see also Domestic violence
see also Homicide
see also Rape
see also Riots and disorders
see also Terrorism
see also Vandalism
see also War
see also War casualties

Virgin Islands
see British Virgin Islands
see U.S. Virgin Islands

Virginia
Appalachian Regional Commission funding, by project and State, planned FY92, annual rpt, 9084–3
Apple production, marketing, and prices, for Appalachia and compared to other States, 1989-92, annual rpt, 1311–13
Banks (insured commercial), Fed Reserve 5th District members financial statements, by State, quarterly rpt, 9389–18
Banks (insured commercial and savings) deposits by instn, State, MSA, and county, as of June 1991, annual regional rpt, 9295–3.2
Blue Ridge Parkway impacts on local economic conditions and employment, by expense type, 1987, 7556–8.4
Blue Ridge Parkway traffic accidents, deaths, and circumstances, 1984-87, 7556–8.2
Coal production and mines by county, prices, productivity, miners, and reserves, by mining method and State, 1990-91, annual rpt, 3164–25
County Business Patterns, 1990: employment, establishments, and payroll, by SIC 2- to 4-digit industry and county, annual State rpt, 2326–6.48
Deaths and rates, by detailed location, cause, and demographic characteristics, 1989, US Vital Statistics annual rpt, 4144–3.1
Economic indicators by State, Fed Reserve 5th District, quarterly rpt, 9389–16
Employment and housing indicators by State, FHLB 4th District, quarterly rpt, 9302–36
Employment, earnings, and hours, by selected SIC 1- to 4-digit industry, State, and for 275 MSAs, 1987-92, 6748–81
Fed Govt spending in States and local areas, by type, State, county, and city, FY91, annual rpt, 2464–3
Fed Govt spending in States, by type, program, agency, and State, FY91, annual rpt, 2464–2
HHS financial aid, by program, recipient, State, and city, FY91, annual regional listing, 4004–3.3
Home health care for Medicare and non-Medicare patients, services use and nursing visits, for Virginia, 1983-85, article, 4652–1.302
Hospital deaths of Medicare patients, actual and expected rates by diagnosis, and hospital characteristics, by instn, FY90 annual State rpt, 4654–14.48

Housing census, 1990: summary unit characteristics, by householder race and age, county, place, and urban-rural location, State rpt, 2471–1.48
Lumber (industrial roundwood) production in Virginia, shipments, and residue volume, by species, product, and location, 1987-89, 1208–138
Military prime contract awards, by contractor, service branch, State, and city, FY91, annual rpt, 3544–22
Mineral Industry Surveys, State reviews of production, 1991, preliminary annual rpt, 5614–6
Multinatl firms US affiliates finances and operations, by industry, country of parent firm, and State, 1987, 2708–48
Physicians, by specialty, age, sex, and location of training and practice, 1990, State rpt, 4116–6.48
Population and housing census, 1990: detailed geographic coverage, State CD-ROM, 2551–9.5
Population and housing census, 1990: population and housing characteristics, detailed geographic coverage, State CD-ROM, 2551–10.57
Population and housing census, 1990: summary characteristics, by county, subdiv, and place, State rpt, 2551–7.48
Population census, 1990: population characteristics and living arrangements, by county, place, and urban-rural location, State rpt, 2531–1.48
Statistical Abstract of US, 1992 annual data compilation, 2324–1
Timber in Virginia, oak decline disease incidence and losses, 1986, 1208–384
Timber in Virginia, resources, growth, and removals, by species, ownership, treatment, and county, 1990-92, series, 1206–6
Water (groundwater) supply, quality, chemistry, and use, 1985 and 1987, State rpt, 5666–28.20
Water supply and quality in streams and lakes, and groundwater levels in wells, by drainage basin, 1990, annual State rpt, 5666–10.43
see also Alexandria, Va.
see also Arlington, Va.
see also Fairfax County, Va.
see also Loudoun County, Va.
see also Newport News, Va.
see also Norfolk, Va.
see also Prince William County, Va.
see also Virginia Beach, Va.
see also under By State in the "Index by Categories"

Virginia Beach, Va.
Housing starts and completions authorized by building permits in 40 MSAs, quarterly rpt, 2382–9

Visakorpi, Tapio
"Small Subgroup of Aggressive, Highly Proliferative Prostatic Carcinomas Defined by p53 Accumulation", 4472–1.322

Visalia, Calif.
Wages by occupation, and benefits for office and plant workers, 1991 survey, periodic MSA rpt, 6785–12.1
see also under By City and By SMSA or MSA in the "Index by Categories"

Visher, Christy
"Comparison of Urinalysis Technologies for Drug Testing in Criminal Justice", 6068–247

Vision
Election polling places accessibility and services availability for aged and disabled, by State, 1990 natl elections, hearing, 21428–11
see also Blind
see also Eye diseases and defects
see also Optometry

Vissage, John S.
"Forest Statistics for Louisiana Parishes, 1991", 1206–35.12

VISTA
Activities and funding of ACTION, by program, FY91, annual rpt, 9024–2

Vital statistics
Data collection for health and vital statistics, and use for planning and evaluation, 1991 biennial conf, 4164–2
Foreign and US health data collection and availability, by country, 1991, biennial listing, 4124–8
Foreign countries economic and social conditions, working paper series, 2326–18
Foreign countries population size, growth rates, and components of change, by country, projected 1990-2020 and trends from 1950, biennial rpt, 2324–9
Health condition and care indicators, 1950s-90 with health improvement and disease prevention goals for 1990, annual data compilation, 4144–11
Natl Vital and Health Statistics Committee activities, FY91, annual narrative rpt, 4164–1
Palau admin, and social, economic, and govtl data, FY91, annual rpt, 7004–6
Statistical Abstract of US, 1992 annual data compilation, 2324–1.2
Survey programs and data collection procedures, Vital and Health Statistics series, 4147–1
Vital and Health Statistics series: advance data rpts, 4146–8
Vital and Health Statistics series and other NCHS rpts, 1990-91, annual listing, 4124–1
Vital and Health Statistics series: methodology, survey design, and data evaluation, 4147–2
Vital and Health Statistics series: natality, marriage, and divorce trends, 4147–21
Vital and Health Statistics series: reprints of advance data rpts, 4147–16
Vital statistics, preliminary 1990-91 and trends from 1960, annual rpt, 4144–7
Vital statistics provisional data, monthly rpt, 4142–1
Vital statistics provisional data, supplements to monthly rpts, series, 4146–5
see also Births
see also Child mortality
see also Deaths
see also Fertility
see also Infant mortality
see also Life expectancy
see also Marriage and divorce

Vitamins and nutrients
Cancer (breast) risk of postmenopausal women relation to dietary fat and other nutrient intake, 1986-89, article, 4472–1.328
Cancer (colorectal) risk relation to diet, for men, 1986-88, article, 4472–1.302
Cancer (colorectal) risk relation to dietary fiber, vitamin C, and beta carotene, 1992 article, 4472–1.358
Cancer (colorectal) risk relation to serum a-tocopherol levels, 1960s-82, article, 4472–1.308
Consumer research, food marketing, legislation, and regulation devs, and consumption and price trends, quarterly journal, 1541–7
Consumption of food, dietary composition, and nutrient intake, natl survey methodology changes and sample results, 1990 rpt, 1358–6
Exports and imports between US and outlying areas, by detailed commodity and mode of transport, 1991, annual rpt, 2424–11
Exports and imports of US, by country and detailed commodity, monthly rpt, 2422–12
Exports and imports of US, by Harmonized System 6-digit commodity and country, 1991, annual rpt, 2424–13
Exports of US, detailed Schedule B commodities with countries of destination, 1991, annual rpt, 2424–10
Folic acid supplements prenatal use to prevent spina bifida and other neural tube birth defects, findings and CDC recommendations, 1992 rpt, 4206–2.64
Food composition, detailed data on nutrients, calories, and waste, for raw, processed, and prepared foods, series, 1356–3
Health condition and behaviors correlation with vitamin supplement use, local area study, 1992 article, 4042–3.373
Manufacturing annual survey, 1990: value of shipments, by SIC 4- to 5-digit product class, 2506–14.1
Maternal and child health indicators and services use, by age, race, and poverty status, 1988, 4478–197
NIH nutrition biomedical and behavioral research and training activities and funding, by inst, FY90, annual rpt, 4434–15
Price indexes (producer), by stage of processing and detailed commodity, monthly rpt, 6762–6
Price indexes (producer), by stage of processing and detailed commodity, monthly 1991, annual rpt, 6764–2
Production and sales of synthetic organic chemicals, and manufacturer listing, by product, 1990, annual rpt, 9884–3
Rice treated with vitamins and other additives, 1988/89, biennial rpt, 1564–11
Shipments, trade, and use of drugs, by product, 1991, annual Current Industrial Rpt, 2506–8.5
Statistical Abstract of US, 1992 annual data compilation, 2324–1.3
see also Cholesterol

Vlahov, David
"Bacterial Infections and Skin Cleaning Prior to Injection Among Intravenous Drug Users", 4042–3.361

Vocational education and training
Condition of Education, detail for elementary, secondary, and higher education, 1920s-91 and projected to 2002, annual rpt, 4824–1

County Business Patterns, 1989: employment, establishments, and payroll, by SIC 2- to 4-digit industry and county, annual State rpt series, 2326–8
County Business Patterns, 1990: employment, establishments, and payroll, by SIC 2- to 4-digit industry and county, annual State rpt series, 2326–6
Digest of Education Statistics, 1992 annual data compilation, 4824–2
Eighth grade class of 1988: educational performance and conditions, characteristics, attitudes, activities, and plans, natl longitudinal survey, series, 4826–9
Elementary and secondary education enrollment, staff, finances, operations, programs, and policies, 1987/88 biennial survey, series, 4836–3
Enrollment, by grade, instn type and control, and student characteristics, 1989 and trends from 1947, annual Current Population Rpt, 2546–1.459
Enrollment in public elementary and secondary schools, and facilities, by State, 1990/91, annual rpt, 4834–17
Enrollment in vocational education, and academic and other credits earned, by subject and student characteristics, high school classes of 1982 and 1987, 4838–50
Enrollment in vocational education, student and teacher characteristics, and outcomes, for secondary and postsecondary instns, 1970s-90, 4828–42
Foreign countries labor conditions, union coverage, and work accidents, annual country rpt series, 6366–4
Homeless adults educational services, program activities, and participation, by State, FY88-89, annual rpt, 4804–39
Homeless persons aid programs of Fed Govt, program descriptions and funding, by agency and State, FY87-91, annual GAO rpt, 26104–21
Homeless persons transitional housing and support services program, outcome relation to client characteristics and services, FY87-90, GAO rpt, 26113–549
Indian education funding of Fed Govt, with enrollment, program grants, and fellowships by State, 1980s-FY91, annual rpt, 14874–1
Juvenile facilities compensatory education programs activities, participant and staff characteristics, and outcomes, 1991 rpts, 4808–40
Juvenile facilities population, by resident characteristics and facility type, late 1970s-89, 6068–250
Juvenile facilities population, by resident characteristics and facility type, 1977-89, annual rpt, 6064–35
Labor laws enacted, by State, 1991, annual article, 6722–1.309
Occupation training completions, and labor demand and turnover, by detailed occupation, 1990 and projected to 2005, biennial rpt, 6744–3
Occupational injury and illness rates, by SIC 2- to 4-digit industry, 1989-90, annual rpt, 6844–7
Occupational injury and illness rates, by SIC 2- to 4-digit industry, 1990, annual rpt, 6844–1
Occupational Outlook Handbook, 1992-93, biennial rpt, 6744–1
Occupational qualification and skill improvement training, workers participating by training source, occupation, age, sex, and race, 1991, 6728–32
Pacific territories population and housing detailed characteristics, by location, 1990 Census of Population and Housing, series, 2551–8
Teachers of vocational education, by subject area and selected characteristics, for public high schools, 1987/88, 4836–3.9
Veterans education benefits and job training, and other VA activities, FY91, annual rpt, 8604–3.3
see also Adult education
see also Apprenticeship
see also Employee development
see also Federal aid to vocational education
see also Industrial arts
see also Manpower training programs
see also Prison work programs
see also Sheltered workshops
see also Vocational guidance
see also Vocational rehabilitation

Vocational guidance
Employment and Training Admin activities, funding, and participant characteristics, by program, FY86-88, annual rpt, 6404–17
Occupational Outlook Handbook, 1992-93, biennial rpt, 6744–1
Occupational Outlook Quarterly, journal, 6742–1
Teachers of vocational education, by subject area and selected characteristics, for public high schools, 1987/88, 4836–3.9

Vocational rehabilitation
Blind-operated vending facilities on Federal and non-Federal property, finances and operations by agency and State, FY91, annual rpt, 4944–2
Disabled persons work experience following OASDI benefit award, by selected characteristics, 1980s, article, 4742–1.312
Disabled workers labor force status, type and cause of disability, and other characteristics, 1970s-89, chartbook, 4948–11
Education (special) enrollment by age, staff, funding, and needs, by type of handicap and State, 1990/91, annual rpt, 4944–4
Expenditures for public welfare by program, FY50s-89, annual article, 4742–1.319
Fed Govt and State rehabilitation activities and funding, FY91, annual rpt, 4944–1
Fed Govt employees compensation costs, and vocational rehabilitation costs and workload, FY82-90, GAO rpt, 26119–381
Govt spending, coverage, and benefits for social welfare programs, late 1930s-90, annual rpt, 4744–3.1
Mentally retarded SSI beneficiaries transitional job training demonstration project participant characteristics, 1985-87, article, 4742–1.301
States vocational rehabilitation agency cases and disposition, by State, FY91 and trends from FY21, annual rpt, 4944–5
Statistical Abstract of US, 1992 annual data compilation, 2324–1.12
Workers compensation laws of States and Fed Govt, 1992 annual rpt, 6504–11
see also Sheltered workshops
see also Veterans rehabilitation

Vogt, Richard L.
"National Survey of State Epidemiologists To Determine the Status of Lyme Disease Surveillance", 4042–3.364

Voith, Richard P.
"Changing Capitalization of CBD-Oriented Transportation Systems: Evidence from Philadelphia, 1970-88", 9387–8.258
"Estimating House Price Appreciation: A Comparison of Methods", 9387–8.284
"Leasing as a Lottery: Implications for Rational Building Surges and Increasing Vacancies", 9387–8.273

Volcanoes
Alaska minerals resources and geologic characteristics, compilation of papers, 1990, annual rpt, 5664–15
Alaska OCS environmental conditions and oil dev impacts, compilation of papers, series, 2176–1
Foreign countries disasters, casualties, damage, and aid by US and others, FY91 and trends from FY64, annual rpt, 9914–12
Incidents and mgmt of disasters and natl security threats, with data by major event and State, 1992 annual rpt, 9434–6
Mount Pinatubo, Philippines, volcanic eruptions, evacuation camps infective disease cases and deaths, 1991, article, 4202–7.320
Natl forests and other land under Forest Service mgmt, acreage by forest and location, 1991, annual rpt, 1204–2
Weather trends and deviations, by world region, 1880s-1990, annual chartbook, 2184–9

Voluntary military service
Budget of DOD, organization, personnel, weapons, and property, by service branch, State, and country, 1992 annual summary rpt, 3504–13
Budget of DOD, personnel needs, costs, and force readiness by service branch, FY93, annual rpt, 3504–1
Enlisted accessions by race, and goals, by sex and service branch, quarterly press release, 3542–7
Enlistments and reenlistment rates, by service branch, FY79-91, annual rpt, 3544–1.2
Enlistments and reenlistment rates, by service branch, quarterly rpt, 3542–14.4
Natl Guard activities, personnel, and facilities, FY91, annual rpt, 3504–22
Reserve forces personnel and equipment strengths, and readiness, by reserve component, FY91, annual rpt, 3544–31
Reserve forces personnel strengths and characteristics, by component, quarterly rpt, 3542–4
see also Selective service

Volunteers
ACTION activities and funding, by program, FY91, annual rpt, 9024–2
Child day care and early childhood education programs availability, demand, use, costs, and provider and enrollee characteristics, 1990 survey, 4808–39
Education data compilation, 1992 annual rpt, 4824–2
Education in Head Start programs, enrollment, funding, and staff, FY91, annual rpt, 4584–5

Foreign countries aid programs of private voluntary agencies, funding, and outlays, by agency, 1990, annual rpt, 9914–9
Forest Service activities and finances, by region and State, FY91, annual rpt, 1204–1
High school and college grads employment status and income, 1992 edition, annual rpt, 4824–2.28
Land Mgmt Bur activities in southwestern US, FY91, annual rpt, 5724–15
Older persons socioeconomic characteristics, 1900s-90 and projected to 2050, biennial chartbook, 12904–1
Peace Corps activities, funding by program, and volunteers, by country, FY93, annual rpt, 9654–1
Statistical Abstract of US, 1992 annual data compilation, 2324–1.12
see also Foster Grandparent Program
see also Retired Senior Volunteer Program
see also Senior Companion Program
see also Student Community Service Program
see also VISTA
see also Voluntary military service

Volunteers in Service to America
see VISTA

Vortac, O. U.
"En Route Air Traffic Controllers' Use of Flight Progress Strips: A Graph-Theoretic Analysis", 7506–10.127

Voting
see Elections

Vroom, Jay J.
"Pesticide Reregistration Dilemma and Its Impact", 1504–9.1

Vroomen, Harry
"Testing for Impacts of Immigration Reform on Farm Employment and Wages", 1561–16.304

Vugia, Duc J.
"Surveillance for Epidemic Cholera in the Americas: An Assessment", 4202–7.310

Vyas, A. D.
"Forecast of Transportation Energy Demand Through the Year 2010", 3008–124

Wade, Alice H.
"Social Security Area Population Projections: 1991", 4706–1.106

Wadsworth, John S.
"Improving Health Care Communication for Persons with Mental Retardation", 4042–3.328

Wage controls
see also Minimum wage

Wage deductions
Child support overdue payments deducted from wages, and employer compliance, by State, FY85-89, 4588–1
Child support overdue payments deducted from wages, interstate enforcement effectiveness, 1991, GAO rpt, 26121–445
see also Employee benefits
see also Social security tax
see also Unemployment insurance tax
see also Withholding tax

Wage surveys
see also Area wage surveys
see also Industry wage surveys
see also National Survey of Professional, Administrative, Technical and Clerical Pay

Wagener, Diane K.
"Trends in Childhood Use of Dental Care Products Containing Fluoride: U.S., 1983-89", 4146–8.222

Wages and salaries
see Agricultural wages
see Earnings, general
see Earnings, local and regional
see Earnings, specific industry
see Educational employees pay
see Federal pay
see Government pay
see Labor costs and cost indexes
see Minimum wage
see Payroll
see Professionals' fees
see State and local employees pay
see Wage deductions

Wagner, Janet
"Economic Dimensions of Household Gift-Giving", 6886–6.90

Wagner, John W.
"Social Security Administration's 10-Percent Sample File of OASDI Beneficiaries", 4742–1.309

Wake Island
Economic, social, political, and geographic summary data, by country, 1992, annual factbook, 9114–2
HHS financial aid, by program, recipient, State, and city, FY91, annual regional listing, 4004–3.9

Wales
see United Kingdom

Walker, James L.
"Haiti Macroeconomic Assessment", 9916–13.3

Walker, Mary B.
"Stochastic Specification in Random Production Models of Cost Minimizing Firms", 9371–10.82

Walkowiak, John T.
"Forest Statistics for Iowa, 1990", 1208–75

Wall coverings
Ceramic floor and wall tiles trade, tariffs, and industry operating data, 1992 rpt, 9885–13.2
Exports and imports between US and outlying areas, by detailed commodity and mode of transport, 1991, annual rpt, 2424–11
Exports and imports of US, by country and detailed commodity, monthly rpt, 2422–12
Exports of US, detailed Schedule B commodities with countries of destination, 1991, annual rpt, 2424–10
Price indexes (producer), by stage of processing and detailed commodity, monthly rpt, 6762–6
Price indexes (producer), by stage of processing and detailed commodity, monthly 1991, annual rpt, 6764–2

Wall, Larry D.
"Choice of Capital Instruments by Banking Organizations", 9371–10.79
"Competition for More Than One Class of Borrowers Using Different Credit-Worthiness Tests", 9371–10.76
"Cost Savings Associated with Bank Mergers", 9371–10.78

Walla Walla, Wash.
Freight (waterborne domestic and foreign) by commodity, traffic, and passengers, by port and waterway, 1989, annual rpt, 3754–3.4

Walnuts
see Nuts

Walsh, Carl E.
"Presidential Popularity, Presidential Policies", 9393–10.17

Walters, W. H.
"Hanford Environmental Dose Reconstruction Project, Literature and Data Review for the Surface-Water Pathway: Columbia River and Adjacent Coastal Areas", 3356–5.8

Wang, Ping
"Money Demand and Relative Prices in Hyperinflations: Evidence from Germany and China", 9371–10.86

War
Black military and civilian DOD personnel, by sex, grade, and period of service, and lists of award recipients, officers, and service academy grads, 1770s-90, 3548–22
Civil War era geographic records for southern US, Natl Archives special collection, 1973 rpt, 9516–1.2
Foreign countries disasters, casualties, damage, and aid by US and others, FY91 and trends from FY64, annual rpt, 9914–12
Participants and casualties in principal US wars, by service branch, 1775-1973, annual rpt, 3544–1.2
Participants and casualties in principal US wars, 1775-1973, annual summary rpt, 3504–13
Participants, deaths, veterans living, and compensation and pension recipients, for each US war, 1775-1991, annual rpt, 8604–2
Statistical Abstract of US, 1992 annual data compilation, 2324–1.11
World War II audiovisual records, Natl Archives special collection, 1981 rpt, 9516–1.3
World War II soldier survey results, questionnaire forms, and related rpts, Natl Archives special collection, 1991 rpt, 9516–1.10
see also Arms control and disarmament
see also Chemical and biological warfare agents
see also Civil defense
see also Military intervention
see also Military invasion and occupation
see also Military science
see also Military strategy
see also National defense
see also Prisoners of war
see also Veterans
see also Veterans benefits and pensions
see also War casualties
see also War crimes
see also War relief

War casualties
Casualties and participants in principal US wars, by service branch, 1775-1973, annual rpt, 3544–1.2
Casualties and participants in principal US wars, 1775-1973, annual summary rpt, 3504–13
Deaths by cause, age, race, and rank, and personnel captured and missing, by service branch, FY91, annual rpt, 3544–40
Deaths, participants, veterans living, and compensation and pension recipients, for each US war, 1775-1991, annual rpt, 8604–2

Foreign countries disasters, casualties, damage, and aid by US and others, FY91 and trends from FY64, annual rpt, 9914–12
Mental illness (post-traumatic stress) among Persian Gulf veterans and VA program use, by site, 1991, annual rpt, 8704–7
Mental illness (post-traumatic stress) among veterans by period of service, and VA treatment and rehabilitation program operations and staff, FY91, annual rpt, 8704–6

War crimes
Kuwait oil fires set by Iraq, pollution levels, disease cases, and US remediation and monitoring spending, 1991 rpt, 9188–117
Kuwait oil fires set by Iraqi forces, air pollution levels by substance and site, as of Mar 1991, 9188–116
Kuwait oil fires set by Iraqi forces, air pollution levels, health effects, intl monitoring activities, and wells affected, 1991, GAO rpt, 26113–566

War prisoners
see Prisoners of war

War relief
Foreign countries disasters, casualties, damage, and aid by US and others, FY91 and trends from FY64, annual rpt, 9914–12
World War I debt to US of foreign govts, by country and program, periodic rpt, 8002–6

Ward, Franklin R.
"California's Forest Products Industry: 1988", 1208–108
"Oregon's Forest Products Industry: 1988", 1208–280

Ward, Nancy I.
"Comparison of Low Birth Weight Among Medicaid Patients of Public Health Departments and Other Providers of Prenatal Care in North Carolina and Kentucky", 4042–3.304

Wards, city
Census Bur data coverage and availability for statistics on counties, cities, and small areas, 1991 rpt, 2326–7.82

Warehouses
Agricultural Stabilization and Conservation Service producer payments, by program and State, 1991, annual table, 1804–12
Alteration and repair spending for commercial and public buildings, by type, size, age, and region, 1989, 2388–4
Arson incidents by whether structure occupied, property value, and arrest rate, by property type, 1991, annual rpt, 6224–2.1
Construction put in place, private and public, by type and region, monthly rpt, annual tables, 2382–4
County Business Patterns, 1989: employment, establishments, and payroll, by SIC 2- to 4-digit industry and county, annual State rpt series, 2326–8
County Business Patterns, 1990: employment, establishments, and payroll, by SIC 2- to 4-digit industry and county, annual State rpt series, 2326–6
Employment, earnings, and hours, by SIC 1- to 4-digit industry, monthly 1989-Feb 1992, annual rpt, 6744–4
Employment of minorities and women, by occupation, SIC 1- to 3-digit industry, State, and MSA, 1991, annual rpt, 9244–1
Energy use in commercial buildings, costs, and conservation, by building characteristics, survey rpt series, 3166–8
Finances of warehouse services, by SIC 2- to 4-digit industry, 1990 survey, annual rpt, 2413–14
Foreign trade zones (US) operations and movement of goods, by zone and commodity, FY90, annual rpt, 2044–30
Input-output structure of US economy, detailed interindustry transactions for 541 industries, and components of final demand, 1982 benchmark data, 2708–17
Multinatl firms US affiliates finances and operations, by industry, country of parent firm, and State, 1987, 2708–48
Occupational injury and illness rates, by SIC 2- to 4-digit industry, 1989-90, annual rpt, 6844–7
Occupational injury and illness rates, by SIC 2- to 4-digit industry, 1990, annual rpt, 6844–1
Oil and fat production, consumption by end use, and stocks, by type, monthly Current Industrial Rpt, 2506–4.4
Statistical Abstract of US, 1992 annual data compilation, 2324–1.21
Tax (income) returns of partnerships, income statement and balance sheet items, by industry group, 1990, annual article, 8302–2.314
Tax (income) returns of sole proprietorships, income statement items, by industry group, 1990, annual article, 8302–2.317; 8302–2.320
Tobacco marketing activity of cooperatives, 1989-91, article, 1122–1.304
Tobacco marketing activity, prices, and sales, by grade, type, market, and State, 1991, annual rpt series, 1319–5
see also Cold storage and refrigeration
see also Grain storage and facilities

Waring, George H.
"Survey of Federally-Funded Marine Mammal Research and Studies, FY74-91", 14734–2

Waring, Kevin, Associates
"Hope Basin Socioeconomic Baseline Study. Alaska Social and Economic Study", 5736–5.16

Warner, Andrew M.
"Did the Debt Crisis Cause the Investment Crisis?", 9366–7.272
"Did the Debt Crisis or the Oil Price Decline Cause Mexico's Investment Collapse?", 9366–7.270
"Does World Investment Demand Determine U.S. Exports?", 9366–7.277

Warren, Debra D.
"Production, Prices, Employment, and Trade in Northwest Forest Industries", 1202–3

Warren, J. Fred
"Dairy Produce, Industry and Trade Summary", 9885–8.3

Warsaw Pact
Military forces reductions and ceilings for NATO and Warsaw Pact under CFE treaty, as of Nov 1990, 9828–1
Military forces reductions and ceilings for NATO and Warsaw Pact under CFE treaty, inspections, and US compliance costs and savings, 1991 hearings, 25388–59
Military spending, arms trade, and force strengths, with govt spending and population, by country, 1979-89, annual rpt, 9824–1

Warshawsky, Mark J.
"Estimates of the Effects of FAS 106 on Corporate Earnings", 9366–6.298
"Factors Contributing to Rapid Growth in National Expenditures on Health Care", 9366–6.296

Warships
see Naval vessels

Washington
see D.C.
see Washington State

Washington County, Md.
Tuberculosis cases, by risk factor, in Washington County, Md, 1975-90, article, 4042–3.319

Washington County, Oreg.
Housing and households characteristics, and unit and neighborhood quality, by MSA location for 11 MSAs, 1986 survey, supplement, 2485–8

Washington Metropolitan Area Transit Authority
Budget of US, authoritative financial statements with appropriations, outlays, and receipts, by category and agency, FY91, annual rpt, 8104–2.2
Budget of US, obligations and authority by function, agency, and program, with summaries and analyses, FY93, annual rpt, 104–2

Washington State
Apple cold storage holdings in Washington, 1989-91, annual rpt, 1631–11
Banks (insured commercial and savings) deposits by instn, State, MSA, and county, as of June 1991, annual regional rpt, 9295–3.6
Birds (northern spotted owl) conservation methods in Pacific Northwest, findings and recommendations, 1990 rpt, 1208–385
Birds (northern spotted owl) conservation methods in Pacific Northwest, timber industry impacts, and Federal and State spending, 1980s-95, 1208–388
Coal production and mines by county, prices, productivity, miners, and reserves, by mining method and State, 1990-91, annual rpt, 3164–25
Coastal areas oil spill in 1988, pollutant levels and impacts on marine biota, by northern Washington site, as of 1990, 5738–38
Coastal areas recreation resources, and impacts of OCS oil and gas dev, for Washington and Oregon, 1983-88, 5738–40
Cranberry production, prices, use, and acreage, for selected States, 1990-91 and forecast 1992, annual rpt, 1621–18.5
Deaths and rates, by detailed location, cause, and demographic characteristics, 1989, US Vital Statistics annual rpt, 4144–3.1
Employment, earnings, and hours, by selected SIC 1- to 4-digit industry, State, and for 275 MSAs, 1987-92, 6748–81
Fed Govt spending in States and local areas, by type, State, county, and city, FY91, annual rpt, 2464–3

Fed Govt spending in States, by type, program, agency, and State, FY91, annual rpt, 2464–2
Fish (salmon) aquaculture activities of Little White Salmon National Fish Hatchery, late 1890s-1980s, 5508–114
Fishing (ocean sport) activities, and catch by species, by angler characteristics and State, 1987-89, annual coastal area rpt, 2166–17.2
Hazelnut production, 1990-92, annual rpt, 1621–18.6
HHS financial aid, by program, recipient, State, and city, FY91, annual regional listing, 4004–3.10
Hospital deaths of Medicare patients, actual and expected rates by diagnosis, and hospital characteristics, by instn, FY90 annual State rpt, 4654–14.49
Housing census, 1990: inventory, occupancy, and costs, State fact sheet, 2326–21.49
Housing census, 1990: summary unit characteristics, by householder race and age, county, place, and urban-rural location, State rpt, 2471–1.49
Indian tribes in Pacific Northwest, OCS oil and gas lease and dev environmental, economic, and cultural impacts, with background data, 1970s-92, 5738–35
Land Mgmt Bur activities and finances, and public land acreage and use, FY91, annual State rpt, 5724–11.2
Lumber (veneer) recovered from Douglas-fir logs and blocks at Oregon and Washington mills, by grade and type, 1981-83 study, 1208–396
Metals (nonferrous) production in 5 western States, and prices, for 5 metals, 1848-1990, 5608–178
Military prime contract awards, by contractor, service branch, State, and city, FY91, annual rpt, 3544–22
Mineral Industry Surveys, State reviews of production, 1991, preliminary annual rpt, 5614–6
Multinatl firms US affiliates finances and operations, by industry, country of parent firm, and State, 1987, 2708–48
Physicians, by specialty, age, sex, and location of training and practice, 1990, State rpt, 4116–6.49
Population and housing census, 1990: detailed geographic coverage, State CD-ROM, 2551–9.9
Population and housing census, 1990: population and housing characteristics, detailed geographic coverage, State CD-ROM, 2551–10.58
Population and housing census, 1990: summary characteristics, by county, subdiv, and place, State rpt, 2551–7.49
Population census, 1990: population characteristics and living arrangements, by county, place, and urban-rural location, State rpt, 2531–1.49
Population, households, employment, income, fuel prices, and electricity demand for Pacific Northwest, alternative forecasts 1991-2010 with trends from 1980, annual rpt, 3224–3.3
Pregnant women smoking, by age and marital status, for Indians in Washington State, mid 1980s, article, 4042–3.306
Radiation and other pollutant releases from DOE contractor research lab and nuclear weapons facilities, monitoring results, 1991 annual site rpt, 3324–2.8
Radiation exposure of population near Hanford, Wash, nuclear plant, with methodology, 1944-91, series, 3356–5
Radioactive low-level waste disposal activities of States and interstate compacts, with data by disposal facility and reactor, 1990, annual rpt, 3004–36
State govt employees comparable worth agreement, compliance costs and indicators of success, for Washington, mid 1980s-93, GAO rpt, 26119–410
Statistical Abstract of US, 1992 annual data compilation, 2324–1
Timber in northwestern US and British Columbia, production, prices, trade, and employment, quarterly rpt, 1202–3
Timber in Pacific Northwest, old-growth forests plant and wildlife population and species diversity, 1991 compilation of papers, 1208–386
Timber in Washington State, acreage and resources by species, ownership class, and county, 1988-89 with harvest trends from 1955, series, 1206–28
Water resources dev projects of Army Corps of Engineers, characteristics, and costs, 1950s-91, biennial State rpt, 3756–2.48
Water supply, and snow survey results, monthly State rpt, 1266–2.9
Water supply, and snow survey results, 1991, annual State rpt, 1264–14.4
see also Kennewick, Wash.
see also King County, Wash.
see also Pierce County, Wash.
see also Richland, Wash.
see also Seattle, Wash.
see also Tacoma, Wash.
see also Vancouver, Wash.
see also Walla Walla, Wash.
see also under By State in the "Index by Categories"

Wasilewski, Edward J., Jr.
"Collective Bargaining in 1992: Contract Talks and Other Activity", 6722–1.306

Waste management
see Hazardous waste and disposal
see Landfills
see Radioactive waste and disposal
see Recycling of waste materials
see Refuse and refuse disposal
see Sewage and wastewater systems

Wastewater treatment
see Sewage and wastewater systems

Watches and clocks
County Business Patterns, 1989: employment, establishments, and payroll, by SIC 2- to 4-digit industry and county, annual State rpt series, 2326–8
County Business Patterns, 1990: employment, establishments, and payroll, by SIC 2- to 4-digit industry and county, annual State rpt series, 2326–6
CPI by component for US city average, and by selected metro area, region, and population size, monthly rpt, 6762–2
Employment, earnings, and hours, by SIC 1- to 4-digit industry, monthly 1989-Feb 1992, annual rpt, 6744–4
Exports and imports between US and outlying areas, by detailed commodity and mode of transport, 1991, annual rpt, 2424–11
Exports and imports of US, by country and detailed commodity, monthly rpt, 2422–12
Exports and imports of US, by Harmonized System 6-digit commodity and country, 1991, annual rpt, 2424–13
Exports and imports of US, by transport mode, country, and SITC 1- to 3-digit commodity, 1991, annual rpt, 2424–12
Exports of US, detailed Schedule B commodities with countries of destination, 1991, annual rpt, 2424–10
Injuries from use of consumer products, by severity, victim age, and detailed product, 1991, annual rpt, 9164–6
Manufacturing annual survey, 1990: finances and operations, by SIC 2- to 4-digit industry, series, 2506–14
Manufacturing census, 1987: concentration of largest firms measured by value added, and for shipments by SIC 2- and 4-digit industry, subject rpt, 2497–6
Manufacturing census, 1987: shipments of manufacturers products, by customer class and SIC 2- and 4-digit industry, subject rpt, 2497–4
Occupational injury and illness rates, by SIC 2- to 4-digit industry, 1989-90, annual rpt, 6844–7
Occupational injury and illness rates, by SIC 2- to 4-digit industry, 1990, annual rpt, 6844–1
OECD trade, total and for 4 major countries, and US trade by country, by commodity, 1980-90, world area rpt series, 9116–1
Price indexes (producer), by stage of processing and detailed commodity, monthly rpt, 6762–6
Price indexes (producer), by stage of processing and detailed commodity, monthly 1991, annual rpt, 6764–2
Science, engineering, and technical employment in manufacturing, by field and industry, 1989, triennial rpt, 9627–23

Water area
Army Corps of Engineers water resources dev projects, characteristics, and costs, 1950s-89, biennial State rpt series, 3756–1
Army Corps of Engineers water resources dev projects, characteristics, and costs, 1950s-91, biennial State rpt series, 3756–2
Coastal and riparian areas environmental conditions, fish, wildlife, use, and mgmt, for individual ecosystems, series, 5506–9
Estuary environmental conditions, research results and methodology, series, 2176–7
Foreign countries economic, social, political, and geographic summary data, by country, 1992, annual factbook, 9114–2
Indian and govt lands under Bur of Indian Affairs mgmt, acreage, leases, and use, 1989, annual rpt, 5704–12
Park natl system and other land under Natl Park Service mgmt, acreage by site, ownership, and region, FY92, semiannual rpt, 5542–1
Park natl system sites acreage and descriptions, 1991, biennial listing, 5544–5
Public lands acreage and use, and Land Mgmt Bur activities and finances, annual State rpt series, 5724–11
Public lands acreage, grants, use, revenues, and allocations, by State, FY91 and trends, annual rpt, 5724–1

Statistical Abstract of US, 1992 annual data compilation, 2324–1.6
Tennessee Valley river control activities, and hydroelectric power generation and capacity, 1990, annual rpt, 9804–7
Water quality, chemistry, hydrology, and other characteristics, local area studies, series, 5666–27
Water supply and quality in streams and lakes, and groundwater levels in wells, by drainage basin, 1990, annual State rpt series, 5666–10
Water supply and quality in streams and lakes, and groundwater levels in wells, by drainage basin, 1990-91, annual CD-ROM, 5664–18
Water supply and quality in streams and lakes, and groundwater levels in wells, by drainage basin, 1991, annual State rpt series, 5666–12
see also Water supply and use

Water fluoridation
Dental caries and baby bottle tooth decay prevalence among Head Start children in southwest US, by characteristics of child and area, 1992 article, 4042–3.317
Health condition and care indicators, 1950s-90 with health improvement and disease prevention goals for 1990, annual data compilation, 4144–11

Water permits
Coastal and riparian areas environmental conditions, fish, wildlife, use, and mgmt, for individual ecosystems, series, 5506–9

Water pollution
Abatement spending by govts, business, and consumers, 1972-90, annual article, 2702–1.321
Abatement spending, capital and operating costs by SIC 2- to 4-digit industry and State, 1990, annual Current Industrial Rpt, 2506–3.6
Agricultural Conservation Program acreage and projects, by State, 1936-90, quinquennial rpt, 1808–1
Agricultural Conservation Program participation and payments, by practice and State, FY91, annual rpt, 1804–7
Agricultural Stabilization and Conservation Service producer payments, by program and State, 1991, annual table, 1804–12
Army Corps of Engineers water resources dev projects, characteristics, and costs, 1950s-89, biennial State rpt series, 3756–1
Army Corps of Engineers water resources dev projects, characteristics, and costs, 1950s-91, biennial State rpt series, 3756–2
Assistance (financial and nonfinancial) of Fed Govt, 1992 base edition, annual listing, 104–5
Birds (least tern and piping plover) and habitat levels of selenium and other pollutants, for Missouri River in South Dakota, 1988-90, 5508–118
Bonneville Power Admin hazardous waste mgmt and environmental protection standards compliance activities, 1991, annual rpt, 3224–6
Coastal and riparian areas environmental conditions, fish, wildlife, use, and mgmt, for individual ecosystems, series, 5506–9
Coastal areas and watersheds pollution indicators, by location, 1980s-90, 2178–35
Disease (waterborne) outbreaks and cases, by type, source, and location, 1989-90, article, 4202–7.301
DOE contractor research lab and nuclear weapons facilities radiation and other pollutant releases, monitoring results, annual site rpt series, 3324–2
Electric utilities privately owned, pollution abatement outlays by type of pollutant and equipment, and firm, 1990, annual rpt, 3164–23
Environmental Quality, status of problems, protection programs, research, and intl issues, 1991 annual rpt, 484–1
EPA pollution control grant program activities, monthly rpt, 9182–8
EPA R&D programs and funding, planned FY92, annual listing, 9184–17
Estuary environmental conditions, research results and methodology, series, 2176–7
Great Lakes Environmental Research Lab activities, FY91 annual rpt, 2144–26
Great Lakes industrial water pollution emissions, comparison of State, EPA, Intl Joint Commission, and Ontario standards, 1991 rpt, 14648–29
Great Lakes Science Advisory Board research activities and water quality goals, FY91, biennial rpt, 14644–6
Great Lakes water quality, and pollution control policy and activities, 1991 biennial rpt, 14644–1
Groundwater pesticide contamination, vulnerability indicators by State and county, 1987-89, GAO rpt, 26131–91
Groundwater supply, quality, chemistry, and use, State and local area rpt series, 5666–28
Groundwater supply, quality, chemistry, other characteristics, and use, regional rpt series, 5666–25
Hazardous waste site remedial action under Superfund, current and proposed sites descriptions and status, periodic listings, series, 9216–3
Health effects of selected pollutants, concentrations in food and environment, sources, human intake, and regulation, series, 9186–8
Health effects of selected pollutants on animals by species and on humans, and environmental levels, series, 5506–14
Industrial hazardous substances releases and reduction methods under EPA regulation, by chemical, source, industry, and location, 1989, annual rpt, 9234–6
Industrial hazardous substances releases and reduction methods under EPA regulation, with chemical stocks and use, facility directory, 1987-89, annual CD-ROM, 9234–7
Industrial water pollution discharge permits, and EPA info system coverage and costs, 1991-92, GAO rpt, 26125–46
Justice Dept enforcement of environmental laws, activities, FY83-92, annual press release, 6004–22
Kuwait oil fires set by Iraq, pollution levels, disease cases, and US remediation and monitoring spending, 1991 rpt, 9188–117
Mink and otter population, breeding, trapping, pollutant levels, and research status, for Great Lakes area, 1991 conf, 14648–27
Natl historic and natural landmarks damaged and threatened, with owner, location, damage type, and recommended remedial action, 1990, annual listing, 5544–16
Pesticide levels and water toxicity indicators, for natl wildlife refuge wetlands in South Dakota, 1990, 5508–117
Quality and supply of water in streams and lakes, and groundwater levels in wells, by drainage basin, 1990, annual State rpt series, 5666–10
Quality and supply of water in streams and lakes, and groundwater levels in wells, by drainage basin, 1990-91, annual CD-ROM, 5664–18
Quality and supply of water in streams and lakes, and groundwater levels in wells, by drainage basin, 1991, annual State rpt series, 5666–12
Quality, chemistry, hydrology, and other characteristics of water, local area studies, series, 5666–27
Radiation and radionuclide concentrations in air, water, and milk, monitoring results by site, quarterly rpt, 9192–5
Radiation exposure of population near commercial reactors, by body site, age group, and selected plant, 1988, annual rpt, 9634–7
Radiation exposure of population near Hanford, Wash, nuclear plant, with methodology, 1944-91, series, 3356–5
Radioactive waste and spent fuel generation, inventory, and disposal, 1960s-90 and projected to 2020, annual rpt, 3364–2
Radionuclide concentrations in air, water, humans, animals, and milk near Nevada and other nuclear test sites, 1990, annual rpt, 9194–17
Radon and other radionuclide levels in air, water, soil, and uranium mill tailings, by site and region, 1950s-80s, compilation of papers, 5668–126
Research on water resources, data collection and analysis activities of USGS Water Resources Div Districts, with project descriptions, series, 5666–26
Rivers dissolved solids and water temperatures, for 6 rivers by monitoring site, monthly rpt, 5662–3
Rural Clean Water Program funding for control of pollution from farming, by region and State, monthly rpt, 1802–14
Salinity control program for Colorado River, participation and payments, FY87-91, annual rpt, 1804–23
Southwestern US streams water quality and fish population impacts of land mgmt and forest fires, 1980s-91, 1208–390
Statistical Abstract of US, 1992 annual data compilation, 2324–1.6
Uranium tailings at inactive mills, remedial action proposals, costs, site characteristics, and environmental, socioeconomic, and health impacts, series, 3356–4
Wetlands acid neutralizing capability for mining runoff, with pollutant levels and site characteristics, for Pennsylvania, 1987-90, 5608–171
see also Eutrophication
see also Food and waterborne diseases
see also Marine pollution

see also Oil spills
Water power
Shipments and firms for fluid power products, by type, 1991, annual Current Industrial Rpt, 2506–12.31
see also Dams
see also Hydroelectric power
Water Resources Council
Budget of US, authoritative financial statements with appropriations, outlays, and receipts, by category and agency, FY91, annual rpt, 8104–2.2
Water resources development
Agricultural and water conservation programs of USDA, cost sharing payments and eligibility requirements, FY88-92, GAO rpt, 26113–572
Agricultural Conservation Program acreage and projects, by State, 1936-90, quinquennial rpt, 1808–1
Agricultural Conservation Program participation and payments, by practice and State, FY91, annual rpt, 1804–7
Agricultural Stabilization and Conservation Service producer payments, by program and State, 1991, annual table, 1804–12
Army Corps of Engineers activities, FY90, annual rpt, 3754–1
Army Corps of Engineers water resources dev projects, characteristics, and costs, 1950s-89, biennial State rpt series, 3756–1
Army Corps of Engineers water resources dev projects, characteristics, and costs, 1950s-91, biennial State rpt series, 3756–2
Army Corps of Engineers water resources dev projects, local sponsors views on cooperation and cost sharing, 1991 survey, GAO rpt, 26113–548
Assistance (block and categorical grants) programs for State and local govts, FY91, biennial listing, 10044–8
Budget of US, obligations and authority by function, agency, and program, with summaries and analyses, FY93, annual rpt, 104–2
Colorado River Storage Project finances and activities in western States, FY91, annual rpt, 5824–3
Conservation of soil and water, USDA funding by program and State, annual rpt, discontinued, 1264–12
Construction put in place (public and private), by type, quarterly rpt, 2042–1.1
Construction put in place, value of new public and private structures, by type, monthly rpt, 2382–4
Electric utilities privately owned, finances and operations, detailed data, 1990, annual rpt, 3164–23
FmHA activities, and loans and grants by program and State, FY91 and trends from FY70, annual rpt, 1184–17
Groundwater supply, quality, chemistry, other characteristics, and use, regional rpt series, 5666–25
Input-output structure of US economy, detailed interindustry transactions for 541 industries, and components of final demand, 1982 benchmark data, 2708–17
Public lands acreage and use, and Land Mgmt Bur activities and finances, annual State rpt series, 5724–11
Reclamation Bur water storage and carriage facilities, capacity, and operating status, as of Sept 1990, biennial listing, 5824–7
Research on water resources, data collection and analysis activities of USGS Water Resources Div Districts, with project descriptions, series, 5666–26
Water Bank program agreements, payments to farmers, and wetlands acreage, by State, monthly rpt, 1802–5
Water Bank Program agreements, payments to farmers, and wetlands acreage, by State, 1972-91, annual rpt, 1804–21
Water quality, chemistry, hydrology, and other characteristics, local area studies, series, 5666–27
Water supply mgmt for surface and groundwater, with groundwater depletion and use by purpose, 1980s, 10048–82
see also Aquaculture
see also Canals
see also Dredging
see also Flood control
see also Hydroelectric power
see also Inland water transportation
see also Irrigation
see also Marine resources
see also Water power
see also Water supply and use
see also Watershed projects
Water supply and use
Army Corps of Engineers activities and projects, FY88 and trends from 1800s, annual rpt, 3754–1.1
Army Corps of Engineers activities and projects, FY89 and trends from 1800s, annual rpt, 3754–1.2
Army Corps of Engineers activities and projects, FY90 and trends from 1800s, annual rpt, 3754–1.3
Army Corps of Engineers water resources dev projects, characteristics, and costs, 1950s-89, biennial State rpt series, 3756–1
Army Corps of Engineers water resources dev projects, characteristics, and costs, 1950s-91, biennial State rpt series, 3756–2
Assistance (financial and nonfinancial) of Fed Govt, 1992 base edition, annual listing, 104–5
Business leaders views on water supply and quality, and use of bottled water and water purification equipment, 1992 survey, article, 9383–19.302
Catfish raised on farms, operations, water use, and acreage, by State, 1990-92, semiannual situation rpt, 1561–15.2
Census of Population and Housing, 1990: summary characteristics, by county, subdiv, and place, State rpt series, 2551–7
Colorado River Basin Federal reservoir and power operations and revenues, 1991-92, annual rpt, 5824–6
Colorado River Storage Project finances and activities in western States, FY91, annual rpt, 5824–3
Colorado water supply, streamflow, precipitation, and reservoir storage, 1992 water year, annual rpt, 1264–13
Consumption of water by end use, well withdrawals, and public supply deliveries, by county, State rpt series, 5666–24
County Business Patterns, 1989: employment, establishments, and payroll, by SIC 2- to 4-digit industry and county, annual State rpt series, 2326–8
County Business Patterns, 1990: employment, establishments, and payroll, by SIC 2- to 4-digit industry and county, annual State rpt series, 2326–6
Criminal sentences for Federal offenses, guidelines by offense and circumstances, series, 17668–1
DC metro area land acquisition and dev projects of Fed Govt, characteristics, funding, and impacts, by agency and project, FY92-96, annual rpt, 15454–1
Developing countries economic and social conditions from 1960s, and Intl Dev Cooperation Agency and AID activities and funding, FY91-93, annual rpt, 9904–4
Environmental Quality, status of problems, protection programs, research, and intl issues, 1991 annual rpt, 484–1
EPA pollution control grant program activities, monthly rpt, 9182–8
Farm production itemized costs, by farm sales size and region, 1991, annual rpt, 1614–3
Freight (waterborne domestic and foreign) by commodity, traffic, and passengers, by port and waterway, 1989, annual rpt, 3754–3
Govt employment and payroll, by function, level of govt, and jurisdiction, annual rpt series, 2466–1
Govt finances, by level of govt, State, and for large cities and counties, annual rpt series, 2466–2
Great Lakes Science Advisory Board research activities and water quality goals, FY91, biennial rpt, 14644–6
Great Lakes water levels, daily and monthly averages by site, 1991 and cumulative from 1900, annual rpt, 2174–3
Groundwater supply, quality, chemistry, and use, State and local area rpt series, 5666–28
Groundwater supply, quality, chemistry, other characteristics, and use, regional rpt series, 5666–25
Housing (rental) units, total, with HUD assistance by program, and eligible for aid, by unit, household, and neighborhood characteristics, and location, 1989, biennial rpt, 5184–11
Housing and households characteristics, and unit and neighborhood quality, by MSA location for 11 MSAs, 1987 survey, supplement, 2485–8
Housing and households detailed characteristics, and unit and neighborhood quality, by location, 1989, biennial rpt supplement, 2485–13
Housing and households detailed characteristics, and unit and neighborhood quality, MSA surveys, series, 2485–6
Housing and population census, 1990: population and housing characteristics, detailed geographic coverage, State CD-ROM series, 2551–10
Input-output structure of US economy, detailed interindustry transactions for 541 industries, and components of final demand, 1982 benchmark data, 2708–17

Iron waterworks compact ductile fittings from PRC at less than fair value, injury to US industry, investigation with background financial and operating data, 1992 rpt, 9886–14.358
Latin America economic and social conditions, resources, trade, and aid, 1992, annual factbook, 9914–14
Minerals offshore lease sales environmental and economic impacts in coastal areas, final statement series, 5736–7
Natl income and product accounts, comprehensive accounts and components, benchmark revisions, 1929-88, 2708–5
Natl income and product accounts, comprehensive accounts and components, *Survey of Current Business*, monthly rpt, 2702–1.28
New Mexico Caballo Resource Area public land mgmt, and grazing, environmental, and leasing activities, FY90-91, annual rpt, 5724–17
Northeastern US water supply, precipitation and stream runoff by station, monthly rpt, 2182–3
Occupational injury and illness rates, by SIC 2- to 4-digit industry, 1989-90, annual rpt, 6844–7
Occupational injury and illness rates, by SIC 2- to 4-digit industry, 1990, annual rpt, 6844–1
Oregon water supply, streamflow by station and reservoir storage, 1992, annual rpt, 1264–9
Pacific territories population and housing detailed characteristics, by location, 1990 Census of Population and Housing, series, 2551–8
Panama Canal water supply and use, FY90-91, annual rpt, 9664–3.2
Public opinion on taxes, spending, and govt efficiency, by respondent characteristics, 1992 survey, annual rpt, 10044–2
Research (agricultural) funding and staffing for USDA, State agencies, and other instns, by topic, FY91, annual rpt, 1744–2
Research and education grants, USDA competitive awards by program and recipient, FY91, annual listing, 1764–1
Research on water resources, data collection and analysis activities of USGS Water Resources Div Districts, with project descriptions, series, 5666–26
Saline water withdrawal and use, for coastal areas, State rpt series, 5666–24
Ship (passenger) sanitary inspection scores, biweekly rpt, 4202–10
Statistical Abstract of US, 1992 annual data compilation, 2324–1.6
Streamflow conditions in US and Puerto Rico, weekly rpt, monthly data, 2182–7
Supply and quality of water in streams and lakes, and groundwater levels in wells, by drainage basin, 1990, annual State rpt series, 5666–10
Supply and quality of water in streams and lakes, and groundwater levels in wells, by drainage basin, 1990-91, annual CD-ROM, 5664–18
Supply and quality of water in streams and lakes, and groundwater levels in wells, by drainage basin, 1991, annual State rpt series, 5666–12
Supply of water in US and southern Canada, streamflow, surface and groundwater conditions, and reservoir levels, by location, monthly rpt, 5662–3
Tax (income) returns of corporations, income and tax items by asset size and detailed industry, 1989, annual rpt, 8304–4; 8304–21
Timber sales of Forest Service, expenses, and operations, by region, State, and natl forest, FY91, annual rpts, 1204–36
Water supply mgmt for surface and groundwater, with groundwater depletion and use by purpose, 1980s, 10048–82
Western US water supply, and snow survey results, annual State rpt series, 1264–14
Western US water supply, and snow survey results, monthly State rpt series, 1266–2
Western US water supply, storage by reservoir and State, and streamflow conditions, as of Oct 1992, annual rpt, 1264–4
Western US water supply, streamflow and reservoir storage forecasts by stream and station, Jan-May monthly rpt, 1262–1
see also Dams
see also Food and waterborne diseases
see also Hydroelectric power
see also Irrigation
see also Reservoirs
see also Water area
see also Water fluoridation
see also Water permits
see also Water pollution
see also Water power
see also Water resources development
see also Watershed projects
see also Weather
see also Wetlands

Watershed projects
Acreage, grants, use, revenues, and allocations, for public lands by State, FY91, annual rpt, 5724–1.2
Agricultural Conservation Program acreage and projects, by State, 1936-90, quinquennial rpt, 1808–1
Agricultural Conservation Program participation and payments, by practice and State, FY91, annual rpt, 1804–7
Army Corps of Engineers activities and projects, FY88 and trends from 1800s, annual rpt, 3754–1.1
Army Corps of Engineers activities and projects, FY89 and trends from 1800s, annual rpt, 3754–1.2
Army Corps of Engineers activities and projects, FY90 and trends from 1800s, annual rpt, 3754–1.3
Army Corps of Engineers water resources dev projects, characteristics, and costs, 1950s-89, biennial State rpt series, 3756–1
Army Corps of Engineers water resources dev projects, characteristics, and costs, 1950s-91, biennial State rpt series, 3756–2
Fires (wild) and acreage burned, by type of land, ownership, cause, region, and State, 1984-90, annual rpt, 1204–4
Forest Service activities and finances, by region and State, FY91, annual rpt, 1204–1.2
Reclamation Bur irrigation activities, finances, and project impacts in western US, 1990, annual rpt, 5824–12

Waterways
see Canals
see Harbors and ports
see Inland water transportation
see Lakes and lakeshores
see Rivers and waterways

Watson, Alan E.
"Effects of the Gates Park Fire on Recreation Choices", 1208–422

Watson, Mark W.
"Business Cycle Durations and Postwar Stabilization of the U.S. Economy", 9375–13.83
"Procedure for Predicting Recessions with Leading Indicators: Econometric Issues and Recent Performance", 9375–13.84

Watson, William D.
"Economic Effects of Western Federal Land-Use Restrictions on U.S. Coal Markets", 5668–125

Wayda, Michael E.
"Index of FAA Office of Aviation Medicine Reports: 1961-91", 7506–10.97

Wayland, Robert H., III
"Overview of Clean Water Legislation", 1504–9.1

Wayne County, Mich.
Housing and households characteristics, unit and neighborhood quality, and journey to work by MSA location, for 11 MSAs, 1985 survey, supplement, 2485–8
Housing and households detailed characteristics, and unit and neighborhood quality, by location, 1989 survey, MSA rpt, 2485–6.2

Wealth
Assets and debts of private sector, balance sheets by segment, 1960-91, semiannual rpt, 9365–4.1
Economic Report of the President for 1992, with economic trends from 1929, annual rpt, 204–1.10
Foreign and US income and capital tax policies, with background data for EC, Japan, and US, mid 1960s-91, article, 9373–1.316
Higher education instn student financial support by parents, by type and funding sources, and student, parent, and instn characteristics, fall 1986, 4846–3.11
Households composition, income, benefits, and labor force status, Survey of Income and Program Participation methodology, working paper series, 2626–10
Households, family, and personal income, wealth, and poverty measures, 1960s-90, Current Population Rpt, chartbook, 2546–6.75
Households net worth distribution under alternative sample weighting systems to account for inconsistency in survey design and response rates, 1992 rpt, 9368–91
Income (household) and wealth distribution by selected characteristics, with foreign comparisons, 1992 compilation of papers, Current Population Rpt, 2546–6.79
Income tax returns of foreign corporations and individuals, and US entities abroad, detailed data compilation, 1970s-89, quinquennial rpt, 8308–31
Minority business Federal procurement set-aside contracts, owners personal assets, 1988, annual rpt, 9764–8
OASDI beneficiary data collection system design compared to earlier surveys, with summary results, 1992 article, 4742–1.313

Older persons economic status compared to other age groups, 1990 and trends from 1947, 4746–26.24
Older persons income by source, for married OASI beneficiaries by work and eligibility pattern of wife, 1982, article, 4746–26.12
Older persons income, net worth, and poverty status, compared to other age groups, 1988-90, article, 4742–1.320
Older population, and health, economic, and other characteristics, with foreign comparisons, 1980s-91 with trends and projections, Current Population Rpt, 2546–2.165
Partnership losses and total income of high-income individuals, by average tax rate, 1985-89, article, 8302–2.313
Personal wealth under alternative measures, by age group, 1984, technical paper, 4746–26.11
Population economic well-being indicators, by selected characteristics and household income and income-to-poverty ratio, 1984, 2546–20.22
Statistical Abstract of US, 1992 annual data compilation, 2324–1.14
Student aid Pell grants and applicants, by tuition, income level, instn type and control, and State, 1990/91, annual rpt, 4804–1
Supplemental Security Income applicants denied benefits because assets exceeded limits by asset type, and later eligibility, 1989, article, 4742–1.317
Tax (estate) returns for nonresident aliens, property and tax data, by estate size and decedent country of residence, 1986, article, 8302–2.310
Tax (estate) returns property and tax data, by size of gross estate and State, 1989-90, article, 8302–2.305
Tax (income) returns of individuals with high incomes, detailed data, 1988, annual rpt, 8304–2
see also Business assets and liabilities, general
see also Business assets and liabilities, specific industry
see also Gross Domestic Product
see also Gross National Product
see also Investments
see also Money supply
see also National income and product accounts
see also Personal and household income
see also Personal debt
see also Poverty
see also Property
see also Savings

Weapons
Arrests, by offense, offender characteristics, and location, 1991, annual rpt, 6224–2.2
Court civil and criminal caseloads for Federal district, appeals, and bankruptcy courts, by type of suit and offense, circuit, and district, 1991, annual rpt, 18204–11
Court civil and criminal caseloads for Federal district, appeals, and special courts, 1991, annual rpt, 18204–8
Crime victimization in cities, suburbs, and rural areas, by offense, circumstances, and victim and offender characteristics, 1987-89, 6066–3.48
Crime victimization rates, by victim and offender characteristics, circumstances, and offense, 1990 survey, annual rpt, 6066–3.47
Crimes, arrests, and rates, by offense, offender characteristics, population size, and jurisdiction, 1991, annual rpt, 6224–2.1; 6224–2.2
Criminal case processing from arrest to sentencing, cases and duration by disposition and offense, for selected cities, 1988, annual rpt, 6064–27
Criminal case processing in Federal district courts, and dispositions, by offense, district, and offender characteristics, 1989, annual data compilation, 6064–29
Criminal case processing in Federal district courts, and dispositions, by offense, 1980-91, annual rpt, 6064–31
Criminal sentences for Federal offenses, guidelines by offense and circumstances, series, 17668–1
Drug (illegal) arrests and related property seizures assisted by Natl Guard, FY89-91, annual rpt, 3504–22
Drug test results at arrest, by drug type, offense, and sex, for selected urban areas, quarterly rpt, 6062–3
Homicides and rate, by weapon, circumstances, and victim characteristics, and years of potential life lost, 1980s, article, 4202–7.315
Input-output structure of US economy, detailed interindustry transactions for 84 industries, and components of final demand, 1987, annual article, 2702–1.316
Juvenile arrests, by sex, race, disposition, and offense, 1990, 6066–27.8
Law enforcement officer assaults and deaths by circumstances, agency, victim and offender characteristics, and location, 1990, annual rpt, 6224–3
Marijuana crop eradication activities of DEA and local agencies, and weapons and assets seized, by State, 1982-91, annual rpt, 6284–4
Police agencies employment, spending, and operations, FY90, 6066–25.44
Police employment, spending, and operations, for State, city, county, and special district agencies, 1990, annual rpt, 6064–39
Prison and parole admissions and releases, sentence length, and time served, by offense and offender characteristics, 1988, annual rpt, 6064–33
Prisoners in Federal and contract instns, by selected characteristics, region, and Federal instn, FY89, annual rpt, 6244–1.1
Prisoners in State and Federal instns, violations by type, 1990, quinquennial rpt, 6068–218
Probation population, by offender characteristics, sentence conditions, whether rearrested, and offense, 1986-89, 6066–19.65
Sheriffs' agencies employment, spending, and operations, FY90, 6066–25.45
Wiretaps authorized, costs, arrests, trials, and convictions, by offense and jurisdiction, 1991, annual rpt, 18204–7
Women in jail, by criminal background and sociodemographic characteristics, with comparisons to men, 1989, 6066–19.66
Youth risk behavior, by level of alcohol use and sex, 1987, article, 4482–1.308
see also Ammunition
see also Arms trade
see also Bombs
see also Chemical and biological warfare agents
see also Firearms
see also Military assistance
see also Military weapons
see also Missiles and rockets
see also Nuclear weapons
see also Torpedoes

Weather
Africa (Sahel) rainfall correlation with northwest Atlantic Ocean hurricanes, 1947-90, 2148–61
Aircraft accidents and circumstances, for US operations of domestic and foreign airlines and general aviation, periodic rpt, 9612–1
Aircraft accidents, casualties, and damage, for commercial operations by detailed circumstances, 1988, annual rpt, 9614–2
Alaska OCS environmental conditions and oil dev impacts, compilation of papers, series, 2176–1
Boat accidents, casualties, and damage, by cause, vessel and operator characteristics, and State, 1991, annual rpt, 7404–1.2
Cattle and calves loss to predators, disease, and other causes, by region and State, 1991, 1618–22
Coastal areas environmental conditions and mgmt, for individual areas, conf series, 2146–8
Coastal currents driven by wind, velocity and direction by station for North America, forecast 1993, annual rpts, 2174–1
Colorado water supply, streamflow, precipitation, and reservoir storage, 1992 water year, annual rpt, 1264–13
Deaths, injuries, and damage from weather phenomena, and storm characteristics, by State, monthly listing, 2152–3
Energy supply, demand, and price forecasts, economic and weather assumptions, quarterly rpt, 3162–34
Environmental Quality, status of problems, protection programs, research, and intl issues, 1991 annual rpt, 484–1
Farmland precipitation and temperature, average by State, monthly 1950-90, biennial rpt, 1544–28
Fires on wildlands, ecology, mgmt, cultural impacts, and historic patterns, 1990 conf, 1208–415
Foreign countries *Background Notes*, summary social, political, and economic data, series, 7006–2
Foreign countries economic, social, political, and geographic summary data, by country, 1992, annual factbook, 9114–2
Forests (aspen) vegetation, climate, and other environmental characteristics, for upper Great Lakes area, 1991 rpt, 1208–418
Grain (feed) yield impacts of El Nino weather events, 1992 article, 1561–4.302
Groundwater supply, quality, chemistry, and use, State and local area rpt series, 5666–28
Groundwater supply, quality, chemistry, other characteristics, and use, regional rpt series, 5666–25

Heating and cooling degree days, by census div, monthly and cumulative for season, monthly rpt, 3162–24.1
Heating and cooling degree days, distribution for commercial buildings by building type, survey rpt series, 3166–8
Heating and cooling degree days, for 45 cities and total US, cumulative for season, weekly rpt, 3162–32.2; 3162–45.2
Heating and cooling degree days weighted by population, by census div and State, with area-weighted temperature and precipitation, monthly rpt, 2152–13
Heating degree days and cold weather rank, by State and region, 1950-80 average, 3168–125
Labor force not at work, unemployed, and working less than 35 hours, by reason, sex, race, region, and State, 1991, annual rpt, 6744–7.1; 6744–7.2
Mariners Weather Log, quarterly journal, 2152–8
Minerals offshore lease sales environmental and economic impacts in coastal areas, final statement series, 5736–7
New Hampshire Hubbard Brook Experimental Forest hydrology and climate data, 1956-89, 1208–410
Northeastern US water supply, precipitation and stream runoff by station, monthly rpt, 2182–3
Ocean weather forecast areas, and broadcast schedules and stations worldwide, as of Sept 1992, annual rpt, 2184–3
Ocean weather forecast broadcast schedules worldwide, periodic rpt, 2182–9
Precipitation, and groundwater and surface water supply and conditions, monthly rpt, 5662–3
Precipitation and temperature, and effect on agriculture, by US region, State, and city, and world area, weekly rpt, 2182–7
Precipitation and temperature for US and foreign locations, major events and anomalies, weekly rpt, 2182–6
Precipitation and temperature forecasts for US and Northern Hemisphere, by location, semimonthly rpt, 2182–1
Railroad accidents, casualties, and damage, by cause, railroad, and State, 1991, annual rpt, 7604–1
Railroad accidents, casualties, circumstances, and railroad involved, 1988, annual rpt, 9614–8
Railroad accidents involving hazardous materials, casualties, and circumstances, 1984-89, 9618–18
Railroad-hwy grade-crossing accidents, detailed data by State and railroad, 1991, annual rpt, 7604–2
Statistical Abstract of US, 1992 annual data compilation, 2324–1.6
Temperature annual and seasonal averages by US region, and departures from normal by world area, 1860s-1990, annual rpt, 3004–33
Timber in southeastern US, resources mgmt and research, 1990 biennial conf papers, 1204–35
Traffic accidents, casualties, circumstances, and characteristics of persons and vehicles involved, 1990, annual rpt, 7764–18
Traffic accidents on rural 2-lane roads related to passing, by circumstances and severity, 1992 article, 7552–3.301
Traffic fatal accidents, deaths, and rates, by circumstances, characteristics of persons and vehicles involved, and location, 1990, annual rpt, 7764–10
Traffic safety research, literature review, with data on accidents and impact of safety measures, 1961-90, 7558–98
Truck accidents, casualties, and damage, by circumstances and characteristics of persons and vehicles involved, 1989, annual rpt, 7554–9
Truck accidents, circumstances, and characteristics of vehicles and persons involved, 1979-86, 7768–124
Unemployed displaced workers, layoffs and recalls by layoff reason, industry, firm size, and State, 2nd half 1988, 6406–6.36
Unemployed displaced workers, layoffs and unemployment insurance claims by reason, industry, selected characteristics, MSA, and State, 1990, annual rpt, 6744–18
Uranium tailings at inactive mills, remedial action proposals, costs, site characteristics, and environmental, socioeconomic, and health impacts, series, 3356–4
Water quality, chemistry, hydrology, and other characteristics, local area studies, series, 5666–27
Weather data for surface and upper air, averages by foreign and US station, monthly rpt, 2152–4
Weather trends and deviations, by world region, 1880s-1990, annual chartbook, 2184–9
Western US water supply, and snow survey results, annual State rpt series, 1264–14
Western US water supply, and snow survey results, monthly State rpt series, 1266–2
Western US water supply, streamflow and reservoir storage forecasts by stream and station, Jan-May monthly rpt, 1262–1
see also Drought
see also Floods
see also Glaciers
see also Global climate change
see also Ice conditions
see also Meteorological satellites
see also Meteorology
see also Storms
see also Weather control
see also Wind energy

Weather Bureau
see National Environmental Satellite, Data, and Information Service
see National Weather Service

Weather control
Glaciology intl research summaries, methodology, and bibls, series, 2156–18

Weather satellites
see Meteorological satellites

Weatherspoon, Anthony
"Production and Sources of Residential Fuelwood from Roundwood in Michigan", 1208–412

Webb, Shwu-Eng H.
"China's Agricultural Marketing System in the 1980's", 1524–4.2
"China's Food Consumption and Production Patterns in the Year 2000: Implications for Trade", 1524–4.2

Weber, Bruce R.
"How Is the Farm Bill Working (Planting Flexibility Opportunities)", 1504–9.1

Webster, Barbara A.
"Assessing Criminal Justice Needs", 6066–20.22

Webster, Linda A.
"Regional and Temporal Trends in the Surveillance of Syphilis, U.S., 1986-90", 4202–7.303

Weidner, Noel
"Tumor Angiogenesis: A New Significant and Independent Prognostic Indicator in Early-Stage Breast Carcinoma", 4472–1.357

Weight
see Body measurements
see Obesity

Weights and measures
Calibration of measurement systems, standard reference materials specifications and availability, 1992 biennial listing, 2214–2
Food products and commodities, weight and volume conversion factors, 1992 rpt, 1508–3
Intl and domestic standards dev for production, controls, and processes in US and EC, 1980s-91, 26358–257
Natl Inst of Standards and Technology rpts, 1991, annual listing, 2214–1
Standards dev, proposals, and policies, for weights, measures, and performance, 1992 annual conf, 2214–7
Statistical Abstract of US, 1992 annual data compilation, 2324–1
Textile products trade regulations of foreign countries, and US exports, by commodity and country, 1989-91, biennial rpt, 2044–18
see also Industrial standards

Weiss, David
"Local Impact of Foreign Trade Zones", 9375–13.86

Weiss, Mary A.
"Structure, Conduct, and Regulation of the Property-Liability Insurance Industry", 9373–3.35

Weiss, Michael D.
"Nonlinear and Chaotic Dynamics: An Economist's Guide", 1502–3.301

Welch, John H.
"Cointegration and Tests of a Classical Model of Inflation in Argentina, Bolivia, Brazil, Mexico, and Peru", 9379–12.91
"Economic Liberalization in the Americas", 9379–2

Welch, W. Pete
"Alternative Geographic Adjustments in Medicare Payment to Health Maintenance Organizations", 4652–1.321

Welfare
see Aid to Families with Dependent Children
see Public welfare programs
see Social security
see State funding for social welfare

Wells, John C.
"Managing Workplace Safety and Health: The Case of Contract Labor in the U.S. Petrochemical Industry", 6608–6

Welniak, Edward J., Jr.
"Money Income of Households, Families, and Persons in the U.S.: 1991", 2546–6.76

Wenner, Mark D.
"Government Intervention in Moroccan Agriculture: Evolution of Subsidy Equivalents and Possible Trade Reform Effects", 1528–329
Wenninger, John
"Small Time Deposits and the Recent Weakness in M2", 9385–1.305
Werner, John L.
"Small Business Administration's Small Business Investment Company Program: A Review of Selected Issues", 25728–44
West Indies
see Caribbean area
West, Jerry
"Profile of Parents of Eighth Graders. National Education Longitudinal Study of 1988", 4826–9.15
West Palm Beach, Fla.
Housing starts and completions authorized by building permits in 40 MSAs, quarterly rpt, 2382–9
Wages by occupation, and benefits for office and plant workers, 1991 survey, periodic MSA rpt, 6785–3.1
see also under By City and By SMSA or MSA in the "Index by Categories"
West Virginia
Appalachian Regional Commission funding, by project and State, planned FY92, annual rpt, 9084–3
Apple production, marketing, and prices, for Appalachia and compared to other States, 1989-92, annual rpt, 1311–13
Banks (insured commercial), Fed Reserve 5th District members financial statements, by State, quarterly rpt, 9389–18
Banks (insured commercial and savings) deposits by instn, State, MSA, and county, as of June 1991, annual regional rpt, 9295–3.2
Coal production and mines by county, prices, productivity, miners, and reserves, by mining method and State, 1990-91, annual rpt, 3164–25
County Business Patterns, 1990: employment, establishments, and payroll, by SIC 2- to 4-digit industry and county, annual State rpt, 2326–6.50
Deaths and rates, by detailed location, cause, and demographic characteristics, 1989, US Vital Statistics annual rpt, 4144–3.1
Economic indicators and components, and Fed Reserve 4th District business and financial conditions, monthly chartbook, 9377–10
Economic indicators by State, Fed Reserve 5th District, quarterly rpt, 9389–16
Employment, earnings, and hours, by selected SIC 1- to 4-digit industry, State, and for 275 MSAs, 1987-92, 6748–81
Fed Govt spending in States and local areas, by type, State, county, and city, FY91, annual rpt, 2464–3
Fed Govt spending in States, by type, program, agency, and State, FY91, annual rpt, 2464–2
HHS financial aid, by program, recipient, State, and city, FY91, annual regional listing, 4004–3.3
Hospital deaths of Medicare patients, actual and expected rates by diagnosis, and hospital characteristics, by instn, FY90 annual State rpt, 4654–14.50
Housing census, 1990: inventory, occupancy, and costs, State fact sheet, 2326–21.50
Housing census, 1990: summary unit characteristics, by householder race and age, county, place, and urban-rural location, State rpt, 2471–1.50
Military prime contract awards, by contractor, service branch, State, and city, FY91, annual rpt, 3544–22
Mineral Industry Surveys, State reviews of production, 1991, preliminary annual rpt, 5614–6
Minerals Yearbook, Vol 2, 1989: State review of production and sales by commodity, and business activity, annual rpt, 5604–16.50
Multinatl firms US affiliates finances and operations, by industry, country of parent firm, and State, 1987, 2708–48
Physicians, by specialty, age, sex, and location of training and practice, 1990, State rpt, 4116–6.50
Population and housing census, 1990: detailed geographic coverage, State CD-ROM, 2551–9.5
Population and housing census, 1990: population and housing characteristics, detailed geographic coverage, State CD-ROM, 2551–10.59
Population and housing census, 1990: summary characteristics, by county, subdiv, and place, State rpt, 2551–7.50
Population census, 1990: population characteristics and living arrangements, by county, place, and urban-rural location, State rpt, 2531–1.50
Statistical Abstract of US, 1992 annual data compilation, 2324–1
Timber in West Virginia, hardwood stands single-tree selection mgmt methods, tree density and growth by species, 1950s-83, 1208–394
Water supply and quality in streams and lakes, and groundwater levels in wells, by drainage basin, 1991, annual State rpt, 5666–12.45
see also Huntington, W.Va.
see also under By State in the "Index by Categories"
Westat, Inc.
"Assessment of the National Science Foundation's 1985-87 College Science Instrumentation Program", 9628–87
"Evaluation of the Asbestos Hazard Emergency Response Act (AHERA): Final Report", 9238–71
"Public School Principal Survey on Safe, Disciplined, and Drug-Free Schools", 4826–1.32
"Scientific and Engineering Research Facilities at Universities and Colleges: 1992", 9624–25
"SEDCAR (Standards for Educational Data Collection and Reporting)", 4828–41
"Unlocking Learning: Chapter 1 in Correctional Facilities. National Study of the Chapter 1 Neglected or Delinquent Program", 4808–40
Western Area Power Administration
Activities of WAPA by plant, financial statements, and sales by customer, FY91, annual rpt, 3254–1
Finances and operations of Federal power admins and electric utilities, 1990, annual rpt, 3164–24.2
Property (real) of DOE owned and leased, by type, subagency, contractor, and site, FY91, annual rpt, 3004–28
Radiation and other pollutant releases from DOE contractor research lab and nuclear weapons facilities, monitoring results, 1992 annual site rpt, 3324–2.14
Western Sahara
Agricultural trade of US, by detailed commodity and country, 1991, semiannual rpt, 1522–4
Economic, social, political, and geographic summary data, by country, 1992, annual factbook, 9114–2
Exports and imports of US, by transport mode, country, and SITC 1- to 3-digit commodity, 1991, annual rpt, 2424–12
Human rights conditions in 170 countries, and US economic and military aid, 1991, annual rpt, 21384–3
Minerals Yearbook, Vol 3, 1989: foreign country review of production, trade, and policy, by commodity, annual rpt, 5604–35.1
Population size, growth rates, and components of change, by country, projected 1990-2020 and trends from 1950, biennial rpt, 2324–9
Refugee migration, and intl aid programs, by world area and country of origin and asylum, 1991, annual rpt, 7004–15
Western Samoa
Agricultural trade of US, by detailed commodity and country, 1991, annual rpt, 1524–8
Agricultural trade of US, by detailed commodity and country, 1991, semiannual rpt, 1522–4
Economic and military aid and loans from US and intl agencies, by program and country, FY46-91, annual rpt, 9914–5
Economic, social, political, and geographic summary data, by country, 1992, annual factbook, 9114–2
Exports and imports of US, by transport mode, country, and SITC 1- to 3-digit commodity, 1991, annual rpt, 2424–12
Exports of US, detailed Schedule B commodities with countries of destination, 1991, annual rpt, 2424–10
Human rights conditions in 170 countries, and US economic and military aid, 1991, annual rpt, 21384–3
Military aid of US, arms sales, and training programs costs and budget requests, by program, world region, and country, FY91-93, annual rpt, 7144–13
Population size, growth rates, and components of change, by country, projected 1990-2020 and trends from 1950, biennial rpt, 2324–9
UN voting record and share of votes in agreement with US, by issue, country, and world area, 1991, annual rpt, 7004–18
Western States
Asian and Pacific Islands Americans social and economic characteristics, for West and total US, 1990-91, Current Population Report, 2546–1.462
Banking industry structure, performance, and financial devs, for Fed Reserve 10th District, 1991, annual rpt, 9381–14
Birds (duck) breeding population, by species, State, and Canada Province, 1991-92 and trends from 1955, annual rpt, 5504–30

Birds (northern spotted owl) conservation methods in Pacific Northwest, findings and recommendations, 1990 rpt, 1208–385
Birds (northern spotted owl) conservation methods in Pacific Northwest, timber industry impacts, and Federal and State spending, 1980s-95, 1208–388
Birds in western US Great Basin sagebrush habitat, population density by species, 1978-83 studies, 1208–402
Bonneville Power Admin hazardous waste mgmt and environmental protection standards compliance activities, 1991, annual rpt, 3224–6
Bonneville Power Admin mgmt of Fed Columbia River Power System, finances and sales, summary data, quarterly rpt, 3222–2
Bonneville Power Admin mgmt of Fed Columbia River Power System, finances, operations, and sales by customer, FY91, annual rpt, 3224–1
Bonneville Power Admin sales, revenues, and rates, by customer and customer type, 1991, semiannual rpt, 3222–1
Coal mining restrictions on public land, impacts on production, costs, and demand, by region, 1985-88 and projected to 2075, 5668–125
Coal production and mines by county, prices, productivity, miners, and reserves, by mining method and State, 1990-91, annual rpt, 3164–25
Colorado River Storage Project finances and activities in western States, FY91, annual rpt, 5824–3
CPI by component for US city average, and by selected metro area, region, and population size, monthly rpt, 6762–2
Dairy prices, by product and selected area, with related marketing data, 1991, annual rpt, 1317–1
Deaths and rates, by cause and selected social, demographic, and employment characteristics, 1979-85, natl longitudinal study, 4478–186
Drought aid of Reclamation Bur, by western State, 1992 press release, 5306–4.17
Economic indicators and cyclical devs and outlook, by Fed Reserve Bank District, periodic rpt, 9362–8
Electric power capacity and use in Pacific Northwest, by energy source, forecast under alternative load and demand cases, 1991-2012, annual rpt, 3224–3
Electric power sales by customer, activities by plant, and financial statements of Western Area Power Admin, FY91, annual rpt, 3254–1
Employment growth by industry div and manufacturing group, Fed Reserve 10th District, 1990-91, annual article, 9381–1.302
Energy supply, demand, and prices, by fuel type and end-use sector, alternative projections by region, 1990-2010, annual rpt, 3164–96
Financial and economic devs, Fed Reserve Bank of Kansas City quarterly journal, 9381–1
Financial and economic devs, Fed Reserve Bank of San Francisco periodic journal, 9393–8
Financial and economic devs, Fed Reserve 10th District, quarterly rpt, 9381–16
Freight (waterborne domestic and foreign) by commodity, traffic, and passengers, by port and waterway, 1989, annual rpt, 3754–3.4
Geothermal resources, power plant generation, capacity, and dev potential, by location, 1988-90 and projected to 2030, 3168–122
HHS financial aid, by program, recipient, State, and city, FY91, annual regional listing, 4004–3.8; 4004–3.9; 4004–3.10
Housing vacancy rates for single and multifamily units and mobile homes in FHLB 10th District, by ZIP code, annual MSA rpt series, 9304–22
Housing vacancy rates for single and multifamily units and mobile homes in FHLB 12th District, by ZIP code, annual MSA rpt series, 9304–21
Hydroelectric power plants, generation, and capacity, for Reclamation Bur projects, 1978-90 and projected to 1995, 5828–14
Indian tribes in Pacific Northwest, OCS oil and gas lease and dev environmental, economic, and cultural impacts, with background data, 1970s-92, 5738–35
Livestock grazing on natl rangeland, BLM mgmt, officials views, 1980s-90, GAO rpt, 26113–567
Lumber prices, by grade and Pacific Northwest species, 1971-90 and projected to 2040, 1208–424
Minerals resources and availability on public lands, State rpt series, 5606–7
Population, households, employment, income, fuel prices, and electricity demand for Pacific Northwest, alternative forecasts 1991-2010 with trends from 1980, annual rpt, 3224–3.3
Radionuclide concentrations in air, water, humans, animals, and milk near Nevada and other nuclear test sites, 1990, annual rpt, 9194–17
Savings instns, FHLB 6th and 11th District and natl cost of funds indexes, and mortgage and Treasury bill rates, monthly rpt, 9302–38
Savings instns, FHLB 10th District members, locations, assets, and deposits, 1992, annual listing, 9304–17
Savings instns, FHLB 11th District shareholder instns, offices, and financial condition, 1992 annual listing, 9304–23
Sheep and wool production, use, and prices, and operations costs and returns, for western US, 1920s-90, 1548–382
Shipborne commerce (domestic) of US, freight by major commodity group, vessel type, and port, 1987-89, annual rpt, 7704–7
Statistical Abstract of US, 1992 annual data compilation, 2324–1
Temperature annual and seasonal averages by US region, and departures from normal by world area, 1860s-1990, annual rpt, 3004–33
Tidal currents, daily time and velocity by station for North America and Asia coasts, forecast 1993, annual rpt, 2174–1.2
Tide height and time daily at coastal points, forecast 1993, annual rpt, 2174–2.2
Timber in northwestern US and British Columbia, production, prices, trade, and employment, quarterly rpt, 1202–3
Timber in Pacific Northwest, old-growth forests plant and wildlife population and species diversity, 1991 compilation of papers, 1208–386
Timber in Rocky Mountain States, production and mill residue, by species, ownership, and county, series, 1206–17
Timber in Rocky Mountains and southwest US, old growth forests ecology, mgmt, and research methods, 1992 conf, 1208–421
Timber in western US, insect and disease infestation from lumber imports from USSR, economic and environmental impacts, 1991 and projected to 2040, 1208–389
Timber insect and disease incidence and damage, 1991, annual regional rpt, 1206–11.1
Timber stumpage prices, for sawtimber sold from natl forests in Pacific Northwest, monthly 1975-89, 1208–387
Uranium tailings at inactive mills, remedial action activities by site, and funding, FY91, annual rpt, 3354–9
Uranium tailings at inactive mills, remedial action proposals, costs, site characteristics, and environmental, socioeconomic, and health impacts, series, 3356–4
Water storage and carriage facilities of Reclamation Bur, capacity, and operating status, as of Sept 1990, biennial listing, 5824–7
Water supply in western US, and snow survey results, annual State rpt series, 1264–14
Water supply in western US, and snow survey results, monthly State rpt series, 1266–2
Water supply in western US, storage by reservoir and State, and streamflow conditions, as of Oct 1992, annual rpt, 1264–4
Water supply in western US, streamflow and reservoir storage forecasts by stream and station, Jan-May monthly rpt, 1262–1
see also under By Region in the "Index by Categories"
see also under names of individual States

Western Union Telegraph Co.
Finances and operations, detail for telegraph firms, 1990, annual rpt, 9284–6.3
Intl telecommunications operations of US carriers, finances, rates, and traffic by service type, firm, and country, 1975-90, annual rpt, 9284–17

Westinghouse Co.
Savannah River nuclear weapons plant operations, Westinghouse Co procurement from govt supply sources, 1990-91, 3006–5.33

Westmoreland County, Pa.
Housing and households characteristics, and unit and neighborhood quality, by MSA location for 11 MSAs, 1986 survey, supplement, 2485–8

Wetlands
Acid neutralizing capability of wetlands for mining runoff, with pollutant levels and site characteristics, for Pennsylvania, 1987-90, 5608–171

Acreage and losses of wetlands, by wetland type, 1970s-80s, 5508–89
Alaska Copper River Delta wetland environmental conditions, 1987, 1208–401
Alaska OCS environmental conditions and oil dev impacts, compilation of papers, series, 2176–1
Birds (duck) population and nesting success in south-central North Dakota, by species, with habitat conditions, 1960s-81, 5508–120
Birds (waterfowl) population, habitat conditions, and migratory flight forecasts, for Canada and US by region, 1992 and trends from 1955, annual rpt, 5504–27
Birds (waterfowl) refuge and breeding area acreage acquired by Fed Govt, and costs, by site and State, FY92, annual rpt, 14784–1
Coastal wetlands mapping projects status, costs, and methods, 1990 conf, 5508–116
Conservation funding for coastal wetlands, by project, 1992 press release, 5306–4.12
Environmental conditions, fish, wildlife, use, and mgmt, for individual coastal and riparian ecosystems, series, 5506–9
Environmental conditions of estuaries, research results and methodology, series, 2176–7
Environmental Quality, status of problems, protection programs, research, and intl issues, 1991 annual rpt, 484–1
Fish and Wildlife Service restoration programs funding, land purchases, and project listing, by State, FY90, annual rpt, 5504–1
Florida wetlands acreage, by wetland type, 1970s-80s, 5508–119
Migratory Bird Conservation Commission wetlands habitat acquisition, funding by State, 1992, press release, 5306–4.13; 5306–4.16
Pesticide levels and water toxicity indicators, for natl wildlife refuge wetlands in South Dakota, 1990, 5508–117
Public lands acreage, grants, use, revenues, and allocations, by State, FY91, annual rpt, 5724–1.2
Soil and plant characteristics in wetlands and riparian areas, series, 5506–10
Water Bank program agreements, payments to farmers, and wetlands acreage, by State, monthly rpt, 1802–5
Water Bank Program agreements, payments to farmers, and wetlands acreage, by State, 1972-91, annual rpt, 1804–21
Wheat acreage enrolled in soils and wetlands conservation programs, and production impacts, by State, 1991, article, 1561–12.302

Whales
see Marine mammals

Wharton, Eric H.
"Timber Industries of Kentucky, 1986", 1206–15.12

Wheat
Acreage of wheat and rye seeded, by State, 1990-92, annual rpt, 1621–30
Acreage of wheat enrolled in soils and wetlands conservation programs, and production impacts, by State, 1991, article, 1561–12.302
Acreage planted and harvested, by crop and State, 1990-91 and planned as of June 1992, annual rpt, 1621–23
Acreage planted, by selected crop and State, 1983-91 and planned 1992, annual rpt, 1621–22
Acreage reduction program compliance, enrollment, and yield on planted acreage, by commodity and State, annual press release series, 1004–20
Agricultural Stabilization and Conservation Service producer payments, by program and State, 1991, annual table, 1804–12
Agricultural Statistics, 1991, annual rpt, 1004–1
Alcoholic beverages production, stocks, materials used, and taxable and tax-free removals, for beer and distilled spirits by State, monthly rpt, 8486–1.1; 8486–1.3
Business statistics, detailed data for major industries and economic indicators, *Survey of Current Business*, monthly rpt, 2702–1.13
Business statistics, detailed data for major industries and economic indicators, 1960-91, *Survey of Current Business* biennial supplement, 2704–1
Canada-US trade agreement issues, with data on Canada fertilizer and agricultural production and trade, 1960s-90s, hearing, 25368–179
CCC certificate exchange activity, by commodity, biweekly press release, 1802–16
CCC financial condition and major commodity program operations, FY63-88, annual chartbook, 1824–2
Consumption, supply, trade, prices, spending, and indexes, by food commodity, 1990, annual rpt, 1544–4
Export licensing, monitoring, and enforcement activities, FY91, annual rpt, 2024–1
Exports and imports (agricultural) commodity and country, prices, and world market devs, monthly rpt, 1922–12
Exports and imports (agricultural) of US, by commodity and country, bimonthly rpt, 1522–1
Exports and imports (agricultural) of US, by detailed commodity and country, 1991, annual rpt, 1524–8
Exports and imports (agricultural) of US, by detailed commodity and country, 1991, semiannual rpt, 1522–4
Exports and imports between US and outlying areas, by detailed commodity and mode of transport, 1991, annual rpt, 2424–11
Exports and imports of US, by country and detailed commodity, monthly rpt, 2422–12
Exports and imports of US, by Harmonized System 6-digit commodity and country, 1991, annual rpt, 2424–13
Exports and imports of US, by transport mode, country, and SITC 1- to 3-digit commodity, 1991, annual rpt, 2424–12
Exports of grains, oilseed products, hides, skins, and cotton, by country, weekly rpt, dropped data, 1922–3
Exports of US, detailed Schedule B commodities with countries of destination, 1991, annual rpt, 2424–10
Farm financial and marketing conditions, forecast 1992, annual chartbook, 1504–8
Farm income, cash marketing receipts ranked by commodity and State, 1990, 1548–385
Farm sector balance sheet, and receipts by detailed commodity, by State, 1986-90, annual rpt, 1544–18
Fed Crop Insurance Corp financial performance, and effect of alternative price forecasts on program costs, 1983-89, GAO rpt, 26131–95
Fertilizer and pesticide use and application rates, by type, crop, and State, 1991, 1616–1.1
Flour milling production by State, stocks, daily capacity, and exports by country, monthly Current Industrial Rpt, 2506–4.1
Foreign and US agricultural production, acreage, and yield for selected crops, forecasts by selected world region and country, FAS monthly circular, 1925–28
Foreign and US agricultural supply and demand indicators, by selected crop, monthly rpt, 1522–5
Foreign and US grain production, prices, trade, stocks, and use, FAS periodic circular series, 1925–2
Foreign and US wheat production, prices, trade, stocks, and use, quarterly situation rpt with articles, 1561–12
Foreign countries agricultural production, prices, and trade, by country, 1980-91 and forecast 1992, annual world area rpt series, 1524–4
Freight (waterborne domestic and foreign) by commodity, traffic, and passengers, by port and waterway, 1989, annual rpt, 3754–3
Futures and options trading volume, by commodity and exchange, FY91, annual rpt, 11924–2
Futures contracts, stocks in deliverable position by type, weekly tables, 11922–4
Futures trading in selected commodities and financial instruments and indexes, for NYC, Chicago, and other markets activity, biweekly rpt, 11922–5
Inspections of grain for domestic use and export, and foreign buyers complaints, FY92, annual rpt, 1294–1
Irrigation projects of Reclamation Bur in western US, crop production and acreage by commodity, State, and project, 1990, annual rpt, 5824–12
Loan support programs of USDA for grains, activity and status by grain and State, monthly rpt, 1802–3
Manufacturing annual survey, 1990: finances and operations, by SIC 2- to 4-digit industry, series, 2506–14
OECD trade, total and for 4 major countries, and US trade by country, by commodity, 1980-90, world area rpt series, 9116–1
Plantings under flexible acreage program provisions, impacts on returns, 1979-81, article, 1561–12.303
Price (season average) forecasts for wheat using futures settlement prices, 1986-92, article, 1561–12.301
Price indexes (producer), by stage of processing and detailed commodity, monthly rpt, 6762–6

Price indexes (producer), by stage of processing and detailed commodity, monthly 1991, annual rpt, 6764–2
Price support and other CCC program outlays, with production and marketing outlook, by commodity, projected 1991-97, annual rpt, 26306–6.171
Prices received and paid by farmers, by commodity and State, monthly rpt, 1629–1
Prices received and paid by farmers, by commodity and State, 1991, annual rpt, 1629–5
Prices received by farmers and production value, by detailed crop and State, 1989-91, annual rpt, 1621–2
Production, farms, acreage, and related data, by selected crop and State, monthly rpt, 1621–1
Production itemized costs, receipts, and returns, by commodity and region, 1975-90, annual rpt, 1544–20
Production itemized costs, receipts, and returns, by crop and State, 1987-89, annual rpt, 1544–24
Production, price, and supply forecasts used for USDA commodity program outlays, accuracy, 1975-88, GAO rpt, 26131–94
Production, prices, trade, and export inspections by US port and country of destination, by grain type, weekly rpt, 1313–2
Production, prices, trade, and marketing, by commodity, current situation and forecast, monthly rpt with articles, 1502–4
Seed varieties patent protection, and wheat farmer profitability of using purchased seed, 1986-89, 1548–388
Soviet Union and US economic and sociodemographic indicators, selected years 1970-90, handbook, 2328–80
Stocks of grain by region and market city, and grain inspected for export, by type, weekly rpt, 1313–4
Stocks of grain on and off farms, by crop, quarterly rpt, 1621–4
Weight and volume conversion factors for agricultural commodities and products, 1992 rpt, 1508–3

Wheeler, Judith C.
"Water Withdrawal and Use in Maryland, 1987", 5666–24.15

Wheelock, David C.
"Monetary Policy in the Great Depression: What the Fed Did, and Why", 9391–1.306

White collar crime
see Fraud

White collar workers
see Area wage surveys
see Business management
see Clerical workers
see Executives and managers
see Industry wage surveys
see Paraprofessionals
see Professional and technical workers

White House
Acreage and descriptions of natl park system sites, 1991, biennial listing, 5544–5
Acreage of land under Natl Park Service mgmt, by site, ownership, and region, FY92, semiannual rpt, 5542–1
Visits in natl park system, by park and State, monthly rpt, 5542–4
Visits in natl park system, by park and State, 1991, annual rpt, 5544–12
see also Executive Office of the President

White House Conference on Library and Information Services
Access, policy, technology, and other info services issues, recommendations, 1991 conf, 15638–16

White, K. D.
"Quality of the Ohio River and Atmospheric Deposition and Its Relation to Corrosion of Lock and Dam Facilities in the Lower Ohio River Basin Near Paducah, Ky.", 5666–27.30

White, Vicky
"Identification and Quantitation of Triamterene in Blood and Urine from a Fatal Aircraft Accident", 7506–10.110

Whiteis, David G.
"Hospital and Community Characteristics in Closures of Urban Hospitals, 1980-87", 4042–3.341

Whitt, Joseph A., Jr.
"Exchange Rate Variability and International Trade", 9371–1.304

Whittaker, Gerald W.
"Life Cycle and Expectations of Farmers", 1541–1.309
"Restricting Pesticide Use: The Impact on Profitability by Farm Size", 1561–16.304

Wholesale Price Index
see Producer Price Index

Wholesale trade
Business statistics, detailed data for major industries and economic indicators, *Survey of Current Business*, monthly rpt, 2702–1.6
Business statistics, detailed data for major industries and economic indicators, 1960-91, *Survey of Current Business* biennial supplement, 2704–1
Census Bur data files and rpts, coverage and availability, 1992 annual listing, 2304–2
Collective bargaining agreements expiring during year, and workers covered, by firm, union, industry group, and State, 1992, annual rpt, 6784–9
County Business Patterns, 1989: employment, establishments, and payroll, by SIC 2- to 4-digit industry and county, annual State rpt series, 2326–8
County Business Patterns, 1990: employment, establishments, and payroll, by SIC 2- to 4-digit industry and county, annual State rpt series, 2326–6
Deaths and rates, by cause and selected social, demographic, and employment characteristics, 1979-85, natl longitudinal study, 4478–186
Employment and Earnings, detailed data, monthly rpt, 6742–2.5
Employment Cost Index and alternative measure of compensation costs, by component, occupation, industry group, union status, and location, 1975-92, annual rpt, 6744–20
Employment, earnings, and hours, by selected SIC 1- to 4-digit industry, State, and for 275 MSAs, 1987-92, 6748–81
Employment, earnings, and hours, by SIC 1- to 4-digit industry, monthly 1989-Feb 1992, annual rpt, 6744–4
Employment, earnings, and hours, monthly press release, 6742–5
Employment of minorities and women, by occupation, SIC 1- to 3-digit industry, State, and MSA, 1991, annual rpt, 9244–1
Employment situation, earnings, hours, and other BLS economic indicators, transcripts of BLS Commissioner's monthly testimony, periodic rpt, 23846–4
Employment, unemployment, and labor force characteristics, by region and census div, 1991, annual rpt, 6744–7.1
Finance companies credit outstanding and leasing activities, by credit type, monthly rpt, 9365–2.7
Financial statements for manufacturing, mining, and trade corporations, by selected SIC 2- to 3-digit industry, quarterly rpt, 2502–1
Foreign-controlled US firms transactions with related foreign persons, by type, industry div, and country, 1988, article, 8302–2.318
Foreign countries economic conditions, policy, and trade practices, by country, 1989-91, annual rpt, 21384–5
Foreign direct investment in US, by industry group and world area, 1989-91, annual article, 2702–1.331
Foreign direct investment in US, major transactions by type, industry, country, and US location, 1990, annual rpt, 2044–20
Foreign direct investment of US, by industry group and world area, 1989-91, annual article, 2702–1.332
Gross State Product by component, industry div, and State, 1977-89, article, 2702–1.303
Income tax returns of foreign corporations and individuals, and US entities abroad, detailed data compilation, 1970s-89, quinquennial rpt, 8308–31
Input-output structure of US economy, detailed interindustry transactions for 541 industries, and components of final demand, 1982 benchmark data, 2708–17
Inventories related to sales, by industry sector, model description and results, late 1960s-91, article, 9389–1.302
Manufacturing census, 1987: shipments of manufacturers products, by customer class and SIC 2- and 4-digit industry, subject rpt, 2497–4
Minority- and woman-owned businesses and owner characteristics, by industry, employment and sales size, and form of ownership, 1987 survey, 2328–59
Multinatl firms US affiliates finances and operations, by industry, country of parent firm, and State, 1987, 2708–48
Multinatl firms US affiliates, finances, and operations, by industry, world area of parent firm, and State, 1989-90, annual rpt, 2704–4
Multinatl US firms and foreign affiliates finances and operations, by industry and country, 1989 benchmark survey, annual rpt, 2704–5
Multinatl US firms foreign affiliates, income statement items by asset size, industry, and country, 1988, biennial article, 8302–2.322
Natl income and product accounts, comprehensive accounts and components, benchmark revisions, 1929-88, 2708–5

Natl income and product accounts, comprehensive accounts and components, *Survey of Current Business*, monthly rpt, 2702–1.29
Occupational injuries, illnesses, and lost workdays, by SIC 2-digit industry, 1990-91, annual press release, 6844–3
Occupational injury and illness rates by circumstances and establishment size, and methodology for computing rates, 1988, industry rpt, 6886–4.4
Occupational injury and illness rates, by SIC 2- to 4-digit industry, 1989-90, annual rpt, 6844–7
Occupational injury and illness rates, by SIC 2- to 4-digit industry, 1990, annual rpt, 6844–1
Pacific territories population and housing detailed characteristics, by location, 1990 Census of Population and Housing, series, 2551–8
Puerto Rico and other US possessions corporations income tax returns, income and tax items, and employment, by selected industry, 1989, article, 8302–2.326
Sales and inventories, by SIC 2- to 3-digit kind of business, monthly rpt, 2413–7
Sales and inventories, monthly rpt, 23842–1.3
SEC registration, firms required to file annual rpts, as of Sept 1991, annual listing, 9734–5
Small Business Admin loan guarantee program participants finances, operations, characteristics, and views, 1991 survey, 9768–25
Small business finances, operations, owner characteristics, and Federal contracts, 1980s-90, annual rpt, 9764–6
Southeastern US employment by industry div, earnings, and hours, for 8 States, quarterly press release, 6942–7
Statistical Abstract of US, 1992 annual data compilation, 2324–1.28
Tax (income) returns filed, by type of filer, selected income items, quarterly rpt, 8302–2.1
Tax (income) returns of corporations, income and tax items by asset size and detailed industry, 1989, annual rpt, 8304–4; 8304–21
Tax (income) returns of corporations with foreign tax credit, income and tax items by industry group, 1988, biennial article, 8302–2.316
Tax (income) returns of partnerships, income statement and balance sheet items, by industry group, 1990, annual article, 8302–2.314
Tax (income) returns of sole proprietorships, income statement items, by industry group, 1990, annual article, 8302–2.317; 8302–2.320
Wage and benefit changes from collective bargaining and mgmt decisions, by industry div, monthly rpt, 6782–1
Wages by occupation, and benefits for office and plant workers, periodic MSA survey rpt series, 6785–12; 6785–16; 6785–17
see also Agricultural marketing
see also Census of Wholesale Trade
see also Industrial purchasing
see also Retail trade
see also Warehouses
see also under By Industry in the "Index by Categories"
see also under names of specific commodities or commodity groups

Wichita, Kans.
Wages by occupation, and benefits for office and plant workers, 1992 survey, periodic MSA rpt, 6785–3.5
see also under By City and By SMSA or MSA in the "Index by Categories"

Widmann, Richard H.
"Ohio Timber Products Output, 1989", 1206–15.11
"Pulpwood Production in the Northeast, 1990", 1204–18

Widows and widowers
Black Americans social and economic characteristics, for South and total US, 1991 and trends from 1950, annual Current Population Rpt, 2546–1.463
Black lung benefits and beneficiaries by recipient type, from 1970, and by State, 1990, annual rpt, 4744–3.7
Census of Population, 1990: population characteristics and living arrangements, by county, place, and urban-rural location, State rpt series, 2531–1
Census of Population, 1990: population characteristics and living arrangements, for Native American, urban, and metro areas, series, 2531–2
Consumer Income, socioeconomic characteristics of persons, families, and households, detailed cross-tabulations, Current Population Rpt series, 2546–6
Deaths and rates, by cause and selected social, demographic, and employment characteristics, 1979-85, natl longitudinal study, 4478–186
Deaths during 1986, decedents health condition, services use, habits, and social, employment, and other characteristics, 4147–20.19
Educational attainment, by social and demographic characteristics and location, 1991 and trends from 1940, biennial Current Population Rpt, 2546–1.460
Farm population, by employment, social, and economic characteristics, and region, 1990, annual Current Population Rpt, 2546–1.458
Foreign and US aged population and characteristics, by country, 1991 and projected to 2020, wallchart, 2328–82
Households and family characteristics, by location, 1991, annual Current Population Rpt, 2546–1.457
Living arrangements, family relationships, and marital status, by selected characteristics, 1991, annual Current Population Rpt, 2546–1.461
Older persons socioeconomic characteristics, 1900s-90 and projected to 2050, biennial chartbook, 12904–1
Pacific territories population and housing detailed characteristics, by location, 1990 Census of Population and Housing, series, 2551–8
Pension plan survivor benefits and coverage of spouses, by income level, age, and sex, 1989, GAO rpt, 26121–450
Population size and components of change, alternative projections 1990-2080 and trends from 1900, annual actuarial rpt, 4706–1.106
Railroad employee benefits program finances and beneficiaries, FY91, annual rpt, 9704–1
Railroad retirement, survivors, unemployment, and health insurance programs, monthly rpt, 9702–2
Single parent families in own and others homes, by financial, housing, and other characteristics, 1989, 2486–1.14
Tax (income) returns of individuals, by filing status, tax item, and income level, 1991, annual article, 8302–2.319
Veterans compensation and pension recipients, for each US war, 1775-1991, annual rpt, 8604–2
Veterans disability and death compensation and pension cases, by type of entitlement and period of service, monthly rpt, 8602–5
Veterans disability and death compensation cases of VA, by entitlement type, period of service, and sex, as of Mar 1992, annual rpt, 8604–13
Veterans disability and death compensation cases of VA, by entitlement type, period of service, sex, age, and State, FY90, annual rpt, 8604–7
Workers compensation laws of States and Fed Govt, 1992 annual rpt, 6504–11
see also Old-Age, Survivors, Disability, and Health Insurance
see also under By Marital Status in the "Index by Categories"

Wilcox, Bruce C., Jr.
"Inward Contaminant Leakage Tests of the S-Tron Corporation Emergency Escape Breathing Device", 7506–10.118

Wilcox, David W.
"Production and Inventory Control at the General Motors Corporation During the 1920s and 1930s", 9375–13.87

Wilcox, James A.
"Measurement and Determinants of Single-Family House Prices", 9373–27.7

Wilderness areas
Acreage and descriptions of natl park system sites, 1991, biennial listing, 5544–5
Acreage and use of public lands, and Land Mgmt Bur activities and finances, annual State rpt series, 5724–11
Acreage, grants, use, revenues, and allocations, for public lands by State, FY91, annual rpt, 5724–1.2
Acreage of land under Forest Service mgmt, by forest and location, 1991, annual rpt, 1204–2
Acreage of land under Natl Park Service mgmt, by site, ownership, and region, FY92, semiannual rpt, 5542–1
Acreage of refuges and other land under Fish and Wildlife Service mgmt, by site and State, as of Sept 1992, annual rpt, 5504–8
Acreage of wilderness areas by State, and Colorado off-road vehicle use, owner expenses, and views on registration fee, 1986-88, hearing, 25318–85
Camping in wilderness areas, impacts on plants and soils, 1979-90 studies, 1208–395
Environmental Quality, status of problems, protection programs, research, and intl issues, 1991 annual rpt, 484–1

Fires (wild) and acreage burned, by type of land, ownership, cause, region, and State, 1984-90, annual rpt, 1204-4
Fires effects on wilderness visitors recreation choices, 1989 local area survey, 1208-422
Fires on wildlands, ecology, mgmt, cultural impacts, and historic patterns, 1990 conf, 1208-415
Forest Service activities and finances, by region and State, FY91, annual rpt, 1204-1.1
Forest Service recreation uses fund outlays by purpose, and wilderness mgmt funds reprogrammed to other activities, FY88-90, GAO rpt, 26113-550
Forests (natl) recreational use, by type of activity and State, 1991, annual rpt, 1204-17
Minerals resources and availability on public lands, State rpt series, 5606-7
New Mexico Caballo Resource Area public land mgmt, and grazing, environmental, and leasing activities, FY90-91, annual rpt, 5724-17
Visits and overnight stays in natl park system, by park and State, monthly rpt, 5542-4
Visits and overnight stays in natl park system, by park and State, 1991, annual rpt, 5544-12

Wildlife and wildlife conservation

Agricultural Conservation Program acreage and projects, by State, 1936-90, quinquennial rpt, 1808-1
Agricultural Conservation Program participation and payments, by practice and State, FY91, annual rpt, 1804-7
Assistance (financial and nonfinancial) of Fed Govt, 1992 base edition, annual listing, 104-5
Bears (grizzly) in Yellowstone Natl Park area, monitoring results, 1991, annual rpt, 5544-4
Cattle and calves loss to predators, disease, and other causes, by region and State, 1991, 1618-22
Coastal and riparian areas environmental conditions, fish, wildlife, use, and mgmt, for individual ecosystems, series, 5506-9
Colorado River Salinity Control Program participation and payments, FY87-91, annual rpt, 1804-23
Colorado River Storage Project finances and activities in western States, FY91, annual rpt, 5824-3
Criminal sentences for Federal offenses, guidelines by offense and circumstances, series, 17668-1
Environmental Quality, status of problems, protection programs, research, and intl issues, 1991 annual rpt, 484-1
Fed Govt spending in States, by type, program, agency, and State, FY91, annual rpt, 2464-2
Fires on wildlands, ecology, mgmt, cultural impacts, and historic patterns, 1990 conf, 1208-415
Fish and Wildlife Service conservation and habitat mgmt activities, FY91, annual narrative rpt, 5504-20
Forest Service activities and finances, by region and State, FY91, annual rpt, 1204-1
Forests (aspen) vegetation, climate, and other environmental characteristics, for upper Great Lakes area, 1991 rpt, 1208-418
Forests (natl) recreational use, by type of activity and State, 1991, annual rpt, 1204-17
Forests (old-growth) ecology, mgmt, and research methods, for Rocky Mountains and southwest US, 1992 conf, 1208-421
Forests inventories use in assessment of wildlife habitats, with data for northern coastal California, as of 1985, 1208-414
Horse and burro wild herd areas in southwestern States, adoptions by State, 1991, annual rpt, 5724-15
Horse and burro wild herd population, and Bur of Land Mgmt removals and disposition, by county, annual State rpt series, 5724-11
Idaho Snake River area birds of prey, rodent, and vegetation distribution and characteristics, research results, 1991, annual rpt, 5724-14
Land Mgmt Bur activities and funding by State, FY90, annual rpt, 5724-13
Land Mgmt Bur activities in southwestern US, FY91, annual rpt, 5724-15
Land under Fish and Wildlife Service mgmt, acreage by site and State, as of Sept 1992, annual rpt, 5504-8
Minerals offshore lease sales environmental and economic impacts in coastal areas, final statement series, 5736-7
Mink population, breeding, trapping, pollutant levels, and research status, for Great Lakes area, 1991 conf, 14648-27
Natl historic and natural landmarks damaged and threatened, with owner, location, damage type, and recommended remedial action, 1990, annual listing, 5544-16
Northeastern US hardwood forests ecology and mgmt, 1992, 1208-405
Otter population, breeding, trapping, pollutant levels, and research status, for Great Lakes area, 1991 conf, 14648-27
Pacific Northwest old-growth forests plant and wildlife population and species diversity, 1991 compilation of papers, 1208-386
Polar bear harvest by Alaska Natives, by village, 1989/90, annual rpt, 5504-12
Pollutants health effects for animals by species and for humans, and environmental levels, for selected substances, series, 5506-14
Public lands acreage and use, and Land Mgmt Bur activities and finances, annual State rpt series, 5724-11
Public lands acreage, grants, use, revenues, and allocations, by State, FY91, annual rpt, 5724-1.2
Radiation and other pollutant releases from DOE contractor research lab and nuclear weapons facilities, monitoring results, annual site rpt series, 3324-2
Radionuclide concentrations in air, water, humans, animals, and milk near Nevada and other nuclear test sites, 1990, annual rpt, 9194-17
Research (agricultural) funding and staffing for USDA, State agencies, and other instns, by topic, FY91, annual rpt, 1744-2
Research on fish and wildlife population, habitat, and mgmt, technical rpt series, 5506-12
Restoration and hunter safety funding of Fish and Wildlife Service, by State, FY92, semiannual press release, 5502-1
Restoration programs of Fish and Wildlife Service, funding, land purchases, and project listing, by State, FY90, annual rpt, 5504-1
Sheep and lamb losses, by type of predator and disease, for western US, 1986, 1548-382
Timber in southeastern US, resources mgmt and research, 1990 biennial conf papers, 1204-35
Timber sales of Forest Service, expenses, and operations, by region, State, and natl forest, FY91, annual rpts, 1204-36
Tropical forests condition, conservation methods, and biological diversity issues, 1992 rpt, 26358-262
Wolf (gray) kills of livestock, and farmer compensation claims and payments, for Minnesota, late 1970s-80s, 5508-115
see also Birds and bird conservation
see also Endangered species
see also Fish and fishing industry
see also Fishing, sport
see also Hunting and fishing licenses
see also Hunting and trapping
see also Marine mammals
see also Marine resources conservation
see also Wildlife refuges
see also Zoological parks

Wildlife refuges

Acreage of land under Forest Service mgmt, by forest and location, 1991, annual rpt, 1204-2
Acreage of land under Natl Park Service mgmt, by site, ownership, and region, FY92, semiannual rpt, 5542-1
Acreage of refuges and other land under Fish and Wildlife Service mgmt, by site and State, as of Sept 1992, annual rpt, 5504-8
Alaska Arctic Natl Wildlife Refuge oil reserves and production, alternative forecasts 1985-2015, 3166-6.64
Army Corps of Engineers water resources dev projects, characteristics, and costs, 1950s-89, biennial State rpt series, 3756-1
Army Corps of Engineers water resources dev projects, characteristics, and costs, 1950s-91, biennial State rpt series, 3756-2
Pesticide levels and water toxicity indicators, for natl wildlife refuge wetlands in South Dakota, 1990, 5508-117
Restoration programs of Fish and Wildlife Service, funding, land purchases, and project listing, by State, FY90, annual rpt, 5504-1
Visits and overnight stays in natl park system, by park and State, 1991, annual rpt, 5544-12
Waterfowl (migratory) refuge and breeding area acreage acquired by Fed Govt, and costs, by site and State, FY92, annual rpt, 14784-1
Wetlands wildlife and migratory bird habitat acquisition, funding by State, 1992, press release, 5306-4.13; 5306-4.16

Wilkinson, James
"Bank Holding Company Performance, 1991", 9381–14

Willamette River
Freight (waterborne domestic and foreign) by commodity, traffic, and passengers, by port and waterway, 1989, annual rpt, 3754–3.4
Water supply and quality in streams and lakes, and groundwater levels in wells, by drainage basin, 1990, annual State rpt series, 5666–10
Water supply and quality in streams and lakes, and groundwater levels in wells, by drainage basin, 1991, annual State rpt series, 5666–12
Water supply in US and southern Canada, streamflow, surface and groundwater conditions, and reservoir levels, by location, monthly rpt, 5662–3

Williams, Allan F.
"Use of Seatbelts in Cars with Automatic Belts", 4042–3.320

Williams, Barbara T.
"Homeowners and Home Improvements: 1987", 2486–1.13

Williams, Christopher
"Projections of National Health Expenditures", 26306–6.175

Williams, Deborah
"Improving the Area Wage Index: The Area Wage Index and the Mix of Occupations Across Areas", 17206–2.31
"Role of Profitability and Community Characteristics in Hospital Closure: An Urban and Rural Analysis", 17206–2.28
"Winners and Losers Under PPS", 17206–2.40

Williams, Donald R.
"Dynamic Analysis of Recent Changes in the Rate of Part-Time Employment", 9377–9.129

Williams, Franklin E.
"U.S. Plumbing Products: An Export Market Plan", 2048–156

Williams, Gerald D.
"Apparent Per Capita Alcohol Consumption: National, State and Regional Trends, 1977-88", 4486–1.11
"Apparent Per Capita Alcohol Consumption: National, State and Regional Trends, 1977-89", 4486–1.15

Williams, Jo A.
"Distribution of Kemp's Ridley Sea Turtles (Lepidochelys kempi) Along the Texas Coast: An Atlas", 2168–132

Williams, Joan
"Natural Sweeteners, Industry and Trade Summary", 9885–8.9

Willits, Susan A.
"Veneer Recovery of Douglas-Fir from the Coast and Cascade Ranges of Oregon and Washington", 1208–396

Wilmington, Del.
CPI by component for US city average, and by region, population size, and for 15 metro areas, monthly rpt, 6762–1
CPI by component for US city average, and by selected metro area, region, and population size, monthly rpt, 6762–2
Wages by occupation, and benefits, for office and plant workers, 1991 survey, periodic MSA rpt, 6785–16.3
see also under By City and By SMSA or MSA in the "Index by Categories"

Wilmington, N.C.
Freight (waterborne domestic and foreign) by commodity, traffic, and passengers, by port and waterway, 1989, annual rpt, 3754–3.1

Wilson, K. E.
"Water Resources Activities of the USGS in Wyoming, Oct. 1989-Sept. 1991", 5666–26.26

Wilson, Robert H.
"Trends in Wage and Salary Inequality, 1967-88", 6722–1.328

Wind
see Meteorology
see Storms
see Weather
see Wind energy

Wind energy
Certification applications filed with FERC, for small power production and cogeneration facilities, FY80-91, annual listing, 3084–13
Electric power plants and capacity, by fuel used, owner, location, and operating status, 1991 and for units planned 1992-2001, annual listing, 3164–36
Pacific Northwest nonutility electric power generation and capacity, by energy source, purchasing utility, and facility, forecasts 1991-2012, annual rpt, 3224–3.4
Supply, demand, and prices, by fuel type and end-use sector, alternative projections 1990-2010, annual rpt, 3164–75
Supply, demand, and prices, by fuel type and end-use sector, projections and underlying assumptions, 1995-2010, annual rpt, 3164–90
Supply, demand, and prices, by fuel type and end-use sector, with foreign comparisons, 1981-90, annual fact book, 3164–76

Windau, Janice
"Fatal Work Injuries: Census for 31 States", 6722–1.338

Windfall profit tax
Collections of excise tax, by source, quarterly rpt, 8302–1
Collections, refunds, and taxes due IRS, by State and region, FY91, annual rpt, 8304–3
Income tax returns of individuals with high incomes, detailed data, 1988, annual rpt, 8304–2
Oil company effective income tax rates, with background income and tax data for domestic and foreign operations, 1977-89, 3168–124
Producers finances and operations, by energy type for US firms domestic and foreign operations, 1990, annual rpt, 3164–44
Tax (excise) collections of IRS, by source, quarterly rpt, 8302–2.1

Windle, Michael
"Alcohol Use and Abuse: Some Findings from the National Adolescent Student Health Survey", 4482–1.302

Wine and winemaking
Brazil table and wine grape production by variety, and wine exports and imports by country, 1991-92, article, 1925–34.341
Business statistics, detailed data for major industries and economic indicators, *Survey of Current Business*, monthly rpt, 2702–1.13
Business statistics, detailed data for major industries and economic indicators, 1960-91, *Survey of Current Business* biennial supplement, 2704–1
Consumption of alcohol, by beverage type, region, and State, 1977-88, annual rpt, 4486–1.11
Consumption of alcohol, by beverage type, region, and State, 1977-89, annual rpt, 4486–1.15
Consumption, supply, trade, prices, spending, and indexes, by food commodity, 1990, annual rpt, 1544–4
County Business Patterns, 1989: employment, establishments, and payroll, by SIC 2- to 4-digit industry and county, annual State rpt series, 2326–8
County Business Patterns, 1990: employment, establishments, and payroll, by SIC 2- to 4-digit industry and county, annual State rpt series, 2326–6
CPI by component for US city average, and by selected metro area, region, and population size, monthly rpt, 6762–2
EC wine trade, with exports by country, 1988-91, article, 1925–34.324
Exports and imports (agricultural) of US, by commodity and country, bimonthly rpt, 1522–1
Exports and imports (agricultural) of US, by detailed commodity and country, 1991, annual rpt, 1524–8
Exports and imports (agricultural) of US, by detailed commodity and country, 1991, semiannual rpt, 1522–4
Exports and imports between US and outlying areas, by detailed commodity and mode of transport, 1991, annual rpt, 2424–11
Exports and imports of US, by country and detailed commodity, monthly rpt, 2422–12
Exports and imports of US, by Harmonized System 6-digit commodity and country, 1991, annual rpt, 2424–13
Exports of US, detailed Schedule B commodities with countries of destination, 1991, annual rpt, 2424–10
Foreign and US fresh and processed fruit, vegetable, and nut production and trade, FAS monthly circular with articles, 1925–34
Fruit (noncitrus) and nut production, prices, and use, by crop and State, 1989-91, annual rpt, 1621–18.1
Grape shipments from California and arrivals by city by mode of transport, prices, and production, by variety, 1970s-90, annual rpt, 1311–25
Grapes crushed and purchased, and grower prices and returns, for California, by type and variety, 1990-91, annual rpt, 1311–30
Hungary vineyard area, wine grape production, and exports by country, 1988-90, article, 1925–34.331
Input-output structure of US economy, detailed interindustry transactions for 541 industries, and components of final demand, 1982 benchmark data, 2708–17
Inventory and supply of wine, by type of wine, source, and selected State, periodic situation rpt with articles, 1561–6
Manufacturing annual survey, 1990: finances and operations, by SIC 2- to 4-digit industry, series, 2506–14

Manufacturing census, 1987: concentration of largest firms measured by value added, and for shipments by SIC 2- and 4-digit industry, subject rpt, 2497–6
Manufacturing census, 1987: shipments of manufacturers products, by customer class and SIC 2- and 4-digit industry, subject rpt, 2497–4
Occupational injury and illness rates, by SIC 2- to 4-digit industry, 1989-90, annual rpt, 6844–7
Occupational injury and illness rates, by SIC 2- to 4-digit industry, 1990, annual rpt, 6844–1
Price indexes (producer), by stage of processing and detailed commodity, monthly rpt, 6762–6
Price indexes (producer), by stage of processing and detailed commodity, monthly 1991, annual rpt, 6764–2
Production, prices, and use of noncitrus fruit and nuts, by crop and State, 1989-91, annual rpt, 1621–18.3
Production, stocks, and taxable and tax-free removals, for wine by State, monthly rpt, 8486–1.2
Tax rates and revenue of State and local govts, by source and State, 1992 and historical trends, annual rpt, 10044–1
Youth alcohol use, knowledge, attitudes, and info sources, series, 4006–10

Winokur, Robert P.
"Publications of the Rocky Mountain Forest and Range Experiment Station, 1980-89", 1208–403

Winston Salem, N.C.
Wages by occupation, and benefits for office and plant workers, 1992 survey, periodic MSA rpt, 6785–3.5

Winter sports
Forest Service activities and finances, by region and State, FY91, annual rpt, 1204–1.1
Forests (natl) recreational use, by type of activity and State, 1991, annual rpt, 1204–17
Injuries from use of consumer products and related activities, by severity and victim age and sex, 1990, annual rpt, 9164–7
Injuries from use of consumer products, by severity, victim age, and detailed product, 1991, annual rpt, 9164–6
Public lands acreage, grants, use, revenues, and allocations, by State, FY91, annual rpt, 5724–1.2

Wiretapping
see Electronic surveillance

Wisconsin
Banks (insured commercial and savings) deposits by instn, State, MSA, and county, as of June 1991, annual regional rpt, 9295–3.3
Business and economic conditions, Fed Reserve 9th District, quarterly journal, 9383–19
Cranberry production, prices, use, and acreage, for selected States, 1990-91 and forecast 1992, annual rpt, 1621–18.5
Dairy prices, by product and selected area, with related marketing data, 1991, annual rpt, 1317–1
Deaths and rates, by detailed location, cause, and demographic characteristics, 1989, US Vital Statistics annual rpt, 4144–3.1
Employment, earnings, and hours, by selected SIC 1- to 4-digit industry, State, and for 275 MSAs, 1987-92, 6748–81
Fed Govt spending in States and local areas, by type, State, county, and city, FY91, annual rpt, 2464–3
Fed Govt spending in States, by type, program, agency, and State, FY91, annual rpt, 2464–2
HHS financial aid, by program, recipient, State, and city, FY91, annual regional listing, 4004–3.5
Hospital deaths of Medicare patients, actual and expected rates by diagnosis, and hospital characteristics, by instn, FY90 annual State rpt, 4654–14.51
Housing census, 1990: inventory, occupancy, and costs, State fact sheet, 2326–21.51
Housing census, 1990: summary unit characteristics, by householder race and age, county, place, and urban-rural location, State rpt, 2471–1.51
Housing vacancy rates for single and multifamily units and mobile homes in FHLB 7th District, by ZIP code, annual MSA rpt series, 9304–18
Lumber (pulpwood) production in 3 North Central States, by species and county, 1990, 1208–397
Military prime contract awards, by contractor, service branch, State, and city, FY91, annual rpt, 3544–22
Mineral Industry Surveys, State reviews of production, 1991, preliminary annual rpt, 5614–6
Minerals Yearbook, Vol 2, 1989: State review of production and sales by commodity, and business activity, annual rpt, 5604–16.51
Mortgage interest fixed and adjustable rates and fees offered by Wisconsin S&Ls, monthly rpt, discontinued, 9302–7
Multinatl firms US affiliates finances and operations, by industry, country of parent firm, and State, 1987, 2708–48
Physicians, by specialty, age, sex, and location of training and practice, 1990, State rpt, 4116–6.51
Population and housing census, 1990: detailed geographic coverage, State CD-ROM, 2551–9.3
Population and housing census, 1990: summary characteristics, by county, subdiv, and place, State rpt, 2551–7.51
Population census, 1990: population characteristics and living arrangements, by county, place, and urban-rural location, State rpt, 2531–1.51
Potato production, acreage, prices, and shipments, for 7 major producer States, and compared to other States, 1970s-92, annual rpt, 1311–29
Savings instns, FHLB 7th District and natl cost of funds indexes, and mortgage rates, monthly rpt, 9302–30
Statistical Abstract of US, 1992 annual data compilation, 2324–1
Timber in Wisconsin, resources and removals by species, forest type, ownership, and county, series, 1206–34
Water supply and quality in streams and lakes, and groundwater levels in wells, by drainage basin, 1990, annual State rpt, 5666–10.46
see also Kenosha, Wis.
see also Milwaukee, Wis.
see also Sheboygan County, Wis.
see also St. Croix County, Wis.
see also under By State in the "Index by Categories"

Withholding tax
Alien nonresidents income from US sources and tax withheld by country and US tax treaty status, detailed data compilation for income tax returns, 1984-88, quinquennial rpt, 8308–31
Alien nonresidents income from US sources and tax withheld by country and US tax treaty status, 1989, annual article, 8302–2.308
Budget of US, authoritative financial statements with appropriations, outlays, and receipts, by category and agency, FY91, annual rpt, 8104–2.2
Collections, enforcement, and litigation activity of IRS, with data by type of tax, region, and State, FY91, annual rpt, 8304–3
Fed Govt agencies delinquent withholding tax accounts, and compared to other taxpayers, 1990, hearing, 21788–206
Final withholding tax systems use in 4 countries, and feasibility of US adoption, with background data, 1986-92, GAO rpt, 26119–400
Foreign countries tax credits on corporate income tax returns, with income and tax items by industry group, 1988, biennial article, 8302–2.316
Foreign partners of US partnerships, detailed data compilation for income tax returns, 1970s-89, quinquennial rpt, 8308–31
Foreign partners of US partnerships, income and tax withheld, by country, 1990, article, 8302–2.324
Natl income and product accounts, comprehensive accounts and components, benchmark revisions, 1929-88, 2708–5
Natl income and product accounts, comprehensive accounts and components, *Survey of Current Business*, monthly rpt, 2702–1.26
Returns and supplemental documents filed, by type, FY91 and projected to FY2000, semiannual rpt, 8302–4
Returns and supplemental documents filed, by type, 1990 and projected to 1999, annual article, 8302–2.304
Returns filed, by type of tax and IRS district, 1990 and projected 1991-98, annual rpt, 8304–24
Returns filed, by type of tax, region, and IRS service center, projected 1991-98 and trends from 1978, annual rpt, 8304–9
Returns filed for individual income tax, detailed data, 1988, annual rpt, 8304–2
Returns of individuals, by filing status, tax item, and income level, 1991, annual article, 8302–2.319
Statements of income tax withholding and related documents filed, by type and IRS service center, 1991 and projected 1992-99, annual rpt, 8304–22
see also Social security tax

Witnesses
Crime victim compensation and support service programs funding, by offense and State, FY88-90, biennial rpt, 6064–37

Criminal sentences for Federal offenses, guidelines by offense and circumstances, series, 17668–1
Felony case processing from arrest to sentencing, cases and duration by disposition and offense, for selected cities, 1988, annual rpt, 6064–27
Immunity requests by Federal prosecutors to US Attorney General, and witnesses involved, data compilation, 1992 annual rpt, 6064–6.5
Marshals Service activities, FY91, annual rpt, 6294–1
Prisoners in Federal and contract instns, by selected characteristics, region, and Federal instn, FY89, annual rpt, 6244–1.1

Witt, L. A.
"Dimensionality and Construct Validity of the Perceptions of Organizational Politics Scale (POPS)", 7506–10.106
"Effects of Subordinate Feedback to the Supervisor and Participation in Decision-Making in the Prediction of Organizational Support", 7506–10.113
"Gender, Equity, and Job Satisfaction", 7506–10.105
"Organizational Goal Congruence and Job Attitudes Revisited", 7506–10.104
"Organizational Politics, Participation in Decision-Making, and Job Satisfaction", 7506–10.117
"Procedural Justice, Occupational Identification, and Organizational Commitment", 7506–10.121

Wixon, Bernard
"Implementing an SSI Model Using the Survey of Income and Program Participation", 4746–26.23
"Rationale for a SIPP-Based Microsimulation Model of SSI and OASDI", 4746–26.23

Wizman, Thierry A.
"Evidence from Tests of the Relation Between Interest-Rate Spreads and Economic Activity", 9385–8.131
"Relative Cost of Capital for Marginal Firms over the Business Cycle", 9385–1.312
"Returns on Capital Assets and Variations in Economic Growth and Volatility: A Model of Bayesian Learning", 9385–8.124
"What Moves Investment? Cash Flows in a Forward-Looking Model of Capital Expenditures", 9385–8.129

Wokutch, Richard E.
"U.S. and Japanese Work Injury and Illness Experience", 6722–1.318

Wolf, gray
see Endangered species

Wolken, John D.
"Banking Markets and the Use of Financial Services by Households", 9362–1.303

Women
AIDS cases by risk group, race, sex, age, State, and MSA, and deaths, quarterly rpt, 4202–9
AIDS knowledge, attitudes, and risk behaviors of women in methadone maintenance programs, effects of life skills training, 1988-89 local area study, article, 4042–3.353
Alcohol use among Mexican American women, by whether immigrant and occupational group, 1992 article, 4482–1.309
Asian and Pacific Islands Americans social and economic characteristics, for West and total US, 1990-91, Current Population Report, 2546–1.462
Black Americans social and economic characteristics, for South and total US, 1991 and trends from 1950, annual Current Population Rpt, 2546–1.463
Black women's labor force status, earnings, and other economic status indicators, and compared to whites, various periods 1939-88, 11048–191
Cancer (brain) risk relation to menopausal status and ovary removal, Germany study, 1992 article, 4472–1.340
Cancer (breast) cases, survival, and death rates, by age, and change by birth cohort, 1970s-90s, article, 4472–1.341
Cancer (breast) death risk by presence of genetic mutations, and family breast cancer history, 1977-82, article, 4472–1.317
Cancer (breast) disease-free survival probability relation to tumor size, histology, and other characteristics, study, 1992 article, 4472–1.335
Cancer (breast) progression relation to loss of chromosomal heterozygosity, 1984-91 local area study, article, 4472–1.310
Cancer (breast) recurrence risk by thymidine kinase levels and estrogen receptor status, 1992 article, 4472–1.355
Cancer (breast) research funding, cases, and deaths, 1970s-90, GAO rpt, 26131–92
Cancer (breast) risk for women relation to incidence among male relatives, 1978-79, article, 4472–1.330
Cancer (breast) risk of postmenopausal women relation to dietary fat and other nutrient intake, 1986-89, article, 4472–1.328
Cancer (breast) risk relation to breast density, for Canada, 1992 article, 4472–1.332
Cancer (breast) risk relation to estrogen replacement therapy use, body mass index, and other risk factors, 1987-89 NYC study, article, 4472–1.350
Cancer (breast) risk relation to radiotherapy treatment for primary breast cancer, study, 1992 article, 4472–1.333
Cancer (breast) screening use relation to cancer anxiety, for high-risk women, 1992 article, 4472–1.301
Cancer (breast) severity relation to HER-2/neu gene amplification and overexpression, 1992 study, 4472–1.337
Cancer (breast) symptoms duration prior to seeking care, for black and white women, by selected characteristics, 1985-86 local area study, article, 4472–1.323
Cancer (breast) tumor genetic mutations, and presence relation to patient survival, 1992 article, 4472–1.329
Cancer (breast) tumor microvessel density and node status relation to patient survival and relapse, local area study, 1992 article, 4472–1.357
Cancer (breast) tumors with genetic mutations, 1992 article, 4472–1.305
Cancer (breast and cervical) deaths and rates by State, and in situ case rates by age, by race, 1970s-86, article, 4202–7.312
Cancer (breast and cervical) screening use and reasons for nonuse, by age, race, income, and State, 1987-89, article, 4202–7.313
Cancer (cervical) and dysplasia rates in Appalachian States, compared to total US, 1986-87, article, 4472–1.327
Cancer (cervical) relapse and metastasis risk related to c-myc gene overexpression and human papillomavirus infection, 1984-88 study, article, 4472–1.348
Cancer (cervical and breast) screening among poor black women, effects of in-home promotion program, 1989-92, article, 4042–3.338
Cancer (liver) risk for women relation to parity and oral contraceptives use, 1985-86, article, 4472–1.331
Cancer (lung) risk relation to environmental smoke exposure, for nonsmoking women, local area study, 1992 article, 4472–1.342
Census of Population and Housing, 1990: detailed geographic coverage, State CD-ROM series, 2551–9
Census of Population and Housing, 1990: population and housing characteristics, detailed geographic coverage, State CD-ROM series, 2551–10
Census of Population and Housing, 1990: summary characteristics, by county, subdiv, and place, State rpt series, 2551–7
Census of Population and Housing, 1990: summary characteristics, households, and land area, by county, subdiv, and place, State rpt series, 2551–1
Census of Population, 1990: population characteristics and living arrangements, by county, place, and urban-rural location, State rpt series, 2531–1
Census of Population, 1990: population characteristics and living arrangements, for Native American, urban, and metro areas, series, 2531–2
Child support and alimony payments, and payments share of income, by selected characteristics of payer and payee, 1988-89, article, 1702–1.305
Crime, criminal justice admin and enforcement, and public opinion, data compilation, 1992 annual rpt, 6064–6
Crimes, arrests, and rates, by offense, offender characteristics, population size, and jurisdiction, 1991, annual rpt, 6224–2.1; 6224–2.2
Deaths and rates, by cause and selected social, demographic, and employment characteristics, 1979-85, natl longitudinal study, 4478–186
Deaths and rates, by detailed location, cause, and demographic characteristics, 1989, US Vital Statistics annual rpt, 4144–3
Developing countries economic, population, and agricultural data, US and other aid sources, and AID activity, country rpt series, 9916–12
Drug (prescription) clinical trials representation of women, and FDA policy guidance, 1988-91, GAO rpt, 26121–486
Drug abuse by mothers, treatment and other services use, referrals, needs, and barriers, for 13 NIDA-funded programs, 1990/91 survey, 4498–76

Drug abuse history and selected other characteristics of women arrestees, for 4 cities, 1988-89, 6068-246
Drug, alcohol, and cigarette use, by selected characteristics, 1991 survey, annual rpt series, 4494-5
Education data, detail for elementary, secondary, and higher education, 1920s-91 and projected to 2002, annual rpt, 4824-1
Educational equity program for women, grants and contracts by project, type, and State, 1988-92, annual rpt, 4804-2
Family members supporting others outside household, by relationship, recipient living arrangements, and provider characteristics, 1988, Current Population Rpt, 2546-20.21
Health condition and care indicators, 1950s-90 with health improvement and disease prevention goals for 1990, annual data compilation, 4144-11
Higher education degrees awarded, by level, field, race, and sex, 1989/90 and trends from 1980/81, annual rpt, 4844-17
Higher education enrollment, by level, race, and sex, fall 1980-90, biennial rpt, 4844-15
Homeless adults educational services, program activities, and participation, by State, FY88-89, annual rpt, 4804-39
Hospital deaths of Medicare patients, actual and expected rates by diagnosis, with hospital characteristics, by instn, FY90, annual State rpt series, 4654-14
Households composition, income, benefits, and labor force status, Survey of Income and Program Participation methodology, working paper series, 2626-10
Income (household) and poverty status under alternative income definitions, by recipient characteristics, 1979-91, annual Current Population Rpt, 2546-6.78
Income (personal) relative to median, by race and selected other characteristics, mid 1960s-89, Current Population Rpt, 2546-6.73
Jail population of women, by criminal background and sociodemographic characteristics, with comparisons to men, 1989, 6066-19.66
Marriage, divorce, and remarriage of women by age, and child living arrangements, by race, 1970s-90, Current Population Rpt, 2546-2.166
Menopause treatment with hormone replacement therapy, use, health risks, and research funding, 1992 rpt, 26358-261
Mexican American obese women participation in weight loss and nutrition education programs, effectiveness, local area study, 1992 article, 4042-3.356
Military service academies prep schools costs and student performance indicators, 1988-90, GAO rpt, 26123-380
Nuclear engineering enrollment and degrees granted by instn and State, and grad placement, by student characteristics, 1991, annual rpt, 3004-5
OASDHI, Medicaid, SSI, and related programs benefits, beneficiary characteristics, and trust funds, selected years 1937-90, annual rpt, 4744-3
Older persons income sources, assets, and health care financing issues, 1991 rpt, 10176-3.4
Older women living alone, income by source, and expenses by type, by marital status, 1988-89, article, 1702-1.301
Pacific territories population and housing detailed characteristics, by location, 1990 Census of Population and Housing, series, 2551-8
Population economic well-being indicators, by selected characteristics and household income and income-to-poverty ratio, 1984, 2546-20.22
Prison and community-based facilities, population, employment, spending, and other characteristics, by State and for Fed Govt, 1990, quinquennial rpt, 6068-218
Prisoners, characteristics, and movements, by State, 1990, annual rpt, 6064-26
Prisoners in Federal and contract instns, by selected characteristics, region, and Federal instn, FY89, annual rpt, 6244-1.1
Radiation protection and health physics enrollment and degrees granted by instn and State, and grad placement, by student characteristics, 1991, annual rpt, 3004-7
Science and engineering employment and education of minorities, women, and disabled, by field, mid 1970s-91, biennial rpt, 9624-20
Science and engineering grad enrollment, by field, source of funds, and characteristics of student and instn, 1990, annual rpt, 9627-7
Science and Engineering Indicators, employment, education, R&D funding, and industry impacts, with foreign comparisons, 1960s-91, biennial rpt, 9624-10
Single parent families in own and others homes, by financial, housing, and other characteristics, 1989, 2486-1.14
Statistical Abstract of US, 1992 annual data compilation, 2324-1
Veteran women population, by period of service, FY70-91, annual rpt, 8604-5.1
Veterans disability and death compensation cases of VA, by entitlement type, period of service, sex, age, and State, FY90, annual rpt, 8604-7
see also Families and households
see also Fertility
see also Mammography
see also Maternal deaths
see also Maternity
see also Maternity benefits
see also Maternity homes
see also Prenatal care
see also Sex discrimination
see also Teenage pregnancy
see also Women-owned businesses
see also Women's employment
see also under By Sex in the "Index by Categories"

Women-Owned Business Enterprise Survey
see Survey of Women-Owned Businesses

Women-owned businesses
Airway facilities and services contract awards of FAA to minority- and woman-owned businesses, FY87-90, annual rpt, 7504-37
DOE contracts and grants, by category, State, and for top contractors, FY91, annual rpt, 3004-21
DOE procurement contract awards to small businesses, by business type and subagency, FY90, annual rpt, 3004-35
Mgmt and financial aid from Minority Business Dev Centers, and characteristics of businesses, by region and State, FY91, annual rpt, 2104-6
Minority business Federal procurement set-aside contracts, by participant race and sex, industry, firm, and State, FY90, annual rpt, 9764-8
NASA procurement contract awards, by type, contractor, State, and country, FY92 with trends from 1961, semiannual rpt, 9502-6
Owner and business characteristics, for minority- and woman-owned firms, by industry, employment and sales size, and form of ownership, 1987 survey, 2328-59
Small Business Admin loan guarantee program participants finances, operations, characteristics, and views, 1991 survey, 9768-25
Small business finances, operations, owner characteristics, and Federal contracts, 1980s-90, annual rpt, 9764-6
Statistical Abstract of US, 1992 annual data compilation, 2324-1.17
see also Survey of Women-Owned Businesses

Women's Bureau
Labor force status, earnings, and other characteristics of women, with comparisons to men, fact sheet series, 6564-1

Women's employment
AFDC beneficiaries demographic and financial characteristics, by State, FY90, annual rpt, 4584-7
Aircraft pilot and nonpilot certificates held and issued, by type of certificate, region, State, and for women, 1990, annual rpt, 7504-1.7
Aircraft pilot and nonpilot certificates held, by type of certificate, age, sex, region, and State, 1991, annual rpt, 7504-2
Apprenticeship programs regulation, participation of minorities and women, and earnings, by occupation, 1990, GAO rpt, 26121-446
Asian and Pacific Islands Americans social and economic characteristics, for West and total US, 1990-91, Current Population Report, 2546-1.462
Athletic depts at NCAA Div I schools, staff by race, and income, by sex and position, 1990/91, GAO rpt, 26121-476
Black Americans social and economic characteristics, for South and total US, 1991 and trends from 1950, annual Current Population Rpt, 2546-1.463
Black and white women's occupational differences, and compared to men, selected years 1940-88, article, 6722-1.321
Black women's labor force status, earnings, and other economic status indicators, and compared to whites, various periods 1939-88, 11048-191
Business statistics, detailed data for major industries and economic indicators, 1960-91, *Survey of Current Business* biennial supplement, 2704-1
Census of Population and Housing, 1990: population and housing characteristics, detailed geographic coverage, State CD-ROM series, 2551-10

Census of Population and Housing, 1990: summary characteristics, by county, subdiv, and place, State rpt series, 2551–7
Child care arrangements of mothers employed and in school, and costs, by age of child and characteristics of mother, 1988, Current Population Rpt, 2546–20.24
Child care arrangements of younger working mothers, and costs, by selected characteristics, 1988, 6726–2.1
Child support payment and visitation practices of absent fathers, and mothers with custody, by employment and other characteristics, 1988, article, 6722–1.329
Dallas-Fort Worth metro area employment, earnings, hours, and CPI changes, late 1970s-91, annual rpt, 6964–2
Disabled women's employment by occupation, and earnings, by race, 1988, fact sheet, 6564–1.2
DOT activities by subagency, budget, and summary accident data, FY89, annual rpt, 7304–1
DOT employment, by subagency, occupation, and selected personnel characteristics, FY91, annual rpt, 7304–18
Drug abuse history and selected other characteristics of women arrestees, for 4 cities, 1988-89, 6068–246
Education data, detail for elementary, secondary, and higher education, 1920s-91 and projected to 2002, annual rpt, 4824–1
Educational attainment, by social and demographic characteristics and location, 1991 and trends from 1940, biennial Current Population Rpt, 2546–1.460
Educational enrollment, by grade, instn type and control, and student characteristics, 1990 and trends from 1947, annual Current Population Rpt, 2546–1.459
Employment and Earnings, detailed data, monthly rpt, 6742–2.5
Employment and economic conditions, alternative BLS projections to 2005 and trends 1975-90, biennial rpt, 6744–19
Employment, earnings, and hours, by SIC 1- to 4-digit industry, monthly 1989-Feb 1992, annual rpt, 6744–4
Employment of minorities and women by industry sector, and govt salaries, by occupation, mid 1960s-90, chartbook, 9248–20
Employment of minorities and women, by occupation, SIC 1- to 3-digit industry, State, and MSA, 1991, annual rpt, 9244–1
Employment part-time of women, transitions by marital status and whether young children present, 1988 and trends from 1978, 6726–2.2
Employment situation, earnings, hours, and other BLS economic indicators, transcripts of BLS Commissioner's monthly testimony, periodic rpt, 23846–4
Employment, unemployment, and labor force characteristics, by region, State, and selected metro area, 1991, annual rpt, 6744–7
Family life and relationships quality and other issues, views of parents and children, 1990 survey, 15528–2
Farm population, by employment, social, and economic characteristics, and region, 1990, annual Current Population Rpt, 2546–1.458
Fed Equal Opportunity Recruitment Program activity, and employment by sex, race, pay grade, and occupational group, FY91, annual rpt, 9844–33
Fed Govt civilian employees demographic and employment characteristics, as of Sept 1991, annual article, 9842–1.301
Fed Govt civilian employees demographic characteristics, by agency, 1990, GAO rpt, 26119–383
Fed Govt employment of minorities, disabled, and veterans, and years of service, by occupation, age, sex, and agency, as of Sept 1990, biennial rpt, 9844–27
Fed Govt employment of minorities, women, and disabled, by agency and occupation, FY90, annual rpt, 9244–10
Food spending of women-headed households, by item and selected characteristics, and compared to other households, 1970s-88, 1548–391
Health care professionals supply and education, by professional and other characteristics, and location, 1960s-92 and projected to 2020, biennial rpt, 4114–8
Households and family characteristics, by location, 1991, annual Current Population Rpt, 2546–1.457
Houston metro area employment, earnings, hours, and CPI changes, 1970s-91, annual rpt, 6964–1
Income (household) and poverty status under alternative income definitions, by recipient characteristics, 1979-91, annual Current Population Rpt, 2546–6.78
Income (household, family, and personal), by source, detailed characteristics, and region, 1991, annual Current Population Rpt, 2546–6.76
IRS employment of minorities and women, compared to Fed Govt and total civilian labor force, FY91, annual rpt, 8304–3.3
Jail population of women, by criminal background and sociodemographic characteristics, with comparisons to men, 1989, 6066–19.66
Labor demand, turnover, and training completions, by detailed occupation, 1990 and projected to 2005, biennial rpt, 6744–3
Labor force status and characteristics of women, 1960s-90, chartbook, 6748–85
Labor force status by race and sex, selected years 1929-91, annual rpt, 204–1.2
Labor force status, by worker characteristics and industry group, 1990-91, annual article, 6722–1.312
Labor force status, earnings, and other characteristics of women, with comparisons to men, fact sheet series, 6564–1
Labor force status, experience, and unemployment duration, by race and sex, 1990-91, annual press release, 6726–1.51
Labor force status of family members and earnings, by family composition and race, quarterly press release, 6742–21
Labor force status of women, by age, race, and family status, quarterly rpt, 6742–17
Labor force, wages, hours, and payroll costs, by major industry group and demographic characteristics, *Survey of Current Business*, monthly rpt, 2702–1.7
Married-couple families income, and spouses labor force participation and hours worked, by income class, 1979 and 1989, 23848–225
Married couples aged 18-25, income and expenses by wife's employment status and family size, 1988-89, article, 1702–1.302
Military and civilian DOD employment of blacks, by sex, grade, and period of service, and lists of award recipients, officers, and service academy grads, 1770s-90, 3548–22
Military officers, enlisted, and reserve personnel, by sex and service branch, FY91 and trends from 1945, annual rpt, 3544–1.2; 3544–1.5
Military personnel deployment in Operation Desert Storm, by sex, race, rank, and service branch, 1990-91, GAO rpt, 26123–394
Military personnel occupational distribution, by race, sex, and service branch, FY90, GAO rpt, 26123–381
Military personnel reductions planned by service branch, and women and minorities affected by Army and Air Force plans, FY90-91, GAO rpt, 26123–373
Military recruits by race, and goals, by sex and service branch, quarterly press release, 3542–7
Military reserve officer and enlisted personnel, by component, FY91, annual rpt, 3544–31.1
Military women personnel on active duty, by rank, grade, and service branch, quarterly rpt, 3542–14.3
NASA minority and women employment, by installation, FY82-91, FY91, annual rpt, 9504–6.2
Navy personnel strengths, accessions, and attrition, detailed statistics, quarterly rpt, 3802–4
NIH research and training grants awarded to women, by recipient characteristics, inst, and host instn, FY90, annual rpt, 4434–18
Nuclear engineering enrollment and degrees by instn and State, and women grads plans and employment, 1991, annual rpt, 3006–8.18
OASDHI coverage of employment and earnings, and social security contributions, by age, sex, race, State, and county, 1988, annual rpt, 4744–29
Older persons income by source, for married OASI beneficiaries by work and eligibility pattern of wife, 1982, article, 4746–26.12
Older women's employment patterns, with background data, 1992 rpt, 6726–2.4
Pacific territories population and housing detailed characteristics, by location, 1990 Census of Population and Housing, series, 2551–8
Physicians, by specialty, age, sex, and location of training and practice, 1990, State rpt series, 4116–6
Population economic well-being indicators, by selected characteristics and household income and income-to-poverty ratio, 1984, 2546–20.22

Postal Service employment and related expenses, FY91, annual rpt, 9864–5.1
Poverty relation to low earnings, by work experience during year, household relationship, sex, race, age, and education, 1960s-90, Current Population Rpt, 2546–6.74
Poverty status of families, by detailed characteristics, 1980 and 1988, GAO rpt, 26131–102
Poverty status of population and families, by detailed characteristics, 1991, annual Current Population Rpt, 2546–6.77
Radiation protection and health physics enrollment and degrees granted by instn and State, and women grads plans and employment, 1991, annual rpt, 3006–8.19
Railroad employee benefits and beneficiaries by type, and railroad employment and payroll, FY90, annual rpt, 9704–2
Science and engineering employment and education of minorities, women, and disabled, by field, mid 1970s-91, biennial rpt, 9624–20
Small Business Admin minority and women employment, and hiring goals, FY91, annual rpt, 9764–9
Southeastern US layoff events and separations, by State, industry div, and reason for separation, 1990-91, press release, 6946–3.25
SSA minority, handicapped, and women employees, by pay grade, FY91, annual rpt, 4704–6
State and local govt employment of minorities and women, by occupation, function, pay level, and State, 1991, annual rpt, 9244–6
Statistical Abstract of US, 1992 annual data compilation, 2324–1.13
Taxes, spending, and govt efficiency, public opinion by respondent characteristics, 1992 survey, annual rpt, 10044–2
Training for job qualification and skill improvement, workers participating by training source, occupation, age, sex, and race, 1991, 6728–32
Training on job for women, duration, costs, and impacts on gender differences in wages, model description and results, 1992 working paper, 6886–6.93
Unemployed displaced workers job search and placement aid effectiveness, relation to previous employment and other characteristics, 1979-87 studies, 15496–1.14
Unemployed displaced workers, layoffs and unemployment insurance claims by reason, industry, selected characteristics, and State, quarterly press release, 6742–23
Unemployed displaced workers, layoffs and unemployment insurance claims by reason, industry, selected characteristics, MSA, and State, 1990, annual rpt, 6744–18
Unemployed persons finding work, by characteristics of worker and new job, aggregate 1986-89, 2546–20.20
Unemployment rates, current data and annual trends, monthly rpt, 23842–1.2
VA employment characteristics and activities, FY91, annual rpt, 8604–3.4
VA health care facilities physicians, dentists, and nurses, by selected employment characteristics and VA district, quarterly rpt, 8602–6
Veteran women's labor force status, by period of service, 1989, article, 6722–1.326
Veteran women's labor force status, by period of service, 1991, biennial press release, 6726–1.49
see also Women-owned businesses
see also under By Sex in the "Index by Categories"

Wood
see Lumber industry and products
see Wood fuel

Wood fuel
California lumber mills, operations, timber use by species and origin, and residue use, by product and county, 1988, 1208–108
China biomass-fired electric power plant feasibility assessment, 1991 rpt, 3308–103
Commercial buildings energy use, costs, and conservation, by building characteristics, survey rpt series, 3166–8
Consumption of wood, waste, and alcohol fuels, by end-use sector and region, 1990, annual rpt, 3164–97
Consumption of wood, waste, and alcohol fuels, by region, and characteristics of wood-burning households, 1981-90, annual rpt, 3164–74.7
Electric power plants and capacity, by fuel used, owner, location, and operating status, 1991 and for units planned 1992-2001, annual listing, 3164–36
Exports and imports between US and outlying areas, by detailed commodity and mode of transport, 1991, annual rpt, 2424–11
Exports and imports of US, by country and detailed commodity, monthly rpt, 2422–12
Exports and imports of US, by Harmonized System 6-digit commodity and country, 1991, annual rpt, 2424–13
Exports and imports of US, by transport mode, country, and SITC 1- to 3-digit commodity, 1991, annual rpt, 2424–12
Exports of US, detailed Schedule B commodities with countries of destination, 1991, annual rpt, 2424–10
Florida industrial roundwood lumber production, by product and county, 1967-89, 1208–352
Freight (waterborne domestic and foreign) by commodity, traffic, and passengers, by port and waterway, 1989, annual rpt, 3754–3
Georgia industrial roundwood lumber production, by product, 1986 and 1989, 1208–393
Housing (rental) units, total, with HUD assistance by program, and eligible for aid, by unit, household, and neighborhood characteristics, and location, 1989, biennial rpt, 5184–11
Housing and households detailed characteristics, and unit and neighborhood quality, MSA surveys, series, 2485–6
Housing energy use, costs, and conservation, and household and housing characteristics, survey rpt series, 3166–7
Iowa timber resources and removals, by species, forest and tree characteristics, ownership, and county, 1988-90 and trends from 1973-74, 1208–75
Michigan fuelwood production, by species, land ownership, survey region, county, and location, 1986, 1208–412
Minnesota fuelwood production, by species, land ownership, and location, 1988, 1208–398
Missouri fuelwood production, by species, land ownership, and location, 1987, 1208–399
Missouri timber resources and removals, by species, forest and tree characteristics, ownership, and county, 1987-89 and trends from 1959, 1208–76
North Central States timber harvest and industrial roundwood production, by product and county, State rpt series, 1206–10
Northeastern US industrial roundwood production by product, State rpt series, 1206–15
Oregon lumber production, and industry operations, by county, 1988, 1208–280
Pacific Northwest nonutility electric power generation and capacity, by energy source, purchasing utility, and facility, forecasts 1991-2012, annual rpt, 3224–3.4
Prices and spending for fuel, by type, end-use sector, and State, 1990, annual rpt, 3164–64
Rocky Mountain States timber and mill residue production, by species, ownership, and county, series, 1206–17
Statistical Abstract of US, 1992 annual data compilation, 2324–1.19
Supply, demand, and prices, by fuel type and end-use sector, with foreign comparisons, 1981-90, annual fact book, 3164–76
TVA biomass energy program, operations, finances, and technological characteristics, series, 9806–9
Virginia industrial roundwood production, shipments, and residue volume, by species, product, and location, 1987-89, 1208–138
Wisconsin timber resources and removals, by species, forest type, ownership, and county, series, 1206–34

Wood, John H.
"Monetary Policy in a Small Open Economy: The Case of Singapore", 9379–1.304

Wood, Suzanne
"American Espionage, 1945-1989", 25428–2

Woodburn, R. Louise
"Estimation of Household Net Worth Using Model-Based and Design-Based Weights: Evidence from the 1989 Survey of Consumer Finances", 9368–91

Woodward, Jeanne M.
"Home Alone in 1989", 2486–1.15
"Housing Characteristics of Recent Movers", 2486–1.12

Woodwell, David A.
"Office Visits to Internists, 1989", 4146–8.214
"Office Visits to Pediatric Specialists, 1989", 4146–8.210

Wool and wool trade
Agricultural Stabilization and Conservation Service mohair programs, 1955-92, annual fact sheet, 1806–4.9
Agricultural Stabilization and Conservation Service producer payments, by program and State, 1991, annual table, 1804–12
Agricultural Stabilization and Conservation Service wool programs, 1955-92, annual fact sheet, 1806–4.11
Agricultural Statistics, 1991, annual rpt, 1004–1
Business statistics, detailed data for major industries and economic indicators, *Survey of Current Business*, monthly rpt, 2702–1.21
Business statistics, detailed data for major industries and economic indicators, 1960-91, *Survey of Current Business* biennial supplement, 2704–1
CCC financial condition and major commodity program operations, FY63-88, annual chartbook, 1824–2
Clothing and shoe production, shipments, trade, and use, by product, periodic Current Industrial Rpt series, 2506–6
County Business Patterns, 1989: employment, establishments, and payroll, by SIC 2- to 4-digit industry and county, annual State rpt series, 2326–8
County Business Patterns, 1990: employment, establishments, and payroll, by SIC 2- to 4-digit industry and county, annual State rpt series, 2326–6
Employment, earnings, and hours, by SIC 1- to 4-digit industry, monthly 1989-Feb 1992, annual rpt, 6744–4
Exports and imports (agricultural) of US, by commodity and country, bimonthly rpt, 1522–1
Exports and imports (agricultural) of US, by detailed commodity and country, 1991, annual rpt, 1524–8
Exports and imports (agricultural) of US, by detailed commodity and country, 1991, semiannual rpt, 1522–4
Exports and imports between US and outlying areas, by detailed commodity and mode of transport, 1991, annual rpt, 2424–11
Exports and imports of dairy, livestock, and poultry products, by commodity and country, FAS monthly circular, 1925–32
Exports and imports of textiles, raw fiber equivalents by product, country, and world region, 1989-90, article, 1561–1.301
Exports and imports of US, by country and detailed commodity, monthly rpt, 2422–12
Exports and imports of US, by Harmonized System 6-digit commodity and country, 1991, annual rpt, 2424–13
Exports and imports of US, by transport mode, country, and SITC 1- to 3-digit commodity, 1991, annual rpt, 2424–12
Exports and imports of wool, for US and other major producers, late 1970s-90, article, 1561–1.304
Exports of US, detailed Schedule B commodities with countries of destination, 1991, annual rpt, 2424–10
Exports of US textiles and apparel, by product group and country, quarterly rpt, 2042–36
Farm sector balance sheet, and receipts by detailed commodity, by State, 1986-90, annual rpt, 1544–18
Foreign countries agricultural production, prices, and trade, by country, 1980-91 and forecast 1992, annual world area rpt series, 1524–4
Foreign countries market conditions for US textile and apparel exports, with domestic industry operations, country rpt series, 2046–15
Imports of textiles, by country of origin, monthly rpt, 2042–27
Imports of textiles, by product and country of origin, monthly rpt series, 2046–8; 2046–9
Imports of textiles under Multifiber Arrangement by product and country, and status of bilateral agreements, 1988-91, annual rpt, 9884–18
Manufacturing annual survey, 1990: finances and operations, by SIC 2- to 4-digit industry, series, 2506–14
Manufacturing census, 1987: concentration of largest firms measured by value added, and for shipments by SIC 2- and 4-digit industry, subject rpt, 2497–6
Manufacturing census, 1987: shipments of manufacturers products, by customer class and SIC 2- and 4-digit industry, subject rpt, 2497–4
Marketing data for livestock, meat, and wool, by species and market, weekly rpt, 1315–1
Occupational injury and illness rates, by SIC 2- to 4-digit industry, 1989-90, annual rpt, 6844–7
Occupational injury and illness rates, by SIC 2- to 4-digit industry, 1990, annual rpt, 6844–1
Price indexes (producer), by stage of processing and detailed commodity, monthly rpt, 6762–6
Price indexes (producer), by stage of processing and detailed commodity, monthly 1991, annual rpt, 6764–2
Prices received and paid by farmers, by commodity and State, monthly rpt, 1629–1
Prices received and paid by farmers, by commodity and State, 1991, annual rpt, 1629–5
Prices, sales, trade, and stocks of wool, and sheep inventory, weekly and biweekly rpt, 1315–2
Production and prices of wool and mohair, by State, 1989-91, annual press release, 1623–6
Production itemized costs, receipts, and returns, by commodity and region, 1988-90, annual rpt, 1544–20
Production, prices, trade, and marketing, by commodity, current situation and forecast, monthly rpt with articles, 1502–4
Production, prices, trade, and use of wool, mohair, and other fibers, periodic situation rpt with articles, 1561–1
Production, trade, sales, stocks, and material used, by product, region, and State, periodic Current Industrial Rpt series, 2506–5
Production, use, and prices, and operations costs and returns, for western US sheep producers, 1920s-90, 1548–382
Science, engineering, and technical employment in manufacturing, by field and industry, 1989, triennial rpt, 9627–23
Weight and volume conversion factors for agricultural commodities and products, 1992 rpt, 1508–3

Worcester, Mass.
Wages by occupation, for office and plant workers, 1991 survey, periodic MSA rpt, 6785–16.2

Work conditions
Air traffic controller job performance and satisfaction impacts of training program, 1984-90, technical rpt, 7506–10.96
Air traffic controller job satisfaction, relation to work conditions and worker characteristics, 1992 technical rpt, 7506–10.117
Aircraft maintenance and inspection operators work conditions, 1989-90 study, technical rpt, 7506–10.99
Education (elementary and secondary) schools, teachers, staff, and enrollment, by selected characteristics, 1987/88-1988/89, 4836–3.10
Education data compilation, 1992 annual rpt, 4824–2
FAA employees job satisfaction and burnout, 1992 technical rpt, 7506–10.103; 7506–10.104
FAA employees job satisfaction, impacts of promotion and pay equity by sex, 1992 technical rpt, 7506–10.105
Fed Govt employees views on work condition, 1991 survey, GAO rpt, 26119–406
Fed Govt Senior Executive Service members views on work environment, 1989 and 1991 surveys, GAO rpt, 26119–402
Fed Govt white collar employees views on work conditions and schedules, 1992 survey, 9848–41
Occupational Outlook Handbook, 1992-93, biennial rpt, 6744–1
Teachers and administrators in private schools, pay, work conditions, and selected characteristics, by school type and affiliation, 1987/88, 4836–3.8
Teachers performance, school conditions, and student characteristics, attitudes, activities, and plans, 1988 8th grade class, natl longitudinal survey, series, 4826–9
Technological devs effect on labor force, composition, and productivity, 1970s-90 and projected to 2005, industry rpt series, 6826–2
see also Agricultural accidents and safety
see also Employee performance and appraisal
see also Job tenure
see also Labor-management relations, general
see also Labor-management relations in government
see also Mine accidents and safety
see also Occupational health and safety

Work incentive programs
AFDC Job Opportunities and Basic Skills Training program high-risk participants, by State and services received, FY91, GAO rpt, 26121–489
AFDC Job Opportunities and Basic Skills Training program State admin, and Unemployed Parent program caseloads and payments by State, 1991 GAO rpt, 26131–96

Assistance (financial and nonfinancial) of Fed Govt, 1992 base edition, annual listing, 104–5
Disabled persons work experience following OASDI benefit award, by selected characteristics, 1980s, article, 4742–1.312
Indians and Alaska Natives organizations AFDC Job Opportunities and Basic Skills Training programs, funding and eligibility, FY91, GAO rpt, 26121–460
Mississippi poverty, hunger, and public welfare program operations and indicators of need, 1991 hearing, 21968–57
Participants characteristics, activities, and funding, for Employment and Training Admin programs, FY86-88, annual rpt, 6404–17
Poor families self-sufficiency aid and Head Start programs, HUD and HHS joint funding by recipient, 1991, press release, 5006–3.83
Supplemental Security Income work incentive programs, participant characteristics, by program, 1982-91, article, 4742–1.305
Tax (income) returns filed, by type of filer, selected income items, quarterly rpt, 8302–2.1

Work stoppages
Business statistics, detailed data for major industries and economic indicators, 1960-91, *Survey of Current Business* biennial supplement, 2704–1
Food stamp recipient household size, composition, income, and income and deductions allowed, summer 1989, annual rpt, 1364–8
Foreign countries labor conditions, union coverage, and work accidents, annual country rpt series, 6366–4
Incidents of stoppages, workers involved, and days idle, 1991 and trends from 1947, annual press release, 6784–12
Labor force, wages, hours, and payroll costs, by major industry group and demographic characteristics, *Survey of Current Business*, monthly rpt, 2702–1.7
Mediation and arbitration activities of Fed Mediation and Conciliation Service, and cases by issue, region, and State, FY85-90, annual rpt, 9344–1
Monthly Labor Review, work stoppages involving 1,000 workers or more, workers involved, and days idle, 6722–1.3
Railroad and airline labor disputes, and Federal mediation activities and caseloads, with data by carrier and union, FY87-88, annual rpt, 9604–1
Replacement workers hired during strikes, and impacts on firm operating capacity, with data for NYC, 1984-88, hearing, 21348–121
Statistical Abstract of US, 1992 annual data compilation, 2324–1.13
Wage and benefit changes from collective bargaining and mgmt decisions, by industry div, monthly rpt, 6782–1

Work-study programs
Assistance and other sources of support, with student expenses and characteristics, by instn type and control, 1987 study, series, 4846–3; 4846–5
Community Service Learning work-study program, earnings and operations, 1986-90, GAO rpt, 26121–449
Fed Govt education funding by agency, program, and recipient type, and instn spending, 1960s-91, annual rpt, 4824–8
Fed Govt share of student aid supplemental grants, loans, and work-study awards, by instn and State, 1992/93, annual listing, 4804–17
Science and engineering grad enrollment, by field, source of funds, and characteristics of student and instn, 1990, annual rpt, 9627–7
Special education programs, enrollment by age, staff, funding, and needs, by type of handicap and State, 1990/91, annual rpt, 4944–4

Work training
see Employee development
see Manpower training programs
see Vocational education and training

Worker adjustment assistance
see Trade adjustment assistance

Worker incentives
see Employee bonuses and work incentives
see Employee ownership

Workers
see Agricultural labor
see Alien workers
see Blue collar workers
see Clerical workers
see Employment and unemployment, general
see Employment and unemployment, local and regional
see Employment and unemployment, specific industry
see Government employees
see Job tenure
see Labor supply and demand
see Migrant workers
see Minority employment
see Occupational testing and certification
see Production workers
see Professional and technical workers
see Sales workers
see Service workers
see Unpaid family workers
see Women's employment
see Work conditions
see Youth employment

Workers compensation
Auto and auto parts trade, production, and labor conditions, for US and compared to Canada and Mexico, 1950s-90, 6366–3.28
Beneficiaries and taxes collected for social insurance programs since 1940, quarterly rpt, 4742–1.4
Benefits under workers compensation, by type of program and insurer, and State, 1988-89, annual article, 4742–1.311
Benefits under workers compensation, costs, coverage, and insurers performance, 1939-88, article, 4742–1.322
Black lung benefits and claims by State, trust fund receipts by source, and disbursements, 1991, annual rpt, 6504–3
Black lung benefits by county, FY91, annual regional listings, 4004–3
Black lung benefits to miners, widows, and dependents, by State, quarterly rpt, 4742–1.3
Black lung trust funds financial condition, monthly rpt, 8102–9.10
Costs (hourly) of labor, by component, industry and occupational group, worker class, and firm size, monthly rpt, annual tables, 6782–1.2
Costs (hourly) of labor, by component, occupational group, industry div, union coverage, and region, 1992, annual rpt, 6744–21
Employee compensation costs, by component, occupation, industry group, union status, and location, 1975-92, annual rpt, 6744–20.2
Expenditures (private) for social welfare, by category, 1970s-90, annual article, 4742–1.323
Expenditures, coverage, and benefits for social welfare programs, late 1930s-90, annual rpt, 4744–3.1; 4744–3.7
Expenditures for health care by businesses, households, and govts, 1965-90, annual article, 4652–1.309
Expenditures for public welfare by program, FY50s-89, annual article, 4742–1.319
Expenditures of Fed Govt in States, by type, program, agency, and State, FY91, annual rpt, 2464–2
Fed Govt civilian employees work-years, pay rates, and benefits use and costs, by agency, FY90, annual rpt, 9844–31
Fed Govt employees compensation costs, and vocational rehabilitation costs and workload, FY82-90, GAO rpt, 26119–381
Fed Govt workers compensation program finances and operations, FY91, annual rpt, 6504–10
Food stamp recipient household size, composition, income, and income and deductions allowed, summer 1989, annual rpt, 1364–8
Foreign countries social security programs coverage, funding, eligibility, and benefits, by country, 1991, biennial rpt, 4746–4.62
Health condition and care indicators, 1950s-90 with health improvement and disease prevention goals for 1990, annual data compilation, 4144–11
Hospital discharges and length of stay, by diagnosis, patient and instn characteristics, procedure performed, and payment source, 1990, annual rpt, 4147–13.112
Income (household, family, and personal), by source, detailed characteristics, and region, 1991, annual Current Population Rpt, 2546–6.76
Natl income and product accounts, comprehensive accounts and components, benchmark revisions, 1929-88, 2708–5
Natl income and product accounts, comprehensive accounts and components, *Survey of Current Business*, monthly rpt, 2702–1.25
Older persons income and sources, by whether OASDI beneficiary, poverty status, and other characteristics, 1990, biennial rpt, 4744–26
Postal Service employment and related expenses, FY91, annual rpt, 9864–5.3
State govt revenue by source, spending and debt by function, and holdings, FY91, annual rpt, 2466–2.6
States workers compensation laws, and Fed Govt provisions, 1992 annual rpt, 6504–11
States workers compensation laws, changes in coverage, benefits, and premium rates, by State, 1991, annual article, 6722–1.310

States workers compensation programs, admin, coverage, benefits, finances, processing, and staff, 1987-90, annual rpt, 6504–9
Statistical Abstract of US, 1992 annual data compilation, 2324–1.12
Traffic accident injury hospitalization, costs, and discharges, by payment source and State, mid 1980s-90, 7768–122
Transit systems finances and operations, by mode, size of fleet and urban area, region, and for 518 systems, 1990, annual rpt, 7884–4

Working women
see Women-owned businesses
see Women's employment

Worksharing
Displaced worker employment and training services, and layoff alternatives, indicators of effectiveness, 1980s, 15498–28
DOT employment, by subagency, occupation, and selected personnel characteristics, FY91, annual rpt, 7304–18

Workshops
see Conferences
see Sheltered workshops

World Bank
see International Bank for Reconstruction and Development
see International Development Association

World Data Center A
see Oceanography

World Meteorological Organization
Weather data for surface and upper air, averages by foreign and US station, monthly rpt, 2152–4

World War II
see War

Worthington, Paula R.
"Investment and Market Imperfections in the U.S. Manufacturing Sector", 9375–13.81

Wrecking and demolition
County Business Patterns, 1989: employment, establishments, and payroll, by SIC 2- to 4-digit industry and county, annual State rpt series, 2326–8
County Business Patterns, 1990: employment, establishments, and payroll, by SIC 2- to 4-digit industry and county, annual State rpt series, 2326–6
Historic and natural natl landmarks damaged and threatened, with owner, location, damage type, and recommended remedial action, 1990, annual listing, 5544–16

Wright, Harlan I.
"Effects of Alcohol on the Male Reproductive System", 4482–1.307

Wright, Randall
"Labor Market in Real Business Cycle Theory", 9383–6.302

Writers and writing
Labor demand, turnover, and training completions, by detailed occupation, 1990 and projected to 2005, biennial rpt, 6744–3
Occupational Outlook Handbook, 1992-93, biennial rpt, 6744–1
see also Journalism

Writing ability
see Language use and ability

Wulfekuhler, Kurt C.
"Finance Companies, Bank Competition, and Niche Markets", 9385–1.309

Wynne, Mark A.
"Analysis of Fiscal Policy in Neoclassical Models", 9379–12.93
"Are Deep Recessions Followed by Strong Recoveries?", 9379–12.82
"Does Aggregate Output Have a Unit Root?", 9379–12.85

Wyoming
Banks (insured commercial and savings) deposits by instn, State, MSA, and county, as of June 1991, annual regional rpt, 9295–3.6
Bears (grizzly) in Yellowstone Natl Park area, monitoring results, 1991, annual rpt, 5544–4
Coal production and mines by county, prices, productivity, miners, and reserves, by mining method and State, 1990-91, annual rpt, 3164–25
County Business Patterns, 1990: employment, establishments, and payroll, by SIC 2- to 4-digit industry and county, annual State rpt, 2326–6.52
Deaths and rates, by detailed location, cause, and demographic characteristics, 1989, US Vital Statistics annual rpt, 4144–3.1
Employment, earnings, and hours, by selected SIC 1- to 4-digit industry, State, and for 275 MSAs, 1987-92, 6748–81
Fed Govt spending in States and local areas, by type, State, county, and city, FY91, annual rpt, 2464–3
Fed Govt spending in States, by type, program, agency, and State, FY91, annual rpt, 2464–2
Financial and economic devs, Fed Reserve 10th District, quarterly rpt, 9381–16
HHS financial aid, by program, recipient, State, and city, FY91, annual regional listing, 4004–3.8
Hospital deaths of Medicare patients, actual and expected rates by diagnosis, and hospital characteristics, by instn, FY90 annual State rpt, 4654–14.52
Housing census, 1990: inventory, occupancy, and costs, State fact sheet, 2326–21.52
Housing census, 1990: summary unit characteristics, by householder race and age, county, place, and urban-rural location, State rpt, 2471–1.52
Land Mgmt Bur activities and finances, and public land acreage and use, FY91, annual State rpt, 5724–11.5
Military prime contract awards, by contractor, service branch, State, and city, FY91, annual rpt, 3544–22
Mineral Industry Surveys, State reviews of production, 1991, preliminary annual rpt, 5614–6
Minerals Yearbook, Vol 2, 1989: State review of production and sales by commodity, and business activity, annual rpt, 5604–16.52
Multinatl firms US affiliates finances and operations, by industry, country of parent firm, and State, 1987, 2708–48
Physicians, by specialty, age, sex, and location of training and practice, 1990, State rpt, 4116–6.52
Population and housing census, 1990: detailed geographic coverage, State CD-ROM, 2551–9.8
Population and housing census, 1990: population and housing characteristics, detailed geographic coverage, State CD-ROM, 2551–10.15
Population and housing census, 1990: summary characteristics, by county, subdiv, and place, State rpt, 2551–7.52
Population census, 1990: population characteristics and living arrangements, by county, place, and urban-rural location, State rpt, 2531–1.52
Statistical Abstract of US, 1992 annual data compilation, 2324–1
Water resources data collection and analysis activities of USGS Water Resources Div District, with project descriptions, 1991 rpt, 5666–26.26
Water salinity control program for Colorado River, participation and payments, FY87-91, annual rpt, 1804–23
Water supply and quality in streams and lakes, and groundwater levels in wells, by drainage basin, 1990, annual State rpt, 5666–10.47
Water supply, and snow survey results, monthly State rpt, 1266–2.10
see also Cheyenne, Wyo.
see also under By State in the "Index by Categories"

X-rays
County Business Patterns, 1989: employment, establishments, and payroll, by SIC 2- to 4-digit industry and county, annual State rpt series, 2326–8
County Business Patterns, 1990: employment, establishments, and payroll, by SIC 2- to 4-digit industry and county, annual State rpt series, 2326–6
Equipment shipments, trade, use, and firms, for electronic medical equipment by product, 1991, annual Current Industrial Rpt, 2506–12.34
Exports and imports between US and outlying areas, by detailed commodity and mode of transport, 1991, annual rpt, 2424–11
Exports and imports of US, by country and detailed commodity, monthly rpt, 2422–12
Exports and imports of US, by Harmonized System 6-digit commodity and country, 1991, annual rpt, 2424–13
Exports of US, detailed Schedule B commodities with countries of destination, 1991, annual rpt, 2424–10
Input-output structure of US economy, detailed interindustry transactions for 541 industries, and components of final demand, 1982 benchmark data, 2708–17
Internist office visits, by characteristics of patient, physician, and visit, 1989, 4146–8.214
Manufacturing finances and operations, by SIC 2- to 4-digit industry, forecast 1992, annual rpt, 2044–28
Medicare and Medicaid beneficiaries and program operations, 1992, annual fact book, 4654–18
Occupational injury and illness rates, by SIC 2- to 4-digit industry, 1989-90, annual rpt, 6844–7
Occupational injury and illness rates, by SIC 2- to 4-digit industry, 1990, annual rpt, 6844–1

Portable X-ray providers profitability effects of Medicare fee schedules, 1991-92, hearing, 25368–178
Price indexes (producer), by stage of processing and detailed commodity, monthly rpt, 6762–6
Price indexes (producer), by stage of processing and detailed commodity, monthly 1991, annual rpt, 6764–2
Radiation from electronic devices, incidents by type of device, and FDA control activities, 1991, annual rpt, 4064–13
see also Mammography

Yates, Eugene B.
"Geohydrology, Water Quality, and Water Budgets of Golden Gate Park and the Lake Merced Area in the Western Part of San Francisco, Calif.", 5666–28.16

Ycas, Martynas A.
"New Beneficiary Data System: The First Phase", 4742–1.313

Yee, Jet
"Assessing Rates of Return to Public and Private Agricultural Research", 1502–3.303

Yellowstone National Park
Bears (grizzly) in Yellowstone Natl Park area, monitoring results, 1991, annual rpt, 5544–4
Fires on wildlands, ecology, mgmt, cultural impacts, and historic patterns, 1990 conf, 1208–415

Yemen
Agricultural trade of US, by detailed commodity and country, 1991, semiannual rpt, 1522–4
AID economic aid to developing countries, obligations and disbursements by country, quarterly rpt, 9912–4
AID loans repayment status and terms by program and country, and status of predecessor agency loans, quarterly rpt, 9912–3
Boycotts (intl) by OPEC and other countries, US firms and individuals cooperation and tax benefits denied, 1990, article, 8302–2.323
Economic and social conditions of developing countries from 1960s, and Intl Dev Cooperation Agency and AID activities and funding, FY91-93, annual rpt, 9904–4
Economic, social, political, and geographic summary data, by country, 1992, annual factbook, 9114–2
Human rights conditions in 170 countries, and US economic and military aid, 1991, annual rpt, 21384–3
Minerals Yearbook, Vol 3, 1989: foreign country review of production, trade, and policy, by commodity, annual rpt, 5604–35.3
Population size, growth rates, and components of change, by country, projected 1990-2020 and trends from 1950, biennial rpt, 2324–9
Refugee migration, and intl aid programs, by world area and country of origin and asylum, 1991, annual rpt, 7004–15
UN voting record and share of votes in agreement with US, by issue, country, and world area, 1991, annual rpt, 7004–18
see also Yemen, North
see also Yemen, South

Yemen Arab Republic
see Yemen, North

Yemen, North
Agricultural trade of US, by detailed commodity and country, 1991, annual rpt, 1524–8
Economic and military aid and loans from US and intl agencies, by program and country, FY46-91, annual rpt, 9914–5
Exports and imports of US, by transport mode, country, and SITC 1- to 3-digit commodity, 1991, annual rpt, 2424–12
Exports of US, detailed Schedule B commodities with countries of destination, 1991, annual rpt, 2424–10
Military spending, arms trade, and force strengths, with govt spending and population, by country, 1979-89, annual rpt, 9824–1

Yemen, South
Agricultural trade of US, by detailed commodity and country, 1991, annual rpt, 1524–8
Economic and military aid and loans from US and intl agencies, by program and country, FY46-91, annual rpt, 9914–5
Exports and imports of US, by transport mode, country, and SITC 1- to 3-digit commodity, 1991, annual rpt, 2424–12
Exports of US, detailed Schedule B commodities with countries of destination, 1991, annual rpt, 2424–10
Military spending, arms trade, and force strengths, with govt spending and population, by country, 1979-89, annual rpt, 9824–1

Yesley, Joel M.
"Study of the Relationships Between Near Midair Collisions (NMAC's), Midair Collisions (MAC's) and Some Potential Causal Factors", 7508–76

Yin, Norman
"Exchange Rate Policy and Shocks to Asset Markets: The Case of Taiwan in the 1980s", 9393–8.303

Yinger, John
"Housing Discrimination Study: Incidence and Severity of Unfavorable Treatment", 5186–16.5
"Housing Discrimination Study: Incidence of Discrimination and Variations in Discriminatory Behavior", 5186–16.7

Yohn, Frederick O.
"What Is the Impact of Pensions on Saving?", 9373–27.5

York, James
"Productivity in Wood Containers", 6722–1.344

York, Pa.
Wages by occupation, for office and plant workers, 1991 survey, periodic MSA rpt, 6785–12.2
see also under By City and By SMSA or MSA in the "Index by Categories"

Young, Allan H.
"Alternative Measures of Change in Real Output and Prices", 2702–1.314

Young, Jennifer
"Summary of Travel Trends: 1990 Nationwide Personal Transportation Survey", 7556–6.2

Young, Timothy M.
"Economic Availability of Woody Biomass Fuel Chips for 13 Southeastern States", 9806–9.13

Youngstown, Ohio
see also under By City and By SMSA or MSA in the "Index by Categories"

Youth
AIDS prevention program for minority youth, interactive videodisc presentation effectiveness, 1992 article, 4042–3.332
AIDS risk behavior of teenage boys, sexual activity, and drug and condom use, 1988, article, 4042–3.313
Alcohol use among youth, relation to risk behavior, by sex, 1987, article, 4482–1.308
Alcohol use and abuse by 8th and 10th graders, by sex, race, Hispanic origin, and grade, 1987, article, 4482–1.302
Alcohol use, knowledge, attitudes, and info sources of youth, series, 4006–10
Asian and Pacific Islands Americans social and economic characteristics, for West and total US, 1990-91, Current Population Report, 2546–1.462
Assistance (financial and nonfinancial) of Fed Govt, 1992 base edition, annual listing, 104–5
Budget of US, House Budget Committee analysis of Bush Admin proposals and economic assumptions, FY93, 21268–42
Census of Population and Housing, 1990: population and housing characteristics, detailed geographic coverage, State CD-ROM series, 2551–10
Census of Population and Housing, 1990: summary characteristics, by county, subdiv, and place, State rpt series, 2551–7
Census of Population, 1990: population characteristics and living arrangements, by county, place, and urban-rural location, State rpt series, 2531–1
Census of Population, 1990: population characteristics and living arrangements, for Native American, urban, and metro areas, series, 2531–2
Contraceptives use at first intercourse, by whether planned and alcohol consumed, for US and Scotland, 1991 article, 4482–1.304
Crime and crime-related issues, public opinion by respondent characteristics, data compilation, 1992 annual rpt, 6064–6.2
Deaths and rates, by cause and selected social, demographic, and employment characteristics, 1979-85, natl longitudinal study, 4478–186
Drivers licenses requirements and admin, by State and Canada Province, as of Jan 1992, biennial rpt, 7554–18
Drug abuse prevention services evaluation, methodological issues, 1991 conf, 4498–78
Drug, alcohol, and cigarette use and attitudes of youth, by substance type and selected characteristics, 1975-91 surveys, annual rpt, 4494–4
Drug, alcohol, and cigarette use and attitudes of youth, by substance type, 1975-91 surveys, press release, 4008–116
Drug, alcohol, and cigarette use, by selected characteristics, 1991 survey, annual rpt series, 4494–5

Drug and alcohol abuse risk indicators among youths in an intervention program, 1991 article, 4482–1.305
Health condition and care indicators, 1950s-90 with health improvement and disease prevention goals for 1990, annual data compilation, 4144–11
Health condition of youth, risk factors, and preventive and treatment services use and availability, 1970s-80s, 26358–234
HHS financial aid, by program, recipient, State, and city, FY91, annual regional listings, 4004–3
Homeless and runaway youth center arrivals, by selected characteristics, data compilation, 1992 annual rpt, 6064–6.6
Homeless youths health conditions and risk behaviors, 1990 local area study, article, 4042–3.344
Homicide and suicide among young black men, by day of week, with comparisons to whites and women, 1979-85, article, 4042–3.323
Indian and Alaska Native youth health condition and behavioral patterns, by sex and grade, 1988-90, 4088–3
Job Training Partnership Act education and worker training program participants, by selected characteristics, 1986-88, 15496–1.15
Latin America young unmarried adults sexual activity, contraceptives use, and AIDS risk knowledge, by sex and country, 1984-91, article, 4202–7.323
Living arrangements, family relationships, and marital status, by selected characteristics, 1991, annual Current Population Rpt, 2546–1.461
Pacific territories population and housing detailed characteristics, by location, 1990 Census of Population and Housing, series, 2551–8
Radiation exposure of population near commercial reactors, by body site, age group, and selected plant, 1988, annual rpt, 9634–7
Statistical Abstract of US, 1992 annual data compilation, 2324–1
Tobacco use by minors, effectiveness of local ordinance enforcing penalties on retailers, 1989-90 local area study, article, 4042–3.336
Traffic accident deaths involving alcohol, by driver and victim blood alcohol levels and other characteristics, 1977-88, annual rpt, 4486–1.12; 4486–1.14
Voting age population, by sex, age, race, and State, forecast 1992 general elections, with votes cast from 1930, Current Population Rpt, 2546–3.170
see also Child mortality
see also Children
see also Elementary and secondary education
see also Foster home care
see also Higher education
see also Juvenile courts and cases
see also Juvenile delinquency
see also Juvenile detention and correctional institutions
see also School dropouts
see also Students
see also Teenage pregnancy
see also Youth employment
see also under By Age in the "Index by Categories"

Youth Conservation Corps
Forest Service employment and human resource program participation, FY91, annual rpt, 1204–1.4

Youth employment
Business statistics, detailed data for major industries and economic indicators, 1960-91, *Survey of Current Business* biennial supplement, 2704–1
Census of Population and Housing, 1990: summary characteristics, by county, subdiv, and place, State rpt series, 2551–7
Condition of Education, detail for elementary, secondary, and higher education, 1920s-91 and projected to 2002, annual rpt, 4824–1
Dallas-Fort Worth metro area employment, earnings, hours, and CPI changes, late 1970s-91, annual rpt, 6964–2
Educational enrollment, by grade, instn type and control, and student characteristics, 1990 and trends from 1947, annual Current Population Rpt, 2546–1.459
Educational performance and conditions, characteristics, attitudes, activities, and plans, 1988 8th grade class, natl longitudinal survey, series, 4826–9
Employment history of younger workers, jobs held and weeks worked since age 18, by age, sex, and race, 1978-90, 6726–2.3
Employment situation, earnings, hours, and other BLS economic indicators, transcripts of BLS Commissioner's monthly testimony, periodic rpt, 23846–4
Employment, unemployment, and labor force characteristics, by region, State, and selected metro area, 1991, annual rpt, 6744–7
High school and college grads and dropouts employment status and income, 1992 edition, annual rpt, 4824–2.28
High school class of 1991: college enrollment, and labor force participation of grads and dropouts, by race and sex, annual press release, 6726–1.46
Houston metro area employment, earnings, hours, and CPI changes, 1970s-91, annual rpt, 6964–1
Labor force status by race and sex, employment by industry div, and unemployment duration and reason, selected years 1929-91, annual rpt, 204–1.2
Labor force status by sex, and employment by class and industry div, for youth by race, summer 1988-92, annual press release, 6744–14
Labor force status by sex and for teens, *Survey of Current Business*, monthly rpt, 2702–1.1
Labor force status, by worker characteristics and industry group, 1990-91, annual article, 6722–1.312
Labor force status of youth, by age, Apr and July 1992 and change from 1991, annual press release, 6744–13
Labor force status of youth, by school enrollment, educational attainment, sex, and race, monthly rpt, 6742–2.1
OASDHI coverage of employment and earnings, and social security contributions, by age, sex, race, State, and county, 1988, annual rpt, 4744–29
Poverty relation to low earnings, by work experience during year, household relationship, sex, race, age, and education, 1960s-90, Current Population Rpt, 2546–6.74
Statistical Abstract of US, 1992 annual data compilation, 2324–1.13
Student guaranteed loan Stafford program, borrowers and likelihood of default by selected characteristics, 1989-90, 26306–3.120
Training for job qualification and skill improvement, workers participating by training source, occupation, age, sex, and race, 1991, 6728–32
Unemployed persons finding work, by characteristics of worker and new job, aggregate 1986-89, 2546–20.20
Unemployment of youth, research based on natl longitudinal surveys, review of studies conducted 1977-88, 6728–42
see also Apprenticeship
see also Child labor

Yucel, Mine K.
"Energy Security: A Comparison of Protectionist Policies", 9379–12.96

Yue, Piyu
"Data Envelopment Analysis and Commercial Bank Performance: A Primer with Applications to Missouri Banks", 9391–1.305
"Microeconometric Approach to Estimating Money Demand: The Asymptotically Ideal Model", 9391–1.303

Yuengert, Andrew M.
"Immigrant Earnings, Relative To What? The Importance of Earnings Function Specification and Comparison Points", 9385–8.143
"Measurement of Efficiency in Life Insurance: Estimates of Mixed Normal-Gamma Error Model", 9385–8.144

Yugoslavia
Agricultural trade of US, by detailed commodity and country, 1991, annual rpt, 1524–8
Agricultural trade of US, by detailed commodity and country, 1991, semiannual rpt, 1522–4
Agricultural trade of US with Eastern Europe, by commodity group and country, 1988-91, 1928–11
AID loans repayment status and terms by program and country, and status of predecessor agency loans, quarterly rpt, 9912–3
Cuba trade, by commodity and country, mid 1980s-91, 9118–8
Economic and military aid and loans from US and intl agencies, by program and country, FY46-91, annual rpt, 9914–5
Economic and social conditions of developing countries from 1960s, and Intl Dev Cooperation Agency and AID activities and funding, FY91-93, annual rpt, 9904–4
Economic conditions, policy, and trade practices, by country, 1989-91, annual rpt, 21384–5
Exports and imports of US, by commodity and country, 1980-90, world area rpt, 9116–1.1
Exports and imports of US, by transport mode, country, and SITC 1- to 3-digit commodity, 1991, annual rpt, 2424–12

Exports and imports of US with Eastern Europe, by commodity and country, 1987-91 and outlook for 1992, 2048–158
Exports, imports, and balances of US for manufactured goods, by SITC 2-digit commodity and country, quarterly rpt, 2042–35
Exports of US, detailed Schedule B commodities with countries of destination, 1991, annual rpt, 2424–10
Human rights conditions in 170 countries, and US economic and military aid, 1991, annual rpt, 21384–3
Imports of goods, services, and investment from US, trade barriers, impacts, and US actions, by country, 1991, annual rpt, 444–2
Military spending, arms trade, and force strengths, with govt spending and population, by country, 1979-89, annual rpt, 9824–1
Population size, growth rates, and components of change, by country, projected 1990-2020 and trends from 1950, biennial rpt, 2324–9
Refugee migration, and intl aid programs, by world area and country of origin and asylum, 1991, annual rpt, 7004–15
Steel imports of US under voluntary restraint agreement, by product, customs district, and country, with US industry operating data, quarterly rpt, 9882–13
Steel trade, by product, country, and customs district, with US industry operating data, 1989-June 1992, semiannual rpt, 9882–15
UN voting record and share of votes in agreement with US, by issue, country, and world area, 1991, annual rpt, 7004–18
see also Bosnia and Herzegovina
see also Croatia
see also Macedonia
see also Montenegro
see also Serbia
see also Slovenia

Zaire
Agricultural trade of US, by detailed commodity and country, 1991, annual rpt, 1524–8
Agricultural trade of US, by detailed commodity and country, 1991, semiannual rpt, 1522–4
AID economic aid to developing countries, obligations and disbursements by country, quarterly rpt, 9912–4
AID loans repayment status and terms by program and country, and status of predecessor agency loans, quarterly rpt, 9912–3
Economic and military aid and loans from US and intl agencies, by program and country, FY46-91, annual rpt, 9914–5
Economic and social conditions of developing countries from 1960s, and Intl Dev Cooperation Agency and AID activities and funding, FY91-93, annual rpt, 9904–4
Economic conditions, income, production, prices, employment, and trade, 1992 periodic country rpt, 2046–4.35
Economic conditions, policy, and trade practices, by country, 1989-91, annual rpt, 21384–5
Economic, social, political, and geographic summary data, by country, 1992, annual factbook, 9114–2
Exports and imports of US, by commodity and country, 1980-90, world area rpt, 9116–1.2
Exports and imports of US, by transport mode, country, and SITC 1- to 3-digit commodity, 1991, annual rpt, 2424–12
Exports of US, detailed Schedule B commodities with countries of destination, 1991, annual rpt, 2424–10
Food supply, needs, and aid for developing countries, status and alternative forecasts, 1992 world area rpt, 1526–8.2
Human rights conditions in 170 countries, and US economic and military aid, 1991, annual rpt, 21384–3
Military spending, arms trade, and force strengths, with govt spending and population, by country, 1979-89, annual rpt, 9824–1
Minerals Yearbook, Vol 3, 1989: foreign country review of production, trade, and policy, by commodity, annual rpt, 5604–35.1
Multinatl US firms foreign affiliates, income statement items by asset size, industry, and country, 1988, biennial article, 8302–2.322
Population size, growth rates, and components of change, by country, projected 1990-2020 and trends from 1950, biennial rpt, 2324–9
Refugee migration, and intl aid programs, by world area and country of origin and asylum, 1991, annual rpt, 7004–15
UN voting record and share of votes in agreement with US, by issue, country, and world area, 1991, annual rpt, 7004–18

Zalewski, Aldon
"Situation and Outlook for Manufactured Agricultural Inputs in Poland", 1561–16.304

Zalokar, Nadja
"Economic Status of Black Women: An Exploratory Investigation", 11048–191

Zambia
Agricultural trade of US, by detailed commodity and country, 1991, annual rpt, 1524–8
Agricultural trade of US, by detailed commodity and country, 1991, semiannual rpt, 1522–4
AID economic aid to developing countries, obligations and disbursements by country, quarterly rpt, 9912–4
AID loans repayment status and terms by program and country, and status of predecessor agency loans, quarterly rpt, 9912–3
Background Notes, summary social, political, and economic data, 1992 rpt, 7006–2.27
Economic and military aid and loans from US and intl agencies, by program and country, FY46-91, annual rpt, 9914–5
Economic and social conditions of developing countries from 1960s, and Intl Dev Cooperation Agency and AID activities and funding, FY91-93, annual rpt, 9904–4
Economic, social, political, and geographic summary data, by country, 1992, annual factbook, 9114–2
Exports and imports of US, by commodity and country, 1980-90, world area rpt, 9116–1.2
Exports and imports of US, by transport mode, country, and SITC 1- to 3-digit commodity, 1991, annual rpt, 2424–12
Exports of US, detailed Schedule B commodities with countries of destination, 1991, annual rpt, 2424–10
Food supply, needs, and aid for developing countries, status and alternative forecasts, 1992 world area rpt, 1526–8.2
Human rights conditions in 170 countries, and US economic and military aid, 1991, annual rpt, 21384–3
Military aid of US, arms sales, and training programs costs and budget requests, by program, world region, and country, FY91-93, annual rpt, 7144–13
Military spending, arms trade, and force strengths, with govt spending and population, by country, 1979-89, annual rpt, 9824–1
Minerals Yearbook, Vol 3, 1989: foreign country review of production, trade, and policy, by commodity, annual rpt, 5604–35.1
Population size, growth rates, and components of change, by country, projected 1990-2020 and trends from 1950, biennial rpt, 2324–9
Refugee migration, and intl aid programs, by world area and country of origin and asylum, 1991, annual rpt, 7004–15
UN voting record and share of votes in agreement with US, by issue, country, and world area, 1991, annual rpt, 7004–18

Zank, Neal S.
"Federal Public Assistance Programs: Coordination and Eligibility Issues", 15498–29

Zaretsky, Adam M.
"How Well Does Unemployment Explain the Low Levels of Consumer Confidence?", 9391–16.304
"Pension Insurance: A Crisis on the Horizon?", 9391–16.309

Zegeer, Charles V.
"Synthesis of Safety Research: Pedestrians", 7558–98.2

Zeile, William J.
"Foreign Direct Investment in the U.S.: Establishment Data for 1987", 2702–1.340

Ziemer, Heidi
"Records Relating to Personal Participation in World War II: "The American Soldier" Surveys", 9516–1.10

Zimbabwe
Agricultural trade of US, by detailed commodity and country, 1991, annual rpt, 1524–8
Agricultural trade of US, by detailed commodity and country, 1991, semiannual rpt, 1522–4
AID economic aid to developing countries, obligations and disbursements by country, quarterly rpt, 9912–4
AID loans repayment status and terms by program and country, and status of predecessor agency loans, quarterly rpt, 9912–3
Economic and military aid and loans from US and intl agencies, by program and country, FY46-91, annual rpt, 9914–5

Economic and social conditions of developing countries from 1960s, and Intl Dev Cooperation Agency and AID activities and funding, FY91-93, annual rpt, 9904–4
Economic, social, political, and geographic summary data, by country, 1992, annual factbook, 9114–2
Exports and imports of US, by commodity and country, 1980-90, world area rpt, 9116–1.2
Exports and imports of US, by transport mode, country, and SITC 1- to 3-digit commodity, 1991, annual rpt, 2424–12
Exports of US, detailed Schedule B commodities with countries of destination, 1991, annual rpt, 2424–10
Food supply, needs, and aid for developing countries, status and alternative forecasts, 1992 world area rpt, 1526–8.2
Human rights conditions in 170 countries, and US economic and military aid, 1991, annual rpt, 21384–3
Military aid of US, arms sales, and training programs costs and budget requests, by program, world region, and country, FY91-93, annual rpt, 7144–13
Military spending, arms trade, and force strengths, with govt spending and population, by country, 1979-89, annual rpt, 9824–1
Minerals Yearbook, Vol 3, 1989: foreign country review of production, trade, and policy, by commodity, annual rpt, 5604–35.1
Multinatl US firms foreign affiliates, income statement items by asset size, industry, and country, 1988, biennial article, 8302–2.322
Population size, growth rates, and components of change, by country, projected 1990-2020 and trends from 1950, biennial rpt, 2324–9
Refugee migration, and intl aid programs, by world area and country of origin and asylum, 1991, annual rpt, 7004–15
UN voting record and share of votes in agreement with US, by issue, country, and world area, 1991, annual rpt, 7004–18

Zinc and zinc industry
Business statistics, detailed data for major industries and economic indicators, *Survey of Current Business*, monthly rpt, 2702–1.16
Business statistics, detailed data for major industries and economic indicators, 1960-91, *Survey of Current Business* biennial supplement, 2704–1
Byproducts of primary metals mining, production and prices by commodity, 1965-90, 5608–170
Castings (nonferrous) shipments, by metal type, 1991, annual Current Industrial Rpt, 2506–10.5
Coin and medal production by denomination, capacity, and facility improvement funding, by mint, with monetary metals purchases, projected FY92-96, hearing, 21248–164
Coin production and monetary metals use and holdings of US Mint, by metal type, FY91, annual rpt, 8204–1
Exports and imports between US and outlying areas, by detailed commodity and mode of transport, 1991, annual rpt, 2424–11
Exports and imports of US, by country and detailed commodity, monthly rpt, 2422–12
Exports and imports of US, by Harmonized System 6-digit commodity and country, 1991, annual rpt, 2424–13
Exports and imports of US, by transport mode, country, and SITC 1- to 3-digit commodity, 1991, annual rpt, 2424–12
Exports of US, detailed Schedule B commodities with countries of destination, 1991, annual rpt, 2424–10
Foreign countries mineral production, reserves, and industry role in domestic economy and world supply, world area and country rpt series, 5606–1
Input-output structure of US economy, detailed interindustry transactions for 541 industries, and components of final demand, 1982 benchmark data, 2708–17
Manufacturing annual survey, 1990: finances and operations, by SIC 2- to 4-digit industry, series, 2506–14
Manufacturing finances and operations, by SIC 2- to 4-digit industry, forecast 1992, annual rpt, 2044–28
Mineral Industry Surveys, commodity review of production, trade, stocks, and use, monthly rpt, 5612–1.27
Mineral Industry Surveys, State reviews of production, 1991, preliminary annual rpt, 5614–6
Minerals Yearbook, Vol 1, 1989: commodity reviews of production, use, trade, prices, and mining operations, annual rpt, 5604–33
Minerals Yearbook, Vol 1, 1990: commodity review of production, reserves, supply, use, and trade, annual rpt, 5604–20.62
Minerals Yearbook, Vol 2, 1989: State reviews of production and sales by commodity, and business activity, annual rpt series, 5604–16
Minerals Yearbook, Vol 2, 1990: State reviews of production and sales by commodity, and business activity, annual rpt series, 5604–22
Minerals Yearbook, Vol 3, 1989: foreign country reviews of production, trade, and policy, by commodity, annual rpt, 5604–35
Mines (metal) and related operations occupational injuries and incidence, employment, and hours, 1990, annual rpt, 6664–3
OECD trade, total and for 4 major countries, and US trade by country, by commodity, 1980-90, world area rpt series, 9116–1
Price indexes (producer), by stage of processing and detailed commodity, monthly rpt, 6762–6
Price indexes (producer), by stage of processing and detailed commodity, monthly 1991, annual rpt, 6764–2
Production and processing losses by State, trade, use, and prices, for zinc, 1850s-1990, 5608–176
Production in 5 western States, and prices, for 5 nonferrous metals, 1848-1990, 5608–178
Production, prices, trade, and foreign and US industry devs, by commodity, bimonthly rpt, 5602–4
Production, prices, trade, use, employment, tariffs, and stockpiles, by mineral, with foreign comparisons, 1987-91, annual rpt, 5604–18
Production, trade, use, and foreign investment in US industry, for minerals, 1985-90 and projected to 2000, annual rpt, 5304–5
Statistical Abstract of US, 1992 annual data compilation, 2324–1.25
Stockpiling of strategic material by Fed Govt, activity, and inventory by commodity, as of Sept 1991, semiannual rpt, 3542–22
Stockpiling of strategic material, inventories and needs, by commodity, 1992, annual rpt, 3544–37

Zinn, Jeffrey A.
"Expected Impacts of Clean Water Legislation on Agriculture", 1504–9.1

ZIP codes
Economic censuses of 1987 and related programs, 1990 CD-ROM, 2326–22.5
Economic censuses of 1987 and related programs, 1990 CD-ROM user guide, 2306–8.5
Mail volume to and from households, use, and views, by class, source, content, and household characteristics, FY87-90, annual rpt, 9864–10
North Central States, FHLB 7th District housing vacancy rates for single and multifamily units and mobile homes, by ZIP code, annual MSA rpt series, 9304–18
West Central States, FHLB 10th District housing vacancy rates for single and multifamily units and mobile homes, by ZIP code, annual MSA rpt series, 9304–22
Western States, FHLB 12th District housing vacancy rates for single and multifamily units and mobile homes, by ZIP code, annual MSA rpt series, 9304–21

Zobeck, Terry S.
"Trends in Alcohol-Related Fatal Traffic Crashes, U.S.: 1977-88", 4486–1.12
"Trends in Alcohol-Related Fatal Traffic Crashes, U.S.: 1977-89", 4486–1.14

Zoning and zoning laws
Housing affordability and availability, impacts of govt land use regulations and rent control, and low income housing condition, 1991 hearing, 21248–174
Real estate assets of failed thrifts, inventory of properties available from Resolution Trust Corp, 1991, semiannual listing, 9722–2.1; 9722–2.7
Real estate assets of failed thrifts, inventory of properties available from Resolution Trust Corp, 1992, semiannual listing, 9722–2.8; 9722–2.14
see also Building permits

Zoological parks
County Business Patterns, 1989: employment, establishments, and payroll, by SIC 2- to 4-digit industry and county, annual State rpt series, 2326–8
County Business Patterns, 1990: employment, establishments, and payroll, by SIC 2- to 4-digit industry and county, annual State rpt series, 2326–6
Licensing and inspection of facilities, and other animal protection activities of USDA, with animals used in research, by State, FY90, annual rpt, 1394–10

Occupational injury and illness rates, by SIC 2- to 4-digit industry, 1989-90, annual rpt, 6844–7
Smithsonian Instn activities and finances, FY91, annual rpt, 29574–1
Zoology
Education in science and engineering, grad programs enrollment by field, source of funds, and characteristics of student and instn, 1990, annual rpt, 9627–7
Marine mammals research, Federal funding by topic, recipient, and agency, FY91, annual rpt, 14734–2
Occupational Outlook Handbook, 1992-93, biennial rpt, 6744–1
Reproduction and population research, Fed Govt funding by project, FY90, annual listing, 4474–9
see also Animals
see also Birds and bird conservation
see also Wildlife and wildlife conservation
see also Zoological parks
Zucker, Robert A.
"Early Developmental Factors and Risk for Alcohol Problems", 4482–1.303
Zuo, Xuejin
"Alternative Samples for Welfare Duration in SIPP: Does Attrition Matter?", 2626–10.148
Zuvekas, Clarence, Jr.
"Costa Rica: The Effects of Structural Adjustment Measures on the Poor, 1982-90", 9916–13.5
"Trends in Per Capita Consumption in Central America, 1969-89", 9916–13.4

Index by Categories

Index by Categories

Geographic Breakdowns	
By Census Division	837
By City	838
By County	841
By Foreign Country	843
By Outlying Area	850
By Region	853
By SMSA or MSA	859
By State	860
By Urban-Rural and Metro-Nonmetro	873
Economic Breakdowns	
By Commodity	875
By Federal Agency	878
By Income	880
By Individual Company or Institution	882
By Industry	888
By Occupation	892
Demographic Breakdowns	
By Age	894
By Disease	899
By Educational Attainment	900
By Marital Status	902
By Race and Ethnic Group	904
By Sex	909

INTRODUCTION

The Index by Categories contains references to all publications, tables, and groups of tables that contain breakdowns of statistical data by any or several of the following 21 standard categories:

GEOGRAPHIC BREAKDOWNS

By Census Division	By Outlying Area
By City	By Region
By County	By SMSA or MSA
By Foreign Country	By State
	By Urban-Rural

ECONOMIC BREAKDOWNS

By Commodity	By Individual Company or Institution
By Federal Agency	By Occupation
By Income	
By Industry	

DEMOGRAPHIC BREAKDOWNS

By Age	By Marital Status
By Disease	By Race and Ethnic Group
By Educational Attainment	By Sex

SUBJECT SUBHEADINGS

Within each of the categories listed above, references have been grouped according to the subject matter of the publication or the statistical content being indexed. Nineteen subheadings have been used for this purpose; they are listed below. The kinds of material referenced under each subheading are noted, as well as cross-references to other, related subheadings.

Agriculture and Food — Covers all agricultural data, including commercial fishing and the fertilizer industry; agricultural credit of all kinds; agricultural land; farm population and labor; and all data on food except retail prices.

See also Natural Resources, Environment, and Pollution, for forestry data, additional conservation data
Prices and Cost of Living, for retail food prices

Banking, Finance, and Insurance — Covers all data on financial institutions and their activities; all banking and insurance data; consumer credit; bankruptcy; securities markets; and money supply, interest rates, and other financial indicators.

See also Other specific subheadings, for Federal insurance programs
Agriculture and Food, for agricultural credit
Government and Defense, for Government debt and securities
Health and Vital Statistics, for health insurance data
Housing and Construction, for mortgage data
Industry and Commerce, for general economic indicators

Communications and Transportation — Covers all data on industries in these sectors, including their finances, employment, occupational safety, and rates and regulation; highway data; Postal Service; all travel and tourism data, including accidents; and propaganda.

See also Energy Resources and Demand, for pipeline data
Industry and Commerce, for equipment and parts manufacturing and trade.

Education — Covers all data on education in general, including schools, faculty, students, graduates, and finances.

See also Government and Defense, for military academies
Health and Vital Statistics, for medical and dental schools and all data on health manpower training
Labor and Employment, for employment training programs, such as CETA and WIN, and for apprenticeships
Science and Technology, for education exclusively in science and engineering
Veterans Affairs, for GI Bill and other veterans' education

Energy Resources and Demand — Covers supply, consumption, and conservation of all types of energy. Includes exploration, extraction, R&D, transportation, distribution, and waste disposal of all energy forms; all data on energy industries; and energy use and costs.

See also Health and Vital Statistics, for accidents and occupational health in energy industries, including mines
Natural Resources, Environment, and Pollution, for additional data exclusively on energy reserves, and for pollution and radioactivity from energy resources
Prices and Cost of Living, for consumer utility bills

Geography and Climate — Covers all data on weather, climate, oceanography, and storms and other natural disasters.

See also Natural Resources, Environment, and Pollution, for data on water supply and land use

Government and Defense — Covers all data on government in general, including activities, finances, programs, and personnel; all data on defense activities and foreign affairs; taxes; coinage; passports; and elections and voting.

See also Other specific subheadings for data on government aid, employment, or regulation in specific areas
Health and Vital Statistics, for military medicine

Health and Vital Statistics—Covers all data on health condition, disease, and disability; occupational health and safety in general; medical care, costs, and insurance; medical facilities; health personnel and their education; and vital statistics.

See also Communications and Transportation, for all transportation accidents, including occupational accidents and health
Labor and Employment, for vocational rehabilitation and other training programs for disabled persons
Public Welfare and Social Security, for data on Medicare, Medicaid, and social security recipients
Veterans Affairs, for data on veterans' health and VA medical facilities

Housing and Construction — Covers all data on housing condition, finance, and occupancy; all data on the construction industry; all mortgages; urban renewal and community development; and government aid for housing or communities.

See also Communications and Transportation, for construction of highways and bridges
Natural Resources, Environment, and Pollution, for construction of dams, sewer plants, etc.

Industry and Commerce — Covers all data on industry in general, including production, finances, payrolls, and profits; productivity; trade and marketing; foreign trade, tariffs, and balance of payments; and economic indicators in general.

See also Other more specific subheadings for data on specific industry sectors
Government and Defense, for corporate income tax data

Labor and Employment — Covers all data on the labor force and employment in general, including characteristics, earnings, hours, working conditions, and employee benefits; unemployment; labor unions; and employment training programs, such as CETA and WIN.

See also Other more specific subheadings for employment and employees in specific disciplines, such as health or science, or in specific industry sectors, such as agriculture or transportation
Industry and Commerce, for general industry data including employment and payrolls

Law Enforcement — Covers all data on crime and the characteristics of criminals; and all data on the criminal justice system, including police, lawyers, courts, prisons, and sentences.

See also Other specific subheadings for civil proceedings and government regulation in specific areas

Natural Resources, Environment, and Pollution—Covers all data on natural resource supply and conservation, including energy reserves, forests, public lands, and wildlife; land use; water supply, dams, and flood control; environmental quality; all types of pollutants; wastes in general, including sewage disposal; oil spills; and radioactivity in the environment.

See also Agriculture and Food, for conservation specifically related to agriculture
Energy Resources and Demand, for additional data on energy reserves, disposal of wastes from energy production, and nuclear power
Health and Vital Statistics, for occupational hazards and for the health effects of pollutants

Population—Covers all data on population size; characteristics of the population in general; demographic groups such as youth, women, or blacks; and migration.

See also Other specific subheadings for data on special population groups such as farmers, veterans, or mortgagors
Health and Vital Statistics, for data on births and deaths

Prices and Cost of Living—Covers prices in general, both wholesale and retail; price indexes; consumer costs; and inflation.

See also Education, for tuition costs
Health and Vital Statistics, for medical costs
Industry and Commerce or other more specific subheadings, for data on production costs, farm value, etc.

Public Welfare and Social Security—Covers everything related to the social security program, including Medicare and disability insurance; everything related to welfare, public assistance, and medical assistance (Medicaid); food stamps and school lunch programs; and social services.

See also Health and Vital Statistics, for data on workers compensation and disabled persons in general
Labor and Employment, for unemployment insurance

Recreation and Leisure—Covers all data on recreation activities and recreation industries. Includes sport fishing, hunting, parks, museums, and the arts; and tourists promotion.

See also Communications and Transportation, for data on travel
Education, for libraries

Science and Technology—Covers activities, private and government funding, employment, and education, exclusively in scientific fields; all data on space programs; and inventions and patents.

See also Agriculture and Food, for agricultural sciences
Energy Resources and Demand, for R&D in energy fields
Geography and Climate, for meteorology, oceanography, etc.

Veterans Affairs—Covers everything that relates exclusively to veterans, including education, health, VA hospitals, housing and VA home loans, employment and employment programs, pensions, and disability payments.

See also Government and Defense, for data on the armed services

USING THE INDEX

In using the Category Index, you must keep in mind that the amount of detail provided in the various tabular breakdowns may vary considerably.

Breakdowns "By sex" or "By urban-rural" are, by definition, complete. Breakdowns "By census division," "By region," or "By State" are generally complete unless specific limitations are noted.

Breakdowns "By race and ethnic group" generally show white and nonwhite or white, black, and other. When substantial data on race/ethnic breakdowns are included, they are indexed specifically in the Index of Subjects and Names (i.e. Black Americans, Asian Americans, Indians, Hispanic Americans) as well as under the category "By race."

The greatest variation in the detail of category breakdowns occurs in such categories as "By city," "By county," "By foreign country," "By industry," "By commodity," and "By occupation." For these categories, we try, whenever possible, to indicate the degree of detail in the notations of content listed under the category terms and in the abstract of the publication.

For further information about using the Category Index, see the User Guide.

For use in conjunction with the Category Index, we have printed several standard classification systems that are frequently used in Federal statistical publications (see p. 1019). These classifications include regions of the U.S., SMSAs, Standard Industrial Classification, and Standard International Trade Classification.

Index by Categories

GEOGRAPHIC BREAKDOWNS

BY CENSUS DIVISION

Agriculture and Food

Cold storage food stocks by commodity and census div, and warehouse space use, by State, monthly rpt, 1631–5

Cold storage food stocks by commodity, and warehouse space use, by census div, 1991, annual rpt, 1631–11

Fertilizer (inorganic) shipments, trade, use, and firms, by product and State, with stocks, 1991, annual Current Industrial Rpt, 2506–8.13

Fertilizer use, by type and State, 1991-92, annual rpt, 9804–30

Rice shipments, by end use, package size, and State of origin and destination, 1960s-89, biennial rpt, 1564–11

Communications and Transportation

Travel to US, by characteristics of visit and traveler, world area of origin, and US destination, 1991 survey, annual rpt, 2904–12

Travel to US, spending by world area of residence, and economic impact, by spending category and State, 1989, 2908–28

Education

Educational attainment, by social and demographic characteristics and location, 1991 and trends from 1940, biennial Current Population Rpt, 2546–1.460

Energy Resources and Demand

Building (commercial) energy use, costs, and conservation, by building characteristics, survey rpt series, 3166–8

Coal and coke supply, demand, movements, prices, and stocks, by end-use sector and State, quarterly rpt, 3162–37

Coal production, reserves, use, and prices by State, exports by country, and employment, 1900s-90, biennial rpt, 3164–79

Coal production, stocks, and shipments, by State of origin and destination, end-use sector, and mode of transport, quarterly rpt, 3162–8

Electric power plants (steam) fuel receipts, costs, and quality, by fuel, plant, utility, and State, 1991, annual rpt, 3164–42

Electric power plants and capacity, by fuel used, owner, location, and operating status, 1991 and for units planned 1992-2001, annual listing, 3164–36

Electric power plants certification applications filed with FERC, for small production and cogeneration facilities, FY80-91, annual listing, 3084–13

Electric power plants natural gas use, by State, 1980 and 1990, annual rpt, 3334–1

Electric power plants production, capacity, sales, and fuel stocks, use, and costs, by State, 1986-90, annual rpt, 3164–11

Electric power plants production, fuel use, stocks, and costs by fuel type, and sales, by State, monthly rpt, with articles, 3162–35

Electric power sales and revenue, by end-use sector, consumption level, and utility, 1990, annual rpt, 3164–91

Housing energy use, costs, and conservation, and household and housing characteristics, survey rpt series, 3166–7

Industrial electric power producers capacity, generation, and sales by industry div and State, and emissions, by census div, 1989-90, article, 3162–35.301

Lighting in commercial buildings, energy use and conservation by building characteristics, 1986, 3166–15.1

Natural gas supply, demand, prices, and distribution, by State, 1986-90 annual rpt, 3164–4

Geography and Climate

Heating and cooling degree days, by census div, monthly and cumulative for season, monthly rpt, 3162–24.1

Heating and cooling degree days weighted by population, by census div and State, with area-weighted temperature and precipitation, monthly rpt, 2152–13

Government and Defense

Military prime contract awards, by category, contractor type, and State, FY89-91, annual rpt, 3544–11

Voting age population, by sex, age, race, and State, forecast 1992 general elections, with votes cast from 1930, Current Population Rpt, 2546–3.170

Health and Vital Statistics

Deaths and rates, by cause, age, sex, marital status, race, and State, 1989, US Vital Statistics advance annual rpt, 4146–5.124

Deaths and rates, by cause and selected social, demographic, and employment characteristics, 1979-85, natl longitudinal study, 4478–186

Health care professionals supply and education, by professional and other characteristics, and location, 1960s-92 and projected to 2020, biennial rpt, 4114–8

Health condition and care indicators, 1950s-90 with health improvement and disease prevention goals for 1990, annual data compilation, 4144–11

Hospital employment and job vacancy rate, by occupation, and instn size and control, 1981-88, annual rpt, 4114–12

Infectious notifiable disease cases, by age, race, and State, and deaths, 1940s-91, annual rpt, 4204–1

Physicians, by specialty, age, sex, and location of training and practice, 1990, State rpt series, 4116–6

Radiation protection and health physics enrollment and degrees granted by instn and State, and grad placement, by student characteristics, 1991, annual rpt, 3004–7

Vital statistics provisional data, monthly rpt, 4142–1

Housing and Construction

Cement (portland) shipments to census divs, quarterly rpt, 2042–1.6

Clay (construction) production and shipments by region and State, trade, and use, by product, quarterly Current Industrial Rpt, 2506–9.2

Construction put in place, value of new public and private structures, by type, monthly rpt, 2382–4

Mobile home placements by structural characteristics, and price, by census div and State, monthly rpt, annual tables, 2382–1

New housing units authorized, by region, State, selected MSA, and permit-issuing place, monthly rpt, 2382–5

New housing units authorized, by State, MSA, and permit-issuing place, 1991, annual rpt, 2384–2

Industry and Commerce

Retail trade sales and inventories, by kind of business, region, and selected State, MSA, and city, monthly rpt, 2413–3

Statistical Abstract of US, 1992 annual data compilation, 2324–1

Labor and Employment

Displaced workers losing job 1987-92, labor force status by employment and other characteristics, as of Jan 1992, biennial press release, 6726–1.48

Employment and Earnings, detailed data, monthly rpt, 6742–2.8

Employment and unemployment, by census region and div, monthly 1978-91, article, 6742–2.303

Employment, unemployment, and labor force characteristics, by region and census div, 1991, annual rpt, 6744–7.1

Labor Relations Natl Board activities, cases, elections conducted, and litigation, FY90, annual rpt, 9584–1

Unemployment, employment, and labor force, by region and State, 1990-91, annual press release, 6726–1.45

Law Enforcement

Assaults and deaths of law enforcement officers, by circumstances, agency, victim and offender characteristics, and location, 1991, annual rpt, 6224–3

Crimes and rates by offense, and law enforcement employment, by population size and jurisdiction, 1991, annual rpt, 6224–2.1; 6224–2.3

Police employment and spending, by population size, metro status, and location, data compilation, 1992 annual rpt, 6064–6.1

Natural Resources, Environment, and Pollution

Electric utilities privately owned, air pollution emissions and abatement equipment by fuel type and State, 1986-90, annual rpt, 3164–11.5

Population

Census of Population, 1990: data adjustment in intercensal data for census undercounts, final decision with data by region and State, 2328–90

Census of Population, 1990: population characteristics and living arrangements, for Native American, urban, and metro areas, series, 2531–2
Income (household, family, and personal), by source, detailed characteristics, and region, 1991, annual Current Population Rpt, 2546–6.76
Income (personal) totals, by region, census div, and State, quarterly article, 2702–1.34
Migration, immigration, and mover characteristics compared to nonmovers, 1987-90, annual Current Population Rpt, 2546–1.456
Migration, population change, and areas losing population, by region, State, and metro-nonmetro location, 1980s and trends from 1940, Current Population Rpt, 2546–2.164
Migration since 1990, mover characteristics by same or different area, and compared to nonmovers, 1991, annual Current Population Rpt, 2546–1.464
Population estimates and projections, by region and State, Current Population Rpt series, 2546–3
Population size, July 1991-92, by region, census div, and State, annual press release, 2324–10
Statistical Abstract of US, 1992 annual data compilation, 2324–1

Public Welfare and Social Security

Medicare reimbursement of hospitals under prospective payment system, and effect on services, finances, and beneficiary payments, 1980-91, annual rpt, 17204–2
Medicare reimbursement of hospitals under prospective payment system, complexity indexes for diagnosis related groups, FY88-90, annual rpt, 17206–2.39
OASDHI, Medicaid, SSI, and related programs benefits, beneficiary characteristics, and trust funds, selected years 1937-90, annual rpt, 4744–3

Science and Technology

Education in science and engineering, grad programs enrollment by field, source of funds, and characteristics of student and instn, 1990, annual rpt, 9627–7
Nuclear engineering enrollment and degrees granted by instn and State, and grad placement, by student characteristics, 1991, annual rpt, 3004–5
R&D and related funding of Fed Govt to higher education and nonprofit instns, by field, instn, agency, and State, FY90, annual rpt, 9627–17
R&D funding by higher education instns and federally funded centers, by field, instn, and State, FY90, annual rpt, 9627–13

BY CITY

Agriculture and Food

Chile fruit exports to US, sales by port of entry, and prices in 5 terminal cities, by commodity, 1990/91, annual rpt, 1311–27
Cotton prices in 7 spot markets, futures prices at NYC exchange, farm prices, and CCC loan stocks, monthly rpt, 1309–1
Fish catch, by species, use, region, State, and major port, 1980s-91, annual rpt, 2164–1.1
Fruit and vegetable imports under quarantine, by crop, country, and port of entry, FY89, annual rpt, 1524–7
Fruit and vegetable shipments, and arrivals by city, by mode of transport and State and country of origin, 1991, annual rpt series, 1311–4
Grain stocks by region and market city, and grain inspected for export, by type, weekly rpt, 1313–4
Grape shipments from California and arrivals by city by mode of transport, prices, and production, by variety, 1970s-90, annual rpt, 1311–25
Meat from Canada inspected and rejected, by US port of entry, 1989-91, hearing, 21368–141
Molasses (feed) wholesale prices by market area, and trade, weekly rpt, 1311–16
Molasses supply, use, wholesale prices by market, and imports by country, 1986-91, annual rpt, 1311–19
Pecan production and prices by State, and US trade by country, late 1980s-91, annual rpt, 1311–28
Potato production, acreage, prices, and shipments, for 7 major producer States, and compared to other States, 1970s-92, annual rpt, 1311–29
Potato production, acreage, shipments, and arrivals, for Maine by variety, and compared to other States and Canada, 1991-92, annual rpt, 1311–26
Salt production capacity, by firm and facility, 1991, annual listing, 5614–30
Tobacco marketing activity, prices, and sales, by grade, type, market, and State, 1991, annual rpt series, 1319–5
Tomato production, acreage, and yield by State, trade and production by country, stocks, shipments, and prices, 1960s-91, 1568–310
Truck rates for fruit and vegetables paid by shippers and receivers, by commodity and city, and fleet itemized costs per mile, weekly rpt, 1311–22

Banking, Finance, and Insurance

Fed Financing Bank holdings and transactions, by borrower, monthly press release, 12802–1
Fed Reserve banks expenses and operations, itemized by service, office, and district, 1991, annual rpt, 9364–11
New England States, FHLB 1st District thrift instns, financial condition, and locations, 1992, annual listing, 9304–26
Savings instns failures, inventory of real estate assets available from Resolution Trust Corp, semiannual listing series, 9722–2
Small Business Admin loans, contract awards, and surety bonds, by firm, State, and city, FY91, annual rpt, 9764–1
West Central States, FHLB 10th District thrifts, locations, assets, and deposits, 1992, annual listing, 9304–17

Communications and Transportation

Air traffic (passenger), and aircraft operations by type, by airport and State, projected FY92-2005 and trends from FY83, annual rpt, 7504–7
Air traffic (passenger and cargo), and departures by aircraft type, by carrier and airport, 1991, annual rpt, 7504–35
Air traffic (passenger and cargo), carrier enplanement shares, and FAA airport improvement program grants, by airport and State, 1990, annual rpt, 7504–48
Air traffic, and passenger and freight enplanements, by airport, 1960s-91 and projected to 2010, hub area rpt series, 7506–7
Air traffic and passengers, for intl routes over north Atlantic, by aviation type and route, alternative forecasts 1992-2010 and trends from 1982, annual rpt, 7504–44
Air traffic and passengers, for intl routes over Pacific, by route, alternative forecasts 1992-2010 and trends from 1980, annual rpt, 7504–51
Air traffic, carriers, craft, airports, and FAA activities, detailed data, 1981-90, annual rpt, 7504–1
Air traffic levels at FAA-operated control facilities, by airport and State, FY91, annual rpt, 7504–27
Aircraft accidents and circumstances, for US operations of domestic and foreign airlines and general aviation, periodic rpt, 9612–1
Aircraft flight service station workload of FAA, pilot briefs, contacts, and flight plans by facility, projected FY92-2002 and trends from FY83, annual rpt, 7504–39
Aircraft handled by instrument flight rule, by user type, FAA traffic control center, and region, FY85-91 and projected to FY2005, annual rpt, 7504–15
Airline consumer complaints by reason, passengers denied boarding, and late flights, by reporting carrier and airport, monthly rpt, 7302–11
Airport capacity improvement projects and funding, traffic, and delays, by major airport, 1988-90 and forecast to 2000, annual rpt, 7504–43
Airport improvement program of FAA, activities and grants by State and airport, FY91, annual rpt, 7504–38
Airport planning and dev project grants of FAA, by airport and location, quarterly press release, 7502–14
Carpool high occupancy vehicle lanes design, enforcement, and use in selected cities, 1991 conf, 7308–204
Coast Guard search and rescue missions, and lives and property lost and saved, by district and assisting unit, FY91, annual rpt, 7404–2
Hwy and road miles and traffic volume, by city, 1991, annual rpt, 7554–1.4
Hwy toll facilities of State and local govts, receipts and disbursements by facility, 1990-91, annual rpt, 7554–1.3
Mexico-US trade agreement impacts on truck traffic at border crossings, Customs Service staff needs, and hwy improvement costs, projected to 2000 with trends from 1986, GAO rpt, 26123–368
Ohio River basin waterway facilities, freight by commodity and port, and recreation, by waterway, 1988-89, annual rpt, 3754–6
Port improvement capital expenditures and financing methods, by region and selected port, 1946-89, 7708–6
Rail rapid transit systems safety, operating, and funding characteristics, 1988-89, 9618–19
Railroad accidents, casualties, circumstances, and railroad involved, 1988, annual rpt, 9614–8
Railroad accidents, casualties, damage, and circumstances, by incident, 1988, annual rpt, 7604–3

Railroad accidents involving hazardous materials, casualties, and circumstances, 1984-89, 9618-18
Shipborne commerce (domestic) of US, freight by major commodity group, vessel type, and port, 1987-89, annual rpt, 7704-7
Shipborne commerce (domestic and foreign) of US, freight by port, 1990, annual rpt, 3754-7
Shipborne trade of US, by type of service, customs district, port, and world area, monthly rpt, 2422-7
St Lawrence Seaway ship, cargo, and passenger traffic, and toll revenue, 1991 and trends from 1959, annual rpt, 7744-2
Telephone local service charges and low-income subsidies, by region, company, and city, 1980s-91, semiannual rpt, 9282-8
Telephone rates for long-distance telephone service, by company, city, and time of day, 1950s-90, annual rpt, 9284-6.7
Transit fare subsidies by employers, participation, and parking costs, by selected city, 1985-92, GAO rpt, 26113-597
Transit systems finances and operations, by mode, size of fleet and urban area, region, and for 518 systems, 1990, annual rpt, 7884-4
Transit systems finances, equipment, and ridership characteristics, 1985-90, biennial rpt, 7884-8
Transit systems grants of Federal Transit Admin, by city and State, FY91, annual rpt, 7884-10
Travel to and from US on US and foreign flag air carriers, by country, world area, and US port, monthly rpt, 7302-2
Travel to US and Canada, market analysis with detailed trip and traveler characteristics, country rpt series, 2906-2
Travel to US, by characteristics of visit and traveler, country, port city, and State of destination, quarterly rpt, 2902-1
Travel to US, by characteristics of visit and traveler, world area of origin, and US destination, 1991 survey, annual rpt, 2904-12
Truck rates for fresh vegetables, by crop, growing area, and market, periodic situation rpt with articles, 1561-11
Truck rates for fruit and vegetables, by growing area and market, weekly 1991, annual rpt, 1311-15
Truck rates for fruit and vegetables paid by shippers and receivers, by commodity and city, and fleet itemized costs per mile, weekly rpt, 1311-22
TV channel allocation and license status, for commercial and noncommercial UHF and VHF stations by market, as of June 1992, semiannual rpt, 9282-6
Waterborne commerce (domestic and foreign) of US, freight by commodity, traffic, and passengers, by port and waterway, 1989, annual rpt, 3754-3

Education

High school dropout rates, and subsequent completion, by student and school characteristics, alternative estimates, 1991, annual rpt, 4834-23

Energy Resources and Demand

Bonneville Power Admin mgmt of Fed Columbia River Power System, finances, operations, and sales by customer, FY91, annual rpt, 3224-1
Bonneville Power Admin sales, revenues, and rates, by customer and customer type, 1991, semiannual rpt, 3222-1
Electric power and industrial plants exempt from oil and gas primary use prohibition, 1991, annual rpt, 3334-1
Electric power sales and revenue, by end-use sector, consumption level, and utility, 1990, annual rpt, 3164-91
Gasoline and other motor fuel use by State, and tax rates by jurisdiction, monthly rpt, 7552-1
Gasoline service stations price competition and divorcement from oil companies, issues with data by firm, city, and State, 1991 hearing, 25528-120
Nuclear reactors for domestic use and export by function and operating status, with owner, operating characteristics, and location, 1991 annual listing, 3354-15
Southeastern Power Admin sales by customer, plants, capacity, and Southeastern Fed Power Program financial statements, FY91, annual rpt, 3234-1
Southwestern Fed Power System financial statements, sales by customer, and operations and costs by project, FY91, annual rpt, 3244-1
TVA electric power purchases and resales, with electricity use, average bills, and rates by customer class, by distributor, 1991, annual tables, 9804-14
TVA electric power purchases of municipal and cooperative distributors, and prices and use by distributor and consumer sector, monthly rpt, 9802-1
Western Area Power Admin activities by plant, financial statements, and sales by customer, FY91, annual rpt, 3254-1

Geography and Climate

Earthquakes and other ground motion, intensity by station, 1990, annual rpt, 5664-14
Great Lakes water levels, daily and monthly averages by site, 1991 and cumulative from 1900, annual rpt, 2174-3
Great Lakes water levels, monthly and annual averages by station, 1860-1990, quinquennial rpt, 2178-1
Heating and cooling degree days, for 45 cities and total US, cumulative for season, weekly rpt, 3162-32.2
Heating degree days for 45 cities and total US, cumulative for season, weekly rpt, 3162-45.2
Statistical Abstract of US, 1992 annual data compilation, 2324-1.6
Tidal currents, daily time and velocity by station for North America and Asia coasts, forecast 1993, annual rpts, 2174-1
Tide height and tidal current velocity daily at Middle Atlantic coastal stations, forecast 1993, annual rpt, 2174-11
Tide height and time daily at coastal points worldwide, forecast 1993, annual rpt series, 2174-2
Weather conditions and effect on agriculture, by US region, State, and city, and world area, weekly rpt, 2182-7
Weather data for surface and upper air, averages by foreign and US station, monthly rpt, 2152-4
Weather events and anomalies, precipitation and temperature for US and foreign locations, weekly rpt, 2182-6
Weather forecasts for US and Northern Hemisphere, precipitation and temperature by location, semimonthly rpt, 2182-1

Government and Defense

Aliens (illegal) held in Immigration and Naturalization Service detention facilities pending hearings, and legal aid requests, 1980s-91, GAO rpt, 26119-409
Aliens admitted to US, by class of admission and for top entry ports and countries, FY90-91, fact sheet, 6266-2.9
Customs collections, by district and port, FY91, annual rpt, 8104-2.2
Fed Govt spending in States and local areas, by type, State, county, and city, FY91, annual rpt, 2464-3.2
Finances of govts, by level of govt, State, and for large cities and counties, annual rpt series, 2466-2
Finances, tax systems and revenue, and fiscal structure, by level of govt and State, 1992 and historical trends, annual rpt, 10044-1
Fiscal condition of State and local govts, with data by State and selected city, 1991 hearing, 21268-44
Immigrant and nonimmigrant visas of US issued and refused, by class, issuing office, and nationality, FY90, annual rpt, 7184-1
Military base support costs by function, and personnel and acreage by installation, by service branch, FY93, annual rpt, 3504-11
Military contracts, payroll, and personnel, by service branch and location, with top 5 contractors and maps, by State and country, FY91, annual rpt, 3544-29
Military in-house commercial activities work-years, by service branch, State, and installation, FY91, annual rpt, 3544-25
Military prime contract awards, by contractor, service branch, State, and city, FY91, annual rpt, 3544-22
Military prime contract awards for R&D to US and foreign nonprofit instns and govt agencies, by instn and location, FY91, annual listing, 3544-17
Military prime contract awards in labor surplus areas, by service branch, State, and area, 1st half FY92, semiannual rpt, 3542-19
Natl Guard emergency response and strengths, by incident and location, FY91, annual rpt, 3504-22
Navy nuclear-powered vessels and support facilities radioactive waste, releases in harbors, and public exposure, 1970s-91, annual rpt, 3804-11

Health and Vital Statistics

AIDS prevention programs for drug abusers and their sexual partners, client characteristics, and outcomes, for selected metro areas, 1989 annual conf, 4494-12
Deaths and rates, by detailed location, cause, and demographic characteristics, 1989, US Vital Statistics annual rpt, 4144-3
Deaths recorded in 121 cities, weekly rpt, 4202-1
Drug abuse indicators for selected metro areas, research results, data collection, and policy issues, 1992 semiannual conf, 4492-5

HHS financial aid, by program, recipient, State, and city, FY91, annual regional listings, 4004–3
Insurance (health) provided by employer, costs and cost factors by industry div and firm size, 1987-91, GAO rpt, 26121–485
NIH grants and contracts, quarterly listing, 4432–1

Housing and Construction

American Housing Survey: unit and households characteristics, unit and neighborhood quality, and journey to work by MSA location, for 11 MSAs, 1987 survey, supplement, 2485–8
American Housing Survey: unit and households detailed characteristics, and unit and neighborhood quality, MSA rpt series, 2485–6
Census of Housing, 1990: summary unit characteristics, by householder race and age, county, place, and urban-rural location, State rpt series, 2471–1
Census of Population and Housing, 1990: detailed geographic coverage, State CD-ROM series, 2551–9
Census of Population and Housing, 1990: population and housing characteristics, detailed geographic coverage, State CD-ROM series, 2551–10
Census of Population and Housing, 1990: summary characteristics, by county, subdiv, and place, State rpt series, 2551–7
Census of Population and Housing, 1990: summary characteristics, households, and land area, by county, subdiv, and place, State rpt series, 2551–1
Homeless persons housing in rehabilitated single occupancy units, funding and characteristics, by city, FY87-91, GAO rpt, 26113–596
Homeless persons housing in rehabilitated single occupancy units, HUD grants by community, 1991, press release, 5006–3.82
Homeless persons housing in rehabilitated single occupancy units, HUD grants by community, 1992, press release, 5006–3.90
Homeless persons transitional housing and support services, HUD grants by community, 1991, press release, 5006–3.80
Homeless persons transitional housing and support services, HUD grants by community, 1992, press release, 5006–3.95
HUD housing and community development programs, press release series, 5006–3
Low income rental housing and homeownership assistance, HUD grants by recipient, FY92, press release, 5006–3.86
Mortgage interest rate differential among cities, and relation to bank market conditions, 1987-88, technical paper, 9366–1.162
New housing units authorized, by region, State, selected MSA, and permit-issuing place, monthly rpt, 2382–5
New housing units authorized, by State, MSA, and permit-issuing place, 1991, annual rpt, 2384–2
North Central States, FHLB 7th District housing vacancy rates for single and multifamily units and mobile homes, by ZIP code, annual MSA rpt series, 9304–18
Public housing drug treatment and anticrime programs, HUD grants by recipient, FY91, press release, 5006–3.81
Public housing drug treatment and anticrime programs, HUD grants by recipient, FY92, press release, 5006–3.99
West Central States, FHLB 10th District housing vacancy rates for single and multifamily units and mobile homes, by ZIP code, annual MSA rpt series, 9304–22
Western States, FHLB 12th District housing vacancy rates for single and multifamily units and mobile homes, by ZIP code, annual MSA rpt series, 9304–21

Industry and Commerce

Exports of US, detailed commodities by country, monthly CD-ROM, 2422–13
Foreign trade zones (US) operations and movement of goods, by zone and commodity, FY90, annual rpt, 2044–30
Imports of US, detailed commodities by country, monthly CD-ROM, 2422–14
Retail trade sales and inventories, by kind of business, region, and selected State, MSA, and city, monthly rpt, 2413–3

Labor and Employment

Employment and Earnings, detailed data, monthly rpt, 6742–2.8
Employment, unemployment, and labor force characteristics, by selected metro area and large city, 1991, annual rpt, 6744–7.3
Unemployment, employment, and labor force, by State, MSA, and city, monthly rpt, 6742–22

Law Enforcement

Aircraft hijackings, on-board explosions, and other crimes, US and foreign incidents, 1986-90, annual rpt, 7504–31
Arrests and criminal case processing through sentencing, cases and duration by disposition and offense, for selected cities, 1988, annual rpt, 6064–27
Arrests, by offense, offender characteristics, and location, data compilation, 1992 annual rpt, 6064–6.4
Assaults and deaths of law enforcement officers, by circumstances, agency, victim and offender characteristics, and location, 1991, annual rpt, 6224–3
Crime Index by population size and region, and offenses by large city, 1st half 1992, semiannual rpt, 6222–1
Crimes and rates by offense, and law enforcement employment, by population size and jurisdiction, 1991, annual rpt, 6224–2.1; 6224–2.3
Crimes, by characteristics of victim and offender, circumstances, and location, data compilation, 1992 annual rpt, 6064–6.3
Drug test results at arrest, by drug type, offense, and sex, for selected urban areas, quarterly rpt, 6062–3
Jail population by sex, race, and for 25 jurisdictions, and instn conditions, 1990-91, annual rpt, 6066–25.48
Police employment, spending, and operations, for State, city, county, and special district agencies, 1990, annual rpt, 6064–39
Terrorism incidents in US, related activity, and casualties, by attack type, target, group, and location, 1991, annual rpt, 6224–6
Women arrestees drug abuse history and selected other characteristics, for 4 cities, 1988-89, 6068–246

Natural Resources, Environment, and Pollution

Acid rain distribution, pH levels, and composition, monitoring results by site, 1989, annual rpt, 9194–20
Air pollution levels, by country and selected city, 1970-90, 9194–1
Air pollution levels for 6 pollutants, and measurements exceeding natl standards, by site, 1990-91, annual rpt, 9194–5
Army Corps of Engineers activities and projects, FY88 and trends from 1800s, annual rpt, 3754–1.1
Army Corps of Engineers activities and projects, FY89 and trends from 1800s, annual rpt, 3754–1.2
Army Corps of Engineers activities and projects, FY90 and trends from 1800s, annual rpt, 3754–1.3
Environmental Quality, status of problems, protection programs, research, and intl issues, 1991 annual rpt, 484–1
Hazardous substances industrial releases and reduction methods under EPA regulation, by chemical, source, industry, and location, 1989, annual rpt, 9234–6
Hazardous waste site remedial action under Superfund, current and proposed sites descriptions and status, periodic listings, series, 9216–3
Hazardous waste site remedial action under Superfund, current and proposed sites priority ranking and status by location, series, 9216–5
Hazardous waste site remedial action under Superfund, EPA records of decision by site, FY90, annual rpt, 9214–5
Military installations hazardous waste site remedial action, activities and funding by site and State, FY91, annual rpt, 3544–36
Minerals resources and availability on public lands, State rpt series, 5606–7
Pollution (air) contributing to global warming, emissions by monitoring site and country, and temperature change by world area and US region, 1860s-1990, annual rpt, 3004–33
Radiation and radionuclide concentrations in air, water, and milk, monitoring results by site, quarterly rpt, 9192–5
Radioactive waste from Navy nuclear-powered vessels and support facilities, releases in harbors, and public exposure, 1970s-91, annual rpt, 3804–11
Radionuclide concentrations in air, water, humans, animals, and milk near Nevada and other nuclear test sites, 1990, annual rpt, 9194–17
Tennessee Valley river control activities, and hydroelectric power generation and capacity, 1990, annual rpt, 9804–7
Timber sales of Forest Service, expenses, and operations, by region, State, and natl forest, FY91, annual rpts, 1204–36
Uranium tailings at inactive mills, remedial action activities by site, and funding, FY91, annual rpt, 3354–9
Uranium tailings at inactive mills, remedial action proposals, costs, site characteristics, and environmental, socioeconomic, and health impacts, series, 3356–4
Water quality, chemistry, hydrology, and other characteristics, local area studies, series, 5666–27

Water resources dev projects of Army Corps of Engineers, characteristics, and costs, 1950s-89, biennial State rpt series, 3756–1
Water resources dev projects of Army Corps of Engineers, characteristics, and costs, 1950s-91, biennial State rpt series, 3756–2
Water supply and quality in streams and lakes, and groundwater levels in wells, by drainage basin, 1990, annual State rpt series, 5666–10
Water supply and quality in streams and lakes, and groundwater levels in wells, by drainage basin, 1990-91, annual CD-ROM, 5664–18
Water supply and quality in streams and lakes, and groundwater levels in wells, by drainage basin, 1991, annual State rpt series, 5666–12
Water supply in northeastern US, precipitation and stream runoff by station, monthly rpt, 2182–3
Water supply in US and southern Canada, streamflow, surface and groundwater conditions, and reservoir levels, by location, monthly rpt, 5662–3
Water supply in western US, streamflow and reservoir storage forecasts by stream and station, Jan-May monthly rpt, 1262–1

Population

Alaska rural areas population characteristics, and energy resources dev effects, series, 5736–5
Census of Population and Housing, 1990: detailed geographic coverage, State CD-ROM series, 2551–9
Census of Population and Housing, 1990: immigrants, by period of entry, citizenship, State, birthplace, and for top cities and counties, press release, 2328–88
Census of Population and Housing, 1990: population and housing characteristics, detailed geographic coverage, State CD-ROM series, 2551–10
Census of Population and Housing, 1990: summary characteristics, by county, subdiv, and place, State rpt series, 2551–7
Census of Population and Housing, 1990: summary characteristics, households, and land area, by county, subdiv, and place, State rpt series, 2551–1
Census of Population, 1990: data adjustment for undercounts, evaluation of advisability, with error rates by race and selected city, hearing, 21628–102
Census of Population, 1990: data adjustment in intercensal data for census undercounts, recommendations with alternative undercount estimates, 2628–36
Census of Population, 1990: population characteristics and living arrangements, by county, place, and urban-rural location, State rpt series, 2531–1
Foreign countries and cities population density, and distribution, life expectancy, and infant mortality by world region, 1991, fact sheet, 2326–17.50
Foreign countries population size, growth rate, and area, for 94 largest cities, 1991 biennial rpt, 2324–9
Immigrants and nonimmigrants admitted to US, alien workers, visitors, deportations, and naturalizations, FY91, annual summary rpt, 6264–7
Immigration to US, alien workers, visitors, deportations, and naturalizations, by country, FY91 and trends from 1820, annual rpt, 6264–2
Income per capita for central cities and suburbs, by city, 1991 hearings, 21308–28
Older population, and health, economic, and other characteristics, with foreign comparisons, 1980s-91 with trends and projections, Current Population Rpt, 2546–2.165
Pacific territories population and housing detailed characteristics, by location, 1990 Census of Population and Housing, series, 2551–8
Refugees from Indochina, arrivals, and departures, by country of origin and resettlement, camp, and ethnicity, monthly rpt, 7002–4
Soviet Union former Republics and Baltic States population size and characteristics, 1989-92, 9118–19
Statistical Abstract of US, 1992 annual data compilation, 2324–1.14
Vietnam population size, components of change, and selected characteristics, 1979, 1989, and projected to 2050, 2326–18.65

Prices and Cost of Living

Cotton prices at selected spot markets, NYC futures prices, and CCC loan rates, 1991/92 and trends from 1944, annual rpt, 1309–2
Dairy prices, by product and selected area, with related marketing data, 1991, annual rpt, 1317–1
Foreign countries living costs, State Dept indexes, housing allowances, and hardship differentials by country and major city, quarterly rpt, 7002–7
Milk order and cooperative prices, by selected area, 1991, annual rpt, 1317–1.5
Poultry and egg prices and marketing, by selected region, State, and city, monthly and weekly 1991, annual rpt, 1317–2

Public Welfare and Social Security

Food aid programs purchases, by commodity, firm, and shipping point or destination, weekly rpt, 1302–3
HHS financial aid, by program, recipient, State, and city, FY91, annual regional listings, 4004–3

Recreation and Leisure

Arts funding, by level of govt, State, and selected city, FY86-92, GAO rpt, 26119–371
Park natl system and other land under Natl Park Service mgmt, acreage by site, ownership, and region, FY92, semiannual rpt, 5542–1

Veterans Affairs

Health care facilities of VA, trainees by detailed program and city, FY91, annual rpt, 8704–4
Health care for veterans, patients, visits, costs, and operating beds, by VA and contract facility, and region, quarterly rpt, 8602–4
Health care professionals of VA, by selected employment characteristics and VA district and duty station, quarterly rpt, 8602–6

BY COUNTY

Agriculture and Food

Cotton acreage planted by State and county, and fiber quality, by variety, 1992, annual rpt, 1309–6
Cotton ginnings, by State and county, seasonal biweekly rpt, 1631–19
Farmland in US owned by foreigners, holdings, acreage, and value by land use, owner country, State, and county, 1991, annual rpt, 1584–3
Irrigated farmland, farm characteristics, and water and fuel sources, by State and leading county, 1950s-88, 1588–122
Japan investment in US farmland and agricultural industries, with data by State and county, late 1960s-90, 1528–332
Labor (hired and contract) costs, by farm type and sales size, and for top States and counties, 1987, article, 1541–1.305
Livestock grazing on public desert areas, acreage, use, fees, and endangered species, 1988-90, GAO rpt, 26113–552

Banking, Finance, and Insurance

Banks (insured commercial and savings) deposits by instn, State, MSA, and county, as of June 1991, annual regional rpt series, 9295–3
Savings instns insured by Savings Assn Insurance Fund, offices, and deposits, by region, State, MSA, and county, 1991, annual rpt, 8434–5

Communications and Transportation

Aircraft registered with FAA, by type and characteristics of aircraft, make, carrier, State, and county, 1991, annual rpt, 7504–3
Commuters, by county of residence and work, for top 10 metro areas, 1990 Census of Population, press release, 2328–84
Hwy scenic routes impacts on local economic conditions, by State, county, and selected byway, late 1980s, 7556–8.1

Energy Resources and Demand

Bonneville Power Admin mgmt of Fed Columbia River Power System, finances, operations, and sales by customer, FY91, annual rpt, 3224–1
Coal production and mines by county, prices, productivity, miners, and reserves, by mining method and State, 1990-91, annual rpt, 3164–25
Coal receipts cost and quality, by electric utility, plant, State, and county, 1991, annual rpt, 3164–42
Wood fuel production in Michigan, by species, land ownership, survey region, county, and location, 1986, 1208–412

Government and Defense

DC metro area land acquisition and dev projects of Fed Govt, characteristics and funding by agency and project, FY92-96, annual rpt, 15454–1
Employment and payroll of county govts, by function and population size, for 424 largest counties, 1991, annual rpt, 2466–1.2
Fed Govt spending in States and local areas, by type, State, county, and city, FY91, annual rpt, 2464–3
Finances of govts, by level of govt, State, and for large cities and counties, annual rpt series, 2466–2
Finances, tax systems and revenue, and fiscal structure, by level of govt and State, 1992 and historical trends, annual rpt, 10044–1
Military prime contract awards in labor surplus areas, by service branch, State, and area, 1st half FY92, semiannual rpt, 3542–19
Tax revenue, by level of govt, type of tax, State, and selected large county, quarterly rpt, 2462–3

Voter registration and verification data storage and retrieval systems use and characteristics, for selected counties, 1992 rpt, 9278–8

Health and Vital Statistics

Alcohol-related deaths, by cause, State, and county, annual averages 1979-80 and 1983-85, 4488–10.4

Deaths and rates, by detailed location, cause, and demographic characteristics, 1989, US Vital Statistics annual rpt, 4144–3.1

Florida cancer incidence impacts of migration, and treatment resources availability, by county, 1980, article, 4042–3.339

Health service areas, indicators of service use, and residents seeking care outside area, under alternative area definitions, 1988-89, 4147–2.113

HHS financial aid, by program, recipient, State, and city, FY91, annual regional listings, 4004–3

Physicians, by specialty, age, sex, and location of training and practice, 1990, State rpt series, 4116–6

Radiation exposure of population near Hanford, Wash, nuclear plant, with methodology, 1944-91, series, 3356–5

Rural areas health care access for counties without hospitals and in which the only hospital closed, 1987-89, 17206–2.30

Housing and Construction

American Housing Survey: unit and households characteristics, unit and neighborhood quality, and journey to work by MSA location, for 11 MSAs, 1987 survey, supplement, 2485–8

Census of Housing, 1990: summary unit characteristics, by householder race and age, county, place, and urban-rural location, State rpt series, 2471–1

Census of Population and Housing, 1990: detailed geographic coverage, State CD-ROM series, 2551–9

Census of Population and Housing, 1990: population and housing characteristics, detailed geographic coverage, State CD-ROM series, 2551–10

Census of Population and Housing, 1990: summary characteristics, by county, subdiv, and place, State rpt series, 2551–7

Census of Population and Housing, 1990: summary characteristics, households, and land area, by county, subdiv, and place, State rpt series, 2551–1

Coastal areas construction authorized by permit, by building type, 1970-89, 2176–8.3

Economic Dev Admin activities, and funding by program, recipient, State, and county, FY91 and cumulative from FY66, annual rpt, 2064–2

HUD housing and community development programs, press release series, 5006–3

Low income rental housing and homeownership assistance, HUD grants by recipient, FY92, press release, 5006–3.86

Mortgages FHA-insured, and foreclosures, by State and county, 1991 and cumulative from 1934, annual rpt, 5144–15

New housing units authorized, by region, State, selected MSA, and permit-issuing place, monthly rpt, 2382–5

New housing units authorized, by State, MSA, and permit-issuing place, 1991, annual rpt, 2384–2

North Central States, FHLB 7th District housing vacancy rates for single and multifamily units and mobile homes, by ZIP code, annual MSA rpt series, 9304–18

West Central States, FHLB 10th District housing vacancy rates for single and multifamily units and mobile homes, by ZIP code, annual MSA rpt series, 9304–22

Western States, FHLB 12th District housing vacancy rates for single and multifamily units and mobile homes, by ZIP code, annual MSA rpt series, 9304–21

Industry and Commerce

County Business Patterns, 1989: employment, establishments, and payroll, by SIC 2- to 4-digit industry and county, annual State rpt series, 2326–8

County Business Patterns, 1990: employment, establishments, and payroll, by SIC 2- to 4-digit industry and county, annual State rpt series, 2326–6

Lumber (industrial roundwood) production and timber harvest for North Central States, by product and county, State rpt series, 1206–10

Lumber (pulpwood) production and mill receipts in North Central States, by species, mill, State, and county, 1990, annual rpt, 1204–19

Lumber (pulpwood) production by species and county, and shipments, by northeastern State, 1990, annual rpt, 1204–18

Lumber (pulpwood) production in 3 North Central States, by species and county, 1990, 1208–397

Lumber mills, operations, log use by species and origin, and residue use, for California by product and county, 1988, 1208–108

Lumber production, and industry operations, for Oregon by county, 1988, 1208–280

Lumber production and mill residue for Rocky Mountain States, by species, ownership, and county, series, 1206–17

Minerals Yearbook, Vol 2, 1989: State reviews of production and sales by commodity, and business activity, annual rpt series, 5604–16

Minerals Yearbook, Vol 2, 1990: State reviews of production and sales by commodity, and business activity, annual rpt series, 5604–22

Labor and Employment

Unemployment, employment, and labor force, by State, MSA, and city, monthly rpt, 6742–22

Law Enforcement

Assaults and deaths of law enforcement officers, by circumstances, agency, victim and offender characteristics, and location, 1991, annual rpt, 6224–3

California jail population and overcrowding by county, and instn construction funding, 1980s, 6066–30.1

Crimes and rates by offense, and law enforcement employment, by population size and jurisdiction, 1991, annual rpt, 6224–2.1; 6224–2.3

Jail population by sex, race, and for 25 jurisdictions, and instn conditions, 1990-91, annual rpt, 6066–25.48

Police employment, spending, and operations, for State, city, county, and special district agencies, 1990, annual rpt, 6064–39

Wiretaps authorized, costs, arrests, trials, and convictions, by offense and jurisdiction, 1991, annual rpt, 18204–7

Natural Resources, Environment, and Pollution

Air pollution levels for 6 pollutants, and measurements exceeding natl standards, by site, 1990-91, annual rpt, 9194–5

Birds (sandhill crane) hunting activity and permits, by State and county, 1990/91-1991/92, annual rpt, 5504–31

Forests (natl) and other lands under Forest Service mgmt, acreage by forest and location, 1991 and historic trends, annual rpt, 1204–2

Forests (natl) revenue share paid to States, and acreage, by forest, county, and congressional district, FY92, annual rpt, 1204–33

Hazardous substances industrial releases and reduction methods under EPA regulation, by chemical, source, industry, and location, 1989, annual rpt, 9234–6

Helium and other components of natural gas, analyses of individual wells and pipelines, 1985-91, annual rpt, 5604–2

Helium and other components of natural gas, analyses of individual wells and pipelines, 1986-90, 5608–132

Oregon railroad grant lands, forest acreage returned to Federal ownership by county, FY91, annual rpt, 5724–1.1

Public lands acreage and use, and Land Mgmt Bur activities and finances, annual State rpt series, 5724–11

Timber in Alabama, acreage and volume by species, forest type, ownership, and county, 1990, series, 1206–30

Timber in Iowa, resources and removals by species, forest and tree characteristics, ownership, and county, 1988-90 and trends from 1973-74, 1208–75

Timber in Louisiana, resources by ownership, forest and tree characteristics, and parish, 1991, series, 1206–35

Timber in Minnesota, acreage, resources, and removals, by ownership, forest and tree characteristics, and county, 1990, series, 1206–24

Timber in Missouri, resources and removals by species, forest and tree characteristics, ownership, and county, 1987-89 and trends from 1959, 1208–76

Timber in Missouri, resources and removals by species, land ownership, and county, 1988-89, series, 1206–3

Timber in Montana outside natl forests, acreage, resources, and mortality by species and ownership class, 1988-89, series, 1206–25

Timber in northeastern US, resources and removals by species, ownership class, and county, State rpt series, 1206–12

Timber in South Carolina, Hurricane Hugo damage by species, damage class, and county, as of 1990, 1208–411

Timber in southern US, resources and removals by species, ownership, State, and county, series, 1206–8

Timber in Tennessee, acreage and resources by species, ownership class, and county, 1989, series, 1206–27

Timber in Virginia, resources, growth, and removals, by species, ownership, treatment, and county, 1990-92, series, 1206–6

Timber in Washington State, acreage and resources by species, ownership class, and county, 1988-89 with harvest trends from 1955, series, 1206–28

Timber in Wisconsin, resources and removals by species, forest type, ownership, and county, series, 1206–34
Timber insect and disease incidence and damage, and control activities, State rpt series, 1206–49
Water (groundwater) pesticide contamination, vulnerability indicators by State and county, 1987-89, GAO rpt, 26131–91
Water (groundwater) supply, quality, chemistry, and use, State and local area rpt series, 5666–28
Water use by end use, well withdrawals, and public supply deliveries, by county, State rpt series, 5666–24

Population

Appalachia population, by State and county, 1980 and 1990, annual rpt, 9084–1
Census of Population and Housing, 1990: detailed geographic coverage, State CD-ROM series, 2551–9
Census of Population and Housing, 1990: immigrants, by period of entry, citizenship, State, birthplace, and for top cities and counties, press release, 2328–88
Census of Population and Housing, 1990: population and housing characteristics, detailed geographic coverage, State CD-ROM series, 2551–10
Census of Population and Housing, 1990: summary characteristics, by county, subdiv, and place, State rpt series, 2551–7
Census of Population and Housing, 1990: summary characteristics, households, and land area, by county, subdiv, and place, State rpt series, 2551–1
Census of Population, 1990: data adjustment in intercensal data for census undercounts, recommendations with alternative undercount estimates, 2628–36
Census of Population, 1990: population characteristics and living arrangements, by county, place, and urban-rural location, State rpt series, 2531–1
Census of Population, 1990: population characteristics and living arrangements, for Native American, urban, and metro areas, series, 2531–2
Income (personal) per capita and by source, and employment, by industry div, State, MSA, and county, 1969-90, annual CD-ROM, 2704–7
Income (personal) per capita and total, by State, MSA, county, and metro-nonmetro location, 1988-90, annual article, 2702–1.317
Pacific territories population and housing detailed characteristics, by location, 1990 Census of Population and Housing, series, 2551–8

Public Welfare and Social Security

AFDC beneficiaries, by State, MSA, and county, as of Feb 1990, annual rpt, 4584–3.6
HHS financial aid, by program, recipient, State, and city, FY91, annual regional listings, 4004–3
Mississippi poverty, hunger, and public welfare program operations and indicators of need, 1991 hearing, 21968–57
OASDHI coverage of employment and earnings, and social security contributions, by age, sex, race, State, and county, 1988, annual rpt, 4744–29
Ohio poverty, hunger, and public welfare program operations and indicators of need, by county, 1991 hearing, 21968–58
Supplemental Security Income payments and beneficiaries, by type of eligibility, State, and county, Dec 1990, annual rpt, 4744–27

Recreation and Leisure

Washington and Oregon coastal areas tourism and recreation facilities and economic impacts, by county, 1983-88, 5738–40.3

Veterans Affairs

VA programs spending, by State, county, and congressional district, FY91, annual rpt, 8604–6

BY FOREIGN COUNTRY

Agriculture and Food

Agricultural Statistics, 1991, annual rpt, 1004–1
Bean (dried) prices by State, market activity, and foreign and US production, use, stocks, and trade, weekly rpt, 1311–17
Bean (dried) production and prices by State, exports and foreign production by country, and USDA food aid purchases, by bean type, 1986-91, annual rpt, 1311–18
Cocoa and cocoa products foreign and US production, prices, and trade, 1980s-93, FAS semiannual circular, 1925–9
Coffee production, trade, and use, by country, with US and intl prices, FAS periodic circular, 1925–5
Cotton production and trade for US and selected countries, FAS periodic circular series, 1925–4
Cotton, wool, and synthetic fiber production, prices, trade, and use, periodic situation rpt with articles, 1561–1
Dairy imports and quotas, by commodity and country of origin, FAS monthly rpt, 1925–31
Dairy production, trade, use, and prices, for US and selected countries, forecast 1992 and trends from 1987, FAS semiannual circular, 1925–10
Developing countries economic, population, and agricultural data, US and other aid sources, and AID activity, country rpt series, 9916–12
Developing countries food supply, needs, and aid, status and alternative forecasts, world area rpt series, 1526–8
Eastern Europe agricultural trade with US, by commodity group and country, 1988-91, 1928–11
Export promotion activities of FAS trade offices, operating costs, and funding by program, by country, 1989-90, GAO rpt, 26123–370
Exports and imports (agricultural) commodity and country, prices, and world market devs, monthly rpt, 1922–12
Exports and imports (agricultural) of US, by commodity and country, bimonthly rpt, 1522–1
Exports and imports (agricultural) of US, by detailed commodity and country, 1991, annual rpt, 1524–8
Exports and imports (agricultural) of US, by detailed commodity and country, 1991, semiannual rpt, 1522–4
Exports and imports (agricultural) of US, outlook and current situation, quarterly rpt, 1542–4
Exports, imports, tariffs, and industry operating data for agricultural, fishery, and forest products, commodity rpt series, 9885–8
Exports of grains, oilseed products, hides, skins, and cotton, by country, weekly rpt, dropped data, 1922–3
Farmland (US) owned by foreigners, by owner country and State, as of Dec 1991, article, 1561–16.302
Farmland in US owned by foreigners, holdings, acquisitions, and disposals by land use, owner type and country, and State, 1991, annual rpt, 1584–2
Farmland in US owned by foreigners, holdings, acreage, and value by land use, owner country, State, and county, 1991, annual rpt, 1584–3
Feed and feed additives production, use, and prices, by commodity, State, and country, various periods 1949-92, 1568–308
Fish (salmon) aquaculture production and exports, by country, 1980s-90, article, 2162–1.301
Fish and shellfish catch and stocks in northwest Atlantic, by species and location, 1887-1991 and forecast to 1993, semiannual conf, 2162–9
Fish and shellfish foreign market conditions for US products, country rpt series, 2166–19
Fish catch by world region, processing, and US trade, 1980-91, semiannual rpt, 1561–15.1
Fish catch, trade, use, and fishery operations, with selected foreign data, by species, 1980s-91, annual rpt, 2164–1
Fish meal and oil production and trade, quarterly tables, 2162–3
Flour milling production by State, stocks, daily capacity, and exports by country, monthly Current Industrial Rpt, 2506–4.1
Flower and foliage shipments from Florida by State and mode of transport, US imports by country, and prices, by variety, mid 1980s-91, annual rpt, 1311–24
Fruit and nut trade, by selected crop and country, periodic situation rpt with articles, 1561–6
Fruit and vegetable imports under quarantine, by crop, country, and port of entry, FY89, annual rpt, 1524–7
Fruit and vegetable shipments, and arrivals by city, by mode of transport and State and country of origin, 1991, annual rpt series, 1311–4
Fruit and vegetable shipments by mode of transport, arrivals, and imports, by commodity and State and country of origin, weekly rpt, 1311–3
Fruit and vegetable shipments by truck, monthly by State and country of origin, and rates weekly by growing area and market, 1991, annual rpt, 1311–15
Fruit shipments, production, and marketing, for Florida, with US trade and prices, by commodity, 1970s-91, annual rpt, 1311–23
Fruit, vegetable, and nut (fresh and processed) foreign and US production and trade, FAS monthly circular with articles, 1925–34
Grain foreign and US production, prices, trade, stocks, and use, FAS periodic circular series, 1925–2

Grain inspected for domestic use and export, foreign buyers complaints, and handling facilities explosions, FY92, annual rpt, 1294–1
Grain production, prices, trade, and export inspections by US port and country of destination, by grain type, weekly rpt, 1313–2
Honey production, prices, trade, stocks, marketing, and CCC honey loan and distribution activities, monthly rpt, 1311–2
Hops production, stocks, use, and US trade by country, monthly rpt, 1313–7
Livestock, meat, poultry, and egg production, prices, trade, and stocks, monthly rpt, 1561–17
Livestock, poultry, and dairy trade, by commodity and country, FAS monthly circular, 1925–32
Livestock, poultry, and products foreign and US production, trade, and use, by selected country, FAS semiannual circular series, 1925–33
Meat and poultry inspection for export and import, by product and country, FY90, annual rpt, 1374–3.3
Meat imports under Meat Import Act, by country of origin, FAS monthly circular, 1925–31
Molasses (feed) wholesale prices by market area, and trade, weekly rpt, 1311–16
Molasses supply, use, wholesale prices by market, and imports by country, 1986-91, annual rpt, 1311–19
Oils, oilseeds, and fats foreign and US production and trade, FAS periodic circular series, 1925–1
Peanut and peanut oil exports of US, and foreign production, by country, 1986-92 and forecast 1993, annual rpt, 1311–5.2
Peanut production and US exports by country, prices, and stocks, weekly rpt, 1311–1
Pecan production and prices by State, and US trade by country, late 1980s-91, annual rpt, 1311–28
PL 480 and CCC export credit sales agreement terms, by commodity and country, FY90, annual rpt, 15344–1.11
Production, acreage, and yield for selected crops, forecasts by selected world region and country, FAS monthly circular, 1925–28
Production, consumption, and policies for selected countries, and US export dev and promotion, monthly journal, 1922–2
Production, prices, and trade of agricultural commodities, by country, 1980-91 and forecast 1992, annual world area rpt series, 1524–4
Research (agricultural) of US, staffing by topic, performing organization, and for 7 countries, FY91, annual rpt, 1744–2.2
Research grants of USDA, by program, subagency, and country, FY92, annual listing, 1954–3
Rice foreign and US production, prices, trade, stocks, and use, periodic situation rpt, 1561–8
Rice market activities, prices, inspections, sales, trade, supply, and use, for US and selected foreign markets, weekly rpt, 1313–8
Seed exports, by type, world region, and country, FAS quarterly rpt, 1925–13
Shrimp catch by region, and US trade by country, 1980-90, article, 1561–15.301
Spice, essential oil, and tea foreign and US production, prices, and trade, FAS annual circular series, 1925–15
Sugar and honey foreign and US production, prices, trade, and use, FAS periodic circular series, 1925–14
Sugar and sugar product imports of US under quota, by country, weekly rpt, 1922–9
Sugar and sweeteners production, prices, trade, supply, and use, quarterly situation rpt with articles, 1561–14
Supply and demand indicators for selected foreign and US crops, monthly rpt, 1522–5
Textile trade, raw fiber equivalents by product, country, and world region, 1989-90, article, 1561–1.301
Tobacco and cigarette production, consumption, and trade, by Eastern European country, 1985-91, article, 1561–10.303
Tobacco and products foreign and US industry review, FAS monthly circular with articles, 1925–16
Tobacco leaf stocks, production, sales, and import inspections by country, by product, quarterly rpt, 1319–3
Tobacco production and US trade, by country, 1986-91, annual rpt, 1319–1
Tobacco production, marketing, use, price supports, and trade, quarterly situation rpt with articles, 1561–10
Tomato production, acreage, and yield by State, trade and production by country, stocks, shipments, and prices, 1960s-91, 1568–310
Tuna production, consumption, trade, and impacts of US dolphin protection embargo, 1989-92, article, 9882–16.303
Wheat and rye foreign and US production, prices, trade, stocks, and use, quarterly situation rpt with articles, 1561–12
Wool trade, for US and other major producers, 1970s-90, article, 1561–1.304

Banking, Finance, and Insurance

Banks (US) and nonbanking firms liabilities to and claims on foreigners, by country, 1989-90, annual rpt, 9364–5.10
Banks (US) foreign branches assets and liabilities, by world region and country, quarterly rpt, 9365–3.7
Capital movements between US and foreign countries, *Treasury Bulletin*, quarterly rpt, 8002–4.13
Debt to US of foreign govts and private obligors, by country and program, periodic rpt, 8002–6
Developing countries debt burden indicators, conversion agreement terms, and swaps for conservation funds, by selected country, 1987-90, hearing, 25368–181
Developing countries debt burden indicators, for 8 countries, alternative projections 1991-2000 and trends from 1974, technical paper, 9366–7.271
Developing countries debt to foreign lenders, and IMF credit outstanding, by country, 1985-91, annual rpt, 9114–7
Dollar exchange rates of 35 currencies, and interest rates and security yields for US and selected foreign countries, weekly chartbook, 9365–1.5
Dollar exchange rates offered by US disbursing offices, by country, quarterly rpt, 8102–6
EC economic integration impacts on financial services, 1992 article, 9391–1.308
European Monetary Union fiscal policy impact on EC govts, with background data, mid 1970s-90, technical paper, 9393–10.18
Exchange rate variability indicators, by selected OECD country, various periods 1959-90, article, 9371–1.304
Exchange settlement daily transactions, by country, 1989 trends from 1986, article, 9391–1.304
Export credit activity of Eximbank and 6 OECD countries, 1990, annual rpt, 9254–3
Fed Financing Bank holdings and transactions, by borrower, monthly press release, 12802–1
Finance (intl) statistics, monthly rpt, 9362–1.3
Financial instns (intl) funds by source and disbursements by purpose, by country, with US policy review, FY90, annual rpt, 15344–1
Financial markets (intl) performance of foreign and US bank and securities firms, finances and competitiveness issues, 1980s, compilation of papers, 9385–10
Futures contracts held by foreigners, by type and country, 1989, article, 8002–4.301
Insurance company finances, by insurance type and firm, with some intl comparisons, 1991 conf, 9373–3.35
Insurance industry financial condition, operations, assets, junk bond holdings, and State regulation, with intl comparisons, 1991 hearings, 25268–79
Interest rate forecasting performance of short- and long-term rate spreads, for US and 6 EC countries, 1950s-91, technical paper, 9385–8.136
Interest rates (long term) relation to rates of return to capital, economic policies, and other factors, US and 4 countries, 1960s-90, article, 9385–1.301
Intl Monetary Fund financial statements, and proposed funding quotas by member country, 1991 hearing, 21248–169
Iraq loans from Banca Nazionale del Lavoro Atlanta office, with purpose and exporting country and company involved, 1991 hearing, 21248–165
Loans and grants for economic and military aid from US and intl agencies, by program and country, FY46-91, annual rpt, 9914–5
Loans of US banks to foreigners at all US and foreign offices, by country group and country, quarterly rpt, 13002–1
Securities (intl) returns, relation to interest rates and other factors, model description, 1992 technical paper, 9385–8.137

Communications and Transportation

Aircraft registered with FAA, by type and characteristics of aircraft, and country, 1991, annual rpt, 7504–3
Airline operations and passenger, cargo, and mail traffic, by type of service, air carrier, State, and country, 1981-90, annual rpt, 7504–1.4
Hazardous material transport cylinder test facilities, certifications by State and country, 1990, annual rpt, 7304–4
Mail (domestic) postal rates, for 14 countries, 1991, annual rpt, 9864–5.1
Panama Canal traffic and tolls, by commodity, flag of vessel, and trade route, FY91, annual rpt, 9664–3.1

Shipbuilding and repair subsidy elimination proposals of US and OECD, impacts on industry and trade, with data on US-flag vessels, 1980s-91, 9886–4.183
Ships in world merchant fleet, tonnage, and new ship construction and deliveries, by vessel type and country, as of Jan 1992, annual rpt, 7704–3
Ships in world merchant fleet, US transfers to foreign firms, and deliveries, by vessel type and country, FY91, annual rpt, 7704–14.1; 7704–14.2
Ships under foreign flag owned by US firms and foreign affiliates, by type, owner, and country of registry and construction, as of July 1991, semiannual rpt, 7702–3
St Lawrence Seaway ship, cargo, and passenger traffic, and toll revenue, 1991 and trends from 1959, annual rpt, 7744–2
Telecommunications finances, rates, and traffic for US carriers intl operations, by service type, firm, and country, 1975-90, annual rpt, 9284–17
Telecommunications industry intl competitiveness, structure, and devs, with background data and foreign comparisons, 1991 rpt, 2808–30
Telephone and telegraph intl operations, revenue, and rates, by world area and country, various dates 1990-91, annual rpt, 9284–6
Travel to and from US, and travel receipts and payments, by world area, with data by country, 1985-90, annual rpt, 2904–10
Travel to and from US, by world area, forecast 1992-93, annual rpt, 2904–9
Travel to and from US on US and foreign flag air carriers, by country, world area, and US port, monthly rpt, 7302–2
Travel to US and Canada, market analysis with detailed trip and traveler characteristics, country rpt series, 2906–2
Travel to US, by characteristics of visit and traveler, country, port city, and State of destination, quarterly rpt, 2902–1
Travel to US, market research data available from US Travel and Tourism Admin, 1992, annual rpt, 2904–15
Travel to US, spending by world area of residence, and economic impact, by spending category and State, 1989, 2908–28

Education

Condition of Education, detail for elementary, secondary, and higher education, 1920s-91 and projected to 2002, annual rpt, 4824–1
Education data for foreign countries, and students enrolled in US higher education instns, 1992 edition, annual rpt, 4824–2.29
Fulbright-Hays academic exchanges, grants by purpose, and foreign govt share of costs, by country, FY91, annual rpt, 10324–1
Math and science proficiency, intl assessment results and other indicators, by selected country, 1960s-80s, 4838–51
Testing costs, achievement scores by selected State, and attendance and testing policies, with foreign comparisons, 1970s-91, 26358–255

Energy Resources and Demand

Coal imports of US electric utilities, by utility and country of origin, 1986-90, annual rpt, 3164–42
Coal trade and average price, by world region, country, and customs district, quarterly rpt, 3162–37
Coal trade flows, by importing and exporting country, alternative projections 1990-2010, annual rpt, 3164–96
Developing countries energy efficiency improvement issues and devs, with data by end use and country, 1980s-90, 26358–260
Energy production by type, and oil trade, and use, by country group and selected country, monthly rpt, 9112–2
Energy production, trade, use, and reserves, and oil and refined products supply and prices, by country, 1981-90, annual rpt, 3164–50
Energy supply, demand, and prices, by fuel type and end-use sector, with foreign comparisons, 1991 and trends from 1949, annual rpt, 3164–74
Energy supply, demand, and prices, by fuel type, end-use sector, and country, detailed data, monthly rpt with articles, 3162–24
Energy supply, demand, and prices, by fuel type, end-use sector, and country, detailed data, monthly 1973-88, 3168–123
Energy use and production, by fuel type, country, and country group, projected 1995-2010 and trends from 1970, annual rpt, 3164–84
Export markets, competitiveness, and promotion, for US energy technology industries, 1992 technical rpt, 3006–13.5
Foreign and US energy supply and demand, by major fuel and end-use sector, 1950s-87 and forecast to 1995, 3166–6.58
Gasoline and diesel fuel tax rates, for US and 7 OECD countries, monthly rpt, 7552–1
Nuclear power generation in US and 20 countries, monthly rpt, 3162–24.10
Nuclear power generation in US and 20 countries, monthly 1973-88, 3168–123.10
Nuclear power plant capacity, availability, and load factors, by plant and foreign country, quarterly journal, annual tables, 3352–4.3
Nuclear power plant safety inspection activities and emergency response procedures of Intl Atomic Energy Agency since 1986 Chernobyl accident, 1991, GAO rpt, 26123–367
Nuclear reactors for domestic use and export by function and operating status, with owner, operating characteristics, and location, 1991 annual listing, 3354–15
Oil crude, gas liquids, and refined products supply, demand, and movement, by PAD district and State, 1991, annual rpt, 3164–2
Oil dependency, energy demand, and efficiency measures, for 6 OECD countries, 1970s-80s, working paper, 9375–13.79
Oil import costs, by crude type and country or group of origin, monthly rpt, 3162–11
Oil import costs, by crude type and country or group of origin, 1991, annual rpt, 3164–85
Oil prices of OPEC and non-OPEC countries, weekly rpt, 3162–32
Oil production, stocks, use, and trade, by selected country and country group, monthly rpt, 3162–42
Oil production, use, stocks, and exports and prices for US, by country, detailed data, monthly rpt with articles, 3162–24
Oil production, use, stocks, and exports and prices for US, by country, detailed data, monthly 1973-88, 3168–123
Oil, refined products, and gas liquids supply, demand, trade, stocks, and refining, by detailed product, State, and PAD district, monthly rpt with articles, 3162–6
Pacific basin countries energy supply and demand, and implications for US trade, country rpt series, 3406–6
South America oil production, investment needs, and exports, for 8 countries, 1980s-90 and projected to 2010, GAO rpt, 26123–396
Soviet Union former Republics and Baltic States energy supply and use, and social, economic, and political indicators, 1989-90, 3168–126
Strategic Petroleum Reserve oil deliveries, by country and State of origin, quarterly rpt, annual data, 3002–13
Transportation energy use, fuel prices, vehicle registrations, and mileage, by selected country, 1950-89, annual rpt, 3304–5.1
Uranium mining and milling industries finances and operations, with selected foreign comparisons, 1970s-90 and projected to 2005, annual rpt, 3164–82

Geography and Climate

Borders (maritime) agreements and claims of coastal countries, series, 7006–8
Disasters, casualties, damage, and aid by US and others, by country, FY91 and trends from FY64, annual rpt, 9914–12
Geographic Notes, foreign countries boundaries, claims, nomenclature, and other devs, quarterly rpt, 7142–3
Oceanographic research and distribution activities of World Data Center A by country, and cruises by ship, 1990, annual rpt, 2144–15
Tide height and time daily at coastal points worldwide, forecast 1993, annual rpt series, 2174–2
Weather conditions and effect on agriculture, by US region, State, and city, and world area, weekly rpt, 2182–7
Weather data for surface and upper air, averages by foreign and US station, monthly rpt, 2152–4
Weather events and anomalies, precipitation and temperature for US and foreign locations, weekly rpt, 2182–6

Government and Defense

Africa (sub-Saharan) economic, social, and political conditions, with US aid by program and country, 1991 rpt, 7008–58
African Dev Foundation dev grants and fellowships, by country, FY84-91, annual rpt, 9034–1
AID activities, finances, and staff, by program and country, FY90, GAO rpt, 26123–382
AID contracts and grants for technical and support services, by instn, country, and State, FY91, annual listing, 9914–7
AID contracts, grants, and cooperative agreements with higher education instns, by project, instn, and country, FY91, annual listing, 9914–6
AID dev projects and socioeconomic impacts, evaluation rpt series, 9916–1
AID economic aid to developing countries, obligations and disbursements by country, quarterly rpt, 9912–4

AID loans repayment status and terms by program and country, and status of predecessor agency loans, quarterly rpt, 9912–3
Aliens admitted to US, by class of admission and for top entry ports and countries, FY90-91, fact sheet, 6266–2.9
Aliens applications for temporary US residency, by occupation, age, sex, marital status, and country, 1988-91, 4808–41
American Battle Monuments Commission activities, expenses, and visitors by site, FY87, annual rpt, 9064–1
Background Notes, foreign countries summary social, political, and economic data, series, 7006–2
Budget deficits share of GDP, for US and 4 OECD countries, 1981 and 1989, GAO rpt, 26109–5
Chiefs of State and Cabinet members, by country, bimonthly listing, 9112–4
Currency (foreign) accounts owned by US under AID admin and by foreign govts with joint AID control, status by program and country, quarterly rpt, 9912–1
Currency (foreign) holdings of US, transactions and balances by program and country, 1st half FY92, semiannual rpt, 8102–7
Currency (foreign) purchases of US with dollars, by country, 1st half FY92, semiannual rpt, 8102–5
Developing countries economic and social conditions from 1960s, and Intl Dev Cooperation Agency and AID activities and funding, FY91-93, annual rpt, 9904–4
Developing countries economic, population, and agricultural data, US and other aid sources, and AID activity, country rpt series, 9916–12
Eastern Europe transition to market economies, tax reform issues, with tax rates, revenue, and govt spending compared to EC, by selected country, late 1960s-91, technical paper, 9366–7.278
Economic and military aid and loans from US and intl agencies, by program and country, FY46-91, annual rpt, 9914–5
Economic and military aid of US, by program and country, and arrearages, selected years 1940-89, annual rpt, 15344–1.1
Economic, social, political, and geographic summary data, by country, 1992, annual factbook, 9114–2
Human rights conditions in 170 countries, and US economic and military aid, 1991, annual rpt, 21384–3
Immigrants admitted to US, by class of admission, country of birth, and MSA of destination, FY91, advance annual rpt, 6264–4
Income tax returns of foreign corporations and individuals, and US entities abroad, detailed data compilation, 1970s-89, quinquennial rpt, 8308–31
Latin America dev grants of Inter-American Foundation by program area, and fellowships by field and instn, by country, FY72-91, annual rpt, 14424–2
Latin America dev grants of Inter-American Foundation by recipient, and fellowships, by country, FY91, annual rpt, 14424–1
Latin America economic and social conditions, resources, trade, and aid, 1992, annual factbook, 9914–14
Middle East arms trade and force strengths, and impacts of voluntary arms trade reductions, by country, mid 1960s-91 and projected to 2002, 26306–6.173
Military aid of US, arms sales, and training, by country, FY50-91, annual rpt, 3904–3
Military aid of US, arms sales, and training programs costs and budget requests, by program, world region, and country, FY91-93, annual rpt, 7144–13
Military spending, arms trade, and force strengths, with govt spending and population, by country, 1979-89, annual rpt, 9824–1
Military weapons trade of 32 countries, 1984-88, hearing, 25408–115
NATO and Warsaw Pact military forces reductions and ceilings under CFE treaty, inspections, and US compliance costs and savings, 1991 hearings, 25388–59
NATO, Japan, and South Korea military spending and indicators of ability to support common defense, by country, 1970s-90, annual rpt, 3544–28
Navy weapons systems parts purchases from foreign suppliers and US contractors, by State and country, 1988, 2026–1.3
OECD members govt budget surplus and deficit, and govt debt privately held, turnover, and selling procedures, FY91, 8008–154
Peace Corps activities, funding by program, and volunteers, by country, FY93, annual rpt, 9654–1
Persian Gulf War allied and other countries cash and in-kind contributions, by type and country, 1990-91, GAO rpt, 26123–371
Persian Gulf War allied countries cash and in-kind contributions, by type and country, and status of DOD accounts, as of Sept 1991, annual GAO rpt, 26104–24
Persian Gulf War costs to US by category and service branch, and offsetting contributions by allied country, monthly rpt, 102–3
Tax (estate) returns for nonresident aliens, property and tax data, by estate size and decedent country of residence, 1986, article, 8302–2.310
Tax (income) brackets simplification under tax reform in US and other countries, fiscal effects, late 1970s-92, working paper, 9377–9.143
Tax (income) returns for foreign corporate activity in US, selected income and tax items, by industry div and selected country, 1988, article, 8302–2.309
Tax (income) returns, income, and tax withheld for foreign partners of US partnerships, by country, 1990, article, 8302–2.324
Tax (income) returns of Foreign Sales Corps, assets, and income and tax items, by industry, country of incorporation, and transaction pricing method, 1987, article, 8302–2.311
Tax (income and capital) policies, with background data, for EC, Japan, and US, mid 1960s-91, article, 9373–1.316
Tax (value added) alternative proposals revenue impacts, with background data and intl comparisons, 1992 rpt, 26306–6.168
Tax withheld and income from US sources for foreign natls not residing in US, by country and tax treaty status, 1989, annual article, 8302–2.308
UN participation of US, and member and nonmember shares of UN budget by country, FY89-91, annual rpt, 7004–5
UN peacekeeping operations costs by mission, and assessment rates by country, 1948-92, GAO rpt, 26123–404
UN voting record and share of votes in agreement with US, by issue, country, and world area, 1991, annual rpt, 7004–18
UNESCO fiscal mgmt, spending, staff, and funding sources, mid 1970s-92, GAO rpt, 26123–84
US govt contingent liabilities and claims paid on federally insured and guaranteed contracts with foreign obligors, by country and program, periodic rpt, 8002–12
US military and civilian personnel and dependents, by service branch and location, FY91, annual rpt, 3544–1
US military and civilian personnel and dependents, by service branch, world area, and country, quarterly rpt, 3542–20
US military base and family housing construction, DOD appropriations by facility, service branch, and location, FY91-93, annual rpt, 3544–39
US military base construction, renovation, and closure, budget requests by project, service branch, State, and country, FY93, annual rpt, 3544–15
US military base support costs by function, and personnel and acreage by installation, by service branch, FY93, annual rpt, 3504–11
US military contracts, payroll, and personnel, by service branch and location, with top 5 contractors and maps, by State and country, FY91, annual rpt, 3544–29
US military deaths, by service branch and country, FY91, annual rpt, 3544–40
US military employment of civilians, by country, quarterly rpt, 3542–16
US military personnel abroad, by service branch, outlying area, and country, quarterly rpt, 3542–14.5
US military personnel abroad, by service branch, world area, and country, quarterly press release, 3542–9
US military presence abroad, by service branch and country, 1992 annual summary rpt, 3504–13
US military prime contract awards for R&D, for top 500 contractors, FY91, annual listing, 3544–4
US military prime contract awards for R&D to US and foreign nonprofit instns and govt agencies, by instn and location, FY91, annual listing, 3544–17
Visa (immigrant) applicants on waiting lists at consular office, by preference class, world region, and for top countries, as of Jan 1992, 7188–1
Visas of US issued and refused to immigrants and nonimmigrants, by class, issuing office, and nationality, FY90, annual rpt, 7184–1

Health and Vital Statistics

Administrative costs for all and public health programs, by selected OECD country, mid 1970s-90, article, 4652–1.325
Allergy and Infectious Diseases Natl Inst activities, grants by recipient and location, and disease cases, FY84-91, annual rpt, 4474–30
Cancer Natl Inst activities, grants by recipient, and cancer deaths and cases, FY91 and trends, annual rpt, 4474–13

Costs, use, and structure of private and public health care delivery, indicators, issues, and foreign comparisons, 1960s-80s, technical paper, 8006–6.1
Dental Research Natl Inst research and training grants, by recipient, FY90, annual listing, 4474–19
Developing countries economic and social conditions from 1960s, and Intl Dev Cooperation Agency and AID activities and funding, FY91-93, annual rpt, 9904–4
Diving (underwater) accidents, illnesses, and deaths, by circumstances, diver characteristics, and location, 1970-90, annual rpt, 2144–29
Expenditures for health care and factors in increase, with background data and foreign comparisons, various periods 1929-90, technical paper, 9366–6.296
Family planning and population activities of AID, grants by project and recipient, and contraceptive shipments, by country, FY91, annual rpt series, 9914–13
Ford Motor Co and foreign subsidiaries employee health care costs, with data on foreign and US health care systems, 1987-90, article, 9882–16.302
Health care system reform issues, insurance coverage and availability, and foreign comparisons, 1991 hearing, 21788–216
Health condition and care indicators, 1950s-90 with health improvement and disease prevention goals for 1990, annual data compilation, 4144–11
Health data collection and availability, by country, 1991, biennial listing, 4124–8
Health, welfare, and research aid from HHS, by program, recipient, and country, FY91, annual listing, 4004–3.10
Heart, Lung, and Blood Natl Inst activities, and grants by recipient and location, FY91 and disease trends from 1940, annual rpt, 4474–15
Infant health, deaths and risk factors, and prevention issues, for US and selected countries, 1990 conf, 4148–28
Infant mortality rate, and births of low birthweight and to teen and older mothers, for US and other countries, 1980s, article, 4652–1.324
Kidney end-stage disease cases, new patients by country, 1984-89, annual rpt, 4654–16.1
Latin America young unmarried adults sexual activity, contraceptives use, and AIDS risk knowledge, by sex and country, 1984-91, article, 4202–7.323
Malaria cases in US, for military personnel and US and foreign natls, and by country of infection, 1966-90, annual rpt, 4205–4
Nurses supply and immigrant status, by country of previous residence, FY82-90, biennial rpt, 4114–8.4
OECD members health care costs, hospital use, resources, and economic and health indicators, by country, 1960s-90, article, 4652–1.322
Physicians from foreign medical schools in US, by admission type and country of origin, 1970s, working paper, 6366–6.2
Refugees, displaced persons, and population affected by famine, CDC recommendations for disease surveillance, control, and prevention, with background data, 1978-91, 4206–2.63
Vaccination needs for intl travel by country, and disease prevention recommendations, 1992 annual rpt, 4204–11
Youth pregnancy, abortion, miscarriage, and birth rates in 11 countries, 1983, 26358–234.2

Housing and Construction

Construction contract awards and billings, by country of contractor and world area of award, 1990, annual article, 2042–1.304

Industry and Commerce

Aluminum plant ownership, capacity, energy and aluminum sources, and startup and closing dates, by US and foreign plant and location, 1990, annual listing, 5604–49
Andean Trade Preference Act duty-free exports from 4 countries to US, and business opportunities, 1989-91, 2048–161
Auto and auto parts trade, production, and labor conditions, for US and compared to Canada and Mexico, 1950s-90, 6366–3.28
Auto industry finances and operations, trade by country, and prices of selected US and foreign models, monthly rpt, 9882–8
Auto parts trade with Japan and other countries, 1985-90 and forecast to 1994, annual rpt, 2004–10
Boycotts (intl) by OPEC and other countries, US firms and individuals cooperation and tax benefits denied, 1990, article, 8302–2.323
Business America, foreign and domestic commerce, and US investment and trade opportunities, biweekly journal, 2042–24
Business cycle (intl) impacts on economic indicators, for industrialized countries, 1950s-80s, working paper, 9383–20.16
Caribbean area duty-free exports to US, and imports from US, by country, and impact on US employment, by commodity, 1991, annual rpt, 6364–2
Caribbean area duty-free exports to US, by commodity and country, with consumer and industry impacts, 1984-91, annual rpt, 9884–20
Caribbean Basin Initiative export and investment incentives, contact listing, bibl, and US imports country, 1983-91, annual rpt, 2044–36
Chemical and energy products trade, tariffs, and industry operating data, commodity rpt series, 9885–11
Clothing exports to US, and domestic and US-owned industry production costs and operations, for Caribbean area and Mexico, impacts of North American Free Trade Agreement, 1992 rpt, 9886–4.186
Communist and transitional economy countries trade with US, by detailed commodity and country, quarterly rpt with articles, 9882–2
Competitiveness (intl) of US industries, with selected foreign and US operating data by major firm and product, series, 2046–12
Cuba trade, by commodity and country, mid 1980s-91, 9118–8
Developing countries economic, population, and agricultural data, US and other aid sources, and AID activity, country rpt series, 9916–12
Eastern Europe export industries dev potential, with trade and industry finances and operations, for 5 countries, 1985-90, 9886–4.179
Eastern Europe imports from US, and trade and dev opportunities, monthly rpt, 2042–33
Eastern Europe trade with US, by commodity and country, 1987-91 and outlook for 1992, 2048–158
EC economic integration impacts on domestic economic conditions and US trade, with background data, 1986-91, 9886–4.181
EC govt subsidies, by industry sector and for Airbus Industrie, by country, 1980s-91, hearing, 21708–132
Economic and monetary trends, compounded annual rates of change and quarterly indicators for US and 7 major industrialized countries, quarterly rpt, 9391–7
Economic and social conditions of foreign countries, working paper series, 2326–18
Economic conditions, and oil supply and demand, for major industrial countries, monthly rpt, 9112–1
Economic conditions, and trade devs and balances, with data by selected country and country group, monthly rpt, 9882–14
Economic conditions in foreign countries and implications for US, periodic country rpt series, 2046–4
Economic conditions, policy, and trade practices, by country, 1989-91, annual rpt, 21384–5
Economic indicators, trade balances, and exchange rates, for selected OECD and Asian countries, 1992 semiannual rpt, 8002–14
Economic, social, political, and geographic summary data, by country, 1992, annual factbook, 9114–2
Electronics and services trade, tariffs, and industry operating data, commodity rpt series, 9885–12
Electronics industry production and labor conditions, in 10 MSAs, EC, and top producer countries, late 1970s-80s, article, 9393–8.307
Export and import balances relation to productivity and capital investment, for selected countries, 1960s-90, working paper, 9393–10.22
Export licensing, monitoring, and enforcement activities, FY91, annual rpt, 2024–1
Exports and imports dependency indexes for total, merchandise, and agricultural products, by country, 1960s-88, 1528–328
Exports and imports of US, by country and detailed commodity, monthly rpt, 2422–12
Exports and imports of US by country, and trade shifts by commodity, 1991, annual rpt, 9884–25
Exports and imports of US, by Harmonized System 6-digit commodity and country, 1991, annual rpt, 2424–13
Exports and imports of US, by selected country, country group, and commodity group, 1991, annual rpt, 2044–37
Exports and imports of US, by transport mode, country, and SITC 1- to 3-digit commodity, 1991, annual rpt, 2424–12
Exports and imports of US, by world area, country, and commodity, *Survey of Current Business*, monthly rpt, 2702–1.9
Exports and imports, trade agreements and relations, and USITC investigations, 1991, annual rpt, 9884–5

Exports, imports, and balances of US, by selected country, country group, and commodity group, preliminary data, monthly rpt, 2042–34
Exports, imports, and balances of US for manufactured goods, by SITC 2-digit commodity and country, quarterly rpt, 2042–35
Exports, imports, and balances of US with major trading partners, by product category, 1987-91, annual chartbook, 9884–21
Exports, imports, and intl competitiveness of US industries, trends and outlook, quarterly rpt with articles, 9882–16
Exports, imports, and trade flows, by country and commodity, with background economic indicators, data compilation, monthly CD-ROM, 2002–6
Exports of US, detailed commodities by country, monthly CD-ROM, 2422–13
Exports of US, detailed Schedule B commodities with countries of destination, 1991, annual rpt, 2424–10
Flows of trade and investment, and economic indicators, for selected countries and country groups, selected years 1946-91, annual rpt, 204–1.9
Footwear production, employment, use, prices, and US trade by country, quarterly rpt, 9882–6
Foreign-controlled US firms transactions with related foreign persons, by type, industry div, and country, 1988, article, 8302–2.318
Foreign direct investment in US by top 10 countries, factors affecting rate of return, and compared to returns for US firms, 1980s-91, article, 2702–1.330
Imports and tariff provisions effect on US industries and products, investigations with background financial and operating data, series, 9886–4
Imports detained by FDA, by reason, product, shipper, brand, and country, monthly listing, 4062–2
Imports injury to US industries from foreign subsidized products and sales at less than fair value, investigations with background financial and operating data, series, 9886–19
Imports injury to US industries from foreign subsidized products, investigations with background financial and operating data, series, 9886–15
Imports injury to US industries from sales at less than fair value, investigations with background financial and operating data, series, 9886–14
Imports of goods, services, and investment from US, trade barriers, impacts, and US actions, by country, 1991, annual rpt, 444–2
Imports of US, detailed commodities by country, monthly CD-ROM, 2422–14
Imports of US given duty-free treatment for value of US material sent abroad, by commodity and country, 1987-90, annual rpt, 9884–14
Imports under Generalized System of Preferences, status, and US tariffs, with trade by country and US economic impacts, for selected commodities, 1987-91, annual rpt, 9884–23
Investment (direct) in US by country, and finances, employment, and acreage owned, by industry group of business acquired or established, 1985-91, annual article, 2702–1.320
Investment (foreign direct) in US, by industry group and world area, 1989-91, annual article, 2702–1.331
Investment (foreign direct) in US, major transactions by type, industry, country, and US location, 1990, annual rpt, 2044–20
Investment (foreign direct) in US, relation to exchange rate and relative labor costs and wealth indicators, for 7 countries, 1980s, working paper, 9373–27.10
Investment (foreign direct) of US, by industry group and world area, 1989-91, annual article, 2702–1.332
Investment (intl) position of US, by component, industry, world region, and country, 1990-91, annual article, 2702–1.323
Latin America and Caribbean country imports from US, by State of origin and country, 1987 and 1990, 2048–160
Latin America economic and social conditions, resources, trade, and aid, 1992, annual factbook, 9914–14
Latin America economic conditions, trade, and foreign aid, working paper series, 9916–13
Latin America exports, investment, debt, and tariffs for 7 countries, and trade and investment policy liberalization issues, mid 1960s-91, 9886–4.184
Lumber (hardwood) exports of US to Europe and Asia, by species and country, 1981-90, 1208–373
Lumber (hardwood) production, prices, employment, and trade, quarterly rpt, 1202–4
Lumber and wood products trade and export promotion of US by country, and trade balance, by commodity, FAS periodic circular, 1925–36
Lumber exports from northwestern US ports, by selected country, quarterly rpt, 1202–3
Machinery and equipment trade, tariffs, and industry operating data, commodity rpt series, 9885–9
Manufacturing trade, tariffs, and industry operating data, commodity rpt series, 9885–10
Mexico trade with US and other countries, foreign investment, and maquiladoras operations, 1980s-91, GAO rpt, 26119–417
Militarily strategic manufacturing industries finances, operations, and intl competitiveness, series, 2026–1
Mineral Industry Surveys, commodity reviews of production, trade, stocks, and use, monthly rpt series, 5612–1
Mineral Industry Surveys, commodity reviews of production, trade, stocks, and use, quarterly rpt series, 5612–2
Mineral Industry Surveys, commodity reviews of production, trade, use, and industry operations, advance annual rpt series, 5614–5
Minerals (strategic) supply and characteristics of individual deposits, by country, commodity rpt series, 5666–21
Minerals and metals trade, tariffs, and industry operating data, commodity rpt series, 9885–13
Minerals foreign and US supply under alternative market conditions, reserves, and background industry data, series, 5606–4
Minerals production, prices, trade, use, employment, tariffs, and stockpiles, by mineral, with foreign comparisons, 1987-91, annual rpt, 5604–18
Minerals production, reserves, and industry role in domestic economy and world supply, world area and country rpt, series, 5606–1
Minerals Yearbook, Vol 1, 1989: commodity reviews of production, use, trade, prices, and mining operations, annual rpt, 5604–33
Minerals Yearbook, Vol 1, 1990: commodity reviews of production, reserves, supply, use, and trade, annual rpt series, 5604–20
Minerals Yearbook, Vol 1, 1991: commodity reviews of production, reserves, supply, use, and trade, annual rpt series, 5604–15
Minerals Yearbook, Vol 3, 1989: foreign country reviews of production, trade, and policy, by commodity, annual rpt, 5604–35
Multinatl firms US affiliates finances and operations, by industry, country of parent firm, and State, 1987, 2702–1.340; 2708–48
Multinatl firms US affiliates finances and operations, by industry div, country of parent firm, and State, 1989-90, annual article, 2702–1.319; 2702–1.337
Multinatl firms US affiliates, finances, and operations, by industry, world area of parent firm, and State, 1989-90, annual rpt, 2704–4
Multinatl firms US affiliates gross product, by component, industry, and country of parent firm, 1987-90, article, 2702–1.342
Multinatl US firms and foreign affiliates finances and operations, by industry and country, 1989 benchmark survey, annual rpt, 2704–5
Multinatl US firms and foreign affiliates finances and operations, by industry and world area, 1988, annual article, 2702–1.329
Multinatl US firms foreign affiliates capital expenditures, by major industry group, world area, and country, 1987-92, semiannual article, 2702–1.312
Multinatl US firms foreign affiliates capital expenditures, by major industry group, world area, and country, 1988-92, semiannual article, 2702–1.335
Multinatl US firms foreign affiliates, income statement items by asset size, industry, and country, 1988, biennial article, 8302–2.322
OECD intl trade position for US and 4 countries, and factors affecting US competition, quarterly pamphlet, 2042–25
OECD trade, total and for 4 major countries, and US trade by country, by commodity, 1980-90, world area rpt series, 9116–1
Overseas Business Reports: economic conditions, investment and export opportunities, and trade practices, country market research rpt series, 2046–6
Plumbing fixtures production, and imports from US and other sources, for 15 countries, 1991 rpt, 2048–156
Production indexes and CPI, for US and 6 OECD countries, current data and annual trends, monthly rpt, 23842–1.7

Services trade of US, direct and among multinatl firms affiliates, by industry and world area, 1986-91, article, 2702–1.336
Statistical Abstract of US, 1992 annual data compilation, 2324–1
Steel imports of US under voluntary restraint agreement, by product, customs district, and country, with US industry operating data, quarterly rpt, 9882–13
Steel trade, by product, country, and customs district, with US industry operating data, 1989-June 1992, semiannual rpt, 9882–15
Technology-intensive industries intl competitiveness, with background data by industry and foreign comparisons, 1960s-91, GAO rpt, 26123–406
Textile and apparel exports of US, by product group and country, quarterly rpt, 2042–36
Textile and apparel foreign market conditions for US exports, with domestic industry operations, country rpt series, 2046–15
Textile imports, by country of origin, monthly rpt, 2042–27
Textile imports, by product and country of origin, monthly rpt series, 2046–8; 2046–9
Textile imports under Multifiber Arrangement by product and country, and status of bilateral agreements, 1988-91, annual rpt, 9884–18
Textile products trade regulations of foreign countries, and US exports, by commodity and country, 1989-91, biennial rpt, 2044–18
Tobacco production and use in Latin America, Canada, and US, and related economic, health, and social issues, 1950s-92, annual rpt, 4204–18

Labor and Employment
Alien workers in US clothing and other industries, and impacts on local economies, with background data, 1990 working paper, 6366–6.6
Employment, unemployment, and productivity indexes, for US and selected OECD countries, Monthly Labor Review, 6722–1.6
Immigrants and legalized aliens, by occupational group and country of birth, preliminary FY91, annual tables, 6264–1
Labor conditions, union coverage, and work accidents in foreign countries, annual country rpt series, 6366–4
Manufacturing hourly compensation costs, by industry and country, series, 6826–3
Manufacturing labor costs and indexes, by selected country, 1991, semiannual rpt, 6822–3
Manufacturing labor productivity and costs, by selected country, 1950s-91, press release, 6726–1.55
Manufacturing labor productivity and unit costs for 14 countries, 1960s-90, article, 6722–1.304
Pension plan finances, participation, and benefits, for 9 OECD countries, with data by firm and worker characteristics, 1990 conf, 6688–2
Population and labor force characteristics, 1940s-90 and projected to 2000, 15496–1.16
Productivity of labor for US and foreign countries, and impacts of investment spending, 1950s-91, article, 9381–1.308
Union membership for 12 countries, 1955-90, article, 6722–1.305

Law Enforcement
Aircraft hijackings, on-board explosions, and other crimes, US and foreign incidents, 1986-90, annual rpt, 7504–31
Aliens (illegal) enforcement activity of Coast Guard, by nationality, 1st half FY92, semiannual rpt, 7402–4
Cocaine trafficking in US and foreign countries, with prices and purity, 1988-90, annual rpt, 6284–5
Drug (illegal) production, eradication, and seizures, by substance, with US aid, by country, 1988-92, annual rpt, 7004–17
Drug (illegal) supply in US by country of origin, abuse, prices, and seizures, by substance, 1991, annual rpt, 6284–2
Heroin trafficking indicators for US, and foreign opium production by country, 1991, annual rpt, 6284–6
Terrorism (intl) incidents, casualties, and attacks on US targets, by attack type and world area, 1991, annual rpt, 7004–13

Natural Resources, Environment, and Pollution
Air pollution levels, by country and selected city, 1970-90, 9194–1
Bismuth reserves, production, and US trade, by country, and US consumption by end use, 1980s-90, 5608–175
Eastern Europe environmental remediation costs, and aid by donor, by country, 1991 hearing, 25368–181
Fish (billfish) tagged and recovered by location, and Japan catch in US waters, 1950-90, annual rpt, 2164–7
Forests (tropical) condition, conservation methods, and biological diversity issues, 1992 rpt, 26358–262
Global climate change impacts on agricultural production and GDP, with data by crop and world area, mid 1970s-86, 1528–326
Pollution (air) contributing to global warming, emissions by monitoring site and country, and temperature change by world area and US region, 1860s-1990, annual rpt, 3004–33

Population
Census of Population and Housing, 1990: immigrants, by period of entry, citizenship, State, birthplace, and for top cities and counties, press release, 2328–88
Developing countries aged population and selected characteristics, 1980s and projected to 2020, country rpt series, 2326–19
Developing countries economic and social conditions from 1960s, and Intl Dev Cooperation Agency and AID activities and funding, FY91-93, annual rpt, 9904–4
Developing countries economic, population, and agricultural data, US and other aid sources, and AID activity, country rpt series, 9916–12
Developing countries population size, life expectancy, and fertility, trends and forecasts, country rpt series, 2326–24
Economic, social, political, and geographic summary data, by country, 1992, annual factbook, 9114–2
Immigrants and nonimmigrants admitted to US, alien workers, visitors, deportations, and naturalizations, FY91, annual summary rpt, 6264–7
Immigrants from Central America in DC, by selected employment and other characteristics, and reasons for migration, 1985-88, working paper, 6366–6.3
Immigration to US, alien workers, visitors, deportations, and naturalizations, by country, FY91 and trends from 1820, annual rpt, 6264–2
Latin America economic and social conditions, resources, trade, and aid, 1992, annual factbook, 9914–14
Older population and characteristics, by country, 1991 and projected to 2020, wallchart, 2328–82
Older population, and health, economic, and other characteristics, with foreign comparisons, 1980s-91 with trends and projections, Current Population Rpt, 2546–2.165
Population density for selected cities and countries, and distribution, life expectancy, and infant mortality by world region, 1991, fact sheet, 2326–17.50
Population size, growth rates, and components of change, by country, projected 1990-2020 and trends from 1950, biennial rpt, 2324–9
Population social and economic conditions in foreign countries, working paper series, 2326–18
Refugee arrivals and resettlement in US, by age, sex, sponsoring agency, State, and country, monthly rpt, 4592–1
Refugee arrivals in US by world area and country of origin, and quotas, monthly rpt, 7002–4
Refugee migration, and intl aid programs, by world area and country of origin and asylum, 1991, annual rpt, 7004–15
Soviet Union former Republics and Baltic States population size and characteristics, 1989-92, 9118–19
Statistical Abstract of US, 1992 annual data compilation, 2324–1

Prices and Cost of Living
Drug (prescription) prices in US and other countries, industry profits, and R&D and marketing spending, 1980s-91 and projected to 2000, 25148–44
Export and import price indexes for goods and services, and dollar exchange rate indexes, quarterly press release, 6762–13
Exports and imports among US, Canada, and Japan related to domestic and foreign prices and income, 1965-87, technical paper, 9366–7.276
Food prices in selected world capitals, monthly rpt, semiannual data, 1922–12
Living costs abroad, State Dept indexes, housing allowances, and hardship differentials by country and major city, quarterly rpt, 7002–7

Public Welfare and Social Security
Social security programs coverage, funding, eligibility, and benefits, by country, 1991, biennial rpt, 4746–4.62
US OASDI beneficiaries abroad, benefits, and eligibility based on intl agreement, by program type and country, 1990, annual rpt, 4744–3.3
Welfare, health, and research aid from HHS, by program, recipient, and country, FY91, annual listing, 4004–3.10

Science and Technology
Ceramics (advanced) research publication releases in 6 countries, by subfield, selected years 1965-90, hearing, 21708–130
NASA procurement contract awards, by type, contractor, State, and country, FY92 with trends from 1961, semiannual rpt, 9502–6

NSF grants and contracts, by field, recipient, and State, FY90, annual rpt, 9624–26
Patent and trademark (US) applications filed and granted, by country, FY88-91, annual rpt, 2244–1.2; 2244–1.3
Patents (US) granted to US and foreign applicants, by applicant and country, 1960s-91, annual rpt, 2244–3
Patents (US) granted to US and foreign applicants, by State and country, FY90-91, annual press release, 2244–2
Science and Engineering Indicators, employment, education, R&D funding, and industry impacts, with foreign comparisons, 1960s-91, biennial rpt, 9624–10
Space launchings and characteristics of craft and flight, by country, 1957-91, annual rpt, 9504–9.1
Spacecraft and satellite launches since 1957, quarterly listing, 9502–2
Standards for production, controls, and processes, domestic and intl dev in US and EC, 1980s-91, 26358–257

BY OUTLYING AREA

Agriculture and Food

Agricultural Stabilization and Conservation Service producer payments, by program and State, 1991, annual table, 1804–12
Agricultural Statistics, 1991, annual rpt, 1004–1
Animal protection, licensing, and inspection activities of USDA, and animals used in research, by State, FY90, annual rpt, 1394–10
Cattle tuberculosis cases and cooperative Federal-State eradication activities, by State, FY90-91, annual rpt, 1394–13
Conservation program of USDA, acreage, projects, participation, and funding, by State, 1936-90, quinquennial rpt, 1808–1
Conservation program of USDA, funding by practice, region and State, monthly rpt, 1802–15
Conservation program of USDA, participation and payments by practice and State, FY91, annual rpt, 1804–7
Fish (processed) production by location, and trade, by species and product, 1988-91, annual rpts, 2166–6
Fishery employment, vessels, plants, and cooperatives, by State, 1990, annual rpt, 2164–1.10
FmHA loans and borrower supervision activities in farm and housing programs, by type and State, monthly rpt, 1182–1
FmHA loans, by type, borrower race, and State, quarterly rpt, 1182–5
FmHA property acquired through foreclosure, acreage, value, and sales, for farm and nonfarm property by State, monthly rpt, 1182–6
Fruit and vegetable imports under quarantine, by crop, country, and port of entry, FY89, annual rpt, 1524–7
Research (agricultural) funding and staffing for USDA, State agencies, and other instns, by topic, FY91, annual rpt, 1744–2
Rice shipments, by end use, package size, and State of origin and destination, 1960s-89, biennial rpt, 1564–11
Tobacco production, prices, stocks, taxes by State, and trade and production by country, 1991, annual rpt, 1319–1

Banking, Finance, and Insurance

Banks (insured commercial and FDIC-insured savings) assets, income, and financial ratios, by asset size and State, quarterly rpt, 13002–3
Banks (insured commercial and savings) deposits by instn, State, MSA, and county, as of June 1991, annual regional rpt series, 9295–3
Banks (insured commercial and savings) finances, by State, 1990, annual rpt, 9294–4
Credit unions federally insured, finances by instn characteristics and State, as of June 1992, semiannual rpt, 9532–6
Credit unions federally insured, finances, 1990-91, annual rpt, 9534–1
Savings instns financial statements, for instns insured by Savings Assn Insurance Fund by FHLB district and State, and for FDIC-insured savings banks, 1989, annual rpt, 8434–1
Savings instns insured by Savings Assn Insurance Fund, finances by profitability group, district, and State, quarterly rpt, 8432–4
Savings instns insured by Savings Assn Insurance Fund, offices, and deposits, by region, State, MSA, and county, 1991, annual rpt, 8434–5
Small Business Admin loans, contract awards, and surety bonds, by firm, State, and city, FY91, annual rpt, 9764–1

Communications and Transportation

Air traffic (passenger), and aircraft operations by type, by airport and State, projected FY92-2005 and trends from FY83, annual rpt, 7504–7
Air traffic (passenger and cargo), and departures by aircraft type, by carrier and airport, 1991, annual rpt, 7504–35
Air traffic (passenger and cargo), carrier enplanement shares, and FAA airport improvement program grants, by airport and State, 1990, annual rpt, 7504–48
Air traffic, carriers, craft, airports, and FAA activities, detailed data, 1981-90, annual rpt, 7504–1
Air traffic levels at FAA-operated control facilities, by airport and State, FY91, annual rpt, 7504–27
Aircraft registered with FAA, by type and characteristics of aircraft, make, carrier, State, and county, 1991, annual rpt, 7504–3
Airport improvement program of FAA, activities and grants by State and airport, FY91, annual rpt, 7504–38
Airport planning and dev project grants of FAA, by airport and location, quarterly press release, 7502–14
DOT planning and safety grants, by program, State, and for 40 SMSAs, FY89, annual rpt, 7304–7
FAA activities and finances, and staff by region, FY90-91, annual rpt, 7504–10
Fed Hwy Admin traffic safety grants, by program and State, FY90, annual rpt, 7764–1.1
Hazardous material transport cylinder test facilities, certifications by State and country, 1990, annual rpt, 7304–4
Hwy Statistics, detailed data by outlying area, 1991, annual rpt, 7554–1.5
Hwy Trust Fund status and net revenues, FY57-90, annual rpt, 7554–24
Port improvement capital expenditures and financing methods, by region and selected port, 1946-89, 7708–6
Shipborne commerce (domestic) of US, freight by major commodity group, vessel type, and port, 1987-89, annual rpt, 7704–7
Telephone and other economic dev loans for rural areas by State, and REA activities and finances, FY91 and trends from FY36, annual rpt, 1244–3
Telephone firms borrowing under Rural Telephone Program, and financial and operating data, by State, 1991, annual rpt, 1244–2
Telephone firms borrowing under Rural Telephone Program, loan activity by State, FY91, annual tables, 1244–8
Telephone lines in residences and businesses, carriage equipment miles, and calls placed, by State, 1990, annual rpt, 9284–6.2
Truck accidents, casualties, and damage, by circumstances and characteristics of persons and vehicles involved, 1989, annual rpt, 7554–9
Urban areas transit systems grants of Federal Transit Admin, by city and State, FY91, annual rpt, 7884–10

Education

Adult literacy and English as a second language programs, Education Dept and State programs, enrollment, and funding, by State, 1988-91, 4808–41
American Historical Assn financial statements, and membership by State, 1990, annual rpt, 29574–2
Bilingual education enrollment, and eligible students not enrolled, by State, 1990-91, annual rpt, 4804–14
Digest of Education Statistics, 1992 annual data compilation, 4824–2
Elementary and secondary education enrollment, teachers, high school grads, and spending, by instn control and State, 1992/93, annual rpt, 4834–19
Elementary and secondary public school agencies, by enrollment size and location, fall 1990, annual listing, 4834–1
Elementary and secondary public school systems enrollment, finances, staff, and high school grads, by State, FY89-90, annual rpt, 4834–6
Elementary and secondary public schools and enrollment, by State, 1990/91, annual rpt, 4834–17
Head Start enrollment, funding, and staff, FY91, annual rpt, 4584–5
Head Start handicapped enrollment, by handicap, State, and for Indian and migrant programs, 1988/89, annual rpt, 4584–4
Higher education enrollment, tuition, control, location, and other instn characteristics, 1991/92, biennial listing, 4844–3
Libraries for blind and handicapped, readership, circulation, staff, funding, and holdings, FY91, annual listing, 26404–3
Natl Education Goals progress indicators, by State, 1992, annual rpt, 15914–1
Special education programs, enrollment by age, staff, funding, and needs, by type of handicap and State, 1990/91, annual rpt, 4944–4

Student guaranteed loans, defaults, and collections, by type of loan, lender, and guarantee agency, with data by State and top lender, FY91, annual rpt, 4804–38
Student loans of Fed Govt in default, losses, and rates, by instn and State, as of June 1991, annual rpt, 4804–18
Student supplemental grants, loans, and work-study awards, Federal share by instn and State, 1992/93, annual listing, 4804–17
Tuition and other student charges, by public and private 2- and 4-year higher education instn, and State, 1991/92, annual listing, 4844–10

Energy Resources and Demand
Conservation aid of Fed Govt to public and nonprofit private instns, by building type and State, 1991, annual rpt, 3304–15
Conservation of energy, State programs aid from Fed Govt, and energy savings, by State, 1990, annual rpt, 3304–1
Housing (low income) energy aid, funding sources, costs, and participation, by State, FY90, annual rpt, 4584–1
Oil company overcharge settlements funds received, and conservation and energy aid spending, by outlying area, 1990, GAO rpt, 26113–564
Oil crude, gas liquids, and refined products supply, demand, and movement, by PAD district and State, 1991, annual rpt, 3164–2
Rural Electrification Admin activities and finances, and loans by State, FY91 and trends from FY36, annual rpt, 1244–3

Geography and Climate
Storms and unusual weather phenomena characteristics, casualties, and property damage, by State, monthly listing, 2152–3

Government and Defense
DOT employment, by subagency, occupation, and selected personnel characteristics, FY91, annual rpt, 7304–18
Election polling places accessibility and services availability for aged and disabled, by State, 1990 natl elections, hearing, 21428–11
Fed Govt spending in States and local areas, by type, State, county, and city, FY91, annual rpt, 2464–3
Fed Govt spending in States, by type, program, agency, and State, FY91, annual rpt, 2464–2
Local govt receipts from Fed Govt in lieu of property taxes on public lands, by State, FY92, annual press release, 5306–4.15
Military and DOD civilian personnel and dependents, by service branch and location, FY91, annual rpt, 3544–1
Military and DOD civilian personnel and dependents, by service branch and US and foreign location, quarterly rpt, 3542–20
Military base and family housing construction, DOD appropriations by facility, service branch, and location, FY91-93, annual rpt, 3544–39
Military base construction, renovation, and closure, budget requests by project, service branch, State, and country, FY93, annual rpt, 3544–15
Military base support costs by function, and personnel and acreage by installation, by service branch, FY93, annual rpt, 3504–11
Military contracts, payroll, and personnel, by service branch and location, with top 5 contractors and maps, by State and country, FY91, annual rpt, 3544–29
Military deaths, by service branch and location, FY91, annual rpt, 3544–40
Military draft registrants by State, FY91, annual rpt, 9744–1
Military in-house commercial activities work-years, by service branch, State, and installation, FY91, annual rpt, 3544–25
Military personnel of DOD abroad, by service branch, world area, and country, quarterly press release, 3542–9
Military personnel of US abroad, by service branch, outlying area, and country, quarterly rpt, 3542–14.5
Military reserve forces personnel strengths and characteristics, by component, quarterly rpt, 3542–4
Votes cast by party, candidate, and State, 1990 natl elections, biennial rpt, 21944–3

Health and Vital Statistics
AIDS cases by risk group, race, sex, age, State, and MSA, and deaths, quarterly rpt, 4202–9
Deaths and rates, by detailed location, cause, and demographic characteristics, 1989, US Vital Statistics annual rpt, 4144–3.2
Disabled persons rehabilitation, Federal and State activities and funding, FY90, annual rpt, 4944–1
Diving (underwater) accidents, illnesses, and deaths, by circumstances, diver characteristics, and location, 1970-90, annual rpt, 2144–29
Fish and shellfish-related disease cases and outbreaks, by cause, species, and State, 1969-87, hearing, 21568–51
Hepatitis cases by infection source, age, sex, race, and State, and deaths, by strain, 1989 and trends from 1966, 4205–2
HHS financial aid, by program, recipient, State, and city, FY91, annual regional listing, 4004–3.2; 4004–3.9
Hospital deaths of Medicare patients, actual and expected rates by diagnosis, with hospital characteristics, by instn, FY90, annual State rpt series, 4654–14
Infectious notifiable disease cases and current outbreaks, by region and State, weekly rpt, 4202–1
Infectious notifiable disease cases, by age, race, and State, and deaths, 1940s-91, annual rpt, 4204–1
Kidney end-stage disease treatment facilities, Medicare enrollment and reimbursement, survival, and patient characteristics, 1984-90, annual rpt, 4654–16
Mental health care facilities, staff, patients, and finances, 1970s-91, biennial rpt, 4094–1
Mines and mills injuries by circumstances, employment, and hours, by type of operation and State, quarterly rpt, 6662–1
Physicians, by specialty, age, sex, and location of training and practice, 1990, State rpt series, 4116–6
Workers compensation laws of States and Fed Govt, 1992 annual rpt, 6504–11

Housing and Construction
Economic Dev Admin activities, and funding by program, recipient, State, and county, FY91 and cumulative from FY66, annual rpt, 2064–2
FmHA property acquired through foreclosure, 1-family homes, value, sales, and leases, by State, monthly rpt, 1182–7
Mortgage originations, by State, 1982-90, annual press release, 5144–21
Mortgages FHA-insured, financial, property, and borrower characteristics, by State, 1991, annual rpt, 5144–1; 5144–25
New housing units authorized, by State, MSA, and permit-issuing place, 1991, annual rpt, 2384–2

Industry and Commerce
Exports and imports between US and outlying areas, by detailed commodity and mode of transport, 1991, annual rpt, 2424–11
Mineral Industry Surveys, commodity reviews of production, trade, stocks, and use, monthly rpt series, 5612–1
Mineral Industry Surveys, commodity reviews of production, trade, stocks, and use, quarterly rpt series, 5612–2
Minerals Yearbook, Vol 1, 1989: commodity reviews of production, use, trade, prices, and mining operations, annual rpt, 5604–33
Minerals Yearbook, Vol 2, 1989: State reviews of production and sales by commodity, and business activity, annual rpt series, 5604–16
Minerals Yearbook, Vol 2, 1990: State reviews of production and sales by commodity, and business activity, annual rpt series, 5604–22
Statistical Abstract of US, 1992 annual data compilation, 2324–1.30
Vending facilities run by blind on Federal and non-Federal property, finances and operations by agency and State, FY91, annual rpt, 4944–2

Labor and Employment
Employment and Earnings, detailed data, monthly rpt, 6742–2.5; 6742–2.6
Employment and Training Admin activities, funding, and participant characteristics, by program, FY86-88, annual rpt, 6404–17
Employment and unemployment, by age, sex, race, marital and family status, industry div, and State, Monthly Labor Review, 6722–1.2
Labor Relations Natl Board activities, cases, elections conducted, and litigation, FY90, annual rpt, 9584–1
Mediation and arbitration activities of Fed Mediation and Conciliation Service, and cases by issue, region, and State, FY85-90, annual rpt, 9344–1
Unemployment insurance programs of States, benefits, coverage, and tax provisions, as of July 1992, semiannual listing, 6402–7
Unemployment insurance programs of States, benefits, coverage, exhaustions, and finances, 1990, annual tables, 6404–10
Unemployment insurance programs of States, comparison of law provisions, as of Jan 1992, semiannual revisions to base edition, 6402–2
Unemployment insurance programs of States, quality appraisal results, FY91, annual rpt, 6404–16
Unemployment insurance trust funds financial condition, by State, monthly rpt, 8102–9.16
Vocational rehabilitation cases of State agencies, by disposition and State, FY91 and trends from FY21, annual rpt, 4944–5

Vocational rehabilitation programs of Fed Govt and States, activities and funding, FY91, annual rpt, 4944–1

Law Enforcement

Assaults and deaths of law enforcement officers, by circumstances, agency, victim and offender characteristics, and location, 1991, annual rpt, 6224–3

Bombing incidents and casualties by target and circumstances, and explosives theft and recovery, by State, 1987-91, annual rpt, 8484–4

Corrupt govt officials prosecuted and convicted, by judicial district and level of govt, 1970-90, annual rpt, 6004–13

Court civil and criminal caseloads for Federal district, appeals, and bankruptcy courts, by type of suit and offense, circuit, and district, 1991, annual rpt, 18204–11

Court civil and criminal caseloads for Federal district, appeals, and special courts, 1991, annual rpt, 18204–8

Crime, criminal justice admin and enforcement, and public opinion, data compilation, 1992 annual rpt, 6064–6

Drug enforcement grants of Fed Govt, and allocations to local govts, by State, FY91, annual rpt, 6064–38

Drug enforcement grants to States, and allocations to local areas, by State, FY87-91, 236–3.1

Drug testing of criminal offenders, grants and program costs by State, FY92, 236–3.3

Office of Justice Programs activities and funding, FY91, annual rpt, 6064–18

Sentences for Federal crimes, guidelines use and results by offense and district, and Sentencing Commission activities, 1991, annual rpt, 17664–1

US attorneys case processing and collections, by case type and Federal district, FY91, annual rpt, 6004–2

Victims of crime, compensation and support service programs funding, by offense and State, FY88-90, biennial rpt, 6064–37

Natural Resources, Environment, and Pollution

Coastal areas environmental mgmt programs of States, activities and Federal funding, FY90-91, biennial rpt, 2174–8

EPA pollution control grant program activities, monthly rpt, 9182–8

Fish and Wildlife Service restoration and hunter safety funding, by State, FY92, semiannual press release, 5502–1

Fish and Wildlife Service restoration programs funding, land purchases, and project listing, by State, FY90, annual rpt, 5504–1

Forests (natl) and other lands under Forest Service mgmt, acreage by forest and location, 1991 and historic trends, annual rpt, 1204–2

Hazardous substances industrial releases and reduction methods under EPA regulation, by chemical, source, industry, and location, 1989, annual rpt, 9234–6

Hazardous waste site remedial action under Superfund, current and proposed sites descriptions and status, periodic listings, series, 9216–3

Hazardous waste site remedial action under Superfund, current and proposed sites priority ranking and status by location, series, 9216–5

Land Mgmt Bur allocations of public land revenues, by State and outlying area, FY91, annual rpt, 5724–1.3

Landmarks (natl historic and natural) damaged and threatened, with owner, location, damage type, and recommended remedial action, 1990, annual listing, 5544–16

Military installations hazardous waste site remedial action, activities and funding by site and State, FY91, annual rpt, 3544–36

Pollution (air) contributing to global warming, emissions by monitoring site and country, and temperature change by world area and US region, 1860s-1990, annual rpt, 3004–33

Timber planting and stand improvement, by ownership and State, FY91, annual rpt, 1204–7

Wastewater treatment and collection facility construction funding needs and Fed Govt grants, by State, 1990 and projected to 2010, biennial rpt, 9204–7

Water resources dev projects of Army Corps of Engineers, characteristics, and costs, 1950s-89, biennial State rpt series, 3756–1

Water resources dev projects of Army Corps of Engineers, characteristics, and costs, 1950s-91, biennial State rpt series, 3756–2

Water supply and quality in streams and lakes, and groundwater levels in wells, by drainage basin, 1990, annual State rpt series, 5666–10

Water supply and quality in streams and lakes, and groundwater levels in wells, by drainage basin, 1990-91, annual CD-ROM, 5664–18

Water supply and quality in streams and lakes, and groundwater levels in wells, by drainage basin, 1991, annual State rpt series, 5666–12

Wildlife refuges and other land under Fish and Wildlife Service mgmt, acreage by site and State, as of Sept 1992, annual rpt, 5504–8

Population

Immigrants and nonimmigrants admitted to US, alien workers, visitors, deportations, and naturalizations, FY91, annual summary rpt, 6264–7

Immigration to US, alien workers, visitors, deportations, and naturalizations, by country, FY91 and trends from 1820, annual rpt, 6264–2

Pacific territories population and housing detailed characteristics, by location, 1990 Census of Population and Housing, series, 2551–8

Refugee arrivals and resettlement in US, by age, sex, sponsoring agency, State, and country, monthly rpt, 4592–1

Refugee arrivals in US by world area of origin and State of settlement, and Federal aid, FY91-92 and proposed FY93 allocations, annual rpt, 7004–16

Statistical Abstract of US, 1992 annual data compilation, 2324–1.30

Public Welfare and Social Security

AFDC beneficiaries by county, payments, application processing and disposition, hearings, and fraud cases, by State, FY90, annual rpt, 4584–3

Assistance to aged, blind, and disabled programs, provisions by outlying area, FY89-90, annual rpt, 4584–8

Fed Govt programs under Ways and Means Committee jurisdiction, finances, operations, and participant characteristics, FY70s-91, annual rpt, 21784–11

Fed Govt spending in States, by type, program, agency, and State, FY91, annual rpt, 2464–2

Food aid program of USDA for women, infants, and children, participants and costs by State and Indian agency, FY90, annual tables, 1364–12

Food aid program of USDA for women, infants, and children, participants by race, State, and Indian agency, 1991, annual rpt, 1364–16

Food aid program of USDA for women, infants, and children, participants, clinics, and costs, by State and Indian agency, monthly tables, 1362–16

Food stamp eligibility and payment errors, by type, recipient characteristics, and State, FY90, annual rpt, 1364–15

HHS financial aid, by program, recipient, State, and city, FY91, annual regional listing, 4004–3.2; 4004–3.9

Homeless persons aid programs of Fed Govt, program descriptions and funding, by agency and State, FY87-91, annual GAO rpt, 26104–21

OASDHI, Medicaid, SSI, and related programs benefits, beneficiary characteristics, and trust funds, selected years 1937-90, annual rpt, 4744–3

School lunch programs food donations processing, contracts, and processors problems with State reporting requirements, with data by State, 1989-91, GAO rpt, 26113–555

Recreation and Leisure

Arts funding, by level of govt, State, and selected city, FY86-92, GAO rpt, 26119–371

Boat registrations, and accidents, casualties, and damage by cause, by vessel characteristics and State, 1991, annual rpt, 7404–1

Historic and natural natl landmarks damaged and threatened, with owner, location, damage type, and recommended remedial action, 1990, annual listing, 5544–16

Historic Preservation Fund grants, by State, FY93, annual press release, 5544–9

Land and Water Conservation Fund allocations for outdoor recreation area dev, by State, FY93, annual table, 5544–15

Park natl system visits and overnight stays, by park and State, 1991, annual rpt, 5544–12

Science and Technology

NSF grants and contracts, by field, recipient, and State, FY90, annual rpt, 9624–26

Patents (US) granted to US and foreign applicants, by State and country, FY90-91, annual press release, 2244–2

Patents granted to US residents, by State, FY88-91, annual rpt, 2244–1.2

R&D and related funding of Fed Govt to higher education and nonprofit instns, by field, instn, agency, and State, FY90, annual rpt, 9627–17

BY REGION

Agriculture and Food

Cattle and calves for beef, ranches, inventory, producers, and returns, by herd size and region, mid 1940s-91, 1568–251
Cattle and calves loss to predators, disease, and other causes, by region and State, 1991, 1618–22
Cattle in beef herds, by region, 1964, 1978, and 1987, article, 1561–7.301
Conservation program of USDA, funding by practice, region and State, monthly rpt, 1802–15
Cooperatives loans, assets, net worth, and assns, for FCS by district, 1990, annual rpt, 1124–1
Cotton fiber and processing test results, by variety, region, State, and production area, 1991, annual rpt, 1309–16
Cotton linters production, stocks, use, and prices, monthly rpt, 1309–10
Cotton, wool, and synthetic fiber production, prices, trade, and use, periodic situation rpt with articles, 1561–1
Cottonseed prices and quality, by State, seasonal weekly rpt, 1309–14
Dairy farms financial statement, by size and region, 1987-90, annual article, 1561–2.301
Economic Indicators of the Farm Sector, itemized production costs, receipts, and returns, by commodity and region, 1975-90, annual rpt, 1544–20
Economic Indicators of the Farm Sector, production inputs, output, and productivity, by commodity and region, 1947-90, annual rpt, 1544–17
Egg production and layer inventory, by State, 1990-91, annual rpt, 1625–7
Egg production by type of product, and eggs broken under Federal inspection by region, monthly rpt, 1625–2
Emergency Conservation Program for farmland damaged by natural disaster, funding by region and State, monthly rpt, 1802–13
Employment of farm hired workers, and earnings, by selected characteristics, 1990, 1598–278
Employment on farms, wages, hours, and perquisites, by State, monthly rpt, 1631–1
Farm Credit System financial statements and loan activity by lender type, and borrower characteristics, 1991, annual rpt, 9264–2
Farmland in US owned by foreigners, holdings, acquisitions, and disposals by land use, owner type and country, and State, 1991, annual rpt, 1584–2
Farms and acreage, by sales size, region, and State, 1990-92, annual rpt, 1614–4
Fertilizer and pesticide use and application rates, by type, crop, and State, series, 1616–1
Finances of farms, debts, assets, and receipts, and lenders financial condition, quarterly rpt with articles, 1541–1
Fish (processed) production by location, and trade, by species and product, 1988-91, annual rpts, 2166–6
Fish catch, trade, use, and fishery operations, with selected foreign data, by species, 1980s-91, annual rpt, 2164–1
Fish Hatchery Natl System activities and deliveries, by species, hatchery, and jurisdiction of waters stocked, FY91, annual rpt, 5504–10
Fruit and vegetable shipments, and arrivals by city, by mode of transport and State and country of origin, 1991, annual rpt series, 1311–4
Fruit, nut, and berry farm income, acreage, prices received, and production costs, by commodity and region, 1987, article, 1561–6.301
Grain production, prices, trade, and export inspections by US port and country of destination, by grain type, weekly rpt, 1313–2
Grain stocks by region and market city, and grain inspected for export, by type, weekly rpt, 1313–4
Grape shipments from California and arrivals by city by mode of transport, prices, and production, by variety, 1970s-90, annual rpt, 1311–25
Honey production, prices, trade, stocks, marketing, and CCC honey loan and distribution activities, monthly rpt, 1311–2
Irrigation projects of Reclamation Bur in western US, crop production and acreage by commodity, State, and project, 1990, annual rpt, 5824–12
Livestock grazing forage demand, and meat supply and demand, indicators, 1960s-90 and projected to 2030, 1208–404
Livestock packers purchases and feeding, and livestock markets, dealers, and sales, by State, 1990, annual rpt, 1384–1
Livestock slaughter, meat production, and slaughter plants, by species and State, 1991, annual rpt, 1623–10
Livestock slaughter under Fed Govt inspection, by livestock type and region, monthly rpt, 1623–9
Loans (farm) at risk of default, lender losses, and selected farm financial indicators, by type of farm and lender, 1984-89, 1548–383
Milk order market prices and detailed operations, by State and market area, 1990-91, annual rpt, 1317–3
Milk order market prices and detailed operations, monthly rpt with articles, 1317–4
Molasses (feed) wholesale prices by market area, and trade, weekly rpt, 1311–16
Molasses supply, use, wholesale prices by market, and imports by country, 1986-91, annual rpt, 1311–19
Mushroom production, sales, and prices, by State, 1966/67-1991/92 and planned 1992/93, annual rpt, 1631–9
Oils, oilseeds, and fats production, prices, trade, and use, periodic situation rpt with articles, 1561–3
Peanut production and US exports by country, prices, and stocks, weekly rpt, 1311–1
Peanut production, prices, stocks, exports, use, inspection, and quality, by region and State, 1982-91, annual rpt, 1311–5
Population on farms, by employment, social, and economic characteristics, and region, 1990, annual Current Population Rpt, 2546–1.458
Potato chip plants and quantity used for chips, by region, 1990-91, annual rpt, 1621–11
Poultry (chicken and turkey) hatchery production, 1990-91, annual rpt, 1625–8
Poultry (chicken, egg, and turkey) production and inventories, monthly rpt, 1625–1
Prices received and paid by farmers, by commodity and State, monthly rpt, 1629–1
Prices received and paid by farmers, by commodity and State, 1991, annual rpt, 1629–5
Production inputs, finances, mgmt, and land value and transfers, periodic situation rpt with articles, 1561–16
Production itemized costs, by farm sales size and region, 1991, annual rpt, 1614–3
Research (agricultural) funding and staffing for USDA, State agencies, and other instns, by topic, FY91, annual rpt, 1744–2
Rice production, practices, costs, and land tenure, by production area, 1988, 1568–309
Shellfish harvest in estuaries, approved and restricted areas, and pollution sources, by estuary, State, and coastal region, 1990, quinquennial rpt, 2178–33
Sugar and sweeteners production, prices, trade, supply, and use, quarterly situation rpt with articles, 1561–14
Tobacco (flue-cured) farms and farm operators, by region and selected characteristics, 1970s-87, 1568–307
Tomato production, acreage, and yield by State, trade and production by country, stocks, shipments, and prices, 1960s-91, 1568–310
Turkey hatcheries egg inventory and poult placements, by region, monthly rpt, 1625–10
Turkeys raised by State, and losses by region, 1990-91, and hatchery plans, 1992, annual rpt, 1625–6
Vegetable production, prices, trade, stocks, and use, for selected fresh and processing crops, periodic situation rpt with articles, 1561–11
Wheat acreage, yield, and profitability impacts of using purchased rather than leftover seed, 1986-88, 1548–388
Women-headed households food spending, by item and selected characteristics, and compared to other households, 1970s-88, 1548–391
Young farm operators acreage owned and rented by region, and method of acquisition of owned acreage, 1992 article, 1541–1.319

Banking, Finance, and Insurance

Banks (FDIC-insured) return on assets, by region and State, 1991, annual rpt, 9294–1
Banks (insured commercial and savings) deposits by instn, State, MSA, and county, as of June 1991, annual regional rpt series, 9295–3
Banks (insured commercial and savings) financial condition and performance, by asset size and region, quarterly rpt, 9292–1
Banks (natl) charters, mergers, liquidations, enforcement cases, and financial performance, with data by instn and State, quarterly rpt, 8402–3
Banks acquisitions of failed and other banks, financial performance relation to asset mix, market concentration, and other factors, 1984-90, article, 9292–4.304
Banks balance sheets, by Fed Reserve District, for major banks in NYC, and for US branches and agencies of foreign banks, weekly rpt, 9365–1.3

Banks failures resolution costs to FDIC, relation to bank financial and other characteristics, 1986-90, article, 9292–4.303
Credit unions (federally-insured) financial performance, by charter type and region, 1st half 1992, semiannual rpt, 9532–7
Credit unions federally insured, finances by instn characteristics and State, as of June 1992, semiannual rpt, 9532–6
Credit unions with low income membership, financial, operating, and membership data, 1982-91, 9536–1.8
Demand deposit velocity changes, by region, 1940s-80s, article, 9389–1.301
Fed Home Loan Banks financial statements, monthly tables, 9442–1
Fed Home Loan Banks financial statements, 1989-91, annual rpt, 9444–1
Fed Natl Mortgage Assn, Fed Home Loan Mortgage Corp, and FHLBs finances, 1991 hearings, 21248–170
Fed Reserve banks expenses and operations, itemized by service, office, and district, 1991, annual rpt, 9364–11
Fed Reserve banks finances and staff, 1991, annual rpt, 9364–1.1
Fed Reserve banks financial statements and performance, by district, 1991-92, annual rpt, 9364–10.3
Financial instns reform issues, with finances, impacts of deposit insurance changes, and views of depositors and bankers, 1991 hearings, 25248–129
Mortgage interest fixed and adjustable rates and fees offered, by region, weekly rpt, 9412–3
Savings instns failure resolution activity and finances of Resolution Trust Corp, with data by asset type, State, region, and instn, monthly rpt, 9722–3
Savings instns failure resolution activity of Resolution Trust Corp, brokered deposits, fees, and interest rates by instn and region, as of July 1991, hearing, 21248–171
Savings instns financial statements, for instns insured by Savings Assn Insurance Fund by FHLB district and State, and for FDIC-insured savings banks, 1989, annual rpt, 8434–1
Savings instns insured by Savings Assn Insurance Fund, finances by profitability group, district, and State, quarterly rpt, 8432–4
Savings instns insured by Savings Assn Insurance Fund, offices, and deposits, by region, State, MSA, and county, 1991, annual rpt, 8434–5
Small Business Admin dev company loan program and debenture sale activity, with data by firm, industry div, State, and region, quarterly rpt, 9762–6
Small Business Admin guaranteed loans issued under regular, certified, and preferred lender programs, selected characteristics, FY83-90, GAO rpt, 26113–581
Small Business Admin loan guarantee program participants finances, operations, characteristics, and views, 1991 survey, 9768–25
Small Business Investment Companies capital holdings, SBA obligation, and ownership, as of July 1992, semiannual listing, 9762–4
Small Business Investment Company program financial performance, findings and recommendations, 1992 rpt, 9768–24
Treasury bill offerings, auction results by Fed Reserve District, and terms, periodic press release series, 8002–7

Communications and Transportation

Air traffic (passenger), and aircraft operations by type, by airport and State, projected FY92-2005 and trends from FY83, annual rpt, 7504–7
Air traffic (passenger and cargo), carrier enplanement shares, and FAA airport improvement program grants, by airport and State, 1990, annual rpt, 7504–48
Air traffic, carriers, craft, airports, and FAA activities, detailed data, 1981-90, annual rpt, 7504–1
Air traffic control and airway facilities staff, by employment and other characteristics, FY90, annual rpt, 7504–41
Air traffic controller academy grads and military hires, training performance, facility assignments, and selected characteristics, 1988, 7506–10.101
Air traffic levels at FAA-operated control facilities, by airport and State, FY91, annual rpt, 7504–27
Air traffic, pilots, airports, and fuel use, forecast FY92-2003 and trends from FY82, annual rpt, 7504–6
Aircraft handled by instrument flight rule, by user type, FAA traffic control center, and region, FY85-91 and projected to FY2005, annual rpt, 7504–15
Aircraft pilot and nonpilot certificates held, by type of certificate, age, sex, region, and State, 1991, annual rpt, 7504–2
Aircraft registered with FAA, by type and characteristics of aircraft, make, carrier, State, and county, 1991, annual rpt, 7504–3
Bridges over navigable waters, with type of bridge and use, owner, dimensions, and location, 1991 regional listing series, 7406–5
Coast Guard search and rescue missions, and lives and property lost and saved, by district and assisting unit, FY91, annual rpt, 7404–2
DOT planning and safety grants, by program, State, and for 40 SMSAs, FY89, annual rpt, 7304–7
FAA activities and finances, and staff by region, FY90-91, annual rpt, 7504–10
Fed Transit Admin grants by State, and oversight, 1988-92, GAO rpt, 26113–600
Hwy construction minority contractor training, funding by region, FY92, annual release, 7554–40
Hwy traffic volume on rural roads and city streets, monthly rpt, 7552–8
Longshore employment in 4 coastal regions, monthly rpt, 7702–1
Mail volume to and from households, use, and views, by class, source, content, and household characteristics, FY87-90, annual rpt, 9864–10
Port improvement capital expenditures and financing methods, by region and selected port, 1946-89, 7708–6
Railroad (Class I) finances and operations, detailed data by firm, class of service, and district, 1990, annual rpt, 9486–5.1
Railroad (Class I) finances and operations, detailed data by firm, class of service, and district, 1991, annual rpt, 9486–6.1
Railroad freight, by commodity and region of origin and destination, 1989, annual rpt, 7604–6
Railroad revenue, income, freight, and rate of return, by Class I freight railroad and district, quarterly rpt, 9482–2
Shipborne commerce (domestic) of US, freight by major commodity group, vessel type, and port, 1987-89, annual rpt, 7704–7
Shipborne trade of US, by type of service, customs district, port, and world area, monthly rpt, 2422–7
Shipbuilding and repair facilities, capacity, and employment, by shipyard, 1991, annual rpt, 7704–9
Telephone firms borrowing under Rural Telephone Program, and financial and operating data, by State, 1991, annual rpt, 1244–2
Telephone local service charges and low-income subsidies, by region, company, and city, 1980s-91, semiannual rpt, 9282–8
Traffic accidents deaths by region, and death rates for miles traveled, monthly rpt, 7762–7
Traffic fatal accidents, circumstances, and characteristics of persons and vehicles involved, 1991, semiannual rpt, 7762–11
Transit systems finances and operations, by mode, size of fleet and urban area, region, and for 518 systems, 1990, annual rpt, 7884–4.2
Travel patterns, personal and household characteristics, and auto use, 1950-90, annual rpt, 3304–5.4
Travel to US and Canada, market analysis with detailed trip and traveler characteristics, country rpt series, 2906–2
Travel to US, by characteristics of visit and traveler, world area of origin, and US destination, 1991 survey, annual rpt, 2904–12
Truck and bus interstate carriers finances and operations, by district, 1990, annual rpt, 9486–5.3
Truck interstate carriers finances and operations, by district, 1990, annual rpt, 9486–5.2
Truck rates for fruit and vegetables, by growing area and market, weekly 1991, annual rpt, 1311–15
Truck transport of property, financial and operating data by region and firm, quarterly rpt, 9482–5
Waterborne commerce (domestic and foreign) of US, freight by commodity, traffic, and passengers, by port and waterway, 1989, annual rpt, 3754–3

Education

Adult education participation, by selected characteristics, 1991 survey, 4826–10.5
American Historical Assn financial statements, and membership by State, 1990, annual rpt, 29574–2
Discrimination in education, natl survey participation and data coverage, school district administrators views, 1991 survey, 4826–1.33
Education data, enrollment, finances, teachers, and other characteristics, by State, 1969-89, 4828–33

Education in science and math, natl assessment of elementary and high school students, 1985/86, series, 4896–6
Educational attainment, by social and demographic characteristics and location, 1991 and trends from 1940, biennial Current Population Rpt, 2546–1.460
Eighth grade class of 1988: educational performance and conditions, characteristics, attitudes, activities, and plans, natl longitudinal survey, series, 4826–9
Elementary and secondary education enrollment, staff, finances, operations, programs, and policies, 1987/88 biennial survey, series, 4836–3
Elementary and secondary students educational performance, and factors affecting proficiency, by selected characteristics, 1990 natl assessments, subject rpt series, 4896–8
Elementary and secondary students educational performance in math, science, reading, and writing, 1969-90, 4898–32
Enrollment and grads of public schools, by region and State, 1984-2002, annual rpt, 4824–4
Enrollment, by grade, instn type and control, and student characteristics, 1989 and trends from 1947, annual Current Population Rpt, 2546–1.459
High school dropout rates, and subsequent completion, by student and school characteristics, alternative estimates, 1991, annual rpt, 4834–23
Indian education funding of Fed Govt, with enrollment, program grants, and fellowships by State, 1980s-FY91, annual rpt, 14874–1
Natl Archives and Records Admin activities, finances, holdings, and staff, FY91, annual rpt, 9514–2
Reading performance and factors affecting proficiency, for elementary and secondary students, 1988 and 1990 natl assessments, 4898–33
Schools safety, discipline, and student drug use, elementary and secondary school principals views, 1991 survey, 4826–1.32
Teachers and administrators in private schools, pay, work conditions, and selected characteristics, by school type and affiliation, 1987/88, 4836–3.8
Vocational education enrollment, student and teacher characteristics, and outcomes, for secondary and postsecondary instns, 1970s-90, 4828–42

Energy Resources and Demand

Coal mining restrictions on public land, impacts on production, costs, and demand, by region, 1985-88 and projected to 2075, 5668–125
Coal production and mines by county, prices, productivity, miners, and reserves, by mining method and State, 1990-91, annual rpt, 3164–25
Coal production by State and region, weekly rpt, 3162–1
Coal production, stocks, and shipments, by State of origin and destination, end-use sector, and mode of transport, quarterly rpt, 3162–8
Coal trade and average price, by world region, country, and customs district, quarterly rpt, 3162–37
Electric power plants (coal-fired) generating capacity and replacement of energy imports, with background data, alternative forecasts 1990-2000, 3166–6.63
Electric power plants and capacity, by fuel used, owner, location, and operating status, 1991 and for units planned 1992-2001, annual listing, 3164–36
Electric power plants production, by North American Electric Reliability Council region, monthly rpt, 3162–35
Electric power plants production, capacity, sales, and fuel stocks, use, and costs, by State, 1986-90, annual rpt, 3164–11
Electric power supply, demand, and trade of Mexico and US, with data by fuel source, utility, and region, 1970s-89 and projected to 2000, 3408–2
Electric utilities conservation programs, peak load reductions, energy savings, and costs, by region, 1989-90 and projected to 2000, article, 3162–35.302
Energy production, dev, and distribution firms revenues and income, quarterly rpt, 3162–38
Energy supply, demand, and prices, by fuel type and end-use sector, alternative projections by region, 1990-2010, annual rpt, 3164–96
Energy supply, demand, and prices, by fuel type and end-use sector, projections and underlying assumptions, 1995-2010, annual rpt, 3164–90
Energy supply, demand, and prices, by fuel type and end-use sector, with foreign comparisons, 1991 and trends from 1949, annual rpt, 3164–74
Fuel oil and kerosene sales and deliveries, by end-use, PAD district, and State, 1990, annual rpt, 3164–94
Heating fuels production, imports, stocks, and prices, by selected PAD district and State, seasonal weekly rpt, 3162–45
Housing (low income) energy aid, funding sources, costs, and participation, by State, FY90, annual rpt, 4584–1
Housing energy use, costs, and conservation, and household and housing characteristics, survey rpt series, 3166–7
Manufacturing energy use and prices, 1988 survey, series, 3166–13
Natural gas interstate pipeline capacity, use, contract deliveries, and prices, by region, State, and firm, 1990, 3168–125
Offshore oil and gas leasing and exploration activity, production, revenue, and environmental studies, by location, quarterly rpt, 5732–1
Offshore oil and gas reserves, geophysical data collection activities and costs, by region, 1976-90, 5738–41
Oil and gas reserves and ultimate recovery, by reservoir characteristics, geologic province, region, and field, 1989, 3166–14.2
Oil crude, gas liquids, and refined products supply, demand, and movement, by PAD district and State, 1991, annual rpt, 3164–2
Oil products prices, sales, and purchases of refiners, processors, and distributors, by product, end-use sector, PAD district, and State, 1991, annual rpt, 3164–85
Oil products sales and purchases of refiners, processors, and distributors, by product, end-use sector, PAD district, and State, monthly rpt, 3162–11
Oil, refined products, and gas liquids supply, demand, trade, stocks, and refining, by detailed product, State, and PAD district, monthly rpt with articles, 3162–6
Rural Electrification Admin loans, and borrower operating and financial data, by distribution firm and State, 1991, annual rpt, 1244–1
Uranium mining and milling industries finances and operations, with selected foreign comparisons, 1970s-90 and projected to 2005, annual rpt, 3164–82
Uranium reserves and industry operations, by region and State, various periods 1966-91, annual rpt, 3164–65.1
Wood, waste, and alcohol fuel use, by end-use sector and region, 1990, annual rpt, 3164–97

Geography and Climate

Temperature annual and seasonal averages by US region, and departures from normal by world area, 1860s-1990, annual rpt, 3004–33
Weather data for farmland, average precipitation and temperature by State, monthly 1950-90, biennial rpt, 1544–28
Weather events and anomalies, precipitation and temperature for US and foreign locations, weekly rpt, 2182–6

Government and Defense

Collective bargaining agreements of Federal employees, coverage, unions, and location, by agency, for contracts expiring 1992, semiannual listing, 9847–1
Customs collections, by district and port, FY91, annual rpt, 8104–2.2
Fed Govt personnel action appeals, decisions of Merit Systems Protection Board by agency and region, FY91, annual rpt, 9494–2
Finances of govts, tax systems and revenue, and fiscal structure, by level of govt and State, 1992 and historical trends, annual rpt, 10044–1
Minority business Federal procurement set-aside contracts, by participant race and sex, industry, firm, and State, FY90, annual rpt, 9764–8
Tax (excise) collections of IRS, by source, region, and State, quarterly rpt, annual table, 8302–1
Tax (income) returns filed, by type, IRS service center, and whether full-paid, refund, and electronically filed, 1990 and projected to 1998, semiannual rpt, 8302–7
Tax (income) withholding and related documents filed, by type and IRS service center, 1991 and projected 1992-99, annual rpt, 8304–22
Tax collection, enforcement, and litigation activity of IRS, with data by type of tax, region, and State, FY91, annual rpt, 8304–3
Tax returns filed, by type of tax and IRS district, 1990 and projected 1991-98, annual rpt, 8304–24
Tax returns filed, by type of tax and IRS region and service center, projected 1991-98 and trends from 1978, annual rpt, 8304–9
Taxes, spending, and govt efficiency, public opinion by respondent characteristics, 1992 survey, annual rpt, 10044–2
Voting age population, by sex, age, race, and State, forecast 1992 general elections, with votes cast from 1930, Current Population Rpt, 2546–3.170

Health and Vital Statistics

Acute and chronic health conditions, disability, absenteeism, and health services use, by selected characteristics, 1990, annual rpt, 4147–10.182

Acute and chronic health conditions, disability, absenteeism, and health services use, by selected characteristics, 1991, annual rpt, 4147–10.183

AIDS and tuberculosis cases in prisons, test results, and control and treatment policies, by location, 1990 survey, annual rpt, 6064–22

AIDS cases among children, hospital use and charges by instn and patient characteristics, and payment source, 1986-87, 4186–6.16

Alcohol-related diagnoses hospital discharges and length of stay, by age, sex, race, and region, 1979-85, 4488–10.5

Alcohol use, by type of beverage, region, and State, 1977-88, annual rpt, 4486–1.11

Alcohol use, by type of beverage, region, and State, 1977-89, annual rpt, 4486–1.15

Child infectious disease cases, and related disability and health care, by disease, health insurance status, and other characteristics, 1988, 4147–10.181

Deaths and rates, by region and State, preliminary 1990-91, US Vital Statistics annual rpt, 4144–7

Dental fluoride products use by children, by frequency of dental visits and selected characteristics, 1983-89, 4146–8.222

Diabetes patients physician office visits, by characteristics of patient, physician, and visit, 1989, 4146–8.212

Disabled persons rehabilitation, Federal and State activities and funding, FY90, annual rpt, 4944–1

Diving (underwater) accidents, illnesses, and deaths, by circumstances, diver characteristics, and location, 1970-90, annual rpt, 2144–29

Drug, alcohol, and cigarette use and attitudes of youth, by substance type and selected characteristics, 1975-91 surveys, annual rpt, 4494–4

Drug, alcohol, and cigarette use, by selected characteristics, 1991 survey, annual rpt series, 4494–5

Fire fighter deaths, by cause, circumstances, and location, 1990, annual rpt, 9434–8

Foreign medical grads in US by age, sex, professional characteristics, State, and country, and US medical school foreign students, 1960s-80s, working paper, 6366–6.2

Health care professionals supply and education, by professional and other characteristics, and location, 1960s-92 and projected to 2020, biennial rpt, 4114–8

Health care services use and costs, methodology and findings of natl survey, series, 4186–8

Health condition and care indicators, 1950s-90 with health improvement and disease prevention goals for 1990, annual data compilation, 4144–11

HHS financial aid, by program, recipient, State, and city, FY91, annual regional listings, 4004–3

Hospital discharges and length of stay, by diagnosis, patient and instn characteristics, procedure performed, and payment source, 1990, annual rpt, 4147–13.112

Hospital discharges and length of stay by region and diagnosis, and procedures performed, by age and sex, 1990, annual rpt, 4146–8.211

Hospital discharges and length of stay under old and new survey designs, by diagnosis, patient and instn characteristics, and procedure, Jan-Mar 1988, 4147–13.110

Hospital discharges by detailed diagnostic and procedure category, primary diagnosis, and length of stay, by age, sex, and region, 1990, annual rpt, 4147–13.111

Hospital discharges, by payment source, diagnosis, patient characteristics, and region, and procedures performed, 1990, 4146–8.221

Hospital employment and job vacancy rate, by occupation, and instn size and control, 1981-88, annual rpt, 4114–12

Indian Health Service and tribal facilities and use, and Indians health and other characteristics, by IHS region, 1980s-90, annual chartbook, 4084–7

Indian Health Service and tribal facility outpatient visits, by type of provider, selected hospital, and service area, FY91, annual rpt, 4084–3

Indian Health Service and tribal hospital admissions, length of stay, beds, and births, by facility and service area, FY90-91, annual rpt, 4084–4

Indian Health Service and tribal hospital capacity, use, and births, by area and facility, quarterly rpt, 4082–1

Indian Health Service, tribal, and contract facilities hospitalization, by diagnosis, age, sex, and service area, FY91, annual rpt, 4084–5

Infectious notifiable disease cases and current outbreaks, by region and State, weekly rpt, 4202–1

Infectious notifiable disease cases, by age, race, and State, and deaths, 1940s-91, annual rpt, 4204–1

Insurance (health) coverage of persons, by insurance type and selected characteristics, 1985-90, 2546–20.23

Kidney end-stage disease treatment facilities approved by Medicare, dialysis and transplant services and ownership, 1991 annual listing, 4654–17

Mental health care facilities, staff, patients, and finances, 1970s-91, biennial rpt, 4094–1

Occupational Safety and Health Admin penalties assessed compared to maximum allowable, by firm size and region, FY89, GAO rpt, 26121–455

Otitis media patients physician office visits, by specialty and characteristics of patient and visit, 1975-90, 4146–8.217

Physicians visits, by patient and practice characteristics, diagnosis, and services provided, 1989, annual rpt, 4147–13.109

Physicians visits, by patient and practice characteristics, diagnosis, and services provided, 1990, advance rpt, 4146–8.215

Rotavirus cases, by region, monthly 1989-May 1991, article, 4202–7.317

Syphilis case rate, by sex, race, and region, 1990, article, 4202–7.303

Housing and Construction

Affordability and availability of housing, impacts of govt land use regulations and rent control, and low income housing condition, 1991 hearing, 21248–174

Alteration and repair of owner-occupied homes, costs and structural, household, financial, and project characteristics, 1987, 2486–1.13

Alteration and repair spending for housing, by type, tenure, region, and other characteristics, quarterly rpt, 2382–7

American Housing Survey: unit and household characteristics of recent movers, and reason for move, by tenure, 1989, 2486–1.12

American Housing Survey: unit and households detailed characteristics, and unit and neighborhood quality, 1989, biennial rpt supplement, 2485–13

Apartment and condominium completions by rent class and sales price, and market absorption rates, quarterly rpt, 2482–2

Apartment completions by region and metro-nonmetro location, and absorption rate, by size and rent class, preliminary 1991, annual Current Housing Rpt, 2484–3

Apartment market absorption rates and characteristics for nonsubsidized furnished and unfurnished units, 1990, annual Current Housing Rpt, 2484–2

Buildings (commercial and public) alteration and repair spending, by type, size, age, and region, 1989, 2388–4

Census of Housing, 1990: median value and rent, by State and region, and compared to 1970 and 1980, fact sheet, 2328–83

Clay (construction) production and shipments by region and State, trade, and use, by product, quarterly Current Industrial Rpt, 2506–9.2

Coastal areas construction authorized by permit, by building type, 1970-89, 2176–8.3

Construction put in place, permits, housing sales, costs, material prices, and employment, quarterly rpt with articles, 2042–1

Construction put in place, value of new public and private structures, by type, monthly rpt, 2382–4

Homeownership values, reasons, and barriers, views by race and tenure, 1992 survey, 9478–1

Housing and households summary characteristics, 1989 and trends, chartbook, 2486–2.1

Migration of households, moving rates by tenure and age, and housing value by mobility status and region, 1989, fact sheet, 2326–17.38

Mortgage delinquencies and properties acquired by Fed Natl Mortgage Assn, by region, 1989-91, annual rpt, 9474–1

Mortgages (conventional) terms at closing, by lender type, with periodic data by district, State, and for 32 MSAs, monthly rpt, 9442–2

Mortgages (conventional) terms at closing, for fixed- and adjustable-rate loans by purpose, FHLB district, State, and selected MSA, 1960s-91, annual rpt, 9444–2

Mortgages FHA-insured, secondary market prices and yields, and interest rates on construction and conventional mortgage loans, by region, monthly press release, 5142–20

New housing starts, by units per structure and metro-nonmetro location, and mobile home placements and prices, by region, monthly rpt, 2382–1

New housing units authorized, by region, State, selected MSA, and permit-issuing place, monthly rpt, 2382–5
New housing units authorized, by State, MSA, and permit-issuing place, 1991, annual rpt, 2384–2
New housing units completed and under construction, by units per structure, region, and inside-outside MSAs, monthly rpt, 2382–2
New single and multifamily units, by structural and financial characteristics, inside-outside MSAs, and region, 1987-91, annual rpt, 2384–1
New single-family houses sold and for sale, by price, stage of construction, months on market, and region, monthly rpt, 2382–3
Real estate supply and demand, housing and commercial property market activity indicators by region, quarterly rpt, 9292–6
Rental housing rehabilitation funding and activities of HUD, by program and region, FY91, annual rpt, 5124–7
Rental housing units, total, with HUD assistance by program, and eligible for aid, by unit, household, and neighborhood characteristics, and location, 1989, biennial rpt, 5184–11
Single parent families in own and others homes, by financial, housing, and other characteristics, 1989, 2486–1.14
Single person and nonfamily households social, economic and housing characteristics, by tenure, 1989, 2486–1.15
Vacant housing characteristics and costs, and occupancy and vacancy rates, by region and metro-nonmetro location, quarterly rpt, 2482–1
Vacant housing characteristics, and occupancy and vacancy rates, by tenure and location, 1960s-91, annual rpt, 2484–1

Industry and Commerce

Auto and auto parts trade, production, and labor conditions, for US and compared to Canada and Mexico, 1950s-90, 6366–3.28
Gross State Product by component, industry div, and State, 1977-89, article, 2702–1.303
Imports detained by FDA, by reason, product, shipper, brand, and country, monthly listing, 4062–2
Lumber production, prices, trade, and employment, for northwestern US and British Columbia, quarterly rpt, 1202–3
Minority Business Dev Centers mgmt and financial aid, and characteristics of businesses, by region and State, FY91, annual rpt, 2104–6
Phosphate rock production, prices, sales, trade, and use, 1992, Mineral Industry Surveys, annual rpt, 5614–20
Retail trade sales and inventories, by kind of business, region, and selected State, MSA, and city, monthly rpt, 2413–3
Small business finances, operations, owner characteristics, and Federal contracts, 1980s-90, annual rpt, 9764–6
Statistical Abstract of US, 1992 annual data compilation, 2324–1
Steel imports of US under voluntary restraint agreement, by product, customs district, and country, with US industry operating data, quarterly rpt, 9882–13
Textile mill production, trade, sales, stocks, and material used, by product, region, and State, periodic Current Industrial Rpt series, 2506–5
Vending facilities run by blind on Federal and non-Federal property, finances and operations by agency and State, FY91, annual rpt, 4944–2

Labor and Employment

Black and white women's occupational differences, and compared to men, selected years 1940-88, article, 6722–1.321
Child care arrangements of mothers employed and in school, and costs, by age of child and characteristics of mother, 1988, Current Population Rpt, 2546–20.24
Employer Cost Index by region, quarterly press release, 6942–8
Employment and Earnings, detailed data, monthly rpt, 6742–2.8
Employment and unemployment, by census region and div, monthly 1978-91, article, 6742–2.303
Employment Cost Index and alternative measure of compensation costs, by component, occupation, industry group, union status, and location, 1975-92, annual rpt, 6744–20
Employment Cost Index and percent change by occupational group, industry div, region, and metro-nonmetro area, quarterly press release, 6782–5
Employment Cost Index changes for nonfarm workers, by occupation, industry div, region, and bargaining status, monthly rpt, 6782–1
Employment cost indexes, by occupation, industry div, and region, Monthly Labor Review, 6722–1.3
Employment, unemployment, and labor force characteristics, by region and census div, 1991, annual rpt, 6744–7.1
Labor Dept activities and funding, by program and State, FY91, annual rpt, 6304–1
Labor hourly costs, by component, occupational group, industry div, union coverage, and region, 1992, annual rpt, 6744–21
Labor Relations Natl Board activities, cases, elections conducted, and litigation, FY90, annual rpt, 9584–1
Mediation and arbitration activities of Fed Mediation and Conciliation Service, and cases by issue, region, and State, FY85-90, annual rpt, 9344–1
Rural areas economic conditions and dev, quarterly journal, 1502–8
Unemployment, employment, and labor force, by region and State, 1990-91, annual press release, 6726–1.45
Vocational rehabilitation cases of State agencies, by disposition and State, FY91 and trends from FY21, annual rpt, 4944–5
Wage inequalities among income classes, regional and other factors, late 1970s-80s, article, 9379–1.307
Wages, hours, and employment by occupation, and benefits, for selected locations, industry survey rpt series, 6787–6

Law Enforcement

Assaults and deaths of law enforcement officers, by circumstances, agency, victim and offender characteristics, and location, 1991, annual rpt, 6224–3
Bombing incidents, casualties, and damage, by target, circumstances, and State, 1991, annual rpt, 6224–5
Cocaine trafficking in US and foreign countries, with prices and purity, 1988-90, annual rpt, 6284–5
Corrupt govt officials prosecuted and convicted, by judicial district and level of govt, 1970-90, annual rpt, 6004–13
Court civil and criminal caseloads for Federal district, appeals, and bankruptcy courts, by type of suit and offense, circuit, and district, 1991, annual rpt, 18204–11
Court civil and criminal caseloads for Federal district, appeals, and special courts, 1991, annual rpt, 18204–8
Crime, criminal justice admin and enforcement, and public opinion, data compilation, 1992 annual rpt, 6064–6
Crime Index by population size and region, and offenses by large city, 1st half 1992, semiannual rpt, 6222–1
Crimes, arrests by offender characteristics, and rates, by offense, and law enforcement employees, by population size and jurisdiction, 1991, annual rpt, 6224–2
Executions by whether habeas corpus used to appeal conviction, and time from crime to execution, with data by race and State, 1977-91, 6008–34
IRS undercover criminal investigations and costs by criminal activity, and success rates, by region, mid 1980s-90, GAO rpt, 26119–394
Juvenile facilities population, by resident characteristics and facility type, late 1970s-89, 6068–250
Juvenile facilities population, by resident characteristics and facility type, 1977-89, annual rpt, 6064–35
Parole and probation population, entries, and exits, by State, 1990, annual rpt, 6066–25.43
Parole decisions, caseloads, and activities of US Parole Commission, FY88-91, annual rpt, 6004–3
Prison and community-based facilities, population, employment, spending, and other characteristics, by State and for Fed Govt, 1990, quinquennial rpt, 6068–218
Prisoners AIDS and tuberculosis cases, test results, and control and treatment policies, by location, 1990 survey, annual rpt, 6064–22
Prisoners and staff in Federal instns, by selected characteristics, region, and instn, FY89, annual rpt, 6244–1
Prisoners, characteristics, and movements, by State, 1990, annual rpt, 6064–26
Prisoners in Federal and State instns by selected characteristics, releases, staff, and instn size, with data by region and State, late 1970s-91, 6068–248
Prisoners in Federal instns, admissions, releases, and recidivism, by region, monthly rpt series, 6242–1
Prosecutors (chief) in State courts, employment characteristics, and felony case prosecution procedures, 1990 survey, 6066–25.46
Sentences for Federal crimes, guidelines use and results by offense and district, and Sentencing Commission activities, 1991, annual rpt, 17664–1
Sentences under Federal mandatory minimum provisions, by defendant characteristics, and views on justice system impacts, FY90, 17668–2

Terrorism incidents in US, related activity, and casualties, by attack type, target, group, and location, 1991, annual rpt, 6224–6
Victimization rates, by victim and offender characteristics, circumstances, and offense, 1990 survey, annual rpt, 6066–3.47
Victimizations of households, by offense, household characteristics, and location, 1975-91, annual rpt, 6066–25.49

Natural Resources, Environment, and Pollution

Acid rain environmental, economic, and health effects, and pollutant emissions, 1985-89 and alternative projections to 2030, 14358–4
Army Corps of Engineers activities and projects, FY88 and trends from 1800s, annual rpt, 3754–1.1
Army Corps of Engineers activities and projects, FY89 and trends from 1800s, annual rpt, 3754–1.2
Army Corps of Engineers activities and projects, FY90 and trends from 1800s, annual rpt, 3754–1.3
Army Corps of Engineers activities, FY90, annual rpt, 3754–1
Birds (mourning dove) population, by hunting and nonhunting State, 1966-92, annual rpt, 5504–15
Birds (waterfowl) hunter harvest, age and sex ratios by species, State, and flyway, 1987-91, annual rpt, 5504–32
Birds (waterfowl) hunter harvest and unretrieved kills, and duck stamps sold, by species, State, Canada Province, and flyway, 1990-91, annual rpt, 5504–28
Birds (waterfowl) population, habitat conditions, and migratory flight forecasts, for Canada and US by region, 1992 and trends from 1955, annual rpt, 5504–27
Birds (woodcock) population in US and Canada from 1968, and hunter harvest, by State, 1992, annual rpt, 5504–11
Coastal and riparian areas environmental conditions, fish, wildlife, use, and mgmt, for individual ecosystems, series, 5506–9
Coastal areas environmental impacts of economic dev and population growth, 1960-80s and projected to 2010, series, 2176–8
Endangered species listing and mgmt activities of Fish and Wildlife Service and Natl Marine Fisheries Service, FY74-91, GAO rpt, 26113–578
Environmental Quality, status of problems, protection programs, research, and intl issues, 1991 annual rpt, 484–1
EPA pollution control grant program activities, monthly rpt, 9182–8
Fires (wild) and acreage burned, by type of land, ownership, cause, region, and State, 1984-90, annual rpt, 1204–4
Fish and shellfish resources and catch, marine mammal and sea turtle population, and mgmt, by species and region, 1988-90, annual rpt, 2164–22
Forest Service activities and finances, by region and State, FY91, annual rpt, 1204–1
Forests (natl) and other lands under Forest Service mgmt, acreage by forest and location, 1991 and historic trends, annual rpt, 1204–2
Forests (natl) revenue, by source, forest, and State, FY91, annual rpt, 1204–34
Hazardous waste site remedial action under Superfund, current and proposed sites priority ranking and status by location, series, 9216–5
Radioactive low-level waste disposal activities of States and interstate compacts, with data by disposal facility and reactor, 1990, annual rpt, 3004–36
Timber improvement program for private land, Fed Govt cost-sharing funds by region and State, monthly rpt, 1802–11
Timber insect and disease incidence and damage, annual regional rpt series, 1206–11
Timber insect and disease incidence and damage, by State, 1990, annual rpt, 1204–8
Timber sales of Forest Service, expenses, and operations, by region, State, and natl forest, FY91, annual rpts, 1204–36
Wastewater treatment and collection facility construction funding needs and Fed Govt grants, by State, 1990 and projected to 2010, biennial rpt, 9204–7
Water (groundwater) supply, quality, chemistry, other characteristics, and use, regional rpt series, 5666–25
Water pollution from farming, funding for control under Rural Clean Water Program by region and State, monthly rpt, 1802–14
Water supply mgmt for surface and groundwater, with groundwater depletion and use by purpose, 1980s, 10048–82

Population

Asian and Pacific Islands Americans social and economic characteristics, for West and total US, 1990-91, Current Population Report, 2546–1.462
Black Americans social and economic characteristics, for South and total US, 1991 and trends from 1950, annual Current Population Rpt, 2546–1.463
Black women's labor force status, earnings, and other economic status indicators, and compared to whites, various periods 1939-88, 11048–191
Census of Population, 1990: data adjustment in intercensal data for census undercounts, final decision with data by region and State, 2328–90
Consumer Income, socioeconomic characteristics of persons, families, and households, detailed cross-tabulations, Current Population Rpt series, 2546–6
Households and family characteristics, by location, 1991, annual Current Population Rpt, 2546–1.457
Immigrants and nonimmigrants admitted to US, alien workers, visitors, deportations, and naturalizations, FY91, annual summary rpt, 6264–7
Immigration to US, alien workers, visitors, deportations, and naturalizations, by country, FY91 and trends from 1820, annual rpt, 6264–2
Income (household) and poverty status under alternative income definitions, by recipient characteristics, 1979-91, annual Current Population Rpt, 2546–6.78
Income (personal) per capita and total, and earnings by industry group, by region and State, 1989-91, annual article, 2702–1.328
Income (personal) per capita, by region compared to total US, alternative model results, 1929-87, working paper, 9387–8.257
Income (personal) relative to median, by race and selected other characteristics, mid 1960s-89, Current Population Rpt, 2546–6.73
Income (personal) totals, by region, census div, and State, quarterly article, 2702–1.34
Income and consumer spending of households, for selected population groups, quarterly journal, 1702–1
Living arrangements, family relationships, and marital status, by selected characteristics, 1991, annual Current Population Rpt, 2546–1.461
Migration, immigration, and mover characteristics compared to nonmovers, 1987-90, annual Current Population Rpt, 2546–1.456
Migration, population change, and areas losing population, by region, State, and metro-nonmetro location, 1980s and trends from 1940, Current Population Rpt, 2546–2.164
Migration since 1990, mover characteristics by same or different area, and compared to nonmovers, 1991, annual Current Population Rpt, 2546–1.464
Older persons socioeconomic characteristics, 1900s-90 and projected to 2050, biennial chartbook, 12904–1
Older population, and health, economic, and other characteristics, with foreign comparisons, 1980s-91 with trends and projections, Current Population Rpt, 2546–2.165
Population economic well-being indicators, by selected characteristics and household income and income-to-poverty ratio, 1984, 2546–20.22
Population estimates and projections, by region and State, Current Population Rpt series, 2546–3
Population size, July 1991-92, by region, census div, and State, annual press release, 2324–10
Poverty status of population and families, by detailed characteristics, 1991, annual Current Population Rpt, 2546–6.77
Statistical Abstract of US, 1992 annual data compilation, 2324–1

Prices and Cost of Living

Consumer Expenditure Survey, spending by category, selected household characteristics, and region, quarterly rpt, 6762–14
CPI by component for US city average, and by region, population size, and for 15 metro areas, monthly rpt, 6762–1
CPI by component for US city average, and by selected metro area, region, and population size, monthly rpt, 6762–2
CPI current statistics, Monthly Labor Review, 6722–1.4
Dairy prices, by product and selected area, with related marketing data, 1991, annual rpt, 1317–1
Energy prices, by fuel type, end-use sector, and region, projected 1991-2030, 3166–6.60
Farm prices received and paid, by commodity and State, 1991, annual rpt, 1629–5

Housing units (1-family) sold, price indexes by region, monthly rpt, quarterly tables, 2382–3.2
Milk order market prices and detailed operations, by State and market area, 1990-91, annual rpt, 1317–3
Milk order market prices and detailed operations, monthly rpt with articles, 1317–4
Poultry and egg prices and marketing, by selected region, State, and city, monthly and weekly 1991, annual rpt, 1317–2
Producer price indexes, by stage of processing and detailed commodity, monthly 1991, annual rpt, 6764–2

Public Welfare and Social Security

Child day care and early childhood education programs availability, demand, use, costs, and provider and enrollee characteristics, 1990 survey, 4808–39
Disability benefit applications under OASDI and SSI, dispositions, awards, and administrative law judge hearing outcomes, by race, 1988, GAO rpt, 26121–459
Food aid program of USDA for women, infants, and children, participants and costs by State and Indian agency, FY90, annual tables, 1364–12
Food aid program of USDA for women, infants, and children, participants by race, State, and Indian agency, 1991, annual rpt, 1364–16
Food aid program of USDA for women, infants, and children, participants, clinics, and costs, by State and Indian agency, monthly tables, 1362–16
HHS financial aid, by program, recipient, State, and city, FY91, annual regional listings, 4004–3
Medicare and Medicaid beneficiaries and program operations, 1992, annual fact book, 4654–18
Medicare beneficiaries knowledge of and experience with physician billing and payment under Medicare, by selected characteristics, 1988-89, 17266–2.1
OASDHI and SSI admin, case processing, staff, and client problems with contacting SSA offices, 1980s-90, hearing, 25148–45

Recreation and Leisure

Fishing (ocean sport) activities, and catch by species, by angler characteristics and State, annual coastal area rpt series, 2166–17
Fishing (ocean sport) catch, by species, mode of fishing, and coastal region, 1991, annual rpt, 2164–1.2
Forests (natl) recreational use, factors affecting regional growth, shift-share analysis, 1992 rpt, 1208–423
Park natl system and other land under Natl Park Service mgmt, acreage by site, ownership, and region, FY92, semiannual rpt, 5542–1.2
Park natl system visits and overnight stays, by park and State, monthly rpt, 5542–4
Park natl system visits and overnight stays, by park and State, 1991, annual rpt, 5544–12

Science and Technology

Higher education instn R&D funding by Fed Govt, indirect costs and effects of alternative reimbursement policies, FY89, GAO rpt, 26113–592

Veterans Affairs

Health care for veterans, patients, visits, costs, and operating beds, by VA and contract facility, and region, quarterly rpt, 8602–4
Health care professionals of VA, by selected employment characteristics and VA district and duty station, quarterly rpt, 8602–6
Health care services sharing contracts among VA and non-VA facilities, by service type and region, FY91, annual rpt, 8704–5
Health care staff of VA, and turnover, by occupation and location, 1991, annual rpt, 8604–8
Hospital compliance with quality assurance standards of accreditation commission, by VA facility and region, 1989-90, GAO rpt, 26121–441

BY SMSA OR MSA

Banking, Finance, and Insurance

Banks (insured commercial and savings) deposits by instn, State, MSA, and county, as of June 1991, annual regional rpt, 9295–3.7
Savings instns insured by Savings Assn Insurance Fund, offices, and deposits, by region, State, MSA, and county, 1991, annual rpt, 8434–5

Communications and Transportation

Airports employment, air cargo shipments by industry, and convention attendance, for Chicago and other locations, mid 1970s-90, working paper, 9375–13.78
Commuters, by county of residence and work, for top 10 metro areas, 1990 Census of Population, press release, 2328–84
DOT planning and safety grants, by program, State, and for 40 SMSAs, FY89, annual rpt, 7304–7

Education

Educational attainment, by social and demographic characteristics and location, 1991 and trends from 1940, biennial Current Population Rpt, 2546–1.460

Government and Defense

Alien workers legal residence applicants share of population, and farm workers share of applicants, by MSA, 1989, working paper, 6366–6.9
Employment and payroll (civilian) of Fed Govt, by pay system and location, 1991, annual rpt, 9844–6.4
Immigrants admitted to US, by class of admission, country of birth, and MSA of destination, FY91, advance annual rpt, 6264–4
State and local govt employees wages by occupation, and benefits, periodic MSA survey rpt series, 6785–15

Health and Vital Statistics

AIDS cases by risk group, race, sex, age, State, and MSA, and deaths, quarterly rpt, 4202–9
Deaths and rates, by detailed location, cause, and demographic characteristics, 1989, US Vital Statistics annual rpt, 4144–3
Drug abuse indicators for selected metro areas, research results, data collection, and policy issues, 1992 semiannual conf, 4492–5
Hospital cost of charity cases and patients bad debts, and relation to operating margin, by selected MSA and urban-rural location, 1980s, 17206–2.32
Hospital deaths of Medicare patients, actual and expected rates by diagnosis and MSA, and methodology, FY90 annual rpt, 4654–14.53
Hospital employees and wages by occupation, and benefits, by region and selected MSA, 1991 survey, 6787–6.254

Housing and Construction

American Housing Survey: unit and households characteristics, MSA fact sheet series, 2485–11
American Housing Survey: unit and households characteristics, unit and neighborhood quality, and journey to work by MSA location, for 11 MSAs, 1987 survey, supplement, 2485–8
American Housing Survey: unit and households detailed characteristics, and unit and neighborhood quality, MSA rpt series, 2485–6
Census of Population and Housing, 1990: population and housing characteristics, detailed geographic coverage, State CD-ROM series, 2551–10
Census of Population and Housing, 1990: summary characteristics, households, and land area, by region, State, MSA, and city, US rpt, 2551–1.1
Construction authorized by building permits, by type of construction, region, State, and MSA, quarterly rpt, 2042–1.3
Homeownership rate for 30 largest metro areas, and direction of change in rate by State, 1989-91, fact sheet, 2326–17.46
Housing vacancy rate, for metro areas with significant changes, by tenure, 1989 and 1991, fact sheet, 2326–17.51
Mortgage purchases, sales, and other activity of Fed Natl Mortgage Assn, 1990, annual rpt, 5184–9
Mortgages (conventional) terms at closing, by lender type, with periodic data by district, State, and for 32 MSAs, monthly rpt, 9442–2
Mortgages (conventional) terms at closing, for fixed- and adjustable-rate loans by purpose, FHLB district, State, and selected MSA, 1960s-91, annual rpt, 9444–2
Mortgages FHA-insured, financial, property, and borrower characteristics, by metro area, 1991, annual rpt, 5144–24
New housing starts and completions authorized by building permits in 40 MSAs, quarterly rpt, 2382–9
New housing units authorized, by region, State, selected MSA, and permit-issuing place, monthly rpt, 2382–5
New housing units authorized, by State, MSA, and permit-issuing place, 1991, annual rpt, 2384–2
North Central States, FHLB 7th District housing vacancy rates for single and multifamily units and mobile homes, by ZIP code, annual MSA rpt series, 9304–18
Vacant housing characteristics, and occupancy and vacancy rates, by tenure and location, 1960s-91, annual rpt, 2484–1
West Central States, FHLB 10th District housing vacancy rates for single and multifamily units and mobile homes, by ZIP code, annual MSA rpt series, 9304–22
Western States, FHLB 12th District housing vacancy rates for single and multifamily units and mobile homes, by ZIP code, annual MSA rpt series, 9304–21

Industry and Commerce
Electronics industry production and labor conditions, in 10 MSAs, EC, and top producer countries, late 1970s-80s, article, 9393–8.307
New England States economic indicators, Fed Reserve 1st District, monthly rpt, 9373–2
Retail trade sales and inventories, by kind of business, region, and selected State, MSA, and city, monthly rpt, 2413–3
Southeastern States, Fed Reserve 6th District, economic indicators by State and MSA, quarterly rpt, 9371–14
Statistical Abstract of US, 1992 annual data compilation, 2324–1

Labor and Employment
Displaced workers, layoffs and unemployment insurance claims by reason, industry, selected characteristics, MSA, and State, 1990, annual rpt, 6744–18
Earnings, annual average percent changes for selected occupational groups, selected MSAs, monthly rpt, 6782–1.1
Employment and Earnings, detailed data, monthly rpt, 6742–2.5; 6742–2.6; 6742–2.8
Employment, earnings, and hours, by selected SIC 1- to 4-digit industry, State, and for 275 MSAs, 1987-92, 6748–81
Employment in manufacturing and nonagricultural industries, by MSA, 1990-91, annual press release, 6946–3.24
Employment, unemployment, and labor force characteristics, by selected metro area and large city, 1991, annual rpt, 6744–7.3
Metalworking machinery and die and tool manufacturing, wages and production workers by occupation, and benefits, by selected MSA, 1990 survey, 6787–6.253
Minority group and women employment, by occupation, SIC 1- to 3- digit industry, State, and MSA, 1991, annual rpt, 9244–1
New England States economic indicators, Fed Reserve 1st District, monthly rpt, 9373–2
North Central States business and economic conditions, Fed Reserve 9th District, quarterly journal, 9383–19
Services (producer) industries in Midwest, employment concentration by industry group, MSA, and urban-rural location, 1970s-89, article, 9375–1.305
Unemployment, by State and metro area, monthly press release, 6742–12
Unemployment, employment, and labor force, by State, MSA, and city, monthly rpt, 6742–22
Wages by occupation, and benefits for office and plant workers, periodic MSA survey rpt series, 6785–3; 6785–12; 6785–16; 6785–17
Wages by occupation, for office and plant workers in selected MSAs, 1991 surveys, annual rpt, 6785–5
Wages by occupation, for office and plant workers in selected MSAs, 1991 surveys, annual summary rpts, 6785–6
Wages, hours, and employment by occupation, and benefits, for selected locations, industry survey rpt series, 6787–6
Wages of workers covered by unemployment insurance, by MSA, 1990-91, annual press release, 6784–17.2

Law Enforcement
Drug (illegal) prices by type and selected metro area, and cocaine and heroin purity, quarterly rpt, 6282–1
Heroin prices and purity in 19 metro areas and Puerto Rico, by world area of origin, quarterly rpt, 6282–2

Natural Resources, Environment, and Pollution
Air pollution levels for 6 pollutants, by source and selected MSA, 1982-91, annual rpt, 9194–1

Population
Census of Population and Housing, 1990: population and housing characteristics, detailed geographic coverage, State CD-ROM series, 2551–10
Census of Population and Housing, 1990: summary characteristics, households, and land area, by region, State, MSA, and city, US rpt, 2551–1.1
Immigrants and nonimmigrants admitted to US, alien workers, visitors, deportations, and naturalizations, FY91, annual summary rpt, 6264–7
Immigration to US, alien workers, visitors, deportations, and naturalizations, by country, FY91 and trends from 1820, annual rpt, 6264–2
Income (personal) per capita and by source, and employment, by industry div, State, MSA, and county, 1969-90, annual CD-ROM, 2704–7
Income (personal) per capita and total, by State, MSA, county, and metro-nonmetro location, 1988-90, annual article, 2702–1.317
Migration, immigration, and mover characteristics compared to nonmovers, 1987-90, annual Current Population Rpt, 2546–1.456
Migration since 1990, mover characteristics by same or different area, and compared to nonmovers, 1991, annual Current Population Rpt, 2546–1.464
Statistical Abstract of US, 1992 annual data compilation, 2324–1

Prices and Cost of Living
CPI and components, relation to CPI of other MSAs, for 4 major MSAs, 1967-92, article, 9373–1.312
CPI by component for US city average, and by region, population size, and for 15 metro areas, monthly rpt, 6762–1
CPI by component for US city average, and by selected metro area, region, and population size, monthly rpt, 6762–2
CPI current statistics, Monthly Labor Review, 6722–1.4
Poultry and egg prices and marketing, by selected region, State, and city, monthly and weekly 1991, annual rpt, 1317–2
Statistical Abstract of US, 1992 annual data compilation, 2324–1.15

Public Welfare and Social Security
AFDC beneficiaries, by State, MSA, and county, as of Feb 1990, annual rpt, 4584–3.6
Medicare payment of physicians, reforms impacts on services, and monitoring methods, 1992 annual rpt, 4004–34

Science and Technology
Small business R&D grants of Fed Govt, by program area, agency, MSA, and State, FY90, annual rpt, 9764–7

BY STATE

Agriculture and Food
Acreage planted and harvested, by crop and State, 1990-91 and planned as of June 1992, annual rpt, 1621–23
Acreage planted, by selected crop and State, 1983-91 and planned 1992, annual rpt, 1621–22
Acreage reduction program compliance, enrollment, and yield on planted acreage, by commodity and State, annual press release series, 1004–20
Agricultural Stabilization and Conservation Service producer payments, by program and State, 1991, annual table, 1804–12
Agricultural Statistics, 1991, annual rpt, 1004–1
Alcoholic beverages and tobacco production, removals, stocks, and material used, by State, monthly rpt series, 8486–1
Animal protection, licensing, and inspection activities of USDA, and animals used in research, by State, FY90, annual rpt, 1394–10
Appalachia food processing firms, employment, and shipments, and farm production, by commodity and State, 1960s-90, 9088–37
Apple production, marketing, and prices, for Appalachia and compared to other States, 1989-92, annual rpt, 1311–13
Bean (dried) prices by State, market activity, and foreign and US production, use, stocks, and trade, weekly rpt, 1311–17
Bean (dried) production and prices by State, exports and foreign production by country, and USDA food aid purchases, by bean type, 1986-91, annual rpt, 1311–18
Catfish raised on farms, operations, water use, and acreage, by State, 1990-92, semiannual situation rpt, 1561–15.2
Cattle and calves for beef and milk, by State, as of July 1992, semiannual press release, 1623–1
Cattle and calves for beef, ranches, inventory, producers, and returns, by herd size and region, mid 1940s-91, 1568–251
Cattle and calves loss to predators, disease, and other causes, by region and State, 1991, 1618–22
Cattle and calves on feed, inventory and marketings by State, monthly release, 1623–2
Cattle tuberculosis cases and cooperative Federal-State eradication activities, by State, FY90-91, annual rpt, 1394–13
Cherry production, by State, 1990-92, annual rpt, 1621–18.2
Citrus production, prices, and use, by commodity and State, 1989/90-1991/92, annual rpt, 1621–18.8
Cold storage food stocks by commodity and census div, and warehouse space use, by State, monthly rpt, 1631–5
Cold storage food stocks by commodity, and warehouse space use, by census div, 1991, annual rpt, 1631–11
Cold storage warehouses and capacity, by State, as of Oct 1991, biennial rpt, 1614–2
Conservation program of USDA, acreage, projects, participation, and funding, by State, 1936-90, quinquennial rpt, 1808–1
Conservation program of USDA, funding by practice, region and State, monthly rpt, 1802–15

Conservation program of USDA, participation and payments by practice and State, FY91, annual rpt, 1804–7
Cooperatives, finances, and membership, by type of service, commodity, and State, 1990, annual rpt, 1124–1
Cotton acreage planted by State and county, and fiber quality, by variety, 1992, annual rpt, 1309–6
Cotton fiber and processing test results, by variety, region, State, and production area, 1991, annual rpt, 1309–16
Cotton fiber grade, staple, and mike, for upland and American pima cotton by State, monthly rpt, 1309–11
Cotton fiber grade, staple, mike, and other quality indicators, for upland cotton by classing office, weekly rpt, 1309–15
Cotton ginnings, by State and county, seasonal biweekly rpt, 1631–19
Cotton quality, by State, 1991, annual rpt, 1309–7
Cotton, wool, and synthetic fiber production, prices, trade, and use, periodic situation rpt with articles, 1561–1
Cottonseed prices and quality, by State, seasonal weekly rpt, 1309–14
Cottonseed quality factors, by State, 1991 crop, annual rpt, 1309–5
Cranberry production, prices, use, and acreage, for selected States, 1990-91 and forecast 1992, annual rpt, 1621–18.5
Dairy cattle, milk production, and grain and other concentrates fed, by State, monthly rpt, 1627–1
Dairy production by commodity, and plants, by State, 1991, annual rpt, 1627–5
Dairy production by State, stocks, prices, and CCC price support activities, by product type, monthly rpt, 1627–3
Dairy production, prices, trade, and use, periodic situation rpt with articles, 1561–2
Economic Indicators of the Farm Sector, balance sheets, and receipts by detailed commodity, by State, 1986-90, annual rpt, 1544–18
Egg production and layer inventory, by State, 1990-91, annual rpt, 1625–7
Emergency Conservation Program for farmland damaged by natural disaster, funding by region and State, monthly rpt, 1802–13
Employment on farms, wages, hours, and perquisites, by State, monthly rpt, 1631–1
Equity of farms, by State, 1990, article, 1541–1.303
Farmland damaged by natural disaster, Emergency Conservation Program aid and participation by State, FY91, annual rpt, 1804–22
Farmland in US owned by foreigners, holdings, acquisitions, and disposals by land use, owner type and country, and State, 1991, annual rpt, 1584–2
Farmland in US owned by foreigners, holdings, acreage, and value by land use, owner country, State, and county, 1991, annual rpt, 1584–3
Farms and acreage, by sales size, region, and State, 1990-92, annual rpt, 1614–4
Farms, production, acreage, and related data, by selected crop and State, monthly rpt, 1621–1
Fed Crop Insurance Corp financial performance, and effect of alternative price forecasts on program costs, 1983-89, GAO rpt, 26131–95
Feed and feed additives production, use, and prices, by commodity, State, and country, various periods 1949-92, 1568–308
Fertilizer (inorganic) shipments, trade, use, and firms, by product and State, with stocks, 1991, annual Current Industrial Rpt, 2506–8.13
Fertilizer and pesticide use and application rates, by type, crop, and State, series, 1616–1
Fertilizer use, by type and State, 1991-92, annual rpt, 9804–30
Finances of farms, assets, liabilities, and debt by lender type, by State, 1960-89, 1548–384
Fish (catfish) raised on farms, inventory, stocks, and production, by major producer State, quarterly rpt, 1631–18
Fish (processed) production by location, and trade, by species and product, 1988-91, annual rpts, 2166–6
Fish (trout) raised on farms, production, sales, prices, and losses, 1991-92, annual rpt, 1631–16
Fish catch, by species, use, region, State, and major port, 1980s-91, annual rpt, 2164–1.1
Fish hatcheries and farms, production, costs, prices, and sales, for catfish and trout, 1970s-92, semiannual situation rpt, 1561–15
Fish Hatchery Natl System activities and deliveries, by species, hatchery, and jurisdiction of waters stocked, FY91, annual rpt, 5504–10
Fishery employment, vessels, plants, and cooperatives, by State, 1990, annual rpt, 2164–1.10
Flour milling production by State, stocks, daily capacity, and exports by country, monthly Current Industrial Rpt, 2506–4.1
Flower and foliage production, sales, prices, and growers, by crop and State, 1990-91 and planting planned 1992, annual rpt, 1631–8
Flower and foliage shipments from Florida by State and mode of transport, US imports by country, and prices, by variety, mid 1980s-91, annual rpt, 1311–24
FmHA activities, and loans and grants by program and State, FY91 and trends from FY70, annual rpt, 1184–17
FmHA loans and borrower supervision activities in farm and housing programs, by type and State, monthly rpt, 1182–1
FmHA loans, by type, borrower race, and State, quarterly rpt, 1182–5
FmHA property acquired through foreclosure, acreage, value, and sales, for farm and nonfarm property by State, monthly rpt, 1182–6
Food (processed) production and stocks by State, shipments, exports, ingredients, and use, periodic Current Industrial Rpt series, 2506–4
Fruit (noncitrus) and nut production, prices, and use, by crop and State, 1989-91, annual rpt, 1621–18.1; 1621–18.3
Fruit and nut production, prices, trade, stocks, and use, by selected crop, periodic situation rpt with articles, 1561–6
Fruit and vegetable shipments, and arrivals by city, by mode of transport and State and country of origin, 1991, annual rpt series, 1311–4
Fruit and vegetable shipments by mode of transport, arrivals, and imports, by commodity and State and country of origin, weekly rpt, 1311–3
Fruit and vegetable shipments by truck, monthly by State and country of origin, and rates weekly by growing area and market, 1991, annual rpt, 1311–15
Fruit and vegetable wholesale prices in NYC by State, and shipments and arrivals by mode of transport, by commodity, weekly rpt, 1311–20
Fruit and vegetable wholesale prices in NYC-Newark, and arrivals by mode of transport, by commodity and State, 1990, annual rpt, 1311–21
Grain stocks on and off farms, by crop, quarterly rpt, 1621–4
Grain support loan programs of USDA, activity and status by grain and State, monthly rpt, 1802–3
Grape shipments from California and arrivals by city by mode of transport, prices, and production, by variety, 1970s-90, annual rpt, 1311–25
Hay (alfalfa and prairie) prices, for selected areas, weekly rpt, 1313–5
Honey production, prices, stocks, and bee colonies, by State, 1990-91, annual rpt, 1631–6
Honey production, prices, trade, stocks, marketing, and CCC honey loan and distribution activities, monthly rpt, 1311–2
Income of farms, cash marketing receipts ranked by commodity and State, 1990, 1548–385
Irrigated farmland, farm characteristics, and water and fuel sources, by State and leading county, 1950s-88, 1588–122
Irrigation projects of Reclamation Bur in western US, crop production and acreage by commodity, State, and project, 1990, annual rpt, 5824–12
Japan investment in US farmland and agricultural industries, with data by State and county, late 1960s-90, 1528–332
Labor (hired and contract) costs, by farm type and sales size, and for top States and counties, 1987, article, 1541–1.305
Livestock grazing on public desert areas, acreage, use, fees, and endangered species, 1988-90, GAO rpt, 26113–552
Livestock grazing on public rangeland, allotments, permits, acreage, and stocking rates, by BLM State office, as of Sept 1991, GAO rpt, 26113–582
Livestock inspected by Fed Govt, by type, weekly rpt, 1315–1
Livestock packers purchases and feeding, and livestock markets, dealers, and sales, by State, 1990, annual rpt, 1384–1
Livestock slaughter and meat production, by livestock type and State, monthly rpt, 1623–9
Livestock slaughter, meat production, and slaughter plants, by species and State, 1991, annual rpt, 1623–10
Meat animal production, prices, receipts, and disposition, by species and State, 1990-91, annual rpt, 1623–8
Milk order market deliveries and producers, by State, 1979-90, article, 1317–4.303
Milk order market deliveries, by State of origin, 1970-90, annual article, 1317–4.301

Milk order market prices and detailed operations, by State and market area, 1990-91, annual rpt, 1317–3
Milk production, use, and receipts, and milk cow inventory, by State, 1989-91, annual rpt, 1627–4
Mink and pelt production, prices, and farms, selected years 1969-92, annual rpt, 1631–7
Mint oil production, yield, and farm prices by State, and NYC spot prices, 1989-92, FAS annual circular, 1925–15.2
Mushroom production, sales, and prices, by State, 1966/67-1991/92 and planned 1992/93, annual rpt, 1631–9
Peaches production, marketing, and prices in 3 southeastern States and Appalachia, 1991, annual rpt, 1311–12
Peanut production and US exports by country, prices, and stocks, weekly rpt, 1311–1
Peanut production, prices, stocks, exports, use, inspection, and quality, by region and State, 1982-91, annual rpt, 1311–5
Pecan production and prices by State, and US trade by country, late 1980s-91, annual rpt, 1311–28
Potato production, acreage, prices, and shipments, for 7 major producer States, and compared to other States, 1970s-92, annual rpt, 1311–29
Potato production, acreage, shipments, and arrivals, for Maine by variety, and compared to other States and Canada, 1991-92, annual rpt, 1311–26
Potato production, prices, stocks, and use, by State, 1980s-91, annual rpt, 1621–11
Potato production, stocks, processing, yields, and harvest losses, by State, periodic rpt, 1621–10
Poultry (broiler) hatcheries eggs set and chicks placed, by State, weekly rpt, 1625–11
Poultry (chicken and turkey) hatchery production, 1990-91, annual rpt, 1625–8
Poultry (chicken, egg, and turkey) production and inventories, monthly rpt, 1625–1
Poultry (chicken, egg, and turkey) production and prices, by State, 1990-91, annual rpt, 1625–5
Poultry slaughtered, by class of bird and State, FY90, annual rpt, 1374–3.2
Poultry slaughtered under Fed Govt inspection, pounds certified, and condemnations by cause, by State, monthly rpt, 1625–3
Prices received and paid by farmers, by commodity and State, monthly rpt, 1629–1
Prices received and paid by farmers, by commodity and State, 1991, annual rpt, 1629–5
Prices received by farmers and production value, by detailed crop and State, 1989-91, annual rpt, 1621–2
Production inputs, finances, mgmt, and land value and transfers, periodic situation rpt with articles, 1561–16
Production itemized costs, receipts, and returns, by crop and State, 1987-89, annual rpt, 1544–24
Research (agricultural) funding and staffing for USDA, State agencies, and other instns, by topic, FY91, annual rpt, 1744–2
Rice foreign and US production, prices, trade, stocks, and use, periodic situation rpt, 1561–8
Rice market activities, prices, inspections, sales, trade, supply, and use, for US and selected foreign markets, weekly rpt, 1313–8
Rice shipments, by end use, package size, and State of origin and destination, 1960s-89, biennial rpt, 1564–11
Sheep and wool production, use, and prices, and operations costs and returns, for western US, 1920s-90, 1548–382
Shellfish harvest in estuaries, approved and restricted areas, and pollution sources, by estuary, State, and coastal region, 1990, quinquennial rpt, 2178–33
South Central States agricultural banks financial ratios, and farm finances and production growth, by State, 1980s-92, annual article, 9391–16.308
Storage facility and equipment loans to farmers under CCC grain program, by State, monthly table, 1802–9
Sugar and sweeteners production, prices, trade, supply, and use, quarterly situation rpt with articles, 1561–14
Swine inventory, value, farrowings, and farms, by State, quarterly release, 1623–3
Timber and orchard damage from natural disaster, USDA restoration aid and program participation by practice and State, FY91, annual rpt, 1804–24
Tobacco marketing activity, prices, and sales, by grade, type, market, and State, 1991, annual rpt series, 1319–5
Tobacco production, marketing, use, price supports, and trade, quarterly situation rpt with articles, 1561–10
Tobacco production, prices, stocks, taxes by State, and trade and production by country, 1991, annual rpt, 1319–1
Tomato production, acreage, and yield by State, trade and production by country, stocks, shipments, and prices, 1960s-91, 1568–310
Turkeys raised by State, and losses by region, 1990-91, and hatchery plans, 1992, annual rpt, 1625–6
Vegetable production, acreage, and yield, current and forecast for selected fresh and processing crops by State, periodic rpt, 1621–12
Vegetable production, prices, trade, stocks, and use, for selected fresh and processing crops, periodic situation rpt with articles, 1561–11
Vegetable production, value, and acreage, for selected fresh and processing crops by State, 1989-91, annual rpts, 1621–25
Wheat acreage enrolled in soils and wetlands conservation programs, and production impacts, by State, 1991, article, 1561–12.302
Wheat and rye acreage seeded, by State, 1990-92, annual rpt, 1621–30
Wheat and rye foreign and US production, prices, trade, stocks, and use, quarterly situation rpt with articles, 1561–12
Wool and mohair production and prices, by State, 1989-91, annual press release, 1623–6

Banking, Finance, and Insurance

Banking system reform impacts on consumers, with background data, 1991 hearing, 21248–167
Banking system reform issues, with top instn finances, fiscal impacts, and views of depositors, bankers, and regulators on deposit insurance, 1991 hearings, 21248–168
Banks (FDIC-insured) return on assets by region, and failed banks, by State, 1991, annual rpt, 9294–1
Banks (insured commercial) financial ratios, by State, 1987-90, annual rpt, 9294–4
Banks (insured commercial and FDIC-insured savings) assets, income, and financial ratios, by asset size and State, quarterly rpt, 13002–3
Banks (insured commercial and savings) deposits by instn, State, MSA, and county, as of June 1991, annual regional rpt series, 9295–3
Banks (insured commercial and savings) finances, by State, 1990, annual rpt, 9294–4
Banks (natl) charters, mergers, liquidations, enforcement cases, and financial performance, with data by instn and State, quarterly rpt, 8402–3
Banks, branches, earnings, assets, and deposits, 1990, annual rpt, 9364–5.11
Banks financial performance in Fed Reserve 10th District, by State, quarterly rpt, 9381–16
Banks mergers antitrust issues, with background financial data by State and selected instn, 1991 hearing, 21248–176
Check-cashing outlets fees by type of check, and legal maximum in regulated States, 1991 article, 9381–1.301
Credit unions federally insured, finances by instn characteristics and State, as of June 1992, semiannual rpt, 9532–6
Credit unions federally insured, finances, 1990-91, annual rpt, 9534–1
Credit unions financial performance and regulation, with background data, 1960s-90, GAO rpt, 26119–364
Fed Natl Mortgage Assn, Fed Home Loan Mortgage Corp, and FHLBs finances, 1991 hearings, 21248–170
Financial instns reform issues, with finances, impacts of deposit insurance changes, and views of depositors and bankers, 1991 hearings, 25248–129
Futures industry registered traders, by type and State, FY91, annual rpt, 11924–2
Insurance (life and health) company failures, and State guaranty fund assessments, by State, 1975-90, GAO rpt, 26119–392
Insurance industry finances, failures, and regulation, with data by firm and State, 1990 hearing, 25528–119
New England States economic indicators, Fed Reserve 1st District, monthly rpt, 9373–2
New England States, FHLB 1st District thrift instns, financial condition, and locations, 1992, annual listing, 9304–26
North Central States business and economic conditions, Fed Reserve 9th District, quarterly journal, 9383–19
Savings instns failure resolution activity and finances of Resolution Trust Corp, with data by asset type, State, region, and instn, monthly rpt, 9722–3
Savings instns failure resolution activity of Resolution Trust Corp, with data by State and instn, and RTC finances, 1990, annual rpt, 9724–1

Savings instns failures, inventory of real estate assets available from Resolution Trust Corp, semiannual listing series, 9722–2
Savings instns financial statements, for instns insured by Savings Assn Insurance Fund by FHLB district and State, and for FDIC-insured savings banks, 1989, annual rpt, 8434–1
Savings instns insured by Savings Assn Insurance Fund, finances by profitability group, district, and State, quarterly rpt, 8432–4
Savings instns insured by Savings Assn Insurance Fund, offices, and deposits, by region, State, MSA, and county, 1991, annual rpt, 8434–5
Small Business Admin dev company loan program and debenture sale activity, with data by firm, industry div, State, and region, quarterly rpt, 9762–6
Small Business Admin direct and guaranteed loans, principal outstanding, and losses, by program, borrower race and sex, and State, 1950s-90, GAO rpt, 26113–554
Small Business Admin guaranteed loans issued under regular, certified, and preferred lender programs, selected characteristics, FY83-90, GAO rpt, 26113–581
Small Business Admin loan guarantee program participants finances, operations, characteristics, and views, 1991 survey, 9768–25
Small Business Admin loans, contract awards, and surety bonds, by firm, State, and city, FY91, annual rpt, 9764–1
Small Business Investment Companies capital holdings, SBA obligation, and ownership, as of July 1992, semiannual listing, 9762–4
South Central States agricultural and small banks financial ratios, by State, as of 1991 and trends from 1985, article, 9391–16.306
Southeastern States, Fed Reserve 5th District insured commercial banks financial statements, by State, quarterly rpt, 9389–18
Southeastern States, Fed Reserve 6th District banks financial ratios, by asset size and State, 1987-91, annual article, 9371–1.305
Trust assets of banks, trust companies, and S&Ls, by type of asset and fund, selected firm, and State, 1991, annual rpt, 13004–1
West Central States, Fed Reserve 10th District banking industry structure, performance, and financial devs, 1991, annual rpt, 9381–14
West Central States, FHLB 10th District thrifts, locations, assets, and deposits, 1992, annual listing, 9304–17

Communications and Transportation

Air traffic (passenger), and aircraft operations by type, by airport and State, projected FY92-2005 and trends from FY83, annual rpt, 7504–7
Air traffic (passenger and cargo), and departures by aircraft type, by carrier and airport, 1991, annual rpt, 7504–35
Air traffic (passenger and cargo), carrier enplanement shares, and FAA airport improvement program grants, by airport and State, 1990, annual rpt, 7504–48
Air traffic, carriers, craft, airports, and FAA activities, detailed data, 1981-90, annual rpt, 7504–1
Air traffic levels at FAA-operated control facilities, by airport and State, FY91, annual rpt, 7504–27
Aircraft accidents and circumstances, for US operations of domestic and foreign airlines and general aviation, periodic rpt, 9612–1
Aircraft flight service station workload of FAA, pilot briefs, contacts, and flight plans by facility, projected FY92-2002 and trends from FY83, annual rpt, 7504–39
Aircraft pilot and nonpilot certificates held, by type of certificate, age, sex, region, and State, 1991, annual rpt, 7504–2
Aircraft registered with FAA, by type and characteristics of aircraft, make, carrier, State, and county, 1991, annual rpt, 7504–3
Airport improvement program of FAA, activities and grants by State and airport, FY91, annual rpt, 7504–38
Airport planning and dev project grants of FAA, by airport and location, quarterly press release, 7502–14
Appalachia hwy system and access roads funding and completion status, by State, quarterly tables, 9082–1
Auto ownership of households, by selected State, 1980 and 1990, 7558–120
Bridge replacement and repair program funding by bridge, and bridge status, by State, 1990, biennial rpt, 7554–27
Bus (intercity) deregulation in 1982, impacts on service, ridership, and State and Federal funding, with background data, 1980s-92, GAO rpt, 26113–583
DOT planning and safety grants, by program, State, and for 40 SMSAs, FY89, annual rpt, 7304–7
Drivers licenses issued and in force by age and sex, fees, and renewal, by license class and State, 1990, annual rpt, 7554–16
Drivers licenses requirements and admin, by State and Canada Province, as of Jan 1992, biennial rpt, 7554–18
FAA activities and finances, and staff by region, FY90-91, annual rpt, 7504–10
Fed Hwy Admin traffic safety grants, by program and State, FY90, annual rpt, 7764–1.1
Fed Transit Admin grants by State, and oversight, 1988-92, GAO rpt, 26113–600
Hazardous material transport accidents, casualties, and damage, by mode of transport, with DOT control activities, 1990, annual rpt, 7304–4
Hwy construction bids and contracts for Federal-aid hwys, by State, 1st half 1992, semiannual rpt, 7552–12
Hwy construction material prices and indexes for Federal-aid system, by type of material and urban-rural location, quarterly rpt, 7552–7
Hwy construction material use by type, and spending, by State, 1940s-91, annual rpt, 7554–29
Hwy funding, costs for completion, and mileage of Federal-aid system, by State, 1989-91 and projected to FY93, 21648–66
Hwy interstate mileage, by completion status and State, as of June 1992, semiannual rpt, 7552–5
Hwy interstate mileage, by route and State, 1991 listing, 7558–111
Hwy safety program funding by State, and accident and death reductions, FY91, annual rpt, 7554–26
Hwy scenic routes impacts on local economic conditions, by State, county, and selected byway, late 1980s, 7556–8.1
Hwy speed averages and vehicles exceeding 55 mph, by State, quarterly rpt, 7552–14
Hwy Statistics, detailed data by State, 1991, annual rpt, 7554–1
Hwy Statistics, summary data by State, 1990-91, annual rpt, 7554–24
Hwy Statistics, summary data with trends and projections, 1992 chartbook, 7554–41
Hwy traffic volume on rural roads and city streets, monthly rpt, 7552–8
Ohio River basin waterway facilities, freight by commodity and port, and recreation, by waterway, 1988-89, annual rpt, 3754–6
Port improvement capital expenditures and financing methods, by region and selected port, 1946-89, 7708–6
Railroad accidents, casualties, and damage, by cause, railroad, and State, 1991, annual rpt, 7604–1
Railroad accidents, casualties, and damage, Fed Railroad Admin activities, and safety inspectors by State, 1990, annual rpt, 7604–12
Railroad employee benefits and beneficiaries by type, and railroad employment and payroll, FY90, annual rpt, 9704–2
Railroad-hwy grade-crossing accidents, detailed data by State and railroad, 1991, annual rpt, 7604–2
Safety belt usage rates, by State, 1990, annual rpt, 7764–1
Telephone and other economic dev loans for rural areas by State, and REA activities and finances, FY91 and trends from FY36, annual rpt, 1244–3
Telephone firms borrowing under Rural Telephone Program, and financial and operating data, by State, 1991, annual rpt, 1244–2
Telephone firms borrowing under Rural Telephone Program, loan activity by State, FY91, annual tables, 1244–8
Telephone lines in residences and businesses, carriage equipment miles, and calls placed, by State, 1990, annual rpt, 9284–6.2
Telephone service subscribership, charges, and local and long distance firm finances and operations, late 1970s-92, semiannual rpt, 9282–7
Tourist spending and economic impacts, for selected tourist areas, 1960s-88, 7556–8.3
Traffic accident injury hospitalization, costs, and discharges, by payment source and State, mid 1980s-90, 7768–122
Traffic accidents, casualties, and rates, by hwy type and State, 1989, annual rpt, 7554–2
Traffic accidents direct and indirect costs, by cost type, payment source, and severity, 1980s, 7558–114
Traffic deaths and speed impacts of speed limits, for States with 55 and 65 mph limits, 1986-90, annual rpt, 7764–15
Traffic fatal accidents, circumstances, and characteristics of persons and vehicles involved, 1991, semiannual rpt, 7762–11
Traffic fatal accidents, deaths, and rates, by circumstances, characteristics of persons and vehicles involved, and location, 1990, annual rpt, 7764–10
Traffic speed and accident impacts of speed limits, for State with 55 and 65 mph limits, 1983-89, 7768–121

Travel to US and Canada, market analysis with detailed trip and traveler characteristics, country rpt series, 2906–2
Travel to US, by characteristics of visit and traveler, country, port city, and State of destination, quarterly rpt, 2902–1
Travel to US, by characteristics of visit and traveler, world area of origin, and US destination, 1991 survey, annual rpt, 2904–12
Travel to US, market research data available from US Travel and Tourism Admin, 1992, annual rpt, 2904–15
Travel to US, spending by world area of residence, and economic impact, by spending category and State, 1989, 2908–28
Truck accidents, casualties, and damage, by circumstances and characteristics of persons and vehicles involved, 1989, annual rpt, 7554–9
Trucks (long combination) hwy use and size restrictions, and accidents, by State, 1980s-90, GAO rpt, 26113–568
Urban areas transit systems and hwys, Federal aid by selected State, aggregate FY76-91, GAO rpt, 26113–570
Urban areas transit systems grants of Federal Transit Admin, by city and State, FY91, annual rpt, 7884–10

Education

Adult education and literacy programs funding, enrollment, and student characteristics and benefits, 1987-90, fact sheet, 4806–4.4
Adult education and literacy programs funding, enrollment by State, and student characteristics and benefits, 1987-90, fact sheet, 4806–4.2
Adult literacy and English as a second language programs, Education Dept and State programs, enrollment, and funding, by State, 1988-91, 4808–41
American Historical Assn financial statements, and membership by State, 1990, annual rpt, 29574–2
Bilingual education enrollment, and eligible students not enrolled, by State, 1990-91, annual rpt, 4804–14
Black higher education instns enrollment, finances, staff, and degrees, by instn and selected student characteristics, 1970s-90, 4848–46
Digest of Education Statistics, 1992 annual data compilation, 4824–2
Education data, enrollment, finances, teachers, and other characteristics, by State, 1969-89, 4828–33
Educational attainment, by social and demographic characteristics and location, 1991 and trends from 1940, biennial Current Population Rpt, 2546–1.460
Elementary and secondary education enrollment, staff, finances, operations, programs, and policies, 1987/88 biennial survey, series, 4836–3
Elementary and secondary education enrollment, teachers, high school grads, and spending, by instn control and State, 1992/93, annual rpt, 4834–19
Elementary and secondary public school agencies, by enrollment size and location, fall 1990, annual listing, 4834–1
Elementary and secondary public school systems enrollment, finances, staff, and high school grads, by State, FY89-90, annual rpt, 4834–6
Elementary and secondary public schools and enrollment, by State, 1990/91, annual rpt, 4834–17
Enrollment and grads of public schools, by region and State, 1984-2002, annual rpt, 4824–4
Enrollment in public elementary and secondary schools, by State, 1980s-93, annual press release, 4804–19
Head Start enrollment, funding, and staff, FY91, annual rpt, 4584–5
Head Start handicapped enrollment, by handicap, State, and for Indian and migrant programs, 1988/89, annual rpt, 4584–4
High school dropout rates, and subsequent completion, by student and school characteristics, alternative estimates, 1991, annual rpt, 4834–23
Higher education enrollment, by level, race, and sex, fall 1980-90, biennial rpt, 4844–15
Higher education enrollment, faculty, finances, and degrees, by instn level and control, and State, FY88, annual rpt, 4844–13
Higher education enrollment, tuition, control, location, and other instn characteristics, 1991/92, biennial listing, 4844–3
Higher education instn revenue by source and spending by function, by State and instn control, FY82-90, annual rpt, 4844–6
Historical Publications and Records Natl Commission grants, by State, FY91, annual rpt, 9514–2
Homeless adults educational services, program activities, and participation, by State, FY88-89, annual rpt, 4804–39
Humanities Natl Endowment activities and grants, FY91, annual rpt, 9564–2
Illiteracy among adults, by State, 1985, 4806–4.3
Indian education funding of Fed Govt, with enrollment, program grants, and fellowships by State, 1980s-FY91, annual rpt, 14874–1
Libraries (public) finances, staff, and operations, by State and population size, 1990, annual rpt, 4824–6
Libraries (public) services for Indians and Hawaii Natives, project listing and funding by tribe and State, FY90, annual rpt, 4874–5
Libraries (research) funding of Education Dept, by project, instn, and State, FY90, annual listing, 4874–2
Libraries for blind and handicapped, readership, circulation, staff, funding, and holdings, FY91, annual listing, 26404–3
Library science training grants for disadvantaged students, by instn and State, FY91, annual listing, 4874–1
Natl Education Goals progress indicators, by State, 1992, annual rpt, 15914–1
Science and math teacher dev project of Education Dept, school district participation by State, 1989/90, GAO rpt, 26121–488
Special education programs, enrollment by age, staff, funding, and needs, by type of handicap and State, 1990/91, annual rpt, 4944–4
Student aid Pell grants and applicants, by tuition, income level, instn type and control, and State, 1990/91, annual rpt, 4804–1
Student guaranteed loan activity, by program, guarantee agency, and State, quarterly rpt, 4802–2
Student guaranteed loans, defaults, and collections, by type of loan, lender, and guarantee agency, with data by State and top lender, FY91, annual rpt, 4804–38
Student loans of Fed Govt in default, losses, and rates, by instn and State, as of June 1991, annual rpt, 4804–18
Student supplemental grants, loans, and work-study awards, Federal share by instn and State, 1992/93, annual listing, 4804–17
Teachers in higher education, and salaries, by faculty rank, sex, instn type and control, and State, 1990/91, annual rpt, 4844–8
Tuition and other student charges, by public and private 2- and 4-year higher education instn, and State, 1991/92, annual listing, 4844–10
Vocational education enrollment, student and teacher characteristics, and outcomes, for secondary and postsecondary instns, 1970s-90, 4828–42
Women's educational equity program grants and contracts, by project, type, and State, 1988-92, annual rpt, 4804–2

Energy Resources and Demand

Coal and coke supply, demand, movements, prices, and stocks, by end-use sector and State, quarterly rpt, 3162–37
Coal mining restrictions on public land, impacts on production, costs, and demand, by region, 1985-88 and projected to 2075, 5668–125
Coal production and mines by county, prices, productivity, miners, and reserves, by mining method and State, 1990-91, annual rpt, 3164–25
Coal production by State and region, weekly rpt, 3162–1
Coal production, reserves, use, and prices by State, exports by country, and employment, 1900s-90, biennial rpt, 3164–79
Coal production, stocks, and shipments, by State of origin and destination, end-use sector, and mode of transport, quarterly rpt, 3162–8
Coal reserves, by type, region, and State, as of Jan 1991, annual rpt, 3164–74.1
Conservation aid of Fed Govt to public and nonprofit private instns, by building type and State, 1991, annual rpt, 3304–15
Conservation of energy, State programs aid from Fed Govt, and energy savings, by State, 1990, annual rpt, 3304–1
Consumption of energy, by detailed fuel type, end-use sector, and State, 1960-90, State Energy Data System annual rpt, 3164–39
DOE contracts and grants, by category, State, and for top contractors, FY91, annual rpt, 3004–21
Electric power demand, and industrial and employment impacts of capacity shortfalls and new power plants, by selected State, 1960s-80s and projected to 2000, hearing, 21248–163
Electric power plants (steam) fuel receipts, costs, and quality, by fuel, plant, utility, and State, 1991, annual rpt, 3164–42
Electric power plants and capacity, by fuel used, owner, location, and operating status, 1991 and for units planned 1992-2001, annual listing, 3164–36

Electric power plants certification applications filed with FERC, for small production and cogeneration facilities, FY80-91, annual listing, 3084–13
Electric power plants natural gas use, by State, 1980 and 1990, annual rpt, 3334–1
Electric power plants production, capacity, sales, and fuel stocks, use, and costs, by State, 1986-90, annual rpt, 3164–11
Electric power plants production, fuel use, stocks, and costs by fuel type, and sales, by State, monthly rpt, with articles, 3162–35
Electric power sales and revenue, by end-use sector, consumption level, and utility, 1990, annual rpt, 3164–91
Electric utilities privately owned, finances and operations, detailed data, 1990, annual rpt, 3164–23
Fed Govt and Indian land oil, gas, and minerals production and revenue, by State, 1991 and trends from 1920, annual rpt, 5734–2
Fuel oil and kerosene sales and deliveries, by end-use, PAD district, and State, 1990, annual rpt, 3164–94
Gasohol and ethanol tax incentives, by State, as of 1991, annual rpt, 3164–97
Gasohol use, and fuel tax exemptions, by State, 1980-91, annual rpt, 3304–5.5
Gasoline and other motor fuel use by State, and tax rates by jurisdiction, monthly rpt, 7552–1
Gasoline service stations price competition and divorcement from oil companies, issues with data by firm, city, and State, 1991 hearing, 25528–120
Geothermal resources, power plant capacity and operating status, leases, and wells, by location, 1960s-95, 3308–87
Geothermal resources, power plant generation, capacity, and dev potential, by location, 1988-90 and projected to 2030, 3168–122
Heating fuels production, imports, stocks, and prices, by selected PAD district and State, seasonal weekly rpt, 3162–45
Housing (low income) energy aid, funding sources, costs, and participation, by State, FY90, annual rpt, 4584–1
Housing (low income) energy aid, program characteristics by assistance type and State, FY91, annual rpt, 4584–2
Hydroelectric power plants retired, characteristics and location, as of 1992, annual listing, 3084–12
Industrial electric power producers capacity, generation, and sales by industry div and State, and emissions, by census div, 1989-90, article, 3162–35.301
Inventions recommended by Natl Inst of Standards and Technology for DOE support, awards, and evaluation status, 1991, annual listing, 2214–5
Natural and supplemental gas production, prices, trade, use, reserves, and pipeline company finances, by firm and State, monthly rpt with articles, 3162–4
Natural gas interstate pipeline capacity, use, contract deliveries, and prices, by region, State, and firm, 1990, 3168–125
Natural gas interstate pipeline company reserves and production, by firm, 1963-91 and deliverability projected to 2011, last issue of annual rpt, 3164–33
Natural gas supply, demand, prices, and distribution, by State, 1986-90 annual rpt, 3164–4
Nuclear reactors for domestic use and export by function and operating status, with owner, operating characteristics, and location, 1991 annual listing, 3354–15
Offshore oil and gas leases, revenue sharing payments by State, 1992 annual press release, 5306–4.14
Offshore oil and gas leasing and exploration activity, production, revenue, and environmental studies, by location, quarterly rpt, 5732–1
Oil and gas reserves, production, and ultimate recovery, by location, with field technical characteristics, series, 3166–14
Oil crude, gas liquids, and refined products supply, demand, and movement, by PAD district and State, 1991, annual rpt, 3164–2
Oil, gas, and gas liquids reserves and production, by State and substate area, 1991, annual rpt, 3164–46
Oil products prices, sales, and purchases of refiners, processors, and distributors, by product, end-use sector, PAD district, and State, 1991, annual rpt, 3164–85
Oil products sales and purchases of refiners, processors, and distributors, by product, end-use sector, PAD district, and State, monthly rpt, 3162–11
Oil, refined products, and gas liquids supply, demand, trade, stocks, and refining, by detailed product, State, and PAD district, monthly rpt with articles, 3162–6
Oil resources recovery impacts of environmental regulation, under alternative oil price, technology, and regulatory assumptions, projected 1990-2015, 3338–2
Rural Electrification Admin activities and finances, and loans by State, FY91 and trends from FY36, annual rpt, 1244–3
Rural Electrification Admin loans, and borrower operating and financial data, by distribution firm and State, 1991, annual rpt, 1244–1
Solar collector and photovoltaic cell shipments by end-use sector and State, and trade, 1990, annual rpt, 3164–62
Southeastern Power Admin sales by customer, plants, capacity, and Southeastern Fed Power Program financial statements, FY91, annual rpt, 3234–1
Uranium mining and milling industries finances and operations, with selected foreign comparisons, 1970s-90 and projected to 2005, annual rpt, 3164–82
Uranium reserves and industry operations, by region and State, various periods 1966-91, annual rpt, 3164–65.1
Western Area Power Admin activities by plant, financial statements, and sales by customer, FY91, annual rpt, 3254–1

Geography and Climate

Heating and cooling degree days weighted by population, by census div and State, with area-weighted temperature and precipitation, monthly rpt, 2152–13
Storms and unusual weather phenomena characteristics, casualties, and property damage, by State, monthly listing, 2152–3
Weather conditions and effect on agriculture, by US region, State, and city, and world area, weekly rpt, 2182–7
Weather data for farmland, average precipitation and temperature by State, monthly 1950-90, biennial rpt, 1544–28

Government and Defense

AID contracts and grants for technical and support services, by instn, country, and State, FY91, annual listing, 9914–7
Appalachia local dev projects, and funding by source, by program and State, FY91, annual rpt, 9084–1
Assistance (formula grants) of Fed Govt, use of adjusted census and intercensal data for allocation, with data by program and State, FY91, 25408–120
Boundary review commission activities in 12 States, 1989, 10048–85
Collective bargaining agreements of Federal employees, coverage, unions, and location, by agency, for contracts expiring 1992, semiannual listing, 9847–1
DOE real property owned and leased, by type, subagency, contractor, and site, FY91, annual rpt, 3004–28
DOT employment, by subagency, occupation, and selected personnel characteristics, FY91, annual rpt, 7304–18
Election (general) Federal and non-Federal party transfers, by State, 1992 House and Senate elections, press release, 9276–1.111; 9276–1.113
Election (presidential) campaign spending limits for candidates, and voting age population, by State, 1992 primary elections, press release, 9276–1.97
Election (senate) campaign spending limits for candidates, and voting age population, by State, 1992 general elections, press release, 9276–1.100
Election campaign finances to FEC, by type of filer, 1990 natl elections, biennial rpt series, 9276–2
Election campaign receipts and spending of congressional candidates, by candidate and State, late 1980s-92, press release, 9276–1.102; 9276–1.103; 9276–1.108; 9276–1.112
Election campaign-related internal communications of firms and assns, spending by organization, location, and candidate, 1991-92, biennial rpt, 9274–3
Election polling places accessibility and services availability for aged and disabled, by State, 1990 natl elections, hearing, 21428–11
Employment and payroll (civilian) of Fed Govt, by pay system and location, 1991, annual rpt, 9844–6.4
Employment and payroll, by function, level of govt, and State, 1991, annual rpt, 2466–1.1
Fed Govt civilian employees retirement, health, and life insurance benefits, coverage and finances of 4 programs, FY86-90, annual rpt, 9844–37
Fed Govt revenues by source and State, *Treasury Bulletin*, quarterly rpt, annual data, 8002–4.1
Fed Govt spending in States and local areas, by type, State, county, and city, FY91, annual rpt, 2464–3
Fed Govt spending in States, by type, program, agency, and State, FY91, annual rpt, 2464–2
Finances of govts, by level of govt, State, and for large cities and counties, annual rpt series, 2466–2

Finances, tax systems and revenue, and fiscal structure, by level of govt and State, 1992 and historical trends, annual rpt, 10044–1
Fiscal condition of State and local govts, with data by State and selected city, 1991 hearing, 21268–44
Gasoline and other motor fuel tax rates, by State, 1981-91, annual table, 7554–32
Local govt receipts from Fed Govt in lieu of property taxes on public lands, by State, FY92, annual press release, 5306–4.15
Mail order sales from out of State, tax revenue losses by State, 1990-92, 10048–84
Military and civilian personnel, by service branch, major installation, and State, as of Sept 1991, annual rpt, 3544–7
Military and DOD civilian personnel, by service branch and State, FY91, annual rpt, 3544–1.1
Military base and family housing construction, DOD appropriations by facility, service branch, and location, FY91-93, annual rpt, 3544–39
Military base construction, renovation, and closure, budget requests by project, service branch, State, and country, FY93, annual rpt, 3544–15
Military base support costs by function, and personnel and acreage by installation, by service branch, FY93, annual rpt, 3504–11
Military budget, organization, personnel, weapons, and property, by service branch, State, and country, 1992 annual summary rpt, 3504–13
Military contracts, payroll, and personnel, by service branch and location, with top 5 contractors and maps, by State and country, FY91, annual rpt, 3544–29
Military deaths, by service branch and home State, FY91, annual rpt, 3544–40
Military draft registrants by State, FY91, annual rpt, 9744–1
Military in-house commercial activities work-years, by service branch, State, and installation, FY91, annual rpt, 3544–25
Military personnel, by age and State, 1990-91, GAO rpt, 26123–391
Military prime contract awards, by category, contractor type, and State, FY89-91, annual rpt, 3544–11
Military prime contract awards, by contractor, service branch, State, and city, FY91, annual rpt, 3544–22
Military prime contract awards, by service branch and State, 1st half FY92, semiannual rpt, 3542–5
Military prime contract awards in labor surplus areas, by service branch, State, and area, 1st half FY92, semiannual rpt, 3542–19
Military reserve forces personnel strengths and characteristics, by component, quarterly rpt, 3542–4
Military spending reductions, economic impacts by defense contractor, industry, State, and congressional district, 1989-90 hearings, 23848–224
Military spending reductions, economic impacts of alternative plans, with data by industry and State, various periods 1949-87, article, 9385–1.313
Military spending reductions, economic impacts of Bush Admin plans by industry and State, FY92-97, 26306–6.167
Minority business Federal procurement set-aside contracts, by participant race and sex, industry, firm, and State, FY90, annual rpt, 9764–8
Minority business Federal procurement set-aside contracts, by State, FY90, GAO rpt, 26113–563
Natl Guard activities, personnel, and facilities, FY91, annual rpt, 3504–22
Navy personnel strengths, accessions, and attrition, detailed statistics, quarterly rpt, 3802–4
Navy weapons systems parts purchases from foreign suppliers and US contractors, by State and country, 1988, 2026–1.3
New England States govt retirement systems investment policy assessment, with system assets and liabilities, by State, 1992 article, 9373–25.301
Senior Executive Service members characteristics, entries, exits, and awards, FY79-91, annual rpt, 9844–36
State and local govt employment of minorities and women, by occupation, function, pay level, and State, 1991, annual rpt, 9244–6
State govt budget balances, balances as share of outlays, and costs of Medicaid coverage expansion, FY89-92, hearing, 21408–129
Tax (estate) returns property and tax data, by size of gross estate and State, 1989-90, article, 8302–2.305
Tax (excise) collections of IRS, by source, region, and State, quarterly rpt, annual table, 8302–1
Tax (income) returns filed, by type of filer, selected income items, quarterly rpt, 8302–2.1
Tax collection, enforcement, and litigation activity of IRS, with data by type of tax, region, and State, FY91, annual rpt, 8304–3
Tax collections of IRS, by type of tax, State, and substate area, FY91, annual rpt, 8104–2.2
Tax collections of State govts by detailed type of tax, and tax rates, by State, FY91, annual rpt, 2466–2.7
Tax revenue, by level of govt, type of tax, State, and selected large county, quarterly rpt, 2462–3
Tree planting on govt land contracted to small businesses, Federal grants, State funding, and projects, by State, FY91, annual rpt, 9764–10
Votes cast by party, candidate, and State, 1990 natl elections, biennial rpt, 21944–3
Voting age population, by sex, age, race, and State, forecast 1992 general elections, with votes cast from 1930, Current Population Rpt, 2546–3.170

Health and Vital Statistics

Abortions by method, patient characteristics, and State, and related deaths, 1970-89, annual article, 4202–7.324
AIDS and tuberculosis cases in prisons, test results, and control and treatment policies, by location, 1990 survey, annual rpt, 6064–22
AIDS cases by risk group, race, sex, age, State, and MSA, and deaths, quarterly rpt, 4202–9
Alcohol-related deaths, by cause, State, and county, annual averages 1979-80 and 1983-85, 4488–10.4
Alcohol use, by type of beverage, region, and State, 1977-88, annual rpt, 4486–1.11
Alcohol use, by type of beverage, region, and State, 1977-89, annual rpt, 4486–1.15
Allergy and Infectious Diseases Natl Inst activities, grants by recipient and location, and disease cases, FY84-91, annual rpt, 4474–30
Appalachian Regional Commission health care services projects by State, and project listing, 1960s-80s, 9088–38
Arson cases, civilian and fire fighter casualties, and property damage, 1986-89, 9438–14
Black lung benefits and claims by State, trust fund receipts by source, and disbursements, 1991, annual rpt, 6504–3
Blind persons by age, older blind persons by State, and State rehabilitation services, 1989, 21148–64
Blue Cross-Blue Shield benefit cost per enrollee compared to Medicare, by selected State, late 1970s-80s, annual rpt, 17266–1.3; 17266–1.7
Cancer (breast and cervical) deaths and rates by State, and in situ case rates by age, by race, 1970s-86, article, 4202–7.312
Cancer (breast and cervical) screening use and reasons for nonuse, by age, race, income, and State, 1987-89, article, 4202–7.313
Cytomegalovirus (congenital) disease cases, by infant, mother, and birth characteristics, type of impairment, State, and Canada Province, 1990-91, 4202–7.314
Deaths and rates, by cause, age, sex, marital status, race, and State, 1989, US Vital Statistics advance annual rpt, 4146–5.124
Deaths and rates, by cause and selected social, demographic, and employment characteristics, 1979-85, natl longitudinal study, 4478–186
Deaths and rates, by detailed location, cause, and demographic characteristics, 1989, US Vital Statistics annual rpt, 4144–3.1
Dental Research Natl Inst research and training grants, by recipient, FY90, annual listing, 4474–19
Disabled persons rehabilitation, Federal and State activities and funding, FY90, annual rpt, 4944–1
Diving (underwater) accidents, illnesses, and deaths, by circumstances, diver characteristics, and location, 1970-90, annual rpt, 2144–29
Fire fighter deaths, by cause, circumstances, and location, 1990, annual rpt, 9434–8
Fires, casualties, losses, and US Fire Admin activities, funding, and training programs, FY91, annual rpt, 9434–7
Fish and shellfish-related disease cases and outbreaks, by cause, species, and State, 1969-87, hearing, 21568–51
Foreign medical grads in US by age, sex, professional characteristics, State, and country, and US medical school foreign students, 1960s-80s, working paper, 6366–6.2
Health care professionals supply and education, by professional and other characteristics, and location, 1960s-92 and projected to 2020, biennial rpt, 4114–8
Health care spending per capita by State, 1990, and relation to income, services availability, rate control, and other factors, 1982, GAO rpt, 26121–444

Health condition and care indicators, 1950s-90 with health improvement and disease prevention goals for 1990, annual data compilation, 4144–11
Health risk behavior, prevalence of 7 habits, by age, State, and other characteristics, 1986-90, article, 4202–7.305
Heart, Lung, and Blood Natl Inst activities, and grants by recipient and location, FY91 and disease trends from 1940, annual rpt, 4474–15
Hepatitis cases by infection source, age, sex, race, and State, and deaths, by strain, 1989 and trends from 1966, 4205–2
HHS financial aid, by program, recipient, State, and city, FY91, annual regional listings, 4004–3
Homicides and rate, by weapon, circumstances, and victim characteristics, and years of potential life lost, 1980s, article, 4202–7.315
Hospital closures in 1990, operating characteristics, current use, and location, annual rpt, 4004–35
Hospital costs per capita in ratesetting States, and HMO enrollment, 1980s-90, article, 4652–1.311
Hospital deaths of Medicare patients, actual and expected rates by diagnosis, with hospital characteristics, by instn, FY90, annual State rpt series, 4654–14
Hospital employment and job vacancy rate, by occupation, and instn size and control, 1981-88, annual rpt, 4114–12
Hospital reimbursement by Medicaid and States rate-setting, adjustments for volume fluctuation, 1991, 17206–2.34
Hospital reimbursement by Medicaid, provisions by State, 1991, 17206–2.35
Infectious notifiable disease cases and current outbreaks, by region and State, weekly rpt, 4202–1
Infectious notifiable disease cases, by age, race, and State, and deaths, 1940s-91, annual rpt, 4204–1
Insurance (health) reforms of States to improve small business access, provisions with background data by State, 1991, GAO rpt, 26121–462
Insurance (health) under multiple employer welfare arrangements, coverage, unpaid claims, and regulation, by State, 1988-91, GAO rpt, 26121–443
Intestinal parasites lab isolations, by State and organism, 1987, article, 4202–7.306
Kidney end-stage disease treatment facilities approved by Medicare, dialysis and transplant services and ownership, 1991 annual listing, 4654–17
Kidney end-stage disease treatment facilities, Medicare enrollment and reimbursement, survival, and patient characteristics, 1984-90, annual rpt, 4654–16
Malaria cases in US, for military personnel and US and foreign natls, and by country of infection, 1966-90, annual rpt, 4205–4
Maternal and child health services block grant beneficiary and taxpayer equity among States, issues, alternative allocation formulas, and background data, 1992 GAO rpt, 26121–454
Mental health care facilities, beds, and bed/population ratios, by instn type and State, 1988, biennial rpt, 4506–3.48
Mental health care facilities partial care services, and patient characteristics, by instn type and State, 1970s-88, 4506–3.51
Mental health care facilities patient episodes, by type of facility and service, and State, 1988 with trends from 1955, 4506–3.50
Mental health care facilities, staff, patients, and finances, 1970s-91, biennial rpt, 4094–1
Mines (coal) and related operations occupational injuries and incidence, employment, and hours, 1990, annual rpt, 6664–4
Mines (metal) and related operations occupational injuries and incidence, employment, and hours, 1990, annual rpt, 6664–3
Mines (nonmetallic minerals) and related operations occupational injuries and incidence, employment, and hours, 1990, annual rpt, 6664–1
Mines (sand and gravel) and related operations occupational injuries and incidence, employment, and hours, 1990, annual rpt, 6664–2
Mines (stone) and related operations occupational injuries and incidence, employment, and hours, 1990, annual rpt, 6664–5
Mines and mills injuries by circumstances, employment, and hours, by type of operation and State, quarterly rpt, 6662–1
NIH grants and contracts, for top 15 States, FY82-91, annual rpt, 4434–9
NIH grants and contracts, quarterly listing, 4432–1
Nursing homes certification requirements, beds, and staff and training needs, by State, 1990, 17206–2.37
Occupational injury and illness rates and lost workdays, for selected industries, 1978-89, compilation of papers, 6728–41
Occupational safety enforcement activities of Federal and State agencies, inspections, closure orders, and violations contested and upheld, FY91, GAO rpt, 26121–461
Physicians, by specialty, age, sex, and location of training and practice, 1990, State rpt series, 4116–6
Physicians payment by Medicare under reasonable charge method, effect of customary charges in selected States, 1987-89, article, 4652–1.307
Radiation protection and health physics enrollment and degrees granted by instn and State, and grad placement, by student characteristics, 1991, annual rpt, 3004–7
Rural areas health care access for counties without hospitals and in which the only hospital closed, 1987-89, 17206–2.30
Soft drink industry occupational injury and illness rate and lost workdays, for 7 States, mid 1970s-90, article, 6722–1.319
Traffic accident deaths involving alcohol, by driver and victim blood alcohol levels and other characteristics, 1977-88, annual rpt, 4486–1.12
Traffic accident deaths involving alcohol, by driver and victim blood alcohol levels and other characteristics, 1977-89, annual rpt, 4486–1.14
Trichinosis cases in US, by type of meat and State, 1987-90, article, 4202–7.304
Vital statistics, preliminary 1990-91, annual rpt, 4144–7
Vital statistics provisional data, monthly rpt, 4142–1
Waterborne disease outbreaks and cases, by type, source, and location, 1989-90, article, 4202–7.301
Workers compensation benefits, by type of program and insurer, and State, 1988-89, annual article, 4742–1.311
Workers compensation coverage, benefits, costs, and insurers performance, 1939-88, article, 4742–1.322
Workers compensation laws of States and Fed Govt, 1992 annual rpt, 6504–11
Workers compensation laws of States, changes in coverage, benefits, and premium rates, by State, 1991, annual article, 6722–1.310
Workers compensation programs of States, admin, coverage, benefits, finances, processing, and staff, 1988-91, annual rpt, 6504–9

Housing and Construction

Census of Housing, 1990: inventory, occupancy, and costs, State fact sheet series, 2326–21
Census of Housing, 1990: median value and rent, by State and region, and compared to 1970 and 1980, fact sheet, 2328–83
Census of Housing, 1990: summary unit characteristics, by householder race and age, county, place, and urban-rural location, State rpt series, 2471–1
Census of Population and Housing, 1990: detailed geographic coverage, State CD-ROM series, 2551–9
Census of Population and Housing, 1990: population and housing characteristics, detailed geographic coverage, State CD-ROM series, 2551–10
Census of Population and Housing, 1990: summary characteristics, by county, subdiv, and place, State rpt series, 2551–7
Census of Population and Housing, 1990: summary characteristics, households, and land area, by county, subdiv, and place, State rpt series, 2551–1
Clay (construction) production and shipments by region and State, trade, and use, by product, quarterly Current Industrial Rpt, 2506–9.2
Coastal areas construction authorized by permit, by building type, 1970-89, 2176–8.3
Construction authorized by building permits, by type of construction, region, State, and MSA, quarterly rpt, 2042–1.3
Disabled persons access to Federal and federally funded facilities, complaints by disposition and State, FY91, annual rpt, 17614–1
Economic Dev Admin activities, and funding by program, recipient, State, and county, FY91 and cumulative from FY66, annual rpt, 2064–2
FmHA property acquired through foreclosure, 1-family homes, value, sales, and leases, by State, monthly rpt, 1182–7
Homeownership rate for 30 largest metro areas, and direction of change in rate by State, 1989-91, fact sheet, 2326–17.46
Low income rental housing in rural areas, FmHA loans and impacts of programs to maintain supply and to deter mortgage prepayment, 1988-91, GAO rpt, 26113–586

Mobile home placements by structural characteristics, and price, by census div and State, monthly rpt, annual tables, 2382–1
Mobile home shipments from manufacturers, by State, monthly rpt, quarterly table, 2382–5
Mortgage originations, by State, 1982-90, annual press release, 5144–21
Mortgages (conventional) terms at closing, by lender type, with periodic data by district, State, and for 32 MSAs, monthly rpt, 9442–2
Mortgages (conventional) terms at closing, for fixed- and adjustable-rate loans by purpose, FHLB district, State, and selected MSA, 1960s-91, annual rpt, 9444–2
Mortgages FHA-insured, and foreclosures, by State and county, 1991 and cumulative from 1934, annual rpt, 5144–15
Mortgages FHA-insured by State, financing costs, and loans in force and claims by loan-to-value ratio, 1970s-80s, hearings, 21248–162
Mortgages FHA-insured, financial, property, and borrower characteristics, by State, 1991, annual rpt, 5144–1; 5144–25
New England States economic indicators, Fed Reserve 1st District, monthly rpt, 9373–2
New housing units authorized, by region, State, selected MSA, and permit-issuing place, monthly rpt, 2382–5
New housing units authorized, by State, MSA, and permit-issuing place, 1991, annual rpt, 2384–2
Paint (lead-based) abatement programs for low- and moderate-income housing, HUD grants to public agencies, 1992 press release, 5006–3.102
Southeastern States, FHLB 4th District, employment and housing indicators by State, quarterly rpt, 9302–36
Vacant housing characteristics, and occupancy and vacancy rates, by tenure and location, 1960s-91, annual rpt, 2484–1

Industry and Commerce

Aluminum plant ownership, capacity, energy and aluminum sources, and startup and closing dates, by US and foreign plant and location, 1990, annual listing, 5604–49
Appalachian Regional Commission funding, by project and State, planned FY92, annual rpt, 9084–3
Auto and auto parts trade, production, and labor conditions, for US and compared to Canada and Mexico, 1950s-90, 6366–3.28
Chemicals (inorganic) production by State, shipments, trade, and use, by product, 1991, annual Current Industrial Rpt, 2506–8.14
Coal industry retirees pension and health trust funds financial condition, employer contributions, and beneficiaries, late 1970s-92, GAO rpt, 26121–469; 26121–471
County Business Patterns, 1989: employment, establishments, and payroll, by SIC 2- to 4-digit industry and county, annual State rpt series, 2326–8
County Business Patterns, 1990: employment, establishments, and payroll, by SIC 2- to 4-digit industry and county, annual State rpt series, 2326–6
Economic indicators forecasts and errors, for Fed Reserve 3rd District by State, 1980s-93, article, 9387–1.303
Enterprise zone programs of States, business investment and jobs created, and incentive programs, by State, 1992 annual rpt, 5124–9
Explosives and blasting agents use, by type, industry, and State, 1991, Mineral Industry Surveys, annual rpt, 5614–22
Exports of States by industry and country, data compilation, monthly CD-ROM, 2002–6
Foreign direct investment in US, major transactions by type, industry, country, and US location, 1990, annual rpt, 2044–20
Foreign trade zones (US) operations and movement of goods, by zone and commodity, FY90, annual rpt, 2044–30
Gross State Product by component, industry div, and State, 1977-89, article, 2702–1.303
Gross State product impacts on govt spending, with data by industry div and State, 1960s-86, working paper, 9377–9.133
Input-output model of BEA, regional multipliers by industry and State, and methodology, 1992 guide, 2708–47
Latin America and Caribbean country imports from US, by State of origin and country, 1987 and 1990, 2048–160
Lumber (industrial roundwood) production and timber harvest for North Central States, by product and county, State rpt series, 1206–10
Lumber (industrial roundwood) production in northeastern US, by product, State rpt series, 1206–15
Lumber (pulpwood) production and mill receipts in North Central States, by species, mill, State, and county, 1990, annual rpt, 1204–19
Lumber (pulpwood) production by species and county, and shipments, by northeastern State, 1990, annual rpt, 1204–18
Lumber (pulpwood) production in 3 North Central States, by species and county, 1990, 1208–397
Lumber (pulpwood and residue) prices, spending, and transport shares by mode, for southeast US, 1989-90, annual rpt, 1204–22
Lumber (veneer) receipts, production, and shipments, by species and southern State, with residue use, 1988, 1208–407
Lumber production and mill residue for Rocky Mountain States, by species, ownership, and county, series, 1206–17
Lumber production by State, trade, and use, by species, with mill stocks, 1991, annual Current Industrial Rpt, 2506–7.4
Lumber production, prices, trade, and employment, for northwestern US and British Columbia, quarterly rpt, 1202–3
Manufacturing annual survey, 1990: finances and operations, by SIC 2- and 3-digit industry and State, 2506–14.3
Manufacturing industries operations and performance, analytical rpt series, 2506–16
Mexico imports from US, by industry and State, 1987-91, 2048–154
Mineral Industry Surveys, commodity reviews of production, trade, stocks, and use, monthly rpt series, 5612–1
Mineral Industry Surveys, commodity reviews of production, trade, stocks, and use, quarterly rpt series, 5612–2
Mineral Industry Surveys, commodity reviews of production, trade, use, and industry operations, advance annual rpt series, 5614–5
Mineral Industry Surveys, State reviews of production, 1991, preliminary annual rpt, 5614–6
Minerals Yearbook, Vol 1, 1989: commodity reviews of production, use, trade, prices, and mining operations, annual rpt, 5604–33
Minerals Yearbook, Vol 1, 1990: commodity reviews of production, reserves, supply, use, and trade, annual rpt series, 5604–20
Minerals Yearbook, Vol 1, 1991: commodity reviews of production, reserves, supply, use, and trade, annual rpt series, 5604–15
Minerals Yearbook, Vol 2, 1989: State reviews of production and sales by commodity, and business activity, annual rpt series, 5604–16
Minerals Yearbook, Vol 2, 1990: State reviews of production and sales by commodity, and business activity, annual rpt series, 5604–22
Minority- and woman-owned businesses and owner characteristics, by industry, employment and sales size, and form of ownership, 1987 survey, 2328–59
Minority Business Dev Centers mgmt and financial aid, and characteristics of businesses, by region and State, FY91, annual rpt, 2104–6
Multinatl firms US affiliates finances and operations, by industry, country of parent firm, and State, 1987, 2708–48
Multinatl firms US affiliates, finances, and operations, by industry, world area of parent firm, and State, 1989-90, annual rpt, 2704–4
New England States economic indicators, Fed Reserve 1st District, monthly rpt, 9373–2
New England States employment growth after recessions, relation to selected economic factors, various periods 1969-90, article, 9373–1.315
North Central States business and economic conditions, Fed Reserve 9th District, quarterly journal, 9383–19
Retail trade sales and inventories, by kind of business, region, and selected State, MSA, and city, monthly rpt, 2413–3
Shoe production, shipments, trade, and use, by product, 1991, annual Current Industrial Rpt, 2506–6.8
Small business finances, operations, owner characteristics, and Federal contracts, 1980s-90, annual rpt, 9764–6
Southeastern States, Fed Reserve 5th District, economic indicators by State, quarterly rpt, 9389–16
Southeastern States, Fed Reserve 6th District, economic indicators by State and MSA, quarterly rpt, 9371–14
Southeastern States, Fed Reserve 8th District banking and economic conditions, quarterly rpt with articles, 9391–16
Statistical Abstract of US, 1992 annual data compilation, 2324–1
Textile mill production, trade, sales, stocks, and material used, by product, region, and State, periodic Current Industrial Rpt series, 2506–5

Vending facilities run by blind on Federal and non-Federal property, finances and operations by agency and State, FY91, annual rpt, 4944–2
West Central States economic indicators, Fed Reserve 10th District, quarterly rpt, 9381–16.2
West Central States, gross State product and growth rates by industry div and State, 1979-89, article, 9381–1.306

Labor and Employment

Collective bargaining agreements expiring during year, and workers covered, by firm, union, industry group, and State, 1992, annual rpt, 6784–9
Displaced worker training programs spending, participation, and placements by State, 1990, GAO rpt, 26121–481
Displaced workers, layoffs and recalls by layoff reason, industry, firm size, and State, 2nd half 1988, 6406–6.36
Displaced workers, layoffs and unemployment insurance claims by reason, industry, selected characteristics, and State, quarterly press release, 6742–23
Displaced workers, layoffs and unemployment insurance claims by reason, industry, selected characteristics, MSA, and State, 1990, annual rpt, 6744–18
Employment and Earnings, detailed data, monthly rpt, 6742–2.5; 6742–2.6; 6742–2.8
Employment and Training Admin activities, funding, and participant characteristics, by program, FY86-88, annual rpt, 6404–17
Employment and unemployment, by age, sex, race, marital and family status, industry div, and State, Monthly Labor Review, 6722–1.2
Employment and unemployment, by State, monthly 1978-91, article, 6742–2.305
Employment and unemployment, for 11 large States, monthly press release, 6742–5
Employment, earnings, and hours, by selected SIC 1- to 4-digit industry, State, and for 275 MSAs, 1987-92, 6748–81
Employment, unemployment, and labor force characteristics, by State, 1991, annual rpt, 6744–7.2
Grocery stores occupational injury and illness rates, and lost workdays by State, 1990, article, 6722–1.339
Job Training Partnership Act education and worker training program participants, by selected characteristics, 1986-88, 15496–1.15
Labor Dept activities and funding, by program and State, FY91, annual rpt, 6304–1
Labor Relations Natl Board activities, cases, elections conducted, and litigation, FY90, annual rpt, 9584–1
Leave for family reasons, State law provisions and employer compliance, for 4 States, 1987-91, hearing, 25548–105
Mediation and arbitration activities of Fed Mediation and Conciliation Service, and cases by issue, region, and State, FY85-90, annual rpt, 9344–1
Metal structural fabrication industry occupational injury and illness rates and lost workdays, by State, 1989, 6722–1.301
Middle Atlantic States economic conditions, Fed Reserve 3rd District, quarterly rpt, 9387–10
Minority group and women employment, by occupation, SIC 1- to 3- digit industry, State, and MSA, 1991, annual rpt, 9244–1
Southeastern States, FHLB 4th District, employment and housing indicators by State, quarterly rpt, 9302–36
Southeastern US employment by industry div, earnings, and hours, for 8 States, quarterly press release, 6942–7
Southeastern US employment conditions, with comparisons to other regions, press release series, 6946–3
Southeastern US textile mill employment, earnings, and hours, for 8 States, quarterly press release, 6942–1
Southwestern US employment by industry div, earnings, and hours, by State, monthly rpt, 6962–2
Trade adjustment aid for workers, petitions by disposition, selected industry, union, and State, monthly rpt, 6402–13
Unemployment, by State and metro area, monthly press release, 6742–12
Unemployment, employment, and labor force, by region and State, 1990-91, annual press release, 6726–1.45
Unemployment, employment, and labor force, by State, MSA, and city, monthly rpt, 6742–22
Unemployment insurance claims and covered unemployment by program, and extended benefit triggers, by State, weekly rpt, 6402–15
Unemployment insurance claims, by program, weekly press release, 6402–14
Unemployment insurance programs of States and Fed Govt, benefits adequacy, and work disincentives, series, 6406–6
Unemployment insurance programs of States, benefits, coverage, and tax provisions, as of July 1992, semiannual listing, 6402–7
Unemployment insurance programs of States, benefits, coverage, exhaustions, and finances, 1990, annual tables, 6404–10
Unemployment insurance programs of States, comparison of law provisions, as of Jan 1992, semiannual revisions to base edition, 6402–2
Unemployment insurance programs of States, quality appraisal results, FY91, annual rpt, 6404–16
Unemployment insurance trust funds financial condition, by State, monthly rpt, 8102–9.16
Vocational rehabilitation cases of State agencies, by disposition and State, FY91 and trends from FY21, annual rpt, 4944–5
Vocational rehabilitation programs of Fed Govt and States, activities and funding, FY91, annual rpt, 4944–1
Wages of workers covered by unemployment insurance, by industry div and State, 1990-91, annual press release, 6784–17.1
Western US employment impacts of changes in California employment, regression results, 1992 article, 9393–8.306

Law Enforcement

Assaults and deaths of law enforcement officers, by circumstances, agency, victim and offender characteristics, and location, 1991, annual rpt, 6224–3
Asset Forfeiture Program of Justice Dept, seizures, finances, and disbursements, FY85-91, annual rpt, 6004–21
Bombing incidents and casualties by target and circumstances, and explosives theft and recovery, by State, 1987-91, annual rpt, 8484–4
Bombing incidents, casualties, and damage, by target, circumstances, and State, 1991, annual rpt, 6224–5
Corrupt govt officials prosecuted and convicted, by judicial district and level of govt, 1970-90, annual rpt, 6004–13
Court civil and criminal caseloads for Federal district, appeals, and bankruptcy courts, by type of suit and offense, circuit, and district, 1991, annual rpt, 18204–11
Court civil and criminal caseloads for Federal district, appeals, and special courts, 1991, annual rpt, 18204–8
Crime, criminal justice admin and enforcement, and public opinion, data compilation, 1992 annual rpt, 6064–6
Crimes, arrests by offender characteristics, and rates, by offense, and law enforcement employees, by population size and jurisdiction, 1991, annual rpt, 6224–2
Criminal case processing in Federal district courts, and dispositions, by offense, district, and offender characteristics, 1989, annual data compilation, 6064–29
Criminal justice systems of States, activities, employment, funding, and data collection, by State, 1970s-91, annual rpt, 6064–40
Driving while intoxicated enforcement incentive grants of Natl Hwy Traffic Safety Admin, by State, 1992 press release, 7306–10.4
Drug abuse treatment, prevention, and enforcement grants by State, and State allocations by program, FY87-90, 6068–252
Drug enforcement grants of Fed Govt, and allocations to local govts, by State, FY91, annual rpt, 6064–38
Drug testing of criminal offenders, grants and program costs by State, FY92, 236–3.3
Electronic monitoring of criminal releases by State, completions, violations, and new offenses, 1989, 6066–20.23
Executions by whether habeas corpus used to appeal conviction, and time from crime to execution, with data by race and State, 1977-91, 6008–34
Expenditures, employment, and payroll, by activity, level of govt, and State, FY90, annual rpt, 6066–25.50
Financial instns fraud and abuse, Justice Dept enforcement activity, staff, and case dispositions by instn type, 1988-92, 6008–35
Juvenile facilities population, by resident characteristics and facility type, late 1970s-89, 6068–250
Juvenile facilities population, by resident characteristics and facility type, 1977-89, annual rpt, 6064–35
Juvenile Justice and Delinquency Prevention Office activities, with background data, FY90, annual rpt, 6064–34
Marijuana crop eradication activities of DEA and local agencies by State, and drug potency and prices, 1982-91, annual rpt, 6284–4
Money laundering investigation activities of States and Fed Govt, and use of IRS large cash transaction rpts, by State, 1985-91, GAO rpt, 26119–430

Office of Justice Programs activities and funding, FY91, annual rpt, 6064–18
Parole and probation population, entries, and exits, by State, 1990, annual rpt, 6066–25.43
Police employment, spending, and operations, for State, city, county, and special district agencies, 1990, annual rpt, 6064–39
Prison and community-based facilities, population, employment, spending, and other characteristics, by State and for Fed Govt, 1990, quinquennial rpt, 6068–218
Prisoners AIDS and tuberculosis cases, test results, and control and treatment policies, by location, 1990 survey, annual rpt, 6064–22
Prisoners and staff in Federal instns, by selected characteristics, region, and instn, FY89, annual rpt, 6244–1
Prisoners, characteristics, and movements, by State, 1990, annual rpt, 6064–26
Prisoners in Federal and State instns by selected characteristics, releases, staff, and instn size, with data by region and State, late 1970s-91, 6068–248
Prisoners in Federal and State instns by sex, admissions, and instn capacity and overcrowding, by State, 1980s-91, annual rpt, 6066–25.47
Sentences for Federal crimes, guidelines use and results by offense and district, and Sentencing Commission activities, 1991, annual rpt, 17664–1
State and local criminal justice spending, by State, 1988-90, 6066–23.7
US attorneys case processing and collections, by case type and Federal district, FY91, annual rpt, 6004–2
Victims of crime, compensation and support service programs funding, by offense and State, FY88-90, biennial rpt, 6064–37
Victims of crime, compensation and support service programs operations, series, 6066–31
Wiretaps authorized, costs, arrests, trials, and convictions, by offense and jurisdiction, 1991, annual rpt, 18204–7

Natural Resources, Environment, and Pollution

Acid rain environmental, economic, and health effects, and pollutant emissions, 1985-89 and alternative projections to 2030, 14358–4
Army Corps of Engineers activities and projects, FY88 and trends from 1800s, annual rpt, 3754–1.1
Army Corps of Engineers activities and projects, FY89 and trends from 1800s, annual rpt, 3754–1.2
Army Corps of Engineers activities and projects, FY90 and trends from 1800s, annual rpt, 3754–1.3
Asbestos in schools, abatement funding and costs by selected State, 1988-91, GAO rpt, 26113–560
Birds (duck) breeding population, by species, State, and Canada Province, 1991-92 and trends from 1955, annual rpt, 5504–30
Birds (mourning dove) population, by hunting and nonhunting State, 1966-92, annual rpt, 5504–15
Birds (sandhill crane) hunting activity and permits, by State and county, 1990/91-1991/92, annual rpt, 5504–31
Birds (waterfowl) hunter harvest, age and sex ratios by species, State, and flyway, 1987-91, annual rpt, 5504–32
Birds (waterfowl) hunter harvest and unretrieved kills, and duck stamps sold, by species, State, Canada Province, and flyway, 1990-91, annual rpt, 5504–28
Birds (waterfowl) population, habitat conditions, and migratory flight forecasts, for Canada and US by region, 1992 and trends from 1955, annual rpt, 5504–27
Birds (woodcock) population in US and Canada from 1968, and hunter harvest, by State, 1992, annual rpt, 5504–11
Coal Surface Mining Reclamation and Enforcement Office activities and funding, by State and Indian tribe, FY91, annual rpt, 5644–1
Coastal and riparian areas environmental conditions, fish, wildlife, use, and mgmt, for individual ecosystems, series, 5506–9
Coastal areas and watersheds pollution indicators, by location, 1980s-90, 2178–35
Coastal areas environmental conditions and mgmt, for individual areas, conf series, 2146–8
Coastal areas environmental impacts of economic dev and population growth, 1960-80s and projected to 2010, series, 2176–8
Coastal areas environmental mgmt programs of States, activities and Federal funding, FY90-91, biennial rpt, 2174–8
Drought aid of Reclamation Bur, by western State, 1992 press release, 5306–4.17
Electric utilities privately owned, air pollution emissions and abatement equipment by fuel type and State, 1986-90, annual rpt, 3164–11.5
Environmental Quality, status of problems, protection programs, research, and intl issues, 1991 annual rpt, 484–1
EPA pollution control grant program activities, monthly rpt, 9182–8
Fires (wild) and acreage burned, by type of land, ownership, cause, region, and State, 1984-90, annual rpt, 1204–4
Fish (striped bass) stocks status on Atlantic coast, and sport and commercial catch by State, 1979-90, annual rpt, 5504–29
Fish and Wildlife Service restoration and hunter safety funding, by State, FY92, semiannual press release, 5502–1
Fish and Wildlife Service restoration programs funding, land purchases, and project listing, by State, FY90, annual rpt, 5504–1
Forest Service activities and finances, by region and State, FY91, annual rpt, 1204–1
Forests (natl) and other lands under Forest Service mgmt, acreage by forest and location, 1991 and historic trends, annual rpt, 1204–2
Forests (natl) revenue, by source, forest, and State, FY91, annual rpt, 1204–34
Forests (natl) revenue share paid to States, and acreage, by forest, county, and congressional district, FY92, annual rpt, 1204–33
Great Lakes Science Advisory Board research activities and water quality goals, FY91, biennial rpt, 14644–6
Hazardous substances industrial releases and reduction methods under EPA regulation, by chemical, source, industry, and location, 1989, annual rpt, 9234–6
Hazardous waste generated, and treated by process, by State, 1987-89 and projected to 2009, hearing, 21408–132
Hazardous waste site remedial action under Superfund, current and proposed sites descriptions and status, periodic listings, series, 9216–3
Hazardous waste site remedial action under Superfund, current and proposed sites priority ranking and status by location, series, 9216–5
Helium and other components of natural gas, analyses of individual wells and pipelines, 1985-91, annual rpt, 5604–2
Helium and other components of natural gas, analyses of individual wells and pipelines, 1986-90, 5608–132
Industrial waste generation, disposal, and regulation, by industry and State, mid 1980s-90, 26358–256
Land Mgmt Bur activities and funding by State, FY90, annual rpt, 5724–13
Land Mgmt Bur activities in southwestern US, FY91, annual rpt, 5724–15
Landmarks (natl historic and natural) damaged and threatened, with owner, location, damage type, and recommended remedial action, 1990, annual listing, 5544–16
Marine mammals research, Federal funding by topic, recipient, and agency, FY91, annual rpt, 14734–2
Metals (nonferrous) production in 5 western States, and prices, for 5 metals, 1848-1990, 5608–178
Military installations hazardous waste site remedial action, activities and funding by site and State, FY91, annual rpt, 3544–36
Minerals production and revenue on Federal and Indian land, by State, 1991 and trends from 1920, annual rpt, 5734–2
Minerals resources and availability on public lands, State rpt series, 5606–7
Nuclear Waste Fund utility payments and liabilities by State, and uranium enrichment customers costs of regulation and waste mgmt, 1991 hearings, 21368–137
Pollution abatement capital and operating costs, by SIC 2- to 4-digit industry and State, 1990, annual Current Industrial Rpt, 2506–3.6
Public lands acreage and use, and Land Mgmt Bur activities and finances, annual State rpt series, 5724–11
Public lands acreage, grants, use, revenues, and allocations, by State, FY91 and trends, annual rpt, 5724–1
Radioactive low-level waste disposal activities of States and interstate compacts, with data by disposal facility and reactor, 1990, annual rpt, 3004–36
Radioactive spent fuel discharges, storage capacity, and inventories, by reactor, 1968-89, 3166–6.62
Radioactive spent fuel storage capacity and inventories, by reactor, as of 1987, 3166–6.59
Radioactive waste and spent fuel generation, inventory, and disposal, 1960s-90 and projected to 2020, annual rpt, 3364–2
Recycling of paper by grade, with newsprint collection, recycling capacity by company, and curbside pickup operations, by State, 1970s-80s and projected to 1995, hearing, 25318–84

Timber improvement program for private land, Fed Govt cost-sharing funds by region and State, monthly rpt, 1802–11
Timber improvement program for private land, participation and payments by State, FY91, annual rpt, 1804–20
Timber in northeastern US, resources and removals by species, ownership class, and county, State rpt series, 1206–12
Timber in southern US, resources and removals by species, ownership, State, and county, series, 1206–8
Timber insect and disease incidence and damage, and control activities, State rpt series, 1206–49
Timber insect and disease incidence and damage, annual regional rpt series, 1206–11
Timber insect and disease incidence and damage, by State, 1990, annual rpt, 1204–8
Timber planting and stand improvement, by ownership and State, FY91, annual rpt, 1204–7
Timber sales of Forest Service, expenses, and operations, by State and natl forest, FY91, annual rpt, 1204–36.3
Wastewater treatment and collection facility construction funding needs and Fed Govt grants, by State, 1990 and projected to 2010, biennial rpt, 9204–7
Wastewater treatment plants construction loan funds for local govts, costs and State officials views by State, projected 1991-2000, GAO rpt, 26113–561
Water (groundwater) pesticide contamination, vulnerability indicators by State and county, 1987-89, GAO rpt, 26131–91
Water (groundwater) supply, quality, chemistry, and use, State and local area rpt series, 5666–28
Water (groundwater) use by purpose and State, and depletion, 1980s, 10048–82
Water pollution from farming, funding for control under Rural Clean Water Program by region and State, monthly rpt, 1802–14
Water quality, chemistry, hydrology, and other characteristics, local area studies, series, 5666–27
Water resources data collection and analysis activities of USGS Water Resources Div Districts, with project descriptions, series, 5666–26
Water resources dev projects of Army Corps of Engineers, characteristics, and costs, 1950s-89, biennial State rpt series, 3756–1
Water resources dev projects of Army Corps of Engineers, characteristics, and costs, 1950s-91, biennial State rpt series, 3756–2
Water supply and quality in streams and lakes, and groundwater levels in wells, by drainage basin, 1990, annual State rpt series, 5666–10
Water supply and quality in streams and lakes, and groundwater levels in wells, by drainage basin, 1990-91, annual CD-ROM, 5664–18
Water supply and quality in streams and lakes, and groundwater levels in wells, by drainage basin, 1991, annual State rpt series, 5666–12
Water supply in western US, and snow survey results, annual State rpt series, 1264–14
Water supply in western US, and snow survey results, monthly State rpt series, 1266–2
Water supply in western US, storage by reservoir and State, and streamflow conditions, as of Oct 1992, annual rpt, 1264–4
Water use by end use, well withdrawals, and public supply deliveries, by county, State rpt series, 5666–24
Water use from Colorado River Basin Project, by State and for Mexico, 1981-85, annual rpt, 5824–6
Wetlands acreage acquired by Fed Govt, and costs, by site and State, FY92, annual rpt, 14784–1
Wetlands acreage, and agreements and payments to farmers under Water Bank Program, by State, 1972-91, annual rpt, 1804–21
Wetlands acreage and losses, by wetland type, 1970s-80s, 5508–89
Wetlands preservation under Water Bank Program, acreage, agreements, and payments, by State, monthly rpt, 1802–5
Wetlands wildlife and migratory bird habitat acquisition, funding by State, 1992, press release, 5306–4.13; 5306–4.16
Wilderness areas acreage by State, and Colorado off-road vehicle use, owner expenses, and views on registration fee, 1986-88, hearing, 25318–85
Wildlife refuges and other land under Fish and Wildlife Service mgmt, acreage by site and State, as of Sept 1992, annual rpt, 5504–8
Zinc production and processing losses by State, trade, use, and prices, 1850s-1990, 5608–176

Population

Census of Population and Housing, 1990: detailed geographic coverage, State CD-ROM series, 2551–9
Census of Population and Housing, 1990: immigrants, by period of entry, citizenship, State, birthplace, and for top cities and counties, press release, 2328–88
Census of Population and Housing, 1990: Indian tribes population size, with data by State, press release, 2328–86
Census of Population and Housing, 1990: population and housing characteristics, detailed geographic coverage, State CD-ROM series, 2551–10
Census of Population and Housing, 1990: summary characteristics, by county, subdiv, and place, State rpt series, 2551–7
Census of Population and Housing, 1990: summary characteristics, households, and land area, by county, subdiv, and place, State rpt series, 2551–1
Census of Population, 1990: data adjustment in intercensal data for census undercounts, final decision with data by region and State, 2328–90
Census of Population, 1990: data adjustment in intercensal data for census undercounts, recommendations with alternative undercount estimates, 2628–36
Census of Population, 1990: population characteristics and living arrangements, for Native American, urban, and metro areas, series, 2531–2
Immigrants and nonimmigrants admitted to US, alien workers, visitors, deportations, and naturalizations, FY91, annual summary rpt, 6264–7
Immigration to US, alien workers, visitors, deportations, and naturalizations, by country, FY91 and trends from 1820, annual rpt, 6264–2
Income (household), by source, detailed characteristics, region, and State, 1991, annual Current Population Rpt, 2546–6.76
Income (median) for 4-person family, by State, 1969 and 1974-89, technical paper, 2626–2.60
Income (personal) per capita and by source, and employment, by industry div, State, MSA, and county, 1969-90, annual CD-ROM, 2704–7
Income (personal) per capita and total, and earnings by industry group, by region and State, 1989-91, annual article, 2702–1.328
Income (personal) per capita and total, by State, MSA, county, and metro-nonmetro location, 1988-90, annual article, 2702–1.317
Income (personal) totals, by region, census div, and State, quarterly article, 2702–1.34
Indian population and Indian-owned firms, by State for North Central States, selected years 1987-90, article, 9383–19.304
Migration, population change, and areas losing population, by region, State, and metro-nonmetro location, 1980s and trends from 1940, Current Population Rpt, 2546–2.164
Older persons socioeconomic characteristics, 1900s-90 and projected to 2050, biennial chartbook, 12904–1
Older population, and health, economic, and other characteristics, with foreign comparisons, 1980s-91 with trends and projections, Current Population Rpt, 2546–2.165
Population estimates and projections, by region and State, Current Population Rpt series, 2546–3
Population size, July 1991-92, by region, census div, and State, annual press release, 2324–10
Poverty status of population and families, by detailed characteristics, 1991, annual Current Population Rpt, 2546–6.77
Refugee arrivals and resettlement in US, by age, sex, sponsoring agency, State, and country, monthly rpt, 4592–1
Refugee arrivals in US by world area of origin and State of settlement, and Federal aid, FY91-92 and proposed FY93 allocations, annual rpt, 7004–16
Statistical Abstract of US, 1992 annual data compilation, 2324–1

Prices and Cost of Living

Dairy prices, by product and selected area, with related marketing data, 1991, annual rpt, 1317–1
Electric power billings for housing, and rankings, by State, as of Jan 1991, annual rpt, 1244–1.6
Energy prices and spending, by fuel type, end-use sector, and State, 1990, annual rpt, 3164–64
Energy prices for housing, by fuel and State, 1990 and forecast 1991-92, 3166–6.61
Farm prices received and paid, by commodity and State, 1991, annual rpt, 1629–5
Farm prices received and production value, by detailed crop and State, 1989-91, annual rpt, 1621–2

Fruit and vegetable wholesale prices in NYC by State, and shipments and arrivals by mode of transport, by commodity, weekly rpt, 1311–20
Fruit and vegetable wholesale prices in NYC, Chicago, and selected shipping points, by crop, 1991, annual rpt, 1311–8
Fruit and vegetable wholesale prices in NYC-Newark, and arrivals by mode of transport, by commodity and State, 1990, annual rpt, 1311–21
Heating oil retail prices, by State, and wholesale prices and dealer margins, monthly rpt, 3162–24.9
Heating oil retail prices, by State, and wholesale prices and dealer margins, monthly 1973-88, 3168–123.9
Milk order market prices and detailed operations, by State and market area, 1990-91, annual rpt, 1317–3
Poultry and egg prices and marketing, by selected region, State, and city, monthly and weekly 1991, annual rpt, 1317–2

Public Welfare and Social Security

AFDC beneficiaries by county, payments, application processing and disposition, hearings, and fraud cases, by State, FY90, annual rpt, 4584–3
AFDC beneficiaries demographic and financial characteristics, by State, FY90, annual rpt, 4584–7
AFDC Job Opportunities and Basic Skills Training program high-risk participants, by State and services received, FY91, GAO rpt, 26121–489
AFDC Job Opportunities and Basic Skills Training program State admin, and Unemployed Parent program caseloads and payments by State, 1991 GAO rpt, 26131–96
AFDC provisions, by State, FY89-90, annual rpt, 4584–8
Black lung benefits to miners, widows, and dependents, by State, quarterly rpt, 4742–1.3
Child abuse and neglect prevention and treatment, and disabled infant protection, grants by State, FY91, annual listing, 4584–6
Child abuse and neglect prevention and treatment, discretionary grants, FY91, annual listing, 4584–9
Child Support Enforcement Program collections for non-AFDC clients, administrative costs, and user fees, by State, with Federal shares of costs, 1990, GAO rpt, 26121–463
Child support overdue payments deducted from wages, and employer compliance, by State, FY85-89, 4588–1
Fed Govt programs under Ways and Means Committee jurisdiction, finances, operations, and participant characteristics, FY70s-91, annual rpt, 21784–11
Fed Govt spending in States, by type, program, agency, and State, FY91, annual rpt, 2464–2
Food aid program of USDA for women, infants, and children, participants and costs by State and Indian agency, FY90, annual tables, 1364–12
Food aid program of USDA for women, infants, and children, participants by race, State, and Indian agency, 1991, annual rpt, 1364–16
Food aid program of USDA for women, infants, and children, participants, clinics, and costs, by State and Indian agency, monthly tables, 1362–16
Food aid program of USDA for women, infants, and children, State contract awards and bid prices for infant formula, late 1980s-91, hearing, 25528–118
Food stamp eligibility and payment errors, by type, recipient characteristics, and State, FY90, annual rpt, 1364–15
Food stamp recipient household size, composition, income, and income and deductions allowed, summer 1989, annual rpt, 1364–8
Foster care programs of States, Federal funding and children served, by State, 1981-89, hearing, 21788–208
HHS financial aid, by program, recipient, State, and city, FY91, annual regional listings, 4004–3
Homeless families in transitional housing, HUD support services grants by recipient, 1991, press release, 5006–3.87
Homeless persons aid by program and Federal agency, and indicators of need, 1990, annual rpt, 14364–1
Homeless persons aid programs of Fed Govt, program descriptions and funding, by agency and State, FY87-91, annual GAO rpt, 26104–21
Medicaid coverage, funding, and costs, with reform recommendations, mid 1960s-92, 10048–83
Medicaid eligibility expansion for prenatal care, coverage, use, and costs, by State, 1990-91, 4008–120
Medicaid impacts on State budgets, and program financing, cost control measures, enrollment, and services coverage, by selected State, 1960s-80s and projected to 1997, 10176–3.6
Medicaid outlay differentials among States, with data by service type and eligibility category, FY89, article, 9373–1.303
Medicaid payment and participation by service type, and cost compared to Medicare, by State, FY89, 17266–1.4
Medicaid spending of States, impacts of cost containment and other factors, with data by eligibility type, mid 1970s-90, working paper, 9373–27.1
Medicare and Medicaid outlays per enrollee, for aged and disabled beneficiaries by State, 1991, annual Current Population Rpt, 2546–6.78
Medicare financial and admin issues, Inspector General rpts, series, 4006–11
Medicare payment of physicians under assigned fee, participation and additional billing, by specialty, service, and State, late 1980s-92, 17266–1.6
Medicare payment of physicians under fee schedule, impacts on charges by specialty and State, 1992 and 1996, hearing, 25368–178
Medicare payment of physicians under fee schedule, methodology with data by procedure and specialty, 1992, annual rpt, 17264–1
Nonprofit charitable organizations finances, with data by State and for top 10 instns, 1988, article, 8302–2.302
Nursing home reimbursement rates of Medicaid, and ratio to private resident payments, by State, FY89, article, 9373–1.311
OASDHI coverage of employment and earnings, and social security contributions, by age, sex, race, State, and county, 1988, annual rpt, 4744–29
OASDHI, Medicaid, SSI, and related programs benefits, beneficiary characteristics, and trust funds, selected years 1937-90, annual rpt, 4744–3
OASDI coverage of State and local govt employees under voluntary Federal-State agreements, 1987, article, 4742–1.315
School lunch programs food donations processing, contracts, and processors problems with State reporting requirements, with data by State, 1989-91, GAO rpt, 26113–555
Single mothers family income, and impacts of child care, govt and child support payments, taxes, and marriage, with data by State, 1970s-91, 21788–212
Supplemental Security Income and Medicaid eligibility and payment provisions, and beneficiaries living arrangements, by State, 1992, annual rpt, 4704–13
Supplemental Security Income child beneficiaries and benefits, by selected characteristics, family income status, and State, 1991, article, 4742–1.316
Supplemental Security Income payments and beneficiaries, by type of eligibility, State, and county, Dec 1990, annual rpt, 4744–27
Supplemental Security Income recipients, by race, sex, living arrangements, age, eligibility, and State, quarterly rpt, 4742–1.2
Supplemental Security Income work incentive programs, participant characteristics, by program, 1982-91, article, 4742–1.305
Tax exempt organizations finances, with data by type, size, State, and for largest organizations, late 1940s-80s, compilation of papers, 8308–35

Recreation and Leisure

Arts funding, by level of govt, State, and selected city, FY86-92, GAO rpt, 26119–371
Boat registrations, and accidents, casualties, and damage by cause, by vessel characteristics and State, 1991, annual rpt, 7404–1
Fishing (ocean sport) activities, and catch by species, by angler characteristics and State, annual coastal area rpt series, 2166–17
Fishing and hunting licenses issued, and costs, by State, FY91, annual tables, 5504–16
Forests (natl) recreational use, by type of activity and State, 1991, annual rpt, 1204–17
Historic and natural natl landmarks damaged and threatened, with owner, location, damage type, and recommended remedial action, 1990, annual listing, 5544–16
Historic Preservation Fund grants, by State, FY93, annual press release, 5544–9
Land and Water Conservation Fund allocations for outdoor recreation area dev, by State, FY93, annual table, 5544–15
Park natl system sites acreage and descriptions, 1991, biennial listing, 5544–5
Park natl system visits and overnight stays, by park and State, 1991, annual rpt, 5544–12

Science and Technology
Animal protection, licensing, and inspection activities of USDA, and animals used in research, by State, FY90, annual rpt, 1394–10
Education in science and engineering, grad programs enrollment by field, source of funds, and characteristics of student and instn, 1990, annual rpt, 9627–7
NASA funding by program and type of performer, and contract awards by State, FY91, annual rpt, 9504–6.2
NASA procurement contract awards, by type, contractor, State, and country, FY92 with trends from 1961, semiannual rpt, 9502–6
NSF grants and contracts, by field, recipient, and State, FY90, annual rpt, 9624–26
Nuclear engineering enrollment and degrees by instn and State, and women grads plans and employment, 1991, annual rpt, 3006–8.18
Nuclear engineering enrollment and degrees granted by instn and State, and grad placement, by student characteristics, 1991, annual rpt, 3004–5
Patents (US) granted to US and foreign applicants, by State and country, FY90-91, annual press release, 2244–2
Patents granted to US residents, by State, FY88-91, annual rpt, 2244–1.2
R&D and related funding of Fed Govt to higher education and nonprofit instns, by field, instn, agency, and State, FY90, annual rpt, 9627–17
R&D funding by higher education instns and federally funded centers, by field, instn, and State, FY90, annual rpt, 9627–13
R&D funding of Fed Govt for large-scale projects, issues and impacts on other research, with data for space station and super collider, 1991 hearings, 21268–43
Radiation protection and health physics enrollment and degrees granted by instn and State, and women grads plans and employment, 1991, annual rpt, 3006–8.19
Science and Engineering Indicators, employment, education, R&D funding, and industry impacts, with foreign comparisons, 1960s-91, biennial rpt, 9624–10.4
Semiconductor materials supply and demand, and semiconductor firms by State, late 1980s and projected to 1993, hearing, 21708–130
Small business R&D grants of Fed Govt, by program area, agency, MSA, and State, FY90, annual rpt, 9764–7
Space station *Freedom* technical characteristics, funding, and contracts by State, 1985-92 and projected 1997-2002, 9508–40

Veterans Affairs
Disability and death compensation cases of VA, by entitlement type, period of service, sex, age, and State, FY90, annual rpt, 8604–7
Health care services of VA, needs, availability, structure, and funding, findings and recommendations, 1991 compilation of papers, 8608–9
Insurance (life) for veterans and servicepersons, finances and coverage by program and State, 1991, annual rpt, 8604–4
Population and characteristics of veterans, and VA hospital and other activities, by State, FY91, annual rpt, 8604–3
VA programs spending, by State, county, and congressional district, FY91, annual rpt, 8604–6

BY URBAN-RURAL AND METRO-NONMETRO

Banking, Finance, and Insurance
Small Business Admin loan guarantee program participants finances, operations, characteristics, and views, 1991 survey, 9768–25

Communications and Transportation
Hwy construction material prices and indexes for Federal-aid system, by type of material and urban-rural location, quarterly rpt, 7552–7
Hwy speed averages and vehicles exceeding 55 mph, by State, quarterly rpt, 7552–14
Hwy Statistics, detailed data by State, 1991, annual rpt, 7554–1
Hwy Statistics, summary data by State, 1990-91, annual rpt, 7554–24
Mail volume to and from households, use, and views, by class, source, content, and household characteristics, FY87-90, annual rpt, 9864–10
Railroad-hwy grade-crossing accidents, detailed data by State and railroad, 1991, annual rpt, 7604–2
Telephone local service charges and low-income subsidies, by region, company, and city, 1980s-91, semiannual rpt, 9282–8
Traffic accidents, casualties, and rates, by hwy type and State, 1989, annual rpt, 7554–2
Traffic accidents, casualties, circumstances, and characteristics of persons and vehicles involved, 1990, annual rpt, 7764–18
Traffic accidents direct and indirect costs, by cost type, payment source, and severity, 1980s, 7558–114
Traffic accidents impacts of roadway lighting, by circumstances, 1991 rpt, 7558–118
Traffic deaths and speed impacts of speed limits, for States with 55 and 65 mph limits, 1986-90, annual rpt, 7764–15
Traffic fatal accidents, alcohol levels of drivers and others, by circumstances and characteristics of persons and vehicles, 1990, annual rpt, 7764–16
Traffic fatal accidents, circumstances, and characteristics of persons and vehicles involved, 1991, semiannual rpt, 7762–11
Traffic fatal accidents, deaths, and rates, by circumstances, characteristics of persons and vehicles involved, and location, 1990, annual rpt, 7764–10
Travel patterns, personal and household characteristics, and auto and public transport use, 1990 survey, series, 7556–6
Truck accidents, circumstances, and characteristics of vehicles and persons involved, 1979-86, 7768–124

Education
Condition of Education, detail for elementary, secondary, and higher education, 1920s-91 and projected to 2002, annual rpt, 4824–1
Digest of Education Statistics, 1992 annual data compilation, 4824–2
Discrimination in education, natl survey participation and data coverage, school district administrators views, 1991 survey, 4826–1.33
Education in science and math, natl assessment of elementary and high school students, 1985/86, series, 4896–6
Educational attainment, by social and demographic characteristics and location, 1991 and trends from 1940, biennial Current Population Rpt, 2546–1.460
Eighth grade class of 1988: educational performance and conditions, characteristics, attitudes, activities, and plans, natl longitudinal survey, series, 4826–9
Elementary and secondary education enrollment, staff, finances, operations, programs, and policies, 1987/88 biennial survey, series, 4836–3
Elementary and secondary public school agencies, by enrollment size and location, fall 1990, annual listing, 4834–1
Elementary and secondary students educational performance, and factors affecting proficiency, by selected characteristics, 1990 natl assessments, subject rpt series, 4896–8
Elementary and secondary students educational performance in math, science, reading, and writing, 1969-90, 4898–32
Enrollment, by grade, instn type and control, and student characteristics, 1989 and trends from 1947, annual Current Population Rpt, 2546–1.459
High school dropout rates, and subsequent completion, by student and school characteristics, alternative estimates, 1991, annual rpt, 4834–23
High school dropouts and rates, and data collection and reporting methods evaluation, 1992 rpt, 4838–49
Libraries (public) finances, staff, and operations, by State and population size, 1990, annual rpt, 4824–6
School districts efficient use of staff, model description and results for Texas, 1987-89, technical paper, 9379–12.80
Vocational education enrollment, and academic and other credits earned, by subject and student characteristics, high school classes of 1982 and 1987, 4838–50
Vocational education enrollment, student and teacher characteristics, and outcomes, for secondary and postsecondary instns, 1970s-90, 4828–42

Energy Resources and Demand
Building (commercial) energy use, costs, and conservation, by building characteristics, survey rpt series, 3166–8
Housing energy use, costs, and conservation, and household and housing characteristics, survey rpt series, 3166–7
Wood fuel production in Michigan, by species, land ownership, survey region, county, and location, 1986, 1208–412
Wood fuel production in Missouri, by species, land ownership, and location, 1987, 1208–399

Government and Defense
Taxes, spending, and govt efficiency, public opinion by respondent characteristics, 1992 survey, annual rpt, 10044–2

Health and Vital Statistics
Acute and chronic health conditions, disability, absenteeism, and health services use, by selected characteristics, 1990, annual rpt, 4147–10.182
Acute and chronic health conditions, disability, absenteeism, and health services use, by selected characteristics, 1991, annual rpt, 4147–10.183

Children (handicapped) with special needs, insurance coverage, and health care services use, by selected characteristics, 1988, 4146–8.216
Deaths and rates, by cause and selected social, demographic, and employment characteristics, 1979-85, natl longitudinal study, 4478–186
Deaths and rates, by detailed location, cause, and demographic characteristics, 1989, US Vital Statistics annual rpt, 4144–3.1
Dental caries and baby bottle tooth decay prevalence among Head Start children in southwest US, by characteristics of child and area, 1992 article, 4042–3.317
Drug, alcohol, and cigarette use and attitudes of youth, by substance type and selected characteristics, 1975-91 surveys, annual rpt, 4494–4
Drug, alcohol, and cigarette use, by selected characteristics, 1991 survey, annual rpt series, 4494–5
Educational attainment relation to health condition and care, indicators by selected characteristics, 1989, 4147–10.180
Fire fighter deaths, by cause, circumstances, and location, 1990, annual rpt, 9434–8
Health care professionals supply and education, by professional and other characteristics, and location, 1960s-92 and projected to 2020, biennial rpt, 4114–8
Health condition and care indicators, 1950s-90 with health improvement and disease prevention goals for 1990, annual data compilation, 4144–11
Hospital closings relation to hospital and community characteristics, by metro-nonmetro location, 1980-87, article, 4042–3.341
Hospital closures in 1990, operating characteristics, current use, and location, annual rpt, 4004–35
Hospital cost of charity cases and patients bad debts, and relation to operating margin, by selected MSA and urban-rural location, 1980s, 17206–2.32
Insurance (health) coverage of persons, by insurance type and selected characteristics, 1985-90, 2546–20.23
Physicians, by specialty, age, sex, and location of training and practice, 1990, State rpt series, 4116–6
Physicians recently graduating, specialties, school debt, and practice settings, and medical school funding sources, 1970s-91, hearing, 21368–135

Housing and Construction

American Housing Survey: unit and household characteristics of recent movers, and reason for move, by tenure, 1989, 2486–1.12
American Housing Survey: unit and households detailed characteristics, and unit and neighborhood quality, 1989, biennial rpt supplement, 2485–13
Apartment and condominium completions by rent class and sales price, and market absorption rates, quarterly rpt, 2482–2
Apartment completions by region and metro-nonmetro location, and absorption rate, by size and rent class, preliminary 1991, annual Current Housing Rpt, 2484–3
Apartment market absorption rates and characteristics for nonsubsidized furnished and unfurnished units, 1990, annual Current Housing Rpt, 2484–2
Census of Housing, 1990: summary unit characteristics, by householder race and age, county, place, and urban-rural location, State rpt series, 2471–1
Census of Population and Housing, 1990: population and housing characteristics, detailed geographic coverage, State CD-ROM series, 2551–10
Housing and households summary characteristics, 1989 and trends, chartbook, 2486–2.1
Mortgages FHA-insured, financial, property, and borrower characteristics, by metro area, 1991, annual rpt, 5144–24
Mortgages FHA-insured, financial, property, and borrower characteristics, by State, 1991, annual rpt, 5144–1; 5144–25
Mortgages FHA-insured, financial, property, and borrower characteristics, 1991, annual rpt, 5144–17; 5144–23
New housing starts and completions, by location inside-outside MSAs, quarterly rpt, 2042–1.2
New housing starts, by units per structure and metro-nonmetro location, and mobile home placements and prices, by region, monthly rpt, 2382–1
New housing units completed and under construction, by units per structure, region, and inside-outside MSAs, monthly rpt, 2382–2
New single and multifamily units, by structural and financial characteristics, inside-outside MSAs, and region, 1987-91, annual rpt, 2384–1
Rental housing units, total, with HUD assistance by program, and eligible for aid, by unit, household, and neighborhood characteristics, and location, 1989, biennial rpt, 5184–11
Single parent families in own and others homes, by financial, housing, and other characteristics, 1989, 2486–1.14
Single person and nonfamily households social, economic and housing characteristics, by tenure, 1989, 2486–1.15
Vacant housing characteristics and costs, and occupancy and vacancy rates, by region and metro-nonmetro location, quarterly rpt, 2482–1
Vacant housing characteristics, and occupancy and vacancy rates, by tenure and location, 1960s-91, annual rpt, 2484–1

Labor and Employment

Child care arrangements of mothers employed and in school, and costs, by age of child and characteristics of mother, 1988, Current Population Rpt, 2546–20.24
Employment and unemployment in metro and nonmetro areas, monthly rpt, quarterly data, 6742–2.9
Employment Cost Index and alternative measure of compensation costs, by component, occupation, industry group, union status, and location, 1975-92, annual rpt, 6744–20
Employment Cost Index and percent change by occupational group, industry div, region, and metro-nonmetro area, quarterly press release, 6782–5
Employment Cost Index changes for nonfarm workers, by occupation, industry div, region, and bargaining status, monthly rpt, 6782–1
Home-based workers by selected characteristics, and views, 1989, article, 1702–1.307
Labor demand in rural areas, job skill and educational requirements impacts of industrial and occupational shifts, 1970s-80s and projected to 2000, article, 1502–7.302
Services (producer) industries in Midwest, employment concentration by industry group, MSA, and urban-rural location, 1970s-89, article, 9375–1.305
Wage differentials among cities related to city size and worker characteristics, 1977-88, article, 9377–1.301
Wages, hours, and employment by occupation, and benefits, for selected locations, industry survey rpt series, 6787–6

Law Enforcement

Arrests, by offense, offender characteristics, and location, data compilation, 1992 annual rpt, 6064–6.4
Assaults and deaths of law enforcement officers, by circumstances, agency, victim and offender characteristics, and location, 1991, annual rpt, 6224–3
Crime, criminal justice admin and enforcement, and public opinion, data compilation, 1992 annual rpt, 6064–6
Crime Index by population size and region, and offenses by large city, 1st half 1992, semiannual rpt, 6222–1
Crimes, arrests by offender characteristics, and rates, by offense, and law enforcement employees, by population size and jurisdiction, 1991, annual rpt, 6224–2
Schools crime victimization, drug availability, and preventive measures, with student views, 1989 survey, 6066–3.46
Victimization rates, by victim and offender characteristics, circumstances, and offense, 1990 survey, annual rpt, 6066–3.47
Victimizations in cities, suburbs, and rural areas, by offense, circumstances, and victim and offender characteristics, 1987-89, 6066–3.48
Victimizations of households, by offense, household characteristics, and location, 1975-91, annual rpt, 6066–25.49

Natural Resources, Environment, and Pollution

Recycling of paper by grade, with newsprint collection, recycling capacity by company, and curbside pickup operations, by State, 1970s-80s and projected to 1995, hearing, 25318–84

Population

Asian and Pacific Islands Americans social and economic characteristics, for West and total US, 1990-91, Current Population Report, 2546–1.462
Black Americans social and economic characteristics, for South and total US, 1991 and trends from 1950, annual Current Population Rpt, 2546–1.463
Black women's labor force status, earnings, and other economic status indicators, and compared to whites, various periods 1939-88, 11048–191
Census of Population and Housing, 1990: population and housing characteristics, detailed geographic coverage, State CD-ROM series, 2551–10

Census of Population, 1990: population characteristics and living arrangements, by county, place, and urban-rural location, State rpt series, 2531–1
Consumer Income, socioeconomic characteristics of persons, families, and households, detailed cross-tabulations, Current Population Rpt series, 2546–6
Costa Rica economic indicators and reform issues, mid 1970s-90, working paper, 9916–13.5
Developing countries population size, life expectancy, and fertility, trends and forecasts, country rpt series, 2326–24
Households and family characteristics, by location, 1991, annual Current Population Rpt, 2546–1.457
Income (household) and poverty status under alternative income definitions, by recipient characteristics, 1979-91, annual Current Population Rpt, 2546–6.78
Income (personal) per capita and total, by State, MSA, county, and metro-nonmetro location, 1988-90, annual article, 2702–1.317
Income (personal) relative to median, by race and selected other characteristics, mid 1960s-89, Current Population Rpt, 2546–6.73
Income and consumer spending of households, for selected population groups, quarterly journal, 1702–1
Living arrangements, family relationships, and marital status, by selected characteristics, 1991, annual Current Population Rpt, 2546–1.461
Migration, population change, and areas losing population, by region, State, and metro-nonmetro location, 1980s and trends from 1940, Current Population Rpt, 2546–2.164
Older population, and health, economic, and other characteristics, with foreign comparisons, 1980s-91 with trends and projections, Current Population Rpt, 2546–2.165
Pacific territories population and housing detailed characteristics, by location, 1990 Census of Population and Housing, series, 2551–8
Population economic well-being indicators, by selected characteristics and household income and income-to-poverty ratio, 1984, 2546–20.22
Poverty status of population and families, by detailed characteristics, 1991, annual Current Population Rpt, 2546–6.77
Soviet Union and US economic and sociodemographic indicators, selected years 1970-90, handbook, 2328–80
Soviet Union former Republics and Baltic States population size and characteristics, 1989-92, 9118–19
Statistical Abstract of US, 1992 annual data compilation, 2324–1

Public Welfare and Social Security

Benefits, beneficiaries, and spells of participation, by aid program and recipient characteristics, 1987-88, Current Population Rpt, 2546–20.25
Child day care and early childhood education programs availability, demand, use, costs, and provider and enrollee characteristics, 1990 survey, 4808–39
Hospital multiple admissions of Medicare beneficiaries, by reason and characteristics of instn and patient, 1985, 4008–117
Hospital reimbursement by Medicare under prospective payment system, rural area instns financial performance and impacts of PPS policy changes, 1991 rpt, 26306–6.164
Medicare beneficiaries knowledge of and experience with physician billing and payment under Medicare, by selected characteristics, 1988-89, 17266–2.1
Medicare payment of physicians, reforms impacts on services, and monitoring methods, 1992 annual rpt, 4004–34
Medicare payment of physicians under assigned fee, participation and additional billing, by specialty, service, and State, late 1980s-92, 17266–1.6
Medicare payment of physicians under fee schedule, methodology with data by procedure and specialty, 1992, annual rpt, 17264–1
Medicare reimbursement of hospitals under prospective payment system, analyses of alternative payment plans, series, 17206–1
Medicare reimbursement of hospitals under prospective payment system, and effect on services, finances, and beneficiary payments, 1980-91, annual rpt, 17204–2
Medicare reimbursement of hospitals under prospective payment system, diagnosis related group code assignment and effects on care and instn finances, series, 4006–7
Medicare reimbursement of hospitals under prospective payment system, impacts on costs, industry structure and operations, and quality of care, series, 17206–2
Medicare reimbursement of hospitals under prospective payment system, methodology, inputs, and data by diagnostic group, 1992 annual rpt, 17204–1

Recreation and Leisure

Park natl system visits and overnight stays, by park and State, monthly rpt, 5542–4

ECONOMIC BREAKDOWNS

BY COMMODITY

Agriculture and Food

Acreage planted and harvested, by crop and State, 1990-91 and planned as of June 1992, annual rpt, 1621–23
Acreage planted, by selected crop and State, 1983-91 and planned 1992, annual rpt, 1621–22
Acreage reduction program compliance, enrollment, and yield on planted acreage, by commodity and State, annual press release series, 1004–20
Agricultural Outlook, production, prices, marketing, and trade, by commodity, forecast and current situation, monthly rpt with articles, 1502–4
Agricultural Stabilization and Conservation Service programs, annual commodity fact sheet series, 1806–4
Agricultural Statistics, 1991, annual rpt, 1004–1
Appalachia food processing firms, employment, and shipments, and farm production, by commodity and State, 1960s-90, 9088–37
Bee colony rentals, and pollinated crop value, by crop, 1989, hearings, 25168–78
Business statistics, detailed data for major industries and economic indicators, *Survey of Current Business*, monthly rpt, 2702–1.13
CCC certificate exchange activity, by commodity, biweekly press release, 1802–16
CCC commodities for sale, and prices, monthly press release, 1802–4
CCC financial condition and major commodity program operations, FY63-88, annual chartbook, 1824–2
CCC loan activities by commodity, and agency operating results, monthly press release, 1802–7
Cold storage food stocks by commodity and census div, and warehouse space use, by State, monthly rpt, 1631–5
Cold storage food stocks by commodity, and warehouse space use, by census div, 1991, annual rpt, 1631–11
Cooperatives finances, aggregate for top 100 assns by commodity group, 1990, annual rpt, 1124–3
Cooperatives, finances, and membership, by type of service, commodity, and State, 1990, annual rpt, 1124–1
Cooperatives finances, operations, activities, and current issues, monthly journal, 1122–1
Developing countries food supply, needs, and aid, status and alternative forecasts, world area rpt series, 1526–8
Economic Indicators of the Farm Sector, balance sheets, and receipts by detailed commodity, by State, 1986-90, annual rpt, 1544–18
Economic Indicators of the Farm Sector, itemized production costs, receipts, and returns, by commodity and region, 1975-90, annual rpt, 1544–20
Economic Indicators of the Farm Sector, production inputs, output, and productivity, by commodity and region, 1947-90, annual rpt, 1544–17
Exports and imports (agricultural) commodity and country, prices, and world market devs, monthly rpt, 1922–12
Exports and imports (agricultural) of US, by commodity and country, bimonthly rpt, 1522–1
Exports and imports (agricultural) of US, by detailed commodity and country, 1991, annual rpt, 1524–8
Exports and imports (agricultural) of US, by detailed commodity and country, 1991, semiannual rpt, 1522–4
Exports and imports (agricultural) of US, outlook and current situation, quarterly rpt, 1542–4
Exports, imports, tariffs, and industry operating data for agricultural, fishery, and forest products, commodity rpt series, 9885–8
Exports of grains, oilseed products, hides, skins, and cotton, by country, weekly rpt, dropped data, 1922–3
Farms, production, acreage, and related data, by selected crop and State, monthly rpt, 1621–1
Fed Crop Insurance Corp financial performance, and effect of alternative price forecasts on program costs, 1983-89, GAO rpt, 26131–95

Fertilizer and pesticide use and application rates, by type, crop, and State, series, 1616–1
Finances of farms, debts, assets, and receipts, and lenders financial condition, quarterly rpt with articles, 1541–1
Financial and marketing conditions of farms, forecast 1992, annual chartbook, 1504–8
Financial condition of farm sector, and prices, supply, and demand by commodity, 1980s-91 and forecast 1992, annual article, 9381–1.303
FmHA guaranteed loan program, characteristics of borrowers, lenders, and loans, FY88, 1548–386
Food (processed) production and stocks by State, shipments, exports, ingredients, and use, periodic Current Industrial Rpt series, 2506–4
Food assistance programs impacts on farm income, by commodity, model description and results, 1989-90, 1548–390
Food composition, detailed data on nutrients, calories, and waste, for raw, processed, and prepared foods, series, 1356–3
Food consumer research, marketing, legislation, and regulation devs, and consumption and price trends, quarterly journal, 1541–7
Food consumption, dietary composition, and nutrient intake, natl survey methodology changes and sample results, 1990 rpt, 1358–6
Food consumption, supply, trade, prices, spending, and indexes, by commodity, 1990, annual rpt, 1544–4
Food processing industry finances and operations, by commodity, 1991, annual rpt, 1544–22
Foreign and US agricultural production, acreage, and yield for selected crops, forecasts by selected world region and country, FAS monthly circular, 1925–28
Foreign and US agricultural supply and demand indicators, by selected crop, monthly rpt, 1522–5
Foreign and US fresh and processed fruit, vegetable, and nut production and trade, FAS monthly circular with articles, 1925–34
Foreign countries agricultural production, consumption, and policies, and US export dev and promotion, monthly journal, 1922–2
Foreign countries agricultural production, prices, and trade, by country, 1980-91 and forecast 1992, annual world area rpt series, 1524–4
Fruit and nut production, prices, and use, annual rpt series, 1621–18
Fruit and nut production, prices, trade, stocks, and use, by selected crop, periodic situation rpt with articles, 1561–6
Fruit and vegetable imports under quarantine, by crop, country, and port of entry, FY89, annual rpt, 1524–7
Fruit and vegetable shipments, and arrivals by city, by mode of transport and State and country of origin, 1991, annual rpt series, 1311–4
Fruit and vegetable shipments by mode of transport, arrivals, and imports, by commodity and State and country of origin, weekly rpt, 1311–3
Fruit and vegetable wholesale prices in NYC by State, and shipments and arrivals by mode of transport, by commodity, weekly rpt, 1311–20
Fruit and vegetable wholesale prices in NYC-Newark, and arrivals by mode of transport, by commodity and State, 1990, annual rpt, 1311–21
Income of farms, cash marketing receipts ranked by commodity and State, 1990, 1548–385
Irrigated farmland, farm characteristics, and water and fuel sources, by State and leading county, 1950s-88, 1588–122
Irrigation projects of Reclamation Bur in western US, crop production and acreage by commodity, State, and project, 1990, annual rpt, 5824–12
Livestock, poultry, and dairy trade, by commodity and country, FAS monthly circular, 1925–32
Livestock, poultry, and products foreign and US production, trade, and use, by selected country, FAS semiannual circular series, 1925–33
Loans (farm) at risk of default, lender losses, and selected farm financial indicators, by type of farm and lender, 1984-89, 1548–383
Mexico agricultural trade with US and Canada, and impacts of North American Free Trade Agreement, 1980s-90, 1528–330
Morocco agricultural subsidies to producers and consumers, by selected commodity, 1970s-90, 1528–329
PL 480 and CCC export credit sales agreement terms, by commodity and country, FY90, annual rpt, 15344–1.11
Price support and other CCC program outlays, with production and marketing outlook, by commodity, projected 1991-97, annual rpt, 26306–6.171
Prices received and paid by farmers, by commodity and State, monthly rpt, 1629–1
Prices received and paid by farmers, by commodity and State, 1991, annual rpt, 1629–5
Prices received by farmers and production value, by detailed crop and State, 1989-91, annual rpt, 1621–2
Production inputs, finances, mgmt, and land value and transfers, periodic situation rpt with articles, 1561–16
Production itemized costs, receipts, and returns, by crop and State, 1987-89, annual rpt, 1544–24
Research (agricultural) funding and staffing for USDA, State agencies, and other instns, by topic, FY91, annual rpt, 1744–2
Rice farms producing other crops, acreage by crop and region, 1988, 1568–309
South Central States agricultural banks financial ratios, and farm finances and production growth, by State, 1980s-92, annual article, 9391–16.308
Soviet Union and US economic and sociodemographic indicators, selected years 1970-90, handbook, 2328–80
Truck rates for fruit and vegetables paid by shippers and receivers, by commodity and city, and fleet itemized costs per mile, weekly rpt, 1311–22
Vegetable production, acreage, and yield, current and forecast for selected fresh and processing crops by State, periodic rpt, 1621–12
Vegetable production, prices, trade, stocks, and use, for selected fresh and processing crops, periodic situation rpt with articles, 1561–11
Vegetable production, value, and acreage, for selected fresh and processing crops by State, 1989-91, annual rpts, 1621–25
Weather conditions and effect on agriculture, by US region, State, and city, and world area, weekly rpt, 2182–7
Weight and volume conversion factors for agricultural commodities and products, 1992 rpt, 1508–3
Women-headed households food spending, by item and selected characteristics, and compared to other households, 1970s-88, 1548–391

Banking, Finance, and Insurance

Futures and options trading volume, by commodity and exchange, FY91, annual rpt, 11924–2
Futures trading in selected commodities and financial instruments and indexes, for NYC, Chicago, and other markets activity, biweekly rpt, 11922–5

Communications and Transportation

Freight and distance hauled, by commodity and mode of transport, selected years 1970-89, annual rpt, 3304–5.6
Ohio River basin waterway facilities, freight by commodity and port, and recreation, by waterway, 1988-89, annual rpt, 3754–6
Panama Canal traffic and tolls, by commodity, flag of vessel, and trade route, FY91, annual rpt, 9664–3.1
Railroad freight, by commodity and region of origin and destination, 1989, annual rpt, 7604–6
Shipborne commerce (domestic) of US, freight by major commodity group, vessel type, and port, 1987-89, annual rpt, 7704–7
St Lawrence Seaway ship, cargo, and passenger traffic, and toll revenue, 1991 and trends from 1959, annual rpt, 7744–2
Truck freight revenue, by commodity, 1990 survey, annual rpt, 2413–14
Truck rates for fruit and vegetables, by growing area and market, weekly 1991, annual rpt, 1311–15
Truck rates for fruit and vegetables paid by shippers and receivers, by commodity and city, and fleet itemized costs per mile, weekly rpt, 1311–22
Waterborne commerce (domestic and foreign) of US, freight by commodity, traffic, and passengers, by port and waterway, 1989, annual rpt, 3754–3

Government and Defense

Military and personal property shipments, passenger traffic, and costs, by service branch and mode of transport, FY91, annual rpt, 3704–15
Military prime contract awards, by detailed procurement category, FY88-91, annual rpt, 3544–18
Prison Industries (Federal) sales, by commodity and Federal agency, FY91, annual rpt, 6244–5
Strategic material stockpile inventories and needs, by commodity, 1992, annual rpt, 3544–37

Strategic material stockpiling by Fed Govt, activity, and inventory by commodity, as of Sept 1991, semiannual rpt, 3542–22
Tax (excise) collections of IRS, by source, quarterly rpt, 8302–1

Health and Vital Statistics

Carcinogens chemistry, sources, environment and health risks, and regulation, by substance and brand, 1991 annual rpt, 4044–15
Injuries from use of consumer products and related activities, by severity and victim age and sex, 1990, annual rpt, 9164–7
Injuries from use of consumer products, by severity, victim age, and detailed product, 1991, annual rpt, 9164–6
Injuries from use of consumer products, related deaths and costs, and recalls by brand, by product type, FY90, annual rpt, 9164–2

Housing and Construction

Building materials production, shipments, and PPI, by type, quarterly rpt, 2042–1.5; 2042–1.6

Industry and Commerce

Andean Trade Preference Act duty-free exports from 4 countries to US, and business opportunities, 1989-91, 2048–161
Business statistics, detailed data for major industries and economic indicators, *Survey of Current Business*, monthly rpt, 2702–1
Business statistics, detailed data for major industries and economic indicators, 1960-91, *Survey of Current Business* biennial supplement, 2704–1
Caribbean area duty-free exports to US, and imports from US, by country, and impact on US employment, by commodity, 1991, annual rpt, 6364–2
Caribbean area duty-free exports to US, by commodity and country, with consumer and industry impacts, 1984-91, annual rpt, 9884–20
China and other Asia countries trade with US, composition and trends, 1980s-91, article, 9385–1.303
China minerals production and trade, by commodity, 1989-90, annual rpt, 5604–38
Communist and transitional economy countries trade with US, by detailed commodity and country, quarterly rpt with articles, 9882–2
Competitiveness (intl) of US industries, with selected foreign and US operating data by major firm and product, series, 2046–12
Consumer holdings of durable goods, by type, in current and constant dollars, 1925-90, annual article, 2702–1.305
Consumer holdings of durable goods, by type, in current and constant dollars, 1988-91, annual article, 2702–1.327
Cuba trade, by commodity and country, mid 1980s-91, 9118–8
Eastern Europe export industries dev potential, with trade and industry finances and operations, for 5 countries, 1985-90, 9886–4.179
Eastern Europe imports from US, and trade and dev opportunities, monthly rpt, 2042–33
Eastern Europe trade with US, by commodity and country, 1987-91 and outlook for 1992, 2048–158
Export and import balances of US, by major commodity group, monthly rpt, 9882–14
Export licensing, monitoring, and enforcement activities, FY91, annual rpt, 2024–1
Exports and imports between US and outlying areas, by detailed commodity and mode of transport, 1991, annual rpt, 2424–11
Exports and imports of US, by country and detailed commodity, monthly rpt, 2422–12
Exports and imports of US by country, and trade shifts by commodity, 1991, annual rpt, 9884–25
Exports and imports of US, by Harmonized System 6-digit commodity and country, 1991, annual rpt, 2424–13
Exports and imports of US, by selected country, country group, and commodity group, 1991, annual rpt, 2044–37
Exports and imports of US, by transport mode, country, and SITC 1- to 3-digit commodity, 1991, annual rpt, 2424–12
Exports and imports, trade agreements and relations, and USITC investigations, 1991, annual rpt, 9884–5
Exports, imports, and balances of US, by selected country, country group, and commodity group, preliminary data, monthly rpt, 2042–34
Exports, imports, and balances of US for manufactured goods, by SITC 2-digit commodity and country, quarterly rpt, 2042–35
Exports, imports, and trade flows, by country and commodity, with background economic indicators, data compilation, monthly CD-ROM, 2002–6
Exports of US, detailed commodities by country, monthly CD-ROM, 2422–13
Exports of US, detailed Schedule B commodities with countries of destination, 1991, annual rpt, 2424–10
Foreign countries economic conditions and implications for US, periodic country rpt series, 2046–4
Foreign trade zones (US) operations and movement of goods, by zone and commodity, FY90, annual rpt, 2044–30
Imports and tariff provisions effect on US industries and products, investigations with background financial and operating data, series, 9886–4
Imports detained by FDA, by reason, product, shipper, brand, and country, monthly listing, 4062–2
Imports, exports, and employment impacts, by SIC 2- to 4-digit industry and commodity, quarterly rpt, 2322–2
Imports injury to US industries from foreign subsidized products, investigations with background financial and operating data, series, 9886–15
Imports injury to US industries from sales at less than fair value, investigations with background financial and operating data, series, 9886–14
Imports of US, detailed commodities by country, monthly CD-ROM, 2422–14
Imports of US given duty-free treatment for value of US material sent abroad, by commodity and country, 1987-90, annual rpt, 9884–14
Imports under Generalized System of Preferences, status, and US tariffs, with trade by country and US economic impacts, for selected commodities, 1987-91, annual rpt, 9884–23
Input-output structure of US economy, detailed interindustry transactions for 84 industries, and components of final demand, 1987, annual article, 2702–1.316
Input-output structure of US economy, detailed interindustry transactions for 541 industries, and components of final demand, 1982 benchmark data, 2708–17
Latin America economic and social conditions, resources, trade, and aid, 1992, annual factbook, 9914–14
Manufacturing annual survey, 1990: value of shipments, by SIC 4- to 5-digit product class, 2506–14.1
Manufacturing census, 1987: concentration of largest firms measured by value added, and for shipments by SIC 2- and 4-digit industry, subject rpt, 2497–6
Manufacturing industry (US) intl competitiveness, trade and economic policies with background data and foreign comparisons, 1991 rpt, 26358–252
Mexico imports from US, by industry and State, 1987-91, 2048–154
Mexico trade with US and other countries, foreign investment, and maquiladoras operations, 1980s-91, GAO rpt, 26119–417
Mexico trade with US, and tariffs, by commodity, impacts of North American Free Trade Agreement and compared to EC expansion to Mediterranean, 1970s-80s, 6366–3.29
Mineral Industry Surveys, commodity reviews of production, trade, stocks, and use, monthly rpt series, 5612–1
Mineral Industry Surveys, commodity reviews of production, trade, stocks, and use, quarterly rpt series, 5612–2
Mineral Industry Surveys, commodity reviews of production, trade, use, and industry operations, advance annual rpt series, 5614–5
Mineral Industry Surveys, State reviews of production, 1991, preliminary annual rpt, 5614–6
Minerals foreign and US supply under alternative market conditions, reserves, and background industry data, series, 5606–4
Minerals production, prices, trade, use, employment, tariffs, and stockpiles, by mineral, with foreign comparisons, 1987-91, annual rpt, 5604–18
Minerals production, reserves, and industry role in domestic economy and world supply, world area and country rpt, series, 5606–1
Minerals resources of Alaska, production, oil and gas leases, reserves, and exploratory wells, with maps and bibl, 1990, annual rpt, 5664–11
Minerals Yearbook, Vol 1, 1989: commodity reviews of production, use, trade, prices, and mining operations, annual rpt, 5604–33
Minerals Yearbook, Vol 1, 1990: commodity reviews of production, reserves, supply, use, and trade, annual rpt series, 5604–20
Minerals Yearbook, Vol 1, 1991: commodity reviews of production, reserves, supply, use, and trade, annual rpt series, 5604–15
Minerals Yearbook, Vol 2, 1989: State reviews of production and sales by commodity, and business activity, annual rpt series, 5604–16

Minerals Yearbook, Vol 2, 1990: State reviews of production and sales by commodity, and business activity, annual rpt series, 5604–22
Minerals Yearbook, Vol 3, 1989: foreign country reviews of production, trade, and policy, by commodity, annual rpt, 5604–35
Multinatl US firms and foreign affiliates finances and operations, by industry and country, 1989 benchmark survey, annual rpt, 2704–5
North America intraindustry trade indexes, for US, Canada, and Mexico, by commodity, 1962-87, 1528–327
OECD trade, total and for 4 major countries, and US trade by country, by commodity, 1980-90, world area rpt series, 9116–1
Overseas Business Reports: economic conditions, investment and export opportunities, and trade practices, country market research rpt series, 2046–6
Romania trade with US, and US import tariff rates, by commodity, 1985-91, GAO rpt, 26119–414
Soviet Union minerals production and exports, by commodity and Republic, 1975-90, annual rpt, 5604–39
Wholesale trade sales and inventories, by SIC 2- to 3-digit kind of business, monthly rpt, 2413–7

Natural Resources, Environment, and Pollution

Global climate change impacts on agricultural production and GDP, with data by crop and world area, mid 1970s-86, 1528–326
Hazardous substances industrial releases and reduction methods under EPA regulation, by chemical, source, industry, and location, 1989, annual rpt, 9234–6

Prices and Cost of Living

Consumer spending, natl income and product account benchmark revisions, 1929-88, 2708–5
Consumer spending, natl income and product accounts, comprehensive accounts and components, *Survey of Current Business*, monthly rpt, 2702–1.25; 2702–1.30
Consumer spending on selected durable goods and services, 1980-90, article, 6722–1.324
CPI by component for US city average, and by region, population size, and for 15 metro areas, monthly rpt, 6762–1
CPI by component for US city average, and by selected metro area, region, and population size, monthly rpt, 6762–2
CPI changes for selected items, 1982-91, annual article, 6722–1.322
CPI current statistics, Monthly Labor Review, 6722–1.4
Department store inventory price indexes, by class of item, monthly table, 6762–7
Export and import price indexes, by selected end-use category, monthly press release, 6762–15
Export and import price indexes for goods and services, and dollar exchange rate indexes, quarterly press release, 6762–13
Farm prices received and paid, by commodity and State, monthly rpt, 1629–1
Farm prices received and paid, by commodity and State, 1991, annual rpt, 1629–5
Farm prices received and production value, by detailed crop and State, 1989-91, annual rpt, 1621–2
Food consumer research, marketing, legislation, and regulation devs, and consumption and price trends, quarterly journal, 1541–7
Food prices (farm-retail), marketing cost components, and industry finances and productivity, 1920s-91, annual rpt, 1544–9
Foreign and US economic conditions, for major industrial countries, monthly rpt, 9112–1
Fruit and vegetable wholesale prices in NYC by State, and shipments and arrivals by mode of transport, by commodity, weekly rpt, 1311–20
Fruit and vegetable wholesale prices in NYC, Chicago, and selected shipping points, by crop, 1991, annual rpt, 1311–8
Fruit and vegetable wholesale prices in NYC-Newark, and arrivals by mode of transport, by commodity and State, 1990, annual rpt, 1311–21
Mail order catalog price changes, and relation to inflation, by item, 1953-87, working paper, 9375–13.76
Price indexes (consumer and producer), by commodity group, selected years 1929-91, annual rpt, 204–1.4
Producer Price Index, by major commodity group and subgroup, and processing stage, monthly press release, 6762–5
Producer price indexes, by stage of processing and detailed commodity, monthly rpt, 6762–6
Producer price indexes, by stage of processing and detailed commodity, monthly 1991, annual rpt, 6764–2
Producer price indexes, changes for selected items by stage of processing, 1987-91, article, 6722–1.323
Statistical Abstract of US, 1992 annual data compilation, 2324–1.15
Survey of Current Business, detailed data for major industries and economic indicators, monthly rpt, 2702–1.4
Texas, Dallas-Ft Worth and Houston MSAs, CPI by major component, monthly rpt, 6962–2

Public Welfare and Social Security

Food aid programs purchases, by commodity, firm, and shipping point or destination, weekly rpt, 1302–3

BY FEDERAL AGENCY

Banking, Finance, and Insurance

Debt delinquent on Federal accounts, cases and collections of Justice Dept and private law firms, pilot project results, FY91, annual rpt, 6004–20
Fed Financing Bank holdings and transactions, by borrower, monthly press release, 12802–1

Communications and Transportation

Air travel by Federal officials aboard military aircraft, trips of 11 officials by reason, with costs and reimbursements, 1989-91, GAO rpt, 26111–78
Air travel by Federal officials and Congress aboard military aircraft, and aircraft inventory characteristics, 1989-91, GAO rpt, 26123–384
Audiovisual activities and spending of Fed Govt, by whether performed in-house and agency, FY91, annual rpt, 9514–1
Auto, bus, and truck fleet of Fed Govt, by agency, FY88, annual rpt, 3304–5.3
Hwy scenic routes and mileage, by govt ownership, land use and usage restrictions, and other characteristics, 1990, 7558–112
Radio frequency assignments for Federal use, by agency, 1st half 1992, semiannual rpt, 2802–1
Shipborne cargo sponsored by Fed Govt, total and US-flag share by agency and program, 1990, annual rpt, 7704–14.3
Transit fare subsidies for Federal employees, costs and participation by agency, 1992, GAO rpt, 26113–601

Education

Expenditures for education by Federal agency, program, and recipient type, and instn spending, 1960s-91, annual rpt, 4824–8
Expenditures for education, by Federal agency, program, and State, FY65-92, annual rpt, 4824–2.27

Energy Resources and Demand

Bonneville Power Admin mgmt of Fed Columbia River Power System, finances, operations, and sales by customer, FY91, annual rpt, 3224–1
Energy use of Fed Govt, by agency and fuel type, FY77-91, annual rpt, 3164–74.1
Finances and operations of Federal power admins and electric utilities, 1990, annual rpt, 3164–24.2

Geography and Climate

Earthquake risk for Federal buildings and employees, by agency and region, 1989, with location and size of major events from 1600s, GAO rpt, 26119–399
Weather services activities and funding, by Federal agency, planned FY92-93, annual rpt, 2144–2

Government and Defense

Administrative law judges, by agency, 1992, GAO report, 26119–428
Advisory committees of Fed Govt, and members, staff, meetings, and costs by agency, FY91, annual rpt, 9454–18
Assets of Fed Govt targeted for disposition, inventories by type, and related employment and contracts, by agency, FY90, GAO rpt, 26119–369
Assistance (financial and nonfinancial) of Fed Govt, 1992 base edition, annual listing, 104–5
Budget of US, authoritative financial statements with appropriations, outlays, and receipts, by agency, FY91, annual rpt, 8104–2
Budget of US, authority rescissions and deferrals, monthly rpt, 102–2
Budget of US, balances of budget authority obligated and unobligated, by function and agency, FY90-93, annual rpt, 104–8
Budget of US, Bush Admin proposals, with detail for defense budgets, and historical data from FY34, FY93, 108–46
Budget of US, House Budget Committee analysis of Bush Admin proposals and economic assumptions, FY93, 21268–42
Budget of US, midsession review of FY93 budget, by function, annual rpt, 104–7
Budget of US, obligations and authority by function, agency, and program, with summaries and analyses, FY93, annual rpt, 104–2

Budget of US, receipts by source, outlays by agency and program, and balances, monthly rpt, 8102–3
Collective bargaining agreements of Federal employees, coverage, unions, and location, by agency, for contracts expiring 1992, semiannual listing, 9847–1
Currency (foreign) holdings of US, transactions and balances by program and country, 1st half FY92, semiannual rpt, 8102–7
DC metro area land acquisition and dev projects of Fed Govt, characteristics and funding by agency and project, FY92-96, annual rpt, 15454–1
Employee and hiree background checks by OPM, efficiency, and Federal agency managers views on timeliness and quality, FY90, GAO rpt, 26119–373
Employee appeals of personnel actions, decisions of Merit Systems Protection Board by agency and region, FY91, annual rpt, 9494–2
Employee incentive awards, costs, and benefits, by award type and agency, FY90, annual rpt, 9844–20
Employees of Fed Govt moonlighting, selected characteristics of 2nd job and Federal position, FY88-90, GAO rpt, 26119–386
Employment (civilian) of Fed Govt, by demographic characteristics and agency, 1990, GAO rpt, 26119–383
Employment (civilian) of Fed Govt, work-years, pay rates, and benefits use and costs, by agency, FY90, annual rpt, 9844–31
Employment (noncareer) of Fed Govt, conversions to career appointments, by pay grade and agency, 1988-89, GAO rpt, 26119–382
Employment and payroll (civilian) of Fed Govt, by agency in DC metro area, total US, and abroad, bimonthly rpt, 9842–1
Employment and payroll (civilian) of Fed Govt, by pay system, agency, and location, 1991, annual rpt, 9844–6.1; 9844–6.2
Employment discrimination complaints, processing and counseling costs, by agency, FY91, GAO rpt, 26119–388
Employment discrimination complaints, processing, and disposition, by complaint type and Federal agency, FY90, annual rpt, 9244–11
Employment recruitment visits at colleges by Federal agencies and private companies, and school officials views, 1991, GAO rpt, 26119–377
Expenditures of Fed Govt in States, by type, program, agency, and State, FY91, annual rpt, 2464–2
Finances of Fed Govt, cash and debt transactions, daily tables, 8102–4
Financial operations of Fed Govt, detailed data, *Treasury Bulletin*, quarterly rpt, 8002–4
Info collection of Fed Govt under Paperwork Reduction Act, respondent burden, OMB reviews, violations, and major info systems proposals, 1981-92, annual rpt, 104–26
Info Security Oversight Office monitoring of Federal security measures and classification actions, FY91, annual rpt, 9454–21
Inspectors General audits and investigations of fraud and abuse, by agency, FY91, annual rpt, 104–29
Investigations of Federal agency and program operations, summaries of findings, as of 1991, annual GAO rpt, 26104–5
Labor Relations Fed Authority and Fed Service Impasses Panel activities, and cases by union, agency, and disposition, FY86-91, annual rpt, 13364–1
Labor unions recognized in Fed Govt, agreements and membership by agency and facility, as of Jan 1991, biennial listing, 9844–14
Loans, loan guarantees, and grants of Fed Govt, administrative costs budget accounting, by program and agency, 1992 rpt, 26306–6.166
Loans of Treasury Dept and Federal Financing Bank to Govt corporations and agencies, outstanding amounts, 1987-91, GAO rpt, 26111–79
Minority group, disabled, and veteran employment in Fed Govt, and years of service, by occupation, age, sex, and agency, as of Sept 1990, biennial rpt, 9844–27
Minority group, women, and disabled employment of Fed Govt, by agency and occupation, FY90, annual rpt, 9244–10
Older population data sources of Fed Govt, interagency forum activities, and contacts, 1989-90, annual rpt, 14324–1
Persian Gulf War allied countries cash and in-kind contributions, by type and country, and status of DOD accounts, as of Sept 1991, annual GAO rpt, 26104–24
Prison Industries (Federal) sales, by commodity and Federal agency, FY91, annual rpt, 6244–5
Puerto Rico statehood referendum proposal, with background data on Federal outlays, economic conditions, and finances of corporations with tax-favored status, 1940s-88, hearing, 21448–46
Senior Executive Service members characteristics, entries, exits, and awards, FY79-91, annual rpt, 9844–36
Senior Executive Service noncareer and Schedule C appointments, by agency, 1990-91, GAO rpt, 26119–412
Small business finances, operations, owner characteristics, and Federal contracts, 1980s-90, annual rpt, 9764–6
Statistical programs of Fed Govt, funding by agency, and BLS programs improvement spending, 1991 hearing, 23848–227
Tax (withholding) delinquent accounts of Federal agencies, and compared to other taxpayers, 1990, hearing, 21788–206
Trust funds of Fed Govt, financial condition, periodic rpt series, 8102–9

Health and Vital Statistics

AIDS prevention and control plans, cases, and Federal funding, 1980s-94, 4048–22
Carcinogens chemistry, sources, environment and health risks, and regulation, by substance and brand, 1991 annual rpt, 4044–15
Disabled persons rehabilitation, Federal and State activities and funding, FY90, annual rpt, 4944–1
Health condition and care indicators, 1950s-90 with health improvement and disease prevention goals for 1990, annual data compilation, 4144–11
Neurosciences research and public policy issues, series, 26356–9
Physical fitness clubs memberships for Federal employees, agency costs, and personnel directors views on OPM guidelines and admin leave use, 1991-92, GAO rpt, 26119–393
Reproduction and population research, Fed Govt funding by project, FY90, annual listing, 4474–9
Youth health promotion and adolescent health training funding by Federal agencies, FY88-90, 26358–234.3

Industry and Commerce

Minority business funding, by program and Federal agency, FY91, annual rpt, 2104–5
Vending facilities run by blind on Federal and non-Federal property, finances and operations by agency and State, FY91, annual rpt, 4944–2

Law Enforcement

Assaults and deaths of law enforcement officers, by circumstances, agency, victim and offender characteristics, and location, 1991, annual rpt, 6224–3
Assaults on law enforcement officers and offenders involved, by agency, data compilation, 1992 annual rpt, 6064–6.3
Asset Forfeiture Program of Justice Dept, seizures, finances, and disbursements, FY85-91, annual rpt, 6004–21
Drug abuse and trafficking reduction programs activities, funding, staff, and Bush Admin budget request, by Federal agency, FY91-93, annual rpt, 234–2
Drug abuse and trafficking reduction programs funding, and Bush Admin budget request, by Federal agency, FY91-93, annual rpt, 234–1
Drug enforcement communications network for Federal agencies, funding for equipment and DOD support, FY88-91 and projected to FY87, GAO rpt, 26123–372
Drug enforcement grants to States, and allocations to local areas, by State, FY87-91, 236–3.1
US attorneys civil cases and amounts involved, and criminal cases declined, by agency, FY91, annual rpt, 6004–2.5; 6004–2.7

Natural Resources, Environment, and Pollution

Alaska oil, gas, and coal reserve acreage, by ownership, 1991 rpt, 5608–174
Environmental Quality, status of problems, protection programs, research, and intl issues, 1991 annual rpt, 484–1
Fish (salmon) conservation spending by organization, and population, for Columbia River basin, 1970-91, GAO rpt, 26113–577
Geological Survey reimbursable program funds from other Federal agencies, by program and agency, FY88-91, annual rpt, 5664–8
Kuwait oil fires set by Iraq, pollution levels, disease cases, and US remediation and monitoring spending, 1991 rpt, 9188–117
Lands (public) disposition and withdrawals from inventory, by agency and State, FY91, annual rpt, 5724–1.2
Marine mammals research, Federal funding by topic, recipient, and agency, FY91, annual rpt, 14734–2
Minerals resources and availability on public lands, State rpt series, 5606–7

Ocean pollution research, monitoring, and resources dev activities of Fed Govt, funding and project descriptions, FY89, annual rpt, 2144–23
Ocean pollution research, monitoring, and resources dev activities of Fed Govt, 5-year plan and funding by agency, FY87-92, triennial rpt, 2148–56

Public Welfare and Social Security

Expenditures of Fed Govt in States, by type, program, agency, and State, FY91, annual rpt, 2464–2
Homeless persons aid by program and Federal agency, and indicators of need, 1990, annual rpt, 14364–1
Homeless persons aid programs of Fed Govt, program descriptions and funding, by agency and State, FY87-91, annual GAO rpt, 26104–21

Science and Technology

Education in science and engineering, grad programs enrollment by field, source of funds, and characteristics of student and instn, 1990, annual rpt, 9627–7
Higher education instn R&D funding by Fed Govt, indirect costs and effects of alternative reimbursement policies, FY89, GAO rpt, 26113–592
Labor force, Federal and university research funding, and educational data, for science and engineering, series, 9626–6
Military prime contract awards for R&D to US and foreign nonprofit instns and govt agencies, by instn and location, FY91, annual listing, 3544–17
Oceanographic research cruise ships characteristics, by higher education instn and Federal agency, 1992, annual listing, 3804–6
Patents granted to Federal agencies, FY82-91, annual rpt, 2244–1.2
R&D and related funding of Fed Govt to higher education and nonprofit instns, by field, instn, agency, and State, FY90, annual rpt, 9627–17
R&D funding by Fed Govt, by detailed function, program, and agency, FY91-93, annual rpt, 9627–9
R&D prime contract awards of DOD, for top 500 contractors, FY91, annual listing, 3544–4
Science and Engineering Indicators, employment, education, R&D funding, and industry impacts, with foreign comparisons, 1960s-91, biennial rpt, 9624–10
Small business R&D grants of Fed Govt, by program area, agency, MSA, and State, FY90, annual rpt, 9764–7
Small business R&D grants of Fed Govt, project sales by type and dev funding by source, by agency and selected firm, 1984-91, GAO rpt, 26113–393
Smithsonian Instn grants and contracts from other agencies, FY90-91, annual rpt, 29574–1
Space and aeronautics activities and budgets, by Federal agency, FY59-91, annual rpt, 9504–9.2
Space programs procurement contract awards of NASA and other agencies, by type, contractor, State, and country, FY92 with trends from 1961, semiannual rpt, 9502–6
Spacecraft launches and other activities of NASA and USSR, with flight data, 1957-91, annual rpt, 9504–6.1

Veterans Affairs

Employment of veterans by Federal agency, and hiring practices, 1988-91, GAO rpt, 26119–391

BY INCOME

Agriculture and Food

Households (farm), by income level, 1989, annual Current Population Rpt, 2546–1.458
Women-headed households food spending, by item and selected characteristics, and compared to other households, 1970s-88, 1548–391

Banking, Finance, and Insurance

Credit cards held by household income, age, and card type, and debt outstanding, with issuer costs and revenue, 1970s-80, article, 9362–1.306
Families financial status, income, net worth, and assets and debt by type, by income and selected characteristics, 1983 and 1989, article, 9362–1.301
Insurance (life) coverage of households, share by income level, 1984, GAO rpt, 26119–389
Small Business Admin loan guarantee program participants finances, operations, characteristics, and views, 1991 survey, 9768–25

Communications and Transportation

Bus (intercity) riders, by income level compared to total US, 1991, GAO rpt, 26113–583
Mail volume to and from households, use, and views, by class, source, content, and household characteristics, FY87-90, annual rpt, 9864–10
Telephone local service charges and low-income subsidies, by region, company, and city, 1980s-91, semiannual rpt, 9282–8
Travel patterns, personal and household characteristics, and auto and public transport use, 1990 survey, series, 7556–6
Travel patterns, personal and household characteristics, and auto use, 1950-90, annual rpt, 3304–5.4
Travel patterns, personal and household characteristics, and auto use, 1990 survey, annual rpt, 7554–1.6
Travel to US and Canada, market analysis with detailed trip and traveler characteristics, country rpt series, 2906–2

Education

Adult education participation, by selected characteristics, 1991 survey, 4826–10.5
American Historical Assn financial statements, and membership by State, 1990, annual rpt, 29574–2
Eighth grade class of 1988: educational performance and conditions, characteristics, attitudes, activities, and plans, natl longitudinal survey, series, 4826–9
Enrollment, by grade, instn type and control, and student characteristics, 1989 and trends from 1947, annual Current Population Rpt, 2546–1.459
High school dropouts and transfers between public and private schools, by instn control, income level, and race, 1990 survey, 4826–10.4
Public housing residents educational attainment, by selected characteristics, 1980s, 5188–132
Student aid and other sources of support, with student expenses and characteristics, by instn type and control, 1987 study, series, 4846–3
Student aid and other sources of support, with student expenses and characteristics, by instn type and control, 1990 triennial study, series, 4846–5
Student aid Pell grants and applicants, by tuition, income level, instn type and control, and State, 1990/91, annual rpt, 4804–1
Student guaranteed loan Stafford program, borrowers and likelihood of default by selected characteristics, 1989-90, 26306–3.120
Undergrad tuition and fees share of family income, by income level, 1964-90, annual rpt, 4824–1
Vocational education enrollment, and academic and other credits earned, by subject and student characteristics, high school classes of 1982 and 1987, 4838–50
Vocational education enrollment, student and teacher characteristics, and outcomes, for secondary and postsecondary instns, 1970s-90, 4828–42

Energy Resources and Demand

Households, housing, and fuel use characteristics, survey rpt series, 3166–7
Housing (low income) energy aid, funding sources, costs, and participation, by State, FY90, annual rpt, 4584–1

Government and Defense

Family income and Federal tax rates, by income level, late 1970s-94, 21788–212
Income tax returns of foreign corporations and individuals, and US entities abroad, detailed data compilation, 1970s-89, quinquennial rpt, 8308–31
Tax (income) returns filed, by type of filer, selected income items, quarterly rpt, 8302–2.1
Tax (income) returns of individuals, by filing status, tax item, and income level, 1991, annual article, 8302–2.319
Tax (income) returns of individuals, detailed data, 1988, annual rpt, 8304–2
Tax (income) returns of individuals, selected income and tax items by income level, preliminary 1990, annual article, 8302–2.307
Tax (income) returns of individuals with foreign earned income, income and tax items by income level and occupation, 1987, article, 8302–2.301
Tax (value added) alternative proposals revenue impacts, with background data and intl comparisons, 1992 rpt, 26306–6.168
Tax rates and revenue of State and local govts, by source and State, 1992 and historical trends, annual rpt, 10044–1
Tax returns filed, by type of tax and IRS region and service center, projected 1991-98 and trends from 1978, annual rpt, 8304–9
Taxes, spending, and govt efficiency, public opinion by respondent characteristics, 1992 survey, annual rpt, 10044–2

Health and Vital Statistics

Acute and chronic health conditions, disability, absenteeism, and health services use, by selected characteristics, 1990, annual rpt, 4147–10.182

Acute and chronic health conditions, disability, absenteeism, and health services use, by selected characteristics, 1991, annual rpt, 4147–10.183
Child infectious disease cases, and related disability and health care, by disease, health insurance status, and other characteristics, 1988, 4147–10.181
Children (handicapped) with special needs, insurance coverage, and health care services use, by selected characteristics, 1988, 4146–8.216
Cytomegalovirus (congenital) disease cases, by infant, mother, and birth characteristics, type of impairment, State, and Canada Province, 1990-91, 4202–7.314
Deaths and rates, by cause and selected social, demographic, and employment characteristics, 1979-85, natl longitudinal study, 4478–186
Disabled workers labor force status, type and cause of disability, and other characteristics, 1970s-89, chartbook, 4948–11
Educational attainment relation to health condition and care, indicators by selected characteristics, 1989, 4147–10.180
Health condition and care indicators, 1950s-90 with health improvement and disease prevention goals for 1990, annual data compilation, 4144–11
Insurance (health) denial by private carriers because of poor health, by selected characteristics, 1987, 4186–8.23
Life expectancy, by sex, income, education, and labor force status, for whites, 1979-85, article, 4042–3.347
Older persons socioeconomic characteristics, 1900s-90 and projected to 2050, biennial chartbook, 12904–1
Youth health condition, risk factors, and preventive and treatment services use and availability, 1970s-80s, 26358–234.3

Housing and Construction

Alteration and repair of owner-occupied homes, costs and structural, household, financial, and project characteristics, 1987, 2486–1.13
American Housing Survey: unit and household characteristics of recent movers, and reason for move, by tenure, 1989, 2486–1.12
American Housing Survey: unit and households characteristics, unit and neighborhood quality, and journey to work by MSA location, for 11 MSAs, 1987 survey, supplement, 2485–8
American Housing Survey: unit and households detailed characteristics, and unit and neighborhood quality, MSA rpt series, 2485–6
American Housing Survey: unit and households detailed characteristics, and unit and neighborhood quality, 1989, biennial rpt supplement, 2485–13
Mortgage applications, dispositions, and secondary loan market sales, by purpose, lender type, and applicant and neighborhood characteristics, 1991, article, 9362–1.307
Mortgages FHA-insured, financial, property, and borrower characteristics, by metro area, 1991, annual rpt, 5144–24
Mortgages FHA-insured, financial, property, and borrower characteristics, by State, 1991, annual rpt, 5144–1
Mortgages FHA-insured, financial, property, and borrower characteristics, 1991, annual rpt, 5144–17; 5144–23
NYC housing supply, occupancy, condition, and household characteristics, by tenure and borough, 1991 triennial survey, 2488–3
Rental housing units, total, with HUD assistance by program, and eligible for aid, by unit, household, and neighborhood characteristics, and location, 1989, biennial rpt, 5184–11

Labor and Employment

Child care arrangements of mothers employed and in school, and costs, by age of child and characteristics of mother, 1988, Current Population Rpt, 2546–20.24
Pension plan survivor benefits and coverage of spouses, by income level, age, and sex, 1989, GAO rpt, 26121–450
Unemployed persons finding work, by characteristics of worker and new job, aggregate 1986-89, 2546–20.20

Law Enforcement

Crime, criminal justice admin and enforcement, and public opinion, data compilation, 1992 annual rpt, 6064–6
Criminal case processing in Federal district courts, and dispositions, by offense, district, and offender characteristics, 1989, annual data compilation, 6064–29
Schools crime victimization, drug availability, and preventive measures, with student views, 1989 survey, 6066–3.46
Victimization rates, by victim and offender characteristics, circumstances, and offense, 1990 survey, annual rpt, 6066–3.47
Victimizations in cities, suburbs, and rural areas, by offense, circumstances, and victim and offender characteristics, 1987-89, 6066–3.48
Victimizations of households, by offense, household characteristics, and location, 1975-91, annual rpt, 6066–25.49

Population

Asian and Pacific Islands Americans social and economic characteristics, for West and total US, 1990-91, Current Population Report, 2546–1.462
Black Americans social and economic characteristics, for South and total US, 1991 and trends from 1950, annual Current Population Rpt, 2546–1.463
Consumer Income, socioeconomic characteristics of persons, families, and households, detailed cross-tabulations, Current Population Rpt series, 2546–6
Family life and relationships quality and other issues, views of parents and children, 1990 survey, 15528–2
Family members supporting others outside household, by relationship, recipient living arrangements, and provider characteristics, 1988, Current Population Rpt, 2546–20.21
Households and family characteristics, by location, 1991, annual Current Population Rpt, 2546–1.457
Households income and consumer spending, for selected population groups, quarterly journal, 1702–1
Households income and poverty rate of persons under alternative income definitions, by recipient characteristics, 1991, annual Current Population Rpt, 2546–6.78
Households income and wealth distribution by selected characteristics, with foreign comparisons, 1992 compilation of papers, Current Population Rpt, 2546–6.79
Households income transition between higher and lower income levels, 1979-88, 8008–156
Indian Health Service and tribal facilities and use, and Indians health and other characteristics, by IHS region, 1980s-90, annual chartbook, 4084–7
Living arrangements, family relationships, and marital status, by selected characteristics, 1991, annual Current Population Rpt, 2546–1.461
Married-couple families income, and spouses labor force participation and hours worked, by income class, 1979 and 1989, 23848–225
Migration, immigration, and mover characteristics compared to nonmovers, 1987-90, annual Current Population Rpt, 2546–1.456
Migration since 1990, mover characteristics by same or different area, and compared to nonmovers, 1991, annual Current Population Rpt, 2546–1.464
Older persons in poverty, by health, nutrition, assistance, and other characteristics, 1990, GAO rpt, 26131–100
Older persons income and sources, by OASDI beneficiary and poverty status, and other characteristics, 1990, biennial chartbook, 4744–25
Older persons income and sources, by whether OASDI beneficiary, poverty status, and other characteristics, 1990, biennial rpt, 4744–26
Older population, and health, economic, and other characteristics, with foreign comparisons, 1980s-91 with trends and projections, Current Population Rpt, 2546–2.165
Pacific territories population and housing detailed characteristics, by location, 1990 Census of Population and Housing, series, 2551–8
Personal income relative to median, by race and selected other characteristics, mid 1960s-89, Current Population Rpt, 2546–6.73
Population economic well-being indicators, by selected characteristics and household income and income-to-poverty ratio, 1984, 2546–20.22
Poverty status of population and families, by detailed characteristics, 1991, annual Current Population Rpt, 2546–6.77

Prices and Cost of Living

Consumer Expenditure Survey, spending by category, selected household characteristics, and region, quarterly rpt, 6762–14
Foreign countries living costs, State Dept indexes, housing allowances, and hardship differentials by country and major city, quarterly rpt, 7002–7

Public Welfare and Social Security

Child care arrangements of younger working mothers, and costs, by selected characteristics, 1988, 6726–2.1
Food stamp eligibility and payment errors, by type, recipient characteristics, and State, FY90, annual rpt, 1364–15

Food stamp recipient household size, composition, income, and income and deductions allowed, summer 1989, annual rpt, 1364–8
Medicare beneficiaries knowledge of and experience with physician billing and payment under Medicare, by selected characteristics, 1988-89, 17266–2.1
OASDHI, Medicaid, SSI, and related programs benefits, beneficiary characteristics, and trust funds, selected years 1937-90, annual rpt, 4744–3
OASDI and SSI benefit overpayments, and overpaid beneficiaries characteristics, late 1970s-90, GAO rpt, 26121–484
OASI benefits, earnings, and tax revenues under alternative eligibility criteria, 1990, technical paper, 4746–26.15
OASI retirement earnings test, liberalization effect on beneficiaries and Federal revenue, 1991 hearing, 21788–215
Older persons income by source, for married OASI beneficiaries by work and eligibility pattern of wife, 1982, article, 4746–26.12
Supplemental Security Income work incentive programs, participant characteristics, by program, 1982-91, article, 4742–1.305

Recreation and Leisure

Fishing (sport) anglers using charter and partyboat services, age, income, and sources of advertising influencing vessel choice, 1974-86, article, 2162–1.301

Veterans Affairs

Health care services of VA, income eligibility and copayment enforcement, and revenue forgone from unreported income, 1987-91, GAO rpt, 26121–479

BY INDIVIDUAL COMPANY OR INSTITUTION

Agriculture and Food

Cooperatives, finances, operations, activities, and membership, commodity rpt series, 1126–1
Cooperatives sales, for 14 coops on *Fortune* 500 list, 1991, article, 1122–1.303
EC economic integration impacts on domestic and intl agricultural conditions, 1990 conf, 1528–325
Fish Hatchery Natl System activities and deliveries, by species, hatchery, and jurisdiction of waters stocked, FY91, annual rpt, 5504–10
Food marketing sector finances, operations, and merger activity, for processors and distributors, 1991, annual rpt, 1544–22
Food retailers after-tax profits, aggregate and for 16 supermarket chains, 1991, annual rpt, 1544–9.3
Foreign countries agricultural research grants of USDA, by program, subagency, and country, FY92, annual listing, 1954–3
Grain handling facility explosions and casualties, by firm, FY92, annual rpt, 1294–1
Japan full and partial ownership of US agricultural industries, listing, 1992 rpt, 1528–332
Lime producing firms and plants, with operating data, 1991, Mineral Industry Surveys, annual listing, 5614–31
Livestock, meat, and wool, market news summary data by animal type and market, weekly rpt, 1315–1
Peat producing firms, with operating data, 1991, Mineral Industry Surveys, annual listing, 5614–32
Poultry Natl Improvement Plan participating hatcheries and birds, by species and disease program, 1992, annual listing, 1394–15
Research (agricultural) funding and staffing for USDA, State agencies, and other instns, by topic, FY91, annual rpt, 1744–2
Research and education grants, USDA competitive awards by program and recipient, FY91, annual listing, 1764–1
Salt production capacity, by firm and facility, 1991, annual listing, 5614–30

Banking, Finance, and Insurance

Automated teller machine network fees, by type and selected network, 1990, working paper, 9387–8.270
Banking system reform impacts on consumers, with background data, 1991 hearing, 21248–167
Banking system reform issues, with top instn finances, fiscal impacts, and views of depositors, bankers, and regulators on deposit insurance, 1991 hearings, 21248–168
Bankruptcy filings with SEC participation, by firm, FY91, annual rpt, 9734–2.4
Banks (insured commercial and savings) deposits by instn, State, MSA, and county, as of June 1991, annual regional rpt series, 9295–3
Banks (natl) charters, mergers, liquidations, enforcement cases, and financial performance, with data by instn and State, quarterly rpt, 8402–3
Banks financial performance indicators, by bank, 1991-92, hearings, 25248–127
Banks financial performance, risk assessment, and regulation, 1991 annual conf papers, 9375–7
Banks in Fed Reserve 3rd District, assets, income, and rates of return, by major instn, quarterly rpt, annual table, 9387–10
Banks mergers and consolidations approved by Fed Reserve Board of Governors, 1991, annual rpt, 9364–1.2
Banks mergers antitrust issues, with background financial data by State and selected instn, 1991 hearing, 21248–176
Banks mergers approved, and assets and offices involved, by instn, 1990, annual rpt, 9294–5
Banks needing FDIC aid, finances and operations, 1991, annual rpt, 9294–1
Bond (junk) holdings of Resolution Trust Corp, quarterly press release, 9722–4
Credit card issuers disclosure of terms and conditions to consumers, with finances and operations, 1991 hearing, 21248–175
Credit unions assets, members, and location, 1992 annual listing, 9534–6
Credit unions failures, assets and losses to Natl Credit Union Share Insurance Fund by asset size and charter, and for largest failures by instn, FY86-91, 9536–1.7
Credit unions federally insured, finances by instn characteristics and State, as of June 1992, semiannual rpt, 9532–6
Credit unions federally insured, finances, mergers, closings, and insurance fund losses and financial statements, FY91, annual rpt, 9534–7
Credit unions federally insured, finances, 1990-91, annual rpt, 9534–1
Credit unions with low income membership, financial, operating, and membership data, 1982-91, 9536–1.8
Deposit insurance coverage of households and small businesses, and value of insurance to banks by instn, 1970s-90, hearing, 21408–126
Eximbank loans for energy-related products and services, by country and firm, 1990, annual rpt, 9254–3
Fed Financing Bank holdings and transactions, by borrower, monthly press release, 12802–1
Fed Govt accounts receivable, delinquent debt cases and collections of Justice Dept and private law firms, pilot project results, FY91, annual rpt, 6004–20
Fed Home Loan Banks financial statements, 1989-91, annual rpt, 9444–1
Finance companies assets, operating ratios, and growth indicators, for top 20 firms, 1980s-90, article, 9385–1.309
Financial instns assets by instn type, and for top 10 finance companies by firm, 1970 and 1990, article, 9391–16.305
Financial instns reform issues, with finances, impacts of deposit insurance changes, and views of depositors and bankers, 1991 hearings, 25248–129
Futures and options trading volume, by commodity and exchange, FY91, annual rpt, 11924–2
Insurance (life and health) company failures, and State guaranty fund assessments, by State, 1975-90, GAO rpt, 26119–392
Insurance company finances, by insurance type and firm, with some intl comparisons, 1991 conf, 9373–3.35
Insurance industry finances, failures, and regulation, with data by firm and State, 1990 hearing, 25528–119
Insurance industry financial condition, operations, assets, junk bond holdings, and State regulation, with intl comparisons, 1991 hearings, 25268–79
Intl financial instns funds by source and disbursements by purpose, by country, with US policy review, FY90, annual rpt, 15344–1
Intl financial markets performance of foreign and US bank and securities firms, finances and competitiveness issues, 1980s, compilation of papers, 9385–10
Investment advisors for trust, employee benefit, and other accounts, assets advised by all and top 10 firms, 1990, annual rpt, 13004–1
Iraq loans from Banca Nazionale del Lavoro Atlanta office, with purpose and exporting country and company involved, 1991 hearing, 21248–165
Mortgage activity impact of lending program for low- and moderate-income neighborhoods in Philadelphia, with background data, 1980s, working paper, 9387–8.266
New England States, FHLB 1st District thrift instns, financial condition, and locations, 1992, annual listing, 9304–26
North Central States, Fed Reserve 9th District members financial data, by State, quarterly journal, 9383–19
North Central States, FHLB 8th District S&Ls, locations, assets, and savings, 1992, annual listing, 9304–9

Pension Benefit Guaranty Corp guaranteed plans, assets and liabilities of top 50 underfunded plans, 1991, annual press release, 9674–2
Pension plans terminated, liabilities, assets, and Pension Benefit Guarantee Corp recoveries and losses, with top 50 underfunded plans, mid 1970s-91, article, 9371–1.302
Savings instns failure resolution activity and finances of Resolution Trust Corp, with data by asset type, State, region, and instn, monthly rpt, 9722–3
Savings instns failure resolution activity of Resolution Trust Corp, assets, deposits, and assets availability and sales, periodic press release, 9722–1
Savings instns failure resolution activity of Resolution Trust Corp, brokered deposits, fees, and interest rates by instn and region, as of July 1991, hearing, 21248–171
Savings instns failure resolution activity of Resolution Trust Corp, with data by State and instn, and RTC finances, 1990, annual rpt, 9724–1
Savings instns failures, inventory of real estate assets available from Resolution Trust Corp, semiannual listing series, 9722–2
Savings instns holdings of low-grade (junk) bonds and relation to stock volatility and deposit interest rates, late 1980s, working paper, 9375–13.69
Securities holdings by shareholder type, and mgmt and executive pay issues, with data by company, 1991 hearing, 25248–130
Securities purchases, sales, and holdings, by issuer and type and ownership of security, monthly listing, 9732–2
Small Business Admin dev company loan program and debenture sale activity, with data by firm, industry div, State, and region, quarterly rpt, 9762–6
Small Business Admin loans, contract awards, and surety bonds, by firm, State, and city, FY91, annual rpt, 9764–1
Small Business Investment Companies capital holdings, SBA obligation, and ownership, as of July 1992, semiannual listing, 9762–4
Stock exchange trading volume, securities listed by type, and finances, by exchange, selected years 1938-90, annual rpt, 9734–2.1; 9734–2.2
Trust assets of banks, trust companies, and S&Ls, by type of asset and fund, selected firm, and State, 1991, annual rpt, 13004–1
West Central States, Fed Reserve 10th District banking industry structure, performance, and financial devs, 1991, annual rpt, 9381–14
West Central States, FHLB 10th District thrifts, locations, assets, and deposits, 1992, annual listing, 9304–17
Western States, FHLB 11th District shareholder instns, offices, and financial condition, 1992 annual listing, 9304–23

Communications and Transportation

Air traffic (passenger), and aircraft operations by type, by airport and State, projected FY92-2005 and trends from FY83, annual rpt, 7504–7
Air traffic (passenger and cargo), and departures by aircraft type, by carrier and airport, 1991, annual rpt, 7504–35
Air traffic (passenger and cargo), carrier enplanement shares, and FAA airport improvement program grants, by airport and State, 1990, annual rpt, 7504–48
Air traffic, and passenger and freight enplanements, by airport, 1960s-91 and projected to 2010, hub area rpt series, 7506–7
Air traffic, capacity, and performance, by carrier and type of operation, monthly rpt, 7302–6
Air traffic, capacity, and performance for medium regionals, by carrier, quarterly rpt, 7302–8
Air traffic, carriers, craft, airports, and FAA activities, detailed data, 1981-90, annual rpt, 7504–1
Air traffic levels at FAA-operated control facilities, by airport and State, FY91, annual rpt, 7504–27
Air traffic, pilots, airports, and fuel use, forecast FY92-2003 and trends from FY82, annual rpt, 7504–6
Aircraft accidents and circumstances, for US operations of domestic and foreign airlines and general aviation, periodic rpt, 9612–1
Aircraft accidents and deaths by carrier, 1980-90, annual rpt, 9614–1
Aircraft accidents, deaths, and circumstances, by carrier and carrier type, preliminary 1991, annual press release, 9614–9
Aircraft engine rotor failures, by carrier and incident characteristics, 1988, annual rpt, 7504–50
Aircraft flight service station workload of FAA, pilot briefs, contacts, and flight plans by facility, projected FY92-2002 and trends from FY83, annual rpt, 7504–39
Aircraft registered with FAA, by type and characteristics of aircraft, make, carrier, State, and county, 1991, annual rpt, 7504–3
Airline consumer complaints by reason, passengers denied boarding, and late flights, by reporting carrier and airport, monthly rpt, 7302–11
Airline finances and operations, summary data, quarterly rpt, 7502–16
Airline finances, by carrier, carrier group, and for total certificated system, quarterly rpt, 7302–7
Airline flight and engine hours, and shutdown rates, by aircraft and engine model, and air carrier, monthly rpt, 7502–13
Airport improvement program of FAA, activities and grants by State and airport, FY91, annual rpt, 7504–38
Airport planning and dev project grants of FAA, by airport and location, quarterly press release, 7502–14
Auto and auto equipment recalls for safety-related defects, by make, monthly listing, 7762–12
Auto engine and power train R&D projects, DOE contracts and funding by recipient, FY91, annual rpt, 3304–17
Auto safety, crash test results by domestic and foreign model, model years 1987-91, 7768–111
Auto safety crash test results, by domestic and foreign model, press release series, 7766–7
Auto safety crash test results by model, and State vehicle inspections, FY89, annual rpt, 7304–1
Bell Operating Companies transmission and network systems dev, and indicators of use, by firm, 1991 rpt, 2808–30
Boats (recreational) and engines recalls for safety-related defects, by make, periodic listing, 7402–5
Bridges over navigable waters, with type of bridge and use, owner, dimensions, and location, 1991 regional listing series, 7406–5
Bus (Class I) passengers and selected revenue data, for individual large carriers, quarterly rpt, 9482–13
Bus finances and operations, by carrier, 1990, annual rpt, 9486–5.3
Coast Guard search and rescue missions, and lives and property lost and saved, by district and assisting unit, FY91, annual rpt, 7404–2
Containers (intermodal) and equipment owned by shipping and leasing companies, inventory by type and size, 1991, annual rpt, 7704–10
Hazardous materials transport violations and DOT penalties assessed, by company, 1990, annual rpt, 7304–4
Hwy construction bids and contracts for Federal-aid hwys, by State, 1st half 1992, semiannual rpt, 7552–12
Maritime Commission activities, case filings by type and disposition, and civil penalties by shipper, FY91, annual rpt, 9334–1
Motor vehicle industry finances, and average fleet fuel economy, by selected firm, 1991 hearings, 21368–138
Parcel deliveries to and from households, carrier preferences, and content, for USPS and competitors, FY87-90, annual rpt, 9864–10
Radio frequency assignments for mobile communications, effects of auctioning frequencies, 1990, 26306–6.169
Railroad (Class I) finances and operations, detailed data by firm, class of service, and district, 1990, annual rpt, 9486–5.1
Railroad (Class I) finances and operations, detailed data by firm, class of service, and district, 1991, annual rpt, 9486–6.1
Railroad (commuter) and other transit systems grants of Fed Transit Admin, FY93, annual rpt, 7884–12
Railroad accidents, casualties, and damage, by cause, railroad, and State, 1991, annual rpt, 7604–1
Railroad accidents, casualties, circumstances, and railroad involved, 1988, annual rpt, 9614–8
Railroad accidents, casualties, damage, and circumstances, by incident, 1988, annual rpt, 7604–3
Railroad accidents involving hazardous materials, casualties, and circumstances, 1984-89, 9618–18
Railroad and airline labor disputes, and Federal mediation activities and caseloads, with data by carrier and union, FY87-88, annual rpt, 9604–1
Railroad-hwy grade-crossing accidents, detailed data by State and railroad, 1991, annual rpt, 7604–2
Railroad retirement annuities in current-payment status and awarded, by last railroad employer, 1984, annual rpt, 9704–2.2

Railroad revenue, income, freight, and rate of return, by Class I freight railroad and district, quarterly rpt, 9482–2
Railroad safety violation claims settled, by carrier, FY91, annual rpt, 7604–10
Shipbuilding and conversion costs for merchant ships by owner and builder, fleet size, and employment, monthly rpt, 7702–1
Shipbuilding and operating subsidies of MarAd, by vessel type and firm, FY91, annual rpt, 7704–14.1; 7704–14.2
Shipbuilding and repair facilities, capacity, and employment, by shipyard, 1991, annual rpt, 7704–9
Ships in US merchant fleet and Natl Defense Reserve Fleet, vessels, tonnage, and owner, as of July 1991, semiannual listing, 7702–2
Ships under foreign flag owned by US firms and foreign affiliates, by type, owner, and country of registry and construction, as of July 1991, semiannual rpt, 7702–3
Ships weather rpts, and gale and wave observations, quarterly journal, 2152–8
Telecommunications fiber optics and copper wire mileage and access lines, and fiber systems investment, by firm, 1985-91, annual rpt, 9284–18
Telecommunications finances, rates, and traffic for US carriers intl operations, by service type, firm, and country, 1975-90, annual rpt, 9284–17
Telephone and telegraph firms detailed finances and operations, 1990, annual rpt, 9284–6
Telephone firms borrowing under Rural Telephone Program, and financial and operating data, by State, 1991, annual rpt, 1244–2
Telephone service subscribership, charges, and local and long distance firm finances and operations, late 1970s-92, semiannual rpt, 9282–7
Transit systems finances and operations, by mode, size of fleet and urban area, region, and for 518 systems, 1990, annual rpt, 7884–4
Transit systems research and training grants to higher education instns, by project, FY92, annual listing, 7884–7
Truck transport of household goods, financial and operating data by firm, quarterly rpt, 9482–14
Truck transport of household goods, performance and disposition of damage claims, for selected carriers, 1991, annual rpt, 9484–11
Truck transport of property, financial and operating data by region and firm, quarterly rpt, 9482–5
Weather (marine) forecast areas, and broadcast schedules and stations worldwide, as of Sept 1992, annual rpt, 2184–3
Weather (marine) forecast broadcast schedules worldwide, periodic rpt, 2182–9

Education

Black colleges grants from HUD for economic and community dev programs, by recipient, 1991, press release, 5006–3.85
Black colleges technical aid programs supporting Community Dev Block Grants, HUD grants by recipient, 1991, press release, 5006–3.78
Black higher education instns enrollment, finances, staff, and degrees, by instn and selected student characteristics, 1970s-90, 4848–46
Correspondence schools guaranteed student loan participation and default rates, FY87-89, GAO rpt, 26121–448
Digest of Education Statistics, 1992 annual data compilation, 4824–2
Educational Resources Info Center (ERIC) data base, foreign and US providers, 1992 biennial listing, 4814–4
Elementary and secondary public school agencies, by enrollment size and location, fall 1990, annual listing, 4834–1
Higher education enrollment, tuition, control, location, and other instn characteristics, 1991/92, biennial listing, 4844–3
Higher education instn endowment funds, for top 100 instns, FY89, annual rpt, 4824–2.25
Humanities Natl Endowment activities and grants, FY91, annual rpt, 9564–2
Libraries (public) services for Indians and Hawaii Natives, project listing and funding by tribe and State, FY90, annual rpt, 4874–5
Libraries (research) funding of Education Dept, by project, instn, and State, FY90, annual listing, 4874–2
Libraries for blind and handicapped, readership, circulation, staff, funding, and holdings, FY91, annual listing, 26404–3
Libraries selected characteristics, for largest public and higher education facilities, 1992 edition, annual rpt, 4824–2.30
Library science training grants for disadvantaged students, by instn and State, FY91, annual listing, 4874–1
Literacy program for preschoolers and parents, Even Start program activities and grants by recipient, FY90, annual listing, 4804–41
Literacy programs in workplaces, project descriptions and Education Dept funding, FY91, annual listing, 4804–40
Student guaranteed loan activity, by program, guarantee agency, and State, quarterly rpt, 4802–2
Student guaranteed loans, defaults, and collections, by type of loan, lender, and guarantee agency, with data by State and top lender, FY91, annual rpt, 4804–38
Student loans of Fed Govt in default, losses, and rates, by instn and State, as of June 1991, annual rpt, 4804–18
Student supplemental grants, loans, and work-study awards, Federal share by instn and State, 1992/93, annual listing, 4804–17
Tuition and other student charges, by public and private 2- and 4-year higher education instn, and State, 1991/92, annual listing, 4844–10
Women's educational equity program grants and contracts, by project, type, and State, 1988-92, annual rpt, 4804–2

Energy Resources and Demand

Alaska minerals resources, production, oil and gas leases, reserves, and exploratory wells, with maps and bibl, 1990, annual rpt, 5664–11
Army Corps of Engineers activities and projects, FY88 and trends from 1800s, annual rpt, 3754–1.1
Army Corps of Engineers activities and projects, FY89 and trends from 1800s, annual rpt, 3754–1.2
Army Corps of Engineers activities and projects, FY90 and trends from 1800s, annual rpt, 3754–1.3
Auto and light truck fuel economy performance by make, standards, and enforcement, 1978-94 model years, annual rpt, 7764–9
Auto fuel economy test results for US and foreign makes, 1993 model year, annual rpt, 3304–11
Bonneville Power Admin mgmt of Fed Columbia River Power System, finances, operations, and sales by customer, FY91, annual rpt, 3224–1
Bonneville Power Admin sales, revenues, and rates, by customer and customer type, 1991, semiannual rpt, 3222–1
Coal imports and prices, total and for individual power plants, by country and State of origin, quarterly rpt, 3162–37.3
Coal production from 10 largest coalbeds, 1990, biennial rpt, 3164–79
Coal production, stocks, and shipments, by State of origin and destination, end-use sector, and mode of transport, quarterly rpt, 3162–8
Conservation aid of Fed Govt to public and nonprofit private instns, by building type and State, 1991, annual rpt, 3304–15
DOE contracts and grants, by category, State, and for top contractors, FY91, annual rpt, 3004–21
Electric power and industrial plants prohibited from oil and gas primary use, exemptions, and gas use by State, 1980-91, annual rpt, 3334–1
Electric power plants (steam) fuel receipts, costs, and quality, by fuel, plant, utility, and State, 1991, annual rpt, 3164–42
Electric power plants and capacity, by fuel used, owner, location, and operating status, 1991 and for units planned 1992-2001, annual listing, 3164–36
Electric power plants certification applications filed with FERC, for small production and cogeneration facilities, FY80-91, annual listing, 3084–13
Electric power plants production and capital costs, operations, and fuel use, by fuel type, plant, utility, and location, 1990, annual rpt, 3164–9
Electric power plants, production and fuel use and costs, by utility and plant, monthly rpt, 3162–35
Electric power sales and revenue, by end-use sector, consumption level, and utility, 1990, annual rpt, 3164–91
Electric power supply, demand, and trade of Mexico and US, with data by fuel source, utility, and region, 1970s-89 and projected to 2000, 3408–2
Electric utilities conservation programs energy savings and spending, with data for top 25 firms, 1990, 3308–106
Electric utilities privately owned, finances and operations, detailed data, 1990, annual rpt, 3164–23
Electric utilities publicly owned, finances and operations, 1990, annual rpt, 3164–24.1
Foreign direct investment in US energy sources by type and firm, and US affiliates operations, as of 1990, annual rpt, 3164–80

Fuel oxygenate supply, blending in gasoline, and plant capacity and use, by PAD district, monthly rpt, 3162–6.4
Geothermal resources, power plant capacity and operating status, leases, and wells, by location, 1960s-95, 3308–87
Geothermal resources, power plant generation, capacity, and dev potential, by location, 1988-90 and projected to 2030, 3168–122
Helium and other components of natural gas, analyses of individual wells and pipelines, 1985-91, annual rpt, 5604–2
Helium and other components of natural gas, analyses of individual wells and pipelines, 1986-90, 5608–132
Hydroelectric power plants, generation, and capacity, for Reclamation Bur projects, 1978-90 and projected to 1995, 5828–14
Hydroelectric power plants retired, characteristics and location, as of 1992, annual listing, 3084–12
Inventions recommended by Natl Inst of Standards and Technology for DOE support, awards, and evaluation status, 1991, annual listing, 2214–5
Natural and supplemental gas production, prices, trade, use, reserves, and pipeline company finances, by firm and State, monthly rpt with articles, 3162–4
Natural gas and liquefied gas trade of US with 5 countries, by US firm, 1955-91, annual article, 3162–4.301
Natural gas interstate pipeline capacity, use, contract deliveries, and prices, by region, State, and firm, 1990, 3168–125
Natural gas interstate pipeline company detailed financial and operating data, by firm, 1990, annual rpt, 3164–38
Natural gas interstate pipeline company reserves and production, by firm, 1963-91 and deliverability projected to 2011, last issue of annual rpt, 3164–33
Natural gas pipeline supply and disposition of 25 major companies, by affiliate and State, 1990, annual rpt, 3164–4
Naval Petroleum and Oil Shale Reserves sales and contract prices, by purchaser and reserve, FY91, annual rpt, 3334–3
Nuclear material inventory discrepancies at DOE and contractor facilities, 1990/91, annual rpt, 3344–2
Nuclear power plant safety standards and research, design, licensing, construction, operation, and finances, with data by reactor, quarterly journal, 3352–4
Nuclear power plant spent fuel discharges and additional storage capacity needed, by reactor, projected 1991-2040, annual rpt, 3354–2
Nuclear reactors for domestic use and export by function and operating status, with owner, operating characteristics, and location, 1991 annual listing, 3354–15
Nuclear Regulatory Commission activities, finances, and staff, with data for individual power plants, FY91, annual rpt, 9634–2
Oil and gas OCS lease sales in Gulf of Mexico, by company and tract, 1990, annual rpt, 5734–8
Oil and gas reserves and production, for top 100 oil and gas fields, 1990, annual rpt, 3164–46
Oil company profits, refinery capacity, gasoline prices, and market share, by firm, 1991 hearing, 25528–120
Oil drawdowns from Strategic Petroleum Reserve during Persian Gulf War, contract deliveries by purchasing firm, 1st quarter 1991, quarterly rpt, supplement, 3002–13
Oil enhanced recovery research contracts of DOE, project summaries, funding, and bibl, quarterly rpt, 3002–14
Oil refinery capacity, openings, closings, and acquisitions by plant, and fuel used by PAD district, 1991, annual rpt, 3164–2.1
Pacific basin countries energy supply and demand, and implications for US trade, country rpt series, 3406–6
Pacific Northwest electric power capacity and use, by energy source, forecast under alternative load and demand cases, 1991-2012, annual rpt, 3224–3
Pacific Northwest nonutility electric power generation and capacity, by energy source, purchasing utility, and facility, forecasts 1991-2012, annual rpt, 3224–3.4
R&D projects and funding of DOE at natl labs, universities, and other instns, periodic summary rpt series, 3004–18
Rural Electrification Admin financed electric power plants, with location, capacity, and owner, as of Jan 1992, annual listing, 1244–6
Rural Electrification Admin loans, and borrower operating and financial data, by distribution firm and State, 1991, annual rpt, 1244–1
Solar photovoltaic R&D sponsored by DOE, projects, funding, and rpts, FY91, annual listing, 3304–20
Southeastern Power Admin sales by customer, plants, capacity, and Southeastern Fed Power Program financial statements, FY91, annual rpt, 3234–1
Southwestern Fed Power System financial statements, sales by customer, and operations and costs by project, FY91, annual rpt, 3244–1
Tennessee Valley river control activities, and hydroelectric power generation and capacity, 1990, annual rpt, 9804–7
TVA electric power purchases and resales, with electricity use, average bills, and rates by customer class, by distributor, 1991, annual tables, 9804–14
TVA electric power purchases of municipal and cooperative distributors, and prices and use by distributor and consumer sector, monthly rpt, 9802–1
Uranium mill capacity by plant, and production, by operating status, 1987-91, annual rpt, 3164–65.1
Uranium mining and milling industries finances and operations, with selected foreign comparisons, 1970s-90 and projected to 2005, annual rpt, 3164–82
Western Area Power Admin activities by plant, financial statements, and sales by customer, FY91, annual rpt, 3254–1

Geography and Climate

Disasters, casualties, damage, and aid by US and others, by country, FY91 and trends from FY64, annual rpt, 9914–12
Oceanographic research and distribution activities of World Data Center A by country, and cruises by ship, 1990, annual rpt, 2144–15

Government and Defense

African Dev Foundation dev grants and fellowships, by country, FY84-91, annual rpt, 9034–1
AID contracts and grants for technical and support services, by instn, country, and State, FY91, annual listing, 9914–7
AID contracts, grants, and cooperative agreements with higher education instns, by project, instn, and country, FY91, annual listing, 9914–6
AID loans repayment status and terms by program and country, and status of predecessor agency loans, quarterly rpt, 9912–3
American Battle Monuments Commission activities, expenses, and visitors by site, FY87, annual rpt, 9064–1
Capitol Architect outlays for salaries, supplies, and services, itemized by payee and function, 2nd half FY91, semiannual rpt, 25922–2
Collective bargaining agreements of Federal employees, coverage, unions, and location, by agency, for contracts expiring 1992, semiannual listing, 9847–1
DC metro area land acquisition and dev projects of Fed Govt, characteristics and funding by agency and project, FY92-96, annual rpt, 15454–1
Developing countries economic and social conditions from 1960s, and Intl Dev Cooperation Agency and AID activities and funding, FY91-93, annual rpt, 9904–4
DOE real property owned and leased, by type, subagency, contractor, and site, FY91, annual rpt, 3004–28
Election campaign finances to FEC, by type of filer, 1990 natl elections, biennial rpt series, 9276–2
Election campaign-related internal communications of firms and assns, spending by organization, location, and candidate, 1991-92, biennial rpt, 9274–3
House of Representatives salaries, expenses, and contingent fund disbursement, detailed listings, quarterly rpt, 21942–1
Indian trust fund overpayments and shortages, by account, 1970s-91, hearing, 21408–131
Insurance (health) coverage of Federal civilian employees, by plan, FY89-90, annual rpt, 9844–37.2
Inter-American Foundation activities, grants by recipient, and fellowships, by country, FY91, annual rpt, 14424–1
Labor unions recognized in Fed Govt, agreements and membership by agency and facility, as of Jan 1991, biennial listing, 9844–14
Latin America dev grants of Inter-American Foundation by program area, and fellowships by field and instn, by country, FY72-91, annual rpt, 14424–2
Latin America dev grants of Inter-American Foundation, project characteristics, area benefits, and investment returns, for 8 projects, 1970s-88, 14428–1
Military and civilian personnel, by service branch, major installation, and State, as of Sept 1991, annual rpt, 3544–7
Military base and family housing construction, DOD appropriations by facility, service branch, and location, FY91-93, annual rpt, 3544–39

Military base construction, renovation, and closure, budget requests by project, service branch, State, and country, FY93, annual rpt, 3544–15
Military base support costs by function, and personnel and acreage by installation, by service branch, FY93, annual rpt, 3504–11
Military contractor debts owed to Fed Govt and deferred, status by service branch and firm, 1980-91, GAO rpt, 26123–400
Military contractor subcontract awards to small and disadvantaged business, by firm and service branch, quarterly rpt, 3542–17
Military contracts, payroll, and personnel, by service branch and location, with top 5 contractors and maps, by State and country, FY91, annual rpt, 3544–29
Military prime contract awards, by contractor, service branch, State, and city, FY91, annual rpt, 3544–22
Military prime contract awards for R&D, for top 500 contractors, FY91, annual listing, 3544–4
Military prime contract awards for R&D to US and foreign nonprofit instns and govt agencies, by instn and location, FY91, annual listing, 3544–17
Military prime contract awards, for top 100 contractors, FY91, annual rpt, 3504–13; 3544–5
Military prisons population and capacity, by service branch and facility, data compilation, 1992 annual rpt, 6064–6.6
Military procurement fraud cases dispositions, fines, and settlements, for top 100 firms, 1981-92, GAO rpt, 26119–423
Military spending reductions, economic impacts by defense contractor, industry, State, and congressional district, 1989-90 hearings, 23848–224
Military training and education programs funding, staff, students, and facilities, by service branch, FY93, annual rpt, 3504–5
Military weapons acquisition costs by system and service branch, DOD budget, FY91-93, annual rpt, 3504–2
Minority business Federal procurement set-aside contracts, by participant race and sex, industry, firm, and State, FY90, annual rpt, 9764–8
NASA funding by program and type of performer, and contract awards by State, FY91, annual rpt, 9504–6.2
Political action committees contributions by party, and finances, by PAC type, 1991-92, press release, 9276–1.106; 9276–1.110
Presidential libraries holdings, use, and costs, by instn, FY91, annual rpt, 9514–2
Semiconductor integrated circuit sales to DOD, for top 10 firms, 1991, GAO rpt, 26113–588
Senate receipts, itemized expenses by payee, and balances, 1st half FY92, semiannual listing, 25922–1
Tax (income) and effective rates on US, foreign, and worldwide income, by company and industry, 1980s, GAO rpt, 26119–289

Health and Vital Statistics

Allergy and Infectious Diseases Natl Inst activities, grants by recipient and location, and disease cases, FY84-91, annual rpt, 4474–30
Cancer Natl Inst activities, grants by recipient, and cancer deaths and cases, FY91 and trends, annual rpt, 4474–13
Carcinogens chemistry, sources, environment and health risks, and regulation, by substance and brand, 1991 annual rpt, 4044–15
Cigarette smoke tar, nicotine, and carbon monoxide content, by brand, 1990, 9408–53
Dental Research Natl Inst research and training grants, by recipient, FY90, annual listing, 4474–19
Drug (prescription) prices charged to VA and Fed Govt, by manufacturer and drug, 1990-91, hearing, 21768–68
Drug (prescription) prices charged to wholesalers, retailers, VA, and Fed Govt, for 29 drugs, 1985-91, GAO rpt, 26121–472
Drug (prescription) prices in Canada and US, by brand and vendor, 1991, GAO rpt, 26121–482
Drug approvals of FDA, by firm, 1985-90, 25148–44
Drug marketing application processing of FDA, by drug, purpose, and producer, 1991, annual rpt, 4064–14
Family planning and population activities of AID, grants by project and recipient, and contraceptive shipments, by country, FY91, annual rpt series, 9914–13
General Medical Sciences Natl Inst activities, budget, and research and training funding by program, FY91, annual rpt, 4474–38
Health Care Financing Admin research activities and grants, by program, FY91, annual listing, 4654–10
Hearing aid performance test results, by make and model, 1992 annual rpt, 8704–3
Heart, Lung, and Blood Natl Inst activities, and grants by recipient and location, FY91 and disease trends from 1940, annual rpt, 4474–15
HHS financial aid, by program, recipient, State, and city, FY91, annual regional listings, 4004–3
Hospital deaths of Medicare patients, actual and expected rates by diagnosis, with hospital characteristics, by instn, FY90, annual State rpt series, 4654–14
Indian Health Service and tribal facility outpatient visits, by type of provider, selected hospital, and service area, FY91, annual rpt, 4084–3
Indian Health Service and tribal hospital admissions, length of stay, beds, and births, by facility and service area, FY90-91, annual rpt, 4084–4
Indian Health Service and tribal hospital capacity, use, and births, by area and facility, quarterly rpt, 4082–1
Insurance (health) private plans to supplement Medicare, loss ratio performance, by firm, 1988-89, GAO rpt, 26121–452
Insurance (health) programs for Federal civilian employees, enrollment, profits, and administrative costs, by plan, 1984-90, GAO rpt, 26119–376
Kidney end-stage disease research of CDC and HCFA, project listing, 1991, annual rpt, 4654–16
NIH grants and contracts, quarterly listing, 4432–1
NIH grants and contracts to top recipients, FY91, annual rpt, 4434–9
NIH research and training grants awarded to women, by recipient characteristics, inst, and host instn, FY90, annual rpt, 4434–18
Northern Mariana Islands, Saipan garment factories occupational health and safety violations and penalties assessed by OSHA, Mar 1992, press release, 6606–3.10
Physicians, by specialty, State of practice, and school of graduation, 1990, State rpt series, 4116–6
Radiation exposure of workers at nuclear power plants and related facilities, by site, 1968-89, annual rpt, 9634–3
Radiation protection and health physics enrollment and degrees granted by instn and State, and grad placement, by student characteristics, 1991, annual rpt, 3004–7
Reproduction and population research, Fed Govt funding by project, FY90, annual listing, 4474–9
Transplants of organs, failures, deaths, and survival rates, by hospital, 1987-89, annual rpt series, 4104–17

Housing and Construction

Disabled persons low income housing capital advances and rental aid of HUD, by recipient, FY92, press release, 5006–3.98
Economic Dev Admin activities, and funding by program, recipient, State, and county, FY91 and cumulative from FY66, annual rpt, 2064–2
Homeless persons housing and support services projects, funding, and clients, by organization, FY87 and FY90, GAO rpt, 26113–593
Homeless persons transitional housing and support services, HUD grants by community, 1992, press release, 5006–3.95
Homeless persons with handicaps, HUD group housing grants by recipient, 1991, press release, 5006–3.79
Homeless persons with handicaps, HUD group housing grants by recipient, 1992, press release, 5006–3.96
HUD funding for community housing groups planning dev, by training organization, 1992, press release, 5006–3.93
HUD grants to aid housing purchase in depressed areas, by recipient, 1991, press release, 5006–3.84
HUD grants to aid purchase of low income housing units, by recipient, 1992, press release, 5006–3.101
HUD grants to aid purchase of multifamily housing units, by recipient, 1992, press release, 5006–3.91
HUD grants to housing organizations to assist first time low income buyers, by recipient, 1992, press release, 5006–3.94
HUD matching grants for neighborhood revitalization and affordable housing, by recipient, 1992, press release, 5006–3.92
Low income rental housing in rural areas, FmHA loans and impacts of programs to maintain supply and to deter mortgage prepayment, 1988-91, GAO rpt, 26113–586
Older persons low income housing capital advances and rental aid of HUD, by recipient, FY91, press release, 5006–3.88
Older persons low income housing capital advances and rental aid of HUD, by recipient, FY92, press release, 5006–3.97
Public and Indian housing tenant assns, HUD project mgmt and operation training grants by recipient, FY91, press release, 5006–3.77

Public and Indian housing tenant assns, HUD project mgmt and operation training grants by recipient, FY92, press release, 5006–3.100

Industry and Commerce

Aluminum plant ownership, capacity, energy and aluminum sources, and startup and closing dates, by US and foreign plant and location, 1990, annual listing, 5604–49

Auto and auto equipment recalls for safety-related defects, by make, quarterly listing, 7762–2

Auto and auto parts trade, production, and labor conditions, for US and compared to Canada and Mexico, 1950s-90, 6366–3.28

Auto industry sales, profits, and loss, by US make, monthly rpt, annual data, 9882–8

Auto parts trade with Japan and other countries, 1985-90 and forecast to 1994, annual rpt, 2004–10

Auto rental age restrictions impacts on military personnel, with personnel by age, and rental receipts by company, 1991, GAO rpt, 26123–391

Auto sales and production of US industry and Japanese assembly plants in US, and imports, 1979-90, article, 6722–1.313

Chemicals (synthetic organic) production, sales, and manufacturer listing, by product, 1990, annual rpt, 9884–3

Competitiveness (intl) of US industries, with selected foreign and US operating data by major firm and product, series, 2046–12

Computers (supercomputers) firms finances, purchases, and market shares, for Japan and US firms, 1991 rpt, 26358–252

Exporters (US) antiboycott law violations and fines by firm, and invitations to boycott by country, FY91, annual rpt, 2024–1

Foreign direct investment in US, major transactions by type, industry, country, and US location, 1990, annual rpt, 2044–20

Imports detained by FDA, by reason, product, shipper, brand, and country, monthly listing, 4062–2

Lumber (pulpwood) production and mill receipts in North Central States, by species, mill, State, and county, 1990, annual rpt, 1204–19

Mexico and US economic and trade impacts of proposed North American Free Trade Agreement, with data on maquiladora plants, 1980s-90, hearings, 21788–210

Mexico trade with US and other countries, foreign investment, and maquiladoras operations, 1980s-91, GAO rpt, 26119–417

Militarily strategic manufacturing industries finances, operations, and intl competitiveness, series, 2026–1

Minerals foreign and US supply under alternative market conditions, reserves, and background industry data, series, 5606–4

Minerals production, reserves, and industry role in domestic economy and world supply, world area and country rpt, series, 5606–1

Minerals Yearbook, Vol 1, 1990: commodity reviews of production, reserves, supply, use, and trade, annual rpt series, 5604–20

Minerals Yearbook, Vol 1, 1991: commodity reviews of production, reserves, supply, use, and trade, annual rpt series, 5604–15

Paper recycling by grade, with newsprint collection, recycling capacity by company, and curbside pickup operations, by State, 1970s-80s and projected to 1995, hearing, 25318–84

Semiconductor and related equipment sales, by US and Japanese firm, 1970s-88, annual rpt, 15034–1.1

Semiconductor industry capital investment and R&D spending under alternative tax proposals, and asset/equity ratios by selected firm, 1980s-91, working paper, 15036–1.2

Steel production of world top 20 firms, 1981 and 1991, semiannual rpt, 9882–15

Tobacco production and use in Latin America, Canada, and US, and related economic, health, and social issues, 1950s-92, annual rpt, 4204–18

Labor and Employment

Alaska rural areas population characteristics, and energy resources dev effects, series, 5736–5

Collective bargaining agreements expiring during year, and workers covered, by firm, union, industry group, and State, 1992, annual rpt, 6784–9

Fed Labor Relations Authority and Fed Service Impasses Panel activities, and cases by union, agency, and disposition, FY86-91, annual rpt, 13364–1

Pension plans health benefits accounting standards changes, and impacts on firm finances, with background data, 1986-89, technical paper, 9366–6.298

Petrochemicals industries contract labor accidents, injuries, safety programs operations, and employee characteristics, 1986-91, 6608–6

Recruitment visits at colleges by Federal agencies and private companies, and school officials views, 1991, GAO rpt, 26119–377

Research contracts of Bur of Intl Labor Affairs, FY83-91, annual listing, 6364–1

Small Business Investment Company funding of selected firms, employment at start of investment and as of 1990, 9768–24

Trade adjustment aid for workers, petitions by disposition, selected industry, union, and State, monthly rpt, 6402–13

Union representation elections conducted by NLRB, results, monthly rpt, 9582–2

Wage and benefit changes from collective bargaining and mgmt decisions, by industry div, monthly rpt, 6782–1

Work stoppages, workers involved, and days idle, 1991 and trends from 1947, annual press release, 6784–12

Law Enforcement

Aircraft hijackings, on-board explosions, and other crimes, US and foreign incidents, 1986-90, annual rpt, 7504–31

Auto theft rates of new cars, by make and model, 1990 model year, annual rpt, 7764–21

Higher education instn law enforcement personnel, and crimes by offense, by instn, 1991, annual rpt, 6224–2.1; 6224–2.3

Prison construction and operating costs, capacity, and inmates, for Federal and State facilities, 1985-89, GAO rpt, 26119–407

Prison employment requirements for new and expanded Federal facilities, by occupation, FY87-95, GAO rpt, 26119–397

Prisoners and staff in Federal instns, by selected characteristics, region, and instn, FY89, annual rpt, 6244–1

Prisoners in Federal instns, admissions, releases, and recidivism, by region, monthly rpt series, 6242–1

Prisons Bur admin offices and correctional instns, facility characteristics, 1992, annual listing, 6244–4

Prisons Bur correctional staff by selected characteristics, and inmates, by facility, data compilation, 1992 annual rpt, 6064–6.1

Research and program evaluation for criminal justice, Natl Inst of Justice grants by recipient, FY91, 6066–20.24

Terrorism (intl) organizations, activities and strengths, listing, 1991, annual rpt, 7004–13

Terrorism incidents in US, related activity, and casualties, by attack type, target, group, and location, 1991, annual rpt, 6224–6

Trials (civil and criminal) of 20 days or more terminated in Federal district courts, case and trial characteristics, 1991, annual rpt, 18204–8.18

Victims of crime, compensation and support service programs funding, by offense and State, FY88-90, biennial rpt, 6064–37

Natural Resources, Environment, and Pollution

EPA R&D programs and funding, FY91, annual listing, 9184–18

Fish (salmon) conservation spending by organization, and population, for Columbia River basin, 1970-91, GAO rpt, 26113–577

Hazardous substances industrial releases and reduction methods under EPA regulation, by chemical, source, industry, and location, 1989, annual rpt, 9234–6

Hazardous substances industrial releases and reduction methods under EPA regulation, with chemical stocks and use, facility directory, 1987-89, annual CD-ROM, 9234–7

Hazardous waste site remedial action under Superfund, current and proposed sites descriptions and status, periodic listings, series, 9216–3

Hazardous waste site remedial action under Superfund, current and proposed sites priority ranking and status by location, series, 9216–5

Indian land ownership, multiple ownership, and Bur of Indian Affairs records maintenance, for 12 reservations, 1991, GAO rpt, 26113–559

Marine mammals research, Federal funding by topic, recipient, and agency, FY91, annual rpt, 14734–2

Nuclear power plant spent fuel discharges, storage capacity, and inventories, by reactor, 1968-89, 3166–6.62

Nuclear power plant spent fuel storage capacity and inventories, by reactor, as of 1987, 3166–6.59

Nuclear weapons facilities of DOE, contractor fees, environmental and safety enforcement activity, and salaries, by contractor and facility, 1987-88, hearing, 21408–127

Ocean pollution research, monitoring, and resources dev activities of Fed Govt, funding and project descriptions, FY89, annual rpt, 2144–23

Radiation exposure of population near commercial reactors, by body site, age group, and selected plant, 1988, annual rpt, 9634–7

Radioactive low-level waste disposal activities of States and interstate compacts, with data by disposal facility and reactor, 1990, annual rpt, 3004–36

Radioactive materials shipments on US hwys, by material type, carrier, and shipper, 1985-90, 3008–129

Radioactive spent fuel deliveries to DOE for disposal, by utility and reactor, projected 1998-2007, annual rpt, 3364–5

Radioactive waste and spent fuel generation, inventory, and disposal, 1960s-90 and projected to 2020, annual rpt, 3364–2

Uranium tailings at inactive mills, remedial action proposals, costs, site characteristics, and environmental, socioeconomic, and health impacts, series, 3356–4

Water storage and carriage facilities of Reclamation Bur, capacity, and operating status, as of Sept 1990, biennial listing, 5824–7

Population

Indian tribes in Pacific Northwest, OCS oil and gas lease and dev environmental, economic, and cultural impacts, with background data, 1970s-92, 5738–35

Prices and Cost of Living

Auto industry finances and operations, trade by country, and prices of selected US and foreign models, monthly rpt, 9882–8

Public Welfare and Social Security

Food aid programs purchases, by commodity, firm, and shipping point or destination, weekly rpt, 1302–3

Foreign countries aid programs of private voluntary agencies, funding, and outlays, by agency, 1990, annual rpt, 9914–9

HHS financial aid, by program, recipient, State, and city, FY91, annual regional listings, 4004–3

Indians and Alaska Natives organizations AFDC Job Opportunities and Basic Skills Training programs, funding and eligibility, FY91, GAO rpt, 26121–460

Nonprofit charitable organizations finances, with data by State and for top 10 instns, 1988, article, 8302–2.302

Nonprofit charitable organizations revenue and assets, for top 10 organizations, 1988, annual article, 8302–2.315

Poor families self-sufficiency aid and Head Start programs, HUD and HHS joint funding by recipient, 1991, press release, 5006–3.83

Refugee arrivals and resettlement in US, by age, sex, sponsoring agency, State, and country, monthly rpt, 4592–1

Tax exempt organizations finances, with data by type, size, State, and for largest organizations, late 1940s-80s, compilation of papers, 8308–35

Recreation and Leisure

Arts Natl Endowment activities and grants, FY91, annual rpt, 9564–3

Historic and natural natl landmarks damaged and threatened, with owner, location, damage type, and recommended remedial action, 1990, annual listing, 5544–16

Museum Services Inst activities and finances, and grants by recipient, FY91, annual rpt, 9564–7

Smithsonian Instn activities, rpts, and funding by donor, FY91, annual rpt, 29574–1.2

Science and Technology

Arkansas govt science agency research grants and industry sponsors matching funds, and Federal R&D aid to higher education instns, mid 1980s-90, hearing, 21708–131

Astronomical tables, time conversion factors, and listing of observatories worldwide, 1993, annual rpt, 3804–7

Education in science and engineering, grad programs enrollment by field, source of funds, and characteristics of student and instn, 1990, annual rpt, 9627–7

Engineering research and education grants of NSF, FY91, annual listing, 9624–24

Labor force, Federal and university research funding, and educational data, for science and engineering, series, 9626–6

NASA procurement contract awards, by type, contractor, State, and country, FY92 with trends from 1961, semiannual rpt, 9502–6

NASA R&D funding to higher education instns, by field, instn, and State, FY91, annual listing, 9504–7

NSF grants and contracts, by field, recipient, and State, FY90, annual rpt, 9624–26

Nuclear engineering enrollment and degrees by instn and State, and women grads plans and employment, 1991, annual rpt, 3006–8.18

Nuclear engineering enrollment and degrees granted by instn and State, and grad placement, by student characteristics, 1991, annual rpt, 3004–5

Oceanographic research cruise ships characteristics, by higher education instn and Federal agency, 1992, annual listing, 3804–6

Patents (US) granted to US and foreign applicants, by applicant and country, 1960s-91, annual rpt, 2244–3

R&D and related funding of Fed Govt to higher education and nonprofit instns, by field, instn, agency, and State, FY90, annual rpt, 9627–17

R&D funding by higher education instns and federally funded centers, by field, instn, and State, FY90, annual rpt, 9627–13

R&D licenses for university activities supported by NSF and NIH, transfer to private firms, related income, and scientists associated with licensees, FY89-90, GAO rpt, 26113–575

Radiation protection and health physics enrollment and degrees granted by instn and State, and women grads plans and employment, 1991, annual rpt, 3006–8.19

Science and Engineering Indicators, employment, education, R&D funding, and industry impacts, with foreign comparisons, 1960s-91, biennial rpt, 9624–10.5

Small business R&D grants of Fed Govt, project sales by type and dev funding by source, by agency and selected firm, 1984-91, GAO rpt, 26113–393

Spacecraft launches and other activities of NASA and USSR, with flight data, 1957-91, annual rpt, 9504–6.1

Technological innovations of industrial and Federal labs, market potential and results of annual *R&D 100* awards competition, 1960s-90, 2218–86

Veterans Affairs

Agent Orange exposure cases at VA health centers, and exemptions from copayment requirements, 1989, GAO rpt, 26121–464

AIDS cases at VA health care centers by sex, race, risk factor, and facility, and AIDS prevention and treatment issues, quarterly rpt, 8702–1

Geriatric Research, Education and Clinical Centers of VA, activities and finances, FY88, annual rpt, 8704–8

Health care facilities of VA, trainees by detailed program and city, FY91, annual rpt, 8704–4

Health care for veterans, patients, visits, costs, and operating beds, by VA and contract facility, and region, quarterly rpt, 8602–4

Health care staff of VA, and turnover, by occupation and location, 1991, annual rpt, 8604–8

Hospital and nursing home use, beds, daily census, and construction projects, by VA facility, FY91, annual rpt, 8604–3

Hospital compliance with quality assurance standards of accreditation commission, by VA facility and region, 1989-90, GAO rpt, 26121–441

Mental illness (post-traumatic stress) among Persian Gulf veterans and VA program use, by site, 1991, annual rpt, 8704–7

Mental illness (post-traumatic stress) among veterans by period of service, and VA treatment and rehabilitation program operations and staff, FY91, annual rpt, 8704–6

Private health care providers payments from VA, by VA clinic, FY90, GAO rpt, 26121–474

VA health care facilities energy use and conservation, by facility, quarterly rpt, 8602–9

BY INDUSTRY

Agriculture and Food

Family farms financial condition, 1970s-88, annual rpt, 1504–4

Banking, Finance, and Insurance

Small Business Admin dev company loan program and debenture sale activity, with data by firm, industry div, State, and region, quarterly rpt, 9762–6

Small Business Admin guaranteed loans issued under regular, certified, and preferred lender programs, selected characteristics, FY83-90, GAO rpt, 26113–581

Small Business Admin loan guarantee program participants finances, operations, characteristics, and views, 1991 survey, 9768–25

Communications and Transportation

Airports employment, air cargo shipments by industry, and convention attendance, for Chicago and other locations, mid 1970s-90, working paper, 9375–13.78

Mail volume to and from households, use, and views, by class, source, content, and household characteristics, FY87-90, annual rpt, 9864–10

Radio frequency assignments for mobile communications, effects of auctioning frequencies, 1990, 26306–6.169

Education
Adult education participation, by selected characteristics, 1991 survey, 4826–10.5
Energy Resources and Demand
Coal receipts and prices at manufacturing plants, by SIC 2-digit industry, quarterly rpt, 3162–37.2
Electric power demand, and industrial and employment impacts of capacity shortfalls and new power plants, by selected State, 1960s-80s and projected to 2000, hearing, 21248–163
Electric power use indexes, by SIC 2- to 4-digit industry, monthly rpt, 9365–2.24
Energy supply, demand, and prices, by fuel type and end-use sector, with foreign comparisons, 1981-90, annual fact book, 3164–76
Industrial electric power producers capacity, generation, and sales by industry div and State, and emissions, by census div, 1989-90, article, 3162–35.301
Manufacturing energy use and prices, by fuel type and industry, 1974-88, 3166–15.3
Manufacturing energy use and prices, 1988 survey, series, 3166–13
Manufacturing sector energy efficiency, by industry, 1980-88, annual rpt, 3164–74.1
Government and Defense
Income tax returns of foreign corporations and individuals, and US entities abroad, detailed data compilation, 1970s-89, quinquennial rpt, 8308–31
Military in-house commercial activities work-years, by service branch, State, and installation, FY91, annual rpt, 3544–25
Military spending reductions, economic impacts by defense contractor, industry, State, and congressional district, 1989-90 hearings, 23848–224
Military spending reductions, economic impacts of alternative plans, with data by industry and State, various periods 1949-87, article, 9385–1.313
Military spending reductions, economic impacts of Bush Admin plans by industry and State, FY92-97, 26306–6.167
Minority business Federal procurement set-aside contracts, by participant race and sex, industry, firm, and State, FY90, annual rpt, 9764–8
Multinatl firms US affiliates income tax compliance issues, with income and tax data by industry group, 1987-89, press release, 8008–155
Puerto Rico and other US possessions corporations income tax returns, income and tax items, and employment, by selected industry, 1989, article, 8302–2.326
Tax (income) and effective rates on US, foreign, and worldwide income, by company and industry, 1980s, GAO rpt, 26119–289
Tax (income) returns filed, by type of filer, selected income items, quarterly rpt, 8302–2.1
Tax (income) returns for foreign corporate activity in US, selected income and tax items, by industry div and selected country, 1988, article, 8302–2.309
Tax (income) returns of corporations, income and tax items by asset size and detailed industry, 1989, annual rpt, 8304–4; 8304–21
Tax (income) returns of corporations, summary data by asset size and industry div, 1989, annual article, 8302–2.321
Tax (income) returns of corporations with foreign tax credit, income and tax items by industry group, 1988, biennial article, 8302–2.316
Tax (income) returns of Foreign Sales Corps, assets, and income and tax items, by industry, country of incorporation, and transaction pricing method, 1987, article, 8302–2.311
Tax (income) returns of Interest Charge-Domestic Intl Sales Corps, assets and selected income and tax items, by detailed industry, 1987, article, 8302–2.312
Tax (income) returns of partnerships, income statement and balance sheet items, by industry group, 1990, annual article, 8302–2.314
Tax (income) returns of sole proprietorships, income statement items, by industry group, 1990, annual article, 8302–2.317; 8302–2.320
Tax (sales) collections of retailers as share of sales, by SIC 2- to 4-digit kind of business, 1990, annual rpt, 2413–5
Health and Vital Statistics
Alaska occupational injury deaths, by cause, occupation, and industry, early 1980s, article, 4042–3.307
Deaths and rates, by cause and selected social, demographic, and employment characteristics, 1979-85, natl longitudinal study, 4478–186
Deaths related to work injuries, by equipment type, circumstances, and OSHA standards violated, series, 6606–2
Hazardous substances occupational exposure, employer compliance with info and training regulations, employer views by firm size and industry div, 1989-91, GAO rpt, 26121–456
Hazardous substances occupational exposure, employer compliance with info and training regulations, inspections, and fines, by firm size and industry div, 1989-91, GAO rpt, 26121–439
Health condition and care indicators, 1950s-90 with health improvement and disease prevention goals for 1990, annual data compilation, 4144–11
Injuries, illnesses, and lost workdays, by industry div and major manufacturing group, Monthly Labor Review, 6722–1.7
Injury and illness rates by SIC 2- to 4-digit industry, and deaths by cause and industry div, 1990, annual rpt, 6844–1
Injury and illness rates, by SIC 2- to 4-digit industry, 1989-90, annual rpt, 6844–7
Insurance (health) coverage, and uninsured workers by industry div, with data by age, race, and marital status, 1989, GAO rpt, 26119–389
Insurance (health) provided by employer, costs and cost factors by industry div and firm size, 1987-91, GAO rpt, 26121–485
Occupational injuries, illnesses, and lost workdays, by SIC 2-digit industry, 1990-91, annual press release, 6844–3
Occupational injury and illness rates by circumstances and establishment size, and methodology for computing rates, industry rpt series, 6886–4
Occupational repetitive motion injury rates by selected industry, with data for California, 1980s, hearing, 21408–128
Housing and Construction
Building materials industry finances and operations, by SIC 4-digit industry, selected years 1977-89, article, 2042–1.302
Economic Dev Admin activities, and funding by program, recipient, State, and county, FY91 and cumulative from FY66, annual rpt, 2064–2
NYC housing supply, occupancy, condition, and household characteristics, by tenure and borough, 1991 triennial survey, 2488–3
Industry and Commerce
Business activity indicators, 1990, annual rpt, 9364–5.9
Business cycle recession and expansion duration indicators, 1850s-1990, working paper, 9375–13.83
Business statistics, detailed data for major industries and economic indicators, *Survey of Current Business*, monthly rpt, 2702–1
Business statistics, detailed data for major industries and economic indicators, 1960-91, *Survey of Current Business* biennial supplement, 2704–1
Capital (fixed), govt and private nonresidential structures and equipment, residential capital, and consumer-owned durable goods, 1925-90, annual article, 2702–1.305
Capital (fixed), govt and private nonresidential structures and equipment, residential capital, and consumer-owned durable goods, 1988-91, annual article, 2702–1.327
Capital expenditures for plant and equipment, by industry div, quarterly rpt, 2042–1.4
Capital expenditures for plant and equipment, by major industry group, quarterly rpt, 2502–2
Capital expenditures for plant and equipment, by major industry group, 1990, annual rpt, 9364–5.6
Capital investment changes relation to changes in costs, by asset type and industry div, late 1950s-80s, article, 9373–1.304
Corporate profits, by industry div, selected years 1929-91, annual rpt, 204–1.7
Corporations financial statements for manufacturing, mining, and trade, by selected SIC 2- to 3-digit industry, quarterly rpt, 2502–1
County Business Patterns, 1989: employment, establishments, and payroll, by SIC 2- to 4-digit industry and county, annual State rpt series, 2326–8
County Business Patterns, 1990: employment, establishments, and payroll, by SIC 2- to 4-digit industry and county, annual State rpt series, 2326–6
EC govt subsidies, by industry sector and for Airbus Industrie, by country, 1980s-91, hearing, 21708–132
Economic censuses of 1987 and related programs, CD-ROM series, 2326–22
Economic conditions and employment, alternative BLS projections to 2005 and trends 1975-90, biennial rpt, 6744–19
Explosives and blasting agents use, by type, industry, and State, 1991, Mineral Industry Surveys, annual rpt, 5614–22

Exports, imports, balances, US consumption, and operations of industries affected, by industry, 1989-91, annual rpt, 9884–25
Finances and operations, by SIC 2- to 4-digit industry, forecast 1992, annual rpt, 2044–28
Foreign-controlled US firms transactions with related foreign persons, by type, industry div, and country, 1988, article, 8302–2.318
Foreign direct investment by method and industry div, and affiliated firms R&D spending, pay, employment, and trade compared to US-owned firms, 1980-90, article, 9391–1.309
Foreign direct investment in US, by industry group and world area, 1989-91, annual article, 2702–1.331
Foreign direct investment in US, major transactions by type, industry, country, and US location, 1990, annual rpt, 2044–20
Foreign direct investment of US, by industry group and world area, 1989-91, annual article, 2702–1.332
Foreign direct investment of US, in oil, selected manufacturing industries, and wholesale trade, by country, 1989-91, annual rpt, 21384–5
Gross State Product by component, industry div, and State, 1977-89, article, 2702–1.303
Gross State product impacts on govt spending, with data by industry div and State, 1960s-86, working paper, 9377–9.133
Imports and tariff provisions effect on US industries and products, investigations with background financial and operating data, series, 9886–4
Imports injury to US industries from foreign subsidized products, investigations with background financial and operating data, series, 9886–15
Imports injury to US industries from sales at less than fair value, investigations with background financial and operating data, series, 9886–14
Input-output model of BEA, regional multipliers by industry and State, and methodology, 1992 guide, 2708–47
Input-output structure of US economy, detailed interindustry transactions for 84 industries, and components of final demand, 1987, annual article, 2702–1.316
Input-output structure of US economy, detailed interindustry transactions for 541 industries, and components of final demand, 1982 benchmark data, 2708–17
Investment (foreign direct) in US by country, and finances, employment, and acreage owned, by industry group of business acquired or established, 1985-91, annual article, 2702–1.320
Investment (intl) position of US, by component, industry, world region, and country, 1990-91, annual article, 2702–1.323
Israel economic conditions, US investment and export opportunities, and trade practices, 1992 rpt, 2008–32
Manufacturing annual survey, 1990: finances and operations, by SIC 2- to 4-digit industry, series, 2506–14
Manufacturing census, 1987: shipments of manufacturers products, by customer class and SIC 2- and 4-digit industry, subject rpt, 2497–4
Manufacturing industries operations and performance, analytical rpt series, 2506–16
Manufacturing output forecasts, performance of regional indexes by SIC 2-digit industry, 1992 working paper, 9375–13.85
Manufacturing production and selected measures of capacity use, for 16 industry groups, monthly rpt, 23842–1.3
Manufacturing production, shipments, inventories, orders, and pollution control costs, periodic Current Industrial Rpt series, 2506–3
Mexico investment spending by industry, and impacts of relative price changes and intl debt crisis, 1980s, technical paper, 9366–7.270
Middle Atlantic States manufacturing output index, monthly rpt, 9387–12
Militarily strategic manufacturing industries finances, operations, and intl competitiveness, series, 2026–1
Minerals production, reserves, and industry role in domestic economy and world supply, world area and country rpt, series, 5606–1
Minority- and woman-owned businesses and owner characteristics, by industry, employment and sales size, and form of ownership, 1987 survcy, 2328–59
Minority Business Dev Centers mgmt and financial aid, and characteristics of businesses, by region and State, FY91, annual rpt, 2104–6
Multinatl firms US affiliates finances and operations, by industry, country of parent firm, and State, 1987, 2702–1.340; 2708–48
Multinatl firms US affiliates finances and operations, by industry div, country of parent firm, and State, 1989-90, annual article, 2702–1.319; 2702–1.337
Multinatl firms US affiliates, finances, and operations, by industry, world area of parent firm, and State, 1989-90, annual rpt, 2704–4
Multinatl firms US affiliates gross product, by component, industry, and country of parent firm, 1987-90, article, 2702–1.342
Multinatl US firms and foreign affiliates finances and operations, by industry and country, 1989 benchmark survey, annual rpt, 2704–5
Multinatl US firms and foreign affiliates finances and operations, by industry and world area, 1988, annual article, 2702–1.329
Multinatl US firms foreign affiliates capital expenditures, by major industry group, world area, and country, 1987-92, semiannual article, 2702–1.312
Multinatl US firms foreign affiliates capital expenditures, by major industry group, world area, and country, 1988-92, semiannual article, 2702–1.335
Multinatl US firms foreign affiliates, income statement items by asset size, industry, and country, 1988, biennial article, 8302–2.322
Natl income and product accounts, comprehensive accounts and components, benchmark revisions, 1929-88, 2708–5
Natl income and product accounts, comprehensive accounts and components, *Survey of Current Business*, monthly rpt, 2702–1.29; 2702–1.30
OPEC members direct investment in US, by industry div, as of 1990, annual rpt, 3164–80
Overseas Business Reports: economic conditions, investment and export opportunities, and trade practices, country market research rpt series, 2046–6
Partnership income and losses impact of 1986 Tax Reform Act, by profit status and selected industry, 1980s, article, 8302–2.313
Philadelphia metro area transit service operations, costs and benefits, and local economic and air pollution impacts, 1970s-90 and projected to 2020, 7308–205
Production and capacity use indexes, by SIC 2- to 4-digit industry, monthly rpt, 9365–2.24
Production indexes, capital investment, and capacity use by industry div, and manufacturers and trade sales and inventories, 1947-90, annual rpt, 204–1.3
Productivity of labor, capital, and other inputs in manufacturing, changes by selected industry, various periods 1949-88, article, 6722–1.345
Recycling in manufacturing industries, fuel savings, and CO2 emissions reductions, 1988 and projected to 1995, hearing, 21368–140
Retail trade sales and inventories, by kind of business, region, and selected State, MSA, and city, monthly rpt, 2413–3
Retail trade sales, by kind of business, advance monthly rpt, 2413–2
Retail trade sales, inventories, purchases, gross margin, and accounts receivable, by SIC 2- to 4-digit kind of business and form of ownership, 1990, annual rpt, 2413–5
Services trade of US, direct and among multinatl firms affiliates, by industry and world area, 1986-91, article, 2702–1.336
Small business finances, operations, owner characteristics, and Federal contracts, 1980s-90, annual rpt, 9764–6
Soviet Union and US economic and sociodemographic indicators, selected years 1970-90, handbook, 2328–80
Statistical Abstract of US, 1992 annual data compilation, 2324–1
Technology-intensive industries intl competitiveness, with background data by industry and foreign comparisons, 1960s-91, GAO rpt, 26123–406
Tennessee Valley economic conditions, and compared to US, alternative projections 1992-2010 and trends from 1929, annual rpt, 9804–27
West Central States, gross State product and growth rates by industry div and State, 1979-89, article, 9381–1.306

Labor and Employment

Alaska rural areas population characteristics, and energy resources dev effects, series, 5736–5
Collective bargaining agreements expiring during year, and workers covered, by firm, union, industry group, and State, 1992, annual rpt, 6784–9
Collective bargaining agreements expiring during year, and workers covered, by industry and level of govt, 1993, annual press release, 6726–1.54
Collective bargaining contract expirations, wage increases, and coverage, by major industry group, 1991, annual article, 6722–1.306

Collective bargaining wage changes and coverage, by industry and whether contract includes escalator clause and lump sum payment, 1982-91, annual article, 6722–1.325
Dallas-Fort Worth metro area employment, earnings, hours, and CPI changes, late 1970s-91, annual rpt, 6964–2
Disabled persons work history before and after SSI application, by age, diagnosis, industry div, and sex, aggregate 1937-87, article, 4742–1.308
Displaced workers, layoffs and recalls by layoff reason, industry, firm size, and State, 2nd half 1988, 6406–6.36
Displaced workers, layoffs and unemployment insurance claims by reason, industry, selected characteristics, and State, quarterly press release, 6742–23
Displaced workers, layoffs and unemployment insurance claims by reason, industry, selected characteristics, MSA, and State, 1990, annual rpt, 6744–18
Displaced workers losing job 1979-89, by industry, as of Jan 1990, article, 6722–1.340
Displaced workers losing job 1987-92, labor force status by employment and other characteristics, as of Jan 1992, biennial press release, 6726–1.48
Earnings by industry group, region, and State, 1989-91, annual article, 2702–1.328
Employment and earnings by industry div, and personal income per capita and by source, by industry div, State, MSA, and county, 1969-90, annual CD-ROM, 2704–7
Employment and Earnings, detailed data, monthly rpt, 6742–2
Employment and economic conditions, alternative BLS projections to 2005 and trends 1975-90, biennial rpt, 6744–19
Employment and GNP, accuracy of BLS forecasts made late 1970s-85, as of 1990, article, 6722–1.335
Employment and unemployment, by age, sex, race, marital and family status, industry div, and State, Monthly Labor Review, 6722–1.2
Employment by industry div and State, monthly press release, 6742–12
Employment Cost Index and alternative measure of compensation costs, by component, occupation, industry group, union status, and location, 1975-92, annual rpt, 6744–20
Employment Cost Index and percent change by occupational group, industry div, region, and metro-nonmetro area, quarterly press release, 6782–5
Employment Cost Index changes for nonfarm workers, by occupation, industry div, region, and bargaining status, monthly rpt, 6782–1
Employment cost indexes, by occupation, industry div, and region, Monthly Labor Review, 6722–1.3
Employment, earnings, and hours, by selected SIC 1- to 4-digit industry, State, and for 275 MSAs, 1987-92, 6748–81
Employment, earnings, and hours, by SIC 1- to 4-digit industry, monthly 1989-Feb 1992, annual rpt, 6744–4
Employment, earnings, and hours, monthly press release, 6742–5
Employment, earnings, hours, and productivity, by industry div, selected years 1946-91, annual rpt, 204–1.2
Employment situation, earnings, hours, and other BLS economic indicators, transcripts of BLS Commissioner's monthly testimony, periodic rpt, 23846–4
Employment, unemployment, and labor force characteristics, by region, State, and selected metro area, 1991, annual rpt, 6744–7
Enterprise zone programs in rural areas, jobs created and saved, and firms participating, by industry, 1986, article, 1502–7.303
Farm population, by employment, social, and economic characteristics, and region, 1990, annual Current Population Rpt, 2546–1.458
Foreign and US manufacturing hourly compensation costs, by industry and country, series, 6826–3
Foreign countries labor conditions, union coverage, and work accidents, annual country rpt series, 6366–4
Home-based workers and hours, by worker characteristics, occupational group and industry div, 1991, press release, 6726–1.52
Houston metro area employment, earnings, hours, and CPI changes, 1970s-91, annual rpt, 6964–1
Imports (duty-free) from Caribbean area, impact on US employment by industry, 1991, annual rpt, 6364–2
Imports, exports, and employment impacts, by SIC 2- to 4-digit industry and commodity, quarterly rpt, 2322–2
Labor demand, turnover, and training completions, by detailed occupation, 1990 and projected to 2005, biennial rpt, 6744–3
Labor force status, by worker characteristics and industry group, 1990-91, annual article, 6722–1.312
Labor force, wages, hours, and payroll costs, by major industry group and demographic characteristics, *Survey of Current Business*, monthly rpt, 2702–1.7
Labor hourly costs, by component, occupational group, industry div, union coverage, and region, 1992, annual rpt, 6744–21
Labor Relations Natl Board activities, cases, elections conducted, and litigation, FY90, annual rpt, 9584–1
Minority group and women employment, by occupation, SIC 1- to 3- digit industry, State, and MSA, 1991, annual rpt, 9244–1
New England States economic indicators, Fed Reserve 1st District, monthly rpt, 9373–2
New England States employment growth after recessions, relation to selected economic factors, various periods 1969-90, article, 9373–1.315
North Central States business and economic conditions, Fed Reserve 9th District, quarterly journal, 9383–19
Occupational changes within firm, by worker characteristics, 1986-87, article, 6742–1.301
Older persons socioeconomic characteristics, 1900s-90 and projected to 2050, biennial chartbook, 12904–1
Pacific territories population and housing detailed characteristics, by location, 1990 Census of Population and Housing, series, 2551–8
Pension plans health benefits accounting standards changes, and impacts on firm finances, with background data, 1986-89, technical paper, 9366–6.298
Productivity of labor, indexes by selected SIC 2- to 4-digit industry, Monthly Labor Review, 6722–1.5
Productivity of labor, indexes of output, hours, and employment by SIC 2- to 4-digit industry, 1967-90, annual rpt, 6824–1
Regional employment mobility index, by industry, aggregate 1969-90, article, 9371–1.306
Rural areas economic conditions and dev, quarterly journal, 1502–8
Schedules of work, and workers with flexible hours and shift work by selected characteristics, 1991, press release, 6726–1.50
Science, engineering, and technical employment by industry and occupation, and degrees awarded, 1970s-90 and projected to 2005, article, 6722–1.314
Services (producer) industries in Midwest, employment concentration by industry group, MSA, and urban-rural location, 1970s-89, article, 9375–1.305
Small business finances, operations, owner characteristics, and Federal contracts, 1980s-90, annual rpt, 9764–6
Southeastern States, Fed Reserve 8th District banking and economic conditions, quarterly rpt with articles, 9391–16
Southeastern US employment by industry div, earnings, and hours, for 8 States, quarterly press release, 6942–7
Southeastern US high technology employment and pay, by industry and State, 1990, press release, 6946–3.23
Southeastern US layoff events and separations, by State, industry div, and reason for separation, 1990-91, press release, 6946–3.25
Southwestern US employment by major industry div, earnings, and hours, by State, monthly rpt, 6962–2
Technological devs effect on labor force, composition, and productivity, 1970s-90 and projected to 2005, industry rpt series, 6826–2
Tenure with current employer compared to 1983, and employment in same occupation in 1990, by sex, age, and race, 1991, press release, 6726–1.47
Trade adjustment aid for workers, petitions by disposition, selected industry, union, and State, monthly rpt, 6402–13
Training for job qualification and skill improvement, workers participating by training source, occupation, age, sex, and race, 1991, 6728–32
Unemployed persons finding work, by characteristics of worker and new job, aggregate 1986-89, 2546–20.20
Unemployed persons finding work by industry div, and earnings, by sector and sex, aggregate 1987-89, fact sheet, 2326–17.47
Union coverage of workers and earnings, by age, sex, race, occupational group, and industry div, monthly rpt, annual article, 6782–1.2

Union coverage of workers and earnings, by age, sex, race, occupational group, and industry div, 1990-91, annual press release, 6726–1.44
Wage and benefit changes from collective bargaining and mgmt decisions, by industry div, monthly rpt, 6782–1
Wages, hourly and weekly averages by industry div, monthly press release, 6742–3
Wages, hours, and employment by occupation, and benefits, for selected locations, industry survey rpt series, 6787–6
Wages of workers covered by unemployment insurance, by industry div and State, 1990-91, annual press release, 6784–17.1
West Central States economic indicators, Fed Reserve 10th District, quarterly rpt, 9381–16.2
Western US employment growth by industry div and manufacturing group, Fed Reserve 10th District, 1990-91, annual article, 9381–1.302
Women's labor force status and characteristics, 1960s-90, chartbook, 6748–85
Women's labor force status, and employment by industry group and occupation, 1990 and projected to 2005, fact sheet, 6564–1.1
Youth labor force status, by sex, race, and industry div, summer 1988-92, annual press release, 6744–14

Law Enforcement

Antitrust criminal enforcement activities of Justice Dept by industry div and offense, sentencing, and labor costs, FY90, GAO rpt, 26119–375

Natural Resources, Environment, and Pollution

Air pollution abatement equipment shipments by industry, and new and backlog orders, by product, 1991, annual Current Industrial Rpt, 2506–12.5
Environmental Quality, status of problems, protection programs, research, and intl issues, 1991 annual rpt, 484–1
Hazardous substances industrial releases and reduction methods under EPA regulation, by chemical, source, industry, and location, 1989, annual rpt, 9234–6
Industrial waste generation, disposal, and regulation, by industry and State, mid 1980s-90, 26358–256
Pollution abatement capital and operating costs, by SIC 2- to 4-digit industry and State, 1990, annual Current Industrial Rpt, 2506–3.6

Population

Census of Population and Housing, 1990: population and housing characteristics, detailed geographic coverage, State CD-ROM series, 2551–10
Income (household, family, and personal), by source, detailed characteristics, and region, 1991, annual Current Population Rpt, 2546–6.76

Prices and Cost of Living

Producer Price Index, by major commodity group and subgroup, and processing stage, monthly press release, 6762–5
Producer Price Index current statistics, Monthly Labor Review, 6722–1.4
Producer price indexes, by stage of processing and detailed commodity, monthly rpt, 6762–6
Producer price indexes, by stage of processing and detailed commodity, monthly 1991, annual rpt, 6764–2

Public Welfare and Social Security

OASDI disabled worker beneficiaries, by diagnostic group and industry div, 1990, annual rpt, 4744–3.4

Science and Technology

Employment of scientists, engineers, and technicians in manufacturing, by field, occupation, and industry, 1989, triennial rpt, 9627–23
Labor force, Federal and university research funding, and educational data, for science and engineering, series, 9626–6
Productivity relation to high technology capital investment, by industry sector, 1940s-80s, technical paper, 9385–8.130
Science and Engineering Indicators, employment, education, R&D funding, and industry impacts, with foreign comparisons, 1960s-91, biennial rpt, 9624–10

BY OCCUPATION

Banking, Finance, and Insurance

Credit unions finances, by occupational membership category, as of June 1992, semiannual rpt, 9532–6
Families financial status, income, net worth, and assets and debt by type, by income and selected characteristics, 1983 and 1989, article, 9362–1.301

Communications and Transportation

Advertising employment, by detailed occupation, 1990, article, 6722–1.341
Air traffic control and airway facilities staff, by employment and other characteristics, FY90, annual rpt, 7504–41
Airline and aviation safety employees drug testing and results, by drug type and occupational group, 1991, semiannual rpt, 7502–17
Postal Service personnel costs, by segment and occupation, FY91, annual rpt, 9864–2
Railroad accidents, casualties, and damage, by cause, railroad, and State, 1991, annual rpt, 7604–1
Railroad and airline labor disputes, and Federal mediation activities and caseloads, with data by carrier and union, FY87-88, annual rpt, 9604–1
Railroad employee benefits and beneficiaries by type, and railroad employment and payroll, FY90, annual rpt, 9704–2
Railroad employment by occupational group, for Class I line-haul railroads, monthly rpt, 9482–3
Railroad employment, earnings, and hours, by occupation for Class I railroads, 1991, annual table, 9484–5
Travel to US and Canada, market analysis with detailed trip and traveler characteristics, country rpt series, 2906–2

Education

Adult education participation, by selected characteristics, 1991 survey, 4826–10.5
College grads labor force status, job degree requirements, and earnings, with data by occupation, 1960s-90, article, 6722–1.330
Degree (PhD) recipients in higher education, by field and selected characteristics, 1979, 1984, and 1989, 4848–44
Educational attainment, by social and demographic characteristics and location, 1991 and trends from 1940, biennial Current Population Rpt, 2546–1.460
Higher education faculty and staff, by occupation, full- and part-time status, sex, and instn type and control, fall 1989, biennial rpt, 4844–18
Special education programs, enrollment by age, staff, funding, and needs, by type of handicap and State, 1990/91, annual rpt, 4944–4

Government and Defense

Aliens applications for temporary US residency, by occupation, age, sex, marital status, and country, 1988-91, 4808–41
DOT employment, by subagency, occupation, and selected personnel characteristics, FY91, annual rpt, 7304–18
Employment (civilian) of Fed Govt, by demographic and employment characteristics, as of Sept 1991, annual article, 9842–1.301
Employment (civilian) of Fed Govt, by occupation, sex, and location, as of Sept 1991, biennial article, 9842–1.302
Employment of minorities, disabled, and veterans in Fed Govt, and years of service, by occupation, age, sex, and agency, as of Sept 1990, biennial rpt, 9844–27
Employment of minorities, women, and disabled in Fed Govt, by agency and occupation, FY90, annual rpt, 9244–10
Equal Opportunity Recruitment Program activity, and Fed Govt employment by sex, race, pay grade, and occupational group, FY91, annual rpt, 9844–33
Military homosexual personnel discharges by pay grade, tenure, race, sex, and occupation, and investigations, by service branch, 1980s-90, GAO rpt, 26123–392
Military reserve forces personnel strengths and characteristics, by component, quarterly rpt, 3542–4
Navy personnel strengths, accessions, and attrition, detailed statistics, quarterly rpt, 3802–4
Senior Executive Service members characteristics, entries, exits, and awards, FY79-91, annual rpt, 9844–36
Small Business Admin minority and women employment, and hiring goals, FY91, annual rpt, 9764–9
State and local govt employees wages by occupation, and benefits, periodic MSA survey rpt series, 6785–15
State and local govt employment of minorities and women, by occupation, function, pay level, and State, 1991, annual rpt, 9244–6
Tax (income) returns of individuals with foreign earned income, income and tax items by income level and occupation, 1987, article, 8302–2.301
Taxes, spending, and govt efficiency, public opinion by respondent characteristics, 1992 survey, annual rpt, 10044–2

Health and Vital Statistics

Alaska occupational injury deaths, by cause, occupation, and industry, early 1980s, article, 4042–3.307
Alcohol use among Mexican American women, by whether immigrant and occupational group, 1992 article, 4482–1.309

Deaths and rates, by cause and selected social, demographic, and employment characteristics, 1979-85, natl longitudinal study, 4478–186
Deaths related to work injuries, by equipment type, circumstances, and OSHA standards violated, series, 6606–2
Disabled persons rehabilitation, Federal and State activities and funding, FY90, annual rpt, 4944–1
Health care professionals supply and education, by professional and other characteristics, and location, 1960s-92 and projected to 2020, biennial rpt, 4114–8
Hospital employees and wages by occupation, and benefits, by region and selected MSA, 1991 survey, 6787–6.254
Hospital employment and job vacancy rate, by occupation, and instn size and control, 1981-88, annual rpt, 4114–12
Indian Health Service employment of Indians and non-Indians, training, hires, and quits, by occupation, FY90, annual rpt, 4084–6
Military health care personnel, and accessions by training source, by occupation, specialty, and service branch, FY90, annual rpt, 3544–24
Mines (coal) and related operations occupational injuries and incidence, employment, and hours, 1990, annual rpt, 6664–4
Mines (metal) and related operations occupational injuries and incidence, employment, and hours, 1990, annual rpt, 6664–3
Mines (nonmetallic minerals) and related operations occupational injuries and incidence, employment, and hours, 1990, annual rpt, 6664–1
Mines (sand and gravel) and related operations occupational injuries and incidence, employment, and hours, 1990, annual rpt, 6664–2
Mines (stone) and related operations occupational injuries and incidence, employment, and hours, 1990, annual rpt, 6664–5
Mines occupational deaths, by circumstances and selected victim characteristics, semiannual rpt series, 6662–3

Housing and Construction

NYC housing supply, occupancy, condition, and household characteristics, by tenure and borough, 1991 triennial survey, 2488–3

Labor and Employment

Alaska rural areas population characteristics, and energy resources dev effects, series, 5736–5
Alien workers in US clothing and other industries, and impacts on local economies, with background data, 1990 working paper, 6366–6.6
Apprenticeship programs regulation, participation of minorities and women, and earnings, by occupation, 1990, GAO rpt, 26121–446
Black and white women's occupational differences, and compared to men, selected years 1940-88, article, 6722–1.321
Child care arrangements of mothers employed and in school, and costs, by age of child and characteristics of mother, 1988, Current Population Rpt, 2546–20.24
Dallas-Fort Worth metro area employment, earnings, hours, and CPI changes, late 1970s-91, annual rpt, 6964–2
Disabled persons work experience following OASDI benefit award, by selected characteristics, 1980s, article, 4742–1.312
Displaced worker employment and training services, and layoff alternatives, indicators of effectiveness, 1980s, 15498–28
Displaced workers losing job 1987-92, labor force status by employment and other characteristics, as of Jan 1992, biennial press release, 6726–1.48
Earnings, annual average percent changes for selected occupational groups, selected MSAs, monthly rpt, 6782–1.1
Employment and Earnings, detailed data, monthly rpt, 6742–2
Employment and economic conditions, alternative BLS projections to 2005 and trends 1975-90, biennial rpt, 6744–19
Employment by occupation, accuracy of BLS forecasts for 1990 made 1980, article, 6722–1.336
Employment by occupation, accuracy of BLS forecasts for 1990 made 1982, article, 6742–1.302
Employment Cost Index and alternative measure of compensation costs, by component, occupation, industry group, union status, and location, 1975-92, annual rpt, 6744–20
Employment Cost Index and percent change by occupational group, industry div, region, and metro-nonmetro area, quarterly press release, 6782–5
Employment Cost Index changes for nonfarm workers, by occupation, industry div, region, and bargaining status, monthly rpt, 6782–1
Employment cost indexes, by occupation, industry div, and region, Monthly Labor Review, 6722–1.3
Employment, unemployment, and labor force characteristics, by region, State, and selected metro area, 1991, annual rpt, 6744–7
Farm population, by employment, social, and economic characteristics, and region, 1990, annual Current Population Rpt, 2546–1.458
Foreign countries labor conditions, union coverage, and work accidents, annual country rpt series, 6366–4
High school and college grads employment status and income, 1992 edition, annual rpt, 4824–2.28
Home-based workers and hours, by worker characteristics, occupational group and industry div, 1991, press release, 6726–1.52
Home-based workers by selected characteristics, and views, 1989, article, 1702–1.307
Houston metro area employment, earnings, hours, and CPI changes, 1970s-91, annual rpt, 6964–1
Immigrants and legalized aliens, by occupational group and country of birth, preliminary FY91, annual tables, 6264–1
Immigrants from Colombia employed in New England textile industry, by selected characteristics, 1960s-80s, working paper, 6366–6.4
Immigration to US, alien workers, visitors, deportations, and naturalizations, by country, FY91 and trends from 1820, annual rpt, 6264–2
Insurance (life) benefits of employer-sponsored plans by plan type, age, occupation, and salary, 1990, article, 6722–1.346
Labor demand, turnover, and training completions, by detailed occupation, 1990 and projected to 2005, biennial rpt, 6744–3
Labor force, wages, hours, and payroll costs, by major industry group and demographic characteristics, *Survey of Current Business*, monthly rpt, 2702–1.7
Labor hourly costs, by component, occupational group, industry div, union coverage, and region, 1992, annual rpt, 6744–21
Labor turnover, job openings, and new hires and wages, pilot survey results, costs, and methodology, 1990-91, 6728–40
Leave benefits in small business compared to larger firms and govts, by occupational group, 1989-90, article, 6722–1.315
Minority group and women employment by industry sector, and govt salaries, by occupation, mid 1960s-90, chartbook, 9248–20
Minority group and women employment, by occupation, SIC 1- to 3- digit industry, State, and MSA, 1991, annual rpt, 9244–1
Occupational changes within firm, by worker characteristics, 1986-87, article, 6742–1.301
Older persons labor force status, income sources, and reasons for not working, with data by occupation, sex, and race, 1989-90 and projected to 2050, 21148–65
Older persons socioeconomic characteristics, 1900s-90 and projected to 2050, biennial chartbook, 12904–1
Pacific territories population and housing detailed characteristics, by location, 1990 Census of Population and Housing, series, 2551–8
Population and labor force characteristics, 1940s-90 and projected to 2000, 15496–1.16
Schedules of work, and workers with flexible hours and shift work by selected characteristics, 1991, press release, 6726–1.50
Science, engineering, and technical employment by industry and occupation, and degrees awarded, 1970s-90 and projected to 2005, article, 6722–1.314
Separations, replacement rates, and related job openings, estimation procedures with data by occupation, age, and sex, late 1980s and projected to 2005, 6748–84
Statistical Abstract of US, 1992 annual data compilation, 2324–1.13
Technological devs effect on labor force, composition, and productivity, 1970s-90 and projected to 2005, industry rpt series, 6826–2
Training for job qualification and skill improvement, workers participating by training source, occupation, age, sex, and race, 1991, 6728–32
Unemployed persons finding work, by characteristics of worker and new job, aggregate 1986-89, 2546–20.20

Unemployment major indicators, by occupational group, monthly press release, 6742–5
Unemployment major indicators, transcripts of BLS Commissioner's monthly testimony, periodic rpt, 23846–4
Union coverage of workers and earnings, by age, sex, race, occupational group, and industry div, monthly rpt, annual article, 6782–1.2
Union coverage of workers and earnings, by age, sex, race, occupational group, and industry div, 1990-91, annual press release, 6726–1.44
Wages and productivity relation to worker age, by sex and occupation, model description and results, 1991 working paper, 9377–9.128
Wages by occupation, and benefits for office and plant workers, periodic MSA survey rpt series, 6785–3; 6785–12; 6785–16; 6785–17
Wages by occupation, for office and plant workers in selected MSAs, 1991 surveys, annual rpt, 6785–5
Wages by occupation, for office and plant workers in selected MSAs, 1991 surveys, annual summary rpts, 6785–6
Wages, hours, and employment by occupation, and benefits, for selected locations, industry survey rpt series, 6787–6
Wages of full- and part-time workers, by selected characteristics, quarterly press release, 6742–20
White collar wages in private industry, by occupation and salary level, 1991, 6787–6.254
Women with disabilities, employment by occupation, and earnings, by race, 1988, fact sheet, 6564–1.2
Women's labor force status and characteristics, 1960s-90, chartbook, 6748–85
Women's labor force status, and employment by industry group and occupation, 1990 and projected to 2005, fact sheet, 6564–1.1

Law Enforcement

Crimes, by characteristics of victim and offender, circumstances, and location, data compilation, 1992 annual rpt, 6064–6.3
Drunk driving arrests, sentencing, and prisoner drinking patterns and other characteristics, 1989, 6066–19.69
Police agencies employment, spending, and operations, FY90, 6066–25.44
Prison and community-based facilities, population, employment, spending, and other characteristics, by State and for Fed Govt, 1990, annual rpt, 6064–26.3
Prison and community-based facilities, population, employment, spending, and other characteristics, by State and for Fed Govt, 1990, quinquennial rpt, 6068–218
Prison employment requirements for new and expanded Federal facilities, by occupation, FY87-95, GAO rpt, 26119–397
Prison staff in Federal instns, by selected characteristics, region, and instn, FY89, annual rpt, 6244–1.2
Public opinion on crime and crime-related issues, by respondent characteristics, data compilation, 1992 annual rpt, 6064–6.2
Sheriffs' agencies employment, spending, and operations, FY90, 6066–25.45

Population

Asian and Pacific Islands Americans social and economic characteristics, for West and total US, 1990-91, Current Population Report, 2546–1.462
Black Americans social and economic characteristics, for South and total US, 1991 and trends from 1950, annual Current Population Rpt, 2546–1.463
Black women's labor force status, earnings, and other economic status indicators, and compared to whites, various periods 1939-88, 11048–191
Census of Population and Housing, 1990: population and housing characteristics, detailed geographic coverage, State CD-ROM series, 2551–10
Consumer Income, socioeconomic characteristics of persons, families, and households, detailed cross-tabulations, Current Population Rpt series, 2546–6
Developing countries aged population and selected characteristics, 1980s and projected to 2020, country rpt series, 2326–19
Migration, immigration, and mover characteristics compared to nonmovers, 1987-90, annual Current Population Rpt, 2546–1.456
Migration since 1990, mover characteristics by same or different area, and compared to nonmovers, 1991, annual Current Population Rpt, 2546–1.464
OASDI beneficiary data collection system design compared to earlier surveys, with summary results, 1992 article, 4742–1.313

Public Welfare and Social Security

Older persons income by source, for married OASI beneficiaries by work and eligibility pattern of wife, 1982, article, 4746–26.12

Science and Technology

NASA Apollo era science and engineering staff background and characteristics, 1958-70, 9508–39
NASA staff characteristics and personnel actions, FY91, annual rpt, 9504–1

Veterans Affairs

Health care facilities of VA, trainees by detailed program and city, FY91, annual rpt, 8704–4
Health care staff of VA, and turnover, by occupation and location, 1991, annual rpt, 8604–8
Labor force status and earnings of Vietnam veterans, by whether served in Southeast Asia, presence and severity of disability, and sociodemographic characteristics, 1989, article, 6722–1.326
Labor force status of Vietnam veterans, by whether served in Southeast Asia, presence and severity of disability, VA programs use, age, race, and occupation, 1991, biennial press release, 6726–1.49

DEMOGRAPHIC BREAKDOWNS

BY AGE

Agriculture and Food

Employment of farm hired workers, and earnings, by selected characteristics, 1990, 1598–278
Farm operators educational attainment, by age, 1890s-1990, article, 1541–1.316
Population on farms, by employment, social, and economic characteristics, and region, 1990, annual Current Population Rpt, 2546–1.458
Tobacco (flue-cured) farms and farm operators, by region and selected characteristics, 1970s-87, 1568–307
Women-headed households food spending, by item and selected characteristics, and compared to other households, 1970s-88, 1548–391
Young farm operators acreage owned and rented by region, and method of acquisition of owned acreage, 1992 article, 1541–1.319

Banking, Finance, and Insurance

Credit cards held by household income, age, and card type, and debt outstanding, with issuer costs and revenue, 1970s-80, article, 9362–1.306
Families financial status, income, net worth, and assets and debt by type, by income and selected characteristics, 1983 and 1989, article, 9362–1.301

Communications and Transportation

Air traffic control and airway facilities staff, by employment and other characteristics, FY90, annual rpt, 7504–41
Aircraft accidents and circumstances, for US operations of domestic and foreign airlines and general aviation, periodic rpt, 9612–1
Aircraft pilot and nonpilot certificates held, by type of certificate, age, sex, region, and State, 1991, annual rpt, 7504–2
Drivers licenses in force, by age, sex, and State, 1990-91, annual rpt, 7554–24
Drivers licenses in force by license type, sex, and age, and fees, by State, 1991, annual rpt, 7554–1.2
Drivers licenses issued and in force by age and sex, fees, and renewal, by license class and State, 1990, annual rpt, 7554–16
Mail volume to and from households, use, and views, by class, source, content, and household characteristics, FY87-90, annual rpt, 9864–10
Railroad employee benefits and beneficiaries by type, and railroad employment and payroll, FY90, annual rpt, 9704–2
Telephone local service charges and low-income subsidies, by region, company, and city, 1980s-91, semiannual rpt, 9282–8
Traffic accidents and casualties, by driver age and sex, 1990, 7768–105
Traffic accidents, casualties, circumstances, and characteristics of persons and vehicles involved, 1990, annual rpt, 7764–18
Traffic fatal accidents, alcohol levels of drivers and others, by circumstances and characteristics of persons and vehicles, 1990, annual rpt, 7764–16
Traffic fatal accidents, circumstances, and characteristics of persons and vehicles involved, 1991, semiannual rpt, 7762–11
Traffic fatal accidents, deaths, and rates, by circumstances, characteristics of persons and vehicles involved, and location, 1990, annual rpt, 7764–10

Travel patterns, personal and household characteristics, and auto and public transport use, 1990 survey, series, 7556–6
Travel patterns, personal and household characteristics, and auto use, 1950-90, annual rpt, 3304–5.4
Travel patterns, personal and household characteristics, and auto use, 1990 survey, annual rpt, 7554–1.6
Travel to US and Canada, market analysis with detailed trip and traveler characteristics, country rpt series, 2906–2
Travel to US, by characteristics of visit and traveler, country, port city, and State of destination, quarterly rpt, 2902–1
Travel to US, by characteristics of visit and traveler, world area of origin, and US destination, 1991 survey, annual rpt, 2904–12
Truck accidents, casualties, and damage, by circumstances and characteristics of persons and vehicles involved, 1989, annual rpt, 7554–9
Truck accidents, circumstances, and characteristics of vehicles and persons involved, 1979-86, 7768–124

Education

Adult education participation, by selected characteristics, 1991 survey, 4826–10.5
Community college attendance, by selected characteristics, 1972 high school class, natl longitudinal study, 1970s-86, 4888–7
Condition of Education, detail for elementary, secondary, and higher education, 1920s-91 and projected to 2002, annual rpt, 4824–1
Degree (PhD) recipients in higher education, by field and selected characteristics, 1979, 1984, and 1989, 4848–44
Digest of Education Statistics, 1992 annual data compilation, 4824–2
Education in science and math, natl assessment of elementary and high school students, 1985/86, series, 4896–6
Educational attainment, by social and demographic characteristics and location, 1991 and trends from 1940, biennial Current Population Rpt, 2546–1.460
Educational enrollment rates, 1960s-91, annual pamphlet, 4824–3
Elementary and secondary education enrollment, staff, finances, operations, programs, and policies, 1987/88 biennial survey, series, 4836–3
Elementary and secondary students educational performance in math, science, reading, and writing, 1969-90, 4898–32
Enrollment, by grade, instn type and control, and student characteristics, 1989 and trends from 1947, annual Current Population Rpt, 2546–1.459
High school dropout rates, and subsequent completion, by student and school characteristics, alternative estimates, 1991, annual rpt, 4834–23
Higher education enrollment by age and instn type, and degrees by level, by sex, 1977/78-1990/91 and alternative projections to 2002/2003, annual rpt, 4824–4
Minority group higher education enrollment, completion, and degrees, by race, sex, and type of instn, 1970s-90, 26306–3.122
Private elementary and secondary schools, students, and staff characteristics, by school type and affiliation, 1987/88, 4836–3.8
Public housing residents educational attainment, by selected characteristics, 1980s, 5188–132
Reading performance and factors affecting proficiency, for elementary and secondary students, 1988 and 1990 natl assessments, 4898–33
Special education programs, enrollment by age, staff, funding, and needs, by type of handicap and State, 1990/91, annual rpt, 4944–4
Student aid and other sources of support, with student expenses and characteristics, by instn type and control, 1987 study, series, 4846–3
Student aid and other sources of support, with student expenses and characteristics, by instn type and control, 1990 triennial study, series, 4846–5
Student aid Pell grants and applicants, by tuition, income level, instn type and control, and State, 1990/91, annual rpt, 4804–1
Student guaranteed loan Stafford program, borrowers and likelihood of default by selected characteristics, 1989-90, 26306–3.120
Teachers of vocational education, by subject area and selected characteristics, for public high schools, 1987/88, 4836–3.9
Vocational education enrollment, student and teacher characteristics, and outcomes, for secondary and postsecondary instns, 1970s-90, 4828–42

Energy Resources and Demand

Coal production, reserves, use, and prices by State, exports by country, and employment, 1900s-90, biennial rpt, 3164–79
Households, housing, and fuel use characteristics, survey rpt series, 3166–7

Government and Defense

Aliens applications for temporary US residency, by occupation, age, sex, marital status, and country, 1988-91, 4808–41
Employment (civilian) of Fed Govt, by demographic characteristics and agency, 1990, GAO rpt, 26119–383
Employment of minorities, disabled, and veterans in Fed Govt, and years of service, by occupation, age, sex, and agency, as of Sept 1990, biennial rpt, 9844–27
Military deaths by cause, age, race, and rank, and personnel captured and missing, by service branch, FY91, annual rpt, 3544–40
Military personnel, by age and State, 1990-91, GAO rpt, 26123–391
Military personnel, by selected characteristics, 1992 annual summary rpt, 3504–13
Military reserve forces personnel strengths and characteristics, by component, quarterly rpt, 3542–4
Navy personnel strengths, accessions, and attrition, detailed statistics, quarterly rpt, 3802–4
Public debt burden on future generations forecast under alternative tax, OASDI, and Medicare policies, 1992 working paper, 9377–9.137
Senior Executive Service members characteristics, entries, exits, and awards, FY79-91, annual rpt, 9844–36
Taxes, spending, and govt efficiency, public opinion by respondent characteristics, 1992 survey, annual rpt, 10044–2
Voting age population, by sex, age, race, and State, forecast 1992 general elections, with votes cast from 1930, Current Population Rpt, 2546–3.170

Health and Vital Statistics

Abortions by method, patient characteristics, and State, and related deaths, 1970-89, annual article, 4202–7.324
Acute and chronic health conditions, disability, absenteeism, and health services use, by selected characteristics, 1990, annual rpt, 4147–10.182
Acute and chronic health conditions, disability, absenteeism, and health services use, by selected characteristics, 1991, annual rpt, 4147–10.183
AIDS cases among children, hospital use and charges by instn and patient characteristics, and payment source, 1986-87, 4186–6.16
AIDS cases by risk group, race, sex, age, State, and MSA, and deaths, quarterly rpt, 4202–9
AIDS patients costs and service use under Medicaid, and service needs, for New Jersey waiver program, 1987-89, article, 4652–1.317
AIDS public knowledge, attitudes, info sources, and testing, 1991 survey, 4146–8.218
Alcohol abuse and dependence prevalence, by age, race, and sex, and diagnostic criteria, 1988, article, 4482–1.306
Alcohol abuse direct and indirect costs, 1985, article, 4482–1.311
Alcohol-related diagnoses hospital discharges and length of stay, by age, sex, race, and region, 1979-85, 4488–10.5
Alcohol-related disorder hospital discharges and length of stay, by diagnosis, sex, age, and race, 1979-89, 4486–1.16
Births and rates, by characteristics of birth, infant, and mother, and presence of maternal risk factors and birth defects, 1989, 4146–5.125
Births of twins, by birth order and weight, gestation period, mothers age, and race, 1950s-88, 4147–21.50
Blind persons by age, older blind persons by State, and State rehabilitation services, 1989, 21148–64
Cancer (breast and cervical) deaths and rates by State, and in situ case rates by age, by race, 1970s-86, article, 4202–7.312
Cancer (breast and cervical) screening use and reasons for nonuse, by age, race, income, and State, 1987-89, article, 4202–7.313
Cancer cases by body site and population characteristics, research results, semimonthly journal, 4472–1
Cancer deaths by age, and cases, by sex, 1988 and 1991, annual rpt, 4474–13
Children (handicapped) with special needs, insurance coverage, and health care services use, by selected characteristics, 1988, 4146–8.216
Cirrhosis of liver deaths, by age, sex, race, and whether alcohol involved, 1988 and trends from 1910, annual rpt, 4486–1.13
Contraceptives use by women, by age and country, 1991 biennial rpt, 2324–9
Costa Rica and Guatemala life expectancy, and death rate by cause and age, by sex, 1984 and trends from 1900, working paper, 2326–18.64

DC metro area drug, alcohol, and tobacco use, user characteristics, and consequences, series, 4496–12
Deaths and rates, by cause, age, sex, marital status, race, and State, 1989, US Vital Statistics advance annual rpt, 4146–5.124
Deaths and rates, by cause, age, sex, race, and State, preliminary 1990-91 and trends from 1960, US Vital Statistics annual rpt, 4144–7
Deaths and rates, by cause and selected social, demographic, and employment characteristics, 1979-85, natl longitudinal study, 4478–186
Deaths and rates, by detailed location, cause, and demographic characteristics, 1989, US Vital Statistics annual rpt, 4144–3
Deaths and rates, provisional data, monthly rpt, 4142–1.2
Deaths during 1986, decedents health condition, services use, habits, and social, employment, and other characteristics, 4147–20.19
Deaths recorded in 121 cities, by age group and for infants, weekly rpt, 4202–1
Dental fluoride products use by children, by frequency of dental visits and selected characteristics, 1983-89, 4146–8.222
Diabetes patients physician office visits, by characteristics of patient, physician, and visit, 1989, 4146–8.212
Digestive diseases (chronic) prevalence, and procedures performed, by disease and patient characteristics, 1989, 4146–8.213
Disability (functional) prevalence and severity, by type of activity needing assistance, age, and sex, 1979-80, 4946–1.1
Disabled persons assistive technology equipment and home accessibility features, use, payment sources, and unmet needs, by age, 1990, 4146–8.219
Disabled persons rehabilitation, Federal and State activities and funding, FY90, annual rpt, 4944–1
Disabled persons with chronic health conditions, prevalence and services use and needs, series, 4946–1
Disabled workers labor force status, type and cause of disability, and other characteristics, 1970s-89, chartbook, 4948–11
Diving (underwater) accidents, illnesses, and deaths, by circumstances, diver characteristics, and location, 1970-90, annual rpt, 2144–29
Drug abuse by mothers, treatment and other services use, referrals, needs, and barriers, for 13 NIDA-funded programs, 1990/91 survey, 4498–76
Drug abuse indicators for selected metro areas, research results, data collection, and policy issues, 1992 semiannual conf, 4492–5
Drug, alcohol, and cigarette use, by selected characteristics, 1991 survey, annual rpt series, 4494–5
Expenditures for health care and factors in increase, with background data and foreign comparisons, various periods 1929-90, technical paper, 9366–6.296
Fire fighter deaths, by cause, circumstances, and location, 1990, annual rpt, 9434–8
Foreign medical grads in US by age, sex, professional characteristics, State, and country, and US medical school foreign students, 1960s-80s, working paper, 6366–6.2
Health care professionals supply and education, by professional and other characteristics, and location, 1960s-92 and projected to 2020, biennial rpt, 4114–8
Health care services use and costs, methodology and findings of natl survey, series, 4186–8
Health condition and care indicators, 1950s-90 with health improvement and disease prevention goals for 1990, annual data compilation, 4144–11
Health risk behavior, prevalence of 7 habits, by age, State, and other characteristics, 1986-90, article, 4202–7.305
Hepatitis cases by infection source, age, sex, race, and State, and deaths, by strain, 1989 and trends from 1966, 4205–2
Homicides and rate, by weapon, circumstances, and victim characteristics, and years of potential life lost, 1980s, article, 4202–7.315
Hospital discharges and length of stay, by diagnosis, patient and instn characteristics, procedure performed, and payment source, 1990, annual rpt, 4147–13.112
Hospital discharges and length of stay by region and diagnosis, and procedures performed, by age and sex, 1990, annual rpt, 4146–8.211
Hospital discharges and length of stay under old and new survey designs, by diagnosis, patient and instn characteristics, and procedure, Jan-Mar 1988, 4147–13.110
Hospital discharges by detailed diagnostic and procedure category, primary diagnosis, and length of stay, by age, sex, and region, 1990, annual rpt, 4147–13.111
Hospital discharges, by payment source, diagnosis, patient characteristics, and region, and procedures performed, 1990, 4146–8.221
Indian Health Service facilities, funding, operations, and Indian health and other characteristics, 1950s-91, annual chartbook, 4084–1
Indian Health Service outpatient services provided, by reason for visit and age, FY90, annual rpt, 4084–2
Indian Health Service, tribal, and contract facilities hospitalization, by diagnosis, age, sex, and service area, FY91, annual rpt, 4084–5
Infectious notifiable disease cases, by age, race, and State, and deaths, 1940s-91, annual rpt, 4204–1
Injuries from use of consumer products and related activities, by severity and victim age and sex, 1990, annual rpt, 9164–7
Injuries from use of consumer products, by severity, victim age, and detailed product, 1991, annual rpt, 9164–6
Injuries from use of consumer products, related deaths and costs, and recalls by brand, by product type, FY90, annual rpt, 9164–2
Insurance (health) coverage, and uninsured workers by industry div, with data by age, race, and marital status, 1989, GAO rpt, 26119–389
Insurance (health) coverage of persons, by insurance type and selected characteristics, 1985-90, 2546–20.23
Internist office visits, by characteristics of patient, physician, and visit, 1989, 4146–8.214
Kidney end-stage disease treatment facilities, Medicare enrollment and reimbursement, survival, and patient characteristics, 1984-90, annual rpt, 4654–16
Life expectancy, and death rates by cause, by sex and age, 1900s-89 and projected to 2080, actuarial rpt, 4706–1.107
LSD trafficking, abuse, and enforcement, and DEA field div activities, 1980s-91, 6288–9
Marriage, divorce, and remarriage of women by age, and child living arrangements, by race, 1970s-90, Current Population Rpt, 2546–2.166
Maternal and child health indicators and services use, by age, race, and poverty status, 1988, 4478–197
Mental health care facilities partial care services, and patient characteristics, by instn type and State, 1970s-88, 4506–3.51
Mental health care facilities, staff, patients, and finances, 1970s-91, biennial rpt, 4094–1
Mental health care of affective disorder patients, by patient and facility characteristics, 1986, 4506–3.49
Mental illness (serious) among adults, functional limitations, govt aid, drugs used, visits to professionals, and other characteristics, 1989, 4146–8.220
Mines occupational deaths, by circumstances and selected victim characteristics, semiannual rpt series, 6662–3
NIH research and training grants awarded to women, by recipient characteristics, inst, and host instn, FY90, annual rpt, 4434–18
Otitis media patients physician office visits, by specialty and characteristics of patient and visit, 1975-90, 4146–8.217
Pediatrician office visits, by characteristics of patient and visit, 1989, 4146–8.210
Physicians, by specialty, age, sex, and location of training and practice, 1990, State rpt series, 4116–6
Physicians visits, by patient and practice characteristics, diagnosis, and services provided, 1989, annual rpt, 4147–13.109
Physicians visits, by patient and practice characteristics, diagnosis, and services provided, 1990, advance rpt, 4146–8.215
Pollutants health effects, concentrations in food and environment, sources, human intake, and regulation, series, 9186–8
Smoking control strategies effectiveness, with data on research funding, smoking prevalence, cancer deaths, and taxation, 1900s-91, 4476–7.1
Traffic accident deaths involving alcohol, by driver and victim blood alcohol levels and other characteristics, 1977-88, annual rpt, 4486–1.12
Traffic accident deaths involving alcohol, by driver and victim blood alcohol levels and other characteristics, 1977-89, annual rpt, 4486–1.14
Transplants of organs, failure and death risk by selected transplant and patient characteristics, 1987-89, annual rpt, 4104–17.1
Tuberculosis cases and rates, by patient characteristics, 1985 and 1990, article, 4202–7.302

Housing and Construction
Alteration and repair of owner-occupied homes, costs and structural, household, financial, and project characteristics, 1987, 2486–1.13
American Housing Survey: unit and household characteristics of recent movers, and reason for move, by tenure, 1989, 2486–1.12
American Housing Survey: unit and households characteristics, unit and neighborhood quality, and journey to work by MSA location, for 11 MSAs, 1987 survey, supplement, 2485–8
American Housing Survey: unit and households detailed characteristics, and unit and neighborhood quality, MSA rpt series, 2485–6
American Housing Survey: unit and households detailed characteristics, and unit and neighborhood quality, 1989, biennial rpt supplement, 2485–13
Census of Housing, 1990: summary unit characteristics, by householder race and age, county, place, and urban-rural location, State rpt series, 2471–1
Census of Population and Housing, 1990: population and housing characteristics, detailed geographic coverage, State CD-ROM series, 2551–10
Homeownership rate, and change in housing tenure, by age, 1980s and projected to 2000, fact sheet, 2326–17.52
Homeownership rates, by household type, householder age and sex, and location, 1960s-91, annual rpt, 2484–1.3
Homeownership rates, by location and age of householder, quarterly rpt, 2482–1
Housing and households summary characteristics, 1989 and trends, chartbook, 2486–2.1
Migration of households, moving rates by tenure and age, and housing value by mobility status and region, 1989, fact sheet, 2326–17.38
Mortgages FHA-insured, financial, property, and borrower characteristics, by metro area, 1991, annual rpt, 5144–24
Mortgages FHA-insured, financial, property, and borrower characteristics, by State, 1991, annual rpt, 5144–1
Mortgages FHA-insured, financial, property, and borrower characteristics, 1991, annual rpt, 5144–17; 5144–23
NYC housing supply, occupancy, condition, and household characteristics, by tenure and borough, 1991 triennial survey, 2488–3
Rental housing units, total, with HUD assistance by program, and eligible for aid, by unit, household, and neighborhood characteristics, and location, 1989, biennial rpt, 5184–11
Single parent families in own and others homes, by financial, housing, and other characteristics, 1989, 2486–1.14
Single person and nonfamily households social, economic and housing characteristics, by tenure, 1989, 2486–1.15

Industry and Commerce
Minority- and woman-owned businesses and owner characteristics, by industry, employment and sales size, and form of ownership, 1987 survey, 2328–59

Labor and Employment
Black and white women's occupational differences, and compared to men, selected years 1940-88, article, 6722–1.321
Disabled persons work experience following OASDI benefit award, by selected characteristics, 1980s, article, 4742–1.312
Disabled persons work history before and after SSI application, by age, diagnosis, industry div, and sex, aggregate 1937-87, article, 4742–1.308
Displaced worker employment and training services, and layoff alternatives, indicators of effectiveness, 1980s, 15498–28
Displaced workers losing job 1987-92, labor force status by employment and other characteristics, as of Jan 1992, biennial press release, 6726–1.48
Employment and Earnings, detailed data, monthly rpt, 6742–2
Employment and economic conditions, alternative BLS projections to 2005 and trends 1975-90, biennial rpt, 6744–19
Employment and Training Admin activities, funding, and participant characteristics, by program, FY86-88, annual rpt, 6404–17
Employment and unemployment, by age, sex, race, marital and family status, industry div, and State, Monthly Labor Review, 6722–1.2
Employment, earnings, and hours, monthly press release, 6742–5
Employment situation, earnings, hours, and other BLS economic indicators, transcripts of BLS Commissioner's monthly testimony, periodic rpt, 23846–4
Home-based workers by selected characteristics, and views, 1989, article, 1702–1.307
Immigrants from Colombia employed in New England textile industry, by selected characteristics, 1960s-80s, working paper, 6366–6.4
Insurance (life) benefits of employer-sponsored plans by plan type, age, occupation, and salary, 1990, article, 6722–1.346
Labor demand, turnover, and training completions, by detailed occupation, 1990 and projected to 2005, biennial rpt, 6744–3
Labor force status by age, sex, and race, accuracy of BLS forecasts made 1970s-80s, as of 1990, article, 6722–1.334
Labor force status, by worker characteristics and industry group, 1990-91, annual article, 6722–1.312
Occupational changes within firm, by worker characteristics, 1986-87, article, 6742–1.301
Occupational separations, replacement rates, and related job openings, estimation procedures with data by occupation, age, and sex, late 1980s and projected to 2005, 6748–84
OECD pension plan finances, participation, and benefits, for 9 countries, with data by firm and worker characteristics, 1990 conf, 6688–2
Pension coverage for State and local govt employees, age and length of service requirements, 1990, biennial rpt, 6784–21
Petrochemicals industries contract labor accidents, injuries, safety programs operations, and employee characteristics, 1986-91, 6608–6
Population and labor force characteristics, 1940s-90 and projected to 2000, 15496–1.16
Poverty relation to low earnings, by work experience during year, household relationship, sex, race, age, and education, 1960s-90, Current Population Rpt, 2546–6.74
Retirement age, and older persons labor force status, by sex, 1950s-90 and projected to 2005, article, 6722–1.332
Schedules of work, and workers with flexible hours and shift work by selected characteristics, 1991, press release, 6726–1.50
Tenure with current employer compared to 1983, and employment in same occupation in 1990, by sex, age, and race, 1991, press release, 6726–1.47
Training for job qualification and skill improvement, workers participating by training source, occupation, age, sex, and race, 1991, 6728–32
Unemployed persons finding work, by characteristics of worker and new job, aggregate 1986-89, 2546–20.20
Unemployment rates, current data and annual trends, monthly rpt, 23842–1.2
Union coverage of workers and earnings, by age, sex, race, occupational group, and industry div, monthly rpt, annual article, 6782–1.2
Union coverage of workers and earnings, by age, sex, race, occupational group, and industry div, 1990-91, annual press release, 6726–1.44
Wages and productivity relation to worker age, by sex and occupation, model description and results, 1991 working paper, 9377–9.128
Wages of full- and part-time workers, by selected characteristics, quarterly press release, 6742–20
Women's labor force status and characteristics, 1960s-90, chartbook, 6748–85
Women's labor force status, by age, race, and family status, quarterly rpt, 6742–17
Younger workers jobs held and weeks worked since age 18, by age, sex, and race, 1978-90, 6726–2.3

Law Enforcement
Assaults and deaths of law enforcement officers, by circumstances, agency, victim and offender characteristics, and location, 1991, annual rpt, 6224–3
Crime, criminal justice admin and enforcement, and public opinion, data compilation, 1992 annual rpt, 6064–6
Crimes, arrests, and rates, by offense, offender characteristics, population size, and jurisdiction, 1991, annual rpt, 6224–2.1; 6224–2.2
Criminal case processing in Federal district courts, and dispositions, by offense, district, and offender characteristics, 1989, annual data compilation, 6064–29
Drug test results at arrest, by drug type, offense, and sex, for selected urban areas, quarterly rpt, 6062–3
Drunk driving arrests, sentencing, and prisoner drinking patterns and other characteristics, 1989, 6066–19.69
Electronic monitoring of criminal releases by State, completions, violations, and new offenses, 1989, 6066–20.23

Fraud and forgery arrests, case dispositions, and sentencing, by age, sex, race, and offense type, 1983-88, 6066–19.64
Juvenile courts drug and alcohol offenses cases, by disposition and offender age, sex, and race, 1985-88, 6066–27.7
Juvenile facilities population, by resident characteristics and facility type, 1977-89, annual rpt, 6064–35
Prison and parole admissions and releases, sentence length, and time served, by offense and offender characteristics, 1988, annual rpt, 6064–33
Prisoners and staff in Federal instns, by selected characteristics, region, and instn, FY89, annual rpt, 6244–1
Prisoners under death sentence, and executions from 1930, by offense, prisoner characteristics, and State, 1990, annual rpt, 6064–26.6
Schools crime victimization, drug availability, and preventive measures, with student views, 1989 survey, 6066–3.46
Sentences for Federal crimes, guidelines use and results by offense and district, and Sentencing Commission activities, 1991, annual rpt, 17664–1
Sentences for Federal crimes, guidelines use and results by offense, 1984-1990, 6066–19.68
Sentences under Federal mandatory minimum provisions, by defendant characteristics, and views on justice system impacts, FY90, 17668–2
Victimization rates, by victim and offender characteristics, circumstances, and offense, 1990 survey, annual rpt, 6066–3.47
Victimizations in cities, suburbs, and rural areas, by offense, circumstances, and victim and offender characteristics, 1987-89, 6066–3.48
Women arrestees drug abuse history and selected other characteristics, for 4 cities, 1988-89, 6068–246
Women in jail, by criminal background and sociodemographic characteristics, with comparisons to men, 1989, 6066–19.66

Natural Resources, Environment, and Pollution

Radiation exposure of population near commercial reactors, by body site, age group, and selected plant, 1988, annual rpt, 9634–7

Population

Alaska rural areas population characteristics, and energy resources dev effects, series, 5736–5
Asian and Pacific Islands Americans social and economic characteristics, for West and total US, 1990-91, Current Population Report, 2546–1.462
Black Americans social and economic characteristics, for South and total US, 1991 and trends from 1950, annual Current Population Rpt, 2546–1.463
Black women's labor force status, earnings, and other economic status indicators, and compared to whites, various periods 1939-88, 11048–191
Census of Population and Housing, 1990: detailed geographic coverage, State CD-ROM series, 2551–9
Census of Population and Housing, 1990: population and housing characteristics, detailed geographic coverage, State CD-ROM series, 2551–10
Census of Population and Housing, 1990: summary characteristics, by county, subdiv, and place, State rpt series, 2551–7
Census of Population and Housing, 1990: summary characteristics, households, and land area, by county, subdiv, and place, State rpt series, 2551–1
Census of Population, 1990: black population undercount, estimates by age and sex, 21628–97
Census of Population, 1990: population characteristics and living arrangements, by county, place, and urban-rural location, State rpt series, 2531–1
Census of Population, 1990: population characteristics and living arrangements, for Native American, urban, and metro areas, series, 2531–2
Consumer Income, socioeconomic characteristics of persons, families, and households, detailed cross-tabulations, Current Population Rpt series, 2546–6
Developing countries population size, life expectancy, and fertility, trends and forecasts, country rpt series, 2326–24
Family members supporting others outside household, by relationship, recipient living arrangements, and provider characteristics, 1988, Current Population Rpt, 2546–20.21
Households and family characteristics, by location, 1991, annual Current Population Rpt, 2546–1.457
Immigrants from Central America in DC, by selected employment and other characteristics, and reasons for migration, 1985-88, working paper, 6366–6.3
Immigration to US, alien workers, visitors, deportations, and naturalizations, by country, FY91 and trends from 1820, annual rpt, 6264–2
Income (household) and poverty status under alternative income definitions, by recipient characteristics, 1979-91, annual Current Population Rpt, 2546–6.78
Income (household) of aged and younger adults, by source, household composition, and age group, 1984 and 1989, article, 4742–1.304
Income (household) of aged and younger adults, by source, household composition, race, and age group, 1984-89, 4746–26.20
Income (personal) relative to median, by race and selected other characteristics, mid 1960s-89, Current Population Rpt, 2546–6.73
Income and consumer spending of households, for selected population groups, quarterly journal, 1702–1
Income, net worth, and poverty status of aged, compared to other age groups, 1988-90, article, 4742–1.320
Indian tribes in Pacific Northwest, OCS oil and gas lease and dev environmental, economic, and cultural impacts, with background data, 1970s-92, 5738–35
Israel economic conditions, US investment and export opportunities, and trade practices, 1992 rpt, 2008–32
Living arrangements, family relationships, and marital status, by selected characteristics, 1991, annual Current Population Rpt, 2546–1.461
Migration, immigration, and mover characteristics compared to nonmovers, 1987-90, annual Current Population Rpt, 2546–1.456
Migration since 1990, mover characteristics by same or different area, and compared to nonmovers, 1991, annual Current Population Rpt, 2546–1.464
OASDI beneficiary data collection system design compared to earlier surveys, with summary results, 1992 article, 4742–1.313
Older persons economic status compared to other age groups, 1990 and trends from 1947, 4746–26.24
Older persons in poverty, by health, nutrition, assistance, and other characteristics, 1990, GAO rpt, 26131–100
Older persons income and sources, by OASDI beneficiary and poverty status, and other characteristics, 1990, biennial chartbook, 4744–25
Older persons income and sources, by whether OASDI beneficiary, poverty status, and other characteristics, 1990, biennial rpt, 4744–26
Older persons population size and characteristics, series, 2326–25
Older persons socioeconomic characteristics, 1900s-90 and projected to 2050, biennial chartbook, 12904–1
Pacific territories population and housing detailed characteristics, by location, 1990 Census of Population and Housing, series, 2551–8
Population economic well-being indicators, by selected characteristics and household income and income-to-poverty ratio, 1984, 2546–20.22
Population size and components of change, alternative projections 1990-2080 and trends from 1900, annual actuarial rpt, 4706–1.106
Population size, by age, selected years 1929-91, annual rpt, 204–1.2
Poverty status of population and families, by detailed characteristics, 1991, annual Current Population Rpt, 2546–6.77
Refugee arrivals and resettlement in US, by age, sex, sponsoring agency, State, and country, monthly rpt, 4592–1
Soviet Union and US economic and sociodemographic indicators, selected years 1970-90, handbook, 2328–80
Soviet Union former Republics and Baltic States population size and characteristics, 1989-92, 9118–19
Statistical Abstract of US, 1992 annual data compilation, 2324–1
Vietnam population size, components of change, and selected characteristics, 1979, 1989, and projected to 2050, 2326–18.65
Wealth (personal) under alternative measures, by age group, 1984, technical paper, 4746–26.11

Prices and Cost of Living

Consumer Expenditure Survey, spending by category, selected household characteristics, and region, quarterly rpt, 6762–14

Public Welfare and Social Security

AFDC beneficiaries demographic and financial characteristics, by State, FY90, annual rpt, 4584–7
Benefits, beneficiaries, and spells of participation, by aid program and recipient characteristics, 1987-88, Current Population Rpt, 2546–20.25

Disability Insurance beneficiaries deaths and survival, by selected characteristics, for persons entitled 1972 and 1985, article, 4742–1.321
Food stamp recipient household size, composition, income, and income and deductions allowed, summer 1989, annual rpt, 1364–8
Medicare and Medicaid beneficiaries and program operations, 1992, annual fact book, 4654–18
Medicare beneficiaries knowledge of and experience with physician billing and payment under Medicare, by selected characteristics, 1988-89, 17266–2.1
Medicare payment of physicians, reforms impacts on services, and monitoring methods, 1992 annual rpt, 4004–34
OASDHI coverage of employment and earnings, and social security contributions, by age, sex, race, State, and county, 1988, annual rpt, 4744–29
OASDHI, Medicaid, SSI, and related programs benefits, beneficiary characteristics, and trust funds, selected years 1937-90, annual rpt, 4744–3
OASDI benefits and beneficiaries, by category, age, and sex, quarterly rpt, 4742–1.1
Older persons care by family members and others, caregiver quit probability related to selected characteristics, 1982, article, 4652–1.305
Poverty status of families, by detailed characteristics, 1980 and 1988, GAO rpt, 26131–102
Supplemental Security Income recipients, by race, sex, living arrangements, age, eligibility, and State, quarterly rpt, 4742–1.2
Supplemental Security Income work incentive programs, participant characteristics, by program, 1982-91, article, 4742–1.305

Recreation and Leisure
Boat accidents, casualties, and damage, by cause, vessel and operator characteristics, and State, 1991, annual rpt, 7404–1.2
Fishing (ocean sport) activities, and catch by species, by angler characteristics and State, annual coastal area rpt series, 2166–17

Science and Technology
Labor force, Federal and university research funding, and educational data, for science and engineering, series, 9626–6
NASA Apollo era science and engineering staff background and characteristics, 1958-70, 9508–39
NASA staff characteristics and personnel actions, FY91, annual rpt, 9504–1
Public knowledge, interest, and expectations for science and technology, 1990 survey, biennial rpt, 9624–10.7
Science and Engineering Indicators, employment, education, R&D funding, and industry impacts, with foreign comparisons, 1960s-91, biennial rpt, 9624–10

Veterans Affairs
Disability and death compensation cases of VA, by entitlement type, period of service, sex, age, and State, FY90, annual rpt, 8604–7
Health care professionals of VA, by selected employment characteristics and VA district, quarterly rpt, 8602–6
Health care services of VA, needs, availability, structure, and funding, findings and recommendations, 1991 compilation of papers, 8608–9
Insurance (life) for veterans and servicepersons, actuarial analyses of VA programs, 1991, annual rpt, 8604–1
Labor force status and earnings of Vietnam veterans, by whether served in Southeast Asia, presence and severity of disability, and sociodemographic characteristics, 1989, article, 6722–1.326
Labor force status of Vietnam veterans, by whether served in Southeast Asia, presence and severity of disability, VA programs use, age, race, and occupation, 1991, biennial press release, 6726–1.49
Mental illness (post-traumatic stress) among veterans by period of service, and VA treatment and rehabilitation program operations and staff, FY91, annual rpt, 8704–6
Population and characteristics of veterans, and VA hospital and other activities, by State, FY91, annual rpt, 8604–3

BY DISEASE

Communications and Transportation
Railroad accidents, casualties, and damage, by cause, railroad, and State, 1991, annual rpt, 7604–1
Railroad employee sickness benefits and beneficiaries, by age, occupation, and disease, 1989/90, annual rpt, 9704–2.3

Education
Head Start handicapped enrollment, by handicap, State, and for Indian and migrant programs, 1988/89, annual rpt, 4584–4
Special education programs, enrollment by age, staff, funding, and needs, by type of handicap and State, 1990/91, annual rpt, 4944–4

Government and Defense
Employment of disabled in Fed Govt, by disability and agency, FY90, annual rpt, 9244–10.2
Employment of minorities, disabled, and veterans in Fed Govt, and years of service, by occupation, age, sex, and agency, as of Sept 1990, biennial rpt, 9844–27

Health and Vital Statistics
Acute and chronic health conditions, disability, absenteeism, and health services use, by selected characteristics, 1990, annual rpt, 4147–10.182
Acute and chronic health conditions, disability, absenteeism, and health services use, by selected characteristics, 1991, annual rpt, 4147–10.183
Alcohol-related disorder hospital discharges and length of stay, by diagnosis, sex, age, and race, 1979-89, 4486–1.16
Births and rates, by characteristics of birth, infant, and mother, and presence of maternal risk factors and birth defects, 1989, 4146–5.125
Child and maternal health condition and services use, indicators by age, race, and poverty status, 1988, 4478–197
Children (handicapped) with special needs, insurance coverage, and health care services use, by selected characteristics, 1988, 4146–8.216
Costa Rica and Guatemala life expectancy, and death rate by cause and age, by sex, 1984 and trends from 1900, working paper, 2326–18.64
Costs (direct and indirect) of disease, by diagnosis, 1990, annual rpt, 4474–15
Death rates by cause, age, and sex, average change 1968-87, annual actuarial rpt, 4706–1.106
Death rates by cause, and life expectancy, by sex and age, 1900s-89 and projected to 2080, actuarial rpt, 4706–1.107
Deaths and rates, by cause, age, sex, marital status, race, and State, 1989, US Vital Statistics advance annual rpt, 4146–5.124
Deaths and rates, by cause and age, preliminary 1990-91, US Vital Statistics annual rpt, 4144–7
Deaths and rates, by cause and selected social, demographic, and employment characteristics, 1979-85, natl longitudinal study, 4478–186
Deaths and rates, by detailed location, cause, and demographic characteristics, 1989, US Vital Statistics annual rpt, 4144–3
Deaths and rates, provisional data, monthly rpt, 4142–1.2
Deaths from 10 leading causes, 1989, annual rpt, 4474–15
Disabled persons rehabilitation, Federal and State activities and funding, FY90, annual rpt, 4944–1
Disabled workers labor force status, type and cause of disability, and other characteristics, 1970s-89, chartbook, 4948–11
Diving (underwater) accidents, illnesses, and deaths, by circumstances, diver characteristics, and location, 1970-90, annual rpt, 2144–29
Educational attainment relation to health condition and care, indicators by selected characteristics, 1989, 4147–10.180
Foreign travel vaccination needs by country, and disease prevention recommendations, 1992 annual rpt, 4204–11
Health condition and care indicators, 1950s-90 with health improvement and disease prevention goals for 1990, annual data compilation, 4144–11
Hospital deaths of Medicare patients, actual and expected rates by diagnosis, with hospital characteristics, by instn, FY90, annual State rpt series, 4654–14
Hospital discharges and length of stay, by diagnosis, patient and instn characteristics, procedure performed, and payment source, 1990, annual rpt, 4147–13.112
Hospital discharges and length of stay by region and diagnosis, and procedures performed, by age and sex, 1990, annual rpt, 4146–8.211
Hospital discharges and length of stay under old and new survey designs, by diagnosis, patient and instn characteristics, and procedure, Jan-Mar 1988, 4147–13.110
Hospital discharges by detailed diagnostic and procedure category, primary diagnosis, and length of stay, by age, sex, and region, 1990, annual rpt, 4147–13.111
Hospital discharges, by payment source, diagnosis, patient characteristics, and region, and procedures performed, 1990, 4146–8.221

Indian Health Service and tribal facilities and use, and Indians health and other characteristics, by IHS region, 1980s-90, annual chartbook, 4084–7
Indian Health Service facilities, funding, operations, and Indian health and other characteristics, 1950s-91, annual chartbook, 4084–1
Indian Health Service outpatient services provided, by reason for visit and age, FY90, annual rpt, 4084–2
Indian Health Service, tribal, and contract facilities hospitalization, by diagnosis, age, sex, and service area, FY91, annual rpt, 4084–5
Infectious notifiable disease cases and current outbreaks, by region and State, weekly rpt, 4202–1
Internist office visits, by characteristics of patient, physician, and visit, 1989, 4146–8.214
Kidney end-stage disease treatment facilities, Medicare enrollment and reimbursement, survival, and patient characteristics, 1984-90, annual rpt, 4654–16
Mental health care facilities, staff, patients, and finances, 1970s-91, biennial rpt, 4094–1
Military health care services costs under Civilian Health and Medical Program of Uniformed Services, for top 10 diagnoses, FY90, annual chartbook, 3504–23.4
Mines (nonmetallic minerals) and related operations occupational injuries and incidence, employment, and hours, 1990, annual rpt, 6664–1
Morbidity and Mortality Weekly Report, infectious notifiable disease cases and deaths, and other public health issues, periodic journal, 4202–7
Morbidity and Mortality Weekly Report, infectious notifiable disease cases by age, race, and State, and deaths, 1940s-91, annual rpt, 4204–1
Occupational injury and illness rates by SIC 2- to 4-digit industry, and deaths by cause and industry div, 1990, annual rpt, 6844–1
OECD members health care costs, hospital use, resources, and economic and health indicators, by country, 1960s-90, article, 4652–1.322
Older persons socioeconomic characteristics, 1900s-90 and projected to 2050, biennial chartbook, 12904–1
Pediatrician office visits, by characteristics of patient and visit, 1989, 4146–8.210
Physicians visits, by patient and practice characteristics, diagnosis, and services provided, 1989, annual rpt, 4147–13.109
Physicians visits, by patient and practice characteristics, diagnosis, and services provided, 1990, advance rpt, 4146–8.215
Soviet Union and US economic and sociodemographic indicators, selected years 1970-90, handbook, 2328–80
Statistical Abstract of US, 1992 annual data compilation, 2324–1.2; 2324–1.3

Labor and Employment

Disabled persons work experience following OASDI benefit award, by selected characteristics, 1980s, article, 4742–1.312
Disabled persons work history before and after SSI application, by age, diagnosis, industry div, and sex, aggregate 1937-87, article, 4742–1.308

Natural Resources, Environment, and Pollution

Pollutants health effects, concentrations in food and environment, sources, human intake, and regulation, series, 9186–8

Public Welfare and Social Security

Disability benefit applications under OASDI and SSI, dispositions, awards, and administrative law judge hearing outcomes, by race, 1988, GAO rpt, 26121–459
Disability Insurance beneficiaries deaths and survival, by selected characteristics, for persons entitled 1972 and 1985, article, 4742–1.321
Hospital multiple admissions of Medicare beneficiaries, by reason and characteristics of instn and patient, 1985, 4008–117
Medicare payment of physicians, reforms impacts on services, and monitoring methods, 1992 annual rpt, 4004–34
Medicare reimbursement of hospitals under prospective payment system, diagnosis related group code assignment and effects on care and instn finances, series, 4006–7
Medicare reimbursement of hospitals under prospective payment system, methodology, inputs, and data by diagnostic group, 1992 annual rpt, 17204–1
OASDHI, Medicaid, SSI, and related programs benefits, beneficiary characteristics, and trust funds, selected years 1937-90, annual rpt, 4744–3
Supplemental Security Income work incentive programs, participant characteristics, by program, 1982-91, article, 4742–1.305

Veterans Affairs

Health care services of VA, needs, availability, structure, and funding, findings and recommendations, 1991 compilation of papers, 8608–9
Hospital discharges by diagnosis, compensation and pension status, and other characteristics, for VA, FY91, annual rpt, 8604–3.2

BY EDUCATIONAL ATTAINMENT

Agriculture and Food

Employment of farm hired workers, and earnings, by selected characteristics, 1990, 1598–278
Farm operators educational attainment, by age, 1890s-1990, article, 1541–1.316
Tobacco (flue-cured) farms and farm operators, by region and selected characteristics, 1970s-87, 1568–307

Banking, Finance, and Insurance

Credit cards held by household income, age, and card type, and debt outstanding, with issuer costs and revenue, 1970s-80, article, 9362–1.306
Families financial status, income, net worth, and assets and debt by type, by income and selected characteristics, 1983 and 1989, article, 9362–1.301

Communications and Transportation

Air traffic control and airway facilities staff, by employment and other characteristics, FY90, annual rpt, 7504–41
Mail volume to and from households, use, and views, by class, source, content, and household characteristics, FY87-90, annual rpt, 9864–10
Travel to US and Canada, market analysis with detailed trip and traveler characteristics, country rpt series, 2906–2

Education

Adult education participation, by selected characteristics, 1991 survey, 4826–10.5
Black higher education instns enrollment, finances, staff, and degrees, by instn and selected student characteristics, 1970s-90, 4848–46
Condition of Education, detail for elementary, secondary, and higher education, 1920s-91 and projected to 2002, annual rpt, 4824–1
Degree (PhD) recipients in higher education, by field and selected characteristics, 1979, 1984, and 1989, 4848–44
Degrees awarded in higher education, by level, field, race, and sex, 1989/90 and trends from 1980/81, annual rpt, 4844–17
Digest of Education Statistics, 1992 annual data compilation, 4824–2
Education in science and math, natl assessment of elementary and high school students, 1985/86, series, 4896–6
Elementary and secondary education enrollment, staff, finances, operations, programs, and policies, 1987/88 biennial survey, series, 4836–3
Elementary and secondary students educational performance in math, science, reading, and writing, 1969-90, 4898–32
Enrollment, by grade, instn type and control, and student characteristics, 1989 and trends from 1947, annual Current Population Rpt, 2546–1.459
High school class of 1991: college enrollment, and labor force participation of grads and dropouts, by race and sex, annual press release, 6726–1.46
Higher education enrollment, by level, race, and sex, fall 1980-90, biennial rpt, 4844–15
Population educational attainment, by social and demographic characteristics and location, 1991 and trends from 1940, biennial Current Population Rpt, 2546–1.460
Private elementary and secondary schools, students, and staff characteristics, by school type and affiliation, 1987/88, 4836–3.8
Public housing residents educational attainment, by selected characteristics, 1980s, 5188–132
Teachers of vocational education, by subject area and selected characteristics, for public high schools, 1987/88, 4836–3.9
Vocational education enrollment, student and teacher characteristics, and outcomes, for secondary and postsecondary instns, 1970s-90, 4828–42

Energy Resources and Demand

Coal production, reserves, use, and prices by State, exports by country, and employment, 1900s-90, biennial rpt, 3164–79

Government and Defense

Military personnel, by selected characteristics, 1992 annual summary rpt, 3504–13
Military personnel on active duty, and reserves, by education, FY91, annual rpt, 3544–1.2; 3544–1.5
Military reserve forces personnel strengths and characteristics, by component, quarterly rpt, 3542–4
Navy personnel strengths, accessions, and attrition, detailed statistics, quarterly rpt, 3802–4

Senior Executive Service members characteristics, entries, exits, and awards, FY79-91, annual rpt, 9844–36
Taxes, spending, and govt efficiency, public opinion by respondent characteristics, 1992 survey, annual rpt, 10044–2

Health and Vital Statistics

AIDS public knowledge, attitudes, info sources, and testing, 1991 survey, 4146–8.218
Births and rates, by characteristics of birth, infant, and mother, and presence of maternal risk factors and birth defects, 1989, 4146–5.125
Deaths and rates, by cause and selected social, demographic, and employment characteristics, 1979-85, natl longitudinal study, 4478–186
Deaths during 1986, decedents health condition, services use, habits, and social, employment, and other characteristics, 4147–20.19
Dental fluoride products use by children, by frequency of dental visits and selected characteristics, 1983-89, 4146–8.222
Disabled persons rehabilitation, Federal and State activities and funding, FY90, annual rpt, 4944–1
Disabled workers labor force status, type and cause of disability, and other characteristics, 1970s-89, chartbook, 4948–11
Drug abuse by mothers, treatment and other services use, referrals, needs, and barriers, for 13 NIDA-funded programs, 1990/91 survey, 4498–76
Drug abuse indicators for selected metro areas, research results, data collection, and policy issues, 1992 semiannual conf, 4492–5
Drug, alcohol, and cigarette use, by selected characteristics, 1991 survey, annual rpt series, 4494–5
Educational attainment relation to health condition and care, indicators by selected characteristics, 1989, 4147–10.180
Health risk behavior, prevalence of 7 habits, by age, State, and other characteristics, 1986-90, article, 4202–7.305
Infant health, deaths and risk factors, and prevention issues, for US and selected countries, 1990 conf, 4148–28
Insurance (health) coverage of persons, by insurance type and selected characteristics, 1985-90, 2546–20.23
Life expectancy, by sex, income, education, and labor force status, for whites, 1979-85, article, 4042–3.347
Marriage, divorce, and remarriage of women by age, and child living arrangements, by race, 1970s-90, Current Population Rpt, 2546–2.166
Mental health care facilities, staff, patients, and finances, 1970s-91, biennial rpt, 4094–1
Mental illness (serious) among adults, functional limitations, govt aid, drugs used, visits to professionals, and other characteristics, 1989, 4146–8.220

Housing and Construction

American Housing Survey: unit and household characteristics of recent movers, and reason for move, by tenure, 1989, 2486–1.12
American Housing Survey: unit and households detailed characteristics, and unit and neighborhood quality, MSA rpt series, 2485–6
NYC housing supply, occupancy, condition, and household characteristics, by tenure and borough, 1991 triennial survey, 2488–3
Rental housing units, total, with HUD assistance by program, and eligible for aid, by unit, household, and neighborhood characteristics, and location, 1989, biennial rpt, 5184–11
Single parent families in own and others homes, by financial, housing, and other characteristics, 1989, 2486–1.14
Single person and nonfamily households social, economic and housing characteristics, by tenure, 1989, 2486–1.15

Industry and Commerce

Minority- and woman-owned businesses and owner characteristics, by industry, employment and sales size, and form of ownership, 1987 survey, 2328–59

Labor and Employment

Black and white women's occupational differences, and compared to men, selected years 1940-88, article, 6722–1.321
Child care arrangements of mothers employed and in school, and costs, by age of child and characteristics of mother, 1988, Current Population Rpt, 2546–20.24
Disabled persons work experience following OASDI benefit award, by selected characteristics, 1980s, article, 4742–1.312
Displaced worker employment and training services, and layoff alternatives, indicators of effectiveness, 1980s, 15498–28
Employment and economic conditions, alternative BLS projections to 2005 and trends 1975-90, biennial rpt, 6744–19
Employment and Training Admin activities, funding, and participant characteristics, by program, FY86-88, annual rpt, 6404–17
Home-based workers by selected characteristics, and views, 1989, article, 1702–1.307
Immigrants from Colombia employed in New England textile industry, by selected characteristics, 1960s-80s, working paper, 6366–6.4
Labor demand, turnover, and training completions, by detailed occupation, 1990 and projected to 2005, biennial rpt, 6744–3
Occupational changes within firm, by worker characteristics, 1986-87, article, 6742–1.301
OECD pension plan finances, participation, and benefits, for 9 countries, with data by firm and worker characteristics, 1990 conf, 6688–2
Petrochemicals industries contract labor accidents, injuries, safety programs operations, and employee characteristics, 1986-91, 6608–6
Population and labor force characteristics, 1940s-90 and projected to 2000, 15496–1.16
Poverty relation to low earnings, by work experience during year, household relationship, sex, race, age, and education, 1960s-90, Current Population Rpt, 2546–6.74
Rural areas job skill and educational requirements, impacts of industrial and occupational shifts, 1970s-80s and projected to 2000, article, 1502–7.302
Training for job qualification and skill improvement, workers participating by training source, occupation, age, sex, and race, 1991, 6728–32
Unemployed persons finding work, by characteristics of worker and new job, aggregate 1986-89, 2546–20.20

Law Enforcement

Crime, criminal justice admin and enforcement, and public opinion, data compilation, 1992 annual rpt, 6064–6
Crimes, by characteristics of victim and offender, circumstances, and location, data compilation, 1992 annual rpt, 6064–6.3
Criminal case processing in Federal district courts, and dispositions, by offense, district, and offender characteristics, 1989, annual data compilation, 6064–29
Drug abuse and trafficking offenders losing Federal benefits under new sentencing guidelines, by selected characteristics, 1990-91, GAO rpt, 26119–398
Drunk driving arrests, sentencing, and prisoner drinking patterns and other characteristics, 1989, 6066–19.69
Prison and parole admissions and releases, sentence length, and time served, by offense and offender characteristics, 1988, annual rpt, 6064–33
Prison staff in Federal instns, by selected characteristics, region, and instn, FY89, annual rpt, 6244–1.2
Prisoners and movements, by offense, location, and selected other characteristics, data compilation, 1992 annual rpt, 6064–6.6
Prisoners under death sentence, and executions from 1930, by offense, prisoner characteristics, and State, 1990, annual rpt, 6064–26.6
Public opinion on crime and crime-related issues, by respondent characteristics, data compilation, 1992 annual rpt, 6064–6.2
Victimization rates, by victim and offender characteristics, circumstances, and offense, 1990 survey, annual rpt, 6066–3.47
Victimizations in cities, suburbs, and rural areas, by offense, circumstances, and victim and offender characteristics, 1987-89, 6066–3.48
Women in jail, by criminal background and sociodemographic characteristics, with comparisons to men, 1989, 6066–19.66

Population

Alaska rural areas population characteristics, and energy resources dev effects, series, 5736–5
Asian and Pacific Islands Americans social and economic characteristics, for West and total US, 1990-91, Current Population Report, 2546–1.462
Black Americans social and economic characteristics, for South and total US, 1991 and trends from 1950, annual Current Population Rpt, 2546–1.463
Black women's labor force status, earnings, and other economic status indicators, and compared to whites, various periods 1939-88, 11048–191
Census of Population and Housing, 1990: population and housing characteristics, detailed geographic coverage, State CD-ROM series, 2551–10

Census of Population and Housing, 1990: summary characteristics, by county, subdiv, and place, State rpt series, 2551–7
Consumer Income, socioeconomic characteristics of persons, families, and households, detailed cross-tabulations, Current Population Rpt series, 2546–6
Costa Rica economic indicators and reform issues, mid 1970s-90, working paper, 9916–13.5
Family members supporting others outside household, by relationship, recipient living arrangements, and provider characteristics, 1988, Current Population Rpt, 2546–20.21
Households and family characteristics, by location, 1991, annual Current Population Rpt, 2546–1.457
Immigrants from Central America in DC, by selected employment and other characteristics, and reasons for migration, 1985-88, working paper, 6366–6.3
Income (household) and poverty status under alternative income definitions, by recipient characteristics, 1979-91, annual Current Population Rpt, 2546–6.78
Income (personal) relative to median, by race and selected other characteristics, mid 1960s-89, Current Population Rpt, 2546–6.73
Income and consumer spending of households, for selected population groups, quarterly journal, 1702–1
Indian Health Service and tribal facilities and use, and Indians health and other characteristics, by IHS region, 1980s-90, annual chartbook, 4084–7
Indian Health Service facilities, funding, operations, and Indian health and other characteristics, 1950s-91, annual chartbook, 4084–1
Israel economic conditions, US investment and export opportunities, and trade practices, 1992 rpt, 2008–32
Living arrangements, family relationships, and marital status, by selected characteristics, 1991, annual Current Population Rpt, 2546–1.461
Migration, immigration, and mover characteristics compared to nonmovers, 1987-90, annual Current Population Rpt, 2546–1.456
Migration since 1990, mover characteristics by same or different area, and compared to nonmovers, 1991, annual Current Population Rpt, 2546–1.464
Older persons socioeconomic characteristics, 1900s-90 and projected to 2050, biennial chartbook, 12904–1
Older population, and health, economic, and other characteristics, with foreign comparisons, 1980s-91 with trends and projections, Current Population Rpt, 2546–2.165
Pacific territories population and housing detailed characteristics, by location, 1990 Census of Population and Housing, series, 2551–8
Population economic well-being indicators, by selected characteristics and household income and income-to-poverty ratio, 1984, 2546–20.22
Poverty status of population and families, by detailed characteristics, 1991, annual Current Population Rpt, 2546–6.77
Statistical Abstract of US, 1992 annual data compilation, 2324–1

Public Welfare and Social Security
Benefits, beneficiaries, and spells of participation, by aid program and recipient characteristics, 1987-88, Current Population Rpt, 2546–20.25
Child care arrangements of younger working mothers, and costs, by selected characteristics, 1988, 6726–2.1
Child care arrangements prior to 1st grade, by setting and parents' educational level, 1991 survey, 4826–10.2
Child support awards, payment status, reasons for nonpayment, and mothers characteristics, by fathers residence in and out of State, 1990, GAO rpt, 26121–442
Child support payment and visitation practices of absent fathers, and mothers with custody, by employment and other characteristics, 1988, article, 6722–1.329
Medicare beneficiaries knowledge of and experience with physician billing and payment under Medicare, by selected characteristics, 1988-89, 17266–2.1
Older persons income by source, for married OASI beneficiaries by work and eligibility pattern of wife, 1982, article, 4746–26.12
Poverty status of families, by detailed characteristics, 1980 and 1988, GAO rpt, 26131–102

Science and Technology
Employment and education of minorities, women, and disabled in science and engineering, by field, mid 1970s-91, biennial rpt, 9624–20
Labor force, Federal and university research funding, and educational data, for science and engineering, series, 9626–6
NASA Apollo era science and engineering staff background and characteristics, 1958-70, 9508–39
NASA staff characteristics and personnel actions, FY91, annual rpt, 9504–1
Nuclear engineering enrollment and degrees by instn and State, and women grads plans and employment, 1991, annual rpt, 3006–8.18
Public knowledge, interest, and expectations for science and technology, 1990 survey, biennial rpt, 9624–10.7
Radiation protection and health physics enrollment and degrees granted by instn and State, and women grads plans and employment, 1991, annual rpt, 3006–8.19

Veterans Affairs
Labor force status and earnings of Vietnam veterans, by whether served in Southeast Asia, presence and severity of disability, and sociodemographic characteristics, 1989, article, 6722–1.326
Mental illness (post-traumatic stress) among veterans by period of service, and VA treatment and rehabilitation program operations and staff, FY91, annual rpt, 8704–6

BY MARITAL STATUS

Agriculture and Food
Employment of farm hired workers, and earnings, by selected characteristics, 1990, 1598–278
Food spending of women-headed households, by item and selected characteristics, and compared to other households, 1970s-88, 1548–391
Population on farms, by employment, social, and economic characteristics, and region, 1990, annual Current Population Rpt, 2546–1.458

Banking, Finance, and Insurance
Families financial status, income, net worth, and assets and debt by type, by income and selected characteristics, 1983 and 1989, article, 9362–1.301

Communications and Transportation
Travel to US and Canada, market analysis with detailed trip and traveler characteristics, country rpt series, 2906–2

Education
Adult education participation, by selected characteristics, 1991 survey, 4826–10.5
Degree (PhD) recipients in higher education, by field and selected characteristics, 1979, 1984, and 1989, 4848–44
Educational attainment, by social and demographic characteristics and location, 1991 and trends from 1940, biennial Current Population Rpt, 2546–1.460
Elementary and secondary education enrollment, staff, finances, operations, programs, and policies, 1987/88 biennial survey, series, 4836–3
Enrollment, by grade, instn type and control, and student characteristics, 1989 and trends from 1947, annual Current Population Rpt, 2546–1.459
Student aid and other sources of support, with student expenses and characteristics, by instn type and control, 1987 study, series, 4846–3
Student aid and other sources of support, with student expenses and characteristics, by instn type and control, 1990 triennial study, series, 4846–5
Student financial support by parents, by type and funding sources, and student, parent, and instn characteristics, fall 1986, 4846–3.11
Student guaranteed loan Stafford program, borrowers and likelihood of default by selected characteristics, 1989-90, 26306–3.120
Teachers and administrators in private schools, pay, work conditions, and selected characteristics, by school type and affiliation, 1987/88, 4836–3.8
Teachers in public schools, demographic and employment characteristics, 1992 annual data compilation, 4824–2.9

Government and Defense
Aliens applications for temporary US residency, by occupation, age, sex, marital status, and country, 1988-91, 4808–41
Tax (income) returns of individuals, by filing status, tax item, and income level, 1991, annual article, 8302–2.319
Tax (income) returns of individuals, detailed data, 1988, annual rpt, 8304–2
Tax rates and revenue of State and local govts, by source and State, 1992 and historical trends, annual rpt, 10044–1
Taxes, spending, and govt efficiency, public opinion by respondent characteristics, 1992 survey, annual rpt, 10044–2

Health and Vital Statistics
Abortions by method, patient characteristics, and State, and related deaths, 1970-89, annual article, 4202–7.324
Cytomegalovirus (congenital) disease cases, by infant, mother, and birth characteristics, type of impairment, State, and Canada Province, 1990-91, 4202–7.314

Deaths and rates, by cause, age, sex, marital status, race, and State, 1989, US Vital Statistics advance annual rpt, 4146–5.124
Deaths and rates, by cause and selected social, demographic, and employment characteristics, 1979-85, natl longitudinal study, 4478–186
Deaths during 1986, decedents health condition, services use, habits, and social, employment, and other characteristics, 4147–20.19
Drug abuse indicators for selected metro areas, research results, data collection, and policy issues, 1992 semiannual conf, 4492–5
Educational attainment relation to health condition and care, indicators by selected characteristics, 1989, 4147–10.180
Health care services use and costs, methodology and findings of natl survey, series, 4186–8
Insurance (health) coverage, and uninsured workers by industry div, with data by age, race, and marital status, 1989, GAO rpt, 26119–389
Insurance (health) coverage of persons, by insurance type and selected characteristics, 1985-90, 2546–20.23
Mental health care facilities, staff, patients, and finances, 1970s-91, biennial rpt, 4094–1

Housing and Construction

Alteration and repair of owner-occupied homes, costs and structural, household, financial, and project characteristics, 1987, 2486–1.13
American Housing Survey: unit and household characteristics of recent movers, and reason for move, by tenure, 1989, 2486–1.12
American Housing Survey: unit and households characteristics, unit and neighborhood quality, and journey to work by MSA location, for 11 MSAs, 1987 survey, supplement, 2485–8
American Housing Survey: unit and households detailed characteristics, and unit and neighborhood quality, MSA rpt series, 2485–6
American Housing Survey: unit and households detailed characteristics, and unit and neighborhood quality, 1989, biennial rpt supplement, 2485–13
Homeownership rate by marital status, and single parents share of family households, by race, 1989, fact sheet, 2326–17.44
Housing and households summary characteristics, 1989 and trends, chartbook, 2486–2.1
Mortgages FHA-insured, financial, property, and borrower characteristics, by metro area, 1991, annual rpt, 5144–24
Mortgages FHA-insured, financial, property, and borrower characteristics, by State, 1991, annual rpt, 5144–1; 5144–25
Mortgages FHA-insured, financial, property, and borrower characteristics, 1991, annual rpt, 5144–17; 5144–23
Rental housing units, total, with HUD assistance by program, and eligible for aid, by unit, household, and neighborhood characteristics, and location, 1989, biennial rpt, 5184–11
Single parent families in own and others homes, by financial, housing, and other characteristics, 1989, 2486–1.14
Single person and nonfamily households social, economic and housing characteristics, by tenure, 1989, 2486–1.15

Industry and Commerce

Minority- and woman-owned businesses and owner characteristics, by industry, employment and sales size, and form of ownership, 1987 survey, 2328–59

Labor and Employment

Child care arrangements of mothers employed and in school, and costs, by age of child and characteristics of mother, 1988, Current Population Rpt, 2546–20.24
Disabled persons work experience following OASDI benefit award, by selected characteristics, 1980s, article, 4742–1.312
Employment and Earnings, detailed data, monthly rpt, 6742–2.2; 6742–2.3; 6742–2.4
Employment and unemployment, by age, sex, race, marital and family status, industry div, and State, Monthly Labor Review, 6722–1.2
Employment, unemployment, and labor force characteristics, by region, State, and selected metro area, 1991, annual rpt, 6744–7
Home-based workers by selected characteristics, and views, 1989, article, 1702–1.307
Immigrants from Colombia employed in New England textile industry, by selected characteristics, 1960s-80s, working paper, 6366–6.4
Labor force status of family members and earnings, by family composition and race, quarterly press release, 6742–21
Labor force, wages, hours, and payroll costs, by major industry group and demographic characteristics, *Survey of Current Business*, monthly rpt, 2702–1.7
Poverty relation to low earnings, by work experience during year, household relationship, sex, race, age, and education, 1960s-90, Current Population Rpt, 2546–6.74
Schedules of work, and workers with flexible hours and shift work by selected characteristics, 1991, press release, 6726–1.50
Unemployed persons finding work, by characteristics of worker and new job, aggregate 1986-89, 2546–20.20
Women's labor force status, by age, race, and family status, quarterly rpt, 6742–17
Women's part-time employment transitions, by marital status and whether young children present, 1988 and trends from 1978, 6726–2.2

Law Enforcement

Criminal case processing in Federal district courts, and dispositions, by offense, district, and offender characteristics, 1989, annual data compilation, 6064–29
Drug abuse and trafficking offenders losing Federal benefits under new sentencing guidelines, by selected characteristics, 1990-91, GAO rpt, 26119–398
Drunk driving arrests, sentencing, and prisoner drinking patterns and other characteristics, 1989, 6066–19.69
Prisoners and movements, by offense, location, and selected other characteristics, data compilation, 1992 annual rpt, 6064–6.6
Prisoners under death sentence, and executions from 1930, by offense, prisoner characteristics, and State, 1990, annual rpt, 6064–26.6
Victimization rates, by victim and offender characteristics, circumstances, and offense, 1990 survey, annual rpt, 6066–3.47
Victimizations in cities, suburbs, and rural areas, by offense, circumstances, and victim and offender characteristics, 1987-89, 6066–3.48
Women arrestees drug abuse history and selected other characteristics, for 4 cities, 1988-89, 6068–246
Women in jail, by criminal background and sociodemographic characteristics, with comparisons to men, 1989, 6066–19.66
Women's labor force status and characteristics, 1960s-90, chartbook, 6748–85

Population

Alaska rural areas population characteristics, and energy resources dev effects, series, 5736–5
Asian and Pacific Islands Americans social and economic characteristics, for West and total US, 1990-91, Current Population Report, 2546–1.462
Black Americans social and economic characteristics, for South and total US, 1991 and trends from 1950, annual Current Population Rpt, 2546–1.463
Black women's labor force status, earnings, and other economic status indicators, and compared to whites, various periods 1939-88, 11048–191
Census of Population and Housing, 1990: detailed geographic coverage, State CD-ROM series, 2551–9
Census of Population and Housing, 1990: population and housing characteristics, detailed geographic coverage, State CD-ROM series, 2551–10
Census of Population, 1990: population characteristics and living arrangements, by county, place, and urban-rural location, State rpt series, 2531–1
Census of Population, 1990: population characteristics and living arrangements, for Native American, urban, and metro areas, series, 2531–2
Consumer Income, socioeconomic characteristics of persons, families, and households, detailed cross-tabulations, Current Population Rpt series, 2546–6
Family members supporting others outside household, by relationship, recipient living arrangements, and provider characteristics, 1988, Current Population Rpt, 2546–20.21
Immigrants from Central America in DC, by selected employment and other characteristics, and reasons for migration, 1985-88, working paper, 6366–6.3
Immigration to US, alien workers, visitors, deportations, and naturalizations, by country, FY91 and trends from 1820, annual rpt, 6264–2
Income (household) of aged and younger adults, by source, household composition, and age group, 1984 and 1989, article, 4742–1.304
Income (household) of aged and younger adults, by source, household composition, race, and age group, 1984-89, 4746–26.20

Income (personal) relative to median, by race and selected other characteristics, mid 1960s-89, Current Population Rpt, 2546–6.73
Income and consumer spending of households, for selected population groups, quarterly journal, 1702–1
Living arrangements, family relationships, and marital status, by selected characteristics, 1991, annual Current Population Rpt, 2546–1.461
Migration, immigration, and mover characteristics compared to nonmovers, 1987-90, annual Current Population Rpt, 2546–1.456
Migration since 1990, mover characteristics by same or different area, and compared to nonmovers, 1991, annual Current Population Rpt, 2546–1.464
OASDI beneficiary data collection system design compared to earlier surveys, with summary results, 1992 article, 4742–1.313
Older persons in poverty, by health, nutrition, assistance, and other characteristics, 1990, GAO rpt, 26131–100
Older persons income and sources, by OASDI beneficiary and poverty status, and other characteristics, 1990, biennial chartbook, 4744–25
Older persons income and sources, by whether OASDI beneficiary, poverty status, and other characteristics, 1990, biennial rpt, 4744–26
Older persons socioeconomic characteristics, 1900s-90 and projected to 2050, biennial chartbook, 12904–1
Older population, and health, economic, and other characteristics, with foreign comparisons, 1980s-91 with trends and projections, Current Population Rpt, 2546–2.165
Pacific territories population and housing detailed characteristics, by location, 1990 Census of Population and Housing, series, 2551–8
Population economic well-being indicators, by selected characteristics and household income and income-to-poverty ratio, 1984, 2546–20.22
Population size and components of change, alternative projections 1990-2080 and trends from 1900, annual actuarial rpt, 4706–1.106
Poverty status of population and families, by detailed characteristics, 1991, annual Current Population Rpt, 2546–6.77
Statistical Abstract of US, 1992 annual data compilation, 2324–1

Public Welfare and Social Security

Benefits, beneficiaries, and spells of participation, by aid program and recipient characteristics, 1987-88, Current Population Rpt, 2546–20.25
Child care arrangements of younger working mothers, and costs, by selected characteristics, 1988, 6726–2.1
Child support payment and visitation practices of absent fathers, and mothers with custody, by employment and other characteristics, 1988, article, 6722–1.329
Food stamp eligibility and payment errors, by type, recipient characteristics, and State, FY90, annual rpt, 1364–15
OASDHI, Medicaid, SSI, and related programs benefits, beneficiary characteristics, and trust funds, selected years 1937-90, annual rpt, 4744–3
Poverty status of families, by detailed characteristics, 1980 and 1988, GAO rpt, 26131–102

Veterans Affairs

Health care services of VA, income eligibility and copayment enforcement, and revenue forgone from unreported income, 1987-91, GAO rpt, 26121–479
Mental illness (post-traumatic stress) among veterans by period of service, and VA treatment and rehabilitation program operations and staff, FY91, annual rpt, 8704–6

BY RACE AND ETHNIC GROUP

Agriculture and Food

Employment of farm hired workers, and earnings, by selected characteristics, 1990, 1598–278
FmHA loans, by type, borrower race, and State, quarterly rpt, 1182–5
Population on farms, by employment, social, and economic characteristics, and region, 1990, annual Current Population Rpt, 2546–1.458
Women-headed households food spending, by item and selected characteristics, and compared to other households, 1970s-88, 1548–391

Banking, Finance, and Insurance

Families financial status, income, net worth, and assets and debt by type, by income and selected characteristics, 1983 and 1989, article, 9362–1.301
Small Business Admin direct and guaranteed loans, principal outstanding, and losses, by program, borrower race and sex, and State, 1950s-90, GAO rpt, 26113–554
Small Business Admin loan guarantee program participants finances, operations, characteristics, and views, 1991 survey, 9768–25

Communications and Transportation

Air traffic control and airway facilities staff, by employment and other characteristics, FY90, annual rpt, 7504–41
Air traffic controller academy grads and military hires, training performance, facility assignments, and selected characteristics, 1988, 7506–10.101
Postal Service employment and related expenses, FY91, annual rpt, 9864–5.1
Telephone local service charges and low-income subsidies, by region, company, and city, 1980s-91, semiannual rpt, 9282–8

Education

Adult education and literacy programs funding, enrollment, and student characteristics and benefits, 1987-90, fact sheet, 4806–4.1; 4806–4.4
Adult education and literacy programs funding, enrollment by State, and student characteristics and benefits, 1987-90, fact sheet, 4806–4.2
Adult education participation, by selected characteristics, 1991 survey, 4826–10.5
Athletic depts at NCAA Div I schools, staff by race, and income, by sex and position, 1990/91, GAO rpt, 26121–476
Black higher education instns enrollment, finances, staff, and degrees, by instn and selected student characteristics, 1970s-90, 4848–46
Community college attendance, by selected characteristics, 1972 high school class, natl longitudinal study, 1970s-86, 4888–7
Condition of Education, detail for elementary, secondary, and higher education, 1920s-91 and projected to 2002, annual rpt, 4824–1
Degree (PhD) recipients in higher education, by field and selected characteristics, 1979, 1984, and 1989, 4848–44
Degrees awarded in higher education, by level, field, race, and sex, 1989/90 and trends from 1980/81, annual rpt, 4844–17
Digest of Education Statistics, 1992 annual data compilation, 4824–2
DOD Dependents Schools basic skills and college entrance test scores, 1991-92, annual rpt, 3504–16
Education in science and math, natl assessment of elementary and high school students, 1985/86, series, 4896–6
Educational attainment, by social and demographic characteristics and location, 1991 and trends from 1940, biennial Current Population Rpt, 2546–1.460
Eighth grade class of 1988: educational performance and conditions, characteristics, attitudes, activities, and plans, natl longitudinal survey, series, 4826–9
Elementary and secondary education enrollment, staff, finances, operations, programs, and policies, 1987/88 biennial survey, series, 4836–3
Elementary and secondary students educational performance, and factors affecting proficiency, by selected characteristics, 1990 natl assessments, subject rpt series, 4896–8
Elementary and secondary students educational performance in math, science, reading, and writing, 1969-90, 4898–32
Enrollment, by grade, instn type and control, and student characteristics, 1989 and trends from 1947, annual Current Population Rpt, 2546–1.459
Enrollment in public elementary and secondary schools, minorities share by group and State, 1990/91, annual rpt, 4834–17
Head Start enrollment, funding, and staff, FY91, annual rpt, 4584–5
High school class of 1991: college enrollment, and labor force participation of grads and dropouts, by race and sex, annual press release, 6726–1.46
High school classes of 1980 and 1982: education, employment, and family characteristics, activities, and attitudes, natl longitudinal study, series, 4826–2
High school dropout rates, and subsequent completion, by student and school characteristics, alternative estimates, 1991, annual rpt, 4834–23
High school dropouts and transfers between public and private schools, by instn control, income level, and race, 1990 survey, 4826–10.4
High school dropouts in Chelsea, Mass, by sex, race, and grade, impacts of Boston University mgmt of local school system, 1988-90, 4808–38

Higher education enrollment, by level, race, and sex, fall 1980-90, biennial rpt, 4844–15
Higher education enrollment, by sex and race, 1976-2000, annual rpt, 4824–4
Higher education enrollment, completion, and degrees, for minorities by race, sex, and type of instn, 1970s-90, 26306–3.122
Private elementary and secondary schools, students, and staff characteristics, by school type and affiliation, 1987/88, 4836–3.8
Public housing residents educational attainment, by selected characteristics, 1980s, 5188–132
Reading performance and factors affecting proficiency, for elementary and secondary students, 1988 and 1990 natl assessments, 4898–33
Student aid and other sources of support, with student expenses and characteristics, by instn type and control, 1987 study, series, 4846–3
Student aid and other sources of support, with student expenses and characteristics, by instn type and control, 1990 triennial study, series, 4846–5
Student guaranteed loan Stafford program, borrowers and likelihood of default by selected characteristics, 1989-90, 26306–3.120
Teachers of vocational education, by subject area and selected characteristics, for public high schools, 1987/88, 4836–3.9
Truman, Harry S, Scholarship Foundation finances, and awards by student characteristics, FY91, annual rpt, 14314–1
Vocational education enrollment, and academic and other credits earned, by subject and student characteristics, high school classes of 1982 and 1987, 4838–50
Vocational education enrollment, student and teacher characteristics, and outcomes, for secondary and postsecondary instns, 1970s-90, 4828–42

Energy Resources and Demand

Coal production, reserves, use, and prices by State, exports by country, and employment, 1900s-90, biennial rpt, 3164–79
Households, housing, and fuel use characteristics, survey rpt series, 3166–7

Government and Defense

DOT employment, by subagency, occupation, and selected personnel characteristics, FY91, annual rpt, 7304–18
Employment (civilian) of Fed Govt, by demographic and employment characteristics, as of Sept 1991, annual article, 9842–1.301
Employment (civilian) of Fed Govt, by demographic characteristics and agency, 1990, GAO rpt, 26119–383
Employment of minorities, disabled, and veterans in Fed Govt, and years of service, by occupation, age, sex, and agency, as of Sept 1990, biennial rpt, 9844–27
Employment of minorities, women, and disabled in Fed Govt, by agency and occupation, FY90, annual rpt, 9244–10
Equal Opportunity Recruitment Program activity, and Fed Govt employment by sex, race, pay grade, and occupational group, FY91, annual rpt, 9844–33
Fed Govt procurement set-aside contracts for minority businesses, by participant race and sex, industry, firm, and State, FY90, annual rpt, 9764–8
IRS employment of minorities and women, compared to Fed Govt and total civilian labor force, FY91, annual rpt, 8304–3.3
Military deaths by cause, age, race, and rank, and personnel captured and missing, by service branch, FY91, annual rpt, 3544–40
Military homosexual personnel discharges by pay grade, tenure, race, sex, and occupation, and investigations, by service branch, 1980s-90, GAO rpt, 26123–392
Military personnel, by selected characteristics, 1992 annual summary rpt, 3504–13
Military personnel deployment in Operation Desert Storm, by sex, race, rank, and service branch, 1990-91, GAO rpt, 26123–394
Military personnel occupational distribution, by race, sex, and service branch, FY90, GAO rpt, 26123–381
Military personnel reductions planned by service branch, and women and minorities affected by Army and Air Force plans, FY90-91, GAO rpt, 26123–373
Military recruits by race, and goals, by sex and service branch, quarterly press release, 3542–7
Military reserve forces personnel strengths and characteristics, by component, quarterly rpt, 3542–4
Military reserve forces personnel strengths, by selected characteristics and reserve component, FY91, annual rpt, 3544–1.5
Military reserve officer and enlisted personnel, by component, FY91, annual rpt, 3544–31.1
Senior Executive Service members characteristics, entries, exits, and awards, FY79-91, annual rpt, 9844–36
Small Business Admin minority and women employment, and hiring goals, FY91, annual rpt, 9764–9
State and local govt employment of minorities and women, by occupation, function, pay level, and State, 1991, annual rpt, 9244–6
Taxes, spending, and govt efficiency, public opinion by respondent characteristics, 1992 survey, annual rpt, 10044–2
Voting age population, by sex, age, race, and State, forecast 1992 general elections, with votes cast from 1930, Current Population Rpt, 2546–3.170

Health and Vital Statistics

Abortions by method, patient characteristics, and State, and related deaths, 1970-89, annual article, 4202–7.324
Acute and chronic health conditions, disability, absenteeism, and health services use, by selected characteristics, 1990, annual rpt, 4147–10.182
Acute and chronic health conditions, disability, absenteeism, and health services use, by selected characteristics, 1991, annual rpt, 4147–10.183
AIDS cases among children, hospital use and charges by instn and patient characteristics, and payment source, 1986-87, 4186–6.16
AIDS cases by risk group, race, sex, age, State, and MSA, and deaths, quarterly rpt, 4202–9
AIDS patients costs and service use under Medicaid, and service needs, for New Jersey waiver program, 1987-89, article, 4652–1.317
AIDS public knowledge, attitudes, info sources, and testing, 1991 survey, 4146–8.218
Alcohol abuse and dependence prevalence, by age, race, and sex, and diagnostic criteria, 1988, article, 4482–1.306
Alcohol-related diagnoses hospital discharges and length of stay, by age, sex, race, and region, 1979-85, 4488–10.5
Alcohol-related disorder hospital discharges and length of stay, by diagnosis, sex, age, and race, 1979-89, 4486–1.16
Births and rates, by characteristics of birth, infant, and mother, and presence of maternal risk factors and birth defects, 1989, 4146–5.125
Births of low birthweight to Indians, compared to whites and blacks, for New York, 1980s, article, 4042–3.359
Births of twins, by birth order and weight, gestation period, mothers age, and race, 1950s-88, 4147–21.50
Cancer (breast and cervical) deaths and rates by State, and in situ case rates by age, by race, 1970s-86, article, 4202–7.312
Cancer (breast and cervical) screening use and reasons for nonuse, by age, race, income, and State, 1987-89, article, 4202–7.313
Cancer cases by body site and population characteristics, research results, semimonthly journal, 4472–1
Child infectious disease cases, and related disability and health care, by disease, health insurance status, and other characteristics, 1988, 4147–10.181
Children (handicapped) with special needs, insurance coverage, and health care services use, by selected characteristics, 1988, 4146–8.216
Cirrhosis of liver deaths, by age, sex, race, and whether alcohol involved, 1988 and trends from 1910, annual rpt, 4486–1.13
Cytomegalovirus (congenital) disease cases, by infant, mother, and birth characteristics, type of impairment, State, and Canada Province, 1990-91, 4202–7.314
DC metro area drug, alcohol, and tobacco use, user characteristics, and consequences, series, 4496–12
Deaths and rates by age, and life expectancy, by sex and race, preliminary 1990-91 and trends from 1950, US Vital Statistics annual rpt, 4144–7
Deaths and rates, by cause, age, sex, marital status, race, and State, 1989, US Vital Statistics advance annual rpt, 4146–5.124
Deaths and rates, by cause and selected social, demographic, and employment characteristics, 1979-85, natl longitudinal study, 4478–186
Deaths and rates, by detailed location, cause, and demographic characteristics, 1989, US Vital Statistics annual rpt, 4144–3
Deaths and rates, provisional data, monthly rpt, 4142–1.2
Deaths during 1986, decedents health condition, services use, habits, and social, employment, and other characteristics, 4147–20.19
Dental fluoride products use by children, by frequency of dental visits and selected characteristics, 1983-89, 4146–8.222
Diabetes patients physician office visits, by characteristics of patient, physician, and visit, 1989, 4146–8.212

Digestive diseases (chronic) prevalence, and procedures performed, by disease and patient characteristics, 1989, 4146–8.213
Disabled persons rehabilitation, Federal and State activities and funding, FY90, annual rpt, 4944–1
Disabled workers labor force status, type and cause of disability, and other characteristics, 1970s-89, chartbook, 4948–11
Drug abuse by mothers, treatment and other services use, referrals, needs, and barriers, for 13 NIDA-funded programs, 1990/91 survey, 4498–76
Drug abuse indicators for selected metro areas, research results, data collection, and policy issues, 1992 semiannual conf, 4492–5
Drug, alcohol, and cigarette use and attitudes of youth, by substance type and selected characteristics, 1975-91 surveys, annual rpt, 4494–4
Drug, alcohol, and cigarette use, by selected characteristics, 1991 survey, annual rpt series, 4494–5
Educational attainment relation to health condition and care, indicators by selected characteristics, 1989, 4147–10.180
Health care professionals supply and education, by professional and other characteristics, and location, 1960s-92 and projected to 2020, biennial rpt, 4114–8
Health care services use and costs, methodology and findings of natl survey, series, 4186–8
Health condition and care indicators, 1950s-90 with health improvement and disease prevention goals for 1990, annual data compilation, 4144–11
Hepatitis cases by infection source, age, sex, race, and State, and deaths, by strain, 1989 and trends from 1966, 4205–2
Homicides and rate, by weapon, circumstances, and victim characteristics, and years of potential life lost, 1980s, article, 4202–7.315
Hospital discharges and length of stay, by diagnosis, patient and instn characteristics, procedure performed, and payment source, 1990, annual rpt, 4147–13.112
Hospital discharges and length of stay under old and new survey designs, by diagnosis, patient and instn characteristics, and procedure, Jan-Mar 1988, 4147–13.110
Hospital discharges, by payment source, diagnosis, patient characteristics, and region, and procedures performed, 1990, 4146–8.221
Infant health, deaths and risk factors, and prevention issues, for US and selected countries, 1990 conf, 4148–28
Infectious notifiable disease cases, by age, race, and State, and deaths, 1940s-91, annual rpt, 4204–1
Insurance (health) coverage, and uninsured workers by industry div, with data by age, race, and marital status, 1989, GAO rpt, 26119–389
Insurance (health) coverage of persons, by insurance type and selected characteristics, 1985-90, 2546–20.23
Internist office visits, by characteristics of patient, physician, and visit, 1989, 4146–8.214
Kidney end-stage disease treatment facilities, Medicare enrollment and reimbursement, survival, and patient characteristics, 1984-90, annual rpt, 4654–16
LSD trafficking, abuse, and enforcement, and DEA field div activities, 1980s-91, 6288–9
Marriage, divorce, and remarriage of women by age, and child living arrangements, by race, 1970s-90, Current Population Rpt, 2546–2.166
Maternal and child health indicators and services use, by age, race, and poverty status, 1988, 4478–197
Medicare payment of physicians, vulnerable beneficiaries services use prior to fee schedule implementation, 1986-90, annual rpt, 17266–1.8
Mental health care facilities partial care services, and patient characteristics, by instn type and State, 1970s-88, 4506–3.51
Mental health care facilities, staff, patients, and finances, 1970s-91, biennial rpt, 4094–1
Mental health care of affective disorder patients, by patient and facility characteristics, 1986, 4506–3.49
Mental illness (serious) among adults, functional limitations, govt aid, drugs used, visits to professionals, and other characteristics, 1989, 4146–8.220
NIH research and training grants awarded to women, by recipient characteristics, inst, and host instn, FY90, annual rpt, 4434–18
Otitis media patients physician office visits, by specialty and characteristics of patient and visit, 1975-90, 4146–8.217
Pediatrician office visits, by characteristics of patient and visit, 1989, 4146–8.210
Physicians visits, by patient and practice characteristics, diagnosis, and services provided, 1989, annual rpt, 4147–13.109
Physicians visits, by patient and practice characteristics, diagnosis, and services provided, 1990, advance rpt, 4146–8.215
Radiation protection and health physics enrollment and degrees granted by instn and State, and grad placement, by student characteristics, 1991, annual rpt, 3004–7
Smoking control strategies effectiveness, with data on research funding, smoking prevalence, cancer deaths, and taxation, 1900s-91, 4476–7.1
Syphilis case rate, by sex, race, and region, 1990, article, 4202–7.303
Transplants of organs, failure and death risk by selected transplant and patient characteristics, 1987-89, annual rpt, 4104–17.1
Tuberculosis cases and rates, by patient characteristics, 1985 and 1990, article, 4202–7.302
Tuberculosis prevention and control among at-risk minority and homeless populations, CDC recommendations, 1992 rpt, 4206–2.55
Youth alcohol use and abuse, by sex, race, Hispanic origin, and grade, 1987, article, 4482–1.302
Youth health condition, risk factors, and preventive and treatment services use and availability, 1970s-80s, 26358–234.2; 26358–234.3

Housing and Construction

Affordability and availability of housing, impacts of govt land use regulations and rent control, and low income housing condition, 1991 hearing, 21248–174
Alteration and repair of owner-occupied homes, costs and structural, household, financial, and project characteristics, 1987, 2486–1.13
American Housing Survey: unit and household characteristics of recent movers, and reason for move, by tenure, 1989, 2486–1.12
American Housing Survey: unit and households characteristics, MSA fact sheet series, 2485–11
American Housing Survey: unit and households characteristics, unit and neighborhood quality, and journey to work by MSA location, for 11 MSAs, 1987 survey, supplement, 2485–8
American Housing Survey: unit and households detailed characteristics, and unit and neighborhood quality, MSA rpt series, 2485–6
American Housing Survey: unit and households detailed characteristics, and unit and neighborhood quality, 1989, biennial rpt supplement, 2485–13
Census of Housing, 1990: inventory, occupancy, and costs, State fact sheet series, 2326–21
Census of Housing, 1990: summary unit characteristics, by householder race and age, county, place, and urban-rural location, State rpt series, 2471–1
Census of Population and Housing, 1990: detailed geographic coverage, State CD-ROM series, 2551–9
Census of Population and Housing, 1990: population and housing characteristics, detailed geographic coverage, State CD-ROM series, 2551–10
Discrimination in housing rental and sales, for blacks and Hispanics in selected metro areas, 1989 study, series, 5186–16
Homeless persons transitional housing and support services program, outcome relation to client characteristics and services, FY87-90, GAO rpt, 26113–549
Homeownership values, reasons, and barriers, views by race and tenure, 1992 survey, 9478–1
Housing and households summary characteristics, 1989 and trends, chartbook, 2486–2.1
Mortgage applications, dispositions, and secondary loan market sales, by purpose, lender type, and applicant and neighborhood characteristics, 1991, article, 9362–1.307
Mortgage applications of minorities, for Boston by disposition and financial characteristics, with problems in analyzing lender disclosure statements, 1990, working paper, 9373–27.15
Mortgages FHA-insured, financial, property, and borrower characteristics, by metro area, 1991, annual rpt, 5144–24
Mortgages FHA-insured, financial, property, and borrower characteristics, by State, 1991, annual rpt, 5144–1; 5144–25
Mortgages FHA-insured, financial, property, and borrower characteristics, 1991, annual rpt, 5144–17; 5144–23

NYC housing supply, occupancy, condition, and household characteristics, by tenure and borough, 1991 triennial survey, 2488–3
Rental housing units, total, with HUD assistance by program, and eligible for aid, by unit, household, and neighborhood characteristics, and location, 1989, biennial rpt, 5184–11
Single parent families in own and others homes, by financial, housing, and other characteristics, 1989, 2486–1.14
Single parent share of family households, and homeownership rate by marital status, by race, 1989, fact sheet, 2326–17.44
Single person and nonfamily households social, economic and housing characteristics, by tenure, 1989, 2486–1.15

Industry and Commerce

Business mgmt and financial aid from Minority Business Dev Centers, and characteristics of businesses, by region and State, FY91, annual rpt, 2104–6
Business owner and business characteristics, for minority- and women-owned firms, by industry, employment and sales size, and form of ownership, 1987 survey, 2328–59

Labor and Employment

Child care arrangements of mothers employed and in school, and costs, by age of child and characteristics of mother, 1988, Current Population Rpt, 2546–20.24
Dallas-Fort Worth metro area employment, earnings, hours, and CPI changes, late 1970s-91, annual rpt, 6964–2
Disabled persons work experience following OASDI benefit award, by selected characteristics, 1980s, article, 4742–1.312
Displaced worker employment and training services, and layoff alternatives, indicators of effectiveness, 1980s, 15498–28
Displaced workers, layoffs and unemployment insurance claims by reason, industry, selected characteristics, and State, quarterly press release, 6742–23
Displaced workers, layoffs and unemployment insurance claims by reason, industry, selected characteristics, MSA, and State, 1990, annual rpt, 6744–18
Displaced workers losing job 1987-92, labor force status by employment and other characteristics, as of Jan 1992, biennial press release, 6726–1.48
Employment and Earnings, detailed data, monthly rpt, 6742–2
Employment and economic conditions, alternative BLS projections to 2005 and trends 1975-90, biennial rpt, 6744–19
Employment and Training Admin activities, funding, and participant characteristics, by program, FY86-88, annual rpt, 6404–17
Employment and unemployment, by age, sex, race, marital and family status, industry div, and State, Monthly Labor Review, 6722–1.2
Employment, earnings, and hours, monthly press release, 6742–5
Employment of minorities and women by industry sector, and govt salaries, by occupation, mid 1960s-90, chartbook, 9248–20
Employment of minorities and women, by occupation, SIC 1- to 3-digit industry, State, and MSA, 1991, annual rpt, 9244–1
Employment situation, earnings, hours, and other BLS economic indicators, transcripts of BLS Commissioner's monthly testimony, periodic rpt, 23846–4
Employment, unemployment, and labor force characteristics, by region, State, and selected metro area, 1991, annual rpt, 6744–7
Family members labor force status and earnings, by family composition and race, quarterly press release, 6742–21
Home-based workers and hours, by worker characteristics, occupational group and industry div, 1991, press release, 6726–1.52
Houston metro area employment, earnings, hours, and CPI changes, 1970s-91, annual rpt, 6964–1
Job Training Partnership Act education and worker training program participants, by selected characteristics, 1986-88, 15496–1.15
Labor demand, turnover, and training completions, by detailed occupation, 1990 and projected to 2005, biennial rpt, 6744–3
Labor force status by age, sex, and race, accuracy of BLS forecasts made 1970s-80s, as of 1990, article, 6722–1.334
Labor force status by race and sex, employment by industry div, and unemployment duration and reason, selected years 1929-91, annual rpt, 204–1.2
Labor force status, by race, detailed Hispanic origin, and sex, quarterly rpt, 6742–18
Labor force status, by worker characteristics and industry group, 1990-91, annual article, 6722–1.312
Labor force status, experience, and unemployment duration, by race and sex, 1990-91, annual press release, 6726–1.51
Labor force, wages, hours, and payroll costs, by major industry group and demographic characteristics, *Survey of Current Business*, monthly rpt, 2702–1.7
Older persons labor force status, income sources, and reasons for not working, with data by occupation, sex, and race, 1989-90 and projected to 2050, 21148–65
Petrochemicals industries contract labor accidents, injuries, safety programs operations, and employee characteristics, 1986-91, 6608–6
Population and labor force characteristics, 1940s-90 and projected to 2000, 15496–1.16
Poverty relation to low earnings, by work experience during year, household relationship, sex, race, age, and education, 1960s-90, Current Population Rpt, 2546–6.74
Schedules of work, and workers with flexible hours and shift work by selected characteristics, 1991, press release, 6726–1.50
Tenure with current employer compared to 1983, and employment in same occupation in 1990, by sex, age, and race, 1991, press release, 6726–1.47
Training for job qualification and skill improvement, workers participating by training source, occupation, age, sex, and race, 1991, 6728–32
Unemployed persons finding work, by characteristics of worker and new job, aggregate 1986-89, 2546–20.20
Unemployment rates, current data and annual trends, monthly rpt, 23842–1.2
Union coverage of workers and earnings, by age, sex, race, occupational group, and industry div, monthly rpt, annual article, 6782–1.2
Union coverage of workers and earnings, by age, sex, race, occupational group, and industry div, 1990-91, annual press release, 6726–1.44
Wages of full- and part-time workers, by selected characteristics, quarterly press release, 6742–20
Women's labor force status and characteristics, 1960s-90, chartbook, 6748–85
Women's labor force status, by age, race, and family status, quarterly rpt, 6742–17
Women's labor force status, earnings, and other characteristics, with comparisons to men, fact sheet series, 6564–1
Women's occupational differences for blacks and whites, and compared to men, selected years 1940-88, article, 6722–1.321
Younger workers jobs held and weeks worked since age 18, by age, sex, and race, 1978-90, 6726–2.3
Youth labor force status, by sex, race, and industry div, summer 1988-92, annual press release, 6744–14

Law Enforcement

Assaults and deaths of law enforcement officers, by circumstances, agency, victim and offender characteristics, and location, 1991, annual rpt, 6224–3
Crime, criminal justice admin and enforcement, and public opinion, data compilation, 1992 annual rpt, 6064–6
Crimes, arrests, and rates, by offense, offender characteristics, population size, and jurisdiction, 1991, annual rpt, 6224–2.1; 6224–2.2
Criminal case processing in Federal district courts, and dispositions, by offense, district, and offender characteristics, 1989, annual data compilation, 6064–29
Drug test results at arrest, by drug type, offense, and sex, for selected urban areas, quarterly rpt, 6062–3
Drunk driving arrests, sentencing, and prisoner drinking patterns and other characteristics, 1989, 6066–19.69
Executions by whether habeas corpus used to appeal conviction, and time from crime to execution, with data by race and State, 1977-91, 6008–34
Fraud and forgery arrests, case dispositions, and sentencing, by age, sex, race, and offense type, 1983-88, 6066–19.64
Jail population by sex, race, and for 25 jurisdictions, and instn conditions, 1990-91, annual rpt, 6066–25.48
Juvenile arrests, by sex, race, disposition, and offense, 1990, 6066–27.8
Juvenile courts drug and alcohol offenses cases, by disposition and offender age, sex, and race, 1985-88, 6066–27.7
Juvenile facilities population, by resident characteristics and facility type, late 1970s-89, 6068–250
Juvenile facilities population, by resident characteristics and facility type, 1977-89, annual rpt, 6064–35

Police agencies employment, spending, and operations, FY90, 6066–25.44
Police employment, spending, and operations, for State, city, county, and special district agencies, 1990, annual rpt, 6064–39
Prison and community-based facilities, population, employment, spending, and other characteristics, by State and for Fed Govt, 1990, quinquennial rpt, 6068–218
Prison and parole admissions and releases, sentence length, and time served, by offense and offender characteristics, 1988, annual rpt, 6064–33
Prisoners and staff in Federal instns, by selected characteristics, region, and instn, FY89, annual rpt, 6244–1
Prisoners, characteristics, and movements, by State, 1990, annual rpt, 6064–26
Prisoners in Federal and State instns by selected characteristics, releases, staff, and instn size, with data by region and State, late 1970s-91, 6068–248
Probation population, by offender characteristics, sentence conditions, whether rearrested, and offense, 1986-89, 6066–19.65
Schools crime victimization, drug availability, and preventive measures, with student views, 1989 survey, 6066–3.46
Sentences for Federal crimes, guidelines use and results by offense and district, and Sentencing Commission activities, 1991, annual rpt, 17664–1
Sentences for Federal crimes, guidelines use and results by offense, 1984-1990, 6066–19.68
Sentences for Federal offenses, guidelines impacts on sentence disparity by offender race and other characteristics, 1985-90, GAO rpt, 26119–415
Sentences under Federal mandatory minimum provisions, by defendant characteristics, and views on justice system impacts, FY90, 17668–2
Sheriffs' agencies employment, spending, and operations, FY90, 6066–25.45
Victimization rates, by victim and offender characteristics, circumstances, and offense, 1990 survey, annual rpt, 6066–3.47
Victimizations in cities, suburbs, and rural areas, by offense, circumstances, and victim and offender characteristics, 1987-89, 6066–3.48
Victimizations of households, by offense, household characteristics, and location, 1975-91, annual rpt, 6066–25.49
Women arrestees drug abuse history and selected other characteristics, for 4 cities, 1988-89, 6068–246
Women in jail, by criminal background and sociodemographic characteristics, with comparisons to men, 1989, 6066–19.66

Natural Resources, Environment, and Pollution

Forest Service employment and human resource program participation, FY91, annual rpt, 1204–1.4

Population

Black Americans social and economic characteristics, for South and total US, 1991 and trends from 1950, annual Current Population Rpt, 2546–1.463
Census of Population and Housing, 1990: detailed geographic coverage, State CD-ROM series, 2551–9
Census of Population and Housing, 1990: population and housing characteristics, detailed geographic coverage, State CD-ROM series, 2551–10
Census of Population and Housing, 1990: summary characteristics, households, and land area, by county, subdiv, and place, State rpt series, 2551–1
Census of Population, 1990: ancestry of US population, by group and State, press release, 2328–87
Census of Population, 1990: data adjustment for undercounts, evaluation of advisability, with error rates by race and selected city, hearing, 21628–102
Census of Population, 1990: data adjustment in intercensal data for census undercounts, recommendations with alternative undercount estimates, 2628–36
Census of Population, 1990: population characteristics and living arrangements, by county, place, and urban-rural location, State rpt series, 2531–1
Census of Population, 1990: population characteristics and living arrangements, for Native American, urban, and metro areas, series, 2531–2
Child living arrangements, and women's marriage and divorce experience, by race, 1970s-90, Current Population Rpt, 2546–2.166
Consumer Income, socioeconomic characteristics of persons, families, and households, detailed cross-tabulations, Current Population Rpt series, 2546–6
Family life and relationships quality and other issues, views of parents and children, 1990 survey, 15528–2
Family members supporting others outside household, by relationship, recipient living arrangements, and provider characteristics, 1988, Current Population Rpt, 2546–20.21
Households and family characteristics, by location, 1991, annual Current Population Rpt, 2546–1.457
Income (household) and poverty status under alternative income definitions, by recipient characteristics, 1979-91, annual Current Population Rpt, 2546–6.78
Income (household) and wealth distribution by selected characteristics, with foreign comparisons, 1992 compilation of papers, Current Population Rpt, 2546–6.79
Income (household) of aged and younger adults, by source, household composition, race, and age group, 1984-89, 4746–26.20
Income (personal) by sex, and poverty status of families and persons, by race, 1970-89, annual rpt, 204–1.1
Income (personal) relative to median, by race and selected other characteristics, mid 1960s-89, Current Population Rpt, 2546–6.73
Income and consumer spending of households, for selected population groups, quarterly journal, 1702–1
Living arrangements, family relationships, and marital status, by selected characteristics, 1991, annual Current Population Rpt, 2546–1.461
Migration, immigration, and mover characteristics compared to nonmovers, 1987-90, annual Current Population Rpt, 2546–1.456
Migration since 1990, mover characteristics by same or different area, and compared to nonmovers, 1991, annual Current Population Rpt, 2546–1.464
Mississippi poverty, hunger, and public welfare program operations and indicators of need, 1991 hearing, 21968–57
Older persons in poverty, by health, nutrition, assistance, and other characteristics, 1990, GAO rpt, 26131–100
Older persons income and sources, by OASDI beneficiary and poverty status, and other characteristics, 1990, biennial chartbook, 4744–25
Older persons income and sources, by whether OASDI beneficiary, poverty status, and other characteristics, 1990, biennial rpt, 4744–26
Older persons population size and characteristics, series, 2326–25
Older persons socioeconomic characteristics, 1900s-90 and projected to 2050, biennial chartbook, 12904–1
Older population, and health, economic, and other characteristics, with foreign comparisons, 1980s-91 with trends and projections, Current Population Rpt, 2546–2.165
Pacific territories population and housing detailed characteristics, by location, 1990 Census of Population and Housing, series, 2551–8
Population economic well-being indicators, by selected characteristics and household income and income-to-poverty ratio, 1984, 2546–20.22
Population size, by race and Hispanic origin, 1992 and projected 2000-2050, press release, 2328–85
Poverty status of population and families, by detailed characteristics, 1991, annual Current Population Rpt, 2546–6.77
Soviet Union and US economic and sociodemographic indicators, selected years 1970-90, handbook, 2328–80
Soviet Union former Republics and Baltic States energy supply and use, and social, economic, and political indicators, 1989-90, 3168–126
Soviet Union former Republics and Baltic States population size and characteristics, 1989-92, 9118–19
Statistical Abstract of US, 1992 annual data compilation, 2324–1
Wage ratios of black women to black men and to white men and women, various periods 1939-88, 11048–191

Public Welfare and Social Security

AFDC beneficiaries demographic and financial characteristics, by State, FY90, annual rpt, 4584–7
Benefits, beneficiaries, and spells of participation, by aid program and recipient characteristics, 1987-88, Current Population Rpt, 2546–20.25
Child care arrangements of younger working mothers, and costs, by selected characteristics, 1988, 6726–2.1
Child day care and early childhood education programs availability, demand, use, costs, and provider and enrollee characteristics, 1990 survey, 4808–39
Child support awards, payment status, reasons for nonpayment, and mothers characteristics, by fathers residence in and out of State, 1990, GAO rpt, 26121–442

Child support payment and visitation practices of absent fathers, and mothers with custody, by employment and other characteristics, 1988, article, 6722–1.329
Disability benefit applications under OASDI and SSI, dispositions, awards, and administrative law judge hearing outcomes, by race, 1988, GAO rpt, 26121–459
Disability Insurance beneficiaries deaths and survival, by selected characteristics, for persons entitled 1972 and 1985, article, 4742–1.321
Food aid program of USDA for women, infants, and children, participants by race, State, and Indian agency, 1991, annual rpt, 1364–16
Food stamp recipient household size, composition, income, and income and deductions allowed, summer 1989, annual rpt, 1364–8
Medicare admin and research, and HCFA affirmative action and accreditation programs, FY87, annual rpt, 4654–5
Medicare and Medicaid beneficiaries and program operations, 1992, annual fact book, 4654–18
Medicare beneficiaries knowledge of and experience with physician billing and payment under Medicare, by selected characteristics, 1988-89, 17266–2.1
Medicare payment of physicians, reforms impacts on services, and monitoring methods, 1992 annual rpt, 4004–34
OASDHI coverage of employment and earnings, and social security contributions, by age, sex, race, State, and county, 1988, annual rpt, 4744–29
OASDHI, Medicaid, SSI, and related programs benefits, beneficiary characteristics, and trust funds, selected years 1937-90, annual rpt, 4744–3
Poverty status of families, by detailed characteristics, 1980 and 1988, GAO rpt, 26131–102
Supplemental Security Income recipients, by race, sex, living arrangements, age, eligibility, and State, quarterly rpt, 4742–1.2
Supplemental Security Income work incentive programs, participant characteristics, by program, 1982-91, article, 4742–1.305

Science and Technology

Education in science and engineering, grad programs enrollment by field, source of funds, and characteristics of student and instn, 1990, annual rpt, 9627–7
Employment and education of minorities, women, and disabled in science and engineering, by field, mid 1970s-91, biennial rpt, 9624–20
Higher education instn undergrad research grants of NSF, administrator and recipient characteristics and views, 1987-89, 9628–86
Labor force, Federal and university research funding, and educational data, for science and engineering, series, 9626–6
NASA Apollo era science and engineering staff background and characteristics, 1958-70, 9508–39
NASA staff characteristics and personnel actions, FY91, annual rpt, 9504–1
Nuclear engineering enrollment and degrees granted by instn and State, and grad placement, by student characteristics, 1991, annual rpt, 3004–5
Science and Engineering Indicators, employment, education, R&D funding, and industry impacts, with foreign comparisons, 1960s-91, biennial rpt, 9624–10

Veterans Affairs

AIDS cases at VA health care centers by sex, race, risk factor, and facility, and AIDS prevention and treatment issues, quarterly rpt, 8702–1
Labor force status and earnings of Vietnam veterans, by whether served in Southeast Asia, presence and severity of disability, and sociodemographic characteristics, 1989, article, 6722–1.326
Labor force status of Vietnam veterans, by whether served in Southeast Asia, presence and severity of disability, VA programs use, age, race, and occupation, 1991, biennial press release, 6726–1.49
Mental illness (post-traumatic stress) among veterans by period of service, and VA treatment and rehabilitation program operations and staff, FY91, annual rpt, 8704–6
VA employment characteristics and activities, FY91, annual rpt, 8604–3.4

BY SEX

Agriculture and Food

Employment of farm hired workers, and earnings, by selected characteristics, 1990, 1598–278
Population on farms, by employment, social, and economic characteristics, and region, 1990, annual Current Population Rpt, 2546–1.458

Banking, Finance, and Insurance

Small Business Admin direct and guaranteed loans, principal outstanding, and losses, by program, borrower race and sex, and State, 1950s-90, GAO rpt, 26113–554
Small Business Admin loan guarantee program participants finances, operations, characteristics, and views, 1991 survey, 9768–25

Communications and Transportation

Air traffic control and airway facilities staff, by employment and other characteristics, FY90, annual rpt, 7504–41
Air traffic controller academy grads and military hires, training performance, facility assignments, and selected characteristics, 1988, 7506–10.101
Aircraft pilot and nonpilot certificates held, by type of certificate, age, sex, region, and State, 1991, annual rpt, 7504–2
Drivers licenses in force, by age, sex, and State, 1990-91, annual rpt, 7554–24
Drivers licenses in force by license type, sex, and age, and fees, by State, 1991, annual rpt, 7554–1.2
Drivers licenses issued and in force by age and sex, fees, and renewal, by license class and State, 1990, annual rpt, 7554–16
FAA employees job satisfaction, impacts of promotion and pay equity by sex, 1992 technical rpt, 7506–10.105
Railroad employee benefits and beneficiaries by type, and railroad employment and payroll, FY90, annual rpt, 9704–2
Traffic accidents and casualties, by driver age and sex, 1990, 7768–105
Traffic accidents, casualties, circumstances, and characteristics of persons and vehicles involved, 1990, annual rpt, 7764–18
Traffic fatal accidents, alcohol levels of drivers and others, by circumstances and characteristics of persons and vehicles, 1990, annual rpt, 7764–16
Traffic fatal accidents, circumstances, and characteristics of persons and vehicles involved, 1991, semiannual rpt, 7762–11
Traffic fatal accidents, deaths, and rates, by circumstances, characteristics of persons and vehicles involved, and location, 1990, annual rpt, 7764–10
Travel patterns, personal and household characteristics, and auto and public transport use, 1990 survey, series, 7556–6
Travel patterns, personal and household characteristics, and auto use, 1950-90, annual rpt, 3304–5.4
Travel to US and Canada, market analysis with detailed trip and traveler characteristics, country rpt series, 2906–2
Travel to US, by characteristics of visit and traveler, world area of origin, and US destination, 1991 survey, annual rpt, 2904–12

Education

Adult education and literacy programs funding, enrollment, and student characteristics and benefits, 1987-90, fact sheet, 4806–4.1; 4806–4.4
Adult education and literacy programs funding, enrollment by State, and student characteristics and benefits, 1987-90, fact sheet, 4806–4.2
Adult education participation, by selected characteristics, 1991 survey, 4826–10.5
American Historical Assn financial statements, and membership by State, 1990, annual rpt, 29574–2
Athletic depts at NCAA Div I schools, staff by race, and income, by sex and position, 1990/91, GAO rpt, 26121–476
Black higher education instns enrollment, finances, staff, and degrees, by instn and selected student characteristics, 1970s-90, 4848–46
Community college attendance, by selected characteristics, 1972 high school class, natl longitudinal study, 1970s-86, 4888–7
Condition of Education, detail for elementary, secondary, and higher education, 1920s-91 and projected to 2002, annual rpt, 4824–1
Degree (PhD) recipients in higher education, by field and selected characteristics, 1979, 1984, and 1989, 4848–44
Degrees awarded in higher education, by level, field, race, and sex, 1989/90 and trends from 1980/81, annual rpt, 4844–17
Digest of Education Statistics, 1992 annual data compilation, 4824–2
DOD Dependents Schools basic skills and college entrance test scores, 1991-92, annual rpt, 3504–16
Education in science and math, natl assessment of elementary and high school students, 1985/86, series, 4896–6
Educational attainment, by social and demographic characteristics and location, 1991 and trends from 1940, biennial Current Population Rpt, 2546–1.460
Eighth grade class of 1988: educational performance and conditions, characteristics, attitudes, activities, and plans, natl longitudinal survey, series, 4826–9

Elementary and secondary education enrollment, staff, finances, operations, programs, and policies, 1987/88 biennial survey, series, 4836–3
Elementary and secondary students educational performance, and factors affecting proficiency, by selected characteristics, 1990 natl assessments, subject rpt series, 4896–8
Elementary and secondary students educational performance in math, science, reading, and writing, 1969-90, 4898–32
Enrollment, by grade, instn type and control, and student characteristics, 1989 and trends from 1947, annual Current Population Rpt, 2546–1.459
High school class of 1991: college enrollment, and labor force participation of grads and dropouts, by race and sex, annual press release, 6726–1.46
High school classes of 1980 and 1982: education, employment, and family characteristics, activities, and attitudes, natl longitudinal study, series, 4826–2
High school dropout rates, and subsequent completion, by student and school characteristics, alternative estimates, 1991, annual rpt, 4834–23
High school dropouts and rates, and data collection and reporting methods evaluation, 1992 rpt, 4838–49
High school dropouts in Chelsea, Mass, by sex, race, and grade, impacts of Boston University mgmt of local school system, 1988-90, 4808–38
Higher education enrollment and degrees awarded, by sex, full- and part-time status, and instn level and control, fall 1991, annual rpt, 4844–16
Higher education enrollment by age and instn type, and degrees by level, by sex, 1977/78-1990/91 and alternative projections to 2002/2003, annual rpt, 4824–4
Higher education enrollment, by level, race, and sex, fall 1980-90, biennial rpt, 4844–15
Higher education faculty and staff, by occupation, full- and part-time status, sex, and instn type and control, fall 1989, biennial rpt, 4844–18
Higher education noncollegiate instns enrollment and program completions, by sex and instn level and control, fall 1990, annual rpt, 4844–19
Indian education funding of Fed Govt, with enrollment, program grants, and fellowships by State, 1980s-FY91, annual rpt, 14874–1
Minority group higher education enrollment, completion, and degrees, by race, sex, and type of instn, 1970s-90, 26306–3.122
Private elementary and secondary schools, students, and staff characteristics, by school type and affiliation, 1987/88, 4836–3.8
Reading performance and factors affecting proficiency, for elementary and secondary students, 1988 and 1990 natl assessments, 4898–33
Student aid and other sources of support, with student expenses and characteristics, by instn type and control, 1987 study, series, 4846–3
Student aid and other sources of support, with student expenses and characteristics, by instn type and control, 1990 triennial study, series, 4846–5
Student guaranteed loan Stafford program, borrowers and likelihood of default by selected characteristics, 1989-90, 26306–3.120
Teachers in higher education, and salaries, by faculty rank, sex, instn type and control, and State, 1990/91, annual rpt, 4844–8
Teachers of vocational education, by subject area and selected characteristics, for public high schools, 1987/88, 4836–3.9
Truman, Harry S, Scholarship Foundation finances, and awards by student characteristics, FY91, annual rpt, 14314–1
Vocational education enrollment, and academic and other credits earned, by subject and student characteristics, high school classes of 1982 and 1987, 4838–50
Vocational education enrollment, student and teacher characteristics, and outcomes, for secondary and postsecondary instns, 1970s-90, 4828–42

Energy Resources and Demand

Coal production, reserves, use, and prices by State, exports by country, and employment, 1900s-90, biennial rpt, 3164–79

Government and Defense

Aliens applications for temporary US residency, by occupation, age, sex, marital status, and country, 1988-91, 4808–41
DOT employment, by subagency, occupation, and selected personnel characteristics, FY91, annual rpt, 7304–18
Employment (civilian) of Fed Govt, by demographic and employment characteristics, as of Sept 1991, annual article, 9842–1.301
Employment (civilian) of Fed Govt, by demographic characteristics and agency, 1990, GAO rpt, 26119–383
Employment (civilian) of Fed Govt, by occupation, sex, and location, as of Sept 1991, biennial article, 9842–1.302
Employment of minorities, disabled, and veterans in Fed Govt, and years of service, by occupation, age, sex, and agency, as of Sept 1990, biennial rpt, 9844–27
Employment of minorities, women, and disabled in Fed Govt, by agency and occupation, FY90, annual rpt, 9244–10
Equal Opportunity Recruitment Program activity, and Fed Govt employment by sex, race, pay grade, and occupational group, FY91, annual rpt, 9844–33
IRS employment of minorities and women, compared to Fed Govt and total civilian labor force, FY91, annual rpt, 8304–3.3
Merit Systems Protection Board activities, staff, and finances, FY91, annual rpt, 9494–5
Military and civilian DOD employment of blacks, by sex, grade, and period of service, and lists of award recipients, officers, and service academy grads, 1770s-90, 3548–22
Military homosexual personnel discharges by pay grade, tenure, race, sex, and occupation, and investigations, by service branch, 1980s-90, GAO rpt, 26123–392
Military personnel, by selected characteristics, 1992 annual summary rpt, 3504–13
Military personnel deployment in Operation Desert Storm, by sex, race, rank, and service branch, 1990-91, GAO rpt, 26123–394
Military personnel occupational distribution, by race, sex, and service branch, FY90, GAO rpt, 26123–381
Military personnel reductions planned by service branch, and women and minorities affected by Army and Air Force plans, FY90-91, GAO rpt, 26123–373
Military recruits by race, and goals, by sex and service branch, quarterly press release, 3542–7
Military reserve forces personnel strengths and characteristics, by component, quarterly rpt, 3542–4
Military reserve forces personnel strengths, by selected characteristics and reserve component, FY91, annual rpt, 3544–1.5
Minority business Federal procurement set-aside contracts, by participant race and sex, industry, firm, and State, FY90, annual rpt, 9764–8
Navy personnel strengths, accessions, and attrition, detailed statistics, quarterly rpt, 3802–4
Public debt burden on future generations forecast under alternative tax, OASDI, and Medicare policies, 1992 working paper, 9377–9.137
Senior Executive Service members characteristics, entries, exits, and awards, FY79-91, annual rpt, 9844–36
Small Business Admin minority and women employment, and hiring goals, FY91, annual rpt, 9764–9
State and local govt employees wages by occupation, and benefits, periodic MSA survey rpt series, 6785–15
State and local govt employment of minorities and women, by occupation, function, pay level, and State, 1991, annual rpt, 9244–6
Taxes, spending, and govt efficiency, public opinion by respondent characteristics, 1992 survey, annual rpt, 10044–2
UNESCO fiscal mgmt, spending, staff, and funding sources, mid 1970s-92, GAO rpt, 26123–84
Voting age population, by sex, age, race, and State, forecast 1992 general elections, with votes cast from 1930, Current Population Rpt, 2546–3.170

Health and Vital Statistics

Acute and chronic health conditions, disability, absenteeism, and health services use, by selected characteristics, 1990, annual rpt, 4147–10.182
Acute and chronic health conditions, disability, absenteeism, and health services use, by selected characteristics, 1991, annual rpt, 4147–10.183
AIDS cases among children, hospital use and charges by instn and patient characteristics, and payment source, 1986-87, 4186–6.16
AIDS cases by risk group, race, sex, age, State, and MSA, and deaths, quarterly rpt, 4202–9
AIDS patients costs and service use under Medicaid, and service needs, for New Jersey waiver program, 1987-89, article, 4652–1.317
AIDS patients costs and service use under Medicaid, for California, 1984-86, article, 4652–1.301
AIDS public knowledge, attitudes, info sources, and testing, 1991 survey, 4146–8.218

AIDS virus-related Medicaid claims and payments, by sex, age, risk group, eligibility, and source of care, for Michigan, mid 1980s, article, 4042–3.348
Alcohol abuse and dependence prevalence, by age, race, and sex, and diagnostic criteria, 1988, article, 4482–1.306
Alcohol abuse direct and indirect costs, 1985, article, 4482–1.311
Alcohol-related diagnoses hospital discharges and length of stay, by age, sex, race, and region, 1979-85, 4488–10.5
Alcohol-related disorder hospital discharges and length of stay, by diagnosis, sex, age, and race, 1979-89, 4486–1.16
Births of twins, by birth order and weight, gestation period, mothers age, and race, 1950s-88, 4147–21.50
Cancer cases by body site and population characteristics, research results, semimonthly journal, 4472–1
Cancer deaths by age, and cases, by sex, 1988 and 1991, annual rpt, 4474–13
Child infectious disease cases, and related disability and health care, by disease, health insurance status, and other characteristics, 1988, 4147–10.181
Children (handicapped) with special needs, insurance coverage, and health care services use, by selected characteristics, 1988, 4146–8.216
Cirrhosis of liver deaths, by age, sex, race, and whether alcohol involved, 1988 and trends from 1910, annual rpt, 4486–1.13
Costa Rica and Guatemala life expectancy, and death rate by cause and age, by sex, 1984 and trends from 1900, working paper, 2326–18.64
DC metro area drug, alcohol, and tobacco use, user characteristics, and consequences, series, 4496–12
Deaths and rates by age, and life expectancy, by sex and race, preliminary 1990-91 and trends from 1950, US Vital Statistics annual rpt, 4144–7
Deaths and rates, by cause, age, sex, marital status, race, and State, 1989, US Vital Statistics advance annual rpt, 4146–5.124
Deaths and rates, by cause and selected social, demographic, and employment characteristics, 1979-85, natl longitudinal study, 4478–186
Deaths and rates, by detailed location, cause, and demographic characteristics, 1989, US Vital Statistics annual rpt, 4144–3
Deaths and rates, provisional data, monthly rpt, 4142–1.2
Diabetes patients physician office visits, by characteristics of patient, physician, and visit, 1989, 4146–8.212
Digestive diseases (chronic) prevalence, and procedures performed, by disease and patient characteristics, 1989, 4146–8.213
Disability (functional) prevalence and severity, by type of activity needing assistance, age, and sex, 1979-80, 4946–1.1
Disabled persons rehabilitation, Federal and State activities and funding, FY90, annual rpt, 4944–1
Disabled persons with chronic health conditions, prevalence and services use and needs, series, 4946–1
Disabled workers labor force status, type and cause of disability, and other characteristics, 1970s-89, chartbook, 4948–11
Diving (underwater) accidents, illnesses, and deaths, by circumstances, diver characteristics, and location, 1970-90, annual rpt, 2144–29
Drug abuse indicators for selected metro areas, research results, data collection, and policy issues, 1992 semiannual conf, 4492–5
Drug, alcohol, and cigarette use and attitudes of youth, by substance type and selected characteristics, 1975-91 surveys, annual rpt, 4494–4
Drug, alcohol, and cigarette use, by selected characteristics, 1991 survey, annual rpt series, 4494–5
Educational attainment relation to health condition and care, indicators by selected characteristics, 1989, 4147–10.180
Foreign countries infant mortality rate and life expectancy, by sex and country, 1991 biennial rpt, 2324–9
Foreign medical grads in US by age, sex, professional characteristics, State, and country, and US medical school foreign students, 1960s-80s, working paper, 6366–6.2
Health care professionals supply and education, by professional and other characteristics, and location, 1960s-92 and projected to 2020, biennial rpt, 4114–8
Health care services use and costs, methodology and findings of natl survey, series, 4186–8
Health condition and care indicators, 1950s-90 with health improvement and disease prevention goals for 1990, annual data compilation, 4144–11
Health risk behavior, prevalence of 7 habits, by age, State, and other characteristics, 1986-90, article, 4202–7.305
Heart disease death rates for US and 31 other countries by sex, 1970s-88, annual rpt, 4474–15
Hepatitis cases by infection source, age, sex, race, and State, and deaths, by strain, 1989 and trends from 1966, 4205–2
Homicides and rate, by weapon, circumstances, and victim characteristics, and years of potential life lost, 1980s, article, 4202–7.315
Hospital discharges and length of stay, by diagnosis, patient and instn characteristics, procedure performed, and payment source, 1990, annual rpt, 4147–13.112
Hospital discharges and length of stay by region and diagnosis, and procedures performed, by age and sex, 1990, annual rpt, 4146–8.211
Hospital discharges and length of stay under old and new survey designs, by diagnosis, patient and instn characteristics, and procedure, Jan-Mar 1988, 4147–13.110
Hospital discharges by detailed diagnostic and procedure category, primary diagnosis, and length of stay, by age, sex, and region, 1990, annual rpt, 4147–13.111
Hospital discharges, by payment source, diagnosis, patient characteristics, and region, and procedures performed, 1990, 4146–8.221
Indian and Alaska Native youth health condition and behavioral patterns, by sex and grade, 1988-90, 4088–3
Indian Health Service and tribal facilities and use, and Indians health and other characteristics, by IHS region, 1980s-90, annual chartbook, 4084–7
Indian Health Service facilities, funding, operations, and Indian health and other characteristics, 1950s-91, annual chartbook, 4084–1
Indian Health Service outpatient services provided, by reason for visit and age, FY90, annual rpt, 4084–2
Indian Health Service, tribal, and contract facilities hospitalization, by diagnosis, age, sex, and service area, FY91, annual rpt, 4084–5
Injuries from use of consumer products and related activities, by severity and victim age and sex, 1990, annual rpt, 9164–7
Insurance (health) coverage of persons, by insurance type and selected characteristics, 1985-90, 2546–20.23
Internist office visits, by characteristics of patient, physician, and visit, 1989, 4146–8.214
Kidney end-stage disease treatment facilities, Medicare enrollment and reimbursement, survival, and patient characteristics, 1984-90, annual rpt, 4654–16
Latin America young unmarried adults sexual activity, contraceptives use, and AIDS risk knowledge, by sex and country, 1984-91, article, 4202–7.323
Life expectancy, and death rates by cause, by sex and age, 1900s-89 and projected to 2080, actuarial rpt, 4706–1.107
Life expectancy, by sex, income, education, and labor force status, for whites, 1979-85, article, 4042–3.347
LSD trafficking, abuse, and enforcement, and DEA field div activities, 1980s-91, 6288–9
Mental health care facilities partial care services, and patient characteristics, by instn type and State, 1970s-88, 4506–3.51
Mental health care facilities, staff, patients, and finances, 1970s-91, biennial rpt, 4094–1
Mental health care of affective disorder patients, by patient and facility characteristics, 1986, 4506–3.49
Mental illness (serious) among adults, functional limitations, govt aid, drugs used, visits to professionals, and other characteristics, 1989, 4146–8.220
Nursing home use risk, and admissions, by sex, projected 1990-2040, article, 1702–1.309
OECD members life expectancy at birth and ages 60 and 80, by sex and country, 1960s-90, article, 4652–1.322
Otitis media patients physician office visits, by specialty and characteristics of patient and visit, 1975-90, 4146–8.217
Pediatrician office visits, by characteristics of patient and visit, 1989, 4146–8.210
Physicians, by specialty, age, sex, and location of training and practice, 1990, State rpt series, 4116–6
Physicians visits, by patient and practice characteristics, diagnosis, and services provided, 1989, annual rpt, 4147–13.109
Physicians visits, by patient and practice characteristics, diagnosis, and services provided, 1990, advance rpt, 4146–8.215
Pollutants health effects, concentrations in food and environment, sources, human intake, and regulation, series, 9186–8
Radiation protection and health physics enrollment and degrees granted by instn and State, and grad placement, by student characteristics, 1991, annual rpt, 3004–7

Retirees health and other characteristics related to Medicare use and charges 2 years later, 1984, article, 4652–1.319
Smoking control strategies effectiveness, with data on research funding, smoking prevalence, cancer deaths, and taxation, 1900s-91, 4476–7.1
Syphilis case rate, by sex, race, and region, 1990, article, 4202–7.303
Traffic accident deaths involving alcohol, by driver and victim blood alcohol levels and other characteristics, 1977-88, annual rpt, 4486–1.12
Traffic accident deaths involving alcohol, by driver and victim blood alcohol levels and other characteristics, 1977-89, annual rpt, 4486–1.14
Tuberculosis cases and rates, by patient characteristics, 1985 and 1990, article, 4202–7.302
Youth alcohol use and abuse, by sex, race, Hispanic origin, and grade, 1987, article, 4482–1.302
Youth health condition, risk factors, and preventive and treatment services use and availability, 1970s-80s, 26358–234.2; 26358–234.3
Youth risk behavior, by level of alcohol use and sex, 1987, article, 4482–1.308

Housing and Construction

Alteration and repair of owner-occupied homes, costs and structural, household, financial, and project characteristics, 1987, 2486–1.13
American Housing Survey: unit and households characteristics, unit and neighborhood quality, and journey to work by MSA location, for 11 MSAs, 1987 survey, supplement, 2485–8
American Housing Survey: unit and households detailed characteristics, and unit and neighborhood quality, 1989, biennial rpt supplement, 2485–13
Homeless persons transitional housing and support services program, outcome relation to client characteristics and services, FY87-90, GAO rpt, 26113–549
Homeownership rates, by household type, householder age and sex, and location, 1960s-91, annual rpt, 2484–1.3
Housing and households summary characteristics, 1989 and trends, chartbook, 2486–2.1
Mortgages FHA-insured, financial, property, and borrower characteristics, by metro area, 1991, annual rpt, 5144–24
Mortgages FHA-insured, financial, property, and borrower characteristics, by State, 1991, annual rpt, 5144–1; 5144–25
Mortgages FHA-insured, financial, property, and borrower characteristics, 1991, annual rpt, 5144–17; 5144–23
NYC housing supply, occupancy, condition, and household characteristics, by tenure and borough, 1991 triennial survey, 2488–3
Rental housing units, total, with HUD assistance by program, and eligible for aid, by unit, household, and neighborhood characteristics, and location, 1989, biennial rpt, 5184–11
Single person and nonfamily households social, economic and housing characteristics, by tenure, 1989, 2486–1.15

Industry and Commerce

Business owner and business characteristics, for minority- and women-owned firms, by industry, employment and sales size, and form of ownership, 1987 survey, 2328–59

Labor and Employment

Alien workers in US clothing and other industries, and impacts on local economies, with background data, 1990 working paper, 6366–6.6
Auto and auto parts trade, production, and labor conditions, for US and compared to Canada and Mexico, 1950s-90, 6366–3.28
Black and white women's occupational differences, and compared to men, selected years 1940-88, article, 6722–1.321
Dallas-Fort Worth metro area employment, earnings, hours, and CPI changes, late 1970s-91, annual rpt, 6964–2
Disabled persons work experience following OASDI benefit award, by selected characteristics, 1980s, article, 4742–1.312
Disabled persons work history before and after SSI application, by age, diagnosis, industry div, and sex, aggregate 1937-87, article, 4742–1.308
Displaced worker employment and training services, and layoff alternatives, indicators of effectiveness, 1980s, 15498–28
Displaced workers, layoffs and unemployment insurance claims by reason, industry, selected characteristics, and State, quarterly press release, 6742–23
Displaced workers losing job 1987-92, labor force status by employment and other characteristics, as of Jan 1992, biennial press release, 6726–1.48
Earnings distribution among and within selected groups, by demographic and employment characteristics, late 1960s-80s, article, 6722–1.328
Employment and Earnings, detailed data, monthly rpt, 6742–2
Employment and economic conditions, alternative BLS projections to 2005 and trends 1975-90, biennial rpt, 6744–19
Employment and Training Admin activities, funding, and participant characteristics, by program, FY86-88, annual rpt, 6404–17
Employment and unemployment, by age, sex, race, marital and family status, industry div, and State, Monthly Labor Review, 6722–1.2
Employment, earnings, and hours, by SIC 1- to 4-digit industry, monthly 1989-Feb 1992, annual rpt, 6744–4
Employment, earnings, and hours, monthly press release, 6742–5
Employment of minorities and women, by occupation, SIC 1- to 3-digit industry, State, and MSA, 1991, annual rpt, 9244–1
Employment situation, earnings, hours, and other BLS economic indicators, transcripts of BLS Commissioner's monthly testimony, periodic rpt, 23846–4
Employment, unemployment, and labor force characteristics, by region, State, and selected metro area, 1991, annual rpt, 6744–7
Family members labor force status and earnings, by family composition and race, quarterly press release, 6742–21
Foreign countries labor conditions, union coverage, and work accidents, annual country rpt series, 6366–4
Home-based workers and hours, by worker characteristics, occupational group and industry div, 1991, press release, 6726–1.52
Home-based workers by selected characteristics, and views, 1989, article, 1702–1.307
Houston metro area employment, earnings, hours, and CPI changes, 1970s-91, annual rpt, 6964–1
Job Training Partnership Act education and worker training program participants, by selected characteristics, 1986-88, 15496–1.15
Labor force status by age, sex, and race, accuracy of BLS forecasts made 1970s-80s, as of 1990, article, 6722–1.334
Labor force status by race and sex, employment by industry div, and unemployment duration and reason, selected years 1929-91, annual rpt, 204–1.2
Labor force status by sex and for teens, *Survey of Current Business*, monthly rpt, 2702–1.1
Labor force status, by worker characteristics and industry group, 1990-91, annual article, 6722–1.312
Labor force status, earnings, and other characteristics of women, with comparisons to men, fact sheet series, 6564–1
Labor force status, experience, and unemployment duration, by race and sex, 1990-91, annual press release, 6726–1.51
Labor force status transition rates, and relation to unemployment rate, by sex, 1980-89, working paper, 9377–9.129
Labor force, wages, hours, and payroll costs, by major industry group and demographic characteristics, *Survey of Current Business*, monthly rpt, 2702–1.7
Minority group labor force status, by race, detailed Hispanic origin, and sex, quarterly rpt, 6742–18
Occupational changes within firm, by worker characteristics, 1986-87, article, 6742–1.301
Occupational separations, replacement rates, and related job openings, estimation procedures with data by occupation, age, and sex, late 1980s and projected to 2005, 6748–84
OECD pension plan finances, participation, and benefits, for 9 countries, with data by firm and worker characteristics, 1990 conf, 6688–2
Older persons labor force status, income sources, and reasons for not working, with data by occupation, sex, and race, 1989-90 and projected to 2050, 21148–65
Pension plan survivor benefits and coverage of spouses, by income level, age, and sex, 1989, GAO rpt, 26121–450
Population and labor force characteristics, 1940s-90 and projected to 2000, 15496–1.16
Poverty relation to low earnings, by work experience during year, household relationship, sex, race, age, and education, 1960s-90, Current Population Rpt, 2546–6.74
Retirement age, and older persons labor force status, by sex, 1950s-90 and projected to 2005, article, 6722–1.332

Schedules of work, and workers with flexible hours and shift work by selected characteristics, 1991, press release, 6726–1.50
Tenure with current employer compared to 1983, and employment in same occupation in 1990, by sex, age, and race, 1991, press release, 6726–1.47
Training for job qualification and skill improvement, workers participating by training source, occupation, age, sex, and race, 1991, 6728–32
Unemployed persons finding work, by characteristics of worker and new job, aggregate 1986-89, 2546–20.20
Unemployed persons finding work by industry div, and earnings, by sector and sex, aggregate 1987-89, fact sheet, 2326–17.47
Unemployment rates, current data and annual trends, monthly rpt, 23842–1.2
Union coverage of workers and earnings, by age, sex, race, occupational group, and industry div, monthly rpt, annual article, 6782–1.2
Union coverage of workers and earnings, by age, sex, race, occupational group, and industry div, 1990-91, annual press release, 6726–1.44
Wages and productivity relation to worker age, by sex and occupation, model description and results, 1991 working paper, 9377–9.128
Wages by occupation, and benefits for office and plant workers, periodic MSA survey rpt series, 6785–12; 6785–16; 6785–17
Wages, hours, and employment by occupation, and benefits, for selected locations, industry survey rpt series, 6787–6
Wages of full- and part-time workers, by selected characteristics, quarterly press release, 6742–20
Younger workers jobs held and weeks worked since age 18, by age, sex, and race, 1978-90, 6726–2.3
Youth labor force status, by sex, race, and industry div, summer 1988-92, annual press release, 6744–14

Law Enforcement

Aircraft hijackings, on-board explosions, and other crimes, US and foreign incidents, 1986-90, annual rpt, 7504–31
Assaults and deaths of law enforcement officers, by circumstances, agency, victim and offender characteristics, and location, 1991, annual rpt, 6224–3
Crime, criminal justice admin and enforcement, and public opinion, data compilation, 1992 annual rpt, 6064–6
Crimes, arrests, and rates, by offense, offender characteristics, population size, and jurisdiction, 1991, annual rpt, 6224–2.1; 6224–2.2
Criminal case processing in Federal district courts, and dispositions, by offense, district, and offender characteristics, 1989, annual data compilation, 6064–29
Drug abuse and trafficking offenders losing Federal benefits under new sentencing guidelines, by selected characteristics, 1990-91, GAO rpt, 26119–398
Drug test results at arrest, by drug type, offense, and sex, for selected urban areas, quarterly rpt, 6062–3
Drunk driving arrests, sentencing, and prisoner drinking patterns and other characteristics, 1989, 6066–19.69
Employment of State and local law enforcement personnel and officers, by sex, population size, census div, and jurisdiction, as of Oct 1991, annual rpt, 6224–2.3
Fraud and forgery arrests, case dispositions, and sentencing, by age, sex, race, and offense type, 1983-88, 6066–19.64
Jail population by sex, race, and for 25 jurisdictions, and instn conditions, 1990-91, annual rpt, 6066–25.48
Jail population of women, by criminal background and sociodemographic characteristics, with comparisons to men, 1989, 6066–19.66
Juvenile arrests, by sex, race, disposition, and offense, 1990, 6066–27.8
Juvenile courts drug and alcohol offenses cases, by disposition and offender age, sex, and race, 1985-88, 6066–27.7
Juvenile facilities population, by resident characteristics and facility type, late 1970s-89, 6068–250
Juvenile facilities population, by resident characteristics and facility type, 1977-89, annual rpt, 6064–35
Police agencies employment, spending, and operations, FY90, 6066–25.44
Police employment, spending, and operations, for State, city, county, and special district agencies, 1990, annual rpt, 6064–39
Prison and community-based facilities, population, employment, spending, and other characteristics, by State and for Fed Govt, 1990, quinquennial rpt, 6068–218
Prison and parole admissions and releases, sentence length, and time served, by offense and offender characteristics, 1988, annual rpt, 6064–33
Prisoners and staff in Federal instns, by selected characteristics, region, and instn, FY89, annual rpt, 6244–1
Prisoners, characteristics, and movements, by State, 1990, annual rpt, 6064–26
Prisoners in Federal and State instns by selected characteristics, releases, staff, and instn size, with data by region and State, late 1970s-91, 6068–248
Prisoners in Federal and State instns by sex, admissions, and instn capacity and overcrowding, by State, 1980s-91, annual rpt, 6066–25.47
Probation population, by offender characteristics, sentence conditions, whether rearrested, and offense, 1986-89, 6066–19.65
Schools crime victimization, drug availability, and preventive measures, with student views, 1989 survey, 6066–3.46
Sentences for Federal crimes, guidelines use and results by offense and district, and Sentencing Commission activities, 1991, annual rpt, 17664–1
Sentences for Federal crimes, guidelines use and results by offense, 1984-1990, 6066–19.68
Sentences under Federal mandatory minimum provisions, by defendant characteristics, and views on justice system impacts, FY90, 17668–2
Sheriffs' agencies employment, spending, and operations, FY90, 6066–25.45
Victimization rates, by victim and offender characteristics, circumstances, and offense, 1990 survey, annual rpt, 6066–3.47
Victimizations in cities, suburbs, and rural areas, by offense, circumstances, and victim and offender characteristics, 1987-89, 6066–3.48

Natural Resources, Environment, and Pollution

Forest Service employment and human resource program participation, FY91, annual rpt, 1204–1.4

Population

Alaska rural areas population characteristics, and energy resources dev effects, series, 5736–5
Asian and Pacific Islands Americans social and economic characteristics, for West and total US, 1990-91, Current Population Report, 2546–1.462
Black Americans social and economic characteristics, for South and total US, 1991 and trends from 1950, annual Current Population Rpt, 2546–1.463
Census of Population and Housing, 1990: detailed geographic coverage, State CD-ROM series, 2551–9
Census of Population and Housing, 1990: population and housing characteristics, detailed geographic coverage, State CD-ROM series, 2551–10
Census of Population and Housing, 1990: summary characteristics, by county, subdiv, and place, State rpt series, 2551–7
Census of Population and Housing, 1990: summary characteristics, households, and land area, by county, subdiv, and place, State rpt series, 2551–1
Census of Population, 1990: black population undercount, estimates by age and sex, 21628–97
Census of Population, 1990: data adjustment in intercensal data for census undercounts, recommendations with alternative undercount estimates, 2628–36
Census of Population, 1990: population characteristics and living arrangements, by county, place, and urban-rural location, State rpt series, 2531–1
Census of Population, 1990: population characteristics and living arrangements, for Native American, urban, and metro areas, series, 2531–2
Consumer Income, socioeconomic characteristics of persons, families, and households, detailed cross-tabulations, Current Population Rpt series, 2546–6
Developing countries aged population and selected characteristics, 1980s and projected to 2020, country rpt series, 2326–19
Developing countries population size, life expectancy, and fertility, trends and forecasts, country rpt series, 2326–24
Family members supporting others outside household, by relationship, recipient living arrangements, and provider characteristics, 1988, Current Population Rpt, 2546–20.21
Foreign and US aged population and characteristics, by country, 1991 and projected to 2020, wallchart, 2328–82
Households and family characteristics, by location, 1991, annual Current Population Rpt, 2546–1.457

Immigrants from Central America in DC, by selected employment and other characteristics, and reasons for migration, 1985-88, working paper, 6366–6.3
Immigration to US, alien workers, visitors, deportations, and naturalizations, by country, FY91 and trends from 1820, annual rpt, 6264–2
Income (household) and poverty status under alternative income definitions, by recipient characteristics, 1979-91, annual Current Population Rpt, 2546–6.78
Income (household) and wealth distribution by selected characteristics, with foreign comparisons, 1992 compilation of papers, Current Population Rpt, 2546–6.79
Income (household) of aged and younger adults, by source, household composition, and age group, 1984 and 1989, article, 4742–1.304
Income (household) of aged and younger adults, by source, household composition, race, and age group, 1984-89, 4746–26.20
Income (personal), by sex and race, 1970-89, annual rpt, 204–1.1
Income (personal) relative to median, by race and selected other characteristics, mid 1960s-89, Current Population Rpt, 2546–6.73
Income and consumer spending of households, for selected population groups, quarterly journal, 1702–1
Israel economic conditions, US investment and export opportunities, and trade practices, 1992 rpt, 2008–32
Living arrangements, family relationships, and marital status, by selected characteristics, 1991, annual Current Population Rpt, 2546–1.461
Migration, immigration, and mover characteristics compared to nonmovers, 1987-90, annual Current Population Rpt, 2546–1.456
Migration since 1990, mover characteristics by same or different area, and compared to nonmovers, 1991, annual Current Population Rpt, 2546–1.464
OASDI beneficiary data collection system design compared to earlier surveys, with summary results, 1992 article, 4742–1.313
Older persons in poverty, by health, nutrition, assistance, and other characteristics, 1990, GAO rpt, 26131–100
Older persons income and sources, by OASDI beneficiary and poverty status, and other characteristics, 1990, biennial chartbook, 4744–25
Older persons income and sources, by whether OASDI beneficiary, poverty status, and other characteristics, 1990, biennial rpt, 4744–26
Older persons population size and characteristics, series, 2326–25
Older persons socioeconomic characteristics, 1900s-90 and projected to 2050, biennial chartbook, 12904–1
Older population, and health, economic, and other characteristics, with foreign comparisons, 1980s-91 with trends and projections, Current Population Rpt, 2546–2.165
Pacific territories population and housing detailed characteristics, by location, 1990 Census of Population and Housing, series, 2551–8
Population economic well-being indicators, by selected characteristics and household income and income-to-poverty ratio, 1984, 2546–20.22
Population size and components of change, alternative projections 1990-2080 and trends from 1900, annual actuarial rpt, 4706–1.106
Poverty status of population and families, by detailed characteristics, 1991, annual Current Population Rpt, 2546–6.77
Refugee arrivals and resettlement in US, by age, sex, sponsoring agency, State, and country, monthly rpt, 4592–1
Soviet Union and US economic and sociodemographic indicators, selected years 1970-90, handbook, 2328–80
Statistical Abstract of US, 1992 annual data compilation, 2324–1
Vietnam population size, components of change, and selected characteristics, 1979, 1989, and projected to 2050, 2326–18.65

Public Welfare and Social Security
AFDC beneficiaries demographic and financial characteristics, by State, FY90, annual rpt, 4584–7
Benefits, beneficiaries, and spells of participation, by aid program and recipient characteristics, 1987-88, Current Population Rpt, 2546–20.25
Disability Insurance beneficiaries deaths and survival, by selected characteristics, for persons entitled 1972 and 1985, article, 4742–1.321
Food stamp recipient household size, composition, income, and income and deductions allowed, summer 1989, annual rpt, 1364–8
Medicare admin and research, and HCFA affirmative action and accreditation programs, FY87, annual rpt, 4654–5
Medicare and Medicaid beneficiaries and program operations, 1992, annual fact book, 4654–18
Medicare beneficiaries knowledge of and experience with physician billing and payment under Medicare, by selected characteristics, 1988-89, 17266–2.1
Medicare payment of physicians, reforms impacts on services, and monitoring methods, 1992 annual rpt, 4004–34
OASDHI coverage of employment and earnings, and social security contributions, by age, sex, race, State, and county, 1988, annual rpt, 4744–29
OASDHI, Medicaid, SSI, and related programs benefits, beneficiary characteristics, and trust funds, selected years 1937-90, annual rpt, 4744–3
OASDI and SSI benefit overpayments, and overpaid beneficiaries characteristics, late 1970s-90, GAO rpt, 26121–484
OASDI benefits and beneficiaries, by category, age, and sex, quarterly rpt, 4742–1.1
OASI benefits, earnings, and tax revenues under alternative eligibility criteria, 1990, technical paper, 4746–26.15
Older persons earnings impacts of 1983 OASI earnings test repeal, 1970-85, technical paper, 4746–26.13
Poverty status of families, by detailed characteristics, 1980 and 1988, GAO rpt, 26131–102
Supplemental Security Income recipients, by race, sex, living arrangements, age, eligibility, and State, quarterly rpt, 4742–1.2
Supplemental Security Income work incentive programs, participant characteristics, by program, 1982-91, article, 4742–1.305

Recreation and Leisure
Fishing (ocean sport) activities, and catch by species, by angler characteristics and State, annual coastal area rpt series, 2166–17

Science and Technology
Education in science and engineering, grad programs enrollment by field, source of funds, and characteristics of student and instn, 1990, annual rpt, 9627–7
Employment and education of minorities, women, and disabled in science and engineering, by field, mid 1970s-91, biennial rpt, 9624–20
Labor force, Federal and university research funding, and educational data, for science and engineering, series, 9626–6
NASA Apollo era science and engineering staff background and characteristics, 1958-70, 9508–39
NASA staff characteristics and personnel actions, FY91, annual rpt, 9504–1
Nuclear engineering enrollment and degrees granted by instn and State, and grad placement, by student characteristics, 1991, annual rpt, 3004–5
Public knowledge, interest, and expectations for science and technology, 1990 survey, biennial rpt, 9624–10.7
Science and Engineering Indicators, employment, education, R&D funding, and industry impacts, with foreign comparisons, 1960s-91, biennial rpt, 9624–10

Veterans Affairs
AIDS cases at VA health care centers by sex, race, risk factor, and facility, and AIDS prevention and treatment issues, quarterly rpt, 8702–1
Disability and death compensation cases of VA, by entitlement type, period of service, and sex, as of Mar 1992, annual rpt, 8604–13
Disability and death compensation cases of VA, by entitlement type, period of service, sex, age, and State, FY90, annual rpt, 8604–7
Hospital discharges by diagnosis, compensation and pension status, and other characteristics, for VA, FY91, annual rpt, 8604–3.2
VA employment characteristics and activities, FY91, annual rpt, 8604–3.4

Index by Titles

Index by Titles

Titles are listed alphabetically in natural word order, as they appear in the Abstracts Section. Titles beginning with numbers (e.g. "1990 Census . . . ") appear at the end of the Index. Where appropriate, alternate word-orders of titles have also been provided.

In addition to publication titles, individual report titles within a publication series are indexed, as are the titles of all periodical articles receiving individual abstracts.

AAFES Annual Report, 1990, 3504–21
AAFES Facts for Vendors, 3504–10
AAFES' Suppliers Handbook, 1991-92, 3504–10
Abortion Surveillance—U.S., 1989, 4202–7.324
Abrasive Materials: Minerals Yearbook, Volume 1, 1990, 5604–20.3
Academic Science and Engineering: Graduate Enrollment and Support, Fall 1990, 9627–7
Academic Science and Engineering: R&D Expenditures, FY90, 9627–13
Academy Preparatory Schools Need a Clearer Mission and Better Oversight. DOD Service Academies, 26123–380
Access Board—1991, Annual Report, U.S. Architectural and Transportation Barriers Compliance Board, 17614–1
Access to Health Insurance: State Efforts To Assist Small Businesses, 26121–462
Accident/Incident Bulletin, 1991: No. 160, 7604–1
Accidents, Fatalities and Rates: Air Carriers and General Aviation, 9614–9
Accidents, Fatalities and Rates Released for U.S. Aviation, 1991, 9614–9
Accidents of Motor Carriers of Property, 7554–9
Accidents Reported by Motor Carriers of Property, 1989, 7554–9
Accountability for Forest Service Funds Needs Improvement. Wilderness Management, 26113–550
Accounting for Prediction Variance in Event Studies, 9366–6.287
Acculturation and Changes in Drinking Patterns Among Mexican-American Women: Implications for Prevention, 4482–1.309
Accumulation of p53 Tumor Suppressor Gene Protein: An Independent Marker of Prognosis in Breast Cancers, 4472–1.317
Accuracy of USDA's Meat Forecasts and Estimates. Short-Term Forecasting, 26131–93
Achievements, 9844–20
Achieving Cost Control in the Hospital Outpatient Department, 4652–1.314
ACIR: The Year in Review, 33rd Annual Report, 10044–3
Acoustic Effects of Oil Production Activities on Bowhead and White Whales Visible During Spring Migration Near Point Barrow, Alaska—1990 Phase: Sound Propagation and Whale Responses to Playbacks of Continuous Drilling Noise from an Ice Platform, as Studied in Pack Ice Conditions, 5738–27
ACP Monthly Progress Report, By State and Area for Period Ending (Date), 1802–15
Acreage, 1621–23
Acreage Reduction Program Enrollment, 1004–20
ACTION Annual Report, FY91, 9024–2
Actions Needed To Improve Participant Support Services. Job Training Partnership Act, 26106–8.15
Active Compensation, Pension and Retirement Cases by Period of Service, 8602–5
Active Corporation Income Tax Returns, July 1989-June 1990. Source Book, Statistics of Income, 8304–21
Active Foreign Agricultural Research Grants, 1992, 1954–3
Activities of EPA Assistance Programs and Interagency-Intergovernmental Agreements, 9182–8
Activities of the Oil Implementation Task Force and Contracts for Field Projects and Supporting Research on Enhanced Oil Recovery, 3002–14
Actuarial Analysis of 1991 Operations for Life Insurance Programs Administered by the Department of Veterans Affairs, 8604–1
Actuarial Notes, 4706–2
Actuarial Status of the Social Security and Medicare Programs, 4742–1.314
Actuarial Studies, 4706–1
Acute Care Treatment, 4208–35
Adequacy of PPS Payment for Medicare Beneficiaries with Hemophilia, 17206–1.13
Adjuvant Radiotherapy and Risk of Contralateral Breast Cancer, 4472–1.333
Administering Social Security by Fiscal Crises: Disabled, Retirees, and Taxpayers Paying the Price, 21148–63
Administration of the Marine Mammal Protection Act of 1972, Annual Report, Jan. 1-Dec. 31, 1990, 5504–12
Administration of the Radiation Control for Health and Safety Act of 1968, Public Law 90-602, 1991 Annual Report, 4064–13
Administration, Use, and Equal Opportunity. Apprenticeship Training, 26121–446
Administrative Costs in Selected Industrialized Countries, 4652–1.325
Administrative Law Judges: Allegations of Interference by the Department of the Interior, 26119–428
Administrative Office of the U.S. Courts, Annual Report of the Director, 1991, 18204–8
Admission, Release, and Movement of Inmates for the Fiscal Year: Bureau of Prisons, 6242–1.3
Admission, Release, and Movement of Inmates for the Month: Bureau of Prisons, 6242–1.2
Adolescent Health, 26358–234
Adolescent Health. Volume II: Background and the Effectiveness of Selected Prevention and Treatment Services, 26358–234.2
Adolescent Health. Volume III: Crosscutting Issues in the Delivery of Health and Related Services, 26358–234.3
Adult Education, FY87. Adult Learning and Literacy Fact Sheet, 4806–4.1
Adult Education Profile for 1990-91, 4826–10.5
Adult Education Program Facts, FY90. Adult Learning and Literacy Fact Sheet, 4806–4.4
Adult Learning and Literacy: Education for Homeless Adults, 1989-90 Report, 4804–39
Adult Learning and Literacy Fact Sheets, 4806–4
Adulterated Imported Foods Are Reaching U.S. Grocery Shelves. Pesticides, 26113–598
Advance Data from Vital and Health Statistics of the Centers for Disease Control/National Center for Health Statistics, 4146–8
Advance Monthly Retail Sales, Current Business Reports, 2413–2
Advance Payment Option Is Not Widely Known or Understood by the Public. Earned Income Tax Credit, 26119–378
Advance Report of Final Mortality Statistics, 1989, 4146–5.124
Advance Report of New Data from the 1989 Birth Certificate, 4146–5.125
Advanced Energy Projects, FY92 Research Summaries, 3004–18.9
Advanced Materials: Minerals Yearbook, Volume 1, 1990, 5604–20.64
Adverse Environmental Conditions: Synthesis of Safety Research, 7558–98.1
Advertising, Industry and Trade Summary, 9885–12.3
Adviser, BLM: New Mexico, Oklahoma, Texas and Kansas, 1991, 5724–15
Advisory Committee on Federal Pay, Annual Report, 10104–1
Advisory Council on Social Security: Issue Analysis Reports, 10176–3
Advisory Council on Social Security: Public Input Reports, 10176–2
Advisory Council on Social Security: Technical and Expert Panel Reports, 10176–1
Aerial Surveys of Endangered Whales in the Alaskan Chukchi and Western Beaufort Seas, 1990, 5738–36
Aeronautics and Space Report of the President, FY91 Activities, 9504–9
Aerospace Industry (Orders, Sales, and Backlog), 1991, Current Industrial Report, 2506–12.22
AFDC Recipient Characteristics Study, 4694–1
AFDC Recipient Characteristics Study, 1990, 4584–7
Affirmative Employment Statistics: Federal Civilian Workforce Statistics, 9844–27
African Development Foundation Funded Projects, 1991, 9034–1
Age and Cohort Effects in PTSD, 8704–6
Agencies' Estimated Costs for Counseling and Processing Discrimination Complaints. Federal Workforce, 26119–388

Agencies' Procurements of Private Health Club Services. Federal Workforce, 26119–393
Agenda for Civil Justice Reform in America, 048–3
AgExporter, 1922–2
Aggregate Reserves of Depository Institutions and Monetary Base, 9365–1
Aggregate Summaries of Annual Surveys of Securities Credit Extension, as of June 28, 1991, 9365–5.1
Aggregates, Directory of Principal Producers in the U.S. in 1991: Mineral Industry Surveys, Annual Advance Summary Supplement, 5614–5.16
Aging America, Trends and Projections, 1991 Edition, 12904–1
Aging Trends, 2326–19
Agrichemical Reduction Policy: Its Effect on Income and Income Distribution, 1502–3.302
Agricultural and Horticultural Machinery, Industry and Trade Summary, 9885–9.3
Agricultural Bank Credit Outlook, 1504–9.1
Agricultural Chemical Usage, 1616–1
Agricultural Conservation Program (ACP) Monthly Progress Report, By State and Area for Period Ending (Date), 1802–15
Agricultural Conservation Program, FY91 Statistical Summary, 1804–7
Agricultural Conservation Program: 55-Year Statistical Summary, 1936 Through 1990, 1808–1
Agricultural Credit Conditions Survey: Federal Reserve Bank of Minneapolis, 9383–11
Agricultural Finance Databook, 9365–3.10
Agricultural Income and Finance Situation and Outlook Report, 1541–1
Agricultural Irrigation and Water Use, 1588–122
Agricultural Land Values and Markets Situation and Outlook Report. Agricultural Resources, 1561–16.302
Agricultural Letter, Federal Reserve Bank of Chicago, 9375–10
Agricultural Maps in the National Archives of the U.S., circa 1860-1930, 9516–1.7
Agricultural Outlook, 1502–4
Agricultural Outlook Conference Proceedings, 1004–16
Agricultural Prices, Monthly Report, 1629–1
Agricultural Prices, 1991 Summary, 1629–5
Agricultural Resources Situation and Outlook Report, 1561–16
Agricultural Stabilization and Conservation Service Commodity Fact Sheets, 1806–4
Agricultural Stabilization and Conservation Service Payments to Producers by State and Program During 1991, 1804–12
Agricultural Statistics Board Catalog, 1992, 1614–1
Agricultural Statistics, 1991, 1004–1
Agricultural Trade Highlights, 1922–12
Agricultural Trade Offices' Role in Promoting U.S. Exports Is Unclear. International Trade, 26123–370
Agricultural Trade Policy and Trade for Central and East Europe, 1928–11
Agriculture and Trade Reports, Situation and Outlook Series, 1524–4
Agriculture in a North American Free Trade Agreement: Analysis of Liberalizing Trade Between the U.S. and Mexico, 1528–330
Agriculture in 1991: The Decline Continues, 9391–16.308
Agriculture Outlook 1992: Panel Discussion on U.S. Sugar Program, 1504–9.1
Agriculture Outlook '92. New Opportunities for Agriculture: Annual Agricultural Outlook Conference Proceedings, 1504–9
Agriculture Outlook '92. New Opportunities for Agriculture: Chartbook, 1504–8
Agriculture Payments: Number of Individuals Receiving 1990 Deficiency Payments and the Amounts, 26113–574
AHCPR Health Technology Assessment Reports, 1991, 4186–10
AID, Congressional Presentation, FY93. Main Volume, 9904–4.1
AID, Congressional Presentation, FY93. Part II, 9904–4.2
AID, Congressional Presentation, FY93. Statistical Annex, 9904–4.3
AID, Congressional Presentation, FY93. Summary Tables, 9904–4.4
AID, Congressional Presentation, FY93. U.S. Trade and Development Program, 9904–4.5
AID Economic Policy Reform Program in Cameroon, 9916–1.76
AID Economic Policy Reform Program in Uganda, 9916–1.77
AID Impact Evaluation Reports, 9916–1
Aid to Nicaragua: U.S. Assistance Supports Economic and Social Development, 26123–398
AID-Financed University Contracts, Grants and Cooperative Agreements Active During the Period Oct. 1, 1987 Through Sept. 30, 1988, 9914–6
AID-Financed University Contracts, Grants and Cooperative Agreements Active During the Period Oct. 1, 1988 Through Sept. 30, 1989, 9914–6
AID-Financed University Contracts, Grants and Cooperative Agreements Active During the Period Oct. 1, 1989 Through Sept. 30, 1990, 9914–6
AID-Financed University Contracts, Grants and Cooperative Agreements Active During the Period Oct. 1, 1990 Through Sept. 30, 1991, 9914–6
AIDS Gram, 8702–1
AIDS in Correctional Facilities, 1990 Update, 6061–22
AIDS Knowledge and Attitudes for January-March 1991. Provisional Data from the National Health Interview Survey, 4146–8.218
AIDS Patient Registry, 8702–1
AIDS Weekly Surveillance Report, 4202–9
AIDS-Related Issues, 26356–6
Air Carrier Aircraft Utilization and Propulsion Reliability Report, 7502–13
Air Carrier Financial Statistics Quarterly, 7302–7
Air Carrier Industry Scheduled Service Traffic Statistics Quarterly, 7302–8
Air Carrier Passenger Enplanements, All Cargo Landings and Apportionments, 1990, 7504–48
Air Carrier Traffic Statistics Monthly, 7302–6
Air Force Comptroller, 3602–1
Air Pollution: Global Pollution from Jet Aircraft Could Increase in the Future, 26113–562
Air Quality in the Detroit-Windsor/Port Huron-Sarnia Region, 14648–28
Air Traffic Control Specialists in the Airway Science Curriculum Demonstration Project 1984-90: Third Summative Evaluation, 7506–10.96
Air Travel Consumer Report: Flight Delays, Mishandled Baggage, Oversales, and Consumer Complaints, 7302–11
Airbus Industrie: An Economic and Trade Perspective, 21708–132
Aircraft Accident Reports: Brief Format, U.S. Civil and Foreign Aviation, 9612–1
Aircraft, Spacecraft, and Related Equipment, Industry and Trade Summary, 9885–9.1
Airport Activity Statistics of Certificated Route Air Carriers, 1991, 7504–35
Airport and Airway Trust Fund, 8102–9.5
Airport Grant Allocations, 7502–14
Airport Improvement Program, 10th Annual Report of Accomplishments, FY91, 7504–38
Alaska Cooperative Snow Survey Data of Federal-State-Private Cooperative Snow Surveys, Water Year 1991, 1264–14.5
Alaska Marine Mammal Tissue Archival Project: Sample Inventory and Results of Analyses of Selected Samples for Organic Compounds and Trace Elements, 2218–87
Alaskan Region Federal Aviation Administration Ten Year Plan, 7504–36
Alaska's Mineral Resources, 1991 Annual Report, 5664–11
Alcohol and Coronary Artery Disease, 4482–1.301
Alcohol Consumption and Sexual Risk-Taking in Adolescents, 4482–1.304
Alcohol Epidemiologic Data System Surveillance Reports, 4486–1
Alcohol Health and Research World, 4482–1
Alcohol Involvement in Fatal Traffic Crashes, 1990, 7764–16
Alcohol, Tobacco, and Firearms: Few Firearms Licensees Had Complaints About Inspections, 26119–429
Alcohol Use and Abuse: Some Findings from the National Adolescent Student Health Survey, 4482–1.302
Alcohol Use and Physically Risky Behavior Among Adolescents, 4482–1.308
Alfalfa Products: Conditions of Competition Between the U.S. and Canadian Industries. Investigation No. 332-310 Under Section 332(g) of the Tariff Act of 1930 as Amended, 9886–4.180
Allais Theory Suggests a Solution and an Explanation for the Equity Premium Puzzle, 9381–10.133
Allegations of Interference by the Department of the Interior. Administrative Law Judges, 26119–428
Allegheny County Case: Metropolitan Organization, 10046–9.2
Allied Burden Sharing Efforts. Persian Gulf, 26123–371
Allocation of Resources and Staffing Levels of the Internal Revenue Service, U.S. Tax Court, and Bureau of Alcohol, Tobacco and Firearms, 21788–217
Allocative Inefficiency in Education, 9379–12.80
All-Payer Ratesetting: Down but Not Out, 4652–1.311
Almond Production, 1621–18.4
Alphabetical Index of Industries and Occupations. 1990 Census of Population and Housing, 2628–1
Alternative Diesel Fuels from Oilseeds, 1504–9.1
Alternative Estimates of Economic Well-Being by Age Using Data on Wealth and Income, 4746–26.11

Alternative Geographic Adjustments in Medicare Payment to Health Maintenance Organizations, 4652–1.321
Alternative Measures of Change in Real Output and Prices, 2702–1.314
Alternative Measures of the Monetary Base: What Are the Differences and Are They Important?, 9391–1.302
Alternative Samples for Welfare Duration in SIPP: Does Attrition Matter?, 2626–10.148
Alternatives to Hospital Care Under Employee Benefit Plans, 6722–1.302
Aluminum, Bauxite, and Alumina: Minerals Yearbook, Volume 1, 1990, 5604–20.4
Aluminum Industry: Mineral Industry Surveys, 5612–1.1
Aluminum Ingot and Mill Products, Current Industrial Report, 2506–10.9
Aluminum: Mineral Industry Surveys, 5612–1.1
American Battle Monuments Commission Annual Report for FY87, 9064–1
American Education at a Glance, 4828–35
American Espionage, 1945-1989, 25428–2
American Historical Association, Annual Report, 1990, 29574–2
American Housing Brief. Housing Profiles, 2485–11
American Housing Survey Data Chart, 1989, 2485–12
American Housing Survey for Selected Metropolitan Areas: 1985, Supplement, 2485–8
American Housing Survey for Selected Metropolitan Areas: 1986, Supplement, 2485–8
American Housing Survey for Selected Metropolitan Areas: 1987, Supplement, 2485–8
American Housing Survey for the Boston Metropolitan Area in 1989, 2485–6.10
American Housing Survey for the Dallas Metropolitan Area in 1989, 2485–6.5
American Housing Survey for the Detroit Metropolitan Area in 1989, 2485–6.2
American Housing Survey for the Fort Worth-Arlington Metropolitan Area in 1989, 2485–6.6
American Housing Survey for the Los Angeles-Long Beach Metropolitan Area in 1989, 2485–6.3
American Housing Survey for the Minneapolis-St. Paul Metropolitan Area in 1989, 2485–6.7
American Housing Survey for the Philadelphia Metropolitan Area in 1989, 2485–6.4
American Housing Survey for the Phoenix Metropolitan Area in 1989, 2485–6.9
American Housing Survey for the San Francisco-Oakland Metropolitan Area in 1989, 2485–6.8
American Housing Survey for the U.S. in 1989, Supplement, 2485–13
American Housing Survey for the Washington Metropolitan Area in 1989, 2485–6.1
American Housing Survey: Housing Data Between the Censuses, 2328–89
American Housing Survey: Metropolitan Areas, 2485–6
American Indian and Alaska Native Areas. 1990 Census of Population: General Population Characteristics, 2531–2.1
American Indian Economic Development, 9383–19.304
American Red Cross Annual Report, 1990-91, 29254–1
American Samoa: Inadequate Management and Oversight Contribute to Financial Problems, 26123–385
American Woodcock Harvest and Breeding Population Status, 1992, 5504–11
America's Agriculture, 2346–1
America's Agriculture: Highlights of U.S. Agricultural Activity, 2346–1.5
America's Agriculture: Part-Time Farmers, 2346–1.6
America's Wars, 8604–2
AMS Food Purchases: Weekly Summary, 1302–3
Amtrak: Information on Amtrak's Operating Expenses, 26113–573
Analyses of Natural Gases, 1986-90, 5608–132
Analyses of Natural Gases, 1991, 5604–2
Analysis and Summary of the 1990 National Scenic Byways Study Inventory, 7558–112
Analysis of Acid Precipitation Samples Collected by State Agencies: January-December 1989, 9194–20
Analysis of Department Store Reference Pricing in Metropolitan Washington, 9408–57
Analysis of Fiscal Policy in Neoclassical Models, 9379–12.93
Analysis of Laws Governing Rights of Mentally Disabled Persons To Reside in Federally Subsidized Housing for the Elderly, 26113–590
Analysis of Major Rental Car Policies. Military Personnel, 26123–391
Analysis of Options To Amend the Public Utility Holding Company Act of 1935. National Energy Strategy, Technical Annex 1, 3006–13.1
Analysis of Options To Increase Exports of U.S. Energy Technology. National Energy Strategy, Technical Annex 5, 3006–13.5
Analysis of Salinity Structure and Stability for Texas Estuaries, 2176–7.26
Analysis of SBA's Preferred Lenders Program. Small Business, 26113–581
Analysis of the Impact of Two Fiscal Policies on the Behavior of a Dynamic Asset Market, 9379–12.97
Analysis of the Maritime Industry and the Effects of 1984 Shipping Act, 9408–54
Analysis of the President's Budgetary Proposals for FY93, 26304–2
Analysis of Transporting Highway Route-Controlled Quantities: An Overview of 1985-90, 3008–129
Analysis Report on Fire Fighter Fatalities, 9434–8
Analytical Report Series. Manufacturing, 2506–16
Andean Trade Initiatives, 1925–34.317
Animal Feeds Compendium, 1568–308
Animal Welfare Enforcement, FY90, Report of the Secretary of Agriculture to the President of the Senate and the Speaker of the House of Representatives, 1394–10
Annual Capacity Report, 3364–5
Annual Energy Outlook 1992 with Projections to 2010, 3164–75
Annual Energy Review, 1991, 3164–74
Annual Environmental Monitoring Report, January-December 1991, Stanford Linear Accelerator Center, Stanford University, 3324–2.11
Annual Environmental Reports on DOE Facilities, 3324–2
Annual Financial Report, FY91, Federal Aviation Administration, 7504–10
Annual Historical Review of FNS Programs, 1364–9
Annual Input-Output Accounts of the U.S. Economy, 1987, 2702–1.316
Annual Intercensal Estimates of the Resident Population of States, 2324–10
Annual Outlook for Oil and Gas, 3164–89
Annual Outlook for U.S. Coal, 3164–68
Annual Outlook for U.S. Electric Power, 3164–81
Annual Prospects for World Coal Trade, 3164–77
Annual RCA Progress Report: National Program for Soil and Water Conservation, 1264–12
Annual Report and Summaries of FY92 Activities: Division of Energy Biosciences, 3004–18.7
Annual Report: Budget Review, 1991-92, 9364–10
Annual Report, Environmental Protection Agency, 9184–20
Annual Report of Energy Purchased by REA Borrowers, 1244–5
Annual Report of Lands Under Control of the U.S. Fish and Wildlife Service, As of Sept. 30, 1992, 5504–8
Annual Report of the Architect of the Capitol for the Period Oct. 1, 1988-Sept. 30, 1989, 25944–1
Annual Report of the Attorney General of the U.S. on the Private Counsel Debt Collection Project for FY91, 6004–20
Annual Report of the Attorney General of the U.S., 1989, 6004–1
Annual Report of the Attorney General of the U.S., 1990, 6004–1
Annual Report of the Attorney General of the U.S., 1991, 6004–1
Annual Report of the Board of Trustees of the Federal Hospital Insurance Trust Fund, 1992, 4654–11
Annual Report of the Board of Trustees of the Federal Old-Age and Survivors Insurance and Disability Insurance Trust Funds, 1992, 4704–4
Annual Report of the Board of Trustees of the Federal Supplementary Medical Insurance Trust Fund, 1992, 4654–12
Annual Report of the Community Relations Service, FY91, 6004–9
Annual Report of the Council of Economic Advisers, 204–1
Annual Report of the Department of Justice Asset Forfeiture Program, FY91, 6004–21
Annual Report of the Director of the Administrative Office of the U.S. Courts, 1991, 18204–8
Annual Report of the Director of the U.S. Mint, FY91, 8204–1
Annual Report of the Federal Trade Commission, FY90, 9404–1
Annual Report of the Librarian of Congress for the Fiscal Year Ending Sept. 30, 1991, 26404–1
Annual Report of the National Advisory Committee on Semiconductors, 15034–1
Annual Report of the Office of Justice Programs, 6064–18
Annual Report of the Postmaster General, FY91, 9864–1

Annual Report of the Register of Copyrights, 26404–2
Annual Report of the Rehabilitation Services Administration on Federal Activities Related to the Administration of the Rehabilitation Act of 1973, as Amended, 4944–1
Annual Report of the Research Grants Program, 1991, Office of Exploratory Research, 9184–18
Annual Report of the Secretary of the Army on Civil Works Activities, 3754–1
Annual Report of the Secretary of the Army on Civil Works Activities, FY88: Volume II, 3754–1.1
Annual Report of the Secretary of the Army on Civil Works Activities, FY89: Volume II, 3754–1.2
Annual Report of the Secretary of the Army on Civil Works Activities, FY90: Volume II, 3754–1.3
Annual Report of the Secretary of the Interior, 1990, 5304–5
Annual Report of the Secretary of Veterans Affairs, FY91, 8604–3
Annual Report of the U.S. Parole Commission, Oct. 1, 1990-Sept. 30, 1991, 6004–3
Annual Report on Hazardous Materials Transportation, 1990, 7304–4
Annual Report on Low-Level Radioactive Waste Management Progress, 3354–14
Annual Report on Low-Level Radioactive Waste Management Progress, 1990, 3004–36
Annual Report on Military Justice, 3504–3
Annual Report on Sharing of Specialized Medical Resources, Pursuant to the Provisions of 38 U.S.C. Section 8153, Secretary of Veterans Affairs, FY91, 8704–5
Annual Report on Strategic Special Nuclear Material Inventory Differences, 3344–2
Annual Report on the Employment of Minorities, Women and People with Disabilities in the Federal Government, FY90, 9244–10
Annual Report on the Impact of the Caribbean Basin Economic Recovery Act on U.S. Industries and Consumers, Seventh Report, 1991, 9884–20
Annual Report on Tobacco Statistics, 1991, 1319–1
Annual Report on Tropical Pacific Subsurface Thermal Data Management, 2154–12
Annual Report Submitted to the Committees on Armed Services of the U.S. Senate and House of Representatives, and to the Secretary of Defense, Secretary of Transportation, and Secretaries of the Army, Navy, and Air Force, Oct. 1, 1990-Sept. 30, 1991, 3504–3
Annual Report to Congress: Indian Civil Service Retirement Act, P.L. 96-135, FY90, 4084–6
Annual Report to Congress of the Marine Mammal Commission, 14734–1
Annual Report to Congress: Office of Civilian Radioactive Waste Management, 3364–1
Annual Report to Congress on Retail Fees and Services of Depository Institutions, 9364–12
Annual Report to Congress on the Community Development Block Grant Program, 1992, 5124–8
Annual Report to Congress on the Effectiveness of the Civil Aviation Security Program, Jan. 1-Dec. 31, 1990, 7504–49
Annual Report to Congress on the Federal Equal Opportunity Recruitment Program, 9844–33
Annual Report to Congress 1991: Energy Information Administration, 3164–29
Annual Report to Congress, 1991: Federal Grain Inspection Service, 1294–1
Annual Report to Congress, 1992: Federal Grain Inspection Service, 1294–1
Annual Report to the Congress, FY91, 26354–3
Annual Report to the Congress of the U.S. from the Director of the Selective Service System, FY91, 9744–1
Annual Report to the Congress on Community Planning and Development Housing Rehabilitation Programs, FY91, 5124–7
Annual Report to the President and the Congress, FY91, on Federal Activities Related to the Rehabilitation Act of 1973 as Amended, 4944–1
Annual Report to the President and the Congress on the State Energy Conservation Program, 1990, 3304–1
Annual Report to the President, FY91, Information Security Oversight Office, 9454–21
Annual Report, 1990, Federal Deposit Insurance Corporation, 9294–1
Annual Report, 1990-91, U.S. National Commission on Libraries and Information Science, 15634–1
Annual Report, 1991, Federal Deposit Insurance Corporation, 9294–1
Annual Review of Aircraft Accident Data, U.S. Air Carrier Operations, 1988, 9614–2
Annual Review of the Chief, National Guard Bureau, FY91, 3504–22
Annual Revision of the U.S. National Income and Product Accounts: Annually, 1989-91; Quarterly, 1989:I-1992:I, 2702–1.324
Annual Sales, Year-End Inventories, Purchases, Gross Margin, and Accounts Receivable, by Kind of Retail Store. 1990 Retail Trade. Current Business Reports, 2413–5
Annual Site Environmental Report for Calendar Year 1991, Western Area Power Administration, 3324–2.14
Annual Site Environmental Report of the Lawrence Berkeley Laboratory, 1991, 3324–2.13
Annual Southwestern Region Pest Conditions Report, 1989, 1206–11.2
Annual Southwestern Region Pest Conditions Report, 1990, 1206–11.2
Annual Southwestern Region Pest Conditions Report, 1991, 1206–11.2
Annual Statistical Digest, 1980-89, 9364–5
Annual Statistical Digest, 1990, 9364–5
Annual Status Report on the Uranium Mill Tailings Remedial Action Program, 3354–9
Annual Summary of Births, Marriages, Divorces, and Deaths: U.S., 1991. Monthly Vital Statistics Report, 4144–7
Annual Survey of Communication Services, 1990. Current Business Reports, 2413–15
Annual Survey of Manufactures, 1990, 2506–14
Annual Test Report, Department of Defense Dependents Schools, 1991-92, 3504–16
Annual Tropical Cyclone Report, 1991, 3804–8
Anti-Drug Abuse Formula Grants: Justice Variable Passthrough Data, 1990, 6066–23.7
Antifriction Bearings, 1991, Current Industrial Report, 2506–12.28
Antimony: Mineral Industry Surveys, 5612–2.1
Antimony: Minerals Yearbook, Volume 1, 1990, 5604–20.5
Antitrust: Information on Criminal Cases, 26119–375
AOML Annual Report, FY91, 2144–19
Apache Helicopter Was Considered Effective in Combat, but Reliability Problems Persist. Operation Desert Storm, 26123–378
Appalachian Highway Program, As Reported by States, 9082–1
Appalachian Highway Program Cumulative Corridor Mileage Summary, 9082–1.3
Appalachian Highway Program Cumulative Mileage Summary, 9082–1.2
Appalachian Highway Program Funding Requirements, 9082–1.1
Appalachian Regional Commission, 1991 Annual Report, 9084–1
Apparel, Current Industrial Report, 2506–6.12
Apparent Consumption of Industrial Explosives and Blasting Agents in the U.S., 1991. Mineral Industry Surveys, 5614–22
Apparent Per Capita Alcohol Consumption: National, State and Regional Trends, 1977-88, 4486–1.11
Apparent Per Capita Alcohol Consumption: National, State and Regional Trends, 1977-89, 4486–1.15
Appearances of Soviet Leaders, 9114–1
Apportionments to States from the Land and Water Conservation Fund, FY93, 5544–15
Apprenticeship Training: Administration, Use, and Equal Opportunity, 26121–446
Approval of Awards to Institutions Participating in the College Work-Study, Supplemental Educational Opportunity Grant, and Perkins Loan Programs: Notification to Members of Congress, 4804–17
Aquaculture Situation and Outlook Report, 1561–15
Architect of the Capitol, Annual Report for the Period Oct. 1, 1988-Sept. 30, 1989, 25944–1
Arctic Fish Habitat Use Investigations: Nearshore Studies in the Alaskan Beaufort Sea, Summer 1990, 5738–37
Arctic Science, Engineering and Education, Awards: FY90, 9626–7.5
Are Deep Recessions Followed by Strong Recoveries?, 9379–12.82
Are Pensions Worth the Cost?, 9373–27.2
Are Small Rural Banks Credit-Constrained? A Look at the Seasonal Borrowing Privilege in the Eighth Federal Reserve District, 9391–1.311
Are There Cost Savings from Bank Mergers?, 9371–1.303
Area Trends in Employment and Unemployment, 6402–1
Area Wage Surveys, 6785–3
Area Wage Surveys: Bull. 3060 Series, 6785–12
Area-Level Predictors of Use of Prenatal Care in Diverse Populations, 4042–3.366

Argonne National Laboratory's Use of Government Supply Sources, 3006–5.29
Arizona Cooperative Snow Survey Data of Federal-State-Private Cooperative Snow Surveys, Water Year 1991, 1264–14.6
Arms Control and Disarmament Agreements, START Treaty Between the U.S.A. and the USSR on the Reduction and Limitation of Strategic Offensive Arms, 9828–26
Army and Air Force Exchange Service Annual Report, 1990, 3504–21
Arrests of Youth, 1990, 6066–27.8
Arsenic in 1991: Mineral Industry Surveys, Annual Review, 5614–5.15
Arson in America: A Profile of 1989 NFIRS, 9438–14
Arts Funding: Public Funding Profiles of the NEA States and Cities, 26119–371
As Threat Declines, NATO Reduces Expenditures. NATO Infrastructure Program, 26123–388
Asbestos in Schools: Evaluation of the Asbestos Hazard Emergency Response Act (AHERA), A Summary Report, 9238–71
Asbestos: Minerals Yearbook, Volume 1, 1991, 5604–15.7
Asbestos Trust Fund, 8102–9.13
ASCS Commodity Fact Sheets, 1806–4
Asia Pacific Energy Series, Country Reports, 3406–6
Asian and Pacific Islander Population in the U.S.: March 1990-91, 2546–1.462
Aspen Ecosystem Properties in the Upper Great Lakes, 1208–418
Aspherical Ophthalmoscopy Lenses from Japan. Determination of the Commission in Investigation No. 731-TA-518 (Final) Under the Tariff Act of 1930, Together with the Information Obtained in the Investigation, 9886–14.343
Assessing Criminal Justice Needs, 6066–20.22
Assessing Economic Impacts to Coastal Recreation and Tourism from Oil and Gas Development in the Oregon and Washington Outer Continental Shelf, 5738–40.2
Assessing Forest Service Recreation Trends with Shift-share Analysis, 1208–423
Assessing Rates of Return to Public and Private Agricultural Research, 1502–3.303
Assessing Removals for North Central Forest Inventories, 1208–419
Assessment and Management of Atlantic and Gulf Menhaden Stocks, 2162–1.303
Assessment of Accuracy of Adjusted Versus Unadjusted 1990 Census Base for Use in Intercensal Estimates, Report of the Committee on Adjustment of Postcensal Estimates, Bureau of the Census, Dept of Commerce, 2628–36
Assessment of Mexico's Environmental Controls for New Companies. U.S.-Mexico Trade, 26119–416
Assessment of Non-Economic Impacts to Coastal Recreation and Tourism Resultant from Oil and Gas Development: A Review of Selected Literature and Example Methodology, 5738–40.1
Assessment of the Economic Status of the Aged, 4746–26.24
Assessment of the National Science Foundation's 1985-87 College Science Instrumentation Program, 9628–87
Assessment of the 50/92 Provision and the U.S. Rice Program, 1561–8.303
Assessment of USDA's Cotton Supply and Demand Estimates, 1561–1.302
Assessment of Using Oil Shale for Power Production in the Hashemite Kingdom of Jordan, 3008–127
Asset Management: Governmentwide Asset Disposition Activities, 26119–369
Asset Pooling and Marketing Practices Add Millions to Contract Costs. Resolution Trust Corporation, 26119–424
Asset Securitization and Secondary Markets, 21248–173
Asset-Backed Commercial Paper Programs, 9362–1.302
Assets and Liabilities of Insured Domestically Chartered and Foreign Related Banking Institutions, 9365–1
Assignment and the Participating Physician Program: An Analysis of Beneficiary Awareness, Understanding, and Experience, 17266–2.1
Assisting Dislocated Workers: Alternatives to Layoffs, and the Role of the Employment Service Under the Economic Dislocation and Worker Adjustment Assistance Act (EDWAA), 15498–28
Assistive Technology Devices and Home Accessibility Features: Prevalence, Payment, Need, and Trends, 4146–8.219
Association Between Brain Tumors and Menopausal Status, 4472–1.340
Association of Overexpression of Tumor Suppressor Protein p53 with Rapid Cell Proliferation and Poor Prognosis in Node-Negative Breast Cancer Patients, 4472–1.329
Assumptions for the Annual Energy Outlook, 1992, 3164–90
Astronomical Almanac for the Year 1993, 3804–7
Atlantic and Gulf Menhaden Purse Seine Fisheries: Origins, Harvesting Technologies, Biostatistical Monitoring, Recent Trends in Fisheries Statistics, and Forecasting, 2162–1.303
Atlas/Data Abstract for the U.S. and Selected Areas, FY91, 3544–29
Atmospheric Sciences Program: Summaries of Research in FY91, 3004–18.4
Attaining Preeminence in Semiconductors: Third Annual Report to the President and the Congress. National Advisory Committee on Semiconductors, 15034–1.4
Attitudes of Patients Toward Smoking by Health Professionals, 4042–3.334
Attorney General of the U.S. Annual Report, 6004–1
Attorney General of the U.S. Annual Report on the Private Counsel Debt Collection Project for FY91, 6004–20
Auctioning Radio Spectrum Licenses, 26306–6.169
Audiovisual Records in the National Archives of the U.S. Relating to World War II, 9516–1.3
Audiovisual Records Relating to Naval History, 9516–1.6
Auto Industry Jobs in the 1980's: A Decade of Transition, 6722–1.313
Auto Parts Advisory Committee, 1991 Annual Report: U.S. Automotive Parts Trade with Japan, 2004–10
Automation Is Restraining but Not Reducing Costs. Postal Service, 26119–395
Automotive Fuel Economy Program, Fifteenth Annual Report to the Congress, 7764–9
Automotive Fuel Economy Program, Sixteenth Annual Report to the Congress, 7764–9
Automotive Technology Development Program 13th Annual Report to Congress, 3304–17
Autonomy of Trade Elasticities: Choice and Consequences, 9366–7.276
Availability and Distribution of Psychiatric Beds, U.S. and Each State, 1988, 4506–3.48
Availability of Federally Owned Minerals for Exploration and Development in Western States, 5606–7
Availability of Intercity Bus Service Continues To Decline. Surface Transportation, 26113–583
Availability of Primary Copper in Market-Economy Countries. A Minerals Availability Appraisal, 5606–4.30
Average Annual Pay, 6784–17
Average Annual Pay by State and Industry, 1991, 6784–17.1
Average Annual Pay Levels in Metropolitan Areas, 1991, 6784–17.2
Average Effective Corporate Income Tax Rates for Petroleum Operations 1977-89, 3168–124
Average Regional End-Use Energy Price Projections to the Year 2030, 3166–6.60
Average Wages for 1985-90 for Indexing Under the Social Security Act, 4706–2.133
Aviation Opportunities for the Decade of the 90's. 17th Annual FAA Aviation Forecast Conference Proceedings, 7504–28
Aviation Research: Information on Funding, Staffing, and Timing of FAA's Research Projects, 26113–565
Aviation Safety Statistics, 7502–15
Aviation System Capacity Plan, 1991-92, 7504–43
Aviation System Capital Investment Plan, 7504–12
Awareness and Use of Blood Cholesterol Tests in 40—74-Year-Olds by Educational Level, 4042–3.335

Back to the Future: Monetary Policy and the Twin Deficits, 9373–27.9
Background Information: National Priorities List, Proposed Rule, 9216–5.5
Background Material and Data on Programs Within the Jurisdiction of the Committee on Ways and Means. Overview of Entitlement Programs. 1992 Green Book, 21784–11
Background Material on Family Income and Benefit Changes, 21788–212
Background Notes on the Countries of the World, 7006–2
Background Paper Series: Physician Payment Review Commission, 17266–2
Background Papers on Drug Abuse Financing and Services Research, 4496–11.1
Back-to-School Forecast, 1992, 4804–19
Bacterial Infections and Skin Cleaning Prior to Injection Among Intravenous Drug Users, 4042–3.361
Balance Sheet Outlook for the Farm Sector in 1992, 1504–9.1
Balance Sheets for the U.S. Economy, 1949-90, 9365–4.1

Balance Sheets for the U.S. Economy, 1960-91, 9365–4.1
Balances of Budget Authority: Budget of the U.S. Government, FY93, 104–8
Banca Nazionale Del Lavoro (BNL), 21248–165
Bank and Thrift Criminal Fraud: Information on Justice's Investigations and Prosecutions, 26119–426
Bank Branching, 9387–8.281
Bank Capital Ratios, Asset Growth, and the Stock Market, 9385–1.311
Bank Credit and Economic Activity: Evidence from the Texas Banking Decline, 9379–14.16
Bank Dividend Patterns, 9292–4.302
Bank Failure Resolutions: Implications for Banking Industry Structure, Conduct and Performance, 9292–4.304
Bank Holding Company Performance, 1991, 9381–14
Bank Mergers, 21248–176
Bank Performance and Regional Economic Growth: Evidence of a Regional Credit Channel, 9377–9.135
Bank Reform?, 1541–1.310
Bank Structure and Competition, Proceedings of the 27th Annual Conference, May 1-3, 1991, Federal Reserve Bank of Chicago. Rebuilding Banking, 9375–7
Bankers Decry New Regulations, But Recognize Need to Protect Deposit Insurance Fund, 9383–19.305
Banking in Computable General Equilibrium Economies, 9383–20.23
Banking in Computable General Equilibrium Economies: Technical Appendices I and II, 9383–20.25
Banking Markets and the Use of Financial Services by Households, 9362–1.303
Banking Review, FDIC, 9292–4
Banking Studies, Federal Reserve Bank of Kansas City, 9381–14
Bankruptcy Administration: Justification Lacking for Continuing Two Parallel Programs, 26119–421
Bargaining Activity in 1993, 6726–1.54
Bargaining Calendar, 1992, 6784–9
Barriers to the Use of Horizontal Drilling Technology. National Energy Strategy, Technical Annex 4, 3006–13.4
Barry M. Goldwater Scholarship and Excellence in Education Foundation, Annual Report for 1991, 10404–1
Base Closures: Long and Costly Process of Reducing the Local National Work Force in Germany, 26123–383
Base Structure Report for FY93, 3504–11
Basic Student Charges at Postsecondary Institutions: Academic Year 1990-91. Tuition and Required Fees and Room and Board Charges at 4-year, 2-Year, and Public Less-than-2-Year Institutions, 4844–10
Basic Student Charges at Postsecondary Institutions: Academic Year 1991-92. Tuition and Required Fees and Room and Board Charges at 4-year, 2-Year, and Public Less-than-2-Year Institutions, 4844–10
Basin Outlook Reports and Federal-State-Private Cooperative Snow Surveys, 1266–2
Bauxite, Alumina, and Aluminum: Minerals Yearbook, Volume 1, 5604–20.4
Bauxite and Alumina: Mineral Industry Surveys, 5612–2.2
BCCI Affair, Part 1, 25388–60
Bean Market News, 1311–17
Bean Market Summary, 1991, 1311–18
BEARFACTS, 2704–7
Beef Cow-Calf Industry, 1964-87; Location and Size, 1568–251
Beer: Monthly Statistical Release, 8486–1.1
Behavior of Uninsured Deposits: Market Discipline or "Too Big To Fail?", 9385–8.126
Behavioral Risk Factor Surveillance, 1986-90, 4202–7.305
Beige Book: Summary of Commentary on Current Economic Conditions by Federal Reserve District, 9362–8
Benchmark Input-Output Accounts of the U.S., 1982, 2708–17
Benchmarking Could Aid OPM's Efforts To Improve Customer Service. OPM Revolving Fund, 26119–373
Benefits and Beneficiaries Under Public Employee Retirement Systems, FY89, 4742–1.318
Benthic Macrofauna of the New York Bight, 1979-89, 2168–128
Better Federal Oversight of Territories' Oil Overcharge Funds Needed. Energy Management, 26113–564
Bettis Atomic Power Laboratory Effluent and Environmental Monitoring Report, 1990, 3324–2.6
BIA and Indian Tribes Are Taking Action To Address Dam Safety Concerns. Indian Programs, 26113–558
Bibliography on Health Indexes, 4122–1
Bibliography on Smoking and Health, 1990, 4204–19
Bibliography on Smoking and Health, 1991, 4204–19
Bid Opening Report: Federal-Aid Highway Construction Contracts, 1991, 7552–12
Bid Opening Report: Federal-Aid Highway Construction Contracts, First Six Months 1992, 7552–12
Bidding for Workers, 6886–6.95
Biennial Report of the U.S. Institute of Peace, 1991, 29594–1
Biennial Report to the Congress on Coastal Zone Management, FY90-91, 2174–8
Big Game Fishing in Northern Gulf of Mexico During 1989, 2164–23
Big Game Fishing in Northern Gulf of Mexico During 1990, 2164–23
Billions of Dollars in Farm Loans Are at Risk. Farmers Home Administration, 26113–569
Binomial Approximation in Financial Models: Computational Simplicity and Convergence, 9377–9.132
Biodegradable Polymers, 1504–9.1
Biological Analysis of Two Management Options for the Atlantic Menhaden Fishery, 2162–1.303
Biological Warfare: Role of Salk Institute in Army's Research Program, 26123–374
Biologics Surveillance, 4205–22
Biology, Oceanography, and Fisheries of the North Pacific Transition Zone and Subarctic Frontal Zone, 2168–131
Biology of Mental Disorders. New Developments in Neuroscience, 26356–9.4
Biomass Energy Development in Yunnan Province, China, Preliminary Evaluation, 3308–103
Birds of a Great Basin Sagebrush Habitat in East-Central Nevada, 1208–402
Bismuth in 1991: Mineral Industry Surveys, Annual Review, 5614–5.10
Bismuth: Mineral Industry Surveys, 5612–2.3
Bismuth—Uses, Supply, and Technology, 5608–175
Black Americans in Defense of Our Nation, 3548–22
Black Lung Benefits Act: Annual Report on Administration of the Act During 1991, 6504–3
Black Lung Disability Trust Fund, 8102–9.10
Black Population in the U.S.: March 1991, 2546–1.463
Bleak Outlook for the U.S. Economy, 9383–6.301
BLM Adviser: New Mexico, Oklahoma, Texas and Kansas, 1991, 5724–15
BLM Facts and Figures for Utah, 1991, 5724–11.4
BLM Facts: Oregon and Washington, 1991, 5724–11.2
BLM in Nevada, 1990 Progress Report, 5724–11.1
BLM in Nevada, 1991 Progress Report, 5724–11.3
BLM in Wyoming, 1991, 5724–11.5
BLM's Hot Desert Grazing Program Merits Reconsideration. Rangeland Management, 26113–552
Block Grant Funds Should Be Distributed More Equitably. Maternal and Child Health, 26121–454
Block Grants: Increases in Set-Asides and Cost Ceilings Since 1982, 26121–466
Blood Supply Safety, 21368–134
BLS Employment Projections for 1990: An Evaluation, 6722–1.335
BLS Establishment Estimates Revised to March 1991 Benchmarks, 6742–2.306
BLS Handbook of Methods, 6888–1
BLS Regional Offices: Contribution to Wage Programs, 6722–1.333
BLS Reports on Labor Market Situation of Vietnam-Era Veterans, 6726–1.49
BLS Reports on Survey of Occupational Injuries and Illnesses in 1991, 6844–3
BLS Working Papers, 6886–6
Blue Thursday? Homicide and Suicide Among Urban 15—24-Year-Old Black Male Americans, 4042–3.323
Board and Care Homes: Elderly at Risk from Mishandled Medications, 26121–447
Board for International Broadcasting, 1992 Annual Report on Radio Free Europe/Radio Liberty, Inc., 10314–1
Board of Governors of the Federal Reserve System Staff Studies, 9366–1
Board of Governors of the Federal Reserve System 78th Annual Report, 1991, 9364–1
Boating Safety Recalls, 7402–5
Boating Statistics, 1991, 7404–1
Bomb Summary, 1991, 6224–5
Bone Marrow Transplants: National Program Has Greatly Increased Pool of Potential Donors, 26121–487
Bonneville Power Administration: Generation and Sales Statistics, 3222–1
Bonneville Power Administration, Quarterly Report, 3222–2
Bonneville Power Administration, 1990 Annual Environmental Report, 3224–6
Bonneville Power Administration, 1991 Annual Report, 3224–1
Bonneville Power Administration, 1991 Site Environmental Report, 3224–6

Boron: Minerals Yearbook, Volume 1, 1991, 5604–15.10
Bottom and Near-Bottom Sediment Dynamics in Norton Sound, Alaska, 2176–1.40
Brazil Textile Market, 2046–15.1
Breast and Cervical Cancer Surveillance, U.S., 1973-87, 4202–7.312
Breast Cancer Beliefs of Women Participating in a Television-Promoted Mammography Screening Project, 4042–3.370
Breast Cancer Risk: Effects of Estrogen Replacement Therapy and Body Mass, 4472–1.350
Breast Cancer Risks in Relatives of Male Breast Cancer Patients, 4472–1.330
Breast Cancer, 1971-91: Prevention, Treatment, and Research, 26131–92
Bridges over the Navigable Waters of the U.S., 7406–5
Bridges over the Navigable Waters of the U.S., Great Lakes, 7406–5.3
Brief History of the Rural Electric and Telephone Programs and Report of the Administrator, FY91, 1244–3
Broadcast Station Totals, 9282–4
Broadwoven Fabrics (Gray), Current Industrial Report, 2506–5.11
Broiler Hatchery, 1625–11
Brokered Deposits and Thrift Institutions, 9379–14.17
Brokered Deposits: Determinants and Implications for Thrift Institutions, 9379–15.301
Brookhaven National Laboratory, Site Environmental Report for 1990, 3324–2.9
Budget Constrained Frontier Measures of Fiscal Equality and Efficiency in Schooling, 9379–12.87
Budget Constraints and Time-Series Evidence on Consumption: Comment, 9371–10.90
Budget Estimates, FY93, 9634–9
Budget in Brief, FY93, Department of Transportation, 7304–10
Budget Issues: 1991 Budget Estimates, What Went Wrong, 26104–23
Budget of the U.S. Government, FY93, 104–2
Budget of the U.S. Government, FY93 Supplement, 108–46
Budget Policy: Prompt Action Necessary To Avert Long-Term Damage to the Economy, 26109–5
Budgeting for Administrative Costs Under Credit Reform, 26306–6.166
Building a New Rural Socialist Order: Implications for Production, Income, and Trade, 1524–4.2
Building Along America's Coasts: 20 Years of Building Permits, 1970-89, 2176–8.3
Building Effective Community Coalitions Against Drugs, 236–3.8
Building Energy Efficiency, 26358–259
Building National Strategies for Rural Economic Development, 1504–9.1
Bulletin of Hardwood Market Statistics, 1202–4
Burden of Caring for Alzheimer's Disease Patients, 4164–2
Bureau for Latin America and Caribbean. Staff Working Papers, 9916–13
Bureau of Indian Affairs' Management of the $2 Billion Indian Trust Fund, 21408–131
Bureau of Indian Affairs Natural Resource Information System Inventory and Production Report, 1988, 5704–12
Bureau of Indian Affairs Natural Resource Information System Inventory and Production Report, 1989, 5704–12
Bureau of Justice Statistics Bulletin, 6066–25
Bureau of Justice Statistics Special Reports, 6066–19
Bureau of Labor Statistics Press Releases, 6726–1
Bureau of Land Management State Offices, Facts and Statistics, 5724–11
Bureau of Mines Metal Industry Indicators, 5602–5
Bureau of Prisons Reports, 6242–1
Burley Tobacco, Summary of 1992 Support Program and Related Information: ASCS Commodity Fact Sheet, 1806–4.6
Burley, 1991 Crop. Tobacco Market Review, 1319–5.1
Business America, 2042–24
Business Cycle Durations and Postwar Stabilization of the U.S. Economy, 9375–13.83
Business Cycle Fluctuations in U.S. Regions and Industries: The Roles of National, Region-Specific, and Industry-Specific Shocks, 9381–10.134
Business, Households, and Governments: Health Care Costs, 1990, 4652–1.309
Business Outlook Survey, Federal Reserve Bank of Philadelphia, 9387–11
Business Review, Federal Reserve Bank of Philadelphia, 9387–1
Business Statistics: 1963-91, 27th Edition, 2704–1
By-catch from the Artisanal Shrimp Trawl Fishery, Gulf of Paria, Trinidad, 2162–1.302
Byproduct Output from the Domestic Primary Copper, Lead, and Zinc Industries, 5608–170

Cadmium in 1991: Mineral Industry Surveys, Annual Review, 5614–5.9
Cadmium: Mineral Industry Surveys, 5612–2.5
Calcium and Calcium Compounds: Minerals Yearbook, Volume 1, 1991, 5604–15.12
Calculating State-Level Estimates of USDA's Farm Income Accounts, 1541–1.313
Calculators and Computers: NAEPfacts, 4896–9.1
Calendar Year Projections: Number of Returns To Be Filed for 1991-98, 8304–9
Calendar Year Projections of Information and Withholding Documents for the U.S. and Service Centers: 1992-99, 8304–22
Calendar Year Return Projections for Districts: 1991-98, 8304–24
California OCS Phase II Monitoring Program: Final Report, 5734–11
California's Forest Products Industry: 1988, 1208–108
Can Retail Depositories Fund Mortgages Profitably?, 9366–6.289
Can the Markov Switching Model Forecast Exchange Rates?, 9381–10.125
Can the Rural Economy Be Competitive? Lessons from the Data, 1504–9.1
Can the States Solve the Health Care Crisis?, 9375–1.308
Can Thymidine Kinase Levels in Breast Tumors Predict Disease Recurrence?, 4472–1.355
Can Unconventional Preferences Explain Risk Premia in the Foreign Exchange Markets?, 9381–10.131
Canada's Broiler Supply Management Program: A Shield from U.S. Price Volatility?, 1502–3.302
Canadian Imports of Horticultural Products, 1925–34.335
Cancer Incidence Among Danish Thorotrast-Exposed Patients, 4472–1.338
Cancer Incidence and Mortality in Workers Exposed to Fluoride, 4472–1.359
Cancer Incidence and Survival Among American Indians Registered for Indian Health Service Care in Montana, 1982-87, 4472–1.347
Cancer Prevention Counseling on Telephone Helplines, 4042–3.325
Cancer Screening Behaviors Among U.S. Women: Breast Cancer, 1987-89, and Cervical Cancer, 1988-89, 4202–7.313
Cancer Screening Intervention Among Black Women in Inner-City Atlanta—Design of a Study, 4042–3.338
Candidate Automated Test Battery for Neuropsychological Screening of Airmen: Design and Preliminary Validation, 7506–10.107
Canned Deciduous Fruit: Semiannual Update, 1925–34.343
Canned Pineapple and Pineapple Juice Situation in Selected World Markets, 1925–34.327
Canola and the Common Market, A Producer's Perspective, 1504–9.1
Capacity and Service on the Interstate Natural Gas Pipeline System, 1990: Regional Profiles and Analyses, 3168–125
Capacity of Refrigerated Warehouses, 1614–2
Capital Adequacy and the Growth of U.S. Banks, 9375–13.88
Capital Costs, Industrial Mix, and the Composition of Business Investment, 9373–1.304
Capital Crunch in New England, 9373–1.309
Capital Crunch: Neither a Borrower Nor a Lender Be, 9373–27.4
Capital Expenditures by Majority-Owned Foreign Affiliates of U.S. Companies, Latest Plans for 1992, 2702–1.335
Capital Expenditures by Majority-Owned Foreign Affiliates of U.S. Companies, Plans for 1992, 2702–1.312
Capital Flight from Debtor Nations When Labor Is Mobile, 9385–8.122
Capital Forbearance and Thrifts: An Ex Post Examination of Regulatory Gambling, 9377–9.140
Capital Investment in Semiconductors: The Lifeblood of the U.S. Semiconductor Industry, 15036–1.2
Capitalization and Portfolio Risk of Insurance Companies, 9373–1.314, 9373–27.3
Capsule Review of DOE Research and Development Laboratories and Field Facilities, 3004–4
Carbon Dioxide and Climate: Summaries of Research, 3004–18.10
Carbon Steel Butt-Weld Pipe Fittings from China and Thailand. Determinations of the Commission in Investigations Nos. 731-TA-520 and 521 (Final) Under the Tariff Act of 1930, Together with the Information Obtained in the Investigations, 9886–14.352

Carcinogens, 1991, Sixth Annual Report, 4044–15
Cardiac Rehabilitation Programs: Heart Transplant, Percutaneous Transluminal Coronary Angioplasty, and Heart Valve Surgery Patients. Health Technology Assessment Report, 1991, 4186–10.8
Caribbean Basin Exporter's Guide, 2044–36
Caribbean Basin Initiative Guidebook, 2044–36
Carload Waybill Statistics, 1989: Territorial Distribution, Traffic and Revenue by Commodity Classes, 7604–6
Carpet and Rugs, 1991, Current Industrial Report, 2506–5.9
Carrier Assignment of Medicare Provider Numbers, 4006–11.1
Cartographic Records in the National Archives of the U.S. Relating to American Indians, 9516–1.4
Cartographic Records in the National Archives of the U.S. Useful for Urban Studies, 9516–1.1
Case Against Adjustment: The 1990 Census, 25408–119
Case of the Missing M2, 9379–1.303, 9379–12.83
Case Studies in Using Data for Better Business Decisions, 2628–33
Case Studies on Electronic Dissemination at Four Agencies. Information Dissemination, 26125–47
Case Study of the Economic Impact of the Blue Ridge Parkway. Final Case Study for the National Scenic Byways Study, 7556–8.4
Case-Control Study of Factors Associated with Failure To Detect Breast Cancer by Mammography, 4472–1.316
Case-Control Study of Factors Associated with Human T-Cell Leukemia Virus Type I Infection in Southern Miyazaki, Japan, 4472–1.319
Caseload Statistics, State Vocational Rehabilitation Agencies, FY91, 4944–5
Catalog of DIOR Reports, 3548–21
Catalog of Federal Domestic Assistance, 1992, 104–5
Catalog of Federal Grant-in-Aid Programs to State and Local Governments, 10044–8
Catalog of Publications of the National Center for Health Statistics, 1990-91, 4124–1
Catalog of Widely Used Code Sets. Data Standards and Guidelines, 2216–2.204
Catalogue of State Medicaid Program Changes, 1991, 4654–19.1
Catalogue of U.S. Geological Survey Strong-Motion Records, 1989, 5664–14
Catalogue of U.S. Geological Survey Strong-Motion Records, 1990, 5664–14
Catfish, 1631–14
Catfish Production, 1631–18
Cattle, 1623–1
Cattle and Calves Death Loss, 1618–22
Cattle on Feed, 1623–2
Causal Model of the Etiology of PTSD, 8704–6
Causality and Correlations of Output and Nominal Variables in a Real Business Cycle Model, 9393–10.19
Causes and Consequences of Structural Changes in U.S. Labor Markets: A Review, 9377–1.304
Causes of Increased Overpayments, 1986-89. Social Security, 26121–484
CBO Papers, 26306–3
CBO Sequestration Report to Congress and the Office of Management and Budget, 26304–6
CBO Studies, 26306–6
CCC Milk Support Program Activities, 1802–2
CDC's Case Definition of AIDS: Implications of the Proposed Revisions, 26356–6.6
Celery, 1621–14
Cement: Mineral Industry Surveys, 5612–1.2
Cement: Minerals Yearbook, Volume 1, 1990, 5604–20.13
Census and You: Monthly News from the U.S. Bureau of the Census, 2302–3
Census Bureau Director Decides Not To Adjust Intercensal Population Estimates, 2328–90
Census Catalog and Guide, 1992, 2304–2
Census, CD-ROM, and You! New Horizons for Microcomputer Users of Census Bureau Data, 2308–64
Census Numbers for Congregations, 2326–7.85
Census of Housing, 1990. General Population Characteristics, 2471–1
Census of Manufactures, 1987. Subject Series. Concentration Ratios in Manufacturing, 2497–6
Census of Manufactures, 1987. Subject Series. Distribution of Sales by Class of Customer, 2497–4
Census of Population and Housing, 199: Guide, 2555–1
Census of Population and Housing, 1990. Alphabetical Index of Industries and Occupations, 2628–1
Census of Population and Housing, 1990. Classified Index of Industries and Occupations, 2628–2
Census of Population and Housing, 1990. Social, Economic, and Housing Characteristics: Pacific Outlying Areas, 2551–8
Census of Population and Housing, 1990. Summary Population and Housing Characteristics, 2551–1
Census of Population and Housing, 1990. Summary Social, Economic, and Housing Characteristics, 2551–7
Census of Population and Housing, 1990. Summary Tape File 1 on CD-ROM, Technical Documentation, 2308–65
Census of Population and Housing, 1990. Summary Tape File 1A Data on CD-ROM, 2551–9
Census of Population and Housing, 1990: Summary Tape File 3 on CD-ROM, Technical Documentation, 2308–68
Census of Population and Housing, 1990: Summary Tape File 3A Data on CD-ROM, 2551–10
Census of Population, 1990. General Population Characteristics, 2531–1, 2531–2
Census of Population, 1990: General Population Characteristics. American Indian and Alaska Native Areas, 2531–2.1
Census of Retail Trade, 1987. Subject Series. Merchandise Line Sales, 2399–3
Census of State Adult Correctional Facilities, 6068–218
Census of State and Federal Correctional Facilities, 1990, 6068–218
Census of U.S. Civil Aircraft, 1990, 7504–3
Census of U.S. Civil Aircraft, 1991, 7504–3
Census Questionnaire Content Bulletins, 1990. We Asked...You Told Us, 2326–23
Center for Population Research, National Institute of Child Health and Human Development: 1991 Progress Report, 4474–33
Center-Specific Graft and Patient Survival Rates, 1991 Report, 4104–17
Central and Eastern Europe: Export Competitiveness of Major Manufacturing and Services Sectors. Investigation No. 332-308, 9886–4.179
Central Banks' Use in East Asia of Money Market Instruments in the Conduct of Monetary Policy, 9366–7.280
Central Liquidity Facility 1991 Annual Report, 9534–5
Central North Pacific Hurricanes—1991, 2152–8.302
Central Questions Remain Unanswered. Sentencing Guidelines, 26119–415
Ceramic Floor and Wall Tiles, Industry and Trade Summary, 9885–13.2
Certification Requirements for Nursing Homes: Final Report, 17206–2.37
CFE Treaty, 25388–59
CFE: Treaty on Conventional Armed Forces in Europe, 9828–1
Challenging Health Care Issues Affecting Older African Americans, 21148–67
CHAMPUS Chartbook of Statistics, 3504–23
Chancroid in the U.S., 1981-90: Evidence for Underreporting of Cases, 4202–7.318
Changes in Cigarette Smoking and Current Smoking Practices Among Adults: U.S., 1978, 4147–16.6
Changes in Collateral Practices Could Reduce the Federal Government's Risk of Loss. Treasury Tax and Loan Accounts, 26111–80
Changes in Energy Intensity in the Manufacturing Sector, 1980-88. Manufacturing Energy Consumption Survey, 3166–13.7
Changes in Family Composition and Income Sources Among the Poor. Poverty Trends, 1980-88, 26131–102
Changes in Family Finances from 1983 to 1989: Evidence from the Survey of Consumer Finances, 9362–1.301
Changes in Farm Credit System Structure, 1541–1.311
Changes in Florida's Industrial Roundwood Products Output, 1987-89, 1208–352
Changes in Monetary Policy Effectiveness: Evidence from Large Macroeconometric Models, 9385–1.306
Changes in Output of Industrial Timber Products in Virginia, 1987-89, 1208–138
Changes in Prices for Selected Drugs. Prescription Drugs, 26121–472
Changes in Schedule B, Statistical Classification of Domestic and Foreign Commodities Exported from the U.S.: 1990. U.S. Foreign Trade, 2428–5.1
Changes in the Incomes of Age Groups, 1984-89, 4742–1.304, 4746–26.20
Changes in Unemployment Insurance Legislation in 1991, 6722–1.311
Changes to the 1990 Edition of Schedule B, Jan. 1, 1993, 2428–5.1
Changing Capitalization of CBD-Oriented Transportation Systems: Evidence from Philadelphia, 1970-88, 9387–8.258

Changing Demographics Cause Shift in Market Share. Statistical Brief, 2326–17.40
Changing Economy of the Tenth District, 9381–1.306
Changing Geographical Patterns of Electronic Components Activity, 9393–8.307
Changing Nation—Its Changing Labor Force, 15496–1.16
Changing Outlook for Feed Grain Trade, 1504–9.1
Changing Patterns in State-Local Finances. Intergovernmental Relations, 26121–457
Changing Public Attitudes on Governments and Taxes, 1992, 10044–2
Changing Public Sector: Shifts in Governmental Spending and Employment, 10048–53
Changing Structure of the U.S. Flour Milling Industry, 1502–3.301
Changing Tobacco User's Dollar, 1561–10.304
Changing Workforce: Demographic Issues Facing the Federal Government, 26119–383
Characteristics and Financial Circumstances of AFDC Recipients, FY90, 4584–7
Characteristics of Apartments Completed: 1991. Current Housing Report, 2484–3
Characteristics of At-Risk Students in NELS:88. National Education Longitudinal Study of 1988, 4826–9.16
Characteristics of Business Owners, 1987 Economic Censuses, 2328–59
Characteristics of Doctorate Recipients: 1979, 1984, and 1989, 4848–44
Characteristics of Farmland Owners and Their Participation in the Farmland Market, 1970-88, 1561–16.302
Characteristics of Federal Grant-in-Aid Programs to State and Local Governments: Grants Funded, FY91, 10044–8
Characteristics of FHA Single-Family Mortgages: Selected Sections of National Housing Act, 1991, 5144–17
Characteristics of Food Stamp Households, Summer 1989, 1364–8
Characteristics of HUD-Assisted Renters and Their Units in 1989, 5184–11
Characteristics of Jobs Provided Through the College Work-Study Program. Student Financial Aid, 26121–449
Characteristics of New Housing: 1991. Current Construction Reports, 2384–1
Characteristics of Physicians, Jan. 1, 1990, 4116–6
Characteristics of Recipients and the Dynamics of Program Participation: 1987-88, 2546–20.25
Characteristics of State Plans for Aid to Families with Dependent Children Under Title IV-A of the Social Security Act, 4584–8, 4694–4
Charities and Other Tax-Exempt Organizations, 1988, 8302–2.315
Chartbook on Work Disability in the U.S., 4948–11
Check-Cashing Outlets in the U.S. Financial System, 9381–1.301
Chernobyl Accident Prompted Worldwide Actions but Further Efforts Needed. Nuclear Power Safety, 26123–367
Cherokee, Navajo, Chippewa, Sioux Top Census Bureau's '90 Tribe List, 2328–86
Cherry Production, 1621–18.2
Chiefs of State and Cabinet Members of Foreign Governments, 9112–4
Child Health Limitations, 4478–197.2
Child Labor: Work Permit and Death and Injury Reporting Systems in Selected States, 26121–451
Child Support Enforcement: Opportunity To Defray Burgeoning Federal and State Non-AFDC Costs, 26121–463
Child-Care Arrangements of Young Working Mothers. Work and Family, 6726–2.1
Children Receiving SSI Payments, December 1991, 4742–1.316
Chile Textile and Apparel Market, 2046–15.2
Chilean Trade: Factors Affecting U.S. Trade and Investment, 26119–408
China: Agriculture and Trade Report, Situation and Outlook Series, 1524–4.2
China: Economic Performance and Outlook, 9114–5
China's Agricultural Marketing System in the 1980's, 1524–4.2
China's Barley: An Analysis of Production, Consumption, and Trade, 1524–4.2
China's Food Consumption and Production Patterns in the Year 2000: Implications for Trade, 1524–4.2
China's Trade with Neighboring Countries Since the Early 1980's, 1524–4.2
Chinese Economy in 1991 and 1992: Pressure To Revisit Reform Mounts, 9114–5
Chinese Fruit Production and Trade, 1925–34.318
Choice of Capital Instruments by Banking Organizations, 9371–10.79
Cholesterol Treatment Practices of Primary Care Physicians, 4042–3.345
Chromium: Mineral Industry Surveys, 5612–1.3
Chromium: Minerals Yearbook, Volume 1, 1990, 5604–20.14
Cigarette Smoking, Alcohol, and Nasopharyngeal Carcinoma: A Case-Control Study Among U.S. Whites, 4472–1.312
Cigarette Smoking and Other Risk Factors for Progression of Precancerous Stomach Lesions, 4472–1.334
Cigarette Use Among Arab Americans in the Detroit Metropolitan Area, 4042–3.360
Cigarettes, Industry and Trade Summary, 9885–8.2
CIR Staff Papers, 2326–18
Circular Mobility, Migrant Communities, and Policy Restrictions: Unauthorized Flows from Mexico, 6366–6.11
Circular, Welded, Non-Alloy Steel Pipes and Tubes from Brazil, the Republic of Korea, Mexico, Romania, Taiwan, and Venezuela. Determinations of the Commission in Investigations Nos. 731-TA-532 through 537 (Final) Under the Tariff Act of 1930, Together with the Information Obtained in the Investigations, 9886–14.361
Citrus Fruits: 1992 Summary, 1621–18.8
City Government Finances: 1989-90, 2466–2.1
Civil Aircraft and Aircraft Engines, Current Industrial Report, 2506–12.24
Civil Service Retirement and Disability Fund, 9844–34
Civil Service Retirement and Disability Fund, An Annual Report To Comply with the Requirements of P.L. 95-595, Sept. 30, 1991, 9844–34
Civil Service Work Force as of Sept. 30, 1991, 9504–1
Civilian Manpower Statistics, 3542–16
Class I Freight Railroads, Selected Earnings Data, 9482–2
Classifications Systems for PPS-Excluded and Non-PPS Providers, 17206–2.29
Classified Index of Industries and Occupations. 1990 Census of Population and Housing, 2628–2
Clay Construction Products, Current Industrial Report, 2506–9.2
Clays: Minerals Yearbook, Volume 1, 1990, 5604–20.15
Clean Air Act of 1990: A Tougher Regulatory Challenge Facing Midwest Industry, 9375–1.304
Clean Air Program Technical Assistance Brief, 7882–3
Clean Coal Technology Demonstration Program, Program Update 1990, 3334–4
Clean Coal Technology Demonstration Program, Program Update 1991, 3334–4
Clean Coal Technology: The New Coal Era, 3334–5, 3338–4
Clearance and Settlement in U.S. Securities Markets, 9366–1.163
Clearinghouse Bibliography on Health Indexes, 4122–1
Clients/Patients with a Principal Diagnosis of Affective Disorder Served in the Inpatient, Outpatient, and Partial Care Programs of Specialty Mental Health Organizations, U.S., 1986, 4506–3.49
Cliff Lake Bench Research Natural Area: Problems Encountered in Monitoring Vegetation Change on Mountain Grasslands, 1208–425
Climate Assessment, a Decadal Review, 2184–9
Climate Change: Economic Implications for World Agriculture, 1528–326
Climate Monitoring and Diagnostics Laboratory, No. 19, Summary Report, 1990, 2144–28
Clinical Correlates of MDR1 (P-glycoprotein) Gene Expression in Ovarian and Small-Cell Lung Carcinomas, 4472–1.345
Closing the Tax Gap: Alternatives to Enforcement. IRS 1991 Research Conference, 8304–25
Closures for Containers, Current Industrial Report, 2506–11.4
Coal Data: A Reference, 3164–79
Coal Distribution, 3162–8
Coal Production, 1991, 3164–25
Coal: Surface Fatalities, Second Half 1991, 6662–3.1
Coal: Underground Fatalities, Second Half 1991, 6662–3.2
Coal-Fired Flow Facility, University of Tennessee Space Institute, Site Environmental Report for 1990, 3324–2.7
Coast Guard Publishes New List of Current Boating Safety Recall Campaigns, 7402–5
Coast Guard SAR Statistics, 7404–2
Coastal Zone Boundary Review Draft National Summary: State Characterization Reports, 2178–35
Cobalt: Mineral Industry Surveys, 5612–1.4
Cobalt: Minerals Yearbook, Volume 1, 1990, 5604–20.16
Cocoa: Foreign Agricultural Service Circular Series. World Cocoa Situation, 1925–9

Coinage Executed During (Month), 8202–1
Cointegration, Aggregate Consumption, and the Demand for Imports: A Structural Econometric Investigation, 9385–8.141
Cointegration and Tests of a Classical Model of Inflation in Argentina, Bolivia, Brazil, Mexico, and Peru, 9379–12.91
Cold Storage, 1631–5
Cold Storage, 1991 Summary, 1631–11
Collective Bargaining in 1992: Contract Talks and Other Activity, 6722–1.306
Collective Bargaining, 1991: Recession Colors Talks, 6722–1.307
College Placement Officials' Views of the Government's Campus Outreach Efforts. Federal Recruiting, 26119–377
Colorado Cooperative Snow Survey Data of Federal-State-Private Cooperative Snow Surveys, Water Year 1990, 1264–14.1
Colorado River Salinity Control Program, From Inception of Program Through Sept. 30, 1991, 1804–23
Colorado River Storage Project and Participating Projects in FY91, 35th Annual Report, 5824–3
Colorado Water Supply Summary, Water Year 1992, 1264–13
Colorado Wilderness Act of 1991, 25318–85
Columbia To Deploy LAGEOS-II, Serve as Technology Testbed: STS-52 Mission, 9506–2.153
Columbium (Niobium) and Tantalum: Minerals Yearbook, Volume 1, 1990, 5604–20.17
Combined Financial Statements: FSLIC-Insured Institutions (Balance Sheet and Income and Expense Statements), 8434–1
Combined Financial Statements: SAIF-Insured Institutions (Balance Sheet and Income and Expense Statements), 1989, 8434–1
Combined Summaries: Technologies To Sustain Tropical Forest Resources and Biological Diversity, 26358–262
Comment on William Poole's Paper "Exchange Rate Management and Monetary Policy Mismanagement: A Study of Germany, Japan, UK, and U.S. After Plaza", 9381–10.124
Comments on the Notice of Proposed Rulemaking for the Medicare Fee Schedule, 17266–2.7
Comments on the President's Budget for FY93, 17266–2.11
Commerce Budget in Brief, FY93, 2004–6
Commerce Publications Update, 2002–1
Commercial Activities Inventory Report and Five Year Review Schedule, FY91, 3544–25
Commercial Bank Information: Implications for the Structure of Banking, 9387–8.264
Commercial Bank Performance, 1991, 9381–14
Commercial Bank Profitability Rises as Interest Margins and Securities Sales Increase, 9371–1.305
Commercial Buildings Energy Consumption and Expenditures, 1989. Commercial Buildings Energy Consumption Survey, 3166–8.10
Commercial Buildings Energy Consumption Survey, 3166–8
Commercial Buildings Energy Consumption Survey: Commercial Buildings Energy Consumption and Expenditures, 1989, 3166–8.10
Commercial Fertilizers, 1991, 9804–30
Commercial Fertilizers, 1992, 9804–30
Commercial Opportunities in Israel: A Report from the U.S./Israel Legal Exchange, Winter 1992, 2008–32
Commissioner of Patents and Trademarks, Annual Report, FY91, 2244–1
Commissioner's Fact Book: Summary of Recent Immigration Data, 6264–7
Commitment to Change: Foundations for Reform, Report of the Advisory Council on Social Security, 10178–1
Commitments and Discharges for the Fiscal Year: Bureau of Prisons, 6242–1.3
Commitments and Discharges for the Month: Bureau of Prisons, 6242–1.2
Commitments of Traders in Futures, 11922–5
Committee for Purchase from the Blind and Other Severely Handicapped Annual Report, 1991, 11714–1
Commodity Credit Corp. Monthly Sales List, 1802–4
Commodity Credit Corporation Charts: A Summary of Data Through Sept. 30, 1988, 1824–2
Commodity Futures Trading Commission, Annual Report, 1991, 11924–2
Commodity Prices and P-Star, 9377–1.303
Communication Equipment, and Other Electronic Systems and Equipment, 1991, Current Industrial Report, 2506–12.35
Communications Network Funding and Requirements Uncertain. Drug Control, 26123–372
Community Development: Neighborhood Reinvestment Corporation Should Improve Program Management, 26113–587
Community Epidemiology Work Group Proceedings, 4492–5
Community Relations Service, FY91 Annual Report, 6004–9
Community-Based AIDS Prevention: Studies of Intravenous Drug Users and Their Sexual Partners. Proceedings of the First Annual NADR National Meeting, 4494–12
Commuting Flows of American Workers Charted by New 1990 Census Computer File, 2328–84
Compact Ductile Iron Waterworks Fittings and Accessories Thereof from the People's Republic of China. Determination of the Commission in Investigation No. 731-TA-621 (Preliminary) Under the Tariff Act of 1930, Together with the Information Obtained in the Investigation, 9886–14.358
Companies Participating in the DOD Subcontracting Program, 3542–17
Companies Receiving the Largest Dollar Volume of Prime Contract Awards, FY91, 3544–5
Companies Typically Charge More in the U.S. than in Canada. Prescription Drugs, 26121–482
Comparing Central Banks' Rulebooks, 9377–1.307
Comparison of Applicants Who Accepted or Declined Federal Job Offers. Federal Recruiting, 26119–387
Comparison of Assistance Programs. Dislocated Workers, 26121–481
Comparison of Individual Characteristics and Death Rates of Disabled-Worker Beneficiaries Entitled in 1972 and 1985, 4742–1.321
Comparison of Low Birth Weight Among Medicaid Patients of Public Health Departments and Other Providers of Prenatal Care in North Carolina and Kentucky, 4042–3.304
Comparison of Methods To Integrate DSM and Supply Resources in Electric-Utility Planning, 3308–100
Comparison of Monetary Policy Operating Procedures in Six Industrial Countries, 9385–1.308
Comparison of Native American Births in Upstate New York with Other Race Births, 1980-86, 4042–3.359
Comparison of Performance on the Shipley Institute of Living Scale, Air Traffic Control Specialist Selection Test, and FAA Academy Screen, 7506–10.126
Comparison of State Unemployment Insurance Laws, 6402–2
Comparison of Urinalysis Technologies for Drug Testing in Criminal Justice, 6068–247
Comparison of U.S. and Mexican Pesticide Standards and Enforcement. Pesticides, 26113–585
Comparison of Vocational and Non-Vocational Public School Teachers of Grades 9 to 12. Schools and Staffing Survey, 4836–3.9
Comparison of Wood Preservatives in Stake Tests: 1991 Progress Report, 1208–391
Comparisons of Independent Statistics on Petroleum Supply, 3162–6.302
Comparisons of Molecular Sieve Oxygen Concentrators for Potential Medical Use Aboard Commercial Aircraft, 7506–10.109
Compendium of Animal Rabies Control, 1992, 4206–2.57
Compendium of Federal Justice Statistics, 1988, 6064–29
Compendium of Federal Justice Statistics, 1989, 6064–29
Compendium of Studies of International Income and Taxes, 1984-88. Statistics of Income, 8308–31
Compendium of Studies of Tax-Exempt Organizations, 1974-87. Statistics of Income, 8308–35
Compensation and Working Conditions, 6782–1
Compensation Varies for Selected Personnel in Athletic Departments. Intercollegiate Athletics, 26121–476
Compensatory Education: Most Chapter 1 Funds in Eight Districts Used for Classroom Services, 26121–478
Competing Economies: America, Europe, and the Pacific Rim, 26358–252
Competition for More Than One Class of Borrowers Using Different Credit-Worthiness Tests, 9371–10.76
Competitive Assessment of the U.S. Power Tool Industry, 2046–12.46
Competitive Assessment of U.S. Industries, 2046–12
Compilation and Interpretation of Water-Quality and Discharge Data for Acidic Mine Waters at Iron Mountain, Shasta County, California, 1940-91, 5666–27.35
Compilations of Advance Data from Vital and Health Statistics. Vital and Health Statistics Series 16, 4147–16
Complete Catalog, 1992-93, Cataloging Distribution Service: Bibliographic Products and Services, 26404–6

Compliance with Joint Commission Accreditation Requirements Is Improving. VA Health Care, 26121–441
Components of City-Size Wage Differentials, 1973-88, 9377–1.301
Composite Index of Coincident Indicators and Alternative Coincident Indexes, 2702–1.322
Composition of Foods, 1356–3
Composition of Foods. Baked Products: Raw, Processed, Prepared, 1356–3.18
Composition of Foods. 1991 Supplement: Raw, Processed, Prepared, 1356–3.17
Composition of Groups Affected by FY91 Force Reductions. Defense Force Management, 26123–373
Composition of U.S. Merchandise Trade, 1987-91, Chartbook, 9884–21
Comprehensive Revision of State Personal Income, 2702–1.328
Comprehensive Revision of the U.S. National Income and Product Accounts: A Review of Revisions and Major Statistical Changes, 2702–1.302
Comprehensive Statement on Postal Operations, 1991, 9864–5
Comptroller General's 1991 Annual Report, 26104–1
Computers and Office and Accounting Machines, 1990, Current Industrial Report, 2506–12.2
Computers and Office and Accounting Machines, 1991, Current Industrial Report, 2506–12.2
Concentration Ratios in Manufacturing. 1987 Census of Manufactures. Subject Series, 2497–6
Concentrations of Hired and Contract Labor Expenses, 1541–1.305
Concerns of the Grain Industry, 1504–9.1
Concordance of Hospital Cancer Registry- and Physician-Collected Data for Patients with Melanoma, 4472–1.354
Concordance of Statistics, 1989, Available in Selected Federal Reserve Publications, 9364–8
Concordance of Statistics, 1990, Available in Selected Federal Reserve Publications, 9364–8
Condition and Recapitalization of the Bank Insurance Fund, 21248–166
Condition of Bilingual Education in the Nation: A Report to the Congress and the President, 4804–14
Condition of Education, 1992, 4824–1
Conduct of Monetary Policy: Report of the Federal Reserve Board Pursuant to the Full Employment and Balanced Growth Act of 1978, P.L. 95-523 and the State of the Economy, 21248–160
Confectionery, 1991, Current Industrial Report, 2506–4.5
Conference on Profiling, 17266–2.10
Conference Series, Federal Reserve Bank of Boston, 9373–3
Confirmatory Factor Analysis of Burnout Dimensions: Correlations with Job Stressors and Aspects of Social Support and Job Satisfaction, 7506–10.103
Confronting Repetitive Motion Illnesses in the Workplace, 21408–128
Congressional Action on Appropriation Request, Department of Defense, 3504–7
Congressional Budget Office, Final Sequestration Report for FY92, 26304–6
Congressional Budget Office, Final Sequestration Report for FY93, 26304–6
Congressional Presentation for Security Assistance Programs, FY93, 7144–13
Congressional Presentation, FY93, AID. Main Volume, 9904–4.1
Congressional Presentation, FY93, AID. Part II, 9904–4.2
Congressional Presentation, FY93, AID. Statistical Annex, 9904–4.3
Congressional Presentation, FY93, AID. Summary Tables, 9904–4.4
Congressional Presentation, FY93, AID. U.S. Trade and Development Program, 9904–4.5
Congressional Presentation, FY93, U.S. International Development Cooperation Agency, 9904–4
Conservation and Protection of Humpback Whales in Hawaii—An Update, 14738–14
Conservation and Renewable Energy. Schools and Hospitals Program Cycle XIII Grants Data: Grants Award Listing, June 25, 1992, 3304–15
Conservation Strategy for the Northern Spotted Owl, 1208–385
Consolidated Federal Funds Report, FY91, 2464–3
Consolidated Federal Funds Report, FY91. Volume I: County Areas, 2464–3.1
Consolidated Federal Funds Report, FY91. Volume II: Subcounty Areas, 2464–3.2
Consolidated Reports of Condition and Income, 9389–18
Construction and Mining Equipment, Industry and Trade Summary, 9885–9.2
Construction Industries: Evaluating Your Firm's Injury and Illness Record, 6886–4.3
Construction Material Trends: Data from the Census and Survey of Manufactures, 2042–1.302
Construction Outlook for 1992, 2042–1.304
Construction Programs (C-1), Department of Defense Budget for FY93, 3544–39
Construction Review, 2042–1
Consumer Attitudes and Business Cycles, 9371–10.69
Consumer Attitudes Toward Labeling, 1504–9.1
Consumer Expenditure Survey: Quarterly Data from the Interview Survey, 6762–14
Consumer Expenditures in 1991, 6726–1.53
Consumer Guide to Uniform Tire Quality Grading, 7764–17
Consumer Income. Current Population Reports. Series P-60, 2546–6
Consumer Installment Credit, 9365–2.6
Consumer Price Index, 6762–1
Consumer, Scientific, Technical, and Industrial Glassware, 1991, Current Industrial Report, 2506–9.3
Consumer Sentiment: Its Causes and Effects, 9393–8.304
Consumer Spending on Durables and Services in the 1980's, 6722–1.324
Consumer Switching Costs, Market Structure and Prices: The Theory and Its Application in the Bank Deposit Market, 9366–6.297
Consumption on the Cotton System and Stocks, Current Industrial Report, 2506–5.8
Consumption on the Cotton System, Current Industrial Report, 2506–5.8
Consumption on the Woolen System and Worsted Combing, Current Industrial Report, 2506–5.2
Containing U.S. Health Care Costs: What Bullet To Bite?, 4652–1.310
Contaminant Evaluation of Interior Least Tern and Piping Plover Eggs and Chicks on the Missouri River, South Dakota, 5508–118
Contaminant Trends in the Southern California Bight: Inventory and Assessment, 2176–3.16
Contingent Foreign Liabilities of the U.S. Government, 8002–12
Contracting Practices with Data Processing Servicers. Depository Institutions, 26119–374
Contractor Accountability at Department of Energy Nuclear Facilities, 21408–127
Contractors Receiving the Largest Dollar Volume of Prime Contract Awards for Research, Development, Test, and Evaluation, FY91, 3544–4
Contracts for Field Projects and Supporting Research on Enhanced Oil Recovery, 3002–14
Control and Security Weaknesses Create Opportunities for Theft. Defense Inventory, 26123–377
Control of Discharges of Toxic Pollutants into the Great Lakes and Their Tributaries: Development of Benchmarks, 14648–29
Control of Disease in Aquaculture: Proceedings of the Nineteenth U.S.-Japan Meeting on Aquaculture, Ise, Mie Prefecture, Japan, 29-30 October 1990, 2164–15
Controlled Foreign Corporations, 1988, 8302–2.322
Controlling Inappropriate Access to Federally Funded Research Results. University Research, 26113–575
Conventional and Conservation Tillage Systems in Soybean Production, 1990, 1561–3.304
Conventional Home Mortgage Rates, 9442–2
Convexity Trap: Pitfalls in Financing Mortgage Portfolios and Related Securities, 9371–1.308
Cooperative Feed and Animal Health Operations, 1126–1.7
Cooperative Financing and Taxation, 1126–1.8
Cooperative Game Fish Tagging Program Annual Newsletter, 1988, 2164–24
Cooperative Game Fish Tagging Program Annual Newsletter, 1989, 2164–24
Cooperative Game Fish Tagging Program Annual Newsletter, 1990, 2164–24
Cooperative Snow Survey Data, 1264–14
Cooperative State-Federal Tuberculosis Eradication Program, Statistical Tables and Status Report, 1394–13
Cooperative Tobacco Warehouses Show Gain in Marketing Activity, 1122–1.304
Co-ops' Net Income Up, Sales Down Slightly in 1991, 1122–1.307
Co-ops' Share of Farm Marketings, Production Supplies at 27 Percent, 1122–1.302
Coordinating Federal Assistance Programs for the Economically Disadvantaged: Recommendations and Background Materials, 15498–29
Coordinating Rural Development with National Strategies, 1504–9.1
Coordinating Water Resources in the Federal System: The Groundwater-Surface Water Connection, 10048–82

Copayment Exemption Procedures Should Be Improved. VA Health Care, 26121–464
Copper in the U.S.: Mineral Industry Surveys, 5612–1.6
Copper: Mineral Industry Surveys, 5612–1.6
Copper: Minerals Yearbook, Volume 1, 1990, 5604–20.18
Copper River Delta Pulse Study: An Interdisciplinary Survey of the Aquatic Habitats, 1208–401
Corporate Foreign Tax Credit, 1988: An Industry Focus, 8302–2.316
Corporate Pensions and Government Insurance: Deja Vu All Over Again?, 9371–1.302
Corporation Income Tax Returns: Statistics of Income, 1988, 8304–4
Corporation Income Tax Returns: Statistics of Income, 1989, 8304–4
Corporation Income Tax Returns, 1989, 8302–2.321
Corps of Engineers' Dredging Program for Small Business Firms. Water Resources, 26113–589
Correctional Populations in the U.S., 1990, 6064–26
Correlation of HER-2/neu Amplification with Expression and with Other Prognostic Factors in 1,103 Breast Cancers, 4472–1.337
Correlation: Textile and Apparel Categories with the Harmonized Tariff Schedule of the U.S., 2044–31
Correspondence Schools' Loan Volume Declines Sharply. Stafford Student Loan Program, 26121–448
Cost and Quality of Fuels for Electric Utility Plants, 1991, 3164–42
Cost and Revenue Analysis, FY91, Rates and Classification Department, 9864–2
Cost Growth Continues on Ship Construction Contracts. Navy Contracting, 26123–401
Cost of Drug Testing, 236–3.3
Cost of Owning and Operating Automobiles, Vans and Light Trucks, 1991, 7554–21
Cost Savings Associated with Bank Mergers, 9371–10.78
Costa Rica: The Effects of Structural Adjustment Measures on the Poor, 1982-90, 9916–13.5
Costs of Highway Crashes, 7558–114
Costs of Producing and Selling Burley Tobacco: 1989, 1990 and Preliminary 1991, 1561–10.301
Costs of Producing and Selling Flue-Cured Tobacco: 1991 and Preliminary 1992, 1561–10.305
Cotton and Wool Situation and Outlook Report, 1561–1
Cotton and Wool Situation and Outlook Yearbook, 1561–1
Cotton: Foreign Agricultural Service Circular Series, 1925–4
Cotton Ginnings, 1631–19
Cotton Manufacturers (Customs Value). U.S. General Imports, 2046–9.4
Cotton Manufacturers. U.S. General Imports, 2046–8.1
Cotton Mill Use in the 1990s, 1504–9.1
Cotton or Man-Made Fiber Manufacturers (Customs Value). U.S. General Imports, 2046–9.8
Cotton or Man-Made Fiber Manufacturers. U.S. General Imports, 2046–8.7
Cotton Price Statistics, 1309–1
Cotton Price Statistics, 1991-92, 1309–2
Cotton Quality: Carryover, 1991, 1309–8
Cotton Quality: Carryover, 1992, 1309–8
Cotton Quality: Crop of 1991, 1309–7
Cotton Varieties Planted, 1992 Crop, 1309–6
Cotton, Wool, Man-Made Fiber, and Vegetable Fiber (Except Cotton) and Silk Blend Textiles. U.S. General Imports, 2042–27
Cottonseed Quality, Crop of 1991, 1309–5
Cottonseed Review, 1309–14
Country and Commodity Allocations Under Public Law 480, Title I/III, 1922–7
Country Development Strategy Statements, 9916–12
Country Exposure Lending Survey, 13002–1
Country Financial Report: Economic Assistance, 9912–4
Country Profile: Switzerland, 1925–16.315
Country Profile: Turkey, 1925–16.313
Country Reports on Economic Policy and Trade Practices, 21384–5
Country Reports on Human Rights Practices for 1991, 21384–3
Country/Regional Profiles, Office of U.S. Foreign Disaster Assistance, 9916–2
County and Metropolitan Area Personal Income, 1988-90, 2702–1.317
County Business Patterns, 1989, 2326–8
County Business Patterns, 1990, 2326–6
County Government Employment: 1991, 2466–1.2
County Government Finances: 1989-90, 2466–2.3
Covariances for Estimated Totals When Comparing Between Years. Vital and Health Statistics Series 2, 4147–2.114
CPI Detailed Report, 6762–2
CRA and the 1990 HMDA Data: Moving Beyond the Impasse, 9371–4
Cranberries, 1621–18.5
Crash Data and Rates for Age-Sex Groups of Drivers, 1990, 7768–105
Credit Union Directory, 9534–6
Credit Union Industry Performance, 1991, 9381–14
Credit Unions: Reforms for Ensuring Future Soundness, 26119–364
Crewing the Merchant Marine for Mobilization, 7708–5
Crime and the Nation's Households, 1991, 6066–25.49
Crime in the U.S., 1991. Uniform Crime Reports, 6224–2
Crime Victimization in City, Suburban, and Rural Areas: A National Crime Victimization Survey Report, 6066–3.48
Criminal Acts Against Civil Aviation, 1990, 7504–31
Criminal Victimization in the U.S., 1990, 6066–3.47
Critical Issues in American Health Care Delivery and Financing Policy, 10176–3.2
Critical Technologies: Materials, 21708–130
Crop Insurance: Inaccurate FCIC Price Forecasts Increase Program Costs, 26131–95
Crop Insurance: Program Has Not Fostered Significant Risk Sharing by Insurance Companies, 26113–556
Crop Production, 1621–1
Crop Sugarbeet and Sugarcane Production and Processing Costs, 1990, 1561–14.303
Crop Values, 1991 Summary, 1621–2
Cross Sections: A Review of Business and Economic Developments Published Quarterly by the Federal Reserve Bank of Richmond, 9389–16
Crude Petroleum, Industry and Trade Summary, 9885–11.4
Crushed Limestone from Mexico. Determination of the Commission in Investigation No. 731-TA-562 (Preliminary) Under the Tariff Act of 1930, Together with the Information Obtained in the Investigation, 9886–14.353
Crushed Stone and Sand and Gravel: Mineral Industry Surveys, 5612–2.20
Cuba: Handbook of Trade Statistics, 9118–8
Cuba's Sugar Industry—Facing a New World Order, 1561–14.302
Cumulative Report on Rescissions and Deferrals, 102–2
Current and Forthcoming Publications, 4822–1
Current Business Reports: Advance Monthly Retail Sales, 2413–2
Current Business Reports: Annual Survey of Communication Services, 1990, 2413–15
Current Business Reports: Monthly Retail Trade Sales and Inventories, 2413–3
Current Business Reports: Monthly Wholesale Trade Sales and Inventories, 2413–7
Current Business Reports: Motor Freight Transportation and Warehousing Survey, 1990, 2413–14
Current Business Reports: 1990 Retail Trade. Annual Sales, Year-End Inventories, Purchases, Gross Margin, and Accounts Receivable, by Kind of Retail Store, 2413–5
Current Construction Reports: Characteristics of New Housing, 1991, 2384–1
Current Construction Reports: Expenditures for Residential Improvements and Repairs, 2382–7
Current Construction Reports: Housing Completions, 2382–2
Current Construction Reports: Housing Starts, 2382–1
Current Construction Reports: Housing Units Authorized by Building Permits, 2382–5
Current Construction Reports: Housing Units Authorized by Building Permits, Annual 1991, 2384–2
Current Construction Reports: New One-Family Houses Sold, 2382–3
Current Construction Reports: New Residential Construction in Selected Metropolitan Statistical Areas, 2382–9
Current Construction Reports: Special Studies. Expenditures for Nonresidential Improvements and Repairs, 1989, 2388–4
Current Construction Reports: Value of New Construction Put in Place, 2382–4
Current Economic Conditions, 9362–8
Current Estimates from the National Health Interview Survey, 1990. Vital and Health Statistics Series 10, 4147–10.182
Current Estimates from the National Health Interview Survey, 1991. Vital and Health Statistics Series 10, 4147–10.183
Current Federal Aid Research Report: Fish, 5504–23
Current Fisheries Statistics, 2166–6
Current Funds Revenues and Expenditures of Institutions of Higher Education: FY81-89, 4844–6

Current Funds Revenues and Expenditures of Institutions of Higher Education: FY82-90, 4844–6
Current Housing Reports. American Housing Survey for Metropolitan Areas, 1989, 2485–6
Current Housing Reports. Characteristics of Apartments Completed: 1991, 2484–3
Current Housing Reports. Housing Vacancies and Homeownership, 2482–1
Current Housing Reports. Market Absorption of Apartments, 2482–2
Current Housing Reports. Market Absorption of Apartments: Annual 1991 Absorptions (Apartments Completed in 1990), 2484–2
Current Housing Reports, Series H-111. Housing Vacancies and Homeownership, Annual Statistics: 1991, 2484–1
Current Housing Reports. Series H-121: Housing Characteristics, 2486–1
Current Housing Reports. Series H-123, 2486–2
Current Housing Reports. Supplement to the American Housing Survey for Selected Metropolitan Areas: 1985, 2485–8
Current Housing Reports. Supplement to the American Housing Survey for Selected Metropolitan Areas: 1986, 2485–8
Current Housing Reports. Supplement to the American Housing Survey for Selected Metropolitan Areas: 1987, 2485–8
Current Industrial Reports: All Manufacturing Industries, 2506–3
Current Industrial Reports: Apparel, 2506–6
Current Industrial Reports: Chemicals and Petroleum Products; Rubber and Plastics, 2506–8
Current Industrial Reports: Food, 2506–4
Current Industrial Reports: Glass, Clay, and Related Products, 2506–9
Current Industrial Reports: Intermediate Metal Products, 2506–11
Current Industrial Reports: Machinery and Equipment; Electrical and Electronics, 2506–12
Current Industrial Reports: Primary Metals, 2506–10
Current Industrial Reports: Textile Mill Products, 2506–5
Current Industrial Reports: Wood, Paper, and Related Products, 2506–7
Current International Trade Position of the U.S., 2042–25
Current Population Reports. Estimates of Median Four-Person Family Income, by State: 1974-89, 2626–2.60
Current Population Reports. Series P-20: Population Characteristics, 2546–1
Current Population Reports. Series P-23: Special Studies, 2546–2
Current Population Reports. Series P-25: Population Estimates and Projections, 2546–3
Current Population Reports. Series P-25: Population Estimates and Projections; Estimates of the Population of the U.S. to (Date), 2542–1
Current Population Reports. Series P-60: Consumer Income, 2546–6
Current Population Reports. Series P-70: Household Economic Studies, 2546–20
Current Status of the Environmental Reserve and the Conservation Compliance Programs: Implications for U.S. Wheat Area, 1561–12.302
Current Taxation of Qualified Pension Plans: Has the Time Come?, 9373–1.305
Current Technical Service Contracts and Grants Active During the Period Oct. 1, 1988 Through Sept. 30, 1989, 9914–7
Current Technical Service Contracts and Grants Active During the Period Oct. 1, 1989 Through Sept. 30, 1990, 9914–7
Current Technical Service Contracts and Grants Active During the Period Oct. 1, 1990 Through Sept. 30, 1991 in Excess of $100,000, 9914–7
Current Water Resources Activities in Ohio, 1991, 5666–26.23
Customs Service: Trade Enforcement Activities Impaired by Management Problems, 26119–420
Cyanide Hazards to Fish, Wildlife, and Invertebrates: A Synoptic Review, 5506–14.4
Czechoslovakia's Changing Health Care System, 4042–3.363

Dabbling Duck Recruitment in Relation to Habitat and Predators at Union Slough National Wildlife Refuge, Iowa. Fish and Wildlife Technical Report, 5506–12.5
Daily Treasury Statement, 8102–4
Dairy, Livestock, and Poultry: Foreign Agricultural Service Circular Series, 1925–33
Dairy, Livestock, and Poultry: U.S. Trade and Prospects. Foreign Agricultural Service Circular Series, 1925–32
Dairy Market Statistics, 1991 Annual Summary, 1317–1
Dairy Monthly Imports: Foreign Agricultural Service Circular Series, 1925–31
Dairy Price Support Program, 1991-92: ASCS Commodity Fact Sheet, 1806–4.8
Dairy Produce, Industry and Trade Summary, 9885–8.3
Dairy Products, 1627–3
Dairy Products, 1991 Summary, 1627–5
Dairy Situation and Outlook Report, 1561–2
Dairy Situation and Outlook Yearbook, 1561–2
Damaged and Threatened National Historic Landmarks, 1990 Section 8 Report, 5544–16.1
Data Bank: Fourth District Thrift Institutions Statistics, Federal Home Loan Bank of Atlanta, 9304–29
Data Book, FY91. National Institute of General Medical Sciences, 4474–38
Data Book, Operating Banks and Branches: Summary of Deposits in All FDIC-Insured Commercial and Savings Banks and U.S. Branches of Foreign Banks, June 30, 1991, 9295–3
Data Compression in Modems Employing CCITT Recommendation V.42 Error Correction. Telecommunications Standard, 2216–2.213
Data Envelopment Analysis and Commercial Bank Performance: A Primer with Applications to Missouri Banks, 9391–1.305
Data Evaluation and Methods Research. Vital and Health Statistics Series 2, 4147–2
Data for Communities, 2326–7.82
Data for Small Communities, 2326–7.82
Data from the National Health Interview Survey. Vital and Health Statistics Series 10, 4147–10
Data from the National Vital Statistics System. Vital and Health Statistics Series 20, 4147–20
Data on Ground-Water Quality, Carson Valley and Topaz Lake Areas, Douglas County, Nevada, for Year Ending September 1987, 5666–28.22
Data on Health Resources Utilization. Vital and Health Statistics Series 13, 4147–13
Data on Natality, Marriage, and Divorce. Vital and Health Statistics Series 21, 4147–21
DDT and Related Compounds and Risk of Pancreatic Cancer, 4472–1.314
Deaths Among Members of the Public Health Service Commissioned Corps, 1965-89, 4042–3.316
Debits and Deposit Turnover at Commercial Banks, 9365–2.5
Debt and Employment Volatility over the Business Cycle, 9366–6.286
Debt Buybacks Signal Sovereign Countries' Creditworthiness: Theory and Tests, 9366–6.294
Debt, Collateral, and U.S. Manufacturing Investment: 1954-80, 9377–9.141
Debt Conversions, 25368–181
Debt Covenants and Renegotiation, 9387–8.272
Debt Investment Securities Held by Banks. Market Value Accounting, 26111–77
Debt Limit Increase; Savings and Loan Costs, 25368–177
Debt Repayment Capacity of Commercial Farm Operators: How Much Debt Can Farmers Afford?, 1541–1.312
Decade of Decisions for Vital and Health Statistics, 1990's: Proceedings of the 1991 Public Health Conference on Records and Statistics, 4164–2
Decennial Census: 1990 Results Show Need for Fundamental Reform, 26119–403
Deciduous Fruit and Table Grape Update: World Apple and Pear Outlook and Southern Hemisphere Focus, 1925–34.307
Decline in American Voter Turnout. Statistical Brief, 2326–17.39
Defaults of Original Issue High-Yield Convertible Bonds, 9373–27.14
Defense Environmental Restoration Program Annual Report to Congress for FY91, 3544–36
Defense Force Management, 26123–392
Defense Force Management: Composition of Groups Affected by FY91 Force Reductions, 26123–373
Defense Force Management: Occupation Distribution and Composition, 26123–381
Defense Force Management. Statistics Related to DOD's Policy on Homosexuality, 26123–392.2
Defense Industries Making Adjustments. Statistical Brief, 2326–17.43
Defense Inventory: Control and Security Weaknesses Create Opportunities for Theft, 26123–377
Defense Procurement Fraud: Information on Plea Agreements and Settlements, 26119–423
Defense Procurement: Need To Improve Internal Controls on Deferred Contractor Debts, 26123–400
Defense Procurement: Trends for 1985-93 in DOD's Spending, Employment, and Contractors, 26123–399

Defense Spending for Counternarcotics Activities for FY89-91. Drug Control, 26123–390
Defense '92: Almanac, 3504–13
Deficit Reduction Act, 21308–28
Deficits and Long-Term Interest Rates: An Empirical Note, 9389–19.33
Delaware Valley Mortgage Plan: An Analysis Using HMDA Data, 9387–8.266
Demand for Land Information System Services: A Theoretical Framework, 1502–3.303
Demand for Older Workers: The Neglected Side of a Labor Market, 4746–14.16, 4746–26.21
Demand, Supply, and Price Outlook for Oxygenated Gasoline, Winter 1992-93, 3162–24.301
Democratic Party Closed Fundraising Gap with Republicans: Parties Show $85 Million Difference Through November 23, 9276–1.113
Demographic Change and the Economy of the Nineties, 23848–226
Demographic Issues Facing the Federal Government. Changing Workforce, 26119–383
Demographic Profile of Participants in Two Gulf of Mexico Inshore Shrimp Fisheries and Their Response to the Texas Closure, 2162–1.301
Demographic Profiles of the Airway Facilities Work Force, Annual Report, FY90 Year-End Data, 7504–41
Denial of SSI Applications Because of Excess Resources, 4742–1.317
Department of Defense Budget for FY93. Construction Programs (C-1), 3544–39
Department of Defense Budget for FY93. Procurement Programs (P-1), 3544–32
Department of Defense Budget for FY93. R, D, T & E Programs (R-1), 3544–33
Department of Defense Dependents Schools, Annual Test Report, School Year 1991-92, 3504–16
Department of Defense Inspector General, Semiannual Report to the Congress, Apr. 1-Sept. 30, 1991, 3542–18
Department of Defense Inspector General, Semiannual Report to the Congress, Oct. 1, 1991-Mar. 31, 1992, 3542–18
Department of Defense Inspector General, Semiannual Report to the Congress, Apr. 1-Sept. 30, 1992, 3542–18
Department of Defense Military Functions, Status of Funds, 3542–3
Department of Defense Prime Contract Awards, FY91, 3542–1
Department of Defense Prime Contract Awards, First Half FY92, 3542–1
Department of Defense Real and Personal Property, 3544–6
Department of Defense Selected Medical Care Statistics, 3542–15
Department of Education: The Eisenhower Math and Science State Grant Program, 26121–488
Department of Education's Race-Specific Scholarship Policy, 21408–130
Department of Energy Annual Procurement and Financial Assistance Report, FY91, 3004–21
Department of Energy Semiannual Report to Congress on Inspector General Audit Reports, 3002–15
Department of Energy's Superconducting Super Collider (SSC) Conventional Construction Program, 3006–5.32
Department of Interior News Releases, 5306–4
Department of Justice Announces Record $2 Billion Year for Environmental Enforcement, 6004–22
Department of Justice Announces Third Straight Record Year for Environmental Enforcement, 6008–37
Department of Justice Asset Forfeiture Program Annual Report, 6004–21
Department of the Treasury News, 8002–7
Department of Transportation News, 7306–10
Department Store Inventory Price Indexes, 6762–7
Dependence on the Persian Gulf, 3166–6.65
Deposit Growth, Nonperforming Assets, and Return on Assets, by County, 9381–14
Deposit Insurance Issues and Depositor Discipline, 21408–126
Depository Institutions: Contracting Practices with Data Processing Servicers, 26119–374
Derelict Ships, 2152–8.304
Derived Annual Estimates of Manufacturing Energy Consumption, 1974-88. Energy Consumption Series, 3166–15.3
Descriptive Compendium. USDA Revenues, 26113–602
Descriptive Epidemiology of Unintentional Residential Fire Injuries in King County, WA, 1984 and 1985, 4042–3.340
Destination Japan: A Business Guide for the 90s, 2048–159
Detailed Characteristics of Private Schools and Staff: 1987-88. Schools and Staffing Survey, 4836–3.8
Detailed Diagnoses and Procedures, National Hospital Discharge Survey, 1990. Vital and Health Statistics Series 13, 4147–13.111
Detecting Colorectal Cancer with a Large Scale Fecal Occult Blood Testing Program, 4042–3.333
Determinants of Long-Term Interest Rates: An Empirical Study of Several Industrial Countries, 9385–1.301
Determinants of Short-term Agricultural Loan Rates at Commercial Banks, 1541–1.307
Determination Letters Issued for Employee Benefit Plans, 8304–23
Determination of a Variable Price Support Schedule as Applied to Agricultural Production Control, 1502–3.301
Determining Margin for Futures Contracts: The Role of Private Interests and the Relevance of Excess Volatility, 9375–1.302
Development and Supermarket Field Testing of Videotaped Nutrition Messages for Cancer Risk Reduction, 4042–3.371
Development of Health Surveillance in Togo, West Africa, 4202–7.322
Development of Recycling Market, 21368–139
Development of the 1991 Manufacturing Energy Consumption Survey. Energy Consumption Series, 3166–15.2
Developments in the Pricing of Credit Card Services, 9362–1.306
Developments in the Spanish Rice Market Since Joining the European Community: Implications for the U.S. Rice Industry, 1561–8.304
Diatomite in 1991: Mineral Industry Surveys, Annual Report, 5614–5.8
Dichotomy Becomes Reality: Ten Years of the Federal Reserve as Regulator and Competitor, 9383–2
Did the Debt Crisis Cause the Investment Crisis?, 9366–7.272
Did the Debt Crisis or the Oil Price Decline Cause Mexico's Investment Collapse?, 9366–7.270
Diesels in Underground Mines: Measurement and Control of Particulate Emissions. Proceedings: Bureau of Mines Information and Technology Transfer Seminar, Minneapolis, Minn., Sept. 29-30, 1992, 5608–177
Dietary Fat and Postmenopausal Breast Cancer, 4472–1.328
Dietary Intake of Fiber and Decreased Risk of Cancers of the Colon and Rectum: Evidence from the Combined Analysis of 13 Case-Control Studies, 4472–1.358
Differences Between Black and White Women with Breast Cancer in Time from Symptom Recognition to Medical Consultation, 4472–1.323
Different Kind of Money Illusion: The Case of Long and Variable Lags, 9377–9.131
Difficulties in Denying Federal Benefits to Convicted Drug Offenders. Drug Control, 26119–398
Digest of Activities, FY91, U.S. Postal Inspection Service, 9864–9
Digest of Education Statistics, 1991, Pocket Digest, 4824–3
Digest of Education Statistics, 1992, 4824–2
Dimensionality and Construct Validity of the Perceptions of Organizational Politics Scale (POPS), 7506–10.106
Directorate for Engineering, FY91 Directory of Awards, 9624–24
Director's Report: A Review of the U.S. Marshals Service in FY91, 6294–1
Directory of Awards, FY89-90, Mechanical and Structural Systems, 9626–7.7
Directory of Companies and Plants Producing Salt in the U.S., 1991, 5614–30
Directory of Companies Required To File Annual Reports with the Securities and Exchange Commission Under the Securities Exchange Act of 1934, Alphabetically and by Industry Groups, Sept. 30, 1991, 9734–5
Directory of Computer Software, 2224–2
Directory of Energy Data Collection Forms, 3164–86
Directory of Energy Information Administration Models, 1992, 3164–87
Directory of ERIC Information Service Providers, 4814–4
Directory of Federally Insured Credit Unions, 9534–6
Directory of Industrial Sand and Gravel Producers in the U.S. in 1990: Mineral Industry Surveys, Annual Advance Summary Supplement, 5614–5.1
Directory of Industrial Sand and Gravel Producers in the U.S. in 1991: Mineral Industry Surveys, Annual Advance Summary Supplement, 5614–5.18
Directory of Library Research and Demonstration Projects 1976-1986: Abstracts of Funded Projects, 4878–5
Directory of Members: Eleventh District—Arizona, California, Nevada, Federal Home Loan Bank of San Francisco, 9304–23

Directory of Operating Small Business Investment Companies, 9762–4
Directory of Postsecondary Institutions, 1991-92, 4844–3
Directory of Postsecondary Institutions, 1991-92. Volume 1: 4-Year and 2-Year, 4844–3.1
Directory of Postsecondary Institutions, 1991-92. Volume 2: Less than 2-Year, 4844–3.2
Directory of Principal Aggregates Producers in the U.S. in 1991: Mineral Industry Surveys, Annual Advance Summary Supplement, 5614–5.16
Directory of Principal Sand and Gravel Producers in the U.S. in 1990: Mineral Industry Surveys, Annual Advance Summary Supplement, 5614–5.6
Directory of Principal U.S. Gem Stone Producers in 1991: Mineral Industry Surveys, Annual Advance Summary Supplement, 5614–5.5
Directory of Public Elementary and Secondary Education Agencies, 1990-91, 4834–1
Directory of Selected Early Childhood Programs, 1991-92, 4944–10
Directory of U.S. Government Software for Mainframes and Microcomputers, 2224–2
Disability Beneficiaries Who Work and Their Experience Under Program Incentives, 4742–1.312
Disability Benefits: Selected Data on Military and VA Recipients, 26121–470
Disability Compensation, Pension and Death Pension Data, 8602–8, 8604–13
Disability in Basic Life Activities Across the Life Span. Disability Statistics Report, 4946–1.1
Disability Risks of Chronic Illnesses and Impairments. Disability Statistics Report, 4946–1.2
Disability Statistics Reports, 4946–1
Disabled SSI Recipients Who Work, 4742–1.308
Disabled Yet Denied: Bureaucratic Injustice, 25148–45
Discovery To Fly Classified Defense Payload: STS-53 Mission, 9506–2.154
Discovery To Loft Satellite To Study Atmosphere, Ozone: STS-48 Mission, 9506–2.144
Dislocated Workers: Comparison of Assistance Programs, 26121–481
Distilled Spirits: Monthly Statistical Release, 8486–1.3
Distribution, Abundance and Behavior of Endangered Whales in the Alaskan Chukchi and Western Beaufort Seas, 1989, 5738–32
Distribution, Abundance and Behavior of Endangered Whales in the Alaskan Chukchi and Western Beaufort Seas, 1991: with a Review, 1982-91, 5738–32
Distribution and Abundance of Fishes and Invertebrates in Gulf of Mexico Estuaries, Volume I: Data Summaries, 2176–7.28
Distribution of Kemp's Ridley Sea Turtles (Lepidochelys kempi) Along the Texas Coast: An Atlas, 2168–132
Distribution of Loans Made by Six Specified Types, By Race or Ethnic Group, 1182–5
Distribution of Obligations by Marital Status, Race, Ethnic Group and Sex, 1182–8
Distribution of Personnel by State and by Selected Locations, Sept. 30, 1991, 3544–7
Distribution of Sales by Class of Customer. 1987 Census of Manufactures, 2497–4
Distribution of Selected Herbicides and Nitrate in the Mississippi River and Its Major Tributaries, April Through June 1991, 5666–27.34
District Agricultural Banks Ride High in the Saddle, 9391–16.306
District Bank Performance in 1991: More Ups than Downs, 9391–16.307
District Banks Navigate Recession's Waters, 9391–16.303
Divers Alert Network. 1990 Report on Diving Accidents and Fatalities, 2144–29
Dividing the Dollars: Issues in Adjusting Decennial Counts and Intercensal Estimates for Funds Distribution, 25408–120
Division of Science Resources Studies Project Summaries, 9624–21
Do Interest Rates Help Predict Inflation?, 9379–1.306
Do U.S. Health Care Costs Affect U.S. International Competitiveness?, 9882–16.302
DOD Commercial Activities Inventory, FY91, 3544–25
DOD Commercial Transportation: Savings Possible Through Better Audit and Negotiation of Rates, 26123–369
DOD Met Need for Chemical Suits and Masks, but Longer Term Actions Needed. Operation Desert Storm, 26123–387
DOD Service Academies: Academy Preparatory Schools Need a Clearer Mission and Better Oversight, 26123–380
DOD Training Fatalities for FY88-91. Military Training, 26123–397
DOD's Policy on Homosexuality. Defense Force Management ALT Defense Force Management. DOD's Policy on Homosexuality, 26123–392.1
DOE Real Property: A Yearly Statistical Handbook, 3004–28
DOE Research and Development Field Facilities Capsule Review, 3004–4
Does Aggregate Output Have a Unit Root?, 9379–12.85
Does California Drive the West? An Econometric Investigation of Regional Spillovers, 9393–8.306
Does the Federal Reserve Affect Asset Prices?, 9375–13.80
Does Veterans' Preference Need Updating? Federal Hiring, 26119–391
Does World Investment Demand Determine U.S. Exports?, 9366–7.277
Dollar Summary of Prime Contract Awards by State, Place, and Contractor, FY91, 3544–22
Domestic Cannabis Eradication/Suppression Program, 1991, 6284–4
Domestic Food Assistance Programs: Measuring Benefits to Producers, 1548–390
Domestic Monitor Program, 6282–2
Domestic Offices, Insured Commercial Bank Assets and Liabilities Consolidated Report of Condition, 9365–3
Domestic Uranium Mining and Milling Industry 1990, Viability Assessment, 3164–82
Domestic Waterborne Trade of the U.S., 1987-89, 7704–7
DOT Employment Facts, A Report to Management, FY91, 7304–18
DRAMs of One Megabit and Above from the Republic of Korea. Determination of the Commission in Investigation No. 731-TA-556 (Preliminary) Under the Tariff Act of 1930, Together with the Information Obtained in the Investigation, 9886–14.348
DRG 14 Validation Update: Specific Cerebrovascular Disorders Except Transient Ischemic Attacks, 4006–7.12
DRG 87: Pulmonary Edema and Respiratory Failure, 4006–7.6
DRG 416: Septicemia, 4006–7.8
DRG 468: Unrelated Operating Room Procedures, 4006–7.7
Driver License Administration Requirements and Fees, 1992, 7554–18
Driver Licenses, 1990, 7554–16
Dropout Rates in the U.S.: 1991, 4834–23
Drug Abuse Prevention Intervention Research: Methodological Issues, 4498–78
Drug Abuse Research: Federal Funding and Future Needs, 26131–99
Drug Abuse Services Research Series, 4496–11
Drug Abuse Treatment in Prisons and Jails, 4498–77
Drug Control: Communications Network Funding and Requirements Uncertain, 26123–372
Drug Control: Defense Spending for Counternarcotics Activities for FY89-91, 26123–390
Drug Control: Difficulties in Denying Federal Benefits to Convicted Drug Offenders, 26119–398
Drug Enforcement and Treatment in Prisons, 1990, 6066–19.70
Drug Enforcement by Police and Sheriffs' Departments, 1990, 6066–19.67
Drug Manufacturing Industry: A Prescription for Profits, 25148–44
Drug Treatment Capacity Expansion Program, 236–3.2
Drug Use Among American High School Students, College Students and Young Adults, 4494–4
Drug Use Forecasting, 6062–3
Drug Use Forecasting (DUF): A Program of the National Institute of Justice Cofunded by the Bureau of Justice Assistance, 6062–3
Drugs and Crime Data, 6066–29
Drugs and Crime Facts, 1991, 6064–30
Drunk Driving, 6066–19.69
Dry Film Photoresist from Japan. Determination of the Commission in Investigation No. 731-TA-622 (Preliminary) Under the Tariff Act of 1930, Together with the Information Obtained in the Investigation, 9886–14.359
Duck Stamp Collection, 1992-93, 5504–25
Dwight D. Eisenhower System of Interstate and Defense Highways: Route Log and Finder List, 7558–111
Dwight D. Eisenhower System of Interstate and Defense Highways Status of Development, 7552–5
Dynamic Analysis of Recent Changes in the Rate of Part-Time Employment, 9377–9.129
Dynamic Impacts of Monetary Policy: An Exercise in Tentative Identification, 9371–10.89
Dynamics of the Trade Balance and the Terms of Trade: The S-Curve, 9377–9.142

Early Corrective Action for Troubled Banks, 9292–4.301
Early Developmental Factors and Risk for Alcohol Problems, 4482–1.303
Early Estimates. National Postsecondary Statistics, Collegiate and Noncollegiate: Fall 1991, 4844–16
Early Estimates. Public and Private Elementary and Secondary Education Statistics, School Year 1991-92, 4834–19
Early Estimates. Public and Private Elementary and Secondary Education Statistics, School Year 1992-93, 4834–19
Early Intervention: Federal Investments Like WIC Can Produce Savings, 26121–458
Earned Income Tax Credit: Advance Payment Option Is Not Widely Known or Understood by the Public, 26119–378
Earnings and Employment Data for Wage and Salary Workers Covered Under Social Security by State and County, 1986, 4744–29
Earnings and Employment Data for Wage and Salary Workers Covered Under Social Security by State and County, 1987, 4744–29
Earnings and Employment Data for Wage and Salary Workers Covered Under Social Security by State and County, 1988, 4744–29
East European Energy: Romania's Energy Needs Persist, 26123–402
Eastern Europe Business Bulletin, 2042–33
Eastern Europe: Struggling To Stay on the Reform Track, 9118–13
Eastern North Pacific Hurricane Season—1991, 2152–8.302
East-West Trade-Statistics Monitoring System: Eleventh Annual Analysis of Manufactured Imports from the Monitored Countries, 9882–2.302
Ebbing Tide Lowers All Boats: Monetary Policy, Inflation, and Social Justice, 9377–1.306
EC Commission Opts for Quota Based Post 1992 EC Banana Regime, 1925–34.316
EC Wine Trade, 1925–34.324
EC 1992: Implications for World Food and Agricultural Trade, 1528–325
Ecological Characterization of the Tampa Bay Watershed, 5506–9.43
Ecology and Management of Northern Hardwood Forests in New England, 1208–405
Ecology: Community Profiles, 5506–9
Econometric Model of Capital Gains Realization Behavior, 8006–6.4
Economic Adjustment After the Cold War, 23848–224
Economic and Budget Outlook: An Update. A Report to the Senate and House Committees on the Budget, 26304–3.3
Economic and Budget Outlook: FY93-97. A Report to the Senate and House Committees on the Budget, 26304–3.1
Economic and Energy Indicators, 9112–1
Economic Availability of Woody Biomass Fuel Chips for 13 Southeastern States, 9806–9.13
Economic Censuses, 1987, CD-ROM Technical Documentation, 2306–8
Economic Censuses, 1987, Characteristics of Business Owners, 2328–59
Economic Censuses, 1987, on CD-ROM, 2326–22
Economic Cost of Alcohol Abuse, 4482–1.311
Economic Costs, Cost-Effectiveness, Financing, and Community-Based Drug Treatment, 4498–80
Economic Development Administration, 1991 Annual Report, 2064–2
Economic Dimensions of Household Gift-Giving, 6886–6.90
Economic Discussion Papers, 6366–3
Economic Effects of Immigrants on Native and Foreign-Born Workers: Complementarity, Substitutability, and Other Channels of Influence, 6366–6.12
Economic Effects of Reduced Defense Spending, 26306–6.167
Economic Effects of the Savings and Loan Crisis, 26306–6.165
Economic Effects of Western Federal Land-Use Restrictions on U.S. Coal Markets, 5668–125
Economic Forecasts for the Pacific Northwest, 3224–5
Economic Growth of OECD Countries, 7144–8
Economic Impact of Travel on Scenic Byways. Final Case Study for the National Scenic Byways Study, 7556–8.1
Economic Impacts of Scenic Byways. Final Case Study for the National Scenic Byways Study, 7556–8.3
Economic Impacts of SEPTA on the Regional and State Economy, 7308–205
Economic Implications of Rising Health Care Costs, 26306–6.174
Economic Indicators, 23842–1
Economic Indicators of the Farm Sector: Costs of Production, 1544–20
Economic Indicators of the Farm Sector: Costs of Production. Livestock and Dairy, 1990, 1544–20.2
Economic Indicators of the Farm Sector: Costs of Production. Major Field Crops, 1990, 1544–20.1
Economic Indicators of the Farm Sector: Production and Efficiency Statistics, 1990, 1544–17
Economic Indicators of the Farm Sector: State Financial Summary, 1990, 1544–18
Economic Liberalization in the Americas, 9379–2
Economic Outlook at Midyear, 23848–230
Economic Outlook, Tennessee Valley Authority, 9804–27
Economic Perspectives: Federal Reserve Bank of Chicago, 9375–1
Economic Profile of the Dallas-Fort Worth Metropolitan Area, 1991, 6964–2
Economic Profile of the Houston Metropolitan Area, 1991, 6964–1
Economic Rents, the Demand for Capital, and Financial Structure, 9373–27.8
Economic Report of the President, Transmitted to the Congress February 1992 Together with the Annual Report of the Council of Economic Advisers, 204–1
Economic Report of the President, 1991, 23844–4
Economic Research Service in 1992, 1504–6
Economic Retirement Studies: An Annotated Bibliography, 4746–26.14
Economic Review, Federal Reserve Bank of Atlanta, 9371–1
Economic Review, Federal Reserve Bank of Cleveland, 9377–1
Economic Review, Federal Reserve Bank of Dallas, 9379–1
Economic Review, Federal Reserve Bank of Kansas City, 9381–1
Economic Review, Federal Reserve Bank of Richmond, 9389–1
Economic Review, Federal Reserve Bank of San Francisco, 9393–8
Economic Status of Black Women: An Exploratory Investigation, 11048–191
Economic Status of Rural Older Americans, 1504–9.1
Economic Status of the Aged, 4742–1.320
Economic Theory and BEA's Alternative Quantity and Price Indexes, 2702–1.315
Economic Transition and U.S. Assistance. Poland and Hungary, 26123–386
Economic Trends, Federal Reserve Bank of Cleveland, 9377–10
Economic Well-Being of Farm Operator Households, 1990, 1541–1.315
Economics Update, Federal Reserve Bank of Atlanta, 9371–15
Economy-Wide Modeling of the Economic Implications of a FTA with Mexico and a NAFTA with Canada and Mexico. Addendum to the Report on Investigation No. 332-317 Under Section 332 of the Tariff Act of 1930, 9886–4.182
Economy-Wide Modeling of the Economic Implications of a FTA with Mexico and a NAFTA with Canada and Mexico. Report on Investigation No. 332-317 Under Section 332 of the Tariff Act of 1930, 9886–4.182
ECP Monthly Progress Report, By State and Area for Period Ending (Date), 1802–13
Ecuador, FY93-94, 9916–12.51
Educating the American Indian/Alaska Native Family, Annual Report to the U.S. Congress, 14874–1
Education and Rural Economic Development: Strategies for the 1990's, 1598–277
Educational and Nonprofit Institutions Receiving Prime Contract Awards for Research, Development, Test, and Evaluation, FY91, 3544–17
Educational Attainment in the U.S.: March 1991 and 1990, 2546–1.460
Educational Attainment of Farm Operators, 1541–1.316
Educational Differences in Health Status and Health Care. Vital and Health Statistics Series 10, 4147–10.180
Effect of a Rating Change on Commercial Paper Outstandings, 9366–6.299
Effect of Changes in Reserve Requirements on Investment and GNP, 9375–13.72
Effect of Immigration Reform on Collective Bargaining in the California Fruit and Vegetable Processing Industry, 6366–6.5
Effect of Marginal Tax Rates on Capital Gains Revenue: Another Look at the Evidence, 8006–6.3
Effect of Price Dispersion on Cost of Living Indexes, 6886–6.82
Effect of the OBRA 1989 Payment Provision for Small Rural Medicare-Dependent Hospitals, 17206–2.42
Effect of the 65 MPH Speed Limit on Travel Speeds and Related Crashes, 7768–121
Effect of Transitional Dynamics on the Distribution of Wealth in a Neoclassical Capital Accumulation Model, 9387–8.261
Effectiveness, Costs, and Cost-Effectiveness of Recruitment Strategies for a Mammographic Screening Program To Detect Breast Cancer, 4472–1.318

Effectiveness of Federal Assistance Programs in Meeting Fiscal Distress, Part I, 21248–172
Effectiveness of Tribal JOBS Programs Unknown. Welfare to Work, 26121–460
Effects of Adopting a Value-Added Tax, 26306–6.168
Effects of Alcohol on the Male Reproductive System, 4482–1.307
Effects of an Oil Spill and Freeze Event on Intertidal Community Structure in Washington, 5738–38.2
Effects of Changing the Tax Treatment of Fringe Benefits. Tax Policy, 26119–389
Effects of Color Vision Deficiency on Detection of Color-Highlighted Targets in a Simulated Air Traffic Control Display, 7506–10.102
Effects of Countercyclical Monetary Policy on Money and Interest Rates: An Evaluation of Evidence from FOMC Documents, 9387–8.259
Effects of Credit Availability, Nonbank Competition, and Tax Reform on Bank Consumer Lending, 9379–12.88
Effects of Environmental Actions on Tuna Trade, 9882–16.303
Effects of FTC Antitrust Challenges on Rival Firms 1981-87: An Analysis of the Use of Stock Returns To Determine the Competitive Effects of Horizontal Mergers, 9408–55
Effects of Greater Economic Integration Within the European Community on the U.S.: Fourth Followup Report. Investigation No. 332-267, 9886–4.181
Effects of Harvest on Feral Rock Dove Survival, Nest Success, and Population Size. Fish and Wildlife Technical Report, 5506–12.4
Effects of Legislating Prompt Corrective Action on the Bank Insurance Fund, 9391–1.312
Effects of Migration on Cancer Incidence and Resources for Prevention and Treatment in Florida, 4042–3.339
Effects of Procedural Differences Between 1977 and 1987 in the Nationwide Food Consumption Survey on Estimates of Food and Nutrient Intakes: Results of the USDA 1988 Bridging Study, 1358–6
Effects of Removing 70- and 71-Year-Olds from Coverage Under the Social Security Earnings Test, 4746–26.13
Effects of Seating Configuration and Number of Type III Exits on Emergency Aircraft Evacuation, 7506–10.124
Effects of Subordinate Feedback to the Supervisor and Participation in Decision-Making in the Prediction of Organizational Support, 7506–10.113
Effects of Tax Changes on Commuter Behavior. Mass Transit, 26113–597
Effects of the Clean Air Act, Amendment of 1990 on the U.S. Coke and Steel Industry and Foreign Trade Balance, 5606–5.10
Effects of the Gates Park Fire on Recreation Choices, 1208–422
Effects of the 65 mph Speed Limit Through 1990, A Report to Congress, 7764–15
Effects of Utility DSM Programs on Risk, 3308–105
Efficiency and Welfare Effects of Tax Reform: Are Fewer Tax Brackets Better Than More?, 9377–9.143
Efficiency in the Savings and Loan Industry, 9387–8.277
Efficient Resolution of Moral Hazard via Capital Market: Monitoring Banks, 9366–6.292
Egg Products, 1625–2
Eggs, Chickens, and Turkeys, 1625–1
EIA Analysis Brief: The Former Soviet Republics, 3168–126
EIA Publications Directory, 1991, 3164–98
EIA Service Reports, 3166–6
Eighth Report to Congress, Health Personnel in the U.S., 1991, 4114–8
Eighth to Tenth Grade Dropouts, 4826–10.3
Eisenhower Math and Science State Grant Program. Department of Education, 26121–488
Elderly Americans: Health, Housing, and Nutrition Gaps Between the Poor and Nonpoor, 26131–100
Elderly at Risk from Mishandled Medications. Board and Care Homes, 26121–447
Election Signature Retrieval Systems, 9278–8
Electric and Hybrid Vehicles Program, 15th Annual Report to Congress for FY91, 3304–2
Electric Consumers Protection Act's Effects on Licensing Hydroelectric Dams. Electricity Regulation, 26113–599
Electric Household Appliances and Certain Heating Equipment, Industry and Trade Summary, 9885–9.4
Electric Housewares and Fans, 1991, Current Industrial Report, 2506–12.15
Electric Lamps, Current Industrial Report, 2506–12.13, 2506–12.33
Electric Lighting Fixtures, 1991, Current Industrial Report, 2506–12.19
Electric Plant Cost and Power Production Expenses, 1990, 3164–9
Electric Power Annual, 1990, 3164–11
Electric Power Monthly, 3162–35
Electric Power Supply and Demand for the Contiguous U.S., Staff Report, 3404–6
Electric Sales and Revenue, 1990, 3164–91
Electric Utility Demand-Side Management, 3162–35.302
Electricity Regulation: Electric Consumers Protection Act's Effects on Licensing Hydroelectric Dams, 26113–599
Electricity Sales Statistics, 9802–1
Electricity Sales Statistics, 1991, 9804–14
Electricity Transmission Access. National Energy Strategy, Technical Annex 3, 3006–13.3
Electric-Utility DSM Programs: Terminology and Reporting Formats, 3308–101
Electric-Utility DSM Programs: 1990 Data and Forecasts to 2000, 3308–106
Electromedical Equipment and Irradiation Equipment (Including X-Ray), 1991, Current Industrial Report, 2506–12.34
Embassies in the Former Soviet Union. Overseas Staffing, 26123–403
Emergency Conservation Program (ECP) Monthly Progress Report, By State and Area for Period Ending (Date), 1802–13
Emergency Conservation Program, FY91 Statistical Summary, 1804–22
Emergency Striped Bass Research Study, Report for 1990, 5504–29
Emerging Importance of Aquaculture, 9391–16.301
Empirical Investigation of Money Demand in the Cash-In-Advance Model Framework, 9387–8.279
Empirical Test of the Incentive Effects of Deposit Insurance: The Case of Junk Bonds at Savings and Loan Associations, 9375–13.69
Employed Persons Who Work at Home, 6726–1.52
Employee Benefits: Financing Health Benefits of Coal Industry Retirees, 26121–469
Employee Benefits: Financing Health Benefits of Retired Coal Miners, 26121–471
Employee Benefits in State and Local Governments, 1990, 6784–21
Employee Benefits: States Need Labor's Help Regulating Multiple Employer Welfare Arrangements, 26121–443
Employee Conduct Standards: Some Outside Activities Present Conflict-of-Interest Issues, 26119–386
Employee Misconduct: Justice Should Clearly Document Investigative Actions, 26119–380
Employee Payments for Health Care Services, 6722–1.348
Employee Tenure and Occupational Mobility in the Early 1990s, 6726–1.47
Employee Turnover and Job Openings Survey: Results of a Pilot Study on the Feasibility of Collecting Measures of Imbalances of Supply and Demand for Labor in an Establishment Survey, 6728–40
Employee Views on Integrity and Willingness To Report Misconduct. Internal Revenue Service, 26119–366
Employer Costs for Employee Compensation, March 1991, 6744–21
Employer Costs for Employee Compensation, March 1992, 6744–21
Employer Layoff and Recall Practices, 6406–6.36
Employer-Based Health Insurance: High Costs, Wide Variation Threaten System, 26121–485
Employers' Experiences in Complying with the Hazard Communication Standard. Occupational Safety and Health, 26121–456
Employment and Earnings, 6742–2, 6744–4
Employment and Earnings Characteristics of Families, 6742–21
Employment and Unemployment Among Youth, Summer 1992, 6744–14
Employment and Unemployment: Area Trends, 6402–1
Employment Cost Index, 6782–5
Employment Cost Index for the South, 6942–8
Employment Cost Indexes and Levels, 1975-91, 6744–20
Employment Cost Indexes and Levels, 1975-92, 6744–20
Employment Data on T.38 Physicians, Dentists and Nurses, 8602–6
Employment Growth in Largest Metropolitan Areas, 1991, 6946–3.24
Employment, Hours, and Earnings, Revised Establishment Data, 6744–4
Employment, Hours, and Earnings, States and Areas, 1987-92, 6748–81
Employment in Perspective: Minority Workers, 6742–18
Employment in Perspective: Women in the Labor Force, 6742–17
Employment Obstacles Experienced by Foreign-Born Workers in New York City Because of the Employer Sanctions Provisions of the Immigration Reform and Control Act of 1986, 6366–6.7

Employment Situation, 6742–5
Employment-Unemployment, Monthly Hearings, 23846–4
En Route Air Traffic Controllers' Use of Flight Progress Strips: A Graph-Theoretic Analysis, 7506–10.127
Encapsulation of Pesticides in Starch, 1504–9.1
Endangered Species Act: Types and Number of Implementing Actions, 26113–578
Endangered Species: Past Actions Taken To Assist Columbia River Salmon, 26113–577
Endogenous Financial Innovation and the Demand for Money, 9389–19.34
End-Stage Renal Disease Payment Policy, 17206–1.17
End-Stage Renal Disease, 1990. Health Care Financing Research Report, 4654–16
Energy and Related Statistics, 2326–7.84
Energy Conservation Indicators, 3164–73
Energy Consumption Series, 3166–15
Energy Efficiency, Technological Change, and the Dieselization of U.S. Agriculture, 1561–16.301
Energy Facts, 1990, 3164–76
Energy, Food Prices Helped Slow Inflation in 1991, 6722–1.322
Energy Information Administration Annual Report to Congress, 1991, 3164–29
Energy Management and Control Quarterly, 8602–9
Energy Management Annual Report, FY91, 9804–26
Energy Management: Better Federal Oversight of Territories' Oil Overcharge Funds Needed, 26113–564
Energy Production and Conservation Act of 1990, 25318–84
Energy Related Inventions Program, A Joint Program of the Department of Energy and the National Institute of Standards and Technology: Status Report, 2214–5
Energy Reports and Testimony: 1990, 26106–10.6
Energy Reports and Testimony: 1991, 26106–10.6
Energy Security: A Comparison of Protectionist Policies, 9379–12.96
Enforcement Accomplishments Report, FY91, 9184–21
Engineer Work Shift Length and Schedule Variability. Railroad Safety, 26113–579
Enhancement of Drug Detection and Identification by Use of Various Derivatizing Reagents on GC-FTIR Analysis, 7506–10.112
Enterprise for the Americas Initiative, 1502–4.301
Environmental Assessment of Remedial Action at the Falls City Uranium Mill Tailings Site, Falls City, Texas, 3356–4.10
Environmental Assessment of Remedial Action at the Gunnison Uranium Mill Tailings Site Near Gunnison, Colo., 3356–4.12
Environmental Assessment of Remedial Action at the Lowman Uranium Mill Tailings Site Near Lowman, Idaho, 3356–4.11
Environmental Challenges and Opportunities, 1504–9.1
Environmental Compliance Summary, U.S. Department of Energy's Hanford Site, 1991, 3324–2.8
Environmental Constraints in East and Southeast Asia: Potential for Changing Patterns of Agricultural Production and Trade, 1524–4.3
Environmental Crisis in the Gulf: The U.S. Response, 9188–117
Environmental Excise Taxes, 1989, 8302–2.303
Environmental Monitoring and Disposal of Radioactive Wastes from U.S. Naval Nuclear-Powered Ships and Their Support Facilities, 1991, 3804–11
Environmental Progress and Challenges: EPA's Update, 9184–16
Environmental Protection Agency, Office of the Inspector General Report to the Congress, 9182–10
Environmental Quality: The Twenty-second Annual Report of the Council on Environmental Quality Together with the President's Message to Congress, 484–1
Environmental Radiation Data, 9192–5
Environmental Research Laboratories Publication Abstracts, FY91, 2144–25
Environmental Tobacco Smoke and Lung Cancer Risk in Nonsmoking Women, 4472–1.342
EPA Aerometric Information Retrieval System (AIRS) Air Quality Subsystem, 9194–5
EPA Publications Bibliography, Quarterly Abstract Bulletin, 9182–5
EPA Research Program Guide, FY92, 9184–17
EPA's Permit Compliance System Could Be Used More Effectively. Water Pollution Monitoring, 26125–46
Epidemiologic Trends in Drug Abuse. Community Epidemiology Work Group Proceedings, December 1991, 4492–5.1
Epidemiologic Trends in Drug Abuse. Community Epidemiology Work Group Proceedings, June 1992, 4492–5.2
Epidemiology and Biostatistics Program, FY91 Report, 4474–29
Epidemiology of Resting Pulse Rate of Persons Ages 25-74—Data from NHANES 1971-74, 4042–3.321
Equatorial Wind, Current and Temperature Data: 108 Degrees West to 140 Degrees West; Apr. 1983-Oct. 1987, 2148–62
Errata: National Income and Product Accounts, 2702–1.307, 2702–1.333
Errata: U.S. Affiliates of Foreign Companies, 2702–1.337
Error Correction in Modems Employing Asynchronous-To-Synchronous Conversion. Telecommunications Standard, 2216–2.212
Escalation and Producer Price Indexes: A Guide for Contracting Parties, 6888–23
Establishing Priorities in Science Funding, 21268–43
Estate Tax Statistics for 1989-90: Data Release, 8302–2.305
Estimated Oil and Gas Reserves, Gulf of Mexico, Dec. 31, 1990, 5734–6
Estimated Oil and Gas Reserves: Pacific Outer Continental Shelf (as of Dec. 31, 1990), 5734–7
Estimates from Two Survey Designs: National Hospital Discharge Survey. Vital and Health Statistics Series 13, 4147–13.110
Estimates of Median Four-Person Family Income, by State: 1974-89, 2626–2.60
Estimates of Mortgage Originations by State, 1982-90, 5144–21
Estimates of Recreation Use in the White River Drainage, Vermont, 1208–400
Estimates of the Effects of FAS 106 on Corporate Earnings, 9366–6.298
Estimates of the Resident Population of States: July 1, 1991 and Apr. 1, 1990, 2324–10
Estimates of the Resident Population of States: July 1, 1992 and July 1, 1991, and Components of Change Since July 1, 1991, 2324–10
Estimates of U.S. Biofuels Consumption, 1990, 3164–97
Estimating a Firm's Age-Productivity Profile Using the Present Value of Workers' Earnings, 9377–9.128
Estimating House Price Appreciation: A Comparison of Methods, 9387–8.284
Estimating Monthly Regional Value Added by Combining Regional Input with National Production Data, 9375–13.85
Estimating the Prevalence of Chronic Fatigue Syndrome and Associated Symptoms in the Community, 4042–3.354
Estimating the Prevalence of Mental Disorders in U.S. Adults from the Epidemiologic Catchment Area Survey, 4042–3.368
Estimating the Probability of Spontaneous Abortion in the Presence of Induced Abortion and Vice Versa, 4042–3.324
Estimation of a Water Budget for the Central Part of the Western San Joaquin Valley, California. Regional Aquifer-System Analysis, 5666–25.14
Estimation of Household Net Worth Using Model-Based and Design-Based Weights: Evidence from the 1989 Survey of Consumer Finances, 9368–91
Ethnicity, Location, Age, and Fluoridation Factors in Baby Bottle Tooth Decay and Caries Prevalence of Head Start Children, 4042–3.317
Europeans Strive To Untangle Rural from Agricultural Policy, 1502–7.301
EUVE Satellite To Explore Newly Opened Window: Extreme Ultraviolet Explorer Mission, 9506–2.149
Evaluating the Accuracy of Sampling-Based Approaches to the Calculation of Posterior Moments, 9383–20.18
Evaluating the Impact of Grassroots Development Funding: An Experimental Methodology Applied to Eight IAF Projects, 14428–1
Evaluating the 1990 Projections of Occupational Employment, 6722–1.336
Evaluating Your Firm's Injury and Illness Record, 6886–4
Evaluation of an Alternative Method for Hiring Air Traffic Control Specialists with Prior Military Experience, 7506–10.101
Evaluation of Head Impact Kinematics for Passengers Seated Behind Interior Walls, 7506–10.120
Evaluation of Labor Force Projections to 1990, 6722–1.334
Evaluation of New Canal Point Sugarcane Clones, 1991-92 Harvest Season, 1704–2
Evaluation of Subjective Poverty Definitions Comparing Results from the U.S. and the Netherlands, 6886–6.84
Evaluation of the Asbestos Hazard Emergency Response Act (AHERA): Final Report, 9238–71
Evaluation of the Asbestos Hazard Emergency Response Act (AHERA): Summary Report, 9238–71

Evaluation of the Effectiveness of Occupant Protection, Federal Motor Vehicle Safety Standard 208, Interim Report, 7768–123
Evaluation of the Low-Income Housing Tax Credit, Final Report, 5188–133
Evaluation of the Oregon Medicaid Proposal, 26358–254
Evaluation of the Small Business Administration's 7(a) Guaranteed Business Loan Program, 9768–25
Evaluation of the Vermont Worksite Smoking Law, 4042–3.375
Evaluation of Winners and Losers Under Medicare's Prospective Payment System, 17206–2.38
Even Start: Abstracts, 1989, 4804–41
Even Start: Abstracts, 1990, 4804–41
Evidence from Tests of the Relation Between Interest-Rate Spreads and Economic Activity, 9385–8.131
Evidence of Improved Inventory Control, 9389–1.302
Evidence on the Size of Banking Markets from Mortgage Loan Rates in Twenty Cities, 9366–1.162
Evolution of Employer-Provided Defined Benefit Pensions, 6722–1.303
Evolution of the U.S. Commercial Paper Market Since 1980, 9362–1.308
Evolution of U.S. Trade with China, 9385–1.303
Ex Ante Risk and Ex Post Collapse of S&Ls in the 1980s, 9375–1.306
Examination of Change in Energy Dependence and Efficiency in the Six Largest Energy Using Countries: 1970-88, 9375–13.79
Examination of Winners and Losers Under Medicare's Prospective Payment System: A Synthesis of the Evidence, 17206–2.36
Excess Mortality in Guatemala: A Comparison of Causes of Death in Guatemala and Costa Rica, 2326–18.64
Exchange Rate Policy and Shocks to Asset Markets: The Case of Taiwan in the 1980s, 9393–8.303
Exchange Rate Variability and International Trade, 9371–1.304
Exclusive Economic Zone Adjacent to Hawaii and Johnston Island. Final Environmental Impact Statement, 5736–7.1
Expanded HMDA Data on Residential Lending: One Year Later, 9362–1.307
Expectations, Demand Shifts, and Milk Supply Response, 1502–3.303
Expected Impacts of Clean Water Legislation on Agriculture, 1504–9.1
Expected Principal Source of Payment for Hospital Discharges: U.S., 1990, 4146–8.221
Expenditures for Food Away from Home, 1702–1.308
Expenditures for Nonresidential Improvements and Repairs, 1989. Current Construction Reports: Special Studies, 2388–4
Expenditures for Residential Improvements and Repairs, Current Construction Reports, 2382–7
Experience of the Stafford Loan Program and Options for Change, 26306–3.120
Experiences in Child Care and Early Childhood Programs of First and Second Graders, 4826–10.2
Experimental Plasma Research Project Summaries, 3004–18.5
Explaining Resource Consumption Among Non-Normal Neonates, 4652–1.303
Explaining the Persistence of the U.S. Trade Deficit in the Late 1980s, 9385–1.302
Exploratory Study of the Relationship Between Hypertension and Diet Diversity Among Saba Islanders, 4042–3.343
Exploring New Methods for Collecting Students' School-Based Writing. NAEP's 1990 Portfolio Study, 4896–8.4
Explosives Incidents Report, 1990, 8484–4
Explosives Incidents Report, 1991, 8484–4
Export Administration Annual Report, FY91, 2024–1
Export Market Report, Textiles and Apparel, 2042–36
Export Markets for U.S. Grain and Products, 1925–2.4
Exposures from Headset Interference Tones, 7506–10.100
Extended Measures of Well-Being, 2546–20.22
Extension System's Commitment to Independent Living for Older Americans, 1504–9.1
Extent and Adequacy of Insurance Coverage for Substance Abuse Services (Institute of Medicine Report: Treating Drug Problems). Volume 1: A Study of the Evolution, Effectiveness, and Financing of Public and Private Drug Treatment Systems, 4496–11.2
Extent and Adequacy of Insurance Coverage for Substance Abuse Services (Institute of Medicine Report: Treating Drug Problems). Volume 2: Commissioned Papers on Historical, Institutional, and Economic Contexts of Drug Treatment, 4496–11.3
External Adjustment in Selected Developing Countries in the 1990s, 9366–7.271
Extramural Trends, FY82-91, 4434–9
Extruded Rubber Thread from Malaysia. Determination of the Commission in Investigation No. 731-TA-527 (Final) Under the Tariff Act of 1930, Together with the Information Obtained in the Investigation, 9886–14.360

FAA Air Traffic Activity, FY91, 7504–27
FAA Aviation Forecast, Annual Conference Proceedings, 7504–28
FAA Aviation Forecasts, 7506–7
FAA Aviation Forecasts: Columbus, 7506–7.43
FAA Aviation Forecasts, FY92-2003, 7504–6
FAA Aviation Forecasts: Seattle-Tacoma Hub, 7506–7.44
FAA Aviation Forecasts: Washington/Baltimore Hub, 7506–7.42
FAA Aviation Industry Drug Test Results, 7502–17
FAA Flight Service Station Facility Level Forecast, FY92-2002, 7504–39
FAA Statistical Handbook of Aviation, 1990, 7504–1
Facilities, 1992, Federal Bureau of Prisons, 6244–4
Fact Book: National Cancer Institute, 4474–13
Fact Sheet, Dept of Defense, Worldwide Military Strength, 3542–9
Fact Sheet: Drug Data Summary, 6066–29.1
Factfinder for the Nation, 2326–7
Factors Affecting Black-White Income Differentials: A Decomposition, 2546–6.79
Factors Affecting Reserves of Depository Institutions and Condition Statement of Federal Reserve Banks, 9365–1
Factors Affecting the Availability and Use of Hemodialysis Facilities, 4652–1.306
Factors Affecting the Demand for Grazed Forage in the U.S., 1208–404
Factors Affecting U.S. Trade and Investment. Chilean Trade, 26119–408
Factors Associated with Rates of Participation in WIC by Eligible Pregnant Women, 4042–3.305
Factors Contributing to Rapid Growth in National Expenditures on Health Care, 9366–6.296
Factors That Affect Construction and Operations Costs. State and Federal Prisons, 26119–407
Facts on Working Women, 6564–1
Failed Bank Resolution and the Collateral Crunch: The Advantages of Adopting Transferable Puts, 9373–27.13
Fall Staff in Postsecondary Institutions, 1989, 4844–18
Fall Water Supply Summary for the Western U.S., 1992, 1264–4
Families on a Treadmill: Work and Income in the 1980s, 23848–225
Families with High Housing Expenditures: A Comparison of Homeowners and Renters, 1702–1.304
Family and Medical Leave Act of 1991, 25548–105
Family Economics Review, 1702–1
Family Versus Individually Oriented Intervention for Weight Loss in Mexican American Women, 4042–3.356
Famine-Affected, Refugee, and Displaced Populations: Recommendations for Public Health Issues, 4206–2.63
Fannie Mae National Housing Survey, 9478–1
Fannie Mae, The U.S.A.s Housing Partner: 1991 Annual Report, 9474–1
Farm and Housing Activity Report, 1182–1
Farm Credit Administration, Annual Report, 1991, 9264–2
Farm Credit System Annual Information Statement, 9264–5.2
Farm Credit System Outlook, 1504–9.1
Farm Credit System, Quarterly Information Statement, 9262–2
Farm Economy Turns Down, 9381–1.303
Farm Equity by State, Ranked Three Ways, 1541–1.303
Farm Financial Performance by Farm Credit District, 1980, 1985, and 1990, 1541–1.317
Farm Income Outlook: Following 1990's Records, 1504–9.1
Farm Labor, 1631–1
Farm Numbers, Land in Farms, 1614–4
Farm Production Expenditures, 1991 Summary, 1614–3
Farm Sector Balance Sheet, Including Operator Households, 1960-89, and Excluding Operator Households, 1974-89: By Sales Class, 1548–387
Farm Sector Balance Sheet, Including Operator Households, 1960-89: U.S. and by State, 1548–384
Farm Storage, Drying Equipment, Wet Storage, Forage and Silage, Hay Storage, and Solar Equipment Loans, 1802–9

Farmer Cooperative Statistics, 1990, 1124–1
Farmer Cooperatives, 1122–1
Farmer Cooperatives in the U.S., 1126–1
Farmer Mac: Can It Help Indebted Farm Operators?, 1541–1.304
Farmer Program (CONACT) Property in Inventory, National Summary, 1182–6
Farmer Response to Changes in Climate: The Case of Corn Production, 1502–3.302
Farmers Home Administration: Billions of Dollars in Farm Loans Are at Risk, 26113–569
Farmers Home Administration Report for FY91, 1184–17
Farmland Prices, Past and Prospective, 1561–16.302
Farmline, 1502–6
Farm-Raised Shrimp: Impacts on U.S. Seafood Trade, 1561–15.301
Fast Response Survey System, 4826–1
Fatal Accident Reporting System, 1990: A Review of Information on Fatal Traffic Crashes in the U.S., 7764–10
Fatal Work Injuries: Census for 31 States, 6722–1.338
Fats and Oils: Oilseed Crushings, Current Industrial Report, 2506–4.3
Fats and Oils: Production, Consumption, and Stocks, Current Industrial Report, 2506–4.4
Fats, Cholesterol, and Sodium Intake in the Diet of Persons 1-74 Years: U.S., 4147–16.6
FBI Fingerprint Identification Automation Program: Issues and Options, 26358–253
FDA Approval Should Be Withheld Until the Mastitis Issue Is Resolved. Recombinant Bovine Growth Hormone, 26131–101
FDA Needs To Ensure More Study of Gender Differences in Prescription Drug Testing. Women's Health, 26121–486
FDA Quarterly Activities Report, 4062–3
FDA Regulations: Sustained Management Attention Needed To Improve Timely Issuance, 26121–453
FDIC Banking Review, 9292–4
Feasibility of Interactive Videodisc Technology To Teach Minority Youth About Preventing HIV Infection, 4042–3.332
FEC Announces 1992 Party Spending Limits—Amounts Range from $110,480 to $2.5 Million, 9276–1.100
FEC Announces 1992 Presidential Spending Limits, 9276–1.97
FEC Approves Matching Funds for 1992 Presidential Candidates, 9276–1.98
FEC Finds Congressional Campaign Spending Up $75 Million as 1992 General Election Approaches, 9276–1.112
FEC Index of Communication Costs, 1989-90, 9274–3
FEC Index of Communication Costs, 1991-92, 9274–3
FEC Releases Mid-Year 1992 PAC Count, 9276–1.107
FEC Releases 1991 Year-End PAC Count, 9276–1.96
FEC Reports on Financial Activity, 9276–2
FEC Reports on Financial Activity, 1989-90: Final Report, Party and Non-Party Political Committees, 9276–2.1
FEC Reports on Financial Activity, 1989-90: Final Report, U.S. Senate and House Campaigns, 9276–2.2
Federal Advisory Committees, Twentieth Annual Report of the President, FY91, 9454–18
Federal Agency Collection and Use of Performance Data. Program Performance Measures, 26119–396
Federal Agency Performance for Minority Business Development, FY90, 2104–5
Federal Agency Performance for Minority Business Development, FY91, 2104–5
Federal Aid in Sport Fish and Wildlife Restoration Funds, 5502–1
Federal Aid in Sport Fish and Wildlife Restoration Programs, 1990, 5504–1
Federal Alternative Fuel Program Light Duty Vehicle Operations, First Annual Report to Congress for FY91, 3304–28
Federal Audiovisual Activity, FY91, 9514–1
Federal Aviation Administration, 29th Annual Financial Report, FY91, 7504–10
Federal Budget Estimates, FY93, 2702–1.310
Federal Buildings: Many Are Threatened by Earthquakes, but Limited Action Has Been Taken, 26119–399
Federal Bureau of Prisons Annual Statistical Report, FY87, 6244–1
Federal Bureau of Prisons Annual Statistical Report, FY88, 6244–1
Federal Bureau of Prisons Annual Statistical Report, FY89, 6244–1
Federal Capital Improvements Program, National Capital Region, FY92-96, 15454–1
Federal Civilian Work Years and Personnel Costs in the Executive Branch for FY91, 9842–1.303
Federal Civilian Workforce Statistics: Affirmative Employment Statistics, 9844–27
Federal Civilian Workforce Statistics, Employment and Trends, 9842–1
Federal Civilian Workforce Statistics: Pay Structure of the Federal Civil Service, Mar. 31, 1991, 9844–6
Federal Civilian Workforce Statistics: Work Years and Personnel Costs, Executive Branch, U.S. Government, FY90, 9844–31
Federal Coastal Wetland Mapping Programs, 5508–116
Federal Communications Commission 56th Annual Report, FY90, 9284–4
Federal Communications Commission 57th Annual Report, FY91, 9284–4
Federal Construction-Related Expenditures: Errata, 2042–1.303
Federal Criminal Case Processing, 1980-90: With Preliminary Data for 1991, 6064–31
Federal Deposit Insurance Corporation 1990 Annual Report, 9294–1
Federal Deposit Insurance Corporation 1990 Merger Decisions, 9294–5
Federal Deposit Insurance Corporation 1991 Annual Report, 9294–1
Federal Disability Insurance Trust Fund, 8102–9.14
Federal Efforts To Enhance the Competitiveness of Small Manufacturers. Technology Transfer, 26113–551
Federal Election Commission, Annual Report, 1991, 9274–1
Federal Emergency Management Agency, U.S. Fire Administration: Report to Congress, FY90, 9434–7
Federal Emergency Management Agency, U.S. Fire Administration: Report to Congress, FY91, 9434–7
Federal Employees' Compensation Act: Need To Increase Rehabilitation and Reemployment of Injured Workers, 26119–381
Federal Employment: How Federal Employees View the Government as a Place To Work, 26119–406
Federal Employment Tax Assessments Against Federal Agencies and Large Internal Revenue Service Accounts Receivable Cases, 21788–206
Federal Energy Regulatory Commission, Annual Qualifying Facilities Report, 3084–13
Federal Energy Regulatory Commission: 1991 Annual Report, 3084–9
Federal Entities with Treasury and Federal Financing Bank Borrowing Authority. Financial Management, 26111–79
Federal Excise Tax Refunds for Contractors of Department of Energy Oak Ridge Field Office, 3006–5.26
Federal Expenditures by State for FY91, 2464–2
Federal Financial Institutions Examination Council: Annual Report, 1991, 13004–2
Federal Financing Bank Activity: Federal Financing Bank News, 12802–1
Federal Financing Bank News: Federal Financing Bank Activity, 12802–1
Federal First-Line Supervisors: How Good Are They?, 9498–15
Federal Forum. Interagency Forum on Aging-Related Statistics, Report 1989-90, 14324–1
Federal Funding and Future Needs. Drug Abuse Research, 26131–99
Federal Grain Inspection Service: Annual Report to Congress, 1991, 1294–1
Federal Grain Inspection Service: Annual Report to Congress, 1992, 1294–1
Federal Health Benefits Program: Stronger Controls Needed To Reduce Administrative Costs, 26119–376
Federal Hiring: Does Veterans' Preference Need Updating?, 26119–391
Federal Home Loan Bank of Atlanta, Quarterly Report, 9302–37
Federal Home Loan Bank of Atlanta, 1991 Annual Report, 9304–1
Federal Home Loan Bank of Boston, Annual Report, 1991, 9304–2
Federal Home Loan Bank of Boston, First District Facts, 9302–4
Federal Home Loan Bank of Boston Membership Directory, 1990, 9304–26
Federal Home Loan Bank of Boston Membership Directory, 1991, 9304–26
Federal Home Loan Bank of Boston Membership Directory, 1992, 9304–26
Federal Home Loan Bank of Boston Quarterly Report, 9302–35
Federal Home Loan Bank of Chicago, Home Mortgage Commitment Rates in Illinois, 9302–6
Federal Home Loan Bank of Chicago, Home Mortgage Commitment Rates in Wisconsin, 9302–7
Federal Home Loan Bank of Chicago Housing Vacancy Survey, 9304–18
Federal Home Loan Bank of Chicago, Index Report, 9302–30
Federal Home Loan Bank of Chicago, 1991 Annual Report, 9304–4
Federal Home Loan Bank of Cincinnati, 1991 Annual Report, 9304–6
Federal Home Loan Bank of Dallas Housing Vacancy Survey, 9304–19

Federal Home Loan Bank of Dallas, 1991 Annual Report, 9304–11
Federal Home Loan Bank of Des Moines, Directory of Bank Services and Membership, 9304–9
Federal Home Loan Bank of Des Moines, 1991 Annual Report, 9304–7
Federal Home Loan Bank of Indianapolis: Possible Adjustable Mortgage Loan Indices, 9302–38
Federal Home Loan Bank of Indianapolis, Quarterly Financial Information Report, 9302–23
Federal Home Loan Bank of New York, Annual Report, 1991, 9304–12
Federal Home Loan Bank of Pittsburgh, 1991 Annual Report, 9304–13
Federal Home Loan Bank of San Francisco, Proceedings of the 15th Annual Conference: Strategies for the Nineties, 9304–24
Federal Home Loan Bank of San Francisco, 1991 Annual Report, 9304–14
Federal Home Loan Bank of San Francisco 1992 Shareholder Directory, Eleventh District: Arizona, California, Nevada, 9304–23
Federal Home Loan Bank of Seattle Housing Vacancy Survey, 9304–21
Federal Home Loan Bank of Seattle, 1991 Annual Report, 9304–15
Federal Home Loan Bank of Topeka, Directory of Members, 9304–17
Federal Home Loan Bank of Topeka Housing Vacancy Survey, 9304–22
Federal Home Loan Bank of Topeka, 1991 Annual Report, 9304–16
Federal Home Loan Bank, Tenth District, Annual Report, 9304–16
Federal Home Loan Banks: Statements of Condition as of (Date), 9442–1
Federal Home Loan Banks 1991 Financial Report, 9444–1
Federal Home Loan Mortgage Corporation Annual Report, 9414–1
Federal Hospital Insurance Trust Fund, 8102–9.15
Federal Hospital Insurance Trust Fund, 1992 Annual Report of the Board of Trustees, 4654–11
Federal Housing Administration, 21248–162
Federal Housing Finance Board, 1990 Annual Summary: Rates and Terms on Conventional Home Mortgages, 9444–2
Federal Housing Finance Board, 1991 Annual Summary: Rates and Terms on Conventional Home Mortgages, 9444–2
Federal Incentive Awards Program: Achievements for FY90, 9844–20
Federal Information Processing Standards Publications, 2216–2
Federal Information Processing Standards Publications (FIPS PUBS) Index, 2216–2.202
Federal Investments Like WIC Can Produce Savings. Early Intervention, 26121–458
Federal Job Training for the Poor May Be More Cost Effective in Rural Areas, 1502–7.305
Federal Judicial Workload Statistics, Dec. 31, 1991, 18204–11
Federal Labor Relations: A Program in Need of Reform, 26119–367
Federal Labor Relations Authority and the Federal Service Impasses Panel, 12th Annual Report, FY90, 13364–1
Federal Labor Relations Authority and the Federal Service Impasses Panel, 13th Annual Report, FY91, 13364–1
Federal Lands: Reasons for and Effects of Inadequate Public Access, 26113–571
Federal Maritime Commission 30th Annual Report, FY91, 9334–1
Federal Meat and Poultry Inspection, FY90, Statistical Summary, 1374–3
Federal Mediation and Conciliation Service, Annual Report, FY90, 9344–1
Federal Milk Order Market Statistics, 1317–4
Federal Milk Order Market Statistics, 1991 Annual Summary, 1317–3
Federal National Mortgage Association 1990 Report to Congress, 5184–9
Federal Nonfarm Business Credit Assistance: An Analysis of Disbursements to Rural Areas, 1548–389
Federal Old Age and Survivors Insurance Trust Fund, 8102–9.2
Federal Old-Age and Survivors Insurance and Disability Insurance Trust Funds, 1992 Annual Report of the Board of Trustees, 4704–4
Federal Personal Income Tax Liabilities and Payments: Revised and Updated Estimates, 1959-91, 2702–1.326
Federal Personnel Research Programs and Demonstration Projects: Catalysts for Change, 9496–2.8
Federal Plan for Meteorological Services and Supporting Research, FY93, 2144–2
Federal Prison Industries, 1991 Annual Report: Service to Government, 6244–3
Federal Processes for Collection and Dissemination. Foreign Technology, 26123–379
Federal Public Assistance Programs: Coordination and Eligibility Issues, 15498–29
Federal R&D Funding by Budget Function, FY91-93, 9627–9
Federal Recruiting: College Placement Officials' Views of the Government's Campus Outreach Efforts, 26119–377
Federal Recruiting: Comparison of Applicants Who Accepted or Declined Federal Job Offers, 26119–387
Federal Research: SEMATECH's Technological Progress and Proposed R&D Program, 26113–588
Federal Research: Small Business Innovation Research Shows Success but Can Be Strengthened, 26113–393
Federal Research: System for Reimbursing Universities' Indirect Costs Should Be Reevaluated, 26113–592
Federal Reserve Annual Statistical Releases, 9365–5
Federal Reserve Bank of Atlanta Economic Review, 9371–1
Federal Reserve Bank of Atlanta Economics Update, 9371–15
Federal Reserve Bank of Atlanta Regional Update, 9371–14
Federal Reserve Bank of Atlanta Working Paper Series, 9371–10
Federal Reserve Bank of Atlanta, 1991 Annual Report, 9371–4
Federal Reserve Bank of Boston Conference Series, 9373–3
Federal Reserve Bank of Boston, New England Economic Indicators, 9373–2
Federal Reserve Bank of Boston, New England Economic Review, 9373–1
Federal Reserve Bank of Boston, 1991 Annual Report, 9373–26
Federal Reserve Bank of Chicago Economic Perspectives, 9375–1
Federal Reserve Bank of Chicago Working Paper Series, 9375–13
Federal Reserve Bank of Chicago, 1991 Annual Report, 9375–5
Federal Reserve Bank of Cleveland Economic Review, 9377–1
Federal Reserve Bank of Cleveland Working Papers, 9377–9
Federal Reserve Bank of Cleveland, 1991 Annual Report, 9377–5
Federal Reserve Bank of Dallas Economic Review, 9379–1
Federal Reserve Bank of Dallas Financial Industry Studies Working Papers, 9379–14
Federal Reserve Bank of Dallas Research Papers, 9379–12
Federal Reserve Bank of Dallas, 1991 Annual Report, 9379–2
Federal Reserve Bank of Kansas City, Banking Studies, 9381–14
Federal Reserve Bank of Kansas City Economic Review, 9381–1
Federal Reserve Bank of Kansas City, Financial Industry Trends, 9381–14
Federal Reserve Bank of Kansas City Regional Economic Digest, 9381–16
Federal Reserve Bank of Kansas City Research Working Papers, 9381–10
Federal Reserve Bank of Kansas City Sponsored Symposium, 9381–13
Federal Reserve Bank of Kansas City, 1991 Annual Report, 9381–3
Federal Reserve Bank of Minneapolis Fedgazette, 9383–19
Federal Reserve Bank of Minneapolis Quarterly Review, 9383–6
Federal Reserve Bank of Minneapolis Staff Reports, 9383–20
Federal Reserve Bank of Minneapolis, 1991 Annual Report, 9383–2
Federal Reserve Bank of New York Quarterly Review, 9385–1
Federal Reserve Bank of New York Research Papers, 9385–8
Federal Reserve Bank of New York, Seventy-seventh Annual Report for the Year Ended Dec. 31, 1991, 9385–2
Federal Reserve Bank of Philadelphia Business Review, 9387–1
Federal Reserve Bank of Philadelphia, Quarterly Regional Economic Report, 9387–10
Federal Reserve Bank of Philadelphia Working Papers, 9387–8
Federal Reserve Bank of Philadelphia, 1991 Annual Report, 9387–3
Federal Reserve Bank of Richmond Economic Review, 9389–1
Federal Reserve Bank of Richmond Working Paper Series, 9389–19
Federal Reserve Bank of Richmond, 1991 Annual Report, 9389–2
Federal Reserve Bank of San Francisco, Annual Report, 1991, 9393–2
Federal Reserve Bank of San Francisco Economic Review, 9393–8
Federal Reserve Bank of San Francisco Working Papers, 9393–10

Federal Reserve Bank of St. Louis Review, 9391–1
Federal Reserve Bank of St. Louis, 1991 Annual Report, 9391–17
Federal Reserve Bulletin, 9362–1
Federal Reserve Monthly Statistical Releases, 9365–2
Federal Reserve Quarterly Statistical Releases, 9365–3
Federal Reserve Semiannual Statistical Releases, 9365–4
Federal Reserve Weekly Statistical Releases, 9365–1
Federal Reserve's First Monetary Policy Report for 1991, 25248–127
Federal Sentencing in Transition, 1986-90, 6066–19.68
Federal Service Impasses Panel, 12th Annual Report, FY90, 13364–1
Federal Service Impasses Panel, 13th Annual Report, FY91, 13364–1
Federal Supplementary Medical Insurance Trust Fund, 8102–9.3
Federal Supplementary Medical Insurance Trust Fund, 1992 Annual Report of the Board of Trustees, 4654–12
Federal Support for Education: FY80-91, 4824–8
Federal Support to Universities and Colleges: FY90, Selected Data Tables, 9626–8.6
Federal Support to Universities, Colleges, and Nonprofit Institutions: FY90, 9627–17
Federal Trade Commission, FY90 Annual Report, 9404–1
Federal Trade Commission Report to Congress for 1989, Pursuant to the Federal Cigarette Labeling and Advertising Act, 9404–4
Federal Transit Administration Grant Assistance Programs, Statistical Summaries, 1991, 7884–10
Federal Transit Administration: 1990 Section 15 Annual Report, 7884–4
Federal Trust Fund Reports, 8102–9
Federal Workforce: Agencies' Estimated Costs for Counseling and Processing Discrimination Complaints, 26119–388
Federal Workforce: Agencies' Procurements of Private Health Club Services, 26119–393
Federal-Aid Highway Construction Materials Usage Factors, 1989-91, 7554–29
Fedgazette, Federal Reserve Bank of Minneapolis, 9383–19
Fee Update and Medicare Volume Performance Standards for 1992, 17266–1.3
Fee Update and Medicare Volume Performance Standards for 1993, 17266–1.7
Feed Situation and Outlook Report, 1561–4
Feed Situation and Outlook Yearbook, 1561–4
Feedback Loops and Economics of Scale: Achieving Export-Led Growth in the Caribbean Basin, 9916–13.2
Feldspar: Mineral Industry Survey, 5612–2.18
Fenvalerate Hazards to Fish, Wildlife, and Invertebrates: A Synoptic Review, 5506–14.5
Ferroalloys: Minerals Yearbook, Volume 1, 1990, 5604–20.20
Ferrosilicon from Argentina, Kazakhstan, the People's Republic of China, Russia, Ukraine, and Venezuela. Determinations of the Commission in Investigation No. 303-TA-23 (Preliminary) and No. 731-TA-565-570 (Preliminary) Under the Tariff Act of 1930, Together with the Information Obtained in the Investigations, 9886–19.84
Fertilizer Materials, Current Industrial Report, 2506–8.2
Fertilizer Materials, 1991, Current Industrial Report, 2506–8.13
Fetal Alcohol Effects Among North American Indians, 4482–1.310
Few Firearms Licensees Had Complaints About Inspections. Alcohol, Tobacco, and Firearms, 26119–429
FHA Home Mortgage Activities, By State and County, 5144–15
FHA Home Mortgage Insurance Operations. State, County and MSA/PMSA, 1988, 5144–15
FHA Home Mortgage Insurance Operations. State, County and MSA/PMSA, 1989, 5144–15
FHA Home Mortgage Insurance Operations. State, County and MSA/PMSA, 1990, 5144–15
FHA Home Mortgage Insurance Operations. State, County and MSA/PMSA, 1991, 5144–15
FHA Home Mortgage Insurance Operations: Volume Statistics for State and County, Year 1984 and Cumulative Through 1984, 5144–15
FHA Homes, 1991, Section 203(b): Characteristics of FHA Home Mortgage Operations, Total Construction by State, 5144–1
FHA National Trends of Home Mortgage Characteristics, Section 203(b) Mortgages Insured, 5144–23
FHA Report of Insurance Operations Under Home Mortgage Programs for (Date): FHA Mortgages Insured, 5142–45
FHA Single Family Trends: Statistical Highlights, 5142–44
FHA Trends of Home Mortgage Characteristics, Section 203b Mortgages Insured, 5144–23
FHA Trends of Home Mortgage Characteristics, Section 203b Mortgages Insured by MSA/PMSA's, 1991, 5144–24
FHA Trends of Home Mortgage Characteristics, Section 203b Mortgages Insured by States, 1991, 5144–25
FHA 1991 Annual Management Report, 5144–26
FHWA Reports Road Construction Costs, 7552–16
Fiber and Processing Tests, Survey of Leading Cotton Varieties: Crop of 1991, 1309–16
Fiber Deployment Update, End of Year 1991, 9284–18
Field Crops Summary, 1991. Agricultural Chemical Usage, 1616–1.1
Field Hearing on Access to Health Care, 21348–123
Field Initiated Studies Program: Abstracts of Funded Projects, 1990-91, 4884–1
Field Studies of Radon in Rocks, Soils, and Water, 5668–126
Fifth National High-Occupancy Vehicle (HOV) Facilities Conference. HOV Facilities: Coming of Age, 7308–204
Fifth Report of the Joint National Committee on Detection, Evaluation, and Treatment of High Blood Pressure (JNC V), 4478–198
Fifty-fifth Annual Report of the National Labor Relations Board, FY90, 9584–1
Fifty-third and Fifty-fourth Annual Report, National Mediation Board, Including the Report of the National Railroad Adjustment Board, FY87-88, 9604–1
Filing Season Statistics, 8302–6
Final Apportionment of Federal Aid in Sport Fish and Wildlife Restoration Funds for FY92, 5502–1
Final Case Study for the National Scenic Byways Study, 7556–8
Final Case Study for the National Scenic Byways Study: Case Study of the Economic Impact of the Blue Ridge Parkway, 7556–8.4
Final Case Study for the National Scenic Byways Study: Economic Impact of Travel on Scenic Byways, 7556–8.1
Final Case Study for the National Scenic Byways Study: Economic Impacts of Scenic Byways, 7556–8.3
Final Case Study for the National Scenic Byways Study: Safety, Traffic and Cost Considerations on Scenic Byways, 7556–8.5
Final Case Study for the National Scenic Byways Study: Study of the Highway Safety Aspects of the Blue Ridge Parkway, 7556–8.2
Final Environmental Impact Statement on Management for the Northern Spotted Owl in the National Forests, 1208–388
Final Environmental Impact Statement on Management for the Northern Spotted Owl in the National Forests: Record of Decision, 1208–388.3
Final Evaluation of the Neighborhood Development Demonstration Program: Final Report, 5188–119
Final Grape Crush Report, 1991 Crop, 1311–30
Final Mortality Statistics, 1989, Advance Report, 4146–5.124
Final OMB Sequestration Report to the President and Congress for FY92, 104–27
Final Passenger Motor Vehicle Theft Data for 1990, 7764–21
Final Report of the SEC Government-Business Forum on Small Business Capital Formation, 9734–4
Final Report on Monitoring Hydrocarbons and Trace Metals in Beaufort Sea Sediments and Organisms, 5738–33
Final Sequestration Report for FY92: A CBO Report to the Congress and the Office of Management and Budget, 26304–6
Final Sequestration Report for FY93: A CBO Report to the Congress and the Office of Management and Budget, 26304–6
Finance and Economics Discussion Series, 9366–6
Finance Companies, 9365–2.7
Finance Companies, Bank Competition, and Niche Markets, 9385–1.309
Finances of Employee-Retirement Systems of State and Local Governments: 1989-90, 2466–2.4
Finances of Selected Public Employee Retirement Systems, 2462–2
Financial Activity of 1992 Congressional Campaigns Soars, 9276–1.108
Financial and Time Costs to Parents of Severely Disabled Children, 4042–3.329
Financial Assistance by Geographic Area, FY91, 4004–3

Financial Characteristics of Vegetable Farms in 1990, 1561-11.304
Financial Condition and Regulation of Insurance Companies, 9373-3.35
Financial Condition of Dairy Farms, 1987-90, 1561-2.301
Financial Condition of SBA's Business Loan Portfolio Is Improving. Small Business, 26113-554
Financial Conditions for the 1990's, 1504-9.1
Financial Efficiency and Aggregate Fluctuations: An Exploration, 9377-1.302
Financial Evolution and the Long-Run Behavior of Velocity: New Evidence from U.S. Regional Data, 9389-1.301
Financial Incentives and Medical Practice: Evidence from Ontario on the Effect of Changes in Physician Fees on Medical Care Utilization, 17266-2.3
Financial Industry Studies, 9379-15
Financial Industry Studies Working Papers: Federal Reserve Bank of Dallas, 9379-14
Financial Industry Trends, Federal Reserve Bank of Kansas City, 9381-14
Financial Information Report, Quarterly, Federal Home Loan Bank of Indianapolis, 9302-23
Financial Integration and the Transmission of Monetary Policy: The Case of France, Germany and Italy, 9385-8.145
Financial Leverage Versus Return on Book Equity at Bank Holding Companies in 1988, 1986, 1980, 9385-8.134
Financial Management: Federal Entities with Treasury and Federal Financing Bank Borrowing Authority, 26111-79
Financial Statistics of Selected Investor-Owned Electric Utilities, 1990, 3164-23
Financial Statistics of Selected Publicly Owned Electric Utilities, 1990, 3164-24
Financial Strength of the Federal Housing Administration, 25248-128
Financial Trends in Federally Insured Credit Unions, Jan. 1-Dec. 31, 1991, 9532-7
Financial Trends in Federally Insured Credit Unions, Jan. 1-June 30, 1992, 9532-7
Financing and Delivery of Long-Term Care Services: A Review of Current Problems and Potential Reform Options, 10176-3.7
Financing Entrepreneurial Business: An Agenda for Action. An Analysis of the Small Business Investment Company Program Together With Findings and Recommendations Concerning Its Effective Operations, 9768-24
Financing Federal-Aid Highways, 7558-107
Financing Health Benefits of Coal Industry Retirees. Employee Benefits, 26121-469
Financing Health Benefits of Retired Coal Miners. Employee Benefits, 26121-471
Finding of No Significant Impact for the Proposed Remedial Action at the Lowman Uranium Mill Site Near Lowman, Idaho, 3356-4.11
Finding of No Significant Impact, Proposed Provision of a Water Supply System, Gunnison Uranium Mill Tailings Site, Gunnison, Colo., 3356-4.12
Finding of No Significant Impact, Proposed Remedial Action: Falls City Uranium Mill Tailings Site, Falls City, Texas, 3356-4.10
Finished Broadwoven Fabric Production, Current Industrial Report, 2506-5.10
FIP Monthly Progress Report, By State and Area for Period Ending (Date), 1802-11
FIPS PUBS Index, 2216-2.202
Fire and the Environment: Ecological and Cultural Perspectives, 1208-415
Fire Ecology of Forests and Woodlands in Utah, 1208-420
Fire-Cured and Dark Air-Cured, 1991 Crop. Tobacco Market Review, 1319-5.2
First Awards Announced Under New "Shelter Plus Care" for the Homeless, 5006-3.89
First District Facts, Federal Home Loan Bank of Boston, 9302-4
First Follow-Up: Dropout Component Data File User's Manual. National Education Longitudinal Study of 1988, 4826-9.17
First Follow-Up: Student Component Data File User's Manual. National Education Longitudinal Study of 1988, 4826-9.14
First Follow-Up: Teacher Component Data File User's Manual. National Education Longitudinal Study of 1988, 4826-9.18
First Year of AIDS Services Delivery Under Title I of the Ryan White CARE Act, 4042-3.352
Fiscal Condition of State and Local Governments, 21268-44
Fiscal Implications of the Transition from Planned to Market Economy, 9366-7.278
Fiscal Policy in Monetary Unions: Implications for Europe, 9393-10.18
Fiscal Year Return Projections for the U.S.: 1992-2000, 8302-4
Fish and Fish Egg Distribution Report of the National Fish Hatchery System, FY91, 5504-10
Fish and Wildlife Service Awards First-ever Coastal Wetlands Grants, 5306-4.12
Fish and Wildlife Technical Reports, 5506-12
Fish and Wildlife '91: A Report to the Nation, 5504-20
Fish Assemblages of Rocky Banks of the Pacific Northwest, Final Report, 5738-39
Fish, Current Federal Aid Research Report, 5504-23
Fish Meal and Oil, 2162-3
Fisheries of the U.S., 1991, 2164-1
Fishermen's Report, Northeast Fisheries Science Center Bottom Trawl Survey, 2164-18
Fixed Reproducible Tangible Wealth in the U.S., Revised Estimates, 2702-1.305
Fixed Reproducible Tangible Wealth in the U.S., 1988-91, 2702-1.327
Flat Glass, Current Industrial Report, 2506-9.6
Flat-Rolled Carbon Steel Products from Argentina, Australia, Austria, Belgium, Brazil, Canada, Finland, France, Germany, Italy, Japan, Korea, Mexico, The Netherlands, New Zealand, Poland, Romania, Spain, Sweden, Taiwan, and the UK. Determinations of the Commission in Investigations Nos. 701-TA-319-354 (Preliminary) and Nos. 731-TA-573-620 (Preliminary) Under the Tariff Act of 1930, Together with the Information Obtained in the Investigations, 9886-19.85
Flight Attendant Duty Time Limitations, 21648-68
Flight Marks Japan's Major Foray into Human Spaceflight: STS-47 Mission, 9506-2.151
"Flight to Quality" in Bank Lending and Economic Activity, 9387-8.283
Floating Ceilings on Deposit Interest Rates, 9366-6.300
Floods of December 1982 to May 1983 in the Central and Southern Mississippi River and the Gulf of Mexico Basins, 5666-27.33
Floriculture and Environmental Horticulture Outlook, 1992, 1504-9.1
Floriculture Crops: 1991 Summary, 1631-8
Florida Wetlands, Status and Trends, 1970's-80's, 5508-119
Flour Milling Products, Current Industrial Report, 2506-4.1
Flow of Funds Accounts, Financial Assets and Liabilities, 9365-3.3
Flow of Funds Accounts, Financial Assets and Liabilities Year-End, 9364-3
Flow of Funds Accounts: Flows and Outstandings, 9365-3.3
Flow of Funds Accounts, Seasonally Adjusted and Unadjusted, 9365-3.3
Flow of Funds Accounts, Seasonally Adjusted Flows, 9365-3.3
Flow of Funds Summary Statistics, 9365-3
Flue-Cured Tobacco Farms: Selected Characteristics, 1568-307
Flue-Cured Tobacco, Summary of 1992 Support Program and Related Information: ASCS Commodity Fact Sheet, 1806-4.4
Flue-Cured, 1991 Crop. Tobacco Market Review, 1319-5.3
Fluid Power Products, Including Aerospace, 1991, Current Industrial Report, 2506-12.31
Fluorescent Lamp Ballasts, Current Industrial Report, 2506-12.14
Fluorspar and Certain Other Mineral Substances, Industry and Trade Summary, 9885-13.1
Fluorspar: Mineral Industry Surveys, 5612-2.10
Followup Audit: Department of Energy's Superconducting Super Collider Program, 3006-5.28
Food and Agricultural Export Directory, 1991, 1924-11
Food and Agricultural Sciences, 1990 Annual Report from the Secretary of Agriculture to the President and the Congress of the U.S., 1004-19
Food and Agriculture Competitively Awarded Research and Education Grants, FY91, 1764-1
Food Assistance: Nutritional Conditions and Program Alternatives in Puerto Rico, 26113-580
Food Assistance: Processing of USDA Commodities Donated to the National School Lunch Program, 26113-555
Food Consumption, Prices, and Expenditures, 1970-90, 1544-4
Food Cost Review, 1991, 1544-9
Food Marketing Review, 1991, 1544-22
Food Price Outlook, 1992, 1504-9.1
Food Review, 1541-7
Food Safety and Quality: USDA Improves Inspection Program for Canadian Meat, but Some Concerns Remain, 26113-595
Food Spending by Female-Headed Households, 1548-391
Footwear, Current Industrial Report, 2506-6.7
Footwear, 1991, Current Industrial Report, 2506-6.8
For Some Cardiac Pacemaker Leads, the Public Health Risks Are Still High. Medical Technology, 26131-103

Forecast of Electricity Use in the Pacific Northwest, 3224–4
Forecast of IFR Aircraft Handled by Air Route Traffic Control Center, FY92-2005, 7504–15
Forecast of Transportation Energy Demand Through the Year 2010, 3008–124
Forecasting Fresh Apple Prices for Selected Months in the Marketing Season, 1561–6.303
Forecasting Industrial Production: Purchasing Managers' Versus Production-Worker Hours Data, 9371–1.301
Forecasting Producer Prices of Rough Rice with Futures Prices, 1561–8.301
Forecasting Season-Average Wheat Prices Using Futures Prices, 1561–12.301
Forecasting the Prices Paid for Farm Inputs, 1561–16.301
Forecasting Turning Points: Is a Two-State Characterization of the Business Cycle Appropriate?, 9379–12.95
Forecasting U.S. Soybean Prices with Futures Prices, 1561–3.303
Foreign Agent Registration: Former Federal Officials Representing Foreign Interests Before the U.S. Government, 26123–134
Foreign Agricultural Service Circular Series: Cocoa. World Cocoa Situation, 1925–9
Foreign Agricultural Service Circular Series: Cotton, 1925–4
Foreign Agricultural Service Circular Series: Cotton. World Cotton Situation, 1925–4.2
Foreign Agricultural Service Circular Series: Dairy, Livestock, and Poultry, 1925–33
Foreign Agricultural Service Circular Series: Dairy, Livestock, and Poultry. U.S. Trade and Prospects, 1925–32
Foreign Agricultural Service Circular Series: Dairy, Livestock, and Poultry. World Livestock Situation, 1925–33.2
Foreign Agricultural Service Circular Series: Dairy, Livestock, and Poultry. World Poultry Situation, 1925–33.1
Foreign Agricultural Service Circular Series: Dairy Monthly Imports, 1925–31
Foreign Agricultural Service Circular Series: Grains, 1925–2
Foreign Agricultural Service Circular Series: Horticultural Products Review, 1925–34
Foreign Agricultural Service Circular Series: Oilseeds, 1925–1
Foreign Agricultural Service Circular Series: Sugar and Honey, 1925–14
Foreign Agricultural Service Circular Series: Tea, Spices and Essential Oils, 1925–15
Foreign Agricultural Service Circular Series: U.S. Seed Exports, 1925–13
Foreign Agricultural Service Circular Series. Wood Products: International Trade and Foreign Markets, 1925–36
Foreign Agricultural Service Circular Series. World Agricultural Production, 1925–28
Foreign Agricultural Service Circular Series: World Coffee Situation, 1925–5
Foreign Agricultural Service Circular Series: World Dairy Situation, 1925–10
Foreign Agricultural Service Circular Series. World Tobacco Situation, 1925–16
Foreign Agricultural Trade of the U.S., 1522–1
Foreign Agricultural Trade of the U.S., FY91 Supplement, 1522–4
Foreign Agricultural Trade of the U.S., CY91 Supplement, 1522–4
Foreign Agricultural Trade of the U.S., 1990: Supplementary Tables, 1524–8
Foreign Agricultural Trade of the U.S., 1991: Supplementary Tables, 1524–8
Foreign Animal Disease Report, 1392–3
Foreign Assistance: A Profile of the Agency for International Development, 26123–382
Foreign Bank Credit to U.S. Corporations: The Implications of Offshore Loans, 9385–1.307
Foreign Bank: Initial Assessment of Certain BCCI Activities in the U.S., 26119–427
Foreign Corporations with Income Effectively Connected with a U.S. Business, 1988, 8302–2.309
Foreign Countries and Plants Certified To Export Meat and Poultry to the U.S., Report of the Secretary of Agriculture to the U.S. Congress, 1374–2
Foreign Currencies Held by the U.S. Government, FY91, 8102–7
Foreign Currencies Held by the U.S. Government, Oct. 1, 1991-Mar. 31, 1992, 8102–7
Foreign Direct Investment in the U.S.: Detail for Historical-Cost Position and Balance of Payments Flows, 1991, 2702–1.331
Foreign Direct Investment in the U.S.: Establishment Data for 1987, 2702–1.340, 2708–48
Foreign Direct Investment in the U.S.: Operations of U.S. Affiliates of Foreign Companies, Preliminary 1990 Estimates, 2704–4
Foreign Direct Investment in the U.S.: Operations of U.S. Affiliates of Foreign Companies, Revised 1989 Estimates, 2704–4
Foreign Direct Investment in the U.S.: 1990 Transactions, 2044–20
Foreign Economic Research, 6364–1
Foreign Economic Trends and Their Implications for the U.S., 2046–4
Foreign Energy Supply Assessment Program Series, 3166–9
Foreign Exchange Intervention by the U.S.: A Review and Assessment of 1985-89, 9391–1.310
Foreign Exchange Rates, 9365–2
Foreign Flag Merchant Ships Owned by U.S. Parent Companies, As of July 1, 1991, 7702–3
Foreign Government and Individual Contributions to the Department of Defense. Operations Desert Shield/Storm, 26104–24
Foreign Labor Trends, 6366–4
Foreign Markets for U.S. Seafood Products, 2166–19
Foreign Military Sales, Foreign Military Construction Sales and Military Assistance Facts, As of Sept. 30, 1991, 3904–3
Foreign Ownership of U.S. Agricultural Land Through Dec. 31, 1991, 1584–2
Foreign Ownership of U.S. Agricultural Land Through Dec. 31, 1991: County-Level Data, 1584–3
Foreign Participation in U.S. Futures Markets Grows, 8002–4.301
Foreign Recipients of U.S. Income, 1989, 8302–2.308
Foreign Recipients of U.S. Partnership Income, 1990: Data Release, 8302–2.324
Foreign Regulations Affecting U.S. Textile and Apparel Exports, 2044–18
Foreign Sales Corporation Statistics for 1987: Data Release, 8302–2.311
Foreign Technology: Federal Processes for Collection and Dissemination, 26123–379
Foreign Trade Barriers, National Trade Estimate Report, 444–2
Foreign-Owned Companies in the U.S.: Malign or Benign?, 9391–1.309
Foreign-Trade Zones Board 51st Annual Report to the Congress of the U.S., 2044–30
Foreign-Trade Zones Board 52nd Annual Report to the Congress of the U.S., 2044–30
Forest Insect and Disease Conditions in the U.S., 1990, 1204–8
Forest Insect and Disease Conditions, Intermountain Region, 1991, 1206–11.1
Forest Pest Conditions Reports: USDA Forest Service Regions, 1206–11
Forest Pest Conditions: State Reports, 1206–49
Forest Pest Management Report: Southwestern Region, 1989, 1206–11.2
Forest Pest Management Report: Southwestern Region, 1990, 1206–11.2
Forest Pest Management Report: Southwestern Region, 1991, 1206–11.2
Forest Resources of Arkansas, 1206–8.13
Forest Resources of Tennessee, 1206–27.11
Forest Resources of the Southern Region, 1206–8
Forest Statistics for Alabama, 1206–30
Forest Statistics for Iowa, 1990, 1208–75
Forest Statistics for Land Outside National Forests in Montana, 1206–25
Forest Statistics for Land Outside National Forests in Southwestern Montana, 1989, 1206–25.12
Forest Statistics for Louisiana Parishes, 1206–35
Forest Statistics for Louisiana Parishes, 1991, 1206–35.12
Forest Statistics for Maryland, 1976 and 1986, 1206–12.16
Forest Statistics for Minnesota, 1990, 1206–24
Forest Statistics for Minnesota's Central Hardwood Unit, 1990, 1206–24.11
Forest Statistics for Minnesota's Prairie Unit, 1990, 1206–24.12
Forest Statistics for Northwest Louisiana Parishes, 1991, 1206–35.11
Forest Statistics for South Delta Louisiana Parishes, 1991, 1206–35.9
Forest Statistics for Southeast Louisiana Parishes, 1991, 1206–35.10
Forest Statistics for Southwest Louisiana Parishes, 1991, 1206–35.8
Forest Statistics for Tennessee, 1206–27
Forest Statistics for the Northeast Region, 1206–12
Forest Statistics for the Northern Mountains of Virginia, 1992, 1206–6.16
Forest Statistics for the Northern Piedmont of Virginia, 1992, 1206–6.15
Forest Statistics for the Southern Mountains of Virginia, 1992, 1206–6.17
Forest Statistics for the Southern Piedmont of Virginia, 1991, 1206–6.14
Forest Statistics for Virginia, 1206–6
Forest Statistics for Virginia, 1992, 1206–6.18
Forest Statistics for West-Central Alabama Counties, 1990, 1206–30.11

Forestry Implications of Water Quality and Wetland Law, 1504–9.1
Forestry Incentives Program (FIP) Monthly Progress Report, By State and Area for Period Ending (Date), 1802–11
Forestry Incentives Program, From Inception of Program Through Sept. 30, 1991, 1804–20
Forgery and Fraud-Related Offenses in 6 States, 1983-88, 6066–19.64
Form Invariance in Biased Sampling Problems, 9371–10.87
Former Federal Officials Representing Foreign Interests Before the U.S. Government. Foreign Agent Registration, 26123–134
Former USSR Agriculture and Trade Report, Situation and Outlook Series, 1524–4.1
Forms 1040, 1040A and 1040EZ by Full-Paid, Other-Than-Full-Paid, Refunds and Electronically-Filed Returns: Projections., 8302–7
Fossil Energy Perspective on Global Climate Change, 3338–3
Fourteen Cooperatives Listed Among Fortune 500, 1122–1.303
Fourteenth Annual Report to Congress on the Implementation of the Individuals with Disabilities Education Act, 4944–4
Fourth District Thrift Institutions Statistics, Data Bank, 9304–29
Framework for Assessing the Effectiveness of Disease and Injury Prevention, 4206–2.53
Freddie Mac, 1991 Annual Report, 9414–1
Free Trade Agreements and the Credibility of Trade Reforms, 9379–1.301
Freedom of Information Activities, Annual Report of the Department of Health and Human Services, 1991, 4004–21
Fresh Apple Trade and Consumption in the Gulf Countries, 1925–34.322
Fresh Fruit and Vegetable Arrival Totals, for 22 Cities, 1311–4.3
Fresh Fruit and Vegetable Arrivals and Shipments, 1991, 1311–4
Fresh Fruit and Vegetable Arrivals in Eastern Cities, by Commodities, States, and Months, 1311–4.1
Fresh Fruit and Vegetable Arrivals in Western Cities, by Commodities, States, and Months, 1311–4.2
Fresh Fruit and Vegetable Prices, 1991: Wholesale Chicago and New York City, F.O.B. Leading Shipping Points, 1311–8
Fresh Fruit and Vegetable Shipments, by Commodities, States, and Months, 1311–4.4
Fresh Fruits, Vegetables and Ornamental Crops. Weekly Summary: Shipments and Arrivals, 1311–3
Fresh Kiwifruit from New Zealand. Determination of the Commission in Investigation No. 731-TA-516 (Final) Under the Tariff Act of 1930, Together with the Information Obtained in the Investigation, 9886–14.345
Fresh or Frozen Fish, Industry and Trade Summary, 9885–8.7
Friction Model of Discount Rate Changes, 9379–14.20
Frozen Fishery Products, Preliminary, 2162–2
Fruit and Nuts Summary, 1991. Agricultural Chemical Usage, 1616–1.3
Fruit and Tree Nuts Situation and Outlook Report, 1561–6
Fruit and Tree Nuts Situation and Outlook Yearbook, 1561–6
Fruit and Vegetable Truck Cost Report, 1272–1
Fruit and Vegetable Truck Rate and Cost Summary, 1991, 1311–15
Fruit and Vegetable Truck Rate Report, 1311–22
Fruits: Production, Use and Value, 1621–18
FTA University Research and Training Program, FY92 Grant Awards, 7884–7
Fuel Oil and Kerosene Sales, 1990, 3164–94
Fueling Development: Energy Technologies for Developing Countries, 26358–260
Fulbright Program 1991, J. William Fulbright Foreign Scholarship Board, Twenty-eighth Annual Report, 10324–1
Full-Time Federal Civilian Employment in White- and Blue-Collar Occupations as of Sept. 30, 1991, 9842–1.302
Functional Cost Analysis, 9364–6
Functional Cost Analysis, 1989 Average Thrift Institutions, 9364–6.1
Functional Cost Analysis, 1990 Average Thrift Institutions, 9364–6.1
Functional Cost Analysis, 1990 National Average Report, Commercial Banks, 9364–6.2
Functional Cost Analysis, 1991 Average Thrift Institutions, 9364–6.1
Functional Cost Analysis, 1991 National Average Report, Commercial Banks, 9364–6.2
Further Evidence Concerning Expense Preference and the Fed, 9387–8.267
Future Financial Resources of the Elderly: A View of Pensions, Savings, Social Security, and Earnings in the 21st Century, 10176–3.3
Future Foods and Fads, 1504–9.1
Future of Agriculture and Trade in the Pacific: An Overview, 1524–4.3
Future of Community Banking: Federal Reserve Bank of St. Louis 1991 Annual Report, 9391–17
Future of Jobs for College Graduates, 6722–1.331
Future Trends in the Food Stamp Program, 1504–9.1
FY85 National DRG Validation Study: Peer Review Organization Coding Accuracy, 4006–7.9
FY90 Federal Agency Performance for Minority Business Development, 2104–5
FY90 U.S. Small Business Administration Annual Report, 9764–1
FY91 Annual Report on In-house Energy Management, 3004–27
FY91 Federal Agency Performance for Minority Business Development, 2104–5
FY91 Guaranteed Student Loan Programs Data Book, 4804–38
FY91 Review of State Formula Grant Strategies. Bureau of Justice Assistance Fact Sheet, 6064–38
FY91 U.S. Small Business Administration Annual Report, 9764–1
FY92 Apportionments to States from the Land and Water Conservation Fund, 5544–15
FY92 EPA Research Program Guide, 9184–17
FY93 Apportionments to States from the Land and Water Conservation Fund, 5544–15
FY93 Budget in Brief, Department of Transportation, 7304–10
FY93 Military Construction Program, 3544–15

Gallium in 1991: Mineral Industry Surveys, Annual Review, 5614–5.12
GAO Reports and Testimony, 26106–10
Gas Mileage Guide, 1993: EPA Fuel Economy Estimates, 3304–11
Gas Supplies of Interstate Natural Gas Pipeline Companies, 1990, 3164–33
Gas Supplies of Interstate Natural Gas Pipeline Companies, 1991, 3164–33
Gasoline Divorcement (Motor Fuel Consumer Protection Act of 1991), 25528–120
GATT Standards Code Activities of the National Institute of Standards and Technology, 1991, 2214–6
Gem Stones, Directory of Principal U.S. Producers in 1991: Mineral Industry Surveys, Annual Advance Summary Supplement, 5614–5.5
Gender Differences in Training, Capital, and Wages, 6886–6.93
Gender, Equity, and Job Satisfaction, 7506–10.105
General Accounting: The Case of Italy, 9377–9.139
General Estimates System 1990: A Review of Information on Police-Reported Traffic Crashes in the U.S., 7764–18
General Housing Characteristics. 1990 Census of Housing, 2471–1
General Management Inspection of the Department of Energy's Nevada Field Office, 3006–5.31
General Population Characteristics. 1990 Census of Population, 2531–1, 2531–2
General Population Characteristics: 1990 Census of Population. American Indian and Alaska Native Areas, 2531–2.1
General Services Administration Annual Report, FY91, 9454–1
General Services Administration Semiannual Report to the Congress, Oct. 1, 1991-Mar. 31, 1992, 9452–8
Generalized Put-Call Parity, 9371–10.67
Generalized System of Preferences, 1925–34.310
Generalized Uncovered Interest Parity Model of Real Exchange Rates, 9393–10.21
Generation and Sales Statistics, FY91, 3222–1
Generation and Sales Statistics, CY91, 3222–1
Geographic Area Statistics. 1990 Annual Survey of Manufactures, 2506–14.3
Geographic Distribution of VA Expenditures, FY91, 8604–6
Geographic Notes, 7142–3
Geographic Profile of Employment and Unemployment, 1991, 6744–7
Geographical Distribution of Assets and Liabilities of Major Foreign Branches of U.S. Banks, 9365–3.7
Geographical Mobility: March 1987-March 1990, 2546–1.456
Geographical Mobility: March 1990-March 1991, 2546–1.464
Geohydrology, Water Quality, and Water Budgets of Golden Gate Park and the Lake Merced Area in the Western Part of San Francisco, Calif., 5666–28.16
Geologic Distributions of U.S. Oil and Gas, 3166–14.2

Geologic Studies in Alaska by the U.S. Geological Survey, 1990, 5664–15
Geological and Geophysical Data Acquisition, Outer Continental Shelf Through FY90, 5738–41
Georgia's Timber Industry—An Assessment of Timber Product Output and Use, 1989, 1208–393
Geothermal Energy in the Western U.S. and Hawaii: Resources and Projected Electricity Generation Supplies, 3168–122
Geothermal Progress Monitor, Report No. 13, 3308–87
Geriatric Education Centers Address Medication Issues Affecting Older Adults, 4042–3.303
Geriatric Research, Education, and Clinical Centers (GRECCs) FY88 Summary of Program Activities, 8704–8
German Housing/Construction Market, 2042–1.306
German, Irish, English, Afro-American Top Census Bureau's '90 Ancestry Lists, 2328–87
German Unification and the European Monetary System: A Quantitative Analysis, 9366–7.275
Germanium: Minerals Yearbook, Volume 1, 1990, 5604–20.23
Germany: A Profile on Consumption and Imports of Fresh Fruits, 1925–34.340
Glaciological Data, 2156–18
Glaciological Data, Passive Microwave Research: Microwave Bibliography Update, 1988-91, 2156–18.24
Glass Containers, Current Industrial Report, 2506–9.4
Glass Fibers, Current Industrial Reports, 2506–9.5
Global Aging: Comparative Indicators and Future Trends, 2328–82
Global Change Research: Summaries of Research in FY92, 3004–18.10
Global Food Assessment: Situation and Outlook Report, 1526–8, 1526–8.2
Global Greening: Marketing U.S. Nursery Products Abroad, 1925–34.306
Global Pollution from Jet Aircraft Could Increase in the Future. Air Pollution, 26113–562
Global Standards: Building Blocks for the Future, 26358–257
Global Trade Talk: U.S. Customs Service Journal for the International Trade Community, 8142–2
Global Versus Country-Specific Productivity Shocks and the Current Account, 9393–10.22
Gloves and Mittens, 1991, Current Industrial Report, 2506–6.4
Glutathione S-Transferase and Epoxide Hydrolase Activity in Human Leukocytes in Relation to Risk of Lung Cancer and Other Smoking-Related Cancers, 4472–1.307
Gold and Silver: Mineral Industry Surveys, 5612–1.10
Gold: Minerals Yearbook, Volume 1, 1990, 5604–20.24
Gold Standard as a Rule, 9377–9.136
Good Quality Care Increases Hospital Profits Under Prospective Payment, 4652–1.316
GOP Continues Fundraising Lead Over Democrats, 9276–1.109
Government Employment, 2466–1
Government Finances Series, 2466–2
Government Finances: 1989-90, 2466–2.2
Government Intervention in Moroccan Agriculture: Evolution of Subsidy Equivalents and Possible Trade Reform Effects, 1528–329
Government Life Insurance Programs for Veterans and Members of the Services, Annual Report, 1991, 8604–4
Government National Mortgage Association (GNMA), Annual Report, 1991, 5144–6
Governmentwide Asset Disposition Activities. Asset Management, 26119–369
GPO Annual Report, 1991, 26204–1
GPO/2001: Vision for a New Millennium, 26208–4
Grain and Feed Market News, Weekly Summary and Statistics, 1313–2
Grain Loan Activity Through (Month), 1802–3
Grain Stocks, 1621–4
Grains: Foreign Agricultural Service Circular Series, 1925–2
Grand and Petit Juror Service in U.S. District Courts, 18204–4
Grand Canyon Protection Act of 1990, 21448–47
Grant Awards, FY89, U.S. Department of Transportation, 7304–7
Great Lakes, Connecting Channels and St. Lawrence River: Water Levels and Depths, 3752–2
Great Lakes Environmental Research Laboratory Annual Report, FY91, 2144–26
Great Lakes Science Advisory Board Report to the International Joint Commission, 1991, 14644–6
Great Lakes Water Levels, 1860-1990, 2178–1
Great Lakes Water Levels, 1991, 2174–3
Great Lakes Water Quality, Sixth Biennial Report, 14644–1
Greater Use of Instrumented Inspection Technology Can Improve Safety. Natural Gas Pipelines, 26113–594
Green Book, 1992. Overview of Entitlement Programs. Background Material and Data on Programs Within the Jurisdiction of the Committee on Ways and Means, 21784–11
Gross Product of U.S. Affiliates of Foreign Direct Investors, 1987-90, 2702–1.342
Gross State Product by Industry, 1977-89, 2702–1.303
Ground-Water Flow System in Indian Wells Valley, Kern, Inyo, and San Bernardino Counties, California, 5666–28.15
Ground-Water Hydrology and Quality in the Lompoc Area, Santa Barbara County, California, 1987-88, 5666–28.17
Groundwater Protection: Measurement of Relative Vulnerability to Pesticide Contamination, 26131–91
Ground-Water Resources of Rhode Island, 5666–28.18
Ground-Water Resources, State, Local, and Regional Studies, 5666–28
Ground-Water Use and Levels in the Southern Coastal Plain of Virginia, 5666–28.20
Ground-Water Use by Public Supply Systems in Tennessee, 1988, 5666–24.14
Group Counseling at STD Clinics To Promote Use of Condoms, 4042–3.376
Growth of America's Elderly in the 1980's. Profiles of America's Elderly, 2326–25.1
Growth of America's Oldest-Old Population. Profiles of America's Elderly, 2326–25.2
Guaranteed Student Loan Programs Data Book, FY91, 4804–38
Guide to Department of Education Programs, 1992, 4804–3
Guide to Economic Censuses and Related Statistics, 2308–5
Guide to Marine Pollution Related Data Collected by Federally Sponsored Projects Identified in the FY84-87 National Marine Pollution Program Catalogs, 2158–51
Guide: 1990 Census of Population and Housing, 2555–1
Guidebook to the Andean Trade Preference Act, 2048–161
Guidelines for the Performance of CD4+ T-Cell Determinations in Persons with Human Immunodeficiency Virus Infection, 4206–2.58
Gulf of Maine: Proceedings of a Seminar Held May 22, 1989, Washington, D.C., 2146–8.1
Gulf of Mexico: Estimated Oil and Gas Reserves, Dec. 31, 1990, 5734–6
Gypsum: Mineral Industry Surveys, 5612–1.31
Gypsum: Minerals Yearbook, Volume 1, 1990, 5604–20.26
Gypsum Mines and Calcining Plants in the U.S. in 1991: Mineral Industry Surveys, Annual Advance Summary Supplement, 5614–5.19

Haiti Macroeconomic Assessment, 9916–13.3
Handbook of Evaluation of Utility DSM Programs, 3308–102
Handbook of Hearing Aid Measurement, 1992, 8704–3
Hanford Environmental Dose Reconstruction Project, 3356–5
Hanford Environmental Dose Reconstruction Project, Ground-Water Contribution to Dose from Past Hanford Operations, 3356–5.7
Hanford Environmental Dose Reconstruction Project, Literature and Data Review for the Surface-Water Pathway: Columbia River and Adjacent Coastal Areas, 3356–5.8
Hanford Site Environmental Report for 1990, 3324–2.8
Harbor Maintenance Trust Fund, 8102–9.12
Harmonized Tariff Schedule of the U.S. (1993) Annotated for Statistical Reporting Purposes, 9886–13
Harry S. Truman Memorial Scholarship Fund: Status of Account, 14312–1
Harry S. Truman Scholarship Foundation, Annual Report, FY91, 14314–1
Hatchery Production, 1991 Summary, 1625–8
Have Regional Per-Capita Incomes Converged?, 9387–8.257
Hay Market News, 1313–5
Hazardous Materials Transportation, 1990 Annual Report, 7304–4
Hazardous Materials: Upgrading of Underground Storage Tanks Can Be Improved To Avoid Costly Cleanups, 26123–395
Hazardous Substance Superfund Trust Fund, 8102–9.6
Hazardous Waste Sites: Descriptions of Sites on Updates to National Priorities List, 9216–3
Hazardous Waste Sites: Descriptions of 22 Sites Proposed for the National Priorities List in July 1991, 9216–3.26

Hazardous Waste Sites: Descriptions of 30 Sites Proposed to the National Priorities List in February 1992, 9216–3.27
Hazards to Fish, Wildlife, and Invertebrates: Synoptic Reviews, 5506–14
Hazelnut Production, 1621–18.6
Hazelnut Situation and Outlook, 1925–34.338
HCFA Statistics, 1992, 4654–18
Health and Demographic Characteristics of Twin Births: U.S., 1988. Vital and Health Statistics Series 21, 4147–21.50
Health and Social Characteristics of the Nonmetro Elderly, 1504–9.1
Health Assessment Document for Talc, 9186–8.38
Health Assessment Document for Vermiculite, 9186–8.37
Health Assessment Documents, 9186–8
Health Benefits of Smoking Cessation: A Report of the Surgeon General, 4204–18
Health Care Costs and Lack of Access to Health Insurance, 25368–180
Health Care Financing Review, 4652–1
Health Care Financing Status Report, Research and Demonstrations in Health Care Financing, 4654–10
Health Care: Most Community and Migrant Health Center Physicians Have Hospital Privileges, 26121–465
Health Care Resource Book, 21788–213
Health Care Spending: Nonpolicy Factors Account for Most State Differences, 26121–444
Health Care Trends, 1702–1.309
Health Hazard Evaluation Report: U.S. West Communications, Phoenix, Ariz.; Minneapolis, Minn.; Denver, Colo., 4248–93
Health, Housing, and Nutrition Gaps Between the Poor and Nonpoor. Elderly Americans, 26131–100
Health Information for International Travel, 1992, 4204–11
Health Insurance and Utilization of Medical Care for Chronically Ill Children with Special Needs: Health of Our Nation's Children, U.S., 1988, 4146–8.216
Health Insurance Coverage, 1987-90, 2546–20.23
Health Insurance for the Unemployed, 21788–209
Health Insurance Options: Reform of Private Health Insurance, 21788–218
Health Insurance Status of Farm Operators, Managers, and Workers, and the President's Health Care Reforms, 1541–1.318
Health Insurance, Use of Health Services, and Health Care Expenditures. National Medical Expenditure Survey, 4186–8.24
Health Insurance: Who Was Covered Between 1987 and 1990? Statistical Brief, 2326–17.49
Health Manpower Statistics, FY90, 3544–24
Health of Our Nation's Children, U.S., 1988. Health Insurance and Utilization of Medical Care for Chronically Ill Children with Special Needs, 4146–8.216
Health of Retired Workers: Survival Status and Medicare Service Use, 4652–1.319
Health Personnel in the U.S., Eighth Report to Congress, 1991, 4114–8
Health Physics/Radiation Protection Enrollments and Degrees, 1991: Appendixes, 3004–7
Health Professions and Nurse Education, 21368–135
Health Risks and Benefits of Contraceptive Use in the U.S., 4164–2
Health Service Areas for the U.S. Vital and Health Statistics Series 2, 4147–2.113
Health Services: The Real Jobs Machine, 6722–1.347
Health, U.S., 4144–11
Health U.S., and Prevention Profile, 1991, 4144–11
Hearing Aids, 1992, 8704–3
Hearing on Appalachia: Poverty Alleviation Strategies, 21968–58
Hearings on H.R. 1, the Civil Rights Act of 1991, 21348–120
Hearings on H.R. 1218, the Privacy for Consumers and Workers Act, 21348–122
Hearings on H.R. 5, the Striker Replacement Bill, 21348–121
Heavy Rail Transit Safety, Annual Report, 7884–5
Heavy-Duty Trucks in Crashes, NASS, 1979-86, 7768–124
Helical Spring Lockwashers from the People's Republic of China and Taiwan. Determinations of the Commission in Investigations Nos. 731-TA-624 and 625 (Preliminary) Under the Tariff Act of 1930, Together with the Information Obtained in the Investigations, 9886–14.362
Helium: Minerals Yearbook, Volume 1, 1990, 5604–20.27
Helium: Minerals Yearbook, Volume 1, 1991, 5604–15.27
Helping Small Business Build America's Future: SBA FY91 Annual Report, 9764–1.1
Helping Small Business Build America's Future: SBA FY91 Guarantees and 8(A) Contracts, 9764–1.2
Hepatitis B Immunization Campaign for Children in the Federated States of Micronesia, 4042–3.357
Hepatitis B Virus: A Comprehensive Strategy for Eliminating Transmission in the U.S. Through Universal Childhood Vaccination. Recommendations of the Immunization Practices Advisory Committee (ACIP), 4206–2.49
Hepatitis Surveillance Report No. 54, 4205–2
Herbicides and Cancer, 4472–1.356
Heroin Price, Purity, and Quantities Seized Over the Past 10 Years. War on Drugs, 26119–404
Heroin Situation: A Status Report, 236–3.5
Heterogeneity for Allelic Loss in Human Breast Cancer, 4472–1.310
High Costs, Wide Variation Threaten System. Employer-Based Health Insurance, 26121–485
High School and Beyond: A National Longitudinal Study for the 1980's, 4826–2
High School and Beyond Fourth Follow-Up Contractor Report, 4826–2.54
High Technology Employment in the Southeast, 6946–3.23
High Tenacity Rayon Filament Yarn from Germany. Determination of the Commission in Investigation No. 731-TA-530 (Final) Under the Tariff Act of 1930, Together with the Information Obtained in the Investigation, 9886–14.350
Higher Education Act, Title II-B. Library Career Training Program, Abstracts of Funded Projects, 1991, 4874–1
Higher Net Income Improves Growth of Largest Co-ops, 1122–1.306
High-Technology Competitiveness: Trends in U.S. and Foreign Performance, 26123–406
Highway and Motor Vehicle Safety, 1990, 7764–1
Highway Bridge Replacement and Rehabilitation Program, 1991: Tenth Report of the Secretary of Transportation to the U.S. Congress, 7554–27
Highway Safety Improvement Programs: 1992 Annual Report of the Secretary of Transportation to the U.S. Congress, 7554–26
Highway Safety Performance, 1989: Fatal and Injury Accident Rates on Public Roads in the U.S., 7554–2
Highway Safety 1990: A Report on Activities Under the Highway Safety Act of 1966, As Amended, 7764–1.1
Highway Statistics, 1991, 7554–1
Highway Trust Fund, 8102–9.7
Hispanic Access to Health Care: Significant Gaps Exist, 26131–97
Hispanic Origin. 1990 Census Questionnaire Content Bulletin, 2326–23.3
Historical Monthly Energy Review, 1973-88, 3168–123
Historical Proportion of New Officers During Benchmark Periods. Service Academies, 26123–389
Historical Trends in the U.S. Cost of Capital, 8006–6.2
Historical Trends: State Education Facts, 1969-89, 4828–33
Historically Black Colleges and Universities Share $1.5 Million in HUD Technical Assistance Funds, 5006–3.78
Historically Black Colleges and Universities, 1976-90, 4848–46
History of the 1987 Economic Censuses, 2628–16
HIV Infection Treatment Costs Under Medicaid in Michigan, 4042–3.348
HIV/AIDS Surveillance, 4202–9
HIV-Infected Men's Practices in Notifying Past Sexual Partners of Infection Risk, 4042–3.310
Hogs and Pigs, 1623–3
Home Activities of 3- to 8-Year-Olds, 4826–10.1
Home Alone in 1989, 2486–1.15
Home and Leisure Injury Prevention, 4208–35
Home Drug Infusion Therapy Under Medicare, 26358–258
Home Mortgage Commitment Rates in Illinois, Federal Home Loan Bank of Chicago, 9302–6
Home Mortgage Commitment Rates in Wisconsin, Federal Home Loan Bank of Chicago, 9302–7
Homelessness: HUD Improperly Restricts Applicants for Supplemental Assistance Program, 26113–593
Homelessness: McKinney Act Programs and Funding Through FY91, 26104–21
Homelessness: Single Room Occupancy Program Achieves Goals, But HUD Can Increase Impact, 26113–596
Homelessness: Transitional Housing Shows Initial Success but Long-term Effects Unknown, 26113–549
Homeowners and Home Improvements: 1987, 2486–1.13

Homeownership: 1989 to 1991. Statistical Brief, 2326–17.46
Homicide Surveillance—U.S., 1979-88, 4202–7.315
Honey, 1631–6
Honey, Summary of 1991-95 Support Program and Related Information: ASCS Commodity Fact Sheet, 1806–4.2, 1806–4.12
Hop Stocks, 1621–8
Hope Basin Socioeconomic Baseline Study Volume I: Final Technical Report. Alaska Social and Economic Study, 5736–5.16
Hope Basin Socioeconomic Baseline Study Volume II: Final Technical Report Summary. Alaska Social and Economic Study, 5736–5.16
Hope Basin Socioeconomic Baseline Study Volume III: NANA Elders Conference and Interview Transcripts. Alaska Social and Economic Study, 5736–5.16
Hops Market News, 1313–7
Horticultural Exports, 1987-91, 1925–34
Horticultural Imports, 1987-91, 1925–34
Horticultural Products Review: Foreign Agricultural Service Circular Series, 1925–34
Hospital and Community Characteristics in Closures of Urban Hospitals, 1980-87, 4042–3.341
Hospital Closure: 1988, 4004–35
Hospital Closure: 1989, 4004–35
Hospital Closure: 1990, 4004–35
Hospital Closures: 1985-88, 17206–2.27
Hospital Readmissions, 4008–117
Hospital Studies Program Research Notes, 4186–6
Hospitals, January 1991. Occupational Wage Survey, 6787–6.254
Hot-Rolled Lead and Bismuth Carbon Steel Products from Brazil, France, Germany, and the UK. Determinations of the Commission in Investigations Nos. 701-TA-314 thru 317 (Preliminary) and 731-TA-522 thru 555 (Preliminary) Under the Tariff Act of 1930, Together with the Information Obtained in the Investigations, 9886–19.82
Hourly Compensation Costs for Production Workers, 6826–3
Hourly Compensation Costs for Production Workers: 40 Manufacturing Industries, 33 Countries or Areas, 1975 and 1980-90, 6826–3.9
House Concurrent Resolution on the Budget, FY93, 21264–2
Household and Family Characteristics: March 1991, 2546–1.457
Household Diary Study, FY89 and FY90, 9864–10
Household Economic Studies. Current Population Reports. Series P-70, 2546–20
Household Income Mobility During the 1980s: A Statistical Assessment Based on Tax Return Data, 8008–156
Household-Based, Nonparametric Test of Demand Theory, 6886–6.88
Housing Characteristics of One-Parent Households: 1989, 2486–1.14
Housing Characteristics of Recent Movers, 2486–1.12
Housing Characteristics, 1990. Residential Energy Consumption Survey, 3166–7.33
Housing Completions, Current Construction Reports, 2382–2
Housing Discrimination Study, 5186–16
Housing Discrimination Study: Analyzing Racial and Ethnic Steering, 5186–16.3
Housing Discrimination Study: Incidence and Severity of Unfavorable Treatment, 5186–16.5
Housing Discrimination Study: Incidence of Discrimination and Variations in Discriminatory Behavior, 5186–16.7
Housing Discrimination Study: Mapping Patterns of Steering for Five Metropolitan Areas, 5186–16.2
Housing Discrimination Study: Methodology and Data Documentation, 5186–16.4
Housing Discrimination Study: Replication of 1977 Study Measures with Current Data, 5186–16.6
Housing Discrimination Study: Synthesis, 5186–16.1
Housing Highlights, 1990, 2326–21
Housing Highlights, 1990: Financial Facts, 2328–83
Housing in America, 1989/90, 2486–2.1
Housing of Single-Parent Families. Statistical Brief, 2326–17.44
Housing Persons with Mental Disabilities with the Elderly. Public Housing, 26113–590
Housing Starts, Current Construction Reports, 2382–1
Housing Units Authorized by Building Permits: Annual 1991. Current Construction Reports, 2384–2
Housing Units Authorized by Building Permits, Current Construction Reports, 2382–5
Housing Vacancies and Home Ownership. Current Housing Reports, 2482–1
Housing Vacancies and Homeownership, Annual Statistics: 1991. Current Housing Reports, Series H-111, 2484–1
Housing Vacancy Rates: 1989-91. Statistical Brief, 2326–17.51
Housing Vacancy Survey, Federal Home Loan Bank of Chicago, 9304–18
Housing Vacancy Survey, Federal Home Loan Bank of Cincinnati, 9304–27
Housing Vacancy Survey, Federal Home Loan Bank of Dallas, 9304–19
Housing Vacancy Survey, Federal Home Loan Bank of Seattle, 9304–21
Housing Vacancy Survey, Federal Home Loan Bank of Topeka, 9304–22
How Accurate Are the Employment Projections in the Occupational Outlook Handbook?, 6742–1.302
How Consumers Spend Their Money. Statistical Brief, 2326–17.42
How Federal Employees View the Government as a Place To Work. Federal Employment, 26119–406
How Federal Milk Order Market Statistics Are Developed and What They Mean, 1317–4.302
How Foreign-Owned Firms Benefit the Eighth District, 9391–16.302
How Important Are Monetary and Fiscal Policy in Explaining Postwar Aggregate U.S. Data? A Vector Autoregressive Approach, 9381–10.132
How Investors Fare. Securities Arbitration, 26119–401
How Is the Farm Bill Working (Planting Flexibility Opportunities), 1504–9.1
How Large Are Economic Forecast Errors?, 9373–1.313
How the 1992 Legislation Will Affect European Financial Services, 9391–1.308
How Well Does Unemployment Explain the Low Levels of Consumer Confidence?, 9391–16.304
How We're Changing: Demographic State of the Nation, 1992, 2546–2.163
How Workers Get Their Training, 6728–32
How Young Farmers Accumulate Farmland, 1541–1.319
H.R. 2440: Credit and Charge Card Disclosure Amendments of 1991, 21248–175
H.R. 2890: To Establish Limits on Prices of Drugs Procured by the Department of Veterans Affairs, 21768–68
HUD Announces Grant Awards Totalling $140 Million To Eliminate Drugs in Public Housing, 5006–3.99
HUD Announces Permanent Housing for Handicapped Homeless Grants for 24 States, 80 Local Projects, 5006–3.79
HUD Announces $20.2 Million for Nehemiah Housing Opportunity Program, 5006–3.84
HUD Announces $43.6 Million for Permanent Housing for Handicapped Homeless in 20 States, 50 Local Projects, 5006–3.96
HUD Announces $106.1 Million in Grants for Transitional Housing for the Homeless, 5006–3.80
HUD Announces $376 Million in Housing Funds To Assist Elderly Families, 5006–3.88
HUD Announces $98 Million in Grants for Transitional Housing for the Homeless, 5006–3.95
HUD Awards $44 Million for Lead-Based Paint Abatement Programs, 5006–3.102
HUD Awards $91.5 Million in Housing Funds To Assist People with Disabilities, 5006–3.98
HUD Awards $14 Million for Technical Assistance To Spur Community Group Involvement in "HOME" Program, 5006–3.93
HUD Awards $366 Million in Housing Funds To Assist Elderly Families, 5006–3.97
HUD Awards $4.5 Million for "Hands On" Activities by Historically Black Colleges and Universities, 5006–3.85
HUD Awards $94.9 Million Under 'HOPE III' To Spur Single-Family Homeownership Programs, 5006–3.94
HUD Improperly Restricts Applicants for Supplemental Assistance Program. Homelessness, 26113–593
HUD Lead-Based Paint Abatement Demonstration (FHA), 5188–131
HUD News: Miscellaneous Press Releases, 5006–3
HUD To Assist 40 Neighborhood Groups in Neighborhood Development Demonstration Program, 5006–3.92
HUD To Award $104 Million in Homeless Funds, 5006–3.82
HUD/HHS To Fund Joint Economic Empowerment Initiative and Head Start Programs, 5006–3.83
Human Factors Evaluation of the Work Environment of Operators Engaged in the Inspection and Repair of Aging Aircraft, 7506–10.99
Human Papillomavirus-Negative Status and c-myc Gene Overexpression: Independent Prognostic Indicators of Distant Metastasis for Early-Stage Invasive Cervical Cancers, 4472–1.348

Hungarian Wine Sector, 1925–34.331
Hurricane Andrew—A Preliminary Look, 2152–8.304
Hurricane Hugo: Effects on South Carolina's Forest Resource, 1208–411
Hydropower 2002: Reclamation's Energy Initiative, 5828–14
Hyperthermia in Conjunction with Cancer Chemotherapy. Health Technology Assessment Report, 1991, 4186–10.7

Ice Patrol—A Titanic Legacy, 2152–8.301
ICL Meeting Presentations, 4208–36
Idaho Cooperative Snow Survey Data of Federal-State-Private Cooperative Snow Surveys, Water Year 1990, 1264–14.3
Idaho Forest Pest Conditions and Program Summary, 1990, 1206–49.1
Idaho Forest Pest Conditions and Program Summary, 1991, 1206–49.4
Identification and Quantitation of Triamterene in Blood and Urine from a Fatal Aircraft Accident, 7506–10.110
Identifying Ability Requirements for Operators of Future Automated Air Traffic Control Systems, 7506–10.122
Identifying Credit Crunches, 9389–19.32
If Properly Implemented, FTA Initiatives Should Improve Oversight. Mass Transit Grants, 26113–600
IGLD 1985: Brochure on the International Great Lakes Datum, 1985, 2178–34
IHS and Tribal Hospital Statistics, 4082–1
Illegal Drug Price/Purity Report, U.S., 6282–1
Immigrant Earnings, Relative To What? The Importance of Earnings Function Specification and Comparison Points, 9385–8.143
Immigrant Links to the Home Country: Implications for Trade, Welfare and Factor Rewards, 9379–12.84
Immigrant Visa Waiting List in the Family-Sponsored and Employment-Based Preferences as of January 1992, 7188–1
Immigrants Admitted by Country or Region of Birth, 6264–4
Immigrants Admitted by Major Occupation Group and Region and Selected Country of Birth, 6264–1
Immigrants and Legalized Aliens Admitted by Country or Region Birth and Major Occupation Group, FY91, 6264–1
Immigration and Naturalization Service Bulletins, 6266–2
Immigration and Naturalization Service 1990 Statistical Yearbook, 6264–2
Immigration and Naturalization Service 1991 Statistical Yearbook, 6264–2
Immigration and Regional Labor Market Performance in the U.S. Apparel Industry, 6366–6.6
Immigration Control: Immigration Policies Affect INS Detention Efforts, 26119–409
Immigration Policies Affect INS Detention Efforts. Immigration Control, 26119–409
Immigration Policy and Colombian Textile Workers in New England, 6366–6.4
Immigration Policy and Research Working Papers, 6366–6
Immigration Reform: The Effects of Employer Sanctions and Legalization on Wages, 6366–6.8
Immigration Statistics: FY91 Advance Report, 6264–4
Immunization: Survey of Recent Research, Volume 5, 4204–16
Impact of a Local Ordinance Banning Tobacco Sales to Minors, 4042–3.336
Impact of Bank Reform Proposals on Consumers, 21248–167
Impact of Demographic, Social, and Economic Change on the Distribution of Income, 2546–6.79
Impact of Deposit Interest Rate Deregulation on Bank Riskiness, 9379–14.15
Impact of Government Deficits on Personal and National Saving Rates, 8006–6.5
Impact of International Visitor Spending on State Economies, 1989, 2908–28
Impact of IRCA on the U.S. Labor Market and Economy, 6366–6.10
Impact of Medicare Payment Policy on Home Health Resources Utilization, 4652–1.302
Impact of Survey and Questionnaire Design on Longitudinal Labor Force Measures, 2626–10.145
Impact of the Clean Air Act on Agriculture, 1504–9.1
Impact of the Current Defense Build-Down, 9385–1.313
Impact of Trade and Environmental Regulations on U.S. Nursery and Greenhouse Producers, 1504–9.1
Imperfect Information and Financial Constraints: New Evidence Using Bank Loan Commitments, 9381–10.128
Implementation of the Chelsea School Project: A Case Study, 4808–38
Implementation of the Individuals with Disabilities Education Act, Fourteenth Annual Report to Congress, 4944–4
Implementation of the U.S.-Canada Free Trade Agreement, 25368–179
Implementing an SSI Model Using the Survey of Income and Program Participation, 4746–26.23
Implications of a Single EC Market for the U.S. Food Manufacturing Sector, 1528–325
Implications of Birth Cohort Patterns in Interpreting Trends in Breast Cancer Rates, 4472–1.341
Implications of Netting Arrangements for Bank Risk in Foreign Exchange Transactions, 9391–1.304
Implications of Proposed National Energy Policy Legislation for Natural Gas, 25318–82
Implications of the Drug Use Forecasting Data for TASC Programs: Female Arrestees, 6068–246
Importance of the Tax System in Determining the Marginal Cost of Funds, 9387–8.278
Imports and Exports of Fishery Products, Annual Summary, 1991, 2166–6.1
Imports from China and Competitive Conditions in the U.S. Market: Further Examination of Product Groups Identified by the East-West Trade Statistics Monitoring System, 9882–2.301
Improvement in IRS' Telephone Assistor Accuracy. Tax Administration, 26119–418
Improving Automobile Fuel Economy: New Standards, New Approaches, 26358–251
Improving Federal Statistics, 23848–227
Improving Health Care Communication for Persons with Mental Retardation, 4042–3.328
Improving Human Resource Programs. Status of Open Recommendations, Part C, 26104–5.3
Improving Justice, General Government, Financial and Information Management, and Evaluation Programs. Status of Open Recommendations, Part D, 26104–5.4
Improving National Security and International Affairs Programs. Status of Open Recommendations, Part A, 26104–5.1
Improving Resources, Community, and Economic Development Programs. Status of Open Recommendations, Part B, 26104–5.2
Improving SBA Loan Collateral Liquidations Would Increase Recoveries. Small Business, 26113–553
Improving the Area Wage Index: The Area Wage Index and the Mix of Occupations Across Areas, 17206–2.31
In Search of a Stable, Short-Run M1 Demand Function, 9389–1.303
In Search of Scale Effects in Trade and Growth, 9383–20.22
In Search of the Liquidity Effect, 9371–10.75
Inaccuracies Found May Lead to Underestimates of Budget Outlays. USDA Commodity Forecasts, 26131–94
Inaccurate FCIC Price Forecasts Increase Program Costs. Crop Insurance, 26131–95
Inadequate Management and Oversight Contribute to Financial Problems. American Samoa, 26123–385
Incentive Conflict in Deposit-Institution Regulation: Evidence from Australia, 9375–13.82
Incentives Maintain Low-Income Housing but Clearer Guidance Needed. Rural Rental Housing, 26113–586
Incidence and Impact of Oak Decline in Western Virginia, 1986, 1208–384
Incidence and Impact of Selected Infectious Diseases in Childhood. Vital and Health Statistics Series 10, 4147–10.181
Incidence of Dysplasia and Carcinoma of the Uterine Cervix in an Appalachian Population, 4472–1.327
Incidence of Non-Hodgkin's Lymphomas in Italy, 4472–1.336
Incidental Catch of Marine Mammals by Foreign and Joint Venture Trawl Vessels in the U.S. EEZ of the North Pacific, 1973-88, 2168–129
Income and Expenditures of Older Widowed, Divorced, and Never-Married Women Who Live Alone, 1702–1.301
Income and Resources of the Population 65 and Over, 4744–25
Income, Assets, and Health Insurance: Economic Resources for Meeting Acute Health Care Needs of the Aged, 4742–1.307
Income of the Aged Chartbook, 1990, 4744–25
Income of the Population 55 and Over, 1990, 4744–26
Income, Poverty, and Wealth in the U.S.: A Chart Book, 2546–6.75
Income Security and Health Care: Economic Implications, 1991-2020. An Expert Panel Report to the Advisory Council on Social Security, 10176–1.3
Income Withholder's Role in Child Support, 4588–1
Increases in Set-Asides and Cost Ceilings Since 1982. Block Grants, 26121–466

Increasing Flower Consumption Through Marketing, 1504–9.1
Increasing Incidence of Cutaneous Melanoma in Queensland, Australia, 4472–1.344
Increasing Incidence of Primary Malignant Brain Tumors: Influence of Diagnostic Methods, 4472–1.309
Increasing Participation by Private Physicians in the EPSDT Program in Rural North Carolina, 4042–3.358
Independent Living Services for the Elderly Blind, 21148–64
Index of Bank Control Share Prices, 9381–14
Index of FAA Office of Aviation Medicine Reports: 1961-91, 7506–10.97
Index of Reports and Testimony: FY91, 26104–17
Index Report, Federal Home Loan Bank of Chicago, 9302–30
Index to the NIPA Tables, 2702–1.304, 2702–1.325
Indexed Bonds as an Aid to Monetary Policy, 9389–2
India: Asia Pacific Energy Series Country Report, 3406–6.10
Indian Civil Service Retirement Act, P.L. 96-135, Annual Report to Congress, FY90, 4084–6
Indian Education: Whose Responsibility? 18th Annual Report to Congress FY91, 14874–1
Indian Health Service and Tribal Hospital Inpatient Workload Summary for FY91 and Comparison with Previous Year, 4084–4
Indian Health Service: Hospital Inpatient Workload Summary and Comparison with Previous Year, 4084–4
Indian Health Service: Regional Differences in Indian Health, 1992, 4084–7
Indian Health Service: Trends in Indian Health, 1992, 4084–1
Indian Nations at Risk: An Educational Strategy for Action, 4808–42.1
Indian Nations at Risk: Listening to the People, 4808–42.2
Indian Nations at Risk Task Force Report, 4808–42
Indian Programs: BIA and Indian Tribes Are Taking Action To Address Dam Safety Concerns, 26113–558
Indian Programs: Profile of Land Ownership at 12 Reservations, 26113–559
Indicators of Comparative East-West Economic Strength, 7144–11
Indicators of Equal Employment Opportunity—Status and Trends, 9248–20
Individual Foreign Earned Income and Tax Credit, 1987, 8302–2.301
Individual Income Tax Returns, Preliminary Data, 1990, 8302–2.307
Individual Income Tax Returns, 1988, 8304–2
Individual Income Tax Returns, 1991: Taxpayer Usage Study, 8302–2.319
Indochinese Refugee Activity and Summary of Refugee Admissions, 7002–4
Indonesia: Asia Pacific Energy Series Country Report, 3406–6.9
Industrial Gases, Current Industrial Report, 2506–8.3
Industrial Gases, 1991, Current Industrial Report, 2506–8.15
Industrial Patent Activity in the U.S., 2244–3
Industrial Patent Activity in the U.S., Part 1: Time Series Profile by Company and Country of Origin, 1969-90, 2244–3.1
Industrial Patent Activity in the U.S., Part 1: Time Series Profile by Company and Country of Origin, 1969-91, 2244–3.1
Industrial Patent Activity in the U.S., Part 2: Alphabetical Listing by Company, 1969-90, 2244–3.2
Industrial Patent Activity in the U.S., Part 2: Alphabetical Listing by Company, 1969-91, 2244–3.2
Industrial Production and Capacity Utilization, 9365–2.24
Industrial Robots, Current Industrial Report, 2506–12.32
Industrial Structure of Job Displacement, 1979-89, 6722–1.340
Industry and Trade Summary Reports: Agriculture, Fisheries, and Forest Products, 9885–8
Industry and Trade Summary Reports: Energy and Chemicals, 9885–11
Industry and Trade Summary Reports: General Manufactures, 9885–10
Industry and Trade Summary Reports: Machinery and Equipment, 9885–9
Industry and Trade Summary Reports: Minerals and Metals, 9885–13
Industry and Trade Summary Reports: Services and Electronic Technology, 9885–12
Industry Output and Job Growth Continues Slow into Next Century, 6744–19
Industry Productivity and High-Tech Investment, 9385–8.130
Industry, Trade, and Technology Review, 9882–16
Industry Wage Survey: Metalworking Machinery Manufacturing, February 1990, 6787–6.253
Industry Wage Surveys, 6787–6
Inefficiency and Productivity Growth in Banking: A Comparison of Stochastic Econometric and Thick Frontier Methods, 9377–9.126
Inflation and Its Variability: A Note?, 9379–12.86
In-Flight Survey of International Air Travelers: Overseas Travelers to the U.S., January-December 1991, 2904–12
In-Flight Survey of International Air Travelers: Profile of Overseas Travelers to U.S.A. Destinations, 2904–12
Influence of Current Judicial Doctrines on the Cost of Purchasing Health Care, 10176–3.5
Influenza Surveillance—U.S., 1991-92, 4202–7.325
Influenza—U.S., 1989-90 and 1990-91 Seasons, 4202–7.316
INFORM Evaluation, 7558–119
Information and Withholding Documents, Projections, U.S. and Service Centers, 8304–22
Information Dissemination: Case Studies on Electronic Dissemination at Four Agencies, 26125–47
Information on Amtrak's Operating Expenses. Amtrak, 26113–573
Information on Costs and Financial Aid to Schools To Control Asbestos. Toxic Substances, 26113–560
Information on Criminal Cases. Antitrust, 26119–375
Information on External Review Organizations. Utilization Review, 26121–490
Information on Federal Participation in Transit Benefit Programs. Mass Transit, 26113–601
Information on Four Federal Banking Agencies. Pay and Benefits, 26119–368
Information on Funding, Staffing, and Timing of FAA's Research Projects. Aviation Research, 26113–565
Information on Justice's Investigations and Prosecutions. Bank and Thrift Criminal Fraud, 26119–426
Information on Plea Agreements and Settlements. Defense Procurement Fraud, 26119–423
Information on the Administration of Workers' Compensation Programs in Each State and D.C., 6504–9
Information on USDA's Water Quality Cost-Share Programs. Water Quality, 26113–572
Information Security Oversight Office, Annual Report to the President, FY91, 9454–21
Information 2000: Library and Information Services for the 21st Century, 15638–16
Inhalation Toxicology Research Institute, Albuquerque, N.Mex., Site Environmental Report, 1990, 3324–2.4
In-house Energy Management Annual Report, FY91, 3004–27
Initial Assessment of Certain BCCI Activities in the U.S.: Foreign Bank, 26119–427
Initial Efforts To Expand State Assistance. Unemployed Parents, 26131–96
Injuries Associated with Selected Consumer Products Treated in Hospital Emergency Departments, 1990, 9164–7
Injury Experience in Coal Mining, 1990, 6664–4
Injury Experience in Metallic Mineral Mining, 1990, 6664–3
Injury Experience in Nonmetallic Mineral Mining (Except Stone and Coal), 1990, 6664–1
Injury Experience in Sand and Gravel Mining, 1990, 6664–2
Injury Experience in Stone Mining, 1990, 6664–5
Injury Surveillance in Developing Countries, 4202–7.308
Inland Waterways Trust Fund, 8102–9.8
Inorganic Acids, Industry and Trade Summary, 9885–11.2
Inorganic Chemicals, Current Industrial Report, 2506–8.1
Inorganic Chemicals, 1991, Current Industrial Report, 2506–8.14
Inpatient Summary Data for Indian Health Service and Tribally-Operated Hospitals, 4082–1
Input-Output Accounts, 2708–17.1
Inputs Situation and Outlook Report. Agricultural Resources, 1561–16.301, 1561–16.304
Inspector General Semiannual Report to the Congress, Department of Transportation, Apr. 1-Sept. 30, 1991, 7302–4
Inspector General Semiannual Report to the Congress, Department of Transportation, Oct. 1, 1991-Mar. 31, 1992, 7302–4
Inspector General's Report to the Congress, Department of Housing and Urban Development. Report No. 27, for the 6-Month Period Ending Mar. 31, 1992, 5002–8
Inspector General's Report to the Congress, Department of Housing and Urban

Development. Report No. 28, for the 6-Month Period Ending Sept. 30, 1992, 5002–8
Inspector General's Semiannual Report to the Congress, U.S. Department of Commerce, Oct. 1, 1991-Mar. 31, 1992, 2002–5
Inspector General's Semiannual Report to the Congress, U.S. Department of Commerce, Sept. 30, 1992, 2002–5
Institute of Museum Services, Annual Report, 1991, 9564–7
Institute of Museum Services Grant Awards, 9564–6
Insulated Wire and Cable, 1991, Current Industrial Report, 2506–10.8
Insurance Companies as Financial Intermediaries: Risk and Return, 9373–3.35
Insurance Company Solvency, 25268–79, 25528–119
Insurance, Industry and Trade Summary, 9885–12.2
Insurance Report, Federal Employees Health Benefits Program, Retired Federal Employees Health Benefits Program, Federal Employees' Group Life Insurance Program, 9844–35
Insurer Failures: Life/Health Insurer Insolvencies and Limitations of State Guaranty Funds, 26119–392
Insurers Whose Loss Ratios Did Not Meet Federal Minimum Standards in 1988-89. Medigap Insurance, 26121–452
Integrated Analysis Supporting the National Energy Strategy: Methodology, Assumptions and Results. National Energy Strategy, Technical Annex 2, 3006–13.2
Integrated Data Base for 1991: U.S. Spent Fuel and Radioactive Waste Inventories, Projections, and Characteristics, 3364–2
Integrated Postsecondary Education Data System Glossary, 4848–47
Integration of Circulation Data in the Beaufort Sea, 2176–1.40
Intellectual Property Rights and the Private Seed Industry, 1548–388
Interagency Council on the Homeless, 1989 Annual Report, 14364–1
Interagency Council on the Homeless, 1990 Annual Report, 14364–1
Interagency Forum on Aging-Related Statistics, Annual Report, 1989-90. Federal Forum, 14324–1
Inter-American Foundation Annual Report, 14424–1
Inter-American Foundation in Numbers: 1971-91, 14424–2
Inter-American Foundation: 1991 in Review, 14424–1
Intercollegiate Athletics: Compensation Varies for Selected Personnel in Athletic Departments, 26121–476
Interest Charge-Domestic International Sales Corporation Statistics for 1987: Data Release, 8302–2.312
Interest Income, Limited Expenses Help Farm Credit System Build Capital Base, 1122–1.301
Intergovernmental Perspective, 10042–1
Intergovernmental Relations: Changing Patterns in State-Local Finances, 26121–457
Interim Report on Social Security and the Federal Budget, 10176–3.1
Interior Secretary Awards $35.1 Million in Historic Preservation Grants, 5544–9
Interior's Monitoring Has Fallen Short of Agency Requirements. Rangeland Management, 26113–567
Intermittent Positive Pressure Breathing (IPPB) Therapy. Health Technology Assessment Report, 1991, 4186–10.6
Intermodal Surface Transportation Efficiency Act of 1991, 7558–117
Internal Combustion Engines, 1991, Current Industrial Report, 2506–12.6
Internal Controls over Computer-Processed Financial Data at Boeing Petroleum Services, 3006–5.27
Internal Net Worth and the Investment Process: An Application to U.S. Agriculture, 9375–13.77
Internal Revenue Report of Excise Taxes, 8302–1
Internal Revenue Service: Employee Views on Integrity and Willingness To Report Misconduct, 26119–366
Internal Revenue Service: Opportunities To Reduce Taxpaper Burden Through Return-Free Filing, 26119–400
Internal Revenue Service, 1991 Advance Annual Report, 8304–3
Internal Revenue Service, 1991 Annual Report, 8304–3
International Boycott Participation, 1990: Data Release, 8302–2.323
International Business Arrangements Used by Cooperatives, 1128–69
International Comparisons of Earnings Inequality for Men in the 1980's, 2546–6.79
International Comparisons of Hourly Compensation Costs for Production Workers in Manufacturing, 1975-90, 6822–3
International Comparisons of Hourly Compensation Costs for Production Workers in Manufacturing, 1991, 6822–3
International Comparisons of Manufacturing Productivity and Unit Labor Cost Trends, 1991, 6726–1.55
International Competitiveness of U.S. Financial Firms: Products, Markets, and Conventional Performance Measures, 9385–10
International Economic Conditions, 9391–7
International Economic Review, 9882–14
International Economic Review Special Edition: Composition of U.S. Merchandise Trade, 1987-91, Chartbook, 9884–21
International Energy Annual, 1990, 3164–50
International Energy Outlook 1992, 3164–84
International Energy Statistical Review, 9112–2
International Environment: Kuwaiti Oil Fires—Chronic Health Risks Unknown but Assessments Are Under Way, 26113–566
International Finance: Annual Report of the Chairman of the National Advisory Council on International Monetary and Financial Policies to the President and to the Congress for FY90, 15344–1
International Finance Discussion Papers, 9366–7
International Health Data Reference Guide, 1991, 4124–8
International Infant Mortality Rankings: A Look Behind the Numbers, 4652–1.324
International Investment Position of the U.S. in 1991, 2702–1.323
International Joint Commission, U.S. and Canada, Activities Report, 14644–3
International Mathematics and Science Assessments: What Have We Learned?, 4838–51
International Monetary Fund, 21248–169
International Narcotics Control Strategy Report, 7004–17
International Oil and Gas Exploration and Development Activities, 3162–43
International Petroleum Statistics Report, 3162–42
International Real Business Cycles, 9383–20.16
International Role of the Dollar, 9381–10.129
International Strategic Minerals Inventory Summary Report. A Regional Assessment of Selected Mineral Commodities in Subequatorial Africa, 5606–1.19
International Strategic Minerals Inventory Summary Reports, 5666–21
International Studies of Atmosphere, Sun Highlight: STS-45 Mission, 9506–2.146
International Taxation: Problems Persist in Determining Tax Effects of Intercompany Prices, 26119–411
International Trade: Agricultural Trade Offices' Role in Promoting U.S. Exports Is Unclear, 26123–370
International Trade and Foreign Markets. Foreign Agricultural Service Circular Series: Wood Products, 1925–36
International Trade: Romanian Trade Data, 26119–414
International Travel To and From the U.S., 1993 Outlook, 2904–9
Interrelation of Child Support, Visitation, and Hours of Work, 6722–1.329
Interstate Child Support: Mothers Report Receiving Less Support from Out-of-State Fathers, 26121–442
Interstate Child Support: Wage Withholding Not Fulfilling Expectations, 26121–445
Interstate Commerce Commission Office of Compliance and Consumer Assistance, Annual Performance Reports for Year Ended Dec. 31, 1991, 9484–11
Interstate Commerce Commission Office of Consumer Protection Annual Performance Reports of Household Goods Carriers Hauling 1,000 or More Shipments for Individual Shippers, 9484–11
Interstate Commerce Commission, 1988 Annual Report, 9484–1
Interstate Commerce Commission, 1989 Annual Report, 9484–1
Interstate Commerce Commission, 1990 Annual Report, 9484–1
Interstate Commerce Commission, 1991 Annual Report, 9484–1
Interstate Cost Estimate, 1991, 21648–66
Interstate Flow of Medicare Funds, 4006–11.4
Intertemporal Asset Pricing Models and the Cross Section of Expected Stock Returns, 9385–8.146
Intervention and the Bid-Ask Spread in G-3 Foreign Exchange Rates, 9377–1.305
Intra-Industry Trade Indexes for Canada, Mexico, and the U.S., 1962-87, 1528–327
Introducing a Broiler Retail Weight Consumption Series, 1561–7.302
Introduction of Seasonally Adjusted State Labor Force Data, 6742–2.305
Inventories of Steel Producing Mills, Current Industrial Report, 2506–10.3

Inventory and Analysis of Federal Population Research, FY90, 4474–9
Inventory and Evaluation of Washington and Oregon Coastal Recreation Resources, 5738–40
Inventory of Agricultural Research, FY91, 1744–2
Inventory of American Intermodal Equipment, 1991, 7704–10
Inventory of Pain Data from the National Center for Health Statistics. Vital and Health Statistics Series 1, 4147–1.27
Inventory of Parks and Recreation Facilities on the Coast of Washington and Oregon, 5738–40.3
Inventory of Power Plants in the U.S., 1991, 3164–36
Inventory of Public Water Supplies in Arkansas, 5666–24.18
Investigation of Passing Accidents on Two-Lane, Two-Way Roads, 7552–3.301
Investigation of Passing Accidents Using the HSIS Data Base, 7552–3.301
Investment and Market Imperfections in the U.S. Manufacturing Sector, 9375–13.81
Inward Contaminant Leakage Tests of the S-Tron Corporation Emergency Escape Breathing Device, 7506–10.118
IRAs and Saving: Evidence from a Panel of Taxpayers, 9381–10.126
IRCA Did Not Do Much to the Labor Market: A Los Angeles County Case Study, 6366–6.9
Iron and Steel Castings, 1991, Current Industrial Report, 2506–10.1
Iron and Steel: Minerals Yearbook, Volume 1, 1990, 5604–20.31
Iron and Steel Scrap: Mineral Industry Surveys, 5612–1.11
Iron and Steel Scrap: Minerals Yearbook, Volume 1, 1990, 5604–20.32
Iron Ore: Mineral Industry Surveys, 5612–1.12
Iron Ore: Minerals Yearbook, Volume 1, 1990, 5604–20.30
Iron Oxide Pigments in 1991: Mineral Industry Surveys, Annual Report, 5614–5.22
IRS Annual Report, 1991, 8304–3
IRS' Efforts To Improve Corporate Compliance. Tax Administration, 26119–405
IRS Estimates of the Aggregate Net Farm Profit (Loss) of Farm Sole Proprietors, 1541–1.320
IRS Undercover Operations Management Oversight Should Be Strengthened. Tax Administration, 26119–394
IRS 1991 Research Conference, 8304–25
Is Real Exchange Rate Variability Caused by Relative Price Changes? An Empirical Investigation, 9381–10.123
Is There Less Assurance in Life Insurance?, 9391–16.310
Issue Analysis Reports, Advisory Council on Social Security, 10176–3
Issues and Policy Proposals Regarding Tax Treatment of Intangible Assets. Tax Policy, 26119–365
Issues in Eastern European Social Security Reform, 8006–6.7
Issues in State Taxation of Banks, 9375–13.68
Jail Construction in California, 6066–30.1
Jail Inmates, 1991, 6066–25.48
Japanese Imports of Horticultural Products from the U.S. and the World, 1989-91, 1925–34.313
Japanese Liberalization of Orange Juice Market Creates New Opportunities, 1925–34.312
Japanese Presence in U.S. Agribusiness, 1528–332
Japan's Construction Market, 2042–1.307
Japan's Tuna Market, 2166–19.11
Job Creation During the Late 1980's: Dynamic Aspects of Employment Growth, 2546–20.20
Job Flight and the Airline Industry: The Economic Impact of Airports on Chicago and Other Metro Areas, 9375–13.78
Job Hazards Underscored in Woodworking Study, 6728–41
Job Market Slid in Early 1991, Then Struggled To Find Footing, 6722–1.312
Job Patterns for Minorities and Women in Private Industry, 1991, 9244–1
Job Patterns for Minorities and Women in State and Local Government, 1991, 9244–6
Job Training Partnership Act, 26106–8
Job Training Partnership Act: Actions Needed To Improve Participant Support Services, 26106–8.15
Jobs Held and Weeks Worked by Young Adults. Work and Family, 6726–2.3
Joint Economic Report, 1992, 23844–2
Joint National Committee on Detection, Evaluation, and Treatment of High Blood Pressure. Fifth Report, 4478–198
Joint Products: The Case of Japanese Demand for Soybean Meal and Oil, 1561–3.305
Joint Report on the Government Securities Market, 8008–154
Journal of Agricultural Economics Research, 1502–3
Journal of the National Cancer Institute, 4472–1
JTPA Education-Coordination Set-Aside: States' Implementation of the Program, 15496–1.15
Just Say Y.E.S.: Matching Adolescents to Appropriate Interventions for Alcohol and Other Drug-Related Problems, 4482–1.305
Justice Drug Grants to States, 236–3.1
Justice Expenditure and Employment, 1990, 6066–25.50
Justice Should Clearly Document Investigative Actions. Employee Misconduct, 26119–380
Justification Lacking for Continuing Two Parallel Programs. Bankruptcy Administration, 26119–421
Juvenile Court Drug and Alcohol Cases: 1985-88, 6066–27.7
Juvenile Justice Bulletin, 6066–27
Juveniles Taken into Custody: FY90 Report, 6064–35
Kemp Announces First HOPE Homeownership Grants for Multifamily Housing Units, 5006–3.91
Key Management Using ANSI X9.17. Computer Security, 2216–2.203
Key Statistics on the Noncollegiate Sector of Postsecondary Education: 1990, 4844–19
Knit Fabric Production, 1991, Current Industrial Report, 2506–5.7
Knolls Atomic Power Laboratory Annual Environmental Monitoring Report, 1990, 3324–2.5
Kuwait Oil Fires: Interagency Interim Report, 9188–116
Kuwaiti Oil Fires—Chronic Health Risks Unknown but Assessments Are Under Way. International Environment, 26113–566
Labor Agreement Expirations in the Federal Service, 9847–1
Labor and the Supreme Court: Significant Issues of 1991-92, 6722–1.308
Labor Demand by Forest Products Industries: A Review, 1208–416
Labor Force Projections: The Baby Boom Moves On, 6744–19
Labor Market Consequences of U.S. Immigration: A Survey, 6366–6.1
Labor Market in Real Business Cycle Theory, 9383–6.302
Laboratory for Energy-Related Health Research, University of California, Davis, Site Environmental Report for 1990, 3324–2.3
Laboratory-Based Surveillance for Rotavirus, U.S., Jan. 1989-May 1991, 4202–7.317
Lamps and Lighting Fittings, Industry and Trade Summary, 9885–10.2
Land Areas of the National Forest System, As of Sept. 30, 1991, 1204–2
Land Ownership and the Regulatory Framework for Oil, Gas, and Coal Leasing in Alaska, 5608–174
Lands Under Control of the U.S. Fish and Wildlife Service, as of Sept. 30, 1992, Annual Report, 5504–8
Language Characteristics and Academic Achievement: A Look at Asian and Hispanic Eighth Graders in National Education Longitudinal Study of 1988, 4826–9.12
Large Class I Household Goods Carriers Selected Earnings Data, 9482–14
Large Class I Motor Carriers of Passengers Selected Earnings Data, 9482–13
Large Class I Motor Carriers of Property Selected Earnings Data, 9482–5
Large Model Comparisons of Monetary Policy Sensitivity, 9385–8.135
Large-Scale Study of Freedom from Smoking Clinics—Factors in Quitting, 4042–3.314
Largest Co-ops Rebound To Post $101 Million Increase in Income, 1122–1.305
Latin America and the Caribbean: Selected Economic and Social Data, 9914–14
Latin America Trade Review: A U.S. Perspective, 2044–34
Law Enforcement Management and Administrative Statistics, 1990: Data for Individual State and Local Agencies with 100 or More Officers, 6064–39
Law Enforcement Officers Killed and Assaulted, 1991, 6224–3
Layers and Egg Production, 1991 Summary, 1625–7
Lead Industry: Mineral Industry Surveys, 5612–1.13
Lead: Mineral Industry Surveys, 5612–1.13
Lead: Minerals Yearbook, Volume 1, 1990, 5604–20.35
Leaders Give Their Schools High Marks, 9383–19.301

Leaf and Cigarette Production and Trade in Central and East Europe, 1561–10.303
Leaking Underground Storage Tanks Trust Fund, 8102–9.11
Leasing as a Lottery: Implications for Rational Building Surges and Increasing Vacancies, 9387–8.273
Legal Restrictions and Welfare in a Simple Model of Money, 9371–10.72
Lessons from Variations in State Medicaid Expenditures, 9373–1.303
Levels of Mathematics Achievement: Initial Performance Standards for the 1990 NAEP Mathematics Assessment. Volume III, Technical Report, 4896–8.6
Library Career Training Program: Abstracts of Funded Projects, 1991, Title II-B, Higher Education Act, 4874–1
Library Programs: Strengthening Research Library Resources Program. Higher Education Act, Title II-C, Abstracts of Funded Projects, 4874–2
Library Resources for the Blind and Physically Handicapped: A Directory with FY91 Statistics on Readership, Circulation, Budget, Staff, and Collections, 26404–3
Library Services for Indian Tribes and Hawaiian Natives Program, Library Services and Construction Act, Title IV, Review of Program Activities, 1990, 4874–5
Life Cycle and Expectations of Farmers, 1541–1.309
Life Expectancy by Employment Status, Income, and Education in the National Longitudinal Mortality Study, 4042–3.347
Life Insurance Benefits in Small Establishments and Government, 6722–1.346
Life Tables for the U.S. Social Security Area: 1900-2080, 4706–1.107
Life/Health Insurer Insolvencies and Limitations of State Guaranty Funds. Insurer Failures, 26119–392
Lighting in Commercial Buildings. Energy Consumption Series, 3166–15.1
LIHEAP Program Activities, 4584–1.1
Lime: Mineral Industry Surveys, 5612–1.15
Lime Plants in the U.S. in 1991: Top Ten Lime Producing States, 5614–31
Limitations in Methods and Procedures To Include the Homeless. 1990 Census, 26119–370
Limited Income Credit Unions, 9536–1.8
Limiting Conventional Arms Exports to the Middle East, 26306–6.173
Limits in the Seas, 7006–8
Liquidity Constraints in Economies with Aggregate Fluctuations: A Quantitative Exploration, 9383–20.19
Liquidity Effects and the Monetary Transmission Mechanism, 9383–20.20
List of Published Soil Surveys, 1264–11
Listing of Latest Car Theft Rates, 7764–21
Literacy and Education Needs in Public and Indian Housing Developments Throughout the Nation: Report to Congress, 5188–132
Literacy Definitions and Estimates. Adult Learning and Literacy Fact Sheet, 4806–4.3
Live Sheep and Meat of Sheep, Industry and Trade Summary, 9885–8.1
Live Swine and Fresh, Chilled, or Frozen Pork, Industry and Trade Summary, 9885–8.5
Liver Cirrhosis Mortality in the U.S., 1973-88, 4486–1.13
Livestock and Poultry Situation and Outlook Report, 1561–7
Livestock and Poultry Update, 1561–17
Livestock, Meat, and Wool Market News, Weekly Summary and Statistics, 1315–1
Livestock Slaughter, 1623–9
Livestock Slaughter, 1991 Summary, 1623–10
Loan and Debenture Activity, 9762–6.1
Loan Contraction Within a Framework of Moral Hazard, 9385–8.133
Loan Growth and Loan Quality: Some Preliminary Evidence from Texas Banks, 9379–1.305
Loan Payment Problems of Farmers in the Mid-1980's, 1548–383
Loan Volume Update Guaranteed Student Loan Programs: Stafford, PLUS, SLS Loans, 4802–2
Loans and Securities at All Commercial Banks, 9365–2
Local Boundary Commissions: Status and Roles in Forming, Adjusting and Dissolving Local Government Boundaries, 10048–85
Local Impact of Foreign Trade Zones, 9375–13.86
Local Sponsors' Views on Corps' Implementation of Project Cost Sharing. Water Resources, 26113–548
Location and Quality Effects of Mergers, 9387–8.268
Long and Costly Process of Reducing the Local National Work Force in Germany. Base Closures, 26123–383
Long Journey Home II: The Second Progress Report on the Department of Veterans Affairs PTSD Clinical Teams Program, 8704–6
Long Journey Home: The First Progress Report on the Department of Veterans Affairs PTSD Clinical Teams Program, 8704–6
Long Range Energy Projections to 2010, 3004–13
Long Staple Cotton Review, 1309–12
Longitudinal Comparison of Charge-Based Weights and Cost-Based Weights, 4652–1.318
Longitudinal Examination of Applicants to the Air Traffic Control Supervisory Identification and Development Program, 7506–10.116
Longitudinal Patterns of California Medicaid Recipients with Acquired Immunodeficiency Syndrome, 4652–1.301
Longitudinal Studies of HIV Infection in Intravenous Drug Users, 4498–79
Longitudinal Study of Aging: 1984-90. Vital and Health Statistics Series 1, 4147–1.28
Longshore and Harbor Workers' Compensation Act: Annual Report on Administration of the Act During FY91, Submitted to Congress 1992, 6504–10
Long-Term Energy Security Interests of the U.S., 21248–163
Long-Term Sequelae of Combat in World War II, Korea and Vietnam: A Comparative Study, 8704–6
Long-Term Strategies for Health Care, 21788–216
Long-Term Unemployed, 21788–207
Low Income Home Energy Assistance Program: Report to Congress, 4694–8
Low Income Home Energy Assistance Program: Report to Congress for FY90, 4584–1
Low Income Home Energy Trends, 1979-89, 4588–2
LSD Situation Report, 6288–9
Luggage and Personal Leather Goods, Current Industrial Report, 2506–6.13
Lumber and Veneer Recovery from Intensively Managed Young-Growth Douglas-Fir, 1208–413
Lumber Production and Mill Stocks, 1991, Current Industrial Report, 2506–7.4
Luxury Excise Tax Issues and Estimated Effects. Tax Policy and Administration, 26119–385

Macadamia Nuts: Economic and Competitive Factors Affecting the U.S. Industry. Report on Investigation No. 332-320 Under Section 332(g) of the Tariff Act of 1930, 9886–4.189
Macroeconomic Policy and Long-Run Growth, 9381–1.308
Macroeconomic Policy Implications of Trade and Currency Zones, 9381–13.1
Magnesium and Magnesium Compounds: Minerals Yearbook, Volume 1, 1990, 5604–20.38
Magnesium from Canada. Determination of the Commission in Investigation No. 701-TA-309 (Final) and No. 731-TA-528 (Final) Under the Tariff Act of 1930, Together with the Information Obtained in the Investigations, 9886–19.86
Magnesium: Mineral Industry Surveys, 5612–2.12
Major Collective Bargaining Settlements in Private Industry, 6782–2
Major Household Appliances, 1991, Current Industrial Report, 2506–12.16
Major Natural Gas Pipelines, Sept. 30, 1990, 3088–21
Major Nondeposit Funds of Commercial Banks, 9365–2
Major Political Parties Increase Non-election Year Activity—Soft Money Coffers Swell to Over $26 Million, 9276–1.101
Major Problems of Data Reliability and Validity Identified. Waste Minimization, 26131–98
Major Statistical Series of the U.S. Department of Agriculture, 1506–1
Major Statistical Series of the U.S. Department of Agriculture, Volume 12: Costs of Production, 1506–1.1
Major Work Stoppages, 1991, 6784–12
Making of the 1990 Farm Bill, 1504–9.1
Making Rural Policy for the 1990's and Beyond: A Federal Government View, 1504–9.1
Making Sense of Economic Indicators: A Consumers' Guide to Indicators of Real Economic Activity, 9375–1.307
Malaria Surveillance, Annual Summary, 1990, 4205–4
Management Information Report: Worker Adjustment Assistance Under the Trade Act of 1974, 6402–13
Management of Persons Exposed to Multidrug-Resistant Tuberculosis, 4206–2.61
Managing Farm Lender Interest Rate Risk with Financial Futures, 1541–1.308

Managing Federal Information Resources, Ninth Annual Report Under the Paperwork Reduction Act of 1980, 104–26
Managing Industrial Solid Wastes from Manufacturing, Mining, Oil and Gas Production, and Utility Coal Combustion, 26358–256
Managing Price Risk with Diammonium Phosphate and Anhydrous Ammonia Futures Contracts, 1561–16.301
Managing Rural Policy in a Federal System of Government, 1504–9.1
Managing Rural Policy Initiatives in the Intergovernmental System, 1504–9.1
Managing the Nation's Public Lands, FY90, 5724–13
Managing Workplace Safety and Health: The Case of Contract Labor in the U.S. Petrochemical Industry, 6608–6
Manganese Availability—Market Economy Countries: 1980's Perspective. A Minerals Availability Appraisal, 5606–4.31
Manganese: Mineral Industry Surveys, 5612–1.16
Man-Made Fiber Manufacturers (Customs Value). U.S. General Imports, 2046–9.2
Man-Made Fiber Manufacturers. U.S. General Imports, 2046–8.3
Manpower Assessment Briefs, 3006–8
Manpower Requirements Report, FY93, 3504–1
Manufactured Abrasives: Mineral Industry Surveys, 5612–2.19
Manufacturers' Pollution Abatement Capital Expenditures and Operating Costs, Advance Report for 1990. Current Industrial Report, 2506–3.6
Manufacturers' Pollution Abatement Capital Expenditures and Operating Costs, Advance Report for 1991, 2506–3.6
Manufacturers' Shipments, Inventories, and Orders, Current Industrial Report, 2506–3.1
Manufacturers' Utilization of Plant Capacity, Advance Report for 4th Quarter 1990, Current Industrial Report, 2506–3.7
Manufacturing: Analytical Report Series, 2506–16
Manufacturing Energy Consumption Survey, 3166–13
Manufacturing Industries: Evaluating Your Firm's Injury and Illness Record, 6886–4.1
Manufacturing Productivity and High-Tech Investment, 9385–1.310
Manufacturing Productivity and Labor Costs in 14 Economies, 6722–1.304
Many Are Threatened by Earthquakes, but Limited Action Has Been Taken. Federal Buildings, 26119–399
Maps and More: Your Guide to Census Bureau Geography, 2308–67
MARAD '91: Annual Report of the Maritime Administration, FY91, 7704–14
Margin Requirements, Price Fluctuations, and Market Participation in Metal and Stock Index Futures, 9385–8.127
Marginal Cost of Funds with Nonseparable Public Spending, 9387–8.265
Marginal Producers Not a Likely Source for Increased U.S. Imports. South American Oil, 26123–396
Marine Accident Reports, Brief Format, 9612–4
Marine Fisheries Review, 2162–1
Marine Mammal Commission: Annual Report to Congress, 1991, 14734–1
Marine Mammal Protection Act of 1972 Annual Report, July 1, 1988-Dec. 31, 1989, 2164–11
Marine Ranching: Proceedings of the Eighteenth U.S.-Japan Meeting on Aquaculture, Port Ludlow, Wash., Sept. 18-19, 1989, 2164–15
Marine Recreational Fishery Statistics Survey, 2166–17
Marine Recreational Fishery Statistics Survey, Atlantic and Gulf Coasts, 1990-91, 2166–17.1
Marine Recreational Fishery Statistics Survey, Pacific Coast, 1987-89, 2166–17.2
Mariners Weather Log, 2152–8
Marital Status and Living Arrangements: March 1991, 2546–1.461
Market Absorption of Apartments: Annual 1991 Absorptions (Apartments Completed in 1990). Current Housing Reports, 2484–2
Market Absorption of Apartments. Current Housing Reports, 2482–2
Market Share Reports Catalog, 2044–6
Market Share Reports: Commodity Series, 2046–13
Market Share Reports: Country Series, 2046–2
Market Structure, Technology, and the Cyclicality of Output, 9375–13.70
Market Value Accounting: Debt Investment Securities Held by Banks, 26111–77
Market Value Accounting for Commercial Banks, 9375–1.301
Marketable Phosphate Rock: Mineral Industry Surveys, 5612–1.30
Marketing Appalachian District Apples, 1991 Crop, 1311–13
Marketing California Grapes for Fresh Use, 1990 Season, 1311–25
Marketing Chile Fruits and Melons, 1311–27
Marketing Florida, Georgia, South Carolina, North Carolina and Appalachian District Peaches, 1991 Crop, 1311–12
Marketing Florida Ornamental Crops, Fresh Flowers and Ferns, Summary 1990, 1311–24
Marketing Florida Ornamental Crops, Fresh Flowers and Ferns, 1991 Season Summary, 1311–24
Marketing Florida Tropical Fruits and Vegetables, Summary 1990-91, 1311–23
Marketing Idaho, Colorado, Minnesota, N. Dakota, Oregon (Malheur County) and Wisconsin Potatoes, 1990 Crop, 1311–29
Marketing in Greece, 2046–6.6
Marketing in Indonesia, 2046–6.4
Marketing in Kenya, 2046–6.7
Marketing in Norway, 2046–6.1
Marketing in Pakistan, 2046–6.5
Marketing in South Africa, 2046–6.8
Marketing in Thailand, 2046–6.9
Marketing in the Netherlands, 2046–6.3
Marketing in the Philippines, 2046–6.2
Marketing Maine Potatoes, 1990 Crop, 1311–26
Marketing Maine Potatoes, 1991 Crop, 1311–26
Marketing Western Potatoes, 1991 Crop, 1311–29
Marriage, Divorce, and Remarriage in the 1990's, 2546–2.166
Mars Observer Ready To Take the Next Step in Mars Exploration, 9506–2.152
Marshall Islands: Status of the Nuclear Claims Trust Fund, 26123–405
Mass Layoffs in the Southeast, 1991, 6946–3.25
Mass Layoffs in 1990, 6744–18
Mass Transit: Effects of Tax Changes on Commuter Behavior, 26113–597
Mass Transit Grants: If Properly Implemented, FTA Initiatives Should Improve Oversight, 26113–600
Mass Transit: Information on Federal Participation in Transit Benefit Programs, 26113–601
Matching USDA Programs with Environmental Needs, 1504–9.1
Materials Flow of Zinc in the U.S., 1850-1990, 5608–176
Materials Sciences Programs, FY85, 3004–18.3
Materials Sciences Programs, FY86, 3004–18.3
Materials Sciences Programs, FY87, 3004–18.3
Materials Sciences Programs, FY88, 3004–18.3
Materials Sciences Programs, FY89, 3004–18.3
Materials Sciences Programs, FY90, 3004–18.3
Materials Sciences Programs, FY91, 3004–18.3
Maternal and Child Health: Block Grant Funds Should Be Distributed More Equitably, 26121–454
Maternal Pregravid Weight, Age, and Smoking Status as Risk Factors for Low Birth Weight Births, 4042–3.367
Maternal-Child Health Data from the NLSY: 1988 Tabulations and Summary Discussion, 4478–197
Mathematical Demonstration of the Pareto Optimality of Pay-As-You-Go Social Security Programs in a Closed Economy, 4746–26.18
Matter of Trust: American Red Cross Annual Report for 1990-91, 29254–1
Maturity and Fecundity in the Rockfishes, Sebastes spp., a Review, 2162–1.302
Maximizing the Market Value of a Firm To Choose Dynamic Policies for Managerial Hiring, Compensation, Firing and Tenuring, 9366–6.293
MBDA Annual Business Assistance Report for FY91, 2104–6
McKinney Act Programs and Funding Through FY91. Homelessness, 26104–21
Measurement and Determinants of Single-Family House Prices, 9373–27.7
Measurement of Efficiency in Life Insurance: Estimates of Mixed Normal-Gamma Error Model, 9385–8.144
Measurement of Relative Vulnerability to Pesticide Contamination. Groundwater Protection, 26131–91
Measurement of Streamflow Gains and Losses on Mission Creek at Santa Barbara, Calif., July and September 1987, 5666–27.29
Measuring Farm and Ranch Business Diversity, 1541–1.314
Measuring Financial Service Output and Prices in Commercial Banking, 6886–6.91
Measuring the Effect of Benefits and Taxes on Income and Poverty: 1979-91, 2546–6.78
Measuring the Value of School Quality, 9379–12.94

Meat Animals Production, Disposition and Income, 1991 Summary, 1623–8
Media Fact Sheet: 1992 Presidential Matching Fund Requests, 9276–1.104
Medicaid Expansions for Prenatal Care: State and Local Implementation, 4008–120
Medicaid Funding Crisis, 21408–129
Medicaid Intergovernmental Trends and Options, 10048–83
Medicaid Payment Methodologies for Inpatient Hospital Services, 17206–2.35
Medicaid spDATA System: Characteristics of Medicaid State Programs, 4654–19
Medicaid spDATA System: Characteristics of Medicaid State Programs. Volume I, National Comparisons, 4654–19.1
Medical Technology: For Some Cardiac Pacemaker Leads, the Public Health Risks Are Still High, 26131–103
Medically Based Programs Serving Maternal Substance Abusers and Their Children: A Survey of NIDA Grantees, 4498–76
Medicare and the American Health Care System, Report to the Congress, June 1992, 17204–2
Medicare Annual Report to Congress, FY87, 4654–5
Medicare Benefits and Financing: Report of the Advisory Council on Social Security, 10178–1
Medicare Hospital Information Report: Analysis of Variation Among Hospitals and Within Geographic Areas, 4654–14.54
Medicare Hospital Information, 1988-90, 4654–14
Medicare Hospital Mortality Information, 4654–14
Medicare Payments for Postoperative Office Visits for Cataract Surgery, 4006–11.3
Medicare Physician Payment Reform Regulations, 25368–178
Medicare Reports, Office of Inspector General, 4006–11
Medicare Volume Performance Standards Recommendation for FY93, 4004–32
Medicare Volume Performance Standards Recommendation, FY92. Report to Congress, 4004–32
Medicare/Medicaid Nursing Home Information, 4654–15
Medicare's Prospective Payment System: A Critical Appraisal, 4652–1.312
Medicare's Share in U.S. Physicians' Revenues, 17266–2.4
Medicare's Skilled Nursing Facility Payment Reform, 17206–1.14
Medigap Insurance: Insurers Whose Loss Ratios Did Not Meet Federal Minimum Standards in 1988-89, 26121–452
Mediterranean Processed Tomato Product Situation and Outlook, 1925–34.326
Medium-Voltage Underground Distribution Cable from Canada. Determination of the Commission in Investigation No. 731-TA-545 (Preliminary) Under the Tariff Act of 1930, Together with the Information Obtained in the Investigation, 9886–14.341
Meeting the Challenge of Multidrug-Resistant Tuberculosis: Summary of a Conference, 4206–2.61
Members of the Federal Home Loan Bank System, 9314–5
Membership Directory, 1990, Federal Home Loan Bank of Boston, 9304–26
Membership Directory, 1991, Federal Home Loan Bank of Boston, 9304–26
Membership Directory, 1992, Federal Home Loan Bank of Boston, 9304–26
Menopause, Hormone Therapy, and Women's Health, 26358–261
Mental Health Statistical Notes, NIMH Survey and Reports Branch, 4506–3
Mental Health, U.S., 4504–9
Mental Health, U.S., 1992, 4094–1
Merchandise Line Sales. 1987 Census of Retail Trade. Subject Series, 2399–3
Merchant Fleets of the World: Oceangoing Steam and Motor Ships of 1,000 Gross Tons and Over, as of Jan. 1, 1991, 7704–3
Merchant Fleets of the World: Oceangoing Steam and Motor Ships of 1,000 Gross Tons and Over, as of Jan. 1, 1992, 7704–3
Mercury in 1990: Mineral Industry Surveys, Annual Review, 5614–5.3
Mercury in 1991: Mineral Industry Surveys, Annual Review, 5614–5.14
Merger Decisions, 1990, Federal Deposit Insurance Corporation, 9294–5
Message from the American Public: A Hearings and Site Visits Report of the Advisory Council on Social Security, 10176–2.1
Message from the American Public: A Report of a National Survey on Health and Social Security by the Advisory Council on Social Security, 10176–2.2
Metal/Nonmetal: Surface Fatalities, Second Half 1991, 6662–3.4
Metal/Nonmetal: Underground Fatalities, Second Half 1991, 6662–3.3
Metalworking Machinery, Current Industrial Report, 2506–12.12
Metalworking Machinery Manufacturing, February 1990, Industry Wage Survey, 6787–6.253
Method for Assessing the Outcomes of Nursing Home Care Using Administrative Databases, 4164–2
Methodology Report for the 1990 National Postsecondary Student Aid Study, 4846–5.2
Metropolitan Areas, 1992, 104–32
Metropolitan Governance: Area Case Studies, 10046–9
Metropolitan Organization: The Allegheny County Case, 10046–9.2
Mexican Citrus Situation, 1925–34.309
Mexico Apparel Market, 2046–15.4
Mexico Textile and Fabric Market, 2046–15.3
Michigan Communities: Services Cut in Response to Fiscal Distress, 26121–483
Microeconometric Approach to Estimating Money Demand: The Asymptotically Ideal Model, 9391–1.303
Mid-Atlantic Manufacturing Index, 9387–12
Mid-Session Review of the Budget, 104–7
Mid-Session Review: The President's Budget and Economic Growth Agenda, 104–7
Migratory Bird Commission Approves Funding for Wetland Conservation Efforts Across North America, 5306–4.13
Migratory Bird Conservation Commission Approves Refuge Additions and Wetlands Projects in the U.S. and Canada, 5306–4.16
Migratory Bird Conservation Commission 1991 Annual Report, 14784–1
Migratory Bird Conservation Commission 1992 Annual Report, 14784–1
Military Aircraft: Policies on Government Officials' Use of 89th Military Airlift Wing Aircraft, 26123–384
Military Aircraft: Travel by Selected Executive Branch Officials, 26111–78
Military Construction Program, FY93, 3544–15
Military Equal Opportunity Assessment, 3704–10
Military Manpower Recruiting and Reenlistment Results for the Active Components, 3542–7
Military Manpower Recruiting Results for the Active Components, 3542–7
Military Manpower Statistics, 3542–14
Military Manpower Training Report, FY93, 3504–5
Military Personnel: Analysis of Major Rental Car Policies, 26123–391
Military Sealift Command, 1991 in Review, 3804–14
Military Strength Figures Summarized by DOD, 3542–2
Military Traffic Management Report, 3702–1
Military Traffic Management Report, FY91, 3704–15
Military Training: DOD Training Fatalities for FY88-91, 26123–397
Milk Production, 1627–1
Milk Production, Disposition and Income, 1991 Summary, 1627–4
Million Dollar Measles Outbreak: Epidemiology, Risk Factors, and a Selective Revaccination Strategy, 4042–3.301
Mine Injuries and Worktime, Quarterly, 6662–1
Mine Safety and Health Administration Fatalities Reports, 6662–3
Mineral Commodities in Subequatorial Africa. Mineral Perspectives, 5606–1.19
Mineral Commodity Summaries, 1992, 5604–18
Mineral Economy of Guinea. Mineral Perspectives, 5606–1.20
Mineral Economy of Mexico. Mineral Perspectives, 5606–1.18
Mineral Industries of Africa. Minerals Yearbook, Volume 3: 1989 International Review, 5604–35.1
Mineral Industries of Asia and the Pacific. Minerals Yearbook, Volume 3: 1989 International Review, 5604–35.2
Mineral Industries of China, 1990, 5604–38
Mineral Industries of the Middle East. Minerals Yearbook, Volume 3: 1989 International Review, 5604–35.3
Mineral Industries of the USSR, 1990, 5604–39
Mineral Industry Surveys: Annual Advance Summaries and Annual Reviews by Commodity, 5614–5
Mineral Industry Surveys: Apparent Consumption of Industrial Explosives and Blasting Agents in the U.S., 1991, 5614–22
Mineral Industry Surveys: Monthly Mineral Surveys, 5612–1
Mineral Industry Surveys: Phosphate Rock 1992 Crop Year, 5614–20
Mineral Industry Surveys: Potash in Crop Years 1991 and 1992, 5614–19
Mineral Industry Surveys: Quarterly Mineral Surveys, 5612–2
Mineral Industry Surveys: U.S. Peat Producers, 1991, 5614–32

Mineral Issues: An Analytical Series, 5606–5
Mineral Perspectives, 5606–1
Mineral Position of the U.S.: Annual Report of the Secretary of the Interior Under the Mining and Minerals Policy Act of 1970, 5304–5
Mineral Revenues 1991: Report on Receipts from Federal and Indian Leases, 5734–2
Minerals Availability Appraisal, 5606–4
Minerals Today, 5602–4
Minerals Yearbook, Volume 3. Annual Chapters by Country, 5604–17
Minerals Yearbook. Volume 3, Annual Preprints by Country, 5604–17
Minerals Yearbook. Volume 3: 1989 International Review, 5604–35
Minerals Yearbook, 1989. Volume 1. Metals and Minerals, 5604–33
Minerals Yearbook, 1989. Volume 2. Annual Chapters by State, 5604–16
Minerals Yearbook, 1989. Volume 3. Area Reports: International, 5604–35
Minerals Yearbook, 1990. Volume 1. Annual Reports by Commodity, 5604–20
Minerals Yearbook, 1990. Volume 2. Annual Reports by State, 5604–22
Minerals Yearbook, 1991. Volume 1. Annual Reports by Commodity, 5604–15
Miners' Views About Why People Go Under Unsupported Roof and How To Stop Them, 5608–173
Minimum Grower Prices and Processing Subsidies for Tomato Products in the EC, 1925–34.336
Mining and Quarrying Trends in the Metals and Industrial Minerals Industries: Minerals Yearbook, Volume 1, 1990, 5604–20.1
Mining Machinery and Mineral Processing Equipment, 1991, Current Industrial Report, 2506–12.4
Minivans from Japan. Determination of the Commission in Investigation No. 731-TA-522 (Final) Under the Tariff Act of 1930, Together with the Information Obtained in the Investigation, 9886–14.351
Mink, 1631–7
Minnesota-Wisconsin Manufacturing Grade Milk Price, 1629–6
Minnesota-Wisconsin Manufacturing Grade Milk, Prices Received, 1991 Summary, 1629–2
Minor Oilseeds: Outlook or Look Out?, 1504–9.1
Minority Business Enterprise (MBE) Program, FY92 Supportive Services Funds Allocation, 7554–40
Minutes and Report of Committee Recommendations: Census Advisory Committee of the American Statistical Association, on Population Statistics, of the American Marketing Association, and of the American Economic Association, 2628–35
Mission, Goals, and Program Plan, Post 1990: National Acid Precipitation Assessment Program. Public Review Draft, 14358–3
Mississippi Revisited: Poverty and Hunger Problems and Prospects, 21968–57
Misspecification Bias in Tests of the Forward Foreign Exchange Rate Unbiasedness Hypothesis, 9371–10.68
MMS Offshore Stats, 5732–1
Modelling the Time Series Behavior of the Aggregate Wage Rate, 9393–10.20
Modern Policing and the Control of Illegal Drugs: Testing New Strategies in Two American Cities, 6068–251
Modernization of the Food Label: An Initial Industry Impression, 1504–9.1
Mohair, Summary of 1992 Support Program and Related Information: ASCS Commodity Fact Sheet, 1806–4.9
Molasses Market News, 1311–16
Molasses Market News, Market Summary, 1991, 1311–19
Molybdenum: Mineral Industry Surveys, 5612–1.17
Molybdenum: Minerals Yearbook, Volume 1, 1990, 5604–20.41
Monetary Policy in a Small Open Economy: The Case of Singapore, 9379–1.304
Monetary Policy in the Great Depression: What the Fed Did, and Why, 9391–1.306
Monetary Policy Objectives, 1992: Summary Report of the Federal Reserve Board, 9362–4
Monetary Policy Report to Congress Pursuant to the Full Employment and Balanced Growth Act of 1978, 9362–4
Monetary Policy Report to Congress, 1992 (July): Testimony by Alan Greenspan, Chairman, Board of Governors of the Federal Reserve System, 9362–4
Monetary Trends, 9391–2
Money Demand and Relative Prices in Hyperinflations: Evidence from Germany and China, 9371–10.86
Money Income of Households, Families, and Persons in the U.S.: 1991, 2546–6.76
Money Laundering: State Efforts To Fight It Are Increasing but More Federal Help Is Needed, 26119–430
Money Laundering: Treasury Civil Case Processing of Bank Secrecy Act Violations, 26119–390
Money Markets and Common Monetary Policy in France, Germany and Italy, 9385–8.140
Money Stock, Liquid Assets, and Debt Measures, 9365–1
Monitor National Marine Sanctuary, 2152–8.304
Monitoring Access of Medicare Beneficiaries: Report to Congress, 17266–1.8
Monitoring Access: Report to Congress, 17266–1.5
Monitoring Hydrocarbons and Trace Metals in Beaufort Sea Sediments and Organisms, Final Report, 5738–33
Monitoring of Olympic National Park Beaches To Determine Fate and Effects of Spilled Bunker C Fuel Oil, 5738–38.1
Monitoring the Financial Liability of Medicare Beneficiaries, 17266–1.6
Montana Cooperative Snow Survey Data of Federal-State-Private Cooperative Snow Surveys, Water Year 1990, 1264–14.2
Montana Forest Pest Conditions and Program Highlights, 1990, 1206–49.2
Montana Forest Pest Conditions and Program Highlights, 1991, 1206–49.3
Montana's Timber Production and Mill Residue, 1988, 1206–17.12
Monthly and Seasonal Weather Outlook, 2182–1
Monthly Awards for Construction Grants for Wastewater Treatment Works, 9202–3
Monthly Benefit Statistics, 9702–2
Monthly Benefit Statistics, Railroad Retirement and Unemployment Insurance Programs, 9702–2
Monthly Bulletin of Lake Levels for the Great Lakes, 3752–1
Monthly Climatic Data for the World, 2152–4
Monthly Cotton Linters Review, 1309–10
Monthly Energy Review, 3162–24
Monthly Import Detention List, 4062–2
Monthly Labor Review, 6722–1
Monthly Motor Fuel Reported by States, 7552–1
Monthly Product Announcement, 2302–6
Monthly Retail Trade, Sales and Inventories, Current Business Reports, 2413–3
Monthly State, Regional and National Heating/Cooling Degree Days Weighted by Population, 2152–13
Monthly Statement of the Public Debt of the U.S., 8242–2
Monthly Statistical Release: Beer, 8486–1.1
Monthly Statistical Release: Distilled Spirits, 8486–1.3
Monthly Statistical Release: Tobacco Products, 8486–1.4
Monthly Statistical Release: Wines, 8486–1.2
Monthly Stumpage Prices for the Pacific Northwest, 1208–387
Monthly Thrift Data, 8432–1
Monthly Traffic Fatality Report, 7762–7
Monthly Treasury Statement of Receipts and Outlays of the U.S. Government, 8102–3
Monthly Vital Statistics Report, Annual Summary of Births, Marriages, Divorces, and Deaths: U.S., 1991, 4144–7
Monthly Vital Statistics Report Provisional Data, 4142–1
Monthly Vital Statistics Report Supplements, 4146–5
Monthly Wholesale Trade: Sales and Inventories, Current Business Reports, 2413–7
Morbidity and Mortality, Weekly Report, 4202–1
Morbidity and Mortality Weekly Report: CDC Surveillance Summaries, 4202–7
Morbidity and Mortality Weekly Report: Recommendations and Reports, 4206–2
Mortality Study of 1.3 Million Persons by Demographic, Social, and Economic Factors: 1979-85 Follow-Up. U.S. National Longitudinal Mortality Study. Second Data Book, 4478–186
Mortgage Lending in Boston: Interpreting HMDA Data, 9373–27.15
Most Chapter 1 Funds in Eight Districts Used for Classroom Services. Compensatory Education, 26121–478
Most Community and Migrant Health Center Physicians Have Hospital Privileges. Health Care, 26121–465
Mothers' Motivations To Participate in a Pregnancy Health Survey, 4042–3.377
Mothers Report Receiving Less Support from Out-of-State Fathers. Interstate Child Support, 26121–442
Motivations for Bank Mergers and Acquisitions: Enhancing the Deposit Insurance Put Option versus Increasing Operating Net Cash Flow, 9371–10.80
Motor Freight Transportation and Warehousing Survey: 1990. Current Business Reports, 2413–14
Motor Vehicle Injury Prevention, 4208–35
Motor Vehicle Safety, 1990: A Report on Activities Under the National Traffic and Motor Vehicle Safety Act of 1966, As

Amended, and the Motor Vehicle Information and Cost Savings Act of 1972, As Amended, 7764–1.2
Motor Vehicles, Model Year 1992, 2702–1.339
Motors and Generators, 1990, Current Industrial Report, 2506–12.17
Motors and Generators, 1991, Current Industrial Report, 2506–12.17
Mourning Dove Breeding Population Status, 1992, 5504–15
Multidrug-Resistant Tuberculosis Challenge to Public Health Efforts To Control Tuberculosis, 4042–3.362
Multifactor Productivity in Manufacturing Industries, 6722–1.345
Multifactor Productivity in Railroad Transportation, 6722–1.337
Multiparametric Prognostic Evaluation of Biological Factors in Primary Breast Cancer, 4472–1.335
Multiple Reserve Requirements: The Case of Small Open Economies, 9371–10.70
Multistage Carcinogenesis: Population-Based Model for Colon Cancer, 4472–1.311
Multistrategy Health Education Program To Increase Mammography Use Among Women Ages 65 and Older, 4042–3.337
Municipal Bond Market, Part II: Problems and Policies, 9373–1.310
Mushroom Supply and Utilization in the U.S., 1561–11.303
Mushrooms, 1631–9
Mutations of p53 Gene in Hepatocellular Carcinoma: Roles of Hepatitis B Virus and Aflatoxin Contamination in the Diet, 4472–1.353
Mutual-to-Stock Conversions by New England Savings Banks: Where Has All the Money Gone?, 9373–1.307

NAEP 1990 Technical Report, 4896–8.5
NAEPfacts, 4896–9
Narrow Fabrics, Current Industrial Report, 2506–5.6
NASA: America's Return to the Red Planet, Mars Observer Press Kit, 9506–2.152
NASA Engineers and the Age of Apollo, 9508–39
NASA: Extreme Ultraviolet Explorer Press Kit, 9506–2.149
NASA FY90 Safety Program Status Report, 9504–4
NASA FY91 Safety Program Status Report, 9504–4
NASA News Press Kits, 9506–2
NASA Office of Inspector General Semiannual Report, Apr. 1-Sept. 30, 1992, 9502–9
NASA Office of Inspector General Semiannual Report, Oct. 1, 1991-Mar. 31, 1992, 9502–9
NASA Pocket Statistics, 9504–6
NASA Procurement Report, FY92, 9502–6
NASA Procurement Report, Oct. 1, 1991-Mar. 31, 1992, 9502–6
NASA: Space Shuttle Mission Spacelab J STS-47 Press Kit, 9506–2.151
NASA: Space Shuttle Mission STS-42 Press Kit, 9506–2.145
NASA: Space Shuttle Mission STS-45 Press Kit, 9506–2.146
NASA: Space Shuttle Mission STS-46 Press Kit, 9506–2.147
NASA: Space Shuttle Mission STS-48 Press Kit, 9506–2.144
NASA: Space Shuttle Mission STS-49 Press Kit, 9506–2.148
NASA: Space Shuttle Mission STS-50 Press Kit, 9506–2.150
NASA: Space Shuttle Mission STS-52 Press Kit, 9506–2.153
NASA: Space Shuttle Mission STS-53 Press Kit, 9506–2.154
NASA-Industry Education Initiative: Education Programs Report, 1991, 9508–41
NASA's University Program Active Projects, FY91, 9504–7
Nation Concerned: Annual Report of the Interagency Council on the Homeless, 14364–1
National Acid Precipitation Assessment Program, 1990 Integrated Assessment Report, 14358–4
National Action Plan To Combat Multidrug-Resistant Tuberculosis, 4206–2.61
National Advisory Committee on Semiconductors Annual Report, 15034–1
National Advisory Council on Educational Research and Improvement 16th Annual Report, FY91, 4814–1
National AIDS Research Consortium Annual Meeting: Community-Based AIDS Prevention, 4494–12
National Air Quality and Emissions Trends Report, 1990, 9194–1
National Air Quality and Emissions Trends Report, 1991, 9194–1
National Airway System, Annual Report, FY90, 7504–37
National Ambulatory Medical Care Survey, 1978 Summary, 4147–16.6
National Ambulatory Medical Care Survey: 1989 Summary. Vital and Health Statistics Series 13, 4147–13.109
National Ambulatory Medical Care Survey: 1990 Summary, 4146–8.215
National Archives and Records Administration, Annual Report for the Year Ended Sept. 30, 1991, 9514–2
National Archives and Records Administration Inventory Series, 9456–3, 9516–2
National Archives and Records Administration, Reference Information Papers, 9516–1
National Assessment of Educational Progress, 1985-86, 4896–6
National Assessment of Educational Progress, 1990, 4896–8
National Cancer Institute Extramural Grant and Contract Awards, 4474–28
National Cancer Institute Fact Book, 4474–13
National Center for Health Statistics, Catalog of Publications, 1990-91, 4124–1
National Center on Child Abuse and Neglect Discretionary Grants: Profiles for FY90, 4584–9
National Center on Child Abuse and Neglect Discretionary Grants: Profiles for FY91, 4584–9
National Center on Child Abuse and Neglect, State Grant Summaries, FY91, 4584–6
National Commission for Employment Policy: Research Report Series, 15496–1
National Commission for Employment Policy: Sixteenth Annual Report, 15494–1
National Committee on Vital and Health Statistics, 1991, 4164–1
National Conference on HOV Systems 1991 HOV Facilities Coming of Age, 7308–204
National Corrections Reporting Program, 1986, 6064–33
National Corrections Reporting Program, 1987, 6064–33
National Corrections Reporting Program, 1988, 6064–33
National Credit Union Administration, Annual Report, 1991, 9534–1
National Credit Union Administration Central Liquidity Facility 1991 Annual Report, 9534–5
National Credit Union Share Insurance Fund, 1991 Annual Report, 9534–7
National Crime Survey, 6066–3
National Crime Victimization Survey, 6066–3
National DRG Validation Study, 4006–7
National DRG Validation Study, FY85: Peer Review Organization Coding Accuracy, 4006–7.9
National DRG Validation Study: Quality of Patient Care in Hospitals, 4006–7.5
National DRG Validation Study, Update: Summary Report, 4006–7.10
National DRG Validation Study, Update: Technical Report, 4006–7.11
National Dropout Statistics Field Test Evaluation, 4838–49
National Drug Control Strategy, 234–1
National Drug Control Strategy, Budget Summary, 234–2
National Economic Trends, 9391–3
National Education Goals Report: Building a Nation of Learners, 15914–1
National Education Longitudinal Study of 1988, 4826–9
National Endowment for the Arts 1991 Annual Report, 9564–3
National Endowment for the Humanities: Twenty-sixth Annual Report, 1991, 9564–2
National Energy Security Act of 1991. Part 14 (Appendixes to Parts 1, 2, 3, and 4), 25318–83
National Energy Strategy (Part 1), 21368–136
National Energy Strategy (Part 2), 21368–137
National Energy Strategy (Part 3), 21368–138
National Energy Strategy (Part 5), 21368–142
National Energy Strategy, Powerful Ideas for America: One Year Later, 3008–128
National Energy Strategy Technical Annexes, 3006–13
National Forest Statement of Receipts, FY91, 1204–34
National Health Accounts: Lessons from the U.S. Experience, 4652–1.323
National Health Interview Survey, 1988, CD-ROM. Vital and Health Statistics Series 10, 4147–10.184
National Heart, Lung, and Blood Institute FY91 Fact Book, 4474–15
National Heart, Lung, and Blood Institute: Sixteenth Report of the Director; Sixteenth Report of the National Heart, Lung, and Blood Advisory Council; and Report of Disease Prevention and Health Promotion Activities, 4474–22
National High School Senior Drug Abuse Survey, 1975-91: Monitoring the Future Survey, 4008–116

National High-Occupancy Vehicle (HOV) Facilities Conference. HOV Facilities: Coming of Age, 7308–204
National Highway Traffic Safety Administration News, 7766–7
National Honey Market News, 1311–2
National Hospital Discharge Survey: Annual Summary, 1989. Vital and Health Statistics Series 13, 4147–13.112
National Hospital Discharge Survey: Annual Summary, 1990. Vital and Health Statistics Series 13, 4147–13.112
National Hospital Discharge Survey. 1990 Summary, 4146–8.211
National Household Survey on Drug Abuse, 4494–5
National Household Survey on Drug Abuse: Population Estimates, 1991, 4494–5.1
National Income and Product Accounts: Errata, 2702–1.307, 2702–1.313, 2702–1.333
National Income and Product Accounts of the U.S., 2708–5
National Income and Product Accounts of the U.S.: Volume 2, 1959-88, 2708–5.1
National Institute of Allergy and Infectious Diseases Profile, FY91, 4474–30
National Institute of Dental Research Programs, FY90 Funds, 4474–19
National Institute of General Medical Sciences, Data Book, FY91, 4474–38
National Institute of Justice: Construction Bulletin, 6066–30
National Institute of Neurological and Communicative Disorders and Stroke Profile, 4474–25
National Institute of Neurological Disorders and Stroke Profile, 4474–25
National Institute of Standards and Technology Publications, 1991 Catalog, 2214–1
National Institute on Drug Abuse Notes, 4492–4
National Institutes of Health New Grants and Awards: Arranged by State, City and Institution, 4432–1
National Juvenile Custody Trends, 1978-89, 6068–250
National Labor Relations Board, Fifty-fifth Annual Report, FY90, 9584–1
National Listing of Medicare Providers Furnishing Kidney Dialysis and Transplant Services, January 1991, 4654–17
National Listing of Providers Furnishing Kidney Dialysis and Transplant Services, 4654–17
National Marine Pollution Program, Federal Plan for Ocean Pollution Research, Development, and Monitoring, 2148–56
National Marine Pollution Program, Summary of Federal Programs and Projects, Update, 2144–23
National Mediation Board 53rd and 54th Annual Report, Including the Report of the National Railroad Adjustment Board, FY87-88, 9604–1
National Medical Expenditure Survey Methods and Research Findings, 4186–8
National Mortality Followback Survey: 1986 Summary, U.S. Vital and Health Statistics Series 20, 4147–20.19
National Ocean Pollution Program. Federal Plan for Ocean Pollution Research, Development, and Monitoring: FY92-96, 2148–56
National Ocean Pollution Program, Summary of Federal Programs and Projects, FY89 Update, 2144–23
National Oceanographic Fleet Operating Schedules, 3804–6
National Oceanographic Fleet Platform Characteristics, 3804–6
National Park Service: Listing of Acreages, 5542–1
National Park Service Monthly Public Use Report, 5542–4
National Park Service Statistical Abstract, 1991, 5544–12
National Parks: Index 1991, 5544–5
National Postsecondary Statistics, Collegiate and Noncollegiate: Early Estimates, Fall 1991, 4844–16
National Poultry Improvement Plan: 1992 Directory of Participants, 1394–15
National Poultry Improvement Plan: 1992 Directory of Participants Handling Egg-Type and Meat-Type Chickens and Turkeys, 1394–15.1
National Poultry Improvement Plan: 1992 Directory of Participants Handling Waterfowl, Exhibition Poultry, and Game Birds, 1394–15.2
National Priorities List, Supplementary Lists and Supporting Materials, 9216–5
National Program Has Greatly Increased Pool of Potential Donors. Bone Marrow Transplants, 26121–487
National Railroad Passenger Corporation, Annual Report, 1991, 29524–1
National Recycling Markets, 21368–140
National Science Foundation, Annual Report, 1991, 9624–6
National Science Foundation Awards, 9626–7
National Security Assessment of the Domestic and Foreign Subcontractor Base: A Study of Three U.S. Navy Weapon Systems, 2026–1.3
National Security Assessment of the U.S. Robotics Industry, 2026–1.1
National Security Assessment of the U.S. Semiconductor Wafer Processing Equipment Industry, 2026–1.2
National Security Assessment of U.S. Industries, 2026–1
National Shellfish Register of Classified Estuarine Waters, 2148–50
National Shellfish Register of Classified Estuarine Waters, 1990, 2178–33
National Small Business Tree Planting Program, 9764–10
National Status and Trends Program for Marine Environmental Quality, 2176–3
National Surveillance System for Sexually Transmitted Diseases in Italy, 4202–7.311
National Survey of State Epidemiologists To Determine the Status of Lyme Disease Surveillance, 4042–3.364
National Toxicology Program, 4044–16
National Toxicology Program: FY91 Annual Plan, 4044–16.2
National Toxicology Program: Review of Current DHHS, DOE, and EPA Research Related to Toxicology, FY91, 4044–16.1
National Trade Data Bank (NTDB): The Export Connection, 2002–6
National Trade Estimate Report on Foreign Trade Barriers, 1992, 444–2
National Transportation Safety Board, 1990 Annual Report to Congress, 9614–1
National Undersea Research Program Program Summary: A Summary of Research Activities, 1987-88, 2144–6
National Urban Mass Transportation Statistics: Section 15 Annual Report, 7884–4
National Veterinary Services Laboratories Summary of Activities, FY91, 1394–17
National Water Conditions, 5662–3
National Wool Market Review, Livestock Division, 1315–2
National Workplace Literacy Program, FY91 Project Abstracts, 4804–40
Nation's Changing Beef Cow Herd, 1561–7.301
Nation's Cooperatives Rebuild Unallocated Equity, 1122–1.308
Nation's Population Projected To Grow by 50 Percent During Next 60 Years, Census Bureau Reports, 2328–85
Nationwide Personal Transportation Survey, 1990, 7556–6
NATO Infrastructure Program: As Threat Declines, NATO Reduces Expenditures, 26123–388
Natural Gas Annual, 1990, 3164–4
Natural Gas Futures Contract Market—The First 2 Years, 3162–4.302
Natural Gas Monthly, 3162–4
Natural Gas Pipelines: Greater Use of Instrumented Inspection Technology Can Improve Safety, 26113–594
Natural Resource Development Program Annual Report, 1991, 9764–10
Natural Sweeteners, Industry and Trade Summary, 9885–8.9
Naval Petroleum and Oil Shale Reserves, FY91 Annual Report of Operations, 3334–3
Naval Petroleum Reserves in California, Site Environmental Report for 1991, 3324–2.10
Navy Contracting: Cost Growth Continues on Ship Construction Contracts, 26123–401
Navy Military Personnel Statistics, 3802–4
NCHS Publication Note: Publications Issued, 4122–2
NCUA Research Studies, 9536–1
NCUA 1991 Yearend Statistics for Federally Insured Credit Unions, 9532–6
NCUA 1992 Midyear Statistics for Federally Insured Credit Unions, 9532–6
Nearly $100 Million Goes to Local Governments for Tax Exempt Federal Lands, 5306–4.15
Need To Improve Internal Controls on Deferred Contractor Debts. Defense Procurement, 26123–400
Need To Increase Rehabilitation and Reemployment of Injured Workers. Federal Employees' Compensation Act, 26119–381
Needle Exchange Programs: Are They Effective?, 236–3.7
Needle Sharing and Participation in the Amsterdam Syringe Exchange Program Among HIV-Seronegative Injecting Drug Users, 4042–3.369
Needs Survey, Report to Congress, 1990: Assessment of Needed Publicly Owned Wastewater Treatment Facilities in the U.S.—Including Federally Recognized Indian Tribes and Alaska Native Villages, 9204–7
Neglected Health Care Needs of Street Youth, 4042–3.344
Neighborhood Reinvestment Corporation Should Improve Program Management. Community Development, 26113–587

NEISS Data Highlights, 9164–7
Neoclassical Model of Seasonal Fluctuations, 9387–8.262
Nepheline Syenite from Canada. Determination of the Commission in Investigation No. 731-TA-525 (Final) Under the Tariff Act of 1930, Together with the Information Obtained in the Investigation, 9886–14.344
Net Cash Income and Selected Characteristics of U.S. Farms Producing Fruits, Tree Nuts, and Berries, 1561–6.301
Net Payments Made to Producers, 1802–10
Nevada Progress Report. BLM Facts and Statistics, 5724–11.1, 5724–11.3
New Beneficiary Data System: The First Phase, 4742–1.313
New BLS Projections: Findings and Implications, 6744–19
New Car Assessment Program Results, Model Years 1987-91, 7768–111
New Crops, New Uses, New Markets: 1992 Yearbook of Agriculture, 1004–18
New Data from the 1989 Birth Certificate, Advance Report, 4146–5.125
New Data on Nonresidential Building Improvements, 2042–1.305
New Demands for Biofuels and Alternative Products, 1504–9.1
New Developments in Neuroscience, 26356–9
New England Economic Indicators, 9373–2
New England Economic Review, 9373–1
New Estimates of Hardwood-Log Exports to Europe and Asia, 1208–373
New International Price Series Published by Nation and Region, 6722–1.327
New Jersey's Medicaid Waiver for Acquired Immunodeficiency Syndrome, 4652–1.317
New Labor Force Data for Census Regions and Divisions, 6742–2.303
New Nonimmigrant Data for 1991—Preliminary, 6266–2.9
New One-Family Houses Sold, Current Construction Reports, 2382–3
New Opportunities for Agriculture, 1504–9.1
New Opportunities for Agriculture. Annual Agricultural Outlook Conference Charts, 1504–8
New Opportunities for Agriculture. Annual Agricultural Outlook Conference Proceedings, 1504–9
New Perspectives in Commuting, Based on Early Data from the 1990 Decennial Census and the 1990 Nationwide Personal Transportation Study, 7558–120
New Publications of the Bureau of Mines, 5602–2
New Publications of the U.S. Geological Survey, 5662–1
New Residential Construction in Selected Metropolitan Statistical Areas, Current Construction Reports, 2382–9
New Results on the Impact of Central-Bank Intervention on Deviations from Uncovered Interest Parity, 9377–9.138
New Seasonal Adjustment Factors for Household Data Series, 6742–2.307
New Seasonal Adjustment Factors for the Establishment Data Series, 6742–2.301
New Steel Rails from Japan, Luxembourg, and the UK. Determination of the Commission in Investigations Nos. 731-TA-557-559 (Preliminary) Under the Tariff Act of 1930, Together with the Information Obtained in the Investigations, 9886–14.349
New Test of Scanning and Monitoring Ability: Methods and Initial Results, 7506–10.108
New York City Housing and Vacancy Survey, 1991, 2488–3
New York City (Hunt's Point) Wholesale Terminal Market Fresh Fruit and Vegetable Prices, 1990, 1311–21
New York City Wholesale Fruit and Vegetable Report, 1311–20
Newest Batch of 65 HOPE Grants, Totalling $31.2 Million, To Help Spur Homeownership for Low-Income Americans, 5006–3.101
News from the Federal Election Commission, 9276–1
Newsprint, Industry and Trade Summary, 9885–8.8
NHTSA Awards $7.2 Million in Grants to States for Drunk Driving Programs, 7306–10.4
NHTSA Releases Additional 1992 Model Year Crash Test Results, 7766–7.32, 7766–7.33, 7766–7.34
NHTSA Releases Crash Test Results Applicable to 71 Model Year 1993 Vehicles, 7766–7.36
NHTSA Releases Crash Test Results Applicable to 77 Model Year 1993 Vehicles, 7766–7.37
NHTSA Releases Final Crash Test Results of 1992 Model Vehicles, 7766–7.35
NHTSA Releases First 1992 Model Year Crash Test Results, 7766–7.29
NHTSA Releases Four Additional 1992 Model Year Crash Test Results, 7766–7.31
NHTSA Releases Three Additional 1992 Model Year Crash Test Results, 7766–7.30
Nickel: Mineral Industry Surveys, 5612–1.20
NIDA Notes, 4492–4
NIH Almanac, 1991, 4434–1
NIH Extramural Trends, FY82-91, 4434–9
NIH Publications List, 4434–2
NIJ Awards in Research and Development and Evaluation: FY91, 6066–20.24
Ninety Years of Salmon Culture at Little White Salmon National Fish Hatchery, 5508–114
Ninety-five Public and Indian Housing Resident Management Organizations Win HUD Grants, 5006–3.77
NIST R&D 100 Awards: A Technology Transfer Study, 2218–86
NIST Standard Reference Materials Catalog, 1992-93, 2214–2
Nitrogen: Minerals Yearbook, Volume 1, 1990, 5604–20.43
NLRB Election Report, 9582–2
NMC Seasonal Performance Summary, 2182–8
NNICC Report, 1991: The Supply of Illicit Drugs to the U.S., 6284–2
No Relief in Sight for the U.S. Economy, 9383–6.303
NOAA Coastal Ocean Program Regional Synthesis Series, 2146–8
NOAA Environmental Digest, Selected Indicators of the U.S. and the Global Environment, 2144–27
NOAA Estuary-of-the-Month Seminar Series, 2146–6
NOAA's Coastal Trends Series, 2176–8
NOAA's Estuarine Living Marine Resources Program. Distribution and Abundance of Fishes and Invertebrates in Gulf of Mexico Estuaries, Volume I: Data Summaries, 2176–7.28
NOAA's National Estuarine Inventory Salinity Characterization: Galveston, Tex., 2176–7.27
NOAA's National Estuarine Inventory Supplement Series. Analysis of Salinity Structure and Stability for Texas Estuaries, 2176–7.26
Nominal Feedback Rules for Monetary Policy: Some Comments, 9379–12.92
Non-Acquired Immune Deficiency Syndrome-Defining Malignancies in a Hospital-Based Cohort of Human Immunodeficiency Virus-Infected Patients: Bordeaux, France, 1985-91, 4472–1.351
Nonagricultural Employment in the Southeast, 6942–7
Noncitrus Fruits and Nuts, 1991 Preliminary, 1621–18.1
Noncitrus Fruits and Nuts: 1991 Summary, 1621–18.3
Nonfarm Prospects Under Agricultural Liberalization, 1502–3.301
Nonfarm Tobacco Industry Regulations, 1561–10.302
Nonferrous Castings, 1991, Current Industrial Report, 2506–10.5
Nonlinear and Chaotic Dynamics: An Economist's Guide, 1502–3.301
Non-Permanent Pavement Markings in Work Zones, 7558–116
Nonpolicy Factors Account for Most State Differences. Health Care Spending, 26121–444
Nonresident Alien Estates, 1986, 8302–2.310
Nonrubber Footwear Quarterly Statistical Report: Report to the Senate Committee on Finance on Investigation No. 332-191, Under Section 332 of the Tariff Act of 1930, 9882–6
Nonutility Power Producers, 3162–35.301
North American Auto Industry at the Onset of Continental Free Trade Negotiations, 6366–3.28
North American Free Trade Agreement: Comparisons with and Lessons from Southern EC Enlargement, 6366–3.29
North American Free Trade Agreement Impact on Horticulture, 1925–34.332
North American Free Trade Agreement (Part 2), 21368–141
North American Free Trade Agreement: U.S.-Mexican Trade and Investment Data, 26119–417
North American Free Trade Agreement: What Is at Stake for U.S. Agriculture?, 9381–1.307
North American Trade Issues, 1504–9.1
North Atlantic Air Traffic Forecasts for the Years 1992-97, 2000, 2005, and 2010, 7504–44
North Atlantic Hurricanes—1991, 2152–8.302
Northeast Fisheries Science Center Bottom Trawl Survey Fishermen's Report, Mar. 2-Apr. 16, 1992, Cape Hatteras-Western Scotian Shelf, 2164–18.1
Northeast Fisheries Science Center Bottom Trawl Survey Fishermen's Report, Sept. 8-Oct. 28, 1992, Cape Hatteras-Gulf of Maine, 2164–18.4
Northeast Fisheries Science Center Sea Scallop Survey Fishermen's Report, Aug. 1-23, 1992, 2164–18.3
Northeast Fisheries Science Center Surf Clam and Ocean Quahog Survey Fishermen's Report, June 8-July 13, 1992, 2164–18.2

Northeast Regional Stock Assessment Workshop Report, 2162–9
Note on Competition, Fixed Costs, and the Profitability of Depository Intermediaries, 9371–10.88
Note on Forward Biases and Equilibrium Foreign Exchange Hedging in a Production Economy, 9371–10.85
Note on Relationships Between Western Sahel Rainfall and U.S. Hurricane Activity, 2148–61
NSF FY90 Awards by State and Institution, 9624–26
NSF Special Reports, 9626–6
NTDB: The Export Connection, 2002–6
NTIA Infrastructure Report: Telecommunications in the Age of Information, 2808–30
Nuclear Engineering Enrollments and Degrees, 1991: Appendixes, 3004–5
Nuclear Engineering Master's Enrollments and Degrees Increased in 1991, While Undergraduate and Doctoral Enrollments and Degrees Decreased, 3006–8.18
Nuclear Facility Decommissioning and Site Remedial Actions: A Selected Bibliography, Volume 12, 3354–12
Nuclear Power Plant Construction Activity, 3164–69
Nuclear Power Safety: Chernobyl Accident Prompted Worldwide Actions but Further Efforts Needed, 26123–367
Nuclear Reactors Built, Being Built, or Planned: 1991, 3354–15
Nuclear Safety Technical Progress Journal, 3352–4
Nuclear Security: Safeguards and Security Weaknesses at DOE's Weapons Facilities, 26113–557
Number of Individuals Receiving 1990 Deficiency Payments and the Amounts. Agriculture Payments, 26113–574
Number of Noncareer SES and Schedule C Employees in Federal Agencies. Political Appointees, 26119–412
Number of Paid Fishing and Hunting License Holders, License Sales, and Cost to Anglers and Hunters, FY91, 5504–16
Number of Returns To Be Filed: Projections for Districts, 8304–24
Number of Returns To Be Filed: Projections, U.S., Regions, and Service Centers, 8304–9
Numerical Modeling of Storm Surges in Norton Sound, 2176–1.40
Numerical Modeling of Storm Surges in the Beaufort and Chukchi Seas, 2176–1.40
Nursing Home Aides Experience Increase in Serious Injuries, 6728–41
Nutrient Content of Foods Important to Health, 1504–9.1
Nutrition Labeling: Phase Two, 1504–9.1
Nutrition Labeling: We're on Our Way, 1504–9.1
Nutritional Conditions and Program Alternatives in Puerto Rico. Food Assistance, 26113–580
Nutritional Status and Dietary Adequacy of Single Homeless Women and Their Children in Shelters, 4042–3.330

Obligations Limitation: Resolution Trust Corporation's Compliance as of (Date), 26102–6
Observation, 2152–8.303
Occupation Distribution and Composition. Defense Force Management, 26123–381
Occupation Trends in Advertising, 1984-90, 6722–1.341
Occupational Advancement from Within, 6742–1.301
Occupational Compensation Survey: Pay and Benefits, State and Local Governments, 6785–15
Occupational Compensation Survey, Summary Reports, 6785–3
Occupational Compensation Surveys: Bulletin 3060 Series, 6785–16
Occupational Compensation Surveys: Bulletin 3065 Series, 6785–17
Occupational Earnings and Wage Trends in Metropolitan Areas, 6785–5
Occupational Earnings in Selected Areas, 6785–6
Occupational Employment Projections, 6744–19
Occupational Fatalities as Found in Reports of OSHA Fatality/Catastrophe Investigations, 6606–2
Occupational Injuries and Illnesses in the U.S. by Industry, 1990, 6844–1
Occupational Injury Prevention, 4208–35
Occupational Outlook Handbook: 1992-93 Edition, 6744–1
Occupational Outlook Quarterly, 6742–1
Occupational Projections and Training Data, 1992 Edition, 6744–3
Occupational Radiation Exposure at Commercial Nuclear Power Reactors and Other Facilities, 1988, 9634–3
Occupational Radiation Exposure at Commercial Nuclear Power Reactors and Other Facilities, 1989, 9634–3
Occupational Radiation Exposure from U.S. Naval Nuclear Propulsion Plants and Their Support Facilities, 1991, 3804–10
Occupational Safety and Health Administration Press Releases, 6606–3
Occupational Safety and Health: Employers' Experiences in Complying with the Hazard Communication Standard, 26121–456
Occupational Safety and Health: Options To Improve Hazard-Abatement Procedures in the Workplace, 26121–461
Occupational Safety and Health: OSHA Action Needed To Improve Compliance with Hazard Communication Standard, 26121–439
Occupational Safety and Health: Penalties for Violations Are Well Below Maximum Allowable Penalties, 26121–455
Occupational Segregation by Race and Sex, 1940-88, 6722–1.321
Occupational Wage Surveys, 6787–6
Oceanographic Data Exchange, 1990, 2144–15
Oceanographic Monthly Summary, 2182–5
Oceanographic Observations in the Inner New York Bight in Support of the 12-Mile Dumpsite Study, 1987-89, 2168–130
Oceanos' Heroes, 2152–8.302
OCS Studies of 1988 Fuel Oil Spill off Washington Coast, 5738–38
OECD Trade Series, 9116–1
OECD Trade with Asia, 9116–1.3
OECD Trade with Mexico and Central America, 9116–1.5
OECD Trade with South America, 9116–1.7
OECD Trade with Sub-Saharan Africa, 9116–1.2
OECD Trade with the Caribbean, 9116–1.4
OECD Trade with the Middle East, 9116–1.6
OECD Trade with the USSR and Eastern Europe, 9116–1.1
Offenders in Juvenile Court, 1988, 6066–27.9
Office for Civil Rights Survey Redesign: A Feasibility Survey, 4826–1.33
Office Furniture, 1990, Current Industrial Report, 2506–7.8
Office Furniture, 1991, Current Industrial Report, 2506–7.8
Office of Aviation Medicine Reports, 7506–10
Office of Basic Energy Sciences, 1991 Summary Report, 3004–18.8
Office of Civilian Radioactive Waste Management, Annual Report to Congress, 3364–1
Office of Energy Research Program Summaries, 3004–18
Office of Exploratory Research, Annual Report of the Research Grants Program, 1991, 9184–18
Office of Housing and Urban Programs Annual Report, FY91, 9914–4
Office of Inspector General Semiannual Report to Congress, Department of Agriculture, 1002–4
Office of Inspector General Semiannual Report to Congress, Department of Defense, 3542–18
Office of Inspector General Semiannual Report to Congress, Department of Energy, 3002–12
Office of Inspector General Semiannual Report to Congress, Department of Health and Human Services, Apr. 1-Sept. 30, 1991, 4002–6
Office of Inspector General Semiannual Report to Congress, Department of Health and Human Services, Oct. 1, 1991-Mar. 31, 1992, 4002–6
Office of Inspector General Semiannual Report to Congress, Department of Health and Human Services, Oct. 1, 1991-Mar. 31, 1992: List of Reports Issued, 4002–6
Office of Inspector General Semiannual Report to Congress, Department of Housing and Urban Development, 5002–8
Office of Inspector General Semiannual Report to Congress, Department of Interior, 5302–2
Office of Inspector General Semiannual Report to Congress, Department of State, 7002–6
Office of Inspector General Semiannual Report to Congress, Department of Transportation, 7302–4
Office of Inspector General Semiannual Report to Congress, Department of Veterans Affairs, 8602–1
Office of Inspector General Semiannual Report to Congress, Environmental Protection Agency, 9182–10
Office of Inspector General Semiannual Report to Congress, General Services Administration, 9452–8
Office of Inspector General Semiannual Report to Congress, NASA, 9502–9
Office of Inspector General Semiannual Report to Congress, National Science Foundation, 9622–1

Office of Inspector General Semiannual Report to Congress, Resolution Trust Corporation, 9722-6
Office of Inspector General Semiannual Report to Congress, U.S. Department of Commerce, 2002-5
Office of Inspector General Semiannual Report to Congress, U.S. Department of Education, 4802-1
Office of Inspector General Semiannual Report to Congress, U.S. Department of Labor, 6302-2
Office of Inspector General Semiannual Report to Congress, U.S. Small Business Administration, 9762-5
Office of Inspector General Semiannual Report to Congress, USIA, 9852-2
Office of Justice Programs, FY91 Annual Report, 6064-18
Office of Juvenile Justice and Delinquency Prevention Annual Report on Missing Children, 1990, 6064-36
Office of Juvenile Justice and Delinquency Prevention Annual Report, 1990, 6064-34
Office of Management and Budget, Final Sequestration Report to the President and Congress for FY92, 104-27
Office of Management and Budget, Sequestration Update Report to the President and Congress, 104-27
Office of National Drug Control Policy Bulletins, 236-3
Office of National Drug Control Policy: White Papers, 236-1
Office of Navajo and Hopi Indian Relocation Program Status, 16002-1
Office of Refugee Resettlement Monthly Data Report, 4592-1, 4692-2
Office of Surface Mining Annual Report, FY91, 5644-1
Office of Technology Assessment, Annual Report to the Congress, FY91, 26354-3
Office of Thrift Supervision Research Papers, 8436-1
Office of U.S. Foreign Disaster Assistance, Annual Report, FY91, 9914-12
Office Visits for Diabetes Mellitus, National Ambulatory Medical Care Survey: U.S., 1977, 4147-16.6
Office Visits for Diabetes Mellitus: U.S., 1989, 4146-8.212
Office Visits for Otitis Media: U.S., 1975-90, 4146-8.217
Office Visits Involving X-rays, National Ambulatory Medical Care Survey: U.S., 1977, 4147-16.6
Office Visits to Internists, 1989, 4146-8.214
Office Visits to Pediatric Specialists, 1989, 4146-8.210
Offices of Drug Evaluation: Statistical Report, 1991, 4064-14
Official Guard and Reserve Manpower: Strengths and Statistics, 3542-4
Official Summary of Security Transactions and Holdings, 9732-2
Offsite Environmental Monitoring Report: Radiation Monitoring Around U.S. Nuclear Test Areas, 1990, 9194-17
Ohio River Navigation System Report, 1990, 3754-6
Ohio Timber Products Output, 1989, 1206-15.11
Oil and Gas Field Code Master List, 1991, 3164-70
Oil Crops Situation and Outlook Report, 1561-3
Oil Crops Situation and Outlook Yearbook, 1561-3
Oil Price Hike in Perspective, 1990, 9391-1.301
Oil Prices and Supplies in the Wake of the Persian Gulf Crisis, 25408-116
Oil Shocks, Monetary Policy, and Economic Activity, 9389-1.304
Oilseeds: Foreign Agricultural Service Circular Series, 1925-1
Oilseeds, Industry and Trade Summary, 9885-8.4
Older Workers in the Labor Market, 21148-65
Old-Growth Forests in the Southwest and Rocky Mountain Regions: Proceedings of a Workshop, 1208-421
OMB Sequestration Report to the President and Congress for FY92, 104-27
OMB Sequestration Update Report to the President and Congress, 104-27
On Markovian Representations of the Term Structure, 9377-9.145
On the Econometrics of World Business Cycles, 9377-9.124
On the Existence and Uniqueness of Nonoptimal Equilibria in Dynamic Stochastic Economies, 9383-20.21
On the Existence of Pareto-Superior Reversals of Dynamically Inefficient Social Security Programs, 4746-26.17
On the Future Erosion of the North American Free Trade Agreement, 9379-12.89
One in Four of Nation's Foreign Born Arrived Since 1985, Census Bureau Says, 2328-88
One State's Response to the Malpractice Insurance Crisis: North Carolina's Rural Obstetrical Care Incentive Program, 4042-3.355
One Trading World, or Many: The Issue of Regional Trading Blocs, 9373-1.308
Operation Desert Storm: Apache Helicopter Was Considered Effective in Combat, but Reliability Problems Persist, 26123-378
Operation Desert Storm: DOD Met Need for Chemical Suits and Masks, but Longer Term Actions Needed, 26123-387
Operation Desert Storm: Race and Gender Comparison of Deployed Forces with All Active Duty Forces, 26123-394
Operation Desert Storm: The Services' Efforts To Provide Logistics Support for Selected Weapon Systems, 26123-375
Operation of the Colorado River Basin 1991, Projected Operations 1992: 21st Annual Report, 5824-6
Operation of the Trade Agreements Program, 9884-5
Operation of TVA Reservoirs: Annual 1990, 9804-7
Operational Impacts of Wider Trucks on Narrow Roadways, 7558-113
Operations Desert Shield/Storm: Foreign Government and Individual Contributions to the Department of Defense, 26104-24
Opinions About the Federal Work Environment. Senior Executive Service, 26119-402
OPM Revolving Fund: Benchmarking Could Aid OPM's Efforts To Improve Customer Service, 26119-373
Opportunities for Using Coal To Replace Imported Energy in Electric Utilities, 3166-6.63
Opportunities To Reduce Taxpaper Burden Through Return-Free Filing. Internal Revenue Service, 26119-400
Opportunities To Teach Better Nutrition, 1504-9.1
Opportunity To Defray Burgeoning Federal and State Non-AFDC Costs. Child Support Enforcement, 26121-463
Optimal Fiscal and Monetary Policy: Some Recent Results, 9383-20.17
Optimal Linear Taxation of Polluting Firms, 9387-8.280
Optimal Venture Capital Solicitation Under a Horizon Constraint, 9371-10.83
Option Pricing with Random Volatilities in Complete Markets, 9371-10.74
Optional Hospital Payment Rates for Private Payers Based on Medicare's Methods (As Specified in H.R. 3626), 17206-1.16
Options That Could Make the Program More Financially Independent. Perkins Student Loans, 26121-440
Options To Improve Hazard-Abatement Procedures in the Workplace. Occupational Safety and Health, 26121-461
Orange Juice Outlook for Selected Countries, 1925-34.308, 1925-34.328
Oregon Water Supply Outlook, 1264-9
Oregon's Forest Products Industry: 1988, 1208-280
Organic Materials: Minerals Yearbook, Volume 1, 1990, 5604-20.65
Organizational Goal Congruence and Job Attitudes Revisited, 7506-10.104
Organizational Politics, Participation in Decision-Making, and Job Satisfaction, 7506-10.117
ORS Working Paper Series, 4746-26
OSHA Action Needed To Improve Compliance with Hazard Communication Standard. Occupational Safety and Health, 26121-439
OSHA Saipan Garment Factory Inspections Bring $559,900 in Penalties, 6606-3.10
Other Tobaccos, Summary of 1992 Support Program: ASCS Commodity Fact Sheet, 1806-4.7
Our Increasingly Populated World. Statistical Brief, 2326-17.50
Our Living Oceans, First Annual Report on the Status of U.S. Living Marine Resources, 2164-22
Our Nation's Highways: Selected Facts and Figures, 7554-41
Outbreak of Bacillus cereus Food Poisoning—Are Caterers Supervised Sufficiently?, 4042-3.350
Outer Continental Shelf Environmental Assessment Program: Final Reports of Principal Investigators, 2176-1
Outer Continental Shelf Oil and Gas Leasing and Production Program: Annual Report FY91, 5734-4
Outer Continental Shelf Statistical Summary, 1989: Leasing by Sale and by Map Area/Block Number, 5734-8
Outer Continental Shelf Statistical Summary, 1990: Leasing by Sale and by Map Area/Block Number, 5734-8
Outlook Charts. Annual Agricultural Outlook Conference, 1504-8
Outlook for Cotton, 1504-9.1
Outlook for Dairy, 1504-9.1
Outlook for Farm Commodity Program Spending, FY92-97, 26306-6.171

Outlook for Genetics Research and Application in Aquaculture, 1504–9.1
Outlook for Horticultural Products, 1504–9.1
Outlook for Poultry and Eggs, 1504–9.1
Outlook for Production Inputs, 1504–9.1
Outlook for Red Meats, 1504–9.1
Outlook for Technology and Labor in Hospitals, 6826–2.8
Outlook for Timber Products, 1504–9.1
Outlook for Tobacco, 1504–9.1
Outlook for U.S. Agricultural Exports, 1542–4
Outlook for U.S. Aquaculture, 1504–9.1
Outlook for U.S. Wheat in 1992 or "A Dry Year in Kansas Is Followed by ...?", 1504–9.1
Outlook Proceedings: Annual Agricultural Outlook Conference, 1004–16, 1504–9
Outlook Story for Oilseeds, 1504–9.1
Outlook 1990-2005, 6744–19
Outpatient Payment Policy Reform, 17206–1.15
Outpatient Surgery: Helping To Contain Health Care Costs, 6722–1.349
Outpatient Surgery: Medicare Payments for Unnecessary and Poor Quality Cataract Surgeries, 4006–11.2
Outpatient Visits by Primary Health Provider, Indian Health Service and Tribally Operated Facilities, FY91, 4084–3
Output and Inflation Components of Medical Care and Other Spending Changes, 4652–1.308
OVC Bulletins, 6066–31
Overdue, 2152–8.304
Overhangs and Hangovers: Coping with the Imbalances of the 1980s, 9385–2
Overseas Business Reports: Marketing in Individual Countries, 2046–6
Overseas Staffing: Embassies in the Former Soviet Union, 26123–403
Oversight Hearing To Review Census Adjustment Decision, 21628–101
Oversight Hearing To Review the Progress of Coverage Evaluation Procedures, 21628–102
Oversight Hearing To Review the 1990 Census Counts, 21628–97
Overview and Inventory of State Requirements for School Coursework and Attendance, 4838–52
Overview of AID Population Assistance, FY91, 9914–13.1
Overview of Clean Water Legislation, 1504–9.1
Overview of Entitlement Programs: 1992 Green Book. Background Material and Data on Programs Within the Jurisdiction of the Committee on Ways and Means, 21784–11
Overview of Home-Based Work: Results from a Regional Research Project, 1702–1.307
Overview of Mark-recovery Studies on Adult and Juvenile Atlantic Menhaden, Brevoortia tyrannus, and Gulf Menhaden, B. patronus, 2162–1.303
Overview of Public Social Welfare Expenditures, FY89, 4742–1.302
Overweight Adults in the U.S., 4147–16.6

PAC Contributions Up 10 Percent for 1992 Races at 18-Month Mark, 9276–1.110
Pacific Air Traffic Forecasts, 1996-2010: Trans-Pacific Market, Top City-Pair Markets, 7504–51
Pacific Marine Environmental Laboratory Summary Report, FY91, 2144–21
Pacific Northwest Loads and Resources Study, Pacific Northwest Economic and Electricity Use Forecast, 1991: Technical Appendix, Volume 1, 3224–3.3
Pacific Northwest Loads and Resources Study, 1991, 3224–3
Pacific Northwest Loads and Resources Study, 1991: Non-Utility Generation Supplement, 3224–3.4
Pacific Northwest Loads and Resources Study, 1991: Technical Appendix, Volume 2, 3224–3.2
Pacific Outer Continental Shelf Region: Production Record by Platform, 1990, 5734–9
Pacific Rim: Agriculture and Trade Report, Situation and Outlook Series, 1524–4.3
Packaging, Transporting, and Burying Low-Level Waste, 3006–5.30
Packers and Stockyards Statistical Report, 1990 Reporting Year, 1384–1
PACS Expense Report, 9364–11
PACS Expense Report, 1989, 9364–11
PACS Expense Report, 1990, 9364–11
PACS Expense Report, 1991, 9364–11
PAC's Give $73 Million to 1991-92 Congressional Campaigns, 9276–1.106
Pads for Woodwind Instrument Keys from Italy. Determination of the Commission in Investigation No. 731-TA-627 (Preliminary) Under the Tariff Act of 1930, Together with the Information Obtained in the Investigation, 9886–14.364
Paint and Allied Products, 1991, Current Industrial Report, 2506–8.16
Paint, Varnish, and Lacquer, Current Industrial Report, 2506–8.4
Paints, Inks, and Related Items, Industry and Trade Summary, 9885–11.3
Pakistan: Asia Pacific Energy Series Country Report, 3406–6.11
Panama Canal Commission, Annual Report, Fiscal Year Ended Sept. 30, 1991, 9664–3
Pantex Plant Site Environmental Report for 1990, 3324–2.1
Parent and Supplemental Student Loans: Volume and Default Trends for FY89-91, 26121–473
Parental Financial Support for Undergraduate Education: 1987 National Postsecondary Student Aid Study, 4846–3.11
Pareto Optimality of Existing Pay-As-You-Go Social Security Programs, 4746–26.16
Parity and Primary Liver Cancer Among Young Women, 4472–1.331
Part of the National Defense Reserve Fleet Is No Longer Needed. Strategic Sealift, 26123–376
Partial Care in Mental Health Organizations, U.S. and Each State, 1988, 4506–3.51
Participant Evaluation and Cost of a Community-Based Health Promotion Program for Elders, 4042–3.342
Participation in Secondary Vocational Education, 1982-87, 4838–50
Partnership Returns, 1990, 8302–2.314
Partnerships, Partners, and Tax Shelters After Tax Reform, 1987-89, 8302–2.313
Part-Time Employment Transitions Among Young Women. Work and Family, 6726–2.2
Passive Microwave Research: Microwave Bibliography Update, 1988-91, 2156–18.24
Past Actions Taken To Assist Columbia River Salmon. Endangered Species, 26113–577
Patents Issued by the Patent and Trademark Office, 2244–2
Patient Care Episodes in Mental Health Organizations, U.S.: Selected Years from 1955 to 1988, 4506–3.50
Pattern of p53 Gene Mutations in Breast Cancers of Women of the Midwestern U.S., 4472–1.305
Patterns of Global Terrorism: 1991, 7004–13
Patterns of HIV Risk and Preventive Behaviors Among Teenage Men, 4042–3.313
Patterns of Use in the Business and Industry Loan Guarantee Program. Rural Development Administration, 26113–591
Pay and Benefits: Information on Four Federal Banking Agencies, 26119–368
Pay Equity: Washington State's Efforts To Address Comparable Worth, 26119–410
Pay Structure of the Federal Civil Service, Mar. 31, 1991, Federal Civilian Workforce Statistics, 9844–6
Paying for Highways, Airways, and Waterways: How Can Users Be Charged?, 26306–6.170
Payments of Child Support and Alimony, 1702–1.305
Payments to Producers by State and Program During 1991, 1804–12
Payments to States from National Forest Receipts, FY91, Adjusted for Spotted Owl Guarantees, 1204–33
Payments to States from National Forest Receipts, FY92, Adjusted for Spotted Owl Guarantees Where Applicable, 1204–33
Peace Corps: Congressional Presentation, 9654–1
Peace Corps of the U.S. Budget Presentation to the U.S. House of Representatives, FY93, 9654–1
Peace Corps of the U.S. Budget Presentation to the U.S. Senate, FY93, 9654–1
Peanut Marketing Summary, 1991 Crop, 1311–5
Peanut Production Practices and Input Use: 1991, 1561–16.304
Peanut Report, 1311–1
Peanut Stocks and Processing, 1621–6
Peanuts, Summary of 1991 Support Program and Related Information: ASCS Commodity Fact Sheet, 1806–4.3
Peat: Minerals Yearbook, Volume 1, 1990, 5604–20.44
Pecan Marketing Summary, 1990 Crop, 1311–28
Pecan Marketing Summary, 1991 Crop, 1311–28
Pedestrians: Synthesis of Safety Research, 7558–98.2
Pediatric AIDS-Related Discharges in a Sample of U.S. Hospitals: Demographics, Diagnoses, and Resource Use, 4186–6.16
Pell Grant End of Year Report, 1990-91, 4804–1
Pell Grant Program, End of Year Report, 4804–1
Penalties for Violations Are Well Below Maximum Allowable Penalties. Occupational Safety and Health, 26121–455
Pension Benefit Guaranty Corporation: Annual Report, 1991, 9674–1
Pension Insurance: A Crisis on the Horizon?, 9391–16.309

Pension Policy: An International Perspective, 6688–2
Pensions Plans: Survivor Benefit Coverage for Wives Increased After 1984 Pension Law, 26121–450
Perceptions of Well-Being Among Three Age Cohorts of Rural Southern Elders, 1504–9.1
Performance of Color-Dependent Tasks of Air Traffic Control Specialists as a Function of Type and Degree of Color Vision Deficiency, 7506–10.123
Performance Optimization and Repowering of Generating Units, 3162–35.303
Performance Profiles of Major Energy Producers, 1990, 3164–44
Perkins Loan Program, Status of Default as of June 30, 1991, 4804–18
Perkins Student Loans: Options That Could Make the Program More Financially Independent, 26121–440
Perlite in 1991: Mineral Industry Surveys, Annual Report, 5614–5.13
Perpetual Signaling with Imperfectly Correlated Costs, 9387–8.271
Persian Gulf: Allied Burden Sharing Efforts, 26123–371
Personal and Household Crimes Rose Less than 2 Percent Last Year, 6068–249
Personnel Practices: Propriety of Career Appointments Granted Former Political Appointees, 26119–382
Personnel Research Highlights Special Report on the Survey of Federal Employees (SOFE), 9848–41
Persons Denied Private Health Insurance Due to Poor Health. National Medical Expenditure Survey, 4186–8.23
Pertussis Vaccination: Acellular Pertussis Vaccine for Reinforcing and Booster Use — Supplementary ACIP Statement. Recommendations of the Immunization Practices Advisory Committee (ACIP), 4206–2.51
Pertussis Vaccination: Acellular Pertussis Vaccine for the Fourth and Fifth Doses of the DTP Series; Update to Supplementary ACIP Statement. Recommendations of the Advisory Committee on Immunization Practices (ACIP), 4206–2.65
Pest Conditions Annual Report, 1989: Southwestern Region, 1206–11.2
Pest Conditions Annual Report, 1990: Southwestern Region, 1206–11.2
Pest Conditions Annual Report, 1991: Southwestern Region, 1206–11.2
Pest Risk Assessment of the Importation of Larch from Siberia and from the Soviet Far East, 1208–389
Pesticide and Toxicity Evaluation of Wetland Waters and Sediments on National Wildlife Refuges in South Dakota, 5508–117
Pesticide Re-registration Dilemma and Its Impact, 1504–9.1, 1504–9.1
Pesticide Review, For USDA State and County Emergency Records, 1804–5
Pesticides: Adulterated Imported Foods Are Reaching U.S. Grocery Shelves, 26113–598
Pesticides: Comparison of U.S. and Mexican Pesticide Standards and Enforcement, 26113–585
Petroleum Marketing Annual, 1990, 3164–85
Petroleum Marketing Annual, 1991, 3164–85
Petroleum Marketing Monthly, 3162–11
Petroleum Supply Annual, 1991, 3164–2
Petroleum Supply Monthly, 3162–6
Pharmaceutical Preparations, Except Biologicals, 1991, Current Industrial Report, 2506–8.5
Pharmaceuticals and Intermediate Chemicals: Identification of Applicable 6-Digit HS Subheadings for Products Covered by the Proposed Uruguay Round Pharmaceutical Agreement. Investigation No. 332-322, 9886–4.185
Philadelphia Research Working Papers, 9387–8
Philippines Fruit and Vegetable Market Situation, 1925–34.303
Phosphate Rock, 1991: Mineral Industry Surveys, Advanced Summary, 5614–5.4
Phosphate Rock, 1992 Crop Year, Mineral Industry Surveys, 5614–20
Photographic Supplies, Industry and Trade Summary, 9885–10.4
Photovoltaic Energy Contract List, FY90, 3304–20.1
Photovoltaic Energy Program Overview, FY91, 3304–20.2
Photovoltaic Energy Program Summary, 3304–20
Physician Cost Experience Under Private Health Insurance Programs, 4652–1.320
Physician Customary Charges and Medicare Payment Experience: Study Findings, 4652–1.307
Physician Fee Schedule Update Recommendation for 1993, 4004–33
Physician Fee Schedule Update Recommendation, 1992. Report to Congress, 4004–33
Physician Payment Review Commission, Annual Report to Congress, 17264–1
Physician Payment Review Commission: Background Paper Series, 17266–2
Physician Payment Review Commission: Reports to Congress, 17266–1
Physician Payment Under Medicaid, 17266–1.4
Pieces of Eight, An Economic Perspective on the 8th District, 9391–16
Pilot Study of AIDS Risk in the General Population, 4042–3.311
Pinellas Plant Site Environmental Report for 1991, 3324–2.12
Pistachio Production, 1621–18.7
Pistachio Situation and Outlook in Selected Countries, 1925–34.345
P.L. 101-237 As It Applies to Debt Waivers and Attorney Fee Restrictions in Regard to Loan Guaranty Indebtedness, 21768–67
Plan and Operation of the NHANES I Epidemiologic Followup Study, 1987. Vital and Health Statistics Series 1, 4147–1.29
Planned R&D Expenditures of Major U.S. Firms: 1990-91, 9626–6.38
Plant and Equipment Expenditures and Plans, 2502–2
Plastic Bottles, Current Industrial Report, 2506–8.10
Plastics Recycling Portends New Wave of Future Exports, 9882–16.301
Platinum-Group Metals: Mineral Industry Surveys, 5612–2.14
Platinum-Group Metals: Minerals Yearbook, Volume 1, 1990, 5604–20.46
Pleasure Travel Markets to North America, 2906–2
Pleasure Travel Markets to North America: Canada. Final Report, 2906–2.24
Pleasure Travel Markets to North America: Canada. Highlights Report, 2906–2.24
Pleasure Travel Markets to North America: Japan. City Market Analysis and City Image Survey, 2906–2.22
Pleasure Travel Markets to North America: Japan. Package Tour Market Analysis and Tour Product Survey, 2906–2.23
Pleasure Travel Markets to North America: South Korea, 2906–2.18
Pleasure Travel Markets to North America: UK and Japan. Highlights Report/Special Edition, 2906–2.19
Pleasure Travel Markets to North America: UK. City Market Analysis and City Image Survey, 2906–2.20
Pleasure Travel Markets to North America: UK, France, West Germany and Japan. Highlights Report, 2906–2.15
Pleasure Travel Markets to North America: UK. Package Tour Market Analysis and Tour Product Survey, 2906–2.21
Pleasure Travel Markets to North America: Venezuela, 2906–2.17
Pleasure Travel Markets to North America: Venezuela and South Korea. Highlights Report, 2906–2.16
Plumbing Fixtures, Current Industrial Report, 2506–11.2
Plywood, Waferboard and Oriented-Strand Board (Formerly "Hardwood Plywood"), Current Industrial Report, 2506–7.1
Pocket Condition of Education, 1992, 4824–10
Poland and Hungary: Economic Transition and U.S. Assistance, 26123–386
Police and Firefighter Pension Plans, 6722–1.350
Policies on Government Officials' Use of 89th Military Airlift Wing Aircraft. Military Aircraft, 26123–384
Policies, Procedures, and Organization of the Federal Home Loan Mortgage Corporation, 5184–8
Policies, Procedures, and Organization of the Federal National Mortgage Association, 5184–9
Policy Implications of Trade and Currency Zones. A Symposium Sponsored by the Federal Reserve Bank of Kansas City, 9381–13.1
Political Appointees: Number of Noncareer SES and Schedule C Employees in Federal Agencies, 26119–412
Poll Respondents Voice Concerns over Region's Water Quality and Quantity, 9383–19.302
Pollution Abatement and Control Expenditures, 1972-90, 2702–1.321
Pollution Abatement Costs and Expenditures, 1989. Current Industrial Report, 2506–3.6
Pollution Abatement Costs and Expenditures, 1990. Current Industrial Report, 2506–3.6
Polysomnography and Sleep Disorder Centers. Health Technology Assessment Report, 1991, 4186–10.9
Population Biology and Life History of the North American Menhadens, Brevoortia spp., 2162–1.303
Population Characteristics. Current Population Reports. Series P-20, 2546–1
Population Dose Commitments Due to Radioactive Releases from Nuclear Power Plant Sites in 1988, 9634–7

Population Estimates and Projections. Current Population Reports. Series P-25, 2546–3
Population Estimates and Projections; Estimates of the Population of the U.S. to (Date). Current Population Reports. Series P-25, 2542–1
Population Trends, 2326–24
Population Trends in the 1980's, 2546–2.164
Port and State Tonnage Reports, 3754–7
Portable Seismographs from Canada. Determination of the Commission in Investigation No. 701-TA-313 (Preliminary) Under the Tariff Act of 1930, Together with the Information Obtained in the Investigation, 9886–15.79
Position Papers from the Third National Injury Control Conference: "Setting the National Agenda for Injury Control in the 1990's," Apr. 22-25, 1991, Denver, Colo., 4208–35
Position Papers from the Third National Injury Control Conference: Setting the National Agenda for Injury Control in the 1990s, Executive Summaries, 4206–2.56
Postal Delivery Scores Improved but Service Is Slower. Revised Delivery Standards, 26119–431
Postal Service: Automation Is Restraining but Not Reducing Costs, 26119–395
Postal Service: Work Hour Allocations to High Growth and Low Growth Post Offices, 26119–379
Post-Louvre Intervention: Did Target Zones Stabilize the Dollar?, 9377–9.134
Postmaster General, FY91 Annual Report, 9864–1
Postmortem Alcohol Production in Fatal Aircraft Accidents, 7506–10.111
Postsecondary Education Facilities Inventory and Classification Manual, 4848–48
Postsecondary Student Outcomes: A Feasibility Study, 4848–45
Potash in Crop Years 1991 and 1992, Mineral Industry Surveys, 5614–19
Potash: Minerals Yearbook, Volume 1, 1990, 5604–20.47
Potassium Hydroxide from Canada, Italy, and the UK. Determinations of the Commission in Investigations Nos. 731-TA-542, 543, and 544 (Preliminary) Under the Tariff Act of 1930, Together with the Information Obtained in the Investigations, 9886–14.339
Potato Stocks, 1621–10
Potatoes, 1621–11
Potential Cumulative Impacts of Environmental Regulatory Initiatives on U.S. Crude Oil Exploration and Production, 3338–2
Potential Effectiveness of the Employment Service in Serving Dislocated Workers Under EDWAA: Evidence from the 1980s, 15496–1.14
Potential Effects of a North American Free Trade Agreement on Apparel Investment in CBERA Countries. Report to the U.S. Trade Representative on Investigation No. 332-321, 9886–4.186
Potential Effects of Mandatory Child Support Programs on Poverty, 6886–6.87
Potential Effects of OCS Oil and Gas Exploration and Development on Pacific Northwest Indian Tribes: Final Technical Report, 5738–35
Potential El Nino Impacts on U.S. Feed Grain Production, 1561–4.302
Potential Merger Synergies Among Large Commercial Banks, 9387–8.256
Potential Oil Production from the Coastal Plain of the Arctic National Wildlife Refuge, Revised Edition, 3166–6.64
Poultry, Industry and Trade Summary, 9885–8.6
Poultry Market Statistics: 1991 Annual Summary, Federal-State Market News in Cooperation with State Departments of Agriculture, 1317–2
Poultry Production and Value, 1991 Summary, 1625–5
Poultry Slaughter, 1625–3
Poverty Guidelines for 1992, 4742–1.310
Poverty in the U.S.: 1991, 2546–6.77
Poverty Trends, 1980-88: Changes in Family Composition and Income Sources Among the Poor, 26131–102
Powerplant and Industrial Fuel Use Act, Annual Report, 3334–1
Powerplant and Industrial Fuel Use Act, Annual Report for Federal Facilities, 3334–2
Practical Information on the Soviet Union, 2048–157
Practice Expenses Under the Medicare Fee Schedule: A Resource-Based Approach, 17266–2.9
Pre- and Postoperative Visits Associated with Surgical Global Services, 17266–2.6
Predicting and Reinforcing Children's Intentions To Wear Protective Helmets While Bicycling, 4042–3.326
Predicting Contemporaneous Output, 9393–8.305
Predicting Needs for Special Education Resources for Mental Retardation from Birth Defects Records, 4042–3.327
Prediction of Release Rates for a Potential Waste Repository at Yucca Mountain, 3368–4
Prefabricated Buildings, Industry and Trade Summary, 9885–10.3
Preliminary Estimates of Age and Sex Compositions of Ducks and Geese Harvested in Comparison with Prior Years, 5504–32
Preliminary Estimates of the Total-System Cost for the Restructured Program: An Addendum to the May 1989 Analysis of the Total-System Life Cycle Cost for the Civilian Radioactive Waste Management Program, 3368–5
Preliminary Estimates of Waterfowl Harvest and Hunter Activity in the U.S. During the 1991 Hunting Season, 5504–28
Preliminary Report on U.S. Production of Selected Synthetic Organic Chemicals, 9882–1
Preliminary Timber Resource Statistics for Southwest Washington, 1206–28.4
Preliminary Timber Resource Statistics for the Olympic Peninsula, Washington, 1206–28.5
Preliminary Timber Resource Statistics for the Puget Sound Area, Washington, 1206–28.6
Preliminary 1991, Final 1987-90. Estimates of Age and Sex Compositions of Harvested Ducks and Geese, 5504–32
Preparation for the 1990 Farm Bill, Part XII, 25168–78
Prescription Drug Advertisements in Medical Journals, 4008–119
Prescription Drugs: Changes in Prices for Selected Drugs, 26121–472
Prescription Drugs: Companies Typically Charge More in the U.S. than in Canada, 26121–482
Preserving the Vital Base: America's Semiconductor Materials and Equipment Industry, 15036–1.1
President Bush's FY93 Budget, 21268–42
President Makes $30 Million in Drought Relief Available to Western States, 5306–4.17
Presidential Candidates Raise $32.8 Million Through January, FEC Report Shows, 9276–1.99
Presidential Election Campaign Fund (Presidential Checkoff System), 21428–10
Presidential Popularity, Presidential Policies, 9393–10.17
President's Council on Integrity and Efficiency: A Progress Report to the President, FY91, 104–29
President's List of Articles Which May Be Designated or Modified as Eligible Articles for Purposes of the U.S. Generalized System of Preferences. Report to the President on Investigation Nos. TA-131-18, 503(a)-23, and 332-319, 9884–23
President's List of Articles Which May Be Designated or Modified as Eligible Articles for Purposes of the U.S. Generalized System of Preferences: Report to the President on Investigation Nos. TA-131-19, 503(a)-24, and 332-331, 9884–23
President's National Urban Policy Report, 5184–7
Prevalence of Artificial Lens Implants in the Civil Airman Population, 7506–10.114
Prevalence of Drug Use in the D.C. Metropolitan Area Household Population: 1990, 4496–12.1
Prevalence of DSM-III-R Alcohol Abuse and Dependence, U.S., 1988, 4482–1.306
Prevalence of Major Digestive Disorders and Bowel Symptoms, 1989, 4146–8.213
Prevention and Control of Influenza: Recommendations of the Immunization Practices Advisory Committee (ACIP), 4206–2.59
Prevention and Control of Tuberculosis Among Homeless Persons: Recommendations of the Advisory Committee for Elimination of Tuberculosis, 4206–2.55
Prevention and Control of Tuberculosis in Migrant Farm Workers: Recommendations of the Advisory Council for the Elimination of Tuberculosis, 4206–2.60
Prevention and Control of Tuberculosis in U.S. Communities with At-Risk Minority Populations: Recommendations of the Advisory Council for the Elimination of Tuberculosis, 4206–2.55
Prevention of Violence and Injuries Due to Violence, 4208–35
Prevention, Treatment, and Research. Breast Cancer, 1971-91, 26131–92
Preview of the 1992 Economic Census, 2308–5
Price of Giving: Taxes, Education, and Econometric Issues, 6886–6.83
Price Projections for Selected Grades of Douglas-Fir, Coast Hem-Fir, Inland Hem-Fir, and Ponderosa Pine Lumber, 1208–424
Price Trends for Federal-Aid Highway Construction, 7552–7

Price-Adjustment Delays in the Secondary Market for Developing Country Debt and the Estimation of Asset Pricing Models, 9385–8.132
Prices Received: Minnesota-Wisconsin Manufacturing Grade Milk, 1991 Summary, 1629–2
Pricing and Promotion of Infant Formula, 25528–118
Pricing Postal Services in a Competitive Environment. U.S. Postal Service, 26119–384
Primary Aluminum Plants, Worldwide, 5604–49
Primary Mortgage Market Survey Results, 9412–3
Prime Contract Awards by Region and State, FY89-91, 3544–11
Prime Contract Awards by Service Category and Federal Supply Classification, FY88-91, 3544–18
Prime Contract Awards by State, FY91, 3542–5
Prime Contract Awards by State, First Half FY92, 3542–5
Prime Contract Awards, First Half FY92, Department of Defense, 3542–1
Prime Contract Awards, FY91, Department of Defense, 3542–1
Prime Contract Awards in Labor Surplus Areas, FY91, 3542–19
Prime Contract Awards in Labor Surplus Areas, First Half FY92, 3542–19
Prime Contract Awards, Size Distribution, FY91, 3544–19
Primer on the Japanese Banking System, 9366–7.273
Principal Threats Facing Communities and Local Emergency Management Coordinators, 9434–6
Prison Expansion: Staffing New Facilities Will Be a Challenge for BOP, 26119–397
Prisoners in 1991, 6066–25.47
Prisons and Prisoners in the U.S., 6068–248
Private Foundation and Charitable Trust Statistics, 1989: Data Release, 8302–2.325
Private Foundations, 1988, 8302–2.302
Private Social Welfare Expenditures, 1972-90, 4742–1.323
Privatizing Social Security: The Chilean Case, 9385–8.123
Probation and Parole, 1990, 6066–25.43
Problems in Restructuring SBA's Minority Business Development Program. Small Business, 26113–563
Problems of Drug Dependence, 1991: Proceeding of the 53rd Annual Scientific Meeting, The Committee on Problems of Drug Dependence, Inc., 4494–11
Problems Persist in Determining Tax Effects of Intercompany Prices. International Taxation, 26119–411
Procedural Justice, Occupational Identification, and Organizational Commitment, 7506–10.121
Procedure for Predicting Recessions with Leading Indicators: Econometric Issues and Recent Performance, 9375–13.84
Proceeding of the 53rd Annual Scientific Meeting, The Committee on Problems of Drug Dependence, Inc.: Problems of Drug Dependence, 1991, 4494–11
Proceedings: Conference on Bank Structure and Competition, Federal Reserve Bank of Chicago, May 1-3, 1991. Rebuilding Banking, 9375–7
Proceedings of the Commission on the Future Structure of Veterans Health Care, 8608–9
Proceedings of the Expert Consultation Meeting on Mink and Otter, 14648–27
Proceedings of the International Collaborative Effort on Perinatal and Infant Mortality, Volume III, 4148–28
Proceedings of the International Conference on Pollution Prevention, 9184–22
Proceedings of the Sixteenth Annual Climate Diagnostics Workshop, 2184–10
Proceedings of the Sixth Biennial Southern Silvicultural Research Conference, 1204–35
Proceedings of the Symposium on Work Zone Traffic Control, 7558–115
Proceedings of the Eighteenth U.S.-Japan Meeting on Aquaculture, Port Ludlow, Wash., Sept. 18-19, 1989: Marine Ranching, 2164–15
Proceedings of the Nineteenth U.S.-Japan Meeting on Aquaculture, Ise, Mie Prefecture, Japan, 29-30 October 1990: Control of Disease in Aquaculture, 2164–15
Proceedings of the 1991 Public Health Conference on Records and Statistics. The 1990's: A Decade of Decisions for Vital and Health Statistics, 4164–2
Proceedings: The 27th Annual Conference on Bank Structure and Competition, May 1-3, 1991, Rebuilding Banking. Federal Reserve Bank of Chicago, 9375–7
Processed Apple Sales, 1986-90: The Effects of Market Factors, 1548–392
Processed Fishery Products, Annual Summary 1988, 2166–6.2
Processed Tomato Production and Stocks Remain High, 1925–34.304
Processing of USDA Commodities Donated to the National School Lunch Program. Food Assistance, 26113–555
Procurement Programs (P-1), Department of Defense Budget for FY93, 3544–32
Procyclical Application of Bank Capital Requirements, 9373–26
Procyclical Labor Productivity, Increasing Returns to Labor, and Labor Hoarding in U.S. Auto Assembly Plant Employment, 6886–6.89
Produce Industry's Challenge To Double Demand for Fresh Vegetables, 1561–11.301
Producer Milk Marketed Under Federal Milk Orders by State of Origin, 1317–4.301
Producer Price Indexes, 6762–5, 6762–6
Producer Price Indexes, Data for 1991, 6764–2
Producer Services: Trends and Prospects for the Seventh District, 9375–1.305
Producer Structure in Federal Milk Order Markets, 1317–4.303
Product Effects of Trade Restrictions in the Japanese Pork Import Market, 1524–4.3
Product Summary Report. Source: National Electronic Injury Surveillance System, U.S. Consumer Product Safety Commission, National Injury Information Clearinghouse, All Products, 1991, 9164–6
Production and Inventory Control at the General Motors Corporation During the 1920s and 1930s, 9375–13.87
Production and Receipts of Veneer Logs in the Southeastern and Midsouth States, 1988, 1208–407
Production and Sources of Residential Fuelwood from Roundwood in Michigan, 1208–412
Production, Prices, Employment, and Trade in Northwest Forest Industries, 1202–3
Production Sharing: U.S. Imports Under Harmonized Tariff Schedule Subheadings 9802.00.60 and 9802.00.80, 1987-90, 9884–14
Productivity and Costs: Preliminary Statistics, 6822–1
Productivity and Costs, Revised Data for Business, Nonfarm Business, and Manufacturing, and Preliminary Measures for Nonfinancial Corporations, 6822–2
Productivity in Crude Oil and Natural Gas Production, 6722–1.316
Productivity in the Nuts and Bolts Industry, 1958-90, 6722–1.343
Productivity in Wood Containers, 6722–1.344
Productivity Measures for Selected Industries and Government Services, 6824–1
Productivity of Brazilian Agriculture: Measurement and Uses, 1528–331
Productivity Shocks and Real Business Cycles, 9375–13.73
Productivity Statistics for Federal Government Functions, FY67-90, 6824–4
Productivity Trends: Prepared Fish and Seafoods Industry, 6722–1.342
Professional Electric Cutting and Sanding/Grinding Tools from Japan. Determination of the Commission in Investigation No. 731-TA-571 (Preliminary) Under the Tariff Act of 1930, Together with the Information Obtained in the Investigation, 9886–14.355
Profile, FY91, National Institute of Allergy and Infectious Diseases, 4474–30
Profile of American Eighth-Grade Mathematics and Science Instruction. National Education Longitudinal Study of 1988, 4826–9.13
Profile of Child Care Settings: Early Education and Care in 1990, 4808–39
Profile of Hired Farmworkers, 1990 Annual Averages, 1598–278
Profile of Land Ownership at 12 Reservations. Indian Programs, 26113–559
Profile of Parents of Eighth Graders. National Education Longitudinal Study of 1988, 4826–9.15
Profile of Participants in FmHA's Guaranteed Farm Loan Programs, 1548–386
Profile of the Agency for International Development. Foreign Assistance, 26123–382
Profile of the Bureau of Land Management's Grazing Allotments and Permits. Rangeland Management, 26113–582
Profile of the "Typical" Federal Civilian Non-Postal Employee, Sept. 30, 1991, 9842–1.301
Profiles in Safety and Health: Eating and Drinking Places, 6728–41
Profiles in Safety and Health: Fabricated Structural Metal, 6722–1.301, 6728–41
Profiles in Safety and Health: Occupational Hazards of Meatpacking, 6728–41
Profiles in Safety and Health: Retail Grocery Stores, 6722–1.339
Profiles in Safety and Health: Roofing and Sheet Metal Work, 6728–41
Profiles in Safety and Health: The Soft Drink Industry, 6722–1.319, 6728–41
Profiles in Safety and Health: Work Hazards of Mobile Homes, 6728–41

Profiles of America's Elderly, 2326–25
Profiles of Foreign Direct Investment in U.S. Energy, 1990, 3164–80
Profiles of Successful Drug Prevention Programs, 4814–2
Profit-Concentration Relationship in Banking, 9366–6.290
Profits and Stock Prices: The Importance of Being Earnest, 9373–1.306
Program Acquisition Costs by Weapon System: Department of Defense Budget for FY93, 3504–2
Program Has Not Fostered Significant Risk Sharing by Insurance Companies. Crop Insurance, 26113–556
Program in Biomedical and Behavioral Nutrition Research and Training, FY89, 13th Annual Report, National Institutes of Health, 4434–15
Program in Biomedical and Behavioral Nutrition Research and Training, FY90, 14th Annual Report, National Institutes of Health, 4434–15
Program in Need of Reform. Federal Labor Relations, 26119–367
Program Performance Measures: Federal Agency Collection and Use of Performance Data, 26119–396
Program Summary Book: A Statistical and Historical Reference for OPE Programs, 4804–28
Programs and Collection Procedures. Vital and Health Statistics Series 1, 4147–1
Progress in the Prevention and Control of Air Pollution, 9194–4
Project Head Start Statistical Fact Sheet, 4584–5, 4604–8
Project Summaries, 9624–21
Projections for Districts: Number of Returns To Be Filed, 8304–24
Projections: Forms 1040, 1040A and 1040EZ by Full-Paid, Other-Than-Full-Paid, Refunds and Electronically-Filed Returns. U.S. and Service Centers, 8302–7
Projections: Number of Returns To Be Filed, 8302–4
Projections, Number of Returns To Be Filed: U.S., Regions, and Service Centers, 8304–9
Projections of Education Statistics to 2002, 4824–4
Projections of Education Statistics to 2002, Pocket Projections, 4824–9
Projections of Education Statistics to 2003, 4824–4
Projections of Information and Withholding Documents for the U.S. and Service Centers, 8304–22
Projections of National Health Expenditures, 26306–6.175
Projections of Returns To Be Filed in CY92-99, 8302–2.304
Projections of the Voting-Age Population, for States: November 1992, 2546–3.170
Promoting Smoking Cessation in the U.S.: Effect of Public Service Announcements on the Cancer Information Service Telephone Line, 4472–1.313
Promotion Activities Under Federal Milk Orders, 1991, 1317–4.304
Prompt Action Necessary To Avert Long-Term Damage to the Economy. Budget Policy, 26109–5
Prompt Payment of Origination Fees Could Reduce Costs. Stafford Student Loans, 26121–467
Proportion of High School Graduates Attending College Sets New Record, 6726–1.46
Proposed Legislation To Authorize a Political Status Referendum in Puerto Rico, Part II, 21448–46
Proposed Marine Mineral Lease Sales: Final Environmental Impact Statements, 5736–7
Proposed Negotiation of a Free Trade Agreement with Mexico, 21788–210
Proposed Refugee Admissions for FY93, Report to the Congress, 7004–16
Propriety of Career Appointments Granted Former Political Appointees. Personnel Practices, 26119–382
Prosecution of Felony Arrests, 1988, 6064–27
Prosecutors in State Courts, 1990, 6066–25.46
Prospective Payment Assessment Commission: Report and Recommendations to the Congress, Mar. 1, 1992, 17204–1
Prospective Payment Assessment Commission: Reports to Congress, 17206–1
Prospective Payment Assessment Commission: Technical Report Series, 17206–2
Prospective Payment for Medicare Hospital Capital: Implications of the Research, 4652–1.313
Prospective Plantings, 1621–22
Prospects for the U.S. Feed Grain Sector, 1504–9.1
Protecting and Enhancing America's Forests and Rangelands: Research Accomplishments, 1204–14
Provider Studies Research Notes, 4186–6
Provisional Legalization Application Statistics, 6262–3
Psychological Distress and Surveillance Behaviors of Women with a Family History of Breast Cancer, 4472–1.301
Public and Private Elementary and Secondary Education Statistics: Early Estimates, School Year 1991-92, 4834–19
Public and Private Elementary and Secondary Education Statistics: Early Estimates, School Year 1992-93, 4834–19
Public Debt News, 8002–7
Public Education Finances: 1989-90, 2466–2.5
Public Elementary and Secondary Schools and Agencies in the U.S. and Outlying Areas: School Year 1990-91, 4834–17
Public Elementary and Secondary State Aggregate Data, for School Year 1990-91 and FY90, 4834–6
Public Employment: 1991, 2466–1.1
Public Finance and Coordination Problems in a Common Currency Area, 9381–10.127
Public Funding Profiles of the NEA States and Cities. Arts Funding, 26119–371
Public Health Reports, 4042–3
Public Health Service: Strategic Plan To Combat HIV and AIDS in the U.S., 4048–22
Public Housing: Housing Persons with Mental Disabilities with the Elderly, 26113–590
Public Input Reports, Advisory Council on Social Security, 10176–2
Public Involvement in Integrated Resource Planning: A Study of Demand-Side Management Collaboratives, 3308–104
Public Land Statistics, 1991, 5724–1
Public Law 480, Concessional Sales Agreements Signed, 1924–6
Public Libraries in the U.S.: 1990, 4824–6
Public Libraries in 50 States and the District of Columbia, 4824–6
Public Pension Dos and Don'ts, 9373–25.301
Public Policy Issues That Challenge the Fresh Fruit and Vegetable Industry for 1992, 1504–9.1
Public Roads, A Journal of Highway Research and Development, 7552–3
Public School Principal Survey on Safe, Disciplined, and Drug-Free Schools, 4826–1.32
Public Social Welfare Expenditures, FY89, 4742–1.319
Public Transportation in the U.S.: Performance and Condition, Report to Congress, 7884–8
Public Water-Supply in Massachusetts, 1986, 5666–24.16
Publications Abstracts, FY91, 2804–3
Publications of the National Institute of Standards and Technology, 1991 Catalog, 2214–1
Publications of the National Science Foundation, 9624–16
Publications of the Rocky Mountain Forest and Range Experiment Station, 1980-89, 1208–403
Publications of the U.S. Geological Survey, 1991, 5664–4
Public-Private Cost Shifts in Nursing Home Care, 9373–1.311
Public-Supply Water Use in Florida, 1987, 5666–24.13
Pulp, Paper, and Board, Current Industrial Report, 2506–7.10
Pulpwood Prices in the Southeast, 1990, 1204–22
Pulpwood Production in the Lake States, 1990, 1208–397
Pulpwood Production in the North-Central Region, 1989, 1204–19
Pulpwood Production in the North-Central Region, 1990, 1204–19
Pulpwood Production in the Northeast, 1990, 1204–18
Pumice and Pumicite in 1991: Mineral Industry Surveys, Annual Report, 5614–5.11
Pumps and Compressors, 1991, Current Industrial Report, 2506–12.8
Purchasing Power Parity and Uncovered Interest Rate Parity: The U.S. 1974-90, 9366–7.279
Purchasing Power Parity Within the U.S., 9373–1.312
Purpose of Admission and Resource Use During Cancer Hospitalizations, 4652–1.304
Putting the Pieces Together: Annual Rural Development Strategy Report, 1004–17

Qualifying Facilities Report: A Cumulative Listing of Filings Made for Qualifying Status for Small Power Production and Cogeneration Facilities, FY80-91, 3084–13
Quality and Risk-Adjusted Cost Function for Banks: Evidence on the "Too-Big-To-Fail" Doctrine, 9387–8.260
Quality Control Annual Report: Food Stamp Program, FY90, 1364–15
Quality Management: Survey of Federal Organizations, 26119–425
Quality of the Ohio River and Atmospheric Deposition and Its Relation to Corrosion of

Lock and Dam Facilities in the Lower Ohio River Basin Near Paducah, Ky., 5666-27.30
Quality-of-Life Assessment: Patient Compliance with Questionnaire Completion, 4472-1.326
Quantifying Management's Role in Bank Survival, 9379-1.302
Quantity and Quality of Stormwater Runoff from Western Daytona Beach, Fla., and Adjacent Areas, 5666-27.28
Quantity-Adjusting Options and Forward Contracts, 9371-10.73
Quarterly Banking Profile, 9292-1
Quarterly Coal Report, 3162-37
Quarterly Financial Information Report, Federal Home Loan Bank of Indianapolis, 9302-23
Quarterly Financial Report for Manufacturing, Mining, and Trade Corporations, 2502-1
Quarterly Industry Review, 7502-16
Quarterly Journal: Comptroller of the Currency, Administrator of National Banks, 8402-3
Quarterly Progress Report, 9182-11
Quarterly Public Assistance Statistics, 4694-7
Quarterly Public Assistance Statistics, FY90, 4584-3
Quarterly Regional Economic Report, Federal Reserve Bank of Philadelphia, 9387-10
Quarterly Report, Federal Home Loan Bank of Boston, 9302-35
Quarterly Report on Program Cost and Schedule, 3362-1
Quarterly Report on the Status of the Steel Industry: Report to the Committee on Ways and Means on Investigation No. 332-226 Under Section 332 of the Tariff Act of 1930, 9882-13
Quarterly Report to the Congress and the Trade Policy Committee: Trade Between the U.S. and China, the Former Soviet Union, Central and Eastern Europe, the Baltic Nations, and Other Selected Countries, 9882-2
Quarterly Review, Federal Reserve Bank of Minneapolis, 9383-6
Quarterly Review, Federal Reserve Bank of New York, 9385-1
Quarterly Speed Monitoring Summary, 7552-14
Quarterly Speed Summary, 7552-14
Quarterly Summary of Federal, State, and Local Tax Revenue, 2462-3
Quarterly Survey of Agricultural Credit Conditions, Eleventh Federal Reserve District, 9379-11
Quarterly Thrift Industry Statistics, 8432-4
Quetelet's Index and Risk of Colon Cancer in College Alumni, 4472-1.339

R, D, T & E Programs (R-1), Department of Defense Budget for FY93, 3544-33
R&D and Internal Finance: A Panel Study of Small Firms in High-Tech Industries, 9375-13.75
Race and Gender Comparison of Deployed Forces with All Active Duty Forces. Operation Desert Storm, 26123-394
Race. 1990 Census Questionnaire Content Bulletin, 2326-23.2
Race/Ethnicity Trends in Degrees Conferred by Institutions of Higher Education: 1980-81 Through 1989-90, 4844-17
Racial Difference in Disability Decisions Warrants Further Investigation. Social Security, 26121-459
Racial Misclassification of Native Americans in a Surveillance, Epidemiology, and End Results Cancer Registry, 4472-1.324
Radiation Exposure of Air Carrier Crewmembers II, 7506-10.98
Radio and Television Receivers, Phonographs, and Related Equipment, 1991, Current Industrial Report, 2506-12.20
Rail Safety Civil Penalty Cases: Agreements Reached and Orders Issued During FY91, 7604-10
Rail-Highway Crossing Accident/Incident and Inventory Bulletin, 1990: No. 13, 7604-2
Rail-Highway Crossing Accident/Incident and Inventory Bulletin, 1991: No. 14, 7604-2
Railroad Accident Reports, Brief Format, 9612-3
Railroad Accident Reports, Brief Format of 1986 Accidents, 9614-8
Railroad Accident Reports, Brief Format of 1987 Accidents, 9614-8
Railroad Accident Reports, Brief Format of 1988 Accidents, 9614-8
Railroad Retirement and Unemployment Insurance Programs. Monthly Benefit Statistics, 9702-2
Railroad Retirement Board, Annual Report, 9704-1
Railroad Safety: Engineer Work Shift Length and Schedule Variability, 26113-579
Railroad Transportation of U.S. Grain to Mexico, 1504-9.1
Randolph-Sheppard Vending Facility Program: Annual Report, FY91, 4944-2
Random-Effects Approach to Attrition Bias in the SIPP Health Insurance Data, 2626-10.147
Rangeland Management: BLM's Hot Desert Grazing Program Merits Reconsideration, 26113-552
Rangeland Management: Interior's Monitoring Has Fallen Short of Agency Requirements, 26113-567
Rangeland Management: Profile of the Bureau of Land Management's Grazing Allotments and Permits, 26113-582
Ranking of States and Commodities by Cash Receipts, 1990, 1548-385
Rare Earths: Minerals Yearbook, Volume 1, 1990, 5604-20.49
Rare-Earth Minerals and Metals: Minerals Yearbook, Volume 1, 5604-20.49
ras Oncogene Activation and Occupational Exposures in Acute Myeloid Leukemia, 4472-1.352
Rates and Terms on Conventional Home Mortgages: FHFB Annual Summary, 9444-2
Rates of Return on Direct Investment, 2702-1.330
Rating Northeasters, 2152-8.301
Rational Expectations and Security Analysts' Earnings Forecasts, 9371-10.84
Rationale for a SIPP-Based Microsimulation Model of SSI and OASDI, 4746-26.23
RCWP Monthly Progress Report, By State and Area for Period Ending (Date), 1802-14
REA Financed Generating Plants, As of Jan. 1, 1992, 1244-6
Reading In and Out of School: Factors Influencing the Literacy Achievement of American Students in Grades 4, 8, and 12, in 1988 and 1990, 4898-33
Real and Personal Property, 3544-6
Real Earnings, 6742-3
Real Effects of Exchange Risk on International Trade, 9371-10.81
Real Effects of Monetary Policy in a World Economy, 9383-20.24
Real Estate Asset Inventory. Resolution Trust Corporation, 9722-2
Real Estate Settlement Procedures Act, 21248-161
Real Exchange Rate and Foreign Direct Investment in the U.S.: Relative Wealth vs. Relative Wage Effects, 9373-27.10
Real Exchange Rate and U.S. Manufacturing Profits: A Theoretical Framework with Some Empirical Support, 9385-8.142
Realignment in Farm Lending: Strategic Issues for the 1990s, 9381-10.122
Reasons for and Effects of Inadequate Public Access. Federal Lands, 26113-571
Rebuilding Banking, 9375-7
Recap of International Travel To and From the U.S. in 1990, 2904-10
Receipts Rise $31.8 Million for '92 Congressional Campaigns, 9276-1.102
Recent Credit Crunch: The Neglected Dimensions, 9391-1.315
Recent Department of Education Publications in ERIC, 4812-1
Recent Developments Affecting the Profitability and Practices of Commercial Banks, 9362-1.305
Recent Growth in the Tennessee Valley and the Near-Term Outlook, 9804-27
Recent Movers. Statistical Brief, 2326-17.38
Recent Publications of the Department of Education, 4812-1
Recent Trends in Afforestation and Reforestation of Nonindustrial Private Pine Forests in Alabama, 1208-409
Recession, Energy Prices Ease Producer Price Inflation, 1991, 6722-1.323
Recession in Historical Perspective, 1990-91, 9373-1.301
Recidivism of Felons on Probation, 1986-89, 6066-19.65
Recombinant Bovine Growth Hormone: FDA Approval Should Be Withheld Until the Mastitis Issue Is Resolved, 26131-101
Recommendations for Prophylaxis Against Pneumocystis carinii Pneumonia for Adults and Adolescents Infected with Human Immunodeficiency Virus, 4206-2.54
Recommendations for the Use of Folic Acid To Reduce the Number of Cases of Spina Bifida and Other Neural Tube Defects, 4206-2.64
Reconciliation Improved SSA Earnings Records, but Efforts Were Incomplete. Social Security, 26121-477
Reconciliation of the U.S.-Canadian Current Account, 2702-1.341
Reconciling Conflicting Data on Jobs for College Graduates, 6722-1.330
Reconnaissance Investigation of Water Quality, Bottom Sediment, and Biota Associated with Irrigation Drainage in the American Falls Reservoir Area, Idaho, 1988-89, 5666-27.24
Reconstruction Finance Corporation: Would It Work Today?, 9381-1.304
Record Number of Patent Applications in FY91, 2244-2
Records and Policies of the Post Office Department Relating to Place-Names, 9516-1.5

Records in the National Archives Relating to the Early Involvement of the U.S. Government in Data Processing, 1880's to 1950's, 9516–1.8
Records of the Accounting Offices of the Department of the Treasury, Record Group 217, 9516–2.2
Records of the Department of the Interior, Record Group 48, 9516–2.1
Records Relating to Personal Participation in World War II: "The American Soldier" Surveys, 9516–1.10
Recoveries on Asset Sales. Resolution Trust Corporation, 26119–372
Recreation Use Report 1991, Servicewide by States, 1204–17
Reducing the Deficit: Spending and Revenue Options. A Report to the Senate and House Committees on the Budget, 26304–3.2
Reductions in the Army Officer Corps, 26306–3.121
Reference Sources, 2326–7.83
Referrals of Participants in an Urban WIC Program to Health and Welfare Services, 4042–3.318
Refined Antimony Trioxide from the People's Republic of China. Determination of the Commission in Investigation No. 731-TA-517 (Final) Under the Tariff Act of 1930, Together with the Information Obtained in the Investigation, 9886–14.342
Reforms for Ensuring Future Soundness. Credit Unions, 26119–364
Refractories, 1991, Current Industrial Report, 2506–9.1
Refrigeration, Air-Conditioning, and Warm Air Heating Equipment, 1991, Current Industrial Report, 2506–12.7
Regional and National Economies Expected To Continue Expansion, 9383–19.303
Regional and Temporal Trends in the Surveillance of Syphilis, U.S., 1986-90, 4202–7.303
Regional Aquifer-System Analysis Program, 5666–25
Regional Economic Digest, Tenth Federal Reserve District, 9381–16
Regional Economic Information System, 1969-90, 2704–7
Regional Employment by Industry: Do Returns to Capital Matter?, 9371–1.306
Regional Multipliers: A User Handbook for the Regional Input-Output Modeling System (RIMS II), 2708–47
Regional Responsiveness of Agricultural Interest Rates to U.S. Treasury Bill Rates, 1541–1.306
Regional Review, Federal Reserve Bank of Boston, 9373–25
Regional Tide and Tidal Current Tables, 1993, New York Harbor to Chesapeake Bay, 2174–11
Regional Update, Federal Reserve Bank of Atlanta, 9371–14
Regional Wage Divergence and National Wage Inequality, 9379–1.307
Register of Copyrights 94th Annual Report, for the Fiscal Year Ending Sept. 30, 1991, 26404–2
Regulations for Implementing the Clinical Laboratory Improvement Amendments of 1988: A Summary, 4206–2.52
Regulatory Framework Has Minimized SIPC's Losses. Securities Investor Protection, 26119–419
Regulatory Reform in Australia and New Zealand, 1524–4.3
Rehabilitation of Persons with Injuries, 4208–35
Rehabilitation Services Administration FY91 Annual Report to the President and the Congress on Federal Activities Related to the Rehabilitation Act of 1973 as Amended, 4944–1
Related Reference Research Information Papers, National Archives Conference on Statistical Research, 9456–1, 9516–1
Relationship Between Family Homelessness, Insurance Coverage, Health Status, and Health Care-Seeking Behavior, 4164–2
Relationship Between Mammographic and Histological Risk Factors for Breast Cancer, 4472–1.332
Relationship Between Personal Income and Adjusted Gross Income: New Estimates for 1989-90 and Revisions for 1959-88, 2702–1.318
Relationship of Diet to Risk of Colorectal Adenoma in Men, 4472–1.302
Relationship of Fixed and Vehicular Lighting to Accidents, 7558–118
Relationship of Polyps to Cancer of the Large Intestine, 4472–1.325
Relative Cost of Capital for Marginal Firms over the Business Cycle, 9385–1.312
Relative Drying Times of 650 Tropical Woods: Estimation by Green Moisture Content, Specific Gravity, and Green Weight Density, 1208–392
Relative Price Movements in Dynamic General Equilibrium Models of International Trade, 9377–9.144
Remarriages of Women 15-44 Years of Age Whose First Marriage Ended in Divorce: U.S., 1976, 4147–16.6
Report and Recommendations to the Congress, Mar. 1, 1992, 17204–1
Report by the Advisory Commission on Regulatory Barriers to Affordable Housing, 21248–174
Report of Center-Specific Graft and Patient Survival Rates, 1991: Executive Summary, 4104–17.1
Report of Center-Specific Graft and Patient Survival Rates, 1991: Heart, Heart Lung, Lung Data, 4104–17.5
Report of Center-Specific Graft and Patient Survival Rates, 1991: Kidney Data, 4104–17.2
Report of Center-Specific Graft and Patient Survival Rates, 1991: Liver Data, 4104–17.3
Report of Center-Specific Graft and Patient Survival Rates, 1991: Pancreas Data, 4104–17.4
Report of Center-Specific Graft and Patient Survival Rates, 1991: User's Guide, 4104–17.6
Report of Mandays for the Month: Bureau of Prisons, 6242–1.4
Report of Railroad Employment, Class I Line-Haul Railroads, 9482–3
Report of the Administrator, FY90, Rural Electrification Administration, 1244–3
Report of the Administrator, FY91, and A Brief History of the Rural Electric and Telephone Programs, 1244–3
Report of the Clerk of the House, 21942–1
Report of the Commission on the Future Structure of Veterans Health Care: The Price of Freedom Is Visible Here, 8608–8
Report of the Epidemiology and Biostatistics Program, FY91, 4474–29
Report of the Forest Service, FY91, 1204–1
Report of the Fourteenth Northeast Regional Stock Assessment Workshop (14th SAW), 2162–9
Report of the Interdepartment Radio Advisory Committee, July 1, 1990-June 30, 1991, 2802–1
Report of the Interdepartment Radio Advisory Committee, July 1-Dec. 31, 1991, 2802–1
Report of the Interdepartment Radio Advisory Committee, Jan. 1-June 30, 1992, 2802–1
Report of the Migratory Bird Conservation Commission for FY91, 14784–1
Report of the Migratory Bird Conservation Commission for FY92, 14784–1
Report of the National Heart, Lung, and Blood Advisory Council, 4474–11
Report of the President to the Congress on the Administration of the Federal Railroad Safety Act of 1970, 7604–12
Report of the Proceedings of the Judicial Conference of the U.S., Sept. 23-24, 1991, 18202–2
Report of the Proceedings of the Judicial Conference of the U.S., Mar. 16, 1992, 18202–2
Report of the Secretary of Agriculture, 1991, 1004–3
Report of the Secretary of Defense to the President and the Congress, 3544–2
Report of the Secretary of the Senate, From Apr. 1-Sept. 30, 1991, 25922–1
Report of the Secretary of the Senate, From Oct. 1, 1991-Mar. 31, 1992, 25922–1
Report of the Thirteenth Northeast Regional Stock Assessment Workshop (13th SAW), 2162–9
Report of the 1987 National Postsecondary Student Aid Study, 4846–3
Report of the 1990 National Postsecondary Student Aid Study, 4846–5
Report of the 77th National Conference on Weights and Measures, 1992, 2214–7
Report on Allied Contributions to the Common Defense, A Report to the U.S. Congress, 3544–28
Report on Applications for Orders Authorizing or Approving the Interception of Wire, Oral, or Electronic Communications (Wiretap Report) for the Period Jan. 1-Dec. 31, 1991, 18204–7
Report on Compliance with the Federal Managers' Financial Integrity Act, Department of Housing and Urban Development, 5004–9
Report on Funding Levels and Allocations of Funds, Report of the Secretary of Transportation to the U.S. Congress Pursuant to Section 3(j) of the Federal Transit Act, As Amended, 7884–12
Report on Medicare Projections by the Health Technical Panel to the 1991 Advisory Council on Social Security, 10176–1.2
Report on Pre-Complaint Counseling and Complaint Processing By Federal Agencies for FY90, 9244–11
Report on Quality Assurance in Non-PPS Settings, 17206–2.41
Report on Quality Changes for 1992 Model Passenger Cars, 6764–3
Report on Quality Changes for 1993 Model Passenger Cars, 6764–3

Report on Survey of U.S. Shipbuilding and Repair Facilities, 1991, 7704–9
Report on Tar, Nicotine, and Carbon Monoxide Content of the Smoke of 534 Varieties of Domestic Cigarettes, 9408–53
Report on the Status of Mass Layoff Actions, 6742–23
Report to Congress: Effects of the 65 mph Speed Limit Through 1990, 7764–15
Report to Congress from the U.S. Office of Special Counsel, FY91, 9894–1
Report to Congress, FY90, Federal Emergency Management Agency, U.S. Fire Administration, 9434–7
Report to Congress, FY91, Federal Emergency Management Agency, U.S. Fire Administration, 9434–7
Report to Congress: Monitoring Changes in Use of, Access to, and Appropriateness of Part B Medicare Services, 4004–34
Report to Congress: Monitoring Utilization of and Access to Services for Medicare Beneficiaries Under Physician Payment Reform, 4004–34
Report to Congress on the Activities and Operations of the Public Integrity Section for 1990, 6004–13
Report to Congress on the Federal Home Loan Mortgage Corporation, 1990, 5184–8
Report to Congress on Voting Practices in the United Nations, 1991, 7004–18
Report to Congress Under the Expedited Funds Availability Act, 1991, 9364–13
Report to Congress: U.S. Gulf Environmental Technical Assistance, 9188–117
Report to Investors of the Farm Credit System, 1991, 9264–5
Report to the Congress and the Trade Policy Committee on Trade Between the U.S. and the Nonmarket Economy Countries, 9882–2
Report to the Congress and the Trade Policy Committee: Trade Between the U.S. and China, the Soviet Union, Central and Eastern Europe, the Baltic Nations, and Other Selected Countries, 9882–2
Report to the Congress on International Economic and Exchange Rate Policy, 8002–14
Report to the Congress on National Defense Stockpile Requirements, 1992, 3544–37
Report to the Congress on Ocean Pollution, Monitoring, and Research, FY90, 2174–9
Report to the Congress on the Tax Treatment of Bad Debts by Financial Institutions, 8008–157
Report to the President and Congress on the Status of Health Personnel in the U.S., 4114–8
Report to the Senate and House Committees on the Budget, 26304–3
Report to the U.S. Congress on Export Credit Competition and the Export-Import Bank of the U.S., For the Period Jan. 1-Dec. 31, 1990, 9254–3
Report to the U.S. Congress on Minority Small Business and Capital Ownership Development, As Required by the Business Opportunity Development Reform Act of 1988, 9764–8
Report: 1991 Survey of Health Occupational Staff, 8604–8
Reported Water Use in Kansas, 1987, 5666–24.17
Reports Concerning Significant Actions of the Office of Personnel Management, 9496–2
Reports of the Office of the Inspector General, Department of Energy, 3006–5
Reports of the Proceedings of the Judicial Conference of the U.S., Held in Washington, D.C., and Asheville, N.C., Mar. 12, 1991 and Sept. 23-24, 1991; Annual Report of the Director of the Administrative Office of the U.S. Courts, 1991, 18204–8
Reports to Congress: Physician Payment Review Commission, 17266–1
Reports to Congress: Prospective Payment Assessment Commission, 17206–1
Representativeness of the Surveillance, Epidemiology, and End Results Program Data: Recent Trends in Cancer Mortality Rates, 4472–1.320
Reproductive Impairments Among Currently Married Couples: U.S, 1976, 4147–16.6
Republican Party Holds Fundraising Edge but Democrats Reduce Gap, 9276–1.111
Republican Party Outpaces Democrats in Fundraising for 15-Month Period in 1992 Cycle, 9276–1.105
Republics of the Former Soviet Union and the Baltic States: An Overview, 9118–19
Reputation Acquisition and Persistence of Moral Hazard in Credit Markets, 9387–8.275
Reregistration of Minor Use Pesticides: Some Observations and Implications, 1561–16.301
Reregistration's Impact on Agriculture, 1504–9.1
Research Experiences for Undergraduates (REU) Program of the National Science Foundation, 9628–86
Research in Brief, 6066–20
Research on WIC Participation Effects on Medicaid Costs, 1504–9.1
Research Paper Series, Office of the Assistant Secretary for Economic Policy, 8006–6
Research Papers, Federal Reserve Bank of Dallas, 9379–12
Research Papers, Federal Reserve Bank of New York, 9385–8
Research Program and Related Opportunities in Science and Engineering Education, 3504–12
Research Reports, SSA, 4746–4
Research Working Papers, Federal Reserve Bank of Kansas City, 9381–10
Reserve Component Programs, FY91: Annual Report of the Reserve Forces Policy Board, 3544–31
Residential Energy Consumption Survey, 3166–7
Residential Energy Consumption Survey: Housing Characteristics, 1990, 3166–7.33
Residential Fuelwood Consumption in the Southeastern U.S., 9806–9.12
Residential Fuelwood Production and Sources from Roundwood in Minnesota, 1988, 1208–398
Residential Fuelwood Production and Sources from Roundwood in Missouri, 1987, 1208–399
Residents of Farms and Rural Areas: 1990, 2546–1.458
Resolution Costs of Bank Failures: An Update of the FDIC Historical Loss Model, 9292–4.303
Resolution Trust Corporation: Asset Pooling and Marketing Practices Add Millions to Contract Costs, 26119–424
Resolution Trust Corporation News Release, 9722–1
Resolution Trust Corporation, Office of Inspector General Semiannual Report to the Congress, Sept. 30, 1991-Mar. 31, 1992, 9722–6
Resolution Trust Corporation, Office of Inspector General Semiannual Report to the Congress, Apr. 1-Sept. 30, 1992, 9722–6
Resolution Trust Corporation Quarterly Performance Data, 9722–5
Resolution Trust Corporation Real Estate Asset Inventory, 9722–2
Resolution Trust Corporation: Recoveries on Asset Sales, 26119–372
Resolution Trust Corporation Refinancing and Restructuring Issues, 21248–171
Resolution Trust Corporation: Survey Results on RTC's Communication and Real Estate Marketing, 26119–422
Resolution Trust Corporation, 1990 Annual Report, 9724–1
Resolution Trust Corporation's Compliance as of (Date). Obligations Limitation, 26102–6
Resource Management Plan and Rangeland Program Summary, Annual Update 1990-91, 5724–17
Respiratory Disease Surveillance in Hungary, 4202–7.319
Response of Market Interest Rates to Discount Rate Changes, 9391–1.314
Restricting Pesticide Use: The Impact on Profitability by Farm Size, 1561–16.304
Restricting Regression Slopes in the Errors-in-Variables Model by Bounding the Error Correlation, 6886–6.96
Restructuring in Centrally-Planned Economies and the Outlook for Sugar, 1504–9.1
Restructuring of the Banking Industry, Part 1, 21248–168
Results of a Survey of ATM Network Pricing, 9387–8.270
Results of Note and Bond Auctions, 8002–7.3
Results of Testing for Intestinal Parasites by State Diagnostic Laboratories, U.S., 1987, 4202–7.306
Results of Three-Year Commercialization Study of the SBIR Program, 9768–23
Results of Treasury's [ ]-Day Bill Auction, 8002–7.4
Results of Treasury's Weekly Bill Auctions, 8002–7.1
Results of Treasury's 52-Week Bill Auction, 8002–7.2
Retail Fees and Services of Depository Institutions, Annual Report to Congress, 9364–12
Retail Trade, 1990. Annual Sales, Year-End Inventories, Purchases, Gross Margin, and Accounts Receivable, by Kind of Retail Store. Current Business Reports, 2413–5
Retired Hydropower Plants in the U.S. (River Basin Code), 3084–12
Retired Plants in the U.S. (By State), 3084–12
Retirement-Age Couples by Type of Wife's Social Security Benefit, 4746–26.12
Retiring Old Cars: Programs To Save Gasoline and Reduce Emissions, 26358–263
Returning Persian Gulf Troops: First Year Findings, 8704–7
Returns on Capital Assets and Variations in Economic Growth and Volatility: A Model of Bayesian Learning, 9385–8.124

Revenue, Pieces and Weight by Classes of Mail and Special Services, 9862–1
Revenue-Restricted Cost Study of 100 Large Banks, 9387–8.274
Review, Federal Reserve Bank of St. Louis, 9391–1
Review Major Alternatives for the Census in the Year 2000, 21628–104
Review of EPA's Capacity Assurance Program, 21408–132
Review of Indian Ocean Fisheries for Skipjack Tuna, Katsuwonus pelamis, and Yellowfin Tuna, Thunnus albacares, 2162–1.301
Review of Literature on Herbicides, Including Phenoxy Herbicides and Associated Dioxins, 8706–1
Review of Literature on Herbicides, Including Phenoxy Herbicides and Associated Dioxins: Analysis of Recent Literature on Health Effects; and Annotated Bibliography of Recent Literature on Health Effects, 8706–1
Review of Mortality in VA Medical Centers. Supplement, 8708–1
Review of State Formula Grant Strategies, FY91. Bureau of Justice Assistance Fact Sheet, 6064–38
Review of Structure-Performance Studies in Grocery Retailing, 9408–56
Review of the Net Revenue Estimates in Robbins and Robbins, "Paying People Not To Work", 4746–26.10
Review of World Salmon Culture, 2162–1.301
Review Progress of Coverage Evaluation and Adjustment Procedures of the 1990 Census, 21628–99
Review the Census Bureau's Proposed Budget for FY92, 21628–98
Review the Role of Local Governments in the 1990 Census and To Hear Recommendations for the 2000 Census, 21628–100
Revised Delivery Standards: Postal Delivery Scores Improved but Service Is Slower, 26119–431
Revised Monthly Retail Sales and Inventories: Jan. 1982-Dec. 1991, 2413–3
Revised Monthly Wholesale Trade: Sales and Inventories, 1986-Mar. 1992, Current Business Report, 2413–7
Revision of Seasonally Adjusted Labor Force Series, 6742–2.302
Revisions in Estimates of Food and Industrial Use for Feed Grains, 1561–4.301
Rhenium in 1990: Mineral Industry Surveys, Annual Review, 5614–5.2
Rhenium in 1991: Mineral Industry Surveys, Annual Review, 5614–5.17
Ricardian Equivalence Under Income Uncertainty, 9387–8.269
Rice Market News, 1313–8
Rice Situation and Outlook Report, 1561–8
Rice Situation and Outlook Yearbook, 1561–8
Rice Stocks, 1621–7
Rice, Summary of 1991 Support Program and Related Information: ASCS Commodity Fact Sheet, 1806–4.1
Rising Inequality in a Salary Survey: Another Piece of the Puzzle, 9377–9.130
Risk Analysis of Planting Flexibility Choices on Rice Farms in the Mississippi River Delta, 1561–8.302
Risk and Return in Banking: Evidence from Bank Stock Returns, 9393–8.301
Risk Aversion, Performance Pay, and the Principal-Agent Problem, 9377–9.127
Risk Factors for Fatal Colon Cancer in a Large Prospective Study, 4472–1.346
Risk Neutral Valuation, Asymmetric Information, and the Efficient Markets Hypothesis, 9371–10.77
RNA Expression of the WT1 Gene in Wilms' Tumors in Relation to Histology, 4472–1.304
Road Damage and Safety Effects of Overweight Trucks Carrying Intermodal Containers, 21648–65
ROD Annual Report, FY90, 9214–5
Role of Bank Capital in Bank Loan Growth: Market and Accounting Measures, 9379–14.19
Role of Basic Research in Economic Competitiveness, 21708–131
Role of Community and Advocacy Organizations During the 1990 Census and in Planning for the 2000 Census, 21628–103
Role of Data-Driven Planning and Coalition Development in Preventing Cardiovascular Disease, 4042–3.302
Role of Foreign Medical Graduates in the Delivery of Health Care in the U.S.: The Immigration Ramifications, 6366–6.2
Role of Monetary Shocks: Evidence from Tests of the Relation Between Interest-Rate Spreads and Economic Activity, 9385–8.131
Role of Profitability and Community Characteristics in Hospital Closure: An Urban and Rural Analysis, 17206–2.28
Role of Real Estate in the New England Credit Crunch, 9373–27.12
Role of Salk Institute in Army's Research Program. Biological Warfare, 26123–374
Role of Specialty Societies and Physicians in the Commission's Evaluation of Relative Work Values, 17266–2.8
Romanian Trade Data. International Trade, 26119–414
Romania's Energy Needs Persist. East European Energy, 26123–402
RTC Inventory of High Yield Securities, 9722–4
RTC Review, 9722–3
Rubber and Plastics Hose and Belting, Current Industrial Report, 2506–8.12
Rubber Mechanical Goods, 1991, Current Industrial Report, 2506–8.17
Rural Areas Gained Doctors During the 1980's, 1502–7.304
Rural Clean Water Program (RCWP) Monthly Progress Report, By State and Area for Period Ending (Date), 1802–14
Rural Conditions and Trends, 1502–8
Rural Development Administration: Patterns of Use in the Business and Industry Loan Guarantee Program, 26113–591
Rural Development Perspectives, 1502–7
Rural Electric Borrowers, 1991 Statistical Report, 1244–1
Rural Electrification Administration, Report of the Administrator, FY90, 1244–3
Rural Hospitals and Medicare's Prospective Payment System, 26306–6.164
Rural Labor Force Trends in China, 1524–4.2
Rural Rental Housing: Incentives Maintain Low-Income Housing but Clearer Guidance Needed, 26113–586
Rural Roads and Bridges, 1276–1
Rural Telephone Bank 19th Annual Report of the Board of Directors, FY90, 1244–4
Rural Telephone Bank 20th Annual Report of the Board of Directors, FY91, 1244–4
Rural Telephone Borrowers, 1991 Statistical Report, 1244–2
Rural Telephone Program: Fiscal Year Statistical Summary, 1244–8
Rye, Summary of 1992 Support Program and Related Information: ASCS Commodity Fact Sheet, 1806–4.10

S. 2726 To Improve U.S. Counterintelligence Measures, 25428–2
Safeguards and Security Weaknesses at DOE's Weapons Facilities. Nuclear Security, 26113–557
Safety and Health Experience of Pilots and Flight Attendants, 6722–1.320
Safety and Health Profiles in Eight Industries, 6728–41
Safety Management Information Statistics (SAMIS) 1990 Annual Report, 7884–13
Safety of Longer Combination Vehicles Is Unknown. Truck Safety, 26113–568
Safety Recall Campaigns, 7762–12
Safety Related Recall Campaigns for Motor Vehicles and Motor Vehicle Equipment, Including Tires, 7762–2
Safety Study: Oversight of Rail Rapid Transit Safety, 9618–19
Safety Study: Transport of Hazardous Materials by Rail, 9618–18
Safety, Traffic and Cost Considerations on Scenic Byways. Final Case Study for the National Scenic Byways Study, 7556–8.5
SAIF-Insured Institutions Combined Financial Statements, 1989, 8434–1
Saint Lawrence Seaway Development Corporation, 1990 Annual Report, 7744–1
Salaries of Full-Time Instructional Faculty on 9- and 10-Month and 11- and 12-Month Contracts in Institutions of Higher Education, 1980-81 Through 1990-91, 4844–8
Sale of Single Family Housing Inventory, 1182–7
Salinity Characterization: Galveston Bay, Tex., 2176–7.27
Sallie Mae, Financing Higher Education: Annual Report, 1991, 9784–1
Salt: Minerals Yearbook, Volume 1, 1990, 5604–20.50
Sample Design: Third National Health and Nutrition Examination Survey. Vital and Health Statistics Series 2, 4147–2.115
Sand and Gravel (Industrial), Directory of Producers in the U.S. in 1990: Mineral Industry Surveys, Annual Advance Summary Supplement, 5614–5.1
Sand and Gravel (Industrial), Directory of Producers in the U.S. in 1991: Mineral Industry Surveys, Annual Advance Summary Supplement, 5614–5.18
Sand and Gravel: Minerals Yearbook, Volume 1, 1990, 5604–20.51
Sand and Gravel (Principal), Directory of Producers in the U.S. in 1990: Mineral Industry Surveys, Annual Advance Summary Supplement, 5614–5.6
Sandhill Crane Harvest and Hunter Activity in the Central Flyway During the 1991-92 Hunting Season, 5504–31

Sanitation Inspections of International Cruise Ships, Summary, 4202–10
SAR Statistics, 1991, U.S. Coast Guard, 7404–2
Satellite Rescue, Spacewalks Mark Endeavour's First Flight: STS-49 Mission, 9506–2.148
Satellite Situation Report, 9502–2
Savannah River Site Environmental Report for 1991, 3324–2.15
Savannah River Site Environmental Report, 1990: Volume I, Environmental Monitoring, Compliance, and Research, 3324–2.2
Savannah River Site Environmental Report, 1990: Volume II, Groundwater Monitoring, 3324–2.2
Savers of Lives, 2152–8.303
Saving and Demographics: Some International Comparisons, 9387–1.302
Savings and Home Financing Source Book, 8434–3
Savings and Loan Institutions Deposits by Market in the Chicago SMSA, 9304–28
Savings and Loan Prosecution Update, 6002–3, 6008–33
Savings Possible Through Better Audit and Negotiation of Rates. DOD Commercial Transportation, 26123–369
SBA Needs To Improve Administrative Practices for Disaster Operations. Small Business, 26113–576
SBA Quarterly Report, 503/504 Economic Development Loan Programs, 9762–6
SBA Rural Development Programs, 21728–79
Schedule B, Statistical Classification of Domestic and Foreign Commodities Exported from the U.S.: 1990. U.S. Foreign Trade, 2428–5
School Crime: A National Crime Victimization Survey Report, 6066–3.46
School Effects on Educational Achievement in Mathematics and Science, 4896–6.7
School Enrollment—Social and Economic Characteristics of Students: October 1990, 2546–1.459
School Lunch and the Dietary Guidelines, 1504–9.1
Schools and Hospitals Program Cycle XIII Grants Data: Grants Award Listing, June 25, 1992. Conservation and Renewable Energy, 3304–15
Schools and Staffing in the U.S.: A Statistical Profile, 1987-88. Schools and Staffing Survey, 4836–3.10
Schools and Staffing Survey, 4836–3
Science and Engineering Indicators, 1991, 9624–10
Science Report: A Summary of Research Supported by NOAA's Office of Undersea Research, 2144–6
Science Report Card, 1990: NAEP's Assessment of Fourth, Eighth, and Twelfth Graders. National Assessment of Educational Progress, 4896–8.3
Scientific and Engineering Research Facilities at Universities and Colleges: 1992, 9624–25
Scientific and Technical Employment, 1990-2005, 6722–1.314
Scientists, Engineers, and Technicians in Manufacturing Industries: 1989, Detailed Statistical Tables, 9627–23
Screening Sigmoidoscopy and Colorectal Cancer Mortality, 4472–1.349
Seafood Safety, 21568–51
Searching for Answers, Annual Evaluation Report on Drugs and Crime: 1991, 6064–32
Seasonal Association Between SIDS Deaths and Kindergarten Absences, 4042–3.331
Seasonal Solow Residuals and Christmas: A Case for Labor Hoarding and Increasing Returns, 9375–13.71
Seasonal Variation in Adolescent Conceptions, Induced Abortions, and Late Initiation of Prenatal Care, 4042–3.372
Seasonality and Equilibrium Business Cycle Theories, 9375–13.74
Second Biennial Report to Congress, U.S. Office of Government Ethics, 9834–1
Second Cancers in Patients with Chronic Lymphocytic Leukemia, 4472–1.343
Second Century of Food Composition Research, 1504–9.1
Second Data Book. A Mortality Study of 1.3 Million Persons by Demographic, Social, and Economic Factors: 1979-85 Follow-Up. U.S. National Longitudinal Mortality Study, 4478–186
Secondary Market Prices and Yields and Interest Rates for Home Loans, 5142–20
Secretary of Agriculture, 1991 Report, 1004–3
Secretary of the Army Annual Report on Civil Works Activities, FY88: Volume II, 3754–1.1
Secretary of the Army Annual Report on Civil Works Activities, FY89: Volume II, 3754–1.2
Secretary of the Army Annual Report on Civil Works Activities, FY90: Volume II, 3754–1.3
Secretary of the Army's Report on Civil Works Activities, 3754–1
Secretary's Annual Report to Congress: U.S. Department of Energy, 1990, 3024–2
Secretary's Semiannual Report to the Congress, Apr. 1-Sept. 30, 1991: Department of Transportation, 7302–12
Secretary's Semiannual Report to the Congress, Oct. 1, 1991-Mar. 31, 1992: Department of Transportation, 7302–12
Secretary's Semiannual Report to the Congress: For the Six Month Period Oct. 1, 1991-Mar. 31, 1992, Pursuant to Section 106 of Public Law 100-504, 5002–11
Secretary's Semiannual Report to the Congress: For the Six Month Period Apr. 1-Sept. 30, 1992, Pursuant to Section 106 of Public Law 100-504, 5002–11
Securities Arbitration: How Investors Fare, 26119–401
Securities Investor Protection: The Regulatory Framework Has Minimized SIPC's Losses, 26119–419
Securitization, Risk, and the Liquidity Problem in Banking, 9366–6.295
Security Assistance Programs, FY93 Congressional Presentation, 7144–13
SEDCAR (Standards for Educational Data Collection and Reporting), 4828–41
SEFC Billfish Program, 1989-90 Report, 2164–7
Segregation Analysis of Esophageal Cancer in 221 High-Risk Chinese Families, 4472–1.315
Seigniorage in the U.S.: How Much Does the U.S. Government Make from Money Production?, 9391–1.307
Selected Borrowings in Immediately Available Funds of Large Commercial Banks, 9365–1
Selected Characteristics of Manufacturing Establishments That Export: 1987. Analytical Report Series, 2506–16.2
Selected Compensation and Pension Data, By State of Residence, FY90, 8604–7
Selected Data from Science Resources Studies: Advance Reports, 9626–8
Selected Data on Academic Science and Engineering R&D Expenditures: FY90, 9626–8.5
Selected Data on Academic Science and Engineering R&D Expenditures: FY91, 9626–8.7
Selected Data on Federal R&D Funding by Budget Function: FY90-92, 9626–8.4
Selected Data on Federal Support to Universities and Colleges: FY89, 9626–8.2
Selected Data on Graduate Students and Postdoctorates in Science and Engineering: Fall 1990, 9626–8.3
Selected Data on Military and VA Recipients. Disability Benefits, 26121–470
Selected Data on Science and Engineering Doctorate Awards: 1990, 9626–8.1
Selected Heating Equipment, Current Industrial Report, 2506–11.6
Selected Highway Statistics and Charts, 1990, 7554–24
Selected Industrial Air Pollution Control Equipment, 1991, Current Industrial Report, 2506–12.5
Selected Instruments and Related Products, 1990, Current Industrial Report, 2506–12.26
Selected Instruments and Related Products, 1991, Current Industrial Report, 2506–12.26
Selected Interest and Exchange Rates: Weekly Series of Charts; and Foreign Exchange Rates, 9365–1.5
Selected Interest Rates, 9365–1, 9365–2.14
Selected Manpower Statistics, FY91, 3544–1
Selected Occupational Fatalities as Found in Reports of OSHA Fatality/Catastrophe Investigations, 6606–2
Selected Occupational Fatalities Related to Marine Cargo Handling as Found in Reports of OSHA Fatality/Catastrophe Investigations, 6606–2.18
Selected Publications of the U.S. International Trade Commission, Through December 1991, 9884–12
Selected Worldwide Marine Weather Broadcasts, 2184–3
Selection Bias and the Diploma Effect, 6886–6.81
Selective Service System, Annual Report of the Director to the Congress of the U.S., 9744–1
Selenium and Tellurium in 1991: Mineral Industry Surveys, Annual Review, 5614–5.20
Self Employed: How Do Farmers Stack Up?, 1541–1.301
SEMATECH's Technological Progress and Proposed R&D Program. Federal Research, 26113–588
Semiannual Canned Pineapple Situation in Thailand and the Philippines, 1925–34.346
Semiannual Report of the Architect of the Capitol, For the Period Apr. 1-Sept. 30, 1991, 25922–2

Semiannual Report of the Inspector General, U.S. Small Business Administration, Covering the Period Apr. 1-Sept. 30, 1991, 9762–5
Semiannual Report of the Inspector General, U.S. Small Business Administration, Covering the Period Oct. 1, 1991-Mar. 31, 1992, 9762–5
Semiannual Report, Office of Inspector General, U.S. Department of Labor, 6302–2
Semiannual Report to Congress on Inspector General Audit Reports, Department of Energy, 3002–15
Semiannual Report to Congress on the Effectiveness of the Civil Aviation Security Program, 7502–5
Semiannual Report to the Congress, VA Office of Inspector General, Apr. 1-Sept. 30, 1992, 8602–1
Semiannual Report to the Congress, VA Office of Inspector General, Oct. 1, 1991-Mar. 31, 1992, 8602–1
Semiconductors, Printed Circuit Boards, and Other Electronic Components, 1991, Current Industrial Report, 2506–12.36
Senior Executive Service: Opinions About the Federal Work Environment, 26119–402
Sentencing Guidelines and Policy Statements, 17668–1
Sentencing Guidelines: Central Questions Remain Unanswered, 26119–415
Sequelae of Traveling Substantial Distances for Prenatal Care and Birthing: The Use of Birth and Linked Birth/Infant Death Records To Assess Racial Differentials in Health Care, 4164–2
Series EE and HH Savings Bonds, Statistical Summary, 8442–1
Serious Mental Illness and Disability in the Adult Household Population: U.S., 1989, 4146–8.220
Serum a-Tocopherol Concentration in Relation to Subsequent Colorectal Cancer: Pooled Data from Five Cohorts, 4472–1.308
Serum Cholesterol Concentrations Among Navajo Indians, 4042–3.309
Serum 2,3,7,8-Tetrachlorodibenzo-p-dioxin Levels of New Zealand Pesticide Applicators and Their Implication for Cancer Hypotheses, 4472–1.303
Service Academies: Historical Proportion of New Officers During Benchmark Periods, 26123–389
Service Life of Treated and Untreated Black Hills Ponderosa Pine Fenceposts, 1208–406
Service Reports, 3166–6
Service to Government: Federal Prison Industries, 1991 Annual Report, 6244–3
Services Cut in Response to Fiscal Distress. Michigan Communities, 26121–483
Services' Efforts To Provide Logistics Support for Selected Weapon Systems. Operation Desert Storm, 26123–375
Services Industries: Evaluating Your Firm's Injury and Illness Record, 6886–4.5
Seventeenth Annual FAA Aviation Forecast Conference Proceedings. Aviation Opportunities for the Decade of the 90's, 7504–28
Sexual Experience and Use of Contraception Among Young Adults in Latin America, 4202–7.323
Shallow Subtidal Survey of the Washington Outer Coast and Olympic National Park To Determine the Distribution, Fate, and Effects of Spilled Bunker C Fuel Oil, 5738–38.3
Shareholder Directory of the Federal Home Loan Bank of San Francisco, 1992, Eleventh District: Arizona, California, Nevada, 9304–23
Shareholder Rights, 25248–130
Sharing of Specialized Medical Resources, FY91, Secretary of Veterans Affairs Annual Report Pursuant to the Provisions of 38 U.S.C. Section 8153, 8704–5
Shark Tagger, Spring 1991, 2164–21
Shark Tagger, 1991 Summary, 2164–21
Sheep Production in 11 Western States, 1548–382
Sheets, Pillowcases, and Towels, Current Industrial Report, 2506–6.6
Sheriffs' Departments, 1990, 6066–25.45
Shifting Fertility Patterns of American Women. Statistical Brief, 2326–17.41
Shipbuilding Trade Reform Act of 1991: Likely Economic Effects of Enactment. Report to the Committee on Ways and Means, on Investigation No. 332-316 Under Section 332(g) of the Tariff Act of 1930, 9886–4.183
Shipwrecks of the Alaskan Shelf and Shore, 5738–34
Shop Towels from Bangladesh. Determination of the Commission in Investigation No. 731-TA-514 (Final) Under the Tariff Act of 1930, Together with the Information Obtained in the Investigation, 9886–14.340
Short-Term Energy Outlook: Quarterly Projections, 3162–34
Short-Term Forecasting: Accuracy of USDA's Meat Forecasts and Estimates, 26131–93
Significant Features of Fiscal Federalism, 1992 Edition, 10044–1
Significant Gaps Exist. Hispanic Access to Health Care, 26131–97
Significant Incidents of Political Violence Against Americans, 1991, 7004–22
Significant Provisions of State Unemployment Insurance Laws, July 7, 1991, 6402–7
Significant Provisions of State Unemployment Insurance Laws, Jan. 5, 1992, 6402–7
Significant Provisions of State Unemployment Insurance Laws, July 5, 1992, 6402–7
Signs of Progress: A Report on Rural America's Revitalization Efforts, 1004–17
Silicon: Mineral Industry Surveys, 5612–1.34
Silicon: Minerals Yearbook, Volume 1, 1990, 5604–20.52
Silver and Gold: Mineral Industry Surveys, 5612–1.10
Silver: Minerals Yearbook, Volume 1, 1990, 5604–20.53
Simulated Economic Impact of TED Regulations on Selected Vessels in the Texas Shrimp Fishery, 2162–1.302
Simulating Aggregate and Distributional Effects of Various Plans for Modifying the Retirement Earnings Test, 4746–26.15
Simulating Smokers' Acceptance of Modifications in a Cessation Program, 4042–3.308
Singapore's Fresh and Processed Vegetable Markets, 1925–34.305
Single Room Occupancy for the Homeless Awards $91 Million in New Competition, 5006–3.90
Single Room Occupancy Program Achieves Goals, But HUD Can Increase Impact. Homelessness, 26113–596
Sir Richard Stone and the Development of National Economic Accounts, 2702–1.309
Situation and Outlook for Manufactured Agricultural Inputs in Poland, 1561–16.304
Sixteenth Annual Report of the National Advisory Council on Educational Research and Improvement, FY91, 4814–1
Sixteenth Annual Report of the National Commission for Employment Policy, 15494–1
Sixth Annual Report on Carcinogens, 4044–15
Sixth Biennial Report on Great Lakes Water Quality, 14644–1
Sixty-Five Plus in America, 2546–2.165
Slag—Iron and Steel: Minerals Yearbook, Volume 1, 1990, 5604–20.33
Slow Recovery in the Third District: Evidence from New Time-Series Models, 9387–1.303
Small Business Administration FY90 National Accomplishment Report and FY91 National Affirmative Employment Program Plan, 9764–9
Small Business Administration National Affirmative Employment, FY91 Accomplishment Report and FY92 Plan Update, 9764–9
Small Business Administration's Small Business Investment Company Program: A Review of Selected Issues, 25728–44
Small Business: Analysis of SBA's Preferred Lenders Program, 26113–581
Small Business: Financial Condition of SBA's Business Loan Portfolio Is Improving, 26113–554
Small Business: Improving SBA Loan Collateral Liquidations Would Increase Recoveries, 26113–553
Small Business Innovation Development Act: Eighth Year Results, 9764–7
Small Business Innovation Research Shows Success but Can Be Strengthened. Federal Research, 26113–393
Small Business: Problems in Restructuring SBA's Minority Business Development Program, 26113–563
Small Business: SBA Needs To Improve Administrative Practices for Disaster Operations, 26113–576
Small Subgroup of Aggressive, Highly Proliferative Prostatic Carcinomas Defined by p53 Accumulation, 4472–1.322
Small Time Deposits and the Recent Weakness in M2, 9385–1.305
Smithsonian Year, 1990, Annual Report of the Smithsonian Institution for the Year Ended Sept. 30, 1990, 29574–1
Smithsonian Year 1990 Supplement: Chronology and Appendices, 29574–1.2
Smithsonian Year, 1991, Annual Report of the Smithsonian Institution for the Year Ended Sept. 30, 1991, 29574–1
Smithsonian Year 1991 Supplement: Chronology and Appendices, 29574–1.2
Smoking and Health in the Americas: A 1992 Report of the Surgeon General, in Collaboration with the Pan American Health Organization, 4204–18
Smoking and Tobacco Control Monographs, 4476–7
Smoking, Drinking, and Illicit Drug Use Among American Secondary School Students, College Students and Young Adults, 1975-91, 4494–4

Smoking, Drinking, and Illicit Drug Use Among American Secondary School Students, College Students and Young Adults, 1975-91. Volume I: Secondary School Students, 4494–4.1

Smoking, Drinking, and Illicit Drug Use Among American Secondary School Students, College Students and Young Adults, 1975-91. Volume II: College Students and Young Adults, 4494–4.2

Smoking During Pregnancy Among Northwest Native Americans, 4042–3.306

Snake River Birds of Prey Area Research and Monitoring Annual Report, 1991, 5724–14

Snow Surveys for Alaska, 1266–2.1

Soaps, Detergents, and Surface-Active Agents, Industry and Trade Summary, 9885–11.1

Social and Economic Studies, Alaska OCS Region, 5736–5

Social, Economic, and Housing Characteristics. 1990 Census of Population and Housing: Pacific Outlying Areas, 2551–8

Social Indicators Study of Alaskan Coastal Villages I. Key Informant Summaries, Volume 1: Schedule A Regions (North Slope, NANA, Calista, Aleutian-Pribilof), 5736–5.17

Social Indicators Study of Alaskan Coastal Villages I. Key Informant Summaries, Volume 2: Schedule B Regions (Bristol Bay, Kodiak, Bering Straits), 5736–5.17

Social Security Administration 1992 Annual Report to the Congress, 4704–6

Social Security Administration's 10-Percent Sample File of OASDI Beneficiaries, 4742–1.309

Social Security and Medicare Policy from the Perspective of Generational Accounting, 9377–9.137

Social Security and Older Workers, 4746–26.22

Social Security and the Future Financial Security of Women, 10176–3.4

Social Security and the Public Debt, 8006–6.6

Social Security Area Population Projections: 1991, 4706–1.106

Social Security Bulletin, 4742–1

Social Security Bulletin, Annual Statistical Supplement, 1991, 4744–3

Social Security: Causes of Increased Overpayments, 1986-89, 26121–484

Social Security Implications of a Reunified Germany, 4742–1.306

Social Security Programs Throughout the World, 1991, 4746–4.62

Social Security: Racial Difference in Disability Decisions Warrants Further Investigation, 26121–459

Social Security: Reconciliation Improved SSA Earnings Records, but Efforts Were Incomplete, 26121–477

Social Security Reform in Four East European Countries, 4742–1.303

Social Security Retirement Test, 21788–215

Social Security Technical Panel Report to the 1991 Advisory Council on Social Security, 10176–1.1

Social Security, Uncertainty Adjustments, and the Consumption Decision, 4746–26.9

Soda Ash and Sodium Sulfate: Mineral Industry Surveys, 5612–1.33

Soda Ash: Minerals Yearbook, Volume 1, 1990, 5604–20.66

Softwood Lumber from Canada. Determination of the Commission in Investigation No. 701-TA-312 (Final) Under Section 703(a) of the Tariff Act of 1930, Together with the Information Obtained in the Investigation, 9886–15.80

SOI Bulletin, 8302–2

Soil-Vegetation Correlations in Wetlands and Riparian Areas, 5506–10

Solar Buildings Research and Development Program Reports, 3306–5

Solar Collector Manufacturing Activity, 1990, 3164–62

Sole Proprietorship Return Preliminary Statistics, 1990: Data Release, 8302–2.317

Sole Proprietorships, 1990, 8302–2.320

Some Economic Aspects of the U.S. Health Care System, 8006–6.1

Some Outside Activities Present Conflict-of-Interest Issues. Employee Conduct Standards, 26119–386

Sorghum Production Practices and Input Use: 1991, 1561–16.304

Source Book, Statistics of Income 1989: Corporation Income Tax Returns with Accounting Periods Ended July 1989-June 1990, 8304–21

Source of Losses to the National Credit Union Share Insurance Fund, 9536–1.7

Source of Payment for the Medical Cost of Motor Vehicle Injuries in the U.S., 7768–122

Source to the Street, Mid-1991 Prices for Cannabis, Cocaine, and Heroin, 6284–7

Sourcebook of Criminal Justice Statistics, 1991, 6064–6

Sources and Nature of Long-Term Memory in the Business Cycle, 9377–9.125

South Africa: Important Competitor for U.S. Deciduous Fruit and Grapes, 1925–34.320

South American Oil: Marginal Producers Not a Likely Source for Increased U.S. Imports, 26123–396

Southeast During the Civil War: Selected War Department Records in the National Archives of the U.S., 9516–1.2

Southeast Regional Economic Report, Federal Home Loan Bank of Atlanta, 9302–36

Southeastern Power Administration, Annual Report, 1991, 3234–1

Southeastern Regional Biomass Energy Program, 9806–9

Southeastern Regional Biomass Energy Program. Six Year Report: 1983-89, 9806–9.11

Southeastern Regional Office Press Releases, 6946–3

Southern Dairy Farmers' Evaluation of Milk Handlers, 1128–67

Southwest Statistical Summary, 6962–2

Southwestern Power Administration FY91 Financial and Statistical Report, 3244–1.2

Southwestern Power Administration: 1991 Annual Report, 3244–1

Southwestern Riparian-Stream Ecosystems: Research Design, Complexity, and Opportunity, 1208–390

Soy Printing Ink, 1504–9.1

Soybean Production Estimates: A Journey Through the Last 27 Years, 1561–3.306

Soybean Quality Issues: Cleaning Practices at Commercial Elevators, 1561–3.302

Soybeans and Minor Oilseeds, Summary of 1991 Support Program and Related Information: ASCS Commodity Fact Sheet, 1806–4.5

Space Station Freedom Media Handbook, 9508–40

Spatial Data Transfer Standard (SDTS). Software Standard, 2216–2.215

Speaking of Kids: A National Survey of Children and Parents, 15528–2

Special Quality Hot-Rolled and Semifinished Carbon and Alloy Steel Products from Brazil. Determination of the Commission in Investigation No. 731-TA-572 (Preliminary) Under the Tariff Act of 1930, Together with the Information Obtained in the Investigation, 9886–14.356

Special Report to the Congress: Mandatory Minimum Penalties in the Federal Criminal Justice System, 17668–2

Special Studies. Current Population Reports. Series P-23, 2546–2

Special Supplemental Food Program for Women, Infants and Children. Program Participation and Expenditures, by State, 1362–16

Special Supplemental Food Program for Women, Infants, and Children. Program Participation and Expenditures, by State, FY89, 1364–12

Special Supplemental Food Program for Women, Infants, and Children: Program Participation and Expenditures, by State, FY90, 1364–12

Special Supplemental Food Program for Women, Infants and Children (WIC), Racial Participation, April 1991, 1364–16

Spent Fuel Pool Maximum Capacities and Inventories for Nuclear Power Plants as of Dec. 31, 1986, 3166–6.59

Spent Fuel Storage Requirements, 1991-2040, 3354–2

Spent Nuclear Fuel Discharges from U.S. Reactors, 1990, 3166–6.62

Spun Yarn Production, 1991, Current Industrial Report, 2506–5.5

SRS Environmental Report for 1991: Summary Pamphlet, 3324–2.15

SSA Research Reports, 4746–4

SSI Recipients by State and County, 4744–27

SSI Work Incentive Participants, September 1991, 4742–1.305

St. Lawrence Seaway: Traffic Report, 1991 Navigation Season, 7744–2

Staff Reports, Federal Reserve Bank of Minneapolis, 9383–20

Staff Studies, Board of Governors of the Federal Reserve System, 9366–1

Staff Working Papers: Bureau for Latin America and Caribbean, 9916–13

Staffing New Facilities Will Be a Challenge for BOP. Prison Expansion, 26119–397

Stafford Student Loan Program: Correspondence Schools' Loan Volume Declines Sharply, 26121–448

Stafford Student Loans: Prompt Payment of Origination Fees Could Reduce Costs, 26121–467

Stainless Steel Butt-Weld Pipe Fittings from Korea and Taiwan. Determinations of the Commission in Investigations Nos. 731-TA-563 and 564 (Preliminary) Under the Tariff Act of 1930, Together with the Information Obtained in the Investigations, 9886–14.354

Stand Development and Yields of Appalachian Hardwood Stands Managed with Single-Tree Selection for at Least 30 Years, 1208–394

State and Federal Motor-Fuel Tax Rates by Years, 1981-91, 7554–32
State and Federal Prisons: Factors That Affect Construction and Operations Costs, 26119–407
State and Local Government Collective Bargaining Settlements, 1991, 6782–6
State and Local Government Collective Bargaining Settlements, First Six Months, 1992, 6782–6
State and Local Government Employment and Payrolls, 6742–4
State and Local Government Fiscal Position in 1991, 2702–1.311
State and Local Government Sector: Long-Term Trends and Recent Fiscal Pressures, 9362–1.309
State and Local Government Workers Covered Under Social Security, 1987, 4742–1.315
State and Local Governments' Reaction to Recession, 9375–1.303
State and Local Pension Fund Financing of Housing: Report to Congress, 5188–134
State and Local Police Departments, 1990, 6066–25.44
State and Metropolitan Area Employment and Unemployment, 6742–12
State and Regional Unemployment in 1991, 6726–1.45
State Assistance Programs for SSI Recipients, 4704–13
State Catalog of FY91 Low Income Home Energy Assistance Program Characteristics, 4584–2
State Catalog of Low Income Home Energy Assistance Program Characteristics, 4694–9
State Discipline of Pharmacists, 4006–8.5
State Efforts To Assist Small Businesses. Access to Health Insurance, 26121–462
State Efforts To Fight It Are Increasing but More Federal Help Is Needed. Money Laundering, 26119–430
State Energy Data Report, Consumption Estimates, 1960-90, 3164–39
State Energy Price and Expenditure Report, 1990, 3164–64
State Energy Price Projections for the Residential Sector, 1991-92, 3166–6.61
State Enterprise Zone Update, 1991 Summaries of the State Enterprise Zone Programs, 5124–9
State Enterprise Zone Update, 1992 Summaries of the State Enterprise Zone Programs, 5124–9
State Enterprise Zones in Nonmetro Areas: Are They Working?, 1502–7.303
State Government Finances: 1991, 2466–2.6
State Government Tax Collections: 1991, 2466–2.7
State Governments: The Effects of Health Care Program Expansion in a Period of Fiscal Stress, 10176–3.6
State Grant Summaries, 4604–14
State Grant Summaries, 1990, 4584–6
State Higher Education Profiles, Fourth Edition: A Comparison of State Higher Education Data for FY88, 4844–13
State Justice Sourcebook of Statistics and Research, 6064–40
State Labor Legislation Enacted in 1991, 6722–1.309
State Licensure and Discipline of Health Professionals, 4006–8
State Mineral Summaries, 1992, 5614–6
State of Native American Youth Health, 4088–3
State of Small Business: A Report of the President, Transmitted to the Congress, 1991, Together with the Annual Report on Small Business and Competition of the U.S. Small Business Administration, 9764–6
State of the Bureau of Prisons, 6244–2
State of the Bureau, 1991, 6244–2
State of the Nation's Child Welfare System, 21788–208
State of the Supermarket Industry, 1504–9.1
State Revolving Funds Insufficient To Meet Wastewater Treatment Needs. Water Pollution, 26113–561
State Strategic Planning Under the Drug Formula Grant Program, 6068–252
State Taxation of Interstate Mail Order Sales, Estimates of Revenue Potential 1990-92, 10048–84
State Water-Data Reports: Hydrologic Records of the U.S. for Water Years 1990-91, 5664–18
State Workers' Compensation: Administration Profiles, 6504–9
State Workers' Compensation Laws, 6502–1, 6504–11
State/EPA Indoor Radon Survey, 9194–19
State-Administered Program—ABE/ESL/ASE: Participant Progress and Separation by Educational Functioning Level, July 1, 1988-June 30, 1989. Adult Learning and Literacy Fact Sheet, 4806–4.2
State-Level Costs of Production: Major Field Crops, 1987-89, 1544–24
State-Level Output Supply and Input Demand Elasticities for Agricultural Commodities, 1502–3.303
Statement of Alan J. Wilensky, Deputy Assistant Secretary (Tax Policy), Department of the Treasury, Before the Subcommittee on Oversight, Committee on Ways and Means, U.S. House of Representatives, Washington, D.C., 8008–155
Statement of Andrew G. McBride, Associate Deputy Attorney General, Concerning the Supreme Court's Decision in Teague v. Lane and the Standard of Review in Federal Habeas Corpus Proceedings, 6008–34
Statement of Foreign Currencies Purchased with Dollars, FY91, 8102–5
Statement of Foreign Currencies Purchased with Dollars, Oct. 1, 1991-Mar. 31, 1992, 8102–5
Statement of Ira Raphaelson, Special Counsel for Financial Institution Fraud, Before the Subcommittee on Consumer and Regulatory Affairs, Committee on Banking, Housing, and Urban Affairs, U.S. Senate, Concerning Efforts To Combat Financial Institution Fraud, 6008–35
Statement on the Posture of the U.S. Army, FY93: Strategic Force, Strategic Vision for the 1990s and Beyond, 3704–13
States Need Labor's Help Regulating Multiple Employer Welfare Arrangements. Employee Benefits, 26121–443
States of the Former Soviet Union: An Updated Overview, 9118–19
States Serve Least Job-Ready While Meeting JOBS Participation Rates. Welfare to Work, 26121–489
Statistical Abstract of the U.S.: 1992, 2324–1
Statistical Abstracts of the Federal Employee Benefit Programs, FY89-90, 9844–37
Statistical Briefs, 2326–17
Statistical Classification of Domestic and Foreign Commodities Exported from the U.S., Schedule B, 1990 Edition. Volumes I and II, Changes Effective Jan. 1, 1993, 2428–5.1
Statistical Comparison of Selected Chemical Constituents in Water from Chemigation and Conventional Irrigation Wells in Kansas, 1987, 5666–28.21
Statistical Compilation of Engineering Features on Bureau of Reclamation Projects, 5824–7
Statistical Needs in Eastern Europe, 6722–1.317
Statistical Notes, NIMH Survey and Reports Branch, 4506–3
Statistical Releases: Bureau of Alcohol, Tobacco and Firearms, 8486–1
Statistical Report, U.S. Attorney's Office, FY91, 6004–2
Statistical Report, U.S. Department of Justice, Federal Bureau of Prisons, 6244–1
Statistical Summary. Federal Meat and Poultry Inspection, FY90, 1374–3
Statistical Summary: Leasing, by Sale, by Tract and by Company, 5734–8
Statistical Summary: Series EE and HH Savings Bonds, 8442–1
Statistical Supplement, Annual Report, U.S. Railroad Retirement Board, 9704–2
Statistical Yearbook of the Immigration and Naturalization Service, 1990, 6264–2
Statistical Yearbook of the Immigration and Naturalization Service, 1991, 6264–2
Statistics for Industry Groups and Industries (Including Capital Expenditures, Inventories, and Supplemental Labor, Fuel, and Electric Energy Costs), 1990 Annual Survey of Manufactures, 2506–14.2
Statistics in Brief, 4826–10
Statistics in Brief, 1991, 2324–1
Statistics of Communications Common Carriers, 9284–6
Statistics of Income Bulletin, 8302–2
Statistics of Income, Compendium of Studies of International Income and Taxes, 1984-88, 8308–31
Statistics of Income, Compendium of Studies of Tax-Exempt Organizations, 1974-87, 8308–35
Statistics of Income, Corporation Income Tax Returns, 1988, 8304–4
Statistics of Income, Corporation Income Tax Returns, 1989, 8304–4
Statistics of Income, Source Book: Active Corporation Income Tax Returns, July 1989-June 1990, 8304–21
Statistics of Interstate Natural Gas Pipeline Companies, 1990, 3164–38
Statistics of the Congressional Election of Nov. 6, 1990, 21944–3
Statistics on Aircraft Gas Turbine Engine Rotor Failures That Occurred in U.S. Commercial Aviation During 1987, 7504–50
Statistics on Aircraft Gas Turbine Engine Rotor Failures That Occurred in U.S. Commercial Aviation During 1988, 7504–50
Statistics on Banking, 1990, 9294–4
Statistics Related to DOD's Policy on Homosexuality. Defense Force Management, 26123–392.2

Status and Trends in Concentrations of Selected Contaminants in Boston Harbor Sediments and Biota, 2176–3.14
Status and Trends in Toxicants and the Potential for Their Biological Effects in Tampa Bay, Fla., 2176–3.15
Status and Trends of Mountain Pine Beetle Populations in the Bear Mountain and White House Gulch Areas on the Harney Ranger District, Black Hills National Forest, South Dakota, 1208–408
Status and Trends of Wetlands in the Conterminous U.S., Mid-1970's to Mid-1980's, 5508–89
Status of Account: Harry S. Truman Memorial Scholarship Fund, 14312–1
Status of Active Foreign Credits of the U.S. Government: Foreign Credits by U.S. Government Agencies, 8002–6
Status of Appalachian Regional Commission Primary Care Projects, 9088–38
Status of FmHA Farmer Programs, 1504–9.1
Status of Foreign Currency Funds Administered by the Agency for International Development, 9912–1
Status of Handicapped Children in Head Start Programs, 4584–4, 4604–1
Status of Health Personnel in the U.S., Seventh Report to the President and Congress, 4114–8
Status of Improvements in Management, Personnel, Financial, and Budgeting Practices. UNESCO, 26123–84
Status of Loan Agreements, 9912–3
Status of Open Recommendations, 26104–5
Status of Open Recommendations, Part A: Improving National Security and International Affairs Programs, 26104–5.1
Status of Open Recommendations, Part B: Improving Resources, Community, and Economic Development Programs, 26104–5.2
Status of Open Recommendations, Part C: Improving Human Resource Programs, 26104–5.3
Status of Open Recommendations, Part D: Improving Justice, General Government, Financial and Information Management, and Evaluation Programs, 26104–5.4
Status of the Nation's Highways and Bridges: Conditions and Performance, and Highway Bridge Replacement and Rehabilitation Program, 7554–27
Status of the Nuclear Claims Trust Fund. Marshall Islands, 26123–405
Status of the Senior Executive Service, 1991, 9844–36
Status of the Social Security and Medicare Programs: A Summary of the 1992 Annual Reports, 4654–8
Status of the World's Nations. Geographic Notes, 7142–3
Status of U.S. Sugar Tariff-Rate Quota, 1922–9
Status of Waterfowl and Fall Flight Forecast, 1992, 5504–27
Status of Wildland Fire Prevention Evaluation in the U.S., 1208–417
Steel Mill Products, 1991, Current Industrial Report, 2506–10.2
Steel: Semiannual Monitoring Report. Special Focus: Privatization in the Latin American Steel Industry. Report to the Committee on Ways and Means on Investigation No. 332-327 Under Section 332 of the Tariff Act of 1930, 9882–15
Steel Shipping Drums and Pails, Current Industrial Report, 2506–11.5
Steel Wire Rope from the Republic of Korea and Mexico. Determinations of the Commission in Investigations Nos. 731-TA-546 and 547 (Preliminary) Under Section 733(a) of the Tariff Act of 1930, Together with the Information Obtained in the Investigations, 9886–14.346
Sticky Prices: New Evidence from Retail Catalogs, 9375–13.76
Stochastic Specification in Random Production Models of Cost Minimizing Firms, 9371–10.82
Stocks of Grain, 11922–4
Stocks of Grain at Selected Terminal and Elevator Sites, 1313–4
Stocks of Wool and Related Fibers, Current Industrial Report, 2506–5.3
Stone: Minerals Yearbook, Volume 1, 1990, 5604–20.55
Storm Data, 2152–3
Straight Baseline Claims: Djibouti and Oman. Limits in the Seas, 7006–8.8
Strange Behavior of the Credit Card Market, 9387–1.301
Strategic and Critical Materials Report to the Congress: Operations Under the Strategic and Critical Materials Stock Piling Act During the Period April-September 1991, 3542–22
Strategic and Critical Minerals in the Midcontinent Region, U.S., 5668–127
Strategic Assessment Reports, 2176–7
Strategic Capital Taxation in Large, Open Economies with Mobile Capital, 9381–10.130
Strategic Force, Strategic Vision for the 1990s and Beyond. A Statement on the Posture of the U.S. Army, FY93, 3704–13
Strategic Industry at Risk: A Report to the President and the Congress from the National Advisory Committee on Semiconductors, 15034–1.1
Strategic Petroleum Reserve Crude Oil Assays, 3338–5
Strategic Petroleum Reserve, Quarterly Report, 3002–13
Strategic Sealift: Part of the National Defense Reserve Fleet Is No Longer Needed, 26123–376
Strategic Special Nuclear Material Inventory Differences, Annual Report, 3344–2
Strategic Targeted Activities for Results System, 9182–11
Strategies for Energy Independence, Part III, 21448–45
Strategies for the Nineties: Proceedings of the Fifteenth Annual Conference, Federal Home Loan Bank of San Francisco, 9304–24
Strategies To Control Tobacco Use in the U.S.: A Blueprint for Public Health Action in the 1990's, 4476–7.1
Strawberry Trade Situation, 1925–34.315
Streamflow Gains and Losses and Selected Flow Characteristics of Cottonwood Creek, North-Central California, 1982-85, 5666–27.31
Strengthening Research Library Resources Program, Abstracts of Funded Projects, 1990, Title II-C, Higher Education Act, 4874–2
Strengthening the Supervision and Regulation of the Depository Institutions, Volume II, 25248–129
Stronger Controls Needed To Reduce Administrative Costs. Federal Health Benefits Program, 26119–376
Strontium: Minerals Yearbook, Volume 1, 1990, 5604–20.67
Structural Approaches to Vector Autoregressions, 9391–1.316
Structural Change in the U.S. Farm Sector, 1974-87: Thirteenth Annual Family Farm Report to Congress, 1504–4
Structure and Regulation of Insurance Markets in Europe, 9373–3.35
Structure, Conduct, and Regulation of the Property-Liability Insurance Industry, 9373–3.35
Structure, Conduct, Performance, and Welfare, 9387–8.276
Structure of Corporate Ownership in Japan, 9366–6.288
Structure of the NAFTA (North American Free Trade Agreement) Negotiations, 1925–34.302
Structuring U.S. Forces After the Cold War: Costs and Effects of Increased Reliance on the Reserves, 26306–6.172
Student Emigration and the Willingness To Pay for Public Schools: A Test of the Publicness of Public High Schools in the U.S., 9379–12.81
Student Financial Aid: Characteristics of Jobs Provided Through the College Work-Study Program, 26121–449
Student Loan Marketing Association Annual Report, 9784–1
Students at Less-Than-4-Year Institutions: 1987 National Postsecondary Student Aid Study, 4846–3.12
Studies in Income Distribution, 4746–14
Studies in the Distribution of Income, 2546–6.79
Study of Cases Decided by the U.S. Merit Systems Protection Board, FY91, 9494–2
Study of Health Care Access in Counties Where the Only Hospital Closed, 17206–2.30
Study of Natural Wetlands Associated with Acid Mine Drainage, 5608–171
Study of the Food and Kindred Products Industry in Appalachia, 9088–37
Study of the Highway Safety Aspects of the Blue Ridge Parkway. Final Case Study for the National Scenic Byways Study, 7556–8.2
Study of the Relationships Between Near Midair Collisions (NMAC's), Midair Collisions (MAC's) and Some Potential Causal Factors, 7508–76
Subequatorial Africa: International Strategic Minerals Inventory Summary Report. Mineral Perspectives, 5606–1.19
Sub-Saharan Africa and the U.S., 7008–58
Success Stories from Drug-Free Schools, A Guide for Educators, Parents and Policymakers, 4814–2
Sugar and Honey: Foreign Agricultural Service Circular Series, 1925–14
Sugar and Sweetener Situation and Outlook Report, 1561–14
Sugar Beets and Sugarcane, 1991-95 Crop, Price Support Program: ASCS Commodity Fact Sheet, 1806–4.13
Sulfanilic Acid from the People's Republic of China. Determination of the Commission in Investigation No. 731-TA-538 (Final) Under the Tariff Act of 1930, Together with the Information Obtained in the Investigation, 9886–14.357

Sulfanilic Acid from the Republic of Hungary and India. Determinations of the Commission in Investigation No. 701-TA-318 (Preliminary) and Nos. 731-TA-560 and 561 (Preliminary) Under the Tariff Act of 1930, Together with the Information Obtained in the Investigations, 9886–19.83
Sulfanilic Acid: Probable Economic Effect of Removal from the List of Eligible Articles Under the U.S. Generalized System of Preferences. Report to the President on Investigation No. 332-330, 9886–4.188
Sulfur Dyes from China, India, and the UK. Determinations of the Commission in Investigations Nos. 731-TA-548, 550, and 551 (Preliminary) Under the Tariff Act of 1930, Together with the Information Obtained in the Investigations, 9886–14.347
Sulfur: Mineral Industry Surveys, 5612–1.23
Sulfur: Minerals Yearbook, Volume 1, 1990, 5604–20.56
Summaries of FY91 Engineering Research, 3004–18.2
Summaries of FY91 Geosciences Research, 3004–18.1
Summaries of FY92 Research in the Chemical Sciences, 3004–18.6
Summaries of Physical Research in the Geosciences, 3004–18.1
Summary and Analysis of International Travel to the U.S., 2902–1
Summary and Analysis of Water-Use Data Collection in Eastern Arkansas, 5666–24.11
Summary of Accidents Investigated by the Federal Railroad Administration, 1988, 7604–3
Summary of Awards, FY87-90, Materials Development, Research, and Informal Science Education, Instructional Materials Development, 9626–7.9
Summary of Awards, FY89, Computer and Computation Research, 9626–7.2
Summary of Awards, FY89, Office of Cross-Disciplinary Activities, 9626–7.8
Summary of Awards, FY90, Advanced Scientific Computing, 9626–7.4
Summary of Awards, FY90, Environmental Biology, Biotic Systems and Resources, 9626–7.6
Summary of Awards, FY90, Information, Robotics, and Intelligent Systems, 9626–7.3
Summary of Awards, FY90, Microelectronic Information Processing Systems, 9626–7.1
Summary of Awards, FY91, Microelectronic Information Processing Systems, 9626–7.10
Summary of Commentary on Current Economic Conditions by Federal Reserve District, 9362–8
Summary of Leading Causes for Outpatient Visits, Indian Health Service Direct and Contract Facilities, FY90, 4084–2
Summary of Loan Activity and Operating Results Through (Month), Issued by CCC, 1802–7
Summary of Medical Programs, 8602–4
Summary of Notifiable Diseases, U.S., 1991, 4204–1
Summary of Recent Immigration Data. Commissioner's Fact Book, 6264–7
Summary of Refugee Admissions, 7002–4
Summary of Reported Water Use for Arkansas Counties, 5666–24.12
Summary of Savings Accounts by Geographic Area, SAIF-Insured Savings Associations, June 30, 1990, 8434–5
Summary of Savings Accounts by Geographic Area, SAIF-Insured Savings Associations, June 30, 1991, 8434–5
Summary of State Appalachian Development Plans and Investment Programs for FY92, 9084–3
Summary of Travel Trends: 1990 Nationwide Personal Transportation Survey, 7556–6.2
Summary of VHA Health Services Training by Major Programs for FY91, 8704–4
Summary of Water Resources Activities of the USGS in Colorado, FY91, 5666–26.24
Summary of Water Resources Activities of the USGS in Iowa, FY90, 5666–26.17
Summary of 1990 Annual Reports of the Medicare Board of Trustees, 4654–8
Summary of 1991 Annual Reports of the Medicare Board of Trustees, 4654–8
Summary Population and Housing Characteristics. 1990 Census of Population and Housing, 2551–1
Summary Report of Observations of Coastal Gill and Trammel Net Fisheries in Central California—Oct. 1, 1984-Mar. 31, 1985, 14738–13
Summary Social, Economic, and Housing Characteristics: 1990 Census of Population and Housing, 2551–7
Summary Tape File 1 on CD-ROM, Technical Documentation: 1990 Census of Population and Housing, 2308–65
Summary Tape File 1A Data on CD-ROM: 1990 Census of Population and Housing, 2551–9
Summary Tape File 3 on CD-ROM, Technical Documentation: 1990 Census of Population and Housing, 2308–68
Summary Tape File 3A Data on CD-ROM: 1990 Census of Population and Housing, 2551–10
Superstructure Icing and Wave Hindcast Statistics in the Navarin and St. George Basin Areas, 2176–1.40
Supplement to Review of Mortality in VA Medical Centers, 8708–1
Supplement to the American Housing Survey for Selected Metropolitan Areas in 1985, 2485–8
Supplement to the American Housing Survey for Selected Metropolitan Areas in 1986, 2485–8
Supplement to the American Housing Survey for Selected Metropolitan Areas: 1987, 2485–8
Supplement to the American Housing Survey for the U.S. in 1989, 2485–13
Supplement to the Annual Energy Outlook, 1992, 3164–96
Supplemental Security Income: State and County Data, 4744–27
Supplemental Tidal Predictions: Anchorage, Nikishka, Seldovia, and Valdez, Alaska, 1993, 2174–2.1
Supplementary Materials: National Priorities List, Proposed Rule, 9216–5.4
Supply of Illicit Drugs to the U.S., the NNICC Report, 1991, 6284–2
Supply Response to Price Changes for Selected Vegetables, 1561–11.302
Supply-Side Consequences of U.S. Fiscal Policy in the 1980s, 9385–1.304, 9385–8.125
Support Networks Among American Families: Who's Helping Out and Who's Being Helped, 1988. Statistical Brief, 2326–17.48
Supporting Analysis Appendix for the World Energy Outlook: Economic and Security Implications, 3166–6.58
Surface Transportation: Availability of Intercity Bus Service Continues To Decline, 26113–583
Surface Water-Quality Assessment of the Lower Kansas River Basin, Kansas and Nebraska: Concentrations of Major Metals and Trace Elements in Streambed Sediments, 1987, 5666–27.26
Surveillance Challenge: Final Stages of Eradication of Poliomyelitis in the Americas, 4202–7.309
Surveillance for Epidemic Cholera in the Americas: An Assessment, 4202–7.310
Surveillance for Measles—New Zealand, 1991, 4202–7.321
Surveillance in Evacuation Camps After the Eruption of Mt. Pinatubo, Philippines, 4202–7.320
Surveillance of Congenital Cytomegalovirus Disease, 1990-91, 4202–7.314
Surveillance of Dracunculiasis, 1981-91, 4202–7.307
Surveillance of Traumatic Occupational Fatalities in Alaska—Implications for Prevention, 4042–3.307
Survey Methods and Statistical Summary of Nonfuel Minerals, 5604–48
Survey Methods and Statistical Summary of Nonfuel Minerals: Minerals Yearbook, Volume 1, 1990, 5604–20.2
Survey Methods and Statistical Summary of Nonfuel Minerals: Minerals Yearbook, Volume 2, 1990, 5604–22.1
Survey of Aviation Medical Examiners: Information and Attitudes About the Pre-Employment and Pre-Appointment Drug Testing Program, 7506–10.115
Survey of Current Business, 2702–1
Survey of Direct U.S. Private Capital Investment in Research and Development Facilities in Japan, 9628–88
Survey of Federal Employees on Misconduct and Protection from Reprisal. Whistleblower Protection, 26119–413
Survey of Federal Organizations. Quality Management, 26119–425
Survey of Federally-Funded Marine Mammal Research and Studies, FY74-91, 14734–2
Survey of Graduates of the Epidemic Intelligence Service as an Approach To Enhancing Ethnic Diversity Among the Nation's Epidemiologists, 4042–3.374
Survey of Health Occupational Staff, 1991 Report, 8604–8
Survey of Income and Program Participation (SIPP): Quality Profile, 2628–34
Survey of Income and Program Participation Users' Guide, 2628–24
Survey of Income and Program Participation Working Paper Series, 2626–10
Survey of Mortgage Lending Activity, 5142–18
Survey of Mortgage Lending Activity, Gross Flows, 5142–30
Survey of Occupational Injuries and Illnesses, 1990, 6844–7
Survey of Plant Capacity, 1990, Current Industrial Report, 2506–3.7

Survey of Real Estate Trends, 9292–6
Survey of Substance Abuse Programs in the Mining Industry, 6668–8
Survey of Terms of Bank Lending Made During (Latest Survey Date), 9365–3
Survey of U.S. Border Infrastructure Needs. U.S.-Mexico Trade, 26123–368
Survey of Visits and Consultations, 17266–2.5
Survey on Waiting List/Preference Rule, Behavioral Problems and Services in Public Housing, 26113–590
Survey Results on RTC's Communication and Real Estate Marketing. Resolution Trust Corporation, 26119–422
Survivor Benefit Coverage for Wives Increased After 1984 Pension Law. Pensions Plans, 26121–450
Suspended-Sediment Budgets for Four Drainage Basins Tributary to Lake Tahoe, California and Nevada, 1984-87, 5666–27.32
Sustained Management Attention Needed To Improve Timely Issuance. FDA Regulations, 26121–453
Sweaters Wholly or in Chief Weight of Manmade Fibers from Hong Kong, the Republic of Korea, and Taiwan. Views on Remand in Investigations Nos. 731-TA-448-450 (Final), 9886–14.363
Switchgear, Switchboard Apparatus, Relays, and Industrial Controls, 1991, Current Industrial Report, 2506–12.11
Symposium Sponsored by the Federal Reserve Bank of Kansas City, 9381–13
Synopsis of Scientific Literature on Phenoxy Herbicides and Associated Dioxins No. 9 (Volumes XIX and XX), 8706–1.5
Synthesis of Safety Research, 7558–98
Synthesis of Safety Research: Adverse Environmental Conditions, 7558–98.1
Synthesis of Safety Research: Pedestrians, 7558–98.2
Synthesis of Seismicity Studies for Western Alaska, 2176–1.40
Synthesis of Soil-Plant Correspondence Data from Twelve Wetland Studies Throughout the U.S., 5506–10.13
Synthetic Organic Chemicals: U.S. Production and Sales, 1990, 9884–3
System for Reimbursing Universities' Indirect Costs Should Be Reevaluated. Federal Research, 26113–592

Tables of Annual Production of Gold, Silver, Copper, Lead and Zinc from the States of California, Idaho, Montana, Nevada, Oregon, Washington: With a Table of Annual Prices, 5608–178
Taiwan, Hong Kong, and Indonesia: Strong Markets for U.S. Apples, 1925–34.347
Talc and Pyrophyllite: Minerals Yearbook, Volume 1, 1990, 5604–20.57
Targeting M2: The Issue of Monetary Control, 9391–1.313
Tax Administration: Improvement in IRS' Telephone Assistor Accuracy, 26119–418
Tax Administration: IRS' Efforts To Improve Corporate Compliance, 26119–405
Tax Administration: IRS Undercover Operations Management Oversight Should Be Strengthened, 26119–394
Tax Fairness: Ensuring Corporate Compliance, 25408–118
Tax Policy and Administration: Luxury Excise Tax Issues and Estimated Effects, 26119–385
Tax Policy and the Macroeconomy: Stabilization, Growth, and Income Distribution, 21788–211
Tax Policy: Effects of Changing the Tax Treatment of Fringe Benefits, 26119–389
Tax Policy: Issues and Policy Proposals Regarding Tax Treatment of Intangible Assets, 26119–365
Tax Policy: 1988 and 1989 Company Effective Tax Rates Higher Than in Prior Years, 26119–289
Taxation and Inflation: A New Explanation for Current Account Imbalances, 9366–7.274
Taxation of Capital Income in a Global Economy: An Overview, 9373–1.316
Tax-Exempt Organization Business Income Tax Return Statistics for 1987: Data Release, 8302–2.306
Tea, Spices and Essential Oils: Foreign Agricultural Service Circular Series, 1925–15
Teaching Adults with Limited English Skills: Progress and Challenges, 4808–41
Team Behavior in the Family: An Analysis of the Rotten Kid Theorem, 6886–6.86
Technical and Expert Panel Reports, Advisory Council on Social Security, 10176–1
Technical Assistance and Safety Programs: FY91 Project Directory, 7884–1
Technical Papers: Census Bureau, 2626–2
Technical Report Series: Prospective Payment Assessment Commission, 17206–2
Technical Reports, Bureau of Justice Statistics, 6066–23
Technological Change and Its Impact on Labor in Four Industries, 6826–2.9
Technology and Productivity Reports Series, 6826–2
Technology Transfer: Federal Efforts To Enhance the Competitiveness of Small Manufacturers, 26113–551
Telecommunications in the Age of Information: NTIA Infrastructure Report, 2808–30
Telephone Rates Update, 9282–8
Television Channel Utilization, 9282–6
Television Receivers and Video Monitors, Industry and Trade Summary, 9885–12.1
Tenant Income Misreporting Deprives Other Families of HUD-Subsidized Housing. Urban Poor, 26121–468
Tennessee Valley Authority: 1991 Annual Report, 9804–1
Tennessee Valley Authority: 1991 Financial Statements, 9804–32
Tenth Annual Report of Accomplishments Under the Airport Improvement Program, FY91, 7504–38
Tenth District: Matching a Nation in Recovery, 9381–1.302
Term Structure Spread and Future Changes in Long and Short Rates: Is There a Puzzle?, 9385–8.136
Terminal Area Forecasts, FY92-2005, 7504–7
Terrorism in the U.S., 1991, 6224–6
Test of the Stability of Early Warning Models of Bank Failures, 9379–14.18
Testing for Antibodies to Human Immunodeficiency Virus Type 2 in the U.S., 4206–2.62
Testing for Impacts of Immigration Reform on Farm Employment and Wages, 1561–16.304
Testing for Nonlinear Dynamics, 6886–6.85
Testing for the Presence of Liquidity Constraints in Post-Secondary Educational Attainment, 6886–6.92
Testing in American Schools: Asking the Right Questions, 26358–255
Tests of Mean-Variance Efficiency of International Equity Markets, 9385–8.137
Texas Upland Cotton Acreage Abandonment and Harvested Yield: A Historical Perspective, 1561–1.303
Textile, Apparel, and Fabric Markets, 2046–15
Textile Plant Employment in the Southeast, 6942–1
Textile Plant Employment in the Southeast, 1991, 6944–1
Textured Yarn Production, 1991, Current Industrial Report, 2506–5.4
Thallium in 1991: Mineral Industry Surveys, Annual Review, 5614–5.7
The Way We Are: The Community College as American Thermometer, 4888–7
The 1990's: A Decade of Decisions for Vital and Health Statistics. Proceedings of the 1991 Public Health Conference on Records and Statistics, 4164–2
Therapeutic Compounds, 1504–9.1
"They Come on Behalf of Their Children": Central American Families in Washington, D.C., 6366–6.3
Third Annual Climate Assessment, 1991, 2184–9
Thirteenth Annual Report of the Federal Labor Relations Authority and the Federal Service Impasses Panel, FY91, 13364–1
Thirteenth Annual Report to Congress on the Automotive Technology Development Program, 3304–17
Thirteenth Annual Report to Congress on the Federal Equal Opportunity Recruitment Program, FY91, 9844–33
Thirty Years of Hydrometeorologic Data at the Hubbard Brook Experimental Forest, New Hampshire, 1208–410
Threshold Cointegration, 9379–12.90
Thrift Industry Cost Structure and Competitive Viability, 8436–1.7
Thrift Industry Performance, 1991, 9381–14
Tidal Current Tables, 2174–1
Tidal Current Tables, 1993: Atlantic Coast of North America, 2174–1.1
Tidal Current Tables, 1993: Pacific Coast of North America and Asia, 2174–1.2
Tide Tables 1993, High and Low Water Predictions, 2174–2
Tide Tables 1993, High and Low Water Predictions: Central and Western Pacific Ocean and Indian Ocean, 2174–2.5
Tide Tables 1993, High and Low Water Predictions: East Coast of North and South America Including Greenland, 2174–2.3
Tide Tables 1993, High and Low Water Predictions: Europe and West Coast of Africa Including the Mediterranean Sea, 2174–2.4
Tide Tables 1993, High and Low Water Predictions: West Coast of North and South America Including the Hawaiian Islands, 2174–2.2
TIGER Questions and Answers, 2628–32

Timber Industries: Northeast Region, 1206–15
Timber Industries of Kentucky, 1986, 1206–15.12
Timber Industry Assessments of Timber Product Output and Use, 1206–10
Timber Industry of Iowa: An Assessment of Timber Product Output and Use, 1988, 1206–10.13
Timber Production and Mill Residues: Intermountain Research Station, 1206–17
Timber Resource of Missouri, 1206–3
Timber Resource of Missouri, Statistical Report, 1989, 1208–76
Timber Resource of Missouri's Eastern Ozarks, 1989, 1206–3.6
Timber Resource of Missouri's Northwest Ozarks, 1989, 1206–3.5
Timber Resource of Missouri's Riverborder, 1989, 1206–3.8
Timber Resource of Missouri's Southwest Ozarks, 1989, 1206–3.7
Timber Resource Statistics for the Chatham Area of the Tongass National Forest, Alaska, 1982, 1206–9.26
Timber Resource Statistics for the Ketchikan Area of the Tongass National Forest, Alaska, 1985, 1206–9.24
Timber Resource Statistics for the Stikine Area of the Tongass National Forest, Alaska, 1984, 1206–9.25
Timber Resource Statistics for Washington, 1206–28
Timber Resources of Minnesota, 1206–24
Timber Resources of the Southern Region, 1206–8
Timber Resources of Wisconsin, 1206–34
Timber Sale Program Annual Report, FY91, 1204–36
Timber Statistics for Alaska, 1206–9
Timberland Resources of the Kenai Peninsula, Alaska, 1987, 1206–9.23
Timeliness of Notification in Infectious Disease Cases, 4042–3.349
Time-Off Benefits in Small Establishments, 6722–1.315
Tin Industry: Mineral Industry Surveys, 5612–1.24
Tin: Mineral Industry Surveys, 5612–1.24
Tin: Minerals Yearbook, Volume 1, 1990, 5604–20.58
Titanic Memorial, 2152–8.301
Titanium: Mineral Industry Surveys, 5612–2.16
Titanium: Minerals Yearbook, Volume 1, 1990, 5604–20.59
To Examine the Future of Our Nation's Infrastructure Needs, 21648–67
To Meet the Needs of the Nations: Staffing the U.S. Civil Service and the Public Service of Canada, 9498–16
Tobacco Market Review, 1319–5
Tobacco Market Review: Burley, 1991 Crop, 1319–5.1
Tobacco Market Review: Fire-Cured and Dark Air-Cured, 1991 Crop, 1319–5.2
Tobacco Market Review: Flue-Cured, 1991 Crop, 1319–5.3
Tobacco Outlook for 1992, 1925–16.304
Tobacco Products: Monthly Statistical Release, 8486–1.4
Tobacco Situation and Outlook Report, 1561–10
Tobacco Situation: Bulgaria, 1925–16.303
Tobacco Situation: European Community, 1925–16.306
Tobacco Situation: Romania, 1925–16.301
Tobacco Stocks, 1319–3
Tobacco Taxes, Employment, and Income, 1504–9.1
Tobin's q, Economic Rents, and the Optimal Stock of Capital, 9373–27.11
Tolerance of Beta Blocked Hypertensives During Orthostatic and Altitude Stresses, 7506–10.119
Tonnage for Selected U.S. Ports in 1990, 3754–7
Top 100 Cooperatives, 1990 Financial Profile, 1124–3
Top 50 Companies with the Largest Unfunded Pension Liability, 9674–2
Total and Net Occupational Separations: A Report on Recent Research, 6748–84
Total Enrollments in Health Physics/Radiation Protection Increased in 1991. Undergraduate and Doctoral Degrees Increased While Master's Degrees Decreased, 3006–8.19
Total Nuclear-Related Employment in 1991 Unchanged from 1989, 3006–8.20
Toward a National Semiconductor Strategy: Regaining Markets in High-volume Electronics. Second Annual Report of the National Advisory Committee on Semiconductors, Volume II, 15034–1.3
Toward a National Semiconductor Strategy. Second Annual Report of the National Advisory Committee on Semiconductors, Volume I, 15034–1.2
Toward the Year 2000: Listening to the Voice of Native America, 17th Annual Report to the U.S. Congress, 14874–1
Toxic Contaminants in the Gulf of Maine, 2176–3.17
Toxic Release Inventory, 9234–7
Toxic Release Inventory CD-ROM Quick User Guide, 9238–70
Toxic Substances: Information on Costs and Financial Aid to Schools To Control Asbestos, 26113–560
Toxics in the Community, National and Local Perspectives: The 1989 Toxics Release Inventory National Report, 9234–6
Toxics Release Inventory National Report, 1989: Toxics in the Community, National and Local Perspectives, 9234–6
Toys and Models, Industry and Trade Summary, 9885–10.1
Tracking Manufacturing: The Survey of Southeastern Manufacturing Conditions, 9371–1.307
Trade Agreements Program, 1991, Annual Report of the President of the U.S., and 1992 Trade Policy Agenda, 444–1
Trade and Employment, 2322–2
Trade and Employment Effects of the Caribbean Basin Economic Recovery Act, 6364–2
Trade Between the U.S. and China, the Former Soviet Union, Central and Eastern Europe, the Baltic Nations, and Other Selected Countries. Quarterly Report to the Congress and the Trade Policy Committee, 9882–2
Trade Dependency Index Tables for Total, Merchandise, and Agricultural Trade, 1960-88, 1528–328
Trade Enforcement Activities Impaired by Management Problems. Customs Service, 26119–420
Trade in Conventional Weapons: The International Arms Bazaar, 25408–115
Trade of NATO Countries with China, 7144–14
Trade of NATO Countries with European CEMA Countries, 7144–5
Trade Patterns of the West, 7144–10
Trade Policy Agenda, 1992, and 1991 Annual Report of the President of the U.S. on the Trade Agreements Program, 444–1
Trade-Weighted Value of the Dollar, 9379–13
Trading Analysis of Nov. 15, 1991, 9738–22
Traffic Fatalities, Semiannual Report, 1991 (January-June), 7762–11
Traffic Fatalities, Preliminary Report, 1991, 7762–11
Traffic Management Progress Report, 3702–1
Traffic Management Progress Report, FY91, 3704–15
Traffic Report, 1991 Navigation Season: St. Lawrence Seaway, 7744–2
Traffic Volume Trends, 7552–8
Training and Employment Report of the Secretary of Labor, 6404–17
Transactions Between Foreign Controlled Corporations and Related Foreign Persons, 1988: Data Release, 8302–2.318
Transit Research Abstracts, Volume 10, 1992, 7884–11
Transitional Employment Training for SSI Recipients with Mental Retardation, 4742–1.301
Transitional Housing Shows Initial Success but Long-term Effects Unknown. Homelessness, 26113–549
Transitions Experienced by 1988 Eighth Graders, 4826–10.4
Transitions to Kindergarten: Final Report of the National Transition Study, 4808–44
Transport Statistics in the U.S. for the Year Ended Dec. 31, 1990. Part 1: Railroads, 9486–5.1
Transport Statistics in the U.S., for the Year Ended Dec. 31, 1990. Part 2: Motor Carriers, Release 1, 9486–5.2
Transport Statistics in the U.S., for the Year Ended Dec. 31, 1990. Part 2: Motor Carriers, Release 2, 9486–5.3
Transport Statistics in the U.S. for the Year Ended Dec. 31, 1991. Part 1: Railroads, 9486–6.1
Transport Statistics in the U.S.: Railroad Companies and Motor Carriers Subject to the Interstate Commerce Act, for the Year Ended Dec. 31, 1990, 9486–5
Transport Statistics in the U.S.: Railroad Companies and Motor Carriers Subject to the Interstate Commerce Act, for the Year Ended Dec. 31, 1991, 9486–6
Transportation Accident Fatalities, Preliminary Statistics, 9614–6
Transportation and Public Utilities Industries: Evaluating Your Firm's Injury and Illness Record, 6886–4.2
Transportation Energy Data Book: Edition 12, 3304–5
Transportation Infrastructure: Urban Transportation Planning Can Better Address Modal Trade-offs, 26113–570
Transportation Reports and Testimony: May 1991-April 1992, 26106–10.7
Trauma Care Systems, 4208–35
Travel Behavior Issues in the 1990's: 1990 Nationwide Personal Transportation Survey, 7556–6.3

Travel by Selected Executive Branch Officials. Military Aircraft, 26111–78
Treasury Bill Rates in the 1970s and 1980s, 9373–27.6
Treasury Bulletin, 8002–4
Treasury, CBO and GAO Reports on FNMA, FHLMC and the Federal Home Loan Bank System, 21248–170
Treasury Civil Case Processing of Bank Secrecy Act Violations. Money Laundering, 26119–390
Treasury Reporting Rates of Exchange, 8102–6
Treasury Tax and Loan Accounts: Changes in Collateral Practices Could Reduce the Federal Government's Risk of Loss, 26111–80
Treaties in Force: A List of Treaties and Other International Agreements of the U.S. in Force on Jan. 1, 1992, 7004–1
Tree Assistance Program, FY91 Statistical Summary, 1804–24
Tree Nut Semiannual Situation and Outlook, 1925–34.311
Tree Planting in the U.S., 1991, 1204–7
Trend and Distribution of Hospital Uncompensated Care Costs, 1980-89, 17206–2.32
Trend Data, 1967-91, 8604–5
Trends and Management of Wolf-Livestock Conflicts in Minnesota, 5508–115
Trends for 1985-93 in DOD's Spending, Employment, and Contractors. Defense Procurement, 26123–399
Trends in Academic Progress: Achievement of U.S. Students in Science, 1969/70-90; Mathematics, 1973-90; Reading, 1971-90; and Writing, 1984-90, 4898–32
Trends in Alcohol-Related Fatal Traffic Crashes, U.S.: 1977-88, 4486–1.12
Trends in Alcohol-Related Fatal Traffic Crashes, U.S.: 1977-89, 4486–1.14
Trends in Alcohol-Related Morbidity Among Short-Stay Community Hospital Discharges, U.S., 1979-89, 4486–1.16
Trends in Breast Feeding, 4147–16.6
Trends in Campsite Condition: Eagle Cap Wilderness, Bob Marshall Wilderness, and Grand Canyon National Park, 1208–395
Trends in Cancer Mortality in 15 Industrialized Countries, 1969-86, 4472–1.306
Trends in Childhood Use of Dental Care Products Containing Fluoride: U.S., 1983-89, 4146–8.222
Trends in Duck Breeding Populations, 1955-92, 5504–30
Trends in Entertainment, 1702–1.303
Trends in Health and Health Care Among Blacks and Hispanics in New York City During the 1980s, 4164–2
Trends in Hospital Personnel 1981-87: From the American Hospital Association Annual Surveys, 4114–12
Trends in Hospital Personnel 1981-88: From the American Hospital Association Annual Surveys, 4114–12
Trends in Income and Wealth of the Elderly in the 1980s, 2546–6.79, 2626–10.144
Trends in LDC External Debt, 1985-91, 9114–7
Trends in Per Capita Consumption in Central America, 1969-89, 9916–13.4
Trends in Racial/Ethnic Enrollment in Higher Education: Fall 1980-Fall 1990, 4844–15
Trends in Relative Income: 1964-89, 2546–6.73
Trends in Retirement Age by Sex, 1950-2005, 6722–1.332
Trends in Telephone Service, 9282–7
Trends in the International Communications Industry, 1975-90, 9284–17
Trends in Total Hospital Financial Performance Under the Prospective Payment System, 4652–1.315
Trends in Transportation, 1702–1.306
Trends in U.S. and Foreign Performance. High-Technology Competitiveness, 26123–406
Trends in Wage and Salary Inequality, 1967-88, 6722–1.328
Trends '91: A Compendium of Data on Global Change, 3004–33
TRI CD-ROM Quick User Guide, 9238–70
Trichinosis Surveillance, U.S., 1987-90, 4202–7.304
Trout Production, 1631–16
Truck Safety: The Safety of Longer Combination Vehicles Is Unknown, 26113–568
Truck Trailers, Current Industrial Report, 2506–12.25
Trust Assets of Financial Institutions, 1989, 13004–1
Trust Assets of Financial Institutions, 1990, 13004–1
Trust Assets of Financial Institutions, 1991, 13004–1
Trust Territory of the Pacific Islands, 1991, 7004–6
Tuberculosis in a Small Semi-Rural County, 4042–3.319
Tuberculosis Morbidity in the U.S.: Final Data, 1990, 4202–7.302
Tumor Angiogenesis: A New Significant and Independent Prognostic Indicator in Early-Stage Breast Carcinoma, 4472–1.357
Tuna: Current Issues Affecting the U.S. Industry. Report to the Committee on Finance, U.S. Senate, on Investigation No. 332-313 Under Section 332(g) of the Tariff Act of 1930 As Amended, 9886–4.187
Tungsten: Mineral Industry Surveys, 5612–1.25
Tungsten: Minerals Yearbook, Volume 1, 1990, 5604–20.60
Turkey Hatchery, 1625–10
Turkeys, 1625–6
Turning Environmental Needs into Farm Opportunities, 1504–9.1
TVA Biomass Fuels Program, 9806–9
TVA Fertilizer Publications, 9804–28
Twelfth Annual Report of the Federal Labor Relations Authority and the Federal Service Impasses Panel, FY90, 13364–1
Twentieth Annual Report of the President on Federal Advisory Committees, FY91, 9454–18
Two Papers on a New SIPP-Based Microsimulation Model of SSI and OASDI: Rationale for a SIPP-Based Microsimulation Model of SSI and OASDI; and Implementing an SSI Model Using the Survey of Income and Program Participation, 4746–26.23
Types and Number of Implementing Actions. Endangered Species Act, 26113–578
UMTA University Research and Training Program, FY91 Awards, 7884–7
Uncertainty and Planting Flexibility Choices on Spring Wheat Farms, 1561–12.303
Uncounted Dead—American Civilians Dying Overseas, 4042–3.315
Undergraduate Enrollment and Completion Among Minorities, 26306–3.122
Understanding Drug Prevention. An Office of National Drug Control Policy White Paper, 236–1.6
Understanding the Market for Charter and Headboat Fishing Services, 2162–1.301
Unemployed Parents: Initial Efforts To Expand State Assistance, 26131–96
Unemployment in States and Local Areas, 6742–22
Unemployment Insurance Claims, 6402–15
Unemployment Insurance Financial Data for 1990, 6404–10
Unemployment Insurance Occasional Papers, 6406–6
Unemployment Insurance Quality Appraisal Results, FY91, 6404–16
Unemployment Insurance Weekly Claims Report, 6402–14
Unemployment Trust Fund, 8102–9.1
Unemployment Trust Fund Activity Summary, 8102–9.16
UNESCO: Status of Improvements in Management, Personnel, Financial, and Budgeting Practices, 26123–84
UNICOR Sales Report, FY91, 6244–5
Uniform Bank Performance Report, State Averages, 13002–3
Uniform Crime Report, 1991 Preliminary Annual Release, 6222–1
Uniform Crime Report, January-June, 1992, 6222–1
Uniform Crime Reports: Crime in the U.S., 1991, 6224–2
Uniform Crime Reports: Law Enforcement Officers Killed and Assaulted, 1991, 6224–3
Union Members in 1991, 6726–1.44
Union Membership Statistics in 12 Countries, 6722–1.305
Union Recognition in the Federal Government: Statistical Summary, Summary Reports Within Agencies, and Listings Within Agencies of Exclusive Recognitions and Agreements, as of January 1991, 9844–14
United Nations: U.S. Participation in Peacekeeping Operations, 26123–404
Universal Health Insurance Coverage Using Medicare's Payment Rates, 26306–6.163
University Research: Controlling Inappropriate Access to Federally Funded Research Results, 26113–575
Unlocking Learning: Chapter 1 in Correctional Facilities. National Study of the Chapter 1 Neglected or Delinquent Program, 4808–40
Unlocking Learning: Chapter 1 in Correctional Facilities. National Study of the Chapter 1 Neglected or Delinquent Program: Descriptive Study Findings, 4808–40.4
Unlocking Learning: Chapter 1 in Correctional Facilities. National Study of the Chapter 1 Neglected or Delinquent Program: Effective Practices Study Findings, 4808–40.3
Unlocking Learning: Chapter 1 in Correctional Facilities. National Study of the Chapter 1 Neglected or Delinquent Program: Final Report, 4808–40.1

Unlocking Learning: Chapter 1 in Correctional Facilities. National Study of the Chapter 1 Neglected or Delinquent Program: Longitudinal Study Findings, 4808–40.2
Unresolved Trade Issues Leave Uncertain Future for U.S. Uranium Industry. Uranium Enrichment, 26113–584
Update on Adult Immunization: Recommendations of the Immunization Practices Advisory Committee (ACIP), 4206–2.48
Upgrading of Underground Storage Tanks Can Be Improved To Avoid Costly Cleanups. Hazardous Materials, 26123–395
Upgrading Workers' Skills Not Sufficient To Jump-Start Rural Economy, 1502–7.302
Upland Cotton, Summary of 1992 Support Program and Related Information: ASCS Commodity Fact Sheet, 1806–4.14
Uranium Enrichment, Annual Report, 3354–7
Uranium Enrichment: Unresolved Trade Issues Leave Uncertain Future for U.S. Uranium Industry, 26113–584
Uranium from the USSR. Determination of the Commission in Investigation No. 731-TA-539 (Preliminary) Under the Tariff Act of 1930, Together with the Information Obtained in the Investigation, 9886–14.337
Uranium Industry Annual, 1991, 3164–65
Uranium Industry of the Commonwealth of Independent States, 3164–65
Uranium Mill Tailings Remedial Action Project, Environmental Assessment, 3356–4
Urban Mass Transportation Administration Grants Assistance Programs, Information Summaries, 7884–10
Urban Poor: Tenant Income Misreporting Deprives Other Families of HUD-Subsidized Housing, 26121–468
Urban Transportation Abstracts, Volume 9, 1990-91, 7884–11
Urban Transportation Planning Can Better Address Modal Trade-offs. Transportation Infrastructure, 26113–570
Uruguay Round Opportunities, 1504–9.1
U.S. Affiliates of Foreign Companies: Errata, 2702–1.337
U.S. Affiliates of Foreign Companies: Operations in 1990, 2702–1.319
U.S. Air Carrier Operations, 1988, Annual Review of Aircraft Accident Data, 9614–2
U.S. Alcohol Epidemiologic Data Reference Manual, 4488–10
U.S. Alcohol Epidemiologic Data Reference Manual. Volume 3: County Alcohol Problem Indicators, 1979-85, 4488–10.4
U.S. Alcohol Epidemiologic Data Reference Manual. Volume 4: Hospital Discharges with Alcohol-Related Conditions, Hospital Discharge Survey, 1979-85, 4488–10.5
U.S. and Japanese Work Injury and Illness Experience, 6722–1.318
U.S. Apple Exports: A World Market Analysis, 1925–34.334
U.S. Architectural and Transportation Barriers Compliance Board, Annual Report, 17614–1
U.S. Arms Control and Disarmament Agency Annual Report to Congress, 1990, 9824–2
U.S. Arms Control and Disarmament Agency Annual Report to Congress, 1991, 9824–2
U.S. Army Corps of Engineers Recreation Study: A Plan Prepared for the Assistant Secretary of the Army (Civil Works), 3758–8
U.S. Army Posture Statement, FY93, 3704–13
U.S. Assistance Supports Economic and Social Development. Aid to Nicaragua, 26123–398
U.S. Attorneys' Statistical Report, FY91, 6004–2
U.S. Automobile Industry: Monthly Report on Selected Economic Indicators. Report to the Subcommittee on Trade, Committee on Ways and Means, on Investigation No. 332-207 Under Section 332 of the Tariff Act of 1930, 9882–8
U.S. Automotive Industry: Monthly Report on Selected Economic Indicators. Report to the Subcommittee on Trade, Committee on Ways and Means, on Investigation No. 332-207 Under Section 332 of the Tariff Act of 1930, 9882–8
U.S. Automotive Parts Trade with Japan: 1991 Annual Report to the Secretary of Commerce, 2004–10
U.S. Business Enterprises Acquired or Established by Foreign Direct Investors in 1991, 2702–1.320
U.S. Cherry Exports to Japan Expand in 1992, 1925–34.339
U.S. Civil Airmen Statistics, 1991, 7504–2
U.S. Claims Court Statistical Report for the Court Year Oct. 1, 1990-Sept. 30, 1991, 18224–1
U.S. Claims Court Statistical Report for the Court Year Oct. 1, 1991-Sept. 30, 1992, 18224–1
U.S. Coast Guard Digest of Law Enforcement Statistics, 7402–4
U.S. Consumer Product Safety Commission, FY90 Annual Report, 9164–2
U.S. Costs in the Persian Gulf Conflict and Foreign Contributions To Offset Such Costs, 102–3
U.S. Cotton Quality Report: Classings Through (Date), 1309–11
U.S. Court of International Trade, Annual Report for Fiscal Year Ending September 1992, 18224–2
U.S. Crude Oil, Natural Gas, and Natural Gas Liquids Reserves, 1991 Annual Report, 3164–46
U.S. Customs Service's Abuse of Overtime Compensation, 21788–214
U.S. Dairy Prospects and Programs, 1504–9.1
U.S. Department of Commerce Annual Report, FY91, 2004–1
U.S. Department of Commerce Office of Inspector General, Semiannual Report to the Congress, Sept. 30, 1992, 2002–5
U.S. Department of Energy: Office of Inspector General, Semiannual Report to Congress, 3002–12
U.S. Department of Energy Posture Statement and FY93 Budget Overview, 3024–5
U.S. Department of Energy, Report to Congress on the Small Business Program, FY90, 3004–35
U.S. Department of Energy, the Secretary's Annual Report to Congress, 1990, 3024–2
U.S. Department of Housing and Urban Development Annual Report, 1990, 5004–10
U.S. Department of Labor Annual Report for FY91, 6304–1
U.S. Department of State Discussion Papers, 7006–7
U.S. Department of State Indexes of Living Costs Abroad, Quarters Allowances, and Hardship Differentials, 7002–7
U.S. Department of State Office of Inspector General: Semiannual Report to the Congress, Oct. 1, 1991-Mar. 31, 1992, 7002–6
U.S. Department of State Office of Inspector General: Semiannual Report to the Congress, Apr. 1-Sept. 30, 1992, 7002–6
U.S. Department of the Interior: Office of Inspector General, Semiannual Report, 5302–2
U.S. Department of Transportation Grant Awards, FY89, 7304–7
U.S. Department of Transportation, 23rd Annual Report, FY89, 7304–1
U.S. Direct Investment Abroad: Detail for Historical-Cost Position and Balance of Payments Flows, 1991, 2702–1.332
U.S. Direct Investment Abroad: Operations of U.S. Parent Companies and Their Foreign Affiliates, Preliminary 1990 Estimates, 2704–5
U.S. Direct Investment Abroad: 1989 Benchmark Survey, Final Results, 2704–5
U.S. Economy into the 21st Century, 6744–19
U.S. Egg and Poultry Statistical Series, 1960-90, 1564–13
U.S. Employment Effects of a North American Free Trade Agreement: A Survey of Issues and Estimated Employment Effects, 6366–3.30
U.S. Energy Industry Financial Developments, 3162–38
U.S. Essential Oil Trade, 1925–15.2
U.S. Export Declaration of Foreign Tobacco Content, 1925–16.307, 1925–16.309
U.S. Export Sales, 1922–3
U.S. Exports and Imports by Harmonized Commodity, 6-Digit Harmonized Commodity by Country, 2424–13
U.S. Exports: Harmonized Schedule B, Commodity by Country, 2424–10
U.S. Exports of Merchandise, 2422–13
U.S. Exports to Latin America and the Caribbean: A State by State Overview 1987-90, 2048–160
U.S. Exports to Mexico: A State-by-State Overview, 1987-91, 2048–154
U.S. Farming Sector Entering the 1990's: Annual Report on the Status of Family Farms, 1504–4
U.S. Financial Data, 9391–4
U.S. Fire Administration Report to Congress, 9434–7
U.S. Foreign Fishery Allocations, 7006–5
U.S. Foreign Trade Highlights, 1991, 2044–37
U.S. Foreign Trade. Schedule B, Statistical Classification of Domestic and Foreign Commodities Exported from the U.S., 2428–5
U.S. Foreign Trade Update: Monthly Analysis for [Date], 2042–34
U.S. Foreign Trade: Waterborne Exports and General Imports. Trade Area, District, Port, Type Service, and U.S. Flag, 2422–7
U.S. Fresh Vegetable Exports, 1925–34.330
U.S. Fruit Industry and the North American Free Trade Agreement, 1561–6.304
U.S. General Imports: Cotton Manufacturers, 2046–8.1

U.S. General Imports: Cotton or Man-Made Fiber Manufacturers, 2046–8.7
U.S. General Imports: Customs Import Value, 2046–9
U.S. General Imports: Man-Made Fiber Manufacturers, 2046–8.3
U.S. General Imports of Cotton Manufacturers (Customs Value), 2046–9.4
U.S. General Imports of Cotton or Man-Made Fiber Manufacturers (Customs Value), 2046–9.8
U.S. General Imports of Cotton, Wool, Man-Made Fiber, and Vegetable Fiber (Except Cotton) and Silk Blend Textiles, 2042–27
U.S. General Imports of Man-Made Fiber Manufacturers (Customs Value), 2046–9.2
U.S. General Imports of Vegetable Fibers (Except Cotton) and Silk Blend Manufacturers (Customs Value), 2046–9.9
U.S. General Imports of Wool Manufacturers (Customs Value), 2046–9.1
U.S. General Imports: Quantity Totals, 2046–8
U.S. General Imports: Vegetable Fibers Manufacturers, 2046–8.6
U.S. General Imports: Wool Manufacturers, 2046–8.2
U.S. Geological Survey Yearbook, FY91, 5664–8
U.S. Government Annual Report, 1991, 8104–2
U.S. Government Printing Office Annual Report, 26204–1
U.S. Gulf Environmental Technical Assistance: Report to Congress, 9188–117
U.S. Health Expenditure Performance: An International Comparison and Data Update, 4652–1.322
U.S. Horticultural Trade with Caribbean Basin Initiative Beneficiary Countries, 1991, 1925–34.329
U.S. Import and Export Price Indexes, 6762–13, 6762–15
U.S. Imports in the 1980s: Some Insights from a Disaggregate Analysis, 9385–8.138
U.S. Imports of Fruits and Vegetables Under Plant Quarantine Regulations, FY89, 1524–7
U.S. Imports of Merchandise, 2422–14
U.S. Imports of Textiles and Apparel Under the Multifiber Arrangement: Annual Report for 1991, 9884–18
U.S. Industrial Outlook, 1992, 2044–28
U.S. Institute of Peace, Biennial Report, 29594–1
U.S. International Air Travel Statistics, 7302–2
U.S. International Development Cooperation Agency, Congressional Presentation, FY93, 9904–4
U.S. International Sales and Purchases of Private Services: U.S. Cross-Border Transactions, 1986-91; and Sales by Affiliates, 1989-90, 2702–1.336
U.S. International Trade Commission, 1991 Annual Report, 9884–1
U.S. International Transactions in 1991, 9362–1.304
U.S. Manufactures Trade Performance, 2042–35
U.S. Market Access in Latin America: Recent Liberalization Measures and Remaining Barriers (With a Special Case Study on Chile). Report to the Committee on Finance of the U.S. Senate on Investigation No. 332-318 Under Section 332 of the Tariff Act of 1930, 9886–4.184
U.S. Marshals Service, Director's Report, FY91, 6294–1
U.S. Merchandise Trade: Exports and General Imports by Country, Standard International Trade Classification Revision 3, Country by Commodity, 2424–12
U.S. Merchandise Trade: Exports, General Imports, and Imports for Consumption, Standard International Trade Classification Revision 3, Commodity by Country, 2422–12
U.S. Merchant Marine Data Sheet, 7702–1
U.S. Merchant Vessel Logbooks, 9516–1.9
U.S. Merit Systems Protection Board Annual Report for FY91, 9494–5
U.S. Military Strengths Worldwide Fact Sheet, as of (Date), 3542–9
U.S. Mint, Annual Report of the Director, 8204–1
U.S. Mint Authorization, the Bureau of Engraving and Printing and the U.S. Secret Service Counterfeit Division, 21248–164
U.S. Multinational Companies: Operations in 1990, 2702–1.329
U.S. National Acid Precipitation Assessment Program: Mission, Goals, and Program Plan, Post 1990, 14358–3
U.S. National Commission on Libraries and Information Science Annual Report, 1990-91, 15634–1
U.S. Natural Gas Imports and Exports, 1991, 3162–4.301
U.S. Nuclear Regulatory Commission, 1991 Annual Report, 9634–2
U.S. Office of Government Ethics, Second Biennial Report to Congress, 9834–1
U.S. Oil and Gas Reserves, 3166–14
U.S. Overseas Loans and Grants and Assistance from International Organizations, 9914–5
U.S. Parole Commission Annual Report, 6004–3
U.S. Participation in Peacekeeping Operations. United Nations, 26123–404
U.S. Participation in the United Nations: Report by the President to the Congress for the Year 1991, 7004–5
U.S. Petroleum Developments: 1991, 3162–6.301
U.S. Petroleum Supply, 3164–2.1
U.S. Petroleum Trade, 1991, 3162–6.303
U.S. Plumbing Products: An Export Market Plan, 2048–156
U.S. Port Development Expenditure Report (1946-89), 7708–6
U.S. Possessions Corporation Returns, 1989: Data Release, 8302–2.326
U.S. Postal Inspection Service: Semiannual Report, 9862–2
U.S. Postal Service Cost Segments and Components, FY91, 9864–4
U.S. Postal Service: Pricing Postal Services in a Competitive Environment, 26119–384
U.S. Processing Snap Bean Industry: A Commodity Highlight, 1561–11.305
U.S. Produce Industry and the North American Free Trade Agreement, 1504–9.1
U.S. Production Trends for High-Protein Soybean Meal, 1561–3.301
U.S. Quality of Cotton Classed Under Smith-Doxey Act, 1309–15
U.S. Railroad Retirement Board Statistical Tables, Data Through FY90, 9704–2
U.S. Railroad Retirement Board, 1992 Annual Report for Fiscal Year Ended Sept. 30, 1991, 9704–1
U.S. Responses to Excessive National Maritime Claims. Limits in the Seas, 7006–8.7
U.S. Rice Distribution Patterns, 1988/89, 1564–11
U.S. Rice Production Practices and Costs, 1988, 1568–309
U.S. Savings Bonds Issued and Redeemed Through (Month), 8242–1
U.S. Secret Service Investigative Activity, FY87-91, 8464–1
U.S. Securities and Exchange Commission Fifty-seventh Annual Report, 1991, 9734–2
U.S. Seed Exports: Foreign Agricultural Service Circular Series, 1925–13
U.S. Sentencing Commission Annual Report, 1991, 17664–1
U.S. Small Business Administration Annual Report, FY90, 9764–1
U.S. Small Business Administration Annual Report: FY90 Guarantees and 8(A) Contracts, 9764–1.2
U.S. Small Business Administration Annual Report, FY91, 9764–1
U.S. Small Business Administration Annual Report: FY91 Guarantees and 8(A) Contracts, 9764–1.2
U.S. Spice Trade, 1925–15.1
U.S. Tax Court Analysis of Cases Closed (By Dockets), Oct. 1, 1990-Sept. 30, 1991, 18224–3
U.S. Tax Court, FY91 Statistical Information, 18224–5
U.S. Tax Court, FY92 Statistical Information, 18224–5
U.S. Textile Imports and Exports, 1561–1.301
U.S. Tobacco Imports, 1561–10.306
U.S. Tobacco Trade, 1984-91, 1925–16.308
U.S. Tomato Statistics, 1960-90, 1568–310
U.S. Trade and Prospects. Foreign Agricultural Service Circular Series: Dairy, Livestock, and Poultry, 1925–32
U.S. Trade Shifts in Selected Commodity Areas, 9882–9
U.S. Trade Shifts in Selected Commodity Areas, Annual Report for 1991, 9884–25
U.S. Trade with Eastern Europe. 1987-91 Highlights and Outlook for 1992, 2048–158
U.S. Trade with Puerto Rico and U.S. Possessions, 2424–11
U.S. Trade with the European Community, 7144–7
U.S. Transportation Deaths Decline Third Year in a Row in 1991, 9614–6
U.S. Underwater Diving Fatality Statistics, 2144–5
U.S. Uranium Enrichment, 1991 Report, 3354–7
U.S. Waterborne Exports and General Imports: Trade Area, District, Port, Type Service, and U.S. Flag, 2422–7
U.S. West Communications: Phoenix, Ariz.; Minneapolis, Minn.; Denver, Colo. Health Hazard Evaluation Report, 4248–93
U.S./Mexico Electricity Trade Study, 3408–2
USA/USSR: Facts and Figures, 2328–80
U.S.-Canada Memorandum of Understanding on Softwood Lumber, 1986, 21728–78
USCGC Tamaroa—Modern Day Lifesavers, 2152–8.303

USDA Announces Final Compliance Figures for 1990 Acreage Reduction Program, 1004–20.1
USDA Announces Final Compliance Figures for 1991 Acreage Reduction Program, 1004–20.3
USDA Announces Final Results of 1991 Program Signup, 1004–20.2
USDA Commodity Forecasts: Inaccuracies Found May Lead to Underestimates of Budget Outlays, 26131–94
USDA Improves Inspection Program for Canadian Meat, but Some Concerns Remain. Food Safety and Quality, 26113–595
USDA Reports Certificate Exchange Activity Through (Date), 1802–16
USDA Revenues: A Descriptive Compendium, 26113–602
USDA's Method of Estimating Fruit and Tree Nut Production, 1561–6.302
Use of Death Certificates for Mesothelioma Surveillance, 4042–3.351
Use of Electronic Monitoring in the U.S.: 1989 Update, 6066–20.23
Use of Equity Positions by Banks: The Japanese Evidence, 9393–8.302
Use of Government Supply Sources at the Savannah River Site, 3006–5.33
Use of Private Providers Should Be Better Controlled. VA Health Care, 26121–474
Use of Restraint Devices To Prevent Collision Injuries and Deaths Among Welfare-Supported Children, 4042–3.312
Use of Seatbelts in Cars with Automatic Belts, 4042–3.320
User Accountability, 236–3.6
User Friendly Facts: A Resource Book, 1992, 2904–15
User's Guide to BEA Information, 2702–1.308, 2704–6
USIA Office of Inspector General Semiannual Report to the Congress, Oct. 1, 1991-Mar. 31, 1992, 9852–2
Using Cluster Analysis as a Tool for Economic and Financial Analysis, 9385–8.128
Using Public Pensions To Balance State and Local Budgets: The Impact on Public Employees, Retirees, and Taxpayers, 21148–66
Using SIPP To Analyze Black-White Differences in Youth Employment, 2626–10.146
Using Switching Models To Study Business Cycle Asymmetries: 1. Overview of Methodology and Application, 9385–8.139
Using the Behavioral Risk Factor Surveillance System To Monitor Year 2000 Objectives Among American Indians, 4042–3.346
USITC Investigations Under Section 332 of the Tariff Act of 1930, 9886–4
USITC Investigations Under Section 733(a) and 735(b) of the Tariff Act of 1930, As Amended, 9886–14
USITC Investigations Under Sections 703(a) and 705(b) of the Tariff Act of 1930, As Amended, 9886–15
USITC Investigations Under Sections 703(a), 733(a), 705(b), and 735(b) of the Tariff Act of 1930, As Amended, 9886–19
U.S.-Mexican Trade and Investment Data. North American Free Trade Agreement, 26119–417
U.S.-Mexico Trade: Assessment of Mexico's Environmental Controls for New Companies, 26119–416
U.S.-Mexico Trade: Survey of U.S. Border Infrastructure Needs, 26123–368
USSR Agriculture and Trade Report, Situation and Outlook Series, 1524–4.1
USSR Construction Sector, 2042–1.301
Usual Weekly Earnings of Wage and Salary Workers, 6742–20
Utah Cooperative Snow Survey Data of Federal-State-Private Cooperative Snow Surveys, Water Year 1991, 1264–14.7
Utilization of IHS and Tribal Direct and Contract General Hospitals, FY90 and U.S. Non-Federal Short-Stay Hospitals, CY89, 4084–5
Utilization of Inpatient Hospital Services by Rural Medicare Beneficiaries, 17206–2.33
Utilization Review: Information on External Review Organizations, 26121–490

VA Health Care: Compliance with Joint Commission Accreditation Requirements Is Improving, 26121–441
VA Health Care: Copayment Exemption Procedures Should Be Improved, 26121–464
VA Health Care: Use of Private Providers Should Be Better Controlled, 26121–474
VA Health Care: Verifying Veterans' Reported Income Could Generate Millions in Copayment Revenues, 26121–479
Vaccinia (Smallpox) Vaccine. Recommendations of the Immunization Practices Advisory Committee (ACIP), 4206–2.50
Validation Study of the Industrial Fuel Chip Supply Simulator (IFCHIPSS), 9806–9.13
Validity of Clinical Color Vision Tests for Air Traffic Control Specialists, 7506–10.125
Value of Cooperative Benefits to Southern Dairy Farmers, 1128–68
Value of Double Leverage, Bank Holding Companies and Capital Regulation, 9366–6.291
Value of Home and Monthly Rent. 1990 Census Questionnaire Content Bulletin, 2326–23.1
Value of New Construction Put in Place, Current Construction Reports, 2382–4
Value of Product Shipments, 1990 Annual Survey of Manufactures, 2506–14.1
Value-Added for the U.S. Agricultural Sector, 1541–1.321
Vanadium: International Strategic Minerals Inventory Summary Report, 5666–21.11
Vanadium: Mineral Industry Surveys, 5612–1.26
Vanadium: Minerals Yearbook, Volume 1, 1990, 5604–20.61
Variation in Medicare Global Service Policies: Relationship to Current Payment and Implications for a Fee Schedule, 17266–2.2
Vector-Autoregression Forecast Models for the Third District States, 9387–8.282
Vegetable Fibers (Except Cotton) and Silk Blend Manufacturers (Customs Value). U.S. General Imports, 2046–9.9
Vegetable Fibers Manufacturers. U.S. General Imports, 2046–8.6
Vegetables, 1621–12
Vegetables and Specialties Situation and Outlook Report, 1561–11
Vegetables and Specialties Situation and Outlook Yearbook, 1561–11
Vegetables, Annual Summary, 1621–25
Vegetables Summary, California, 1990. Agricultural Chemical Usage, 1616–1.2
Vegetables: 1991 Preliminary Acreage, Yield, and Production, 1621–25.1
Vegetables: 1991 Summary, 1621–25.2
Vending Machines (Coin-Operated), 1991, Current Industrial Report, 2506–12.10
Veneer Recovery of Douglas-Fir from the Coast and Cascade Ranges of Oregon and Washington, 1208–396
Verifying Veterans' Reported Income Could Generate Millions in Copayment Revenues. VA Health Care, 26121–479
Vermiculite in 1991: Mineral Industry Surveys, Annual Report, 5614–5.21
Vessel Inventory Report, As of July 1, 1991, 7702–2
Veterans Affairs, Annual Report of the Secretary, FY91, 8604–3
Veterans Benefits Under Current Educational Programs, 8604–9
VHSIC Hardware Description Language (VHDL). Software Standard, 2216–2.214
Victim Programs To Serve Native Americans, 6066–31.1
Victims of Crime Act of 1984 As Amended: A Report to Congress by the Attorney General, 6064–37
Vietnam Population Dynamics and Prospects, 2326–18.65
Vietnam-Era Cohort: Employment and Earnings, 6722–1.326
Visa Office, 1990 Report, 7184–1
Vital and Health Statistics Series 1: Program and Collection Procedures, 4147–1
Vital and Health Statistics Series 2: Data Evaluation and Methods Research, 4147–2
Vital and Health Statistics Series 10: Data from the National Health Interview Survey, 4147–10
Vital and Health Statistics Series 13: Data on Health Resources Utilization, 4147–13
Vital and Health Statistics Series 16: Compilations of Advance Data from Vital and Health Statistics, 4147–16
Vital and Health Statistics Series 20: Data from the National Vital Statistics System, 4147–20
Vital and Health Statistics Series 21: Data on Natality, Marriage, and Divorce, 4147–21
Vital Link to Trade in Tree Fruit Between Mexico and California Is Transportation, 1504–9.1
Vital Statistics of the U.S., 1989. Volume II: Mortality, Part B, 4144–3
Vitamin Supplement Use and Its Correlates Among Elderly Japanese Men Residing on Oahu, HI, 4042–3.373
Vocational Education in the U.S.: 1969-90, 4828–42
Volume Adjustments Used in State Medicaid Programs and Rate Setting Systems, 17206–2.34
Volume and Default Trends for FY89-91. Parent and Supplemental Student Loans, 26121–473
Voluntary Foreign Aid Programs, Report of American Voluntary Agencies Engaged in Overseas Relief and Development Registered with the Agency for International Development, 1992, 9914–9
Voting Accessibility for the Elderly and Handicapped Act, 21428–11

Voting Practices in the United Nations, FY91, Report to Congress, 7004–18

Wage and Compensation Changes in Settlements, 1991, 6722–1.325
Wage Statistics of Class I Railroads in the U.S., 1991, 9484–5
Wage Withholding Not Fulfilling Expectations. Interstate Child Support, 26121–445
Wages, Family Background, and Endogenous Schooling, 6886–6.94
Wages in the South, 6942–8
Wagner's Hypothesis: A Local Perspective, 9377–9.133
Walnut Situation and Outlook, 1925–34.344
Wanted and Unwanted Births Reported by Mothers 15-44 Years of Age: U.S., 1976, 4147–16.6
War on Drugs: A Progress Report, 236–3.4
War on Drugs: Heroin Price, Purity, and Quantities Seized Over the Past 10 Years, 26119–404
War Zone Stress Among Returning Persian Gulf Troops: A Preliminary Report, 8704–7
War Zone Traumas and PTSD Symptomatology, 8704–6
Washington Cooperative Snow Survey Data of Federal-State-Private Cooperative Snow Surveys, 1264–14.4
Washington, D.C., Metropolitan Area Drug Study Technical Reports, 4496–12
Washington State's Efforts To Address Comparable Worth. Pay Equity, 26119–410
Waste Management Facility Annual Dangerous Waste Report, 1991, 3224–6
Waste Minimization: Major Problems of Data Reliability and Validity Identified, 26131–98
Wastepaper Recycling and the Future Timber Market, 1504–9.1
Water Bank Program: Compilation of Status of Agreements, 1802–5
Water Bank Program: From Inception of Program Through Sept. 30, 1991, 1804–21
Water, Land, and Related Data: 1990 Summary Statistics, 5824–12
Water Pollution Monitoring: EPA's Permit Compliance System Could Be Used More Effectively, 26125–46
Water Pollution: State Revolving Funds Insufficient To Meet Wastewater Treatment Needs, 26113–561
Water Quality in the Upper Floridan Aquifer in the Vicinity of Drainage Wells, Orlando, Fla., 5666–28.19
Water Quality: Information on USDA's Water Quality Cost-Share Programs, 26113–572
Water Quality of Fountain and Monument Creeks, South-Central Colorado, with Emphasis on Relation of Water Quality to Stream Classifications, 5666–27.25
Water Resources Activities in Florida, 1990-91, 5666–26.18
Water Resources Activities in New York, FY89, 5666–26.22
Water Resources Activities, North Dakota District, FY90, 5666–26.20
Water Resources Activities of the Mississippi District, 1990-91, 5666–26.27
Water Resources Activities of the USGS in Montana, Oct. 1989-Sept. 1991, 5666–26.21
Water Resources Activities of the USGS in South Dakota, FY89-90, 5666–26.16
Water Resources Activities of the USGS in Wyoming, Oct. 1989-Sept. 1991, 5666–26.26
Water Resources Activities of the USGS: Selected States, 5666–26
Water Resources Data for (State), Water Year 1990, 5666–10
Water Resources Data for (State), Water Year 1991, 5666–12
Water Resources Development by the U.S. Army Corps of Engineers in (State), 1989, 3756–1
Water Resources Development by the U.S. Army Corps of Engineers in (State), 1991, 3756–2
Water Resources Investigations in Pennsylvania: Programs and Activities of the USGS, 1990-91, 5666–26.25
Water Resources Investigations in Puerto Rico and the U.S. Virgin Islands, 1986-88, 5666–26.19
Water Resources: Local Area Studies, 5666–27
Water Resources: Local Sponsors' Views on Corps' Implementation of Project Cost Sharing, 26113–548
Water Resources: The Corps of Engineers' Dredging Program for Small Business Firms, 26113–589
Water Supply Outlook and Summary for Oregon, Oct. 1, 1992, 1264–9
Water Supply Outlook for Arizona, 1266–2.2
Water Supply Outlook for Colorado, 1266–2.3
Water Supply Outlook for Idaho, 1266–2.4
Water Supply Outlook for Nevada, 1266–2.6
Water Supply Outlook for New Mexico, 1266–2.11
Water Supply Outlook for Oregon, 1266–2.7
Water Supply Outlook for the Northeastern U.S., 2182–3
Water Supply Outlook for the Western U.S., 1262–1
Water Supply Outlook for Utah, 1266–2.8
Water Supply Outlook for Washington, 1266–2.9
Water Supply Outlook for Wyoming, 1266–2.10
Water Treatment Technology Costs Associated with Offshore Oil and Gas Production, 3166–6.66
Water Use in the St. Jones River Basin, Kent County, Delaware, 1983-86, 5666–24.10
Water Use: Selected States, 5666–24
Water Withdrawal and Use in Maryland, 1987, 5666–24.15
Waterborne Commerce of the U.S., 3754–3
Waterborne-Disease Outbreaks, 1989-90, 4202–7.301
Waterfowl Production on the Woodworth Station in South-central North Dakota, 1965-81, 5508–120
Water-Level and Pumpage Data for Las Vegas Valley, Clark County, Nevada, 1986-90, 5666–28.23
Water-Quality Trends in New Jersey Streams, 5666–27.27
We Asked...You Told Us. 1990 Census Questionnaire Content Bulletins, 2326–23
Weather in U.S. Agriculture: Monthly Temperature and Precipitation by State and Farm Production Region, 1950-90, 1544–28
Weekly Climate Bulletin, 2182–6
Weekly Coal Production, 3162–1
Weekly Consolidated Condition Report of Large Commercial Banks in the U.S., 9365–1.3
Weekly Petroleum Status Report, 3162–32
Weekly Weather and Crop Bulletin, 2182–7
Weighing Costs and Benefits of Adequate Prenatal Care for 12,023 Births in Missouri's Medicaid Program, 1988, 4042–3.365
Weights, Measures, and Conversion Factors for Agricultural Commodities and Their Products, 1508–3
Welded Stainless Steel Pipes from the Republic of Korea and Taiwan. Determinations of the Commission in Investigations Nos. 731-TA-540 and 541 (Preliminary) Under the Tariff Act of 1930, Together with the Information Obtained in the Investigations, 9886–14.338
Welded Stainless Steel Pipes from the Republic of Korea and Taiwan. Determinations of the Commission in Investigations Nos. 731-TA-540-541 (Final) Under the Tariff Act of 1930, Together with the Information Obtained in the Investigations, 9886–14.365
Welfare to Work: Effectiveness of Tribal JOBS Programs Unknown, 26121–460
Welfare to Work: States Serve Least Job-Ready While Meeting JOBS Participation Rates, 26121–489
Western Area Power Administration, 1991 Annual Report, 3254–1
Western North Pacific Typhoons—1991, 2152–8.303
Wetlands: Status and Trends in the Conterminous U.S. Mid-1970's to Mid-1980's, 5508–89
What About (Hurricane) Bob?, 2152–8.301
What Do Early Warning Models Tell Us About Asset Risk and Bank Failures?, 9379–15.302
What Do I Need To Map Out 1990 Census Data?, 2308–66
What Is the Impact of Pensions on Saving?, 9373–27.5
What Moves Investment? Cash Flows in a Forward-Looking Model of Capital Expenditures, 9385–8.129
What Past Recoveries Say About the Outlook for New England, 9373–1.315
What Researchers Have Learned from the National Longitudinal Surveys About Youth Unemployment, 6728–42
Wheat Situation and Outlook Report, 1561–12
Wheat Situation and Outlook Yearbook, 1561–12
When a Bank's Not a Bank—Nonbanks in the Financial Marketplace, 9391–16.305
When Do Regulators Close Banks? When Should They?, 9387–8.263
Where Have All the Data Gone?, 2152–8.302
Where the Jobs Were: Job Creation in the Late 1980's. Statistical Brief, 2326–17.47
Whistleblower Protection: Survey of Federal Employees on Misconduct and Protection from Reprisal, 26119–413
White Papers. Office of National Drug Control Policy, 236–1
Who Could Own Homes in the Year 2000? Statistical Brief, 2326–17.52
Who Makes Do-It-Yourself Home Improvements? Statistical Brief, 2326–17.45

Wholesale and Retail Trade Industries: Evaluating Your Firm's Injury and Illness Record, 6886–4.4
Who's Helping Out? Support Networks Among American Families: 1988, 2546–20.21
Who's Minding the Kids? Child Care Arrangements: Fall 1988, 2546–20.24
Why Do Some Caregivers of Disabled and Frail Elderly Quit?, 4652–1.305
Why Does the Paper-Bill Spread Predict Real Economic Activity?, 9375–13.67
Why New England Went the Way of Texas Rather than California, 9373–1.302
Why State Medicaid Costs Vary: A First Look, 9373–27.1
Why U.S. Farm Income Is Record High, 1541–1.302
Wild Card Option in T-Bond Futures Is Relatively Worthless, 9371–10.71
Wilderness Management: Accountability for Forest Service Funds Needs Improvement, 26113–550
Wildfire Statistics, 1984-90, 1204–4
Wildlife and Vegetation of Unmanaged Douglas-Fir Forests, 1208–386
Wildlife Habitats of the North Coast of California: New Techniques for Extensive Forest Inventory, 1208–414
Will the Real Price of Housing Drop Sharply in the 1990s?, 9381–1.305
Wine Sector in Brazil, 1925–34.341
Wines: Monthly Statistical Release, 8486–1.2
Winners and Losers Under PPS, 17206–2.40
Winners of the Secretary's Award for Innovations in Health Promotion and Disease Prevention, 4042–3.322
Winter Fuels Report, 3162–45
Winter Wheat and Rye Seedings, 1621–30
Wire Ropes Used for Hoisting in U.S. Mines, 5608–172
Wiring Devices and Supplies, 1990, Current Industrial Report, 2506–12.18
Wiring Devices and Supplies, 1991, Current Industrial Report, 2506–12.18
Wisconsin's Timberland Plantations, 1983, 1206–34.9
Within DRG Case Complexity Change in FY90, 17206–2.39
Wollastonite and Zeolites: Minerals Yearbook, Volume 1, 1990, 5604–20.68
Women and Minorities in Science and Engineering: An Update, 9624–20
Women in Jail, 1989, 6066–19.66
Women in NIH Extramural Grant Programs, FY81-90, 4434–18
Women Methadone Patients Taught Skills To Reduce Heterosexual HIV Transmission, 15-Month Followup, 4042–3.353
Women with Work Disabilities, 6564–1.2
Women Workers: Outlook to 2005, 6564–1.1
Women's Educational Equity Act Program: Report of Activities, 1988-92, 4804–2
Women's Health: FDA Needs To Ensure More Study of Gender Differences in Prescription Drug Testing, 26121–486
Wood Products: Foreign Agricultural Service Circular Series. International Trade and Foreign Markets, 1925–36
Wood Products: International Trade and Foreign Markets. Annual Statistical Trade Issue. Foreign Agricultural Service, 1925–36
Wool and Mohair, 1623–6
Wool Manufacturers (Customs Value). U.S. General Imports, 2046–9.1
Wool Manufacturers. U.S. General Imports, 2046–8.2
Wool, Summary of 1992 Support Program and Related Information: ASCS Commodity Fact Sheet, 1806–4.11
Work and Family, 6726–2
Work Experience of the Population in 1991, 6726–1.51
Work Hour Allocations to High Growth and Low Growth Post Offices. Postal Service, 26119–379
Work Patterns of Women Near Retirement. Work and Family, 6726–2.4
Work Permit and Death and Injury Reporting Systems in Selected States. Child Labor, 26121–451
Work Years and Personnel Costs, Executive Branch, U.S. Government, FY90. Federal Civilian Workforce Statistics, 9844–31
Worker Displacement Increased Sharply in Recent Recession, 6726–1.48
Worker Rights in U.S. Policy, 1991, 6366–4.11
Workers' Compensation: Coverage, Benefits, and Costs, 1989, 4742–1.311
Workers' Compensation: State Enactments in 1991, 6722–1.310
Workers' Compensation: 1984-88 Benchmark Revisions, 4742–1.322
Workers on Flexible and Shift Schedules, 6726–1.50
Workers with Low Earnings: 1964-90, 2546–6.74
Workforce Quality and Federal Procurement: An Assessment, 9498–17
Working Group Report on Primary Prevention of Hypertension, 4478–198
Working Paper Series, Federal Reserve Bank of Atlanta, 9371–10
Working Paper Series, Federal Reserve Bank of Boston, 9373–27
Working Paper Series, Federal Reserve Bank of Chicago, 9375–13
Working Paper Series, Federal Reserve Bank of Richmond, 9389–19
Working Papers, Federal Reserve Bank of Cleveland, 9377–9
Working Papers, Federal Reserve Bank of San Francisco, 9393–10
Working Papers of the National Advisory Committee on Semiconductors, 15036–1
Working Women: A Chartbook, 6748–85
Workplace Literacy: Reshaping the American Workforce, 4808–43
World Agricultural Production: Foreign Agricultural Service Circular Series, 1925–28
World Agricultural Supply and Demand Estimates, 1522–5
World Agriculture Current Trends and Perspectives, 1522–3
World Agriculture Situation and Outlook Report, 1522–3
World Almond Situation in Selected Countries, 1925–34.337
World and U.S. Agricultural Outlook, 1504–9.1
World Cigarette Production and Trade, 1925–16.312
World Citrus Situation, 1925–34.301
World Cocoa Situation. Foreign Agricultural Service Circular Series: Cocoa, 1925–9
World Coffee Situation: Foreign Agricultural Service Circular Series, 1925–5
World Cotton Situation, 1925–4.2
World Cotton Situation: World Cotton Statistical Supplement, 1967/68-1991/92, 1925–4.3
World Cotton Situation: World Cotton Statistical Supplement, 1967-91, 1925–4.3
World Cotton Statistical Supplement, 1967/68-1991/92, 1925–4.3
World Cotton Statistical Supplement, 1967-91, 1925–4.3
World Dairy Situation: Foreign Agricultural Service Circular Series, 1925–10
World Data Center A, Oceanography: Oceanographic Data Exchange, 1990, 2144–15
World Factbook, 1992, 9114–2
World Fresh Citrus Situation, 1925–34.323
World Fresh Deciduous Fruit Update, 1925–34.342
World Grain Outlook, 1504–9.1
World Grain Situation and Outlook, 1925–2.1
World Grain Trade Prospects: an Australian Perspective, 1504–9.1
World Honey Situation, 1925–14.1
World Kiwifruit Production and Trade Situation in Selected Countries, 1925–34.314
World Livestock Situation. Foreign Agricultural Service Circular Series: Dairy, Livestock, and Poultry, 1925–33.2
World Military Expenditures and Arms Transfers, 1990, 9824–1
World Oilseed Situation and Outlook, 1925–1.1
World Outlook for Canned Deciduous Fruit, 1925–34.319
World Population Profile: 1991, 2324–9
World Poultry Situation. Foreign Agricultural Service Circular Series: Dairy, Livestock, and Poultry, 1925–33.1
World Raisin Situation, 1925–34.321, 1925–34.348
World Refugee Report: A Report Submitted to the Congress as Part of the Consultations on FY92 Refugee Admissions to the U.S., 7004–15
World Refugee Report: A Report Submitted to the Congress as Part of the Consultations on FY93 Refugee Admissions to the U.S., 7004–15
World Sugar Situation and Outlook, 1925–14.2, 1925–14.3
World Tea Situation, 1925–15.3
World Tobacco Prices, 1990, 1925–16.305
World Tobacco Situation: Foreign Agricultural Service Circular Series, 1925–16
World Trade in Canned Mushrooms for Selected Countries, 1925–34.333
World Unmanufactured Tobacco Production, 1925–16.302, 1925–16.310
World Unmanufactured Tobacco Supply and Distribution, 1925–16.311
World Unmanufactured Tobacco Trade, 1925–16.314
World View on Sugar Trade and Prices, 1504–9.1, 1561–14.301
World Wine Situation, 1925–34.325
World Wool Trade During the 1980's, 1561–1.304
Worldwide Cocaine Situation, 1990, 6284–5
Worldwide Heroin Situation, 1990, 6284–6
Worldwide Heroin Situation, 1991, 6284–6

Worldwide Manpower Distribution, by Geographical Area, 3542–20
Worldwide Marine Radiofacsimile Broadcast Schedules, 2182–9
World-Wide Materials, Life Science Studies Highlight: STS-42 Mission, 9506–2.145
Worldwide Reports on AID Population Programs, FY91, 9914–13
Worldwide U.S. Active Duty Military Personnel Casualties, Oct. 1, 1979-Dec. 31, 1991, 3544–40
Would Monetary Policy Be Effective if the OASDI Trust Funds Held Most Treasury Debt?, 4746–26.19

Year in Trade, Operation of the Trade Agreements Program, 43d Report, 1991, 9884–5
Yearbook of Agriculture, 1992: New Crops, New Uses, New Markets, 1004–18
Yellowstone Grizzly Bear Investigations, Annual Report of the Interagency Study Team, 1991, 5544–4
Young Husband-Wife Households with Children, 1702–1.302
Youth and Alcohol, 4006–10
Youth and Alcohol: Controlling Alcohol Advertising That Appeals to Youth, 4006–10.5
Youth and Alcohol: Laws and Enforcement. Is the 21-Year-Old Drinking Age a Myth?, 4006–10.4
Youth Labor Force Expected To Be Smaller This Summer, 6744–13
Yukon Delta Oceanography and Meteorology, 2176–1.40

Zinc Industry: Mineral Industry Surveys, 5612–1.27
Zinc: Mineral Industry Surveys, 5612–1.27
Zinc: Minerals Yearbook, Volume 1, 1990, 5604–20.62
Zirconium and Hafnium: Minerals Yearbook, Volume 1, 1990, 5604–20.63
Zirconium: International Strategic Minerals Inventory Summary Report, 5666–21.12

$1.46 Billion in Funds Now Available for Low Income Housing, 5006–3.86
$10.8 Million in McKinney Act Funds Awarded for Comprehensive Services to Homeless Families, 5006–3.87
15-Month Followup of Women Methadone Patients Taught Skills To Reduce Heterosexual HIV Transmission, 4042–3.353
19th Annual Report of the Board of Directors of the Rural Telephone Bank, FY90, 1244–4
20th Annual Report of the Board of Directors of the Rural Telephone Bank, FY91, 1244–4
30th Annual Report for FY91, Federal Maritime Commission, 9334–1
35th Annual Report, Colorado River Storage Project and Participating Projects in FY91, 5824–3
$35.1 Million in Historic Preservation Grants Apportioned, 5544–9
$45.5 Million Goes to Six Coastal States in 1992 8(g) Payment, 5306–4.14
48th Shuttle Mission To Be Longest, Focus on Weightlessness: STS-50 Mission, 9506–2.150
49th Shuttle Flight To Test Feasibility of Tethered Satellite: STS-46 Mission, 9506–2.147
51st Annual Report of the Foreign-Trade Zones Board to the Congress of the U.S., For the Fiscal Year Ended Sept. 30, 1989, 2044–30
52nd Annual Report of the Foreign-Trade Zones Board to the Congress of the U.S., For the Fiscal Year Ended Sept. 30, 1990, 2044–30
$55 Million Jump in Receipts Reported by Congressional Campaigns, 9276–1.103
56th Annual Report, FY90. Federal Communications Commission, 9284–4
57th Annual Report, FY91, Federal Communications Commission, 9284–4
57th Annual Report of the U.S. Securities and Exchange Commission, FY91, 9734–2
78th Annual Report, 1991, Board of Governors of the Federal Reserve System, 9364–1
94 Resident Management Groups Share $4.6 Million To Help Tenants Manage Their Own Public Housing Communities, 5006–3.100
94th Annual Report of the Register of Copyrights, For the Fiscal Year Ending Sept. 30, 1991, 26404–2
100 Companies Receiving the Largest Dollar Volume of Prime Contract Awards, FY91, 3544–5
$140 Million To Fight Drugs in Public Housing Announced, 5006–3.81
500 Contractors Receiving the Largest Dollar Volume of Prime Contract Awards for Research, Development, Test, and Evaluation, FY91, 3544–4

1,200 Bits Per Second Two-Wire Duplex Modems for Data Communications Use on Telephone-Type Circuits. Telecommunications Standard, 2216–2.205
1978 Summary: National Ambulatory Medical Care Survey, 4147–16.6
1982 Benchmark Input-Output Accounts of the U.S., 2708–17
1984-90 Wildfire Statistics, 1204–4
1985 American Housing Survey for Metropolitan Areas, Supplement, 2485–8
1986 American Housing Survey for Metropolitan Areas, Supplement, 2485–8
1986 U.S.-Canada Memorandum of Understanding on Softwood Lumber, 21728–78
1987 American Housing Survey for Metropolitan Areas, Supplement, 2485–8
1987 Census of Manufactures. Subject Series, Concentration Ratios in Manufacturing, 2497–6
1987 Census of Manufactures. Subject Series. Distribution of Sales by Class of Customer, 2497–4
1987 Census of Retail Trade: Subject Series. Merchandise Line Sales, 2399–3
1987 Economic Censuses, CD-ROM Technical Documentation, 2306–8
1987 Economic Censuses, Characteristics of Business Owners, 2328–59
1987 Economic Censuses on CD-ROM, 2326–22
1988 and 1989 Company Effective Tax Rates Higher Than in Prior Years. Tax Policy, 26119–289
1988 National Health Interview Survey, CD-ROM. Vital and Health Statistics Series 10, 4147–10.184
1989 American Housing Survey for Metropolitan Areas, 2485–6
1989 Annual Report of the Attorney General of the U.S., 6004–1
1989 Annual Report of the Interagency Council on the Homeless, 14364–1
1989 Carload Waybill Statistics: Territorial Distribution, Traffic and Revenue by Commodity Classes, 7604–6
1989 Impact of International Visitor Spending on State Economies, 2908–28
1989-90 Report of the SEFC Billfish Program, 2164–7
1990 AFDC Recipient Characteristics Study, 4584–7
1990 Annual Report, FDIC, 9294–1
1990 Annual Report of the Attorney General of the U.S., 6004–1
1990 Annual Report of the Interagency Council on the Homeless, 14364–1
1990 Annual Report on Low-Level Radioactive Waste Management Progress, 3004–36
1990 Annual Report on the Food and Agricultural Sciences, From the Secretary of Agriculture to the President and the Congress of the U.S., 1004–19
1990 Annual Report, Resolution Trust Corporation, 9724–1
1990 Annual Survey of Manufactures, 2506–14
1990 Bibliography on Smoking and Health, 4204–19
1990 Census: Limitations in Methods and Procedures To Include the Homeless, 26119–370
1990 Census of Housing: General Housing Characteristics, 2471–1
1990 Census of Population and Housing. Alphabetical Index of Industries and Occupations, 2628–1
1990 Census of Population and Housing. Classified Index of Industries and Occupations, 2628–2
1990 Census of Population and Housing: Guide, 2555–1
1990 Census of Population and Housing: Social, Economic, and Housing Characteristics. Pacific Outlying Areas, 2551–8
1990 Census of Population and Housing: Summary Population and Housing Characteristics, 2551–1
1990 Census of Population and Housing: Summary Social, Economic, and Housing Characteristics, 2551–7
1990 Census of Population and Housing: Summary Tape File 1 on CD-ROM, Technical Documentation, 2308–65
1990 Census of Population and Housing: Summary Tape File 1A Data on CD-ROM, 2551–9
1990 Census of Population and Housing: Summary Tape File 3 on CD-ROM, Technical Documentation, 2308–68

1990 Census of Population and Housing: Summary Tape File 3A Data on CD-ROM, 2551–10
1990 Census of Population: General Population Characteristics, 2531–1, 2531–2
1990 Census of Population: General Population Characteristics. American Indian and Alaska Native Areas, 2531–2.1
1990 Census of State and Federal Correctional Facilities, 6068–218
1990 Census Questionnaire Content Bulletins. We Asked...You Told Us, 2326–23
1990 Clean Air Act: A Tougher Regulatory Challenge Facing Midwest Industry, 9375–1.304
1990 Crop Sugarbeet and Sugarcane Production and Processing Costs, 1561–14.303
1990 Effluent and Environmental Monitoring Report for the Bettis Atomic Power Laboratory, 3324–2.6
1990 Housing Highlights, 2326–21
1990 Housing Highlights: Financial Facts, 2328–83
1990 Merger Decisions, 9294–5
1990 National Shellfish Register of Classified Estuarine Waters, 2178–33
1990 Nationwide Personal Transportation Survey, 7556–6
1990 Needs Survey, Report to Congress: Assessment of Needed Publicly Owned Wastewater Treatment Facilities in the U.S.—Including Federally Recognized Indian Tribes and Alaska Native Villages, 9204–7
1990 Ohio River Navigation System Report, 3754–6
1990 Oil Price Hike in Perspective, 9391–1.301
1990 Report of the President to the Congress on the Administration of the Federal Railroad Safety Act of 1970, 7604–12
1990 Report of the Visa Office, 7184–1
1990 Report on Diving Accidents and Fatalities, Divers Alert Network, 2144–29
1990 Report to Congress on the Federal Home Loan Mortgage Corporation, 5184–8
1990 Report to Congress on the Federal National Mortgage Association, 5184–9
1990 Results Show Need for Fundamental Reform. Decennial Census, 26119–403
1990 Science Report Card: NAEP's Assessment of Fourth, Eighth, and Twelfth Graders. National Assessment of Educational Progress, 4896–8.3
1990 Section 8 Report on Damaged and Threatened National Historic Landmarks and National Natural Landmarks, 5544–16
1990 Statistical Yearbook of the Immigration and Naturalization Service, 6264–2
1990 Summary: National Hospital Discharge Survey, 4146–8.211
1990 Summary Statistics: Water, Land, and Related Data, 5824–12
1990 Update: AIDS in Correctional Facilities, 6064–22
1990-91 Pell Grant End of Year Report, 4804–1
1990-91 Recession in Historical Perspective, 9373–1.301
1991 Accidents, Fatalities and Rates Released for U.S. Aviation, 9614–9
1991 Annual Report, Appalachian Regional Commission, 9084–1
1991 Annual Report, Economic Development Administration, 2064–2
1991 Annual Report, FDIC, 9294–1
1991 Annual Report of the Attorney General of the U.S., 6004–1
1991 Annual Report, Office of Housing and Urban Programs, 9914–4
1991 Annual Report on Alaska's Mineral Resources, 5664–11
1991 Annual Report on the Administration of the Radiation Control for Health and Safety Act of 1968, Public Law 90-602, 4064–13
1991 Annual Tropical Cyclone Report, 3804–8
1991 Bibliography on Smoking and Health, 4204–19
1991 BLM Facts and Figures for Utah, 5724–11.4
1991 Budget Estimates: What Went Wrong. Budget Issues, 26104–23
1991 Catalogue of State Medicaid Program Changes, 4654–19.1
1991 Domestic Cannabis Eradication/Suppression Program, 6284–4
1991 Economic Report of the President, 23844–4
1991 Federal Transit Administration Grant Assistance Programs, Statistical Summaries, 7884–10
1991 in Review: Inter-American Foundation, 14424–1
1991 Interstate Cost Estimate, 21648–66
1991 New York City Housing and Vacancy Survey, 2488–3
1991 Pacific Northwest Loads and Resources Study, 3224–3
1991 Pacific Northwest Loads and Resources Study: Non-Utility Generation Supplement, 3224–3.4
1991 Pacific Northwest Loads and Resources Study, Pacific Northwest Economic and Electricity Use Forecast, 1991: Technical Appendix, Volume 1, 3224–3.3
1991 Pacific Northwest Loads and Resources Study: Technical Appendix, Volume 2, 3224–3.2
1991 Promotion Activities Under Federal Milk Orders, 1317–4.304
1991 Recreation Use Report, Servicewide by States, 1204–17
1991 Report, Great Lakes Science Advisory Board Report to the International Joint Commission, 14644–6
1991 Report of Center-Specific Graft and Patient Survival Rates, 4104–17
1991 Report to Congress Under the Expedited Funds Availability Act, 9364–13
1991 Report to Investors of the Farm Credit System, 9264–5
1991 SAR Statistics, U.S. Coast Guard, 7404–2
1991 Statistical Report, Rural Electric Borrowers, 1244–1
1991 Statistical Report, Rural Telephone Borrowers, 1244–2
1991 Statistical Yearbook of the Immigration and Naturalization Service, 6264–2
1991 Statistics in Brief, 2324–1
1991 Traffic Fatalities, Preliminary Report, 7762–11
1991 Traffic Fatalities, Semiannual Report, 7762–11
1991 Trust Territory of the Pacific Islands, 7004–6
1991-92 Aviation System Capacity Plan, 7504–43
1991-92 Dairy Price Support Program: ASCS Commodity Fact Sheet, 1806–4.8
1991-92 Directory of Postsecondary Institutions, 4844–3
1991-92 Directory of Selected Early Childhood Programs, 4944–10
1992 Agricultural Statistics Board Catalog, 1614–1
1992 Annual Report of Foreign Agricultural Research Grants, 1954–3
1992 Annual Report of the Board of Trustees of the Federal Hospital Insurance Trust Fund, 4654–11
1992 Annual Report of the Board of Trustees of the Federal Old-Age and Survivors Insurance and Disability Insurance Trust Funds, 4704–4
1992 Annual Report of the Board of Trustees of the Federal Supplementary Medical Insurance Trust Fund, 4654–12
1992 Annual Report on Highway Safety Improvement Programs, Report of the Secretary of Transportation to the U.S. Congress, 7554–26
1992 Annual Report to Congress on Community Planning and Development Housing Rehabilitation Programs, 5124–7
1992 Back-to-School Forecast, 4804–19
1992 Catalog of Federal Domestic Assistance, 104–5
1992 Driver License Administration Requirements and Fees, 7554–18
1992 Fall Water Supply Summary for the Western U.S., 1264–4
1992 Filing Season Statistics, 8302–6
1992 Floriculture and Environmental Horticulture Outlook, 1504–9.1
1992 Food Price Outlook, 1504–9.1
1992 Green Book. Overview of Entitlement Programs. Background Material and Data on Programs Within the Jurisdiction of the Committee on Ways and Means, 21784–11
1992 Guide to Department of Education Programs, 4804–3
1992 HCFA Statistics, 4654–18
1992 Joint Economic Report, 23844–2
1992 Monetary Policy Objectives: Summary Report of the Federal Reserve Board, 9362–4
1992 National Trade Estimate Report on Foreign Trade Barriers, 444–2
1992 Report to the Congress on National Defense Stockpile Requirements, 3544–37
1992 Shareholder Directory of the Federal Home Loan Bank of San Francisco, Eleventh District: Arizona, California, Nevada, 9304–23
1992 Status of Waterfowl and Fall Flight Forecast, 5504–27
1992 Trade Policy Agenda and 1991 Annual Report of the President of the U.S. on the Trade Agreements Program, 444–1
1992 U.S. Industrial Outlook, 2044–28
1992 Yearbook of Agriculture: New Crops, New Uses, New Markets, 1004–18
1993 Gas Mileage Guide: EPA Fuel Economy Estimates, 3304–11
1993 Outlook: International Travel To and From the U.S., 2904–9

2,400 Bits Per Second Four-Wire Duplex and Two-Wire Half-Duplex Modems for Data

Communications Use on Telephone-Type Circuits. Telecommunications Standard, 2216–2.207
2,400 Bits Per Second Two-Wire Duplex Modems for Data Communications Use on Telephone-Type Circuits. Telecommunications Standard, 2216–2.206

4,800 and 9,600 Bits Per Second Two-Wire Duplex Modems for Data Communications Use on Telephone-Type Circuits. Telecommunications Standard, 2216–2.209
4,800 Bits Per Second Four-Wire Duplex and Two-Wire Half-Duplex Modems for Data Communications Use on Telephone-Type Circuits. Telecommunications Standard, 2216–2.208

9,600 Bits Per Second Four-Wire Duplex Modems for Data Communications Use on Telephone-Type Circuits. Telecommunications Standard, 2216–2.210

12,000 and 14,400 Bits Per Second Four-Wire Duplex Modems for Data Communications Use on Telephone-Type Circuits. Telecommunications Standard, 2216–2.211

Index by Agency Report Numbers

Index by Agency Report Numbers

Agency report number practices vary from agency to agency, and from publication to publication within an agency. Sometimes a number is noted on the publication, sometimes it is not. In the following list an attempt is made to include every agency report number available in the form in which it appears on the publication.

Those publications covered that did not have identifiable assigned numbers are not included in the list.

EXECUTIVE OFFICE OF THE PRESIDENT

OMB 93-05 ... 104–32
ONDCP Bull. 1 ... 236–3.1
ONDCP Bull. 2 ... 236–3.2
ONDCP Bull. 3 ... 236–3.3
ONDCP Bull. 4 ... 236–3.4
ONDCP Bull. 5 ... 236–3.5
ONDCP Bull. 6 ... 236–3.6
ONDCP Bull. 7 ... 236–3.7
ONDCP Bull. 8 ... 236–3.8

DEPARTMENT OF AGRICULTURE

ACS Res. Rpt. 97 ... 1128–67
ACS Res. Rpt. 99 ... 1128–68
ACS Res. Rpt. 100 ... 1128–69
ACS Service Rpt. 31 ... 1124–1
AER 647 ... 1528–326
AER 649 ... 1548–383
AER 653 ... 1568–307
AER 654 ... 1548–388
AER 656 ... 1568–308
AER 657 ... 1544–22
AER 658 ... 1598–278
AER 659 ... 1568–251
AER 662 ... 1544–9
AFO-(nos.) ... 1541–1
Ag 3(10-92) ... 1631–16
AgCh 1(92) ... 1616–1.1
— 1616–1.2
— 1616–1.3
Agric. Hndbk. 8,
1991 Supp ... 1356–3.17
Agric. Hndbk. 8-18 ... 1356–3.18
Agric. Hndbk. 671 ... 1506–1
Agric. Hndbk. 697 ... 1508–3
Agric. Info. Bull. 638 ... 1588–122
AO-(nos.) ... 1502–4
APHIS 41-35-006 ... 1394–10
APHIS 91-45-003 ... 1394–13.3
APHIS 91-55-008 ... 1394–15.1
APHIS 91-55-009 ... 1394–15.2
Aq 2(date) ... 1631–18
AQUA 8 ... 1561–15
AQUA 9 ... 1561–15
AR-(nos.) ... 1561–16
Biological Evaluation
R2-92-04 ... 1208–408
CEP-16R ... 1802–15
CEP-18R ... 1802–13
CEP-25R ... 1802–14
Cooperative Info. Rpt. 1,
Section 9 ... 1126–1.8
Cooperative Info. Rpt. 1,
Section 21 ... 1126–1.7
CoSt 1(date) ... 1631–5
CoSt 1(2-92) ... 1631–11
CoSt 2(1-92) ... 1614–2
CrPr 2-1(date) ... 1621–1
CrPr 2-2(date) ... 1621–1
CrPr 2-2(6-92) ... 1621–23
CrPr 2-3(1-92) ... 1621–30
CrPr 2-4(3-92) ... 1621–22
CWS-(nos.) ... 1561–1
Da 1-1(date) ... 1627–1
Da 1-2(92) ... 1627–4
Da 2-1(92) ... 1627–5
Da 2-6(date) ... 1627–3
DS-(nos.) ... 1561–2
ECIFS 10-2 ... 1544–18
ECIFS 10-3 ... 1544–17
ECIFS 10-4 ... 1544–20.1
ECIFS 10-5 ... 1544–20.2
EMG (nos.) ... 1925–2.4
ERS Staff Rpt. AGES
9133 ... 1528–325
ERS Staff Rpt. AGES
9150 ... 1548–382
ERS Staff Rpt. AGES
9153 ... 1598–277
ERS Staff Rpt. AGES
9160 ... 1548–386
ERS Staff Rpt. AGES
9201 ... 1504–8
ERS Staff Rpt. AGES
9202 ... 1504–9
ERS Staff Rpt. AGES
9204 ... 1524–8
ERS Staff Rpt. AGES
9206 ... 1528–327
ERS Staff Rpt. AGES
9208 ... 1528–329
ERS Staff Rpt. AGES
9209 ... 1524–7
ERS Staff Rpt. AGES
9211 ... 1584–2
ERS Staff Rpt. AGES
9214 ... 1548–389
ERS Staff Rpt. AGES
9217 ... 1584–3
ERS Staff Rpt. AGES
9218 ... 1548–390
ERS Staff Rpt. AGES
9219 ... 1528–331
ERS Staff Rpt. AGES
9221 ... 1548–392
FAER 244 ... 1528–332
FATS-92 ... 1524–8
FC (nos.) ... 1925–4.2
FCB (nos.) ... 1925–9
FCB 1-92 ... 1925–9.1
FCB 2-92 ... 1925–9.2
FCOF (nos.) ... 1925–5
FD 1-92 ... 1925–10
FD-MI (nos.) ... 1925–31
FDLP (nos.) ... 1925–32
FdS-(nos.) ... 1561–4
FFVS (nos.) ... 1925–13
FG (nos.) ... 1925–2.1
FHORT (nos.) ... 1925–34
FL&P 1-92 ... 1925–33.1
FL&P 2-92 ... 1925–33.2
FL&P 3-92 ... 1925–33.1
FL&P 4-91 ... 1925–33.2
FL&P 4-92 ... 1925–33.2
FMOS (nos.) ... 1317–4
FOP (nos.) ... 1925–1
FrNt 1-3(92) ... 1621–18.1
— 1621–18.3
FrNt 2-4(6-92) ... 1621–18.2
FrNt 3-1(92) ... 1621–18.8
FrNt 4(8-92) ... 1621–18.5
FrNt 5(8-92) ... 1621–18.6
FrNt 7(6-92) ... 1621–18.4
FrNt 8(8-92) ... 1621–18.7
FS 1-92 ... 1925–14.2
FS 2-92 ... 1925–14.3
FS 3-91 ... 1925–14.1
FS-383 ... 1204–2
FSIS-14 ... 1374–3
FT (nos.) ... 1925–16
FTEA 1-92 ... 1925–15.1
FTEA 2-92 ... 1925–15.2
FTEA 3-92 ... 1925–15.3
FVAS-1(1991) ... 1311–4.1
FVAS-2(1991) ... 1311–4.2
FVAS-3(1991) ... 1311–4.3
FVAS-4(1991) ... 1311–4.4
Gen. Tech. Rpt.
FPL-GTR-71 ... 1208–392
Gen. Tech. Rpt. INT-287 ... 1208–420
Gen. Tech. Rpt. NE-(nos.) ... 1202–4
Gen. Tech. Rpt. NE-141 ... 1208–410
Gen. Tech. Rpt. NE-159 ... 1208–405
Gen. Tech. Rpt.
PNW-GTR-282 ... 1208–401
Gen. Tech. Rpt.
PNW-GTR-285 ... 1208–386
Gen. Tech. Rpt. RM-208 ... 1208–403
Gen. Tech. Rpt. RM-210 ... 1208–404
Gen. Tech. Rpt. RM-213 ... 1208–421
Gen. Tech. Rpt. SE-69 ... 1208–415
Gen. Tech. Rpt. SE-70 ... 1204–35
GFA 3 ... 1526–8.2
GrLg 6 (date) ... 1621–6
GrLg 11-1(date) ... 1621–4
GrLg 11-3(date) ... 1621–7
Hny 1(2-92) ... 1631–6
LPS-(nos.) ... 1561–7
LvGn 2(3-92) ... 1623–6
LvGn 3(7-92) ... 1631–7
M92T2 ... 1311–23
M91T23 ... 1311–24
Misc. Pub. 1495 ... 1208–389
Misc. Pub. 1497 ... 1924–11
MtAn 1-1(92) ... 1623–8
MtAn 1-2(date) ... 1623–9
MtAn 1-2-1(92) ... 1623–10
MtAn 2-1(date) ... 1623–2
MtAn 2(2-92) ... 1623–1.1
MtAn 2(5-92) ... 1618–22
MtAn 2(7-92) ... 1623–1.2
MtAn 4(date) ... 1623–3
NFCS Rpt. No. 87-M-1 ... 1358–6
NFR-(nos.) ... 1541–7
OCS-(nos.) ... 1561–3
P&SA 92-1 ... 1384–1
Pot 1-2(date) ... 1621–10
Pot 6(9-92) ... 1621–11
Pou 1-1(date) ... 1625–1
Pou 1-1-1(92) ... 1625–8
Pou 2-1(date) ... 1625–3

Pou 2-2 ... 1625–11
Pou 2-4(92) ... 1625–7
Pou 2-5(date) ... 1625–2
Pou 3(date) ... 1625–10
Pou 3-1(92) ... 1625–5
Pou 3-2(1-92) ... 1625–6
Pr 1(date) ... 1629–1
Pr 1-3(92) ... 1629–5
Pr 1-4(92) ... 1629–2
Pr 2(92) ... 1621–2
R-3 90-9 ... 1206–11.2
R-3 91-5 ... 1206–11.2
R-3 92-1 ... 1206–11.2
REA Informational Pub. 100-2 ... 1244–3
REA Informational Pub. 100-7 ... 1244–3
REA Informational Pub. 200-2 ... 1244–6
REA Informational Pub. 201-1 ... 1244–1
REA Informational Pub. 300-4 ... 1244–2
REA Informational Pub. 300-5 ... 1244–8
REA Informational Pub. 400-2 ... 1244–4
Res. Note FPL-RN-02 ... 1208–391
Res. Note INT-402 ... 1208–422
Res. Note INT-404 ... 1208–423
Res. Note NC-356 ... 1208–397
Res. Note SE-364 ... 1204–22
Res. Paper FPL-RP-510 ... 1208–416
Res. Paper INT-452 ... 1208–402
Res. Paper INT-453 ... 1208–395
Res. Paper INT-454 ... 1208–425
Res. Paper NC-298 ... 1208–417
Res. Paper NC-299 ... 1208–419
Res. Paper NC-300 ... 1208–418
Res. Paper NE-655 ... 1208–394
Res. Paper NE-658 ... 1208–400
Res. Paper NE-659 ... 1208–373
Res. Paper PNW-RP-436 ... 1208–387
Res. Paper PNW-RP-437 ... 1208–413
Res. Paper PNW-RP-439 ... 1208–396
Res. Paper PNW-RP-440 ... 1208–414
Res. Paper PNW-RP-447 ... 1208–424
Res. Paper RM-299 ... 1208–390
Res. Paper RM-300 ... 1208–406
Res. Paper SE-284 ... 1208–411
Resource Bull. INT-75 ... 1206–25.12
Resource Bull. INT-77 ... 1206–17.12
Resource Bull. NC-114 ... 1206–3.5
Resource Bull. NC-115 ... 1206–3.6
Resource Bull. NC-116 ... 1206–3.7
Resource Bull. NC-118 ... 1206–3.8
Resource Bull. NC-119 ... 1208–76
Resource Bull. NC-122 ... 1208–412
Resource Bull. NC-126 ... 1206–10.13
Resource Bull. NC-132 ... 1208–399
Resource Bull. NC-133 ... 1208–398
Resource Bull. NC-134 ... 1204–19
Resource Bull. NC-135 ... 1206–24.11
Resource Bull. NC-136 ... 1208–75
Resource Bull. NC-137 ... 1206–34.9
Resource Bull. NC-138 ... 1206–24.12
Resource Bull. NC-140 ... 1204–19
Resource Bull. NE-107 ... 1206–12.16
Resource Bull. NE-120 ... 1206–15.12
Resource Bull. NE-121 ... 1206–15.11
Resource Bull. NE-123 ... 1204–18
Resource Bull. PNW-RB-177 ... 1206–28.4
Resource Bull. PNW-RB-178 ... 1206–28.5
Resource Bull. PNW-RB-179 ... 1206–28.6
Resource Bull. PNW-RB-180 ... 1206–9.23
Resource Bull. PNW-RB-181 ... 1208–108
Resource Bull. PNW-RB-183 ... 1208–280
Resource Bull. PNW-RB-184 ... 1206–9.24
Resource Bull. PNW-RB-185 ... 1206–9.25
Resource Bull. PNW-RB-186 ... 1206–9.26
Resource Bull. SE-121 ... 1208–407
Resource Bull. SE-123 ... 1208–384
Resource Bull. SE-124 ... 1206–6.14
Resource Bull. SE-125 ... 1208–352
Resource Bull. SE-126 ... 1208–393
Resource Bull. SE-127 ... 1206–6.15
Resource Bull. SE-128 ... 1206–6.16
Resource Bull. SE-129 ... 1208–138
Resource Bull. SE-130 ... 1206–6.17
Resource Bull. SE-131 ... 1206–6.18
Resource Bull. SO-150 ... 1206–30.11
Resource Bull. SO-160 ... 1206–27.11
Resource Bull. SO-161 ... 1206–35.8
Resource Bull. SO-162 ... 1206–35.10
Resource Bull. SO-163 ... 1206–35.9
Resource Bull. SO-164 ... 1208–409
Resource Bull. SO-167 ... 1206–35.11
Resource Bull. SO-168 ... 1206–35.12
Resource Bull. SO-169 ... 1206–8.13
Rpt. Code 691 ... 1182–5
Rpt. No. 91-2 ... 1206–49.1
— 1206–49.2
Rpt. No. 92-1 ... 1206–49.4
Rpt. No. 92-2 ... 1206–49.3
RS-(nos.) ... 1561–8
RS-92-1 ... 1524–4.1
RS-92-2 ... 1524–4.3
RS-92-3 ... 1524–4.2
RSED-OD-1011 ... 1954–3
Semiannual Rpt. 26 ... 1002–4
Semiannual Rpt. 27 ... 1002–4
Semiannual Rpt. 28 ... 1002–4
SpCr 2(9-92) ... 1621–8
SpCr 6-1(3-92) ... 1621–8
SpCr 6-1(92) ... 1631–8
SpCr 8(date) ... 1631–14
SpSy (date) ... 1631–1
SpSy 3(7-92) ... 1614–4
SpSy 8(92) ... 1614–3
SSR-(v.nos. & nos.) ... 1561–14
Stat. Bull. 826 ... 1548–384
Stat. Bull. 831 ... 1548–387
Stat. Bull. 832 ... 1548–385
Stat. Bull. 833 ... 1564–13
Stat. Bull. 834 ... 1544–28
Stat. Bull. 835 ... 1528–328
Stat. Bull. 836 ... 1564–11
Stat. Bull. 837 ... 1568–309
Stat. Bull. 838 ... 1544–24
Stat. Bull. 839 ... 1317–3
Stat. Bull. 840 ... 1544–4
Stat. Bull. 841 ... 1568–310
Sugar Import Notice (nos.-yr.) ... 1922–9
Supp. 3-92 ... 1925–4.3
Supp. 7-91 ... 1925–4.3
Tech. Bull. 1806 ... 1548–391
TFS-(nos.) ... 1561–6
TOB-(nos.) ... 1319–3
TOB-FL-35 ... 1319–5.3
TOB-LA-35 ... 1319–5.2
TOB-LA-36 ... 1319–5.1
TS-(nos.) ... 1561–10
TVS-(nos.) ... 1561–11
Vg 1-1(date) ... 1621–12
Vg 1-2(92) ... 1621–25.2
Vg 2-1(date) ... 1621–12
Vg 2-1-1(date) ... 1621–14
Vg 2-1-2(8-92) ... 1631–9
Vg 3-1(date) ... 1621–12
Vg 3-1(1-92) ... 1621–25.1
WAP-(nos.) ... 1925–28
WASDE-(nos.) ... 1522–5
WIC-1-89 ... 1364–12
WIC-1-90 ... 1364–12
WIC-2-89 ... 1364–12
WIC-2-90 ... 1364–12
WP(nos.) ... 1925–36
WS-(nos.) ... 1561–12
WS-(yr.-nos.) ... 1311–3

DEPARTMENT OF COMMERCE

Census AG88-PP-3(R) ... 2346–1.6
Census AG88-PP-4 ... 2346–1.5
Census AHB-88-8 ... 2485–11.2
Census AHB-88-11 ... 2485–11.1
Census AHB-89-1 ... 2485–11.3
Census AHB-89-2 ... 2485–11.4
Census AHB-89-3 ... 2485–11.5
Census AHB-89-4 ... 2485–11.8
Census AHB-89-5 ... 2485–11.6
Census AHB-89-6 ... 2485–11.9
Census AHB-89-7 ... 2485–11.7
Census AHB-89-8 ... 2485–11.10
Census AHB-89-9 ... 2485–11.11
Census AHB-89-10 ... 2485–11.12
Census AHB-89-11 ... 2485–11.13
Census AR87-2 ... 2506–16.2
Census BC-90 ... 2413–15
Census BR-(yr.-nos.) ... 2413–3
Census BR-90-A ... 2413–5
Census BR-91-RV ... 2413–3
Census BT-90 ... 2413–14
Census BW-(yr.-nos.) ... 2413–7
Census BW-91-RV ... 2413–7
Census C20-(yr.-nos.) ... 2382–1
Census C21-(yr.-nos.) ... 2382–9
Census C22-(yr.-nos.) ... 2382–2
Census C25-(yr.-nos.) ... 2382–3
Census C25-91-A ... 2384–1
Census C30-(yr.-nos.) ... 2382–4
Census C40-(yr.-nos.) ... 2382–5
Census C40-91-A ... 2384–2
Census C50-(yr.)-Q(nos.) ... 2382–7
Census CB (yr.-nos.) ... 2413–2
Census CB91-346 ... 2324–10
Census CB92-242 ... 2328–85
Census CB92-244 ... 2328–86
Census CB92-259 ... 2328–87
Census CB92-260 ... 2328–88
Census CB92-267 ... 2328–84
Census CB92-275 ... 2328–90
Census CB92-276 ... 2324–10
Census CBO-87-1 ... 2328–59
Census CBP-89-1 ... 2326–8.1
Census CBP-90-2 ... 2326–6.2
Census CBP-90-4 ... 2326–6.4
Census CBP-90-8 ... 2326–6.8
Census CBP-90-11 ... 2326–6.11
Census CBP-90-14 ... 2326–6.14
Census CBP-90-15 ... 2326–6.15
Census CBP-90-17 ... 2326–6.17
Census CBP-90-18 ... 2326–6.18
Census CBP-90-19 ... 2326–6.19
Census CBP-90-21 ... 2326–6.21
Census CBP-90-23 ... 2326–6.23
Census CBP-90-25 ... 2326–6.25
Census CBP-90-26 ... 2326–6.26
Census CBP-90-27 ... 2326–6.27
Census CBP-90-28 ... 2326–6.28
Census CBP-90-29 ... 2326–6.29

Census CBP-90-30 .... 2326–6.30
Census CBP-90-31 .... 2326–6.31
Census CBP-90-33 .... 2326–6.33
Census CBP-90-35 .... 2326–6.35
Census CBP-90-36 .... 2326–6.36
Census CBP-90-37 .... 2326–6.37
Census CBP-90-41 .... 2326–6.41
Census CBP-90-42 .... 2326–6.42
Census CBP-90-43 .... 2326–6.43
Census CBP-90-44 .... 2326–6.44
Census CBP-90-46 .... 2326–6.46
Census CBP-90-47 .... 2326–6.47
Census CBP-90-48 .... 2326–6.48
Census CBP-90-50 .... 2326–6.50
Census CBP-90-52 .... 2326–6.52
Census CD90-1A-(nos.) 2551–9
Census CD90-1A-1 .... 2551–9.1
Census CD90-1A-2-1 .... 2551–9.2
Census CD90-1A-2-2 .... 2551–9.2
Census CD90-1A-3-1 .... 2551–9.3
Census CD90-1A-3-2 .... 2551–9.3
Census CD90-1A-3-3 .... 2551–9.3
Census CD90-1A-4-1 .... 2551–9.4
Census CD90-1A-4-2 .... 2551–9.4
Census CD90-1A-5-1 .... 2551–9.5
Census CD90-1A-5-2 .... 2551–9.5
Census CD90-1A-5-3 .... 2551–9.5
Census CD90-1A-6 .... 2551–9.6
Census CD90-1A-7-1 .... 2551–9.7
Census CD90-1A-7-2 .... 2551–9.7
Census CD90-1A-8 .... 2551–9.8
Census CD90-1A-9-1 .... 2551–9.9
Census CD90-1A-9-2 .... 2551–9.9
Census CD90-3A-2 .... 2551–10.2
Census CD90-3A-5/992-3 .... 2551–10.5
Census CD90-3A-6 .... 2551–10.6
Census CD90-3A-7 .... 2551–10.7
Census CD90-3A-9 .... 2551–10.9
Census CD90-3A-10 .... 2551–10.10
Census CD90-3A-11/992-2 .... 2551–10.11
Census CD90-3A-12 .... 2551–10.12
Census CD90-3A-13 .... 2551–10.13
Census CD90-3A-14 .... 2551–10.14
Census CD90-3A-15 .... 2551–10.15
Census CD90-3A-24 .... 2551–10.24
Census CD90-3A-25 .... 2551–10.25
Census CD90-3A-26 .... 2551–10.26
Census CD90-3A-36/992-2 .... 2551–10.36
Census CD90-3A-37/992-2 .... 2551–10.37
Census CD90-3A-38 .... 2551–10.38
Census CD90-3A-39 .... 2551–10.39
Census CD90-3A-40 .... 2551–10.40
Census CD90-3A-43 .... 2551–10.43
Census CD90-3A-51 .... 2551–10.51
Census CD90-3A-52 .... 2551–10.52
Census CD90-3A-57 .... 2551–10.57
Census CD90-3A-58 .... 2551–10.58
Census CD90-3A-59 .... 2551–10.59
Census CFF No. 5(Rev.) 2326–7.83
Census CFF No. 20(Rev.) 2326–7.84
Census CFF No. 22(Rev.) 2326–7.82
Census CH-S-1-3 .... 2326–21.3
Census CH-S-1-4 .... 2326–21.4
Census CH-S-1-5 .... 2326–21.5
Census CH-S-1-7 .... 2326–21.7
Census CH-S-1-12 .... 2326–21.12
Census CH-S-1-14 .... 2326–21.14
Census CH-S-1-15 .... 2326–21.15
Census CH-S-1-16 .... 2326–21.16
Census CH-S-1-17 .... 2326–21.17
Census CH-S-1-18 .... 2326–21.18
Census CH-S-1-20 .... 2326–21.20
Census CH-S-1-21 .... 2326–21.21
Census CH-S-1-23 .... 2326–21.23
Census CH-S-1-24 .... 2326–21.24
Census CH-S-1-25 .... 2326–21.25
Census CH-S-1-26 .... 2326–21.26
Census CH-S-1-27 .... 2326–21.27
Census CH-S-1-28 .... 2326–21.28
Census CH-S-1-29 .... 2326–21.29
Census CH-S-1-30 .... 2326–21.30
Census CH-S-1-31 .... 2326–21.31
Census CH-S-1-33 .... 2326–21.33
Census CH-S-1-35 .... 2326–21.35
Census CH-S-1-36 .... 2326–21.36
Census CH-S-1-37 .... 2326–21.37
Census CH-S-1-38 .... 2326–21.38
Census CH-S-1-39 .... 2326–21.39
Census CH-S-1-41 .... 2326–21.41
Census CH-S-1-42 .... 2326–21.42
Census CH-S-1-43 .... 2326–21.43
Census CH-S-1-44 .... 2326–21.44
Census CH-S-1-46 .... 2326–21.46
Census CH-S-1-49 .... 2326–21.49
Census CH-S-1-50 .... 2326–21.50
Census CH-S-1-51 .... 2326–21.51
Census CH-S-1-52 .... 2326–21.52
Census CH-S-1-53 .... 2326–21.53
Census CH-S-1-55 .... 2326–21.55
Census CH-S-2 2328–83
Census CIR Staff Paper No. 65 .... 2326–18.65
Census CIR Staff Paper No. 66 .... 2326–18.64
Census CPH-R-3 2628–1
Census CPH-R-4 2628–2
Census EC92-PR-1 2308–5
Census FES/91 2464–2
Census FT447/91-A 2424–10
Census FT895/91-A 2424–11
Census FT925/(date) 2422–12
Census FT927/91-A 2424–12
Census FT947/91-A 2424–13
Census GE91-1 .... 2466–1.1
Census GE91-4 .... 2466–1.2
Census GF90-2 .... 2466–2.4
Census GF90-4 .... 2466–2.1
Census GF90-5 .... 2466–2.2
Census GF90-8 .... 2466–2.3
Census GF90-10 .... 2466–2.5
Census GF91-1 .... 2466–2.7
Census GF91-3 .... 2466–2.6
Census GR (yr.-nos.) 2462–2
Census GT (yr.-nos.) 2462–3
Census H-111-(yr.-nos.) 2482–1
Census H-111-91-A 2484–1
Census H-121-91-2 .... 2486–1.12
Census H-121-92-1 .... 2486–1.13
Census H-121-92-2 .... 2486–1.14
Census H-121-92-4 .... 2486–1.15
Census H-123/91-1 .... 2486–2.1
Census H-130-(yr.-nos.) 2482–2
Census H-130-91-A 2484–2
Census H-131-91-A 2484–3
Census H-151-89-1 2485–13
Census H-170-89-3 .... 2485–6.10
Census H-170-89-4 .... 2485–6.5
Census H-170-89-5 .... 2485–6.2
Census H-170-89-6 .... 2485–6.6
Census H-170-89-7 .... 2485–6.3
Census H-170-89-9 .... 2485–6.7
Census H-170-89-12 .... 2485–6.9
Census H-170-89-18 .... 2485–6.1
Census H-170-89-33 .... 2485–6.4
Census H-170-89-39 .... 2485–6.8
Census H-171-85 2485–8
Census H-171-86 2485–8
Census H-171-87 2485–8
Census M3-1(yr.-nos.) 2506–3.1
Census M20 A(yr.-nos.) 2506–4.1
Census M20 J(yr.-nos.) 2506–4.3
Census M20 K(yr.-nos.) 2506–4.4
Census M32 G(yr.-nos.) 2506–9.4
Census M33 J(yr.-nos.) 2506–10.3
Census M33 2(yr.-nos.) 2506–10.9
Census M36 D(yr.-nos.) 2506–12.13
Census M37 G(yr.-nos.) 2506–12.24
Census M37 L(yr.-nos.) 2506–12.25
Census M90(AS)-1 .... 2506–14.2
Census M90(AS)-2 .... 2506–14.1
Census M90(AS)-3 .... 2506–14.3
Census MA20 D(91)-1 .... 2506–4.5
Census MA22 F.1(91)-1 .... 2506–5.4
Census MA22 F.2(91)-1 .... 2506–5.5
Census MA22 K(91)-1 .... 2506–5.7
Census MA22 Q(91)-1 .... 2506–5.9
Census MA23 D(91)-1 .... 2506–6.4
Census MA24 T(91)-1 .... 2506–7.4
Census MA25 H(90)-1 .... 2506–7.8
Census MA25 H(91)-1 .... 2506–7.8
Census MA28 A(91)-1 .... 2506–8.14
Census MA28 B(91)-1 .... 2506–8.13
Census MA28 C(91)-1 .... 2506–8.15
Census MA28 F(91)-1 .... 2506–8.16
Census MA28 G(91)-1 .... 2506–8.5
Census MA30 C(91)-1 .... 2506–8.17
Census MA31 A(91)-1 .... 2506–6.8
Census MA32 C(91)-1 .... 2506–9.1
Census MA32 E(91)-1 .... 2506–9.3
Census MA33 A(91)-1 .... 2506–10.1
Census MA33 B(91)-1 .... 2506–10.2
Census MA33 E(91)-1 .... 2506–10.5
Census MA33 L(91)-1 .... 2506–10.8
Census MA35 F(91)-1 .... 2506–12.4
Census MA35 J(91)-1 .... 2506–12.5
Census MA35 L(91)-1 .... 2506–12.6
Census MA35 M(91)-1 .... 2506–12.7
Census MA35 N(91)-1 .... 2506–12.31
Census MA35 P(91)-1 .... 2506–12.8
Census MA35 Q(91)-1 .... 2506–12.28
Census MA35 R(90)-1 .... 2506–12.2
Census MA35 R(91)-1 .... 2506–12.2
Census MA35 U(91)-1 .... 2506–12.10
Census MA36 A(91)-1 .... 2506–12.11
Census MA36 E(91)-1 .... 2506–12.15
Census MA36 F(91)-1 .... 2506–12.16
Census MA36 H(90)-1 .... 2506–12.17
Census MA36 H(91)-1 .... 2506–12.17
Census MA36 K(90)-1 .... 2506–12.18
Census MA36 K(91)-1 .... 2506–12.18
Census MA36 L(91)-1 .... 2506–12.19
Census MA36 M(91)-1 .... 2506–12.20
Census MA36 P(91)-1 .... 2506–12.35
Census MA36 Q(91)-1 .... 2506–12.36
Census MA36 R(91)-1 .... 2506–12.34
Census MA37 D(91)-1 .... 2506–12.22
Census MA38 B(90)-1 .... 2506–12.26
Census MA38 B(91)-1 .... 2506–12.26
Census MA200 (89)-1 .... 2506–3.6
Census MA200 (90)-1 .... 2506–3.6
Census MA200 (91)-1 .... 2506–3.6
Census MC87-S-4 2497–4
Census MC87-S-6 2497–6
Census MQ22 D(yr.-nos.) 2506–5.2
Census MQ22 P(yr.-nos.) 2506–5.8
Census MQ22 T(yr.-nos.) 2506–5.11
Census MQ23 A(yr.-nos.) 2506–6.12
Census MQ23 X(yr.-nos.) 2506–6.6
Census MQ28 A(yr.-nos.) 2506–8.1
Census MQ28 B(yr.-nos.) 2506–8.2
Census MQ28 C(yr.-nos.) 2506–8.3
Census MQ28 F(yr.-nos.) 2506–8.4
Census MQ31 A(yr.-nos.) 2506–6.7
Census MQ32 A(yr.-nos.) 2506–9.6
Census MQ32 D(yr.-nos.) 2506–9.2
Census MQ34 E(yr.-nos.) 2506–11.2
Census MQ34 H(yr.-nos.) 2506–11.4
Census MQ34 K(yr.-nos.) 2506–11.5
Census MQ35 W(yr.-nos.) 2506–12.12
Census MQ36 B(yr.-nos.) 2506–12.33

Census MQ36 C(yr.-nos.) 2506–12.14
Census MQ-C1(90)-1 .... 2506–3.7
Census P-20, No. 456 .... 2546–1.456
Census P-20, No. 457 .... 2546–1.458
Census P-20, No. 458 .... 2546–1.457
Census P-20, No. 459 .... 2546–1.462
Census P-20, No. 460 .... 2546–1.459
Census P-20, No. 461 .... 2546–1.461
Census P-20, No. 462 .... 2546–1.460
Census P-20, No. 463 .... 2546–1.464
Census P-20, No. 464 .... 2546–1.463
Census P-23, No. 175 .... 2546–2.164
Census P-23, No. 177 .... 2546–2.163
Census P-23, No. 178 .... 2546–2.165
Census P-23, No. 180 .... 2546–2.166
Census P-25, No. 1080 2542–1
Census P-25, No. 1081 2542–1
Census P-25, No. 1082 2542–1
Census P-25, No. 1083 2542–1
Census P-25, No. 1084 2542–1
Census P-25, No. 1085 .... 2546–3.170
Census P-25, No. 1086 2542–1
Census P-25, No. 1087 2542–1
Census P-25, No. 1088 2542–1
Census P-25, No. 1089 2542–1
Census P-25, No. 1090 2542–1
Census P-25, No. 1091 2542–1
Census P-25, No. 1093 2542–1
Census P-25, No. 1094 2542–1
Census P-60, No. 177 .... 2546–6.73
Census P-60, No. 178 .... 2546–6.74
Census P-60, No. 179 .... 2546–6.75
Census P-60, No. 180 .... 2546–6.76
Census P-60, No. 181 .... 2546–6.77
Census P-60, No. 182-RD 2546–6.78
Census P-60, No. 183 .... 2546–6.79
Census P-70, No. 26 .... 2546–20.22
Census P-70, No. 27 .... 2546–20.20
Census P-70, No. 28 .... 2546–20.21
Census P-70, No. 29 .... 2546–20.23
Census P-70, No. 30 .... 2546–20.24
Census P-70, No. 31 .... 2546–20.25
Census PA-92-1 .... 2326–19.7
Census PA-92-2 .... 2326–19.8
Census PESVY (yr.-nos.) 2502–2
Census PPT/92-1 .... 2326–24.1
Census PPT/92-2 .... 2326–24.2
Census PPT/92-3 .... 2326–24.3
Census Pub. Bull. B-3 .... 2428–5.1
Census QFR-(yr.-nos.) 2502–1
Census SB-91-6 .... 2326–17.41
Census SB-91-7 .... 2326–17.42
Census SB-91-15 .... 2326–17.44
Census SB-91-17 .... 2326–17.38
Census SB-91-20 .... 2326–17.40
Census SB-91-23 .... 2326–17.39
Census SB-92-1 .... 2326–17.43
Census SB-92-3 .... 2326–17.47
Census SB-92-4 .... 2326–17.45
Census SB-92-5 .... 2326–17.48
Census SB-92-7 .... 2326–17.46
Census SB-92-8 .... 2326–17.49
Census SB-92-9 .... 2326–17.50
Census SB-92-10 .... 2326–17.52
Census SB-92-11 .... 2326–17.51
Census SIPP Working Paper Series, No. 9101 .... 2626–10.144
Census SIPP Working Paper Series, No. 9102 .... 2626–10.145
Census SIPP Working Paper Series, No. 9103 .... 2626–10.146
Census SIPP Working Paper Series, No. 9104 .... 2626–10.147
Census SIPP Working Paper Series, No. 9105 .... 2626–10.148
Census Tech. Paper 61 .... 2626–2.60
Census TM-(yr.-nos.) 2322–2
Census TM-985(yr.-nos.) 2422–7
Census WP/91 2324–9
Census 1990 CH-1-2 .... 2471–1.2
Census 1990 CH-1-3 .... 2471–1.3
Census 1990 CH-1-4 .... 2471–1.4
Census 1990 CH-1-5 .... 2471–1.5
Census 1990 CH-1-6 .... 2471–1.6
Census 1990 CH-1-7 .... 2471–1.7
Census 1990 CH-1-8 .... 2471–1.8
Census 1990 CH-1-9 .... 2471–1.9
Census 1990 CH-1-10 .... 2471–1.10
Census 1990 CH-1-11 .... 2471–1.11
Census 1990 CH-1-12 .... 2471–1.12
Census 1990 CH-1-13 .... 2471–1.13
Census 1990 CH-1-14 .... 2471–1.14
Census 1990 CH-1-15 .... 2471–1.15
Census 1990 CH-1-16 .... 2471–1.16
Census 1990 CH-1-17 .... 2471–1.17
Census 1990 CH-1-18 .... 2471–1.18
Census 1990 CH-1-19 .... 2471–1.19
Census 1990 CH-1-20 .... 2471–1.20
Census 1990 CH-1-21 .... 2471–1.21
Census 1990 CH-1-22 .... 2471–1.22
Census 1990 CH-1-23 .... 2471–1.23
Census 1990 CH-1-24 .... 2471–1.24
Census 1990 CH-1-25 .... 2471–1.25
Census 1990 CH-1-26 .... 2471–1.26
Census 1990 CH-1-27 .... 2471–1.27
Census 1990 CH-1-28 .... 2471–1.28
Census 1990 CH-1-29 .... 2471–1.29
Census 1990 CH-1-30 .... 2471–1.30
Census 1990 CH-1-31 .... 2471–1.31
Census 1990 CH-1-32 .... 2471–1.32
Census 1990 CH-1-33 .... 2471–1.33
Census 1990 CH-1-34 .... 2471–1.34
Census 1990 CH-1-35 .... 2471–1.35
Census 1990 CH-1-36 .... 2471–1.36
Census 1990 CH-1-37 .... 2471–1.37
Census 1990 CH-1-38 .... 2471–1.38
Census 1990 CH-1-39 .... 2471–1.39
Census 1990 CH-1-40 .... 2471–1.40
Census 1990 CH-1-41 .... 2471–1.41
Census 1990 CH-1-42 .... 2471–1.42
Census 1990 CH-1-43 .... 2471–1.43
Census 1990 CH-1-44 .... 2471–1.44
Census 1990 CH-1-45 .... 2471–1.45
Census 1990 CH-1-46 .... 2471–1.46
Census 1990 CH-1-47 .... 2471–1.47
Census 1990 CH-1-48 .... 2471–1.48
Census 1990 CH-1-49 .... 2471–1.49
Census 1990 CH-1-50 .... 2471–1.50
Census 1990 CH-1-51 .... 2471–1.51
Census 1990 CH-1-52 .... 2471–1.52
Census 1990 CP-1-2 .... 2531–1.2
Census 1990 CP-1-3 .... 2531–1.3
Census 1990 CP-1-4 .... 2531–1.4
Census 1990 CP-1-5 .... 2531–1.5
Census 1990 CP-1-6 .... 2531–1.6
Census 1990 CP-1-7 .... 2531–1.7
Census 1990 CP-1-8 .... 2531–1.8
Census 1990 CP-1-9 .... 2531–1.9
Census 1990 CP-1-1A 2531–2.1
Census 1990 CP-1-10 .... 2531–1.10
Census 1990 CP-1-11 .... 2531–1.11
Census 1990 CP-1-12 .... 2531–1.12
Census 1990 CP-1-13 .... 2531–1.13
Census 1990 CP-1-14 .... 2531–1.14
Census 1990 CP-1-15 .... 2531–1.15
Census 1990 CP-1-16 .... 2531–1.16
Census 1990 CP-1-17 .... 2531–1.17
Census 1990 CP-1-18 .... 2531–1.18
Census 1990 CP-1-19 .... 2531–1.19
Census 1990 CP-1-20 .... 2531–1.20
Census 1990 CP-1-21 .... 2531–1.21
Census 1990 CP-1-22 .... 2531–1.22
Census 1990 CP-1-23 .... 2531–1.23
Census 1990 CP-1-24 .... 2531–1.24
Census 1990 CP-1-25 .... 2531–1.25
Census 1990 CP-1-26 .... 2531–1.26
Census 1990 CP-1-27 .... 2531–1.27
Census 1990 CP-1-28 .... 2531–1.28
Census 1990 CP-1-29 .... 2531–1.29
Census 1990 CP-1-30 .... 2531–1.30
Census 1990 CP-1-31 .... 2531–1.31
Census 1990 CP-1-32 .... 2531–1.32
Census 1990 CP-1-33 .... 2531–1.33
Census 1990 CP-1-34 .... 2531–1.34
Census 1990 CP-1-35 .... 2531–1.35
Census 1990 CP-1-36 .... 2531–1.36
Census 1990 CP-1-37 .... 2531–1.37
Census 1990 CP-1-38 .... 2531–1.38
Census 1990 CP-1-39 .... 2531–1.39
Census 1990 CP-1-40 .... 2531–1.40
Census 1990 CP-1-41 .... 2531–1.41
Census 1990 CP-1-42 .... 2531–1.42
Census 1990 CP-1-43 .... 2531–1.43
Census 1990 CP-1-44 .... 2531–1.44
Census 1990 CP-1-45 .... 2531–1.45
Census 1990 CP-1-46 .... 2531–1.46
Census 1990 CP-1-47 .... 2531–1.47
Census 1990 CP-1-48 .... 2531–1.48
Census 1990 CP-1-49 .... 2531–1.49
Census 1990 CP-1-50 .... 2531–1.50
Census 1990 CP-1-51 .... 2531–1.51
Census 1990 CP-1-52 .... 2531–1.52
Census 1990 CP-1-53 .... 2531–1.53
Census 1990 CP-1-55 .... 2531–1.54
Census 1990 CPH-1-1 .... 2551–1.1
Census 1990 CPH-1-53 .... 2551–1.53
Census 1990 CPH-5-2 .... 2551–7.2
Census 1990 CPH-5-3 .... 2551–7.3
Census 1990 CPH-5-4 .... 2551–7.4
Census 1990 CPH-5-5 .... 2551–7.5
Census 1990 CPH-5-6 .... 2551–7.6
Census 1990 CPH-5-7 .... 2551–7.7
Census 1990 CPH-5-8 .... 2551–7.8
Census 1990 CPH-5-9 .... 2551–7.9
Census 1990 CPH-5-10 .... 2551–7.10
Census 1990 CPH-5-11 .... 2551–7.11
Census 1990 CPH-5-12 .... 2551–7.12
Census 1990 CPH-5-13 .... 2551–7.13
Census 1990 CPH-5-14 .... 2551–7.14
Census 1990 CPH-5-15 .... 2551–7.15
Census 1990 CPH-5-16 .... 2551–7.16
Census 1990 CPH-5-17 .... 2551–7.17
Census 1990 CPH-5-18 .... 2551–7.18
Census 1990 CPH-5-19 .... 2551–7.19
Census 1990 CPH-5-20 .... 2551–7.20
Census 1990 CPH-5-21 .... 2551–7.21
Census 1990 CPH-5-22 .... 2551–7.22
Census 1990 CPH-5-23 .... 2551–7.23
Census 1990 CPH-5-24 .... 2551–7.24
Census 1990 CPH-5-25 .... 2551–7.25
Census 1990 CPH-5-26 .... 2551–7.26
Census 1990 CPH-5-27 .... 2551–7.27
Census 1990 CPH-5-28 .... 2551–7.28
Census 1990 CPH-5-29 .... 2551–7.29
Census 1990 CPH-5-30 .... 2551–7.30
Census 1990 CPH-5-31 .... 2551–7.31
Census 1990 CPH-5-32 .... 2551–7.32
Census 1990 CPH-5-33 .... 2551–7.33
Census 1990 CPH-5-34 .... 2551–7.34
Census 1990 CPH-5-35 .... 2551–7.35
Census 1990 CPH-5-36 .... 2551–7.36
Census 1990 CPH-5-37 .... 2551–7.37
Census 1990 CPH-5-38 .... 2551–7.38
Census 1990 CPH-5-39 .... 2551–7.39
Census 1990 CPH-5-40 .... 2551–7.40
Census 1990 CPH-5-41 .... 2551–7.41
Census 1990 CPH-5-42 .... 2551–7.42
Census 1990 CPH-5-43 .... 2551–7.43
Census 1990 CPH-5-44 .... 2551–7.44
Census 1990 CPH-5-45 .... 2551–7.45
Census 1990 CPH-5-46 .... 2551–7.46

Census 1990 CPH-5-47 ... 2551–7.47
Census 1990 CPH-5-48 ... 2551–7.48
Census 1990 CPH-5-49 ... 2551–7.49
Census 1990 CPH-5-50 ... 2551–7.50
Census 1990 CPH-5-51 ... 2551–7.51
Census 1990 CPH-5-52 ... 2551–7.52
Census 1990 CPH-6-AS ... 2551–8.1
Census 1990 CPH-6-CNMI ... 2551–8.2
Census 1990 CPH-6-G ... 2551–8.3
Census 1990 CPH-6-P ... 2551–8.4
Census 1990 CPH-I-15 ... 2308–66
Census 1990 CPH-R-1A ... 2555–1.1
Census 1990 CQC-4 ... 2326–23.2
Census 1990 CQC-7 ... 2326–23.3
Census 1990 CQC-11 ... 2326–23.1
ELMR Rpt. No. 10 ... 2176–7.28
FCM P1-1992 ... 2144–2
FET 91-68 ... 2046–4.1
FET 91-69 ... 2046–4.2
FET 91-70 ... 2046–4.3
FET 91-71 ... 2046–4.4
FET 91-72 ... 2046–4.5
FET 91-73 ... 2046–4.6
FET 91-74 ... 2046–4.7
FET 91-75 ... 2046–4.8
FET 91-76 ... 2046–4.9
FET 91-77 ... 2046–4.10
FET 92-01 ... 2046–4.11
FET 92-02 ... 2046–4.12
FET 92-03 ... 2046–4.13
FET 92-04 ... 2046–4.14
FET 92-05 ... 2046–4.15
FET 92-06 ... 2046–4.16
FET 92-07 ... 2046–4.17
FET 92-08 ... 2046–4.18
FET 92-09 ... 2046–4.19
FET 92-10 ... 2046–4.20
FET 92-11 ... 2046–4.21
FET 92-12 ... 2046–4.22
FET 92-13 ... 2046–4.23
FET 92-14 ... 2046–4.24
FET 92-15 ... 2046–4.25
FET 92-16 ... 2046–4.26
FET 92-17 ... 2046–4.27
FET 92-18 ... 2046–4.28
FET 92-19 ... 2046–4.29
FET 92-20 ... 2046–4.30
FET 92-21 ... 2046–4.31
FET 92-22 ... 2046–4.32
FET 92-23 ... 2046–4.33
FET 92-24 ... 2046–4.34
FET 92-25 ... 2046–4.35
FET 92-26 ... 2046–4.36
FET 92-27 ... 2046–4.37
FET 92-28 ... 2046–4.38
FET 92-29 ... 2046–4.39
FET 92-30 ... 2046–4.40
FET 92-31 ... 2046–4.41
FET 92-32 ... 2046–4.42
FET 92-33 ... 2046–4.43
FET 92-34 ... 2046–4.44
FET 92-35 ... 2046–4.45
FET 92-36 ... 2046–4.46
FET 92-37 ... 2046–4.47
FET 92-38 ... 2046–4.48
FET 92-39 ... 2046–4.49
FET 92-40 ... 2046–4.50
FET 92-41 ... 2046–4.51
FET 92-42 ... 2046–4.52
FET 92-43 ... 2046–4.53
FET 92-44 ... 2046–4.54
FET 92-45 ... 2046–4.55
FET 92-46 ... 2046–4.56
FET 92-47 ... 2046–4.57
FET 92-48 ... 2046–4.58
FET 92-49 ... 2046–4.59
FET 92-50 ... 2046–4.60
FET 92-51 ... 2046–4.61
FET 92-52 ... 2046–4.62
FET 92-53 ... 2046–4.63
FET 92-54 ... 2046–4.64
FET 92-55 ... 2046–4.65
FIPS PUB 19-2 ... 2216–2.204
FIPS PUB 162 ... 2216–2.205
FIPS PUB 163 ... 2216–2.206
FIPS PUB 164 ... 2216–2.207
FIPS PUB 165 ... 2216–2.208
FIPS PUB 166 ... 2216–2.209
FIPS PUB 167 ... 2216–2.210
FIPS PUB 168 ... 2216–2.211
FIPS PUB 169 ... 2216–2.212
FIPS PUB 170 ... 2216–2.213
FIPS PUB 171 ... 2216–2.203
FIPS PUB 172 ... 2216–2.214
FIPS PUB 173 ... 2216–2.215
GD-24 ... 2156–18.24
NEFSC Ref. Doc. 91-05 ... 2168–130
NEFSC Ref. Doc. 92-02 ... 2162–9
NEFSC Ref. Doc. 92-07 ... 2162–9
NIST Pub. List 58 ... 2216–2.202
NIST Spec. Pub. 260 ... 2214–2
NIST Spec. Pub. 845 ... 2214–7
NIST/SP-305/23 ... 2214–1
NISTIR 4731 ... 2218–87
NISTIR 4829 ... 2214–6
NISTIR 4898 ... 2214–5.1
NISTIR 4899 ... 2214–5.2
NOAA CFS (nos.) FF ... 2162–2
NOAA CFS (nos.) FM ... 2162–3
NOAA CFS 8803 ... 2166–6.2
NOAA CFS 9100 ... 2164–1
NOAA CFS 9102 ... 2166–6.1
NOAA CFS 9204 ... 2166–17.1
NOAA CFS 9205 ... 2166–17.2
NOAA Coastal Ocean Program Regional Synthesis Series No. 1 ... 2146–8.1
NOAA DR ERL PMEL-35 ... 2148–62
NOAA TM ERL AOML-68 ... 2148–61
NOAA TM NMFS-F/SPO-1 ... 2164–22
NOAA TM NMFS-SEFC-242 ... 2164–24
NOAA TM NMFS-SEFC-258 ... 2164–24
NOAA TM NMFS-SEFC-273 ... 2164–23
NOAA TM NMFS-SEFC-289 ... 2164–23
NOAA TM NMFS-SEFC-290 ... 2164–7
NOAA TM NMFS-SEFC-295 ... 2164–24
NOAA TM NMFS-SWR-026 ... 2166–19.11
NOAA TM NOS OMA 56 ... 2176–3.14
NOAA TM NOS OMA 58 ... 2176–3.15
NOAA TM NOS ORCA 62 ... 2176–3.16
NOAA TR NMFS 103 ... 2168–128
NOAA TR NMFS 104 ... 2168–129
NOAA TR NMFS 105 ... 2168–131
NOAA TR NMFS 106 ... 2164–15
NOAA TR NMFS 110 ... 2168–132
NOAA TR NMFS 111 ... 2164–15
NTIA Spec. Pub. 91-26 ... 2808–30
OBR 92-01 ... 2046–6.1
OBR 92-02 ... 2046–6.2
OBR 92-03 ... 2046–6.5
OBR 92-04 ... 2046–6.3
OBR 92-05 ... 2046–6.4
OBR 92-06 ... 2046–6.6
OBR 92-07 ... 2046–6.8
OBR 92-08 ... 2046–6.7
OBR 92-09 ... 2046–6.9
PAT 92-1 ... 2244–2
TQ 2200 ... 2046–8.7
TQ 2205 ... 2046–9.8
TQ 2300 ... 2046–8.1
TQ 2305 ... 2046–9.4
TQ 2400 ... 2046–8.2
TQ 2405 ... 2046–9.1
TQ 2496 ... 2042–27
TQ 2600 ... 2046–8.3
TQ 2605 ... 2046–9.2
TQ 2800 ... 2046–8.6
TQ 2805 ... 2046–9.9
WDCA-OC-91-2 ... 2144–15

DEPARTMENT OF DEFENSE

C-1 ... 3544–39
CHAMPUS 5400.2-CB ... 3504–23
CRC No. 531-6690 ... 3504–10
DOD 4100.33-INV ... 3544–25
FAD 748/(yr.) ... 3542–3
L02 ... 3542–15
L03 ... 3544–29
M01 ... 3544–1
M02 ... 3544–7
M03 ... 3542–14
M04 ... 3542–16
M05 ... 3542–20
M06 ... 3544–24
M07 ... 3544–40
NAVPERS 15658 ... 3802–4
News Release 36-92 ... 3544–15
NT-92-1 ... 3804–11
NT-92-2 ... 3804–10
P01 ... 3544–5
P02 ... 3544–4
P03 ... 3542–1
P04 ... 3544–17
P05 ... 3542–19
P06 ... 3544–11
P07 ... 3544–18
P08 ... 3544–19
P09 ... 3542–5
P14 ... 3542–17
P-1 ... 3544–32
R-1 ... 3544–33
RCS:DD-M(Q) 493 ... 3704–15
RP-53 ... 3804–6
WRSC-WCUS-89-1 ... 3754–3.1
WRSC-WCUS-89-2 ... 3754–3.2
WRSC-WCUS-89-3 ... 3754–3.3
WRSC-WCUS-89-4 ... 3754–3.4
WRSC-WCUS-89-5 ... 3754–3.5

DEPARTMENT OF EDUCATION

Campus-Based Programs Rpt. No. 93-1 ... 4804–17
Data Series DR-CCD/SAS-91/92-1.1 ... 4834–19
ED/OBEMLA 92-10 ... 4804–14
ED/OERI 91-24 ... 4814–2
ED/OERI 92-2 ... 4814–4
ED/OERI 92-25 ... 4874–5
ED/OERI 92-27 ... 4874–2
ED/OERI 92-29 ... 4884–1
ED/OERI 92-31 ... 4812–1
ED/OESE 92-51 ... 4804–2
ED/OIG 92-5 ... 4802–1

ED/OIG 93-2 4802–1
ED/OPE 92-5 4804–18
ED/OPP 92-19 R 4808–44
ED/OSERS 91-12 4948–11
ED/OSERS 92-20 4944–1
ED/OUS 91-26 4808–40
ED/OUS 91-42 4808–38
ED/OUS 91-44 4808–39
ERIC 92-5002 4814–4
ERIC 92-5003 4812–1
LP 92-4742 4874–2
LP 92-4760 4878–5
LP 92-4762 4874–1
LP 92-4765 4874–5
NAEP Rpt. 21-T-01 4898–32
NCES 91-222 .... 4826–10.5
NCES 91-384 4848–44
NCES 91-490 4824–4
NCES 91-667 4838–50
NCES 92-004 .... 4826–10.1
NCES 92-005 .... 4826–10.2
NCES 92-006 .... 4826–10.3
NCES 92-007 .... 4826–1.32
NCES 92-011 4838–51
NCES 92-013 4848–45
NCES 92-014 4844–6
NCES 92-022 4828–41
NCES 92-023 .... 4826–10.4
NCES 92-024 4844–15
NCES 92-028 4824–6
NCES 92-030 .... 4826–9.14
NCES 92-031 4834–17
NCES 92-032 4834–19
NCES 92-033 4834–6
NCES 92-039 4844–17
NCES 92-040 4844–16
NCES 92-041 4844–6
NCES 92-042 .... 4826–9.16
NCES 92-050 4844–8
NCES 92-051 4838–49
NCES 92-054-1 .... 4844–3.1
NCES 92-054-2 .... 4844–3.2
NCES 92-060 .... 4896–9.1
NCES 92-064 .... 4896–8.3
NCES 92-066 .... 4896–6.7
NCES 92-067 .... 4896–8.5
NCES 92-077 .... 4826–2.54
NCES 92-079 .... 4836–3.8
NCES 92-080 .... 4846–5.2
NCES 92-081 4848–47
NCES 92-083 .... 4826–9.17
NCES 92-088 .... 4826–9.14
NCES 92-090 4844–19
NCES 92-093 4828–33
NCES 92-096 4824–1
NCES 92-097 4824–2
NCES 92-100 4834–1
NCES 92-120 .... 4836–3.10
NCES 92-129 4834–23
NCES 92-130 .... 4826–1.33
NCES 92-156 4844–10
NCES 92-165 4848–48
NCES 92-193 4824–10
NCES 92-206 .... 4846–3.12
NCES 92-218 4824–4
NCES 92-223 4844–18
NCES 92-316 4844–10
NCES 92-347 4844–13
NCES 92-390 .... 4846–3.11
NCES 92-479 .... 4826–9.12
NCES 92-486 .... 4826–9.13
NCES 92-488 .... 4826–9.15
NCES 92-489 4824–9
NCES 92-640 4848–46
NCES 92-641 4824–8
NCES 92-663 4838–52
NCES 92-666 .... 4836–3.9
NCES 92-669 4828–42
NCES 92-693 4824–3
NCES 92-696 4828–35
NCES 93-032 4834–19
NCES 93-085 .... 4826–9.18
NIDRR Rpt. 1 .... 4946–1.1
NIDRR Rpt. 2 .... 4946–1.2
OR 92-3003 4884–1
Perkins Loan Program Rpt. 42 4804–18
PIP 91-908 4814–2
Rpt. No. 21-TR-20 .... 4896–8.5
RSA-IM-92-21 4944–5
RSA-IM-92-30 4944–2

DEPARTMENT OF ENERGY

ANL/ESD-9 3008–124
BNL-52322 .... 3324–2.9
CNEAF/NAFD/88-01 .... 3166–6.59
DOE/AD-0029 3004–28
DOE/AD-0034 P 3004–27
DOE/BC-(yr./nos.) 3002–14
DOE/BP-801 3222–2
DOE/BP-1738 .... 3224–3.1
DOE/BP-1739 .... 3224–3.2
DOE/BP-1753 3224–1
DOE/BP-1806 .... 3224–3.3
DOE/BP-1891 .... 3224–3.4
DOE/BU-0002 3004–35
DOE/CE-0019/12 3304–11
DOE/CE-0351 3304–28
DOE/CE-0532 3308–87
DOE/CE-0347P 3304–17
DOE/CH-10093-94 .... 3304–20.1
DOE/CH-10093-129 .... 3304–20.2
DOE/CR-0007 3024–5
DOE/DP-00539/063 9194–17
DOE/EA-0353 .... 3356–4.11
DOE/EA-0376 .... 3356–4.12
DOE/EA-0468 .... 3356–4.10
DOE/EIA-0035(date) 3162–24
DOE/EIA-0035(73-88) 3168–123
DOE/EIA-0064(90) 3164–79
DOE/EIA-0095(91) 3164–36
DOE/EIA-0109(yr./nos.) 3162–6
DOE/EIA-0118(91) 3164–25
DOE/EIA-0121(yr./nos.) 3162–37
DOE/EIA-0125(yr./nos.) 3162–8
DOE/EIA-0130(yr./nos.) 3162–4
DOE/EIA-0131(90) 3164–4.3
DOE/EIA-0131(90)/1 .... 3164–4.1
DOE/EIA-0131(90)/2 .... 3164–4.2
DOE/EIA-0145(90) 3164–38
DOE/EIA-0149(91) 3164–98
DOE/EIA-0167(90) 3164–33
DOE/EIA-0167(91) 3164–33
DOE/EIA-0173(91) 3164–29
DOE/EIA-0174(90) 3164–62
DOE/EIA-0191(91) 3164–42
DOE/EIA-0202/(nos.) 3162–34
DOE/EIA-0206(90) 3164–44
DOE/EIA-0208(yr./nos.) 3162–32
DOE/EIA-0214(90) 3164–39
DOE/EIA-0216(91) 3164–46
DOE/EIA-0218(nos.) 3162–1
DOE/EIA-0219(90) 3164–50
DOE/EIA-0226(yr./nos.) 3162–35
DOE/EIA-0249(91) 3164–86
DOE/EIA-0293(92) 3164–87
DOE/EIA-0314(90) 3166–7.33
DOE/EIA-0318(89) 3166–8.10
DOE/EIA-0340(91)/1 .... 3164–2.1
DOE/EIA-0340(91)/2 .... 3164–2.2
DOE/EIA-0348(90) 3164–11
DOE/EIA-0370(91) 3164–70
DOE/EIA-0376(90) 3164–64
DOE/EIA-0380(yr./nos.) 3162–11
DOE/EIA-0383(92) 3164–75
DOE/EIA-0384(91) 3164–74
DOE/EIA-0437(90)/1 3164–23
DOE/EIA-0437(90)/2 3164–24
DOE/EIA-0455(90) 3164–9
DOE/EIA-0466(90) 3164–80
DOE/EIA-0469(90) 3164–76
DOE/EIA-0477(90) 3164–82
DOE/EIA-0478(91) 3164–65
DOE/EIA-0484(92) 3164–84
DOE/EIA-0487(90) 3164–85
DOE/EIA-0487(91) 3164–85
DOE/EIA-0520 (yr./nos.) 3162–42
DOE/EIA-0527(92) 3164–90
DOE/EIA-0535(90) 3164–94
DOE/EIA-0538 (yr./nos.) 3162–45
DOE/EIA-0540(90) 3164–91
DOE/EIA-0544 3168–122
DOE/EIA-0548(90) 3164–97
DOE/EIA-0550 3168–124
DOE/EIA-0552(80-88) 3166–13.7
DOE/EIA-0554(92) 3164–96
DOE/EIA-0555(92)/1 .... 3166–15.1
DOE/EIA-0555(92)/2 .... 3166–15.2
DOE/EIA-0555(92)/3 .... 3166–15.3
DOE/EIA-0555(92)/4 .... 3166–15.4
DOE/EIA-0556 3168–125
DOE/EIA-0557 .... 3166–14.2
DOE/EM-0001 3354–9
DOE/EM-0059P 3004–36
DOE/ER-0143/3 .... 3004–18.3
DOE/ER-0144/10 .... 3004–18.6
DOE/ER-0295 .... 3004–18.3
DOE/ER-0348 .... 3004–18.3
DOE/ER-0389 .... 3004–18.3
DOE/ER-0447P 3004–18.3
DOE/ER-0483P 3004–18.3
DOE/ER-0507P 3004–18.8
DOE/ER-0512T 3004–18.4
DOE/ER-0528P 3004–18.1
DOE/ER-0529P 3004–18.2
DOE/ER-0537P 3004–18.3
DOE/ER-0550T 3004–18.5
DOE/ER-0558T 3004–18.9
DOE/ER-0562P 3004–18.7
DOE/ER-0565T 3004–18.10
DOE/FE-(nos.) 3002–13
DOE/FE-0164 3338–3
DOE/FE-0245 3338–5
DOE/FE-0193P 3338–4
DOE/FE-0217P 3334–5
DOE/FE-0219P 3334–4
DOE/FE-0247P 3334–4
DOE/FE-0254P 3334–3
DOE/FE-61679P-H1 3338–2
DOE/IE-0020P 3408–2
DOE/IG-0001(92) 3002–12
DOE/IG-0002(92) 3002–12
DOE/IG-0305 .... 3006–5.28
DOE/IG-0308 .... 3006–5.30
DOE/IG-0310 .... 3006–5.31
DOE/IG-0313 .... 3006–5.32
DOE/OSTI-4500-R75 .... 3324–2.9
DOE/OSTI-8200-R55 3354–15
DOE/PR-0020 3004–21
DOE/RL-91-44 3354–2
DOE/RW-0006, Rev. 7 3364–2
DOE/RW-0188(nos.) 3362–1
DOE/RW-0249P 3364–5
DOE/RW-0295P 3368–5
DOE/RW-0331P 3364–5
DOE/RW-0335P 3364–1
DOE/S-0010P(91) 3024–2
DOE/S-0084P 3006–13.1
DOE/S-0085P 3006–13.3
DOE/S-0086P 3006–13.2

DOE/S-0088P 3006–13.4
DOE/S-0093P 3002–15
DOE/S-0096P 3006–13.5
DOE/S-0101P 3002–15
DOE/SA-0007P 3344–2
DOE/ST-0002P 3004–4
DOE/SWP-9201 .... 3244–1.1
ER-B-92-01 .... 3006–5.26
ER-B-92-04 .... 3006–5.29
ER-B-92-07 .... 3006–5.33
ER-BC-92-01 .... 3006–5.27
ES/ER/TM-20 3354–12
KAPL-4726 .... 3324–2.5
LBL-27170(1992) 3324–2.13
LBL-27767 3368–4
LMF-131 .... 3324–2.4
Manpower Assessment Brief 18 .... 3006–8.18
Manpower Assessment Brief 19 .... 3006–8.19
Manpower Assessment Brief 20 .... 3006–8.20
MHSMP-91-06 .... 3324–2.1
MMSC-EM-92047 .... 3324–2.12
ORNL-6643 3008–127
ORNL-6710 3304–5
ORNL/CDIAC-46 3004–33
ORNL/CON-336 3308–102
ORNL/CON-337 3308–101
ORNL/CON-341 3308–100
ORNL/CON-344 3308–104
ORNL/CON-346 3308–105
ORNL/CON-347 3308–106
ORNL/TM-11791 3308–103
PNL-7930 .... 3324–2.8
PNL-7978 HEDR 3356–5.7
PNL-8083 HEDR 3356–5.8
SAND-92-0391C 3008–129
SLAC-404 .... 3324–2.11
SR/CNEAF/92-01 .... 3166–6.62
SR/EDID/91-03 .... 3166–6.60
SR/EMEU/91-04 .... 3166–6.61
SR/EPD/87-01 .... 3166–6.63
SR/ICID/87-01 .... 3166–6.58
SR/ICID/88-01 .... 3166–6.65
SR/RNGD/87-01 .... 3166–6.64
SR/RNGD/92-01 .... 3166–6.66
TTC-1193 3008–129
WAPD-RC/E(EE)-1562 .... 3324–2.6
WP/16151-6 .... 3324–2.14
WSRC-IM-91-28 .... 3324–2.2
WSRC-TR-92-186 .... 3324–2.15
WSRC-TR-92-186-1 .... 3324–2.15

DEPARTMENT OF HEALTH AND HUMAN SERVICES

Actuarial Note No. 133 .... 4706–2.133
Actuarial Study No. 106 .... 4706–1.106
Actuarial Study No. 107 .... 4706–1.107
ADM (yr.)-151 4482–1
ADM 91-1740 .... 4488–10.4
ADM 91-1752 4494–12
ADM 91-1761 4498–78
ADM 91-1777 .... 4496–11.1
ADM 91-1786 4498–79
ADM 91-1823 4498–80
ADM 92-1778 .... 4496–11.2
ADM 92-1884 4498–77
ADM 92-1886 .... 4506–3.48
ADM 92-1887 .... 4494–5.1
ADM 92-1888 4494–11
ADM 92-1897 .... 4506–3.49
ADM 92-1898 .... 4496–11.3
ADM 92-1911 .... 4506–3.50
ADM 92-1918 .... 4492–5.1
ADM 92-1919 .... 4496–12.1
ADM 92-1939 .... 4506–3.51
ADM 92-1958 .... 4492–5.2
AHCPR 13 .... 4186–8.23
AHCPR 14 .... 4186–8.24
AHCPR Pub. No. 92-0013 .... 4186–10.6
AHCPR Pub. No. 92-0014 .... 4186–10.7
AHCPR Pub. No. 92-0015 .... 4186–10.8
AHCPR Pub. No. 92-0016 .... 4186–8.23
AHCPR Pub. No. 92-0017 .... 4186–8.24
AHCPR Pub. No. 92-0027 .... 4186–10.9
AHCPR Pub. No. 92-0031 .... 4186–6.16
Biologics Surveillance, No. 93 4205–22
CDC (yr.)-8017 4202–1
— 4202–7
— 4206–2
CDC 90-8017 4204–1
CDC 91-8391 4204–16
CDC 91-8399 4204–19
CDC 92-8280 4204–11
CDC 92-8399 4204–19
CDC 92-8419 4204–18
DHHS (yr.)-1225 4122–1
Drug Abuse Svcs. Res. Series, No. 1 .... 4496–11.1
Drug Abuse Svcs. Res. Series, No. 2 .... 4496–11.2
Drug Abuse Svcs. Res. Series, No. 3 .... 4496–11.3
HCFA 02178 .... 4654–19.1
HCFA 03318 4654–17
HCFA 03323 4654–10
HCFA 03328 4654–16
HCFA 03333 4654–18
Health Technology Assessment Rpt. No. 1: 1991 .... 4186–10.6
Health Technology Assessment Rpt. No. 2: 1991 .... 4186–10.7
Health Technology Assessment Rpt. No. 3: 1991 .... 4186–10.8
Health Technology Assessment Rpt. No. 4: 1991 .... 4186–10.9
Hepatitis Surveillance, No. 54 4205–2
HETA 89-299-2230 4248–93
HRS-P-OD 90-4 4114–12
HRS-P-OD 92-1 4114–8
Mental Health Stat. Note No. 202 .... 4506–3.48
Mental Health Stat. Note No. 203 .... 4506–3.49
Mental Health Stat. Note No. 204 .... 4506–3.50
Mental Health Stat. Note No. 205 .... 4506–3.51
NIDA Res. Mono. 107 4498–78
NIDA Res. Mono. 109 4498–79
NIDA Res. Mono. 113 4498–80
NIDA Res. Mono. 118 4498–77
NIDA Res. Mono. 119 4494–11
NIH (v.nos.&nos.) 4472–1
NIH 90-2092 4434–15
NIH 91-5 4434–1
NIH 91-2092 4434–15
NIH 91-3094 4474–22
NIH 92-7 4434–2
NIH 92-3297 4478–186
NIH 92-3316 .... 4476–7.1
NIH 93-3480 .... 4494–4.1
NIH 93-3481 .... 4494–4.2
OAI-01-89-89020 .... 4006–8.5
OAI-09-88-00870 .... 4006–7.5
OAI-12-88-01170 .... 4006–7.7
OAI-12-88-01180 .... 4006–7.8
OAI-12-88-01200 .... 4006–7.6
OAI-12-88-01220 4008–117
ODAM 6-89 4114–12
OEI-01-90-00482 4008–119
OEI-04-89-01810 4004–35
OEI-04-90-02440 4004–35
OEI-04-91-00560 4004–35
OEI-06-89-00871 .... 4006–11.1
OEI-06-90-00160 4008–120
OEI-09-88-01005 .... 4006–11.2
OEI-09-88-01007 .... 4006–11.3
OEI-09-91-00650 .... 4006–10.4
OEI-09-91-00654 .... 4006–10.5
OEI-12-89-00190 .... 4006–7.10
OEI-12-89-00191 .... 4006–7.11
OEI-12-89-00192 .... 4006–7.12
OEI-12-89-89220 .... 4006–11.4
OEI-12-90-00660 .... 4006–7.9
ORS Working Paper 40 .... 4746–26.9
ORS Working Paper 41 .... 4746–26.10
ORS Working Paper 42 .... 4746–26.11
ORS Working Paper 43 .... 4746–26.12
ORS Working Paper 44 .... 4746–26.13
ORS Working Paper 45 .... 4746–26.14
ORS Working Paper 46 .... 4746–26.15
ORS Working Paper 47 .... 4746–26.16
ORS Working Paper 48 .... 4746–26.17
ORS Working Paper 49 .... 4746–26.18
ORS Working Paper 50 .... 4746–26.19
ORS Working Paper 51 .... 4746–26.20
ORS Working Paper 52 .... 4746–26.21
ORS Working Paper 53 .... 4746–26.22
ORS Working Paper 54 .... 4746–26.23
ORS Working Paper 55 .... 4746–26.24
OS 91-12 4004–3
PHS (yr.)-1120 4142–1
PHS (yr.)-1309-(nos.) 4122–2
PHS (yr.)-50193 4042–3
PHS 91-1250, No. 210 .... 4146–8.211
PHS 91-1507 .... 4147–10.180
PHS 91-1508 .... 4147–10.181
PHS 91-1865 .... 4147–16.6
PHS 92-1007 4124–8
PHS 92-1102 4144–3
PHS 92-1120, Vol. 40, No. 13 4144–7
PHS 92-1120, Vol. 40, No. 12, Supp 4146–5.125
PHS 92-1120, Vol. 40, No. 8, Supp 4146–5.124
PHS 92-1205 4164–1
PHS 92-1214 4164–2
PHS 92-1232 4144–11
PHS 92-1250, No. 208 .... 4146–8.210
PHS 92-1250, No. 209 .... 4146–8.214
PHS 92-1250, No. 211 .... 4146–8.212
PHS 92-1250, No. 212 .... 4146–8.213
PHS 92-1250, No. 213 .... 4146–8.215
PHS 92-1250, No. 214 .... 4146–8.217
PHS 92-1250, No. 215 .... 4146–8.216
PHS 92-1250, No. 216 .... 4146–8.218
PHS 92-1250, No. 217 .... 4146–8.219
PHS 92-1250, No. 218 .... 4146–8.220
PHS 92-1252 4148–28
PHS 92-1301 4124–1
PHS 92-1303 .... 4147–1.29
PHS 92-1304 .... 4147–1.28
PHS 92-1308 .... 4147–1.27
PHS 92-1386 .... 4147–2.113
PHS 92-1387 .... 4147–2.115
PHS 92-1388 .... 4147–2.114
PHS 92-1509 .... 4147–10.182
PHS 92-1770 .... 4147–13.112
PHS 92-1771 .... 4147–13.109
PHS 92-1772 .... 4147–13.110

PHS 92-1773 ..... 4147–13.112
PHS 92-1774 ..... 4147–13.111
PHS 92-1856 ..... 4147–20.19
PHS 92-1928 ..... 4147–21.50
PHS 93-1250, No. 219 ..... 4146–8.222
PHS 93-1250, No. 220 ..... 4146–8.221
PHS 93-1512 ..... 4147–10.183
PHS Bibliography Series No. 45 4204–19
Provider Studies Res. Note 16 ..... 4186–6.16
SMA 92-1942 4094–1
Smoking and Tobacco Control Monograph No. 1 ..... 4476–7.1
SSA 11-11536 ..... 4706–1.107
SSA 11-11553 ..... 4706–1.106
SSA 13-11700 4742–1
— 4744–3
SSA 13-11727 4744–25
SSA 13-11776, No. 15 ..... 4746–14.16
SSA 13-11784 4744–29
SSA 13-11787-11796 4744–29
SSA 13-11871 4744–26
SSA 13-11976 4744–27
SSA 17-002 4704–13
SSA 61-006 ..... 4746–4.62
Surveillance Rpt. 16 ..... 4486–1.11
Surveillance Rpt. 17 ..... 4486–1.12
Surveillance Rpt. 18 ..... 4486–1.13
Surveillance Rpt. 19 ..... 4486–1.14
Surveillance Rpt. 20 ..... 4486–1.15
Surveillance Rpt. 21 ..... 4486–1.16
Vital and Health Statistics Series 1, No. 26 ..... 4147–1.27
Vital and Health Statistics Series 1, No. 27 ..... 4147–1.29
Vital and Health Statistics Series 1, No. 28 ..... 4147–1.28
Vital and Health Statistics Series 2, No. 112 ..... 4147–2.113
Vital and Health Statistics Series 2, No. 113 ..... 4147–2.115
Vital and Health Statistics Series 2, No. 114 ..... 4147–2.114
Vital and Health Statistics Series 10, CD-ROM No. 2 ..... 4147–10.184
Vital and Health Statistics Series 10, No. 179 ..... 4147–10.180
Vital and Health Statistics Series 10, No. 180 ..... 4147–10.181
Vital and Health Statistics Series 10, No. 181 ..... 4147–10.182
Vital and Health Statistics Series 10, No. 184 ..... 4147–10.183
Vital and Health Statistics Series 13, No. 109 ..... 4147–13.112
Vital and Health Statistics Series 13, No. 110 ..... 4147–13.109
Vital and Health Statistics Series 13, No. 111 ..... 4147–13.110
Vital and Health Statistics Series 13, No. 112 ..... 4147–13.112
Vital and Health Statistics Series 13, No. 113 ..... 4147–13.111
Vital and Health Statistics Series 16, No. 6 ..... 4147–16.6
Vital and Health Statistics Series 20, No. 19 ..... 4147–20.19
Vital and Health Statistics Series 21, No. 50 ..... 4147–21.50

DEPARTMENT OF HOUSING AND URBAN DEVELOPMENT

HUD 91-38 ..... 5006–3.77
HUD 91-44 ..... 5006–3.78
HUD 91-46 ..... 5006–3.79
HUD 91-51 ..... 5006–3.80
HUD 91-54 ..... 5006–3.83
HUD 91-58 ..... 5006–3.81
HUD 91-60 ..... 5006–3.82
HUD 91-61 ..... 5006–3.84
HUD 91-69 ..... 5006–3.85
HUD 92-03 ..... 5006–3.86
HUD 92-05 ..... 5006–3.87
HUD 92-17 ..... 5006–3.88
HUD 92-22 5144–21
HUD 92-35 ..... 5006–3.89
HUD 92-51 ..... 5006–3.91
HUD 92-53 ..... 5006–3.90
HUD 92-57 ..... 5006–3.92
HUD 92-61 ..... 5006–3.93
HUD 92-63 ..... 5006–3.94
HUD 92-65 ..... 5006–3.95
HUD 92-66 ..... 5006–3.96
HUD 92-67 ..... 5006–3.97
HUD 92-68 ..... 5006–3.98
HUD 92-69 ..... 5006–3.99
HUD 92-71 ..... 5006–3.100
HUD 92-72 ..... 5006–3.101
HUD 92-83 ..... 5006–3.102
HUD 329-PA(19) 5004–10
HUD 1059-CPD(2) 5124–9
HUD 1059-CPD(3) 5124–9
HUD 1285-OS(3) 5002–11
HUD 1285-OS(4) 5002–11
HUD 1296-GNMA 5144–6
HUD 1304-H(3) 5144–26
HUD 1357-IG 5002–8
HUD 1378-IG 5002–8
HUD-1316-PDR 5188–131
HUD-1318-PDR 5186–16.1
HUD-1325-PDR 5186–16.3
HUD-1326-PDR 5186–16.7
HUD-1327-PDR 5186–16.5
HUD-1328-PDR 5186–16.2
HUD-1329-PDR 5186–16.6
HUD-1330-PDR 5186–16.4
HUD-1346-PDR 5184–11
HUD-1352-PDR 5188–119
HUD-0005809 5184–9
HUD-0005810 5184–8
R33SECA 5142–45
RR:250-Areas 5144–24
RR:250 Book (States) 5144–1
RR:250-Sections 5144–17
RR:250-States 5144–25
RR:250-U.S 5144–23
RR:S0117 5144–15

DEPARTMENT OF INTERIOR

BIA Rpt. 55-38-X 5704–12
Biological Rpt. 2 ..... 5506–14.5
Biological Rpt. 85(1.23) 5506–14.4
Biological Rpt. 90(17) 5508–114
Biological Rpt. 90(18) 5508–116
Biological Rpt. 90(19) 5506–10.13
BLM-ID-PT-92-005-4351 5724–14
BLM-NM-GI-92-003-4730 5724–15
BLM-NM-PT-92-005-4410 5724–17
BLM-NV-GI-92-001-1120 ..... 5724–11.1
BLM-NV-GI-92-150-1120 ..... 5724–11.3
BLM-OR-AE-92-03-1792 ..... 5724–11.2
BLM-SC-PT-92-011+1165 5724–1
BLM-WY-AE-92-006-4830 ..... 5724–11.5
Bur. Mines IC 9292 5608–170
Bur. Mines IC 9299 5608–172
Bur. Mines IC 9300 5608–173
Bur. Mines IC 9301 5608–132
Bur. Mines IC 9310 ..... 5606–4.30
Bur. Mines IC 9312 5608–175
Bur. Mines IC 9318 5604–2
Bur. Mines IC 9327 ..... 5606–4.31
Bur. Mines Open File Rpt. 41-91 5608–174
Contaminant Hazard Reviews Rpt. 23 ..... 5506–14.4
Contaminant Hazard Reviews Rpt. 24 ..... 5506–14.5
Contaminant Rpt. No. R6/804P/91 5508–117
Fish and Wildlife Resource Pub. 181 5508–115
Fish and Wildlife Tech. Rpt. 31 ..... 5506–12.4
Fish and Wildlife Tech. Rpt. 32 ..... 5506–12.5
Fish Distribution Rpt. 26 5504–10
FWS Resource Pub. 180 5508–120
GS List (nos.) 5662–1
GS Water-Data Rpt. AK-90-1 ..... 5666–10.2
GS Water-Data Rpt. AL-91-1 ..... 5666–12.1
GS Water-Data Rpt. AZ-90-1 ..... 5666–10.3
GS Water-Data Rpt. HI-90-1 ..... 5666–10.10
GS Water-Data Rpt. MN-90-1 ..... 5666–10.22
GS Water-Data Rpt. MN-90-2 ..... 5666–10.22
GS Water-Data Rpt. ND-90-1 ..... 5666–10.33
GS Water-Data Rpt. NV-90-1 ..... 5666–10.27
GS Water-Data Rpt. NV-91-1 ..... 5666–12.27
GS Water-Data Rpt. NY-91-1 ..... 5666–12.31
GS Water-Data Rpt. NY-91-2 ..... 5666–12.31
GS Water-Data Rpt. NY-91-3 ..... 5666–12.31
GS Water-Data Rpt. OK-90-1 ..... 5666–10.35
GS Water-Data Rpt. PA-90-1 ..... 5666–10.37
GS Water-Data Rpt. PA-90-2 ..... 5666–10.37
GS Water-Data Rpt. PA-90-3 ..... 5666–10.37
GS Water-Data Rpt. TX-90-1 ..... 5666–10.41
GS Water-Data Rpt. TX-90-2 ..... 5666–10.41
GS Water-Data Rpt. TX-90-3 ..... 5666–10.41
GS Water-Data Rpt. UT-91-1 ..... 5666–12.42
GS Water-Data Rpt. VA-90-1 ..... 5666–10.43
GS Water-Data Rpt. VA-90-2 ..... 5666–10.43
GS Water-Data Rpt. WI-90-1 ..... 5666–10.46
GS Water-Data Rpt. WV-91-1 ..... 5666–12.45
GS Water-Data Rpt. WY-90-1 ..... 5666–10.47
IC 9324 5608–177
MMS 90-0024 OCS Rpt 5734–8
MMS 90-0029

EIS/EA, Vol. I 5736–7.1
MMS 90-0029
EIS/EA, Vol. II 5736–7.1
MMS 90-0051 OCS Study 5738–32
MMS 90-0054 OCS Study 5738–33
MMS 90-0061 OCS Study 5738–38.1
MMS 90-0073 OCS Study 5738–38.3
MMS 91-0002 OCS Study 5738–38.2
MMS 91-0010 OCS Rpt 5734–8
MMS 91-0017 OCS Study 5738–36
MMS 91-0037 OCS Study 5738–27
MMS 91-0045 OCS Study 5738–40.1
MMS 91-0046 OCS Study 5738–40.2
MMS 91-0047 OCS Study 5738–40.3
MMS 91-0052 OCS Study 5738–39
MMS 91-0056 OCS Study 5738–35
MMS 91-0079 OCS Rpt 5734–6
MMS 91-0083 OCS Study 5734–11
MMS 91-0084 OCS Study 5736–5.16
MMS 91-0085 OCS Study 2176–1.40
MMS 91-0087 OCS Rpt 5734–7
MMS 91-0091 Stat. Rpt 5734–9
MMS 91-0092 OCS Rpt 5738–41
MMS 92-0002 OCS Rpt 5738–34
MMS 92-0011 OCS Study 5738–37
MMS 92-0029 OCS Study 5738–32
MMS 92-0031 OCS Study 5736–5.17
MMS 92-0059 OCS Rpt 5734–4
MMS Tech. Rpt. 148 .... 5736–5.16
MMS Tech. Rpt. 151 .... 5736–5.17
USGS Bull. 1971 5668–126
USGS Bull. 1989-A-C 5668–127
USGS Bull. 1999 5664–15
USGS Circ. 930-K 5666–21.11
USGS Circ. 930-L 5666–21.12
USGS Circ. 1042 5668–125
USGS Circ. 1072 5664–11
USGS Circ. 1084 5664–14
USGS Circ. 1093 5664–14
USGS Open-File Rpt.
61-91 5608–178
USGS Open-File Rpt.
72-92 5608–176
USGS Open-File Rpt.
90-122 .... 5666–26.19
USGS Open-File Rpt.
90-146 .... 5666–28.22
USGS Open-File Rpt.
90-376 .... 5666–26.22
USGS Open-File Rpt.
90-572 .... 5666–24.15
USGS Open-File Rpt.
90-581 .... 5666–27.26
USGS Open-File Rpt.
90-583 .... 5666–26.17
USGS Open-File Rpt.
90-596 .... 5666–24.13
USGS Open-File Rpt.
91-78 .... 5666–26.18
USGS Open-File Rpt.
91-86 .... 5666–24.16
USGS Open-File Rpt.
91-91 .... 5666–26.16
USGS Open-File Rpt.
91-96 .... 5666–26.23
USGS Open-File Rpt.
91-176 .... 5666–24.14
USGS Open-File Rpt.
91-187 .... 5666–28.20
USGS Open-File Rpt.
91-188 .... 5666–26.20
USGS Open-File Rpt.
91-191 .... 5666–26.21
USGS Open-File Rpt.
91-199 .... 5666–28.18
USGS Open-File Rpt.
91-203 .... 5666–24.12
USGS Open-File Rpt.
91-210 .... 5666–26.24
USGS Open-File Rpt.
91-212 .... 5666–24.17
USGS Open-File Rpt.
91-214 .... 5666–26.25
USGS Open-File Rpt.
91-226 .... 5666–26.26
USGS Open-File Rpt.
91-234 .... 5666–26.27
USGS Open-File Rpt.
91-247 .... 5666–24.18
USGS Open-File Rpt.
91-496 .... 5666–28.23
USGS Open-File Rpt.
92-478 5664–18
USGS Water-Supply Paper
2362 .... 5666–27.33
USGS/WRD/HD-91/236 .... 5666–10.43
USGS/WRD/HD-91/239 .... 5666–10.37
USGS/WRD/HD-91/247 .... 5666–10.33
USGS/WRD/HD-91/248 .... 5666–10.43
USGS/WRD/HD-91/254 .... 5666–10.47
USGS/WRD/HD-91/292 .... 5666–10.46
USGS/WRD/HD-91/293 .... 5666–10.22
USGS/WRD/HD-91/294 .... 5666–10.41
USGS/WRD/HD-91/295 .... 5666–10.41
USGS/WRD/HD-91/296 .... 5666–10.41
USGS/WRD/HD-91/299 .... 5666–10.37
USGS/WRD/HD-91/300 .... 5666–10.37
USGS/WRD/HD-91/301 .... 5666–10.27
USGS/WRD/HD-91/302 .... 5666–10.22
USGS/WRD/HD-91/303 .... 5666–10.35
USGS/WRD/HD-91/304 .... 5666–10.10
USGS/WRD/HD-91/305 .... 5666–10.2
USGS/WRD/HD-92/233 .... 5666–10.3
USGS/WRD/HD-92/255 .... 5666–12.1
USGS/WRD/HD-92/260 .... 5666–12.27
USGS/WRD/HD-92/269 .... 5666–12.42
USGS/WRD/HD-92/279 .... 5666–12.45
USGS/WRD/HD-92/290 .... 5666–12.31
USGS/WRD/HD-92/292 .... 5666–12.31
USGS/WRD/HD-92/302 .... 5666–12.31
Water-Resources
Investigations Rpt.
88-4132 .... 5666–27.25
Water-Resources
Investigations Rpt.
89-4191 .... 5666–28.15
Water-Resources
Investigations Rpt.
90-4002 .... 5666–27.28
Water-Resources
Investigations Rpt.
90-4046 .... 5666–27.27
Water-Resources
Investigations Rpt.
90-4080 .... 5666–28.16
Water-Resources
Investigations Rpt.
90-4094 .... 5666–24.10
Water-Resources
Investigations Rpt.
90-4120 .... 5666–27.24
Water-Resources
Investigations Rpt.
90-4175 .... 5666–28.19
Water-Resources
Investigations Rpt.
90-4177 .... 5666–24.11
Water-Resources
Investigations Rpt.
91-4002 .... 5666–27.29
Water-Resources
Investigations Rpt.
91-4049 .... 5666–28.21
Water-Resources
Investigations Rpt.
91-4050 .... 5666–27.30
Water-Resources
Investigations Rpt.
91-4054 .... 5666–27.32
Water-Resources
Investigations Rpt.
91-4160 .... 5666–27.35
Water-Resources
Investigations Rpt.
91-4163 .... 5666–27.34
Water-Resources
Investigations Rpt.
91-4172 .... 5666–28.17
Water-Resources
Investigations Rpt.
91-4192 .... 5666–25.14
Water-Resources
Investigations Rpt.
92-4009 .... 5666–27.31

DEPARTMENT OF JUSTICE

DEA-92012 6284–7
DEA-92014 6288–9
DEA-92031 6284–6
INS Bull. 9 .... 6266–2.9
M-338 6264–7
NCJ-125097 .... 6066–30.1
NCJ-129671 6068–246
NCJ-130474 6064–29
NCJ-130582 6064–36
NCJ-130583 6064–34
NCJ-130758 6064–35
NCJ-130914 6064–27
NCJ-131645 .... 6066–3.46
NCJ-131649 6068–250
NCJ-131651 .... 6066–20.23
NCJ-132073 .... 6066–27.7
NCJ-132291 6064–33
NCJ-132397 6068–247
NCJ-132445 .... 6066–19.64
NCJ-133011 .... 6066–27.8
NCJ-133013 .... 6066–27.9
NCJ-133018 .... 6066–23.7
NCJ-133283 .... 6066–25.45
NCJ-133284 .... 6066–25.44
NCJ-133285 .... 6066–25.43
NCJ-133785 6068–251
NCJ-133963 .... 6066–31.1
NCJ-134126 .... 6066–3.47
NCJ-134177 .... 6066–19.65
NCJ-134371 6064–30
NCJ-134436 6064–39
NCJ-134500 .... 6066–25.46
NCJ-134505 .... 6066–19.67
NCJ-134724 .... 6066–19.70
NCJ-134726 .... 6066–25.48
NCJ-134727 .... 6066–19.68
NCJ-134728 .... 6066–19.69
NCJ-134729 .... 6066–25.47
NCJ-134730 6064–29
NCJ-134732 .... 6066–19.66
NCJ-134928 6064–33
NCJ-134929 6064–33
NCJ-134946 6064–26
NCJ-135777 .... 6066–25.50
NCJ-135943 .... 6066–3.48
NCJ-136317 .... 6066–20.24
NCJ-136396 .... 6066–20.22
NCJ-136610 6068–252
NCJ-136945 6064–31
NCJ-136950 .... 6066–25.49
NCJ-137002 6068–248
NCJ-137003 6068–218
NCJ-137369 6064–6
NCJ-137991 6064–40

Release 91-476 6008–33

DEPARTMENT OF LABOR

BLS Bull. 2385 6748–85
BLS Bull. 2389 6744–20
BLS Bull. 2390 .... 6787–6.253
BLS Bull. 2392 .... 6787–6.254
BLS Bull. 2395 6744–18
BLS Bull. 2396 6784–9
BLS Bull. 2398 6784–21
BLS Bull. 2399 6844–1
BLS Bull. 2400 6744–1
BLS Bull. 2401 6744–3
BLS Bull. 2402 6744–19
BLS Bull. 2404 .... 6826–2.8
BLS Bull. 2406 6824–1
BLS Bull. 2407 6728–32
BLS Bull. 2409 .... 6826–2.9
BLS Bull. 2410 6744–7
BLS Bull. 2411 6748–81
BLS Bull. 2413 6744–20
BLS Bull. 2414 6888–1
BLS Bull. 3060-31 .... 6785–12.1
BLS Bull. 3060-32 .... 6785–12.1
BLS Bull. 3060-33 .... 6785–12.1
BLS Bull. 3060-34 .... 6785–12.1
BLS Bull. 3060-35 .... 6785–12.2
BLS Bull. 3060-36 .... 6785–12.2
BLS Bull. 3060-37 .... 6785–12.2
BLS Bull. 3060-38 .... 6785–12.2
BLS Bull. 3060-39 .... 6785–12.2
BLS Bull. 3060-40 .... 6785–12.3
BLS Bull. 3060-41 .... 6785–12.3
BLS Bull. 3060-42 .... 6785–16.1
BLS Bull. 3060-43 .... 6785–16.1
BLS Bull. 3060-44 .... 6785–16.1
BLS Bull. 3060-45 .... 6785–12.4
BLS Bull. 3060-46 .... 6785–16.2
BLS Bull. 3060-47 .... 6785–16.3
BLS Bull. 3060-48 .... 6785–16.3
BLS Bull. 3060-49 .... 6785–16.3
BLS Bull. 3060-50 .... 6785–16.3
BLS Bull. 3060-51 .... 6785–16.3
BLS Bull. 3060-52 .... 6785–16.3
BLS Bull. 3060-53 .... 6785–16.3
BLS Bull. 3060-54 .... 6785–16.3
BLS Bull. 3060-55 .... 6785–16.3
BLS Bull. 3060-56 .... 6785–16.4
BLS Bull. 3060-57 .... 6785–16.4
BLS Bull. 3060-58 .... 6785–16.4
BLS Bull. 3060-59 .... 6785–16.4
BLS Bull. 3060-60 .... 6785–16.4
BLS Bull. 3060-61 .... 6785–16.4
BLS Bull. 3060-62 .... 6785–16.5
BLS Bull. 3060-63 .... 6785–16.5
BLS Bull. 3060-64 .... 6785–16.6
BLS Bull. 3065-1 .... 6785–17.1
BLS Bull. 3065-2 .... 6785–17.1
BLS Bull. 3065-3 .... 6785–17.1
BLS Bull. 3065-4 .... 6785–17.1
BLS Bull. 3065-5 .... 6785–17.1
BLS Bull. 3065-6 .... 6785–17.1
BLS Bull. 3065-7 .... 6785–17.1
BLS Bull. 3065-8 .... 6785–17.2
BLS Bull. 3065-9 .... 6785–17.2
BLS Bull. 3065-10 .... 6785–17.2
BLS Bull. 3065-11 .... 6785–17.2
BLS Bull. 3065-12 .... 6785–17.2
BLS Bull. 3065-13 .... 6785–17.3
BLS Bull. 3065-14 .... 6785–17.3
BLS Bull. 3065-15 .... 6785–17.3
BLS Bull. 3065-16 .... 6785–17.3
BLS Bull. 3065-17 .... 6785–17.3
BLS Bull. 3065-18 .... 6785–17.3
BLS Bull. 3065-19 .... 6785–17.3
BLS Bull. 3065-20 .... 6785–17.3
BLS Rpt. (nos.) 6742–17
BLS Rpt. 807 6888–23
BLS Rpt. 808 .... 6886–4.1
BLS Rpt. 811 .... 6886–4.2
BLS Rpt. 812 .... 6886–4.3
BLS Rpt. 813 .... 6886–4.4
BLS Rpt. 814 .... 6886–4.5
BLS Rpt. 817 6822–3
BLS Rpt. 820 .... 6726–2.1
BLS Rpt. 824 .... 6726–2.2
BLS Rpt. 825 6822–3
BLS Rpt. 827 .... 6726–2.3
BLS Rpt. 828 6728–42
BLS Rpt. 830 .... 6726–2.4
BLS Summary 91-6 .... 6785–5.2
BLS Summary 91-11 .... 6785–5.1
BLS Summary 92-1 6844–7
BLS Summary 92-5 .... 6785–6.1
BLS Working Paper 212 .... 6886–6.81
BLS Working Paper 213 .... 6886–6.82
BLS Working Paper 214 .... 6886–6.83
BLS Working Paper 215 .... 6886–6.84
BLS Working Paper 216 .... 6886–6.85
BLS Working Paper 217 .... 6886–6.86
BLS Working Paper 218 .... 6886–6.87
BLS Working Paper 219 .... 6886–6.88
BLS Working Paper 220 .... 6886–6.89
BLS Working Paper 221 .... 6886–6.90
BLS Working Paper 222 .... 6886–6.91
BLS Working Paper 223 .... 6886–6.92
BLS Working Paper 224 .... 6886–6.93
BLS Working Paper 225 .... 6886–6.94
BLS Working Paper 226 .... 6886–6.95
BLS Working Paper 227 .... 6886–6.96
BLS/LAUS/MR-(yr./nos.) 6742–22
Econ. Discussion Paper 38 .... 6366–3.28
Econ. Discussion Paper 39 .... 6366–3.29
Econ. Discussion Paper 40 .... 6366–3.30
Econ. Discussion Paper 41 6364–2
Fact Sheet 92-1 .... 6564–1.1
Fact Sheet 92-2 .... 6564–1.2
FLT 91-44 .... 6366–4.1
FLT 91-45 .... 6366–4.2
FLT 91-46 .... 6366–4.3
FLT 91-47 .... 6366–4.4
FLT 91-48 .... 6366–4.5
FLT 91-49 .... 6366–4.6
FLT 91-50 .... 6366–4.7
FLT 91-51 .... 6366–4.8
FLT 91-52 .... 6366–4.9
FLT 91-53 .... 6366–4.10
FLT 91-54 .... 6366–4.11
FLT 91-55 .... 6366–4.12
FLT 91-56 .... 6366–4.13
FLT 91-57 .... 6366–4.14
FLT 91-58 .... 6366–4.15
FLT 91-59 .... 6366–4.16
FLT 91-60 .... 6366–4.17
FLT 91-61 .... 6366–4.18
FLT 92-1 .... 6366–4.19
FLT 92-2 .... 6366–4.20
FLT 92-3 .... 6366–4.21
FLT 92-4 .... 6366–4.22
FLT 92-5 .... 6366–4.23
FLT 92-6 .... 6366–4.24
FLT 92-7 .... 6366–4.25
FLT 92-8 .... 6366–4.26
FLT 92-9 .... 6366–4.27
FLT 92-10 .... 6366–4.28
FLT 92-11 .... 6366–4.29
FLT 92-12 .... 6366–4.30
FLT 92-13 .... 6366–4.31
FLT 92-14 .... 6366–4.32
FLT 92-15 .... 6366–4.33
FLT 92-16 .... 6366–4.34
FLT 92-17 .... 6366–4.35
FLT 92-18 .... 6366–4.36
FLT 92-19 .... 6366–4.37
FLT 92-20 .... 6366–4.38
FLT 92-21 .... 6366–4.39
FLT 92-22 .... 6366–4.40
FLT 92-23 .... 6366–4.41
FLT 92-24 .... 6366–4.42
FLT 92-25 .... 6366–4.43
FLT 92-26 .... 6366–4.44
FLT 92-27 .... 6366–4.45
FLT 92-28 .... 6366–4.46
FLT 92-29 .... 6366–4.47
FLT 92-30 .... 6366–4.48
FLT 92-31 .... 6366–4.49
FLT 92-32 .... 6366–4.50
FLT 92-33 .... 6366–4.51
FLT 92-34 .... 6366–4.52
FLT 92-35 .... 6366–4.53
Immigration Policy and Res. Working Paper 1 .... 6366–6.1
Immigration Policy and Res. Working Paper 2 .... 6366–6.2
Immigration Policy and Res. Working Paper 3 .... 6366–6.3
Immigration Policy and Res. Working Paper 4 .... 6366–6.4
Immigration Policy and Res. Working Paper 5 .... 6366–6.5
Immigration Policy and Res. Working Paper 7 .... 6366–6.6
Immigration Policy and Res. Working Paper 8 .... 6366–6.7
Immigration Policy and Res. Working Paper 9 .... 6366–6.8
Immigration Policy and Res. Working Paper 10 .... 6366–6.9
Immigration Policy and Res. Working Paper 11 .... 6366–6.10
Immigration Policy and Res. Working Paper 13 .... 6366–6.11
Immigration Policy and Res. Working Paper 16 .... 6366–6.12
IR 1201 6664–3
IR 1202 6664–1
IR 1203 6664–5
IR 1204 6664–2
IR 1205 6664–4
UIPL 2-92 6404–10
UIPL 39-92 6404–10
Unemployment Insurance Occasional Paper No. 92-3 .... 6406–6.36
USDL (yr.-nos.) 6742–3
— 6742–12
— 6742–20
— 6742–21
— 6742–23
— 6822–2
USDL 90-585 6764–3
USDL 91-292 6744–21
USDL 92-53 6784–12
USDL 92-61 .... 6726–1.44
USDL 92-78 .... 6726–1.45
USDL 92-115 6782–6
USDL 92-172 .... 6606–3.10
USDL 92-255 .... 6726–1.49
USDL 92-295 6744–13
USDL 92-386 .... 6726–1.47
USDL 92-391 6744–21
USDL 92-395 .... 6726–1.46
USDL 92-491 .... 6726–1.50
USDL 92-530 .... 6726–1.48
USDL 92-543 6782–6
USDL 92-588 6744–14
USDL 92-631 .... 6784–17.1
USDL 92-632 .... 6726–1.52
USDL 92-644 .... 6726–1.51
USDL 92-722 6764–3

USDL 92-731 6844–3
USDL 92-738 .... 6726–1.53
USDL 92-739 .... 6726–1.54
USDL 92-740 .... 6784–17.2
USDL 92-752 .... 6726–1.55

DEPARTMENT OF STATE

Limits in the Seas, No. 112 .... 7006–8.7
Limits in the Seas, No. 113 .... 7006–8.8
Pub. 7669 .... 7006–2.20
Pub. 7748 .... 7006–2.23
Pub. 7753 .... 7006–2.6
Pub. 7759 .... 7006–2.8
Pub. 7768 .... 7006–2.21
Pub. 7798 .... 7006–2.14
Pub. 7841 .... 7006–2.27
Pub. 7906 .... 7006–2.19
Pub. 7932 .... 7006–2.13
Pub. 7961 .... 7006–2.4
Pub. 7968 .... 7006–2.1
Pub. 7974 .... 7006–2.3
Pub. 7998 .... 7006–2.16
Pub. 8010 .... 7006–2.22
Pub. 8013 .... 7006–2.7
Pub. 8022 .... 7006–2.11
Pub. 8097 .... 7006–2.17
Pub. 8132 .... 7006–2.5
Pub. 8169 .... 7006–2.25
Pub. 8184 .... 7006–2.15
Pub. 8228 .... 7006–2.26
Pub. 8874 .... 7006–2.1
— 7006–2.5
— 7006–2.8
Pub. 8933 .... 7006–2.2
Pub. 8963 .... 7006–2.12
Pub. 9375 .... 7006–2.18
Pub. 9433 7004–1
Pub. 9823 7184–1
Pub. 9867 7002–6
Pub. 9895 7004–15
Pub. 9935 7004–6
Pub. 9951 7004–18
Pub. 9953 7004–22
Pub. 9963 7004–13
Pub. 9998 7004–15
Pub. 10014 7002–6
Visa Bull. 9A 7188–1

DEPARTMENT OF TRANSPORTATION

Accident/Incident Bull. 160 7604–1
COMDTPUB 16590.3a 7406–5.3
COMDTPUB P16107.6 7404–2
COMDTPUB P16754.5 7404–1
DOT-FAA 42-92 7502–17
DOT-FAA-AM-91-18 .... 7506–10.96
DOT-FAA-AM-92-1 .... 7506–10.97
DOT-FAA-AM-92-2 .... 7506–10.98
DOT-FAA-AM-92-3 .... 7506–10.99
DOT-FAA-AM-92-4 .... 7506–10.100
DOT-FAA-AM-92-5 .... 7506–10.101
DOT-FAA-AM-92-6 .... 7506–10.102
DOT-FAA-AM-92-7 .... 7506–10.103
DOT-FAA-AM-92-8 .... 7506–10.104
DOT-FAA-AM-92-9 .... 7506–10.105
DOT-FAA-AM-92-10 .... 7506–10.106
DOT-FAA-AM-92-11 .... 7506–10.107
DOT-FAA-AM-92-12 .... 7506–10.108
DOT-FAA-AM-92-13 .... 7506–10.113
DOT-FAA-AM-92-14 .... 7506–10.114
DOT-FAA-AM-92-15 .... 7506–10.115
DOT-FAA-AM-92-16 .... 7506–10.116
DOT-FAA-AM-92-17 .... 7506–10.117
DOT-FAA-AM-92-18 .... 7506–10.118
DOT-FAA-AM-92-19 .... 7506–10.119
DOT-FAA-AM-92-20 .... 7506–10.120
DOT-FAA-AM-92-21 .... 7506–10.121
DOT-FAA-AM-92-22 .... 7506–10.109
DOT-FAA-AM-92-23 .... 7506–10.110
DOT-FAA-AM-92-24 .... 7506–10.111
DOT-FAA-AM-92-25 .... 7506–10.112
DOT-FAA-AM-92-26 .... 7506–10.122
DOT-FAA-AM-92-27 .... 7506–10.124
DOT-FAA-AM-92-28 .... 7506–10.123
DOT-FAA-AM-92-29 .... 7506–10.125
DOT-FAA-AM-92-30 .... 7506–10.126
DOT-FAA-AM-92-31 .... 7506–10.127
DOT-FAA-APO-92-1 7504–6
— 7504–37
DOT-FAA-APO-92-5 7504–7
DOT-FAA-APO-92-6 7504–15
DOT-FAA-ASC-91-1 7504–43
DOT-FAA-ASV-91-1 7508–76
DOT-FAA-CT-90/19 7504–50
DOT-FAA-CT-91/28 7504–50
DOT HS (nos.) 7762–2
DOT HS 807 710 7764–9
DOT HS 807 764 7768–121
DOT HS 807 770 7764–17
DOT HS 807 781 7764–18
DOT HS 807 784 7762–11
DOT HS 807 786 7764–16
DOT HS 807 794 7764–10
DOT HS 807 800 7768–122
DOT HS 807 821 7762–11
DOT HS 807 822 .... 7764–1.2
DOT HS 807 823 .... 7764–1.1
DOT HS 807 863 7768–124
DOT-T-92-03 7308–205
DOT-VNTSC-FTA-92-2 7884–13
FAA (nos.-yr.) 7502–14
FAA-APO 92-2 7504–28
FAA-APO-91-9 .... 7506–7.42
FAA-APO-91-10 7504–39
FAA-APO-91-11 .... 7506–7.43
FAA-APO-92-8 .... 7506–7.44
FHWA-ED-90-023 .... 7556–8.1
FHWA-ED-90-038 .... 7556–8.2
FHWA-ED-90-040 .... 7556–8.3
FHWA-ED-90-043 .... 7556–8.4
FHWA-MC-90-018 7554–9
FHWA-PD-91-008 .... 7556–8.5
FHWA-PD-91-014 7558–112
FHWA-PD-92-017 7552–12
FHWA-PD-93-011 7552–12
FHWA-PL-(yr.)-005 7552–8
FHWA-PL-92-002 7554–16
FHWA-PL-92-004 7554–41
FHWA-PL-92-008 7558–117
FHWA-PL-92-013 7554–18
FHWA-PL-92-016 7558–107
FHWA-PL-92-019 7554–21
FHWA-PL-92-025 7554–1
FHWA-PL-92-026 7558–120
FHWA-PL-92-027 .... 7556–6.2
FHWA-RD-90-103 7558–113
FHWA-RD-91-055 7558–114
FHWA-RD-91-075 .... 7558–119.1
FHWA-RD-91-076 .... 7558–119.2
FHWA-RD-92-007 7558–116
FHWA-SA-91-019 7558–118
FHWA-SA-91-034 .... 7558–98.2
FHWA-SA-92-003 7554–2
FHWA-SA-92-013 7554–26
FHWA-TS-89-046 .... 7558–98.1
FHWA-TS-91-003 7558–115
FTA-DC-26-0003-92-1 7884–11
FTA-MA-06-0194-92-01 7884–13
FTA-TTS-5-92-1 7884–1
HEP-23/11-90(1M)QE 7556–8.5
HNG-22 7554–40
HPM-10/6-92(150M)E 7554–21
HPM-40/7-92(10M)E 7556–6.2
HPM-40/7-92(700)QE 7558–120
HPM-40/9-92(50M)E 7554–41
HPP-24/R1-92(25M)E 7558–117
HPP-24/R12-91(50M)E 7558–117
HPP-24/12-91(5M)E 7558–117
HSR-30/2-92(625)QR 7558–114
HTA-121/6-92(700)QE 7558–98.2
MA-RD-840-90013 7708–5
MF-205 7554–32
NHTSA 06-92 .... 7766–7.29
NHTSA 11-92 .... 7766–7.30
NHTSA 15-92 .... 7766–7.31
NHTSA 20-92 .... 7766–7.32
NHTSA 23-92 .... 7766–7.33
NHTSA 32-92 .... 7766–7.34
NHTSA 36-92 .... 7766–7.35
NHTSA 48-92 .... 7306–10.4
NHTSA 53-92 .... 7766–7.36
NHTSA 65-92 .... 7766–7.37
NRM-21 7764–9
Tech. Assistance Brief Bulletin (nos.) 7882–3
Transportation Res. Circ. 384 7308–204
UMTA-DC-06-0651 7884–11
UMTRIS 1990 7884–11
UMTRIS 1991 7884–11

DEPARTMENT OF TREASURY

ATF P3320-4 8484–4
B(nos.) 8002–7
IR-92-(nos.) 8302–6
IR-92-6 8304–23
IRS Doc. 6149(Rev.11-91) 8304–24
IRS Doc. 6186(Rev.10-91) 8304–9
IRS Doc. 6187(Rev.8-91) 8302–7
IRS Doc. 6292(Rev.4-92) 8302–4
IRS Doc. 6961(Rev.4-92) 8304–22
IRS Doc. 7302(Rev.3-92) 8304–25
IRS Pub. 16(Rev.10-92) 8304–4
IRS Pub. 16(Rev.11-91) 8304–4
IRS Pub. 55(Rev.9-92) 8304–3
IRS Pub. 1053(Rev.5-92) 8304–21
IRS Pub. 1136(date) 8302–2
IRS Pub. 1267(Rev. 9/91) 8308–31
IRS Pub. 1304(Rev.9-91) 8304–2
IRS Pub. 1416(7-91) 8308–35
NB-1746 8008–155
Res. Paper 92-01 .... 8436–1.7
Res. Paper 9001 .... 8006–6.1
Res. Paper 9002 .... 8006–6.2
Res. Paper 9003 .... 8006–6.3
Res. Paper 9004 .... 8006–6.4
Res. Paper 9101 .... 8006–6.5
Res. Paper 9102 .... 8006–6.6
Res. Paper 9201 .... 8006–6.7
Rpt. Symbol 76 .... 8486–1.3

DEPARTMENT OF VETERANS AFFAIRS

RCS 10-0161 8704–4
Semiannual Rpt. 27 8602–1
Semiannual Rpt. 28 8602–1
1B 11-78 8704–3
1B 11-78a 8704–3

INDEPENDENT AGENCIES

Central Intelligence Agency

ALA 92-10033	9118–8
DI EEI (yr.-nos.)	9112–1
DI IESR (yr.-nos.)	9112–2
EUR 92-10016	9118–13
LDA CS (yr.-nos.)	9112–4
Ref. Aid IR 92-10004	9116–1.6
Ref. Aid IR 92-10005	9116–1.1
Ref. Aid IR 92-10006	9116–1.5
Ref. Aid IR 92-10007	9116–1.7
Ref. Aid IR 92-10008	9116–1.4
Ref. Aid IR 92-10009	9116–1.2
Ref. Aid IR 92-10010	9116–1.3
Ref. Aid OSE 92-10002	9118–19
Ref. Aid OSE 92-10017	9118–19
Ref. Aid RTT 92-10018	9116–1.6
Ref. Aid RTT 92-10019	9116–1.1
Ref. Aid RTT 92-10020	9116–1.5
Ref. Aid RTT 92-10021	9116–1.7
Ref. Aid RTT 92-10022	9116–1.4
Ref. Aid RTT 92-10023	9116–1.2
Ref. Aid RTT 92-10024	9116–1.3
Ref. Aid RTT 92-10031	9114–7

Environmental Protection Agency

EPA 300/R92-008	9184–21
EPA 402-R-(yr.-nos.)	9192–5
EPA 430/09-91-024	9204–7
EPA 450/R-92-001	9194–1
EPA 450/4-91-023	9194–1
EPA 540/8-91-067	9214–5
EPA 560/4-91-012	9238–71
EPA 560/4-91-013	9238–71
EPA 560/4-91-014	9234–6
EPA 600/R-92-021	9184–18
EPA 600/4-91-030	9194–17
EPA 600/8-91-037	9186–8.37
EPA 600/8-91-217	9186–8.38
EPA 600/9-91-025	9184–17
EPA Pub. 9320.7-04I	9216–5.5
EPA Pub. 9320.7-05I	9216–5.4
EPA Pub. 9320.7-07I	9216–3.26
—	9216–3.27
EPA Pub. 9355.6-04	9214–5

Federal Deposit Insurance Corp.

P-1400-105-90	9294–4
P-7700-01-91	9295–3.1
P-7700-02-91	9295–3.2
P-7700-03-91	9295–3.3
P-7700-04-91	9295–3.4
P-7700-05-91	9295–3.5
P-7700-06-91	9295–3.6
P-7700-07-91	9295–3.7

Federal Home Loan Mortgage Corp.

Pub. 159	9414–1

Federal National Mortgage Association

CA 012U03/92	9474–1
CA 123U05/92	9478–1

Federal Reserve Bank of Atlanta

Working Paper 91-9	9371–10.67
Working Paper 91-10	9371–10.68
Working Paper 91-11	9371–10.69
Working Paper 91-12	9371–10.70
Working Paper 91-13	9371–10.71
Working Paper 91-14	9371–10.72
Working Paper 91-15	9371–10.73
Working Paper 91-16	9371–10.74
Working Paper 91-17	9371–10.75
Working Paper 91-18	9371–10.76
Working Paper 92-1	9371–10.77
Working Paper 92-2	9371–10.78
Working Paper 92-3	9371–10.79
Working Paper 92-4	9371–10.80
Working Paper 92-5	9371–10.81
Working Paper 92-6	9371–10.82
Working Paper 92-7	9371–10.83
Working Paper 92-8	9371–10.84
Working Paper 92-9	9371–10.85
Working Paper 92-10	9371–10.86
Working Paper 92-11	9371–10.87
Working Paper 92-12	9371–10.88
Working Paper 92-13	9371–10.89
Working Paper 92-14	9371–10.90

Federal Reserve Bank of Boston

Conf. Series No. 35	9373–3.35
Working Paper 91-1	9373–27.1
Working Paper 91-2	9373–27.2
Working Paper 91-3	9373–27.3
Working Paper 91-4	9373–27.4
Working Paper 91-5	9373–27.5
Working Paper 91-6	9373–27.6
Working Paper 91-7	9373–27.7
Working Paper 91-8	9373–27.8
Working Paper 92-1	9373–27.9
Working Paper 92-2	9373–27.10
Working Paper 92-3	9373–27.11
Working Paper 92-4	9373–27.12
Working Paper 92-5	9373–27.13
Working Paper 92-6	9373–27.14
Working Paper 92-7	9373–27.15

Federal Reserve Bank of Chicago

WP-1991-16	9375–13.67
WP-1991-17	9375–13.68
WP-1991-18	9375–13.69
WP-1991-19	9375–13.70
WP-1991-20	9375–13.71
WP-1991-21	9375–13.72
WP-1991-22	9375–13.73
WP-1991-23	9375–13.74
WP-1991-25	9375–13.75
WP-1991-26	9375–13.76
WP-1991-27	9375–13.77
WP-1992-1	9375–13.78
WP-1992-2	9375–13.79
WP-1992-3	9375–13.80
WP-1992-4	9375–13.81
WP-1992-5	9375–13.82
WP-1992-6	9375–13.83
WP-1992-7	9375–13.84
WP-1992-8	9375–13.85
WP-1992-9	9375–13.86
WP-1992-10	9375–13.87
WP-1992-11	9375–13.88

Federal Reserve Bank of Cleveland

Working Paper 9115	9377–9.124
Working Paper 9116	9377–9.125
Working Paper 9117	9377–9.126
Working Paper 9118	9377–9.127
Working Paper 9119	9377–9.128
Working Paper 9120	9377–9.129
Working Paper 9121	9377–9.130
Working Paper 9122	9377–9.131
Working Paper 9201	9377–9.132
Working Paper 9202	9377–9.133
Working Paper 9203	9377–9.134
Working Paper 9204	9377–9.135
Working Paper 9205	9377–9.136
Working Paper 9206	9377–9.137
Working Paper 9207	9377–9.138
Working Paper 9208	9377–9.139
Working Paper 9209	9377–9.140
Working Paper 9210	9377–9.141
Working Paper 9211	9377–9.142
Working Paper 9212	9377–9.143
Working Paper 9213	9377–9.144
Working Paper 9214	9377–9.145

Federal Reserve Bank of Dallas

FIS Working Paper 1-92	9379–14.17
FIS Working Paper 2-92	9379–14.18
FIS Working Paper 3-92	9379–14.19
FIS Working Paper 4-91	9379–14.15
FIS Working Paper 4-92	9379–14.20
FIS Working Paper 5-91	9379–14.16
Res. Paper 9118	9379–12.80
Res. Paper 9119	9379–12.81
Res. Paper 9201	9379–12.82
Res. Paper 9202	9379–12.83
Res. Paper 9203	9379–12.84
Res. Paper 9204	9379–12.85
Res. Paper 9205	9379–12.86
Res. Paper 9206	9379–12.87
Res. Paper 9207	9379–12.88
Res. Paper 9208	9379–12.89
Res. Paper 9209	9379–12.90
Res. Paper 9210	9379–12.91
Res. Paper 9211	9379–12.92
Res. Paper 9212	9379–12.93
Res. Paper 9213	9379–12.94
Res. Paper 9214	9379–12.95
Res. Paper 9215	9379–12.96
Res. Paper 9216	9379–12.97

Federal Reserve Bank of Kansas City

RWP 91-01	9381–10.122
RWP 91-02	9381–10.123
RWP 91-03	9381–10.124
RWP 91-04	9381–10.125
RWP 91-05	9381–10.126
RWP 91-06	9381–10.127
RWP 91-07	9381–10.128
RWP 91-08	9381–10.129
RWP 92-01	9381–10.130
RWP 92-02	9381–10.131
RWP 92-03	9381–10.132
RWP 92-04	9381–10.133
RWP 92-05	9381–10.134

Federal Reserve Bank of Minneapolis

Staff Rpt. 146 .... 9383–20.16
Staff Rpt. 147 .... 9383–20.17
Staff Rpt. 148 .... 9383–20.18
Staff Rpt. 149 .... 9383–20.19
Staff Rpt. 150 .... 9383–20.20
Staff Rpt. 151 .... 9383–20.21
Staff Rpt. 152 .... 9383–20.22
Staff Rpt. 153 .... 9383–20.23
Staff Rpt. 154 .... 9383–20.24
Staff Rpt. 155 .... 9383–20.25

Federal Reserve Bank of New York

Res. Paper 9126 .... 9385–8.122
Res. Paper 9127 .... 9385–8.123
Res. Paper 9128 .... 9385–8.124
Res. Paper 9129 .... 9385–8.125
Res. Paper 9130 .... 9385–8.126
Res. Paper 9131 .... 9385–8.127
Res. Paper 9132 .... 9385–8.128
Res. Paper 9201 .... 9385–8.129
Res. Paper 9202 .... 9385–8.130
Res. Paper 9203 .... 9385–8.131
Res. Paper 9204 .... 9385–8.132
Res. Paper 9205 .... 9385–8.133
Res. Paper 9206 .... 9385–8.134
Res. Paper 9207 .... 9385–8.135
Res. Paper 9208 .... 9385–8.136
Res. Paper 9209 .... 9385–8.137
Res. Paper 9210 .... 9385–8.138
Res. Paper 9211 .... 9385–8.139
Res. Paper 9212 .... 9385–8.140
Res. Paper 9213 .... 9385–8.141
Res. Paper 9214 .... 9385–8.142
Res. Paper 9215 .... 9385–8.143
Res. Paper 9216 .... 9385–8.144
Res. Paper 9217 .... 9385–8.145
Res. Paper 9218 .... 9385–8.146

Federal Reserve Bank of Philadelphia

Working Paper 91-17 .... 9387–8.256
Working Paper 91-18 .... 9387–8.257
Working Paper 91-19 .... 9387–8.258
Working Paper 91-20 .... 9387–8.259
Working Paper 91-21 .... 9387–8.260
Working Paper 91-22 .... 9387–8.261
Working Paper 91-23 .... 9387–8.262
Working Paper 91-24 .... 9387–8.263
Working Paper 92-1 .... 9387–8.264
Working Paper 92-2 .... 9387–8.265
Working Paper 92-3 .... 9387–8.266
Working Paper 92-4 .... 9387–8.267
Working Paper 92-5 .... 9387–8.268
Working Paper 92-6 .... 9387–8.269
Working Paper 92-7 .... 9387–8.270
Working Paper 92-8 .... 9387–8.271
Working Paper 92-9 .... 9387–8.272
Working Paper 92-10 .... 9387–8.273
Working Paper 92-11 .... 9387–8.274
Working Paper 92-12 .... 9387–8.275
Working Paper 92-13 .... 9387–8.276
Working Paper 92-14 .... 9387–8.277
Working Paper 92-15 .... 9387–8.278
Working Paper 92-16 .... 9387–8.279
Working Paper 92-17 .... 9387–8.280
Working Paper 92-18 .... 9387–8.281
Working Paper 92-19 .... 9387–8.282
Working Paper 92-20 .... 9387–8.283
Working Paper 92-21 .... 9387–8.284

Federal Reserve Bank of Richmond

Pub. No. P-1 9389–2
Working Paper 92-1 .... 9389–19.32
Working Paper 92-2 .... 9389–19.33
Working Paper 92-3 .... 9389–19.34

Federal Reserve Bank of San Francisco

Working Paper 92-01 .... 9393–10.17
Working Paper 92-02 .... 9393–10.18
Working Paper 92-03 .... 9393–10.19
Working Paper 92-04 .... 9393–10.20
Working Paper 92-05 .... 9393–10.21
Working Paper 92-06 .... 9393–10.22

Federal Reserve Board of Governors

C.2 .... 9365–5.1
C.9 .... 9365–4.1
E.2 9365–3
E.11 .... 9365–3.7
E.15 .... 9365–3.10
E.16 9365–3
Finance and Economics Discussion Series, No. 172 .... 9366–6.286
Finance and Economics Discussion Series, No. 173 .... 9366–6.287
Finance and Economics Discussion Series, No. 174 .... 9366–6.288
Finance and Economics Discussion Series, No. 175 .... 9366–6.289
Finance and Economics Discussion Series, No. 176 .... 9366–6.290
Finance and Economics Discussion Series, No. 177 .... 9366–6.291
Finance and Economics Discussion Series, No. 178 .... 9366–6.292
Finance and Economics Discussion Series, No. 179 .... 9366–6.293
Finance and Economics Discussion Series, No. 180 .... 9366–6.294
Finance and Economics Discussion Series, No. 181 .... 9366–6.295
Finance and Economics Discussion Series, No. 182 .... 9366–6.296
Finance and Economics Discussion Series, No. 183 .... 9366–6.297
Finance and Economics Discussion Series, No. 184 .... 9366–6.298
Finance and Economics Discussion Series, No. 185 .... 9366–6.299
Finance and Economics Discussion Series, No. 186 .... 9366–6.300
FRB 1/1-50-0592 9364–12
FRB 1/1-1500-0292 .... 9366–1.162
FRB 1/1-2000-0292 C 9364–10
FRB 1/1-2500-0392 .... 9366–1.163
FRB 1-50-0591 9364–12
FRB 1-1700-1191-C 9364–5
FRB 1-1700-1291 9364–8
FRB 1-3000-0491 9364–8
FRB 1-3000-0491C 9364–5
FRB 1-12500-0492C 9364–1
FRB 4-4000-0292 9362–4
G.5 9365–2
G.6 .... 9365–2.5
G.7 9365–2
G.10 9365–2
G.13 .... 9365–2.14
G.17 .... 9365–2.24
G.19 .... 9365–2.6
G.20 .... 9365–2.7
H.3 9365–1
H.4.1 9365–1
H.4.2 .... 9365–1.3
H.5 9365–1
H.6 9365–1
H.8 9365–1
H.10 .... 9365–1.5
H.15 9365–1
Intl. Finance Discussion Paper 416 .... 9366–7.270
Intl. Finance Discussion Paper 417 .... 9366–7.271
Intl. Finance Discussion Paper 418 .... 9366–7.272
Intl. Finance Discussion Paper 419 .... 9366–7.273
Intl. Finance Discussion Paper 420 .... 9366–7.274
Intl. Finance Discussion Paper 421 .... 9366–7.275
Intl. Finance Discussion Paper 422 .... 9366–7.276
Intl. Finance Discussion Paper 423 .... 9366–7.277
Intl. Finance Discussion Paper 424 .... 9366–7.278
Intl. Finance Discussion Paper 425 .... 9366–7.279
Intl. Finance Discussion Paper 426 .... 9366–7.280
K.7 9366–7
Staff Study 162 .... 9366–1.162
Staff Study 163 .... 9366–1.163
Z.1 .... 9365–3.3
Z.7 9365–3
Z.11 9366–6

Interstate Commerce Commission

Statement A-300 9484–5
Statement M-350 9482–3

National Aeronautics and Space Administration

NASA SP-4104 9508–39
NASA TM-105457 9504–7
NP-158 9508–41
Release 91-136 .... 9506–2.144
Release 92-XX 9506–2.149
Release 92-32 .... 9506–2.146
Release 92-48 .... 9506–2.148
Release 92-81 .... 9506–2.150
Release 92-95 .... 9506–2.147
Release 92-128 .... 9506–2.151
Release 92-142 .... 9506–2.152
Release 92-153 .... 9506–2.153
Release 92-185 .... 9506–2.154

Release 92-211 .... 9506–2.145

National Archives and Records Administration

Natl Archives Inventory Series No. 13 .... 9516–2.1
Natl Archives Inventory Series No. 14 .... 9516–2.2
Ref. Info. Paper 68 .... 9516–1.1
Ref. Info. Paper 69 .... 9516–1.2
Ref. Info. Paper 70 .... 9516–1.3
Ref. Info. Paper 71 .... 9516–1.4
Ref. Info. Paper 72 .... 9516–1.5
Ref. Info. Paper 73 .... 9516–1.6
Ref. Info. Paper 75 .... 9516–1.7
Ref. Info. Paper 76 .... 9516–1.8
Ref. Info. Paper 77 .... 9516–1.9
Ref. Info. Paper 78 .... 9516–1.10

National Credit Union Administration

NCUA 8060 9532–6
NCUA 8602 9534–6
NCUA Letter No. 133 9532–7
NCUA Letter No. 138 9532–7
Res. Study 15 .... 9536–1.7
Res. Study 17 .... 9536–1.8

National Labor Relations Board

ER(nos.) 9582–2

National Science Foundation

NSB 91-1 9624–10
NSF 90-58 9628–86
NSF 90-132 .... 9626–7.1
NSF 91-2 9624–26
NSF 91-4 .... 9626–7.5
NSF 91-5 .... 9626–7.4
NSF 91-23 .... 9626–7.3
NSF 91-45 .... 9626–7.2
NSF 91-61 9624–16
NSF 91-66 .... 9626–7.7
NSF 91-76 .... 9626–7.8
NSF 91-96 .... 9626–7.9
NSF 91-114 .... 9626–7.6
NSF 91-306 .... 9626–6.38
NSF 91-310 .... 9626–8.1
NSF 91-312 9628–88
NSF 91-316 .... 9626–8.2
NSF 91-318 .... 9626–8.5
NSF 91-319 .... 9626–8.4
NSF 91-320 .... 9626–8.3
NSF 92-1 9624–6
NSF 92-36 .... 9626–7.10
NSF 92-55 9624–24
NSF 92-73 9624–16
NSF 92-303 9624–20
NSF 92-310 .... 9626–8.6
NSF 92-312 9627–23
NSF 92-318 9627–9
NSF 92-321 9627–13
NSF 92-323 9627–7
NSF 92-324 9627–17
NSF 92-325 9624–25
NSF 92-329 .... 9626–8.7
Semiannual Rpt. 6 9622–1
Semiannual Rpt. 7 9622–1

National Transportation Safety Board

NTSB/AAB-(yr.-nos.) 9612–1
NTSB/ARC-91/01 9614–2
NTSB/MAB-(yr.-nos.) 9612–4
NTSB/RAB-89/01 9614–8
NTSB/RAB-89-02 9614–8
NTSB/RAB-92/01 9614–8
NTSB/SS-91/01 9618–18
NTSB/SS-91/02 9618–19
SB 92-03 9614–9
SB 92-28 9614–6

Nuclear Regulatory Commission

NUREG-0713, Vol. 10 9634–3
NUREG-0713, Vol. 11 9634–3
NUREG-1100, Vol. 8 9634–9
NUREG-1145, Vol. 8 9634–2
NUREG/CR-2850, Vol. 10 9634–7
PNL-4221 9634–7

Office of Personnel Management

MW (nos.) 9842–1
OLRWP 91-05 9844–14
OLRWP 91-6 9847–1
OLRWP 92-6 9847–1
OPM/SASD/EEO-90/1 9844–27
OPM/SASD/PAY-91/1 9844–6
OPM/SASD/WKYRS-90/1 9844–31
PSOG 90-06 9844–31
PSOG 90-71 9844–27
PSOG 91-33 9844–6
RI 10-27 9844–34
SES 92-07 9844–36

Pension Benefit Guaranty Corp.

PBGC 93-02 9674–2

Resolution Trust Corp.

RTC 1400-001-90 9724–1

Small Business Administration

Vol. I: 40-00.10 .... 9764–1.1
Vol. I: 40-00.12 .... 9764–1.1
Vol. II: 40-00.11 .... 9764–1.2
Vol. II: 40-00.13 .... 9764–1.2

Tennessee Valley Authority

Bull. Y-225 9804–30
Bull. Y-230 9804–30
Circ. Z-69 .... 9804–28.1
Circ. Z-289 .... 9806–9.11
Circ. Z-309 .... 9806–9.12
Circ. Z-69A 9804–28.2
Monthly Rpt. (nos.) 9802–1
Tech. Rpt. No. 29-1-54 9804–7
TVA/LR/NRM-89/1/supp 9806–9.13
TVA/LR/NRM-89/1 .... 9806–9.13
TVA/NFERC-91/15 9804–30
TVA/NFERC-92/8 9804–30
TVA/NFERC/BIO-92/5 .... 9806–9.12
TVA/P&E/EU&DR-(yr./nos.) 9802–1
TVA/WR-92/11 9804–7

U.S. Information Agency

OIG Issue 92-I 9852–2

U.S. International Development Cooperation Agency

AID Impact Evaluation Rpt. No. 78 .... 9916–1.76
AID Impact Evaluation Rpt. No. 79 .... 9916–1.77
AID Staff Working Paper No. 2 .... 9916–13.2
AID Staff Working Paper No. 3 .... 9916–13.3
AID Staff Working Paper No. 4 .... 9916–13.4
AID Staff Working Paper No. 5 .... 9916–13.5
CIMS-116 9914–7
CONG-R-0105 9914–5
PD-ABD-616 .... 9916–12.59
PD-ABD-671 .... 9916–12.60
PD-ABD-749 .... 9916–12.61
PD-ABD-839 .... 9916–12.62
PD-ABD-893 .... 9916–12.63
PD-ABD-955 .... 9916–12.67
PD-ABD-967 .... 9916–12.66
PD-ABD-980 .... 9916–12.69
PD-ABE-005 .... 9916–12.65
PD-ABE-031 .... 9916–12.64
PD-ABE-107 .... 9916–12.70
PN-AAX-251 .... 9916–1.76
PN-AAX-252 .... 9916–1.77
PN-ABD-855 .... 9916–12.51
PN-ABH-609 .... 9916–12.52
PN-ABH-855 .... 9916–12.53
PN-ABH-856 .... 9916–12.54
PN-ABI-275 .... 9916–12.56
PN-ABJ-409 .... 9916–12.57
PN-ABJ-956 .... 9916–12.55
PN-ABK-006 .... 9916–12.58
PN-ABK-018 .... 9916–12.48
PN-ABK-020 .... 9916–12.49
PN-ABK-046 .... 9916–12.50
PN-ABL-330 .... 9916–12.71
PN-ABL-415 .... 9916–12.68
PN-ABL-681 .... 9916–12.72
W-209 9912–4
W-213 9912–1
W-224 9912–3
W-442 9914–6
W-443 9914–7

U.S. International Trade Commission

SOC Series C/P (yr.-nos.) 9882–1
USITC Pub. (nos.) 9882–2
— 9882–6
— 9882–13
USITC Pub. 2426 (GM-1) 9885–10.1
USITC Pub. 2430 (ME-1) 9885–9.1
USITC Pub. 2445 (ET-1) 9885–12.1
USITC Pub. 2446 .... 9886–4.179
USITC Pub. 2449 .... 9886–13.1
USITC Pub. 2452 .... 9886–4.179
USITC Pub. 2456 (SV-1) 9885–12.2
USITC Pub. 2458 (CH-1) 9885–11.1
USITC Pub. 2459 (AG-1) 9885–8.1
USITC Pub. 2462 (AG-2) 9885–8.2
USITC Pub. 2469 9884–14

USITC Pub. 2470 9884–3
USITC Pub. 2471 .... 9886–14.337
USITC Pub. 2472 .... 9886–4.180
USITC Pub. 2474 .... 9886–14.338
USITC Pub. 2475 (MM-1) 9885–13.1
USITC Pub. 2476 (GM-2) 9885–10.2
USITC Pub. 2477 (AG-3) 9885–8.3
USITC Pub. 2478 (AG-4) 9885–8.4
USITC Pub. 2482 .... 9886–14.339
USITC Pub. 2484 9884–12
USITC Pub. 2487 .... 9886–14.340
USITC Pub. 2489 .... 9886–14.341
USITC Pub. 2490 9884–1
USITC Pub. 2491 9884–23
USITC Pub. 2495 .... 9886–4.183
USITC Pub. 2496 .... 9886–15.79
USITC Pub. 2497 .... 9886–14.342
USITC Pub. 2498 .... 9886–14.343
USITC Pub. 2501 .... 9886–4.181
USITC Pub. 2502 .... 9886–14.344
USITC Pub. 2504 (MM-2) 9885–13.2
USITC Pub. 2505 (ME-2) 9885–9.2
USITC Pub. 2507 .... 9886–4.185
USITC Pub. 2508 .... 9886–4.182
USITC Pub. 2509 (CH-2) 9885–11.2
USITC Pub. 2510 .... 9886–14.345
USITC Pub. 2511 (AG-5) 9885–8.5
USITC Pub. 2512 .... 9886–19.82
USITC Pub. 2513 .... 9886–14.346
USITC Pub. 2514 .... 9886–14.347
USITC Pub. 2516 .... 9886–4.182
USITC Pub. 2517 9884–25
USITC Pub. 2519 .... 9886–14.348
USITC Pub. 2520 (AG-6) 9885–8.6
USITC Pub. 2520 (AG-7) 9885–8.7
USITC Pub. 2521 .... 9886–4.184
USITC Pub. 2523 (GM-3) 9885–10.3
USITC Pub. 2524 .... 9886–14.349
USITC Pub. 2525 .... 9886–14.350
USITC Pub. 2526 .... 9886–19.83
USITC Pub. 2528 .... 9886–14.352
USITC Pub. 2529 .... 9886–14.351
USITC Pub. 2530 .... 9886–15.80
USITC Pub. 2533 .... 9886–14.353
USITC Pub. 2534 .... 9886–14.354
USITC Pub. 2535 .... 9886–19.84
USITC Pub. 2536 .... 9886–14.355
USITC Pub. 2537 .... 9886–14.356
USITC Pub. 2540 (GM-4) 9885–10.4
USITC Pub. 2541 .... 9886–4.186
USITC Pub. 2542 .... 9886–14.357
USITC Pub. 2545 (AG-8) 9885–8.9
USITC Pub. 2546 (ME-3) 9885–9.3
USITC Pub. 2547 .... 9886–4.187
USITC Pub. 2548 (CH-3) 9885–11.3
USITC Pub. 2549 .... 9886–19.85
USITC Pub. 2550 .... 9886–19.86
USITC Pub. 2551 (AG-9) 9885–8.8
USITC Pub. 2552 .... 9886–14.358
USITC Pub. 2553 9884–20
USITC Pub. 2554 9884–5
USITC Pub. 2555 .... 9886–14.359
USITC Pub. 2558 9882–15
USITC Pub. 2559 .... 9886–14.360
USITC Pub. 2561 9884–18
USITC Pub. 2562 .... 9886–4.188
USITC Pub. 2564 .... 9886–14.361
USITC Pub. 2565 .... 9886–14.362
USITC Pub. 2567 .... 9886–13.2
USITC Pub. 2569 (SV-2) 9885–12.3
USITC Pub. 2570 (ME-4) 9885–9.4
USITC Pub. 2573 .... 9886–4.189
USITC Pub. 2577 .... 9886–14.363
USITC Pub. 2578 (CH-4) 9885–11.4
USITC Pub. 2582 9884–23
USITC Pub. 2583 .... 9886–14.364
USITC Pub. 2585 .... 9886–14.365

SPECIAL BOARDS, COMMITTEES, AND COMMISSIONS

Advisory Commission on Intergovernmental Relations

A-118 10048–82
A-119 10048–83
M-178 10048–53
M-179 10048–84
M-180-II 10044–1.2
M-180 .... 10044–1.1
M-181 .... 10046–9.2
M-182 10044–8
M-183 10048–85
S-21 10044–2

Federal Financial Institutions Examination Council

Rpt. E.16(126) 13002–1

Federal Labor Relations Authority

FLRA Doc. 1401 13364–1

National Advisory Council on Indian Education

ED/OESE 91-24 14874–1
ED/OESE 92-33 14874–1

National Commission for Employment Policy

Res. Rpt. 91-02 .... 15496–1.14
Res. Rpt. 91-03 .... 15496–1.15
Res. Rpt. 91-04 .... 15496–1.16
Rpt. 29 15494–1
Spec. Rpt. 30 15498–28
Spec. Rpt. 31 15498–29

Physician Payment Review Commission

Background Paper No. 89-1 .... 17266–2.1
Background Paper No. 89-2 .... 17266–2.2
Background Paper No. 89-3 .... 17266–2.3
Background Paper No. 89-4 .... 17266–2.4
Background Paper No. 91-1 .... 17266–2.5
Background Paper No. 91-6 .... 17266–2.7
Background Paper No. 91-7 .... 17266–2.8
Background Paper No. 92-1 .... 17266–2.9
Background Paper No. 92-2 .... 17266–2.10
Background Paper No. 92-6 .... 17266–2.11
Rpt. to Congress No. 91-3 .... 17266–1.3
Rpt. to Congress No. 91-4 .... 17266–1.4
Rpt. to Congress No. 91-5 .... 17266–1.5
Rpt. to Congress No. 92-3 .... 17266–1.6
Rpt. to Congress No. 92-4 .... 17266–1.7
Rpt. to Congress No. 92-5 .... 17266–1.8

Prospective Payment Assessment Commission

C-89-04 .... 17206–1.13
C-92-01 .... 17206–1.14
C-92-02 .... 17206–1.15
C-92-03 .... 17206–1.16
C-92-04 .... 17206–1.17
E-91-01 .... 17206–2.29
E-91-02 .... 17206–2.30
E-91-03 .... 17206–2.33
E-91-04 .... 17206–2.34
E-91-05 .... 17206–2.35
E-91-06 .... 17206–2.36
E-92-01 .... 17206–2.37
E-92-02 .... 17206–2.38
E-92-03 .... 17206–2.41
E-92-04 .... 17206–2.39
I-91-01 .... 17206–2.27
I-91-02 .... 17206–2.28
I-91-03 .... 17206–2.31
I-91-04 .... 17206–2.32
I-92-01 .... 17206–2.40
I-92-02 .... 17206–2.42

CONGRESS

Congressional Committees

H. Doc. 102-279 4704–4
H. Doc. 102-280 4654–11
H. Doc. 102-281 4654–12
H. Rpt. 102-450 21264–2
S. Doc. 102-10, Pt. 1 .... 25922–1.1
S. Doc. 102-10, Pt. 2 .... 25922–1.2
S. Doc. 102-12 25922–2
S. Doc. 102-19, Pt. 1 .... 25922–1.1
S. Doc. 102-19, Pt. 2 .... 25922–1.2
S. Hrg. 101-181 23844–4
S. Hrg. 101-259, Pt. 12 25168–78
S. Hrg. 101-928 25318–84
S. Hrg. 101-1049 25248–128
S. Hrg. 101-1215 23848–224
S. Hrg. 101-1236 25368–177
S. Hrg. 101-1259 25368–179
S. Hrg. 101-1288 25528–119
S. Hrg. 101-1290 25148–45
S. Hrg. 101-1293 25428–2
S. Hrg. 101-1294 25408–116
S. Hrg. 102-5, Pt. 14 25318–83
S. Hrg. 102-55 25248–127
S. Hrg. 102-57 25318–82
S. Hrg. 102-58 25548–105
S. Hrg. 102-84, Pt. 1 25368–180
S. Hrg. 102-127 25268–79
S. Hrg. 102-135 25528–118
S. Hrg. 102-150 25408–115
S. Hrg. 102-184 23848–227
S. Hrg. 102-206 25528–120
S. Hrg. 102-234 25368–181
S. Hrg. 102-249, Pt. 40 .... 23846–4.34
S. Hrg. 102-249, Pt. 41 .... 23846–4.35
S. Hrg. 102-249, Pt. 42 .... 23846–4.36
S. Hrg. 102-261 25408–118
S. Hrg. 102-288 25388–59
S. Hrg. 102-313 25368–178
S. Hrg. 102-339 23848–230
S. Hrg. 102-350, Pt. 1 25388–60
S. Hrg. 102-429 25248–129
S. Hrg. 102-453 25318–85
S. Hrg. 102-461 25248–130
S. Hrg. 102-498 25408–119
S. Prt. 102-44 25728–44
S. Prt. 102-50 25148–44
S. Prt. 102-55 23848–226
S. Prt. 102-83 25408–120
S. Pub. 101-15 25944–1

S. Rpt. 102-266 23844–2

General Accounting Office

GAO/AFMD-(nos.) 26102–6
GAO/AFMD-92-10 26111–77
GAO/AFMD-92-51 26111–78
GAO/AFMD-92-54 26111–80
GAO/AFMD-92-66 FS 26111–79
GAO/GGD-91-85 26119–364
GAO/GGD-91-88 26119–365
GAO/GGD-91-101 26119–367
GAO/GGD-91-112 FS 26119–366
GAO/GGD-91-137 BR 26119–368
GAO/GGD-91-139 FS 26119–369
GAO/GGD-92-1 26119–370
GAO/GGD-92-9 26119–385
GAO/GGD-92-18 26119–373
GAO/GGD-92-19 26119–374
GAO/GGD-92-21 FS 26119–375
GAO/GGD-92-26 26119–378
GAO/GGD-92-30 26119–381
GAO/GGD-92-31 26119–380
GAO/GGD-92-34 26119–386
GAO/GGD-92-35 FS 26119–371
GAO/GGD-92-36 FS 26119–372
GAO/GGD-92-37 26119–376
GAO/GGD-92-38 26119–383
GAO/GGD-92-43 26119–389
GAO/GGD-92-44 26119–392
GAO/GGD-92-46 26119–390
GAO/GGD-92-48 BR 26119–377
GAO/GGD-92-49 26119–384
GAO/GGD-92-51 26119–382
GAO/GGD-92-52 26119–391
GAO/GGD-92-54 BR 26119–379
GAO/GGD-92-56 26119–398
GAO/GGD-92-58 26119–395
GAO/GGD-92-61 BR 26119–387
GAO/GGD-92-62 26119–399
GAO/GGD-92-63 26119–402
GAO/GGD-92-64 FS 26119–388
GAO/GGD-92-65 26119–396
GAO/GGD-92-66 26119–393
GAO/GGD-92-73 26119–407
GAO/GGD-92-74 26119–401
GAO/GGD-92-75 26119–397
GAO/GGD-92-79 26119–394
GAO/GGD-92-81 BR 26119–405
GAO/GGD-92-85 26119–409
GAO/GGD-92-87 BR 26119–410
GAO/GGD-92-88 BR 26119–400
GAO/GGD-92-89 26119–411
GAO/GGD-92-91 26119–406
GAO/GGD-92-93 26119–415
GAO/GGD-92-94 26119–403
GAO/GGD-92-95 FS 26119–404
GAO/GGD-92-96 26119–427
GAO/GGD-92-101 FS 26119–412
GAO/GGD-92-106 26119–408
GAO/GGD-92-109 26119–419
GAO/GGD-92-111 26119–289
GAO/GGD-92-113 26119–416
GAO/GGD-92-114 26119–414
GAO/GGD-92-120 FS 26119–413
GAO/GGD-92-123 26119–420
GAO/GGD-92-131 26119–417
GAO/GGD-92-133 26119–421
GAO/GGD-92-134 BR 26119–422
GAO/GGD-92-135 FS 26119–423
GAO/GGD-92-139 FS 26119–418
GAO/GGD-93-1 26119–430
GAO/GGD-93-2 26119–424
GAO/GGD-93-6 26119–428
GAO/GGD-93-9 BR 26119–425
GAO/GGD-93-10 FS 26119–426
GAO/GGD-93-11 BR 26119–429
GAO/GGD-93-12 26119–431
GAO/HRD-92-5 26121–454
GAO/HRD-92-6 26121–440
GAO/HRD-92-8 26121–439
GAO/HRD-92-18 26121–458
GAO/HRD-92-19 26121–441
GAO/HRD-92-35 26121–453
GAO/HRD-92-36 26121–444
GAO/HRD-92-39 FS 26121–442
GAO/HRD-92-40 26121–443
GAO/HRD-92-43 26121–446
GAO/HRD-92-44 FS 26121–451
GAO/HRD-92-45 26121–447
GAO/HRD-92-48 26121–455
GAO/HRD-92-49 26121–450
GAO/HRD-92-54 26121–452
GAO/HRD-92-56 26121–459
GAO/HRD-92-58 FS 26121–466
GAO/HRD-92-60 26121–468
GAO/HRD-92-61 26121–467
GAO/HRD-92-62 FS 26121–448
GAO/HRD-92-63 BR 26121–456
GAO/HRD-92-65 BR 26121–445
GAO/HRD-92-67 BR 26121–460
GAO/HRD-92-72 BR 26121–449
GAO/HRD-92-77 26121–464
GAO/HRD-92-81 26121–477
GAO/HRD-92-87 FS 26121–457
GAO/HRD-92-90 26121–462
GAO/HRD-92-91 26121–463
GAO/HRD-92-98 26121–465
GAO/HRD-92-105 26121–461
GAO/HRD-92-106 26121–470
GAO/HRD-92-107 26121–484
GAO/HRD-92-109 26121–474
GAO/HRD-92-110 26121–482
GAO/HRD-92-121 26121–476
GAO/HRD-92-124 .... 26106–8.15
GAO/HRD-92-125 26121–485
GAO/HRD-92-128 26121–472
GAO/HRD-92-130 FS 26121–471
GAO/HRD-92-136 FS 26121–478
GAO/HRD-92-137 FS 26121–469
GAO/HRD-92-138 FS 26121–473
GAO/HRD-92-142 26121–483
GAO/HRD-92-153 BR 26121–481
GAO/HRD-92-159 26121–479
GAO/HRD-93-2 26121–489
GAO/HRD-93-11 26121–487
GAO/HRD-93-17 26121–486
GAO/HRD-93-22 FS 26121–490
GAO/HRD-93-25 26121–488
GAO/IMTEC-92-6 FS 26125–47
GAO/IMTEC-92-58 BR 26125–46
GAO/NSIAD-91-321 26123–375
GAO/NSIAD-92-03 26123–376
GAO/NSIAD-92-28 26123–367
GAO/NSIAD-92-29 26123–372
GAO/NSIAD-92-31 26123–373
GAO/NSIAD-92-33 26123–374
GAO/NSIAD-92-56 26123–368
GAO/NSIAD-92-57 26123–380
GAO/NSIAD-92-60 26123–377
GAO/NSIAD-92-61 26123–369
GAO/NSIAD-92-62 26123–383
GAO/NSIAD-92-64 26123–385
GAO/NSIAD-92-65 26123–370
GAO/NSIAD-92-71 26123–371
GAO/NSIAD-92-82 26123–390
GAO/NSIAD-92-85 26123–381
GAO/NSIAD-92-90 26123–389
GAO/NSIAD-92-98 .... 26123–392.1
GAO/NSIAD-92-98 S 26123–392.2
GAO/NSIAD-92-101 26123–379
GAO/NSIAD-92-102 26123–386
GAO/NSIAD-92-111 FS 26123–394
GAO/NSIAD-92-113 26123–134
GAO/NSIAD-92-116 26123–387
GAO/NSIAD-92-117 26123–395
GAO/NSIAD-92-133 26123–384
GAO/NSIAD-92-144 26104–24
GAO/NSIAD-92-146 26123–378
GAO/NSIAD-92-148 26123–382
GAO/NSIAD-92-172 26123–84
GAO/NSIAD-92-174 26123–388
GAO/NSIAD-92-198 26123–400
GAO/NSIAD-92-203 26123–398
GAO/NSIAD-92-213 FS 26123–397
GAO/NSIAD-92-214 26123–391
GAO/NSIAD-92-218 26123–401
GAO/NSIAD-92-227 26123–396
GAO/NSIAD-92-229 26123–405
GAO/NSIAD-92-236 26123–406
GAO/NSIAD-92-247 26123–404
GAO/NSIAD-92-257 26123–402
GAO/NSIAD-92-274 BR 26123–399
GAO/NSIAD-92-306 26123–403
GAO/OCG-92-1 26104–23
GAO/OCG-92-2 26109–5
GAO/OP-92-1 A 26104–5.1
GAO/OP-92-1 B 26104–5.2
GAO/OP-92-1 C 26104–5.3
GAO/OP-92-1 D 26104–5.4
GAO/OPA-91-15 26104–17
GAO/PEMD-91-16 26131–93
GAO/PEMD-91-24 26131–94
GAO/PEMD-92-4 26131–95
GAO/PEMD-92-5 26131–99
GAO/PEMD-92-6 26131–97
GAO/PEMD-92-8 26131–91
GAO/PEMD-92-11 26131–96
GAO/PEMD-92-12 26131–92
GAO/PEMD-92-16 26131–98
GAO/PEMD-92-20 26131–103
GAO/PEMD-92-26 26131–101
GAO/PEMD-92-29 26131–100
GAO/PEMD-92-34 26131–102
GAO/RCED-91-84 .... 26106–10.6
GAO/RCED-91-200 26113–549
GAO/RCED-92-5 26113–553
GAO/RCED-92-11 FS 26113–548
GAO/RCED-92-12 26113–552
GAO/RCED-92-24 26113–564
GAO/RCED-92-25 26113–556
GAO/RCED-92-30 26113–551
GAO/RCED-92-33 26113–550
GAO/RCED-92-35 26113–561
GAO/RCED-92-37 26113–393
GAO/RCED-92-39 26113–557
GAO/RCED-92-49 26113–554
GAO/RCED-92-50 26113–558
GAO/RCED-92-51 26113–567
GAO/RCED-92-57 FS 26113–560
GAO/RCED-92-66 26113–568
GAO/RCED-92-67 26113–555
GAO/RCED-92-68 26113–563
GAO/RCED-92-72 26113–562
GAO/RCED-92-80 BR 26113–566
GAO/RCED-92-81 26113–590
GAO/RCED-92-86 26113–569
GAO/RCED-92-96 BR 26113–559
GAO/RCED-92-104 26113–575
GAO/RCED-92-108 FS 26113–565
GAO/RCED-92-112 26113–570
GAO/RCED-92-114 26113–580
GAO/RCED-92-116 BR 26113–571
GAO/RCED-92-120 .... 26106–10.6
GAO/RCED-92-124 26113–581
GAO/RCED-92-126 26113–583
GAO/RCED-92-131 BR 26113–578
GAO/RCED-92-133 26113–579
GAO/RCED-92-139 FS 26113–572
GAO/RCED-92-140 26113–585
GAO/RCED-92-144 26113–576

GAO/RCED-92-150 26113–586
GAO/RCED-92-163 FS 26113–574
GAO/RCED-92-173 BR 26113–577
GAO/RCED-92-174 26113–587
GAO/RCED-92-177 FS 26113–573
GAO/RCED-92-194 26113–584
GAO/RCED-92-197 26113–591
GAO/RCED-92-200 26113–593
GAO/RCED-92-203 26113–592
GAO/RCED-92-205 26113–598
GAO/RCED-92-213 FS 26113–582
GAO/RCED-92-215 26113–596
GAO/RCED-92-223 BR 26113–588
GAO/RCED-92-224 .... 26106–10.7
GAO/RCED-92-237 26113–594
GAO/RCED-92-239 BR 26113–589
GAO/RCED-92-243 26113–597
GAO/RCED-92-246 26113–599
GAO/RCED-92-250 26113–595
GAO/RCED-93-8 26113–600
GAO/RCED-93-19 FS 26113–602
GAO/RCED-93-25 26113–601
GAO/RCED-93-39 26104–21

Office of Technology Assessment

OTA-A-530 26354–3
OTA-BA-538 .... 26356–9.4
OTA Background Paper 8 .... 26356–6.6
OTA-BP-BA-88 26358–261
OTA-BP-H-89 .... 26356–6.6
OTA-BP-O-82 26358–256
OTA-BP-TCT-84 26358–253
OTA-E-504 26358–251
OTA-E-516 26358–260
OTA-E-517 26358–260
OTA-E-518 26358–259
OTA-E-536 26358–263
OTA-F-515 26358–262
OTA-H-466 .... 26358–234.2
OTA-H-467 .... 26358–234.3
OTA-H-509 26358–258
OTA-H-510 26358–258
OTA-H-531 26358–254
OTA-H-532 26358–254
OTA-ITE-498 26358–252
OTA-ITE-499 26358–252
OTA-SET-519 26358–255
OTA-SET-520 26358–255
OTA-TCT-512 26358–257

QUASI-OFFICIAL AGENCIES

American National Red Cross

ARC 501 29254–1

Index by Superintendent of Documents Numbers

Index of Superintendent of Documents Numbers

This index presents, in shelf list order, the Superintendent of Documents (SuDocs) Classification Numbers of publications abstracted by ASI in this Annual, and provides references from SuDoc Numbers to ASI accession numbers.

A1.1:991	1004–3
A1.1/3:991-2	1002–4
A1.1/3:992	1002–4
A1.1/3:992-2	1002–4
A1.2:Ou8/992	1504–9
A1.10:992	1004–18
A1.34:826	1548–384
A1.34:831	1548–387
A1.34:832	1548–385
A1.34:833	1564–13
A1.34:834	1544–28
A1.34:835	1528–328
A1.34:837	1568–309
A1.34:838	1544–24
A1.34:841	1568–310
A1.34/4:970-90	1544–4
A1.36:1806	1548–391
A1.38:1497	1924–11
A1.47:991	1004–1
A1.75:638	1588–122
A1.75:647	1504–4
A1.76:(nos.)	1356–3
A1.76:8-18/992	1356–3.18
A1.76:8/991/supp	1356–3.17
A1.76:671/(v.nos.)	1506–1
A1.76:671/v.12/rev	1506–1.1
A1.76:697	1508–3
A1.101:(date)	1802–4
A1.107:647	1528–326
A1.107:649	1548–383
A1.107:653	1568–307
A1.107:654	1548–388
A1.107:656	1568–308
A1.107:658	1598–278
A1.107:659	1568–251
A1.107/2:991	1544–9
A1.107/3:991	1544–22
A1.116:R88/2/990	1244–4
A1.116:R88/2/991	1244–4
A13.1/3:991	1204–1
A13.10:991	1204–2
A13.32/2:984-90	1204–4
A13.52/2:990	1204–8
A13.52/11:989	1206–11.2
A13.52/11:990	1206–11.2
A13.52/11:991	1206–11.2
A13.52/12:991	1206–11.1
A13.66/13:(date)	1202–3
A13.78:FLP-RP-510	1208–416
A13.78:INT-452	1208–402
A13.78:INT-453	1208–395
A13.78:INT-454	1208–425
A13.78:NC-298	1208–417
A13.78:NC-299	1208–419
A13.78:NC-300	1208–418
A13.78:NE-655	1208–394
A13.78:NE-658	1208–400
A13.78:NE-659	1208–373
A13.78:PNW-RP-436	1208–387
A13.78:PNW-RP-437	1208–413
A13.78:PNW-RP-439	1208–396
A13.78:PNW-RP-440	1208–414
A13.78:PNW-RP-447	1208–424
A13.78:RM-299	1208–390
A13.78:RM-300	1208–406
A13.78:SE-284	1208–411
A13.79:INT-402	1208–422
A13.79:INT-404	1208–423
A13.79:NC-356	1208–397
A13.79/2:990	1204–22
A13.79/3:(date)	1202–4
A13.80:INT-(nos.)	1206–17
—	1206–25
A13.80:INT-75	1206–25.12
A13.80:INT-77	1206–17.12
A13.80:NC-(nos.)	1206–3
—	1206–10
—	1206–24
—	1206–34
A13.80:NC-114	1206–3.5
A13.80:NC-115	1206–3.6
A13.80:NC-116	1206–3.7
A13.80:NC-118	1206–3.8
A13.80:NC-119	1208–76
A13.80:NC-122	1208–412
A13.80:NC-126	1206–10.13
A13.80:NC-132	1208–399
A13.80:NC-133	1208–398
A13.80:NC-135	1206–24.11
A13.80:NC-136	1208–75
A13.80:NC-137	1206–34.9
A13.80:NC-138	1206–24.12
A13.80:NE-(nos.)	1206–12
—	1206–15
A13.80:NE-107	1206–12.16
A13.80:NE-120	1206–15.12
A13.80:NE-121	1206–15.11
A13.80:PNW-(nos.)	1206–28
A13.80:PNW-RB-(nos.)	1206–9
A13.80:PNW-RB-177	1206–28.4
A13.80:PNW-RB-178	1206–28.5
A13.80:PNW-RB-179	1206–28.6
A13.80:PNW-RB-180	1206–9.23
A13.80:PNW-RB-181	1208–108
A13.80:PNW-RB-183	1208–280
A13.80:PNW-RB-184	1206–9.24
A13.80:PNW-RB-185	1206–9.25
A13.80:PNW-RB-186	1206–9.26
A13.80:SE-(nos.)	1206–6
A13.80:SE-121	1208–407
A13.80:SE-123	1208–384
A13.80:SE-124	1206–6.14
A13.80:SE-125	1208–352
A13.80:SE-126	1208–393
A13.80:SE-127	1206–6.15
A13.80:SE-128	1206–6.16
A13.80:SE-129	1208–138
A13.80:SE-130	1206–6.17
A13.80:SE-131	1206–6.18
A13.80:SO-(nos.)	1206–8
—	1206–27
—	1206–30
—	1206–35
A13.80:SO-150	1206–30.11
A13.80:SO-160	1206–27.11
A13.80:SO-161	1206–35.8
A13.80:SO-162	1206–35.10
A13.80:SO-163	1206–35.9
A13.80:SO-164	1208–409
A13.80:SO-167	1206–35.11
A13.80:SO-168	1206–35.12
A13.80:SO-169	1206–8.13
A13.80/3:990	1204–18
A13.80/5:989	1204–19
A13.80/5:990	1204–19
A13.88:FPL-GTR-71	1208–392
A13.88:INT-287	1208–420
A13.88:NE-141	1208–410
A13.88:NE-159	1208–405
A13.88:(no.)	1204–14
A13.88:PNW-GTR-282	1208–401
A13.88:PNW-GTR-285	1208–386
A13.88:RM-208	1208–403
A13.88:RM-210	1208–404
A13.88:RM-213	1208–421
A13.88:SE-69	1208–415
A13.88:SE-70/v.1,2	1204–35
A13.109:991	1204–7
A57.38:list/991	1264–11
A57.46:(date)	1266–2.2
A57.46/4:(date)	1266–2.6
A57.46/5:(date)	1266–2.7
A57.46/6:(date)	1266–2.8
A57.46/6-3:991	1264–14.7
A57.46/7:(date)	1266–2.9
A57.46/7-2:991	1264–14.4
A57.46/8:992	1264–4
A57.46/10:(date)	1266–2.10
A57.46/11:(date)	1266–2.4
A57.46/12-2:(date)	1262–1
A57.46/13:(date)	1266–2.1
A57.46/13-3:991	1264–14.5
A57.46/18:(date)	1266–2.11
A57.46/19:(date)	1266–2.3
A57.46/19-2:990	1264–14.1
A67.7/3:(v.nos.&nos.)	1922–2
A67.18:(ltrs.-nos.)	1925–2
A67.18:(nos.)	1925–4
A67.18:EMG(nos.)	1925–2.4
A67.18:FC(nos.)	1925–4.2
A67.18:FCOF(nos.)	1925–5
A67.18:FD-MI(nos.)	1925–31
A67.18:FD1-92	1925–10
A67.18:FDLP(nos.)	1925–32
A67.18:FFVS(nos.)	1925–13
A67.18:FG(nos.)	1925–2.1
A67.18:FHORT(nos.)	1925–34
A67.18:FL&P(nos.)	1925–33
A67.18:FL&P1-92	1925–33.1
A67.18:FL&P2-92	1925–33.2
A67.18:FL&P3-92	1925–33.1
A67.18:FL&P4-91	1925–33.2
A67.18:FL&P4-92	1925–33.2
A67.18:FOP(nos.)	1925–1
—	1925–1.1
A67.18:FS(nos.)	1925–14
A67.18:FS1-92	1925–14.2
A67.18:FS2-92	1925–14.3
A67.18:FS3-91	1925–14.1
A67.18:FT(nos.)	1925–16
A67.18:FTEA(nos.)	1925–15
A67.18:FTEA1-92	1925–15.1

A67.18:FTEA2-92 .... 1925–15.2
A67.18:FTEA3-92 .... 1925–15.3
A67.18:WAP(nos.) 1925–28
A67.18:WP(nos.) 1925–36
A67.18/2:(yr.) 1925–9
A67.18/2:992 .... 1925–9.1
A67.18/2:992-2 .... 1925–9.2
A67.40:(date) 1922–3
A67.42/2:(nos.) 1922–9
A67.45:(nos.) 1922–12
A68.1:990 1244–3
A68.1:991 1244–3
A68.1/2:991 1244–1
A68.1/3:991 1244–2
A68.1/4:(yr.) 1244–5
A68.2:P69/991 1244–6
A77.245:(v.nos.&nos.) 1702–1
A82.76:(yr.) 1804–5
A82.82/2:(CT) 1806–4
A82.82/2:B92/992 .... 1806–4.6
A82.82/2:D14/991-92 .... 1806–4.8
A82.82/2:F67/992 .... 1806–4.4
A82.82/2:H75/991-95/summ 1806–4.2
A82.82/2:H75/991-95/ summ 2 .... 1806–4.12
A82.82/2:M72/992/rev 1806–4.9
A82.82/2:P31/991 .... 1806–4.3
A82.82/2:R36/991 .... 1806–4.1
A82.82/2:R98/992 .... 1806–4.10
A82.82/2:So9/991 .... 1806–4.5
A82.82/2:Su3/2/992 .... 1806–4.13
A82.82/2:T55/992 .... 1806–4.7
A82.82/2:Up4/992 .... 1806–4.14
A82.82/2:W88/992 .... 1806–4.11
A82.83/2:(date) 1802–7
A82.89/2:991 1804–7
A82.92:991 1804–20
A82.93:991 1804–22
A82.94:991 1804–21
A82.95:(date) 1802–2
A82.96/2:(date) 1802–16
A82.97:(date) 1802–3
A82.311:988 1824–2
A84.2:H62/992 1184–17
A88.10:(v.nos.&nos.) 1311–1
A88.11:(v.nos.&nos.) 1309–11
A88.11:64/9 1309–8
A88.11:65/8 1309–7
A88.11:65/9 1309–8
A88.11/3:(v.nos.&nos.) 1309–10
A88.11/9:(v.nos.&nos.) 1309–1
A88.11/9:73/13 1309–2
A88.11/13:992 1309–6
A88.11/15:991 1309–5
A88.11/20:(v.nos.&nos.) 1309–12
A88.11/23:(v.nos.&nos.) 1309–15
A88.12/22:(nos.) 1311–3
A88.12/22-3:991 1311–8
A88.12/31:991 .... 1311–4.1
A88.12/31-2:991 .... 1311–4.2
A88.12/31-3:991 .... 1311–4.4
A88.12/31-4:991 .... 1311–4.3
A88.14/11:(nos.) 1317–4
A88.14/11-2:991 1317–3
A88.16/4:(v.nos.&nos.) 1315–1
A88.18/4-2:(v.nos.&nos.) 1313–2
A88.18/9:(v.nos.&nos.) 1313–8
A88.19:(v.nos.&nos.) 1311–2
A88.23:(v.nos.&nos.) 1311–16
A88.34:(date) 1319–3
A88.34/5:991 .... 1319–5.1
A88.34/6:991 .... 1319–5.3
A88.34/8:991 .... 1319–5.2
A88.42/3:(v.nos.&nos.) 1309–14
A88.57:(nos.) 1302–3
A92.9/3:991 1625–5
A92.9/4:(date) 1625–2
A92.9/5:(date) 1625–3
A92.9/6:991 1625–8
A92.9/13:991 1625–7
A92.9/16:(date) 1625–1
A92.9/17:992 1625–6
A92.9/17-2:(date) 1625–10
A92.10:(date) 1627–1
A92.10/2:991 1627–4
A92.10/5:991 1627–5
A92.10/7:(date) 1627–3
A92.11:(date) 1621–12
A92.11/2-2:991 .... 1621–18.1
A92.11/2-3:991 .... 1621–18.3
A92.11/4:989-91 1621–11
A92.11/6:992 .... 1621–18.5
A92.11/8:992 .... 1621–18.8
A92.11/10-2:991 .... 1621–25.2
A92.11/10-4:(date) 1621–14
A92.11/10-5:992 1631–9
A92.11/10-6:991 .... 1621–25.1
A92.11/11:(date) 1621–10
A92.12:(date) 1631–1
A92.14:(date) 1621–6
A92.15:(date) 1621–4
A92.16:(date) 1629–1
A92.16/2:991 1629–5
A92.16/3:991 1629–2
A92.17:991 1623–8
A92.18:991 1623–10
A92.18/3:(date) 1623–9
A92.18/6:(date) 1623–2
A92.18/6-2:(date) 1623–1
A92.18/6-2:992 .... 1623–1.1
A92.18/6-2:992-2 .... 1623–1.2
A92.18/7:(date) 1623–3
A92.18/11:992 1631–7
A92.21:(date) 1631–5
A92.21/2:991 1631–11
A92.21/3:991 1614–2
A92.24:(date) 1621–1
A92.24/2:992 1621–22
A92.24/3:991 1621–2
A92.24/4:990(summary) 1621–1
A92.29/5:992 1623–6
A92.30:992 1621–8
A92.30:992-2 1621–8
A92.32:991 1631–8
A92.35/2:992 1614–1
A92.39:992 1621–23
A92.40:991 1614–3
A92.42:992 1621–30
A92.43:(date) 1621–7
A92.44:(date) 1631–14
A92.46:(date) 1625–11
A92.47:(nos.) 1631–19
A93.2:Ec7/3/992 1504–6
A93.9/8:(nos.) 1541–1
A93.10/2:(nos.) 1502–4
A93.11:(nos.) 1561–12
A93.11/2:(nos.) 1561–4
A93.11/2-2:992(yearbook) 1561–4
A93.11/2-3:992(yearbook) 1561–12
A93.11/3:(nos.) 1561–8
A93.12/2:(nos.) 1561–11
A93.12/2-3:991(yearbook); A93.12/2-3:992(yearbook) 1561–11
A93.12/3:(nos.) 1561–6
A93.12/3-2:992(yearbook) 1561–6
A93.13:(nos.) 1561–2
A93.13/2-2:992(yearbook) 1561–2
A93.16/3:(nos.) 1541–7
A93.17/7:(date) 1522–1
A93.17/7-2:991 1522–4
A93.17/7-3:991 1522–4
A93.17/7-4:990 1524–8
A93.17/7-4:991 1524–8
A93.23/2:(nos.) 1561–3
A93.23/2-2:992(yearbook) 1561–3
A93.24/2:(nos.) 1561–1
A93.25:(nos.) 1561–10
A93.26:(v.nos.&nos.) 1502–3
A93.27:244 1528–332
A93.29/2-7:992 .... 1524–4.1
A93.29/2-11:992 .... 1524–4.2
A93.29/2-19:992 .... 1524–4.3
A93.29/3:(nos.) 1522–5
A93.31/3:(date) 1561–14
A93.33/2:(v.nos.&nos.) 1502–6
A93.41/2:(v.nos.&nos.) 1502–7
A93.41/3:(v.nos.&nos.) 1502–8
A93.43:(date) 1542–4
A93.44:AGES9133 1528–325
A93.44:AGES9150 1548–382
A93.44:AGES9153 1598–277
A93.44:AGES9160 1548–386
A93.44:AGES9201 1504–8
A93.44:AGES9206 1528–327
A93.44:AGES9208 1528–329
A93.44:AGES9211 1584–2
A93.44:AGES9214 1548–389
A93.44:AGES9217 1584–3
A93.44:AGES9218 1548–390
A93.44:AGES9219 1528–331
A93.44:AGES9221 1548–392
A93.44/3:989 1524–7
A93.45/2:990 .... 1544–20.1
A93.45/5:990 1544–17
A93.45/6:990 1544–18
A93.46:(nos.) 1561–7
A93.46/2:(date) 1561–17
A93.47:(nos.) 1561–16
A93.51:988/89 1564–11
A94.14:991 1744–2
A101.17:(v.nos.&nos.) 1392–3
A101.22/2:990 1394–10
A101.27:991 1394–17
A104.1:992 1294–1
A106.42:991 1764–1
A108.10:(nos.) 1272–1
A109.10:97 1128–67
A109.10:99 1128–68
A109.10:100 1128–69
A109.10/2:(nos./sec.) 1126–1
A109.10/2:1/sec.9 .... 1126–1.8
A109.10/2:1/sec.21 .... 1126–1.7
A109.11:(v.nos.&nos.) 1122–1
A109.11/2:990 1124–1
A110.13:14/990 1374–3
A110.14:991 1374–2
AA1.1:991 9024–2
AC1.16:990 9824–1
AE1.101:991 9514–2
AE1.102:Am3/3 .... 9516–1.10
AE1.110/5:991 9514–1
C1.1:991 2004–1
C1.1/2:992 2002–5
C1.1/2:992-2 2002–5
C1.1/3:991 2104–6
C1.2:H81/3 2328–89
C1.2:Is7 2008–32
C1.24/3:(v.nos.&nos.) 2002–1
C1.39:993 2004–6
C1.88:(date) 2002–6
C3.2:Ag4 .... 2326–19.7
C3.2:Ag4/2 .... 2326–19.8

C3.2:Ag8/10/992 .... 2346–1.6
C3.2:Ag8/11 .... 2346–1.5
C3.2:C33/45 2308–66
C3.2:C37/992 2328–59
C3.2:C73/11 2308–64
C3.2:El2/5 .... 2326–25.1
C3.2:El2/5/992 .... 2326–25.2
C3.2:F11/6 2328–80
C3.2:G29/4 2308–67
C3.2:G51 2328–82
C3.2:P81/23/kenya 2326–24.1
C3.6/2:C33/8/990/PT.A 2555–1.1
C3.6/2:C33/8/990/PT.(ltrs.) 2555–1
C3.24/9-6:990 .... 2506–14.1
C3.24/9-7:990 .... 2506–14.2
C3.24/9-9:990 .... 2506–14.3
C3.24/9-12:(nos.) 2506–16
C3.24/9-12:87-2 .... 2506–16.2
C3.24/12:MC87-S-4 2497–4
C3.24/12:MC87-S-6 2497–6
C3.133:(nos.) 2413–7
C3.133/2:986-92(summary) .. 2413–7
C3.134:992 2324–1
C3.134/2-2:991 2324–1
C3.138/3:(nos.) 2413–3
C3.138/3-2:990 2413–5
C3.138/3-3:982-91(summary) 2413–3
C3.138/3-5:990 2413–14
C3.138/4:(nos.) 2413–2
C3.140/2-4:991 .... 2466–1.1
C3.140/2-5:991 .... 2466–1.2
C3.145/6:(date/nos.) 2462–3
C3.150:B/990/rev.3 .... 2428–5.1
C3.158:(ltrs.-nos.) 2506–3
— 2506–4
— 2506–5
— 2506–6
— 2506–7
— 2506–8
— 2506–9
— 2506–10
— 2506–11
— 2506–12
C3.158:M3-1(yr.-nos.) 2506–3.1
C3.158:M20A(yr.-nos.) 2506–4.1
C3.158:M20J(yr.-nos) 2506–4.3
C3.158:M20K(yr.-nos.) 2506–4.4
C3.158:M22P(yr.-nos.) 2506–5.8
C3.158:M32G(yr.-nos.) 2506–9.4
C3.158:M33D(yr.-nos.) 2506–10.9
C3.158:M33J(yr.-nos.) 2506–10.3
C3.158:M36D(yr.-nos.) 2506–12.13
C3.158:M37G(yr.-nos.) 2506–12.24
C3.158:M37L(yr.-nos.) 2506–12.25
C3.158:MA20D(91)-1 .... 2506–4.5
C3.158:MA22F.1(91)-1 .... 2506–5.4
C3.158:MA22F.2(91)-1 .... 2506–5.5
C3.158:MA22G(yr.)-1 .... 2506–5.6
C3.158:MA22K(91)-1 .... 2506–5.7
C3.158:MA22M(yr.)-1 .... 2506–5.3
C3.158:MA22Q(91)-1 .... 2506–5.9
C3.158:MA22S(yr.)-1 .... 2506–5.10
C3.158:MA23D(91)-1 .... 2506–6.4
C3.158:MA24F(yr.)-1 .... 2506–7.1
C3.158:MA24T(91)-1 .... 2506–7.4
C3.158:MA25H(90)-1/rev 2506–7.8
C3.158:MA25H(91)-1 .... 2506–7.8
C3.158:MA26A(yr.)-1 .... 2506–7.10
C3.158:MA28A(91)-1 .... 2506–8.14
C3.158:MA28B(91)-1 .... 2506–8.13
C3.158:MA28C(91)-1 .... 2506–8.15
C3.158:MA28F(91)-1 .... 2506–8.16
C3.158:MA28G(91)-1 .... 2506–8.5
C3.158:MA30A(yr.)-1 .... 2506–8.7
C3.158:MA30B(yr.)-1 .... 2506–8.12
C3.158:MA30C(91)-1 .... 2506–8.17
C3.158:MA30E(yr.)-1 .... 2506–8.10
C3.158:MA31A(91)-1 .... 2506–6.8
C3.158:MA31C(yr.)-1 .... 2506–6.13
C3.158:MA32C(91)-1 .... 2506–9.1
C3.158:MA32E(91)-1 .... 2506–9.3
C3.158:MA32J(yr.)-1 .... 2506–9.5
C3.158:MA33A(91)-1 .... 2506–10.1
C3.158:MA33B(91)-1 .... 2506–10.2
C3.158:MA33E(91)-1 .... 2506–10.5
C3.158:MA33L(91)-1 .... 2506–10.8
C3.158:MA34N(yr.)-1 .... 2506–11.6
C3.158:MA35F(91)-1 .... 2506–12.4
C3.158:MA35J(91)-1 .... 2506–12.5
C3.158:MA35L(91)-1 .... 2506–12.6
C3.158:MA35M(91)-1 .... 2506–12.7
C3.158:MA35N(91)-1 .... 2506–12.31
C3.158:MA35P(91)-1 .... 2506–12.8
C3.158:MA35Q(91)-1 .... 2506–12.28
C3.158:MA35R(90)-1 .... 2506–12.2
C3.158:MA35R(91)-1 .... 2506–12.2
C3.158:MA35U(91)-1 .... 2506–12.10
C3.158:MA35X(yr.)-1 .... 2506–12.32
C3.158:MA36A(91)-1 .... 2506–12.11
C3.158:MA36E(91)-1 .... 2506–12.15
C3.158:MA36F(91)-1 .... 2506–12.16
C3.158:MA36H(90)-1 .... 2506–12.17
C3.158:MA36H(91)-1 .... 2506–12.17
C3.158:MA36K(90)-1 .... 2506–12.18
C3.158:MA36K(91)-1 .... 2506–12.18
C3.158:MA36L(91)-1 .... 2506–12.19
C3.158:MA36M(91)-1 .... 2506–12.20
C3.158:MA36P(91)-1 .... 2506–12.35
C3.158:MA36Q(91)-1 .... 2506–12.36
C3.158:MA36R(91)-1 .... 2506–12.34
C3.158:MA37D(91)-1 .... 2506–12.22
C3.158:MA38B(90)-1 .... 2506–12.26
C3.158:MA38B(91)-1 .... 2506–12.26
C3.158:MA200(89)-1/final 2506–3.6
C3.158:MA200(90)-1/ advance 2506–3.6
C3.158:MA200(90)-1/final 2506–3.6
C3.158:MA200(91)-1/ advance 2506–3.6
C3.158:MQ-C1(90)-1/ advance 2506–3.7
C3.158:MQ-C1(90)-1/final 2506–3.7
C3.158:MQ22D(yr.-nos.) 2506–5.2
C3.158:MQ22T(yr.-nos.) 2506–5.11
C3.158:MQ23A(yr.-nos.) 2506–6.12
C3.158:MQ23X(yr.-nos.) 2506–6.6
C3.158:MQ28A(yr.-nos.) 2506–8.1
C3.158:MQ28B(yr.-nos.) 2506–8.2
C3.158:MQ28C(yr.-nos.) 2506–8.3
C3.158:MQ28F(yr.-nos.) 2506–8.4
C3.158:MQ31A(yr.-nos.) 2506–6.7
C3.158:MQ32A(yr.-nos.) 2506–9.6
C3.158:MQ32D(yr.-nos.) 2506–9.2
C3.158:MQ34E(yr.-nos.) 2506–11.2
C3.158:MQ34H(yr.-nos.) 2506–11.4
C3.158:MQ34K(yr.-nos.) 2506–11.5
C3.158:MQ35W(yr.-nos.) 2506–12.12
C3.158:MQ36B(yr.-nos.) 2506–12.33
C3.158:MQ36C(yr.-nos.) 2506–12.14
C3.163/3:992 2304–2
C3.163/7:(date) 2302–6
C3.164:447/991 2424–10
C3.164:925/(nos.) 2422–12
C3.164:927/991 2424–12
C3.164:947/991 2424–13
C3.164:985-(nos.) 2422–7
C3.164:985/991 2424–11
C3.183/3-6:990 2413–15
C3.186:P-20/459 .... 2546–1.462
C3.186:P-20/464 .... 2546–1.463
C3.186:P-23/175 .... 2546–2.164
C3.186:P-23/177 .... 2546–2.163
C3.186:P-23/178 .... 2546–2.165
C3.186:P-23/180 .... 2546–2.166
C3.186:P-60/177 .... 2546–6.73
C3.186:P-60/178 .... 2546–6.74
C3.186:P-60/179 .... 2546–6.75
C3.186:P-60/182-RD 2546–6.78
C3.186:P-60/183 .... 2546–6.79
C3.186:P-70/2/(nos.) 2546–20
C3.186:P-70/2/26 .... 2546–20.22
C3.186:P-70/2/27 .... 2546–20.20
C3.186:P-70/2/28 .... 2546–20.21
C3.186:P-70/2/29 .... 2546–20.23
C3.186:P-70/2/30 .... 2546–20.24
C3.186:P-70/2/31 .... 2546–20.25
C3.186/2:991 .... 2546–6.76
C3.186/6:991 .... 2546–1.461
C3.186/7:(nos.) 2542–1
C3.186/12:990 .... 2546–1.459
C3.186/17:991 .... 2546–1.457
C3.186/18:990 .... 2546–1.456
C3.186/18:991 .... 2546–1.464
C3.186/22:991 .... 2546–6.77
C3.186/23:990-91 .... 2546–1.460
C3.186/25:990 .... 2546–1.458
C3.186/26:992 .... 2546–3.170
C3.191/2-2:989-90 .... 2466–2.4
C3.191/2-3:991 .... 2466–2.6
C3.191/2-4:989-90 .... 2466–2.2
C3.191/2-5:989-90 .... 2466–2.1
C3.191/2-7:989-90 .... 2466–2.3
C3.191/2-8:991 .... 2466–2.7
C3.191/2-10:989-90 .... 2466–2.5
C3.204/3-(nos.):989 2326–8
C3.204/3-(nos.):990 2326–6
C3.204/3-1:989 .... 2326–8.1
C3.204/3-2:990 .... 2326–6.2
C3.204/3-4:990 .... 2326–6.4
C3.204/3-8:990 .... 2326–6.8
C3.204/3-11:990 .... 2326–6.11
C3.204/3-14:990 .... 2326–6.14
C3.204/3-15:990 .... 2326–6.15
C3.204/3-17:990 .... 2326–6.17
C3.204/3-18:990 .... 2326–6.18
C3.204/3-19:990 .... 2326–6.19
C3.204/3-21:990 .... 2326–6.21
C3.204/3-23:990 .... 2326–6.23
C3.204/3-25:990 .... 2326–6.25
C3.204/3-26:990 .... 2326–6.26
C3.204/3-27:990 .... 2326–6.27
C3.204/3-28:990 .... 2326–6.28
C3.204/3-29:990 .... 2326–6.29
C3.204/3-30:990 .... 2326–6.30
C3.204/3-31:990 .... 2326–6.31
C3.204/3-33:990 .... 2326–6.33
C3.204/3-35:990 .... 2326–6.35
C3.204/3-36:990 .... 2326–6.36
C3.204/3-37:990 .... 2326–6.37
C3.204/3-41:990 .... 2326–6.41
C3.204/3-42:990 .... 2326–6.42
C3.204/3-43:990 .... 2326–6.43
C3.204/3-44:990 .... 2326–6.44
C3.204/3-46:990 .... 2326–6.46
C3.204/3-47:990 .... 2326–6.47
C3.204/3-48:990 .... 2326–6.48
C3.204/3-50:990 .... 2326–6.50
C3.204/3-52:990 .... 2326–6.52
C3.205/3:WP/91 2324–9
C3.205/8:(nos.-yr.) 2326–17
C3.205/8:91-6 .... 2326–17.41
C3.205/8:91-7 .... 2326–17.42

C3.205/8:91-15 2326–17.44
C3.205/8:91-17 2326–17.38
C3.205/8:91-20 2326–17.40
C3.205/8:91-23 2326–17.39
C3.205/8:92-1 2326–17.43
C3.205/8:92-3 2326–17.47
C3.205/8:92-4 2326–17.45
C3.205/8:92-5 2326–17.48
C3.205/8:92-7 2326–17.46
C3.205/8:92-8 2326–17.49
C3.205/8:92-9 2326–17.50
C3.205/8:92-10 2326–17.52
C3.205/8:92-11 2326–17.51
C3.212:(nos.) 2626–2
C3.212:61 2626–2.60
C3.215:H-111-(nos.) 2482–1
C3.215:H-111/91-A 2484–1
C3.215:H-121/(nos.) 2486–1
C3.215:H-121/91-2 2486–1.12
C3.215:H-121/92-1 2486–1.13
C3.215:H-121/92-2 2486–1.14
C3.215:H-121/92-4 2486–1.15
C3.215:H-123/(nos.) 2486–2
C3.215:H-123/91-1 2486–2.1
C3.215:H-130-(nos.) 2482–2
C3.215:H-130/91-A 2484–2
C3.215:H-131/91-A 2484–3
C3.215:H-151-89-1 2485–13
C3.215:H-170/(yr.-nos.) 2485 6
C3.215:H-170/89-3 2485–6.10
C3.215:H-170/89-4 2485–6.5
C3.215:H-170/89-5 2485–6.2
C3.215:H-170/89-6 2485–6.6
C3.215:H-170/89-7 2485–6.3
C3.215:H-170/89-9 2485–6.7
C3.215:H-170/89-12 2485–6.9
C3.215:H-170/89-18 2485–6.1
C3.215:H-170-89-33 2485–6.4
C3.215:H-170/89-39 2485–6.8
C3.215/2:C20-(nos.) 2382–1
C3.215/3:C30-(nos.) 2382–4
C3.215/4:C40-(nos.) 2382–5
C3.215/4:C40/91-A 2384–2
C3.215/8:C50-(nos.) 2382–7
C3.215/8:989 2388–4
C3.215/9:C25-(nos.) 2382–3
C3.215/9-3:991 2384–1
C3.215/13:C22-(nos.) 2382–2
C3.215/15:C21-(nos.) 2382–9
C3.215/16:985 2485–8
C3.215/16:986 2485–8
C3.215/16:987 2485–8
C3.215/20:(yr.-nos.) 2485–11
C3.215/20:88-8 2485–11.2
C3.215/20:88-11 2485–11.1
C3.215/20:89-1 2485–11.3
C3.215/20:89-2 2485–11.4
C3.215/20:89-3 2485–11.5
C3.215/20:89-4 2485–11.8
C3.215/20:89-5 2485–11.6
C3.215/20:89-6 2485–11.9
C3.215/20:89-7 2485–11.7
C3.215/20:89-8 2485–11.10
C3.215/20:89-9 2485–11.11
C3.215/20:89-10 2485–11.12
C3.215/20:89-11 2485–11.13
C3.223/6:990CP-1-(nos.) 2531–1
C3.223/6:990CP-1-2 2531–1.2
C3.223/6:990CP-1-3 2531–1.3
C3.223/6:990CP-1-4 2531–1.4
C3.223/6:990CP-1-5 2531–1.5
C3.223/6:990CP-1-6/sec.1-3.. 2531–1.6
C3.223/6:990CP-1-7 2531–1.7
C3.223/6:990CP-1-8 2531–1.8
C3.223/6:990CP-1-9 2531–1.9
C3.223/6:990CP-1-10 2531–1.10
C3.223/6:990CP-1-11/sec.1,2 2531–1.11
C3.223/6:990CP-1-12 2531–1.12
C3.223/6:990CP-1-13 2531–1.13
C3.223/6:990CP-1-14 2531–1.14
C3.223/6:990CP-1-15 2531–1.15
C3.223/6:990CP-1-16 2531–1.16
C3.223/6:990CP-1-17 2531–1.17
C3.223/6:990CP-1-18 2531–1.18
C3.223/6:990CP-1-19 2531–1.19
C3.223/6:990CP-1-20 2531–1.20
C3.223/6:990CP-1-21 2531–1.21
C3.223/6:990CP-1-22 2531–1.22
C3.223/6:990CP-1-23 2531–1.23
C3.223/6:990CP-1-24 2531–1.24
C3.223/6:990CP-1-25 2531–1.25
C3.223/6:990CP-1-26 2531–1.26
C3.223/6:990CP-1-27 2531–1.27
C3.223/6:990CP-1-28 2531–1.28
C3.223/6:990CP-1-29 2531–1.29
C3.223/6:990CP-1-30 2531–1.30
C3.223/6:990CP-1-31 2531–1.31
C3.223/6:990CP-1-32/sec.1,2 2531–1.32
C3.223/6:990CP-1-33 2531–1.33
C3.223/6:990CP-1-34/sec.1,2 2531–1.34
C3.223/6:990CP-1-35 2531–1.35
C3.223/6:990CP-1-36 2531–1.36
C3.223/6:990CP-1-37 2531–1.37
C3.223/6:990CP-1-38 2531–1.38
C3.223/6:990CP-1-39 2531–1.39
C3.223/6:990CP-1-40/sec.1,2 2531–1.40
C3.223/6:990CP-1-41 2531–1.41
C3.223/6:990CP-1-42 2531–1.42
C3.223/6:990CP-1-43 2531–1.43
C3.223/6:990CP-1-44 2531–1.44
C3.223/6:990CP-1-45/sec.1,2 2531–1.45
C3.223/6:990CP-1-46 2531–1.46
C3.223/6:990CP-1-47 2531–1.47
C3.223/6:990CP-1-48 2531–1.48
C3.223/6:990CP-1-49 2531–1.49
C3.223/6:990CP-1-50 2531–1.50
C3.223/6:990CP-1-51 2531–1.51
C3.223/6:990CP-1-52 2531–1.52
C3.223/6:990CP-1-53 2531–1.53
C3.223/6:990CP-1-55 2531–1.54
C3.223/6-2:990CP-1-1A 2531–2.1
C3.223/18:990CPH-1-(nos.) .. 2551–1
C3.223/18:990CPH-1-1 2551–1.1
C3.223/18:990CPH-1-53 2551–1.53
C3.223/22:90-R-3 2628–1
C3.223/22:90-R-4 2628–2
C3.223/23:990CPH-5-(nos.) .. 2551–7
C3.223/23:990CPH-5-(nos.)/errata 2551–7.55
C3.223/23:990CPH-5-2 2551–7.2
C3.223/23:990CPH-5-3 2551–7.3
C3.223/23:990CPH-5-4 2551–7.4
C3.223/23:990CPH-5-5 2551–7.5
C3.223/23:990CPH-5-6 2551–7.6
C3.223/23:990CPH-5-7 2551–7.7
C3.223/23:990CPH-5-8 2551–7.8
C3.223/23:990CPH-5-9 2551–7.9
C3.223/23:990CPH-5-10 2551–7.10
C3.223/23:990CPH-5-11 2551–7.11
C3.223/23:990CPH-5-12 2551–7.12
C3.223/23:990CPH-5-13 2551–7.13
C3.223/23:990CPH-5-14 2551–7.14
C3.223/23:990CPH-5-15 2551–7.15
C3.223/23:990CPH-5-16 2551–7.16
C3.223/23:990CPH-5-17 2551–7.17
C3.223/23:990CPH-5-18 2551–7.18
C3.223/23:990CPH-5-19 2551–7.19
C3.223/23:990CPH-5-20 2551–7.20
C3.223/23:990CPH-5-21 2551–7.21
C3.223/23:990CPH-5-22 2551–7.22
C3.223/23:990CPH-5-23 2551–7.23
C3.223/23:990CPH-5-24 2551–7.24
C3.223/23:990CPH-5-25 2551–7.25
C3.223/23:990CPH-5-26 2551–7.26
C3.223/23:990CPH-5-27 2551–7.27
C3.223/23:990CPH-5-28 2551–7.28
C3.223/23:990CPH-5-29 2551–7.29
C3.223/23:990CPH-5-30 2551–7.30
C3.223/23:990CPH-5-31 2551–7.31
C3.223/23:990CPH-5-32 2551–7.32
C3.223/23:990CPH-5-33 2551–7.33
C3.223/23:990CPH-5-34 2551–7.34
C3.223/23:990CPH-5-35 2551–7.35
C3.223/23:990CPH-5-36 2551–7.36
C3.223/23:990CPH-5-37 2551–7.37
C3.223/23:990CPH-5-38 2551–7.38
C3.223/23:990CPH-5-39 2551–7.39
C3.223/23:990CPH-5-40 2551–7.40
C3.223/23:990CPH-5-41 2551–7.41
C3.223/23:990CPH-5-42 2551–7.42
C3.223/23:990CPH-5-43 2551–7.43
C3.223/23:990CPH-5-44 2551–7.44
C3.223/23:990CPH-5-45 2551–7.45
C3.223/23:990CPH-5-46 2551–7.46
C3.223/23:990CPH-5-47 2551–7.47
C3.223/23:990CPH-5-48 2551–7.48
C3.223/23:990CPH-5-49 2551–7.49
C3.223/23:990CPH-5-50 2551–7.50
C3.223/23:990CPH-5-51 2551–7.51
C3.223/23:990CPH-5-52 2551–7.52
C3.223/23:990CPH-6-(ltrs.) .. 2551–8
C3.223/23:990CPH-6-AS 2551–8.1
C3.223/23:990CPH-6-CNMI 2551–8.2
C3.223/23:990CPH-6-G 2551–8.3
C3.223/23:990CPH-6-P 2551–8.4
C3.224/3:990CH-1-(nos.) 2471–1
C3.224/3:990CH-1-2 2471–1.2
C3.224/3:990CH-1-3 2471–1.3
C3.224/3:990CH-1-4 2471–1.4
C3.224/3:990CH-1-5 2471–1.5
C3.224/3:990CH-1-6 2471–1.6
C3.224/3:990CH-1-7 2471–1.7
C3.224/3:990CH-1-8 2471–1.8
C3.224/3:990CH-1-9 2471–1.9
C3.224/3:990CH-1-10 2471–1.10
C3.224/3:990CH-1-11 2471–1.11
C3.224/3:990CH-1-12 2471–1.12
C3.224/3:990CH-1-13 2471–1.13
C3.224/3:990CH-1-14 2471–1.14
C3.224/3:990CH-1-15 2471–1.15
C3.224/3:990CH-1-16 2471–1.16
C3.224/3:990CH-1-17 2471–1.17
C3.224/3:990CH-1-18 2471–1.18
C3.224/3:990CH-1-19 2471–1.19
C3.224/3:990CH-1-20 2471–1.20
C3.224/3:990CH-1-21 2471–1.21
C3.224/3:990CH-1-22 2471–1.22
C3.224/3:990CH-1-23 2471–1.23
C3.224/3:990CH-1-24 2471–1.24
C3.224/3:990CH-1-25 2471–1.25
C3.224/3:990CH-1-26 2471–1.26
C3.224/3:990CH-1-27 2471–1.27
C3.224/3:990CH-1-28 2471–1.28
C3.224/3:990CH-1-29 2471–1.29
C3.224/3:990CH-1-30 2471–1.30
C3.224/3:990CH-1-31 2471–1.31
C3.224/3:990CH-1-32 2471–1.32
C3.224/3:990CH-1-33 2471–1.33
C3.224/3:990CH-1-34 2471–1.34
C3.224/3:990CH-1-35 2471–1.35
C3.224/3:990CH-1-36 2471–1.36

C3.224/3:990CH-1-37 .... 2471–1.37
C3.224/3:990CH-1-38 .... 2471–1.38
C3.224/3:990CH-1-39 .... 2471–1.39
C3.224/3:990CH-1-40 .... 2471–1.40
C3.224/3:990CH-1-41 .... 2471–1.41
C3.224/3:990CH-1-42 .... 2471–1.42
C3.224/3:990CH-1-43 .... 2471–1.43
C3.224/3:990CH-1-44 .... 2471–1.44
C3.224/3:990CH-1-45 .... 2471–1.45
C3.224/3:990CH-1-46 .... 2471–1.46
C3.224/3:990CH-1-47 .... 2471–1.47
C3.224/3:990CH-1-48 .... 2471–1.48
C3.224/3:990CH-1-49 .... 2471–1.49
C3.224/3:990CH-1-50 .... 2471–1.50
C3.224/3:990CH-1-51 .... 2471–1.51
C3.224/3:990CH-1-52 .... 2471–1.52
C3.224/3-8:CH-S-1-(nos.) 2326–21
C3.224/3-8:CH-S-1-3............ 2326–21.3
C3.224/3-8:CH-S-1-4............ 2326–21.4
C3.224/3-8:CH-S-1-5............ 2326–21.5
C3.224/3-8:CH-S-1-7............ 2326–21.7
C3.224/3-8:CH-S-1-12........... 2326–21.12
C3.224/3-8:CH-S-1-14........... 2326–21.14
C3.224/3-8:CH-S-1-15........... 2326–21.15
C3.224/3-8:CH-S-1-16........... 2326–21.16
C3.224/3-8:CH-S-1-17........... 2326–21.17
C3.224/3-8:CH-S-1-18........... 2326–21.18
C3.224/3-8:CH-S-1-20........... 2326–21.20
C3.224/3-8:CH-S-1-21........... 2326–21.21
C3.224/3-8:CH-S-1-23........... 2326–21.23
C3.224/3-8:CH-S-1-24........... 2326–21.24
C3.224/3-8:CH-S-1-25........... 2326–21.25
C3.224/3-8:CH-S-1-26........... 2326–21.26
C3.224/3-8:CH-S-1-27........... 2326–21.27
C3.224/3-8:CH-S-1-28........... 2326–21.28
C3.224/3-8:CH-S-1-29........... 2326–21.29
C3.224/3-8:CH-S-1-30........... 2326–21.30
C3.224/3-8:CH-S-1-31........... 2326–21.31
C3.224/3-8:CH-S-1-33........... 2326–21.33
C3.224/3-8:CH-S-1-35........... 2326–21.35
C3.224/3-8:CH-S-1-36........... 2326–21.36
C3.224/3-8:CH-S-1-37........... 2326–21.37
C3.224/3-8:CH-S-1-38........... 2326–21.38
C3.224/3-8:CH-S-1-39........... 2326–21.39
C3.224/3-8:CH-S-1-41........... 2326–21.41
C3.224/3-8:CH-S-1-42........... 2326–21.42
C3.224/3-8:CH-S-1-43........... 2326–21.43
C3.224/3-8:CH-S-1-44........... 2326–21.44
C3.224/3-8:CH-S-1-46........... 2326–21.46
C3.224/3-8:CH-S-1-49........... 2326–21.49
C3.224/3-8:CH-S-1-50........... 2326–21.50
C3.224/3-8:CH-S-1-51........... 2326–21.51
C3.224/3-8:CH-S-1-52........... 2326–21.52
C3.224/3-8:CH-S-1-53........... 2326–21.53
C3.224/3-8:CH-S-1-55........... 2326–21.55
C3.224/3-8:CH-S-2/fin 2328–83
C3.238:(v.nos.& nos.)............ 2302–3
C3.242:(nos.)........................... 2462–2
C3.252:(nos.)........................... 2326–7
C3.252:5/992 .... 2326–7.83
C3.252:20/991 .... 2326–7.84
C3.252:22/991 .... 2326–7.82
C3.252:22/991/supp 2326–7.85
C3.253/2:EC92-PR-1............. 2308–5
C3.253/3:987 2628–16
C3.255/3:RC87-S-(nos.) 2399–3
C3.266:991 2464–2
C3.266/2:991/v.(nos.) 2464–3
C3.266/2:991/v.1 .... 2464–3.1
C3.266/2:991/v.2 .... 2464–3.2
C3.267:(yr.-nos.)...................... 2502–1
C3.269:TM-(date)..................... 2322–2
C3.270:H81 2485–12
C3.272:CQC-(nos.)................. 2326–23
C3.272:CQC-4 .... 2326–23.2
C3.272:CQC-7 .... 2326–23.3
C3.272:CQC-11 .... 2326–23.1
C3.277:Ec7/987/CD/(v.nos./ rel.nos.) 2326–22
C3.277:Ec7/987/CD/v.1/rel. 1A 2326–22.1
C3.277:Ec7/987/CD/v.1/rel. 1B.. 2326–22.2
C3.277:Ec7/987/CD/v.1/rel. 1C.. 2326–22.3
C3.277:Ec7/987/CD/v.1/rel. 1D 2326–22.4
C3.277:Ec7/987/CD/v.2/rel. 2A 2326–22.5
C3.277:Ec7/987/doc/(v.nos./ rel.nos.) 2306–8
C3.277:Ec7/987/doc./v.1/rel. 1A 2306–8.1
C3.277:Ec7/987/doc./v.1/rel. 1B................................ 2306–8.2
C3.277:Ec7/987/doc./v.1/rel. 1C................................ 2306–8.3
C3.277:Ec7/987/doc./v.1/rel. 1D 2306–8.4
C3.277:Ec7/987/doc./v.2/rel. 2A 2306–8.5
C3.278/2:(date)...................... 2422–14
C3.278/3:(date)...................... 2422–13
C3.279:T62 2628–32
C3.282:990/doc.................... 2308–65
C3.282:990/east-north-cen./v. 1.................................... 2551–9.3
C3.282:990/east-north-cen./v. 2 .... 2551–9.3
C3.282:990/east-north-cen./v. 3 .... 2551–9.3
C3.282:990/east-south 2551–9.6
C3.282:990/middle-Atl./v.1 .. 2551–9.2
C3.282:990/middle-Atl./v.2 .. 2551–9.2
C3.282:990/mount 2551–9.8
C3.282:990/New-England...... 2551–9.1
C3.282:990/Pacific/v.1 .... 2551–9.9
C3.282:990/Pacific/v.2 .... 2551–9.9
C3.282:990/(region)/v.(nos.) 2551–9
C3.282:990/south-Atl./v.1 .... 2551–9.5
C3.282:990/south-Atl./v.2 .... 2551–9.5
C3.282:990/south-Atl./v.3 .... 2551–9.5
C3.282:990/west-north/v.1 .... 2551–9.4
C3.282:990/west-north/v.2 .... 2551–9.4
C3.282:990/west-south/v.1 .... 2551–9.7
C3.282:990/west-south/v.2 .... 2551–9.7
C3.282/2:CD90-3A-(nos.)...... 2551–10
C3.282/2:CD90-3A-2 .... 2551–10.2
C3.282/2:CD90-3A-5/992-3.. 2551–10.5
C3.282/2:CD90-3A-6 .... 2551–10.6
C3.282/2:CD90-3A-7 .... 2551–10.7
C3.282/2:CD90-3A-9 .... 2551–10.9
C3.282/2:CD90-3A-10 .... 2551–10.10
C3.282/2:CD90-3A-11/992-2 2551–10.11
C3.282/2:CD90-3A-12 .... 2551–10.12
C3.282/2:CD90-3A-13 .... 2551–10.13
C3.282/2:CD90-3A-14 .... 2551–10.14
C3.282/2:CD90-3A-15 .... 2551–10.15
C3.282/2:CD90-3A-24 .... 2551–10.24
C3.282/2:CD90-3A-25 .... 2551–10.25
C3.282/2:CD90-3A-26 .... 2551–10.26
C3.282/2:CD90-3A-36/992-2 2551–10.36
C3.282/2:CD90-3A-37/992-2 2551–10.37
C3.282/2:CD90-3A-38 .... 2551–10.38
C3.282/2:CD90-3A-39 .... 2551–10.39
C3.282/2:CD90-3A-40 .... 2551–10.40
C3.282/2:CD90-3A-43 .... 2551–10.43
C3.282/2:CD90-3A-51 .... 2551–10.51
C3.282/2:CD90-3A-52 .... 2551–10.52
C3.282/2:CD90-3A-57 .... 2551–10.57
C3.282/2:CD90-3A-58 .... 2551–10.58
C3.282/2:CD90-3A-59 .... 2551–10.59
C3.282/2:990/doc 2308–68
C3.288:92-2.......................... 2326–24.2
C3.288:92-3.......................... 2326–24.3
C13.10:260/992-93................. 2214–2
C13.10:305/supp.23 2214–1
C13.10/3:992 2214–7
C13.52:(nos.)......................... 2216–2
C13.52:19-2........................... 2216–2.204
C13.52:58/991/index............. 2216–2.202
C13.52:162 .... 2216–2.205
C13.52:163 .... 2216–2.206
C13.52:164 .... 2216–2.207
C13.52:165 .... 2216–2.208
C13.52:166 .... 2216–2.209
C13.52:167 .... 2216–2.210
C13.52:168 .... 2216–2.211
C13.52:169 .... 2216–2.212
C13.52:170 .... 2216–2.213
C13.52:171 .... 2216–2.203
C13.52:172 .... 2216–2.214
C13.52:173 .... 2216–2.215
C13.58:4829 2214–6
C13.72:(nos.)......................... 2214–5
C13.72:4898 .... 2214–5.1
C13.72:4899 .... 2214–5.2
C21.1/2:991 2244–1
C46.1:991 2064–2
C47.2:(CT) 2906–2
C47.2:C16/3 .... 2906–2.24
C47.2:F91/992 2904–15
C47.2:T69/5/990 2904–10
C47.2:T69/13 .... 2906–2.16
C47.2:T69/14 .... 2906–2.17
C47.2:T69/15 .... 2906–2.18
C47.15:(date) 2902–1
C51.11/2:992 2224–2
C55.2:C61/2/991 2184–10
C55.2:D56/991...................... 2144–27
C55.2:P76/7 2144–23
C55.2:Un2/(yr.) 2144–5
C55.8:M33/3 2158–51
C55.12:P1-992 2144–2
C55.13:NMFS103 2168–128
C55.13:NMFS104 2168–129
C55.13:NMFS105 2168–131
C55.13:NMFS106 2164–15
C55.13:NMFS110 2168–132
C55.13:NMFS111 2164–15
C55.13/2:NMFS-F/SPO-1 2164–22
C55.13/2:NMFS-SEFC-242 .. 2164–24
C55.13/2:NMFS-SEFC-273 .. 2164–23
C55.13/2:NMFS-SEFC-289 .. 2164–23
C55.13/2:NMFS-SEFC-290 .. 2164–7
C55.13/2:NMFS-SEFC-295 .. 2164–24
C55.13/2:NMFS-SWR-026.... 2166–19.11
C55.13/2:NOSOMA56 .... 2176–3.14
C55.13/2:NOSOMA58 .... 2176–3.15
C55.29:987-88....................... 2144–6
C55.32:990-91/v.(nos.) 2174–8
C55.32:990-91/v.1 .... 2174–8.1
C55.32:990-91/v.2 .... 2174–8.2
C55.49:(nos.)......................... 2146–6
C55.49/2:(nos.)...................... 2146–8
C55.49/2:1 .... 2146–8.1
C55.102:M33/2/(date) 2182–9
C55.109:(v.nos.&nos.) 2182–1
C55.113/2:(v.nos.&nos.) 2182–3
C55.119:992 2184–3
C55.123/2:(v.nos.&nos.) 2182–5
C55.129/2:(yr./nos.) 2182–6

C55.196:(date) 2182–8
C55.209:(v.nos.&nos.) 2182–7
C55.211:(v.nos.&nos.) 2152–4
C55.212:(v.nos.&nos.) 2152–3
C55.219/3:(nos.) 2154–12
C55.220/3:990 2144–15
C55.220/6:(nos.) 2156–18
C55.220/6:24 .... 2156–18.24
C55.287/60-2:(date) 2152–13.1
C55.287/60-3:(date) 2152–13.2
C55.299/2:(v.nos.&nos.) 2152–8
C55.309/2-2:991 2164–1
C55.309/2-3:990-91 .... 2166–17.1
C55.309/2-4:991(summary) .. 2162–2
C55.309/2-5:987-89 .... 2166–17.2
C55.309/2-7:(nos.) 2162–3
C55.309/2-8:(nos.) 2162–2
C55.309/2-9:988 .... 2166–6.2
C55.309/2-10:991 .... 2166–6.1
C55.310:(v.nos.&nos.) 2162–1
C55.327:988-89 2164–11
C55.402:B86 .... 2176–8.3
C55.402:Es8/5 2178–33
C55.402:M33/2/992 .... 2176–3.17
C55.420/2:860-990 2178–1
C55.420/2:991 2174–3
C55.421:993 .... 2174–2.2
C55.421/2:993 .... 2174–2.3
C55.421/3:993 .... 2174–2.4
C55.421/4:993 .... 2174–2.5
C55.425:993 .... 2174–1.1
C55.425/2:993 .... 2174–1.2
C55.425/3:993 2174–11
C55.432:993 .... 2174–2.1
C55.433:(nos.) 2176–1
C55.433:74 .... 2176–1.40
C55.439:990 2174–9
C55.616:P96/991 2144–25
C55.618:19 2144–28
C59.2:F76/7 2708–48
C59.2:In7/2 2708–17
C59.2:In8/4/989/final 2704–5
C59.8:R26/2/992 2708–47
C59.8:Us2/992 2704–6
C59.11:(v.nos.&nos.) 2702–1
C59.11/3:992 2704–1
C59.11/5:(yr.)/v.(nos.) 2708–5
C59.11/5:959-88/v.2 .... 2708–5.1
C59.20:989/rev 2704–4
C59.20:990/prelim 2704–4
C59.20/2:990/prelim 2704–5
C59.24:992/CD 2704–7
C60.2:T23 2808–30
C60.13:P96/991 2804–3
C60.15:991 2802–1
C60.15:991-2 2802–1
C60.15:992 2802–1
C61.2:(CT) 2044–6
— 2046–12
C61.2:F76/992 2044–18
C61.2:M57/2 2048–154
C61.2:P87 .... 2046–12.46
C61.2:T31/993 2044–31
C61.2:T67/11 2048–158
C61.8:An2 2048–161
C61.8:C19/3 2044–36
C61.8:J27 2048–159
C61.11:Au7/2/992 .... 2046–4.25
C61.11:B22/992 .... 2046–4.62
C61.11:B41/992 .... 2046–4.30
C61.11:B43/992 .... 2046–4.15
C61.11:B73/992 .... 2046–4.28
C61.11:B91/991 .... 2046–4.2
C61.11:B91/992 .... 2046–4.56
C61.11:B92/992 .... 2046–4.12
C61.11:C33/992 .... 2046–4.11
C61.11:C34/991-2 .... 2046–4.3
C61.11:C44/992 .... 2046–4.64
C61.11:C76/992 .... 2046–4.43
C61.11:C82/992 .... 2046–4.23
C61.11:C99/992 .... 2046–4.54
C61.11:D41/992 .... 2046–4.40
C61.11:F49/992 .... 2046–4.31
C61.11:F84/992 .... 2046–4.38
C61.11:G11/992 .... 2046–4.36
C61.11:G31/992 .... 2046–4.24
C61.11:G81/992 .... 2046–4.18
C61.11:G94/991 .... 2046–4.7
C61.11:H75/992 .... 2046–4.59
C61.11:Ic2/992 .... 2046–4.49
C61.11:In2/2/992 .... 2046–4.47
C61.11:In2/992 .... 2046–4.14
C61.11:In2/992-2 .... 2046–4.55
C61.11:Ir2/992 .... 2046–4.21
C61.11:It1/992 .... 2046–4.29
C61.11:K42/991 .... 2046–4.10
C61.11:K59/992 .... 2046–4.53
C61.11:M29/2/992 .... 2046–4.17
C61.11:M29/3/992 .... 2046–4.22
C61.11:M44/2/991 .... 2046–4.6
C61.11:M44/2/992 .... 2046–4.51
C61.11:M87/992 .... 2046–4.61
C61.11:N15/992 .... 2046–4.37
C61.11:N38/992 .... 2046–4.60
C61.11:N56/2/991 .... 2046–4.4
C61.11:N56/992 .... 2046–4.39
C61.11:N83/992 .... 2046–4.42
C61.11:P17/992 .... 2046–4.19
C61.11:P53/991-2 .... 2046–4.8
C61.11:P83/992 .... 2046–4.45
C61.11:R94/991 .... 2046–4.9
C61.11:Se5/991 .... 2046–4.5
C61.11:Se5/992 .... 2046–4.50
C61.11:Si6/992 .... 2046–4.65
C61.11:So8a/991 .... 2046–4.1
C61.11:So8a/992 .... 2046–4.44
C61.11:Sp1/992 .... 2046–4.32
C61.11:Sr3/992 .... 2046–4.52
C61.11:Su2/992 .... 2046–4.46
C61.11:Sw2/992 .... 2046–4.26
C61.11:Sw3/992 .... 2046–4.33
C61.11:Sw6/992 .... 2046–4.20
C61.11:Sw6/992-2 .... 2046–4.48
C61.11:Sy8/992 .... 2046–4.27
C61.11:T13/992 .... 2046–4.63
C61.11:T32/992 .... 2046–4.16
C61.11:T32/992-2 .... 2046–4.58
C61.11:T57/992 .... 2046–4.13
C61.11:T84/992 .... 2046–4.57
C61.11:Ug1/992 .... 2046–4.34
C61.11:Un3/992 .... 2046–4.41
C61.11:Z1/992 .... 2046–4.35
C61.12:(yr.-nos.) 2046–6
C61.12:92-01 .... 2046–6.1
C61.12:92-02 .... 2046–6.2
C61.12:92-03 .... 2046–6.5
C61.12:92-04 .... 2046–6.3
C61.12:92-05 .... 2046–6.4
C61.12:92-06 .... 2046–6.6
C61.12:92-07 .... 2046–6.8
C61.12:92-08 .... 2046–6.7
C61.12:92-09 .... 2046–6.9
C61.18:(v.nos.&nos.) 2042–24
C61.24:991 2024–1
C61.25/2:990 2044–20
C61.28/2:991 2044–37
C61.34:992 2044–28
C61.37:(v.nos.&nos.) 2042–1
C61.38:(yr.) 2044–34
C61.43:(v.nos.&nos.) 2042–33
CC1.1:990 9284–4
CC1.1:991 9284–4
CC1.35:990-91 9284–6
D1.1:992 3544–2
D1.1/3-2:991 3544–31
D1.2:B56/991 3548–22
D1.19:990-91 3504–3
D1.33/4:991 3548–21
D1.57:991 3544–5
D1.57/2:991 3544–4
D1.57/3:(date) 3542–7
D1.57/3:991-2 3542–1
D1.57/3:992 3542–1
D1.57/3-5:991 3544–19
D1.57/4:988-91 3544–18
D1.57/5:989-91 3544–11
D1.57/6:991-2 3542–5
D1.57/6:992 3542–5
D1.57/7:991-2 3542–19
D1.57/7:992 3542–19
D1.57/8:991 3544–17
D1.57/9:(date) 3542–17
D1.58/2:(yr.) 3544–6
D1.58/4:991 3544–29
D1.61:(date) 3542–14
D1.61/2:(date) 3542–16
D1.61/3:(date) 3542–20
D1.61/4:991 3544–1
D1.61/5:991 3544–7
D1.61/6:991 3544–40
D1.62:(date) 3542–15
D1.62/2:990 3544–24
D1.64:991 3544–25
D1.66:991 3904–3
D1.82:991 3504–23
D1.85:993 7144–13
D1.94:991-2 3542–22
D1.97:991 3544–36
D2.15/3:992 3504–13
D12.1:991 3504–22
D103.1:(yr.)/v.(nos.) 3754–1
D103.1:988/v.2 .... 3754–1.1
D103.1:989/v.2 .... 3754–1.2
D103.1:990/v.2 .... 3754–1.3
D103.1/2:989/(pt.nos.) 3754–3
D103.1/2:989/pt.1 .... 3754–3.1
D103.1/2:989/pt.2 .... 3754–3.2
D103.1/2:989/pt.3 .... 3754–3.3
D103.1/2:989/pt.4 .... 3754–3.4
D103.1/2:989/pt.5 .... 3754–3.5
D103.2:R24/9/v.(nos.) 3758–8
D103.2:R24/9/v.1 .... 3758–8.1
D103.2:R24/9/v.2 .... 3758–8.2
D103.35/(nos.):989 3756–1
D103.35/(nos.):991 3756–2
D103.35/10:991 .... 3756–2.11
D103.35/12:991 .... 3756–2.13
D103.35/13:991 .... 3756–2.14
D103.35/14:991 .... 3756–2.15
D103.35/19:991 .... 3756–2.20
D103.35/21:991 .... 3756–2.22
D103.35/26:991 .... 3756–2.27
D103.35/27:991 .... 3756–2.28
D103.35/35:991 .... 3756–2.36
D103.35/37:991 .... 3756–2.38
D103.35/42:989 .... 3756–1.43
D103.35/47:991 .... 3756–2.48
D103.35/51:991 .... 3756–2.9
D103.116:(date) 3752–1
D203.33:991 3804–6
D208.25:(date) 3802–4
D213.8:993 3804–7

D216.1:991 3804–14
D220.11:991 3804–8
D301.73:(v.nos.&nos.) 3602–1
E1.1:990 3024–2
E1.2:St8/tech.(nos.) 3006–13
E1.2:St8/tech.1 3006–13.1
E1.2:St8/tech.2 3006–13.2
E1.2:St8/tech.3 3006–13.3
E1.2:St8/tech.4 3006–13.4
E1.2:St8/tech.5 3006–13.5
E1.2:St8/992 3008–128
E1.15/2:992 3344–2
E1.19:(nos.) 3004–18
E1.19:0143/3 3004–18.3
E1.19:0144/10 3004–18.6
E1.19:0295 3004–18.3
E1.19:0348 3004–18.3
E1.19:0389 3004–18.3
E1.19:0447P 3004–18.3
E1.19:0483P 3004–18.3
E1.19:0507P 3004–18.8
E1.19:0512T 3004–18.4
E1.19:0528P 3004–18.1
E1.19:0529P 3004–18.2
E1.19:0537P 3004–18.3
E1.19:0550T 3004–18.5
E1.19:0558T 3004–18.9
E1.19:0562P 3004–18.7
E1.19:0565T 3004–18.10
E1.20/2:0376 3356–4.12
E1.27:990 3304–1
E1.28:DOE/OSTI-8200-R55 3354–15
E1.28:SERI/SP-(nos.) 3306–5
E1.35/4:991 3004–21
E1.36/2:991 3354–7
E1.45/2:991 3304–2
E1.48:0305 3006–5.28
E1.48:0308 3006–5.30
E1.48:0310 3006–5.31
E1.48:0313 3006–5.32
E1.50/2:991 3004–27
E1.60:0093P 3002–15
E1.60:0101P 3002–15
E1.68/2:0249P 3364–5
E1.68/2:0295P 3368–5
E1.68/2:0331P 3364–5
E1.68/2:0335P 3364–1
E1.68/2-6:(date) 3362–1
E1.81:(nos.) 3004–13
E1.84:0164 3338–3
E1.84:0217P/992 3334–5
E1.84:0245 3338–5
E1.84:0247P 3334–4
E1.84:61679P-H1/v.(nos.) 3338–2
E1.84:61679P-H1/v.1 3338–2.1
E1.84:61679P-H1/v.2 3338–2.2
E1.84/2:991 3334–3
E1.89:0019/12 3304–11
E1.89:0347P 3304–17
E1.89:0351 3304–28
E1.89:0532 3308–87
E1.90/2:(date) 3002–13
E1.93:(v.nos.&nos.) 3352–4
E1.95:991 3234–1
E1.95/2:991 3244–1.1
E2.1:991 3084–9
E2.12/3:980-91 3084–13
E2.15:G21/990 3088–21
E3.1:991 3164–29
E3.1/2:991 3164–74
E3.1/4:992 3164–75
E3.1/4:992/supp 3164–96
E3.1/4-3:992 3164–90
E3.2:B52 3164–97
E3.2:G29 3168–122
E3.2:H62/2 3168–123
E3.2:N21/5 3168–125
E3.2:T19/2 3168–124
E3.9:(date) 3162–24
E3.11:(yr./nos.) 3162–4
E3.11/2-2:990/supp 3164–4.3
E3.11/2-2:990/v.(nos.) 3164–4
E3.11/2-2:990/v.1 3164–4.1
E3.11/2-2:990/v.2 3164–4.2
E3.11/4:(yr./nos.) 3162–1
E3.11/5:(date) 3162–6
E3.11/5-5:991/v.(nos.) 3164–2
E3.11/5-5:991/v.1 3164–2.1
E3.11/5-5:991/v.2 3164–2.2
E3.11/5-6:(date) 3162–42
E3.11/7:(date) 3162–8
E3.11/7-3:991 3164–25
E3.11/7-7:990 3164–79
E3.11/7-8:(yr.) 3164–68
E3.11/7-9:(yr.) 3164–77
E3.11/7-10:(yr.) 3164–89
E3.11/9:(yr./nos.) 3162–37
E3.11/11-3:990 3164–94
E3.11/15-2:991 3164–42
E3.11/17-8:(date) 3162–35
E3.11/17-10:990 3164–11
E3.11/20:990 3164–50
E3.11/20-3:992 3164–84
E3.11/20-4:(date) 3162–43
E3.13/4:(yr./nos.) 3162–11
E3.13/4-2:990 3164–85
E3.13/4-2:991 3164–85
E3.17/4-2:990 3164–9
E3.17/6:(yr.) 3164–69
E3.18/4-2:990 3164–23
E3.18/4-3:990 3164–24
E3.19/2:990 3164–62
E3.22:990 3164–91
E3.25:990 3164–38
E3.25/2:990 3164–33
E3.25/2:991 3164–33
E3.26/5:(nos.) 3166–6
E3.26/5:CNEAF/92-01 3166–6.62
E3.26/5:EDID/91-03 3166–6.60
E3.26/5:EMEU/91-04 3166–6.61
E3.26/5:EPD/87-01 3166–6.63
E3.26/5:ICID/87-01 3166–6.58
E3.26/5:ICID/88-01 3166–6.65
E3.26/5:NAFD/88-01 3166–6.59
E3.26/5:RNGD/87-01 3166–6.64
E3.26/5:RNGD/92-01 3166–6.66
E3.27:991 3164–98
E3.29:991 3164–36
E3.31:(nos.) 3162–34
E3.32:(date) 3162–32
E3.32/3:(yr./nos.) 3162–45
E3.34:991 3164–46
E3.34/2:991 3164–70
E3.37:990 3164–44
E3.42:960-90 3164–39
E3.42/3:990 3164–64
E3.43/2-2:989 3166–8.10
E3.43/3:990 3166–7.33
E3.45:991 3164–86
E3.46/3:990 3164–82
E3.46/5:991 3164–65
E3.47:(yr.) 3164–73
E3.48:992 3164–87
E3.49:990 3164–76
E3.50:(yr.) 3164–81
E3.52:990 3164–80
E3.54/2:980-88 3166–13.7
E3.56:(nos.) 3162–38
E5.1:991 3224–1
E5.1/2:(date) 3222–2
E5.14:991 3222–1
E5.14:991-2 3222–1
E6.1:991 3254–1.1
E6.1:991/app 3254–1.2
ED1.2:Ab8 4804–41
ED1.2:Ab8/990 4804–41
ED1.2:Ad9/4 4808–41
ED1.2:C42 4808–38
ED1.2:C43/8/v.(nos.) 4808–39
ED1.2:C43/8/v.1 4808–39.1
ED1.2:C43/8/v.2 4808–39.2
ED1.2:C81/2/descrip 4808–40.4
ED1.2:C81/2/effect 4808–40.3
ED1.2:C81/2/final 4808–40.1
ED1.2:C81/2/longit 4808–40.2
ED1.2:D26/6 4828–41
ED1.2:D63/8/991 4948–11
ED1.2:F45/2 4884–1
ED1.2:G76/2/990-91 4804–1
ED1.2:H75/989-90 4804–39
ED1.2:In8/4/992 4848–47
ED1.2:K57 4808–44
ED1.2:L71/2 4808–43
ED1.2:N21/6 4808–42.1
ED1.10/2:992 4804–3
ED1.14:93-1 4804–17
ED1.18:990 4874–2
ED1.18/3-2:990 4874–5
ED1.18/4:991 4874–1
ED1.26:992 4802–1
ED1.26:992-2 4802–1
ED1.29/2:(yrs.) 4804–28
ED1.30/2:C43 4944–10
ED1.30/2:Ed8/992 4814–4
ED1.32:992 4944–4
ED1.40/4:991 4804–18
ED1.44:988-92 4804–2
ED1.84:(nos.) 4946–1
ED1.84:1 4946–1.1
ED1.84:2 4946–1.2
ED1.102:As7/4 4896–8.5
ED1.102:Ex7 4896–8.4
ED1.102:M42/v.3 4896–8.6
ED1.102:T72/3 4898–32
ED1.109:992 4824–1
ED1.111/2:990-91 4834–1
ED1.111/4:991-92/v.(nos.) 4844–3
ED1.111/4:991-92/v.1 4844–3.1
ED1.111/4:991-92/v.2 4844–3.2
ED1.116/3:988 4844–13
ED1.120:991-2002 4824–4
ED1.120:992-2003 4824–4
ED1.210:991 4944–1
ED1.302:(CT) 4896–9
ED1.302:B56 4848–46
ED1.302:C12 4896–9.1
ED1.302:C68/3 4888–7
ED1.302:Ed8/4/992 4828–35
ED1.302:Ed8/10 4828–42
ED1.302:H62/969-89 4828–33
ED1.302:L26 4826–9.12
ED1.302:P75/4 4824–10
ED1.302:P75/992 4824–9
ED1.302:P96/2 4834–19
ED1.302:P96/2/992-93 4834–19
ED1.302:R22/2 4898–33
ED1.302:Sch6/6 4896–6.7
ED1.302:Sch6/7 4836–3.10
ED1.302:Sci1 4896–8.3
ED1.302:St2/2 4844–16
ED1.302:St9/5 4848–45
ED1.308:D83 4826–9.17

ED1.308:St9/v.1 4826–9.14
ED1.308:St9/v.2 4826–9.14
ED1.308:T22/2 4826–9.18
ED1.326:991/pocket 4824–3
ED1.326:992 4824–2
ED1.328:F31/980-91 4824–8
ED1.328:Ra11/980-990 4844–15
ED1.328/3:C37/4 4848–44
ED1.328/3:El2/2 4834–6
ED1.328/3:El2/3 4834–17
ED1.328/3:F96/981-89 4844–6
ED1.328/3:F96/982-90 4844–6
ED1.328/3:K52 4844–19
ED1.328/3:L61/2 4824–6
ED1.328/3:P93 4836–3.8
ED1.328/3:P96/2 4826–1.32
ED1.328/3:Sa3 4844–8
ED1.328/3:St1 4844–18
ED1.328/3:T72 4844–17
ED1.328/4:C43 4826–10.2
ED1.328/4:D83 4826–10.3
ED1.328/4:H75 4826–10.1
ED1.328/4:T68 4826–10.4
ED1.328/5:C37 4826–9.16
ED1.328/5:P94 4826–9.13
ED1.328/5:P94/2 4826–9.15
ED1.328/5:St9 4844–10
ED1.328/5:St9/991-92 4844–10
ED1.328/5:V85 4836–3.9
ED1.328/5:V85/2 4838–50
ED1.328/6:In8 4838–52
ED1.328/6:M42 4838–51
ED1.328/7:M56 4846–5.2
ED1.329:991 4834–23
EP1.1/5:992 9182–10
EP1.2:(CT) 9184–16
EP1.21/7:(nos.) 9182–5
EP1.23/5:600/4-91/030 9194–17
EP1.23/6:(nos.) 9184–22
EP1.23/6-2:992 9184–17
EP1.23/9:(nos.) 9186–8
EP1.23/9:600/8-91/037 9186–8.37
EP1.23/9:600/8-91/217 9186–8.38
EP1.53:990-91 9194–5
EP1.56:(yr.-nos.) 9202–3
EP2.2:W28/13/990 9204–7
EP4.22/2:990 9194–1
EP4.22/2:991 9194–1
EP5.18/2:989 9234–6
EP5.22:T65/987-90/CD 9234–7
EP5.22:T65/987-90/doc 9238–70
FCA1.1:991 9264–2
FEM1.2:T41 9434–6
FHL1.31:(yr.) 9314–5
FM1.1:990 9344–1
FMC1.1:991 9334–1
FR1.1:991 9364–1
FR1.2:C74/990 9364–8
FR1.2:C74/991 9364–8
FR1.2:F96/7/(yrs.) 9364–3
FR1.3:(v.nos.&nos.) 9362–1
FR1.16:(date) 9365–1.3
FR1.17:(date) 9365–2.5
FR1.26:(date) 9365–2.7
FR1.32/6:(date) 9365–2.14
FR1.36:(date) 9365–2.6
FR1.51:(nos.) 9366–1
FR1.51:162 9366–1.162
FR1.51:163 9366–1.163
FR1.56:(date) 9365–3.3
FR1.62:(nos.) 9366–7
FR1.62:416 9366–7.270
FR1.62:417 9366–7.271
FR1.62:418 9366–7.272
FR1.62:419 9366–7.273
FR1.62:420 9366–7.274
FR1.62:421 9366–7.275
FR1.62:422 9366–7.276
FR1.62:423 9366–7.277
FR1.62:424 9366–7.278
FR1.62:425 9366–7.279
FR1.62:426 9366–7.280
FT1.1:990 9404–1
FT1.2:C48/2/989 9404–4
FTZ1.1:989 2044–30
FTZ1.1:990 2044–30
GA1.1:991 26104–1
GA1.13:AFMD-(nos.) 26102–6
GA1.13:AFMD-92-51 26111–78
GA1.13:AFMD-92-54 26111–80
GA1.13:AFMD-92-66FS 26111–79
GA1.13:GGD-91-85 26119–364
GA1.13:GGD-91-88 26119–365
GA1.13:GGD-91-101 26119–367
GA1.13:GGD-91-112FS 26119–366
GA1.13:GGD-91-137BR 26119–368
GA1.13:GGD-91-139FS 26119–369
GA1.13:GGD-92-1 26119–370
GA1.13:GGD-92-9 26119–385
GA1.13:GGD-92-10 26111–77
GA1.13:GGD-92-18 26119–373
GA1.13:GGD-92-19 26119–374
GA1.13:GGD-92-21FS 26119–375
GA1.13:GGD-92-26 26119–378
GA1.13:GGD-92-30 26119–381
GA1.13:GGD-92-31 26119–380
GA1.13:GGD-92-34 26119–386
GA1.13:GGD-92-35FS 26119–371
GA1.13:GGD-92-36FS 26119–372
GA1.13:GGD-92-37 26119–376
GA1.13:GGD-92-38 26119–383
GA1.13:GGD-92-43 26119–389
GA1.13:GGD-92-44 26119–392
GA1.13:GGD-92-46 26119–390
GA1.13:GGD-92-48BR 26119–377
GA1.13:GGD-92-49 26119–384
GA1.13:GGD-92-51 26119–382
GA1.13:GGD-92-52 26119–391
GA1.13:GGD-92-54BR 26119–379
GA1.13:GGD-92-56 26119–398
GA1.13:GGD-92-58 26119–395
GA1.13:GGD-92-61BR 26119–387
GA1.13:GGD-92-62 26119–399
GA1.13:GGD-92-63 26119–402
GA1.13:GGD-92-64FS 26119–388
GA1.13:GGD-92-65 26119–396
GA1.13:GGD-92-66 26119–393
GA1.13:GGD-92-73 26119–407
GA1.13:GGD-92-74 26119–401
GA1.13:GGD-92-75 26119–397
GA1.13:GGD-92-79 26119–394
GA1.13:GGD-92-81BR 26119–405
GA1.13:GGD-92-85 26119–409
GA1.13:GGD-92-87BR 26119–410
GA1.13:GGD-92-88BR 26119–400
GA1.13:GGD-92-89 26119–411
GA1.13:GGD-92-91 26119–406
GA1.13:GGD-92-93 26119–415
GA1.13:GGD-92-94 26119–403
GA1.13:GGD-92-95FS 26119–404
GA1.13:GGD-92-96 26119–427
GA1.13:GGD-92-101FS 26119–412
GA1.13:GGD-92-106 26119–408
GA1.13:GGD-92-109 26119–419
GA1.13:GGD-92-111 26119–289
GA1.13:GGD-92-113 26119–416
GA1.13:GGD-92-114 26119–414
GA1.13:GGD-92-120FS 26119–413
GA1.13:GGD-92-123 26119–420
GA1.13:GGD-92-131 26119–417
GA1.13:GGD-92-133 26119–421
GA1.13:GGD-92-134BR 26119–422
GA1.13:GGD-92-135FS 26119–423
GA1.13:GGD-92-139FS 26119–418
GA1.13:GGD-93-1 26119–430
GA1.13:GGD-93-2 26119–424
GA1.13:GGD-93-6 26119–428
GA1.13:GGD-93-9BR 26119–425
GA1.13:GGD-93-10FS 26119–426
GA1.13:GGD-93-11BR 26119–429
GA1.13:GGD-93-12 26119–431
GA1.13:HRD-(nos.) 26106–8
GA1.13:HRD-92-5 26121–454
GA1.13:HRD-92-6 26121–440
GA1.13:HRD-92-8 26121–439
GA1.13:HRD-92-18 26121–458
GA1.13:HRD-92-19 26121–441
GA1.13:HRD-92-35 26121–453
GA1.13:HRD-92-36 26121–444
GA1.13:HRD-92-39FS 26121–442
GA1.13:HRD-92-40 26121–443
GA1.13:HRD-92-43 26121–446
GA1.13:HRD-92-44FS 26121–451
GA1.13:HRD-92-45 26121–447
GA1.13:HRD-92-48 26121–455
GA1.13:HRD-92-49 26121–450
GA1.13:HRD-92-54 26121–452
GA1.13:HRD-92-56 26121–459
GA1.13:HRD-92-58FS 26121–466
GA1.13:HRD-92-60 26121–468
GA1.13:HRD-92-61 26121–467
GA1.13:HRD-92-62FS 26121–448
GA1.13:HRD-92-63BR 26121–456
GA1.13:HRD-92-65BR 26121–445
GA1.13:HRD-92-67BR 26121–460
GA1.13:HRD-92-72BR 26121–449
GA1.13:HRD-92-77 26121–464
GA1.13:HRD-92-81 26121–477
GA1.13:HRD-92-87FS 26121–457
GA1.13:HRD-92-90 26121–462
GA1.13:HRD-92-91 26121–463
GA1.13:HRD-92-98 26121–465
GA1.13:HRD-92-105 26121–461
GA1.13:HRD-92-106 26121–470
GA1.13:HRD-92-107 26121–484
GA1.13:HRD-92-109 26121–474
GA1.13:HRD-92-110 26121–482
GA1.13:HRD-92-121 26121–476
GA1.13:HRD-92-124 26106–8.15
GA1.13:HRD-92-125 26121–485
GA1.13:HRD-92-128 26121–472
GA1.13:HRD-92-130FS 26121–471
GA1.13:HRD-92-136FS 26121–478
GA1.13:HRD-92-137FS 26121–469
GA1.13:HRD-92-138FS 26121–473
GA1.13:HRD-92-142 26121–483
GA1.13:HRD-92-153BR 26121–481
GA1.13:HRD-92-159 26121–479
GA1.13:HRD-93-2 26121–489
GA1.13:HRD-93-11 26121–487
GA1.13:HRD-93-17 26121–486
GA1.13:HRD-93-22FS 26121–490
GA1.13:HRD-93-25 26121–488
GA1.13:IMTEC-92-6FS 26125–47
GA1.13:IMTEC-92-58BR 26125–46
GA1.13:NSIAD-91-321 26123–375
GA1.13:NSIAD-92-03 26123–376
GA1.13:NSIAD-92-28 26123–367
GA1.13:NSIAD-92-29 26123–372
GA1.13:NSIAD-92-31 26123–373
GA1.13:NSIAD-92-33 26123–374
GA1.13:NSIAD-92-56 26123–368

GA1.13:NSIAD-92-57 26123–380
GA1.13:NSIAD-92-60 26123–377
GA1.13:NSIAD-92-61 26123–369
GA1.13:NSIAD-92-62 26123–383
GA1.13:NSIAD-92-64 26123–385
GA1.13:NSIAD-92-65 26123–370
GA1.13:NSIAD-92-71 26123–371
GA1.13:NSIAD-92-82 26123–390
GA1.13:NSIAD-92-85 26123–381
GA1.13:NSIAD-92-90 26123–389
GA1.13:NSIAD-92-98 26123–392.1
GA1.13:NSIAD-92-98S 26123–392.2
GA1.13:NSIAD-92-101 26123–379
GA1.13:NSIAD-92-102 26123–386
GA1.13:NSIAD-92-111FS 26123–394
GA1.13:NSIAD-92-113 26123–134
GA1.13:NSIAD-92-116 26123–387
GA1.13:NSIAD-92-117 26123–395
GA1.13:NSIAD-92-133 26123–384
GA1.13:NSIAD-92-144 26104–24
GA1.13:NSIAD-92-146 26123–378
GA1.13:NSIAD-92-148 26123–382
GA1.13:NSIAD-92-172 26123–84
GA1.13:NSIAD-92-174 26123–388
GA1.13:NSIAD-92-198 26123–400
GA1.13:NSIAD-92-203 26123–398
GA1.13:NSIAD-92-213FS 26123–397
GA1.13:NSIAD-92-214 26123–391
GA1.13:NSIAD-92-218 26123–401
GA1.13:NSIAD-92-227 26123–396
GA1.13:NSIAD-92-229 26123–405
GA1.13:NSIAD-92-236 26123–406
GA1.13:NSIAD-92-247 26123–404
GA1.13:NSIAD-92-257 26123–402
GA1.13:NSIAD-92-274BR 26123–399
GA1.13:NSIAD-92-306 26123–403
GA1.13:OCG-92-1 26104–23
GA1.13:OCG-92-2 26109–5
GA1.13:PEMD-91-16 26131–93
GA1.13:PEMD-91-24 26131–94
GA1.13:PEMD-92-4 26131–95
GA1.13:PEMD-92-5 26131–99
GA1.13:PEMD-92-6 26131–97
GA1.13:PEMD-92-8 26131–91
GA1.13:PEMD-92-11 26131–96
GA1.13:PEMD-92-12 26131–92
GA1.13:PEMD-92-16 26131–98
GA1.13:PEMD-92-20 26131–103
GA1.13:PEMD-92-26 26131–101
GA1.13:PEMD-92-29 26131–100
GA1.13:PEMD-92-34 26131–102
GA1.13:RCED-91-200 26113–549
GA1.13:RCED-92-5 26113–553
GA1.13:RCED-92-11FS 26113–548
GA1.13:RCED-92-12 26113–552
GA1.13:RCED-92-24 26113–564
GA1.13:RCED-92-25 26113–556
GA1.13:RCED-92-30 26113–551
GA1.13:RCED-92-33 26113–550
GA1.13:RCED-92-35 26113–561
GA1.13:RCED-92-37 26113–393
GA1.13:RCED-92-39 26113–557
GA1.13:RCED-92-49 26113–554
GA1.13:RCED-92-50 26113–558
GA1.13:RCED-92-51 26113–567
GA1.13:RCED-92-57FS 26113–560
GA1.13:RCED-92-66 26113–568
GA1.13:RCED-92-67 26113–555
GA1.13:RCED-92-68 26113–563
GA1.13:RCED-92-72 26113–562
GA1.13:RCED-92-80BR 26113–566
GA1.13:RCED-92-81 26113–590
GA1.13:RCED-92-86 26113–569
GA1.13:RCED-92-96BR 26113–559
GA1.13:RCED-92-104 26113–575
GA1.13:RCED-92-108FS 26113–565
GA1.13:RCED-92-112 26113–570
GA1.13:RCED-92-114 26113–580
GA1.13:RCED-92-116BR 26113–571
GA1.13:RCED-92-124 26113–581
GA1.13:RCED-92-126 26113–583
GA1.13:RCED-92-131BR 26113–578
GA1.13:RCED-92-133 26113–579
GA1.13:RCED-92-139FS 26113–572
GA1.13:RCED-92-140 26113–585
GA1.13:RCED-92-144 26113–576
GA1.13:RCED-92-150 26113–586
GA1.13:RCED-92-163FS 26113–574
GA1.13:RCED-92-173BR 26113–577
GA1.13:RCED-92-174 26113–587
GA1.13:RCED-92-177FS 26113–573
GA1.13:RCED-92-194 26113–584
GA1.13:RCED-92-197 26113–591
GA1.13:RCED-92-200 26113–593
GA1.13:RCED-92-203 26113–592
GA1.13:RCED-92-205 26113–598
GA1.13:RCED-92-213FS 26113–582
GA1.13:RCED-92-215 26113–596
GA1.13:RCED-92-223BR 26113–588
GA1.13:RCED-92-237 26113–594
GA1.13:RCED-92-239BR 26113–589
GA1.13:RCED-92-243 26113–597
GA1.13:RCED-92-246 26113–599
GA1.13:RCED-92-250 26113–595
GA1.13:RCED-93-8 26113–600
GA1.13:RCED-93-19FS 26113–602
GA1.13:RCED-93-25 26113–601
GA1.13:RCED-93-39 26104–21
GA1.13/18:992/pt.A 26104–5.1
GA1.13/18:992/pt.(ltrs.) 26104–5
GA1.13/18:992/pt.B 26104–5.2
GA1.13/18:992/pt.C 26104–5.3
GA1.13/18:992/pt.D 26104–5.4
GA1.16/3-2:991 26104–17
GP1.1:991 26204–1
GP1.2:V82 26208–4
GS1.1:991 9454–1
GS1.1/3:992 9452–8
H20.7009:v.40/RR-12 4206–2.48
H20.7009:v.40/RR-13 4206–2.49
H20.7009:v.40/RR-14 4206–2.50
HE1.1/2:991-2 4002–6
HE1.1/2:992 4002–6
HE1.2:M46/18 4006–11.1
HE1.57:region(nos.)/991 4004–3
HE1.57:1/991 4004–3.1
HE1.57:2/991 4004–3.2
HE1.57:3/991 4004–3.3
HE1.57:4/991 4004–3.4
HE1.57:5/991 4004–3.5
HE1.57:6/991 4004–3.6
HE1.57:7/991 4004–3.7
HE1.57:8/991 4004–3.8
HE1.57:9/991 4004–3.9
HE1.57:10/991 4004–3.10
HE3.1:992 4704–6
HE3.2:In2/6 4744–25
HE3.3:(v.nos.&nos.) 4742–1
HE3.3/3:991 4744–3
HE3.19:(nos.) 4706–1
HE3.19:106 4706–1.106
HE3.19:107 4706–1.107
HE3.19/2:(nos.) 4706–2
HE3.19/2:133 4706–2.133
HE3.49/3:991 4746–4.62
HE3.71:990 4744–27
HE3.75:990 4744–26
HE3.77:992 4704–13
HE20.23:991 4044–16.1
HE20.23/2:991 4044–16.2
HE20.23/4:991/summ 4044–15
HE20.23/4:991/v.1,2 4044–15
HE20.30:(v.nos.&nos.) 4042–3
HE20.3009:992 4434–2
HE20.3016:991 4434–1
HE20.3034:(date) 4432–1
HE20.3036:989 4434–15
HE20.3036:990 4434–15
HE20.3055:982-91 4434–9
HE20.3161:(v.nos.&nos.) 4472–1
HE20.3174:991 4474–13
HE20.3176/3:(yr.) 4474–28
HE20.3176/4:(yr.) 4474–28
HE20.3178:991 4474–29
HE20.3202:M84/2/979-85 4478–186
HE20.3211:(yr.) 4474–11
HE20.3211/2:16 4474–22
HE20.3216:991 4474–15
HE20.3252:P94/991 4474–30
HE20.3351/3:991 4474–33
HE20.3362/2:990 4474–9
HE20.3401/3:990 4474–19
HE20.3508:G94/991 4474–25
HE20.4017:(date) 4062–2
HE20.4033:(nos.) 4062–3
HE20.4202:St2/991 4064–14
HE20.6208/13:991 4124–8
HE20.6209:1/(nos.) 4147–1
HE20.6209:1/26 4147–1.27
HE20.6209:1/27 4147–1.29
HE20.6209:1/28 4147–1.28
HE20.6209:2/(nos.) 4147–2
HE20.6209:2/112 4147–2.113
HE20.6209:2/113 4147–2.115
HE20.6209:2/114 4147–2.114
HE20.6209:10/179 4147–10.180
HE20.6209:10/180 4147–10.181
HE20.6209:13/110 4147–13.109
HE20.6209:13/111 4147–13.110
HE20.6209:16/(nos.) 4147–16
HE20.6209:16/6 4147–16.6
HE20.6209:20/(nos.) 4147–20
HE20.6209:20/19 4147–20.19
HE20.6209:21/(nos.) 4147–21
HE20.6209:21/50 4147–21.50
HE20.6209/3:(nos.) 4146–8
HE20.6209/3:208 4146–8.210
HE20.6209/3:209 4146–8.214
HE20.6209/3:210 4146–8.211
HE20.6209/3:211 4146–8.212
HE20.6209/3:212 4146–8.213
HE20.6209/3:213 4146–8.215
HE20.6209/3:214 4146–8.217
HE20.6209/3:215 4146–8.216
HE20.6209/3:216 4146–8.218
HE20.6209/3:217 4146–8.219
HE20.6209/3:218 4146–8.220
HE20.6209/3:219 4146–8.222
HE20.6209/3:220 4146–8.221
HE20.6209/4:990 4147–10.182
HE20.6209/4:991 4147–10.183
HE20.6209/4-3:10/2/CD 4147–10.184
HE20.6209/7:989 4147–13.112
HE20.6209/7:990 4147–13.112
HE20.6209/9:990 4147–13.111
HE20.6210:989/v.2/pt.B 4144–3
HE20.6211:991 4164–1
HE20.6214:991 4164–2
HE20.6216/2-2:(date) 4122–1
HE20.6216/3:(date) 4122–2
HE20.6216/4:990-91 4124–1
HE20.6217:(v.nos.&nos.) 4142–1

HE20.6217:(v.nos.&nos.)/supp	4146–5
HE20.6217:v.40/8/supp	4146–5.124
HE20.6217:v.40/12/supp	4146–5.125
HE20.6217:v.40/13	4144–7
HE20.6223:991	4144–11
HE20.6512/7:991/4	4186–10.9
HE20.6514:(nos.)	4186–6
HE20.6514:16	4186–6.16
HE20.6517/2:4	4186–8.23
HE20.6617:(CT)/990	4116–6
HE20.6617:All b/990	4116–6.1
HE20.6617:All s/990	4116–6.2
HE20.6617:Ar4i/990	4116–6.3
HE20.6617:Ar4k/990	4116–6.4
HE20.6617:C12/990	4116–6.5
HE20.6617:C71/990	4116–6.6
HE20.6617:C76/990	4116–6.7
HE20.6617:D37/990	4116–6.8
HE20.6617:D63/990	4116–6.9
HE20.6617:F66/990	4116–6.10
HE20.6617:G29/990	4116–6.11
HE20.6617:H31/990	4116–6.12
HE20.6617:Id1/990	4116–6.13
HE20.6617:Il6/990	4116–6.14
HE20.6617:In2/990	4116–6.15
HE20.6617:Io9/990	4116–6.16
HE20.6617:K13/990	4116–6.17
HE20.6617:K41/990	4116–6.18
HE20.6617:L93/990	4116–6.19
HE20.6617:M28/990	4116–6.20
HE20.6617:M36/990	4116–6.21
HE20.6617:M38/990	4116–6.22
HE20.6617:M58/990	4116–6.23
HE20.6617:M66/990	4116–6.24
HE20.6617:M69i/990	4116–6.25
HE20.6617:M69o/990	4116–6.26
HE20.6617:M76/990	4116–6.27
HE20.6617:N27/990	4116–6.28
HE20.6617:N41/990	4116–6.29
HE20.6617:N42h/990	4116–6.30
HE20.6617:N42j/990	4116–6.31
HE20.6617:N42m/990	4116–6.32
HE20.6617:N42y/990	4116–6.33
HE20.6617:N81c/990	4116–6.34
HE20.6617:N81d/990	4116–6.35
HE20.6617:Oh3/990	4116–6.36
HE20.6617:Ok4/990	4116–6.37
HE20.6617:Or3/990	4116–6.38
HE20.6617:P38/990	4116–6.39
HE20.6617:R34/990	4116–6.41
HE20.6617:So8c/990	4116–6.42
HE20.6617:So8d/990	4116–6.43
HE20.6617:T25/990	4116–6.44
HE20.6617:T31/990	4116–6.45
HE20.6617:Ut1/990	4116–6.46
HE20.6617:V59/990	4116–6.47
HE20.6617:V81/990	4116–6.48
HE20.6617:W27/990	4116–6.49
HE20.6617:W52v/990	4116–6.50
HE20.6617:W75/990	4116–6.51
HE20.6617:W99/990	4116–6.52
HE20.7009:(v.nos.&nos.)	4202–1
—	4206–2
HE20.7009:v.41/RR-1	4206–2.51
HE20.7009:v.41/RR-2	4206–2.52
HE20.7009:v.41/RR-3	4206–2.53
HE20.7009:v.41/RR-4	4206–2.54
HE20.7009:v.41/RR-5	4206–2.55
HE20.7009:v.41/RR-6	4206–2.56
HE20.7009:v.41/RR-7	4206–2.57
HE20.7009:v.41/RR-8	4206–2.58
HE20.7009:v.41/RR-9	4206–2.59
HE20.7009:v.41/RR-10	4206–2.60
HE20.7009:v.41/RR-11	4206–2.61
HE20.7009:v.41/RR-12	4206–2.62
HE20.7009:v.41/RR-13	4206–2.63
HE20.7009:v.41/RR-14	4206–2.64
HE20.7009:v.41/RR-15	4206–2.65
HE20.7009:40/53	4204–1
HE20.7009/2:(v.nos.&nos.)	4202–7
HE20.7011/6:992	4205–2
HE20.7011/8:990	4205–4
HE20.7011/37:93	4205–22
HE20.7011/38:(date)	4202–9
HE20.7311/2:v.5	4204–16
HE20.7315:992	4204–11
HE20.7502:In5/2	4208–35
HE20.7511:(date)	4202–10
HE20.7610/2:990	4204–19
HE20.7610/2:991	4204–19
HE20.7614:992	4204–18
HE20.8116:(nos.)	4506–3
HE20.8116:202	4506–3.48
HE20.8116:203	4506–3.49
HE20.8116:204	4506–3.50
HE20.8116:205	4506–3.51
HE20.8137:992	4094–1
HE20.8202:(CT)	4492–5
—	4494–5
HE20.8202:H81/2/991	4494–5.1
HE20.8202:Sm7/2/v.(nos.)	4494–4
HE20.8202:Sm7/2/v.1	4494–4.1
HE20.8202:Sm7/2/v.2	4494–4.2
HE20.8216:107	4498–78
HE20.8216:109	4498–79
HE20.8216:113	4498–80
HE20.8216:118	4498–77
HE20.8216/5:991	4494–11
HE20.8217/4:(date)	4492–4
HE20.8235:(nos.)	4496–11
HE20.8235:1	4496–11.1
HE20.8235:2/v.1	4496–11.2
HE20.8235:3/v.2	4496–11.3
HE20.8236:(nos.)	4496–12
HE20.8236:1	4496–12.1
HE20.8308:All/8/v.(nos.)	4488–10
HE20.8308:All/8/v.3/979-85	4488–10.4
HE20.8308:All/8/v.4	4488–10.5
HE20.8309:(v.nos.&nos.)	4482–1
HE20.9202:C33/exec.summ	4104–17.1
HE20.9202:C33/heart	4104–17.5
HE20.9202:C33/kidney	4104–17.2
HE20.9202:C33/liver	4104–17.3
HE20.9202:C33/pan	4104–17.4
HE20.9202:C33/user	4104–17.6
HE20.9310:992	4114–8
HE20.9313:981-87	4114–12
HE20.9313:981-88	4114–12
HE20.9414:990	4084–6
HE20.9421:992	4084–1
HE20.9422:992	4084–7
HE22.16/2:991	4654–10
HE22.18:(v.nos.&nos.)	4652–1
HE22.18/2:991(supplement)	4652–1
HE22.19/2:R29/990	4654–16
HE22.21:985	4654–5
HE22.21:986	4654–5
HE22.21:987	4654–5
HE22.25:991	4654–17
HE22.34:988-90/tech.supp	4654–14.53
HE22.34:988-90/v.(nos.)	4654–14
HE22.34:988-90/v.1	4654–14.1
HE22.34:988-90/v.2	4654–14.2
HE22.34:988-90/v.3	4654–14.3
HE22.34:988-90/v.4	4654–14.4
HE22.34:988-90/v.5	4654–14.5
HE22.34:988-90/v.6	4654–14.5
HE22.34:988-90/v.7	4654–14.6
HE22.34:988-90/v.8	4654–14.7
HE22.34:988-90/v.9	4654–14.8
HE22.34:988-90/v.10	4654–14.9
HE22.34:988-90/v.11	4654–14.10
HE22.34:988-90/v.12	4654–14.11
HE22.34:988-90/v.13	4654–14.12
HE22.34:988-90/v.14	4654–14.13
HE22.34:988-90/v.15	4654–14.14
HE22.34:988-90/v.16	4654–14.15
HE22.34:988-90/v.17	4654–14.16
HE22.34:988-90/v.18	4654–14.17
HE22.34:988-90/v.19	4654–14.18
HE22.34:988-90/v.20	4654–14.19
HE22.34:988-90/v.21	4654–14.20
HE22.34:988-90/v.22	4654–14.21
HE22.34:988-90/v.23	4654–14.22
HE22.34:988-90/v.24	4654–14.23
HE22.34:988-90/v.25	4654–14.24
HE22.34:988-90/v.26	4654–14.25
HE22.34:988-90/v.27	4654–14.26
HE22.34:988-90/v.28	4654–14.27
HE22.34:988-90/v.29	4654–14.28
HE22.34:988-90/v.30	4654–14.29
HE22.34:988-90/v.31	4654–14.30
HE22.34:988-90/v.32	4654–14.31
HE22.34:988-90/v.33	4654–14.32
HE22.34:988-90/v.34	4654–14.33
HE22.34:988-90/v.35	4654–14.34
HE22.34:988-90/v.36	4654–14.35
HE22.34:988-90/v.37	4654–14.36
HE22.34:988-90/v.38	4654–14.37
HE22.34:988-90/v.39	4654–14.38
HE22.34:988-90/v.40	4654–14.39
HE22.34:988-90/v.41	4654–14.40
HE22.34:988-90/v.42	4654–14.41
HE22.34:988-90/v.43	4654–14.42
HE22.34:988-90/v.44	4654–14.43
HE22.34:988-90/v.45	4654–14.44
HE22.34:988-90/v.46	4654–14.45
HE22.34:988-90/v.47	4654–14.45
HE22.34:988-90/v.48	4654–14.46
HE22.34:988-90/v.49	4654–14.47
HE22.34:988-90/v.50	4654–14.48
HE22.34:988-90/v.51	4654–14.49
HE22.34:988-90/v.52	4654–14.50
HE22.34:988-90/v.53	4654–14.51
HE22.34:988-90/v.54	4654–14.52
HE22.35:(CT)/(yrs.)	4654–15
HE22.509:992	4654–18
HE23.1002:St2/3/991	4584–5
HE23.1012:990	4584–4
HE25.15:990	4584–3
HH1.1:990	5004–10
HH1.1/2:992	5002–8
HH1.1/2:992-2	5002–8
HH1.1/6:992	5002–11
HH1.1/6:992-2	5002–11
HH1.2:C73/32	5004–9
HH1.2:D63/(nos.)	5186–16
HH1.2:D63/14	5186–16.1
HH1.2:D63/15	5186–16.2
HH1.2:D63/16	5186–16.3
HH1.2:D63/17	5186–16.4
HH1.2:D63/18	5186–16.5
HH1.2:D63/19	5186–16.6
HH1.2:D63/20	5186–16.7
HH1.2:L46/8	5188–131.1
HH1.2:L46/8/v.1/app.A-H	5188–131.2
HH1.2:L46/8/v.2/app.I-P	5188–131.3
HH1.37:991	5144–6
HH1.75:991	5184–7
HH1.99:(date)	5142–18

HH1.99/2:(date) 5142–30
HH1.99/2-2:982-90 5144–21
HH1.99/3:(date) 5142–20
HH2.1:991 5144–26
HH2.24/4:991 5144–1
HH2.24/5:991 5144–15
HH2.24/7:991 5144–17
I1.1/7:992 5302–2
I1.1/7:992-2 5302–2
I1.96/3:990 5304–5
I19.1:991 5664–8
I19.3:1971 5668–126
I19.3:1989-A-C 5668–127
I19.4/2:(nos.) 5666–21
I19.4/2:930-K 5666–21.11
I19.4/2:930-L 5666–21.12
I19.4/2:1042 5668–125
I19.4/4:991 5664–11
I19.4/6:989 5664–14
I19.4/6:990 5664–14
I19.4/8:990 5664–15
I19.13:2362 5666–27.33
I19.14:991 5664–4
I19.14/4:(nos.) 5662–1
I19.42:(date) 5662–3
I19.42/4:88-4132 5666–27.25
I19.42/4:90-596 5666–24.13
I19.42/4:90-4002 5666–27.28
I19.42/4:90-4046 5666–27.27
I19.42/4:90-4094 5666–24.10
I19.42/4:90-4120 5666–27.24
I19.42/4:90-4175 5666–28.19
I19.42/4:90-4177 5666–24.11
I19.42/4:91-4002 5666–27.29
I19.42/4:91-4049 5666–28.21
I19.42/4:91-4050 5666–27.30
I19.42/4:91-4054 5666–27.32
I19.42/4:91-4160 5666–27.35
I19.42/4:91-4172 5666–28.17
I19.42/4:91-4192 5666–25.14
I19.42/4:92-4009 5666–27.31
I19.53/2:(nos.) 5666–10
— 5666–12
I19.53/2:AK-90-1 5666–10.2
I19.53/2:AL-91-1 5666–12.1
I19.53/2:AZ-90-1 5666–10.3
I19.53/2:HI-90-1 5666–10.10
I19.53/2:MN-90-1 5666–10.22
I19.53/2:MN-90-2 5666–10.22
I19.53/2:ND-90-1 5666–10.33
I19.53/2:NV-90-1 5666–10.27
I19.53/2:NV-91-1 5666–12.27
I19.53/2:NY-91-1 5666–12.31
I19.53/2:NY-91-2 5666–12.31
I19.53/2:NY-91-3 5666–12.31
I19.53/2:OK-90-1 5666–10.35
I19.53/2:PA-90-1 5666–10.37
I19.53/2:PA-90-2 5666–10.37
I19.53/2:PA-90-3 5666–10.37
I19.53/2:TX-90-1 5666–10.41
I19.53/2:TX-90-2 5666–10.41
I19.53/2:TX-90-3 5666–10.41
I19.53/2:UT-91-1 5666–12.42
I19.53/2:VA-90-1 5666–10.43
I19.53/2:VA-90-2 5666–10.43
I19.53/2:WI-90-1 5666–10.46
I19.53/2:WV-91-1 5666–12.45
I19.53/2:WY-90-1 5666–10.47
I19.76:90-122 5666–26.19
I19.76:90-146 5666–28.22
I19.76:90-376 5666–26.22
I19.76:90-572 5666–24.15
I19.76:90-581 5666–27.26
I19.76:90-583 5666–26.17
I19.76:91-78 5666–26.18
I19.76:91-86 5666–24.16
I19.76:91-91 5666–26.16
I19.76:91-96 5666–26.23
I19.76:91-176 5666–24.14
I19.76:91-187 5666–28.20
I19.76:91-188 5666–26.20
I19.76:91-191 5666–26.21
I19.76:91-199 5666–28.18
I19.76:91-203 5666–24.12
I19.76:91-210 5666–26.24
I19.76:91-212 5666–24.17
I19.76:91-214 5666–26.25
I19.76:91-226 5666–26.26
I19.76:91-234 5666–26.27
I19.76:91-247 5666–24.18
I19.76:91-496 5666–28.23
I19.76:92-478/CD 5664–18
I27.1/4:990 5824–12
I27.2:H99/6 5828–14
I27.2:St7/3/990 5824–7
I27.71:991-92 5824–6
I27.71/2:991 5824–3
I28.2:C44/2/990 5604–38
I28.2:M66/22 5614–6
I28.2:Us7/2 5604–39
I28.5/2:(nos.) 5602–2
I28.27:9292 5608–170
I28.27:9299 5608–172
I28.27:9300 5608–173
I28.27:9301 5608–132
I28.27:9310 5606–4.30
I28.27:9312 5608–175
I28.27:9327 5606–4.31
I28.27/2:991 5604–2
I28.28/2:(date) 5612–1.15
I28.29:(date) 5612–1.2
I28.32:(date) 5612–1.31
I28.37:989/v.1 5604–33
I28.37:989/v.3/africa 5604–35.1
I28.37:989/v.3/asia/pacific 5604–35.2
I28.37:989/v.3/mid.east 5604–35.3
I28.37:989/v.3/(regions) 5604–35
I28.37/a:(CT)/990 5604–20
I28.37/a:(CT)/991 5604–15
I28.37/a:Ab84/990 5604–20.3
I28.37/a:Al82/2/990 5604–20.4
I28.37/a:An87/990 5604–20.5
I28.37/a:As15/991 5604–15.7
I28.37/a:B645/991 5604–15.10
I28.37/a:C126/2/991 5604–15.12
I28.37/a:C332/990 5604–20.13
I28.37/a:C468/2/990 5604–20.14
I28.37/a:C579/990 5604–20.15
I28.37/a:C632/990 5604–20.16
I28.37/a:C723/2/990 5604–20.17
I28.37/a:C766/990 5604–20.51
I28.37/a:C793/990 5604–20.18
I28.37/a:F417/990 5604–20.20
I28.37/a:G317/990 5604–20.23
I28.37/a:G563/16/990 5604–20.24
I28.37/a:G998/990 5604–20.26
I28.37/a:H367/990 5604–20.27
I28.37/a:H367/991 5604–15.27
I28.37/a:Ir6/2/990 5604–20.32
I28.37/a:Ir6/3/990 5604–20.30
I28.37/a:Ir6/5/990 5604–20.31
I28.37/a:L469/990 5604–20.35
I28.37/a:M274/6/990 5604–20.38
I28.37/a:M664/2/990 5604–20.1
I28.37/a:M739/990 5604–20.41
I28.37/a:N73/(yr.) 5604–48
I28.37/a:N638/990 5604–20.43
I28.37/a:P329/990 5604–20.44
I28.37/a:P696/990 5604–20.46
I28.37/a:P847/990 5604–20.47
I28.37/a:R182/990 5604–20.49
I28.37/a:Sa37/990 5604–20.50
I28.37/a:Sa56/990 5604–20.51
I28.37/a:Si34/990 5604–20.52
I28.37/a:Si39/3/990 5604–20.53
I28.37/a:Sl1/990 5604–20.33
I28.37/a:So16/5/990 5604–20.66
I28.37/a:St72/2/990 5604–20.55
I28.37/a:St72/3/990 5604–20.55
I28.37/a:St89/990 5604–20.67
I28.37/a:Su5/990 5604–20.56
I28.37/a:Su7/990 5604–20.2
— 5604–22.1
I28.37/a:T49/990 5604–20.58
I28.37/a:T53/990 5604–20.59
I28.37/a:T143/990 5604–20.57
I28.37/a:T834/990 5604–20.60
I28.37/a:V26/990 5604–20.61
I28.37/a:W83/990 5604–20.68
I28.37/a:Z66/990 5604–20.62
I28.37/a:Z68/990 5604–20.63
I28.37/a2:(CT)/(yr.) 5604–17
I28.37/a2:(CT)/989 5604–16
I28.37/a2:(CT)/990 5604–22
I28.37/a2:Al1b/990 5604–22.2
I28.37/a2:Al1s/990 5604–22.3
I28.37/a2:Ar4i/990 5604–22.4
I28.37/a2:Ar4k/990 5604–22.5
I28.37/a2:C12/990 5604–22.6
I28.37/a2:C71/990 5604–22.7
I28.37/a2:C76/990 5604–22.8
I28.37/a2:D37/990 5604–22.9
I28.37/a2:F66/990 5604–22.10
I28.37/a2:Id1/990 5604–22.13
I28.37/a2:Il6/990 5604–22.14
I28.37/a2:In2/990 5604–22.15
I28.37/a2:M69o/990 5604–22.26
I28.37/a2:W52v/989 5604–16.50
I28.37/a2:W75/989 5604–16.51
I28.37/a2:W99/989 5604–16.52
I28.37/2:(CT) 5606–1
I28.53:(date) 5612–1.11
I28.54:(date) 5612–1.16
I28.58/2:(date) 5612–1.17
I28.59/2:(date) 5612–1.6
I28.61/2:(date) 5612–1.10
I28.63:(date) 5612–1.23
I28.66:(date) 5612–1.12
I28.69:(date) 5612–1.27
I28.70:(date) 5612–2.10
I28.73:(date) 5612–1.25
I28.75:(date) 5612–1.34
I28.76:(date) 5612–1.4
I28.77:(date) 5612–2.14
I28.78:(date) 5612–1.26
I28.80:(date) 5612–2.2
I28.82/2:(date) 5612–2.16
I28.84:(date) 5612–1.3
I28.85:(date) 5612–1.1
I28.87:(date) 5612–1.13
I28.92:(date) 5612–1.20
I28.95:(date) 5612–2.1
I28.96:(date) 5612–1.24
I28.101:(date) 5612–2.12
I28.102:(date) 5612–2.5
I28.103:(date) 5612–2.3
I28.111/2:(date) 5612–2.18
I28.112:991 5614–22
I28.118/4:(date) 5612–2.20
I28.119:991/advance 5614–5.4
I28.119/2:992 5614–20
I28.119/3:(date) 5612–1.30

I28.120/2:991-92 5614–19
I28.134/2:991 5614–30
I28.135/2:(date) 5612–1.33
I28.146:991/advance/supp. 5614–5.1
I28.148:992 5604–18
I28.149/2:(date) 5602–4
I28.151:Id1 .... 5606–7.7
I28.156/2:991 .... 5606–5.10
I28.171:(date) 5612–2.19
I28.173:(date) 5602–5
I29.94:991 5544–4
I29.103:991 5544–5
I29.114:991 5544–12
I29.117/2:990 .... 5544–16.1
I49.1:991 5504–20
I49.2:C76/4 5508–118
I49.2:P43/3 5508–117
I49.2:W53/14/update 5508–89
I49.2:W53/16 5508–119
I49.29/3:990 5504–1
I49.66:180 5508–120
I49.69:991 5504–10
I49.84:990 5504–12
I49.89/2:(nos.) 5506–14
I49.89/2:85/(1.23) 5506–14.4
I49.89/2:90(17) 5508–114
I49.89/2:90(18) 5508–116
I49.89/2:90(19) 5506–10.13
I49.89/2:92(2) 5506–14.5
I49.93:992-93 5504–25
I49.94:(yr.) 5504–23
I49.100:(nos.) 5506–12
I49.100:31 .... 5506–12.4
I49.100:32 .... 5506–12.5
I49.100/3:992 5504–27
I49.102:992 5504–8
I49.103:990 5504–29
I49.106:991 5504–28
I49.106/2:992 5504–30
I49.106/3:991 5504–32
I49.106/4:991-92 5504–31
I49.106/5:992 5504–15
I49.106/6:992 5504–11
I53.1/2:991 5724–1
I53.12/2:990 5724–13
I53.39:991 5724–14
I53.43:991 .... 5724–11.4
I53.43/2:991 .... 5724–11.2
I53.43/3:991 .... 5724–11.5
I53.43/4:990 .... 5724–11.1
I53.43/4:991 .... 5724–11.3
I53.43/5:991 5724–15
I71.1:991 5644–1
I72.12/2:91-0084/v.1 .... 5736–5.16
I72.12/2:91-0084/v.2 .... 5736–5.16
I72.12/2:91-0084/v.3 .... 5736–5.16
I72.12/2:92-011 5738–37
I72.12/3:91-0079 5734–6
I72.12/3:92-0002 5738–34
I72.12/3-2:991 5734–4
I72.12/3-4:0091 5734–9
I72.12/7:P11/990 5734–7
I72.13:991 5734–2
I72.18:(date&nos.) 5732–1
IC1.1:988 9484–1
IC1.1:989 9484–1
IC1.1:990 9484–1
IC1.1:991 9484–1
IC1.2:M85/6/991 9484–11
IC1.25:990/pt.(nos.) 9486–5
IC1.25:990/pt.1 .... 9486–5.1
IC1.25:990/pt.2/release1 .... 9486–5.2
IC1.25:990/pt.2/release2 .... 9486–5.3
IC1.25:991/pt.(nos.) 9486–6
IC1.25:991/pt.1 .... 9486–6.1
IC1ste.25/3-2:(date) 9482–3
ITC1.1:991 9884–1
ITC1.2:In2/2 .... 9885–12.2
ITC1.2:In2/3 .... 9885–8.3
ITC1.9/3:991 9884–12
ITC1.10:(yr.)/[supp. nos.] 9886–13
ITC1.10:992/supp.1 .... 9886–13.1
ITC1.10:993 .... 9886–13.2
ITC1.10/3:987-90/prod 9884–14
ITC1.12:(nos.) 9886–4
— 9886–14
— 9886–15
— 9886–19
ITC1.12:TA-131-18, 503(a)-23, 332-319 9884–23
ITC1.12:TA-131-19,503(a)-24, 332-331 9884–23
ITC1.12:303-TA-23(prelim.), 731-TA-565-570(prelim.) 9886–19.84
ITC1.12:332-267/992 .... 9886–4.181
ITC1.12:332-308 .... 9886–4.179
ITC1.12:332-308/summ 9886–4.179
ITC1.12:332-310 .... 9886–4.180
ITC1.12:332-313 .... 9886–4.187
ITC1.12:332-316 .... 9886–4.183
ITC1.12:332-317 .... 9886–4.182
ITC1.12:332-317/addendum 9886–4.182
ITC1.12:332-318 .... 9886–4.184
ITC1.12:332-320 .... 9886–4.189
ITC1.12:332-321 .... 9886–4.186
ITC1.12:332-322 .... 9886–4.185
ITC1.12:332-330 .... 9886–4.188
ITC1.12:701-TA-309(final), 731-TA-528(final) 9886–19.86
ITC1.12:701-TA-312(final) 9886–15.80
ITC1.12:701-TA-313(prelim.) 9886–15.79
ITC1.12:701-TA-314-317(prelim.),731-TA-522-555(prelim.) 9886–19.82
ITC1.12:701-TA-318(prelim.), 731-TA-560-561(prelim.) 9886–19.83
ITC1.12:701-TA-319-354(prelim.),731-TA-573-620(prelim.) 9886–19.85
ITC1.12:731-TA-448-450(final)/remand 9886–14.363
ITC1.12:731-TA-514(final) 9886–14.340
ITC1.12:731-TA-516(final) 9886–14.345
ITC1.12:731-TA-517(final) 9886–14.342
ITC1.12:731-TA-518(final) 9886–14.343
ITC1.12:731-TA-520-521(final) 9886–14.352
ITC1.12:731-TA-522(final) 9886–14.351
ITC1.12:731-TA-525(final) 9886–14.344
ITC1.12:731-TA-527(final) 9886–14.360
ITC1.12:731-TA-530(final) 9886–14.350
ITC1.12:731-TA-532-537(final) 9886–14.361
ITC1.12:731-TA-538(final) 9886–14.357
ITC1.12:731-TA-539(prelim.) 9886–14.337
ITC1.12:731-TA-540-541(final) 9886–14.365
ITC1.12:731-TA-540-541(prelim.) 9886–14.338
ITC1.12:731-TA-542-544(prelim.) 9886–14.339
ITC1.12:731-TA-545(prelim.) 9886–14.341
ITC1.12:731-TA-546-547(prelim.) 9886–14.346
ITC1.12:731-TA-548,550-551 (prelim.) 9886–14.347
ITC1.12:731-TA-556(prelim.) 9886–14.348
ITC1.12:731-TA-557-559(prelim.) 9886–14.349
ITC1.12:731-TA-562(prelim.) 9886–14.353
ITC1.12:731-TA-563-564(prelim.) 9886–14.354
ITC1.12:731-TA-571(prelim.) 9886–14.355
ITC1.12:731-TA-572(prelim.) 9886–14.356
ITC1.12:731-TA-621(prelim.) 9886–14.358
ITC1.12:731-TA-622(prelim.) 9886–14.359
ITC1.12:731-TA-624-625(prelim.) 9886–14.362
ITC1.12:731-TA-627(prelim.) 9886–14.364
ITC1.13:(nos.) 9882–2
ITC1.14:990 9884–3
ITC1.14/2:(nos.) 9882–1
ITC1.15/2:991 9884–25
ITC1.16/3:(date) 9882–8
ITC1.21/2:(date) 9882–6
ITC1.24:991 9884–5
ITC1.27:(date) 9882–13
ITC1.29:(date) 9882–14
ITC1.29/2:987-91 9884–21
ITC1.30:991 9884–18
ITC1.32:991 9884–20
J1.1:989 6004–1
J1.1:990 6004–1
J1.1:991 6004–1
J1.14/7:991 6224–2
J1.14/7-2:991/prelim 6222–1
J1.14/7-2:992 6222–1
J1.14/7-6:991 6224–3
J1.14/7-7:991 6224–5
J1.14/22:991 6224–6
J1.87:991 6064–18
J16.1:991 6244–2
J16.5:991 6244–3
J16.23/5:987 6244–1
J16.23/5:988 6244–1
J16.23/5:989 6244–1
J16.31:992 6244–4
J21.2/10:990 6264–2
J21.2/10:991 6264–2
J21.20:991 6264–4
J23.1:991 6004–9
J24.22:991 6284–2
J24.25:991 6284–4
J26.2:T71 6068–246
J27.1:990-91 6004–3
J28.15/2-3:(yr./nos.) 6062–3
J28.23:Ac7/3/990/update 6064–22
J28.24:(CT) 6066–20
J28.24:As2/992 .... 6066–20.22
J28.24:R31 .... 6066–20.24
J28.24/3:D84 6068–252
J28.24/3:Ur3 6068–247
J28.29:991 6064–32
J29.2:C26/980-90 6064–31
J29.2:C86/10 .... 6066–3.48
J29.2:D84/991 6064–30
J29.2:P93/3 6068–248
J29.2:Sch6 .... 6066–3.46
J29.9/2:990 .... 6066–3.47
J29.9/4:988 6064–27
J29.9/6:991 6064–6
J29.11:Sh5 .... 6066–25.45
J29.11/2:990 .... 6066–25.50
J29.11/5:991 .... 6066–25.48
J29.11/6:990 .... 6066–25.43
J29.11/7:991 .... 6066–25.47
J29.11/8:991 .... 6066–25.49
J29.11/13:986 6064–33
J29.11/13:987 6064–33
J29.11/13:988 6064–33
J29.13:D84/4 .... 6066–19.67
J29.13:D84/5 .... 6066–19.70
J29.13:D84/992 .... 6066–19.69

J29.13:F76 .... 6066–19.64
J29.13:J19 .... 6066–19.66
J29.13:Se5/3 .... 6066–19.68
J29.15:(CT) 6066–23
J29.15:J98/990 .... 6066–23.7
J29.16:990 6068–218
J29.17:990 6064–26
J29.20:988 6064–29
J29.20:989 6064–29
J31.2:J98 6068–250
J31.10:991 6004–2
J32.1:990 6064–34
J32.2:Ar6 .... 6066–27.8
J32.10:C83/4 .... 6066–27.7
J32.10:J98/988 .... 6066–27.9
J32.17:990 6064–36
J32.18:990 6064–35
Ju10.1/2:991 18204–8
Ju10.10:991-2 18202–2
Ju10.10:992 18202–2
Ju10.13:(yr.) 18204–4
Ju10.19:991 18204–7
Ju10.21:991 18204–11
L1.1:991 6304–1
L1.2:P38/11 6688–2
L1.74:991-92 6302–2
L1.74:992 6302–2
L1.79:(yr.-nos.) 6606–3
L1.79:92-172 .... 6606–3.10
L1.121/13:C43/991 .... 6785–16.1
L1.121/18:N42/991 .... 6785–16.1
L1.122/43:C81/992 .... 6785–3.5
L2.2:(CT) 6826–3
L2.2:C73/8/991 .... 6826–3.8
L2.2:C73/8/991-2 .... 6826–3.9
L2.2:Oc1/49 .... 6785–15.1
L2.2:Su7/2/990 6844–7
L2.3:(nos.) 6826–2
L2.3:2385 6748–85
L2.3:2389 6744–20
L2.3:2392 .... 6787–6.254
L2.3:2402 6744–19
L2.3:2404 .... 6826–2.8
L2.3:2407 6728–32
L2.3:2409 .... 6826–2.9
L2.3:2411 6748–81
L2.3:2413 6744–20
L2.3:2414 6888–1
L2.3/3:M56 .... 6787–6.253
L2.3/4:992-93 6744–1
L2.3/4-2:992 6744–3
L2.3/8:992 6784–9
L2.3/10-2:990 6784–21
L2.3/11:990 6844–1
L2.3/12:991 6744–7
L2.3/20:992 6824–1
L2.3/36:990 6744–18
L2.6:(v.nos.&nos.) 6722–1
L2.38/3:(date) 6762–2
L2.38/3-2:(date) 6762–1
L2.41/2:(v.nos.&nos.) 6742–2
L2.41/2-2:992 6744–4
L2.41/4:(date) 6742–4
L2.41/9:(date) 6742–22
L2.41/11:(date) 6742–17
L2.41/11-2:(date) 6742–18
L2.44:(v.nos.&nos.) 6782–1
L2.45/2:(date) 6782–2
L2.45/3:991 6784–12
L2.45/4:991-2 6782–6
L2.45/4:992 6782–6
L2.53/2:(date) 6742–5
L2.60/3:(date) 6762–13
L2.61:(date) 6762–6
L2.61/10:(date) 6762–5
L2.61/11:991 6764–2
L2.70/4:(v.nos.&nos.) 6742–1
L2.71:(nos.) 6726–2
— 6886–4
L2.71:807 6888–23
L2.71:808 .... 6886–4.1
L2.71:811 .... 6886–4.2
L2.71:812 .... 6886–4.3
L2.71:813 .... 6886–4.4
L2.71:814 .... 6886–4.5
L2.71:820 .... 6726–2.1
L2.71:824 .... 6726–2.2
L2.71:827 .... 6726–2.3
L2.71:830 .... 6726–2.4
L2.79:(date) 6762–7
L2.86:(nos.) 6785–5
L2.86:91-6 .... 6785–5.2
L2.86:91-11 .... 6785–5.1
L2.111/5:(date) 6742–12
L2.115:(date) 6742–3
L2.117:(date) 6782–5
L2.118/2:(yr.-nos.) 6742–21
L2.119:(date) 6822–1
— 6822–2
L2.119/2:990 6824–4
L2.120:92-255 .... 6726–1.49
L2.120:92-295 6744–13
L2.120:92-386 .... 6726–1.47
L2.120:92-395 .... 6726–1.46
L2.120:92-491 .... 6726–1.50
L2.120:92-530 .... 6726–1.48
L2.120:92-588 6744–14
L2.120:92-632 .... 6726–1.52
L2.120:92-644 .... 6726–1.51
L2.120:92-752 .... 6726–1.55
L2.120/2:991 .... 6726–1.45
L2.120/2-3:991 .... 6784–17.1
L2.120/2-4:991 .... 6784–17.2
L2.120/2-5:991 .... 6726–1.53
L2.120/2-7:992 6764–3
L2.120/2-7:993 6764–3
L2.120/2-8:993 .... 6726–1.54
L2.120/2-11:991 6844–3
L2.120/2-12:991 .... 6726–1.44
L2.120/2-13:991 6744–21
L2.120/2-13:992 6744–21
L2.121/1:H92/992 .... 6785–17.1
L2.121/5:An1/991 .... 6785–16.3
L2.121/5:L89/991 .... 6785–16.6
L2.121/5:Sa5d/991 .... 6785–16.3
L2.121/5:Sa5f/992 .... 6785–17.3
L2.121/5:V82/991 .... 6785–12.1
L2.121/6:D43/991 .... 6785–16.4
L2.121/7:D19/992 .... 6785–17.1
L2.121/7:N42b/992 .... 6785–17.2
L2.121/8:W68/991 .... 6785–16.3
L2.121/9:M58/991 .... 6785–16.3
L2.121/9:T15/991 .... 6785–16.3
L2.121/13:C35/991 .... 6785–12.2
L2.121/13:D35/991 .... 6785–12.2
L2.121/14:El5/991 .... 6785–16.5
L2.121/14:G19/992 .... 6785–17.1
L2.121/14:In2/991 .... 6785–12.1
L2.121/15:D27/992 .... 6785–17.1
L2.121/17:Ev1/992 .... 6785–17.2
L2.121/17:L93/991 .... 6785–16.3
L2.121/20:B21/991 .... 6785–12.2
L2.121/21:B65/991 .... 6785–16.1
L2.121/21:B65/992 .... 6785–17.3
L2.121/21:L43/991 .... 6785–16.3
L2.121/21:W89/991 .... 6785–16.2
L2.121/22:D48/991 .... 6785–16.4
L2.121/23:Sa2c/992 .... 6785–17.2
L2.121/24:J13/992 .... 6785–17.1
L2.121/25:Sa21/992 .... 6785–17.2
L2.121/26:B49/991 .... 6785–16.3
L2.121/30:B45/992 .... 6785–17.3
L2.121/30:M58/991 .... 6785–12.3
L2.121/30:N42/992 .... 6785–17.1
L2.121/30:T72/991 .... 6785–12.3
L2.121/32:N18/991 .... 6785–16.4
L2.121/32:P86/991 .... 6785–16.4
L2.121/32:R58/991 .... 6785–16.4
L2.121/35:C49/992 .... 6785–17.3
L2.121/35:C72/991 .... 6785–16.3
L2.121/37:P83/991 .... 6785–12.1
L2.121/38:P53/991 .... 6785–16.5
L2.121/38:P68/992 .... 6785–17.1
L2.121/38:Y8/991 .... 6785–12.2
L2.121/42:M51/991 .... 6785–12.4
L2.121/42:N17/992 .... 6785–17.3
L2.121/43:D16/991 .... 6785–16.4
L2.121/43:H81/992 .... 6785–17.3
L2.121/43:Sa5a/2/991 .... 6785–12.1
L2.121/44:Sa3/991 .... 6785–12.2
L2.121/44:Sa3/992 .... 6785–17.3
L2.121/51:D63/992 .... 6785–17.2
L2.122/1:D74/991 .... 6785–3.4
L2.122/1:M71/992 .... 6785–3.6
L2.122/3:T79/992 .... 6785–3.3
L2.122/4:P65/991 .... 6785–3.4
L2.122/5:Sa3/992 .... 6785–3.3
L2.122/5:V24/992 .... 6785–3.3
L2.122/7:C76/991 .... 6785–3.4
L2.122/9:F77/991 .... 6785–3.1
L2.122/9:N81/992 .... 6785–3.5
L2.122/9:Or5/992 .... 6785–3.6
L2.122/10:C72/992 .... 6785–3.6
L2.122/10:Sa9/992 .... 6785–3.5
L2.122/14:B62/991 .... 6785–3.4
L2.122/16:T62/992 .... 6785–3.5
L2.122/16:W63/992 .... 6785–3.5
L2.122/18:B32/992 .... 6785–3.6
L2.122/21:W52/991 .... 6785–3.4
L2.122/24:C72/992 .... 6785–3.6
L2.122/28:R29/991 .... 6785–3.4
L2.122/30:At6/992 .... 6785–3.6
L2.122/31:Al1/991 .... 6785–3.4
L2.122/32:Al1/991 .... 6785–3.1
L2.122/32:P86/991 .... 6785–3.4
L2.122/33:G85/992 .... 6785–3.5
L2.122/35:M31/2/991 .... 6785–3.4
L2.122/38:H24/991 .... 6785–3.4
L2.122/39:P94/992 .... 6785–3.5
L2.122/40:C72/992 .... 6785–3.6
L2.122/42:C56/992 .... 6785–3.5
L2.122/42:K77/991 .... 6785–3.4
L2.122/50:C42/992 .... 6785–3.5
L2.122/53:P96/991 .... 6785–3.2
L2.126:(date) 6742–20
L2.130:991-2 6822–3
L2.130:992 6822–3
L29.15:(nos.) 6366–3
L29.15:38 .... 6366–3.28
L29.15:39 .... 6366–3.29
L29.15:40 .... 6366–3.30
L29.15:41 6364–2
L29.16:(CT) 6366–4
L29.16:Au7/2/990-91 .... 6366–4.18
L29.16:Au7/990-91 .... 6366–4.3
L29.16:B22/990-91 .... 6366–4.1
L29.16:B22/991-92 .... 6366–4.47
L29.16:B41/990-91 .... 6366–4.19
L29.16:B41/991-92 .... 6366–4.30
L29.16:B73/990-91 .... 6366–4.16
L29.16:C16/991 .... 6366–4.32
L29.16:C44/990-92 .... 6366–4.50

L29.16:C82/991 .... 6366–4.33
L29.16:C99/991-92 .... 6366–4.41
L29.16:D41/991 .... 6366–4.24
L29.16:D41/991-92 .... 6366–4.48
L29.16:Egy9/991 .... 6366–4.26
L29.16:F49/990-91 .... 6366–4.14
L29.16:F84/991-92 .... 6366–4.49
L29.16:G31/990-91 .... 6366–4.5
L29.16:G81/991-92 .... 6366–4.35
L29.16:G99/991 .... 6366–4.39
L29.16:H75/2/991-92 .... 6366–4.40
L29.16:H75/990-91 .... 6366–4.12
L29.16:H89 .... 6366–4.28
L29.16:Ic2/991-92 .... 6366–4.53
L29.16:In2/2/990-91 .... 6366–4.25
L29.16:Ir2/991-92 .... 6366–4.31
L29.16:Is7/990-91 .... 6366–4.6
L29.16:Is7/991-92 .... 6366–4.42
L29.16:It1/990-91 .... 6366–4.23
L29.16:J22/990 .... 6366–4.4
L29.16:J27/991 .... 6366–4.29
L29.16:J76/991 .... 6366–4.38
L29.16:K96/991-92 .... 6366–4.37
L29.16:M57/991-92 .... 6366–4.51
L29.16:M82/990-91 .... 6366–4.20
L29.16:N38/990-91 .... 6366–4.9
L29.16:N38/991-92 .... 6366–4.45
L29.16:N83/989-91 .... 6366–4.15
L29.16:P19/990-91 .... 6366–4.7
L29.16:P19/991 .... 6366–4.27
L29.16:P53/990-91 .... 6366–4.22
L29.16:P83/990-91 .... 6366–4.21
L29.16:So8a/991 .... 6366–4.34
L29.16:Sp1/990-91 .... 6366–4.10
L29.16:Sr3/991-92 .... 6366–4.43
L29.16:Sw3/991-92 .... 6366–4.36
L29.16:Sw6/990-91 .... 6366–4.2
L29.16:T13/990-91 .... 6366–4.8
L29.16:T13/991-92 .... 6366–4.52
L29.16:T83/990-91 .... 6366–4.13
L29.16:Un3/2/990-91 .... 6366–4.17
L29.16:Un3/2/991-92 .... 6366–4.46
L29.16:Ur8/991-92 .... 6366–4.44
L29.16:W89/2 .... 6366–4.11
L36.2:W89/4/992 6504–11
L36.13:991 6504–3
L36.16:991 6504–9
L36.18:991 6504–10
L36.114/3:(nos.) 6564–1
L36.114/3:92-1 .... 6564–1.1
L36.114/3:92-2 .... 6564–1.2
L37.12/2-2:(date) 6402–14
L37.13:(date) 6402–1
L37.20:(nos.) 6406–6
L37.20:92-3 .... 6406–6.36
L37.23:992 6404–17
L37.210:991-2 6402–7
L37.210:992 6402–7
L37.210:992-2 6402–7
L37.212:991/rev.2 6402–2
L37.213:991 6404–16
L38.2:Su1/2 6668–8
L38.10:1201 6664–3
L38.10:1202 6664–1
L38.10:1203 6664–5
L38.10:1205 6664–4
L38.10/2:990 6664–2
L38.16:(date) 6662–1
L38.19/2:991-2 .... 6662–3.3
L38.19/3:991-2 .... 6662–3.4
L38.20/2:991-2 .... 6662–3.2
L38.20/3:991-2 .... 6662–3.1
LC1.1:991 26404–1
LC3.1:991 26404–2
LC19.16:992 26404–3
LC30.27/2:992-93 26404–6
LR1.1:990 9584–1
LR1.16:(nos.) 9582–2
MS1.1:991 9494–5
MS1.2:C49/2 9498–16
MS1.2:M89/4 9498–17
MS1.2:Su7/2 9498–15
MS1.15:991 9494–2
MS1.16:992 .... 9496–2.8
NAS1.15:991 9504–7
NAS1.21:4104 9508–39
NAS1.30:992 9502–6
NAS1.30:992-2 9502–6
NAS1.40:(v.nos.&nos.) 9502–2
NAS1.52:991 9504–9
NAS1.57:990 9504–4
NAS1.57:991 9504–4
NCU1.1:991 9534–1
NCU1.9/2:991 9532–6
NCU1.9/3:992 9532–6
NCU1.16:992 9534–6
NCU1.17:991 9534–5
NCU1.18:991 9534–7
NCU1.19:138 9532–7
NCU1.21:(nos.) 9536–1
NCU1.21:15 .... 9536–1.7
NCU1.21:17 .... 9536–1.8
NF2.1:991 9564–3
NF3.1:991 9564–2
NMB1.1:987-88 9604–1
NS1.1:991 9624–6
NS1.13/5:991-2 9624–16
NS1.13/5:992 9624–16
NS1.18/4:991-93 9627–9
NS1.22:Ex7 .... 9626–6.38
NS1.22:Sci2/12/989 9627–23
NS1.22/3:990 9627–13
NS1.22/4:990 9627–7
NS1.28/2:991 9624–10
NS1.30/2:990 9627–17
NS1.30/2-2:989 .... 9626–8.2
NS1.30/2-2:990 .... 9626–8.6
NS1.39/2:(yr.) 9624–21
NS1.49:992 9624–20
NS1.53:992 9624–25
NS1.55:Ac1/990 .... 9626–8.5
NS1.55:G75/990 .... 9626–8.3
P1.1:991 9864–1
P4.6:991 9864–2
PM1.2:Se5/4/991 9844–36
PM1.10/2:P29/991 9844–6
PM1.10/2-3:990 9844–27
PM1.10/4:990 9844–31
PM1.15:(nos.) 9842–1
PM1.26:991 9844–20
PM1.42:991 9844–33
PM1.47:991 9844–14
Pr41.8/3:991 104–29
Pr41.9:992 204–1
Pr41.10:991 9454-18
PrEx1.2:(CT) 236–1
PrEx1.2:C64 .... 236–1.7
PrEx1.2:D84/992 234–1
PrEx1.2:D84/992/budget 234–2
PrEx1.3/2:(nos.) 236–3
PrEx1.3/2:1 .... 236–3.1
PrEx1.3/2:2 .... 236–3.2
PrEx1.3/2:3 .... 236–3.3
PrEx1.3/2:4 .... 236–3.4
PrEx1.3/2:5 .... 236–3.5
PrEx1.3/2:6 .... 236–3.6
PrEx1.3/2:7 .... 236–3.7
PrEx1.3/2:8 .... 236–3.8
PrEx2.2:Se6/4 104–27
PrEx2.8:993 104–2
PrEx2.8:993/supp 108–46
PrEx2.20:992 104–5
PrEx2.25:9 104–26
PrEx2.31:993 104–7
PrEx3.10/7-2:(yr.) 9114–1
PrEx3.11/2:(nos.) 9112–4
PrEx3.14:(nos.) 9112–2
PrEx3.14/2:(nos.) 9112–1
PrEx3.15:992 9114–2
PrEx8.109:992-96 2148–56
PrEx9.10:992 444–2
PrEx9.11:991-92 444–1
PrEx14.1:992 484–1
RR1.1:991 9704–1
RR1.13:(nos.) 9702–2
S1.1/4:990 7184–1
S1.1/7:992 7004–15
S1.1/7:993 7004–15
S1.1/8:992 7004–18
S1.2:In2/991 7004–22
S1.2:N16/3/992 .... 7004–17.1
S1.70/7:991 7004–6
S1.70/8:991 7004–5
S1.71/5:Af8/8 7008–58
S1.76/4:(date) 7002–7
S1.119/4:(nos.) 7142–3
S1.119/5:(nos.) 7006–8
S1.119/5:112 .... 7006–8.7
S1.119/5:113 .... 7006–8.8
S1.123:(CT) 7006–2
S1.123:As7/992 .... 7006–2.18
S1.123:B14/991 .... 7006–2.7
S1.123:C14/2/992 .... 7006–2.22
S1.123:C34/992 .... 7006–2.20
S1.123:C43/992 .... 7006–2.16
S1.123:C73/992 .... 7006–2.12
S1.123:C82/992 .... 7006–2.21
S1.123:C99/2/992 .... 7006–2.13
S1.123:D71/991 .... 7006–2.8
S1.123:G11/991 .... 7006–2.1
S1.123:G93/992 .... 7006–2.14
S1.123:H75/2/992 .... 7006–2.15
S1.123:Ir2/991 .... 7006–2.3
S1.123:M29/991 .... 7006–2.6
S1.123:M44/2/992 .... 7006–2.25
S1.123:N83/992 .... 7006–2.26
S1.123:P17/992 .... 7006–2.23
S1.123:P19/992 .... 7006–2.11
S1.123:Q1/992 .... 7006–2.19
S1.123:Sw6/991 .... 7006–2.5
S1.123:T15/992 .... 7006–2.17
S1.123:T32/991 .... 7006–2.4
S1.123:Un34n/991 .... 7006–2.2
S1.123:Z1/992 .... 7006–2.27
S1.123/2:991/4 .... 7006–2.9
S1.123/2:992/1 .... 7006–2.10
S1.123/2:992/2 .... 7006–2.24
S1.123/2:992/3 .... 7006–2.28
S1.138:991 7004–13
S9.14:992 7004–1
S18.2:C19/2 9914–14
S18.2:C19/2/992 9914–14
S18.2:Ov2/945-91 9914–5
S18.19:991 9914–9
S18.52:(nos.) 9916–1
S18.52:78 .... 9916–1.76
S18.52:79 .... 9916–1.77
SBA1.1:990 .... 9764–1.1
SBA1.1:991 .... 9764–1.1
SBA1.1/2:991 9764–6

SBA1.1/3:991-2 9762–5
SBA1.1/3:992 9762–5
SBA1.1/4:991 9764–7
SBA1.2:Ac2 9764–9
SBA1.2:Ac2/update 9764–9
SBA1.2:B86/3 9768–23
SBA1.2:B96/10/[app.] 9768–25
SBA1.2:D49/4 9764–10
SBA1.2:F49/5 9768–24
SBA1.2:M66/5 9764–8
SBA1.13/4:Op2/991-2 9762–4
SBA1.13/4:Op2/992 9762–4
SBA1.27/2:(date) 9762–6
SBA1.36/2:G93/991 .... 9764–1.2
SE1.1:991 9734–2
SE1.9:(v.nos.&nos.) 9732–2
SE1.27:991 9734–5
SE1.35/2:992 9734–4
SI1.1:990 .... 29574–1.1
SI1.1:990/supp 29574–1.2
SI1.1:991 .... 29574–1.1
SI1.1:991/supp 29574–1.2
SI4.1:990 29574–2
T1.2:Se2/7 8008–154
T1.45/2:(date) 8002–6
T1.45/3:(date) 8002–12
T12.18:(v.nos.&nos.) 8402–3
T17.28:(date) 8142–2
T22.1:991 8304–3
T22.2:P94/14/991-98 8304–9
T22.2/15:6149/991 8304–24
T22.2/15:6292/922 8302–4
T22.2/15:6292/991-2 8302–4
T22.2/15:6961/992 8304–22
T22.2/15:7302/992 8304–25
T22.35/2:In8/984-88 8308–31
T22.35/4:(v.nos.&nos.) 8302–2
T22.35/5:988 8304–4
T22.35/5:989 8304–4
T22.35/5-2:989 8304–21
T22.35/8:988 8304–2
T28.1:991 8204–1
T28.12:(date) 8202–1
T34.9:987-91 8464–1
T63.101/2:991 .... 8104–2.1
T63.101/2-2:991 .... 8104–2.2
T63.103/2:(date) 8002–4
T63.113/2:(date) 8102–3
T63.113/2-2:(date) 8102–4
T63.118/2:991-2 8102–7
T63.118/2:992 8102–7
T63.118/3:991-2 8102–5
T63.118/3:992 8102–5
T63.121:(date) 8102–6
T63.209/8-3:(date) 8242–1
T63.215:(date) 8242–2
T70.9/2:(date) 8486–1.4
T70.9/3:(date) 8486–1.3
T70.9/4:(date) 8486–1.1
T70.9/5:(date) 8486–1.2
T70.11:990 8484–4
T70.11:991 8484–4
T71.7/2:(nos.) 9442–2
T71.17:(yr.) 8434–3
T71.19:989 8434–1
T71.20:(v.nos.&nos.) 9722–3
T71.21:(date) 8432–1
TD1.1:989 7304–1
TD1.1/3:991-2 7302–4
TD1.1/3:992 7302–4
TD1.2:B85/993 7304–10
TD1.20/10:92-03 7308–205
TD1.39:989 7304–7
TD1.40:(date) 7302–2
TD1.40/3:989(summary) 7302–2
TD1.46:991 7304–18
TD1.54:(date) 7302–11
TD1.101:990 9614–1
TD1.109/13:(yr.-nos.) 9612–1
TD1.112/5:89/01 9614–8
TD1.112/5:89/02 9614–8
TD1.112/5:92/01 9614–8
TD1.113/5:988 9614–2
TD1.127:91/01 9618–18
TD1.127:91/02 9618–19
TD2.2:D83/2/990 7554–16
TD2.2:Sci6 7558–112
TD2.19:(v.nos.&nos.) 7552–3
TD2.23:990/charts 7554–24
TD2.23:991 7554–1
TD2.30/4:91-003 7558–115
TD2.30/13:92-003 7554–2
TD2.46/2:(date) 7552–1
TD2.47:991-2 7552–12
TD2.47:992 7552–12
TD2.49:(date) 7552–7
TD2.50:(date) 7552–8
TD2.58:992 7554–26
TD2.60:991 7554–21
TD2.61:992 7554–18
TD2.310:989 7554–9
TD3.14:989 7604–6
TD3.103:160 7604–1
TD3.109:990 7604–2
TD3.109:991 7604–2
TD3.111:988 7604–3
TD4.2:St2/2/991 7504–2
TD4.2/10:991 7504–12
TD4.14:991 7504–35
TD4.18:990 7504–3
TD4.18:991 7504–3
TD4.19:991 7504–27
TD4.20:990 7504–1
TD4.41:991 7504–10
TD4.56:(yr.) 7504–36
TD4.57:92-2 7504–28
TD4.57:92-5 7504–7
TD4.57/2:(nos.) 7506–7
TD4.57/2:91-9 .... 7506–7.42
TD4.57/2:91-11 .... 7506–7.43
TD4.57/2:92-8 .... 7506–7.44
TD4.57/2:992-2003 7504–6
TD4.57/3:990 7504–37
TD4.59:(date) 7502–13
TD4.61:991 7504–38
TD4.65:990 7504–41
TD4.210:(yr.-nos.) 7506–10
TD4.210:91-18 .... 7506–10.96
TD4.210:92-1 .... 7506–10.97
TD4.210:92-2 .... 7506–10.98
TD4.210:92-3 .... 7506–10.99
TD4.210:92-4 .... 7506–10.100
TD4.210:92-5 .... 7506–10.101
TD4.210:92-6 .... 7506–10.102
TD4.210:92-7 .... 7506–10.103
TD4.210:92-8 .... 7506–10.104
TD4.210:92-9 .... 7506–10.105
TD4.210:92-10 .... 7506–10.106
TD4.210:92-11 .... 7506–10.107
TD4.210:92-12 .... 7506–10.108
TD4.210:92-13 .... 7506–10.113
TD4.210:92-14 .... 7506–10.114
TD4.210:92-15 .... 7506–10.115
TD4.210:92-16 .... 7506–10.116
TD4.210:92-17 .... 7506–10.117
TD4.210:92-18 .... 7506–10.118
TD4.210:92-19 .... 7506–10.119
TD4.210:92-20 .... 7506–10.120
TD4.210:92-21 .... 7506–10.121
TD4.210:92-22 .... 7506–10.109
TD4.210:92-23 .... 7506–10.110
TD4.210:92-24 .... 7506–10.111
TD4.210:92-25 .... 7506–10.112
TD4.210:92-26 .... 7506–10.122
TD4.210:92-27 .... 7506–10.124
TD4.210:92-28 .... 7506–10.123
TD4.210:92-29 .... 7506–10.125
TD4.210:92-30 .... 7506–10.126
TD4.210:92-31 .... 7506–10.127
TD4.810:990 7504–49
TD5.2:(nos.) 7406–5
TD5.2:B76/great lakes/991 .... 7406–5.3
TD5.11:991 7404–1
TD5.50:991 7404–2
TD6.1:990 7744–1
TD7.2:Un3/991 7884–7
TD7.2:Un3/992 7884–7
TD7.9:991 7884–1
TD7.17:(nos.) 7884–5
TD7.18:992 7884–8
TD8.2:C85/25 7768–105
TD8.8:T51/3/992 7764–17
TD8.9/2:(date) 7762–2
TD8.12:990 .... 7764–1.2
TD8.12/2:990 .... 7764–1.1
TD8.26:990 7764–9
TD8.26:991 7764–9
TD8.27:990 7764–10
TD9.15:990 7304–4
TD10.9/2:(date) 7302–8
TD10.9/3:(date) 7302–6
TD10.9/4:(date) 7302–7
TD11.1:991 7704–14
TD11.2:P83/3 7708–6
TD11.10:(date) 7702–1
TD11.11:991-2 7702–2
TD11.14:991 7704–3
TD11.14:992 7704–3
TD11.16:991-2 7702–3
TD11.19:987-89 7704–7
TD11.25:991 7704–9
TD11.31:991 7704–10
VA1.1:991 8604–3
VA1.2:L62/12/991 8604–1
VA1.2:P94/8/pts.1-4 8608–9
VA1.2/11:991 8604–6
VA1.20/2:H41/v.(nos.) 8706–1
VA1.20/2:H41/v.17,18 .... 8706–1.4
VA1.20/2:H41/v.19,20 .... 8706–1.5
VA1.20/2:H41/v.19,20/syn. no. 9 .... 8706–1.5
VA1.22:11-78a/992 8704–3
VA1.22/3:992 8704–3
VA1.43/5:(date) 8602–4
VA1.46:991 8604–4
VA1.55:27 8602–1
VA1.55:28 8602–1
VA1.71:967-91 8604–5
VA1.75:(date) 8602–6
VA1.82:(date) 8602–9
VA1.88:990 8604–7
VA1.92:988 8704–8
Y1.1/3:S.pub.101-15 25944–1
Y1.1/3:102-10/pt.1 .... 25922–1.1
Y1.1/3:102-10/pt.2 .... 25922–1.2
Y1.1/3:102-12 25922–2
Y1.1/3:102-19/pt.1 .... 25922–1.1
Y1.1/3:102-19/pt.2 .... 25922–1.2
Y1.1/5:102-266 23844–2
Y1.1/7:(nos.) 21942–1
Y1.1/8:102-450 21264–2
Y3.Ad9/8:1/991 10044–3

Y3.Ad9/8:2B66 10048–85
Y3.Ad9/8:2M46/3.................. 10048–83
Y3.Ad9/8:2M56/7.................. 10046–9.2
Y3.Ad9/8:2W29/2.................. 10048–82
Y3.Ad9/8:11/(v.nos.&nos.).... 10042–1
Y3.Ad9/8:17/992.................. 10044–2
Y3.Ad9/8:18/992/v.(nos.) 10044–1
Y3.Ad9/8:18/992/v.1 .... 10044–1.1
Y3.Ad9/8:18/992/v.2 .... 10044–1.2
Y3.Ad9/8:20/991.................. 10044–8
Y3.Ad9/11:1/(yr.) 10104–1
Y3.Af8:2/P94 9034–1
Y3.Ap4/2:1/991................... 9084–1
Y3.B27:1/991 17614–1
Y3.B78:1/992 10314–1
Y3.C73/5:1/991.................... 11924–2
Y3.C73/5:9-3/(date) 11922–5
Y3.C73/5:10/(date) 11922–4.3
Y3.C76/3:1/990.................... 9164–2
Y3.C76/3:7-3/990 9164–7
Y3.Ed8/10:1/992.................. 15914–1
Y3.El2/3:1/991 9274–1
Y3.El2/3:15-2/989-90 9274–3
Y3.El2/3:15-2/991-92 9274–3
Y3.El2/3:15/989-90/final rpt 9276–2.2
Y3.El2/3:15/989-90/v.1-4 .... 9276–2.1
Y3.Em7/3:1/16 15494–1
Y3.Em7/3:9/30 15498–28
Y3.Em7/3:9/31 15498–29
Y3.Em7/3:10/(nos.)............... 15496–1
Y3.Em7/3:10/91-02............... 15496–1.14
Y3.Em7/3:10/91-03............... 15496–1.15
Y3.Em7/3:10/91-04............... 15496–1.16
Y3.Eq2:2C83/990 9244–11
Y3.Eq2:2In2/991 9248–20
Y3.Eq2:12-4/991 9244–6
Y3.Eq2:12-5/990 9244–10
Y3.Eq2:12-7/991 9244–1
Y3.F31/8:1/990 9294–1
Y3.F31/8:1/991 9294–1
Y3.F31/8:22/991/v.(nos.)...... 9295–3
Y3.F31/8:22/991/v.1............. 9295–3.1
Y3.F31/8:22/991/v.2............. 9295–3.2
Y3.F31/8:22/991/v.3............. 9295–3.3
Y3.F31/8:22/991/v.4............. 9295–3.4
Y3.F31/8:22/991/v.5............. 9295–3.5
Y3.F31/8:22/991/v.6............. 9295–3.6
Y3.F31/8:22/991/v.7............. 9295–3.7
Y3.F31/15:2Ag4/2/991 12904–1
Y3.F31/21-3:1/990 13364–1
Y3.F31/21-3:1/991 13364–1
Y3.F49:1/991 13004–2
Y3.F76/4:1/991 10324–1
Y3.H75:1/990........................ 14364–1
Y3.In2/10:1/990 14874–1
Y3.In2/10:1/991 14874–1
Y3.In8/25:1/991 14424–1
Y3.In8/28:1/(yr.) 14644–3
Y3.In8/28:12/991/rev 14644–6
Y3.In8/31:2In8..................... 14358–4
Y3.In8/31:2M69.................... 14358–3
Y3.L61:1/990-91 15634–1
Y3.M33/3:1/991 14734–1
Y3.M58:1/991 14784–1
Y3.M58:1/992 14784–1
Y3.N21/16:1/990................... 15344–1
Y3.N88:1/991........................ 9634–2
Y3.N88:10-2/993-94/v.8........ 9634–9
Y3.N88:10-5/988 9634–3
Y3.N88:10-5/989 9634–3
Y3.N88:25/2850/v.10 9634–7
Y3.P19/2:1/991 9664–3
Y3.P29:1/992 17204–1
Y3.P29:3/992 17204–2
Y3.P31:1/991 29594–1
Y3.P38/2:1/991 9674–1
Y3.P97:1/991 11714–1
Y3.R31/2:15/(yr.)/v.(nos.) 9722–2
Y3.R31/2:15/991-2/v.1.......... 9722–2.1
Y3.R31/2:15/991-2/v.2/pt.1 9722–2.2
Y3.R31/2:15/991-2/v.2/pt.2 9722–2.3
Y3.R31/2:15/991-2/v.2/pt.3 9722–2.4
Y3.R31/2:15/991-2/v.2/pt.4 9722–2.5
Y3.R31/2:15/991-2/v.2/pt.5 9722–2.6
Y3.R31/2:15/991-2/v.3......... 9722–2.7
Y3.R31/2:15/992/v.1 .... 9722–2.8
Y3.R31/2:15/992/v.2/pt.1 .... 9722–2.9
Y3.R31/2:15/992/v.2/pt.2 .... 9722–2.10
Y3.R31/2:15/992/v.2/pt.3 .... 9722–2.11
Y3.R31/2:15/992/v.2/pt.4 .... 9722–2.12
Y3.R31/2:15/992/v.2/pt.5 .... 9722–2.13
Y3.R31/2:15/992/v.3 .... 9722–2.14
Y3.Se4:1/991 9744–1
Y3.Se5:1/991 17664–1
Y3.Se5:2P37 17668–2
Y3.Se5:8G94/app.C/992........ 17668–1.9
Y3.Se5:8G94/992.................. 17668–1.9
Y3.Se5/3:(CT) 15036–1
Y3.Se5/3:1/(yr.).................. 15034–1
Y3.Se5/3:1/990/v.1 .... 15034–1.2
Y3.Se5/3:1/990/v.2 .... 15034–1.3
Y3.Se5/3:1/991 .... 15034–1.4
Y3.Se5/3:2In8...................... 15036–1.2
Y3.Se5/3:2P92 .... 15036–1.1
Y3.T22/2:1/991 26354–3
Y3.T22/2:2Ad7/2/v.(nos.) 26358–234
Y3.T22/2:2Ad7/2/v.2 .... 26358–234.2
Y3.T22/2:2Ad7/2/v.3 .... 26358–234.3
Y3.T22/2:2Au8/7 26358–251
Y3.T22/2:2B57/10................. 26356–9.4
Y3.T22/2:2C23..................... 26358–263
Y3.T22/2:2D84/6 26358–258
Y3.T22/2:2D84/6/summ 26358–258
Y3.T22/2:2Ec7 26358–252
Y3.T22/2:2Ec7/summ........... 26358–252
Y3.T22/2:2En2/15 26358–259
Y3.T22/2:2F31/4.................. 26358–253
Y3.T22/2:2F95/4.................. 26358–260
Y3.T22/2:2F95/4/summ........ 26358–260
Y3.T22/2:2G51/3 26358–257
Y3.T22/2:2H88/3 .... 26356–6.6
Y3.T22/2:2In2/5 26358–256
Y3.T22/2:2M46/16 26358–254
Y3.T22/2:2M46/16/summ 26358–254
Y3.T22/2:2M52 26358–261
Y3.T22/2:2T28..................... 26358–255
Y3.T22/2:2T28/summ........... 26358–255
Y3.T22/2:2T75/3/summ........ 26358–262
Y3.T25:Ec7/2/989................. 9804–27
Y3.T25:Ec7/2/990................. 9804–27
Y3.T25:Ec7/2/991................. 9804–27
Y3.T25:Ec7/2/992/[supp.] 9804–27
Y3.T25:1/991 9804–1
Y3.T25:2F41/23/991............ 9804–30
Y3.T25:2F41/23/992............ 9804–30
Y3.T25:4-2/Z-289 .... 9806–9.11
Y3.T25:4-2/Z-309 .... 9806–9.12
Y3.T25:13/(nos.) 9802–1
Y3.T25:13-2/991 9804–14
Y3.W58/20:2In3/summ.......... 15638–16
Y4.Ag4:S.hrg.101-1290 25148–45
Y4.Ag4:S.prt.102-50............. 25148–44
Y4.Ag4/2:Af8...................... 21148–67
Y4.Ag4/2:B61/4................... 21148–64
Y4.Ag4/2:P96/2................... 21148–66
Y4.Ag4/2:So1/44................. 21148–63
Y4.Ag4/2:W89/7 21148–65
Y4.Ag8/3:S.hrg.101-259/pt. 12 25168–78
Y4.B22/1:101-138 21248–162
Y4.B22/1:101-164 21248–161
Y4.B22/1:101-183 21248–163
Y4.B22/1:102-3 21248–160
Y4.B22/1:102-17 21248–165
Y4.B22/1:102-19 21248–167
Y4.B22/1:102-23/pt.1 21248–168
Y4.B22/1:102-24 21248–164
Y4.B22/1:102-26 21248–166
Y4.B22/1:102-33 21248–170
Y4.B22/1:102-48 21248–169
Y4.B22/1:102-52 21248–172
Y4.B22/1:102-57 21248–174
Y4.B22/1:102-66 21248–173
Y4.B22/1:102-70 21248–171
Y4.B22/1:102-72 21248–176
Y4.B22/1:102-74 21248–175
Y4.B22/3:S.hrg.101-1049 25248–128
Y4.B22/3:S.hrg.102-55 25248–127
Y4.B22/3:S.hrg.102-429/v.2 .. 25248–129
Y4.B22/3:S.hrg.102-461 25248–130
Y4.B85/3:P92/3/993............. 21268–42
Y4.B85/3:102-3-2.................. 21268–43
Y4.B85/3:102-16 21268–44
Y4.C73/7:S.hrg.102-127 25268–79
Y4.D63/1:102-4 21308–28
Y4.Ec7:D39/3 23848–226
Y4.Ec7:Ec7/(date) 23842–1
Y4.Ec7:Ec7/67/991............... 23848–230
Y4.Ec7:Em7/12/pt.(nos.) 23846–4
Y4.Ec7:Em7/12/pt.40........... 23846–4.34
Y4.Ec7:Em7/12/pt.41........... 23846–4.35
Y4.Ec7:Em7/12/pt.42........... 23846–4.36
Y4.Ec7:F31/13..................... 23848–227
Y4.Ec7:P92/7....................... 23844–4
Y4.Ec7:W19/3 23848–224
Y4.Ed8/1:102-2 21348–120
Y4.Ed8/1:102-19 21348–121
Y4.Ed8/1:102-57 21348–122
Y4.Ed8/1:102-84 21348–123
Y4.En2:S.hrg.101-928 25318–84
Y4.En2:S.hrg.102-5/pt.14 25318–83
Y4.En2:S.hrg.102-57 25318–82
Y4.En2:S.hrg.102-453 25318–85
Y4.En2/3:102-7 21368–134
Y4.En2/3:102-18 21368–135
Y4.En2/3:102-29 21368–136
Y4.En2/3:102-37 21368–137
Y4.En2/3:102-42 21368–139
Y4.En2/3:102-56 21368–140
Y4.En2/3:102-59 21368–138
Y4.En2/3:102-71 21368–142
Y4.En2/3:102-88 21368–141
Y4.F49:S.hrg.101-1236 25368–177
Y4.F49:S.hrg.101-1259 25368–179
Y4.F49:S.hrg.102-84/pt.1 25368–180
Y4.F49:S.hrg.102-234 25368–181
Y4.F49:S.hrg.102-313 25368–178
Y4.F76/1-15:991 21384–3
Y4.F76/1-16:990 9824–2
Y4.F76/1-16:991 9824–2
Y4.F76/2:S.hrg.102-288 25388–59
Y4.F76/2:S.hrg.102-350/pt.1 25388–60
Y4.F76/2:S.prt.102-80........... 21384–5
Y4.G74/7:C82/8 21408–127
Y4.G74/7:D44/2 21408–126
Y4.G74/7:Ed8/9 21408–130
Y4.G74/7:En8/21 21408–132
Y4.G74/7:Il6 21408–128
Y4.G74/7:In2/5 21408–131
Y4.G74/7:M46/10.................. 21408–129
Y4.G74/9:S.hrg.101-1294 25408–116
Y4.G74/9:S.hrg.102-150 25408–115
Y4.G74/9:S.hrg.102-261 25408–118

Y4.G74/9:S.hrg.102-498	25408–119
Y4.G74/9:S.prt.102-83	25408–120
Y4.H81/3:P92/5/corr	21428–10
Y4.H81/3:V94/13	21428–11
Y4.H89:102-5	21968–57
Y4.H89:102-7	21968–58
Y4.In8/14:101-34/pt.3	21448–45
Y4.In8/14:101-74	21448–47
Y4.In8/14:101-81/pt.2	21448–46
Y4.In8/19:S.hrg.101-1293	25428–2
Y4.J89/2:S.hrg.101-1288	25528–119
Y4.J89/2:S.hrg.102-135	25528–118
Y4.J89/2:S.hrg.102-206	25528–120
Y4.L11/4:S.hrg.102-58	25548–105
Y4.M53:102-17	21568–51
Y4.P84/10:102-2	21628–97
Y4.P84/10:102-4	21628–98
Y4.P84/10:102-5	21628–99
Y4.P84/10:102-17	21628–100
Y4.P84/10:102-19	21628–102
Y4.P84/10:102-21	21628–101
Y4.P84/10:102-25	21628–104
Y4.P84/10:102-32	21628–103
Y4.P96/11:101-71	21648–65
Y4.P96/11:101-87	21648–67
Y4.P96/11:102-3	21648–68
Y4.P96/11:102-10	21648–66
Y4.Sci2:102/K	21708–132
Y4.Sci2:102/26	21708–130
Y4.Sci2:102/38	21708–131
Y4.Sm1:102-3	21728–78
Y4.Sm1:102-15	21728–79
Y4.Sm1/2:S.prt.102-44	25728–44
Y4.V64/3:102-3	21768–67
Y4.V64/3:102-21	21768–68
Y4.W36:WMCP102-30	21788–212
Y4.W36:WMCP102-31	21788–213
Y4.W36:10-4/992	21784–11
Y4.W36:101-127	21788–206
Y4.W36:102-2	21788–207
Y4.W36:102-4	21788–208
Y4.W36:102-12	21788–209
Y4.W36:102-19	21788–210
Y4.W36:102-28	21788–215
Y4.W36:102-29	21788–214
Y4.W36:102-33	21788–216
Y4.W36:102-34	21788–218
Y4.W36:102-50	21788–217
Y10.2:(CT)	26306–6
Y10.2:Ar5/7	26306–6.173
Y10.2:B85/29	26306–6.166
Y10.2:C67	26306–6.172
Y10.2:Ec7/6	26306–6.165
Y10.2:Ec7/7	26306–6.174
Y10.2:F22/5/992	26306–6.171
Y10.2:H34/6	26306–6.163
Y10.2:H53/2	26306–6.170
Y10.2:H81/8	26306–6.164
Y10.2:P94/4	26306–6.175
Y10.2:R11	26306–6.169
Y10.2:T19/9	26306–6.168
Y10.13:992	26304–3.1
Y10.13:992/pt.2	26304–3.2
Y10.17:992	26304–3.3
Y10.19:993	26304–2

Guide to Selected Standard Classifications

Guide to Selected Standard Classifications

(This guide outlines the major standard classification systems used by various Federal agencies to arrange and present social and economic statistical data.)

Census Regions and Divisions	1019
Outlying Areas of the U.S.	1019
Standard Federal Administrative Regions	1019
Farm Production Regions	1019
Federal Reserve Districts	1020
Federal Home Loan Bank Districts	1020
Bureau of Labor Statistics Regions (and Regional Offices)	1020
Metropolitan Statistical Areas	1021
Consolidated Metropolitan Statistical Areas	1022
Cities with Population over 100,000	1023
Consumer Price Index Cities	1023
Standard Industrial Classification	1024
Standard Occupational Classification	1032
Standard International Trade Classification, Revision 3	1035

Census Regions and Divisions

CENSUS REGIONS SHOWING DIVISIONS INCLUDED IN EACH:

Northeast
New England, Middle Atlantic

Midwest
East North Central, West North Central

South
South Atlantic, East South Central, West South Central

West
Mountain, Pacific

CENSUS DIVISIONS SHOWING STATES INCLUDED IN EACH:

New England
Maine, New Hampshire, Vermont, Massachusetts, Rhode Island, Connecticut

Middle Atlantic
New York, New Jersey, Pennsylvania

East North Central
Ohio, Indiana, Illinois, Michigan, Wisconsin

West North Central
Minnesota, Iowa, Missouri, North Dakota, South Dakota, Nebraska, Kansas

South Atlantic
Delaware, Maryland, District of Columbia, Virginia, West Virginia, North Carolina, South Carolina, Georgia, Florida

East South Central
Kentucky, Tennessee, Alabama, Mississippi

West South Central
Arkansas, Louisiana, Oklahoma, Texas

Mountain
Montana, Idaho, Wyoming, Colorado, New Mexico, Arizona, Utah, Nevada

Pacific
Washington, Oregon, California, Alaska, Hawaii

Outlying Areas of the United States

American Samoa
Guam
Northern Mariana Islands
Puerto Rico
Republic of Palau
Virgin Islands

Standard Federal Administrative Regions

Region I
Connecticut, Maine, Massachusetts, New Hampshire, Rhode Island, and Vermont

Region II
New Jersey, New York, Puerto Rico, and the Virgin Islands

Region III
Delaware, District of Columbia, Maryland, Pennsylvania, Virginia, and West Virginia

Region IV
Alabama, Florida, Georgia, Kentucky, Mississippi, North Carolina, South Carolina, and Tennessee

Region V
Illinois, Indiana, Michigan, Minnesota, Ohio, and Wisconsin

Region VI
Arkansas, Louisiana, New Mexico, Oklahoma, and Texas

Region VII
Iowa, Kansas, Missouri, and Nebraska

Region VIII
Colorado, Montana, North Dakota, South Dakota, Utah, and Wyoming

Region IX
American Samoa, Arizona, California, Guam, Hawaii, and Nevada

Region X
Alaska, Idaho, Oregon, and Washington

Farm Production Regions

National agricultural data are frequently grouped into 10 farm production regions, covering the 48 contiguous States. Alaska, Hawaii, and Puerto Rico are each shown separately, if included.

Appalachian
Kentucky, North Carolina, Tennessee, Virginia, West Virginia

Corn Belt
Illinois, Indiana, Iowa, Missouri, Ohio

Delta States
Arkansas, Louisiana, Mississippi

Lake States
Michigan, Minnesota, Wisconsin

Mountain
Arizona, Colorado, Idaho, Montana, Nevada, New Mexico, Utah, Wyoming

Northeast
Connecticut, Delaware, Maine, Maryland, Massachusetts, New Hampshire, New Jersey, New York, Pennsylvania, Rhode Island, Vermont

Northern Plains
Kansas, Nebraska, North Dakota, South Dakota

Pacific
California, Oregon, Washington

Southeast
Alabama, Florida, Georgia, South Carolina

Southern Plains
Oklahoma, Texas

Federal Reserve Districts

District 1 (Boston)
Maine, Massachusetts, New Hampshire, Rhode Island, Vermont; most of Connecticut

District 2 (New York)
New York, Puerto Rico, Virgin Islands; portions of New Jersey; Fairfield Co., Connecticut

District 3 (Philadelphia)
Delaware; portions of New Jersey and Pennsylvania

District 4 (Cleveland)
Ohio; portions of Kentucky, Pennsylvania, West Virginia

District 5 (Richmond)
District of Columbia, Maryland, North & South Carolina, Virginia; portions of West Virginia

District 6 (Atlanta)
Alabama, Florida, Georgia; portions of Louisiana, Mississippi, Tennessee

District 7 (Chicago)
Iowa; portions of Michigan, Illinois, Indiana, Wisconsin

District 8 (St. Louis)
Arkansas; portions of Kentucky, Illinois, Indiana, Mississippi, Missouri, Tennessee

District 9 (Minneapolis)
Minnesota, Montana, North & South Dakota; portions of Michigan and Wisconsin

District 10 (Kansas City)
Colorado, Kansas, Nebraska, Oklahoma Wyoming; portions of Missouri, New Mexico

District 11 (Dallas)
Texas; portions of Louisiana, New Mexico

District 12 (San Francisco)
Alaska, Arizona, California, Guam, Hawaii, Idaho, Nevada, Oregon, Utah, Washington

Federal Home Loan Bank Districts

District 1 (Boston)
Connecticut, Maine, Massachusetts, New Hampshire, Rhode Island, and Vermont

District 2 (New York)
New Jersey, New York, Puerto Rico, and Virgin Islands

District 3 (Pittsburgh)
Delaware, Pennsylvania, and West Virginia

District 4 (Atlanta)
Alabama, District of Columbia, Florida, Georgia, Maryland, North Carolina, South Carolina, and Virginia

District 5 (Cincinnati)
Kentucky, Ohio, and Tennessee

District 6 (Indianapolis)
Indiana and Michigan

District 7 (Chicago)
Illinois and Wisconsin

District 8 (Des Moines)
Iowa, Minnesota, Missouri, North Dakota, and South Dakota

District 9 (Dallas)
Arkansas, Louisiana, Mississippi, New Mexico, and Texas

District 10 (Topeka)
Colorado, Kansas, Nebraska, and Oklahoma

District 11 (San Francisco)
Arizona, Nevada, and California

District 12 (Seattle)
Alaska, Hawaii, Guam, Idaho, Montana, Oregon, Utah, Washington, and Wyoming

Bureau of Labor Statistics Regions (And Regional Offices)

Region 1: New England (Boston)
Connecticut, Maine, Massachusetts, New Hampshire, Rhode Island, Vermont

Region 2: Middle Atlantic Region (New York)
New Jersey, New York, Puerto Rico, Virgin Islands

Region 3: Mideast Region (Philadelphia)
Delaware, District of Columbia, Maryland, Pennsylvania, Virginia, West Virginia

Region 4: Southeast Region (Atlanta)
Alabama, Florida, Georgia, Kentucky, Mississippi, North Carolina, South Carolina, Tennessee

Region 5: North Central Region (Chicago)
Illinois, Indiana, Michigan, Minnesota, Ohio, Wisconsin

Region 6: Southwest Region (Dallas)
Arkansas, Louisiana, New Mexico, Oklahoma, Texas

Region 7 and 8: Mountain-Plains Region (Kansas City)
Colorado, Iowa, Kansas, Missouri, Montana, Nebraska, North Dakota, South Dakota, Utah, Wyoming

Region 9 and 10: Pacific Region (San Francisco)
Alaska, American Samoa, Arizona, California, Guam, Hawaii, Idaho, Nevada, Oregon, Trust Territory of the Pacific Islands, Washington

Metropolitan Statistical Areas

Metropolitan Statistical Areas (MSAs) were developed to enable all Federal statistical agencies to use the same boundaries in publishing urban data.

MSA listings are updated annually to reflect changes in inclusion standards or demographic data. The following list, which is current as of Dec. 1992, includes both MSAs and Primary MSAs (PMSAs). Consolidated Metropolitan Statistical Areas (CMSAs), which consist of adjacent PMSAs are listed separately below.

In July 1983 this MSA system replaced a system based on the Standard Metropolitan Statistical Area (SMSA). SMSA titles in use through June 1983 are listed in the ASI 1980–84 Cumulative Index.

Area Code	Area Title
0040	Abilene, TX
0060	Aguadilla, PR
0080	Akron, OH
0120	Albany, GA
0160	Albany-Schenectady-Troy, NY
0200	Albuquerque, NM
0220	Alexandria, LA
0240	Allentown-Bethlehem-Easton, PA
0280	Altoona, PA
0320	Amarillo, TX
0360	Anaheim-Santa Ana, CA (See Orange County, CA)
0380	Anchorage, AK
0400	Anderson, IN (See Indianapolis, IN)
0405	Anderson, SC (See Greenville-Spartanburg-Anderson, SC)
0440	Ann Arbor, MI
0450	Anniston, AL
0460	Appleton-Oshkosh-Neenah, WI
0470	Arecibo, PR
0480	Ashville, NC
0500	Athens, GA
0520	Atlanta, GA
0560	Atlantic-Cape May, NJ
0600	Augusta-Aiken, GA-SC
0620	Aurora-Elgin, IL (See Chicago, IL)
0640	Austin-San Marcos, TX
0680	Bakersfield, CA
0720	Baltimore, MD
0730	Bangor, ME
0740	Barnstable-Yarmouth, MA (new)
0760	Baton Rouge, LA
0780	Battle Creek, MI (See Kalamazoo-Battle Creek, MI)
0840	Beaumont-Port Arthur, TX
0845	Beaver County, PA (See Pittsburgh, PA)
0860	Bellingham, WA
0870	Benton Harbor, MI
0875	Bergen-Passaic, NJ (See New York-Newark, NY-NJ-PA)
0880	Billings, MT
0920	Biloxi-Gulfport-Pascagoula, MS
0960	Binghamton, NY
1000	Birmingham, AL
1010	Bismarck, ND
1020	Bloomington, IN
1040	Bloomington-Normal, IL
1080	Boise City, ID
1120	Boston, MA-NH-ME-CT
1125	Boulder-Longmont, CO
1140	Bradenton, FL (See Sarasota-Bradenton, FL)
1145	Brazoria, TX
1150	Bremerton, WA
1160	Bridgeport, CT
1170	Bristol, CT (See Hartford, CT)
1200	Brockton, MA
1240	Brownsville-Harlingen-San Benito, TX
1260	Bryan-College Station, TX
1280	Buffalo-Niagara Falls, NY
1300	Burlington, NC (See Greensboro-Winston Salem-High Point, NC)
1305	Burlington, VT
1310	Caguas, PR
1320	Canton-Massillon, OH
1350	Casper, NY
1360	Cedar Rapids, IA
1400	Champaign-Urbana, IL
1440	Charleston-North Charleston, SC
1480	Charleston, WV
1520	Charlotte-Gastonia-Rock Hill, NC-SC
1540	Charlottesville, VA
1560	Chattanooga, TN-GA
1580	Cheyenne, WY
1600	Chicago, IL
1620	Chico-Paradise, CA
1640	Cincinnati, OH-KY-IN
1660	Clarksville-Hopkinsville, TN-KY
1680	Cleveland-Lorain-Elyria, OH
1720	Colorado Springs, CO
1740	Columbia, MO
1760	Columbia, SC
1800	Columbus, GA-AL
1840	Columbus, OH
1880	Corpus Christi, TX
1900	Cumberland, MD-WV
1920	Dallas, TX
1930	Danbury, CT
1950	Danville, VA
1960	Davenport-Moline-Rock Island, IA-IL
2000	Dayton-Springfield, OH
2020	Daytona Beach, FL
2030	Decatur, AL
2040	Decatur, IL
2080	Denver, CO
2120	Des Moines, IA
2160	Detroit, MI
2180	Dothan, AL
2190	Dover, DE (new)
2200	Dubuque, IA
2240	Duluth-Superior, MN-WI
2281	Dutchess County, NY
2290	Eau Claire, WI
2320	El Paso, TX
2330	Elkhart-Goshen, IN
2335	Elmira, NY
2340	Enid, OK
2360	Erie, PA
2400	Eugene-Springfield, OR
2440	Evansville-Henderson, IN-KY
2480	Fall River, MA-RI (See Providence-Fall River-Warwick, RI-MA)
2520	Fargo-Moorhead, ND-MN
2560	Fayetteville, NY
2580	Fayetteville-Springdale-Rogers, AR
2600	Fitchburg, Leominster, MA (See Boston, MA-NH-ME-CT)
2640	Flint, MI
2650	Florence, AL
2655	Florence, SC
2670	Fort Collins-Loveland, CO
2680	Fort Lauderdale, FL
2700	Fort Myers-Cape Coral, FL
2710	Fort Pierce-Port St. Lucie, FL
2720	Fort Smith, AR-OK
2750	Fort Walton Beach, FL
2760	Fort Wayne, IN
2800	Forth Worth-Arlington, TX
2840	Fresno, CA
2880	Gadsden, AL
2900	Gainesville, FL
2920	Galveston-Texas City, TX
2960	Gary, IN
2975	Glens Falls, NY
2980	Goldsboro, NC (new)
2985	Grand Forks, ND-MN
3000	Grand Rapids-Muskegon-Holland, MI
3040	Great Falls, MT
3060	Greeley, CO
3080	Green Bay, WI
3120	Greensboro-Winston-Salem-High Point, NC
3150	Greenville, NC (new)
3160	Greenville-Spartanburg-Anderson, SC
3180	Hagerstown, MD
3200	Hamilton-Middletown, OH
3240	Harrisburg, Lebanon-Carlisle, PA
3280	Hartford, CT
3290	Hickory-Morgantown, NC
3320	Honolulu, HI
3350	Houma, LA
3360	Houston, TX
3400	Huntington-Ashland, WV-KY-OH
3440	Huntsville, AL
3480	Indianapolis, IN
3500	Iowa City, IA
3520	Jackson, MI
3560	Jackson, MS
3580	Jackson, TN
3600	Jacksonville, FL
3605	Jacksonville, NC
3610	Jamestown, NY
3620	Janesville-Beloit, WI
3640	Jersey City, NJ (See New York-Newark, NY-NJ-PA)
3660	Johnson City-Kingsport-Bristol, TN-VA
3680	Johntown, PA
3690	Joliet, IL (See Chicago, IL)
3710	Joplin, MO
3720	Kalamazoo-Battle Creek, MI
3740	Kankakee, IL
3760	Kansas City, MO-KS
3800	Kenosha, WI
3810	Killeen-Temple, TX
3840	Knoxville, TN
3850	Kokomo, IN
3870	La Crosse, WI-MN
3880	Lafayette, LA
3920	Lafayette, IN
3960	Lake Charles, LA
3965	Lake County, IL (See Chicago, IL)
3980	Lakeland-Winter Haven, FL
4000	Lancaster, PA
4040	Lansing-East Lansing, MI
4080	Laredo, TX
4100	Las Cruces, NM
4120	Las Vegas, NV-AZ
4150	Lawrence, KS
4160	Lawrence-Haverhill, MA-NH (See Boston, MA-NH-ME-CT)
4200	Lawton, OK
4240	Lewiston-Auburn, ME
4280	Lexington, KY
4320	Lima, OH
4360	Lincoln, NE
4400	Little Rock-North Little Rock, AR
4420	Longview-Marshall, TX
4440	Lorain-Elyria, OH (See Cleveland-Lorain-Elyria, OH)
4480	Los Angeles-Long Beach, CA
4520	Louisville, KY-IN
4560	Lowell, MA-NH (See Boston, MA-NH-ME-CT)
4600	Lubbock, TX
4640	Lynchburg, VA
4680	Macon, GA
4720	Madison, WI
4760	Manchester, NH (See Boston, MA-NH-ME-CT)

4800	Mansfield, OH
4840	Mayaguez, PR
4880	McAllen-Edinburg, Mission, TX
4890	Medford-Ashland, OR
4900	Melbourne-Titusville-Palm Bay, FL
4920	Memphis, TN-AR-MS
4940	Merced, CA
5000	Miami, FL
5015	Middlesex-Somerset-Hunterdon, NJ (See New York-Newark, NY-NJ-PA)
5020	Middletown, CT (See Hartford, CT)
5040	Midland, TX (See Odessa-Midland, TX)
5080	Milwaukee, Waukesha, WI
5120	Minneapolis, St. Paul, MN-WI
5160	Mobile, AL
5170	Modesto, CA
5190	Monmouth-Ocean, NJ (See New York-Newark, NY-NJ-PA)
5200	Monroe, LA
5240	Montgomery, AL
5280	Muncie, IN
5320	Muskegon, MI (See Grand Rapids-Muskegon-Holland, MI)
5330	Myrtle Beach, SC (new)
5345	Naples, FL
5350	Nashua, NH
5360	Nashville, TN
5380	Nassau-Suffolk, NY (See New York-Newark, NY-NJ-PA)
5400	New Bedford, MA (See Boston, MA-NH-ME-CT)
5440	New Britain, CT (See Hartford, CT)
5480	New Haven-Meriden, CT
5520	New London-Norwich, CT-RI
5560	New Orleans, LA
5600	New York-Newark, NY-NJ-PA
5640	Newark, NJ (See New York-Newark, NY-NJ-PA)
5700	Niagara Falls, NY (See Buffalo-Niagara Falls, NY)
5720	Norfolk-Virginia Beach-Newport News, VA-NC
5760	Norwalk, CT (See Stamford-Norwalk, CT)
5775	Oakland, CA
5790	Ocala, FL
5800	Odessa-Midland, TX
5880	Oklahoma City, OK
5910	Olympia, WA
5920	Omaha, NE-IA
5945	Orange County, CA
5950	Orange County, NY
5960	Orlando, FL
5990	Owensboro, KY
6000	Oxnard-Ventura, CA (See Ventura, CA)
6015	Panama City, FL
6020	Parkersburg-Marietta, WV-OH
6025	Pascagoula, MS (See Biloxi-Gulfport-Pascagoula, MS)
6060	Pawtucket-Woonsocket-Attleboro, RI-MA (See Providence-Fall River-Warwick, RI-MA)
6080	Pensacola, FL
6120	Peoria-Pekin, IL
6160	Philadelphia, PA-NJ
6200	Phoenix-Mesa, AZ
6240	Pine Bluff, AR
6280	Pittsburgh, PA
6320	Pittsfield, MA
6360	Ponce, PR
6400	Portland, ME
6440	Portland-Vancouver, OR-WA
6450	Portsmouth-Dover-Rochester, NH-ME (See Boston, MA-NH-ME-CT)
6460	Poughkeepsie, NY (See Dutchess County, NY)
6480	Providence-Fall River-Warwick, RI-MA
6520	Provo-Orem, UT
6560	Pueblo, CO
6580	Punta Gorda, FL (new)
6600	Racine, WI
6640	Raleigh-Durham-Chapel Hill, NC
6660	Rapid City, SD
6680	Reading, PA
6690	Redding, CA
6720	Reno, NV
6740	Richland-Kemmewick-Pasco, WA
6760	Richmond-Petersburg, VA
6780	Riverside-San Bernardino, CA
6800	Roanoke, VA
6820	Rochester, MN
6840	Rochester, NY
6880	Rockford, IL
6895	Rocky Mount, NC
6920	Sacramento, CA
6960	Saginaw-Bay City-Midland, MI
6980	St. Cloud, MN
7000	St. Joseph, MO
7040	St. Louis, MO-IL
7080	Salem, OR
7090	Salem-Gloucester, MA (See Boston, MA-NH-ME-CT)
7120	Salinas, CA
7160	Salt Lake City-Ogden, UT
7200	San Angelo, TX
7240	San Antonio, TX
7320	San Diego, CA
7360	San Francisco, CA
7400	San Jose, CA
7440	San Juan-Bayamon, PR
7460	San Luis Obispo-Atascadero-Paso Robles, CA (new)
7480	Santa Barbara-Santa Maria-Lompoc, CA
7485	Santa Cruz-Watsonville, CA
7490	Santa Fe, NM
7500	Santa Rosa, CA
7510	Sarasota-Bradenton, FL
7520	Savannah, GA
7560	Scranton-Wilkes-Barre-Hazleton, PA
7600	Seattle-Bellevue-Everett, WA
7610	Sharon, PA
7620	Sheboygan, WI
7640	Sherman-Denison, TX
7680	Shreveport-Bossier City, LA
7720	Sious City, IA-NE
7760	Sioux Falls, SD
7800	South Bend, IN
7840	Spokane, WA
7880	Springield, IL
7920	Springfield, MO
8000	Springfield, MA
8040	Stamford-Norwalk, CT
8050	State College, PA
8080	Steubenville, Weirton, OH-WV
8120	Stockton-Lodi, CA
8140	Sumter, SC
8160	Syracuse, NY
8200	Tacoma, WA
8240	Tallahassee, FL
8280	Tampa-St. Petersburg-Clearwater, FL
8320	Terre Haute, IN
8360	Texarkana, TX-Texarkana, AR
8400	Toledo, OH
8440	Topeka, KS
8480	Trenton, NJ
8520	Tucson, AZ
8560	Tulsa, OK
8600	Tuscaloosa, AL
8640	Tyler, TX
8680	Utica-Rome, NY
8720	Vallejo-Fairfield-Napa, CA
8725	Vancouver, WA (See Portland-Vancouver, OR-WA)
8735	Ventura, CA
8750	Victoria, TX
8760	Vineland-Millville-Bridgeton, NJ
8780	Visalia-Tulare-Porterville, CA
8800	Waco, TX
8840	Washington, DC-MD-VA-WV
8880	Waterbury, CT
8920	Waterloo-Cedar Falls, IA
8940	Wausau, WI
8960	West Palm Beach-Boca Raton, FL
9000	Wheeling, WV-OH
9040	Wichita, KS
9080	Wichita Falls, TX
9140	Williamsport, PA
9160	Wilmington-Newark, DE-MD
9200	Wilmington, NC
9240	Worcester, MA (See Boston, MA-NH-ME-CT)
9260	Yakima, WA
9270	Yolo, CA
9280	York, PA
9320	Youngstown-Warren, OH
9340	Yuba City, CA
9360	Yuma, AZ

Consolidated Metropolitan Statistical Areas

Area Code	Area Title
07	Boston-Brockton-Nashua, MA-NH-ME-CT
14	Chicago-Gary-Kenosha, IL-IN-WI
21	Cincinnati-Hamilton, OH-KY-IN
28	Cleveland-Akron, OH
31	Dallas-Fort Worth, TX
34	Denver-Boulder-Greeley, CO
35	Detroit-Ann Arbor-Flint, MI
42	Houston-Galveston-Brazoria, TX
49	Los Angeles-Riverside-Orange County, CA
56	Miami-Fort Lauderdale, FL
63	Milwaukee-Racine, WI
70	New York-Northern New Jersey-Long Island, NY-NJ-CT-PA
77	Philadelphia-Wilmington-Atlantic City, PA-NJ-DE-MD
79	Portland-Salem, OR-WA
82	Sacramento-Yolo, CA
84	San Francisco-Oakland-San Jose, CA
87	San Juan-Caguas-Arecibo, PR
91	Seattle-Tacoma-Bremerton, WA
97	Washington-Baltimore, DC-MD-VA-WV

Cities With Population Over 100,000

1990 Rank and Population

1	New York, NY	7,322,564
2	Los Angeles, CA	3,485,398
3	Chicago, IL	2,783,726
4	Houston, TX	1,630,553
5	Philadelphia, PA	1,585,577
6	San Diego, CA	1,110,549
7	Detroit, MI	1,027,974
8	Dallas, TX	1,006,877
9	Phoenix, AZ	983,403
10	San Antonio, TX	935,933
11	San Jose, CA	782,248
12	Indianapolis, IN	741,952
13	Baltimore, MD	736,014
14	San Francisco, CA	723,959
15	Jacksonville, FL	672,971
16	Columbus, OH	632,910
17	Milwaukee, WI	628,088
18	Memphis, TN	610,337
19	Washington, DC	606,900
20	Boston, MA	574,283
21	Seattle, WA	516,259
22	El Paso, TX	515,342
23	Nashville-Davidson, TN	510,784
24	Cleveland, OH	505,616
25	New Orleans, LA	496,938
26	Denver, CO	467,610
27	Austin, TX	465,622
28	Fort Worth, TX	447,619
29	Oklahoma City, OK	444,719
30	Portland, OR	437,319
31	Kansas City, MO	435,146
32	Long Beach, CA	429,433
33	Tucson, AZ	405,390
34	St. Louis, MO	396,685
35	Charlotte, NC	395,934
36	Atlanta, GA	394,017
37	Virginia Beach, VA	393,069
38	Albuquerque, NM	384,736
39	Oakland, CA	372,242
40	Pittsburgh, PA	369,879
41	Sacramento, CA	369,365
42	Minneapolis, MN	368,383
43	Tulsa, OK	367,302
44	Honolulu, HI	365,272
45	Cincinnati, OH	364,040
46	Miami, FL	358,548
47	Fresno, CA	354,202
48	Omaha, NE	335,795
49	Toledo, OH	332,943
50	Buffalo, NY	328,123
51	Wichita, KS	304,011
52	Santa Ana, CA	293,742
53	Mesa, AZ	288,091
54	Colorado Springs, CO	281,140
55	Tampa, FL	280,015
56	Newark, NJ	275,221
57	St. Paul, MN	272,235
58	Louisville, KY	269,063
59	Anaheim, CA	266,406
60	Birmingham, AL	265,968
61	Arlington, TX	261,721
62	Norfolk, VA	261,229
63	Las Vegas, NV	258,295
64	Corpus Christi, TX	257,453
65	St. Petersburg, FL	238,629
66	Rochester, NY	231,636
67	Jersey City, NJ	228,537
68	Riverside, CA	226,505
69	Anchorage, AK	226,338
70	Lexington-Fayette, KY	225,366
71	Akron, OH	223,019
72	Aurora, CO	222,103
73	Baton Rouge, LA	219,531
74	Stockton, CA	210,943
75	Raleigh, NC	207,951
76	Richmond, VA	203,056
77	Shreveport, LA	198,525
78	Jackson, MS	196,637
79	Mobile, AL	196,278
80	Des Moines, IA	193,187
81	Lincoln, NE	191,972
82	Madison, WI	191,262
83	Grand Rapids, MI	189,126
84	Yonkers, NY	188,082
85	Hialeah, FL	188,004
86	Montgomery, AL	187,106
87	Lubbock, TX	186,206
88	Greensboro, NC	183,521
89	Dayton, OH	182,044
90	Huntington Beach, CA	181,519
91	Garland, TX	180,650
92	Glendale, CA	180,038
93	Columbus, GA	179,278
94	Spokane, WA	177,196
95	Tacoma, WA	176,664
96	Little Rock, AR	175,795
97	Bakersfield, CA	174,820
98	Fremont, CA	173,339
99	Fort Wayne, IN	173,072
100	Newport News, VA	170,045
101	Worcester, MA	169,759
102	Knoxville, TN	165,121
103	Modesto, CA	164,730
104	Orlando, FL	164,693
105	San Bernardino, CA	164,164
106	Syracuse, NY	163,860
107	Providence, RI	160,728
108	Salt Lake City, UT	159,936
109	Huntsville, AL	159,789
110	Amarillo, TX	157,615
111	Springfield, MA	156,983
112	Irving, TX	155,037
113	Chattanooga, TN	152,466
114	Chesapeake, VA	151,976
115	Kansas City, KS	149,767
116	Fort Lauderdale, FL	149,377
117	Glendale, AZ	148,134
118	Warren, MI	144,864
119	Winston-Salem, NC	143,485
120	Garden Grove, CA	143,050
121	Oxnard, CA	142,216
122	Tempe, AZ	141,865
123	Bridgeport, CT	141,686
124	Paterson, NJ	140,891
125	Flint, MI	140,761
126	Springfield, MO	140,494
127	Hartford, CT	139,739
128	Rockford, IL	139,426
129	Savannah, GA	137,560
130	Durham, NC	136,611
131	Chula Vista, CA	135,163
132	Reno, NV	133,850
133	Hampton, VA	133,793
134	Ontario, CA	133,179
135	Torrance, CA	133,107
136	Pomona, CA	131,723
137	Pasadena, CA	131,591
138	New Haven, CT	130,474
139	Scottsdale, AZ	130,069
140	Plano, TX	128,713
141	Oceanside, CA	128,398
142	Lansing, MI	127,321
143	Lakewood, CO	126,481
144	Evansville, IN	126,272
145	Boise, ID	125,738
146	Tallahassee, FL	124,773
147	Laredo, TX	122,899
148	Hollywood, FL	121,697
149	Topeka, KS	119,883
150	Pasadena, TX	119,363
151	Moreno Valley, CA	118,779
152	Sterling Heights, MI	117,810
153	Sunnyvale, CA	117,229
154	Gary, IN	116,646
155	Beaumont, TX	114,323
156	Fullerton, CA	114,144
157	Peoria, IL	113,504
158	Santa Rosa, CA	113,313
159	Eugene, OR	112,669
160	Independence, MO	112,301
161	Overland Park, KS	111,790
162	Hayward, CA	111,498
163	Concord, CA	111,348
164	Alexandria, VA	111,183
165	Orange, CA	110,658
166	Santa Clarita, CA	110,642
167	Irvine, CA	110,330
168	Elizabeth, NJ	110,002
169	Inglewood, CA	109,602
170	Ann Arbor, MI	109,592
171	Vallejo, CA	109,199
172	Waterbury, CT	108,961
173	Salinas, CA	108,777
174	Cedar Rapids, IA	108,751
175	Erie, PA	108,718
176	Escondido, CA	108,635
177	Stamford, CT	108,056
178	Salem, OR	107,786
179	Abilene, TX	106,654
180	Macon, GA	106,612
181	El Monte, CA	106,209
182	South Bend, IN	105,511
183	Springfield, IL	105,227
184	Allentown, PA	105,090
185	Thousand Oaks, CA	104,352
186	Portsmouth, VA	103,907
187	Waco, TX	103,590
188	Lowell, MA	103,439
189	Berkeley, CA	102,724
190	Mesquite, TX	101,484
191	Rancho Cucamonga, CA	101,409
192	Albany, NY	101,082
193	Livonia, MI	100,850
194	Sioux Falls, SD	100,814
195	Simi Valley, CA	100,217

Consumer Price Index Cities

Consumer Price Index data are collected for the following Metropolitan Statistical Areas:

Anchorage, AK
Atlanta, GA
Baltimore, MD
Boston-Lawrence-Salem, MA-NH
Buffalo-Niagara Falls, NY
Chicago-Gary-Lake County, IL-IN-WI
Cincinnati-Hamilton, OH-KY-IN
Cleveland-Akron-Lorain, OH
Dallas-Fort Worth, TX
Denver-Boulder, CO
Detroit-Ann Arbor, MI
Honolulu, HI
Houston-Galveston-Brazoria, TX
Kansas City, MO-KS
Los Angeles-Anaheim-Riverside, CA
Miami-Fort Lauderdale, FL
Milwaukee, WI
Minneapolis-St. Paul, MN-WI
New Orleans, LA
N.Y. Northern N.J.-Long Island, NY-NJ-CT
Phi.-Wilmington-Trenton, PA-NJ-DE-MD
Pittsburgh-Beaver Valley, PA
Portland-Vancouver, OR-WA
St. Louis-East St. Louis, MO-IL
San Diego, CA
San Francisco-Oakland-San Jose, CA
Seattle-Tacoma, WA
Tampa-St. Petersburg-Clearwater, FL
Washington, DC-MD-VA

Standard Industrial Classification

The Standard Industrial Classification (SIC) was developed to classify industrial establishments by the type of activity in which they are engaged, for the purpose of promoting uniformity and comparability of statistical data collected by Federal and State agencies, trade associations, and others. The classification system is at 4 levels: industry divisions, major groups, groups, and individual industries—represented by 1- to 4-digit codes. The following list is taken from the 1987 *Standard Industrial Classification Manual,* which revises the 1972 edition and 1977 supplement. For description of the 1987 Manual, see 108-4 in ASI 1987 Annual.

Group and Industry Code

AGRICULTURE, FORESTRY, AND FISHING

01 AGRICULTURAL PRODUCTION—CROPS

011 Cash Grains
0111 Wheat
0112 Rice
0115 Corn
0116 Soybeans
0119 Cash grains, nec

013 Field Crops, Except Cash Grains
0131 Cotton
0132 Tobacco
0133 Sugarcane and sugar beets
0134 Irish potatoes
0139 Field crops, except cash grains, nec

016 Vegetables and Melons
0161 Vegetables and melons

017 Fruits and Tree Nuts
0171 Berry crops
0172 Grapes
0173 Tree nuts
0174 Citrus fruits
0175 Deciduous tree fruits
0179 Fruits and tree nuts, nec

018 Horticultural Specialties
0181 Ornamental nursery products
0182 Food crops grown under cover

019 General Farms, Primarily Crop
0191 General farms, primarily crop

02 AGRICULTURAL PRODUCTION—LIVESTOCK

021 Livestock, Except Dairy and Poultry
0211 Beef cattle feedlots
0212 Beef cattle, except feedlots
0213 Hogs
0214 Sheep and goats
0219 General livestock, nec

024 Dairy Farms
0241 Dairy farms

025 Poultry and Eggs
0251 Broiler, fryer, and roaster chickens
0252 Chicken eggs
0253 Turkeys and turkey eggs
0254 Poultry hatcheries
0259 Poultry and eggs, nec

027 Animal Specialties
0271 Fur-bearing animals and rabbits
0272 Horses and other equines
0273 Animal aquaculture
0279 Animal specialties, nec

029 General Farms, Primarily Animal
0291 General farms, primarily animal

07 AGRICULTURAL SERVICES

071 Soil Preparation Services
0711 Soil preparation services

072 Crop Services
0721 Crop planting and protecting
0722 Crop harvesting
0723 Crop preparation services for market
0724 Cotton ginning

074 Veterinary Services
0741 Veterinary services for livestock
0742 Veterinary services, specialties

075 Animal Services, Except Veterinary
0751 Livestock services, exc. veterinary
0752 Animal specialty services

076 Farm Labor and Management Services
0761 Farm labor contractors
0762 Farm management services

078 Landscape and Horticultural Services
0781 Landscape counseling and planning
0782 Lawn and garden services
0783 Ornamental shrub and tree services

08 FORESTRY

081 Timber Tracts
0811 Timber tracts

083 Forest Products
0831 Forest products

085 Forestry Services
0851 Forestry services

09 FISHING, HUNTING, AND TRAPPING

091 Commercial Fishing
0912 Finfish
0913 Shellfish
0919 Miscellaneous marine products

092 Fish Hatcheries and Preserves
0921 Fish hatcheries and preserves

097 Hunting, Trapping, Game Propagation
0971 Hunting, trapping, game propagation

MINING

10 METAL MINING

101 Iron Ores
1011 Iron ores

102 Copper Ores
1021 Copper ores

103 Lead and Zinc Ores
1031 Lead and zinc ores

104 Gold and Silver Ores
1041 Gold ores
1044 Silver ores

106 Ferroalloy Ores, Except Vanadium
1061 Ferroalloy ores, except vanadium

108 Metal Mining Services
1081 Metal mining services

109 Miscellaneous Metal Ores
1094 Uranium-radium-vanadium ores
1099 Metal ores, nec

12 COAL MINING

122 Bituminous Coal and Lignite Mining
1221 Bituminous coal and lignite—surface
1222 Bituminous coal—underground

123 Anthracite Mining
1231 Anthracite mining

124 Coal Mining Services
1241 Coal mining services

13 OIL AND GAS EXTRACTION

131 Crude Petroleum and Natural Gas
1311 Crude petroleum and natural gas

132 Natural Gas Liquids
1321 Natural gas liquids

138 Oil and Gas Field Services
1381 Drilling oil and gas wells
1382 Oil and gas exploration services
1389 Oil and gas field services, nec

14 NONMETALLIC MINERALS, EXCEPT FUELS

141 Dimension Stone
1411 Dimension stone

142 Crushed and Broken Stone
1422 Crushed and broken limestone
1423 Crushed and broken granite
1429 Crushed and broken stone, nec

144 Sand and Gravel
1442 Construction sand and gravel
1446 Industrial sand

145 Clay, Ceramic, & Refractory Minerals
1455 Kaolin and ball clay
1459 Clay and related minerals, nec

147 Chemical and Fertilizer Minerals
1474 Potash, soda, and borate minerals
1475 Phosphate rock
1479 Chemical and fertilizer mining, nec

148 Nonmetallic Minerals Services
1481 Nonmetallic minerals services

149 Miscellaneous Nonmetallic Minerals
1499 Miscellaneous nonmetallic minerals

CONSTRUCTION

15 GENERAL BUILDING CONTRACTORS

152 Residential Building Construction
1521 Single-family housing construction
1522 Residential construction, nec

153 Operative Builders
1531 Operative builders

154 Nonresidential Building Construction
1541 Industrial buildings and warehouses
1542 Nonresidential construction, nec

16 HEAVY CONSTRUCTION, EX. BUILDING

161 Highway and Street Construction
1611 Highway and street construction

162 Heavy Construction, Except Highway
1622 Bridge, tunnel, & elevated highway
1623 Water, sewer, and utility lines
1629 Heavy construction, nec

17 SPECIAL TRADE CONTRACTORS

171 Plumbing, Heating, Air-Conditioning
1711 Plumbing, heating, air-conditioning

172 Painting and Paper Hanging
1721 Painting and paper hanging

173 Electrical Work
1731 Electrical work

174 Masonry, Stonework, and Plastering
1741 Masonry and other stonework
1742 Plastering, drywall, and insulation
1743 Terrazzo, tile, marble, mosaic work

175 Carpentry and Floor Work
1751 Carpentry work
1752 Floor laying and floor work, nec

176 Roofing, Siding, and Sheet Metal Work
1761 Roofing, siding, and sheet metal work

177 Concrete Work
1771 Concrete work

178 Water Well Drilling
1781 Water well drilling

179 Misc. Special Trade Contractors
1791 Structural steel erection
1793 Glass and glazing work
1794 Excavation work
1795 Wrecking and demolition work
1796 Installing building equipment, nec
1799 Special trade contractors, nec

MANUFACTURING

20 FOOD AND KINDRED PRODUCTS

201 Meat Products
2011 Meat packing plants
2013 Sausages and other prepared meats
2015 Poultry slaughtering and processing

202 Dairy Products
2021 Creamery butter
2022 Cheese, natural and processed
2023 Dry, condensed, evaporated products
2024 Ice cream and frozen desserts
2026 Fluid milk

203 Preserved Fruits and Vegetables
2032 Canned specialties
2033 Canned fruits and vegetables
2034 Dehydrated fruits, vegetables, soups
2035 Pickles, sauces, and salad dressings
2037 Frozen fruits and vegetables
2038 Frozen specialties, nec

204 Grain Mill Products
2041 Flour and other grain mill products
2043 Cereal breakfast foods
2044 Rice milling
2045 Prepared flour mixes and doughs
2046 Wet corn milling
2047 Dog and cat food
2048 Prepared feeds, nec

205 Bakery Products
2051 Bread, cake, and related products
2052 Cookies and crackers
2053 Frozen bakery products, except bread

206 Sugar and Confectionery Products
2061 Raw cane sugar
2062 Cane sugar refining
2063 Beet sugar
2064 Candy & other confectionery products
2066 Chocolate and cocoa products
2067 Chewing gum
2068 Salted and roasted nuts and seeds

207 Fats and Oils
2074 Cottonseed oil mills
2075 Soybean oil mills
2076 Vegetable oil mills, nec
2077 Animal and marine fats and oils
2079 Edible fats and oils, nec

208 Beverages
2082 Malt beverages
2083 Malt
2084 Wines, brandy, and brandy spirits
2085 Distilled and blended liquors
2086 Bottled and canned soft drinks
2087 Flavoring extracts and syrups, nec

209 Misc. Food and Kindred Products
2091 Canned and cured fish and seafoods
2092 Fresh or frozen prepared fish
2095 Roasted coffee
2096 Potato chips and similar snacks
2097 Manufactured ice
2098 Macaroni and spaghetti
2099 Food preparations, nec

21 TOBACCO PRODUCTS

211 Cigarettes
2111 Cigarettes

212 Cigars
2121 Cigars

213 Chewing and Smoking Tobacco
2131 Chewing and smoking tobacco

214 Tobacco Stemming and Redrying
2141 Tobacco stemming and redrying

22 TEXTILE MILL PRODUCTS

221 Broadwoven Fabric Mills, Cotton
2211 Broadwoven fabric mills, cotton

222 Broadwoven Fabric Mills, Manmade
2221 Broadwoven fabric mills, manmade

223 Broadwoven Fabric Mills, Wool
2231 Broadwoven fabric mills, wool

224 Narrow Fabric Mills
2241 Narrow fabric mills

225 Knitting Mills
2251 Women's hosiery, except socks
2252 Hosiery, nec
2253 Knit outerwear mills
2254 Knit underwear mills
2257 Weft knit fabric mills
2258 Lace & warp knit fabric mills
2259 Knitting mills, nec

226 Textile Finishing, Except Wool
2261 Finishing plants, cotton
2262 Finishing plants, manmade
2269 Finishing plants, nec

227 Carpets and Rugs
2273 Carpets and rugs

228 Yarn and Thread Mills
2281 Yarn spinning mills
2282 Throwing and winding mills
2284 Thread mills

229 Miscellaneous Textile Goods
2295 Coated fabrics, not rubberized
2296 Tire cord and fabrics
2297 Nonwoven fabrics
2298 Cordage and twine
2299 Textile goods, nec

23 APPAREL AND OTHER TEXTILE PRODUCTS

231 Men's and Boys' Suits and Coats
2311 Men's and boys' suits and coats

232 Men's and Boys' Furnishings
2321 Men's and boys' shirts
2322 Men's & boys' underwear & nightwear
2323 Men's and boys' neckwear
2325 Men's and boys' trousers and slacks
2326 Men's and boys' work clothing
2329 Men's and boys' clothing, nec

233 Women's and Misses' Outerwear
2331 Women's & misses' blouses & shirts
2335 Women's, juniors', & misses' dresses
2337 Women's and misses' suits and coats
2339 Women's and misses' outerwear, nec

234 Women's and Children's Undergarments
2341 Women's and children's underwear
2342 Bras, girdles, and allied garments

235 Hats, Caps, and Millinery
2353 Hats, caps, and millinery

236 Girls' and Children's Outerwear
2361 Girls' & children's dresses, blouses
2369 Girls' and children's outerwear, nec

237 Fur Goods
2371 Fur goods

238 Miscellaneous Apparel and Accessories
2381 Fabric dress and work gloves
2384 Robes and dressing gowns
2385 Waterproof outerwear
2386 Leather and sheep-lined clothing
2387 Apparel belts
2389 Apparel and accessories, nec

239 Misc. Fabricated Textile Products
2391 Curtains and draperies
2392 Housefurnishings, nec
2393 Textile bags
2394 Canvas and related products
2395 Pleating and stitching
2396 Automotive and apparel trimmings
2397 Schiffli machine embroideries
2399 Fabricated textile products, nec

24 LUMBER AND WOOD PRODUCTS

241 Logging
2411 Logging

242 Sawmills and Planing Mills
2421 Sawmills and planing mills, general
2426 Hardwood dimension & flooring mills
2429 Special product sawmills, nec

243 Millwork, Plywood & Structural Members
2431 Millwork
2434 Wood kitchen cabinets
2435 Hardwood veneer and plywood
2436 Softwood veneer and plywood
2439 Structural wood members, nec

244 Wood Containers
2441 Nailed wood boxes and shook
2448 Wood pallets and skids
2449 Wood containers, nec

245 Wood Buildings and Mobile Homes
2451 Mobile homes
2452 Prefabricated wood buildings

249 Miscellaneous Wood Products
2491 Wood preserving
2493 Reconstituted wood products
2499 Wood products, nec

25 FURNITURE AND FIXTURES

251 Household Furniture
2511 Wood household furniture
2512 Upholstered household furniture
2514 Metal household furniture
2515 Mattresses and bedsprings
2517 Wood TV and radio cabinets
2519 Household furniture, nec

252 Office Furniture
2521 Wood office furniture
2522 Office furniture, except wood

253 Public Building & Related Furniture
2531 Public building & related furniture

254 Partitions and Fixtures
2541 Wood partitions and fixtures
2542 Partitions and fixtures, except wood

259 Miscellaneous Furniture and Fixtures
2591 Drapery hardware & blinds & shades
2599 Furniture and fixtures, nec

26 PAPER AND ALLIED PRODUCTS

261 Pulp Mills
2611 Pulp mills

262 Paper Mills
2621 Paper mills

263 Paperboard Mills
2631 Paperboard mills

265 Paperboard Containers and Boxes
2652 Setup paperboard boxes
2653 Corrugated and solid fiber boxes
2655 Fiber cans, drums & similar products
2656 Sanitary food containers
2657 Folding paperboard boxes

267 Misc. Converted Paper Products
2671 Paper coated & laminated, packaging
2672 Paper coated and laminated, nec
2673 Bags: plastics, laminated, & coated
2674 Bags: uncoated paper & multiwall
2675 Die-cut paper and board
2676 Sanitary paper products
2677 Envelopes
2678 Stationery products
2679 Converted paper products, nec

27 PRINTING AND PUBLISHING

271 Newspapers
2711 Newspapers

272 Periodicals
2721 Periodicals

273 Books
2731 Book publishing
2732 Book printing

274 Miscellaneous Publishing
2741 Miscellaneous publishing

275 Commercial Printing
2752 Commercial printing, lithographic
2754 Commercial printing, gravure
2759 Commercial printing, nec

276 Manifold Business Forms
2761 Manifold business forms

277 Greeting Cards
2771 Greeting cards

278 Blankbooks and Bookbinding
2782 Blankbooks and looseleaf binders
2789 Bookbinding and related work

279 Printing Trade Services
2791 Typesetting
2796 Platemaking services

28 CHEMICALS AND ALLIED PRODUCTS

281 Industrial Inorganic Chemicals
2812 Alkalies and chlorine
2813 Industrial gases
2816 Inorganic pigments
2819 Industrial inorganic chemicals, nec

282 Plastics Materials and Synthetics
2821 Plastics materials and resins
2822 Synthetic rubber
2823 Cellulosic manmade fibers
2824 Organic fibers, noncellulosic

283 Drugs
2833 Medicinals and botanicals
2834 Pharmaceutical preparations
2835 Diagnostic substances
2836 Biological products exc. diagnostic

284 Soap, Cleaners, and Toilet Goods
2841 Soap and other detergents
2842 Polishes and sanitation goods
2843 Surface active agents
2844 Toilet preparations

285 Paints and Allied Products
2851 Paints and allied products

286 Industrial Organic Chemicals
2861 Gum and wood chemicals
2865 Cyclic crudes and intermediates
2869 Industrial organic chemicals, nec

287 Agricultural Chemicals
2873 Nitrogenous fertilizers
2874 Phosphatic fertilizers
2875 Fertilizers, mixing only
2879 Agricultural chemicals, nec

289 Miscellaneous Chemical Products
2891 Adhesives and sealants
2892 Explosives
2893 Printing ink
2895 Carbon black
2899 Chemical preparations, nec

29 PETROLEUM AND COAL PRODUCTS

291 Petroleum Refining
2911 Petroleum refining

295 Asphalt Paving and Roofing Materials
2951 Asphalt paving mixtures and blocks
2952 Asphalt felts and coatings

299 Misc. Petroleum and Coal Products
2992 Lubricating oils and greases
2999 Petroleum and coal products, nec

30 RUBBER AND MISC. PLASTICS PRODUCTS

301 Tires and Inner Tubes
3011 Tires and inner tubes

302 Rubber and Plastics Footwear
3021 Rubber and plastics footwear

305 Hose & Belting & Gaskets & Packing
3052 Rubber & plastics hose & belting
3053 Gaskets, packing and sealing devices

306 Fabricated Rubber Products, NEC
3061 Mechanical rubber goods
3069 Fabricated rubber products, nec

308 Miscellaneous Plastics Products, NEC
3081 Unsupported plastics film & sheet
3082 Unsupported plastics profile shapes
3083 Laminated plastics plate & sheet
3084 Plastics pipe
3085 Plastics bottles
3086 Plastics foam products
3087 Custom compound purchased resins
3088 Plastics plumbing fixtures
3089 Plastics products, nec

31 LEATHER AND LEATHER PRODUCTS

311 Leather Tanning and Finishing
3111 Leather tanning and finishing

313 Footwear Cut Stock
3131 Footwear cut stock

314 Footwear, Except Rubber
3142 House slippers
3143 Men's footwear, except athletic
3144 Women's footwear, except athletic
3149 Footwear, except rubber, nec

315 Leather Gloves and Mittens
3151 Leather gloves and mittens

316 Luggage
3161 Luggage

317 Handbags and Personal Leather Goods
3171 Women's handbags and purses
3172 Personal leather goods, nec

319 Leather Goods, NEC
3199 Leather goods, nec

32 STONE, CLAY, AND GLASS PRODUCTS

321 Flat Glass
3211 Flat glass

322 Glass and Glassware, Pressed or Blown
3221 Glass containers
3229 Pressed and blown glass, nec

323 Products of Purchased Glass
3231 Products of purchased glass

324 Cement, Hydraulic
3241 Cement, hydraulic

325 Structural Clay Products
3251 Brick and structural clay tile
3253 Ceramic wall and floor tile
3255 Clay refractories
3259 Structural clay products, nec

326 Pottery and Related Products
3261 Vitreous plumbing fixtures
3262 Vitreous china table & kitchenware
3263 Semivitreous table & kitchenware
3264 Porcelain electrical supplies
3269 Pottery products, nec

327 Concrete, Gypsum, and Plaster Products
3271 Concrete block and brick
3272 Concrete products, nec
3273 Ready-mixed concrete
3274 Lime
3275 Gypsum products

328 Cut Stone and Stone Products
3281 Cut stone and stone products

329 Misc. Nonmetallic Mineral Products
3291 Abrasive products
3292 Asbestos products
3295 Minerals, ground or treated
3296 Mineral wool
3297 Nonclay refractories
3299 Nonmetallic mineral products, nec

33 PRIMARY METAL INDUSTRIES

331 Blast Furnace and Basic Steel Products
3312 Blast furnaces and steel mills
3313 Electrometallurgical products
3315 Steel wire and related products
3316 Cold finishing of steel shapes
3317 Steel pipe and tubes

332 Iron and Steel Foundries
3321 Gray and ductile iron foundries
3322 Malleable iron foundries
3324 Steel investment foundries
3325 Steel foundries, nec

333 Primary Nonferrous Metals
3331 Primary copper
3334 Primary aluminum
3339 Primary nonferrous metals, nec

334 Secondary Nonferrous Metals
3341 Secondary nonferrous metals

335 Nonferrous Rolling and Drawing
3351 Copper rolling and drawing
3353 Aluminum sheet, plate, and foil
3354 Aluminum extruded products
3355 Aluminum rolling and drawing, nec
3356 Nonferrous rolling and drawing, nec
3357 Nonferrous wiredrawing & insulating

336 Nonferrous Foundries (Castings)
3363 Aluminum die-castings
3364 Nonferrous die-casting exc. aluminum
3365 Aluminum foundries
3366 Copper foundries
3369 Nonferrous foundries, nec

339 Miscellaneous Primary Metal Products
3398 Metal heat treating
3399 Primary metal products, nec

34 FABRICATED METAL PRODUCTS

341 Metal Cans and Shipping Containers
3411 Metal cans
3412 Metal barrels, drums, and pails

342 Cutlery, Handtools, and Hardware
3421 Cutlery
3423 Hand and edge tools, nec
3425 Saw blades and handsaws
3429 Hardware, nec

343 Plumbing and Heating, Except Electric
3431 Metal sanitary ware
3432 Plumbing fixture fittings and trim
3433 Heating equipment, except electric

344 Fabricated Structural Metal Products
3441 Fabricated structural metal
3442 Metal doors, sash, and trim
3443 Fabricated plate work (boiler shops)
3444 Sheet metal work
3446 Architectural metal work
3448 Prefabricated metal buildings
3449 Miscellaneous metal work

345 Screw Machine Products, Bolts, Etc.
3451 Screw machine products
3452 Bolts, nuts, rivets, and washers

346 Metal Forgings and Stampings
3462 Iron and steel forgings
3463 Nonferrous forgings
3465 Automotive stampings
3466 Crowns and closures
3469 Metal stampings, nec

347 Metal Services, NEC
3471 Plating and polishing
3479 Metal coating and allied services

348 Ordnance and Accessories, NEC
3482 Small arms ammunition
3483 Ammunition, exc. for small arms, nec
3484 Small arms
3489 Ordnance and accessories, nec

349 Misc. Fabricated Metal Products
3491 Industrial valves
3492 Fluid power valves & hose fittings
3493 Steel springs, except wire
3494 Valves and pipe fittings, nec
3495 Wire springs
3496 Misc. fabricated wire products
3497 Metal foil and leaf
3498 Fabricated pipe and fittings
3499 Fabricated metal products, nec

35 INDUSTRIAL MACHINERY AND EQUIPMENT

351 Engines and Turbines
3511 Turbines and turbine generator sets
3519 Internal combustion engines, nec

352 Farm and Garden Machinery
3523 Farm machinery and equipment
3524 Lawn and garden equipment

353 Construction and Related Machinery
3531 Construction machinery
3532 Mining machinery
3533 Oil and gas field machinery
3534 Elevators and moving stairways
3535 Conveyors and conveying equipment
3536 Hoists, cranes, and monorails
3537 Industrial trucks and tractors

354 Metalworking Machinery
3541 Machine tools, metal cutting types
3542 Machine tools, metal forming types
3543 Industrial patterns
3544 Special dies, tools, jigs & fixtures
3545 Machine tool accessories
3546 Power-driven handtools
3547 Rolling mill machinery
3548 Welding apparatus
3549 Metalworking machinery, nec

355 Special Industry Machinery
3552 Textile machinery
3553 Woodworking machinery
3554 Paper industries machinery
3555 Printing trades machinery
3556 Food products machinery
3559 Special industry machinery, nec

356 General Industrial Machinery
3561 Pumps and pumping equipment
3562 Ball and roller bearings
3563 Air and gas compressors
3564 Blowers and fans
3565 Packaging machinery
3566 Speed changers, drives, and gears
3567 Industrial furnaces and ovens
3568 Power transmission equipment, nec
3569 General industrial machinery, nec

357 Computer and Office Equipment
3571 Electronic computers
3572 Computer storage devices
3575 Computer terminals
3577 Computer peripheral equipment, nec
3578 Calculating and accounting equipment
3579 Office machines, nec

358 Refrigeration and Service Machinery
3581 Automatic vending machines
3582 Commercial laundry equipment
3585 Refrigeration and heating equipment
3586 Measuring and dispensing pumps
3589 Service industry machinery, nec

359 Industrial Machinery, NEC
3592 Carburetors, pistons, rings, valves
3593 Fluid power cylinders & actuators
3594 Fluid power pumps and motors
3596 Scales and balances, exc. laboratory
3599 Industrial machinery, nec

36 ELECTRONIC & OTHER ELECTRIC EQUIPMENT

361 Electric Distribution Equipment
3612 Transformers, except electronic
3613 Switchgear and switchboard apparatus

362 Electrical Industrial Apparatus
3621 Motors and generators
3624 Carbon and graphite products
3625 Relays and industrial controls
3629 Electrical industrial apparatus, nec

363 Household Appliances
3631 Household cooking equipment
3632 Household refrigerators and freezers
3633 Household laundry equipment
3634 Electric housewares and fans
3635 Household vacuum cleaners
3639 Household appliances, nec

364 Electric Lighting and Wiring Equipment
3641 Electric lamps
3643 Current-carrying wiring devices
3644 Noncurrent-carrying wiring devices
3645 Residential lighting fixtures
3646 Commercial lighting fixtures
3647 Vehicular lighting equipment
3648 Lighting equipment, nec

365 Household Audio and Video Equipment
3651 Household audio and video equipment
3652 Prerecorded records and tapes

366 Communications Equipment
3661 Telephone and telegraph apparatus
3663 Radio & TV communications equipment
3669 Communications equipment, nec

367 Electronic Components and Accessories
3671 Electron tubes
3672 Printed circuit boards
3674 Semiconductors and related devices
3675 Electronic capacitors
3676 Electronic resistors
3677 Electronic coils and transformers
3678 Electronic connectors
3679 Electronic components, nec

369 Misc. Electrical Equipment & Supplies
3691 Storage batteries
3692 Primary batteries, dry and wet
3694 Engine electrical equipment
3695 Magnetic and optical recording media
3699 Electrical equipment & supplies, nec

37 TRANSPORTATION EQUIPMENT

371 Motor Vehicles and Equipment
3711 Motor vehicles and car bodies
3713 Truck and bus bodies
3714 Motor vehicle parts and accessories
3715 Truck trailers
3716 Motor homes

372 Aircraft and Parts
3721 Aircraft
3724 Aircraft engines and engine parts
3728 Aircraft parts and equipment, nec

373 Ship and Boat Building and Repairing
3731 Ship building and repairing
3732 Boat building and repairing

374 Railroad Equipment
3743 Railroad equipment

375 Motorcycles, Bicycles, and Parts
3751 Motorcycles, bicycles, and parts

376 Guided Missiles, Space Vehicles, Parts
3761 Guided missiles and space vehicles
3764 Space propulsion units and parts
3769 Space vehicle equipment, nec

379 Miscellaneous Transportation Equipment
3792 Travel trailers and campers
3795 Tanks and tank components
3799 Transportation equipment, nec

38 INSTRUMENTS AND RELATED PRODUCTS

381 Search and Navigation Equipment
3812 Search and navigation equipment

382 Measuring and Controlling Devices
3821 Laboratory apparatus and furniture
3822 Environmental controls
3823 Process control instruments
3824 Fluid meters and counting devices
3825 Instruments to measure electricity
3826 Analytical instruments
3827 Optical instruments and lenses
3829 Measuring & controlling devices, nec

384 Medical Instruments and Supplies
3841 Surgical and medical instruments
3842 Surgical appliances and supplies
3843 Dental equipment and supplies
3844 X-ray apparatus and tubes
3845 Electromedical equipment

385 Ophthalmic Goods
3851 Ophthalmic goods

386 Photographic Equipment and Supplies
3861 Photographic equipment and supplies

387 Watches, Clocks, Watchcases & Parts
3873 Watches, clocks, watchcases & parts

39 MISCELLANEOUS MANUFACTURING INDUSTRIES

391 Jewelry, Silverware, and Plated Ware
3911 Jewelry, precious metal
3914 Silverware and plated ware
3915 Jewelers' materials & lapidary work

393 Musical Instruments
3931 Musical instruments

394 Toys and Sporting Goods
3942 Dolls and stuffed toys
3944 Games, toys, and children's vehicles
3949 Sporting and athletic goods, nec

395 Pens, Pencils, Office, & Art Supplies
3951 Pens and mechanical pencils
3952 Lead pencils and art goods
3953 Marking devices
3955 Carbon paper and inked ribbons

396 Costume Jewelry and Notions
3961 Costume jewelry
3965 Fasteners, buttons, needles, & pins

399 Miscellaneous Manufactures
3991 Brooms and brushes
3993 Signs and advertising specialities
3995 Burial caskets
3996 Hard surface floor coverings, nec
3999 Manufacturing industries, nec

TRANSPORTATION AND PUBLIC UTILITIES

40 RAILROAD TRANSPORTATION

401 Railroads
4011 Railroads, line-haul operating
4013 Switching and terminal services

41 LOCAL AND INTERURBAN PASSENGER TRANSIT

411 Local and Suburban Transportation
4111 Local and suburban transit
4119 Local passenger transportation, nec

412 Taxicabs
4121 Taxicabs

413 Intercity and Rural Bus Transportation
4131 Intercity & rural bus transportation

414 Bus Charter Service
4141 Local bus charter service
4142 Bus charter service, except local

415 School Buses
4151 School buses

417 Bus Terminal and Service Facilities
4173 Bus terminal and service facilities

42 TRUCKING AND WAREHOUSING

421 Trucking & Courier Services, Ex. Air
4212 Local trucking, without storage
4213 Trucking, except local
4214 Local trucking with storage
4215 Courier services, except by air

422 Public Warehousing and Storage
4221 Farm product warehousing and storage
4222 Refrigerated warehousing and storage
4225 General warehousing and storage
4226 Special warehousing and storage, nec

423 Trucking Terminal Facilities
4231 Trucking terminal facilities

43 U.S. POSTAL SERVICE

431 U.S. Postal Service
4311 U.S. Postal Service

44 WATER TRANSPORTATION

441 Deep Sea Foreign Trans. of Freight
4412 Deep sea foreign trans. of freight

442 Deep Sea Domestic Trans. of Freight
4424 Deep sea domestic trans. of freight

443 Freight Trans. on the Great Lakes
4432 Freight trans. on the Great Lakes

444 Water Transportation of Freight, NEC
4449 Water transportation of freight, nec

448 Water Transportation of Passengers
4481 Deep sea passenger trans., ex. ferry
4482 Ferries
4489 Water passenger transportation, nec

449 Water Transportation Services
4491 Marine cargo handling
4492 Towing and tugboat service
4493 Marinas
4499 Water transportation services, nec

45 TRANSPORTATION BY AIR

451 Air Transportation, Scheduled
4512 Air transportation, scheduled
4513 Air courier services

452 Air Transportation, Nonscheduled
4522 Air transportation, nonscheduled

458 Airports, Flying Fields, & Services
4581 Airports, flying fields, & services

46 PIPELINES, EXCEPT NATURAL GAS

461 Pipelines, Except Natural Gas
4612 Crude petroleum pipelines
4613 Refined petroleum pipelines
4619 Pipelines, nec

47 TRANSPORTATION SERVICES

472 Passenger Transportation Arrangement
4724 Travel agencies
4725 Tour operators
4729 Passenger transport arrangement, nec

473 Freight Transportation Arrangement
4731 Freight transportation arrangement

474 Rental of Railroad Cars
4741 Rental of railroad cars

478 Miscellaneous Transportation Services
4783 Packing and crating
4785 Inspection & fixed facilities
4789 Transportation services, nec

48 COMMUNICATIONS

481 Telephone Communications
4812 Radiotelephone communications
4813 Telephone communications, exc. radio

482 Telegraph & Other Communications
4822 Telegraph & other communications

483 Radio and Television Broadcasting
4832 Radio broadcasting stations
4833 Television broadcasting stations

484 Cable and Other Pay TV Services
4841 Cable and other pay TV services

489 Communications Services, NEC
4899 Communications services, nec

49 ELECTRIC, GAS, AND SANITARY SERVICES

491 Electric Services
4911 Electric services

492 Gas Production and Distribution
4922 Natural gas transmission
4923 Gas transmission and distribution
4924 Natural gas distribution
4925 Gas production and/or distribution

493 Combination Utility Services
4931 Electric and other services combined
4932 Gas and other services combined
4939 Combination utilities, nec

494 Water Supply
4941 Water supply

495 Sanitary Services
4952 Sewerage systems
4953 Refuse systems
4959 Sanitary services, nec

496 Steam and Air-Conditioning Supply
4961 Steam and air-conditioning supply

497 Irrigation Systems
4971 Irrigation systems

WHOLESALE TRADE

50 WHOLESALE TRADE—DURABLE GOODS

501 Motor Vehicles, Parts, and Supplies
5012 Automobiles and other motor vehicles
5013 Motor vehicle supplies and new parts
5014 Tires and tubes
5015 Motor vehicle parts, used

502 Furniture and Homefurnishings
5021 Furniture
5023 Homefurnishings

503 Lumber and Construction Materials
5031 Lumber, plywood, and millwork
5032 Brick, stone, & related materials
5033 Roofing, siding, & insulation
5039 Construction materials, nec

504 Professional & Commercial Equipment
5043 Photographic equipment and supplies
5044 Office equipment
5045 Computers, peripherals & software

5046 Commercial equipment, nec
5047 Medical and hospital equipment
5048 Ophthalmic goods
5049 Professional equipment, nec

505 Metals and Minerals, Except Petroleum
5051 Metals service centers and offices
5052 Coal and other minerals and ores

506 Electrical Goods
5063 Electrical apparatus and equipment
5064 Electrical appliances, TV & radios
5065 Electronic parts and equipment

507 Hardware, Plumbing & Heating Equipment
5072 Hardware
5074 Plumbing & hydronic heating supplies
5075 Warm air heating & air-conditioning
5078 Refrigeration equipment and supplies

508 Machinery, Equipment, and Supplies
5082 Construction and mining machinery
5083 Farm and garden machinery
5084 Industrial machinery and equipment
5085 Industrial supplies
5087 Service establishment equipment
5088 Transportation equipment & supplies

509 Miscellaneous Durable Goods
5091 Sporting & recreational goods
5092 Toys and hobby goods and supplies
5093 Scrap and waste materials
5094 Jewelry & precious stones
5099 Durable goods, nec

51 WHOLESALE TRADE—NONDURABLE GOODS

511 Paper and Paper Products
5111 Printing and writing paper
5112 Stationery and office supplies
5113 Industrial & personal service paper

512 Drugs, Proprietaries, and Sundries
5122 Drugs, proprietaries, and sundries

513 Apparel, Piece Goods, and Notions
5131 Piece goods & notions
5136 Men's and boys' clothing
5137 Women's and children's clothing
5139 Footwear

514 Groceries and Related Products
5141 Groceries, general line
5142 Packaged frozen foods
5143 Dairy products, exc. dried or canned
5144 Poultry and poultry products
5145 Confectionery
5146 Fish and seafoods
5147 Meats and meat products
5148 Fresh fruits and vegetables
5149 Groceries and related products, nec

515 Farm-Product Raw Materials
5153 Grain and field beans
5154 Livestock
5159 Farm-product raw materials, nec

516 Chemicals and Allied Products
5162 Plastics materials & basic shapes
5169 Chemicals & allied products, nec

517 Petroleum and Petroleum Products
5171 Petroleum bulk stations & terminals
5172 Petroleum products, nec

518 Beer, Wine, and Distilled Beverages
5181 Beer and ale
5182 Wine and distilled beverages

519 Misc. Nondurable Goods
5191 Farm supplies
5192 Books, periodicals, & newspapers
5193 Flowers & florists' supplies
5194 Tobacco and tobacco products
5198 Paints, varnishes, and supplies
5199 Nondurable goods, nec

RETAIL TRADE

52 BUILDING MATERIALS & GARDEN SUPPLIES

521 Lumber and Other Building Materials
5211 Lumber and other building materials

523 Paint, Glass, and Wallpaper Stores
5231 Paint, glass, and wallpaper stores

525 Hardware Stores
5251 Hardware stores

526 Retail Nurseries and Garden Stores
5261 Retail nurseries and garden stores

527 Mobile Home Dealers
5271 Mobile home dealers

53 GENERAL MERCHANDISE STORES

531 Department Stores
5311 Department stores

533 Variety Stores
5331 Variety stores

539 Misc. General Merchandise Stores
5399 Misc. general merchandise stores

54 FOOD STORES

541 Grocery Stores
5411 Grocery stores

542 Meat and Fish Markets
5421 Meat and fish markets

543 Fruit and Vegetable Markets
5431 Fruit and vegetable markets

544 Candy, Nut, and Confectionery Stores
5441 Candy, nut, and confectionery stores

545 Dairy Products Stores
5451 Dairy products stores

546 Retail Bakeries
5461 Retail bakeries

549 Miscellaneous Food Stores
5499 Miscellaneous food stores

55 AUTOMOTIVE DEALERS & SERVICE STATIONS

551 New and Used Car Dealers
5511 New and used car dealers

552 Used Car Dealers
5521 Used car dealers

553 Auto and Home Supply Stores
5531 Auto and home supply stores

554 Gasoline Service Stations
5541 Gasoline service stations

555 Boat Dealers
5551 Boat dealers

556 Recreational Vehicle Dealers
5561 Recreational vehicle dealers

557 Motorcycle Dealers
5571 Motorcycle dealers

559 Automotive Dealers, NEC
5599 Automotive dealers, nec

56 APPAREL AND ACCESSORY STORES

561 Men's & Boys' Clothing Stores
5611 Men's & boys' clothing stores

562 Women's Clothing Stores
5621 Women's clothing stores

563 Women's Accessory & Specialty Stores
5632 Women's accessory & specialty stores

564 Children's and Infants' Wear Stores
5641 Children's and infants' wear stores

565 Family Clothing Stores
5651 Family clothing stores

566 Shoe Stores
5661 Shoe stores

569 Misc. Apparel & Accessory Stores
5699 Misc. apparel & accessory stores

57 FURNITURE AND HOMEFURNISHINGS STORES

571 Furniture and Homefurnishings Stores
5712 Furniture stores
5713 Floor covering stores
5714 Drapery and upholstery stores
5719 Misc. homefurnishings stores

572 Household Appliance Stores
5722 Household appliance stores

573 Radio, Television, & Computer Stores
5731 Radio, TV, & electronic stores
5734 Computer and software stores
5735 Record & prerecorded tape stores
5736 Musical instrument stores

58 EATING AND DRINKING PLACES

581 Eating and Drinking Places
5812 Eating places
5813 Drinking places

59 MISCELLANEOUS RETAIL

591 Drug Stores and Proprietary Stores
5912 Drug stores and proprietary stores

592 Liquor Stores
5921 Liquor stores

593 Used Merchandise Stores
5932 Used merchandise stores

594 Miscellaneous Shopping Goods Stores
5941 Sporting goods and bicycle shops
5942 Book stores
5943 Stationery stores
5944 Jewelry stores
5945 Hobby, toy, and game shops
5946 Camera & photographic supply stores
5947 Gift, novelty, and souvenir shops
5948 Luggage and leather goods stores
5949 Sewing, needlework, and piece goods

596 Nonstore Retailers
5961 Catalog and mail-order houses
5962 Merchandising machine operators
5963 Direct selling establishments

598 Fuel Dealers
5983 Fuel oil dealers
5984 Liquefied petroleum gas dealers
5989 Fuel dealers, nec

599 Retail Stores, NEC
5992 Florists
5993 Tobacco stores and stands
5994 News dealers and newsstands
5995 Optical goods stores
5999 Miscellaneous retail stores, nec

FINANCE, INSURANCE, AND REAL ESTATE

60 DEPOSITORY INSTITUTIONS

601 Central Reserve Depositories
6011 Federal reserve banks
6019 Central reserve depository, nec

602 Commercial Banks
6021 National commercial banks
6022 State commercial banks
6029 Commercial banks, nec

603 Savings Institutions
6035 Federal savings institutions
6036 Savings institutions, except federal

606 Credit Unions
6061 Federal credit unions
6062 State credit unions

608 Foreign Bank & Branches & Agencies
6081 Foreign bank & branches & agencies
6082 Foreign trade & international banks

609 Functions Closely Related to Banking
6091 Nondeposit trust facilities
6099 Functions related to deposit banking

61 NONDEPOSITORY INSTITUTIONS

611 Federal & Fed.-Sponsored Credit
6111 Federal & fed.-sponsored credit

614 Personal Credit Institutions
6141 Personal credit institutions

615 Business Credit Institutions
6153 Short-term business credit
6159 Misc. business credit institutions

616 Mortgage Bankers and Brokers
6162 Mortgage bankers and correspondents
6163 Loan brokers

62 SECURITY AND COMMODITY BROKERS

621 Security Brokers and Dealers
6211 Security brokers and dealers

622 Commodity Contracts Brokers, Dealers
6221 Commodity contracts brokers, dealers

623 Security and Commodity Exchanges
6231 Security and commodity exchanges

628 Security and Commodity Services
6282 Investment advice
6289 Security & commodity services, nec

63 INSURANCE CARRIERS

631 Life Insurance
6311 Life insurance

632 Medical Service and Health Insurance
6321 Accident and health insurance
6324 Hospital and medical service plans

633 Fire, Marine, and Casualty Insurance
6331 Fire, marine, and casualty insurance

635 Surety Insurance
6351 Surety insurance

636 Title Insurance
6361 Title insurance

637 Pension, Health, and Welfare Funds
6371 Pension, health, and welfare funds

639 Insurance Carriers, NEC
6399 Insurance carriers, nec

64 INSURANCE AGENTS, BROKERS, & SERVICE

641 Insurance Agents, Brokers, & Service
6411 Insurance agents, brokers, & service

65 REAL ESTATE

651 Real Estate Operators and Lessors
6512 Nonresidential building operators
6513 Apartment building operators
6514 Dwelling operators, exc. apartments
6515 Mobile home site operators
6517 Railroad property lessors
6519 Real property lessors, nec

653 Real Estate Agents and Managers
6531 Real estate agents and managers

654 Title Abstract Offices
6541 Title abstract offices

655 Subdividers and Developers
6552 Subdividers and developers, nec
6553 Cemetery subdividers and developers

67 HOLDING AND OTHER INVESTMENT OFFICES

671 Holding Offices
6712 Bank holding companies
6719 Holding companies, nec

672 Investment Offices
6722 Management investment, open-end
6726 Investment offices, nec

673 Trusts
6732 Educational, religious, etc. trusts
6733 Trusts, nec

679 Miscellaneous Investing
6792 Oil royalty traders
6794 Patent owners and lessors
6798 Real estate investment trusts
6799 Investors, nec

SERVICES

70 HOTELS AND OTHER LODGING PLACES

701 Hotels and Motels
7011 Hotels and motels

702 Rooming and Boarding Houses
7021 Rooming and boarding houses

703 Camps and Recreational Vehicle Parks
7032 Sporting and recreational camps
7033 Trailer parks and campsites

704 Membership-Basis Organization Hotels
7041 Membership-basis organization hotels

72 PERSONAL SERVICES

721 Laundry, Cleaning, & Garment Services
7211 Power Laundries, family & commercial
7212 Garment pressing & cleaners' agents
7213 Linen supply
7215 Coin-operated laundries and cleaning
7216 Drycleaning plants, except rug
7217 Carpet and upholstery cleaning
7218 Industrial launderers
7219 Laundry and garment services, nec

722 Photographic Studios, Portrait
7221 Photographic studios, portrait

723 Beauty Shops
7231 Beauty shops

724 Barber Shops
7241 Barber shops

725 Shoe Repair and Shoeshine Parlors
7251 Shoe repair and shoeshine parlors

726 Funeral Service and Crematories
7261 Funeral service and crematories

729 Miscellaneous Personal Services
7291 Tax return preparation services
7299 Miscellaneous personal services, nec

73 BUSINESS SERVICES

731 Advertising
7311 Advertising agencies
7312 Outdoor advertising services
7313 Radio, TV, publisher representatives
7319 Advertising, nec

732 Credit Reporting and Collection
7322 Adjustment & collection services
7323 Credit reporting services

733 Mailing, Reproduction, Stenographic
7331 Direct mail advertising services
7334 Photocopying & duplicating services
7335 Commercial photography
7336 Commercial art and graphic design
7338 Secretarial & court reporting

734 Services to Buildings
7342 Disinfecting & pest control services
7349 Building maintenance services, nec

735 Misc. Equipment Rental & Leasing
7352 Medical equipment rental
7353 Heavy construction equipment rental
7359 Equipment rental & leasing, nec

736 Personnel Supply Services
7361 Employment agencies
7363 Help supply services

737 Computer and Data Processing Services
7371 Computer programming services
7372 Prepackaged software
7373 Computer integrated systems design
7374 Data processing and preparation
7375 Information retrieval services
7376 Computer facilities management
7377 Computer rental & leasing
7378 Computer maintenance & repair
7379 Computer related services, nec

738 Miscellaneous Business Services
7381 Detective & armored car services
7382 Security systems services
7383 News syndicates
7384 Photofinishing laboratories
7389 Business services, nec

75 AUTO REPAIR, SERVICES, AND PARKING

751 Automotive Rentals, No Drivers
7513 Truck rental and leasing, no drivers
7514 Passenger car rental
7515 Passenger car leasing
7519 Utility trailer rental

752 Automobile Parking
7521 Automobile parking

753 Automotive Repair Shops
7532 Top & body repair & paint shops
7533 Auto exhaust system repair shops
7534 Tire retreading and repair shops
7536 Automotive glass replacement shops
7537 Automotive transmission repair shops
7538 General automotive repair shops
7539 Automotive repair shops, nec

754 Automotive Services, Except Repair
7542 Carwashes
7549 Automotive services, nec

76 MISCELLANEOUS REPAIR SERVICES

762 Electrical Repair Shops
7622 Radio and television repair
7623 Refrigeration service and repair
7629 Electrical repair shops, nec

763 Watch, Clock, and Jewelry Repair
7631 Watch, clock, and jewelry repair

764 Reupholstery and Furniture Repair
7641 Reupholstery and furniture repair

769 Miscellaneous Repair Shops
7692 Welding repair
7694 Armature rewinding shops
7699 Repair services, nec

78 MOTION PICTURES

781 Motion Picture Production & Services
7812 Motion picture & video production
7819 Services allied to motion pictures

782 Motion Picture Distribution & Services
7822 Motion picture and tape distribution
7829 Motion picture distribution services

783 Motion Picture Theaters
7832 Motion picture theaters, ex drive-in
7833 Drive-in motion picture theaters

784 Video Tape Rental
7841 Video tape rental

79 AMUSEMENT & RECREATION SERVICES

791 Dance Studios, Schools, and Halls
7911 Dance studios, schools, and halls

792 Producers, Orchestras, Entertainers
7922 Theatrical producers and services
7929 Entertainers & entertainment groups

793 Bowling Centers
7933 Bowling centers

794 Commercial Sports
7941 Sports clubs, managers, & promoters
7948 Racing, including track operation

799 Misc. Amusement, Recreation Services
7991 Physical fitness facilities
7992 Public golf courses
7993 Coin-operated amusement devices
7996 Amusement parks
7997 Membership sports & recreation clubs
7999 Amusement and recreation, nec

80 HEALTH SERVICES

801 Offices & Clinics of Medical Doctors
8011 Offices & clinics of medical doctors

802 Offices and Clinics of Dentists
8021 Offices and clinics of dentists

803 Offices of Osteopathic Physicians
8031 Offices of osteopathic physicians

804 Offices of Other Health Practitioners
8041 Offices and clinics of chiropractors
8042 Offices and clinics of optometrists
8043 Offices and clinics of podiatrists
8049 Offices of health practitioners, nec

805 Nursing and Personal Care Facilities
8051 Skilled nursing care facilities
8052 Intermediate care facilities
8059 Nursing and personal care, nec

806 Hospitals
8062 General medical & surgical hospitals
8063 Psychiatric hospitals
8069 Specialty hospitals exc. psychiatric

807 Medical and Dental Laboratories
8071 Medical laboratories
8072 Dental laboratories

808 Home Health Care Services
8082 Home health care services

809 Health and Allied Services, NEC
8092 Kidney dialysis centers
8093 Specialty outpatient clinics, nec
8099 Health and allied services, nec

81 LEGAL SERVICES

811 Legal Services
8111 Legal services

82 EDUCATIONAL SERVICES

821 Elementary and Secondary Schools
8211 Elementary and secondary schools

822 Colleges and Universities
8221 Colleges and universities
8222 Junior colleges

823 Libraries
8231 Libraries

824 Vocational Schools
8243 Data processing schools
8244 Business and secretarial schools
8249 Vocational schools, nec

829 Schools & Educational Services, NEC
8299 Schools & educational services, nec

83 SOCIAL SERVICES

832 Individual and Family Services
8322 Individual and family services

833 Job Training and Related Services
8331 Job training and related services

835 Child Day Care Services
8351 Child day care services

836 Residential Care
8361 Residential care

839 Social Services, NEC
8399 Social services, nec

84 MUSEUMS, BOTANICAL, ZOOLOGICAL GARDENS

841 Museums and Art Galleries
8412 Museums and art galleries

842 Botanical and Zoological Gardens
8422 Botanical and zoological gardens

86 MEMBERSHIP ORGANIZATIONS

861 Business Associations
8611 Business associations

862 Professional Organizations
8621 Professional organizations

863 Labor Organizations
8631 Labor organizations

864 Civic and Social Associations
8641 Civic and social associations

865 Political Organizations
8651 Political organizations

866 Religious Organizations
8661 Religious organizations

869 Membership Organizations, NEC
8699 Membership organizations, nec

87 ENGINEERING & MANAGEMENT SERVICES

871 Engineering & Architectural Services
8711 Engineering services
8712 Architectural services
8713 Surveying services

872 Accounting, Auditing, & Bookkeeping
8721 Accounting, auditing, & bookkeeping

873 Research and Testing Services
8731 Commercial physical research
8732 Commercial nonphysical research
8733 Noncommercial research organizations
8734 Testing laboratories

874 Management and Public Relations
8741 Management services
8742 Management consulting services
8743 Public relations services
8744 Facilities support services
8748 Business consulting, nec

88 PRIVATE HOUSEHOLDS

881 Private Households
8811 Private households

89 SERVICES, NEC

899 Services, NEC
8999 Services, nec

PUBLIC ADMINISTRATION

91 EXECUTIVE, LEGISLATIVE, AND GENERAL

911 Executive Offices
9111 Executive offices

912 Legislative Bodies
9121 Legislative bodies

913 Executive and Legislative Combined
9131 Executive and legislative combined

919 General Government, NEC
9199 General government, nec

92 JUSTICE, PUBLIC ORDER, AND SAFETY

921 Courts
9211 Courts

922 Public Order and Safety
9221 Police protection
9222 Legal counsel and prosecution
9223 Correctional institutions
9224 Fire protection
9229 Public order and safety, nec

93 FINANCE, TAXATION, & MONETARY POLICY

931 Finance, Taxation, & Monetary Policy
9311 Finance, taxation, & monetary policy

94 ADMINISTRATION OF HUMAN RESOURCES

941 Admin. of Educational Programs
9411 Admin. of educational programs

943 Admin. of Public Health Programs
9431 Admin. of public health programs

944 Admin. of Social & Manpower Programs
9441 Admin. of social & manpower programs

945 Administration of Veterans' Affairs
9451 Administration of veterans' affairs

95 ENVIRONMENTAL QUALITY AND HOUSING

951 Environmental Quality
9511 Air, water, & solid waste management
9512 Land, mineral, wildlife conservation

953 Housing and Urban Development
9531 Housing programs
9532 Urban and community development

96 ADMINISTRATION OF ECONOMIC PROGRAMS

961 Admin. of General Economic Programs
9611 Admin. of general economic programs

962 Regulation, Admin. of Transportation
9621 Regulation, admin. of transportation

963 Regulation, Admin. of Utilities
9631 Regulation, admin. of utilities

964 Regulation of Agricultural Marketing
9641 Regulation of agricultural marketing

965 Regulation Misc. Commercial Sectors
9651 Regulation misc. commercial sectors

966 Space Research and Technology
9661 Space research and technology

97 NATIONAL SECURITY AND INTL. AFFAIRS

971 National Security
9711 National security

972 International Affairs
9721 International affairs

NONCLASSIFIABLE ESTABLISHMENTS

99 NONCLASSIFIABLE ESTABLISHMENTS

999 Nonclassifiable Establishments
9999 Nonclassifiable establishments

Standard Occupational Classification

The Standard Occupational Classification was developed to provide a standardized system of job descriptions and classification codes for all occupations performed for pay or profit, for use in the presentation and analysis of statistical data about occupations. The classification system is at 4 levels, with division titles, 2- and 3-digit occupation group codes, and 4-digit unit group codes. The classification was used in the 1980 Census of Population and in Labor Department programs.

The classification is presented in the revised 1980 *Standard Occupational Classification Manual,* from which the following list is taken (for description, see ASI 1981 Annual, 2088-2).

Occupation Group Code

EXECUTIVE, ADMINISTRATIVE AND MANAGERIAL OCCUPATIONS

11 Officials and Administrators, Public Administration
- 111 Legislators
- 112 Chief Executives and General Administrators
- 113 Officials and Administrators, Government Agencies

12-13 Officials and Administrators, Other
- 121 General Managers and Other Top Executives
- 122 Financial Managers
- 123 Personnel and Labor Relations Managers
- 124 Purchasing Managers
- 125 Managers; Marketing, Advertising, and Public Relations
- 126 Managers; Engineering, Mathematics, and Natural Sciences
- 127 Managers; Social Sciences and Related Fields
- 128 Administrators; Education and Related Fields
- 131 Managers; Medicine and Health
- 132 Production Managers, Industrial
- 133 Construction Managers
- 134 Public Utilities Managers
- 135 Managers; Service Organizations
- 136 Managers; Mining, Quarrying, Well Drilling, and Similar Operations
- 137 Managers; Administrative Services
- 139 Officials and Administrators; Other, Not Elsewhere Classified

14 Management Related Occupations
- 141 Accountants, Auditors, and Other Financial Specialists
- 142 Management Analysts
- 143 Personnel, Training, and Labor Relations Specialists
- 144 Purchasing Agents and Buyers
- 145 Business and Promotion Agents
- 147 Inspectors and Compliance Officers
- 149 Management Related Occupations, Not Elsewhere Classified

ENGINEERS, SURVEYORS AND ARCHITECTS

16 Engineers, Surveyors and Architects
- 161 Architects
- 162-3 Engineers
- 164 Surveyors and Mapping Scientists

NATURAL SCIENTISTS AND MATHEMATICIANS

17 Computer, Mathematical, and Operations Research Occupations
- 171 Computer Scientists
- 172 Operations and Systems Researchers and Analysts
- 173 Mathematical Scientists

18 Natural Scientists
- 184 Physical Scientists
- 185 Life Scientists

SOCIAL SCIENTISTS, SOCIAL WORKERS, RELIGIOUS WORKERS, AND LAWYERS

19 Social Scientists and Urban Planners
- 191 Social Scientists
- 192 Urban and Regional Planners

20 Social, Recreation, and Religious Workers
- 203 Social and Recreation Workers
- 204 Religious Workers

21 Lawyers and Judges
- 211 Lawyers
- 212 Judges

TEACHERS, LIBRARIANS, AND COUNSELORS

22 Teachers; College, University and Other Postsecondary Institution

23 Teachers, Except Postsecondary Institution
- 231 Prekindergarten and Kindergarten Teachers
- 232 Elementary School Teachers
- 233 Secondary School Teachers
- 235 Teachers; Special Education
- 236 Instructional Coordinators
- 239 Adult Education and Other Teachers, Not Elsewhere Classified

24 Vocational and Educational Counselors

25 Librarians, Archivists, and Curators
- 251 Librarians
- 252 Archivists and Curators

HEALTH DIAGNOSING AND TREATING PRACTITIONERS

26 Physicians and Dentists
- 261 Physicians
- 262 Dentists

27 Veterinarians

28 Other Health Diagnosing and Treating Practitioners
- 281 Optometrists
- 283 Podiatrists
- 289 Health Diagnosing and Treating Practitioners, Not Elsewhere Classified

REGISTERED NURSES, PHARMACISTS, DIETITIANS, THERAPISTS, AND PHYSICIAN'S ASSISTANTS

29 Registered Nurses

30 Pharmacists, Dietitians, Therapists, and Physician's Assistants
- 301 Pharmacists
- 302 Dietitians
- 303 Therapists
- 304 Physician's Assistants

WRITERS, ARTISTS, ENTERTAINERS, AND ATHLETES

32 Writers, Artists, Performers, and Related Workers
- 321 Authors
- 322 Designers
- 323 Musicians and Composers
- 324 Actors and Directors
- 325 Painters, Sculptors, Craft-Artists and Artist-Printmakers
- 326 Photographers
- 327 Dancers
- 328 Performers, Not Elsewhere Classified
- 329 Writers, Artists, and Related Workers; Not Elsewhere Classified

33 Editors, Reporters, Public Relations Specialists, and Announcers
- 331 Editors and Reporters
- 332 Public Relations Specialists and Publicity Writers
- 333 Radio, Television and Other Announcers

34 Athletes and Related Workers

HEALTH TECHNOLOGISTS AND TECHNICIANS

36 Health Technologists and Technicians
- 362 Clinical Laboratory Technologists and Technicians
- 363 Dental Hygienists
- 364 Health Record Technologists and Technicians
- 365 Radiologic Technologists and Technicians
- 366 Licensed Practical Nurses
- 369 Health Technologists and Technicians, Not Elsewhere Classified

TECHNOLOGISTS AND TECHNICIANS, EXCEPT HEALTH

37 Engineering and Related Technologists and Technicians
- 371 Engineering Technologists and Technicians
- 372 Drafting Occupations
- 373 Surveying and Mapping Technicians

38 Science Technologists and Technicians
- 382 Biological Technologists and Technicians, Except Health
- 383 Chemical and Nuclear Technologists and Technicians
- 384 Mathematical Technicians
- 389 Science Technologists and Technicians, Not Elsewhere Classified

39 Technicians; Except Health, Engineering, and Science
- 392 Air Traffic Controllers
- 393 Radio and Related Operators
- 396 Legal Technicians
- 397 Programmers
- 398 Technical Writers
- 399 Technicians, Not Elsewhere Classified

MARKETING AND SALES OCCUPATIONS

40 Supervisors; Marketing and Sales Occupations
- 401 Supervisors; Sales Occupations, Insurance, Real Estate, and Business Services
- 402 Supervisors; Sales Occupations, Commodities Except Retail
- 403 Supervisors; Sales Occupations, Retail

41 Insurance, Securities, Real Estate, and Business Service Sales Occupations
- 412 Insurance, Real Estate, and Securities Sales Occupations
- 415 Business Service Sales Occupations

42 Sales Occupations, Commodities Except Retail
- 421 Sales Engineers
- 423 Technical Sales Workers and Service Advisors
- 424 Sales Representatives

43 Sales Occupations, Retail
- 434-5 Salespersons, Commodities
- 436 Sales Occupations; Other

44 Sales Related Occupations
- 444 Appraisers and Related Occupations
- 445 Demonstrators, Promoters, and Models
- 446 Shoppers
- 447 Auctioneers
- 449 Sales Occupations; Other, Not Elsewhere Classified

ADMINISTRATIVE SUPPORT OCCUPATIONS, INCLUDING CLERICAL

45 Supervisors; Administrative Support Occupations, Including Clerical

46-47 Administrative Support Occupations, Including Clerical
- 461 Computer and Peripheral Equipment Operators
- 462 Secretaries, Stenographers and Typists
- 463 General Office Occupations
- 464 Information Clerks
- 466 Correspondence Clerks and Order Clerks
- 469 Record Clerks
- 471 Financial Record Processing Occupations
- 472 Duplicating, Mail and Other Office Machine Operators
- 473 Communications Equipment Operators
- 474 Mail and Message Distributing Occupations
- 475 Material Recording, Scheduling, and Distributing Clerks
- 478 Adjusters, Investigators, and Collectors
- 479 Miscellaneous Administrative Support Occupations, Including Clerical

SERVICE OCCUPATIONS

50 Private Household Occupations
- 502 Day Workers
- 503 Launderers and Ironers
- 504 Cooks, Private Household
- 505 Housekeepers and Butlers
- 506 Child Care Workers, Private Household
- 507 Private Household Cleaners and Servants
- 509 Private Household Occupations, Not Elsewhere Classified

51 Protective Service Occupations
- 511 Supervisors; Service Occupations, Protective
- 512 Firefighting and Fire Prevention Occupations
- 513 Police and Detectives
- 514 Guards

52 Service Occupations, Except Private Household and Protective
- 521 Food and Beverage Preparation and Service Occupations
- 523 Health Service Occupations
- 524 Cleaning and Building Service Occupations, Except Private Household
- 525-6 Personal Service Occupations

AGRICULTURAL, FORESTRY AND FISHING OCCUPATIONS

55 Farm Operators and Managers
- 551 Farmers (Working Proprietors)
- 552 Farm Managers

56 Other Agricultural and Related Occupations
- 561 Farm Occupations, Except Managerial
- 562 Related Agricultural Occupations

57 Forestry and Logging Occupations
- 571 Supervisors; Forestry and Logging Workers
- 572 Forestry Workers, Except Logging
- 573 Timber Cutting and Related Occupations
- 579 Logging Occupations, Not Elsewhere Classified

58 Fishers, Hunters, and Trappers
- 583 Fishers
- 584 Hunters and Trappers

MECHANICS AND REPAIRERS

60 Supervisors; Mechanics and Repairers

61 Mechanics and Repairers
- 611 Vehicle and Mobile Equipment Mechanics and Repairers
- 613 Industrial Machinery Repairers
- 614 Machinery Maintenance Occupations
- 615 Electrical and Electronic Equipment Repairers
- 616 Heating, Air-Conditioning, and Refrigeration Mechanics
- 617 Miscellaneous Mechanics and Repairers

CONSTRUCTION AND EXTRACTIVE OCCUPATIONS

63 Supervisors; Construction and Extractive Occupations
- 631 Supervisors; Construction
- 632 Supervisors; Extractive Occupations

64 Construction Trades
- 641 Brickmasons, Stonemasons, and Hard Tile Setters
- 642 Carpenters and Related Workers
- 643 Electricians and Power Transmission Installers
- 644 Painters, Paperhangers, and Plasterers
- 645 Plumbers, Pipefitters and Steamfitters
- 646-7 Other Construction Trades

65 Extractive Occupations
- 652 Drillers, Oil Well
- 653 Explosive Workers
- 654 Mining Machine Operators
- 656 Extractive Occupations, Not Elsewhere Classified

PRECISION PRODUCTION OCCUPATIONS

67 Supervisors; Precision Production Occupations

68 Precision Production Occupations
- 681-2 Precision Metal Workers
- 683 Precision Woodworkers
- 684 Precision Printing Occupations
- 685 Precision Textile, Apparel and Furnishings Workers
- 686 Precision Workers; Assorted Materials
- 687 Precision Food Production Occupations
- 688 Precision Inspectors, Testers, and Related Workers

69 Plant and System Operators
- 691 Water and Sewage Treatment Plant Operators
- 692 Gas Plant Operators
- 693 Power Plant Operators
- 694 Chemical Plant Operators
- 695 Petroleum Plant Operators
- 696 Miscellaneous Plant or System Operators

PRODUCTION WORKING OCCUPATIONS

71 Supervisors; Production Occupations

73-74 Machine Setup Operators
- 731-2 Metalworking and Plastic Working Machine Setup Operators
- 733 Metal Fabricating Machine Setup Operators
- 734 Metal and Plastic Processing Machine Setup Operators
- 743 Woodworking Machine Setup Operators
- 744 Printing Machine Setup Operators
- 745 Textile Machine Setup Operators
- 746-7 Assorted Materials: Machine Setup Operators

75-76 Machine Operators and Tenders
- 751-2 Metalworking and Plastic Working Machine Operators and Tenders
- 753 Metal Fabricating Machine Operators and Tenders
- 754 Metal and Plastic Processing Machine Operators and Tenders
- 763 Woodworking Machine Operators and Tenders
- 764 Printing Machine Operators and Tenders
- 765 Textile, Apparel and Furnishings Machine Operators and Tenders
- 766-7 Machine Operators and Tenders; Assorted Materials

77 Fabricators, Assemblers, and Hand Working Occupations
- 771 Welders and Solderers
- 772 Assemblers
- 774 Fabricators, Not Elsewhere Classified
- 775 Hand Working Occupations

78 Production Inspectors, Testers, Samplers, and Weighers
- 782 Production Inspectors, Checkers and Examiners
- 783 Production Testers
- 784 Production Samplers and Weighers
- 785 Graders and Sorters, Except Agricultural
- 787 Production Expediters

TRANSPORTATION AND MATERIAL MOVING OCCUPATIONS

81 Supervisors; Transportation and Material Moving Occupations
- 811 Supervisors; Motorized Equipment Operators
- 812 Supervisors; Material Moving Equipment Operators

82 Transportation Occupations
- 821 Motor Vehicle Operators
- 823 Rail Transportation Occupations
- 824 Water Transportation Occupations
- 825 Airplane Pilots and Navigators
- 828 Transportation Inspectors

83 Material Moving Occupations, Except Transportation
- 831 Material Moving Equipment Operators

HANDLERS, EQUIPMENT CLEANERS, HELPERS AND LABORERS

85 Supervisors; Handlers, Equipment Cleaners, Helpers, and Laborers

86 Helpers
- 861 Helpers; Machine Operators and Tenders
- 862 Helpers; Fabricators and Inspectors
- 863 Helpers; Mechanics and Repairers
- 864 Helpers; Construction Trades
- 865 Helpers; Extractive Occupations

87 Handlers, Equipment Cleaners and Laborers
- 871 Construction Laborers
- 872 Freight, Stock, and Material Movers; Hand
- 873 Garage and Service Station Related Occupations
- 874 Parking Lot Attendants
- 875 Vehicle Washers and Equipment Cleaners
- 876 Miscellaneous Manual Occupations

MILITARY OCCUPATIONS

91 Military Occupations

MISCELLANEOUS OCCUPATIONS

99 Miscellaneous Occupations

Standard International Trade Classification, Revision 3

The Standard International Trade Classification (SITC) is a statistical classification of commodities in world trade, developed by the United Nations to facilitate international comparison of commodity trade data. The classification is at 5 levels: sections, divisions, groups, subgroups, and items—represented by 1- to 5-digit codes.

SITC Revision 3 was published in 1986. An earlier classification scheme, Revision 2, was published in 1975.

The 1- to 3-digit codes of Revision 3 are listed below. For Revision 2 codes, see ASI 1989 Annual Index volume.

Section, Division, and Group Codes

0 FOOD AND LIVE ANIMALS

00 Live Animals Other Than Animals of Division 03
- 001 Live animals other than animals of division 03

01 Meat and Meat Preparations
- 011 Meat of bovine animals, fresh, chilled or frozen
- 012 Other meat and edible meat offal, fresh, chilled or frozen (except meat and meat offal unfit or unsuitable for human consumption)
- 016 Meat and edible meat offal, salted, in brine, dried or smoked; edible flours and meals of meat or meat offal
- 017 Meat and edible meat offal, prepared or preserved, n.e.s.

02 Dairy Products and Birds' Eggs
- 022 Milk and cream and milk products other than butter or cheese
- 023 Butter and other fats and oils derived from milk
- 024 Cheese and curd
- 025 Eggs, birds', and egg yolks, fresh, dried or otherwise preserved, sweetened or not; egg albumin

03 Fish (Not Marine Mammals), Crustaceans, Molluscs and Aquatic Invertebrates, and Preparations Thereof
- 034 Fish, fresh (live or dead), chilled or frozen
- 035 Fish, dried, salted or in brine; smoked fish (whether or not cooked before or during the smoking process)
- 036 Crustaceans, molluscs and aquatic invertebrates, whether in shell or not, fresh (live or dead), chilled, frozen, dried, salted or in brine; crustaceans, in shell, cooked by steaming or boiling in water
- 037 Fish, crustaceans, molluscs and other aquatic invertebrates, prepared or preserved, n.e.s.

04 Cereals and Cereal Preparations
- 041 Wheat (including spelt) and meslin, unmilled
- 042 Rice
- 043 Barley, unmilled
- 044 Maize (not including sweet corn) unmilled
- 045 Cereals, unmilled (other than wheat, rice, barley, and maize)
- 046 Meal and flour of wheat and flour of meslin
- 047 Other cereal meals and flours
- 048 Cereal preparations and preparations of flour or starch of fruits or vegetables

05 Vegetables and Fruit
- 054 Vegetables, fresh, chilled, frozen or simply preserved (including dried leguminous vegetables); roots, tubers and other edible vegetable products, n.e.s., fresh or dried
- 056 Vegetables, roots and tubers, prepared or preserved, n.e.s.
- 057 Fruit and nuts (not including oil nuts), fresh or dried
- 058 Fruit, preserved, and fruit preparations (excluding fruit juices)
- 059 Fruit juices (including grape must) and vegetable juices, unfermented and not containing added spirit, whether or not containing added sugar or other sweetening matter

06 Sugars, Sugar Preparations and Honey
- 061 Sugars, molasses and honey
- 062 Sugar confectionery

07 Coffee, Tea, Cocoa, Spices, and Manufactures Thereof
- 071 Coffee and coffee substitutes
- 072 Cocoa
- 073 Chocolate and other food preparations containing cocoa, n.e.s.
- 074 Tea and mate
- 075 Spices

08 Feeding Stuff for Animals (Not Including Unmilled Cereals)
- 081 Feeding stuff for animals (not including unmilled cereals)

09 Miscellaneous Edible Products and Preparations
- 091 Margarine and shortening
- 098 Edible products and preparations, n.e.s.

1 BEVERAGES AND TOBACCO

11 Beverages
- 111 Non-alcoholic beverages, n.e.s.
- 112 Alcoholic beverages

12 Tobacco and Tobacco Manufactures
- 121 Tobacco, unmanufactured; tobacco refuse
- 122 Tobacco, manufactured (whether or not containing tobacco substitutes)

2 CRUDE MATERIALS, INEDIBLE, EXCEPT FUELS

21 Hides, Skins and Furskins, Raw
- 211 Hides and skins (except furskins), raw
- 212 Furskins, raw (including heads, tails, paws and other pieces or cuttings, suitable for furriers' use), other than hides and skins of group 211

22 Oil Seeds and Oleaginous Fruits
- 222 Oil seeds and oleaginous fruits of a kind used for the extraction of "soft" fixed vegetable oils (excluding flours and meals)
- 223 Oil seeds and oleaginous fruits, whole or broken, of a kind used for the extraction of other fixed vegetable oils (including flours and meals of oil seeds or oleaginous fruit, n.e.s.)

23 Crude Rubber (Including Synthetic and Reclaimed)
- 231 Natural rubber, balata, gutta percha, guayule, chicle and similar natural gums, in primary forms (including latex) or in plates, sheets or strip
- 232 Synthetic rubber; reclaimed rubber; waste, parings and scrap of unhardened rubber

24 Cork and Wood
- 244 Cork, natural, raw and waste (including natural cork in blocks or sheets)
- 245 Fuel wood (excluding wood waste) and wood charcoal
- 246 Wood in chips or particles and wood waste
- 247 Wood in the rough or roughly squared
- 248 Wood, simply worked, and railway sleepers of wood

25 Pulp and Waste Paper
- 251 Pulp and waste paper

26 Textile Fibres (Other Than Wool Tops and Other Combed Wool) and Their Wastes (Not Manufactured Into Yarn or Fabric)
- 261 Silk
- 263 Cotton
- 264 Jute and other textile bast fibres, n.e.s., raw or processed but not spun; tow and waste of these fibres (including yarn waste and garnetted stock)
- 265 Vegetable textile fibres (other than cotton and jute), raw or processed but not spun; waste of these fibres
- 266 Synthetic fibres suitable for spinning
- 267 Other man-made fibres suitable for spinning and waste of man-made fibres
- 268 Wool and other animal hair (including wool tops)
- 269 Worn clothing and other worn textile articles; rags

27 **Crude Fertilizers, Other Than Those of Division 56, and Crude Minerals (Excluding Coal, Petroleum and Precious Stones)**
- 272 Fertilizers, crude, other than those of division 56
- 273 Stone, sand and gravel
- 274 Sulphur and unroasted iron pyrites
- 277 Natural abrasives, n.e.s. (including industrial diamonds)
- 278 Other crude minerals

28 **Metalliferous Ores and Metal Scrap**
- 281 Iron ore and concentrates
- 282 Ferrous waste and scrap; remelting ingots of iron or steel
- 283 Copper ores and concentrates; copper mattes, cement copper
- 284 Nickel ores and concentrates; nickel mattes, nickel oxide, sinters and other intermediate products of nickel metallurgy
- 285 Aluminium ores and concentrates (including alumina)
- 286 Ores and concentrates of uranium or thorium
- 287 Ores and concentrates of base metals, n.e.s.
- 288 Non-ferrous base metal waste and scrap, n.e.s.
- 289 Ores and concentrates of precious metals; waste, scrap and sweepings of precious metals (other than of gold)

29 **Crude Animal and Vegetable Materials, n.e.s.**
- 291 Crude animal materials, n.e.s.
- 292 Crude vegetable materials, n.e.s.

3 MINERAL FUELS, LUBRICANTS AND RELATED MATERIALS

32 **Coal, Coke and Briquettes**
- 321 Coal, whether or not pulverized, but not agglomerated
- 322 Briquettes, lignite and peat
- 325 Coke and semi-coke (including char) of coal, of lignite or of peat, whether or not agglomerated; retort carbon

33 **Petroleum, Petroleum Products and Related Materials**
- 333 Petroleum oils and oils obtained from bituminous minerals, crude
- 334 Petroleum oils and oils obtained from bituminous minerals (other than crude); preparations, n.e.s., containing by weight 70% or more of petroleum oils or of oils obtained from bituminous minerals, these oils being the basic constituents of the preparations
- 335 Residual petroleum products, n.e.s. and related materials

34 **Gas, Natural and Manufactured**
- 342 Liquefied propane and butane
- 343 Natural gas, whether or not liquefied
- 344 Petroleum gases and other gaseous hydrocarbons, n.e.s.
- 345 Coal gas, water gas, producer gas and similar gases, other than petroleum gases and other gaseous hydrocarbons

35 **Electric Current**
- 351 Electric current

4 ANIMAL AND VEGETABLE OILS, FATS AND WAXES

41 **Animal Oils and Fats**
- 411 Animal oils and fats

42 **Fixed Vegetable Fats and Oils, Crude, Refined or Fractionated**
- 421 Fixed vegetable fats and oils, "soft", crude, refined or fractionated
- 422 Fixed vegetable fats and oils, crude, refined or fractionated, other than "soft"

43 **Animal or Vegetable Fats and Oils, Processed; Waxes of Animal or Vegetable Origin; Inedible Mixtures or Preparations of Animal or Vegetable Fats or Oils, n.e.s.**
- 431 Animal or vegetable fats and oils, processed, waxes, and inedible mixtures or preparations of animal or vegetable fats or oils, n.e.s.

5 CHEMICALS AND RELATED PRODUCTS, N.E.S.

51 **Organic Chemicals**
- 511 Hydrocarbons, n.e.s., and their halogenated, sulphonated, nitrated or nitrosated derivatives
- 512 Alcohols, phenols, phenol-alcohols, and their halogenated, sulphonated, nitrated or nitrosated derivatives
- 513 Carboxylic acids and their anhydrides, halides, peroxides and peroxyacids; their halogenated, sulphonated, nitrated or nitrosated derivatives
- 514 Nitrogen-function compounds
- 515 Organo-inorganic compounds, heterocyclic compounds, nucleic acids and their salts
- 516 Other organic chemicals

52 **Inorganic Chemicals**
- 522 Inorganic chemical elements, oxides and halogen salts
- 523 Metallic salts and peroxysalts, of inorganic acids
- 524 Other inorganic chemicals; organic and inorganic compounds of precious metals
- 525 Radio-active and associated materials

53 **Dyeing, Tanning and Colouring Materials**
- 531 Synthetic organic colouring matter and colour lakes, and preparations based thereon
- 532 Dyeing and tanning extracts, and synthetic tanning materials
- 533 Pigments, paints, varnishes and related materials

54 **Medicinal and Pharmaceutical Products**
- 541 Medicinal and pharmaceutical products, other than medicaments of group 542
- 542 Medicaments (including veterinary medicaments)

55 **Essential Oils and Resinoids and Perfume Materials; Toilet, Polishing and Cleansing Preparations**
- 551 Essential oils, perfume and flavour materials
- 553 Perfumery, cosmetics or toilet preparations (excluding soaps)
- 554 Soap, cleansing and polishing preparations

56 **Fertilizers (Other Than Those of Group 272)**
- 562 Fertilizers (other than those of group 272)

57 **Plastics in Primary Forms**
- 571 Polymers of ethylene, in primary forms
- 572 Polymers of styrene, in primary forms
- 573 Polymers of vinyl chloride or of other halogenated olefins, in primary forms
- 574 Polyacetals, other polyethers and epoxide resins, in primary forms; polycarbonates, alkyd resins and other polyesters, in primary forms
- 575 Other plastics, in primary forms
- 579 Waste, parings and scrap, of plastics

58 **Plastics in Non-primary Forms**
- 581 Tubes, pipes and hoses of plastics
- 582 Plates, sheets, film, foil and strip, of plastics
- 583 Monofilament of which any cross-sectional dimension exceeds 1 mm, rods, sticks and profile shapes, whether or not surface-worked but not otherwise worked, of plastics

59 **Chemical Materials and Products, n.e.s.**
- 591 Insecticides, rodenticides, fungicides, herbicides, anti-sprouting products and plant-growth regulators, disinfectants and similar products, put up in forms or packings for retail sale or as preparations or articles (e.g., sulphur-treated bands, wicks and candles, and fly-papers)
- 592 Starches, inulin and wheat gluten; albuminoidal substances; glues
- 593 Explosives and pyrotechnic products
- 597 Prepared additives for mineral oils and the like; prepared liquids for hydraulic transmission; anti-freezing preparations and prepared de-icing fluids; lubricating preparations
- 598 Miscellaneous chemical products, n.e.s.

6 MANUFACTURED GOODS CLASSIFIED CHIEFLY BY MATERIAL

61 **Leather, Leather Manufactures, n.e.s., and Dressed Furskins**
- 611 Leather
- 612 Manufactures of leather or of composition leather, n.e.s.; saddlery and harness
- 613 Furskins, tanned or dressed (including heads, tails, paws and

other pieces or cuttings), unassembled, or assembled (without the addition of other materials), other than those of heading 848.3

62 Rubber Manufactures, n.e.s.
- 621 Materials of rubber (e.g., pastes, plates, sheets, rods, thread, tubes, of rubber)
- 625 Rubber tyres, interchangeable tyre treads, tyre flaps and inner tubes for wheels of all kinds
- 629 Articles of rubber, n.e.s.

63 Cork and Wood Manufactures (Excluding Furniture)
- 633 Cork manufactures
- 634 Veneers, plywood, particle board, and other wood, worked, n.e.s.
- 635 Wood manufactures, n.e.s.

64 Paper, Paperboard, and Articles of Paper Pulp, of Paper or of Paperboard
- 641 Paper and paperboard
- 642 Paper and paperboard, cut to size or shape, and articles of paper or paperboard

65 Textile Yarn, Fabrics, Made-Up Articles, n.e.s., and Related Products
- 651 Textile yarn
- 652 Cotton fabrics, woven (not including narrow or special fabrics)
- 653 Fabrics, woven, of man-made textile materials (not including narrow or special fabrics)
- 654 Other textile fabrics, woven
- 655 Knitted or crocheted fabrics (including tubular knit fabrics, n.e.s., pile fabrics and open-work fabrics), n.e.s.
- 656 Tulles, lace, embroidery, ribbons, trimmings and other small wares
- 657 Special yarns, special textile fabrics and related products
- 658 Made-up articles, wholly or chiefly of textile materials, n.e.s.
- 659 Floor coverings, etc.

66 Non-Metallic Mineral Manufactures, n.e.s.
- 661 Lime, cement, and fabricated construction materials (except glass and clay materials)
- 662 Clay construction materials and refractory construction materials
- 663 Mineral manufactures, n.e.s.
- 664 Glass
- 665 Glassware
- 666 Pottery
- 667 Pearls, precious and semi-precious stones, unworked or worked

67 Iron and Steel
- 671 Pig iron, spiegeleisen, sponge iron, iron or steel granules and powders and ferro-alloys
- 672 Ingots and other primary forms, of iron or steel; semi-finished products of iron or steel
- 673 Flat-rolled products, of iron or non-alloy steel, not clad, plated or coated
- 674 Flat-rolled products of iron or non-alloy steel, clad, plated or coated
- 675 Flat-rolled products of alloy steel
- 676 Iron and steel bars, rods, angles, shapes and sections (including sheet piling)
- 677 Rails and railway track construction material, of iron or steel
- 678 Wire of iron or steel
- 679 Tubes, pipes and hollow profiles, and tube or pipe fittings, of iron or steel

68 Non-Ferrous Metals
- 681 Silver, platinum and other metals of the platinum group
- 682 Copper
- 683 Nickel
- 684 Aluminium
- 685 Lead
- 686 Zinc
- 687 Tin
- 689 Miscellaneous non-ferrous base metals employed in metallurgy, and cermets

69 Manufactures of Metals, n.e.s.
- 691 Structures and parts of structures, n.e.s., of iron, steel or aluminium
- 692 Metal containers for storage or transport
- 693 Wire products (excluding insulated electrical wiring) and fencing grills
- 694 Nails, screws, nuts, bolts, rivets and the like, of iron, steel, copper or aluminium
- 695 Tools for use in the hand or in machines
- 696 Cutlery
- 697 Household equipment of base metal, n.e.s.
- 699 Manufactures of base metal, n.e.s.

7 MACHINERY AND TRANSPORT EQUIPMENT

71 Power Generating Machinery and Equipment
- 711 Steam or other vapour generating boilers, super-heated water boilers, and auxiliary plant for use therewith; and parts thereof
- 712 Steam turbines and other vapour turbines, and parts thereof, n.e.s.
- 713 Internal combustion piston engines, and parts thereof, n.e.s.
- 714 Engines and motors, non-electric (other than those of groups 712, 713 and 718); parts, n.e.s. of these engines and motors
- 716 Rotating electric plant and parts thereof, n.e.s.
- 718 Other power generating machinery and parts thereof, n.e.s.

72 Machinery Specialized for Particular Industries
- 721 Agricultural machinery (excluding tractors) and parts thereof
- 722 Tractors (other than those of headings 744.14 and 744.15)
- 723 Civil engineering and contractors' plant and equipment
- 724 Textile and leather machinery, and parts thereof, n.e.s.
- 725 Paper mill and pulp mill machinery, paper cutting machines and other machinery for the manufacture of paper articles; parts thereof
- 726 Printing and bookbinding machinery, and parts thereof
- 727 Food-processing machines (excluding domestic)
- 728 Other machinery and equipment specialized for particular industries, and parts thereof, n.e.s.

73 Metalworking Machinery
- 731 Machine-tools working by removing metal or other material
- 733 Machine-tools for working metal, sintered metal carbides or cermets, without removing material
- 735 Parts, n.e.s., and accessories suitable for use solely or principally with the machines falling within headings 731 and 733 (including work or tool holders, self-opening dieheads, dividing heads and other special attachments for machine-tools); tool holders for any type of tool for working in the hand
- 737 Metalworking machinery (other than machine-tools), and parts thereof, n.e.s.

74 General Industrial Machinery and Equipment, n.e.s., and Machine Parts, n.e.s.
- 741 Heating and cooling equipment and parts thereof, n.e.s.
- 742 Pumps for liquids, whether or not fitted with a measuring device; liquid elevators; parts for such pumps and liquid elevators
- 743 Pumps (other than pumps for liquids), air or other gas compressors and fans; ventilating or recycling hoods incorporating a fan, whether or not fitted with filters; centrifuges; filtering or purifying apparatus; and parts thereof
- 744 Mechanical handling equipment, and parts thereof, n.e.s.
- 745 Other non-electrical machinery, tools and mechanical apparatus, and parts thereof, n.e.s.
- 746 Ball or roller bearings
- 747 Taps, cocks, valves and similar appliances, for pipes, boiler shells, tanks, vats and the like (including pressure reducing valves and thermostatically controlled valves)
- 748 Transmission shafts (including cam shafts and crank shafts) and cranks; bearing housings and plain shaft bearings; gears and gearing; ball screws; gear boxes and other speed changers (including torque converters); flywheels and pulleys (including pulley blocks); clutches and shaft couplings (including universal joints); and parts thereof
- 749 Non-electric parts and accessories of machinery, n.e.s.

75 Office Machines and Automatic Data Processing Machines
- 751 Office machines
- 752 Automatic data processing machines and units thereof; magnetic or optical readers, machines for transcribing data onto data media in coded form and machines for processing such data, n.e.s.
- 759 Parts and accessories (other than covers, carrying cases and the like) suitable for use solely or principally with machines falling within groups 751 and 752

76 Telecommunications and Sound Recording and Reproducing Apparatus and Equipment
- 761 Television receivers (including

video monitors and video projectors), whether or not combined, in the same housing, with radio-broadcast receivers or sound or video recording or reproducing apparatus
762 Radio-broadcast receivers, whether or not combined, in the same housing, with sound recording or reproducing apparatus or a clock
763 Sound recorders or reproducers; television image and sound recorders or reproducers; prepared unrecorded media
764 Telecommunications equipment, n.e.s.; and parts, n.e.s., and accessories of apparatus falling within division 76

77 Electrical Machinery, Apparatus and Appliances, n.e.s., and Electrical Parts Thereof (Including Non-Electrical Counterparts, n.e.s. of Electrical Household Type Equipment)
771 Electric power machinery (other than rotating electric plant of heading 716), and parts thereof
772 Electrical apparatus for switching or protecting electrical circuits or for making connections to or in electrical circuits (e.g., switches, relays, fuses, lightning arresters, voltage limiters, surge suppressors, plugs and sockets, lampholders and junction boxes); electrical resistors (including rheostats and potentiometers), other than heating resistors; printed circuits; boards, panels (including numerical control panels), consoles, desks, cabinets and other bases, equipped with two or more apparatus for switching, protecting or for making connections to or in electrical circuits, for electric control or the distribution of electricity (excluding switching apparatus of heading 764.1)
773 Equipment for distributing electricity, n.e.s.
774 Electro-diagnostic apparatus for medical, surgical, dental or veterinary sciences and radiological apparatus
775 Household type, electrical and non-electrical equipment, n.e.s.
776 Thermionic, cold cathode or photo-cathode valves and tubes (e.g., vacuum or vapour or gas filled valves and tubes, mercury arc rectifying valves and tubes, cathode-ray tubes, television camera tubes); diodes, transistors and similar semi-conductor devices; photosensitive semi-conductor devices; light emitting diodes; mounted piezo-electric crystals; electronic integrated circuits and microassemblies; and parts thereof
778 Electrical machinery and apparatus, n.e.s.

78 Road Vehicles (Including Air-Cushion Vehicles)
781 Motor cars and other motor vehicles principally designed for the transport of persons (other than public-transport type vehicles), including station wagons and racing cars
782 Motor vehicles for the transport of goods and special purpose motor vehicles
783 Road motor vehicles, n.e.s.
784 Parts and accessories of the motor vehicles of groups 722, 781, 782 and 783
785 Motorcycles (including mopeds) and cycles, motorized and non-motorized; invalid carriages
786 Trailers and semi-trailers; other vehicles, not mechanically propelled; specially designed and equipped transport containers

79 Other Transport Equipment
791 Railway vehicles (including hover-trains) and associated equipment
792 Aircraft and associated equipment; spacecraft (including satellites) and spacecraft launch vehicles; and parts thereof
793 Ships, boats (including hovercraft) and floating structures

8 MISCELLANEOUS MANUFACTURED ARTICLES

81 Prefabricated Buildings; Sanitary, Plumbing, Heating and Lighting Fixtures and Fittings, n.e.s.
811 Prefabricated buildings
812 Sanitary, plumbing and heating fixtures and fittings, n.e.s.
813 Lighting fixtures and fittings, n.e.s.

82 Furniture and Parts Thereof; Bedding, Mattresses, Mattress Supports, Cushions and Similar Stuffed Furnishings
821 Furniture and parts thereof; bedding, mattresses, mattress supports, cushions and similar stuffed furnishings

83 Travel Goods, Handbags and Similar Containers
831 Trunks, suit-cases, vanity-cases, executive-cases, brief-cases, school satchels, binocular cases, camera cases, musical instrument cases, spectacle cases, gun cases, holsters and similar containers; travelling bags, toilet bags, rucksacks, handbags, shopping-bags, wallets, purses, map-cases, cigarette-cases, tobacco-pouches, tool bags, sports bags, bottle-cases, jewellery boxes, powder-boxes, cutlery cases and similar containers, of leather or of composition leather, of plastic sheeting, of textile materials, of vulcanized fibre or of paperboard, or wholly or mainly covered with such materials; travel sets for personal toilet, sewing or shoe or clothes cleaning

84 Articles of Apparel and Clothing Accessories
841 Men's or boys' coats, jackets, suits, blazers, trousers, shorts, shirts, underwear, knitwear and similar articles of textile fabrics, not knitted or crocheted (other than those of heading 845.2 or 845.6)
842 Women's and girls' coats, capes, jackets, suits, blazers, trousers, shorts, shirts, underwear and similar articles of textile fabrics, not knitted or crocheted (other than those of heading 845.2 or 845.6)
843 Men's or boys' coats, capes, jackets, suits, blazers, trousers, shorts, shirts, underwear, nightwear and similar articles of textile fabrics, knitted or crocheted (other than those of heading 845.2 or 845.6)
844 Women's or girls' coats, capes, jackets, suits, blazers, trousers, shorts, shirts, underwear, nightwear and similar articles of textile fabrics, knitted or crocheted (other than those of heading 845.2 or 845.6)
845 Articles of apparel, of textile fabrics, whether or not knitted or crocheted, n.e.s.
846 Clothing accessories, of textile fabrics, whether or not knitted or crocheted (other than those for babies)
848 Articles of apparel and clothing accessories of other than textile fabrics; headgear of all materials

85 Footwear
851 Footwear

87 Professional, Scientific and Controlling Instruments and Apparatus, n.e.s.
871 Optical instruments and apparatus, n.e.s.
872 Instruments and appliances, n.e.s., for medical, surgical, dental or veterinary purposes
873 Meters and counters, n.e.s.
874 Measuring, checking, analysing and controlling instruments and apparatus, n.e.s.

88 Photographic Apparatus, Equipment and Supplies and Optical Goods, n.e.s.; Watches and Clocks
881 Photographic apparatus and equipment, n.e.s.
882 Photographic and cinematographic supplies
883 Cinematograph film, exposed and developed, whether or not incorporating sound track or consisting only of sound track
884 Optical goods, n.e.s.
885 Watches and clocks

89 Miscellaneous Manufactured Articles, n.e.s.
891 Arms and ammunition
892 Printed matter
893 Articles, n.e.s. of plastics
894 Baby carriages, toys, games and sporting goods
895 Office and stationery supplies, n.e.s.
896 Works of art, collectors' pieces and antiques
897 Jewellery, goldsmiths' and silversmiths' wares, and other articles of precious or semi-precious materials, n.e.s.

898 Musical instruments and parts and accessories thereof; records, tapes and other sound or similar recordings (excluding goods of groups 763, 882 and 883)
899 Miscellaneous manufactured articles, n.e.s.

9 COMMODITIES AND TRANSACTIONS NOT CLASSIFIED ELSEWHERE IN THE SITC

91 Postal Packages Not Classified According to Kind
911 Postal packages not classified according to kind

93 Special Transactions and Commodities Not Classified According to Kind
931 Special transactions and commodities not classified according to kind

96 Coin (Other Than Gold Coin), Not Being Legal Tender
961 Coin (other than gold coin), not being legal tender

97 Gold, Non-Monetary (Excluding Gold Ores and Concentrates)
971 Gold, non-monetary (excluding gold ores and concentrates)